Dillon's sell Books

A bookshop ▓▓▓▓▓ ned for people who care about b▓▓▓▓, we now have one of the largest stocks of books (including paperbacks and secondhand and antiquarian books) in the U.K.

We specialize in importing books from the United States, and from other places abroad.

Lists of recent and forthcoming books are available in many subjects, and recent comprehensive catalogues include African Arts, Statistics, Urban and Regional Planning and Sociology. Write, telephone, or call in for all your book needs.

Dillon's University Bookshop Ltd., 1, Malet Street, London, WC1E 7JB
01–636 1577

Our flag flies for all who go to sea

The Flying Angel is well known to seafarers the world over

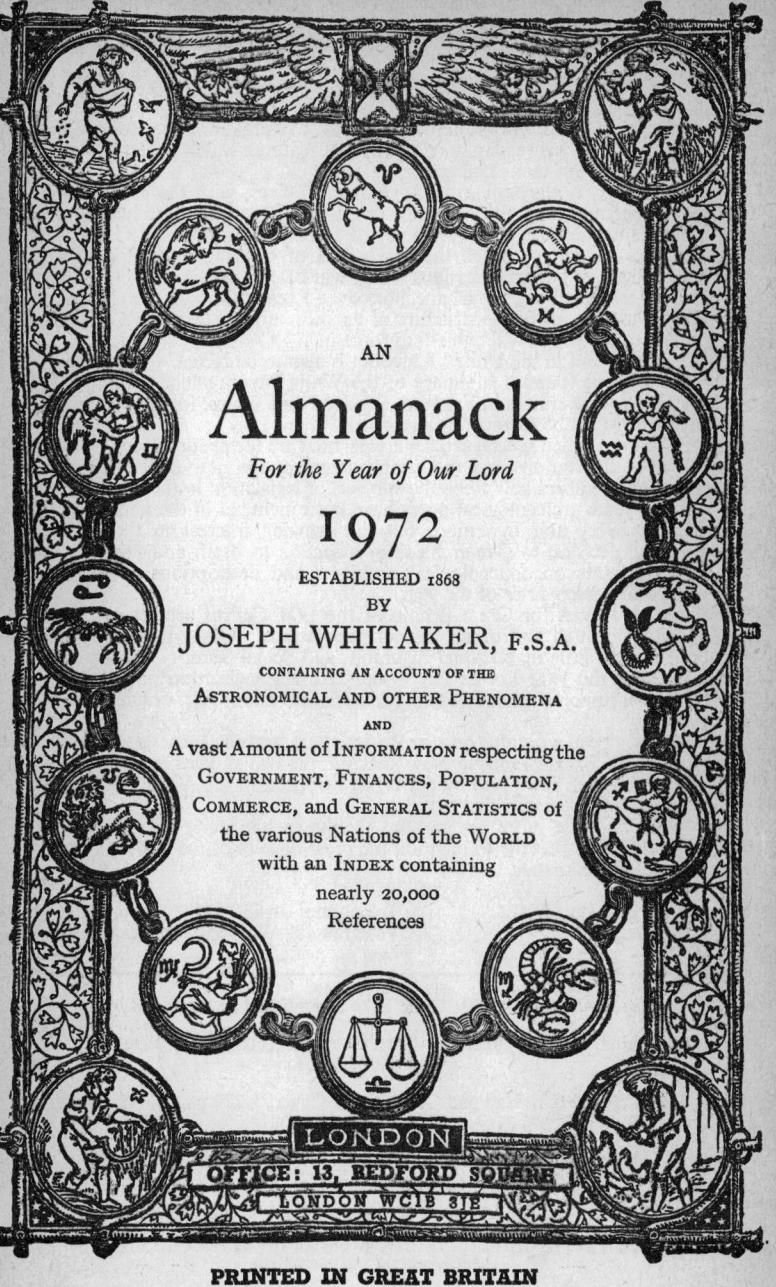

AN

Almanack

For the Year of Our Lord

1972

ESTABLISHED 1868

BY

JOSEPH WHITAKER, F.S.A.

CONTAINING AN ACCOUNT OF THE
ASTRONOMICAL AND OTHER PHENOMENA

AND

A vast Amount of INFORMATION respecting the
GOVERNMENT, FINANCES, POPULATION,
COMMERCE, and GENERAL STATISTICS of
the various Nations of the WORLD
with an INDEX containing
nearly 20,000
References

LONDON

OFFICE: 13, BEDFORD SQUARE
LONDON WC1B 3JE

PRINTED IN GREAT BRITAIN

PREFACE TO THE 104TH ANNUAL VOLUME
(1972)

In introducing the 104th annual volume of "Whitaker", the Editor seeks to call the attention of his readers to a number of features which reflect the events of a year which has seen many changes.

There has been a regrouping of Government offices, with the establishment of the new Departments of the Environment and of Trade and Industry, and the additional responsibilities of the Ministry of Defence. In the Law Courts section of the Almanack will be noted the first stages of the transformation of the old system of assizes and quarter sessions which will be completed in 1972.

In his Budget statement, the Chancellor of the Exchequer explained his proposals for widespread reforms of the structure of taxation, and a special article deals with these innovations, which will come into force in 1973.

Local government in the United Kingdom is also to be recast, and among Topics of the Day will be found a summary of the White Papers which set out the plans for the new two-tier system in England, Scotland and Wales, for which Bills will be brought forward in the forthcoming session.

Other topics to which special articles are devoted are the proposals for independent commercial radio stations and the establishment of the new British Library, two matters which are also likely to be the subjects of legislation in the near future.

For many years archæological notes have been included in the annual article on Science, Discovery and Invention, but the growing interest in the subject has prompted the decision to give archæology a section to itself, and this new feature includes comments on archæological problems and descriptions of some of the more important discoveries of the year.

Preliminary figures for Great Britain of the 1971 Census are set out, including county, city, borough and urban district populations. Other topical information includes the new scale of National Insurance and Social Security benefits and contributions, and the 1971 Forces Pay Code. Among legislation passed during the year, the most important item was the Industrial Relations Act, which is considered in detail.

The year has been a notable one for British sport, and the successes of the M.C.C. in Australia, the British Lions in New Zealand, the British Isles team in the Walker Cup, and the British crews, led by the Prime Minister, in the Admiral's Cup, are all recorded and appropriately illustrated.

In expressing once more his grateful thanks to his many correspondents, the Editor would like especially to mention the press officers of the public corporations for their valuable assistance.

13 BEDFORD SQUARE, W.C.1.   Telephone: 01-636 4748
    October, 1971   Telegrams: " Whitmanack, London, W.C.1."

Note—" WHITAKER " for 1972 is published in three editions:

Library Edition, Leather Binding with 16 Coloured Maps, 1,220 pages—£3.00 *net.*
(SBN 85021 052 6)

Complete Edition, Red and Green Cloth Cover, 1,220 pages—£2.00 *net.*
(SBN 85021 050 X)

Shorter Edition, Orange Paper Cover, 692 pages—95p. *net.*
(SBN 85021 051 8)

© 1971 J. Whitaker & Sons, Ltd.

MADE AND PRINTED IN GREAT BRITAIN BY WILLIAM CLOWES & SONS, LIMITED
LONDON, BECCLES AND COLCHESTER

TABLE OF CONTENTS

	PAGES
Index	ix–xx, 1–81
Occurrences during Printing	82
Foreign Exchange Rates	83–84
Abbreviations in Common Use	85–88
THE CALENDAR YEAR 1972	89–137
ASTRONOMY	138–169
The Structure of the Universe	152–155
The Solar System	156–162
The Earth	163–164
Artificial Satellites and Space Probes	165–169
Royal Observatories	169
TIDAL CONSTANTS AND PREDICTIONS	170–184
CHRONOLOGICAL NOTES	184–193
Easy Reference Calendar	194–197
THE WORLD	198–203
The Largest Cities, etc	204–207
Rulers of Foreign Countries	208–209
THE UNITED KINGDOM:—	
Tables of Sovereigns, etc	210–213
Princes of Wales	214
The Royal Family, etc	214–219
Precedence in England	219
Royal Households, etc	220–225
The Peerage	226–256
The Privy Council	257–258
Orders of Chivalry	259–302
The Victoria Cross, George Cross	302–304
Decorations and Medals	305
The British Constitution	306
The House of Parliament	307–308
Officers of Parliament	309
Parliamentary Procedure, etc	310–311
Government by Party	312
Her Majesty's Ministry	313
Cabinet Ministers (1939–1971)	314–315
Parliamentary Parties	316
Votes Cast, 1955–1971	317
The House of Commons	318–348
Parliamentary Summary, 1970–1971	349–359
Public Acts of 1970–1971	359–361
Government and Public Offices	362–437
Commissions, etc	437–438
National Trusts, etc	438–440
Banks, Savings, etc	440–448
Law Courts and Offices	449–458
Defence	459–472
The Churches	473–491
National Insurance, etc	492–499
National Health Service	500–501
Education Directory	502–547
Events of 1970–1971	548–574
Illustrations	549–564
Obituary of 1970–1971	574–575
Centenaries of 1972 and 1973	576–577
Bank Holidays, etc	578
STATISTICS	579–621
Food Imports, etc	579
Agriculture	580–582
The Post Office	582
Fuel and Power, etc	583–584
World Trade; British Trade	585–587
Motor Vehicle Production	587–588
Transport:—	
Air Statistics; U.K. Airports	588–590
Roads	591
Railways	592–593
Shipping	594–598
Population and Vital Statistics	599–600
Causes of Death	601–602
Criminal Statistics	602–603
Building; New Towns; Immigration	604–605
Employment, Work Stoppages, etc	606–608
United Kingdom Finance	609–620
Taxation Reform	620–621

	PAGES
LOCAL GOVERNMENT	622–625
NATIONAL PARKS	626–627
The British Isles (Map)	628
THE KINGDOM OF ENGLAND	629–633
London	634–653
Houses Open to the Public	653–654
Museums and Art Galleries	655–657
Principal English Cities, etc	657–663
Municipal Directories	664–670
LOCAL PARTY REPRESENTATION	671–673
THE PRINCIPALITY OF WALES	674–676
THE KINGDOM OF SCOTLAND	677–686
Scottish Law Courts, etc	683–684
Scottish Municipal Directory	685–686
NEW TOWNS IN GREAT BRITAIN	687
NORTHERN IRELAND	688–691
ISLE OF MAN, CHANNEL ISLANDS	691–692

And in "Complete Edition" and "Library Edition"

THE BRITISH COMMONWEALTH OF NATIONS:—	
Area, Population, Government, etc.	693–694
CANADA	695–706
AUSTRALIA	707–729
NEW ZEALAND	730–735
OTHER INDEPENDENT STATES	735–775
ASSOCIATED STATES, COLONIES, ETC	775–790
COMMONWEALTH UNIVERSITIES	790–793
IRELAND (and Republic of Ireland)	794–797
THE UNITED STATES	798–812
THE UNITED NATIONS	812–816
FOREIGN COUNTRIES	817–976
EUROPEAN FREE TRADE ASSOCIATION	976
EUROPEAN COMMUNITY	977–981
INTERNATIONAL ORGANIZATIONS	981–982
PASSPORTS; CURRENCIES	983–988
RETROSPECT OF SPORT	989–1013
TOPICS OF THE DAY:—	
The Industrial Relations Act; Independent Radio Broadcasting; The British Library; Reorganization of Local Government	1014–1019
MORTGAGE INTEREST & REPAYMENTS	1020
LITERATURE OF THE YEAR	1021–1025
DRAMATIC SUMMARY	1025–1026
SCIENCE AND INVENTION	1027–1042
ARCHÆOLOGY IN 1970–71	1043–1047
EDUCATION IN THE UNITED KINGDOM	1048–1053
THE NOBEL PRIZES	1054
BRITISH ARCHITECTURE, 1970–71	1055–1059
THE QUEEN'S AWARD TO INDUSTRY	1059–1060
WEATHER	1061–1070
PUBLISHERS AND BOOK PRODUCTION	1071–1073
ANNUAL REFERENCE BOOKS	1074–1076
NEWSPAPERS, NEWS AGENCIES, ETC	1077–1086
CLUBS AND CLUB HOUSES	1087–1093
SOCIETIES AND INSTITUTIONS	1094–1121
EMPLOYERS' ASSOCIATIONS, ETC.	1122–1124
TRADE UNIONS	1125–1128
RESEARCH ASSOCIATIONS, INSTITUTES	1129–1131
CHARITABLE BEQUESTS OF THE YEAR	1132–1133
LIFE ASSURANCE; LIFE TABLES	1134–1149
FRIENDLY AND BUILDING SOCIETIES	1150–1157
UNIT TRUSTS	1158–1160
LEGAL NOTES	1161–1181
PROBATE OFFICES	1181–1182
SELECTIVE EMPLOYMENT TAX	1182–1184
INCOME TAX	1185–1191
STAMP DUTIES; PURCHASE TAX	1191–1195
POSTAL REGULATIONS	1196–1209
BRITISH MONETARY UNITS, ETC.	1210–1211
HALL MARKS	1212–1213
WEIGHTS AND MEASURES, ETC	1214–1220

PAGE

A.A., The.................1096
A.A.A...................1013
  Championships...........995
Aachen (Germany)..........866
Aarhus (Denmark)..........852
A.B.A....................1013
  Championships..........1010
Abbey National Building Society
                  1152
Abbreviations.............85–8
Aberavon, M.P.............325
Aberdare, 675; M.P........325
ABERDEEN, CITY OF....680–1, 685
  Bishops............484, 487
  County of City....(Note) 679
  Customs and Excise......377
  Lord Provost...........681
  Members of Parliament...325
  Population.........680, 685
  Research Establishments
              424, 432
  Sheriff................684
  University.........511, 512
Aberdeenshire..........679–80
  Members of Parliament...325
  Sheriff, etc............684
Abergavenny..............675
Aberration Constant......145
Abertillery, 675; M.P.....325
Aberystwyth..............675
  National Library........405
  University College....510, 512
Abha (Asir)..............935
Abidjan (Ivory Coast)..199, 892
Abingdon, 664; M.P.......325
Abney Park Cemetery......644
Abortions, Deaths from....601
Absolute Temperature....1216
Abu Dhabi (Trucial States)..950
ABYSSINIA (Ethiopia)..199, 855–6
Academic Awards, Council for
           512, 1051
Academies of Art.....1094, 1095
Accession Day........89, 94, 218
Accident Insurance Companies
            1145–8
ACCIDENTS (1970–71) 568–9
  Air 568, 569
  Deaths in...........591, 602
  Fires, Explosions 568, 569
  Investigation Branch (Trade)
             430
  Prevention Society......1115
  Railway............569, 592
  Road...................591
  Shipping...............569
  Statistics (N.H.S.).....1157
Accountancy (Training).....517
Accountants' Societies....1095
Accra (Ghana)........199, 742
  Bishops............482, 488
Accrington, 664; M.P......325
Acheson, Dean, Obit........82
Achill Island (Co. Mayo)...794
Aconcagua (Andes) 205, 206, 853
Acre (Measure)...........1214
Acres and Hectares.......1218
Acting, Schools of.........521
Acton, M.P...............325
Acts of Parliament........306
  How dated.............186
  "Local"................623

PAGE

Acts of Parliament—continued
  Public (1970–71)......359–61
  Queen's Printer.........426
Actuarial Training........517
Actuary, The Government...390
A.D.....................188
Addis Ababa (Ethiopia)..199, 856
Addison, Joseph, Centenary
           106, 577
ADDRESS, MODE OF:—
  Apostolic Delegate......487
  Archbishop (C. of E.)
        227, 473, 478
    (R.C.).................487
  Baron..................237
  Baroness (Own Right)....249
  Baronet................262
  Bishop (C. of E.).......237
    (R.C.).................487
  Cardinal...............487
  Countess (Own Right)....249
  Courtesy Title Holder....256
  Dame...................301
  Duke...................227
  Earl...................229
  Heir to Peerage........256
  Knight.................262
  Lord Lieutenant.....(Note) 631
  Malaysian Titleholders...758
  Marquess...............227
  Moderator, Gen. Assembly.484
  Pope, The..............487
  Privy Councillor....(Note) 258
  Rt. Hon. (Prefix)...(Note) 258
  Royal, Duke............226
  Viscount...............234
Adelaide (S. Australia)
     203, 714, 724
  Archbishop (R.C.).......490
  Bishop.................487
  Newspapers............1085
Adélie Land (Antarctic)....717
Adelphi, Strand...........643
Aden (Yemen P.D.R.)
     201, 973, 974
  British Embassy.........974
Adjutant General......459, 463
Administration (Education)...519
  Counties........622, 632, 675
  Staff College...........519
Administrators of Assize...453–4
Admirals.................461
  Pay, 467; Pensions 472
Admiral's Cup (1971)......571
  (Illus.)................561
Admirals of the Fleet 461, 467, 472
Admiralty Islands..........715
Admiralty Marshal's Office..452
  Registry...............452
Adoption of Children
     1161, 1163, 1169
  Registers.............1161
ADRIAN, THE LORD.130, 238, 1093
  Cambridge University....504
  Order of Merit.........260
Adult Education
    502–13; 517–37, 1051
  Authorities..........511–2
  Centres................513
  Colleges...............512
  Universities Council....511
  University Depts........512

PAGE

ADVENT SUNDAY..89; (Note) 189
  (1972)................134
  (1968–77).............189
Adventists, Seventh Day....486
Advice, Legal.....1173, 1174
Advocates, Faculty of......524
Advocates' Library.........405
Aegean Islands (Greece)....870
Aerodromes Civil 590
  Traffic Statistics.......588
Aeronautics:—
  Education..............517
  Museum................411
Aerospace Division (Dept. of
  Trade).................432
  Minister for........313, 428
Afars and Issas Territory.199, 864
A.F.C....................305
Affiliation Orders......603, 1168
Afforestation............389
AFGHANISTAN...........201, 817–8
  British Embassy........818
  Cabinet................817
  Currency...............984
  Embassy................817
  Government.............817
AFRICA (Continent)......198, 199
  Areas Below Sea Level....1128
  Countries..............199
  Events (1971).........573
  Highest Point..........206
  Population.............198
  R.C. Church.........488–9
Afternoon defined.........186
Agaña (Guam)............810
Agartala (Tripura, India)...753
Agency Shop Agreements
  (Indust. Relations Act) .1014
Agra (Uttar Pradesh)......752
Agreements (Stamp Duty)...1191
AGRICULTURAL:—
  Advisory Service........365
  Bureaux, Commonwealth
          368–9
  Colleges..........517, 1051
  Credits Department......404
  Economics Divisions...362–3
  Engineering (Educ.).....521
    Research Station......1131
  Estimates...........610–11
  Executive Chairmen......368
  Fertilizers (Imports)....586
  Holdings...............580
    Acts............1171, 1172
    by Product 580
  Institutes..............368
  Land Divisions........364–5
    Service..............364–5
  Price Guarantees....581, 610
  Production (U.K.).......580–1
  Research Council
     362, 368, 611, 1130
    Institutes..........1130–1
  Scientific Services (Scot.)...424
  Societies..........581, 1095
  Subsidies..............610
  Training Board..........535
  Vehicle Licences........591
  Workers (U.K.)........581–2
AGRICULTURE.............580–2
  Act (1970)............359
  Crop Acreage..........580

PAGE

AGRICULTURE—*continued*
Crops of 1971............582
Department, Scotland...423-4
Development Commission. 378
E.E.C. Progress..........979
Experimental Stations....365-6
Farming Income...........581
Farms (Number)..........580
Guaranteed Prices........581
Harvests................580
Livestock Statistics......580
Ministry of, *see below*
Numbers Employed in..581-2
Organization (U.N.)......814
Standard Man-days.......580
Value of Output.........581
Welsh Department.......367
**AGRICULTURE, FISHERIES AND
FOOD:—**
Minister of......313, 315, 362
Ministry..............362-8
Divisional/Regional Offices
367
Estimates...............610
Staff Numbers, etc......608
Under Secretaries.313, 362-4
Ahmednagar (Maharashtra)..751
Aides de Camp to H.M......220
AIR:—
Accidents..........568, 569
Aides de Camp..........220
British Airways Corporations
371-2
Chief Marshals..........465
Commodores, Pay, etc....468
Corporations, Strikes (1971)
570
Distances from London...1131
Divns. (Dept. of Trade)....432
Estimates...............612
Events (1970-71).........572
Force, *see* ROYAL
Freight Statistics.....588, 595
Industrial Training Board..535
Mail Services...1197-8, 1206-9
Marshals..............465-6
Pay, etc...............468
Members (Min. of Defence)..453
Mobility Forces (R.A.F.)...458
Parcel Rates...........1206-9
Passenger Statistics......588
Registration Board.......369
Safety Directorate........429
Secretary..........459, 465
Service Regiment.........465
Traffic.................588
Controllerate.........429
Training Colleges........517
Corps Cadets..........612
Transport:—
Licensing Board....369, 434
Statistics..........588-90
(U.S.A.)............808
U.K. Overseas Forces......458
Vice-Marshals..........466
Pay and Pensions....468, 472
Aircraft Carriers...........462
Types in Use..........589
Airdrie, 685; M.P.........330
Aireborough..............668
Air Force Cross...........305
Airlines, British..........589
Operating Statistics......588

PAGE

Airports:—
Authority, British........371
Irish Republic...........797
United Kingdom.........590
Trade Statistics......595
Traffic at...........588
Airways Letters...........1200
Ajman (Trucial State)......951
Akola (Maharashtra).......751
Alabama (State)..........800
Alabama Claim (1872)....576
Aland Archipelago (Finland)..857
Alaska (U.S.A.)...*(Map)* 799; 800
ALBANIA......202, 818, 984
Labour (Communist) Party.818
Albany Herald............369
Alberta...200, 695, 697, 700-1
London Office...........701
Albert Hall, Royal........650
Albert Medal............305
Albion, H.M.S..........462
Aldeburgh..............664
Aldergrove (Belfast) Airport..590
Aldermen.............622
City of London......637-8
G.L.C.............634-5
Alderney..............692
Aldershot, 664; M.P.......325
Aldridge-Brownhills.......668
Aleppo (Syria)...........948
Alexander Barracks, Pirbright
1056-7
Alexandria (U.A.R.)....204, 957
Pharos Lighthouse........202
Alfred the Great, King
210, 630, 663
Alfreton................668
Algae Culture Centre.......415
ALGERIA
199, 818-20; *(Map)* 819; 863
British Embassy......819-20
Cabinet............818-9
Embassy............819
Government.........819
Trade..............819
Algiers..............199, 819
Distance by Air........1131
Algol (Binary Star)........153
Minima Times (1972)
90, 94, 98, etc.; 138
ALIENS:—
Department (Home Office).396
Naturalization..........1163
Status of.............1164
Alimony (Legal Notes)....1166
Allahabad (Uttar Pradesh)..752
Alloa.................685
All Saints Day.........130, 225
All Saints (Birmingham), M.P.327
All Souls College, Oxford...502
All Souls Day............130
Alma Ata (Kazakhstan)..201, 966
Alnwick Castle...........653
Alps, The.......206, 888, 946
Alps, Southern (N.Z.).......731
Altrincham, 664; M.P.......325
Alva.................685
A.M. and P.M.........141, 186
Amazon River.....206, 830, 853
Ambassadors, British....818-976
Salaries, etc..........817
Ambassadors, Foreign (London)
817-975

PAGE

Ambassadors—*continued*
Precedence.............219
Amenity Beds (N.H.S.)......501
America (Continent)........198
Countries and Capitals.....200
See also CENTRAL, NORTH,
SOUTH
AMERICAN:—
Banks....441, 442, 443, 444
Embassy (London)......802-3
See also UNITED STATES
AMERY, RT. HON. J.:—
Govt. Hospitality Fund....390
Member of Parliament....328
Minister for Housing..313, 384
Offices held...........315
Privy Councillor.........257
Amindivi Islds. (India)......753
Amman (Jordan).....201, 896
Ampère (Measure).......1215
Amravati (Maharashtra).....751
Amsterdam (Netherlands)
202, 915
Distance by Air........1131
Amundsen, Roald, Centenary
114, 577
ANARE.................717
Anatolia (Turkey).........953
Ancient Monuments:—
Boards..............395
Report, 1970........1043-4
Commissions........394-5
Division (Environment Dept.)
386
Andaman Islands........752
Sea...............203
Andes, The......205, 821, 828,
837, 843, 853, 923, 969
Andhra Pradesh (State)....749
ANDORRA............202, 820
Andover..............664
Andromeda Nebula.....152, 155
Angel Falls (Venezuela).....207
Anglesey.....626, 674, 675, 676
Member of Parliament....325
Angling................1009
Anglo-Saxons.......630, 674
Angola (Port W. Africa)
199, 929, 984
Anguilla (West Indies)....787-8
Angular Measure.........1215
Angus................679-80
Members of Parliament...325
Sheriff..............684
Animal Health Division (Min.
of Agriculture).......365
Research Bureaux.......368
Animals Acts (1970-71)..360, 361
Animals, Gestation Periods..1124
Ankara (Turkey)...201, 202, 204,
954
Annaba (Algeria)..........819
Annan...............685
Annobon Island (Eq. Guinea).854
Annual Reference Books..1074-6
Annual Register, The......1074
Annuities, Immediate....1137-8
To Royal Family........224
Annunciation, The.........98
New Year's Day........186
Anomalistic Year.........145
Antananarivo (Madagascar)
199, 906
ANTARCTIC, THE..........717

Pages 693-1220 are omitted from the Shorter Edition

PICKFORDS
HEAVY HAULAGE LIMITED
GREAT CAMBRIDGE ROAD, ENFIELD, MIDDLESEX

BIRMINGHAM
Wood Lane, Erdington
021-373 5211/5

BIRTLEY
Durham Road, Barley Mow, Co. Durham
Birtley 2766

BRISTOL
128 Easton Rd., Bristol BS5 OEU   *Bristol* 557072

CARDIFF
358 Newport Road, CF3 7YL   *Cardiff* 34321

DERBY
Alfreton Road, DE2 4AS
Derby 46167 & 48026

EDINBURGH
8 Gylemuir Road, Corstorphine   031-334 2381/2

GLASGOW
2600 London Road, Mount Vernon, Glasgow E.2   041-778 5561/5

IPSWICH
Wright Road, Ipswich, Suffolk, IP3 9RW.
Ipswich 77323 & 75446

LEEDS
Gelderd Road, LS12 6DQ
Leeds 630471/3

LEICESTER
Wharf Way, Leicester Rd., Glen Parva, Leicester, LE2 9TB
Wigston 2317/8

LINCOLN
Ropewalk, Lincoln
Lincoln 20386/7

LIVERPOOL
199 Great Howard Street, Liverpool L5 9SJ
051-207 3151

LONDON
Coronation Rd,Park Royal, NW10 7PX 01-965 6171/3
2 Blaker Road, High Street, Stratford, E15 2NG
01-534 4590/9

LUTON
Kingsway, Luton, Beds., LU4 8EL   *Luton* 51483/5

MANCHESTER
Manchester Rd., Kearsley, Bolton BL4 8RL.
Farnworth 72821/72826

ORPINGTON
Leeson's Hill, St. Paul's Cray, Orpington, Kent
Orpington 31341 & 21916

PETERBOROUGH
Peterborough Road, Whittlesey. Nr. Peterborough, PE7 1PD
Whittlesey 2284 & 3302

PRESTON
Chorley Road, Walton-le-Dale, Lancs. PR5 4JP } *Preston* 53206/7

RUGBY
Market Street
Rugby 4801 & 4940

SHEFFIELD
Brightside Lane, S9 2SJ
Sheffield 41264/6

SOUTHAMPTON
Belvidere Wharf, Belvidere Rd, Southampton SO1 1QY
Southampton 21316/7

STAFFORD
Common Road
Stafford 52446/7

STOCKTON-ON-TEES
Church Road, Stockton-on-Tees, Teesside TS18 2LY
Stockton-on-Tees 64028/9

WALSALL
Pleck Rd.   *Walsall* 21404/5

Attached Company: WESTFIELD TRANSPORT LIMITED,
Westfield House, Southwell Road West, Mansfield, Notts.   Mansfield 26136

PAGE

ANTARCTIC, THE—*continued*
Australian...............717
New Zealand...........735
Norwegian.............919
Survey, British........415
Treaty (1959)..........717
Antigua (West Indies)
200, 694, 786–7
Antilles, Netherlands
200, 786, 915–6
Antiquities Museum, Scotland 414
Antisana, Mt...........205, 853
ANTRIM................691
High Sheriff...........691
Members of Parliament
325, 688
Anzac Day.............102
Apennines (Italy)........888
Apia (Samoa)........203, 775
Apogee and Perigee....90, 94, 98
Defined...............138
Apollo 14 Spacecraft......572
Apollo 15 Mission (1971)....572,
1027
Lunar Vehicle (*Illus.*)....556
Apostolic Delegates......487–90
Apothecaries, Soc. of....640, 1096
Hall..................646
Apothecaries' Weight......1215
Apparent Solar Time
138, 140, 141
Appeal Courts.....307, 449, 450
Lords Justices of.........449
Appleby................664
Approved School Orders....603
Aquatic Sports........1009–10
ARABIA..............201, 820
Area, etc..............820
Language and Literature...820
Seaports..............934
See also BAHRAIN; KUWAIT;
OMAN; QATAR; SAUDI
ARABIA; TRUCIAL STATES;
YEMEN REPUBLICS
Aral, Lake.............205
Ararat, Mt. (Armenia)...205, 968
Arbitration (Education).....517
Tribunals.............383–4
Arbitrators, Official.........458
Arbroath...............685
ARCHAEOLOGY IN 1970–71.1043–7
Aerial Photos. in.......1044
Degrees...............517
Societies.........1096, 1121–2
Archangel (U.S.S.R.)........964
ARCHBISHOPS......227, 473, 478
Commonwealth.......480–2
How addressed.......227, 487
In House of Lords.......307
Precedence............219
Resigned..............483
Roman Catholic......487–90
Archdeacons..........473–9
Archers, Royal Company of .223
Arches, Court of..........484
Architects' Registration Council
1096
Societies..............1096
ARCHITECTURE IN 1970–71.1055–9
Museum, 412; Periods of..577
Schools of...........517–8
Archives, The Queen's......220
Administration (Educ.)....525
City of London..........422

PAGE

Archives—*continued*
Hist. MSS. Commission..421–2
House of Lords.........421
National Register of......421
Parliamentary..........421
Public Records Advisory
Council............421
Offices.........421, 422
Scottish..............422
ARCTIC, THE:—
Bishop...............480
Ocean............203, 982
Ardrossan..............685
Ardwick (Manchester), M.P...339
Area Electricity Boards...381–2
Gas Boards............390
Area, Measures of.........1214
Conversion Table.....1218
ARGENTINA
200, 574, 820–3; (*Map*) 821
Agriculture...........821–2
British Embassy........822–3
Cabinet...............820
Communications........822
Currency..............984
Embassy............820–1
Government............821
Mineral Production.......822
Nobel Prizes..........1054
Production and Industry.821–2
Shipping Owned.........596
Trade.............585, 822
Argyll................679–80
Bishops..........484, 487
Members of Parliament...325
Sheriff, etc............684
Ariel (Satellite)..........158
Ariel 3 Satellite..........169
Aries, First Point of
91, 95, 99, etc.; 138, 140, 141, 150
Arizona (State)..........800
Arkansas (State)..........800
Armadale...............685
ARMAGH, COUNTY........691
Archbishops........485, 487
High Sheriff...........691
Members of Parliament
325, 688
Armagh, Urban District...691
Armed Forces (U.K.).....458–72
Pay, 467–71; Pensions....472
Quartering Changes......471
ARMENIA (U.S.S.R.)
201, 961, 968
Armistice Day............130
Armour School (R.A.C.)....521
Arms, College of.....369, 644
Kings of..........259–61, 369
of Scotland...........679
Armstrong-Jones, *see* SNOWDON
Armstrong, Louis, Obituary..574
ARMY, THE..............463–5
A.D.C.'s General........220
Air Corps.............465
Brit. Forces Broadcasting...578
Cadets (Nos.)..........612
Chief of Staff..........459
Clubs in London......1087–9
Combat Forces (1972).....458
Constitution.........464–5
Decorations and Medals..302–5
Director, W.R.A.C.......459
Divisions (1972).......464–5
Estimates.............612

PAGE

ARMY, THE—*continued*
Field Marshals...........463
General Officers........463–4
Infantry Depôts, Divisions
464–5
Institute of Education......521
Judge Advocate General....456
Medical College..........527
Military Education......520–1
Military Secretary........459
National Museum........652
Nursing Services (Director).459
Pay.................471
Officers (Number)........612
Pay:—
Cadets..............469
Officers.............467
Other Ranks..........469
Women's Services....470, 471
Pensions, etc...........472
Quartering Charges.......471
Ranks (and Equivalents)...1020
Record Offices........464–5
Reserves (Personnel)
465, 565, 612
School of Music.........529
Services..............465
Strength (Personnel).......612
T. & A.V.R............465
Training Schools......520–1
Victoria Cross Awards....302–4
Arnhem (Netherlands).......915
Arnold................668
Arno River (Italy).........888
ART:—
Colleges of.....510, 518, 1051
Commissions........369–70
Courtauld Institute of.....508
Diplomas and Degrees.....518
Galleries
647, 648, 649, 651, 655–7
Admission Charge......566
Cost...............611
National............370, 371
Queen's Gallery.......643
Standing Commission....409
Library, National........412
Royal Academies...1094, 1095
V. and A. Museum........412
Artificers (R.N.), Pay, etc....468
Artificial Satellites......165–9
Artillery, Royal..........464
Arts Council........1086, 1096
Cost to Taxpayers....1086
Arts, Royal Society of......1115
Arundel, 664; Bishop (R.C.)..487
Castle...............653
Member of Parliament....325
Ascension Day..89, 106, 189, 225
Island.............199, 785
Ascot Office............221
Races..............999
Ashanti (Ghana).........742
Ashes regained (1971)...571, 1000
M.C.C. Team (*Portrait*)....563
Ashfield (Notts.), M.P.......325
Ashford, 668; M.P.........325
Ashington..............668
Ashkhabad (Turkmenistan)
201, 968
Ashmolean Museum.......657
Keeper..............502
Aston-in-Makerfield.......668

PAGE

Ashton under Lyne..........664
  Member of Parliament.....326
Ash Wednesday
        89, 188; (*Note*) 189
  (1972)..................94
  (1968–77)..............189
  Red Letter Day.........225
ASIA (Continent).......198, 201
  Area below Sea Level....1128
  Countries and Capitals....201
  Highest Point............206
  Population...............198
  Roman Catholic Church
              489–90
  S.E.A.T.O..............981–2
  Standard Time...........143
Asir (Saudi Arabia).........935
Asmara (Eritrea)...........856
ASSAM (India).............749
Assault Ships (R.N.).........462
Assaults (Criminal Statistics)..602
Assay Office Marks......1212–3
Assizes (Eng. & Wales), *see*
  Crown Courts
Associated Board (Music).....529
Associated (Commonwealth)
  States..........694, 786–90
Association Football........1005
  Leagues 1005, 1013
Association of Commonwealth
  Universities.............511
ASSURANCE AND INSURANCE
              1134–48
Assurance, Endowment...1141–3
  Industrial, Commissioner...390
Assyria (Iraq)..............884
Asteroids..................159
Aston, Bishop of...........474
  Member of Parliament.....327
Aston in Birmingham, Uni-
  versity of...............510
Astor of Hever, Lord, Obit...574
Astronomers Royal.....146, 169
ASTRONOMICAL SECTION ..90–169
  Introductory Notes.....138–42
  Constants...............145
  Ephemeris..............1074
  Museum................412
  Observatories............169
  Phenomena (1972)
       90, 94, 98; 148–9
  Twilight.....91, 95, 99; 139
Astronomy, Degrees in.....518
  Notes............1030, 1039
  Societies..............1096
Astrophysical Measurements
             152–3
Astrophysics Degrees.......518
Asuncion (Paraguay) 200, 922
Aswan Dam (U.A.R.)...573, 956
Athenaeum Club (London)..1087
Athens (Greece)....202, 204, 871
  British School...........1098
  Distance by Air..........1131
Atherton (Lancs.)...........668
ATHLETICS...............989–97
  A.A.A. Championships....995
  Associations............1013
  English Schools..........996
  European Championships
    (1971) 994
  Indoor Championships....994
  G.B. *v.* France (1971).....994–5
  v. G.D.R. (1971).........994

PAGE

ATHLETICS—*continued*
  Indoor Championships.....996
  International Matches....994–5
  Junior Championships....996
  Olympic Records.........989
  Oxford v. Cambridge.996, 997
  Records..............989–93
    National...............993
    U.K. (All-comers).....992–3
    Women's...989, 991, 992–3
    World................990–1
ATHLONE, H.R.H. COUNTESS OF
              216
  Birthday...............216
  Dame Grand Cross.......301
  Victoria and Albert Order..261
Atlanta (U.S.A.)...........204
Atlantic Ocean.............203
  Time..................143
Atlas Mountains (Morocco)..911
Atmosphere (Measure)......584
ATOMIC ENERGY:—
  Agency, International.....814
  Authority..............371
  Act (1971)..............360
  Community (Euratom)....981
  Divn. (Dept. of Trade)....431
Atomic Time..............142
Attendance Allowances (Soc.
  Security)...............498
Attercliffe (Sheffield), M.P....344
Attica Prison Riot, 1971......573
ATTORNEY GENERAL......313, 405
  of Duchy of Cornwall....378
  of Duchy of Lancaster....378
  of Northern Ireland.......689
Auckland (Durham), Arch-
  deacon...............478
Auckland (New Zealand)....734
  Archbishop (R.C.)........490
  Bishop (C. of E.)........481
Audit Department..........387
  Overseas..............416
Auditor General...........387
Auditors, Local Govt........385
Augsburg (Germany)........866
Aurora Australis......161, 917
  Borealis.........161, 917
AUSTRALIA, COMMONWEALTH
  OF 203,
    693, 707–29 (*Map*) 708
  Air Mail Rates.....1197, 1206
    Passengers to...........588
  Antarctic...............717
  Archbishops..........481, 490
  Area and Population
         203, 707, 708
  Army.................710–11
  Banks.........441, 443, 712
  Births, Deaths, etc.........707
  Bishops.............481, 490
  Boys' Schools..........542–3
  British High Commission
             709–10
  British Immigrants........605
  Broadcasting............714
  Butter Production........712
  Cabinet................709
  Capital Territory .203, 707, 714
  Census (1961–66)........707
  Chief Justice............710
  Civil Aviation...........714
  Climate................709
  Communications.........714

PAGE

AUSTRALIA, COMMONWEALTH
  OF—*continued*
  Currency...........711, 984
  Day.................89, 90
  Defence..............710–11
  Emigrants to U.K........605
  Exchange Rate.......83, 611
  Exports..............713–4
  Finance................711
  Flag..................709
  Food Exports to U.K....713–4
  Gold Production.........712
  Government............709
  Governor General........709
  High Commissioners...709–10
  Highest Point...........206
  House (London)......643, 709
  House of Representatives ..710
  Immigration............707
  Imports and Exports....713–4
  Judicature..............710
  Lawn Tennis...........1007
  Livestock Statistics.......712
  Manufactures...........712
  M.C.C. Tour (1970–71)..571,
              1000
  Methodists in...........707
  Minerals...........709, 712
  Motor Vehicles..........714
  National Day............709
    Welfare Fund 711, 712
  Natural Gas Deposits......709
  Navy..................710
  Newspapers...........1085
  Nobel Prizes...........1054
  Northern Territory......714–5
  Oilfields................709
  Parcel Post to..........1206
  Parliament.............710
  Physical Features......708–9
  Population.........203, 707
  Posts and Telegraphs......714
  Prime Minister.......572, 709
  Production.............712
  Public Debt.............711
  R.A.A.F...............711
  Races and Religions......707
  Railways...............714
  R.C. Church........490, 707
  Repatriation Benefits...711–2
  Revenue and Expenditure..711
  Rivers...............708–9
  Seaports (Traffic)........714
  Senate................710
  Shipbuilding............597
  Shipping...............714
  Social Welfare..........711
  Standard Time..........143
  State Finance...........712
  States of............717–29
  Telegram Rates to.......1206
  Telephone Rates to......1205
  Television Stations.......714
  Territories...........714–7
  Test Matches (1970–71) ..571,
              1000
    English Team (*Portrait*) ..563
  Trade............585, 713–4
    Commissioners.........729
    Unions..............713
    with U.K...........713–4
  Trusteeships............694
  U.K. Immigrants........605
  Universities............790

Pages 693–1220 *are omitted from the* Shorter Edition

PAGE

AUSTRALIA, COMMONWEALTH
OF—*continued*
Victoria Cross Awards...302–4
Wheat Production.......712
Wool Production........712
Australian Alps.........726
Australopithecus.........185
AUSTRIA...202, 823–4; (*Map*) 823
British Embassy.........826
Currency...........824, 984
Embassy.............823
Exchange Rate......83, 824
Expectation of Life......1149
Finance and Trade...585, 824
Government..........823–4
Nobel Prizes...........1054
Revaluation, 1971........574
Telephone Rates to......1205
Automobile Association....1096
Autumn Defined........187–8
Equinox.......89, 122, 187
Avebury (Wilts.)....630, 653
See also AIR; CIVIL AVIATION
Average Earnings (U.K.)....617
Avoirdupois Weight......1215
AVON, EARL OF........229
Birthday.............110
Chancellor, B'ham Univ....509
Knight of the Garter......259
Offices held (Eden)....308, 314
Portrait..............552
Privy Councillor........257
Trinity House..........435
Aycliffe (New Town)....605, 687
Aylesbury.............664
Member of Parliament....326
Ayr 685; M.P............326
Ayrshire............679–80
Members of Parliament....326
Sheriff, etc............684
Azerbaidjan (U.S.S.R.)
201, 961, 967
Aznam, El (Algeria).......819
Azores Islands (Portuguese)...929

BAALBEK (LEBANON)........902
Babel, Tower of (Iraq).....884
Babies' Birth Weights.....1031
Heartbeat Monitors.....1033
Babylon...............884
Hanging Gardens........202
Bacon, Sir Edmund:—
Knight of the Garter.....259
Lord Lieutenant........632
Premier Baronet........264
Bacup...............664
Baden-Wurttemberg.......866
Badminton, 1007–8; School..544
Baffin Bay............982
Baffin Land............697
Baghdad (Iraq)...201, 204, 884
Distance by Air........1131
Pact...............982
BAHAMAS (West Indies)
200, 775–6, 786
Bishop (R.C.)..........488
Currency............984
Finance and Trade.......776
Government...........776
Summer Time..........142
BAHRAIN ISLANDS....201, 824–5
Council of State........824
Currency............984
Baikal, Lake.......205, 965

PAGE

Baku (Azerbaidjan).....201, 967
Bala, Lake (Wales).........674
Balboa Heights......200, 811
Balearic Islands (Spain).....941
Balkhash, Lake.........205
Ballarat (Victoria).......727
Ballet School, Royal......520
Balliol College, Oxford....502
Ballot Act (1872).........576
Ballymena............691
Baltic Exchange......643, 1096
Baltic Sea, Area, etc.......203
Baltimore (Maryland)....204, 800
Bamako (Mali)......199, 907
Banbury, 664; M.P........326
Banff...............685
Banffshire...........679–80
Member of Parliament....326
Sheriff, etc............684
Bangalore (Mysore)........751
Bangkok (Thailand) 201, 204, 949
Distance by Air........1131
Bangla Desh...........765
Bangor..............675
Bishop of............480
Colleges of Education....532
Party Representation....673
N. Wales Univ. College
510, 512
Theological Colleges..536, 537
Bangor (Co. Down).......691
Bangui (Central African
Republic)........199, 836
Bankers' Clearing House...440–1
Bank Holidays (U.K.).(*Notes*) 90,
98, 102, 106, 114, 118; 190
(1972–74).........578, 663
Postal Arrangements......1204
Banking (Education)........518
Bank Notes..........1210–11
Circulation (1971).......1210
New Series...........1210
Scottish, etc..........1211
BANK OF ENGLAND.....440, 643
Note Issue...........440
Bank of New Zealand......442
of Scotland.........442
Bank Rate.......566, 567, 615
Bankruptcy:—
Cases (1970).........1160
Dept, (Dept. of Trade)....430
Dept. (High Court)......451
Official Receivers......451
BANKS.........440–6, 448
Clearing Banks
442, 443, 444, 445, 446
Committee...........446
Hours of opening.......441
Inter-Bank Computer
Bureau...........440
Lending Freed (1971)....567
Savings Banks........448
Banks Islds. (N. Hebrides)....781
Bannockburn, Battle of....678
Banns, Publication of..1174, 1176
Banstead............668
BAOR...............458
Baptist Central Church.....491
Church.............486
Colleges............537
BARBADOS (W. Indies)
200, 693, 735–6
Bishop..............481

PAGE

BARBADOS (W. Indies)—*continued*
Distance by Air.........1131
High Commissions.......735
Trade..............736
Commissioner.........729
BARBER, RT. HON. A.P.L.:—
Chancellor of the Exchequer
313, 314, 432
Member of Parliament....325
Offices Held........314, 315
Privy Councillor........257
Barbers' Hall (London)....646
Barbuda (Antigua).....200, 787
Barcelona (Spain)....204, 941
Distance by Air........1131
Barclays Bank.........442
Bar Council..........1096
Bareilly (Uttar Pradesh)....752
Barent's Sea..........982
Bargemaster, The Queen's...221
Bari (Italy).......890, 891
Barking.............642
Bishop of (Chelmsford)....474
Member of Parliament....326
Party Strengths........671
Barkston Ash, M.P........326
Barley Harvests......580, 582
Prices.............581
Barnardo's Homes.......1097
Barnes Bridge.........643
Barnet, 642; M.P.........326
Party Strengths........671
Penny Rate..........624
Barnsley, 664; M.P........326
Barnstaple............664
Archdeacon (Exeter)....475
Baron, Premier (Mowbray)...245
do. Irish (Kingsale).....245
do. Scottish (Forbes)....241
Baronesses:—
How addressed.........249
in Own Right.......249–50
Life Peeresses.........252
Baronet, Premier (Bacon)...264
do. Gt. Britain (Dashwood)
271
do. Irish (Coote).......270
Baronetcies Extinct (1970–71).300
BARONETS...........262–300
Badge.............262
Council............1097
How addressed........262
Precedence......219, 682
BARONS...........237–49
By Courtesy.........256
Coronets...........237
How addressed........237
Life Peers.........250–2
Minors............226
Number of...........226
Precedence......219, 682
Barons Court, M.P........326
Barony, Premier (De Ros)...250
Barra Island..........677
Barranquilla (Colombia)....844
Barrhead............685
Barrow in Furness.......664
Member of Parliament....326
Barry, 675 M.P...........326
Basildon.......605, 668, 687
Basingstoke...........664
Archdeacon (Winchester)..473
Member of Parliament.....326

Pages 693–1220 are omitted from the Shorter Edition

PAGE

Basle (Switzerland).........947
  Distance by Air.........1131
Basrah (Iraq)..............884
Basseterre (St. Kitts).....200, 787
Bassetlaw, M.P.............326
Bass Strait................708
Bastia (Corsica)...........863
Bata (Rio Muni)............854
Bath and Wells, Bishop .237, 473
Bath, City of..............664
  Member of Parliament.....326
  Royal School.............544
  University...............510
Bathgate...................685
Bath, Order of the.........259
    King of Arms...........259
    Knights...........262–300
    Women admitted (1970)..548
Bathurst (Gambia)......199, 741
Batinah (Oman).............919
Batley, 664; M.P...........326
Battersea Bridge...........643
  Dogs Home...............1102
  Members of Parliament....326
Batting Averages....1000, 1003
Battle of Britain, 864; Day...122
Baudouin, King.......208, 825
  Knight of the Garter.....259
Bavaria (Germany)..........866
B.B.C......................371
  Home Services (Cost) (*Note*) 610
  Time Signals.............142
B.C. and A.D...............188
B.E.A......................589
  Loans Outstanding........614
  Route Distances.........1131
Beardsley, Aubrey, Centenary
                       118, 577
Bearsden...................685
Beating the Bounds.........189
BEAUFORT, DUKE OF..........227
  Knight of the Garter.....259
  Lord Lieut., Gloucestershire 632
  Master of the Horse......220
  Privy Councillor.........257
  Royal Victorian Chain....260
Beaufort Scale............1211
Beaumaris..................675
Bebington, 664; M.P........326
Beccles....................664
Bechuanaland, *see* BOTSWANA
Beckenham, M.P.............326
Becket, Thomas......189, 658
Bede College, Durham.......507
BEDFORD....................664
  Bishop of (St. Albans)...477
  College (London Univ.)...508
  Colleges of Education....531
  Member of Parliament.....326
Bedfordshire............631–3
  Members of Parliament....326
Bedlingtonshire............668
Bedouin Race (U.A.R.)....955
Bedwellty, 675; M.P........327
Bedworth...................668
" Beehive " Star Cluster...155
Beer, Public Spending on...618
Beersheba (Israel).........887
Beeston and Stapleford.....669
Behring Strait.............982
Beirut (Lebabon)......201, 902
  Distance by Air.........1131
BELFAST, CITY OF...202, 690, 691
  Airport.................590

BELFAST, CITY OF—*continued*
  Clubs...................1092
  High Sheriff.............691
  Inn of Court.............524
  Local Govt. Electors.....625
  Lord Lieutenant..........691
  Lord Mayor...............690
  Members of Parliament
                       327, 688
  Newspapers........1077, 1085
  Passport Office..........983
  Population...............690
  Queen's University ..511, 512
  Recorder.................690
  Riots (1970–71).......567–8
    (*Illus.*).............553
  Schools..................541
  Shipping Statistics......595
  Stock Exchange..........1053
  Sunrise Times.93, 97, 101, etc.
  University...............511
  Weather Information.....1086
BELGIUM
      202, 825–8; (*Map*) 826; 863
  Air Passengers to........588
  British Embassy..........828
  Cabinet................825–6
  Canals...................827
  Communications..........827
  Currency..........827, 984
  Education................827
  Embassy..................826
  European Community..977–81
  Exchange Rate............827
  Finance..................827
  Government...............826
  King of the Belgians ..208, 825
  Language and Literature..827
  Nobel Prizes.......827, 1054
  Production.............826–7
  Shipbuilding.............597
  Shipping.................596
  Telephone Rates to.....1205
  Trade...............585, 827
  Visitors Passports to....983
Belgrade (Yugoslavia)..202, 976
Belize (Brit. Honduras) 777
Belmopan (Brit. Honduras)
                       200, 777
Belorussia.......202, 961, 966
Belper, M.P................327
Benares (Uttar Pradesh)....752
Bendigo (Australia)........727
Benefices Act Court........458
Benelux Countries..825–8, 913–6
Benenden School............544
Benevolent Societies..1095–1120
Benfleet...................669
BENGAL, W. (India).........752
Benghazi (Libya)...........904
Ben Nevis...........206, 677
Bentley with Arksey........669
Bentley, W.O., Obituary....574
Bergamo (Italy)............891
Bergen (Norway)............919
Berkshire...............631–3
BERLIN...........202, 204, 866
  Brigade (British)........458
  British Commandant.......869
  Distance by Air.........1131
  Governing Mayor..........867
Bermondsey, M.P............327
BERMUDA...........200, 776–7
  Currency.................984

BERMUDA—*continued*
  Distance by Air.........1131
  Finance and Trade........777
Bernal, Prof. J. D., Obit....574
Berne (Switzerland)....202, 947
Berwick on Tweed...........664
  Member of Parliament.....327
Berwickshire.............679–80
  Member of Parliament.....327
  Sheriff..................684
Bessarabia.................961
Betelgeuse (Star)..........152
Beth Din...................486
Bethnal Green, M.P.........327
    Museum.................412
Betjeman, Sir John.........265
  Hist. Monuments Commission
                         394
Betting, Gaming Offences....602
Beverley...................664
Bewdley....................664
Bexhill....................664
Bexley, 642; M.P...........327
  Party Strengths..........671
Bhopal (Madhya Pradesh)....750
Bhubaneswar (Orissa).......751
Bhutan................201, 828
" Big Ben "........308, 645
Biggin Hill Aerodrome......590
Bihar (State).........749–50
Bilbao (Spain).............941
Billericay, M.P............327
Billiards (1970–71).......1011
Billion (U.K. and U.S.A.)..1216
Bill of Rights........311, 421
Bills, Parliamentary..306, 307
  (1970–71)............349–59
Bilston, M.P...............327
Binary Stars...............153
Bingley....................669
Biographies of 1970–71....1021
Biological Research Board..408
Biology (Education)........519
Birds, Close Season.......1213
Birkbeck College...........508
Birkenhead.................664
  Bishop (Chester)........479
  Member of Parliament.....327
Birkenhead, Earl of, Centenary
                       114, 577
BIRMINGHAM........657–8, 664
  Airport.................590
  Archaeological Society..1121
  Archbishop (R.C.)........487
  Bishop of...........237, 474
  City Polytechnic.........534
  Clubs..................1090
  Colleges of Education....532
  Customs and Excise.......377
  Hall Marks.............1213
  London Rail Fare........593
  Lord Mayor..............658
  Members of Parliament....327
  Motorways...............591
  Museums.................655
  Newspapers.............1077
  Party Strengths.........671
  Penny Rate..............624
  Polytechnic Music School..529
  Population..........657, 664
  Probate Registry.......1181
  Stipendiary........455, 658
  Sunrise Times 93, 97, 101, etc.
  Teaching Hospitals......527

BIRMINGHAM—*continued*
Town Clerk..............658
Universities.....509, 510, 512
Weather (Monthly)....1065-7
Birth Abroad or at Sea.....1161
Birth Certificates..........1162
BIRTHDAYS:—
Admirals of the Fleet......461
Field Marshals............463
Foreign Rulers.......208-9
Marshals of the R.A.F....465
Royal Family........89, 225
Various........90, 94, 98, etc.
Birth Rate (United Kingdom) 600
Births:—
Notable (1872).............577
Registered (1960-70).....600
Registrar-General.........418
N. Ireland................689
Scotland.................426
Registration of........1161-2
Birth Weights (Sci. Notes)...1031
Bishop Auckland..........669
Member of Parliament......327
Bishopbriggs...............685
BISHOPS (C. of E.)....237, 473-82
Abroad................480-2
House of................480
How addressed...........237
in House of Lords..226, 237, 307
Missionary................482
Precedence................219
Resigned.................483
Suffragan...........473-82
Bishops (R.C.)............487
How addressed...........487
Bishops (Scottish)........484
(Welsh)..................480
Bishops Stortford.........669
Bisley, 1013; Results (1971)..1010
Bismarck Archipelago.......715
Bissau (Port. Guinea)...199, 929
Bissextile Year.......186, 192
Blackburn................664
Bishop...........237, 478
Member of Parliament....327
Blackfriars Bridge, London...643
Blackheath (London)......650
Blackley (Manchester), M.P...339
Blackpool.................664
Airport.................590
Members of Parliament..327-8
Black Rod Usher...221, 259, 309
N. Ireland..............688
Blackwall Tunnels......648-9
Blackwood Class Frigates...462
Blairgowrie and Rattray...685
Blandford Forum..........664
Blantyre (Malawi)..........757
Blaydon, 669; M.P...........328
Blenheim Palace...........653
Bletchley.................669
Blida (Algeria)...........819
BLIND:—
Associations............1097
Income Tax Allowances...1189
Literature (Postage)......1201
Pensions.................498
Teachers' Training........534
Wills in Braille..........1179
Wireless Licences for....1204
Bliss, Sir Arthur..........265
Companion of Honour....261

Bliss, Sir Arthur—*continued*
Master of the Queen's Music
..........................221
Portrait.................559
Bloemfontein (O.F.S.)......938
Blood Research Units......407
Blue Nile River.......855, 942
Blue Rod Usher..........260
Blues and Royals..........464
Blum, Leon, Centenary......577
Blundeston Prison (Governor)
..........................398
Blyth, 664; M.P..........328
B.O.A.C.................589
Loans Outstanding......614
Route Distances........1131
Boadicea..................630
Statue of.........643, 647
Board, Lillian, Obituary....574
Board of Customs and Excise
.......................376-8
Board of Green Cloth......222
Board of Inland Revenue
....................410-4, 610
Board of Referees, Income
Tax Acts.................458
Board of Trade, President
...............313, 314, 428
Boat Race, The....1010, 1011
Boccaccio..................891
Bochum (Germany)........866
Bodleian Library.....502, 1073
Bodmin...................664
Archdeacon (Truro)......478
Member of Parliament....328
Body Temperature........1216
Bognor Regis.............669
Bogotá (Colombia).200, 204, 846
Boiling Point.............1214
Boldon....................669
BOLIVIA...200, 828-9; (*Map*) 830
British Embassy...........829
Communications........828-9
Currency........829, 984
Embassy..................828
Production...............828
Bologna (Italy).......890, 891
Bolsover, M.P..............328
Bolton...................664
Members of Parliament...328
Bolts, " Tell-Torq " (Sci. Notes)
.........................1040
BOMBAY............204, 751
Archbishop (R.C.)......489
Distance by Air.......1131
University..............791
Bonallack, M. F..........1006
Portrait.................562
Bône (Algeria) *see* Annaba
Bo'ness..................685
Bonn (W. Germany)
.............202, 866, 868
Bonnyrig and Lasswade...685
BOOK:—
Exports................1072
League, National.......1110
Post.....................1196
Production..............1072
Publishers............1072-2
Books:—
Educational..........1022-3
Micro (Science Notes)....1036
of 1970-71..........1021-5
Public Spending on......618

BOOKS—*continued*
Published in 1970.......1073
Published in 1872........576
Registration of.........1073
Sizes of................1217
Bookseller, The......1073, 1081
Booksellers' Associations...1097
Boot and Shoe:—
Consumer Expenditure...618
Exports and Imports......587
Bootle, 664; M.P..........328
Bordeaux (France).........863
Border, Penrith and, M.P...342
Borneo, *see* Kalimantan
Bornholm Island (Denmark)..851
BOROUGHS (E. & W.) 664-8, 675
Average Rates...........624
Borough Councils.......622
County Boroughs
.............622, 664-8, 675
Electors (Number).......622
Incorporation Dates...664-8
London...................642
Number of..............622
Parliamentary.........325-48
Party Strengths......671-3
Boroughs (N. Ireland).....691
Boroughs (Wales).........675
Borstal Governors.....398-9
Bosphorus (Turkey).......953
Boston (Lincolnshire).....664
Member of Parliament....336
Boston (Massachusetts)..204, 800
Bosworth, M.P............328
Botanic Gardens, Kew
...............367-8, 649
Botany Dept. (Natural History
Museum).............411
Bothwell, M.P............328
BOTSWANA......199, 693, 736-7
Cabinet.................736
Trade...................737
High Commissions......736
Tribal Composition......736
Boult, Sir Adrian, Birthday..102
Companion of Honour...265
Boundary Commission (Local
Government)...........1018
Bounty, The Royal........224
Bournemouth.............664
Airport.................590
London Rail Fare........593
Members of Parliament...328
Weather (Monthly)....1065-7
Bowes Museum............655
Bowling (Bowls)..........1011
(Cricket)............1000-3
Averages (1971)...1000, 1003
Bow Street Court..........455
Boxing (1971) 1010-11
Posts..................1204
Boxing Day (*Note*)........134
Box Railway Tunnel......207
Boycott, G. (*Portrait*).....563
Boyd-Orr, Lord, Obituary...574
Boy Scouts, *see* Scouts Association
Boys:—
National Insurance Contribu-
tions.................499
Boys' Brigade...........1097
Boys' Clubs.............1098
Schools............537-44
Overseas............542-4
Brackley.................664

Pages 693–1220 are omitted from the Shorter Edition

PAGE

Bracknell (New Town)..605, 687
Bradbury, Lord, Centenary...577
Braddock, Mrs. E. M., Obit..574
BRADFORD, CITY OF.....658, 664
  Bishop of................478
  Building Societies........1153
  Lord Mayor..............658
  Members of Parliament...328
  Museums................655
  Party Strengths...........671
  Population............658, 664
  University of.........510, 513
Bradwell, Bishop of (Chelmsford)................474
Bragg, Sir Lawrence, Obit...574
Brahmaputra River..........206
Braille, Wills in............1179
Braintree and Bocking......669
Branderburgh..............686
Brandt, Hr. Willy...........866
Brasenose College, Oxford...502
Brasilia (Brazil).........200, 831
Brasov (Rumania)...........932
Bratislava (Czechoslovakia)..850
BRAZIL...200, 829-32; (Map) 830
  British Embassy.........831-2
  Capital..................831
  Communications.........831
  Currency................984
  Embassy................829
  Exchange Rate......83, 831
  Finance and Trade....585, 831
  Government.............830
  Language and Literature..831
  Production............830-1
  Shipbuilding............597
  Shipping...............596
Brazzaville (Congo)....199, 844
Bread, Expenditure on.....618
Breakspear, Nicholas.......209
Brechin..................685
  Bishop................484
Brechou (C.I.).............692
Brecknockshire............675
Brecon................675, 676
  Beacons (National Park)..626
  Bishop of................480
  Member of Parliament...328
Bredbury and Romiley......669
Breeders, Leading..........998
Bremen (Germany)..........866
  Land...................866
Brent....................642
  Party Strengths...........671
  Penny Rate..............624
Brentford, M.P............328
Brentwood...............669
  Bishop (R.C.)............487
Brescia (Italy).............891
Brest (France)............863
Brethren, The.............486
Brewing Courses..........519
Brezhnev, L. I.............959
Bridge of Allan............685
BRIDGES, FAMOUS..........206
  in London..............643
Bridgeton, M.P............334
Bridgetown (Barbados)..200, 735
Bridgwater, 664; M.P.......328
Bridlington, 664; M.P.......328
Bridport..................664
Brierley Hill, M.P..........328
Brigade of Gurkhas........465
Brigadiers, Pay, etc........467

PAGE

Brigg, M.P................328
Brighouse, 664; M.P........328
Brighton.................664
  London Rail Fare........593
  Marina Project..........568
  Members of Parliament...328
  Museums................655
  Polytechnic.............534
Brightside (Sheffield), M.P...344
Brisbane (Queensland)
          203, 714, 722
  Archbishops........481, 490
  Distance by Air.........1131
BRISTOL, CITY OF..........658
  Airport.................590
  Bishop of...........237, 474
  Clubs..................1090
  Colleges of Education....532
  Customs and Excise......377
  London Rail Fare........593
  Lord Mayor............658
  Members of Parliament...328
  Museums................655
  Party Strengths...........671
  Penny Rate.............624
  Polytechnic.............535
  Population............658, 664
  Probate Registry........1181
  Rateable Value..........664
  Schools of Architecture..518
  Sheriff.................658
  Shipping...............595
  Sunrise Times..93, 97, 101, etc.
  Teaching Hospitals......527
  Theological Colleges..536, 537
  Tide Tables...........172-83
  University.........509, 512
Britannia, H.M.S..........462
Britannia R.N. College......520
BRITISH ACADEMY.........1098
British Airports Authority
    371, 590, 613, 614
British Airways Corporations
    371-2, 589
  Route Distances......1131
British Antarctic Survey.....415
British Archæology (1970-71)
    1043-7
British Architecture, New 1055-9
British Army of the Rhine...458
British Association........1098
  Meeting (1971).....1032-3
British Astronomical Association................138
British Book Production....1072
British Books in Print......1074
British Broadcasting Corporation.................371
British Car Production..587, 588
British Citizenship......1162-4
British Columbia
    200, 695, 697, 701-2
  Agent-General..........701
  Government.............701
  Production, etc........701-2
  Province (C. of E.).......480
  Royal Visit (1971)........548
    (*Illus.*)...............549
BRITISH COMMONWEALTH OF
  NATIONS...........693-793
Air Mail Services
    1197-8, 1206-9
Area and Population......693

PAGE

BRITISH COMMONWEALTH OF
  NATIONS—*continued*
Associated States..694, 786-90
Citizenship........693, 1162-4
Colonial Development.....694
Colonies and Protectorates
    775-86
Commercial Representatives
    729
Currencies.............984-8
Defence................694
Emigration Statistics......605
Events in 1970-71....... 572
Finance................694
Former Members........694
Gas Corporation (1973)...567
Government.............693
Immigration from........605
Judicature............693-4
Member Countries.......693
Nationality.............693
Population.............693
Postage Rates..........1196
Prime Ministers' Meetings..693
Republics (List).........693
R.C. Church.........487-90
Shipbuilding............597
Shipping 595, 596
States........693-775; 785-90
Statute of Westminster....693
Telephone Rates........1205
Trade Commissioners....729
Trusteeships............694
Universities...........790-3
BRITISH CONSTITUTION, THE:—
  Cabinet...........306, 313
  Commission on.........437
  Councillors of State......306
  Crown.................306
  Executive..............306
  Leader of the Opposition..306
  Legislature........306-61
  Local Government....622-5
  Parliament.........306-61
  Party Government.......312
  Prime Minister...306, 313, 314
  Proceedings against Crown
    1164
British Council....438, 610, 1098
  Representatives Abroad
    818-976
British Embassies Abroad.818-976
British Empire Medal......305
British Empire Order......261
  Dames..............301-2
  Knights............262-300
British European Airways...371
  Loans Outstanding....613
British Forces Broadcasting
  Service.................578
BRITISH HONDURAS....200, 777-8
  Currency...............984
  Finance and Trade.......777
  Government.............778
British Industry, Confederation of................1124
British Kings and Queens....212
British Legion, Royal......1098
  Scotland..............1098
British Library, The.....565-6,
    1017-18
British Lions in N.Z. (1971)...571
  Team Portrait...........564
British Medical Association..1098

Pages 693–1220 are omitted from the Shorter Edition

British Export Board 440

PAGE

British Monetary Units..1210–11
BRITISH MUSEUM....409–10, 1017
  Copyright Library......1073
  Cost (1971–72)......409, 611
  Natural History .410–11, 611
  Staff Numbers, etc.....608
British National Export
  Council............439–40
British Nationality......1162–4
BRITISH OVERSEAS AIRWAYS

371–2
  Boeing Dispute........570
  Finance............589
  Loans Outstanding.....613
British Passports...........983
  Postgraduate Medical Federa-
  tion.................527
British Railways Board
      372, 571, 592
  Loans Outstanding.....614
  See also RAILWAY
British Red Cross.........1098
British Savings Bonds ...353, 447
British Schools Abroad.....1098
British Solomon Islands
      203, 782–3
British Standards Institution
      439, 1099
British Standard Time aband-
  oned......146, 350–1, 565
British Steel Corporation....372
  Loans Outstanding
      613, 614
  Strike (1971)........570
British Thermal Unit......584
British Tourist Authority...372
British Transport Docks Board
      372, 584
  Loans........613, 614
British Virgin Islands......778
British Visitors' Passports...983
British Waterways Board
      372, 613, 614
Britten, Benjamin:—
  Companion of Honour....261
  Order of Merit........260
Brixton:—
  Gaol (Governor).........398
  Member of Parliament....337
Brno (Czechoslovakia)......850
BROADCASTING:—
  B.B.C...............371
    Cost (1971–72).........610
  British Forces Service....578
  Independent Radio.....1016–7
  Licences........371, 579, 1204
    Revenue............609
  Television Licences......1204
Broadstairs and St. Peters...669
Bromley (Kent)..........642
  Archdeacon (Rochester)...477
  Member of Parliament....329
  Party Strengths........671
Brompton Oratory.........491
Bromsgrove.............669
  Member of Parliament....329
Bronchitis, Deaths from....601
Bronze Age, The..........185
Bronze Coinage..........1210
Bruce, Robert........213, 678
Bruges (Belgium)..........827
BRUNEI (Borneo)..201, 778–9, 984
  British High Commission..779
  Currency..............779

PAGE

Brunel University..........510
Brunswick (Germany)......866
BRUSSELS (Belgium).202, 826, 827
  Distance by Air.........1131
Bryant, Sir Arthur........267
  Companion of Honour....261
Brythons (Iron Age).....630, 678
Buchanan Fund (Natl. Debt) 615
Buchan's Weather Spells....1211
Bucharest (Rumania)
      202, 204, 932
Buckhaven and Methil.....685
Buckie.................685
Buckingham............664
  Bishop of (Oxford).......476
  Member of Parliament....329
Buckingham Palace........643
Buckinghamshire........631–3
  Members of Parliament...329
Buckland Abbey.........653
Budapest (Hungary) 202, 204, 878
  Distance by Air.........1131
Buddhist Calender.........193
BUDGET OF U.K. (1971–72)
  351–4, 566, 609–12, 620–1
  By Classes............610–2
Buenos Aires.......200, 204, 822
Buffalo (U.S.A.)........204, 800
BUILDING:—
  Agency, National.......1124
  Bankruptcies (1970)......1160
  Company Profits........619
  Education..............519
  Frozen Foundations (Science
    Notes)............1032
  Industrial Training Bd.....535
  Numbers Employed in....606
  Public, Ministry for, *see*
    ENVIRONMENT
  Statistics................604
BUILDING SOCIETIES......1151–7
  Business (1970).........1151
  Designated............1152
  Interest Rates ..1020, 1151–2
  Mergers (1970)........1151
  Number..............1151
  Registrar..............390
  Statistics (1970)....1151, 1152
  Treasury Loans.........615
  Trustee Status..........1152
  Yearbook............1074
Buildings, Highest........203
  Historic, Councils........394
  Public, London......643–9
Bujumbura (Burundi)...199, 835
Bulawayo (Rhodesia)......784
BULGARIA 202, 832–3; (*Map*) 832
  British Embassy.........833
  Cabinet...............832
  Communist Party.......832
  Currency..............984
  Embassy..............832
  Finance and Trade...585, 833
  Production, etc.........833
Bulwark, H.M.S.........462
BURGHS, SCOTTISH....625, 685–6
  Electors (Number)......625
  Royal................685–6
    Convention of.......422
  Town Councils.........625
Burglary Statistics.........602
Burials (Legal Notes)......1165
BURMA ..201; (*Map* 746); 834–5
  Area, etc..............834

PAGE

BURMA—*continued*
  British Embassy.........835
  Communications........835
  Currency..............984
  Education.............834
  Embassy.............834
  Exchange Rate..........83
  Government...........834
  Production, etc.......834–5
  States...............834
  Trade with U.K.........835
Burnham Beeches......650–1
  Cttee. (Teachers' Pay)....1050
Burnley..............664
  Bishop of (Blackburn)....478
  Member of Parliament....329
Burntisland.............685
Burn Treatments (Sci. Notes)
      1036–7
Burton on Trent.........664
  Member of Parliament....329
Burundi............199, 835, 984
Bury (Lancs.)...........664
  (and Radcliffe), M.P......329
Bury St. Edmunds........664
  Member of Parliament....329
Busby, Sir Matthew.....106, 267
Bus Company, National....414
Bushel (Measure).....809, 1214
  Conversions......1215, 1218
Bushey................669
Bushy Park.............651
Business Degrees, etc........519
  Journals..............1081–4
  Library, City...........644
  Names Registry 620
  Premises (Law)....1171, 1172
  Reply Service...........1201
  Statistics Office (Dept. of
    Trade)...............430
  Studies Schl., London.519, 1058
Bute..................679–80
  Member of Parliament....326
  Sheriff, etc.............684
BUTLER OF SAFFRON WALDEN,
  LORD...................250
  Birthday...............134
  Chancellor:—
    Univ. of Essex.........509
    Univ. of Sheffield 509
  Companion of Honour....261
  Inter-Parliamentary Union.317
  Knight of the Garter.....259
  Master, Trinity College....505
  Offices Held.........314, 315
  Privy Councillor........257
Butler Act (Education).....1048
Buxton...............664
By-elections, Writs for.....310
BY-ELECTION VOTING:—
  (1959–71), Total Votes....317
  (1970):—
    Enfield, W. (Nov. 19)
      333, 565
    St. Marylebone (Oct. 22)
      343. 565
  (1971):—
    Arundel & Shoreham
      (April 1)........325, 566
    Bromsgrove(May 27)329, 566
    Goole (May 22)....334, 566
    Greenwich (July 8).335, 567
    Hayes & Harlington (June
      18)............335, 566

Pages 693–1220 are omitted from the Shorter Edition

PAGE

By-Election Voting—*continued*
Liverpool, Scotland
(April 1)........339, 566
Macclesfield (Sept. 30)...567
Southampton, Itchen
(May 27)........344, 566
Stirling and Falkirk (Sept 16)
567
Widnes (Sept. 23) 567
Byssinosis Benefit............497
Board................393

Cabinet, The..........306, 313
Ministers................313
Office.......... 372, 608, 610
Origin of................312
Secretary of............372
Cabinet Rank, Ministers of...313
Cabinets (1939–71).......314–5
Cable and Wireless Ltd......372
Measure................578
Cabot, Sebastion............697
Cadet Colleges........520, 521
Caerleon Legionary Museum.414
Caernarvon................675
Member of Parliament....329
Caernarvonshire......675, 676
Caerphilly, 675; M.P......329
Cagliari (Sardina)......890, 891
Cainozoic Period............184
Cairo (U.A.R.)...199, 204, 956–7
Distance by Air........1131
Caithness................679–80
Member of Parliament....329
Sheriff................684
Caius College, Cambridge...505
Calcutta..........204, 752
Archbishop (R.C.)......489
Distance by Air........1131
University................791
Calcutta Cup (Rugby)....1004
Calderon de la Barca......940
Caledonia, New............203
Calendar (1972 and 1973)...89
Any Year (1753–2000)...194–7
Buddhist................193
Chinese................193
Christian..............188–90
Coptic................193
Ethiopian................193
Greek................193
Gregorian................188
India................193
Japanese................193
Jewish................190–1
Julian................188
Moslem................193
New Style................188
Old Style................188
Roman................192
Year................186
Calendar Line................143
Calgary (Alberta)............701
Cali (Colombia)............844
California................800
Calley, Lt. William........572
Callisto (Satellite)............158
Calne................664
Calvinistic Methodists....485–6
Camberley, Frimley and......669
Camberley Staff College......520
Camberwell Green Magistrates'
Court................455
Camberwell, M.P.'s............329

PAGE

Cambodia, *see* Khmer Republic
Camborne-Redruth........669
Member of Parliament....333
Cambrian Academy, Royal.1094
Cambridge, City of....658, 664
Clubs................1090
Member of Parliament....329
Population..........658, 664
Theological Colleges..536, 537
Cambridgeshire............631–3
Member of Parliament....329
Cambridgeshire, The.........999
Cambridge University....504–7
Colleges................505
Copyright Library......1073
Cricket................1002
Extra-Mural Studies......512
Fitzwilliam Museum......655
Press..........1022, 1071
Professors............505–7
Students (Number)......504
Teaching Hospitals......527
Terms (Dates)............504
v. Oxford (Sports)......1011
Women's Colleges......505
Camden................642
Party Strengths........671
Penny Rate............624
Cameroon (Republic)
199, 835–6; (*Map*) 836;984
British Embassy........836
Embassy................835
Campbell, Rt Hon. G.T.C.:—
Member of Parliament....340
Privy Councillor........257
Secretary of State.313, 315, 423
Campbell Island (N.Z.)..730, 734
Campbeltown................685
Campion Hall, Oxford......503
Canada
200, 693, 695–706; (*Map*) 696
Agriculture................700
Air Force................699
Mail Rates to....1197, 1206
Passengers to............588
Archbishops........480, 487
Area, etc................695
Army................699
Banks
441, 442, 444, 445, 446, 699
Births................699
Bishops........480, 488
Boys' Schools............542
British High Commission..698
Cabinet................697–8
Canada House, London....643
Capital................705
Census (1966)............695
Civil Aviation............700
Climate................697
Communications............700
Currency............83, 984
Deaths................699
Debt................699
Defence................699
Divorces................699
Dominion Day...89, 114, 697
Education................699
Emigration Statistics......605
Exchange Rate............83
Eskimo Population........695
Finance................699
Fisheries................700

PAGE

Canada—*continued*
Flag................697
French Population........695
Fur Farming............700
Government............697–8
Governor-General........697
Grain Crops............700
High Commissioners......698
History................697
House of Commons........698
Immigration............695
Indian Population........695
Judicature............698–9
Lakes................205
Languages................699
Leader of the Opposition..698
Legislature............698
Live Stock............700
Marriages................699
Medal................305
Mineral Production......700
Motor Vehicles (Number)..700
Mountains................697
National Day............697
Navy................699
Newspapers............1085
Nobel Prizes............1054
Parcel Rates to..........1206
Peerage (De Longueuil)...240
Physiography............697
Polar Regions............697
Population........200, 695
Prime Minister............697
Production............700
Province of (C. of E.)......480
Provinces....695, 697, 700–6
Public Debt............699
Racial Origins............695
Railways................700
Religious Statistics........695
Revenue and Expenditure..699
R.C. Church........487–8, 695
Senate................698
Shipbuilding............597
Ship Canals............700
Shipping..........596, 700
Standard Time............143
Summer Time............142
Telegraph Rates to......1206
Telephone Rates to......1205
Territories................700
Trade..........585, 699–700
Commissioners........729
with U.K......699, 700
United Church............485
U.K. Immigrants....605, 695
Universities....695, 699, 790–1
Victoria Cross Awards...302–4
Vital Statistics............699
Canals:—
Belgium................827
Board, British............372
Canada................700
of the World............206
Panama................206
Suez................206
U.K................629
U.S.A................811–2
U.S.S.R................964
Canary Islands (Spain)......941
Canberra (Australia)....203, 714
Archbishop (R.C.)......490
Population (1970)........707
Canberra, S.S................598

Pages 693–1220 are omitted from the Shorter Edition

PAGE

Cancer Deaths (1969, 1970)...601
  Research, etc. Societies...1099
  (1971)...........1029-30
Candlemas...........(Note) 94
Cannock, 669; M.P........329
Cannock Chase...........626
Canoeing (1971)...........1011
Canonbury Tower.........643
Canons Residentiary.....473-9
Canopus...................151
CANTERBURY, CITY OF.658-9, 664
  Member of Parliament....329
  Royal Museum...........655
  Sheriff...............659
Canterbury Diocese.......473
  Cathedral.............659
CANTERBURY PROVINCE....473-8
  Archbishop.........227, 473
    Precedence..........219
    Privy Councillor......257
    Residence...........646
  Ecclesiastical Courts.....484
  Vicar-General..........473
Canton (China)......204, 842
Canton Island (Pacific)
    782, 798, 810
Canvey Island...........669
Capacity, Measures of...1214-5
  Conversion Table......1218
Cape Breton Island........704
Capella..................151
CAPE OF GOOD HOPE.......936
Cape Town..........199, 938
  Archbishop............481
Cape Verde Islands.199, 929, 984
Capital Duty............1192
  Gains (Income Tax)
    352, 566, 1186
  Receipts...............609
Capitals, World........199-203
Captain-General for Scotland.223
Caracas (Venezuela).200, 204, 971
Carat Marks (Gold Wares)..1213
Caratacus (Caractacus)...630, 674
CARDIFF, CITY OF..202, 675, 676
  Archbishop............487
  Clubs................1090
  Institute of Science and
    Technology...........510
  Lord Mayor............676
  Members of Parliament....329
  National Museum........413
    Schl. of Medicine......510
    Sports Centre.........530
  Newspapers...........1077
  Party Strengths.........673
  Population.........675, 676
  S. Wales Univ. College....510
  Stipendiary........455, 676
  Teaching Hospitals......527
  University Colleges...510, 512
  Weather (Monthly)....1065-7
  Welsh Office........436-7
Cardigan................675
Cardiganshire......675, 676
  Member of Parliament....329
Cardinals, College of......487
Caribbean Sea...........203
Carisbrooke Castle Museum..655
CARLISLE................664
  Bishop...........237, 478
  Member of Parliament....329
Carlton, 669; M.P.........329
Carlyle's House..........643

Carmarthen..............675
  Member of Parliament....329
Carmarthenshire....675, 676
Carnegie Trusts, etc...513, 1099
Carnoustie..............685
Carolina, N. and S........800
Caroline Islands (U.S.A.)
    203, 810, 811
Carpathian Mountains......965
CARR, RT HON. L. R.:—
  Member of Parliament....340
  Privy Councillor........800
  Secretary of State.313, 315, 382
Carrickfergus...........691
CARRINGTON, LORD:—
  Birthday..............110
  Privy Councillor........257
  Secretary of State.313, 315, 459
Carshalton, M.P..........329
Carver, Sir Michael........268
  Chief of General Staff....459
Casablanca (Morocco)......912
Casey Station, Antarctic....717
Cash on Delivery........1200
Caspian Sea.............205
Castilian Language........940
Castle Ashby............653
Castle Douglas...........685
Castleford..............664
Castle Howard...........653
Castles Open to Public....653-4
Castries (St. Lucia)....200, 788
Catania (Sicily)..........891
Catchment Boards........625
Caterham and Warlingham..669
Catering (Prof. Educ.)...521, 523
Cathcart (Glasgow), M.P....334
Cathedral Organists.....473-80
Cathedrals, London....490, 491
Catholic Central Library...643-4
Catholic Church, see ROMAN
    CATHOLIC CHURCH
Catholic Herald............1078
Cattle (U.K.)............580
  Gestation Periods......1124
  Herds (Number).......580
Caucasus, The......198, 205
Causes of Death (1969, 1970)
    601-2
Cavalry Regiments........464
Cavendish Collegiate Society,
    Cambridge............505
Cayenne (Fr. Guiana)....200, 863
C.B.I...................1124
Cayman Islands (W. Indies)
    200, 787
Cebu (Philippines)......925, 926
Celebes, see Sulawesi
Celestial Equator..........150
  Phenomena (1972)......148-9
Cemeteries (London)......644
Cenotaph (Whitehall)......644
Cenozoic Period..........184
Censuses, Office of.....418-9
CENSUS OF POPULATION:—
  Northern Ireland........688
  United Kingdom.566, 567, 599
Centenaries (1972)......576-7
  (1973)...............577
  Various......90, 94, 98, etc
Centigrade Thermometer..1216
Centimetre and Inch......1218
C.E.N.T.O...............982
Central Africa, Archbishop...482

CENTRAL AFRICAN REPUBLIC
    199, 836; (Map) 836
CENTRAL AMERICA...........200
Central Bank of India......442
Central Chancery..........222
  Criminal Court.........453
  Trials in 1970-71......569
  Electricity Generating Board
    381
  European Time..........143
  Institutions (Further Educ.) 1052
  Midwives Boards........530
  Office of Information....400-1
  Statistical Office........372
  Treaty Organization......982
Cepheid Variable Stars..153, 154
Ceramics Museum (V. & A.).412
Cereals Divisions (Ministry of
    Agriculture)...........363
  Home grown, Authority..1131
  Imports, etc........579, 586
  Production (U.K.).......580
Ceres (Minor Planet)......159
Certificate of Posting....1198
Certificate of Secondary
    Education..........1049-50
Certificates, Birth, etc......1162
Cesarewitch, The 999
Ceuta (Spanish Morocco) 199, 941
CEYLON ...201, 572, 693, 737-9
  Area and Population.....737
  Banks................738
  Cabinet..............738
  Climate..............737
  Communications........739
  Currency.............984
  Exchange Rate.........83
  Finance..............738
  Government.........737-8
  Governor-General.......738
  High Commissions......738
  Judicature............738
  Legislature...........738
  Production...........738
  Races and Religions.....737
  Rivers...............737
  Trade............585, 738
  Commissioner.........729
  Universities...........791
C.G.S................459, 463
CHAD, REPUBLIC OF,
    199, 836-7; (Map) 917
Chadderton..............669
CHAIRMEN OF:—
  County Councils
    632, 676, 691
  Urban District Councils
    668-70
  Ways and Means.......309
Chalfont St. Giles.........652
CHAMBERLAIN, THE LORD....220
Chamberlain, Lord Great...406
Champion Stakes..........999
Chancellor:—
  County Palatine.........378
  Duchy of Lancaster...313, 378
    Precedence..........219
  of the Exchequer.313, 314, 432
    Master of the Mint....408
    Precedence..........219
    Residence...........308
Chancery Court of York....484
  Division.............449

Pages 693–1220 are omitted from the Shorter Edition

PAGE

Chancery—*continued*
  Division—*continued*
    Judges.................449
    Chambers............451
    Offices...............451
    Registrars............451
    Sheriff Court of.........683
    Visitors..............452
Chandigarh (India) . 750, 751, 752
CHANNEL ISLANDS...........692
  Airports...............590
  Bank Holidays ...(*Notes*) 90,
    106; 190, 578, 663
    Notes...............1211
  Education Officers.........516
  Summer Time..........142
Chapels Royal.........221, 222
Chaplain-Gen. to the Forces..459
Chaplain of the Fleet.........459
Chaplains to the Queen 221, 222–3
Chard.....................664
Charing Cross Hospital.....525
Charitable Bequests.....1132–3
  Societies (Various)....1095–1120
  Employment Tax Refund
    1183–4
Charity Commission....373, 611
Charleroi (Belgium).........827
Charlestown (Nevis).........787
Charlotte Amalie (Virgin Islands)
    200, 811
Charlottetown (P.E.I.)....200, 705
Charlton House (Greenwich).651
Charterhouse School........538
  London.................644
Chartwell, Kent 653
CHATAWAY, RT. HON. C. J.:—
  Birthday.................90
  Member of Parliament....330
  Minister of Posts......313, 419
  Privy Councillor.........257
Chatham..................664
  Member of Parliament....343
Chatham Islands (N.Z.)......730
Chatsworth, Derbyshire.....653
Cheadle and Gatley.........669
Cheadle, M.P.............329
Cheam, Sutton and, M.P....346
Cheetham (Manchester), M.P.339
CHELMSFORD...............664
  Bishop.............237, 474
  Member of Parliament....330
CHELSEA:—
  See also Kensington and
    Chelsea
  Bridge..................643
  College of Science and Tech-
    nology...............508
  Member of Parliament....330
  Physic Garden.........644
  Royal Hospital.........644
CHELTENHAM...............664
  Archdeacon (Gloucester)..475
  College.................538
  Colleges of Education.....532
  Gold Cup.............999
  Ladies' College.........544
  Member of Parliament....330
Chelyabinsk (U.S.S.R.).....965
Chemical Engineering (Educa-
  tion)..............521–2
Chemicals Divn. (Dept. of
  Trade)................431

PAGE

Chemicals:—
  Exports and Imports......586
Chemistry Degrees, etc.....519
  Museum...............411
  Nobel Prizes...........1054
  Royal Institute.........519
Chemists, N.H.S. (Number)..500
Chengtu (China)...........842
Cheops, Pyramid of........202
Chequers.............308, 651
Cheques Clearing House...440–1
Chertsey, 669; M.P........330
Chesapeake Bay Bridge–Tunnel
    206
Cheshire...............631–3
Cheshunt................669
CHESTER..................664
  Bishop.............237, 479
  Crown Court Circuit......454
  Member of Parliament....330
Chester Cup.............999
Chesterfield.............664
  Archdeacon (Derby)......474
  Member of Parliament....330
Chester Herald...........369
Chester-le-Street..........669
  Member of Parliament....330
Cheveley Park Stakes......999
Cheviot Hills..........629, 677
Chicago..............204, 800
  Distance by Air........1131
Chichester...............664
  Bishop.............237, 474
  Clerk of the Closet......221
  Harbour.............626
  Member of Parliament....330
Chief Constables....633, 676, 680
Chief Inspector of Taxes....403
Chief Insurance Officer (Natl.
  Insurance)............393
Chief of Defence Staff......459
Chief Secretary, Treasury 313, 433
Chiefs of Staff:—
  Air..............459, 465
  Army (C.G.S.).......459, 463
  Royal Navy........459, 461
Chiefs, Scottish.........681–2
Chigwell, 669; M.P........330
Child Care (Cost).........624
CHILDREN:—
  Adoption of...1161, 1163, 1169
  Anti-Cruelty Societies
    1110, 1114
  Birthweights (Sci. Notes)..1031
  British Nationality.....1162–3
  Cruelty (Statistics)........602
  Custody of (Divorce) 1166, 1167
  Family Allowances.......498
  Guardians' Allowances....494
  Handicapped (Schools)....1049
  Illegitimate, 1162; In Care.1157
  Income Tax Allowances
    353, 566, 1187–8
  Juvenile Courts..........455
    Crime Statistics....602, 603
  Legitimacy of...........1168
  Maintenance Orders....1166–7
  Save the Children Fund...1116
  Special Allowances (National
    Insurance).........494, 496
  Unit Trust Holdings......1158
Children's Homes (Statistics) 1157
Passports................983

PAGE

CHILE.200, 573; (*Map*) 821; 837–9
  British Embassy..........839
  Cabinet................837
  Currency...............984
  Earthquake (1971).......569
  Embassy...............837
  Exchange Rate.......83, 838
  Finance and Trade.....585, 838
  Government............837
  Nobel Prizes...........838
  Production, etc........837–8
  Trade with U.K.........838
Chiltern Hills............626
Chiltern Hundreds.........310
Chimborazo, Mt. (Andes)
    205, 853
CHINA....201, 839–43; (*Map*) 839
  Armed Forces..........841
  British Charge d'Affaires...843
  Calendar.............193
  Cities................842
  Communications........842
  Communist Party........839
  Currency.........841, 984
  Education.............841
  Government..........840–1
  Industrial Production......842
  Language and Literature...841
  London Office.........839
  Mandarin Dialect.......841
  Population......201, 839–40
  Production, etc.......841–2
  Provinces.............840
  Religions.............841
  Trade with U.K.........842
Chinese Art Foundation.....647
Chippenham.............665
  Member of Parliament....330
Chipping Norton..........665
Chiropody (Education) 528
Chislehurst, M.P..........330
Chiswick Bridge.........643
  Member of Parliament....328
Chittagong (Pakistan)......766
CHIVALRY, ORDERS OF....259–61
  Central Chancery.......259
Chorley, 665; M.P........330
Chosun, *see* Korea
Chou-en-Lai.............839
Christ, The Birth of.........188
Christchurch (Hampshire)..665
  Member of Parliament....328
Christchurch (N.Z.)........734
  Bishops............481, 490
Christ Church (Oxford).....502
  Dean and Chapter.......476
Christian Chronology....188–90
  Festivals....90, 94, 98; 138, 189
  Scientists.............486
Christianity in Britain
    630, 674, 678
  in Ireland.............794
Christie, Agatha (*Portrait*)...559
Christmas Day.......89, 134
  Posts................1204
  Quarter Day . .(*Notes*) 94, 134
Christmas Island (Australian)..716
Christ's Coll., Cambridge....505
Christ's Hospital Schools 538, 544
CHRONOLOGICAL NOTES...184–97
Chrysler Building (N. York)..203
Chungking (China).....204, 842
CHURCH:—
  Commissioners.........373

12

Fight cancer with a will

When testators ask your advice, please remind them of the urgent work of the Imperial Cancer Research Fund. In the Fund's up-to-date laboratories trained minds are using every weapon of modern science to fight all forms of cancer, including leukaemia.

Now one of the world's great research centres, the I.C.R.F. relies entirely on public support. The cancer problem *must* be solved. Please help now.

Please write for further information to:
The Secretary, I.C.R.F. (Dept. 179)
PO Box 123, Lincoln's Inn Fields, London WC2A 3PX

IMPERIAL CANCER RESEARCH FUND

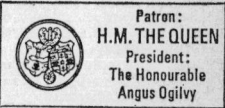

Patron:
H.M. THE QUEEN
President:
The Honourable
Angus Ogilvy

Lincoln's Inn Fields Laboratories

AH 5

"Don't answer back!"

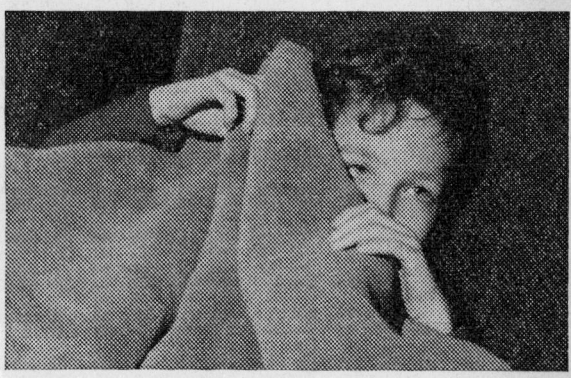

Next time you get impatient with your own child (and who doesn't?) remember Peter. His mother would give anything if only he *would* answer back. For Peter is emotionally disturbed and refuses to talk at all—even to her.
ICAA has a school for children like Peter. Help us to help them—and hundreds more children, with all kinds of sickness or handicap.
Donations, covenants, legacies gratefully received by
**The Lord Grenfell, Hon. Treasurer, Invalid Children's Aid Association,
126 Buckingham Palace Road, London, SW1W 9SB   Tel: 01–730 9891**
REMEMBER—*ICAA* HELPS CHILDREN WITH *ALL* HANDICAPS

PAGE

CHURCH—continued
Education Corporation....544
Music, Royal School of....529
Schools Company.........544
Churches, London........490–1
Churchill, Sir Winston......90
Offices held..........314, 315
Churchill College, Cambridge 505
CHURCH IN WALES..........480
Theological Colleges......536
CHURCH OF ENGLAND.....473–84
Archbishops.....227, 473, 478
Archdeacons...........473–9
Beneficed Clergy......473–80
Bishops......237, 473–82
Abroad.............480–2
Resigned.............483
Canons Residentiary....473–9
Church House...........480
Clergy.............473–80
Colleges of Education....532–4
Commissioners..........373
Deans and Chapters....473–9
Dioceses.............473–80
Ecclesiastical Courts......484
Estates Commissioners....373
General Synod....480, 548
House of Bishops, etc....480
In Australia.............707
In Canada.............695
Marriages.............1174
Missionary Bishops.......482
Newspapers...........1078
Primate of All England....473
Primate of England......478
Schools.............1048
Societies.............1100
Theological Colleges......536
Vicars General..........484
CHURCH OF IRELAND.......485
CHURCH OF SCOTLAND......484
Ecclesiastical Household..222–3
General Assembly.......484
In London.............491
Lord High Commissioner..484
Moderator.............484
Theological Colleges......536
C.I.D.................456
Cigarettes, Public Spending..618
Cinema Admissions, Takings.579
Public Spending.........618
Cincinnati (U.S.A.)........204
Cinque Ports.............204
Circuits of Judges (Crown
Courts)...........453–4
Circular Measures........1215
Circumcision, The.........90
Cirencester, M.P.........330
Cisterns, Capacity of.......1216
Cities, Counties of (Scotland)
(Note) 679
Cities, English.....657–63, 664–8
Party Representation..671–3
Largest.............204
Northern Irish.......690, 691
Electors (Number)....625
Scottish.............680–1
Electors (Number)....625
United States..........800
Welsh.............675
Citizenship, British...693, 1162–4
Loss of.............1163–4
City and Guilds Institute....534

PAGE

CITY OF LONDON.....622, 637–40
Aldermen.............637–8
Banks...............440–6
Bridges.............643
Buildings.............643–9
Business Library.........644
Chamberlain.........637, 639
Chief Commoner........637
City's Estate...........637
City University.........510
Clerk of the Peace........639
Clubs...............1087–9
Commissioner of Police....639
Committees...........637
Common Council......638–9
Elections.......(Note) 134
Common Sergeant....637, 639
Deputies.............638–9
Exchequer Grants........640
Finances.............640
Freemen's Guild........663
Government.........637–40
Guildhall, 645; Courts......456
History.............637
Irish Society.........637, 1106
Judges.............639
Justice Rooms..........456
Livery Companies......640–2
Halls.............646
Lord Mayor.........568, 637
Lord Mayor's Day
(Note) 130; 187, 637
Mansion House Court......456
Markets...........637, 639
Mayor's Court.....(Note) 639
Member of Parliament.....330
Museum of London.......411
Officers.............639
Parks, Commons, etc..650, 651
Penny Rate............624
Police...........457, 584
Population.............637
Rateable Value.........640
Rates (1971–72).........640
per Head............624
Recorder...........637, 639
Records Office..........422
Remembrancer.........639
Roman Remains.......647–8
St. Paul's Cathedral......490
Schools...........538, 546, 639
Secondary.............639
Sheriffs....(Note) 110; 637, 638
Town Clerk.........637, 639
Under Sheriffs..........453
Wards.............637–8
Civic Trust.............1120
CIVIL AVIATION..........588–90
Air Registration Board...369
Air Safety Directorate...429
Authority proposed....571
Cost of.............610
Divns. (Dept. of Trade)
429–30
Industrial Training Bd....535
Licensing Board........369
Organization, U.N.......816
Civil Courts, Legal Aid in
1172–3, 1173–4
Civil Defence (Cost)....610, 624
Training School.......397
Civil Engineering (Education) 522
Civil Estimates, *see* Supply
Estimates

PAGE

Civilization, Stages of.....185–6
Civil List..........224, 375, 566
Civil Parishes...........622
CIVIL SERVICE, THE......362–437
College.............374
Commissioners.........374
Department.........373–4
Cost.............608, 610
Head of the...........374
Minister for..........373
Staff Statistics.........608
Civil Twilight............139
(1972).........91, 95, 99
Civil Year.............186
Clackmannan.........679–80
Member of Parliament....345
Sheriff.............684
Clacton.............669
Clans, Scottish (Chiefs)....681–2
Clapham (Wandsworth), M.P. 347
Clare College, Cambridge....505
Hall, Cambridge Univ....505
Clarenceux King of Arms....369
Clark, Lord............250
Brit. Museum Trustee....409
Companion of Honour....261
University of York......509
Clark, Sir Wilfrid le Gros,
Obituary............574
Clay Pigeon Shooting.....1010
Clearing Banks
442, 443, 444, 445, 446
Cleethorpes...........665
Cleopatra's Needle........647
Clergy, Diocesan........473–80
House of.............480
Clerkenwell Court........455
Clerical Workers, Average
Earnings.............617
Clerk of the Closet........221
Clerk of the House of Commons
310
Clerk of the Parliaments
309, 310, 449
Clerks of the Cheque......222
Clerks of County Councils
633, 635, 676, 680
Clerks of the Peace:—
England...........(Note) 633
Scotland.............680
Cleveland:—
Archdeacon (York).......478
Member of Parliament....330
Cleveland (Ohio)......204, 800
Clifton, Bishop (R.C.).....487
Clinical Research Board....408
Units.............407–8
Clitheroe, 665; M.P........330
Clogher, Bishops (C. of I.)..485
Clore, Sir Charles.........269
Portrait............559
Closed Shop (Industrial Relations
Act).............1014
Close Times (Game)
(Notes) 94, 122; 1213
Clothing, Expenditure on...618
Imports, etc..........587
Clothworkers' Company....640
CLUBS:—
England and Wales....1087–93
London.............1087–9
Northern Ireland...1092, 1093
Scotland.........1091–2, 1093
Yacht.............1092–3

Pages 693–1220 are omitted from the Shorter Edition

PAGE

Clwyd (New Welsh County)
................1019
Clydebank................685
CLYDE, THE LORD:—
Lord President, Court of
Session................683
Privy Councillor.........257
Clyde River................677
Erskine Bridge opened (1971)
................548
Port Authority..........435
Clydesdale Bank..........443
C.N.A.A................1051
COAL:—
Board, National........414
Financial Results.......583
Consumer Expenditure....618
Divn. (Dept. of Trade)....431
European Community.....978
Exports and Imports.....586
Open Cast Production....583
Production.............583
Coalition Ministry (1940-45)
314-5
Prime Ministers.........308
Coalville................669
Coastal Sedimentation Unit..415
Coastguard, H.M.........793
Coatbridge, 685; M.P.....330
COBHAM, VISCOUNT........234
Knight of the Garter......259
Lord Lieut., Worcestershire 632
Lord Steward............220
Privy Councillor.........257
Cochran, Sir Charles B.,
Centenary..........122, 577
Cockenzie and Port Seton....685
COCOS (KEELING) ISLANDS...716
COD Services..............1200
Co-educational Schools
537, 541, 542
Cohen of Birkenhead, Lord..240
Chancellor, Hull Univ.....509
Coimbatore (Tamil Nadu)...752
Coinage of the U.K....1210-11
Denominations.......1211
Illustrated............558
Legal Tender........1210
of Foreign Countries...984-8
Colchester................665
Bishop (Chelmsford)....474
Member of Parliament....330
Museum................655
Coldest Day..............1064
Coldest Places...........1064
Cold Spells, Buchan's......1211
Coleraine................691
Coleridge, Samuel Taylor,
Centenary..........126, 577
Coll and Tiree Islds......677
Collective Bargaining (Industrial
Relations Act)......1014-5
College of Arms........369, 644
of Cardinals..........487
of Chaplains..........221
of Law...............525
Colleges of Education
532-4, 1050, 1052
Domestic Science......521
Colne, 665; M.P..........340
Colne Valley, 669; M.P....330
Cologne (Germany)........866
COLOMBIA (Republic)..200, 843-4
British Embassy..........844

PAGE

COLOMBIA (Republic)—*continued*
Currency................984
Embassy................843
Finance and Trade....585, 844
Government..........843-4
Production, etc..........844
Colombo (Ceylon)....201, 738
Archbishop (R.C.).......489
Distance by Air.........1131
COLONIES AND PROTECTORATES
775-86
British Nationality....1162-4
Crown Agents...........375
Development Funds......694
Overseas Income Tax Office
417
Colony Defined...........694
Colorado River (U.S.A.)....206
Colorado (State)..........800
Colossus of Rhodes.......202
Colour Television Licences
Number........371, 579
Columbia, District of....800, 803
Columbus Day (U.S.A.)
(*Note*) 126
Colwyn Bay..............675
Comets..............156, 162
Commanders in Chief (R.N.) 461
Commando Ships (R.N.)
458, 462
Commerce, Colleges of...519-20
Commercial Education...519-20
Guarantee Department....387
Commissionaires, Corps of..1101
Commissioner of Police....456
Commissioners:—
Countryside............375
of Crown Estate........375
of Northern Lighthouses..435
Commission for Industrial
Relations............1016
for New Towns..........687
Commissions of the Peace
(Secretary)...........450
Royal, etc.............437
Common Market, European
357-9, 978-81
see also EUROPEAN ECONOMIC
COMMUNITY
Common (Marriage) Licence
1174
COMMONS, HOUSE OF, *see* HOUSE
Commonwealth (1649-1660)..212
COMMONWEALTH:—
See also British Common-
wealth
Agricultural Institutes....368-9
Day................(*Note*) 110
Development Corporation..374
Institute..........412-3, 644
Member States......693, 694
Office, *see* FOREIGN AND
COMMONWEALTH
Parliamentary Association
317; (*Note*) 612
Secretariat........375, 982
Societies......1098, 1101, 1114
Universities...........790-3
Association..............511
War Graves Commission
435-6, 610
Communications Museum...411
COMMUNIST PARTY:—
Albania................818

PAGE

COMMUNIST PARTY—*continued*
Bulgaria................832
China..................839
Czechoslovakia..........848
Germany, East..........869
Great Britain..........1101
Hungary................876
North Korea............899
North Vietnam..........973
Outer Mongolia.........910
Poland.................926
Rumania..............930-1
U.S.S.R...............959
Yugoslavia............974-5
Community:—
Programmes Dept. (Home
Office)..............395
Relations Commission.....437
Comoro Archipelago....864, 984
COMPANIES:—
Court..................451
Dept. (Dept. of Trade)....430
Directors, Bankruptcies (1970)
1160
Dividends (U.K.)..........620
Income and Interest......620
Net Trading Profits......619
Registered (G.B.)........620
Registrar of............430
Registration Offices...620, 683
Registrations (1970).....620
Taxation (Exchequer Receipts)
620
Companions of Honour.....261
Precedence............219
Compass Needle..........163-4
Compensation:—
Board (Criminal Injuries)..438
Commission, Foreign......437
Postal.............1199-1200
Tribunal...............457
Comprehensive:—
Insurance Policies.......1134
Schools................1049
Compton Castle...........653
Comptroller and Auditor...387
of the Household........220
Computer Science Degrees...520
Institute of (London
University)...........508
Computers:—
Assembling by..........1037
Divn. (Dept. of Trade)....431
Conakry (Guinea)......199, 873
Concepción (Chile).......838
Concorde, Divn. (Dept. of Trade)
432
Condominium Defined......694
Confederation of British
Industry..............1124
Confinement Grants (National
Insurance)............494
Confirmation (Probate)....1181
Congleton................665
CONGO, REPUBLIC OF
199; (*Map*) 836; 844
CONGOLESE REPUBLIC
199, 844-6; (*Map*) 845
British Embassy..........846
Currency............845, 984
Embassy................845
Government.............845
Production, etc..........845

Pages 693–1220 are omitted from the Shorter Edition

+ Committee on Invisible Exports
as Director Dr. P. E. STONHAM Page 373

PAGE

Congo River..............206
CONGREGATIONAL:—
Church...........486, 491
Colleges...........536, 537
Union (Scotland).........486
Connacht (Counties).........795
Connecticut (State).........800
Connemara, Mts. (Ireland)......794
CONSERVATIVE PARTY:—
Cabinets............314–5
Central Office..........1101
G.L.C. Strength.........635
Local Council Strengths..671–3
Majorities.............316
Origin of Name.........312
Prime Ministers....308, 314
Strength (1918–71)......316
Votes Cast (1955–70).....317
Whips...............312
Consett, 669: M.P..........330
Consolidated Fund:—
Standing Services.........609
Surplus Disposal........613
Conspicuous Gallantry Medal
305
Constable of the Tower . 224, 649
Constabulary............584
H.M. Chief Inspectors.397, 425
Royal Ulster...........689
Special........457, 584
Constant Attendance Allowances
498
Constantine, Lord, Obituary..574
Constantine (Algeria).......819
Constantinople, see Istanbul
Constellations
90, 94, 98, etc.; 138
Constituencies, Parliamentary
325–48; 350, 565
Construction, see BUILDING
Consular Dept. (Diplomatic
Service)................388
Constitution, Commission on
437
Construction Divns. (Environ-
ment)................386
Minister for..........313, 384
See also BUILDING
Consulates, General (London)
821–975
Consumer Expenditure. 618, 619
Price Index...........1195
Continental Telephone Rates
1204, 1205
Continents, The............198
Contracts of Employment....1014
Contracts, Stamp Duty....1192
Contributory Pensions....494–5
Rates.................499
Controlled Schools........1048
Conveners, Scottish........680
Convention of Royal Burghs.422
Conversion Tables, Metric..1218
Conversion of St. Paul.......90
Convertible Currency Reserves
584
Conveyances, Stamp Duty.1192–3
Conveyancing (Scotland) Act,
1970.................1180
Conway, 675; M.P..........330
Conway, H.M.S............530
Cook Islands (N.Z.)
203, 730, 734–5

Cook, Mt. (New Zealand)
206, 731
Cookery, Schools of.........521
Coolidge, Calvin, Centenary .577
Co-operative Societies......1101
Copenhagen......202, 204, 852
Distance by Air.........1131
Coptic Calendar..........193
Copyright...............1073
Dept. (Dept. of Trade)....1073
Government (H.M.S.O.)....426
Libraries.....405, 409–10, 1073
Office (Dept. of Trade)....418
Corby (New Town)
605, 669, 687
Cordilleras, Mts. (Colombia).843
Cordoba (Argentina).......822
CORFIELD, CAPT.
RT. HON. F. V.:—
Member of Parliament....334
Minister for Aerospace
313, 428
Privy Councillor.........257
Corisco Islands (Eq. Guinea)..854
Cork City...............797
Corn Harvests............580
Cornwall........626–7, 631–3
Archdeacon (Truro)......478
Duchy of............378
Duke of, see PRINCE OF WALES
Members of Parliament....330
Coronation Chair.........490
Cup...............999
Dates.............1047
Day............110, 225
Mark (Plate)..........1213
Corporation of London...637–40
See also CITY; LONDON
Corporation Tax
349, 353, 565, 566, 610, 621
Act (1970)............359
Commons Debate (1970)
350, 609
Receipts (1970).........349
Corpus Christi (1972).......89
Corpus Christi College:—
Cambridge............505
Oxford..............502
Correcting for the Press..1219–20
Corsham Court..........653
Corsica (France)............863
Cosmos Satellites.......167–9
COSTA RICA
200, 846–7; (Map) 846
British Embassy.........847
Currency..........846, 984
Embassy.............846
Finance.............846
Cost of Living Index.......1195
Cotopaxi, Mt.......205, 853
Cotswold Hills......627, 629
Council of Europe......982, 988
Industrial Design.......439
Legal Education.........524
Council on Tribunals.......434
Councillors, Local Govt......622
Councillors of State.........306
Countesses, Own Right.....249
Counties, English:—
Administrative...........631
Acreage..............631
Geographical..........631
New (List) 1019
Officials..............633

Counties, English—*continued*
Population.............631
Rates and Values........631
Reorganization.........1018
Counties of Cities.....(*Note*) 679
Counties, Scottish.......679–80
Counties, Welsh......675, 1019
Country Houses Open to Public
653–4
Countryside Commissions...375
County Agricultural:—
Advisers.............365
Committees...........368
County Boroughs.........664–8
Average Rates.........624
Councils.............622
Education Officers....515–6
Electors (Numbers).....622
Local Government Act
(1958)..............622
Number of............622
Party Representation....671–3
County Clerks (Scotland)....680
County Councils.........622
Chairmen.............632
Clerks of.............633
Constitution of.........622
Number of............625
Scotland...........624–5
Treasurers of......633, 676
County Courts..........452–3
Cost of.............610
Judges............452–3
Staff Numbers.........608
Statistics............453
County Cricket........1002–3
County Education Authorities
514–5; 516–7
County Hall (London).......644
County Palatine of Durham..378
County Schools..........1048
County Treasurers......633, 676
Courtauld Institute of Art....508
COURT:—
Central Criminal.........453
of Appeal............449
(Criminal Division)....450
of Arches............484
of Bankruptcy........451
of Chancery..........449
of Faculties..........484
of Justice, European....978
of Protection.........452
of Session............683
of the Lord Lyon.....369, 681
Restrictive Practices......452
Supreme.........449–50
Courtesy Titles......227–50, 256
COURTS:—
Courts Act (1971).........360
Crown Courts........453–4
Ecclesiastical..........484
Courts-Martial Appeals Office
451
Coutts Bank............443
Covenants, Income Tax....1190
Covent Garden..........646
Market Authority...375, 614
Royal Opera..........650
COVENTRY.........659, 665
Bishop of...........237, 474
Members of Parliament....330
Party Strengths..........671
Population............659

A+ *Pages 693–1220 are omitted from the* Shorter Edition

PAGE

COVENTRY—*continued*
Probate Registry........1181
Coventry Stakes.........999
Cowdenbeath............685
Cowdrey, M. C., Portrait ..563
Cowes, 629; R.Y.S.......1092
Crab Nebula.............155
Craigavon (N. Ireland)....691
Craighton (Glasgow), M.P...334
Craig, Gordon, Centenary 90, 577
Cranfield Inst. of Technology 510
Cranwell, R.A.F. College....521
Craven, Archdeacon (Bradford)
............478
Crawley.........605, 669, 687
Crayford, Erith and, M.P....333
Crediton, Bishop of (Exeter)..475
Cremation (Legal Notes)....1165
Crematoria (London)......644
Crete (Greece)...........870
Crewe, 665; M.P..........331
CRICKET.........571, 1000–4
Ashes Winners (1971).....563
Averages (1971) 1000, 1003
County Championship Table
............1002
County Champions (1873–71)
............1004
England:—
v. Australia 1000
v. India (1971).........1001
v. Pakistan (1971)......1001
Gillette Cup (1971).......1002
John Player League (1971) 1002
Lord's................1088
M.C.C..........1013, 1088
Memorial Gallery (Lord's)..646
N.Z. *v.* England........1000
Records...............1002
S.A. Tour Compensation...571
Test Matches.........1000–2
Universities and Schools...1002
W. Indies *v.* India (1971)
............1000–1
Crieff.................685
Criminal Appeal Divn. (High
Court)..............450
Office...............451
Courts.............453–4
Circuits............453–4
Legal Aid in.........1173
Damage Act (1971)......361
Dept. (Home Office).....395
Divn. (Ct. of Appeal).....450
Injuries Compensation Board
............438
Investigation Depts....456, 457
Justice Act (1967)........417
Statistics...........602–3
Trials, 1970–71..........569
Crofters Commission......424
Cromarty............679–80
Cromwell Museum (Hunting-
don)...............655
Crook and Willington......669
Crop Husbandry Advisers...365
Crop Prices.............581
Production............582
Crosby, 665; M.P..........331
Cross Country Running....997
Cross of Chelsea, Lord....240
Lord of Appeal..........449

PAGE

CROWN:—
Agent (Scotland)........683
Agents for Overseas Govern-
ments...............375
Colonies............775–86
Courts......360, 453–4, 571
Equerry...............222
Estate Commissioners .375, 611
(Scotland)...........683
Jewels, Keeper.........649
Office...............451
(Scotland)...........683
of India Order.........261
Proceedings Against 1164
Croydon............622, 642
Bishop of (Canterbury)...473
Members of Parliament...331
Party Strengths.........671
Cruelty (Divorce)........1167
Cruelty to Animals Inspectors 399
Cruelty to Children, Preven-
tion Societies......1110, 1114
Cruisers, R.N..........462
Crystal Palace..........636
CUBA
200, 206, 786, 847–8; (*Map*) 847
British Embassy.........848
Currency.........848, 984
Embassy.............847
Government........847–8
Trade...............848
Cubic Measure..........1214
Conversion Table......1218
Cuckfield.............669
Cuillins (Skye)..........678
Culloden, Battle of.......678
Cumberland........631–3, 685
Cumbernauld (New Town)
605, 685, 687
Cumnock and Holmhead...685
Cunobelinus...........674
Cupar...............685
Cupro-Nickel Coinage....1210
Cup-Winners' Cup, European
1005
Currencies, National....984–8
Revaluations (1971).....574
Currency, British......1210–11
Notes..............1211
Custody of Children (Divorce)
1166, 1167
Custom House (London)....644
CUSTOMS AND EXCISE BOARD
376–8
Collectors..........377–8
Estimates............610
Revenue from.........609
Staff Numbers, etc......608
Cutty Sark (Greenwich)....651
Cwmbran (New Town)
605, 675, 687
Cyclades Islands (Greece)....870
Cycling, 1011–12; Casualties..591
Cylinder Measure.......1215
CYPRUS, REPUBLIC OF
202, 693, 739–40
Bishop (R.C.).........489
British Bases..........740
Currency............984
Finance and Trade......740
Government...........739
High Commissions 739
Cyrillic Alphabet........963

PAGE

CZECHOSLOVAKIA
202, 848–9; (*Map*) 849
British Embassy.........850
Cabinet..............848
Communist Party.......848
Currency.........850, 984
Embassy.............849
Finance and Trade....585, 850
Government...........849
Language and Literature
849–50

DACCA (Pakistan)..........767
Dadra and Nagar Haveli
(India)..............753
Dagenham, M.P..........331
DAHOMEY (Republic of)
199, 850–1; (*Map*) 957; 984
Dail Eireann..........795, 796
Daily Newspapers......1077–8
Daily Sketch merged (1971)...570
Daily Telegraph.........1077
Dairy Advisory Officers....365
Produce, Imports.......586
Dakar (Senegal).......199, 936
Dakota, N. and S.........800
Daladier, Edouard Obituary..574
Dalai Lama (Tibet).......842
Dalbeattie.............685
Dalkeith..............685
Dallas (Texas).......204, 800
Daman (Damão, India).....753
Damascus (Syria)..201, 947, 948
Dames:—
Commanders.........301–2
Grand Cross.........301–2
How addressed........301
Precedence...........301
Danang (Vietnam).......972
Dancing, Schools of......520
Daniels, Bebe. Obituary 574
Dante (Italy)............891
Danube River..........206
Dardanelles (Turkey).....953
Dar es Salaam (Tanzania) 199, 770
Archbishop...........482
Distance by Air.......1131
University............793
Darling River......708, 717
Darlington, 665; M.P......331
Dartford.............665
Member of Parliament...331
Dartmoor............629
National Park.........626
Prison Governor.......398
Dartmouth............665
R.N. College.........520
Darvel..............685
Darwen, 665; M.P........331
Darwin (Australia)..203, 714, 715
Distance by Air.......1131
Darwin and Down House...651
Darwin College, Cambridge .505
Datapost Service.......1201
Date Letters on Plate..1212, 1213
Date Line.............143
Datel Services (Telex)....1204
Davao (Philippines).......926
Daventry.............665
DAVIES, RT. HON. J.E.H.:—
Member of Parliament....337
President, Bd. of Trade....428
Privy Councillor........257
Secretary of State..313, 314, 428

PAGE

Davis Base (Antarctic)......717
Davis Cup (Lawn Tennis) ...571,
    1007
Dawes, John (*Portrait*).......564
Dawley (Shropshire).........669
DAY, THE..................186
    Battle of Britain..........122
    Coldest..................1064
    Commonwealth Day(*Note*).110
    Divisions of the..........186
    Hottest..................1064
    Jewish...................191
    Julian....................89
    Longest......(*Note*) 110; 186-7
    Lord Mayor's..(*Note*) 130; 187
    New Year's Day
        89; (*Note*) 90; 186
    New Zealand Day....(*Note*) 94
    of Atonement..(*Note*) 122; 191
    Shortest......(*Note*) 134; 187
    Sidereal...............141, 163
    Solar.................140, 141
    Twelfth Day..............90
    Wettest..................1064
Daylight Saving Time.......142
Days from Month to Month...84
    Names of the.............186
    Red Letter................225
    Saints' Days...94, 98, 102, etc.
D.C.M......................305
"D" Day....................110
Dead Letter Office.........1199
Dead Sea (Israel)...........886
Deaf, Societies for........1102
    Teachers' Training Schools.534
Deal.......................665
DEAN:—
    of Chapel Royal...........222
    of Chapels Royal..........221
    of Christ Church..........502
    of Guernsey........473, 692
    of Jersey..........473, 692
    of St. Paul's.............473
    of the Thistle............222
    of Westminster...........473
    of Windsor...............476
Dean of Dioceses........473-9
Dearne.....................669
Dearne Valley, M.P.........331
Death:—
    Benefits (Friendly Societies)
        1150-1
    Industrial Injuries Insurance
        497
    Causes of,.............601-2
    Certificates.............1162
    Estate Duty 352, 566, 609, 1193
        Offices..........402, 404
    Grant (National Insurance)
        495-6
    Rates (U.K.)..............600
Deaths:—
    Abroad or at Sea 1164
    By Violence........591, 602
    Registered (1960-70)....600
    Registrar-General........418
        (Scotland)...........426
    Registration of........1164-5
Deaths, Notable (1970-71)
        82, 574-5
    (1872)..................576
    (1873)..................577
Death Valley, U.S.A....801, 1128
Debrett's Peerage..........1074

PAGE

Debt, Imprisonment for......452
    Local Government....624, 625
DEBT, NATIONAL............440
    Office....................414
    Overseas (Repayments)...352
Decimal Coinage...566, 1210-11
    Denominations (Value, etc.)
        1211
        (*Illustration*)...........558
    Wages Table.............1184
Declination defined..........150
    Magnetic................164
Decoration and Medals....302-5
Decree Absolute (Divorce)..1166
Dedham Vale Designated
    Area.....................627
Deeds of Covenant (duty
    abolished, 1971).........352
Deemsters (I.O.M.).........692
Deepest Lake...............965
    Ocean...................203
Deer Act (Close Times).....1213
Dee River..................674
    Scotland................677
DEFENCE:—
    Bonds...................614
    Central Admin. Cost.....612
    Combat Formations (1971).458
    Estimates............349, 612
    Far East Policy..........565
    Minister of State....313, 459
    Ministry of...........459-61
        Buildings (Cost)......611
        Staff Numbers, etc....608
        Under Secretaries
            313, 459, 460
    North Atlantic Treaty
        Organization 981
    Procurement Executive....460
        Minister for....313, 459
    Reserve Forces (Strengths)..612
    Secretary of State.313, 315, 459
    Services...............459-72
        Married Quarters (Rents)
            471
        Pay and Pensions 467-72, 567
        Staff, Chief of......459, 461
        Studies, Royal College...459
        Training Schools.....520-1
De Gaulle, Gen. C..........209
    Funeral (1970) (*Illus.*)......552
    Obituary.....130, 573, 574
    Portrait..................552
Deimos (Satellite).......158, 159
Delaware (State)............800
Delhi (City)........201, 204, 745
    Archbishop (R.C.)........489
    Distance by Air..........1131
Delhi (Territory)............752
DE L'ISLE, VISCOUNT.......235
    Knight of the Garter......259
    National Portrait Gallery...370
    Penshurst Place..........654
    Privy Councillor.........257
    St. Michael and St. George
        Order..................260
    Victoria Cross...........303
Denbigh, 675; M.P.........331
Denbighshire.........675, 676
DENMARK. 202, 851-2; (*Map*) 851
    British Embassy..........852
    Cabinet..................851
    Currency.................984
    Embassy..................851

PAGE

DENMARK—*continued*
    Exchange Rate............83
    Finance and Trade...585, 852
    Government...............851
    Language and Literature...851
    Nobel Prizes........851, 1054
    Outlying Islands.........852
    Shipbuilding.............597
    Telephone Rates to......1205
    Trade with U.K...........852
DENNING, LORD............240
    Birthday.................90
    Master of the Rolls......449
    Privy Councillor.........257
Denny and Dunipace........685
Denominational Schools....1048
Dental:—
    Council, General........1102
    Dept. (Min. of Health)....393
    Education...............521
    Hospital, Royal..........526
    Service (N.H.S.).........500
        Charges increased (1970).565
        Statistics.............1157
Denton.....................669
Dentures, N.H.S. (Charges)..500
Denver (U.S.A.)............800
Department:—
    for National Savings......415
    of Education and Science
        378-81
    of Employment........382-4
    of the Environment.....384-7
    of Health and Social Security
        391-3
    of Trade and Industry...428-32
Dependent Relatives Allowance
    (Income Tax)............1188
Deposit Friendly Societies...1150
Deposits (Election), Forfeited .311
Deptford, M.P..............331
De-rating.................623
Derby......................665
    Bishop of.........237, 474
    Members of Parliament....331
    Museum.................655
Derby, The (Race).........998
Derbyshire.............631-3
    Members of Parliament....331
De Ros, Premier Barony....250
Derry, Bishops........485, 487
Desertion (Legal Notes)
        1166, 1167
    Child Care Statistics......1157
Design, Industrial, Council of 439
Designs, Registration of....418
Destroyers, R.N............462
Detention Centres..........399
Detroit (Michigan)......204, 800
    Distance by Air..........1131
De Valera, Eamon..126, 208, 795
    Chancellor, Nat. Univ. of
        Ireland..............511
Development:—
    Association, International...815
    Commission..............378
    Corporations.............687
    Department, Scottish....425-6
    Divns. (Environment Dept.)
        385, 386
    Economic (N.E.D.O.).....414
    Minister for.........313, 384

PAGE

Development—*continued*
Town and Country Planning
............1177–8
Devizes....................665
Member of Parliament....331
DEVLIN, LORD..............240
High Steward, Camb. Univ.
............504
Judicial Committee........449
Privy Councillor..........257
Devonport, M.P...........342
DEVONSHIRE, DUKE OF......227
Chancellor, Manchester Univ.
............508
Chatsworth...............653
Privy Councillor..........257
DEVONSHIRE.........627, 631–3
Members of Parliament....331
National Park............627
Dewhurst Stakes..........999
Dewsbury, 665; M.P........331
D.F.C....................305
D.F.M....................305
Dhofar (Oman).........919–20
Diabetes, Deaths from.....601
Diaghilev, Serge, Centenary..577
Diameter Measure.........1215
Diamond Sculls...........1010
Diana, Temple of..........202
DIARY OF EVENTS (1970–71)
548; 564–574
Dickens House, London.....644
Diesel Engines, Underwater..1041
Diesel Locomotives........592
Dietectics (Education)......521
Dijon (France)............863
DILHORNE, VISCOUNT........235
Lord of Appeal...........449
Offices Held.............314
Privy Councillor..........257
Dili (Timor)..........210, 929
Dingwall.................685
Dioceses (C. of E.).....473–80
Dione (Satellite)..........158
DIPLOCK, LORD............241
Lord of Appeal...........449
Privy Councillor..........257
Diplomatic Service, H.M..387–9
Cost...................610
Departmental Heads...388–9
Head of.................388
List...................1074
Marshals of........221–2, 389
Messengers.............389
Staff Numbers...........608
Dip-poles, Magnetic......164
Direct Grant Schools......1048
Directors Bankrupt (1970)..1160
Director of Prosecutions....456
Disabled Persons' Attendance
Allowances............498
Disablement Benefit......496–7
Discovery and Invention
(1970–71)..........1028–42
Diseases, Deaths from....601–2
Dissolution of Parliament...310
Dates..................316
Distances by Air..........1131
Measures of............1214
Nautical...............578
of the Horizon..........207
of the Moon............158
of Stars................152

PAGE

Distinguished Conduct Medal
305
Flying Cross.............305
Medal................305
Service Cross...........305
Medal................305
Order.................304
District Land Registries...404–5
DISTRICT OF COLUMBIA..800, 803
District Probate Registries
452, 1181
Diu (India)..............753
Diving Championships.....1009
DIVORCE...............1165–7
Court, *see* Family Division
Custody of Children 1166, 1167
Grounds for............1166
Legal Aid.........1167, 1172
Maintenance..........1166–7
Queen's Proctor.434, 450, 1166
Reconciliation Proceedings
1166
Reform Act.............1166
Separation Orders......1166–7
Statistics (U.K.)..........600
(U.S.A.)..............798
Summary Jurisdiction ..1166–7
Djakarta (Indonesia) 201, 204, 881
Dnepropetrovsk (Ukraine)..966
Dock Labour Board........414
Dockland Settlements......513
Docks Authorities.....372, 419
Finance and Traffic.....584
Docks (London)...........419
Dr. Johnson's House 644–5
Doctors (N.H.S.).........500
Dodecanese (Greece)......870
Dog Days (*Note*).......114; 187
Doggett's Coat and Badge
651, 1010
Dogs, Gestation Period....1124
Dogs Home, Battersea.....1102
Doha (Qatar)........201, 930
d'Oliveira, B. L. (*Portrait*)..563
Dollar, American......806, 987
Canadian..............984
Domestic Employees, S.E.T. 1184
Food Expenditure.......618
Science Training.........521
Service, Spending on.....618
Dominica (West Indies)
200, 694, 789–90
Dominical Letters.........188
DOMINICAN REPUBLIC..200, 852–3
British Embassy.........853
Currency...............984
Embassy...............852
Finance and Trade.......853
Dominican Citizenship...1162–4
Day (Canada)...........89
Doncaster...............665
Archdeacon (Sheffield)...479
Colleges of Education....532
Member of Parliament....331
Races.................999
Donetsk (Ukraine).......966
DONOVAN, LORD...........241
Birthday...............110
Lord of Appeal..........449
Privy Councillor.........257
Don Valley, M.P..........331
Dorchester..............665
Bishop of (Oxford).......476

PAGE

Dorking.................669
Bishop of (Guildford).....475
Member of Parliament....331
Dorneywood House........651
Dorset............627, 631–3
Archdeacon (Salisbury)...477
Members of Parliament....331
Dortmund (Germany)......866
Douala (Cameroon Repub.)..836
Double Summer Time......146
Douglas (I.O.M.).........692
Dover...............204, 665
Bishop of (Canterbury)....473
Member of Parliament....331
Shipping...............595
Down, County...........691
Bishops............485, 487
High Sheriff............691
Members of Parliament 332, 688
Downing College, Cambridge 505
Street.................308
Dragoon Guards..........464
Drakensberg Mountains....937
Drama, The (1970–71)....1025–6
Drama Schools of.........521
Dram Weight............1215
Drapers' Company........640
Drawing Paper Sizes......1216
Dresden (E. Germany).....869
Drink, Expenditure on.....618
Driving Licences..........1209
Droitwich...............665
Dromore, Bishops......485, 487
Drowning Deaths (1969, 1970)
602
Droylsden...............669
Drugs and Medicines (N.H.S.) 500
Dangerous (Classes of)...361
Inspectorate............399
Misuse Act (1971).......361
Drumalbyn, Lord.........241
Minister without Portfolio.313
D.S.C...................305
D.S.O...................304
Dubai (Trucial States)....950–1
DUBLIN, CITY OF........202, 797
Airport................797
British Embassy.........795
Distance by Air.........1131
National University.......511
Trinity College.......511, 1073
DUCHESS OF GLOUCESTER....217
Birthday...............217
Crown of India..........261
Dame Grand Cross.......301
Household..............224
DUCHESS OF KENT......217, 548
Chancellor, Leeds Univ....509
Duchy of Cornwall........378
Duchy of Lancaster.......378
See also CHANCELLOR
Duck Egg Prices..........581
Dudley.................665
Archdeacon (Worcester)..478
Member of Parliament....332
Duisberg (Germany)......866
DUKE OF CORNWALL, *see* PRINCE
OF WALES
DUKE OF EDINBURGH, H.R.H.
212, 217, 218, 226
Academic Awards Council.512
Admiral of the Fleet......461
Birthday....89, 110, 217, 225

Pearson's Fresh Air Fund

Patron : HER MAJESTY THE QUEEN

Please help some of the thousands of needy or neglected children in Britain to be as happy as these.

£3 will ensure a week's holiday for them in the country or at the seaside

PLEASE ALSO REMEMBER CHILDREN IN YOUR WILL

Donations to :

81 DENISON HOUSE, 296, VAUXHALL BRIDGE ROAD, LONDON, S.W.1

PAGE

DUKE OF EDINBURGH—*continued*
Chancellor:—
Edinburgh University . . . 511
Salford University 510
University of Wales 510
Diary (1970–71) 548; 565
Duchy of Cornwall 378
Field Marshal 463
Financial Provision for 224
Grand Master, British Empire
Order 261
Guild of Air Pilots 640
Household 223
Knight of the Garter 259
Knight of the Thistle 259
Marriage 218
Marshal of the R.A.F. 465
Master Mariner 641
Master, Trinity House 435
Order of Merit 260
Pacific Tour (1971) 548
Precedence 219, 682
President, C.C.P.R. 530
Private Secretary 223
Privy Councillor 257
Royal Commission (1851) . . . 422
DUKE OF FIFE 216, 227, 233
Succession to the Throne . . . 219
DUKE OF GLOUCESTER . . . 217, 226
Birthday 98, 217, 226
Field Marshal 463
Financial Provision for 224
Great Master (Bath) 259
Household 224
Knight of Garter, St. Patrick
and Thistle Orders 259
Marshal of the R.A.F. 465
Patron, Service Clubs 466
Precedence 219, 682
Privy Councillor 257
Residences 217
Royal Victorian Chain 260
Succession to Throne 219
Trinity House 435
Duke of Kent (1902–42) 217
DUKE OF KENT 126, 217, 226
Birthday 217
Grand Master, St Michael and
St. George Order 260
Household 224
Succession to Throne 219
War Graves Commission 436
Duke of Rothesay . . . 218, 682
See also PRINCE OF WALES
DUKE OF WINDSOR
217, 226, 259, 463, 465
DUKES 227
Coronets 227
How Addressed 227
Number of 226
Precedence 219, 682
Royal 226
Dukinfield 665
Dulwich 651
College 651
Member of Parliament 329
Dumbarton 685
"Dumb-bell" Nebula 155
Dumfries 685
Member of Parliament 332
Dumfriesshire 679–80
Sheriff, etc. 684
Dunbar 685

PAGE

Dunbartonshire 679–80
Members of Parliament 332
Sheriff, etc. 684
Dunblane 685
DUNDEE, CITY OF . . 681, 685, 1019
County of City (*Note*) 679
Lord Provost 681
Members of Parliament 332
Sheriff, etc. 684
University of 511, 512
Weather (Monthly) . . . 1065–7
DUNDEE, EARL OF 230
Hereditary Standard Bearer 222
Privy Councillor 257
Dunedin (N.Z.) 734
Bishops 481, 490
Dunfermline 685
Member of Parliament 332
Dunipace, Denny and 685
Dunkeld, Bishop (R.C.) 487
Dunkirk 860
Dún Laoghaire 797
Tide Tables 172–83
Dunoon 685
Duns 685
Dunstable 665
Dunwich, Bishop (St. Edmunds-
bury) 477
Durban (S. Africa) 938
DURHAM, CITY OF 665
Bishop of 237, 478
Colleges of Education 532
Members of Parliament 332
Party Strengths 671
University 507, 512
Durham, County 631–3
Palatinate 378
Probate Offices 1181
Dushanbe (U.S.S.R.) . . 201, 968
Düsseldorf (Germany) 866
Distance by Air 1131
Dutch, *see* NETHERLANDS
Duty Marks (Plate) 1213
Dwelling Houses, *see* HOUSING
Dyfed (New Welsh County)
1019
Dyfed Powys Constabulary . . 676
Dynasties, British 213
English 210–11

EALING 642
Members of Parliament . . . 332
Party Strengths 671
Penny Rate 624
Earl Haig Fund (Scotland) . . 1102
Earl Marshal 227, 369, 644
EARL OF ST. ANDREWS 217
Birthday 217
Succession to Throne 219
EARLS 229–34
By Courtesy 256
Coronets 229
How addressed 229
Minors 226
Number of 226
Precedence 219, 682
Earnings, Average 617
EARTH, THE:—
Age 184
Area 198
Circumference 198
Density 163
Diameter 157, 198
Dimensions of 163

PAGE

EARTH, THE—*continued*
Distance from Moon 158
Distance from Sun 198
Ecliptic 163
Equator 163, 198
Equatorial Radius 145
Geological Periods 184–5
Inclination 163
Magnetic Storms 164
Orbital Speed 163, 198
Plane of Ecliptic 163
Polar Axis 163
Diameter 198
Radius 145
Rotation 141, 157, 198
Period 163
Satellites, *see below*
Seasons 163, 187–8
Shape 163
Sidereal Period 157
Terrestrial Magnetism . . . 163–4
Tides 163
Velocity 163, 198
See also WORLD
Earthquakes (1971) 568, 569
EARTH SATELLITES 165–9
Designation of 169
Heights and Speeds 166
Launchings (1957–71) . . . 166–9
(1970–71) 167–8
Observation of 169
Orbital Variations 165–6
Orbits 165
Retardation 165–9
Eas-Coul-Aulin (Waterfall)
207, 677
Easington, M.P. 332
Easington, M.P. 332
EAST AFRICA:—
Portuguese 929
Railways Administration . . . 756
Universities 792
East Anglia, University of . . . 509
Eastbourne, 665; M.P. 332
Weather (Monthly) 1065–7
EASTER DAY 188–9
Any Year (1753–2000) . . 194–7
(1972) 89, 102
(1968–77) 189
(1500–2000) 190
Earliest and Latest .(*Note*) 189
Fixed 189
Easter Island (Pacific) 837
Easter Law Sittings (1972)
102, 106, 449
Eastern Association 486
Eastern Germany 869–70
East Grinstead, M.P. 332
East Ham, M.P.'s 332
East Kilbride (New Town)
605, 685, 687
Eastleigh, 665; M.P. 332
East Lothian 679–80
Member of Parliament 327
East Midlands Airport 590
East Pakistan 765, 767
Civil War (1971) 572
(*Illus.*) 555
Cyclone Disaster (1970) . . 568
(*Illus.*) 555
East Retford 665
East Riding 631–3
Archdeacon 478
East Suffolk 631–3
East Sussex 631–3

Pages 693–1220 are omitted from the Shorter Edition

	PAGE
Ebbw Vale................675
Member of Parliament....332
Eccles, 665; M.P............332
ECCLES, VISCOUNT..........235
Paymaster General...313, 418
Privy Councillor..........257
ECCLESIASTICAL:—
Commissioners..........373
Courts..................484
Household.......221, 222–3
Patronage, Secretary for...450
Echo Satellites...............166
ECLIPSES (1972):—
Jupiter's Satellites.........147
Moon...................148
Sun.....................148
Eclipse Stakes...............999
Eclipse Year...............145
Eclipsing Variable Stars......153
Ecliptic, The...........150, 163
Defined.................141
Obliquity (1972)..........145
Economic Development Office 414
Planning Bd., Chairman .385–6
Economics Divns. (Dept. of Trade)................430
(Environment)..........384
ECSC.....................978
ECUADOR.. 200, 853–4; (Map) 923
British Embassy...........854
Currency..........854, 984
Embassy................853
Exchange Rate........83, 854
EDEN, SIR JOHN..........273
Member of Parliament....328
Minister for Industry .313, 428
Eden, Garden of (Iraq).......884
Edgbaston, M.P..........327
Edge Hill (Liverpool), M.P...338
EDINBURGH, CITY OF 202, 680, 685, 1019
Airport.................590
Archbishop (R.C.).........487
Art Galleries.............371
Banks................442–6
Bishops.................484
Castle, Governor.....222, 463
Clubs..............1091, 1093
Colleges of Education......532
County of City.....(Note) 679
Court of Session.........683
Customs and Excise.......377
Duke of, *see* DUKE
General Register House....422
Office..............426
Government Offices....423–6
Hall Marks on Plate......1213
Law Courts.............683
London Rail Fare.........593
Lord Provost............680
Members of Parliament.332–3
Newspapers............1077
Occultations Visible (1972)148–9
Population..........680, 685
Procurator Fiscal..........684
Royal Observatory........169
Scottish Academy......1094
Society.............1116
Schools...........541, 547
Scottish Central Library....606
Scottish Office..........423–6
Sheriff, etc.............684

EDINBURGH, CITY OF—*continued*
Theological Colleges...536, 537
Tide Tables (Leith).....172–83
University...........511, 512
Settlement.............513
Weather Information Service (Monthly)..........1065–7
Edmonton, Bishop of (London) 473
Edmonton, M.P............333
Edmonton (Alberta)....200, 701
Edrich, J. H. (*Portrait*).....563
Archbishop (R.C.).......487
EDUCATION IN U.K....1048–53
Adult....502–13, 517–37, 1051
Boys' Schools........537–44
Central Advisory Councils.1048
Colleges of 531, 532–4, 1050, 1052
C.N.A.A................1051
Cost.............611, 624
Curriculum and Exams Council....1049–50, 1053
Degrees in.............531–2
Directory...........502–47
Eleven-plus Selection.....1049
England and Wales....1048–51
Extra-Mural Studies......512
Further Education System 1050–1
(Scotland).............1052
General Certificate..1049–50
Girls' Schools........544–7
Headmasters' Conference..538
Schools.......538–41; 542–4
Inner London Authority...635
Inspectorate.......380–1, 1048
Local Authorities 514–7, 1048, 1050
Northern Ireland........1052
Officers..............514–7
Polytechnics......534–5, 1051
Professional.........517–37
Public Schools.......537–44
Scotland............1051–2
Scottish Certificate of....1052
Education Department....424
Secondary, Certificate of 1049–50
Secretary of State, *see* EDUCATION AND SCIENCE
Societies..............1103
Technical............534–6
Theological Colleges...536–7
Training Colleges......532–4
Universities and Colleges 502–12, 1052–3
Awards..............566
University Grants Cttee...435
Voluntary Agencies.....1048
Youth Service.........1051
EDUCATIONAL:—
Centres, Adult..........513
Settlements.............513
Trusts.............513–4
EDUCATION AND SCIENCE DEPT. OF............378–81, 622
Estimates................611
Secretary of State.313, 315, 378
Staff Numbers, etc.........608
Under Secretaries....313, 378

EDWARD VII (1901–1910) 130, 212, 214
Edward Medal...........305
EDWARD VIII (1936).....212, 217
See also DUKE OF WINDSOR
EFTA... 585; (*Note*) 868; 976
Trade with U.K..........976
Egg Imports, 579; Prices.....581
Eggs Division (M. of Agric.).363
Egham...................669
Eiffel Tower...............203
Eindhoven (Netherlands)....915
EIRE, *see* IRELAND, REPUBLIC OF
Eisteddfod................674
Elba (Italy)................888
Election Deposits, Forfeited...311
Election Petitions..........310
Office................458
Elections, Local Government 622–3
Elections, Parliamentary (1955–70)..................317
Electoral Divisions..........623
Electors, Local Government 622, 625
Parliamentary (Numbers) 325–48
Registration of...........1178
Electrical Engineering (Educ.).522
Exports.................587
ELECTRICITY:—
Authorities............381–2
Finance................583
Loans Outstanding..613, 614
Consumer Expenditure....618
Council.............381, 614
Divn. (Dept. of Trade)....431
Generating Board.........381
Industrial Training Bd......535
Measures........584, 1215
Production..............583
Strike (1970)............570
Electric Locomotives 592
Motors, High Temperature 1033–4
Electronics:—
Divn. (Trade Dept.).......431
Engineering (Educ.)......522
National Council........1124
Elgin....................685
Elizabeth (1558–1603).......211
Ellesmere Port............665
Ellice Islands (Pacific).......782
Eltham...................651
Elworthy, Sir Charles........273
Governor, Windsor Castle. 221
Marshal of the R.A.F.....465
Royal Commission (1851) .422
Ely......................669
Ely, Isle of..............631–3
Bishop of..........237. 475
Member of Parliament.....337
Ely Place, London..........645
Embankments, Thames......648
Embassies.....796, 802–3, 817–96
Ember Days...............189
Emigration................605
Emmanuel College, Cambridge, 505
Empire Gallantry Medal(*Note*) 304
State Building...........203
Employees (U.K.), Number of 606

DEFIANCE IN PUTNEY.

Down in the wilds of Putney there's a hospital full of men and women from all over Britain with a variety of crippling illnesses and one common quality. Defiance.

Our patients are incurable—as yet, in the present state of medical knowledge. They suffer from things like rheumatoid arthritis and multiple sclerosis and Parkinson's disease. They know they're incurable and they fight their disabilities with a defiance that would warm the cockles of your heart.

But, you may say, if they're all incurable, I'm wasting my money.

Not so. For the Royal Hospital and Home is a home as well as a hospital, and the more legacies we get and the more donations you send us, the more of a home we can make it.

The Royal Hospital and Home is *not* state-aided, either; without your help this war being waged down in Putney may well be lost.

The Appeals Secretary,
The Royal Hospital &
Home for Incurables,
Dept. W.A.1, 136 West Hill,
Putney, London S.W.15

PAGE

EMPLOYERS:—
Associations......1122–3, 1124
Registrar of............1015
Registration and Conduct
(Indust. Relations Act)
1015
Contributions (National
Insurance)...495, 499, 618
EMPLOYMENT:—
Average Wages, etc.......617
Collective Bargaining...1014–5
Contracts of............1014
Income from............616
Industrial Relations Act
354–7, 1014–6
Promotion, Local........610
Regional Premium.......349
(Selective) Tax 566, 610, 1182–4
Statistics..........606–8
Strikes (1970–71)......569–71
Unfair Dismissal........1014
EMPLOYMENT, DEPT. OF...382–4
Estimates (1971–72).......610
Gazette...............1082
Minister of State....313, 382–4
Secretary of State.313, 315, 382
Staff Statistics.........608
Under Secretaries........313
Enceladus (Satellite)......158
Enderbury Island (Pacific)782, 810
Endowment Assurances...1141–3
Bonuses............1138–9
Friendly Societies......1150–1
E.N.E.A.................982
Enfield.................642
Members of Parliament....333
Party Strengths.........671
Penny Rate.............624
ENGINEERING:—
College (R.N.)...........520
Degrees, etc..........521–2
Group Apprenticeship....536
Industrial Training Board..535
Institutions, Council of....522
Museums...........411, 412
Societies..............1103
Strikes (1969 & 1970).....607
Engineers, Royal..........464
England, Church of, see CHURCH
ENGLAND, KINGDOM OF...629–73
(Map)..............628
Ancient Monuments Board 395
Anglo-Saxons............630
Area and Population..202, 629
Christianity Introduced...630
Cities........634–42, 657–63
Climate................629
Coldest Month...........629
Counties.............631–3
Highest Point (Scafell).206, 629
High Sheriffs of Counties..632
Historical Monuments Com-
mission...............394
Historic Buildings Council. 394
History................630
Islands................629
Keeper of the Records.....421
Kings and Queens......210–11
Lakes..................629
Local Govt. Reorganization
568, 1018
Mountains..............629
Municipal Directory...664–70
New Towns.............687

PAGE

ENGLAND, KINGDOM OF—*continued*
Norman Conquest.......630
Patron Saint............673
Peers of................226
Population (1971).........629
Precedence in...........219
Premier Barony..........250
Presbyterian Church.......484
Primate................478
Rainfall................629
Rivers.................629
Roman Conquest........630
Sunniest Months........629
Test Matches.....1000, 1001
ENGLAND AND WALES:—
Map................628
Adult Colleges..........512
Aerodromes............590
Ages of Population.......600
Agricultural Holdings.....580
Area, etc..............599
Bank Holidays (1972–74)
190, 663
Borough Councils........622
Building Statistics........604
Causes of Death (1969, 1970)
601–2
Census (1801–1971)......599
Child Care Statistics......1157
County Boroughs........622
County Councils.........622
Crimes and Trials 569
Criminal Statistics......602–3
Crown Revenues.........375
Divorce Statistics........600
Education.........1048–51
Authorities..........514–6
Cost of...........611, 624
Directory..........502–47
Electricity Boards......381–2
Expectation of Life.......1149
Income from Employment.616
Judicature...........449–56
Jury Service............1170
Law Sittings............449
Local Government......622–4
Party Strengths.......671–3
Motorways..............591
Police (Strength)........584
Population (1801–1971)....599
Age Distribution........600
Public Holidays..........190
Quarter Days........(Note) 94
Rateable Value..........624
Rates Levied (Total)......624
River Authorities.........625
Roads (Length).........591
Roman Catholic Church....487
Rural District Councils.....622
Spring Holiday. (Note) 106; 578
Urban District Councils....622
Weather in 1970–71....1061–4
Weather Values (1970–71) .1064
English Channel..........629
English-speaking Union.....1103
Enham Village Centre......1103
Entertainments, Public Spend-
ing on................618
Entomology Museum (Natural
History)...............411
Enugu (Nigeria).........763
Environmental Pollution, Royal
Commission on..........437

PAGE

Environmental Research
Council 415–6
ENVIRONMENT, DEPT. OF THE
384–7, 565, 622
Estimates (1971–72).......611
Secretary of State.313, 315, 384
Staff Strength, Cost......608
Envoys, see Ambassadors;
Ministers
Eolian Islands (Italy)........891
Epact...............89, 187
Ephemeris Time 141–2
Ephesus, Temple of Diana...202
Epiphany............90, 188
Episcopal Church in Scotland.484
Theological College.......536
Episcopal Sees (C. of E.)...473–82
Epochs and Calendars.....186–97
Epping Forest...........651
Epping, M.P.............333
Epsom.................665
Member of Parliament....333
Races...........998, 999
Equalization Grants (Local
Government)...........623
Equation of Time, Daily
91, 95, 99; 141
Equator, The............198
Celestial..............150
Magnetic.............164
Equatorial Guinea....199, 854
Equerries, H.M..........222
Duke of Edinburgh.......223
Duke of Gloucester.......224
Equinoctial Year......186, 187–8
Equinoxes.............89
Autumnal.........122, 187
Spring...........98, 187
Erevan (Armenia)......201, 968
Erie, Lake..............205
Erith (and Crayford), M.P....333
Eritrea (Ethiopia)..........855
"ERNIE"..............446
Eros (Planet)............159
Erskine Bridge opened (1971).548
Ervine, St. John, Obituary ...574
Esher, 669; M.P..........333
Essen (Germany)..........866
Essex...............631–3
Members of Parliament...333
Probate Offices........1181
University of...........509
Estate Duty:—
Offices..........402, 404
Rates...........566, 1193
Revenue.............609
Starting Point raised (1971).352
Estate Management (Educ.).522–3
Estimates:—
Defence Services 612
Supply...........610–12
ESTONIA (U.S.S.R.).202, 961, 968
ETHIOPIA. 199; (Map) 855; 855–6
British Embassy.........856
Calendar..............193
Currency.........856, 984
Education.............856
Embassy..............855
Emperor..........208, 855
Exchange Rate......83, 856
Finance and Trade.......856
Government............855
Etna, Mt...............205

Pages 693–1220 *are omitted from the* Shorter Edition

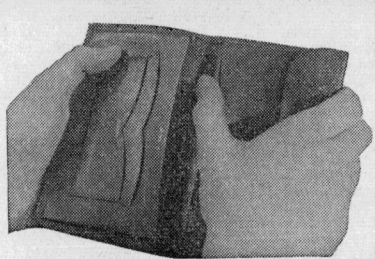

PAGE

Eton College..........539, 651
  v. Harrow (Cricket).....1002
Eton Fives.................1008
Eton, M.P..................333
Euphrates River (Iraq)..206, 883
  (Syria)..................947
Euratom....................981
Eurocontrol (Cost)..........982
Europa (Satellite)...........158
EUROPE (Continent)....198, 202
  Air Mail Rates...1197, 1206–9
  Passengers to............588
  Areas and Populations.....202
  Areas below Sea Level.....1128
  British Holiday Statistics...448
  Common Market, *see* EURO-
   PEAN ECONOMIC COMMUNITY
  Council of.................988
  Countries and Capitals.....202
  Highest Point.............206
  Population.................198
  Standard Time............143
  Telephone Charges to.....1205
  Service (STD).........1204
  Trade Statistics..........585
EUROPEAN:—
  Airways Corporation..371, 589
  Athletics (1971)........994–5
  Atomic Energy Community
     981
  Boxing Champions.......1011
  Coal and Steel Community.978
  Commission...............977
  Community............977–81
  Council of Ministers......977
  Court of Justice...........978
  Cup-Winners' Cup.......1005
EUROPEAN ECONOMIC COM-
  MUNITY:—
  Agriculture Policy........979
  British Delegation to......981
  Entry Terms............574
  White Paper
     357–9, 558, 567
  Economic Policy......979–80
  Enlargement..............978
  Finance..................981
  Industrial Policy..........980
  Member States...........977
  Regional Policy..........980
  Social Policy.............980
  Trade............585, 978–9
   with U.K...............979
  Transport Policy..........980
  Tariff....................979
EUROPEAN:—
  Football Competitions....1005
  Free Trade Association 976, 982
  Trade (1968–70).........585
  Information Service.......977
  Nuclear Energy Agency....982
  Parliament............977–8
  Space Research Organization
     982
  Theatre, Ground Forces....458
  Time.....................143
Evangelical Union..........486
Evening Newspapers....1077–8
Evening Stars.......91, 95, 99
EVENTS OF THE YEAR..548; 565–74
  Latest...................574
Everest, Mt........205, 206, 913
Evesham...................665

PAGE

Examinations, Secondary Schl.
     1049–50
Examiners, Supreme Court....450
Exchange (Liverpool), M.P...339
Exchange (Manchester), M.P..339
EXCHANGE RATES..........83–4
Exchequer and Audit Dept.
    387, 608, 610
Exchequer Assets (1970)....614–5
Exchequer, Chancellor of the,
  see CHANCELLOR
Exchequer Court (Scotland)..683
Excise, Board of..........376–8
Executive, The.............313
Executors of Wills..........1180
EXETER.....................665
  Bishop of............237, 475
  Member of Parliament......333
  University.............509, 512
Exeter College, Oxford......502
Exeter, Marquess of.........228
  Grand Almoner...........220
Exhibition of 1851 Committee
    422
Exhibitions, Museum.....409–14
Exmoor National Park......626
Exmouth...................669
Expectation of Life.........1149
Explosives Inspectorate (Home
  Office)...................396
EXPORTS:—
  Credits Department......387
  Divns. (Dept. of Trade)....429
  from U.K..............586–7
  National Council......439–40
  Queen's Award......1059–60
  Restrictions (Postal).....1198
  Transit Ports.............595
Express Postal Services.1200, 1201
Extragalactic Nebulae.....154–5
Extra-Mural Studies Depts....512
Extra-terrestrial Life........1034
Eye Services (N.H.S.)...501, 1157
Eye (Suffolk), 665; M.P.....333

FACTORIES, INSPECTORS OF.....383
Faculae (Solar)..............156
Faculties, Court of..........484
Faculty of Advocates........524
Fahrenheit Thermometer....1216
Failsworth.................669
Fair Isle...................678
Falkirk, 685; M.P............345
FALKLAND ISLANDS. .200, 779, 984
Falling Stars (Meteors)....161–2
Falls, Capt. Cyril, Obituary . .574
Falls, Deaths from (1970).....602
Falls of Glomach...........677
Falmouth, 665; M.P..........333
Famagusta (Cyprus).....739, 740
Family Allowances..........498
  Cost of.............498, 611
  Income Tax............1188
Family Division (High Court) 450
  Judges.................450
  Probate Offices 451–2, 1181–2
  Doctor Service (N.H.S.)...500
Family Income Supplement
  349, 350, 359, 498, 565, 566
Family Law Reform Act (1969)
    1168, 1169, 1176
  Names of Peers........252–6
FAO.......................814
Far East, The..............201

PAGE

Fareham, 669; M.P.........334
Farming:—
  Bankruptcies (1970).....1160
  Income.............581, 618
  Institutes (Educ.).........1051
  Statistics..............580–2
Farms (Number).............582
Farnborough...............669
Farnham, 669; M.P..........333
Farnworth, 665; M.P........333
Faröe (Sheep Islands)...852, 984
Fathom (Measure)..........578
Fat Stock:—
  Divisions (Min. of Agric.)..363
  Prices...................581
Faversham, 665; M.P........333
Feasts, Movable...........189
Feather, Victor.............102
  Gen. Secretary, T.U.C....1125
Felixstowe, Shipping........595
Fellahin Race (U.A.R.).......955
Felling....................669
Feltham, M.P...............333
Fencing...................1008
Ferens Art Gallery..........655
Fermanagh, County.........691
  High Sheriff..............691
  M.P. (Westminster).......333
  M.P.'s (Belfast)...........688
Fernando Póo (Eq. Guinea)..854
Festival Hall................636
Festivals, Religious:—
  Christian...........138, 188–90
  Jewish..................191
  Moslem.................193
Fettes College.........541, 548
Fez (Morocco)..............912
Fiction of 1970–71.........1025
Fidei Defensor (Record)......421
Field Marshals..............463
  Pay, 467; Pensions.......472
Fife.....................679–80
  Members of Parliament....333
  Sheriff, etc...............684
FIJI.............203, 693, 740–1
  Cabinet..................740
  Communications.........741
  Currency................984
  Finance and Trade.......740
  Government.............740
  High Commissions.......740
  S. Pacific University......791
FINANCE:—
  Act (1971)............620–1
  Bank Controls freed (1971).567
  Bank of England.........440
  Bank Rate.....566, 567, 615
  Bankruptcies (1962–70)...1160
  Banks and Banking.440–6, 448
  Bill (1971), Debates......351–4
  Budget (1971).....351–4, 566
  Estimates............609–12
  Surplus.................609
  Consumer Expenditure....618
  Price Index.............1195
  Corporation Tax Reform..621
  Defence Estimates........612
  Estate Duty....566, 609, 1193
  Financial Year........(*Note*) 98
  Food Subsidies...........610
  Foreign Exchange Rates...83–4
  Income Tax..........1185–91
  International Banks......815–6

Pages 693–1220 are omitted from the Shorter Edition

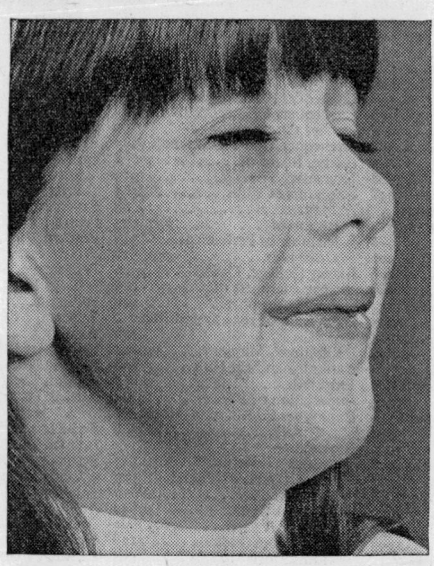

Janet has no fear of the dark–now

Janet has lost her sight, but once again she is like any other little girl – happy and mischievous. Her parents knew they could rely on the RNIB. The RNIB help the blind of all ages, help nearly all the 116,000 blind of Britain.

With their Sunshine Homes and Schools for blind babies and children, rehabilitation centres for the newly blind and homes for the elderly. And with braille literature, Talking Books and many other special aids for the blind.

For all this, the RNIB need donations and legacies. Please give generously.

RNIB THE ROYAL NATIONAL INSTITUTE
FOR THE BLIND
224 GREAT PORTLAND ST., LONDON W1N 6AA
Registered in accordance with the National Assistance Act 1948

PAGE

FINANCE—*continued*
Local Government......623–4
National Debt..........613–5
National Insurance....492–9
National Loans Fund....613
Overseas Debt Repaid.....352
Overseas Loans Guaranteed.614
Personal Incomes......616–8
Public Sector Expenditure
349, 616–9
Purchasing Power of £....1195
Revenue and Expenditure
609–12
Selective Employment Tax
1182–4
Stock Exchanges
648, 1053, 1117
Supply Estimates...609, 610–12
Taxation Reform (1973) 620–1
Revenue................609
U.K. Official Reserves.....584
Unit Trusts............1158–60
Financial Secretary of the
Treasury..........313, 433
Financial Times............1077
Financial Year..........(*Note*) 98
Finchley, M.P..............333
Fine Art Commissions...369–70
FINLAND...202, 856–8; (*Map*) 856
British Embassy..........858
Cabinet..................856
Currency..........858, 984
Embassy.................857
Finance and Trade..585, 857–8
Nobel Prizes........857, 1054
Shipbuilding............597
Shipping.................596
Finsbury, M.P..............344
Fireballs...............161–2
Fire Insurance:—
Companies............1145–8
Due.(*Notes*) 90, 102, 114, 126
Rates................1134
Fire Salvage Corps........1116
Fire Service:—
Colleges...............396
Cost to Ratepayers........624
Departments......396, 425
London..................636
Fires in 1970–71.....568, 569
First and Principal ADC....220
First-class Mail..........1047
First Lord of the Treasury 313, 432
First Point of Aries
91, 95, 99; 138, 140, 141, 150
First Sea Lord..........459, 461
FISH:—
Consumer Expenditure... 618
Imports and Exports.....586
Landed (1970)..........582
Fisheries Boards....394, 437
Department............363
Development Authorities..625
Commission.........378
Estimates.............611
Grants, etc.............611
Laboratories........363, 424
Minister of....313, 315, 362
(Scotland) Dept.......423–4
Fishermen (Numbers)........582
Fishing (Angling) Records...1009
Fishmongers' Company......640
Hall....................646

PAGE

Fitzwilliam College, Cambridge
505
Museum......505, 655
Fives (1971)..............1008
Fixed Easter..............189
Fixed Stars, *see* STARS—Mean
Places
Flag Officers (R.N.).......461
Flags, Flying of..........225
Flags, National 818–976
Flamsteed, John..........146
House, Greenwich........651
Flat Racing......998, 999
Fleet, H.M. (1972)........462
Admirals of the.........461
Submarines.............462
Fleet (Hants.).............669
Fleetwood..................665
Flegrean Islds. (Italy).......891
Fleming, Peter, Obituary....574
Flint (Wales)..............675
Flintshire, 675, 676; M.P.'s..333
Floating Debt (U.K.)........614
Florence (Italy).........890, 891
Florida (State)...........800
Florin, The...............1210
Flying Schools.............517
Folio Defined..............1217
Folkestone 204, 665; M.P...333
FOOD:—
Civil Estimates...........610
Divisions (Min. of Agric.)..364
Expenditure, National....618
Exports and Imports...579, 586
Minister of, and Ministry, *see*
AGRICULTURE
Organization (U.N.)......814
Side Effects of 1040
Subsidies................610
FOOTBALL:—
Association Football......1005
Associations............1013
Disaster (1971); 568; (*Illus.*) 554
European...............1005
Events (1970–71)........571
F.A. Cup (1971)....571, 1005
Rugby League...........1004
Rugby Union...........1004
World Cup 1005
Footwear, Imports, etc.....587
Forces' Clubs............466
Pay and Pensions.......467–72
Ford Prison (Governor).....398
FOREIGN AND COMMONWEALTH
OFFICE.............387–9
Estimated (1971–72)....610
Minister of State....313, 388
Passports.............983
Secretary of State...313, 387
(1939–71)..........314
Under Secretaries...313, 388
Foreign Compensation Com-
mission.............437
FOREIGN COUNTRIES
199–203, 817–976
Air Mail Letters.....1197–8
Parcels...........1206–9
Ambassadors.......817–975
Capitals....199–203, 818–976
Car Production 587
Consulates.........821–975
Currencies.........984–8
Distances by Air.......1131
Events (1970–71)....572–4

PAGE

FOREIGN COUNTRIES—*continued*
Exchange Rates........83–4
Flags.............818–976
National Days.90, 94, 98, etc.
Postage Rates to......1196
Rulers..............208–9
Shipbuilding...........597
Shipping Arrivals, etc....595
Owned, etc........596
Summer Time..........142
Telephone Rates to.....1205
Foreign Service Messengers...389
Salaries...............817
Forestry Commission.......389
Cost to Taxpayers......611
Commonwealth Institute...368
Education.............523
Training Board..........535
Forfar (Angus).............685
Forfeited Election Deposits...311
Formby (Lancs.)...........669
Formosa (Taiwan)...201, 843, 985
Forms of Address, *see* ADDRESS
Forres.................685
Fort de France (Martinique)
200, 862
Forth River................677
Bridges................206
Fort Lamy (Chad) ...199, 837
Foulness, Airport Site......566
Fowey (with St. Austell).....667
Fox Hunting Season...(*Note*) 130
Franc (France)............862
FRANCE..202, 858–64; (*Map*) 860
Air Passengers to 588
Area, etc...............859
British Council..........863
British Embassy..........863
Cabinet................858
Capital............202, 863
Car Production........587
Cathedrals.............862
Cities.................863
Communications.........862
Constitution (Fifth Repub-
lic)...............860–1
Currency..........862, 985
Defence................861
Departments.......859, 862–3
Education............861–2
Embassy.............858–9
European Community...977–81
Events (1970–71).........573
Exchange Rate......83, 862
Fifth Republic......209, 860–1
Finance.................862
Government.........859–61
Harvests (1970)..........861
Language and Literature...861
Nobel Prizes......861, 1054
Overseas Depts., etc....862–3
Population............202, 859
Presidents 208, 209, 858, 859–61
Prime Minister..........858
Production and Industry...861
Railways, Roads..........862
Regions, etc. (Population)...859
Secretaries of State........858
Shipbuilding............597
Shipping..........596, 862
Telegram, Parcel, Telephone
Rates to......1205, 1206
Trade............585, 862
Universities.............862

PAGE

FRANCE—continued
v. G.B. (Athletics)......994–5
Visitors' Passports to......983
France, S.S....................598
Franchise, The..............1178
Francophone Countries......863
Frankfurt (Germany).......866
Franklin (N.W.T., Canada)...700
Franks, Lord................251
   Chancellor, Univ. of East
     Anglia....................509
   Privy Councillor...........257
   Provost, Worcester Coll....503
Fraserburgh..................685
Fraud Statistics..............602
Fredericton (New Brunswick)
                200, 703
   Archbishop.................480
Frederik IX, King
       208, 259, 260, 851
Free Church of England.....486
Free Handicap (Newmarket) 999
Freemen's Guilds...... 663, 1104
Freetown (Sierra Leone).199, 767
Free Trade Association......976
Freezing Point..............1216
Freight Corporation, National
                389–90
   Integration Council........390
Fremantle (W. Australia).714, 729
FRENCH COMMUNITY......863–4
   Currency...................985
French Guiana........ 863, 985
   Polynesia..................203
   West Indies........200, 862–3
French-speaking States.......863
Freshwater Fisheries Lab.....424
Friendly Societies 1150–1
   Act (1971)................1151
   Registries........390, 611, 1150
Friends (Quakers)...........486
   House (London)............491
   Marriage Law.............1174
Frigates, R.N................462
Frimley and Camberley.....669
FRUIT:—
   Consumer Expenditure... 618
   Imports and Exports...579, 586
   Picking Machine (Science
     Notes)...................1035
   Statistics (U.K.). 580
Frunze (Kirghizia)...... 201, 968
Fry, C.B., Centenary.........577
Fuel and Power:—
   Consumer Expenditure... 618
   Divns. (Dept. of Trade)....431
   Electricity Measures.......1215
   Manpower Employed......606
   Measures...................584
   Oil Consumption (U.K.)...584
   Statistics................583–4
   Technology (Education)....523
Fujairah (Trucial State).....951
Fujiyama, Mt................205
Fukuoka (Japan)............895
Fulham, Bishop of (London).473
   Member of Parliament.....333
   Palace.....................645
Fulwood (Lancs.)............669
Funchal (Madeira)..........929
Funen Isld. (Denmark).......851
Furniture, Exports, etc.... 587
   Industrial Training Bd....535
   Public Spending on....... 618

PAGE

Further Education:—
   Branches 1050–1, 1052
   Statistics 1050, 1051
Fylde, Members of Parliament
              341, 344

GABOON, Republic of
     199; (Map) 836; 864
Gaborone (Botswana) ...199, 736
Gaelic Speakers (1961)......677
Gainsborough, M.P..........333
Galactic Nebulae............154
Galactic Pole, North........145
   Star Clusters..............153
Galápagos Islands (Ecuador) ..853
Galashiels...................685
Galaţi (Rumania)............932
Galaxies, External.........154–5
   4C$_3$1·04 1039
Galaxy, The.................154
Gale Measures..............1211
   Warning Service (Coastguard)
               793
Galilee (Israel)..............886
Galle (Ceylon)...............738
Gallon (Measure)...........1214
   U.S........................809
Gallons and Litres..........1218
Galloway, Bishops......484, 487
   Member of Parliament....334
   Sheriff.....................684
Galston.......................685
GAMBIA, THE.....199, 693, 741–2
   Currency...................985
   Finance and Trade........742
   Government................741
   High Commissions.........741
   Trade Commissioner.......729
Gambier Islds. (Pacific)......864
Game (Close Times)........1213
Gaming Board...............390
Ganges Delta Cyclone (1970)..568
   (Illus.)....................555
Gangtok (Sikkim)...........753
Ganymede (Satellite)........158
Goals........................398
Garages Bankrupt (1970) ...1160
Garden of Eden (Iraq).......884
Gardner Arts Centre (Brighton)
               1059
Garforth (W. Yorks.)........669
Garibaldi (Italy)............889
Garston (Liverpool), M.P....339
Garter, Order of the........259
   King of Arms.........259, 369
   Knights of the............259
      Precedence..............219
   Ladies of the..............259
GAS:—
   Boards.....................390
   Consumer Expenditure....618
   Corporation (proposal)....567
   Council....................390
      Finance.................583
   Loans Outstanding .613, 614
   Divn. (Dept. of Trade)....431
   Imports (1969–70)........586
   Industrial Training Board..535
   Measures...................584
   Production.................583
Gateshead, 665; M.P.'s......334
Gatley, Cheadle and........
GATT....................816, 982
Gatwick Airport 588, 590

PAGE

Gawber (Yorks), Glasshouse
   Sites....................1046–7
G.C.E....................1049–50
Gdańsk (Poland)............927
Geelong (Victoria).........727
Geffrye Museum............645
Gelligaer...................675
Gelsenkirchen (Germany)....866
Geminid Meteors......135, 162
Genealogists, Society of
             1104, 1162
GENERAL:—
   Certificate of Education 1049–50
   Council of the Bar........1096
   Dental Council............1102
GENERAL ELECTION (1970)....317
   Forfeited Deposits........311
   Small Majorities..........324
   Votes Cast......317, 325–48
General Elections (1955–70)...317
GENERAL:—
   Medical Council..........1108
   Nursing Councils........1111
   Officers.................463–4
   Pay, 467; Pensions.......472
   Optical Council...........1111
   Rate Act, 1967.......623, 624
   Register Office, see Population
     Censuses, Office of
   Register Office (Edinburgh)
                426
Genetic Research Units......407
Geneva (Switzerland).......947
   Distance by Air..........1131
Genoa (Italy)..........890, 891
Gentlemen-at-Arms........222
Gentlemen Ushers
     220–1, 259–61, 309
Geographical Society, Royal
               1104
Geological Periods........184–5
   Sciences, Institute of......415
Geology Degrees............523
   Museum...................415
Geophysics Museum........412
GEORGE V (1910–36)
    90, 212, 214, 216, 217
GEORGE VI (1936–52)
    134, 212, 217, 218
   George Cross......304, 1189
George-Brown, Lord...251, 358
   In My Way..............1024
   Offices held...........314, 315
George Inn, Southwark.....645
George Medal...............305
George Town (Cayman).....787
Georgetown (Guyana)...200, 744
George Town (Penang).....201
Georgia (U.S.A.)............800
Georgia (U.S.S.R.) .201, 961, 966
German Grand Prix........1012
Germany..202, 864–70 (Map) 865
Germany, Eastern........869–70
   Communist Party.........869
   Council of State..........869
   Currency...................985
   Regions....................869
   Trade......................585
   v. G.B. (Athletics), 1971....994
GERMANY, FEDERAL REPUBLIC OF
      202, 866–9
   Agriculture................867
   Air Passengers to.........588
   British Embassy.........868–9

PAGE

GERMANY, FEDERAL REPUBLIC OF
—*continued*
Cabinet..................866
Car Production..........587
Chancellor..............866
Communications.........868
Currency...........867, 985
Education...............868
Embassy................866
European Community..977–81
Finance.................867
Exchange Rate...........83
Government...........866–7
Industrial Production....867
Labour Statistics........867
Länder.................866
Language and Literature..866
Nobel Prizes.....868, 1054
Parcel Post Rates to.....1207
Political Parties........866–7
Population..........202, 866
President...............866
Production Statistics.....867
Shipbuilding............597
Shipping...............596
Telephone Rates to......1205
Trade...........585, 867–8
   with U.K.............868
Visitors' Passports to....983
Vital Statistics..........866
Gestation, Periods of.....1124
GHANA
      199, 693, 742–3; (*Map*) 957
Cabinet.................742
Communications.........743
Currency...............985
Finance and Trade.....743–4
Government.............742
High Commissions.......743
Production, etc..........743
Regional Chief Executives
                      742–3
Trade Commissioner.....729
Universities............791
Volta River Project......743
Ghent (Belgium).........827
Giant's Causeway........794
GIBRALTAR........202, 779–80
Air Mail Rates.........1197
Bishops............482, 487
Currency...............985
Distance by Air.........1131
Government.............780
Gifts, Stamp Duty.......1194
GILBERT AND ELLICE ISLANDS
                     203, 782
Gillingham (Kent)........665
Member of Parliament.....334
Gipsy Moth IV (Greenwich)..651
Girl Guides Association...1105
Girls:—
Brigade, The.............1105
Clubs, etc..............1105
National Insurance
   Contributions..........499
Public Day School Trust...545
Schools..............544–7
   Yearbook............1075
Girton College, Cambridge..505
Girvan..................685
Glamorgan..........675, 676
Polytechnic, Pontypridd...535
Probate Offices.........1181
Proposed Counties 1019

PAGE

GLASGOW, CITY OF......680, 685
Airport.................590
Archbishop (R.C.).......487
Bishop.................484
Clubs.............1091–2, 1093
Colleges of Education....532
County of City.....(*Note*) 679
Football Disaster (1971)...568
   (*Illus.*)............554
London Rail Fare........593
Lord Provost...........680
Members of Parliament...334
Newspapers............1077
Passport Office.........983
Population.........680, 685
Procurator Fiscal........684
School of Art...........518
Schools...........541, 547
Sheriffs, etc............684
Shipping...............595
Stipendiary Magistrates...683
Sunrise Times .93, 97, 101, etc.
Theological Colleges..536, 537
Trade..................595
University...........511, 512
Weather (Monthly)....1065–7
Glastonbury.............665
Tor, Excavations.......1045–6
Glenrothes (New Town).605, 687
Globular Star Clusters......153
Glossop.................665
Gloucester..............665
Bishop of.........237, 475
Member of Parliament....334
Gloucestershire........631–3
Members of Parliament...334
G.M.T.............140–1, 143
G.N.P. Statistics.........616
Goa (India).............753
Gobi (Mongolia).........910
Godalming..............665
Goddard, Lord, Obituary ..574
   (*Portrait*)...........560
Godmanchester, Huntingdon
   and.................666
Godthaab (Greenland)....852
Golborne...............669
GOLD:—
Coins.................1210
Cup (Ascot)............999
Extraction Process......1035
Reserves (U.K.).........584
Sticks............220, 223
U.S.A. Holdings........806
Wares (Hall-Marks)....1212–3
Golden Gate Bridge........206
Golden Number......89, 187
Goldsmiths' Company and Hall
                     640, 646
College................513
Hall-Marks...........1212–3
Golf...............571, 1006
Unions, etc...........1013
Gonville and Caius College,
   Cambridge............505
Good Friday (1972)....89, 98
Posts, etc...........1200, 1204
Good Housekeeping.........1079
Goods Vehicle Licences....591
Production and Exports..587
Goole, 665; M.P.........334
Gorbals (Glasgow), M.P....334
Gorky (R.S.F.S.R.)........965
Gorton (Manchester), M.P....339

PAGE

Gosforth.................669
Gosport; 665; M.P.........334
Gothenburg (Sweden)......945
Gough Island (Tristan)....785
Gourock................685
Govan, M.P..............334
Governing Bodies Association
   (Boys' Schools').......537
GOVERNMENT, THE:—
British Commonwealth....693
British Constitution......306
Cabinet................313
Local Government......622–5
Party Government........312
Prime Minister...313, 314, 432
Sovereign, The..........306
Government Actuary....390, 612
Chemist...............432
Copyright..............426
Hospitality Fund......390, 612
Information Dept.......400–1
GOVERNMENT OFFICES....362–428
Buildings (Cost)..........611
Northern Ireland.........689
Reorganization (1970)....565
Staff Numbers, etc........608
Union Jack Flown.........225
Government of Ireland Act...688
Government Printing Office..426
Government Publications...426
Whips.................312
Governors-General.........693
Gower, M.P..............334
Gozo (Malta).........202, 760
Grace and Favour Residences.651
Graduated Pensions....492, 495
Contracting out.........495
Contributions......495, 499
Rates of Pension........495
Graduate Society (Durham) . 507
Grammar Schools........1049
Gramophone Records Produc-
   tion and Sales)........579
Grampian Hills...........677
Grand Almoner...........220
Grand Challenge Cup.....1009
Grand National (1971).....999
Grand Prix de Paris.......999
Grands Prix Motor Races...1012
Grand Turk.........200, 788
Grangemouth............685
Grantham...............665
Bishop of (Lincoln)......476
Member of Parliament....334
Grass Harvests..........582
Grassland Advisers (Min of
   Agric.)...............365
Graveney Boat Find (1970)..1046
Graves Art Gallery........657
Gravesend..............665
Member of Parliament....334
Gray's Inn..........524, 646
Graz (Austria)...........824
Great Barrier Reef........708
Great Bear, Lake.........205
GREAT BRITAIN, *see* UNITED
   KINGDOM
Greater London:—
See also LONDON
Area and Population......634
Boroughs..............642
Electors (Number).......622
Life Expectation Table....1149
Planning Authorities......635

Pages 693–1220 are omitted from the Shorter Edition

Thank you

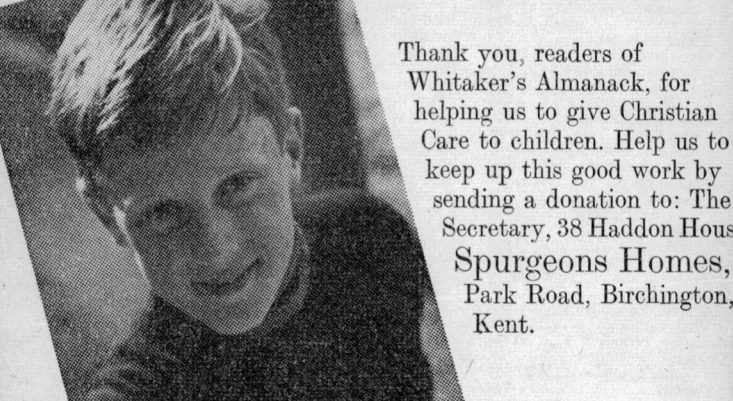

PAGE

Greater London Council ..634–6
  Aldermen..............634–5
  Chairman............632, 634
  Chief Officers...........635
  County Hall..............644
  Finance.................636
  Members..............634–5
  Rent Increases (1971–3)...568
  Services..............635–6
Great Grimsby.............665
  Bishop of (Lincoln).......476
  Member of Parliament......335
Great Marlborough Street
    Court.................455
"Great" Nebula............155
Great Seal (Scotland)......682
Great Slave Lake..........205
Great Yarmouth............668
  Member of Parliament......348
GREECE 202; (*Map*) 870; 870–2
  British Embassy........871–2
  Cabinet.................870
  Communications..........871
  Currency............871, 985
  Defence.................871
  Embassy................870
  Exchange Rate........83, 871
  Government..........869–70
  Language and Literature...871
  Production..............871
  Religion................871
  Shipping................596
  Trade, 585; with U.K....871
Green Cloth, Board of......222
Green Jackets, The Royal...465
Greenland.............206, 852
Green Line Coach Fares.....593
Greenock.................685
  Member of Parliament......334
  Tide Tables......171, 172–83
Green Park (London)........649
Green Rod, Usher of the....259
GREENWICH............642, 651
  Hospital................651
  Magistrates' Court........455
  Mean Time
                140–1, 142, 143, 169
    Resumed (1971)....350–1
  Member of Parliament......335
  National Maritime Museum
                            413
  Occultations Visible (1972)
                            143–9
  Party Strengths..........671
  Royal Naval Colleges......520
  Royal Observatory...169, 651
  Sidereal Time............141
  Tunnel.................649
Gregorian Calendar........188
Grenada (West Indies)
                200, 694, 786, 788
Grenadines (Windward Islands)
                            788
Grenoble (France)..........863
Grey College (Durham Univ.)
                            507
Greyfriars Hall (Oxford Univ.)503
Grey of Naunton, Lord......251
  Governor, N. Ireland.....688
Grimond, Rt. Hon. J.:—
  Chancellor, University of
    Kent..................510
  Member of Parliament.....341
Grimsby, *see* Great Grimsby

PAGE

Grocers Bankrupt (1970)....1160
Grocers Company...........640
Gross National Product(U.K.)616
Group Captains, Pay, etc....468
Grouse Shooting.(*Notes*), 118, 134
Guadalajara (Mexico)....204, 909
Guadeloupe......200, 862–3, 985
GUAM......203, 798, 800, 810
Guarantees (Stamp Duty)....1193
Guardian, The...........1077
Guardians' Allowances......494
  Cost..................496
Guardianship Act, 1971.....359
  Court Orders...........603
Guards, Division, The......464
  Depôt Buildings, Pirbright
                            1056–7
GUATEMALA 200, 872; (*Map*) 875
  Currency............872, 985
Guatemala (City)...........872
Guayaquil (Ecuador)........854
Guayra Falls (Brazil).......207
Guernsey.................692
  Dean (Winchester).......473
  Population..............599
Guiana, French........200, 863
Guiana, Netherlands...200, 915–6
Guided Missile Destroyers...462
Guildford.................665
  Bishop of..........237, 475
  Member of Parliament.....335
  Museum................655
Guildhall.................645
  Justice Rooms...........456
  Library.................645
  Museum..............411, 648
  School of Music.........529
Guilds (Livery Companies).640–2
GUINEA, REPUBLIC OF
            199, 872–3; (*Map*) 873
  British Embassy..........873
  Cabinet.................872
  Currency................985
  Government...........872–3
Guinea, Equatorial, *see* Equa-
    torial Guinea
Guinea, Portuguese.....929, 987
"Guineas, The"............999
Gujarat (State), India......750
Gulf Stream (Norway).......917
Gurkhas, Brigade of........465
Gustaf VI, Adolf, King
            209, 216, 259, 260, 943
GUYANA........200, 693, 744–5
  Archbishop..............481
  Currency................985
  Finance and Trade.......745
  Government..............744
  High Commissions.......744
  Judicature..............744
  Trade Commissioner.....729
  University...............791
Guy's Hospital............525
Gwent, Gwynedd (New Welsh
    Counties)............1019
Gwynedd Police Authority...676

HABERDASHERS' COMPANY....640
H.A.C...................645
Hackney (Borough)........642
  Members of Parliament
                        335, 345
  Party Strengths.........671
Hackney Carriage Licences..1209

PAGE

Haddington...............685
Hadrian's Wall........630, 678
Hague The (Netherlands)
                        202, 915
  British Embassy..........915
  Intl. Court of Justice.....813
Haifa (Israel).............887
Hailé Selassié, Emperor..208, 855
  Knight of the Garter......259
  Royal Victorian Chain....260
Haileybury School.........539
HAILSHAM OF ST. MARYLEBONE,
    LORD.................251
  Birthday................126
  Lord High Chancellor.313, 314
  Privy Councillor.........257
  Speaker, House of Lords...309
Haiphong (Vietnam)........973
HAITI...................200;
    574, 786, 863, 873–5; (*Map*) 874
  British Embassy..........875
  Currency............874, 985
Halesowen................665
  (Oldbury and), M.P......341
Halfpenny, New......1210, 1211
    (*Illus.*)..............558
Halicarnassus (Mausoleum)..202
HALIFAX.................665
  Archdeacon (Wakefield)...480
  Member of Parliament.....335
Halifax Building Society....1154
Halifax (Nova Scotia)..200, 704
Hallam, M.P..............344
Hallamshire, High Sheriff...632
  Master Cutler...........662
Halley, Edmund...........146
Halley's Comet............162
Hall Green, M.P...........327
Hall-Marks on Plate.....1212–3
Hallowmas.........(*Note*) 130
  Eve...................126
HALSBURY, EARL OF........231
  Chancellor, Brunel Univ...510
  Museums Commission....409
Haltemprice, 669; M.P......335
Hamburg............204, 866
  Land.................866
Ham House, Richmond .412, 651
Hamilton (Bermuda)...200, 777
Hamilton (Lanarkshire).....685
  Member of Parliament.....335
Hamilton (N.Z.)...........734
Hamilton (Ontario).........705
HAMILTON, DUKE OF........227
  Chancellor, St. Andrews
    University............510
  Hereditary Keeper.......222
  Knight of the Thistle.....259
  Premier Peer of Scotland...227
  Privy Councillor.........257
  Royal Company of Archers
                            223
  Royal Victorian Chain.....260
Hammersmith.............642
  Bridge................643
  Hospital...............526
  Member of Parliament.....335
  Party Strengths 671
Hampshire..........627, 631–3
  Probate Offices 1181
Hampstead:—
  Archdeacon of...........473
  Heath.................576
  Member of Parliament....335

Pages 693–1220 *are omitted from the* Shorter Edition

PAGE
Hampton Court Palace......651
Handicapped Children (Spec.
  Schools)................1049
Handsworth, M.P...........327
Hanging Gardens...........202
Hanoi (N. Vietnam)....201, 973
Hanover (Germany)........866
  House of................212
"Hansard"........307, 426, 1080
  Editors................309
  Society................1105
Harbin (China)........204, 842
Harborough, M.P...........335
Harewood House...........654
Haringey................642
  Party Strengths........671
Harkness, Edward S. (Pilgrim
  Trust)................438
Harlington, M.P...........335
Harlow...........605, 669, 687
Harold II................630
Harpenden................669
Harris (Scotland)..........677
HARRIS, SIR ARTHUR T....278
  Marshal of the R.A.F....465
Harrogate................665
  Member of Parliament...335
Harrow................642, 652
  Members of Parliament...335
  Municipal Offices....(Note) 642
  Party Strengths........671
Harrow School......539, 548
  Eton v. Harrow (Cricket).1002
Hartlepool................665
  Member of Parliament...335
Harvard University........809
Harvest Moon....(Note) 122; 161
Harvests of 1971..........582
Harwich................665
  Member of Parliament...335
  Shipping................595
Haryana (State)..........750
Haslingden................665
Hasluck, Sir Paul..........278
  Governor-Gen., Australia .709
Hastings............204, 665
  Archdeacon (Chichester)..474
  Battle of................630
  Member of Parliament...335
  Weather (Monthly)....1065–7
Hatfield (New Town)..605, 687
  Polytechnic..............535
Hatfield College (Durham)..507
  House................654
Havana (Cuba)....200, 204, 848
Havant and Waterloo......669
Haverfordwest............675
Havering................642
  Party Strengths........671
HAWAII................800, 802
Hawick................685
Hayes and Harlington, M.P..335
Hazel Grove and Bramhall..669
Headmasters............538–44
  Conference............538
  Schools......538–41; 542–4
  Independent Schools Society
                        541–2
HEALTH:—
  Insurance, National........496
  Laboratories..........419–20
  Scottish Department....424–5
  Service, *see* NATIONAL HEALTH
    SERVICE

PAGE
HEALTH—*continued*
  Services, Local (Cost)......624
  WHO................815
HEALTH AND SOCIAL SECURITY,
  DEPT. OF....391–3, 492, 622
  Estimates (1971–72)........611
  Health Divisions........392–3
  Minister of State.....313, 391
  Secretary of State.313, 315, 391
  Staff Numbers, Cost......608
  Under Secretaries.....313, 391
Heanor................669
Heartbeat Monitors (Science
  Notes)................1033
Heart Diseases, Deaths from..601
HEATH, RT. HON. E. R. G.:—
  Admiral's Cup...........571
    (*Illus.*)............561
  Birthday................114
  First Lord of the Treasury
                      313, 432
  Inter-Parliamentary Union.317
  Member of Parliament....327
  Offices Held............315
  Portraits............552, 561
  Prime Minister....308, 313, 314
  Privy Councillor.........257
Heath Robinson, W.,
  Centenary..............577
Heathrow Airport (London)
                      590, 595
  Traffic Statistics........588
Hebburn................669
Hebrew Calendar........190–1
Hebrides, The............678
Hebrides, New......203, 781–2
Hectares and Acres........1218
Hectolitres and Bushels....1215
Hedingham Castle..........654
Heeley (Sheffield), M.P......344
Heenan, Cardinal..........487
Heights above Sea Level....206
Heirs, Titles Borne by......256
Heirs to Titles........227–50
Hejaz (Arabia)..........934–5
Hejira Years..............193
Helensburgh............685
Helicopter Stations........590
Hellenes, Kings of the......870
Helsinki (Finland)......202, 858
  Distance by Air........1131
Helston................665
Hemel Hempstead..605, 665, 687
  Member of Parliament...335
Hemsworth, M.P...........335
Hendon, M.P.'s............335
Hengist and Horsa..........630
Henley on Thames..........665
  Grand Challenge Cup....1009
  Member of Parliament...335
  Regatta............1009–10
Henry VIII..............211
Heralds................369
  College............369, 644
  Scottish................369
Herbert, Sir Alan..........278
  Companion of Honour....261
Hercules, Pillars of........911
Hereditary:—
  Keepers (Scotland)......222
  Lord High Constable..222, 249
  Master of the Household...222

PAGE
Hereditary—*continued*
  Standard Bearer (Scotland)
                      222, 230
Hereford................666
  Bishop........237, 475
  Member of Parliament...335
Herefordshire..........631–3
HER MAJESTY'S FLEET......462
HER MAJESTY'S MINISTERS...313
Hermes (Minor Planet)......159
Hermes, H.M.S............462
Herne Bay..............669
Herring Industry Board....394
  Statistics (1970)........582
Herriott, Edouard, Centenary
                      114, 577
Herstmonceux, Royal
  Observatory............169
Hertford................666
  Bishop of (St. Albans)....477
  Member of Parliament...336
Hertford College, Oxford...502
Hertfordshire..........631–3
  Archaeological Societies...1121
  Members of Parliament..335–6
Hessen (*Land*, Germany)....866
Heston and Isleworth, M.P...336
Hexham:—
  Bishop (R.C.)............487
  Member of Parliament...336
Heysham................666
Heythrop College (London
  University)............508
Heywood, 666; M.P.........336
Hidalgo (Minor Planet)....159
Higham Ferrers..........666
HIGH COMMISSIONERS:—
  Australia, 709; Canada, 698;
  New Zealand, 732; other
  Commonwealth Countries
                      735–75
  Precedence............219
High Constable (Scotland)
                      222, 249
High Court of Justice....449–50
  Circuits of Judges....453–4
  Judges................449–50
Highest Buildings..........203
  Mountains..............205
Highgate Cemetery..........644
Highgate School............539
Highlands, The............677
  Development Board......394
High Peak, M.P............336
High Sheriffs....632, 676, 691
High Water (1972)......172–83
Highways Act (1971)........361
  Authorities............591
  Divns. (Environment Dept.)
                        385
High Wycombe..........666
Hilary Law Sittings (1972)
                      90, 98
Hillhead, M.P............334
Hillingdon..............642
  Party Strengths........671
HILL OF LUTON, LORD.....251
  Birthday..............90
  Chairman, B.B.C........371
Hillsborough, M.P..........343
Himachal Pradesh (India)....754
Himalaya Mountains........205
Hinckley................669

PAGE

Hindley....................669
HINTON OF BANKSIDE, LORD . .251
  Bath University of Tech-
    nology................510
Hire Purchase (Law).....1167-8
  Controls Removed (1971)
                357, 567
Hirohito, Emperor.....208, 892
Historical MSS. Commission
                    421-5
  Monuments, Royal
    Commissions..........394-5
  Records (Scotland).......422
  Research, Institute of......508
  Year, The...............186
Historic Buildings Councils...394
Historic Houses Open.....653-4
Hitchin, 669; M.P........336
Hitler, Adolf.........864, 865
H.M.S.O.................426-7
Hobart (Tasmania)..203, 714, 725
  Archbishop (R.C.).........490
Hockey....................1004
  Associations............1013
Hoddesdon (Herts.)..........670
Hokkaido Island (Japan).....893
Holborn, M.P...............336
Holford, Lord..............251
  Historic Buildings Council.394
  Trustee, British Museum....409
Holiday Posts..............1204
  Resorts, Weather at....1065-7
Holidays:—
  Bank..................190
  with Pay (Legal Notes)..1177
Holland, *see* NETHERLANDS
Holland (Lincolnshire).....631-3
  Member of Parliament......336
Holland Park (London).....650
Holloway Prison, Governor..398
Holmhead, Cumnock and....685
Holograph Will (Scots Law).1180
Holy Days and Saint Days ...189
Holy Innocents'............134
HOLYOAKE, RT. HON. K. J.:—
  Companion of Honour....261
  Prime Minister, New Zealand
                    731
  Privy Councillor.........257
Holy See, The...........968-9
Home Affairs (1970-71)..565-72
Home and Health Department
  Scottish..............424-5
Home-grown Cereals Authority
                    1124
Homeless Children (Statistics)
                    1157
Homeless Children's Society.1105
HOME, RT. HON. SIR
  ALEXANDER DOUGLAS:—
  Birthday................279
  Chancellor, Heriot-Watt
    University.............511
  Inter-Parliamentary Union .317
  Knight of the Thistle......259
  Member of Parliament......342
  Offices Held..........308, 314
  Privy Councillor..........257
  Royal Coy. of Archers....223
  Secretary of State.313, 314, 387
HOME OFFICE.....395-400, 622
  Computer Depts..........397
  Estimates..............610
  Ministers of State.....313, 395

PAGE

HOME OFFICE—*continued*
  Nationality Dept..........396
  Scientific Dept...........399
  Secretary of State.313, 314, 395
  Staff Numbers, etc........608
  Telecommunications......397
  Under Secretaries.313, 395, 396
Homicide Statistics.........602
Honduras, British.....200, 777-8
  Bishop................481
HONDURAS, REPUBLIC
    200, 875-6; (*Map*) 875
  British Embassy..........876
  Currency...........876, 985
  Embassy...............875
  Trade..................876
HONG KONG.........201, 780-1
  Air Letter Rates.........1197
  Bishops............482, 489
  Climate................780
  Commander, British Forces 463
  Currency...........781, 985
  Distance by Air.........1131
  Finance and Trade....585, 781
  Government.............781
  Leased Territory.........694
  London Office...........781
  New Territory...........780
  Production.............781
  Summer Time...........142
  Trade Commissioner......729
  Universities............791
Honiara (Solomon Islands) . .782
Honiton, 666; M.P.........336
Honours (Political) Scrutiny
  Committee............418
Honshû (Japan).......206, 893
Horizon, Distances of......207
Horncastle, M.P...........336
Hornchurch, M.P..........336
Horniman Museum.........645
Hornsey, M.P............336
Horse Guards, Whitehall.....645
HORSE RACES..........998, 999
  Totalisator Board........400
Horse Shoe Falls (Guyana)....744
Horse Show, International ...1011
Horsham..................670
  Bishop of (Chichester) 474
  Member of Parliament......336
Horticultural Society, Royal ..115
Horticulture (Education).....517
  Advisers, Divisions. .364, 365-6
  Experimental Stations....365-6
Hospitality Fund, Govt......390
Hospitals (N.H.S.)..........501
  Boards........393-4, 425, 501
  Cost..................611
  Divns. (Dept of Health)....392
  Scottish Trust...........359
  Statistics..............1157
Hospitals (Teaching)...501, 525-8
Hotelkeeping, Degrees, etc. . .523
  Training Board..........535
Hottest Day and Place......1064
Houghton le Spring........670
  Member of Parliament......336
Hounslow.................642
  Party Strengths.........671
Hours of Work, Average....617
  in U.S.A...............807
Household Cavalry.........464
Household Expenditure......618
Households, Royal......220-4

PAGE

Housekeeper Allowance (In-
  come Tax)..........1188-9
House of Bishops..........480
  of Clergy..............480
HOUSE OF COMMONS.......645
  Alphabetical List......318-24
  By-Elections (1959-71)....317
    See also BY-ELECTIONS
    (1970-71)
  Chairmen of Committees. .309
  Clerk of.............309, 310
  Committees...........310-11
  Debates...............310
  Deputy Chairman........309
  Election Petitions........310
  Estimates..............610
  European Community De-
    bate (1971)........357-9
  General Election (1970)....316
  General Elections (1950-70) 317
  Hansard.......307, 426, 1080
  Hours of Meeting........310
  Industrial Relations Debates
    (1971).............354-5
  Journals (Access).........421
  Leader................313
  Longest Sitting.........307
  Majorities (1833-1970)....316
  Members............318-48
    Number.............307-8
  Northern Ireland........688
    Officers...............309
  Origin of..............307
  Parliamentary Summary349-59
  Payment of Members
           307; (*Note*) 610
  Pensions for M.P.'s.......307
  Political Parties.......312, 316
  Previous Question.........311
  Privileges of M.P.'s........311
  Procedure............310-11
  Public Bills.............306
  Question Time..........310
  Quorum...............310
  Records...............421
  Redistribution of Seats
    (1970)..............350
  Resignation of Members...310
  Serjeant at Arms.........309
  Speaker.......307, 309, 351, 565
  Speakers since 1660......306
  Strangers' Gallery........645
  Suspension of Members....311
  Vacant Seats............310
  Whips.................312
  Women Members........316
House of Laity.............480
HOUSE OF LORDS..........645
  Bills..................307
  Clerk of the Parliaments
           309, 310, 449
  Composition............307
  Court of Appeal.........307
  Debates...............310
  Estimates..............610
  Expenses of Members.....307
  Hours of Meeting........310
  Industrial Relations Debates
    (1971).............355-6
  Judicial Authority........694
  Leader................313
  Life Peers............250-2
  Longest Sitting.........307
  Lord Chairman.........309

PAGE

HOUSE OF LORDS—*continued*
Lord High Chancellor
308, 313, 449
Office..................450
Lords of Appeal..........449
Money Bills..............307
Numbers.................307
Officers.................309
Parliamentary Summary 349-59
Privileges...............311
Procedure.............310-11
Quorum.................310
Records Office...........421
Speaker................308
Whips..................312
HOUSE OF WINDSOR
212, 216, 218-9
House, British Royal. 210-3,217-9
Houses, Local Authority.....604
HOUSES OF PARLIAMENT
307-8, 645, 649
Houses Open to Public....653-4
HOUSING:—
Acts...................1152
Building Societies.....1151-7
Corporation.............439
Cost:—
to Ratepayers......604, 624
to Taxpayers......604, 611
Divns. (Environment Dept.) 386
G.L.C. Rents increased....568
Insurance..............1134
Landlord and Tenant...1171-2
Loans..................614
Minister for.........313, 384
Ministry, *see* ENVIRONMENT,
DEPT. OF
Mortgage Interest Rates..1020
National Building Agency 1124
New Towns..............687
Personal Expenditure......618
Planning Law.........1177-8
Rates Differential........623
Registration of Title......404
Regulated Tenancies....1172
Rent Acts............1171-2
Rebates Policy.........565
Slum Clearance...........604
Societies Finance Corpora-
tion..................439
Statistics............604, 635
Houston (U.S.A.).....204, 800
Hove, 666; M.P.........336
Howden (Yorks), M.P.....336
Howrah (W. Bengal).......752
Hoylake................670
Huascaran, Mt. (Peru)...205, 923
Hucknall................670
Huddersfield.............666
Members of Parliament....336
Polytechnic.............535
Weather (Monthly)....1065-7
Hudson Bay..............203
Hué (Vietnam)............972
Hughenden Manor.........652
Hughes Hall, Cambridge....505
Hugh Town (Scilly Islands)..629
HULL, CITY OF......659, 666
Bishop of (York).........478
Colleges of Education....533
Ferens Art Gallery.......655
Lord Mayor.............666
Members of Parliament....336
Party Representation......672

PAGE

HULL, CITY OF—*continued*
Probate Registry.........1181
Shipping................595
Stipendiary..........455, 659
Tidal Tables.........172-83
University.........509, 512
Weather (Monthly)....1065-7
Hulme, Bishop (Manchester).479
Humane Society, Royal....1115
Humber Bridge Plan........568
HUNGARY..202, 876-8; (*Map*) 877
British Embassy...........878
Cabinet................876
Communist Party........876
Currency..........878, 985
Embassy................876
Finance and Trade....585, 878
Government.............877
Nobel Prizes............1054
Production, etc..........877
Hungerford Bridge.........643
HUNT, LORD.......110, 251
Chairman, Parole Board...418
Hunters' Moon (1972) .(*Note*) 126
Huntington and Godman-
chester................666
Bishop (Ely).............475
Cromwell Museum........655
Huntingdonshire........631-3
Members of Parliament....336
Huntly.................685
Hurdling (Athletics).....989-97
Huron, Lake.............205
Hurricane Measure........1211
Hussar Regiments.........464
Hutchinson, A.S., Obituary..574
Huyton with Roby.........670
Member of Parliament....336
Hyades Star Cluster.....153, 155
Hyde, 666; M.P..........345
Hyde Park..........224, 649
Hyderabad (Andhra Pradesh) .749
Hydrology, Institute of....415
Hyperion (Satellite).......158
Hythe (Kent)............666
Member of Parliament....333

IAPETUS (SATELLITE)..........158
I.B.A. Radio Stations 1016-7
Ibadan (Nigeria)...........763
Iberian Peninsula.. 928, 939-40
Ibrox Park Disaster (1971)...568
(*Illus*)..............554
I.B.R.D.................815
ICAO.............816, 982
Ice Age, The............184
ICELAND
202, 206, 878-9; (*Map*) 878
British Embassy...........879
Currency..........879, 985
Embassy................878
Exchange Rate........83, 879
Nobel Prize.............1054
Ice Skating.............1010
Idaho (State)............800
Ides (Roman Calendar).....192
Ife (Nigeria)............763
Ifni (Morocco)...........941
Iguaçú Falls.............830
I.L.E.A........515, 635, 1048
Ilford, M.P.'s...........336
Ilkeston, 666; M.P........337
Illegitimacy (Legal Notes)
1162, 1168

PAGE

Illegitimacy—*continued*
Children in Care........1157
Property Rights (Law)
1168, 1169
Illingworth, R. (*Portrait*).....563
Illinois (State)............800
IMCO...............816, 982
IMF.................815-6
Immediate Annuities.....1137-8
Immigrants in Schools (Statis-
tics)..................1049
Immigration Branch Appeals
Adjudicator............458
Branch, Home Office 396
Immigration Statistics......605
Immingham, Shipping......595
IMPERIAL:—..
College (Science and Tech-
nology)...............508
Institute, *see* Common-
wealth Institute
Service Medal............305
Service Order............261
War Museum........413, 611
Imphal (Manipur, India)....753
IMPORTS (1969-70)......586-7
Ince, M.P..............337
Inch and Centimetre.......1218
Inchon (Korea)..........899
INCOMES:—
Companies (U.K.)........620
Personal...............616-8
Disposable............618
Distribution:—
by Ranges...........617
by Sources......616, 618-9
Self-employed Persons...618
Table.................1184
Income Supplements (Soc.
Security)...............498
INCOME TAX...565, 566, 1185-91
Acts...............350, 359
Age Relief/Exemption....1189
Allowances.......621, 1187-9
Annuities Relief........1189
Board of Referees........458
Building Society Interest
1189, 1020
Capital Gains.......352, 1186
Child Allce. raised (1971)...353
Covenants.............1190
Dependent Relatives Allce.1188
Double Taxation Relief ..1190
Earned Income Allowance..1189
Exempt Income.........1187
Housekeeper Allowance.1188-9
Life Assurance Premiums .1189
Married Couples (Tables)
1186, 1187, 1188
Overseas Territories Office..417
P.A.Y.E.........616, 1191
Personal Allowance......1187
Incomes...............617
Personal Tax (1973) .353, 620-1
Post-War Credits.........1190
Reform (1973)..........620-1
Residents Abroad.......1190
Revenue from...........609
Schedules...........1185-7
Settlement Incomes.......1190
Short-term Gains........1186
Single Persons...........1185
Small Income Relief......1189

PAGE

INCOME TAX—*continued*
Special Commissioners.....404
Specimen Tables.......1185–8
Standard Rate......349, 1185
Sub-contractors.........352
Tax Reserve Certificates..1191
Unified Tax (1973)......620–1
Year.....(*Note*) 102, 186; 1185
Incubation, Periods of.....1124
Indefatigable Sea School.....530
Independence Day (U.S.A.)
114, 802
Independent:—
Methodists.............485
Newspapers.........1077–85
Schools....537, 538–42, 1048–9
Independent Broadcasting
Authority 1016
Radio................1016–7
Independents (Congregationalists)
486
INDEPENDENT TELEVISION
AUTHORITY.............400
INDIA:—
Calendar Eras............193
Crown of, Order.........261
Star of, Order..........260
Indiana (State).............800
Indian Empire Order.........260
Knights...........262–300
Indian Museum (V. and A.)..412
Indian Ocean..............203
Indian-Pacific Railway,
Australia...............714
India Office Library.....388, 389
INDIA, REPUBLIC OF
201, 693, 745–53; (*Map*) 746
Cabinet..........745, 747
Capital.................745
Communications.........747
Council of States........747
Currency................985
Defence.................747
Education...............748
Events (1970–71)........572
Exchange Rate............83
Finance..............748–9
High Commissions........747
Immigrants from.........605
Industrial Production....748
Institutes of Technology..791
Judicature..............747
Languages...............747
Legislature.............747
Nobel Prizes...........1054
Population..............745
Protectorate............753
Republic Day............745
Revenue and Expenditure
748–9
Roman Catholic Church 489
States...............749–53
Territories..........752–3
Test Matches (1971)
571, 1000, 1001–2
Trade..............585, 748
Commissioners.........729
With U.K...........748
Universities.......748, 791–2
Indo-China............(*Map*) 972
INDONESIA, REPUBLIC OF
201, 879–81; (*Map*) 879
British Embassy.........881
Cabinet................879

PAGE

INDONESIA, REPUBLIC OF
—*continued*
Currency..........880, 985
Embassy.................879
Finance...............880
Government............880
Production, etc........880
Trade, 585; with U.K...880
INDUSTRIAL:—
Arbitration Board......1016
Associations.....1122–3, 1124
Assurance Commissioner...390
Award, Queen's.....1059–60
Companies............1136
Court.......383, 1015, 1016
Design Council.........439
Development Org. (U.N.)
813
Diseases Insurance......497
Disputes (1970–71)....569–71
Divisions (Dept. of Trade)
430
Employment..........606–8
Group (Dept. of Trade)..431–2
Health Centre.........383
Hours and Wages, Average..617
Injuries:—
Advisory Council......393
Insurance..........496–7
Contributions...496, 499
Finance............497
Research Unit........407
Museum.............411–2
Newspapers.........1081–4
Property Department 418, 1073
Rehabilitation Units....382
INDUSTRIAL RELATIONS ACT,
1971....354–7, 565, 1014–6
Code of Practice......1016
Collective Bargaining 1014–5
Commission.437, 1015, 1016
Court................1016
Departments..........382
Investigations.......1015
Protest Demonstrations..570
Secret Ballots.......1016
Trade Unions.........1015
Unfair Practices.....1015
Workers' Rights......1014
INDUSTRIAL:—
Research Associations 1129–30
Safety Cttee., Museum....383
Standards Institution.430, 1090
Stoppages (1959–70)...606–7
Training Act.......382, 1051
Boards.............535–6
Foundation...........536
Tribunals....383, 457–8, 1016
Industry:—
Confederation of British..1124
Dept. of Trade and....428–32
Minister for.........313, 428
Queen's Award to....1059–60
Inertia-selling (prevention)
Act.,.................360
Infantry Divisions.......464–5
Infants, Marriage of (Law)..1176
Schools, *see* Primary
Infestation Control (Agric.)
364
Influenza, Deaths from 601
Information, Central Office of
400–1, 608, 612

PAGE

Injuries:—
Criminal (Compensation
Bd.)..................438
Industrial (Advisory
Council)............393
Insurance, Industrial....496–7
INLAND POSTAGE.........1196
INLAND REVENUE:—
Board.............401–4
Estimates............610
Receipts.............609
Staff Numbers, etc......608
Valuation Offices....403, 404
Inland Telegrams......1202
Inner London Boroughs....642
Education Authority
515, 635, 1048
Inner Temple........524, 645
Innsbruck (Austria).........824
Inns of Court....524, 645–6
Senate of 524
Insolvency Statistics......1160
Inspectors of Taxes......403
Institutional Management
(Educ.)..............523
INSTITUTIONS (Various) 1094–1120
INSURANCE:—
Comprehensive Policies...1134
Dept. (Dept. of Trade)...430
Diplomas, etc.........523
Directory of Companies
1154–8
Divns. (Health & Social
Security)............391
Fire................1134
Friendly Societies....1150–1
Industrial Injuries....496–7
Life...............1134–48
National, *see* NATIONAL
INSURANCE
New Business (1970)....1144–5
Personal Spending on....618
Policies Issued (1970)...1144–5
Stamp Duty.........1193
Postal..........1196, 1200
Insured Box Post.........1196
Inter-Bank Computer Bureau
440
Inter-Cities Fairs Cup......1005
Interest Rates:—
Banks...............615
Building Societies......1020
Intergovernmental Maritime
Organization......816, 982
INTERNATIONAL:—
Affairs (Events)........572–4
Athletics...........994–5
Atomic Energy Agency...814
Cost to Taxpayers.....982
Banks............615, 815–6
Civil Aviation Organization
816
Court of Justice........813
Cross Country Running..997
Development Association 815
Express Post..........1201
Finance Corporation..615, 815
Football..........1004, 1005
Labour Organization.....814
Measures...........1214
Monetary Fund.........815
U.K. Drawings........584
Organizations......976, 981–2
U.K. Subscriptions.....982

PAGE

INTERNATIONAL—*continued*
Paper Sizes..............1217
System,Weights and Measures...............809–10
Telecommunication Union.816
Telegrams...............1202
Telephones...1203, 1204, 1205
Trade (GATT)............816
Inter-Parliamentary Union
317, 612
Intestacy (Legal Notes)...1169–70
Invalidity Benefit (Nat. Ins.)..493
Invention, Natl. Library of..410
Inverkeithing..............686
Inverness.................686
Member of Parliament....337
Inverness-shire..........679–80
Sheriff, etc.............684
Inverurie.................686
Investment Grants (Cost)....610
Io(Satellite)..............158
Ionian Islands (Greece)......870
Iowa (State)..............800
Ipoh (Perak)..............201
Ipswich..................666
Bishop...........237, 477
Member of Parliament....337
Museums................655
Ipswich (Queensland)......722
IRAN (Persia)
201, 881–3; (*Map*) 881
British Embassy..........883
Currency...........882, 985
Defence................882
Embassy................881
Exchange Rate......84, 882
Finance.................882
Government............881–2
Language, etc............882
Oil Industry............882
Production..............882
Shahanshah..208, 260, 881, 883
IRAQ (Mesopotamia)
201; (*Map*) 881; 883–5
British Embassy..........885
Cabinet................883
Currency...........884, 985
Early Civilization.........884
Embassy................884
Finance and Trade....585, 884
Government.............884
Production..............884
Revolution Cmd. Council 883
IRELAND.............206, 794
Banks....441, 444, 445, 446
Church of..............485
Climate................794
History................794
Patron Saint............673
Population........688, 795
Provinces........688–91; 795
Universities......511, 796
IRELAND, NORTHERN, *see*
NORTHERN IRELAND
IRELAND, REPUBLIC OF.202, 795–7
Agriculture.............797
Archbishops............485
Area, etc..............795
Bishops................485
British Citizenship...693, 1162
Embassy...............795
Cabinet................795
Census (1966)...........795
Chief Justice............796

PAGE

IRELAND, REPUBLIC OF—*continued*
Constitution.............795
Counties...............795
Currency...............985
Defence................796
Education..............796
Embassy...............795
Finance................796
Government...........795–6
Judiciary...............796
Legislature..........795, 796
National University.......511
Nobel Prizes...........1054
Parliamentary Secretaries...795
Political Parties..........795
Population........202, 795
Postage Rates..........1196
President..........208, 795
Prime Minister (*Taoiseach*)..795
Production..............797
Provinces..............795
Public Debt............796
Railways...............797
Religion...............796
Revenue and Expenditure..796
Senate................795
Shipping...............797
Trade............585, 797
    with U.K...........797
Vital Statistics..........795
Irish Academy, Royal......1094
Irish Newspapers....1077, 1085
Irish Society, The.....637, 1106
Irlam (Lancs.)...........670
Iron Age, The.........185–6
IRON AND STEEL:—
Divn. (Dept. of Trade)....431
Exports and Imports......587
Industrial Training Board..535
Ironmongers' Company....640
Irvine.........605, 686, 687
Ischia (Italy)............891
Isfahan (Iran)...........883
ISLAM:—
Kaaba, The (Hejaz).......935
Mosque of the Prophet (Medina)............935
Islamabad (Pakistan)......765
Islands, largest..........206
Islay (Hebrides)......677, 678
Isle of Ely, *see* ELY
Isle of Man, *see* MAN
Isle of Thanet, M.P........337
Isle of Wight....627, 629, 631–3
Archdeacon (Portsmouth)..477
Member of Parliament....337
Isles of Scilly............629
Isleworth (Heston and), M.P..336
Islington, 642; M.P.'s....337
Party Strengths.........671
Penny Rate.............624
I.S.O..................260
Isogonic Lines...........164
ISRAEL, REPUBLIC OF
201, 885–7; (*Map*) 885
Air Letter Rates........1197
Antiquities.............886
British Embassy..........887
Cabinet................885
Communications........886–7
Currency..........886, 985
Education..............886
Embassy...............885
Exchange Rate..........84

PAGE

ISRAEL, REPUBLIC OF—*continued*
Government.............886
Immigration.............886
Production and Industry...887
Regions................886
Trade, 585; with U.K.....887
Istanbul (Turkey)...204, 953, 954
I.T.A., *see* INDEPENDENT
ITALY....202, 887–92; (*Map*) 888
Agriculture.............891
Air Passengers to........588
British Embassy........891–2
Cabinets (1948–1971).....889
Car Production..........587
Communications.........891
Council of Ministers......887
Currency..........890, 985
Defence................889
Education..............891
Embassy...............888
European Community..977–81
Exchange Rate........83, 890
Government.............889
Language and Literature...891
Nobel Prizes......891, 1054
President..........208, 889
Production...........890–1
Regions..............889–90
Shipbuilding............597
Shipping...............596
Telephone Rates to......1205
Tourist Traffic..........891
Trade, 585, 891; with U.K. 891
Universities.............891
Visitors' Passports to.....983
Itchen, M.P..............344
ITU...................816
IVORY COAST, REPUBLIC OF
199 (*Map*) 873; 892, 985
British Embassy..........892
Embassy...............892
Iwo (Nigeria)............763
Izmir (Turkey)...........954

JACOBITE RISING...........678
Jaffa (Israel)............887
Jaffa (Ceylon)...........738
Jaipur (Rajasthan).......751
Jakarta (Batavia), *see* DJAKARTA
JAMAICA....200, 693, 753–4, 786
Air Letter Rates........1197
Bishops...........481, 488
Cabinet................754
Currency...............985
Distance by Air........1131
Finance and Trade.......754
High Commissions.......754
Production..............754
Trade, 585; Commissioner 729
JAMES I and VI....212, 213, 678
Jamestown (St. Helena)..199, 785
Jammu.................753
Jan Mayen Island (Svalbard)..919
Janus (Satellite).........158
(Zodiac)...............90
JAPAN.....201, 892–5; (*Map*) 893
British Embassy..........895
Cabinet..............892–3
Calendar..............193
Car Production..........587
Currency..........895, 985
Defence Forces..........894
Distance by Air........1131
Education............894–5

Pages 693–1220 are omitted from the Shorter Edition

PAGE

JAPAN—*continued*
Embassy................803
Emperor...........208, 892
Exchange Rate.......... 83
Finance................895
Government..........893-4
Language and Literature...895
Nobel Prizes...........1054
Population.............893
Production.............894
Shipbuilding...........597
Shipping..............596
Trade.............585, 895
Vital Statistics.........893
Jarrow.................666
  Bishop of (Durham)......478
  Member of Parliament....337
Java (Indonesia).......206, 880
Jedburgh...............686
Jeddah (Hejaz)..........935
JELLICOE, EARL..........231
  Leader, H. of Lords......313
  Lord Privy Seal....313, 406
  Privy Councillor........257
Jersey.................692
  Airport...............590
  Dean (Winchester)......473
  Population.............599
Jerusalem (Israel)....201, 886, 887
  British School........1098
Jesselton, *see* Kota Kinabalu
Jesus College (Cambridge)....505
  (Oxford)............502
JEWISH:—
  Calendar............190-1
  Marriages (Law)....1174, 1175
  Museum...............646
  Newspapers...........1078
  New Year (5733) 89; (*Note*) 122
  Passover..........(*Note*) 102
  Pentecost........(*Note*) 106
  Societies............1106
JEWS, THE..............486
  College..............537
Jibuti (Afars Territory)...199, 864
Jockey Club, 998; Cup Stakes.999
Jockeys, Winning........998
Johannesburg (Transvaal).....938
  Bishop...............481
  Distance by Air........1131
John O'Groats...........677
Johnson, Samuel (Museum) 644-5
Johnstone..............686
JOHORE (Malaysia)........201
Jones, Lady Sarah Armstrong.219
JORDAN (Hashemite Kingdom
  of....201; (*Map*) 885; 895-7
  British Embassy.......896-7
  Currency.............985
  Embassy..............896
  Finance and Trade......896
Jordan River............886
Jordans (Bucks).........652
JOSEPH, SIR KEITH.........281
  Member of Parliament....338
  Privy Councillor........257
  Secretary of State.313, 315, 391
Journalism (Education)......524
Juan Fernandez Islands (Chile)
                       837
Jubilee Handicap..........999
Judge Advocate General......456
  of the Fleet...........450

PAGE

JUDGES:—
  Central Criminal Court....453
  Circuits of...........453-4
  City of London.....456, 639
  County Court.........452-3
  Divorce (Family Divn.).....450
  Ecclesiastical........484
  High Court.........449-50
  Northern Ireland......689-90
  Precedence...........219
  Salaries.........449, 450
  Scottish............683-4
Judicial Committee........449
Judicial Separations (Law)
                  1166, 1167
  (1969)..............600
Judiciary (Scotland)......683-4
JULIANA, QUEEN.......208, 913
  Lady of the Garter......220
  Royal Victorian Chain....260
Julian Calendar..........188
  Day.................89
  Period...........89, 187
Julius Caesar........192, 630
Jumping (Athletics).....989-97
Jungfrau (Switzerland).....946
Junior Lords of the Treasury
                  313, 322
Juno (Planet)...........159
Junto, The.............312
JUPITER...............159-60
  Atmosphere..........159-60
  Distance, etc..........157
  Monthly
  91, 95, 99, etc.; 93, 97, 101, etc.
  Phenomena (1972)
          90, 94, 98, etc.
  Radio Emissions........160
  Satellites........147, 158, 160
Jupiter Olympus (Statue)....202
Jura, Island of (Hebrides)....678
Jury Service...........1170-1
  Allowances...........1170
Justice, International Court of
                      813
Jutland (Denmark).........851
Juvenile Courts (London)....455
  Crime............602, 603

K2 (KARAKORAM MTS.).......205
Kabishah Year............193
Kabul (Afghanistan).....201, 818
Kaieteur Fall (Guyana).....744
Kalends...............192
Kalgoorlie (W. Australia)....729
Kalimantan (Indonesia)......880
Kaliningrad (U.S.S.R.).......961
Kaliyuga Era............193
Kamet, Mt.............205
Kampala (Uganda).....199, 773
Kandahar (Afghanistan)....818
Kandy (Ceylon)..........738
Kano (Nigeria)..........763
Kanpur (India)..........752
Kansas City (U.S.A.)...204, 800
Kansas (State)..........800
Kaohsiung (Formosa).......843
KARACHI (Pakistan)....204, 767
  Archbishop (R.C.).......489
  Distance by Air........1131
Kara Sea..............982
Kashmir...............753
Kassel (Germany)........866
Katmandu (Nepal).....201, 913

PAGE

Katowice (Poland).........927
Kawasaki (Japan)..........895
Kawthooli State (Burma)....834
Kaya State (Burma)........834
KAZAKHSTAN.......201, 961, 966
  Minerals.............966
Kazan (U.S.S.R.).........965
Keats House (Hampstead)....646
Keble College, Oxford......502
Kedah (Malaya)..........201
Keele University......509, 512
Keelung (Formosa)........843
Keeper of the Jewel House...221
  of the Privy Purse......220
  of the Records.........421
    (Scotland)...........422
  of the Swans..........221
Keewatin (N.W.T., Canada)..700
Keighley, 666; M.P........337
Keith.................686
Kelantan (State), Malaysia...201
Kelham Theological College..536
Kelso.................686
Kelvingrove, M.P.........334
Kemptown (Brighton), M.P..328
Kendal................666
Kenilworth (Warwicks)....670
Kensal Green Cemetery.....644
Kensington:—
  Bishop of (London)......473
  Gardens..............649
  Members of Parliament....337
  Palace..........646, 651
    London Museum........411
Kensington and Chelsea....642
  Party Strengths........671
  Penny Rate...........624
Kent..............627, 631-3
  University of (Canterbury).510
Kentucky (State)..........800
Ken Wood..............650
KENYA......199, 693, 755-6, 985
  Cabinet..............755
  Finance and Trade.......756
  High Commissions.......755
  Immigrants............605
  Production............755
  Trade Commissioner.....729
  University............792
Kerala (State)...........750
Kermadec Islands (N.Z.).730, 734
Kesteven (Lincs.).......631-3
Kettering, 666; M.P.......337
Kew (Surrey)...........651
  Bridge...............643
  Gardens...........367-8, 649
  Weather Observations.1068-70
Keyes, Lord, Centenary.126, 577
Keys, House of..........692
Khaibar Oasis (Hejaz)......935
Kharkov (Ukraine)........966
Khartoum (Sudan)......199, 943
  Distance by Air........1131
KHMER REPUBLIC
  201, 897-8; (*Maps*) 746,972
  British Embassy........898
  Change of Name.....573, 897
  Embassy..............897
Khon Cataracts..........207
Khyber Pass (Afghanistan)...818
Kidderminster...........666
  Member of Parliament....337
Kidsgrove.............670

PAGE

Kiel (Germany).............866
Canal....................206
Kiev (Ukraine).....202, 204, 965
Kigali (Rwanda)........199, 932
KILBRANDON, LORD.........243
Lord of Appeal...........449
Privy Councillor.........257
Kilimanjaro, Mt....205, 206, 770
Killarney, Lake of..........794
Killiecrankie...............678
Kilmarnock, 686; M.P.......337
Kilmore, Bishops......485, 487
Kilogram, The.............1215
Kilograms and Pounds.1215, 1218
Kilometres and Miles...1214, 1218
Kilsyth...................686
Kilwinning................686
Kincardine............679–80
Member of Parliament....325
Sheriff, etc.............684
Kinchinjanga, Mt........205
King George V Dock......647
King George and Queen
Elizabeth Stakes......999
King's College:—
Cambridge.............505
London................508
King's College Hospital..525–6
King's Division (Army)...464–5
King's Lynn..............666
Member of Parliament....337
Kings and Queens:—
England...........210–11
Foreign Countries....208–9
Scotland.............213
United Kingdom......212
Kings of Arms......259–61, 369
Kingston (Jamaica)....200, 753
(Norfolk Island)....203, 716
Kingston upon Thames......642
Bishop (Southwark)....477
Member of Parliament...337
Party Strengths.......671
Polytechnic..........535
Kingston upon Hull, see HULL
Kingstown (St. Vincent).200, 789
Kingswood...............670
Kinross.............625, 686
Member of Parliament....342
Kinross-shire..........679–80
Sheriff, etc............684
Kinshasa (Congolese Republic)
199, 204, 846
Kirghizia (Kirghizhstan)
201, 961, 967–8
Kirkby..................670
Kirkby in Ashfield........670
Kirkcaldy...............686
Member of Parliament....337
Kirkcudbright............686
Kirkcudbrightshire.....679–80
Kirkdale (Liverpool), M.P....339
Kirkintilloch............686
Kirkwall............677, 686
Kirriemuir..............686
Kishinev (Moldavia)....202, 967
Kita-Kyushu (Japan)......895
Kitchener Memorial Fund....514
Kluchevskaya, Mt........205
Knaresborough, Bishop of
(Ripon)..............479
Knebworth House.........654
Kneller Hall.............650

Knighthood, Orders of....259–61
Central Chancery......222
Knight of Kerry (Fitzgerald)..274
KNIGHTS:—
Bachelor..........262–300
Badge.................262
How Addressed.........262
Commanders, Gd. Cdrs. and
Gd. Cross.......262–300
How Addressed........262
of the Garter...........259
of St. Patrick...........259
of the Thistle....259, 682
of Windsor............225
Precedence............219
Knots and M.P.H..........578
Knutsford, M.P...........337
Kobé (Japan).......204, 895
Kolhapur (Maharashtra)....751
Korea People's Republic...899
Communist Party......899
KOREA, REPUBLIC OF
201; (Map) 898; 899
British Embassy.........899
Currency.........899, 986
Embassy...............899
Kosciusko, Mt....206, 708, 717
Kosygin, A. N......959, 961
Kota Kinabalu (Sabah)..201, 758
Kowloon (Hong Kong)....780
Kraków (Poland)........927
Krefeld (Germany).......866
Kroomdrai, Anthropological
Discoveries.........185
Kuala Lumpur (Malaya)
201, 489, 758
Distance by Air........1131
Kuching (Sarawak)...201, 758
Kuibyshev (R.S.F.S.R.)....965
Kuria Muria Islds. (Aden)...974
Kurile Islands............961
Kuwait (State)....201, 899–901
British Embassy.......900–1
Currency........900, 986
Distance by Air.........1131
Embassy...............899
Government........899–900
Oil Production.........900
Trade with U.K.........900
Kyoto (Japan)......204, 895
Kyushu (Japan)..........893

LABORATORIES, NATIONAL....432
Fisheries................363
Infestation Control......364
Marine Research........424
Plant Pathology.........366
Public Health.......419–20
Salmon Fisheries.......363
Veterinary.............366
LABOUR:—
Average Wages, etc.......617
Employers' Associations
1122–3; 1124
Employment Statistics...606–8
Events (1970–71)....569–71
Hours and Wages.......617
I.L.O..................814
Independent Tribunals...383–4
Legal Notes............1177
Minister of (1939–68).....315
National Dock Labour
Board.............414
Parliamentary Party.......312

LABOUR—continued
Statistics.............606–8
Division..............383
Strikes in 1970–71...606, 607
Trade Unions........1125–8
Unemployment Statistics...606
LABOUR PARTY, THE.......1107
Cabinets............314–5
G.L.C. Strength.........635
Local Council Strengths..671–3
Majorities.............316
Prime Ministers.....308, 314
Strength (1918–1970)....316
Votes Cast (1955–70).....317
Whips.................312
Labrador (Newfoundland)....704
Laccadive Islands (India)....753
Lacock Abbey............654
Lacrosse................1004
Ladies' Clubs (London)...1087–9
Ladies in Waiting.........224
of the Bedchamber...220, 223
of the Garter...........259
Ladoga, Lake............205
Lady Day.....(Notes), 94, 98, 186
Lady Margaret Hall (Oxford).503
Lady of the Thistle........259
Ladywood (B'ham), M.P.....327
Lae (New Guinea)......715, 716
"Lagoon" Nebula.........155
Lagos (Nigeria).....199, 763
Archbishop (R.C.)......488
Bishops...............482
Lahore (Pakistan).........767
Laing Art Gallery.........656
Laity, House of...........480
Lake, Deepest............965
Lake District National Park...626
Lake Portchartrain Causeway,
U.S.A.............206
Lakes, English............629
Irish (Loughs)..........794
Largest..........205, 794
Scottish (Lochs).........677
Welsh................674
Lambeth (Borough).........642
Magistrates' Court.......455
Members of Parliament..337–8
Palace................646
Party Strengths.........671
Penny Rate............624
Lambeth Bridge..........643
Lammas............(Notes), 94, 118
Lampeter (Borough).......675
St. David's College......510
Lanark (Burgh)..........686
Member of Parliament....338
Lanarkshire...........679–80
Members of Parliament...338
Sheriff, etc............684
Lancashire............631–3
Archæological Societies...1121
Lancaster (Borough).......666
Bishop (Blackburn).....478
Bishop (R.C.)..........487
Member of Parliament....338
Lancaster, Duchy of.......378
See also CHANCELLOR
Lancaster, House of.........211
Lancaster, Univ. of.........509
Lanchester Polytechnic......535
LAND:—
Below Sea Level........1128
Commission (Dissolution)...360

PAGE

LAND—*continued*
Court, Scottish............683
Development (Law)....1177–8
Divisions (Agric.).......364–5
Drainage Authorities.....625
Registry...........404–5, 608
Revenues, Crown........375
Landlord and Tenant (Law)
1171–2
Land's End.............629
to John o' Groats......677
Lands Tribunal.......434, 457
Langstone (Portsmouth), M.P. 342
Languages, Degrees, etc.....524
LAOS (Indo-China)
201, 901; (*Map*) 972
British Embassy..........901
Currency...............986
Embassy...............901
La Paz (Bolivia)..........829
Larceny Statistics.........602
Largest Cities............204
Islands...............206
Lakes................205
Ships Afloat...........598
Largs.................686
Larnaca (Cyprus).........739
Larne.................691
Las Palmas (Canaries).....941
Lasswade, Bonnyrigg and...685
LATEST EVENTS............82
Latin America............198
Latitude, Degrees of.......198
LATVIA (U.S.S.R.)..202, 961, 967
Launceston (Cornwall).....666
(Tasmania)...........725
Lausanne (Switzerland)......947
Laval (Quebec).............706
University..............790
Law, College of...........525
Law Commission..........452
Scotland...............683
LAW COURTS AND OFFICES:—
England and Wales.....449–56
Holidays................190
Jury Service...........1170–1
Legal Aid Scheme......1172–4
London.............453, 455
Northern Ireland......689, 690
Scotland..............683–4
Witnesses' Allowances ..1170
Law Degrees, etc..........524
Law List................1075
Law Lords............226, 449
Scottish...........(*Note*) 683
LAW NOTES............1161–81
Lawn Tennis............1007
Law Officers' Departments...405
Offices (Holidays).........190
Reform Act (1971).........361
Sittings (Eng. and Wales)...90,
94, 98, 106, 114, 126, 134,
189, 449
Law Society............524–5
Legal Aid...........1172–3
Scotland..............525
Statute Law Committee...427
Leader:—
Greater London Council...634
H. of Commons.......313, 419
House of Lords.......313, 406
of the Opposition....306, 313
Leamington..............666
Member of Parliament.....347

PAGE

Leander Class Frigates........462
Leap Year..............186, 188
Leases (Legal Notes)........1172
Stamp Duty...........1193–4
Leatherhead.............670
LEBANON, REPUBLIC OF
201; (*Map*) 885; 902
British Embassy..........902
Currency............902, 986
Embassy...............902
Finance and Trade........902
Lee Conservancy Board.....625
Lee, Sir Frank, Obituary.....574
LEEDS, CITY OF......659, 666
Archdeacon (Ripon)......479
Bishop (R.C.)...........477
Building Societies.......1154
Colleges of Education.....533
Lord Mayor............659
Members of Parliament....338
Museums, etc........655–6
Party Strengths..........672
Penny Rate.............624
Polytechnic............535
Probate Registry........1181
Roundhay Park Centenary..576
Stipendiary.......455, 659
Teaching Hospitals......527
University.........509, 512
Settlement............513
Leek, M.P..............338
Le Fanu, Sir Michael, Obit...575
Legacies, Lapsed.........1180
Legal Advice............1173
Scotland..............1174
Legal Aid............1172–4
Cost of...............610
Eligibility.............1172
Excepted Causes........1172
Legal Education........524–5
Council of............524
Legal Events (1970–71)......571
LEGAL NOTES..........1161–81
Tender...........567, 1210
Year..................186
Legislation, How Initiated....306
Public Acts (1970–71)...359–61
See also PARLIAMENT
Legitimacy (Legal Notes) ...1168
Le Havre (France)..........863
LEICESTER, CITY OF..659–60, 666
Bishop..............237, 475
Building Societies.......1154
City Polytechnic........535
Lord Mayor............660
Members of Parliament....338
Party Strengths..........672
Museums..............656
Probate Registry........1181
University.........509, 512
Leicestershire..........631–3
Leicester Square (London)...645
Leigh (Lancashire)..........666
Member of Parliament....338
Leighton-Linslade (Beds.)....670
Leinster (Counties)........
Leipzig (E. Germany)......869
Leisure Activities (U.K.)....491
Leith, M.P................332
Tidal Predictions.....172–83
Lemass, Sean, Obituary.....575
Length, Measures of.......1214
Conversion Table......1218
Leningrad.........204, 964, 965

PAGE

Lent (Period)............188
(1971).............(*Note*) 94
Leominster, 666; M.P......338
Lerwick............678, 686
Leslie..................686
Leslie, Sir Shane, Obituary ..575
LESOTHO.........199, 693, 756
Bishops...............481
Cabinet...............756
High Commissions.......756
Trade Commissioner......729
University.............792
Letchworth.............670
Letter Postage......566, 1196
Air Mail............1197–8
Airway Service.........1200
Railway Service........1200
Rates since 1897.......1047
Letters of Administration
(Wills).............1180
Leukemia Research Unit.....408
Leven.................686
Lever Art Gallery..........657
Leverhulme Trust Fund......514
Lewes.................666
Bishop (of Chichester)...474
Member of Parliament....338
Museums..............656
Prison (Governor).......398
Lewisham..............642
Archdeacon (Southwark)...477
Members of Parliament....338
Party Strengths..........671
Lewis with Harris.........678
Leyhill Prison (Governor)...398
Leyland...............670
Leyte (Philippines)........925
Leyton, M.P.............338
Lhasa (Tibet)............842
Liberal Party:—
Local Council Strengths..671–3
Majorities.............316
Organisation..........1107
Origin of Name.........312
Prime Ministers........308
Strength (1918–70)......316
Votes Cast (1955–70)....317
Whips................312
Liberal Unionists.........312
Liberation Day (Channel Islds.)
190
LIBERIA, REPUBLIC OF
199; (*Map*) 873; 903
British Embassy..........903
Currency...........903, 986
Embassy...............903
Shipping Registered......596
Libra, First Point of.......150
Librarianship (Education)....525
Libraries Branch (Dept. of Educ.)
379
Libraries, Copyright....405, 1073
in London.........644, 645
National....380, 405–6, 409–10
Library Association.......525
Libreville (Gaboon)....199, 864
LIBYA...199, 903–5; (*Map*) 904
Antiquities............
British Embassy........904–5
Currency...........904, 986
Embassy...............903
Government............904
Libyan Desert (Egypt)..956, 1128

PAGE

LICENCES................1204
Broadcast Receiving...566, 579
Driving................1209
Expiry of..........(*Note*) 134
Marriage................1174
Motor Vehicles......591, 1209
Lichfield..................666
Bishop of........237, 475
Member of Parliament.....338
LIECHTENSTEIN........202, 905
Liège (Belgium)............827
Lieutenant-Generals.......463
Lieutenant, H.M......(*Note*) 631
LIFE ASSURANCE......1134-48
Annuities...........1137-8
Average Premiums....1140
Bonuses............1138-9
Companies.........1135-6
Directory.........1145-8
Endowment........1141-3
Industrial Companies....1136
New Business (1970)..1144-5
Policies in Force......1136
Premiums.........1140-1
Statistics..........1135-6
Valuations..........1134
Without-profit Policies
                   1140-1
Lifeboats (R.N.L.I.)......1115
Life Expectation Tables....1149
Extra-terrestrial......1033
Guards, The..........464
Peerages Act (1958).....307
Peeresses (Number).......226
Peers.............250-2
Number of.............226
Light Division (Army).......465
Lighthouse Authorities.....435
Lighting-up Times....138, 140
Light, Velocity of....145, 152
Light Year................152
Lille (France)............863
Lilongwe (Malawi)........757
Lima (Peru)....200, 204, 924
Limassol (Cyprus).......739
Limerick (City)..........797
Limón (Costa Rica)......847
Limpopo River (S. Africa)...937
Linacre College, Oxford....502
Lincoln City..............666
Bishop..........237, 476
Member of Parliament....338
Museums, etc.........656
Lincoln College, Oxford....502
Lincolnshire.........622, 631-3
Lincoln Handicap.........999
Lincoln's Inn........524, 645-6
Lincoln's Inn Fields.......646
Lindsey (Lincolnshire)....631-3
Line Islands (Pacific)......782
Liners, Largest..........598
LINLEY, VISCOUNT........233
Birthday................
Succession to Throne.....219
Linlithgow (Burgh).........686
Linz (Austria)............824
Lion and the Unicorn......224
Lipari (Italy)............891
Lisbon (Portugal)......202, 929
Distance by Air........1131
Lisburn..................691
Liskeard..................666
Lister   Institute   (London
University)............508

PAGE

Liston, "Sonny", Obituary ..575
LISTOWEL, EARL OF........231
Lord Chairman.........309
Privy Councillor..........257
Literature (Nobel Prizes)....1054
LITERATURE OF THE YEAR...1021-5
Litherland................670
Lithuania (U.S.S.R.)
                202, 961, 967
Litre (Measure)......1214, 1215
Litres and Gallons.........1218
LIVERPOOL, CITY OF.....660, 666
Airport..................590
Archbishop (R.C.)........487
Bishop..........237, 479
Clubs..................1091
Colleges of Education.531, 533
Customs and Excise......377
Docks..................660
Education Settlements....513
Girls' Schools...........545
London Rail Fare........593
Lord Mayor.............660
Medical Schools.........527
Members of Parliament...338-9
Mersey Tunnels.........660
(*Illus.*)...............550
Newspapers...........1077
Party Strengths.........672
Passport Office..........983
Penny Rate.............624
Polytechnic..............535
Population........660, 666
Probate Registry........1181
Railway Fares..........593
Shipping................595
Stipendiary......455, 660
Teaching Hospitals.....527-8
Tide Tables...........172-83
University.........509, 512
Walker Art Gallery......656
Weather (Monthly)....1065-7
Livery Companies (Guilds).640-2
Halls..................646
Livestock (U.K.).........580
Advisers (Min. of Agric.)...365
Divns. (Min. of Agric.)....363
Livestock Imports.........586
Prices................581
Livingston (New Town).605, 687
Ljubljana (Yugoslavia).....976
Llandovery..............675
Llanelli, 675 ; M.P.........339
Llanidloes...............675
Lloyd, Harold, Obituary ...575
LLOYD, RT. HON. J. S. B.:—
Birthday................114
Cambridge University....504
Companion of Honour....261
Speaker, H. of Commons
           306, 309, 351, 565
Lloyd's............646, 1107
Lloyd's Bank.............444
Lloyd's Register...596-8, 1107
Llwchwr................675
Llwycoed Crematorium....1055
Loan Board (Public Works)
                   420-1
Loanhead................686
"Local" Acts............623
Local Archaeological Socs.
                   1121-2
Local Education Authorities
           514-7, 1048, 1050

PAGE

Local Employment Promotion
(Cost)..................610
LOCAL GOVERNMENT.......622-5
Acts............622, 623-4
Auditors................385
Boundary Commission....1018
Capital Receipts.........624
Chief Officers........635, 639
Children in Care........1157
Committees and Staff..623, 639
Debts...........624, 625
De-Rating.............623
Divisions (Environment
Dept.)................385
Election Petitions Office...458
Elections, 622-3; (1971)....568
Electors.........622, 625
England.............664-73
Equalization Grants......623
Events (1970-71).........568
Exchequer Grants....611, 623-4
Expenditure (1968-69)....624
Finance...........623-4
Functions and Services
           623, 635-6, 637
Health, Welfare Services...501
Highway Authorities......591
Housing Statistics.....604, 635
Loans.......420, 624, 625
London........622, 634-42
Minister for........313, 384
Ministry, *see* ENVIRONMENT
Municipal Airports.......590
Northern Ireland........625
Party Representation...671-3
Rates..................623
England.............664-70
English Counties........631
London, 640; Boroughs..642
Northern Ireland........691
Scotland.........679, 685-6
Wales..................675
Rating Act (1971).........361
Receipts................624
Reorganization....568, 1018-9
Scotland.............624-5
Selective Employment Pay-
ments................1184
Social Services..........501
Societies..............1107
Statutory Appointments...623
Trading Services.........624
Training Board..........536
Voters' Qualifications....1178
Welfare Services........501
Local Health Sces. (Cost)...624
Local Loans Fund Advances
Outstanding...........615
Local Precedence.........219
Sidereal Time..........141
Lochgelly................686
Lochgilphead............686
Lochs, Scottish..........677
Locomotives, Statistics.....592
Lodz (Poland)............927
Lombardy (Italy).........890
Lomé (Togo).......199, 950
LONDON:—
Airports................590
Authority................371
Third............565, 566
Traffic Statistics....588, 595
Ambulance Service......636
American Embassy......802-3

PAGE

LONDON—*continued*
Archdeacon of............473
Art Galleries............370–1
Schools.................518
Banker's Clearing House.440–1
Banks.................440–6
Hours of Opening......441
Bishop of
237, 257, 261, 473, 645
Boroughs................642
Average Rates..........624
Education Officers......515
Inner.................642
Party Strengths........671
Rateable Values........642
Boys' Schools........538–41
Bridges.................643
Buildings.............643–9
Business Studies School
519, 1058
Cathedrals...........490, 491
Cemeteries...............644
Churches..............490–1
Church of Scotland......491
City of, *see* p. 13 of Index
Clubs.................1087–9
Coach Fares...............593
College of Music.........529
Colleges of Education..531, 533
Consulates in.........821–975
Customs and Excise......377
Date-marks on Plate.....1213
Dental Schools...........521
Distances by Air from...1131
Docks...................419
Education Authorities 515, 1048
Statistics...............635
Electricity Board.........381
Exhibitions, etc..........650
Fire Brigade..............636
Foreign Embassies in..817–975
Gardens.............649–50
Gazette Office......426, 1079
Girls' Schools...........546
Government..........634–42
Act (1963)............634
Greater London Council
622, 634–6
High Sheriff.............632
High Water, Exceptional ..163
Hospital, The.............526
Hospitals..............525–7
Housing Authorities......635
Juvenile Courts..........455
Libraries in .405, 409–13, 643–4
Licensing Statistics......636
Livery Companies......640–2
Local Government.622, 634–42
Lord Lieutenant..........632
Lord Mayor.......568, 637
Magistrates' Courts.......455
Main Drainage...........636
Mayors.................642
Medical Officers.........639
Schools.............525–7
M.P. (City of Westminster) 330
Metropolitan Hospital Bds..393
Monuments...............647
Museums........409–13, 611
News Agencies..........1085
Newspaper Offices
1077, 1078–85
Parks............636, 649–50
Parochial Charities......514

PAGE

LONDON—*continued*
Passport Office..........983
Picture Galleries......370–1
Planetarium.............650
Police................456–7
Polytechnics.............535
Population.......202, 204
Port of..........419, 647
Postal Arrangements.....1204
Prisons.................398
Rail and Coach Fares....593
Rainfall.............1068–70
Rateable Values.........642
Rates of..........640, 642
Roads Authority......635–6
Roman Remains.......647–8
Sailing Clubs..........1092
St. Paul's Cathedral......473
Saluting Stations........224
School of Economics.....508
Schools of Architecture...518
Shipping...............595
Offices...............594
Societies...........1107–8
South Central Petty Sessions
455
Sunrise and Sunset (Daily)
93, 97, 101, etc.
Sunshine Records.....1068–70
Taxi Fares.............571
Teaching Hospitals....525–7
Theatres.............1025–6
Theological Colleges..536, 537
Tide Tables.........172–83
Tower of.......224, 649
Town Clerks............639
Trade.................595
Traffic Authority......635–6
Transport Executive.....406
Underground Fares.....593
Universities......507–8, 510
University of London...507–8
Extra-Mural Dept......512
Medical Schools....525–7
Water Supplies.........408
Weather Forecast Service. 1086
Records............1068–70
Zoological Gardens. 650, 1120
LONDON, GREATER.....631–3
Administrative County..631–3
Council.............634–6
Lord Lieutenant.........632
LONDONDERRY, CITY OF..690–1
Local Govt. Electors......625
Lord Lieutenant.........691
Member of Parliament 339, 688
Riots (1970–71).....567, 568
(*Illus.*)...............553
LONDONDERRY, COUNTY...691
High Sheriff.............691
Lord Lieutenant.........691
Members of Parliament...688
Long Benton............670
Long Eaton.............670
Longest:—
Day.......(*Note*) 110; 186–7
Railway Tunnels.........207
Rivers................206
LONGFORD, EARL OF........232
Knight of the Garter......259
Longitude, Degrees of......198
Longleat House............654
Longmore, Sir Arthur, Obit...575
Long Tons.......809, 1215, 1218

PAGE

Lonsdale, Dame Kathleen,
Obituary................575
Lonsdale, M.P............340
Lord Advocate.........313, 406
Precedence............682
Lord Advocate's Dept......406
Lord Chairman...........309
Lord Chamberlain.........220
Lord Chamberlain's Office...220
Lord Chancellor, *see* Lord High
Chancellor
Lord Chief Justice.......449, 571
Precedence............219
Lord Chief Justice (N.Ireland).689
Lord Clerk Register.......682
Lord Great Chamberlain.....406
Lord High Chancellor
308, 313, 427, 449
(1939–71)..............314
Office.................450
Precedence.......219, 682
Lord High Commissioner
(Church of Scotland)484, 682
Lord High Constable 222, 249,682
Lord High Treasurer.......432
Lord Howe Island (N.S.W.)...720
Lord Justice Clerk........683
General, 682......(*Note*) 683
Lord Lyon King of Arms
222, 259, 369, 682
LORD MAYOR, THE.....568, 637
City University..........510
Election Day......(*Note*) 122
Lord Mayor's Day
(*Note*) 130; 187, 225, 637
Precedence............219
Lord Mayors.....658–63, 664–8
Lord President of the Council,
258, 313, 314, 419
Judicial Committee......449
Precedence............219
Lord President (Court of Ses-
sion)..................683
Lord Privy Seal......313, 406
Civil Service Dept....374
Precedence..........219
Lord Provosts......680–1, 682
Lords by Courtesy........256
Lords Commissioners of the
Treasury...............432
Lord's Cricket Ground
646, 1000, 1088
Lords, House of, *see* HOUSE
Lords in Waiting.....220, 312
Lords Justices..........449
Lords Lieutenant:—
England................632
Northern Ireland.......691
Precedence.......219, 682
Scotland..............679
Title and Duties....(*Note*) 631
Wales.................676
Lords of Appeal.........449
Precedence............219
Lords of Session......682, 683
Lords of the Treasury.......313
Lord Steward...........220
Lord Treasurer's Remembrancer
683
Lord Warden, Cinque Ports..204
Stannaries............378
Lorengau (Admiralty Islands). 715
Los Angeles (California) .204, 800
Lossiemouth.................686

PAGE

Lothians, The............679–80
Sheriff...................684
Loughborough............666
Archdeacon (Leicester)....475
Member of Parliament....339
University of Technology..510
Louisiana (State)......568, 800
Lourenço Marques (Mozam-
bique)............199, 929
Louth (Lincolnshire).........666
Member of Parliament....339
Lower Saxony.............866
Lowestoft, 666; M.P.........339
Loyalty Islands (Oceania)....864
Luanda (Angola)......199, 929
Lübeck (Germany).........866
Lublin (Poland)............927
Lubumbashi (Congolese Repub-
lic) 846
Luce, Sir David, Obituary ...575
Lucknow (Uttar Pradesh)....752
Lucy Cavendish Collegiate
Society, Cambridge....505
Luderitz (S.W. Africa)......939
Ludlow:—
Archdeacon (Hereford)....475
Member of Parliament....339
Lunacy:—
Chancery Visitors........452
Court of Protection......452
Lunakhod 1 Spacecraft....1028–9
Lunar Craters (*Ranger* probes) 161
Lunar Cycle..............187
Lunar Eclipses, 161; (1972)....148
Rover (1971), 572; (*Illus.*) .556
Terminator..............139
Luna Spacecraft (1971)..573, 1028
Lunik Satellites............166
Lunt Fort (Coventry).......1045
Lurgan..................691
Lusaka (Zambia)........199, 774
Luton, 666; M.P.........339
Luton Hoo...............654
LUXEMBURG, GRAND DUCHY
202, 905
British Embassy..........905
Currency...........905, 986
Embassy................905
European Community..977–81
Luzon (Philippines) 206, 925
Lydd....................666
Lyme Regis...............666
Lymington...............666
Lynn, Bishop of (Norwich)...476
Lyon King of Arms, see LORD
LYON
Lyons (France)............863
Lytham St. Annes..........666

MACAU (PORTUGUESE)
201, 929, 986
Macclesfield..............666
Archdeacon (Chester)....479
Member of Parliament....339
McCracken, Esther, Obit ...575
Macduff.................686
Macedonia (Greece)........870
McGill University..........790
Machinery Exports.........587
Machine Tools Divn. (Dept. of
Trade)...............431
Mackail, Denis, Obituary 575
Mackay Fund (Natl. Debt)...615

PAGE

Mackenzie (N.W.T., Canada) .700
Mackenzie River........206, 697
McKinley, Mt. (Alaska)
205, 206, 801
Maclean, The Lord..........220
Chief Scout...............1117
Knight of the Thistle......259
Lord Lieutenant..........679
Royal Coy. of Archers......223
MACMILLAN, RT. HON. H.:—
Birthday..................94
Chancellor, Oxford Univ...502
Offices Held.......308, 314, 315
Portrait..................552
Privy Councillor..........257
Macquarie Island (Antarctic) .717
MADAGASCAR (Malagasy Re-
public).......199, 206, 905–6
British Embassy..........906
Currency................986
Embassy.................906
Language................863
Madame Tussaud's Exhibition 650
Madeira Islands (Portugal)...929
Madhya Pradesh..........750
Madras City.........204, 752
Archbishop (R.C.).......489
University..............792
Madras (State), see Tamil Nadu
Madrid (Spain)....202, 204, 941
Distance by Air..........1131
Madurai (Tamil Nadu)......752
Maesteg.................675
Magazines..............1078–81
Postage................1196
Public Spending on.......618
Magdalen College, Oxford...502
Magdalene College, Cambridge
505
Magellanic Clouds..........155
Magistrates Courts:—
Approved School Orders .603
Indictable Offences......602
Legal Aid in............1173
London................455
Matrimonial Cases ...1166–7
Non-Criminal Orders...603
Statistics..............602
Magistrates, Stipendiary....455
Scotland (Glasgow).....683
Magna Carta..............652
Magnetic Declination......164
Dip-poles...............164
Equator................164
Magnetism, Terrestrial...163–4
Maharashtra (State), India .750–1
Admin. Divisions........750
Area, etc................750
Communications.......750–1
Production, etc..........751
Mahé Island (Seychelles)....785
Mahon (Minorca)..........941
Maidenhead..............666
Maidstone...............666
Bishop (Canterbury).....473
Member of Parliament....339
Maine (State).............800
Mainland (Orkneys).......677
(Shetlands)............678
Maintenance Orders........603
Majorca (Balearic Islands)...941
Major-Generals........463–4
Majorities, Parliamentary....314
Small..................326

PAGE

Makassar (Indonesia)........881
Malacca (State), Malaysia....201
Málaga (Spain)............941
Malagasy Republic, see MADA-
GASCAR
MALAWI........199, 693, 757
Bishop.................482
Cabinet................757
Currency...............986
Finance and Trade........757
High Commissioners......757
Trade Commissioner......729
University (Limbe).......792
Malawi, Lake.......205, 757
Malay Sea................203
MALAYSIA..201, 585, 693, 758–60
Area and Population......758
Cabinet................758
Climate................758
Currency...............986
Defence................759
Exchange Rate...........83
Government............758
High Commissions.......758
Judicature..............759
Languages..............758
Legislature.............759
Modes of Address........758
Prime Minister..........758
Production, etc........759–60
Religion................758
States..................201
Supreme Head..........758
Trade..................760
Commissioner.......729
with U.K.............760
Universities............792
Maldive Islands......201, 906
Maldon, 666; M.P..........339
Malé (Maldives).......201, 906
Malegaon (Maharashtra)....751
Male Leisure Activities.......491
MALI (Republic)
199, 906–7; (*Map*) 907; 986
British Embassy..........907
Malmesbury.............666
Bishop of (Bristol).......474
Malmö (Sweden).........945
MALTA........202, 693, 760–1
Air Mail Rates..........1197
Archbishop (R.C.).......487
Cabinet................760
Currency...............986
Distance by Air..........1131
Education..............761
Finance and Trade........761
Government............760
High Commissions...760, 761
Judicature..............761
Knights of.............760
Prime Minister......572, 760
Royal University.........792
Trade Commissioner......729
Malton (Thirsk and), M.P....346
Malvern, 670; Hills.........627
Malvern, Visct., Obituary...575
Management (Education)....519
Institutional..........523
Managua (Nicaragua)....200, 916
Manama (Bahrain)..201, 824, 825
MANCHESTER, CITY OF..660, 666
Airport................590
Art Galleries...........656
Bishop..........237, 479

Pages 693–1220 *are omitted from the* Shorter Edition

PAGE

MANCHESTER, CITY OF—*continued*
Clubs.....................1091
College of Music.....529, 533
Colleges of Education.....533
Institute of Science.......508
London Rail Fare.........593
Lord Mayor..............660
Members of Parliament....339
Museums................656
National Westminster Bank
   Building...........1058-9
Newspapers.............1077
Party Strengths..........672
Patent Office............418
Penny Rate.............624
Polytechnic.............535
Probate Registry.......1181
Ship Canal........206, 660
Shipping...............595
Stipendiary........455, 660
Sunrise Times..93, 97, 101, etc.
Teaching Hospitals......527
Theological Colleges...536, 537
University..........508, 512
Weather (Monthly).....1065-7
Manchester College, Oxford.537
Man, Cultural Stages.....185-6
Mandalay (Burma).........835
Mandarin Dialect (China)....841
Mangotsfield..............670
Manila (Philippines) 201, 204, 925
Manipur (India)............753
MAN, ISLE OF...........691-2
  Airport................590
  Bank Notes.............1211
  Bishop of............237, 479
  Census (1901-71).........599
  Lieutenant-Governor......692
  Lighthouse Authority.....435
  T.T. Races.............1012
  Tynwald Day...(*Note*) 114, 692
Manitoba.....200, 695, 697, 702
Mannheim (Germany)......866
Manor Houses Open......653-4
Manpower, Distribution of...606
  Economics, Office of..406, 565
Man, Prehistoric..........185
Mansfield, 666; M.P.........339
Mansfield College, Oxford
         503, 537
Mansfield Woodhouse......670
Mansion House..............646
Manufactures, Numbers En-
  gaged in................606
Manuscripts (Historical) Com-
  mission................421
Maori Population (N.Z.).....730
Mao Tse-tung............839
Maps in *Whitaker*, *see* Notice
  at head of Preface, p. vi
Mar, Earl of (Premier Earl of
  Scotland)................232
Maracaibo (Venezuela)......970
Maracaibo, Lake.....205, 970
Marble Hill (Twickenham)...650
  House...................652
Marchmont Herald..........369
Margate.................666
  Smallest Rainfall.......1064
  Weather (Monthly).....1065-7
Mariana (Marianne) Islands
        203, 810, 811
Trench (Pacific)...........203

PAGE

Marie Galante (French W.
  Indies)...........862, 863
Marina Fall (Guyana).....744
MARINE:—
  Division (Dept. of Trade)..430
  Engineering (Education)....522
  Environmental Research,
    Institute of...........415
  Insurance Companies...1145-8
  Laboratories............424
Mariner Spacecraft (1971)....572
Marines, Royal............462
Maritime Consultative
  Organization............816
  Joint Training School.....520
  Museum, National.......413
  Studies (Degrees)........529
Markets, London......375, 646
Marlborough.............666
  College................539
  House............646-7, 651
Marlborough Street Court...455
Marple (Cheshire)........670
Marquesas Islands (Oceania)..864
Marquesses............227-8
  By Courtesy............256
  Coronets...............227
  How Addressed.........227
  Number of..............226
  Precedence......219, 682
Marrakesh (Morocco)......912
Marre, Sir Alan............285
  Council on Tribunals......434
  Paritry. Commr. for
    Administration........417
MARRIAGE:—
  Acts.................1174-7
  Certificates.......1162, 1175
  Licence Offices.........484
  Licences...............1174
  Matrimonial Orders (1970).603
  Minimum Age..........1176
  Notice of............1174-5
  Nullity of
    600, 1165-6, 1167, 1176
    Act (1971)............361
  Prohibited Degrees......1176
  Rates (U.K.)............600
Marriages (Legal Notes)...1174-7
  By Banns.............1174
  Church of England......1174
  Common Licence......1174
  Consanguinity, etc......1176
  Dissolved (1969)........600
  Family Law Reform Act..1176
  Fees............1174, 1175
  in Registered Buildings....1174
  in Scotland...........1176-7
  Irregular, Scotland.....1176-7
  Jewish............1174, 1175
  of Minors.............1176
  Polygamous (Nat. Ins.)....361
  Quaker........1174, 1175
  Registered (1960-70).....600
  Register Office.........1174
  Registrar-General.......418
    Scotland............426
  Registrar's Certificate....1174
    Fees...............1175
  Solemnization.........1175
  Special Licence.........1174
  Survey (Science Notes)....1034
Married Quarters (Army, etc.)
         471

PAGE

MARS................140, 158-9
  Atmosphere.............159
  Distance, etc...........157
  Monthly
    91, 95, 99; 92, 96, 100, etc.
  Occulted (1972)......148, 149
  Phenomena (1972)...90, 94, 98
  Satellites..........158, 159
Marseilles (France)..........863
Marshal, Diplomatic Corps...221
Marshall Islands.......203, 811
Marshals of the R.A.F.......465
  Pay, 468; Pensions.......472
Martin, R. J., Obituary......575
Martinique (Fr. W. Indies)
       200, 862, 986
Martinmas........(*Notes*) 94, 130
Maryhill, M.P............334
Maryland (State)...........800
Marylebone C.C. (Lord's) *see*
  M.C.C.
  Police Court............455
Mary Queen of Scots........213
Maseru (Lesotho).....199, 756
Masonic Year............186
Massachusetts (State).......800
Massawa (Ethiopia).........856
Mass, Measures of........1215
Master and Servant (Law)...1177
Master-General of the Ordance
       460, 463
Master Gunner............224
Master of the Horse....220, 227
  of the Household.........222
  of the Queen's Music......221
  of the Rolls.......421, 449
    Precedence.............219
  of the Temple...........491
  Worker of the Mint.......408
Masters of the Supreme Court
       451
Maternity Benefits (National
  Insurance).............494
  Cost..................496
Mathematics Degrees.......525
Matlock..................670
Matrah (Oman)...........920
Matrimonial Causes Act....1165
Matrons-in-Chief (Nursing
  Services)..............459
Matsu Island (Formosa)......843
Matterhorn..........888, 946
Matthews, Sir Stanley....94, 285
MAUDLING, RT. HON. R.:—
  Birthday................98
  Member of Parliament....326
  Privy Councillor.........257
  Secretary of State.313, 314, 395
Maundy Money..........1210
  Thursday...........98, 188
Maurice, F. D., Centenary
      102, 576
MAURITANIA (Republic of)
  199; (*Map*) 873; 907, 986
MAURITIUS.....199, 693, 761-3
  Bishop.................482
  Currency...............986
  Dependencies..........762-3
  Distance by Air.........1131
  Finance and Trade.......762
  Government.............762
  High Commissions......762
  University..............792
Mausolus, Tomb of........202

Pages 693–1220 are omitted from the Shorter Edition

PAGE

Mawson (Antarctic)........717
Maybole.................686
Maybray-King, Lord....106, 251
Privy Councillor.........257
Mayors:—
English............622, 664–8
London Boroughs........642
Northern Irish...........691
Welsh.................675
Mazzini, Guiseppe, Centenary
98, 576
Mbabane (Swaziland)....199, 769
M.C....................305
M.C.C..........1000, 1013, 1088
Australian Tour (1970–71).1000
Team Portrait.........563
Mean and Sidereal Time...146
Mean Time, Greenwich....140–1
Measures:—
Nautical...............578
Wind Forces............1211
Meat Division (Ministry of
Agriculture)...........363
Imports..........579, 586
Personal Expenditure on..618
Mecca (Hejas)............935
Mechanical Engineering (Educ.)
522
Museum..............412
Mechanicians (R.N.), Pay....468
Medals and Decorations....302–5
Medan (Indonesia)..........881
Medellin (Colombia)........844
MEDICAL:—
Council, General........1108
Directory.............1075
Divns. (Dept. of Health)...392
Education...........525–8
Teaching Hospitals...525–8
Household, H.M....221–2, 223
Licensing Corporations....528
Officers of Health....633, 676
Research Council..406–8, 611
Units...............407–8
Schools.........520, 525–8
Services (N.H.S.)......500, 501
Techniques (Science Notes)
1029–30, 1031, 1033, 1036–7,
1039–40
Technology (Training)....528
Medicine, Degrees.........528
Nobel Prizes..........1054
Royal Colleges..........528
Supplementary Professions.528
Tropical, Research Board..408
Medicines (N.H.S.)........500
Medina (Hejaz)...........935
Mediterranean Sea......163, 203
Meganthropus............185
Meknès (Morocco).........912
MELBOURNE (Victoria)
203, 204, 714, 726, 727
Archbishops........481, 490
Newspapers...........1085
Melcombe Regis (Weymouth)
668
Melilla (Spanish Presidios).199, 941
Melton, M.P............339
MEMBERS OF PARLIAMENT 318–48
Alphabetical List....318–24
Northern Ireland.........688
Payment of............307
Small Majorities.........324
Suspension of...........311

PAGE

Memel (Lithuania)..........961
Men, Death Rate (U.K.)....600
Menai Bridge............674
Menevia (Wales), Bishop of..487
Mental Welfare Commission
(Scotland)............425
MENZIES, RT. HON. SIR ROBERT
286
Birthday............134
Companion of Honour....261
Knight of the Thistle.....259
Lord Warden, Cinque Ports.204
Privy Councillor.........257
Mercers Company.........640
Hall.................646
MERCHANT NAVY:—
Decorations and Medals....305
Largest Ships...........598
Maritime Museum........413
Shipbuilding Statistics....597
Training..............599
Merchant Shipping......595–8
Merchant Taylors' Company.640
Schools..............539
MERCURY...........140, 157–8
Monthly 91, 95, 99; 92, 96, 100
Phenomena......90, 94, 98
Meriden (Warwicks), M.P....339
Merionethshire......675, 676
Member of Parliament.....339
Merit, Order of.......260, 548
Mermaid Theatre........1026
Mersey Tunnels..........660
2nd Tunnel opened.......548
(*Illus.*).............550
Merthyr Tydfil..........675
Member of Parliament....340
Party Strengths.........673
Stipendiary............455
Merton (London Borough)..642
Party Strengths.........671
Merton and Morden, M.P....340
Merton College, Oxford....502
Mesopotamia, *see* IRAQ
Messina (Sicily)..........891
Mesozoic Periods.........184
Metallurgy (Education)....528
Metals, Exports and Imports..587
Metalwork, Museum of.....412
Meteoric Dust...........156
Meteorites.............162
Meteorological:—
Observations........1068–70
Office..............460–1
Organization World......816
Summary (1970–71)....1061–4
METEORS.............161–2
Meteor Showers (1972)
119, 135, 162
Methil, Buckhaven and.....685
Methodist Church, The.....485
Churches in London......491
Colleges..............536
New Connexion.........485
World Council.........485
Methodists in Australia....707
Metonic Cycle........187, 191
Metre, The.............1214
Metres and Yards........1218
Metrication Board........408
Metric Weights, etc......1214–5
Système Internationale
809–10

PAG

METROPOLITAN:—
Counties (1975).........101
Hospital Boards..........39
Magistrates............45
Police............456–7, 58
Water Board...........40
Meuse River (Belgium)....82
Mews Dept., Royal........22
MEXICO..200, 907–9; (*Map*) 90
British Embassy.........90
Cabinet..............90
Communications.........90
Currency..........909, 98
Embassy.............90
Exchange Rate..........8
Finance and Trade....585, 90
Government............90
Language and Literature...90
Production, etc.........908—0
Mexico City.....200, 204, 90
Miami (U.S.A.)......204, 80
Michaelmas.......(*Notes*) 94, 12
Law Sittings......126, 13.
Michigan (State).........80
Michigan, Lake..........20
Micro Books (Sci. Notes)...103
Micro Meteorites.........16
Middle East Defined.......20
Air Passengers to......58.
Bishops (C. of E.)......48
Middle Park Stakes.......99
Middlesbrough:—
Bishop (R. C.)..........48
Members of Parliament...34.
Shipping Statistics.......59.
Middlesex:—
Archdeacon of..........47
Hospital.............52
Middle Temple.......524, 64
Middleton..............66
Bishop (Manchester)....48
Member of Parliament...34
Midland Bank...........44
Midland Circuit (Crown Cts.) 45
Midlands Stock Exchange...105
Midlothian...........679–8(
Member of Parliament...34
Midnight Sun (Norway)....91
Midsummer Day..(*Notes*) 94, 11
Mid-Ulster, M.P.........34
Midway Islands (U.S.A.) 798, 81
Midwives Boards.........53
College of............110
Milan (Italy).....204, 890, 89
Distance by Air........113
Miles and Kilometres..1214, 121
Miles, Comparative Table....8.
Milford Haven (Shipping)...59
Military:—
Air Traffic Org..........45
Colleges............520–
Cross...............30
Knights of Windsor......22
Medal..............30
Salary.............467–7
Secretary..........459, 46
Milk Divisions (Min. of
Agric.)............36
Wholesale Price........58
Milky Way, The.........1
Million (U.K. and U.S.A.)..121
Millilitre.............121
Milngavie.............68

Pages 693–1220 are omitted from the Shorter Edition

PAGE

Milton Keynes (New Town)
605, 687
Millwall Docks............647
Milwaukee (U.S.A.).....204, 800
Mimas (Satellite)............158
Minch, The.................678
Mindanao (Philippines).....925
Mindoro (Philippines).....925
Mineralogy Museum (Natural
History).................411
Minerals Divn. (Dept. of
Trade)..................431
Mines Inspectorate (Dept. of
Trade)..................431
Safety Research Estab.....432
Minesweepers (R.N.)........462
Minicoy Islds. (India).......753
Minima Gorge (Colombia)..843
Minima of Algol
90, 94, 98; 138
MINING:—
Anti-Fire Bacteria.....1031
Coal Production......... 583
Degrees, etc.............528
Engineering Training.....528
Museum.................411
National Coal Board......414
Numbers Engaged in 606
Strikes (1969–70)......569, 607
Ministers and Envoys...817–976
Precedence.............219
Ministers of Cabinet Rank...313
of the Crown Acts.........306
MINISTERS OF STATE:—
Defence..............313, 459
Procurement.......313, 459
Employment.........313, 382
Foreign and Cwlth....313, 388
Health and Soc. Security
313, 391
Home Affairs........313, 395
Scottish Office.......313, 423
Treasury............313, 433
Welsh Affairs.......313, 433
Minister without Portfolio....313
Ministries (1939–71)......314–5
(1970–71)...............313
MINISTRY OF:—
Agriculture, etc.........362–8
Defence..............459–61
Posts and Telecommunica-
tions..................419
Minneapolis (U.S.A.).......204
Minnesota (State)..........800
Minorca (Balearics).........941
Minor Planets..............159
Minors (Guardianship) Act,
1971...................359
Family Law Reform Act .1176
Minors in Peerage..........226
Minos, Palace of............870
Minsk (Belorussia)......202, 966
MINT, THE ROYAL............408
Output..................1210
Minyaa Konka (China).....205
Miranda (Satellite)..........158
Missionary Bishops..........482
Colleges................536–7
Mississippi River......206, 801
State..................568, 800
Missouri River.........206, 801
State...................800
Mistress of the Robes........220
Mitcham, M.P.............340

PAGE

Modena (Italy) 891
Moderator:—
Calvinistic Methodists.....486
Church of Scotland...484, 682
Presbyterian Churches.....484
Modes of Address (Various),
see ADDRESS
Mogadishu (Somalia)....199, 936
Moldavia (U.S.S.R.) 202, 961, 967
Molecular Time Scale.......142
Molucca Islands (Indonesia)..880
Mombasa (Kenya)..........755
MONACO (Principality)...202, 910
Consulate-General..........910
Grand Prix.............1012
Monetary Fund, International
815–6
Units........984–8, 1210–11
MONEY:—
Bills...............306, 307
Exchange Rates.........83–4
Foreign Currencies.......984–8
Legal Tender.......567, 1210
Purchasing Power of £...1195
Money Orders...........1201–2
Mongolia (Outer)
201; (Map) 839; 910–11
British Embassy..........911
Communist Party.........910
Embassy...............910
Production, etc.........910–11
Monifieth.................686
Monmouth................675
Bishop of..............480
Member of Parliament......340
Monmouthshire........675, 676
Ancient Monuments Com-
mission..............394–5
Monopolies Commission.....409
Monrovia (Liberia)......199, 903
Montacute House...........654
Montana (State)...........800
Mont Blanc..205, 206, 888, 946
Monte Carlo (Monaco).....910
Monte Rosa...........888, 946
Monterrey (Mexico).....204, 909
Montevideo (Uruguay)
200, 204, 959
Montgomery (Borough).....675
MONTGOMERY OF ALAMEIN,
VISCT..................236
Birthday.............130, 463
Field Marshal.............463
Knight of the Garter.......259
Montgomeryshire......675, 676
Member of Parliament......340
Month, The..............186
Length of............186
Monthly Notes........90, 94, 98
Mountpellier (France) 863
Montreal............204, 706
Archbishop (R.C.)........487
Montrose.................686
Montserrat (West Indies).200, 787
Monuments Boards 395
Commissions.........394–5
Division (Environment)...386
London................647
Schedule Nos. (1970)....1044
MOON, THE................161
Age...............92, 96, 100
Apogee (1972)....92, 96, 100
Apollo 15 Landing (1971)
1027, 1028

PAGE

MOON, THE—continued
Conjunctions (Monthly)
90, 94, 98
Craters....................161
Declination........92, 96, 100
Diameter..................161
Distance from Earth.......158
Eclipses 161; (1972) 90, 114, 148
Epact................89, 187
Equatorial Parallax........145
Explorations (1971)
1027, 1028–9
Harvest Moon......161, 122
Horizontal Parallax
92, 96, 100; 139
Hunter's Moon......(Note) 126
Libration.................161
Lunakhod 1 Landing (1971)
1028–9
Lunar Cycle.........187, 191
Terminator............139
Rover Vehicle (Illus.).....556
Metonic Cycle...........187
Moonrise and Moonset.....139
Calculation Method.....145
Tables.........92, 96, 100
Occultations of Stars
148–9, 161
Paschal Full Moon.......188–9
Perigee (1972).......90, 94, 98
Phase (Daily)......92, 96, 100
Phases
90, 94, 98; 138, 139, 161
Phenomena (1972).....90, 94, 98
Position Angle..92, 96, 100; 139
Revolution Period......158, 161
Right Ascension.....92, 96, 100
Rotation Period...........161
Selenographic Colong.
92, 96, 100; 139
Semi-Diameter.....92, 96, 100
Transit......92, 96, 100; 139–40
Moore, Henry:—
Companion of Honour.....261
National Gallery Trustee...370
Order of Merit...........260
Moravian Church...........486
Moray............624, 679–80
Bishop.................484
Sheriff.................684
Moray and Nairn, M.P.....340
Morden College, Blackheath..650
Morden, Merton and, M.P....340
Morecambe, 666; M.P.......340
Weather (Monthly)....1065–7
Morley...................666
(Batley and), M.P.........326
Morning Cloud (Illus.)........561
Morning Defined...........186
Morning Stars........91, 95, 99
MOROCCO
199, 573, 911–3; (Map) 911
British Embassy..........913
Cabinet.................911
Currency............912, 986
Embassy...............911
Exchange Rate...........84
Finance and Trade....585, 912
Government..............912
Production, etc.,.........912
Spanish Possessions.......942
Morpeth, 666; M.P........340
MORRIS OF BORTH-Y-GEST, LORD
245

PAGE

MORRIS OF BORTH-Y-GEST, LORD
—*continued*
  Commissary, Cambridge
    University............504
  Lord of Appeal..........449
  Privy Councillor..........258
  University of Wales......510
Mortgage Business (1970)...1151
  Interest Rates.....1020, 1151–2
  Repayment Table........1020
Mortgages, Stamp Duty
  abolished...........352, 566
Moscow..........202, 204, 965
  British Embassy..........964
  Distance by Air..........1131
Moslem Calendar..........193
  New Year (1392)..89; (*Note*) 94
Mossley................666
Moss Side (Manchester), M.P..339
Mosul (Iraq)............884
Motherwell..............686
  Bishop (R.C.)..........487
  Member of Parliament....340
Motor Cycles:—
  Licences.............1209
  Number Registered......591
Motor Cycling (1971).....1012
Motor Industry Disputes..570, 607
Motoring, Personal Spending
  on.................618
Motor Racing...........1012
Motorships (Statistics)......597
MOTOR VEHICLES:—
  Accident Casualties.......591
  Acts (1970–71).....359–60, 361
  Driving Licences........1195
  Excise Act (1970)..359–60, 1209
  Flywheel Propelled.....1035–6
  Foreign Car Production....587
  Insurance Companies..1145–8
  Licences.......591, 603, 1209
  Lighting-up Times....138, 140
  Numbers Licensed....591, 603
  Personal Spending on.....618
  Petrol Statistics.........584
  Production..........587–8
    Numbers Employed.....606
  Safety Belts..........1030
  (Scotland), Number......603
  Tax Receipts..........609
  Top-selling Cars........588
Motorways.............591
Mottram, R. H., Obituary
             102, 575
Mountain Ash............675
Mountains, Highest........205
  of Mourne...........794
MOUNTBATTEN OF BURMA, EARL
            215, 232
  Admiral of the Fleet......461
  Birthday...........215, 461
  Gold Stick...........220
  Knight of the Garter......259
  Order of Merit.........260
  Privy Councillor........258
  Trinity House.........435
Mourne Mountains (Ireland)..794
Movable Feasts (1968–77)....189
Mozambique (Port E. Africa)
         199, 929, 986
Muckle Flugga...........678
MUHAMMAD:—
  Birthplace (Hejaz).......935
  Flight of (Hejira)........193

PAGE

Mull, Island of.........677, 678
Munich (Germany)..........866
  Distance by Air.........1131
MUNICIPAL:—
  Aerodromes...........590
  Affairs (1970–71)........568
  Corporations Act........622
  Elections (1971)........568
  See also LOCAL GOVERNMENT;
    RATES
MUNICIPAL DIRECTORY:—
  England............664–70
  Northern Ireland........691
  Scotland...........685–6
  Wales..............675
Municipal:—
  Election Petitions Office....458
  Party Representation....671–3
  Yearbook...........1075
Munster (Counties)........795
Münster (Germany)........866
Murbat (Dhofar, Oman)....920
Murchison Meteorite (Science
  Notes)..............1033
Murcia (Spain)...........941
Murder.........602, 603, 803
  "Abnormal" and "Normal"
             603
  Motives for (1970).......603
  Trials (1970–71).........569
Murmansk (U.S.S.R.).....964
Murray River
    206, 708, 717, 722, 726
Murray of Newhaven, Lord..251
  Southampton University...509
Murrumbidgee River.......717
Muscat (Oman)........201, 920
Museums.....409–14, 415, 644,
    645, 646, 648, 649, 655–7
  Admission Charges
        350, 565, 566
  Cost to Taxpayers.......611
  Industrial Safety.........383
  Standing Commission....409
MUSIC:—
  Associated Board........529
  Colleges and Schools.....529
  Degrees, etc.........528–9
  Pimlico School......1057–8
  Royal Academy, etc......529
Musselburgh............686
Mysore (State)..........571
Mzuzu (Malawi).........757

NAGALAND (INDIA).......751
Nagar Haveli (India).......753
Nagoya (Japan).....204, 805
Nagpur (Maharashtra).....751
Nairn......624, 625, 679–80, 686
  Sheriff..............684
Nairn (Moray and), M.P.....340
Nairobi (Kenya).....199, 755
  Archbishops.......482, 488
  Distance by Air.........1131
  University...........792
Nanda Devi, Mt..........205
Nanga Parbat, Mt.........205
Nanking (China)....204, 842
Nantes (France)..........863
Nantwich, M.P...........340
Naples (Italy)....204, 890, 891
  Distance by Air.........1131
Napoleon I.............784
Nash, Ogden, Obituary.....575

PA

Nasik (Maharashtra)........7.
Nassau (Bahamas)...200, 775, 7°
  Bishop..............4°
  Distance by Air.........11.
NATAL................9°
National Academic Awards
  Council...........512, 10,
National Air Traffic Control-
  lerate...............4°
  Army Museum..........6
  Art Library............4
  Athletics Records........9°
  Banks.............444°
  Building Agency........11
  Bus Company......414, 6
  Central Library.........4
NATIONAL COAL BOARD......4
  Chairman.........414, 5
  Financial Results......566 5
  Loans Outstanding....613, 6
National:—
  Colleges (Further Education)
          10
  Council for Art Diplomas..5
  Cross Country Running....9
  Cup-Winners' Cup......10
  Days.........90, 94, 98, 0
NATIONAL DEBT.........613
  Amount (1900–71).....6
  Cost of.............6
  Floating Debt..........4
  Office..............4
  Reduction Funds........6
  Repayment......352, 357, 6
National:—
  Development Bonds......6
  Dock Labour Board......4
  Economic Development Offi
          4
  Engineering Laboratory....4
  Export Council.......439–
  Freight Corporation
        389–90, 6
  Fund..............6
  Galleries (Cost)........6
  Gallery..........370, 6
    of Scotland..........6
NATIONAL HEALTH SERVICE
    391, 393–4, 50°
  Acts...............3
  Amenity Beds.........5
  Contributions...496, 499, 5
  Cost..........500, 611, 6
  Hospital Boards.......393
  Statistics............11
  Prescription Charges..349, 3
  Statistics............1
  Tribunals............
National Hunt Committee....
  Income of U.K. (1960–70)..
  Industrial Relations Court..1
  Institute of Oceanography..
NATIONAL INSURANCE......49°
  Acts..............361,
  Advisory Committee.....
  Benefits..........492–6,
  Chief Insurance Officer....
  Claims (1969)..........
  Commissioner.........
  Contributions..492, 499,
    Increased (1971).......
  Contributors (Number)...
  Contributory Pensions.49
  Cost............496,

PAGE

NATIONAL INSURANCE—*continued*
Divns. (Soc. Security)....391
Earnings-related Supplement......................493
Employers' Contributions 618
Exchequer Supplement...492
Finance.........496, 497
Funds..................496
Graduated Pensions Scheme 492, 495
Contributions......499
Industrial Injuries....496–7
Invalidity Benefit......493
Joint Authorities......393
Maternity Benefits.....494
Payments..............496
Sickness Benefit........493
Tribunals.............434
Unemployment Benefit..493
Widows' Benefits......494
NATIONAL:—
Lending Library, Science and Technology....380, 405–6
Liberal Party............312
Libraries
405–6, 409–10, 1017, 1073
Loans Fund....(*Note*) 609; 613
Assets (1970)........614–5
Maritime Museum....413, 611
Meterological Service....460–1
Monuments Record......394
Museum of Antiquities (Scotland)..........414
Museum of Wales....413–4
Parks.........375, 626–7
Physical Laboratory...142, 432
Playing Fields Association.1112
Police Computer Unit.....397
Portrait Gallery.......370, 611
Scottish...........371
Ports Council............414
Railway Museum........571
Reference Library of Science 419
Register of Archives......421
Road Relay (Athletics)....997
National Savings...........352–3
Bank.................448
Certificates....353, 447, 614
Committees............415
Dept. for.....415, 608, 612
Stock Register..........447
National Sea Training School................530
Societies............1109–10
Sports Centre...........636
Theatre Board..........428
Trusts..........438, 1110
Properties Open....653–4
Westminster Bank......445
Manchester H.Q. (Architecture)..........1058–9
Nationality, British...693, 1162–4
Dept. (Home Office).....396
Nationalized Industries, *see*
PUBLIC CORPORATIONS
Nationwide Bldg. Society...1155
N.A.T.O................981
Cost to U.K............982
Natural Environment Research Council.........415–6, 986
Natural History Museum..410–11
Naturalization Law......1163

Nature Conservancy........415
Nauru, Republic of.203, 693, 763
Nautical Almanac..........1075
Office..................169
·Colleges.................530
Measures................578
Studies (Degrees)........529
Twilight..91, 95, 99, etc.; 139
NAVAL:—
Architecture (Education) ...522
Colleges.................520
Estimates................612
Reserve (Personnel)......612
Secretary..............459
Navy List................1075
Nazareth (Israel)..........886
Neandertal Discoveries.....185
Neap Tides.............163
Near East, The..........201
Air Force (R.A.F.).....458
Neath, 675; M.P........340
Nebraska (State)..........800
Nebulae..............154–5
Negev, The (Israel)........886
Negri Semblian (Malaysia)....201
Nejd (Saudi Arabia)........934
Nelson Monument (London).647
Nelson (Lancashire).......666
Nelson and Colne, M.P....340
Nelson (N.Z.), Bishop......481
NELSON OF STAFFORD, LORD ...245
Chancellor, University of Aston in Birmingham ...510
Neolithic Age...........185
NEPAL (Kingdom).......201, 913
British Embassy..........913
Currency...............986
Embassy...............913
Neptune............140, 160–1
Distance, etc............157
Monthly.....93, 97, 101, etc.
Satellites........158, 160–1
Nereid (Satellite)...........158
NETHERLANDS, KINGDOM OF THE...202, 913–6; (*Map*) 914
Air Passengers to.........588
Area, etc..............914
British Embassy..........915
Cabinet...............914
Colonies..............915–6
Currency.......915, 986
Defence...............915
Education.............915
Embassy..............914
European Community..977–81
Exchange Rate......83, 915
Finance and Trade....585, 915
Government.........914–5
Nobel Prizes............1054
Queen Juliana......208, 913
Royal Family.........913–4
Shipbuilding...........597
Shipping..............596
Telephone Rates to.....1205
Visitors' Passports to......983
Netherlands West Indies
200, 786, 915–6, 986
Nevada (State)...........800
Neville's Cross College......507
Nevis (West Indies).....200, 787
Newark................666
Archdeacon (Southwell)....480
Member of Parliament....340
Newark (U.S.A.)......204, 800

Newbattle Abbey College....512
New Brunswick Province
200, 695, 697, 702–3
Newburn.................670
Newbury, 666; M.P........340
New Caledonia.........203, 864
Newcastle (N.S.W.).......720
Newcastle under Lyme......666
Member of Parliament....340
NEWCASTLE UPON TYNE..660, 666
Bishops.........237, 479, 487
Colleges of Education......533
Customs and Excise......377
Laing Art Gallery........656
Lord Mayor............660
Members of Parliament....340
Party Strengths..........672
Polytechnic............535
Population.............660
Probate Registry.........1181
Sunrise Times......93, 97, 101
Teaching Hospitals.......527
University.........508–9, 512
New College, London......508
Oxford...............502
New Forest, M.P..........340
NEWFOUNDLAND
200, 206, 695, 697, 703–4
Bishop...............480
New Guinea Island
203, 206, 694, 715
see also Papua–New Guinea
Bishop...............481
New Hall, Cambridge......505
Newham (Borough).......642
Party Strengths..........671
New Hampshire (State).....800
New Hebrides.......203, 781–2
New Jersey (State).........800
Newmarket Races.........999
New Mexico (State).......800
Newmilns and Greenholm...686
Newnham College,
Cambridge...........505
New Orleans (Louisiana)....800
New Penny, The...........1211
Newport (I.O.W.).......629, 666
Newport (Mon.).........675
Member of Parliament....340
Party Strengths..........673
Passport Office.........983
Newport-on-Tay..........686
New Providence (Bahamas) ..775
New Romney............666
Newry.................691
News Agencies (London)....1085
New Scientist............1080
Newson, Sir John, Obit.....575
NEW SOUTH WALES
203, 707, 717–20
Agent-General (London)...718
Agriculture.............719
Archbishop.............481
Banking...............719
Bishop...............481
Dependency............720
Education.............719
Finance..........712, 719
Government............718
Judicature.............718
Legislature.............718
Manufactures...........719
Posts, Telegraphs, etc......720
Production and Industry...719

Pages 693–1220 are omitted from the Shorter Edition

PAGE

NEW SOUTH WALES—*continued*
Public Debt..............719
Religions...............717
Schools.................542
Trade...................719
Unions..................719
Transport............719-20
University..............790
Newspaper Offices......1077-85
Press Directory........1076
Societies..............1110
Strikes (1970-71) .569, 570, 571
Newspapers:—
Air Mail Rates.......1197-8
Circulations..........1077-8
Postage............1196, 1201
Press Council..........1086
Principal Daily.......1077-8
Provincial...........1077-8
Public Spending on.....618
Religious..............1078
Sunday.................1078
Newstead Abbey (Museum) . 657
New Style Calendar.......188
Newtownabbey (Co. Antrim)
691
Newton Aycliffe, *see* AYCLIFFE
Newton, M.P.............340
Newton le Willows......670
Newtownards............691
Newtown (Wales)........605
NEW TOWNS (U.K.)......687
Commission for........687
Divn. (Environment
Dept.).............386
Loans Outstanding....614
Progress (Statistics)......605
New University of Ulster....511
New Year, Christian 89; (*Note*) 90
New Year, Jewish
89; (*Note*) 122; 191
Moslem...........89; (*Note*) 94
New Year's Day..........186
NEW YORK (City)......204, 800
Bridges................206
Distance by Air........1131
New York (State)........800
NEW ZEALAND
203, 693, 730-5; (*Map*) 731
Agriculture............734
Air Force..............733
Air Mail Rates to...1198, 1208
Archbishops............490
Army...................733
Banking................733
Banks..............441, 445
Bishops...........481, 490
Boys' Schools..........543
British High Commission. 732
British Lions (1971)...571, 1004
Team Portrait......564
Cabinet...............731-2
Capital................734
Climate................731
Communications.........734
Currency...............986
Day................89; (*Note*) 94
Defence...............732-3
Education..............733
Emigrants to U.K........605
Exchange Rate...........83
Finance................733
Government............731-2
Governor-General.......731

PAGE

NEW ZEALAND—*continued*
High Commissions........732
Highest Point..........206
Islands....206, 730, 731, 734-5
Judicature.............732
Legislature............732
Maori Population.......730
Mountains..............731
Navy...................733
Newspapers.............1085
Parcel Post to.........1208
Population.............730
Production, etc........734
Public Debt............733
Races and Religions.....730
Representatives Abroad....732
Revenue and Expenditure..733
Ross Dependency........735
Standard Time..........143
Telegram Rates to......1208
Telephone Rates to.....1205
Test Matches (1971).....1000
Trade..............585, 734
Commissioners........729
Transport..............734
Trust Territories......735
U.K. Immigrants........605
Universities and Colleges
733, 792
Victoria Cross Awards...302-4
Vital Statistics.......730
Wool Production........734
Next-of-Kin (Legal Notes)
1169-70
Niagara Falls...........207
Niamey (Niger).....199, 917
Nicea, Council of.......188
NICARAGUA . 200, (*Map*) 875; 916
British Embassy........916
Currency...............986
Embassy................916
Nice (France)..........863
Nicobar Islands (India)..752
Nicosia (Cyprus)...202, 739
Distance by Air........1131
Niemeyer, Sir Otto, Obit... 575
NIGER, REPUBLIC OF
199, 916-7; (*Map*) 917
Currency...........917, 986
Niger River............206
NIGERIA, FEDERATION OF
199, 693, 763-5; (*Map*) 917
Bishops................482
Climate................763
Commissioners..........764
Currency...............986
Finance and Trade...585, 765
Government.............764
High Commissions.......764
Judicature.............764
Military Council.......764
Production and Industry..765
State Governors........764
Transport..............764
Universities...........792
Night and Day..........186
Nightingale Islands (Tristan). 785
Nile River.........206, 956
Nile Valley, The......942, 955-6
Early Civilization......185
Nineveh (Iraq).........884
Niue Island (N.Z.)..203, 730, 735
NIXON, RICHARD M.:—
Birthday................90

PAGE

NIXON, RICHARD M.—*continued*
Diary (1970-71)......548, 572
President, U.S.A..209, 801, 802
Noah's Ark (Armenia)......968
Nobel Prizes...........1054
Non-Contributory Pensions..498
Nones (Roman Calendar)....192
Norfolk...............631-3
Archdeacon of..........476
Coast..................627
Members of Parliament....341
NORFOLK, DUKE OF........227
Ascot Office...........221
Earl Marshal........369, 644
Knight of the Garter....259
Lord Lieutenant, Sussex....632
Premier Duke and Earl...227
Privy Councillor.......258
Royal Victorian Chain...260
Trinity House..........435
Norfolk Island (Australia)203, 716
Norman Conquest.....630, 692
Normandy, Dukedom of....692
Normandy, House of......210
Normanton, M.P.........341
Norroy and Ulster King of
Arms.............259, 369
Norse Language..........918
NORTH AMERICA (Continent) .198
Countries and Capitals.....200
Highest Point..........206
NORTHAMPTON........605, 666
Archdeacon (Peterborough) 476
Bishop (R.C.)..........487
Member of Parliament....341
Northamptonshire.......631-3
Members of Parliament....341
North Atlantic Treaty
Organization.......981, 982
North Berwick..........686
North Carolina (State)...800
North Dakota (State)....800
North-Eastern Circuit
(Crown Courts)......453
Northern Circuit (Crown
Courts)............454
NORTHERN IRELAND......688-91
Aerodromes.............590
Agent in London........689
Archbishop.............485
Area, etc........202, 599, 688
Bank Holidays
(*Notes*) 98, 114, 190, 663
Bishops................485
Boys' Schools..........541
Building Statistics.....604
Cabinet...............688-9
Census (1971).......599, 688
Clubs..............1092, 1093
Constitution...........688
Counties...............691
Customs and Excise......378
Dept. (Home Office).....396
Divorce Statistics......600
Education..............1052
Authorities.........516-7
Electors (Number)......625
Events (1969-70)......567-8
Exchequer, Payments to....600
Expectation of Life....1149
Finance................690
Fisheries..............690
Flags of...............690

PAGE

NORTHERN IRELAND—*continued*
G.O.C. (Army)............463
Government............688–9
Offices................689
Governor..............688
H.M. Lieutenants........691
High Sheriffs...........691
Holiday Posts..........1204
House of Commons......688
Income from Employment.616
Inn of Court............524
Judicature............689–90
Legislature............688
Local Government......625
London Office..........689
Manufactures..........690
M.P.'s (Belfast)........688
Methodist Church.......485
Minerals..............690
Municipal Directory.....691
Newspapers...........1085
Parliament............688
Parliamentary Secretaries..689
Party Strengths........688
Passport Office.........688
Population......599, 600, 688
Density..............688
Presbyterian Church.....484
Prime Minister...566, 567, 688
Privy Council..........688
Production............690
Quarter Days.......(*Note*) 94
Quarter Sessions.......690
Railways.............690
Recorders............690
Registrar-General......689
Religions.............690
Riots (1970–71)......567–8
(*Illus.*).............553
Roman Catholic Church...487
Seaports.............690
Senate...............688
Speakers, Parliamentary...688
Sunrise and Sunset (Daily)
93, 97, 101, etc.
Supreme Court.........610
Technical Colleges......535
Theological Colleges.....536
Trade................690
U.K. Representative in...689
Universities......511, 1052
Northern Lighthouses.....435
Northern Lights (Norway)..917
Northern School of Music...529
Northern Stock Exchange...1053
Northern Territory (Australia)
203, 707, 714–5
NORTHERN VIETNAM....972–3
Northfield (B'ham), M.P....327
Northfleet.............670
North Fylde, M.P........341
North Galactic Pole......145
North London Police Court...455
North-Rhine Westphalia....866
North Riding..........631–3
North Sea............203
Northstead, Manor of.....310
Northumberland........631–3
Archdeacon of (Newcastle).479
Coast...............627
National Park.........626
NORTHUMBERLAND, DUKE OF..227
Knight of the Garter.....259
Lord Lieutenant........632

PAGE

NORTHUMBERLAND, DUKE OF
—*continued*
Medicine Research Cncl....406
Newcastle University......508
Syon House............652
North West Territories
(Canada)........200, 695
Northwich, M.P.........341
Northwood, M.P.........343
Norton, Sir Peter Hill-....288
Admiral of the Fleet......461
Chief of Defence Staff....459
NORWAY, KINGDOM OF
202, 917–9; (*Map*) 918
Antarctica............919
British Embassy.........919
Cabinet..............917
Currency.............986
Education............918
Embassy.............917
Exchange Rate.........83
Finance and Trade..585, 918–9
Government...........918
Language and Literature...918
Nobel Prizes.......918, 1054
Shipbuilding..........597
Shipping........596, 918
Telephone Rates to.....1205
Norwegian Deep (Arctic)..982
NORWICH, CITY OF...660–1, 666
Bishop............237, 476
London Rail Fare........593
Lord Mayor...........661
Members of Parliament...341
Museums.............656
Party Strengths........672
Population............661
Probate Registry.......1181
Sheriff..............661
Norwood, M.P..........337
Note Issue (U.K.)........440
NOTTINGHAM, CITY OF..661, 666
Archdeacon (Southwell)....480
Bishop (R.C.).........487
Colleges of Education.....533
Lord Mayor...........661
Members of Parliament...341
Museums and Galleries...656–7
Party Strengths........672
Population............661
Probate Registry.......1181
Trent Polytechnic.......535
University........509, 512
Weather (Monthly)....1065–7
Nottinghamshire......631–3
Nouakchott (Mauritania) 199, 907
Noumea (New Caledonia)
203, 864
Novae (Stars)...........153
NOVA SCOTIA (Canada)
200, 695, 697, 704
Novels of 1970–71.......1025
Novosibirsk (R.S.F.S.R.)...965
Nubian Race (U.A.R.).....955
Nuclear:—
Installations Inspectorate..431
Strategic Force (U.K.)....458
Nuffield College, Oxford...502
Foundation...........514
Nuku'alofa (Tonga).......775
Nullity of Marriage
600, 1165–6, 1167
Act (1971)............361
Numerals, Roman........192

PAGE

Nuneaton, 666; M.P........341
Nunthorpe Stakes........999
Nuremberg (Germany)....866
Nursery Schools.........1049
Nurses:—
National Council of......530
Training of............530
Nursing:—
Central Midwives' Board..530
Degrees, etc............530
Divn. (Dept. of Health)...393
General Councils.......1111
Royal College of.......530
Nutation (Sidereal Time) 141, 145

OAKS, THE (RACE)........999
Oases (U.A.R.)..........956
Oats Harvests, Prices 580, 581, 582
Oban................686
Oberhausen (Germany)....866
Oberon (Satellite).......158
Oberon Class Submarines..462
Obituary (1970–71)...82, 574–5
OBSERVATORIES:—
Cambridge Univ., Director 505
Royal...............169
Observer Corps, Royal.....466
Occultation Defined.......161
Occultations (1972).....148–9
of Stars.............161
Occupational:—
Pensions (1975)........567
Therapy (Training).....528
OCCURRENCES DURING PRINTING
82
Ocean Areas and Depths.203, 982
Ocean Island (Pacific)......782
OCEANIA........198, 203
Countries............203
Highest Point.........206
R.C. Church..........490
Oceanography, National
Institute of............415
Octavo Defined........1217
Odense (Denmark)........852
Odessa (Ukraine)....964, 966
Offa's Dike............630
Office of :—
Manpower Economics.....406
Population Censuses....418–9
the Umpire...........384
Officers Cadets, Pay of.....469
Officers:—
Ranks (Equivalents).....1020
Pay and Pensions...467–72
Quartering Charges.....471
Offices and Shops Act.....1177
Official Periodicals
1079, 1080, 1082, 1083
Referees (Supreme Ct.)219, 450
Solicitor (Supreme Court)..451
Ogmore, M.P...........341
Ogmore and Garw.......675
Ohm (Measure).........1215
Ohio (State)............800
Oil:—
Imports (U.K.)..........586
Production (U.K.)........584
Tankers, Largest........598
Okehampton...........666
Oklahoma (State)........800
Olav V, King
209, 216, 219, 259, 260, 917

PAGE

Old Age Pensions
352, 494–5, 498, 566
Old and New Style..........188
Oldbury (and Halesowen), M.P.
341
Oldest City (Damascus).....947
Oldham, 666; M.P.'s........341
Old Street Court...........455
Old Vic (1970–71)..........1026
Olympiads..................193
Olympic Games (1972)..571, 989
Athletic Records.........989
Swimming Records....1012–3
O.M........................260
Omagh (Co. Tyrone).......691
OMAN (Arabia)......201, 919–20
British Embassy..........920
Currency..........920, 986
Finance and Trade........920
Omar Khayyám.............882
Ombudsman, see Parliamentary
Commissioner
One Thousand Guineas......999
ONTARIO (Canada) 200, 697, 704–5
Agent-General............705
Province (C. of E.)......480
Ontario, Lake.............205
Oosterschelde Bridge......206
Open Golf Champions......1006
Openshaw (Manchester), M.P.
339
Open University...........510
Opera House, Covent Garden 650
Ophthalmic Optics, Degrees..530
Services (N.H.S.)....510, 1157
Oporto (Portugal).........929
Opposition, Leader of the 306, 313
Number of the...........316
Whips...................312
Optical Council, General..1111
Optics Degrees etc.........530
Oran (Algeria)............819
Orange Free State.........937
Orange River (S. Africa)..937
Order of Merit............260
of St. John........305, 648
of St. Michael and St. Geo. 260
of St. Patrick..........259
of the Bath.............259
of the British Empire...261
of the Companions of
Honour.................261
of the Crown of India...261
of the Garter...........259
of the Indian Empire....260
of the Star of India....260
of the Thistle..........259
of Victoria and Albert..261
Orders of Chivalry......259–61
Central Chancery........222
Knights..............262–300
Ordnance Factories (Cost)..612
Master-General of..460, 463
Survey.......416, 608, 611
Oregon (State)............800
Organists, Roy. College of..529
Oriel College, Oxford.....508
Oriental Studies School....508
Orinoco River (Venezuela)..969
Orissa (State)............751
Orkney...........677, 679–80
Bishop..................484
Member of Parliament....341
Sheriff.................684

PAGE

Ormskirk, 670; M.P........341
Orontes River.........902, 947
Orphans, Guardians' Allow-
ances...................494
Orpington, M.P............341
Orthoptics (Training).....528
Osaka (Japan).......204, 895
Osborne House.............654
Oslo (Norway)......202, 919
Distance by Air........1131
Ossett....................667
Ostend (Belgium)..........827
Osteopathy, London Coll....530
Osterley Park.............652
Ostrava (Czechoslovakia)...850
Oswestry, M.P.............341
OTTAWA............200, 705
Archbishop (R.C.)........487
Ouagadougou (Upper Volta)
189, 958
Outer Mongolia........910–11
Outward Bound Trust......1111
Overnight Telegrams......1202
Overseas Aid (Cost).......610
Airways...............371–2
Audit Department........416
Debt Repayments....352, 357
OVERSEAS DEVELOPMENT
ADMINISTRATION..416–7, 608
Minister for.........313, 416
Estimates...............610
Under Secretaries........313
Overseas Income Tax Office..417
Information Dept.......400–1
Loans Guaranteed........614
Money Orders...........1202
Parcel Rates.........1206–9
Surveys Directorate......417
Telegraph Rates..1202, 1206–9
Telephones......1904, 1205
Oxford, Bishop of......237, 476
OXFORD CITY......661, 667
Ashmolean Museum.......657
Clubs..................1091
London Rail Fare........593
Lord Mayor..............661
Member of Parliament....341
Party Strengths.........672
Polytechnic.............535
Population..............661
Probate Registry.......1181
Ruskin School of Art....518
Theological Colleges..536, 537
Weather (Monthly)....1065–7
Oxfordshire............631–3
OXFORD UNIVERSITY..502–4, 661
Appointments Committee,
Secretary..............502
Colleges and Halls......502–3
Copyright Library......1073
Extra-Mural Studies.....512
Hebdomadal Council.....502
Professors............503–4
Teaching Hospitals......527
Terms (Dates)..........502
Undergraduates (Number). 502
Women's Colleges........503
OXFORD v. CAMBRIDGE...1011
Athletics..........996, 997
Boat Race.............1010
Cricket..........1002, 1011
Football..............1004

PAGE

OXFORD v. CAMBRIDGE—continued
Lawn Tennis...........1007
Swimming..............1009
Oyster Season Opens...(Note) 118

PACIFIC ISLANDS:—
British...........203, 782–3
French............203, 864
Japanese................893
U.S.A...................810
W. Pacific High Commission
782
Pacific Ocean.............203
Time....................143
Trust Territory (U.S.A.)
798, 810, 811
Paddington, M.P.'s......341–2
Padua (Italy).........890, 891
PAGE, R. G.:—
Member of Parliament....331
Minister for Local Govt.
313, 384
Pago Pago (Samoa).....203, 811
Pahang (State), Malaysia....201
Paisley...................686
Bishop (R.C.)...........487
Member of Parliament....342
PAKISTAN, REPUBLIC OF
201, 693; (Map) 746; 765–7
Civil War (1971)........572
(Illus.)................555
Cyclone Disaster (1970)..568
(Illus.)................555
Currency..........766, 986
Education...............766
Events (1970–71)..568, 572, 765
Exchange Rate............83
Finance.................766
Government..............765
High Commissions........766
Immigrants from.........605
Legal Framework Order
(1970).................765
Production..............766
Provinces.............766–7
R.C. Church.............489
Seaports................766
Trade...........585, 766
Commissioners..........729
Universities..........792–3
Palace of Westminster.....306
Palæolithic Age...........185
Palæontology Museum (Natural
History)................411
Palæozoic Periods.........184
Palatine County (Durham)..378
Palembang (Indonesia).....881
Palermo (Sicily).......890, 891
PALESTINE, see ISRAEL
Pallas (Minor Planet).....159
Palma (Majorca)..........941
Palmerston North (N.Z.)...734
Palm Sunday.........98, 188
Pamekesan (Indonesia).....881
Panaji (Nova Goa, India)..753
PANAMA, REPUBLIC OF
200; (Map) 846; 920–1
British Embassy.........921
Currency..........921, 986
Embassy.................920
Shipping Registered.....596
PANAMA CANAL......206, 811–2
PANAMA CANAL ZONE
200, 798, 811–2

Pages 693–1220 are omitted from the Shorter Edition

	PAGE
Panama City	921
Pantelleria Island	891
PAPAL STATE, THE, *see* VATICAN	
Papeete (Fr. Polynesia)	203, 864
Paperbacks in Print	1083
Paper:—	
Compost (Science Notes)	1037
Imports and Exports	586, 587
Industrial Training Bd.	535
Measures	1216–7
Paper Sizes, International	1217
PAPUA—NEW GUINEA	
	203, 694, 715–6
Finance and Trade	716
University	793
Parachute Regiment	465
PARAGUAY, REPUBLIC OF	
200; (*Map*) 830;	921–2
British Embassy	922
Communications	922
Currency	922, 986
Embassy	921
Government	922
Paramaribo (Neth. W. Indies)	
	200, 916
Paraña River	821, 830, 921
Paranthropus	185
PARCEL POST	582, 1196
Compensation for Loss	1200
Imports and Exports	587
Inland Rates	1196
Overseas Rates	1206–9
Postage Forward Service	1201
Railway Parcels	1200
PARIS	202, 204, 863
British Embassy	863
Distance by Air	1131
District of	863
Grand Prix	999
Parish Councils	622
Meetings	622
Park (Sheffield), M.P.	344
Parkhurst Prison, Governor	398
Parks:—	
London	636, 649–50
National (List)	626–7
Countryside Commission	375
PARLIAMENT, HOUSES OF	
	306–61, 645
Adjournment of	311
Bill of Rights	311
Bills	306
Buildings	308
Candidates' Deposits	311
Closure	311
Debates	310
(1970–71)	349–59
Dissolution	307, 310
Dates	316
Duration of	307, 316
Election Petitions Office	458
European Community	
Debates (1971)	357–9
Freedom of Speech	311
Government Whips	312
Guillotine	311, 355
Hansard	307
Hours of Meeting	310
House of Commons, *see*	
HOUSE	
Majorities, 1833–1970	316
Small	324
Members of	318–48
Money Bills	306

	PAGE
PARLIAMENT, HOUSES OF	
—*continued*	
Officers of	309
Palace of Westminster	308
Parties in	316
Party Government	312
Payment of Members	307
Peers of	226
Press Gallery	310
Private Bills	306
Privileges	311
Procedure	310–11
Prorogation	310
Public Acts (1970–71)	359–61
Queen's Printer	426
Record Office	421
Record Sittings	307
Sessional Orders	310
Standing Orders	310
Union Jack Flown	225, 308
Voters' Qualifications	1178
Westminster Hall	649
Women Members	316
Writs	310
PARLIAMENTARY:—	
Associations	317
Commissioner for Adminis-	
tration	417, 610
Constituencies	325–48, 350
Redistribution	565
Counsel	417
Debates (Hansard)	1080
Elections (1955–70)	317
Electors	325–48
Labour Party	1112
Printing Press	426
Private Secretaries	362–436
Salaries	307
Secretaries	306, 313, 362–433
Summary	349–59
Whips	312
Parliament Hill	650
Square	645
Parliaments, Clerk of the	309, 449
Parliaments since 1852	316
Parole Board	417–8
Parsec (Astronomical measure)	152
Parties, Parliamentary	312, 316
Partridge Shooting (*Notes*)	94, 1222
Party Government	312
Party Representation (Local)	
	671–3
Paschal Full Moon	188–9
Passenger:—	
Movement by Air	588
Ships, Largest	598
Vehicle Production	587–8
Passover (Jewish Festival)	191
Passport Offices	389, 983
Passports	983
Fees increased (1970)	349, 565
Patent Agency (Education)	530
PATENT OFFICE	418
Library	410
Appeal Tribunals	457
Number Sealed (1970)	418
Patna (Bihar)	749
Patron Saints	673, 794
Pavilion (Brighton), M.P.	328
P.A.Y.E.	616, 1191
Paymaster-General	313, 418
Office (Crawley)	418
Peace Commissions, Secretary	450
Peace, Nobel Prize	1054

	PAGE
Peak District National Park	626
PEARCE, LORD	246
Chairman, Press Council	1086
Judicial Committee	449
Privy Councillor	258
Pears Cyclopedia	1076
PEARSON, LORD	246
Lord of Appeal	246
Privy Councillor	258
Pearson, Rt. Hon. Lester:—	
Order of Merit	260, 548
Privy Councillor	258
Peckham, M.P.	329
Peculiars, Court of	484
Peebles	686
Peeblesshire	679–80
Member of Parliament	343
Sheriff	684
PEERAGE, THE	226–56
Contractions and Symbols	226
Disclaimers	226, 307
Life Peerages Act	307
Peerages Extinct (1970–71)	226
Peeresses In Own Right	249–50
Peeresses, Life	252, 307
Number of	226
Surnames	252–6
PEERS	226–56
Irish (H. of Commons)	307
Life Peers	226, 250–2
Minors	226
Number of	226
Surnames of	252–6
Trial of	307
Peking (China)	201, 204, 842
Anthropological Discoveries	
	185
Pelagian Islands	891
Pembroke	675
College (Cambridge)	505
(Oxford)	502
Pembrokeshire	675, 676
Member of Parliament	342
National Park	626
Penang (Malaysia)	201
Penarth (Glam.)	675
Penicuik	686
Penistone, M.P.	342
Pennine Chain	629
Pennsylvania (State)	800
Penny, New (decimal)	1211
(*Illus.*)	558
Penny Post (1897–1918)	1047
Penny Rate, Product of	624
Penrith, Bishop of (Carlisle)	478
Member of Parliament	342
Penryn (Cornwall)	667
Penshurst Place	654
PENSIONS:—	
Appeals Tribunal	458
Blind Persons	498
Contributory	494–5
Rates	499
Cost of	496
Defence Services	490
Disablement	496–7
Graduated	492
Non-Contributory	498
Occupational (1975)	567
Retirement	494–5, 498
Increased (1971) 352, 565, 566	
Supplementary (Social	
Security)	498
Victoria Cross	302

Pages 693–1220 are omitted from the Shorter Edition

PAGE

PENSIONS—*continued*
War.....................611
Widows'.................494
Women's Services.........472
Pentecost................106
Jewish...........(*Note*) 106; 191
Pentlands, M.P.............332
Pentonville Prison (Governor) 398
Penzance.................667
Perak (Malaysia)...........201
Percival David Foundation...647
Performing Right Tribunal...458
Perigee and Apogee....90, 94, 98
Defined................138
Periodicals.............1078–81
Periods of Gestation......1124
Perlis (Malaysia)..........201
Perry Barr, M.P............327
Perseid Meteors:—
Maxima (1972)...........119
Showers................162
PERSIA, *see* IRAN
PERSIAN GULF STATES:—
Bahrain...............824–5
British Resident.......825
Kuwait..............899–901
Oman................919–20
Qatar...............929–30
Saudi Arabia..........934–5
Trucial States........950–1
Personal Expenditure..618, 619
Personal Incomes........616–9
in U.S.A...............805
Personal Property Defined...1179
Social Services...........501
Tax................353, 354
Perth (Scotland)...........686
Member of Parliament....342
Perth (Western Australia) 203, 729
Archbishops.............490
Distance by Air.........1131
Newspapers.............1085
Perthshire..........624, 679–80
Members of Parliament....342
Sheriff, etc.............684
PERU, REPUBLIC OF
200, 922–4; (*Map*) 923
British Embassy..........924
Currency................986
Embassy................922
Exchange Rate............84
Finance and Trade.....585, 924
Government..............923
Production..............923
Petroleum:—
Divn. (Dept. of Trade)....431
Imports................586
Industrial Training Board..535
Measures...............584
Tankers, Largest.........598
U.K. Consumption, etc....584
Petsamo................961
Petty Session Courts (London) 455

PAGE

Petworth House...........654
PEYTON, RT. HON. J. W. W.:—
Member of Parliament....348
Minister for Transport
Industries........313, 384
Privy Councillor.........258
Pharmaceutical Dept. (Min. of
Health)...............393
Pharmacy, School of (London
University)............508
Training, etc............530
Pharos (Alexandria).....202, 957
Phases of the Moon
90, 94, 98, etc.; 138
Pheasant Shooting. (*Notes*) 94, 126
Philadelphia (U.S.A.)....204, 800
PHILIPPINES, REPUBLIC OF THE
201, 924–6; (*Map*) 924
British Embassy..........926
Cabinet................924
Currency............925, 986
Embassy................924
Exchange Rate............84
Finance and Trade........925
Language and Literature..925
Principal Islands.........925
Trade..................585
Phnom Penh (Khmer Repub.)
201, 898
Phobos (Satellite)........158
Phoebe (Satellite)..158, 159, 160
Phoenix Islds. (Pacific)....782
Photography Training......530
Physical Laboratory, National 142
Recreation, Central Council
430, 636, 1112
Physical Training Colleges...531
Physicians, Royal Colleges..1112
Physicians to H.M......221, 223
Physicians to the Household..223
Physics, Degrees, etc.......519
Museum...............411
Nobel Prizes............1054
Physiology, Nobel Prize....1054
Physiotherapy Training.....528
Picketing (Industrial Relations
Act).................1016
Picture Galleries, London
370–1
Piedmont (Italy)..........890
Pietermaritzburg (Natal)....938
Pigs:—
Number of (1971).........580
Prices................581
Pik Communizmu..........205
Pilgrims, The............1112
Pilgrim Trust..........438–9
Pilkington, Lord...........251
Chancellor, Loughborough
Univ................510
Pillars of Hercules.........911
Piltdown Skull...........185
Pimlico Music School....1057–8
Pirbright Guards Depôt...1056–7
Pitcairn Islands (Pacific)....783
Pithecanthropus..........185
Pittsburgh (Pennsylvania)
205, 800
Pius, Wall of.............678
P.L.A..............419, 647
Plaid Cymru............1119
Votes Cast (1964–70).....317
Planetarium, London......650
Planetary Nebulae.........154

PAGE

Planets, The....140, 156, 157–61
Conjunctions (Monthly)
90, 94, 98 etc.
Minor...............159
Phases Defined.........140
Transit..............140
Planning, Town and Country
1177–8
Degrees, Diplomas......537
Departments....425–6, 635
Officers (Environment)
385, 386
Plantagenet, House of....210–11
Plant Health Inspectorate...366
Plant Pathology:—
Advisers..............365
Laboratory.............366
Plants Divisions (Agric.)...364
Plastic Containers, Soluble..1039
Plate, Hall Marks on....1212–3
Player Sunday League (Cricket)
1002
Playing Fields Association...1112
Plays of 1970–71.......1025–6
Pleiades Star Cluster...153, 155
Occultation (1972).....148
Pleistocene Period......184–5
Plesianthropus..........185
Ploiesti (Rumania).........932
Plovdiv (Bulgaria).........833
Plowden Report, 1967....1048
Plow Monday............188
PLUTO.................161
Distance, etc...........157
PLYMOUTH...........661, 667
Bishops...........475, 487
Lord Mayor...........661
Members of Parliament...342
Museums, etc..........657
Party Strengths.........672
Polytechnic............535
Weather (Monthly)...1065–7
Plymouth (Montserrat)..200, 787
Plzen (Czechoslovakia)....850
P.M. and A.M.......141, 186
Pneumoconiosis Benefit....497
Board................393
Deaths from............601
Research Units.........408
Pneumonia, Deaths from....601
Poets' Corner............490
Poetry in 1970–71........1023
Poets Laureate......221, 1026
Point à Petre (Guadeloupe)
200, 863
Poisoning, Deaths by.......602
POLAND, REPUBLIC OF
202, 926–7; (*Map*) 926
British Embassy..........927
Cabinet................926
Communist Party........926
Currency............927, 987
Embassy................926
Exchange Rate......84, 927
Finance and Trade........927
Government...........926–7
Nobel Prizes........927, 1054
Shipbuilding............597
Shipping...............596
Trade..................585
Polaris................151
Polaris Submarines....458, 462
Polar Medals............305
Poles, Magnetic..........164

Pages 693–1220 *are omitted from the* Shorter Edition

PAGE

POLICE:—
Cadet Corps (London).....456
City of London..........457
College, Basingstoke.....397
Computer Unit..........397
Cost of.............610, 624
Courts (London).........455
Department (Home Office)
396–7
H.M. Inspectors......397, 425
Laboratory.............457
Medals................305
Metropolitan...........456–7
Courts..............455
Royal Ulster Constabulary.689
Scotland Yard......456–7, 584
Statistics..............584
Welsh Authorities........676
Political Honours Scrutiny
Committee............418
Parties................316
Survey (1970–71)......565–8
Politics, Books on (1970–71).1024
Pollok (Glasgow), M.P.....334
Polo....................1008
Pollution, R. Commission on 437
Polwarth, Lord............246
Chancellor, Aberdeen Univ.
511
Polynesia, French.......203, 864
Polytechnics (Further Educ.)
534–5, 1050, 1051
London.................535
POMPIDOU, GEORGES...573, 574
Birthday...........114, 208
President of France
208, 209, 858
Pondicherry (India).........753
Pontefract, 667; M.P........342
Bishop (Wakefield).......480
Ponte Salazar (Portugal)...206
Pontine Archipelago (Italy)...891
Pontypool, 675; M.P........342
Pontypridd, 675; M.P........342
Stipendiary............455
Poole, 667; M.P...........342
Yacht Clubs............1092
Poona (India).............751
POPE, HIS HOLINESS THE
209, 487, 968
Birthday................122
Popes, Election of...........487
List of (1700–1971)........209
Poplar, M.P...............342
Popacatapetl, Mt............205
Population:—
Census (1971)....566, 567, 599
Censuses, Office of
418–9, 608, 612
Density of.............199, 203
Po River..................888
Porpoise Class Submarines...462
Portadown (N. Ireland)......691
PORTAL OF HUNGERFORD,
VISCOUNT:—
Obituary............102, 575
Portrait.................560
Port au Prince (Haiti)
200, 874, 875
Port Authorities........372, 435
Port Blair (Andamans).......752
Portchartrain Causeway, U.S.A.
206
Port Elizabeth (S. Africa)....938

PAGE

Port Glasgow..............686
PORTLAND, DUKE OF........227
Chancellor, Nottingham
University...........509
Knight of the Garter......259
Port Louis (Mauritius)...199, 762
Port Moresby (Papua)...203, 716
PORT OF LONDON..........647
Authority..............419
Port of Spain (Trinidad)
200, 771
Archbishop (R.C.).........487
Porto Novo (Dahomey) .199, 851
Port Pirie (S. Australia).....724
Portrait Galleries, National..370
Portree (Skye).............678
Ports Council, National.....414
Divn. (Dept. of Environment)
386
PORTSMOUTH..........661–2, 667
Airport................590
Bishops.........237, 477, 487
Lord Mayor............662
Members of Parliament....342
Party Representation......672
Polytechnic............535
Port Talbot..............675
PORTUGAL, REPUBLIC OF
202, 927–9; (*Map*) 939
British Embassy..........929
Cabinet................927
Currency............928, 987
Embassy..............927–8
Exchange Rate......83, 928
Finance................928
Government............928
Language, etc..........928
Nobel Prizes...........1054
Production.............928
Provinces Overseas......929
Trade...........585, 928–9
Portuguese East Africa....929
Guinea...........199, 929, 987
Timor...........929, 987
Postage, Public Spending on .618
Rates (1897–1971)......1047
Stamps...............1201
Postal Charges Increased (1971)
566
Insurance Rates........1200
Orders...............1202
POSTAL REGULATIONS (U.K.)
1196–1209
Postal Strike (1971).......570
(*Illus.*)............557
Postal Union, Universal....816
Post Cards.........1196, 1201
Airmail..............1197–8
Post Restante...........1199
Postgate, Raymond, Obit....575
Post Graduate Medical Schools
527
Teaching Hospitals......526–7
POST OFFICE..........419, 614
Chairman....419, 565, 566
Corporation Established .582
Financial Results.........582
Loans Outstanding......613
Radio Time Signals......142
Strike (1971)...........570
(*Illus.*)............557
Tower (London)........203
Post Offices Always Open
1202, 1204

PAGE

Posts and Telecommunications:—
Minister of....313, 419, 1017
Ministry of..............419
(Cost)...............610
Post-War Credits.........1190
Potato Farms (No.)........580
Harvests, Prices...580, 581, 582
Potsdam Agreement......865–6
Potters Bar..............670
Poultry Advisers (Min. of
Agric.)...............365
Farms (Number).........580
Gestation Periods.......1124
Statistics (U.K.).........580
Pound, Purchasing Power of
1195
Pound Weight Conversion
Table...............1218
Power of Attorney (Stamp Duty)
1194
Power Station Strike (1970). .570
Powys (Planned Welsh
County)..............1019
Poynings' Law............794
Poznán (Poland)...........927
Praesepe Star Cluster.....153, 155
Prager Spy Case (1971)......569
Prague................202, 850
Distance by Air..........1131
Praia (Cape Verde Islands)
199, 929
Praslin Isld. (Seychelles).....785
Precedence in England......219
in Scotland............682–3
Local (England and Wales).219
Preceptors, College of......1112
Precession 141; Defined.....150
(1972)...............145
Prehistoric Man...........185
Premier Baron:—
England (Mowbray)......245
Ireland (Kingsale)........244
Scotland (Forbes)........241
Premier Baronet:—
England (Bacon)........264
Gt. Britain (Dashwood)...271
Ireland (Coote).........270
Scotland (Roxburghe)....227
Premier Barony (England)...250
Premier Duke (Norfolk).....227
Ireland (Leinster).......227
Scotland (Hamilton)....227
Premier Earl (Norfolk-Arundel)
227
England (Shrewsbury)....233
Ireland (by date-Leinster)..227
(on roll-Shrewsbury) .233
Scotland (Mar).........232
Premier Marquess:—
England (Winchester)....228
Ireland (Leinster).......227
Scotland (Huntly).......228
Premier Peer (Norfolk).....227
Ireland (Leinster).......227
Scotland (Hamilton)....227
Premier Viscount:—
England (Hereford)......235
Ireland (Gormanston)....235
Premium Savings Bonds
352, 446, 614
Premiums (Endowment Assur-
ance)..............1142–3
(Life Assurance).......1140–1
Preparatory Schools.......1049

Pages 693–1220 *are omitted from the* Shorter Edition

PAGE

Presbyterian Churches.484, 485–6
Colleges.................536
Presbyterians in Australia....707
in Canada.................695
Prescriptions (N.H.S.)..500, 1157
President, Board of Trade
313, 428
Family Divn. (High Ct.)....450
Presidents, American....801, 802
Foreign.................208–9
French.................209
Royal Academy.........1094
Society (1660–1971).....1093
U.S. Senate.............803
PRESS, THE.............1077–85
Association.......1085, 1113
Circulations..........1077–8
Clubs (London).....1088, 1089
Correcting for the...1219–20
Council................1086
Reporting Agencies.....1085
Secretary, H.M..........220
PRESTON................667
Members of Parliament....342
Prestonpans.............686
Prestwich (Lancashire)....667
Member of Parliament....340
Prestwick (Ayrshire)......686
Airport................590
Weather (Monthly)....1065–7
Prices Index............1195
Primary Schools.....1049, 1052
Improvement Finance....567
Plowden Report........1048
Primate of All England....473
of Australia............481
of Canada.............480
of England.............478
of Ireland.............485
of Scotland (Primus).....484
PRIME MINISTER, THE 313, 314, 432
Minister for the Civil
Service................373
Office of.....306, 312, 315
Precedence.......219, 682
Residences.............308
Prime Ministers (Historical Lists)
308, 314
Primitive Methodists.......485
Primus, The (Scotland).....484
PRINCE ANDREW............218
Birthday.....89, 94, 218, 225
Precedence..........219, 682
PRINCE EDWARD............218
Birthday.....89, 98, 218, 225
Precedence..........219, 682
PRINCE EDWARD ISLAND
200, 695, 697, 705
Prince Henry's Room........647
PRINCE OF WALES...214, 218, 226
Birthday...99, 130, 218, 225
Councillor of State........306
Diary (1970–71).....548; 565
Household.............223
Knight of the Garter......259
Parachute Jump (Illus.)....551
Portrait................552
Precedence.............219
Succession to Throne......219
Prince of Wales (Title)..214, 674
Prince of Wales's Division...465

PAGE

Prince Philip, The, see DUKE
OF EDINBURGH
Princes of Wales..........214
PRINCESS ALEXANDRA....217, 548
Birthday................217
Chancellor, Univ. of Lan-
caster................509
Dame Grand Cross.......301
Household.............224
Succession to Throne.....219
Princess Andrew of
Greece............215, 216
PRINCESS ANNE............218
Birthday....89, 118, 218, 225
Diary (1970–71).....548; 565
Household.............223
PRINCESS MARGARET.....218–9
Birthday.....118, 219, 225
Crown of India..........261
Dame Grand Cross.......301
Diary (1970–71).....548; 565
Financial Provision for.....224
Household.............224
Keele University.........509
Marriage...............219
Residence..............219
Succession to Throne.....219
Principal Probate Registry
451, 1181
Principé Island (Port.
Guinea)...........199, 929
Printed Paper Post...1196, 1197–8
Printing Degrees, etc........531
Industrial Training Board..535
Paper Sizes.............1216
PRIOR, RT. HON. J. M. L.:—
Member of Parliament....339
Minister of Agriculture
313, 315, 362
Privy Councillor.........258
PRISONS:—
Cost of................610
Dept. (Home Office)....397–9
England and Wales.......398
Governors.............398
Scotland...............425
Parole Board.........417–8
Private Bills (Parliament)....306
Private Building (1945–71)...604
Private Companies (G.B.)....620
Secretary to H.M.........220
PRIVY COUNCIL, THE......257–8
Judicial Committee.449, 693
Lord President
258, 313, 314, 419
Northern Ireland........688
Office..............419, 610
Registrar..............449
Privy Councillors........257–8
How Addressed...(Note) 258
Precedence..........219, 682
Privy Purse.............224
Office.................220
Probate................1180
Probate Divn. (High Court),
see Family Division.
Probate Offices.........1181–2
Registries.....451–2, 1180
Probation Dept. (Home Office)
399
Orders................603
Proceedings against Crown..1164
Procurator-General.........433
Procurators Fiscal (Scotland)..684

PAGE

Production Engineering
(Educ.)................521
Professional:—
Abbreviations..........85–8
Boxing..............1010–11
Education...........517–37
Newspapers..........1081–4
Professors:—
Cambridge University...505–7
Oxford University.....503–4
Prohibited Articles (Postal)..1198
Proof Correcting.......1219–20
Property, Real and Personal.1179
Prorogation of Parliament....310
Prosecutions Branch.......456
Protection, Court of.......452
Protectorated Defined......694
Protectorates, British.....775–86
Protection, Court of......452
Protozoa Culture Centre.....415
Provan (Glasgow), M.P.......334
Province of Canterbury....473–8
Province of York........478–80
Provosts of Dioceses....473–80
Provosts (Scottish Burghs)..685–6
Prussia, East (U.S.S.R.).....961
Psychiatric Social Work 531
Psychiatry Research Units....408
Public Accounts, Auditor-
General................387
Acts of Parliament
(1970–71)............359–61
Public Buildings London...643–9
Public Companies (U.K.)....620
PUBLIC CORPORATIONS:—
Loans (1970–71)......613, 614
S.E.T. Payments........1183
Trading Results (1970–71):—
Airlines...............589
Buses.................571
Coal.............566, 583
Docks Board...........584
Electricity.............583
Gas..................583
Post Office.............582
Rail..................592
Public Health Acts........622
Laboratories.........419–20
Services (Cost)....624, 640
Holidays...............190
Offices.........362–438, 608
Parks, London........649–50
Prosecutions Dept........456
Record Offices....421, 422, 611
Scotland.............422
Records, Advisory Council.421
Schools...537, 538–41, 1048–9
Associations..........1113
Boys.............537–44
Girls.............544–7
Overseas.........542–4
Scotland.............1051
Service Vehicles, Driving
Permits..............1209
Number Licensed......591
Spending...............618
Trustee Office......420, 608
Works Loan Board.....420–1
Publishers, Principal.....1071–2
Association......1072, 1113
Training Board.........535
Pudsey, 667; M.P.........342
PUERTO RICO
200, 786, 798, 800, 810–11

Pages 693–1220 *are omitted from the* Shorter Edition

PAGE

Pulsars (Radio Astronomy)...155
Punakha (Bhutan).......201, 828
Punch......................1080
Punjab (India)..............751
Purchase Tax............1194-5
Reduced (1971).......357, 567
Purification..........94, 225
Purple Rod Usher...........261
Pursuivants................369
Pusan (Korea)..............899
Putney Bridge..............643
Putney, M.P................347
Pwllheli...................675
Pyongyang (Korea)......201, 899
Pyramid of Sun, etc........908
Pyramids (Egypt)......202, 956

Q.A.R.A.N.C..........470, 471
QATAR (Sheikhdom)
201, 572, 929-30, 987
Currency.................930
Oil Production...........930
Quadragesima...............188
Quakers (Friends)..........486
Marriage Law......1174, 1175
Quantock Hills.............627
Quarter Days
(*Notes*) 94, 110, 122, 134; 189
Quarter-Master General..459, 463
Quarter Sessions abolished
360, 571; (*Note*) 632
Quarto Defined.............1217
Quasars (Astronomy)........155
Quebec (City)..............706
QUEBEC (Province)
200, 695, 697, 705-6
Agent-General............706
Archbishops..............487
Bishops..................480
Production, etc..........706
QUEEN, H. M. THE..212, 218, 681
Accession.........89, 94, 225
Air Equerries............222
Army.....................463
Birthday......89, 102, 218, 225
Official Date (1972)
89; (*Note*) 110; 224
Bodyguard.........222, 223
British Columbia Tour.....548
(*Illus.*)..............549
British Commonwealth....693
Civil List..........224, 566
Coronation......110, 218, 225
Crown of India...........261
Diary (1970-71)......548; 565
Ecclesiastical Household...221
Family...................218
Grace and Favour
Residences.............651
Hon. Physicians (Civil)....224
Household.............220-3
in Scotland..........222-3
Indian Empire Order......260
Ladies of the Bedchamber..220
Marriage.................218
Mistress of the Robes......220
Order of the Bath........259
of the British Empire....261
of the Garter..........259
of St. Michael and St.
George..............260
of St. Patrick..........259
of the Thistle.........259
Portraits..........549, 550

PAGE

QUEEN, H.M. THE—*continued*
Private Secretary.........220
Privy Purse, 224; Office...220
Royal Air Force..........465
Royal Navy...............461
Observer Corps.........466
Victorian Chain........260
Order.................260
Star of India Order......260
Title..................218
Wedding Day........130, 225
Queen Alexandra...........216
Army Nursing Corps......465
Nursing Services (Directors) 459
Pay.................471
Queenborough-in-Sheppey...667
QUEEN ELIZABETH THE
QUEEN MOTHER
212, 217, 218, 301
Birthday....89, 118, 218, 225
Chancellor, Dundee Univ..511
London Univ...........507
Crown of India..........261
Diary (1970-71)......548; 565
Financial Provision for...224
Household...............223
Lady of the Garter.......259
Lady of the Thistle......259
Residences..............259
Royal Victorian Chain....260
Royal Victorian Order....260
Queen Elizabeth I (1558-
1603)................211
Queen Elizabeth College
(London University).....508
Queen Elizabeth Hall, London 636
Queen Elizabeth II, S.S......598
Queen Mary...............217
Queen Mary College, London 508
Queens:—
British..................212
English..............210-11
Scottish................213
Queen's Archives, Keeper...220
Award to Industry.....1059-60
Queen's Bench Division...449-50
Judges..............449-50
Offices...............451
Queen's Birthday.........225
Official Date
(*Note*) 110; 224, 225
Queens' College, Cambridge .505
Queen's College, Oxford.....502
Queen's Division (Army)....464
Queen's Flight, Captain of...222
Queen's Gallery (Buckingham
Palace)...............643
Queen's House, Greenwich...413
Queen's Institute (Nursing)..1113
Queen's Messengers........389
Queen's Police and Fire
Service Medals.........305
Queen's Printer...........426
Queen's Prize (Bisley).....1010
Queen's Proctor...434, 450, 1166
Queen's Remembrancer....451
Queen's University (Belfast)
511, 512
Queensferry...............686
QUEENSLAND.....203, 707, 720-2
Agent-General............721
Agriculture..............721
Archbishop...............481
Banks....................722

PAGE

QUEENSLAND—*continued*
Bishops..................481
Broadcasting.............722
Climate..................720
Communications...........722
Education................721
Finance.............712, 721-2
Government...........720-1
Judicature...............721
Legislature..............721
Minerals.................721
Population...............720
Production and Industry...721
Religions................720
Schools..................543
Seaports.................722
Trade....................722
Queen Victoria (1837-1901)
212, 576
Family of............214-6
Quemoy Isld. (Formosa)....843
Quezon City (Philippines)..925
Quinquagesima........94, 188
Quintal, The............1215
Quito (Ecuador)....200, 853, 854

RABAT (MOROCCO).....199, 912
Rabaul (New Britain).......716
Raby Castle...............654
Race Horse Owners, Trainers,
etc.....................998
RACE RELATIONS:—
Board...................421
Commission..............437
Institute..............1113
Races (Horse), Winners....998-9
Rackets................1008
Radcliffe................667
Bury and, M.P...........329
RADCLIFFE, VISCOUNT.......236
Chancellor, Warwick Univ.
509
Judicial Committee.......449
Privy Councillor.........258
Radian Measure..........1215
RADIO:—
Independent.......566, 1016-7
Licences...............1204
Abolished (1971).......579
Sets (Prodn. and Sales)....579
Stars...................155
Time Signals............142
See also BROADCASTING;
TELEVISION
Radiography, Radiotherapy
Training...............528
Radiotelegrams.........1202-3
Radiotelephone Service.....1203
Radnor, M.P...............328
Radnorshire..........675, 676
"Railex" Postal Services...1200
RAILWAY:—
Accidents...........569, 592
Average Earnings.........592
Board, British...........372
Division (Environment Dept)
386
Engines (Number)........592
Fares (1971)........571, 593
Public Spending on....618
Finance.................592
Freight Authorities....389-90
Traffic.................592
Letters...............1200

Pages 693-1220 *are omitted from the* Shorter Edition

RAILWAY—*continued*
Locomotive Types.......592
Mileage (U.K.)...........592
Museum, National.......571
Offences.................602
Parcel Service...........1200
Premises Act............1177
Regions.................592
Societies................1114
Staff Strength...........592
Statistics...............592
Tunnels, Longest.......207
Work-to-rule (1971)......570
Rainfall, Greatest.......1064
Records....1064, 1065–70
Rain, Inch of.............1216
Rajasthan (India)........751
Ramadân (Notes)..126, 130; 193
Ramsgate................667
Rangoon (Burma)..201, 204, 835
Distance by Air........1131
Ranjitsinhji, K. S., Centenary.577
Ranks, Service (Equivalents).1020
Rarotonga (N.Z.)...........735
Ras al Kaimah (Trucial States)
  951

RATEABLE VALUES:—
England and Wales........624
English Boroughs......664–8
English Counties........631
London Boroughs........642
Northern Ireland.........691
Scotland................625
Scottish Burghs........685–6
Scottish Counties.......679
Urban Districts......668–70
Wales.................675

RATES, LOCAL GOVERNMENT..623
Acts...................361
Average...625, 631, 675, 679
City of London..........640
Deficiency Grants.......623
Differentials, 1971–72...623
Empty Property.........623
England and Wales.......624
English Boroughs.....664–8
English Counties........631
General Rate Act (1967)
  623, 624
Government Property
  433, 612
London Boroughs......642
Northern Ireland........691
Per Head..............624
Product of 1p...........624
Receipts from......624, 625
Scotland...............625
Scottish Burghs, etc....685–6
Scottish Counties........679
Small Income Rebates....623
Support Grants...611, 623–4
Urban Districts......668–70
Valuation...............623
Welsh Boroughs, etc.....675
Welsh Counties........675
Rathbone, Eleanor, Centenary
  106, 577
Rattigan, Sir Terence........291
Portrait...............559
Rattray, Blairgowrie and...685
Rawalpindi (Pakistan)...201, 765
Bishop (R.C.)...........489

RAWLINSON, RT. HON. SIR
  PETER:—
Attorney-General.313, 315, 405
Privy Councillor.........258
Raw Materials, Imports...586–7
Rawtenstall...............667
Rayleigh................670
READING.................667
Bishop (of Oxford)......476
Member of Parliament....342
Party Strengths.........672
University........509, 512
Real Property Defined......1179
Rear-Admiral of the U.K....220
Rear-Admirals...........461
Réaumur Thermometer....1216
Receipts (Legal Notes).....1177
Recife (Brazil)...........831
Reconciliation Proceedings
  (Divorce)...............1166
Recorded Postal Delivery...1198
Recorders.............454–5
City of London..........639
How Addressed.........454
Northern Ireland........690
Record Offices:—
Army................464–5
Public.............421, 422
Record Players (Production, etc.)
  579
Records, Athletic, etc....989–93
Recreational Spending (1970).618
Redbridge (London Borough)
  642
Party Strengths.........671
Redcliffe-Maud, Lord.....251
University, Coll., Oxford..503
Red Deer Commission....424
Redditch............605, 670
New Town Site.........687
Redirection, Postal........1199
Red Letter Days......189, 225
Red Sea (Area, etc.).......203
Redundancy Payments
  (Taxation)...........1187
Administration.........382
Referees (Income Tax Acts)..458
Reference Books, Annual.1074–6
Calendar..............194–7
Laboratories...........420
Reformed Episcopal Church..486
Refraction Table..........146
Regent's Park............404
College, Oxford....503, 537
Zoological Gardens.....650
Reggio Calabria (Italy)....891
Regiments, Infantry 464–5
Regina (Saskatchewan)..200, 706
Regional Colleges (Further
  Education)..........1050–1
Regional Hospital Boards
  393–4, 501
Scotland...............425
Registered Envelopes......1201
Registrar-General (E. & W.).418
Scotland........426, 1162
Registrar of Companies....620
Registration, Electoral.....1178
of Title...............404
Registration, Postal...1199, 1200
Registry of Friendly Societies.390
Regnal Years.............186
REID, LORD..............246
Companion of Honour....261

REID, LORD—*continued*
Lord of Appeal..........449
Privy Councillor.........258
Statute Law Committee....427
Reigate, 667; M.P.........342
Reims (France)............863
Reith, Sir John, Obituary .. 575
Relay Racing..........989–97
Records...........989–93
Religious, Denominations...486
Newspapers...........1078
Remand Centres..........399
Remedial Gymnastics (Training)
  528
"Remedy, The"..........1210
Remembrance Sunday
  89; (*Note*) 130; 225
Remembrancer, Queen's....683
Removal Terms, Scotland....190
Renaissance Architecture
  (Period)...............577
Renfrew (Burgh).........686
Renfrewshire.........679–80
Members of Parliament..342–3
Sheriff, etc.............684
Rennes (France)...........863
Rent Acts...............1171–2
Rent and Rates, Personal
  Expenditure on........618
Rent Rebates Policy.......565
Reply Coupons (Postal)....1199
Reporting Agencies (London)
  1085
Representation Acts..307–8, 1178
Repton, Bishop (Derby)....474
REPUBLIC OF IRELAND, *see*
  IRELAND, REPUBLIC OF
"Rescue" (Archaeological Soc.)
  1043
Rescue Stations (Coastguard).793
Research Associations, Industrial
  1129–30
Councils (Expenditure).....349
Institutes, Agricultural..1130–1
Medical Council......406–8
(Science) Council........423
Vessels Unit............415
Residential Colleges, Adult...512
Nurseries.............1157
Restoration, The...........212
Restrictive Practives Commission
  409
Court.................452
Registrar..............611
Trading Agreements
Registrar..............422
Retailing Bankruptcies (1970)
  1160
Retail Prices, Index of......1195
Retirement:—
Benefits (H.M. Forces).....472
Pensions...........352, 494–5
Contribution Rates.....499
Cost...........352, 496
Women's.............495
Réunion, La......199, 862
Reuters Ltd.............1085
Revenue of U.K..........609
Reviews, Offices of.....1078–81
Reykjavik (Iceland)....202, 879
Rhea (Satellite).........158
Rheumatism Research Units.408
Rhine, British Army of the..458
Rhineland Palatinate........866

PAGE

Rhode Island (State)........800
Rhodes, Colossus of........202
RHODESIA.......199, 693, 783–4
Rhondda, 675; M.P..........343
Rhyl......................675
Riau (Indonesia)...........880
R.I.B.A..............517, 1096
Ricardo, David, Centenary
                      102, 577
Richmond College (London
    University)............508
Richmond Herald............369
Richmond upon Thames 642, 652
    Member of Parliament....343
    Party Strengths........671
Richmond (Yorks)...........667
    Archdeacon (Ripon)......479
    Member of Parliament....343
Rickmansworth..............670
Rifle Associations........1013
    Shooting..............1010
Riga (Latvia)........202, 967
Right Ascension............150
Right Honourable (Prefix)
             (*Note*) 258
"Ring" Nebula........154, 155
Rio de Janeiro........204, 831
Rio Muni (Eq. Guinea)......854
Rio Negro River (Uruguay).958
Ripon.....................667
    Bishop...........237, 479
    Member of Parliament....343
RIPPON, RT. HON. A. G. F.:—
    Birthday..............106
    Chancellor, Duchy of
       Lancaster......313, 378
    London University......507
    Member of Parliament....336
    Offices held......314, 315
    Portrait..............558
    Privy Councillor......258
River Authorities..........625
Rivers, Longest............206
Riyadh (Saudi Arabia)
             201, 934, 935
ROAD:—
    Accidents.............591
    Casualties, 602; (1951–70) .591
ROADS:—
    Cost to Ratepayers......624
       to Taxpayers.........611
    Divisions (Environment) .385
    Exchequer Grants for....591
    Expenditure on.........591
    Freight Authorities.....389–90
    Greater London........635–6
    Highways Act (1971)......361
       Authorities..........591
    Maintenance Expenditure .591
    New Construction.......591
    "Principal Roads".......591
Road Town (Brit. Virgin Islds.)
             200, 778
Robbery Statistics.........602
Robbins, Lord..............251
    Chancellor, Univ. of Stirling
                        511
    Companion of Honour.....261
    Natl. Gallery Trustee....370
ROBENS OF WOLDINGHAM, LORD
             251, 359
    Bank of England........440
    Chancellor, Univ. of Surrey
                        510

PAGE

ROBENS OF WOLDINGHAM, LORD
    —*continued*
    Safety and Health Cttee....383
Robes, Mistress of the......220
Robinson, W. Heath,
    Centenary........106, 577
Rochdale..................667
    Archdeacon (Manchester)..479
    Member of Parliament....343
Rochester.................667
    (and Chatham), M.P......343
    Bishop......220, 237, 477
Rockhampton (Queensland)..722
Rocky Mountains......697, 801
Rodrigues Islands (Mauritius)
             762–3
Roedean School............546
Rogation Days.............189
Rogation Sunday.106; (*Note*) 189
Rolls-Royce Crisis (1970)
       565, 566, 572, 573
    Purchase Act..........359
    Redundancies (1971)....570
Roman Britain......630, 678
Roman Calendar............192
ROMAN CATHOLIC CHURCH
             487–90
    Boys' Schools.......538–40
    Churches (London).....491
    Girls' Schools.......544–7
    Holy See............968–9
    Newspapers..........1078
    Schools............1048
    Societies..........1099
    Theological Colleges 537
    Training Colleges 532–4
    Westminster Cathedral...491
ROMAN:—
    Indiction.......89, 187
    London.............647–8
    Numerals............192
Rome....202, 204, 889, 891
    British Embassy......891–2
       School.............1098
    Distance by Air........1131
    Romford, M.P..........343
    Romiley, Bredbury and..669
Romsey..................667
Roraima, Mt......744, 969
Rosario (Argentina)........822
Roseau (Dominica).....200, 789
Ross and Cromarty......679–80
    Member of Parliament....337
    Sheriff..............684
Ross Dependency (N.Z.)
       203, 730, 735
Rossendale, M.P...........343
Rotary International.......1114
Rothamsted Experimental
    Station.............1131
Rothenstein, Sir W., Centenary
             99, 577
Rotherham, 667; M.P........343
Rotherhithe Tunnel........648
Rother Valley, M.P.........343
Rothesay.................686
Rothesay Class Frigates....462
Rothesay Herald...........369
Rothwell.................670
Rotterdam................915
Rouble (U.S.S.R.).........963
Rowing.........1009–10, 1011
Rowley Regis, M.P.........343

PAGE

Roxburgh..............679–80
    (and Selkirk), M.P.......343
    Sheriff..............684
Royal Academy of Arts..1094
    Schools..............518
Royal Academy of Music...529
ROYAL AIR FORCE:—
    Air Members..........459
       Secretary.....459, 465
       Support Command....458
    Chaplain in Chief......459
    Chief of Staff.....459, 465
    Clubs (London).......1088
    Colleges.............521
    Director, W.R.A.F......459
    Estimates............612
    G.P. Combat Forces.....458
    Joint Use Airfields.....590
    Judge Advocate........456
    Maritime Operations
       Training............520
    Marshals.............465
    Medals and Decorations..302–5
    Memorial (Runnimede)...652
    Officers (Number)......612
    Pay:—
       Aircrew........469, 470
       Ground Tradesmen....469
       Officer Cadets......469
       Officers...........468
    Pensions.............472
    Principal A.D.C.'s......220
    Quartering Charges.....471
    Relative Rank........1020
    Reserves (Personnel)....612
    School of Education.....521
    Societies...........1114
    Staff College.........521
    Strength (Personnel)....612
    Strike Command........458
    Victoria Cross Awards...302–4
ROYAL:—
    Albert Hall......439, 650
    Almonry..............220
    Armoured Corps........464
       Centre, Bovington....521
    Arms, The............224
    Artillery............464
    Assent........306, 307
    Automobile Club......1088
    Botanic Gardens (Kew)
             367–8, 649
    Bounty...............224
    Burghs.............685–6
    Conventions..........422
    Cambrian Academy.....1094
    College of Art.........510
       of Music............529
       of Nursing.........530
       Organists...........529
       of Veterinary Surgeons .1114
    Commission (1851)....422, 514
    Commissions..........437
       Cost to Taxpayers....610
    Commonwealth Society...1114
    Company of Archers.....223
    Corps of Transport.....465
    Dental Hospital.......526
       School..............521
    Drawing Society........518
ROYAL DUKES.............226
    Precedence......219, 682
Royal Engineers...........464
    Exchange, Cornhill.....648

Pages 693–1220 are omitted from the Shorter Edition

PAGE

ROYAL—*continued*
Family Annuities..........224
  Events (1970–71)....548; 565
Festival Hall..........636, 650
Fine Art Commissions..369–70
Free Hospital..............526
Geographical Society.648, 1104
Holloway College........508
Horticultural Society........650
Hospital School, Holbrook
                 1115
Households..............220–4
Houses, British...210–3, 217–9
Institute of British Archi-
  tects..................517
Institutions............1114–6
Irish Academy............1094
ROYAL MARINES.........462
  General Officers..........462
  Pay and Pensions
         467, 468, 472
  School of Music..........529
Royal Mews Department
          222, 643
  Military Academy........520
  College of Science......520
  School of Music..........529
ROYAL MINT, THE........408
  Output................1210
ROYAL NAVY:—
  Admirals..............461
  Chaplain of the Fleet......459
  Chiefs of Staff..........461
  Colleges, etc...........520
  Commanders-in-Chief......461
  Director, W.R.N.S......459
  Dockyards (Managers)....460
  Engineering College......520
  Estimates..............612
  First and Principal A.D.C..220
  First Sea Lord..........459
  Flag Officers..........461
  G.P. Combat Forces......458
  Joint Maritime Training....520
  Marriages Act..........1176
  Medals and Decorations..302–5
  Medical School..........520
  Naval Secretary........459
  Nursing Service, Pay......471
  Officers (Number)........612
  Pay:—
    Officers..............467
    Seaman Branch/R.M......468
  Principal Ships (1972)......462
  Quartering Charges......471
  Rear Admirals..........461
  Reserve (Strength)........612
  Retirement Benefits......472
  Royal Marines..........462
  Sea Lords..........459, 461
  Staff College..........520
  Strength (Personnel)......612
  Vice-Admirals..........461
  Victoria Cross Awards..302–4
ROYAL:—
  Observatories..........169
  Observer Corps..........466
  Opera, Covent Garden....650
  Ordnance Factories (Cost)..612
  Ranks (and Equivalents)..1020
  Red Cross..............305
  Salutes................224
  School of Church Music...529
  Scottish Academy........1094

ROYAL—*continued*
  Scottish Academy of Music 529
  Scottish Museum.....414, 611
  Signals................464
  Societies..............1114–6
  Society, The..........1115
    Presidents (1660–1971)..1093
  Society of Arts..........1115
  Standard, When Flown....225
  Tank Regiment..........464
  Titles................218
  Ulster Academy..........1095
    Constabulary..........689
  United Service Institution..1116
  Veto..................306
  Victorian Chain..........260
    Medal..............305
    Order..............260
    Dames..............301–2
    Knights..........262–300
  Visits (1971)..............548
    (*Illus.*)..........549, 550
  Voluntary Services, Women's
          1120
  Yacht Squadron.........1092
Royston, M.P............336
R.S.F.S.R...201, 202, 961, 964–5
  Production, etc..........965
Rubber Imports and Exports.586
  Industrial Training Board..535
Rubicon, The (Italy).........888
Rugby, 667; M.P............343
Rugby Fives..............1008
Rugby Football...........1004
  British Lions in N.Z....1004
  Team Portrait..........564
  Union................1013
Rugby School..............540
Rugeley (Staffs.)..........670
Ruislip-Northwood, M.P....343
Rulers of Foreign Countries
        208–9
RUMANIA, 202, 930–2; (*Map*) 931
  British Embassy..........932
  Communist Party......930–1
  Council of Ministers......930
  Currency........932, 987
  Embassy..............931
  Exchange Rate......84, 932
  Finance and Trade....585, 932
  Government..........931
  Language and Literature..931
  Production, etc..........931
RUNCORN, 670; M.P......343
  New Town........605, 687
Runnimede..............652
Running (Athletics).....989–97
Rupert's Land, Province of..480
Rural Development Com-
  mission..............378
Rural District Councils......622
Rural Districts, Average Rates
        624
  Electors (Number)......622
Rushcliffe, M.P............343
Ruskin School of Art........518
Russell, Bertrand, Centenary
        105, 577
Russia (R.S.F.S.R.)
    201, 202, 961, 964–5
Russians in U.K.
  Expulsions (1971)......567
Ruthenia................961
Rutherglen, 686; M.P......343

PAGE

Rutland................631–3
  (and Stamford), M.P......343
RWANDA (Republic)199, 932, 987
  Bishop................482
Ryde..................667
Ryder Cup (Golf)..........1006
Rye Harvests, Prices....580, 581
Rye (Sussex)............667
  Member of Parliament....343
Ryukyu Islands..........894

SAARBRUCKEN (Germany)..866
Saarland (Germany)........866
Sabah (Malaysia)..........201
Sacred College of Cardinals..487
Safety Belts, Automatic....1030–1
Safety Dept. (Employment)..383
  Divn. (Dept. of Trade)....431
Saffron Walden............667
  Member of Parliament....343
Sahara (Spanish).....199, 941–2
Saigon (Vietnam)..201, 204, 972
Sailing Clubs............1092–3
St. Aidan's College........507
St. Alban................630
St. Albans..........652, 667
  Bishop............237, 477
  Member of Parliament....343
St. Andrew..........130, 673
St. Andrew's Day......89, 225
St. Andrews..............686
  Archbishop............487
  Bishop................484
  Royal and Ancient......1013
  University......510–11, 512
St. Anne's (Alderney)......692
St. Anne's College, Oxford...503
St. Antony's College, Oxford 502
St. Asaph, Bishop..........480
St. Austell with Fowey......667
St. Barnabas........110, 225
St. Bartholomew..........118
St. Bartholomew's Hospital..526
St. Benet's Hall, Oxford.....503
St. Catharine's College, Cam-
  bridge..............505
St. Catherine's College Oxford
        502
St. Chad's College..........507
St. Columba's Pont Street....491
St. Cross College, Oxford....502
St. Cuthbert's Society......507
St. David................673
St. David's, Bishop........480
St. David's Coll., Lampeter..510
St. David's Day......89, 98, 225
St. Denis (Réunion).....199, 862
St. Dunstan's............1116
St. Edmund Hall, Oxford....503
St. Edmondsbury, Bishop of
      237, 477
St. Edmund's House, Cam-
  bridge..............505
St. George................673
St. George's Channel........674
St. George's Chapel, Windsor
      476, 653
St. George's Day....89, 102, 225
St. George's, Grenada...200, 788
St. George's Hospital......526
ST. HELENA....199, 784–5
St. Helens, 667; M.P........343
St. Helier (Jersey)..........692
St. Hilda's College, Oxford...503

Pages 693–1220 *are omitted from the* Shorter Edition

PAGE

t. Hild's College, Durham...507
t. Hugh's College, Oxford..503
t. Ives (Cornwall)..........667
  Member of Parliament...343
t. James......106, 114, 225
t. James's Palace......648, 651
t. James's Park......649–50
  Master Gunner........224
t. John....................134
t. John Baptist......110, 225
t. John (New Brunswick)...703
t. John of Jerusalem:—
  Association and Brigade...1116
  Order of........305, 648
t. John's (Antigua).....200, 787
t. John's (Newfoundland)
                200, 704
  Archbishop (R.C.)......487
t. John's College:—
  Cambridge...............505
  Durham..................507
  Oxford..................503
t. John's Gate, Clerkenwell..648
t. Jude, St. Simon and..126, 225
t. Kitts-Nevis (W. Indies)
     200, 694, 786, 787
t. Lawrence River.....206, 697
t. Leger, The (Race).......999
t. Louis (Missouri)....204, 800
t. Lucia (W. Indies)
     200, 694, 786, 788–9
t. Luke..............126, 225
t. Luke's Summer..........187
t. Mark.............102, 225
t. Martin's Summer........188
t. Mary College, Durham...526
t. Mary's Hospital........526
t. Marylebone, M.P........343
t. Matthew................122
t. Matthias..........94, 225
t. Michael and All Angels..122
t. Michael and St. George
    Order...............260
    Dames...............301–2
    Knights............262–300
t. Michael's Mount........654
t. Pancras, M.P.'s....336, 344
t. Patrick........673, 794
  Order of............259
t. Patrick's Day......89, 98
t. Paul, Conversion of...90, 225
t. Paul's Cathedral....203, 490
  Dean and Chapter......473
t. Paul de Luanda.....199, 929
t. Paul's School.........540
t. Peter...........110, 225
t. Peter Port (Guernsey)....692
t. Peter's College, Oxford..503
t. Philip and St. James..106, 225
t. Pierre (French)....200, 864
t. Simon and St. Jude..126, 225
t. Sophia, Mosque.........954
t. Stephen................134
t. Swithin's Day..........114
t. Thomas..........134, 225
t. Thomas's Hospital......526
t. Tomé...........199, 987
t. Vincent (W. Indies)
    200, 694, 786, 788
aints Days................189
  Number of..............189
  Patron..................673
aipan (Mariana Islds.)......811
aka Era Revised...........193

PAGE

Sakhalin (R.S.F.S.R.).......961
Saladin, Tomb of (Damascus).947
Salaries, Average (U.K.)....617
  Reckoner..............1184
Sale (Cheshire), 667; M.P....325
Salerno (Italy)............891
SALFORD....................667
  Bishop (R.C.)..........487
  Members of Parliament...344
  Stipendiary............455
  University.............510
SALISBURY..................667
  Bishop............237, 477
  Cathedral.............203
  Member of Parliament...344
SALISBURY, MARQUESS OF....228
  Chancellor, Liverpool
    University..........509
  Order of the Garter....259
  Hist. MSS. Commission..421
  Hist. Monuments Commis-
    sion................394
  Inter-Parliamentary Union.317
  Offices Held...........314
  Privy Councillor.......258
Salisbury (Rhodesia)...199, 784
  Archbishop (R.C.)......488
Salmon, Close Time...(Note) 122
  Fisheries Laboratory...363
Salonika (Greece).........871
Salop...................631–3
  Archdeacon (Lichfield)..476
Saltash....................667
Saltcoats..................686
Salters' Company..........640
Salutes, Royal............224
SALVADOR, REPUBLIC OF
    200; (Map) 875; 932–3
  British Embassy........933
  Currency..........933, 986
  Embassy................932
  Exchange Rate...........84
  Finance and Trade......933
  Government.............933
Salvador (Brazil).........831
Salvage Corps, Fire......1116
Salvation Army............486
Salween River....206, 834, 948
Salyut Space Station...1027, 1028
Salzburg (Austria)........824
Samarkand (Ubezkistan)....966
Samoa, E. (U.S.A.)
    203, 798, 800, 810, 811
SAMOA, WESTERN......203, 775
Samos 2 (Satellite).......165
Sana'a (Yemen)............973
San Cristobal (Galápagos)..853
Sandhurst (R.M.A.)........520
San Diego (U.S.A.)........204
Sandown Park, Eclipse Stakes 999
Sands of Dee..............674
Sandwich..................667
San Fernando (Trinidad)...771
San Francisco (California) 204, 800
  Distance by Air.......1131
  Transbay Bridge.......206
San José (Costa Rica)...200, 847
San Juan (Puerto Rico)..200, 811
SAN MARINO......202, 933–4
San Salvador.........200, 933
Santa Cruz (Canaries).....941
Santa Isabel (Eq. Guinea) 199, 854
Santiago (Chile)....200, 204, 838
Santo Domingo........200, 853

PAGE

São Paulo (Brazil)......204, 831
São Tomé (Portugese)......929
Sapporo (Japan)...........895
Saptarshi Era.............193
Sarajevo (Yugoslavia).....976
SARAWAK...................201
Sardinia............888, 890
Sark (Channel Island).....692
Sarum, Archdeacon.........477
SASKATCHEWAN
    200, 695, 697, 706
  Agent-General.........706
  Bishop................480
Saskatoon (Canada)........706
Satellites, Artificial....165–9
  Disintegrated (1958–70)..169
SATURN................140, 160
  Distance, etc..........157
  Monthly.91, 95, 99; 93, 97, 101
  Phenomena (1972)...90, 94, 98
  Rings.............140, 160
  Satellites........158, 160
SAUDI ARABIA
    201, 934–5; (Map) 934
  British Embassy........935
  Cabinet................934
  Communications........935
  Currency..........935, 987
  Embassy................934
  Finance and Trade......935
  King...................209
  Seaports, etc..........934
  Trade with U.K.........953
Save As You Earn..352–3, 447–8
SAVINGS:—
  Banks..................448
  Bonds, British.....353, 447
  Budget Changes (1971)..352–3
  Certificates......353, 614
  Committees.............415
  Department........415, 612
  Personal (1960–70).....619
  Premium Bonds..........449
  Unit Trusts........1158–60
Saxe-Coburg, House of.....212
Saxon Kings of England....210
Saxony (Germany).....866, 869
S.A.Y.E...........352–3, 447–8
Scafell Pike........206, 629
Scapa Flow................677
Scarborough...............667
  Member of Parliament...344
  Weather (Monthly)....1065–7
Scarborough (Tobago)......771
Scarlet Rod Usher.........259
Scheldt River (Belgium)...826
Schleswig-Holstein........866
Scholarships, University..1053
School Leaving Age.......1048
  Meals................1049
    Charges.........349, 565
  System Eng. & Wales)
             1048–50
SCHOOLS:—
  Athletics..............996
  Boys'..............537–44
  Branch (Dept. of Educ.)...379
  Categories of.......1048–9
  Class Sizes (1969–70)...1048
  Co-Educational...537, 541, 542
  Council.......1049–50, 1053
  Extensions, etc. (Finance)
             565, 567
  Girls'..............544–7

PAGE

SCHOOLS—*continued*
Immigrant Pupils........1049
in Brit. Commonwealth .542-4
Independent...........1048-9
H.M.C..............538-41
Soc. of Headmasters...541-2
Inner London............635
Inspectors of.......380-1, 424
Number of Pupils..1049, 1050
Secondary Examinations..1049
Sixth-form Pupils.........1050
Statistics.............1049
Teachers (No.)...........1050
SCIENCE:—
Branch (Educ. & Science)..380
See also EDUCATION AND
SCIENCE
SCIENCE, DISCOVERY AND
INVENTION (1971)....1027-42
Science, Imperial College of..508
Science Museum......411-2, 611
Birmingham...........655
Library............412
National Lending Library
380, 405-6, 1017
Reference Library........410
Research Council......423
Cost..............611
Science, Royal Military Coll-
ege of 520
Scilly Islands.............629
Weather (Monthly)....1065-7
SCOTLAND, KINGDOM OF
(*Map*) 628; 677-86
Adoption Acts..........1161
Adult Education Institute ..512
Agricultural Holdings
(Numbers)............580
Airports...............590
Ancient Monuments Board
395
Archaeological Socs......1122
Archbishops (R.C.).......487
Area and Population
202, 599, 677
Association Football......1005
Astronomer Royal........169
Bank Holidays
(*Notes*) 90, 106, 118
(1972-74).........190, 663
Banks...............442-6
Hours of Opening
441, 442-6
Births Registration....1161-2
Bishops...........484, 487
Boys' Schools..........541
Building Statistics........604
Burgh Directory......685-6
Census (1801-1971)..599, 677
Chief Constables........680
Christianity............678
Church of Scotland.......484
Cities and Burghs.680-1, 685-6
Civil Estimates........610-2
Clan Chiefs..........681-2
Clerks of the Peace......680
Climate..............677
Clubs.........1091-2, 1093
Coat of Arms..........679
Colleges of Education.....1052
Conveners............680
Council on Tribunals......434
Counties...........679-80
of Cities ....625; (*Note*) 679

PAGE

SCOTLAND, KINGDOM OF—*continued*
Counties—*continued*
Population (1971)......679
Rates and Values.......679
County Clerks..........680
Countryside Commission ..375
Court of Session.........683
Criminal Statistics........603
Crown Revenues........375
Customs and Excise....377-9
Deaths (Legal Notes)..1164-5
Dept. of Agriculture...423-4
of Employment........383
Development Department
425-6
District Councils.........625
Divorce (Legal Notes)....1167
Statistics.............600
Education...........1051-2
Authorities........516-7
Department..........424
Electricity Boards........382
Episcopal Church........484
Expectation of Life......1149
Exports..............677
Faculty of Advocates.....524
Finance...........610-2
Fine Art Commission.....370
Fiscals..............684
Football........1004, 1005
Gaelic Speakers.........677
Girls' Schools..........547
Gold Stick............223
Government Offices....423-6
Hereditary Standard Bearer.230
High Constable....222, 249
Highest Point..........206
Highlands............677
Historical Monuments
Commission..........395
Historic Buildings Council .394
History..............678
Holiday and Term Days...190
Holiday Posts.........1204
Home and Health Dept.
424-5, 610
Housing, Cost.........611
Hydro-Electric Board......382
Income from Employment.616
Industries.......677, 680-1
Information Office........423
Inland Revenue Dept....403-4
Inspectors of Schools......424
Insurance Companies...1145-8
Intestacy (Legal Notes)1169-70
Irregular Marriages....1176-7
Islands...........677-8
Judiciary...........683-4
Jury Service........1170-1
Juvenile Crime.........603
Keeper of the Records.....422
Keeper of the Registers....422
Kings and Queens....213, 678
Knights of the Thistle.....259
Landlord and Tenant.....1172
Law Courts.........683-4
Reform Act, 1968........1169
Legal Aid and Advice...1173-4
Education.......524, 525
Notes............1161-81
Legitimation Law....1168-9
Life Expectation Table.....1149
Local Authorities (Number)
625

PAC

SCOTLAND, KINGDOM OF—*continu*
Local Government 624-
Electors..............62
Reorganization.......101
Lord Advocate..........3
Lord High Constable..222, 24
Lord Lyon.............36
Lord Provosts......625, 680-
Lords Lieutenant........22
Lords of Session........68
Lowlands............67
Marriages (Legal Notes).1176-
Master of the Household...22
Members of Parliament
325-47, 6
Mental Welfare Commission
42
Minister of State.....313, 42
Moderator............48
Motor Vehicles (Number)..6c
Mountains............67
Murder (Statistics) 6c
Museums.............4
Galleries........371, 6
Health Service (Cost)...5c
Library......405, 611, 10
Trust............438, 111
Newspapers...........107
New Towns............68
New Year's Day.........18
Northernmost Point......6
Patron Saint..........6
Peerage.............22
Physiography........677-
Police (Strength)........58
Population........599, 600, 6
Density.............6
(1801-1971).........59
Precedence Table.......682-
Premier Baron (Forbes)...24
Baronet (Roxburghe)...22
Earl (Mar)..........23
Marquess (Huntly)....22
Peer (Hamilton).......22
Primus.............48
Prison Governors 4
Procurators-Fiscal.......68
Provosts.........625, 685-
Public Holidays.........19
Schools..........1051-
Pursuivants...........36
Queen's Bodyguard.....22
Queen's Household.....222-
Rateable Value.........6
Rates and Values...679, 685-
Rates Levied..........6
Records Offices........42
Regional Hospital Boards..4
Registers Department.....4
Registers of Births, etc...42
Registrar-General.......42
Rivers..............6
Roads (Cost)......591, 6
Roman Catholic Church...48
Royal Arms............
Burghs........422, 685-
Household..........222-
Scottish Academy......109
St. Andrew's Day..89, 130, 32
Schools and Pupils....1051-
Scottish Office.........423-
Secretary of State.313, 315, 42
Sheriffs and Clerks......68

Pages 693-1220 are omitted from the Shorter Edition

	PAGE
SCOTLAND, KINGDOM OF—*continued*	
Silver Sticks	223
Societies	1094–1120
Solicitor-General	313, 406
Stuart Kings	678
Sunrise Tables (56°)	91, 95, 99
Technical Colleges	535
Term Days	
(*Notes*) 94, 106, 130; 189, 190	
Theological Colleges	536, 537
Town Clerks	685–6
Councils	625
Universities	510–11, 1052
Extra-Mural Depts.	512
Waterfalls	677
Weather in 1970–71	1064
Wills (Legal Notes)	1180–1
Yacht Clubs	1093
Scotland (Liverpool), M.P.	339
Scotland Yard	456–7
Scots, The	678
Scotstoun (Glasgow), M.P.	334
Scottish Central Library	406
Certificate of Education	1052
Departments, Estimates	
	610, 611, 612
Development Dept.	425–6
Estimates	611
Division (Army)	464
Education Dept.	424
Estimates	611
Hospital Trust Act	359
Kings and Queens	213
Land Court	683
Law Agents	1107
Commission	683
Nationalist Vote (1950–70)	317
Office	423–6
Minister of State	313, 423
Staff Numbers, etc.	608
Under Secretaries	313, 423–5
Periodicals	1080
Record Office	422, 611
Regional Development Divn.	
	423
Savings Committee	415
Stock Exchange	1053
Societies, etc.	1116–7
Transport Groups	613
T.U.C.	1125
Scout Association	1117
Sculling	1010
Sculpture Galleries, etc.	412
Scunthorpe	667
Seabed Waste Disposal	1038
Seabirds, Decontamination of	
	1037
Sea Cadets (Strength)	612
Sea Depth Detectors	1038–9
Sea Fisheries Inspectors	424
Laboratory	363
Seaham	670
Sea Level, Areas below	1128
Heights Above	206
Sea Lords	459, 461
Seamen, Training Schools	530
Sea of Okhotsk	203
Seaports	199–204
British	595
Authorities	372, 435, 484
National Ports Council	414
Seasons, The	163, 187–8
E.A.T.O.	981–2
Seaton Valley	670

	PAGE
Seattle (U.S.A.)	204
Secondary Education	1049
Certificate of	1049–50
Policy Change (1970)	1049
Modern Schools	1049
Schools	1052
N. Ireland	1052
Second-class Mail	1047
Secretaries of State	314
Precedence	219
SECRETARY OF STATE:—	
Defence	313, 459
Education and Science	313, 378
Employment and Produc-	
tivity	313, 382
Environment	313, 384
Foreign and Cwlth. Affairs	
	313, 387
Home Affairs	313, 395
Scotland	313, 423
Social Services	313, 391
Trade and Industry	313, 428
Wales	313, 436
Secretary of State (U.S.A.)	807
Secret Service (Cost)	612
Security Council (U.N.)	813
Sedgefield, M.P.	344
Seeds Divn. (Min. of Agric.)	364
Inspectorate (Min. of Agric.)	
	366
Segrave, Edmond, Obit.	98, 575
Selangor (Malaysia)	201
SELECTIVE EMPLOYMENT TAX	
	566, 1182–4
Abolition (1973)	353
Cost	1182
Premium	1182–3
Rates	1182
Receipts	609
Reduced (1971)	353
Refunds	
(*Note*) 609; 1183, 1184	
Selkirk	679–80, 686
Member of Parliament	343
Sheriff	684
Sell's Directories	1076
Selly Oak (B'ham), M.P.	327
SELNEC (Metropolitan	
Counties)	1018
Selwyn College, Cambridge	505
Senate of the Inns of Court	524
SENEGAL (Republic	
199; (*Map*) 873; 935–6	
British Embassy	935
Embassy	935
Seoul (Korea)	201, 204, 899
Separation, Judicial	
	600, 1166, 1167
Septuagesima	89, 90, 188
Serengeti, National Park (Tan-	
ganyika)	770
Serjeants at Arms	221, 309
Serjeant Surgeon, H.M.	221
SERVICE PAY	467–71, 567
Retirement Benefits	472
Services' Clubs	466
Service Ranks	1020
Service Voters	1178
S.E.T., *see* SELECTIVE	
Setif (Algeria)	819
Sevenoaks, M.P.	344
Seventh Day Adventists	486
Seven Wonders of the World	202

	PAGE
Severn River	206, 629, 674
Bridge	206, 629
Railway Tunnel	207, 629
Seville (Spain)	941
Sexagesima	94, 188
Sexual Offences (Statistics)	602
Seychelles	199, 785–6
Currency	987
Sfax (Tunisia)	952
Shaftesbury	667, 1117
Shah Jehan Mosque	486
Shanghai (China)	204, 842
Shannon Airport	797
Shannon River	794
Shan State (Burma)	834
Sharjah (Trucial States)	951
SHAWCROSS, LORD	252
Chancellor, Univ. of Sussex	509
London University	507
Privy Councillor	258
Sheep Farms (Number)	580
Sheep Numbers, Prices	580
SHEFFIELD, CITY OF	662, 667
Bishop	237, 479
Colleges of Education	534
Hall-Marks	1213
London Rail Fare	593
Lord Mayor	662
Master Cutler	662
Members of Parliament	344
Museums and Galleries	667
Newspapers	1077
Party Representation	672
Penny Rate	624
Polytechnic	535
Population	662, 667
Probate Registry	1181
Teaching Hospitals	527
University	509, 512
Weather (Monthly)	1065–7
Shenyang (China)	204, 842
Sherborne, Bishop (Salisbury)	477
Sherfield, Lord	247
Reading University	509
Sheriff Court of Chancery	683
Sheriffs:—	
Expenses of	(*Note*) 612
London	637, 638
Nominated	(*Note*) 130
Northern Ireland	691
Scottish Counties	682, 684
Sherwood, Bishop of	480
Shetland (Zetland)	678, 679–80
Shettleston, M.P.	334
Shikoku (Japan)	893
Shillong (Assam)	749
Shipbuilding :—	
Credit Scheme Loans	575, 615
Numbers Employed	606
Statistics	597
Strikes (1969–70)	607
Training Board	536
Ship Canals	629, 811–2, 827
of the World	206
Shipley, 670; M.P.	344
SHIPPING	595–8
Accidents	569
Baltic Exchange	1096
Claims Tribunal	457
Classification	597
H.M. Fleet (1972)	462
IMCO	816
Insurance Companies	1145–8
Largest Ships Afloat	598

PAGE

SHIPPING—*continued*
Lighthouses.............435
Lloyd's Register...596–8, 1107
Movements.............595
Museum................411
Policy Divn. (Dept. of Trade)
                            430
Radiotelephone Service...1203
Registered (1970)........597
Seaports........199–204, 595
Trinity House...........435
Wrecks at Sea.......568, 569
Ships, Largest...........598
Launched (1970).........597
Sholapur (Maharashtra).....751
Shooting (1971)..........1010
Pheasant, etc.........(Note) 94
Shooting Stars........161–2
Shops Act, 1963.........1177
Shoreditch, M.P..........344
Shoreham, M.P...........325
Shortest Day.....(Note) 134; 187
Short Tons..........809, 1215
Conversion Table........1218
Show Jumping (1971)......1011
Shrewsbury..............667
Bishop (Lichfield).......476
(R.C.)................487
Member of Parliament....344
Shropshire (Salop).....631–3
Hills..................627
Shrove Tuesday..........94
Shwe Dagon Pagoda......835
Siam *see* THAILAND
Sian (China)............842
Sicily.............888, 890
Sickness Benefit (N.H.I.)....493
Cost.................496
Friendly Societies....1150–1
Sidereal Time......138, 141, 146
Monthly.........91, 95, 99
Year................145
Sidi-bel-Abbes (Algeria)......819
Sidney Sussex College, Cam-
bridge.................505
SIERRA LEONE
        199, 693, 767–8; (*Map*) 873
Archbishop.............482
Currency...............987
Events (1967–71).....573, 773
Government.............767
High Commissioners.....768
Judicature.............768
Republican Status (1971)...767
Trade Commissioners.....729
University.............793
Sierra Madre (Mexico)......907
Signals, Royal..........464
Signet, Writers to........1120
Signs of the Zodiac...90, 94, 98
Sikkim (Himalayas)........753
Silchester.............630
Silver:—
Coinage...............1210
Goblets, Henley........1010
Jubilee Marks..........1213
Plate, Hall-Marks.....1212–3
Silver Stick (Scotland).....223
Silverstone (Brit. Grand Prix) 1012
Simla (Himachal Pradesh)....753
Simonds, Visct., Obituary....575
Simon of Glaisdale, Lord....247
Lord of Appeal.........449
Privy Councillor........258

PAGE

Simplon Tunnel............207
Sinai Peninsula (Egypt).......955
Sinanthropus.............185
Singapore...201, 204, 693, 768–9
Air Letter Rates........1198
Area, etc..............768
Bishops...............482
Currency...............987
Distance by Air........1131
Finance and Trade...585, 769
Government.............768
High Commissions.......769
Judicature.............769
Population.............768
Production, etc.........769
Universities...........793
Sires, Winning..........998
Sirius (Star)..........151
Sittingbourne...........670
Skating..........998, 1010
Skelmersdale with Holland
                 605, 670, 687
Skikda (Algeria)..........819
Skinners' Company........640
Skipton, M.P............344
Skopje (Yugoslavia).......976
Skye, Isle of......677, 678
Skyscrapers.............203
Slade School of Art.......518
Slim, Visct., Obituary...134, 575
Portrait...............560
Slough, 667; M.P.........333
Slum Clearance..........604
Small Heath (B'ham), M.P....327
Small Holdings (U.K.)......580
Small Packets Post....1196, 1201
Smethwick, M.P..........344
Smith, F. E., *see* Birkenhead,
Earl of
Smoke Removal (Sci. Notes)
                        1032–3
Snails Desert (Sci. Notes)....1031
Snooker................1011
SNOWDON, EARL OF..98, 219, 233
Snowdon Mountain.....206, 674
Snowdonia National Park....626
Snowshill Manor.........654
Soane, Sir John..........643
Soane's Museum..........648
Social Insurance (U.K.).....492–9
Socialist Party..........1117
Social Science Research Council
                         611
Social Security:—
Departments..........391–2
Non-contributory Benefits.498
Supplementary Benefits:—
Commission.....497, 498
Departments.......391, 392
Social Services, Secretary of
State for......313, 315, 391
Social Studies, Books on
(1970–71)............1025
Social Surveys, Office of......418
Work (Educ.)...........531
Services Group.........424
SOCIETIES AND INSTITUTIONS
                      1094–1120
Archæological........1121–2
Society Islands (Oceania)....864
Society of Friends (Quakers)
                     486, 491
Sodor and Man (Name)......678
Bishop........237, 479, 691

PAG

Sofia (Bulgaria)........202, 83
SOLAR:—
Apex.................14
Cycle...........89, 187, 19
Eclipses...............16
Motion................14
Parallax..............14
System..............156–6
Elements of (Table).....15
Time.................13
Soldering, Ultrasonic (Science
Notes)..............1040
Sol-fa College of Music.....52
Solicitor-General......313, 40
Scotland........313, 68
Solicitor, Official (Supreme
Court)...............45
Solicitors' Education, etc...524–
Solicitors in Supreme Courts,
Scotland............III
Solihull, 667; M.P..........34
Solomon Islands (Australia).715–
(U.K.).........203, 782–
Solstice, Summer
        89, 110, 186, 18
Winter......89, 134, 187, 18
Solway Coast..............62
SOMALIA (Republic)
  199; (*Map*) 855, 936, 98
Embassies...............93
Somerset Herald...........36
Somerset House..418, 451–2, 64
Somerset................631–
Glastonbury Tor Excavations
                    1045–
Members of Parliament....34
Somerville College, Oxford...50
Soulbury, Visct., Obituary...57
SOUTH AFRICA (Republic)
  199, 936–8; (*Map*) 93
Air Letter Rates.........119
Passengers to.........58
Archbishops............48
Bishops...............48
Boys' Schools..........54
British Embassy.........93
Cabinet...............93
Communications........937–
Currency...........938, 98
Embassy................93
Exchange Rate.......83, 93
Gold Production.........93
Government.............93
Minerals..............93
Nobel Prizes...........105
Population.........199, 93
Production, etc.........93
Trade................58
  with U.K............93
Southall, M.P............34
SOUTH AMERICA (Continent)
                     198, 20
Countries and Capitals...20
H.M.C. Schools.........54
Highest Point...........20
SOUTHAMPTON........662, 66
Airport...............59
Art Gallery............65
Customs and Excise......37
Members of Parliament...34
Party Strengths........6;
Population.............66
Shipping..............59
University......509, 512, 53

Pages 693–1220 are omitted from the Shorter Edition

PAGE

SOUTHAMPTON—*continued*
  Weather (Monthly)....1065–7
  Information Service....1086
  Yacht Clubs..........1092–3
SOUTH AUSTRALIA
                    203, 707, 722–5
  Agent-General..........723
  Agriculture............723
  Area and Population.....722
  Banking................723
  Climate................722
  Communications...723, 725
  Education..............723
  Finance............712, 725
  Government.............722
  Judicature.............723
  Legislature............723
  Production, etc........723
  Trade..............724, 725
  Transport..............723
South Bank Polytechnic....535
South Carolina (State)......800
South Dakota (State)......800
South-East Asia Treaty Organ-
    ization..............981–2
    Cost.................982
South Eastern Circuit......454
Southend-on-Sea...........667
  Airport................590
  Members of Parliament....344
SOUTHERN RHODESIA, *see*
    RHODESIA
Southern Uplands..........677
SOUTHERN VIETNAM......971–2
Southern Yemen, *see* YEMEN
    REPUBLICS
South Fylde, M.P..........344
Southgate, M.P............344
South Georgia.............779
South Metropolitan Cemetery 644
South of Scotland Electricity
    Board................382
South Pacific Commission...982
Southport, 667; M.P.......345
South Shields.............667
  Member of Parliament....345
SOUTHWARK................642
  Archbishops (R.C.)......487
  Bishops..........237, 477
  Bridge.................643
  Cathedral..............490
  George Inn.............645
  Member of Parliament....345
  Party Strengths........671
Southwell, Bishop of....237, 480
South West Africa...199, 938–9
South Western Magistrates'
    Court................455
Southwold................667
Sovereign (Coin)..........1210
Soviet Embassy............961
Soviet Russia...201, 202, 959–68
  See also U.S.S.R.
Sowerby, M.P.............345
Soyuz 11 Spacecraft (1971)
                573, 1027, 1028
Space Division (Dept. of Trade)
                         432
  Flights (1971).......1027–29
  Probes...............165–9
  Stations..............1028
SPAIN (State)
  202; (*Map*) 939; 939–942
  Air Passengers to........588

PAGE

SPAIN (State)—*continued*
  British Embassy..........941
  Cabinet.................939
  Colonies.........199, 941–2
  Currency...........940, 987
  Embassy................939
  Exchange Rate......83, 940
  Finance................940
  Government.............940
  Language and Literature...940
  Nobel Prizes.....940, 1054
  Production, etc........940–1
  Shipbuilding...........597
  Shipping...............596
  Trade............585, 941
    with U.K.............941
Spanish Guinea, *see* EQUATORIAL
    GUINEA
Morocco...........199, 942
Sparkbrook, M.P...........327
Speaker, H. of Commons
                309, 311, 351, 565
  Contested Elections....351
  First..................307
  (1660–1971)............306
  Precedence.......219, 311
Speaker, H. of Lords....308, 309
Special Air Service Regiment 465
Special Commissioners (Income
    Tax)..................404
Special Constabulary....457, 484
  Strength...............584
Special Delivery (Postal)....1200
Specialists, Medical (N.H.S.)..508
Special (Marriage) Licences...1174
  Schools...............1049
Specialists, Medical (N.H.S.)..501
Spectacles (N.H.S.).........501
  Numbers Paid for........1157
Spectroscopic Binary Stars...153
Speech Therapy Training......531
Speed (Nautical) Measures....578
Speed of Light.......145, 152
Spelthorne, M.P...........345
Spenborough, 667; M.P.......328
Spence, Sir Basil..........295
  Order of Merit..........260
  Royal Academician......1094
Spey River................677
Sphinx, The (Egypt).........956
Spitsbergen Archipelago.....919
Sporting Life.............1077
SPORTS:—
  Athletics............989–97
  Clubs (London).......1087–9
  Council................571
  Diary (1970–71)........571
  Representative Bodies...1013
  Results and Records..989–1013
Springburn (Glasgow), M.P....334
Spring Defined............187
  Equinox.........89, 98, 187
  Holiday (1972)..........106
  (1972–74)..............190
  Tides.................163
Sputnik Satellites........165
Squadron Leaders, Pay, etc
                        468, 472
Square Measure...........1214
  Conversion Table.......1218
Squash Rackets (1970–71)...1008
Staff College, Camberley.....520

PAGE

STAFFORD.................667
  Bishop (Lichfield).......476
  Member of Parliament....345
Staffordshire.............631–3
  Archaeological Societies...1121
  Polytechnic, N. Staffs....535
  Stipendiary Magistrates....455
Stage, The (1970–71).....1025–6
Staines..................670
Stalybridge, 667; M.P.......345
Stamford, 667: M.P.........343
STAMP DUTIES........1191–4
  Budget Changes (1971)
                    352, 566
  Inland Revenue
    Divisions 402
    Revenue from........609
Stamps, Postage...........1201
Standards Divn. (Dept. of
    Trade)................430
Standards Institution, British
                439, 1099
Standard Time.............143
  British (abandoned, 1971)
                         350–1
Standing Commission,
    Museums and Galleries ..409
Stanley (Durham)..........670
Stanley (Falkland Islds.)...200, 779
Stannaries, Lord Warden....378
Stansted Airport..........590
  Traffic Statistics......588
Stapleford, Beeston and....669
Staple Inn................646
Star and Garter Home......1117
Star of India Order........260
  Knights............262–300

STARS..................152–5
  Absolute Magnitude......152
  Brightness.............152
  Chemical Composition...153
  Clusters and Nebulae..153, 155
  Colour Measurement....152–3
  Distances.............152
  Double................153
  Hot...................154
  Interstellar Gas......153–4
  Luminosity............1039
  Magnitudes............152
  Mean Places (1972)....150–1
  Morning and Evening..
                91, 95, 99
  Occultation Defined....161
  Occultations (1972)...148–9
  Populations I and II....154
  Radii.................153
  Size Measurements.....153
  Spectra.............152–3
  Spectral Colours.....152–3
  Surface Temperatures...152
  Variable.........153, 154
Star Time, *see* Sidereal Time
State Airlines (Finance)....589
State Airports............590
State Expenditure 349, 609, 610–12
State Governors (U.S.A.)....800
State Mgmt. Scheme (Scot.)..568
STATE VISITS (1970–71)....548
Stationers' Hall....641, 646, 1073
Stationery Office, H.M.
                426–7, 608, 612
Statistical Office, Central....372

PAGE   PAGE   PAGE

STATISTICS:—

United Kingdom

Agriculture..............580–2
(Production, Finance, Labour)
Air Corporations; Air
   Traffic..............588–9
Building Progress..........604
Civil Service..............608
Entertainment Items......579
(Production, Sales; Cinema
Statistics; Television
Viewing)
FINANCE:—
Bankruptcies..........1160
Building Societies.....1151–9
Companies...........619–20
Friendly Societies.......1150
Gross National Product...616
Life Assurance......1134–45
National Debt........613–5
National Revenue and
  Expenditure (Supply
  Estimates)...........610–12
Official Reserves (Gold, etc.) 584
Personal Sector........616–9
Public Corporations
   582, 583, 584, 589
Unit Trusts..........1158–60
Food Imports..........579, 587
Fuel and Power........583, 584

Holidays................1160
Immigration.............605
Leisure Activities..........491
Motor Vehicles:—
Production and Export by
  Quantity............587
Top-ten Car Sales........588
Population..........599, 600
Railways................592
Roads..................591
Shipping..............595–8
(Foreign Trade Movement;
Ships Registered; Launched;
Largest Ships)
TRADE:—
Value by Classes.......587–8
Volume and Value by Ports 595
Trade Unions............1125
Unemployment...........606
Universities............1052
Vital Statistics..........600

Great Britain

Book Production and Exports
   1072, 1073
Docks (Traffic, Finance)...584
LABOUR..............606–7
(Employment; Unemploy-
ment; Work Stoppages)

England & Wales

Building Progress...........604

Causes of Death...........601
Child Welfare...........1157
Crime................602–3
Divorce................600
Education............1048–51
Local Government
  624, 631, 640, 642, 664–70
National Health Service...1157
New Towns..............605
Police..................584
Population Census........599
  Age Distribution........600
Weather.........1064, 1065–70
Wales
Local Government........675
Scotland
Building Progress..........604
Crime..................603
Divorce................600
Education............1051–2
Local Government 625, 679, 685–6
National Health Service...1157
New Towns..............605
Police..................584
Weather................1064
Northern Ireland
Building Progress..........604
Education..............1052
Finance, Production, Trade...690
Local Government......625, 691
Population....599, 600, 688, 691

Statute Law Committee....427
Statute of Westminster
   693, 697, 731
Statutory Publications Office .427
Steamship Statistics.........598
Stechford, M.P............327
STEEL:—
Community, European....978
Corporation, British......372
Exports and Imports......587
Industrial Training Bd....535
Strike (1971)............570
Stellar System.........152–5
Steele, Richard, Centenary...577
Stepney, Bishop of (London) .473
  Member of Parliament...345
Sterkfontein Discoveries.....185
Stevenage......605, 670, 687
Stevenston..............686
Stewart Islands (N.Z.)......730
Stewarton (Ayrshire).......686
Still Births, Registration of
   1161, 1162
Stipendiary Magistrates
   658, 659, 660
Glasgow................683
London................455
Stirling, 686; M.P.........345
University of............511
Stirlingshire..........679–80
Members of Parliament...345
Sheriff, etc............684
Stock Exchanges..........1053
London........648, 1117
Holidays..............190
Stockholm (Sweden) 202, 204, 945
Distance by Air..........1131
Stockport................667
Bishop (Chester)........479
Members of Parliament...345
Stockton-on-Tees, M.P.....345
Stoke Newington, M.P.....345

STOKE ON TRENT......662, 667
Members of Parliament...345
Stipendiary Magistrate....455
Stoke Poges.............652
Stolen Goods (Crime Statistics)
   602
Stone Age, The...........185
Stone (Staffs.), M.P........345
Stonehaven.............686
Stonehenge.............630
Stone's Justices' Manual...1076
Stoppages of Work 569–71, 606–7
Storm Force Measure......1211
Storms, Magnetic..........164
Stornoway..........678, 686
Stourbridge.............667
Stow, Archdeacon (Lincoln)..476
Stranraer...............686
Strasbourg (France).........863
STRATFORD UPON AVON 662–3, 667
Member of Parliament....345
Strathclyde..............678
University of............511
Stravinsky, Igor, Obituary
   102, 575
Portrait................560
Streatham, M.P..........347
Stretford, 667; M.P........345
Strike Command (R.A.F.)..458
Strikes, Industrial (1970–71) 569–71
in 1959–70............606–7
Stroud, M.P.............345
Structural Engineering (Educ.) 522
Stuart, House of..........212
Sub-contractors (Income Tax) 352
Suburban Rail and Coach
  Fares................593
Submarine Fleet (R.N.).....462
Subsidies, Food...........581
Succession (Legal Notes) 1169–70
Succession (Scotland).......1180
Succession to the Throne.....219

SUDAN....199, 942–3; (Map) 942
British Embassy...........943
Currency.........943, 987
Education............942–3
Embassy...............942
Sudbury................667
Member of Parliament...345
Suez (U.A.R.)............957
Suez Canal..............206
Shares................615
Suffolk..........622, 631–3
Archdeacon of..........477
Suffragan Bishops......473–82
Resigned..............483
Sugar Beet......580, 581, 582
Board................428
Loans Outstanding.....614
Division (Min. of Agric.)...363
Imports (1967–70).......579
and Exports............586
Suicide Statistics........601–2
Sulawesi (Indonesia)........880
Sumatra.............206, 880
Summer Defined...........187
Solstice......89, 110, 186, 187
Time..................142
Acts..................146
Duration of..........350–1
(1972)........(Notes) 98, 126
Summerson, Sir John........295
Historical Mss. Commission 421
Monuments Commission 394
Historic Buildings Council .391
National Portrait Gallery...374
Public Records Council....420
SUN, THE..............156–7
Age of................156
Aurorae...............161
Autumnal Equinox......122
Corona................157
Declination........91, 95, 99

PAGE

SUN, THE—*continued*
Diameter...........153, 157
Eclipses...............161
(1972).........90, 114, 148
Enters Signs of Zodiac
90, 94, 98
Faculae................156
Longitude (Monthly).90, 94, 98
Mass..................157
Motion................145
Right Ascension 91, 95, 99; 138
Rotation...............156
Period...............157
Solar Apex.............145
Cycle................89
Flares...............157
System............156–62
Spring Equinox.........98
Summer Solstice........110
Sunspots.......156–7, 164
Temperatures of........156
Transit.......91, 95, 99; 138
Variable Rotation.......156
Winter Solstice........134
Sunbury-on-Thames.......670
Sunday Letters (A–G) 89, 188, 190
Sunday Newspapers......1078
Sunday Postal Arrangements 1204
Sundays after Trinity....189
SUNDERLAND..........667
Civic Centre..........1055
Members of Parliament...345
Polytechnic...........535
Royal Visit (1970)......548
Sundial Time......140, 141
Sunrise and Sunset....138–9
Legal Definition........138
Local Mean Time (1972)
91, 95, 99; 93, 97, 101; 144
Sunshine Hours (1970–71)..1064
Records...........1065–70
Superannuation Dept. (Inland
Revenue)............402
Superior, Lake..........205
Supernovae (Stars)......153
Supplementary Benefits (Social
Security)..........497–8
Commission...391, 497, 498
Cost..................611
Departments...........391
Family Income Suppt.....498
Recipients and Scales....498
Supply Estimates......609–12
Supreme Allied Commander
(Europe)............981
SUPREME COURT........449–50
Central Office.........451
Conveyancing Counsel....450
Estimates.............610
Northern Ireland.......689
Offices............450–1
Official Referees.......450
Solicitor.............451
Staff Numbers, etc......608
Taxing Office..........451
Surbiton, M.P..........345
Surface Measure........1214
Surgeons, Royal Colls. of..1118
Surgeons, to H.M......221, 223
Surinam (Neth. W. Indies)
200, 915–6
Currency..............987
Surnames of Peers....252–6

PAGE

Surrey..........627, 631–3
Archdeacon (Guildford)...475
Members of Parliament..345–6
University of...........510
Surtax..566, 1185, 1189–90, 1191
Office (Inland Revenue)...403
Abolition (1973)....353, 621
Rates................1190
Revenue from..........609
Surveying (Education)....522–3
Surveys, Social, Office of..418–9
Survivorship (Wills).....1181
Sussex...........622, 631–3
Downs...............627
University of..........509
Arts Centre..........1059
Sutherland.........679–80
Member of Parliament...329
Sheriff..............684
Sutton and Cheam, M.P.....346
Sutton (London Borough)...642
Party Strengths.......671
Sutton Coldfield.......667
Member of Parliament...346
Sutton in Ashfield.......670
Sutton (Plymouth), M.P....342
Suva (Fiji)........203, 740
Svalbard (Norway).......919
Sverdlovsk (R.S.F.S.R.)...965
Swadlincote............670
Swanborough, Baroness
(Marchioness of Reading)
Obituary.............575
Swan Hunter Strike (1971)...570
Swans, Keeper of the......221
SWANSEA.......673, 675, 676
Member of Parliament...346
Population............676
Shipping.............595
Transit Trade.........595
University College...510, 512
Swansea and Brecon, Bishop. 480
SWAZILAND...199, 693, 769–70
SWEDEN (Kingdom)
202, 943–5; (Map) 944
British Embassy........945
Cabinet............943–4
Communications........944
Currency........945, 987
Education............945
Embassy..............945
Exchange Rate.....83, 945
Finance and Trade...585, 945
Language and Literature 944–5
Nobel Prizes.........1054
Production............944
Shipbuilding..........597
Shipping.............596
Telephone Rates to....1205
Swedenborg Centenary.....577
Swimming............1009
Olympic Records....1012–3
Swindon.............1009
Archdeacon (Bristol)....474
Member of Parliament...346
Swinton and Pendlebury...667
SWITZERLAND
202, 945–7; (Map) 946
Air Passengers to.......588
Alps.................946
British Embassy........947
Communications........946
Currency........946, 987
Education............946

PAGE

SWITZERLAND—*continued*
Embassy..............945
Exchange Rate..........83
Finance and Trade...585, 947
French-speakers, Number..863
Government...........946
Lakes................946
Language and Literature.946–7
Nobel Prizes......947, 1054
President........209, 945
Revaluation (1971)......574
Sword of State Usher.....221
SYDNEY (N.S.W.)
203, 204, 714, 719, 720
Archbishops......481, 490
Distance by Air.......1131
Harbour Bridge....206, 720
Newspapers..........1085
Schools..............542
University............790
Syon House (Brentford)...652
SYRIA .201, 573 (Map) 885; 947–8
Currency........948, 987
Exchange Rate..........84
Government...........947
Trade...............948
Szczecin (Poland)......927

TABERNACLES, FEAST OF......191
Table Mountain (S. Africa)..937
Table Tennis.........1008
Tabriz (Iran)..........883
Tadjikistan......201, 961, 968
Taegu (Korea).........899
Tahiti (Fr. Polynesia)....864
Taichung (Formosa)......843
Tainan (Formosa).......843
Taipei (Formosa)...201, 204, 843
Taiwan, *see* FORMOSA
Taiyuan (China)........842
Taiz (Yemen).......201, 973
Taj Mahal (Agra).......752
Tallinn (Estonia)....202, 968
Tamatave (Madagascar)....906
Tamerlane's Mausoleum
(Tashkent)...........966
Tamil Nadu (India).....751–2
Tampere (Finland).......858
Tamworth (Staffordshire)..667
(Lichfield and), M.P......338
T. and A.V.R. Forces
465, 565, 612
Tanganyika, Lake........205
Tanga (Tanzania).......770
Tangier..........911, 912
Tankers, Largest........598
Tannu Tuva (Mongolia).....961
TANZANIA......199, 693, 770–1
Archbishop...........482
Bishops..............482
Cabinet..............771
Currency.............987
Government.........770–1
High Commissions......771
Production, etc........771
Trade Commissioner.....729
Taranto (Italy).......890, 891
Tara, Kingdom of.......794
Tarawa Island (Gilberts)...782
Tariff Divn. (Dept. of Trade).430
Tashkent (Uzbekistan)...201, 966
Tasman Glacier (N.Z.).....731
TASMANIA......203, 707, 724–5
Agent General.........724

74 TA · Index · TI [1972

TASMANIA—*continued*
Archbishop (R.C.).......490
Bishop.................481
Education..............725
Finance.............712, 725
Government............724
Judicature...........724-5
Legislature............724
Production, etc.........725
Schools...............543
Summer Time..........142
Tate Gallery......370-1, 568, 611
Taungs Discoveries......185
Taunton..............667
Bishop (Bath and Wells)..473
Member of Parliament....346
Tavistock, M.P.........346
Taxation...........1182-95
Reform (1973)......353, 620-1
Revenue from.........609
Taxes and Stamp Duties..1182-95
Inspectors of..........403
Taxicabs, Licences......1209
Taxpayers, Number of....617
Tax Reductions (1971)....357
Tax Reserve Certificates..1191
Tay River.............677
Bridges..........206, 677
Tbilisi (Georgia)......201, 967
T.D....................305
Teachers:—
Branches (Dept. of
  Education)...........380
Numbers (1970).......1050
Qualifications........1050
Salaries.............1050
Scotland.............1052
Societies............1118
Training.............1050
Colleges......531, 532-4
Teaching:—
Degrees in Education...531-2
Hospitals......501, 525-8
Post-Graduate......526-7
TECHNICAL EDUCATION...534-6
Central Institutions
  (Scotland)...........535
City and Guilds Institute.534
Northern Ireland......535
Scotland.............535
Technical Newspapers...1081-4
Schools..............1049
TECHNOLOGY:—
Diploma in...........512
Queen's Award to Industry
                1059-60
Natl. Lending Library
            380, 405-6
Queen's Award to Industry
                1059-60
Universities of........510
TEESSIDE..............667
Party Strengths.......673
Penny Rate...........624
Polytechnic..........535
Educational Settlements..513
Tegucigalpa (Honduras)..200, 879
Tehran (Iran)......201, 204, 862
Distance by Air......1131
Tekufah (Equinox).....191
Tel Aviv-Jaffa (Israel)..887
Distance by Air......1131
Telecommunications:—
Cable and Wireless......372

Telecommunications—*continued*
I.T.U.................816
Minister of........313, 419
Ministry.............419
Telegrams:—
Inland..............1202
International....1202, 1206-9
Radiotelegrams.....1202-3
Telegraph Money Orders...1201
TELEPHONES............1203
International..1203, 1204, 1206
Radiotelephone Service...1203
Teleprinter Services...1203-4
TELEVISION:—
Independent Television
  Authority...........400
Licence Fees.........566
Licences........371, 1204
Sets (Production and Sales).579
Viewing (U.K.)....491, 1106
Telex (G.P.O.).......1203-4
Datel Services........1204
Telford, Salop (New Town)
                605, 687
Temperance Societies....1118
TEMPERATURE:—
Averages (1968-71)....1064
Conversions.........1216
Measures of.........1216
Records......1064, 1065-70
  (1970-71).......1068-70
Temple, The...........645
Temple Church.....491, 645
Temple of Diana.......202
TEMPLER, SIR GERALD....296
Birthday.............122
Field Marshal.........463
Gold Stick...........220
Knight of the Garter...259
Lord Lieutenant......632
National Portrait Gallery..370
Tenancies, Regulated....1172
Rent Acts........1171-2
Tenant, Landlord and (Law)
                1171-2
Tenby................675
Tennessee (State)......800
Tennis...............1007
Lawn...............1007
Table..............1008
Tenterden............667
Tequendama Fall (Colombia)
Term Days (Scotland)...189
Terrestrial Magnetism...163-4
Observatories........164
Terriss, Ellaline, Obituary...575
Territorial and Army Volunteer
  Reserve..465, 565, 612
Territorial Army Decorations.305
Territorial Titles, Scottish..681-2
Test Matches (1970-71)...1000-3
  M.C.C. Team (*Portrait*)..563
Test (Southampton), M.P...344
Tethys (Satellite).....158
Tewkesbury...........668
Bishop (Gloucester)...475
(Cirencester and), M.P...330
Texas (State)........800
TEXTILES:—
Divn. (Dept. of Trade)...431
Education in.........536
Exports and Imports..586, 587
Museum.............412

TEXTILES—*continued*
Numbers Employed......606
THAILAND (Siam)
  201, 948-9; (*Maps*) 746, 972
British Embassy.......949
Communications......949
Currency........949, 987
Embassy............948
Exchange Rate......84, 949
Production, etc.......949
Thames, The......206, 629
Bridges............643
Conservancy.....428, 625
Docks.............647
Embankments.......648
High Water (1972)....163
Magistrates' Court....455
Polytechnic.........535
Rowing Events.....1009-10
Tunnels...........648-9
Valley Constabulary (*Note*) 633
Thana (Maharashtra).....751
Thanet, Isle of M.P....337
Thanksgiving Day (U.S.A.)
                (*Note*) 130
THATCHER, RT. HON.
  MARGARET H.:—
Member of Parliament....333
Privy Councillor......258
Secretary of State.313, 315, 378
Theatre Board, National...428
Theatres in London...1025-6
Theft (Statistics)......602
Theological Colleges...536-7
Thermal Unit Defined...584
Thermometer Comparisons.1216
Thetford.............668
Bishop (Norwich)....476
Thirsk and Malton, M.P...346
Thistle, Order of the....259
Dean..............222
Thornton Cleveleys.....670
Thorshavn (Faröes).....852
Three-dimensional X-rays...1038
Three Kings Isld. (N.Z.)..730, 734
Throne, Succession to....219
Throwing (Athletics)..989, 991-6
Records....989, 991, 992, 993
Thurrock, 670; M.P......346
Thurso..............686
Tiberias, Lake (Israel)..886
Tiber River (Italy).....888
TIBET...............842
Tichborne Claim (1872)...577
TIDAL:—
Constants..........170-1
Predictions........172-84
Tides, The...........163
Tientsin (China)....204, 842
Tigris River (Iraq)....883-4
Tilbury Docks........647
Tillicoultry.........686
Timber Imports, etc.....586
TIME...............140-3
Apparent Sidereal.....140
Solar........138, 140, 141
Astronomical and Atomic..142
B.S.T. ended......350-1, 565
Central European......143
Chronological Notes...184-97
Civil..............141
Double Summer.......146
Ephemeris.........141-2

Pages 693-1220 are omitted from the Shorter Edition

PAGE

TIME—*continued*
Equation of
    91, 95, 99; 138, 141
European...............143
Geological Periods......184-5
Greenwich Mean...140-1, 142
In Various Countries......143
Legal Definition..........143
Lighting-up........138, 140
Mean and Sidereal....138, 146
Solar..................141
Measurements of
    184-5, 186-97
Radio Signals System......142
Sidereal........91, 95, 99, 141
Signals................142
Solar..................140
Standard...............143
(1968-71)............146
Summer Time .142, 146, 350-1
(1972)..............98, 126
Sundial Time............140
Universal...............141
Co-ordinated..........142
Winter Time............142
Times, The................1077
Supplements, etc........1080
Timișoara (Rumania)......932
Timor (Portuguese).201, 929, 987
Tipton, Rowley Regis and,
  M.P...................343
Tirana (Albania).....202, 818
Tiruchirapalli (Tamil Nadu)..752
Titan (Satellite)........158, 160
Titania (Satellite)............158
Titanic Disaster............102
Tithe Redemption Annuities.401
Office...............403
Title, Registration of.......404
Titles, Heirs to........227-50
Titles of Courtesy.........256
Titles, Scottish (Chiefs)....681-2
Tito, Marshal......209, 974
Tiverton, 668; M.P........346
Tizi-Ouzou (Algeria).......819
Tobago (W. Indies).....200, 771
Tobruk (Libya)............904
Todd, Lord...............252
Christ's Coll., Cambridge..505
Univ. of Strathclyde......511
Todmorden................668
Togo (Republic)
  199, 949-50, 987; (*Map*) 957
Tokelau Islands (N.Z.)...730, 735
Tokyo (Japan)......201, 204, 895
Distance by Air..........1131
Tomb of Mausolus.........202
Tonbridge................670
Bishop of (Rochester)....477
Member of Parliament....346
TONGA.......203, 693, 775, 987
Tonnages, Gross and Net....578
Tons, Avoirdupois.........1215
Long and Short
    809, 1215, 1218
Metric...............1218
TOPICS OF THE DAY....1014-19
Torbay....................668
Party Strengths........673
Tories and Whigs..........312
TORONTO (Ontario).200, 204, 705
Torquay, M.P............346
Torres Islands (N. Hebrides)..781

PAGE

Torrington, 668; M.P.......346
Torry Marine Laboratory...424
Research Station..........432
Tory Prime Ministers......308
Totalisator Board..........400
Totnes....................668
Member of Parliament...346
Tottenham, M.P..........346
Tourism, Development of
  (Cost).................610
Tourist Authority, British...372
Expenditure in U.K......618
Tower Bridge............643
Court................455
Tower Hamlets..........642
Party Strengths........671
Tower Hill..............649
Tower of London.........649
Keeper, Jewel House...221
Officers..............224
Royal Salutes.........224
TOWN AND COUNTRY
PLANNING:—
Cost to Ratepayers........624
Degrees, Diplomas......537
Departments...........425-6
Legal Notes..........1177-8
Minister of, and Ministry,
see Housing and Local
Government
Officers.................385
TOWN CLERKS:—
England...............664-8
English Cities........658-63
London Boroughs.......642
Northern Ireland.....690, 691
Scotland.............685-6
Wales................675
Town Councils (Scotland)...625
Townsend, Mt. (N.S.W.)...717
Towns, New..............687
Townsville (Queensland)...722
Toxteth (Liverpool), M.P....339
Trade and Industry..........1084
TRADE AND INDUSTRY, DEPT.
OF...........428-32, 565
Central Group........430-1
Exports Guarantees Dept.
    387
Industrial Divisions......430
Group.............431-2
Property Dept..418, 1073
Ministers..............428
Regional Organization..429
Research Grants......1129
Secretary of State...313, 428
Staff Numbers, etc......608
Supply Estimates........610
Trade Group..........428-9
Under Secretaries...313, 428
Weights and Measures...1214
Trade, Board of, President....428
TRADE, BRITISH............586-7
Associations 1122-3, 1124
Budget Statement (1971)...352
Commissioners...........729
Commission Service......387
Export Promotion....387, 610
Descriptions Act, 1968....1168
Journals..............1081-4
Marks, Statistics........418
Minister for.......313, 428
National Export Council...594
Secretary of State ...313, 428

PAGE

TRADE, BRITISH—*continued*
Shipping...............595
Movements............595
Statistics...............595
Trade Union Congress (1971)
    570
TRADE UNIONS..........1125-8
Membership (Industrial
Relations Act)......1014
Registrar of...........1015
Registration and Conduct
(Industrial Relations Act)
    1015
U.S.A................807
TRADE, WORLD.............585
G.A.T.T..............816
Trading Agreements, Restric-
tive, Registrar's Office...422
Trafalgar Day............126
Square..............643, 645
Monuments...........647
Traffic:—
Dept. (Metropolitan Police)
    456
Offences..............602
Traherne, Sir Cennydd.....259
Knight of the Garter....259
Lord Lieutenant.........676
Train Accidents, *see* RAILWAY
Trainers, Winning.........998
Training Boards, Industrial.535-6
Colleges...............531
Ships................530
Tranent.................686
Transbay Bridge..........206
Transcarpathia (U.S.S.R.)...961
Transfers, Stamp Duty....1192-3
Transfiguration, The........118
TRANSJORDAN, *see* JORDAN
TRANSPORT:—
Airways Corporations.....589
Company Profits........619
Divns. (Environment Dept.)385
Docks Board......372, 584
Events (1970-71).........571
Holding Company
    432, 613, 614
Industrial Training Board..535
Industries Divns. (Environ-
ment)...........386-7, 611
Minister for.......313, 384
London Transport Executive
Ministry, *see* Environment
    406
Museum..............411
Numbers Engaged in....606
Railways..............592
Board...............372
Roads...............591
Services (Cost)........611
Shipping............595-8
Lines................594
Strikes (1969-70).......607
Tribunal..........434, 458
Waterways Board......372
Trans-Siberian Railway....964
TRANSVAAL, THE...........937
Travel, Public Spending on..618
Treasurer of the Household..220
Precedence............219
Treasurer to H.M.........220
TREASURY, THE...........432-3
Administrative Cost......610
Chief Secretary......313, 433

Pages 693–1220 are omitted from the Shorter Edition

PAGE

TREASURY, THE—*continued*
Financial Secretary.... 313, 433
First Lord............ 313, 432
Junior Lords.......... 313, 432
Lords Commissioners.......432
Minister of State...... 313, 433
Notes..................... 1211
Parliamentary Secretary.....433
Permanent Secretaries......433
Representative Abroad....433
Senior Lords............ 313
Solicitor......... 433–4, 608
Staff Numbers, etc.........608
Under-Secretaries.........433
Valuer....................433
Tree Biology, Institution of..415
Trengganu (State), Malaya...201
Trevelyan College (Durham
Univ.)..................507
Trials, Criminal (1970–71)...569
Tribal Class Frigates........462
Tribunals, Council on........434
Industrial, etc. 457–8
Trieste....................890
"Trifid" Nebula..............155
Tring Zoological Museum....410
TRINIDAD AND TOBAGO
200, 693, 771–2, 987
Bishop..................482
Distance by Air..........1131
High Commissions.........772
Trade..............585, 772
Commissioner...........729
Trinity College:—
Cambridge................505
Dublin............ 511, 1073
of Music.................529
Oxford...................503
Trinity Hall, Cambridge.....505
TRINITY HOUSE..............435
Trinity Law Sittings.....106, 114
Trinity Sunday
89, 106; (Note) 189
Tripoli (Libya)........ 199, 904
Tristan da Cunha........ 199, 785
Triton (Satellite)........158, 160
Troon......................686
Tropical:—
Medicine Research Board..408
Year............... 145, 186–7
Troy Weight...............1215
Trucial States (Arabia).201, 950–1
British Political Agents....951
Oil Concessions..........950
Trade with U.K...........951
Truck Acts (Legal Notes)...1177
Trudeau, Rt. Hon. P. E.:—
Birthday..................126
Prime Minister, Canada...697
Trunk Roads..............591
Truro (Cornwall)..........668
Bishop............ 237, 478
Member of Parliament.....346
Trustee Savings Banks......448
Trustee, The Public........420
Tsetse Fly Research....1039–40
T.T. Races (I.O.M.)........1012
Tuberculosis, Deaths from..601
Research Units..........408
Tubman, W. V. S., Obituary
575
T.U.C....................1125
Tudor, Architecture........557
House of 211

PAGE

Tunbridge Wells............668
Tunis (City)........... 199, 952
TUNISIA (Republic)... 199, 951–2
Currency..........951, 987
Exchange Rate...........84
Production, etc...........951
Trade....................585
Tunnels, Longest..........207
Turf, The (Retrospect).....998–9
Turin (Italy)...... 204, 890, 891
TURKEY
201, 202, 574, 952–4 (*Map*) 952
Council of Ministers........952
Currency..........954, 987
Exchange Rate...........84
Finance..................954
Language and Literature....953
Production, etc...........953
Trade............585, 954
Turkmenistan (U.S.S.R.)
201, 961, 968
Turks and Caicos Islands.200, 788
Turner House Art Gallery....414
Turnhouse (Edinburgh) Airport
590
Turton (Lancs.)...........670
Tuscany (Italy)............890
Tussaud's Exhibition.......650
Tuva (U.S.S.R.)...........961
Tweed River...............677
Tweeds (Textiles)..........678
Twelfth Day................90
Tweedsmuir of Belhelvie,
Baroness.............252
Minister of State.... 313, 423
Twickenham, M.P...........346
Twilight Defined...........139
(1971)............ 91, 95, 99
Stages of................139
Two Thousand Guineas......999
Tyldesley (Lancs.).........670
Tynemouth, 668; M.P.......346
Tynwald.................691–2
Day (I.O.M.).......(*Note*) 114
Tyrone, County............691
High Sheriff.............691
M.P.'s............ 333, 688

U.C.C.A...................1052
UGANDA... 199, 573, 693, 772–3
Bishops..................482
Council of Ministers......773
Currency.................987
Events (1971)............773
High Commissioners......773
Trade Commissioner......729
University of E. Africa.....793
Uist Islands...............677
Ukraine......... 202, 961, 965–6
Ulan Bator (Mongolia)..201, 911
Ulhasnagar (Maharashtra)....751
ULSTER.................688–91
Counties.................795
Events (1970–71)........567–8
King of Arms........259, 369
Mid, M.P................340
New University of........511
Royal Academy..........1095
Umbriel (Satellite).........158
Umpire, Office of..........384
UNCTAD.................813
Undergraduates, Number of
502–11
Underground Railway Fares.593

PAGE

Under Secretaries:—
Parliamentary.... 313, 362–433
Permanent.......... 362–436
Unemployment:—
Assistance................498
Benefit..................493
Cost..................496
Waiting Period..........493
Earnings-related Benefits...493
Peak Figures (1971)... 567, 606
Statistics.......... 493, 606
UNESCO........... 814–5, 982
UNICEF....................813
UNIDO....................813
Unified Tax System (1973).620–1
Unionist Party............312
Central Office........1101
Majorities...........316
Union Jack................224
Service Clubs, etc........466
When Flown............225
Unitarian Churches.........486
Unitarian College..........537
UNITED ARAB REPUBLIC
199, 954–7; (*Map*) 955
Agriculture...............956
British Embassy..........957
Cabinet...............954–5
Currency......... 956, 987
Embassy................955
Government.............956
President............ 573, 954
Pyramids................202
Trade....................585
With U.K..............956
United Church of Canada....485
UNITED KINGDOM, THE
(*Map*) 628; 693
Ages of Population........600
Agriculture............580–2
Air Passenger Movement...588
Airports............ 371, 590
Traffic.................588
Area, etc................599
Army..................463–5
Athletics Records........992–3
Atomic Energy Authority
360, 371
Bank Holidays
(*Notes*) 90, 98, 118, 663
Banks............... 440–6; 663
Baronetage.......... 262–300
Birth Rates..............600
Book Production.........1072
Budget (1971–72)...351–4, 566
Building Statistics........604
Census (1801–1971).......599
Citizenship........ 693, 1162–4
Civil Estimates, *see* Supply
Estimates
Coinage......... 987, 1210–11
(*Illus.*).................558
Colonies and Protectorates
775–86
Companies......... 619, 620
Constitutional Commission.437
Crop Acreage............580
Death Rates.............600
Defence...............458–72
Estimates..............612
Education............1048–53
Directory............502–47
Emigration Statistics......605
Events (1970–71)...548; 565–72

PAGE

UNITED KINGDOM, THE—*continued*
Executive................313
Exports............352, 586-7
External Debt............614
Farming Income............581
Finance................609-21
Flag............224, 225
Food Imports........579, 586
Foreign Trade Movements .595
Gold Reserves............584
Government............313
Gross National Product
(1960-70) 616
Harvests............580, 582
Holiday Statistics...........448
Housing Statistics..........604
Immigration in 1970 605
Imports and Exports
352, 579, 586-7
Income and Expenditure
609-12, 616
International Subscriptions..982
Kings and Queens.........212
Legislature............306-61
Local Government
622-5, 1018-9
Marriage Rates...........600
Merchant Shipping Owned 596
Mobile (Defence) Force....458
Monetary Units....987, 1210-11
Motor Vehicle Production
587-8
National Debt.........613-5
Income (1960-70)......616
Newspapers...........1077-84
Nobel Prizes............1054
Official Periodicals
1079, 1080, 1082, 1083
Reserves (Gold, etc.).....584
Overseas Loans (*Note*) 615
Parliament............306-61
Passport Regulations.....983
Peerage.............226-56
Personal Expenditure..618, 619
Income Statistics.....616-9
Population (1971) 202, 599
Age Distribution........600
Census (1971) ..566, 567, 599
Future................599
Postal Guide........1196-1209
Prime Minister
308, 313, 314, 432
Prime Ministers (1721-1971)
308
Principal Clubs.......1087-93
Production Statistics......579
Public Debt............613-5
Revenue and Expenditure
609-12
Royal Family..........217-9
Seaports................595
Shipbuilding............597
Shipping.........594, 595-8
Registered............597
Summer Time (1972)
(*Note*) 98, 126; 142
Supply Estimates.......610-12
Taxation 620-21, 1182-95
Television Viewing (Hrs.) .1160
Trade.........585, 586-7, 595
with U.S.A...........806
Unemployment...........606
Universities............502-11
Vital Statistics...........600

PAGE

UNITED KINGDOM, THE—*continued*
Weather in 1970-71...1061-70
Weights and Measures...1214-5
United Nations Association..1119
UNITED NATIONS ORGANIZATION
812-6
Children's Fund.........813
Cost to U.K........813, 982
Educational Organization
814-5
General Assembly....812-3
International Agencies. 814-6
Court................813
Member Nations........812
Secretariat............813
Security Council........813
Trade and Development
(UNCTAD) 813
Trusteeship Council......813
U.K. Representatives......814
UNITED STATES
200, 798-812; (*Map*) 799
Agriculture..............807
Air Force...............804
Air Mail Rates to....1198, 1209
Passengers to.........588
Transport............808
American Currency Holdings
806
Area............200, 798, 800
Army.................804
Athletics Records........990-2
Average Earnings, etc....807
Banks..........442, 443, 444
Bridges................206
British Embassy.........812
Budget................805
Cabinet................802
Cable Charges to........1209
Capital................803
Car Sales (1960-69)......587
Census (1970)..........798
Cities................800
Civil Aviation...........808
Colleges and Schools.....809
Congress..............803
Constitution...........802
Cost of Living..........805
Criminal Statistics......803
Currency..........806, 987
Defence...............803-4
Commands............804
Distance by Air..........1131
Divorce Statistics........798
Education System.........809
Embassy..............802-3
Employment, etc.........807
Events (1970-71)........572
Exchange Rate...........83
Exports (1970)..........806
Federal Debt............805
Finance (1970-71).......805
Flag..................802
Foreign-born Population...804
Government............802
Departments Reorganized
802
Highest Point............801
House of Representatives...803
Immigration Statistics......798
Imports (1970)..........806
Independence Day........114
Island Possessions ..200, 810-11
Judicature..............803

PAGE

UNITED STATES—*continued*
Labour Statistics..........807
Largest Cities............800
Largest Ship............598
Lawn Tennis............1007
Life Expectation Table....1149
Livestock Statistics.......807
Measures (Conversion)....1218
Minerals............801, 807
Minimum Wages.........807
Moon Landings (1971)....572
Motor Vehicles..........808
Mountains.............801
Naturalizations..........798
Navy.................804
Negro Population.........798
Nobel Prizes............1054
Oil Production...........807
Outlying Possessions
800, 810-12
Pacific Trust Territories
810, 811
Parcel Rates from U.K....1209
Personal Incomes.........805
Population (1970) 798
National Origins........804
of Voting Age........803
States, etc............800
President, The..........802
Presidents (1789-1971)....801
Production, etc..........807
Railway Statistics........808
Revenue and Expenditure. 805
Rivers................801
Roads................808
School System...........809
Secretary of State........802
Senate................803
Shipbuilding...........597
Shipping..........596, 808
Social Welfare (Cost)......804
Space Flights (1970-71)
572, 1027-8
Standard Time...........143
State Capitals............800
States and Territories......800
Supreme Court..........803
Telegram Rates to....1206-9
Telephone Rates to.......1205
Territories, etc...........800
Thanksgiving Day...(*Note*) 130
Trade Statistics......585, 806
Trade with U.K..........806
Tri-Star Programme......572
Unemployment..........807
Universities............809
Vice-President...........802
Vital Statistics..........798
Wages in 1971..........807
Weights and Measures..809-10
West Indian Islands........200
United States, S.S.........598
Unit Trusts..........1158-60
Instruments (Stamp Duty)
1194
Managers Association...1158
Savings Schemes.......1158
Service Charges.......1158
Value of Funds.....1158-60
Universal Co-ordinated Time.142
Universal Postal Union......816
Time..............141
Universe, Structure of the..152-5

Pages 693-1220 *are omitted from the* Shorter Edition

PAGE

UNIVERSITIES (U.K.)
　　　　502–11, 1052–3
　Admissions Council......1052
　Branch (Dept. of Educ.)....380
　Commonwealth.........790–3
　　Association of.....511, 1101
　Cost to Taxpayers...611, 1053
　Cricket..............1002
　Extra-Mural Depts........512
　Income, etc..............1053
　Open University....510, 1052
　Rugby................1004
　Staff (Statistics)...........1052
　Students (Number)......1052
　U.S.A................809

UNIVERSITY:—
　Adult Education Council...511
　Athletics...........996, 997
　Awards............566, 1053
　Boat Race.............1010
　Buildings, New....1058, 1059
　Clubs (London).......1087–9
　College Hospital.........526
　Colleges....502–3, 504, 507
　　Cambridge......505, 513
　　Dublin...............511
　　Durham..............507
　　London.............508
　　Oxford...........502–3
　　Wales...............510
　Degrees Awarded........1052
　Extra-Mural Depts........512
　Grants...............1053
　　Committee....435, 1053
　Medical Schools.......525–8
　Professors:—
　　Cambridge......505–7
　　Oxford.........503–4
　Schools of Architecture..517–8
　Settlements..............513
　Students (Number)...502–11
　Swimming........1009, 1011
　Terms............502, 504
Unknown Warrior..........490
Unsolicited Goods Act (1971).360
Unst (Zetland)............678
Upjohn, Lord, Obituary...90, 575
Upper Clyde Shipbuilders
　　　　　　　566, 567

UPPER VOLTA
　199, 957–8; (Map) 957; 987
Ural Mountains......198, 964–5
URANUS.............140, 160
　Distance, etc...........157
　Monthly.......93, 97, 101
　Satellites..............158
URBAN DISTRICTS:—
　Average Rates...........624
　Councils...............622
　England............668–70
　Northern Ireland.........691
　Wales.................675
Urmston................670
URUGUAY
　200; (Map) 821; 958–9
　British Embassy..........959
　Cabinet...............958
　Currency..........959, 987
　Embassy...............958
　Exchange Rate...........84
Uruguay River.............958
Ushaw College, Durham
　University................507

PAGE

Ushers, Gentlemen
　220–1, 259–61, 309
Ussher's Notation..........186
U.S.S.R.
　201, 202, 959–68; (Map) 960
　Area, etc..........198, 961
　British Embassy..........964
　Communist Party.........959
　Council of Ministers......961
　Currency..........963, 987
　Defence...............963
　Diplomats Expelled...82, 567
　Education..............963
　Embassy...............964
　Ethnical Composition...961–2
　Exchange Rate.......84, 963
　Government.......959, 961
　Industries............963–4
　Language and Literature...963
　Local Government........962
　Military Strength........963
　Ministries (Number).......961
　Nationalities.........961–2
　Nobel Prizes..........1054
　Oil...................965
　Population......198, 961–2
　Presidium........959, 961
　Production..........963–4
　Railways..............964
　Religion............962–3
　Shipping..............596
　Space Flights (1971)
　　　　1027, 1028–9
　Standard Time......143, 963
　Trade.................585
　　with U.K...........964
　Urbanization...........961
Utah (State).............800
U.T.C..................142
Uttar Pradesh (State)......752
Uxbridge, M.P............346
Uzbekistan......201, 961, 966

VADUZ (LIECHTENSTEIN)..202, 905
Vagrancy Offences.........602
Valencia (Spain)...........941
Valletta (Malta)......202, 760
Valparaiso (Chile)..........838
Valuation (Rating)..........623
　Offices (Inland Revenue)
　　　　　403, 404
Value Added Tax....353, 566, 621
Value of the £...........1195
Vancouver City...........702
Van Mildert Coll. (Durham)..507
Varanasi (Benares).........752
Variable Stars........153, 154
VATICAN CITY STATE..202, 968–9
Vauxhall, M.P............338
Vehicles Divn. (Dept. of Trade)
　　　　　　431
Velocity of Earth......163, 198
　of Light..............145
VENEZUELA
　200, 969–71; (Map) 969
　British Embassy..........971
　Currency..........971, 987
　Embassy...............969
　Exchange Rate.......84, 971
　Trade............585, 971
Venice (Italy)..........890, 891
　Distance by Air........1131

PAGE

VENUS................140, 158
　Distance, etc...........157
　Monthly 91, 95, 99; 92, 96, 100
　Phenomena (1972)...90, 94, 98
　Spacecraft Landing (1971)..573
Vermont (State)...........800
Vernal Equinox...........871
Verrazano Narrows Bridge...206
Verulamium.........630, 652
Vesta (Planet)...........159
Vesuvius, Mt............205
Veterinary Degrees, etc......537
　Division (Min. of Agric.)..366
　Laboratories (Min. of Agric.)
　　　　　　366
　Royal College.........1114
Vicar-General, Canterbury..473
　York...............478
Vice-Admiral of the U.K....220
Vice-Admirals............461
Vice-Chamberlain, The......220
Victoria and Albert Museum
　　　　412, 611
　Order................261
Victoria (B.C.)......200, 702
　Hong Kong.......201, 780
　Seychelles........199, 786
Victoria Cross.......302–4, 1189
　First award......110, 302
Victoria Falls (Rhodesia)...207
Victorian Chain, Royal......260
　Order, Royal...........260
　Dames............301–2
　Knights.........262–300
Victoria Nyanza, Lake......205
VICTORIA, QUEEN..90, 106, 212
　Family of...........214–6
VICTORIA (State) .203, 707, 725–7
　Agent-General..........726
　Archbishop.............481
　Bishops..............481
　Education.............726
　Finance............712, 727
　Government............726
　Judicature............726
　Murchison Meteorite....1033
　Production and Trade...726–7
　Schools...............543
Victory, H.M.S...........662
　Logbook of.............421
Vienna (Austria)....202, 204, 824
　Distance by Air........1131
Vientiane (Laos)......201, 901
VIETNAM
　201, 971–3; (Map) 972
　Currency..........987, 988
　U.S. Repatriations........572
Vila (New Hebrides)...203, 782
Vilnius (Lithuania)....202, 967
Vindolanda Fort, etc......1044
Vintners' Company.....640, 646
Violence Statistics.........602
Virginia (State)...........800
Virgin Islands (British)...200, 778
　(U.S.A.)...200, 798, 800, 811
Virus Research Units.......408
Viscounts...........234–7
　By Courtesy...........256
　Coronets..............234
　How addressed..........234
　Number of............226
　Precedence.......219, 682
Vision Research Unit.......408
Visitors' Passports.........983

Pages 693–1220 are omitted from the Shorter Edition

PAGE

Vital Statistics..............600
Volcanoes 205
Volga River................206
Volt (Measure)..............1215
Volume, Measures of......1214
    Conversion Table....1218
" Volunteers " Reserve (Army)
                    465, 565, 612
Voluntary Dispositions (Stamp
    Duty)................1194
Vostok (Coldest Place)......1064
Voters, Local Government....622
Voters' Qualifications......1178
Votes Cast (1955–71).......317
V.R.D.....................305

WADHAM COLLEGE, OXFORD. 503
Wages:—
    Average........592, 617
        in U.S.A...........807
    Councils Act..........1177
    Legal Notes...........1177
    Table................1184
    U.K. Total............618
Wakefield.................
    Bishop........237, 480
    Member of Parliament....346
Wake Island (U.S.A.)..798, 810
WALES, PRINCIPALITY OF..674–6
    (Map).................628
    Ancient Monuments Board 395
    Archbishop of..........480
    Area...........202, 599
    Association Football..1005
    Bishops........480, 487
    Boroughs......675, 676
        Party Representation...673
    Calvinistic Church....485–6
    Capital...............676
    Chief Constables......676
    Church in Wales.......480
    County Officials......676
    Crown Court Circuit...454
    Dept. of Agriculture...367
        of Employment......383
    Education Authorities..514–6
        Inspectorate.......381
        Office for.........380
    Flag..................674
    Football..............1004
    Highest Point.........206
    High Sheriffs.........676
    Historical Monuments Com-
        mission...........394–5
    Historic Buildings Council 394
    History...............674
    Lakes.................674
    Language..............674
    Local Government.622–4, 1019
    Lords Lieutenant......676
    Mayors.........675, 676
    Medical Officers of Health .676
    Minister of State....313, 436
    National Library...405, 1073
        Museums..........413–4
        Parks.........626, 627
        Sports Centre......530
    New Town..............687
    Patron Saint..........673
    Population............674
    Prince of, see PRINCE
    Princes...............214
    Rateable Values.......675
    River Authorities.....625

WALES—continued
    Rugby Football........1004
    Secretary of State....313, 436
    Sovereigns and Princes...214
    Teaching Hospitals.....527
    Town Clerks...........675
    University of....510, 512
WALKER, RT. HON. P. E.:—
    Member of Parliament...348
    Privy Councillor.......258
    Secretary of State.313, 315, 384
Walker Art Gallery.........656
Walker Cup (Golf)....571, 1006
    Team Portrait.........562
Walking (Athletics)
                989, 991, 993, 997
Wallace Collection.....371, 611
Wallasey, 668; M.P........346
Wall Brook, Roman Remains 648
Wallingford................668
Wallis Islands (French)....864
Wallsend...................668
    Member of Parliament...346
Walpole, Sir Robert 308, 312, 315
Walsall....................668
    Members of Parliament...346
Waltham Abbey.............652
    Forest................642
        Party Strengths....671
Walthamstow, M.P.'s.......347
Walton and Weybridge......670
Walton le Dale............670
Walton (Liverpool), M.P....339
Wandsworth................642
    Bridge................643
    Member of Parliament...347
    Party Strengths.......671
Wanstead and Woodford, M.P.
                        347
Warburg Institute (Lond.
    Univ.).................508
War Graves Commission..435–6
    Medals and Stars......305
    Museum Imperial.......413
Wareham...................668
Warley....................668
Warlingham................669
WAR OF 1914–1918.........130
    Pensions (Nos., Cost) (Note) 611
    Victoria Cross Awards...302–4
WAR OF 1939–45..........864–5
    Declaration...........122
    Pensions (Nos., Costs) (Note) 611
    Victoria Cross Awards...302–4
War Pensions Dept.........391
Warrington.........605, 668
    Bishop (Liverpool)....479
    Member of Parliament...347
Warsaw (Poland)...202, 204, 927
    Distance by Air.......1131
Warwick...................668
    Archdeacon (Coventry)..474
    Castle................654
    Member of Parliament...347
    University of......509–10
Warwickshire............631–3
Washington, D.C.
            200, 204, 800, 803
    British Embassy.......812
Washington (Co. Durham)
                605, 670, 687
Washington International
    (Race)................999
Washington (State)........800

Water Divining (Sci. Notes)
                    1037–8
Waterfalls, Highest.......207
Waterford (Eire)..........797
Waterloo Bridge..........643
    Day..................110
Waterloo, Havant and......669
Water Measures.........1215–6
Water:—
    Resources Board.......436
    Supply Division (Min. of
        Agric.)...........365
Waterways Board, British...372
Watford, 668; M.P.........347
Watling Street............630
Watt (Measure)...........1215
Wavertree, M.P...........339
Waves, Submarine.........1035
Ways and Means Committee,
    Chairman.........309, 311
Weather:—
    Buchan's Periods......1211
    Information Service...1086
    of 1970–71.........1061–4
    Values (1968–71)......1064
Watches (Coastguard).....793
Wednesbury, M.P..........347
Weekly Wages Table.......1184
Weight, Measures of......1215
WEIGHTS AND MEASURES..1214–5
    Act (1963)...........1214
    American..........809–10
    Book Sizes...........1217
    Conversion Tables....1218
    Dept. (Dept. of Trade)..430
    Metric.............1214–5
    Metrication Board.....408
    Paper Sizes........1216–7
    Système Internationale .809–10
Weir, Sir John, Obit......575
Welbeck College...........521
Welfare:—
    Divn. (Dept. of Employment)
                        383
    Services (Local)......501
Wellingborough, 670; M.P..347
Wellington College........540
    Museum...............649
Wellington (N.Z.).....203, 734
    Archbishop (R.C.).....490
    Bishop (C. of E.).....481
Wells.....................668
    Member of Parliament...347
Wells, Bath and, Bishop.237, 473
Wells Street Court........455
Welsh, The...............674
    Education Office......380
    Flag.................674
    Folk Museum..........413
    Nationalist Vote (1959–70)..317
    National Opera Company..361
    Office.............436–7
        Estimates.........611
        Minister of State..313, 436
        Secretary of State..313, 436
        Staff Numbers, etc...608
        Under Secretaries...436
Welshpool................675
Welwyn Garden City
                605, 670, 687
Wembley, M.P.'s..........347
Wesley, John............485
Wesley House, Cambridge..536
Wesleyan Methodists......485

Pages 693–1220 are omitted from the Shorter Edition

PAGE

Wesleyan Reform Union....485
Wesley's Chapel (London)....491
Wessex............210, 630, 663
WEST AFRICA:—
  Archbishop...............482
  Portuguese...............929
  Spanish...............941–2
West Bengal (State)........752
West Bridgford............670
West Bromwich, 668; M.P...347
Westbury, M.P............347
West Cumberland, Archdeacon
  (Carlisle)...............479
West Derby (L'pool), M.P...339
WESTERN AUSTRALIA
  203, 707; (*Map*) 708; 727–9
  Agent-General (London)...728
  Agriculture...............728
  Bishops...............481
  Education...............728
  Finance............712, 729
  Government...............728
  Judicature...............728
  Legislature...............728
  Production, etc...........728
  Schools...............543
  Trade...............729
Western Circuit (Crown Courts)
  454
  European Union...........982
  Fleet, C.-in-C............461
WESTERN GERMANY, *see*
  GERMANY, FEDERAL
  REPUBLIC OF
Western Isles...............678
  Member of Parliament....347
Western Pacific High Commis-
  sion...............782
Western Samoa........693, 775
Westfield College...........508
West Ford Satellite.........166
West Ham:—
  Members of Parliament....347
Westhoughton, M.P.........347
West Indian Islands.........969
WEST INDIES, BRITISH..200, 786
  Act (1967)...............694
  Archbishop...............481
  Associated States.....786–90
  Bishops..........481–2, 488
  Boys' Schools...........544
  British Govt. Representa-
    tive...............786
  Currency...............988
  Immigrants from........605
  London Office...........786
  Supreme Court...........786
  Test Matches (1971)...1000–1
  University...............793
WEST INDIES:—
  French........200, 786, 862–3
  Netherlands ...200, 786, 915–6
  U.S.A...............810–11
  Venezuela...............969
West Irian (Indonesia).......880
Westland Heliport...........588
West London Police Court....455
West Lothian............679–80
  Member of Parliament....347
West Mercia Police Authority
  (*Note*) 633
WESTMINSTER...............642
  Abbey...............490
    Dean and Chapter....473

PAGE

WESTMINSTER—*continued*
  Archbishop (R.C.).........487
  Cathedral...............491
  Hall...............649
  Hospital...............526
  Member of Parliament....330
  Palace of............308, 645
  Party Strengths.........671
  Penny Rate...............624
  School...............541
Westminster College, Cambridge
  536
Westminster, Duke of.......227
Westmorland............631–3
  Archdeacon (Carlisle)....479
  Member of Parliament....347
Weston-super-Mare........668
  Member of Parliament....347
West Pakistan............765–6
  New Provinces......765, 766
Westphalia...............866
West Riding............631–3
West Suffolk............631–3
West Sussex............631–3
West Virginia (State).......800
Wettest Place (Assam).....1064
Weymouth...............668
  Weather (Monthly)......1065–7
Wheat Farms (Number)....580
  Harvests............580, 582
  Imports (1967–70).......579
  Prices...............581
Whickham...............670
Whig Prime Ministers......308
Whigs and Tories......312, 316
Whips, Parliamentary......312
Whipsnade Zoo...........650
Whitaker, Sir Cuthbert.....577
Whitaker's Cumulative Book List
  1084
Whitburn...............686
Whitby (Scarborough and),
  M.P...............344
Whitechapel Art Gallery....649
Whitefield (Lancs.)........670
White Fish Authority.......437
Whitehall Monuments......647
Whitehaven, 668; M.P......347
Whitehead, Sir Edgar, Obit...575
Whitehorse (Yukon) ...200, 700
WHITELAW, RT. HON. W. S. I.:—
  Leader, H. of Commons
  313, 419
  Lord President
  258, 313, 314, 419
  Member of Parliament....342
White Nile River...........942
White Tower, The..........649
Whitley Bay...............668
Whitstable...............670
Whit Sunday 89; (*Note*) 106; 189
Whitsunday (Scotland)
  (*Notes*) 94, 106
Whitworth Gallery,
  Manchester...............656
WHO...............815, 982
Who's Who...............1076
  Marriages Survey from...1034
Wick...............686
Widgery, Lord...............249
  Lord Chief Justice....449, 571
  Privy Councillor.........258
Widnes, 668; M.P...........347

PAGE

Widows' Benefits (Nat. Ins.)..494
  Cost...............496
  Damages (amendment Act).361
Wiesbaden (Germany)......866
Wigan, 668; M.P...........348
Wight, Isle of, *see* Isle of Wight
Wightman Cup (Lawn Tennis)
  1007
Wigston...............670
Wigtownshire............679–80
Wilberforce, Lord..........249
  High Steward, Oxford Univ.
  502
  Lord of Appeal...........449
  Privy Councillor.........258
Wild Birds (Close Season)...1213
Willemstad (Curaçao)....200, 916
Willesden:—
  Bishop...............473
  Members of Parliament....348
William the Conqueror..210, 663
Willington, Crook and......669
WILLS (Legal Notes)....1178–81
  Application for Probate...1180
  Dependants' Maintenance..1179
  Execution of............1179–80
  Lapsed Legacies.........1180
  Proved...............1180
  Public Trustee...........420
  Residuary Legatees.......1179
  Revocation of............1180
  Scots Law...............1180–1
  Survivorship...............1181
  Testamentary Capacity...1180
  Where to Find...........1180
  Witnesses...............1179
WILSON, RT. HON. J. H.:—
  Birthday...............98
  Chancellor, Univ. of Brad-
    ford...............510
  Inter-Parliamentary Union.317
  Leader of the Opposition
  306, 313
  Member of Parliament....336
  Offices held............308, 314
  Portrait (1970)...........552
  Privy Councillor.........258
  Trinity House...........435
Wilton, 668; House.........654
Wiltshire...............631–3
Wimbledon, Lawn Tennis...1007
  Member of Parliament....348
WINCHESTER......630, 663, 668
  Bishop of........237, 473
    Order of the Garter....259
  College...............541, 663
  Member of Parliament....348
  Prison (Governor)........398
Wind Force Measures.......1211
Windhoek (S.W. Africa).199, 939
WINDSOR CASTLE.........652–3
  Constable and Governor...221
  Military Knights.........225
Windsor Castle, S.S........598
Windsor, Dean and Chapter..476
Windsor, Duke of, *see* DUKE
Windsor Herald............369
WINDSOR, HOUSE OF
  212, 216, 218–9
Windsor, Lady Helen.......217
Windsor (Ontario).........705
Windsor (Royal Borough)...668
  Member of Parliament....348
Wind Speed Readings...1068–70

	PAGE
WINDWARD ISLANDS	788
Portuguese	929
Wing Commanders, Pay, etc.	468, 472
Wingfield Sculls	1010
Winning Jockeys, Owners, Sires and Trainers	998
Winnipeg (Manitoba)	200, 702
Archbishops	487
Lake	205
Winsford (Cheshire)	670
Winter Defined	188
Solstice	89, 134, 187, 188
Time	142
Wireless, *see* BROADCASTING; RADIO	
Wirral, 670; M.P.	348
Wisbech	668
Wisden Cricketers' Almanack	1076
Wishaw, Motherwell and	686
Withington, M.P.	339
Witnesses' Allowances (Law Courts)	1170
Wives of Baronets and Knights, How Addressed	262
WMO	816, 982
Woburn Abbey	654
Woking, 670; M.P.	348
Wokingham, 668; M.P.	348
Wolfson College, Oxford	703
Wolverhampton	668
Colleges of Education	534
Members of Parliament	348
Polytechnic	535
WOMEN:—	
A.A.A. Championships	995-6
Annuity Rates	1137-8
Athletics	989, 991-7
Records	989, 991-3
Average Wages, etc.	617
British Nationality	1162-4
Clubs	1087-92
Colleges	503, 505
of Education	531
Cricket Association	1013
Cross Country Running	997
Crown of India	261
Dames Commanders	301-2
Dames Grand Cross	301-2
Death Rate (U.K.)	600
Domestic Science Schools	521
Employment Statistics	606
Expectation of Life	1149
George Cross	304
Golf Champions	1006
Union	1013
Graduated Pensions	495
Hockey	1004
Income Tax	1185, 1187
Reliefs	1189
Leisure Activities	491
Life Peeresses	252, 307
Magazines, etc.	1078-81
Maintenance Orders	1166-7
Maternity Benefits	494
Members of Parliament	316
National Insurance	492-9
Contributions	492, 499
Newspapers	1078-81
Number of (U.K.)	599
of the Bedchamber	220, 223
Peeresses	249-50
Police (Number)	584
Population (1970)	600
WOMEN—*continued*	
Precedence	219, 301
Retirement Pensions	495
Royal Voluntary Service	400, 1120
Selective Employment Tax	1182-4
Service Pay	467, 470, 471
Pensions	472
Ranks	1020
Societies	1120
Swimming	1009
Television Viewing (Hrs.)	1160
Transport Service (FANY)	1120
T.U.C. Members	1125
Unemployment	606
Benefit	493
University Colleges	503, 505
Settlements	513
Students (Number)	1052
Victoria and Albert Order	261
Widows' Benefits	494
Wives' Passports	983
Y.W.C.A.	1120
Women's Cricket Association	1013
Services (Strengths)	612
Clubs	466
Pay, etc.	470-2
Wonders of the World	202
Woodard Corporation Schools	538, 539, 541, 542, 547
Woodbridge (Sudbury and), M.P.	345
Woodford (Wanstead and), M.P.	347
Wood Green, M.P.	348
Wood, Imports	586, 587
WOOD, RT. HON. R. F.:—	
Member of Parliament	328
Minister for Overseas Development	313, 416
Privy Councillor	258
Woodside (Glasgow), M.P.	334
Woodstock	668
Wool:—	
Industrial Training Board	536
Prices	581
Woolsack, The	308
Woolwich, Bishop of (Southwark)	477
Magistrates' Court	455
Members of Parliament	348
Woolwich Equitable Bldg. Soc.	1157
WORCESTER	668
Bishop	237, 478
Member of Parliament	348
Worcester College, Oxford	503
Worcestershire	631-3
Members of Parliament	348
Work, Average Hours of	617
Workers' Educational Association	1051, 1120
Working Men's College	513
Working Population (1970-71)	606
Workington, 668; M.P.	348
Workmen's Compensation Acts	496
Supplementation Board	393
Works Dept., *see* ENVIRONMENT	
Worksop	668
Work Stoppages	569-71, 606-7
WORLD, THE:—	
Area and Population	198
Areas below Sea Level	1128
Athletics Records	990-1
Bank	815
Continents	198
Cup (Football)	1005
Currencies	984-8
Future Population	198
Health Organization	815
Highest Buildings	203
Highest Points	206
Lakes	205
Land Area	198
Largest Cities	204
Islands	206
Meteorological Organization	816
Mountains	205
Oceans and Seas	203
Oldest City	947
Population	198
Railway Tunnels	207
Rivers	206
Seven Wonders	202
Ship Canals	206
Trade	585
Volcanoes	205
Water Area	198
Waterfalls	207
Weather Extremes	1064
Worsley	670
Worthing, 668; M.P.	348
Weather (Monthly)	1065-7
Wrecks and Losses at Sea	568, 569
Wrekin, The, M.P.	348
Wrestling	1008
Wrexham, 675; M.P.	348
Writers to the Signet	1120
Writing Paper Sizes	1216
Writs of Summons	310
Wroxeter	630
W.R.V.S.	400, 1120
Wuhan (China)	204, 842
Wycliffe Hall, Oxford	536
Wycombe, M.P.	348
Wye College, London Univ.	508
Wye River	674
Wyoming (State)	800
Wythenshawe, M.P.	339
X-RAYS, 3-DIMENSIONAL	1038
YACHT CLUBS	1092-3
Yale University	809
Yangtse River	206
Yaoundé (Cameroon)	199, 836
Yardley, M.P.	327
Yard (Measure)	1214
Yards and Metres	1218
Yarmouth, Great	668
Member of Parliament	348
Year 1972, The	89
Year 1973, The	89
YEAR, THE	186
Anomalistic	145
Bissextile	186
Calendar	186
Civil	186
Eclipse	145
Equinoctial	186
Financial	(*Note*) 98
Historical	186

PAGE

YEAR, THE—*continued*
Income Tax...(*Note*) 102; 1185
Jewish..........(*Note*) 122; 191
Leap...........................186
Length of.....................145
Light Year....................152
Masonic.......................186
Moslem.......193; (*Note*) 94
of Confusion..................192
Regnal........................186
Sidereal......................145
Tropical..........145, 186–7
YEMEN REPUBLICS (Arabia)
201, 973–4
British Embassy:—
Aden......................974
Sana'a....................973
Currencies....................988
Embassy (P.D.R.)..............973
Legation (Arab. Repub.)...973
Yeomen of the Guard..........222
Yeovil, 668; M.P.............348
Y.M.C.A.....................1120
Yokohama (Japan)......204, 895
Yom Kippur.....(*Note*) 122; 191
YORK.....................663, 668
London Rail Fare.............593
Lord Mayor...................663
Member of Parliament....348
Minster......................439
Museums and Galleries....657
Party Strengths..............673
Population...................663
Probate Registry.........1181
Sheriff......................663
University...................509
Weather (Monthly)....1065–7

PAGE

York Herald.................369
York, House of..............211
YORK, PROVINCE OF.....478–80
Archbishop.........227, 478
Precedence............219
Privy Councillor......258
Univ. of York.........509
Chancery Court..............484
Dioceses..............478–90
Ecclesiastical Courts.......484
Vicar-General's Office.......484
Yorkshire.........622, 631–3
Archæological Societies...1121
Bank Ltd...................446
Moors......................629
National Parks.............626
Post (Leeds)..............1077
New Building..............1056
Yosemite Waterfalls (U.S.A.).207
Youth Employment Service..382
Hostels Association......1120
Leaders..................1051
Service (Education)......1051
YUGOSLAVIA
202, 974–6; (*Map*) 975
British Embassy............976
Communist League.....974–5
Currency...........976–988
Embassy 975
Exchange Rate...............84
Finance and Trade...585, 976
Government.................975
Languages..................975
Production, etc.........975–6
Seaports...................976
Shipbuilding...............597
Shipping...................596
Yukon River................206

PAGE

YUKON TERRITORY..200, 695, 700
Y.W.C.A...................1120

ZAGREB (YUGOSLAVIA)......976
Zambesi River...............206
ZAMBIA, REPUBLIC OF
199, 693, 774–5
Cabinet....................774
Currency...................988
Finance and Trade..........775
High Commissions...........774
Government.................774
University..................793
Zanzibar...................770
Bishop...................482
Zaragoza (Spain)...........941
Zeeland (Denmark)..........851
Zetland (Shetland)...678, 679–80
(Orkney and), M.P.......341
Sheriff..................684
Zodiac, Signs of the...90, 94, 98
Sun enters...............89
Zodiacal Light...95, 99, 123, 161
Zomba (Malawi).......199, 757
Zone Standard Time.........143
Zoological Gardens....650, 1120
Museums...........410, 411
Societies................1120
Zoroastrian Calendar.......193
Zuckerman, Lord...........252
Environmental Pollution
Commission 437
Museum Trustee.........419
Order of Merit.........260
Zululand (Natal)...........937
Zürich (Switzerland)......947

Pages 693–1220 *are omitted from the* Shorter Edition

OCCURRENCES DURING PRINTING

The Royal House. Oct. 5.—Emperor Hirohito and Empress Nagako of Japan arrived in London on State Visit; the Queen held State banquet for them at Buckingham Palace; the visitors remained in London till Oct. 8.

Home Affairs. Oct. 4.—Labour Party Conference at Brighton voted by 5,073,000 to 1,032,000 against entry into Common Market on terms negotiated by Government.
Oct. 5.—Electricity Council announced deficit for year of £56,000,000; spokesman said that large increase in charges would take place early in 1972, and even larger one was likely later in the year. Central Electricity Generating Board also showed deficit—of £14,000,000.
Oct. 8.—Labour Party Conference passed resolution in favour of nationalization of all banks, insurance companies and building societies.
Frederick Joseph Sewell, who had been arrested in North London on previous day, was charged at Blackpool with murder of Superintendent Richardson on Aug. 23.
Oct. 12.—Gas Council announced that prices would rise by 5 per cent. in January 1972.
Oct. 13.—Conservative party conference at Brighton voted by 2,474 to 324 in favour of British entry to Common Market.
Lord Carrington told Conservative conference that two new destroyers, four frigates and other smaller vessels would be ordered, and that four infantry battalions, including the 1st Argyll and Sutherland Highlanders, would be re-formed.

Overseas. Oct. 8.—In retaliation for British expulsion of Soviet officials, Soviet Government ordered 5 Britons to leave Russia and banned 13 more from re-entering; they also cancelled Sir Alec Douglas-Home's proposed visit to Moscow in Feb. 1972.
Oct. 16.—Four tons of arms and ammunition, understood to be intended for I.R.A., were seized at Schiphol airport in Netherlands, where they had been flown in from Prague.

Accidents. Oct. 2.—B.E.A. Vanguard plane *en route* for Salzburg crashed in Belgium with loss of 63 lives.

Sport. Oct. 3.—Mill Reef, winner of the Derby, Eclipse Stakes and King George VI and Queen Elizabeth Stakes, won Prix de l'Arc de Triomphe at Longchamps by three lengths in record time.

Obituary. Oct. 12.—Dean Acheson, former U.S. Secretary of State, aged 78.

FOREIGN EXCHANGE RATES
A. London Market Rates

Country	Denomination	1939 Average Rate to £ (approx.)	September 30, 1971 Middle Rates
Austria	Schilling	—	59·85
Belgium	Franc	26·49 *Belgas*	116·92½
Canada	Dollar	4·545	2·50½
Denmark	Krone	22·26	18·07½
Finland	Markka	217½	10·33½
France	Franc	176·10	13·73½
Germany (Federal Republic of)	D. Mark	—	8·24
Greece	Drachma	545	74·10
Italy	Lira	85	1,520½
Japan	Yen	1/2d.†	820
Netherlands	Florin	8·34	8·36½
Netherlands West Indies	Florin	8·34	4·60
Norway	Krone	19·45	17·05
Portugal	Escudo	110·07	68·12½
Spain	Peseta	42·45	171·75
Sweden	Krona	18·59	12·47½
Switzerland	Franc	19·87	9·82
U.S.A.	Dollar	4·485	2·48½

B. Scheduled Territories

Country	Denomination	1939 Average Rate to £ (approx.)	September 30, 1971 Middle Rates
Australia	Australian $	A.£1·2525	2·1471½
Bahamas	Bahamas $	—	2·48½
Barbados	East Caribbean $	—	4·80
Bermuda	Bermuda $	—	2·4
British Honduras	British Honduras $	—	4·0
Ceylon	Rupee	13·38	14·236
Cyprus	Cyprus £	—	Par
Ghana	Cedi	—	2·45
Hongkong	Hong Kong $	—	14·572
Iceland	Krona	—	214½
India	Rupee	13·38	5·37½
Jamaica	Jamaica $	—	2·0
Jordan	Dinar	Par	0·857
Kenya	Shilling	—	17·1429
Kuwait	Dinar	—	0·85715
Libya	Dinar	—	0·848
Malawi	Kwacha	—	2·0
Malaysia	Malaysia $	8·571	7·36875
Malta	Maltese £	—	0·9756
New Zealand	New Zealand $	£1·2425	2·1429½
Nigeria	Nigerian £	—	0·85712
Pakistan	Rupee	—	8·75
South Africa	Rand	S.A.£1	1·7728
Tanzania	Shilling	—	17·685
Trinidad	Trinidad and Tobago $	—	4·80
Uganda	Shilling	—	17·1429
Yemen P.D.R.	Yemen Dinar	—	N/A
Zambia	Kwacha	—	1·71425

C. Other Rates

Country	Denomination	1939 Average Rate to £ (approx.)	September 30, 1971 Middle Rates
Algeria	Dinar	—	11·85
Argentina	Peso	19	12·40
Bolivia	Bolivian Peso	141·50	28·45
Brazil	New Cruzeiro	82	13·60
Bulgaria	Lev	375	2·81*
Burma	Kyat (Rupee)	13·38	8·75
Chile	Escudo	116½	N/A
China	Renmimbi	4½	5·908
Colombia	Peso	7·59	50*
Congolese Republic	Zaire	—	686⅝
Costa Rica	Colon	25·16	N/A
Cuba	Peso	4·386	2·48½
Czechoslovakia	Koruna	—	17·28*
Ecuador	Sucre	66	60
Ethiopia	Ethiopian $	—	5·90

* Indicates that other rates are also obtainable, varying according to the nature of the transaction.
† One shilling and two pence.   § Per £100 London.

C*

Country	Denomination	1939 Average Rate to £ (approx.)	September 30, 1971 Middle Rates
Germany (East)	*Ostmark*	—	10
Guatemala	*Quetzal*	4·386	248½
Guinea	Franc	—	N/A
Haiti	*Gourde*	22·4	12·42½
Honduras (Republic of)	*Lempira*	8⅜	4·97
Hungary	*Forint*	20¾	28·18 ★
Indonesia	*Rupiah*	—	1031·3★
Iran	*Rial*	80·50 (Persian)	188
Iraq	*Dinar*	Par	0·859
Israel	*Israel £*	Par	10·41
Lebanon	*Lebanon £*	9·65	7·815
Madagascar	*M.G. Franc*	175 (F. Fr.)	686⅝
Mexico	*Peso*	—	30·85
Morocco	*Dirham*	176·10 (F. Fr.)	12·42
Nicaragua	*Cordoba*	24	17·40
Paraguay	*Guarani*	—	305
Peru	*Sol*	24½	105
Philippines	*Peso*	—	16·15
Poland	*Zloty*	23½	9·6★
Rumania	*Lev (Lei)*	655	43·2★
Salvador	*Colon*	11·20	6·20
Saudi Arabia	*Ryal*	—	11·56
Sudan	*Sudan £*	97½§	N/A
Syria	*Syrian £*	—	10⅞
Thailand	*Baht*	10·91	51·95
Tunisia	*Tunisian Dinar*	—	1·275
Turkey	*T. Lira*	—	35·9375
United Arab Republic	*Egyptian £*	97½§	N/A
Uruguay	*Peso*	9	600
U.S.S.R.	*Rouble*	23·75	2·20
Venezuela	*Bolivar*	14·15	11·12
Vietnam (South)	*Piastre*	—	N/A
Yugoslavia	*New Yugoslav Dinar*	197½	36

See Notes, p. 83.

A TABLE OF THE NUMBER OF DAYS FROM ANY DAY IN ONE MONTH TO THE SAME IN ANY OTHER MONTH IN ORDINARY YEARS

	Jan.	Feb.	Mar.	April	May	June	July	Aug.	Sept.	Oct.	Nov.	Dec.
January	365	31	59	90	120	151	181	212	243	273	304	334
February	334	365	28	59	89	120	150	181	212	242	273	303
March	306	337	365	31	61	92	122	153	184	214	245	275
April	275	306	334	365	30	61	91	122	153	183	214	244
May	245	276	304	335	365	31	61	92	123	153	184	214
June	214	245	273	304	334	365	30	61	92	122	153	183
July	184	215	243	274	304	335	365	31	62	92	123	153
August	153	184	212	243	273	304	334	365	31	61	92	122
September	122	153	181	212	242	273	303	334	365	30	61	91
October	92	123	151	182	212	243	273	304	335	365	31	61
November	61	92	120	151	181	212	242	273	304	334	365	30
December	31	62	90	121	151	182	212	243	274	304	335	365

THE ENGLISH MILE COMPARED WITH OTHER EUROPEAN MEASURES

	English Mile	English Geog. M.	French Kilom.	German Geog. M.	Russian Verst	Austrn. Mile	Dutch Ure	Norweg. Mile	Swedish Mile	Danish Mile	Swiss Stunde
English Statute Mile	1·000	0·868	1·609	0·217	1·508	0·212	0·289	0·142	0·151	0·213	0·335
English Geog. Mile	1·153	1·000	1·855	0·250	1·738	0·245	0·333	0·164	0·169	0·246	0·386
Kilometre	0·621	0·540	1·000	0·135	0·937	0·132	0·180	0·088	0·094	0·133	0·208
German Geog. Mile	4·610	4·000	7·420	1·000	6·953	0·978	1·333	0·657	0·694	0·985	1·543
Russian Verst	0·663	0·575	1·067	0·144	1·000	0·141	0·192	0·094	0·100	0·142	0·222
Austrian Mile	4·714	4·089	7·586	1·022	7·112	1·000	1·363	0·672	0·710	1·006	1·578
Dutch Ure	3·458	3·000	5·565	0·750	5·215	0·734	1·000	0·493	0·520	0·738	1·157
Norwegian Mile	7·021	6·091	11·299	1·523	10·589	1·489	2·035	1·000	1·057	1·499	2·350
Swedish Mile	6·644	5·764	10·692	1·441	10·019	1·409	1·921	0·948	1·000	1·419	2·224
Danish Mile	4·682	4·062	7·536	1·016	7·078	0·994	1·354	0·667	0·705	1·000	1·567
Swiss Stunde	2·987	2·592	4·808	0·648	4·505	0·634	0·864	0·425	0·449	0·638	1·000

Ψ = Seaport.

A

A.A., Automobile Association.
A.A.A., Amateur Athletic Association.
A.A.C.C.A., *Associate* of Association of Certified and Corporate Accountants.
A.A.I., of Chartered Auctioneers' and Estate Agents' Institute.
A. and M., (Hymns) Ancient and Modern.
A.B., Able-bodied Seaman.
A.B.C., Alphabet (also Aerated Bread Company).
a.c., alternating current.
a/c., accounts.
A.C. (*Ante Christum*), B.C.
A.C.A., *Associate* of Inst. of Chartered Accountants (of England and Wales).
A.C.C.S.—of the Corporation of Secretaries.
A.C.I.S.—of the Chartered Institute of Secretaries.
A.C.W.A.—of the Institute of Cost and Works Accountants.
A.D. (*Anno Domini*), In the year of our Lord.
A.D.C., Aide-de-Camp.
Ad lib. (*ad libitum*), At pleasure.
A.F.C., Air Force Cross.
A.F.M., Air Force Medal.
A.H. (*Anno Hegirae*), In the year of the Hejira.
A.I.A., *Associate* of the Institute of Actuaries.
A.I.B.—of Bankers.
A.I.C.S.—of Chartered Shipbrokers.
A.I.M.T.A.—of Munic. Treas. and Accountants.
A. Inst.P.—of Physics.
A.I.Q.S.—of Quantity Surveyors.
A.K.C.—of King's College.
A.L. (*Anno Lucis*), in the year of Light.
A.L.A., *Associate* of the Library Association.
A.L.C.D.—of London College of Divinity.
A.M.(*Ante meridiem*), Before noon.
A.M. (*Anno mundi*), In the year of the world.
A.M.D.G. (*Ad majorem Dei Gloriam*), To the greater glory of God.
A.M.I.Chem.E.—*Associate Member* of Institution of Chemical Engineers.
A.M.I.E.E.—Do. Electrical Engineers.
A.N.A.R.E., Australian National Antarctic Research Expeditions.
A.N.Z.A.C., Australian and New Zealand Army Corps.
A.O.C., Air Officer Commanding.
A.R.A., *Associate* of Royal Academy.
A.R.A.M.—of Royal Academy of Music.
A.R.B.S.—of the Royal Society of British Sculptors.

A.R.C.A.—of Royal Coll. of Arts.
A.R.C.M.—of Royal College of Music.
A.R.C.O.—of Organists.
A.R.I.B.A.—of Royal Institute of British Architects.
A.R.I.C.—of Royal Institute of Chemistry.
A.R.I.C.S.—of Chartered Institution of Chartered Surveyors.
A.R.P.S.—of Royal Photographic Society.
A.R.R.C.—of Royal Red Cross.
A.R.W.S.—of Royal Society of Painters in Water Colours.
A.S.V.A.—of Inc. Society of Valuers and Auctioneers.
A.S.A., Amateur Swimming Association.
A.S.D.I.C., Anti-Submarine Detector Indicator Committee.
A.S.L.I.B., Association of Special Libraries and Information Bureaux.
A.T.A., Air Transport Auxiliary.
A.T.C., Air Training Corps.
A.U.C. (*Ab urbe condita*). In the year from the foundation of Rome.
A.W.O.L., Absent Without Leave.

B

B.A., *Bachelor* of Arts.
B.Arch.—of Architecture.
B.Ch. (or Ch.B.)—of Surgery.
B.C.L.—of Civil Law.
B.Com.—of Commerce.
B.D.—of Divinity.
B.D.S. (or B.Ch.D.)—of Dental Surgery.
B.Ed.—of Education.
B.Eng.—of Engineering.
B.Litt.—of Literature *or* of Letters.
B.Phil.—of Philosophy.
B.Sc.—of Science.
B.V.M.S.—of Veterinary Medicine and Surgery.
B.A.O.R., British Army of the Rhine.
B.B., Boys' Brigade.
B.B.C., British Broadcasting Corporation.
B.C., Before Christ.
B.D.A., British Dental Assocn.
B.E.A., British European Airways.
B.E.M., British Empire Medal.
B.M.A., British Medical Assocn.
B.N.C., Brasenose College (Oxon.).
B.O.A.C., British Overseas Airways.
B.Pharm., Bachelor of Pharmacy.
B.R.C.S., British Red Cross Society.
B.S.T., British Standard Time.
Bt., Baronet.
B.Th.U., British Thermal Unit.
B.V.M., Blessed Virgin Mary.

C

C.—Conservative.
ca. (*circa*), about.

C.A., Chartered Accountant (*Scottish Institute*).
Cantab., Cambridge.
Cantuar., Canterbury.
Cap. (Chapter), Number of Act of Parliament.
C.B., Companion of the Bath.
C.B.E., Commander of Order of British Empire.
C.B.I., Confederation of British Industry.
c.c., cubic centimetres.
C.C., County Council.
C.C.F., Combined Cadet Force.
C.E., Civil Engineer.
C.E.N.T.O., Central Treaty Organisation.
C.E.T., Central European Time.
C. of E., Church of England.
cf. (*confer*), Compare.
C.F., Chaplain to the Forces.
C.G.M., Conspicuous Gallantry Medal.
C.G.S., Centimetre - gramme - second (system).
C.H., Companion of Honour.
Ch. Ch., Christ Church.
C.I., Lady of Imperial Order of the Crown of India.
C.I., Channel Islands.
C.I.A., Central Intelligence Agency.
C.I.D., Criminal Investigation Department.
C.I.E., Companion, Order of Indian Empire.
C.I.F. (usually cif.), Cost, Insurance and Freight.
C.I.G.S., Chief of Imperial General Staff.
C.-in-C., Commander-in-Chief.
C.I.O., Congress of Industrial Organizations (U.S.A.).
C.L.B., Church Lads' Brigade.
C.M. (*Chirurgiae Magister*), Master of Surgery.
C.M.G., Companion, Order of St. Michael and St. George.
C.M.S., Church Missionary Society.
C.N.A.A., Council for National Academic Awards.
C.O., Commanding Officer.
C.O.D., Cash on delivery.
C.O.I.—Central Office of Information.
C.P.R.E.—Council for Preservation of Rural England.
C.S.I., Companion, Order of Star of India.
C.T.C., Cyclists' Touring Club.
C.V.O., Commander, Royal Victorian Order.
cwt., Hundredweight.

D

D.B.E., Dame Commander of Order of British Empire.
d.c., direct current.
D.C., District of Columbia.
D.C.L., *Doctor* of Civil Law.
D.D.—of Divinity.
D.D.S.—of Dental Surgery.
D.Litt.—of Letters, *or* of Literature.

D.Phil.—of Philosophy.

D.Sc.—of Science.

D.Th.—of Theology.

D.C.M., Distinguished Conduct Medal.

D.C.M.G.—Dame Commander, Order of St. Michael and St. George.

D.C.V.O.—Dame Commander of the Royal Victorian Order.

D.D.T., dichlorodiphenyltrichloroethane (insecticide).

del. (*delineavit*), He (she) drew it.

D.F.C., Distinguished Flying Cross.

D.F.M., Distinguished Flying Medal.

D.G. (*Dei gratia*), By the Grace of God.

D.I.C., *Diploma of the Imperial College.*

D.P.H.—in Public Health.

D.P.M.—in Psychological Medicine.

D.T.M.—in Tropical Medicine.

D.L., Deputy-Lieutenant.

D.N.B., Dictionary of National Biography.

Do. (ditto), The same. (Italian, *detto*).

D.O.M., *Dominus Omnium Magister* (God the Master of All).

D.S.C., Distinguished Service Cross.

D.S.M., Do. Medal.

D.S.O., Companion of Distinguished Service Order.

D.V. (*Deo volente*), God willing.

dwt., Pennyweight.

E

E. and O.E., Errors and omissions excepted.

E.C., East Central District.

E.C.S.C., European Coal and Steel Community.

E.D., Efficiency Decoration.

E.E.C., European Economic Community.

E.F.T.A., European Free Trade Association.

e.g. (*exempli gratia*), for the sake of example.

E.M.A., European Monetary Agreement.

E.R., Elizabetha Regina, or Edwardus Rex.

E.R.D., Emergency Reserve Decoration.

etc. (*et cetera*). And the other things.

et seq. (*et sequentia*). And the following.

ex lib. (*ex libris*), from the books of.

F

F.A., Football Association.

F.A.C.A., *Fellow* of Association of Certified Accountants.

F.A.I., of Chartered Auctioneers' and Estate Agents Institute.

F.B.A.—of the British Academy.

F.C.A.—of Institute of Chartered Accountants (of England and Wales).

F.C.C.S.—of Corporation of Secretaries.

F.C.G.I.—of City and Guilds Institute.

F.C.I.A.—of Corporation of Insurance Agents.

F.C.I.B.—of Corporation of Insurance Brokers.

F.C.I.I.—of the Chartered Insurance Institute.

F.C.I.S.—of the Chartered Institute of Secretaries.

F.C.P.—of the College of Preceptors.

F.C.W.A.—of the Institute of Cost and Works Accountants.

F.G.S.—of the Geological Society.

F.H.S.—of the Heraldry Society.

F.I.A.—of the Institute of Actuaries.

F.I.Arb.—of Arbitrators.

F.I.B.—of Bankers.

F.I.C.E.—of Institution of Civil Engineers.

F.I.C.S.—of Chartered Shipbrokers.

F.I.M.T.A.—of Munic. Treas. and Accountants.

F.Inst.P.—of Physics.

F.I.Q.S.—of Quantity Surveyors.

F.J.I.—of Journalists.

F.L.A., Fellow of Library Assocn.

F.L.A.S.—of Land Agents Society.

F.L.S.—of the Linnean Society.

F.P.S.—of the Pharmaceutical Society.

F.R.A.I.—of Royal Anthropological Institute.

F.R.A.M.—of Royal Academy of Music.

F.R.A.S.—of the Royal Astronomical Society.

F.R.Ae.S.—of Royal Aeronautical Society.

F.R.B.S.—of the Royal Society of British Sculptors.

F.R.C.M.—of the Royal College of Music.

F.R.C.O.—of Royal College of Organists.

F.R.C.O.G.—of Royal College of Obstetricians and Gynaecologists.

F.R.C.P., F.R.C.P.Ed., and F.R.C.P.I.—of the Royal College of Physicians of London, of Edinburgh, and in Ireland respectively.

F.R.C.P.S.G.—of the Royal Faculty of Physicians and Surgeons of Glasgow.

F.R.C.S.—of Royal College of Surgeons of England.

F.R.C.S.Ed., ditto of Edinburgh; F.R.C.S.I., of Ireland.

F.R.C.V.S.—of Royal College of Veterinary Surgeons.

F.R.Econ.S.—of Roy. Economic Society.

F.R.G.S.—of the Royal Geographical Society.

F.R.H.S.—of the Royal Horticultural Society.

F.R.Hist.Soc., ditto Historical.

F.R.I.B.A.—of the Royal Institute of British Architects.

F.R.I.C.—of the Royal Institute of Chemistry.

F.R.I.C.S.—of the Royal Institution of Chartered Surveyors.

F.R.M.S.—of Royal Microscopical Society.

F.R. Met. S.—of Royal Meteorological Society.

F.R.N.S.—of Royal Numismatic Society.

F.R.P.S.—of Royal Photographic Society.

F.R.S.—of the Royal Society.

F.R.S.E., ditto of Edinburgh.

F.R.S.A.—of the Royal Society of Arts.

F.R.S.L.—Do. Literature.

F.S.A.—of the Society of Antiquaries.

F.S.S.—Do. Statistical Society.

F.S.V.A.—Do. Valuers and Auctioneers.

F.Z.S.—of the Zoological Society.

F.A.N.Y., First Aid Nursing Yeomanry.

F.A.O., Food and Agriculture Organization.

fcp., Foolscap.

F.D. (*Fidei Defensor*) Defender of the Faith.

Fec. (*fecit*), He did it (or made it).

F.H., Fire Hydrant.

F.I.D.O., Fog Investigation Dispersal Operations.

fl. (*floruit*), he, or she, flourished.

F.O., Flying Officer; Foreign Office.

FOB (usually f.o.b.), Free on board.

G

G.A.T.T., General Agreement on Tariffs and Trade.

G.B.E., Knight or Dame Grand Cross of British Empire.

G.C., George Cross.

G.C.B., Knight Grand Cross of the Bath.

G.C.I.E., Knight Grand Commander of Indian Empire.

G.C.M.G., Knight (or Dame) Grand Cross of St. Michael and St. George.

G.C.S.I., Knight Grand Commander of Star of India.

G.C.V.O., Knight or Dame Grand Cross of Royal Victorian Order.

G.H.Q., General Headquarters.

G.L.C., Greater London Council.

G.M., George Medal.

G.M.T., Greenwich Mean Time.

G.O.C., General Officer Commanding.

G.P.O., General Post Office.

G.R. (*Georgius Rex*), King George.

G.R.C.M., Graduate of the Royal College of Music.

G.R.S.M., Graduate of the Royal Schools of Music (Royal Academy and Royal College).

G.S.O., General Staff Officer.

H

H.A.C., Honble. Artillery Coy.

H.C.F., Highest Common Factor.

H.E., His Excellency.

H.E.H., His [Her] Exalted Highness.

H.H., His [Her] Highness.

H.I.H., His [Her] Imperial Highness.
H.I.M., His [Her] Imperial Majesty.
H.J.S. (*Hic jacet sepultus*), Here lies buried. *cf.* H.S.E.
H.M., His, or Her, Majesty.
H.M.A.S., Her Majesty's Australian Ship.
H.M.L., Her Majesty's Lieutenant.
H.M.S., Her Majesty's Ship.
H.M.S.O., Her Majesty's Stationery Office.
h.p., horse power.
H.Q., Headquarters.
H.R.H., His [Her] Royal Highness.
H.S.E. (*Hic sepultus est*), Here lies buried. *cf.* H.J.S.
H.S.H., His [Her] Serene Highness.

I

I.A., Indian Army.
Ibid. (*ibidem*), In the same place.
IBRD., Internat. Bank for Reconstruction and Development.
I.C.B.M., Inter-Continental ballistic missile.
I.C.S., Indian Civil Service.
Id. (*idem*), The same.
I.C.A.O., International Civil Aviation Organization.
i.d.c., Graduate of Imperial Defence College.
i.e. (*id est*), That is.
IFC, International Finance Corporation.
I.H.S. (*Iesus Hominum Salvator*), Jesus the Saviour of Mankind; originally, these were the Greek Capital letters, IHΣ.
I.L.O., International Labour Organization.
I.L.P., Independent Labour Party.
IMCO., Inter - Governmental Maritime Consultative Organization.
IMF, International Monetary Fund.
I.M.S., Indian Medical Service.
Incog. (*incognito*), Unknown.
In loc (*in loco*), In its place.
I.N.R.I. (*Iesus Nazarenus Rex Iudaeorum*), Jesus of Nazareth King of the Jews.
Inst. (instant), current month.
I.O.M., Isle of Man.
I.O.U., I owe you.
I.O.W., Isle of Wight.
I.Q., Intelligence Quotient.
IRBM., Intermediate - range ballistic missile.
I.S.O., Imperial Service Order.
I.T.A., Independent Television Authority.
I.T.O., International Trade Organization.
I.T.U., International Telecommunication Union.

J

J., Judge.
J.P., Justice of the Peace.

K

K.B.E. Knight Commander of Order of British Empire.
K.C.B.—Do. the Bath.
K.C.I.E.—Do. Indian Empire.

K.C.M.G.—Do. St. of Michael and St. George.
K.C.S.I.—Do. the Star of India.
K.C.V.O.—Do. Royal Victorian Order.
K.G., Knight of the Garter.
k.o., knock out (boxing).
K.P., Knight of St. Patrick.
K.T., Knight of the Thistle.
Kt., Knight Bachelor.

L

L., Liberal.
Lab., Labour.
L.A.C., London Athletic Club.
L.A.H., *Licentiate* of Apothecaries' Hall, Dublin.
L.C.P., Do. of College of Preceptors.
L.D.S., Do. in Dental Surgery.
L.M., Do. in Midwifery.
L.M.S.S.A. Do. in Medicine and Surgery, Soc. of Apothecaries.
L.R.A.M., Do. of Royal Acad. of Music.
L.R.C.P., Do. of the Roy. Coll. of Physicians.
L.R.C.P.Ed., ditto Edinburgh.
L.R.C.S.Ed.—of Roy. Coll. Surg., Edinburgh.
L.R.F.P.S.G., Do. of the Royal Faculty of Physicians and Surgeons of Glasgow.
L.S.A., Do. of Society of Apothecaries.
L.Th., Licenciate in Theology.
L.T.M., Do. of Tropical Medicine.
Lat., Latitude.
lb. (*libra*). Pound weight.
L.C.C., London County Council.
L.C.J., Lord Chief Justice.
L.C.M., Least Common Multiple.
Lit., Literally.
Litt.D., Doctor of Letters.
L.J., Lord Justice.
LL.B., Bachelor of Laws.
LL.D., Doctor of Laws.
LL.M., Master of Laws.
L.S. (*loco sigilli*), Place of the Seal.
L s d. (*Librae, solidi, denarii*), Pounds, shillings, pence.
L.T.A., Lawn Tennis Association.
Ltd., Limited Liability.
LXX., Septuagint.

M

M.A., *Master* of Arts.
M.Ch.—of Surgery.
M.Ch.D.—of Dental Surgery.
M.S.—of Surgery.
M.Sc.—of Science.
M.Th.—of Theology.
M.B., Bachelor of Medicine.
M.D., Doctor of ditto.
M.B.E., *Member* of British Empire Order.
M.E.C.—of Executive Council.
M.I.Chem.E.—of Institution of Chemical Engineers.
M.I.C.E.—of Institution of Civil Engineers.
M.I.E.E.—of Institution of Electrical Engineers.
M.I.Mar.E.—of Institute of Marine Engineers.
M.I.Mech.E.—of Institution of Mechanical Engineers.
M.Inst.Met.—of Institute of Metals.

M.Inst.T.—of Institute of Transport.
M.J.I.—of Journalists.
M.L.A., *Member* of Legislative Assembly.
M.L.C., ditto Council.
M.N., Merchant Navy.
M.P., Member of Parliament (also Military Police).
M.P.S. — of Pharmaceutical Society.
M.R.C.P.—of Royal College of Physicians.
M.R.C.S.—of Royal College of Surgeons.
M.R.C.V.S.—of Royal College of Veterinary Surgeons.
M.V.O.—of Royal Victorian Order.
M.C., Military Cross.
M.C.C., Marylebone Cricket Club.
M.F.H., Master of Fox Hounds.
Mgr., Monsignor.
Min. Plenip., Minister Plenipotentiary.
Mlle., Mademoiselle.
M.M., Military Medal (also MM., Messieurs).
Mme., Madame.
M.O.H., Medical Officer of Health.
m.p.h., Miles per hour.
MS., manuscript (pl. MSS.).
Mus. D.[B.] Doctor, [Bachelor], of Music.

N

N.A.A.F.I., Navy, Army and Air Force Institutes.
N.A.T.O., North Atlantic Treaty Organization.
N.B. (*Nota bene*), Note well.
N.C.B., National Coal Board.
N.C.O., Non - commissioned Officer.
n.d., no date (of books).
N.D.P.S., National Data Processing Service.
Nem. con. (*Nemine contradicente*), No one contradicting.
N.F.U. — National Farmers' Union.
No. (*Numero*), Number.
N.P., Notary Public.
Non seq. (*non sequitur*), It does not follow.
N.R.A., National Rifle Association.
N.S., Nova Scotia.
N.S.P.C.C., National Society for the Prevention of Cruelty to Children.
N.S.W., New South Wales.
N.T., New Testament.
N.U.J., *National Union* of Journalists.
N.U.R.—of Railwaymen.
N.U.S.—of Students.
N.W.P.[T.], North West Provinces [Territory].
N.Y., New York.
N.Z., New Zealand.

O

O.B.E., Officer of British Empire Order.
ob., or *obiit.* died.

O.C., Officer Commanding.

O.E.C.D., Organisation for Economic Co-operation and Development.

O.E.D., Oxford English Dictionary.

O.H.M.S., On Her Majesty's Service.

O.M., Order of Merit (and member of).

O.P., Opposite Prompt side (of Theatre), Out of Print (of books).

op. cit. (*opere citato*), in the work cited.

O.S., Old Style.

O.S.B., Order of St. Benedict.

O.T., Old Testament.

O.U.D.S., Oxford University Dramatic Society.

Oxon., Oxford; Oxfordshire.

Oz., Ounce.

P

P.A., Press Association.

P.C., Privy Councillor.

P.E.N. (*Club*), Poets, Essayists, Novelists.

p.f.c., Passed Flying College.

Ph.D., Doctor of Philosophy.

pinx(it), he (or she) painted it.

P.L.A., Port of London Authority.

P.M. (*post meridiem*), Afternoon (also *post mortem*).

P.M.G., Postmaster-General.

P.N.E.U., Parents' National Educational Union.

p.p., or per pro. (*per procurationem*)—by proxy.

Pro tem. (*pro tempore*), For the time being.

Prox. (*proximo*), Next month.

P.S. (*Post scriptum*), Postscript.

p.s.c., Passed Staff College.

P.T., Physical Training.

P.T.O., Please turn over.

Q

Q.C., Queen's Counsel.

Q.e.d. (*quod erat demonstrandum*), which was to be proved.

Q.H.C., Honorary Chaplain to the Queen; Q.H.P., ditto Physician; Q.H.S., ditto Surgeon; Q.H.D.S., ditto Dental Surgeon; Q.H.N.S., ditto Nursing Sister.

Q.M.G., Quartermaster-General.

Q.S., Quarter Sessions.

Q.S.O., Quasi-stellar object (quasar).

q.v. (*quod vide*), " which see ".

R

R.A., *Royal* Artillery or Royal Academy (or Academician).

R.A.C.—Armoured Corps (also Royal Automobile Club).

R.A.D.C.—Army Dental Corps.

R.A.E.C.—Army Educational Corps.

R.Ae.S., Royal Aeronautical Society.

R.A.F.—Air Force.

R.A.M.—Academy of Music.

R.A.M.C.—Army Medical Corps.

R.A.N.—Australian Navy.

R.A.P.C.—Army Pay Corps.

R.A.O.C.—Army Ordnance Corps.

R.A.V.C.—Army Veterinary Corps.

R.B.A.—Society of British Artists.

R.B.S.—Society of British Sculptors.

R.C.N.—Canadian Navy.

R.C.N.C.—Corps of Naval Constructors.

R.C.T.—Corps of Transport.

R.D.—Naval Reserve Decoration, or Rural Dean.

R.E.—Engineers.

R.E.M.E.—Electrical and Mechanical do.

R.H.A.—Horse Artillery or—Hibernian Academy.

R.I.A.—Irish Academy.

R.M.—Marines.

R.M.A.—Military Academy.

R.M.S.—Mail Steamer.

R.N.—Navy; R.N.R., Naval Reserve; R.N.V.R., Naval Volunteer Reserve.

R.O.I.—Institute of Oil Painters.

R.P.—Society of Portrait Painters.

R.P.C.—Pay Corps.

R.Sigs.—Signals.

R.S.A.—Scottish Academician.

R.S.P.C.A.—Society for the Prevention of Cruelty to Animals.

R.W.S.—Water Colour Society.

R.Y.S.—Yacht Squadron.

R.C., Roman Catholic.

R.D., Refer to drawer (banking).

R.D.C., Rural District Council.

R.D.I., Designer for Industry of the Royal Society of Arts.

R.I.P. (*Requiescat in pace*), May he (she) rest in peace.

Ro. (*recto*), On the right-hand page. (*See* Vo.)

R.O.C., Royal Observer Corps.

r.p.m., revolutions per minute.

R.R.C., Lady of Royal Red Cross.

R.S.V.P. (*Répondez, s'il vous plaît*), Answer, if you please.

R.V., Revised Version (of Bible).

S

Sc.D., Doctor of Science.

S.E.A.T.O.—South East Asia Treaty Organization.

S.E.T., Selective Employment Tax.

S.H.A.P.E.—Supreme Headquarters, Allied Powers, Europe.

Sic, So written.

S.J., Society of Jesus.

S.O.S. (" Save Our Souls ") Distress Signal.

s.p. (*sine prole*), Without issue.

S.P.C.K., Society for Promoting Christian Knowledge.

S.P.Q.R. (*Senatus Populusque Romanus*), The Senate and People of Rome.

S.R.N., State Registered Nurse.

S.S.A.F.A., Soldiers', Sailors', and Airmen's Families Assocn.

S.S.C., Solicitor in the Supreme Court (Scotland).

Stet, Let it stand.

S.T.P. (=D.D.), *Sacrae Theologiae Professor*.

T

T.A.N., Twilight all night.

t.b., Tuberculosis.

T.D., Territorial Decoration.

T.C.D., Trinity College, Dublin.

T.N.T., Trinitrotoluene (explosive).

Toc. H., Talbot House.

T.U.C., Trades Union Congress.

U

Ult. (*ultimo*), in the preceding month.

U.D.C., Urban District Council.

U.K., United Kingdom.

U.N.A.C., United Nations Appeal for Children.

U.N.E.S.C.O., United Nations Educational, Scientific and Cultural Organization.

U.N.O., United Nations Organization.

U.P.U., Universal Postal Union.

U.S.A. or U.S., United States of America.

U.S.C.L., United Society for Christian Literature.

U.S.S.R., Union of Soviet Socialist Republics.

V

v. (*versus*), Against.

V.A., Victoria and Albert Order or Vicar Apostolic.

V.A.D., Voluntary Aid Detachment.

V.C., Victoria Cross.

V.D., Vol. Officers' Decoration.

Ven., Venerable.

Verb. sap. (*Verbum sapienti satis est*), A word to the wise is enough.

V.I.P., Very Important Person.

Viz. (*videlicet*), Namely.

Vo. (*verso*), On the left-hand page. (*See* Ro.)

V.R., Victoria Regina.

V.R.D.—Volunteer Reserve Decoration.

W

W.A.A.F., now W.R.A.F., Women's Auxiliary Air Force.

W.H.O., World Health Organization.

W.M.O. World Meteorological Organization.

W.O., Warrant Officer.

W.R.A.C., Woman's Royal Army Corps.

W.R.A.F., Women's Royal Air Force.

W.R.N.S., Women's Royal Naval Service.

W.R.V.S., Women's Royal Voluntary Service.

W.S., Writer to the Signet.

Y

Y.M.C.A., Young Men's Christian Association.

Y.W.C.A., Young Women's do.

BEING BISSEXTILE OR LEAP YEAR

Golden Number	.. .. ..	XVI
Epact	.. .. ..	14
Dominical Letter	.. .. ..	BA
Solar Cycle	.. .. ..	21
Roman Indiction	.. .. ..	10
Julian Period	.. .. ..	6685
Julian Day, Jan. 1 (begins at noon)		2441318
New Year's Day (Saturday)	..	Jan. 1
Australia Day	.. ..	,, 26
Septuagesima Sunday	.. ..	,, 30
Accession of Queen Elizabeth II		Feb. 6
New Zealand Day	.. ..	,, 6
Ash Wednesday	.. ..	,, 16
Moslem New Year (1392)	..	,, 16
Prince Andrew's Birthday (1960)		,, 19
St. David's Day	.. ..	Mar. 1
Prince Edward's Birthday (1964)		,, 10
St. Patrick's Day	.. ..	,, 17
Good Friday	.. .. ..	,, 31

Easter Day	.. .. ..	Apr. 2
The Queen's Birthday (1926) ..		,, 21
St. George's Day	.. ..	,, 23
Ascension Day	.. ..	May 11
Whit Sunday	.. ..	,, 21
Trinity Sunday	.. ..	,, 28
Corpus Christi	.. ..	June 1
Queen's Official Birthday	..	,, 3
Duke of Edinburgh's Birthday (1921)		,, 10
Dominion Day, Canada (1867)		July 1
The Queen Mother's Birthday (1900)		Aug. 4
Princess Anne's Birthday (1950)		,, 15
Jewish New Year (5733)	..	Sept. 9
Remembrance Sunday ..	..	Nov. 12
Prince of Wales's Birthday (1948)		,, 14
St. Andrew's Day	.. ..	,, 30
First Sunday in Advent	..	Dec. 3
Christmas Day (Monday)	..	,, 25

Spring Equinox	Sun enters Sign Aries	March	20d 12h
Summer Solstice	,, ,, ,, Cancer	June	21d 07h
Autumn Equinox	,, ,, ,, Libra	Sept.	22d 23h
Winter Solstice	,, ,, ,, Capricornus	Dec.	21d 18h

G.M.T.

CALENDAR FOR THE YEAR 1972

January
Su. — 2 9 16 23 30
M. — 3 10 17 24 31
Tu. — 4 11 18 25 —
W. — 5 12 19 26 —
Th. — 6 13 20 27 —
F. — 7 14 21 28 —
S. 1 8 15 22 29 —

February
Su. .. — 6 13 20 27
M. .. — 7 14 21 28
Tu. .. 1 8 15 22 29
W. .. 2 9 16 23 —
Th. .. 3 10 17 24 —
F. .. 4 11 18 25 —
S. .. 5 12 19 26 —

March
Su. .. — 5 12 19 26
M. .. — 6 13 20 27
Tu. .. — 7 14 21 28
W. .. 1 8 15 22 29
Th. .. 2 9 16 23 30
F. .. 3 10 17 24 31
S. .. 4 11 18 25 —

April
Su. — 2 9 16 23 30
M. — 3 10 17 24 —
Tu. — 4 11 18 25 —
W. — 5 12 19 26 —
Th. — 6 13 20 27 —
F. — 7 14 21 28 —
S. 1 8 15 22 29 —

May
Su. .. — 7 14 21 28
M. .. 1 8 15 22 29
Tu. .. 2 9 16 23 30
W. .. 3 10 17 24 31
Th. .. 4 11 18 25 —
F. .. 5 12 19 26 —
S. .. 6 13 20 27 —

June
Su. .. — 4 11 18 25
M. .. — 5 12 19 26
Tu. .. — 6 13 20 27
W. .. — 7 14 21 28
Th. .. 1 8 15 22 29
F. .. 2 9 16 23 30
S. .. 3 10 17 24 —

July
Su. — 2 9 16 23 30
M. — 3 10 17 24 31
Tu. — 4 11 18 25 —
W. — 5 12 19 26 —
Th. — 6 13 20 27 —
F. — 7 14 21 28 —
S. 1 8 15 22 29 —

August
Su. .. — 6 13 20 27
M. .. — 7 14 21 28
Tu. .. 1 8 15 22 29
W. .. 2 9 16 23 30
Th. .. 3 10 17 24 31
F. .. 4 11 18 25 —
S. .. 5 12 19 26 —

September
Su. .. — 3 10 17 24
M. .. — 4 11 18 25
Tu. .. — 5 12 19 26
W. .. — 6 13 20 27
Th. .. — 7 14 21 28
F. .. 1 8 15 22 29
S. .. 2 9 16 23 30

October
Su. .. 1 8 15 22 29
M. .. 2 9 16 23 30
Tu. .. 3 10 17 24 31
W. .. 4 11 18 25 —
Th. .. 5 12 19 26 —
F. .. 6 13 20 27 —
S. .. 7 14 21 28 —

November
Su. .. — 5 12 19 26
M. .. — 6 13 20 27
Tu. .. — 7 14 21 28
W. .. 1 8 15 22 29
Th. .. 2 9 16 23 30
F. .. 3 10 17 24 —
S. .. 4 11 18 25 —

December
Su. .. — 3 10 17 24 31
M. .. — 4 11 18 25 —
Tu. .. — 5 12 19 26 —
W. .. — 6 13 20 27 —
Th. .. — 7 14 21 28 —
F. .. 1 8 15 22 29 —
S. .. 2 9 16 23 30 —

CALENDAR FOR THE YEAR 1973

January
Su. — 7 14 21 28
M. 1 8 15 22 29
Tu. 2 9 16 23 30
W. 3 10 17 24 31
Th. 4 11 18 25 —
F. 5 12 19 26 —
S. 6 13 20 27 —

February
Su. .. — 4 11 18 25
M. .. — 5 12 19 26
Tu. .. — 6 13 20 27
W. .. — 7 14 21 28
Th. .. 1 8 15 22 —
F. .. 2 9 16 23 —
S. .. 3 10 17 24 —

March
Su. .. — 4 11 18 25
M. .. — 5 12 19 26
Tu. .. — 6 13 20 27
W. .. — 7 14 21 28
Th. .. 1 8 15 22 29
F. .. 2 9 16 23 30
S. .. 3 10 17 24 31

April
Su. — 1 8 15 22 29
M. — 2 9 16 23 30
Tu. — 3 10 17 24 —
W. — 4 11 18 25 —
Th. — 5 12 19 26 —
F. — 6 13 20 27 —
S. — 7 14 21 28 —

May
Su. .. — 6 13 20 27
M. .. — 7 14 21 28
Tu. .. 1 8 15 22 29
W. .. 2 9 16 23 30
Th. .. 3 10 17 24 31
F. .. 4 11 18 25 —
S. .. 5 12 19 26 —

June
Su. .. — 3 10 17 24
M. .. — 4 11 18 25
Tu. .. — 5 12 19 26
W. .. — 6 13 20 27
Th. .. — 7 14 21 28
F. .. 1 8 15 22 29
S. .. 2 9 16 23 30

July
Su. — 8 15 22 29
M. 2 9 16 23 30
Tu. 3 10 17 24 31
W. 4 11 18 25 —
Th. 5 12 19 26 —
F. 6 13 20 27 —
S. 7 14 21 28 —

August
Su. .. — 5 12 19 26
M. .. — 6 13 20 27
Tu. .. — 7 14 21 28
W. .. 1 8 15 22 29
Th. .. 2 9 16 23 30
F. .. 3 10 17 24 31
S. .. 4 11 18 25 —

September
Su. .. — 2 9 16 23 30
M. .. — 3 10 17 24 —
Tu. .. — 4 11 18 25 —
W. .. — 5 12 19 26 —
Th. .. — 6 13 20 27 —
F. .. — 7 14 21 28 —
S. .. 1 8 15 22 29 —

October
Su. .. — 7 14 21 28
M. .. 1 8 15 22 29
Tu. .. 2 9 16 23 30
W. .. 3 10 17 24 31
Th. .. 4 11 18 25 —
F. .. 5 12 19 26 —
S. .. 6 13 20 27 —

November
Su. .. — 4 11 18 25
M. .. — 5 12 19 26
Tu. .. — 6 13 20 27
W. .. — 7 14 21 28
Th. .. 1 8 15 22 29
F. .. 2 9 16 23 30
S. .. 3 10 17 24 —

December
Su. .. — 2 9 16 23 30
M. .. — 3 10 17 24 31
Tu. .. — 4 11 18 25 —
W. .. — 5 12 19 26 —
Th. .. — 6 13 20 27 —
F. .. — 7 14 21 28 —
S. .. 1 8 15 22 29 —

Day of Month	Week		

Janus, god of the portal, facing two ways, past and future.

Sun's Longitude 300° ♒ 20ᵈ 23ʰ

1	S.	Circumcision. Sir E. Lutyens d. 1944
2	S.	2nd Sunday after Christmas. A. W. Kinglake d.
3	M.	James Elroy Flecker d. 1915　　　　[1891
4	Tu.	Visct. Waverley d. 1958. T. S. Eliot d. 1965
5	W.	Sir Edward Shackleton d. 1922
6	Th.	Epiphany. Twelfth Day
7	F.	Sir Frederick Gibberd b. 1908. Gerald Durrell b.
8	S.	Lord Baden-Powell d. 1941　　　　[1925
9	S.	1st Sunday after Epiphany. Richard M. Nixon b.
10	M.	Mary Russell Mitford d. 1855　　　　[1913
11	Tu.	HILARY LAW SITTINGS BEGIN
12	W.	Nevil Shute d. 1960. Lord Tovey d. 1971
13	Th.	James Joyce d. 1941. Wickham Steed d. 1956
14	F.	Cardinal Manning d. 1892. Lewis Carroll d. 1898
15	S.	Lord Hill of Luton b. 1904
16	S.	2nd S. after Epiphany. Gordon Craig b. 1872**
17	M.	Sir Compton Mackenzie b. 1883
18	Tu.	Rudyard Kipling d. 1936. Hugh Gaitskell d. 1963
19	W.	Ciudad Rodrigo 1812
20	Th.	George V d. 1936. Sir John Soane d. 1837
21	F.	Lenin d. 1924. George Orwell d. 1950
22	S.	Queen Victoria d. 1901. David Garrick d. 1779
23	S.	3rd S. after Epiphany. Lord Denning b. 1899
24	M.	Sir W. Churchill d. 1965. St. John Ervine d. 1971
25	Tu.	Conversion of St. Paul. Robert Burns b. 1759
26	W.	Australia Day. Cardinal Heenan b. 1905.
27	Th.	Verdi d. 1901. Lord Upjohn d. 1971
28	F.	W. B. Yeats d. 1939. Gen. Weygand d. 1965
29	S.	Sir William Rothenstein b. 1872**
30	S.	Septuagesima Charles I d. 1649　　　[d. 1933
31	M.	Christopher Chataway b. 1931. John Galsworthy

(G.M.T.)
PHENOMENA

January 1ᵈ 14ʰ Mercury at greatest western elongation (23°).

3ᵈ Perihelion (147,000,000 kilometres).

6ᵈ 19ʰ Mercury in conjunction with Jupiter. Mercury 0°·8 N.

14ᵈ 04ʰ Jupiter in conjunction with the Moon. Jupiter 4°N.

14ᵈ 20ʰ Mercury in conjunction with the Moon. Mercury 3°N.

16ᵈ 11ʰ Annular eclipse of the Sun. *See* p. 148.

19ᵈ 08ʰ Venus in conjunction with the Moon. Venus 4° S.

22ᵈ 11ʰ Mars in conjunction with the Moon. Mars 5° S.

25ᵈ 10ʰ Saturn in conjunction with the Moon. Saturn 7° S.

30ᵈ 11ʰ Total eclipse of the Moon. *See* p. 148.

CONSTELLATIONS

The following constellations are near the meridian at

	d h		d h
Dec.	1 24	Dec.	16 23
Jan.	1 22	Jan.	16 21
Feb.	1 20	Feb.	15 19

Draco (below the Pole), Ursa Minor (below the Pole), Camelopardus, Perseus, Auriga, Taurus, Orion, Eridanus and Lepus.

MINIMA OF ALGOL

d	h	d	h
1	02	18	07
3	23	21	04
6	20	24	01
9	17	26	22
12	14	29	18
15	10		

(G.M.T.)
PHASES OF THE MOON

	d h m
☾ Last Quarter	8 13 31
● New Moon	16 10 52
☽ First Quarter	23 09 29
○ Full Moon	30 10 58

	d h
Apogee (404,460 kilometres)	9 04
Perigee (370,020 „)	22 05

Mean Longitude of Ascending Node on January 1, 307°.

MONTHLY NOTES

Jan. 1. New Year's Day. Bank Holiday in Scotland and in the Channel Islands.

6. Dividends on Consols, etc., due. Christmas Fire Insurances must be paid.

NATIONAL DAYS.—Jan. 1, Haiti; Cuba; Sudan; Cameroon; 4, Burma; 26, Australia (*see above*); India.

** Centenary

THE SUN s.d. 16'·2

Day	Right Ascension	Dec. −	Equation of time	Rise 52°	Rise 56°	Transit	Set 52°	Set 56°	Sidereal Time	Transit of First Point of Aries (G.M.T.)
	h m s	° '	m s	h m	h m	h m	h m	h m	h m s	h m s
1	18 42 03	23 06	− 3 02	8 08	8 32	12 03	15 58	15 35	6 39 01	17 18 08
2	18 46 28	23 01	− 3 30	8 08	8 32	12 04	15 59	15 36	6 42 58	17 14 12
3	18 50 53	22 56	− 3 58	8 08	8 31	12 04	16 00	15 37	6 46 54	17 10 16
4	18 55 17	22 50	− 4 26	8 08	8 31	12 05	16 01	15 39	6 50 51	17 06 20
5	18 59 41	22 44	− 4 54	8 08	8 31	12 05	16 03	15 40	6 54 48	17 02 24
6	19 04 05	22 38	− 5 21	8 08	8 30	12 06	16 04	15 41	6 58 44	16 58 29
7	19 08 28	22 31	− 5 47	8 07	8 30	12 06	16 05	15 43	7 02 41	16 54 33
8	19 12 51	22 23	− 6 14	8 07	8 29	12 06	16 06	15 44	7 06 37	16 50 37
9	19 17 13	22 15	− 6 39	8 06	8 28	12 07	16 08	15 46	7 10 34	16 46 41
10	19 21 35	22 07	− 7 04	8 06	8 28	12 07	16 09	15 47	7 14 30	16 42 45
11	19 25 56	21 59	− 7 29	8 05	8 27	12 08	16 10	15 49	7 18 27	16 38 49
12	19 30 17	21 49	− 7 53	8 05	8 26	12 08	16 12	15 51	7 22 23	16 34 53
13	19 34 37	21 40	− 8 17	8 04	8 25	12 08	16 13	15 52	7 26 20	16 30 57
14	19 38 56	21 30	− 8 40	8 03	8 24	12 09	16 15	15 54	7 30 17	16 27 00
15	19 43 15	21 19	− 9 02	8 03	8 23	12 09	16 16	15 56	7 34 13	16 23 05
16	19 47 34	21 09	− 9 24	8 02	8 22	12 10	16 18	15 58	7 38 10	16 19 09
17	19 51 51	20 57	− 9 45	8 01	8 21	12 10	16 19	16 00	7 42 06	16 15 14
18	19 56 08	20 46	−10 05	8 00	8 20	12 10	16 21	16 02	7 46 03	16 11 18
19	20 00 24	20 34	−10 24	7 59	8 18	12 11	16 23	16 03	7 49 59	16 07 22
20	20 04 40	20 22	−10 44	7 58	8 17	12 11	16 24	16 05	7 53 56	16 03 26
21	20 08 54	20 09	−11 02	7 57	8 15	12 11	16 26	16 07	7 57 52	15 59 30
22	20 13 08	19 56	−11 19	7 56	8 14	12 11	16 28	16 09	8 01 49	15 55 34
23	20 17 21	19 42	−11 36	7 55	8 13	12 12	16 29	16 11	8 05 46	15 51 38
24	20 21 34	19 28	−11 52	7 53	8 11	12 12	16 31	16 14	8 09 42	15 47 42
25	20 25 45	19 14	−12 07	7 52	8 10	12 12	16 33	16 16	8 13 39	15 43 46
26	20 29 56	18 59	−12 21	7 51	8 08	12 12	16 35	16 18	8 17 35	15 39 50
27	20 34 06	18 44	−12 34	7 49	8 06	12 12	16 37	16 20	8 21 32	15 35 54
28	20 38 15	18 29	−12 47	7 48	8 05	12 13	16 38	16 22	8 25 28	15 31 58
29	20 42 23	18 14	−12 59	7 47	8 03	12 13	16 40	16 24	8 29 25	15 28 03
30	20 46 31	17 58	−13 10	7 45	8 01	12 13	16 42	16 26	8 33 22	15 24 07
31	20 50 38	17 41	−13 20	7 44	7 59	12 13	16 44	16 28	8 37 18	15 20 11

Duration of Civil (C), Nautical (N), and Astronomical (A), Twilight (in minutes)

Lat. °	Jan. 1 C	N	A	Jan. 11 C	N	A	Jan. 21 C	N	A	Jan. 31 C	N	A
52	41	84	125	40	82	123	38	80	120	37	78	117
56	47	96	141	45	93	138	43	85	134	41	87	130

ASTRONOMICAL NOTES

MERCURY is a morning star, magnitude − 0·1, for the first few days of the month, visible for a short while above the south-east horizon around the time of beginning of morning civil twilight. For the remainder of the month it is unsuitably placed for observation. Mercury is close to Jupiter on the mornings of the 6th and 7th, passing only 0°·8N. of it on the evening of the 6th.

VENUS is a brilliant evening star, magnitude − 3·5, and visible in the S.W. sky after sunset. At the beginning of the month Venus is visible for almost two hours after sunset but by the end of the month this has increased to three hours. The crescent Moon will be near Venus on the evenings of the 18th and 19th.

MARS is an evening star, its magnitude decreasing during the month from +0·5 to +1·0. Although moving closer to the Sun this is offset by its northward motion in declination so that it is visible until about the same time (23ʰ) throughout the month. Mars is in Pisces.

JUPITER is a difficult morning star, magnitude − 1·4, visible for a very short while at the beginning of morning civil twilight, low above the S.E. horizon. On the morning of the 14th the old crescent Moon passes 4°S. of Jupiter.

SATURN is a prominent evening star, magnitude +0·1, in the constellation of Taurus.

ECLIPSE. An annular eclipse of the Sun occurs on the 16th. See page 148 for details.

ECLIPSE. A total eclipse of the Moon occurs on the 30th. See page 148 for details.

THE MOON

Day	R.A.	Dec.	Hor. Par.	Semi-diam.	Sun's Co-long.	P.A. of Bright Limb	Phase	Age	Rise 52°	Rise 56°	Transit	Set 52°	Set 56°
	h m	°	′	′	°	°		d	h m	h m	h m	h m	h m
1	6 51	+25·0	58·5	15·9	87	48	100	14·2	16 40	16 14	0 13	8 51	9 18
2	7 50	+22·0	57·8	15·8	99	97	98	15·2	18 02	17 43	1 09	9 20	9 40
3	8 44	+17·8	57·1	15·6	111	106	95	16·2	19 22	19 09	2 01	9 41	9 55
4	9 34	+12·9	56·3	15·4	123	111	89	17·2	20 38	20 30	2 48	9 57	10 06
5	10 21	+ 7·6	55·7	15·2	136	113	82	18·2	21 50	21 48	3 32	10 10	10 14
6	11 05	+ 2·1	55·1	15·0	148	115	74	19·2	23 01	23 04	4 14	10 22	10 21
7	11 49	− 3·4	54·6	14·9	160	115	65	20·2	··	··	4 54	10 33	10 28
8	12 32	− 8·6	54·3	14·8	172	114	55	21·2	0 11	0 19	5 34	10 45	10 36
9	13 16	−13·5	54·2	14·8	184	112	46	22·2	1 21	1 34	6 16	10 59	10 45
10	14 01	−17·9	54·3	14·8	196	109	37	23·2	2 33	2 51	6 59	11 17	10 57
11	14 49	−21·7	54·5	14·9	209	105	28	24·2	3 45	4 09	7 46	11 39	11 14
12	15 40	−24·5	54·9	15·0	221	100	20	25·2	4 55	5 25	8 35	12 11	11 40
13	16 34	−26·3	55·4	15·1	233	94	12	26·2	6 01	6 35	9 28	12 54	12 20
14	17 30	−26·8	56·0	15·3	245	87	7	27·2	6 57	7 30	10 23	13 52	13 18
15	18 28	−25·9	56·6	15·4	257	79	2	28·2	7 40	8 10	11 19	15 03	14 34
16	19 25	−23·5	57·3	15·6	269	67	0	29·2	8 13	8 36	12 13	16 23	16 00
17	20 20	−19·8	57·9	15·8	282	259	0	0·5	8 37	8 54	13 06	17 47	17 31
18	21 14	−14·9	58·4	15·9	294	250	3	1·5	8 56	9 07	13 56	19 11	19 02
19	22 06	− 9·3	58·7	16·0	306	246	8	2·5	9 11	9 17	14 45	20 35	20 32
20	22 57	− 3·1	59·0	16·1	318	244	15	3·5	9 25	9 26	15 33	21 59	22 01
21	23 48	+ 3·3	59·2	16·1	330	244	24	4·5	9 40	9 35	16 22	23 23	23 32
22	0 39	+ 9·5	59·3	16·1	343	245	34	5·5	9 55	9 45	17 12	··	··
23	1 32	+15·2	59·2	16·1	355	248	45	6·5	10 14	9 58	18 05	0 49	1 04
24	2 28	+20·1	59·1	16·1	7	252	57	7·5	10 39	10 16	19 01	2 16	2 38
25	3 26	+23·9	59·0	16·1	19	258	68	8·5	11 12	10 43	20 00	3 41	4 10
26	4 27	+26·2	58·7	16·0	31	264	78	9·5	12 00	11 26	21 00	4 58	5 31
27	5 29	+26·8	58·4	15·9	43	271	86	10·5	13 02	12 29	22 00	6 01	6 35
28	6 30	+25·8	58·0	15·8	55	277	93	11·5	14 17	13 48	22 57	6 48	7 17
29	7 29	+23·2	57·6	15·7	68	283	98	12·5	15 37	15 15	23 50	7 21	7 44
30	8 24	+19·5	57·1	15·5	80	285	100	13·5	16 58	16 42	··	7 44	8 01
31	9 15	+14·8	56·5	15·4	92	117	100	14·5	18 16	18 06	0 39	8 02	8 13

MERCURY ☿

Day	R.A.	Dec. −	Diam.	Phase	Transit		Day	R.A.	Dec. −	Diam.	Phase	Transit	
	h m	°	″		h m			h m	°	″		h m	
1	17 05	20·8	7	62	10 26	Mercury is too close to the Sun for observation	16	18 26	23·4	5	85	10 48	Mercury is too close to the Sun for observation
4	17 18	21·5	6	69	10 28		19	18 44	23·5	5	88	10 56	
7	17 33	22·2	6	74	10 31		22	19 04	23·5	5	90	11 03	
10	17 50	22·7	6	79	10 36		25	19 23	23·2	5	92	11 11	
13	18 07	23·1	6	82	10 42		28	19 43	22·8	5	94	11 19	
16	18 26	23·4	5	85	10 48		31	20 04	22·1	5	95	11 28	

VENUS ♀   MARS ♂

Day	R.A.	Dec. −	Diam.	Phase	Transit	5° high W 52°	5° high W 56°	Day	R.A.	Dec. +	Diam.	Phase	Transit	5° high W 52°	5° high W 56°
	h m	°	″		h m	h m	h m		h m	°	″		h m	h m	h m
1	20 55	19·3	12	86	14 17	17 52	17 27	1	0 13	1·2	8	87	17 32	23 07	23 05
6	21 20	17·4	13	85	14 22	18 10	17 48	6	0 24	2·6	8	87	17 24	23 06	23 05
11	21 44	15·4	13	83	14 26	18 28	18 10	11	0 36	4·0	7	88	17 17	23 05	23 06
16	22 08	13·3	13	82	14 30	18 46	18 30	16	0 48	5·3	7	88	17 09	23 05	23 06
21	22 31	10·9	13	81	14 33	19 04	18 50	21	1 00	6·7	7	88	17 01	23 04	23 06
26	22 54	8·5	14	80	14 36	19 20	19 10	26	1 12	8·0	7	89	16 54	23 03	23 07
31	23 16	6·0	14	78	14 39	19 37	19 29	31	1 25	9·3	6	89	16 46	23 02	23 07

SUNRISE AND SUNSET (G.M.T.)

Day	London a.m.	London p.m.	Bristol a.m.	Bristol p.m.	Birmingham a.m.	Birmingham p.m.	Manchester a.m.	Manchester p.m.	Newcastle a.m.	Newcastle p.m.	Glasgow a.m.	Glasgow p.m.	Belfast a.m.	Belfast p.m.
	h m	h m	h m	h m	h m	h m	h m	h m	h m	h m	h m	h m	h m	h m
1	8 06	4 01	8 16	4 11	8 18	4 02	8 26	3 59	8 32	3 47	8 48	3 53	8 48	4 07
2	8 06	4 02	8 16	4 12	8 18	4 03	8 25	4 00	8 31	3 48	8 48	3 54	8 47	4 08
3	8 06	4 03	8 16	4 13	8 18	4 04	8 25	4 01	8 31	3 49	8 47	3 55	8 47	4 09
4	8 06	4 04	8 16	4 14	8 18	4 06	8 25	4 03	8 31	3 51	8 47	3 57	8 47	4 11
5	8 06	4 05	8 15	4 16	8 18	4 07	8 25	4 04	8 31	3 52	8 47	3 58	8 47	4 12
6	8 06	4 06	8 15	4 17	8 17	4 08	8 24	4 05	8 30	3 53	8 46	3 59	8 46	4 13
7	8 05	4 07	8 15	4 18	8 17	4 10	8 24	4 07	8 30	3 55	8 46	4 01	8 46	4 15
8	8 05	4 09	8 15	4 19	8 16	4 11	8 23	4 08	8 29	3 56	8 45	4 02	8 45	4 16
9	8 04	4 10	8 14	4 21	8 16	4 12	8 23	4 09	8 28	3 58	8 44	4 04	8 44	4 18
10	8 04	4 11	8 14	4 22	8 15	4 14	8 22	4 11	8 28	3 59	8 44	4 05	8 44	4 19
11	8 03	4 12	8 13	4 23	8 14	4 15	8 21	4 12	8 27	4 01	8 43	4 07	8 43	4 21
12	8 03	4 14	8 13	4 25	8 14	4 17	8 21	4 14	8 26	4 03	8 42	4 09	8 42	4 23
13	8 02	4 15	8 12	4 26	8 13	4 18	8 20	4 15	8 25	4 04	8 41	4 10	8 41	4 24
14	8 01	4 17	8 11	4 28	8 13	4 20	8 19	4 17	8 24	4 06	8 40	4 12	8 40	4 26
15	8 01	4 18	8 11	4 29	8 12	4 21	8 19	4 18	8 23	4 08	8 39	4 14	8 39	4 28
16	8 00	4 20	8 10	4 30	8 11	4 23	8 18	4 20	8 22	4 09	8 38	4 16	8 38	4 29
17	7 59	4 21	8 09	4 32	8 10	4 24	8 17	4 21	8 21	4 11	8 37	4 18	8 37	4 31
18	7 58	4 23	8 08	4 33	8 09	4 26	8 16	4 23	8 20	4 13	8 36	4 20	8 36	4 33
19	7 57	4 25	8 07	4 35	8 08	4 28	8 15	4 25	8 19	4 15	8 34	4 21	8 35	4 35
20	7 56	4 26	8 06	4 37	8 07	4 29	8 14	4 27	8 18	4 17	8 33	4 23	8 34	4 37
21	7 55	4 28	8 05	4 38	8 06	4 31	8 13	4 28	8 16	4 18	8 31	4 25	8 33	4 38
22	7 54	4 30	8 04	4 40	8 05	4 33	8 11	4 30	8 15	4 20	8 30	4 27	8 31	4 40
23	7 53	4 31	8 03	4 41	8 04	4 34	8 10	4 32	8 14	4 22	8 29	4 29	8 30	4 42
24	7 51	4 33	8 01	4 43	8 02	4 36	8 09	4 34	8 12	4 25	8 27	4 32	8 29	4 44
25	7 50	4 35	8 00	4 45	8 01	4 38	8 07	4 36	8 11	4 27	8 26	4 34	8 27	4 46
26	7 49	4 37	7 59	4 47	8 00	4 40	8 06	4 38	8 09	4 29	8 24	4 36	8 26	4 48
27	7 47	4 39	7 57	4 49	7 58	4 42	8 04	4 40	8 07	4 31	8 22	4 38	8 24	4 50
28	7 46	4 40	7 56	4 50	7 57	4 43	8 03	4 42	8 06	4 33	8 21	4 40	8 23	4 52
29	7 45	4 42	7 55	4 52	7 56	4 45	8 01	4 44	8 04	4 35	8 19	4 42	8 21	4 54
30	7 43	4 44	7 53	4 54	7 54	4 47	8 00	4 46	8 03	4 37	8 17	4 44	8 19	4 56
31	7 42	4 46	7 52	4 56	7 53	4 49	7 58	4 48	8 01	4 39	8 15	4 46	8 17	4 58

JUPITER ♃   SATURN ♄

Day	R.A.	Dec. −	5° high East 52°	5° high East 56°	Transit	R.A.	Dec. +	Transit	5° high West 52°	5° high West 56°
	h m	°	h m	h m	h m	h m	°	h m	h m	h m
1	17 27	22·8	7 42	8 17	10 46	3 55	18·2	21 12	4 18	4 31
11	17 36	22·9	7 13	7 48	10 17	3 53	18·2	20 31	3 37	3 49
21	17 45	23·0	6 44	7 19	9 46	3 52	18·2	19 51	2 56	3 09
31	17 54	23·1	6 14	6 49	9 16	3 51	18·2	19 11	2 17	2 29

Equatorial diameter of Jupiter 32″; of Saturn 20″.   Diameters of Saturn's rings 44″ and 18″.

URANUS ⛢   NEPTUNE ♆

Day	R.A.	Dec. −	10° high in East 52°	10° high in East 56°	Transit	R.A.	Dec. −	10° high in East 52°	10° high in East 56°	Transit
	h m	° ′	h m	h m	h m	h m	° ′	h m	h m	h m
1	13 07·7	6 29	2 10	2 23	6 28	16 09·7	19 24	6 44	7 23	9 29
11	13 08·4	6 33	1 32	1 45	5 49	16 11·0	19 27	6 06	6 46	8 51
21	13 08·6	6 34	0 53	1 06	5 10	16 12·1	19 29	5 28	6 08	8 13
31	13 08·5	6 33	0 13	0 27	4 30	16 13·0	19 31	4 50	5 30	7 34

Diameter 4″.   Diameter 2″.

Februa, Roman festival of Purification.

Sun's Longitude 330° ♓ 19d 13h

Day of Month	Week	
1	Tu.	Sir Stanley Matthews b. 1915
2	W.	**Purification.** Candlemas
3	Th.	Woodrow Wilson d. 1924. Sir Albert Richardson
4	F.	Carlyle d. 1881. Lord Shawcross b. 1902 [d. 1964
5	S.	Visct. Samuel d. 1963. H. M. Bateman d. 1970
6	☉	**Sexagesima.** QUEEN'S ACCESSION, 1952
7	M.	Charles Dickens b. 1812
8	Tu.	Sir Leslie O'Brien b. 1908. Sir Victor Gollancz d.
9	W.	Marquess of Exeter b. 1905 [1967
10	Th.	Harold Macmillan b. 1894. Edgar Wallace d. 1932
11	F.	E. W. Swanton b. 1907. Sir Vivian Fuchs b. 1908
12	S.	Kant b. 1804. Lily Langtry d. 1929
13	☉	**Quinquagesima.** Herbert Strudwick d. 1970
14	M.	Capt. Cook d. 1779. Kenneth Horne d. 1969
15	Tu.	Shrove Tuesday. Lord Dowding d. 1970
16	W.	**Ash Wednesday.** Lord Franks b. 1905
17	Th.	Albert, King of the Belgians d. 1934
18	F.	Luther d. 1546. Sir Arthur Bryant b. 1899
19	S.	PRINCE ANDREW BORN, 1960
20	☉	**1st Sunday in Lent.** Dr. R. W. Stopford b. 1901
21	M.	W. H. Auden b. 1907. Lord Florey d. 1968
22	Tu.	George Washington b. 1732. John Mills b. 1908
23	W.	Keats d. 1821. Sir Edward Elgar d. 1934
24	Th.	**St. Matthias**
25	F.	Thomas Moore d. 1852. Sir John Tenniel d. 1914
26	S.	Sir Christopher Wren d. 1723. W. R. Inge d. 1954
27	☉	**2nd Sunday in Lent.** Lawrence Durrell b. 1912
28	M.	Visct. Hailsham b. 1872**. Henry James d. 1916
29	Tu.	E. F. Benson d. 1940

(G.M.T.)

PHENOMENA

February 10d 23h Jupiter in conjunction with the Moon. Jupiter 3° N.

17d 07h Mercury in superior conjunction with the Sun.

18d 04h Venus in conjunction with the Moon. Venus 5° S.

20d 00h Mars in conjunction with the Moon. Mars 5° S.

21d 16h Saturn in conjunction with the Moon. Saturn 7° S.

CONSTELLATIONS

The following constellations are near the meridian at

	d	h		d	h
Jan.	1	24	Jan.	16	23
Feb.	1	22	Feb.	15	21
Mar.	1	20	Mar.	16	19

Draco (below the Pole), Camelopardus, Auriga, Taurus, Gemini, Orion, Canis Minor, Monoceros, Lepus, Canis Major and Puppis (Argo).

MINIMA OF ALGOL

d	h	d	h
1	15	15	23
4	12	18	20
7	09	21	17
10	06	24	14
13	03	27	11

MONTHLY NOTES

Feb. 1. Pheasant and partridge shooting ends.
    16. Lent begins (ends midnight April 1). Moslem New Year (A.H. 1392).

QUARTER DAYS (England, Wales and Northern Ireland)

Lady Day	March 25	*Michaelmas*	September 29
Midsummer	June 24	*Christmas*	December 25

SCOTTISH TERM DAYS

Candlemas	February 2	*Lammas*	August 1
Whitsunday	May 15	*Martinmas*	November 11

Removal Terms are May 28 and November 28.

NATIONAL DAYS.—*Feb.* 4, Ceylon; 6, New Zealand; 18, The Gambia, Nepal; 25, Kuwait; 27, Dominican Republic.

** Centenary.

(G.M.T.)

PHASES OF THE MOON

	d	h	m
☾ Last Quarter	7	11	11
● New Moon	15	00	29
☽ First Quarter	21	17	20
○ Full Moon	29	03	12

	d	h
Apogee (404,580 kilometres)	6	01
Perigee (365,170 ,,)	17	19

Mean Longitude of Ascending Node on February 1, 305°.

s.d. 16'·2

Day	Right Ascension	Dec. —	Equation of Time	Rise 52°	Rise 56°	Transit	Set 52°	Set 56°	Sidereal Time	Transit of First Point of Aries (G.M.T.)
	h m s	° '	m s	h m	h m	h m	h m	h m	h m s	h m s
1	20 54 44	17 25	−13 29	7 42	7 58	12 14	16 46	16 30	8 41 15	15 16 15
2	20 58 49	17 08	−13 37	7 41	7 56	12 14	16 48	16 33	8 45 11	15 12 19
3	21 02 53	16 51	−13 45	7 39	7 54	12 14	16 49	16 35	8 49 08	15 08 23
4	21 06 56	16 33	−13 52	7 38	7 52	12 14	16 51	16 37	8 53 04	15 04 27
5	21 10 59	16 15	−13 58	7 36	7 50	12 14	16 53	16 39	8 57 00	15 00 31
6	21 15 01	15 57	−14 03	7 34	7 48	12 14	16 55	16 41	9 00 57	14 56 35
7	21 19 02	15 39	−14 08	7 33	7 46	12 14	16 57	16 44	9 04 54	14 52 39
8	21 23 02	15 20	−14 11	7 31	7 44	12 14	16 59	16 46	9 08 51	14 48 43
9	21 27 01	15 02	−14 14	7 29	7 42	12 14	17 01	16 48	9 12 47	14 44 48
10	21 31 00	14 42	−14 17	7 27	7 40	12 14	17 02	16 50	9 16 44	14 40 52
11	21 34 58	14 23	−14 18	7 25	7 37	12 14	17 04	16 52	9 20 40	14 36 56
12	21 38 55	14 03	−14 18	7 24	7 35	12 14	17 06	16 55	9 24 37	14 33 00
13	21 42 52	13 44	−14 18	7 22	7 33	12 14	17 08	16 57	9 28 33	14 29 04
14	21 46 47	13 24	−14 17	7 20	7 31	12 14	17 10	16 59	9 32 30	14 25 08
15	21 50 42	13 03	−14 16	7 18	7 29	12 14	17 12	17 01	9 36 26	14 21 12
16	21 54 36	12 43	−14 13	7 16	7 26	12 14	17 14	17 03	9 40 23	14 17 16
17	21 58 30	12 22	−14 10	7 14	7 24	12 14	17 15	17 05	9 44 20	14 13 20
18	22 02 22	12 01	−14 06	7 12	7 22	12 14	17 17	17 08	9 48 16	14 09 24
19	22 06 14	11 40	−14 02	7 10	7 19	12 14	17 19	17 10	9 52 13	14 05 28
20	22 10 06	11 19	−13 57	7 08	7 17	12 14	17 21	17 12	9 56 09	14 01 33
21	22 13 56	10 57	−13 51	7 06	7 15	12 14	17 23	17 14	10 00 06	13 57 37
22	22 17 46	10 36	−13 44	7 04	7 12	12 14	17 25	17 16	10 04 02	13 53 41
23	22 21 35	10 14	−13 37	7 02	7 10	12 14	17 27	17 19	10 07 59	13 49 45
24	22 25 24	9 52	−13 29	7 00	7 07	12 13	17 28	17 21	10 11 55	13 45 49
25	22 29 12	9 30	−13 20	6 58	7 05	12 13	17 30	17 23	10 15 52	13 41 53
26	22 32 59	9 08	−13 11	6 55	7 03	12 13	17 32	17 25	10 19 49	13 37 57
27	22 36 46	8 45	−13 01	6 53	7 00	12 13	17 34	17 27	10 23 45	13 34 01
28	22 40 32	8 23	−12 51	6 51	6 58	12 13	17 36	17 29	10 27 42	13 30 05
29	22 44 18	8 00	−12 40	6 49	6 55	12 13	17 38	17 31	10 31 38	13 26 09

Duration of Civil (C), Nautical (N), and Astronomical (A), Twilight (in minutes)

Lat. °	Feb. 1 C	N	A	Feb. 11 C	N	A	Feb. 21 C	N	A	Feb. 28 C	N	A
52	37	77	117	35	75	114	34	74	113	34	73	112
56	41	86	130	39	83	126	38	81	125	38	81	124

ASTRONOMICAL NOTES

MERCURY is unsuitably placed for observation, superior conjunction occurring on the 17th.

VENUS is a brilliant evening star, magnitude −3·6, visible for several hours in the western sky after sunset. It is moving rapidly northwards during the month so that it will be seen low above the W.S.W. horizon before setting, at the beginning of the month but by the end of the month the corresponding position will be W.N.W. The crescent Moon will be near Venus on the evenings of the 17th and 18th.

MARS is an evening star, magnitude +1·1, still visible in the western sky until about 23ʰ each evening. During the month Mars moves from Pisces to Aries.

JUPITER is a morning star, magnitude −1·5, visible low in the S.E. sky before dawn. The old crescent Moon is near Jupiter on the morning of the 11th.

SATURN is a prominent evening star, magnitude +0·3, in the constellation of Taurus. The rings of Saturn are a beautiful sight even in small telescopes and now their width extends just beyond the polar limbs of the planet itself. Also visible in such instruments is Saturn's largest satellite, Titan, magnitude +8½.

ZODIACAL LIGHT. The evening cone may be observed in the western sky after the end of twilight from the beginning of the month to the 16th. This faint phenomenon is only visible in the absence of both moonlight and artificial lighting.

THE MOON

Day	R.A.	Dec.	Hor. Par.	Semi-diam.	Sun's Co-long.	P.A. of Bright Limb	Phase	Age	Rise 52°	Rise 56°	Transit	Set 52°	Set 56°
	h m	°	'	'	°	°		d	h m	h m	h m	h m	h m
1	10 03	+ 9·6	55·9	15·2	104	117	97	15·5	19 30	19 26	1 25	8 16	8 22
2	10 49	+ 4·1	55·4	15·1	116	118	93	16·5	20 43	20 43	2 07	8 28	8 30
3	11 33	− 1·4	54·9	15·0	128	118	88	17·5	21 53	21 59	2 49	8 40	8 37
4	12 16	− 6·8	54·5	14·9	140	117	81	18·5	23 04	23 15	3 29	8 52	8 45
5	13 00	−11·9	54·3	14·8	152	115	72	19·5	..		4 10	9 05	8 53
6	13 45	−16·5	54·2	14·8	165	113	64	20·5	0 15	0 31	4 53	9 21	9 04
7	14 32	−20·5	54·3	14·8	177	109	54	21·5	1 26	1 48	5 38	9 41	9 18
8	15 22	−23·6	54·5	14·9	189	104	45	22·5	2 37	3 05	6 26	10 08	9 40
9	16 14	−25·8	55·0	15 0	201	99	36	23·5	3 45	4 17	7 16	10 45	10 12
10	17 09	−26·8	55·5	15·1	213	93	26	24·5	4 45	5 19	8 10	11 35	11 01
11	18 05	−26·4	56·3	15·3	226	87	18	25·5	5 33	6 05	9 04	12 40	12 08
12	19 02	−24·6	57·0	15·5	238	82	11	26·5	6 10	6 37	9 59	13 56	13 30
13	19 58	−21·4	57·8	15·8	250	77	5	27·5	6 38	6 59	10 53	15 19	15 00
14	20 54	−16·9	58·6	16·0	262	76	1	28·5	7 00	7 14	11 46	16 45	16 33
15	21 47	−11·5	59·2	16·1	274	152	0	29·5	7 17	7 25	12 36	18 11	18 05
16	22 40	− 5·3	59·7	16·3	286	236	1	1·0	7 32	7 35	13 26	19 38	19 38
17	23 32	+ 1·2	60·0	16·3	299	239	5	2·0	7 47	7 44	14 16	21 05	21 11
18	0 24	+ 7·7	60·0	16·4	311	241	12	3·0	8 02	7 54	15 07	22 33	22 45
19	1 18	+13·8	59·9	16·3	323	244	21	4·0	8 21	8 06	16 00	..	..
20	2 14	+19·0	59·6	16·2	335	248	31	5·0	8 43	8 23	16 56	0 02	0 21
21	3 13	+23·1	59·2	16·1	347	254	42	6·0	9 14	8 47	17 55	1 29	1 55
22	4 13	+25·7	58·8	16·0	0	260	53	7·0	9 57	9 25	18 55	2 49	3 21
23	5 15	+26·8	58·3	15·9	12	267	64	8·0	10 54	10 20	19 54	3 56	4 29
24	6 15	+26·1	57·8	15·7	24	273	74	9·0	12 04	11 33	20 51	4 46	5 17
25	7 14	+24·0	57·2	15·6	36	279	83	10·0	13 21	12 57	21 44	5 23	5 48
26	8 09	+20·6	56·7	15·5	48	283	90	11·0	14 40	14 22	22 34	5 49	6 08
27	9 00	+16·3	56·3	15·3	60	285	95	12·0	15 58	15 46	23 20	6 08	6 21
28	9 48	+11·3	55·8	15·2	73	282	99	13·0	17 13	17 07	..	6 23	6 31
29	10 34	+ 6·0	55·3	15·1	85	230	100	14·0	18 26	18 24	0 03	6 36	6 40

MERCURY ☿

Day	R.A.	Dec. −	Diam.	Phase	Transit	Day	R.A.	Dec. −	Diam.	Phase	Transit
	h m	°	"		h m		h m	°	"		h m
1	20 10	21·8	5	95	11 30	16	21 54	15·0	5	100	12 15
4	20 31	20·9	5	97	11 39	19	22 14	12·9	5	100	12 24
7	20 51	19·7	5	98	11 48	22	22 35	10·7	5	99	12 33
10	21 12	18·4	5	99	11 57	25	22 56	8·3	5	97	12 42
13	21 33	16·8	5	99	12 06	28	23 16	5·8	5	94	12 50
16	21 54	15·0	5	100	12 15	31	23 36	3·1	5	88	12 58

Mercury is too close to the Sun for observation (left)

Mercury is too close to the Sun for observation (right)

VENUS ♀

Day	R.A.	Dec.	Diam.	Phase	Transit	5° high W 52°	56°
	h m	°	"		h m	h m	h m
1	23 20	− 5·5	14	78	14 39	19 40	19 32
6	23 42	− 2·9	15	76	14 41	19 56	19 51
11	0 03	− 0·3	15	75	14 43	20 11	20 08
16	0 25	+ 2·4	15	73	14 45	20 27	20 26
21	0 46	+ 5·0	16	72	14 46	20 41	20 42
26	1 07	+ 7·5	16	70	14 48	20 56	20 59
31	1 28	+10·0	17	68	14 49	21 10	21 15

MARS ♂

Day	R.A.	Dec. +	Diam.	Phase	Transit	5° high W 52°	56°
	h m	°	"		h m	h m	h m
1	1 27	9·6	6	89	16 45	23 02	23 07
6	1 39	10·9	6	89	16 37	23 02	23 07
11	1 52	12·1	6	90	16 30	23 01	23 08
16	2 04	13·3	6	90	16 23	23 00	23 08
21	2 17	14·5	6	90	16 16	22 59	23 08
26	2 30	15·6	6	91	16 09	22 59	23 09
31	2 43	16·6	5	91	16 03	22 58	23 09

SUNRISE AND SUNSET (G.M.T.)

Day	London a.m. h m	London p.m. h m	Bristol a.m. h m	Bristol p.m. h m	Birmingham a.m. h m	Birmingham p.m. h m	Manchester a.m. h m	Manchester p.m. h m	Newcastle a.m. h m	Newcastle p.m. h m	Glasgow a.m. h m	Glasgow p.m. h m	Belfast a.m. h m	Belfast p.m. h m
1	7 41	4 48	7 50	4 58	7 52	4 51	7 57	4 50	8 00	4 41	8 14	4 48	8 16	5 00
2	7 39	4 50	7 49	5 00	7 50	4 53	7 55	4 52	7 58	4 43	8 12	4 51	8 14	5 03
3	7 38	4 51	7 47	5 01	7 48	4 55	7 53	4 54	7 56	4 45	8 10	4 53	8 12	5 05
4	7 37	4 53	7 46	5 03	7 46	4 57	7 51	4 56	7 54	4 47	8 08	4 55	8 10	5 07
5	7 35	4 55	7 44	5 05	7 44	4 59	7 49	4 58	7 52	4 49	8 06	4 57	8 08	5 09
6	7 33	4 57	7 42	5 07	7 43	5 01	7 48	5 00	7 50	4 51	8 04	4 59	8 07	5 11
7	7 32	4 58	7 41	5 08	7 41	5 03	7 46	5 02	7 48	4 54	8 02	5 02	8 05	5 13
8	7 30	5 00	7 39	5 10	7 39	5 05	7 44	5 04	7 46	4 56	8 00	5 04	8 03	5 15
9	7 28	5 02	7 38	5 12	7 37	5 07	7 42	5 06	7 44	4 58	7 58	5 06	8 01	5 17
10	7 26	5 04	7 36	5 14	7 35	5 08	7 40	5 07	7 42	5 00	7 56	5 08	7 59	5 19
11	7 24	5 05	7 34	5 15	7 33	5 10	7 38	5 09	7 40	5 02	7 54	5 10	7 57	5 21
12	7 23	5 07	7 32	5 17	7 32	5 12	7 37	5 11	7 38	5 04	7 52	5 12	7 55	5 23
13	7 21	5 09	7 31	5 19	7 30	5 14	7 35	5 13	7 36	5 06	7 50	5 14	7 53	5 25
14	7 19	5 11	7 29	5 21	7 28	5 16	7 33	5 15	7 34	5 08	7 48	5 16	7 51	5 27
15	7 17	5 13	7 27	5 23	7 26	5 18	7 31	5 17	7 32	5 10	7 46	5 18	7 49	5 29
16	7 15	5 15	7 25	5 25	7 24	5 20	7 29	5 19	7 29	5 12	7 43	5 20	7 47	5 31
17	7 13	5 16	7 23	5 26	7 22	5 21	7 27	5 21	7 27	5 14	7 41	5 22	7 45	5 33
18	7 11	5 18	7 21	5 28	7 20	5 23	7 25	5 23	7 25	5 17	7 39	5 25	7 43	5 35
19	7 09	5 20	7 19	5 30	7 18	5 25	7 22	5 25	7 22	5 19	7 36	5 27	7 40	5 37
20	7 07	5 22	7 17	5 32	7 16	5 27	7 20	5 27	7 20	5 21	7 34	5 29	7 38	5 39
21	7 05	5 24	7 15	5 34	7 14	5 29	7 18	5 29	7 18	5 23	7 32	5 31	7 36	5 41
22	7 03	5 26	7 13	5 36	7 12	5 31	7 16	5 31	7 16	5 25	7 29	5 33	7 33	5 43
23	7 01	5 28	7 11	5 38	7 10	5 33	7 14	5 33	7 14	5 27	7 27	5 36	7 31	5 46
24	6 59	5 29	7 09	5 39	7 08	5 34	7 11	5 35	7 11	5 29	7 24	5 38	7 28	5 48
25	6 57	5 31	7 07	5 41	7 06	5 36	7 09	5 37	7 09	5 31	7 22	5 40	7 26	5 50
26	6 54	5 33	7 04	5 43	7 03	5 38	7 07	5 39	7 07	5 33	7 20	5 42	7 24	5 52
27	6 52	5 35	7 02	5 45	7 01	5 40	7 04	5 41	7 04	5 35	7 17	5 44	7 21	5 54
28	6 50	5 37	7 00	5 47	6 59	5 42	7 02	5 43	7 02	5 37	7 15	5 46	7 19	5 56
29	6 48	5 39	6 58	5 49	6 57	5 44	7 00	5 45	6 59	5 39	7 12	5 48	7 17	5 58

JUPITER ♃　　　　SATURN ♄

Day	R.A. h m	Dec. − °	5° high East 52° h m	5° high East 56° h m	Transit h m	R.A. h m	Dec. + °	Transit h m	5° high West 52° h m	5° high West 56° h m
1	17 55	23·1	6 11	6 46	9 13	3 51	18·2	19 07	2 13	2 25
11	18 03	23·1	5 40	6 15	8 42	3 52	18·3	18 28	1 34	1 47
21	18 11	23·1	5 08	5 43	8 10	3 53	18·4	17 50	0 57	1 09
31	18 18	23·0	4 35	5 10	7 37	3 55	18·5	17 13	0 20	0 33

Equatorial diameter of Jupiter 34″; of Saturn 19″. Diameters of Saturn's rings 42″ and 17″.

URANUS ♅　　　　NEPTUNE ♆

Day	R.A. h m	Dec. − ° ′	10° high in East 52° h m	10° high in East 56° h m	Transit h m	R.A. h m	Dec. − ° ′	10° high in East 52° h m	10° high in East 56° h m	Transit h m
1	13 08·5	6 33	0 09	0 23	4 27	16 13·1	19 31	4 47	5 26	7 31
11	13 08·0	6 30	23 25	23 39	3 47	16 13·8	19 33	4 08	4 48	6 52
21	13 07·3	6 25	22 45	22 58	3 07	16 14·3	19 33	3 29	4 09	6 13
31	13 06·2	6 18	22 04	22 17	2 26	16 14·5	19 33	2 50	3 30	5 34

Diameter 4″.　　　　Diameter 2″.

Day of Month	Week		

Mars, Roman god of battle.

Sun's Longitude 0° ♈ 20ᵈ 12ʰ

1	W.	St. David's Day. Michael Flanders b. 1922
2	Th.	John Wesley d. 1791. Horace Walpole d. 1797
3	F.	Sir Sidney Lee d. 1926
4	S.	Dunkirk Pact signed 1947
5	☉	3rd Sunday in Lent. James I d. 1625
6	M.	Cologne captured 1945 [1930
7	Tu.	Reginald Maudling b. 1917. Earl of Snowdon b.
8	W.	William III d. 1702. Sir Thomas Beecham d. 1961
9	Th.	V. M. Molotov b. 1890
10	F.	Prince Edward born, 1964. Mazzini d. 1872**
11	S.	Harold Wilson b. 1916. Earl Beatty d. 1935
12	☉	4th Sunday in Lent. Sun Yat Sen d. 1925
13	M.	Sir Frank Worrell d. 1967 [1965
14	Tu.	Karl Marx d. 1883. Sir Frederick Browning d.
15	W.	Lord Salter b. 1881. Visct. Chandos b. 1893
16	Th.	Lord Beveridge d. 1963. Thomas E. Dewey d. 1971
17	F.	St. Patrick's Day. Bobby Jones b. 1902
18	S.	Sir Robert Walpole d. 1745
19	☉	5th Sunday in Lent. Earl of Balfour d. 1930
20	M.	Sir Isaac Newton d. 1727. Sir Michael Redgrave b.
21	Tu.	Aboukir 1801 [1908
22	W.	Goethe d. 1832. Nicholas Monsarrat b. 1910
23	Th.	Roger Bannister b. 1929. Visct. Maugham d. 1958
24	F.	Queen Mary d. 1953. J. M. Synge d. 1909
25	S.	Annunciation. Lady Day
26	☉	6th Sunday in Lent. Palm Sunday
27	M.	James Callaghan b. 1912. Capt. Scott d. 1912
28	Tu.	Dame Flora Robson b. 1902. Edmond Segrave d.
29	W.	Hilary Law Sittings End [1971
30	Th.	Maundy Thursday. Visct. Radcliffe b. 1899
31	F.	Good Friday

(G.M.T.)
PHENOMENA
March 9ᵈ 16ʰ Jupiter in conjunction with the Moon. Jupiter 3° N.

14ᵈ 10ʰ Mercury at greatest eastern elongation (18°).

16ᵈ 20ʰ Mercury in conjunction with the Moon. Mercury 2° S.

18ᵈ 18ʰ Venus in conjunction with the Moon. Venus 3° S.

19ᵈ 14ʰ Mars in conjunction with the Moon. Mars 4° S.

20ᵈ 01ʰ Saturn in conjunction with the Moon. Saturn 6° S.

20ᵈ 12ʰ Vernal Equinox.

21ᵈ 05ʰ Pluto at opposition.

31ᵈ 12ʰ Mercury in inferior conjunction with the Sun.

CONSTELLATIONS
The following constellations are near the meridian at

	d	h		d	h
Feb.	1	24	Feb.	15	23
Mar.	1	22	Mar.	16	21
April	1	20	April	15	19

Cepheus (below the Pole), Camelopardus, Lynx, Gemini, Cancer, Leo, Canis Minor, Hydra, Monoceros, Canis Major and Puppis (Argo).

MINIMA OF ALGOL

d	h	d	h
1	07	18	12
4	04	21	09
7	01	24	06
9	22	27	03
12	19	30	00
15	15		

(G.M.T.)
PHASES OF THE MOON

	d	h	m
☾ Last Quarter	8	07	05
● New Moon	15	11	35
☽ First Quarter	22	02	12
○ Full Moon	29	20	05

	d	h
Apogee (405,340 kilometres)	4	19
Perigee (360,060 ,,)	16	21

Mean Longitude of Ascending Node on March 1, 303°.

Summer Time in 1972 (see p. 142).—Begins: March 19 at 2 a.m. G.M.T. Ends: October 29 at 2 a.m. G.M.T.

MONTHLY NOTES
Mar. 1. Auditors of Boroughs, Eng. and W., to be elected.
    17. Bank Holiday in Northern Ireland.
    25. Lady Day. Quarter Day. Accounts of Local Government Authorities, Eng. and W., to be made up to 31st.
    31. Financial Year 1971–72 ends.

National Days.—*Mar.* 1, Wales (*see above*); 3, Morocco; 6, Ghana; 11, Denmark; 12, Mauritius; 17, Irish Republic; 23, Pakistan; 25, Greece.

** Centenary

Day	Right Ascension	Dec.	Equation of Time	Rise 52°	Rise 56°	Transit	Set 52°	Set 56°	Sidereal Time	Transit of First Point of Aries (G.M.T.)
	h m s	° '	m s	h m	h m	h m	h m	h m	h m s	h m s
1	22 48 03	−7 38	−12 28	6 47	6 53	12 12	17 39	17 34	10 35 35	13 22 13
2	22 51 48	−7 15	−12 17	6 45	6 50	12 12	17 41	17 36	10 39 31	13 18 18
3	22 55 32	−6 52	−12 04	6 42	6 48	12 12	17 43	17 38	10 43 28	13 14 22
4	22 59 15	−6 29	−11 51	6 40	6 45	12 12	17 45	17 40	10 47 24	13 10 26
5	23 02 59	−6 06	−11 38	6 38	6 42	12 12	17 46	17 42	10 51 21	13 06 30
6	23 06 42	−5 43	−11 24	6 36	6 40	12 11	17 48	17 44	10 55 17	13 02 34
7	23 10 24	−5 19	−11 10	6 33	6 37	12 11	17 50	17 46	10 59 14	12 58 38
8	23 14 06	−4 56	−10 55	6 31	6 35	12 11	17 52	17 48	11 03 11	12 54 42
9	23 17 48	−4 32	−10 41	6 29	6 32	12 11	17 53	17 50	11 07 07	12 50 46
10	23 21 29	−4 09	−10 25	6 27	6 30	12 10	17 55	17 52	11 11 04	12 46 50
11	23 25 10	−3 45	−10 10	6 24	6 27	12 10	17 57	17 55	11 15 00	12 42 54
12	23 28 51	−3 22	−9 54	6 22	6 24	12 10	17 59	17 57	11 18 57	12 38 58
13	23 32 31	−2 58	−9 38	6 20	6 22	12 09	18 00	17 59	11 22 53	12 35 03
14	23 36 11	−2 35	−9 21	6 17	6 19	12 09	18 02	18 01	11 26 50	12 31 07
15	23 39 51	−2 11	−9 05	6 15	6 16	12 09	18 04	18 03	11 30 46	12 27 11
16	23 43 31	−1 47	−8 48	6 13	6 14	12 09	18 06	18 05	11 34 43	12 23 15
17	23 47 10	−1 23	−8 31	6 11	6 11	12 08	18 07	18 07	11 38 40	12 19 19
18	23 50 49	−1 00	−8 13	6 08	6 09	12 08	18 09	18 09	11 42 36	12 15 23
19	23 54 28	−0 36	−7 56	6 06	6 06	12 08	18 11	18 11	11 46 33	12 11 27
20	23 58 07	−0 12	−7 38	6 04	6 03	12 07	18 13	18 13	11 50 29	12 07 31
21	0 01 46	+0 12	−7 20	6 01	6 01	12 07	18 14	18 15	11 54 26	12 03 35
22	0 05 25	+0 35	−7 02	5 59	5 58	12 07	18 16	18 17	11 58 22	11 59 39
23	0 09 03	+0 59	−6 44	5 57	5 55	12 07	18 18	18 19	12 02 19	11 55 44
24	0 12 41	+1 23	−6 26	5 54	5 53	12 06	18 20	18 21	12 06 15	11 51 48
25	0 16 20	+1 46	−6 08	5 52	5 50	12 06	18 21	18 23	12 10 12	11 47 52
26	0 19 58	+2 10	−5 50	5 50	5 48	12 06	18 23	18 25	12 14 09	11 43 56
27	0 23 36	+2 33	−5 31	5 47	5 45	12 05	18 25	18 27	12 18 05	11 40 00
28	0 27 15	+2 57	−5 13	5 45	5 42	12 05	18 26	18 29	12 22 02	11 36 04
29	0 30 53	+3 20	−4 55	5 43	5 39	12 05	18 28	18 31	12 25 58	11 32 08
30	0 34 31	+3 43	−4 36	5 41	5 37	12 04	18 30	18 34	12 29 55	11 28 12
31	0 38 10	+4 07	−4 18	5 38	5 34	12 04	18 31	18 36	12 33 51	11 24 16

THE SUN s.d. 16'.1

Duration of Civil (C), Nautical (N), and Astronomical (A), Twilight (in minutes)

Lat. °	Mar. 1 C	N	A	Mar. 11 C	N	A	Mar. 21 C	N	A	Mar. 31 C	N	A
52	34	73	112	34	73	113	34	74	116	34	76	120
56	38	81	124	37	80	125	37	82	129	38	84	136

ASTRONOMICAL NOTES

MERCURY is visible as an evening star from the beginning of the month to about the 25th, magnitude −1·2 to +2·0. It may be seen above the western horizon around the end of evening civil twilight. Under very good conditions on the evening of the 16th the thin crescent Moon, only 31 hours old, may be seen passing about 2° N. of Mercury. For observers in the British Isles this appearance of Mercury is the *only* evening one during the year.

VENUS is a brilliant evening star, magnitude −3·8, visible in the western sky for several hours after sunset. On the evening of the 18th the crescent Moon passes 3° N. of Venus.

MARS is an evening star, magnitude +1·5. The combined effect of its northward motion and decreasing elongation from the Sun means that it is still visible until nearly 23ʰ every evening. During the month Mars passes from Aries into Taurus.

JUPITER is a morning star, magnitude −1·7 and by the end of the month is visible by 03ʰ, low above the S.E. horizon. The Moon, one day after Last Quarter, is near on the morning of the 9th.

SATURN is a prominent evening star, magnitude +0·4, in the constellation of Taurus. Mars is approaching Saturn and passes N. of it on April 1st.

ZODIACAL LIGHT. The evening cone may be observed in the western sky after the end of twilight from the beginning of the month to the 16th. This faint phenomenon is only visible in the absence of both moonlight and artificial lighting.

THE MOON

Day	R.A.	Dec.	Hor. Par.	Semi-diam.	Sun's Co-long.	P.A. of Bright Limb	Phase	Age	Rise 52°	Rise 56°	Transit	Set 52°	Set 56°
	h m	°	′	′	°	°		d	h m	h m	h m	h m	h m
1	11 19	+ 0·4	54·9	15·0	97	134	99	15·0	19 37	19 40	0 44	6 48	6 47
2	12 02	− 5·0	54·6	14·9	109	125	97	16·0	20 48	20 56	1 25	7 00	6 54
3	12 46	− 10·2	54·3	14·8	121	121	92	17·0	21 58	22 12	2 06	7 13	7 02
4	13 31	− 15·0	54·1	14·8	133	117	86	18·0	23 10	23 29	2 48	7 27	7 12
5	14 17	− 19·2	54·1	14·7	145	113	79	19·0	··	··	3 32	7 46	7 25
6	15 06	− 22·6	54·2	14·8	158	108	71	20·0	0 21	0 46	4 19	8 10	7 44
7	15 56	− 25·1	54·5	14·8	170	103	62	21·0	1 29	1 59	5 07	8 42	8 11
8	16 49	− 26·4	54·9	15·0	182	97	53	22·0	2 31	3 05	5 59	9 25	8 51
9	17 44	− 26·6	55·5	15·1	194	91	43	23·0	3 24	3 57	6 52	10 22	9 49
10	18 40	− 25·3	56·2	15·3	206	85	33	24·0	4 05	4 34	7 46	11 32	11 03
11	19 35	− 22·8	57·1	15·6	218	80	24	25·0	4 37	5 00	8 39	12 50	12 28
12	20 30	− 18·9	58·0	15·8	231	76	15	26·0	5 01	5 18	9 31	14 13	13 58
13	21 24	− 13·9	58·9	16·1	243	74	8	27·0	5 20	5 31	10 22	15 39	15 30
14	22 17	− 8·0	59·8	16·3	255	76	3	28·0	5 36	5 42	11 13	17 06	17 03
15	23 10	− 1·6	60·4	16·5	267	95	0	29·0	5 52	5 52	12 04	18 34	18 37
16	0 03	+ 5·1	60·8	16·6	279	216	1	0·5	6 09	6 02	12 56	20 05	20 14
17	0 58	+ 11·5	60·9	16·6	292	235	4	1·5	6 25	6 14	13 50	21 36	21 53
18	1 55	+ 17·2	60·7	16·5	304	242	9	2·5	6 47	6 29	14 47	23 08	23 31
19	2 55	+ 21·9	60·3	16·4	316	249	17	3·5	7 16	6 51	15 46	··	··
20	3 57	+ 25·0	59·7	16·3	328	256	27	4·5	7 55	7 25	16 48	0 33	1 03
21	5 00	+ 26·5	59·0	16·1	341	263	38	5·5	8 49	8 15	17 48	1 47	2 20
22	6 01	+ 26·2	58·2	15·9	353	270	49	6·5	9 56	9 24	18 47	2 44	3 15
23	7 01	+ 24·4	57·5	15·7	5	276	60	7·5	11 11	10 45	19 41	3 24	3 51
24	7 56	+ 21·4	56·8	15·5	17	281	70	8·5	12 29	12 10	20 31	3 53	4 14
25	8 48	+ 17·3	56·2	15·3	29	285	79	9·5	13 47	13 33	21 18	4 14	4 29
26	9 37	+ 12·5	55·7	15·2	41	287	86	10·5	15 01	14 53	22 01	4 30	4 40
27	10 22	+ 7·3	55·2	15·0	54	287	93	11·5	16 14	16 11	22 43	4 44	4 49
28	11 07	+ 1·9	54·8	14·9	66	284	97	12·5	17 24	17 26	23 23	4 56	4 57
29	11 50	− 3·5	54·5	14·8	78	269	99	13·5	18 35	18 41	··	5 08	5 04
30	12 34	− 8·7	54·2	14·8	90	182	100	14·5	19 45	19 57	0 04	5 21	5 12
31	13 18	− 13·6	54·1	14·7	102	133	99	15·5	20 56	21 13	0 46	5 35	5 22

MERCURY ☿

Day	R.A.	Dec.	Diam.	Phase	Transit	5° high W 52°	5° high W 56°	Day	R.A.	Dec. +	Diam.	Phase	Transit	5° high W 52°	5° high W 56°
	h m	°			h m	h m	h m		h m	°			h m	h m	h m
1	23 30	− 4·0	5	90	12 56	18 06	18 00	16	0 46	7·6	8	38	13 11	19 19	19 22
4	23 49	− 1·3	6	84	13 03	18 28	18 24	19	0 52	8·8	8	26	13 04	19 16	19 20
7	0 07	+ 1·3	6	74	13 09	18 47	18 45	22	0 53	9·3	9	16	12 53	19 07	19 11
10	0 23	+ 3·8	6	64	13 13	19 03	19 03	25	0 51	9·2	10	8	12 37	18 50	18 54
13	0 37	+ 5·9	7	50	13 14	19 14	19 16	28	0 45	8·3	11	2	12 19	18 27	18 30
16	0 46	+ 7·6	8	38	13 11	19 19	19 22	31	0 37	7·2	11		12 00	18 00	18 03

VENUS ♀

MARS ♂

Day	R.A.	Dec. +	Diam.	Phase	Transit	5° high W 52°	5° high W 56°	Day	R.A.	Dec. +	Diam.	Phase	Transit	5° high W 52°	5° high W 56°
	h m	°	″		h m	h m	h m		h m	°	″		h m	h m	h m
1	1 24	9·5	17	68	14 49	21 07	21 12	1	2 40	16·4	5	91	16 04	22 58	23 09
6	1 45	11·9	18	66	14 50	21 21	21 28	6	2 54	17·5	5	92	15 57	22 57	23 05
11	2 06	14·3	18	64	14 52	21 35	21 44	11	3 07	18·4	5	92	15 51	22 56	23 0
16	2 28	16·4	19	62	14 53	21 49	22 00	16	3 20	19·3	5	92	15 45	22 55	23 0
21	2 49	18·5	20	60	14 55	22 02	22 15	21	3 34	20·2	5	93	15 38	22 53	23 0
26	3 10	20·3	21	58	14 56	22 14	22 29	26	3 47	20·9	5	93	15 32	22 52	23 0
31	3 32	22·0	22	55	14 58	22 25	22 42	31	4 01	21·7	5	93	15 26	22 50	23 0

SUNRISE AND SUNSET (G.M.T.)

Day	London a.m. h m	London p.m. h m	Bristol a.m. h m	Bristol p.m. h m	Birmingham a.m. h m	Birmingham p.m. h m	Manchester a.m. h m	Manchester p.m. h m	Newcastle a.m. h m	Newcastle p.m. h m	Glasgow a.m. h m	Glasgow p.m. h m	Belfast a.m. h m	Belfast p.m. h m
1	6 46	5 40	6 56	5 50	6 55	5 46	6 58	5 47	6 57	5 42	7 10	5 51	7 15	6 00
2	6 44	5 42	6 54	5 52	6 52	5 47	6 55	5 48	6 54	5 43	7 07	5 53	7 12	6 01
3	6 42	5 44	6 51	5 54	6 50	5 49	6 53	5 50	6 52	5 45	7 05	5 55	7 10	6 03
4	6 40	5 46	6 49	5 56	6 47	5 51	6 50	5 52	6 49	5 47	7 02	5 57	7 07	6 05
5	6 38	5 47	6 47	5 57	6 45	5 53	6 48	5 54	6 47	5 49	6 59	5 59	7 05	6 07
6	6 36	5 49	6 45	5 59	6 43	5 55	6 46	5 56	6 45	5 51	6 57	6 01	7 03	6 09
7	6 33	5 50	6 43	6 00	6 40	5 57	6 43	5 58	6 42	5 53	6 54	6 03	7 00	6 11
8	6 31	5 52	6 41	6 02	6 38	5 59	6 41	6 00	6 40	5 55	6 52	6 05	6 58	6 13
9	6 29	5 54	6 39	6 04	6 36	6 00	6 39	6 01	6 37	5 57	6 49	6 07	6 55	6 15
10	6 27	5 55	6 36	6 05	6 34	6 02	6 37	6 03	6 35	5 59	6 47	6 09	6 53	6 17
11	6 24	5 57	6 34	6 07	6 31	6 04	6 34	6 05	6 32	6 02	6 44	6 12	6 50	6 20
12	6 22	5 59	6 32	6 09	6 29	6 06	6 32	6 07	6 29	6 04	6 41	6 14	6 47	6 22
13	6 20	6 00	6 30	6 10	6 27	6 07	6 30	6 09	6 27	6 06	6 39	6 16	6 45	6 24
14	6 17	6 02	6 27	6 12	6 24	6 09	6 27	6 11	6 24	6 08	6 36	6 18	6 42	6 26
15	6 15	6 04	6 25	6 14	6 22	6 11	6 25	6 12	6 22	6 09	6 33	6 20	6 40	6 27
16	6 13	6 06	6 23	6 16	6 20	6 13	6 22	6 14	6 19	6 11	6 31	6 22	6 37	6 29
17	6 11	6 07	6 21	6 17	6 18	6 14	6 20	6 16	6 17	6 13	6 28	6 24	6 35	6 31
18	6 08	6 09	6 18	6 19	6 15	6 16	6 17	6 18	6 14	6 15	6 26	6 26	6 32	6 33
19	6 06	6 11	6 16	6 21	6 13	6 18	6 15	6 20	6 12	6 17	6 23	6 28	6 30	6 35
20	6 04	6 13	6 14	6 23	6 11	6 20	6 12	6 22	6 09	6 19	6 20	6 30	6 27	6 37
21	6 01	6 14	6 11	6 24	6 08	6 21	6 10	6 24	6 07	6 21	6 18	6 32	6 25	6 39
22	5 59	6 16	6 09	6 26	6 06	6 23	6 07	6 26	6 04	6 23	6 15	6 34	6 22	6 41
23	5 57	6 18	6 07	6 28	6 04	6 25	6 05	6 27	6 02	6 24	6 12	6 36	6 20	6 42
24	5 54	6 20	6 04	6 30	6 01	6 27	6 03	6 29	6 00	6 26	6 10	6 38	6 18	6 44
25	5 52	6 21	6 02	6 31	5 59	6 28	6 00	6 31	5 57	6 28	6 07	6 40	6 15	6 46
26	5 50	6 23	6 00	6 33	5 57	6 30	5 58	6 33	5 55	6 30	6 05	6 42	6 13	6 48
27	5 47	6 25	5 57	6 34	5 54	6 32	5 55	6 35	5 52	6 32	6 02	6 44	6 10	6 50
28	5 45	6 26	5 55	6 36	5 52	6 33	5 53	6 36	5 49	6 34	5 59	6 46	6 07	6 52
29	5 43	6 28	5 53	6 38	5 50	6 35	5 51	6 38	5 46	6 36	5 56	6 48	6 04	6 54
30	5 41	6 30	5 51	6 39	5 48	6 37	5 49	6 40	5 44	6 38	5 54	6 51	6 02	6 57
31	5 39	6 31	5 49	6 41	5 45	6 38	5 46	6 41	5 41	6 40	5 51	6 53	5 59	6 58

JUPITER ♃   SATURN ♄

Day	R.A. h m	Dec. − °	5° high East 52° h m	5° high East 56° h m	Transit h m	R.A. h m	Dec. + °	Transit h m	5° high West 52° h m	5° high West 56° h m
1	18 17	23·0	4 38	5 13	7 40	3 54	18·5	17 16	0 24	0 36
11	18 23	23·0	4 04	4 40	7 07	3 57	18·7	16 39	23 44	23 57
21	18 28	23·0	3 30	4 05	6 33	4 00	18·8	16 03	23 09	23 22
31	18 32	22·9	2 54	3 29	5 57	4 04	19·1	15 28	22 35	22 48

Equatorial diameter of Jupiter 37″; of Saturn 18″. Diameters of Saturn's rings 40″ and 17″.

URANUS ♅   NEPTUNE ♆

Day	R.A. h m	Dec. − ° ′	10° high in East 52° h m	10° high in East 56° h m	Transit h m	R.A. h m	Dec. − ° ′	10° high in East 52° h m	10° high in East 56° h m	Transit h m
1	13 06·3	6 19	22 08	22 21	2 30	16 14·5	19 33	2 54	3 34	5 38
11	13 05·1	6 11	21 26	21 39	1 50	16 14·6	19 33	2 15	2 55	4 59
21	13 03·6	6 02	20 45	20 57	1 09	16 14·4	19 32	1 35	2 15	4 19
31	13 02·1	5 52	20 03	20 15	0 28	16 13·9	19 30	0 55	1 35	3 39

Diameter 4″.   Diameter 2″.

D+

Aperire, to open. Earth opens to receive seed.

Sun's Longitude 30° ♉ 20ᵈ 00ʰ

Day of Month	Week	
1	S.	F. D. Maurice d. 1872★★. R.A.F. formed 1918
2	℞.	**𝕰𝖆𝖘𝖙𝖊𝖗 𝕯𝖆𝖞**
3	M.	Easter Monday [1950
4	Tu.	Oliver Goldsmith d. 1774. Sir Cuthbert Whitaker d.
5	W.	John Wisden d. 1884. Gen MacArthur d. 1964
6	Th.	Raphael d. 1520. Igor Stravinsky d. 1971
7	F.	Wordsworth b. 1770. C. H. Dodd b. 1884
8	S.	Sir Adrian Boult b. 1889. Henry Ford d. 1947
9	℞.	**1st 𝕾𝖚𝖓𝖉𝖆𝖞 𝖆𝖋𝖙𝖊𝖗 𝕰𝖆𝖘𝖙𝖊𝖗.** Lord David Cecil b. 1902
10	M.	Victor Feather b. 1908. Swinburne d. 1909
11	Tu.	Easter Law Sittings Begin
12	W.	Chaliapin d. 1938. F. D. Roosevelt d. 1945
13	Th.	Sir Arthur Harris b. 1892. Eric Kennington d. 1960
14	F.	Handel d. 1759. Arnold Toynbee b. 1889
15	S.	*Titanic* lost 1912. R. H. Mottram d. 1971
16	℞.	**2nd 𝕾𝖚𝖓𝖉𝖆𝖞 𝖆𝖋𝖙𝖊𝖗 𝕰𝖆𝖘𝖙𝖊𝖗.** Charlie Chaplin b. 1889
17	M.	Benjamin Franklin d. 1790
18	Tu.	H. A. L. Fisher d. 1940. Albert Einstein d. 1955
19	W.	David Ricardo b. 1772★★. Dr. Adenauer d. 1967
20	Th.	Edouard Manet d. 1883
21	F.	Queen Elizabeth II Born, 1926
22	S.	Visct. Portal of Hungerford d. 1971
23	℞.	**3rd 𝕾𝖚𝖓𝖉𝖆𝖞 𝖆𝖋𝖙𝖊𝖗 𝕰𝖆𝖘𝖙𝖊𝖗.** St. George's Day
24	M.	Jack Hulbert b. 1892. Sir Richard Woolley b. 1906
25	Tu.	**𝕾𝖙. 𝕸𝖆𝖗𝖐.** Anzac Day
26	W.	Defoe d. 1730
27	Th.	Emerson d. 1882. C. Day Lewis b. 1904
28	F.	Mussolini d. 1945
29	S.	Jeremy Thorpe b. 1929
30	℞.	**4th 𝕾𝖚𝖓𝖉𝖆𝖞 𝖆𝖋𝖙𝖊𝖗 𝕰𝖆𝖘𝖙𝖊𝖗.** Queen Juliana b. 1909

(G.M.T.)

PHENOMENA

April 1ᵈ 07ʰ Mars in conjunction with Saturn. Mars 3° N.

6ᵈ 00ʰ Uranus at opposition.

6ᵈ 05ʰ Jupiter in conjunction with the Moon. Jupiter 2° N.

8ᵈ 00ʰ Venus at greatest eastern elongation. (46°).

8ᵈ 11ʰ Venus in conjunction with Saturn. Venus 5° N.

12ᵈ 16ʰ Mercury in conjunction with the Moon. Mercury 5° S.

16ᵈ 14ʰ Saturn in conjunction with the Moon. Saturn 6° S.

17ᵈ 02ʰ Venus in conjunction with the Moon. Venus 0°·1 N.

17ᵈ 04ʰ Mars in conjunction with the Moon. Mars 3°S.

22ᵈ 20ʰ Venus in conjunction with Mars. Venus 3° N.

28ᵈ 12ʰ Mercury at greatest western elongation (27°).

CONSTELLATIONS

The following constellations are near the meridian at

	d	h		d	h
Mar.	1	24	Mar.	16	23
April	1	22	April	15	21
May	1	20	May	16	19

Cepheus (below the Pole), Cassiopeia (below the Pole), Ursa Major, Leo Minor, Leo, Sextant, Hydra and Crater.

(G.M.T.)

PHASES OF THE MOON

		d	h	m
☾ Last Quarter	......	6	23	44
● New Moon	....	13	20	31
☽ First Quarter	......	20	12	45
○ Full Moon	....	28	12	44

			d	h
Apogee (406,130 kilometres)			1	07
Perigee (357,270	,,	)	14	06
Apogee (406,460	,,	)	28	10

Mean Longitude of Ascending Node on April 1, 302°.

MINIMA OF ALGOL

d	h	d	h	d	h	d	h	d	h	d	h
1	20	7	14	13	08	19	01	24	19	30	13
4	17	10	11	16	04	21	22	27	16		

See note on *Summer Time*, p. 98.

MONTHLY NOTES

April 1. Refreshment House Licences to be renewed.
   3. Bank and General Holiday, England, Wales and N. Ireland.
   5. Income Tax Year (1971–72) ends.
   6. Lady Day Fire Insurances must be paid.
   30. First day of Jewish Passover.

National Days.—*April* 4, Hungary, Senegal; 19, Israel (1972 only) 23, England (*see* above); 27, Sierra Leone, Togo; 29, Japan; 30, Netherlands.

★★ Centenary

Day	Right Ascension	Dec. +	Equation of Time	Rise 52°	Rise 56°	Transit	Set 52°	Set 56°	Sidereal Time	Transit of First Point of Aries (G.M.T.)
	h m s	° ′	m s	h m	h m	h m	h m	h m	h m s	h m s
1	0 41 48	4 30	− 4 00	5 36	5 32	12 04	18 33	18 38	12 37 48	11 20 20
2	0 45 27	4 53	− 3 42	5 34	5 29	12 04	18 35	18 40	12 41 44	11 16 24
3	0 49 05	5 16	− 3 24	5 31	5 26	12 03	18 37	18 42	12 45 41	11 12 29
4	0 52 44	5 39	− 3 07	5 29	5 24	12 03	18 38	18 44	12 49 38	11 08 33
5	0 56 23	6 02	− 2 49	5 27	5 21	12 03	18 40	18 46	12 53 34	11 04 37
6	1 00 02	6 24	− 2 32	5 24	5 19	12 02	18 42	18 48	12 57 31	11 00 41
7	1 03 42	6 47	− 2 15	5 22	5 16	12 02	18 43	18 50	13 01 27	10 56 45
8	1 07 22	7 10	− 1 58	5 20	5 13	12 02	18 45	18 52	13 05 24	10 52 49
9	1 11 02	7 32	− 1 41	5 18	5 11	12 02	18 47	18 54	13 09 20	10 48 53
10	1 14 42	7 54	− 1 25	5 15	5 08	12 01	18 49	18 56	13 13 17	10 44 57
11	1 18 22	8 16	− 1 09	5 13	5 06	12 01	18 50	18 58	13 17 13	10 41 01
12	1 22 03	8 38	− 0 53	5 11	5 03	12 01	18 52	19 00	13 21 10	10 37 05
13	1 25 44	9 00	− 0 38	5 09	5 00	12 01	18 54	19 02	13 25 07	10 33 09
14	1 29 26	9 22	− 0 23	5 06	4 58	12 00	18 55	19 04	13 29 03	10 29 14
15	1 33 07	9 44	− 0 08	5 04	4 55	12 00	18 57	19 06	13 33 00	10 25 18
16	1 36 50	10 05	+ 0 07	5 02	4 53	12 00	18 59	19 08	13 36 56	10 21 22
17	1 40 32	10 26	+ 0 21	5 00	4 50	12 00	19 00	19 10	13 40 53	10 17 26
18	1 44 15	10 47	+ 0 34	4 58	4 48	11 59	19 02	19 12	13 44 49	10 13 30
19	1 47 58	11 08	+ 0 48	4 56	4 45	11 59	19 04	19 14	13 48 46	10 09 34
20	1 51 42	11 29	+ 1 01	4 53	4 43	11 59	19 06	19 16	13 52 42	10 05 38
21	1 55 26	11 49	+ 1 13	4 51	4 40	11 59	19 07	19 18	13 56 39	10 01 42
22	1 59 10	12 10	+ 1 25	4 49	4 38	11 58	19 09	19 20	14 00 36	9 57 46
23	2 02 55	12 30	+ 1 37	4 47	4 36	11 58	19 11	19 22	14 04 32	9 53 50
24	2 06 40	12 50	+ 1 48	4 45	4 33	11 58	19 12	19 24	14 08 29	9 49 54
25	2 10 26	13 09	+ 1 59	4 43	4 31	11 58	19 14	19 26	14 12 25	9 45 59
26	2 14 12	13 29	+ 2 09	4 41	4 28	11 58	19 16	19 28	14 16 22	9 42 03
27	2 17 59	13 48	+ 2 19	4 39	4 26	11 58	19 17	19 30	14 20 18	9 38 07
28	2 21 46	14 07	+ 2 29	4 37	4 24	11 57	19 19	19 32	14 24 15	9 34 11
29	2 25 34	14 26	+ 2 37	4 35	4 21	11 57	19 21	19 34	14 28 11	9 30 15
30	2 29 22	14 44	+ 2 46	4 33	4 19	11 57	19 22	19 36	14 32 08	9 26 19

THE SUN s.d. 16′·0

Duration of Civil (C), Nautical (N), and Astronomical (A), Twilight (in minutes)

Lat. °	Apr. 1 C	Apr. 1 N	Apr. 1 A	Apr. 11 C	Apr. 11 N	Apr. 11 A	Apr. 21 C	Apr. 21 N	Apr. 21 A	Apr. 30 C	Apr. 30 N	Apr. 30 A
52	34	76	121	35	79	128	37	84	138	39	89	152
56	38	85	137	40	90	148	42	96	167	44	105	200

ASTRONOMICAL NOTES

MERCURY is unsuitably placed for observation.

VENUS is a brilliant evening star, magnitude −4·0, dominating the western sky for several hours after sunset. By the end of the month Venus is visible until about 23ʰ. During the first half of the month Venus will be seen passing north of Saturn and by the middle of the month is passing 9° N. of Aldebaran. On the evenings of the 16th and 17th the Moon will be near Venus. At the beginning of the month Venus is about 7° west of Mars and this distance gradually diminishes, Venus passing 3° N. of Mars on the 22nd.

MARS is an evening star, magnitude +1·7. The planet is in Taurus and only slightly fainter than Aldebaran. On the 1st it is only 3° N. of Saturn.

JUPITER is a conspicuous morning star, magnitude −1·9, visible in the S.E. sky, though never visible at any great altitude due to its negative declination of −23°. On the morning of the 6th the gibbous Moon passes 2° S. of Jupiter.

SATURN is a prominent evening star, magnitude +0·4, in the constellation of Taurus. Mars passes 3° N. of Saturn on the 1st. Venus passes 5° N. of Saturn on the 8th.

URANUS is at opposition on the 6th, in the constellation of Virgo, about 7° N.W. of Spica. It is barely visible to the naked eye as its magnitude is +5·7 but it is easily located with only small optical aid. Telescopically it shows a slightly greenish disc 4″ in diameter.

THE MOON

Day	R.A.	Dec.	Hor. Par.	Semi-diam.	Sun's Co-long.	P.A. of Bright Limb	Phase	Age	Rise 52°	Rise 56°	Tran-sit	Set 52°	Set 56°
	h m	°	′	′	°	°		d	h m	h m	h m	h m	h m
1	14 04	−17·9	54·0	14·7	114	121	96	16·5	22 07	22 30	1 29	5 52	5 34
2	14 52	−21·5	54·0	14·7	127	114	91	17·5	23 16	23 44	2 14	6 14	5 50
3	15 42	−24·3	54·2	14·8	139	108	85	18·5	..	..	3 02	6 43	6 14
4	16 34	−26·0	54·4	14·8	151	101	78	19·5	0 20	0 52	3 52	7 22	6 50
5	17 28	−26·4	54·8	14·9	163	95	69	20·5	1 16	1 49	4 44	8 13	7 40
6	18 22	−25·6	55·4	15·1	175	88	60	21·5	2 00	2 31	5 36	9 16	8 46
7	19 16	−23·6	56·1	15·3	187	83	50	22·5	2 35	3 00	6 28	10 29	10 04
8	20 10	−20·3	56·9	15·5	200	78	40	23·5	3 01	3 21	7 19	11 48	11 29
9	21 02	−15·8	57·9	15·8	212	74	30	24·5	3 22	3 36	8 09	13 10	12 58
10	21 54	−10·5	58·8	16·0	224	72	20	25·5	3 39	3 47	8 59	14 34	14 28
11	22 46	− 4·4	59·8	16·3	236	72	12	26·5	3 55	3 58	9 49	16 00	16 00
12	23 39	+ 2·1	60·6	16·5	248	75	5	27·5	4 10	4 08	10 40	17 28	17 34
13	0 33	+ 8·7	61·1	16·7	261	87	1	28·5	4 27	4 19	11 33	19 00	19 13
14	1 30	+14·8	61·4	16·7	273	181	0	0·1	4 48	4 33	12 30	20 34	20 54
15	2 30	+20·0	61·3	16·7	285	235	2	1·1	5 14	4 53	13 30	22 06	22 32
16	3 33	+23·8	60·9	16·6	297	249	7	2·1	5 50	5 22	14 33	23 28	
17	4 38	+25·9	60·2	16·4	310	258	14	3·1	6 39	6 07	15 36	..	0 00
18	5 42	+26·3	59·4	16·2	322	266	24	4·1	7 43	7 12	16 38	0 34	1 06
19	6 44	+24·8	58·5	15·9	334	274	34	5·1	8 59	8 31	17 35	1 22	1 50
20	7 42	+22·0	57·6	15·7	346	280	44	6·1	10 18	9 57	18 28	1 55	2 17
21	8 36	+18·1	56·8	15·5	358	284	55	7·1	11 36	11 21	19 16	2 19	2 36
22	9 25	+13·5	56·0	15·3	11	288	65	8·1	12 52	12 42	20 00	2 37	2 48
23	10 12	+ 8·4	55·4	15·1	23	289	74	9·1	14 05	14 00	20 42	2 52	2 58
24	10 56	+ 3·1	54·9	15·0	35	290	82	10·1	15 15	15 16	21 23	3 04	3 06
25	11 39	− 2·3	54·5	14·8	47	288	89	11·1	16 25	16 30	22 03	3 16	3 14
26	12 23	− 7·5	54·2	14·8	59	285	94	12·1	17 35	17 45	22 44	3 29	3 22
27	13 07	−12·4	54·0	14·7	72	277	98	13·1	18 45	19 00	23 27	3 43	3 31
28	13 52	−16·9	54·0	14·7	84	250	100	14·1	19 56	20 17	..	3 59	3 42
29	14 40	−20·6	54·0	14·7	96	151	100	15·1	21 06	21 32	0 12	4 20	3 58
30	15 29	−23·6	54·1	14·7	108	119	98	16·1	22 11	22 42	0 59	4 46	4 20

MERCURY ☿

Day	R.A.	Dec. +	Diam.	Phase	Transit		Day	R.A.	Dec. +	Diam.	Phase	Transit	
	h m	°	″		h m			h m	°	″		h m	
1	0 34	6·7	11	0	11 53	Mercury is too close to the Sun for observation	16	0 16	0·6	10	22	10 37	Mercury is too close to the Sun for observation
4	0 26	5·1	11	2	11 33		19	0 20	0·4	9	28	10 30	
7	0 20	3·6	11	6	11 15		22	0 26	0·6	9	33	10 25	
10	0 15	2·2	11	11	11 00		25	0 34	1·0	8	38	10 22	
13	0 14	1·3	10	16	10 47		28	0 44	1·8	8	43	10 20	
16	0 16	0·6	10	22	10 37		31	0 56	2·8	8	48	10 20	

VENUS ♀

Day	R.A.	Dec. +	Diam.	Phase	Transit	5° high W 52°	5° high W 56°
	h m	°	″		h m	h m	h m
1	3 36	22·3	22	55	14 58	22 28	22 45
6	3 57	23·7	23	52	15 00	22 38	22 57
11	4 18	24·9	24	49	15 01	22 46	23 07
16	4 38	25·9	26	46	15 01	22 53	23 15
21	4 58	26·7	28	43	15 01	22 57	23 21
26	5 16	27·2	29	40	14 59	22 59	23 23
31	5 33	27·5	32	36	14 56	22 58	23 23

MARS ♂

Day	R.A.	Dec. +	Diam.	Phase	Transit	5° high W 52°	5° high W 56°
	h m	°	″		h m	h m	h m
1	4 04	21·8	5	93	15 25	22 50	23 06
6	4 17	22·4	5	94	15 19	22 47	23 05
11	4 31	23·0	5	94	15 13	22 45	23 03
16	4 45	23·4	4	94	15 08	22 42	23 01
21	4 59	23·8	4	95	15 02	22 39	22 58
26	5 13	24·1	4	95	14 56	22 35	22 55
31	5 27	24·4	4	95	14 51	22 31	22 52

SUNRISE AND SUNSET (G.M.T.)

Day	London a.m. h m	London p.m. h m	Bristol a.m. h m	Bristol p.m. h m	Birmingham a.m. h m	Birmingham p.m. h m	Manchester a.m. h m	Manchester p.m. h m	Newcastle a.m. h m	Newcastle p.m. h m	Glasgow a.m. h m	Glasgow p.m. h m	Belfast a.m. h m	Belfast p.m. h m
1	5 37	6 33	5 47	6 42	5 43	6 40	5 44	6 43	5 39	6 42	5 49	6 55	5 57	7 00
2	5 35	6 35	5 45	6 44	5 40	6 42	5 41	6 45	5 36	6 44	5 46	6 57	5 54	7 02
3	5 32	6 36	5 42	6 46	5 38	6 44	5 39	6 47	5 34	6 46	5 43	6 59	5 52	7 04
4	5 30	6 38	5 40	6 47	5 35	6 46	5 36	6 49	5 31	6 48	5 41	7 01	5 49	7 06
5	5 28	6 39	5 38	6 49	5 33	6 48	5 34	6 51	5 29	6 50	5 38	7 03	5 47	7 08
6	5 25	6 41	5 35	6 51	5 31	6 50	5 32	6 53	5 27	6 52	5 36	7 05	5 45	7 10
7	5 23	6 43	5 33	6 52	5 28	6 51	5 29	6 54	5 24	6 54	5 33	7 07	5 42	7 11
8	5 21	6 44	5 31	6 54	5 26	6 53	5 27	6 56	5 21	6 56	5 30	7 09	5 40	7 13
9	5 19	6 46	5 29	6 56	5 24	6 55	5 24	6 58	5 19	6 58	5 28	7 11	5 37	7 15
10	5 16	6 48	5 26	6 58	5 21	6 57	5 22	7 00	5 16	7 00	5 25	7 13	5 35	7 17
11	5 14	6 49	5 24	6 59	5 19	6 58	5 20	7 02	5 14	7 02	5 23	7 15	5 33	7 19
12	5 12	6 51	5 22	7 01	5 17	7 00	5 17	7 04	5 11	7 04	5 20	7 17	5 30	7 21
13	5 10	6 53	5 20	7 03	5 15	7 02	5 15	7 05	5 09	7 05	5 17	7 19	5 27	7 23
14	5 07	6 54	5 17	7 04	5 12	7 03	5 12	7 07	5 06	7 07	5 15	7 21	5 24	7 25
15	5 05	6 56	5 15	7 06	5 10	7 05	5 10	7 09	5 04	7 09	5 12	7 23	5 22	7 27
16	5 03	6 58	5 13	7 08	5 08	7 07	5 08	7 11	5 02	7 11	5 10	7 25	5 20	7 29
17	5 01	6 59	5 11	7 09	5 06	7 08	5 05	7 13	4 59	7 13	5 07	7 27	5 17	7 31
18	4 59	7 01	5 09	7 11	5 04	7 10	5 03	7 15	4 57	7 15	5 05	7 29	5 15	7 33
19	4 57	7 03	5 07	7 13	5 02	7 12	5 01	7 17	4 54	7 17	5 02	7 31	5 13	7 35
20	4 54	7 05	5 04	7 15	4 59	7 14	4 58	7 18	4 51	7 19	5 00	7 33	5 10	7 36
21	4 52	7 06	5 02	7 16	4 57	7 15	4 56	7 20	4 49	7 21	4 57	7 35	5 08	7 38
22	4 50	7 08	5 00	7 18	4 55	7 17	4 54	7 22	4 47	7 23	4 55	7 37	5 06	7 40
23	4 48	7 10	4 58	7 20	4 53	7 19	4 52	7 24	4 45	7 25	4 53	7 39	5 04	7 42
24	4 46	7 11	4 56	7 21	4 51	7 20	4 50	7 25	4 42	7 27	4 50	7 41	5 01	7 44
25	4 44	7 13	4 54	7 23	4 49	7 22	4 48	7 27	4 40	7 29	4 48	7 43	4 59	7 46
26	4 42	7 15	4 52	7 24	4 47	7 24	4 46	7 29	4 38	7 31	4 46	7 45	4 57	7 48
27	4 40	7 16	4 50	7 26	4 45	7 26	4 44	7 31	4 36	7 33	4 44	7 47	4 55	7 50
28	4 38	7 18	4 48	7 27	4 43	7 28	4 42	7 32	4 34	7 34	4 42	7 48	4 53	7 51
29	4 37	7 20	4 47	7 29	4 40	7 29	4 39	7 34	4 31	7 36	4 39	7 50	4 50	7 53
30	4 35	7 21	4 45	7 30	4 35	7 31	4 37	7 36	4 29	7 38	4 37	7 52	4 48	7 55

JUPITER ♃

Day	R.A. h m	Dec. − °	5° high East 52° h m	5° high East 56° h m	Transit h m
1	18 32	22.9	2 50	3 25	5 54
11	18 35	22.9	2 13	2 48	5 17
21	18 36	22.9	1 35	2 10	4 39
31	18 36	22.9	0 56	1 31	3 59

SATURN ♄

Day	R.A. h m	Dec. + °	Transit h m	5° high West 52° h m	5° high West 56° h m
1	4 04	19.1	15 24	22 31	22 45
11	4 08	19.3	14 49	21 58	22 11
21	4 13	19.5	14 14	21 24	21 38
31	4 18	19.8	13 40	20 51	21 05

Equatorial diameter of Jupiter 40″; of Saturn 17″. Diameters of Saturn's rings 38″ and 16″.

URANUS ⛢

Day	R.A. h m	Dec. − ° ′	Transit h m	10° high in West 52° h m	10° high in West 56° h m
1	13 01.9	5 51	0 24	4 45	4 33
11	13 00.3	5 41	23 39	4 05	3 53
21	12 58.7	5 32	22 58	3 25	3 13
31	12 57.3	5 23	22 17	2 45	2 33

Diameter 4″.

NEPTUNE ♆

Day	R.A. h m	Dec. − ° ′	10° high in East 52° h m	10° high in East 56° h m	Transit h m
1	16 13.9	19 30	0 51	1 31	3 35
11	16 13.3	19 28	0 11	0 50	2 56
21	16 12.4	19 26	23 26	0 10	2 15
31	16 11.5	19 23	22 46	23 25	1 35

Diameter 2″.

Maia, goddess of growth and increase.

Sun's Longitude 60° Ⅱ 20ᵈ 23ʰ

Day of Month	Week	
1	M.	**St. Philip and St. James.** Addison b. 1672★★
2	Tu.	Leonardo da Vinci d. 1519
3	W.	Thomas Hood d. 1845
4	Th.	Sir Osbert Sitwell d. 1969
5	F.	Napoleon d. 1821. Lord Fisher of Lambeth b. 1887
6	S.	Edward VII d. 1910. Sir Alan Cobham b. 1894
7	☉	**5th Sunday after Easter. Rogation Sunday**
8	M.	J. S. Mill d. 1873. Harry S. Truman b. 1884
9	Tu.	OFFICIAL END OF WAR IN EUROPE, 1945
10	W.	Sir H. M. Stanley d. 1904.
11	Th.	**Ascension Day.** Earl of Chatham d. 1778
12	F.	Eleanor Rathbone b. 1872★★. John Masefield d.
13	S.	Lord Crowther b. 1907. Nansen d. 1930 [1967
14	☉	**Sunday after Ascension.** Sir Rider Haggard d. 1925
15	M.	Joseph Whitaker b. 1895. Visct. Snowden d. 1937
16	Tu.	Albuera 1811. H. E. Bates b. 1905
17	W.	Talleyrand d. 1838. Nigel Balchin d. 1970
18	Th.	Bertrand Russell b. 1872★★. George Meredith d.
19	F.	EASTER LAW SITTINGS END [1909
20	S.	Lord Harlech b. 1918. Sir Max Beerbohm d. 1956
21	☉	**Whit Sunday. Pentecost**
22	M.	Victor Hugo d. 1885
23	Tu.	Edmund Rubbra b. 1901. Sir Hugh Casson b. 1910
24	W.	Queen Victoria b. 1819
25	Th.	Lord Maybray-King b. 1901
26	F.	Queen Mary b. 1867. Sir Matt Busby b. 1909
27	S.	Hubert Humphrey b. 1911
28	☉	**Trinity Sunday.** Geoffrey Rippon b. 1924
29	M.	Charles II b. 1630. Lord Goddard d. 1971
30	Tu.	TRINITY LAW SITTINGS BEGIN
31	W.	W. Heath Robinson b. 1872★★. Jutland 1916

(G.M.T.)

PHENOMENA

May 3ᵈ 12ʰ Jupiter in conjunction with the Moon. Jupiter 2° N.

11ᵈ 11ʰ Venus at greatest brilliancy.

11ᵈ 19ʰ Mercury in conjunction with the Moon. Mercury 8° S.

14ᵈ 06ʰ Saturn in conjunction with the Moon. Saturn 5° S.

15ᵈ 20ʰ Venus in conjunction with the Moon. Venus 2° N.

15ᵈ 20ʰ Mars in conjunction with the Moon. Mars 1° S.

17ᵈ 06ʰ Venus in conjunction with Mars. Venus 3° N.

25ᵈ 00ʰ Neptune at opposition.

30ᵈ 15ʰ Jupiter in conjunction with the Moon. Jupiter 2° N.

31ᵈ 08ʰ Saturn in conjunction with the Sun.

CONSTELLATIONS

The following constellations are near the meridian at

	d h		d h
April 1	24	April 15	23
May 1	22	May 16	21
June 1	20	June 15	19

Cepheus (below the Pole), Cassiopeia (below the Pole), Ursa Minor, Ursa Major, Canes Venatici, Coma Berenices, Bootes, Leo, Virgo, Crater, Corvus and Hydra.

ALGOL

ALGOL is inconveniently situated for observation during May.

(G.M.T.)

PHASES OF THE MOON

	d	h	m
☾ Last Quarter	6	12	26
● New Moon	13	04	08
☽ First Quarter	20	01	16
○ Full Moon	28	04	28

	d	h
Perigee (357,460 kilometres)	12	17
Apogee (406,140 ″)	25	15

Mean Longitude of Ascending Node on May 1, 300°.

See note on *Summer Time*, p. 98.

MONTHLY NOTES

May 1. Bank Holiday, Scotland.
    9. Half-Quarter Day. Bank and General Holiday, Channel Islands.
  15. Whitsunday (Scotland). Scottish Term Day.
  19. Jewish Pentecost (Feast of Weeks) begins.
  28. Removal Day, Scotland.
  29. Bank and General Holiday, England, Wales and N. Ireland.

NATIONAL DAYS.—*May* 9, Czechoslovakia; 11, Laos; 14, Paraguay; 17, Norway; 25, Argentine Republic, Jordan; 26, Guyana; 27, Afghanistan; 31, South Africa.

★★ Centenary.

Day	Right Ascension	Dec. +	Equation of Time	Rise 52°	Rise 56°	Transit	Set 52°	Set 56°	Sidereal Time	Transit of First Point of Aries (G.M.T.)
	h m s	° ′	m s	h m	h m	h m	h m	h m	h m s	h m s
1	2 33 11	15 03	+ 2 53	4 31	4 17	11 57	19 24	19 38	14 36 04	9 22 23
2	2 37 00	15 21	+ 3 01	4 29	4 14	11 57	19 26	19 40	14 40 01	9 18 27
3	2 40 50	15 38	+ 3 07	4 27	4 12	11 57	19 27	19 42	14 43 58	9 14 31
4	2 44 41	15 56	+ 3 13	4 25	4 10	11 57	19 29	19 44	14 47 54	9 10 35
5	2 48 32	16 13	+ 3 19	4 24	4 08	11 57	19 31	19 46	14 51 51	9 06 39
6	2 52 23	16 30	+ 3 24	4 22	4 06	11 57	19 32	19 48	14 55 47	9 02 44
7	2 56 15	16 47	+ 3 28	4 20	4 04	11 56	19 34	19 50	14 59 44	8 58 48
8	3 00 08	17 03	+ 3 32	4 18	4 01	11 56	19 36	19 52	15 03 40	8 54 52
9	3 04 01	17 20	+ 3 35	4 16	3 59	11 56	19 37	19 54	15 07 37	8 50 56
10	3 07 55	17 36	+ 3 38	4 15	3 57	11 56	19 39	19 56	15 11 34	8 47 00
11	3 11 50	17 51	+ 3 40	4 13	3 55	11 56	19 40	19 58	15 15 30	8 43 04
12	3 15 45	18 06	+ 3 41	4 11	3 53	11 56	19 42	20 00	15 19 27	8 39 08
13	3 19 41	18 21	+ 3 42	4 10	3 51	11 56	19 44	20 02	15 23 23	8 35 12
14	3 23 37	18 36	+ 3 43	4 08	3 50	11 56	19 45	20 04	15 27 20	8 31 16
15	3 27 34	18 50	+ 3 42	4 06	3 48	11 56	19 47	20 06	15 31 16	8 27 20
16	3 31 31	19 04	+ 3 42	4 05	3 46	11 56	19 48	20 08	15 35 13	8 23 24
17	3 35 29	19 18	+ 3 40	4 03	3 44	11 56	19 50	20 09	15 39 09	8 19 29
18	3 39 28	19 32	+ 3 38	4 02	3 42	11 56	19 51	20 11	15 43 06	8 15 33
19	3 43 27	19 45	+ 3 36	4 01	3 40	11 56	19 53	20 13	15 47 03	8 11 37
20	3 47 26	19 57	+ 3 33	3 59	3 39	11 56	19 54	20 15	15 50 59	8 07 41
21	3 51 26	20 10	+ 3 29	3 58	3 37	11 57	19 56	20 17	15 54 56	8 03 45
22	3 55 27	20 22	+ 3 25	3 57	3 36	11 57	19 57	20 18	15 58 52	7 59 49
23	3 59 28	20 34	+ 3 21	3 55	3 34	11 57	19 58	20 20	16 02 49	7 55 53
24	4 03 30	20 45	+ 3 16	3 54	3 32	11 57	20 00	20 22	16 06 45	7 51 57
25	4 07 32	20 56	+ 3 10	3 53	3 31	11 57	20 01	20 23	16 10 42	7 48 01
26	4 11 34	21 06	+ 3 04	3 52	3 30	11 57	20 02	20 25	16 14 38	7 44 05
27	4 15 37	21 17	+ 2 58	3 51	3 28	11 57	20 04	20 27	16 18 35	7 40 09
28	4 19 41	21 27	+ 2 51	3 50	3 27	11 57	20 05	20 28	16 22 32	7 36 14
29	4 23 45	21 36	+ 2 43	3 49	3 26	11 57	20 06	20 30	16 26 28	7 32 18
30	4 27 49	21 45	+ 2 35	3 48	3 24	11 57	20 07	20 31	16 30 25	7 28 22
31	4 31 54	21 54	+ 2 27	3 47	3 23	11 58	20 09	20 32	16 34 21	7 24 26

THE SUN   s.d. 15′·8

Duration of Civil (C), Nautical (N), and Astronomical (A), Twilight (in minutes)

Lat. °	May 1 C	N	A	May 11 C	N	A	May 21 C	N	A	May 31 C	N	A
52	39	90	154	41	97	179	44	106	T.A.N.	46	116	T.A.N.
56	45	106	209	49	121	T.A.N.	53	143	T.A.N.	57	T.A.N.	T.A.N.

ASTRONOMICAL NOTES

MERCURY is unsuitably placed for observation.

VENUS is a brilliant evening star, magnitude −4·2, visible for a noticeably shortening interval after sunset. At the beginning of the month Venus attains the unusually high declination of +27½°, about 4° N. of the ecliptic. The crescent phase of Venus is a beautiful sight in even a small telescope and particularly during this month as the fraction illuminated decreases from 36% to only 9%, whilst at the same time its diameter increases from 32″ to 53″. The crescent Moon passes 2° S. of Venus and only 1° N. of Mars on the evening of the 15th.

MARS is an evening star, magnitude +1·9, and no longer a very conspicuous object. During the month Mars passes from Taurus into Gemini. On the evening of the 15th the crescent Moon passes between Mars and Venus.

JUPITER is a conspicuous morning star, magnitude −2·1, and by the end of the month visible well before midnight. Even from southern England, however, its maximum altitude will never be greater than 16°. The gibbous Moon passes 2° S. of Jupiter on the 3rd and again on the 30th.

SATURN is an evening star, magnitude +0·3, at the beginning of the month, low above the W.N.W. horizon at about 20ʰ. It is moving towards the Sun and is lost in the evening twilight before the middle of the month: conjunction occurs on the 31st.

NEPTUNE is at opposition on the 25th, in the constellation of Scorpius, very close to υ Scorpii (4ᵐ·3). Neptune is so slow moving that it is within about 2° of this star throughout the year.

THE MOON

Day	R.A.	Dec.	Hor. Par.	Semi-diam.	Sun's Co-long.	P.A. of Bright Limb	Phase	Age	Rise 52°	Rise 56°	Transit	Set 52°	Set 56°
	h m	°	′	′	°	°		d	h m	h m	h m	h m	h m
1	16 21	−25·5	54·2	14·8	120	107	94	17·1	23 09	23 42	1 48	5 22	4 51
2	17 14	−26·2	54·5	14·9	132	99	89	18·1	23 57	..	2 40	6 10	5 37
3	18 08	−25·7	54·9	15·0	145	91	83	19·1	..	0 28	3 31	7 09	6 38
4	19 02	−24·0	55·4	15·1	157	85	75	20·1	0 34	1 01	4 23	8 17	7 51
5	19 54	−21·1	56·1	15·3	169	79	66	21·1	1 03	1 24	5 13	9 32	9 12
6	20 46	−17·1	56·8	15·5	181	75	55	22·1	1 25	1 40	6 02	10 51	10 36
7	21 36	−12·1	57·7	15·7	193	71	45	23·1	1 43	1 53	6 50	12 11	12 02
8	22 27	−6·5	58·6	16·0	206	70	34	24·1	1 59	2 04	7 38	13 33	13 30
9	23 17	−0·3	59·4	16·2	218	69	24	25·1	2 14	2 14	8 26	14 57	15 00
10	0 09	+6·0	60·2	16·4	230	71	15	26·1	2 29	2 24	9 17	16 25	16 34
11	1 04	+12·2	60·9	16·6	242	76	7	27·1	2 48	2 36	10 11	17 56	18 12
12	2 02	+17·8	61·3	16·7	255	86	2	28·1	3 11	2 53	11 09	19 29	19 52
13	3 04	+22·2	61·3	16·7	267	136	0	29·1	3 41	3 17	12 12	20 58	21 28
14	4 09	+25·1	61·1	16·6	279	241	1	0·8	4 25	3 55	13 17	22 14	22 46
15	5 16	+26·2	60·5	16·5	291	259	5	1·8	5 24	4 52	14 21	23 12	23 42
16	6 21	+25·4	59·7	16·3	304	270	11	2·8	6 38	6 08	15 23	23 52	..
17	7 22	+22·9	58·8	16·0	316	277	20	3·8	7 59	7 35	16 19	..	0 17
18	8 19	+19·2	57·8	15·8	328	283	29	4·8	9 20	9 03	17 10	0 21	0 39
19	9 11	+14·7	56·9	15·5	340	287	39	5·8	10 39	10 27	17 57	0 41	0 54
20	9 59	+9·6	56·1	15·3	352	290	49	6·8	11 54	11 48	18 40	0 58	1 05
21	10 44	+4·2	55·4	15·1	5	292	59	7·8	13 05	13 04	19 22	1 11	1 14
22	11 28	−1·1	54·8	14·9	17	292	69	8·8	14 15	14 19	20 02	1 24	1 22
23	12 12	−6·4	54·4	14·8	29	290	77	9·8	15 25	15 34	20 43	1 36	1 30
24	12 55	−11·3	54·1	14·8	41	288	85	10·8	16 35	16 49	21 25	1 50	1 39
25	13 40	−15·9	54·0	14·7	54	284	91	11·8	17 45	18 04	22 09	2 05	1 50
26	14 27	−19·8	54·0	14·7	66	278	96	12·8	18 56	19 20	22 56	2 24	2 04
27	15 16	−22·9	54·1	14·7	78	266	99	13·8	20 03	20 32	23 45	2 49	2 24
28	16 08	−25·1	54·3	14·8	90	218	100	14·8	21 04	21 36	..	3 23	2 53
29	17 01	−26·1	54·5	14·9	102	116	99	15·8	21 55	22 27	0 36	4 07	3 34
30	17 55	−25·8	54·9	15·0	114	97	97	16·8	22 35	23 03	1 28	5 03	4 31
31	18 49	−24·4	55·3	15·1	127	87	93	17·8	23 06	23 29	2 19	6 09	5 42

MERCURY ☿

Day	R.A.	Dec. +	Diam.	Phase	Transit	Day	R.A.	Dec. +	Diam.	Phase	Transit
	h m	°	″		h m		h m	°	″		h m
1	0 56	2·8	8	48	10 20	16	2 14	10·9	6	72	10 39
4	1 09	4·1	7	53	10 21	19	2 33	12·9	6	77	10 47
7	1 23	5·6	7	57	10 24	22	2 54	14·9	6	83	10 57
10	1 39	7·2	7	62	10 28	25	3 17	17·0	5	88	11 08
13	1 56	9·0	6	67	10 33	28	3 41	18·9	5	93	11 20
16	2 14	10·9	6	72	10 39	31	4 07	20·8	5	97	11 35

Mercury is too close to the Sun for observation

Mercury is too close to the Sun for observation

VENUS ♀

Day	R.A.	Dec. +	Diam.	Phase	Transit	5° high W 52°	5° high W 56°
	h m	°	″		h m	h m	h m
1	5 33	27·5	32	36	14 56	22 58	23 23
6	5 48	27·6	34	32	14 52	22 54	23 19
11	6 01	27·5	37	28	14 44	22 46	23 10
16	6 11	27·3	40	24	14 35	22 34	22 58
21	6 18	26·9	43	19	14 21	22 17	22 41
26	6 21	26·3	47	14	14 04	21 56	22 18
31	6 20	25·6	50	10	13 43	21 29	21 50

MARS ♂

Day	R.A.	Dec. +	Diam.	Phase	Transit	5° high W 52°	5° high W 56°
	h m	°	″		h m	h m	h m
1	5 27	24·4	4	95	14 51	22 31	22 51
6	5 42	24·5	4	96	14 45	22 26	22 46
11	5 56	24·6	4	96	14 39	22 21	22 41
16	6 10	24·6	4	96	14 34	22 15	22 35
21	6 24	24·5	4	97	14 28	22 09	22 29
26	6 38	24·4	4	97	14 22	22 02	22 22
31	6 52	24·1	4	97	14 17	21 55	22 14

SUNRISE AND SUNSET (G.M.T.)

Day	London a.m. h m	London p.m. h m	Bristol a.m. h m	Bristol p.m. h m	Birmingham a.m. h m	Birmingham p.m. h m	Manchester a.m. h m	Manchester p.m. h m	Newcastle a.m. h m	Newcastle p.m. h m	Glasgow a.m. h m	Glasgow p.m. h m	Belfast a.m. h m	Belfast p.m. h m
1	4 33	7 23	4 43	7 32	4 36	7 33	4 35	7 38	4 27	7 40	4 35	7 54	4 46	7 57
2	4 31	7 24	4 41	7 34	4 34	7 35	4 33	7 40	4 24	7 42	4 32	7 56	4 44	7 59
3	4 29	7 26	4 39	7 35	4 32	7 36	4 31	7 42	4 22	7 44	4 30	7 58	4 42	8 01
4	4 27	7 27	4 37	7 37	4 30	7 38	4 29	7 43	4 20	7 46	4 28	8 00	4 40	8 02
5	4 26	7 29	4 36	7 39	4 29	7 40	4 27	7 45	4 18	7 48	4 26	8 02	4 38	8 04
6	4 24	7 30	4 34	7 40	4 27	7 41	4 25	7 47	4 16	7 50	4 24	8 04	4 36	8 06
7	4 22	7 32	4 32	7 42	4 25	7 43	4 23	7 49	4 14	7 52	4 22	8 06	4 34	8 08
8	4 20	7 34	4 30	7 44	4 23	7 45	4 21	7 50	4 12	7 53	4 19	8 08	4 31	8 10
9	4 18	7 35	4 28	7 45	4 21	7 46	4 19	7 52	4 10	7 55	4 17	8 10	4 29	8 12
10	4 17	7 37	4 27	7 47	4 20	7 48	4 17	7 54	4 08	7 57	4 15	8 12	4 27	8 14
11	4 15	7 38	4 25	7 48	4 18	7 49	4 16	7 56	4 06	7 59	4 13	8 14	4 26	8 16
12	4 13	7 40	4 23	7 50	4 16	7 51	4 14	7 58	4 04	8 01	4 11	8 16	4 24	8 18
13	4 12	7 42	4 22	7 52	4 15	7 53	4 12	7 59	4 02	8 03	4 09	8 18	4 22	8 19
14	4 10	7 43	4 20	7 53	4 13	7 54	4 10	8 01	4 01	8 05	4 08	8 20	4 20	8 21
15	4 08	7 45	4 18	7 55	4 11	7 56	4 09	8 03	3 59	8 07	4 06	8 22	4 19	8 23
16	4 07	7 46	4 17	7 56	4 10	7 57	4 07	8 04	3 57	8 08	4 04	8 24	4 17	8 24
17	4 05	7 48	4 16	7 58	4 08	7 59	4 05	8 06	3 55	8 10	4 02	8 25	4 15	8 26
18	4 04	7 49	4 14	7 59	4 07	8 00	4 04	8 07	3 54	8 12	4 00	8 27	4 14	8 28
19	4 03	7 51	4 13	8 01	4 06	8 02	4 03	8 09	3 52	8 13	3 58	8 29	4 12	8 29
20	4 01	7 52	4 12	8 02	4 04	8 03	4 01	8 10	3 51	8 15	3 57	8 31	4 11	8 31
21	4 00	7 54	4 11	8 04	4 03	8 05	4 00	8 12	3 49	8 17	3 55	8 33	4 09	8 33
22	3 59	7 55	4 10	8 05	4 02	8 06	3 59	8 13	3 48	8 18	3 54	8 34	4 08	8 34
23	3 57	7 56	4 08	8 06	4 00	8 07	3 57	8 14	3 46	8 20	3 52	8 36	4 06	8 36
24	3 56	7 58	4 07	8 08	3 59	8 09	3 56	8 16	3 44	8 22	3 50	8 38	4 04	8 38
25	3 55	7 59	4 06	8 09	3 58	8 10	3 55	8 17	3 43	8 23	3 49	8 39	4 03	8 39
26	3 54	8 00	4 05	8 10	3 57	8 11	3 54	8 19	3 42	8 25	3 48	8 41	4 02	8 41
27	3 54	8 02	4 04	8 11	3 55	8 13	3 52	8 20	3 40	8 26	3 46	8 43	4 00	8 42
28	3 52	8 03	4 03	8 12	3 54	8 15	3 51	8 22	3 39	8 28	3 45	8 44	3 59	8 44
29	3 51	8 04	4 02	8 14	3 53	8 16	3 50	8 23	3 38	8 29	3 44	8 46	3 58	8 45
30	3 51	8 05	4 01	8 15	3 52	8 17	3 49	8 24	3 37	8 30	3 42	8 47	3 57	8 46
31	3 50	8 07	4 00	8 16	3 51	8 18	3 48	8 26	3 36	8 32	3 41	8 48	3 56	8 48

JUPITER ♃

Day	R.A. h m	Dec. − °	5° high East 52° h m	5° high East 56° h m	Transit h m
1	18 36	22·9	0 56	1 31	3 59
11	18 34	22·9	0 15	0 50	3 18
21	18 32	23·0	23 29	0 09	2 36
31	18 28	23·0	22 47	23 22	1 53

SATURN ♄

Day	R.A. h m	Dec. + °	Transit h m	5° high West 52 h m	5° high West 56° h m
1	4 18	19·8	13 40	20 51	21 05
11	4 23	20·0	13 06	20 18	20 33
21	4 29	20·2	12 32	19 46	20 00
31	4 34	20·4	11 58	19 13	19 28

Equatorial diameter of Jupiter 44″; of Saturn 15″. Diameters of Saturn's rings 37″ and 16″.

URANUS ♅

Day	R.A. h m	Dec. − ° ′	Transit h m	10° high in West 52° h m	10° high in West 56° h m
1	12 57·3	5 23	22 17	2 45	2 33
11	12 56·0	5 15	21 37	2 06	1 54
21	12 54·9	5 08	20 56	1 26	1 14
31	12 54·0	5 04	20 16	0 46	0 34

Diameter 4″.

NEPTUNE ♆

Day	R.A. h m	Dec. − ° ′	Transit h m	10° high in West 52° h m	10° high in West 56° h m
1	16 11·5	19 23	1 35	4 21	3 41
11	16 10·5	19 20	0 55	3 41	3 02
21	16 09·3	19 17	0 14	3 01	2 22
31	16 08·2	19 14	23 30	2 21	1 42

Diameter 2″.

D*

Junius, Roman *gens* (family).

♊ *Sun's Longitude* 90° ♋ 21^{d} 07^{h}

Day of Month	Day of Week	
1	Th.	Sir Hugh Walpole d. 1941. Leslie Howard d. 1943
2	F.	Coronation Day (1953)
3	S.	George V b. 1865. Pope John XXIII d. 1963
4	S.	**1st Sunday after Trinity.** George III b. 1738
5	M.	Lord Kitchener d. 1916
6	Tu.	Lord Carrington b. 1919. "D" Day 1944
7	W.	J. B. Morton b. 1893. E. M. Forster d. 1970
8	Th.	Sarah Siddons d. 1831. Sir Joseph Paxton d. 1865
9	F.	Charles Dickens d. 1870
10	S.	Duke of Edinburgh Born 1921
11	S.	**2nd Sunday after Trinity. St. Barnabas**
12	M.	Earl of Avon b. 1897. John Ireland d. 1962
13	Tu.	Lord Donovan b. 1898
14	W.	Mrs. Pankhurst d. 1928. J. L. Baird d. 1946
15	Th.	Alcock and Brown's Atlantic Flight, 1919
16	F.	Marlborough d. 1722. Lord Reith d. 1971
17	S.	Addison d. 1719. Visct. Alanbrooke d. 1963
18	S.	**3rd Sunday after Trinity.** Waterloo Day
19	M.	Sir James Barrie d. 1937
20	Tu.	William IV d. 1837
21	W.	Inigo Jones d. 1652. First **V.C.** won, 1854†
22	Th.	Lord Hunt b. 1910. Peter Pears b. 1910
23	F.	Sir Leonard Hutton b. 1916. Sir C. Oman d. 1946
24	S.	**St. John Baptist.** Midsummer Day
25	S.	**4th Sunday after Trinity.** Korean War began
26	M.	George IV d. 1830. Gilbert White d. 1793 [1950
27	Tu.	Cherbourg captured 1944
28	W.	William Whitelaw b. 1918. Treaty of Versailles
29	Th.	**St. Peter.** Paderewski d. 1941 [1919
30	F.	Elizabeth Barrett Browning d. 1861

† See p. 302.

(G.M.T.)

PHENOMENA

June 4^{d} 21^{h} Mercury in superior conjunction with the Sun.

13^{d} 13^{h} Mars in conjunction with the Moon. Mars 0°·7 N.

17^{d} 15^{h} Venus in inferior conjunction with the Sun.

21^{d} 07^{h} Summer Solstice.

24^{d} 21^{h} Jupiter at opposition.

26^{d} 15^{h} Jupiter in conjunction with the Moon. Jupiter 2° N.

28^{d} 16^{h} Mercury in conjunction with Mars. Mercury 0°·3 N.

CONSTELLATIONS

The following constellations are near the meridian at

	d	h		d	h
May	1	24	May	16	23
June	1	22	June	15	21
July	1	20	July	16	19

Cassiopeia (below the Pole), Ursa Minor, Draco, Ursa Major, Canes Venatici, Bootes, Corona, Serpens, Virgo and Libra.

ALGOL

Algol is inconveniently situated for observation during June.

(G.M.T.)

PHASES OF THE MOON

	d	h	m
☾ Last Quarter......	4	21	22
● New Moon.......	11	11	30
☽ First Quarter......	18	15	41
○ Full Moon........	26	18	46

	d	h
Perigee (360,400 kilometres)	10	00
Apogee (405,260 „)	22	03

Mean Longitude of Ascending Node on June 1, 299°.

See note on *Summer Time*, p. 98.

MONTHLY NOTES

June 3. Queen's Official Birthday. Commonwealth Day.
15. World Children's Day.
21. Longest day.
24. Midsummer Day. Quarter Day. Sheriffs of London to be elected by the Liverymen.

National Days—*June* 1, Tunisia; 2, Italy; 4, Tonga; 10, Portugal; 12, Philippines; 17, Iceland; 23, Luxemburg; 30, Congolese Republic.

Day	Right Ascension	Dec. +	Equation of Time	Rise 52°	Rise 56°	Transit	Set 52°	Set 56°	Sidereal Time	Transit of First Point of Aries (G.M.T.)
	h m s	° ′	m s	h m	h m	h m	h m	h m	h m s	h m s
1	4 35 59	22 02	+ 2 18	3 46	3 22	11 58	20 10	20 34	16 38 18	7 20 30
2	4 40 05	22 10	+ 2 09	3 45	3 21	11 58	20 11	20 35	16 42 14	7 16 34
3	4 44 11	22 18	+ 2 00	3 44	3 20	11 58	20 12	20 36	16 46 11	7 12 38
4	4 48 18	22 25	+ 1 50	3 44	3 19	11 58	20 13	20 38	16 50 07	7 08 42
5	4 52 25	22 32	+ 1 39	3 43	3 18	11 58	20 14	20 39	16 54 04	7 04 46
6	4 56 32	22 39	+ 1 29	3 42	3 17	11 59	20 15	20 40	16 58 01	7 00 50
7	5 00 39	22 45	+ 1 18	3 42	3 17	11 59	20 16	20 41	17 01 57	6 56 54
8	5 04 47	22 50	+ 1 06	3 41	3 16	11 59	20 17	20 42	17 05 54	6 52 59
9	5 08 55	22 55	+ 0 55	3 41	3 15	11 59	20 17	20 43	17 09 50	6 49 03
10	5 13 04	23 00	+ 0 43	3 40	3 15	11 59	20 18	20 44	17 13 47	6 45 07
11	5 17 12	23 05	+ 0 31	3 40	3 14	12 00	20 19	20 45	17 17 43	6 41 11
12	5 21 21	23 09	+ 0 19	3 40	3 14	12 00	20 20	20 46	17 21 40	6 37 15
13	5 25 30	23 12	+ 0 06	3 40	3 13	12 00	20 20	20 46	17 25 36	6 33 19
14	5 29 39	23 16	− 0 07	3 39	3 13	12 00	20 21	20 47	17 29 33	6 29 23
15	5 33 49	23 18	− 0 19	3 39	3 13	12 00	20 21	20 48	17 33 30	6 25 27
16	5 37 58	23 21	− 0 32	3 39	3 13	12 01	20 22	20 48	17 37 26	6 21 31
17	5 42 08	23 23	− 0 45	3 39	3 12	12 01	20 22	20 49	17 41 23	6 17 35
18	5 46 17	23 24	− 0 58	3 39	3 12	12 01	20 23	20 49	17 45 19	6 13 39
19	5 50 27	23 26	− 1 11	3 39	3 12	12 01	20 23	20 50	17 49 16	6 09 43
20	5 54 36	23 26	− 1 24	3 39	3 13	12 02	20 23	20 50	17 53 12	6 05 48
21	5 58 46	23 27	− 1 37	3 39	3 13	12 02	20 24	20 50	17 57 09	6 01 52
22	6 02 56	23 27	− 1 50	3 40	3 13	12 02	20 24	20 51	18 01 05	5 57 56
23	6 07 05	23 26	− 2 03	3 40	3 13	12 02	20 24	20 51	18 05 02	5 54 00
24	6 11 14	23 25	− 2 16	3 40	3 14	12 02	20 24	20 51	18 08 59	5 50 04
25	6 15 24	23 24	− 2 29	3 41	3 14	12 03	20 24	20 51	18 12 55	5 46 08
26	6 19 33	23 22	− 2 41	3 41	3 14	12 03	20 24	20 51	18 16 52	5 42 12
27	6 23 42	23 20	− 2 54	3 41	3 15	12 03	20 24	20 50	18 20 48	5 38 16
28	6 27 51	23 17	− 3 06	3 42	3 16	12 03	20 24	20 50	18 24 45	5 34 20
29	6 31 59	23 14	− 3 18	3 43	3 16	12 03	20 23	20 50	18 28 41	5 30 24
30	6 36 08	23 11	− 3 30	3 43	3 17	12 04	20 23	20 49	18 32 38	5 26 28

The Sun s.d. 15′·8

Duration of Civil (C), Nautical (N), and Astronomical (A), Twilight (in minutes)

Lat. °	June 1 C	N	A	June 11 C	N	A	June 21 C	N	A	June 30 C	N	A
52	47	117	T.A.N.	48	125	T.A.N.	49	128	T.A.N.	49	125	T.A.N.
56	58	T.A.N.	T.A.N.	61	T.A.N.	T.A.N.	63	T.A.N.	T.A.N.	62	T.A.N.	T.A.N.

ASTRONOMICAL NOTES

MERCURY is unsuitably placed for observation, superior conjunction occurring on the 4th.

VENUS is a bright evening star, magnitude $-3\frac{1}{2}$, but only visible for a short while after sunset in the W.N.W. sky for the first week of the month. It then moves rapidly westwards, through inferior conjunction on the 17th, not being visible again until it reappears as a morning star at the beginning of July.

MARS is a difficult evening star, magnitude $+2\cdot0$, but only visible for a short while low above the W.N.W. horizon. Before the end of the month Mars is lost in the long evening twilight.

JUPITER is now visible throughout the hours of darkness as opposition occurs on the 24th. Its magnitude is $-2\cdot2$ so that even low down, it is a conspicuous object, in Sagittarius. On the afternoon of the 26th the Full Moon passes 2° S. of Jupiter.

This opposition occurs when Jupiter is so close to the ecliptic that, to an observer on Jupiter a rare phenomenon would be visible (though only telescopically)—that of the Earth passing in front of the Sun.

SATURN is unsuitably placed for observation.

THE MOON

Day	R.A.	Dec.	Hor. Par.	Semi-diam.	Sun's Co-long.	P.A. of Bright Limb	Phase	Age	Rise 52°	Rise 56°	Transit	Set 52°	Set 56°
	h m	°	′	′	°	°		d	h m	h m	h m	h m	h m
1	19 42	−21.7	55.8	15.2	139	81	87	18.8	23 29	23 47	3 10	7 22	7 01
2	20 33	−17.9	56.3	15.3	151	75	79	19.8	23 48	..	3 59	8 39	8 23
3	21 24	−13.2	56.9	15.5	163	71	70	20.8	..	0 00	4 46	9 57	9 47
4	22 13	− 7.9	57.6	15.7	175	69	60	21.8	0 04	0 11	5 33	11 16	11 12
5	23 02	− 2.0	58.3	15.9	188	67	49	22.8	0 19	0 21	6 20	12 37	12 38
6	23 52	+ 4.1	59.1	16.1	200	68	38	23.8	0 34	0 30	7 08	14 00	14 07
7	0 44	+10.2	59.8	16.3	212	70	27	24.8	0 50	0 42	7 58	15 27	15 40
8	1 39	+15.8	60.3	16.4	224	73	17	25.8	1 10	0 56	8 53	16 57	17 16
9	2 38	+20.6	60.7	16.5	237	79	9	26.8	1 36	1 15	9 52	18 26	18 53
10	3 41	+24.1	60.8	16.6	249	88	3	27.8	2 13	1 45	10 55	19 49	20 20
11	4 46	+25.9	60.7	16.5	261	111	0	28.8	3 04	2 32	12 00	20 56	21 27
12	5 53	+25.9	60.3	16.4	273	251	0	0.5	4 11	3 40	13 04	21 45	22 12
13	6 56	+24.0	60.3	16.2	286	272	3	1.5	5 31	5 05	14 04	22 19	22 40
14	7 56	+20.7	58.8	16.0	298	281	9	2.5	6 55	6 35	14 59	22 44	22 59
15	8 51	+16.3	57.9	15.8	310	287	16	3.5	8 17	8 04	15 49	23 02	23 12
16	9 42	+11.2	57.0	15.5	322	291	24	4.5	9 36	9 28	16 35	23 17	23 22
17	10 29	+ 5.8	56.2	15.3	335	293	34	5.5	10 50	10 48	17 18	23 30	23 30
18	11 15	+ 0.3	55.5	15.1	347	294	44	6.5	12 02	12 04	17 59	23 43	23 39
19	11 59	− 5.0	54.9	15.0	359	293	53	7.5	13 13	13 20	18 40	23 56	23 47
20	12 43	−10.1	54.5	14.8	11	292	63	8.5	14 23	14 35	19 22	..	23 57
21	13 27	−14.8	54.2	14.8	23	289	72	9.5	15 33	15 51	20 06	0 11	..
22	14 14	−18.9	54.1	14.7	36	286	80	10.5	16 44	17 07	20 51	0 29	0 10
23	15 02	−22.2	54.2	14.8	48	281	87	11.5	17 53	18 21	21 40	0 51	0 28
24	15 53	−24.6	54.3	14.8	60	275	93	12.5	18 56	19 28	22 30	1 22	0 53
25	16 46	−25.9	54.6	14.9	72	268	97	13.5	19 51	20 23	23 22	2 02	1 30
26	17 40	−26.0	55.0	15.0	84	255	99	14.5	20 35	21 05	..	2 55	2 23
27	18 35	−24.8	55.4	15.1	97	120	100	15.5	21 09	21 33	0 15	3 59	3 30
28	19 29	−22.4	55.8	15.2	109	83	99	16.5	21 35	21 53	1 06	5 11	4 48
29	20 21	−18.8	56.3	15.3	121	75	95	17.5	21 55	22 08	1 56	6 28	6 11
30	21 12	−14.3	56.8	15.5	133	71	89	18.5	22 12	22 20	2 45	7 47	7 35

MERCURY ☿

Day	R.A.	Dec. +	Diam.	Phase	Transit		Day	R.A.	Dec. +	Diam.	Phase	Transit	
	h m	°	″		h m			h m	°	″		h m	
1	4 16	21.3	5	98	11 40	Mercury is too close to the Sun for observation	16	6 35	25.1	5	86	13 00	Mercury is too close to the Sun for observation
4	4 43	22.9	5	100	11 56		19	7 00	24.7	6	81	13 13	
7	5 12	24.0	5	99	12 12		22	7 24	24.0	6	75	13 25	
10	5 40	24.8	5	96	12 29		25	7 46	23.1	6	70	13 35	
13	6 08	25.2	5	92	12 45		28	8 06	21.9	6	64	13 42	
16	6 35	25.1	5	86	13 00		31	8 24	20.6	7	58	13 48	

VENUS ♀   MARS ♂

Day	R.A.	Dec. +	Diam.	Phase	Transit	5° high W 52°	56°	Day	R.A.	Dec. +	Diam.	Phase	Transit	5° high W 52°	56°
	h m	°	″		h m	h m	h m		h m	°	″		h m	h m	h m
1	6 19	25.5	51	9	13 38	21 23	21 44	1	6 55	24.1	4	97	14 16	21 53	22 12
6	6 12	24.6	54	5	13 11	20 50	21 10	6	7 08	23.7	4	97	14 09	21 45	22 04
11	6 02	23.5	57	2	12 41	20 13	20 31	11	7 22	23.3	4	98	14 04	21 37	21 55
16	5 49	22.3	58	0	12 09	19 33	19 50	16	7 36	22.8	4	98	13 58	21 27	21 45
21	5 36	21.1	58	1	11 36	18 53	19 08	21	7 49	22.3	4	98	13 51	21 18	21 35
26	5 24	19.9	56	3	11 05	18 15	18 29	26	8 03	21.7	4	98	13 45	21 08	21 24
31	5 16	19.0	53	6	10 37	17 43	17 56	31	8 16	21.0	4	99	13 39	20 57	21 12

SUNRISE AND SUNSET (G.M.T.)

Day	London a.m.	London p.m.	Bristol a.m.	Bristol p.m.	Birmingham a.m.	Birmingham p.m.	Manchester a.m.	Manchester p.m.	Newcastle a.m.	Newcastle p.m.	Glasgow a.m.	Glasgow p.m.	Belfast a.m.	Belfast p.m.
	h m	h m	h m	h m	h m	h m	h m	h m	h m	h m	h m	h m	h m	h m
1	3 49	8 08	3 59	8 17	3 50	8 20	3 47	8 27	3 35	8 33	3 40	8 50	3 55	8 49
2	3 48	8 09	3 58	8 18	3 49	8 21	3 46	8 28	3 34	8 34	3 39	8 51	3 54	8 50
3	3 47	8 10	3 57	8 19	3 48	8 22	3 45	8 29	3 33	8 35	3 38	8 52	3 53	8 51
4	3 47	8 11	3 57	8 20	3 48	8 23	3 44	8 30	3 32	8 37	3 37	8 54	3 52	8 52
5	3 46	8 12	3 56	8 21	3 47	8 24	3 44	8 31	3 31	8 38	3 36	8 55	3 52	8 53
6	3 45	8 12	3 55	8 22	3 46	8 25	3 43	8 32	3 30	8 39	3 35	8 56	3 51	8 54
7	3 45	8 13	3 55	8 23	3 46	8 26	3 42	8 33	3 30	8 40	3 35	8 57	3 50	8 55
8	3 44	8 14	3 54	8 24	3 45	8 27	3 42	8 34	3 29	8 41	3 34	8 58	3 50	8 56
9	3 44	8 15	3 54	8 24	3 45	8 27	3 41	8 35	3 28	8 42	3 33	8 59	3 49	8 57
10	3 43	8 16	3 53	8 25	3 44	8 28	3 41	8 36	3 28	8 43	3 33	9 00	3 49	8 58
11	3 43	8 16	3 53	8 26	3 44	8 29	3 40	8 37	3 27	8 44	3 32	9 01	3 48	8 59
12	3 43	8 17	3 53	8 27	3 44	8 30	3 40	8 38	3 27	8 45	3 32	9 02	3 48	9 00
13	3 43	8 17	3 53	8 27	3 44	8 30	3 39	8 38	3 26	8 45	3 31	9 02	3 47	9 00
14	3 42	8 18	3 52	8 28	3 43	8 31	3 39	8 39	3 26	8 46	3 31	9 03	3 47	9 01
15	3 42	8 19	3 52	8 28	3 43	8 31	3 39	8 40	3 26	8 47	3 31	9 04	3 47	9 02
16	3 42	8 19	3 52	8 29	3 43	8 32	3 39	8 40	3 26	8 47	3 31	9 04	3 47	9 02
17	3 42	8 19	3 52	8 29	3 43	8 32	3 39	8 41	3 26	8 48	3 30	9 05	3 47	9 03
18	3 42	8 20	3 52	8 30	3 43	8 33	3 39	8 41	3 26	8 48	3 30	9 05	3 47	9 03
19	3 42	8 20	3 52	8 30	3 43	8 33	3 39	8 41	3 26	8 48	3 30	9 06	3 47	9 03
20	3 42	8 20	3 52	8 30	3 43	8 33	3 39	8 42	3 26	8 49	3 31	9 06	3 47	9 04
21	3 42	8 21	3 52	8 31	3 43	8 34	3 39	8 42	3 26	8 49	3 31	9 06	3 47	9 04
22	3 43	8 21	3 53	8 31	3 44	8 34	3 39	8 42	3 26	8 49	3 31	9 07	3 47	9 04
23	3 43	8 21	3 53	8 31	3 44	8 34	3 39	8 42	3 26	8 49	3 31	9 07	3 47	9 04
24	3 43	8 21	3 53	8 31	3 44	8 34	3 40	8 42	3 27	8 49	3 32	9 07	3 48	9 04
25	3 44	8 21	3 54	8 31	3 45	8 34	3 40	8 42	3 27	8 49	3 32	9 07	3 48	9 04
26	3 44	8 21	3 54	8 31	3 45	8 34	3 41	8 42	3 28	8 49	3 32	9 07	3 49	9 04
27	3 44	8 21	3 54	8 31	3 45	8 34	3 41	8 42	3 28	8 49	3 33	9 06	3 49	9 04
28	3 45	8 21	3 55	8 31	3 46	8 34	3 42	8 42	3 29	8 49	3 34	9 06	3 50	9 04
29	3 46	8 21	3 56	8 31	3 47	8 34	3 42	8 42	3 29	8 49	3 34	9 06	3 50	9 04
30	3 46	8 21	3 56	8 30	3 47	8 33	3 43	8 41	3 30	8 48	3 35	9 05	3 51	9 03

JUPITER ♃   SATURN ♄

Day	R.A.	Dec. −	Transit	5° high West 52°	5° high West 56°	R.A.	Dec. +	Transit	
	h m	°	h m	h m	h m	h m	°	h m	
1	18 27	23·1	1 49	4 51	4 16	4 35	20·4	11 55	Saturn is too
11	18 23	23·1	1 05	4 06	3 31	4 40	20·6	11 21	close to the
21	18 17	23·2	0 20	3 21	2 45	4 45	20·8	10 47	Sun for
31	18 12	23·2	23 31	2 36	2 00	4 51	21·0	10 13	observation

Equatorial diameter of Jupiter 46″; of Saturn 15″.   Diameters of Saturn's rings 37″ and 17″.

URANUS ♅   NEPTUNE ♆

Day	R.A.	Dec. −	Transit	10° high in West 52°	10° high in West 56°	R.A.	Dec. −	Transit	10° high in West 52°	10° high in West 56°
	h m	° ′	h m	h m	h m	h m	° ′	h m	h m	h m
1	12 54·0	5 03	20 12	0 42	0 30	16 08·1	19 14	23 26	2 17	1 38
11	12 53·5	5 00	19 33	23 59	23 47	16 07·0	19 11	22 45	1 37	0 58
21	12 53·3	5 00	18 53	23 19	23 08	16 06·0	19 09	22 05	0 57	0 19
31	12 53·4	5 01	18 14	22 40	22 28	16 05·1	19 06	21 25	0 17	23 35

Diameter 4″   Diameter 2″

Day of Month	Week			(G.M.T.) PHENOMENA

Julius Caesar, formerly *Quintilis*, 5th month (from March). Sun's Longitude 120° ♌ 22ᵈ 18ʰ

(G.M.T.)
PHENOMENA
July   5ᵈ   Aphelion
(152,000,000 kilometres).
8ᵈ 12ʰ Saturn in conjunction with the Moon. Saturn 5° S.
8ᵈ 18ʰ Venus in conjunction with the Moon. Venus 8° S.
10ᵈ 20ʰ Total eclipse of the Sun. *See* p. 148.
10ᵈ 23ʰ Mercury at greatest eastern elongation (26°).
12ᵈ 07ʰ Mars in conjunction with the Moon. Mars 2° N.
12ᵈ 21ʰ Mercury in conjunction with the Moon. Mercury 1° N.
23ᵈ 16ʰ Jupiter in conjunction with the Moon. Jupiter 2° N.
24ᵈ 00ʰ Venus at greatest brilliancy.
26ᵈ 07ʰ Partial eclipse of the Moon. *See* p. 148.
29ᵈ 15ʰ Mercury in conjunction with Mars. Mercury 6° S.

1	S.	Dominion Day, Canada. Gettysburg 1863
2	☉.	**5th Sunday after Trinity.** Tchekov d. 1904
3	M.	Joel Chandler Harris d. 1908
4	Tu.	Independence Day, U.S.A.
5	W.	Edouard Herriot b. 1872**. Georges Pompidou b.
6	Th.	Edward VI d. 1553. Sedgmoor 1685 [1911
7	F.	Dame Laura Knight d. 1970. Sir Allen Lane d.
8	S.	Shelley d. 1822. Alec Waugh b. 1898 [1970
9	☉.	**6th Sunday after Trinity.** Edward Heath b. 1916
10	M.	Lord Fisher d. 1920. Albert Chevalier d. 1923
11	Tu.	Paul Nash d. 1946. Sir John Rothenstein b. 1901
12	W.	Earl of Birkenhead (F. E. Smith) b. 1872**
13	Th.	Marat d. 1793. Lord Clark b. 1903
14	F.	Fête Nationale, France
15	S.	St. Swithin's Day. Massacre of Cawnpore 1957
16	☉.	**7th Sunday after Trinity.** Roald Amundsen b.
17	M.	Whistler d. 1903. Sir A. Munnings d. 1959. [1872**
18	Tu.	Jane Austen d. 1817
19	W.	A. J. Cronin b. 1896. John Bratby b. 1928
20	Th.	G. M. Trevelyan d. 1962. Iain Macleod d. 1970
21	F.	First men landed on Moon, 1969
22	S.	St. Mary Magdalen. Mackenzie King d. 1950
23	☉.	**8th Sunday after Trinity**
24	M.	Harold Raymond b. 1887
25	Tu.	**St. James.** Blériot's Channel Flight, 1909
26	W.	George Borrow d. 1881. Lord Thorneycroft b.1909
27	Th.	John Dalton d. 1844. Dr. Salazar d. 1970
28	F.	Selwyn Lloyd b. 1904. Earl of Cromer b. 1918
29	S.	Joseph Grimond b. 1913. Sir John Barbirolli d.1970
30	☉.	**9th Sunday after Trinity.** Henry Moore b. 1898
31	M.	Trinity Law Sittings End

CONSTELLATIONS

The following constellations are near the meridian at

	d	h		d	h
June	1	24	June	15	23
July	1	22	July	16	21
Aug.	1	20	Aug.	16	19

Ursa Minor, Draco, Corona, Hercules, Lyra, Serpens, Ophiuchus, Libra, Scorpius and Sagittarius.

MINIMA OF ALGOL

d	h	d	h
2	14	19	19
5	11	22	16
8	08	25	13
11	05	28	10
14	02	31	07
16	23		

(G.M.T.)
PHASES OF THE MOON

		d	h	m
☾	Last Quarter	4	03	25
●	New Moon	10	19	39
☽	First Quarter	18	07	46
○	Full Moon	26	07	24

Perigee (365,100 kilometres) 7 23
Apogee (404,410   ,,   ) 19 20

Mean Longitude of Ascending Node on July 1, 297°.

See note on *Summer Time*, p. 98.

MONTHLY NOTES

July 1. Special Sessions for Licences to deal in Game to be held this month.
  3. Dog Days begin (end Aug. 15).
  5. Dividends due.   Tynwald Day, Isle of Man.
  8. Midsummer Fire Insurances to be paid.
  12. Bank and General Holiday, Northern Ireland.
  15. Latest date for receiving corrections for next year's "Whitaker."

National Days.—*July* 1, Canada, Burundi, Rwanda; 4, United States; 5, Venezuela; 6, Malawi; 11, Mongolia; 14, France, Iraq; 18, Spain; 20, Colombia; 21, Belgium; 22, Poland; 23 Ethiopia, U.A.R.; 26, Liberia; 28, Peru.
    ** Centenary.

Day	Right Ascension	Dec. +	Equation of Time	Rise 52°	Rise 56°	Transit	Set 52°	Set 56°	Sidereal Time	Transit of First Point of Aries (G.M.T.)
	h m s	° ′	m s	h m	h m	h m	h m	h m	h m s	h m s
1	6 40 16	23 07	− 3 42	3 44	3 18	12 04	20 23	20 49	18 36 35	5 22 33
2	6 44 24	23 03	− 3 53	3 44	3 19	12 04	20 23	20 49	18 40 31	5 18 37
3	6 48 32	22 59	− 4 04	3 45	3 20	12 04	20 22	20 48	18 44 28	5 14 41
4	6 52 39	22 54	− 4 15	3 46	3 20	12 04	20 22	20 47	18 48 24	5 10 45
5	6 56 47	22 48	− 4 26	3 47	3 21	12 05	20 21	20 47	18 52 21	5 06 49
6	7 00 53	22 42	− 4 36	3 48	3 22	12 05	20 21	20 46	18 56 17	5 02 53
7	7 05 00	22 36	− 4 46	3 49	3 24	12 05	20 20	20 45	19 00 14	4 58 57
8	7 09 06	22 30	− 4 56	3 50	3 25	12 05	20 20	20 44	19 04 10	4 55 01
9	7 13 12	22 23	− 5 05	3 51	3 26	12 05	20 19	20 44	19 08 07	4 51 05
10	7 17 17	22 15	− 5 14	3 52	3 27	12 05	20 18	20 42	19 12 04	4 47 09
11	7 21 22	22 08	− 5 22	3 53	3 28	12 05	20 17	20 41	19 16 00	4 43 13
12	7 25 27	21 59	− 5 30	3 54	3 30	12 06	20 16	20 40	19 19 57	4 39 17
13	7 29 31	21 51	− 5 38	3 55	3 31	12 06	20 16	20 39	19 23 53	4 35 22
14	7 33 35	21 42	− 5 45	3 56	3 33	12 06	20 15	20 38	19 27 50	4 31 26
15	7 37 38	21 33	− 5 51	3 57	3 34	12 06	20 14	20 37	19 31 46	4 27 30
16	7 41 40	21 23	− 5 57	3 58	3 36	12 06	20 13	20 35	19 35 43	4 23 34
17	7 45 42	21 13	− 6 03	4 00	3 37	12 06	20 12	20 34	19 39 39	4 19 38
18	7 49 44	21 03	− 6 08	4 01	3 39	12 06	20 10	20 33	19 43 36	4 15 42
19	7 53 45	20 52	− 6 12	4 02	3 40	12 06	20 09	20 31	19 47 33	4 11 46
20	7 57 45	20 41	− 6 16	4 03	3 42	12 06	20 08	20 30	19 51 29	4 07 50
21	8 01 45	20 30	− 6 19	4 05	3 43	12 06	20 07	20 28	19 55 26	4 03 54
22	8 05 44	20 18	− 6 22	4 06	3 45	12 06	20 06	20 27	19 59 22	3 59 58
23	8 09 43	20 06	− 6 24	4 08	3 47	12 06	20 04	20 25	20 03 19	3 56 02
24	8 13 41	19 54	− 6 26	4 09	3 48	12 06	20 03	20 23	20 07 15	3 52 07
25	8 17 38	19 41	− 6 27	4 10	3 50	12 06	20 01	20 22	20 11 12	3 48 11
26	8 21 35	19 28	− 6 27	4 12	3 52	12 06	20 00	20 20	20 15 08	3 44 15
27	8 25 31	19 15	− 6 27	4 13	3 54	12 06	19 58	20 18	20 19 05	3 40 19
28	8 29 27	19 01	− 6 26	4 15	3 55	12 06	19 57	20 16	20 23 02	3 36 23
29	8 33 22	18 47	− 6 24	4 17	3 57	12 06	19 55	20 14	20 26 58	3 32 27
30	8 37 17	18 33	− 6 22	4 18	3 59	12 06	19 54	20 12	20 30 55	3 28 31
31	8 41 11	18 18	− 6 19	4 19	4 01	12 06	19 52	20 11	20 34 51	3 24 35

Duration of Civil (C), Nautical (N), and Astronomical (A), Twilight (in minutes)

Lat. °	July 1 C	N	A	July 11 C	N	A	July 21 C	N	A	July 31 C	N	A
52	48	124	T.A.N.	T.A.N.	46	116	T.A.N.	44	107	T.A.N.	41	98	180
56	61	T.A.N.	T.A.N.	T.A.N.	58	T.A.N.	T.A.N.	53	144	T.A.N.	49	122	T.A.N.

ASTRONOMICAL NOTES

MERCURY is unsuitably placed for observation.

VENUS is a brilliant morning star, magnitude −4·1, and by the end of the month is visible for two hours in the eastern sky before sunrise. The old crescent Moon will be near Venus on the mornings of the 8th and 9th.

MARS is unsuitably placed for observation.

JUPITER is an evening star magnitude −2·2 and still visible for most of the night. The gibbous Moon passes 2° S. of Jupiter on the afternoon of the 23rd. The four Galilean satellites of Jupiter are easily visible with only small optical aid. Eclipses and shadow transits of these satellites are given on page 147.

SATURN is too close to the Sun for the first week or ten days of the month but then becomes a morning star, magnitude +0·3. By the end of the month it is visible low above the E.N.E. horizon shortly after 01^h.

ECLIPSE. A total eclipse of the Sun occurs on the 10th. A partial phase is visible from the British Isles. See page 148 for details.

ECLIPSE. A partial eclipse of the Moon occurs on the 26th. See page 148 for details.

THE MOON

Day	R.A.	Dec.	Hor. Par.	Semi-diam.	Sun's Co-long.	P.A. of Bright Limb	Phase	Age	Rise 52°	Rise 56°	Transit	Set 52°	Set 56°
	h m	°	′	′	°	°		d	h m	h m	h m	h m	h m
1	22 01	− 9·0	57·4	15·6	145	67	82	19·5	22 26	22 30	3 32	9 06	8 59
2	22 50	− 3·3	57·9	15·8	158	66	73	20·5	22 41	22 39	4 18	10 25	10 24
3	23 39	+ 2·7	58·4	15·9	170	65	63	21·5	22 56	22 49	5 04	11 46	11 51
4	0 30	+ 8·7	58·9	16·0	182	67	52	22·5	23 14	23 02	5 53	13 09	13 20
5	1 22	+14·3	59·4	16·2	194	69	40	23·5	23 37	23 18	6 44	14 35	14 52
6	2 18	+19·3	59·7	16·3	207	73	29	24·5	··	23 42	7 40	16 02	16 26
7	3 18	+23·1	60·0	16·3	219	79	19	25·5	0 07	··	8 39	17 26	17 56
8	4 22	+25·5	60·1	16·4	231	85	11	26·5	0 50	0 20	9 42	18 39	19 11
9	5 26	+26·1	59·9	16·3	243	93	5	27·5	1 49	1 17	10 45	19 35	20 05
10	6 31	+25·0	59·6	16·2	256	102	1	28·5	3 03	2 34	11 47	20 16	20 40
11	7 32	+22·2	59·1	16·1	268	268	0	0·2	4 26	4 03	12 45	20 44	21 02
12	8 29	+18·2	58·5	15·9	280	287	2	1·2	5 50	5 34	13 38	21 05	21 18
13	9 22	+13·3	57·7	15·7	292	292	6	2·2	7 12	7 01	14 26	21 22	21 29
14	10 12	+ 7·8	56·9	15·5	305	294	12	3·2	8 30	8 25	15 11	21 36	21 38
15	10 58	+ 2·3	56·1	15·3	317	296	20	4·2	9 44	9 44	15 54	21 49	21 47
16	11 43	− 3·3	55·5	15·1	329	296	28	5·2	10 56	11 01	16 36	22 02	21 55
17	12 28	− 8·5	54·9	15·0	341	295	37	6·2	12 08	12 18	17 18	22 16	22 05
18	13 13	−13·4	54·5	14·9	354	293	47	7·2	13 19	13 34	18 01	22 33	22 17
19	13 59	−17·7	54·3	14·8	6	290	56	8·2	14 29	14 50	18 46	22 54	22 32
20	14 47	−21·3	54·2	14·8	18	286	66	9·2	15 39	16 05	19 33	23 21	22 54
21	15 37	−24·0	54·3	14·8	30	281	74	10·2	16 45	17 15	20 22	23 57	23 26
22	16 29	−25·7	54·6	14·9	42	276	82	11·2	17 43	18 16	21 14	··	··
23	17 23	−26·2	55·0	15·0	55	270	89	12·2	18 32	19 03	22 07	0 45	0 12
24	18 18	−25·4	55·4	15·1	67	264	94	13·2	19 10	19 36	22 59	1 45	1 14
25	19 12	−23·3	56·0	15·3	79	260	98	14·2	19 38	19 59	23 50	2 55	2 29
26	20 06	−20·0	56·5	15·4	91	263	100	15·2	20 01	20 16	··	4 12	3 52
27	20 58	−15·6	57·1	15·6	103	64	99	16·2	20 19	20 28	0 40	5 32	5 18
28	21 49	−10·5	57·6	15·7	116	64	97	17·2	20 34	20 39	1 28	6 52	6 44
29	22 38	− 4·7	58·1	15·8	128	63	92	18·2	20 49	20 49	2 16	8 10	8 10
30	23 28	+ 1·3	58·5	15·9	140	63	85	19·2	21 04	20 59	3 03	9 34	9 37
31	0 18	+ 7·4	58·8	16·0	152	64	76	20·2	21 21	21 10	3 51	10 56	11 05

MERCURY ☿

Day	R.A.	Dec. +	Diam.	Phase	Transit		Day	R.A.	Dec. +	Diam.	Phase	Transit	
	h m	°	″		h m			h m	°	″		h m	
1	8 24	20·6	7	58	13 48	Mercury is	16	9 25	13·7	9	34	13 48	Mercury is
4	8 40	19·2	7	53	13 52	too close to	19	9 31	12·5	9	29	13 42	too close to
7	8 54	17·8	7	49	13 54	the Sun	22	9 34	11·5	10	23	13 32	the Sun
10	9 06	16·4	8	44	13 54	for	25	9 34	10·8	10	18	13 21	for
13	9 17	15·0	8	39	13 52	observation	28	9 32	10·3	11	13	13 06	observation
16	9 25	13·7	9	34	13 48		31	9 27	10·2	11	8	12 49	

VENUS ♀

Day	R.A.	Dec. +	Diam.	Phase	5° high E 52°	5° high E 56°	Transit
	h m	°	″		h m	h m	h m
1	5 16	19·0	53	6	3 31	3 18	10 37
6	5 11	18·3	50	10	3 11	2 58	10 13
11	5 11	18·0	46	15	2 53	2 41	9 53
16	5 14	17·9	43	20	2 37	2 25	9 37
21	5 21	18·0	39	24	2 23	2 11	9 25
26	5 31	18·2	36	29	2 12	2 00	9 15
31	5 43	18·5	34	33	2 03	1 50	9 07

MARS ♂

Day	R.A.	Dec. +	Diam.	Phase	Transit	
	h m	°	″		h m	
1	8 16	21·0	4	99	13 39	
6	8 29	20·3	4	99	13 32	Mars is
11	8 42	19·5	4	99	13 25	too close to
16	8 55	18·6	4	99	13 19	the Sun
21	9 08	17·7	4	99	13 12	for
26	9 20	16·8	4	99	13 05	observation
31	9 33	15·8	4	99	12 57	

SUNRISE AND SUNSET (G.M.T.)

Day	London a.m.	London p.m.	Bristol a.m.	Bristol p.m.	Birmingham a.m.	Birmingham p.m.	Manchester a.m.	Manchester p.m.	Newcastle a.m.	Newcastle p.m.	Glasgow a.m.	Glasgow p.m.	Belfast a.m.	Belfast p.m.
	h m	h m	h m	h m	h m	h m	h m	h m	h m	h m	h m	h m	h m	h m
1	3 47	8 21	3 57	8 30	3 48	8 33	3 44	8 41	3 31	8 48	3 36	9 05	3 52	9 03
2	3 47	8 20	3 57	8 30	3 48	8 33	3 44	8 41	3 32	8 48	3 37	9 05	3 52	9 03
3	3 48	8 20	3 58	8 29	3 49	8 32	3 45	8 40	3 33	8 47	3 38	9 04	3 53	9 02
4	3 49	8 19	3 59	8 29	3 50	8 32	3 46	8 40	3 33	8 46	3 38	9 03	3 54	9 02
5	3 50	8 19	4 00	8 28	3 51	8 31	3 47	8 39	3 34	8 46	3 39	9 03	3 55	9 01
6	3 51	8 18	4 01	8 28	3 52	8 31	3 48	8 39	3 35	8 45	3 40	9 02	3 56	9 01
7	3 52	8 18	4 02	8 27	3 53	8 30	3 49	8 38	3 37	8 44	3 42	9 01	3 57	9 00
8	3 53	8 17	4 03	8 27	3 54	8 30	3 50	8 37	3 38	8 43	3 43	9 00	3 58	8 59
9	3 54	8 17	4 04	8 26	3 55	8 29	3 51	8 36	3 39	8 43	3 44	9 00	3 59	8 58
10	3 55	8 16	4 05	8 25	3 56	8 28	3 52	8 35	3 40	8 41	3 45	8 58	4 00	8 57
11	3 56	8 15	4 06	8 24	3 57	8 27	3 53	8 35	3 41	8 41	3 46	8 57	4 01	8 57
12	3 57	8 14	4 07	8 24	3 58	8 26	3 55	8 34	3 43	8 40	3 48	8 56	4 03	8 56
13	3 58	8 14	4 08	8 23	3 59	8 26	3 56	8 33	3 44	8 39	3 49	8 55	4 04	8 55
14	3 59	8 13	4 09	8 22	4 00	8 25	3 57	8 32	3 45	8 38	3 51	8 54	4 05	8 54
15	4 00	8 12	4 10	8 21	4 01	8 24	3 58	8 31	3 46	8 37	3 52	8 53	4 06	8 53
16	4 01	8 11	4 11	8 20	4 03	8 22	4 00	8 29	3 48	8 35	3 54	8 51	4 08	8 51
17	4 02	8 10	4 13	8 19	4 04	8 21	4 01	8 28	3 49	8 34	3 55	8 50	4 09	8 50
18	4 03	8 08	4 14	8 18	4 05	8 20	4 02	8 27	3 51	8 33	3 57	8 49	4 11	8 49
19	4 04	8 07	4 15	8 17	4 07	8 19	4 04	8 26	3 52	8 31	3 58	8 47	4 12	8 47
20	4 06	8 06	4 16	8 16	4 08	8 17	4 05	8 24	3 54	8 30	4 00	8 46	4 14	8 46
21	4 07	8 05	4 18	8 15	4 10	8 16	4 07	8 23	3 55	8 28	4 01	8 44	4 15	8 44
22	4 08	8 04	4 19	8 14	4 11	8 15	4 08	8 22	3 57	8 27	4 03	8 43	4 17	8 43
23	4 10	8 02	4 20	8 12	4 13	8 13	4 10	8 20	3 59	8 25	4 05	8 41	4 19	8 41
24	4 11	8 01	4 22	8 11	4 14	8 12	4 11	8 19	4 00	8 23	4 06	8 39	4 20	8 39
25	4 12	7 59	4 23	8 09	4 15	8 10	4 12	8 17	4 02	8 22	4 08	8 38	4 22	8 38
26	4 14	7 58	4 24	8 08	4 17	8 09	4 14	8 16	4 04	8 20	4 10	8 36	4 24	8 36
27	4 15	7 56	4 26	8 06	4 18	8 07	4 15	8 14	4 05	8 19	4 11	8 34	4 25	8 35
28	4 17	7 55	4 27	8 05	4 20	8 06	4 17	8 13	4 07	8 17	4 13	8 32	4 27	8 33
29	4 19	7 53	4 29	8 03	4 22	8 04	4 19	8 11	4 09	8 15	4 15	8 30	4 29	8 31
30	4 20	7 52	4 30	8 02	4 23	8 03	4 20	8 10	4 10	8 13	4 17	8 28	4 30	8 30
31	4 21	7 50	4 31	8 00	4 24	8 01	4 22	8 08	4 12	8 12	4 19	8 27	4 32	8 28

JUPITER ♃   SATURN ♄

Day	R.A.	Dec. −	Transit	5° high West 52°	5° high West 56°	R.A.	Dec. +	5° high East 52°	5° high East 56°	Transit
	h m	°	h m	h m	h m	h m	°	h m	h m	h m
1	18 12	23·2	23 31	2 36	2 00	4 51	21·0	2 55	2 39	10 13
11	18 06	23·3	22 46	1 51	1 15	4 56	21·1	2 20	2 04	9 38
21	18 02	23·3	22 02	1 06	0 30	5 01	21·2	1 44	1 29	9 04
31	17 58	23·3	21 19	0 23	23 42	5 05	21·3	1 09	0 53	8 29

Equatorial diameter of Jupiter 46″; of Saturn 17″.   Diameters of Saturn's rings 38″ and 17″.

URANUS ♅   NEPTUNE ♆

Day	R.A.	Dec. −	Transit	10° high in West 52°	10° high in West 56°	R.A.	Dec. −	Transit	10° high in West 52°	10° high in West 56°
	h m	° ′	h m	h m	h m	h m	° ′	h m	h m	h m
1	12 53·4	5 01	18 14	22 40	22 28	16 05·1	19 06	21 25	0 17	23 35
11	12 53·9	5 04	17 35	22 01	21 49	16 04·3	19 05	20 45	23 33	22 55
21	12 54·6	5 09	16 56	21 22	21 10	16 03·7	19 03	20 05	22 52	22 16
31	12 55·7	5 17	16 18	20 43	20 31	16 03·3	19 03	19 25	22 14	21 36

Diameter 4″   Diameter 2″

DAY OF		
Month	Week	

Julius Caesar *Augustus*,
formerly *Sextilis*, 6th
month (from March).

Sun's Longitude 150° ♍ 23ᵈ 01ʰ

1	Tu.	Queen Anne d. 1714.　Lord Dilhorne b. 1905
2	W.	Blenheim 1704.　Hindenburg d. 1934
3	Th.	Grinling Gibbons d. 1721.　Joseph Conrad d. 1924
4	F.	QUEEN ELIZABETH THE QUEEN MOTHER BORN 1900
5	S.	Hans Christian Andersen d. 1875
6	☉	10th Sunday after Trinity.　Transfiguration
7	M.	Sir Rabindranath Tagore d. 1941
8	Tu.	George Canning d. 1827.　Visct. Bracken d. 1958
9	W.	Capt Marryat d. 1848.　Léonide Massine b. 1896
10	Th.	Sir Arthur Porritt b. 1900
11	F.	Cardinal Newman d. 1890
12	S.	William Blake d. 1827.　Ian Fleming d. 1964
13	☉	11th Sunday after Trinity.　Sir Basil Spence b. 1907
14	M.	Richard Jefferies d. 1887.　Leonard Woolf d. 1969
15	Tu.	PRINCESS ANNE BORN 1950
16	W.	Thomas Fuller d. 1661.　Andrew Marvell d. 1678
17	Th.	Balzac d. 1850.　Frederick the Great d. 1786
18	F.	Basil Cameron b. 1884.　W. H. Hudson d. 1922
19	S.	James Watt d. 1819.　Diaghilev d. 1929
20	☉	12th Sunday after Trinity.　Cardinal Griffin d. 1956
21	M.	PRINCESS MARGARET BORN 1930
22	Tu.	Warren Hastings d. 1818.　Lord Salisbury d. 1903
23	W.	William Wallace d. 1305
24	Th.	St. Bartholomew.　Aubrey Beardsley b. 1872★★
25	F.	Faraday d. 1867.　Paris liberated 1944
26	S.	Ralph Vaughan Williams d. 1958
27	☉	13th Sunday after Trinity.　Lyndon B. Johnson b.
28	M.	Leigh Hunt d. 1859.　Gen. Botha d. 1919　[1908
29	Tu.	Lord Casey b. 1890.　Mary Clare d. 1970
30	W.	Denis Healey b. 1917.　Sir J. J. Thomson d. 1940
31	Th.	Bunyan d. 1688.　Sir Bernard Lovell b. 1913

(G.M.T.)
PHENOMENA

August 5ᵈ 00ʰ Saturn in
conjunction with the Moon.
Saturn 5° S.

5ᵈ 20ʰ Venus in con-
junction with the Moon.
Venus 7° S.

7ᵈ 20ʰ Mercury in in-
ferior conjunction with the
Sun.

19ᵈ 22ʰ Jupiter in con-
junction with the Moon.
Jupiter 2° N.

25ᵈ 15ʰ Mercury at
greatest western elongation
(18°).

27ᵈ 02ʰ Venus at greatest
western elongation (46°).

CONSTELLATIONS

The following constel-
lations are near the meridian at

d h	d h
July 1 24	July 16 23
Aug. 1 22	Aug. 16 21
Sept. 1 20	Sept. 15 19

Draco, Hercules, Lyra,
Cygnus, Sagitta, Ophiu-
chus, Serpens, Aquila and
Sagittarius.

MINIMA OF ALGOL

d h	d h
3 03	20 08
6 00	23 05
8 21	26 02
11 18	28 23
14 15	31 20
17 12	

PHASES OF THE MOON
(G.M.T.)

	d h m
☾ Last Quarter	2 08 02
● New Moon	9 05 26
☽ First Quarter	17 01 09
○ Full Moon	24 18 22
☾ Last Quarter	31 12 48

	d h
Perigee (369,370 kilometres)	3 15
Apogee (405,240 ,,)	16 15
Perigee (367,830 ,,)	28 20

Mean Longitude of Ascending
Node on August 1, 295°.

See note on *Summer Time*, p. 98.

MONTHLY NOTES

Aug. 1. Lammas.　Scottish Term Day.
　5. Oyster season opens.
　7. Bank Holiday, Scotland.
　11. Half-Quarter Day, Eng. and W.
　12. Grouse shooting begins.
　28. Bank and General Holiday, England, Wales and N. Ireland.

NATIONAL DAYS.—*Aug.* 1, Switzerland, Dahomey; 6, Bolivia;
7, Ivory Coast, Jamaica (1972 only); 9, Singapore; 10, Ecuador;
15, Korea; 17, Gaboon, Indonesia; 23, Rumania; 25, Uruguay;
31, Malaysia, Trinidad and Tobago.

★★ Centenary

Day	Right Ascension	Dec. +	Equation of Time	Rise 52°	Rise 56°	Transit	Set 52°	Set 56°	Sidereal Time	Transit of First Point of Aries (G.M.T.)
	h m s	° ′	m s	h m	h m	h m	h m	h m	h m s	h m s
1	8 45 04	18 03	− 6 16	4 21	4 03	12 06	19 51	20 09	20 38 48	3 20 39
2	8 48 57	17 48	− 6 12	4 22	4 05	12 06	19 49	20 07	20 42 44	3 16 43
3	8 52 49	17 33	− 6 08	4 24	4 07	12 06	19 47	20 04	20 46 41	3 12 47
4	8 56 40	17 17	− 6 03	4 25	4 08	12 06	19 45	20 02	20 50 37	3 08 52
5	9 00 31	17 01	− 5 57	4 27	4 10	12 06	19 44	20 00	20 54 34	3 04 56
6	9 04 22	16 44	− 5 51	4 29	4 12	12 06	19 42	19 58	20 58 31	3 01 00
7	9 08 11	16 28	− 5 44	4 30	4 14	12 06	19 40	19 56	21 02 27	2 57 04
8	9 12 01	16 11	− 5 37	4 32	4 16	12 06	19 38	19 54	21 06 24	2 53 08
9	9 15 49	15 54	− 5 29	4 33	4 18	12 05	19 36	19 52	21 10 20	2 49 12
10	9 19 37	15 36	− 5 21	4 35	4 20	12 05	19 34	19 49	21 14 17	2 45 16
11	9 23 25	15 19	− 5 12	4 37	4 22	12 05	19 32	19 47	21 18 13	2 41 20
12	9 27 12	15 01	− 5 02	4 38	4 24	12 05	19 30	19 45	21 22 10	2 37 24
13	9 30 58	14 43	− 4 52	4 40	4 26	12 05	19 29	19 42	21 26 06	2 33 28
14	9 34 44	14 24	− 4 41	4 42	4 28	12 05	19 27	19 40	21 30 03	2 29 32
15	9 38 29	14 06	− 4 30	4 43	4 30	12 04	19 25	19 38	21 34 00	2 25 37
16	9 42 14	13 47	− 4 18	4 45	4 32	12 04	19 23	19 35	21 37 56	2 21 41
17	9 45 58	13 28	− 4 05	4 46	4 34	12 04	19 21	19 33	21 41 53	2 17 45
18	9 49 41	13 09	− 3 52	4 48	4 36	12 04	19 18	19 31	21 45 49	2 13 49
19	9 53 24	12 49	− 3 39	4 50	4 38	12 04	19 16	19 28	21 49 46	2 09 53
20	9 57 07	12 29	− 3 25	4 51	4 40	12 03	19 14	19 26	21 53 42	2 05 57
21	10 00 49	12 10	− 3 10	4 53	4 42	12 03	19 12	19 23	21 57 39	2 02 01
22	10 04 31	11 50	− 2 55	4 55	4 44	12 03	19 10	19 21	22 01 35	1 58 05
23	10 08 12	11 29	− 2 40	4 56	4 46	12 03	19 08	19 18	22 05 32	1 54 09
24	10 11 53	11 09	− 2 24	4 58	4 47	12 02	19 06	19 16	22 09 29	1 50 13
25	10 15 33	10 48	− 2 08	4 59	4 49	12 02	19 04	19 13	22 13 25	1 46 17
26	10 19 13	10 28	− 1 51	5 01	4 51	12 02	19 01	19 11	22 17 22	1 42 22
27	10 22 52	10 07	− 1 34	5 03	4 53	12 01	18 59	19 08	22 21 18	1 38 26
28	10 26 31	9 46	− 1 17	5 04	4 55	12 01	18 57	19 06	22 25 15	1 34 30
29	10 30 10	9 24	− 0 59	5 06	4 57	12 01	18 55	19 03	22 29 11	1 30 34
30	10 33 48	9 03	− 0 41	5 08	4 59	12 01	18 53	19 01	22 33 08	1 26 38
31	10 37 27	8 41	− 0 22	5 09	5 01	12 00	18 50	18 58	22 37 04	1 22 42

THE SUN   s.d. 15′·8

Duration of Civil (C), Nautical (N), and Astronomical (A), Twilight (in minutes)

Lat. °	Aug. 1 C	N	A	Aug. 11 C	N	A	Aug. 21 C	N	A	Aug. 31 C	N	A
52	41	97	177	39	89	153	37	83	138	35	79	127
56	48	120	T.A.N.	45	106	205	42	96	166	40	89	147

ASTRONOMICAL NOTES

MERCURY is unsuitably placed for observation at first, inferior conjunction occurring on the 7th. During the second half of the month it is a morning star, magnitude +1·5 to −0·6. It is then visible low above the eastern horizon around the time of beginning of morning civil twilight.

VENUS is a brilliant morning star, magnitude −4·1, dominating the eastern sky for several hours before sunrise. The old crescent Moon is near Venus on the mornings of the 5th and 6th. Venus can be seen in daylight if one knows exactly where to look for it and occasions such as these when the Moon is near to the planet and can be used as a guide, should assist the observer to locate it—shortly after sunrise would be the best time to look.

MARS is unsuitably placed for observation.

JUPITER is an evening star, magnitude −2·1, almost stationary in the extreme western part of Sagittarius. By the end of the month it is no longer visible after 22ʰ. On the evening of the 19th the gibbous Moon passes 2° S. of Jupiter.

SATURN is a morning star, magnitude +0·4, in the constellation of Taurus. The old crescent Moon passes 5° N. of Saturn just before they rise on the night of the 4th–5th.

METEORS. The maximum of the famous Perseid meteor shower occurs during the night of the 11th–12th. Fortunately the Moon is only 2¾ᵈ old and sets at 20ʰ so that it will not interfere with observation.

THE MOON

Day	R.A.	Dec.	Hor. Par.	Semi-diam.	Sun's Co-long.	P.A. of Bright Limb	Phase	Age	Rise 52°	Rise 56°	Transit	Set 52°	Set 56°
	h m	°	′	′	°	°		d	h m	h m	h m	h m	h m
1	1 10	+13·1	59·1	16·1	164	66	65	21·2	21 42	21 25	4 41	12 21	12 36
2	2 05	+18·2	59·2	16·1	177	70	54	22·2	22 09	21 46	5 34	13 47	14 09
3	3 03	+22·3	59·3	16·2	189	75	42	23·2	22 46	22 17	6 31	15 11	15 39
4	4 04	+25·0	59·4	16·2	201	81	31	24·2	23 37	23 05	7 32	16 26	16 58
5	5 07	+26·1	59·3	16·1	213	87	21	25·2	··	··	8 33	17 27	17 58
6	6 10	+25·6	59·1	16·1	225	93	13	26·2	0 44	0 13	9 34	18 13	18 39
7	7 11	+23·4	58·7	16·0	238	99	6	27·2	2 02	1 36	10 32	18 45	19 06
8	8 09	+19·8	58·3	15·9	250	101	2	28·2	3 25	3 05	11 27	19 09	19 23
9	9 03	+15·2	57·8	15·7	262	77	0	29·2	4 47	4 34	12 17	19 27	19 36
10	9 53	+10·0	57·1	15·6	274	306	1	0·8	6 07	5 59	13 03	19 42	19 47
11	10 41	+ 4·4	56·5	15·4	287	301	4	1·8	7 23	7 21	13 47	19 56	19 55
12	11 27	− 1·2	55·9	15·2	299	300	8	2·8	8 37	8 40	14 30	20 09	20 04
13	12 12	− 6·7	55·3	15·1	311	298	15	3·8	9 49	9 57	15 12	20 23	20 13
14	12 57	−11·7	54·8	14·9	323	296	22	4·8	11 01	11 14	15 55	20 38	20 24
15	13 43	−16·3	54·5	14·8	336	293	31	5·8	12 12	12 31	16 39	20 57	20 38
16	14 31	−20·1	54·3	14·8	348	289	40	6·8	13 23	13 47	17 26	21 22	20 57
17	15 20	−23·2	54·3	14·8	0	285	50	7·8	14 30	14 59	18 14	21 54	21 24
18	16 11	−25·2	54·4	14·8	12	280	59	8·8	15 32	16 04	19 04	22 36	22 04
19	17 04	−26·1	54·7	14·9	25	274	68	9·8	16 24	16 56	19 56	23 30	22 59
20	17 59	−25·7	55·2	15·0	37	269	77	10·8	17 06	17 35	20 49	··	··
21	18 53	−24·1	55·8	15·2	49	264	85	11·8	17 39	18 02	21 40	0 36	0 08
22	19 47	−21·3	56·5	15·4	61	260	91	12·8	18 04	18 21	22 31	1 50	1 28
23	20 40	−17·3	57·2	15·6	73	258	96	13·8	18 24	18 36	23 21	3 09	2 53
24	21 31	−12·3	57·9	15·8	85	264	99	14·8	18 41	18 47	··	4 31	4 20
25	22 22	− 6·7	58·5	15·9	98	266	100	15·8	18 56	18 58	0 09	5 53	5 48
26	23 13	− 0·6	59·0	16·1	110	53	98	16·8	19 11	19 08	0 57	7 15	7 16
27	0 04	+ 5·6	59·4	16·2	122	58	93	17·8	19 28	19 19	1 46	8 40	8 47
28	0 57	+11·6	59·6	16·2	134	62	87	18·8	19 48	19 33	2 37	10 06	10 19
29	1 52	+17·0	59·6	16·2	146	66	78	19·8	20 13	19 52	3 30	11 33	11 52
30	2 50	+21·3	59·5	16·2	159	71	67	20·8	20 47	20 20	4 27	12 58	13 24
31	3 50	+24·4	59·3	16·2	171	77	56	21·8	21 33	21 02	5 26	14 17	14 47

MERCURY ☿

Day	R.A.	Dec. +	Diam.	Phase	Transit	Day	R.A.	Dec. +	Diam.	Phase	5° high E 52°	5° high E 56°	Transit
	h m	°	″		h m		h m	°	″		h m	h m	h m
1	9 25	10·3	11	6	12 43	Mercury is too close to the Sun for observation	16	8 49	14·4	10	10	4 28	4 19	11 09
4	9 17	10·7	11	3	12 23		19	8 49	15·3	9	19	4 12	4 02	10 58
7	9 08	11·4	11	1	12 02		22	8 54	15·9	8	28	4 02	3 52	10 52
10	8 59	12·3	10	1	11 42		25	9 03	16·1	7	40	3 59	3 48	10 50
13	8 53	13·4	10	5	11 24		28	9 17	15·9	7	54	4 02	3 52	10 52
16	8 49	14·4	10	10	11 09		31	9 34	15·2	6	66	4 11	4 01	10 58

VENUS ♀

Day	R.A.	Dec. +	Diam.	Phase	5° high E 52°	5° high E 56°	Transit
	h m	°	″		h m	h m	h m
1	5 45	18·6	33	33	2 01	1 48	9 06
6	6 00	18·9	31	37	1 54	1 41	9 01
11	6 16	19·2	29	41	1 49	1 36	8 58
16	6 34	19·4	27	44	1 46	1 32	8 56
21	6 53	19·4	26	47	1 45	1 31	8 55
26	7 12	19·3	24	50	1 45	1 32	8 55
31	7 33	19·1	23	52	1 48	1 35	8 56

MARS ♂

Day	R.A.	Dec. +	Diam.	Phase	Transit	
	h m	°	″		h m	
1	9 35	15·6	4	—	12 56	Mars is too close to the Sun for observation
6	9 48	14·5	4	—	12 49	
11	10 00	13·4	4	—	12 41	
16	10 12	12·3	4	—	12 34	
21	10 24	11·1	4	—	12 26	
26	10 36	10·0	4	—	12 18	
31	10 48	8·8	4	—	12 10	

SUNRISE AND SUNSET (G.M.T.)

Day	London a.m.	London p.m.	Bristol a.m.	Bristol p.m.	Birmingham a.m.	Birmingham p.m.	Manchester a.m.	Manchester p.m.	Newcastle a.m.	Newcastle p.m.	Glasgow a.m.	Glasgow p.m.	Belfast a.m.	Belfast p.m.
	h m	h m	h m	h m	h m	h m	h m	h m	h m	h m	h m	h m	h m	h m
1	4 23	7 49	4 33	7 59	4 26	8 00	4 23	8 06	4 14	8 10	4 21	8 25	4 33	8 26
2	4 24	7 47	4 34	7 57	4 27	7 58	4 25	8 04	4 16	8 08	4 23	8 23	4 35	8 24
3	4 26	7 45	4 36	7 55	4 29	7 56	4 27	8 02	4 18	8 05	4 25	8 20	4 37	8 22
4	4 27	7 43	4 37	7 53	4 30	7 54	4 28	8 00	4 19	8 03	4 26	8 18	4 38	8 20
5	4 29	7 42	4 39	7 52	4 32	7 53	4 30	7 59	4 21	8 02	4 28	8 16	4 40	8 18
6	4 31	7 40	4 41	7 50	4 34	7 51	4 32	7 57	4 23	8 00	4 30	8 14	4 42	8 16
7	4 32	7 38	4 42	7 48	4 35	7 49	4 34	7 55	4 25	7 58	4 32	8 12	4 44	8 14
8	4 34	7 37	4 44	7 46	4 37	7 47	4 35	7 53	4 26	7 56	4 34	8 10	4 46	8 12
9	4 35	7 35	4 45	7 44	4 38	7 45	4 37	7 51	4 28	7 54	4 36	8 08	4 48	8 10
10	4 37	7 33	4 47	7 42	4 40	7 43	4 39	7 48	4 30	7 51	4 38	8 05	4 50	8 07
11	4 39	7 31	4 49	7 40	4 42	7 41	4 41	7 46	4 32	7 49	4 40	8 03	4 52	8 05
12	4 40	7 29	4 50	7 39	4 44	7 39	4 43	7 44	3 34	7 47	4 42	8 01	4 54	8 03
13	4 42	7 28	4 52	7 37	4 46	7 37	4 45	7 42	4 36	7 44	4 44	7 58	4 55	8 01
14	4 43	7 26	4 53	7 35	4 47	7 35	4 46	7 40	4 38	7 42	4 46	7 56	4 57	7 59
15	4 45	7 24	4 55	7 33	4 49	7 33	4 48	7 38	4 40	7 40	4 48	7 54	4 59	7 57
16	4 46	7 22	4 56	7 31	4 51	7 31	4 50	7 36	4 42	7 38	4 50	7 52	5 01	7 55
17	4 48	7 20	4 58	7 29	4 52	7 29	4 51	7 34	4 43	7 36	4 51	7 50	5 02	7 53
18	4 49	7 17	4 59	7 27	4 54	7 26	4 53	7 31	4 45	7 33	4 53	7 48	5 04	7 50
19	4 51	7 15	5 01	7 25	4 56	7 24	4 55	7 29	4 47	7 31	4 55	7 45	5 06	7 48
20	4 52	7 13	5 02	7 23	4 57	7 22	4 56	7 27	4 49	7 29	4 57	7 43	5 08	7 46
21	4 54	7 11	5 04	7 21	4 59	7 20	4 58	7 25	4 51	7 26	4 59	7 40	5 10	7 43
22	4 56	7 09	5 06	7 19	5 01	7 18	5 00	7 23	4 53	7 24	5 01	7 38	5 11	7 41
23	4 57	7 07	5 07	7 17	5 02	7 16	5 01	7 21	4 55	7 21	5 03	7 35	5 13	7 39
24	4 59	7 05	5 09	7 15	5 04	7 14	5 03	7 19	4 56	7 19	5 04	7 33	5 15	7 37
25	5 00	7 03	5 10	7 13	5 05	7 12	5 05	7 16	4 58	7 16	5 06	7 30	5 17	7 34
26	5 02	7 00	5 12	7 10	5 07	7 09	5 07	7 14	5 00	7 14	5 08	7 28	5 19	7 32
27	5 04	6 58	5 14	7 08	5 09	7 07	5 08	7 12	5 02	7 12	5 10	7 25	5 20	7 29
28	5 05	6 56	5 15	7 06	5 10	7 05	5 10	7 09	5 04	7 09	5 12	7 23	5 22	7 27
29	5 07	6 54	5 17	7 04	5 12	7 03	5 12	7 07	5 06	7 07	5 14	7 20	5 24	7 24
30	5 09	6 52	5 19	7 02	5 14	7 01	5 14	7 04	5 08	7 04	5 16	7 18	5 26	7 22
31	5 10	6 49	5 20	6 59	5 15	6 58	5 15	7 02	5 09	7 02	5 18	7 15	5 28	7 19

JUPITER ♃

Day	R.A. h m	Dec. − °	Transit h m	5° high West 52° h m	5° high West 56° h m
1	17 57	23·3	21 15	0 19	23 38
11	17 55	23·4	20 33	23 33	22 56
21	17 54	23·4	19 53	22 52	22 15
31	17 54	23·4	19 13	22 13	21 36

SATURN ♄

R.A. h m	Dec. + °	5° high East 52° h m	5° high East 56° h m	Transit h m
5 05	21·3	1 05	0 49	8 25
5 09	21·4	0 29	0 13	7 50
5 13	21·4	23 49	23 34	7 14
5 15	21·5	23 13	22 57	6 37

Equatorial diameter of Jupiter 43″; of Saturn 18″. Diameters of Saturn's rings 40″ and 18″.

URANUS ⛢

Day	R.A. h m	Dec. − ° ′	Transit h m	10° high in West 52° h m	10° high in West 56° h m
1	12 55·8	5 17	16 14	20 39	20 27
11	12 57·2	5 26	15 37	20 00	19 48
21	12 58·8	5 37	14 59	19 21	19 09
31	13 00·7	5 49	14 21	18 43	18 30

Diameter 4″

NEPTUNE ♆

R.A. h m	Dec. − ° ′	Transit h m	10° high in West 52° h m	10° high in West 56° h m
16 03·2	19 03	19 21	22 10	21 32
16 03·0	19 03	18 42	21 30	20 53
16 03·1	19 04	18 02	20 51	20 13
16 03·3	19 05	17 23	20 12	19 34

Diameter 2″

Day of		
Month	Week	

Septem (seven), 7th month of Roman (pre-Julian) Calendar.

Sun's Longitude 180° ♎ 22ᵈ23ʰ

Month	Week	
1	F.	Louis XIV d. 1715. Sir Richard Steele d. 1729
2	S.	Lord George-Brown b. 1914
3	☉.	**14th Sunday after Trinity.** Britain at War 1939
4	M.	Grieg d. 1907. Albert Schweitzer d. 1965
5	Tu.	John Wisden b. 1826
6	W.	Reginald McKenna d. 1943
7	Th.	Queen Elizabeth I b. 1533. King Baudouin b. 1930
8	F.	Richard Strauss d. 1949
9	S.	Allied Landing at Salerno 1943
10	☉.	**15th S. after Trinity.** Treaty of St. Germain 1919
11	M.	Sir Gerald Templer b. 1898. J. C. Smuts d. 1950
12	Tu.	Maurice Chevalier b. 1888
13	W.	General Wolfe d. 1759. Sir Robert Robinson b.
14	Th.	Wellington d. 1852. Angus Ogilvie b. 1928 [1886
15	F.	Battle of Britain Day
16	S.	Sir Ronald Ross d. 1932. Sir James Jeans d. 1946
17	☉.	**16th Sunday after Trinity.** Sir Francis Chichester
18	M.	Hazlitt d. 1830. Greta Garbo b. 1905 [b. 1901
19	Tu.	Sir David Low d. 1963
20	W.	Sibelius d. 1957. Yvonne Arnaud d. 1958
21	Th.	**St. Matthew.** Sir Walter Scott d. 1832
22	F.	Boulogne reoccupied 1944
23	S.	Wilkie Collins d. 1889. Sigmund Freud d. 1939
24	☉.	**17th Sunday after Trinity.** Sir Alan Herbert b.
25	M.	Sir Charles B. Cochran b. 1872★★ [1890
26	Tu.	Pope Paul VI b. 1897. W. H. Davies d. 1940
27	W.	Degas d. 1917. Adelina Patti d. 1919
28	Th.	Louis Pasteur d. 1895. President Nasser d. 1970
29	F.	**St Michael and All Angels**
30	S.	Sir Michael Adeane b. 1910. Calais reoccupied 1944

(G.M.T.)

PHENOMENA

September 1ᵈ 09ʰ Saturn in conjunction with the Moon. Saturn 5° S.

3ᵈ 23ʰ Venus in conjunction with the Moon. Venus 2° S.

7ᵈ 11ʰ Mars in conjunction with the Sun.

16ᵈ 08ʰ Jupiter in conjunction with the Moon. Jupiter 2° N.

19ᵈ 20ʰ Mercury in superior conjunction with the Sun.

22ᵈ 23ʰ Autumnal Equinox.

24ᵈ 21ʰ Pluto in conjunction with the Sun.

28ᵈ 16ʰ Saturn in conjunction with the Moon. Saturn 4° S.

CONSTELLATIONS

The following constellations are near the meridian at

	d	h		d	h
Aug.	1	24	Aug.	16	23
Sept.	1	22	Sept.	15	21
Oct.	1	20	Oct.	16	19

Draco, Cepheus, Lyra, Cygnus, Vulpecula, Sagitta, Delphinus, Equuleus, Aquila, Aquarius and Capricornus.

MINIMA OF ALGOL

d	h	d	h
3	16	18	00
6	13	20	21
9	10	23	18
12	07	26	15
15	04	29	12

See note on *Summer Time*, p. 98.

(G.M.T.)

PHASES OF THE MOON

		d	h	m
●	New Moon	7	17	28
☽	First Quarter	15	19	13
○	Full Moon	23	04	07
☾	Last Quarter	29	19	16

	d	h
Apogee (404,900 kilometres)	13	10
Perigee (362,680 ")	25	07

Mean Longitude of Ascending Node on September 1, 294°.

MONTHLY NOTES

Sept. 1. Partridge shooting begins. Salmon close-time begins.
9. Jewish New Year (A.M. 5733).
18. Yom Kippur (Jewish Day of Atonement).
23. Harvest Moon.
27. Sheriffs of London to be sworn in.
29. Michaelmas. Quarter day. Lord Mayor of London elected.

NATIONAL DAYS.—*Sept.* 1, Libya; 6, Swaziland; 7, Brazil; 9, Bulgaria; 15, Costa Rica, El Salvador, Honduras, Nicaragua; 16, Mexico; 18, Chile; 21, Malta; 22, Mali; 23, Saudi Arabia; 30, Botswana.

★★ Centenary

Day	Right Ascension	Dec.	Equation of Time	Rise 52°	Rise 56°	Transit	Set 52°	Set 56°	Sidereal Time	Transit of First Point of Aries (G.M.T.)
							THE SUN s.d. 15'·9			
	h m s	° '	m s	h m	h m	h m	h m	h m	h m s	h m s
1	10 41 04	+8 20	− 0 03	5 11	5 03	12 00	18 48	18 56	22 41 01	1 18 46
2	10 44 42	+7 58	+ 0 16	5 12	5 05	12 00	18 46	18 53	22 44 58	1 14 50
3	10 48 19	+7 36	+ 0 35	5 14	5 07	11 59	18 44	18 50	22 48 54	1 10 54
4	10 51 56	+7 14	+ 0 54	5 16	5 09	11 59	18 41	18 48	22 52 51	1 06 58
5	10 55 33	+6 52	+ 1 14	5 17	5 11	11 59	18 39	18 45	22 56 47	1 03 02
6	10 59 09	+6 29	+ 1 34	5 19	5 13	11 58	18 37	18 43	23 00 44	0 59 07
7	11 02 46	+6 07	+ 1 54	5 21	5 15	11 58	18 34	18 40	23 04 40	0 55 11
8	11 06 22	+5 45	+ 2 15	5 22	5 17	11 58	18 32	18 37	23 08 37	0 51 15
9	11 09 58	+5 22	+ 2 35	5 24	5 19	11 57	18 30	18 35	23 12 33	0 47 19
10	11 13 34	+4 59	+ 2 56	5 26	5 21	11 57	18 27	18 32	23 16 30	0 43 23
11	11 17 09	+4 36	+ 3 17	5 27	5 23	11 57	18 25	18 29	23 20 27	0 39 27
12	11 20 45	+4 14	+ 3 38	5 29	5 25	11 56	18 23	18 27	23 24 23	0 35 31
13	11 24 20	+3 51	+ 3 59	5 30	5 27	11 56	18 20	18 24	23 28 20	0 31 35
14	11 27 56	+3 28	+ 4 20	5 32	5 29	11 55	18 18	18 21	23 32 16	0 27 39
15	11 31 31	+3 05	+ 4 42	5 34	5 31	11 55	18 16	18 19	23 36 13	0 23 43
16	11 35 06	+2 41	+ 5 03	5 35	5 33	11 55	18 13	18 16	23 40 09	0 19 47
17	11 38 41	+2 18	+ 5 24	5 37	5 35	11 54	18 11	18 13	23 44 06	0 15 52
18	11 42 17	+1 55	+ 5 46	5 39	5 36	11 54	18 09	18 11	23 48 02	0 11 56
19	11 45 52	+1 32	+ 6 07	5 40	5 38	11 54	18 06	18 08	23 51 59	0 08 00
20	11 49 27	+1 09	+ 6 28	5 42	5 40	11 53	18 04	18 05	23 55 56	0 04 04
21	11 53 02	+0 45	+ 6 50	5 44	5 42	11 53	18 02	18 03	23 59 52	{ 0 00 08 / 23 56 12
22	11 56 38	+0 22	+ 7 11	5 45	5 44	11 53	17 59	18 00	0 03 49	23 52 16
23	12 00 13	−0 01	+ 7 32	5 47	5 46	11 52	17 57	17 57	0 07 45	23 48 20
24	12 03 48	−0 25	+ 7 53	5 48	5 48	11 52	17 55	17 55	0 11 42	23 44 24
25	12 07 24	−0 48	+ 8 14	5 50	5 50	11 52	17 52	17 52	0 15 38	23 40 28
26	12 11 00	−1 12	+ 8 35	5 52	5 52	11 51	17 50	17 49	0 19 35	23 36 32
27	12 14 36	−1 35	+ 8 55	5 54	5 54	11 51	17 48	17 47	0 23 31	23 32 37
28	12 18 12	−1 58	+ 9 16	5 55	5 56	11 51	17 46	17 44	0 27 28	23 28 41
29	12 21 49	−2 22	+ 9 36	5 57	5 58	11 50	17 44	17 42	0 31 24	23 24 45
30	12 25 26	−2 45	+ 9 55	5 58	6 00	11 50	17 41	17 39	0 35 21	23 20 49

Duration of Civil (C), Nautical (N), and Astronomical (A), Twilight (in minutes)

Lat. °	Sept. 1 C	N	A	Sept. 11 C	N	A	Sept. 21 C	N	A	Sept. 30 C	N	A
52	35	79	127	34	76	120	34	74	115	34	73	113
56	39	89	146	38	84	135	37	82	129	37	80	126

ASTRONOMICAL NOTES

MERCURY is only visible as a difficult morning star, magnitude −0·7 to −1·1, low above the E.S.E. horizon, at the time of beginning of morning civil twilight, for the first few days of the month. On the mornings of the 4th and 5th Mercury is only about 1° from Regulus, Mercury being noticeably the brighter object. For the remainder of the month Mercury is too close to the Sun for observation, superior conjunction occurring on the 19th.

VENUS is a brilliant morning star, magnitude −3·8, visible in the eastern sky for several hours before sunrise. The old crescent Moon is near the planet on the morning of the 4th.

MARS is unsuitably placed for observation, conjunction occurring on the 7th.

JUPITER is an evening star, magnitude −1·8. The Moon, just after First Quarter, is near on the evenings of the 15th and 16th.

SATURN is a morning star, magnitude +0·3, in the constellation of Taurus. The Moon (at Last Quarter) is near on the mornings of the 28th and 29th.

ZODIACAL LIGHT. The morning cone may be seen in the eastern sky before twilight commences, from the 6th to the 21st. This faint phenomenon can only be seen in the absence of both moonlight and artificial lighting.

THE MOON

Day	R.A.	Dec.	Hor. Par.	Semi-diam.	Sun's Co-long.	P.A. of Bright Limb	Phase	Age	Rise 52°	Rise 56°	Transit	Set 52°	Set 56°
	h m	°	'	'	°	°		d	h m	h m	h m	h m	h m
1	4 52	+25.9	59.1	16.1	183	84	45	22.8	22 34	22 03	6 27	15 22	15 53
2	5 54	+25.7	58.7	16.0	195	90	34	23.8	23 48	23 20	7 27	16 11	16 39
3	6 55	+24.0	58.3	15.9	207	96	24	24.8	..	..	8 25	16 47	17 09
4	7 52	+20.9	57.9	15.8	220	101	15	25.8	1 08	0 46	9 20	17 13	17 30
5	8 47	+16.6	57.4	15.6	232	103	8	26.8	2 29	2 13	10 10	17 33	17 44
6	9 37	+11.7	56.9	15.5	244	103	3	27.8	3 48	3 38	10 57	17 49	17 55
7	10 25	+6.3	56.4	15.4	256	91	1	28.8	5 04	5 00	11 42	18 03	18 04
8	11 12	+0.7	55.9	15.2	269	345	0	0.3	6 19	6 19	12 25	18 16	18 13
9	11 57	−4.8	55.4	15.1	281	311	2	1.3	7 31	7 37	13 07	18 30	18 22
10	12 42	−10.0	55.0	15.0	293	303	5	2.3	8 44	8 54	13 50	18 45	18 33
11	13 28	−14.7	54.6	14.9	305	298	10	3.3	9 55	10 11	14 34	19 03	18 45
12	14 15	−18.8	54.3	14.8	317	294	17	4.3	11 06	11 28	15 19	19 25	19 02
13	15 04	−22.1	54.2	14.8	330	289	25	5.3	12 15	12 41	16 07	19 53	19 20
14	15 54	−24.5	54.2	14.8	342	283	33	6.3	13 18	13 49	16 56	20 31	20 00
15	16 46	−25.7	54.4	14.8	354	278	42	7.3	14 14	14 46	17 47	21 20	20 48
16	17 40	−25.8	54.7	14.9	6	272	52	8.3	15 00	15 30	18 38	22 20	21 50
17	18 33	−24.7	55.2	15.0	19	266	62	9.3	15 36	16 01	19 29	23 29	23 04
18	19 26	−22.3	55.9	15.2	31	261	71	10.3	16 04	16 24	20 20	..	..
19	20 19	−18.8	56.7	15.4	43	258	80	11.3	16 26	16 40	21 09	0 45	0 26
20	21 11	−14.3	57.5	15.7	55	255	88	12.3	16 44	16 54	21 58	2 04	1 51
21	22 02	−9.0	58.4	15.9	67	255	94	13.3	17 01	17 05	22 46	3 25	3 18
22	22 53	−3.0	59.2	16.1	79	261	98	14.3	17 17	17 15	23 36	4 48	4 47
23	23 44	+3.3	59.8	16.3	92	309	100	15.3	17 33	17 27	..	6 13	6 18
24	0 38	+9.4	60.3	16.4	104	44	99	16.3	17 52	17 40	0 27	7 41	7 51
25	1 34	+15.2	60.5	16.5	116	58	95	17.3	18 16	17 58	1 21	9 10	9 27
26	2 32	+20.0	60.4	16.5	128	66	89	18.3	18 48	18 24	2 18	10 40	11 03
27	3 34	+23.5	60.1	16.4	140	73	80	19.3	19 31	19 02	3 18	12 03	12 32
28	4 37	+25.5	59.7	16.3	152	80	70	20.3	20 29	19 58	4 20	13 14	13 45
29	5 40	+25.7	59.2	16.1	165	88	59	21.3	21 39	21 11	5 22	14 09	14 38
30	6 41	+24.3	58.5	16.0	177	94	48	22.3	22 57	22 34	6 21	14 48	15 12

MERCURY ☿

Day	R.A.	Dec. +	Diam.	Phase	5° high E 52°	5° high E 56°	Transit	Day	R.A.	Dec.	Diam.	Phase	Transit	
	h m	°	"		h m	h m	h m		h m	°	"		h m	
1	9 40	14.9	6	69	4 15	4 06	11 00	16	11 25	+5.6	5	99	11 47	Mercury is too close to the Sun for observation
4	10 00	13.7	6	80	4 30	4 22	11 09	19	11 46	+3.3	5	100	11 55	
7	10 21	12.0	5	88	4 49	4 42	11 18	22	12 05	+0.9	5	100	12 03	
10	10 43	10.1	5	94	5 09	5 04	11 28	25	12 25	−1.5	5	99	12 10	
13	11 04	7.9	5	97	5 30	5 27	11 38	28	12 43	−3.8	5	98	12 17	
16	11 25	5.6	5	99	5 50	5 49	11 47	31	13 01	−6.0	4	97	12 23	

VENUS ♀   MARS ♂

Day	R.A.	Dec. +	Diam.	Phase	5° high E 52°	5° high E 56°	Transit	Day	R.A.	Dec. +	Diam.	Phase	Transit	
	h m	°	"		h m	h m	h m		h m	°	"		h m	
1	7 37	19.0	23	53	1 49	1 35	8 56	1	10 51	8.5	4	—	12 09	Mars is too close to the Sun for observation
6	7 58	18.5	21	55	1 53	1 40	8 58	6	11 03	7.3	4	—	12 01	
11	8 20	17.8	20	58	1 59	1 47	9 00	11	11 14	6.0	4	—	11 53	
16	8 42	16.9	20	60	2 06	1 55	9 02	16	11 26	4.7	4	—	11 45	
21	9 04	15.8	19	62	2 15	2 05	9 05	21	11 38	3.5	4	—	11 37	
26	9 27	14.5	18	64	2 25	2 16	9 07	26	11 50	2.2	4	—	11 29	
31	9 49	13.1	17	66	2 35	2 28	9 10	31	12 02	0.9	4	—	11 21	

SUNRISE AND SUNSET (G.M.T.)

Day	London a.m. h m	London p.m. h m	Bristol a.m. h m	Bristol p.m. h m	Birmingham a.m. h m	Birmingham p.m. h m	Manchester a.m. h m	Manchester p.m. h m	Newcastle a.m. h m	Newcastle p.m. h m	Glasgow a.m. h m	Glasgow p.m. h m	Belfast a.m. h m	Belfast p.m. h m
1	5 12	6 47	5 22	6 57	5 17	6 56	5 17	7 00	5 11	7 00	5 20	7 13	5 30	7 17
2	5 13	6 45	5 23	6 55	5 18	6 54	5 19	6 57	5 13	6 57	5 22	7 10	5 32	7 14
3	5 15	6 43	5 25	6 53	5 20	6 52	5 21	6 55	5 15	6 54	5 24	7 07	5 34	7 12
4	5 17	6 40	5 27	6 50	5 22	6 49	5 23	6 52	5 17	6 52	5 26	7 05	5 36	7 09
5	5 18	6 38	5 28	6 48	5 23	6 47	5 24	6 50	5 19	6 49	5 28	7 02	5 37	7 07
6	5 20	6 36	5 30	6 46	5 25	6 44	5 26	6 47	5 21	6 47	5 30	7 00	5 39	7 04
7	5 22	6 34	5 32	6 43	5 27	6 42	5 28	6 45	5 23	6 44	5 32	6 57	5 41	7 02
8	5 23	6 32	5 33	6 41	5 29	6 40	5 30	6 43	5 25	6 41	5 34	6 54	5 43	7 00
9	5 25	6 30	5 35	6 39	5 31	6 37	5 32	6 40	5 27	6 39	5 36	6 52	5 45	6 57
10	5 27	6 27	5 37	6 36	5 32	6 35	5 33	6 38	5 28	6 37	5 38	6 49	5 46	6 55
11	5 28	6 25	5 38	6 34	5 34	6 32	5 35	6 35	5 30	6 34	5 40	6 46	5 48	6 52
12	5 30	6 23	5 40	6 32	5 36	6 30	5 37	6 33	5 32	6 32	5 42	6 44	5 50	6 50
13	5 31	6 20	5 41	6 30	5 37	6 27	5 38	6 30	5 34	6 29	5 44	6 41	5 52	6 47
14	5 32	6 18	5 42	6 28	5 39	6 25	5 40	6 28	5 36	6 26	5 46	6 38	5 54	6 44
15	5 34	6 16	5 44	6 26	5 41	6 23	5 42	6 26	5 38	6 24	5 48	6 36	5 56	6 41
16	5 36	6 13	5 46	6 23	5 42	6 20	5 43	6 23	5 40	6 21	5 50	6 33	5 58	6 39
17	5 37	6 11	5 47	6 21	5 44	6 18	5 45	6 21	5 42	6 18	5 52	6 30	6 00	6 36
18	5 39	6 09	5 49	6 19	5 46	6 16	5 47	6 19	5 43	6 16	5 53	6 28	6 02	6 34
19	5 40	6 06	5 50	6 16	5 47	6 13	5 48	6 16	5 45	6 14	5 55	6 25	6 03	6 31
20	5 42	6 04	5 52	6 14	5 49	6 11	5 50	6 14	5 47	6 11	5 57	6 22	6 05	6 29
21	5 44	6 02	5 54	6 12	5 51	6 09	5 52	6 11	5 49	6 08	5 59	6 20	6 07	6 26
22	5 45	5 59	5 55	6 09	5 52	6 06	5 54	6 09	5 51	6 06	6 01	6 17	6 09	6 24
23	5 47	5 57	5 57	6 07	5 54	6 04	5 56	6 06	5 53	6 03	6 03	6 14	6 11	6 21
24	5 48	5 55	5 58	6 05	5 55	6 02	5 57	6 04	5 54	6 01	6 05	6 12	6 12	6 19
25	5 50	5 52	6 00	6 02	5 57	5 59	5 59	6 01	5 56	5 58	6 07	6 09	6 14	6 16
26	5 52	5 50	6 02	6 00	5 59	5 57	6 01	5 59	5 58	5 56	6 09	6 06	6 16	6 14
27	5 54	5 48	6 04	5 58	6 01	5 55	6 03	5 56	6 00	5 53	6 11	6 04	6 18	6 11
28	5 55	5 46	6 05	5 56	6 02	5 53	6 05	5 54	6 02	5 51	6 13	6 01	6 20	6 09
29	5 57	5 44	6 07	5 54	6 04	5 51	6 06	5 52	6 03	5 48	6 15	5 59	6 21	6 06
30	5 58	5 41	6 08	5 51	6 05	5 48	6 08	5 49	6 05	5 46	6 17	5 56	6 23	6 04

JUPITER ♃   SATURN ♄

Day	R.A. h m	Dec. − °	Transit h m	5° high West 52° h m	5° high West 56° h m	R.A. h m	Dec. + °	5° high East 52° h m	5° high East 56° h m	Transit h m
1	17 54	23·4	19 10	22 09	21 32	5 16	21·5	23 09	22 53	6 34
11	17 55	23·4	18 32	21 31	20 54	5 18	21·5	22 31	22 15	5 56
21	17 57	23·5	17 56	20 54	20 18	5 19	21·5	21 53	21 37	5 18
31	18 02	23·5	17 20	20 19	19 42	5 20	21·5	21 14	20 58	4 40

Equatorial diameter of Jupiter 39″; of Saturn 19″. Diameters of Saturn's rings 42″ and 19″.

URANUS ♅   NEPTUNE ♆

Day	R.A. h m	Dec. − ° ′	Transit h m		R.A. h m	Dec. − ° ′	Transit h m	10° high in West 52° h m	10° high in West 56° h m
1	13 00·9	5 50	14 18	Uranus is too	16 03·4	19 05	17 20	20 08	19 30
11	13 02·9	6 03	13 40	close to the	16 03·9	19 07	16 41	19 29	18 51
21	13 05·1	6 16	13 03	Sun for	16 04·6	19 10	16 02	18 50	18 12
31	13 07·4	6 31	12 26	observation	16 05·5	19 13	15 24	18 11	17 32

Diameter 4″   Diameter 2″

		Octo (eight), 8th month of Roman (pre-Julian) Calendar. Sun's Longitude 210° ♏ 23ᵈ 08ʰ

Month / Week

1   ♋.   18th Sunday after Trinity.   Landseer d. 1873.
2   M.   MICHAELMAS LAW SITTINGS BEGIN
3   Tu.   William Morris d. 1896.   Sir Arnold Bax d. 1953
4   W.   Rembrandt d. 1669.   Lord Keyes b. 1872★★.
5   Th.   Sir Frank Francis b. 1901
6   F.   Tennyson d. 1892.   Walter Hagen d. 1969
7   S.   Sir Hubert Parry d. 1918.   Marie Lloyd d. 1922

8   ♋.   19th Sunday after Trinity.   Pierre Trudeau b. 1919
9   M.   Duke of Kent b. 1935.   Lord Hailsham b. 1907
10   Tu.   Edouard Daladier d. 1970
11   W.   Camperdown 1797
12   Th.   Christopher Soames b. 1920.   Sonja Henie d. 1969
13   F.   Sir Henry Irving d. 1905.   Sir Stanley Unwin d. 1968
14   S.   James II b. 1633.   Eamon de Valera b. 1882

15   ♋.   20th Sunday after Trinity.   Lord Snow b. 1905
16   M.   Nuremberg executions 1946
17   Tu.   Chopin d. 1849
18   W.   St. Luke.   Lord Shinwell b. 1884
19   Th.   Swift d. 1745.   Lord Rutherford d. 1937
20   F.   Grace Darling d. 1842.   Herbert Hoover d. 1964
21   S.   TRAFALGAR DAY (1805)

22   ♋.   21st Sunday after Trinity.   Lord Carson d. 1935
23   M.   Cézanne d. 1906.   W. G. Grace d. 1915
24   Tu.   Franz Lehar d. 1948
25   W.   George II d. 1760.   S. T. Coleridge b. 1772★★
26   Th.   Hogarth d. 1764
27   F.   Sir Oliver Leese b. 1894
28   S.   St. Simon and St. Jude.   John Locke d. 1704

29   ♋.   22nd ♋. after Trinity.   Wilfred Rhodes b.1877
30   M.   Bonar Law d. 1923.   Dame Rose Macaulay d. 1958
31   Tu.   Hallowmas Eve.   Augustus John d. 1961

(G.M.T.)

PHENOMENA

October 3ᵈ 18ʰ Venus in conjunction with the Moon. Venus 3° N.

8ᵈ 16ʰ Mercury in conjunction with the Moon. Mercury 5° N.

11ᵈ 23ʰ Uranus in conjunction with the Sun.

13ᵈ 21ʰ Jupiter in conjunction with the Moon. Jupiter 2° N.

25ᵈ 23ʰ Saturn in conjunction with the Moon. Saturn 4° S.

CONSTELLATIONS

The following constellations are near the meridian at

	d	h		d	h
Sept.	1	24	Sept.	15	23
Oct.	1	22	Oct.	16	21
Nov.	1	20	Nov.	15	19

Ursa Major (below the Pole), Cepheus, Cassiopeia, Cygnus, Lacerta, Andromeda, Pegasus, Capricornus, Aquarius and Piscis Austrinus.

MINIMA OF ALGOL

d	h	d	h
2	09	19	13
5	05	22	10
8	02	25	07
10	23	28	04
13	20	31	01
16	17		

(G.M.T.)

PHASES OF THE MOON

	d	h	m
● New Moon	7	08	08
☽ First Quarter	15	12	55
○ Full Moon	22	13	25
☾ Last Quarter	29	04	41

	d	h
Apogee (405,920 kilometres)	11	03
Perigee (358,310 ,,)	23	12

Mean Longitude of Ascending Node on October 1, 292°.

MONTHLY NOTES

Oct. 2. Pheasant shooting begins.
     9. Ramadân begins (A.H. 1392).
    12. Columbus Day, U.S.A.
    14. Michaelmas Fire Insurances must be paid.
    22. Hunter's Moon.
    29. *Summer Time* ends at 2 a.m. G.M.T.

NATIONAL DAYS.—Oct. 1, China, Cyprus, Nigeria; 2, Guinea; 4, Lesotho; 9, Uganda, Khmer Republic; 10, Fiji; 14, Madagascar, Yemen P.D.R.; 21, Somalia; 24, Zambia; 26, Austria; Iran; 29, Turkey.

★★ Centenary

Day	Right Ascension	Dec. —	Equation of Time	Rise 52°	Rise 56°	Transit	Set 52°	Set 56°	Sidereal Time	Transit of First Point of Aries (G.M.T.)
	h m s	° '	m s	h m	h m	h m	h m	h m	h m s	h m s
1	12 29 03	3 08	+10 15	6 00	6 02	11 50	17 38	17 36	0 39 18	23 16 53
2	12 32 40	3 32	+10 34	6 02	6 04	11 49	17 36	17 34	0 43 14	23 12 57
3	12 36 18	3 55	+10 53	6 03	6 06	11 49	17 34	17 31	0 47 11	23 09 01
4	12 39 56	4 18	+11 11	6 05	6 08	11 49	17 31	17 28	0 51 07	23 05 05
5	12 43 34	4 41	+11 30	6 07	6 10	11 48	17 29	17 26	0 55 04	23 01 09
6	12 47 13	5 04	+11 47	6 08	6 12	11 48	17 27	17 23	0 59 00	22 57 13
7	12 50 52	5 27	+12 05	6 10	6 14	11 48	17 25	17 21	1 02 57	22 53 18
8	12 54 32	5 50	+12 22	6 12	6 16	11 47	17 22	17 18	1 06 53	22 49 22
9	12 58 11	6 13	+12 38	6 14	6 18	11 47	17 20	17 16	1 10 50	22 45 26
10	13 01 52	6 36	+12 55	6 15	6 20	11 47	17 18	17 13	1 14 47	22 41 30
11	13 05 33	6 59	+13 10	6 17	6 22	11 47	17 16	17 10	1 18 43	22 37 34
12	13 09 14	7 21	+13 25	6 19	6 24	11 46	17 13	17 08	1 22 40	22 33 38
13	13 12 56	7 44	+13 40	6 21	6 26	11 46	17 11	17 05	1 26 36	22 29 42
14	13 16 38	8 06	+13 54	6 22	6 28	11 46	17 09	17 03	1 30 33	22 25 46
15	13 20 21	8 28	+14 08	6 24	6 30	11 46	17 07	17 00	1 34 29	22 21 50
16	13 24 05	8 50	+14 21	6 26	6 32	11 46	17 05	16 58	1 38 26	22 17 54
17	13 27 49	9 13	+14 34	6 28	6 35	11 45	17 02	16 55	1 42 22	22 13 58
18	13 31 33	9 34	+14 46	6 29	6 37	11 45	17 00	16 53	1 46 19	22 10 03
19	13 35 18	9 56	+14 57	6 31	6 39	11 45	16 58	16 50	1 50 16	22 06 07
20	13 39 04	10 18	+15 08	6 33	6 41	11 45	16 56	16 48	1 54 12	22 02 11
21	13 42 50	10 39	+15 18	6 35	6 43	11 45	16 54	16 46	1 58 09	21 58 15
22	13 46 37	11 01	+15 28	6 36	6 45	11 44	16 52	16 43	2 02 05	21 54 19
23	13 50 25	11 22	+15 37	6 38	6 47	11 44	16 50	16 41	2 06 02	21 50 23
24	13 54 13	11 43	+15 45	6 40	6 49	11 44	16 48	16 38	2 09 58	21 46 27
25	13 58 03	12 03	+15 52	6 42	6 51	11 44	16 46	16 36	2 13 55	21 42 31
26	14 01 52	12 24	+15 59	6 43	6 53	11 44	16 44	16 34	2 17 51	21 38 35
27	14 05 43	12 44	+16 05	6 45	6 56	11 44	16 42	16 31	2 21 48	21 34 39
28	14 09 34	13 05	+16 10	6 47	6 58	11 44	16 40	16 29	2 25 45	21 30 43
29	14 13 26	13 25	+16 15	6 49	7 00	11 44	16 38	16 27	2 29 41	21 26 48
30	14 17 19	13 45	+16 18	6 50	7 02	11 44	16 36	16 25	2 33 38	21 22 52
31	14 21 13	14 04	+16 21	6 52	7 04	11 44	16 34	16 22	2 37 34	21 18 56

THE SUN   s.d. 16'·1

Duration of Civil (C), Nautical (N), and Astronomical (A), Twilight (in minutes)

Lat. °	Oct. 1 C	N	A	Oct. 11 C	N	A	Oct. 21 C	N	A	Oct. 31 C	N	A
52	34	73	113	34	73	112	34	74	113	36	75	114
56	37	80	125	37	80	124	38	81	124	40	83	126

ASTRONOMICAL NOTES

MERCURY is unsuitably placed for observation. VENUS is a brilliant morning star, magnitude −3·6, still visible in the eastern sky for several hours before sunrise. The old crescent Moon is near Venus on the mornings of the 3rd and 4th, while Venus itself is approaching Regulus, passing 0°·3 S. of that star only a few hours before it rises on the 5th.

MARS is unsuitably placed for observation for most of the month. By the end of the month, under very good conditions, it may be glimpsed low above the E.S.E. horizon at about 06ʰ. Its magnitude is +2·0.

JUPITER is an evening star, magnitude −1·7. The crescent Moon passes 2° S. of Jupiter on the evening of the 13th.

SATURN is a morning star, magnitude +0·1, in the constellation of Taurus. The gibbous Moon passes 4° N. of Saturn late on the 25th.

THE MOON

Day	R.A.	Dec.	Hor. Par.	Semi-diam.	Sun's Co-long.	P.A. of Bright Limb	Phase	Age	Rise 52°	Rise 56°	Transit	Set 52°	Set 56°
	h m	°	'	'	°	°		d	h m	h m	h m	h m	h m
1	7 40	+21·5	57·9	15·8	189	100	37	23·3	..	..	7 16	15 17	15 35
2	8 34	+17·5	57·3	15·6	201	104	27	24·3	0 17	0 00	8 07	15 38	15 51
3	9 25	+12·8	56·8	15·5	213	106	18	25·3	1 36	1 24	8 54	15 55	16 03
4	10 13	+7·6	56·2	15·3	226	107	11	26·3	2 51	2 45	9 39	16 10	16 13
5	10 59	+2·2	55·7	15·2	238	105	5	27·3	4 05	4 04	10 22	16 24	16 22
6	11 44	−3·2	55·3	15·1	250	97	2	28·3	5 17	5 21	11 04	16 37	16 31
7	12 29	−8·4	54·9	15·0	262	62	0	29·3	6 29	6 38	11 46	16 52	16 42
8	13 14	−13·3	54·5	14·9	274	326	1	0·7	7 40	7 54	12 30	17 09	16 54
9	14 01	−17·5	54·3	14·8	287	304	3	1·7	8 51	9 11	13 15	17 30	17 09
10	14 49	−21·1	54·1	14·7	299	295	7	2·7	10 01	10 25	14 01	17 56	17 31
11	15 39	−23·7	54·0	14·7	311	288	12	3·7	11 06	11 35	14 50	18 30	18 01
12	16 31	−25·2	54·1	14·7	323	281	19	4·7	12 05	12 36	15 40	19 14	18 43
13	17 23	−25·7	54·3	14·8	336	275	27	5·7	12 54	13 24	16 30	20 09	19 39
14	18 16	−24·9	54·6	14·9	348	269	35	6·7	13 33	13 59	17 20	21 14	20 47
15	19 08	−23·0	55·1	15·0	0	263	45	7·7	14 03	14 25	18 10	22 25	22 04
16	20 00	−20·0	55·8	15·2	12	259	55	8·7	14 27	14 44	18 58	23 40	23 25
17	20 50	−16·0	56·6	15·4	24	255	65	9·7	14 46	14 58	19 46	..	..
18	21 41	−11·1	57·5	15·7	36	252	74	10·7	15 03	15 10	20 34	0 58	0 49
19	22 31	−5·5	58·5	15·9	49	252	83	11·7	15 19	15 21	21 22	2 19	2 14
20	23 21	+0·6	59·4	16·2	61	253	91	12·7	15 36	15 32	22 12	3 41	3 43
21	0 14	+6·8	60·2	16·4	73	258	96	13·7	15 54	15 45	23 05	5 07	5 14
22	1 09	+12·8	60·8	16·6	85	280	99	14·7	16 16	16 01		6 37	6 50
23	2 08	+18·1	61·2	16·7	97	33	100	15·7	16 45	16 24	0 02	8 08	8 28
24	3 10	+22·2	61·2	16·7	109	63	97	16·7	17 25	16 57	1 03	9 38	10 04
25	4 15	+24·8	60·9	16·6	122	75	91	17·7	18 18	17 48	2 06	10 57	11 28
26	5 20	+25·6	60·3	16·4	134	84	83	18·7	19 27	18 58	3 11	12 00	12 30
27	6 24	+24·6	59·6	16·2	146	92	74	19·7	20 45	20 20	4 13	12 47	13 12
28	7 25	+22·1	58·8	16·0	158	98	63	20·7	22 06	21 47	5 11	13 19	13 39
29	8 21	+18·3	57·9	15·8	170	103	52	21·7	23 26	23 13	6 04	13 43	13 57
30	9 13	+13·7	57·1	15·6	182	107	41	22·7	..	..	6 53	14 02	14 11
31	10 02	+8·6	56·4	15·4	195	109	31	23·7	0 42	0 35	7 38	14 17	14 22

MERCURY ☿

Day	R.A.	Dec. −	Diam.	Phase	Transit	Day	R.A.	Dec. −	Diam.	Phase	Transit
	h m	°	"		h m		h m	°	"		h m
1	13 01	6·0	5	97	12 23	16	14 28	16·0	5	89	12 51
4	13 19	8·2	5	96	12 29	19	14 45	17·6	5	86	12 56
7	13 37	10·3	5	94	12 35	22	15 02	19·2	5	84	13 00
10	13 54	12·3	5	93	12 40	25	15 18	20·5	6	81	13 05
13	14 11	14·2	5	91	12 45	28	15 34	21·7	6	77	13 09
16	14 28	16·0	5	89	12 51	31	15 50	22·8	6	72	13 13

Mercury is too close to the Sun for observation   Mercury is too close to the Sun for observation

VENUS ♀

Day	R.A.	Dec. +	Diam.	Phase	5° high E 52°	5° high E 56°	Transit
	h m	°	"		h m	h m	h m
1	9 49	13·1	17	66	2 35	2 28	9 10
6	10 12	11·4	17	68	2 46	2 40	9 13
11	10 34	9·7	16	70	2 58	2 54	9 15
16	10 56	7·7	16	72	3 11	3 08	9 18
21	11 18	5·7	15	74	3 24	3 23	9 20
26	11 41	3·5	15	75	3 37	3 38	9 23
31	12 03	1·3	14	77	3 51	3 54	9 25

MARS ♂

Day	R.A.	Dec.	Diam.	Phase	5° high E 52°	5° high E 56°	Transit
	h m	°	"		h m	h m	h m
1	12 02	+0·9	4	−	5 50	5 53	11 22
6	12 13	−0·5	4	−	5 49	5 53	11 14
11	12 25	−1·8	4	−	5 48	5 53	11 06
16	12 37	−3·1	4	−	5 47	5 53	10 58
21	12 49	−4·4	4	−	5 46	5 53	10 50
26	13 01	−5·6	4	−	5 46	5 54	10 43
31	13 13	−6·9	4	−	5 45	5 55	10 35

SUNRISE AND SUNSET (G.M.T.)

Day	London a.m. h m	London p.m. h m	Bristol a.m. h m	Bristol p.m. h m	Birmingham a.m. h m	Birmingham p.m. h m	Manchester a.m. h m	Manchester p.m. h m	Newcastle a.m. h m	Newcastle p.m. h m	Glasgow a.m. h m	Glasgow p.m. h m	Belfast a.m. h m	Belfast p.m. h m
1	6 00	5 38	6 10	5 48	6 07	5 45	6 10	5 46	6 07	5 43	6 19	5 53	6 25	6 01
2	6 02	5 36	6 12	5 46	6 09	5 43	6 12	5 44	6 09	5 41	6 21	5 51	6 27	5 59
3	6 03	5 34	6 13	5 44	6 10	5 41	6 13	5 42	6 11	5 38	6 23	5 48	6 29	5 56
4	6 05	5 32	6 15	5 42	6 12	5 38	6 15	5 39	6 13	5 35	6 25	5 45	6 31	5 53
5	6 07	5 30	6 17	5 40	6 14	5 36	6 17	5 37	6 15	5 33	6 27	5 43	6 33	5 51
6	6 08	5 27	6 18	5 37	6 15	5 34	6 18	5 35	6 17	5 30	6 29	5 40	6 35	5 48
7	6 10	5 25	6 20	5 35	6 17	5 32	6 20	5 33	6 19	5 28	6 31	5 38	6 37	5 46
8	6 12	5 23	6 21	5 33	6 19	5 29	6 22	5 30	6 21	5 25	6 33	5 35	6 39	5 43
9	6 14	5 21	6 23	5 31	6 21	5 27	6 24	5 28	6 23	5 23	6 35	5 33	6 41	5 41
10	6 15	5 19	6 24	5 29	6 23	5 24	6 26	5 25	6 25	5 20	6 37	5 30	6 43	5 38
11	6 17	5 17	6 26	5 27	6 25	5 22	6 28	5 23	6 27	5 18	6 39	5 27	6 45	5 36
12	6 19	5 14	6 28	5 24	6 26	5 20	6 29	5 21	6 28	5 16	6 41	5 25	6 46	5 34
13	6 20	5 12	6 30	5 22	6 28	5 17	6 31	5 18	6 30	5 13	6 43	5 22	6 48	5 31
14	6 22	5 10	6 31	5 20	6 30	5 15	6 33	5 16	6 32	5 11	6 45	5 20	6 50	5 29
15	6 23	5 08	6 33	5 18	6 32	5 13	6 35	5 14	6 34	5 08	6 47	5 17	6 52	5 27
16	6 25	5 06	6 35	5 16	6 34	5 11	6 37	5 11	6 36	5 06	6 49	5 15	6 54	5 24
17	6 27	5 03	6 37	5 13	6 36	5 08	6 39	5 09	6 39	5 03	6 52	5 12	6 56	5 22
18	6 28	5 01	6 38	5 11	6 37	5 06	6 41	5 07	6 41	5 01	6 54	5 10	6 58	5 20
19	6 30	4 59	6 40	5 09	6 39	5 04	6 43	5 04	6 43	4 58	6 56	5 07	7 00	5 17
20	6 32	4 57	6 42	5 07	6 41	5 02	6 45	5 02	6 45	4 56	6 58	5 05	7 02	5 15
21	6 34	4 55	6 44	5 05	6 43	5 00	6 47	5 00	6 47	4 54	7 00	5 03	7 04	5 13
22	6 35	4 53	6 45	5 03	6 44	4 58	6 48	4 58	6 48	4 52	7 02	5 00	7 06	5 10
23	6 37	4 51	6 47	5 01	6 46	4 56	6 50	4 55	6 50	4 49	7 04	4 58	7 08	5 08
24	6 39	4 49	6 49	4 59	6 48	4 54	6 52	4 53	6 52	4 47	7 06	4 55	7 10	5 05
25	6 41	4 47	6 51	4 57	6 50	4 52	6 54	4 51	6 54	4 45	7 08	4 53	7 12	5 03
26	6 42	4 45	6 52	4 55	6 51	4 50	6 56	4 49	6 56	4 43	7 10	4 51	7 14	5 01
27	6 44	4 43	6 54	4 53	6 53	4 48	6 58	4 47	6 59	4 40	7 13	4 48	7 16	4 59
28	6 46	4 41	6 56	4 51	6 55	4 46	7 00	4 45	7 01	4 38	7 15	4 46	7 18	4 57
29	6 48	4 39	6 58	4 49	6 57	4 44	7 02	4 42	7 03	4 36	7 17	4 44	7 20	4 55
30	6 49	4 37	6 59	4 47	6 58	4 42	7 03	4 41	7 05	4 34	7 19	4 42	7 22	4 53
31	6 51	4 35	7 01	4 45	7 00	4 40	7 05	4 39	7 07	4 32	7 21	4 40	7 24	4 51

JUPITER ♃

Day	R.A. h m	Dec. − °	Transit h m	5° high West 52° h m	5° high West 56° h m
1	18 02	23·5	17 20	20 19	19 42
11	18 08	23·5	16 46	19 45	19 08
21	18 14	23·5	16 13	19 12	18 35
31	18 21	23·4	15 41	18 40	18 04

SATURN ♄

R.A. h m	Dec. + °	5° high East 52° h m	5° high East 56° h m	Transit h m
5 20	21·5	21 14	20 58	4 40
5 19	21·5	20 35	20 19	4 00
5 18	21·4	19 55	19 39	3 20
5 16	21·4	19 14	18 58	2 38

Equatorial diameter of Jupiter 36″; of Saturn 20″. Diameters of Saturn's rings 44″ and 20″.

URANUS ♅

Day	R.A. h m	Dec. − ° ′	Transit h m	
1	13 07·4	6 31	12 26	Uranus is too
11	13 09·7	6 45	11 49	close to the
21	13 12·1	6 59	11 12	Sun for
31	13 14·4	7 13	10 35	observation

Diameter 4″

NEPTUNE ♆

R.A. h m	Dec. − ° ′	Transit h m	
16 05·5	19 13	15 24	Neptune is too
16 06·6	19 16	14 46	close to the
16 07·9	19 20	14 07	Sun for
17 09·2	19 24	13 30	observation

Diameter 2″

Novem (nine), 9th month of Roman (pre-Julian) Calendar.

Sun's Longitude 240° ♐ 22^{d} 05^{h}

Day of Month	Day of Week	
1	W.	**All Saints.** Edmund Blunden b. 1896
2	Th.	All Souls' Day. G. B. Shaw d. 1950
3	F.	J. G. Winant d. 1947. Matisse d. 1954
4	S.	Mendelssohn d. 1847. Sir John Dill d. 1944
5	S.	**23rd S. after Trinity.** Guy Fawkes Day (1605)
6	M.	Michael Stewart b. 1906. Sir J. Forbes Robertson
7	Tu.	Norman Shaw d. 1912 [d. 1937
8	W.	Allied Landing in North Africa 1942
9	Th.	Edward VII b. 1841. Gen. de Gaulle d. 1970
10	F.	Richard Burton b. 1925. Kemal Ataturk d. 1938
11	S.	ARMISTICE DAY 1918. Roy Jenkins b. 1920
12	S.	**24th Sunday after Trinity.** Mrs. Gaskell d. 1865
13	M.	Francis Thompson d. 1907
14	Tu.	PRINCE OF WALES BORN 1948
15	W.	Sir Sacheverell Sitwell b. 1897
16	Th.	Gustavus Adolphus d. 1632. Clark Gable d. 1960
17	F.	Visct. Montgomery of Alamein b. 1887
18	S.	T. P. O'Connor d. 1929. Clifford Bax d. 1962
19	S.	**25th Sunday after Trinity.** Charles I b. 1600
20	M.	QUEEN'S WEDDING DAY (1947)
21	Tu.	Gen. Hertzog d. 1942
22	W.	Benjamin Britten b. 1913. John F. Kennedy d. 1963
23	Th.	Richard Hakluyt d. 1616. Sir A. Pinero d. 1934
24	F.	Clemenceau d. 1929. Lilian Baylis d. 1937
25	S.	Isaac Watts d. 1748. Dame Myra Hess d. 1965
26	S.	**26th Sunday after Trinity.** Coventry Patmore d.
27	M.	Eugene O'Neill d. 1952 [1896
28	Tu.	Enid Blyton d. 1968
29	W.	Prince Rupert d. 1682. Sir George Robey d. 1954
30	Th.	**St. Andrew.** Lord Adrian b. 1889

(G.M.T.)

PHENOMENA

November 2^{d} 23^{h} Venus in conjunction with the Moon. Venus 7° N.

4^{d} 11^{h} Mars in conjunction with the Moon. Mars 6° N.

5^{d} 10^{h} Mercury at greatest eastern elongation (23°).

8^{d} 04^{h} Mercury in conjunction with the Moon. Mercury 0°·5 N.

10^{d} 13^{h} Jupiter in conjunction with the Moon. Jupiter 0°·9 N.

22^{d} 07^{h} Saturn in conjunction with the Moon. Saturn 4° S.

26^{d} 04^{h} Mercury in inferior conjunction with the Sun.

27^{d} 03^{h} Neptune in conjunction with the Sun.

CONSTELLATIONS

The following constellations are near the meridian at

	d	h		d	h
Oct.	1	24	Oct.	16	23
Nov.	1	22	Nov.	15	21
Dec.	1	20	Dec.	16	19

Ursa Major (below the Pole), Cepheus, Cassiopeia, Andromeda, Pegasus, Pisces, Aquarius and Cetus.

MINIMA OF ALGOL

d	h	d	h
2	22	17	06
5	18	20	02
8	15	22	23
11	12	25	20
14	09	28	17

(G.M.T.)

PHASES OF THE MOON

	d	h	m
● New Moon	6	01	21
☽ First Quarter	14	05	01
○ Full Moon	20	23	07
☾ Last Quarter	27	17	45

	d	h
Apogee (406,570 kilometres)	7	13
Perigee (356,520 „)	21	00

Mean Longitude of Ascending Node on November 1, 290°.

MONTHLY NOTES

Nov. 1. Hallowmas. Fox-hunting begins.
7. Ramadân ends (A.H. 1392).
11. Martinmas. Scottish Term Day. Lord Mayor's Day. County Sheriffs, England and Wales, for next year, nominated.
12. Remembrance Sunday.
23. Thanksgiving Day, U.S.A.
29. Removal Day, Scotland.

NATIONAL DAYS.—*Nov.* 1, Algeria, Vietnam; 3, Panama; 7, U.S.S.R.; 11, Sweden; 22, Lebanon; 28, Mauritania; 29, Yugoslavia; 30, Barbados, Scotland (*see* above).

Day	Right Ascension	Dec. —	Equation of Time	Rise 52°	Rise 56°	Transit	Set 52°	Set 56°	Sidereal Time	Transit of First Point of Aries (G.M.T.)
	h m s	° ′	m s	h m	h m	h m	h m	h m	h m s	h m s
1	14 25 07	14 24	+16 23	6 54	7 06	11 44	16 32	16 20	2 41 31	21 15 00
2	14 29 03	14 43	+16 24	6 56	7 08	11 44	16 30	16 18	2 45 27	21 11 04
3	14 32 59	15 02	+16 25	6 58	7 10	11 44	16 29	16 16	2 49 24	21 07 08
4	14 36 56	15 20	+16 25	7 00	7 13	11 44	16 27	16 14	2 53 20	21 03 12
5	14 40 54	15 39	+16 23	7 01	7 15	11 44	16 25	16 12	2 57 17	20 59 16
6	14 44 52	15 57	+16 21	7 03	7 17	11 44	16 23	16 10	3 01 14	20 55 20
7	14 48 52	16 15	+16 18	7 05	7 19	11 44	16 22	16 08	3 05 10	20 51 24
8	14 52 52	16 32	+16 15	7 07	7 21	11 44	16 20	16 06	3 09 07	20 47 28
9	14 56 53	16 50	+16 10	7 09	7 23	11 44	16 18	16 04	3 13 03	20 43 33
10	15 00 55	17 07	+16 05	7 10	7 25	11 44	16 17	16 02	3 17 00	20 39 37
11	15 04 58	17 23	+15 58	7 12	7 27	11 44	16 15	16 00	3 20 56	20 35 41
12	15 09 01	17 40	+15 51	7 14	7 30	11 44	16 14	15 58	3 24 53	20 31 45
13	15 13 06	17 56	+15 43	7 16	7 32	11 44	16 12	15 56	3 28 49	20 27 49
14	15 17 11	18 12	+15 35	7 18	7 34	11 44	16 11	15 55	3 32 46	20 23 53
15	15 21 17	18 27	+15 25	7 19	7 36	11 45	16 09	15 53	3 36 43	20 19 57
16	15 25 24	18 43	+15 15	7 21	7 38	11 45	16 08	15 51	3 40 39	20 16 01
17	15 29 32	18 57	+15 03	7 23	7 40	11 45	16 07	15 49	3 44 36	20 12 05
18	15 33 41	19 12	+14 51	7 25	7 42	11 45	16 05	15 48	3 48 32	20 08 09
19	15 37 50	19 26	+14 39	7 26	7 44	11 45	16 04	15 46	3 52 29	20 04 13
20	15 42 00	19 40	+14 25	7 28	7 46	11 46	16 03	15 45	3 56 25	20 00 18
21	15 46 11	19 53	+14 11	7 30	7 48	11 46	16 02	15 43	4 00 22	19 56 22
22	15 50 23	20 07	+13 55	7 31	7 50	11 46	16 00	15 42	4 04 18	19 52 26
23	15 54 36	20 19	+13 39	7 33	7 52	11 46	15 59	15 40	4 08 15	19 48 30
24	15 58 49	20 32	+13 22	7 35	7 54	11 47	15 58	15 39	4 12 12	19 44 34
25	16 03 03	20 44	+13 05	7 36	7 56	11 47	15 57	15 38	4 16 08	19 40 38
26	16 07 18	20 55	+12 46	7 38	7 57	11 47	15 56	15 37	4 20 05	19 36 42
27	16 11 34	21 06	+12 27	7 39	7 59	11 48	15 56	15 35	4 24 01	19 32 46
28	16 15 51	21 17	+12 07	7 41	8 01	11 48	15 55	15 34	4 27 58	19 28 50
29	16 20 08	21 28	+11 46	7 42	8 03	11 48	15 54	15 33	4 31 54	19 24 54
30	16 24 26	21 38	+11 25	7 44	8 05	11 49	15 53	15 32	4 35 51	19 20 58

Duration of Civil (C), Nautical (N), and Astronomical (A), Twilight (in minutes)

Lat. °	Nov. 1 C	N	A	Nov. 11 C	N	A	Nov. 21 C	N	A	Nov. 30 C	N	A
52	36	75	115	37	78	117	38	80	120	39	82	123
56	40	84	127	41	87	130	43	90	134	45	93	137

ASTRONOMICAL NOTES

MERCURY is unsuitably placed for observation, inferior conjunction occurring on the 26th.

VENUS is a brilliant morning star, magnitude −3·5, still visible in the south-eastern sky for over 2 hours before sunrise. The old crescent Moon is near on the morning of the 3rd. Venus is moving rapidly eastwards and passes 4° N. of Spica late on the 17th.

MARS is a difficult morning star, magnitude +1·9, visible for a short while low above the E.S.E. horizon at about 06ʰ. On the morning of the 4th Mars passes 3° N. of Spica and is itself overtaken by the old crescent Moon later in the morning.

JUPITER is an evening star, magnitude −1·5, but by the end of the month is only visible for a short while, low in the S.W. sky after the end of evening civil twilight. On the evening of the 10th the Moon will be seen only a few degrees to the left of Jupiter.

SATURN is a prominent morning star, magnitude −0·2, in the constellation of Taurus. It is increasing in brightness as it moves towards opposition, and by the end of the month is visible shortly after 17ʰ. On the morning of the 22nd the gibbous Moon is near Saturn.

THE MOON

Day	R.A.	Dec.	Hor. Par.	Semi-diam.	Sun's Co-long.	P.A. of Bright Limb	Phase	Age	Rise 52°	Rise 56°	Transit	Set 52°	Set 56°
	h m	°	′	′	°	°		d	h m	h m	h m	h m	h m
1	10 48	+ 3.3	55.8	15.2	207	110	22	24.7	1 56	1 53	8 21	14 31	14 31
2	11 33	− 2.0	55.2	15.1	219	109	15	25.7	3 08	3 10	9 03	14 45	14 40
3	12 18	− 7.3	54.8	14.9	231	106	9	26.7	4 18	4 26	9 45	14 59	14 50
4	13 03	−12.1	54.5	14.8	243	101	4	27.7	5 29	5 41	10 27	15 15	15 02
5	13 49	−16.5	54.2	14.8	256	88	1	28.7	6 40	6 57	11 12	15 35	15 16
6	14 36	−20.1	54.0	14.7	268	26	0	29.7	7 49	8 12	11 58	15 59	15 36
7	15 26	−23.0	53.9	14.7	280	306	1	0.9	8 56	9 23	12 46	16 31	16 03
8	16 17	−24.8	53.9	14.7	292	289	3	1.9	9 57	10 27	13 35	17 12	16 42
9	17 09	−25.5	54.0	14.7	304	279	8	2.9	10 49	11 19	14 25	18 03	17 33
10	18 02	−25.0	54.2	14.8	317	272	13	3.9	11 31	11 59	15 15	19 04	18 37
11	18 54	−23.4	54.6	14.9	329	265	20	4.9	12 03	12 27	16 04	20 13	19 50
12	19 45	−20.7	55.0	15.0	341	260	29	5.9	12 29	12 47	16 52	21 25	21 08
13	20 35	−17.1	55.7	15.2	353	255	38	6.9	12 49	13 03	17 39	22 40	22 28
14	21 23	−12.6	56.4	15.4	5	252	48	7.9	13 07	13 15	18 25	23 56	23 49
15	22 12	− 7.4	57.3	15.6	17	250	58	8.9	13 23	13 26	19 11	..	..
16	23 00	− 1.7	58.2	15.9	30	249	69	9.9	13 38	13 37	19 58	1 14	1 13
17	23 51	+ 4.3	59.2	16.1	42	250	78	10.9	13 55	13 49	20 48	2 36	2 40
18	0 43	+10.2	60.1	16.4	54	253	87	11.9	14 15	14 03	21 42	4 01	4 11
19	1 40	+15.7	60.8	16.6	66	258	94	12.9	14 40	14 22	22 41	5 30	5 47
20	2 40	+20.4	61.3	16.7	78	270	98	13.9	15 14	14 50	23 44	7 01	7 24
21	3 45	+23.8	61.5	16.8	90	355	100	14.9	16 01	15 32	..	8 28	8 56
22	4 52	+25.3	61.3	16.7	102	73	98	15.9	17 05	16 35	0 50	9 42	10 12
23	5 59	+25.0	60.8	16.6	115	87	90	16.9	18 22	17 56	1 55	10 37	11 05
24	7 03	+23.0	60.1	16.4	127	96	87	17.9	19 46	19 25	2 58	11 17	11 39
25	8 02	+19.5	59.2	16.1	139	102	78	18.9	21 09	20 55	3 55	11 45	12 01
26	8 58	+15.0	58.2	15.9	151	107	68	19.9	22 29	22 20	4 47	12 06	12 17
27	9 48	+ 9.9	57.3	15.6	163	110	58	20.9	23 45	23 41	5 35	12 23	12 29
28	10 36	+ 4.5	56.4	15.4	175	112	47	21.9	..	..	6 19	12 38	12 39
29	11 22	− 0.9	55.7	15.2	187	112	37	22.9	0 58	0 59	7 02	12 52	12 49
30	12 07	− 6.2	55.1	15.0	200	111	28	23.9	2 09	2 15	7 44	13 06	12 58

MERCURY ☿

Day	R.A.	Dec. −	Diam.	Phase	Transit	Day	R.A.	Dec. −	Diam.	Phase	Transit
	h m	°	″		h m		h m	°	″		h m
1	15 55	23.1	6	71	13 14	16	16 43	24.3	8	30	13 00
4	16 09	23.8	6	66	13 16	19	16 40	23.6	9	18	12 44
7	16 22	24.4	7	57	13 17	22	16 30	22.4	10	7	12 21
10	16 33	24.7	7	51	13 15	25	16 15	20.8	10	0	11 54
13	16 40	24.7	8	41	13 10	28	15 59	19.1	10	2	11 27
16	16 43	24.3	8	30	13 00	31	15 46	17.6	9	11	11 03

Mercury is too close to the Sun for observation

Mercury is too close to the Sun for observation

VENUS ♀

Day	R.A.	Dec.	Diam.	Phase	5° high E 52°	5° high E 56°	Transit
	h m	°	″		h m	h m	h m
1	12 07	+ 0.9	14	77	3 54	3 57	9 26
6	12 30	− 1.4	14	79	4 09	4 12	9 29
11	12 52	− 3.7	14	80	4 23	4 30	9 31
16	13 15	− 5.9	13	82	4 39	4 48	9 34
21	13 38	− 8.2	13	83	4 54	5 05	9 38
26	14 01	−10.4	13	84	5 11	5 24	9 41
31	14 25	−12.5	13	85	5 27	5 42	9 45

MARS ♂

Day	R.A.	Dec. −	Diam.	Phase	5° high E 52°	5° high E 56°	Transit
	h m	°	″		h m	h m	h m
1	13 16	7.2	4	−	5 45	5 55	10 33
6	13 28	8.4	4	−	5 44	5 55	10 26
11	13 40	9.7	4	−	5 44	5 56	10 19
16	13 53	10.9	4	−	5 44	5 57	10 12
21	14 05	12.0	4	−	5 44	5 59	10 04
26	14 18	13.2	4	−	5 44	6 00	9 58
31	14 31	14.3	4	−	5 44	6 02	9 51

SUNRISE AND SUNSET (G.M.T.)

Day	London a.m. h m	London p.m. h m	Bristol a.m. h m	Bristol p.m. h m	Birmingham a.m. h m	Birmingham p.m. h m	Manchester a.m. h m	Manchester p.m. h m	Newcastle a.m. h m	Newcastle p.m. h m	Glasgow a.m. h m	Glasgow p.m. h m	Belfast a.m. h m	Belfast p.m. h m
1	6 53	4 34	7 03	4 44	7 02	4 38	7 07	4 37	7 09	4 30	7 23	4 38	7 26	4 49
2	6 55	4 32	7 05	4 42	7 04	4 36	7 09	4 35	7 11	4 28	7 25	4 36	7 28	4 47
3	6 57	4 30	7 06	4 40	7 06	4 35	7 11	4 34	7 13	4 26	7 27	4 34	7 30	4 45
4	6 59	4 29	7 08	4 39	7 08	4 33	7 13	4 32	7 15	4 24	7 29	4 32	7 32	4 43
5	7 00	4 27	7 10	4 37	7 10	4 31	7 15	4 30	7 17	4 22	7 31	4 30	7 34	4 41
6	7 02	4 25	7 11	4 35	7 12	4 29	7 17	4 28	7 19	4 20	7 33	4 28	7 36	4 39
7	7 04	4 24	7 13	4 34	7 14	4 27	7 19	4 26	7 21	4 18	7 35	4 26	7 38	4 37
8	7 06	4 22	7 15	4 32	7 16	4 25	7 21	4 24	7 23	4 16	7 37	4 24	7 40	4 35
9	7 07	4 20	7 17	4 30	7 17	4 24	7 22	4 23	7 25	4 14	7 39	4 22	7 41	4 34
10	7 09	4 19	7 18	4 29	7 19	4 22	7 24	4 21	7 27	4 12	7 41	4 20	7 43	4 32
11	7 11	4 17	7 20	4 27	7 21	4 20	7 26	4 19	7 29	4 10	7 43	4 18	7 45	4 30
12	7 12	4 16	7 22	4 26	7 23	4 19	7 28	4 17	7 31	4 08	7 46	4 16	7 48	4 28
13	7 14	4 14	7 24	4 24	7 25	4 17	7 30	4 16	7 33	4 07	7 48	4 14	7 50	4 26
14	7 16	4 13	7 26	4 23	7 27	4 16	7 32	4 14	7 35	4 05	7 50	4 13	7 52	4 25
15	7 17	4 11	7 27	4 21	7 28	4 14	7 34	4 13	7 37	4 04	7 52	4 11	7 54	4 23
16	7 19	4 10	7 29	4 20	7 30	4 13	7 36	4 11	7 39	4 02	7 54	4 09	7 56	4 21
17	7 21	4 09	7 31	4 19	7 32	4 12	7 38	4 09	7 41	4 00	7 56	4 07	7 58	4 19
18	7 23	4 07	7 33	4 17	7 34	4 10	7 40	4 08	7 43	3 59	7 58	4 06	8 00	4 18
19	7 24	4 06	7 34	4 16	7 35	4 09	7 42	4 07	7 45	3 57	8 00	4 04	8 02	4 17
20	7 26	4 05	7 36	4 15	7 37	4 08	7 43	4 05	7 47	3 56	8 02	4 03	8 03	4 15
21	7 28	4 04	7 38	4 14	7 39	4 07	7 45	4 04	7 49	3 54	8 04	4 01	8 05	4 14
22	7 29	4 02	7 39	4 13	7 40	4 05	7 47	4 03	7 51	3 53	8 06	4 00	8 07	4 13
23	7 31	4 01	7 41	4 12	7 42	4 04	7 49	4 01	7 53	3 51	8 08	3 58	8 09	4 11
24	7 33	4 00	7 43	4 11	7 44	4 03	7 51	4 00	7 55	3 50	8 10	3 57	8 11	4 10
25	7 34	3 59	7 44	4 10	7 45	4 02	7 52	3 59	7 56	3 49	8 12	3 56	8 12	4 09
26	7 36	3 58	7 46	4 09	7 47	4 01	7 54	3 58	7 58	3 48	8 13	3 55	8 14	4 08
27	7 37	3 58	7 47	4 08	7 48	4 01	7 55	3 58	8 00	3 47	8 15	3 53	8 16	4 07
28	7 39	3 57	7 49	4 07	7 50	4 00	7 57	3 57	8 01	3 46	8 17	3 52	8 17	4 06
29	7 40	3 56	7 50	4 07	7 51	3 59	7 58	3 56	8 03	3 45	8 19	3 51	8 19	4 05
30	7 42	3 55	7 52	4 06	7 53	3 58	8 00	3 55	8 05	3 44	8 21	3 50	8 21	4 04

JUPITER ♃

Day	R.A. h m	Dec. − °	Transit h m	5° high West 52° h m	5° high West 56° h m
1	18 22	23.4	15 38	18 37	18 00
11	18 30	23.4	15 07	18 06	17 30
21	18 38	23.3	14 36	17 37	17 00
31	18 47	23.1	14 06	17 07	16 32

SATURN ♄

R.A. h m	Dec. + °	5° high East 52° h m	5° high East 56° h m	Transit h m
5 16	21.4	19 10	18 54	2 34
5 14	21.3	18 28	18 12	1 53
5 11	21.3	17 46	17 31	1 10
5 07	21.2	17 04	16 48	0 28

Equatorial diameter of Jupiter 34"; of Saturn 20". Diameters of Saturn's rings 46" and 21".

URANUS ♅

Day	R.A. h m	Dec. − ° ′	10° high in East 52° h m	10° high in East 56° h m	Transit h m
1	13 14·6	7 15	6 18	6 33	10 31
11	13 16·8	7 28	5 43	5 57	9 54
21	13 18·9	7 40	5 07	5 21	9 17
31	13 20·8	7 52	4 30	4 45	8 40

NEPTUNE ♆

R.A. h m	Dec. − ° ′	Transit h m	
16 09·4	19 24	13 26	Neptune is too
16 10·9	19 28	12 48	close to the
16 12·4	19 33	12 10	Sun for
16 14·0	19 37	11 32	observation

Diameter 4"   Diameter 2"

E+

Day of		Decem (ten), 10th month of Roman (pre-Julian) Calendar. *Sun's Longitude* 270° ♑ 21ᵈ 18ʰ ♑
Month	Week	
1	F.	Queen Alexandra b. 1844
2	S.	Dame Irene Vanbrugh b. 1872★★.
3	☉.	**1st Sunday in Advent.** Lord Carron d. 1969
4	M.	Cardinal Richelieu d. 1642. John Gay d. 1732
5	Tu.	Mozart d. 1791. Dumas père d. 1870
6	W.	Trollope d. 1882. Baroness Horsbrugh d. 1969
7	Th.	Pearl Harbour 1941
8	F.	De Quincey d. 1859
9	S.	Lord Butler of Saffron Walden b. 1902
10	☉.	**2nd Sunday in Advent.** Alfred Nobel d. 1896
11	M.	Accession of George VI 1936
12	Tu.	Robert Browning d. 1889. Douglas Fairbanks d.
13	W.	Dr. Johnson d. 1784 [1939
14	Th.	George VI b. 1895. Visct. Slim d. 1970
15	F.	Izaak Walton d. 1683. H. M. Abrahams b. 1899
16	S.	Sir Noël Coward b. 1899. Somerset Maugham d. 1965
17	☉.	**3rd Sunday in Advent.** Lord Ismay d. 1965
18	M.	Dame Gladys Cooper b. 1889. Willy Brandt b. 1913
19	Tu.	J. M. W. Turner b. 1851
20	W.	Sir R. Menzies b. 1894. Sir John Squire d. 1958
21	Th.	**St. Thomas.** MICHAELMAS LAW SITTINGS END
22	F.	Dame Peggy Ashcroft b. 1907. Richard Dimbleby
23	S.	Earl of Halifax d. 1959 [d. 1965
24	☉.	**4th Sunday in Advent.** Christmas Eve
25	M.	**Christmas Day.**
26	Tu.	**St. Stephen.** Visct. Amory b. 1899
27	W.	**St. John.** Sir William Russell Flint d. 1969
28	Th.	**Holy Innocents.** Lord Macaulay d. 1859
29	F.	Eden Philpotts d. 1960
30	S.	Pablo Casals b. 1876. Ruth Draper d. 1956
31	☉.	**1st Sunday after Christmas.** Sir Frank Benson [d. 1939

(G.M.T.)

PHENOMENA

December 3ᵈ 06ʰ Venus in conjunction with the Moon. Venus 7° N.

3ᵈ 06ʰ Mars in conjunction with the Moon. Mars 5° N.

3ᵈ 23ʰ Venus in conjunction with Mars. Venus 1°·3 N.

4ᵈ 12ʰ Mercury in conjunction with the Moon. Mercury 7° N.

8ᵈ 06ʰ Jupiter in conjunction with the Moon. Jupiter 0°·3 N.

9ᵈ 02ʰ Saturn at opposition.

14ᵈ 06ʰ Mercury at greatest western elongation (21°).

19ᵈ 15ʰ Saturn in conjunction with the Moon. Saturn 4° S.

21ᵈ 18ʰ Winter Solstice.

CONSTELLATIONS

The following constellations are near the meridian at

	d	h		d	h
Nov.	1	24	Nov.	15	23
Dec.	1	22	Dec.	16	21
Jan.	1	20	Jan.	16	19

Ursa Major (below the Pole), Ursa Minor (below the Pole), Cassiopeia, Andromeda, Perseus, Triangulum, Aries, Taurus, Cetus and Eridanus.

MINIMA OF ALGOL

d	h	d	h
1	14	18	19
4	11	21	15
7	07	24	12
10	04	27	09
13	01	30	06
15	22		

(G.M.T.)

PHASES OF THE MOON

	d	h	m
● New Moon	5	20	24
☽ First Quarter	13	18	36
○ Full Moon	20	09	45
☾ Last Quarter	27	10	27

	d	h
Apogee (406,560 kilometres)	4	14
Perigee (358,040 ,,)	19	13
Apogee (405,950 ,,)	31	22

Mean Longitude of Ascending Node on December 1, 289°.

MONTHLY NOTES

Dec. 9. Grouse and Black Game Shooting ends.
15. Notices to owners and occupiers affected by private Bills in Parliament must be delivered.
17. Common Council Elections, City of London.
22. Shortest day.
25. Quarter day.
26. Boxing Day. General Holiday, England, Wales and Northern Ireland.
31. Various licences expire.

NATIONAL DAYS.—Dec. 5, Thailand; 6, Finland; 9–10, Tanzania; 11, Upper Volta; 12, Kenya.
★★ Centenary

Day	THE SUN						s.d. 16'·3			Sidereal Time	Transit of First Point of Aries (G.M.T.)
	Right Ascension	Dec. −	Equation of Time	Rise		Transit	Set				
				52°	56°		52°	56°			
	h m s	° ′	m s	h m	h m	h m	h m	h m	h m s	h m s	
1	16 28 44	21 47	+ 11 03	7 45	8 06	11 49	15 52	15 31	4 39 47	19 17 02	
2	16 33 04	21 56	+ 10 40	7 46	8 08	11 50	15 52	15 30	4 43 44	19 13 07	
3	16 37 23	22 05	+ 10 17	7 48	8 10	11 50	15 51	15 30	4 47 41	19 09 11	
4	16 41 44	22 14	+ 9 53	7 49	8 11	11 50	15 51	15 29	4 51 37	19 05 15	
5	16 46 05	22 21	+ 9 28	7 51	8 13	11 51	15 50	15 28	4 55 34	19 01 19	
6	16 50 27	22 29	+ 9 03	7 52	8 14	11 51	15 50	15 28	4 59 30	18 57 23	
7	16 54 49	22 36	+ 8 38	7 53	8 16	11 52	15 49	15 27	5 03 27	18 53 27	
8	16 59 12	22 42	+ 8 12	7 54	8 17	11 52	15 49	15 26	5 07 23	18 49 31	
9	17 03 35	22 49	+ 7 45	7 56	8 18	11 52	15 49	15 26	5 11 20	18 45 35	
10	17 07 58	22 54	+ 7 18	7 57	8 20	11 53	15 49	15 26	5 15 16	18 41 39	
11	17 12 22	23 00	+ 6 50	7 58	8 21	11 53	15 49	15 25	5 19 13	18 37 43	
12	17 16 47	23 04	+ 6 23	7 59	8 22	11 54	15 49	15 25	5 23 10	18 33 47	
13	17 21 12	23 09	+ 5 54	8 00	8 23	11 54	15 49	15 25	5 27 06	18 29 52	
14	17 25 37	23 12	+ 5 26	8 01	8 24	11 55	15 49	15 25	5 31 03	18 25 56	
15	17 30 02	23 16	+ 4 57	8 02	8 25	11 55	15 49	15 25	5 34 59	18 22 00	
16	17 34 27	23 19	+ 4 28	8 03	8 26	11 56	15 49	15 25	5 38 56	18 18 04	
17	17 38 53	23 21	+ 3 59	8 03	8 27	11 56	15 49	15 25	5 42 52	18 14 08	
18	17 43 19	23 23	+ 3 30	8 04	8 28	11 57	15 49	15 25	5 46 49	18 10 12	
19	17 47 45	23 25	+ 3 00	8 05	8 29	11 57	15 50	15 26	5 50 45	18 06 16	
20	17 52 11	23 26	+ 2 31	8 05	8 29	11 58	15 50	15 26	5 54 42	18 02 20	
21	17 56 38	23 26	+ 2 01	8 06	8 30	11 58	15 50	15 27	5 58 39	17 58 24	
22	18 01 04	23 27	+ 1 31	8 06	8 30	11 59	15 51	15 27	6 02 35	17 54 28	
23	18 05 30	23 26	+ 1 01	8 07	8 31	11 59	15 51	15 28	6 06 32	17 50 32	
24	18 09 57	23 25	+ 0 31	8 07	8 31	12 00	15 52	15 28	6 10 28	17 46 36	
25	18 14 23	23 24	+ 0 02	8 08	8 31	12 00	15 53	15 29	6 14 25	17 42 41	
26	18 18 49	23 22	− 0 28	8 08	8 32	12 01	15 53	15 30	6 18 21	17 38 45	
27	18 23 16	23 20	− 0 58	8 08	8 32	12 01	15 54	15 30	6 22 18	17 34 49	
28	18 27 42	23 17	− 1 27	8 08	8 32	12 02	15 55	15 31	6 26 15	17 30 53	
29	18 32 08	23 14	− 1 57	8 08	8 32	12 02	15 56	15 32	6 30 11	17 26 57	
30	18 36 33	23 11	− 2 26	8 08	8 32	12 03	15 57	15 33	6 34 08	17 23 01	
31	18 40 59	23 07	− 2 55	8 08	8 32	12 03	15 58	15 34	6 38 04	17 19 05	

Duration of Civil (C), Nautical (N), and Astronomical (A), Twilight (in minutes)

Lat °	Dec. 1			Dec. 11			Dec. 21			Dec. 31		
	C	N	A	C	N	A	C	N	A	C	N	A
52	40	82	123	41	84	125	41	85	126	41	84	125
56	45	93	138	47	96	141	47	97	142	47	96	141

ASTRONOMICAL NOTES

MERCURY is a morning star, magnitude +1·5 to -0·3, for most of the month. It is visible low above the E.S.E. horizon around the time of beginning of morning civil twilight. During the last week of the month it is too close to the Sun for observation.

VENUS is a bright morning star, magnitude −3·4. Even by the end of the month it is still visible for an hour in the S.E. sky before sunrise, though no longer so high in the sky as it was previously. At the beginning of the month Venus is close to Mars passing 1°·3 N. of it late on the 3rd, while on the morning of the 3rd the old crescent Moon passes 5° S. of Mars and 7° S. of Venus.

MARS is a morning star, magnitude +1·8. Although not visible before about 06ʰ the time available for observation is lengthening due to the later time of sunrise. Mars is in Libra. The old crescent Moon passes 5° S. of Mars on the morning of the 3rd.

JUPITER is an evening star, magnitude −1·5 but only seen at a low altitude above the S.W. horizon at the end of the evening civil twilight. The crescent Moon will be near Jupiter on the evenings of the 7th and 8th. After the middle of the month it is too close to the Sun for observation.

SATURN is at opposition on the 9th, magnitude −0·3, and thus visible all night. It is in Taurus. Shortly before sunset on the 19th the gibbous Moon passes 4° N. of Saturn.

METEORS. The maximum of the well-known Geminid meteor shower occurs during the night of the 12th–13th. The Moon, at First Quarter, sets at about 23 hours and so will provide little interference with observation.

THE MOON

Day	R.A.	Dec.	Hor. Par.	Semi-diam.	Sun's Co-long.	P.A. of Bright Limb	Phase	Age	Rise 52°	Rise 56°	Transit	Set 52°	Set 56°
	h m	°	′	′	°	°	°	d	h m	h m	h m	h m	h m
1	12 51	−11·1	54·6	14·9	212	109	20	24·9	3 20	3 31	8 26	13 22	13 09
2	13 37	−15·6	54·3	14·8	224	106	13	25·9	4 30	4 46	9 10	13 40	13 2:
3	14 24	−19·4	54·1	14·7	236	101	7	26·9	5 40	6 01	9 55	14 03	13 4:
4	15 13	−22·4	53·9	14·7	248	94	3	27·9	6 47	7 13	10 42	14 32	14 0?
5	16 04	−24·4	53·9	14·7	261	80	1	28·9	7 50	8 20	11 31	15 10	14 4:
6	16 56	−25·4	54·0	14·7	273	336	0	0·2	8 45	9 16	12 22	15 59	15 2?
7	17 49	−25·2	54·2	14·8	285	279	1	1·2	9 30	9 59	13 12	16 58	16 2?
8	18 41	−23·8	54·4	14·8	297	268	4	2·2	10 05	10 30	14 02	18 04	17 4?
9	19 32	−21·3	54·8	14·9	309	260	9	3·2	10 33	10 53	14 50	19 15	18 5?
10	20 22	−17·9	55·2	15·0	321	255	15	4·2	10 54	11 09	15 36	20 28	20 1?
11	21 11	−13·6	55·7	15·2	334	251	23	5·2	11 12	11 22	16 21	21 43	21 3?
12	21 58	− 8·7	56·3	15·4	346	249	32	6·2	11 28	11 33	17 06	22 58	22 5?
13	22 46	− 3·3	57·1	15·5	358	247	42	7·2	11 43	11 44	17 51	..	..
14	23 34	+ 2·4	57·9	15·8	10	247	52	8·2	11 59	11 54	18 38	0 15	0 1?
15	0 23	+ 8·2	58·7	16·0	22	248	63	9·2	12 16	12 07	19 28	1 35	1 4?
16	1 16	+13·7	59·6	16·2	34	251	74	10·2	12 37	12 22	20 22	2 59	3 1?
17	2 13	+18·6	60·3	16·4	47	255	83	11·2	13 06	12 44	21 21	4 27	4 4?
18	3 14	+22·5	60·9	16·6	59	261	91	12·2	13 45	13 18	22 25	5 54	6 2?
19	4 20	+24·8	61·2	16·7	71	269	97	13·2	14 39	14 09	23 31	7 14	7 4?
20	5 27	+25·4	61·2	16·7	83	287	100	14·2	15 51	15 22	..	8 20	8 4?
21	6 33	+24·1	60·9	16·6	95	88	99	15·2	17 14	16 50	0 36	9 09	9 3?
22	7 36	+21·1	60·3	16·4	107	101	96	16·2	18 41	18 23	1 38	9 43	10 0?
23	8 35	+16·8	59·5	16·2	119	107	91	17·2	20 05	19 54	2 34	10 08	10 2?
24	9 29	+11·7	58·5	15·9	131	111	83	18·2	21 26	21 20	3 26	10 27	10 3?
25	10 20	+ 6·2	57·6	15·7	144	113	74	19·2	22 42	22 42	4 13	10 43	10 4?
26	11 07	+ 0·7	56·6	15·4	156	114	64	20·2	23 56	..	4 58	10 58	10 5?
27	11 53	− 4·8	55·8	15·2	168	114	54	21·2	..	0 00	5 41	11 12	11 0?
28	12 39	− 9·9	55·1	15·0	180	113	44	22·2	1 08	1 17	6 23	11 27	11 1?
29	13 24	−14·5	54·6	14·9	192	110	35	23·2	2 19	2 33	7 07	11 45	11 3?
30	14 11	−18·5	54·3	14·8	204	107	26	24·2	3 29	3 48	7 52	12 06	11 4?
31	15 00	−21·7	54·1	14·7	217	103	18	25·2	4 37	5 02	8 38	12 33	12 0?

MERCURY ☿

Day	R.A.	Dec. −	Diam.	Phase	5° high E 52°	5° high E 56°	Transit	Day	R.A.	Dec. −	Diam.	Phase	5° high E 52°	5° high E 56°	Transit
	h m	°	″		h m	h m	h m		h m	°	″		h m	h m	h m
1	15 46	17·6	9	11	7 19	7 42	11 03	16	16 06	18·8	6	67	6 51	7 16	10 2
4	15 39	16·9	9	23	6 56	7 17	10 45	19	16 20	19·8	6	74	7 01	7 28	10 3
7	15 39	16·7	8	37	6 43	7 05	10 34	22	16 36	20·7	6	79	7 13	7 42	10 3
10	15 44	17·1	7	49	6 40	7 02	10 28	25	16 53	21·7	5	83	7 26	7 57	10 4
13	15 53	17·8	7	60	6 43	7 06	10 26	28	17 11	22·5	5	87	7 39	8 13	10 4
16	16 06	18·8	6	67	6 51	7 16	10 27	31	17 30	23·2	5	90	7 52	8 28	10 5

VENUS ♀

Day	R.A.	Dec. −	Diam.	Phase	5° high E 52°	5° high E 56°	Transit
	h m	°	″		h m	h m	h m
1	14 25	12·5	12	85	5 27	5 42	9 45
6	14 49	14·4	12	87	5 44	6 02	9 50
11	15 13	16·3	12	88	6 01	6 21	9 55
16	15 38	18·0	12	89	6 18	6 41	10 00
21	16 04	19·4	12	90	6 34	7 00	10 06
26	16 30	20·7	11	91	6 50	7 19	10 12
31	16 56	21·7	11	92	7 05	7 36	10 19

MARS ♂

Day	R.A.	Dec. −	Diam.	Phase	5° high E 52°	5° high E 56°	Transit
	h m	°	″		h m	h m	h m
1	14 31	14·3	4	−	5 44	6 02	9 51
6	14 44	15·4	4	−	5 44	6 04	9 44
11	14 58	16·4	4	−	5 45	6 05	9 38
16	15 11	17·4	4	−	5 45	6 07	9 32
21	15 25	18·3	4	−	5 45	6 09	9 26
26	15 38	19·1	4	−	5 46	6 11	9 20
31	15 52	19·9	4	−	5 46	6 13	9 14

SUNRISE AND SUNSET (G.M.T.)

Day	London a.m.	London p.m.	Bristol a.m.	Bristol p.m.	Birmingham a.m.	Birmingham p.m.	Manchester a.m.	Manchester p.m.	Newcastle a.m.	Newcastle p.m.	Glasgow a.m.	Glasgow p.m.	Belfast a.m.	Belfast p.m.
	h m	h m	h m	h m	h m	h m	h m	h m	h m	h m	h m	h m	h m	h m
1	7 43	3 54	7 53	4 05	7 54	3 57	8 01	3 54	8 06	3 43	8 22	3 49	8 22	4 03
2	7 45	3 54	7 55	4 05	7 56	3 57	8 03	3 54	8 08	3 42	8 24	3 48	8 24	4 02
3	7 46	3 53	7 56	4 04	7 57	3 56	8 04	3 53	8 10	3 42	8 26	3 48	8 26	4 02
4	7 47	3 53	7 57	4 04	7 59	3 55	8 06	3 52	8 11	3 41	8 27	3 47	8 28	4 01
5	7 49	3 52	7 58	4 03	8 00	3 55	8 07	3 52	8 13	3 40	8 29	3 46	8 29	4 00
6	7 50	3 52	8 00	4 03	8 01	3 54	8 08	3 51	8 14	3 40	8 30	3 46	8 30	4 00
7	7 51	3 52	8 01	4 02	8 03	3 54	8 10	3 51	8 16	3 39	8 32	3 45	8 32	3 59
8	7 52	3 52	8 02	4 02	8 04	3 53	8 11	3 50	8 17	3 38	8 33	3 44	8 33	3 58
9	7 54	3 51	8 03	4 02	8 05	3 53	8 12	3 50	8 18	3 38	8 34	3 44	8 34	3 58
10	7 55	3 51	8 04	4 02	8 06	3 53	8 13	3 50	8 19	3 38	8 36	3 44	8 35	3 58
11	7 56	3 51	8 05	4 02	8 08	3 53	8 15	3 50	8 21	3 38	8 37	3 43	8 37	3 58
12	7 57	3 51	8 06	4 02	8 09	3 53	8 16	3 50	8 22	3 38	8 38	3 43	8 38	3 58
13	7 58	3 51	8 07	4 02	8 10	3 53	8 17	3 50	8 23	3 38	8 39	3 43	8 39	3 58
14	7 59	3 51	8 08	4 02	8 11	3 53	8 18	3 50	8 24	3 38	8 40	3 43	8 40	3 58
15	8 00	3 52	8 09	4 02	8 12	3 53	8 19	3 50	8 25	3 38	8 41	3 43	8 41	3 58
16	8 01	3 52	8 10	4 02	8 12	3 53	8 19	3 50	8 25	3 38	8 42	3 43	8 41	3 58
17	8 01	3 52	8 10	4 02	8 13	3 53	8 20	3 50	8 26	3 38	8 43	3 43	8 42	3 58
18	8 02	3 52	8 11	4 02	8 14	3 53	8 21	3 50	8 27	3 38	8 44	3 43	8 43	3 58
19	8 03	3 53	8 12	4 03	8 15	3 54	8 22	3 50	8 28	3 38	8 45	3 44	8 44	3 58
20	8 03	3 53	8 12	4 03	8 15	3 54	8 22	3 51	8 28	3 39	8 45	3 44	8 44	3 59
21	8 04	3 53	8 13	4 03	8 16	3 54	8 23	3 51	8 29	3 39	8 46	3 45	8 45	3 59
22	8 04	3 54	8 13	4 04	8 16	3 55	8 24	3 52	8 30	3 40	8 46	3 45	8 46	4 00
23	8 05	3 54	8 14	4 04	8 17	3 55	8 24	3 52	8 30	3 40	8 47	3 46	8 46	4 00
24	8 05	3 55	8 14	4 05	8 17	3 56	8 24	3 53	8 30	3 41	8 47	3 46	8 46	4 01
25	8 06	3 56	8 15	4 06	8 18	3 57	8 25	3 54	8 31	3 42	8 47	3 47	8 47	4 02
26	8 06	3 56	8 15	4 06	8 18	3 57	8 25	3 54	8 31	3 42	8 48	3 48	8 47	4 02
27	8 06	3 57	8 15	4 07	8 18	3 58	8 25	3 55	8 31	3 43	8 48	3 48	8 47	4 03
28	8 06	3 58	8 15	4 08	8 18	3 59	8 25	3 56	8 31	3 44	8 48	3 49	8 47	4 04
29	8 06	3 59	8 16	4 09	8 18	4 00	8 25	3 57	8 31	3 45	8 48	3 50	8 47	4 05
30	8 06	4 00	8 16	4 10	8 18	4 01	8 26	3 58	8 32	3 46	8 48	3 51	8 48	4 06
31	8 06	4 01	8 16	4 11	8 18	4 02	8 25	3 59	8 31	3 47	8 48	3 52	8 47	4 07

JUPITER ♃   SATURN ♄

Day	R.A.	Dec. −	Transit	5° high West 52°	5° high West 56°	R.A.	Dec. +	Transit	5° high West 52°	5° high West 56°
	h m	°	h m	h m	h m	h m	°	h m	h m	h m
1	18 47	23·1	14 06	17 07	16 32	5 07	21·2	0 28	7 47	8 03
11	18 57	22·9	13 36	16 39	16 04	5 04	21·2	23 40	7 04	7 19
21	19 06	22·7	13 06	16 12	15 37	5 00	21·1	22 58	6 21	6 36
31	19 16	22·5	12 37	15 45	15 11	4 57	21·0	22 15	5 38	5 53

Equatorial diameter of Jupiter 32″; of Saturn 21″.   Diameters of Saturn's rings 47″ and 21″.

URANUS ♅   NEPTUNE ♆

Day	R.A.	Dec. −	10° high in East 52°	10° high in East 56°	Transit	R.A.	Dec. −	Transit	
	h m	° ′	h m	h m	h m	h m	° ′	h m	
1	13 20·8	7 52	4 30	4 45	8 40	16 14·0	19 37	11 32	Neptune is too
11	13 22·5	8 01	3 54	4 09	8 02	16 15·5	19 40	10 55	close to the
21	13 23·9	8 09	3 16	3 32	7 24	16 17·0	19 44	10 17	Sun for
31	13 25·0	8 16	2 39	2 54	6 46	16 18·5	19 47	9 39	observation

Diameter 4″   Diameter 2″

INTRODUCTION TO ASTRONOMICAL SECTION

GENERAL

The astronomical data are given in a form suitable for those who practise naked-eye astronomy or use small telescopes. No attempt has been made to replace the *Astronomical Ephemeris* for professional astronomers. Positions of the heavenly bodies are given only to the degree of accuracy required by amateur astronomers for setting telescopes, or for plotting on celestial globes or star atlases. Where intermediate positions are required, linear interpolation may be employed.

All data are, unless otherwise stated, for 0h G.M.T., or the midnight at the beginning of the day named.

(*See notes on British Summer Time, p. 142*).

Definitions of the terms used cannot be given in an ephemeris of this nature. They must be sought in astronomical literature and text-books. Probably the best source for the amateur is Norton's *Star Atlas* (Gall and Inglis, 15th edition, 1964; £1.05.), which contains an excellent introduction to observational astronomy, and the finest series of star maps yet produced for showing stars visible to the naked eye. Certain more extended ephemerides are available in the British Astronomical Association Handbook, an annual very popular among amateur astronomers. (Secretary: Burlington House, Piccadilly, London, W.1.)

A special feature has been made of the times when the various heavenly bodies are visible in the British Isles. Since two columns, calculated for latitudes 52° and 56°, are devoted to risings and settings, the range 50° to 58° can be covered by interpolation and extrapolation. The times given in these columns are G.M.T.'s for the meridian of Greenwich. An observer west of this meridian must add his longitude (in time) and vice versa.

In accordance with the usual convention in astronomy, + and − indicate respectively north and south latitudes or declinations.

PAGE I OF EACH MONTH

The Zodiacal signs through which the Sun is passing during each month are illustrated. The date of transition from one sign to the next, to the nearest hour, is also given.

The FASTS AND FESTIVALS in black-letter type are those so given in the Prayer Book. The line immediately to the right of the Day of Week is shown heavy when the Law Courts are sitting in London.

Under the heading PHENOMENA will be found particulars of the more important conjunctions of the Sun, Moon and planets with each other, and also the dates of eclipses and other astronomical phenomena of special interest.

The CONSTELLATIONS listed each month are those that are near the meridian at the beginning of the month at 22h local mean time. Allowance must be made for Summer Time if necessary. The fact that any star crosses the meridian 4m earlier each night or 2h earlier each month may be used, in conjunction with the lists given each month, to find what constellations are favourably placed at any moment. The table preceding the list of constellations may be extended indefinitely at the rate just quoted.

Times of MINIMA OF ALGOL are approximate times of the middle of the period of diminished light (*see* p. 153).

The principal PHASES OF THE MOON are the G.M.T.'s when the difference between the longitude of the Moon and that of the Sun is 0°, 90°, 180° or 270°. The times of perigee and apogee are those when the Moon is nearest to, and farthest from the Earth, respectively. The nodes or points of intersection of the Moon's orbit and the ecliptic make a complete retrograde circuit of the ecliptic in about 19 years. From a knowledge of the longitude of the ascending node and the inclination, whose value does not vary much from 5°, the path of the Moon among the stars may be plotted on a celestial globe or star atlas.

The MONTHLY NOTES are self-explanatory.

PAGE II OF EACH MONTH

The Sun's semi-diameter, in arc, is given once a month.

The right ascension given is that of the true Sun. The right ascension of the mean Sun is obtained by applying the equation of time, with the sign given, to the right ascension of the true Sun, or, more easily, by applying 12h to the column Sidereal Time. The direction in which the equation of time has to be applied in different problems is a frequent source of confusion and error. Apparent Solar Time is equal to the Mean Solar Time plus the Equation of Time. For example at noon on Aug. 8 the Equation of Time is $-5^m\ 33^s$ and thus at 12h Mean Time on that day the Apparent Time is $12^h - 5^m\ 33^s = 11^h\ 54^m\ 27^s$.

The Greenwich Sidereal Time at 0h and the Transit of the First Point of Aries (which is really the mean time when the sidereal time is 0h) are used for converting mean time to sidereal time and vice versa.

The G.M.T. of transit of the Sun at Greenwich may also be taken as the L.M.T. of transit in any longitude. It is independent of latitude. The G.M.T. of transit in any longitude is obtained by adding the longitude to the time given if west, and vice versa.

The legal importance of SUNRISE and SUNSET is that the Road Traffic Act, 1956, defines Lighting-up Time for vehicles as being from half an hour after sunset to half an hour before sunrise throughout the year. In all laws and regulations "sunset" refers to the local sunset, i.e. the time at which the Sun sets at the place in question. This common-sense interpretation has been upheld by legal tribunals. Thus the necessity for providing for different latitudes and longitudes, as already described, is evident.

The times of SUNRISE and SUNSET are those when the Sun's upper limb, as affected by refraction, is on the true horizon of an observer at sea-level. Assuming the mean refraction to be 34', and the Sun's semi-diameter to be 16', the time given is that when the true zenith distance of the Sun's centre is 90° + 34' + 16' or 90° 50', or, in other words, when the depression of the Sun's

centre below the true horizon is 50'. The upper limb is then 34' below the true horizon, but is brought there by refraction. It is true, of course, that an observer on a ship might see the Sun for a minute or so longer, because of the dip of the horizon, while another viewing the sunset over hills or mountains would record an earlier time. Nevertheless, the moment when the true zenith distance of the Sun's centre is 90° 50' is a precise time dependent only on the latitude and longitude of the place, and independent of its altitude above sea-level, the contour of its horizon, the vagaries of refraction or the small seasonal change in the Sun's semi-diameter; this moment is suitable in every way as a definition of sunset (or sunrise) for all statutory purposes.

It is well known that light reaches us before sunrise and also continues to reach us for some time after sunset. The interval between darkness and sunrise or sunset and darkness is called twilight. Astronomically speaking, twilight is considered to begin or end when the Sun's centre is 18° below the horizon, as no light from the Sun can then reach the observer. As thus defined twilight may last several hours; in high latitudes at the solstices the depression of 18° is not reached, and twilight lasts from sunset to sunrise.

The need for some sub-division of twilight was met some years ago by dividing the gathering darkness into four steps.

(1) *Sunrise or Sunset*, defined as above.

(2) *Civil twilight*, which begins or ends when the Sun's centre is 6° below the horizon. This marks the time when operations requiring daylight may commence or must cease. In England it varies from about 30 to 60 minutes after sunset.

(3) *Nautical twilight*, which begins or ends when the Sun's centre is 12° below the horizon. This marks the time when it is, to all intents and purposes, completely dark.

(4) *Astronomical twilight*, which begins or ends when the Sun's centre is 18° below the horizon. This marks theoretical perfect darkness. It is not of practical importance, especially if nautical twilight is tabulated.

To assist observers the durations of civil, nautical and astronomical twilights are given at intervals of ten days. The beginning of a particular twilight is found by subtracting the duration from the time of sunrise, while the end is found by adding the duration to the time of sunset. Thus the beginning of astronomical twilight in latitude 52°, on the Greenwich meridian, on March 11 is found as $06^h 24^m - 113^m = 04^h 31^m$ and similarly the end of civil twilight as $17^h 57^m + 34^m = 18^h 31^m$.

The letters T.A.N. are printed when twilight lasts all night.

Lighting-up time is a crude attempt to approximate to civil twilight over the British Isles.

Under the heading ASTRONOMICAL NOTES will be found notes describing the position and visibility of the planets and also of other phenomena; these are intended to guide naked-eye observers, or those using small telescopes.

PAGE III OF EACH MONTH

The Moon moves so rapidly among the stars that its position is given only to the degree of accuracy that permits linear interpolation. The right ascension and declination are geocentric, i.e. for an imaginary observer at the centre of the Earth. To an observer on the surface of the Earth the position is always different, as the altitude is always less on account of parallax which may reach 1°.

The lunar terminator is the line separating the bright from the dark part of the Moon's disk. Apart from irregularities of the lunar surface, the terminator is elliptical, because it is a circle seen in projection. It becomes the full circle forming the limb, or edge, of the Moon at New and Full Moon. The selenographic longitude of the terminator is measured from the mean centre of the visible disk, which may differ from the visible centre by as much as 8°, because of libration.

Instead of the longitude of the terminator the Sun's selenographic colongitude is tabulated. It is numerically equal to the selenographic longitude of the morning terminator, measured eastward from the mean centre of the disk. Thus its value is approximately 270° at New Moon, 360° at First Quarter, 90° at Full Moon and 180° at Last Quarter.

The Position Angle of the Bright Limb is the position angle of the midpoint of the illuminated limb, measured eastwards from the north point on the disk. The column PHASE shows the percentage of the area of the Moon's disk illuminated; this is also the illuminated percentage of the diameter at right angles to the line of cusps. The terminator is a semi-ellipse whose major axis is the line of cusps, and whose semi-minor axis is determined by the tabulated percentage; from New Moon to Full Moon the east limb is dark, and vice versa.

The times given as moonrise and moonset are those when the upper limb of the Moon is on the horizon of an observer at sea-level. The Sun's horizontal parallax is about 9", and is negligible when considering sunrise and sunset, but that of the Moon averages about 57'. Hence the computed time represents the moment when the true zenith distance of the Moon is 90° 50' (as for the Sun) minus the horizontal parallax. The time required for the Sun or Moon to rise or set is about four minutes (except in high latitudes).

The tables have been constructed for the meridian of Greenwich, and for latitudes 52° and 56°. They give Greenwich Mean Time (G.M.T.) throughout the year. To obtain the G.M.T. of the phenomenon as seen from any other latitude and longitude, first interpolate or extrapolate for latitude by the usual rules of proportion. To the time thus found the longitude (expressed in time) is to be *added* if west (as it usually is in Great Britain) or *subtracted* if east. If the longitude is expressed in degrees and minutes of arc, it must be converted to time at the rate of $1° = 4^m$ and $15' = 1^m$.

The G.M.T. of transit of the Moon over the meridian of Greenwich is given: these times are independent of latitude, but must be corrected for longitude. For places in the British Isles it suffices

to add the longitude if west, and vice versa. For more remote places a further correction is necessary because of the rapid movement of the Moon relative to the stars. The entire correction is conveniently determined by first finding the west longitude λ of the place. If the place is in west longitude, λ is the ordinary west longitude; if the place is in east longitude λ is the complement to 24h (or 360°) of the longitude, and will be greater than 12h (or 180°). The correction then consists of two positive portions, namely λ and the fraction $\lambda/24$ (or $\lambda°/360$) multiplied by the difference between consecutive transits. Thus for Sydney, N.S.W., the longitude is 10h 05m east, so $\lambda = $ 13h 55m and the fraction $\lambda/24$ is 0.58. The transit on the local date 1972 Oct. 11 is found as follows:

	d	h	m
G.M.T. of transit at Greenwich....	Oct. 10	14	01
λ		13	55
$0.58 \times (14^h\ 50^m - 14^h\ 01^m)$			28
G.M.T. of transit at Sydney........		11 04	24
Corr. to N.S.W. Standard Time....		10	00
Local standard time of transit		11 14	24

It is evident, of course, that for any given place the quantities λ and the correction to local standard time may be combined permanently, being here 23h 55m.

Positions of Mercury are given for every third day, and those of Venus and Mars for every fifth day; they may be interpolated linearly. The column PHASE shows the illuminated percentage of the disk. In the case of the inner planets this approaches 100 at superior conjunction and 0 at inferior conjunction. When the phase is less than 50 the planet is crescent-shaped or horned; for greater phases it is gibbous. In the case of the exterior planet Mars, the phase approaches 100 at conjunction and opposition, and is a minimum at the quadratures.

Since the planets cannot be seen when on the horizon, the actual times of rising and setting are not given; instead, the time when the planet has an apparent altitude of 5° has been tabulated. The phenomenon tabulated is the one that occurs between sunset and sunrise; unimportant exceptions to this rule may occur because changes are not made during a month, except in the case of Mercury. The times given may be interpolated for latitude and corrected for longitude as in the case of the Sun and Moon.

The G.M.T. at which the planet transits the Greenwich meridian is also given. The times of transit are to be corrected to local meridians in the usual way, as already described.

PAGE IV OF EACH MONTH

The G.M.T.'s of Sunrise and Sunset may be used not only for these phenomena, but also for Lighting-up Times, which, under the Road Traffic Act, 1956, are from half an hour after sunset to half an hour before sunrise throughout the year.

The particulars for the four outer planets resemble those for the planets on Page III of each month, except that, under Uranus and Neptune, times when the planet is 10° high instead of 5° high are given; this is because of the inferior brightness of these planets. The polar diameter of Jupiter is about 3″ less than the equatorial diameter, while that of Saturn is about 2″ less. The diameters given for the rings of Saturn are those of the major axis (in the plane of the planet's equator) and the minor axis respectively. The former has a small seasonal change due to the slightly varying distance of the Earth from Saturn, but the latter varies from zero when the Earth passes through the ring plane every 15 years to its maximum opening half-way between these periods. The rings were completely closed on three occasions in 1966 and were open at their widest extent in the middle of 1958.

TIME

From the earliest ages, the natural division of time into recurring periods of day and night has provided the practical time scale for the everyday activities of mankind. Indeed, if any alternative means of time measurement is adopted, it must be capable of adjustment so as to remain in general agreement with the natural time scale defined by the diurnal rotation of the Earth on its axis. Ideally the rotation should be measured against a fixed frame of reference; in practice it must be measured against the background provided by the celestial bodies. If the Sun is chosen as the reference point, we obtain Apparent Solar Time, which is the time indicated by a sundial. It is not a uniform time, but is subject to variations which amount to as much as a quarter of an hour in each direction. Such wide variations cannot be tolerated in a practical time scale, and this has led to the concept of Mean Solar Time in which all the days are of exactly the same length and equal to the average length of the Apparent Solar Day.

The positions of the stars in the sky are specified in relation to a fictitious reference point in the sky known as the First Point of Aries (or the Vernal Equinox). It is therefore convenient to adopt this same reference point when considering the rotation of the Earth against the background of the stars. The time scale so obtained is known as Apparent Sidereal Time.

Greenwich Mean Time

The daily rotation of the Earth on its axis causes the Sun and the other heavenly bodies to appear to cross the sky from East to West. It is convenient to represent this relative motion as if the Sun really performed a daily circuit around a fixed Earth. Noon in Apparent Solar Time may then be defined as the time at which the Sun transits across the observer's meridian. In Mean Solar Time, noon is similarly defined by the meridian transit of a fictitious Mean Sun moving uniformly in the sky with the same average speed as the true Sun. Mean Solar Time observed on the meridian of the transit circle telescope of the Royal Observatory at Greenwich is called Greenwich Mean Time (G.M.T.) The mean solar day is

divided into 24 hours and, for astronomical and other scientific purposes, these are numbered 0 to 23, commencing at midnight. Civil time is usually reckoned in two periods of 12 hours, designated a.m. (before noon) and p.m. (after noon).

Universal Time

Before January 1, 1925, G.M.T. was reckoned in 24 hours commencing at noon: since that date it has been reckoned from midnight. In view of the risk of confusion in the use of the designation G.M.T. before and after 1925, the International Astronomical Union recommended in 1928 that astronomers should, for the present, employ the term Universal Time, U.T. (or Weltzeit, W.Z.) to denote G.M.T. measured from Greenwich Mean Midnight.

In precision work it has now become necessary to take account of small variations, hitherto negligible, in Universal Time. These arise from small irregularities in the rotation of the Earth. Observed astronomical time is designated U.T.o. Observed time corrected for the effects of the motion of the poles (giving rise to a "wandering" in longitude) is designated U.T.1. There is also a seasonal fluctuation in the rate of rotation of the Earth arising from meteorological causes, often called the annual fluctuation. U.T.1 corrected for this effect is designated U.T.2, and provides a time scale free from short-period fluctuations. It is still subject to small secular and irregular changes.

Apparent Solar Time

As has been mentioned, the time shown by a sundial is called Apparent Solar Time. It differs from Mean Solar Time by an amount known as the Equation of Time, which is the total effect of two causes which make the length of the apparent solar day non-uniform. One cause of variation is that the orbit of the Earth is not a circle, but an ellipse, having the Sun at one focus. As a consequence, the angular speed of the Earth in its orbit is not constant; it is greatest at the beginning of January when the Earth is nearest the Sun. The other cause is due to the obliquity of the ecliptic; the plane of the equator (which is at right-angles to the axis of rotation of the Earth) does not coincide with the ecliptic (the plane defined by the apparent annual motion of the Sun around the celestial sphere) but is inclined to it at an angle of $23°\ 27'$. As a result, the apparent solar day is shorter than average at the equinoxes and longer at the solstices. From the combined effects of the components due to obliquity and eccentricity, the equation of time reaches its maximum values in February (-14 mins.) and early November ($+16$ mins.). It has a zero value on four dates during the year, and it is only on these dates (approx. April 15, June 14, Sept. 1, and Dec. 25) that a sundial shows Mean Solar Time.

Sidereal Time

A sidereal day is the duration of a complete rotation of the Earth with reference to the First Point of Aries. The term sidereal (or "star") time is perhaps a little misleading since the time scale so defined is not exactly the same as that which would be defined by successive transits of a selected star, as there is a small progressive motion between the stars and the First Point of Aries due to the pre-

cession of the Earth's axis. This makes the length of the sidereal day shorter than the true period of rotation by 0·008 seconds. Superimposed on this steady precessional motion are small oscillations called nutation, giving rise to fluctuations in apparent sidereal time amounting to as much as 1·2 seconds. It is therefore customary to employ Mean Sidereal Time, from which these fluctuations have been removed. The conversion of G.M.T. to Greenwich sidereal time (G.S.T.) may be performed by adding the value of the G.S.T. at 0^h on the day in question (page II of each month) to the G.M.T. converted to sidereal time using the table on p. 146.

Example. To find the G.S.T. at $2^h\ 41^m\ 11^s$ G.M.T. on Aug. 8

	h	m	s
G.S.T. at 0^h	21	06	24
G.M.T.	2	41	11
Acceleration for 2^h			20
„ „ $41^m\ 11^s$			7
Sum = G.S.T. =	23	48	02

If the observer is not on the Greenwich meridian then his longitude, measured positively westwards from Greenwich, must be subtracted from the G.S.T. to obtain Local Sidereal Time (L.S.T.). Thus, in the above example, an observer 5^h east of Greenwich, or 19° west, would find his L.S.T. as $4^h\ 48^m\ 02^s$.

Ephemeris Time

In the study of the motions of the Sun, Moon and planets, observations taken over an extended period are used in the preparation of tables giving the apparent position of the body each day. A table of this sort is known as an ephemeris, and may be used in the comparison of current observations with tabulated positions. A detailed examination of the observations made over the past 300 years shows that the Sun, Moon and planets appear to depart from their predicted positions by amounts proportional to their mean motions. The only satisfactory explanation is that the time scale to which the observations were referred was not uniform as had been supposed. Since the time scale was based on the rotation of the Earth, it follows that this rotation is subject to irregularities. The fact that the discrepancies between the observed and ephemeris positions were proportional to the mean motions of the bodies made it possible to secure agreement by substituting a revised time scale and recomputing the ephemeris positions. The time scale which brings the ephemeris into agreement with the observations has been named Ephemeris Time (E.T.).

The new unit of time has been defined in terms of the apparent annual motion of the Sun. Thus the second is now defined in terms of the annual motion of the Earth in its orbit around the Sun ($1/31556925·9747$ of the Tropical Year for 1900 January 0 at 12h. E.T.) instead of in terms of the diurnal rotation of the Earth on its axis ($1/86\ 400$ of the Mean Solar Day). In many branches of scientific work other than astronomy there has been a demand for a unit of time that is invariable, and the second of Ephemeris time was adopted by the Comité International des Poids et

E*

Mésures in 1956.   The length of the unit has been chosen to provide general agreement with U.T. throughout the 19th and 20th centuries.   During 1972 the estimated difference E.T.—U.T. is 42 seconds.   The precise determination of E.T. from astronomical observations is a lengthy process, as the accuracy with which a single observation of the Sun can be made is far less than that obtainable in, for instance, a comparison between clocks.   It is therefore necessary to average the observations over an extended period.   Largely on account of its faster motion, the position of the Moon may be observed with greater accuracy, and a close approximation to Ephemeris Time may be obtained by comparing observations of the Moon with its ephemeris position.   Even in this case, however, the requisite standard of accuracy can only be achieved by averaging over a number of years.

Atomic Time

The fundamental standards of time and frequency must be defined in terms of a periodic motion adequately uniform, enduring and susceptible of measurement.   This has led in the past to the adoption of standards based on the observed motions in the Solar System.   Recent progress has made it possible to consider the use of other natural standards, such as atomic or molecular oscillations. The oscillations so far employed are not in fact continuous periodic motions such as the revolution of the electrons in their orbits around the nuclei. The continuous oscillations are generated in an electrical circuit, the frequency of which is then compared or brought into coincidence with the frequency characteristic of the absorption or emission by the atoms or molecules when they change between two selected energy levels.   At the National Physical Laboratory regular comparisons have been made since the middle of 1955 between quartz clocks of high stability and a frequency defined by atoms of caesium.   The standard has proved of great value in the precise calibration of frequencies and time intervals: it has also been possible to build up a scale of " atomic time " by using continuously-running quartz clocks calibrated in terms of the caesium frequency standard.   Because of the high precision attained in the comparisons, cumulative errors in the integrated time scale do not become serious in the course of a few years, and the atomic time scale may thus be compared with the astronomical time scale.

Radio Time Signals

The establishment of a uniform time system by the assessment of the performance of standard clocks in terms of astronomical observations is the work of a national observatory, and standard time is then made generally available by means of radio time signals.   In the United Kingdom, the Royal Greenwich Observatory is responsible for the legal standard of time, and controls the " 6-pips " radio signals emitted by the British Broadcasting Corporation.   Signals by land line from the Observatory correct the Post Office Speaking Clock, TIM.

For survey and scientific purposes in which the highest accuracy is required, special signals are transmitted from the Post Office Radio Station at Rugby.   The International Signals, consisting of a five-minute series of pips, one-tenth of a second long, with the pips at the minutes lengthened for identification, are radiated at 02.54–03.00, 08.54–09.00, 14.54–15.00, 20.54–21.00 from GBR (16 kHz) and associated H.F. transmitters.   The seconds pulses superposed on the MSF standard frequency transmissions, which consists of five cycles of a 1,000 c.p.s. tone, are derived from the same master control at the transmitting station, and are radiated for ten minutes in each quarter-hour on $2\frac{1}{2}$, 5, and 10 MHz for 24 hours per day, and continuously on 60 kHz.   The carrier frequencies of all the MSF transmissions, and of GBR, are closely controlled, and measured regularly at the National Physical Laboratory in terms of the caesium atomic resonance.   The time signals, derived from the same master oscillator, and thus rigidly locked to the carrier frequencies, are monitored regularly at the Royal Greenwich Observatory.   A uniform rate is maintained throughout the year and, if corrections are required to keep the time signals in agreement with UTz, a step adjustment of 100 milliseconds is made on all transmissions on the first day of a month.   Since April 1960 the Rugby service has been run in close co-operation with the time services of the United States.   By mutual agreement, the rates are adjusted to correspond, and the signals are synchronized.   Any necessary adjustments are made simultaneously in the U.K. and U.S.A. services.   The American transmissions concerned are: WWV (Beltsville) $2\frac{1}{2}$, 5, 10, 15, 20, 25 MHz; WWVH (Hawaii) 5, 10, 15 MHz; NBA (Canal Zone) 18 kHz.   Other national Observatories have agreed to some measure of co-ordination.

From 1972, January 1, the universal co-ordinated time (UTC), disseminated by the Royal Greenwich Observatory and other observatories, may be as much as 0·7ˢ different from Greenwich Mean Time before any correction (which will then be of one second precisely) is applied.

SUMMER TIME

In the United Kingdom, Summer Time, one hour in advance of G.M.T. will be kept between 02ʰ G.M.T. on the day following the third Saturday in March and 02ʰ G.M.T. on the day following the fourth Saturday in October.   Thus, in 1972, Summer Time will be in force between March 19 and October 29.

Variations from the standard time of some countries occurs during part of the year: they are decided annually and are usually referred to as Summer Time or Daylight Saving Time.   These variations occur in:

British Commonwealth.—Bahamas; British Honduras; Canada; Channel Islands; Hong Kong; Tasmania.

Foreign Countries.—Albania; Brazil; Chile; parts of China; Cuba; Dominican Republic; Egypt; Formosa; Iceland; Irish Republic; Italy; Macau; Morocco; Norway; Pescadores Is.; Poland; Sudan; parts of U.S.A.; Syria; Tunisia; Turkey.

In British Honduras and the Dominican Republic the variation occurs in winter and is called Winter Time.

STANDARD TIME

In the year 1880 it was enacted by statute that the word " time ", when it occurred in any legal document relating to Great Britain, was to be interpreted, unless otherwise specifically stated, as the Mean Time of the Greenwich meridian.* Since the year 1883 the system of Standard Time by Zones has been gradually accepted, and now almost throughout the world a Standard Time which differs from that of Greenwich by an integral number of hours, either fast or slow, is used.

The large territories of the United States, Canada and U.S.S.R. are divided into zones approximately $7\frac{1}{2}°$ on either side of central meridians. The important ones are given below; there are in addition zones from 5 to 13 hours fast in the U.S.S.R. centred at 60° E. to 180° E.

Fast on Greenwich Time

12 hrs. F...Fiji, Gilbert and Ellice Is., New Zealand, Marshall Is., Caroline Is. (east of 160° E.).

$11\frac{1}{2}$ „ F...Norfolk I., Nauru I.

11 „ F...New Caledonia, New Hebrides, Santa Cruz and Solomon Is., Truk, Ponape, Sakhalin.

10 „ F...Victoria, N.S.W. (except Broken Hill Area), Queensland, Tasmania, British New Guinea, Admiralty Islds., Caroline Islds. (west of 160° E.), Australian Capital Territory, Mariana Islds.

$9\frac{1}{2}$ „ F...South Australia, Northern Territory of Australia, N.S.W. (Broken Hill Area).

9 „ F...Japan, Schouten Islds., Kurile Islds., Manchuria, Korea, West Irian (Indonesia).

$8\frac{1}{2}$ „ F...Molucca Islds.

8 „ F...China (coast), Hong Kong, Philippine Is., Macau, Timor, Western Australia, Sulawesi (Celebes), Kalimantan†, Formosa, Pescadores Islds., Malaysia, Vietnam (south).

$7\frac{1}{2}$ „ F...Singapore.

7 „ F...Sumatra, Java, Christmas I. (Indian Ocean), Thailand, Khmer Republic, Laos, Vietnam (north).

$6\frac{1}{2}$ „ F...Burma, Cocos-Keeling Islds.

6 „ F...Pakistan (East).

$5\frac{1}{2}$ „ F...India, Ceylon, Laccadive Islds., Andaman and Nicobar Islds.

5 „ F...Chagos Archipelago, Pakistan (West).

4 „ F...Mauritius, Seychelles, Réunion, U.S.S.R., 40° E. to 52°30′ E.

$3\frac{1}{2}$ „ F...Iran.

3 „ F...U.S.S.R. west of 40° E., Iraq, Ethiopia, Yemen (Dem. Repub.), Socotra I., Somali Republic, Comoro Islds., Madagascar, Uganda, Kenya, Tanzania.

2 „ F...Turkey, Greece, Bulgaria, Rumania, Finland, Israel, Jordan, U.A.R., Syria, Cyprus, Rhodesia.

E. European Malawi, South Africa, Mozambique, Sudan, Congolese Republic, Crete, Lebanon, Libya, Zambia, Botswana, Lesotho.

1 hr. F...Sweden, Norway, Denmark, Netherlands, Belgium, Germany, France, Luxemburg, Spain, Gibraltar, Monaco, Balearic Islds., Poland, Austria,

Central- Hungary, Switzerland, Italy, Czecho-
European slovakia, Yugoslavia, Albania, Tunisia, Nigeria, Malta, Sicily, Central African Republic, Cameroon Republic, Republic of Congo, Angola, Spitsbergen, Algeria, Dahomey, Corsica, Sardinia, Portugal, Niger.

Greenwich..The United Kingdom, Republic of
Time Ireland, Faroe, Channel Is., Algeria, Morocco, Iceland, Mauritania, Sierra Leone, Ivory Coast, Ifni, Ghana, Principe I., St. Helena, Gambia, Canary Is., Ascension I., Tangier, São Tomé, Rio de Oro, Madeira, Mali, Senegal.

Slow on Greenwich Time

1 hr. S...Azores, Portuguese Guinea.

2 hrs. S...Cape Verde Is., Fernando Noronha I., Scoresby Sound, South Georgia.

3 „ S...Greenland (excluding Scoresby Sound and Thule),Eastern Brazil,Argentina.

$3\frac{1}{2}$ „ S...Newfoundland, Dutch Guiana, Uruguay.

$3\frac{3}{4}$ „ S...Guyana.

4 „ S...Canada east of 68° W., Greenland
Atlantic. (Thule Area), Puerto Rico, Lesser Antilles, Central Brazil, Falkland Islds., Paraguay, Bermuda, Bolivia, French Guiana, Chile, Curaçao I., Venezuela, Labrador.

5 „ S...Canada from 68° W. to 85° W. (north)
Eastern. or 90° W. (south), Eastern States of U.S.A., Jamaica, Bahama Islds., Haiti, Peru, Panama, W. Brazil, Colombia, Cayman Is., Ecuador, Dominican Republic, Cuba.

6 hrs. S...Central parts of U.S.A., Canada from
Central. 85° W. to 102° W., Costa Rica, Salvador, Honduras, part of Mexico, Guatemala, Nicaragua.

7 hrs. S...Canada from 102° W. to 120° W.,
Mountain. Mountain States of U.S.A., part of Mexico.

8 hrs. S...Canada west of 120° W., Alaska,
Pacific. (south-east coast), Western States of U.S.A., part of Mexico, Yukon (east of 138° W.).

9 hrs. S...Alaska 137° W. to 141° W., Yukon (west of 138° W.).

10 „ S...Alaska from 141° W. to 161° W., Low Archipelago, Austral and Society Islds., Hawaii, Fanning I., Christmas Islds. (Pacific Ocean).

11 „ S...Aleutian Islds., Alaska (west coast), Samoa, Midway Islds.

In the Tonga Islands the time 13h fast and in Chatham Is. 12h 45m fast on Greenwich is used, as the Date line is to the East of them.

Liberia keeps a time of $0^h\ 44^m\ 30^s$ slow on G.M.T.

THE DATE OR CALENDAR LINE

The line where the change of date occurs is a modification of the 180th meridian, and is drawn so as to include islands of any one group on the same side of the line, or for political reasons. It is indicated by joining up the following nine points:

Lat.	Long.	Lat.	Long.	Lat.	Long.
60° S.	180°	15° S.	$172\frac{1}{2}°$ W.	53° N.	170° E.
51° S.	180°	5° S.	180°	$65\frac{1}{2}°$ N.	169° W.
45° S.	$172\frac{1}{2}°$ W.	48° N.	180°	75° N.	180°

* Summer Time is the " legal " time during the period in which its use is ordained. † Formerly Indonesian Borneo.

RISING AND SETTING TIMES

Table 1. Hour Angle

Dec.	Latitude and Declination of Opposite Signs						0°	Latitude and Declination of Same Signs					
	50°	45°	40°	30°	20°	10°		10°	20°	30°	40°	45°	50°
°	h m	h m	h m	h m	h m	h m	h m	h m	h m	h m	h m	h m	h m
0	6 00	6 00	6 00	6 00	6 00	6 00	6 00	6 00	6 00	6 00	6 00	6 00	6 00
1	5 55	5 56	5 57	5 58	5 59	5 59	6 00	6 01	6 01	6 02	6 03	6 04	6 05
2	5 50	5 52	5 53	5 55	5 57	5 58	6 00	6 02	6 03	6 05	6 07	6 08	6 10
3	5 45	5 48	5 50	5 53	5 56	5 58	6 00	6 02	6 04	6 07	6 10	6 12	6 15
4	5 40	5 44	5 46	5 51	5 54	5 57	6 00	6 03	6 06	6 09	6 14	6 16	6 20
5	5 36	5 40	5 43	5 48	5 52	5 56	6 00	6 04	6 08	6 12	6 17	6 20	6 24
6	5 31	5 36	5 39	5 46	5 51	5 56	6 00	6 04	6 09	6 14	6 21	6 24	6 29
7	5 26	5 32	5 36	5 44	5 50	5 55	6 00	6 05	6 10	6 16	6 24	6 28	6 34
8	5 21	5 27	5 33	5 41	5 48	5 54	6 00	6 06	6 12	6 19	6 27	6 33	6 39
9	5 16	5 23	5 29	5 39	5 47	5 53	6 00	6 07	6 13	6 21	6 31	6 37	6 44
10	5 11	5 19	5 26	5 37	5 45	5 53	6 00	6 07	6 15	6 23	6 34	6 41	6 49
11	5 06	5 15	5 22	5 34	5 44	5 52	6 00	6 08	6 16	6 26	6 38	6 45	6 54
12	5 01	5 11	5 19	5 32	5 42	5 51	6 00	6 09	6 18	6 28	6 41	6 49	6 59
13	4 56	5 06	5 15	5 29	5 40	5 51	6 00	6 09	6 20	6 31	6 45	6 54	7 04
14	4 51	5 02	5 12	5 27	5 39	5 50	6 00	6 10	6 21	6 33	6 48	6 58	7 09
15	4 46	4 58	5 08	5 24	5 38	5 49	6 00	6 11	6 22	6 36	6 52	7 02	7 14
16	4 40	4 53	5 04	5 22	5 36	5 48	6 00	6 12	6 24	6 38	6 56	7 07	7 20
17	4 35	4 49	5 00	5 19	5 35	5 48	6 00	6 12	6 25	6 41	7 00	7 11	7 25
18	4 29	4 44	4 57	5 17	5 33	5 47	6 00	6 13	6 27	6 43	7 03	7 16	7 31
19	4 23	4 39	4 53	5 14	5 31	5 46	6 00	6 14	6 29	6 46	7 07	7 21	7 37
20	4 17	4 35	4 49	5 11	5 30	5 45	6 00	6 15	6 30	6 49	7 11	7 25	7 43
21	4 11	4 30	4 44	5 09	5 28	5 44	6 00	6 16	6 32	6 51	7 16	7 30	7 49
22	4 04	4 25	4 40	5 06	5 26	5 44	6 00	6 16	6 34	6 54	7 20	7 35	7 56
23	3 58	4 19	4 36	5 03	5 24	5 43	6 00	6 17	6 36	6 57	7 24	7 41	8 02
24	3 52	4 14	4 32	5 00	5 23	5 42	6 00	6 18	6 37	7 00	7 28	7 46	8 08
25	3 45	4 09	4 28	4 58	5 21	5 41	6 00	6 19	6 39	7 02	7 32	7 51	8 15
26	3 38	4 03	4 24	4 55	5 19	5 40	6 00	6 20	6 41	7 05	7 36	7 57	8 22
27	3 30	3 57	4 19	4 52	5 17	5 39	6 00	6 21	6 43	7 08	7 41	8 03	8 30
28	3 23	3 51	4 14	4 48	5 15	5 38	6 00	6 22	6 45	7 12	7 46	8 09	8 37
29	3 15	3 45	4 09	4 45	5 14	5 38	6 00	6 22	6 46	7 15	7 51	8 15	8 45

SUNRISE AND SUNSET

The local mean time of sunrise or sunset (as defined on page 138) may be found by determining the appropriate hour angle from the table above and applying it to the time of transit given in the ephemeris for each month. The hour angle is negative for sunrise and positive for sunset. A small correction to the hour angle, which always has the effect of increasing it numerically, is necessary to allow for the Sun's semi-diameter (16′) and for refraction (34′). This correction may be obtained from Table 2. The resulting local mean time may be converted into the standard time of the country by taking the difference between the longitude of the standard meridian of the country and that of the place, and adding it to the local mean time if the place is west of the standard meridian, and subtracting it if the place is east of the standard meridian.

Example.—Required the N.Z. Mean Time (12ʰ fast on G.M.T.) of sunset on May 24 at Auckland. The latitude is 36° 50′ south (or minus) and the longitude 11ʰ 39ᵐ east. Taking the declination as +20°·7, we find

	h m
Tabular entry for 30° Lat. and Dec. 20°, opposite signs	+ 5 11
Proportional part for 6° 50′ of Lat.	− 15
Proportional part for 0°·7 of Dec.	− 3
Correction (Table 2)	+ 6
Hour angle	4 59
Sun transits	11 57
Longitudinal correction	+ 21
N.Z. Mean Time	17 17

Table 2. Correction for Refraction and Semi-Diameter

Latitude	Declination			
	0°	10°	20°	29°
°	m	m	m	m
0	4	4	4	5
20	4	4	5	5
30	5	5	5	6
40	5	6	6	7
50	6	6	7	9

MOONRISE AND MOONSET

It is possible to calculate the times of moonrise and moonset using Table 1 though the method is more complicated because the apparent motion of the Moon is much more rapid than that of the Sun.

Table 3. Longitude Correction

X / A	40^m	45^m	50^m	55^m	60^m	65^m	70^m
h	m	m	m	m	m	m	m
1	2	2	2	2	3	3	3
2	3	4	4	5	5	5	6
3	5	6	6	7	8	8	9
4	7	8	8	9	10	11	12
5	8	9	10	11	13	14	15
6	10	11	13	14	15	16	18
7	12	13	15	16	18	19	20
8	13	15	17	18	20	22	23
9	15	17	19	21	23	24	26
10	17	19	21	23	25	27	29
11	18	21	23	25	28	30	32
12	20	23	25	28	30	33	35
13	22	24	27	30	33	35	38
14	23	26	29	32	35	38	41
15	25	28	31	34	38	41	44
16	27	30	33	37	40	43	47
17	28	32	35	39	43	46	50
18	30	34	38	41	45	49	53
19	32	36	40	44	48	51	55
20	33	38	42	46	50	54	58
21	35	39	44	48	53	57	61
22	37	41	46	50	55	60	64
23	38	43	48	53	58	62	67
24	40	45	50	55	60	65	70

Notation

φ = latitude of observer
λ = longitude of observer (measured positively towards the west)
T_{-1} = time of transit of Moon on previous day
T_0 = time of transit of Moon on day in question
T_1 = time of transit of Moon on following day
δ_0 = approximate declination of Moon
δ_R = declination of Moon at moonrise
δ_S = declination of Moon at moonset
h_0 = approximate hour angle of Moon
h_R = hour angle of Moon at moonrise
h_S = hour angle of Moon at moonset
t_R = time of moonrise
t_S = time of moonset

The parallax of the Moon, about $57'$, is near to the sum of the semi-diameter and refraction but has the opposite effect on these times. It is thus convenient to neglect all three quantities in the method outlined below.

METHOD

1. With arguments φ, δ_0 enter Table 1 on p. 144 to determine h_0 where h_0 is negative for moonrise and positive for moonset.

2. Form approximate times from
$$t_R = T_0 + \lambda + h_0$$
$$t_S = T_0 + \lambda + h_0$$

3. Determine δ_R, δ_S for times t_R, t_S respectively.

4. Re-enter Table 1 on p. 144 with—
   (a) arguments φ, δ_R to determine h_R
   (b) arguments φ, δ_S to determine h_S

5. Form $t_R = T_0 + \lambda + h_R + AX$
$$t_S = T_0 + \lambda + h_S + AX$$
where $A = (\lambda + h)$
$X = (T_0 - T_{-1})$ if $(\lambda + h)$ is negative
and $X = (T_1 - T_0)$ if $(\lambda + h)$ is positive
AX is the respondent in Table 3.

Example.—To find the times of moonrise and moonset at Vancouver ($\varphi = +49°$, $\lambda = +8^h 12^m$) on 1972 October 10. The starting data (from p. 128) are

$$
\begin{aligned}
& \quad\quad h \quad m \\
T_{-1} &= 13 \quad 15 \\
T_0 &= 14 \quad 01 \\
T_1 &= 14 \quad 50 \\
\delta_0 &= -21°
\end{aligned}
$$

1. $h_0 = \pm 4^h 15^m$

2. Approximate values
$$
\begin{aligned}
t_R &= 10^d 14^h 01^m + 8^h 12^m + (-4^h 15^m) \\
&= 10^d 17^h 58^m \\
t_S &= 10^d 14^h 01^m + 8^h 12^m + (+4^h 15^m) \\
&= 11^d 02^h 28^m
\end{aligned}
$$

3. $\delta_R = -23°.1$
$\delta_S = -23°.9$

4. $h_R = -4^h 01^m$
$h_S = +3^h 57^m$

5. $t_R = 10^d 14^h 01^m + 8^h 12^m - 4^h 01^m + 8^m$
$= 10^d 18^h 20^m$
$t_S = 10^d 14^h 01^m + 8^h 12^m + 3^h 57^m + 25^m$
$= 11^d 02^h 35^m$

To get the L.M.T. of the phenomenon the longitude is subtracted from the G.M.T. thus
Moonrise $= 10^d 18^h 20^m - 8^h 12^m = 10^d 10^h 08^m$
Moonset $= 11^d 02^h 35^m - 8^h 12^m = 10^d 18^h 23^m$

ASTRONOMICAL CONSTANTS

Solar Parallax	$8''.794$
Precession for the year 1972	$50''.272$
„ in R.A.	$3^s.074$
„ in Declination	$20''.041$
Constant of Nutation	$9''.21$
Constant of Aberration	$20''.496$
Mean Obliquity of Ecliptic (1972)	$23° 26' 35''$
Moon's Equatorial Hor. Parallax	$57' 02''.70$
Velocity of Light in vacuo *per sec.*	299792.5 km.
Solar motion *per sec.*	20.0 km.
Equatorial radius of the Earth	6378.160 km.
Polar radius of the Earth	6356.775 km.

North Galactic Pole R.A. $12^h 49^m$ (1950.0).
(I.A.U. *Standard*). Dec. $27°.4$ N.
Solar Apex R.A. $18^h 06^m$ Dec. $+30°$.
Length of Year...Tropical 365.24220
(*In Mean* Sidereal 365.25636
Solar Days) Anomalistic 365.25964
(Perihelion to Perihelion)
Eclipse 346.6200

	d h m s
Length of Month New Moon to New	29 12 44 02·9
(*Mean Values*) Sidereal	27 07 43 11·5
Anomalistic	27 13 18 33·2
(Perigee to Perigee)	

MEAN AND SIDEREAL TIME

MEAN REFRACTION

h	m s	h	m s	m s	s
1	0 10	13	2 08	0 00	0
2	0 20	14	2 18	3 02	1
3	0 30	15	2 28	9 07	2
4	0 39	16	2 38	15 13	3
5	0 49	17	2 48	21 18	4
6	0 59	18	2 57	27 23	5
				33 28	6
7	1 09	19	3 07	39 34	7
8	1 19	20	3 17	45 39	8
9	1 29	21	3 27	51 44	9
10	1 39	22	3 37	57 49	10
11	1 48	23	3 47	60 00	
12	1 58	24	3 57		

Acceleration

h	m s	h	m s	m s	s
1	0 10	13	2 08	0 00	0
2	0 20	14	2 18	3 03	1
3	0 29	15	2 27	9 09	2
4	0 39	16	2 37	15 15	3
5	0 49	17	2 47	21 21	4
6	0 59	18	2 57	27 28	5
				33 34	6
7	1 09	19	3 07	39 40	7
8	1 19	20	3 17	45 46	8
9	1 28	21	3 26	51 53	9
10	1 38	22	3 36	57 59	10
11	1 48	23	3 46	60 00	
12	1 58	24	3 56		

Retardation

Alt.	Ref.	Alt.	Ref.
° '		° '	
1 20	21	4 30	10
1 30	20	5 06	9
1 41	19	5 50	8
1 52	18	6 44	7
2 05	17	7 54	6
2 19	16	9 27	5
2 35	15	11 39	4
2 52	14	15 00	3
3 12	13	20 42	2
3 34	12	32 20	1
4 00	11	62 17	0
4 30		90 00	

The length of a sidereal day in mean time is $23^h 56^m 04^s.09$. Hence 1^h M.T.$=1^h+9^s.86$ S.T. and 1^h S.T.$=1^h-9^s.83$ M.T.

To convert an interval of mean time to the corresponding interval of sidereal time, enter the acceleration table with the given mean time (taking the hours and the minutes and seconds separately) and add the acceleration obtained to the given mean time. To convert an interval of sidereal time to the corresponding interval of mean time, take out the retardation for the given sidereal time and subtract.

The columns for the minutes and seconds of the argument are in the form known as Critical Tables. To use these tables, find in the appropriate left-hand column the two entries between which the given number of minutes and seconds lies; the quantity in the right-hand column between these two entries is the required acceleration or retardation. Thus the acceleration for $11^m 26^s$ (which lies between the entries $9^m 07^s$ and $15^m 13^s$) is 2^s. If the given number of minutes and seconds is a tabular entry, the required acceleration or retardation is the entry in the right-hand column *above* the given tabular entry; e.g. the retardation for $45^m 46^s$ is 7^s.

Example.—Convert $14^h 27^m 35^s$ from S.T. to M.T.

	h	m	s
Given S.T.	14	27	35
Retardation for 14^h		2	18
Retardation for $27^m 35^s$			5
Corresponding M.T.	14	25	12

For further explanation, see p. 141.

The refraction table is also in the form of a critical table.

THE SUMMER TIME ACTS

In 1916 an Act ordained that during a defined period of that year the legal time for general purposes in Great Britain should be one hour in advance of Greenwich Mean Time. The practice was stabilized (until the war) by the *Summer Time Acts,* 1922 to 1925, which enacted that "For the purposes of this Act, the period of summer time shall be taken to be the period beginning at two o'clock, Greenwich Mean Time, in the morning of the day next following the third Saturday in April, or, if that day is Easter Day, the day next following the second Saturday in April and ending at two o'clock, Greenwich Mean Time, in the morning of the day next following the first Saturday in October."

During the Second World War the duration of Summer Time was extended and in the years 1941-45 and in 1947, Double Summer Time (2 hrs. in advance of Greenwich Mean Time) was in force.

Summer Time was extended in each year from 1948 to 1952 and again in 1961–1964, by Order in Council.

The duration of Summer Time during the last few years is given in the following table.

1953 Apr. 19—Oct. 4	1961 Mar. 26—Oct. 29
1954 Apr. 11—Oct. 3	1962 Mar. 25—Oct. 28
1955 Apr. 17—Oct. 2	1963 Mar. 31—Oct. 27
1956 Apr. 22—Oct. 7	1964 Mar. 22—Oct. 25
1957 Apr. 14—Oct. 6	1965 Mar. 21—Oct. 24
1958 Apr. 20—Oct. 5	1966 Mar. 20—Oct. 23
1959 Apr. 19—Oct. 4	1967 Mar. 19—Oct. 29
1960 Apr. 10—Oct. 2	1968 Feb. 18—Oct. 27

British Standard Time, also one hour ahead of G.M.T., was kept between 1968 Oct. 27–1971 Oct. 31. In 1972 Summer Time will be in force from March 19 to October 29.

ASTRONOMERS ROYAL

John Flamsteed, first Astronomer Royal	1675–1719
Edmund Halley	1720–1742
James Bradley	1742–1762
Nathaniel Bliss	1762–1764
Nevil Maskelyne	1765–1811
John Pond	1811–1835

Sir George Biddell Airy	1835–1881
Sir William Henry Mahoney Christie	1881–1910
Sir Frank Watson Dyson	1910–1933
Sir Harold Spencer Jones	1933–1955
Sir Richard van der Riet Woolley	1955–1971

PHENOMENA OF JUPITER'S SATELLITES, 1972

G.M.T.	Sat.	Phen.	G.M.T.	Sat.	Phen.	G.M.T.	Sat.	Phen.	G.M.T.	Sat.	Phen.
January			*May*			*July*			*September*		
d h m			d h m			d h m			d h m		
19 7 18	II	Ec.D.	3 3 43	II	Sh.I.	6 2 47	II	Sh.I.	2 21 14	II	Ec.R.
25 7 12	II	Ec.D.	5 4 09	I	Ec.D.	6 23 58	I	Sh.I.	7 22 10	I	Ec.R.
28 7 35	II	Sh.E.	6 1 19	I	Sh.I.	7 2 13	I	Sh.E.	8 19 29	I	Sh.E.
			6 3 32	I	Sh.E.	7 23 26	I	Ec.R.	13 19 31	IV	Ec.D.
February			12 0 31	II	Ec.D.	8 0 13	II	Ec.R.	13 21 52	IV	Ec.R.
2 6 16	I	Sh.I.	13 3 12	I	Sh.I.	14 1 52	I	Sh.I.	15 19 10	I	Sh.I.
4 7 29	II	Sh.I.	14 0 31	I	Ec.D.	15 1 20	I	Ec.R.	15 19 14	III	Sh.I.
10 5 50	III	Ec.D.	17 2 19	III	Sh.E.	15 22 36	I	Sh.E.	15 21 24	I	Sh.E.
18 6 43	I	Sh.E.	19 3 07	II	Ec.D.	16 21 20	II	Sh.E.	18 20 38	II	Sh.E.
20 6 50	II	Ec.D.	21 0 48	II	Sh.E.	17 0 12	III	Ec.R.	22 21 06	I	Sh.I.
25 6 25	I	Sh.I.	21 23 35	I	Sh.I.	22 22 16	I	Sh.I.	23 20 29	I	Ec.R.
28 6 34	III	Sh.E.	22 1 49	I	Sh.E.	23 0 31	I	Sh.E.	25 20 29	II	Sh.I.
			24 3 23	III	Sh.I.	23 21 13	II	Sh.I.	27 18 24	II	Ec.D.
March			28 0 40	II	Sh.I.	23 21 43	I	Ec.R.			
4 5 38	I	Ec.D.	28 3 22	II	Sh.E.	23 23 55	II	Sh.E.			
5 4 58	I	Sh.E.	29 1 28	I	Sh.I.	30 0 11	I	Sh.I.	*October*		
12 4 40	I	Sh.I.	29 3 43	I	Sh.E.	30 23 38	I	Ec.R.	1 19 44	I	Sh.E.
16 3 50	II	Ec.D.				30 23 47	II	Sh.I.	3 20 18	III	Ec.R.
17 4 28	III	Ec.R.	*June*			31 20 55	I	Sh.E.	8 19 25	I	Sh.I.
20 3 53	I	Ec.D.	4 3 14	II	Sh.I.				9 18 48	I	Ec.R.
24 5 37	III	Ec.D.	6 0 40	I	Ec.D.				13 17 46	II	Sh.E.
25 4 16	II	Sh.E.	7 0 06	I	Sh.E.				17 18 04	I	Sh.E.
27 5 46	I	Ec.D.	11 1 13	III	Ec.D.	*August*			20 17 36	II	Sh.I.
28 5 07	I	Sh.E.	13 0 14	II	Ec.D.	1 21 24	II	Ec.R.	21 18 28	III	Sh.E.
			13 2 33	I	Ec.D.	2 21 13	IV	Sh.I.	24 17 45	I	Sh.I.
April			13 23 45	I	Sh.I.	2 22 27	IV	Sh.E.	25 17 49	IV	Sh.E.
1 4 10	II	Sh.I.	14 2 00	I	Sh.E.	3 22 19	III	Sh.E.	28 19 15	III	Sh.I.
4 4 48	I	Sh.I.	20 2 51	II	Ec.D.	7 20 35	I	Sh.I.	29 18 10	II	Ec.R.
11 3 35	III	Sh.I.	21 1 40	I	Sh.I.	7 22 50	I	Sh.E.			
12 4 01	I	Ec.D.	21 21 39	II	Sh.I.	9 0 02	II	Ec.R.			
13 3 22	I	Sh.I.	21 22 18	III	Sh.I.	10 23 13	III	Sh.I.	*November*		
17 3 26	II	Ec.R.	21 22 56	I	Ec.D.	14 22 31	I	Sh.I.	1 19 03	I	Ec.R.
20 3 03	I	Sh.I.	22 0 21	II	Sh.E.	15 21 56	I	Ec.R.	9 18 18	I	Sh.E.
26 3 50	II	Sh.E.	22 22 23	I	Sh.E.	17 20 57	II	Sh.E.	14 17 33	II	Sh.I.
28 2 16	I	Ec.D.	28 23 16	III	Sh.I.	21 20 14	III	Ec.R.	15 17 05	III	Ec.D.
29 1 25	III	Ec.D.	29 0 13	II	Sh.I.	23 21 09	I	Sh.E.	16 17 59	I	Sh.I.
29 1 38	I	Sh.E.	29 2 17	III	Sh.E.	24 20 49	II	Sh.I.	17 17 22	I	Ec.R.
29 4 20	III	Ec.R.	29 2 55	II	Sh.E.	28 21 05	III	Ec.D.	21 17 21	II	Sh.I.
			29 22 03	I	Sh.I.	30 20 50	I	Sh.I.			
			30 0 18	I	Sh.E.	31 20 15	I	Ec.R.			
			30 21 31	I	Ec.R.				*December*		
			30 21 36	II	Ec.R.				6 16 53	IV	Ec.R.

Jupiter's satellites transit across the disk from east to west, and pass behind the disk from west to east. The shadows that they cast also transit across the disk. With the exception at times of Satellite IV, the satellites also pass through the shadow of the planet, i.e. they are eclipsed. Just before opposition the satellite disappears in the shadow to the west of the planet, and reappears from occultation on the east limb. Immediately after opposition the satellite is occulted at the west limb, and reappears from eclipse to the east of the planet. At times approximately two to four months before and after opposition, both phases of eclipses of Satellite III may be seen. When Satellite IV is eclipsed, both phases may be seen.

The list of phenomena gives most of the eclipses and shadow transits visible in the British Isles under favourable conditions.

Ec. = Eclipse	R = Reappearance	
Sh. = Shadow transit	I = Ingress	
D = Disappearance	E = Egress	

The times given in these predictions are strictly for the centre of the satellite. Observers will appreciate that as the satellite is of considerable size the immersion and emersion phases are not instantaneous. Even when the satellite enters or leaves the shadow along a radius of the shadow the phase can last for several minutes. With satellite IV grazing phenomena can occur so that the light from the satellite may fade and brighten again without a complete eclipse taking place.

CELESTIAL PHENOMENA FOR OBSERVATION IN 1972

ECLIPSES, 1972

There will be four eclipses during 1972, two of the Sun and two of the Moon.

Penumbral eclipses are not mentioned in this section as they are so difficult to observe.

1. An annular eclipse of the Sun on January 16. The track of the annular eclipse crosses part of Antarctica. A parallel eclipse is visible from the south of South America, Antarctica and a small part of south-west Australia. The eclipse begins at $08^h 45^m$ and ends at $13^h 20^m$. The duration of the annular phase nowhere exceeds 2^m.

2. A total eclipse of the Moon on January 30. The beginning is visible from the north-eastern part of Asia, the eastern coast of Australia, New Zealand, the Pacific Ocean, the arctic regions, North America, South America except the extreme eastern part, while the end is visible from Asia (except the south-western part), Australia, New Zealand, the Pacific Ocean and North America except the eastern part, and the arctic regions. The eclipse begins at $09^h 11^m$ and ends at $12^h 35^m$. It is total between $10^h 35^m$ and $11^h 12^m$.

3. A total eclipse of the Sun on July 10. The path of totality starts on the east coast of Sakhalin Island and then passes through extreme N.E. Siberia, northern Alaska, northern Canada and Nova Scotia before ending in mid-Atlantic. The partial phase will be visible from N.E. Asia including northern Japan, the whole of N. America (except most of Mexico), central America, northern South America, Greenland, Iceland, and part of northern and western Europe including Scandinavia and the British Isles. The eclipse begins at $17^h 19^m$ and ends at $22^h 13^m$. Totality begins at $18^h 29^m$ and ends at $21^h 03^m$. The maximum duration of totality is $2^m 36^s$.

4. A partial eclipse of the Moon on July 26. The eclipse is visible from New Zealand, Antarctica, eastern Australia, most of the Pacific Ocean, North America, South America, and N.W. Africa. The eclipse begins at $05^h 55^m$ and ends at $08^h 36^m$. At the time of maximum eclipse 0·55 of the Moon's diameter is obscured.

OCCULTATIONS OF STARS

The list on the opposite page includes all the occultations visible under favourable conditions in the British Isles. Disappearances of stars down to magnitude 6·5 are normally included, and re-appearances to 6·0 magnitude. No occultation is included unless the star is at least 10° above the horizon and the Sun sufficiently far below the horizon to permit the star to be seen with the naked eye or in a small telescope. The altitude limit is reduced from 10° to 2° for stars and planets brighter than magnitude 2·0 and such occultations are also predicted in daylight.

The column Phase shows whether a disappearance (D) or reappearance (R) is to be observed. The column headed "El. of Moon" gives the elongation of the Moon from the Sun, in degrees. The elongation increases from 0° at New Moon

to 180° at Full Moon and on to 360° (or 0°) at New Moon again. Times and position angles (P), reckoned from the north point in the direction north, east, south, west, are given for Greenwich (Lat. 51° 29′, Long. 0°) and Edinburgh (Lat. 55° 56′, Long. 3° 11′ west). The coefficients a and b are the variations in the G.M.T. for each degree of longitude (positive to the west) and latitude (positive to the north) respectively: they enable approximate times (to within about 1^m generally) to be found for any point in the British Isles. If the point of observation is $\Delta\lambda$ degrees west and $\Delta\phi$ degrees north, the approximate time is found by adding $a.\Delta\lambda + b.\Delta\phi$ to the given G.M.T.

As an illustration the disappearance of 101 Piscium on November 18 at Liverpool will be found from both Greenwich and Edinburgh.

	Greenwich	Edinburgh
	°	°
Longitude	0·0	+3·2
Long. of Liverpool	+3·0	+3·0
$\Delta\lambda$	+3·0	−0·2
Latitude	+51·5	+55·9
Lat. of Liverpool	+53·4	+53·4
$\Delta\phi$	+1·9	−2·5
	h m	h m
G.M.T.	21 08·9	21 07·4
$a.\Delta\lambda$	−4·5	+0·2
$b.\Delta\phi$	+0·8	−2·0
	21 05·2	21 05·6

If the occultation is given for one station but not the other, the reason for the suppression is given by the following code.

No occn. = star not occulted.

Low = star's altitude less than 10° (2° for bright stars and planets).

Sun = Sun not sufficiently below the horizon.

Graze = occultation is of very short duration.

It will be noticed that in some cases the coefficients a and b are not given: this is because the occultation is so short that prediction for other places by means of these coefficients would not be reliable.

OCCULTATIONS 1972

The series of occultations of some of the stars of the Pleiades continues into 1972. The evening of March 19 will be a particularly favourable occasion to view such events with the Moon only 25 per cent. illuminated.

Antares will be occulted twice, on May 1 and again on September 14, though on the latter occasion the event occurs in daylight.

Mars will be occulted on May 15.

Occultation Observations.—Observations of the times of these occultations are made by both amateurs and professionals. Such observations are later analyzed to yield accurate positions of the

Moon: this is one method of determining the difference between ephemeris time and universal time.

Many of the observations made by amateurs are obtained with the use of a stop-watch which is compared with a time signal immediately after the observation. Thus an accuracy of about one-fifth of a second is obtainable, though the observer's personal equation may amount to one-third or one-half of a second.

OCCULTATIONS OF STARS BY THE MOON, 1972

Date	Star	Mag.	Phase	El. of Moon	GREENWICH				EDINBURGH			
					G.M.T.	a	b	P	G.M.T.	a	b	P
				°	h m	m	m	°	h m	m	m	°
Jan. 24	26 Arietis........	6·1	D	98	Low	..	..	..	1 14·6	−0·1	−0·6	50
25	χ Tauri d........	5·5	D	123	21 32·3	−1·4	−0·7	89	21 26·5	−1·3	−0·1	75
27	+25° 879........	6·3	D	138	2 56·1	+0·4	−2·1	135	2 47·4	+0·2	−2·1	129
27	125 Tauri........	5·0	D	139	4 05·6	+0·4	−1·6	119	3 59·5	+0·3	−1·7	116
28	+24° 1343......	6·5	D	152	3 46·4	+0·3	−2·1	139	3 37·9	+0·2	−2·1	135
Feb. 19	47 B. Arietis.....	6·5	D	66	21 16·4	−0·4	−0·8	65	21 12·0	−0·5	−0·5	52
Mar. 7	65 B. Scorpii.....	5·6	R	259	Low	−1·6	−0·2	291	Low	..	..	..
19	16 Tauri........	5·4	D	61	19 18·9	−1·3	+1·3	30	No occn.	..	..	..
19	17 Tauri........	3·8	D	61	19 05·3	−1·0	−0·7	74	18 59·8	−1·0	−0·3	61
19	23 Tauri........	4·2	D	61	19 47·8	−0·5	−2·3	118	19 36·8	−0·6	−1·8	105
19	η Tauri........	3·0	D	62	20 14·6	−0·5	−1·4	89	20 07·0	−0·6	−1·1	79
19	η Tauri........	3·0	R	62	21 14·4	−0·3	−1·2	261	21 07·4	−0·3	−1·5	269
19	27 Tauri d.......	3·8	D	62	20 58·5	−0·2	−1·9	108	20 49·8	−0·3	−1·7	98
19	28 Tauri........	5·2	D	62	20 57·7	−0·3	−1·4	90	20 50·5	−0·4	−1·3	81
26	43 Leonis........	6·3	D	150	23 28·2	−1·3	−1·4	114	23 18·8	−1·2	−1·1	112
Apr. 3	1 Scorpii........	4·8	R	229	4 14·5	−1·7	−0·2	233	Low	..	..	..
18	52 B. Geminorum .	6·4	D	71	21 15·4	−0·9	−0·8	63	21 09·0	−1·0	−0·7	57
May 1	α Scorpii d.......	1·2	D	210	3 05·6	−1·5	−0·3	58	2 59·7	−1·4	−0·3	54
1	α Scorpii d.......	1·2	R	210	4 12·0	−1·6	−1·6	308	4 00·4	−1·4	−1·4	315
15	Mars..........	1·9	D	38	20 43·6	..	..	172	20 33·2	+0·9	−2·9	165
15	Mars..........	1·9	R	38	21 01·8	..	..	212	20 58·5	−0·6	−0·5	219
19	83 B. Leonis.....	5·9	D	90	22 41·5	−0·3	−1·9	116	22 32·0	−0·4	−1·9	115
June 2	ν Capricorni......	5·3	D	236	2 22·4	−1·8	+0·5	294	Sun	..	..	..
30	29 Capricorni.....	5·5	D	218	0 27·6	−0·6	+2·1	185	0 33·9	−0·7	+1·7	193
Aug. 22	ν Capricorni......	5·3	D	155	23 11·2	−1·4	0·0	73	23 07·3	−1·2	+0·1	64
30	ε Arietis d........	4·6	R	249	3 23·0	−1·2	+1·3	243	3 24·3	−1·1	+0·9	258
30	104 B. Tauri.....	5·5	R	260	Low	..	..	..	22 13·9	+0·4	+1·4	254
Sept. 1	98 Tauri d.......	5·6	R	275	0 45·2	+0·9	+3·2	198	0 59·1	+0·4	+2·4	216
14	α Scorpii d.......	1·2	D	75	14 23·9	−0·6	+0·3	140	Low	..	..	..
14	α Scorpii d.......	1·2	R	75	15 26·5	−1·9	+1·2	244	15 26·3	−1·6	+1·2	246
26	μ Arietis d.......	5·7	R	218	4 01·0	−1·1	+2·1	204	4 03·9	−1·0	+0·9	223
30	87 B. Geminorum .	5·8	R	272	3 09·7	−1·2	−0·1	308	3 04·0	−1·2	−0·9	328
Oct. 18	170 B. Aquarii....	6·1	D	127	19 06·6	−1·2	+1·2	57	19 08·8	−0·9	+1·3	50
20	22 B. Piscium.....	6·5	D	142	0 49·5	−0·7	−0·5	62	0 46·0	−0·6	−0·1	47
26	118 Tauri d......	5·9	R	228	3 06·3	−1·5	−0·1	274	3 00·6	−1·3	−0·5	288
27	63 Geminorum....	5·3	R	253	23 55·7	−0·4	+0·9	291	23 57·9	−0·4	+0·7	306
Nov. 13	−15° 5908........	6·4	D	82	17 00·6	−1·0	+1·2	35	17 02·8	−0·8	+1·1	26
15	6 G. Piscium.....	6·2	D	109	22 51·1	−0·5	+0·1	41	22 51·3	−0·3	+0·6	23
17	136 B. Piscium...	6·5	D	135	22 22·1	−1·3	−0·2	74	22 18·7	−1·0	+0·3	59
18	101 Piscium......	6·2	D	149	21 08·9	−1·5	+0·4	88	21 07·4	−1·1	+0·8	74
22	132 Tauri.......	5·0	D	205	19 21·4	0·0	+1·1	282	19 26·0	−0·1	+1·0	293
22	412 B. Tauri.....	6·0	R	206	No occn.	..	..	..	22 15·9	+0·1	+3·8	209
23	5 Geminorum.....	5·9	R	210	5 07·3	−0·2	−2·8	328	4 52·9	0·0	−3·6	340
23	44 Geminorum....	5·9	R	221	23 47·8	−1·4	−2·1	338	No occn.	..	..	..
27	π Leonis........	4·9	R	262	5 27·3	−1·1	−1·2	314	5 18·8	−0·9	−1·1	321
Dec. 13	22 B. Piscium.....	6·5	D	88	17 00·6	−2·3	−0·7	107	17 43·9	−1·6	+0·2	91
13	κ Piscium.......	4·9	D	89	20 33·3	−1·0	+0·9	27	20 37·6	−0·2	+1·8	7
13	9 Piscium.......	6·4	D	89	20 28·0	−1·0	−0·3	62	20 24·8	−0·8	+0·1	47
24	o Leonis d.......	3·8	D	231	4 46·2	−1·6	−0·7	90	4 38·7	−1·5	−0·4	85
24	o Leonis d.......	3·8	R	231	5 45·9	−0·5	−2·2	334	5 34·9	−0·4	−2·1	337

NAME	Mag.	R.A	Dec.	Spectrum
		h m	° ′	
α Andromedæ *Alpheratz*	2·1	0 06·9	+28 56	Aop
β Cassiopeiæ *Caph*	2·4	0 07·7	+59 00	F5
γ Pegasi *Algenib*	2·9	0 11·8	+15 02	B2
α Phœnicis	2·4	0 24·9	−42 27	K0
α Cassiopeiæ *Schedar*	2·3	0 38·9	+56 23	K0
β Ceti *Diphda*	2·2	0 42·2	−18 08	K0
γ Cassiopeiæ★	Var.	0 55·0	+60 34	Bop
β Andromedæ *Mirach*	2·4	1 08·2	+35 28	M0
δ Cassiopeiæ	2·8	1 24·0	+60 05	A5
α Eridani *Achernar*	0·6	1 36·7	−57 23	B5
β Arietis *Sheratan*	2·7	1 53·1	+20 40	A5
γ Andromedæ *Almak*........	2·3	2 02·2	+42 12	K0
α Ursæ Minoris *Polaris*	2·1	2 04·9	+89 08	F8
α Arietis *Hamal*	2·2	2 05·6	+23 20	K2
β Persei *Algol*★	Var.	3 06·3	+40 51	B8
α Persei *Mirfak*..........	1·9	3 22·3	+49 46	F5
η Tauri *Alcyone*	3·0	3 45·8	+24 01	B5p
α Tauri *Aldebaran*	1·1	4 34·3	+16 27	K5
β Orionis *Rigel*	0·3	5 13·2	− 8 14	B8p
α Aurigæ *Capella*	0·2	5 14·6	+45 58	G0
γ Orionis *Bellatrix*	1·7	5 23·6	+ 6 20	B2
β Tauri *Elnath*	1·8	5 24·5	+28 35	B8
δ Orionis	2·5	5 30·6	− 0 19	B0
α Leporis..................	2·7	5 31·5	−17 50	F0
Orionis..................	1·7	5 34·8	− 1 13	B0
ζ Orionis	2·0	5 39·3	− 1 57	B0
κ Orionis	2·2	5 46·4	− 9 41	B0
α Orionis *Betelgeuse*★	Var.	5 53·7	+ 7 24	M0
β Aurigæ *Menkalinan*........	2·1	5 57·5	+44 57	Aop
β Canis Majoris *Mirzam*......	2·0	6 21·5	−17 56	B1
α Carinæ *Canopus*	−0·9	6 23·3	−52 41	F0
γ Geminorum *Alhena*.......	1·9	6 36·1	+16 25	A0
α Canis Majoris *Sirius*.....	−1·6	6 43·9	−16 41	A0
ε Canis Majoris	1·6	6 57·5	−28 56	B1
δ Canis Majoris	2·0	7 07·3	−26 21	F8p
α Geminorum *Castor*	1·6	7 32·8	+31 57	A0
α Canis Minoris *Procyon*.......	0·5	7 37·8	+ 5 18	F5
β Geminorum *Pollux*	1·2	7 43·6	+28 06	K0
ζ Puppis	2·3	8 02·6	−39 55	Od
γ Velorum	1·9	8 08·7	−47 15	Oap
ε Carinæ.................	1·7	8 21·9	−59 25	K0
δ Velorum	2·0	8 43·9	−54 36	A0
λ Velorum *Suhail*	2·2	9 07·0	−43 19	K5
β Carinæ...............	1·8	9 12·9	−69 36	A0
ι Carinæ.................	2·2	9 16·3	−59 09	F0
α Hydræ *Alphard*..........	2·2	9 26·2	− 8 32	K2
α Leonis *Regulus*........	1·3	10 06·9	+12 06	B8
γ Leonis *Algeiba*	2·6	10 18·4	+19 59	K0
β Ursæ Majoris *Merak*	2·4	11 00·2	+56 32	A0
α Ursæ Majoris *Dubhe*	1·9	11 02·0	+61 54	K0

★ γ Cassiopeiæ, 1971 mag. 2·7.   β Persei, mag. 2·2 to 3·5.
α Orionis, mag. 0·1 to 1·2.

The positions of heavenly bodies on the celestial sphere are defined by two co-ordinates, right ascension and declination, which are analogous to longitude and latitude on the surface of the Earth. If we imagine the plane of the terrestrial equator extended indefinitely, it will cut the celestial sphere in a great circle known as the celestial equator. Similarly the plane of the Earth's orbit, when extended, cuts in the great circle called the ecliptic. The two intersections of these circles are known as the First Point of Aries and the First Point of Libra. If from any star a perpendicular be drawn to the celestial equator, the length of this perpendicular is the star's declination. The arc, measured eastwards along the equator from the First Point of Aries to the foot of this perpendicular, is the right ascension. An alternative definition of right ascension is that it is the angle at the celestial pole (where the Earth's axis, if prolonged, would meet the sphere) between the great circles to the First Point of Aries and to the star.

The plane of the Earth's equator has a slow movement, so that our reference system for right ascension and declination is not fixed. The consequent alteration in these quantities from year to year is called precession. In right ascension it is an increase of about 3ˢ a year for equatorial stars, and larger or smaller amounts for stars near the pole. In declination it varies between +20″ and −20″ according to the right ascension of the star.

A star or other body crosses the meridian when the sidereal time is equal to its right ascension. The altitude is then a maximum, and may be deduced by remembering that the altitude of the elevated pole is numerically equal to the latitude, while that of the equator at its intersection with the meridian is equal to the co-latitude, or complement of the latitude.

MEAN PLACES OF STARS, 1972·0

NAME	Mag.	R.A.	Dec.	Spectrum
		h m	° ′	
δ Leonis	2·6	11 12·6	+20 41	A3
β Leonis *Denebola*............	2·2	11 47·6	+14 44	A2
γ Ursæ Majoris *Pheeda*..	2·5	11 52·4	+53 51	Ao
γ Corvi....................	2·8	12 14·4	−17 23	B8
α Crucis..................	1·0	12 25·0	−62 57	B1
γ Crucis..................	1·6	12 29·6	−56 57	M3
γ Centauri...............	2·4	12 40·0	−48 48	Ao
γ Virginis................	2·9	12 40·2	− 1 18	Fo
ε Crucis.................	1·5	12 46·1	−59 32	B1
ε Ursæ Majoris *Alioth*..	1·7	12 52·8	+56 07	Aop
α Canum Venaticorum......	2·9	12 54·7	+38 28	Aop
ζ Ursæ Majoris *Mizar* ..	2·4	13 22·8	+55 04	A2p
α Virginis *Spica*...........	1·2	13 23·7	−11 01	B2
η Ursæ Majoris *Alkaid*...	1·9	13 46·4	+49 27	B3
β Centauri *Hadar*........	0·9	14 01·8	−60 14	B1
ζ Centauri................	2·3	14 05·0	−36 14	Ko
α Bootis *Arcturus*.........	0·2	14 14·4	+19 20	Ko
α Centauri *Rigil Kent*...	0·1	14 37·7	−60 43	Go
ε Bootis.................	2·7	14 43·8	+27 11	Ko
β Ursæ Minoris *Kochab*..	2·2	14 50·8	+74 16	K5
α Coronæ Borealis *Alphecca*.	2·3	15 33·5	+26 48	Ao
δ Scorpii.................	2·5	15 58·7	−22 33	Bo
β Scorpii.................	2·9	16 03·8	−19 44	B1
α Scorpii *Antares*........	1·2	16 27·7	−26 22	Mo
α Trianguli Australis....	1·9	16 45·7	−68 59	K2
ε Scorpii................	2·4	16 48·3	−34 15	Ko
α Herculis*..............	Var.	17 13·4	+14 25	M3
λ Scorpii................	1·7	17 31·7	−37 05	B2
α Ophiuchi *Rasalhague*......	2·1	17 33·6	+12 35	A5
θ Scorpii................	2·0	17 35·3	−42 59	Fo
κ Scorpii................	2·5	17 40·5	−39 01	B2
λ Draconis...............	2·4	17 56·0	+51 29	K5
ε Sagittarii *Kaus Australis*	1·9	18 22·3	−34 24	Ao
α Lyræ *Vega*.............	0·1	18 36·0	+38 45	Ao
σ Sagittarii.............	2·1	18 53·5	−26 20	B3
β Cygni *Albireo*.........	3·2	19 29·6	+27 54	Ko
α Aquilæ *Altair*.........	0·9	19 49·4	+ 8 48	A5
β Capricorni.............	3·2	20 19·4	−14 52	Go
λ Cygni.................	2·3	20 21·2	+40 10	F8p
α Pavonis................	2·1	20 23·4	−56 50	B3
α Cygni *Deneb*..........	1·3	20 40·5	+45 11	A2p
α Cephei *Alderamin*......	2·6	21 17·9	+62 28	A5
ε Pegasi.................	2·5	21 42·8	+ 9 45	Ko
δ Capricorni.............	3·0	21 45·5	−16 15	A5
α Gruis..................	2·2	22 06·5	−47 06	B5
δ Cephei*................	Var.	22 28·1	+58 16	*
β Gruis..................	2·2	22 41·0	−47 02	M3
α Piscis Austrini *Fomalhaut* ...	1·3	22 56·1	−29 46	A3
β Pegasi *Scheat*.........	2·6	23 02·4	+27 56	Mo
α Pegasi *Markab*........	2·6	23 03·4	+15 03	Ao

*α Herculis, mag. 3·1 to 3·9.
  δ Cephei, mag. 3·7 to 4·4, Spectrum F5 to Go.

Thus in London (Lat. 51° 30′) the meridian altitude of *Sirius* is found as follows:

	°	′
Altitude of equator.....	38	30
Declination south......	16	40
Difference............	21	50

The altitude of *Capella* (Dec. +45° 58′) at lower transit is:

	°	′
Altitude of pole........	51	30
Polar distance of star ..	44	02
Difference.............	7	28

The brightness of a heavenly body is denoted by its magnitude. Omitting the exceptionally bright stars *Sirius* and *Canopus*, the twenty brightest stars are of the first magnitude, while the faintest stars visible to the naked eye are of the sixth magnitude. The magnitude scale is a precise one, as a difference of five magnitudes represents a ratio of 100 to 1 in brightness. Typical second magnitude stars are *Polaris* and the stars in the Belt of Orion. The scale is most easily fixed in memory by comparing the stars with Norton's *Star Atlas* (see page 138). The stars *Sirius* and *Canopus* and the planets Venus and Jupiter are so bright that their magnitudes are expressed by negative numbers. A small telescope will show stars down to the ninth or tenth magnitude, while stars fainter than the twentieth magnitude may be photographed by long exposures with the largest telescopes.

Some of the astronomical information in this ALMANACK has been taken from the *Astronomical Ephemeris*, and is published here by arrangement with, and with the permission of, the Controller of H.M. Stationery Office.

THE STRUCTURE OF THE UNIVERSE

The Solar System, although occupying a volume of space large by terrestrial standards, is only a very tiny fraction of the whole Universe. The Sun itself is just one of the millions of stars which make up our Galaxy, and our Galaxy is just one of the millions of galaxies which are distributed through the visible Universe. All these stars and galaxies are in motion, many of them with enormous velocities; yet they are so remote that to the naked eye they present almost the same configurations for a period of many thousands of years, and even with telescopic aid the measurement of their motions is a delicate matter. The nearest star is about 250,000 times as far away as the Sun, the Great Nebula in Andromeda, one of the few galaxies visible to the naked eye, is over 500,000 times as far away as the nearest star, and the largest telescopes can penetrate to a distance of at least 500 times that of the Andromeda Nebula. It is convenient to express astronomical distances in terms of the time that light takes to accomplish the journey. Light travels at the rate of 300,000 kilometres a second; it takes $1\frac{1}{4}$ seconds to reach us from the Moon, our nearest neighbour in space; just over 8 minutes to reach us from the Sun; four years from the nearest star; two million years from the Andromeda Nebula, and over 1000 million years from the most distant bodies yet photographed. We therefore talk about a star as being so many light years distant. Astronomers also use another unit of distance, the parsec. 1 parsec equals 3.26 light years.

THE STARS

The stars are classed according to their apparent brightness in magnitudes. A few of the brightest stars are brighter than the first magnitude. Stars as faint as the sixth magnitude can be seen by the naked eye. The 200-inch telescope, the world's largest, on Mount Palomar in California, can photograph stars of the 23rd magnitude, which is about 650 million times fainter than the first magnitude. This large range in the apparent brightness of the stars is due to a combination of two factors. The first of these is distance. According to a standard law of optics, the apparent brightness of any given luminous object is inversely proportional to the square of its distance away. Thus, if two similar stars are at distances one of which is 10 times the other, the more distant star will appear to be 100 times fainter than the nearer star. The second factor affecting the apparent brightness of a star is its real intrinsic brightness. There are many different kinds of stars; some are very large luminous objects, others are small and faint.

The distances of the stars can be determined in a variety of ways. The direct trigonometric method consists in measuring the minute difference of direction of the star as seen from opposite sides of the Earth's orbit; this is always done photographically. The distances of about 15,000 stars have been measured in this way, but the method has very little accuracy for distances greater than about 250 light years. For more distant stars, distances may be estimated from a study of their spectra. The distances of some double and variable stars can

be found from their special characteristics. A star is said to be at a distance of one parsec if the radius of the Earth's orbit round the Sun subtends an angle of one second of arc at the star.

When the distance of any star has been determined, and its apparent magnitude measured, the real intrinsic brightness of the star may be determined. As a convenient convention, astronomers adopt as the " absolute magnitude " of a star (or other object) that apparent magnitude which the star would have if it were moved from its real position to a distance of ten parsecs. Conversely, if the absolute magnitude of a star is known by spectroscopic or other methods, and its apparent magnitude is observed, its distance may be calculated.

STELLAR SPECTRA

A large number of stars have been examined spectroscopically, and it is found that their spectra fall, with very few exceptions, into a sequence of types, denoted by the letters O, B, A, F, G, K, M; the types merge imperceptibly one into the next. O and B stars, exemplified by the three stars which form *Orion's* belt, have spectra showing helium and hydrogen lines. A stars, like *Sirius*, are characterized by very strong hydrogen lines. F, G and K stars, like *Procyon*, our *Sun*, and *Arcturus*, respectively, have spectra showing large numbers of metallic lines, and hydrogen lines much weaker than in A stars. Finally, the M stars, like *Betelgeuse*, show very complex molecular spectra, chiefly of titanium oxide. This sequence of spectral types O to M is essentially a temperature sequence, the O stars being the hottest and the M stars the coolest. Approximate values of the surface temperatures of the stars are, a value for the middle of each type being quoted in degrees Centigrade: O, $30,000°$; B, $18,000°$; A, $10,000°$; F, $7000°$; G, $5500°$; K, $4500°$; M, $3000°$. This sequence is also one of colour, the O stars being the bluest and the M stars the reddest. The colour of a star is capable of precise definition and measurement; there is a very close correlation between colour and surface temperature, and between colour and spectral type. The latter correlation is so good that for many astrophysical purposes colour measurements are used instead of spectral types.

When the spectral types (or colours) of a large number of stars are correlated with their absolute magnitudes, a surprising result emerges. The sequence O to M is one of decreasing absolute brightness. Approximate values of the absolute magnitudes of the stars are, a value for the middle of each type being quoted: O, -4; B, -2; A, $+1$; F, $+3$; G, $+5$; K, $+7$; M, $+11$. A graphical illustration of this relation between spectral type and absolute magnitude is known as the Hertzsprung-Russell Diagram (or, when colours are used instead of spectral types, as a colour-magnitude diagram). The relationship represented by this diagram is one of the corner stones of modern astrophysics. The above series of stars of types O to M and absolute magnitude decreasing from -4

to $+11$, or fainter, is known as the "main sequence", and a large proportion of all known stars are members of this sequence. A relatively small proportion of the stars of spectral types O to M do not belong to the main sequence. Closer examination of the spectra of these stars reveals slight differences between their spectra and ordinary stars of nominally the same type on the main sequence. These differences are sufficiently characteristic to enable the two types of stars to be segregated spectroscopically without independent knowledge of their absolute magnitudes. These stars are found to be brighter than the corresponding main sequence stars of the same types. Most of those of types G, K and M have absolute magnitudes about o; many of those of types O to F and a few of types G to M are still brighter, with absolute magnitudes ranging from -4 to -7. The exceptional brightness of these stars is believed to be due to their sizes: those with absolute magnitudes about o are called giants, those of -4 to -7 are called supergiants.

The sizes of the stars have been determined mostly by theoretical calculation. In very few cases direct determinations have been made by means of an interferometer, and sizes can also be inferred from observations of some eclipsing binary stars. The Sun is 1,392,000 kilometres in diameter. The main sequence is found to be a sequence of diminishing radii; an O star has a radius of about 20 times that of the Sun, while an average M star has a radius of one-third of the Sun. The giant stars of types G to M have radii between 10 and 100 times the Sun; supergiants have radii between 30 and 1000 times the Sun.

It is possible to determine the chemical composition of a star from a study of its spectrum. This has been done for main sequence stars and for giants and supergiants. All these stars appear to be of similar chemical composition, about 80 per cent by numbers of atoms being hydrogen, most of the remainder helium, heavier elements being less than one per cent of the total. All the differences between types O to M and main sequence, giant and supergiant stars can be accounted for by variations of surface temperature and of size (affecting the spectrum through the surface gravity).

A few stars cannot be classified according to the standard sequence O to M. Among these those classified as R and N stars show strong bands of carbon compounds instead of the titanium oxide of M stars, and the S stars show zirconium oxide instead of titanium oxide. A number of still less common types of stars show anomalous lines of strontium, barium, manganese, silicon, europium, lanthanum and other elements. The reasons for all these peculiarities are not known; it is probable that many of them are genuine differences from the standard chemical composition of the majority of the stars.

DOUBLE STARS

Many stars which appear single to the naked eye are found to be double in the telescope. These are frequently found to be in orbital motion round one another in periods varying from about one year to many thousands of years. Some binary stars are so close together that they cannot be seen separately even in large telescopes; their binary nature is revealed by the spectroscope. The varying motions of the stars in their orbits can be detected by the Doppler shifts of lines in their spectra. Some spectroscopic binaries, as they are called, are of special interest in that during their orbital motion the two components periodically eclipse each other, and the combined light of the two stars will vary. This happens when the Earth is nearly in the plane of the binary star orbits. Such binaries are called eclipsing variables, of which the best known is *Algol*, or β Persei.

VARIABLE STARS

We have already referred to the eclipsing variables, whose light variation is due to a geometrical cause. Some single stars vary in light. These include Cepheid variables, with periods of from a few hours up to about fifty days, long-period variables with periods of from a hundred to a thousand days, and numerous types of variable stars in which the periods and light fluctuations are entirely irregular. Many of these variations are attributed to pulsation of the stars by alternate expansion and contraction. The Cepheids are of particular interest because of the period-luminosity relation: the longer the period of a Cepheid the brighter is its mean absolute magnitude. An observation of the period of variation of the star immediately tells us its absolute magnitude and thence its distance.

Novæ are stars whose light increases by 10 to 15 magnitudes in a few days, and then fades gradually to normal brightness, reached a year or two later. The cause of the brightening is the sudden expansion of the star, but the reason for this is unknown. Supernovæ are stars whose brightness increases by up to 20 magnitudes; they are believed to be caused by the explosion of the whole star.

STAR CLUSTERS

Stars frequently occur in clusters; two types of clusters are known. The first, called open (or galactic) clusters, are groups of up to two or three hundred stars; the second, globular clusters, contain over one hundred thousand stars. The open clusters are found mainly in the neighbourhood of the Milky Way, the globular clusters avoid the Milky Way. Several open clusters are visible to the naked eye: the Pleiades, the Hyades and Praesepe are the best known of these. The colour-magnitude diagrams of open clusters are generally similar to those of nearby single stars; the most important difference is that when a cluster contains blue O and B stars it does not also contain red giant stars. The colour-magnitude diagrams of globular clusters are very similar among themselves, but differ greatly from the diagrams of galactic clusters and nearby stars. The main sequence does not exist in any globular cluster for stars of types O, B and A; red giants are present in all the clusters, and they range up to absolute magnitude -3. There is an additional sequence of stars with absolute magnitudes about o which is quite unlike any sequence in the diagrams for nearby stars.

INTERSTELLAR MATTER

The space between the stars is not empty; it contains a mixture of gas and dust which serves to

dim the light of distant objects and tends to make them appear redder than normal. Very distant objects may be obscured completely if they lie in or near the plane of the Milky Way. The density of interstellar gas averages one atom in each cubic centimetre; this may be compared with a density 26 million million million times as great in ordinary air at normal pressure and temperature. As is the case for cosmic material in general, hydrogen predominates in interstellar gas. In addition to this widely distributed matter, there are denser clouds of gas and dust existing locally. These are frequently in evidence as dark clouds in front of a brighter stellar background. Some clouds have hot stars embedded, and the interstellar gas may then shine either by reflection of the starlight or it may be heated until it glows and emits its own characteristic light. Such dense glowing clouds are termed galactic nebulæ. Sometimes the cloud is more regular in shape and is excited by one star; such clouds are termed planetary nebulæ, and the Ring Nebula in Lyra is an excellent example of these objects. Planetary nebulæ are among the denser interstellar formations; their densities range up to 20,000 atoms per cubic centimetre. Hot stars can make ordinary interstellar gas glow even when the density is low; the spherical region of glowing gas surrounding a hot star is termed an ionized-hydrogen region. These regions are of particular interest for the study of the Galaxy and of extragalactic nebulæ because they are relatively bright and can be seen at large distances.

THE GALAXY

A cursory glance at the sky is sufficient to show that the fainter stars are concentrated towards the region of the Milky Way. This implies that the stars form a flattened system, which extends farther in the direction of the Milky Way than it does at right angles to it. It is now known that this system, called the Galaxy, is about 100,000 light years in diameter, and has a thickness of less than 5000 light years. The Milky Way is the centre plane of the system. We in the Solar System are situated at about 27,000 light years from the centre, and not far from the central plane. All the objects mentioned earlier, single and multiple stars, variable stars, novæ and supernovæ, galactic and globular clusters, interstellar gas, dust and galactic and planetary nebulæ, form part of the Galaxy. The distribution of these various objects in the Galaxy is not all alike. The hot O and B stars, galactic clusters and interstellar matter are closely concentrated towards the Milky Way plane, mostly lying within 300 light years on either side of the plane. The stars of types A to M tend to be less closely concentrated to the plane; globular clusters show hardly any concentration, forming a nearly spherical distribution stretching to over 30,000 light years from the plane. Most Cepheid variables with periods of more than a day are closely concentrated to the galactic plane; those with periods of less than a day have a distribution similar to that of globular clusters.

The Galaxy has a spiral structure similar to that of some extragalactic nebulæ. This structure was first shown by studying the positions of O and B

stars; these trace out spiral arms. Radio astronomers subsequently found that interstellar neutral hydrogen gas emits radio waves on 21 centimetres wavelength. Studies of this radio radiation have enabled the density and distribution of interstellar hydrogen to be determined. The hydrogen gas is found to be situated along the same spiral arms as the O and B stars. Indeed, there is remarkably close correlation between O and B stars and interstellar matter.

Observations by both optical and radio methods have proved that the whole Galaxy is rotating about an axis through its centre perpendicular to the galactic plane. The period of rotation varies with distance from the centre, an average value being 200 million years. The total mass of the Galaxy is about 100 thousand million times the mass of the Sun.

STELLAR POPULATIONS

The two different types of colour-magnitude (or Hertzsprung-Russell) diagram mentioned above appear to apply not only to star clusters but to other objects in our Galaxy and in other galaxies. There seems little doubt that there are two fundamentally different types of stellar population. Population I has a colour-magnitude diagram similar to that of nearby stars and open clusters. Population II has a diagram similar to that for globular clusters. Population I includes both open clusters, longer-period Cepheid variables and supergiant stars, and is intimately associated with interstellar matter; it occurs prominently in the spiral structure of our Galaxy, and is generally concentrated towards the galactic plane. Population II includes the globular clusters, short-period Cepheids and other objects, tends to avoid the spiral structure of the Galaxy, has little or no interstellar dust associated with it, but may be associated with interstellar hydrogen gas, and is not concentrated towards the galactic plane. All the available evidence suggests that Population II stars are old objects, with ages averaging 5000 million years, while Population I stars are much younger, with ages in a few cases of only a few million years. Population II stars have lower content of metals relative to hydrogen than Population I stars.

EXTRAGALACTIC NEBULÆ

Outside our own Galaxy there are large numbers of objects having a more or less hazy appearance on photographs. These are the extragalactic nebulæ, also known as external galaxies. Some show well-defined spiral structure, some are elliptical in form with no marked structural features, and some are irregular in form. The spiral nebulæ consist of central bulge surrounded by spiral arms embedded in a disk-shaped structure. The elliptical nebulæ and the central bulges of the spiral nebulæ are believed to be composed of stars of Population II. The spiral arms are composed of Population I and some Population II, together with large quantities of gas and dust. The presence of dust is evident because of the dark patches of absorption which are a feature of the photographs of spiral nebulæ; the presence of hydrogen gas has been proved by the observation of regions of glowing gas and by the reception of radio waves on 21 centimetres wavelength. In a few of the nearer galaxies individual

NEBULAE, CLUSTERS AND GALAXIES

Designation	Name	Type	Mag.	R.A. (1950·0)	Dec. (1950·0)	Angular Size
				h m	°	′ ′
N.G.C. 104.......	47 Tucanae	GC	4	0 22	−72·4	42×42
M.31	Andromeda (Nebula)......	G	4	0 40	+41·0	160×40
Nubecula Minor...		—	—	0 50	−73·9	(10 sq. deg.)
M.33.............		G	7	1 31	+30·4	60×40
H. VI. 33, 34.....	Double Cluster............	OC	4	2 18	+56·9	2(36×36)
M.45.............	Pleiades.................	OC	—	3 45	+23·9	90×60
	Hyades.................	OC	—	4 26	+15·8	180×180
Nubecula Major...		—	—	5 25	−69·3	(42 sq. deg.)
M.1.............	" Crab " nebula..........	PN	10	5 32	+22·0	6×4
M.42............	" Great " nebula..........	N	6	5 33	− 5·4	66×60
N.G.C. 2070.....	30 Doradus.............	OC+N	—	5 39	−69·1	—
M.44............	" Praesepe " or " Beehive ".	OC	4	8 37	+20·2	90×90
N.G.C. 3372.....	η Carinae...............	N	—	10 43	−59·4	80×80
N.G.C. 4755.....	κ Crucis.................	OC	—	12 51	−60·1	10×10
	ω Centauri..............	GC	3	13 24	−47·1	45×45
M.3.............		GC	6	13 40	+28·6	19×19
M.13............		GC	6	16 40	+36·6	23×23
M.7.............		OC	5	17 51	−34·8	50×50
M.20............	" Trifid " nebula.........	N	8	17 59	−23·0	29×27
M.8.............	" Lagoon " nebula........	N	5	18 01	−24·4	90×40
M.57............	" Ring " nebula..........	PN	9	18 52	+33·0	1×1
M.55............		GC	5	19 37	−31·0	15×15
M.27............	" Dumb-bell " nebula.....	PN	8	19 57	+22·6	8×4

Types: N—Nebula.   PN—Planetary Nebula. OC—Open Cluster. GC—Globular Cluster. G—Galaxy.

stars have been observed, and comparison with stars in our own Galaxy provides estimates of the distances and sizes of the galaxies. Many of them are found to be comparable with our own Galaxy—with diameters of 100,000 light years and masses 100 thousand million times the Sun. The two Magellanic Clouds are the nearest galaxies to our own, their distances being about 140,000 light years. The best known external galaxy is the Great Nebula in Andromeda, at a distance of 2,000,000 light years; this spiral nebula is believed to be similar to our own Galaxy in size and stellar content. Extragalactic nebulæ frequently occur in large clusters, each containing hundreds of nebulæ. Many extragalactic nebulæ are in rotation in a manner similar to our own Galaxy and with comparable periods.

RADIO SOURCES

In addition to the 21 centimetre hydrogen radiation received from interstellar gas, radio noise is received on other wavelengths. Some of this originates in well-known objects; one important source of radio noise is the Crab Nebula, which is known to be the remains of the supernova of A.D. 1054. Some extragalactic nebulæ are also sources of radio noise, but many of the apparently isolated sources, " radio stars ", do not seem to coincide with any visible stars or nebulæ. Recently several sources have been discovered which exhibit extremely regular variations in radio " brightness ", with incredibly short periods (of the order of 1 second). These sources are now called " pulsars ".

QUASARS

The observation of occultations of radio sources by the Moon has led to the accurate determination of the positions of these radio sources. Thus it has been possible to use large optical telescopes with small angular fields of view and high magnifications to photograph these positions. This has led to the discovery of a new type of object called a quasar (or quasi-stellar object or QSO). On a photographic plate such objects appear almost stellar, so they are not readily identified without the help of information from the radio astronomers. Spectroscopic examination of four of them shows that, like external galaxies, they have enormous velocities of recession. Such velocities imply great distances, yet no ordinary star (or even supergiant) would be detectable at even a fraction of these distances. The answer to the question ' what are quasars? ' is not yet known with any certainty but the current explanation is that they are radio sources with the shape of a star but many millions of times larger, with unusually high ultra-violet radiation and sometimes with large red shifts. Already several dozen quasars are known.

COSMOLOGY

The large scale problems of the Universe are concerned with the motions and distribution of the extragalactic nebulæ through the observable region of space. It has been found that in spite of the tendency of galaxies to cluster together, on a still larger scale the galaxies are distributed remarkably uniformly. Observations have shown that distant galaxies have spectra showing " red-shifts ", which have been interpreted as Doppler shifts due to velocities of recession; all the distant galaxies appear to be moving away from us with velocities proportional to their distance. This suggests that the whole Universe is in expansion. One theory postulates a gigantic initial explosion some 5,000 million years ago. Another postulates a steady state, with continuous creation of matter producing new galaxies which eventually force the existing ones to continually increasing distances. Some recent observations suggest that the latter theory is no longer tenable.

THE SOLAR SYSTEM

The Sun is one of the millions of stars that make up the Universe. The energy that it radiates in the form of light and heat is maintained by nuclear reactions among the atoms in its interior. It is surrounded by an immense number of comparatively cold planets and comets, together with smaller particles that give rise to meteors and the zodiacal light.

The planets are solid bodies revolving about the Sun in elliptical orbits with the Sun at one focus, and at distances related to the periodic times in accordance with Kepler's third law: the squares of the periodic times vary as the cubes of the semi-major axes. All revolve in the same direction, the orbits being only slightly inclined to the plane of the ecliptic in which the Earth moves round the Sun. As seen from the Earth, therefore, the planets are always near the ecliptic, moving in general from west to east round the sky. Once in every such revolution the planet appears to become stationary and then retrograde, forming a looped path which is a consequence of the Earth's own orbital movement.

The nine major planets, of which the earth is one, are of special interest, the five that are visible to the naked eye having been known from the earliest times. Six have satellites or moons revolving round them. These, like the planets themselves, are not self-luminous, but shine by the reflected light of the Sun. Notes on these bodies are given in the following pages. The thousands of minor planets that are also known, although of less interest to the observer, afford many problems to the mathematical astronomer. Comets are also members of the solar system; their orbits are inclined at all angles to the ecliptic, and are generally highly eccentric, reaching out to immense distances in space. The light of a comet is not due entirely to reflected sunlight, but partly to fluorescence caused by selective absorption of solar radiation. The return of a comet of short period may be predicted with some accuracy, but most comets appear quite unexpectedly. Meteoric dust appears to have a common origin with the comets, since some meteor showers have been shown to follow the orbits of certain comets.

THE SUN

The Sun is the ultimate source of most of the chemical energy available on the Earth. Hence the origin of that energy, which reaches the Earth in the form of light and heat from within the Sun, is of particular interest. The spectral distribution of the light from the Sun's surface indicates a temperature of about $5,700°$ C., but a relatively short distance inside the surface the temperature reaches $1,000,000°$ and deeper in the interior, near the centre, it is believed to be in the region of $14,000,000°$. Now the constitution of the Sun is similar to that of the Earth, as is shown by similarities in the chemical spectra of solar and terrestrial sources; but at these high temperatures the atoms become stripped of their outer layers of electrons. In this highly " ionized " state the substance of the Sun acts in much the same way as a " perfect gas "

does on the Earth, even though the density is high. Furthermore, the thermal velocities are sufficiently great for nuclear collisions to take place. Nuclear energy can be released in the Sun by a variety of collision-processes, in each of which the light atoms of hydrogen, by far the most abundant element, are ultimately combined into the heavier atoms of helium. This energy, released almost entirely in the central regions, is transmitted by radiation and convection to the cooler outer layers of the Sun and thence to outer space, a very small proportion of it falling on the Earth. It is possible to infer with some certainty, by considering the Sun as a typical star, that this process has been going on for about three thousand million years and that it may be expected to continue similarly for perhaps a further ten thousand million years.

As viewed in a low-power telescope provided with heavily absorbing filters, the Sun presents various features. Over most of its surface a fine mottling can be seen under good observing conditions. This " granulation " is visible evidence of a turbulent convective layer near the surface. Much more noticeable surface-markings called sunspots appear sporadically in the equatorial zones of the Sun and up to latitudes of $40°$–$50°$ north and south. These sunspots, which are sometimes visible to the naked eye, provide direct evidence of the rotation of the Sun on an axis which is inclined about $7°$ to the line joining the poles of the ecliptic. They also indicate that the Sun does not rotate as a solid body but somewhat faster in equatorial regions than at higher latitudes. Its mean sidereal rotation-period is about 25 days but the motion of the Earth in its orbit around the Sun results in an apparent rotation-period, as viewed from the Earth, of approximately 27 days. Associated with sunspots are bright regions called faculae but these can not be seen when the spot is near the centre of the disk.

Sunspots vary in size from small dark specks barely visible in a telescope, but actually with an area of about a million square miles, to large dark markings several thousand times as great. The largest spot ever measured (April 1947) covered 18,000 million square kilometres at its greatest, or approximately 0·7 per cent. of the Sun's visible surface. Correspondingly, sunspots have lifetimes ranging from a few hours in the case of some of the smallest, to many weeks in the case of the most persistent spots, which are often regular in shape but not as a rule particularly large. The frequency of spots varies in a definite eleven-year cycle, though the number of spots may vary considerably in a haphazard way from week to week in a particular year. One of the observed properties of spots during the 11-year cycle is that high latitudes, north and south, are predominant towards the beginning of a cycle, while later on there is a gradual drift of the most densely occupied zones towards the equator. In addition, a strong magnetic-field is found to be associated with sunspots, as well as certain systematic drifts in the solar layers there. These and other observed properties, such as concern the detailed structure and movements of spots

ELEMENTS OF THE SOLAR SYSTEM

Orb	Mean Distance from Sun		Sidereal Period	Synodic Period	Inclination of Orbit to Ecliptic	Diameter	Mass compared with Earth	Period of Rotation on Axis
	Radii of Earth's Orbit	Millions of kilometres						
			y d	Days	° ′	km.		d h m
Sun.............	...	...	... ...		... ...	1,392,000	333,434	25 09
Mercury.........	0·39	58	88	116	7 00	4,840	0·04	59
Venus	0·72	108	225	584	3 24	12,300	0·83	244
Earth.............	1·00	150	1 0	...	... ...	12,756eq.	1·00	23 56
Mars.............	1·52	228	1 322	780	1 51	6,790	0·11	24 37
Jupiter...........	5·20	778	11 315	399	1 18	{142,800eq. 133,500p.	318	{ 9 50 9 56
Saturn	9·54	1427	29 167	378	2 29	{119,300eq. 107,700p.	95	{10 14 10 38
Uranus..........	19·19	2870	84 6	370	0 46	47,100	15	10 49
Neptune.........	30·07	4497	164 288	367	1 46	51,000	17	15 48
Pluto.............	39·46	5950	247 255	367	17 09	5,900?	0·06?	6 09 17?

must be explained by any comprehensive physical theory of sunspots. At present no generally accepted theory exists, though it seems clear that the magnetic field of the spot inhibits convection in the turbulent layers near the Sun's surface and so produces local cooling.

The Table below gives dates of recent maxima and minima of the sunspot cycles. It will be seen that the intervals between successive maxima (or minima) vary considerably from the average value of 11·1 years.

Maxima		Minima	
1837·2	1907·0	1843·5	1913·6
1848·1	1917·6	1856·0	1923·6
1860·1	1928·4	1867·2	1933·8
1870·6	1937·4	1878·9	1944·2
1883·9	1947·5	1889·6	1954·3
1894·1	1957·9	1901·7	1964·7
	1968·9		

The 1957 sunspot maximum was unusual in its absence of giant spots, the intense activity being due to a very large number of smaller spots

Other features of the Sun may be detected in light of wavelengths other than those of normal integrated visual light. With the light from the centre of strong spectral absorption lines such as Hα, the C-line of hydrogen, or the H and K lines of calcium, bright regions can almost always be seen around sunspots and these regions occasionally become exceptionally bright for periods of an hour, or thereabouts. This is the phenomenon of the " solar flare ", and its occurrence may be otherwise detected upon the Earth by immediate changes in propagation-conditions for long-distance radio-communication (changes in the ionosphere caused by a sudden increase in ionizing radiation) or, in the case of large flares, by the subsequent occurrence, a day or two later, of a magnetic storm. A very few large flares have had associated with them increases, occurring a few minutes later, of the high-energy cosmic-ray flux detected at the earth's surface.

Also visible in monochromatic wavelengths are the prominences, which extend outwards from the Sun's surface into its tenuous outer regions, called the corona. At the limb prominences appear as bright forms, often arched or branching, while against the Sun's disk they appear as dark filaments. The corona itself can normally only be observed in its brightest regions by using light from certain bright spectral lines in special instruments at a high altitude on the Earth. At lower altitudes, and in the outer corona at high altitudes, scattered sky-light is too great. However, when the Sun is obscured by the Moon at a total solar eclipse, the whole corona becomes easily seen. As well as the bright lines, it shows a weak continuous spectrum. It is also found that the corona has characteristically different appearances at sunspot maximum and sunspot minimum and that it frequently shows streamers extending outwards several million km. When observed with radio wavelengths in the range 10 cm. to 5 m. the corona is normally detected, as well as short-lived emissions from disturbed regions around sunspots.

MERCURY

Mercury is the smallest planet and the nearest to the Sun. Because it moves in an orbit between the Sun and the Earth, it is never far west or east of the Sun. If east, it appears as an evening star; if west as a morning star. The extremes of these apparent excursions are known as Greatest Elongations; their times and extent, measured by the angular distance from the Sun, are given on the first page of each month under the heading PHENOMENA. The great ellipticity of the orbit of Mercury causes the amount of these elongations to vary from 18° to 28°. The planet is best placed for naked-eye observation some days before eastern elongation on spring evenings, or after western elongation on autumn mornings, though in Great Britain at these times its actual distance from the Sun is near its minimum. In the southern hemisphere the conditions are, of course, reversed.

In a telescope, Mercury shows phases to the Earth like the Moon, resembling her at first quarter when at eastern elongation, and at last quarter when at western elongation. The planet is exceedingly difficult to observe telescopically and is best scrutin-

THE SATELLITES

Name	Star Mag.	Mean distance from Primary	Sidereal Period of Revolution	Name	Star Mag.	Mean distance from Primary	Sidereal Period of Revolution
Earth		km.	d h m	*Saturn*		km.	d h m
Moon	—	384,400	27 07 43	Janus............	14	159,000	17 58
				Mimas	12	186,000	22 37
Mars				Enceladus.......	12	238,000	1 08 53
Phobos...........	11	9,400	7 39	Tethys	11	295,000	1 21 18
Deimos...........	12	23,500	1 06 18	Dione...........	11	378,000	2 17 41
				Rhea............	10	527,000	4 12 25
Jupiter				Titan............	8½	1,222,000	15 22 42
V. Unnamed....	13	181,000	11 57	Hyperion........	15	1,483,000	21 06 38
I. Io..........	5½	422,000	1 18 28	Iapetus..........	11	3,560,000	79 07 56
II. Europa.......	5½	671,000	3 13 14	Phoebe..........	14	12,950,000	550
III. Ganymede....	5	1,070,000	7 03 43	*Uranus*			
IV. Callisto......	6	1,883,000	16 16 32	Miranda........	17	130,000	1 10 00
VI. Unnamed....	15	11,480,000	251	Ariel............	14	192,000	2 12 29
X. „	19	11,720,000	254	Umbriel.........	14½	267,000	4 03 28
VII. „	18	11,740,000	260	Titania..........	14	438,000	8 16 56
XII. „	18	21,200,000	620	Oberon..........	14	586,000	13 11 07
XI. „	19	22,600,000	692	*Neptune*			
VIII. „	17	23,500,000	739	Triton..........	13½	355,000	5 21 03
IX. „	18½	23,600,000	745	Nereid..........	19½	5,562,000	359 10 00

ized with large apertures in full daylight. A recent map of the surface, made by Antoniadi, confirms in its essential features one made last century by Schiaparelli; these observers agree that Mercury always turns the same face to the Sun. Different results have been obtained by recent radar observations which are supported by theoretical investigations. The question of whether Mercury has an atmosphere cannot be regarded as settled.

VENUS

Venus, next from the Sun, has a diameter only four or five hundred kilometres less than that of the Earth. Its apparent movement with regard to the Sun is similar to that of Mercury, but, owing to the greater size of its orbit, its elongations extend as far as 47°. Venus is the brightest planet and is several times brighter than any star; it can often be seen in full daylight with the naked eye.

Apart from the beauty of its phases, Venus is a disappointing object in the telescope, its extensive atmosphere being so highly reflective, probably owing to cloud, that its true surface can never be observed. Vague dusky shadings may be seen or imagined, but conspicuous markings are both rare and evanescent.

Photographs of Venus in violet light were taken by Kuiper in 1950 and 1954 with the 2-metre reflector of the McDonald Observatory in Texas, and show that the surface of the planet is banded, three or more dark and bright bands being noted lying in a direction perpendicular to the terminator. These bands have been attributed to zones of ascending and descending currents in the atmosphere of Venus. Assuming that the bands are parallel to the equator, Kuiper deduced the position of the pole of Venus at $3^h 32^m$, $+81°$, which is in Cepheus. The equator of Venus is therefore tilted at an angle of about 32° to its orbit. Recent radar observations have provided the unexpected value for the period of rotation given on p. 157.

The spectrum of the atmosphere above the re-flecting layer reveals a considerable amount of carbon dioxide, but no oxygen; such might also be the conditions on the Earth, were it not for the constant absorption of carbon dioxide by vegetation and its replacement by oxygen. A remarkable feature of the upper atmosphere is the absence of all trace of water vapour.

MARS

Mars, the first planet whose orbit is exterior to that of the Earth, is a little larger than Mercury. Oppositions occur at intervals of about 2 years 2 months, but owing to the eccentricity of the orbit the opposition distance varies between 56 and 100 million kilometres. The most favourable approaches unfortunately take place when the planet is low in the sky for northern observers; but when, as in 1956, one occurs in the early autumn, the distance may be less than 65 million kilometres and the planet just north of the equator. It is only within two or three months of opposition that Mars is near enough for its surface to be successfully studied with a telescope; even at these times only the coarser details are likely to be recognized with instruments of less than 15 cm. aperture.

Except for Mercury, Mars is the only planet whose true surface we are able to see. This exhibits many well-defined markings, most of which are permanent, and from these the rotation period has been well determined; it is about 41½ minutes longer than that of the Earth. The axis of rotation is inclined at about 24° to the plane of the orbit. There are white spots at the poles which are deposited during the winter of each hemisphere and melt or evaporate during the summer. It is most probable that these consist of thick deposits of hoar frost, and the infra-red absorption spectra of the polar caps support this view. The major portion of the surface is of a featureless orange hue, which gives rise to the ruddy appearance of Mars. But there abound large areas, often with sharp boundaries, of a blue-grey colour. The latter were once thought to be seas; but it is now known that

there are no large sheets of open water, and some regard areas of vegetation as their most likely interpretation, especially as they undergo change of tint. It has been claimed that these changes follow the Martian seasons; but as 15 or 17 years must elapse between the times when we can study Mars under similar conditions, it cannot yet be confirmed that there are any changes of a truly seasonal character apart from the waxing and waning of the polar caps.

The controversy over the canal-like markings on Mars has ended with the successful close range photography of the surface by Mariner 4. The photographs show a surface covered with craters, but no "canals".

Mars has an atmosphere believed to be considerably less dense than our own. The spectroscope has been unable to establish that it contains either oxygen or water vapour, which can therefore be present only in minute proportions. Recently, however, about the same amount of carbon dioxide has been detected as is found in our own atmosphere.

Mars has two faint satellites, Phobos and Deimos, which were discovered by Asaph Hall in 1877.

THE MINOR PLANETS

Moving in orbits which in general lie between those of Mars and Jupiter, are a large number of small bodies called minor planets or asteroids. It is estimated that at least 50,000 come within reach of present instruments. Scores of them are now found every year by photographing the sky. Their orbits are calculated as observations accrue, and when the results are reliable enough the new planets are given permanent numbers, and usually also names, by a central authority—now at the Cincinnati Observatory, U.S.A. At present there are over 1600 on the permanent list, and several dozen are likely to be added each year; and always there are many still under investigation. All are faint—none has ever been seen by an unaided eye except, just possibly, Vesta.

These celestial bodies are probably little more than masses of rock revolving round the Sun. The first four, found early in the 19th century, are also the largest: Ceres, 670 kilometres in diameter, Pallas, 450, Juno 240, and Vesta 385 kilometres.

The periodic times of the revolutions about the Sun vary considerably around an average of 4½ years, but interesting groups and gaps occur among the values for these times owing to disturbances of the orbits caused by the attraction on these bodies of the massive planet Jupiter. Although some of the orbits are nearly circular, others are very elongated ovals (ellipses); and though the inclinations of their planes to the ecliptic are mostly less than 20°, several exceed 30°, including Pallas 35°. The highest known, 43°, is that of Hidalgo. This planet has also the longest period, 14 years, and travels out as far as Saturn's orbit. On the other hand Icarus, discovered in 1949, comes within the orbit of Mercury, and three others Apollo, Adonis and Hermes, within that of Venus. Another, Eros, is of importance because in some circumstances it can be within 21 million kilometres of the Earth. This happened in 1931 when carefully planned photo-graphic recording of the planet and the surrounding stars enabled measurements of its distance to be made, and hence a new value of the distance of the Sun from the Earth to be deduced.

Similarly, certain other minor planets with suitable orbits can be used for special purposes, as in the precise measurement of the equinox and equator, or in finding the masses of Mercury or Venus.

JUPITER

Jupiter, the largest planet, has a volume over 1000 times that of the Earth, but a density only one-quarter of ours. Its oblate shape is so marked, owing to its great size and rapid rotation, as to be obvious in quite small telescopes.

The characteristic surface features of Jupiter are bright zones separated by dusky belts, running practically parallel to the planet's equator. With telescopes of moderate size some of these may be resolved into finer detail, consisting of spots, wisps, streaks, etc., but the general banded appearance still remains. When the period of rotation is determined by timing objects such as these as they cross the planet's central meridian, it is found that spots within about 10° of the equator indicate a period of approximately $9^h 50\frac{1}{2}^m$, while most of those in higher latitudes give periods between $9^h 55^m$ and $9^h 56^m$, the transition from the shorter to the longer being usually quite abrupt. When the rotation periods are examined in greater detail, it is found that the surface may be divided into many zones, each having a particular period characteristic of its latitude, but that the distribution in latitude of the various periods is quite haphazard. This differs from the Sun, whose rotation is also fastest at the equator, for whereas a definite formula connects the periods of solar spots with their latitude, no such law can be found for Jupiter. Actually the fastest moving spots are confined to a narrow strip in latitude about $+25°$; the last outbreak of such spots occurred in 1939.

Few Jovian markings have any degree of permanence, having generally lost their individuality after a few months. Two objects, however, form notable exceptions. The well-known "Bay" or "Hollow" in the South Equatorial Belt, which is so closely associated with the Great Red Spot, made famous in 1878–80 by its darkness and colour, is known to have existed from 1831 and the Red Spot itself may be identical with a similar object first depicted in the 17th century and followed for many years. The physical nature of the Red Spot is a mystery; its long duration suggests some connection with the solid surface, but the non-uniformity of its period of rotation seems to rule out this explanation. The other feature displaying considerable permanence is known as the South Tropical Disturbance, which has the same latitude as the Red Spot. Its rotation period is somewhat shorter than that of the latter; since its first detection in 1901 it has overtaken and passed the Red Spot eight times.

The spectroscope shows that Jupiter's atmosphere contains ammonia and considerable quantities of methane (marsh gas). The main constituents are unknown, but it is probable that hydrogen and helium abound and that the light clouds of the

surface are due to minute droplets or crystals of ammonia, the surface temperature having been found by measurement to be of the order — 120° C., which is not far from the calculated value. It has been suggested that this atmosphere is very deep; but if so, the pressure at depths below 100 kilometres or so must be such as to give it the properties of a liquid rather than a gas. A recent theory is that it may be dense enough to support in flotation a light solid body at some depth below the surface, and that what we see as the Red Spot may be a manifestation in the atmosphere above it of thermal changes in such a solid.

Jupiter has four principal satellites—the first celestial objects discovered by telescope by Galileo. The two inner major satellites are about the size of our Moon, while the two outer are about as large as Mercury. A fifth, very much smaller and fainter and nearer to Jupiter, was discovered visually by Barnard in 1892; this satellite has the most rapid motion of any in the solar system. Seven other satellites have been discovered photographically but all are minute objects; the four outermost of these have retrograde motion and are so greatly disturbed by the solar attractions that their orbits are not even approximately elliptical.

Intense but irregular bursts of radio noise were detected at the Carnegie Institute at Washington in January 1955, on wavelengths of 13·5 and 10 metres; these signals were received only during the few minutes while Jupiter was crossing the aerial beam. Some evidence indicates that there is a connection between the position of the satellite Io and these radio bursts.

SATURN

This planet is unique because of its encircling ring system, which makes it a very beautiful object in even a small telescope. There are two bright rings and an inner dusky one, which is transparent enough for the body of the planet to be seen through it. The dark line separating the two outer rings is known as Cassini's division in honour of its discoverer. The rings lie almost exactly in one plane, which is inclined at 27° to the planet's orbit and is sensibly that of its equator. It has been proved theoretically that the rings consist of a vast swarm of small individual particles, each pursuing its own orbit like a satellite around Saturn; this has been confirmed observationally by the spectroscope. This makes even more remarkable the extreme thinness of the rings, which is illustrated every 15 years, when the plane of the rings passes through the Earth; they then become almost completely invisible even in the greatest telescopes. Thus they cannot present when edgewise a width of more than a very few kilometres.

From the few spots that have been observed on Saturn's surface, the rotation period at the equator is about 10h 15m, in higher latitudes 10h 38m has been found in the northern hemisphere and 10h 37m in the southern. There is thus some analogy with Jupiter, but we are ignorant of the behaviour of intermediate zones.

The density of Saturn is less than three-quarters that of water; the oblateness is even more marked than is Jupiter's, the equatorial diameter exceeding

the polar by about one part in nine. The general appearance of the disk is banded, but the dusky belts are fewer and wider than those on Jupiter and present less contrast with the brighter zones. The atmosphere is known to contain methane and ammonia.

Among the more interesting results obtained from measurements of infra-red absorption spectra with the 2-metre reflector of the McDonald Observatory in Texas are those of the constitution of Saturn's rings and the five inner satellites. The only substance which gives similar absorption bands to those observed would appear to be frost deposited on a material at very low temperatures. The absorption curve is quite characteristic, and seems to be governed by the size of the frost crystals. Similar curves are given by the polar caps of Mars, but not by snow or ice. Estimates of the masses of Saturn's rings and of the five inner satellites show that their densities cannot be far from unity, and it is provisionally suggested that they are all composed of ice. Evaporation will be negligible at the low temperatures prevailing, and the small particles of which the ring is composed will suffer little or no loss.

Saturn has ten satellites, of which the largest, Titan, is easily seen with a small telescope. Titan is the largest satellite in the solar system, and the only one which shows definite evidence of possessing an atmosphere. The seven innermost satellites revolve nearly in the plane of the rings. When the rings are seen edgewise, these inner satellites may transit the planet or be eclipsed in the same manner as those of Jupiter. The faint outermost satellite, Phœbe, has a retrograde motion.

URANUS

This planet was discovered by William Herschel at Bath in 1781, and so has completed only two revolutions since its discovery. It is only just visible to the naked eye, but in a telescope is distinguishable by its disk, which is quite obvious, though less than 4″ in diameter, and by the different quality of its light. The two outer and brighter of its four main satellites were found by Herschel in 1787; the two inner by Lassell in 1851. Their movement is retrograde in a plane inclined 82° to the plane of the ecliptic. A fifth satellite was discovered by Kuiper in 1948. The period of rotation of Uranus has been determined spectroscopically to be 10¾ hours; the direction is the same as that of the satellites.

NEPTUNE

This planet is a telescopic object of about the 8th magnitude, presenting a disk of well over 2″ in diameter. A rotation period of 15·8 hours, inferred spectroscopically, is now generally adopted for the planet.

The planet was found in 1846 as a result of calculations, made independently by J. C. Adams and Le Verrier, which gave the position of an unknown planet which was responsible for perturbations of the motion of Uranus. The planet was found near the indicated place by Galle of the Berlin Observatory. Neptune has two satellites, of which the inner, Triton, revolves about Neptune in a retrograde direction at a distance a little less than that of the Moon from the Earth.

The other satellite revolves in the normal direction in a period of about a year. Its orbit is remarkably eccentric, and the satellite's distance from Neptune varies from 1,300,000 to over 10 million kilometers.

PLUTO

The outermost planet of the solar system was discovered photographically at the Lowell Observatory in March 1930, as a result of a systematic search for a trans-Neptunian planet. The existence of such a planet had been suggested many years before, and although the predicted elements of the orbit differ in some respects from the facts, yet these predictions were undoubtedly responsible for the ultimate discovery. The planet was called Pluto, and would appear to be small, with a mass possibly much less than that of the Earth. It would also appear to be a poor reflector of the Sun's light, since it shines only as a star of the 14th-15th magnitude.

THE MOON

The Moon is the Earth's satellite, and although its motion is highly complicated, it may be considered to revolve about the Earth in an elliptical orbit inclined about 5° to the plane of the ecliptic. Owing to perturbations, the ellipse is continually varying in shape, and the whole orbit twists round in space so that the nodes, or points where the orbit intersects the ecliptic, move in a retrograde direction, making one complete revolution in 18·6 years.

The Moon, whose diameter is 3,476 kilometres, rotates in the same time that it revolves ($27^d 7^h 43^m$) so that the same face is always presented to the Earth. The tilt of its axis, and the variable speed in the orbit, cause it to undergo an apparent swaying motion called libration, which enables us, in the long run, to see rather more than an exact half of the lunar surface. In a telescope this surface shows many objects of great beauty and interest, the rugged ranges of mountains, the craters and plains forming an impressive picture of jet-black shadows and bright highlights. Recent photographs obtained from the successful *Ranger* series of lunar probes show craters as small as a metre in diameter. On July 21, 1969, the first men (Americans) landed on the Moon and returned with samples of lunar rock and dust for subsequent laboratory analysis.

The revolution of the Moon about the Earth with reference to the Sun takes rather longer than a sidereal revolution, so that the phases of the Moon repeat themselves in a period that varies slightly about a mean of 29½ days. Each month the Moon passes in front of all stars in its path. Such an *occultation* causes the light of the star to be extinguished instantly. This, together with the sharpness and intensity of the shadows on the Moon, indicates a complete lack of atmosphere. Eclipses occur at two "seasons" of the year, when the Moon is near one of its nodes and in line with the Earth and the Sun. A lunar eclipse takes place when the Full Moon passes through the Earth's shadow, and is visible over half the Earth at any one time. A solar eclipse takes place when the New Moon passes in front of the Sun, and is visible only from a rather small area of the Earth.

As a result of its eastward movement among the stars the Moon rises later each day by a variable amount that depends on the inclination of its apparent path to the observer's horizon. When this angle is small, the Moon rises at much the same time for several days in succession. Although this occurs each month, it is most noticeable in high latitudes at the Full Moon nearest to the Autumnal Equinox. This is the Harvest Moon.

THE AURORA BOREALIS (AND AUSTRALIS)

An aurora is the visible counterpart of a marked disturbance of the Earth's magnetic field (a " magnetic storm ") apparently due to the action of a stream of electrified particles shot earthwards from localized regions of the Sun, such as that of a big sunspot. The glow of auroral patches, arches or streamers results from the action of this solar stream upon the constituent gases of the Earth's upper atmosphere. The usual height of the lower limit of the auroral luminescence is about 100 kilometres; upwards, it may extend to 500 kilometres or higher. Auroræ are very frequent in the so-called auroral zones (magnetic latitude about 67°) ; they are most frequent for the Earth as a whole near sunspot maximum. Although the solar origin of great displays (e.g. January 25, 1938 and January 24-26, 1949) can be traced to particular sunspots with solar flares, many lesser auroral displays cannot be thus associated. However, their solar origin is evidenced by their tendency to recur at intervals of 27 days, the time required for the Sun to turn once on its axis with respect to the Earth.

THE ZODIACAL LIGHT

This faint phenomenon of the late evening or early morning sky can be seen only when the air is sufficiently clear, the sky quite dark, and the ecliptic making a fairly steep angle with the horizon. It then appears as a cone of faint light stretching up from the position of the Sun (below the horizon) in the direction of the ecliptic, with its apex anything from 60° to 110° from the Sun. In our latitudes it is best seen after sunset in spring and before sunrise in the autumn, when its brightest parts may appear brighter than the Galaxy.

Occasionally, under very good conditions, an extension of the Cone may be traced right round the ecliptic. This is known as the Zodiacal Band. The Gegenschein or " Counter-glow " may also be detected as a widening of the band at the anti-solar point.

Recent work shows that the zodiacal cloud is a continuation of the Sun's corona, and that much of this fine dust must fall on the earth every day. The particles are much too small, however, to become visible (by incandescence) as they fall through the atmosphere, and there is evidence to show that they settle in the form of micro-meteorites. These probably act as centres of condensation in the formation of rain.

METEORS

The scattered particles which move in streams about the Sun give rise to occasional showers of meteors ("shooting-stars") or fireballs—bodies that differ only in size. They are visible in varying numbers every night, being sometimes so abundant

as to be quite spectacular. Often on a particular date or dates, meteors radiate from the same part of the heavens every year. This is because a stream of particles more or less dense, is moving in an orbit that intersects that of the Earth. The orbits of some of these streams, Lyrids, Pons-Winneckeids, Perseids, Giacobinids, Leonids, are known to be closely similar to those of certain comets, but modern work on the measurement of meteor velocities by photographic and radar methods has given very different results for the other streams. Thus the Geminids and the November Taurids have been shown by Whipple (from photographic results) to have small but eccentric orbits, more like those of minor planets. The radar methods of studying meteors have the advantage of being equally useful in daylight, and unaffected by cloud. Besides making measurements of the major showers noted above, the radar technique has shown the presence of a number of extensive showers in daylight hours, particularly in the summer months. These also show the same type of small eccentric orbit as those determined by Whipple.

METEOR SHOWERS

Date	Radiant		Name
	R.A.	Dec.	
	°	°	
January 3.........	232	+52	Quadrantids
April 20–22.......	271	+33	Lyrids*
May 2–6..........	336	0	η Aquarids*
June 27–30........	213	+53	Pons-Winneckeids*
August 10–13.....	46	+58	Perseids
October 9........	262	+54	Giacobinids*
October 18–23....	96	+15	Orionids*
November 14–15..	152	+22	Leonids*
December 10–13..	112	+32	Geminids
December 22	217	+76	Bečvár's Stream*

* Not plentiful each year.

The real paths of a great number of meteors have been computed, and the average heights found to be about 110 kilometres at the beginning and about 75 kilometres at the end. The speeds vary from 15 to 80 km. per second. Fireballs, or very bright meteors, appear at all times of the year unexpectedly so that they are often imperfectly noted and computation of their flight is not practicable.

Fireballs would seem to have a different origin from the ordinary shooting star, and probably arise from the belt of minor planets. The largest fireballs, when not completely consumed, land on the earth as meteorites. The largest meteorite found weighs 30 tons, and considerable collections are to be seen in our museums. Very large falls were recorded in Siberia in 1908 and 1947, while craters (formed presumably by large meteorites) are found in Arizona, Ungava and elsewhere. A number of meteorites have been found at Barwell, Leicestershire, as the result of two exploding fireballs on 24 December, 1965. At the other end of the scale are the micro-meteorites which are too small to become incandescent in the atmosphere and which drift slowly down to the earth's surface.

Above is a list of the nights when meteor showers may be expected, with the radiant points from which the meteors diverge. The dates given are those when the meteors are likely to be most abundant. In some cases, e.g. the Perseids, the apparition lasts beyond these limiting dates, and the position of the radiant, which changes from night to night, is given for the date of maximum.

COMETS

A comet is distinguished from other bodies in the solar system by its appearance: a hazy luminous patch moving in the sky, more or less round and usually brighter in the centre, sometimes with a star-like nucleus there; and from it not infrequently extends a tail which may, in bright comets, reach a length of as much as 150 million kilometres—a fine spectacle. Most comets are found accidentally and few observers search for these objects. One of the few is G. E. D. Alcock of Peterborough, Northants, who, after searching unsuccessfully for six years, found two new comets in August, 1959, within the space of 5 days. Two naked-eye comets which appeared in 1957 (Comet Arend–Roland in April, and Comet Mrkos in August) aroused considerable interest.

Although generally large in volume, a comet is small in mass, probably less than one-millionth that of the Earth even in the largest comets—the centre being composed mainly of an aggregation of pieces of matter mostly of sizes between that of pebbles and fine dust, but probably containing also a solid core a few kilometres in diameter. According to a recent theory, the earthy material is held together by various " ices "—masses of frozen gases such as ammonia, carbon dioxide and methane —which, on approaching the Sun, begin to evaporate. The pressure of the Sun's radiation is great enough to repel these gases, together with fine dust, and thus form a tail. As the comet approaches the Sun, it grows brighter and as it recedes it grows fainter again, the tail now preceding it in its journey away from the Sun.

Most comets follow paths which are very elongated ovals (ellipses) and return to the Sun, if at all, only after hundreds or thousands of years. The arrival of such comets cannot therefore be predicted. A few dozen comets, however, mostly too faint ever to be seen with the unaided eye, move in smaller ellipses which are sufficiently accurately known to enable predictions to be made of their returns. The most famous and brightest of these periodic comets is Halley's comet whose spectacular appearances about every 75 years have been traced back over more than 2000 years— it is next due early in 1986. Two very faint comets are known which travel in nearly circular orbits and, on this account, come within reach for photographic observation every year: Schwassmann-Wachmann (1), designated 1925 II, and Oterma. The former is of special interest, not only because its orbit is the only known one lying wholly between Jupiter and Saturn, but on account of the unexpected outbursts in brightness it occasionally manifests.

THE EARTH

The shape of the Earth is that of an oblate spheroid or solid of revolution whose meridian sections are ellipses not differing much from circles, whilst the sections at right angles are circles. The length of the equatorial axis is about 12,756 kilometres, and that of the polar axis 12,714 kilometres. The mean density of the Earth is 5·5 times that of water, although that of the surface layer is less. The Earth and Moon revolve about their common centre of gravity in a lunar month; this centre in turn revolves round the Sun in a plane known as the ecliptic, that passes through the Sun's centre. The Earth's equator is inclined to this plane at an angle of 23½°. This tilt is the cause of the seasons. In mid-latitudes, and when the Sun is high above the Equator, not only does the high noon altitude make the days longer, but the Sun's rays fall more directly on the Earth's surface; these effects combine to produce summer. In equatorial regions the noon altitude is large throughout the year, and there is little variation in the length of the day. In higher latitudes the noon altitude is lower, and the days in summer are appreciably longer than those in winter.

The average velocity of the Earth in its orbit is 30 kilometres a second. It makes a complete rotation on its axis in about $23^h 56^m$ of mean time, which is the sidereal day. Because of its annual revolution round the Sun, the rotation with respect to the Sun, or the solar day, is more than this by about four minutes (see p. 140). The extremity of the axis of rotation, or the North Pole of the Earth, is not rigidly fixed, but wanders over an area roughly 20 metres in diameter.

THE TIDES

The tides are caused by the attraction of the Moon for the waters of the Earth, while a similar but smaller effect is due to the Sun. Normally there are two high tides every day, about 12½ hours apart. They thus occur about 50 minutes later than those of the previous day, corresponding to the $24^h 50^m$ interval between consecutive meridian passages of the Moon. Briefly, a high tide occurs when the Moon is near the meridian because the attraction on the water is greater than on the solid earth. On the other side of the Earth the water is farther from the Moon than the solid earth and thus is less strongly attracted to the Moon and a second high tide occurs at this point. The height of the tide varies considerably. The highest, called Spring Tides, always occur about the time of New or Full Moon, when the lunar and solar attractions act together. At Neap Tides, which occur about First and Last Quarter, the rise and fall is only about half as much as at Spring Tide.

The tidal flow of water across the Earth is greatly modified by the shape of the coastlines and other geographical conditions. The complicated motion of the Moon, its changing position north or south of the equator, and its varying distance from the Earth, all add small variations; it is thus impossible to predict tides theoretically. Tide-tables for any place are always constructed from an analysis of past observations of times and heights. It is found that the height can be expressed as the sum of a series of periodic terms, which can be carried forward. (See pages 170–184.)

High water does not necessarily occur at the same time as the meridian passage of the Moon, nor do springs and neaps necessarily occur on the same day as the phases stated. Thus at London Bridge the tide is high when the Moon is somewhat west of the meridian, while Spring Tides occur about 2½ days after New or Full Moon.

The shape and depth of a channel or estuary very greatly modify the nature of the tides. At some places one of the daily tides becomes so small as to be negligible, while in other channels (e.g. Southampton Water) the high tides are doubled. The difference between high and low water, or range of the tide, may vary from a small amount, as in the land-locked Mediterranean, up to 13 metres in the Severn Estuary and 16 metres in the Bay of Fundy.

As the energy involved in this tidal flow is considerable, various schemes for harnessing tidal energy have been evolved. As a consequence of the friction caused by tidal flow, the Earth's period of rotation is increasing by about a thousandth of a second every century. Although very small at present, this effect was greater in the past, and has played a considerable part in the history of the Earth–Moon system.

High Water in the Thames, 1972
Occasions when predicted height at London Bridge is 23·9 feet or more

February...16–18	August.....26–28
March.....16–19	September..23–27
April......14–17	October....22–26
May.......14–16	November.21–34

TERRESTRIAL MAGNETISM

In the earliest years of experimental science it was known that a bar of iron rubbed with a piece of the commonly occurring iron ore, magnetite or lodestone, was subject to a directing force causing it to take up a constant direction when freed from other restraint. Before the 12th century, voyagers were using this mysterious property to guide themselves, their method being to place a light magnetized needle in a reed floated on water. From this primitive device the Mariner's compass subsequently developed. That the direction, though roughly north to south, is by no means accurately so, was known to the Chinese before A.D. 1000.

William Gilbert gave the first approximately correct explanation of the then known facts. In the proximity of the Earth magnetized needles behave much as if the Earth itself were a large magnetized sphere. It was soon found that the direction of the force in a particular locality slowly changed. Henry Gellibrand, observing near Greenwich in 1634, found the direction to be about 4° east of north, whereas there was undoubted evidence that in 1580 it had been about 11° east in the same neighbourhood. In 1722, Graham, the clockmaker found that the direction oscillated slowly through a small angle every day. In the

British Isles the movement is eastwards till about 08^h U.T., then rather quickly westwards till about 14^h U.T., after which there is a gradual return eastwards. The amplitude may be as much as $15'$ in the summer.

A magnetic compass points along the horizontal component of a magnetic line of force. These directions converge on the " magnetic dip-poles ". At these poles a freely suspended magnetized needle would become vertical. Not only do the positions of these poles change with time, but their exact location is ill-defined, particularly so in the case of the north dip-pole where the lines of force, on the north side of it, instead of converging radially, tend to bunch into a channel. Although it is therefore unrealistic to attempt to specify the locations of the dip-poles exactly, the present adopted positions are $76^\circ \cdot 0$ N., $101^\circ \cdot 0$ W. and $66^\circ \cdot 5$ S., $140^\circ \cdot 0$ E. The two magnetic dip-poles are thus not antipodal, the line joining them passing the centre of the Earth at a distance of about $1,100$ kilometres. The distances of the magnetic dip-poles from the north and south geographic poles are about $1,600$ and $2,700$ kilometres respectively.

There is also a " magnetic equator ", at all points of which the vertical force is nil and a magnetized needle remains horizontal. This line runs between 2° and 10° north of the geographical equator in the eastern hemisphere, turns sharply south off the West African coast, and crosses South America through Brazil, Bolivia and Peru; it re-crosses the geographical equator in mid-Pacific.

Reference has already been made to secular changes in the Earth's field. The following table indicates the changes in magnetic declination (or variation of the compass). Similar, though much smaller, changes have occurred in " dip " or magnetic inclination. Secular changes differ throughout the world. Although the London observations strongly suggest a cycle of several hundred years, an exact repetition is unlikely.

London		Greenwich	
1580	$11^\circ 15'$ E.	1850	$22^\circ 24'$ W.
1622	$6 \ 00$ E.	1907	$16 \ 00$ W.
1660	$0 \ 00$	1929	$12 \ 23$ W.
1720	$13 \ 00$ W.	1946	$9 \ 38$ W.
1815	$24 \ 27$ W.	1965	$7 \ 29$ W.

In order that up-to-date information on the variation of the compass may be available, many governments publish magnetic charts on which there are lines (called isogonic) passing through all places at which specified values of declination will be found at the date of the chart.

In the British Isles, isogonic lines now run from north-east to south-west, making an angle of about 15° with the meridians. Though there are considerable local deviations due to mineralogical causes, a rough value of magnetic declination may be obtained by assuming that at 50° N. on the meridian of Greenwich, the value in 1972 is $6^\circ 36'$ west and allowing an increase of $14'$ for each degree of latitude northwards and one of $31'$ for each degree of longitude westwards. For example, at 53° N., 5° W., declination will be about $6^\circ 36' + 42' + 155'$, i.e. $9^\circ 53'$ west. The average annual change at the present time is about $4'$ decrease.

The number of magnetic observatories now approaches 200—widely scattered over the globe. In Great Britain three are maintained by the Government: at Hartland, North Devon, at Eskdalemuir in Dumfriesshire, Scotland, and at Lerwick, Shetland Islands, while a fourth is maintained by Stonyhurst College, Lancashire. Some recent annual mean values of the magnetic elements for Hartland are given below.

The normal worldwide terrestrial magnetic field corresponds approximately to that of a very strong small bar magnet near the centre of the Earth but with appreciable smooth spatial departures. The origin and slow secular change of the normal field is not yet fully understood but is generally ascribed to electric currents associated with fluid motions within the Earth's core. Superposed on the normal field are local and regional anomalies whose magnitudes may in places exceed that of the normal field; these are due to the influence of mineral deposits in the Earth's crust. A small proportion of the field is of external origin, mostly associated with electric currents in the ionosphere. The configuration of the external field and the ionization of the atmosphere depend on the incident particle and radiation flux. There are, therefore, short-term and non-periodic as well as diurnal, 27-day, seasonal and 11-year periodic changes in the magnetic field, dependent upon the position of the Sun and the degree of solar activity.

Year	Declination West	Dip or Inclination	Horizontal Force	Vertical Force
	$^\circ \quad '$	$^\circ \quad '$	oersted	oersted
1940	12 30	66 55	0·1839	0·4315
1945	11 46	66 55	0·1843	0·4326
1950	11 06	66 54	0·1848	0·4334
1955	10 30	66 49	0·1859	0·4340
1960	9 59	66 44	0·1871	0·4350
1965	9 30	66 34	0·1887	0·4354
1970	9 06	66 26	0·1903	0·4364

Magnetic Storms. Occasionally—sometimes with great suddenness—the Earth's magnetic field is subject for several hours to marked disturbance. In extreme cases, departures in field intensity as much as one tenth the normal value are experienced. In many instances, such disturbances are accompanied by widespread displays of aurorae, marked changes in the incidence of cosmic rays, an increase in the reception of ' noise ' from the Sun at radio frequencies together with rapid changes in the ionosphere and induced electric currents within the earth which adversely affect radio and telegraphic communications. The disturbances are generally ascribed to flux changes in the stream of neutral and ionized particles which emanates from the Sun and through which the Earth is continuously passing. Some of these changes are associated with visible eruptions on the Sun, usually in the region of sunspots. There is a marked tendency for disturbances to recur after intervals of about 27 days, the apparent period of rotation of the Sun on its axis, which is consistent with the sources being located on particular areas of the Sun.

ARTIFICIAL SATELLITES AND SPACE PROBES

The progress of rocket research during the last war led to the development by the Germans in 1944 of the V.2 rocket which, if fired vertically, attained a height of 180 km. Before the end of the decade the U.S. rocket engineers had increased this maximum height to 400 km by using a two-stage rocket, the first stage being a V.2 and the second a WAC Corporal. Plans for using multistage rockets to put artificial satellites into orbit around the earth during the International Geophysical Year (July 1957–December 1958) were announced by both the U.S. and the U.S.S.R. Such projects also called for an immense effort in establishing optical, radio, and radar tracking facilities around the world.

The historic event which heralded the Space Age occurred on October 4, 1957, when the U.S.S.R. successfully injected a "sputnik" into an orbit inclined at 65° to the earth's equator. One month later "Sputnik 2" was also put into orbit, carrying a dog that survived the ascent trajectory and lived for several days orbiting the earth. The rate of satellite launching has increased since 1957 and by the end of 1960 the number of artificial satellites in orbit around the Earth exceeded the number of natural satellites known to be in the Solar System. All the satellites launched up to the end of 1960 have been sent up in the same direction as the rotation of the Earth, i.e., eastwards. Thus they are able to start with the benefit of the Earth's rotational velocity at the particular launching site. This is why these satellites always appear to move in an easterly direction. However, the first satellite launching of 1961 (*Samos 2*) achieved a retrograde orbit.

Satellite Orbits

To consider the orbit of an artificial satellite it is best to imagine that one is looking at the Earth from a distant point in space. The Earth would then be seen to be rotating about its axis inside the orbit described by the rapidly revolving satellite. The inclination of a satellite orbit to the Earth's equator (which generally remains almost constant throughout the satellite's lifetime) gives at once the maximum range of latitudes over which the satellite passes. Thus a satellite whose orbit has an inclination of 53° will pass overhead all latitudes between 53° S. and 53° N., but would never be seen in the zenith of any place nearer the poles than these latitudes. If we consider a particular place on the earth, whose latitude is less than the inclination of the satellite's orbit then the Earth's rotation carries this place under first the northbound part of the orbit and then, later on, under the southbound portion of the orbit, these two occurrences being always less than 12 hours apart for satellites moving in direct orbits (i.e. to the east). For satellites in retrograde orbits the words "northbound" and "southbound" should be interchanged in the preceding statement. As the value of the latitude of the observer increases and approaches the value of the inclination of the orbit, so this interval gets shorter until (when the latitude is equal to the inclination) only one overhead passage occurs each day.

Orbital Variations

The relatively simple picture described above is unfortunately complicated by the considerable variations in the shape, orientation and size of the orbit during a satellite's lifetime. The major variations are due to the Earth's oblateness and to air-drag. A third cause, radiation pressure from the Sun, is noticeable only on large satellites of extremely low density.

The oblate shape of the Earth—the equatorial diameter is 43 km longer than the polar diameter —has two marked effects on a satellite orbit. It causes a regression of the nodes, amounting to several degrees a day for close satellites. Thus from a point in space, the whole orbit is seen to twist around the Earth, making a complete turn of 360° within a few months. This regression, which may also be described as the rotation of the orbital plane around the Earth's axis, is in the opposite direction to the satellite's motion, i.e. the orbit of a satellite with a direct motion regresses to the west. The actual amount of the regression depends, first, on the inclination of the orbit to the equator, being greatest at low inclinations and zero for a true polar orbit (inclination 90°). It is also dependent on the distance of the satellite from the Earth, being greatest for small orbits. At the distance of the Moon the regression is only 19° *a year*.

The orbit of *Samos 2* is extremely interesting from this point of view as its regression is to the east at almost an identical rate with the movement of the Sun. Thus there is hardly any change in the area of visibility over a long period of time.

The other effect the Earth's oblateness has on a satellite orbit is to cause a rotation of the line of apsides (i.e. the line joining the perigee and apogee points of the orbit). The rate of the rotation is dependent on the inclination of the orbit, and also on the distance of the satellite, again being greater for close satellites than for more distant ones. The value of this rotation has its greatest positive value (i.e. it moves forward along the orbit in the same direction as the satellite) at the equator and becomes zero at an inclination of 63°·4. As the inclination moves from 63°·4 to 90° the value increases again numerically, but with the opposite sign, the motion of the line of apsides being backwards along the orbit.

Even at heights of several hundred kilometres there is still sufficient atmosphere to cause a retarding effect on satellites. Although air-drag will have most effect around the perigee point the actual result is to reduce the height of the apogee point with hardly any change in perigee height and thus to decrease the eccentricity of the orbit until, in the final stage of a satellite's life-time, the orbit is almost circular. Unfortunately the air density at perigee height is not constant. It alters as the perigee moves from daylight into darkness and from darkness into daylight, and also as the latitude of perigee changes

Period		Height, kilometres	Velocity km per hour	Period		Height, kilometres	Velocity km per hour
h	m			h	m		
1	28	182	28,077	3	40	5,700	20,686
1	32	380	27,663	3	50	6,064	20,382
1	36	575	27,274	4	00	6,428	20,096
1	40	766	26,905	5	00	8,473	18,655
1	44	954	26,556	6	00	10,393	17,555
1	48	1,141	26,224	7	00	12,207	16,676
1	52	1,326	25,907	8	00	13,937	15,950
1	56	1,508	25,606	9	00	15,596	15,335
2	00	1,688	25,318	10	00	17,194	14,806
2	04	1,867	25,043	11	00	18,739	14,344
2	08	2,042	24,779	12	00	20,529	13,934
2	12	2,216	24,526	13	00	21,699	13,567
2	16	2,390	24,283	14	00	23,120	13,235
2	20	2,560	24,050	15	00	24,509	12,934
2	24	2,729	23,826	16	00	25,865	12,659
2	28	2,897	23,609	17	00	27,195	12,406
2	32	3,064	23,400	18	00	28,498	12,171
2	36	3,228	23,199	19	00	29,779	11,954
2	40	3,392	23,004	20	00	31,036	11,751
2	50	3,795	22,544	21	00	32,272	11,562
3	00	4,189	22,117	22	00	33,490	11,384
3	10	4,577	21,723	23	00	34,689	11,217
3	20	4,958	21,354	24	00	35,871	11,059
3	30	5,332	21,010				

due to the rotation of the line of apsides. There is already some evidence that the atmospheric density varies with the sunspot cycle. In addition unpredictable short-period variations in the output of solar radiation may also occur and these have the effect of increasing the air density at any given height. Thus the air-drag on a satellite is by no means a constant factor and this is the reason why it is not possible to forecast accurately the position of a satellite for any considerable period of time. There is also some retardation due to electrified particles but this effect may be included with the air-drag.

Radiation pressure from the Sun only has any appreciable effect on large satellites of extremely low density such as the 30 metre diameter balloon, Echo 1. For such satellites, however, this effect can be severe, and for heights greater than a few hundred kilometres, it can equal or even surpass that due to air drag. The effect on the orbit is very much more complicated than that due to air-drag, and even the signs of the variations can change period-ically with time. Thus it is possible for the eccentricity to increase rather than decrease, with an increase in apogee height and a decrease in perigee height.

For close artificial satellites the gravitational attractions of the Sun and Moon are many thousand times weaker than that of the Earth's equatorial bulge and need only be considered in an extremely precise analysis of observational material.

Height and Velocity

The mean height of a satellite above the Earth's surface, which is determined by its orbital velocity, is related to its period of revolution around the Earth as is shown by the table above. This table is only strictly valid for circular orbits.

As the orbit shrinks due to air drag, both the me height and the period decrease so that the retardi effect of air drag actually causes the satellite move faster, though in a smaller orbit.

Satellite Launchings, 1957-71

Many different types of orbit have been achiev though the vast majority have had a direct motio The majority of the Russian satellite orbits have h inclinations of 65° or 49° and orbits entirely belo 2000 kilometres in height. An important exce tion was Lunik 3 whose original inclination was ? and initial apogee height 470,000 km. This satell orbited the Moon on its first revolution, returni with the first photographs of the other side of t Moon, which were transmitted back to the Ear when near perigee.

The American satellites have been injected in orbits of various inclinations. The early Explore and Vanguards are in orbits of inclination abo 28-35° while near-polar orbits were achieved wi the Discoverers. Other series of launchings su as the Transit, Tiros and Echo put satellites orbits of intermediate inclinations. In contrast the heavy, but short-lived, Russian satellites, number of those launched by the U.S. have be very small and have been put in larger orbits whi have given them considerably longer life-times.

One launching project has caused great contr versy amongst astronomers. This is the so-call "West Ford" project, involving the launching a Midas satellite into a polar orbit, carrying dispenser. The dispenser contains several hundr million small needles and these are released after t Midas has been successfully injected into a selec orbit. The needles form a belt around the Ear which is used as a reflector for radio signals. T first attempt (1961 α δ) failed but the seco (1963-14) has been successful. [continued on p. 1

ARTIFICIAL SATELLITES LAUNCHED IN 1970–71

Designation	Satellites	Launch date	i	P	e	Perigee height (km)
			°	m		
1970–		1970				
26	Cosmos 331, rocket	April 8	65·0	89·8	0·009	206
27	Vela 11, Vela 12, rocket	April 8	32·4	6729	0·005	111,210
28	Cosmos 332, rocket	April 11	74·1	100·0	0·000	755
29	Apollo 13*, rocket, LEM 7	April 11	(lunar trajectory)			
30	Cosmos 333, rocket, capsule........	April 15	81·3	89·1	0·001	219
31	?	April 15	111·0	89·7	0·019	130
32	Intelsat 3G, rocket	April 23	0·2	1436·2	0·000	35,772
33	Cosmos 334, rocket	April 23	70·9	92·1	0·016	272
34	China 1, rocket	April 24	68·4	114·1	0·125	441
35	Cosmos 335, rocket	April 24	48·4	91·0	0·011	250
36	Cosmos 336–343, rocket	April 25	74·0	115·5	0·002	1,464
37	Meteor 4, rocket	April 28	81·2	98·1	0·006	625
38	Cosmos 344, rocket	May 12	72·9	89·8	0·010	202
39	Cosmos 345, rocket	May 20	51·8	89·1	0·006	192
40	? , capsule	May 20	83·0	88·6	0·006	162
41	Soyuz 9, rocket	June 1	51·6	88·5	0·004	176
42	Cosmos 346, rocket	June 10	51·7	89·2	0·006	197
43	Cosmos 347, rocket	June 12	48·4	107·9	0·122	216
44	Cosmos 348, rocket	June 13	71·0	93·1	0·033	201
45	Cosmos 349, rocket	June 17	65·4	89·8	0·010	199
46	? , rocket	June 19	28·2	588·9	0·719	178
47	Meteor 5, rocket	June 23	81·2	102·2	0·004	831
48	?	June 25	108·9	89·7	0·020	129
49	Molniya 1 P, rocket, launcher rocket, launcher	June 26	65·4	704·7	0·740	448
50	Cosmos 350, rocket	June 26	51·7	89·0	0·004	202
51	Cosmos 351, rocket	June 27	71·0	91·9	0·015	270
52	Cosmos 352, rocket	July 7	51·8	89·5	0·007	207
53	Cosmos 353, rocket	July 9	65·4	89·4	0·006	204
54	?	July 23	60·0	90·0	0·018	158
55	Intelsat 3H, rocket	July 23	28·0	642·7	0·730	282
56	Cosmos 354, rocket	July 28	49·6	87·5	0·003	134
57	Intercosmos 3, rocket	August 7	48·4	99·7	0·077	200
58	Cosmos 355, rocket	August 7	65·4	89·7	0·009	199
59	Cosmos 356, rocket	August 10	82·0	92·6	0·025	231
60	Venus 7, launcher rocket, launcher	August 17	(on path to Venus)			
61	?	August 18	111·0	89·7	0·016	151
62	Skynet 2, rocket	August 19	28·0	636·5	0·729	270
63	Cosmos 357, rocket	August 19	71·0	92·0	0·015	272
64	Cosmos 358, rocket	August 20	74·0	95·2	0·002	515
65	Cosmos 359, launcher rocket, platform	August 22	51·1	95·6	0·049	208
66	?	August 26	75·0	94·5	0·001	484
67	Oscar 6, rocket	August 27	90·0	107·0	0·018	955
68	Cosmos 360, rocket, capsule	August 29	65·0	89·6	0·007	209
69	? , rocket	September 1	28·5	88·0	0·001	179
70	? , rocket	September 3	98·7	101·3	0·008	764
71	Cosmos 361, rocket, capsule	September 8	72·9	89·6	0·007	209
72	Luna 16, launcher rocket, launcher	September 12	(soft landed on Moon)			
73	Cosmos 362, rocket	September 16	71·0	95·7	0·040	270
74	Cosmos 363, rocket	September 17	65·0	89·5	0·007	208
75	Cosmos 364, rocket, capsule	September 22	65·4	89·5	0·007	202
76	Cosmos 365, launch platform, rocket	September 25	49·7	87·5	0·003	133
77	Molniya 1Q, launcher, launcher rocket, rocket	September 29	65·5	706·1	0·739	480
78	Cosmos 366, rocket	October 1	65·0	89·5	0·007	204
79	Cosmos 367, rocket, platform	October 3	65·3	104·5	0·007	922
80	Cosmos 368, rocket	October 8	65·0	90·6	0·015	204

Designation	Satellites	Launch date	i	P	e	Perigee height (km
1970-		1970	°	m		
81	*Cosmos 369, rocket*	October 8	70·9	92·3	0·018	26
82	*Cosmos 370, rocket*	October 9	64·9	89·4	0·006	20
83	Cosmos 371, rocket	October 12	74·0	99·9	0·000	75
84	*Intercosmos 4, rocket*	October 14	48·4	93·6	0·029	25
85	Meteor 6, rocket	October 15	81·2	97·5	0·002	62
86	*Cosmos 372, rocket*	October 16	74·1	100·8	0·001	78
87	*Cosmos 373, rocket*	October 20	62·9	94·8	0·005	47
88	*Zond 8, launcher rocket*	October 20	(lunar trajectory)			
89	Cosmos 374, rocket	October 23	63·0	112·3	0·105	52
90	*?*	October 23	111·1	89·8	0·020	13
91	Cosmos 375, rocket	October 30	62·8	111·8	0·102	52
92	*Cosmos 376, rocket, capsule*	October 30	65·4	89·4	0·006	20
93	*?*	November 6	26·3	635·1	0·727	30
94	*OFO 1, rocket*	November 9	37·4	92·6	0·016	30
95	*Luna 17, launcher rocket, launcher*	November 10	(soft landed on Moon)			
96	Cosmos 377, rocket	November 11	65·0	89·4	0·006	20
97	Cosmos 378, rocket	November 17	74·0	104·9	0·102	23
98	*?* , capsule	November 18	83·0	88·7	0·004	18
99	*Cosmos 379, rocket, platform*	November 24	51·6	88·7	0·003	19
100	*Cosmos 380, rocket*	November 24	82·0	102·2	0·091	19
101	Molniya 1 R, *launcher rocket, launcher, rocket*	November 27	65·5	707·1	0·740	47
102	Cosmos 381, rocket	December 2	74·0	104·9	0·003	90
103	Cosmos 382, rocket, platform	December 2	51·5	142·8	0·262	30
104	*Cosmos 383, rocket*	December 3	65·4	89·3	0·006	20
105	*Cosmos 384, rocket, capsule*	December 10	72·9	89·5	0·007	20
106	NOAA 1, rocket	December 11	101·9	114·9	0·003	1,42
107	Explorer 42, rocket	December 12	3·0	95·3	0·003	52
108	Cosmos 385, rocket	December 12	74·0	104·8	0·000	97
109	PEOLE 1, rocket	December 12	15·0	98·4	0·008	63
110	*Cosmos 386, rocket, capsule*	December 15	65·0	89·4	0·005	21
111	Cosmos 387, rocket	December 16	74·0	95·3	0·001	52
112	Cosmos 388, rocket	December 18	71·0	92·3	0·017	27
113	Cosmos 389, rocket	December 18	81·2	98·1	0·003	64
114	Molniya 1 S, *launcher rocket, launcher, rocket*	December 25	65·0	711·8	0·740	49
1971-		1971				
01	*Cosmos 390, rocket, capsule*	January 12	65·0	89·3	0·005	20
02	Cosmos 391, rocket	January 14	70·9	95·3	0·039	26
03	Meteor 7, rocket	January 20	81·2	97·6	0·002	62
04	*Cosmos 392, rocket*	January 21	65·0	89·3	0·006	20
05	*?*	January 21	110·9	90·1	0·021	13
06	Intelsat 4 A, rocket	January 26	28·3	638·7	0·718	54
07	Cosmos 393, rocket	January 26	71·0	92·1	0·016	27
08	Apollo 14*, rocket, LEM 8	January 31	32·6	88·1	0	18
09	NATO 2, rocket	February 3	27·8	587·5	0·713	29
10	Cosmos 394, rocket	February 9	65·8	96·5	0·003	57
11	Tansei	February 16	29·7	105·9	0·008	98
12	Calsphere 3–5, rockets	February 17	98·8	100·9	0·005	76
13	Cosmos 395, rocket	February 17	74·0	95·4	0·001	52
14	*Cosmos 396, rocket, capsule*	February 18	65·4	89·4	0·006	20
15	Cosmos 397, rocket	February 25	65·7	113·5	0·105	57
16	*Cosmos 398, rocket, platform*	February 26	51·6	88·9	0·005	18
17	*Cosmos 399, rocket, capsule*	March 3	65·0	89·3	0·006	20
18	China 2, rocket	March 3	69·9	106·2	0·105	26
19	Explorer 43, rocket, rocket	March 13	28·8	5,628	0·937	23
20	Cosmos 400, rocket	March 18	65·8	105·0	0·002	98

An interesting feature of some of the Cosmos satellites in 65° orbits is that after 8 days in orbit they return to Earth (Russia) in a controlled re-entry through the atmosphere

A third Anglo-American satellite, Ariel 3, was launched on May 5, 1967 and has been of great interest to visual observers. Sets of mirrors and highly reflective solar cells on its sides cause the observer to see a series of flashes and the observations are used to determine the direction of the axis of rotation of the satellite.

Apart from their names, *e.g.* Cosmos 6 Rocket or Injun 3, the satellites are also classified according to their date of launch. Thus 1961 α refers to the launching of Samos 2. The next satellite launching was 1961 β and so on. A number following the Greek letter is intended to indicate the relative brightness of the satellites put in orbit. From the beginning of 1963 the Greek letters are replaced by numbers and the numbers by roman letters e.g. 1963-01A. In this table are given the designation and names of the main objects in orbit (in the order A, B, C ... etc.), the launch date and some initial orbital data. These are the inclination to the equator (i), the nodal period of revolution (P), the eccentricity, e, and the perigee height. The names of those satellites which have already disintegrated in the Earth's atmosphere or returned to the Earth's surface are printed in *italics*. A satellite which carried a human being is indicated by an asterisk.

Since the last edition of *Whitaker's Almanack* the following satellites launched in the years 1958-70 have disintegrated in the Earth's atmosphere:—

1961α2	1962ζ2	1963-30D	1965-53A
1966-39B	1967-20B	1967-42A	1967-42B
1967-72B	1968-04A	1968-41A	1968-57A
1968-57F	1968-81B	1968-84A	1968-86A
1969-64B	1969-82A	1969-94A	1969-94B
1969-97A	1969-108A	1970-20A	1970-20B

Some American satellites are of military significance and details of their orbits are not disclosed. This is the reason for the gaps in the table.

Observation of Satellites

The regression of the orbit around the Earth causes alternate periods of visibility and invisibility, though this is of little concern to the radio or radar observer. To the visual observer the following cycle of events normally occurs (though the cycle may start in any position): invisibility, morning observations before dawn, invisibility, evening observations after dusk, invisibility, morning observations before dawn, and so on. With reasonably high satellites and for observers in high latitudes around the summer solstice the evening observations follow the morning observations without interruption as sunlight passing over the polar regions can still illuminate satellites which are passing over temperate latitudes at local midnight. At the moment all satellites rely on sunlight to make them visible though a satellite with a flashing light has been suggested for a future launching. The observer must be in darkness or twilight in order to make any useful observations and the durations of twilight and the sunrise, sunset times given on page II of each month will be a useful guide.

Some of the satellites are visible to the naked eye and much interest has been aroused by the spectacle of a bright satellite disappearing into the Earth's shadow. The event is even more fascinating telescopically as the disappearance occurs gradually as the satellite traverses the Earth's penumbral shadow, and during the last few seconds before the eclipse is complete the satellite may change colour (under suitable atmospheric conditions) from yellow to red. This is because the last rays of sunlight are refracted through the denser layers of our atmosphere before striking the satellite.

Some satellites rotate about one or more axes so that a periodic variation in brightness is observed. This was particularly noticeable in several of the U.S.S.R. satellites.

Satellite research has already provided some interesting results. Among them may be mentioned a revised value of the Earth's oblateness, 1/298·2, and the discovery of the Van Allen radiation belts.

ROYAL OBSERVATORIES

Royal Greenwich Observatory
Herstmonceux, Sussex

The Royal Observatory was established at Greenwich in 1675 by Charles II for improving methods of navigation. Latterly the growth of London, with its smoke and bright lights, seriously hampered astronomical observations there, and it was decided in 1946 to move the telescopes to Herstmonceux Castle in Sussex. The removal was completed by 1958. The meridian of zero longitude still passes through the old site, which now houses the Department of Navigation and Astronomy of the National Maritime Museum.

At the Observatory astronomical measurements are made of the positions, motions and distances of the heavenly bodies, and of such physical characteristics as their luminosities, masses and temperatures. Two meridian instruments and six equatorially-mounted telescopes are devoted to this work, and the Isaac Newton telescope, a 98-inch reflector for the use of any qualified British astronomer, was completed in 1967. The Observatory is responsible for the time service of the United Kingdom and the time zones of the world are based on Greenwich Mean Time.

Astronomer Royal, Sir Richard Woolley, O.B.E., Sc.D., F.R.S.

H.M. Nautical Almanac Office

The *Nautical Almanac* was first published for 1767 by the Board of Longitude. The Office is now a branch of the Royal Greenwich Observatory. Annual publications—Astronomical Ephemeris, Nautical Almanac, Air Almanac, Star Almanac.

Royal Observatory
Blackford Hill, Edinburgh 9

The Observatory, founded by the Astronomical Institution in 1818 on Calton Hill, was moved to its present site in 1896. Its work, which is closely linked to that of the Astronomy Department of Edinburgh University, is concerned with the physics of stars and interstellar matter and the structure and evolution of the Galaxy. Observational data are secured with four telescopes on Blackford Hill and one at an outstation at Monte Porzio, Italy. Satellite tracking is pursued at a second outstation in Peeblesshire. Much of the work of the Observatory is directed to the design and construction of new instruments and to the introduction of automation into astronomy.

Astronomer Royal for Scotland and Regius Professor of Astronomy in the University of Edinburgh, Prof. H. A. Brück, C.B.E., D.Phil, Ph.D.

TIDAL CONSTANTS

THE TIME OF HIGH WATER *at the undermentioned Ports and Places may be* approximately *found by taking the appropriate Time of High Water at the Standard Port* (as shown on pp. 172, 173, etc.) *and adding thereto the quantities annexed. The columns headed " Springs " and " Neaps " show the height of the tide above datum for Mean High Water Springs and Mean High Water Neaps respectively.*

Tidal data is no longer available for a number of places which formerly appeared in the list below. These places (with the name of the substitute now recorded) are: *Air Point* (Mostyn Quay); *Ardrishaig* (East Loch Tarbert); *Arisaig* (Loch Moidart); *Ayr Pt.*, I.o.M. (Peel); *Beachy Head* (Eastbourne); *Beaumaris* (Menai Bridge); *Brielle* (Scheveningen); *Broughty Ferry* (Newburgh); *Burryport* (Whiteford Lighthouse); *Caen* (Cayeux); *Caernarvon* (Llanddwyn Isld.); *Dumbarton* (Bowling); *Dumfries* (Port Carlisle); *Fareham* (Itchenor); *Fifeness* (Anstruther Easter); *Glasson Dock* (Tarn Pt.); *Gravesend* (Tilbury Dock); *Greenwich* (R. Albert Dock); *Hythe* (Totland Bay); *Lancaster* (Duddon Bar); *Lynmouth* (Porlock Bay); *Nash Pt.* (Chepstow); *Needles Pt.* (Freshwater Bay); *Neath* (Porthcawl); *Nore Lt.* (Chatham); *Port Harrington* (Hestan Islet); *Portishead* (Avonmouth); *St. Agnes* (Coverack); *St. Mary's* (Sennen Cove); *Start Pt.* (Lulworth Cove); *Stockton* (Seaham); *Sutton Bridge* (Blacktoft); *Torbay* (Torquay); *Woolwich* (Hammersmith Br.); *Worms Head* (Ferryside); *Honfleur Harbour* (Duclair).

Port	Diff.	Springs	Neaps	Port	Diff.	Springs	Neaps
	h. m.	ft.	ft.		h. m.	ft.	ft.
Aberdeen..........Leith	− 1 16	12·3	9·5	Coverack..........Bristol	− 1 59	17·4	13·7
Aberdovey.......Liverpool	− 3 16	15·7	12·4	★Cowes (West)....London	− 2 28	13·9	11·4
Aberystwyth....Liverpool	− 3 34	15·6	12·2	Cromarty..........Leith	− 2 51	13·9	11·2
Aldeburgh........London	− 3 6	9·3	8·7	Cromer............Hull	− 0 34	16·1	12·5
Alderney..........London	+5 32	21·6	16·3	Dartmouth......London	+4 28	15·8	11·8
Alloa..............Leith	+0 46	18·3	13·9	Deal..............London	− 2 27	20·1	16·3
Amlwch.........Liverpool	− 0 40	—	—	Devonport Dock..London	+4 0	18·2	14·4
Anstruther Easter....Leith	− 0 22	17·7	14·0	Dieppe............London	− 3 8	30·0	23·3
Antwerp..........London	+1 20	17·7	14·8	Dingle Harbour..Liverpool	+5 30	11·4	8·5
Appledore.........Bristol	− 1 24	24·8	16·6	Donegal Harbour...L'pool	− 5 26	11·9	8·9
Arbroath..........Leith	− 0 30	15·8	12·7	Douglas.........Liverpool	− 0 4	22·8	17·8
Ardrossan.......Greenock	− 0 20	9·2	7·6	Dover.............London	− 2 42	21·9	17·5
★Arundel..........London	− 1 8	10·3	7·1	Duclair...........London	− 0 42	25·7	21·1
Avonmouth........Bristol	0 0	42·2	31·6	Duddon Bar.....Liverpool	+0 3	26·8	20·5
Ayr.............Greenock	− 0 20	9·5	8·2	Dunbar............Leith	− 0 8	16·1	13·1
Ballycotton......Bristol	− 1 41	12·4	9·9	Dundalk (Pile Lt.)..L'pool	+0 13	16·1	12·8
Banff.............Leith	− 2 41	10·6	8·3	Dundee............Leith	+0 15	15·5	12·1
Bantry Harbour...L'pool	+5 31	12·1	9·6	Dungeness........London	− 2 56	24·1	18·7
Bardsey Island...L'pool	− 3 23	14·4	11·3	Dunkirk.........London	− 1 57	19·0	15·5
Barmouth......Liverpool	− 3 9	16·1	12·8	Eastbourne.......London	− 2 52	22·3	16·8
Barnstaple Bridge....B'tol	− 1 7	13·4	4·6	East Loch Tarbert. G'nock	− 0 5	10·9	9·8
Barrow.........Liverpool	+0 5	28·8	22·0	Exmouth.........London	+4 50	13·1	9·2
Barry Island......Bristol	− 0 25	35·8	26·9	Eyemouth..........Leith	− 0 20	14·9	11·8
Belfast...........London	− 2 48	11·4	9·7	Falmouth.........London	+3 30	17·4	13·7
Berwick...........Leith	− 0 1	15·4	12·4	Ferryside.........Bristol	− 1 0	25·7	19·3
Bideford.........Bristol	− 1 24	19·5	11·9	Filey Bay.........Leith	+1 51	15·5	12·5
Blacktoft...........Hull	+0 38	17·3	11·6	Fishguard......Liverpool	− 4 9	15·5	11·2
Blakeney...........Hull	+0 28	10·2	7·0	Flushing.........London	− 0 37	15·6	12·7
Blyth.............Leith	+0 51	14·8	11·0	Folkestone.......London	− 2 44	22·1	16·5
Boscastle.........Bristol	− 1 39	22·8	17·5	Formby Pt......Liverpool	− 0 21	28·1	22·3
Boulogne.........London	− 2 48	29·1	23·4	Fowey.............London	+3 48	17·7	14·0
Bowling.........Greenock	+0 24	12·3	10·2	Fraserburgh........Leith	− 2 16	11·8	9·2
Brest.............London	+2 25	24·3	18·9	★†Freshwater Bay..London	− 4 33	7·0	5·9
Bridgwater Bar....Bristol	0 0	16·0	6·2	Galway Bay.....Liverpool	+6 15	15·5	11·5
Bridlington.......Leith	+2 4	17·5	13·3	Glasgow........Greenock	+0 27	13·3	10·8
Bridport..........London	+4 32	12·6	8·7	Goole.............Hull	+1 12	18·3	11·9
Brighton..........London	− 2 52	19·2	14·6	Granton Pier......Leith	0 0	17·7	14·3
Buckie............Leith	− 2 54	11·7	9·7	Granville.........London	+4 32	42·0	31·2
Bude Haven......Bristol	− 1 34	22·8	17·5	Grimsby...........Hull	− 0 29	20·6	16·1
Burntisland.......Leith	0 0	17·7	14·3	Hammersmith Bdge. Lond	+0 38	—	—
Calais............London	− 2 25	22·7	18·4	Hartlepool........Leith	+0 59	15·8	12·4
Campbeltown....Greenock	− 0 32	8·9	7·5	Harwich...........London	− 2 18	13·2	11·0
Cape Cornwall.....Bristol	− 2 17	—	—	Hastings..........London	− 2 47	23·0	17·5
Cardiff...........Bristol	− 0 7	37·6	28·0	Haverfordwest...Liverpool	− 4 36	6·9	1·5
Cardigan.......Liverpool	− 4 7	15·5	11·6	Havre, Le........London	− 4 0	25·5	20·9
Carmarthen Bar...Bristol	− 0 39	8·9	3·0	Hestan Islet....Liverpool	+0 25	27·0	20·5
Cayeux...........London	− 3 00	33·0	25·4	Hilbre Island....Liverpool	− 0 20	28·5	21·5
Chatham (N. Lock).London	− 1 4	19·8	16·1	Holyhead.......Liverpool	− 0 54	16·7	12·8
Chepstow.........Bristol	+0 20	—	—	Hook of Holland..London	+0 19	6·7	5·6
Cherbourg.........London	− 6 4	20·3	15·7	★†Hurst Point.....London	− 3 43	7·5	6·1
Chester.........Liverpool	+1 5	13·7	5·5	Ilfracombe.......Bristol	− 1 9	28·3	21·4
Chichester Harbour . Lond	− 2 30	16·2	13·0	Inveraray.......Greenock	+0 11	11·0	10·1
★†Christchurch Hbr...Lond	− 4 58	8·0	6·6	Invergordon......Leith	− 2 41	14·1	10·9
Cobh...........Liverpool	− 5 59	12·0	9·2	Ipswich..........London	− 1 43	13·9	11·1

★ Approximate figures only, owing to abnormality of tides in the area.
† 1st H.W. (Springs).

Port	Diff. h. m.	Springs ft.	Neaps ft.	Port	Diff. h. m.	Springs ft.	Neaps ft.
Itchenor.........*London*	−2 21	16·6	13·1	Ramsgate Harbour..*Lond*	−2 22	16·2	12·6
Kinsale Harbour. *Liverpool*	−6 11	13·1	10·6	Ribble Lt. House...*L'pool*	−0 4	27·0	19·7
Kirkcudbright.. *Liverpool*	+0 15	23·1	18·0	Rosslare Harbour...*L'pool*	−5 29	5·7	4·3
Kirkwall. ......*Leith*	−4 11	8·5	6·2	Rosyth............*Leith*	+0 6	17·7	14·0
Lamlash.......*Greenock*	−0 26	9·1	7·6	R.A. Dock.......*London*	−0 25	23·3	19·4
Lerwick Harbour....*Leith*	−3 46	5·9	4·3	Ryde ....*London*	−2 28	14·9	12·2
Limerick.....*Liverpool*	−4 40	19·3	14·7	St. Helier......*London*	+4 47	36·3	26·7
Littlehampton Bar.*London*	−2 38	16·6	12·9	St. Ives........*Bristol*	−2 9	22·8	17·8
Lizard...........*Bristol*	−2 14	17·4	13·8	St. Malo......*London*	+4 26	39·5	29·6
Llanddwyn Island..*L'pool*	−1 47	14·1	11·0	St. Peter Port...*London*	+4 53	29·4	22·1
Llanelli Bar ......*Bristol*	−0 52	25·5	19·2	Salcombe......*London*	+4 5	17·3	13·6
Loch Long....*Greenock*	−0 5	11·0	9·4	Saltash.........*London*	+4 9	18·3	14·5
Loch Moidart....*Greenock*	+5 49	14·2	10·1	Scarborough....*Leith*	+1 49	16·6	13·0
Londonderry....*London*	−5 41	8·2	6·0	Scheveningen...*London*	−0 28	6·8	5·6
Looe (East).....*London*	+3 50	17·7	13·9	Seaham.......*Leith*	+0 54	14·9	11·6
Lossiemouth.......*Leith*	−2 58	12·0	9·6	Selsey Bill......*London*	−2 33	17·4	13·9
Lowestoft......*London*	−4 26	7·1	5·9	Sennen Cove...*Bristol*	−2 26	20·0	15·7
*Lulworth Cove..*London*	+5 5	—	—	Sharpness......*Bristol*	+0 42	30·4	19·1
Lundy Island......*Bristol*	−1 19	22·8	17·3	Sheerness......*London*	−1 19	18·8	15·6
Lyme Regis....*London*	+4 50	12·7	8·8	Shoreham Harbour..*Lond*	−2 45	18·4	14·2
*†Lymington..*London*	−3 23	8·5	6·9	Silloth.........*Liverpool*	+0 35	31·3	23·7
Lynn Road....*Hull*	+0 4	2·1	17·0	††Southampton...*London*	−2 55	14·9	12·3
Margate Pier....*London*	−2 4	15·4	13·0	Southend.......*London*	−1 29	19·0	15·7
Maryport......*Liverpool*	+0 24	27·0	20·7	Southwold......*London*	−3 51	8·1	7·0
Menai Bridge....*Liverpool*	−0 25	24·3	19·1	Spurn Head....*Hull*	−0 37	20·0	15·5
Mevagissey....*London*	−3 48	17·7	14·0	Stirling........*Leith*	+1 12	8·6	4·2
Middlesbrough....*Leith*	+1 10	17·2	13·5	Stonehaven....*Leith*	−1 6	13·7	10·8
Milford Haven....*Liverpool*	−5 12	23·0	17·2	Stornoway....*Liverpool*	−4 28	14·1	10·5
Minehead Pier.....*Bristol*	No data	34·8	26·0	Stranraer.......*Greenock*	−0 20	9·2	7·5
Montrose.......*Leith*	−0 16	14·8	11·6	Stromness.....*Leith*	−5 22	10·3	7·5
Morecambe.....*Liverpool*	+0 1	28·5	22·3	Sunderland.....*Leith*	+0 52	15·5	12·1
Mostyn Quay....*Liverpool*	−0 10	28·7	22·7	*†Swanage......*London*	−5 18	5·4	4·2
Mull of Galloway.*Gr'nock*	−1 1	—	—	Swansea Bay......*Bristol*	−0 43	29·3	21·8
Newburgh......*Leith*	+0 51	13·6	9·8	Tarn Point.....*Liverpool*	+0 5	26·5	20·3
Newcastle on Tyne..*Leith*	−0 55	15·7	12·0	Tay River Bar....*Leith*	−0 18	15·3	11·9
Newhaven.....*London*	−2 57	21·5	16·9	Tees River Bar....*Leith*	+1 9	16·7	12·9
Newport (Mon.)...*Bristol*	−0 10	39·7	29·7	Teignmouth....*London*	+4 32	15·6	11·8
Newquay.......*Bristol*	−1 59	22·4	17·3	Tenby........*Bristol*	−1 3	25·4	19·0
New Quay (Card.).*L'pool*	−3 41	15·5	11·9	Thurso.......*Leith*	−3 56	14·3	10·6
North Shields....*Leith*	−0 52	14·8	11·3	Tilbury Docks....*London*	−0 59	21·2	17·7
North Sunderland....*Leith*	+0 6	15·2	11·6	Tobermory....*Liverpool*	−5 24	13·3	9·6
Oban........*Greenock*	+5 45	11·3	8·1	Torquay.......*London*	+4 35	14·0	10·0
Orfordness......*London*	−2 51	9·3	8·8	*†Totland Bay....*London*	−3 58	7·4	6·1
Ostend........*London*	−1 33	16·4	13·5	Troon........*Greenock*	−0 20	9·1	7·3
Padstow.......*Bristol*	−1 49	22·3	16·8	Truro........*London*	+3 38	17·4	13·7
Peel (I.O.M.)....*Liverpool*	−0 4	18·0	14·2	Tynemouth Bar....*Leith*	+0 57	15·0	11·2
Pembroke Dock .*Liverpool*	−5 12	23·0	17·2	Ushant.......*London*	+2 20	24·6	19·1
Penzance.......*Bristol*	−2 16	18·4	14·5	Valentia Harbour...*L'pool*	+5 28	11·6	8·7
Peterhead.......*Leith*	−1 56	11·7	9·3	Walton on Naze...*London*	−0 17	13·8	11·4
Plymouth B'water.*London*	+3 54	18·1	14·3	Waterford Hbr..*Liverpool*	−5 46	13·8	11·3
†*Poole (Entrance).*London*	−5 8	5·6	4·3	Weston S. Mare...*Bristol*	−0 25	38·9	29·3
Porlock Bay.....*Bristol*	−0 52	31·6	24·1	Wexford ......*Liverpool*	−5 6	5·7	4·5
Port Carlisle.....*Liverpool*	+0 52	—	—	Whitby.......*Leith*	+1 23	16·0	12·2
Portmadoc....*Liverpool*	−3 8	16·6	13·1	Whiteford Lt. Hse..*Bristol*	−0 55	27·1	20·3
Port Patrick.....*Liverpool*	0 0	12·5	10·0	Whitehaven ....*Liverpool*	+0 2	26·2	20·0
Port Talbot.....*Bristol*	−0 54	29·1	21·9	Wick.............*Leith*	−3 26	10·4	7·6
Porthcawl......*Bristol*	−0 49	29·9	21·8	Wisbech........*Hull*	+0 7	22·6	16·5
Portland Bill......*London*	+4 50	9·7	7·0	Workington ....*Liverpool*	+0 9	26·8	20·4
Portland B'water..*London*	+5 5	7·0	4·5	Worthing ......*London*	−2 38	18·2	14·2
Portsmouth......*London*	−2 28	15·4	12·5	Yarmouth Roads..*London*	−5 1	7·1	5·8
Preston........*Liverpool*	0 0	27·3	21·0	*††Yarmth (I.O.W.)..*Lond*	−2 58	8·4	6·5
Pwllheli........*Liverpool*	−3 18	16·2	12·3	Ymuiden.......*London*	+1 13	6·9	5·5
Ramsey (I.O.M.)...*L'pool*	+0 4	22·8	18·0	Youghal........*Liverpool*	−5 53	12·9	10·4

* Approximate figures only, owing to abnormality of tides in area. † 1st H.W. (Springs). †† 1st H.W. — No data available

The Standard Ports referred to in the heading are given in italic.

EXAMPLE.—Required times of high water at Stranraer on January 16, 1972:—

(a) *Morning Tide.*

Appropriate time of high water at *Greenock*	0054 hrs. (Jan. 16)
Tidal difference.........	−0020 hrs.
H.W. at *Stranraer* ...	0034 hrs.

(b) *Afternoon Tide.*

Appropriate time of high water at *Greenock*.....	1315 hrs. (Jan. 16)
Tidal difference.........	−0020 hrs.
H.W. at *Stranraer* ...	1255 hrs.

JANUARY, 1972

High Water at the undermentioned Places (C.E.T.★)—

Day of Month	Day of Week	LONDON BRIDGE †Datum of Predictions 10.50 ft. below Mn.	Ht.	Aft.	Ht.	LIVERPOOL †Datum of Predictions 14.54 ft. below Mn.	Ht.	Aft.	Ht.	BRISTOL (Avonmouth) †Datum of Predictions 20.11 ft. below Mn.	Ht.	Aft.	Ht.	HULL (Salend) †Datum of Predictions 10.68 ft. below Mn.	Ht.	Aft.	Ht.	GREENOCK †Datum of Predictions 4.80 ft. below Mn.	Ht.	Aft.	Ht.	LEITH AND GRANTON †Datum of Predictions 8.92 ft. below Mn.	Ht.	Aft.	Ht.	DUN LAOGHAIRE †Datum of Predictions 1.43 ft. above Mn.	Ht.	Aft.	Ht.
1	S	243	20.9	15 6	22.3	—	—	1221	28.4	821	41.1	2048	41.2	717	21.0	1929	21.5	121	10.5	1313	11.4	326	17.4	1555	17.5	010	11.9	1228	12.7
2	S	326	21.2	1550	22.6	046	27.8	13 5	28.6	9 6	41.7	2133	41.3	8 6	21.1	2012	21.6	213	10.5	14 0	11.8	415	17.6	1630	17.7	057	11.9	1313	12.9
3	M	4 6	21.8	1633	22.7	130	27.6	1346	28.6	948	41.8	2213	40.8	850	20.8	2051	21.5	3 1	10.4	1445	12.1	5 0	17.5	17 5	17.5	144	11.7	1359	12.9
4	Tu	444	21.8	1712	22.4	212	27.2	1427	28.0	1026	41.2	2250	39.7	930	20.4	2126	21.1	344	10.3	1527	12.2	542	17.1	18 1	17.1	229	11.4	1445	12.7
5	W	521	21.7	1751	21.9	253	26.4	15 5	27.4	11 2	40.0	2325	38.2	424	10.2	2159	20.7	424	10.2	16 7	12.0	624	16.6	1843	16.4	313	11.0	1531	12.3
6	Th	556	21.9	1829	21.4	333	25.5	1544	26.2	1135	38.4	2358	36.4	1041	19.0	2232	20.0	5 1	9.9	1646	11.6	7 5	15.6	1926	15.1	358	10.6	1615	11.8
7	F	631	20.7	19 9	20.4	413	24.6	1624	24.9	—	—	12 8	36.5	1116	18.1	23 8	19.2	538	9.7	1727	11.0	747	14.8	20 8	15.1	445	10.1	17 3	11.1
8	S	713	20.0	1956	19.7	456	23.3	17 8	23.5	031	34.5	1243	34.4	1157	17.3	2354	18.1	618	9.4	1812	10.3	831	14.2	2052	14.5	536	9.7	1755	10.4
9	S	8 8	19.2	2051	19.1	545	22.3	1758	22.3	1 3	33.6	1326	32.4	—	—	12 4	16.6	7 2	9.1	19 3	9.7	919	13.8	2142	14.0	635	9.4	1857	9.9
10	M	913	18.7	2151	18.9	644	21.6	19 7	21.5	159	31.1	1423	30.9	048	17.1	1353	16.3	759	8.9	20 3	9.4	1014	13.7	2241	13.8	739	9.6	20 3	9.7
11	Tu	1018	18.5	2249	18.9	753	21.6	2029	21.5	3 5	30.4	1535	30.4	2 3	16.3	15 7	16.2	9 0	8.9	21 3	9.4	1118	13.7	2350	13.8	839	9.6	2159	9.8
12	W	1120	18.7	2347	19.1	9 1	21.3	2130	22.3	420	30.9	1652	31.4	328	16.3	1611	17.0	1018	9.0	2213	9.4	—	—	1227	14.1	931	10.1	2159	10.1
13	Th	—	—	1223	19.1	959	23.6	2216	23.3	535	32.8	18 0	33.5	438	17.4	1714	18.0	1112	9.2	2311	9.6	057	14.1	1323	14.6	1017	10.7	2245	10.5
14	F	047	19.6	1323	19.9	1047	25.0	2310	24.7	635	35.3	1859	36.5	537	19.0	1758	19.0	1156	10.0	—	—	154	14.1	1414	15.3	1058	11.2	2327	10.9
15	S	141	20.4	1412	20.9	1129	26.4	—	—	727	37.8	1948	38.3	627	19.8	1834	20.0	0 5	9.7	1236	10.3	244	15.5	1450	16.8	1136	11.8	—	—
16	S	229	21.2	1457	22.0	011	27.0	1211	27.7	811	39.9	2031	40.2	712	19.8	1913	20.8	054	9.8	1315	10.8	328	16.3	1538	16.8	0 7	11.2	1215	12.2
17	M	313	22.0	1540	22.8	031	27.7	1250	28.5	853	41.5	2113	41.6	753	20.5	1952	21.5	140	9.9	1354	11.4	4 7	17.0	1616	17.8	046	11.5	1253	12.6
18	Tu	353	22.7	1620	23.4	111	28.0	1326	29.5	933	42.6	2154	42.4	833	21.0	2029	22.1	226	10.0	1434	11.4	444	17.4	1653	17.8	126	11.6	1334	12.6
19	W	431	23.0	17 0	23.4	151	28.1	14 6	29.8	1014	43.0	2235	42.4	911	21.1	21 7	22.4	3 9	10.2	1515	11.7	522	17.5	1733	17.7	2 6	11.7	1415	13.0
20	Th	5 6	22.9	1739	23.1	229	28.0	1446	29.7	1054	42.8	2315	41.7	948	21.0	2146	22.4	352	10.5	1557	12.0	6 2	17.2	1816	17.8	249	11.7	1459	13.1
21	F	541	22.7	1819	22.4	3 6	27.3	1526	29.0	1133	41.7	2352	40.3	1028	20.5	2227	22.1	433	10.8	1640	12.0	647	16.7	19 3	17.1	335	11.5	1546	12.9
22	S	619	22.4	19 2	21.5	350	26.7	16 3	27.9	—	—	1252	37.6	11 5	19.7	2312	21.3	512	10.9	1725	11.7	735	16.5	1952	16.9	423	11.2	1637	12.4
23	S	7 3	22.0	1953	20.6	444	25.5	17 5	26.4	031	38.2	1346	35.1	1157	18.8	—	—	553	10.7	1815	11.1	827	15.5	2045	16.2	520	10.8	1737	11.8
24	M	757	21.2	2057	19.7	541	24.2	18 7	24.7	116	35.8	1452	33.4	0 5	20.1	1256	17.8	637	9.9	1914	10.4	925	15.0	2145	15.6	626	10.4	1848	11.1
25	Tu	9 7	20.4	2213	19.2	654	23.3	1928	23.7	218	33.7	15 1	33.6	113	18.8	1412	17.3	731	9.8	2032	9.7	1034	14.2	23 2	15.2	740	10.3	20 7	10.7
26	W	1031	19.9	2330	19.1	815	23.3	2054	23.7	341	33.0	1633	33.6	248	18.0	1533	17.5	848	9.6	2327	9.4	1151	14.8	—	—	852	10.5	2123	10.7
27	Th	1158	20.0	—	—	934	24.4	22 7	24.7	511	34.4	1750	35.5	411	18.6	1645	18.3	1017	9.6	—	—	024	15.3	13 4	15.3	955	11.0	2228	11.0
28	F	043	19.5	1312	20.6	1037	25.6	23 5	25.8	627	36.5	19 3	37.8	524	19.9	1745	19.5	1125	10.0	1219	10.7	135	15.8	1458	16.8	1051	11.5	2324	11.2
29	S	143	20.1	1410	21.3	1128	27.0	2353	26.7	727	38.9	1956	39.7	624	19.9	1836	20.5	0 9	9.8	1310	11.3	233	16.5	1543	17.3	1139	12.1	—	—
30	S	232	20.7	1457	21.8	—	—	1215	28.0	815	40.7	2039	40.9	713	20.6	1920	21.2	1 3	10.1	13 7	11.6	323	17.0	1623	17.6	010	11.4	1223	12.4
31	M	313	21.8	1538	22.1	035	27.4	1251	28.6	856	41.5	2118	41.5	755	21.0	1958	21.6	2 8	10.1	1354	11.6	4 7	17.3	1623	17.6	051	11.5	13 4	12.7

★ All times shown are Central European Time; to obtain Greenwich Mean Time, subtract one hour.   † Difference of height in feet from Ordnance Datum (Newlyn).   † Difference of height in feet from ... Ordnance Datum (Dublin).

FEBRUARY, 1972

High Water at the undermentioned Places (C.E.T.*)—

Day of Month	Day of Week	LONDON BRIDGE † Datum 10·50 ft. below				LIVERPOOL † Datum 14·54 ft. below				BRISTOL (Avonmouth) † Datum 20·11 ft. below				HULL (Saltend) † Datum 10·68 ft. below				GREENOCK † Datum 4·80 ft. below				LEITH§ AND GRANTON † Datum 8·92 ft. below				DUN LAOGHAIRE ‡ Datum 1·43 ft. above			
		Mn. h.m.	Ht. ft.	Aft. h.m.	Ht. ft.	Mn. h.m.	Ht. ft.	Aft. h.m.	Ht. ft.	Mn. h.m.	Ht. ft.	Aft. h.m.	Ht. ft.	Mn. h.m.	Ht. ft.	Aft. h.m.	Ht. ft.	Mn. h.m.	Ht. ft.	Aft. h.m.	Ht. ft.	Mn. h.m.	Ht. ft.	Aft. h.m.	Ht. ft.	Mn. h.m.	Ht. ft.	Aft. h.m.	Ht. ft.
1	Tu	350	21·7	1615	22·2	114	27·7	1328	28·8	932	42·2	2153	41·4	832	21·0	2031	21·8	249	10·2	1433	11·9	444	17·3	1659	17·6	130	11·4	1344	12·7
2	W	424	22·0	1651	22·1	151	27·6	14 3	28·6	10 5	41·9	2226	40·8	9 5	20·7	2111	21·7	327	10·2	1512	12·0	519	17·0	1735	17·3	2 5	11·3	1421	12·6
3	Th	457	22·1	1724	21·9	225	27·2	1436	28·0	1038	41·1	2254	39·7	935	20·4	2130	21·4	4 0	10·2	1546	11·9	553	16·4	1810	16·7	240	11·1	1459	12·2
4	F	528	22·0	1757	21·6	257	26·5	15 7	27·0	11 3	39·8	2320	38·2	10 4	19·8	2159	20·8	430	10·1	1619	11·6	627	15·8	1846	16·1	317	10·7	1537	11·7
5	S	6 1	21·7	1832	21·2	329	25·5	1538	25·7	1138	38·0	2345	36·3	1033	19·1	2231	20·0	5 0	10·0	1653	11·1	7 2	15·1	1922	15·5	355	10·3	1615	11·0
6	S	639	21·1	1912	20·5	4 3	24·3	1612	24·2	1155	35·8	—	—	11 1	18·1	23 8	18·7	530	9·9	1731	10·5	739	14·5	20 0	14·8	435	9·7	1657	10·3
7	M	726	20·1	1958	19·6	442	23·0	1657	22·8	013	34·1	1227	33·3	1140	17·0	2354	17·2	647	9·6	1815	9·9	820	13·9	2044	13·9	522	9·5	1749	9·6
8	Tu	820	19·0	2053	18·6	534	21·8	1756	21·2	050	31·9	1312	31·0	—	—	1239	15·9	647	9·3	1917	9·4	910	13·5	2143	13·3	624	9·2	1849	9·2
9	W	922	18·0	2154	17·8	643	21·0	1916	20·5	140	30·0	1419	29·3	0 1	15·8	1357	15·3	742	9·0	20 8	9·1	1015	13·3	23 1	13·1	737	9·6	2020	9·1
10	Th	1028	17·4	23 0	17·6	8 6	21·1	2047	21·0	3 8	29·3	1554	29·4	243	15·2	1547	15·7	858	8·9	2246	9·2	1137	13·3	—	—	847	9·6	2128	9·6
11	F	1142	17·6	—	—	923	22·5	2158	22·6	447	30·8	1727	31·8	518	17·3	1726	18·3	1032	9·2	—	—	026	13·4	1253	13·9	945	10·2	2223	10·8
12	S	015	18·2	1257	18·8	1021	24·4	2249	24·5	6 7	33·9	1837	35·2	652	20·0	1853	20·9	1132	9·7	2351	9·5	133	14·2	1351	14·9	1031	11·3	23 8	10·8
13	S	129	19·5	1351	20·1	11 6	26·4	2331	26·2	7 5	37·4	2013	39·5	732	21·2	1933	22·4	—	—	1216	10·3	225	15·3	1438	15·9	1115	11·7	2347	11·4
14	M	2 9	21·2	1437	—	1147	28·2	—	—	754	40·4	2031	43·2	8 9	22·6	2011	23·6	041	9·7	1257	10·8	3 9	16·3	1518	17·0	1154	12·3	—	—
15	Tu	252	22·6	1519	23·3	011	27·7	1226	29·6	834	42·7	2054	44·3	848	22·1	2049	23·6	126	9·7	1338	11·3	347	17·2	1555	17·9	026	11·8	1232	12·9
16	W	333	23·5	16 0	23·9	051	28·8	13 7	30·7	956	44·3	2135	44·4	925	22·0	2128	23·5	211	10·1	1421	11·7	422	17·8	1631	18·5	1 3	12·1	1312	13·3
17	Th	4 9	24·0	1639	24·0	132	29·4	1347	31·1	937	45·3	2216	44·7	10 3	21·4	22 8	22·8	253	10·5	15 3	12·1	459	18·0	1711	18·7	143	12·1	1353	13·5
18	F	445	24·1	1718	23·8	213	29·5	1427	30·8	1031	45·0	2255	44·0	1042	20·4	2246	21·8	333	10·8	1544	12·3	539	17·8	1755	18·5	223	12·4	1437	13·4
19	S	521	23·8	1758	22·4	250	28·9	15 7	29·8	1114	43·7	2332	42·1	1127	19·1	2346	19·8	410	11·2	1625	12·3	623	17·2	1841	18·0	3 7	12·2	1533	13·1
20	S	6 1	23·2	1840	22·4	331	27·7	1550	28·2	1150	42·1	—	—	057	18·0	1341	16·5	447	11·3	17 6	12·4	710	16·5	1930	17·1	355	11·6	1615	12·4
21	M	647	22·3	1929	20·1	417	26·0	1641	26·0	0 6	39·2	1227	37·9	237	17·0	1516	16·5	524	11·1	1756	11·5	811	15·9	2024	16·1	450	11·5	1715	11·5
22	Tu	741	21·1	2029	19·3	514	24·2	1747	23·8	046	35·9	1315	34·3	412	17·4	1635	17·5	6 6	10·5	1851	10·6	9 0	14·8	2130	15·1	557	10·4	1830	10·6
23	W	848	20·0	2143	18·3	626	22·6	1912	22·4	142	32·8	1431	31·6	524	18·5	1735	18·9	656	9·8	20 0	9·2	1013	14·2	2254	14·5	716	10·0	1958	10·1
24	Th	1011	19·2	23 3	18·3	755	22·3	2048	22·8	312	31·1	1617	31·1	614	19·9	1822	20·1	8 7	9·1	2215	9·1	1141	14·3	—	—	837	10·7	2122	10·6
25	F	1140	19·3	—	—	927	23·4	22 4	23·9	459	32·1	1750	34·0	656	20·4	19 1	20·0	947	9·5	2338	9·1	023	14·8	13 0	15·8	947	10·7	2228	10·6
26	S	021	18·9	1257	20·2	1030	25·1	2258	25·4	620	35·6	1854	37·0	732	20·9	1934	21·5	1125	9·7	—	—	1325	15·5	14 0	15·8	1044	11·4	2331	11·0
27	S	124	20·1	1353	21·3	1118	26·7	2341	26·6	717	38·6	1943	39·4					030	9·5	1238	10·3	227	16·2	1449	16·6	1131	11·9	—	—
28	M	212	21·1	1439	22·0	1157	27·8	—	—	8 1	40·6	2022	40·8					119	9·8	1257	10·4	311	16·7	1529	17·1	011	11·3	1211	12·3
29	Tu	252	21·8	1518	22·3	018	27·4	1232	28·5	837	41·7	2055	41·5	732	20·9	1934	21·5	150	10·0	1337	11·3	349	17·0	16 4	17·4	035	11·4	1247	12·5

* All times shown are Central European Time: to obtain Greenwich Mean Time, subtract one hour. † Difference of height in feet from Ordnance Datum (Newlyn). ‡ Difference of height in feet from Ordnance Datum (Ireland). (*See notes, p. 184.*) § *See note, p. 175.*

F*

MARCH, 1972

High Water at the undermentioned Places (C.E.T.*)—

Day of Month	Day of Week	LONDON BRIDGE † Datum of Predictions 10·50 ft. below Mn. h.m.	Ht. ft.	Aft. h.m.	Ht. ft.	LIVERPOOL † Datum of Predictions 14·54 ft. below Mn. h.m.	Ht. ft.	Aft. h.m.	Ht. ft.	BRISTOL (Avonmouth) † Datum of Predictions 20·11 ft. below Mn. h.m.	Ht. ft.	Aft. h.m.	Ht. ft.	HULL (Saltend) † Datum of Predictions 10·68 ft. below Mn. h.m.	Ht. ft.	Aft. h.m.	Ht. ft.	GREENOCK † Datum of Predictions 4·80 ft. below Mn. h.m.	Ht. ft.	Aft. h.m.	Ht. ft.	LEITH§ AND GRANTON † Datum of Predictions 8·92 ft. below Mn. h.m.	Ht. ft.	Aft. h.m.	Ht. ft.	DUN LAOGHAIRE † 1·43 ft. above Mn. h.m.	Ht. ft.	Aft. h.m.	Ht. ft.
1	W	3 28	22·3	15 53	22·4	0 52	27·8	13 5	28·7	9 8	42·1	21 26	41·6	8 4	21·1	20 4	21·7	2 26	10·0	14 15	11·5	4 21	17·0	16 35	17·4	1 6	11·4	13 21	12·5
2	Th	4 31	22·5	16 25	22·3	1 24	27·9	13 35	28·6	9 38	41·9	21 55	41·3	8 34	21·9	20 32	21·7	2 59	10·1	14 49	11·5	4 51	16·8	17 5	17·2	1 37	11·3	13 55	12·3
3	F	5 0	22·4	16 54	22·1	1 54	27·7	14 4	28·0	10 5	41·2	22 21	40·3	9 1	21·9	20 59	21·5	3 29	10·1	15 19	11·4	5 19	16·5	17 30	16·8	2 6	11·2	14 27	11·9
4	S	5 33	22·1	17 23	22·0	2 22	27·1	14 31	27·2	10 29	40·0	22 44	39·0	9 28	20·4	21 28	20·5	3 55	10·2	15 48	11·1	5 49	15·9	18 0	16·2	2 38	11·0	15 0	11·4
5	S	6 9	21·6	17 55	21·1	2 49	26·2	14 58	26·0	10 51	38·3	23 5	37·2	9 54	19·7	21 59	20·0	4 20	10·2	16 19	10·8	6 21	15·4	18 42	15·5	3 11	10·7	15 35	10·8
6	M	6 50	20·6	19 11	20·1	3 19	25·1	15 29	24·5	11 14	36·2	23 29	35·0	10 23	18·8	22 33	18·7	4 47	10·1	16 54	10·3	6 55	14·8	19 19	14·7	3 49	10·3	16 14	10·2
7	Tu	7 34	19·4	19 56	18·8	3 54	23·8	16 10	22·9	11 43	33·8			10 56	17·7	23 16	17·2	5 20	9·9	17 36	9·6	7 33	14·1	20 3	13·9	4 33	9·8	17 3	9·6
8	W	8 25	18·2	20 50	17·6	4 43	22·4	17 7	21·4	0 2	32·7	12 23	31·4	11 39	16·4			5 59	9·6	18 25	9·4	8 21	13·5	21 1	13·2	5 30	9·4	18 10	9·0
9	Th	9 28	17·3	22 0	17·0	5 49	21·2	18 28	20·4	0 52	30·5	13 26	29·3	0 17	15·6	12 45	15·4	6 48	9·6	19 36	9·0	9 27	13·0	22 25	12·8	6 41	9·2	19 36	8·9
10	F	10 53	17·2	23 34	17·5	7 14	21·0	20 5	20·7	2 12	29·1	15 3	28·9	1 18	14·8	14 24	15·4	7 50	8·9	20 34	8·8	10 52	13·0	23 55	13·2	8 4	9·4	20 56	9·4
11	S			12 22	18·5	8 42	22·3	21 26	22·4	4 3	30·1	16 53	31·4	3 40	15·5	15 50	16·4	9 37	8·9	22 23	8·9			12 20	13·6	9 8	10·1	21 55	10·1
12	S	0 47	19·3	13 21	20·6	9 48	24·3	22 21	24·6	5 35	33·6	18 8	35·3	4 48	17·1	16 51	18·1	11 11	9·5	23 31	9·3	1 4	14·1	13 20	14·7	10 1	10·9	22 41	10·6
13	M	1 38	21·2	14 4	22·4	10 37	26·6	23 4	26·7	6 37	37·5	19 2	39·0	5 39	18·8	17 41	20·0	0 18	9·7	12 33	9·9	1 57	15·3	14 9	16·0	10 46	11·5	23 22	11·6
14	Tu	2 22	22·9	14 52	23·6	11 20	28·6	23 45	28·4	7 25	40·0	19 47	41·5	6 24	20·4	18 25	21·5	1 11	9·9	13 14	10·5	2 41	16·4	14 50	17·2	11 27	12·5	23 59	12·7
15	W	3 2	24·1	15 33	24·6			12 0	30·2	8 8	43·3	20 28	43·9	7 4	21·6	19 7	22·9	1 44	10·1	13 55	10·7	3 19	17·3	15 28	18·2			12 7	13·1
16	Th	3 40	24·7	16 13	24·0	0 26	29·6	12 43	31·5	8 50	45·0	21 8	45·4	7 43	22·4	19 47	23·7	2 41	10·7	14 50	11·0	3 55	18·0	16 5	18·9	0 36	12·5	12 47	13·5
17	F	4 19	24·8	16 53	24·5	1 7	30·2	13 24	31·5	9 33	45·8	21 53	45·4	8 21	22·6	20 27	24·0	3 19	10·7	15 28	11·2	4 33	18·3	16 47	19·1	1 14	12·6	13 30	13·6
18	S					1 48	30·1	14 6	31·0	10 14	45·5	22 33	44·6	8 59	22·4	21 8	23·7	3 55	10·8	16 5	11·1	5 14	18·1	17 32	18·8	1 56	12·6	14 15	13·4
19	S	5 1	24·5	17 34	22·5	2 28	29·6	14 48	29·6	10 53	43·9	23 10	42·4	9 37	21·7	21 51	22·7	3 43	11·4	16 8	12·0	6 0	17·5	18 21	18·0	2 41	12·4	15 4	12·9
20	M	5 46	23·7	18 19	22·3	3 10	28·0	15 33	27·7	11 31	41·0	23 45	39·3	10 16	20·6	22 38	21·2	4 19	11·5	16 52	12·1	6 49	16·6	19 14	17·0	3 31	11·9	15 8	12·1
21	Tu	6 35	22·4	19 0	21·9	3 56	26·1	16 26	25·3			12 9	37·3	11 0	19·2	23 34	19·2	4 58	11·3	17 40	11·9	7 42	15·6	20 12	15·8	4 26	11·3	17 1	11·1
22	W	7 31	21·0	19 57	18·9	4 51	24·1	17 34	23·1	0 26	35·6	12 58	33·5	11 56	17·5			5 40	10·7	18 35	11·0	8 42	14·7	21 21	14·7	5 34	10·6	18 19	10·2
23	Th	8 37	19·9	21 15	18·2	6 9	22·5	19 3	21·9	1 23	31·5	14 15	30·7	0 51	17·3	13 17	16·2	6 31	9·9	19 54	10·3	9 58	14·0	22 47	14·3	6 56	10·2	19 51	9·8
24	F	9 52	18·9	22 31	18·0	7 44	22·1	20 38	22·3	2 53	30·6	16 1	30·7	2 31	16·5	14 55	16·1	7 38	9·9	20 54	8·4			11 50	14·0	8 20	10·2	21 14	10·1
25	S	11 15	19·0	23 51	19·0	9 12	23·1	21 50	23·7	4 41	32·0	17 30	33·3	3 59	17·0	16 14	17·1	9 5	8·8	22 21	8·3	0 11	14·7	12 44	14·8	9 30	10·7	22 16	10·5
26	S			12 31	19·9	10 14	24·0	22 40	25·2	5 59	35·1	18 32	36·8	5 2	18·1	17 11	18·9	10 11	9·4	23 28	8·9	1 2	15·6	13 43	15·6	10 26	11·3	23 3	10·9
27	M	0 54	20·2	13 27	21·4	10 58	26·4	23 19	26·4	6 53	38·0	19 17	38·8	5 49	19·1	17 55	19·6	11 1	9·4			2 6	16·3	14 26	16·3	11 12	11·6	23 39	11·2
28	Tu	1 44	21·5	14 17	22·4	11 34	27·3	23 57	27·2	7 35	39·9	19 54	40·8	6 28	20·0	18 31	20·4	0 1	9·3	11 54	10·0	2 48	16·4	15 5	16·8	11 50	12·0		
29	W	2 26	22·4	14 51	22·8			12 6	28·0	8 9	40·8	20 26	40·8	7 0	20·5	19 4	20·6	0 47	9·6	12 34	10·5	3 26	16·7	15 37	17·0	0 11	11·3	12 24	12·1
30	Th	3 2	22·8	15 26	22·9	0 24	27·8	12 37	28·0	8 40	40·8	20 56	40·5	7 32	20·9	19 33	21·2	1 21	9·8	13 12	10·9	3 52	16·7	16 36	17·1	0 37	11·4	12 54	12·1
31	F	3 35	22·8	15 56	22·5	0 54	27·8	13 6	27·9	9 8	40·9	21 24	40·8	8 0	21·0	20 3	21·2	1 54	9·9	13 48	11·0	4 14	16·9	16 35	16·9	1 4	11·4	13 26	11·8

* All times shown are Central European Time = British Summer Time, in force from March 19 (0200 hrs G.M.T.) to October 29 (0200 hrs) G.M.T., 1972. To obtain Greenwich Mean Time, subtract one hour. † Difference of height in feet from Ordnance Datum. (*See notes*, p.184.) § *See note*, p. 175.

APRIL, 1972

High Water at the undermentioned Places (C.E.T.*)—

Day of Month	Day of Week	LONDON BRIDGE † Datum of Predictions 10·50 ft. below				LIVERPOOL † Datum of Predictions 14·54 ft. below				BRISTOL (Avonmouth) † Datum of Predictions 20·11 ft. below				HULL (Salend) † Datum of Predictions 10·68 ft. below				GREENOCK † Datum of Predictions 4·80 ft. below				LEITH AND GRANTON § Datum of Predictions 8·92 ft. below				DUN LAOGHAIRE † Datum of Predictions 1·43 ft. above			
		Mn. h.m.	Ht. ft.	Aft. h.m.	Ht. ft.	Mn. h.m.	Ht. ft.	Aft. h.m.	Ht. ft.	Mn. h.m.	Ht. ft.	Aft. h.m.	Ht. ft.	Mn. h.m.	Ht. ft.	Aft. h.m.	Ht. ft.	Mn. h.m.	Ht. ft.	Aft. h.m.	Ht. ft.	Mn. h.m.	Ht. ft.	Aft. h.m.	Ht. ft.	Mn. h.m.	Ht. ft.	Aft. h.m.	Ht. ft.
1	S	4 5	22·6	16 22	22·3	1 23	27·6	13 34	27·5	9 34	40·4	21 49	40·1	8 28	20·9	20 33	20·9	2 53	10·0	14 49	10·7	4 46	16·4	17 5	16·6	1 33	11·3	13 56	11·5
2	S	4 33	22·3	16 49	22·2	1 50	27·2	14 1	26·7	9 58	39·4	22 13	38·9	8 54	20·5	21 3	20·4	3 18	10·1	15 17	10·5	5 15	16·1	17 38	16·0	2 3	11·2	14 30	11·5
3	M	5 5	22·0	17 19	21·9	2 17	26·5	14 28	25·8	10 20	37·9	22 33	37·2	9 20	19·9	21 35	19·8	3 42	10·2	15 47	10·4	5 40	15·6	18 12	15·5	2 38	10·9	15 5	10·6
4	Tu	5 41	21·5	17 54	21·4	2 47	25·6	15 1	24·5	10 44	36·0	22 59	35·3	9 47	19·2	22 10	18·4	4 9	10·2	16 23	10·0	6 21	15·0	18 51	14·8	3 16	10·6	15 47	10·1
5	W	6 19	20·9	18 32	20·6	3 23	24·4	15 43	23·1	11 15	33·8	23 34	33·2	10 19	18·3	22 53	17·1	4 43	10·1	17 6	9·7	7 0	14·8	19 38	14·0	4 1	10·2	16 36	9·6
6	Th	7 2	20·0	19 13	19·5	4 11	23·1	16 40	21·7	11 57	31·7			11 0	17·2			5 23	9·9	17 56	9·3	7 50	13·8	20 40	13·3	4 54	9·6	17 40	9·2
7	F	7 48	19·1	20 3	18·5	5 15	21·7	17 57	20·9	0 24	33·3	13 1	30·1	0 4	15·9	12 0	16·3	6 11	9·5	18 51	9·0	8 55	13·3	21 55	13·0	6 0	9·6	18 59	9·1
8	S	8 48	18·3	21 9	17·7	6 35	21·8	19 26	21·2	1 41	30·1	14 35	29·8	2 56	15·6	16 10	18·4	7 8	9·1	19 59	8·7	10 14	13·3	23 16	13·4	7 15	9·7	20 19	9·5
9	S	10 10	18·1	22 39	18·0	8 8	22·9	20 45	22·8	3 25	31·0	16 16	32·2	4 7	17·1	17 15	20·2	8 38	9·0	21 49	8·8	11 45	13·9			8 26	10·3	21 21	10·2
10	M	11 40	19·3			9 26	24·6	21 56	24·9	4 56	34·2	17 32	35·9	5 49	20·4	17 53	22·9	10 20	9·5	23 44	9·3	0 24	14·3	12 38	14·9	9 25	11·1	22 51	11·7
11	Tu	0 2	19·6	12 45	21·2	10 21	26·8	22 50	26·7	6 3	37·8	18 27	39·3	6 33	21·6	19 22	24·5	11 15	10·0			1 5	15·3	14 16	17·3	10 14	11·8	23 29	13·0
12	W	1 0	21·0	13 37	22·8	11 4	28·7	23 36	28·6	6 58	40·9	19 15	41·6	7 14	22·5	19 22	25·2	0 8	10·1	12 2	10·7	2 5	16·5	14 57	18·8	11 39	13·0		
13	Th	1 48	23·1	14 22	23·6	11 43	30·1			7 38	43·0	19 58	43·6	7 54	22·5	20 52	23·0	0 56	10·4	12 43	10·8	3 25	18·0	15 39	19·6	0 48	12·6	12 22	13·3
14	F	2 31	24·2	15 5	23·9	0 43	30·3	12 30	30·8	8 16	44·4	20 44	44·5	8 34	22·5	21 39	23·0	1 45	10·8	13 25	10·9	4 18	18·3	16 25	19·6	1 39	13·7	13 7	13·3
15	S	3 14	24·9	15 47	23·8	1 26	30·0	13 9	30·9	8 52	44·6	21 28	44·7	9 57	21·7	21 39	23·0	2 19	11·2	13 7	13·7	4 51	18·0	17 14	19·6	2 19	12·5	13 57	13·0
16	S	3 58	24·9	16 29	23·3	2 9	29·3	13 49	30·1	9 28	44·1	22 11	43·8	10 43	22·5	21 39	20·4	3 15	10·9	15 18	17·4	5 39	17·5	18 6	18·7	3 11	12·1	14 49	12·4
17	M	4 44	24·8	17 14	22·7	2 54	27·9	14 33	28·8	10 3	43·0	22 52	41·9	12 17	21·7	21 39	18·7	4 51	11·5	16 24	17·6	6 31	17·3	19 0	17·8	4 9	11·5	15 47	11·8
18	Tu	5 34	23·8	18 2	21·7	3 42	26·2	15 22	26·9	10 35	43·0	23 32	39·0	9 57	21·7	21 39	17·8	4 51	10·8	17 14	17·6	6 31	16·7	20 3	16·8	5 16	10·9	16 50	10·8
19	W	6 27	22·6	18 53	20·6	4 34	24·4	16 18	24·9	11 17	40·2			10 43	19·3	21 39	16·7	5 39	11·2	18 6	16·8	7 20	15·7	20 57	15·7	4 9	11·0	16 50	10·8
20	Th	7 23	21·2	19 47	19·5	5 54	23·0	18 46	22·1	0 16	35·8	12 52	33·6	0 42	17·2	12 52	16·6	6 31	10·0	19 46	8·2	8 28	14·8	22 25	14·4	6 34	10·5	19 33	9·8
21	F	8 23	19·8	20 48	18·6	7 19	22·6	20 10	22·4	1 13	33·0	14 3	31·3	2 5	16·4	14 18	16·3	7 18	9·2	21 52	8·2	9 38	14·3	23 40	14·6	7 54	10·5	20 49	10·0
22	S	9 23	18·9	21 56	18·2	8 40	23·1	21 18	23·8	2 33	31·5	15 32	31·1	3 24	16·6	16 34	16·9	9 9	8·8	23 40	8·6	10 57	14·2	23 40	14·0	9 3	10·8	21 47	10·4
23	S	10 43	18·9	23 11	18·7	9 41	24·5	22 18	24·8	4 4	32·3	16 52	33·0	4 24	17·3	17 53	18·3	10 30	9·1			0 42	15·1	13 9	14·3	9 58	11·4	22 32	10·8
24	M	11 56	19·9			10 27	25·9	22 48	25·8	5 25	34·5	17 53	35·5	5 12	18·3	17 17	19·6	0 45	9·4	12 58	10·0	1 23	15·6	13 55	15·2	10 44	11·4	23 9	11·0
25	Tu	0 18	19·9	12 54	21·2	11 7	26·8	23 22	26·6	6 14	36·8	18 40	37·5	5 51	18·3	17 17	19·6	1 19	9·5	13 33	10·2	2 43	15·9	14 33	16·2	11 26	11·5	23 39	11·0
26	W	1 11	21·3	13 41	22·3	11 41	26·8	23 53	27·0	6 58	38·3	19 19	38·8	6 25	19·9	18 31	20·1	0 45	9·6	14 58	16·4	2 47	16·0	15 37	16·5	11 55	11·5		
27	Th	1 55	22·3	14 21	22·8			12 8	26·9	7 34	39·1	19 53	39·4	6 58	20·4	19 38	20·3	0 45	9·4	13 14	16·5	3 47	16·3	16 34	16·5	0 34	11·3	12 27	11·4
28	F	2 34	22·7	14 55	22·8	0 24	27·2	12 30	26·9	8 7	39·4	20 25	39·8	7 29	20·4	19 38	20·8	1 49	9·7	13 47	16·3	4 16	16·5	16 58	16·5	0 34	11·4	12 58	11·2
29	S	3 8	22·6	15 24	22·5	0 55	27·3	13 0	26·6	8 38	39·4	20 54	39·8	7 29	20·3	20 38	20·4	1 49	10·1	16 18	16·5	23 9				0 34	11·4	12 58	11·2
30	S	3 39	22·3	15 51	22·3			13 0	26·6	9 7	39·1	21 23	39·4	7 58	20·5	20 38	20·1	4 16	16·3	16 34	16·4			23 39		1	11·0	13 31	11·0

* All times shown are Central European Time = British Summer Time. To obtain Greenwich Mean Time, subtract one hour.
† Datum of Predictions from Ordnance Datum. Difference of height in feet from Ordnance Datum. (See notes, p. 184.) § To obtain depth of water over the sill at the entrance to the Imperial Dock, Leith, the constant of 12·60 ft. should be added to the above predictions.

MAY, 1972

High Water at the undermentioned Places (C.E.T.*)—

Day of Month	Day of Week	LONDON BRIDGE † Datum of Predictions 10·50 ft. below				LIVERPOOL † Datum of Predictions 14·54 ft. below				BRISTOL (Avonmouth) † Datum of Predictions 20·11 ft. below				HULL (Salend) † Datum of Predictions 10·68 ft. below				GREENOCK † Datum of Predictions 4·86 ft. below				LEITH§ AND GRANTON † Datum of Predictions 8·92 ft. below				DUN LAOGHAIRE † Datum of Predictions r·43 ft. above			
		Mn. h.m.	Ht. ft.	Aft. h.m.	Ht. ft.	Mn. h.m.	Ht. ft.	Aft. h.m.	Ht. ft.	Mn. h.m.	Ht. ft.	Aft. h.m.	Ht. ft.	Mn. h.m.	Ht. ft.	Aft. h.m.	Ht. ft.	Mn. h.m.	Ht. ft.	Aft. h.m.	Ht. ft.	Mn. h.m.	Ht. ft.	Aft. h.m.	Ht. ft.	Mn. h.m.	Ht. ft.	Aft. h.m.	Ht. ft.
1	M	4 10	22·0	16 19	22·1	1 25	27·0	13 38	26·1	9 34	38·4	21 49	38·5	8 26	20·3	20 47	19·6	2 43	10·0	14 49	9·8	4 47	16·1	17 16	16·1	1 36	11·3	14 5	10·7
2	Tu	4 43	21·7	16 51	21·9	1 55	26·6	14 10	25·4	10 7	37·2	22 16	37·1	8 54	19·5	21 22	19·0	3 9	10·1	15 23	9·6	5 21	15·8	17 54	15·6	2 12	11·2	14 45	10·4
3	W	5 19	21·4	17 26	21·6	2 28	25·9	14 46	24·5	10 30	35·7	22 46	35·6	9 24	19·4	22 0	18·2	3 39	10·2	16 2	9·5	5 58	15·4	18 36	15·0	2 53	11·0	15 29	10·5
4	Th	5 57	20·7	18 07	20·5	3 7	25·1	15 31	23·6	11 6	34·2	23 25	34·0	9 58	18·9	22 44	17·7	4 15	10·2	16 47	9·5	6 41	14·8	19 24	13·9	3 39	10·7	16 18	9·8
5	F	6 38	20·7	18 43	20·4	3 55	24·2	16 27	22·7	11 52	32·7			10 41	18·2	23 39	16·5	4 57	10·1	17 36	9·3	7 31	14·4	20 21	13·9	4 30	10·5	17 16	9·5
6	S	7 25	20·2	19 32	19·7	4 54	23·5	17 35	22·2	0 10	32·7	12 52	31·8	11 38	17·5			5 44	9·9	18 29	9·1	8 31	14·1	21 25	13·7	5 28	10·3	18 26	9·5
7	S	8 23	19·6	20 35	19·2	6 3	23·3	18 50	22·4	1 2	31·8	14 12	31·8	0 49	16·0	12 51	17·2	6 39	9·6	19 31	8·9	9 47	14·1	22 33	14·1	6 34	10·6	19 38	9·8
8	M	9 39	19·3	21 56	19·3	7 16	23·9	20 2	23·5	2 5	32·8	15 37	33·6	2 10	16·3	14 13	17·7	7 56	9·6	21 0	8·9	10 48	14·5	23 39	14·6	7 43	10·6	20 42	10·4
9	Tu	11 3	20·4	23 17	20·5	8 24	25·2	21 5	25·3	3 22	33·0	16 50	36·3	3 22	17·7	15 25	18·8	9 33	9·6	22 14	9·3	11 53	15·3			8 46	11·2	21 34	11·0
10	W			12 11	21·7	9 24	26·8	21 58	26·8	4 41	35·1	17 52	41·0	4 23	19·0	16 27	20·2	11 29	10·6	23 51	10·1			12 50	16·2	9 40	11·8	22 20	11·7
11	Th	0 22	21·9	12 56	23·0	10 17	28·2	22 47	28·2	5 51	37·9	18 50	43·3	5 14	20·0	17 21	21·4			12 21	11·0	0 37	15·5	13 42	17·1	10 29	12·3	23 2	12·3
12	F	1 17	22·3	13 42	23·6	11 7	29·2	23 34	29·1	6 47	40·2	19 41	44·3	5 59	21·3	18 3	22·3	0 37	10·5	13 13	11·6	1 27	17·1	14 30	17·9	11 16	12·6	23 42	12·5
13	S	2 7	22·9	14 24	24·1	12 0	29·7			7 84	41·8	20 20	43·5	6 47	21·8	18 43	22·6	1 20	11·1	14 4	11·0	2 17	17·6	15 18	18·5			12 2	12·7
14	S	2 55	24·0	15 27	24·1	0 22	29·5	12 45	29·6	8 46	43·2	21 0	43·1	7 31	22·0	19 23	22·6	2 8	11·3	14 53	10·9	3 4	17·9	16 1	18·2	0 26	12·7	12 51	12·7
15	M	3 44	24·6	16 12	24·1	1 8	28·9	13 34	28·0	9 26	43·1	21 40	41·7	8 15	21·8	20 3	21·9	2 51	11·6	15 41	10·9	3 52	17·5	16 47	17·6	1 12	12·6	13 43	12·4
16	Tu	4 34	24·6	16 59	23·6	1 55	28·9	14 23	26·0	10 2	42·4	22 15	42·7	8 59	21·4	20 45	21·2	3 34	11·8	16 30	10·8	4 32	17·6	17 18	18·0	2 3	12·6	14 38	11·9
17	W	5 25	23·6	17 54	23·3	2 43	27·9	15 14	24·0	10 39	39·8	22 55	39·3	9 44	20·7	21 26	20·4	4 18	11·6	17 17	10·5	5 16	17·8	17 54	18·2	2 57	12·3	15 36	11·3
18	Th	6 16	22·6	18 34	22·3	3 33	26·6	16 9	22·5	11 19	39·8	23 24	39·3	10 31	19·7	22 20	19·2	5 4	11·1	18 6	10·2	6 0	16·8	18 40	16·9	3 55	11·9	16 37	10·7
19	F	7 7	21·4	19 24	20·3	4 28	25·3	17 9	23·7			12 4	36·9	11 22	18·6			5 55	11·1	19 0	9·6	7 1	15·4	19 46	15·9	4 57	11·4	17 46	10·2
20	S	8 1	20·0	20 16	19·3	5 30	24·1	18 15	22·9	0 10	36·9	12 44	34·8	0 18	17·5	12 19	17·6	6 55	11·1	19 47	8·4	8 8	15·3	20 45	15·1	6 0	11·1	18 51	9·9
21	S	8 59	19·1	21 16	18·6	6 39	23·3	19 25	22·7	1 1	34·7	13 34	32·6	1 24	17·0	13 26	17·0	6 55	9·5	20 50	8·2	9 9	14·7	21 48	14·6	7 1	10·7	19 11	9·9
22	M	10 3	18·8	22 23	18·7	7 50	23·3	20 30	23·1	2 2	33·2	14 48	32·6	2 29	16·3	14 36	16·6	8 13	9·5	20 50	8·2	10 9	14·5	22 53	14·5	7 18	10·7	20 1	8·9
23	Tu	11 11	19·3	23 31	19·4	8 56	24·3	21 24	24·0	3 12	32·8	15 57	34·0	3 31	16·6	15 39	17·3	9 34	8·8	21 54	8·7	11 21	14·5			8 25	10·6	21 8	10·1
24	W			12 16	20·1	9 46	24·4	22 4	24·8	4 22	33·6	16 59	34·0	4 24	17·1	16 28	18·6	10 31	9·3	22 46	9·3			12 21	14·8	9 22	10·7	22 4	10·4
25	Th	0 32	20·5	13 4	20·4	10 29	25·4	22 48	25·6	5 21	34·8	17 57	35·5	5 10	18·3	17 10	18·6	0 7	9·4	13 13	9·5	0 47	15·1	13 12	15·1	10 9	10·8	22 32	10·7
26	F	1 22	21·5	13 46	21·6	11 6	25·4	23 24	26·1	6 11	35·8	18 37	36·7	5 52	19·1	17 48	19·1	0 42	9·7	13 53	10·0	1 31	15·2	13 55	15·4	10 50	10·9	23 6	11·0
27	S	2 5	21·9	14 23	22·1	11 41	25·7	23 58	26·6	6 55	36·8	19 17	37·7	6 30	19·6	18 24	19·5	1 16	9·7	14 34	9·6	2 10	15·5	14 34	15·6	11 27	10·9	23 36	11·2
28	S	2 43	22·0	14 55	22·1			12 16	25·9	7 34	37·4	19 55	38·4	7 1	19·9	18 58	19·5	1 46	9·8	15 11	9·8	2 45	15·8	15 11	15·9			12 0	11·3
29	M	3 18	22·1	15 27	22·0	0 32	26·8	12 50	25·9	8 14	38·0	20 31	38·8	7 34	20·0	19 33	19·5	2 16	9·7	15 48	9·7	3 19	16·0	15 48	16·1	0 7	11·3	12 34	10·8
30	Tu	3 53	21·7	16 0	21·7	1 6	26·9	13 24	25·3	8 46	36·3	21 4	38·9	8 7	20·0	20 4	19·3	2 16	9·8	16 25	9·6	3 53	16·0	16 25	16·0	0 40	11·4	13 10	10·7
31	W	4 29	21·6	16 36	21·8	1 40	26·8	14 0	25·5	9 20	38·5	21 38	38·5	8 39	19·9	20 38	18·9	2 46	10·0	17 2	9·2	5 5	16·1	17 42	15·9	1 16	11·5	13 48	10·6

* All times shown are Central European Time = British Summer Time. To obtain Greenwich Mean Time, subtract one hour.   † Difference of height
in feet from Ordnance Datum (Newlyn). ‡ Difference of height in feet from Ordnance Datum (Ireland). *(See notes, p. 184.)*   § *See note, p. 175.*

JUNE, 1972

High Water at the undermentioned Places (C.E.T.*)—

Day of Month	Day of Week	LONDON BRIDGE † Datum of Predictions 10·50 ft. below				LIVERPOOL † Datum of Predictions 14·54 ft. below				BRISTOL (Avonmouth) † Datum of Predictions 20·11 ft. below				HULL (Salena) † Datum of Predictions 10·68 ft. below				GREENOCK † Datum of Predictions 4·80 ft. below				LEITH§ AND GRANTON † Datum of Predictions 8·92 ft. below				DUN LAOGHAIRE ‡ Datum of Predictions 1·43 ft. above			
		Mn. h.m.	Ht. ft.	Aft. h.m.	Ht. ft.	Mn. h.m.	Ht. ft.	Aft. h.m.	Ht. ft.	Mn. h.m.	Ht. ft.	Aft. h.m.	Ht. ft.	Mn. h.m.	Ht. ft.	Aft. h.m.	Ht. ft.	Mn. h.m.	Ht. ft.	Aft. h.m.	Ht. ft.	Mn. h.m.	Ht. ft.	Aft. h.m.	Ht. ft.	Mn. h.m.	Ht. ft.	Aft. h.m.	Ht. ft.
1	Th	5 6	21·5	1711	21·7	216	26·5	1439	25·0	1030	36·6	2247	36·8	912	19·8	2157	18·6	319	9·2	1550	9·2	544	15·9	1823	15·5	236	11·4	1512	10·3
2	F	544	21·5	1746	21·5	256	26·2	1523	24·5	11 9	35·7	2327	35·9	949	19·6	2239	18·1	357	9·4	1635	9·4	627	15·6	19 9	15·1	320	11·4	16 0	10·2
3	S	624	21·3	1825	21·2	342	25·7	1613	24·1	1145	34·9	—	—	1032	19·3	2236	17·6	439	9·4	1722	9·5	715	15·3	1959	14·7	4 7	11·3	1653	10·1
4	Su	710	21·1	1911	20·9	433	25·3	1713	23·7	013	34·9	1244	34·3	1033	19·0	—	—	525	9·3	1810	9·4	9 5	15·2	2053	14·6	5 0	11·2	1753	10·0
5	M	8 4	20·7	20 8	20·6	537	25·0	1820	23·7	013	34·6	1346	34·1	1128	18·7	1223	18·7	617	9·1	19 4	9·3	0 6	15·2	2255	14·3	559	11·6	1858	10·1
6	Tu	911	20·5	2119	20·5	744	25·4	2026	25·0	217	34·7	1456	34·1	028	17·1	1332	18·7	722	9·8	2010	9·1	1110	15·5	—	—	7 5	11·0	20 2	10·4
7	W	1029	20·6	2238	21·0	850	26·4	2128	26·1	330	35·6	16 7	36·2	238	17·5	1445	19·0	845	9·7	2124	9·6	054	15·8	1315	16·6	811	11·2	21 0	10·9
8	Th	1139	21·4	—	—	953	26·7	2224	27·2	441	37·1	1713	37·8	344	18·4	1554	19·8	958	9·9	2225	9·9	148	16·6	1412	17·2	911	11·5	2159	11·4
9	F	055	22·2	1241	21·7	1048	27·8	2316	28·1	545	38·7	1814	39·4	443	19·4	1658	20·6	1058	10·1	2318	9·9	239	17·1	15 7	17·7	1059	12·0	2239	11·9
10	S	154	22·5	1337	22·1	1134	28·4	—	—	645	40·0	1910	40·6	536	20·4	1757	21·2	010	10·4	1255	10·3	330	17·5	1543	17·9	054	12·1	1259	12·1
11	Su	248	22·8	1429	21·7	0 7	28·7	1234	28·6	741	41·0	20 4	41·4	627	21·1	1849	21·6	1 0	10·8	1352	10·2	420	17·7	1652	17·6	1150	12·1	—	—
12	M	339	23·0	16 1	22·1	056	28·9	1324	28·6	834	41·5	2055	42·0	716	21·5	1949	21·6	149	11·1	1445	10·1	5 1	17·7	1743	17·5	010	12·5	1241	12·0
13	Tu	427	23·2	1646	22·4	144	28·8	14 8	28·3	925	41·7	2144	42·0	8 4	21·5	2041	21·5	236	11·6	1535	10·0	650	16·5	1832	16·9	059	12·7	1334	11·8
14	W	514	23·1	1729	22·4	227	28·4	1450	27·8	1013	41·3	2230	41·5	849	21·3	2120	21·0	321	11·8	1622	9·8	6 5	16·5	1921	16·1	151	12·7	1427	11·6
15	Th	6 0	22·5	1812	21·9	3 7	27·4	1530	26·9	1058	40·1	2313	40·3	933	20·5	2215	20·2	4 5	11·7	17 7	9·5	741	15·8	20 2	15·3	244	12·6	1520	11·2
16	F	645	21·4	1854	21·0	350	25·8	1550	25·8	1142	38·5	2355	38·5	1017	19·7	2259	19·2	449	11·5	1753	9·0	831	15·2	2057	15·3	337	12·3	1615	11·1
17	S	731	20·3	1939	20·1	4 5	26·3	1639	24·6	1224	36·5	—	—	1057	19·7	2343	18·1	535	11·0	1841	8·5	925	14·6	2158	14·2	432	11·8	1712	11·0
18	Su	820	19·5	2031	19·3	455	23·9	1732	23·1	037	36·7	13 7	34·7	031	17·1	1230	17·8	625	10·7	1937	8·4	1022	14·3	2255	14·2	530	11·3	1815	9·9
19	M	916	19·0	2133	18·9	549	23·9	1828	22·9	121	34·8	1335	34·2	125	16·4	1330	17·2	722	9·9	2045	8·3	1122	14·3	2353	14·5	632	10·7	1919	9·9
20	Tu	1017	19·0	2238	19·0	649	23·1	1929	22·9	213	33·3	1451	32·3	226	16·3	1439	16·8	829	8·8	2151	8·4	1222	14·3	—	—	735	10·3	2019	9·7
21	W	1118	19·5	—	—	856	22·9	2125	23·5	313	32·5	1552	32·3	332	16·4	1546	17·0	935	8·7	2245	8·7	10 2	14·2	2353	14·2	837	10·1	2111	10·0
22	Th	—	—	1217	20·1	950	23·4	2214	24·4	417	32·5	1654	33·1	428	17·4	1646	17·6	1032	8·8	2330	9·0	1222	14·3	2353	14·2	931	10·1	2155	10·3
23	F	045	20·2	13 9	20·6	1037	24·4	2256	25·7	518	33·3	1751	34·1	516	18·9	1739	18·8	1123	9·0	—	—	045	14·5	1317	14·5	1018	10·2	2333	10·7
24	S	137	20·8	1353	21·0	1037	25·6	2336	26·0	614	34·4	1843	35·8	6 0	18·9	1827	18·8	011	9·4	1210	9·0	134	14·8	14 6	14·9	11 0	10·8	2310	11·0
25	Su	221	21·4	1434	21·4	1157	25·3	—	—	7 4	35·7	1929	37·2	639	19·9	19 9	19·3	048	9·7	1254	8·9	218	15·2	1451	15·3	1137	10·5	2344	11·3
26	M	3 1	21·5	1513	21·8	013	26·7	1235	25·8	749	36·9	2012	38·3	717	19·9	1954	19·7	123	9·7	1337	8·9	259	15·7	1533	15·8	020	11·6	1252	10·7
27	Tu	340	21·8	1551	22·1	049	26·8	1312	26·1	831	37·9	2051	39·1	752	20·0	2033	19·8	156	9·9	1418	8·9	337	16·1	1613	16·2	057	11·8	1331	10·8
28	W	419	22·1	1628	22·2	050	27·2	1312	26·1	910	38·6	2129	39·6	828	20·6	2111	19·8	156	9·9	1418	8·9	414	16·5	1650	16·5	135	11·9	1411	10·9
29	Th	457	22·3	17 3	22·2	419	22·1	1650	26·3	949	38·9	22 7	39·6	9 3	20·8	2148	19·7	230	10·1	15 0	9·0	453	16·7	1728	16·5	216	12·0	1453	10·9
30	F	457	22·3	17 3	22·3	2 4	27·7	1439	26·3	1027	38·8	2245	39·3	9 3	20·8	2148	19·7	3 7	10·4	1542	9·2	529	16·7	18 7	16·3	—	—	—	—

* All times shown are Central European Time = British Summer Time. To obtain Greenwich Mean Time, subtract one hour.
† Difference of height in feet from Ordnance Datum (Newlyn). ‡ Difference of height in feet from Ordnance Datum (Ireland). (See notes, p. 184.)
§ See note, p. 175.

JULY, 1972

High Water at the undermentioned Places (C.E.T.★)—

Day of Month	Day of Week	LONDON BRIDGE † Datum of Predictions 10·50 ft. below — Mn. h.m.	Ht. ft.	Aft. h.m.	Ht. ft.	LIVERPOOL † Datum of Predictions 14·54 ft. below — Mn. h.m.	Ht. ft.	Aft. h.m.	Ht. ft.	BRISTOL (Avonmouth) † Datum of Predictions 20·11 ft. below — Mn. h.m.	Ht. ft.	Aft. h.m.	Ht. ft.	HULL (Salend) † Datum of Predictions 10·68 ft. below — Mn. h.m.	Ht. ft.	Aft. h.m.	Ht. ft.	GREENOCK † Datum of Predictions 4·80 ft. below — Mn. h.m.	Ht. ft.	Aft. h.m.	Ht. ft.	LEITH§ AND GRANTON † Datum of Predictions 8·92 ft. below — Mn. h.m.	Ht. ft.	Aft. h.m.	Ht. ft.	DUN LAOGHAIRE ‡ Datum of Predictions r·43 ft. above — Mn. h.m.	Ht. ft.	Aft. h.m.	Ht. ft.
1	S	5 34	22·2	17 36	22·0	2 43	27·7	15 10	26·1	11 1	38·4	23 24	38·8	9 41	20·8	22 26	19·4	3 45	10·7	16 24	9·5	6 11	16·6	18 49	16·0	2 59	12·1	15 37	10·9
2	S	6 12	22·0	18 12	21·9	3 25	27·5	15 54	25·7	11 47	37·8			10 20	20·7	23 7	18·9	4 26	10·9	17 7	9·8	6 56	16·4	19 34	15·6	3 44	12·1	16 25	10·8
3	M	6 54	21·6	18 53	21·8	4 12	27·0	16 42	25·1	0 4	37·9	12 29	36·9	11 5	20·0	23 54	18·3	5 10	10·8	17 49	9·8	7 44	16·1	20 24	15·3	4 34	11·9	17 19	10·6
4	Tu	7 42	21·1	19 43	21·5	5 2	26·3	17 38	24·6	0 49	36·9	13 17	35·8	11 57	19·8			5 58	10·5	18 35	9·7	8 36	15·9	21 18	15·0	5 28	11·6	18 20	10·4
5	W	8 41	20·5	20 46	21·1	6 2	25·5	18 42	24·2	1 42	35·8	14 16	35·0	0 58	17·7	12 59	19·2	6 55	10·2	19 28	9·4	9 32	15·6	22 18	15·0	6 32	11·3	19 27	10·4
6	Th	9 55	20·1	22 5	20·8	7 10	25·0	19 53	24·1	2 51	35·1	15 28	35·0	1 58	17·7	14 14	18·9	8 6	9·6	20 35	9·2	10 38	15·5	23 25	15·0	7 42	11·0	20 31	10·7
7	F	11 11	20·1	23 37	20·9	8 25	25·0	21 5	25·1	4 8	35·5	16 44	36·0	3 12	18·0	15 34	18·6	9 27	9·4	21 50	9·3	11 50	15·5			8 52	11·0	21 31	11·1
8	S	11 11	20·1			9 37	25·6	22 7	25·8	5 24	36·7	17 56	37·5	4 20	18·7	16 48	19·5	10 43	9·5	22 56	9·6	0 32	15·4	13 2	15·9	9 56	11·2	22 26	11·6
9	S	0 44	21·2	13 26	20·5	10 40	26·5	23 7	27·3	6 33	38·3	19 0	39·2	5 21	19·7	17 54	20·3	11 50	9·5	23 55	10·0	1 35	16·0	14 7	16·5	10 53	11·4	23 15	12·0
10	M	1 50	21·6	14 21	20·8	11 35	27·3	23 58	28·0	7 33	39·7	19 56	40·6	6 16	20·6	18 53	20·9	0 49	10·6	13 48	9·6	2 32	16·7	15 5	17·1	11 46	11·6		
11	Tu	2 45	21·9	15 8	21·3			12 25	27·8	8 26	40·8	20 46	41·7	7 7	21·3	19 45	21·4	1 39	11·1	14 40	9·7	3 23	17·2	15 56	17·6	0 3	12·4	12 36	11·7
12	W	3 33	22·4	15 50	21·8	0 45	28·8	13 10	29·0	9 14	41·4	21 34	42·1	7 54	21·8	20 32	21·4	2 26	11·5	15 25	9·7	4 11	17·6	16 44	17·7	0 51	12·7	13 24	11·6
13	Th	4 16	22·6	16 30	22·3	1 30	29·0	13 57	29·0	9 58	41·5	22 14	42·1	8 36	21·6	21 14	21·4	3 10	11·7	16 7	9·7	4 56	17·7	17 27	17·3	1 39	12·4	14 11	11·5
14	F	4 57	22·6	17 8	22·4	2 13	28·7	14 40	28·6	10 39	40·9	22 53	41·3	9 14	21·8	21 52	20·5	3 51	11·7	16 45	9·6	5 40	17·4	18 9	17·0	2 25	12·8	14 57	11·3
15	S	5 37	22·6	17 45	22·4	2 54	28·1	15 21	28·0	11 17	39·7	23 29	39·9	9 50	21·2	22 28	19·2	4 30	11·7	17 25	9·6	6 23	16·9	18 52	16·2	3 13	12·5	15 43	11·0
16	S	6 16	22·6	18 21	22·4	3 33	27·6	16 1	27·1	11 54	38·6			11 5	19·7	23 3	19·2	5 8	10·9	17 58	9·4	7 7	15·3	19 34	15·4	4 2	12·4	16 30	10·5
17	M	6 55	22·0	19 0	22·0	4 13	26·7	16 43	26·0	0 3	38·0	12 30	37·0	11 39	18·6			5 58	10·9	18 39	9·1	7 52	15·4	20 24	14·7	4 48	11·4	17 20	10·1
18	Tu	7 37	22·0	19 48	21·0	4 56	25·6	17 29	24·8	0 35	35·9	13 5	34·0	0 25	16·9	12 30	17·4	6 37	9·4	19 27	8·5	8 36	14·7	21 14	13·8	5 40	10·7	18 16	9·7
19	W	8 27	19·6	20 46	19·4	5 46	24·2	18 23	23·2	1 13	33·6	13 43	33·2	1 23	16·6	13 38	16·3	7 31	8·8	20 30	8·3	9 24	14·1	21 53	13·8	6 39	10·0	19 18	9·5
20	Th	9 24	19·1	21 51	18·9	6 47	23·1	19 27	22·2	2 1	31·6	14 40	30·9	2 35	16·5	14 58	16·0	8 35	8·5	21 47	8·7	10 31	13·7	22 52	13·6	7 46	9·6	20 20	9·6
21	F	10 24	18·8	22 56	18·7	7 59	22·5	20 37	22·2	3 7	30·5	15 51	30·8	3 46	16·5	16 20	16·6	9 44	8·6	22 54	8·7	11 31	13·5			8 47	9·8	21 15	10·0
22	S	11 27	18·8			9 12	22·9	21 43	23·0	4 23	30·8	17 5	32·1	4 45	17·6	17 29	17·6	10 51	8·7	23 52	9·0	0 1	13·8	12 42	13·8	9 47	9·8	22 4	10·5
23	S	0 7	18·9	12 33	19·2	10 11	23·9	22 30	24·4	5 36	32·4	18 12	34·3	5 35	18·4	18 13	18·5	11 55	8·9			1 3	14·2	13 42	14·3	10 34	10·1	22 43	11·0
24	M	1 12	19·5	13 30	20·0	10 58	24·2	23 15	25·5	6 39	34·6	19 13	36·6	6 18	19·6	18 58	19·6	0 26	9·8	13 23	9·3	1 56	14·8	14 34	15·1	11 17	10·5	23 22	11·5
25	Tu	2 1	20·5	14 16	20·9	11 39	25·4	23 54	26·4	7 30	36·8	19 53	38·6	6 58	20·4	19 38	20·3	1 3	10·1	14 6	9·1	2 41	15·9	15 19	15·8	11 55	10·9	23 59	11·8
26	W	2 43	21·5	14 58	21·7			12 17	26·4	8 14	38·7	20 35	40·4	7 36	21·0	20 16	20·8	1 40	10·1	14 47	9·1	3 21	16·5	15 57	16·5			12 32	11·2
27	Th	3 24	22·4	15 37	22·2	0 31	28·0	12 55	27·7	8 55	40·0	21 14	41·4	8 12	21·8	20 52	21·0	2 16	10·8	15 28	9·8	3 57	17·0	16 33	17·0	0 36	12·3	13 9	11·4
28	F	4 3	23·1	16 13	23·1	1 8	28·8	13 33	27·9	9 34	41·6	21 54	42·0	8 48	22·1	21 31	21·0	2 55	11·0	16 7	9·8	4 32	17·4	17 8	17·1	1 14	12·8	13 48	11·6
29	S	4 41	23·3	16 48	23·1	1 46	29·2	14 11	27·9	10 14	41·6	22 33	42·0	9 25	22·2	22 4	20·5	3 33	11·1	16 46	9·8	5 9	17·6	17 45	17·1	1 54	12·8	14 28	11·7
30	S	5 18	23·1	17 20	22·9	2 25	29·3	14 50	27·7	10 53	41·3	23 10	41·5	10 3	22·0	22 42	20·0	4 13	11·1	17 6	9·8	5 50	17·6	18 25	16·8	2 36	12·9	15 9	11·6
31	M	5 54	22·6	17 55	22·7	3 4	28·9	15 30	27·1	11 30	40·4	23 47	40·1	10 3	22·0			4 13	11·1	16 46	9·4	6 34	17·3	19 6	16·3	3 19	12·6	15 55	11·4

★ All times shown are Central European Time = British Summer Time. To obtain Greenwich Mean Time, subtract one hour.   † Difference of height in feet from Ordnance Datum (Newlyn).   ‡ Difference of height in feet from Ordnance Datum (Ireland).   (*See notes*, p. 184.)   § *See note*, p. 175.

AUGUST, 1972

High Water at the undermentioned Places (C.E.T.*)—

Day of Month	Day of Week	London Bridge † Datum of Predictions 10·50 ft. below				Liverpool † Datum of Predictions 14·54 ft. below				Bristol (Avonmouth) † Datum of Predictions 20·11 ft. below				Hull (Salted) † Datum of Predictions 10·68 ft. below				Greenock † Datum of Predictions 4·80 ft. below				Leith and Granton † Datum of Predictions 8·92 ft. below				Dun Laoghaire ‡ 4·3 ft. above			
		Mn. h.m	Ht. ft	Aft. h.m	Ht. ft	Mn. h.m	Ht. ft	Aft. h.m	Ht. ft	Mn. h.m	Ht. ft	Aft. h.m	Ht. ft	Mn. h.m	Ht. ft	Aft. h.m	Ht. ft	Mn. h.m	Ht. ft	Aft. h.m	Ht. ft	Mn. h.m	Ht. ft	Aft. h.m	Ht. ft	Mn. h.m	Ht. ft	Aft. h.m	Ht. ft
1	Tu	633	21·9	1834	22·3	346	28·0	1614	26·1	—	—	12 7	38·7	1044	21·4	2325	19·2	455	11·2	1725	10·3	721	16·9	1958	15·7	4 7	12·5	1657	11·1
2	W	718	21·0	1922	21·7	434	26·7	17 6	25·0	026	38·1	1248	36·5	1133	20·4	—	—	540	10·8	1816	10·1	811	16·3	2051	15·2	5 2	11·9	1747	10·8
3	Th	812	20·0	2022	20·9	534	25·2	1811	23·9	113	35·7	1342	34·4	017	18·3	1234	19·2	633	10·1	1855	9·6	9 9	15·5	2152	14·7	6 7	11·3	1857	10·5
4	F	924	19·2	2142	20·1	647	24·0	1930	23·5	219	33·8	1457	33·3	125	17·5	1335	18·1	738	9·3	1956	9·1	1020	15·1	23 7	14·6	724	10·6	2011	10·6
5	S	1045	18·9	2311	20·0	813	23·7	2054	24·1	348	33·4	1628	34·0	248	17·1	1530	18·4	910	8·8	2123	9·0	1144	15·0	—	—	844	10·6	2119	11·5
6	S	—	—	1204	19·3	933	24·5	22 5	25·5	507	35·0	1750	36·3	4 7	18·1	1654	20·0	1047	9·0	2250	9·9	025	15·0	13 3	15·5	955	10·9	2219	11·5
7	M	037	20·5	1311	20·1	1038	25·8	2301	27·0	630	37·4	1850	38·8	513	19·4	1754	21·5	1158	9·0	2352	9·9	132	15·7	14 7	16·3	1055	11·2	2357	12·1
8	Tu	144	21·5	1414	20·9	1130	27·4	2349	28·3	728	39·6	1949	40·9	6 8	20·6	1848	22·9	—	—	1254	9·4	229	16·5	15 2	17·0	1144	11·5	—	—
9	W	236	22·1	1454	21·6	—	—	1214	27·8	816	41·0	2034	42·1	656	21·6	1933	21·5	044	10·5	1342	9·4	317	17·2	1548	17·4	040	12·9	1228	11·7
10	Th	319	22·5	1533	22·2	031	28·9	1326	28·3	858	41·8	2113	42·7	737	22·2	2013	22·3	131	11·0	1426	9·6	359	17·7	1629	17·6	130	13·0	1348	11·7
11	F	359	22·6	1611	22·5	111	29·2	1336	28·3	936	41·9	2150	42·6	814	22·4	2048	21·3	215	11·3	15 6	9·6	438	17·8	17 6	17·4	2 3	13·3	1425	11·7
12	S	436	22·6	1644	22·6	148	29·0	1411	27·9	1011	41·5	2224	41·9	847	22·3	2119	20·9	255	11·5	1542	9·7	515	17·6	1742	17·0	244	12·6	15 4	11·3
13	S	510	22·4	1716	22·5	223	28·4	1448	27·2	1044	40·5	2254	40·6	918	21·9	2151	20·3	332	11·5	1614	9·7	553	17·1	1818	16·3	323	12·1	1544	10·9
14	M	543	22·2	1749	22·2	256	27·4	1519	26·1	1113	38·9	2321	38·7	948	21·0	2220	19·5	4 8	10·8	1645	9·7	632	16·3	1855	15·5	4 5	11·4	1625	10·4
15	Tu	616	21·6	1835	21·7	329	26·0	1552	24·9	1139	36·9	2347	36·3	1019	20·2	2239	18·6	438	10·0	1716	9·3	711	15·5	1929	14·8	449	10·9	1713	10·0
16	W	653	21·0	19 9	20·8	4 4	24·4	1623	23·6	—	—	12 6	34·6	1055	19·0	2339	17·5	514	10·0	1751	9·3	750	14·7	2014	14·0	541	9·9	1812	9·6
17	Th	737	20·3	2017	19·9	448	22·8	1657	22·3	017	33·7	1240	33·2	—	—	1138	17·4	556	9·5	1832	8·9	835	14·0	2101	13·6	649	9·4	1922	9·5
18	F	830	19·2	2134	18·6	545	21·3	1827	21·4	059	31·1	1333	30·2	038	16·4	1243	16·0	645	8·9	1923	8·6	931	13·3	2158	13·3	8 8	9·3	2030	9·9
19	S	931	18·3	2259	17·9	7 3	20·6	1947	21·4	2 1	29·2	1448	29·3	150	15·3	14 3	15·3	743	8·5	2030	8·4	1046	13·0	2315	13·3	918	9·6	2127	10·4
20	S	1039	17·8	2329	17·8	833	21·0	2101	22·4	330	29·0	1622	30·4	259	15·5	1553	15·9	855	8·2	2159	8·5	—	—	12 5	13·3	1052	10·9	2235	11·1
21	M	1159	18·8	—	—	944	22·4	2210	24·2	5 3	31·0	1743	33·3	411	16·8	1659	17·2	1026	8·4	2317	9·0	031	13·8	1319	14·0	1130	11·4	2256	11·8
22	Tu	046	18·8	1315	19·4	1035	24·2	2250	26·0	614	34·3	1844	36·6	5 5	18·3	1750	18·7	1132	8·7	—	—	131	14·4	1412	15·0	—	—	12 6	11·9
23	W	136	20·1	1355	20·9	1116	25·9	2328	27·6	7 7	37·4	1931	39·4	552	19·8	1833	20·0	0 2	9·5	1220	8·9	218	15·6	1456	16·0	010	12·2	1242	12·2
24	Th	219	21·7	1433	22·3	1153	27·3	—	—	751	40·0	2014	41·6	632	21·2	1907	20·6	041	10·0	13 3	9·0	258	16·6	1534	16·9	048	13·3	1319	12·4
25	F	259	23·1	1511	23·3	0 6	29·0	1231	28·4	831	41·9	2051	43·2	711	22·2	1950	21·0	120	10·8	1345	9·2	333	17·4	16 5	17·5	128	13·5	1358	12·5
26	S	338	23·9	1547	23·9	044	30·0	13 9	29·1	9 5	42·9	2129	44·1	749	23·0	2026	20·7	159	10·8	1426	9·5	4 8	18·1	1641	17·8	210	13·5	1441	12·6
27	S	416	24·2	1622	24·1	123	30·4	1347	29·3	952	43·7	2209	44·2	826	23·4	2101	20·9	239	11·2	15 6	9·9	445	18·4	1720	17·8	255	13·3	1526	12·1
28	M	453	23·7	1657	23·9	2 3	30·4	1434	29·0	9 3	43·7	2137	43·3	9 3	23·3	2137	21·5	318	11·4	1544	10·3	527	18·3	18 2	17·4	337	13·1	16 8	11·6
29	Tu	531	23·1	1735	23·4	242	29·7	15 5	28·9	942	42·8	2235	42·0	942	22·8	2235	20·8	358	11·5	1621	10·7	612	17·9	1847	16·7	345	12·7	1618	11·6
30	W	611	22·0	1818	22·7	324	28·3	1549	26·6	1021	42·8	2257	41·2	1025	21·3	2257	19·7	440	11·3	17 0	10·7	7 1	17·2	1936	16·0	442	12·0	1720	11·1
31	Th	656	20·8	19 9	21·6	413	26·4	1642	25·0	1115	20·3	2349	18·5	1115	20·3	2349	18·5	526	10·7	1741	10·4	755	16·3	2031	15·2	—	—	—	—

*All times shown are Central European Time = British Summer Time. To obtain Greenwich Mean Time, subtract one hour. † Difference of height in feet from Ordnance Datum (Newlyn). ‡ Difference of height in feet from Ordnance Datum (Ireland). (See notes, p. 184.) § See note, p. 175.

Tidal Predictions [1972

SEPTEMBER, 1972

High Water at the undermentioned Places (C.E.T.*)—

Day of Month	Day of Week	LONDON BRIDGE † Datum of Predictions 10·50 ft. below				LIVERPOOL † Datum of Predictions 14·54 ft. below				BRISTOL (Avonmouth) † Datum of Predictions 20·11 ft. below				HULL (Salend) † Datum of Predictions 10·68 ft. below				GREENOCK † Datum of Predictions 4·80 ft. below				LEITH AND GRANTON † Datum of Predictions 8·92 ft. below				DUN LAOGHAIRE ‡ Datum of Predictions 1·43 ft. above			
		Mn. h.m.	Ht. ft.	Aft. h.m.	Ht.	Mn. h.m.	Ht. ft.	Aft. h.m.	Ht.	Mn. h.m.	Ht. ft.	Aft. h.m.	Ht. ft.	Mn. h.m.	Ht. ft.	Aft. h.m.	Ht.	Mn. h.m.	Ht. ft.	Aft. h.m.	Ht.	Mn. h.m.	Ht. ft.	Aft. h.m.	Ht.	Mn. h.m.	Ht. ft.	Aft. h.m.	Ht.
1	F	7 50	19·6	20 11	20·4	5 15	24·4	17 50	23·5	2 50	35·0	13 16	33·6	1 0	17·3	12 20	18·7	6 18	9·8	18 29	9·8	8 57	15·3	21 38	14·6	5 52	11·1	18 34	10·7
2	S	9 0	18·7	21 13	19·6	6 30	23·0	19 18	22·9	3 59	32·3	14 38	31·9	2 33	17·1	13 54	17·7	7 24	8·9	19 29	9·2	10 16	14·7	23 0	14·4	7 17	10·5	19 56	10·7
3	S	10 21	18·4	22 59	19·5	8 11	22·9	20 50	23·7	5 40	33·8	16 23	32·9	3 57	18·0	15 22	17·7	9 28	8·3	21 9	8·8	11 45	14·8	—		8 43	10·5	21 10	11·2
4	M	11 43	19·0	—		9 33	24·2	21 1	25·4	7 17	34·2	17 47	36·0	5 15	19·4	17 45	20·0	11 2	8·6	22 51	9·2	0 22	14·9	13 1	15·5	9 55	10·9	22 12	11·8
5	Tu	0 23	20·4	12 53	20·3	10 32	25·8	22 53	27·1	8 24	37·4	18 48	39·2	5 20	8·3	16 31	20·0	12 0	9·0	23 48	9·3	1 28	15·8	14 1	16·3	10 51	11·4	23 2	12·4
6	W	1 27	21·7	13 47	21·5	11 18	27·2	23 35	28·3	9 16	40·5	19 34	41·4	6 36	21·8	19 10	21·4	0 33	10·4	13 23	9·5	2 20	16·6	14 50	17·0	11 35	11·8	23 45	12·4
7	Th	2 16	22·6	14 31	22·4	11 57	28·0	—		10 5	42·5	20 16	43·4	7 13	22·3	19 45	21·4	0 33	10·9	14 14	9·6	3 4	17·3	15 31	17·3	—		12 13	12·1
8	F	2 58	23·1	15 9	22·9	0 12	28·9	12 33	28·5	10 48	44·2	21 1	44·2	7 46	22·5	20 16	21·4	1 56	11·1	14 37	9·6	3 41	17·7	16 7	17·5	0 24	13·1	12 46	12·1
9	S	3 35	23·2	15 45	23·1	0 47	29·1	13 7	28·5	11 29	44·2	21 42	44·0	8 16	22·5	20 45	21·3	2 34	11·2	15 10	9·9	4 15	17·7	16 39	17·3	1 3	13·1	13 18	12·0
10	S	4 10	23·0	16 17	23·0	1 20	28·9	13 39	28·2	9 30	42·0	21 12	41·7	8 45	21·9	21 13	20·7	3 6	11·2	15 40	9·9	4 48	17·5	17 10	16·9	1 35	12·5	13 51	11·9
11	M	4 40	22·8	16 48	22·8	1 51	28·2	14 0	27·6	9 40	40·7	22 17	40·4	9 14	21·2	21 40	20·1	3 36	10·9	16 7	9·9	5 21	17·0	17 42	16·3	2 11	12·5	14 24	11·7
12	Tu	5 9	22·5	17 18	22·5	2 20	27·3	14 38	26·7	10 33	39·3	22 41	38·2	9 45	20·2	22 8	19·2	4 6	10·5	16 35	9·7	5 56	16·4	18 15	15·7	2 48	11·9	15 0	11·3
13	W	5 38	22·2	17 54	21·9	2 49	26·0	15 5	25·5	10 56	37·3	23 4	36·2	10 19	18·9	22 41	18·2	4 40	10·0	17 9	9·3	6 32	15·6	18 50	15·0	3 25	11·3	15 39	10·9
14	Th	6 12	21·7	18 34	21·1	3 21	24·5	15 34	24·1	11 17	35·0	23 33·7		11 11	17·4	23 42	17·0	5 21	9·5	17 49	9·3	7 10	14·8	19 28	14·4	4 6	10·5	16 23	10·5
15	F	6 52	20·8	19 19	20·0	4 1	22·8	16 31	22·7	11 51	33·6	—		11 11	17·4	—		4 55	9·9	17 28	10·0	7 55	14·0	20 14	13·8	4 55	9·9	17 28	10·0
16	S	7 36	19·8	20 16	18·7	4 58	21·3	17 36	21·5	0 10	31·2	12 39	30·3	0 25	16·0	13 37	15·7	4 55	9·4	18 26	9·8	8 53	13·3	21 15	13·3	5 59	9·4	18 26	9·8
17	S	8 29	18·3	21 13	17·6	6 16	20·3	18 58	21·0	1 10	29·0	13 54	28·5	1 57	15·6	15 18	15·6	7 4	9·3	19 41	10·0	10 10	12·9	22 33	13·3	7 23	9·3	19 41	10·0
18	M	9 38	17·5	22 39	17·4	7 51	20·6	20 24	22·2	2 11	30·0	14 54	29·8	3 27	16·7	16 26	17·1	8 40	9·7	20 48	10·4	11 35	13·2	23 53	13·7	8 40	9·7	20 48	10·4
19	Tu	11 12	17·7	—		9 11	22·3	21 30	24·1	2 45	35·4	15 16	37·0	4 28	18·4	17 17	18·8	9 37	10·5	21 40	11·4	—		12 45	14·1	9 37	10·5	21 40	11·4
20	W	0 6	18·5	12 26	19·2	10 4	24·4	22 18	26·2	4 29	39·7	17 12	33·1	5 17	20·2	18 0	20·3	10 23	11·0	22 25	12·2	0 57	14·6	13 40	15·1	10 23	11·0	22 25	12·2
21	Th	1 1	20·4	13 16	21·0	10 45	26·3	22 58	28·1	5 45	34·5	18 14	37·0	6 1	21·7	18 40	21·2	11 0	11·9	23 4	12·9	1 47	15·7	14 24	16·2	11 0	11·9	23 4	12·9
22	F	1 47	22·2	13 59	22·6	11 24	28·1	23 37	29·7	6 38	38·2	19 4	43·1	6 41	22·9	19 18	22·2	11 36	12·5	23 42	13·4	2 27	16·5	15 3	17·2	11 36	12·5	23 42	13·4
23	S	2 29	23·6	14 39	23·9	12 3	29·2	—		7 23	41·4	19 43	45·1	7 21	23·7	19 56	22·5	—		12 13	13·1	3 4	17·9	15 38	17·9	—		12 13	13·1
24	S	3 9	24·4	15 17	24·6	0 17	30·7	12 42	30·0	8 4	44·3	20 24	44·2	8 1	23·9	20 33	23·0	0 20	13·8	12 49	13·1	3 41	18·6	16 15	18·2	0 20	13·8	12 49	13·1
25	M	3 47	24·6	15 54	24·8	0 59	31·1	13 23	30·0	8 45	44·3	21 6	45·1	8 41	23·7	21 10	22·9	1 1	13·9	13 29	13·1	4 21	18·6	16 54	18·2	1 1	13·9	13 29	13·1
26	Tu	4 26	24·2	16 35	24·8	1 40	30·8	14 3	29·6	9 27	44·8	21 48	45·5	9 24	22·9	21 56	21·2	1 46	13·7	14 12	13·0	5 4	18·8	17 39	17·8	1 46	13·7	14 12	13·0
27	W	5 7	23·4	17 19	24·1	2 23	29·7	14 45	28·5	10 18	44·3	22 39	43·8	10 13	21·2	22 31	21·2	2 35	13·3	15 1	12·6	5 53	18·2	18 27	17·0	2 35	13·3	15 1	12·6
28	Th	5 50	22·3	18 8	23·0	3 7	28·0	15 30	26·9	10 47	42·5	23 9	40·4	11 6	19·9	23 33	18·6	3 28	12·8	15 56	12·1	6 46	17·3	19 19	16·2	3 28	12·8	15 56	12·1
29	F	6 39	20·9	19 2	21·2	4 0	25·9	16 25	25·0	11 25	39·8	23 49	38·0	6 199		23 7	18·6	4 29	11·8	17 15	11·5	7 44	15·2	20 19	15·3	4 29	11·8	17 15	11·5
30	S	7 35	19·7	20 7	20·3	5 6	23·8	17 38	23·4	0 39	34·4	13 33·3		12 18	18·3	—		5 42	11·0	18 17	11·1	8 52	15·2	22 28	14·7	5 42	11·0	18 17	11·1

* All times shown are Central European Time = British Summer Time. To obtain Greenwich Mean Time, subtract one hour. † Difference of height in feet from Ordnance Datum (Newlyn). ‡ Difference of height in feet from Ordnance Datum (Ireland). (See notes, p. 184.) § See note, p. 175.

OCTOBER, 1972

High Water at the undermentioned Places (C.E.T.*)—

Day of Month	Day of Week	LONDON BRIDGE †Datum of Predictions 10·50 ft. below				LIVERPOOL †Datum of Predictions 14·54 ft. below				BRISTOL (Avonmouth) †Datum of Predictions 20·11 ft. below				HULL (Salnee) †Datum of Predictions 10·68 ft. below				GREENOCK †Datum of Predictions 4·80 ft. below				LEITH§ AND GRANTON †Datum of Predictions 8·92 ft. below				DUN LAOGHAIRE †Datum of Predictions 1·43 ft. above			
		Mn. h.m.	Ht. ft.	Aft. h.m.	Ht. ft.	Mn. h.m.	Ht. ft.	Aft. h.m.	Ht. ft.	Mn. h.m.	Ht. ft.	Aft. h.m.	Ht. ft.	Mn. h.m.	Ht. ft.	Aft. h.m.	Ht. ft.	Mn. h.m.	Ht. ft.	Aft. h.m.	Ht. ft.	Mn. h.m.	Ht. ft.	Aft. h.m.	Ht. ft.	Mn. h.m.	Ht. ft.	Aft. h.m.	Ht. ft.

* All times shown are Central European Time = British Summer Time, in force from March 19, (0200 hrs. G.M.T.) to October 29 (0200 hrs. G.M.T.), 1972. To obtain Greenwich Mean Time, subtract one hour.   † Difference of height in feet from Ordnance Datum. (*See notes*, p. 184.)

§ *See note*, p. 175.

NOVEMBER, 1972

High Water at the undermentioned Places (C.E.T.*)—

Day of Month	Day of Week	LONDON BRIDGE † Datum of Predictions 10·50 ft. below				LIVERPOOL † Datum of Predictions 14·54 ft. below				BRISTOL (*Avonmouth*) † Datum of Predictions 20·11 ft. below				HULL (*Salend*) † Datum of Predictions 10·68 ft. below				GREENOCK † Datum of Predictions 4·80 ft. below				LEITH AND GRANTON † Datum of Predictions 8·92 ft. below				DUN LAOGHAIRE ‡ Datum of Predictions 1·43 ft. above			
		Mn. h.m.	Ht. ft.	Aft. h.m.	Ht.	Mn. h.m.	Ht. ft.	Aft. h.m.	Ht.	Mn. h.m.	Ht. ft.	Aft. h.m.	Ht.	Mn. h.m.	Ht. ft.	Aft. h.m.	Ht.	Mn. h.m.	Ht. ft.	Aft. h.m.	Ht.	Mn. h.m.	Ht. ft.	Aft. h.m.	Ht.	Mn. h.m.	Ht. ft.	Aft. h.m.	Ht.
1	W	1041	19·2	2328	20·1	851	23·9	2115	25·0	427	33·6	1655	35·3	3	2	1557	18·1	1025	8·9	22 1	9·4			1214	15·6	919	11·1	2130	12·0
2	Th	1151	20·2			940	25·2	2205	26·1	530	36·1	1753	37·7	4 5	17·8	1648	19·0	1110	9·3	2257	9·8			13 0	16·1	10 9	11·5	2221	12·3
3	F	030	21·3	1248	21·6	1029	26·3	2246	26·8	620	38·1	1838	39·3	455	19·7	1730	19·8	1146	9·6	2341	10·2	131	16·3	1355	16·4	1049	11·8	23 3	12·4
4	S	120	22·5	1336	22·6	11 5	27·1	2321	27·2	7 1	39·6	1917	40·1	530	20·3	1810	20·5	213	10·2	1734	10·6	213	16·7	1434	16·6	1120	12·0	2339	12·4
5	S	2	23·2	1417	23·1	1139	27·6			737	40·2	1952	40·1	614	20·7	1840	20·9	249	16·8	1539	16·8	253	17·0	1539	16·8	1153	12·1		
6	M	239	23·4	1454	23·4	1211	27·8	2354	27·3	813	40·2	2023	40·1	649	20·8	1912	21·1	322	16·8	1539	16·8	322	16·8	1539	16·8	0 12	12·2	1222	12·2
7	Tu	311	23·2	1527	23·2	026	27·2	1242	27·8	841	40·3	2054	39·7	724	20·7	1942	21·1	355	16·6	1610	16·7	355	16·6	1610	16·7	044	11·9	1251	12·2
8	W	338	22·8	1559	22·8	057	26·8	1313	27·6	910	39·8	2122	38·6	758	20·4	2010	20·8	428	16·6	1641	16·5	428	16·6	1641	16·5	116	11·6	1323	12·1
9	Th	4 5	22·2	1631	22·4	127	26·3	1343	27·7	937	38·5	2149	37·7	833	19·9	2039	20·5	5 3	16·3	1714	16·3	5 3	16·3	1714	16·3	151	11·3	1359	11·9
10	F	435	22·2	1705	21·9	158	25·6	1415	26·4	5 3	37·6	2217	36·5	540	15·8	1750	15·8	540	15·8	1750	15·8	209	10·9	1439	11·7	350	10·9	1439	11·7
11	S	5 9	21·8	1742	21·4	232	24·7	1451	25·6	1028	36·4	2249	34·6	621	15·2	1831	15·3	621	15·2	1831	15·3	311	10·6	1521	11·4	311	10·6	1521	11·4
12	S	544	21·3	1823	20·9	313	23·8	1538	24·7	1102	34·4	2331	33·0	7 7	14·6	1918	14·8	358	10·3	16 0	11·2	358	10·3	16 0	11·2				
13	M	622	20·7	1904	20·3	4 4	22·7	1635	23·4	1153	33·0			8 0	14·1	2011	14·5	452	10·2	17 8	11·0	452	10·2	17 8	11·0				
14	Tu	7 6	20·0	1956	19·6	5 6	22·1	1732	23·4	0 4	33·8	1254	34·1	859	13·9	2113	14·4	557	9·9	18 6	10·9	557	9·9	18 6	10·9				
15	W	8 3	19·4	2104	19·5	612	22·6	1843	23·6	130	31·4	1400	34·2	10 5	14·0	2218	14·6	7 8	10·1	1913	11·1	7 8	10·1	1913	11·1				
16	Th	916	19·2	2227	19·1	730	23·8	1952	24·5	3 0	32·4	1540	33·8	1110	14·5	2321	15·2	8·4	10·0	2017	11·1	8 4	10·0	2017	11·1				
17	F	1043	20·0	2338	21·4	852	25·0	2150	25·9	418	34·8	1653	36·6			1353	15·3	956	10·0	2214	12·6	956	10·0	2214	12·6				
18	S					932	26·0	2150	26·7	523	37·7	1751	39·3	021	16·0	13 4	15·3	1039	10·4	2250	13·0	1039	10·4	2250	13·0				
19	S	036	22·6	1249	22·9	1022	27·7	2241	28·8	617	40·4	1844	41·5	019	17·7	1328	15·3	114	16·9	1353	17·0	1120	13·0	2336	13·2				
20	M	216	23·3	1341	23·8	1110	28·9	2331	29·6	7 7	42·0	1934	42·7	2 4	17·7	1439	17·6	2 4	17·7	1439	17·6			12 1	13·3				
21	Tu	3 2	23·2	1421	24·5	020	29·9	1244	30·1	756	43·2	2023	43·7	253	18·3	1513	18·3	253	18·3	1513	18·3	023	13·0	1246	13·4				
22	W	3 2	23·0	1501	24·5	110	30·6	1332	29·8	845	43·8	2112	43·4	342	18·6	1613	18·3	342	18·6	1613	18·3	17 3	18·1	1336	13·4				
23	Th	348	24·0	1539	24·5	159	30·8	1420	29·1	932	43·7	2205	42·4	434	18·6	17 3	18·1	527	17·7	1755	17·7	2 7	17·4	1429	13·2				
24	F	435	23·9	1539	24·3	249	28·9	1430	27·9	1022	42·7	2248	41·5	527	18·5	1755	17·7	621	17·5	1850	17·0	3 4	16·8	1525	12·9				
25	S	523	23·6	1753	23·6	250	27·6	1539	26·6	11 0	41·0	2336	39·6	5 2	16·6	1650	16·3	718	16·6	1947	16·3	4 4	11·5	1626	12·4				
26	S	612	22·8	1845	22·4	343	26·1	16 5	25·2	1057	39·1	2354	39·0	5 2	10·3	1748	9·8	816	15·8	2046	15·5	511	10·9	1733	12·0				
27	M	7 3	20·1	1939	21·4	441	24·7	17 2	25·2	058	18·1	1255	19·0	918	15·2	2149	15·2	624	10·5	1845	11·6	624	10·5	1845	11·6				
28	Tu	854	19·3	2138	19·4	545	23·6	18 7	24·2	221	33·1	1447	33·7	9 8	15·2	2254	15·2	738	10·6	1955	11·4	738	10·6	1955	11·4				
29	W	959	19·0	2250	19·5	654	23·1	1919	23·7	2 8	17·7	1744	17·2	1024	15·0	2254	15·1	738	10·6	1955	11·4	738	10·6	1955	11·4				
30	Th					8 3	23·3	2028	23·9	331	33·5	1558	33·9	2 8	17·7	1744	17·2	1130	15·1	2358	15·3	842	10·6	2058	11·4				

* All times shown are Central European Time: to obtain Greenwich Mean Time, subtract one hour.　　† Difference of height in feet from Ordnance Datum (Newlyn).　　‡ Difference of height in feet from Ordnance Datum (Ireland).　(*See notes*, p. 184.)　§ *See note*, p. 175.

DECEMBER, 1972

High Water at the undermentioned Places (C.E.T.*)—

Day of Month	Day of Week	LONDON BRIDGE † Datum of Predictions 10.50 ft. below				LIVERPOOL † Datum of Predictions 14.54 ft. below				BRISTOL (Avonmouth) † Datum of Predictions 20.11 ft. below				HULL (Salend) † Datum of Predictions 10.68 ft. below				GREENOCK † Datum of Predictions 4.80 ft. below				LEITH§ AND GRANTON † Datum of Predictions 8.92 ft. below				DUN LAOGHAIRE ‡ Datum of Predictions 1.43 ft. above			
		Mn. h.m.	Ht. ft.	Aft. h.m.	Ht. ft.	Mn. h.m.	Ht. ft.	Aft. h.m.	Ht. ft.	Mn. h.m.	Ht. ft.	Aft. h.m.	Ht. ft.	Mn. h.m.	Ht. ft.	Aft. h.m.	Ht. ft.	Mn. h.m.	Ht. ft.	Aft. h.m.	Ht. ft.	Mn. h.m.	Ht. ft.	Aft. h.m.	Ht. ft.	Mn. h.m.	Ht. ft.	Aft. h.m.	Ht. ft.
1	F	11 8	19.4	2350	20.3	9 3	24.0	2126	24.4	437	33.9	17 2	35.0	316	17.8	16 5	17.9	1026	9.2	2212	9.6	053	15.5	1328	15.3	935	10.9	2151	11.5
2	S	1212	20.5	—	—	952	24.9	2213	25.0	534	35.4	1756	36.2	415	18.3	1653	18.7	711	9	23 3	9.9	140	15.8	1418	15.6	1020	11.3	2237	11.5
3	S	045	21.3	1252	21.6	1034	25.7	2254	25.9	623	36.8	1842	37.1	5 4	18.8	1735	19.5	1149	9.9	2349	10.1	221	15.9	1439	16.1	1056	11.5	2317	11.5
4	M	130	22.0	1335	22.3	7 6	26.4	2337	25.9	7 6	37.9	1924	37.9	549	19.2	1813	20.1	—	—	1227	10.1	221	15.9	15 8	16.1	1128	11.7	2351	11.5
5	Tu	210	22.3	1415	22.7	1148	26.1	—	—	743	38.7	20 1	38.5	631	19.8	1848	20.5	031	10.2	13 1	10.4	3 0	16.1	1515	16.3	12 0	11.9	—	—
6	W	244	22.3	1453	22.5	0 6	26.1	1222	27.3	821	39.3	2036	38.7	719	19.8	1921	20.6	110	10.1	1338	10.5	337	16.3	1549	16.5	025	11.3	1231	12.0
7	Th	315	22.5	1543	22.5	044	25.9	1255	27.5	854	39.5	2114	38.8	750	19.9	1953	20.6	148	10.0	1338	10.6	413	16.4	1622	16.6	134	11.1	13 4	12.0
8	F	347	22.3	1617	22.3	040	26.2	1328	27.4	926	39.2	2141	38.1	828	19.7	2024	20.6	224	9.8	1439	10.6	449	16.4	1657	16.7	134	11.1	1341	12.1
9	S	420	22.0	1653	22.1	147	25.9	14 1	27.2	957	38.5	2213	37.4	9 5	19.5	2056	20.5	3 0	9.7	1511	10.8	525	16.4	1733	16.4	251	10.8	1419	12.0
10	S	455	21.8	1729	21.8	222	25.4	1437	26.8	1029	37.6	2243	36.5	942	19.1	2131	20.3	338	9.7	1546	10.8	6 4	15.8	18 3	16.1	251	10.8	15 0	11.9
11	M	529	21.5	18 6	21.8	3 0	24.9	1517	26.3	11 5	36.7	2326	35.6	1020	18.8	2211	20.0	547	10.0	1757	10.7	645	15.4	1856	15.5	335	10.6	1544	11.8
12	Tu	6 4	21.2	1846	21.4	344	24.3	16 2	25.7	1145	35.8	—	—	11 1	18.1	2254	19.1	2 4	18.7	1511	18.1	731	15.0	1943	15.5	420	10.5	1628	11.7
13	W	644	20.8	1932	20.8	435	23.7	1655	25.1	011	34.7	1 5	33.9	547	19.0	1757	20.7	5 2	9.9	18 4	10.4	823	14.7	2036	15.3	517	10.3	1725	11.5
14	Th	734	20.4	2145	20.5	533	23.3	1756	24.7	1 5	33.9	1333	34.2	2 4	18.7	1511	15.1	634	9.9	1854	10.4	920	14.6	2133	15.3	620	9.3	1828	11.4
15	F	837	20.2	23 1	20.5	639	23.3	19 4	24.7	210	33.6	1446	34.2	730	9.8	20 6	10.3	547	10.0	1757	10.7	1021	14.7	2235	15.4	727	10.5	1935	11.4
16	S	956	20.4	—	—	748	23.1	2028	25.2	326	34.3	1553	35.4	2 4	18.7	1511	15.1	730	9.8	20 6	10.3	1125	15.1	234	15.8	830	10.9	204	11.6
17	S	1115	21.2	1 7	20.7	856	23.1	2122	26.2	440	35.0	17 7	37.3	328	19.1	16 3	19.2	950	10.0	2233	10.6	045	16.3	1326	15.6	927	11.4	2140	11.9
18	M	0 7	21.7	1247	21.7	957	23.9	2216	27.1	547	36.5	18 2	39.4	428	20.0	1713	20.5	1049	10.2	2335	10.6	145	17.0	1426	16.4	11 3	11.7	2234	12.0
19	Tu	1 7	21.7	1327	22.3	1052	24.7	2316	27.5	647	38.2	18 7	40.6	531	20.8	1824	21.4	1143	10.9	—	—	245	17.6	15 2	17.7	11 3	11.7	2335	12.4
20	W	2 3	21.8	1425	22.7	1144	25.2	—	—	743	41.8	20 3	42.0	630	21.5	1852	22.0	034	10.9	1235	11.4	335	18.1	16 2	18.2	1148	12.9	—	—
21	Th	254	21.7	1517	22.5	010	28.8	1233	29.7	835	44.9	21 3	43.1	725	22.0	1940	22.5	131	10.9	1327	11.8	420	18.3	1651	18.3	015	12.5	1236	13.2
22	F	340	21.6	16 6	22.4	1 0	28.7	1325	29.6	923	43.5	2238	43.1	818	22.4	2027	22.6	226	10.9	1447	12.2	426	18.3	15 5	18.1	1 6	12.4	1326	13.3
23	S	425	21.1	1653	22.2	150	28.1	1438	28.7	1010	43.4	2238	42.9	9 7	22.9	2112	22.6	318	10.8	155	12.5	516	18.2	1740	18.1	158	12.4	1417	13.3
24	S	510	21.0	1739	22.4	237	28.1	1455	28.9	1054	42.5	2322	40.9	954	21.9	2154	21.9	4 6	10.7	1551	12.5	6 4	17.7	1830	17.6	250	11.9	15 9	13.1
25	M	553	22.4	1825	22.4	325	27.0	1541	27.7	1136	40.9	—	—	1038	20.4	2237	21.1	451	10.5	1656	12.2	654	16.9	1920	16.8	344	11.3	15 9	13.1
26	Tu	637	20.7	1911	22.1	413	25.7	1629	26.3	0 4	38.9	1259	38.8	1122	19.2	2320	20.0	534	10.1	1721	11.7	745	16.0	20 1	16.0	440	11.0	17 0	12.1
27	W	722	20.7	20 0	20.2	5 4	24.5	1720	24.9	045	36.5	1319	36.5	12 8	17.8	—	—	618	9.7	18 9	10.9	837	15.2	201	15.3	541	10.5	18 2	11.5
28	Th	811	19.7	2053	19.4	558	23.2	1819	23.4	129	34.4	1346	34.3	0 4	17.8	13 3	17.0	7 8	9.3	1910	10.8	933	14.6	23 3	14.5	648	10.5	1910	10.6
29	F	910	19.7	2154	19.1	7 2	22.6	1926	23.1	221	32.6	1444	32.6	147	16.5	14 4	16.6	811	9.0	20 7	10.6	1033	14.3	23 1	14.5	755	10.1	2018	10.6
30	S	1015	19.4	2255	19.3	8 6	22.5	2036	22.9	324	31.9	1548	31.9	215	16.5	1512	16.6	924	9.0	2117	10.5	1136	14.3	9 3	14.3	855	10.1	2119	10.5
31	S	1125	19.4	2359	19.4	—	—	2136	23.0	433	31.7	17 2	32.5	215	16.8	1512	17.3	1027	9.3	2222	9.4	0	14.5	1237	14.6	946	10.5	2211	10.5

* All times shown are Central European Time: to obtain Greenwich Mean Time, subtract one hour. † Difference of height in feet from Ordnance Datum (Newlyn). ‡ Difference of height in feet from Ordnance Datum (Ireland). (See notes, p. 184). § See note, p. 175.

NOTES ON TIDAL PREDICTIONS

Changes in Chart Datum

During recent years the Department of the Hydrographer of the Navy has been carrying out a survey of tidal levels. On the conclusion of each section of the survey the Department is taking the opportunity to regularize the sequence of chart datums so that eventually chart datums throughout the British Isles will approximate to the Lowest Astronomical Tide, *i.e.* the lowest level which can be predicted to occur under average meteorological conditions and under any combination of meteorological conditions.

In some cases the changes in chart datum will be appreciable (perhaps as much as 3 feet) and the resulting predictions will appear to give heights of tide quite different from those of previous years. In such cases there has been no change in the tidal conditions, but simply an apparent change due to the fact that the new heights have been measured from a different level.

It will be found that, where such datum changes have been made, the relationship between Ordnance Datum and the datum of the predictions will also have been altered. In order to compare the predictions for one year with those of another year for which the datum has been altered, it is necessary to refer both years to the same datum. Ordnance Datum (Newlyn) is a convenient datum to which tidal heights may thus be referred.

Example.—In 1965, at Devonport, the highest predicted high water was 17·6 feet above chart datum; chart datum for that year was 8·9 feet below Ordnance Datum (Newlyn). In 1966 the highest predicted high water was 19·6 feet above chart datum, while chart datum for this year was altered to 10·6 feet below Ordnance Datum (Newlyn). To compare these two maximum predicted levels we must reduce both to Ordnance Datum (Newlyn), with the following results:—

$$1965 \quad 17·6 - 8·9 = +8·7$$
$$1966 \quad 19·6 - 10·6 = +9·0$$

Thus it will be seen that the highest prediction for 1966 is only 0·3 ft. higher than for 1965.

The datum of the predictions for each port to be found in the headings of each of the preceding pages is unchanged from those quoted in *Whitaker*, 1971, with the exception of the datum from Leith and Granton which is reduced for 1972 predictions by 0·03 ft. to 8·9 ft. below Ordnance Datum (Newlyn).

Tidal predictions for London Bridge, Liverpool, Bristol, Hull, Greenock and Leith are supplied by the Institute of Coastal Oceanography and Tides, copyright reserved. Tidal predictions for Dún Laoghaire are based upon data supplied by the Institute of Coastal Oceanography and Tides, copyright reserved.

Chronological Notes

TIME MEASURES

Kelvin (1883) estimated the age of the earth's crust at 20–400 million years. Study of radioactivity has since shown cooling to have been slower. Holmes and others gave 1,500–2,000 million years as the age of the oldest known rocks. Jeffreys suggests an age not exceeding 8,000 million years for the separate existence of the earth, which, probably with other related planets, separated from the sun after a star-collision. Very early rocks, almost without traces of fossils, are variously named in North America and Europe and account for a period down to about 500 million years ago.

PALÆOZOIC (Old Animal Life) PERIODS include:—

Cambrian, Ordovician and Silurian rocks, all named from Wales (Cambria, Ordovices, Silures, the two latter ancient Celtic peoples). These rocks account for about 200 million years and there then followed a major phase of mountain-building, called *Caledonian* because studied early in Scotland, characterized by N.E.–S.W. lines of hills and valleys in several areas.

Devonian, including the Old Red Sandstone.

Carboniferous, including Mountain Limestone, Millstone Grit and Coal Measures.

These rocks account for about 100 million years and then there followed a major phase of mountain-building called *Hercynian* because widespread in W. Germany and adjacent areas. In Britain there are E.–W. lines of hills and valleys, and some N.–S.

MESOZOIC (Middle Forms of Life) PERIODS include:—

Permian rocks, widespread in Perm district, U.S.S.R. *Triassic,* including New Red Sandstone. *Jurassic,* important in the Jura Mts. *Cretaceous,* including the Greensands and the Chalk of England. In the Mesozoic, modern large land groups of animals, reptiles, birds and mammals first appear, but almost no modern genera or species of animals are known.

CAINOZOIC or CENOZOIC (Recent forms of Life) PERIODS include :—

Eocene. A few existing genera or species *Oligocene.* A minority of existing forms. *Miocene.* Approach to a balance of existing and extinct forms. *Pliocene.* A majority of existing forms. *Pleistocene.* A very large majority of existing forms. *Holocene.* Existing forms only, save for a few exterminated by man. In the last 50 million years, from the Miocene through the Pliocene, the Alpine-Himalayan and the circum-Pacific phases of mountain building reached their climax.

During the Pleistocene period icesheets repeatedly locked up masses of water as land ice, its weight depressed the land, but the locking up of water lowered sea-level by 100–200 metres. Milankovitch has worked out variations of radiation theoretically receivable from the sun and has reached conclusions not very markedly different as to dates from those of Penck who studied sediments, and both can fit into Deperet's scheme based on study of river terraces. Milankovitch gives 600,000 years for the Pleistocene.

Phases of the Pleistocene:—

(*a*) Early Glaciations (probably 2), Gunz glaciations of Penck's Alpine series. About 600 to 500 thousand years ago.

(*b*) An interglacial phase with high sea level, Milazzian terraces (of Deperet's series) around the Mediterranean. About 500,000 years ago.

(*c*) A second pair of Glaciations, the Mindel of Penck's series. About 500 to rather before 400 thousand years ago.

(*d*) A long interglacial phase with high sea level, but less high than during (*b*). Tyrrhenian terraces around the Mediterranean. From about 400 to about 200 thousand years ago.

(*e*) The penultimate series of glaciations (probably 3), the Riss of Penck's series. About 200 to 150 thousand years ago.

(*f*) An interglacial phase with fairly high sea level, less high than during (*d*). Monastirian terraces around the Mediterranean. From about 150 to about 120 thousand years ago.

(*g*) The ultimate series of glaciations (probably 3, preceded perhaps by a cool phase), the Wurm of Penck's series. From about 115 to rather more than 20 thousand years ago.

(*h*) The last glacial retreat merging into the Holocene period about 10,000 or 8,000 years ago.

MAN IN THE PLEISTOCENE

In the East African Miocene have been found by Hopwood and Leakey fragmentary remains of apes with possible human links in thigh bone characters.

In S. Africa at Taungs, Sterkfontein and Kroomdraai have been found remains of *Australopithecus*, *Plesianthropus* and *Paranthropus*, possibly linked with early man in limb characters and some features of skull and teeth though the brains are small and rather ape-like. The cave deposits in which they occur are supposed to be late Pliocene or early Pleistocene

Java and Peking finds began with Dubois' discovery (1892) of an imperfect skull cap, some teeth and a possibly related femur indicating the erect posture. Later finds by von Koenigswald and by Weidenreich (1937–41) have emphasized the human relationship of the Java specimens, and also give evidence of gigantism (the name *Meganthropus* has been used). The specimens are usually given a Middle Pleistocene age. Oppenoorth (1932) discovered robust skulls and human Pleistocene bones on a terrace of the Solo river, Java. Twelve specimens from Chou Kou Tien near Peking studied by Black and Weidenreich and called *Sinanthropus* are broadly like the Java finds; the name *Pithecanthropus* had better be used for all.

A jaw from Mauer, Heidelberg, found 1902, and dated to the mid Pleistocene is very large but human in form. A skull cap from Neandertal near Düsseldorf, Germany, has been under discussion for 100 years. It and later found congeners belong to the onset of the 4th series of Glaciations (Penck's Wurm). The best preserved of these skulls is that of La Chapelle aux Saints (France) with very strong brow-ridges. Related skulls of rather earlier date from Steinheim, Ehringsdorf, Krapina and elsewhere are less specialized and more akin to modern man. Skulls from Sacco Pastore and Circeo in Italy are related to the Neandertal group.

Mt. Carmel, Palestine, has yielded to Professor Dorothy Garrod and Dr. McCown several mid- or late Pleistocene specimens apparently related both to modern types and to the Neandertal group.

A skull from Galilee, and a skull from Kabwe (formerly Broken Hill), Zambia, are related to the Neandertal group.

Recently Oakley has estimated the age of Pleistocene fossil bones from their fluorine content. The back part of a skull from Swanscombe, N. Kent, has in this way been dated to the mid Pleistocene. Its discoverer, Marston, has won widespread support for his view linking it with modern types.

Controversy over the Piltdown skull and jaw is ended. The skull was dated by Oakley's method as late Pleistocene, or later, so the old name *Eoanthropus* is inappropriate. The ape-like jaw was found to be modern and to have nothing to do with the skull.

With the last retreat of the ice sheets it seems that the Neandertal group, and probably the Pithecanthropus group, became extinct. Well-known specimens of man of modern type with diversity of form have been found at Combe Capelle, Cro-Magnon, Chancelade and elsewhere in the later Pleistocene in France and others in Czechoslovakia.

HUMAN CULTURAL STAGES

Until about 8 or 7 thousand years ago men lived by hunting and collecting. In the middle of the Pleistocene they already made finely shaped hand axes (Abbevillean and Acheulian) from stone cores by chipping off flakes, using flint, chert, obsidian, rhyolite, quartzite, etc. in many regions, and these cultures spread from Africa to Spain, France and Britain during some interglacial periods. Apparently the men hunted and made pitfalls for animals as Leakey has shown at Olorgesailie in Kenya, while women and children collected. Fire was used very early. In the continental interior of Eurasia rough stone flakes were long used rather than shaped stone cores and apparently in cold periods at any rate this culture spread west to Britain. In the later part of the Riss-Wurm interglacial, stone flakes became finer especially in regions where contact was made with makers of core-tools, and in some groups both cores and flakes were used.

With the last retreat of the ice-sheets stone flakes became the dominant tools, with diverse types suited to scraping, boring, sawing, etc.—Aurignacian, followed in France by Solutrian, in which long leaf-like flakes were treated as cores and shaped very skilfully by pressing off flakes. The Magdalenian stage next following used flakes but specialized in implements of bone, horn and ivory. In some areas the Aurignacian grades into the Magdalenian and this seems to be largely the case in parts of Britain. All the above cultures are often grouped as Palæolithic.

About 8 or 7 thousand years ago people in S.W. Asia began to cultivate cereals on river mud laid down by annual floods, thus keeping the soil fertile and allowing durable settlement with concomitant advances in mud brick construction, pot-making, stone grinding, which had begun earlier and gave an improved control of shape, carpentering, weaving and other inventions. In all this development the Nile valley was early concerned and its regular floods from summer rains in Abyssinia could be managed to give such an advantage that Egypt gained a unique primacy in early history. Domestication of animals was added very early to cultivation of crops, most probably as a source of milk, flesh, leather, sinews, etc. Neolithic Culture was thus characterized by stone axes shaped by grinding or rubbing, by cultivation, usually by domestic animals, often by durable settlements and a variety of arts and crafts.

Especially after the practice of castration of surplus male animals was introduced, domestic beasts were used for work, notably for pulling a modified hoe to scratch the drying surface of river-mud and so keep it from caking too hard. This is the early plough, valuable in lands where plant food in the soil is drawn up nearly to the surface as moisture rises and evaporates. Animals were also used as porters and tractors.

Heating stones in fires, probably for water-heating, led to the discovery of impure copper and the invention of bronze (standardized at about 10 per cent. tin and 90 per cent. copper) at the beginning of the Bronze Age in S.W. Asia and/or Egypt. By that time, about 5,000 years ago, cities and trade were developing and the basic arts were spreading to the Indus basin, the Mediterranean and the loess areas of Central Europe. Western Europe on the one hand and N. China on the other were affected somewhat later but more than 4,000 years ago; and China rapidly advanced to a high skill in pottery and bronze. Over 3,000 years ago in Anatolia the smelting of iron was developed, and it spread thence in the next centuries, beginning the Iron Age. Iron nails and tools made possible larger boats, houses, furniture and especially larger ploughs, working

deeper into the earth and so suited to cooler lands, where plant food was often deep in the soil because evaporation was not very strong and rain might occur at every season. So the farmer needed to bring up the deeper layers to the surface in north-west Europe. With the spread of iron, especially about 2,000 to 1,000 years ago, northwest Europe emerged from its former low status and went ahead, still more after houses were improved with more privacy, chimneys and beds.

The evolution of culture in the Americas is much discussed. Early drifts of hunters viâ Alaska may have occurred in the late Pleistocene. Probably a good deal of Neolithic culture (stone implements, pottery, etc.) spread by the same route to America about or after 5,000 years ago but did not take Asiatic cereals or domestic animals. America also received contributions to its life by maritime routes especially following the North Pacific currents.

TIME MEASUREMENT AND CALENDARS

MEASUREMENTS OF TIME

Measurements of Time.—These are based on the time taken by the earth to rotate on its axis (*Day*); by the moon to revolve round the earth (*Month*); and by the earth to revolve round the sun (*Year*). From these, which are not commensurable, certain average or mean intervals have been adopted for ordinary use. Of these the first is the *Day*, which begins at midnight and is divided into 24 hours of 60 minutes, each of 60 seconds. The hours are counted from midnight up to 12 at noon (when the sun crosses the meridian), and these hours are designated A.M. (*ante meridiem*); and again from noon up to 12 at midnight, which hours are designated P.M. (*post meridiem*), except when the *Twenty-four Hour* reckoning is employed. The 24-hour reckoning ignores A.M. and P.M., and the hours are numbered 0 to 23 from midnight to midnight.

Colloquially the 24 hours are divided into *day* and *night*, day being the time while the sun is above the horizon (including the four stages of twilight defined on p. 139). Day is subdivided further into *morning*, the early part of daytime, ending at noon; *afternoon* from noon to 6 p.m. and *evening*, which may be said to extend from 6 p.m. until midnight. *Night*, the dark period between day and day, begins at the close of Astronomical Twilight (*see* p. 139) and extends beyond midnight to sunrise the next day.

The names of the *Days*—Sunday, Monday, Tuesday (Tiw=God of War), Wednesday (Woden or Odin), Thursday (Thor), Friday (Frig=wife of Odin), and Saturday are derived from Old English translations or adaptations of the Roman names (Sol, Luna, Mars, Mercurius, Jupiter, Venus and Saturnius).

The *Week* is a period of 7 days.

The *Month* in the ordinary calendar is approximately the twelfth part of a year, but the lengths of the different months vary from 28 (or 29) days to 31.

The Year.—The *Equinoctial* or *Tropical Year* is the time that the earth takes to revolve round the sun from equinox to equinox, or 365·2422 mean solar days. The *Calendar Year* consists of 365 days, but a year the date of which is divisible by 4, without remainder, is called *bissextile* (see Roman Calendar) or *Leap Year* and consists of 366 days, one day being added to the month February, so that a year "leaps over" a day of the week. The last year of a century is not a leap year unless its number is divisible by 400 (*e.g.* the years 1800 and 1900 had only 365 days).

The Historical Year.—Before the year 1752, two Calendar systems were in use in England. The Civil or Legal Year began on March 25, while the Historical Year began on January 1. Thus the Civil or Legal date 1658 March 24, was the same day as 1659 March 24 Historical; and a date in that portion of the year is written as: March 24 165⅞, the lower figure showing the Historical year.

The Masonic Year.—Two dates are quoted in warrants, dispensations etc., issued by the United Grand Lodge of England, those for the current year being expressed as *Anno Domini* 1972—*Anno Lucis* 5972. This *Year of Light* is based on the Book of Genesis I: 3, the 4000 year difference being derived from *Ussher's Notation*, published in 1654, which placed the Creation of the World in 4,000 B.C.

Regnal Years.—These are the years of a sovereign's reign, and each begins on the anniversary of his or her accession: *e.g.* Regnal year 20 of the present Queen began on Feb. 6, 1971. The system was used for dating Acts of Parliament until 1962. The *Summer Time Act* of 1925, for example, is quoted as 15 and 16 Geo. V. c. 64, because it became law in the session which extended over part of both of these regnal years. The regnal years of Edward VII began on January 22, which was the day of Queen Victoria's death in 1901, so that Acts passed in that reign are, in general, quoted with only one year number, but year 10 of the series ended on May 6, 1910, being the day on which King Edward died, and Acts of the Parliamentary Session 1910 are headed 10 Edw. VII. and 1 Geo. V.; Acts passed in 1936 were dated 1 Edw. VIII. and 1 Geo. VI.; Acts passed in 1952 were dated 16 Geo. VI. and 1 Elizabeth II. An Act to effect the dating of Acts of Parliament by the calendar year, Parl. No. 1, 1963, received the Royal Assent on July 19, 1962.

New Year's Day.—In England in the seventh century, and as late as the thirteenth, the year was reckoned from Christmas Day, but in the twelfth century the Anglican Church began the year with the Feast of The Annunciation of the Blessed Virgin (Lady Day) on March 25 and this practice was adopted generally in the fourteenth century. The Civil or Legal year in the British Dominions (exclusive of Scotland), as opposed to the Historical, which already began on Jan. 1, began with "Lady Day" until 1751. But in and since 1752 the civil year has begun with Jan. 1. Certain dividends are still paid by the Bank of England on dates based on Old Style. The Income Tax year begins on April 6 (the New Style equivalent of March 25, Old Style) in accordance with Act of Parliament (39 Geo. III. 1798). New Year's Day in *Scotland* was changed from March 25 to Jan. 1 in 1600. On the Continent of Europe Jan. 1 was adopted as the first day of the year by Venice in 1522, Germany in 1544, Spain, Portugal, and the Roman Catholic Netherlands in 1556. Prussia, Denmark and Sweden in 1559, France 1564, Lorraine 1579, Protestant Netherlands 1583, Russia 1725, Tuscany 1751.

The Longest Day.—The longest day measured from sunrise to sunset at any place is the day on which the Sun attains its greatest distance from the Equator, north or south, accordingly as the place is in the northern or southern hemisphere; in other words, it is the day of the Calendar on which a Solstice falls. If a Solstice falls on June 21 late in the day, by Greenwich Time, that day will be the longest of the year at Greenwich, though it may be by only a second of time or a fraction

thereof, but it will be on June 22 (local date) in Japan, and therefore June 22 will be the longest day there and at places in Eastern longitudes.

But leaving this question of locality and confining consideration to Greenwich, the Solstices are events in the Tropical Year whose length is 365¼ days less about 11 minutes, and therefore, if a Solstice happens late on June 21 in one year, it will be nearly six hours later in the next, or early on June 22, and that will be the longest day. This delay of the Solstice is not permitted to continue because the extra day in Leap Year brings it back a day in the Calendar, and at the present time three of the four years in the Leap Year cycle have the longest day on June 21, one on June 22 (1971, then 1975). By the end of the century the longest day will fall each year on June 21.

Because of the 11 minutes above mentioned the additional day in Leap Year brings the Solstice back too far by 44 minutes, and the time of the Solstice in the calendar is earlier as the century progresses. In the year 2000 the Summer Solstice reaches its earliest date for 100 years, *i.e.*, June 21^d 02^h.

To remedy this the last year of a century is in most cases not a Leap Year, and the omission of the extra day puts the date of the Solstice later by about six hours too much, compensation for which is made by making the fourth centennial year a Leap Year.

The Shortest Day.—Similar considerations apply to the shortest day of the year, or the day of the Winter Solstice. At the present time one year of the Leap Year cycle has the shortest day on Dec. 21 (1972, then 1976) and the rest on Dec. 22, but in roughly the last quarter of the century the shortest day will fall on Dec. 21 in two years of each four and on Dec. 22 in the remaining two years. In the year 2000 the Winter Solstice reaches its earliest date, *i.e.*, Dec. 21^d 13^h. The difference due to locality also prevails in the same sense as for the longest day.

At Greenwich the Sun sets at its earliest by the clock about ten days before the shortest day, which is a circumstance that may require explanation. The daily change in the time of sunset is due in the first place to the Sun's movement southwards at this time of year, which diminishes the interval between the Sun's southing or Apparent noon, and its setting, and, secondly, because of the daily decrease of the Equation of Time subtractive from Apparent time, which causes the time of Apparent noon to be continuously later, day by day, and so in a measure counteracts the first effect. The rates of the resulting daily acceleration and retardation are not equal, nor are they uniform, but are such that their combination causes the date of earliest sunset to be Dec. 13 or 14 at Greenwich. In more southerly latitudes the effect of the movement of the Sun is less, and the change in the time of sunset depends on that of the Equation of Time to a greater degree, and the date of earliest sunset is earlier than it is at Greenwich.

Lord Mayor's Day.—The Lord Mayor of London was previously elected on the Feast of St. Simon and St. Jude (Oct. 28), and from the time of Edward I, at least, was presented to the King or to the Barons of the Exchequer on the following day, except that day be a Sunday.

The day of election was altered to Oct. 16 in 1346, and after some further changes was fixed for Michaelmas Day in 1546, but the ceremonies of admittance and swearing-in of the Lord Mayor continued to take place on Oct. 28 and 29 respectively until 1751. In 1752, when Sept. 3 was reckoned as Sept. 14 at the reform of the Calendar, the Lord Mayor was continued in office until Nov. 8, the " New Style " equivalent of Oct. 28. The Lord Mayor is now presented to the Lord Chief Justice at the Royal Courts of Justice, on the second Saturday in November to make the final declaration of office, having been sworn in at Guildhall on the preceding day.

Dog Days.—The days about the heliacal rising of the Dog Star, noted from ancient times as the hottest and most unwholesome period of the year in the Northern Hemisphere. Their incidence has been variously calculated as depending on the Greater or Lesser Dog Star (Sirius or Procyon) and their duration has been reckoned as from 30 to 54 days. A generally accepted period is from July 3 to August 15.

Metonic (Lunar, or Minor) *Cycle.*—In the year 432 B.C. Meton, an Athenian astronomer, found that 235 Lunations are very nearly, though not exactly equal in duration to 19 Solar Years, and, hence, after 19 years the Phases of the Moon recur on the same days of the month (nearly). The dates of Full Moon in a cycle of nineteen years were inscribed in *figures of gold* on public monuments in Athens, and the number showing the position of a year in the Cycle is called the *Golden Number* of that year.

Solar (or Major) *Cycle.*—A period of twenty-eight years, in any corresponding year of which the days of the week recur on the same day of the month.

Julian Period.—Proposed by Joseph Scaliger in 1582. The period is 7980 Julian years, and its first year coincides with the year 4713 B.C. 7980 is the product of the number of years in the Solar Cycle, the Metonic Cycle and the cycle of the Roman Indication (28 × 19 × 15).

Roman Indication.—A period of fifteen years, instituted for fiscal purposes about A.D. 300.

Epact.—The age of the calendar Moon, diminished by one day, on January 1, in the ecclesiastical lunar calendar.

THE FOUR SEASONS

SPRING, the first season of the year, is defined astronomically to begin in the *Northern Hemisphere* at the Vernal Equinox when the Sun enters the sign Aries (*i.e.* about March 21) and crosses the Equator, thus causing day and night to be of equal length all over the world; and to terminate at the Summer Solstice. In *Great Britain*, Spring in popular parlance comprises the months of February, March and April; in *North America* the months of March, April and May. In the *Southern Hemisphere* Spring corresponds with Autumn in the Northern Hemisphere.

SUMMER, the second and warmest season, begins astronomically at the Summer Solstice when the Sun enters the sign Cancer (about June 21). The Sun then attains its greatest northern declination and appears to stand still, the times of sunrise and sunset and the consequent length of the day showing no variation for several days together, before and after the Longest Day (June 21 or 22). Summer terminates at the Autumnal Equinox. In popular parlance Summer in *Great Britain* includes the months of May, June, July and August, Mid-summer Day being June 24. In *North America* the season includes the months of June, July and August.

AUTUMN, the third season, begins astronomically at the Autumnal Equinox (*i.e.*, about September 21) when the Sun enters the sign Libra, the beginning of which sign is at the intersection of the Equator and the Ecliptic, the point in the sky where the Sun crosses from N. to S. of the Equator and causes the length of day and night to be equal all over the world. In *Great Britain* it is popularly held to include the months of September and October. A warm period sometimes occurs round about St. Luke's Day (Oct. 18) and is known as "St. Luke's Summer." In *North America*,

Autumn, or "The Fall," comprises September, October and November. Autumn ends at the Winter Solstice. In the *Southern Hemisphere* it corresponds with Spring of the Northern Hemisphere.

WINTER, the fourth and coldest season, begins astronomically at the Winter Solstice (*i.e.* about Dec. 21) when the Sun enters the sign Capricornus, and ends at the Vernal Equinox. In *Great Britain*

the season is popularly held to comprise the months of November, December and January, midwinter being marked by the Shortest Day. A warm period sometimes occurs round about Martinmas (Nov. 11) and is known as "St. Martin's Summer." In *North America* the season includes the months of December, January and February. In the *Southern Hemisphere* it corresponds with Summer of the Northern Hemisphere.

THE CHRISTIAN CALENDAR

In the Christian chronological system the years are distinguished by cardinal numbers before or after the Incarnation, the period being denoted by the letters B.C. (Before Christ) or, more rarely, A.C. (*Ante Christum*), and A.D. (*Annus Domini*). The correlative dates of the epoch are the 4th year of the 194th Olympiad, the 753rd year from the Foundation of Rome, A.M. 3761 (Jewish Chronology), and the 4714th year of the Julian Period. This was introduced into Italy in the sixth century, and though first used in France in the seventh it was not universally established there until about the eighth century. It has been said that the system was introduced into England by St. Augustine (A.D. 596), but was probably not generally used until some centuries later. It was ordered to be used by the Bishops at the Council of Chelsea, A.D. 816. The actual date of the birth of Christ is somewhat uncertain. Dec. 25, 4 B.C., is supported by several lines of argument.

Old and New Style.—In the Julian Calendar all the centennial years were Leap Years, and for this reason towards the close of the sixteenth century there was a difference of 10 days between the tropical and calendar years; or, in other words, the equinox fell on March 11 of the Calendar, whereas at the time of the Council of Nicaea, A.D. 325, it had fallen on March 21. In 1582 Pope Gregory ordained that Oct. 5th should be called Oct. 15th, and that of the end-century years only the fourth should be a Leap Year (*see* p. 186). This change was adopted by Italy, France, Spain, and Portugal in 1582 ; by Prussia, the German Roman Catholic States, Switzerland, Holland, and Flanders on Jan. 1, 1583. Poland 1586, Hungary 1587, the German and Netherland Protestant States and Denmark 1700, Sweden (gradually) by the omission of eleven leap days, 1700–1740; Great Britain and her Dominions (including the North American Colonies) in 1752, by the omission of eleven days (Sept. 3 being reckoned as Sept. 14). This *Gregorian Calendar* was adopted by Japan in 1872, China in 1912, Bulgaria in 1915, Turkey and Soviet Russia in 1918, by Yugoslavia and Rumania in 1919, and by Greece in February, 1923. The Russian, Greek, Serbian and Rumanian Churches did not abandon the Julian Calendar until May, 1923, when the Gregorian, slightly modified, was adopted. The *difference* between the Old and New Styles was 11 days after 1752, 12 days after 1800, and has been 13 days since 1900. It happened that a change of the beginning of the year from March 25 to January 1 was made in England in 1752, the year in which the change from Julian to Gregorian Calendar was made, and for that reason the words Old and New Style have been used in a sense which is not strictly correct, but is nevertheless expressive.

The Dominical Letter is one of the letters A–G which are used to denote the Sundays in successive years. If the first day of the year is a Sunday the letter is A; if the second, B; the third, C; and so on. Leap year requires two letters, the first for Jan. 1—Feb. 29, the second for March 1—Dec. 31.

Epiphany.—The Feast of the Epiphany, commemorating the manifestation of the infant Jesus to the Gentiles, later became associated with the offering of gifts by the Magi. The day was of exceptional importance from the time of the Council of Nicaea (A.D. 325) as the primate of Alexandria was charged at every Epiphany Feast with the announcement in a letter to the Churches of the date of the forthcoming Easter. The day was of considerable importance in Britain as it influenced dates, ecclesiastical and lay, *e.g.* Plow Monday, when work was resumed in the fields, falls upon the Monday in the first full week after the Epiphany.

Lent.—The Teutonic word *Lent*, which denotes the Fast preceding Easter, originally meant no more than the Spring season; but from Anglo-Saxon times, at least, it has been used as the equivalent of the more significant Latin term *Quadragesima*, meaning the "Forty Days" or, more literally, the fortieth day. As early as the fifth century some of the Fathers of the Church put forward the view that the forty days Fast is of Apostolic origin, but this is not supported or believed by modern scholars; and it appears to some that it dates from the early years of the fourth century. There is some suggestion that the Fast was kept originally for only forty hours. *Ash Wednesday* is the first day of Lent, which ends at midnight before Easter Day.

Sexagesima and Septuagesima.—It has been suggested that the unmeaning application of the names *Sexagesima* and *Septuagesima* to the second and third Sundays before Lent was made by analogy with the names *Quadragesima* and *Quinquagesima*. Another less likely conjecture is that *Septuagesima* means the seventieth day before the Octave of Easter. It is not certain whether the name *Quinquagesima* is due to the fact that the Sunday in question is the fiftieth day before Easter (reckoned inclusive) or was simply formed on the analogy of *Quadragesima* (*New English Dictionary*).

Palm Sunday commemorates the triumphal entry of Our Lord into Jerusalem (when palm is not available) by branches of willow gathered for use in the decoration of churches on that day.

Maundy Thursday, the day before Good Friday, the name itself being a corruption of *dies mandati* (day of the mandate) when Christ washed the feet of the disciples and gave them the mandate to love one another.

Easter-Day is the first Sunday after the full moon which happens upon, or next after, the 21st day of March; and if the full moon happens upon a Sunday, Easter-Day is the Sunday after. This definition is contained in an Act of Parliament (24 Geo. II., cap. 23), and explanation is given in the preamble to the Act that the day of Full Moon depends on certain tables that have been prepared. These are the tables whose essential points are given in the early pages of the Book of Common Prayer. The Moon referred to is not the real moon of the heavens, but a hypothetical Moon on whose "Full" the date of Easter depends, and the

lunations of this "Calendar" Moon consist of twenty-nine and thirty days alternately with certain necessary modifications to make the date of its Full agree as nearly as possible with that of the real Moon, which is known as the *Paschal Full Moon*.

A Fixed Easter.—As at present ordained, Easter falls on one of 35 days—(March 22–April 25). On June 15, 1928, the House of Commons agreed to a motion for the third reading of the Bill that Easter Day shall, in the Calendar year next but one after the commencement of the Act and in all subsequent years, be *the first Sunday after the second Saturday in April.* Easter would thus fall between April 9 and 15, both inclusive—that is, on the second or third Sunday in April. A clause in the Bill provided that before it shall come into operation regard shall be had to any opinion expressed officially by the various Christian Churches. Efforts were being made during 1971 by the World Council of Churches to secure a unanimous choice of date for Easter by its 239 member Churches. Press reports suggested the second Sunday in April as their most likely choice.

Holy Days and Saints Days were the normal factors in early times for settling the dates of future and recurrent appointments, *e.g.* the *Quarter Days* in England and Wales are the Feast of the Nativity, the Feast of the Annunciation, the Feast of St. John the Baptist and the Feast of St. Michael and All the Holy Angels, while *Term Days* in Scotland are Candlemas (Feast of the Purification), Whitsunday (a fixed date), Lammas (Loaf Mass) and Martinmas (St. Martin's Day). *Law Sittings* in England and Wales commence on the Feast of St. Hilary and the term which begins on Old Michaelmas Day ends on the feast of St. Thomas the Apostle.

The number of Saints commemorated in the Calendar of the Book of Common Prayer is 73, but (with the exception of All Saints' Day) "days" are appointed only for those whose names are mentioned in Scripture. *Red Letter Days* (*see also* p. 225) were Holy Days and Saints Days indicated in early ecclesiastical calendars by letters printed in red ink. The days to be distinguished in this way were finally approved at the Council of Nicaea, A.D. 325,

and special services are set apart for them in the Book of Common Prayer.

Rogation Days.—These are the Monday, Tuesday and Wednesday preceding Ascension Day, "Holy Thursday", and in the fifth century were ordered by the Church to be observed as Public Fasts with solemn processions and supplications. The processions were discontinued as religious observances at the Reformation, but survive in the ceremony known as "Beating the Parish Bounds".

Ember Days.—The Ember Days at the Four Seasons are the Wednesday, Friday and Saturday after (1) the First Sunday in lent, (2) the Feast of Pentecost, (3) September 14, (4) December 13.

Whit Sunday.—It is generally said that this name is a variant of White Sunday, and was so called from the albs or white robes of the newly baptized. But other derivations have been suggested.

Trinity Sunday.—The Festival in honour of the Trinity is observed on the Sunday following Whit Sunday, and subsequent Sundays are reckoned in the Church of England as "after Trinity"; in the Roman Catholic Church Sundays are reckoned "after Pentecost".

Thomas Becket, called by his contemporaries Thomas of London (*born* 1118; *murdered* Dec. 29, 1170), was consecrated Archbishop of Canterbury on the Sunday after Whit Sunday and his first act was to ordain that the day of his consecration should be held as a new festival in honour of the Holy Trinity. The observance thus originated spread from Canterbury throughout the whole of Christendom.

Advent Sunday is the Sunday nearest to St. Andrew's Day, Nov. 30, which allows three Sundays between Advent and Christmas Day in all cases. The Sunday preceding Advent is the 27th after Trinity if Easter falls on one of the days, March 22–26 inclusive. It is the 22nd after Trinity when Easter Day is on April 24 or 25. If the date of Easter were determined as proposed (*see Fixed Easter*) there would generally be 24 Sundays after Trinity, the number being 25 only in the years when Easter fell on April 9. With a Fixed Easter there would never be a sixth Sunday after Epiphany. There would be a fifth Sunday when Easter Day fell on April 15 or April 14, the year being a leap year.

A TABLE OF THE MOVABLE FEASTS FOR 10 YEARS—1968–77

Year	Ash Wednesday	Easter	Ascension	Whit Sunday	Sundays after Trinity	Advent
1968.......	Feb. 28	April 14	May 23	June 2	xxiv	Dec. 1
1969.......	Feb. 19	April 6	May 15	May 25	xxv	Nov. 30
1970.......	Feb. 11	March 29	May 7	May 17	xxvi	Nov. 29
1971.......	Feb. 24	April 11	May 20	May 30	xxiv	Nov. 28
1972.......	Feb. 16	April 2	May 11	May 21	xxvi	Dec. 3
1973.......	March 7	April 22	May 31	June 10	xxiii	Dec. 2
1974.......	Feb. 27	April 14	May 23	June 2	xxiv	Dec. 1
1975.......	Feb. 12	March 30	May 8	May 18	xxvi	Nov. 30
1976.......	March 3	April 18	May 27	June 6	xxiii	Nov. 28
1977.......	Feb. 23	April 10	May 19	May 29	xxiv	Nov. 27

NOTES CONCERNING TABLE OF MOVABLE FEASTS

Ash Wednesday (first Day in *Lent*) can fall at earliest on February 4 and at latest on March 10.
Easter Day can fall at earliest on March 22 and at latest on April 25.
Ascension Day can fall at earliest on April 30 and at latest on June 3.
Whit Sunday can fall at earliest on May 10 and at latest on June 13.
Rogation Sunday is the Sunday next before *Holy Thursday* (Ascension Day).
Trinity Sunday is the Sunday next after *Whit Sunday*.
Corpus Christi falls on the Thursday next after *Trinity Sunday*.
There are not less than xxii and not more than xxvii *Sundays after Trinity*.
Advent Sunday is the Sunday nearest to November 30.

A TABLE OF EASTER DAYS AND SUNDAY LETTERS, 1500 TO 2000.

	1500—1599	1600—1699	1700—1799	1800—1899	1900—2000	
d Mar. 22	1573	1668	1761	1818		d Mar. 22
e " 23	1505-16	1600	1788	1845-56	1913	e " 23
f " 24		1611-95	1706-99		1940	f " 24
g " 25	1543-54	1627-38-49	1722-33-44	1883-94	1951	g " 25
A " 26	1559-70-81-92	1654-65-76	1749-58-69-80	1815-26-37	1967-78-89	A " 26
b Mar. 27	1502-13-24-97	1608-87-92	1785-96	1842-53-64	1910-21-32	b Mar. 27
c " 28	1529-35-40	1619-24-30	1703-14-25	1869-75-80	1937-48	c " 28
d " 29	1551-62	1635-46-57	1719-30-41-52	1807-12-91	1959-64-70	d " 29
e " 30	1567-78-89	1651-62-73-84	1746-55-66-77	1823-34	1902-75-86-97	e " 30
f " 31	1510-21-32-83-94	1605-16-78-89	1700-71-82-93	1839-50-61-72	1907-18-29-91	f " 31
g April 1	1526-37-48	1621-32	1711-16	1804-66-77-88	1923-34-45-56	g April 1
A " 2	1553-64	1643-48	1727-38-52(NS)	1809-20-93-99	1961-72	A " 2
b " 3	1575-80-86	1659-70-81	1743-63-68-74	1825-31-36	1904-83-88-94	b " 3
c " 4	1507-18-91	1602-13-75-86-97	1708-79-90	1847-58	1915-20-26-99	c " 4
d " 5	1523-34-45-56	1607-18-29-40	1702-13-24-95	1801-63-74-85-96	1931-42-53	d " 5
e April 6	1539-50-61-72	1634-45-56	1729-35-40-60	1806-17-28-90	1947-58-69-80	e April 6
f " 7	1504-77-88	1667-72	1751-65-76	1822-33-44	1901-12-85-96	f " 7
g " 8	1509-15-20-99	1604-10-83-94	1705-87-92-98	1849-55-60	1917-28	g " 8
A " 9	1531-42	1615-26-37-99	1710-21-32	1871-82	1939-44-50	A " 9
b " 10	1547-58-69	1631-42-53-64	1726-37-48-57	1803-14-87-98	1955-66-77	b " 10
c April 11	1501-12-63-74-85-96	1658-69-80	1762-73-84	1819-30-41-52	1909-71-82-93	c April 11
d " 12	1506-17-28	1601-12-91-96	1789	1846-57-68	1903-14-25-36-98	d " 12
e " 13	1533-44	1623-28	1707-18	1800-73-79-84	1941-52	e " 13
f " 14	1555-60-66	1639-50-61	1723-34-45-54	1805-11-16-95	1963-68-74	f " 14
g " 15	1571-82-93	1655-66-77-88	1750-59-70-81	1827-38	1900-06-79-90	g " 15
A April 16	1503-12-25-36-87-98	1609-20-82-93	1704-75-86-97	1843-54-65-76	1911-22-33-95	A April 16
b " 17	1530-41-52	1625-36	1715-20	1808-70-81-92	1927-38-49-60	b " 17
c " 18	1557-68	1647-52	1731-42-56	1802-13-24-97	1954-65-76	c " 18
d " 19	1500-79-84-90	1663-74-85	1747-67-72-78	1829-35-40	1908-81-87-92	d " 19
e " 20	1511-22-95	1606-17-79-90	1701-12-83-94	1851-62	1919-24-30	e " 20
f April 21	1527-38-49	1622-33-44	1717-28	1867-78-89	1935-46-57	f April 21
g " 22	1565-76	1660	1739-53-64	1810-21-32	1962-73-84	g " 22
A " 23	1508	1671		1848	1905-16-2000	A " 23
b " 24	1519	1603-14-98	1709-91	1859		b " 24
c " 25	1546	1641	1736	1886	1943	c " 25

PUBLIC HOLIDAYS

BANK HOLIDAYS IN ENGLAND, WALES, NORTHERN IRELAND AND THE CHANNEL ISLANDS ARE (1972):—Easter Monday (April 3), Spring Holiday (May 29), August Bank Holiday (August 28); and December 26; (1973) April 23; May 28; August 27 and Dec. 26; (1974) April 15; May 27; August 26; and Dec. 26.

New Year's Day and Liberation Day (May 9) are bank and public holidays in the Channel Islands.

Banks are also closed on Good Friday and Christmas Day and on all Saturdays.

The Stock Exchange is closed on Bank Holidays, Good Friday, Christmas Day and New Year's Day; and on Saturdays throughout the year.

Custom House and Docks, as *Banks*; with the Queen's Birthday (when decreed).

Excise and Stamp Offices, as *Banks*; with Whit Tuesday and Coronation Day, if and when decreed.

Law Offices.—Good Friday, Easter Monday and Tuesday, Spring Bank Holiday (*see* col. 1), Christmas Day, and first week-day after Christmas.

BANK HOLIDAYS IN SCOTLAND ARE (1972): New Year's Day (Jan. 1); May 1; and August 7; (1973) Jan. 1; May 7 and August 6; (1974) Jan. 1; May 6; and August 5.

Banks in Scotland are also closed on Good Friday, Christmas Day and on Saturdays.

Scotland has special *Term* (*Quarter*) *Days:*—Candlemas, Feb. 2; Whitsunday, May 15 (Fixed date); Lammas, Aug. 1; and Martinmas, Nov. 11; the *Removal Terms* are May 28 and Nov. 28.

THE JEWISH CALENDAR

Origin.—The story in the Book of Genesis that the Flood began on the seventeenth day of the second month; that after the end of 150 days the waters were abated; and that on the seventeenth day of the seventh month the Ark rested on Mount Ararat, indicates a calendar of some kind and that the writers recognized 30 days as the length of a lunation. There is other mention of months by their ordinal numbers in the Book of Genesis and in establishing the rite of the Passover Moses spoke of *Abib* as the month when the Israelites came out from Egypt and Abib was to be the first month of

the year. In the First Book of Kings three months are mentioned by name, Zif the second month, Ethanim the seventh and Bul the eighth, but these are not names now in use. After the Dispersion, Jewish communities were left in considerable doubt as to the times of Fasts and Festivals, and this led to the formation of the Jewish Calendar as used to-day, which, it is said by some, was done in A.D. 358 by Rabbi Hillel II, a descendant of Gamaliel —though some assert that it did not happen until much later. This calendar is luni-solar, and is based on the lengths of the lunation and of the

tropical year as found by Hipparchus (*Circ.* 120 B.C.) which differ little from those adopted at the present day. The year 5732 A.D. (1971–72) is the 13th year of the 302nd *Metonic* (Minor or Lunar) *Cycle* of 19 years and the 20th year of the 205th *Solar* (or Major) *Cycle* of 28 years since the Era of the Creation, which the Jews hold to have occurred at the time of the Autumnal Equinox in the year known in the Christian Calendar as 3760 B.C. (954 of the Julian Period) and the epoch or starting point of Jewish Chronology corresponds to Oct. 7, 3761 B.C. At the beginning of each Solar Cycle the *Tekufah* of Nisan (the vernal equinox) returns to the same day and to the same hour.

The hour is divided into 1080 *minims* and the month between one new Moon and the next is reckoned as 29 days, 12 hours, 793 minims. The normal calendar year, called a Common Regular year, consists of 12 months of 30 days and 29 days alternately. Since 12 months such as these comprise only 354 days, in order that each of them shall not diverge greatly from an average place in the solar year, a thirteenth month is occasionally added after the fifth month of the Civil year (which commences on the first day of month Tishri), or as the penultimate month of the Ecclesiastical (which commences on the first day of month Nisan), the years when this happens being called Embolismic. Of the 19 years that form a Metonic cycle, 7 are embolismic; they occur at places in the cycle indicated by the numbers 3, 6, 8, 11, 14, 17, 19, these places being chosen so that the accumulated excesses of the solar years should be as small as possible. The first of each month is called the day of New Moon, though it is not necessarily the day of astronomical New Moon, that being the day on which conjunction of Sun and Moon occurs, but there is generally a difference of a day or two. In practice, in a month which follows one of 30 days, the day preceding its first day is also observed as a day of New Moon. The dates in the Christian calendar of the first days of the months depend on that of the first of Tishri, which therefore controls the dates of fasts and festivals in the Jewish year. For certain ceremonial reasons connected with these, the first of Tishri must not

fall on a Sunday, Wednesday or Friday, and if this should happen as the result of the computation it is postponed to the next day in the Christian calendar. Also, if the New Moon of Tishri falls on any day of the week at noon or later than noon, then the following day is to be taken for the celebration of that New Moon and is Tishri 1, provided that it is not one of the forbidden days, in which case there is a further postponement of a day. These rules and others have been considered in detail, and finally a calendar scheme has been drawn up in which a Jewish year is of one of the following six types: Common Deficient (353 days), Common Regular (354 days), Common Abundant (355 days), Embolismic Deficient (383 days), Embolismic Regular (384 days), or Embolismic Abundant (385 days).

The Regular year has an alternation of 30 and 29 days. In an Abundant year, whether Common or Embolismic, Marcheshvan, the second month of the Civil year, has 30 days instead of 29; in Deficient years Kislev, the third month, has 29 instead of 30. The additional month in Embolismic years which is called Adar I., and precedes the month called Adar in Common years and Adar II., or Ve-Adar, in Embolismic, always has 30 days, but neither this, nor the other variations mentioned, is allowed to change the number of days in the other months which still follow the alternation of the normal twelve. In Embolismic years the month intercalated precedes Adar and usurps its name, but the usual Adar festivals are kept in Ve-Adar.

These are the main features of the Jewish Calendar which must be considered permanent, because as a Jewish law it cannot be altered except by a great Synhedrion.

The Jewish day begins between sunset and nightfall. The time used is that of the meridian of Jerusalem, which is 2h. 21m. in advance of Greenwich Mean Time. Rules for the beginning of Sabbaths and Festivals were laid down for the latitude of London in the eighteenth century and hours for nightfall are now fixed annually by the Chief Rabbi.

Jewish Calendar 5732–5734

Jewish Month			A.M. 5732			A.M. 5733			A.M. 5734	
Tishri	1	..	1971 September 20	..	1972	September 9	..	1973	September 27	
Marcheshvan	1	..	October 20	..		October 9	..		October 27	
Kislev	1	..	November 19	..		November 7	..		November 26	
Tebet	1	..	December 18	..		December 6	..		December 26	
Shebat	1	..	1972 January 17	..	1973	January 4	..	1974	January 24	
Adar	1	..	February 16	..		February 3	..		February 23	
Ve-Adar	1	..	..	..		March 5	..		..	
Nisan	1	..	March 16	..		April 3	..		March 24	
Iyar	1	..	April 15	..		May 3	..		April 23	
Sivan	1	..	May 14	..		June 1	..		May 22	
Tammuz	1	..	June 13	..		July 1	..		June 21	
Ab	1	..	July 12	..		July 30	..		July 20	
Elul	1	..	August 11	..		August 29	..		August 19	

A.M. 5732 (known as 732 in the short system) is a Common Abundant year of 12 months, 50 Sabbath and 355 days. A.M. 5733 (733) is an Embolismic Deficient year of 13 months, 55 Sabbaths and 383 days. A.M. 5734 (734) is a Common Abundant year of 12 months, 51 Sabbaths and 355 days.

Jewish Fasts and Festivals

Tishri	1	Rosh Hoshanah (New Year).
,,	3	*Fast of Gedaliah.
,,	10	Yom Kippur (Day of Atonement).
,,	15–22	Succoth (Feast of Tabernacles).
,,	21	Hoshana Rabba.
,,	22	Solemn Assembly.
,,	23	Rejoicing of the Law.
Kislev	25	Dedication of the Temple.

Tebet	10	Fast of Tebet.
Adar	13	§Fast of Esther.
,,	14	Purim.
,,	15	Shushan Purim.
Nisan	15–21	Passover. [Weeks].
Sivan	6 and 7	Shavuot (Pentecost or Feast of
Tammuz	17	*Fast of Tammuz.
Ab	9	*Fast of Ab.

NOTES.—* If these dates fall on the Sabbath the Fast is kept on the following day.

§ This fast is observed on Adar 11 (or Ve-Adar 11 in Embolismic years) if Adar 13 falls on a Sabbath.

THE ROMAN CALENDAR

Roman historians adopted as an epoch the Foundation of Rome, which is believed to have happened in the year 753 B.C., and the ordinal number of the years in Roman reckoning is followed by the letters A.U.C. (*Ab Urbe Condita*), so that the year 1972 is 2725 A.U.C. (MMDCCXXV). The Calendar that we know has developed from one established by Romulus, who is said to have used a year of 304 days divided into ten months, beginning with March, to which Numa added January and February, making the year consist of 12 months of 30 and 29 days alternately, with an additional day so that the total was 355. It is also said that Numa ordered an intercalary month of 22 or 23 days in alternate years, making 90 days in eight years, to be inserted after Feb. 23, but there is some doubt as to the origination and the details of the intercalation in the Roman Calendar, though it is certain that some scheme of this kind was inaugurated and not fully carried out, for in the year 46 B.C. Julius Cæsar, who was then Pontifex

Maximus, found that the Calendar had been allowed to fall into some confusion. He therefore sought the help of the Egyptian astronomer Sosigenes, which led to the construction and adoption (45 B.C.) of the Julian Calendar, and, by a slight alteration, to the Gregorian now in use. The year 46 B.C. was made to consist of 445 days. and is called the *Year of Confusion*. In the Roman (Julian) Calendar the days of the month were counted backwards from three fixed points, or days. and an intervening day was said to be so many days *before* the next coming point, the first *and* last being counted. These three points were (1) the Kalends; (2) the Nones; and (3) the Ides. Their positions in the months and the method of counting from them will be seen in the table below. The year containing 366 days was called *bissextilis annus*, as it had a doubled sixth day (*bissextus dies*) before the March Kalends on Feb. 24—*ante diem sextum Kalendas Martias*, or VI Kal. Mart.

Present Days of the Month	March, May, July, October have thirty-one days	January, August, December have thirty-one days	April, June, September, November have thirty days	February has twenty-eight days, and in Leap Year twenty-nine
1	Kalendis.	Kalendis.	Kalendis.	Kalendis.
2	VI. ⎫	IV. ⎫ Ante	IV. ⎫ Ante	IV. ⎫ Ante
3	V. ⎬ Ante	III. ⎬ Nonas.	III. ⎬ Nonas.	III. ⎬ Nonas.
4	IV. ⎭ Nonas.	Pridie Nonas.	Pridie Nonas.	Pridie Nonas.
5	III. ⎭	Nonis.	Nonis.	Nonis.
6	Pridie Nonas.	VIII. ⎫	VIII.	VIII.
7	Nonis.	VII.	VII.	VII.
8	VIII. ⎫	VI. ⎫ Ante	VI. ⎫ Ante	VI. ⎫ Ante
9	VII. ⎬ Ante	V. ⎬ Idus.	V. ⎬ Idus.	V. ⎬ Idus.
10	VI. ⎬ Ante	IV.	IV.	IV.
11	V. ⎭ Idus.	III. ⎭	III. ⎭	III. ⎭
12	IV. ⎫	Pridie Idus.	Pridie Idus.	Pridie Idus.
13	III. ⎭	Idibus.	Idibus.	Idibus.
14	Pridie Idus.	XIX. ⎫	XVIII. ⎫	XVI. ⎫
15	Idibus.	XVIII.	XVII.	XV.
16	XVII. ⎫	XVII.	XVI.	XIV.
17	XVI.	XVI.	XV.	XIII.
18	XV.	XV.	XIV.	XII.
19	XIV.	XIV.	XIII.	XI.
20	XIII.	XIII.	XII.	X.
21	XII.	XII.	XI.	IX.
22	XI.	XI.	X.	VIII.
23	X. ⎬ Ante Kalendas (of the month following)	X. ⎬ Ante Kalendas (of the month following)	IX. ⎬ Ante Kalendas (of the month following)	VII. ⎬ Ante Kalendas Martias
24	IX.	IX.	VIII.	VI.
25	VIII.	VIII.	VII.	V.
26	VII.	VII.	VI.	IV.
27	VI.	VI.	V.	III.
28	V.	V.	IV. ⎭	Pridie Kalendas Martias.
29	IV.	IV.	III.	
30	III. ⎭	III. ⎭	Pridie Kalendas (of the month following).	
31	Pridie Kalendas (of the month following).	Pridie Kalendas (of the month following).		

ROMAN NUMERALS

1	I	9	IX	17	XVII	70	LXX	600	DC
2	II	10	X	18	XVIII	80	LXXX	700	DCC
3	III	11	XI	19	XIX	90	XC	800	DCCC
4	IV	12	XII	20	XX	100	C	900	CM
5	V	13	XIII	30	XXX	200	CC	1000	M
6	VI	14	XIV	40	XL	300	CCC	1500	MD
7	VII	15	XV	50	L	400	CD	1900	MCM
8	VIII	16	XVI	60	LX	500	D	2000	MM

Other Examples: 43=XLIII; 66=LXVI; 98=XCVIII.
339=CCCXXXIX; 619=DCXIX; 988=CMLXXXVIII; 996=CMXCVI.
1674=MDCLXXIV; 1962=MCMLXII.
A bar placed over a numeral has the effect of multiplying the number by 1,000, *e.g.*:
6,000=V̄I; 16,000=X̄V̄I; 160,000=C̄L̄X; 666,000=D̄C̄L̄X̄V̄I.

THE MOSLEM CALENDAR

The basic date of the Moslem Calendar is the *Hejira*, or Flight of Muhammad from Mecca to Medina, the corresponding date of which is A.D. 622, July 16, in the Julian Calendar. Hejira years are used principally in Iran, Turkey, Arabia, Egypt, in certain parts of India and in Malaya. The system was adopted about A.D. 632, commencing from the first day of the month preceding the Hejira. The years are purely lunar and consist of 12 months containing in alternate sequence 30 or 29 days, with the intercalation of one day at the end of the 12th month at stated intervals in each cycle of 30 years, the object of the intercalation being to reconcile the date of the first of the month with the date of the actual New Moon. Some adherents still take the date of the evening of the first visibility of the crescent as that of the first of the month. In each cycle of 30 years 19 are common and contain 354 days and 11 are intercalary (355 days), the latter being called *kabishah*.

The mean length of the Hejira year is 354 days, 8 hours, 48 minutes and the period of mean lunation is 29 days, 12 hours, 44 minutes.

To ascertain if a Hejira year is common or *kabishah* divide it by 30; the quotient gives the number of completed cycles and the remainder shows the place of the year in the current cycle. If the remainder is 2, 5, 7, 10, 13, 16, 18, 21, 24, 26 or 29 the year is *kabishah* and consists of 355 days.

Hejira year 1391 gives a quotient of 46 with remainder 11 and is a common year, as is 1392 with remainder 12. A.H. 1393 (remainder 13) is *kabishah*.

Hejira Years 1391 and 1392

Name and Length of Month	A.H. 1391	A.H. 1392
Muharram (30)...	1971 Feb. 27	1972 Feb. 16
Safar (29)	Mar. 29	Mar. 17
Rabía I (30)......	April 27	April 15
Rabía II (29)......	May 27	May 15
Jumâda I (30).....	June 25	June 13
Jumâda II (29)....	July 25	July 13
Rajab (30).......	Aug. 23	Aug. 11
Shaabân (29).....	Sept. 22	Sept. 10
Ramadân (30)....	Oct. 21	Oct. 9
Shawwâl (29)....	Nov. 20	Nov. 8
Dhû 'l-Qa'da (30)	Dec. 19	Dec. 7
Dhû 'l-Hijja (29 or 30)............	1972 Jan. 18	1973 Jan. 6

NOTE.—A.H. 1393 (*kabishah* year of 355 days) begins on 1973, February 4.

OTHER EPOCHS AND CALENDARS

China.—Until the year A.D. 1911 a Lunar Calendar was in force in China, but with the establishment of the Republic the Government adopted the Gregorian Calendar, and the new and old systems were used simultaneously by the people for several years. Since 1930 the publication and use of the old Calendar have been banned by the Government, and an official Chinese Calendar, corresponding with the European and Western system, is compiled, but the old Lunar Calendar is still in use to some extent in China. The old Chinese Calendar, with a cycle of 60 years, is still in use in Tibet, Hong Kong, Singapore, Malaysia and elsewhere in South-East Asia.

Ethiopia.—In the Coptic Calendar, which is used in part by the population of Egypt and Ethiopia, the year is made up of 12 months of 30 days each, followed, in general, by 5 complementary days. Every fourth year is an Intercalary or Leap year and in these years there are 6 complementary days.

The Intercalary year of the Coptic Calendar immediately precedes the Leap year of the Julian Calendar. The Era is that of Diocletian or the Martyrs, the origin of which is fixed at A.D. 284, Aug. 29 (Julian date).

Greece.—Ancient Greek chronology was reckoned in *Olympiads*, cycles of 4 years corresponding with the periodic Olympic Games held on the plain of Olympia in Elis once in 4 years, the intervening years being the first, second, etc., of the Olympiad which received the name of the victor at the Games. The first recorded Olympiad is that of Choroebus, 776 B.C.

India.—In addition to the Moslem reckoning there are six eras used in India. The principal astronomical system was the *Kaliyuga Era*, which appears to have been adopted in the fourth century A.D. It began on Feb. 18, 3102 B.C. The chronological system of Northern India, known as the *Vikrama Samvat Era*, prevalent in Western India, began on Feb. 23, 57 B.C. The year A.D. 1972 is, therefore, the year 2029 of the Vikrama Era.

The *Saka Era* of Southern India dating from March 3, A.D. 78, was declared the uniform national calendar of the Republic of India with effect from March 22, 1957, to be used concurrently with the Gregorian Calendar. As revised, the year of the new *Saka Era* begins at the spring equinox, with five successive months of 31 days and seven of 30 days in ordinary years; six months of each length in leap years. The year A.D. 1972 is 1894 of the revised *Saka Era*.

In the Hills, the *Saptarshi Era* dates from the moment when the Saptarshi, or saints, were translated and became the stars of the Great Bear in 3076 B.C.

The *Buddhists* reckoned from the death of Buddha in 543 B.C. (the actual date being 487 B.C.); and the epoch of the *Jains* was the death of Vardhamana, the founder of their faith, in 527 B.C.

Iran.—The chronology of Iran (Persia) is the Era of Hejira, which began on A.D. 622, July 16. The *Zoroastrian Calendar* was used in pre-Moslem days and is still employed by Zoroastrians in Iran and India (Parsees) with era beginning A.D. 632, June 16.

Japan.—The Japanese Calendar is the Gregorian, and is essentially the same as that in use by Western nations, the years, months and weeks being of the same length and beginning on the same days as those of the Western Calendar. The numeration of the years is different, for Japanese chronology is based on a system of epochs or periods, each of which begins at the accession of an Emperor or other important occurrence, the method being not unlike the former British system of Regnal years, but differing from it in the particular that each year of a period closes on Dec. 31. The Japanese scheme begins about A.D. 650 and the three latest epochs are defined by the reigns of Emperors, whose actual names are not necessarily used:—

Epoch Meiji	from 1868 Oct. 13	to 1912 July 31
,, Taishō	,, 1912 Aug. 1	to 1926 Dec. 25
,, Shōwa	,, 1926 Dec. 26	

Hence the year Shōwa 47 begins 1972 Jan. 1. The months are not named. They are known as First Month, Second Month, etc., first month being the equivalent to January. The days of the week are Nichiyōbi (Sun-day), Getsuyōbi (Moon-day), Kayōbi (Fire-day), Suiyōbi (Water-day), Mokuyōbi (Wood-day), Kinyōbi (Metal-day), Doyōbi (Earth-day).

EASY REFERENCE CALENDAR

for any year between 1753 and 2000 together with the dates of Easter in each of those years
TO SELECT THE CORRECT CALENDAR FOR ANY YEAR consult the INDEX below

INDEX TO CALENDARS

Year		Year		Year		Year		Year		Year	
1753	C	1795	I	1836	L★	1877	C	1918	E	1959	I
1754	E	1796	L★	1837	A	1878	E	1919	G	1960	L★
1755	G	1797	A	1838	C	1879	G	1920	J★	1961	A
1756	J★	1798	C	1839	E	1880	J★	1921	M	1962	C
1757	M	1799	E	1840	H★	1881	M	1922	A	1963	E
1758	A	1800	G	1841	K	1882	A	1923	C	1964	H★
1759	C	1801	I	1842	M	1883	C	1924	F★	1965	M
1760	F★	1802	K	1843	A	1884	F★	1925	I	1966	A
1761	I	1803	M	1844	D★	1885	I	1926	K	1967	C
1762	K	1804	B★	1845	G	1886	K	1927	M	1968	D★
1763	M	1805	E	1846	I	1887	M	1928	B★	1969	G
1764	B★	1806	G	1847	K	1888	B★	1929	E	1970	I
1765	E	1807	I	1848	N★	1889	E	1930	G	1971	K
1766	G	1808	L★	1849	C	1890	G	1931	I	1972	N★
1767	I	1809	A	1850	E	1891	I	1932	L★	1973	C
1768	L★	1810	C	1851	G	1892	L★	1933	A	1974	E
1769	A	1811	E	1852	J★	1893	A	1934	C	1975	G
1770	C	1812	H★	1853	M	1894	C	1935	E	1976	J★
1771	E	1813	K	1854	A	1895	E	1936	H★	1977	M
1772	H★	1814	M	1855	C	1896	H★	1937	K	1978	A
1773	K	1815	A	1856	F★	1897	K	1938	M	1979	C
1774	M	1816	D★	1857	I	1898	M	1939	A	1980	F★
1775	A	1817	G	1858	K	1899	A	1940	D★	1981	I
1776	D★	1818	I	1859	M	1900	C	1941	G	1982	K
1777	G	1819	K	1860	B★	1901	E	1942	I	1983	M
1778	I	1820	N★	1861	E	1902	G	1943	K	1984	B★
1779	K	1821	C	1862	G	1903	I	1944	N★	1985	E
1780	N★	1822	E	1863	I	1904	L★	1945	C	1986	G
1781	C	1823	G	1864	L★	1905	A	1946	E	1987	I
1782	E	1824	J★	1865	A	1906	C	1947	G	1988	L★
1783	G	1825	M	1866	C	1907	E	1948	J★	1989	A
1784	J★	1826	A	1867	E	1908	H★	1949	M	1990	C
1785	M	1827	C	1868	H★	1909	K	1950	A	1991	E
1786	A	1828	F★	1869	K	1910	M	1951	C	1992	H★
1787	C	1829	I	1870	M	1911	A	1952	F★	1993	K
1788	F★	1830	K	1871	A	1912	D★	1953	I	1994	M
1789	I	1831	M	1872	D★	1913	G	1954	K	1995	A
1790	K	1832	B★	1873	G	1914	I	1955	M	1996	D★
1791	M	1833	E	1874	I	1915	K	1956	B★	1997	G
1792	B★	1834	G	1875	K	1916	N★	1957	E	1998	I
1793	E	1835	I	1876	N★	1917	C	1958	G	1999	K
1794	G									2000	N★

★ Leap Year.

A

```
            January             May             September
Su ...  1  8 15 22 29        7 14 21 28          3 10 17 24
M. ...  2  9 16 23 30     1  8 15 22 29          4 11 18 25
Tu. ..  3 10 17 24 31     2  9 16 23 30          5 12 19 26
W. ..   4 11 18 25        3 10 17 24 31          6 13 20 27
Th. ..  5 12 19 26        4 11 18 25             7 14 21 28
F. ..   6 13 20 27        5 12 19 26          1  8 15 22 29
S. ..   7 14 21 28        6 13 20 27          2  9 16 23 30

            February            June            October
Su ...  5 12 19 26        4 11 18 25          1  8 15 22 29
M. ...  6 13 20 27        5 12 19 26          2  9 16 23 30
Tu. ..  7 14 21 28        6 13 20 27          3 10 17 24 31
W. ..1  8 15 22           7 14 21 28          4 11 18 25
Th. ..2  9 16 23       1  8 15 22 29          5 12 19 26
F. ..3 10 17 24        2  9 16 23 30          6 13 20 27
S. ..4 11 18 25        3 10 17 24             7 14 21 28

            March               July            November
Su ...  5 12 19 26        2  9 16 23 30          5 12 19 26
M. ...  6 13 20 27        3 10 17 24 31          6 13 20 27
Tu. ..  7 14 21 28        4 11 18 25             7 14 21 28
W. ..1  8 15 22 29        5 12 19 26          1  8 15 22 29
Th. ..2  9 16 23 30       6 13 20 27          2  9 16 23 30
F. ..3 10 17 24 31        7 14 21 28          3 10 17 24
S. ..4 11 18 25        1  8 15 22 29          4 11 18 25

            April               August          December
Su ...  2  9 16 23 30      6 13 20 27          4 11 18 25
M. ...  3 10 17 24         7 14 21 28          5 12 19 26
Tu. ..  4 11 18 25      1  8 15 22 29          6 13 20 27
W. ..   5 12 19 26      2  9 16 23 30          7 14 21 28
Th. ..  6 13 20 27      3 10 17 24 31       1  8 15 22 29
F. ..   7 14 21 28      4 11 18 25          2  9 16 23 30
S. ..1  8 15 22 29      5 12 19 26          3 10 17 24 31
```

B (Leap year)

```
            January             May             September
Su ...  1  8 15 22 29     6 13 20 27          2  9 16 23 30
M. ...  2  9 16 23 30     7 14 21 28          3 10 17 24
Tu. ..  3 10 17 24 31  1  8 15 22 29          4 11 18 25
W. ..   4 11 18 25     2  9 16 23 30          5 12 19 26
Th. ..  5 12 19 26     3 10 17 24 31          6 13 20 27
F. ..   6 13 20 27     4 11 18 25             7 14 21 28
S. ..   7 14 21 28     5 12 19 26          1  8 15 22 29

            February            June            October
Su ...  5 12 19 26        3 10 17 24          7 14 21 28
M. ...  6 13 20 27        4 11 18 25       1  8 15 22 29
Tu. ..  7 14 21 28        5 12 19 26       2  9 16 23 30
W. ..1  8 15 22 29        6 13 20 27       3 10 17 24 31
Th. ..2  9 16 23          7 14 21 28       4 11 18 25
F. ..               1  8 15 22 29          5 12 19 26
S. ..4 11 18 25        2  9 16 23 30          6 13 20 27

            March               July            November
Su ...  4 11 18 25        1  8 15 22 29          4 11 18 25
M. ...  5 12 19 26        2  9 16 23 30          5 12 19 26
Tu. ..  6 13 20 27        3 10 17 24 31          6 13 20 27
W. ..   7 14 21 28        4 11 18 25             7 14 21 28
Th. ..1  8 15 22 29       5 12 19 26          1  8 15 22 29
F. ..2  9 16 23 30        6 13 20 27          2  9 16 23 30
S. ..3 10 17 24 31        7 14 21 28          3 10 17 24

            April               August          December
Su ...  1  8 15 22 29      5 12 19 26          2  9 16 23 30
M. ...  2  9 16 23 30      6 13 20 27          3 10 17 24 31
Tu. ..  3 10 17 24         7 14 21 28          4 11 18 25
W. ..   4 11 18 25      1  8 15 22 29          5 12 19 26
Th. ..  5 12 19 26      2  9 16 23 30          6 13 20 27
F. ..   6 13 20 27      3 10 17 24 31          7 14 21 28
S. ..   7 14 21 28      4 11 18 25          1  8 15 22 29
```

Easter Days

March 26.	1758 1769 1815 1826 1837 1967 1978
April 2.	1809 1893 1899 1961. [1989.
April 9.	1871 1882 1939 1950.
April 16.	1775 1786 1797 1843 1854 1865 1911
April 23.	1905. [1922 1933 1995.

Easter Days

April 1.	1804 1888 1956.
April 8.	1792 1860 1928.
April 22.	1764 1832 1984.

CALENDAR TABLES
C – F

C

Day	Jan	May	Sep	Feb	June	Oct	Mar	July	Nov	Apr	Aug	Dec
Su..	7 14 21 28	6 13 20 27	2 9 16 23 30	4 11 18 25	3 10 17 24	7 14 21 28	4 11 18 25	1 8 15 22 29	4 11 18 25	1 8 15 22 29	5 12 19 26	2 9 16 23 30
M...	1 8 15 22 29	7 14 21 28	3 10 17 24	5 12 19 26	4 11 18 25	1 8 15 22 29	5 12 19 26	2 9 16 23 30	5 12 19 26	2 9 16 23 30	6 13 20 27	3 10 17 24 31
Tu..	2 9 16 23 30	1 8 15 22 29	4 11 18 25	6 13 20 27	5 12 19 26	2 9 16 23 30	6 13 20 27	3 10 17 24 31	6 13 20 27	3 10 17 24	7 14 21 28	4 11 18 25
W...	3 10 17 24 31	2 9 16 23 30	5 12 19 26	7 14 21 28	6 13 20 27	3 10 17 24 31	7 14 21 28	4 11 18 25	7 14 21 28	4 11 18 25	1 8 15 22 29	5 12 19 26
Th..	4 11 18 25	3 10 17 24 31	6 13 20 27	1 8 15 22	7 14 21 28	4 11 18 25	1 8 15 22 29	5 12 19 26	1 8 15 22 29	5 12 19 26	2 9 16 23 30	6 13 20 27
F...	5 12 19 26	4 11 18 25	7 14 21 28	2 9 16 23	1 8 15 22 29	5 12 19 26	2 9 16 23 30	6 13 20 27	2 9 16 23 30	6 13 20 27	3 10 17 24 31	7 14 21 28
S...	6 13 20 27	5 12 19 26	1 8 15 22 29	3 10 17 24	2 9 16 23 30	6 13 20 27	3 10 17 24 31	7 14 21 28	3 10 17 24	7 14 21 28	4 11 18 25	1 8 15 22 29

Easter Days

March 25.	1883	1894	1951.				
April 1.	1866	1877	1923	1934	1945.		
April 8.	1787	1798	1849	1855	1917.		
April 15.	1759	1770	1781	1827	1838	1900	1906
	1979	1990.					
April 22.	1753	1810	1821	1962	1973.		

D (Leap year)

Day	Jan	May	Sep	Feb	June	Oct	Mar	July	Nov	Apr	Aug	Dec
Su..	7 14 21 28	5 12 19 26	1 8 15 22 29	4 11 18 25	2 9 16 23 30	6 13 20 27	3 10 17 24 31	7 14 21 28	3 10 17 24	7 14 21 28	4 11 18 25	1 8 15 22 29
M...	1 8 15 22 29	6 13 20 27	2 9 16 23 30	5 12 19 26	3 10 17 24	7 14 21 28	4 11 18 25	1 8 15 22 29	4 11 18 25	1 8 15 22 29	5 12 19 26	2 9 16 23 30
Tu..	2 9 16 23 30	7 14 21 28	3 10 17 24	6 13 20 27	4 11 18 25	1 8 15 22 29	5 12 19 26	2 9 16 23 30	5 12 19 26	2 9 16 23 30	6 13 20 27	3 10 17 24 31
W...	3 10 17 24 31	1 8 15 22 29	4 11 18 25	7 14 21 28	5 12 19 26	2 9 16 23 30	6 13 20 27	3 10 17 24 31	6 13 20 27	3 10 17 24	7 14 21 28	4 11 18 25
Th..	4 11 18 25	2 9 16 23 30	5 12 19 26	1 8 15 22 29	6 13 20 27	3 10 17 24 31	7 14 21 28	4 11 18 25	7 14 21 28	4 11 18 25	1 8 15 22 29	5 12 19 26
F...	5 12 19 26	3 10 17 24 31	6 13 20 27	2 9 16 23	7 14 21 28	4 11 18 25	1 8 15 22 29	5 12 19 26	1 8 15 22 29	5 12 19 26	2 9 16 23 30	6 13 20 27
S...	6 13 20 27	4 11 18 25	7 14 21 28	3 10 17 24	1 8 15 22 29	5 12 19 26	2 9 16 23 30	6 13 20 27	2 9 16 23 30	6 13 20 27	3 10 17 24 31	7 14 21 28

Easter Days

March 24.	1940.			
March 31.	1872.			
April 7.	1776	1844	1912	1996.
April 14.	1816	1968.		

E

Day	Jan	May	Sep	Feb	June	Oct	Mar	July	Nov	Apr	Aug	Dec
Su..	6 13 20 27	5 12 19 26	1 8 15 22 29	3 10 17 24	2 9 16 23 30	6 13 20 27	3 10 17 24 31	7 14 21 28	3 10 17 24	7 14 21 28	4 11 18 25	1 8 15 22 29
M...	7 14 21 28	6 13 20 27	2 9 16 23 30	4 11 18 25	3 10 17 24	7 14 21 28	4 11 18 25	1 8 15 22 29	4 11 18 25	1 8 15 22 29	5 12 19 26	2 9 16 23 30
Tu..	1 8 15 22 29	7 14 21 28	3 10 17 24	5 12 19 26	4 11 18 25	1 8 15 22 29	5 12 19 26	2 9 16 23 30	5 12 19 26	2 9 16 23 30	6 13 20 27	3 10 17 24 31
W...	2 9 16 23 30	1 8 15 22 29	4 11 18 25	6 13 20 27	5 12 19 26	2 9 16 23 30	6 13 20 27	3 10 17 24 31	6 13 20 27	3 10 17 24	7 14 21 28	4 11 18 25
Th..	3 10 17 24 31	2 9 16 23 30	5 12 19 26	7 14 21 28	6 13 20 27	3 10 17 24 31	7 14 21 28	4 11 18 25	7 14 21 28	4 11 18 25	1 8 15 22 29	5 12 19 26
F...	4 11 18 25	3 10 17 24 31	6 13 20 27	1 8 15 22	7 14 21 28	4 11 18 25	1 8 15 22 29	5 12 19 26	1 8 15 22 29	5 12 19 26	2 9 16 23 30	6 13 20 27
S...	5 12 19 26	4 11 18 25	7 14 21 28	2 9 16 23	1 8 15 22 29	5 12 19 26	2 9 16 23 30	6 13 20 27	2 9 16 23 30	6 13 20 27	3 10 17 24 31	7 14 21 28

Easter Days

March 24.	1799.					
March 31.	1771	1782	1793	1839	1850	1861
	[1907	1918	1929	1991.		
April 7.	1765	1822	1833	1901	1985.	
April 14.	1754	1805	1811	1895	1963	1974.
April 21.	1867	1878	1889	1935	1946	1957.

F (Leap year)

Day	Jan	May	Sep	Feb	June	Oct	Mar	July	Nov	Apr	Aug	Dec
Su..	6 13 20 27	4 11 18 25	7 14 21 28	3 10 17 24	1 8 15 22 29	5 12 19 26	2 9 16 23 30	6 13 20 27	2 9 16 23 30	6 13 20 27	3 10 17 24 31	7 14 21 28
M...	7 14 21 28	5 12 19 26	1 8 15 22 29	4 11 18 25	2 9 16 23 30	6 13 20 27	3 10 17 24 31	7 14 21 28	3 10 17 24	7 14 21 28	4 11 18 25	1 8 15 22 29
Tu..	1 8 15 22 29	6 13 20 27	2 9 16 23 30	5 12 19 26	3 10 17 24	7 14 21 28	4 11 18 25	1 8 15 22 29	4 11 18 25	1 8 15 22 29	5 12 19 26	2 9 16 23 30
W...	2 9 16 23 30	7 14 21 28	3 10 17 24	6 13 20 27	4 11 18 25	1 8 15 22 29	5 12 19 26	2 9 16 23 30	5 12 19 26	2 9 16 23 30	6 13 20 27	3 10 17 24 31
Th..	3 10 17 24 31	1 8 15 22 29	4 11 18 25	7 14 21 28	5 12 19 26	2 9 16 23 30	6 13 20 27	3 10 17 24 31	6 13 20 27	3 10 17 24	7 14 21 28	4 11 18 25
F...	4 11 18 25	2 9 16 23 30	5 12 19 26	1 8 15 22 29	6 13 20 27	3 10 17 24 31	7 14 21 28	4 11 18 25	7 14 21 28	4 11 18 25	1 8 15 22 29	5 12 19 26
S...	5 12 19 26	3 10 17 24 31	6 13 20 27	2 9 16 23	7 14 21 28	4 11 18 25	1 8 15 22 29	5 12 19 26	1 8 15 22 29	5 12 19 26	2 9 16 23 30	6 13 20 27

Easter Days

March 23.	1788	1856.
April 6.	1760	1828 1980.
April 13.	1884	1952.
April 20.	1924.	

CALENDAR TABLES

G – J

G

	January	May	September
Su. ..	5 12 19 26	4 11 18 25	7 14 21 28
M. ..	6 13 20 27	5 12 19 26	1 8 15 22 29
Tu...	7 14 21 28	6 13 20 27	2 9 16 23 30
W. ..	1 8 15 22 29	7 14 21 28	3 10 17 24
Th...	2 9 16 23 30	1 8 15 22 29	4 11 18 25
F. ..	3 10 17 24 31	2 9 16 23 30	5 12 19 26
S. ..	4 11 18 25	3 10 17 24 31	6 13 20 27

	February	June	October
Su. ..	2 9 16 23	1 8 15 22 29	5 12 19 26
M. ..	3 10 17 24	2 9 16 23 30	6 13 20 27
Tu...	4 11 18 25	3 10 17 24	7 14 21 28
W. ..	5 12 19 26	4 11 18 25	1 8 15 22 29
Th...	6 13 20 27	5 12 19 26	2 9 16 23 30
F. ..	7 14 21 28	6 13 20 27	3 10 17 24 31
S. ..	1 8 15 22	7 14 21 28	4 11 18 25

	March	July	November
Su. ..	9 16 23 30	6 13 20 27	2 9 16 23 30
M. ..	3 10 17 24 31	7 14 21 28	3 10 17 24
Tu...	4 11 18 25	1 8 15 22 29	4 11 18 25
W. ..	5 12 19 26	2 9 16 23 30	5 12 19 26
Th...	6 13 20 27	3 10 17 24 31	6 13 20 27
F. ..	7 14 21 28	4 11 18 25	7 14 21 28
S. ..	1 8 15 22 29	5 12 19 26	1 8 15 22 29

	April	August	December
Su. ..	6 13 20 27	10 17 24 31	7 14 21 28
M. ..	7 14 21 28	4 11 18 25	1 8 15 22 29
Tu...	1 8 15 22 29	5 12 19 26	2 9 16 23 30
W. ..	2 9 16 23 30	6 13 20 27	3 10 17 24 31
Th...	3 10 17 24	7 14 21 28	4 11 18 25
F. ..	4 11 18 25	1 8 15 22 29	5 12 19 26
S. ..	5 12 19 26	2 9 16 23 30	6 13 20 27

Easter Days

March 23. 1845 1913.
March 30. 1755 1766 1777 1823 1834 1902 1975 1986 1997.
April 6. 1806 1817 1890 1947 1958 1969.
April 13. 1800 1873 1879 1941.
April 20. 1783 1794 1851 1862 1919 1930.

H (Leap year)

	January	May	September
Su. ..	5 12 19 26	3 10 17 24 31	6 13 20 27
M. ..	6 13 20 27	4 11 18 25	7 14 21 28
Tu...	7 14 21 28	5 12 19 26	1 8 15 22 29
W. ..	1 8 15 22 29	6 13 20 27	2 9 16 23 30
Th...	2 9 16 23 30	7 14 21 28	3 10 17 24
F. ..	3 10 17 24 31	1 8 15 22 29	4 11 18 25
S. ..		2 9 16 23 30	5 12 19 26

	February	June	October
Su. ..	2 9 16 23	7 14 21 28	4 11 18 25
M. ..	3 10 17 24	1 8 15 22 29	5 12 19 26
Tu...	4 11 18 25	2 9 16 23 30	6 13 20 27
W. ..	5 12 19 26	3 10 17 24	7 14 21 28
Th...	6 13 20 27	4 11 18 25	1 8 15 22 29
F. ..	7 14 21 28	5 12 19 26	2 9 16 23 30
S. ..	1 8 15 22 29	6 13 20 27	3 10 17 24 31

	March	July	November
Su. ..	1 8 15 22 29	5 12 19 26	1 8 15 22 29
M. ..	2 9 16 23 30	6 13 20 27	2 9 16 23 30
Tu...	3 10 17 24 31	7 14 21 28	3 10 17 24
W. ..	4 11 18 25	1 8 15 22 29	4 11 18 25
Th...	5 12 19 26	2 9 16 23 30	5 12 19 26
F. ..	6 13 20 27	3 10 17 24 31	6 13 20 27
S. ..	7 14 21 28	4 11 18 25	7 14 21 28

	April	August	December
Su. ..	5 12 19 26	2 9 16 23 30	6 13 20 27
M. ..	6 13 20 27	3 10 17 24 31	7 14 21 28
Tu...	7 14 21 28	4 11 18 25	1 8 15 22 29
W. ..	1 8 15 22 29	5 12 19 26	2 9 16 23 30
Th...	2 9 16 23 30	6 13 20 27	3 10 17 24
F. ..	3 10 17 24	7 14 21 28	4 11 18 25
S. ..	4 11 18 25	1 8 15 22 29	5 12 19 26

Easter Days

March 29. 1812 1964.
April 5. 1896.
April 12. 1868 1936.
April 19. 1772 1840 1908 1992.

I

	January	May	September
Su. ..	4 11 18 25	3 10 17 24 31	6 13 20 27
M. ..	5 12 19 26	4 11 18 25	7 14 21 28
Tu...	6 13 20 27	5 12 19 26	1 8 15 22 29
W. ..	7 14 21 28	6 13 20 27	2 9 16 23 30
Th...	1 8 15 22 29	7 14 21 28	3 10 17 24
F. ..	2 9 16 23 30	1 8 15 22 29	4 11 18 25
S. ..	3 10 17 24 31	2 9 16 23 30	5 12 19 26

	February	June	October
Su. ..	1 8 15 22	7 14 21 28	4 11 18 25
M. ..	2 9 16 23	1 8 15 22 29	5 12 19 26
Tu...	3 10 17 24	2 9 16 23 30	6 13 20 27
W. ..	4 11 18 25	3 10 17 24	7 14 21 28
Th...	5 12 19 26	4 11 18 25	1 8 15 22 29
F. ..	6 13 20 27	5 12 19 26	2 9 16 23 30
S. ..	7 14 21 28	6 13 20 27	3 10 17 24 31

	March	July	November
Su. ..	1 8 15 22 29	5 12 19 26	1 8 15 22 29
M. ..	2 9 16 23 30	6 13 20 27	2 9 16 23 30
Tu...	3 10 17 24 31	7 14 21 28	3 10 17 24
W. ..	4 11 18 25	1 8 15 22 29	4 11 18 25
Th...	5 12 19 26	2 9 16 23 30	5 12 19 26
F. ..	6 13 20 27	3 10 17 24 31	6 13 20 27
S. ..	7 14 21 28	4 11 18 25	7 14 21 28

	April	August	December
Su. ..	5 12 19 26	2 9 16 23 30	6 13 20 27
M. ..	6 13 20 27	3 10 17 24 31	7 14 21 28
Tu...	7 14 21 28	4 11 18 25	1 8 15 22 29
W. ..	1 8 15 22 29	5 12 19 26	2 9 16 23 30
Th...	2 9 16 23 30	6 13 20 27	3 10 17 24
F. ..	3 10 17 24	7 14 21 28	4 11 18 25
S. ..	4 11 18 25	1 8 15 22 29	5 12 19 26

Easter Days

March 22. 1761 1818.
March 29. 1807 1891 1959 1970.
April 5. 1795 1801 1863 1874 1885 1931 1942 1953.
April 12. 1789 1846 1857 1903 1914 1925 1998.
April 19. 1767 1778 1829 1835 1981 1987.

J (Leap year)

	January	May	September
Su. ..	4 11 18 25	2 9 16 23 30	5 12 19 26
M. ..	5 12 19 26	3 10 17 24 31	6 13 20 27
Tu...	6 13 20 27	4 11 18 25	7 14 21 28
W. ..	7 14 21 28	5 12 19 26	1 8 15 22 29
Th...	1 8 15 22 29	6 13 20 27	2 9 16 23 30
F. ..	2 9 16 23 30	7 14 21 28	3 10 17 24
S. ..	3 10 17 24 31	1 8 15 22 29	4 11 18 25

	February	June	October
Su. ..	1 8 15 22 29	6 13 20 27	3 10 17 24 31
M. ..	2 9 16 23	7 14 21 28	4 11 18 25
Tu...	3 10 17 24	1 8 15 22 29	5 12 19 26
W. ..	4 11 18 25	2 9 16 23 30	6 13 20 27
Th...	5 12 19 26	3 10 17 24	7 14 21 28
F. ..	6 13 20 27	4 11 18 25	1 8 15 22 29
S. ..	7 14 21 28	5 12 19 26	2 9 16 23 30

	March	July	November
Su. ..	7 14 21 28	4 11 18 25	7 14 21 28
M. ..	1 8 15 22 29	5 12 19 26	1 8 15 22 29
Tu...	2 9 16 23 30	6 13 20 27	2 9 16 23 30
W. ..	3 10 17 24 31	7 14 21 28	3 10 17 24
Th...	4 11 18 25	1 8 15 22 29	4 11 18 25
F. ..	5 12 19 26	2 9 16 23 30	5 12 19 26
S. ..	6 13 20 27	3 10 17 24 31	6 13 20 27

	April	August	December
Su. ..	4 11 18 25	1 8 15 22 29	5 12 19 26
M. ..	5 12 19 26	2 9 16 23 30	6 13 20 27
Tu...	6 13 20 27	3 10 17 24 31	7 14 21 28
W. ..	7 14 21 28	4 11 18 25	1 8 15 22 29
Th...	1 8 15 22 29	5 12 19 26	2 9 16 23 30
F. ..	2 9 16 23 30	6 13 20 27	3 10 17 24 31
S. ..	3 10 17 24	7 14 21 28	4 11 18 25

Easter Days

March 28. 1880 1948.
April 4. 1920.
April 11. 1784 1852.
April 18. 1756 1824 1976.

CALENDAR TABLES
K – N

K

	January	May	September
Su...	3 10 17 24 31	2 9 16 23 30	5 12 19 26
M...	4 11 18 25	3 10 17 24 31	6 13 20 27
Tu...	5 12 19 26	4 11 18 25	7 14 21 28
W...	6 13 20 27	5 12 19 26	1 8 15 22 29
Th...	7 14 21 28	6 13 20 27	2 9 16 23 30
F... 1	8 15 22 29	7 14 21 28	3 10 17 24
S... 2	9 16 23 30	1 8 15 22 29	4 11 18 25

	February	June	October
Su...	7 14 21 28	6 13 20 27	3 10 17 24 31
M... 1	8 15 22	7 14 21 28	4 11 18 25
Tu...	2 9 16 23	1 8 15 22 29	5 12 19 26
W...	3 10 17 24	2 9 16 23 30	6 13 20 27
Th...	4 11 18 25	3 10 17 24	7 14 21 28
F...	5 12 19 26	4 11 18 25	1 8 15 22 29
S...	6 13 20 27	5 12 19 26	2 9 16 23 30

	March	July	November
Su...	7 14 21 28	4 11 18 25	7 14 21 28
M... 1	8 15 22 29	5 12 19 26	1 8 15 22 29
Tu...	2 9 16 23 30	6 13 20 27	2 9 16 23 30
W...	3 10 17 24 31	7 14 21 28	3 10 17 24
Th...	4 11 18 25	1 8 15 22 29	4 11 18 25
F...	5 12 19 26	2 9 16 23 30	5 12 19 26
S...	6 13 20 27	3 10 17 24 31	6 13 20 27

	April	August	December
Su...	4 11 18 25	1 8 15 22 29	5 12 19 26
M...	5 12 19 26	2 9 16 23 30	6 13 20 27
Tu...	6 13 20 27	3 10 17 24 31	7 14 21 28
W...	7 14 21 28	4 11 18 25	1 8 15 22 29
Th... 1	8 15 22 29	5 12 19 26	2 9 16 23 30
F... 2	9 16 23 30	6 13 20 27	3 10 17 24
S... 3	10 17 24	7 14 21 28	4 11 18 25

Easter Days

March 28.	1869 1875 1937.
April 4.	1779 1790 1847 1858 1915 1926 1999.
April 11.	1762 1773 1819 1830 1841 1909 1971 1982 1993.
April 18.	1802 1813 1897 1954 1965.
April 25.	1886 1943.

L (Leap year)

	January	May	September
Su...	3 10 17 24 31	1 8 15 22 29	4 11 18 25
M...	4 11 18 25	2 9 16 23 30	5 12 19 26
Tu...	5 12 19 26	3 10 17 24 31	6 13 20 27
W...	6 13 20 27	4 11 18 25	7 14 21 28
Th...	7 14 21 28	5 12 19 26	1 8 15 22 29
F... 1	8 15 22 29	6 13 20 27	2 9 16 23 30
S... 2	9 16 23 30	7 14 21 28	3 10 17 24

	February	June	October
Su...	7 14 21 28	5 12 19 26	2 9 16 23 30
M... 1	8 15 22 29	6 13 20 27	3 10 17 24 31
Tu...	2 9 16 23	7 14 21 28	4 11 18 25
W...	3 10 17 24	1 8 15 22 29	5 12 19 26
Th...	4 11 18 25	2 9 16 23 30	6 13 20 27
F...	5 12 19 26	3 10 17 24	7 14 21 28
S...	6 13 20 27	4 11 18 25	1 8 15 22 29

	March	July	November
Su...	6 13 20 27	3 10 17 24 31	6 13 20 27
M...	7 14 21 28	4 11 18 25	7 14 21 28
Tu... 1	8 15 22 29	5 12 19 26	1 8 15 22 29
W...	2 9 16 23 30	6 13 20 27	2 9 16 23 30
Th...	3 10 17 24 31	7 14 21 28	3 10 17 24
F...	4 11 18 25	1 8 15 22 29	4 11 18 25
S...	5 12 19 26	2 9 16 23 30	5 12 19 26

	April	August	December
Su...	3 10 17 24	7 14 21 28	4 11 18 25
M...	4 11 18 25	1 8 15 22 29	5 12 19 26
Tu...	5 12 19 26	2 9 16 23 30	6 13 20 27
W...	6 13 20 27	3 10 17 24 31	7 14 21 28
Th...	7 14 21 28	4 11 18 25	1 8 15 22 29
F... 1	8 15 22 29	5 12 19 26	2 9 16 23 30
S... 2	9 16 23 30	6 13 20 27	3 10 17 24 31

Easter Days

March 27.	1796 1864 1932.
April 3.	1768 1836 1904 1988.
April 17.	1808 1892 1960.

M

	January	May	September
Su...	2 9 16 23 30	1 8 15 22 29	4 11 18 25
M...	3 10 17 24 31	2 9 16 23 30	5 12 19 26
Tu...	4 11 18 25	3 10 17 24 31	6 13 20 27
W...	5 12 19 26	4 11 18 25	7 14 21 28
Th...	6 13 20 27	5 12 19 26	1 8 15 22 29
F...	7 14 21 28	6 13 20 27	2 9 16 23 30
S... 1	8 15 22 29	7 14 21 28	3 10 17 24

	February	June	October
Su...	6 13 20 27	5 12 19 26	9 16 23 30
M... 1	7 14 21 28	6 13 20 27	3 10 17 24 31
Tu... 1	8 15 22	7 14 21 28	4 11 18 25
W...	2 9 16 23	1 8 15 22 29	5 12 19 26
Th...	3 10 17 24	2 9 16 23 30	6 13 20 27
F...	4 11 18 25	3 10 17 24	7 14 21 28
S...	5 12 19 26	4 11 18 25	1 8 15 22 29

	March	July	November
Su...	6 13 20 27	3 10 17 24 31	6 13 20 27
M...	7 14 21 28	4 11 18 25	7 14 21 28
Tu... 1	8 15 22 29	5 12 19 26	1 8 15 22 29
W...	2 9 16 23 30	6 13 20 27	2 9 16 23 30
Th...	3 10 17 24 31	7 14 21 28	3 10 17 24
F...	4 11 18 25	1 8 15 22 29	4 11 18 25
S...	5 12 19 26	2 9 16 23 30	5 12 19 26

	April	August	December
Su...	3 10 17 24	7 14 21 28	4 11 18 25
M...	4 11 18 25	1 8 15 22 29	5 12 19 26
Tu...	5 12 19 26	2 9 16 23 30	6 13 20 27
W...	6 13 20 27	3 10 17 24 31	7 14 21 28
Th...	7 14 21 28	4 11 18 25	1 8 15 22 29
F... 1	8 15 22 29	5 12 19 26	2 9 16 23 30
S... 2	9 16 23 30	6 13 20 27	3 10 17 24 31

Easter Days

March 27.	1785 1842 1853 1910 1921.
April 3.	1763 1774 1825 1831 1983 1994.
April 10.	1757 1803 1814 1887 1898 1955 1966.
April 17.	1870 1881 1927 1938 1949. [1977.
April 24.	1791 1859.

N (Leap year)

	January	May	September
Su...	2 9 16 23 30	7 14 21 28	3 10 17 24
M...	3 10 17 24 31	1 8 15 22 29	4 11 18 25
Tu...	4 11 18 25	2 9 16 23 30	5 12 19 26
W...	5 12 19 26	3 10 17 24 31	6 13 20 27
Th...	6 13 20 27	4 11 18 25	7 14 21 28
F...	7 14 21 28	5 12 19 26	1 8 15 22 29
S... 1	8 15 22 29	6 13 20 27	2 9 16 23 30

	February	June	October
Su...	6 13 20 27	4 11 18 25	1 8 15 22 29
M...	7 14 21 28	5 12 19 26	2 9 16 23 30
Tu... 1	8 15 22	6 13 20 27	3 10 17 24 31
W...	2 9 16 23	7 14 21 28	4 11 18 25
Th...	3 10 17 24	1 8 15 22 29	5 12 19 26
F...	4 11 18 25	2 9 16 23 30	6 13 20 27
S...	5 12 19 26	3 10 17 24	7 14 21 28

	March	July	November
Su...	5 12 19 26	2 9 16 23 30	5 12 19 26
M...	6 13 20 27	3 10 17 24 31	6 13 20 27
Tu...	7 14 21 28	4 11 18 25	7 14 21 28
W... 1	8 15 22 29	5 12 19 26	1 8 15 22 29
Th...	2 9 16 23 30	6 13 20 27	2 9 16 23 30
F...	3 10 17 24 31	7 14 21 28	3 10 17 24
S...	4 11 18 25	1 8 15 22 29	4 11 18 25

	April	August	December
Su...	2 9 16 23 30	6 13 20 27	3 10 17 24 31
M...	3 10 17 24	7 14 21 28	4 11 18 25
Tu...	4 11 18 25	1 8 15 22 29	5 12 19 26
W...	5 12 19 26	2 9 16 23 30	6 13 20 27
Th...	6 13 20 27	3 10 17 24 31	7 14 21 28
F... 1	7 14 21 28	4 11 18 25	1 8 15 22 29
S... 2	9 16 23 30	5 12 19 26	2 9 16 23 30

Easter Days

March 26.	1780.
April 2.	1820 1972.
April 9.	1944.
April 16.	1876.
April 23.	1848 1916 2000.

The World

The *Superficial Area* of the Earth is estimated to be 196,836,000 square miles, of which 55,786,000 square miles are Land and 141,050,000 square miles Water. The *Diameter* of the Earth at the Equator is 7,926 English miles, and at the Poles 7,900 English miles. The Equatorial *Circumference* is 24,901·8 English miles, divided into 360 Degrees of Longitude, each of 69·17 English (or 60 Geographical) miles; these Degrees are measured from the Meridian of Greenwich, and numbered East and West of that point to meet in the Antipodes at the 180th Degree. Distance North and South of the Equator is marked by Parallels of Latitude, which proceed from zero (at the Equator) to 90° at the Poles.

The *velocity* of a given point of the Earth's surface at the Equator exceeds 1,000 miles an hour (24,901·8 miles in 24 hours); the Earth's velocity in its orbit round the Sun is about 66,600 miles an hour (584,000,000 miles in 365¼ days). The Earth is distant from the Sun 93,000,000 miles, on the average.

AREA AND POPULATION

The total population of the world in June, 1969, was estimated by the *United Nations Statistical Office* at 3,552,000,000 compared with 3,003,000,000 in 1960 and 2,070,000,000 in 1930. Figures of areas in the following table are of land area and inland water, but exclude uninhabited polar regions and some uninhabited islands. Figures for Europe and Asia exclude U.S.S.R. which is shown separately. Figures for Oceania exclude Hawaii which is included with North America, being the 50th State of U.S.A.

Continent, etc.	Area		Estimated Population, 1969
	Sq. miles '000	Sq. km. '000	
Europe......	1,903	4,929	460,000,000
Asia*.......	10,661	27,611	1,988,000,000
U.S.S.R.....	8,649	22,402	240,000,000
Africa......	11,683	30,258	345,000,000
America.....	16,241	42,063	500,000,000
Oceania.....	3,286	8,510	18,900,000
Total.....	52,422	135,773	3,552,000,000

* Excludes U.S.S.R. (shown separately); includes European and Asiatic Turkey.

A United Nations report (*The Future Growth of World Population*) in 1958, pointed out that the population of the world had increased since the beginning of the 20th Century at an unprecedented rate: in 1850 it was estimated at 1,094,000,000 and in 1900 at 1,550,000,000, an increase of 42 per cent. in 50 years. By 1925 it had risen to 1,907,000,000—23 per cent. in 25 years—and by 1950 it had reached 2,500,000,000, an increase of 31 per cent. in 25 years. Levels of population and the trend in distribution of the population by continents as forecast for the years 1975 and 2000 were:—

	1975		2000	
Continent	Estimated Population	Per cent.	Estimated Population	Per cent.
Europe‡...	751	19·6	947	15·1
Asia*......	2,210	57·7	3,870	61·8
Africa.....	303	7·9	517	8·2
N. America.	240	6·3	312	5·0
Latin America†.	303	7·9	592	9·4
Oceania ...	21	0·5	29	0·5
World.....	3,828	100	6,267	100

[millions]

* Excluding U.S.S.R. † Mexico and the remainder of America south of U.S.A. ‡ Including U.S.S.R.

THE CONTINENTS

Europe (including European Russia) forms about one-fourteenth of the land surface of the globe. Its length from the North Cape, 71° 12′ N., to Cape Matapan, in the south of Greece, 36° 23′ N. is about 2,400 miles, and its breadth from Cape St Vincent to the Urals is about 3,300 miles. The political boundary between Europe and Asia extends some distance beyond the Urals, to include the mining regions; in the south-east it follows the valley of the Manych, north of the Caucasus.

Asia (including Asiatic Russia) extends over nearly one-third of the land surface of the globe. The distance between its extreme longitudes, the west coast of Asia Minor (26° E.) and the East Cape (170° W.), is 6,000 miles. The extreme latitudes, Cape Chelyuskin (78° 30″ N.) and Cape Bulus (76 miles north of the Equator), are 5,350 miles apart. Asia is bounded by the ocean on all sides except the west. The Isthmus of Suez connects it with Africa. The land boundary between Europe and Asia is formed on the west mainly by the Ural Mountains and the Ural River. In the south-west the valley of the Manych, which stretches from the Caspian Sea to the mouth of the Don, is now taken as the line between the two continents, although the Caucasus was formerly considered as belonging to Europe. The islands of the archipelago which lie in the south-east between the continents of Asia and Australia may be divided into two groups by a line passing east of Timor, Timor Laut, the Kei Islands and the Moluccas.

Africa is about three times the area of Europe. Its extreme longitudes are 17° W. at Cape Verde and 51° 27′ 52″ E. at Ras Hafun. The extreme latitudes are Cape Blanco in 37° N. and Cape Agulhas in 35° S., at a distance of about 5,000 miles. It is surrounded by seas on all sides, except in the narrow isthmus through which is cut the Suez Canal, and may be considered as a great peninsula of the Eurasian continent.

North America, including Mexico, is a little less than twice the size of Europe. Its extreme longitudes extend from a little west of 170° W. to 52½° W. in the east of Newfoundland, and its extreme latitudes from about 80° N. lat. to 15° N. lat. in the south of Mexico. It is surrounded by seas on all sides except in the south, where it joins the Isthmian States of *Central America*, which have an area of about 200,000 square miles. The area of the *West Indies* is about 65,000 square miles, a little more than half that of the United Kingdom. They extend from about 27° N. latitude to 10° N. latitude.

South America is a little more than 1¾ times the size of Europe. The extreme longitudes are Cape Branco 35° W. and Punta Parina 81° W., and the extreme latitudes, Punta Gallinas, 12½° N. and Cape Horn 56° S. South America is surrounded by the ocean, except where it is joined to Central America by the narrow isthmus through which is cut the Panama Canal.

Oceania extends over an area 1½ times the size of Europe, from Australia (in the West) to the most easterly islands of Polynesia, and from New Zealand (in the south) to the Sandwich Islands (Hawaii) in the north.

The appended tables of area and population are based on such information as is immediately available. With regard to areas it will be realized that no complete survey of many countries has yet been either achieved or even undertaken and that consequently accurate area figures are not available. In addition, among the results of the war of 1939-1945 is a readjustment of boundaries which have not yet been definitely settled.

The populations given hereunder are derived from various sources; some have as their basis an authenticated census; some are official and some are unofficial estimates. In certain cases where later information becomes available during printing the new figures are given in the overseas sections of the ALMANACK. What has been said about the survey of many of the world's countries applies equally to the question of census.

AFRICA

Ψ Seaport.

COUNTRY	Area Sq. Miles	Population	Per Sq. Mile	Capital	Population of Capital
Afars and Issas Territory..	9,000	81,000	9	Ψ Jibouti...............	62,000
Algeria	856,000	13,547,000	16	Ψ Algiers..............	943,000
Angola.................	488,000	5,430,000	11	Ψ St. Paul de Luanda....	346,763
Botswana..............	220,000	629,000	3	Gaborone...........	18,000
Burundi...............	10,700	3,475,000	325	Bujumbura..........	70,000
Cameroon.............	183,000	5,836,000	32	Yaoundé............	180,000
Cape Verde Islands.....	1,516	250,000	165	Ψ Praia...............	6,000
Central African Republic	234,000	1,518,000	6	Bangui.............	301,793
Chad..................	488,000	3,510,000	7	Fort Lamy..........	45,600
Congo.................	130,000	915,000	7	Brazzaville.........	136,000
Congolese Republic....	906,000	17,100,000	19	Kinshasa...........	1,300,000
Dahomey..............	47,000	2,640,000	56	Ψ Porto Novo.........	85,000
Egypt, see U.A.R.					
Equatorial Guinea......	11,000	286,000	26	Ψ Santa Isabel........	9,000
Ethiopia (Abyssinia)....	400,000	24,769,000	62	Addis Ababa........	644,190
Gaboon................	101,400	630,000	6	Ψ Libreville.........	31,000
Gambia...............	4,000	374,000	93	Ψ Bathurst..........	27,809
Ghana................	92,000	8,546,000	93	Ψ Accra.............	633,800
Guinea...............	97,000	3,890,000	40	Ψ Conakry..........	120,000
Ivory Coast...........	189,000	4,195,000	22	Ψ Abidjan...........	400,000
Kenya................	225,000	10,890,000	48	Nairobi............	480,000
Lesotho..............	11,700	970,000	83	Maseru............	14,000
Liberia..............	43,000	1,150,000	27	Ψ Monrovia..........	110,000
Libya................	810,000	1,869,000	2	Ψ Tripoli............	331,947
Madagascar...........	228,000	6,600,000	29	Antananarivo.......	364,496
Malawi...............	45,000	4,530,000	101	Zomba.............	19,666
Mali.................	465,000	4,929,000	11	Bamako............	150,000
Mauritania...........	419,000	1,140,000	3	Nouakchott........	18,000
Mauritius, etc........	805	834,000	1,036	Ψ Port Louis........	139,681
Morocco..............	180,000	15,525,000	86	Ψ Rabat............	469,000
Mozambique..........	298,000	7,376,000	25	Ψ Lourenço Marques...	441,363
Niger................	484,000	4,016,000	8	Niamey............	60,000
Nigeria..............	357,000	66,174,000	185	Ψ Lagos.............	700,000
Portuguese Guinea.....	14,000	530,000	38	Ψ Bissau............	6,000
Réunion..............	1,000	436,000	436	St. Denis..........	65,614
Rhodesia.............	151,000	5,190,000	34	Salisbury..........	400,000
Rwanda..............	10,000	3,500,000	350	Kigali.............	4,273
St. Helena...........	47	4,722	100	Ψ Jamestown........	1,475
Ascension..........	38	1,527	40	Ψ Georgetown.......	..
Tristan da Cunha.....	45	280	6	Ψ Edinburgh........	..
St. Tomé & Príncipe...	372	66,000	177	Ψ São Tomé.........	3,187
Senegal..............	78,000	3,780,000	48	Ψ Dakar............	500,000
Seychelles...........	156	51,000	327	Ψ Victoria..........	11,000
Sierra Leone.........	28,000	2,512,000	90	Ψ Freetown.........	85,000
Somalia.............	246,000	2,730,000	11	Ψ Mogadishu........	200,000
South Africa.........	472,000	21,282,000	45 {	Pretoria...........	422,590
				Ψ Cape Town	807,211
S.W. Africa..........	318,000	610,000	2	Windhoek..........	60,000
Spanish Presidios:—				..	..
Ceuta..............	5	88,000	..		
Melilla.............	72	77,000	..		
Sahara.............	125,000	63,000	..	Villa Cisneros.......	250
Sudan...............	977,000	15,312,000	16	Khartoum..........	124,000
Swaziland...........	6,700	451,000	67	Mbabane...........	14,000
Tanzania............	363,000	12,508,000	34	Ψ Dar-es-Salaam	272,743
Togo................	21,000	1,857,000	88	Lomé..............	100,000
Tunisia.............	45,000	5,027,000	112	Ψ Tunis............	784,787
Uganda.............	94,000	9,764,000	104	Kampala...........	331,000
United Arab Republic..	386,000	34,000,000	88	Cairo.............	5,126,000
Upper Volta.........	100,000	5,330,000	53	Ouagadougou........	110,000
Zambia	291,000	4,054,000	14	Lusaka............	238,000

AMERICA

Country	Area Sq. Miles	Population	Per Sq. Mile	Capital	Population of Capital
North America					
Canada†	3,560,000	20,401,000	6	Ottawa............	536,00
Alberta............	249,000	1,553,000	6	Edmonton............	435,00
British Columbia......	359,000	2,056,000	6	Ψ Victoria............	173,45
Manitoba............	212,000	981,000	5	Winnipeg............	535,00
New Brunswick.......	28,000	627,000	22	Ψ Fredericton........	22,46
Newfoundland.......	143,000	513,000	4	Ψ St. John's........	90,83
Nova Scotia.........	20,000	764,000	38	Ψ Halifax........	198,19
Ontario............	344,000	7,425,000	22	Toronto........	2,366,00
Prince Edward Island...	2,000	109,000	55	Ψ Charlottetown........	18,50
Quebec............	524,000	6,005,000	11	Ψ Quebec........	193 98
Saskatchewan........	220,000	961,000	4	Regina........	143,00
Yukon Territory......	205,000	15,000	..	Whitehorse........	4,77
Northwest Territories..	1,253,000	31,000	..	Ottawa........	536,00
Mexico............	758,000	48,313 000	64	Mexico City........	8,000,00
St. Pierre and Miquelon.	93	5,000	54	Ψ St. Pierre........	3,50
United States*.........	3,554,000	203,166,000	57	Washington, D.C.....	2,861,12
Central America and the West Indies					
Anguilla..............	35	5,810	166		....
Antigua and Barbuda...	170	65,000	382	Ψ St. John's........	25,00
Bahamas............	4,400	169,900	38	Ψ Nassau........	112,00
Barbados............	166	254,000	1,530	Ψ Bridgetown........	12,43
Bermuda............	21	53,000	2,524	Ψ Hamilton........	3,00
British Honduras.......	8,900	122,000	14	Belmopan........	3,00
Cayman Islands........	100	10,652	107	Ψ George Town........	3,00
Costa Rica..........	19,300	1,685,000	87	San José........	205 65
Cuba..............	44,000	8,553,000	194	Ψ Havana........	1,755,36
Dominica............	290	74,000	255	Ψ Roseau........	11,92
Dominican Republic...	19,000	4,012,000	212	Santa Domingo........	823,00
Grenada............	133	105,000	790	Ψ St. George's........	8,40
Guadeloupe..........	688	323,000	469	Ψ Pointe à Pitre........	39,00
Guatemala..........	42,000	5,014,000	119	Guatemala........	572,90
Haiti..............	10,000	4,768,000	477	Ψ Port au Prince........	300,00
Honduras............	43,000	2,535,000	59	Tegucigalpa........	225,00
Jamaica............	4,400	1,861,000	423	Ψ Kingston........	555,11
Martinique..........	400	332,000	83	Ψ Fort de France........	60,60
Montserrat..........	39	15,000	385	Ψ Plymouth........	3,00
Netherlands Antilles....	394	220,000	558	Ψ Willemstad........	45,00
Nicaragua...........	57,000	1,984,000	35	Managua........	300,00
Panama............	31,900	1,425,000	45	Ψ Panama City........	418,00
Panama Canal Zone....	647	51,000	79	Ψ Balboa Heights........	3,95
Puerto Rico..........	3,400	2,712,000	798	Ψ San Juan........	455,42
St. Kitts-Nevis........	136	51,000	375	Ψ Basseterre........	13,05
St. Lucia............	238	110,000	462	Ψ Castries........	40,00
St. Vincent..........	150	92,000	613	Ψ Kingstown........	23,00
(El) Salvador.........	7,700	3,390,000	440	San Salvador........	340,00
Trinidad and Tobago...	1,980	1,010,000	510	Ψ Port of Spain........	93,95
Turks and Caicos Islds. .	166	6,000	36	Ψ Grand Turk........	2,33
Virgin Islands:—					
British..............	59	10,500	178	Ψ Road Town........	2,18
U.S.................	133	63,000	474	Ψ Charlotte Amalie.....	11,00
South America					
Argentina............	1,080,000	23,360,000	21	Ψ Buenos Aires........	7,200,000
Bolivia............	415,000	4,658,000	11	La Paz............	553,00
Brazil............	3,289,000	93,000,000	28	Brasília........	544,86
Chile............	290,000	8,835,000	30	Santiago........	2,100,00
Colombia............	440,000	22,000,000	50	Bogotá........	2,000,00
Ecuador............	226,000	5,890,000	26	Quito........	483,84
Falkland Islands.......	4,700	2,045	..	Ψ Stanley........	1,05
Guiana, French.......	35,000	48,000	1	Ψ Cayenne........	20,00
Netherlands' (Surinam) .	54,000	389,000	7	Ψ Paramaribo........	120,00
Guyana	83,000	714,000	9	Ψ Georgetown........	168,00
Paraguay............	157,000	2,314,000	15	Ψ Asunción........	437,00
Peru............	531,000	13,600,000	26	Lima........	2,500,00
Uruguay	72,000	2,852,000	40	Ψ Montevideo........	1,173,11
Venezuela	352,000	10,399,000	30	Caracas........	2,064,00

★ The 50 States and Federal *District of Columbia* at the 1970 Census; for area and population of in
dividual States *see* main article.   Ψ Seaport.   † For total areas (including freshwater), see p. 69

ASIA

The expressions " The Near East," " The Middle East " and " The Far East " often appear in the Press of English-speaking countries, but have no definite boundaries. The following limits have been suggested:— *Near East* (Turkey to Iran) 25°–60° E. long., *Middle East* (Baluchistan to Burma) 60°–100° E. long., *Far East* (Thailand to Japan) 100°–160° E. long. Ψ Seaport.

COUNTRY	Area Sq. miles	Population	Per Sq. Mile	Capital	Population of Capital
Afghanistan.............	250,000	16,516,000	66	Kabul................	450,000
Bahrain.................	213	207,000	972	Ψ Manama.............	89,608
Bhutan.................	18,000	770,000	43	Punakha.............	..
Brunei..................	2,226	130,000	58	Ψ Brunei..............	41,000
Burma..................	262,000	27,584,000	105	Ψ Rangoon............	1,758,731
Ceylon..................	25,000	12,240,000	490	Ψ Colombo............	551,200
China...................	4,300,000	732,000,000	170	Peking..............	4,010,000
Formosa (Taiwan)....	13,800	14,746,000	1,069	Taipei..............	1,769,568
Macau................	5	*260,000	..	Ψ Macau.............	157,175
Hong Kong............	398	3,951,000	..	Ψ Victoria............	767,000
India..................	1,262,000	536,984,000	426	Delhi...............	3,780,423
Indonesia..............	735,000	118,000,000	160	Ψ Djakarta............	4,750,000
Iran (Persia)..........	628,000	28,448,000	45	Tehran..............	3,150,000
Iraq....................	172,000	9,465,800	55	Baghdad............	2,696,000
Israel..................	8,000	2,919,000	365	Jerusalem...........	283,000
Japan..................	143,000	103,265,000	722	Tokyo..............	11,403,744
Jordan.................	30,000	2,300,000	76	Amman.............	542,000
Khmer Republic......	70,000	6,701,000	96	Ψ Phnom Penh.......	1,500,000
Korea:—					
North Korea........	48,000	13,300,000	277	Pyongyang..........	286,000
South Korea........	38,000	31,738,000	817	Seoul...............	3,794,959
Kuwait.................	5,800	733,000	126	Ψ Kuwait.............	300,000
Laos....................	90,000	2,700,000	30	Vientiane...........	162,297
Lebanon................	4,300	2,645,000	615	Ψ Beirut..............	555,000
Malaysia...............	128,000	10,434,000	82	Kuala Lumpur......	500,000
Johore..............	7,330	1,274,000	174	Johore Bahru.......	..
Kedah..............	3,640	955,000	265	Alor Star...........	..
Kelantan...........	5,765	681,000	118	Kota Bahru.........	..
Malacca............	640	404,000	631	Ψ Malacca............	..
Negri Sembilan.....	2,570	479,000	186	Seremban...........	..
Pahang.............	13,900	503,000	36	Kuantan............	..
Penang.............	400	777,000	1,942	Ψ George Town......	234,930
Perak..............	8,100	1,563,000	193	Ipoh...............	125,776
Perlis..............	310	121,000	390	Kangar.............	..
Sabah..............	29,000	656,000	23	Kota Kinabalu......	41,830
Sarawak............	48,000	977,000	20	Ψ Kuching...........	63,491
Selangor...........	3,166	1,629,000	515	Kuala Lumpur......	500,000
Trengganu..........	5,000	406,000	81	Kuala Trengganu....	..
Maldive Islands........	115	114,000	991	Ψ Malé...............	13,610
Mongolia (Outer)......	600,000	1,240,000	2	Ulan Bator.........	195,300
Nepal..................	54,000	10,845,000	201	Katmandu..........	224,867
Oman..................	82,000	750,000	9	Ψ Muscat............	7,650
Pakistan................	366,000	111,830,000	306	Rawalpindi.........	340,175
Philippine Islds........	115,000	39,079,000	340	Ψ Manila.............	2,989,300
Qatar..................	4,000	130,000	33	Doha...............	100,000
Saudi Arabia..........	927,000	7,200,000	8	Riyadh.............	300,000
Singapore..............	225	*2,975,000	..		..
Syria...................	71,000	6,294,000	89	Damascus...........	599,000
Thailand (Siam).......	198,000	34,738,000	176	Ψ Bangkok...........	1,577,003
Timor, Eastern........	7,329	590,000	81	Ψ Dili...............	7,000
Trucial States.........	32,000	185,000	6		..
Turkey in Asia,†	285,000	32,501,000	..	Ankara.............	1,440,779
U.S.S.R. (Asia).......		58,964,000	..		..
R.S.F.S.R. (Asia)..	6,640,000	*See* Europe			
Armenia (Hyastan)...	11,000	2,492,000	227	Erevan.............	767,000
Azerbaidjan..........	33,000	5,117,000	155	Ψ Baku..............	1,261,000
Georgia.............	27,000	4,686,000	174	Tbilisi.............	839,000
Turkmenistan.......	188,000	2,159,000	11	Ashkhabad..........	253,000
Uzbekistan..........	158,000	11,960,000	76	Tashkent...........	1,385,000
Tadjikistan.........	54,000	2,900,000	55	Dushanbe...........	374,000
Kazakhstan.........	1,064,000	12,849,000	12	Alma Ata..........	730,000
Kirghizia...........	77,000	2,933,000	38	Frunze.............	431,000
Vietnam:—					
Northern Zone.......	63,000	21,340,000	339	Hanoi..............	800,000
Southern Zone.......	66,000	17,867,000	271	Ψ Saigon.............	2,500,000
Yemen.................	74,000	5,000,000	68	Taiz...............	20,000
Yemen P.D.R..........	60,000	1,250,000	21	Ψ Aden..............	150,000

* Population subject to wide fluctuations. † Total, incl. European parts: Area, 294,200 sq. miles; population, 35,666,549.

EUROPE AND THE MEDITERRANEAN

COUNTRY	Area Sq. Miles	Population	Per Sq. Mile	Capital	Population of Capital
Albania..............	10,700	2,075,000	194	Tirana..............	50,000
Andorra..............	180	19,000	106	Andorra La Vella.....	2,500
Austria..............	32,000	7,391,000	231	Vienna..............	1,643,100
Belgium..............	11,800	9,691,000	821	Brussels..............	1,077,035
Bulgaria..............	43,000	8,524,000	198	Sofia..............	868,200
Cyprus..............	3,500	633,000	181	Nicosia..............	115,000
Czechoslovakia......	54,000	14,467,000	268	Prague..............	1,030,330
Denmark..............	17,000	4,879,000	287	Ψ Copenhagen..........	1,199,010
Finland..............	130,000	4,706,000	36	Ψ Helsinki..............	526,896
France..............	213,000	50,770,000	238	Paris..............	2,590,000
Germany:—					
Federal Republic of Germany ‡	96,000	59,378,000	619	Bonn..............	299,376
Eastern Germany......	41,400	15,993,000	386	East Berlin..............	1,200,000
Gibraltar..............	2	28,000	..	Ψ Gibraltar..............	20,000
Greece..............	51,000	8,736,000	171	Athens..............	1,852,709
Hungary..............	36,000	10,344,000	287	Budapest..............	2,007,000
Iceland..............	40,500	204,000	5	Ψ Reykjavik..............	81,354
Irish Republic	26,600	2,944,000	111	Ψ Dublin..............	568,772
Italy..............	131,000	54,683,000	417	Rome..............	2,778,872
Liechtenstein..........	65	22,000	338	Vaduz..............	4,070
Luxemburg..........	1,000	340,000	340	Luxemburg..........	76,143
Malta and Gozo........	122	322,000	2,639	Ψ Valletta..............	15,547
Monaco..............	½	24,000	..	Monaco..............	2,422
Netherlands..............	13,500	13,077,000	969 {	The Hague.............. / Ψ Amsterdam..............	576,160 / 845,821
Norway..............	125,000	3,892,000	31	Ψ Oslo..............	486,972
Poland..............	121,000	32,889,000	272	Warsaw..............	1,308,100
Portugal§..............	35,700	9,560,000	268	Ψ Lisbon..............	820,000
Rumania..............	91,600	20,010,000	218	Bucharest..............	1,511,388
San Marino..............	23	19,000	826	San Marino..............	2,000
Spain..............	197,000	33,290,000	169	Madrid..............	3,150,000
Sweden..............	173,000	8,014,000	46	Ψ Stockholm..............	1,306,762
Switzerland..............	16,000	6,270,000	392	Berne..............	166,800
Turkey in Europe......	9,200	3,166,000	344	Ankara..............	1,440,779
THE UNITED KINGDOM†	93,026	55,521,534	597 }	Ψ London..............	7,379,014
England..............	50,053	45,870,062	916 }		
Wales..............	7,969	2,723,596	342	Ψ Cardiff..............	278,221
Scotland..............	29,798	5,227,706	171	Ψ Edinburgh..............	467,650
Northern Ireland......	5,206	1,525,187	278	Ψ Belfast..............	385,900
U.S.S.R. (Europe)......		179,407,000	..		
R.S.F.S.R.*......	1,970,000	130,079,000	66	Moscow..............	7,061,000
Ukraine..............	232,000	47,126,000	203	Kiev..............	1,632,000
Belorussia..............	80,000	9,002,000	113	Minsk..............	916,000
Moldavia..............	13,000	3,569,000	275	Kishinev..............	357,000
Estonia..............	17,400	1,356,000	78	Ψ Tallinn..............	363,000
Latvia..............	25,000	2,364,000	95	Ψ Riga..............	733,000
Lithuania..............	26,000	3,128,000	120	Vilnius..............	329,000
Vatican City State......	109 *acres*	1,000	..	Vatican City..............	1,000
Yugoslavia..............	99,000	21,500,000	217	Belgrade..............	1,204,000

* Total population, Europe and Asia.   † *Land* areas are shown for U.K. and parts (*total area* U.K., 94,216 sq. m.); populations at 1971 Census (prelim.) except Belfast.   ‡ Data include West Berl § Data include Madeira (314 sq. miles) and the Azores (922 sq. miles).   Ψ Seaport.

THE SEVEN WONDERS OF THE WORLD

I. THE PYRAMIDS OF EGYPT.—From Gizeh (near Cairo) to a southern limit 60 miles distant. The olde is that of Zoser, at Saggara, built about 2,700 B.C. The Great Pyramid of Cheops covers more th 12 acres and was originally 481 ft. in height and 756 × 756 ft. at the base.

II. THE HANGING GARDENS OF BABYLON.—Adjoining Nebuchadnezzar's palace, 60 miles south Baghdad. Terraced gardens, ranging from 75 to 300 ft. above ground level, watered from stora tanks on the highest terrace.

III. THE TOMB OF MAUSOLUS.—At Halicarnassus, in Asia Minor. Built by the widowed Que Artemisia about 350 B.C. The memorial originated the term mausoleum.

IV. THE TEMPLE OF DIANA AT EPHESUS.—Ionic temple erected about 350 B.C. in honour of the godde and burned by the Goths in A.D. 262.

V. THE COLOSSUS OF RHODES.—A bronze statue of Apollo, set up about 280 B.C. According to lege it stood at the harbour entrance of the seaport of Rhodes.

VI. THE STATUE OF JUPITER OLYMPUS.—At Olympia in the plain of Ellis, constructed of marble inl with ivory and gold by the sculptor Phidias, about 430 B.C.

VII. THE PHAROS OF ALEXANDRIA.—A marble watch tower and lighthouse on the island of Pharos in t harbour of Alexandria.

OCEANIA

COUNTRY	Area Sq. Miles	Population	Per Sq. Mile	Capital	Population of Capital
Australia..............	2,968,000	12,713,000	4	Canberra............	139,800
New South Wales.....	309,000	4,624,000	15	Ψ Sydney..............	2,780,310
Queensland...........	667,000	1,820,000	3	Ψ Brisbane............	813,300
South Australia.......	380,000	1,178,000	3	Adelaide............	762,800
Tasmania.............	26,000	396,000	15	Ψ Hobart.............	127,260
Victoria..............	88,000	3,481,000	40	Ψ Melbourne..........	2,110,168
Western Australia.....	976,000	1,001,000	1	Perth..............	635,500
Northern Territory ...	520,000	74,000	..	Ψ Darwin.............	32,943
Norfolk Island........	15	1,240	83	Ψ Kingston...........	..
British Solomon Is......	11,500	161,000	14	Ψ Honiara............	3,536
Fiji..................	7,100	524,000	74	Ψ Suva..............	54,157
French Polynesia......	2,500	109,000	44	Ψ Papeete............	15,220
Gilbert and Ellice Is.....	360	54,000	150	Tarawa.............	10,616
Guam................	209	87,000	416	Agaña..............	..
Mariana, Caroline and Marshall Islands†	687	101,592	148	Saipan.............	..
Nauru...............	8	7,000	875	Ψ Nauru.............	..
New Caledonia.......	7,200	98,000	14	Ψ Noumea............	12,000
New Hebrides.........	5,700	86,000	15	Ψ Vila...............	5,500
New Zealand..........	104,000	2,867,000	28	Ψ Wellington	301,300
Cook Islands ...... }	200	{ 21,000	..	Avarua.............	..
Niue.............. }		5,302	..	Alofi..............	956
Ross Dependency......	160,000	262	..		..
Papua and New Guinea.	178,000	2,523,000	14	Ψ Port Moresby.......	13,590
Samoa:—					
Eastern..............	76	28,000	368	Ψ Pago Pago..........	1,251
Western.............	1,097	131,000	129	Ψ Apia..............	25,000
Tonga, etc.............	270	87,000	322	Ψ Nukualofa..........	9,202

† Trust Territory of the Pacific Islands.   Ψ Seaport

OCEAN AREAS AND DEPTHS

The greatest known Ocean Depth (in the Pacific, off the Philippines, 36,198 feet) is not much greater than the greatest land height (in the Himalayas); but the mean depth of the Ocean floor exceeds 12,000 feet, while the mean height of the surface of the land area of the Earth above sea level is only 2,300 feet. The following table gives the areas of the principal oceans and seas, with the greatest known depth of each:—

Oceans

Name	Area of Basin (sq. miles)	Greatest Depth (feet)
Pacific..........	63,986,000	Mariana Trench 36,198
Atlantic........	31,530,000	Porto Rico Trench, 27,498
Indian..........	28,350,000	Diamantina, 26,400
Arctic..........	5,541,600	17,850

Seas

Name	Area of Basin (sq. miles)	Greatest Depth (feet)
Malay..........	3,137,000	Kei Trench, 21,342
Caribbean......	1,770,170	Cayman, 23,000
Mediterranean...	1,145,000	Matapan, 14,435
Bering.........	878,000	Buldir Trough, 13,422
Okhotsk........	582,000	Kurile Trough, 11,154
East China......	480,000	*about* 10,500
Hudson Bay....	472,000	*about* 1,500
Japan...........	405,000	*about* 10,200
Andaman.......	305,000	*about* 11,000
North Sea......	221,000	Skaggerak, 1,998
Red Sea........	178,000	20° N., 7,254
Baltic..........	158,000	*about* 1,300

THE HIGHEST BUILDINGS

	Feet
Empire State, N.Y. U.S.A...............	1,472
Chrysler Building N.Y., U.S.A...........	1,046
Eiffel Tower, Paris (originally)	985
60 Wall Tower, N.Y., U.S.A...........	950
Bank of Manhattan, N.Y., U.S.A.	927
Rockefeller Centre, N.Y., U.S.A.	850
Woolworth's, N.Y., U.S.A..............	792
City Bank Farmers' Trust, 20 Exchange Place, N.Y., U.S.A................	741
Toronto-Dominion Bank Tower, Toronto	740

	Feet
Metropolitan Life Building, Madison Avenue, N.Y., U.S.A.................	700
500 Fifth Avenue, N.Y., U.S.A...........	697
Chanin, Lexington Avenue and 42nd Street, N.Y., U.S.A......................	680
Husky Tower, Calgary, Alberta..........	626
Post Office Tower, England	580
Pyramid of Cheops, Egypt	450
Salisbury Cathedral (Spire), England......	404
St. Paul's Cathedral (Cross), England	365

THE LARGEST CITIES OF THE WORLD

Ψ = Seaport	Population★	Ψ = Seaport	Population★
Ψ New York, U.S.A. (1970)	11,528,649	Ψ Houston, U.S.A. (1970)	1,985,031
TOKYO, Japan (1971)	11,403,744	Ψ Karachi, Pakistan (1961)	1,916,000
MEXICO CITY, Mexico (1970)	8,000,000	Ψ Alexandria, U.A.R. (1969)	1,900,000
Ψ LONDON, England (1971)	7,379,014	Ψ Newark, U.S.A. (1970)	1,856,556
Ψ BUENOS AIRES, Argentina (1960)	7,200,000	ATHENS, Greece (1961)	1,852,709
MOSCOW, U.S.S.R. (1969)	7,061,000	Ψ Canton, China (1957)	1,840,000
Ψ Los Angeles, U.S.A. (1970)	7,032,075	Ψ Hamburg, Germany (1969)	1,817,073
Ψ Chicago, U.S.A. (1970)	6,978,947	Minneapolis, U.S.A. (1970)	1,813,647
Ψ Shanghai, China (1957)	6,900,000	TAIPEI, Formosa (1970)	1,769,568
São Paulo, Brazil (1970)	5,901,533	Ψ RANGOON, Burma (1970)	1,758,731
Ψ Bombay, India (1971)	5,850,000	Ψ HAVANA, Cuba (1970)	1,755,360
CAIRO, U.A.R. (1971)	5,126,000	Ψ Barcelona, Spain (1969)	1,750,000
Ψ Philadelphia, U.S.A. (1970)	4,817,914	Milan, Italy (1971)	1,713,539
Ψ DJAKARTA, Indonesia (1969)	4,750,000	VIENNA, Austria (1970)	1,643,100
Ψ Rio de Janeiro, Brazil (1970)	4,296,782	Kiev, U.S.S.R. (1969)	1,632,000
Ψ Detroit, U.S.A. (1970)	4,199,931	Ψ BANGKOK, Thailand (1966)	1,577,003
PEKING, China (1957)	4,010,000	Dallas, U.S.A. (1970)	1,555,950
Ψ Leningrad, U.S.S.R. (1969)	3,950,000	Harbin, China (1957)	1,552,000
SEOUL, Korea (1966)	3,794,959	BUCHAREST, Rumania (1966)	1,511,388
DELHI, India (1969)	3,780,423	Ψ Lushun-Dairen, China (1957)	1,508,000
Tientsin, China (1957)	3,220,000	Guadalajara, Mexico (1970)	1,500,000
Berlin, Germany (1969)	3,218,256	Ψ PHNOM PENH, Khmer Repub. (1970)	1,500,000
MADRID, Spain (1969)	3,150,000	ANKARA, Turkey (1970)	1,440,779
TEHRAN, Iran (1970)	3,150,000	Ψ Pusan, Korea (1966)	1,425,703
Ψ Calcutta, India (1971)	3,141,180	Ψ Seattle, U.S.A. (1970)	1,421,869
Ψ San Francisco, U.S.A. (1970)	3,109,519	Anaheim, U.S.A. (1970)	1,420,386
Ψ MANILA, Philippines (1969)	2,989,300	Kyoto, Japan (1971)	1,415,880
Ψ Osaka, Japan (1971)	2,980,409	Nanking, China (1957)	1,409,000
WASHINGTON, U.S.A. (1970)	2,861,123	Ψ Milwaukee, U.S.A. (1970)	1,403,887
Ψ Sydney, Australia (1969)	2,780,310	Atlanta, U.S.A. (1970)	1,390,164
ROME, Italy (1971)	2,778,872	Tashkent, U.S.S.R. (1969)	1,385,000
Ψ Boston, U.S.A. (1970)	2,753,700	Cincinnati, U.S.A. (1970)	1,384,911
BAGHDAD, Iraq (1970)	2,696,000	Ψ Casablanca, Morocco (1969)	1,363,000
PARIS, France (1969)	2,590,000	Paterson, U.S.A. (1970)	1,358,794
LIMA, Peru (1969)	2,500,000	Ψ San Diego, U.S.A. (1970)	1,357,854
Ψ SAIGON, S. Vietnam (1968)	2,500,000	Ψ Buffalo, U.S.A. (1970)	1,349,211
Ψ Madras, India (1971)	2,470,289	Munich, Germany (1969)	1,326,331
Shenyang, China (1957)	2,411,000	Sian, China (1957)	1,310,000
Pittsburgh, U.S.A. (1970)	2,401,245	WARSAW, Poland (1970)	1,308,100
Ψ Toronto, Canada (1970)	2,366,000	Ψ STOCKHOLM, Sweden (1970)	1,306,762
St. Louis, U.S.A. (1970)	2,363,017	KINSHASA, Congolese Repub. (1971)	1,300,000
Ψ Istanbul, Turkey (1970)	2,312,751	Lahore, Pakistan (1961)	1,296,477
Ψ Yokohama, Japan (1971)	2,273,029	Ψ Kobé, Japan (1971)	1,294,373
Ψ Montreal, Canada (1970)	2,225,420	Ψ Naples, Italy (1971)	1,278,051
Wuhan, China (1957)	2,146,000	Ψ Miami, U.S.A. (1970)	1,267,792
Chungking, China (1957)	2,121,000	Ψ Baku, U.S.S.R. (1969)	1,261,000
Ψ Melbourne, Australia (1966)	2,110,168	Kansas City, U.S.A. (1970)	1,256,649
SANTIAGO, Chile (1964)	2,100,000	Hyderabad, India (1963)	1,251,119
Ψ SINGAPORE (1970)	2,074,507	Ψ Belo Horizonte, Brazil (1970)	1,232,708
Ψ Baltimore, U.S.A. (1970)	2,070,670	Denver, U.S.A. (1970)	1,227,529
Ψ Cleveland, U.S.A. (1970)	2,064,194	BELGRADE, Yugoslavia (1970)	1,204,000
CARACAS, Venezuela (1968)	2,064,000	Monterrey, Mexico (1970)	1,200,000
Ψ Nagoya, Japan (1971)	2,037,952	Ψ COPENHAGEN, Denmark (1969)	1,199,010
BUDAPEST, Hungary (1969)	2,007,000	Turin, Italy (1971)	1,190,688
BOGOTA, Colombia (1968)	2,000,000	MONTEVIDEO, Uruguay (1963)	1,173,114

★ *See* paragraph 2, p. 199. U.S.A.—Populations of the largest cities are those of the standard metropolitan statistical areas at the Census of 1970.

THE CINQUE PORTS

As their name implies the Cinque Ports were originally 5 in number, Hastings, New Romney, Hythe, Dover and Sandwich. They were in existence before the Norman Conquest and were the Anglo-Saxon successors to the Roman system of coast defence organized from the Wash to Spithead to resist Saxon onslaughts. William the Conqueror reconstituted them and granted peculiar jurisdiction, most of which was abolished in 1855. Only jurisdiction in Admiralty still survives.

At some time after the Conquest the "ancient towns" of Winchelsea and Rye were added with equal privileges. The other members of the Confederation, known as Limbs, are:—Lydd, Faversham, Folkestone, Deal, Tenterden, Margate and Ramsgate.

The Barons of the Cinque Ports have the ancient privilege of attending the Coronation Ceremony and are allotted special places in Westminster Abbey.

Lord Warden, Rt. Hon. Sir Robert Menzies, K.T., C.H., Q.C.

Judge, Court of Admiralty, Sir Henry Barnard.

Registrar, James A. Johnson, New Bridge House, Dover.

Lord Wardens since 1904

Marquess Curzon	1904
The Prince of Wales	1905
Earl Brassey	1908
Earl Beauchamp	1913
Marquess of Reading	1934
Marquess of Willingdon	1936
Sir Winston Churchill	1941
Sir Robert Menzies	1965

THE WORLD'S LAKES

Name	Country	Length (Miles)	Area. (Sq. Miles)	Name	Country	Length (Miles)	Area (Sq. Miles)
Caspian Sea	Asia	680	170,000	Amadjuak	Baffin Land	75	4,000
Superior	North America	383	31,820	Onega	U.S.S.R.	145	3,800
Victoria Nyanza	Africa	200	26,200	Eyre	Australia	..	3,700
Aral	U.S.S.R.	205	24,400	Rudolf	Africa	185	3,500
Huron	North America	247	23,010	Titicaca	South America	120	3,200
Michigan	North America	321	22,400	Athabasca	Canada	100	3,058
Malawi	Africa	350	14,200	Nicaragua	Central America	195	3,000
Tanganyika	Africa	420	12,700	Gairdner	Australia	..	3,000
Great Bear	Canada	175	11,660	Van	Asia Minor	80	2,500
Baikal	U.S.S.R.	330	11,580	Reindeer	Canada	160	2,444
Great Slave	Canada	325	11,170	Torrens	Australia	130	2,400
Erie	North America	241	9,940	Koko-Nor	Tibet	68	2,300
Winnipeg	Canada	260	9,398	Issyk-Kul	U.S.S.R.	115	2,250
Maracaibo	South America	..	8,296	Vänern	Sweden	93	2,150
Ontario	North America	193	7,540	Winnipegosis	Canada	122	2,086
Balkhash	U.S.S.R.	323	7,050	Bangweolo	Africa	150	2,000
Ladoga	U.S.S.R.	125	7,000	Nipigon	Canada	70	1,870
Chad	Africa	..	6,000	Manitoba	Canada	191	1,817
Nettilling	Baffin Land	120	5,000				

VOLCANOES OF THE WORLD

Volcano	Locality	Height in Feet	Volcano	Locality	Height in Feet
Cotopaxi	Ecuador	19,612	Nyamuragira	Congo	10,150
Kluchevskaya	U.S.S.R.	16,130	Villarica	Chile	9,325
Mount Wrangel	U.S.A.	14,000	Ruapehu	New Zealand	9,175
Mauna Loa	Hawaii	13,675	Paricutin	Mexico	9,000
Cameroons	W. Cameroon	13,350	Asama	Japan	8,200
Erebus	Antarctic Continent	12,200	Ngauruhoe	New Zealand	7,515
Nyiragongo	Congo	11,560	Hecla	Iceland	5,100
Etna	Sicily	11,121	Kilauea	Hawaii	4,090
Iliamna	Aleutian Islands, U.S.A.	11,000	Vesuvius	Italy	3,700
Chillan	Chile	10,500	Stromboli	Lipari Islands, Italy	3,000

QUIESCENT

Llullaillaco	Chile	20,244	Tristan da Cunha	South Atlantic	6,000
Demavend	Iran	18,600	Pelée	Martinique, W. Indies	4,430
Pico de Teyde	Teneriffe	12,180	Tarawera	New Zealand	3,646
Semerou	Indonesia	12,050	Soufrière	St. Vincent Is., W.I.	3,000
Haleakala	Hawaii	10,032	Krakatoa	Sunda Strait	2,600
Guntur	Indonesia	7,300	Two-Shma	Japan	2,480
Tongariro	New Zealand	6,458			

BELIEVED EXTINCT

Aconcagua	Chile and Argentina	22,976	Popocatapetl	Mexico	17,540
Chimborazo	Ecuador	20,500	Orizaba	Mexico	17,400
Kilimanjaro	Tanganyika	19,340	Karisimbi	Congo	15,020
Antisana	Ecuador	18,850	Mikeno	Congo	14,780
Elbruz	Caucasus	18,526	Fujiyama	Japan	12,395

THE HIGHEST MOUNTAINS

The following list contains the principal peaks of such ranges as the Himalayas and the Andes, and the highest mountains in other ranges.

Name	Range	Height in Feet	Name	Range	Height in Feet
EVEREST	Himalayas	29,028	North Peak	Alaska	19,370
K 2	Karakoram	28,250	Kilimanjaro	Tanganyika	19,340
Kinchinjanga	Himalayas	28,146	Antisana	Andes	18,850
Nanga Parbat	Himalayas	26,629	Demavend	Elbruz	18,600
Nanda Devi	Himalayas	25,645	Elbruz	Caucasus	18,526
Kamet	Himalayas	25,447	Tolima	Andes	18,320
Minyaa Konka	China	24,900	Mount St. Elias	Alaska	18,008
Pik Communizmu	Pamirs	24,590	Popocatapetl	S. Madre	17,540
Pik Pobedy	Tian Shan	24,410	Orizaba	S. Madre	17,400
Aconcagua	Andes	22,976	Foraker	Alaska	17,395
Huascaran	Andes	22,211	Ararat	Armenia	17,160
Nandakhat	Himalayas	21,690	Mount Lucania	Yukon	17,150
Sorata (Illampu)	Andes	21,500	King's Peak	Yukon	17,130
Sajama	Andes	21,480	Sangay	Andes	17,124
Illimani	Andes	21,221	Koshtan Tau	Caucasus	17,096
Huandoy	Andes	20,855	Kenya	Kenya	17,058
Chimborazo	Andes	20,500	Vinson Massif	Ellsworth	16,860
McKinley	Alaska	20,320	Ruwenzori	Uganda	16,800
Llullaillaco	Andes	20,244	Carstensz	New Guinea	16,500
Mount Logan	Yukon	19,850	Kluchevskaya	Miakovski	16,130
Cotopaxi	Andes	19,612	Mont Blanc	Alps	15,782

G*

THE LONGEST RIVERS

River	Outflow	Length in Miles
Nile	Mediterranean	4,160
Amazon	Atlantic	4,050
Missouri-Mississippi-Red Rock	Gulf of Mexico	3,710
Yangtze	North Pacific	3,400
Yenisei	Arctic	3,300
Congo	Atlantic	3,000
Lena	Arctic	2,800
Mekong	China Sea	2,800
Obi	Arctic	2,700
Niger	Gulf of Guinea	2,600
Hwang-ho	North Pacific	2,600
Amur	,, ,,	2,500
Paraná	Atlantic	2,450
Volga	Caspian Sea	2,400
Mackenzie	Beaufort Sea	2,300
Yukon	Bering Sea	2,000
Arkansas	Mississippi	2,000
Madeira	Amazon	2,000
Colorado	Gulf of California	2,000
St. Lawrence	Gulf of St. Lawrence	1,800
Rio Grande del Norte	Gulf of Mexico	1,800
São Francisco	Atlantic	1,800
Salween	Gulf of Martaban	1,800
Danube	Black Sea	1,725
Euphrates	Persian Gulf	1,700
Indus	Arabian Sea	1,700
Brahmaputra	Bay of Bengal	1,680
Zambesi	Indian Ocean	1,633
Murray	Indian Ocean	1,609
Severn	Bristol Channel	220
Thames	North Sea	210

SOME FAMOUS BRIDGES

Among the outstanding *suspension bridges* of the World are the Verrazano Narrows Bridge, New York (main span, 4,260 ft.); the Golden Gate Bridge, San Francisco (4,200 ft.); Mackinac Bridge, Michigan (3,800 ft.); George Washington Bridge, New York (3,500 ft.); the Ponte Salazar (Tagus Bridge, Portugal (3,323 ft.); Forth Road Bridge, Scotland (3,300 ft.); Severn Bridge, England and Wales (3,240 ft.); Tacoma Bridge, Washington, U.S.A. (2,800 ft.) and the Orinoco Bridge, Venezuela (2,336 ft.); Lengths shown above are all those of the main or longest span.

The Transbay Bridge (*suspension and cantilever*), crossing San Francisco Bay from Oakland to San Francisco is 7½ miles long, with spans of 2,310 ft. each.

Among important *steel arch* bridges are the Bayonne Bridge, from New Jersey to Staten Island, U.S.A. (1,652 ft.); Sydney Harbour Bridge, Australia (1,650 ft.); the Runcorn-Widnes Bridge, England (1,082 ft.); and the Glen Canyon Bridge over the Colorado River, U.S.A. (1,028 ft.). Major *concrete trestle* bridges include the Lake Portchartrain Causeway, U.S.A. of 2,170 spans extending 24 miles; the Oosterscheldebrug, Netherlands, 3½ miles long, and the Tay Road Bridge in Scotland (42 spans), 7,365 ft. long. Gladesville Bridge, Sydney, Australia, is a *concrete arch* bridge of 1,000 ft. span.

The Chesapeake Bay Bridge-Tunnel (17·6 miles long) joining Cape Charles, Virginia, to Chesapeake Beach has 12·5 miles of *concrete trestle* bridge.

PRINCIPAL HEIGHTS ABOVE SEA LEVEL

	Feet
Europe: Alps—Mont Blanc	15,782
England: Scafell Pike	3,210
Wales: Snowdon	3,560
Scotland: Ben Nevis	4,406
Ireland: Carrantuohill	3,414
Asia: Everest	29,028
Africa: Kilimanjaro	19,340
North America: McKinley	20,320
South America: Aconcagua	22,976
Australia: Kosciusko	7,328
New Zealand: Cook	12,349
Oceania: Carstensz, Indonesia	16,500
Antarctica: Vinson Massif	16,860

THE LARGEST ISLANDS

Name of Island	Ocean	Area in Sq. miles	Name of Island	Ocean	Area in Sq. miles
Greenland (Danish)	Arctic	827,300	Prince Albert (Canadian)	Arctic	60,000
New Guinea (Australian-Indonesian)	Pacific	347,450	South Island, N.Z.	Pacific	58,500
Borneo (various)	,,	307,000	Java (Indonesian)	Indian	48,400
Baffin Land (Canadian)	Arctic	231,000	North Island, N.Z.	Pacific	44,500
Madagascar	Indian	228,000	Cuba (Independent)	Atlantic	44,000
Sumatra (Indonesian)	Indian	163,000	Newfoundland (Canadian)	Atlantic	42,750
Great Britain	Atlantic	88,745	Luzon (Philippines)	Pacific	41,000
Honshū (Japanese)	Pacific	87,500	Ellesmere (Canadian)	Arctic	41,000
Celébes (Indonesian)	Indian	73,000	Iceland (Independent)	Atlantic	40,000
			Mindanao (Philippines)	Pacific	37,000
			Ireland	Atlantic	32,600

GREAT SHIP CANALS OF THE WORLD

Canal	Opened year	Length, miles	Depth, feet	Width,§ feet
Amsterdam (Netherlands)	1876	16½	23	88
Corinth (Greece)	1893	4	26·25	72
Elbe and Trave (Germany)	1900	41	10	72
Gota (Sweden)*	1832	115	10	47
Kiel (Germany)†	1895	61	45	150
Manchester (England)	1894	35·5	28–30	120
Panama (U.S.A.)	1914	50·5	45	300
Princess Juliana (Netherlands)	1935	20	16	52
Sault Ste. Marie (U.S.A.)	1855	1·6	22	100
Sault Ste. Marie (Canada)	1895	1·11	20·25	142
Suez (Egypt)	1869	100	34	197
Welland (Canada)‡	1887	26·75	25	200

* Reconstructed 1916.   † Reconstructed 1914.   ‡ Reconstructed 1929–30.   § At the bottom.

WATERFALLS OF THE WORLD

In order of height

Fall	Locality	Height in Feet
Angel Falls	Venezuela	3,212
Ribbon Fall	Yosemite, U.S.A.	1,612
Upper Yosemite	Yosemite, U.S.A.	(a) 1,430
Gavarnie	Pyrenees	1,385
Wollomombie	New South Wales	(b) 1,100
Staubbach	Switzerland	980
Vettisfoss	Norway	856
King Edward VIII	Guyana	840
Gersoppa	Mysore, India	(c) 830
Sutherland	New Zealand	(d) 815
Kaieteur (Köituök)	Guyana	741
Kalambo	Tanzania	(e) 704
Maletsunyane	Lesotho	630
Bridalveil	Yosemite, U.S.A.	620
Nevada	Yosemite, U.S.A.	594
Skjeggedalsfoss	Norway	525
Eas-Coul-Aulin	Scotland	(f) 511

In order of volume

Fall	Locality	Width in Yards
Khon Cataracts (1)	Indo-China	15,840
Guayra (2)	Brazil	5,300
Victoria (3)	Rhodesia—Zambia	1,760
Niagara (4)	Canada— U.S.A.	1,200

On the basis of annual flow the Guayra Falls in Brazil are the most spectacular, with a flow of 470,000 cubic feet per second (annual average).

NOTES.—(a) Out of a total fall of 2,565 ft.;
(b) 1,700 ft.; (c) 960 ft.; (d) 1,904 ft.;
(e) 3,000 ft; (f) 658 ft.
(1) Height, 50–70 ft.; (2) 90–130 ft.;
(3) 236–354 ft.; (4) 158–175 ft.

LONGEST RAILWAY TUNNELS

E.R. = Eastern Region; L.M.R. = London Midland Region;
S.R. = Southern Region; W.R. = Western Region

United Kingdom

		Miles	Yards
Severn	W.R.	4	628
Totley	L.M.R.	3	950
Standedge	E.R.	3	66
Woodhead	L.M.R.	3	66
Sodbury	W.R.	2	924
Disley	L.M.R.	2	346
Bramhope	E.R.	2	241
Ffestiniog	L.M.R.	2	338
Cowburn	L.M.R.	2	182
Sevenoaks	S.R.	1	1693
Rhondda	W.R.	1	1683
Morley	E.R.	1	1609
Box	W.R.	1	1452
Catesby	L.M.R.	1	1240
Dove Holes	L.M.R.	1	1224
Littleborough (Summit)	L.M.R.	1	1125
Vict. Waterloo (Liverpool)	L.M.R.	1	946
Ponsbourne	E.R.	1	924
Polhill	S.R.	1	851
Queensbury	E.R.	1	741
Merthyr	W.R.	1	737
Kilsby	L.M.R.	1	666
Bleamoor	L.M.R.	1	869
Shepherd's Well	S.R.	1	609
Gildersome	E.R.	1	571
Strood	S.R.	1	569
Clayton	S.R.	1	499
Oxted	S.R.	1	501
Sydenham	S.R.	1	381
Drewton	E.R.	1	354

		Miles	Yards
Merstham New (Quarry)	S.R.	1	353
Wapping	L.M.R.	1	351
Mersey	Mersey	1	350
Greenock	Scottish Region	1	351
Bradway	E.R.	1	267
Sough	L.M.R.	1	255
Watford, New	L.M.R.	1	230
Caerphilly	W.R.	1	173
Llangyfelach	W.R.	1	192
Abbot's Cliff	S.R.	1	182
Corby	L.M.R.	1	166
Halton	L.M.R.	1	176
Wenvoe	W.R.	1	107
Sapperton	W.R.	1	100
Sharnbrook	L.M.R.	1	100

(The London Underground *Northern Line* between Morden and East Finchley by the City Branch serves 25 stations and uses tunnels totalling 17½ miles in length).

The World

		Miles	Yards
Simplon	Switzerland–Italy	12	560
Apennine	Italy	11	880
St. Gotthard	Switzerland	9	550
Lötschberg	Switzerland	9	130
Mont Cenis	Italy	8	870
Cascade	United States	7	1410
Arlberg	Austria	6	650
Moffat	United States	6	200
Shimizu	Japan	6	70

DISTANCE OF THE HORIZON

The limit of distance to which one can see varies with the height of the spectator. The greatest distance at which an object on the surface of the sea, or of a level plain, can be seen by a person whose eyes are at a height of 5 feet from the same level is about 3 miles. At a height of 20 feet the range is increased to nearly 6 miles, and an approximate rule for finding the range of vision for small heights is to increase the square root of the number of feet that the eye is above the level surface by a third of itself, the result being the distance of the horizon in miles, but is slightly in excess of that in the table below, which is computed by a more precise formula. The table may be used conversely to show the distance of an object of given height that is just visible from a point in the surface of the earth or sea. Refraction is taken into account both in the approximate rule and in the Table.

At a height of	the range is	At a height of	the range is	At a height of	the range is
5 ft.	2·9 miles	500 ft.	29·5 miles	4,000 ft.	83·3 miles
20 ,,	5·9 ,,	1,000 ,,	41·6 ,,	5,000 ,,	93·1 ,,
50 ,,	9·3 ,,	2,000 ,,	58·9 ,,	20,000 ,,	186·2 ,,
100 ,,	13·2 ,,	3,000 ,,	72·1 ,,		

RULERS OF FOREIGN COUNTRIES

Country	Ruler	Born	Acceded
Afghanistan	Mohamed Zahir Shah, *King*	Oct. 15, 1914	Nov. 8, 1933
Algeria	Col. Houari Boumedienne, *President, Council of Revolution*	..	June 19, 1965
Argentine Republic	Lt.-Gen. Alejandro Agustín Lanusse, *President*	..	Mar. 26, 1971
Austria	Franz Jonas, *President*	1899	May 23, 1965
Bahrain	Khalifa bin Sulman, *Shaik*	1932	Dec. 16, 1961
Belgium	Baudouin, *King*	Sept. 7, 1930	July 17, 1951
Bhutan	Jigme Dorji Wangchuk, *King*	1929	March 1952
Bolivia	Gen. Hugo Banzer, *President*	1928	Aug. 22, 1971
Brazil	Gen. Emilio Garrastazú Medici, *President*	..	Oct. 30, 1969
Bulgaria	Todor Zhivkov, *Chairman, Council of State*	..	July 7, 1971
Burma	Gen. Ne Win, *Chairman, Revolutionary Govt*	..	Mar. 2, 1962
Burundi	Col. Micombero Michel, *President*	..	Nov. 28, 1966
Cameroon	Ahmadou Ahidjo, *President*	..	May 5, 1960
Cent. African Rep.	Gen. Jean Bedel Bokassa, *President*	..	Jan. 1, 1966
Chad	Francois Tombalbaye, *President*	..	Aug. 11, 1960
Chile	Dr. Salvador Allende, *President*	..	Nov. 4, 1970
China	*Chairman* (vacant)	..	
Colombia	Misael Pastrana (Borrero), *President*	..	Aug. 7, 1970
Congo*	Maj. Marien Ngoabi, *President, Revolutionary Council*	..	Jan. 1, 1969
Congolese Republic	Maj.-Gen. Joseph Mobutu, *President*	..	Nov. 25, 1965
Costa Rica	José Figures Ferrer, *President*	1907	May 8, 1970
Cuba	Dr. Osvaldo Dorticos Torrado, *President*	..	July 17, 1959
Czechoslovakia	Ludwig Svoboda, *President*	Nov. 25, 1895	Mar. 30, 1968
Dahomey	Hubert Maga, *President*	..	May 7, 1970
Denmark	Frederik IX, *King*	Mar. 11, 1899	April 20, 1947
Dominican Republic	Joaquin Balaguer, *President*	Sept. 1, 1907	July 1, 1966
Ecuador	Dr. José Maria Velasco (Ibarra), *President*	1893	Sept. 1, 1968
Equatorial Guinea	Francisco Macias Nguema, *President*	1925	Oct. 12, 1968
Ethiopia	Hailé Selassie, *Emperor*	July 23, 1892	April 2, 1930
Finland	Dr. U. K. Kekkonen, *President*	1900	Feb. 15, 1956
Formosa	Gen. Chiang Kai-Shek, *President*	1887	1948
France	Georges Jean Raymond Pompidou, *President*	July 5, 1911	June 20, 1969
Gabon	Albert-Bernard Bongo, *President*	..	Dec. 1967
Germany (Fed.Rep.)	Dr. Gustav W. Heinemann, *Federal President*	July 23, 1899	July 1 1969
Germany (Eastern)	W. Ulbricht, *Chairman, Council of State*	..	Sept. 12, 1960
Greece	Constantine XIII, *King of the Hellenes*	June 2, 1940	Mar. 6, 1964
Guatemala	Col. Carlos Araña Osorio, *President*	1918	July 1, 1970
Guinea	Ahmed Sékou Touré, *President*	..	Jan. 1961
Haiti	Jean Claude Duvalier, *President*	1951	April 21, 1971
Honduras	Dr. Ramon Ernesto Croz, *President*	..	June 6, 1971
Hungary	Pál Losonczi, *President*	..	April 1967
Iceland	Dr. Kristian Eldjarn, *President*	1917	Aug. 1, 1968
Indonesia	Gen. Soeharto, *President*	June 9, 1921	Mar. 28, 1968
Iran	Shahpoor Mohammed Reza Pahlevi, *Shah*	Oct. 26, 1919	Sept. 16, 1941
Iraq	Ahmad Hasan al-Bakr, *President*	..	July 17, 1968
Irish Republic	Eamon de Valéra, *President*	Oct. 14, 1882	June 25, 1959
Israel	Zalman Shazar, *President*	1889	May 22, 1963
Italy	Giuseppe Saragat, *President*	1898	Dec. 28, 1964
Ivory Coast	Felix Houphouët-Boigny, *President*	..	Nov. 27, 1960
Japan	Hirohito, *Emperor*	April 29, 1901	Dec. 25, 1926
Jordan	Hussein, *King*	Nov. 14, 1935	Aug. 11, 1952
Khmer Republic	Cheng Heng, *Head of State*	..	Mar. 1970
Korea, South	Park, Chung Hee, *President*	..	Mar. 22, 1962
Kuwait	Sabah as-Salem as Sabah, *Amir*	1915	Nov. 24, 1965
Laos	Savang Vatthana, *King*	1907	Nov. 1. 1959
Lebanon	Suleiman Franjieh, *President*	..	Aug. 17, 1970
Liberia	William Richard Tolbert, *President (provisional)*	1913	July 23, 1971
Libya	Col. Muammer El Qadhafi, *Chairman of Revolutionary Cmd. Council*	..	Sept. 1, 1969
Liechtenstein	Franz Joseph II., *Prince*	Aug. 16, 1906	Aug. 25, 1938
Luxemburg	Jean, *Grand Duke*	Jan. 5, 1921	Nov. 1964
Madagascar	Philibert Tsiranana, *President*	..	June 26, 1960
Maldives	Amir Ibrahim Nasir, *President*	..	
Mali	Lt. Moussa Traore, *Chairman, Nat. Lib. Cttee*	1937	Nov. 20, 1968
Mauritania	Moktar Ould Dadda, *President*	..	Nov. 28, 1958
Mexico	Luis Ec verria (Alvarez), *President*	..	Dec. 1, 1970
Monaco	Rainier, *Prince*	May 31, 1923	May 9, 1949
Morocco	Hassan II, *King*	July 9, 1929	Feb. 26. 1961
Nepal	Mahendra Bir Bikram Shah, *King*	1920	Mar. 13, 1955
Netherlands	Juliana, *Queen*	April 30, 1909	Sept. 4, 1948

*Formerly French Congo.

RULERS OF FOREIGN COUNTRIES—*continued*

Country	Ruler	Born	Acceded
Nicaragua	Anastasio Somoza Debayle, *President*	..	May 1, 1967
Niger	Diori, Hamani *President*	..	Nov. 9, 1960
Norway	Olav V., *King*	July 2, 1903	Sept. 21, 1957
Oman	Qabas bin Said, *Sultan*	..	July 23, 1970
Panama	Demetrio Lakas, *President, Govt. Junta*	..	1969
Paraguay	Gen. Alfredo Stroessner, *President*	..	Aug. 15, 1954
Peru	Gen. Juan Velasco Alvarado, *President*	1910	Oct. 3, 1968
Philippine Islands	Ferdinand Marcos, *President*	1917	Dec. 30, 1965
Poland	Jósef Cyrankiewicz, *Chairman of Council of State.*	..	Dec. 3, 1970
Portugal	Americo D. Rodrigues Tomás, *President*	..	Aug. 9, 1958
Qatar	Ahmed al Thani, *Shaikh*	..	Oct. 24, 1960
Rumania	Nicolai Ceauşescu, *President*	1918	Dec. 9, 1967
Rwanda	Grégoire Kayibanda, *President*	1925	July 1, 1962
Salvador	Fidel Sanchez Hernandez, *President*	..	July 1, 1967
Saudi Arabia	Faisal bin Abdul Aziz, *King*	1904	Nov. 2, 1964
Senegal	Leopold Senghor, *President*	..	Sept. 5, 1960
Somalia	Gen. Mohammed Siyad (*Chairman, Revolutionary Council*)	..	Oct. 21, 1969
South Africa	Johannes Jacobus Fouché, *President*	1898	April 10, 1968
Spain	General Francisco Franco Bahamonde, *Regent*	Dec. 4, 1892	Aug. 9, 1939
Sudan	Col. Jaafar Mohammed al Nemery (*Chairman, Revolutionary Council*)	..	May 25, 1969
Sweden	Gustaf VI Adolf *King*	Nov. 1, 1882	Oct. 29, 1950
Switzerland	Rudolf Gnägi, *President*	..	Jan. 1, 1971
Syria	Lt. Gen. Hafez al Assad, *President*	1928	Mar. 14, 1971
Thailand	Bhumibol Adulyadej, *King*	Dec. 5, 1927	June 9, 1946
Togo	General Etienne Eyadéma, *President*	1937	April 14, 1967
Tunisia	Habib Bourguiba, *President*	..	July 25, 1957
Turkey	Gen. Cevdet Sunay, *President*	1900	Mar. 28, 1966
United Arab Rep.	Anwar Sadat, *President*	..	Oct. 15, 1970
United States	Richard M. Nixon, *President*	Jan. 9, 1913	Jan. 20, 1969
Upper Volta	Lt. Col. Sangoulé Lamizana, *Head of State*	..	Jan. 3, 1966
Uruguay	Jorge Pacheco Areco, *President*	1920	Dec. 6, 1967
U.S.S.R.	Nikolai V. Podgorny, *President*	1903	Dec. 9, 1965
Vatican City State	Paul VI, *Pope*	Sept. 26, 1897	June 21, 1963
Venezuela	Dr. Rafael Caldera Rodriguez, *President*	1916	Mar. 11, 1969
Vietnam, North	Ton Duc Thang, *President*	1889	Sept. 24, 1969
Vietnam, South	Nguyen van Thieu, *President*	..	June 19, 1965
Yemen P.D.R.	Salim Robaya Ali (*Chairman, Presidential Council*)	..	..
Yugoslavia	Josip Broz Tito, *President*	May 25, 1892	Jan. 13, 1953

PRESIDENTS OF THE FRENCH REPUBLIC

Acceded

Committee of Public Defence	4 Sept. 1870
Louis Adolphe Thiers	31 Aug. 1871
Marshal MacMahon	24 May, 1873
Jules Grévy	30 Jan. 1879
Sadi Carnot (assass.: 14 June, 1894).	3 Dec. 1887
Jean Casimir Périer	27 June, 1894
François Félix Faure	17 Jan. 1895
Emile Loubet	18 Feb. 1899
Armand Fallières	18 Jan. 1906
Raymond Poincaré	17 Jan. 1913
Paul Deschanel	18 Feb. 1920
Alexandre Millerand	20 Sept. 1920
Gaston Doumergue	13 June, 1924
Paul Doumer (assass.: 7 May, 1932).	13 June, 1931
Albert Lebrun (deposed 1940)	10 May, 1932
Maréchal Pétain, "Vichy" nominee,	11 July, 1940

[After the liberation of Paris, General Charles de Gaulle entered the capital and formed a provisional government on Sept. 10, 1944. This was regarded as a continuation of the *Third Republic.*]

Acceded

Charles de Gaulle, *born* 1890	Sept. 10, 1944
Félix Gouin	Jan. 23, 1946
Georges Bidault, *born* 1899	June 2, 1946

[A new Constitution (*Fourth Republic*), adopted on Oct. 13, 1946, and amended in 1954, was in force until 1958.]

Acceded

Vincent Auriol, *born* 1884	Jan. 16, 1947
René Coty, *born* 1882	Jan. 17, 1954

[The *Fifth French Republic* came into being on October 5, 1958, after the approval of its constitution by a national referendum in September, 1958.]

Charles de Gaulle, *born* 1890	Jan. 8, 1959
Georges Pompidou, *born* 1911	June 20, 1969

POPES FROM 1700

Sovereign Pontiff	Family Name	Elected	Sovereign Pontiff	Family Name	Elected
Clement XI	Albani	1700	Pius IX	Mastai-Ferretti	1846
Innocent XIII	Conti	1721	Leo XIII	Pecci	1878
Benedict XIII	Orsini	1724	Pius X	Sarto	1903
Clement XII	Corsini	1730	Benedict XV	della Chiesa	1914
Benedict XIV	Lambertini	1740	Pius XI	Ratti	1922
Clement XIII	Rezzonico	1758	Pius XII	Pacelli	1939
Clement XIV	Ganganelli	1769	John XXIII	Roncalli	1958
Pius VI	Braschi	1775	Paul VI	Montini	1963
Pius VII	Chiaramonti	1800			
Leo XII	della Genga	1823			
Pius VIII	Castiglioni	1829			
Gregory XVI	Cappellari	1831			

Adrian IV (Nicholas Breakspear, the only Englishman elected Pope) was born at Langley, near St. Albans; elected Pope, on the death of Anastasius IV, 1154; died 1159.

ENGLISH KINGS AND QUEENS A.D. 827 TO 1603

Name	DYNASTY	MARRIED	Access.	Died	Age	R.gnd. Yrs.
	Saxons and Danes					
EGBERT	King of Wessex and all England		827	839	—	12
ETHELWULF	Son of Egbert		839	858	—	19
{ETHELBALD	Son of Ethelwulf		858	860	—	2
{ETHELBERT	Son of Ethelwulf		858	866	—	8
ETHELRED	Son of Ethelwulf		866	871	—	5
ALFRED THE GREAT	Son of Ethelwulf	Ealhswith of Gaini	871	899	52	30
EDWARD THE ELDER	Son of Alfred the Great	1, Egwyn; 2, Elfled; 3, Eadgifu	901	925	55	24
ATHELSTAN	Eldest son of Edward the Elder (by 1)		925	940	45	15
EDMUND	Third son of Edward the Elder (by 3)	1, Elgiva; 2, Ethelfled	940	946	25	6
EDRED	Fourth son of Edward the Elder (by 3)		946	955	32	9
EDWY	Son of Edmund (by 1)	1, Ethelfled; 2, Elfthryth	955	959	18	3
EDGAR	Second son of Edmund (by 1)	1, Elgiva; 2, Elfthryth	959	975	32	17
EDWARD THE MARTYR	Son of Edgar (by 1)		975	978	17	4
ETHELRED II	Younger son of Edgar (by 2)	1, Elfgifu; 2, Emma, dau. of Richard, Duke of Normandy	978	1016	48	37
EDMUND IRONSIDE	Eldest son of Ethelred II (by 1)	...........[1]	1016	1016	27	0
CANUTE THE DANE	By conquest and election	1, Elfgifu of Delar; 2, Emma, widow of Ethelred	1017	1035	40	18
HAROLD I	Son of Canute (by 1)		1035	1040	—	5
HARDICANUTE	Son of Canute (by 2)		1040	1042	24	2
EDWARD THE CONFESSOR	Son of Ethelred II (by 2)	Edith, dau. of Earl Godwin	1042	1066	62	24
HAROLD II	Son of Earl Godwin		1066	1066	44	0
	The House of Normandy					
WILLIAM I	Obtained the Crown by Conquest	Matilda, dau. of Baldwin, Count of Flanders.	1066	1087	60	21
WILLIAM II	Third son of William I	(Died unmarried)	1087	1100	43	13
HENRY I	Youngest son of William I	1st Matilda, dau. of Malcolm Canmore, K. of Scotland; 2nd Adelicia, dau. of Godfrey, D. of Louvaine.	1100	1135	67	35
STEPHEN	Third son of Stephen, Count of Blois, by Adela, fourth dau. of William I.	Matilda, dau. of Eustace, Count of Boulogne.	1135	1154	50	19
	The House of Plantagenet					
HENRY II	Son of Geoffrey Plantagenet by Matilda, only dau. of Henry I; his grandmother, Matilda of Scotland, was a lineal descendant of Alfred and of Egbert.	Eleanor, dau. of D. of Guienne and divorced Queen of Louis VII of France.	1154	1189	56	35
RICHARD I	Eldest surviving son of Henry II	Berengaria, dau. of Sancho VI, K. of Navarre.	1189	1199	42	10
JOHN	Sixth and youngest son of Henry II	1st Avisa, dau. of E. of Gloucester, divorced upon grounds of consanguinity; 2nd Isabella dau. of Aymer, Count of Angoulême.	1199	1216	50	17
HENRY III	Eldest son of John	Eleanor, dau. of Raymond, Count of Provence.	1216	1272	65	56
EDWARD I	Eldest son of Henry III	1st Eleanor, dau. of Ferdinand III, K. of Castile; 2nd Margaret, dau. of Philip III, the Hardy, K. of France.	1272	1307	68	35
EDWARD II	Eldest surviving son of Edward I	Isabella, dau. of Philip IV, the Fair, K. of France	1307	1327	43	20

Name	DYNASTY	MARRIED	Access.	Died	Age	R.gnd.
						Yrs.
EDWARD III	Eldest son of Edward II.	Philippa, dau. of William, Count of Holland and Hainault.	1327	1377	65	50
RICHARD II	Son of the Black Prince, eldest son of Edward III.	1st Anne, dau. of Emp. Charles IV; 2nd Isabel, dau. of Charles VI of France.	1377	dep. 1399 (d. 1400)	34	22
	The House of Lancaster					
HENRY IV	Son of John of Gaunt, 4th son of Edward III.	1st Mary de Bohun, dau. of the E. of Hereford; 2nd Joanna of Navarre, widow of John de Montford, D. of Bretagne.	1399	1413	47	13
HENRY V	Eldest son of Henry IV	Katherine, dau. of Charles VI, K. of France..	1413	1422	34	9
HENRY VI	Only son of Henry V, (died 1471)	Margaret of Anjou, dau. of René, D. of Anjou.	1422	dep. 1461	49	39
	The House of York					
EDWARD IV	Son of Richard, grandson of Edmund, fifth son of Edward III; and of Anne, great-grand-daughter of Lionel, third son of Edward III.	Elizabeth Widvile (or Woodville), dau. of Sir Richard Widvile and widow of Sir John Grey of Groby.	1461	1483	41	22
EDWARD V	Eldest son of Edward IV	(Died unmarried)	1483	1483	13	0
RICHARD III	Younger brother of Edward IV	Anne, dau. of the E. of Warwick, and widow of Edward, Prince of Wales, s. of Henry VI.	1483	1485	35	2
	The House of Tudor					
HENRY VII	Son of Edmund, eldest son of Owen Tudor, by Katherine, widow of Henry V; his mother, Margaret Beaufort, was great-grand-daughter of John of Gaunt.	Elizabeth, dau. of Edward IV.	1485	1509	53	24
HENRY VIII	Only surviving son of Henry VII.	1st Katharine of Aragon, widow of his elder brother Arthur, (divorced); 2nd Anne, dau. of Sir Thomas Boleyn, (beheaded); 3rd Jane, dau. of Sir John Seymour, (died in childbirth of a son, aff. Edward VI); 4th Anne, sister of William, D. of Cleves, (divorced); 5th Katharine Howard, niece of the Duke of Norfolk, (beheaded); 6th Katharine, dau. of Sir Thomas Parr and widow of Edward Nevill, Lord Latimer.	1509	1547	56	38
EDWARD VI	Son of Henry VIII by Jane Seymour.	(Died unmarried)	1547	1553	16	6
JANE	Grand-daughter of Mary, younger sister of Henry VIII, (beheaded Feb. 12, 1554).	Lord Guilford Dudley	1553	1554	17	14 days
MARY I	Daughter of Henry VIII by Katharine of Aragon.	Philip II of Spain.	1553	1558	43	5
ELIZABETH I	Daughter of Henry VIII by Anne Boleyn.	(Died unmarried)	1558	1603	69	44

BRITISH KINGS AND QUEENS FROM 1603

Name	DYNASTY	MARRIED	Access.	Died	Age	R.gnd. Yrs.
JAMES I (VI OF SCOT.)	*The House of Stuart* Son of Mary, Queen of Scots, granddaughter of James IV and Margaret, daughter of Henry VII.	Anne, dau. of Frederick II of Denmark.....	1603	1625	59	22
CHARLES I	Only surviving son of James I.........	Henrietta-Maria, dau. of Henry IV of France. *declared May 19, 1649*	1625	Beh.1649	48	24
	Commonwealth *Oliver Cromwell, Lord Protector, 1653–8* *Richard Cromwell, Lord Protector, 1658–9*					
CHARLES II	Eldest son of Charles I, (restored 1660)...	The Infanta Catharine of Portugal, dau. of John IV and sister of Alphonso VI.	1649	1685	55	36
JAMES II (VII OF SCOT.)	Second son of Charles I (interregnum, Dec. 11, 1688—Feb. 13, 1689)	1st Lady Anne Hyde, dau. of Edward, E. of Clarendon, who died before James ascended the throne; 2nd Mary Beatrice Eleanor d'Este, dau. of Alphonso, D. of Modena.	1685	Dep.1688 Dec.1701	68	3
WILLIAM III and	Son of William Prince of Orange and grandson of Charles I........	....	168.	1702	51	13
MARY II	Eldest daughter of James II...........	....		1694	33	6
ANNE	Second daughter of James II...........	Prince George of Denmark.........	1702	1714	49	12
GEORGE I	*The House of Hanover* Son of Elector of Hanover, by Sophia, daughter of Elizabeth, daughter of James I	Sophia Dorothea, dau. of George William, D. of Celle.	1714	1727	67	13
GEORGE II	Only son of George I.............	Wilhelmina Caroline, dau. of John Frederick, Margrave of Brandenburg-Anspach.	1727	1760	77	33
GEORGE III	Grandson of George II............	Charlotte Sophia, dau. of Charles Lewis Frederick, D. of Mecklenburg-Strelitz.	1760	1820	81	59
GEORGE IV	Eldest son of George III, (Regent from February 5, 1811)	Caroline Amelia Elizabeth, dau. of Charles William Ferdinand, D. of Brunswick-Wolfenbuttel, by Augusta, eldest sister of George III.	1820	1830	67	10
WILLIAM IV	Third son of George III...........	Amelia Adelaide Louisa Theresa Caroline, dau. of George Frederick Charles, D. of Saxe-Meiningen.	1830	1837	71	7
VICTORIA	Daughter of Edward, 4th son of George III.	Francis Albert Augustus Charles Emmanuel, D. of Saxe, Pr. of Saxe-Coburg and Gotha.	1837	1901	81	63
EDWARD VII	*The House of Saxe-Coburg* Eldest son of Victoria..........	Princess Alexandra of Denmark.........	1901	1910	68	9
GEORGE V	*The House of Windsor* Surviving son of Edward VII......	H.S.H. Princess Victoria Mary of Teck....	1910	1936	70	25
EDWARD VIII	Eldest son of George V (abdicated 1936).	(Mrs. Wallis Warfield, June 3, 1937.)	1936	—	—	325 days
GEORGE VI	Second son of George V...........	The Lady Elizabeth Angela Marguerite, dau. of 14th Earl of Strathmore and Kinghorne (HER MAJESTY QUEEN ELIZABETH THE QUEEN MOTHER).	1936	1952	56	15
ELIZABETH II	Elder daughter of George VI.........	Philip, son of Prince Andrew of Greece (H.R.H. THE DUKE OF EDINBURGH).	1952	WHOM GOD PRESERVE.		

SCOTTISH KINGS AND QUEENS A.D. 1057 TO 1603

SOVEREIGN	MARRIED	Access.	Died
MALCOLM III (CANMORE)	*1st* Ingibiorg, widow of Thorfinn, Earl of Orkney; *2nd* Margaret, sister of Edgar the Atheling.	1057	1093
DONALD BÁN	....	1093	—
DUNCAN II	Brother of Malcolm Canmore	1094	1094
DONALD BÁN	Son of Malcolm Canmore, by first marriage.	1094	1097
EDGAR	(Restored)	1097	1107
ALEXANDER I	Died unmarried	1107	1124
DAVID I	Sybilla, natural daughter of Henry I of England. Matilda, daughter of Waltheof, Earl of Northumbria	1124	1153
MALCOLM IV (THE MAIDEN) ..	widow of Simon, Earl of Northampton. Died unmarried	1153	1165
WILLIAM I (THE LION)	Ermengarde, daughter of Richard, Viscount of Beaumont	1165	1214
ALEXANDER II	*1st* Joanna, daughter of King John; *and* Mary, daughter of Ingelram de Coucy (*Picardy*).	1214	1249
ALEXANDER III	*1st* Margaret, daughter of Henry III of England; *and* Joleta, daughter of the Count de Dreux.	1249	1286
MARGARET, MAID OF NORWAY	Died unmarried	1286	1290
JOHN BALIOL	Isabella, daughter of Donald, Earl of Mar; *2nd* Elizabeth de Burgh, sister of Earl of Ulster.	1292	1296
ROBERT I (BRUCE)	*1st* Isabella, daughter of Donald, Earl of Mar; *2nd* Elizabeth de Burgh, sister of Earl of Ulster.	1306	1329
DAVID II	*1st* Joanna, daughter of Edward II of England; *2nd* Margaret, widow of Sir John Logie (divorced, 1369).	1329	1371
ROBERT II (STEWART)	*1st* Elizabeth, dau., of Sir Robert Mure (or More) of Rowallan; *2nd* Euphemia, dau., of Hugh, Earl of Ross, widow of John, Earl of Moray.	1371	1390
ROBERT III	Annabella, daughter of Sir John Drummond of Stobhall, niece of Margaret Logie.	1390	1406
JAMES I	Jane Beaufort, daughter of John, Earl of Somerset, 4th son of John of Gaunt and grandson of Edward III of England.	1406	1437
JAMES II	Mary, daughter of Arnold, Duke of Gueldres	1437	1460
JAMES III	Margaret, daughter of Christian I of Denmark Norway and Sweden.	1460	1488
JAMES IV	Margaret Tudor, daughter of Henry VII.	1488	1513
JAMES V	*1st* Madeleine, daughter of Francis I of France; *2nd* Mary of Lorraine, daughter of Duc de Guise, widow of Duc de Longueville.	1513	1542
MARY	*1st* Francis, Dauphin of France; *2nd* Henry, Lord Darnley; *3rd* James, Earl of Bothwell.	1542	158,
JAMES VI (Ascended the Throne [of England 1603)	Anne, daughter of Frederick II of Denmark	1567	1625

WELSH SOVEREIGNS AND PRINCES

WALES was ruled by Sovereign Princes from the "earliest times" until the death of Llywelyn in 128:
The first English Prince of Wales was the son of Edward I, and was born in Caernarvon town on April 2;
1284. According to a discredited legend, he was presented to the Welsh chieftains as their Prince, i
fulfilment of a promise that they should have a Prince who "could not speak a word of English" an
should be native born. This son, who afterwards became Edward II, was created "Prince of Wales an
Earl of Chester" at the famous Lincoln Parliament on February 7, 1301. The title Prince of Wales is born
after individual conferment and is not inherited at birth; it was conferred on Prince Charles by He
Majesty the Queen on July 26, 1958. He was invested at Caernarvon on July 1, 1969.

INDEPENDENT PRINCES, A.D. 844 to 1282		ENGLISH PRINCES, SINCE A.D. 1301	
Rhodri the Great	844–878	Edward, b. 1284 (Edwd. II), cr. Pr. of Wales	130
Anarawd, son of Rhodri	878–916	Edward the Black Prince, s. of Edward III..	134
Hywel Dda, the Good	916–950	Richard (Richard II), s. of the Black Prince	137
Iago ab Idwal (or Ieuaf)	950–979	Henry of Monmouth (Henry V)	139
Hywel ab Ieuaf, the Bad	979–985	Edward of Westminster, son of Henry VI..	145
Cadwallon, his brother	985–986	Edward of Westminster (Edward V)	147
Maredudd ab Owain ap Hywel Dda	986–999	Edward, son of Richard III (d. 1484)	148
Cynan ap Hywel ab Ieuaf	999–1008	Arthur Tudor, son of Henry VII	148
Llewelyn ap Sitsyhlt	1018–1023	Henry Tudor (Hen. VIII), s. of Henry VII.	150
Iago ab Idwal ap Meurig	1023–1039	Henry Stuart, son of James I (d. 1612)	161
Gruffydd ap Llywelyn ap Seisyll	1039–1063	Charles Stuart (Charles I), s. of James I	161
Bleddyn ap Cynfyn	1063–1075	Charles (Charles II), son of Charles I	163
Trahaern ap Caradog	1075–1081	James Francis Edward, "The Old Pretender" (d. 1766)	168
Gruffydd ap Cynan ab Iago	1081–1137	George Augustus (Geo. II), s. of George I.	171
Owain Gwynedd	1137–1170	Frederick Lewis, s. of George II (d. 1751) .	172
Dafydd ab Owain Gwynedd	1170–1194	George William Frederick (George III)	175
Llywelyn Fawr, the Great	1194–1240	George Augustus Frederick (George IV)	176
Dafydd ap Llywelyn	1240–1246	Albert Edward (Edward VII)	184
Llywelyn ap Gruffydd ap Llywelyn	1246–1282	George (George V)	190
		Edward (Edward VIII)	191
		Charles Philip Arthur George	195

THE FAMILY OF QUEEN VICTORIA

QUEEN VICTORIA was *born* May 24, 1819; *succeeded* to the Throne June 20, 1837; *married* Feb. 10, 184c
Albert, PRINCE CONSORT (*born* Aug. 26, 1819, *died* Dec. 14, 1861); *died* Jan. 22, 1901. Her Majesty had issue:—

1. H.R.H. Princess Victoria (*Princess Royal*), born Nov. 21, 1840, married 1858, Frederick, German Emperor; died Aug. 5, 1901, leaving issue:—

(1) H.I.M. William II., *German Emperor* 1888–1918, born Jan. 27, 1859, died June 4, 1941, having married Princess Augusta Victoria of Schleswig-Holstein-Sonderburg-Augustenburg (born 1858, died 1921), and secondly, Princess Hermine of Reuss (born 1887, died 1947). The late German Emperor's family:—

(a) The late Prince William (*Crown Prince* 1888–1918), born May 6, 1882, married Duchess Cecilia of Mecklenburg-Schwerin (who died May 6, 1954); died July 20, 1951. (The Crown Prince's children:—Prince Wilhelm, born July 4, 1906, died 1940; Prince Louis Ferdinand, born Nov. 9, 1907, married (1938) Grand Duchess Kira (died Sept. 8, 1967), daughter of Grand Duke Cyril of Russia (and has issue four sons and two daughters); Prince Hubertus, born Sept. 30, 1909, died April 8, 1950; Prince Frederick George, born Dec. 19, 1911, died April 1966; Princess Alexandrine Irene, born April 7, 1915; Princess Cecilia, born Sept. 5, 1917).

(b) The late Prince Eitel Frederick, born July 7, 1883, married Duchess Sophie of Oldenburg (marriage dissolved 1926); died Dec. 7, 1942.

(c) The late Prince Adalbert (born July 14, 1884, died Sept. 22, 1948), married Duchess Adelaide of Saxe-Meiningen. (Prince Adalbert's children:—Princess Victoria Marina, born Sept. 11, 1917; Prince William Victor, born Feb. 15, 1919.)

(d) The late Prince Augustus William, born Jan. 29, 1887, married Princess Alexandra of Schleswig-Glucksburg (marriage dissolved 1920); died March, 1949. (Prince Augustus's son is Prince Alexander, born Dec. 26, 1912.)

(e) The late Prince Oscar, born July 27, 1888, married Countess von Ruppin, died Jan. 27, 1958 (Prince Oscar's children:—Prince Oscar, bor. July 12, 1915, died 1939; Prince Burchard, bor. Jan. 8, 1917; Princess Herzeleida, born Dec. 25 1918; Prince William, born Jan. 30, 1922).

(f) The late Prince Joachim, born Dec. 17 1890, married Princess Marie of Anhalt, July 17, 1920 (leaving issue).

(g) Princess Victoria, born Sept. 13, 1892 married (1913) the then reigning Duke of Bruns wick. (Princess Victoria's children:—Prince Ernest, born March 18, 1914, married Princes Ortrud von Glucksburg, 1951; Prince George born March 25, 1915; Princess Frederica, bor April 18, 1917, married Paul I., King of th Hellenes (*see p.* 215); Prince Christian Oskar born Sept 1, 1919; Prince Welf Heinrich, bor March 11, 1923, married Princess Alexandra o Ysemburg, 1960).

(2) The late Princess Charlotte, born July 24 1860, married (1878) the late Duke of Saxe-Mein ingen, died Oct. 1, 1919. (Princess Charlotte' daughter, Princess Feodora, born May 12, 1879 married (1898) the late Prince Henry XXX. o Reuss, died Aug. 26, 1945).

(3) The late Prince Henry, born Aug. 14, 1862 married (1888) the late Princess Irene of Hesse, died April 20, 1929 (issue, Prince Waldemar, bor. March 20, 1889, died May 2, 1945; Prince Sigis mund, born Nov. 27, 1896).

(4) The late Princess Victoria, born April 12 1866, married firstly (1890) Prince Adolphus o Schaumburg-Lippe, secondly (1927) Alexande Zubkov, died Nov. 13, 1929.

(5) The late Princess Sophia, born June 14, 1870

married (1889) the late Constantine, *King of the Hellenes*, died Jan. 13, 1932, leaving issue:—

(*a*) The late George II., *King of the Hellenes* 1922–24 and 1935–47, born July 7, 1890, married Princess Elisabeth of Roumania (marriage dissolved 1935); died April 1, 1947.

(*b*) The late Alexander, *King of the Hellenes* 1917–1920, born Aug. 1, 1893, married (1919) Aspasia Manos; died Oct. 25, 1920, leaving issue Princess Alexandra (born 1921) who married, March 20, 1944, King Petar II. of Yugoslavia.

(*c*) Princess Helena, born May 2, 1896, married (1921) late King Carol of Roumania, (marriage dissolved 1928), having issue, King Michael, G.C.V.O., born Oct. 25, 1921, married (1948) Princess Anne of Bourbon Parma, and has issue, Princess Marguerite, born March 26, 1949, Princess Helene, born Nov. 15, 1950, and Princess Irina, born Feb. 28, 1953.

(*d*) The late Paul (*Paul I., King of the Hellenes*), born Dec. 4, 1901, acceded April 1, 1947, married Jan. 9, 1938, Princess Frederica of Brunswick (*see* p. 214); and died Mar. 6, 1964, leaving issue Constantine (*Constantine XIII.*), born June 2, 1940, married, Sept. 18, 1964, H.R.H. Princess Anne-Marie of Denmark, and has issue; Sophia, born Nov. 2, 1938, married (1962) Don Juan Carlos, Prince of Spain, and has issue; and Irene, born May 11, 1942.

(*e*) Princess Eirene, born Feb. 13, 1904, married (1939) the Duke of Aosta, and has issue.

(*f*) Princess Catherine, born May 4, 1913, married (1947) Major R. C. A. Brandram and has issue.

(6) The late Princess Margarete, born April 22, 1872, married (1893) the late Prince Frederick Charles of Hesse, died Jan. 21, 1954 (issue the late Prince Frederick William, born 1893, died 1916; the late Prince Maximilian, born 1894, died 1914; Prince Philipp, born 1896, married (1925) Princess Mafalda, daughter of King Victor Emmanuel III. of Italy (and has issue, Prince Maurice, born 1926, and Prince Henry, born 1927); Prince Wolfgang, born 1896; Prince Richard, born May 14, 1901).

2. H.M. KING EDWARD VII. (*see* p. 216).

3. H.R.H. Princess Alice, born April 25, 1843, married Prince Louis (afterwards reigning Grand Duke) of Hesse; died Dec. 14, 1878. Issue:—

(i) Victoria Alberta, born April 5, 1863, married Admiral of the Fleet the late Marquess of Milford Haven, died Sept. 24, 1950, leaving issue:—

(*a*) Alice (*H.R.H. Princess Andrew of Greece*), born Feb. 25, 1885, married Prince Andrew of Greece; died Dec. 5, 1969, leaving issue (*see* p. 217).

(*b*) Lady Louise Mountbatten (*Queen of Sweden*), born July 13, 1889; married Nov. 3, 1923, H.R.H. The Crown Prince of Sweden, now King Gustaf VI. Adolf; died March 7, 1965.

(*c*) George, Marquess of Milford Haven, G.C.V.O., born Nov. 6, 1892, Capt. R.N., married (1916) Countess Nadejda (died Jan. 22, 1963), daughter of late Grand Duke Michael of Russia; died April 8, 1938, leaving issue:—Lady Elizabeth, born 1917; David Michael, Marquess of Milford Haven, O.B.E., D.S.C., Lieutenant, R.N. ret.), born 1919, died April 14, 1970, leaving issue, George Ivar Louis, *Marquess of Milford Haven, b.* 1961; Lord Ivar Mountbatten, *b.* 1963.

(*d*) Louis, Admiral of the Fleet Earl Mountbatten of Burma, K.G., P.C., G.C.B., O.M., G.C.S.I., G.C.I.E., G.C.V.O., D.S.O., born June 25, 1900, Personal A.D.C. to the Queen, Governor of the Isle of Wight; married July 18, 1922, Edwina Cynthia Annette (died Feb. 20, 1960), daughter of Lord Mount Temple, and has issue two daughters, the Lady Patricia (Lady Brabourne), born 1924 and the Lady Pamela Hicks, born 1929.

(ii) Elizabeth Fedorovna (*Grand Duchess Sergius of Russia*), born Nov. 1, 1864; died July 1918.

(iii) Irene (*Princess Henry of Prussia*), born July 11, 1866, married the late Prince Henry of Prussia, and died Nov. 11, 1953 (*see* p. 214).

(iv) Ernest Ludwig, Grand Duke of Hesse, born Nov. 25, 1868, died Oct. 9, 1937, having married (1905) Princess Eleonore of Solms-Hohensolmslich, with issue (*a*) George, Grand Duke of Hesse, born Nov. 8, 1906, married Princess Cecilie of Greece and Denmark (*see* p. 217); *accidentally killed* (with mother, wife and two sons) Nov. 16, 1937; (*b*) Ludwig, Grand Duke of Hesse, born Nov. 20, 1908, married (Nov. 17, 1937) Margaret, daughter of 1st Lord Geddes; died May 30, 1968.

(v) Alix (*Tsaritsa of Russia*), born June 6, 1872, married (Nov. 25, 1894) the late Nicholas II. (*Tsar of All the Russias*), assassinated July 16, 1918, with the Tsar and their issue (Grand Duchess Olga; Grand Duchess Tatiana; Grand Duchess Marie; Grand Duchess Anastasia, and the Tsarevitch).

(vi) Mary, born May 24, 1874, died Nov. 15, 1878.

4. Admiral of the Fleet H.R.H. Prince Alfred, *Duke of Edinburgh*, born Aug. 6, 1844, married Jan. 2, 1874, Marie Alexandrovna (died Oct. 25, 1920), only daughter of Alexander II., Emperor of Russia; succeeded as *Duke of Saxe-Coburg and Gotha*, Aug. 22, 1893; died July 30, 1900, leaving issue:—

(1) Alfred (*Prince of Saxe-Coburg*), born Oct. 15, 1874, died Feb. 6, 1899.

(2) Marie (*Queen of Roumania*), born Oct. 29, 1875, married (1893) the late King Ferdinand of Roumania; died July 18, 1938, having issue:—

(*a*) King Carol II. of Roumania, K.G., born Oct. 15, 1893, married (1921) Princess Helena of Greece (*see* col. 1), died April 4, 1953.

(*b*) Elisabeth (*Queen of the Hellenes*), born Oct. 11, 1894, married (1921) the late King George II of the Hellenes, died Nov. 15, 1956.

(*c*) Marie, born Jan. 8, 1900, married (1922) the late King Alexander of Yugoslavia, died June 22, 1961 (having issue:—Petar, King of Yugoslavia, born Sept. 6, 1923, married (1944) Princess Alexandra of Greece died Nov. 5, 1970, having issue, Prince Alexander, born July 17, 1945; Prince Tomislav, born Jan. 19, 1928, married (1957) Princess Margarita of Baden (*see* p. 217) and has issue, Prince Nicholas, born 1958; Prince Andrej, born 1929, married 1956, Princess Christina of Hesse).

(*d*) H.R.H. Prince Nicolas, born Aug. 7, 1903.

(*e*) H.R.H. Princess Ileana, born Jan. 5, 1909; married 1st, Archduke Anton of Austria (having issue:—Stephan, born Aug. 15, 1932); 2nd, Dr. Stefan Issarescu.

(*f*) Prince Mircea, born Jan. 3, 1913, died 1916.

(3) Victoria, born Nov. 25, 1876, married (1894) Grand Duke of Hesse and (1905) the late Grand Duke Cyril of Russia; died March 2, 1936, having issue:—

(*a*) Marie, born Feb. 2, 1907, married (1925) Prince Friedrich Carl of Leiningen, died Oct. 27, 1951.

(*b*) Kira Cyrillovna, born May 22, 1909, married (1938) Prince Ludwig of Germany, died Sept. 8, 1967.

(*c*) Vladimir Cyrillovitch, born Aug. 17, 1917, married (1948) Princess Leonide Bagration-Moukhransky, and has issue, a daughter.

(4) Alexandra, born Sept. 1, 1878, married (1896) the late Prince of Hohenlohe Langenburg; died April 16, 1942, leaving issue:—

(*a*) Gottfried, born March 24, 1897; died May 11, 1960.

(*b*) Maria (*Princess Friedrich of Holstein-Glucksburg*), born Jan. 18, 1899; died Nov. 8, 1967.

(c) Princess Alexandra, born April 2, 1901; died Oct. 26, 1963.

(d) Princess Irma, born July 4, 1902.

(5) Princess Beatrice, born April 20, 1884, married (1909) Infante Alfonso Maria of Orleans, died July 13, 1966, leaving issue.

5. H.R.H. Princess Helena Augusta Victoria, born May 25, 1846, married July 5, 1866, General H.R.H. *Prince Christian of Schleswig-Holstein* (died Oct. 28, 1917); died June 9, 1923. Issue:—

(i) H.H. Prince Christian Victor, born April 14, 1867, died Oct. 29, 1900.

(ii) H.H. Prince Albert, born Feb. 26, 1869, died April 27, 1931.

(iii) H.H. Princess Helena Victoria, born May 3, 1870; died March 13, 1948.

(iv) H.H. Princess Marie Louise, born Aug. 12, 1872; died Dec. 8, 1956.

(v) H.H. Prince Harold, born May 12, died May 20, 1876.

6. H.R.H. Princess Louise, born March 18, 1848, married March 21, 1871, the Marquess of Lorne, afterwards the 9th Duke of Argyll K.G.; died Dec. 3, 1939, without issue.

7. Field Marshal H.R.H. Prince Arthur, *Duke of Connaught*, born May 1, 1850, married March 13, 1879, H.R.H. Princess Louisa of Prussia (died March 14, 1917); died Jan. 16, 1942. Issue:—

(i) H.R.H. Princess Margaret, born Jan. 15, 1882, married H.R.H. the Crown Prince of Sweden, now KING GUSTAF VI. ADOLF, K.G., G.C.B., G.C.V.O., died May 1, 1920, leaving issue:—

(a) Duke of Westerbotten, born April 22, 1906, married (1932) Princess Sybil of Saxe-Coburg-Gotha, died Jan. 26, 1947, leaving issue one son, now the Crown Prince of Sweden, and 4 daughters.

(b) Duke of Upland (Count Sigvard Bernadotte), born June 7, 1907.

(c) Princess Ingrid (*Queen of Denmark*), born March 28, 1910, married (1935) the Crown Prince (now King Frederick IX.) of Denmark, and has issue 3 daughters.

(d) Duke of Halland, born Feb. 28, 1912.

(e) Duke of Dalecarlia, born Oct. 31, 1916.

(ii) Major-Gen. H.R.H. Prince Arthur, born Jan. 13, 1883; married Oct. 15, 1913, H.H. the Duchess of Fife; died Sept. 12, 1938, leaving issue (see below).

(iii) H.R.H. Princess Patricia (*Lady Patricia Ramsay*) V.A., C.I., born March 17, 1886, married Feb. 27, 1919, Adm. Hon. Sir Alexander Ramsay, G.C.V.O., K.C.B., D.S.O., having issue Alexander Arthur Alfonso David, born Dec. 21, 1919.

8. H.R.H. Prince Leopold, *Duke of Albany*, born April 7, 1853, married Princess Helena of Waldeck (died Sept. 1, 1922); died March 28, 1884. Issue:—

(i) H.R.H. Princess Alice (*Countess of Athlone*), V.A., G.C.V.O., G.B.E., Commandant in Chief Women's Transport Service. Chancellor of the University of the West Indies, born Feb. 25, 1883, married Feb. 10, 1904, Maj.-Gen. the Earl of Athlone (who died Jan. 16, 1957), having issue:—

(a) Lady May Helen Emma, born Jan. 23, 1906, married (1931) Sir Henry Abel-Smith, K.C.V.O., D.S.O., and has issue a son and 2 daughters.

(b) The late *Viscount Trematon*, born 1907, died April 15, 1928.

(ii) Charles Edward, *Duke of Saxe-Coburg-Gotha* (1900–1918), born July 19, 1884, married (1905) Princess Victoria of Schleswig-Holstein, died March 6, 1954, leaving surviving issue 2 sons and 2 daughters.

9. H.R.H. Princess Beatrice, born April 14, 1857, married July 23, 1885, H.R.H. Prince Henry of Battenberg (born Oct. 5, 1858, died Jan. 20, 1896); died Oct. 26, 1944, leaving issue:—

(i) Alexander, *Marquess of Carisbrooke*, born Nov. 23, 1886, married Lady Irene Denison (died July 15, 1956); died Feb. 23, 1960, leaving issue a daughter, Lady Iris Mountbatten, born Jan. 13, 1920.

(ii) Victoria Eugénie, V.A., born Oct. 24, 1887, married May 31, 1906, His late Majesty Alfonso XIII. (*King of Spain* 1886–1931; born 1886, died 1941), died April 15, 1969, leaving issue.

(iii) Major Lord Leopold Mountbatten, G.C.V.O., born May 21, 1889; died April 23, 1922.

(iv) Maurice, born Oct. 3, 1891; died of wounds received in action, Oct. 27, 1914.

THE FAMILY OF KING EDWARD VII

KING EDWARD VII., eldest son of Queen Victoria, *born* Nov. 9, 1841; *married* March 10, 1863, Her Royal Highness Princess Alexandra, eldest daughter of King Christian IX. of Denmark; *succeeded* to the Throne Jan. 22, 1901; *died* May 6, 1910. Issue:—

1. H.R.H. Prince ALBERT VICTOR, *Duke of Clarence and Avondale and Earl of Athlone*, born Jan. 8, 1864, died Jan. 14, 1892.

2. H.M. KING GEORGE V. (*see p. 217*). Assumed by Royal Proclamation (June 17, 1917) for his House and Family as well as for all descendants in the male line of Queen Victoria who are subjects of these Realms, the name of WINDSOR; died Jan. 20, 1936, having had issue (*see p. 217*).

3. H.R.H. LOUISE, *Princess Royal*, born Feb. 20, 1867; married July 27, 1889, 1st Duke of Fife (who died Jan. 29, 1912); died Jan. 4, 1931. Issue:—

(i) H.H. Princess Alexandra, Duchess of Fife (*H.R.H. Princess Arthur of Connaught*), born May 17, 1891; married Oct. 15, 1913, H.R.H. the late Prince Arthur; died Feb. 26, 1959. Issue:—

Alastair Arthur, Duke of Connaught, born Aug. 9, 1914; died April 26, 1943.

(ii) H.H. Princess Maud, born April 3, 1893;

married Nov. 12, 1923, 11th Earl of Southesk; died Dec. 14, 1945, leaving issue:—

The Duke of Fife, born Sept. 23, 1929; married (1956) Hon. Caroline Dewar (marriage dissolved, 1966) and has issue.

4. H.R.H. Princess VICTORIA, born July 6, 1868; died Dec. 3, 1935.

5. H.R.H. Princess MAUD, born Nov. 26, 1869; married July 22, 1896, Haakon VII., King of Norway, who died Sept. 21, 1957; died Nov. 20, 1938. Issue:—

H.M. Olav V., K.G., K.T., G.C.B., G.C.V.O., KING OF NORWAY, born July 2, 1903, *married* March 21, 1929, H.R.H. Princess Marthe of Sweden (who died April 5, 1954). Issue:—

(a) H.R.H. Princess Ragnhild, born June 9, 1930.

(b) H.R.H. Princess Astrid, born Feb. 12, 1932.

(c) H.R.H. Harald, Crown Prince of Norway, G.C.V.O., born Feb. 21, 1937.

THE FAMILY OF PRINCE ANDREW OF GREECE

Prince Andrew of Greece, *born* Feb. 2, 1882; *married* Princess Alice of Battenberg (*H.R.H. Princess Andrew of Greece*), who *died* Dec. 5, 1969 (*see p. 215*); *died* Dec. 2, 1944, having had issue:—

(1) Princess Margarita, born April 17, 1905, married Prince Gottfried of Hohenlohe-Langenburg (*see p. 215*), and has issue, Prince Kraft, *born* 1935, Princess Beatrix, *born* 1936, Prince George, *born* 1938; Prince Ruprecht and Prince Albrecht, *born* 1944.

(2) Princess Theodora, *born* May 30, 1906, *married* Prince Berthold of Baden (who *died* Oct. 27, 1963, *died* Oct. 16, 1969, leaving issue, Princess Margarita, *born* 1932 (married, 1957, Prince Tomislav of Yugoslavia (see p. 215)), Prince Max, *born* 1933, Prince Louis, *born* 1937.

(3) Princess Cecilie, *born* June 22, 1911, *married* George, Grand Duke of Hesse, accidentally killed with husband and two sons, Nov. 16, 1937 (*see* p. 215).

(4) Princess Sophie, *born* June 26, 1914, *married* (i) Prince Christopher of Hesse (who died, 1944, leaving issue, Princess Christina, *born* 1933, Princess Dorothea, *born* 1934, Prince Charles, *born* 1937, Prince Rainer, *born* 1939, Princess Clarissa, *born* 1944); *married* (ii) Prince George of Hanover, and has further issue.

(5) Prince Philip (*H.R.H. the Prince Philip, Duke of Edinburgh*), *born* June 10, 1921 (*see* p. 218).

THE FAMILY OF KING GEORGE V

KING GEORGE V, second son of King Edward VII, *born* June 3, 1865; *married* July 6, 1893, Her Serene Highness Princess Victoria Mary Augusta Louise Olga Pauline Claudine Agnes (Queen Mary), *succeeded* to the throne May 6, 1910; *died* Jan. 20, 1936. Queen Mary died March 24, 1953. Issue:—

H.R.H. THE DUKE OF WINDSOR (EDWARD Albert Christian George Andrew Patrick David) K.G., K.T., K.P., G.C.B., G.C.S.I., G.C.M.G., G.C.I.E., G.C.V.O., G.B.E., I.S.O., M.C., F.R.S., Royal Victorian Chain, Admiral of the Fleet, Field Marshal, Marshal of the Royal Air Force, *born* June 23, 1894, *succeeded* to the Throne as KING EDWARD VIII., Jan. 20, 1936; *abdicated* Dec. 11, 1936; *married* June 3, 1937, Mrs. Wallis Warfield (The Duchess of Windsor). *Resident abroad.*

H.M. KING GEORGE VI (Albert Frederick Arthur George) *born* at York Cottage, Sandringham, Dec.14, 1895; *married* April 26, 1923, to Lady Elizabeth Angela Marguerite (HER MAJESTY QUEEN ELIZABETH THE QUEEN MOTHER), daughter of the 14th Earl of Strathmore and Kinghorne, *succeeded* to the throne Dec. 11, 1936; *crowned* in Westminster Abbey, May 12, 1937; *died* Feb. 6, 1952, having had issue (*see* p. 218).

H.R.H. THE PRINCESS ROYAL (Victoria Alexandra Alice Mary), *born* April 25, 1897, *married* Feb. 28, 1922, the 6th Earl of Harewood (*born* Sept. 9, 1882; *died* May 24, 1947), died at Harewood House, Yorks., March 28, 1965, leaving issue:—

(1) George Henry Hubert, *7th Earl of Harewood*, *born* Feb. 7, 1923; *married*, firstly, Sept. 29, 1949, Maria Donata (Marion), daughter of the late Erwin Stein (marriage dissolved 1967), and has issue, David Henry George, Viscount Lascelles, *born* Oct. 21, 1950; Hon. James Edward Lascelles, *born* Oct. 5, 1953; Hon. Robert Jeremy Hugh Lascelles, *born* Feb. 14, 1955; secondly, July 31, 1967, Mrs. Patricia Elizabeth Tuckwell, and has issue, Mark Hubert, *born* July 5, 1964. (2) Hon. Gerald David Lascelles, *born* Aug. 21, 1924, *married* July 15, 1952, Miss Angela Dowding, and has issue, Henry Ulick, *born* May 19, 1953.

H.R.H. THE DUKE OF GLOUCESTER (HENRY William Frederick Albert), Duke of Gloucester, Earl of Ulster and Baron Culloden, High Steward of Windsor, K.G., P.C., K.T., K.P., Great Master of the Most Honourable Order of the Bath, G.C.M.G. G.C.V.O., LL.D., F.R.S., Royal Victorian Chain; Personal A.D.C. to the Queen; Grand Prior of the Order of St. John of Jerusalem; Field Marshal, Marshal of the Royal Air Force, Colonel Scots Guards, Col.-in-Chief 10th Hrs., R. Innis. Fus., Gloster Regt., Gordons, Rifle Bde., Royal Corps of Transport, Royal Winnipeg Rifles, Royal Canadian Army Service Corps, Royal Australian Army Service Corps, Royal New Zealand Army Service Corps, Deputy Colonel-in-Chief, Royal Green Jackets, Hon. Col. Camb. U.O.T.C. and 245th (Ulster) L.A.A. Regt., R.A. (T.A.) and Ceylon Light Infantry, Hon. Commodore, R.N.R.; *born* March 31, 1900, *married* Nov. 6, 1935, Lady Alice Montagu-Douglas-Scott, daughter of the 7th Duke of Buccleuch (H.R.H. the Duchess of Gloucester, C.I., G.C.V.O., G.B.E., Grand Cordon of Al Kamal, Colonel-in-Chief the Royal Hussars (Prince of Wales's Own), the King's Own Scottish Borderers, Deputy Colonel-in-Chief, Royal Anglian Regt., Air Chief Commandant W.R.A.F., *born* Dec. 25, 1901); and has issue, H.R.H. Prince WILLIAM Henry Andrew Frederick, *born*, Dec. 18, 1941; H.R.H. Prince RICHARD Alexander Walter George, *born* Aug. 26, 1944. *Residences*— York House, St. James's Palace, S.W.1; Barnwell Castle, Northamptonshire.

H.R.H. THE DUKE OF KENT (GEORGE Edward Alexander Edmund), Duke of Kent, Earl of St. Andrews and Baron Downpatrick, *born* Dec. 20, 1902, *married* Nov. 29, 1934, H.R.H. Princess Marina of Greece and Denmark (*born* Nov. 30, O.S., 1906; *died* Aug. 27, 1968). Killed on Active Service, Aug. 25, 1942, leaving issue:—

(1) H.R.H. Prince EDWARD George Nicholas Paul Patrick, *Duke of Kent*, G.C.M.G., G.C.V.O., *born* Oct. 9, 1935, Major The Royal Scots Greys, Personal A.D.C. to the Queen, Colonel-in-Chief, Royal Regiment of Fusiliers, *married* June 8, 1961, Katharine Lucy Mary, Controller Commandant, Women's Royal Army Corps, Hon. Major-General, Colonel-in-Chief Army Catering Corps, daughter of Sir William Worsley, Bt., and has issue, George Philip Nicholas, Earl of St. Andrews, *born* June 26, 1962; Helen Marina Lucy (Lady Helen Windsor), *born* April 28, 1964; Nicholas Charles Edward Jonathan (Lord Nicholas Windsor) *born* July 25, 1970.

(2) H.R.H. Princess ALEXANDRA Helen Elizabeth Olga Christabel, G.C.V.O., *born* Dec. 25, 1936, Colonel-in-Chief, 17th/21st Lancers, Deputy Colonel-in-Chief, The Light Infantry, Hon. Colonel North Irish Horse, Air Chief Commandant, Princess Mary's Royal Air Force Nursing Service, *married*, April 24, 1963, Hon. Angus Ogilvy, son of the 12th Earl of Airlie, *born* Sept. 14, 1928, and his issue, James Robert Bruce, *born* Feb. 29, 1964 and Marina Victoria Alexandra, *born* July 31, 1966. *Residence of Princess Alexandra*—Thatched House Lodge, Richmond Park, Surrey.

(3) H.R.H. Prince MICHAEL George Charles Franklin, *born* July 4, 1942, Captain, Royal Hussars. *Residence of the Duke of Kent*—Coppins, Iver, Bucks.

H.R.H. PRINCE JOHN, *born* July 12, 1905; *died* Jan. 18, 1919.

Ɯbe Ibouse of Ɯindsor

Her Most Excellent Majesty ELIZABETH THE SECOND (Elizabeth Alexandra Mary of Windsor), by the Grace of God, of the United Kingdom of Great Britain and Northern Ireland and of Her other Realms and Territories Queen, Head of the Commonwealth, Defender of the Faith, Sovereign of the British Orders of Knighthood and Sovereign Head of the Order of St. John, Lord High Admiral of the United Kingdom, Captain General of the Royal Regiment of Artillery, and the Honourable Artillery Company, Colonel-in-Chief of the Life Guards, the Blues and Royals (Royal Horse Guards and 1st Dragoons), The Royal Scots Dragoon Guards (Carabiniers and Greys), the 16th/5th The Queen's Royal Lancers, the Royal Tank Regiment, the Corps of Royal Engineers, the Grenadier Guards, the Coldstream Guards, the Scots Guards, the Irish Guards, the Welsh Guards, the Royal Welsh Fusiliers, the Queen's Lancashire Regiment, the Argyll and Sutherland Highlanders, the Royal Green Jackets, Royal Malta Artillery, R.A.O.C., Captain-General, Combined Cadet Force, Captain-General, Royal Canadian Artillery, Royal Regiment of Australian Artillery, Colonel-in-Chief, the Regiment of Canadian Guards, Royal Canadian Engineers, King's Own Calgary Regiment, Royal 22e Regiment, Governor-General's Foot Guards, Canadian Grenadier Guards, the Royal New Brunswick Regt. (Carleton and York), Le Régiment de la Chaudière, the 48th Highlanders of Canada, Argyll and Sutherland Highlanders of Canada, Royal Canadian Ordnance Corps, Royal Australian Engineers, Royal Australian Infantry Corps, Royal Australian Army Ordnance Corps, Royal Australian Army Nursing Corps, Captain-General, Royal New Zealand Artillery, Royal New Zealand Armoured Corps, Colonel-in-Chief, Royal New Zealand Engineers, Royal New Zealand Infantry Regiment, Colonel-in-Chief, the Nigerian Army, Royal Sierra Leone Military Forces, Ghana Regiment of Infantry, Malawi Rifles, Air Commodore-in-Chief, R.A.A.F., R.A.F. Regiment, Royal Observer Corps, Royal Canadian Air Force Auxiliary, Australian Citizen Air Force, Commandant-in-Chief, Royal Air Force College, Cranwell, Hon. Commissioner, Royal Canadian Mounted Police, Master of the Merchant Navy and Fishing Fleets, Head of the Civil Defence Corps, Head of the National Hospital Service Reserve.

Elder daughter of His late Majesty King George VI and of Her Majesty Queen Elizabeth the Queen Mother; *born* at 17 Bruton Street, London, W.1, April 21, 1926, *succeeded* to the throne February 6, 1952, *crowned* June 2, 1953; having *married*, November 20, 1947, in Westminster Abbey, Philip, Duke of Edinburgh, Earl of Merioneth and Baron Greenwich (H.R.H. The Prince Philip, Duke of Edinburgh), K.G., P.C., K.T., O.M., G.B.E., Admiral of the Fleet, Field Marshal, Marshal of the Royal Air Force, Admiral of the Fleet, Royal Australian Navy, Field Marshal, Australian Military Forces, Marshal of the Royal Australian Air Force, Admiral of the Fleet, Royal New Zealand Navy, Captain General, Royal Marines, Colonel-in-Chief, The Queen's Royal Irish Hussars, The Duke of Edinburgh's Royal Regiment (Berkshire and Wiltshire), Queen's Own Highlanders (Seaforth and Camerons), The Corps of Royal Electrical and Mechanical Engineers, The Royal Canadian Regiment, Royal Corps of Australian Electrical and Mechanical Engineers, Colonel of the Welsh Guards, Hon. Colonel, Edinburgh and Heriot-Watt Universities Officers' Training Corps, Admiral, Sea Cadet Corps, Royal Canadian Sea Cadets, Colonel-in-Chief, Army Cadet Force, Royal Canadian Army Cadets, Australian Cadet Corps, Cameron Highlanders of Ottawa (Militia), Queen's Own Cameron Highlanders (Militia) (Canadian), Seaforth Highlanders (Militia) (Canadian), Hon. Colonel, Trinidad and Tobago Regiment, Air Commodore-in-Chief Air Training Corps, Royal Canadian Air Cadets, Master of the Corporation of Trinity House, Ranger of Windsor Park. *See p. 217.*

CHILDREN OF HER MAJESTY

H.R.H. THE PRINCE OF WALES (CHARLES Philip Arthur George), Prince of Wales and Earl of Chester, Duke of Cornwall and Duke of Rothesay, Earl of Carrick and Baron Renfrew, Lord of the Isles and Great Steward of Scotland, K.G., Colonel-in-Chief, Royal Regiment of Wales, *born* at Buckingham Palace, November 14, 1948.

H.R.H. PRINCESS ANNE ELIZABETH ALICE LOUISE, Colonel-in-Chief 14th/20th King's Hussars and Worcestershire and Sherwood Foresters' Regiment, *born* at Clarence House, August 15, 1950.

H.R.H. PRINCE ANDREW ALBERT CHRISTIAN EDWARD, *born* at Buckingham Palace, Feb. 19, 1960.

H.R.H. PRINCE EDWARD ANTONY RICHARD LOUIS, *born* at Buckingham Palace, March 10 1964.

MOTHER OF HER MAJESTY

H.M. QUEEN ELIZABETH THE QUEEN MOTHER (Elizabeth Angela Marguerite) (daughter of the 14th Earl of Strathmore and Kinghorne), Lady of the Garter, Lady of the Thistle, Order of the Crown of India, Grand Master of the Royal Victorian Order, Dame Grand Cross of the Order of the British Empire, Royal Victorian Chain, Doctor of Civil Law, Doctor of Literature, Colonel-in-Chief 1st the Queen's Dragoon Guards, The Queen's Own Hussars, 9th/12th Royal Lancers (Prince of Wales's), Royal Anglian Regiment, Black Watch (Royal Highland Regiment), The Light Infantry, The King's Regiment R.A.M.C., Royal Australian Army Medical Corps, Royal Canadian Army Medical Corps, Toronto Scottish Regiment, Hon. Colonel The Royal Yeomanry Regiment, University of London O.T.C. Commandant-in-Chief R.A.F. Central Flying School, W.R.A.F., W.R.A.C., W.R.N.S.; Air Chief Commandant, Women's Royal Australian Air Force. *Born* Aug. 4, 1900, *married* April 26, 1923, Prince Albert Frederick Arthur George of Windsor, Duke of York, who *succeeded* to the throne as King GEORGE V Dec. 11, 1936, and *died* February 6, 1952.

Residences.—Clarence House, St. James's, S.W.1.; Castle of Mey, Caithness, Scotland.

SISTER OF HER MAJESTY

H.R.H. PRINCESS MARGARET ROSE (The Princess Margaret, Countess of Snowdon), C.I., G.C.V.O., Colonel-in-Chief, 15th/19th the King's Royal Hussars, The Royal Highland Fusiliers (Princess Margaret's Own Glasgow and Ayrshire Regiment), Queen Alexandra's Royal Army Nursing Corps, Women's Royal Australian Army Corps, The Highland Light Infantry of Canada (Militia), Princess Louise Fusiliers, Deputy Colonel-in-Chief, Royal Anglian Regiment, Commandant-in-Chief, St. John Ambulance Brigade Cadets

Dame Grand Cross of the Order of St. John of Jerusalem, President of the Girl Guides Association; *born* at Glamis Castle, Angus, Scotland, Aug. 21, 1930; *married* May 6, 1960, Antony Charles Robert Armstrong-Jones, G.C.V.O. (*born* March 7, 1930), son of the late Ronald Armstrong Jones, Q.C. and the Countess of Rosse, *created* Earl of Snowdon, 1961, Constable of Caernarvon Castle; and has issue, David Albert Charles, Viscount Linley, *born* Nov. 3, 1961; Sarah Frances Elizabeth (Lady Sarah Armstrong-Jones), *born* May 1, 1964.

Residence—Kensington Palace, W.8.

ORDER OF SUCCESSION TO THE THRONE

The Queen's sons and daughter are in the order of succession to the throne, and after the Princess Margaret and her son and daughter, the Duke of Gloucester and his sons; then the Duke of Kent, his sons and daughter, his brother and his sister and her son and daughter, then the Earl of Harewood and his sons and the Hon. Gerald Lascelles and his son; then the Duke of Fife, son of the late Countess of Southesk, and his son and daughter; then King Olav of Norway and his children, then the children and grandchildren of the second daughter of the late Duke of Saxe-Coburg (his eldest daughter, the late Queen Marie of Roumania, having formally renounced on her marriage all possibility of claim to the British Throne); then the children of the third daughter (the late Princess Alexandra of Hohenlohe-Langenburg); then the children of the eldest son of the late Princess Margaret of Connaught (Crown Princess of Sweden), her other sons and her daughter (Queen Ingrid of Denmark) and her children; then the younger daughter of the first Duke of Connaught and Strathearn (Lady Patricia Ramsay) and her son; then the Princess Alice (Countess of Athlone) and her daughter and grandchildren.

Precedence in England

The Sovereign.
The Prince Philip, Duke of Edinburgh.
The Prince of Wales, The Prince Andrew, The Prince Edward
The Duke of Gloucester.
The Duke of Windsor.
Archbishop of Canterbury.
Lord High Chancellor.
Archbishop of York.
The Prime Minister.
Lord President of the Council.
Speaker of the House of Commons.
Lord Privy Seal.
High Commissioners of Commonwealth Countries and Ambassadors of Foreign States.
Dukes, according to their Patents of Creation:
(1) Of England; (2) of Scotland; (3) of Great Britain; (4) of Ireland; (5) those created since the Union.
Ministers and Envoys.
Eldest sons of Dukes of Blood Royal.
Marquesses, in same order as Dukes.
Dukes' eldest Sons.
Earls, in same order as Dukes.
Younger sons of Dukes of Blood Royal.
Marquesses' eldest Sons.
Dukes' younger Sons.
Viscounts, in same order as Dukes.
Earls' eldest Sons.
Marquesses' younger Sons.
Bishops of London, Durham and Winchester.
All other English Bishops, according to their seniority of Consecration.
Secretaries of State, if of the degree of a Baron.
Barons, in same order as Dukes.
Treasurer of H.M.'s Household.
Comptroller of H.M.'s Household.
Vice-Chamberlain of H.M.'s Household.
Secretaries of State under the degree of Baron.

Viscounts' eldest Sons.
Earls' younger Sons.
Barons' eldest Sons.
Knights of the Garter if Commoners.
Privy Councillors if of no higher rank.
Chancellor of the Exchequer.
Chancellor of the Duchy of Lancaster.
Lord Chief Justice of England.
Master of the Rolls.
President of the Probate Court.
The Lords Justices of Appeal.
Judges of the High Court.
Vice-Chancellor of County Palatine of Lancaster.
Viscounts' younger Sons.
Barons' younger Sons.
Sons of Life Peers.
Baronets of either Kingdom, according to date of Patents.
Knights of the Thistle if Commoners.
Knights Grand Cross of the Bath.
Members of the Order of Merit.
Knights Grand Commanders of the Star of India.
Knights Grand Cross of St. Michael and St. George.
Knights Grand Commanders of the Indian Empire.
Knights Grand Cross of the Royal Victorian Order.
Knights Grand Cross of Order of the British Empire.
Companions of Honour.
Knights Commanders of the above Orders.
Knights Bachelor.
Official Referees of The Supreme Court.
Judges of County Courts and Judges of the Mayor's and City of London Court.
Companions and Commanders e.g. C.B.; C.S.I.; C.M.G.; C.I.E.; C.V.O.; C.B.E.; D.S.O.; M.V.O. (4th); O.B.E.; I.S.O.
Eldest Sons of younger Sons of Peers.
Baronets' eldest Sons.

Eldest Sons of Knights in the same order as their Fathers.
M.V.O. (5th); M.B.E.
Younger Sons of the younger Sons of Peers.
Baronets' younger Sons.
Younger Sons of Knights in the same order as their Fathers.
Naval, Military, Air, and other Esquires by Office.

WOMEN

Women take the same rank as their husbands or as their eldest brothers; but the daughter of a Peer marrying a Commoner retains her title as Lady or Honourable. Daughters of Peers rank next immediately after the wives of their elder brothers, and before their younger brothers' wives. Daughters of Peers marrying Peers of lower degree take the same order of precedency as that of their husbands; thus the daughter of a Duke marrying a Baron becomes of the rank of Baroness only, while her sisters married to commoners retain their rank and take precedence of the Baroness. Merely official rank on the husband's part does not give any similar precedence to the wife.

For Dames Grand Cross, *see* pp. 301–302.

LOCAL PRECEDENCE

ENGLAND AND WALES.—No written code of county or city order of precedence has been promulgated, but in Counties the Lord Lieutenant stands first, and secondly (normally) the Sheriff, and therefore in Cities and Boroughs the Lord Lieutenant has social precedence over the Mayor; but at City or Borough functions the Lord Mayor or Mayor will preside. At Oxford and Cambridge the High Sheriff takes precedence of the Vice-Chancellor.

SCOTLAND.—*See* Index.

The Queen's Household

Lord Chamberlain, The Lord Maclean, K.T., K.B.E. ⟩ GCVO 6/72

Lord Steward, The Viscount Cobham, K.G., P.C., G.C.M.G., T.D.

Master of the Horse, The Duke of Beaufort, K.G., P.C., G.C.V.O.

Treasurer of the Household, H. E. Atkins, M.P.

Comptroller of the Household, R. E. Eyre, M.P.

Vice-Chamberlain, J. More, M.P.

Administrative Adviser, Sir Basil Smallpeice, K.C.V.O.

Gold Sticks, Field-Marshal Sir Gerald Templer, K.G., G.C.B., G.C.M.G., K.B.E., D.S.O.; Admiral of the Fleet the Earl Mountbatten of Burma, K.G., P.C., G.C.B., O.M., G.C.S.I., G.C.I.E., G.C.V.O., D.S.O., A.D.C.

Vice-Admiral of the United Kingdom, Admiral Sir Peter Reid, G.C.B., C.V.O.

Rear-Admiral of the United Kingdom, Admiral Sir Alexander Bingley, G.C.B., O.B.E.

First and Principal Naval Aide-de-Camp, Admiral Sir Horace Law, K.C.B. O.B.E., D.S.C.

Aides-de-Camp General, General Sir Michael Carver, G.C.B., C.B.E., D.S.O., M.C.; General Sir Desmond Fitzpatrick, G.C.B., D.S.O., M.B.E., M.C.; General Sir John Mogg, K.C.B., C.B.E., D.S.O.; General Sir Antony Read, K.C.B., C.B.E., D.S.O., M.C.

Air Aides-de-Camp, Air Chief Marshal Sir Brian Burnett, G.C.B., D.F.C., A.F.C.; Air Chief Marshal Sir Denis Spotswood, G.C.B., C.B.E., D.S.O., D.F.C.

Mistress of the Robes, The Duchess of Grafton, D.C.V.O.

Ladies of the Bedchamber, The Countess of Leicester, C.V.O.; The Marchioness of Abergavenny, C.V.O.; The Countess of Cromer (*temporary*).

Women of the Bedchamber, Lady Margaret Hay, D.C.V.O.; Lady Rose Baring, C.V.O.; Hon. Mary Morrison, C.V.O.; Lady Susan Hussey, C.V.O.

Extra Women of the Bedchamber, Hon. Mrs. Andrew Elphinstone, C.V.O.; Lady Abel Smith, C.V.O.; Mrs. John Dugdale.

THE PRIVATE SECRETARY'S OFFICE
Buckingham Palace, S.W.1.

Private Secretary to the Queen, Lt.-Col. Rt. Hon. Sir Michael Adeane, G.C.B., G.C.V.O.

Assistant Private Secretaries to the Queen, Lt.-Col. Hon. Sir Martin Charteris, K.C.V.O., C.B., O.B.E.; P. B. C. Moore, C.M.G.; W. Heseltine, C.V.O.

Defence Services Secretary, Major-General C. Blair, O.B.E., M.C.

Press Secretary, W. Heseltine, C.V.O.

Assistant Press Secretaries, Miss Anne Hawkins, M.V.O.; L. R. V. Bryant (*temp.*).

Chief Clerk, Miss Jean Taylor, M.V.O.

Secretary to the Private Secretary, A. C. Neal, M.V.O., B.E.M.

Clerks, Miss O. M. Short, M.V.O.; Miss J. F. Munro, M.V.O.; Miss C. W. Austin, M.V.O.; Miss D. King; Miss W. M. Balcomb, M.V.O.; Miss A. M. Downes, M.V.O. (*Press*); Miss F. M. Simpson, M.V.O. (*Press*); Miss J. Kirby, M.V.O.; Miss S. Reid; Miss A. Vaughan-Neil (*Press*).

The Queen's Archives,
Norman Tower, Windsor Castle.

Keeper of the Queen's Archives, Lt.-Col. Rt. Hon. Sir Michael Adeane, G.C.B., G.C.V.O.

Assistant Keeper, R. C. Mackworth-Young, C.V.O.

Registrar, Miss Jane Langton, M.V.O.

Assistant Registrars, Mrs. G. de Bellaigue; Miss F. Dimond.

Historical Adviser, Sir John Wheeler-Bennett, K.C.V.O., C.M.G., O.B.E.

DEPARTMENT OF THE KEEPER OF THE PRIVY PURSE AND TREASURER TO THE QUEEN
Buckingham Palace, S.W.1.

Keeper of the Privy Purse and Treasurer to the Queen, Brigadier the Lord Tryon, G.C.V.O., K.C.B., D.S.O.

Privy Purse Office

Assistant Keeper of the Privy Purse, Major J. R. Maudslay, C.V.O., M.B.E.

Chief Accountant, Edmund F. Grove, M.V.O.

Clerk to the Keeper of the Privy Purse, D. Waters, M.V.O.

Accountant, Peter Wright, M.V.O.

Clerks, Miss J. Boutwood; Miss S. Hume.

Land Agent, Sandringham, Julian Loyd.

Resident Factor, Balmoral, Col. W. G. McHardy, M.B.E., M.C.

Land Steward, Royal Farms, Windsor (R. Reeks).

Consulting Engineers, J. Fraser (*Balmoral*); Sir Ralph Freeman, C.V.O., C.B.E. (*Sandringham*).

Treasurer's Office.

Deputy Treasurer to the Queen, R. D. Wood, V.R.D.

Chief Accountant and Paymaster, Charles Warner, M.V.O.

Accountant, F. R. Mintram.

Establishment Officer, Miss E. S. Colquhoun, M.V.O., M.B.E.

Royal Almonry

High Almoner, The Rt. Rev. the Lord Bishop of Rochester.

Hereditary Grand Almoner, The Marquess of Exeter, K.C.M.G.

Sub-Almoner, Rev. Canon J. S. D. Mansel, M.A. F.S.A.

Secretary, Peter Wright, M.V.O.

THE LORD CHAMBERLAIN'S OFFICE
St. James's Palace, S.W.1.

Comptroller, Lt.-Col. E. C. W. Penn, C.V.O., O.B.E., M.C.

Assistant Comptroller, Lt.-Col. J. F. D. Johnston, M.V.O., M.C.

Secretary, R. J. Hill, M.V.O., M.B.E.

Assistant Secretary, D. V. G. Buchanan, M.V.O.

Registrar, J. E. P. Titman, M.V.O.

State Invitation Assistant, Lt.-Col. A. A. Blacoe, M.C.

Clerks, Mrs. J. Bevan; M. Bishop; Mrs. G. Cousland; Miss M. Fisher, M.V.O., B.E.M.; Miss M. Greiner; Miss J. Hoos; Miss H. Mellor; Miss L. Nicholson; Miss G. Trentham.

Permanent Lord in Waiting, Lt.-Col. The Lord Nugent, G.C.V.O., M.C.

Lords in Waiting, The Earl of Westmorland, K.C.V.O.; The Lord Hamilton of Dalzell, M.C.; The Lord Denham; The Lord Mowbray; The Earl Ferrers.

Gentlemen Ushers, H. L. Carron Greig; Capt. Michael Neville Tufnell, D.S.C., R.N.; General Sir Rodney Moore, G.C.V.O., K.C.B., C.B.E., D.S.O.; Air Marshal Sir Maurice Heath, K.B.E., C.B.; Lt.-Cmdr. John Arundell Holdsworth, O.B.E., R.N.; Col. William Henry Gerard Leigh, M.V.O.; Vice-Admiral Sir Ronald Brockman, K.C.B., C.S.I., C.I.E., C.B.E.; Group Capt. the Hon. Peter Beckford Rutgers Vanneck, O.B.E., A.F.C.; Lt.-Col. Julian Tolver Paget.

Extra Gentlemen Ushers, Capt. Andrew Yates, M.V.O., R.N.; Major Thomas Harvey, C.V.O., D.S.O.; Ernest Frederick Orby Gascoigne, T.D.; Brig. Charles Richard Britten, O.B.E., M.C.; Air Vice-Marshal Sir Ranald Reid, K.C.B., D.S.O., M.C.; Esmond Butler; Sir Austin Strutt, K.C.V.O., C.B.; Col. Sir Geoffrey Codrington, K.C.V.O., C.B., C.M.G., D.S.O., O.B.E., T.D.; Capt. Philip Lloyd Neville, C.V.O., R.N.; Col. John Sidney North FitzGerald, C.V.O., M.B.E., M.C.; Maj.-Gen. Frederick George Beaumont-Nesbitt, C.V.O., C.B.E., M.C.; Maj.-Gen. Sir Cyril Harry Colquhoun, K.C.V.O., C.B., O.B.E.; Lt.-Col. Sir John Mandeville Hugo, K.C.V.O., O.B.E.; Brigadier Richard Frank Sherlock Gooch, D.S.O., M.C.; Sir John Mitchell Henry Wilson, Bt., K.C.V.O.; Nicholas William Bridge; William Richard Cumming, C.V.O.

Gentleman Usher to the Sword of State, General Sir William Stirling, G.C.B., C.B.E., D.S.O.

Gentleman Usher of the Black Rod, Admiral Sir Frank Twiss, K.C.B., D.S.C.

Serjeants at Arms R. J. Hill, M.V.O., M.B.E.; C. G. R. Warner, M.V.O.; T. J. Barnham, M.V.O.

Constable & Governor of Windsor Castle, Marshal of the Royal Air Force Sir Charles Elworthy, G.C.B., C.B.E., D.S.O., M.V.O., D.F.C., A.F.C.

Deputy Constable and Lieutenant Governor, Maj-Gen. Sir Edmund Hakewill-Smith, K.C.V.O., C.B., C.B.E. M.C

Keeper of the Jewel House, Tower of London, Maj.-Gen. W. D. M. Raeburn, C.B., D.S.O., M.B.E.

Surveyor of the Queen's Pictures, Professor Sir Anthony Frederick Blunt, K.C.V.O., F.S.A.

Deputy Surveyor of the Queen's Pictures, Oliver Nicholas Millar, C.V.O., F.S.A., F.B.A.

Librarian, R. C. Mackworth-Young, C.V.O.

Librarian Emeritus, Sir Owen Morshead, G.C.V.O., K.C.B., D.S.O., M.C.

Curator of the Print Room, Miss J. Sherwood.

Surveyor of the Queen's Works of Art, Francis Watson, C.V.O., F.S.A.

Deputy Surveyor, Geoffrey de Bellaigue, M.V.O.

Master of the Queen's Music, Sir Arthur Bliss, K.C.V.O., C.H., MUS.D., Ll.D.

Poet Laureate, Cecil Day Lewis, C.B E.

Bargemaster, H. A. Barry, M.V.O.

Keeper of the Swans, F. J. Turk.

Caretaker of St. James's Palace, H. C. Phillips, M.B.E.

ASCOT OFFICE
St. James's Palace, S.W.1.

Her Majesty's Representative at Ascot, The Duke of Norfolk, K.G., P.C., G.C.V.O., G.B.E., T.D.

Secretary, Miss A. Ainscough, M.V.O.

ECCLESIASTICAL HOUSEHOLD
The College of Chaplains.

Clerk of the Closet The Bishop of Chichester.

Deputy Clerk of the Closet, Rev. Canon J. S. D. Mansel, M.A., F.S.A.

Chaplains to the Queen, Rev. Canon P. L. Gillingham, M.V.O., M.A.; Ven. J. F. Richardson, M.A.; Rev. H. D. Anderson, M.V.O., B.D.; Ven. E. J. G. Ward, M.V.O., M.A.; Rev. C. J. Brown, O.B.E. M.A.; Ver. D H. Booth M.B.E. M.A.; Rev. J. R. W. Stott, M.A.; Rev. S. A. Williams, M.A.; Ven. W. S. Hayman, M.A.; Canon T. J. Pugh, T.D., M.A.; Canon H. C. Blackburne, M.A.; Rev. C. E. M. Roderick, M.A.; Ven. S. F. Linsley; Canon C. H. G. Hopkins, M.A.; Canon W. Garlick, M.A., B.SC.; Canon J. P. Pelloe, M.A.; Rev. L. S. R. Badham, M.A.; Very Rev. W. F. Morley, M.A., B.D.; Ven. B. Stratton, M.A.;

Ven. J. F. Lister, M.A.; Ven. L. W. Harland, M.B.E., M.A.; Rev. J. G. Downward, M.A.; Canon E. Saxon, B.A., B.D.; Canon R. S. O. Stevens, B.SC., M.A.; Rev. P. T. Ashton, M.V.O., M.A.; Rev. A. H. H. Harbottle, M.A.; Canon G. H. G. Hewitt, M.A.; Canon E. M. Pilkington, M.A.; Canon G. R. Sansbury, M.A.; Ven. H. Johnson, M.A.; Ven. J. R. Youens, C.B., O.B.E., M.C.; Preb. D. M. Lynch, M.A.; Rev. R. L. Roberts, M.A.; Canon L. L. Rees.

Extra Chaplains, Rev. M. F. Foxell, K.C.V.O., M.A.; Rev. P. T. B. Clayton, C.H., M.C., D.D., M.A.; Ven. A. S. Bean, M.B.E., M.A., D.D.

Chapels Royal

Dean of the Chapels Royal, The Bishop of London.

Sub-Dean of the Chapel Royal, Rev. Canon J. S. D. Mansel, M.A., F.S.A.

Priests in Ordinary Rev. G. R. Dunstan, M.A. F.S.A.; Rev. R. Simpson, M.A.; Rev. J. F. M. Llewellyn, M.A.

Deputy Priests, Rev. C. T. H. Dams, M.A.; Rev. C. J. A. Hickling, M.A.

Organist, Choirmaster and Composer, W. H. Gabb, M.V.O., F.R.C.O., A.R.C.M.

Domestic Chaplain—Buckingham Palace, Rev. Canon J. S. D. Mansel, M.A., F.S.A.

Domestic Chaplain—Windsor Castle, The Dean of Windsor.

Domestic Chaplain—Sandringham, Rev. A. Glendining.

Chaplain—Royal Chapel, Windsor Great Park Rev. A. H. H. Harbottle M.A.

Chaplain—Hampton Court Palace, Rev. F. V. A. Boyse, M.A.

Chaplain—Tower of London, Rev. J. G. Nicholls.

Organist and Choirmaster—Hampton Court Palace, Gordon Reynolds, A.R.C.M.

MEDICAL HOUSEHOLD

Physicians, Sir Ronald Bodley Scott, K.C.V.O., D.M., F.R.C.P.; Miss M. G. Blackie, M.D., M.B., B.S., M.R.C.S., L.R.C.P.; R. I. S. Bayliss, M.D., F.R.C.P.

Physician-Paediatrician, Sir Wilfrid Sheldon, K.C.V.O., M.D., F.R.C.P.

Serjeant Surgeon Sir Ralph Marnham, K.C V.O., M.Chir., F.R.C.S.

Surgeons, Sir Edward Muir, M.S., F.R.C.S.; E. G. Tuckwell, M.Ch., F.R.C.S.

Surgeon Oculist, Sir Allen Goldsmith, K.C.V.O., M.B., B.S., F.R.C.S., L.R.C.P.

Extra Surgeon Oculist, Sir Stewart Duke-Elder, G.C.V.O., D.SC, Ph.D., M.D., F.R.C.S., F.R.C.P.

Orthopædic Surgeon, Sir Henry Osmond-Clarke, K.C.V.O., C.B.E., F.R.C.S.

Extra Orthopædic Surgeon, Sir Reginald Watson-Jones, F.R.C.S., F.R.C.S.E., M.Ch.Orth., B.SC.

Surgeon Gynaecologist, Sir John Peel, K.C.V.O., F.R.C.S., F.R.C.O.G.

Surgeon Dentist, Sir Alan McLeod, K.C.V.O., F.D.S., R.C.S.(ENG.), D.D.S.

Aurist, J. C. Hogg, C.V.O., F.R.C.S.

Physician to the Household, J. C. Batten, M.D., F.R.C.P.

Surgeon to the Household, H. E. Lockhart-Mummery, M.D., M.Chir., F.R.C.S.

Surgeon Oculist to the Household, S. J. H. Miller, M.D., F.R.C.S.

Apothecary to the Household, Ralph Southward, M.B., Ch.B., F.R.C.P.

Surgeon Apothecary to the Household at Windsor, J. P. Clayton, M.B., B.Chir., M.R.C.S., L.R.C.P.

Surgeon Apothecary to the Household at Sandringham, H. K. Ford, M.B., B.S., D.Obst., R.C.O.G.

Coroner of the Queen's Household, A. G. Davies, M.B., B.S., M.R.C.S., L.R.C.P.

Marshal of the Diplomatic Corps, Maj.-Gen. Hon. Sir Michael Fitzalan-Howard, K.C.V.O., C.B., C.B.E., M.C.

Vice-Marshal, A. L. Mayall, C.M.G., C.V.O.

CENTRAL CHANCERY
OF THE ORDERS OF KNIGHTHOOD
8 Buckingham Gate, S.W.1.

Secretary, Maj.-Gen. P. B. Gillett, C.B., O.B.E
Chief Clerk, G. A. Harris, M.V.O., M.B.E.
Clerks, D. Morrison, M.V.O.; M. G. P. Kelly; Miss A. A. Hamersley, M.V.O.; Miss E. Spooner; Mrs. E. Rogers, M.V.O.; Mrs. A. M. Hughes, M.V.O.; Mrs. H. Hill.

The Honorable Corps of Gentlemen at Arms
St. James's Palace, S.W.1.

Captain, The Earl St. Aldwyn, P.C., K.B.E., T.D.; *Lieutenant*, Col. Sir Robert Gooch, Bt., D.S.O.; *Standard Bearer*, Col. Sir John Carew Pole, Bt., D.S.O., T.D.; *Clerk of the Cheque & Adjutant*, Col. H. N. Clowes, D.S.O., O.B.E.; *Harbinger*, Lt.-Col. J. Chandos-Pole, O.B.E.

Gentlemen of the Corps

Brigadiers, R. B. T. Daniell, D.S.O.; J. O. E. Vande-leur, D.S.O.; Hon. R. G. Hamilton-Russell, D.S.O.; J. E. Swetenham, D.S.O.
Colonels, C. Mitford-Slade; S. Enderby, D.S.O., M.C.; K. E. Savill, D.S.O.; G. J. Kidston-Mont-gomerie, D.S.O., M.C.; P. F. I. Reid, O.B.E.; R. J. V. Crichton, M.C.; P. Pardoe.
Lieutenant-Colonels, R. S. G. Perry, D.S.O.; Hon. M. G. Edwardes, M.B.E.; P. J. Clifton, D.S.O.; Sir William Lowther, Bt., O.B.E.; H. A. Hope, O.B.E., M.C.; T. C. Sinclair, O.B.E., M.C.; N. H. R. Speke, M.C.; C. E. J. Eagles, R.M.; D. A. St. G. Laurie, O.B.E., M.C.; P. Hodgson; R. Steele, M.B.E.; W. S. P. Lithgow.
Majors, D. S. Allhusen; The Lord Templemore; Sir Guy Carne Rasch, Bt.; D. A. Jamieson, 𝒱ℭ.

The Queen's Bodyguard of the Yeomen of the Guard
St. James's Palace, S.W.1.

Captain, Col. the Viscount Goschen, O.B.E.; *Lieutenant*, Lt.-Col. J. D. Hornung, O.B.E., M.C.; *Clerk of the Cheque and Adjutant*, Col. H. T. Brassey, O.B.E., M.C.; *Ensign*, Col. A. B. Pemberton, M.B.E.; *Exons*, Capt. Sir Charles McGrigor, Bt.; Major B. M. H. Shand, M.C.

MASTER OF THE HOUSEHOLD'S
DEPARTMENT
Board of Green Cloth.
Buckingham Palace, S.W.1.

Master of the Household, Brig. G. P. Hardy-Roberts, C.B., C.B.E.
Deputy Master of the Household, Lt.-Col. the Lord Plunket, C.V.O.
Chief Clerk, T. J. Barnham, M.V.O.
Deputy Chief Clerk, G. H. Franklin, M.V.O.
Assistants to the Master of the Household, M. D. Tims, M.V.O.; R. Winship.
Senior Clerk, S. S. Haims, M.V.O.
Clerks, Mrs. S. Linfoot; Miss J. Fowler; Miss C. Morris; Miss M. Childs.
Superintendent, Windsor Castle, Major W. Nash, M.B.E.
Palace Steward, J. Walton.
Chief Housekeeper, Miss V. Martin.

ROYAL MEWS DEPARTMENT
Buckingham Palace, S.W.1.

Crown Equerry, Lt.-Col. John Mansel Miller, C.V.O., D.S.O., M.C.
Equerries, Lt.-Col. the Lord Plunket, C.V.O.;

Lt.-Cdr. J. C. K. Slater, R.N.; Capt. Sir Brian Barttelot, Bt. (*temp*.).

Extra Equerries, Vice-Admiral Sir Conolly Abel-Smith, G.C.V.O., C.B.; Lt.-Col. Rt. Hon. Sir Michael Adeane, G.C.B., G.C.V.O.; Col. Sir John Renton Aird, Bt., M.V.O., M.C.; Rt. Hon. Sir James Ulick Francis Canning Alexander, G.C.B., G.C.V.O., C.M.G., O.B.E.; Vice-Adm. P. W. B. Ashmore, C.B., M.V.O., D.S.C.; Cdr. Colin Buist, C.V.O., R.N.; Lt.-Col. Hon. Sir Martin Michael Charles Charteris, K.C.V.O., C.B., O.B.E.; Cdr. Sir Dudley Colles, K.C.B., K.C.V.O., O.B.E., R.N.; Cdr. Sir Richard Colville, K.C.V.O., C.B., D.S.C., R.N.; Vice-Admiral Sir Peter Dawnay, K.C.V.O., C.B., D.S.C.; Major Sir Geoffrey Eastwood, K.C.V.O.; C.B.E.; Air Vice-Marshal Sir Edward Fielden, G.C.V.O., C.B., D.F.C., A.F.C.; Sir Edward William Spencer Ford, K.C.B., K.C.V.O.; Brigadier Walter Douglas Campbell Greenacre, C.B., D.S.O., M.V.O.; Capt. Lord Claud Hamilton, G.C.V.O., C.M.G., D.S.O.; Brig. Geoffrey Paul Hardy-Roberts, C.B., C.B.E.; Lt.-Col. John Frederick Dame Johnston, M.V.O., M.C.; Rt. Hon. Sir Alan Las-celles, G.C.B., G.C.V.O., C.M.G., M.C.; Major the Earl of Leicester, M.V.O.; Major Sir Mark Vane Milbank, Bt., K.C.V.O., M.C.; Air Commodore Dennis Mitchell, C.V.O., D.F.C., A.F.C.; Rear-Adm. Sir Patrick John Morgan, K.C.V.O., C.B., D.S.C.; Lt.-Col. Ririd Myddleton, M.V.O.; Lt.-Col. the Lord Nugent, G.C.V.O., M.C.; Lt.-Col. Eric Charles William MacKenzie Penn, C.V.O., O.B.E., M.C.; Cdr. Sir Philip John Row, K.C.V.O., O.B.E., R.N.; Brig. Walter Morley Sale, C.V.O., O.B.E.; Maj.-Gen. Sir Arthur Guy Salisbury-Jones, G.C.V.O., C.M.G., C.B.E., M.C.; Group Capt. Peter Wooldridge Townsend, C.V.O., D.S.O., D.F.C.; Air Commodore Archie Little Winskill, C.B.E., D.F.C. (*Captain of the Queen's Flight*); Rear-Adm. R. J. Trowbridge.

Veterinary Surgeon, Peter Scott Dunn, M.R.C.V.S.
Hon. Veterinary Surgeon, A. C. Fraser, PH.D., B.V.SC., M.R.C.V.S.
Supt. Royal Mews, Buckingham Palace, Major W. Phelps, M.B.E.
Comptroller of Stores, J. W. McNelly, M.V.O.
Chief Clerk, M. Carlisle.

HER MAJESTY'S HOUSEHOLD
IN SCOTLAND

Hereditary Lord High Constable, The Countess of Erroll.
Hereditary Master of the Household, The Duke of Argyll, T.D.
Lyon King of Arms, Sir James Grant, K.C.V.O., W.S.
Hereditary Standard-Bearer, The Earl of Dundee, P.C.
Hereditary Keepers:—
  Holyrood, The Duke of Hamilton and Brandon, P.C., K.T., G.C.V.O., A.F.C.
  Falkland, Maj. M. D. D. Crichton-Stuart, M.C.
  Stirling, The Earl of Mar and Kellie.
Keeper of Dumbarton Castle, Admiral Sir Angus Cunninghame Graham of Gartmore, K.B.E., C.B.
Governor of Edinburgh Castle, Lieut.-Gen. Sir Henry Leask, K.C.B., D.S.O., O.B.E.
Dean of the Order of the Thistle, Very Rev. H. C. Whitley, D.D., M.A., PH.D.
Dean of the Chapel Royal, Very Rev. J.B. Longmuir, T.D., D.D., M.A., B.L.
Chaplains in Ordinary, Very Rev. H. O. Douglas, C.B.E., M.A., D.D.; Rev. R. W. V. Selby Wright, C.V.O., T.D., D.D., F.R.S.A., F.S.A.(Scot.); Very Rev. H. C. Whitley, D.D., M.A., PH.D.; Rev. A. Nicol, M.A.; Very Rev. W. R. Sanderson, D.D.; Rev. W. H. Rogan, D.D.; Very Rev. R. L. Small,

O.B.E., D.D.; Rev. W. J. Morris, B.A., B.D., Ph.D.; Rev. G. T. H. Reid, M.C., M.A., D.D.

Extra Chaplains, Very Rev. J. Hutchinson Cockburn, D.D.; Rev. T. B. Stewart Thomson, M.C., T.D., D.D.; Rev. J. Lamb, C.V.O., D.D., Very Rev. J. A. Fraser, M.B.E., T.D., D.D.; Very Rev. the Lord Macleod of Fuinary, M.C., D.D.; Very Rev. Prof. J. S. Stewart, D.D.; Rev. Prof. E. P. Dickie, M.C., D.D.; Very Rev. A. N. Davidson, D.D.

Domestic Chaplain, Balmoral, Rev. R. H. G. Budge, M.V.O., M.A.

Historiographer, J. D. Mackie, C.B.E., M.C., Ll.D.

Botanist, Harold R. Fletcher, Ph.D., D.SC., F.R.S.C.

Painter and Limner, Stanley Cursiter, C.B.E., R.S.A., F.R.S.E., R.S.W.

Sculptor, Benno Schotz, R.S.A.

Astronomer, H. A. Brück, C.B.E., Ph.D.

Physicians in Scotland, Prof. W. I. Card, M.D., F.R.C.P.; Prof. K. W. Donald, D.S.C., M.A., M.D., F.R.C.P.E., F.R.C.P., F.R.S.E.; Prof. Kenneth Lowe, M.D., F.R.C.P.

Extra Physicians in Scotland, Prof. Sir Stanley Davidson, M.D., F.R.C.P., F.R.S.E.; Prof. Sir Derrick Dunlop, M.D., F.R.C.P., F.R.C.P.E., F.R.S.E.

Surgeons in Scotland, Prof. Sir John Bruce, C.B.E., T.D., F.R.C.S.E.; Prof. D. M. Douglas, M.B.E., Ch.M., F.R.C.S.

Extra Surgeons in Scotland, George G. Bruce, M.D., Ch.B., F.R.C.S.E., L.R.C.P.; Prof. Sir Charles Illingworth, C.B.E., M.D., F.R.C.S.E.

Surgeon Oculist in Scotland, Prof. G. I. Scott, C.B.E., M.A., P.R.C.S.Ed., M.R.C.P.Ed., F.R.S.E.

Surgeon Dentist in Scotland, John Crawford Shiach, F.D.S., L.R.C.P.E., L.R.C.S.E., L.R.F.P.S.

Surgeon Apothecary to the Household at Balmoral, Sir George Proctor Middleton, K.C.V.O., M.B., Ch.B.

Surgeon Apothecary to the Household at Holyroodhouse, D. G. Illingworth, M.D., F.R.C.P., Ch.B.

THE QUEEN'S BODYGUARD FOR SCOTLAND
The Royal Company of Archers.
Archers' Hall, Edinburgh.

Captain General and Gold Stick for Scotland, Col. the Duke of Buccleuch and Queensberry, P.C., K.T., G.C.V.O., T.D.

Captains, Wing-Comdr. the Earl of Haddington, K.T., M.C., T.D.; Brigadier T. Grainger Stewart, C.B., M.C., T.D.; Col. the Earl of Stair, C.V.O., M.B.E.; The Lord Elphinstone.

Lieutenants, Major Sir Hugh Rose, Bt., T.D.; Air Commodore the Duke of Hamilton and Brandon, P.C., K.T., G.C.V.O. A.F.C.; Major Rt. Hon. Sir Alexander Douglas-Home, K.T., M.P.; Brigadier the Lord Stratheden and Campbell, C.B.E.

Ensigns, Major Sir Ian Forbes-Leith, Bt., M.B.E.; The Earl of Dalkeith, V.R.D., M.P.; Admiral Sir Angus Cunninghame Graham, K.B.E., C.B.; Lt.-Col. Sir John E. Gilmour, Bt., D.S.O., T.D., M.P.

Brigadiers, The Earl of Mansfield; Major Sir Alastair Blair, K.C.V.O., T.D.; Col. The Lord Clydesmuir, C.B., M.B.E., T.D.; The Lord Maclean, K.T., K.B.E.; Major Sir Hew Hamilton-Dalrymple, Bt. (*Adjutant*); Major The Earl of Wemyss and March, K.T.; The Earl of Airlie; Lt.-Gen. Sir William Turner, K.B.E., C.B., D.S.O.; Major The Earl of Dalhousie, K.T., C.B.E., M.C.; Capt. I. M. Tennant; Maj.-Gen. The Earl Cathcart, D.S.O., M.C.; Capt. N. E. F. Dairymple-Hamilton, M.B.E., D.S.C., R.N.; The Earl of Haddo, C.B.E.

Adjutant, Major Sir Hew Hamilton-Dalrymple, Bt.

Surgeon, Lt.-Col. D. N. Nicholson, T.D., M.B., F.R.C.P.E.

Chaplain, Very Rev. J. B. Longmuir, T.D., D.D.

President of the Council and Silver Stick for Scotland, Wing-Comdr. the Earl of Haddington, K.T., M.C., T.D.

Vice-President, Brigadier T. Grainger Stewart, C.B., M.C., T.D.

Secretary, Capt. G. W. Burnet.

Treasurer, Col. G. R. Simpson, D.S.O., T.D.

HOUSEHOLD OF THE PRINCE PHILIP, DUKE OF EDINBURGH
Private Secretary, Cdr. W. B. Willett, O.B.E., M.V.O., D.S.C., R.N.

Treasurer, Lord Rupert Nevill.

Equerry, Major B. J. Herman., R.M.

Extra Equerries, Rear-Admiral Sir Christopher Bonham-Carter, G.C.V.O., C.B.; J. B. V. Orr, C.V.O.

Temporary Equerries, Capt. T. P. Donkin, M.B.E., R.N.; Capt. M. P. R. Barnes.

Chief Clerk and Accountant, L. A. J. Treby, M.V.O., M.B.E., B.E.M.

HOUSEHOLD OF QUEEN ELIZABETH THE QUEEN MOTHER
Lord Chamberlain, Major the Earl of Dalhousie, K.T., G.B.E., M.C.

Comptroller, The Lord Adam Gordon, K.C.V.O., M.B.E.

Private Secretary and Equerry, Lt.-Col. Sir Martin Gilliat, K.C.V.O., M.B.E.

Treasurer and Equerry, Major Sir Ralph Anstruther, Bt., C.V.O., M.C.

Equerry, Major the Hon. Sir Francis Legh, K.C.V.O.

Press Secretary and Extra Equerry, Major Arthur J. S. Griffin, M.V.O.

Asst. Private Secretary and Extra Equerry, Capt. Alastair S. Aird, M.V.O.

Extra Equerries, The Lord Sinclair, M.V.O.; Maj. Raymond Seymour.

Equerry (Tempy.), Capt. I. W. Farquhar.

Apothecary to the Household, Ralph Southward, M.B., Ch.B., F.R.C.P.

Surgeon-Apothecary to the Household (Royal Lodge, Windsor), J. P. Clayton, M.A., M.B., B.Chir., M.R.C.S., L.R.C.P.

Mistress of the Robes, The Duchess of Abercorn D.C.V.O.

Ladies of the Bedchamber, The Countess Spencer, D.C.V.O., O.B.E.; The Dowager Viscountess Hambleden, D.C.V.O.

Extra Ladies of the Bedchamber, The Dowager Countess of Halifax, C.I., D.C.V.O.; The Dowager Lady Harlech, D.C.V.O.; The Dowager Countess of Scarbrough, D.C.V.O.

Women of the Bedchamber, The Lady Jean Rankin, D.C.V.O.; The Hon. Mrs. John Mulholland, D.C.V.O.; Ruth, Lady Fermoy, C.V.O., O.B.E.; Mrs. Patrick Campbell-Preston.

Extra Women of the Bedchamber, The Lady Victoria Wemyss, C.V.O.; The Hon. Mrs. Geoffrey Bowlby, C.V.O.; The Lady Delia Peel, D.C.V.O.; The Lady Katharine Seymour, D.C.V.O.; The Lady Elizabeth Basset.

Clerk Comptroller, M. Blanch, M.V.O.

Clerk Accountant, J. P. Kyle.

Clerks, Miss L. A. Gosling; Miss A. M. Sheppard; Mrs. R. Beattie.

HOUSEHOLD OF THE PRINCE OF WALES
Private Secretary and Equerry, Sqn.-Ldr. D. J. Checketts, C.V.O.

Temporary Equerry, Lt. D. F. Wilson.

HOUSEHOLD OF THE PRINCESS ANNE
Ladies in Waiting, Miss Mary Dawnay; Miss Rowena Brassey.

HOUSEHOLD OF THE PRINCESS MARGARET, COUNTESS OF SNOWDON

Treasurer, Major The Hon. Sir Francis Legh, K.C.V.O.
Private Secretary, Lt.-Col. F. J. Burnaby-Atkins.
Personal Secretary, Miss M. M. Brown, M.V.O.
Lady in Waiting, The Hon. Hoyer-Millar (*temp.*).
Extra Ladies in Waiting, The Lady Elizabeth Cavendish; Mrs. Alastair Aird; Mrs. Robin Benson; The Lady Juliet Townsend; The Hon. Mrs. Wills; Mrs. Jocelyn Stevens; The Lady Anne Tennant.

THE DUKE AND DUCHESS OF GLOUCESTER'S HOUSEHOLD

Private Secretary to the Duke of Gloucester and Equerry, Maj. Sir Michael Hawkins, K.C.V.O., M.B.E.
Private Secretary to the Duchess of Gloucester and Equerry, Lt.-Col. S. C. M. Bland, M.V.O.
Equerry, Capt. N. M. L. Barne.
Extra Equerries, Lt.-Col. Sir Howard Kerr, K.C.V.O., C.M.G., O.B.E.; Maj. N. B. Chamberlayne-Macdonald, M.V.O.
Ladies in Waiting, Miss Jean Maxwell Scott, C.V.O.; The Hon. Jane Walsh; Miss Diana Harrison (*temp.*).
Extra Ladies in Waiting, The Lady Cecily Vesey; Miss Dorothy Meynell, C.V.O.; Mrs. Cedric Holland, C.V.O.

THE DUKE AND DUCHESS OF KENT'S HOUSEHOLD

Treasurer, Sir Philip Hay, K.C.V.O., T.D
Private Secretary, Lieut.-Cdr. Richard Buckley, M.V.O., R.N.
Ladies in Waiting, Mrs. Alan Henderson; Miss Rosemary Pugh (*temp.*).

HOUSEHOLD OF PRINCESS ALEXANDRA

Lady in Waiting, The Lady Mary Fitzalan-Howard.
Extra Lady in Waiting and Secretary, Miss Mona Mitchell.
Extra Ladies in Waiting, The Hon. Lady Rowley; Mrs. Timothy Colman; The Lady Caroline Waterhouse.
Extra Equerry, Maj. P. C. Clarke, C.V.O.

HONORARY PHYSICIANS TO THE QUEEN (CIVIL)

(Appointed for three years from Nov. 1, 1968)
C. Bainbridge, O.B.E., *Senior Administrative Medical Officer, Western Regional Hospital Board in Scotland;* T. A. Lloyd Davies, M.D., F.R.C.P., *Senior Medical Inspector of Factories, Dept. of Employment and Productivity;* J. A. B. Gray, SC.D., *Secretary, Medical Research Council;* F. N. Marshall, M.D., *Senior Administrative Medical Officer, Manchester Regional Hospital Board;* R. C. M. Pearson, M.D.(Ed.), *Medical Officer of Health, Newcastle upon Tyne;* W. E. Thomas, *County Medical Officer of Health, Glamorgan County Council.*

THE QUEEN'S BIRTHDAY, 1972

The date for the observance of the Queen's Birthday in 1972, both at home and abroad, will be Saturday, June 3 (Customs and Excise Department and certain dock companies, June 24.).

ROYAL SALUTES

On the Anniversaries of the Birth, Accession and Coronation of the Sovereign a salute of 62 guns is fired on the wharf at the Tower of London.

On extraordinary and triumphal occasions, such as on the occasion of the Sovereign opening, proroguing or dissolving Parliament in Person, or when passing through London in procession, except when otherwise ordered, 41 guns only are fired.

On the occasion of the birth of a Royal infant, a salute of 41 guns is fired from the two Saluting Stations in London, *i.e.* Hyde Park and the Tower of London.

Constable of the Royal Palace and Fortress of London, Field-Marshal Sir Richard Hull, G.C.B., D.S.O. (1970).

Lieutenant of the Tower of London, Lieut.-Gen. Sir Richard Goodwin, K.C.B., C.B.E., D.S.O.

Major, Resident Governor and Keeper of the Jewel House, Maj-Gen. W. D. M. Raeburn, C.B., D.S.O., M.B.E.

Master Gunner of St. James's Park, Field-Marshal Sir Geoffrey Baker, G.C.B., C.M.G., C.B.E., M.C. (1970).

THE ROYAL ARMS

QUARTERLY.—1st and 4th *gules,* three lions passant guardant in pale or (*England*); 2nd *or,* a lion rampant within a double tressure flory counterflory *gules* (*Scotland*); 3rd *azure,* a harp *or,* stringed *argent* (*Ireland*): the whole encircled with the Garter.

SUPPORTERS.—*Dexter:* a lion rampant guardant *or,* imperially crowned. *Sinister:* a unicorn *argent,* armed crined and unguled *or,* gorged with a coronet composed of crosses patées and fleurs de lis, a chain affixed passing between the forelegs and reflexed over the back.

BADGES.—The red and white rose united (*England*), a thistle (*Scotland*); a harp *or,* the strings *argent,* with a shamrock leaf *vert* (*Ireland*); upon a mount *vert,* a dragon passant wings elevated *gules* (*Wales*).

THE UNION JACK

The national flag of the United Kingdom is the Union Flag, generally known as the Union Jack, the name deriving from the use of the Union Flag on the jack-staff of naval vessels. It is a combination of the cross of the patron saint of England, St. George (*cross gules in a field argent*), the cross of the patron saint of Scotland, St. Andrew (*saltire argent in a field azure*) and a cross similar to that of St. Patrick, patron saint of Ireland (*saltire gules in a field argent*). The Union Flag was first introduced in 1606 after the union of England and Scotland, the cross of St. Patrick being added in 1801.

ANNUITIES TO THE ROYAL FAMILY

The annuities payable to Her Majesty are known as the *Civil List,* which is granted by Parliament upon the recommendation of a Select Committee. The Civil List of King George VI amounted to £410,000. A Select Committee appointed to consider the Civil List in May, 1952, made the following recommendations, which were embodied in the Civil List Consolidated Fund (Appropriation) Act, which received the Royal Assent on Aug. 1. The annual provision made for Her Majesty the Queen and other members of the Royal Family under the Acts of 1937 and 1952 is as follows:—

Her Majesty's Privy Purse	£60,000	Queen Elizabeth the Queen Mother ..	£70,000
Salaries of Household	185,000	The Duke of Edinburgh	40,000
Expenses of Household	121,800	The Duke of Gloucester	35,000
Royal Bounty, alms and special services	13,200	The Princess Margaret	15,000
Supplementary Provision	95,000		
	£475,000		

These payments are separately charged on the Consolidated Fund, and do not form part of the Civil List.

THE FLYING OF FLAGS

Days for hoisting the Union Flag on Government and Public Buildings (from 8 A.M. to sunset).

February 6 (1952).—Her Majesty's Accession.
February 19 (1960).—Birthday of Prince Andrew.
March 1.—St. David's Day (in Wales only).
March 10 (1964).—Birthday of Prince Edward.
March 31 (1900).—Birthday of Duke of Gloucester.
April 21 (1926).—Birthday of Her Majesty the Queen.
April 23.—St. George's Day (in England only). Where a building has two or more flagstaffs the Cross of St. George may be flown in addition to the Union Jack but not in a superior position.
June 2 (1953).—Coronation Day.
June 3.—Queen's Official Birthday, 1972.
June 10 (1921) Birthday of the Duke of Edinburgh.
Aug. 4 (1900).—Birthday of Her Majesty Queen Elizabeth the Queen Mother.
Aug. 15 (1950).—Birthday of the Princess Anne.
Aug. 21 (1930).—Birthday of the Princess Margaret.
Nov. 12.—Remembrance Sunday, 1972.
Nov. 14 (1948).—Birthday of the Prince of Wales.
Nov. 20 (1947).—Her Majesty's Wedding Day.
Nov. 30.—St. Andrew's Day (in Scotland only).
And on the occasion of the opening and closing of Parliament by the Queen, flags should be flown on public buildings in the Greater London area, whether or not Her Majesty performs the ceremony in person.

The only additions to the above list will be those notified to the Ministry of Public Building and Works by Her Majesty's command and communicated by the Ministry to the other Departments. The list applies equally to Government and Public Buildings in London and elsewhere in the United Kingdom. In cases where it has been the practice to fly the Union Jack daily, *e.g.* on some Custom Houses, that practice may continue.

Flags will be flown at half-mast on the following occasions:—

(a) From the announcement of the death up to the funeral of the Sovereign, except on Proclamation Day, when they are hoisted right up from 11 a.m. to sunset.

(b) The funerals of members of the Royal Family, subject to special commands from Her Majesty in each case.

(c) The funerals of Foreign Rulers, subject to special commands from Her Majesty in each case.

(d) The funerals of Prime Ministers and ex-Prime Ministers of the United Kingdom.

(e) Other occasions by special command of Her Majesty.

On occasions when days for flying flags coincide with days for flying flags at half mast the following rules will be observed. Flags will be flown: (a) although a member of the Royal Family, or a near relative of the Royal Family, may be lying dead, unless special commands be received from Her Majesty to the contrary, and (b) although it may be the day of the funeral of a Foreign Ruler. If the body of a very distinguished subject is lying at a Government Office the flag may fly at half mast on that office until the body has left (provided it is a day on which the flag would fly) and then the flag is to be hoisted right up. On all other Public Buildings the flag will fly as usual.

The *Royal Standard* is only to be hoisted when the Queen is actually present in the building, and never when Her Majesty is passing in procession.

RED-LETTER DAYS

Scarlet Robes are worn by the Judges of the Queen's Bench Division on *Red-Letter Days* at the sittings of a Criminal Court or of the Court of Appeal (Criminal Divn.) and on all State Occasions.

RED-LETTER DAYS AND STATE OCCASIONS, 1972.			
Jan. 25. Conversion of St. Paul.	*May* 1. St. Philip and St. James.	*Aug.* 4. Birthday of Queen Elizabeth the Queen Mother.	
Feb. 2. Purification.	" 11. Ascension Day.		
" 6. Queen's Accession.	*June* 2. Coronation Day.	*Oct.* 18. St. Luke.	
" 16. Ash Wednesday.	" 3. Queen's Official Birthday.	" 28. St. Simon and St. Jude.	
" 24. St. Matthias.	" 10. Birthday of the Duke of Edinburgh.	*Nov.* 1. All Saints.	
Mar. 25. Annunciation.	" 11. St. Barnabas.	" 11. Lord Mayor's Day.	
Apr. 21. Queen's Birthday.	" 24. St. John the Baptist.	" 14. Birthday of the Prince of Wales.	
" 25. St. Mark.	" 29. St. Peter.	" 30. St. Andrew.	
	July 25. St. James.	*Dec.* 21. St. Thomas.	

THE MILITARY KNIGHTS OF WINDSOR

Founded in 1348 after the Wars in France to assist English Knights, who, having been prisoners in the hands of the French had become impoverished by the payments of heavy ransoms. They received a pension and quarters in Windsor Castle. Edward III founded the Order of the Garter later in the same year, incorporating the Knights of Windsor and the College of St. George into its foundation and raising the number of Knights to 26 to correspond with the number of the Knights of the Garter. Known later as the Alms Knights or Poor Knights of Windsor, their establishment was reduced under the will of King Henry VIII to 13 and Statutes were drawn up by Queen Elizabeth I.

In 1833 King William IV changed their designation to The Military Knights and granted them their present uniform which consists of a scarlet tail-coat with white cross sword-belt, crimson sash and cocked hat with plume. The badges are the Shield of St. George and the Star of the Order of the Garter. The Knights receive a small stipend in addition to their Army pensions and quarters in Windsor Castle. They take part in all ceremonies of the Noble Order of the Garter and attend Sunday morning service in St. George's Chapel as representatives of the Knights of the Garter.

Applications for appointment should be made to The Military Secretary, Ministry of Defence, Army Dept.

Governor, Maj.-Gen. Sir Edmund Hakewill Smith, K.C.V.O., C.B., C.B.E., M.C.

Military Knights, Colonel R. F. Squibb, M.C.; Brigadier E. K. B. Furze, D.S.O., O.B.E., M.C.; Brigadier W. P. A. Robinson, M.A.; Major R. W. Garnett, M.B.E.; Brigadier A. A. Crook, D.S.O.; Lt.-Colonel R. J. L. Penfold; Lt.-Colonel L. W. Giles, O.B.E., M.C.; Lt.-Colonel H. G. Duncombe, D.S.O.; Lt.-Colonel R. W. Dobbin, O.B.E.; Major H. Smith, M.B.E.; Lt.-Colonel A. R. Clark, M.C.; Major C. A. Harvey.

The Peerage

THE PEERAGE AND ITS DEGREES

The rules which govern the creation and succession of Peerages are extremely complicated. There were separate Peerages of England, of Scotland, and of Ireland, until the unions of the three countries: of England and Scotland, forming Great Britain, in 1707; and of Great Britain and Ireland, forming the United Kingdom, in 1801. Some Scottish Peers received additional Peerages of Great Britain or of the United Kingdom, since 1707; and some Irish Peers additional Peerages of the United Kingdom since 1801.

All Peers of England, Scotland, Great Britain, or the United Kingdom who are of full age and of British nationality are entitled to seats in the House of Lords. But Peers of Ireland who have no additional United Kingdom Peerage are not entitled to sit, although they are eligible for election to the House of Commons and to vote (if of voting age) in Parliamentary elections (which other Peers are not). The two Archbishops and 24 of the 41 diocesan Bishops of the Church of England also have seats in the House of Lords.

Certain ancient Peerages pass on death to the nearest heir, male or female, and several are now held by women who are thus Peeresses in their own Right. They are entitled to sit in the House of Lords if they are of full age and British nationality.

Since 1876 the Crown has conferred non-hereditary or Life Peerages in the degree of Baron on eminent judges to enable them to carry out the judicial function of the House of Lords. They are known as Law Lords. Under an Act passed in 1958 the Crown may confer Life Peerages on men and women giving them, in the degree of Baron or Baroness, seats in the House of Lords.

In 1963 an Act was passed enabling Peers to disclaim their Peerages for life: living Peers, within 12 months after the passing of the Act (July 31, 1963), future Peers within 12 months (one month if an M.P.) after the date of their succession, or of attaining their majority if later.

No fees for Dignities have been payable since 1937. No hereditary Peerages have been created since 1965.

PEERAGES EXTINCT SINCE THE LAST ISSUE

VISCOUNTCIES—Portal of Hungerford (cr. 1946); Simonds (cr. 1954).
BARONIES—Bilsland (cr. 1950); Boyd-Orr (cr. 1949); Glentanar (cr. 1916); Goddard (cr. 1944) (Law Life Peerage); Tovey (cr. 1946); Upjohn (cr. 1963) (Law Life Peerage).

DISCLAIMER OF PEERAGES

The following peers have disclaimed their peerages under the Peerage Act, 1963: Earl of Durham; Earl of Home; Earl of Sandwich; Viscount Hailsham; Viscount Stansgate; Lord Altrincham; Lord Beaverbrook; Lord Fraser of Allander; Lord Monkswell; Lord Southampton.

PEERS WHO ARE MINORS
(As at Jan. 1, 1972)

MARQUESS (1): Milford Haven (b. 1961).

EARLS (4): Belmore (b. 1951); Craven (b. 1957); Lovelace (b. 1951); Woolton (b. 1958).

VISCOUNT (1): Astor (b. 1951).

BARONS (5): Brocket (b. 1952); Fairfax of Cameron (b. 1956); Latham (b. 1954) Londesborough (b. 1959); Wedgwood (b. 1954).

CONTRACTIONS AND SYMBOLS

Contractions and Symbols.—S. or I. appended to the date of creation denotes a *Scottish* or *Irish* title, the further addition of a * implies that the Peer in question holds also an *Imperial* title, which is specified (after the name) by its more definite description as *Engl.*, *Brit.*, or *U.K.* When both titles are alike, as in the case of Argyll, this star is appended to the conjoined date below, and it then denotes that such date is that of the imperial creation. The mark ° signifies that there is no " of " in the Marquessate or Earldom so designated; *b.* signifies born; *s.*, succeeded; *m.*, married; *w.*, widower or widow; M., minor.

NUMBERS OF THE PEERAGE

	Hereditary	Minors	No Seat	Life or Term	In House of Lords
Royal Dukes	5	—	—	—	5
Archbishops	—	—	—	2	2
Dukes	26	—	—	—	26
Marquesses	38	1	—	—	37
Earls	199	4	21	—	174
Viscounts	131	1	15	—	115
Bishops	—	—	17	24	24
Barons (and Scots Lords)	504	5	36	20	483
Peeresses in own Right	21	—	1	—	20
Life Peers (under 1958 Act)	—	—	—	165	165
Life Peeresses (under 1958 Act)	—	—	—	25	25
Totals	924	11	90	236	1,076

ROYAL DUKES

Style, His Royal Highness the Duke of ——.
Addressed as, Sir, or more formally, May it please your Royal Highness.

1947 *Edinburgh,* The Prince Philip, Duke of Edinburgh, K.G., P.C., K.T., O.M., G.B.E., *b.* 1921, *m.* (*see* pp. 217 and 218).

1337 *Cornwall,* Charles, Prince of Wales, Duke of Cornwall (*Scottish Duke, Rothesay,* 1398), K.G., *b.* 1948, (*see* p. 217).

1928 *Gloucester,* Henry, Duke of Gloucester, K.G., P.C., K.T., K.P., etc., *b.* 1900, *m.* (*see* p. 217).

1934 *Kent* (2nd), Edward, Duke of Kent, G.C.M.G., G.C.V.O., *b.* 1935, *s.* 1942, *m.* (*see* p. 217).

1936 *Windsor,* Edward, Duke of Windsor, K.G., K.T., K.P., etc., *b.* 1894, *m.* (*see* p. 217).

ARCHBISHOPS

Style, The Most Rev. His Grace the Lord Archbishop of ——.
Addressed as, My Lord Archbishop; or, Your Grace.

Trans.	
1961	*Canterbury* (100th), Arthur Michael Ramsey, P.C., D.D., *b.* 1904, *m.* Consecrated Bishop of Durham, 1952, translated to York, 1956.
1961	*York* (93rd), Frederick Donald Coggan, P.C., D.D., *b.* 1909, *m. Consecrated Bishop of Bradford,* 1956

DUKES

Style, His Grace the Duke of ——. *Addressed as,* My Lord Duke; or, Your Grace. The eldest sons of Dukes and Marquesses take, by courtesy, their father's second title. The other sons and the daughters are styled Lord Edward, Lady Caroline, etc.

Created.	*Title, Order of Succession, Name, etc.*	*Eldest Son or Heir.*
1868 1.★	*Abercorn* (4th), James Edward Hamilton (5th *Brit. Marq.,* 1790, and 13th *Scott. Earl,* 1606, both *Abercorn*), *b.* 1904, *s.* 1953, *m.*	Marquess of Hamilton, *b.* 1934.
1701 S. 1892★ }	*Argyll,* Ian Douglas Campbell, T.D. (11th *Scottish* and 4th *U.K. Duke, Argyll*), *b.* 1903, *s.* 1949.	Marquess of Lorne, *b.* 1937.
1703 S.	*Atholl* (10th), George Iain Murray, *b.* 1931, *s.* 1957.	Arthur S. P. M. *b.* 1899.
1682	*Beaufort* (10th), Henry Hugh Arthur FitzRoy Somerset, K.G., P.C., G.C.V.O., Royal Victorian Chain, *b.* 1900, *s.* 1924, *m.* (Master of the Horse).	David R. S., *b.* 1928.
1694	*Bedford* (13th), John Robert Russell, *b.* 1917, *s.* 1953, *m.*	Marquess of Tavistock, *b.* 1940.
1663 S.★	*Buccleuch* (8th) & (10th) Queensberry (1706), Walter John Montagu-Douglas-Scott, P.C., K.T., G.C.V.O., T.D. (7th *Engl. Earl, Doncaster,* 1662), *b.* 1894, *s.* 1935, *m.*	Earl of Dalkeith, M.P. *b.* 1923.
1694	*Devonshire* (11th), Andrew Robert Buxton Cavendish, P.C., M.C., *b.* 1920, *s.* 1950, *m.*	Marquess of Hartington, *b.* 1944.
1900	*Fife* (3rd), James George Alexander Bannerman Carnegie, *b.* 1929, *s.* 1959. (see p. 216)	Earl of Macduff, *b.* 1961.
1675	*Grafton* (11th), Hugh Denis Charles FitzRoy, *b.* 1919, *s.* 1970, *m.*	Earl of Euston, *b.* 1947.
1643 S.★	*Hamilton* (14th), Douglas Douglas-Hamilton, P.C., K.T., G.C.V.O., A.F.C., Royal Victorian Chain (*Premier Peer of Scotland;* 11th *Brit. Duke, Brandon,* 1711), *b.* 1903, *s.* 1940, *m.*	Marquess of Douglas and Clydesdale, *b.* 1938.
1766 1.★	*Leinster* (7th), Edward FitzGerald (*Premier Duke, Marquess and Earl of Ireland;* 7th *Brit. Visct., Leinster,* 1747), *b.* 1892, *s.* 1922, *m.*	Marquess of Kildare, *b.* 1914.
1719	*Manchester* (10th), Alexander George Francis Drogo Montagu, O.B.E., *b.* 1902, *s.* 1947, *m.*	Visct. Mandeville, *b.* 1929.
1702	*Marlborough* (10th), John Albert Edward William Spencer-Churchill, *b.* 1897, *s.* 1934, *w.*	Marquess of Blandford, *b.* 1926.
1707 S.★	*Montrose* (7th), James Angus Graham (5th *Brit. Earl, Graham,* 1722), *b.* 1907, *s.* 1954, *m.*	Marquess of Graham, *b.* 1935.
1756	*Newcastle* (under Lyme) (9th), Henry Edward Hugh Pelham-Clinton-Hope, O.B.E., *b.* 1907, *s.* 1941, *m.*	Edward C. *Pelham-Clinton, b.* 1920.
1483	*Norfolk* (16th), Bernard Marmaduke Fitzalan-Howard, K.G., P.C., G.C.V.O., G.B.E., Royal Victorian Chain *Premier Duke and Earl;* 13th *Scott. Baron, Herries,* 1489), *b.* 1908, *s.* 1917, *m.* (*Earl Marshal*).	Lord Howard of Glossop, M.B.E., *b.* 1885 (see p. 243) (to Dukedom); to Herries Barony, Lady Anne F.-H., *b.* 1938.
1766	*Northumberland* (10th), Hugh Algernon Percy, K.G., T.D., F.R.S., *b.* 1914, *s.* 1940, *m.*	Earl Percy, *b.* 1953.
1716	*Portland* (7th), William Arthur Henry Cavendish-Bentinck, K.G., T.D., (3rd *U.K. Baron, Bolsover,* 1880) *b.* 1893, *s.* 1943, *m.*	Major Sir Ferdinand W. C.-B., K.B.E., C.M.G., *b.* 1888.
1675	*Richmond* (9th) & *Gordon* (4th, 1876), Frederick Charles Gordon-Lennox (9th *Scott. Duke, Lennox,* 1675), *b.* 1904, *s.* 1935, *m.*	Earl of March and Kinrara, *b.* 1929.
1707 S.★	*Roxburghe* (9th), George Victor Robert John Innes-Ker (4th *U.K. Earl, Innes,* 1837), *b.* 1913, *s.* 1932, *m.* (*Premier Baronet of Scotland*).	Marquess of Bowmont, *b.* 1954.
1703	*Rutland* (10th), Charles John Robert Manners, C.B.E., *b.* 1919, *s.* 1940, *m.*	Marquess of Granby, *b.* 1959.
1684	*St. Albans* (13th), Charles Frederic Aubrey de Vere Beauclerk, O.B.E., *b.* 1915, *s.* 1964, *m.*	Earl of Burford, *b.* 1939.
1547	*Somerset* (18th), Percy Hamilton Seymour, *b.* 1910, *s.* 1954, *m.*	Lord Seymour, *b.* 1952.
1833	*Sutherland* (6th), John Sutherland Egerton (5th *U.K. Earl Ellesmere,* 1846), *b.* 1915, *s.* 1963, *m.*	Cyril R. E., *b.* 1905.
1814	*Wellington* (7th), Gerald Wellesley, K.G. (8th *Irish Earl, Mornington,* 1746), *b.* 1885, *s.* 1943, *w.*	Brig. Marquess Douro, M.V.O.,O.B.E.,M.C., *b.*1915.
1874	*Westminster* (5th), Robert George Grosvenor, T.D., *b.* 1910, *s.* 1967, *m.*	Earl Grosvenor, *b.* 1951.

MARQUESSES

Style, The Most Hon. the Marquess of ——. *Addressed as,* My Lord Marquess.
In titles marked ° the " of " is *not* used. For the style of Marquesses' sons and daughters, see under " DUKES," above.

| 1915 | *Aberdeen and Temair* (3rd), Dudley Gladstone Gordon, D.S.O., (9th *Scott. Earl, Aberdeen,* 1682), *b.* 1883, *s.* 1965, *m.* | Earl of Haddo, C.B.E., T.D. *b.* 1908. |

Created.	Title, Order of Succession, Name, etc.	Eldest Son or Heir.
1876	*Abergavenny* (5th), John Henry Guy Larnach-Nevill, O.B.E., b. 1914, s. 1954, m.	Lord Rupert N. b. 1923.
1821	*Ailesbury* (7th), Chandos Sidney Cedric Brudenell-Bruce, b. 1904, s. 1961, m.	Viscount Savernake, b. 1926.
1831	*Ailsa* (7th), Archibald David Kennedy, O.B.E. (19th *Scott. Earl, Cassillis*, 1509), b. 1925, s. 1957, m.	Earl of Cassillis, b. 1956.
1815	*Anglesey* (7th), George Charles Henry Victor Paget, b. 1922, s. 1947, m.	Earl of Uxbridge, b. 1950.
1789	*Bath* (6th), Henry Frederick Thynne, E.D., b. 1905, s. 1946, m.	Viscount Weymouth, b. 1932.
1826	*Bristol* 6th), Victor Frederick Cochrane Hervey, b. 1915, s. 1960, m.	Earl Jermyn, b. 1954.
1796	*Bute* (6th), John Crichton-Stuart (11th *Scott. Earl, Dumfries*, 1663), b. 1933, s. 1956, m.	Earl of Dumfries, b. 1958.
1917	*Cambridge* (2nd), George Francis Hugh Cambridge, G.C.V.O., b. 1895, s. 1927, m.	(None.)
1812	°*Camden* (5th), John Charles Henry Pratt, b. 1899, s. 1943, m.	Earl of Brecknock, b. 1930.
1815	*Cholmondeley* (6th), George Hugh Cholmondeley, M.C. (10th *Irish Viscount, Cholmondeley*, 1661), b. 1919, s. 1968, m. (Lord Great Chamberlain).	Earl of Rocksavage, b. 1960.
1816 I.*	°*Conyngham* (6th), Frederick William Burton Conyngham (6th *U.K. Baron, Minster*, 1821), b. 1890, s. 1918, m.	Earl of Mount Charles, b. 1924.
1791 I.*	*Donegall* (6th), Edward Arthur Donald St. George Hamilton Chichester (6th *Brit. Baron, Fisherwick*, 1790), b. 1903, s. 1904, m.	Lord Templemore, b. 1916 (see p. 248).
1789 I.*	*Downshire* (7th), Arthur Wills Percy Wellington Blundell Trumbull Sandys Hill (7th *Brit. Earl, Hillsborough*, 1772), b. 1894, s. 1918, m.	A. Robin I. H., b. 1929.
1888	*Dufferin & Ava* (5th), Sheridan Frederick Terence Hamilton-Temple-Blackwood (11th *Irish Baron, Dufferin & Clandeboye*, 1800), b. 1938, s. 1945, m.	(None to Marquessate), to Irish Barony, Sir Francis E. T. *Blackwood*, Bt., b. 1901.
1801.*	*Ely* (8th) Charles John Tottenham (8th *U.K. Baron, Loftus*, 1801), b. 1913, s. 1969, m.	Viscount Loftus, b. 1943.
1801	*Exeter* (6th), David George Brownlow Cecil, K.C.M.G., b. 1905, s. 1956, m.	Lord Martin C., b. 1909.
1800 I.*	*Headfort* (6th), Thomas Geoffrey Charles Michael Taylour (4th *U.K. Baron, Kenlis*, 1831), b. 1932, s. 1960, m.	Earl of Bective, b. 1959.
1793	*Hertford* (8th), Hugh Edward Conway Seymour (9th *Irish Baron, Conway*, 1712), b. 1930, s. 1940, m.	Earl of Yarmouth, b. 1953.
1599 S.*	*Huntly* (12th), Douglas Charles Lindsay Gordon (*Premier Marquess of Scotland* (4th *U.K. Baron, Meldrum*, 1815), b. 1908, s. 1937.	Earl of Aboyne, b. 1944.
1784	*Lansdowne* (8th), George John Charles Mercer Nairne Petty-Fitzmaurice, P.C. (8th *Irish Earl, Kerry*, 1722), b. 1912, s. 1944, m.	Earl of Shelburne, b. 1941.
1902	*Linlithgow* (3rd), Charles William Frederick Hope, M.C. (10th *Scott. Earl, Hopetoun*, 1703), b. 1912, s. 1952, m.	Earl of Hopetoun, b. 1946.
1816 I.*	*Londonderry* (9th), Alexander Charles Robert Vane-Tempest-Stewart (6th *U.K. Earl, Vane*, 1823), b. 1937, s. 1955.	Francis C. J. *Vane-Tempest*, b. 1911.
1701 S.*	*Lothian* (12th), Peter Francis Walter Kerr (6th *U.K. Baron, Ker*, 1821), b. 1922, s. 1940, m.	Earl of Ancram, b. 1945.
1917	*Milford Haven* (4th), George Ivar Louis Mountbatten, b. 1961, s. 1970, M.	Lord Ivar M, b. 1963.
1838	*Normanby* (4th), Oswald Constantine John Phipps, M.B.E. (8th *Irish Baron, Mulgrave*, 1767), b. 1912, s. 1932, m.	Earl of Mulgrave, b. 1954.
1812	*Northampton* (6th), William Bingham Compton, D.S.O., b. 1885, s. 1913, m.	Earl Compton, b. 1946.
1825 I.*	*Ormonde* (7th), James Hubert Theobald Charles Butler, M.B.E. (7th *U.K. Baron, Ormonde*, 1821), b. 1899, s. 1971, m.	(None to Marquessate; to Earldoms of Ormonde and Ossory Visct. Mountgarret (see p. 236).
1682 S.	*Queensberry* (12th), David Harrington Angus Douglas, b. 1929, s. 1954, m.	Lord Gawain D., b. 1948.
1926	*Reading* (3rd), Michael Alfred Rufus Isaacs, M.B.E., M.C., T.D., b. 1916, s. 1960, m.	Viscount Erleigh, b. 1942.
1789	*Salisbury* (5th), Robert Arthur James Gascoyne-Cecil, K.G., P.C., b. 1893, s. 1947, m.	Viscount Cranborne, b. 1916.
1800 I.*	*Sligo* (10th), Denis Edward Browne (10th *U.K. Baron, Monteagle*, 1806), b. 1908, s. 1952, m.	Earl of Altamont, b. 1939.
1787	°*Townshend* (7th), George John Patrick Dominic Townshend, b. 1916, s. 1921, m.	Viscount Raynham, b. 1945.
1694 S.*	*Tweeddale* (12th), David George Montagu Hay (3rd *U.K. Baron, Tweeddale*, 1881), b. 1921, s. 1967, m.	Earl of Gifford, b. 1947.
1789 I.*	*Waterford* (8th), John Hubert de la Poer Beresford (8th *Brit. Baron, Tyrone*, 1786), b. 1933, s. 1934, m.	Earl of Tyrone, b. 1958.
1936	*Willingdon* (2nd), Inigo Brassey Freeman-Thomas, b. 1899, s. 1941 m.	(None.)
1551	*Winchester* (18th), Nigel George Paulet (*Premier Marquess of England*), b. 1942, s. 1968.	Timothy G. P., b. 1944.
1892	*Zetland* (3rd), Lawrence Aldred Mervyn Dundas (5th *U.K. Earl of Zetland*, 1838, 6th *Brit. Baron Dundas*, 1794), b. 1908, s. 1961, m.	Earl of Ronaldshay, b. 1937.

EARLS

Style (see also note, p. 258). The Right Hon. the Earl of ——. *Addressed as*, My Lord. The eldest sons of Earls take, by courtesy, their father's second title, the younger sons being styled the Hon. *e.g.* the Hon. John ——, but the daughters Lady Elizabeth ——, etc. Where marked ° the " of " is not used.

Created.	Title, Order of Succession, Name, etc.	Eldest Son or Heir.
1639 S.	Airlie (13th), David George Coke Patrick Ogilvy, *b.* 1926, *s.* 1968, *m.*	Lord Ogilvy, *b.* 1958.
1696	Albemarle (9th), Walter Egerton George Lucian Keppel, M.C., *b.* 1882, *s.* 1942. *m.*	Viscount Bury, *b.* 1965.
1952	°Alexander of Tunis (2nd), Shane William Desmond Alexander, *b.* 1935, *s.* 1969, *m.*	Hon. Brian J. A., *b.* 1939.
1826	°Amherst (5th), Jeffery John Archer Amherst, M.C., *b.* 1896, *s.* 1927.	Hon. Humphrey W. *A.*, *b* 1903.
1892	Ancaster (3rd), Gilbert James Heathcote-Drummond-Willoughby, K.C.V.O., T.D. (26th *E. Baron Willoughby de Eresby*, 1313), *b.* 1907, *s.* 1951, *m.*	(To Earldom, none; to Barony, Lady Nancy *H.-D.-W.*, *b.* 1934.)
1789 I.	°Annesley (9th), Robert Annesley, *b.* 1900, *s.* 1957, *m.*	Viscount Glerawly, *b.* 1924.
1785 I.	Antrim (8th), Randal John Somerled McDonnell, K.B.E., *b.* 1911, *s.* 1932, *m.*	Viscount Dunluce, *b.* 1935.
1762 I.*	Arran (8th), Arthur Strange Kattendyke David Archibald Gore (4th *U.K. Baron Sudley*, 1884), *b.* 1910, *s.* 1958, *m.*	Viscount Sudley, *b.* 1938.
1955	°Attlee (2nd), Martin Richard Attlee, *b.* 1927, *s.* 1967, *m.*	Viscount Prestwood, *b.* 1956.
1961	Avon (1st), (Robert) Anthony Eden, K.G., P.C., M.C., *b.* 1897, *m.*	Viscount Eden, O.B.E., T.D., *b.* 1930.
1714	Aylesford (11th), Charles Ian Finch-Knightley. *b.* 1918, *s.* 1958, *m.*	Lord Guernsey, *b.* 1947.
1937	°Baldwin of Bewdley (3rd), Arthur Windham Baldwin, *b.* 1904, *s.* 1958, *m.*	Viscount Corvedale, *b.* 1938.
1922	Balfour (4th) Gerald Arthur James Balfour, *b.* 1925, *s.* 1968, *m.*	Eustace A. G. B., *b.* 1921.
1800 I.	Bandon (5th), Percy Ronald Gardner Bernard, G.B.E., C.B., C.V.O., D.S.O., *b.* 1904, *s.* 1924, *m.*	Maj. Hon. Charles B. A. *B.*, C.B.E., *b.* 1904 (Twin).
1772	°Bathurst (8th), Henry Allen John Bathurst, *b.* 1927, *s.* 1943, *m.*	Lord Apsley, *b.* 1961.
1919	°Beatty (2nd), David Field Beatty, D.S.C., *b.* 1905, *s.* 1936, *m.*	Viscount Borodale, *b.* 1946.
1815	°Beauchamp (8th), William Lygon, *b.* 1903, *s.* 1938, *m.*	Reginald A. L., *b.* 1904.
1797 I.	Belmore (8th), John Armar Lowry-Corry, *b.* 1951, *s.* 1960, M.	Sir Henry C. *L.*-C., M.C., *b.* 1887.
1739 I.) 1937*	Bessborough (2nd), Frederick Edward Neuflize Ponsonby, (10th *Irish Earl Bessborough*), *b.* 1913, *s.* 1956. *m.*	Arthur M.L. *P.*, *b* 1912 (to Irish Earldom only).
1922	Birkenhead (2nd), Frederick Winston Furneaux Smith, T.D., *b.* 1907, *s.* 1930, *m.*	Viscount Furneaux, *b.* 1936.
1815	Bradford (7th), Gerald Michael Orlando Bridgeman, T.D., *b.* 1911, *s.* 1957, *m.*	Viscount Newport, *b.* 1947.
1677 S.	Breadalbane and Holland (10th), John Romer Boreland Campbell, *b.* 1919, *s.* 1959. *m.*	(None.)
1469 S.*	Buchan (16th), Donald Cardross Flower Erskine. (7th *U.K. Baron Erskine*), *b.* 1899, *s.* (to Barony), 1957, (to Earldom) 1960, *m.*	Lord Cardross, *b.* 1930.
1746	Buckinghamshire (9th), Vere Frederick Cecil Hobart-Hampden, *b.* 1901, *s.* 1963.	Cyril L. *H.*-H., *b.* 1902.
1800	°Cadogan (7th), William Gerald Charles Cadogan, M.C. *b.* 1914, *s.* 1933, *m.*	Viscount Chelsea, *b.* 1937.
1878	°Cairns (5th), David Charles Cairns, K.C.V.O., C.B., *b.* 1909, *s.* 1946, *m.*	Viscount Garmoyle, *b.* 1939.
1543 S.	Caithness (20th), Malcolm Ian Sinclair, *b.* 1948, *s.* 1965.	Sir John R. N. B. *S.*, Bt., *b.* 1928.
1800 I.	Caledon (6th) Denis James Alexander, *b.* 1920, *s.* 1968, *m.*	Viscount Alexander, *b.* 1955.
1661	Carlisle (12th), Charles James Ruthven Howard, M.C., *b.* 1923, *s.* 1963, *m.*	Viscount Morpeth, *b.* 1949.
1793	Carnarvon (6th), Henry George Alfred Marius Victor Francis Herbert, *b.* 1898, *s.* 1923.	Lord Porchester, *b.* 1924.
1748 I.*	Carrick (9th), Brian Stuart Theobald Somerset Caher Butler (3rd *U.K. Baron, Butler*, 1912), *b.* 1931, *s.* 1957. *m.*	Viscount Ikerrin, *b.* 1953.
1800 I.	°Castle Stewart(8th),Arthur Patrick Avondale Stuart, *b.* 1928, *s.* 1961, *m.*	Viscount Stuart, *b.* 1953.
1814	°Cathcart (6th), Alan Cathcart, D.S.O., M.C. (15th *Scott. Baron, Cathcart*), *b.* 1919, *s.* 1927, *m.*	Lord Greenock, *b.* 1952.
1647 I.	Cavan (12th), Michael Edward Oliver Lambart, T.D., *b.* 1911, *s.* 1950, *m.*	Roger C. *L.*, *b.* 1944.
1827	°Cawdor (6th), Hugh John Vaughan Campbell, *b.* 1932, *s.* 1970, *m.*	Viscount Emlyn, *b.* 1962.
1801	Chichester (9th), John Nicholas Pelham, *b.* 1944, *s.* 1944.	Richard A. H. *P.*, *b.* 1952.
1803 I.*	Clancarty (7th), Greville Sydney Rochfort Le Poer Trench (6th *U.K. Visct. Clancarty*, 1823), *b.* 1902, *s.* 1971, *m.*	Hon. William F. B. *Le P. T.*, *b.* 1911.
1776 I.*	Clanwilliam (6th), John Charles Edmund Carson Meade (4th *U.K. Baron Clanwilliam*, 1828), *b.* 1914, *s.* 1953, *m.*	John H. *M.*, *b.* 1919.

H+

Created.	Title, Order of Succession, Name, etc.	Eldest Son or Heir.

1776   *Clarendon* (7th), George Frederick Laurence Villiers, *b.* 1933, *s.* 1955.   Hon. Nicholas *V.*, *b.* 1916.

1620 I.*   *Cork & Orrery* (1660), Patrick Reginald Boyle (13th *Irish Earl* and 9th *Brit. Baron, Boyle of Marston,* 1711), *b.* 1910, *s.* 1967, *m.*   Lt.-Cdr. John W. *B.*, D.S.C., *b.* 1916.

1850   *Cottenham* (8th), Kenelm Charles Everard Digby Pepys, *b.* 1948, *s.* 1968.   Samuel G. L. *P*, *b.* 1915.

1762 I.*   *Courtown* (8th), James Montagu Burgoyne Stopford, O.B.E., T.D. (7th *Brit. Baron, Saltersford,* 1796), *b.* 1908, *s.* 1957, *m.*   Viscount Stopford, *b.* 1954.

1697   *Coventry* (11th), George William Coventry, *b.* 1934, *s.* 1940.   Viscount Deerhurst, *b.* 1957.

1857   *Cowley* (6th), Richard Francis Wellesley, *b.* 1946, *s.* 1968.   Hon. Garret G. *W.*, *b.* 1934.

1892   *Cranbrook* (4th), John David Gathorne-Hardy, C.B.E., *b.* 1900, *s.* 1915, *m.*   Lord Medway, *b.* 1933.

1801   *Craven* (7th), Thomas Robert Douglas Craven, *b.* 1957, *s.* 1965, M.   Hon. Simon G. *C.*, *b.* 1961.

1398 S.*   *Crawford* (28th) *and Balcarres* (11th), David Alexander Robert Lindsay, K.T., G.B.E. (*Premier Earl on Union Roll* and 4th *U.K. Baron, Wigan,* 1826), *b.* 1900, *s.* 1940, *m.*   Lord Balniel, M.P., *b.* 1927.

1861   *Cromartie* (4th), Roderick Grant Francis Mackenzie, M.C., *b.* 1904, *s.* 1962, *m.*   Viscount Tarbat, *b.* 1948.

1901   *Cromer* (3rd) George Rowland Stanley Baring, P.C., K.C.M.G., M.B.E., *b.* 1918, *s.* 1953.   Viscount Errington, *b.* 1946.

1633 S.*   *Dalhousie* (16th) Simon Ramsay, K.T., G.B.E., M.C. (4th *U.K. Baron, Ramsay,* 1875), *b.* 1914, *s.* 1950, *m.*   Lord Ramsay, *b.* 1946.

1725 I.*   *Darnley* (10th), Peter Stuart Bligh (19th *English Baron, Clifton of Leighton Bromswold,* 1608), *b.* 1915, *s.* 1955.   Hon. Adam I. S. *B.*, *b.* 1941.

1711   *Dartmouth* (9th), Gerald Humphry Legge, *b.* 1924, *s.* 1962, *m.*   Viscount Lewisham, *b.* 1949.

1761   °*De La Warr* (9th), Herbrand Edward Dundonald Brassey Sackville, P.C., G.B.E., *b.* 1900, *s.* 1915, *m.*   Lord Buckhurst, *b.* 1921.

1622   *Denbigh* (11th) *and Desmond* (10th), William Rudolph Michael Feilding (10th *Irish Earl, Desmond,* 1622), *b.* 1943, *s.* 1966, *m.*   Viscount Feilding, *b.* 1970.

1485   *Derby* (18th) Edward John Stanley, M.C., *b.*, 1918, *s.* 1948, *m.*   Hon. Richard *S.*, *b.* 1920.

1553   *Devon* (17th), Charles Christopher Courtenay, *b.* 1916, *s.* 1935, *m.*   Lord Courtenay, *b.* 1942.

1800 I.*   *Donoughmore* (7th), John Michael Henry Hely-Hutchinson, (7th *U.K. Visct. Hutchinson,* 1821), *b.* 1902, *s.* 1948, *m.*   Viscount Suirdale, *b.* 1927.

1661 I.*   *Drogheda* (11th), Charles Garrett Moore, K.B.E. (2nd *U.K. Baron, Moore,* 1954), *b.* 1910, *s.* 1957, *m.*   Viscount Moore, *b.* 1937.

1837   *Ducie* (6th), Basil Howard Moreton, *b.* 1917, *s.* 1952, *m.*   Lord Moreton, *b.* 1951.

1860   *Dudley* (4th), William Humble David Ward, *b.* 1920, *s.* 1969, *m.*   Viscount Ednam, *b.* 1947.

1660 S.*   *Dundee* (11th), Henry James Scrymgeour-Wedderburn, P.C. (1st *U.K. Baron, Glassary,* 1954) *b.* 1902, *s.* 1924 (*claim admitted,* 1953), *m.* (*Hereditary Standard Bearer, Scotland*).   Lord Scrymgeour, *b.* 1949.

1669 S.   *Dundonald* (14th), Ian Douglas Leonard Cochrane, *b.* 1918, *s.* 1958, *m.*   Lord Cochrane, *b.* 1961.

1686 S.*   *Dunmore* (9th), John Alexander Murray (4th *U.K. Baron, Dunmore,* 1831), *b.* 1939, *s.* 1962, *m.*   Reginald A. *M.*, *b.* 1911.

1822 I.   *Dunraven and Mount Earl* (7th), Thady Windham Thomas Wyndham-Quin, *b.* 1939, *s.* 1965, *m.*   Capt. Hon. Valentine M. *W.-Q.*, R.N., *b.* 1890.

1837   *Effingham* (6th), Mowbray Henry Gordon Howard (16th *E. Baron, Howard of Effingham,* 1553), *b.* 1905, *s.* 1946, *m.*   David P. M. A. *H.*, *b.* 1939.

1507 S. 1859* }   *Eglinton* (18th) *& (9th) Winton* (1600), Archibald George Montgomerie (6th *U.K. Earl Winton,* 1859), *b.* 1939, *s.* 1966, *m.*   Lord Montgomerie, *b.* 1966.

1733 I.*   *Egmont* (11th), Frederick George Moore Perceval (9th *Brit. Baron, Lovel & Holland,* 1762), *b.* 1914, *s.* 1932, *m.*   Viscount Perceval, *b.* 1934.

1821   *Eldon* (4th), John Scott, G.C.V.O., *b.* 1899, *s.* 1926, *w.*   Viscount Encombe, *b.* 1937.

1633 S.*   *Elgin* (11th), *& Kincardine* (15th) (1647), Andrew Douglas Alexander Thomas Bruce, (4th *U.K. Baron, Elgin,* 1849), *b.* 1924, *s.* 1968, *m.*   Lord Bruce, *b.* 1961.

1789 I.*   *Enniskillen* (6th), David Lowry Cole, M.B.E., (4th *U.K. Baron, Grinstead,* 1815), *b.* 1918, *s.* 1963, *m.*   Viscount Cole, *b.* 1942.

1781 I.*   *Erne* (6th), Henry George Victor John Crichton (3rd *U.K. Baron, Fermanagh,* 1876), *b.* 1937, *s.* 1940, *m.*   Viscount Crichton, *b.* 1971.

1661   *Essex* (9th), Reginald George de Vere Capell, T.D., *b.* 1906, *s.* 1966, *m.*   Robert E. de V. *C.*, *b.* 1920.

1711   °*Ferrers* (13th), Robert Washington Shirley, *b.* 1929, *s.* 1954, *m.*   Viscount Tamworth, *b.* 1952.

1628 I.*   *Fingall* (12th), Oliver James Horace Plunkett, M.C. (19th *I. Baron, Killeen,* 1449) (5th *U.K. Baron, Fingall,* 1831), *b.* 1896, *s.* 1929, *m.*   (None to Earldom or U.K. Barony), to Irish Barony Lord Dunsany (*see p. 241*).

1746*   °*Fitzwilliam* (8th) William Thomas George Wentworth-Fitzwilliam (10th *Irish Earl, Fitzwilliam,* 1716), *b.* 1904, *s.* 1952, *m.*   (None.)

Created.	Title, Order of Succession, Name, etc.	Eldest Son or Heir.
1789	°*Fortescue* (6th), Denzil George Fortescue, M.C., T.D., *b.* 1893, *s.* 1958, *m.*	Viscount Ebrington, *b.* 1922.
1841	*Gainsborough* (5th), Anthony Gerard Edward Noel, *b.* 1923, *s.* 1927.	Viscount Campden, *b.* 1950.
1623 S.*	*Galloway* (12th), Randolph Algernon Ronald Stewart (5th *Brit. Baron, Stewart of Garlies, 1796*), *b.* 1892, *s.* 1920, *m.*	Lord Garlies, *b.* 1928.
1703 S.*	*Glasgow* (9th), David William Maurice Boyle, C.B., D.S.C. (3rd *U.K. Baron, Fairlie, 1897*), *b.* 1910, *s.* 1963, *m.*	Viscount Kelburn, *b.* 1939.
1806 I.*	*Gosford* (7th). Charles David Alexander John Sparrow Acheson (5th *U.K. Baron, Worlingham, 1835*), *b.* 1942, *s.* 1966.	Hon. Patrick B. V. M. *A., b.* 1915.
1945	*Gowrie* (2nd), Alexander Patrick Greysteel Hore-Ruthven (3rd *U.K. Baron, Ruthven of Gowrie, 1919*), *b.* 1939, *s.* 1955, *m.*	Viscount Ruthven, *b.* 1964.
1684 I.*	*Granard* (9th) Arthur Patrick Hastings Forbes, A.F.C. (4th *U. K. Baron, Granard, 1806*), *b.* 1915, *s.* 1948, *m.* [*m.*	Hon. John *F., b.* 1920.
1833	°*Granville* (5th), Granville James Leveson-Gower, M.C., *b.* 1918, *s.* 1953.	Lord Leveson, *b.* 1959.
1806	°*Grey* (6th), Richard Fleming George Charles Grey, *b.* 1939, *s.* 1963, *m.*	Philip K. G., *b.* 1940.
1752	*Guilford* (9th), Edward Francis North, *b.* 1933, *s.* 1949, *m.*	Lord North, *b.* 1971.
1619 S.	*Haddington* (12th), George Baillie-Hamilton, K.T., M.C., T.D., *b.* 1894, *s.* 1917, *m.*	Lord Binning, *b.* 1941.
1919	°*Haig* (2nd), George Alexander Eugene Douglas Haig, O.B.E. *b.* 1918, *s.* 1928, *m.*	Viscount Dawick, *b.* 1961.
1944	*Halifax* (2nd), Charles Ingram Courtenay Wood (4th *U.K. Viscount, Halifax, 1866*), *b.* 1912, *s.* 1959, *m.*	Lord Irwin, *b.* 1944.
1898	*Halsbury* (3rd), John Anthony Hardinge Giffard, F.R.S., *b.* 1908, *s.* 1943, *m.*	Viscount Tiverton, *b.* 1934.
1754	*Hardwicke* (9th), Philip Grantham Yorke, *b.* 1906, *s.* 1936, *m.*	Viscount Royston, *b.* 1938.
1812	*Harewood* (7th), George Henry Hubert Lascelles, *b.* 1923, *s.* 1947, *m.* (See also p. 217).	Viscount Lascelles, *b.* 1950.
1742	*Harrington* (11th), William Henry Leicester Stanhope (8th *U.K. Viscount, Stanhope of Mahon, 1717*), *b.* 1922, *s.* 1929, *m.*	Viscount Petersham, *b.* 1945.
1809	*Harrowby* (6th), Dudley Ryder, *b.* 1892, *s.* 1956, *m.*	Viscount Sandon, *b.* 1922.
1821	°*Howe* (6th), Edward Richard Assheton Curzon, C.B.E., *b.* 1908, *s.* 1964, *m.*	Chambré G. W. P. *C., b.* 1898.
1529	*Huntingdon* (15th), Francis John Clarence Westenra Plantagenet Hastings, *b.* 1901, *s.* 1939, *m.*	David F. G. *H., b.* 1909.
1885	*Iddesleigh* (4th), Stafford Henry Northcote, *b.* 1932, *s.* 1970, *m.*	Viscount St. Cyres, *b.* 1957.
1750	*Ilchester* (9th), Maurice Vivian de Touffreville Fox-Strangways, *b.* 1920, *s.* 1970, *m.*	Hon. Raymond G. *F.-S., b.* 1921.
1929	*Inchcape* (3rd), Kenneth James William Mackay, *b.* 1917, *s.* 1939, *m.*	Viscount Glenapp, *b.* 1943.
1919	*Iveagh* (3rd), Arthur Francis Benjamin Guinness, *b.* 1937, *s.* 1967, *m.*	Viscount Elveden, *b.* 1969.
1925	°*Jellicoe* (2nd), George Patrick John Rushworth Jellicoe, P.C., D.S.O., M.C., *b.* 1918, *s.* 1935, *m.*	Viscount Brocas, *b.* 1950.
1697	*Jersey* (9th), George Francis Child-Villiers (12th *Irish Visct., Grandison, 1620*), *b.* 1910, *s.* 1923, *m.*	Viscount Villiers, *b.* 1948.
1822 I.	*Kilmorey* (5th), Francis Jack Richard Patrick Needham, *b.* 1915, *s.* 1961, *m.*	Richard F. *N., b.* 1942.
1866	*Kimberley* (4th), John Wodehouse, *b.* 1924, *s.* 1941.	Lord Wodehouse, *b.* 1951.
1768 I.	*Kingston* (11th), Barclay Robert Edwin King-Tenison, *b.* 1943, *s.* 1948, *m.*	Capt. R. D. *King-Harman*, D.S.O., D.S.C., R.N., *b.*1311.
1633 S.*	*Kinnoull* (15th), Arthur William George Patrick Hay (9th *Brit. Baron, Hay of Pedwardine, 1711*), *b.* 1935, *s.* 1938, *m.*	Viscount Dupplin, *b.* 1962.
1914	°*Kitchener of Khartoum* (3rd). Henry Herbert Kitchener, *b.* 1919. *s.* 1937.	Hon. Charles E. *K., b.* 1920.
1756 I.	*Lanesborough* (9th), Denis Anthony Brian Butler, *b.* 1918, *s.* 1959.	Lt.-Cdr. Terence B. J. D. *B., b.* 1913.
1624 S.	*Lauderdale* (17th), Patrick Francis Maitland, *b.* 1911, *s.* 1968, *m.*	Viscount Maitland, *b.* 1937.
1837	*Leicester* (5th), Thomas William Edward Coke, M.V.O., *b.* 1908, *s.* 1949, *m.*	Anthony L. *C., b.* 1909.
1641 S.	*Leven* (14th) & (13th) *Melville* (1690), Alexander Robert Leslie-Melville, *b.* 1924, *s.* 1947, *m.*	Lord Balgonie, *b.* 1954.
1831	*Lichfield* (5th), Thomas Patrick John Anson, *b.* 1939, *s.* 1960.	Geoffrey R. *A. b.* 1929.
1803 L.*	*Limerick* (6th), Patrick Edmund Pery (6th *U.K. Baron, Foxford, 1815*), *b.* 1930, *s.* 1967, *m.*	Viscount Glentworth, *b.* 1963.
1633 S.	*Lindsay* (14th), William Tucker Lindesay-Bethune, *b.* 1901, *s.* 1943.	Viscount Garnock, *b.* 1926.
1626	*Lindsey* (14th) *and Abingdon* (9th) (1682), Richard Henry Rupert Bertie, *b.* 1931, *s.* 1963, *m.*	Lord Norreys of Rycote, *b.* 1958.
1776 I.	*Lisburne* (8th), John David Malet Vaughan, *b.* 1918, *s.* 1965, *m.*	Viscount Vaughan, *b.* 1945.
1822 I.*	*Listowel* (5th), William Francis Hare, P.C., G.C.M.G. (3rd *U.K. Baron, Hare, 1869*), *b.* 1906, *s.* 1931, *m.*	Viscount Ennismore, *b.* 1964.
1905	*Liverpool* (5th), Edward Peter Bertram Savile Foljambe, *b.* 1944, *s.* 1969, *m.*	

Created.	Title, Order of Succession, Name, etc.	Eldest Son or Heir.

1945 — °Lloyd George of Dwyfor (3rd), Owen Lloyd George, b. 1924, s. 1968, m. — Viscount Gwynnedd, b. 1951.

1785 I.* — Longford (7th), Francis Aungier Pakenham, K.G., P.C. (6th *U.K. Baron, Silchester*, 1821; 1st U.K. *Baron, Pakenham*, 1945), b. 1905, s. 1961, m. — Lord Silchester, b. 1933.

1807 — Lonsdale (7th), James Hugh William Lowther, b. 1922, s. 1953. m. — Viscount Lowther, b. 1949.

1838 — Lovelace (5th), Peter Axel William Locke King (12th *British Baron, King*, 1725), b. 1951, s. 1964, M. — (None.)

1795 I.* — Lucan (7th), Richard John Bingham (3rd *U.K. Baron, Bingham*, 1934), b. 1934, s. 1964, m. — Lord Bingham, b. 1967.

1880 — Lytton (4th), Noel Anthony Scawen Lytton (17th *English Baron, Wentworth*, 1529), b. 1900, s. 1951, m. — Viscount Knebworth, b. 1950.

1721 — Macclesfield (7th), George Loveden William Henry Parker, b. 1888, s. 1896, m. — Viscount Parker, b. 1914.

1800 — Malmesbury (6th), William James Harris, T.D., b. 1907, s. 1950, m. — Viscount FitzHarris, b. 1946.

1776 & 1792 — Mansfield and Mansfield (7th), Mungo David Malcolm Murray (13th *Scott, Chaworth, Stormont*, 1621), b. 1900, s. 1935, m. — Viscount Stormont, b. 1930.

1404 S. — Mar (30th), James Clifton of Mar (*Premier Earl of Scotland*), b. 1914, s. 1965, m. — The Mistress of Mar, b. 1940.

1565 S. — Mar (13th) & (14th) Kellie (1616), John Francis Hervey Erskine, b. 1921, s. 1955, m. — Lord Erskine, b. 1949.

1785 I. — Mayo (10th), Terence Patrick Bourke, b. 1929, s. 1962, m. — Lord Naas, b. 1953.

1627 I.* — Meath (14th), Anthony Windham Normand Brabazon (5th *U.K. Baron, Chaworth*, 1831), b. 1910, s. 1949, m. — Lord Ardee, b. 1941.

1766 I. — Mexborough (7th), John Raphael Wentworth Savile, b. 1906, s. 1945, m. — Viscount Pollington, b. 1931.

1920 — Midleton (2nd), George St. John Brodrick, M.C. (10th *Irish Viscount, Midleton*, 1717), b. 1888, s. 1942. m. — (None to Earldom), to Irish Viscountcy, Trevor L. B., b. 1903.

1813 — Minto (5th), Victor Gilbert Lariston Garnet Elliot-Murray-Kynynmound, b. 1891, s. 1914, m. — Viscount Melgund, M.B.E., b. 1928.

1562 S.* — Moray (19th) (Archibald) John Morton Stuart (11th *Brit. Baron, Stuart of Castle Stuart*, 1796), b. 1894, s. 1943, w. — Lord Doune, b. 1928.

1815 — Morley (6th), John St. Aubyn Parker, b. 1923, s. 1962, m. — Visct. Boringdon, b. 1956.

1458 S. — Morton (21st), Sholto Charles John Hay Douglas, b. 1907, s. 1935. — Hon. John C. S. D., b. 1927.

1947 — Mountbatten of Burma (1st), Louis Francis Albert Victor Nicholas Mountbatten, K.G., P.C., G.C.B., O.M., G.C.S.I., G.C.I.E., G.C.V.O., D.S.O., b. 1900, w. (*Personal A.D.C. to the Queen*), Admiral of the Fleet. (See also p. 215.) — Baroness Brabourne, b. 1924 (see pp. 215 and 239).

1789 — Mount Edgcumbe (7th), Edward Piers Edgcumbe, b. 1903, s. 1965, m. — George A. V. E., b. 1907.

1831 — Munster (5th), Geoffrey William Richard Hugh FitzClarence, P.C., K.B.E., b. 1906, s. 1928, m. — Edward C. FitzC., b. 1899.

1805 — °Nelson (7th), Henry Edward Joseph Horatio Nelson, b. 1894, s. 1957. — Hon. George J. H. N., b. 1905.

1827 I. — Norbury (6th), Noel Terence Graham-Toler, b 1939, s. 1955, m. — Viscount Glandine, b. 1967.

1806 I.* — Normanton (6th), Shaun James Christian Welbore Ellis Agar (4th *U.K. Baron, Somerton*, 1873), b. 1945, s. 1967, m. — Hon. Mark S. A. A., b. 1948.

1647 S. — Northesk (12th), John Douglas Carnegie, b. 1895, s. 1963, w. — Lord Rosehill, b. 1926.

1801 — Onslow (7th), Michael William Coplestone Onslow, b. 1938, s. 1971, m. — Viscount Cranley, b. 1967.

1925 — Oxford & Asquith (2nd), Julian Edward George Asquith, K.C.M.G., b. 1916, s. 1928, m. — Viscount Asquith of Morley, b. 1952.

1929 — Peel (3rd), William James Robert Peel (4th *U.K. Viscount Peel*, 1895), b. 1947, s. 1969. — Hon Robert M. A. P., b. 1950.

1551 — Pembroke (17th) & (14th) Montgomery (1605), Henry George Charles Alexander Herbert, b. 1939, s. 1969, m. —

1605 S. — Perth (17th), John David Drummond, P.C., b. 1907, s. 1951, m. — Viscount Strathallan, b. 1935.

1905 — Plymouth (3rd), Other Robert Ivor Windsor-Clive (15th *English Baron, Windsor*, 1529), b. 1923, s. 1943, m. — Viscount Windsor, b. 1951.

1785 I. — Portarlington (7th), George Lionel Yuill Seymour Dawson-Damer, v. 1938, s. 1959, m. — Viscount Carlow, b. 1965.

1743 — Portsmouth (9th), Gerard Vernon Wallop, b. 1898, s. 1943, m. — Viscount Lymington, b. 1923.

1706 — °Poulett (8th), George Amias Fitzwarrine Poulett, b. 1909, s. 1918, w. — (None.)

1804 — Powis (5th), Edward Robert Henry Herbert, C.B.E., T.D. (6th *Irish Baron, Clive*, 1762), b. 1889, s. 1952, m. — Hon. Christian V. C. H., b. 1904.

1765 — Radnor (8th) Jacob Pleydell-Bouverie, b. 1927, s. 1968, m. — Viscount Folkestone, b. 1955.

1831 I.* — Ranfurly (6th), Thomas Daniel Knox, K.C.M.G. (7th *U.K. Baron, Ranfurly*, 1826), b. 1913, s. 1933, m. — Gerald F. N. K. b. 1929.

1771 I. — Roden (9th), Robert William Jocelyn, b. 1909, s. 1956, m. — Viscount Jocelyn. b. 1938.

1601 — Romney (6th), Charles Marsham, b. 1892, s. 1933, m. — Michael H. M., b. 1910.

Created.	Title, Order of Succession, Name, etc.	Eldest Son or Heir.

1703 S.★   *Rosebery* (6th), Albert Edward Harry Mayer Archibald Primrose, P.C., K.T., D.S.O., M.C. (2nd *U.K. Earl of Midlothian*, 1911), *b.* 1882 *s.* 1929, *m.* — Lord Primrose, *b.* 1929

1806 I.   *Rosse* (6th), Laurence Michael Harvey Parsons, M.B.E., *b.* 1906, *s.* 1918, *m.* — Lord Oxmantown, *b.* 1936

1801   *Rosslyn* (6th), Anthony Hugh Francis Harry St. Clair-Erskine, *b.* 1917, *s.* 1939 — Lord Loughborough, *b.* 1958.

1457 S.   *Rothes* (20th), Malcolm George Dyer Edwardes Leslie, *b.* 1902, *s.* 1927, *m.* — Lord Leslie, *b.* 1932.

1861   °*Russell* (4th), John Conrad Russell, *b.* 1921, *s.* 1970. — Hon. Conrad S. R. R., *b.* 1937.

1915   *St. Aldwyn* (2nd), Michael John Hicks-Beach, P.C., K.B.E. T.D., *b.* 1912, *s.* 1916, *m.* — Viscount Quenington, *b.* 1950.

1815   *St. Germans* (9th), Nicholas Richard Michael Eliot, *b.* 1914, *s.* 1960, *m.* — Lord Eliot, *b.* 1941.

1690   *Scarbrough* (12th), Richard Aldred Lumley, (13th *Irish Visct.*, *Lumley*, 1628), *b.* 1932, *s.* 1969, *m.*

1701 S.   *Seafield* (13th), Ian Derek Francis Ogilvie-Grant-Studley-Herbert, *b.* 1939, *s.* 1969, *m.* — Visct. Reidhaven, *b.* 1963.

1771 I.★   *Sefton* (7th), Hugh William Osbert Molyneux (6th *U.K. Baron*, *Sefton*, 1831), *b.* 1898, *s.* 1930, *w.* — (None.)

1882   *Selborne* (3rd), Roundell Cecil Palmer, P.C., C.H., *b.* 1887, *s.* 1942, *w.* — Viscount Wolmer, *b.* 1940.

1646 S.   *Selkirk* (7th) (George) Nigel Douglas-Hamilton, P.C., G.C.M.G., G.B.E., A.F.C., Q.C., *b.* 1906, *s.* 1940 *m.* — The Master of Selkirk, *b.* 1939.

1672   *Shaftesbury* (10th), Anthony Ashley-Cooper, *b.* 1938, *s.* 1961, *m.* — Hon. John P. H. N. A.-C., *b.* 1915.

1756 I.★   *Shannon* (9th), Richard Bentinck Boyle (8th *Brit. Bn. Carleton* 1786), *b.* 1924, *s.* 1963, *m.* — Viscount Boyle, *b.* 1960.

1442   *Shrewsbury* (21st) & *Waterford* (I. 1446), John George Charles Henry Alton Alexander Chetwynd Chetwynd-Talbot (*Premier Earl of England and Ireland*; *Earl Talbot*, 1784), *b.* 1914, *s.* 1921, *m.* — Viscount Ingestre, *b.* 1952.

1961   *Snowdon* (1st), Antony Charles Robert Armstrong-Jones, G.C.V.O., *b.* 1930, *m.* (*See also* p. 219.) — Viscount Linley, *b.* 1961 (*see* p. 219).

1880   °*Sondes* (5th), Henry George Herbert Milles-Lade, *b.* 1940, *s.* 1970, *m.*

1633 S.★   *Southesk* (11th), Charles Alexander Carnegie, K.C.V.O. (3rd *U.K. Baron, Balinhard*, 1869), *b.* 1893, *s.* 1941, *m.* — The Duke of Fife, *b.* 1929 (*see* pp. 216 and 227).

1765   °*Spencer* (7th), Albert Edward John Spencer, T.D., *b.* 1892, *s.* 1922, *m.* — Viscount Althorp, M.V.O., *b.* 1924

1703 S.★   *Stair* (13th), John Aymer Dalrymple, C.V.O., M.B.E. (6th *U.K. Baron*, *Oxenfoord* 1841), *b.* 1906, *s.* 1961. *m* — Viscount Dalrymple, *b.* 1961.

1628   *Stamford* (10th), Roger Grey, *b.* 1896, *s.* 1910. — (None.)

1821   *Stradbroke* (4th), John Anthony Alexander Rous, *b.* 1903, *s.* 1947, *m.* — Hon. Keith R., *b.* 1907.

1847   *Strafford* (7th), Robert Cecil Byng, *b.* 1904 *s.* 1951, *m.* — Viscount Enfield, *b.* 1936.

1937   *Strathmore* (3rd), Timothy Patrick Bowes-Lyon (16th *Scottish Earl, Strathmore & Kinghorne* 1606), *b.* 1918, *s.* 1949, *w.* — Fergus M. C. B.-L., *b.* 1928.

1603   *Suffolk* (21st) & (14th) *Berkshire* (1626), Michael John James George Robert Howard, *b.* 1935, *s.* 1941. — Hon. Maurice H., *b.* 1936.

1955   *Swinton* (1st), Philip Cunliffe-Lister, P.C., G.B.E., C.H., M.C., *b.* 1884, *m.* — Lord Masham, *b.* 1937

1714   *Tankerville* (8th), Charles Augustus Ker Bennet, *b.* 1897, *s.* 1931, *m.* — Lord Ossulston, *b.* 1921.

1822   °*Temple of Stowe* (7th), Ronald Stephen Brydges Temple-Gore-Langton, *b.* 1910, *s.* 1966. — Hon. Evelyn A. T.-G.-L., D.S.O., *b.* 1884.

1815   *Verulam* (6th), John Grimston (10th *Irish Visct.*, *Grimston*, 1719; 15th *Scot. Baron, Forrester of Corstorphine* 1633),*b.* 1912, *s.* 1960, *m.* — Viscount Grimston, *b.* 1951.

1729   °*Waldegrave* (12th), Geoffrey Noel Waldegrave, K.G., T.D., *b.* 1905, *s.* 1936, *m.* — Viscount Chewton, *b.* 1940.

1759   *Warwick* & °*Brooke* (1746), Charles Guy Fulke Greville (7th *Earl Brooke* and 7th *Earl of Warwick*), *b.* 1911, *s.* 1928, *m.* — Lord Brooke, *b.* 1934.

1633 S.★   *Wemyss* (12th) & (8th) *March* (1697), Francis David Charteris, K.T. (5th *U.K. Baron, Wemyss*, 1821), *b.* 1912, *s.* 1937, *m.* — Lord Neidpath, *b.* 1948.

1621 I.   *Westmeath* (12th), Gilbert Charles Nugent, *b.* 1880, *s.* 1933, *w.* — Lord Delvin, *b.* 1928.

1624   *Westmorland* (15th), David Anthony Thomas Fane, K.C.V.O., *b.* 1924, *s.* 1948, *m.* — Lord Burghersh, *b.* 1951.

1876   *Wharncliffe* (4th), Alan James Montagu-Stuart-Wortley-Mackenzie, *b.* 1935, *s.* 1953, *m.* — Alan R. *Montagu-Stuart Wortley*, *b.* 1927.

1793 I.   *Wicklow* (8th), William Cecil James Philip John Paul Forward-Howard, *b.* 1902, *s.* 1946, *m.* — Cecil A. *F.-H.*, *b.* 1909

1801   *Wilton* (7th), Seymour William Arthur John Egerton *b.* 1921, *s.* 1927, *m.* — Lord Ebury, *b.* 1934 (*see* p. 241).

1628   *Winchilsea* (16th) & (11th) *Nottingham* (1681), Christopher Denys Stormont Finch-Hatton, *b.* 1936, *s.* 1950, *m.* — Viscount Maidstone, *b.* 1967

1766 I.   °*Winterton* (7th), Robert Chad Turnour, *b.* 1915, *s.* 1962, *m.* — Cecil N. T., *b.* 1919

1956   *Woolton* (3rd), Simon Frederick Marquis, *b.* 1958, *s.* 1969, *M.* — (None.)

Created.	Title, Order of Succession, Name, etc.	Eldest Son or Heir.
1837	*Yarborough* (7th), John Edward Pelham, *b.* 1920, *s.* 1966, *m.*	Lord Worsley, *b.* 1963.
1922	*Ypres* (3rd), John Richard Charles Lambart French, *b.* 1921, *s.* 1948, *m.*	(None.)

VISCOUNTS

Style (*see* note, p. 258), The Right Hon. the Viscount ——. *Addressed as,* My Lord. The eldest sons of Viscounts and Barons have no distinctive title; they, as well as their brothers and sisters, are styled the Hon. Robert, Hon. Mary, &c.

1945	*Addison* (2nd), Christopher Addison, *b.* 1904, *s.* 1951, *m.*	Hon. Michael A., *b.* 1914.
1946	*Alanbrooke* (2nd), Thomas Brooke, *b.* 1920, *s.* 1963.	Hon. Alan V. H. B., *b.* 1932.
1919	*Allenby* (2nd), Dudley Jaffray Hynman Allenby, *b.* 1903, *s.* 1936, *m.*	Hon. Michael A., *b.* 1931.
1911	*Allendale* (3rd), Wentworth Hubert Charles Beaumont, *b.* 1922, *s.* 1956, *m.*	Hon. Wentworth P. I. B., *b.* 1948.
1960	*Amory* (1st), Derick Heathcoat Amory, K.G., P.C., G.C.M.G., *b.* 1899.	(None.)
1642 S.	*Arbuthnott* (16th *Viscount of Arbuthnott*), John Campbell Arbuthnott, D.S.C., *b.* 1924, *s.* 1966, *m.*	Master of Arbuthnott, *b.* 1950.
1751 I.	*Ashbrook* (10th), Desmond Llowarch Edward Flower, M.B.E., *b.* 1905, *s.* 1936, *m.*	Hon. Michael F., *b.* 1935.
1917	*Astor* (4th), William Waldorf Astor, *b.* 1951, *s.* 1966, M.	Hon. David A., *b.* 1912.
1781 I.	*Bangor* (7th), Edward Henry Harold Ward, *b.* 1905, *s.* 1950.	Hon. William M. D. W., *b.* 1948.
1720 I.★	*Barrington* (11th), Patrick William Daines Barrington (5th *U.K. Baron Shute*, 1880), *b.* 1908, *s.* 1960.	Hon. Rupert E. S. B., D.S.O., *b.* 1877.
1925	*Bearsted* (3rd), Marcus Richard Samuel, T.D., *b.* 1909, *s.* 1948, *m.*	Hon. Peter S., M.C., T.D., *b.* 1911.
1963	*Blakenham* (1st), John Hugh Hare, P.C., O.B.E., *b.* 1911, *m.*	Hon. Michael J. H., *b.* 1938.
1935	*Bledisloe* (2nd), Benjamin Ludlow Bathurst, Q.C., *b.* 1899, *s.* 1958, *m.*	Hon. Christopher H. L. B., *b.* 1934.
1712	*Bolingbroke & St. John* (6th), Vernon Henry St. John, *b.* 1896, *s.* 1899.	Capt. Geoffrey R. St. J., M.C., *b.* 1889.
1960	*Boyd of Merton* (1st), Alan Tindal Lennox-Boyd, P.C., C.H., *b.* 1904, *m.*	Hon. Simon D. R. N. L.-B., *b.* 1939.
1717 I.★	*Boyne* (10th), Gustavus Michael George Hamilton-Russell (4th *U.K. Baron, Brancepeth*, 1866), *b.* 1931, *s.* 1942, *m.*	Hon. Michael G. S. H.-R., *b.* 1965.
1929	*Brentford* (3rd), Lancelot William Joynson-Hicks, *b.* 1902, *s.* 1958, *m.*	Hon. Crispin W. J.-H., *b.* 1933.
1929	*Bridgeman* (2nd), Robert Clive Bridgeman, K.B.E., C.B., D.S.O., M.C., *b.* 1896, *s.* 1935, *m.*	Hon. Geoffrey B., M.C., *b.* 1898.
1868	*Bridport* (4th), Alexander Nelson Hood (7th *Duke of Brontë in Sicily and 6th Irish Baron, Bridport* 1794), *b.* 1948, *s.* 1969.	(None to Viscountcy), to Barony, Lord St. Audries, *b.* 1893 (*See* p. 247).
1952	*Brookeborough* (1st), Basil Stanlake Brooke, K.G., P.C. (N.I.), C.B.E., M.C., *b.* 1888, *w.*	Hon. John W. B., *b.* 1922.
1932	*Buckmaster* (2nd), Owen Stanley Buckmaster, *b.* 1890, *s.* 1934, *m.*	Hon. Martin S. B., *b.* 1921.
1939	*Caldecote* (2nd), Robert Andrew Inskip, D.S.C., *b.* 1917, *s.* 1947, *m.*	Hon. Piers J. H. I., *b.* 1947.
1941	*Camrose* (2nd), (John) Seymour Berry, T.D., *b.* 1909, *s.* 1954.	Lord Hartwell, M.B.E., T.D., *b.* 1911 (*see* p. 251).
1954	*Chandos* (1st), Oliver Lyttelton, K.G., P.C., D.S.O., M.C., *b.* 1893, *m.*	Hon. Antony A. L., *b.* 1920.
1916	*Chaplin* (3rd), Anthony Freskyn Charles Hamby Chaplin, *b.* 1906. *s.* 1949, *m.*	(None.)
1665 I.	*Charlemont* (11th), Charles St. George Caulfeild (15th *Irish Baron, Caulfeild of Charlemont*, 1620), *b.* 1884, *s.* 1967; *m.*	Richard W. St. G. C., *b.* 1887.
1921	*Chelmsford* (3rd), Frederic Jan Thesiger, *b.* 1931, *s.* 1970, *m.*	Hon. Frederic C. P. T., *b.* 1962.
1717 I.	*Chetwynd* (10th), Adam Richard John Casson Chetwynd, T.D., *b.* 1935, *s.* 1965, *m.*	Hon. Adam D. C., *b.* 1969.
1911	*Chilston* (3rd), Eric Alexander Akers-Douglas, *b.* 1910, *s.* 1947, *w.*	Alastair G. A.-D., *b.* 1946.
1902	*Churchill* (2nd), Victor Alexander Spencer, *b.* 1890, *s.* 1934, *w.*	Hon. Victor G. S., *b.* 1934.
1781 I.★	*Clifden* (8th), (Arthur) Victor Agar-Robartes, M.C. (8th *Brit. Baron, Mendip*, 1791), *b.* 1887, *s.* 1966 *m.*	None to Viscountcy; to Barony, Earl of Normanton (*see* p. 232).
1718	*Cobham* (10th), Charles John Lyttelton, K.G., P.C., G.C.M.G. (7th *Irish Baron, Westcote*, 1766), *b.* 1909, *s.* 1949, *m.* (Lord Steward)	Hon. John W. L. L., *b.* 1943.
1902	*Colville of Culross* (4th), John Mark Alexander Colville (13th *Scott. Baron, Colville of Culross*, 1766), *b.* 1933, *s.* 1945, *m.*	Master of Colville, *b.* 1959.
1827	*Combermere* (5th), Michael Wellington Stapleton-Cotton, *b.* 1929, *s.* 1969, *m.*	Hon. Thomas R. W. S.-C., *b.* 1969.
1917	*Cowdray* (3rd), Weetman John Churchill Pearson (3rd *U.K. Baron, Cowdray*, 1910), *b.* 1910, *s.* 1933, *m.*	Hon. Michael P., *b.* 1944.
1927	*Craigavon* (2nd), James Craig, *b.* 1906, *s.* 1940, *m.*	Hon. Janric C., *b.* 1944.
1886	*Cross* (3rd), Assheton Henry Cross, *b.* 1920, *s.* 1932, *m.*	(None.)

Created.	Title, Order of Succession, Name, etc.	Eldest Son or Heir.
1943	Daventry (2nd), Robert Oliver FitzRoy, b. 1893, s. 1962, m.	Cdr. Hon. John M. *FitzRoy-Newdegate*, b. 1897.
1937	Davidson (2nd), John Andrew Davidson, b. 1928, s. 1970, m.	Hon. Malcolm W. M. D., b. 1934.
1956	De L'Isle (1st), William Philip Sidney, ℣℃., K.G., P.C., G.C.M.G., G.C.V.O., (6th Baron De L'Isle and Dudley, 1835), b. 1909, m.	Hon. Philip S., b. 1945.
1776 I.	De Vesci (6th), John Eustace Vesey (7th Irish Baron, Knapton, 1750), b. 1919, s. 1958, m.	Hon. Thomas E. V., b. 1955.
1917	Devonport (2nd), Gerald Chester Kearley, b. 1890, s. 1934, m.	Hon. Terence K., b. 1944.
1964	Dilhorne (1st), Reginald Edward Manningham-Buller, P.C. (Lord of Appeal), b. 1905, m.	Hon. John M., M.-B., b. 1932.
1622 I.	Dillon (20th), Michael Eric Dillon, b. 1911, s. 1946, m.	Hon. Charles D., b. 1945.
1785 I.	Doneraile (9th), Richard St. John St. Leger, b. 1923, s. 1957, m.	Hon. Richard A. St. L., b. 1946.
1680 I.*	Downe (11th), John Christian George Dawnay (4th U.K. Baron, Dawnay, 1897), b. 1935, s. 1965, m.	Hon. Richard D., b. 1967.
1959	Dunrossil (2nd), John William Morrison, b. 1926, s. 1961, m.	Hon. Andrew W. R. M., b. 1953.
1964	Eccles (1st), David McAdam Eccles, P.C., K.C.V.O., b. 1904, m.	Hon. John D. E., b. 1931.
1897	Esher (4th), Lionel Gordon Baliol Brett, C.B.E., b. 1913, s. 1963, m.	Hon. Christopher L. B. B., b. 1936.
1816	Exmouth (10th), Paul Edward Pellew, b. 1940, s. 1970, m.	Hon. Peter I. P., b. 1942.
1620 S.	Falkland (14th), Lucius Henry Plantagenet Cary (Premier Scottish Viscount on the Roll), b. 1905, s. 1961, m.	Master of Falkland, b. 1935.
1720	Falmouth (9th), George Hugh Boscawen (26th Eng. Baron, Le Despencer, 1264), b. 1919, s. 1962, m.	Hon. Evelyn A. H. B., b. 1955.
1918	Furness (2nd), William Anthony Furness, b. 1929, s. 1940.	(None.)
1720 I.*	Gage (6th), Henry Rainald Gage, K.C.V.O. (5th Brit. Baron, Gage, 1790), b. 1895, s. 1912, m.	Hon. George J. St. C. G., b. 1932.
1727 I.*	Galway (10th), William Arundell Monckton (4th U.K. Baron, Monckton, 1887), b. 1894, s. 1971, m.	Edmund S. M., b. 1900.
1478 I.*	Gormanston (17th), Jenico Nicholas Dudley Preston (Premier Viscount of Ireland; 5th U.K. Baron, Gormanston, 1868), b. 1939, s. 1940.	Hon. Robert Shaw-Preston, b. 1915.
1816 I.	Gort (7th), Standish Robert Gage Prendergast Vereker, M.C., b. 1888, s. 1946, m.	Colin L. P. V., b. 1916.
1900	Goschen (3rd), John Alexander Goschen, O.B.E., b. 1906, s. 1952. m.	Hon. Giles J. H. G., b. 1965.
1849	Gough (5th), Shane Hugh Maryon Gough, b. 1941, s. 1951.	(None.)
1937	Greenwood (2nd), David Henry Hamar Greenwood, b. 1914, s. 1948.	Hon. Michael G. H. G., b. 1923.
1946	Hall 2nd), (William George) Leonard Hall, b. 1913, s. 1965, m.	(None.)
1891	Hambleden (4th), William Herbert Smith, b. 1930, s. 1948, m.	Hon. William H. S., b. 1955.
1884	Hampden (5th), David Francis Brand, b. 1902, s. 1965, m.	Hon. Anthony D. B., b. 1937.
1936	Hanworth (2nd), David Bertram Pollock, b. 1916, s. 1936, m.	Hon. David P., b. 1946.
1791 I.	Harberton (9th), Henry Ralph Martyn Pomeroy, b. 1908, s. 1956.	Hon. Thomas De V. P., b. 1910.
1917	Harcourt (2nd), William Edward Harcourt, K.C.M.G., O.B.E., b. 1908, s. 1922, w.	(None.)
1846	Hardinge (4th), Caryl Nicholas Charles Hardinge, M.B.E., b. 1905, s. 1924, m.	Hon. Henry N. H., b. 1929.
1791 I.	Hawarden (8th), Robert Leslie Eustace Maude, b. 1926, s. 1958, m.	Hon. Robert C. W. L., M., b. 1961.
1960	Head (1st), Antony Henry Head, P.C., G.C.M.G., C.B.E., M.C., b. 1906, m.	Hon. Richard A. H., b. 1937.
1550	Hereford (18th), Robert Milo Leicester Devereux (Premier Viscount of England), b. 1932, s. 1952, m.	Rupert M. D., b. 1907.
1842	Hill (7th), Gerald Rowland Clegg-Hill, b. 1904, s. 1957, m.	Hon. Antony R. C-H., b. 1931.
1796	Hood (6th), Samuel Hood, G.C.M.G. (6th Irish Baron, Hood, 1782), b. 1910, s. 1933.	Hon. Alexander L. H., b. 1914.
1956	Ingleby (1st), Martin Raymond Peake, b. 1926, s. 1966, m.	Hon. Richard M. H. P., b. 1953.
1945	Kemsley (2nd), (Geoffrey) Lionel Berry, b. 1909, s. 1968, m.	Hon. Denis G. B. T.D., b. 1911.
1911	Knollys (3rd), David Francis Dudley Knollys, b. 1931, s. 1966, m.	Hon. Patrick N. M. K., b. 1962.
1895	Knutsford (4th), Thurstan Holland-Hibbert, b. 1888, s. 1935, w.	Hon. Julian H.-H., b. 1920.
1945	Lambert (2nd), George Lambert, T.D., b. 1909, s. 1958, m.	Hon. Michael J. L., b. 1912.
1954	Leathers (2nd), Frederick Alan Leathers, b. 1908, s. 1965, m.	Hon. Christopher G. L., b. 1941.
1922	Leverhulme (3rd), Philip William Bryce Lever, T.D., b. 1915, s. 1949, m.	(None.) [1949.
1781 I.	Lifford (8th), Alan William Wingfield Hewitt, b. 1900, s. 1954, m.	Hon. Edward J. W. H., b.
1921	Long (4th), Richard Gerard Long, b. 1929, s. 1967, m.	Hon James R. L., b. 1960.
1957	Mackintosh of Halifax (2nd), John Mackintosh, b. 1921, s. 1964, m.	Hon. John C. M., b. 1958.

Created.	Title, Order of Succession, Name, &c.	Eldest Son or Heir.
1955	Malvern (2nd), John Godfrey Huggins, b. 1922, s. 1971, m.	Hon. Ashley K. G. H., b. 1949.
1945	Marchwood (2nd) Peter George Penny, M.B.E., b. 1912, s. 1955, m.	Hon. David G. S. P., b. 1936.
1942	Margesson (2nd) Francis Vere Hampden Margesson, b. 1922, s. 1965, m.	Hon. Richard F. D. M., b. 1960.
1660 I.*	Massereene (13th) & (6th) Ferrard (1797), John Clotworthy Talbot Foster Whyte-Melville Skeffington (6th U.K. Baron, Oriel, 1821), b. 1914, s. 1956, m.	Hon. John D. C. W. M. S., b. 1940.
1939	Maugham (2nd), Robert Cecil Romer Maugham, b. 1916, s. 1958.	(None.)
1802	Melville (9th), Robert David Ross Dundas, b. 1937, s. 1971.	
1916	Mersey (3rd), Edward Clive Bigham, b. 1906, s. 1956, m.	Master of Nairne, b. 1934.
1962	Mills (2nd), Roger Clinton Mills, b. 1919, s. 1968, m.	Hon. Christopher P.R. M b. 1956.
1716 I.	Molesworth (11th), Richard Gosset Molesworth, b. 1907, s. 1961, m.	Hon. Robert B. K. M., b. 1959.
1801 I.*	Monck (6th), Henry Wyndham Stanley Monck, O.B.E., (3rd U.K. Baron, Monck, 1866), b. 1905, s. 1927, m.	Hon. Charles S. M., b. 1953.
1957	Monckton of Brenchley (2nd), Gilbert Walter Riversdale Monckton, C.B., O.B.E., M.C., b. 1915, s. 1965, m.	Hon. Christopher W. M., b. 1952.
1935	Monsell (2nd), Henry Bolton Graham Eyres-Monsell, b. 1905, s. 1969.	(None.)
1946	Montgomery of Alamein (1st), Bernard Law Montgomery, K.G., G.C.B., D.S.O., Field Marshal, b. 1887, w.	Hon. David M., b. 1928.
1550 I.*	Mountgarret (17th), Richard Henry Piers Butler (4th U.K. Baron, Mountgarret, 1911), b. 1936, s. 1966, m.	Hon. Piers J. R. B., b. 1961.
1964	Muirshiel (1st), John Scott Maclay, P.C., C.H., C.M.G., b. 1905, m.	(None.)
1952	Norwich (2nd), John Julius Cooper, b. 1929, s. 1954, m.	Hon. Jason C. D. B. C., b. 1959.
1873	Portman (9th), Edward Henry Berkeley Portman, b. 1934, s. 1967, m.	Hon. Christopher E. B. P., b. 1958.
1743 I.*	Powerscourt (9th) Mervyn Patrick Wingfield, (3rd U.K. Baron, Powerscourt, 1885), b. 1905, s. 1947, m.	Hon. Mervyn W., b. 1935.
1962	Radcliffe (1st), Cyril John Radcliffe, P.C., G.B.E., b. 1899, m. (Lord of Appeal, retired).	(None.)
1900	Ridley (4th), Matthew White Ridley, T.D., b. 1925, s. 1964, m.	Hon. Matthew W. R. b. 1958.
1960	Rochdale (1st), John Durival Kemp, O.B.E., T.D. (2nd U.K. Baron, Rochdale, 1913), b. 1906, s. 1945, m.	Hon. St. John K., b. 1938.
1919	Rothermere (2nd), Esmond Cecil Harmsworth, b. 1898, s. 1940, m.	Hon. Vere H., b. 1925.
1937	Runciman of Doxford (2nd), Walter Leslie Runciman, O.B.E., A.F.C. (3rd, U.K. Baron, Runciman, 1933), b. 1900, s. 1949, m.	Hon. Walter G. R., b. 1934.
1918	St. Davids (2nd), Jestyn Reginald Austen Plantagenet Philipps, b. 1917, s. 1938, m.	Hon. Colwyn P., b. 1939.
1801	St.Vincent (7th), Ronald George James Jervis, b. 1905, s. 1940, m.	Hon. Edward R. J. J., b. 1951.
1937	Samuel (2nd), Edwin Herbert Samuel, C.M.G., b. 1898, s. 1963, m.	Hon. David H. S., b. 1922.
1911	Scarsdale (2nd), Richard Nathaniel Curzon, T.D. (6th Brit. Baron, Scarsdale, 1761), b. 1898, s. 1925, m.	Francis J. N. C., b. 1924. [1945.
1905	Selby (4th), Michael Guy John Gully, b. 1942, s. 1959, m.	Hon. James E. H. G. G., b.
1805	Sidmouth (6th), Raymond Anthony Addington, b. 1887, s. 1953, m.	Hon. John T. A., b. 1914.
1940	Simon (2nd), John Gilbert Simon, C.M.G., b. 1902, s. 1954, m.	Hon. Jan D. S., b. 1940.
1960	Slim (2nd), John Douglas Slim, b. 1927, s. 1970, m.	Hon. Mark W. R. S., b. 1960.
1954	Soulbury (2nd), James Herwald Ramsbotham, b. 1915, s. 1971, w.	Hon. Peter E. R., C.M.G., b. 1919.
1776 I.	Southwell (7th), Pyers Anthony Joseph Southwell, b. 1930, s. 1960, m.	Hon. Richard A. P. S., b. 1956.
1938	Stonehaven (2nd), (James) Ian Baird, b. 1908, s. 1941, m.	Hon. Michael B., b. 1939.
1959	Stuart of Findhorn (2nd), David Randolph Moray Stuart, b. 1924, s. 1971, m.	Hon. James D. S., b. 1948.
1806 I.	Templetown (5th), Henry Augustus George Mountjoy Heneage Upton, b. 1894, s. 1939, m.	Hon. Henry U., b. 1917.
1957	Tenby (2nd), David Lloyd George, b. 1922, s. 1967.	Hon. William L. G., b. 1927.
1952	Thurso (2nd), Robin Macdonald Sinclair, b. 1922, s. 1970, m.	Hon. John A. S., b. 1953.
1721	Torrington (11th), Timothy Howard St. George Byng, b. 1943, s. 1961.	John L. B., M.C., b. 1919.
1936	Trenchard (2nd), Thomas Trenchard, M.C., b. 1923, s. 1956, m.	Hon. Hugh T., b. 1951.
1921	Ullswater (2nd), Nicholas James Christopher Lowther, b. 1942, s. 1949.	
1621 I.	Valentia (14th), Francis Dighton Annesley, M.C., b. 1888, s. 1951 (claim established, 1959), m.	Hon. Richard J. D. A., b. 1929.

Created.	Title, Order of Succession, Name, etc.	Eldest Son or Heir.
1960	Ward of Witley (1st), George Reginald Ward, P.C., b. 1907, m.	Hon. Anthony G. H. W., b. 1943.
1964	Watkinson (1st), Harold Arthur Watkinson, P.C., C.H., b. 1910, m.	(None.)
1952	*Waverley (2nd), David Alastair Pearson Anderson, b. 1911, s. 1958, m.	Hon. John D. F. A., b. 1949.
1938	Weir (2nd), (James) Kenneth Weir, C.B.E., b. 1905, s. 1959, m.	Hon. William K. J. W., b. 1933.
1918	Wimborne (3rd), Ivor Fox-Strangways Guest (4th U.K. Baron, Wimborne, 1880), b. 1939, s. 1967, m.	Hon. Ivor M. V.G., b. 1968.
1923	Younger of Leckie (3rd), Edward George Younger, O.B.E., T.D., b. 1906, s. 1946, m.	Hon. George Y., M.P. b. 1931.

BISHOPS

Style, The Right Rev. the Lord Bishop of ——. *Addressed as,* My Lord.
[Those marked * always sit; of the others, except †Sodor and Man, 21 sit by date, those awaiting admission in order shown (in parentheses)].

Apptd.
Entd. Lords

1961	*London (114th), Robert Wright Stopford, P.C., C.B.E., D.D., b. 1901, cons. 1955, trans. 1956 and 1961, m.	1961
1966	*Durham (90th), Ian Thomas Ramsey, D.D., b. 1915, cons. 1966, m.	1966
1961	*Winchester (93rd), Sherard Falkner Allison, D.D., b. 1907, cons. 1951, trans. 1961, m.	1958
1960	Bath & Wells (73rd), Edward Barry Henderson, D.S.C., D.D., b. 1910, cons. 1955, m.	1969
1969	Birmingham (5th), Laurence Ambrose Brown, M.A., b. 1907, cons. 1960, m.	(7)
1960	Blackburn (4th), Charles Robert Claxton, D.D., b. 1903, cons. 1946, m.	1967
	Bradford (vacant)	
1958	Bristol (52nd), Oliver Stratford Tomkins, D.D., b. 1908, cons. 1959, m.	1963
1967	Carlisle (63rd), Sydney Cyril Bulley, M.A., b. 1907, cons. 1959	(4)
1971	Chelmsford (6th), Albert John Trillo, M.Th., B.D., A.K.C., b. 1915, cons. 1963, m.	(14)
1955	Chester (37th), Gerald Alexander Ellison, D.D., b. 1910, cons. 1950, m.	1960
1958	Chichester (98th), Roger Plumpton Wilson, D.D., b. 1905, cons. 1949, trans. 1958, m.	1955
1956	Coventry (5th), Cuthbert Killick Norman Bardsley, C.B.E., D.D., b. 1907, cons. 1947	1962
1969	Derby (4th), Cyril William Johnston Bowles, M.A., b. 1916, cons. 1969, m.	(6)
1964	Ely (65th), Edward James Keymer Roberts, D.D., b. 1908, cons. 1956, trans. 1962 and 1964, m.	(1)
1949	Exeter (67th), Robert Cecil Mortimer, D.D., b. 1902, cons. 1949, m.	1955
1962	Gloucester (36th), Basil Tudor Guy, M.A., b. 1910, cons. 1957, m.	1971
1961	Guildford (5th), George Edmund Reindorp, D.D., b. 1911, cons. 1961, m.	1969
1961	Hereford (102nd), Mark Allin Hodson, B.A., b. 1907, cons. 1956, m.	1970
1953	Leicester (3rd), Ronald Ralph Williams, D.D., b. 1906, cons. 1953, m.	1959
1953	Lichfield (95th), Arthur Stretton Reeve, D.D., b. 1907, cons. 1953, m.	1959
1956	Lincoln (68th), Kenneth Riches, D.D., b. 1908, cons. 1952, m.	1962
1966	Liverpool (5th) Stuart Yarworth Blanch, M.A., b. 1918, cons. 1966, m.	(2)
1970	Manchester (8th), Patrick Campbell Rodger, M.A., b. 1920, cons. 1970, m.	(9)
1957	Newcastle (8th), Hugh Edward Ashdown, D.D., b. 1904, cons. 1957, m.	1962
1971	Norwich (69th), Maurice Arthur Ponsonby Wood, M.A., cons. 1971, m.	(15)
1971	Oxford (39th), Kenneth John Woollcombe, M.A., b. 1924, cons. 1971	(11)
1961	Peterborough (34th), Cyril Eastaugh, M.C., M.A., b. 1897, cons. 1949, m.	1970
1960	Portsmouth (5th), John Henry Lawrence Phillips, D.D., b. 1910, cons. 1960, m.	1966
1959	Ripon (9th), John Richard Humpidge Moorman, D.D., b. 1905, cons. 1959, m.	1964
1961	Rochester (104th), Richard David Say, D.D., b. 1914, cons. 1961, m.	1969
1970	St. Albans (7th), Robert Alexander Kennedy Runcie, M.C., M.A., b. 1921, cons. 1970, m.	(8)
1966	St. Edmundsbury & Ipswich (6th), Leslie Wilfrid Brown, D.D., b. 1912, cons. 1953, m.	(3)
1963	Salisbury (74th), Joseph Edward Fison, D.D., b. 1906, cons. 1963, m.	1971
1971	Sheffield (4th), William Gordon Fallows, M.A., b. 1913, cons. 1968, m.	(13)
1966	†Sodor & Man (76th), George Eric Gordon, M.A., b. 1905, cons. 1966, w.	
1959	Southwark (6th), Arthur Mervyn Stockwood, D.D., b. 1913, cons. 1959	1963
1970	Southwell (7th), John Denis Wakeling, M.C., M.A., b. 1918, cons. 1970, m.	(10)
1959	Truro (10th), John Maurice Key, D.D., b. 1905, cons. 1947, m.	1965
1968	Wakefield (8th), Eric Treacy, M.B.E., b. 1907, cons. 1961, m.	(5)
1971	Worcester (110th), Robert Wylmer Woods, K.C.V.O., M.A., b. 1914, cons. 1971, m.	(12)

BARONS

Style (see note, p. 258) The Right Hon. the Lord ——.
Addressed as, My Lord.

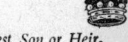

Created.	Title, Order of Succession, Name, etc.	Eldest Son or Heir.
1911	Aberconway (3rd), Charles Melville McLaren, b. 1913, s. 1953.	Hon. Henry C. McL., b. 1948.
1873	Aberdare (4th), Morys George Lyndhurst Bruce, b. 1919, s. 1957, m.	Hon. Alastair J. L. B., b. 1947.

H*

Created.	Title, Order of Succession, Name, etc.	Eldest Son or Heir.
1835	*Abinger* (8th), James Richard Scarlett, b. 1914, s. 1943, m.	Hon. James H. S., b. 1959.
1869	*Acton* (3rd), John Emerich Henry Lyon-Dalberg-Acton, C.M.G., M.B.E., b. 1907, s. 1924, m.	Hon. Richard L.-D.-A., b. 1941.
1887	*Addington* (4th), Raymond Egerton Hubbard, b. 1884, s. 1966, w.	James H., b. 1930.
1955	*Adrian* (1st), Edgar Douglas Adrian, O.M., M.D., F.R.S., b. 1889, w.	Hon. Richard H. A., b.1927.
1921	*Ailwyn* (3rd), Eric William Edward Fellowes, C.B.E., b. 1887, s. 1936, m.	Hon. Carol A. F., T.D., b. 1896.
1907	*Airedale* (4th) Oliver James Vandeleur Kitson, b. 1915, s. 1958.	(None.)
1896	*Aldenham* (5th), and (3rd) *Hunsdon of Hunsdon* (1923), Antony Durant Gibbs, b. 1922, s. 1969, m.	Hon. Vicary T. G., b. 1948
1962	*Aldington* (1st), Toby Austin Richard William Low, P.C., K.C.M.G., C.B.E., D.S.O., T.D., b. 1914, m.	Hon. Charles H. S. L., b. 1948.
1902	*Allerton* (3rd), George William Lawies Jackson, b. 1903, s. 1925. m.	Hon. Edward L. J.,b. 1928.
1929	*Alvingham* (2nd), Robert Guy Eardley Yerburgh, b. 1926, s. 1955, m.	Hon. Robert R. G. Y., b. 1956.
1892	*Amherst of Hackney* (3rd), William Alexander Evering Cecil, C.B.E., b. 1912, s. 1919, m.	Hon. William C., b. 1940.
1881	*Ampthill* (3rd), John Hugo Russell, C.B.E., b. 1896, s. 1935, m.	Hon. Geoffrey R., b. 1921.
1929	*Amulree* (2nd), Basil William Sholto Mackenzie, M.D.,b.1900, s. 1942	(None.)
1947	*Amwell* (2nd), Frederick Norman Montague, b. 1912, s. 1966, m.	Hon. Keith N. M., b. 1943.
1863	*Annaly* (5th), Luke Robert White, b. 1927, s. 1970.	Hon. Luke R. W., b. 1954.
1949	*Archibald* (1st), George Archibald, C.B.E. b. 1898, m.	Hon. George Christopher A., b. 1926.
1903	*Armstrong* (2nd), William John Montagu Watson-Armstrong, b. 1892, s. 1941, m.	Hon. William H. C. J. R. W.-A., b. 1919.
1885	*Ashbourne* (3rd), Edward Russell Gibson, C.B., D.S.O., b. 1901, s. 1942, m	Hon. Edward B. G. G., b. 1933.
1835	*Ashburton* (6th), Alexander Francis St. Vincent Baring, K.G., K.C.V.O., b. 1898, s. 1938, m.	Hon. John F. H. B., b. 1928.
1892	*Ashcombe* (4th), Henry Edward Cubitt, b. 1924, s. 1962.	Maj. Hon. Archibald E. C., b. 1901.
1911	*Ashton of Hyde* (2nd), Thomas Henry Raymond Ashton, b. 1901, s. 1933, m.	Hon. Thomas J. A., b. 1926.
1800 I.	*Ashtown* (5th), Dudley Oliver Trench, O.B.E., b. 1901, s. 1966, w.	Christopher O. T., b. 1931.
1956	*Astor of Hever* (2nd), Gavin Astor, b. 1918, s. 1971, m.	Hon. John J. A., b. 1946.
1789 I. } 1793* }	*Auckland* (9th), Ian George Eden (9th *Brit. Baron, Auckland*), b. 1926, s. 1957, m.	Hon. Robert I. B. E., b. 1962.
1900	*Avebury* (4th), Eric Reginald Lubbock, b. 1928, s. 1971. m.	Hon. Lyulph A. J. L., b. 1954.
1718 I.	*Aylmer* (9th), John Frederick Whitworth Aylmer, b. 1880, s. 1923, m.	Hon. Kenneth A. A., b. 1883.
1929	*Baden-Powell* (3rd), Robert Crause Baden-Powell, b. 1936, s. 1962, m.	Hon. David M. B.-P., b. 1940.
1780	*Bagot* (7th), Harry Eric Bagot, b. 1894, s. 1961, w.	Reginald W. B., b. 1897.
1953	*Baillieu* (2nd), William Latham Baillieu, b. 1915, s. 1967, m.	Hon. James W. L. B., b. 1950.
1607 S.	*Balfour of Burleigh* (8th), Robert Bruce, b. 1927, s. 1967.	Master of Burleigh, b. 1930.
1945	*Balfour of Inchrye* (1st), Harold Harington Balfour, P.C., M.C., b. 1897, m.	Hon. Ian B., b. 1924.
1924	*Banbury of Southam* (2nd), Charles William Banbury, b. 1915, s. 1936.	Hon. Charles W. B., b. 1953.
1698	*Barnard* (11th), Harry John Neville Vane, T.D., b. 1923, s. 1964, m.	Hon. Henry F. C. V., b. 1959.
1922	*Barnby* (2nd), Francis Vernon Willey, C.M.G., C.B.E., M.V.O., T.D., b. 1884, s. 1929, m.	(None.)
1887	*Basing* (4th), George Lutley Sclater-Booth, T.D., b. 1903, s. 1969, m.	Hon. Neil L. S.-B., b. 1939
1647 S.	*Belhaven & Stenton* (13th), Robert Anthony Carmichael Hamilton, b. 1927, s. 1961, m.	Master of Belhaven, b. 1953.
1848 I.	*Bellew* (5th), Edward Henry Bellew, M.B.E., b. 1889, s. 1935, w.	Hon. Bryan B., M.C., b.1890.
1856	*Belper* (4th), (Alexander) Ronald George Strutt, b. 1912, s. 1956.	Hon. Richard H. S., b. 1941.
1938	*Belstead* (2nd), John Julian Ganzoni, b. 1932, s. 1958.	(None.)
1922	*Bethell* (4th), Nicholas William Bethell, b. 1938, s. 1967.	Hon. James N. B., b. 1967.
1938	*Bicester* (3rd), Angus Edward Vivian Smith, b. 1932, s. 1968.	Hugh C. V. S., b. 1934.
1903	*Biddulph* (3rd), Michael William John Biddulph, b. 1898, s. 1949, m.	Hon. Robert M. C. B., b. 1931.
1938	*Birdwood* (3rd), Mark William Ogilvie Birdwood, b. 1938, s. 1962, m.	(None).
1958	*Birkett* (2nd), Michael Birkett, b. 1929, s. 1962, m.	(None.)
1935	*Blackford* (2nd), Glyn Keith Murray Mason, C.B.E., D.S.O., b. 1887, s. 1947, m.	Hon. Keith M., D.F.C., b. 1923.

Created	Title, Order of Succession, Name, etc.	Eldest Son or Heir.
1907	Blyth (3rd), Ian Audley James Blyth, b. 1905, s. 1943, m.	Hon. Anthony B., b. 1931.
1797	Bolton (7th), Richard William Algar Orde-Powlett, b. 1929, s. 1963, m.	Hon. Harry A. N. O.-P., b. 1954.
1922	Borwick (4th), James Hugh Myles Borwick, M.C., b. 1917, s. 1961, m.	Hon. George S. B., b. 1922.
1761	Boston (8th), Cecil Eustace Irby, M.C., b. 1897, s. 1958.	Gerald H. B. I., M.B.E., b. 1897.
1942	Brabazon of Tara (2nd), Derek Charles Moore-Brabazon, C.B.E., b. 1910, s. 1964, m.	Hon. Ivon A. M.-B., b. 1946.
1880	Brabourne (7th), John Ulick Knatchbull, b. 1924, s. 1943, m.	Hon. Norton K., b. 1947.
1925	Bradbury (2nd), John Bradbury, b. 1914, s. 1950, m.	Hon. John B., b. 1940.
1962	Brain (2nd), Christopher Langdon Brain, b. 1926, s. 1966, m.	Hon. Michael C. B., D.M., b. 1928.
1938	Brassey of Apethorpe (3rd), David Henry Brassey, T.D., b. 1932, s. 1967, m.	Hon. Edward B., b. 1964.
1788	Braybrooke (9th), Henry Seymour Neville, b. 1897, s. 1943, m.	Hon. Robin N., b. 1932.
1529	Braye (7th), Thomas Adrian Verney-Cave, b. 1902, s. 1952, m.	Hon. Penelope M. V.-C., b. 1941.
1958	Brecon (1st), David Vivian Penrose Lewis, P.C., b. 1905, m.	(None.)
1957	Bridges (2nd), Thomas Edward Bridges, b. 1927, s. 1969, m.	Hon. Mark T. B., b. 1954.
1945	Broadbridge (2nd), Eric Wilberforce Broadbridge, b. 1895, s. 1952, w.	Hon. Peter H. B., b. 1938.
1933	Brocket (3rd), Charles Ronald George Nall-Cain, b. 1952, s. 1967, M.	Richard P. C. N.-C., b. 1953.
1860	Brougham and Vaux (5th), Michael John Brougham, b. 1938, s. 1967.	Hon. David B., b. 1940.
1945	Broughshane (2nd), Patrick Owen Alexander Davison, b. 1903, s. 1953, m.	Hon. Alexander D., b. 1936.
1776	Brownlow (6th), Peregrine Francis Adelbert Cust, b. 1899, s. 1927, m.	Hon. Edward C., b. 1936.
1942	Bruntisfield (1st), Victor Alexander George Anthony Warrender, M.C., b. 1899, m.	Hon. John R. W., M.C., b. 1921.
1950	Burden (2nd), Philip William Burden, b. 1916, s. 1970, m.	Hon. Andrew P. B., b. 1959.
1529	Burgh (7th), Alexander Peter Willoughby Leith, b. 1935, s. 1959, m.	Hon. Alexander G. D. L., b. 1958.
1903	Burnham (5th), William Edward Harry Lawson, b. 1920, s. 1963, m.	Hon. Hugh J. F. L., b. 1931.
1897	Burton (3rd), Michael Evan Victor Baillie, b. 1924, s. 1962, m.	Hon. Evan B., b. 1949.
1643	Byron (11th), Rupert Frederick George Byron, b. 1903, s. 1949, m.	Richard G. G. B., D.S.O., b. 1899.
1937	Cadman (3rd), John Anthony Cadman, b. 1938, s. 1966.	Hon. James R. C., b. 1944.
1796	Calthorpe (10th), Peter Waldo Somerset Gough-Calthorpe, b. 1927, s. 1945, m.	(None.)
1945	Calverley (3rd), Charles Rodney Muff, b. 1946, s. 1971.	Hon. Peter R. M., b. 1953.
1383	Camoys (6th), (Ralph Robert Watts) Sherman Stonor, b. 1913, s. 1968, m.	Hon. Ralph T. C. G. S., b. 1940.
1715 I.	Carbery (10th), John Evans Carberry, b. 1892, s. 1898, m.	Peter R. H. Evans-Freke, b. 1920.
1834 I. 1838 * }	Carew (6th), William Francis Conolly-Carew, C.B.E. (6th U.K. Baron, Carew, 1838), b. 1905, s. 1927, m.	Hon. Patrick Thomas C.-C., b. 1938.
1916	Carnock (3rd), Erskine Arthur Nicolson, D.S.O., b. 1884, s. 1952, w.	Hon. David H. A. N., b. 1920.
1796 I. 1797 * }	Carrington (6th), Peter Alexander Rupert Carington, P.C., K.C.M.G., M.C. (6th Brit. Baron, Carrington, 1797), b. 1919, s. 1938, m.	Hon. Rupert F. J. C., b. 1948.
1812 I.	Castlemaine (7th), John Michael Schomberg Staveley Handcock, b. 1904, s. 1954, m.	Hon. Roland T. J. H., b. 1943.
1936	Catto (2nd), Stephen Gordon Catto, b. 1923, s. 1959, m.	Hon. Innes G. C., b. 1950.
1918	Cawley (3rd), Frederick Lee Cawley, b. 1913, s. 1954, m.	Hon. John F. C., b. 1946.
1937	Chatfield (2nd), Ernle David Lewis Chatfield, b. 1917, s. 1967, m.	
1858	Chesham (5th), John Charles Compton Cavendish, P.C., b. 1916, s. 1952, m.	Hon. Nicholas C., b. 1941.
1945	Chetwode (2nd), Philip Chetwode, b. 1937, s. 1950, m.	Hon. Roger C., b. 1968.
1887	Cheylesmore (4th), Francis Ormond Henry Eaton, D.S.O., b. 1893, s. 1925, m.	(None.)
1945	Chorley (1st), Robert Samuel Theodore Chorley, Q.C., b. 1895, m.	Hon. Roger C., b. 1930.
1858	Churston (4th), Richard Francis Roger Yarde-Buller, V.R.D., b. 1910, s. 1930, m.	Hon. John Y.-B., b. 1934.
1946	Citrine (1st), Walter McLennan Citrine, P.C., G.B.E., b. 1887, m.	Hon. Norman C., b. 1914.
1800 I.	Clanmorris (7th), John Michael Ward Bingham, b. 1908, s. 1960, m.	Hon. Simon J. W. B., b. 1937.
1672	Clifford of Chudleigh (13th), Lewis Hugh Clifford, O.B.E., b. 1916, s. 1964, m.	Hon. Thomas H. C., b. 1948.
1299	Clinton (22nd), Gerard Neville Mark Fane Trefusis, b. 1934, title called out of abeyance 1965, m.	Hon. Charles P. R. F. T., b. 1962.
1955	Clitheroe (1st), Ralph Assheton, P.C., b. 1901, m.	Hon. Ralph J. A., b. 1929
1919	Clwyd (2nd), (John) Trevor Roberts, b. 1900, s. 1955, m.	Hon. John A. R., b. 1935

Created.	Title, Order of Succession, Name, etc.	Eldest Son or Heir.
1947	Clydesmuir (2nd) Ronald John Bilsland Colville, C.B., M.B.E., T.D., b. 1917, s. 1954, m.	Hon. David R. C., b. 1949.
1960	Cobbold (1st), Cameron Fromanteel Cobbold, K.G., P.C., G.C.V.O., b. 1904, m.	Hon. David A. F. C., b. 1937.
1919	Cochrane of Cults (3rd), Thomas Charles Anthony Cochrane, b. 1922, s. 1968.	Hon. R. H. Vere, C. b. 1926.
1951	Cohen, Lionel Leonard Cohen, P.C., b. 1888, w. (Lord of Appeal, retired).	(Law Life Peerage.)
1956	Cohen of Birkenhead (1st), Henry Cohen, M.D., D.SC., Ll.D., F.R.C.P., F.S.A., b. 1900.	(None.)
1954	Coleraine (1st), Richard Kidston Law, P.C. b. 1901, m.	Hon. James M.B. L., b.1931.
1873	Coleridge (4th), Richard Duke Coleridge, K.B.E., b. 1905, s. 1955, m.	Hon. William D. C., b. 1937.
1946	Colgrain (2nd), Donald Swinton Campbell, M.C., b. 1891. s. 1954, m.	Hon. David C., b. 1920.
1917	Colwyn (3rd), (Ian) Anthony Hamilton Smith, b. 1942, s. 1966, m.	Hon. Craig, P. S., b. 1968.
1956	Colyton (1st), Henry Lennox D'Aubigne Hopkinson, P.C., C.M.G., b. 1902, m.	Hon. Nicholas H. E. H., b. 1932.
1955	Conesford (1st), Henry George Strauss, Q.C., b. 1892, w.	(None.)
1841	Congleton (8th), Christopher Patrick Parnell, b. 1930, s. 1967, m.	Hon. John P. C. P., b. 1959
1927	Cornwallis (2nd), Wykeham Stanley Cornwallis, K.C.V.O., K.B.E., M.C., b. 1892, s. 1935, w.	Hon. Fiennes C., b. 1921
1874	Cottesloe (4th), John Walgrave Halford Fremantle, G.B.E., T.D., b. 1900, s. 1956, m.	Hon. John T. F., b. 1927.
1914	Cozens-Hardy (4th), Herbert Arthur Cozens-Hardy, O.B.E., b. 1907, s. 1956.	(None.)
1920	Craigmyle (3rd), Thomas Donald Mackay Shaw, b. 1923, s. 1944, m.	Hon. Thomas C. S., b. 1960.
1899	Cranworth (3rd), Philip Bertram Gurdon, b. 1940, s. 1964, m.	Son, b. 1970.
1959	Crathorne (1st), Thomas Lionel Dugdale, P.C., T.D., b. 1897, w.	Hon. Charles J. D., b. 1939.
1892	Crawshaw (4th), William Michael Clifton Brooks, b. 1933, s. 1946.	Hon. David B., b. 1934.
1940	Croft (2nd), Michael Henry Glendower Page Croft, b. 1916, s. 1947, m.	Hon. Bernard W. H. P. C. b. 1949.
1797 I.	Crofton (5th), Edward Blaise Crofton, b. 1926, s. 1942, w.	Hon.Charles E.P.C., b.1949.
1375	Cromwell (6th), David Godfrey Bewicke-Copley, b. 1929, s. 1966, m.	Hon. Godfrey J. B.-C., b. 1960.
1947	Crook (1st), Reginald Douglas Crook, b. 1901, m.	Hon. Douglas C., b. 1925.
1971	Cross of Chelsea, (Arthur) Geoffrey (Neale) Cross, P.C., b. 1904, m. (Lord of Appeal).	(Law Life Peerage.)
1920	Cullen of Ashbourne (2nd), Charles Borlase Marsham Cokayne, M.B.E., b. 1912, s. 1932, m.	Hon. Edmund C. b. 1916.
1914	Cunliffe (3rd), Roger Cunliffe, b. 1932, s. 1963, m.	Hon. Henry C., b. 1962.
1927	Daresbury (2nd), Edward Greenall, b. 1902, s. 1933, w.	Hon. Edward G. G., b. 1928.
1924	Darling (2nd), Robert Charles Henry Darling, b. 1919, s. 1936, m.	Hon. Robert D., b. 1944.
1946	Darwen (2nd), Cedric Percival Davies, b. 1915, s. 1950, m.	Hon. Roger M. D., b. 1933.
1923	Daryngton (2nd), Jocelyn Arthur Pike Pease, b. 1908, s. 1949.	(None.)
1932	Davies (3rd), David Davies, b. 1940, s. 1944.	Hon.Jonathan H. D., b. 1944.
1812 I.	Decies (6th), Arthur George Marcus Douglas de la Poer Beresford, b. 1915, s. 1944, m.	Hon. Marcus de la P.B., b. 1948.
1299	De Clifford (26th), Edward Southwell Russell, O.B.E., E.D., b. 1907 s. 1909.	Hon. John R., b. 1928.
1851	De Freyne (7th), Francis Arthur John French, b. 1927. s. 1935, m.	Hon. Fulke C. J. A. F., b. 1957.
1821	Delamere (4th), Thomas Pitt Hamilton Cholmondeley, b. 1900, s. 1931, m.	Hon. Hugh G. C., b. 1934.
1700	De Longueuil (10th) (Peerage of Canada), Ronald Charles Grant, b. 1888, s. 1938, m.	Hon. Raoul G., b. 1919.
1838	De Mauley (6th), Gerald John Ponsonby, b. 1921, s. 1962, m.	Hon. Thomas M. P., b. 1930.
1937	Denham (2nd), Bertram Stanley Mitford Bowyer, b. 1927, s. 1948, m.	Hon. Richard G. B., b. 1959.
1834	Denman (5th), Charles Spencer Denman, M.C., b. 1916, s. 1971, m.	Hon. Richard T. S. D., b. 1946.
1957	Denning, Alfred Thompson Denning, P.C., b. 1899, m. (Master of the Rolls).	(Law Life Peerage.)
1885	Deramore (6th), Richard Arthur de Yarburgh-Bateson, b. 1911, s. 1964, m.	(None.)
1887	De Ramsey (3rd), Ailwyn Edward Fellowes, T.D., b. 1910, s. 1925, m.	Hon. John A. F., b. 1942.
1881	Derwent (4th), Patrick Robin Gilbert Vanden-Bempde-Johnstone, b. 1901, s. 1949, m.	Hon. Robin V.-B.-J., b. 1930.
1831	De Saumarez (6th), James Victor Broke Saumarez, b. 1924, s. 1969, m.	Hon. Eric D. S., b. 1956.
1910	De Villiers (3rd), Arthur Percy De Villiers, b. 1911, s. 1934, m.	Hon. Alexander C. de V., b. 1940.
1961	Devlin, Patrick Arthur Devlin, P.C., F.B.A., b. 1905, m. (Lord of Appeal, retired).	(Law Life Peerage.)
1930	Dickinson (2nd), Richard Clavering Hyett Dickinson, b. 1926, s. 1943, m.	Hon. Martin H. D., b. 1961.

Created.	Title, Order of Succession, Name, etc.	Eldest Son or Heir.
1620 I. } 1765* }	Digby (12th), Edward Henry Kenelm Digby, (6th *Brit. Baron, Digby*), b. 1924, s. 1964, m.	Hon. Henry N. K. D., b. 1954.
1968	Diplock, (William John) Kenneth Diplock, P.C., b. 1907, m. (Lord of Appeal).	(Law Life Peerage).
1964	Donovan, Terence Norbert Donovan, P.C., b. 1898, m. (Lord of Appeal).	(Law Life Peerage.)
1615	Dormer (15th), Charles Walter James Dormer, b. 1903, s. 1922, m.	Hon. Joseph D., b. 1914.
1950	Douglas of Barloch (1st), Francis Campbell Ross Douglas, K.C.M.G., b. 1889, m.	(None.)
1943	Dowding (2nd), Derek Hugh Tremenheere Dowding, b. 1919, s. 1970, m.	Hon. Piers H. T. D., b. 1948.
1963	Drumalbyn (1st), Niall Malcolm Stewart Macpherson, P.C., b. 1908, m.	(None.)
1439	Dudley (13th), Ferdinando Dudley Henry Lea Smith, b. 1910, s. 1936	Hon. Mrs. Guy Wallace, b. 1907.
1929	Dulverton (2nd), (Frederick) Anthony Hamilton Wills, T.D., b. 1915, s. 1956, m.	Hon. Gilbert M. H. W., b. 1944.
1800 I.	Dunalley (6th), Henry Desmond Graham Prittie, b. 1912, s. 1948, m.	Hon. Henry P., b. 1948.
1324 I.	Dunboyne (28th), Patrick Theobald Tower Butler, b. 1917, s. 1945, m.	Hon. John F. B., b. 1951.
1802	Dunleath (4th), Charles Edward Henry John Mulholland, T.D., b. 1933, s. 1956, m.	Sir Michael H. M., Bt., b. 1915.
1439 I.	Dunsany (19th), Randal Arthur Henry Plunkett, b. 1906, s. 1957, m.	Hon. Edward P., b. 1939.
1780	Dynevor (9th), Richard Charles Uryan Rhys, b. 1935, s. 1962, m.	Hon. Hugo G. U. R., b.1966.
1928	Ebbisham (2nd) Rowland Roberts Blades, T.D., b. 1912, s. 1953, m.	(None.)
1857	Ebury (6th), Francis Egerton Grosvenor, b. 1934, s. 1957.	Hon. Julian F. M. G., b. 1959.
1643 S.	Elibank (13th), James Alastair Frederick Campbell Erskine-Murray, b. 1902, s. 1962.	Alan D'A. E.-M., b. 1923.
1802	Ellenborough (8th), Richard Edward Cecil Law, b. 1926, s. 1945, m.	Hon. Rupert E. H. L., b. 1955.
1509 S.*	Elphinstone (17th), John Alexander Buller-Fullerton-Elphinstone, (3rd *U.K. Baron* Elphinstone, 1885), b. 1914, s. 1955.	Rev. the Hon. A. C. V. B.-F.-E., b. 1918.
1934	Elton (1st), Godfrey Elton, b. 1892, m.	Hon. Rodney E., b. 1930.
1964	Erroll of Hale (1st), Frederick James Erroll, P.C., T.D., b. 1914, m.	(None.)
1964	Erskine of Rerrick (1st), John Maxwell Erskine, G.B.E., b. 1893, m.	Maj. Hon. Iain M. E., b. 1926.
1932	Essendon (2nd), Brian Edmund Lewis, b. 1903. s. 1944, m.	(None.)
1627 S.	Fairfax of Cameron (14th), Nicholas John Albert Fairfax, b. 1956, s. 1964, M.	Hon. Hugh N. T. F., b. 1958.
1961	Fairhaven (2nd), Henry Rogers Broughton, b. 1900, s. 1966, m.	Hon. Ailwyn H. G. B., b. 1936.
1916	Faringdon (2nd), Alexander Gavin Henderson, b. 1902, s. 1934.	Charles M. H., b. 1937.
1756 I.	Farnham (12th), Barry Owen Somerset Maxwell, b. 1931, s. 1957, m.	Hon. Simon K. M., b. 1933.
1856 I.	Fermoy (5th), Edmund James Burke Roche, b. 1939, s. 1955, m.	Hon. Patrick M. R., b. 1967.
1826	Feversham (6th), Charles Anthony Peter Duncombe, b. 1945, s. 1963, m.	Hon. Jasper O. S, D., b. 1968.
1798 I.	ffrench (7th), Peter Martin Joseph Charles John ffrench, b. 1926, s. 1955, m.	Hon. Robuck J. P. C. M. ff., b. 1956.
1909	Fisher (3rd), John Vavasseur Fisher, D.S.C. b. 1921, s. 1955.	Hon. Patrick V. F., b. 1953.
1295	Fitzwalter (21st), Fitzwalter Brook Plumptre, b. 1914, called out of abeyance, 1953, m.	Hon. Julian B. P., b. 1952.
1776	Foley (8th), Adrian Gerald Foley, b. 1923, s. 1927, m.	Hon. Thomas H. F., b.1961.
1445 S.	Forbes (22nd), Nigel Ivan Forbes, K.B.E. (*Premier Baron of Scotland*), b. 1918, s. 1953, m.	Master of Forbes, b. 1946.
1821	Forester (7th), Cecil George Wilfrid Weld-Forester, b. 1899, s. 1932, m.	Hon. George C. B. W.-F., b. 1938.
1922	Forres (3rd), John Archibald Harford Williamson, b. 1922, s. 1954, m.	Hon. Alastair S. G. W., b. 1946.
1959	Forster of Harraby (1st), John Forster, K.B.E., Q.C., b. 1888, m.	(None.)
1917	Forteviot (3rd), Henry Evelyn Alexander Dewar, M.B.E., b. 1906, s. 1947, m.	Hon. J. J. Evelyn D., b. 1938.
1946	Fraser of North Cape (1st), Bruce Austin Fraser, G.C.B., K.B.E., Admiral of the Fleet, b. 1888.	(None.)
1951	Freyberg (2nd), Paul Richard Freyberg, O.B.E., M.C., b. 1923, s. 1963, m.	Hon. Valerian B. F., b. 1970.
1917	Gainford (2nd), Joseph Pease, T.D., b. 1889, s. 1943, m.	Hon. Joseph P., b. 1921.
1818 I.	Garvagh (5th), (Alexander Leopold Ivor) George Canning, b. 1920, s. 1956, m.	Hon. Spencer G S. de R. C., b. 1953.

Created.	Title, Order of Succession, Name, etc.	Eldest Son or Heir.
1942	Geddes (2nd), Ross Campbell Geddes, K.B.E., b. 1907, s. 1954, m.	Hon. Euan M. R. G., b. 1937.
1876	Gerard (4th), Robert William Frederick Alwyn Gerard, b. 1918, s. 1953.	Rupert C. F. G., M.B.E., b. 1916.
1876	Gerard (4th), Robert William Frederick Alwyn Gerard, b. 1918, s. 1953.	Lt.-Col. Charles R. T. M. G., D.S.O., O.B.E., b. 1894.
1824	Gifford (6th), Anthony Marice Gifford, b. 1940, s. 1961, m.	Hon. Thomas A. G., b. 1967.
1917	Gisborough (3rd), Thomas Richard John Long Chaloner, b. 1927, s. 1951, m.	Hon. Thomas P. L. C., b. 1961.
1960	Gladwyn (1st), (Hubert Miles) Gladwyn Jebb, G.C.M.G., G.C.V.O., C.B., b. 1900, m.	Hon. Miles A. J., b. 1931.
1899	Glanusk (4th), David Russell Bailey, b. 1917, s. 1948, m.	Hon. Christopher B., b. 1942.
1918	Glenarthur (3rd), Matthew Arthur, O.B.E., b. 1909, s. 1942, m.	Hon. Simon M. A., b. 1944.
1921	Glenavy (3rd), Patrick Gordon Campbell, b. 1913, s. 1963, m.	Hon. Michael C., b. 1924.
1911	Glenconner (2nd), Christopher Grey Tennant, b. 1899, s. 1920, m.	Hon. Colin T., b. 1926.
1964	Glendevon (1st), John Adrian Hope, P.C., b. 1912, m.	Hon. Julian J. S. H., b. 1950.
1922	Glendyne (3rd), Robert Nivison, b. 1926, s. 1967, m.	Hon. John N., b. 1960.
1939	Glentoran (2nd), Daniel Stewart Thomas Bingham Dixon, P.C., (N.I.), b. 1912, s. 1950, m.	Hon. Thomas R. V. D., b. 1935.
1956	Godber (1st), Frederick Godber, b. 1888, m.	(None.)
1909	Gorell (4th), Timothy John Radcliffe Barnes, b. 1927, s. 1963, m.	Hon. Ronald A. H. B., b. 1931.
1953	Grantchester (1st), Alfred Jesse Suenson-Taylor, O.B.E., b. 1893, m.	Hon. Kenneth S.-T., b. 1921.
1782	Grantley (7th), John Richard Brinsley Norton, M.C., b. 1923, s. 1954, m.	Hon. Richard W. B. N., b. 1956.
1794 I.	Graves (8th), Peter George Wellesley Graves, b. 1911, s. 1963, m.	Evelyn P. G., b. 1926.
1445 S.	Gray (22nd), Angus Diarmid Ian Campbell-Gray, b. 1931, s. 1946, m.	Master of Gray, b. 1964.
1950	Greenhill (2nd), Stanley Ernest Greenhill, M.D., b. 1917, s. 1967, m.	Hon. Malcolm G., b. 1924.
1927	Greenway (3rd), Charles Paul Greenway, b. 1917, s. 1963, m.	Hon. Ambrose C. D. G. b. 1941.
1902	Grenfell (2nd), Pascoe Christian Victor Francis Grenfell, b. 1905, s. 1925, m.	Hon. Julian G., b. 1935.
1944	Gretton (2nd), John Frederic Gretton, O.B.E., b. 1902, s. 1947, m.	Hon. John H. G., b. 1941.
1869	Greville (4th), Ronald Charles Fulke Greville, b. 1912, s. 1952.	(None.)
1955	Gridley (2nd), Arnold Hudson Gridley, b. 1906, s. 1965, m. 1956.	Hon. Richard D. A. G., b. 1925.
1964	Grimston of Westbury (1st), Robert Villiers Grimston, b. 1897, m.	Hon. Robert W. S. G., b. 1925.
1880	Grimthorpe (4th), Christopher John Beckett, O.B.E., b. 1915, s. 1963, m.	Hon. Edward J. B., b. 1954.
1961	Guest, Christopher William Graham Guest, P.C., b. 1901, m. (Lord of Appeal, retired).	(Law Life Peerage.)
1945	Hacking (2nd), Douglas Eric Hacking, b. 1910. s. 1950, m.	Hon. Douglas D. H., b. 1938.
1950	Haden-Guest (2nd), Stephen Haden-Guest, b. 1902, s. 1960, m.	Hon. Richard H.-G., b. 1904.
1957	Hailes (1st), Patrick George Thomas Buchan-Hepburn, P.C., G.B.E., C.H., b. 1901, m.	(None.)
1886	Hamilton of Dalzell (3rd), John D'Henin Hamilton, M.C., b. 1911, s. 1952, m.	Hon. James L. H., b. 1938.
1874	Hampton (5th), Humphrey Arthur Pakington, O.B.E., b. 1888, s. 1962, w.	Hon. Richard H. R. P., b. 1925.
1939	Hankey (2nd), Robert Maurice Alers Hankey, K.C.M.G., K.C.V.O., b. 1905, s. 1963, m.	Hon. Donald R. A. H., b. 1938.
1958	Harding of Petherton (1st), John Harding, G.C.B., C.B.E., D.S.O., M.C., Field Marshal, b. 1896, m.	Capt. Hon. John C. H., b. 1928.
1910	Hardinge of Penshurst (3rd), George Edward Charles Hardinge, b. 1921, s. 1960, m.	Hon. Julian A. H., b. 1945.
1877	Harlech (5th), (William) David Ormsby-Gore, P.C., K.C.M.G., b. 1918, s. 1964, m.	Hon. Julian H. O.-G., b. 1940.
1939	Harmsworth (2nd), Cecil Desmond Bernard Harmsworth, b. 1903, s. 1948, m.	Hon. Eric H., b. 1905.
1815	Harris (5th), George St. Vincent Harris, M.C. b. 1889, s. 1932. m.	Hon. George R. H., b. 1920.
1954	Harvey of Tasburgh (2nd), Peter Charles Oliver Harvey, b. 1921, s. 1968, m.	Hon. John W. H., b. 1923.
1295	Hastings (22nd), Edward Delaval Henry Astley, b. 1912, s. 1956, m.	Hon. Delaval T. H. A., b. 1960.
1835	Hatherton (6th), John Walter Stuart Littleton, b. 1906, s. 1969, m.	Hon. Thomas C. T. L., T.D., b. 1907.
1776	Hawke (9th), Bladen Wilmer Hawke, b. 1901, s. 1939, m.	Hon. Julian H., b. 1901.
1927	Hayter (3rd), George Charles Hayter Chubb, b. 1911, s. 1967, m.	Hon. George W. M. C., b. 1943.

Created.	Title, Order of Succession, Name, etc.	Eldest Son or Heir.
1945	Hazlerigg (2nd), Arthur Grey Hazlerigg, M.C., b. 1910, s. 1949, m.	Hon. Arthur G. H., b. 1951.
1797 I.	Headley (7th), Charles Rowland Allanson-Winn, b. 1902, s. 1969, m.	Hon. John R. A.-W., b. 1934.
1943	Hemingford (2nd), Dennis George Ruddock Herbert, b. 1904, s. 1947, m.	Hon. Dennis H., b. 1934.
1906	Hemphill (5th), Peter Patrick Fitzroy Martyn Hemphill-Martyn, b. 1928, s. 1957, m.	Hon. Charles A. M. H-M., b. 1954.
1945	Henderson (1st), William Watson Henderson, P.C., b. 1891.	(None.)
1799 I.*	Henley (7th), Michael Francis Eden (5th U.K. Baron, Northington, 1885), b. 1914, s. 1962, m.	Hon. Oliver M. R. E., b. 1953.
1800 I.*	Henniker (7th), John Ernest de Grey Henniker-Major (3rd U.K. Baron, Hartismere, 1866), b. 1883, s. 1956, w.	Hon. Sir John P. E. C. H.-M., K.C.M.G., C.V.O., M.C., b. 1916.
1886	Herschell (3rd), Rognvald Richard Farrer Herschell, b. 1923, s. 1929, m.	(None.)
1935	Hesketh (3rd) Thomas Alexander Fermor-Hesketh, b. 1950, s. 1955.	Hon. Robert F.-H., b. 1951.
1828	Heytesbury (5th), William Leonard Frank Holmes à Court, b. 1906, s. 1949, w.	Hon. Francis H. à C., b. 1931.
1955	Heyworth (1st), Geoffrey Heyworth, b. 1894, m.	(None.)
1886	Hillingdon (4th), Charles Hedworth Mills, b. 1922, s. 1952, m.	Hon. Charles J. M., b. 1951.
1886	Hindlip (5th), Henry Richard Allsopp, b. 1912, s. 1966, m.	Hon. Charles H. A., b. 1940.
1950	Hives (2nd), John Warwick Hives, b. 1913, s. 1965, m.	Hon. Peter A. H., b. 1921.
1960	Hodson, Francis Lord Charlton Hodson, P.C., M.C., b. 1895, w. (Lord of Appeal, retired).	(Law Life Peerage.)
1912	Hollenden (2nd), Geoffrey Hope Hope-Morley, b. 1885, s. 1929, m.	Gordon H. H.-M., b. 1914.
1897	Holm Patrick (3rd), James Hans Hamilton, b. 1928, s. 1942, m.	Hon. H. J. D. H., b. 1955.
1933	Horder (2nd), Thomas Mervyn Horder, b. 1911, s. 1955.	(None.)
1797 I.	Hotham (8th), Henry Durand Hotham, b. 1940, s. 1967.	Hon. Peter W. H., b. 1944.
1881	Hothfield (4th), Thomas Sackville Tufton, b. 1916, s. 1961.	Lt.-Col. George W. A. T., T.D., b. 1904.
1597	Howard de Walden (9th), John Osmael Scott-Ellis (5th U.K. Baron, Seaford, 1826), b. 1912, s. 1946, m.	Co-heiresses. To U.K. Barony, W. F. Ellis, b. 1912.
1869	Howard of Glossop (3rd), Bernard Edward Fitzalan-Howard, M.B.E., b. 1885, s. 1924, m.	Maj.-Gen. Hon. Miles F. F.-H., C.B., C.B.E., M.C., b. 1915.
1930	Howard of Penrith (2nd), Francis Philip Howard, b. 1905, s. 1939, m.	Hon. Philip H., b. 1945.
1960	Howick of Glendale (1st), Evelyn Baring, G.C.M.G., K.C.V.O., b. 1903, m.	Hon. Charles E. B., b. 1937.
1796 I.	Huntingfield (6th), Gerard Charles Arcedeckne Vanneck, b. 1915, s. 1969, m.	Hon. Joshua C. V., b. 1954.
1950	Hurcomb (1st), Cyril William Hurcomb, G.C.B., K.B.E., b. 1883, w.	(None.)
1866	Hylton (5th), Raymond Hervey Jolliffe, b. 1932, s. 1967, m.	Hon. William H. M. J., b. 1967.
1933	Iliffe (2nd), Edward Langton Iliffe, b. 1908, s. 1960, m.	Robert P. R. I, b. 1944.
1543 I.	Inchiquin (17th), Phaedrig Lucius Ambrose O'Brien (O'Brien of Thomond), b. 1900, s. 1968, m.	Hon. Fionn M. O'B., b. 1903.
1962	Inchyra (1st), Frederick Robert Hoyer Millar, G.C.M.G., C.V.O., b. 1900, m.	Hon. Robert H. M., b. 1953.
1964	Inglewood (1st), William Morgan Fletcher-Vane, T.D., b. 1909, m.	Hon. W. Richard F.-V., b. 1951.
1946	Inman (1st), Philip Albert Inman, P.C., b. 1892, m.	(None.)
1919	Inverforth (2nd), Andrew Alexander Morton Weir, b. 1897, s. 1955, m.	Hon. Andrew C. R. W., b. 1932.
1941	Ironside (2nd), Edmund Oslac Ironside, b. 1924, s. 1959, m.	Hon. Charles E.G. I., b. 1956.
1952	Jeffreys (2nd), Mark George Christopher Jeffreys, b. 1932, s. 1960, m.	Hon. Christopher H. M. J., b. 1957.
1924	Jessel (2nd), Edward Herbert Jessel, C.B.E. b. 1904, s. 1950, m.	(None.)
1906	Joicey (4th), Michael Edward Joicey, b. 1925, s. 1966, m.	Hon. James M. J., b. 1953.
1937	Kenilworth (3rd), John Davenport Siddeley, b. 1924, s. 1971, m.	Hon. John R. S., b. 1951.
1935	Kennet (2nd), Wayland Hilton Young, b. 1923, s. 1960, m.	Hon. W. A. Y., b. 1957.
1776 I. } 1886* }	Kensington (7th), William Edwardes (4th U.K. Baron, Kensington), b. 1904, s. 1938.	Hugh I. E., b. 1933.
1951	Kenswood (2nd), John Michael Howard Whitfield, b. 1930, s. 1963, m.	Hon. Michael C. W., b. 1955.
1788	Kenyon (5th), Lloyd Tyrell-Kenyon, b. 1917, s. 1927, m.	Hon. Lloyd T.-K., b. 1947.
1947	Kershaw (4th), Edward John Kershaw, b. 1936, s. 1962, m.	Hon. Donald A. K., b. 1915.
1943	Keyes (2nd), Roger George Bowlby Keyes, b. 1919, s. 1945, m.	Hon. Charles W. P. K., b. 1951.
1909	Kilbracken (3rd), John Raymond Godley, D.S.C., b. 1920, s. 1950.	Hon. Christopher J. G., b. 1945.
1971	Kilbrandon, Charles James Dalrymple Shaw, P.C., b. 1906, m. (Lord of Appeal).	(Law Life Peerage).
1900	Killanin (3rd), Michael Morris, M.B.E., T.D., b. 1914, s. 1927, m.	Hon. George R. F. M., b. 1947.

Created.	Title, Order of Succession, Name, etc.	Eldest Son or Heir.
1943	Killearn (2nd), Graham Curtis Lampson, *b.* 1919, *s.* 1964, *m.*	Hon. Victor M. G. A. L., *b.* 1941.
1789 I.	Kilmaine (6th), John Francis Archibald Browne, C.B.E., *b.* 1902, *s.* 1946, *m.*	Hon. John D. H. B., *b.* 1948.
1831	Kilmarnock (6th), Gilbert Allan Rowland Boyd, M.B.E., *b.* 1903, *s.* 1941, *m.*	Hon. Alastair B., *b.* 1927.
1941	Kindersley (2nd), Hugh Kenyon Molesworth Kindersley, C.B.E., M.C., *b.* 1899, *s.* 1954, *m.*	Hon. Robert H. M. K., *b.* 1929.
1223 I.	Kingsale (35th), John de Courcy (*Premier Baron of Ireland*), *b.* 1941, *s.* 1969.	Nevinson R. de C., *b.* 1920.
1682 S. 1860* }	*Kinnaird* (12th), Kenneth FitzGerald Kinnaird, K.T., K.B.E. (4th U.K. Baron, *Kinnaird*), *b.* 1880, *s.* 1923, *w.*	Master of Kinnaird, *b.* 1912.
1902	Kinross (3rd), John Patrick Douglas Balfour, *b.* 1904, *s.* 1939.	Hon. David A. B., T.D., *b.* 1906.
1951	Kirkwood (3rd) David Harvie Kirkwood, PH.D., *b.* 1931, *s.* 1970, *m.*	Hon. James S. K., *b.* 1937.
1800 I.	Langford (9th), Geoffrey Alexander Rowley-Conway, O.B.E., *b.* 1912, *s.* 1953, *m.*	Hon. Owen G. R-C., *b.* 1958.
1942	Latham (2nd), Dominic Charles Latham, *b.* 1954, *s.* 1970, *M.*	Hon. Anthony L., *b.* 1954.
1431	Latymer (7th), Thomas Burdett Money-Coutts, *b.* 1901, *s.* 1949, *m.*	Hon. Hugo N. M.-C., *b.* 1926.
1869	*Lawrence* (5th), David John Downer Lawrence, *b.* 1937, *s.* 1968.	(None.)
1947	Layton (2nd), Michael John Layton, *b.* 1912, *s.* 1966, *m.*	Hon. Geoffrey M. L., *b.* 1947.
1859	Leconfield (6th), John Edward Reginald Wyndham, M.B.E., (1st U.K. Baron, *Egremont*, 1963), *b.* 1920, *s.* 1967, *m.*	Hon. John M. S. W., *b.* 1948.
1839	Leigh (4th), Rupert William Dudley Leigh, *b.* 1908, *s.* 1938, *m.*	Hon. John P. L., *b.* 1935.
1962	Leighton of St. Mellons (2nd), (John) Leighton Seager, *b.* 1922, *s.* 1963, *m.*	Hon. Robert W. H. L. S., *b.* 1955.
1797	Lilford (7th), George Vernon Powys, *b.* 1931, *s.* 1949, *m.*	Frank L. P., *b.* 1902.
1945	Lindsay of Birker (2nd), Michael Francis Morris Lindsay, *b.* 1909, *s.* 1952, *m.*	Hon. James F. L., *b.* 1945.
1758 I.	Lisle (7th), John Nicholas Horace Lysaght, *b.* 1903, *s.* 1919, *m.*	Hon. Horace L., *b.* 1908.
1925	Lloyd (2nd), Alexander David Frederick Lloyd, M.B.E., *b.* 1912, *s.* 1941, *m.*	Hon. Charles G. D. L., *b.* 1949.
1895	Loch (3rd), George Henry Compton Loch, *b.* 1916, *s.* 1942, *m.*	Hon. Spencer L., M.C., *b.* 1920.
1850	Londesborough (9th), Richard John Denison, *b.* 1959, *s.* 1968, *M.*	(None.)
1541 I.	Louth (16th), Otway Michael James Oliver Plunkett, *b.* 1929, *s.* 1950, *m.*	Hon. Jonathan O.P. *b.* 1952.
1458 S. 1837* }	Lovat (15th), Simon Christopher Joseph Fraser, D.S.O., M.C., T.D. (4th U.K. Baron, *Lovat*), *b.* 1911, *s.* 1933, *m.*	Master of Lovat, *b.* 1939.
1946	Lucas of Chilworth (2nd), Michael William George Lucas, *b.* 1926, *s.* 1967, *m.*	Hon. Simon W. L., *b.* 1957.
1929	Luke (2nd), Ian St. John Lawson-Johnston, *b.* 1905, *s.* 1943, *m.*	Hon. Arthur L.-J., *b.* 1933.
1839	Lurgan (4th), William George Edward Brownlow, *b.* 1902, *s.* 1937.	John D. C. B., O.B.E., *b.* 1911.
1914	Lyell (3rd), Charles Lyell, *b.* 1939, *s.* 1943.	(None.)
1945	Lyle of Westbourne (2nd), Charles John Leonard Lyle, *b.* 1905, *s.* 1954, *w.*	(None.)
1859	Lyveden (5th), Sidney Munro Vernon, *b.* 1888, *s.* 1969, *w.*	Hon. Ronald C. V., *b.* 1918.
1959	MacAndrew (1st), Charles Glen MacAndrew, P.C., T.D., *b.* 1888, *m.*	Hon. Colin N. G. MacA. *b.* 1919.
1955	McCorquodale of Newton (1st), Malcolm Stewart McCorquodale, P.C., K.C.V.O., *b.* 1901, *w.*	(None.)
1947	MacDermott, John Clarke MacDermott, P.C., M.C., *b.* 1896, *m.* (Lord Chief Justice of Northern Ireland, retired.	(Law Life Peerage.)
1776 I.	Macdonald (8th) Godfrey James Macdonald, *b.* 1947, *s.* 1970, *m.*	
1949	Macdonald of Gwaenysgor (2nd), Gordon Ramsay Macdonald, *b.* 1915, *s.* 1966, *m.*	Hon. Kenneth M., *b.* 1921.
1937	McGowan (3rd), Harry Duncan Cory McGowan, *b.* 1938, *s.* 1966, *m.*	Hon. Dominic J. W. Mc. G., *b.* 1951.
1922	Maclay (3rd), Joseph Paton Maclay, *b.* 1942, *s.* 1969.	Hon. David M. M., *b.* 1944.
1955	McNair (1st), Arnold Duncan McNair, C.B.E., Q.C., Ll.D., F.B.A., *b.* 1885, *w.*	Hon. John McN., *b.* 1913.
1951	Macpherson of Drumochter (2nd), James Gordon Macpherson, *b.* 1924, *s.* 1965, *m.*	Hon. Thomas I. M., *b.* 1948.
1937	Mancroft (2nd), Stormont Mancroft Samuel Mancroft, K.B.E., T.D., *b.* 1914, *s.* 1942, *m.*	Hon. Benjamin L. S. M., *b.* 1957.
1807	Manners (4th), Francis Henry Manners, M.C., *b.* 1897, *s.* 1927, *m.*	Hon. John R. C. M., *b.* 1923.
1922	Manton (3rd), Joseph Rupert Eric Robert Watson, *b.* 1924, *s.* 1968, *m.*	Hon. Miles R. M. W., *b.* 1958.

Created.	Title Order of Succession, Name, etc.	Eldest Son or Heir.
1908	Marchamley (3rd), John William Tattersall Whiteley, b. 1922, s. 1949, m.	Hon. William F. W., b. 1968.
1965	Margadale (1st), John Granville Morrison, T.D., b. 1906, m.	Hon. Harry James I. M., T.D., b. 1930.
1961	Marks of Broughton (2nd), Michael Marks, b. 1920, s. 1964.	Hon. Simon R. M., b. 1950.
1930	Marley (2nd), Godfrey Pelham Leigh Aman, b. 1913, s. 1952, m.	(None.)
1964	Martonmere (1st), (John) Roland Robinson, P.C., K.C.M.G., b. 1907, m.	Hon. Richard A. G. R., b. 1935.
1776 I.	Massy (9th), Hugh Hamon John Somerset Massy, b. 1921, s. 1958, m.	Hon. David H. S. M., b. 1947.
1935	May (3rd), Michael St. John May, b. 1931, s. 1950, m.	Hon. Jasper B. St. J. M., b. 1965.
1928	Melchett (3rd), Julian Edward Alfred Mond, b. 1925, s. 1949, m.	Hon. Peter R. H. M., b. 1948.
1925	Merrivale (3rd), Jack Henry Edmond Duke, b. 1917, s. 1951, m.	Hon. Derek J. P. D., b. 1948.
1911	Merthyr (3rd), William Brereton Couchman Lewis, P.C., K.B.E., T.D., b. 1901, s. 1932, m.	Hon. Trevor O. L., b. 1935.
1919	Meston (2nd), Dougall Meston, b. 1894, s. 1943, m.	Hon. James M., b. 1950.
1838	Methuen (4th), Paul Ayshford Methuen, R.A., b. 1886, s. 1932, w.	Hon. Anthony P. M., b. 1891.
1905	Michelham (2nd), Herman Alfred Stern, b. 1900, s. 1919, w.	Hon. Jack Michelham, b. 1903.
1711	Middleton (12th), (Digby) Michael Godfrey John Willoughby, M.C., b. 1921, s. 1970, m.	Hon. Michael C. J. W., b. 1948.
1939	Milford (2nd), Wogan Philipps, b. 1902, s. 1962, m	Hon. Hugo J. L. P., b. 1929.
1933	Milne (2nd), George Douglass Milne, b. 1909, s. 1948, m.	Hon. George M., b. 1941.
1951	Milner of Leeds (2nd), Michael Milner, b. 1923, s. 1967, m.	Hon. Richard J. M., b. 1959.
1947	Milverton (1st), Arthur Frederick Richards, G.C.M.G., b. 1885, m.	Hon. Fraser R., b. 1930.
1873	Moncreiff (5th), Harry Robert Wellwood Moncreiff, b. 1915, s. 1942, m.	Hon. Rhoderick H. W. M., b. 1954.
1884	Monk Bretton (3rd), John Charles Dodson, b. 1924, s. 1933, m.	Hon. Christopher M. D., b. 1958.
1728	Monson (11th), John Monson, b. 1932, s. 1958, m.	Hon. Nicholas J. M., b. 1955.
1885	Montagu of Beaulieu (3rd), Edward John Barrington Douglas-Scott-Montagu, b. 1926, s. 1929, m.	Hon. Ralph D-S-M., b. 1961.
1839	Monteagle of Brandon (6th), Gerald Spring Rice, b. 1926, s. 1946, m.	Hon. Charles I. S. R., b. 1953.
1943	Moran (1st), Charles McMoran Wilson, M.C., M.D., b. 1882, m.	Hon. Richard J. M. W., C.M.G., b. 1924.
1918	Morris (2nd), Michael William Morris, b. 1903, s. 1935.	Hon. Michael M., b. 1937.
1960	Morris of Borth-y-Gest, John William Morris, P.C., C.B.E., M.C., b. 1896. (Lord of Appeal.)	(Law Life Peerage.)
1950	Morris of Kenwood (2nd), Philip Geoffry Morris, b. 1928, s. 1954, m.	Hon. Jonathan D. M. b. 1968.
1945	Morrison (2nd), Dennis Morrison, b. 1914, s. 1953, m.	(None.)
1947	Morton of Henryton, Fergus Dunlop Morton, P.C., M.C., b. 1887, m. (Lord of Appeal, retired).	(Law Life Peerage.)
1831	Mostyn (5th), Roger Edward Lloyd Lloyd-Mostyn, M.C., b. 1920, s. 1965, m.	Hon. Llewellyn R. L.-M., b. 1948.
1933	Mottistone (4th), David Peter Seely, b. 1920, s. 1966, m.	Hon. Peter J. P. S., b. 1949.
1945	Mountevans (2nd), Richard Andvord Evans, b. 1918, s. 1957, m.	Hon. Edward P. B. E., b. 1943.
1283	Mowbray (26th), Segrave (27th) (1283), & Stourton (23rd) (1448), Charles Edward Stourton (Premier Baron of England), b. 1923, s. 1965, m.	Hon. Edward W. S. S., b. 1953.
1932	Moyne (2nd), Bryan Walter Guinness, b. 1905, s. 1944, m.	Hon. Jonathan G., b. 1930.
1929	Moynihan (3rd), Antony Patrick Andrew Cairnes Berkeley Moynihan, b. 1936, s. 1965.	Hon. Colin B. M., b. 1955.
1781 I.	Muskerry (8th), Hastings Fitzmaurice Tilson Deane, b. 1907, s. 1966, m.	Hon. Robert F. D., b. 1948.
1627 S.*	Napier and Ettrick (14th), Francis Nigel Napier (5th U.K. Baron, Ettrick, 1872), b. 1930, s. 1954, m.	Master of Napier, b. 1962.
1868	Napier of Magdala (5th), (Robert) John Napier, O.B.E., b. 1904, s. 1948, m.	Hon. Robert N., b. 1940.
1940	Nathan (2nd), Roger Carol Michael Nathan, b. 1922, s. 1963, m.	Hon. Rupert H. B. N., b. 1957.
1960	Nelson of Stafford (2nd), Henry George Nelson, b. 1917, s. 1962, m.	Hon. Henry R. G. N., b. 1943.
1959	Netherthorpe (1st), James Turner, b. 1908, m.	Hon. Andrew T., b. 1936.
1940	Newall (2nd), Francis Storer Eaton Newall, b. 1930, s. 1963, m.	Hon. Richard H. E. N., b. 1961.
1776 I.	Newborough (7th), Robert Charles Michael Vaughan Wynn, D.S.C., b. 1917, s. 1965.	Hon. Robert V. W., b. 1949.
1892	Newton (4th), Peter Richard Legh, b. 1915, s. 1960, m.	Hon. Richard T. L., b. 1950.
1930	Noel-Buxton (2nd), Rufus Alexander Buxton, b. 1017, s. 1048, m.	Hon. Martin C. B., b. 1940.
1957	Norrie (1st), (Charles) Willoughby (Moke) Norrie, G.C.M.G., G.C.V.O., C.B., D.S.O., M.C., b. 1893, m.	Hon. George W. M. N., b. 1936.
1884	Northbourne (4th), Walter Ernest Christopher James, b. 1896, s. 1932, m.	Hon. Christopher G. W. J., b. 1926.
1866	Northbrook (5th), Francis John Baring, b. 1915, s. 1947, m.	Hon. Francis T. B., b. 1951.

Created.	Title, Order of Succession, Name, etc.	Eldest Son or Heir.
1878	Norton (7th), John Arden Adderley, O.B.E., b. 1915, s. 1961, m.	Hon. James N. A. A., b.1947.
1960	Nugent (1st), Terence Edward Gascoigne Nugent, G.C.V.O., M.C., b. 1895, m.	(None.)
1906	Nunburnholme (3rd), Charles John Wilson, b. 1904, s. 1924, m.	Hon. Ben Charles W., b. 1928.
1950	Ogmore (1st), David Rees Rees-Williams, P.C., T.D., b. 1903, m.	Hon. Gwilym R.-W., b. 1931.
1870	O'Hagan (4th), Charles Towneley Strachey, b. 1945, s. 1961, m.	Hon. Richard T. S., b.1950.
1868	O'Neill (4th), Raymond Arthur Clanaboy O'Neill, b. 1933, s. 1944, m.	Hon. Shane S. O'N., b. 1965.
1836 I.*	Oranmore and Browne (4th), Dominick Geoffrey Edward Browne (2nd U.K. Baron Mereworth, 1926), b. 1901, s. 1927, m.	Hon. Dominick G. T. B., b. 1929.
1868	Ormathwaite (6th), John Arthur Charles Walsh, b. 1912, s. 1944.	(None.)
1933	Palmer (3rd), Raymond Cecil Palmer, O.B.E., b. 1916, s. 1950, m.	Hon. Gordon W. N. P., O.B.E., b. 1918.
1958	Parker of Waddington, Hubert Lister Parker, P.C., b. 1900, m. (Lord Chief Justice of England, retired).	(Law Life Peerage.)
1914	Parmoor (2nd), Alfred Henry Seddon Cripps, b. 1882. s. 1941.	Hon. Frederick H. C., D.S.O., T.D., b. 1885.
1962	Pearce, Edward Holroyd Pearce, P.C., b. 1901, m. (Lord of Appeal, retired).	(Law Life Peerage.)
1965	Pearson, Colin Hargreaves Pearson, P.C., C.B.E., b. 1899, m. (Lord of Appeal).	(Law Life Peerage.)
1937	Pender (3rd), John Willoughby Denison-Pender, b. 1933, s. 1965, m.	Hon. Henry J. R. D.-P., b. 1968.
1866	Penrhyn (6th), Malcolm Frank Douglas-Pennant, D.S.O., M.B.E., b. 1908, s. 1967, m.	Hon. Nigel D.-P., b. 1909.
1909	Pentland (2nd), Henry John Sinclair, b. 1907, s. 1925, m.	(None.)
1603	Petre (17th), Joseph William Lionel Petre, b. 1914, s. 1915, m.	Hon. John P., b. 1942.
1918	Phillimore (3rd), Robert Godfrey Phillimore, b. 1939, s. 1947.	Hon. Claud P., b., 1911.
1945	Piercy (2nd), Nicholas Pelham Piercy, b. 1918, s. 1966, m.	Hon. James W. P., b. 1946.
1827	Plunket (7th), Patrick Terence William Span Plunket, C.V.O., b. 1923, s. 1938.	Hon. Robin P., b. 1925.
1831	Poltimore (6th), Hugh de Burgh Warwick Bampfylde, b. 1888, s. 1967, m.	Mark C. B., b. 1957.
1690 S.	Polwarth (10th), Henry Alexander Hepburne-Scott, T.D., b. 1916. s. 1944, m.	Master of Polwarth, b.1947.
1930	Ponsonby of Shulbrede (2nd), Matthew Henry Hubert Ponsonby, b. 1904, s. 1946, m.	Hon. Thomas A. P., b. 1930.
1958	Poole (1st), Oliver Brian Sanderson Poole, P.C., C.B.E. T.D., b. 1911, m.	Hon. David C. P., b. 1945.
1852	Raglan (5th), FitzRoy John Somerset, b. 1927, s. 1964.	Hon. Geoffrey S., b. 1932.
1957	Rank (1st), Joseph Arthur Rank, b. 1888, m.	(None.)
1932	Rankeillour (4th), Peter St. Thomas More Henry Hope, b. 1935, s. 1967.	Michael R. H., b. 1940.
1953	Rathcavan (1st), (Robert William) Hugh O'Neill, P.C., b. 1883, m.	Hon. Phelim R. H. O'N., M.P., b. 1909.
1916	Rathcreedan (2nd), Charles Patrick Norton, T.D.,b. 1905, s. 1930, m.	Hon. Christopher J. N., b. 1949.
1868 I.	Rathdonnell (5th), Thomas Benjamin McClintock-Bunbury, b. 1938, s. 1959, m.	Hon. William L. McC-B., b. 1966.
1911	Ravensdale (3rd), Nicholas Mosley, M.C., b. 1923, s. 1966, m.	Hon. Shaun N. M., b. 1949.
1821	Ravensworth (8th), Arthur Waller Liddell, b. 1924, s. 1950, m.	Hon. Thomas A. H. L., b. 1954.
1821	Rayleigh (5th), John Arthur Strutt, b. 1908, s. 1947, m.	Hon. Charles S., b. 1910.
1937	Rea (2nd) Philip Russell Rea, P.C., O.B.E., b. 1900, s. 1948, m.	John N. R., b. 1928.
1628 S.	Reay (14th), Hugh William Mackay, b. 1937, s. 1963, m.	Master of Reay, b. 1965.
1902	Redesdale (5th), Clement Napier Bertram Freeman-Mitford, b. 1932, s. 1963, m.	Hon. Rupert B. F.-M., b. 1967.
1948	Reid, James Scott Cumberland Reid, P.C., C.H., b. 1890, m. (Lord of Appeal).	(Law Life Peerage.)
1940	Reith (2nd), Christopher John Reith, b. 1928, s. 1971, m.	
1928	Remnant (3rd), James Wogan Remnant, b. 1930, s. 1967, m.	Hon. Philip J. R., b. 1954.
1806 I.	Rendlesham (8th), Charles Anthony Hugh Thellusson, b. 1915, m. 1943, m.	Hon. Charles W. B. T., b. 1954.
1933	Rennell (2nd), Francis James Rennell Rodd, K.B.E., C.B., b. 1895, s. 1941, m.	Hon. Gustaf G. R., O.B.E., b. 1905.
1964	Renwick (1st), Robert Burnham Renwick, K.B.E., b. 1904, m.	Hon. Harry A. R., b. 1935.
1885	Revelstoke (4th), Rupert Baring, b. 1911, s. 1934.	Hon. John B., b. 1934.
1905	Ritchie of Dundee (3rd), John Kenneth Ritchie, P.C., b. 1902, s. 1948, w.	Hon. Colin R., b. 1908.
1935	Riverdale (2nd), Robert Arthur Balfour, b. 1901, s. 1957, m.	Hon. Mark R. B., b. 1927.
1961	Robertson of Oakridge (1st), Brian Hubert Robertson, G.C.B., G.B.E., K.C.M.G., K.C.V.O., D.S.O., M.C., b. 1896, m.	Hon. William R. R., b. 1930.
1938	Roborough (2nd), Massey Henry Edgcumbe Lopes, b. 1903, s.1938, m.	Hon. Henry L., b. 1940.
1931	Rochester (2nd), Foster Charles Lowry Lamb, b. 1916, s. 1955, m.	Hon. David C. L., b. 1944.

Created.	Title, Order of Succession, Name, etc.	Eldest Son or Heir.

1034   *Rockley* (2nd), Robert William Evelyn Cecil, *b.* 1901, *s.* 1941, *m.* — Hon. James H. C., *b.* 1934.

1782   *Rodney* (8th), George Bridges Harley Guest Rodney, *b.* 1891, *s.* 1909, *w.* — Hon. John F. R., *b.* 1920.

1651 S.   *Rollo* (13th), Eric John Stapylton Rollo (4th *U.K. Baron, Dunning,* 1869), *b.* 1915, *s.* 1947, *m.* — Master of Rollo, *b.* 1943.

1866   *Romilly* (4th), William Gaspard Guy Romilly, *b.* 1899, *s.* 1905, *m.* — (None.)

1959   *Rootes* (2nd), William Geoffrey Rootes, *b.* 1917, *s.* 1964, *m.* — Hon. Nicholas G. R., *b.* 1951.

1796 I.   *Rossmore* (7th), William Warner Westenra (6th *U.K. Baron, Rossmore*), *b.* 1931, *s.* 1958. — (None.)
1838*

1939   *Rotherwick* (2nd), (Herbert) Robin Cayzer, *b.* 1912, *s.* 1958, *m.* — Hon. H. Robin C., *b.* 1954.

1885   *Rothschild* (3rd), Nathaniel Mayer Victor Rothschild, G.M., F.R.S., *b.* 1910, *s.* 1937, *m.* — Hon. Nathaniel R., *b.* 1936.

1911   *Rowallan* (2nd), Thomas Godfrey Polson Corbett, K.T., K.B.E., M.C., T.D., *b.* 1895, *s.* 1933, *m.* — Hon. Arthur C., *b.* 1919.

1947   *Rugby* (2nd) Alan Loader Maffey, *b.* 1913, *s.* 1969, *m.* — Hon. John R. M., *b.* 1949.

1945   *Rusholme* (1st), Robert Alexander Palmer, *b.* 1890. — (None.)

1919   *Russell of Liverpool* (2nd), Edward Frederick Langley Russell, C.B.E., M.C., T.D., *b.* 1895, *s.* 1920, *m.* — Hon. Langley G. H. R., M.C., *b.* 1922.

1876   *Sackville* (6th), Lionel Bertrand Sackville-West, *b.* 1913, *s.* 1965, *w.* — Hugh R. I. S.-W., M.C., *b.* 1919.

1911   *St. Audries* (2nd), Alexander Peregrine Fuller-Acland-Hood, *b.* 1893, *s.* 1917. — (None.)

1964   *St. Helens* (1st), Michael Henry Colin Hughes-Young, *b.* 1912, *w.* — Hon. Richard F. H.-Y., *b.* 1945.

1559   *St. John of Bletso* (19th), John Moubray Russell St. John, *b.* 1917, *s.* 1934. — Comdr. Oliver *St. J.*, D.S.C., R.N., *b.* 1914.

1935   *St. Just* (2nd), Peter George Grenfell, *b.* 1922, *s.* 1941, *m.* — (None.)

1852   *St. Leonards* (3rd), Frank Edward Sugden, *b.* 1890, *s.* 1908. — John G. S., *b.* 1950.

1887   *St. Levan* (3rd), Francis Cecil St. Aubyn, *b.* 1895, *s.* 1940, *m.* — Hon. John F. A. *St. A.,* D.S.C., *b.* 1919.

1885   *St. Oswald* (4th), Rowland Denys Guy Winn, M.C., *b.* 1916, *s.* 1957, *m.* — Hon. Derek E. A. *W.*, *b.* 1919.

1953   *Salter* (1st), (James) Arthur Salter, P.C., G.B.E., K.C.B., *b.* 1881, *w.* — (None.)

1445 S.   *Saltoun* (19th), Alexander Arthur Fraser, M.C., *b.* 1886, *s.* 1933, *m.* — Hon. Flora M. *Ramsay*, *b.* 1930.

1960   *Sanderson of Ayot* (1st), Basil Sanderson, M.C., *b.* 1894, *w.* — Hon. Alan L. S., *b.* 1931.

1945   *Sandford* (2nd), Rev. John Cyril Edmondson, D.S.C. *b.* 1920, *s.* 1959, *m.* — Hon. James J. M. E., *b.* 1949.

1871   *Sandhurst* (5th), (John Edward) Terence Mansfield, D.F.C., *b.* 1920, *s.* 1964, *m.* — Hon. Guy R. J. M., *b.* 1949.

1802   *Sandys* (7th), Richard Michael Oliver Hill, *b.* 1931, *s.* 1961. — Marcus T. H., *b.* 1931.

1888   *Savile* (3rd), George Halifax Lumley-Savile, *b.* 1919, *s.* 1931. — Hon. Henry L. T. L.-S., *b.* 1923.

1447   *Saye and Sele* (21st), Nathaniel Thomas Allen Twisleton-Wykeham-Fiennes, *b.* 1920, *s.* 1968, *m.* — Hon. Richard I., *T.-W.-F.*, *b.* 1959.

1932   *Selsdon* (3rd), Malcolm McEacharn Mitchell-Thomson, *b.* 1937, *s.* 1963, *m.* — Hon. Callum M. M. *M.-T.*, *b.* 1969.

1916   *Shaughnessy* (3rd), William Graham Shaughnessy, *b.* 1922, *s.* 1938, *m.* — Hon. Patrick J. S., *b.* 1944.

1783 I.   *Sheffield* (8th), Thomas Henry Oliver Stanley (8th *U.K. Baron,* — Hon. Richard O. S., *b.* 1956.
1839*   *Stanley of Alderley* and 7th *U.K. Baron Eddisbury,* 1848), *b.* 1927, *s.* 1971, *m.*

1946   *Shepherd* (2nd), Malcolm Newton Shepherd, P.C., *b.* 1918, *s.* 1954, *m.* — Hon. Grahame G. S., *b.* 1949.

1784   *Sherborne* (7th), Charles Dutton, *b.* 1911, *s.* 1949, *m.*, *b.* 1969. — Hon. George E. D., *b.* 1912.

1964   *Sherfield* (1st), Roger Mellor Makins, G.C.B., G.C.M.G., *b.* 1904, *m.* — Hon. Christopher M., *b.* 1942.

1902   *Shuttleworth* (4th), Charles Ughtred John Kay-Shuttleworth, M.C., *b.* 1917, *s.* 1942, *m.* — Hon. Charles G. N. S., *b.* 1948.

1950   *Silkin* (1st), Lewis Silkin, P.C., C.H., *b.* 1889, *w.* — Hon. Arthur S., *b.* 1916.

1963   *Silsoe* (1st), (Arthur) Malcolm Trustram Eve, G.B.E., M.C., T.D., Q.C., *b.* 1894, *m.* — Hon. David M. T. E., *b.* 1930.

1971   *Simon of Glaisdale,* Jocelyn Edward Salis Simon, P.C., *b.* 1911, *m.* — (Law Life Peerage.)
(*Lord of Appeal.*)

1947   *Simon of Wythenshawe* (2nd), Roger Simon, *b.* 1913, *s.* 1960, *m.* — Hon. Matthew S., *b.* 1955.

1449 S.   *Sinclair* (17th), Charles Murray Kennedy St. Clair, M.V.O., *b.* 1914, *s.* 1957, *m.* — The Master of Sinclair, *b.* 1968.

1957   *Sinclair of Cleeve* (1st), Robert John Sinclair, K.C.B., K.B.E., *b.* 1893, *m.* — Maj. Hon. John R. K. S., M.B.E., *b.* 1919.

1919   *Sinha* (3rd), Sudhindro Prosannho Sinha, *b.* 1920, *s.* 1967. — Hon. A. K. S., *b.* 1930.

1828   *Skelmersdale* (6th), Lionel Bootle-Wilbraham, D.S.O., M.C., *b.* 1896, *s.* 1969, *m.* — Hon. Roger B.-*W.*, *b.* 1945.

1916   *Somerleyton* (3rd), Savile William Francis Crossley, *b.* 1928, *s.* 1959, *m.* — Hon. Richard N. C., *b.* 1932.

1784   *Somers* (8th), John Patrick Somers Cocks, *b.* 1907, *s.* 1953, *m.* — Philip S. S. C., *b.* 1948.

1917   *Southborough* (3rd), Francis John Hopwood, *b.* 1897, *s.* 1960, *m.* — Hon. Francis M. H., *b.* 1922.

Created.	Title. Order of Succession, Name, etc.	Eldest Son or Heir.
1959	Spens (1st), William Patrick Spens, P.C., K.B.E., Q.C., b. 1885, m.	Hon. William G. M. S., M.B.E., b. 1914.
1640	Stafford (14th), Basil Francis Nicholas Fitzherbert, b. 1926, s. 1941, m.	Hon. Francis M. W. F., b. 1954.
1938	Stamp (3rd), Trevor Charles Stamp, b. 1907, s. 1941, m.	Hon. Trevor S., b. 1935.
1318	Strabolgi (11th), David Montague de Burgh Kenworthy, b. 1914, s. 1953.	Rev. the Hon. Jonathan M. A. K., b. 1916.
1911	Strachie (2nd), Edward Strachey, b. 1882, s. 1936, w.	(None.)
1954	Strang (1st), William Strang, G.C.B., G.C.M.G., M.B.E., b. 1893, m.	Hon. Colin S., b. 1922.
1628	Strange (15th), John Drummond, b. 1900, title called out of abeyance 1964, m.	Three co-heiresses.
1955	Strathalmond (2nd), William Fraser, C.M.G., O.B.E., T.D., b. 1916, s. 1970, m.	Hon. William R. F., b. 1947.
1936	Strathcarron (2nd), David William Anthony Blyth Macpherson, b. 1924, s. 1937, m.	Hon. Ian D. P. M., b. 1949.
1955	Strathclyde (1st), Thomas Dunlop Galbraith, P.C., b. 1891, m.	Hon. Thomas G. D. G., M.P., b. 1917.
1900	Strathcona and Mount Royal (4th), Donald Euan Palmer Howard, b. 1923, s. 1959, m.	Hon. Donald A. H., b. 1961.
1836	Stratheden & Campbell (1841) (4th), Alastair Campbell, C.B.E., b. 1899, s. 1918, m.	Maj. Hon. Gavin C., b. 1901.
1884	Strathspey (5th), Donald Patrick Trevor Grant, b. 1912, s. 1948, m.	Hon. James P. G., b. 1943.
1838	Sudeley (7th), Merlyn Charles Sainthill Hanbury-Tracy, b. 1939, s. 1941.	Ninian J. H.-T., b. 1910.
1786	Suffield (11th), Anthony Philip Harbord-Hamond, M.C., b. 1922, s. 1951, m.	Hon. Charles A. A. H.-H., b. 1953.
1893	Swansea (4th), John Hussey Hamilton Vivian, b. 1925, s. 1934, m.	Hon. Richard A. H. V., b. 1957.
1907	Swaythling (3rd), Stuart Albert Samuel Montagu, O.B.E., b. 1898, s. 1927, m.	Hon. David C. M., b. 1928.
1919	Swinfen (2nd), Charles Swinfen Eady, b. 1904, s. 1919, m.	Hon. Roger M. E., b. 1938.
1935	Sysonby (3rd), John Frederick Ponsonby, b. 1945, s. 1956.	(None.)
1831 I. } 1856* }	Talbot of Malahide (7th), Milo John Reginald Talbot, C.M.G. (4th U.K. Baron, Talbot de Malahide), b. 1912, s. 1948.	Reginald S. V. T., b. 1897 (to Irish Barony).
1946	Tedder (2nd), John Michael Tedder, Sc.D., Ph.D., D.Sc., b. 1926, s. 1967, m.	Hon. Robin J. T., b. 1955.
1797I.	Teignmouth (7th), Frederick Maxwell Aglionby Shore, D.S.C., b. 1920, s. 1964, m.	(None.)
1831	Templemore (5th), Dermot Richard Claud Chichester, b. 1916, s. 1953, m.	Hon. Arthur P. C., b. 1952.
1884	Tennyson (4th), Harold Christopher Tennyson, b. 1919, s. 1951	Lieut.-Com. Hon. Mark A. T., D.S.C., R.N., b. 1920.
1918	Terrington (4th), (James Allen) David Woodhouse, b. 1915, s. 1961, m.	Hon. C. Montague W., D.S.O., O.B.E., M.P., b. 1917.
1940	Teviot (2nd), Charles John Kerr, b. 1934, s. 1968, m.	
1616	Teynham (19th), Christopher John Henry Roper-Curzon, D.S.O., D.S.C., b. 1896, s. 1936, m.	Hon. John C. I. R.-C., b. 1928.
1964	Thomson of Fleet (1st), Roy Herbert Thomson, G.B.E., b. 1894, w	Hon. Kenneth R. T., b. 1923.
1792	Thurlow (8th), Francis Edward Hovell-Thurlow-Cumming-Bruce, K.C.M.G., b. 1912, s. 1971, m.	Hon. Roualeyn R. H.-T.-C.-B., b. 1952.
1876	Tollemache (4th), John Edward Hamilton Tollemache, M.C., b. 1910, s. 1955, m.	Hon. Timothy J. E. T., b. 1939.
1564 S.	Torphichen (13th), John Gordon Sandilands, b. 1886, s. 1915, m.	Master of Torphichen, b. 1917.
1947	Trefgarne (2nd), David Garro Trefgarne, b. 1941, s. 1960, m.	Hon. George G. T., b. 1970.
1921	Trevethin (3rd) and Oaksey (1st), Geoffrey Lawrence, P.C., D.S.O., T.D. (1st U.K. Baron, Oaksey, 1947), b. 1880 s. 1959, m.	Hon. John G. T. L., b. 1929.
1880	Trevor (4th), Charles Edwin Hill-Trevor, b. 1928, s. 1950, m.	Hon. Nevill E. H.-T., b. 1931.
1461 I.	Trimlestown (10th), Charles Aloysius Barnewall, b. 1899, s. 1937, w.	Hon. Anthony B., b. 1928.
1940	Tryon (2nd), Charles George Vivian Tryon, G.C.V.O., K.C.B., D.S.O., b. 1906, s. 1940, m.	Hon. Anthony T., b. 1940.
1950	Tucker (Frederick) James Tucker, P.C., b. 1888 (Lord of Appeal, retired).	(Law Life Peerage.)
1935	Tweedsmuir (2nd), John Norman Stuart Buchan, C.B.E., C.D., b. 1911, s. 1940, m.	Hon. William B., b. 1916.
1946	Uvedale of North End (1st). Ambrose Edgar Woodall, M.D., F.R.C.S., b. 1885, m.	(None.)
1523	Vaux of Harrowden (9th), Rev. Peter Hugh Gordon Gilbey, b. 1914, s. 1958.	Hon. John H. P. G. b. 1915.
1800 I.	Ventry (7th), Arthur Frederick Daubeney Olav Eveleigh-de-Moleyns, b. 1898, s. 1936.	Andrew W. D. De M. b., 1943.
1762	Vernon (10th), John Lawrence Venables-Vernon, b. 1923, s. 1963, m.	Visct. Harcourt (see p. 235).
1922	Vestey (3rd), Samuel George Armstrong Vestey, b. 1941, s. 1954, m.	Mark W. V., b. 1943.
1841	Vivian (5th), Anthony Crespigny Claude Vivian, b. 1906, s. 1940, m.	Hon. Nicholas V., b. 1935.

Created.	Title, Order of Succession, Name, etc.	Eldest Son or Heir.
1963	*Wakefield of Kendal* (1st), (William) Wavell Wakefield, b. 1898, m.	(None.)
1934	*Wakehurst* (3rd), (John) Christopher Loder, b. 1925, s. 1970, m.	Hon. Timothy W. L., b. 1928.
1723	*Walpole* (9th), Robert Henry Montgomerie Walpole, b. 1913, s. 1931, m.	Hon. Robert H. W., b. 1938.
1780	*Walsingham* (9th), John de Grey, M.C., b. 1925, s. 1965, m.	Hon. Robert de G., b. 1969.
1936	*Wardington* (2nd), Christopher Henry Beaumont Pease, b. 1924, s. 1950, m.	Hon. William S. P., b. 1925.
1792 I.	*Waterpark* (7th), Frederick Caryll Phillip Cavendish, b. 1926, s. 1948, m.	Hon. Roderick A. C., b. 1959.
1942	*Wedgwood* (4th), Piers Anthony Weymouth Wedgwood, b. 1954, s. 1970 M.	Hon. John W., M.D., b. 1919.
1861	*Westbury* (5th), David Alan Bethell, M.C., b. 1922, s. 1961, m.	Hon. Richard N. B., b. 1950.
1944	*Westwood* (2nd), William Westwood, b. 1907, s. 1953, m.	Hon. William G. W., b. 1944.
1971	*Widgery*, John Passmore Widgery, P.C., O.B.E., T.D., b. 1911, m. (*Lord Chief Justice of England*).	(Law Life Peerage.)
1935	*Wigram* (2nd), (George) Neville (Clive) Wigram, M.C., b. 1915, s. 1960, m.	Hon. Andrew F. C. W., b. 1949.
1964	*Wilberforce*, Richard Orme Wilberforce, P.C., C.M.G., O.B.E., b. 1907, m. (*Lord of Appeal.*)	(Law Life Peerage.)
1491	*Willoughby de Broke* (20th), John Henry Peyto Verney, M.C., A.F.C., b. 1896, s. 1923, m.	Hon. Leopold D. V., b. 1938.
1946	*Wilson* (2nd), Patrick Maitland Wilson, b. 1915, s. 1964, m.	(None.)
1937	*Windlesham* (3rd), David James George Hennessy, b. 1932, s. 1962, m.	Hon. James R. H., b. 1968.
1951	*Wise* (2nd), John Clayton Wise, b. 1923, s. 1968, m.	Hon. Christopher J. C. W., b. 1948.
1869	*Wolverton* (5th), Nigel Reginald Victor Glyn, b. 1904, s. 1932.	Jeremy C. G., b. 1930.
1928	*Wraxall* (2nd), George Richard Lawley Gibbs, b. 1928, s. 1931.	Hon. Eustace H. B. G., b. 1929.
1915	*Wrenbury* (3rd), John Burton Buckley, b. 1927, s. 1940, m.	Hon. William E. B., b. 1966.
1838	*Wrottesley* (5th), Richard John Wrottesley, M.C., b. 1918, s. 1962, m.	Clifton H. L. de V. W., b. 1968.
1919	*Wyfold* (3rd), Hermon Robert Fleming Hermon-Hodge, b. 1915, s. 1942.	(None.)
1829	*Wynford* (8th), Robert Samuel Best, M.B.E., b. 1917, s. 1943, m.	Hon. John P. R. B., b. 1950.
1308	*Zouche* (18th), James Assheton Frankland, b. 1943, s. 1965.	Hon. Roger N. F., b. 1909.

X 1970 LORD WHEATLEY

Peeresses in Their Own Right

Peerages are occasionally granted immediately to ladies of distinction or the widows of distinguished men; but frequently the instances falling under this heading are the result of regular inheritance in lines which are open to females in default of males. A Peeress in her Own Right retains her title after marriage, and if her husband's rank is the superior she is designated by the two titles jointly, the inferior one last: her hereditary claim still holds good in spite of any marriage whether higher or lower. No rank held by a woman can confer any title or even precedence upon her husband but the rank of a Peeress in her Own Right is inherited by her eldest son (or perhaps daughter), to whomsoever she may have been married.

COUNTESSES IN THEIR OWN RIGHT.—*Style*, The Countess of —— Addressed as, My Lady.

Created.	Title, Name, etc.	Eldest Son or Heir.
1643 S.	*Dysart*, Wenefryde Agatha Greaves, b. 1889, s. 1935, w.	Lady Rosamund G., b. 1914.
1452 S.	*Erroll*, Diana Denyse Hay (*Hereditary Lord High Constable and Knight Marischal of Scotland*), b. 1926, s. 1941, m.	Lord Hay, b. 1948.
1677 S.	*Kintore*, Ethel Sydney Baird (*Dowager Viscountess Stonehaven*), b. 1874, s. 1966, w.	Visct. Stonehaven, b. 1908 (see p. 236).
1633 S.	*Loudoun*, Barbara Huddleston Abney-Hastings, b. 1919, s. 1960, m.	Lord Mauchline, b. 1942.
1660 S.	*Newburgh*, Maria Sofia Giuseppina Gravina di Ramacca (*Princess Giustiniani-Bandini*), b. 1889, s. 1941, w.	Prince Giulio Rospigliosi, b. 1907.
1235 S.	*Sutherland*, Elizabeth Millicent Sutherland, b. 1921, s. 1963, m.	Lord Strathnaver, b. 1947.

BARONESSES IN THEIR OWN RIGHT.—*Style*, The Baroness ——. Addressed as, My Lady.

Created.	Title, Name, etc.	Eldest Son or Heir.
1313	*Audley*, Rosina Lois Veronica Tuchet-Macnamee, b. 1911, s. 1963, m.	Richard M. T. Souter, b. 1914.
1309	*Beaumont*, Mona Josephine Tempest Fitzalan-Howard, O.B.E. (*Baroness Howard of Glossop*), b. 1894, s. 1896, m.	Maj.-Gen. Hon. Miles F. F.-H, C.B., C.B.E., M.C., b. 1915.
1421	*Berkeley*, Mary Lalle Foley-Berkeley, b. 1905, title called out of abeyance, 1967.	Hon Cynthia E. Gueterbock, b. 1909.

Created.	Title, Name, etc.	Eldest Son or Heir.
1455	*Berners,* Vera Ruby Williams, *b.* 1901, *s.* 1950, *m.*	Two co-heiresses.
1307	*Dacre,* Rachel Leila Douglas-Home, *b.* 1929, *title called out of abeyance,* 1970.	Hon. James T. A. *D.-H., b.* 1952.
1332	*Darcy de Knayth,* Davina Marcia Ingrams, *b.* 1938, *s.* 1943, *w.*	Hon. Caspar D. *I., b.* 1962.
1264	*De Ros,* Georgiana Angela Maxwell, *b.* 1933, *s.* 1958, *m.* (Premier Barony of England).	Hon. Peter *M., b.* 1958.
1602 S.	*Kinloss,* Beatrice Mary Grenville Freeman-Grenville, *b.* 1922, *s.* 1944, *m.*	Master of Kinloss, *b.* 1953.
1663	*Lucas of Crudwell* (*Scottish Baroness, Dingwall* 1609), Anne Rosemary Palmer, *b.* 1919, *s.* 1958, *m.*	Hon. Ralph M. *P., b.* 1951.
1681 S.	*Nairne,* Katherine Evelyn Constance Bigham (*Viscountess Mersey*), *b.* 1912, *s.* 1944. *m.*	Master of Nairne, *b.* 1934.
1945	*Portal of Hungerford,* Rosemary Ann Portal, *b.* 1923, *s.* 1971.	Hon. Mavis E. A. *P., b.* 1926.
1651 S.	*Ruthven of Freeland,* Bridget Helen Monckton, C.B.E. (*Bridget, Viscountess Monckton of Brenchley*), *b.* 1896, *s.* 1956, *w.*	Earl of Carlisle, M.C., *b.* 1923 (*see p.* 229).
1489 S.	*Sempill,* Ann Moira Sempill, *b.* 1920, *s.* 1965, *m.*	Master of Sempill, *b.* 1949.
1299	*Strange of Knokin,* (1426) Hungerford and (1445) De Moleyns, Elizabeth Philipps (*Dowager Viscountess St. Davids*), *b.* 1884, *s.* 1921, *w.*	Viscount St. Davids, *b.* 1917. (*see p.* 236).
1544	*Wharton,* Elizabeth Dorothy Vintcent, *b.* 1906, *s.* 1969.	Nicholas H., *Kemeys-Tynte, b.* 1903.

LIFE PEERS
Created under Life Peerages Act, 1958
BARONS

1961	*Alport,* Cuthbert James McCall Alport, P.C., T.D., *b.* 1912, *m.*	
1965	*Annan,* Noel Gilroy Annan, O.B.E., *b.* 1916, *m.*	
1970	*Ardwick,* John Cowburn Beavan, *b.* 1910, *m.*	
1964	*Arwyn,* Arwyn Randall Arwyn, *b.* 1897, *m.*	
1967	*Aylestone,* Herbert William Bowden P.C., C.B.E., *b.* 1905, *m.*	
1963	*Balerno,* Alick Drummond Buchanan-Smith, C.B.E., T.D., D.SC., F.R.S.E., *b.* 1898, *w.*	
1968	*Balogh,* Thomas Balogh, *b.* 1905.	
1967	*Beaumont of Whitley,* Rev. Timothy Wentworth Beaumont, *b.* 1928, *m*	
1965	*Beeching,* Richard Beeching, PH.D., *b.* 1913, *m.*	
1969	*Bernstein,* Sidney Lewis Bernstein, *b.* 1899, *m.*	
1964	*Beswick,* Frank Beswick, P.C., *b.* 1912.	
1968	*Black,* William Rushton Black, *b.* 1893, *m.*	
1969	*Blackett,* Patrick Maynard Stuart Blackett, O.M., C.H., F.R.S., *b.* 1897, *m.*	
1971	*Blake,* Robert Norman William Blake, F.B.A., *b.* 1916, *m.*	
1964	*Blyton,* William Reid Blyton, *b.* 1899, *m.*	
1958	*Boothby,* Robert John Graham Boothby, K.B.E., *b.* 1900, *m.*	
1964	*Bourne,* Geoffrey Kemp Bourne, G.C.B., K.B.E., C.M.G., *b.* 1902, *m.*	
1964	*Bowden,* Bertram Vivian Bowden, PH.D., *b.* 1910, *w.*	
1970	*Boyle of Handsworth,* Edward Charles Gurney Boyle, P.C., *b.* 1923.	
1965	*Brock,* Russell Claude Brock, F.R.C.S., *b.* 1903, *m.*	
1964	*Brockway,* (Archibald) Fenner Brockway, *b.* 1888, *m.*	
1966	*Brooke of Cumnor,* Henry Brooke, P.C., C.H., *b.* 1903, *m.*	
1964	*Brown,* Wilfred Banks Duncan Brown, P.C., M.B.E., *b.* 1908, *m.*	
1966	*Buckton,* Samuel Storey, *b.* 1896, *w.*	
1970	*Burntwood,* Julian Ward Snow, *b.* 1910, *m.*	
1965	*Butler of Saffron Walden,* Richard Austen Butler, K.G., P.C., C.H., *b.* 1902, *m.*	
1964	*Byers,* (Charles) Frank Byers, O.B.E., *b.* 1915, *m.*	
1965	*Caccia,* Harold Anthony Caccia, G.C.M.G., G.C.V.O., *b.* 1905, *m.*	
1966	*Campbell of Eskan,* John Middleton Campbell, *b.* 1912, *m.*	
1964	*Caradon,* Hugh Mackintosh Foot, P.C., G.C.M.G., K.C.V.O., O.B.E. *b.* 1907, *m.*	
1960	*Casey,* Richard Gardiner Casey, K.G., P.C., G.C.M.G., C.H., D.S.O., M.C., *b.* 1890, *m.*	
1964	*Chalfont,* Alun Arthur Gwynne Jones, P.C., O.B.E., M.C., *b.* 1919, *m.*	
1962	*Champion,* Arthur Joseph Champion, P.C., *b.* 1897, *m.*	
1963	*Chelmer,* Eric Cyril Boyd Edwards, M.C., T.D., *b.* 1914. *m.*	
1969	*Clark,* Kenneth Mackenzie Clark, C.H., K.C.B., F.B.A., *b.* 1903, *m.*	
1965	*Cole,* George James Cole, *b.* 1906, *m.*	
1964	*Collison,* Harold Francis Collison, C.B.E., *b.* 1909, *m.*	
1966	*Cooper of Stockton Heath,* John Cooper, *b.* 1908.	
1961	*Coutanche,* Alexander Moncrieff Coutanche, *b.* 1892, *m.*	
1959	*Craigton,* Jack Nixon Browne, P.C., C.B.E., *b.* 1904.	
1968	*Crowther,* Geoffrey Crowther, *b.* 1907. *m.*	
1970	*Davies of Leek,* Harold Davies, P.C., *b.* 1904, *m.*	
1967	*Delacourt-Smith,* Charles George Percy Smith, P.C., *b.* 1917, *m.*	
1970	*Diamond,* John Diamond, P.C., *b.* 1907, *m.*	
1967	*Donaldson of Kingsbridge,* John George Stuart Donaldson, O.B.E., *b.* 1907.	
1967	*Douglass of Cleveland,* Harry Douglass, *b.* 1902, *m.*	
1968	*Energlyn,* William David Evans, PH.D., *b.* 1912, *m.*	
1967	*Evans of Hungershall,* Benjamin Ifor Evans, D.Lit., *b.* 1899, *m*	
1958	*Ferrier,* Victor Ferrier Noel-Paton, E.D., *b.* 1900, *m.*	
1961	*Fisher of Lambeth,* Most Rev. Geoffrey Francis Fisher, P.C., G.C.V.O., Royal Victorian Chain, D.D., *b.* 1887, *m.*	
1967	*Fiske,* William Geoffrey Fiske, C.B.E., *b.* 1905, *m.*	

1970   *Fletcher*, Eric George Molyneux Fletcher, P.C., Ll.D., *b.* 1903, *m.*
1967   *Foot*, John Mackintosh Foot, *b.* 1909, *m.*
1962   *Franks*, Oliver Shewell Franks, P.C., G.C.M.G., K.C.B., C.B.E., F.B.A, *b.* 1905, *m.*
1958   *Fraser of Lonsdale*, (William Jocelyn) Ian Fraser, C.H., C.B.E., *b,* 1897, *m.*
1966   *Fulton*, John Scott Fulton, *b.* 1902, *m.*
1964   *Gardiner*, Gerald Austin Gardiner, P.C., *b.* 1900, *m.*
1969   *Garner*, (Joseph John) Saville Garner, G.C.M.G., *b.* 1908, *m.*
1967   *Garnsworthy*, Charles James Garnsworthy, O.B.E., *b.* 1907.
1958   *Geddes of Epsom*, Charles John Geddes, C.B.E., *b.* 1897, *m.*
1970   *George-Brown*, George Alfred George-Brown, P.C., *b.* 1914, *m.*
1965   *Goodman*, Arnold Abraham Goodman, *b.* 1915.
1969   *Gore-Booth*, Paul Henry Gore-Booth, G.C.M.G., K.C.V.O., *b.* 1909, *m.*
1967   *Granville of Eye*, Edgar Louis Granville, *b,* 1899, *m.*
1958   *Granville-West*, Daniel Granville West, *b.* 1904, *m.*
1970   *Greenwood of Rossendale*, (Arthur William James) Anthony Greenwood, P.C., *b.* 1911, *m.*
1968   *Grey of Naunton*, Ralph Francis Alnwick Grey, G.C.M.G., K.C.V.O., O.B.E., *b.* 1910, *m.* (Governor of Northern Ireland).
1970   *Hailsham of St. Marylebone*, Quintin McGarel Hogg, P.C., *b.* 1907, *m.* (Lord High Chancellor).
1970   *Hamnett*, Cyril Hamnett, *b.* 1906, *w.*
1968   *Hartwell*, (William) Michael Berry, M.B.E., T.D., *b.* 1911, *m.*
1971   *Harvey of Prestbury*, Arthur Vere Harvey, C.B.E., *b.* 1906, *m.*
1968   *Helsby*, Laurence Norman Helsby, G.C.B., K.B.E., *b.* 1908, *m.*
1967   *Heycock*, Llewellyn Heycock, C.B.E., *b.* 1905, *m.*
1963   *Hill of Luton*, Charles Hill, P.C., M.D., *b.* 1904, *m.*
1965   *Hilton of Upton*, Albert Victor Hilton, *b.* 1908, *m.*
1965   *Hinton of Bankside*, Christopher Hinton, K.B.E., F.R.S., *b.* 1901, *m.*
1967   *Hirshfield*, Desmond Barel Hirshfield, *b.* 1913, *m.*
1965   *Holford*, William Graham Holford, R.A., *b.* 1907, *m.*
1970   *Hoy*, James Hutchison Hoy, P.C., *b.* 1909, *m.*
1961   *Hughes*, William Hughes, P.C., C.B.E., *b.* 1911, *m.*
1966   *Hunt*, (Henry Cecil) John Hunt, C.B.E., D.S.O., *b.* 1910, *m.*
1962   *Ilford*, Geoffrey Clegg Hutchinson, M.C., T.D., Q.C., *b.* 1893, *m.*
1968   *Jacques*, John Henry Jacques, *b.* 1905, *m.*
1959   *James of Rusholme*, Eric John Francis James, *b.* 1909, *m.*
1970   *Janner*, Barnett Janner, *b.* 1892, *m.*
1965   *Kahn*, Richard Ferdinand Kahn, C.B.E., F.B.A., *b.* 1905.
1970   *Kearton*, (Christopher) Frank Kearton, O.B.E., F.R.S., *b.* 1911, *m.*
1966   *Kilmany*, William John St. Clair Anstruther-Gray, P.C., M.C., *b.* 1905, *m.*
1965   *Kings Norton*, Harold Roxbee Cox, Ph.D., *b.* 1902, *m.*
1964   *Leatherland*, Charles Edward Leatherland, O.B.E., *b.* 1898.
1961   *Lindgren*, George Samuel Lindgren, *b.* 1900, *m.*
1964   *Llewelyn-Davies*, Richard Llewelyn-Davies, *b.* 1912, *m.*
1965   *Lloyd of Hampstead*, Dennis Lloyd, Ll.D., *b.* 1915, *m.*
1966   *McFadzean*, William Hunter McFadzean, *b.* 1903, *m.*
1971   *Maclean*, Charles Hector Fitzroy Maclean, K.T., K.B.E., *b.* 1916, *m.* (Lord Chamberlain).
1967   *McLeavy*, Frank McLeavy, *b.* 1899, *m.*
1967   *MacLeod of Fuinary*, Very Rev. George Fielden MacLeod, M.C., D.D., *b.* 1895, *m.*
1966   *Maelor*, Thomas William Jones, *b.* 1898, *m.*
1967   *Mais*, Alan Raymond Mais, O.B.E., T.D., E.R.D., *b.* 1911, *m.*
1971   *Maybray-King*, Horace Maybray King, Ph.D., *b.* 1901, *m.*
1961   *Molson*, (Arthur) Hugh (Elsdale) Molson, P.C., *b.* 1903, *m.*
1967   *Morris of Grasmere*, Charles Richard Morris, K.C.M.G., *b.* 1898, *m.*
1966   *Moyle*, Arthur Moyle, C.B.E., *b.* 1894, *m.*
1971   *Moyola*, James Dawson Chichester-Clark, P.C. (N.I.), *b.* 1923, *m.*
1964   *Murray of Newhaven*, Keith Anderson Hope Murray, K.C.B., Ph.D., *b.* 1903.
1966   *Nugent of Guildford*, (George) Richard (Hodges) Nugent, P.C., *b.* 1907, *m.*
1964   *Oakshott*, Hendrie Dudley Oakshott, M.B.E., *b.* 1904, *m.*
1971   *Olivier*, Laurence Kerr Olivier, *b.* 1907, *m.*
1970   *O'Neill of the Maine*, Terence Marne O'Neill, P.C. (N.I.), *b.* 1914, *m.*
1971   *Orr-Ewing*, (Charles) Ian Orr-Ewing, O.B.E., *b.* 1912, *m.*
1966   *Pargiter*, George Albert Pargiter, C.B.E., *b.* 1897, *m.*
1961   *Peddie*, James Mortimer Peddie, M.B.E., *b.* 1906, *m.*
1967   *Penney*, William George Penney, O.M., K.B.E., Ph.D., D.Sc., F.R.S., *b.* 1909, *m.*
1968   *Pilkington*, William Henry (Harry) Pilkington, *b.* 1905, *m.*
1967   *Platt*, Robert Platt, M.D., *b.* 1900, *m.*
1959   *Plowden*, Edwin Noel Plowden, K.C.B., K.B.E., *b.* 1907, *m.*
1966   *Popplewell*, Ernest Popplewell, C.B.E., *b.* 1899, *m.*
1967   *Redcliffe-Maud*, John Primatt Redcliffe Maud, G.C.B., C.B.E., *b.* 1906, *m.*
1966   *Redmayne*, Martin Redmayne, P.C., D.S.O., T.D., *b.* 1910, *m.*
1970   *Reigate*, John Kenyon Vaughan-Morgan, P.C., *b.* 1905, *m.*
1964   *Rhodes*, Hervey Rhodes, P.C., D.F.C., *b.* 1895, *m.*
1970   *Rhyl*, (Evelyn) Nigel (Chetwoode) Birch, P.C., O.B.E., *b.* 1906, *m.*
1966   *Ritchie-Calder*, (Peter) Ritchie Calder, C.B.E., *b.* 1906, *m.*
1959   *Robbins*, Lionel Charles Robbins, C.H., C.B., F.B.A., *b.* 1898, *m.*
1961   *Robens of Woldingham*, Alfred Robens, P.C., *b.* 1910, *m.*
1969   *Roberthall*, Robert Lowe Roberthall, K.C.M.G., C.B., *b.* 1901, *m.*
1970   *Rosenheim*, Max Leonard Rosenheim, K.B.E., M.D., *b.* 1908.

1964 *Royle*, Charles Royle, *b.* 1896, *m.*
1962 *Sainsbury*, Alan John Sainsbury, *b.* 1902, *m.*
1964 *Segal*, Samuel Segal, *b.* 1902, *m.*
1958 *Shackleton*, Edward Arthur Alexander Shackleton, P.C., O.B.E., *b.* 1911, *m.*
1959 *Shawcross*, Hartley William Shawcross, P.C., Q.C., *b.* 1902, *m.*
1970 *Shinwell*, Emanuel Shinwell, P.C., C.H., *b.* 1884, *w.*
1966 *Sieff*, Israel Moses Sieff, *b.* 1889, *w.*
1970 *Slater*, Joseph Slater, B.E.M., *b.* 1904, *m.*
1964 *Snow*, Charles Percy Snow, C.B.E., *b.* 1905, *m.*
1965 *Soper*, Rev. Donald Oliver Soper, Ph.D., *b.* 1903, *m.*
1964 *Sorensen*, Reginald William Sorensen, *b.* 1891, *m.*
1969 *Stokes*, Donald Gresham Stokes, T.D., *b.* 1914, *m.*
1958 *Stonham*, Victor John Collins, P.C., O.B.E., *b.* 1903, *m.*
1966 *Stow Hill*, Frank Soskice, P.C., Q.C., *b.* 1902, *m.*
1964 *Tangley*, Edwin Savory Herbert, K.B.E., *b.* 1899, *m.*
1971 *Tanlaw*, Simon Brooke Mackay, *b.* 1934, *m.*
1958 *Taylor*, Stephen James Lake Taylor, M.D., *b.* 1910, *m.*
1968 *Taylor of Gryfe*, Thomas Johnston Taylor, *b.* 1912, *m.*
1966 *Taylor of Mansfield*, Harry Bernard Taylor, *b.* 1895, *m.*
1967 *Tayside*, David Lauchlan Urquhart, O.B.E., *b.* 1914.
1971 *Thomas*, (William) Miles (Webster) Thomas, D.F.C., *b.* 1897, *m.*
1967 *Thorneycroft*, (George Edward) Peter Thorneycroft, P.C., *b.* 1909, *m.*
1962 *Todd*, Alexander Robertus Todd, D.SC., D.Phil., F.R.S., *b.* 1907, *m.*
1968 *Trevelyan*, Humphrey Trevelyan, G.C.M.G., C.I.E., O.B.E., *b.* 1905, *m.*
1964 *Wade*, Donald William Wade, *b.* 1904, *m.*
1961 *Walston*, Henry David Leonard George Walston, *b.* 1912, *m.*
1965 *Wells-Pestell*, Reginald Alfred Wells-Pestell, *b.* 1910, *m.*
1970 *Wheatley*, John Wheatley, P.C., *b.* 1908, *m.*
1967 *Wigg*, George Edward Cecil Wigg, P.C., *b.* 1900, *m.*
1962 *Williamson*, Thomas Williamson, C.B.E., *b.* 1897, *m.*
1964 *Willis*, Edward Henry Willis, *b.* 1918, *m.*
1969 *Wilson of Langside*, Henry Stephen Wilson, P.C., Q.C., *b.* 1916, *m.*
1965 *Winterbottom*, Ian Winterbottom, *b.* 1913. *m.*
1967 *Woolley*, Harold Woolley, C.B.E., *b.* 1905, *m.*
1968 *Wright of Ashton under Lyne*, Lewis Tatham Wright, C.B.E., *b.* 1903.
1964 *Wynne-Jones*, William Francis Kenrick Wynne-Jones, *b.* 1903, *w.*
1971 *Zuckerman*, Solly Zuckerman, O.M., K.C.B., F.R.S., M.D., D.SC., *b.* 1904, *m.*

BARONESSES

1970 *Bacon*, Alice Martha Bacon, P.C., C.B.E., *b.* 1911.
1967 *Birk*, Alma Birk, *b.* 1921, *m.*
1964 *Brooke of Ystradfellte*, Barbara Muriel Brooke, D.B.E., *b.* 1908, *m.*
1962 *Burton of Coventry*, Elaine Frances Burton, *b.* 1904.
1958 *Elliot of Harwood*, Katharine Elliot, D.B.E., *b.* 1903, *w.*
1964 *Emmet of Amberley*, Evelyn Violet Elizabeth Emmet, *b.* 1899, *w.*
1964 *Gaitskell*, Anna Dora Gaitskell, *w.*
1965 *Hylton-Foster*, Audrey Pellew Hylton-Foster, *b.* 1908, *w.*
1970 *Lee of Asheridge*, Janet Bevan, P.C., *b.* 1904, *w.*
1967 *Llewelyn-Davies of Hastoe*, Annie Patricia Llewelyn-Davies, *m.*
1971 *Macleod of Borve*, Evelyn Macleod, *w.*
1970 *Masham of Ilton*, Susan Lilian Primrose Cunliffe-Lister, *b.* 1935. *m.*
1964 *Northchurch*, Frances Joan Davidson, D.B.E. (*Dowager Viscountess Davidson*), *b.* 1894, *w.*
1964 *Phillips*, Norah Mary Phillips, *b.* 1910, *w.*
1965 *Plummer*, Beatrice Plummer, *b.* 1903, *w.*
1971 *Seear*, (Beatrice) Nancy Seear, *b.* 1913.
1967 *Serota*, Beatrice Serota, *b.* 1919, *m.*
1966 *Sharp*, Evelyn Adelaide Sharp, G.B.E., *b.* 1903.
1965 *Spencer-Churchill*, Clementine Ogilvy Spencer Churchill, G.B.E., *b.* 1885, *w.*
1966 *Stocks*, Mary Danvers Stocks, LL.D., Litt.D., *b.* 1891, *w.*
1961 *Summerskill*, Edith Summerskill, P.C., C.H., *b.* 1901, *m.*
1970 *Tweedsmuir of Belhelvie*, Priscilla Jean Fortescue Buchan, *b.* 1915, *m.*
1970 *White*, Eirene Lloyd White, *b.* 1909, *m.*
1958 *Wootton of Abinger*, Barbara Frances Wright, *b.* 1897, *w.*
1971 *Young*, Janet Mary Young, *m.*

Surnames of Peers and Peeresses differing from their Titles

Abney Hastings — *Lou-don*
Acheson—*Gosford*
Adderley—*Norton*
Addington—*Sidmouth*
Agar—*Normanton*
Agar Robartes—*Clifden*
Akers Douglas—*Chilston*
Alexander—*Alexander of Tunis*

Alexander—*Caledon*
Allanson Winn—*Headley*
Allsopp—*Hindlip*
Aman—*Marley*
Anderson—*Waverley*
Annesley—*Valentia*
Anson—*Lichfield*
Anstruther-Gray—*Kilmany**

Armstrong Jones—*Snow-don*
Arthur—*Glenarthur*
Ashley Cooper—*Shaftesbury*
Ashton—*Ashton of Hyde*
Asquith—*Oxford & A.*
Assheton—*Clitheroe*
Astley—*Hastings*
Astor—*Astor of Hever*

Bailey—*Glanusk*
Baillie—*Burton*
Baillie Hamilton—*Haddington*
Baird—*Kintore*
Baird—*Stonehaven*
Baldwin — *Baldwin of Bewdley*
Balfour—*Kinross*
Balfour—*Riverdale*

* Life Peer created under Life Peerages Act, 1958.

Balfour — Balfour of Inchrye
Bampfylde—Poltimore
Banbury — Banbury of Southam
Baring—Ashburton
Baring—Cromer
Baring—Howick of Glendale
Baring—Northbrook
Baring—Revelstoke
Barnes—Gorell
Barnewall—Trimlestown
Bathurst—Bledisloe
Beauclerk—St. Albans
Beaumont—Allendale
Beaumont—Beaumont of Whitley*
Beavan—Ardwick*
Beckett—Grimthorpe
Eennet—Tankerville
Beresford—Decies
Beresford—Waterford
Bernard—Bandon
Berry—Camrose
Berry—Hartwell*
Berry—Kemsley
Bertie—Lindsey
Best—Wynford
Bethell—Westbury
Bevan—Lee of Asheridge*
Bewicke Copley—Cromwell
Bigham—Mersey
Bigham—Nairne
Bingham—Clanmorris
Bingham—Lucan
Birch—Rhyl*
Blades—Ebbisham
Bligh—Darnley
Bootle Wilbraham — Skelmersdale
Boscawen—Falmouth
Bourke—Mayo
Bowden—Aylestone*
Bowes Lyon—Strathmore
Bowyer—Denham
Boyd—Kilmarnock
Boyle—Boyle of Handsworth
Boyle—Cork and Orrery
Boyle—Glasgow
Boyle—Shannon
Brabazon—Meath
Brand—Hampden
Brassey — Brassey of Apethorpe
Brett—Esher
Bridgeman—Bradford
Brodrick—Midleton
Brooke—Alanbrooke
Brooke—Brooke of Cumnor*
Brooke—Brooke of Ystradfellte*
Brooke—Brookeborough
Brooks—Crawshaw
Brougham — Brougham and Vaux
Broughton—Fairhaven
Browne—Craigton*
Browne—Kilmaine
Browne — Oranmore and Browne
Browne—Sligo
Brownlow—Lurgan

Bruce—Aberdare
Bruce—Balfour of Burleigh
Bruce — Elgin and Kincardine
Brudenell Bruce — Ailesbury
Buchan—Tweedsmuir
Buchan—Tweedsmuir of Belhelvie*
Buchan-Hepburn—Hailes
Buchanan-Smith — Balerno*
Buckley—Wrenbury
Burton—Burton of Coventry*
Butler—Butler of Saffron Walden*
Butler—Carrick
Butler—Dunboyne
Butler—Lanesborough
Butler—Mountgarret
Butler—Ormonde
Buxton—Noel-Buxton
Byng—Strafford
Byng—Torrington
Calder—Ritchie-Calder*
Campbell—Argyll
Campbell — Breadalbane and Holland
Campbell—Campbell of Eskan*
Campbell—Cawdor
Campbell—Colgrain
Campbell—Glenavy
Campbell—Stratheden and Campbell
Campbell Gray—Gray
Canning—Garvagh
Capell—Essex
Carberry—Carbery
Carington—Carrington
Carnegie—Fife
Carnegie—Northesk
Carnegie—Southesk
Cary—Falkland
Caulfeild—Charlemont
Cavendish—Chesham
Cavendish—Devonshire
Cavendish—Waterpark
Cavendish Bentinck — Portland
Cayzer—Rotherwick
Cecil—Amherst of Hackney
Cecil—Exeter
Cecil—Rockley
Chaloner—Gisborough
Charteris—Wemyss and March
Chetwynd Talbot — Shrewsbury
Chichester—Donegall
Chichester — Templemore
Chichester Clark — Moyola*
Child Villiers—Jersey
Cholmondeley — Delamere
Chubb—Hayter
Clegg Hill—Hill
Clifford — Clifford of Chudleigh
Cochrane — Cochrane of Cults
Cochrane—Dundonald

Cocks—Somers
Cohen—Cohen of Birkenhead
Cokayne — Cullen of Ashbourne
Coke—Leicester
Cole—Enniskillen
Collins—Stonham*
Colville—Clydesmuir
Colville—Colville of Culross
Compton—Northampton
Conolly Carew—Carew
Cooper—Norwich
Cooper—Cooper of Stockton Heath*
Corbett—Rowallan
Courtenay—Devon
Cox—Kings Norton*
Craig—Craigavon
Crichton—Erne
Crichton Stuart—Bute
Cripps—Parmoor
Cross—Cross of Chelsea
Crossley—Somerleyton
Cubitt—Ashcombe
Cunliffe Lister—Masham of Ilton*
Cunliffe Lister—Swinton
Curzon—Howe
Curzon—Scarsdale
Cust—Brownlow
Dalrymple—Stair
Davidson—Northchurch*
Davies—Darwen
Davies—Davies of Leek*
Davison—Broughshane
Dawnay—Downe
Dawson Damer — Portarlington
De Courcy—Kingsale
De Grey—Walsingham
De Yarburgh Bateson—Deramore
Deane—Muskerry
Denison—Londesborough
Denison Pender—Pender
Devereux—Hereford
Dewar—Forteviot
Dixon—Glentoran
Dodson—Monk Bretton
Donaldson—Donaldson of Kingsbridge*
Douglas—Douglas of Barloch
Douglas—Morton
Douglas—Queensberry
Douglas Hamilton — Hamilton
Douglas Hamilton — Selkirk
Douglas Home—Dacre
Douglas Pennant—Penrhyn
Douglas Scott Montagu—Montagu of Beaulieu
Douglass—Douglass of Cleveland*
Drummond—Perth
Drummond—Strange
Dugdale—Crathorne
Duke—Merrivale
Duncombe—Feversham
Dundas—Melville
Dundas—Zetland

Dutton—Sherborne
Eady—Swinfen
Eaton—Cheylesmore
Eden—Auckland
Eden—Avon
Eden—Henley
Edgcumbe—Mount Edgcumbe
Edmondson—Sandford
Edwardes—Kensington
Edwards—Chelmer*
Egerton—Sutherland
Egerton—Wilton
Eliot—St. Germans
Elliot—Elliot of Harwood*
Elliot—Minto
Emmet—Emmet of Amberley*
Erroll—Erroll of Hale
Erskine—Buchan
Erskine—Erskine of Rerrick
Erskine—Mar & Kellie
Erskine Murray—Elibank
Evans—Everglyn*
Evans—Evans of Hungershall*
Evans—Mountevans
Eve—Silsoe
Eveleigh de Moleyns—Ventry
Eyres Monsell—Monsell
Fane—Westmorland
Feilding—Denbigh
Fellowes—Ailwyn
Fellowes—De Ramsey
Fermor Hesketh—Hesketh
Finch Hatton—Winchilsea
Finch Knightley—Aylesford
Fisher—Fisher of Lambeth*
Fitzalan Howard—Beaumont
Fitzalan Howard — Howard of Glossop
Fitzalan Howard—Norfolk
FitzClarence—Munster
FitzGerald—Leinster
Fitzherbert—Stafford
FitzRoy—Daventry
FitzRoy—Grafton
Fletcher Vane—Inglewood
Flower—Ashbrook
Foley Berkeley—Berkeley
Foljambe— Liverpool
Foot—Caradon*
Forbes—Granard
Forster—Forster of Harraby
Forward Howard — Wicklow
Fox Strangways — Ilchester
Frankland—Zouche
Fraser—Fraser of Lonsdale*
Fraser—Lovat
Fraser—Saltoun
Fraser—Strathalmond
Freeman Grenville—Kinloss
Freeman Mitford — Redesdale

* Life Peer created under Life Peerages Act, 1958

Freeman Thomas—*Willingdon*
Fremantle—*Cottesloe*
French—*De Freyne*
French—*Ypres*
Fuller Acland Hood—*St. Audries*
Galbraith—*Strathclyde*
Ganzoni—*Belstead*
Gascoyne Cecil—*Salisbury*
Gathorne Hardy—*Cranbrook*
Geddes—*Geddes of Epsom**
Gibbs—*Aldenham*
Gibbs—*Wraxall*
Gibson—*Ashbourne*
Giffard—*Halsbury*
Gilbey—*Vaux of Harrowden*
Glyn—*Wolverton*
Godley—*Kilbracken*
Gordon—*Aberdeen*
Gordon—*Huntly*
Gordon Lennox—*Richmond*
Gore—*Arran*
Gough Calthorpe—*Calthorpe*
Graham—*Montrose*
Graham Toler—*Norbury*
Grant—*De Longueuil*
Grant—*Strathspey*
Granville—*Granville of Eye**
Greaves—*Dysart*
Greenall—*Daresbury*
Greenwood—*Greenwood of Rossendale**
Grenfell—*St. Just*
Greville—*Warwick*
Grey—*Grey of Naunton**
Grey—*Stamford*
Grimston—*Grimston of Westbury*
Grimston—*Verulam*
Grosvenor—*Ebury*
Grosvenor—*Westminster*
Guest—*Wimborne*
Guinness—*Iveagh*
Guinness—*Moyne*
Gully—*Selby*
Gurdon—*Cranworth*
Gwynne Jones—*Chalfont**
Hamilton—*Abercorn*
Hamilton—*Belhaven and Stenton*
Hamilton — *Hamilton of Dalzell*
Hamilton — *Holm Patrick*
Hamilton Russell—*Boyne*
Hamilton Temple Blackwood—*Dufferin*
Hanbury Tracy—*Sudeley*
Handcock—*Castlemaine*
Harbord Hamond — *Suffield*
Harding—*Harding of Petherton*
Hardinge — *Hardinge of Penshurst*
Hare—*Blakenham*
Hare—*Listowel*

Harmsworth — *Rothermere*
Harris—*Malmesbury*
Harvey—*Harvey of Prestbury**
Harvey—*Harvey of Tasburgh*
Hastings—*Huntingdon*
Hay—*Erroll*
Hay—*Kinnoull*
Hay—*Tweeddale*
Heathcote Drummond Willoughby—*Ancaster*
Hely Hutchinson—*Donoughmore*
Henderson—*Faringdon*
Hennessy—*Windlesham*
Henniker Major — *Henniker*
Hepburne Scott — *Polwarth*
Herbert—*Carnarvon*
Herbert—*Hemingford*
Herbert—*Pembroke*
Herbert—*Powis*
Herbert—*Tangley**
Hermon Hodge—*Wyfold*
Hervey—*Bristol*
Hewitt—*Lifford*
Hicks Beach—*St. Aldwyn*
Hill—*Downshire*
Hill—*Hill of Luton**
Hill—*Sandys*
Hill Trevor—*Trevor*
Hinton—*Hinton of Bankside**
Hilton—*Hilton of Upton**
Hobart Hampden—*Buckinghamshire*
Hogg—*Hailsham of St. Marylebone**
Holland Hibbert—*Knutsford*
Holmes à Court—*Heytesbury*
Hood—*Bridport*
Hope—*Glendevon*
Hope—*Linlithgow*
Hope—*Rankeillour*
Hope Morley—*Hollenden*
Hopkinson—*Colyton*
Hopwood — *Southborough*
Hore Ruthven—*Gowrie*
Hovell Thurlow Cumming Bruce—*Thurlow*
Howard—*Carlisle*
Howard—*Effingham*
Howard—*Howard of Penrith*
Howard—*Strathcona*
Howard—*Suffolk*
Hoyer Millar—*Inchyra*
Hubbard—*Addington*
Huggins—*Malvern*
Hughes Young — *St. Helens*
Hutchinson—*Ilford**
Ingrams—*Darcy de Knayth*
Innes Ker—*Roxburghe*
Inskip—*Caldecote*
Irby—*Boston*
Isaacs—*Reading*
Jackson—*Allerton*

James—*James of Rusholme**
James—*Northbourne*
Jebb—*Gladwyn*
Jervis—*St. Vincent*
Jocelyn—*Roden*
Jolliffe—*Hylton*
Jones—*Maelor**
Joynson Hicks—*Brentford*
Kaye Shuttleworth — *Shuttleworth*
Kearley—*Devonport*
Kemp—*Rochdale*
Kennedy—*Ailsa*
Kenworthy—*Strabolgi*
Keppel—*Albemarle*
Kerr—*Lothian*
Kerr—*Teviot*
King—*Lovelace*
King—*Maybray King**
King Tenison—*Kingston*
Kitchener — *Kitchener of Khartoum*
Kitson—*Airedale*
Knatchbull—*Brabourne*
Knox—*Ranfurly*
Lamb—*Rochester*
Lambart—*Cavan*
Lampson—*Killearn*
Larnach Nevill — *Abergavenny*
Lascelles—*Harewood*
Law—*Coleraine*
Law—*Ellenborough*
Lawrence—*Trevethin and Oaksey*
Lawson—*Burnham*
Lawson Johnston—*Luke*
Le Poer Trench—*Clancarty*
Legge—*Dartmouth*
Legh—*Newton*
Leith—*Burgh*
Lennox Boyd—*Boyd of Merton*
Leslie—*Rothes*
Leslie Melville—*Leven*
Lever—*Leverhulme*
Leveson Gower—*Granville*
Lewis—*Brecon*
Lewis—*Essendon*
Lewis—*Merthyr*
Liddell—*Ravensworth*
Lindesay Bethune — *Lindsay*
Lindsay—*Crawford*
Lindsay — *Lindsay of Birker*
Littleton—*Hatherton*
Llewelyn-Davies—*Llewelyn-Davies of Hastoe**
Lloyd—*Lloyd of Hampstead**
Lloyd George — *Lloyd George of Dwyfor*
Lloyd George—*Tenby*
Lloyd Mostyn—*Mostyn*
Loder—*Wakehurst*
Lopes—*Roborough*
Low—*Aldington*
Lowry Corry—*Belmore*
Lowther—*Lonsdale*

Lowther—*Ullswater*
Lubbock—*Avebury*
Lumley—*Scarbrough*
Lumley Savile—*Savile*
Lygon—*Beauchamp*
Lyle—*Lyle of Westbourne*
Lyon Dalberg Acton— *Acton*
Lysaght—*Lisle*
Lyttelton—*Chandos*
Lyttelton — *Cobham (Viscountcy)*
McClintock Bunbury— *Rathdonnell*
McCorquodale—*McCorquodale of Newton*
Macdonald — *Macdonald of Gwaenysgor*
McDonnell—*Antrim*
Mackay—*Inchcape*
Mackay—*Reay*
Mackay—*Tanlaw**
Mackenzie—*Amulree*
Mackintosh—*Mackintosh of Halifax*
McLaren—*Aberconway*
Macleod — *Macleod of Borve**
MacLeod—*MacLeod of Fuinary**
Maclay—*Muirshiel*
Macnamee—*Audley*
Macpherson—*Drumalbyn*
Macpherson — *Macpherson of Drumochter*
Macpherson—*Strathcarron*
Maffey—*Rugby*
Maitland—*Lauderdale*
Makins—*Sherfield*
Manners—*Rutland*
Manningham Buller— *Dilhorne*
Mansfield—*Sandhurst*
Marks—*Marks of Broughton*
Marquis—*Woolton*
Marsham—*Romney*
Martyn Hemphill—*Hemphill—Hemphill*
Mason—*Blackford*
Maud—*Redcliffe-Maud**
Maude—*Hawarden*
Maxwell—*De Ros*
Maxwell—*Farnham*
Meade—*Clanwilliam*
Milles Lade—*Sondes*
Mills—*Hillingdon*
Milner—*Milner of Leeds*
Mitchell Thomson — *Selsdon*
Molyneux—*Sefton*
Monckton—*Galway*
Monckton—*Monckton of Brenchley*
Monckton—*Ruthven of Freeland*
Mond—*Melchett*
Money-Coutts—*Latymer*
Montagu—*Manchester*
Montagu—*Swaythling*
Montagu Douglas Scott —*Buccleuch*
Montagu Stuart Wortley Mackenzie—*Wharncliffe*

* Life Peer created under Life Peerages Act, 1958.

Montague—Amwell
Montgomerie—Eglinton
Montgomery — Montgomery of Alamein
Moore—Drogheda
Moore Brabazon—Brabazon of Tara
Moreton—Ducie
Morris—Killanin
Morris — Morris of Borth-y-Gest
Morris—Morris of Grasmere★
Morris—Morris of Kenwood
Morrison—Dunrossil
Morrison—Margadale
Morton—Morton of Henryton
Mosley—Ravensdale
Mountbatten—Edinburgh
Mountbatten — Milford Haven
Mountbatten—Mountbatten of Burma
Muff—Calverley
Mulholland—Dunleath
Murray—Atholl
Murray—Dunmore
Murray—Mansfield and Mansfield
Murray—Murray of Newhaven★
Nall Cain—Brocket
Napier — Napier and Ettrick
Napier — Napier of Magdala
Needham—Kilmorey
Nelson—Nelson of Stafford
Neville—Braybrooke
Nicolson—Carnock
Nivison—Glendyne
Noel—Gainsborough
Noel Paton—Ferrier★
North—Guilford
Northcote—Iddesleigh
Norton—Grantley
Norton—Rathcreedan
Nugent — Nugent of Guildford★
Nugent—Westmeath
O'Brien—Inchiquin
Ogilvy—Airlie
O'Neill—O'Neill of the Maine★
O'Neill—Rathcavan
Orde Powlett—Bolton
Ormsby Gore—Harlech
Paget—Anglesey
Pakenham—Longford
Pakington—Hampton
Palmer—Lucas of Crudwell
Palmer—Rusholme
Palmer—Selborne
Parker—Macclesfield
Parker—Morley
Parker—P. of Waddington
Parnell—Congleton
Parsons—Rosse
Paulet—Winchester
Peake—Ingleby
Pearson—Cowdray
Pease—Daryngton
Pease—Gainford

Pease—Wardington
Pelham—Chichester
Pelham—Yarborough
Pelham Clinton Hope—Newcastle
Pellew—Exmouth
Penny—Marchwood
Pepys—Cottenham
Perceval—Egmont
Percy—Northumberland
Pery—Limerick
Petty Fitzmaurice—Lansdowne
Philipps—Milford
Philipps—St. Davids [kin
Philipps—Strange of Knophipps—Normanby
Pleydell Bouverie—Radnor
Plumptre—Fitzwalter
Plunkett—Dunsany
Plunkett—Fingall
Plunkett—Louth
Pollock—Hanworth
Pomeroy—Harberton
Ponsonby—Bessborough
Ponsonby—De Mauley
Ponsonby—P. of Shulbrede
Ponsonby—Sysonby
Portal—Portal of Hungerford
Powys—Lilford
Pratt—Camden
Preston—Gormanston
Primrose—Rosebery
Prittie—Dunalley
Ramacca—Newburgh
Ramsay—Dalhousie
Ramsbotham—Soulbury
Rees Williams—Ogmore
Rhys—Dynevor
Richards—Milverton
Ritchie—Ritchie of Dundee   [ingham★
Robens—Robens of Wold-
Roberts—Clwyd
Robertson—Robertson of Oakridge
Robinson—Martonmere
Roche—Fermoy
Rodd—Rennell
Roper Curzon—Teynham
Rous—Stradbroke
Rowley Conway—Langford
Runciman — Runcanim of Doxford
Russell—Ampthill
Russell—Bedford
Russell—De Clifford
Russell—R. of Liverpool
Ryder—Harrowby
Sackville—De La Warr
Sackville West—Sackville
St. Aubyn—St. Levan
St. Clair—Sinclair
St. Clair Erskine—Rosslyn
St. John—St. J. of Bletso
St. John—Bolingbroke and St. John
St. Leger—Doneraile
Samuel—Bearsted
Sanderson — Sanderson of Ayot

Sandilands—Torphichen
Saumarez—De Saumarez
Savile—Mexborough
Scarlett—Abinger
Sclater Booth—Basing
Scott—Eldon   [Walden
Scott Ellis—Howard de
Scrymgeour Wedderburn—Dundee
Seager—Leighton of St. Mellons
Seely—Mottistone
Seymour—Hertford
Seymour—Somerset
Shaw—Craigmyle
Shaw—Kilbrandon
Shirley—Ferrers
Shore—Teignmouth
Siddeley—Kenilworth
Sidney—De L'Isle
Simon—Simon of Glaisdale
Simon—Simon of Wythenshawe
Sinclair—Caithness
Sinclair—Pentland
Sinclair—Sinclair of Cleeve
Sinclair—Thurso
Skeffington—Massereene
Smith—Bicester
Smith—Birkenhead
Smith—Colwyn
Smith—Delacourt-Smith★
Smith—Dudley (Barony)
Smith—Hambleden
Snow—Burntwood★
Somerset—Beaufort
Somerset—Raglan
Soskice—Stow Hill★
Spencer—Churchill
Spencer Churchill — Marlborough
Spring Rice—Monteagle of Brandon
Stanhope—Harrington
Stanley—Derby
Stanley—Sheffield
Stapleton Cotton—Combermere
Stern—Michelham
Stewart—Galloway
Stonor—Camoys
Stopford—Courtown
Storey—Buckton★
Stourton—Mowbray
Strachey—O'Hagan
Strachey—Strachie
Strauss—Conesford
Strutt—Belper
Strutt—Rayleigh
Stuart—Castle Stewart
Stuart—Moray
Stuart—Stuart of Findhorn
Studley Herbert — Seafield
Suenson Taylor—Grantchester
Sugden—St. Leonards
Talbot—T. de Malahide
Taylor—Taylor of Gryfe★
Taylor—Taylor of Mansfield★
Taylour—Headfort

Temple Gore Langton—Temple of Stowe
Tennant—Glenconner
Thellusson—Rendlesham
Thesiger—Chelmsford
Thomson—Thomson of Fleet
Thynne—Bath
Tottenham—Ely
Trefusis—Clinton
Trench—Ashtown
Tufton—Hothfield
Turner—Netherthorpe
Turnour—Winterton
Twisleton-Wykeham-Fiennes—Saye and Sele
Tyrrell Kenyon—Kenyon
Upton—Templetown
Urquhart—Tayside★
Vanden Bempde Johnstone—Derwent
Vane—Barnard
Vane Tempest Stewart—Londonderry
Vanneck—Huntingfield
Vaughan—Lisburne
Vaughan Morgan—Reigate★
Vavasseur Fisher—Fisher
Venables Vernon—Vernon
Vereker—Gort
Verney—Willoughby de Broke
Verney Cave—Braye
Vernon—Lyveden
Vesey—De Vesci
Villiers—Clarendon
Vintcent—Wharton
Vivian—Swansea
Wakefield—Wakefield of Kendal
Wallop—Portsmouth
Walsh—Ormathwaite
Ward—Bangor
Ward—Dudley (Earldom)
Ward—Ward of Witley
Warrender — Bruntisfield
Watson—Manton
Watson Armstrong — Armstrong
Weir—Inverforth
Weld Forester—Forester
Wellesley—Cowley
Wellesley—Wellington
Wentworth Fitzwilliam—Fitzwilliam
West—Granville-West★
Westenra—Rossmore
White—Annaly
Whiteley—Marchamley
Whitfield—Kenswood
Willey—Barnby
Williams—Berners
Williamson—Forres
Willoughby—Middleton
Wills—Dulverton
Wilson—Moran
Wilson—Nunburnholme
Wilson—Wilson of Langside★
Windsor—Cornwall
Windsor—Gloucester
Windsor—Kent

Windsor Clive — *Plymouth*
Wingfield—*Powerscourt*
Winn—*St. Oswald*
Winn—*Headley*
Wodehouse—*Kimberley*

Wood—*Halifax*
Woodall — *Uvedale of North End*
Woodhouse— *Terrington*
Wright—*Wootton of Abinger*★

Wright—*Wright of Ashton under Lyne*★
Wyndham—*Leconfield*
Wyndham Quin—*Dunraven*
Wynn—*Newborough*

Yarde Buller—*Churston*
Yerburgh—*Alvingham*
Yorke—*Hardwicke*
Young—*Kennet*
Younger—*Y. of Leckie*

Courtesy Titles (*in actual existence in* 1972)

Holders of Courtesy Titles are addressed in the same manner as holders of substantive titles

From this list it will be seen that, for example, the " Marquess of Blandford " is heir to the Dukedom of Marlborough, and " Viscount Althorp " to the Earldom of Spencer. *Titles of second heirs are also given, and the Courtesy Title of the father of a second heir is indicated by ★; e.g.,* Earl of Sunderland, *eldest son of* ★Marquess of Blandford.

In addition, the heir, and sometimes the second heir, to some Scottish peerages is usually styled " The Master of ——"; *e.g.,* " The Master of Falkland " *is heir to* Viscount Falkland; *and* " The Master of Lindsay " *is eldest son of* ★Lord Balniel, *heir to the* Earl of Crawford and Balcarres. *Users of this style are not included here.*

Marquesses.

★Blandford—*Marlborough*
Bowmont & Cessford—*Roxburghe*
Clydesdale—*Hamilton*
★°Douro—*Wellington*
Graham—*Montrose*
Granby—*Rutland*
★Hamilton—*Abercorn*
★Hartington—*Devonshire*
★Kildare—*Leinster*
★Lorne—*Argyll*
★Tavistock—*Bedford*

Earls.

Aboyne—*Huntly*
Altamont—*Sligo*
Ancram—*Lothian*
Bective—*Headfort*
★Brecknock—*Camden*
★Burford—*St. Albans*
Burlington—★*Hartington*
Campbell and Cowal—*—*★*Lorne*
Cassillis—*Ailsa*
Compton—*Northampton*
★Dalkeith—*Buccleuch*
Dumfries—*Bute*
Euston—*Grafton*
Gifford—*Tweeddale*
°Grosvenor—*Westminster*
°★Hopetoun—*Linlithgow*
°Jermyn—*Bristol*
Macduff—*Fife*
★March and Kinrara—*Richmond*
Mornington—★*Douro*
★Mount Charles—*Conyngham*
Mulgrave—*Normanby*
Offaly—★*Kildare*
°Percy—*Northumberland*
Rocksavage — *Cholmondeley*
★Ronaldshay—*Zetland*
St. Andrews—*Kent*
Shelburne—*Lansdowne*
Sunderland—★*Blandford*
Tyrone—*Waterford*
Uxbridge—*Anglesey*
Wiltshire—*Winchester*
Yarmouth—*Hertford*

Viscounts.

Aithrie—★*Hopetoun*
Alexander—*Caledon*
Althorp—*Spencer*
Asquith—*Oxford & Asquith*
Bayham—★*Brecknock*
Boringdon—*Morley*
Borodale—*Beatty*
Boyle—*Shannon*
Brocas—*Jellicoe*
Bury—*Albemarle*
Campden—*Gainsborough*
Carlow—*Portarlington*
Chelsea—*Cadogan*
Chewton—*Waldegrave*
Cole—*Enniskillen*
Corvedale—*Baldwin of Bewdley*
Cranborne—*Salisbury*
Cranley—*Onslow*
Crichton—*Erne*
Dalrymple—*Stair*
Dawick—*Haig*
Deerhurst—*Coventry*
Dunluce—*Antrim*
Dupplin—*Kinnoull*
Ebrington—*Fortescue*
Eden—*Avon*
Ednam—*Dudley*
Elveden—*Iveagh*
Emlyn—*Cawdor*
Encombe—*Eldon*
Ennismore—*Listowel*
Enfield—*Strafford*
Erleigh—*Reading*
Errington—*Cromer*
Feilding—*Denbigh*
FitzHarris—*Malmesbury*
Folkestone—*Radnor*
Furneaux—*Birkenhead*
Garmoyle—*Cairns*
Garnock—*Lindsay*
Glandine—*Norbury*
Glenapp—*Inchcape*
Glentworth—*Limerick*
Glerawly—*Annesley*
Grimston—*Verulam*
Gwynnedd—*Lloyd George of Dwyfor*
Ikerrin—*Carrick*
Ingestre—*Shrewsbury*

Jocelyn—*Roden*
Kelburn—*Glasgow*
Knebworth—*Lytton*
Lascelles—*Harewood*
Lewisham—*Dartmouth*
Linley—*Snowdon*
Loftus—*Ely*
Lowther—*Lonsdale*
Lymington—*Portsmouth*
Maidstone— *Winchilsea and Nottingham*
Maitland—*Lauderdale*
Mandeville—*Manchester*
Melgund—*Minto*
Moore—*Drogheda*
Morpeth—*Carlisle*
Newport—*Bradford*
Parker—*Macclesfield*
Perceval—*Egmont*
Petersham—*Harrington*
Pollington—*Mexborough*
Prestwood—*Attlee*
Quenington—*St. Aldwyn*
Raynham—*Townshend*
Reidhaven—*Seafield*
Royston—*Hardwicke*
Ruthven of Canberra—*Gowrie*
St. Cyres—*Iddesleigh*
Sandon—*Harrowby*
Savernake—*Ailesbury*
Slane—★*Mount Charles*
Stopford—*Courtown*
Stormont—*Mansfield*
Stralone—*Hamilton*
Strathallan—*Perth*
Stuart—*Castle Stewart*
Sudley—*Arran*
Surdale—*Donoughmore*
Tamworth—*Ferrers*
Tarbat—*Cromartie*
Tiverton—*Halsbury*
Vaughan—*Lisburne*
Villiers—*Jersey*
Weymouth—*Bath*
Windsor—*Plymouth*
Wolmer—*Selborne*

Barons (Lord —)

Apsley—*Bathurst*
Ardee—*Meath*
Balgonie—*Leven & Melville*

Balniel—*Crawford*
Bingham—*Lucan*
Binning—*Haddington*
Brooke—*Warwick*
Bruce—*Elgin*
Buckhurst—*De La Warr*
Burghersh—*Westmorland*
Cardross—*Buchan*
Cochrane—*Dundonald*
Courtenay—*Devon*
Delvin—*Westmeath*
Doune—*Moray*
Dundas—★*Ronaldshay*
Eliot—*St. Germans*
Erskine—*Mar & Kellie*
Eskdaill—★*Dalkeith*
Garlies—*Galloway*
Greenock—*Cathcart*
Guernsey—*Aylesford*
Hay—*Erroll*
Howland—★*Tavistock*
Irwin—*Halifax*
Leslie—*Rothes*
Leveson—*Granville*
Loughborough—*Rosslyn*
Masham—*Swinton*
Mauchline—*Loudoun*
Medway—*Cranbrook*
Montgomerie—*Eglinton and Winton*
Moreton—*Ducie*
Naas—*Mayo* [March
Neidpath—*Wemyss & Norreys of Rycote—Lindsey & Abingdon*
North—*Guilford*
Ogilvy—*Airlie*
Ossulston—*Tankerville*
Oxmantown—*Rosse*
Porchester—*Carnarvon*
Primrose—*Rosebery*
Ramsay—*Dalhousie*
Rosehill—*Northesk*
Scrymgeour—*Dundee*
Settrington—★*March and Kinrara*
Seymour—*Somerset*
Silchester—*Longford*
Strathnaver—*Sutherland*
Vere of Hanworth—★*Burford*
Wodehouse—*Kimberley*
Worsley—*Yarborough*

THE PRIVY COUNCIL

The Privy Council consists of certain eminent persons whose names are given below. Members of the Cabinet must be Privy Councillors, and they principally form the active Privy Council. The Council is summoned as such to act " with others " upon the demise of the Crown, and many matters are referred by the Sovereign to Committees of the Council, some of which are standing Committees, and others constituted to deal with particular cases, *e.g.*, the Judicial Committee.

H.R.H. the Prince Philip, Duke of Edinburgh..... 1951
H.R.H. the Duke of Gloucester........... 1925

Adeane, Sir Michael...... 1953
Ademola, Sir Adetokunbo 1963
Adermann, Sir Charles ... 1966
Aldington, Lord......... 1954
Alexander, Sir Ulick..... 1952
Alport, Lord............ 1960
Amery, Julian.......... 1960
Amory, Viscount....... 1953
Anthony, John Douglas... 1971
Atkinson, Sir Fenton...... 1968
Avon, Earl of........... 1934
Avonside, Lord........ 1962
Aylestone, Lord........ 1962
Azikiwe, Nnamdi........ 1960
Bacon, Lady............ 1966
Baker, Sir George....... 1971
Baker, Philip J. Noel-.... 1945
Balfour of Inchrye, Lord.. 1941
Barber, Anthony........ 1963
Barnes, Alfred.......... 1945
Barrow, Errol.......... 1969
Barrowclough, Sir Harold 1954
Barwick, Sir Garfield.... 1964
Beadle, Sir Hugh....... 1964
Beaufort, Duke of....... 1936
Beaumont, Sir John..... 1944
Benn, Anthony Wedg-wood 1964
Beswick, Lord 1968
Bevins, John Reginald.... 1959
Blakenham, Viscount..... 1955
Bottomley, Arthur George 1952
Boyd of Merton, Viscount 1951
Boyle of Handsworth, Lord.............. 1962
Brecon, Lord 1960
Brooke of Cumnor, Lord.. 1955
Brown, Lord 1970
Buccleuch and Queens-berry, Duke of....... 1937
Buckley, Sir Denys...... 1970
Bustamante, Sir Alexander 1964
Butler of Saffron Walden, Lord 1939
Cairns, Sir David....... 1970
Callaghan, Leonard James 1964
Calwell, Arthur Augustus. 1967
Campbell, Gordon....... 1970
Campbell, Sir Ronald Ian. 1950
Canterbury, The Arch-bishop of 1956
Caradon, Lord.......... 1968
Carpenter, John Boyd-... 1954
Carr, Robert........... 1963
Carrington, Lord 1959
Casey, Lord............ 1939
Castle, Barbara Anne..... 1964
Chalfont, Lord 1964
Champion, Lord......... 1967
Chandos, Viscount....... 1940
Chataway, Christopher... 1970
Chesham, Lord.......... 1964
Citrine, Lord........... 1940
Clayden, Sir John........ 1963

Clitheroe, Lord 1944
Clyde, Lord 1951
Cobbold, Lord.......... 1959
Cobham, Viscount 1957
Cohen, Lord............ 1946
Coleraine, Lord......... 1943
Colyton, Lord.......... 1952
Corfield, Frederick...... 1970
Cousins, Frank 1964
Craigton, Lord.......... 1961
Crathorne, Lord........ 1951
Cromer, Earl of......... 1966
Crosland, Anthony...... 1965
Cross of Chelsea, Lord.... 1969
Crossman, Richard...... 1964
Danckwerts, Sir Harold... 1961
Darling, George......... 1966
Davies, Sir Edmund..... 1966
Davies, John........... 1970
Davies, Sir William Arthian 1961
Davies of Leek, Lord..... 1969
Deedes, William Francis.. 1962
de Freitas, Sir Geoffrey .. 1967
Delacourt-Smith, Lord.... 1969
De La Warr, Earl........ 1936
De L'Isle, Viscount...... 1951
Dell, Edmund.......... 1970
Denning, Lord.......... 1948
Devlin, Lord........... 1960
Devonshire, Duke of..... 1964
Diamond, Lord 1965
Diefenbaker, John 1957
Dilhorne, Viscount...... 1954
Diplock, Lord.......... 1961
Dixon, Sir Owen........ 1951
Donovan, Lord.......... 1960
Drumalbyn, Lord....... 1962
du Cann, Edward........ 1964
Dundee, Earl of......... 1959
Eccles, Viscount........ 1951
Ennals, David.......... 1970
Erroll of Hale, Lord 1960
Fadden, Sir Arthur 1942
Fernyhough, Ernest...... 1970
Ferris, Sir Robert Grant-.. 1971
Fisher of Lambeth, Lord.. 1939
Fletcher, Lord.......... 1967
Foot, Sir Dingle........ 1967
Forde, Francis Michael.... 1944
Franks, Lord........... 1949
Fraser, Hugh........... 1962
Fraser, Thomas......... 1964
Freeman, John.......... 1966
Gardiner, Lord 1964
George-Brown, Lord..... 1951
Gibbs, Sir Humphrey..... 1969
Glendevon, Lord........ 1959
Godber, Joseph Bradshaw. 1963
Gorton, John Grey 1968
Grant, Lord 1958
Greenwood of Rossendale, Lord.............. 1964
Gresson, Sir Kenneth 1963
Griffiths, James 1945
Grimond, Joseph........ 1961
Guest, Lord 1961
Gunter, Raymond James . 1964
Hailes, Lord........... 1951
Hailsham of St. Maryle-bone, Lord......... 1956

Hamilton and Brandon, Duke of.............. 1940
Harlech, Lord........... 1957
Harrison, Sir Eric John... 1952
Hart, Judith........... 1967
Hasluck, Sir Paul....... 1966
Head, Viscount......... 1951
Heald, Sir Lionel....... 1954
Healey, Denis Winston... 1964
Heath, Edward......... 1955
Henderson, Lord........ 1950
Herbison, Margaret...... 1964
Hill of Luton, Lord...... 1955
Hodson, Lord 1951
Holyoake, Sir Keith Jacka. 1954
Home, Sir Alexander Douglas-........... 1951
Houghton, Douglas 1964
Hoy, Lord 1969
Hughes, Lord........... 1970
Hughes, Cledwyn........ 1966
Inman, Lord............ 1947
Irvine, Sir Arthur....... 1970
Irving, Sydney.......... 1969
Isaacs, George Alfred..... 1945
James, Sir Morrice....... 1968
Jay, Douglas........... 1952
Jellicoe, Earl........... 1963
Jenkins, Roy Harris...... 1964
Jones, Aubrey.......... 1955
Jones, Sir Elwyn........ 1964
Joseph, Sir Keith, Bt...... 1962
Karminski, Sir Seymour.. 1967
Kilbrandon, Lord........ 1971
Kilmany, Lord.......... 1962
Kitto, Sir Frank........ 1963
Kotelawala, Sir John..... 1954
Lansdowne, Marquess of.. 1964
Lascelles, Sir Alan....... 1943
Lee, Frederick.......... 1964
Lee of Asheridge, Lady.... 1966
Lever, Harold.......... 1969
Listowel, Earl of........ 1946
Lloyd, Geoffrey William.. 1943
Lloyd, Selwyn.......... 1951
London, The Bishop of... 1961
Longford, Earl of........ 1948
MacAndrew, Lord....... 1952
McBride, Sir Philip...... 1959
McCarthy, Sir Thaddeus.. 1968
McCorquodale of Newton, Lord.............. 1945
MacDermott, Lord....... 1947
MacDonald, Malcolm..... 1935
McEwen, Sir John....... 1953
McKell, Sir William 1948
McMahon, William...... 1966
Macmillan, Harold....... 1942
McTiernan, Sir Edward... 1963
Marples, Alfred Ernest.... 1957
Marquand, Hilary Adair.. 1949
Marsh, Richard William... 1966
Marshall, John Ross...... 1966
Martonmere, Lord....... 1962
Mason, Roy............ 1968
Maudling, Reginald 1955
Maybray-King, Lord...... 1965
Megaw, Sir John........ 1969
Mellish, Robert......... 1967
Menzies, Sir Douglas..... 1963
Menzies, Sir Robert...... 1937

Merthyr, Lord..........	1964	Rhodes, Lord...........	1969	Stow Hill, Lord.........	1948
Milligan, Lord.........	1955	Rhyl, Lord.............	1955	Strathclyde, Lord	1953
Molson, Lord...........	1956	Rippon, Geoffrey.......	1962	Strauss, George Russell...	1947
Morris of Borth-y-Gest, Lord.................	1951	Ritchie of Dundee, Lord..	1965	Summerskill, Lady	1949
Morris, John...........	1970	Robens of Woldingham, Lord.................	1951	Swinton, Earl of	1922
Morton of Henryton, Lord	1944	Roberts, Goronwy......	1968	Thatcher, Mrs. Margaret...	1970
Mountbatten of Burma, Earl	1947	Robinson, Kenneth	1964	Thomas, George........	1968
Muirshiel, Viscount......	1952	Rosebery, Earl of	1945	Thomas, Peter John Mitchell...................	1964
Mulley, Frederick William	1964	Ross, William..........	1964	Thomson, George Morgan.	1966
Munster, Earl of........	1954	Russell, Sir Charles.......	1962	Thorneycroft, Lord.......	1951
Nkrumah, Kwame......	1959	Sachs, Sir Eric..........	1966	Thorpe, Jeremy..........	1967
Noble, *Cdr.* Sir Allan.....	1956	St. Aldwyn, Earl	1959	Touche, Sir Gordon......	1959
Noble, Michael.........	1962	St. Laurent, Louis Stephen	1946	Tredgold, Sir Robert.....	1957
Norfolk, Duke of	1936	Salisbury, Marquess of....	1940	Trevethin and Oaksey, Lord.................	1944
North, Sir Alfred.......	1966	Salmon, Sir Cyril........	1964	Tucker, Lord...........	1945
Nugent of Guildford, Lord.	1962	Salter, Lord............	1941	Turner, Sir Alexander....	1968
Nutting, Harold Anthony	1954	Sandys, Duncan	1944	Turton, Sir Robert Hugh.	1955
O'Brien, Sir Leslie.......	1970	Selborne, Earl of........	1929	Walker, Patrick Gordon-.	1950
Ogmore, Lord	1951	Selkirk, Earl of.........	1955	Walker, Peter..........	1970
Ormerod, Sir Benjamin...	1957	Sellers, Sir Frederic.....	1957	Walsh, Sir Cyril.........	1971
Orr, Sir Alan...........	1971	Shackleton, Lord........	1966	Wand, *Rt. Rev.* John William Charles.......	1943
Owen, Sir William......	1963	Shakespeare, Sir Geoffrey, Bt.................	1945	Ward of Witley, Viscount	1957
Pannell, Charles	1964	Shawcross, Lord	1946	Waterhouse, *Capt.* Charles	1944
Parker of Waddington, Lord..............	1954	Shearer, Hugh..........	1969	Watkinson, Viscount.....	1955
Pearce, Lord...........	1957	Shepherd, Lord	1965	Welensky, Sir Roy.......	1960
Pearson, Lord..........	1961	Shinwell, Lord..........	1945	Wheatley, Lord	1947
Pearson, Lester	1963	Shore, Peter	1967	Whitelaw, William (Lord President).........	1967
Peart, Thomas Frederick	1964	Short, Edward Watson ...	1964	Widgery, Lord..........	1968
Perth, Earl of..........	1957	Silkin, Lord	1945	Wigg, Lord.............	1964
Peyton, John...........	1970	Silkin, John............	1966	Wilberforce, Lord	1964
Phillimore, Sir Henry ...	1968	Simon of Glaisdale, Lord..	1961	Wild, Sir Richard.......	1966
Pickthorn, Sir Kenneth ..	1964	Slesser, Sir Henry	1929	Willey, Frederick Thomas	1964
Poole, Lord	1963	Smith, Sir Derek Colclough Walker-, Bt..........	1957	Williams, Eric..........	1964
Powell, Enoch..........	1960	Smith, Dame Patricia Hornsby-...........	1959	Willink, Sir Henry, Bt....	1943
Prentice, Reginald Ernest..	1966	Smith, Sir Reginald Dorman-............	1939	Wills, Eustace George....	1967
Prior, James...........	1970	Smyth, Sir John, Bt......	1962	Willmer, Sir Henry Gordon	1958
Pym, Francis...........	1970	Soames, Christopher.....	1958	Wilson, James Harold....	1947
Radcliffe, Viscount......	1949	Spens, Lord............	1953	Wilson, of Langside, Lord.	1967
Ramgoolam, Sir Seewoosagur...................	1971	Stable, Sir Wintringham	1965	Windeyer, Sir Victor.....	1963
Ramsden, James........	1963	Stamp, Sir Blanshard.....	1971	Winn, Sir Rodger	1965
Rathcavan, Lord	1937	Stephenson, Sir John......	1971	Wood, Richard Frederick.	1959
Rawlinson, Sir Peter	1964	Stewart, Michael	1964	Woodburn, Arthur.......	1947
Rea, Lord..............	1962	Stonehouse, John Thomas.	1968	Woodcock, George.......	1967
Redmayne, Lord........	1959	Stonham, Lord..........	1969	Wooding, Sir Hugh......	1966
Reid, Lord.............	1941	Stott, Lord	1964	Wylie, Norman	1970
Reigate, Lord..........	1961			York, The Archbishop of.	1961
Renton, Sir David	1962			Younger, Kenneth......	1951

Clerk of the Council, Sir Godfrey Agnew, K.C.V.O.   *Deputy Clerk of the Council,* N. E. Leigh, C.V.O.

THE PREFIX RIGHT HONOURABLE

"Right Honourable."—By long established custom, or courtesy, members of Her Majesty's Most Honourable Privy Council are entitled to be designated "The Right Honourable," but, in practice, this prefix is sometimes absorbed in other designations; for example, a Prince of the Blood admitted a Privy Councillor remains "His Royal Highness"; a Duke remains "His Grace"; a Marquess is still styled "Most Honourable". The style of all other Peers, whether Privy Councillors or not, is "Right Honourable", although it is more usual to describe them with the prefix "The", omitting the more elaborate styles. A Privy Councillor who is not a Peer should be addressed as The Right (or Rt.) Hon. ——. A Peer below the rank of Marquess who is a Privy Councillor should be addressed as The Right (or Rt.) Hon. the Lord (or Earl or Viscount) ——, P.C., or, less elaborately, The Lord (or Earl or Viscount) ——P.C.

THE MOST NOBLE ORDER OF THE GARTER (1348)—K.G.

Ribbon, Garter Blue. *Motto,* Honi soit qui mal y pense (*Shame on him who thinks evil of it*)
The number of Knights Companions is limited to 24.
SOVEREIGN OF THE ORDER—THE QUEEN
H.R.H. The Prince of Wales
Ladies of the Garter—H.M. QUEEN ELIZABETH THE QUEEN MOTHER, 1936.

H.M. THE QUEEN OF THE NETHERLANDS, 1958.

ROYAL KNIGHTS

H.R.H. the Prince Philip, Duke of Edinburgh, 1947.
H.R.H. the Duke of Gloucester, 1021.
H.R.H. the Duke of Windsor, 1936.

EXTRA KNIGHTS

H.M. King Leopold III, 1935.
H.M. the King of Denmark, 1951.
H.M. the King of Sweden, 1954.
H.I.M. the Emperor of Ethiopia, 1954.
H.M. the King of Norway, 1959.
H.M. the King of the Belgians, 1963.
H.I.M. the Emperor of Japan, 1971.
H.R.H. Prince Paul of Yugoslavia, 1939.

KNIGHTS COMPANIONS

The Duke of Norfolk, 1937.
The Duke of Beaufort, 1937.
The Marquess of Salisbury, 1946.
The Earl Mountbatten of Burma, 1946.
The Viscount Montgomery of Alamein, 1946.
The Duke of Portland, 1948.
The Duke of Wellington, 1951.
The Earl of Avon, 1959. [1959.
The Duke of Northumberland,
Sir Gerald Templer, 1963.
The Viscount Cobham, 1964.
The Viscount Brookeborough, 1965.
The Viscount Amory, 1968.
The Viscount De L'Isle, 1968.
The Lord Casey, 1969.

The Lord Ashburton, 1969.
The Viscount Chandos, 1970.
The Lord Cobbold, 1970.
Sir Edmund Bacon, Bt., 1970.
Sir Cennydd Traherne, 1970.
The Earl of Longford, 1971.
The Earl Waldegrave, 1971.
The Lord Butler of Saffron Walden, 1971.
Prelate, The Bishop of Winchester.
Chancellor, The Marquess of Salisbury, K.G., P.C.
Register, The Dean of Windsor.
Garter King of Arms, Sir Anthony Richard Wagner, K.C.V.O.
Gentleman Usher of the Black Rod, Admiral Sir Frank Roddam Twiss, K.C.B., D.S.C.
Secretary, Hon. Sir George Rothe Bellew, K.C.B., K.C.V.O.

THE MOST ANCIENT AND MOST NOBLE ORDER OF THE THISTLE (1687)—K.T.

Ribbon, Green. *Motto,* Nemo me impune lacessit (*No one provokes me with impunity*)
The number of Knights Companions is limited to 16.
SOVEREIGN OF THE ORDER—THE QUEEN

Lady of the Thistle—H.M. QUEEN ELIZABETH THE QUEEN MOTHER, 1937

ROYAL KNIGHTS

H.R.H. the Prince Philip, Duke of Edinburgh, 1952.
H.R.H. the Duke of Gloucester, 1933.
H.R.H. the Duke of Windsor, 1922.

EXTRA KNIGHT

H.M. the King of Norway, 1962.

KNIGHTS COMPANIONS

The Earl of Rosebery, 1947.
The Duke of Buccleuch and Queensberry, 1949.

The Duke of Hamilton and Brandon, 1951.
The Earl of Haddington, 1951.
The Earl of Crawford and Balcarres, 1955.
Sir John Stirling of Fairburn, 1956.
The Lord Kinnaird, 1957.
The Lord Rowallan, 1957.
Sir Alexander Douglas-Home, 1962.
Sir Robert Menzies, 1963.
Sir James Robertson, 1965.
The Earl of Wemyss and March, 1966.

The Lord Maclean, 1969.
The Earl of Dalhousie, 1971.
Sir Richard O'Connor, 1971.
Chancellor, The Duke of Buccleuch and Queensberry, P.C., K.T., G.C.V.O., T.D.
Dean, The Very Rev. H. C. Whitley, M.A. Ph.D.
Lord Lyon King of Arms and Secretary, Sir James Monteith Grant, K.C.V.O., W.S.
Usher of the Green Rod, Sir Reginald Graham of Larbert, Bt., VC, O.B.E.

THE MOST ILLUSTRIOUS ORDER OF SAINT PATRICK (1783)—K.P.

Ribbon, Sky Blue. *Motto,* Quis separabit? (*Who shall separate*) (No conferments since 1934)
SOVEREIGN OF THE ORDER—THE QUEEN
ROYAL KNIGHTS

H.R.H. the Duke of Gloucester, 1934.   H.R.H. the Duke of Windsor, 1927.

Norroy and Ulster King of Arms Registrar and Officer of the Order, R. P. Graham-Vivian, M.V.O., M.C.

THE MOST HONOURABLE ORDER OF THE BATH (1725)

Ribbon, Crimson. *Motto,* Tria juncta in uno (*Three joined in one*). (Remodelled 1815, and enlarged thirteen times since. The Order is divided into civil and military divisions.)

G.C.B. Mil.   G.C.B. Civ.   K.C.B. Mil.   K.C.B. Civ.   C.B. Mil.

THE SOVEREIGN; *Great Master and First or Principal Knight Grand Cross,* Field Marshal H.R.H. the Duke of Gloucester, K.G., P.C., K.T., K.P., G.C.B., G.C.M.G., G.C.V.O.; *Dean of the Order,* The Dean of Westminster; *Bath King of Arms,* General Sir Richard Goodbody, G.C.B., K.B.E., D.S.O.; *Registrar and Secretary,* Air Marshal Sir Anthony Selway, K.C.B., D.F.C.; *Genealogist,* Sir Anthony Wagner, K.C.V.O.; *Gentleman Usher of the Scarlet Rod,* Rear-Admiral C. D. Madden, C.B., C.B.E., M.V.O., D.S.C.; *Deputy Secretary,* The Secretary of the Central Chancery of the Orders of Knighthood; *Chancery.* Central Chancery of the Orders of Knighthood, 8 Buckingham Gate, S.W.1.—G.C.B., Knight (or Dame) Grand Cross; K.C.B., Knight Commander; D.C.B., Dame Commander; C.B., Companion. Women became eligible for the Order from Jan. 1, 1971.

THE ORDER OF MERIT (1902)—O.M. *Ribbon*, Blue and Crimson.

This Order is designed as a special distinction for eminent men and women—without conferring a knighthood upon them. The Order is limited in numbers to 24, with the addition of foreign honorary members. Membership is of two kinds, Military and Civil, the badge of the former having crossed swords, and the latter oak leaves. Membership is denoted by the suffix O.M., which follows the first class of the Order of the Bath and precedes the letters designating membership of the inferior classes of the Bath and all classes of the lesser Orders of Knighthood.

O.M. Mil.   O.M.Civ.

H.R.H. THE DUKE OF EDINBURGH (1968).

The Lord Adrian, 1942.
Sir Robert Robinson, 1949.
Wilder Graves Penfield, 1953.
Sir (Frank) Macfarlane Burnet, 1958.
Graham Vivian Sutherland, 1960.
Sir Basil Urwin Spence, 1962.
Sir Owen Dixon, 1963.

Henry Spencer Moore, 1963.
Edward Benjamin Britten, 1965.
Dorothy Hodgkin, 1965.
The Earl Mountbatten of Burma, 1965.
The Lord Blackett, 1967.
Sir William Turner Walton, 1967.
Ben Nicholson, 1968.
The Lord Zuckerman, 1968.

Malcolm MacDonald, 1969.
The Lord Penney, 1969.
Sir Geoffrey Ingram Taylor, 1969.
Dame Veronica Wedgwood, 1969.
John Cawte Beaglehole, 1970.
Sir Isaiah Berlin, 1971.
Sir George Edwards, 1971.
Lester Pearson, 1971.

Honorary Member, Dr. Sarvepalli Radhakrishnan, 1963.
Secretary and Registrar, (vacant).

THE MOST EXALTED ORDER OF THE STAR OF INDIA (1861).

Ribbon, Light Blue, with White Edges.   *Motto*, Heaven's Light our Guide.

THE SOVEREIGN; *Registrar*, The Secretary of the Central Chancery of the Orders of Knighthood; G.C.S.I., Knight Grand Commander; K.C.S.I., Knight Commander; C.S.I., Companion. No conferments since 1947.

G.C.S.I.

THE MOST DISTINGUISHED ORDER OF ST. MICHAEL AND ST. GEORGE (1818).

Ribbon Saxon Blue, with Scarlet centre. *Motto*, Auspicium melioris ævi (Token of a better age).

THE SOVEREIGN; *Grand Master*, H.R.D. The Duke of Kent, G.C.M.G., G.C.V.O.; *Prelate*, The Bishop of Worcester; *Chancellor*, The Viscount De L'Isle, *V.C.*, K.G., P.C., G.C.M.G., G.C.V.O., *Secretary*, Sir Denis Greenhill, K.C.M.G., O.B.E.; *Registrar*, The Lord Gore-Booth, G.C.M.G., K.C.V.O.; *King of Arms*, The Lord Inchyra, G.C.M.G., C.V.O.; *Gentleman Usher of the Blue Rod*, Sir George Beresford Stooke, K.C.M.G.; *Dean*, The Dean of St. Paul's; *Deputy Secretary*, Maj.-Gen. P. B. Gillett, C.B., O.B.E. *Chancery*, Central Chancery of the Orders of Knighthood, 8 Buckingham Gate, S.W.1.—G.C.M.G., Knight (or Dame), Grand Cross; K.C.M.G., Knight Commander; D.C.M.G., Dame Commander; C.M.G., Companion.

THE MOST EMINENT ORDER OF THE INDIAN EMPIRE (1868).

Ribbon, Imperial Purple. *Motto*, Imperatricis auspiciis (*Under the auspices of the Empress*).

THE SOVEREIGN; *Registrar*, The Secretary of the Central Chancery of the Orders of Knighthood; G.C.I.E., Knight Grand Commander; K.C.I.E., Knight Commander; C.I.E., Companion. No conferments since 1947.

G.C.I.E

THE ROYAL VICTORIAN ORDER (1896).

Ribbon, Blue, with Red and White Edges. *Motto*, Victoria.

THE SOVEREIGN; *Grand Master*, H.M. Queen Elizabeth the Queen Mother; *Chancellor*, The Lord Chamberlain; *Secretary*, The Keeper of the Privy Purse; *Registrar*, The Secretary of the Central Chancery of the Orders of Knighthood; *Chaplain*, The Rev. R. L. Roberts; G.C.V.O., Knight or Dame Grand Cross; K.C.V.O., Knight Commander; D.C.V.O., Dame Commander; C.V.O., Commander; M.V.O., Member, marked 4th or 5th Class.

THE ROYAL VICTORIAN CHAIN (1902).

Founded by King Edward VII, in 1902. It confers no precedence on its holders.

H.M. THE QUEEN

H.M. QUEEN ELIZABETH THE QUEEN MOTHER (1937).

H.R.H. the Duke of Windsor (1921).
H.R.H. the Duke of Gloucester (1932).
Lord Fisher of Lambeth (1949).
The Duke of Norfolk (1953).
The Duke of Beaufort (1953).
The Duke of Hamilton and Brandon (1964).
H.M. The King of Sweden (1923).

H.I.M. The Emperor of Ethiopia (1930).
H.R.H. Prince Paul of Yugoslavia (1934).
H.M. King Leopold III (1937).
H.I.M. The Shahanshah of Iran (1948).
H.M. The Queen of the Netherlands (1950).
H.M. The King of Norway (1955).

H.M. The King of Denmark (1957).
H.M. The King of Thailand (1960).
H.M. The King of Nepal (1961).
H.I.H. The Crown Prince of Ethiopia (1965).
H.M. The King of Jordan (1966) ·
Field Marshal Ayub Khan (1966).
H.M. King Faisal of Saudi Arabia (1967).

THE MOST EXCELLENT ORDER OF THE BRITISH EMPIRE (1917).

Ribbon, Rose pink edged with pearl grey with vertical pearl stripe in centre (Military Division) : without vertical pearl stripe (Civil Division). *Motto*, For God and the Empire.

G.B.E.   **K.B.E.**

The SOVEREIGN: *Grand Master*, H.R.H. the Prince Philip, Duke of Edinburgh, K.G., P.C., K.T., O.M., G.B.E.; *Prelate*, The Bishop of London; *King of Arms*, Lieut.-Gen. Sir George Gordon Lennox, K.B.E., C.B., C.V.O., D.S.O.; *Registrar*, The Secretary of the Central Chancery of the Orders of Knighthood. *Secretary*, The Permanent Secretary to the Civil Service Department; *Dean*, The Dean of St. Paul's; *Gentleman Usher of the Purple Rod*, Sir Robert Bellinger, G.B.E.; *Sub-Dean* (vacant). *Chancery*, Central Chancery of the Orders of Knighthood, 8 Buckingham Gate, S.W.1. G.B.E., Knight or Dame Grand Cross; K.B.E., Knight Commander; D.B.E., Dame Commander; C.B.E., Commander; O.B.E., Officer; M.B.E., Member. The Order was divided into *Military* and *Civil* divisions in Dec. 1918.

ORDER OF THE COMPANIONS OF HONOUR (June 4, 1917)—C.H.

Ribbon, Carmine, with Gold Edges.

This Order consists of one Class only and carries with it no title. It ranks after the 1st Class of the Order of the British Empire, *i.e.*, Knights and Dames Grand Cross (Mil. and Civ. Div.). The number of awards is limited to 65 (excluding honorary members) and the Order is open to both sexes. *Secretary and Registrar*, The Secretary of the Central Chancery of the Orders of Knighthood.

Ashton, Sir Frederick, 1970.
Best, Charles Herbert, 1971.
Blackett, The Lord, 1965.
Bliss, Sir Arthur, 1971.
Boult, Sir Adrian, 1969.
Boyd of Merton, The Viscount, 1960.
Britten, Edward Benjamin, 1953.
Brooke of Cumnor, The Lord, 1964.
Bryant, Sir Arthur, 1967.
Butler of Saffron Walden, The Lord, 1954.
Casey, The Lord, 1944.
Cecil, Lord David Gascoyne, 1949.
Chadwick, Sir James, 1970.
Clark, The Lord, 1959.
Clayton, Rev. Philip T. B., 1933.
Dodd, Rev. Charles Harold, 1961.
Fraser of Lonsdale, The Lord, 1953.
Gorton, John Grey, 1971.
Greene, Graham, 1966.
Griffiths, Rt. Hon. James, 1966.

Hailes, The Lord, 1962.
Hartley, *Brig.-Gen.* Sir Harold, 1967.
Herbert, Sir Alan, 1970.
Hill, *Prof.* Archibald Vivian, 1946.
Holyoake, Rt. Hon. Sir Keith, 1963.
Houghton, Rt. Hon. Douglas, 1967.
Kotelawala, Rt. Hon. Sir John, 1956.
Lloyd, Rt. Hon. Selwyn, 1962.
McEwen, Rt. Hon. Sir John, 1969.
Mann, Arthur Henry, 1941.
Matthews, Very Rev. Walter Robert, 1962.
Menzies, Rt. Hon. Sir Robert, 1951.
Moore, Henry Spencer, 1955.
Muirshiel, The Viscount, 1962.
Payne, The Rev. Ernest Alexander, 1968.
Rahman, Tunku Abdul, 1960.

Reid, The Lord, 1967.
Richards, *Prof.* Ivor Armstrong, 1964.
Robbins, The Lord, 1968.
Selborne, The Earl of, 1945.
Shinwell, The Lord, 1965.
Silkin, The Lord, 1965.
Stewart, Rt. Hon. Michael, 1969.
Summerskill, The Baroness, 1966
Swinton, The Earl of, 1943.
Thorndike, Dame Sybil, 1970.
Toynbee, *Prof.* Arnold Joseph, 1956.
Walker, Rt. Hon. Patrick Christien Gordon, 1968.
Watkinson, The Viscount, 1962.
Wheeler, Sir Mortimer, 1967.
Williams, Rt. Hon. Eric, 1969.
Honorary Members, M. René Massigli, 1954; M. Paul-Henri Spaak, 1963; Lee Kuan Yew, 1970; Dr. Joseph Luns, 1971.

THE ROYAL ORDER OF VICTORIA AND ALBERT (for Ladies)—V.A.

Instituted in 1862, and enlarged in 1864, 1865, and 1880, but no conferments have been made since 1902. Badge, a medallion of Queen Victoria and the Prince Consort, surmounted by a crown, which is attached to a bow of white moiré ribbon. The honour does not confer any rank or title upon the recipient.

FIRST CLASS
H.R.H. the Princess Alice, Countess of Athlone.

SECOND CLASS
Lady Victoria Patricia Helena Ramsay.

THE IMPERIAL ORDER OF THE CROWN OF INDIA (for Ladies)—C.I.

Instituted Dec. 31, 1877. Badge, the royal cipher in jewels within an oval, surmounted by an Heraldic Crown and attached to a bow of light blue watered ribbon, edged white. The honour does not confer any rank or title upon the recipient. No conferments have been made since 1947.

H.M. THE QUEEN, 1947.
H.M. Queen Elizabeth the Queen Mother, 1931.
H.R.H. the Princess Margaret, Countess of Snowdon, 1947.
H.R.H. the Duchess of Gloucester, 1937.

Lady Victoria Patricia Helena Ramsay, 1911.
Dorothy Evelyn Augusta, Dowager Countess of Halifax, 1926.
H.H. Maharani of Travancore, 1929.

Doreen Geraldine, Dowager Baroness Brabourne, 1937.
Eugenie Marie, Countess Wavell, 1943.
Florence Amery, 1945.

THE IMPERIAL SERVICE ORDER (1902) —I.S.O.

Ribbon, Crimson, with Blue Centre.

Appointment of Companion of this Order shall be open to those members of the Civil Services whose eligibility shall be determined by the grade held by such persons. The Order consists of the SOVEREIGN and Companions (not exclusively male) to a number not exceeding 1325 of whom 750 may belong to the Home Civil Services and 575 to Overseas Civil Services. *Secretary*, the Permanent Secretary to the Civil Service Department. *Registrar*, The Secretary of the Central Chancery of the Orders of Knighthood, 8 Buckingham Gate, S.W.1.

Baronets, Knights Grand Cross, Knights Grand Commanders Knights Commanders and Knights Bachelor

Badge of Baronets
of England, Great Britain, U.K.,
(and Ireland marked I.).

Badge of Baronets
of Scotland or Nova Scotia
(marked s.).

NOTES CONCERNING BARONETS

Clause II. of the Royal Warrant of February 8, 1910, ordains as follows:—" That no person whose name is not entered upon the Official Roll shall be received as a Baronet, or shall be addressed or mentioned by that title in any Civil or Military Commission, Letters Patent or other official document." When an obelisk (†) precedes a name it indicates that, *at the time of going to press*, the Baronet concerned has not been registered on the Official Roll of the Baronetage. The date of creation of the Baronetcy is given in parenthesis ( ).

Baronets are addressed as " Sir "(with Christian name) and in writing as " Sir Robert *A*—, Bt." Baronets' wives are addressed (formally) as " Your Ladyship " or " Lady *A*—," without any Christian name unless a daughter of a Duke, Marquess or Earl, in which case " The Lady Mary *A*— "; if daughter of a Viscount or Baron " The Hon. Lady *A*—."

NOTES CONCERNING KNIGHTS GRAND CROSS, ETC.

Knights Grand Cross, Knights Grand Commanders and Knights Commanders are addressed in the same manner as Baronets (*q.v.*), but in writing the appropriate initials (G.C.B., K.C.B., &c.) are appended to surname after "Bt." if they are also baronets or in place of "Bt." if they are not. Knights Bachelor are addressed as " Sir —— (first or Christian name) "and in writing as " Sir —— *B*—." The wife of a Knight Grand Cross, Knight Grand Commander, Knight Commander or Knight Bachelor is addressed as stated for the wife of a Baronet.

NOTES CONCERNING KNIGHTS BACHELOR

The Knights Bachelor do not constitute a Royal Order, but comprise the surviving representation of the ancient State Orders of Knighthood. The Register of Knights Bachelor, instituted by James I. in the 17th century, lapsed, and in 1908 a voluntary Association under the title of "The Society of Knights" (now "The Imperial Society of Knights Bachelor " by Royal command) was formed with the primary objects of continuing the various registers dating from 1257 and obtaining the uniform registration of every created Knight Bachelor. In 1926 a design for a badge to be worn by Knights Bachelor was approved and adopted, a miniature reproduction being shown above. The Officers of the Society are:—*Knight Principal*, Sir Anthony Wagner, K.C.V.O., *Deputy Knight Principal*, Hon. Sir George Bellew, K.C.B., K.C.V.O.; *Hon. Registrar*, Sir John Weir Russell; *Clerk*, Mrs. Rodney; *Registry and Library*, 21 Old Buildings, Lincoln's Inn, W.C.2.

BARONETAGE AND KNIGHTAGE

(Revised to Aug. 13, 1971)
Peers are not included in this list.

A full entry in italic type indicates that the recipient of a Knighthood died during the year in which the honour was conferred. The name is included for purposes of record.

Aarons, Sir Daniel Sidney, Kt., O.B.E., M.C.

Aarvold, *His Hon.* Sir Carl Douglas, Kt., O.B.E., T.D.

Abayomi, Sir Kofo Adekunle, Kt.

Abbott, *Very Rev.* Eric Symes, K.C.V.O., D.D.

Abbott, *Hon.* Sir Myles John, Kt.

Abdy, Sir Robert Henry Edward, Bt. (1850).

Abell, Sir Anthony Foster, K.C.M.G.

Abell, Sir George Edmond Brackenbury, K.C.I.E. O.B.E.

Abercromby, *Maj.* Sir Robert Alexander, Bt., M.C. (S. 1636).

Abrahall, Sir Theo Chandos Hoskyns-, Kt., C.M.G.

Abrahams, Sir Charles, K.C.V.O.

Acheson, Sir James Glasgow, Kt., C.I.E.

Ackner, *Hon.* Sir Desmond James Conrad, Kt.

Ackroyd, Sir Cuthbert Lowell, Bt. (1956).

Acland, *Capt.* Sir Hubert Guy Dyke, Bt., D.S.O., R.N. (1890).

Acland, Sir (Hugh) John (Dyke), K.B.E.

Acland, Sir Richard Thomas Dyke, Bt. (1644).

Acutt, Sir Keith Courtney, K.B.E.

Adair, *Maj.-Gen.* Sir Allan Henry Shafto, Bt., K.C.V.O., C.B., D.S.O., M.C. (1838).

Adam, *Hon.* Sir Alistair Duncan Grant, Kt.

Adam, *General* Sir Ronald Forbes, Bt., G.C.B., D.S.O., O.B.E. (1917).

Adams, Sir Ernest Charles, Kt., C.B.E.

Adams, *Hon.* Sir Francis Boyd, Kt.

Adams, Sir Grantley Herbert, Kt., C.M.G., Q.C.

Adams, Sir Maurice Edward, K.B.E.

Adams, Sir Philip George Doyne, K.C.M.G.

Adams, Sir Walter, Kt., C.M.G., O.B.E.

Adamson, Sir Kenneth Thomas, Kt., C.M.G.

Adcock, Sir Robert Henry, Kt., C.B.E.

Addis, Sir William, K.B.E., C.M.G.

Adeane, *Lt.-Col.* Rt. Hon. Sir Michael Edward, G.C.B., G.C.V.O.

Adeane, *Col.* Sir Robert Philip Wyndham, Kt., O.B.E.

Ademola, *Rt. Hon.* Sir Adetokunbo Adegboyega, K.B.E.

Adermann, *Rt. Hon.* Sir Charles Frederick, K.B.E.

Adjaye, Sir Edward Otchere Asafu-, Kt.

Adrien, Sir Maurice Latour-, Kt.

Agnew, Sir Fulque Melville Gerald Noel, Bt. (S 1629).

Agnew, Sir (John) Anthony Stuart, Bt. (1895).

Agnew, Sir Norris Montgomerie, Kt., C.B.E.

Agnew, *Cdr.* Sir Peter Garnett, Bt. (1957).

Agnew, Sir (William) Godfrey, K.C.V.O.

Ainley, Sir (Alfred) John, Kt., M.C.

Ainscough, Sir Thomas Martland, Kt., C.B.E.

Ainsworth, Sir John Francis, Bt. (1917).

Aird, *Col.* Sir John Renton, Bt., M.V.O., M.C. (1901).

Airey, *Lt.-Gen.* Sir Terence Sydney, K.C.M.G., C.B., C.B.E.

Aitchison, Sir Charles Walter de Lancey, Bt. (1938).

Aitchison, *Capt.* Sir David, K.C.V.O.

Aitken, Sir Arthur Percival Hay, Kt.

Aitken, Sir (John William) Maxwell, Bt., D.S.O., D.F.C. (1916).

Aitken, Sir Robert Stevenson, Kt., M.D., D.phil.

Albu, Sir George, Bt. (1912).

Alderson, Sir Harold George, Kt., M.B.E.

Aldington, Sir Geoffrey William, K.B.E., C.M.G.

Alexander, Sir Charles Gundry, Bt. (1945).

Alexander, Sir Claud Hagart-, Bt. (1886).

Alexander, Sir Desmond William Lionel Cable, Bt. (1809).

Alexander, Sir Douglas Hamilton, Bt. (1921).

Alexander, Sir Norman Stanley, Kt., C.B.E.

Alexander, *Maj. Rt.Hon.* Sir Ulick, G.C.B., G.C.V.O., C.M.G., O.B.E.

Alexander, Sir William Picken, Kt., ph.D.

Alford, Sir Robert Edmund, K.B.E., C.M.G.

Algie, *Hon.* Sir Ronald Macmillan, Kt.

Allan, Sir Henry Ralph Moreton Havelock-, Bt. (1858).

Allan, Sir Robert George, Kt., C.I.E.

Allcroft, Sir Philip Montefiore Magnus-, Bt., C.B.E. (1917).

Allen, Sir Donald Richard, Kt., O.B.E., M.C.

Allen, Sir Douglas Albert Vivian, K.C.B.

Allen, Sir Peter Christopher, Kt.

Allen, Sir Philip, G.C.B.

Allen, Sir Richard Hugh Sedley, K.C.M.G.

Allen, Sir Roger, K.C.M.G.

Allen, *Prof.* Sir Roy George Douglas, Kt., C.B.E., D.Sc., F.B.A.

Allen, Sir (William) Denis, G.C.M.G., C.B.

Allen, Sir William Kenneth Gwynne, Kt.

Alleyne, *Capt.* Sir John Meynell, Bt., D.S.O., D.S.C., R.N. (1769).

Allison, Sir Charles William, Kt., C.B.E.

Allitt, Sir John William, Kt., M.B.E.

Allum, Sir John Andrew Charles, Kt., C.B.E.

Aluwihare, Sir Richard, K.C.M.G., C.B.E.

Amcotts, *Lt.-Col.* Sir Weston Cracroft-, Kt., M.C.

Ameer Ali, Sir Torick, Kt.

Ames, Sir Cyril Geraint, Kt.

Amies, *Prof.* Sir Arthur Barton Pilgrim, Kt., C.M.G.

Amory, Sir John Heathcoat-, Bt. (1874).

Anderson, Sir Austin Innes, Kt.

Anderson, Sir Colin Skelton, K.B.E.

Anderson, Sir David Stirling, Kt., Ph.D.

Anderson, Sir Donald Forsyth, Kt.

Anderson, Sir Donald George, Kt., C.B.E.

Anderson, Sir Duncan Law, K.B.E., T.D.

Anderson, Sir Edward Arthur, Kt.

Anderson, Sir Gilmour Menzies, Kt., C.B.E.

Anderson, *General* Sir John D'Arcy, G.B.E., K.C.B., D.S.O.

Anderson, *Maj.-Gen.* Sir John Evelyn, K.B.E.

Anderson, Sir John Muir, Kt., C.M.G.

Anderson, Sir Kenneth, K.B.E., C.B.

Anderson, *Hon.* Sir Kenneth McColl, Kt.

Anderson, *Lt.-Gen.* Sir Richard Neville, K.C.B., C.B.E., D.S.O.

Andrew, *Rev.* Sir (George) Herbert, K.C.M.G., C.B.

Andrewes, Sir Christopher Howard, Kt., M.D., F.R.S.

Andrewes, *Admiral* Sir William Gerrard, K.B.E., C.B., D.S.O.

Andrews, Sir Edwin Arthur Chapman-, K.C.M.G., O.B.E.

Andrews, Sir (William) Linton, Kt.

Angas, Sir John Keith, Kt.

Ankole, The Omugabe of, Kt.

Annamunthodo, *Prof.* Sir Harry, Kt., F.R.C.S.

Ansell, *Col.* Sir Michael Picton, Kt., C.B.E., D.S.O.

Ansett, Sir Reginald Myles, K.B.E.

Anson, Sir (George) Wilfrid, Kt.

Anson, *Capt.* Sir Peter, Bt., R.N. (1831).

Ansorge, Sir Eric Cecil, Kt., C.S.I., C.I.E.

Anstice, *Vice-Adm.* Sir Edmund Walter, K.C.B.

Anstruther, Sir Ralph Hugo, Bt. C.V.O., M.C. (S 1694).

Anstruther, Sir Windham Eric Francis Carmichael-, Bt. (S. 1700; G.B. 1798).

Anthony, Sir Michael Mobolaji Bank-, K.B.E.

Antrobus, Sir Philip Coutts, Bt. (1815).

Arbuthnot, Sir Hugh Fitzgerald, Bt. (1823).

Arbuthnot, Sir John Sinclair-Wemyss, Bt., M.B.E., T.D. (1964).

Archdale, *Comdr.* Sir Edward Folmer, Bt. D.S.C., R.N. (1928).

Archer, Sir Clyde Vernon Harcourt, Kt.

Archey, Sir Gilbert Edward, Kt., C.B.E.

Arkell, *Capt.* Sir (Thomas) Noel, Kt.

Armer, Sir (Isaac) Frederick, K.B.E., C.B., M.C.

Armitage, *General* Sir (Charles) Clement, K.C.B., C.M.G., D.S.O.

Armitage, Sir Robert Perceval, K.C.M.G., M.B.E.

Armstrong, Sir Andrew St. Clare, Bt. (1841).

Armstrong, Sir Thomas Henry Wait, Kt., D.MUS.

Armstrong, Sir William, G.C.B., M.V.O.

Armytage, *Capt.* Sir (John) Lionel, Bt. (1738).

Arnold, Sir William Henry, Kt., C.B.E.

Arnott, Sir John Robert Alexander, Bt. (1896).

Arnott, *Prof.* Sir (William) Melville, Kt., T.D., M.D.

Arrowsmith, Sir Edwin Porter, K.C.M.G.

Arthur, Sir Basil Malcolm, Bt. (1841).

Arthur, Sir Geoffrey George, K.C.M.G.

Arthur, Sir (Oswald) Raynor, K.C.M.G., C.V.O.

Arundell, *Brig.* Sir Robert Duncan Harris, K.C.M.G., O.B.E.

Arup, Sir Ove Nyquist, Kt., C.B.E.

Ashbridge, Sir Noel, Kt.

Ashburnham, Sir Denny Reginald, Bt. (1661).

Ashby, Sir Eric, Kt., D.SC., F.R.S.

Ashenheim, Sir Neville Noel, Kt., C.B.E.

Ashmore, *Admiral* Sir Edward Beckwith, K.C.B., D.S.C.

Ashton, Sir (Arthur) Leigh (Bolland), Kt.

Ashton, Sir Frederick William Mallandaine, Kt., C.H., C.B.E.

Ashton, Sir Hubert, Kt., M.B.E.

Ashwin, Sir Bernard Carl, K.B.E., C.M.G.

Ashworth, *Hon.* Sir John Percy, Kt., M.B.E.

Aske, Sir Conan, Bt., (1922).

Astbury, Sir George, Kt.

Astley, Sir Francis Jacob Dugdale, Bt. (1821).

Aston, *Hon.* Sir William John, K.C.M.G.

Atkins, *Prof.* Sir Hedley John Barnard, K.B.E., D.M., F.R.C.S.

Atkinson, *Rt. Hon.* Sir Fenton, Kt.

Atkinson, Sir (John) Kenneth, Kt.

Atkinson, *Maj.-Gen.* Sir Leonard Henry, K.B.E.

Attygalle, *Hon.* Sir Nicholas, Kt.

Auchinleck, *Field Marshal* Sir Claude John Eyre, G.C.B., G.C.I.E., C.S.I., D.S.O., O.B.E.

Austin, Sir John (Byron Fraser), Bt. (1894).

Austin, Sir John Worroker, Kt.

Austin, Sir Thomas, K.C.I.E.

Axon, Sir Albert Edwin, K.B.E.

Ayer, *Prof.* Sir Alfred Jules, Kt., F.B.A.

Aykroyd, Sir William Miles, Bt., M.C. (1920).

Aykroyd, Sir Cecil William, Bt. (1929).

Aylmer, Sir Felix, Kt., O.B.E.

Aylmer, Sir Fenton Gerald, Bt. (1622).

Babington, *Rt. Hon.* Sir Anthony Brutus, Kt., Q.C.

Backhouse, Sir Jonathan Roger, Bt. (1901).

Bacon, Sir Edmund Castell, Bt. K.G., K.B.E., T.D. *Premier Baronet of England* (1611 and 1627).

Bacon, Sir Ranulph Robert Maunsell, Kt.

Baddeley, Sir John Beresford, Bt. (1922).

Badenoch, Sir (Alexander) Cameron, K.C.I.E., C.S.I.

Bagge, Sir John Alfred Picton, Bt. (1867).

Bagnall, *Hon.* Sir William Arthur, Kt., M.B.E.

Bagrit, Sir Leon, Kt.

Bailey, Sir Derrick Thomas Louis, Bt., D.F.C. (1919).

Bailey, Sir Donald Coleman, Kt., O.B.E.

Bailey, *Prof.* Sir Harold Walter, Kt., D.Phil., F.B.A.

Bailey, Sir Kenneth Hamilton, Kt., C.B.E.

Baillie, Sir Gawaine George Hope, Bt. (1823).

Bairamian, *Hon.* Sir Vahe Robert, Kt.

Baird, Sir David Charles, Bt. (1809).

Baird, *Prof.* Sir Dugald, Kt., M.D.

Baird, Sir James Richard Gardiner, Bt., M.C. (S. 1695).

Baker, *Air Marshal* Sir Brian Edmund, K.B.E., C.B., D.S.O., M.C., A.F.C.

Baker, *Field-Marshal* Sir Geoffrey Harding, G.C.B., C.M.G., K.C.B., M.C.

Baker, *Rt. Hon.* Sir George Gillespie, Kt., O.B.E.

Baker, Sir Humphrey Dodington Benedict Sherston-, Bt. (1796).

Baker, *Prof.* Sir John Fleetwood, Kt., O.B.E., Sc.D., F.R.S.

Baker, *Air Chief Marshal* Sir John Wakeling, G.B.E., K.C.B., M.C., D.F.C.

Baker, Sir Rowland, Kt., O.B.E.

Baker, Sir (Stanislaus) Joseph, Kt., C.B.

Balcon, Sir Michael, Kt.

Baldwin, *Air Marshal* Sir John Eustace Arthur, K.B.E., C.B., D.S.O.

Balfour, Sir John, G.C.M.G., G.B.E.

Balfour, *Lt.-Gen.* Sir Philip Maxwell, K.B.E., C.B., M.C.

Balfour, *General* Sir (Robert George) Victor FitzGeorge-, K.C.B., C.B.E., D.S.O., M.C.

Ball, *Air Vice-Marshal* Sir Benjamin, K.B.E., C.B.

Ball, Sir Nigel Gresley, Bt. (1911).

Balmer, Sir Joseph Reginald, Kt.

Banks, *Maj.-Gen.* Sir Donald, K.C.B., D.S.O., M.C., T.D.

Banks, Sir John Garnett, Kt., C.B.E.

Banks, Sir Maurice Alfred Lister, Kt.

Banner, Sir George Knowles Harmood-, Bt. (1924).

Bannerman, *Lt.-Col.* Sir Donald Arthur Gordon, Bt. (S. 1682).

Banwell, Sir (George) Harold, Kt.

Barber, Sir Herbert William, Kt.

Barber, *Lt.-Col.* Sir William Francis, Bt., T.D. (1960).

Barclay, Sir Colville Herbert Sanford, Bt. (S. 1668).

Barclay, Sir Roderick Edward, G.C.V.O., K.C.M.G.

Barford, Sir Leonard, Kt.

Baring, Sir Charles Christian, Bt. (1911).

Barker, Sir Alwyn Bowman, Kt., C.M.G.

Barker, Sir Charles Frederic James, Kt., M.B.E.

Barker, *General* Sir Evelyn Hugh, K.C.B., K.B.E., D.S.O., M.C.

Barker, Sir William, K.C.M.G., O.B.E.

Barlow, Sir Christopher Hilaro, Bt. (1803).

Barlow, Sir John Denman, Bt. (1907).

Barlow, Sir Robert, Kt.

Barlow, Sir Thomas Erasmus, Bt., D.S.C. (1902).

Barnard, Sir (Arthur) Thomas, Kt., C.B., O.B.E.

Barnard, *Vice-Adm.* Sir Geoffrey, K.C.B., C.B.E., D.S.O.

Barnard, *Capt.* Sir George Edward, Kt.

Barnard, Sir Henry William, Kt.

Barnes, Sir Denis Charles, K.C.B.

Barnes, Sir William Lethbridge Gorell-, K.C.M.G., C.B.

Barnett, Sir Ben Lewis, K.B.E., C.B., M.C.

Barnett, *Air Chief Marshal* Sir Denis Hensley Fulton, G.C.B., C.B.E., D.F.C.

Barnett, Sir Oliver Charles, Kt., C.B.E., Q.C.

Barnewall, Sir Reginald Robert, Bt. (I. 1623).

Barraclough, *Air Marshal* Sir John, K.C.B., C.B.E., D.F.C., A.F.C.

Barraclough, *Brig.* Sir John Ashworth, Kt., C.M.G., D.S.O., O.B.E., M.C.

Barran, Sir David Haven, Kt.

Barran, Sir John Leighton, Bt. (1895).

Barratt, Sir Sydney, Kt.

Barrett, Sir Arthur George, Kt.

Barrie, Sir Walter, Kt.

Barrington, Sir Charles Bacon, Bt. (1831).

Barritt, Sir David Thurlow, Kt.

Barrow, Sir Malcolm Palliser, Kt.

Barrow, Sir Richard John Uniacke, Bt. (1835).

Barrowclough, *Rt. Hon.* Sir Harold Eric, K.C.M.G. C.B., D.S.O., M.C., E.D.

Barry, Sir Patrick Redmond Joseph, Kt., M.C.

Barry, Sir Rupert Rodney Francis Tress, Bt., M.B.E. (1809).

Barter, Sir Percy, Kt., C.B.

Bartlett, *Lt.-Col.* Sir Basil Hardington, Bt. (1913).

Barttelot, Sir Brian Walter de Stopham, Bt. (1875).

Barwick, *Rt. Hon.* Sir Garfield Edward John, G.C.M.G.

Barwick, Sir Richard Llewellyn, Bt. (1912).

Baskett, *Prof.* Sir Ronald Gilbert, Kt., O.B.E.

Bassett, Sir Walter Eric, K.B.E., M.C.

Basten, Sir Henry Bolton, Kt., C.M.G.

Bastyan, *Lt.-Gen.* Sir Edric Montague, K.C.M.G., K.C.V.O., K.B.E., C.B.

Bate, Sir William Edwin, Kt. O.B.E.

Bateman, Sir Cecil Joseph, K.B.E.

Bateman, Sir Charles Harold, K.C.M.G., M.C.

Bates, Sir Alfred, Kt., M.C.

Bates, *Maj.-Gen.* Sir (Edward) John (Hunter), K.B.E., C.B., M.C.

Bates, Sir Geoffrey Voitelin, Bt., M.C. (1880).

Bates, Sir John David, Kt., C.B.E., V.R.D.

Bates, Sir (John) Dawson, Bt. (1937).

Bates, Sir (Julian) Darrell, Kt., C.M.G., C.V.O.

Batho, Sir Maurice Benjamin, Bt., (1928).

Bathurst, Sir Frederick Peter Methuen Hervey-, Bt. (1818).

Batterbee, Sir Harry Fagg, G.C.M.G., K.C.V.O.

Baulkwill, Sir (Reginald) Pridham, Kt., C.B.E.

Bawden, Sir Frederick Charles, Kt., F.R.S.

Baxter, *Prof.* Sir John Philip, K.B.E., C.M.G.

Bayly, *Vice-Adm.* Sir Patrick Uniacke, K.B.E., C.B., D.S.C.

Baynes, Sir William Edward Colston, Bt., M.C. (1801).

Bazley, Sir Thomas Stafford, Bt. (1869).

Bazl-ul-lah, *Sahib Bahadur* K. B., Sir Muhammad, Kt., C.I.E., O.B.E.

Beadle, Sir Gerald Clayton, Kt., C.B.E.

Beadle, *Rt. Hon.* Sir (Thomas) Hugh (William), Kt., C.M.G., O.B.E.

Beale, *Hon.* Sir (Oliver) Howard, K.B.E., Q.C.

Beale, Sir William Francis, Kt., O.B.E.

Beamish, *Col.* Sir Tufton Victor Hamilton, Kt., M.C., M.P.

Bean, Sir Edgar Layton, Kt., C.M.G.

Bean, *Hon.* Sir George Joseph, Kt., O.B.E.

Beauchamp, Sir Brograve Campbell, Bt. (1911).

Beauchamp, Sir Christopher Radstock Proctor-, Bt. (1745).

Beauchamp, Sir Douglas Clifford, Bt. (1918).

Beaumont, Sir George (Howland Francis), Bt. (1661).

Beaumont, *Rt. Hon.* Sir John William Fisher, Kt., Q.C.

Beaumont, Sir Richard Ashton, K.C.M.G., O.B.E.

Becher, Sir William Fane Wrixon Bt., M.C. (1831).

Becker, Sir Jack Ellerton, Kt.

Beckett, Sir Eric Frederick, Kt., C.B.E.

Beckett, *Capt.* Sir (Martyn) Gervase, Bt., M.C., (1921).

Bedingfeld, *Capt.* Sir Edmund George Felix Paston-, Bt. (1661).

Bednall, *Maj.-Gen.* Sir Peter, K.B.E., C.B., M.C.

Beecham, Sir Adrian Welles, Bt. (1914).

Beeley, Sir Harold, K.C.M.G., C.B.E.

Beetham, Sir Edward Betham, K.C.M.G., C.V.O., O.B.E.

Beevor, Sir Thomas Agnew, Bt. (1784).

Begg, *Admiral of the Fleet* Sir Varyl Cargill, G.C.B., D.S.O., D.S.C.

Beharrell, Sir (George) Edward, Kt.

Behrens, Sir Leonard Frederick, Kt., C.B.E.

Beit, Sir Alfred Lane, Bt. (1924).

Beith, Sir John Greville Stanley, K.C.M.G.

Bell, Sir Arthur Capel Herbert, Kt.

Bell, Sir Douglas James, Kt., C.B.E.

Bell, Sir Frederick (Archibald), Kt., O.B.E., M.C.

Bell, Sir Gawain Westray, K.C.M.G., C.B.E.

Bell, Sir John Lowthian, Bt. (1885).

Bell, Sir Stanley, Kt., O.B.E.

Bell, Sir William Hollin Dayrell Morrison-, Bt. (1905).

Bellew, Sir Arthur John Grattan-, Kt., C.M.G., Q.C.

Bellew, *Hon.* Sir George Rothe, K.C.B., K.C.V.O., F.S.A.

Bellew, Sir Henry Charles Grattan-, Bt. (1838).

Bellinger, Sir Robert Ian, G.B.E.

Bellingham, Sir Roger Carroll Patrick Stephen, Bt. (1796).

Bemrose, Sir (John) Maxwell, Kt.

Benn, *Capt.* Sir (Patrick Ion) Hamilton, Bt. (1920).

Benn, Sir John Andrews, Bt. (1914).

Bennett, Sir Albert Edward, Kt.

Bennett, Sir Frederic Mackarness, Kt., M.P.

Bennett, Sir Hubert, Kt.

Bennett, Sir John Wheeler Wheeler-, K.C.V.O., C.M.G., O.B.E.

Bennett, Sir Ronald Wilfrid Murdoch, Bt. (1929).

Bennett, Sir Thomas Penberthy, K.B.E.

Bennett, Sir William Gordon, Kt.

Benson, Sir Arthur Edward Trevor, G.C.M.G.

Benson, *Rev.* Sir (Clarence) Irving, Kt., C.B.E.

Benson, Sir George, Kt.

Benson, Sir Henry Alexander, G.B.E.

Benstead, Sir John, Kt., C.B.E.

Benthall, Sir (Arthur) Paul, K.B.E.

Bentinck, *Maj.* Sir Ferdinand William Cavendish-, K.B.E., C.M.G.

Berar, H.H. the Prince of, G.C.I.E., G.B.E.

Berendsen, Sir Carl August, K.C.M.G.

Berlin, Sir Isaiah, Kt., O.M., C.B.E.

Bernard, Sir Dallas Gerald Mercer, Bt. (1954).

Berney, *Capt.* Sir Thomas Reedham, Bt., M.C. (1620).

Berrill, Sir Kenneth Ernest, K.C.B.

Berry, Sir (Henry) Vaughan, Kt.

Berryman, *General* Sir Frank Horton, K.C.V.O., C.B., C.B.E., D.S.O.

Berthoud, Sir Eric Alfred, K.C.M.G.

Best, Sir John Victor Hall, Kt.

Bethune, Sir Alexander Maitland Sharp, Bt. (S 1683).

Betjeman, Sir John, Kt., C.B.E.

Bevan, Sir David Martyn Evans, Bt. (1958).

Bevan, *Rear-Adm.* Sir Richard Hugh Loraine, K.B.E., C.B., D.S.O., M.V.O.

Beverley, *Vice-Adm.* Sir (William) York (La Roche), K.B.E., C.B.

Bevir, Sir Anthony, K.C.V.O., C.B.E.

Bhagchand Soni, *Rai Bahadur* Sir Seth, Kt., O.B.E.

Bibby, *Maj.* Sir (Arthur) Harold, Bt., D.S.O. (1959).

Biddulph, Sir Francis Henry, Bt. (1664).

Biggart, *Prof.* Sir (John) Henry, Kt., C.B.E., D.SC., M.D., F.R.C.P.

Bigge, Sir John Amherst Selby-, Bt., O.B.E., (1919).

Biggs, *Vice-Adm.* Sir Hilary Worthington, K.B.E., C.B., D.S.O.

Biggs, Sir Lionel William, Kt.

Bing, Sir Rudolf Franz Josef, K.B.E.

Bingen, Sir Eric Albert, Kt.

Bingley, *Admiral* Sir Alexander Noel Campbell, G.C.B., O.B.E.

Binney, Sir George, Kt., D.S.O.

Binns, Sir Arthur Lennon, Kt., C.B.E., M.C.

Bird, *Lt.-Gen.* Sir Clarence August, K.C.I.E., C.B., D.S.O.

Bird, Sir Cyril Pangbourne, Kt.

Bird, Sir Hugh Stonehewer-, K.C.M.G., O.B.E.

Bird, Sir Richard Geoffrey Chapman, Bt. (1922).

Birkin, Sir Charles Lloyd, Bt. (1905).

Birkmyre, Sir Henry, Bt. (1921).

Birley, Sir Robert, K.C.M.G., F.S.A.

Bishop, Sir (Frank) Patrick, Kt., M.B.E.

Bishop, Sir Harold, Kt., C.B.E.

Bishop, *Instructor Rear-Adm.*, Sir William Alfred, K.B.E., C.B.

Bishop, *Maj.-Gen.* Sir William Henry Alexander, K.C.M.G., C.B., C.V.O., O.B.E.

Bishop, Sir William Poole, Kt., C.M.G.

Black, Sir Cyril Wilson, Kt.

Black, Sir Harold, Kt.

Black, Sir Robert Andrew Stransham, Bt. (1922).

Black, Sir Robert Brown, G.C.M.G. O.B.E.

Blackall, Sir Henry William Butler, Kt., Q.C.

Blackburn, *Lt.-Col.* Sir Charles Bickerton, K.C.M.G., O.B.E., M.D.

Blackburn, Sir Thomas, Kt.

Blackburne, Sir Kenneth William, G.C.M.G., G.B.E

Blacker, *Lt.-Gen.* Sir Cecil Hugh, K.C.B., O.B.E., M.C.

Blackett, Sir George William, Bt. (1673).

Blackwell, Sir Basil Henry, Kt.

Blackwood, Sir Francis Elliot Temple, Bt. (1819).

Blackwood, Sir Robert Rutherford, Kt.

Blagden, Sir John Ramsay, Kt., O.B.E., T.D.

Blair, *Maj.* Sir Alastair Campbell, K.C.V.O., T.D.

Blair, Sir James Hunter-, Bt. (1786).

Blair, *Col.* Sir Patrick James, K.B.E., D.S.O., T.D.

Blake, *Cdr.* Sir Cuthbert Patrick, Bt., D.S.O., R.N. (1772).

Blake, Sir (Francis) Michael, Bt. (1907).

Blake, Sir Thomas Richard Valentine, Bt. (I 1622).

Blaker, Sir Reginald, Bt., T.D. (1919).

Blakiston, Sir Arthur Frederick, Bt., M.C. (1763).

Bland, Sir (George) Nevile (Maltby), K.C.M.G., K.C.V.O.

Bland, Sir Henry Armand, Kt., C.B.E.

Blennerhassett, Sir Marmaduke Adrian Francis William, Bt. (1809).

Bligh, Sir Edward Clare, Kt.

Bliss, Sir Arthur, K.C.V.O., C.H. MUS.D., LL.D.

Blois, Sir Charles Nicholas Gervase, Bt. (1686).

Blomefield, Sir Thomas Edward Peregrine, Bt. (1807).

Bloomfield, *Hon.* Sir John Stoughton, Kt., Q.C.

Blosse, Sir David Edward Lynch-, Bt. (1622).

Blount, Sir Edward Robert, Bt. (1642).

Blundell, Sir Edward Denis, K.B.E.

Blundell, Sir Michael, K.B.E.

Blunden, Sir William, Bt. (1766).

Blunt, *Prof.* Sir Anthony Frederick, K.C.V.O., F.B.A.

Blunt, Sir Richard David Harvey, Bt. (1720).

Blyde, Sir Henry Ernest, K.B.E.

Board, Sir (Archibald) Vyvyan, Kt., D.S.O., M.C.

Bodilly, *Hon.* Sir Jocelyn, Kt., V.R.D.

Boevey, Sir Thomas Michael Blake Crawley-, Bt. (1784).

Boileau, Sir Gilbert George Benson, Bt. (1838).

Boland, Sir (Edward) Rowan, Kt., C.B.E., M.D.

Boles, Sir Jeremy John Fortescue, Bt. (1922).

Bollers, *Hon.* Sir Harold Brodie Smith, Kt.

Bolte, *Hon.* Sir Henry Edward, K.C.M.G.

Bolton, Sir George Lewis French, K.C.M.G.

Bolton, Sir Ian Frederick Cheney, Bt., K.B.E. (1927).

Bonallack, Sir Richard Frank, Kt., C.B.E.

Bonar, Sir Herbert Vernon, Kt., C.B.E.

Bonham, *Maj.* Sir Antony Lionel Thomas, Bt. (1852).

Bonsor, Sir Bryan Cosmo, Bt., M.C., T.D. (1925).

Boord, Sir Richard William, Bt. (1896).

Boos, Sir Werner James, Kt., C.B.E.

Booth, Sir Douglas Allen, Bt. (1916).

Booth, Sir G. Arthur W., K.B.E.

Booth, Sir Michael Savile Gore-, Bt. (1 1760).

Boothby, Sir Hugo Robert Brooke, Bt. (1660).

Boreel, Sir Francis David, Bt. (1645).

Bornu, The Waziri of, K.C.M.G., C.B.E.

Borthwick, Sir John Thomas, Bt. M.B.E. (1908).

Borwick, *Lt.-Col.* Sir Thomas Faulkner, Kt., C.I.E., D.S.O.

Bossom, *Maj.* Hon. Sir Clive, Bt., M.P. (1953).

Boswall, Sir Thomas Houstoun-, Bt. (1836).

Bouchier, *Air Vice-Marshal* Sir Cecil Arthur, K.B.E., C.B., D.F.C.

Boughey, Sir Richard James, Bt. (1798).

Boult, Sir Adrian Cedric, Kt., C.H., D.Mus.

Boulton, Sir Edward John, Bt. (1944).

Boulton, Sir Harold Hugh Christian, Bt. (1905).

Bourke, *Maj.* Sir (Edward Alexander) Henry Legge-, K.B.E., M.P.

Bourke, *Hon.* Sir Paget John, Kt.

Bourne, Sir Frederick Chalmers, K.C.S.I., C.I.E.

Boustead, *Col.* (Sir John Edmund) Hugh, K.B.E., C.M.G., D.S.O., M.C.

Bovell, Sir (Conrad Swire) Kerr, Kt., C.M.G.

Bovenschen, Sir Frederick Carl, K.C.B., K.B.E.

Bowater, *Lt. Col.* Sir Ian Frank, G.B.E., D.S.O., T.D.

Bowater, Sir Noel Vansittart, Bt., G.B.E., M.C. (1939).

Bowater, Sir (Thomas) Dudley (Blennerhassett), Bt. (1914).

Bowden, Sir Frank, Bt. (1915).

Bowen, Sir Thomas Frederic Charles, Bt. (1921).

Bower, Sir John Dykes, Kt., C.V.O.

Bower, Sir Frank, Kt., C.B.E.

Bower, Sir John Reginald Hornby Nott-, K.C.V.O.

Bower, *Air Marshal* Sir Leslie William Clement, K.C.B., D.S.O., D.F.C.

Bower, *Lt.-Gen.* Sir Roger Herbert, K.C.B., K.B.E.

Bower, Sir (William) Guy Nott-, K.B.E., C.B.

Bowes, Sir (Harold) Leslie, K.C.M.G., C.B.E.

Bowker, Sir (Reginald) James, G.B.E., K.C.M.G.

Bowlby, Sir Anthony Hugh Mostyn, Bt. (1923).

Bowman, Sir James, Bt., K.B.E. (1961).

Bowman, Sir John Paget, Bt. (1884).

Boxer, *Air Vice-Marshal* Sir Alan Hunter Cachemaille, K.C.V.O., C.B., D.S.O., D.F.C.

Boyce, Sir Robert Charles Leslie, Bt. (1916).

Boyd, Sir Alexander Walter, Bt. (1916).

Boyd, *Brig.* Sir John Smith Knox, Kt., O.B.E., M.D., F.R.S.

Boyes, Sir Brian Gerald Barratt-, K.B.E.

Boyle, *Marshal of the Royal Air Force* Sir Dermot Alexander, G.C.B., K.C.V.O., K.B.E., A.F.C.

Brabin, *Hon.* Sir Daniel James, Kt., M.C.

Bracegirdle, *Rear-Adm.* Sir Leighton Seymour, K.C.V.O., C.M.G., D.S.O.

Bradbury, *Surgeon Vice-Adm.* Sir Eric Blackburn, K.B.E., C.B.

Bradford, Sir Edward Alexander Slade, Bt. (1902).

Bradlaw, *Prof.* Sir Robert Vivian, Kt., C.B.E.

Bradley, *Air Marshal* Sir John Stanley Travers, K.C.B., C.B.E.

Bradley, Sir Kenneth Granville, Kt., C.M.G.

Bradman, Sir Donald George, Kt.

Brain, Sir (Henry) Norman, K.B.E., C.M.G.

Braithwaite, Sir John Bevan, Kt.

Brancker, *His Hon.* Sir (John Eustace) Theodore, Kt., Q.C.

Brand, *Hon.* Sir David, K.C.M.G.

Brand, Sir (William) Alfred, Kt., C.B.E.

Brandon, *Hon.* Sir Henry Vivian, Kt., M.C.

Branigan, Sir Patrick Francis, Kt., Q.C.

Branson, *Col.* Sir Douglas Stephenson, K.B.E., C.B., D.S.O., M.C., T.D.

Bray, *General* Sir Robert Napier Hubert Campbell, G.B.E., K.C.B., D.S.O.

Brayley, Sir John Desmond, Kt., M.C.

Brearley, Sir Norman, Kt., C.B.E., D.S.O., M.C. A.F.C.

Brebner, Sir Alexander, Kt., C.I.E.

Brechin, Sir (Herbert) Archbold, K.B.E.

Brett, *Hon.* Sir Lionel, Kt.

Brickwood, Sir Rupert Redvers, Bt. (1927).

Bridge, *Hon.* Sir Nigel Cyprian, Kt.

Bridgeford, *Lt.-Gen.* Sir William, K.B.E., C.B., M.C.

Bridgeman, Hon. Sir Maurice Richard, K.B.E.

Briercliffe, Sir Rupert, Kt., C.M.G., O.B.E., M.D.

Briggs, Sir (Alfred) George (Ernest), Kt.

Briggs, *Hon.* Sir Francis Arthur, Kt.

Brightman, *Hon.* Sir John Anson, Kt.

Brimelow, Sir Thomas, K.C.M.G., O.B.E.

Brinckman, *Col.* Sir Roderick Napoleon, Bt. D.S.O., M.C. (1831).

Brinton, *Maj.* Sir (Esme) Tatton (Cecil), Kt., M.P.

Brisco, Sir Donald Gilfrid, Bt. (1782).

Briscoe, Sir John Leigh Charlton, Bt., D.F.C. (1910).

Brise, Sir John Archibald Ruggles-, Bt., C.B., O.B.E., T.D. (1935).

Bristow, *Hon.* Sir Peter Henry Rowley, Kt.

Brittain, Sir Harry, K.B.E., C.M.G.

Broad, *Lt.-Gen.* Sir Charles Noel Frank, K.C.B., D.S.O.

Broadbent, Sir William Francis, Bt. (1893

Broadhurst, *Air Chief Marshal* Sir Harry, G.C.B., K.B.E., D.S.O., D.F.C., A.F.C.

Broadley, Sir Herbert, K.B.E.

Broadmead, Sir Philip Mainwaring, K.C.M.G., M.C.

Brocklebank, Sir John Montague, Bt. (1885).

Brocklehurst, Sir Philip Lee, Bt., T.D. (1903).

Brockman, *Vice-Adm.* Sir Ronald Vernon, K.C.B., C.S.I., C.I.E., C.B.E.

Brodie, Sir Benjamin David Ross, Bt. (1834).

Brodie, *Very Rev.* Sir Israel, K.B.E.

Brogan, *Prof.* Sir Denis William, Kt.

Bromet, *Air Vice-Marshal* Sir Geoffrey Rhodes, K.B.E., C.B., D.S.O.

Bromhead, *Lt.-Col.* Sir Benjamin Denis Gonville, Bt., O.B.E. (1806).

Bromley, Sir Rupert Charles, Bt. (1757).

Bromley, Sir Thomas Eardley, K.C.M.G.

Brook, Sir Dryden, Kt.

Brooke, *Maj.* Sir George Cecil Francis, Bt. (1903).

Brooke, *Maj.* Sir John Weston, Bt. (1919).

Brooke, Sir (Norman) Richard (Rowley), Kt.

Brooke, Sir Richard Christopher, Bt. (1662).

Brookes, Sir Raymond Percival, Kt.

Brooksbank, Sir (Edward) William, Bt. (1919).

Broughton, Sir Alfred Davies Devonsher, Kt., M.P.

Broughton, *Air Marshal* Sir Charles, K.B.E., C.B.

Broughton, Sir Evelyn Delves, Bt. (1661).

Broun, Sir Lionel John Law, Bt. (s 1686).

Brown, Sir Allen Stanley, Kt., C.B.E.

Brown, Sir (Arthur James) Stephen, K.B.E.

Brown, *Lt.-Col.* Sir (Charles Frederick) Richmond, Bt. (1863).

Brown, Sir Charles James Officer, Kt., M.D.

Brown, Sir (Cyril) Maxwell (Palmer), K.C.B., C.M.G.

Brown, Sir David, Kt.

Brown, Sir Edward Joseph, Kt., M.B.E., M.P.

Brown, Sir (Frederick Herbert) Stanley, Kt., C.B.E.

Brown, Sir James Raitt, Kt.

Brown, Sir John Douglas Keith, Kt.

Brown, Sir Kenneth Alfred Leader, Kt.

Brown, *Air Vice-Marshal* Sir Leslie Oswald, K.C.B., C.B.E., D.S.C., A.F.C.

Brown, *Lt.-Col.* Sir Norman Seddon Seddon-, Kt., T.D.

Brown, *Hon.* Sir Ralph Kilner, Kt., O.B.E., T.D.

Brown, Sir Raymond Frederick, Kt., O.B.E.

Brown, *Air Commodore* Sir Vernon Sydney, Kt., C.B., O.B.E.

Brown, Sir William Brian Pigott-, Bt. (1903).

Brown, Sir William Robson-, Kt.

Browne, Sir (Edward) Humphrey, Kt., C.B.E.

Browne, *Hon.* Sir Patrick Reginald Evelyn, Kt., O.B.E., T.D.

Brownjohn, *General* Sir Nevil Charles Dowell, G.B.E., K.C.B., C.M.G., M.C.

Brownrigg, Sir Nicholas (Gawen), Bt. (1816).

Bruce, Sir Arthur Atkinson, K.B.E., M.C.

Bruce, Sir (Francis) Michael Ian, Bt. (s 1628).

Bruce, Sir Hervey James Hugh, Bt. (1804).

Bruce, *Hon.* Sir (James) Roualeyn Hovell - Thurlow - Cumming -, Kt.

Bruce, *Prof.* Sir John, Kt., C.B.E., T.D.

Brundrett, Sir Frederick, K.C.B., K.B.E.

Brune, Sir Humphrey Ingelram Prideaux, K.B.E., C.M.G.

Brunner, Sir Felix John Morgan, Bt. (1895).

Brunton, Sir (Edward Francis) Lauder, Bt. (1908).

Bruxner, *Lt.-Col. Hon.* Sir Michael Frederick, K.B.E., D.S.O.

Bryan, Sir Andrew Meikle, Kt.

Bryant, Sir Arthur Wynne Morgan, Kt., C.H., C.B.E.

Bryce, *Hon.* Sir William Gordon, Kt., C.B.E.

Buchan, Sir John, Kt., C.M.G.

Buchanan, Sir Charles James, Bt. (1878).

Buchanan, Sir George Hector Macdonald Leith-, Bt. (1775).

Buchanan, Sir John Cecil Rankin, K.C.M.G., M.D.

Buchanan, *Maj.-Gen.* Sir Kenneth Gray, Kt., C.B., C.M.G., D.S.O.

Buchanan, *Maj.* Sir Reginald Narcissus Macdonald-, K.C.V.O., M.B.E., M.C.

Bucher, *General* Sir Roy, K.B.E., C.B., M.C.

Buckley, *Rt. Hon.* Sir Denys Burton, Kt., M.B.E.

Budd, *Hon.* Sir Harry Vincent, Kt.

Buckley, *Rear-Adm.* Sir Kenneth Robertson, K.B.E.

Bulkeley, Sir Richard Harry David Williams-, Bt. (1661).

Bull, Sir George, Bt. (1922).

Bullard, Sir Edward Crisp, Kt., Ph.D., SC.D., F.R.S.

Bullard, Sir Reader William, K.C.B., K.C.M.G., C.I.E.

Bullock, Sir Christopher Llewellyn, K.C.B., C.B.E.

Bullock, Sir Ernest, Kt., C.V.O., MUS.D.

Bullus, Sir Eric Edward, Kt., M.P.

Bunbury, Sir (John) William Napier, Bt. (1681).

Bunbury, Sir (Richard David) Michael Richardson-, Bt. ((1787).

Bunting, Sir (Edward) John, Kt., C.B.E.

Burbidge, Sir John Richard Woodman, Bt. (1916).

Burbury, *Hon.* Sir Stanley Charles, K.B.E.

Burder, Sir John Henry, Kt.

Burdett, Sir Savile Aylmer, Bt. (1665).

Burke, Sir Aubrey Francis, Kt., O.B.E.

Burke, Sir Thomas Stanley, Bt. (1 1797)

Burman, Sir (John) Charles, Kt.

Burne, Sir Lewis Charles, Kt., C.B.E., A.F.C.

Burnet, Sir (Frank) Macfarlane, O.M., K.B.E., M.D., F.R.S.

Burnett, *Air Chief Marshal* Sir Brian Kenyon, G.C.B., D.F.C., A.F.C.

Burnett, *Maj.* Sir David Humphery, Bt., M.B.E., T.D. (1913).

Burney, Sir Anthony George Bernard, Kt., O.B.E.

Burney, Sir Cecil Denniston, Bt. (1921).

Burns, Sir Alan Cuthbert, G.C.M.G.

Burns, Sir Charles Ritchie, K.B.E., M.D.

Burns, Sir John Crawford, Kt.

Burns, *Maj.-Gen.* Sir (Walter Arthur) George, K.C.V.O., C.B., D.S.O., O.B.E., M.C.

Burrell, *Vice-Adm.* Sir Henry Mackay, K.B.E., C.B.

Burrell, Sir Walter Raymond, Bt., C.B.E., T.D. (1774).

Burrough, *Admiral* Sir Harold Martin, G.C.B., K.B.E., D.S.O.

Burrows, Sir Bernard Alexander Brocas, G.C.M.G.

Burrows, Sir Frederick John, G.C.S.I., G.C.I.E.

Burrows, Sir (Robert) John (Formby), Kt.

Burt, Sir Cyril Lodowic, Kt., D.SC., LL.D.

Burton, Sir Geoffrey Pownall, K.C.S.I., K.C.I.E.

Burton, *Air Marshal* Sir Harry, K.C.B., C.B.E., D.S.O.

Busby, Sir Matthew, Kt., C.B.E.

Bush, *Admiral* Sir John Fitzroy Duyland, G.C.B., D.S.C.

Busk, Sir Douglas Laird, K.C.M.G.

Bustamante, *Rt. Hon.* Sir (William) Alexander, Kt.

Butland, Sir Jack Richard, K.B.E.

Butler, Sir James Ramsay Montagu, Kt., M.V.O., D.LITT.

Butler, *General* Sir Mervyn Andrew Haldane, K.C.B., C.B.E., D.S.O., M.C.

Butler, Sir Nevile Montagu, K.C.M.G., C.V.O.

Butler, Sir (Reginald) Michael (Thomas), Bt. (1922).

Butler, *Lt.-Col.* Sir Thomas Pierce, C.V.O., D.S.O., O.B.E. (1628).

Butlin, Sir William Edmund, Kt., M.B.E.

Butt, Sir (Alfred) Kenneth Dudley, Bt. (1929).

Butterfield, Sir Harry Durham, Kt., C.B.E.

Butterfield, *Prof.* Sir Herbert, Kt., F.B.A.

Buxton, Sir Thomas Fowell Victor, Bt. (1840).

Buzzard, *Rear-Adm.* Sir Anthony Wass, Bt., C.B., D.S.O., O.B.E. (1929).

Byass, *Col.* Sir Geoffrey Robert Sidney, Bt., T.D. (1926).

Byrne, Sir Clarence Askew, Kt., O.B.E., D.S.C.

Byrnes, *Hon.* Sir Percy Thomas, Kt.

Cabot, Sir Daniel Alfred Edmund, Kt.

Cade, *Air Vice-Marshal* Sir Stanford, K.B.E., C.B.

Cader, Sir Hussein Hassanaly Abdool, Kt., C.B.E.

Cadwallader, Sir John, Kt.

Cadzow, Sir Norman James Kerr, Kt., V.R.D.

Caffyn, *Brig.* Sir Edward Roy, K.B.E., C.B., T.D.

Cahn, Sir Albert Jonas, Bt. (1934).

Caine, Sir Derwent Hall, Bt. (1937).

Caine, Sir Sydney, K.C.M.G.

Cairncross, Sir Alexander Kirkland, K.C.M.G.

Cairns, *Rt. Hon.* Sir David Arnold Scott, Kt.

Cakobau, *Ratu* Sir Etuate Tuivanuavou Tugi, K.B.E., M.C., E.D.

Calder, Sir John Alexander, K.C.M.G.

Caldicott, *Hon.* Sir John Moore, K.B.E., C.M.G.

Caldwell, *Surgeon Vice-Adm.* Sir Eric Dick, K.B.E., C.B.

Cailander, *Lt.-Gen.* Sir Colin Bishop, K.C.B., K.B.E., M.C.

Calthorpe, *Brig.* Sir Richard Hamilton Anstruther-Gough-, Bt., C.B.E., (1929).

Cameron, *Lt.-Gen.* Sir Alexander Maurice, K.B.E., C.B., M.C.

Cameron, Sir Cornelius, Kt., C.B.E.

Cameron, *Hon.* Sir John, Kt., D.S.C., Q.C. (Lord Cameron).

Cormack, Sir Magnus Cameron, K.B.E.

Camilleri, *His Hon.* Sir Luigi Antonio, Kt, LL.D.

Campbell, *Maj.-Gen.* Sir (Alexander) Douglas, K.B.E., C.B., D.S.O., M.C.

†Campbell, Sir Bruce Colin Patrick, Bt. (S 1804).

Campbell, Sir Clifford Clarence, G.C.M.G., G.C.V.O.

Campbell, Sir Colin, Kt., O.B.E.

Campbell, Sir Colin Moffat, Bt., M.C. (S 1668).

Campbell, *Prof.* Sir David, Kt., M.C., M.D., LL.D., F.R.S.E.

Campbell, *Col.* Sir Guy Theophilus Halswell, Bt., O.B.E., M.C. (1815).

Campbell, *Maj.-Gen.* Sir Hamish Manus, K.B.E., C.B.

Campbell, *Vice-Adm.* Sir Ian Murray Robertson, K.B.E., C.B., D.S.O.

Campbell, Sir Ian Vincent Hamilton, Bt., C.B. (1831).

Campbell, Sir Ilay Mark, Bt. (1808).

Campbell, Sir John Johnston, Kt.

Campbell, Sir Matthew, K.B.E., C.B., F.R.S.E.

Campbell, Sir Ralph Abercromby, Kt.

Campbell, Sir Robin Auchinbreck, Bt. (S. 1628).

Campbell, *Rt. Hon.* Sir Ronald Ian, G.C.M.G., C.B.

Campbell, Sir Thomas Cockburn-, Bt. (1821).

Campbell, *Lt.-Col.* Sir Walter Fendall, K.C.I.E.

Campion, Sir Harry, Kt., C.B., C.B.E.

Cantley, *Hon.* Sir Joseph Donaldson, Kt., O.B.E.

Cantlie, Sir Keith, Kt., C.I.E.

Cantlie, *Lt.-Gen.* Sir Neil, K.C.B., K.B.E., M.C.

Capper, Sir (William) Derrick, Kt.

Carberry, Sir John Edward Doston, Kt.

Carden, *Lt.-Col.* Sir Henry Christopher, Bt., O.B.E. (1887).

Carden, Sir John Craven, Bt. (1787).

Cardus, Sir Neville, Kt., C.B.E.

Carew, Sir Thomas Palk, Bt. (1661).

Carlill, *Vice-Adm.* Sir Stephen Hope, K.B.E., C.B., D.S.O.

Carmichael, Sir David Peter William Gibson-Craig-, Bt. (S 1702 and 1831).

Carmichael, Sir John, K.B.E.

Carnac, Sir Henry George Crabbe Rivett-, Bt. (1836).

Caroe, Sir Olaf Kirkpatrick, K.C.S.I., K.C.I.E.

Carpenter, Sir Eric Ashton, Kt., O.B.E.

Carr, *Air Marshal* Sir (Charles) Roderick, K.B.E., C.B., D.F.C., A.F.C.

Carr, Sir (Frederick) Bernard, Kt., C.M.G.

Carr, *Air Marshal* Sir John Darcy Baker-, K.B.E., C.B., A.F.C.

Carr, Sir William Emsley, Kt.

Carreras, *Lt.-Col.* Sir James, Kt., M.B.E.

Carrington, Sir William Speight, Kt.

Carroll, Sir Alfred Thomas, K.B.E.

Carroll, Sir John Anthony, K.B.E., Ph.D., F.R.S.E.

Carter, Sir (Arthur) Desmond Bonham-, Kt., T.D.

Carter, *Rear-Adm.* Sir Christopher Douglas Bonham-, G.C.V.O., C.B.

Carter, Sir John, Kt., Q.C.

Carter, *Admiral* Sir Stuart Sumner Bonham-, G.C.B., C.V.O., D.S.O.

Carter, *His Hon.* Sir Walker Kelly, Kt., Q.C.

Cartland, Sir George Barrington, Kt., C.M.G.

Carver, *General* Sir (Richard) Michael (Power), G.C.B., C.B.E., D.S.O., M.C.

Cary, Sir (Arthur Lucius) Michael, K.C.B.

Cary, Sir Robert Archibald, Bt., M.P. (1955).

Cash, Sir Thomas James, K.B.E., C.B.

Cassel, Sir Harold Felix, Bt., Q.C. (1920).

Cassels, *Field Marshal* Sir (Archibald) James Halkett, G.C.B., K.B.E., D.S.O.

Cassels, Sir James Dale, Kt.

Cassidy, Sir Jack Evelyn, Kt.

Casson, Sir Hugh Maxwell, Kt., R.A., F.R.I.B.A.

Catherwood, Sir Henry Frederick Ross, Kt.

Catlin, *Prof.* Sir George Edward Gordon, Kt., Ph.D.

Catling, Sir Richard Charles, Kt., C.M.G., O.B.E.

Cator, Sir Geoffrey Edmund, Kt., C.M.G.

Caulfield, *Hon.* Sir Bernard, Kt.

Cave, Sir Charles Edward Coleridge, Bt. (1896).

Cave, Sir Robert Cave-Browne-, Bt. (1641).

Cawley, Sir Charles Mills, Kt., C.B.E., Ph.D.

Cawthorn, *Maj.-Gen.* Sir Walter Joseph, Kt., C.B., C.I.E., C.B.E.

Cayley, Sir Digby William David, Bt. (1661).

Cayzer, Sir James Arthur, Bt. (1904).

Cayzer, Sir (William) Nicholas, Bt. (1921).

Cazalet, *Vice-Adm.* Sir Peter Grenville Lyon, K.B.E., C.B., D.S.O., D.S.C.

Chacksfield, *Air Vice-Marshal* Sir Bernard Albert, K.B.E., C.B.

Chadwick, Sir James, Kt., C.H., M.D., F.R.S.

Chadwick, Sir John Edward, K.C.M.G.

Chadwick, Sir Robert Burton Burton-, Bt. (1935).

Chain, *Prof.* Sir Ernest Boris, Kt., F.R.S., Ph.D., D.Phil.

Chalk, *Hon.* Sir Gordon William Wesley, K.B.E.

Chamberlain, Sir Henry Wilmot, Bt. (1828).

Chamberlain, *Hon.* Sir Reginald Roderic St. Clair, Kt.

Chamberlin, Sir Michael, Kt., O.B.E.

Chambers, Sir (Stanley) Paul, K.B.E., C.B., C.I.E.

Chamier, *Air Commodore* Sir (John) Adrian, Kt., C.B., C.M.G., D.S.O., O.B.E.

Champion, *Prof.* Sir Harry George, Kt., C.I.E., D.SC.

Champion, *Rev.* Sir Reginald Stuart, K.C.M.G., O.B.E.

Champneys, *Capt.* Sir Weldon Dalrymple-, Bt., C.B. (1910).

Chance, Sir Roger James Ferguson, Bt., M.C. (1900).

Chance, Sir (William) Hugh (Stobart), Kt., C.B.E.

Chancellor, Sir Christopher John, Kt., C.M.G.

Chaplin, Sir George Frederick, Kt., C.B.E.

Chapman, Sir Robert Macgowan, Bt., C.B.E., T.D. (1958).

Chapman, *Air Chief Marshal* Sir Ronald Ivelaw-, G.C.B., K.B.E., D.F.C., A.F.C.

Chapman, *Hon.* Sir Stephen. Kt.

Charles, Sir Noel Hughes Havelock, Bt., K.C.M.G., M.C. (1928).

Charley, Sir Philip Belmont, Kt.

Charlton, *Commodore* Sir William Arthur, Kt., D.S.C.

Charrington, Sir John, Kt.

Charteris, *Lt.-Col. Hon.* Sir Martin Michael Charles, K.C.V.O., C.B., O.B.E.

Chau, Sir Sik-nin, Kt., C.B.E.

Chau, Sir Tsun-nin, Kt., C.B.E.

Chaytor, Sir William Henry Clervaux, Bt. (1831).

Cheetham, Sir Nicolas John Alexander, K.C.M.G.

Chegwidden, Sir Thomas Sidney, Kt., C.B. C.V.O.

Cheshire, *Air Chief Marshal* Sir Walter Graemes, G.B.E., K.C.B.

Chesterman, Sir Dudley Ross, Kt., Ph.D.

Chesterton, Sir Oliver Sidney, Kt., M.C.

Chetwynd, Sir (Arthur Henry) Talbot, Bt., O.B.E., M.C. (1795).

Cheyne, Sir Joseph Lister Watson, Bt. (1908).

Chichester, Sir (Edward) John, Bt. (1641).

Chichester, Sir Francis Charles, K.B.E.

Chick, Sir (Alfred) Louis, K.B.E.

Chiesman, Sir Walter Eric, Kt., C.B., M.D.

Child, Sir Coles John Jeremy, Bt. (1919).

Chilton, *Air Marshal* Sir (Charles) Edward, K.B.E., C.B.

Chilton, *Brig.* Sir Frederick Oliver, Kt., C.B.E., D.S.O.

Chinoy, Sir Sultan Meherally, Kt.

Chisholm, Sir Henry, Kt., C.B.E.

Chitham, Sir Charles Carter, Kt., C.I.E.

Chitty, Sir Thomas Willes, Bt. (1924).

Cholmeley, Sir Montague John, Bt. (1896).

Chrimes, Sir (William) Bertram, Kt., C.B.E.

Christie, *Hon.* Sir Harold George, Kt., C.B.E.

Christie, Sir William, K.C.I.E., C.S.I., M.C.

Christison, *Gen.* Sir (Alexander Frank) Philip, Bt., G.B.E., C.B., D.S.O., M.C. (1871).

Christopher, Sir George Perrin, Kt.

Christophers, *Col.* Sir Samuel Rickard, Kt., C.I.E., O.B.E., F.R.S.

Christopherson, Sir Derman Guy, Kt., O.B.E., D.Phil., F.R.S.

Church, *Brig.* Sir Geoffrey Selby, Bt., C.B.E., M.C., T.D. (1901).

Cilento, Sir Raphael West, Kt., M.D.

Clague, *Col. Hon.* Sir John Douglas, Kt., C.B.E., M.C., T.D.

Clancy, *Hon.* Sir John Sydney James, K.B.E., C.M.G.

Clark Sir Andrew Edmund James, Bt., M.B.E., M.C., Q.C. (1883).

Clark, *Capt.* Sir George Anthony, Bt. (1917).

Clark, Sir George Norman, Kt., D.Litt.

Clark, Sir (Gordon) Colvin Lindesay, K.B.E., C.M.G., M.C.

Clark, Sir Henry Laurence Urling, Kt.

Clark, Sir John Allen, Kt.

Clark, Sir Stewart Stewart-, Bt. (1918).

Clark, Sir Thomas, Bt. (1886).

Clark, Sir (Thomas) Fife, Kt.,C.B.E.

Clarke, *Maj.-Gen.* Sir (Edward Montagu) Campbell K.B.E., C.B.

Clarke, Sir Ellis Emmanuel Innocent, Kt., C.M.G.

Clarke, Sir Frederick Joseph, Kt.

Clarke, Sir (Henry) Ashley, G.C.M.G., G.C.V.O.

Clarke, Sir Henry Osmond Osmond-, K.C.V.O., C.B.E.

Clarke, Sir Humphrey Orme, Bt. (1831).

Clarke, Sir Percy Selwyn Selwyn-, K.B.E., C.M.G., M.C., M.D.

Clarke, Sir Richard William Barnes, K.C.B., O.B.E.

Clarke, Sir Rupert William John, Bt., M.B.E. (1882).

Clauson, Sir Gerard Leslie Makins, K.C.M.G., O.B.E.

Clavering, Sir Albert, Kt., O.B.E.

Clay, Sir Charles Travis, Kt., C.B.

Clay, Sir Henry Felix, Bt. (1841).

Clayden, *Rt. Hon.* Sir (Henry) John, Kt.

Claye, *Prof.* Sir Andrew Moynihan, Kt., M.D.

Clayson, Sir Eric Maurice, Kt.

Clayton, Sir Arthur Harold, Bt., D.S.C. (1732).

Clayton, *Air Marshal* Sir Gareth Thomas Butler, K.C.B., D.F.C.

Clayton, *Col. Hon.* Sir Hector Joseph Richard, Kt., E.D.

Cleary, Sir Joseph Jackson, Kt.

Clee, Sir (Charles) Beaupré Bell, Kt., C.S.I., C.I.E.

Clegg, Sir Alexander Bradshaw, Kt.

Clegg, Sir Cuthbert Barwick, Kt.

Cleland, *Brig.* Sir Donald Mackinnon, Kt., C.B.E.

Clements, Sir John Selby, Kt., C.B.E.

Clerk, Sir John Dutton, Bt., C.B.E., V.R.D. (s 1679).

Clerke, Sir John Edward Longueville, Bt. (1660).

Clifford, Sir (Geoffrey) Miles, K.B.E., C.M.G., E.D.

Clifford, Sir Roger Charles Joseph Gerrard, Bt. (1887).

Clore, Sir Charles, Kt.

Cloutman, *His Hon.* Sir Brett Mackay, Kt., V.C., M.C., Q.C.

Clutterbuck, *Vice-Adm.* Sir David Granville, K.B.E., C.B.

Clutterbuck, Sir (Peter) Alexander, G.C.M.G., M.C.

Coate, *Maj.-Gen.* Sir Raymond Douglas, K.B.E., C.B.

Coates, Sir Albert Ernest, Kt., O.B.E., M.D.

Coates, *Maj.* Sir Clive Milnes-, Bt., O.B.E. (1911).

Coates, Sir Frederick Gregory Lindsay, Bt. (1921).

Coats, Sir Alastair Francis Stuart, Bt. (1905).

Cobham, Sir Alan John, K.B.E., A.F.C.

Cochrane, Sir Desmond Oriel Alastair George Weston, Bt. (1903).

Cochrane, *Rear-Adm.* Sir Edward Owen, K.B.E.

Cochrane, *Air Chief Marshal Hon.* Sir Ralph Alexander, G.B.E., K.C.B., A.F.C.

Cockburn, Sir John Elliot, Bt. (s 1671).

Cockburn, Sir Robert, K.B.E., C.B., Ph.D.

Cocker, Sir William Wiggins, Kt., C.B.E.

Cockerell, Sir Christopher Sydney, Kt., C.B.E., F.R.S.

Cockram, Sir John, Kt.

Cocks, Sir (Thomas George) Barnett, K.C.B., O.B.E.

Codrington, Sir Christopher William Gerald Henry, Bt. (1876).

Codrington, *Col.* Sir Geoffrey Ronald, K.C.V.O., C.B., C.M.G., D.S.O., O.B.E., T.D.

Codrington, Sir William Alexander, Bt. (1721).

Coghill, *Capt.* Sir (Marmaduke Nevill) Patrick (Somerville), Bt. (1778).

Cohen, Sir Bernard Nathaniel Waley-, Bt. (1961).

Cohen, Sir Edgar Abraham, K.C.M.G.

Cohen, Sir Edward, Kt.

Cohen, Sir Jack, Kt., O.B.E.

Cohen, Sir John Edward, Kt.

Cohen, Sir Karl Cyril, Kt., C.B.E.

Cohen, Sir Rex Arthur Louis, K.B.E.

Coldstream, Sir George Phillips, K.C.B., K.C.V.O., Q.C.

Coldstream, *Prof.* Sir William Menzies. Kt., C.B.E.

Cole, *Lt.-Gen.* Sir George Sinclair, K.C.B., C.B.E.

Cole, Sir Noel, Kt.

Coleman, *Lieut.-Gen.* Sir (Cyril Frederick) Charles, K.C.B., C.M.G., D.S.O., O.B.E.

Coles, Sir Arthur William, Kt.

Coles, Sir Edgar Barton, Kt.

Coles, Sir George James, Kt., C.B.E.

Coles, Sir Kenneth Frank, Kt.

Coles, *Air Marshal* Sir William Edward, K.B.E., C.B., D.S.O., D.F.C., A.F.C.

I*

Colfox, Sir (William) John, Bt. (1939).

Colles, *Cmdr.* (S.) Sir (Ernest) Dudley, K.C.B., K.C.V.O., O.B.E., R.N.

Collett, Sir Ian Seymour, Bt. (1934).

Collett, Sir (Thomas) Kingsley, Kt., C.B.E.

Collier, *Air Vice-Marshal* Sir (Alfred) Conrad, K.C.B., C.B.E.

Collier, Sir Laurence, K.C.M.G.

Collingwood, *Lt.-Gen.* Sir (Richard) George, K.B.E., C.B., D.S.O.

Collins, Sir Charles Henry, Kt., C.M.G.

Collins, Sir Geoffrey Abdy, Kt.

Collins, *Vice-Adm.* Sir John Augustine, K.B.E., C.B.

Collins, Sir William Alexander Roy, Kt., C.B.E.

Colman, Sir Michael Jeremiah, Bt. (1907).

Colquhoun, *Maj.-Gen.* Sir Cyril Harry, K.C.V.O., C.B., O.B.E.

Colquhoun of Luss, Sir Ivar Iain, Bt. (1786).

Colt, Sir Edward William Dutton, Bt. (1694).

Colthurst, Sir Richard La Touche, Bt. (1744).

Colville, Sir (Henry) Cecil, Kt.

Colville, *Cmdr.* Sir Richard, K.C.V.O., C.B., D.S.C., R.N. (ret.).,

Compston, *Vice-Adm.* Sir Peter Maxwell, K.C.B.

Compton, Sir Edmund Gerald, G.C.B., K.B.E.

Conant, Sir Roger John Edward, Bt., C.V.O. (1954).

Connell, Sir Charles, Kt.

Connell, Sir Charles Gibson, Kt.

Connolly, Sir Willis Henry, Kt., C.B.E.

Conroy, Sir Diarmaid William, Kt., C.M.G., O.B.E., T.D., Q.C.

Constable, Sir Henry Marmaduke Strickland-, Bt. (1641).

Constantine, *Air Chief Marshal* Sir Hugh Alex, K.B.E., C.B., D.S.O.

Constantine, Sir Theodore, Kt., C.B.E., T.D.

Cook, Sir Francis Ferdinand Maurice, Bt. (1886).

Cook, Sir James Wilfred, Kt., D.Sc., Ph.D., F.R.S.

Cook, Sir William Richard Joseph, K.C.B., F.R.S.

Cooke, Sir Charles Arthur John, Bt. (1661).

Cooke, *Air Marshal* Sir Cyril Bertram, K.C.B., C.B.E.

Cooke, Sir Henry Frank, Kt.

Cooke, Sir John Fletcher-, Kt., C.M.G.

Cooke, Sir Leonard, Kt., O.B.E.

Cooke, *Hon.* Sir Samuel Burgess Ridgway, Kt.

Coomaraswamy, Sir Velupillai, Kt., C.M.G.

Cooper, *Maj.* Sir Charles Eric Daniel, Bt. (1863).

Cooper, Sir Francis Ashmole, Bt., Ph.D. (1905).

Cooper, Sir (Harold) Stanford, Kt.

Cooper, Sir (Henry) Guy, Kt., M.C., D.C.M.

Cooper, Sir Patrick Graham Astley, Bt. (1821).

Cooper, *Hon.* Sir Walter Jackson, Kt., M.B.E.

Cooper, *Prof.* Sir (William) Mansfield, Kt.

Coote, *Capt.* Sir Colin Reith, Kt., D.S.O.

Coote, *Rear-Adm.* (E.) Sir John Ralph, Bt., C.B., C.B.E., D.S.C., *Premier Baronet of Ireland* (I 1621).

Cope, Sir Mordaunt Leckonby, Bt., M.C. (1611).

Cope, Sir (Vincent) Zachary, Kt., M.D.

Copland, Sir Douglas Berry, K.B.E., C.M.G., D.SC.

Coppleson, Sir Lionel Wolfe, Kt.

Corah, Sir John Harold, Kt.

Corbet, Sir John Vincent, Bt., M.B.E. (1808).

Cordingley, *Air Vice-Marshal* Sir John Walter, K.C.B., K.C.V.O., C.B.E.

Cormack, Sir Magnus Cameron, K.B.E.

Corfield, Sir Conrad Laurence, K.C.I.E., C.S.I., M.C.

Cornwall, *General* Sir James Handyside Marshall-, K.C.B., C.B.E., D.S.O., M.C.

Corry, *Lt.-Col.* Sir Henry Charles Lowry-, Kt., M.C.

Corry, Sir James Perowne Ivo Myles, Bt. (1885).

Cory, Sir Clinton James Donald, Bt. (1919).

Coryton, *Air Chief Marshal* Sir (William) Alec, K.C.B., K.B.E., M.V.O., D.F.C.

Coslett, *Air Marshal* Sir (Thomas) Norman, K.C.B., O.B.E.

Costar, Sir Norman Edgar, K.C.M.G.

Costello, Sir Leonard Wilfred James, Kt., C.B.E.

Cotter, *Lt.-Col.* Sir Delaval James Alfred, Bt., D.S.O. (I. 1763).

Cotterell, Sir Richard Charles Geers, Bt. C.B.E., T.D. (1805).

Cotton, Sir Charles Andrew, K.B.E.

Cotton, Sir John Richard, K.C.M.G., O.B.E.

Cottrell, Sir Alan Howard, Kt. Ph.D., F.R.S.

Cottrell, Sir Edward Baglietto, Kt., C.B.E.

Cotts, Sir (Robert) Crichton Mitchell, Bt. (1921).

Couchman, *Admiral* Sir Walter Thomas, K.C.B., C.V.O., D.S.O., O.B.E.

Coulson, Sir John Eltringham, K.C.M.G.

Couper, Sir Guy, Bt. (1841).

Courtney, *Air Chief Marshal* Sir Christopher Lloyd, G.B.E., K.C.B., D.S.O.

Coutts, Sir Walter Fleming, G.C.M.G., M.B.E.

Covell, *Maj.-Gen.* Sir Gordon, C.I.E., M.D.

Cowan, Sir Christopher George Armstrong, Kt.

Coward, Sir Noel Peirce, Kt.

Cowley, *Lt.-Gen.* Sir John Guise, K.B.E., C.B.

Cowper, Sir Norman Lethbridge, Kt., C.B.E.

Cowperthwaite, Sir John James, K.B.E., C.M.G.

Cox, Sir Christopher William Machell, G.C.M.G.

Cox, Sir (Ernest) Gordon, K.B.E., T.D., D.SC., F.R.S.

Cox, Sir Geoffrey Sandford, Kt., C.B.E.

Cox, Sir (George) Trenchard, Kt., C.B.E., F.S.A.

Cox, Sir Herbert Charles Fahie, Kt.

Cox, Sir John William, Kt., C.B.E.

Crabbe, Sir Cecil Brooksby, Kt.

Craddock, Sir (George) Beresford, Kt.

Craddock, *Lt.-Gen.* Sir Richard Walter, K.B.E., C.B., D.S.O.

Craddock, Sir Walter Merry, Kt., D.S.O., M.C.

Craig, Sir Arthur John Edward, Kt.

Craig, Sir John Herbert Mc-Cutcheon, K.C.V.O., C.B., Ll.D.

Cramer, *Hon.* Sir John Oscar, Kt.

Crane, Sir Harry Walter Victor, Kt., O.B.E.

Craster, Sir John Montagu, Kt.

Craufurd, Sir Robert James, Bt. (1781).

Craven, *Air Marshal* Sir Robert Edward, K.B.E., C.B., D.F.C.

Crawford, Sir (Archibald James) Dirom, Kt.

Crawford, *Brig.* Sir Douglas Inglis, Kt., C.B., D.S.O., T.D.

Crawford, Sir Frederick, G.C.M.G., O.B.E.

Crawford, Sir John Grenfell, Kt., C.B.E.

Crawford, Sir (Robert) Stewart, K.C.M.G., C.V.O.

Crawford, Sir (Walter) Ferguson, K.B.E., C.M.G.

Crawford, *Vice-Adm.* Sir William Godfrey, K.B.E., C.B., D.S.C.

Crawshaw, *Hon.* Sir (Edward) Daniel (Weston), Kt.

Creagh, *Maj.-Gen.* Sir (Kilner) Rupert Brazier-, K.B.E., C.B., D.S.O.

Creasy, *Admiral of the Fleet* Sir George Elvey, G.C.B., C.B.E., D.S.O., M.V.O.

Creasy, Sir Gerald Hallen, K.C.M.G., K.C.V.O., O.B.E.

Creedy, Sir Herbert James, G.C.B., K.C.V.O.

Cresswell, *Rev.* Cyril Leonard, K.C.V.O.

Cresswell, *Prof.* Sir Keppel Archibald Cameron, Kt., C.B.E.

Cresswell, Sir Michael Justin, K.C.M.G.

Crichton, Sir Andrew James Maitland-Makgill-, Kt.

Crichton, *Hon.* Sir (John) Robertson (Dunn), Kt.

Crichton, Sir Robert, C.B.E.

Cripps, Sir Cyril Thomas, Kt., M.B.E.

Crisp, Sir (John) Peter, Bt. (1913).

Crisp, *Hon.* Sir Malcolm Peter, Kt.

Critchett, Sir Ian (George Lorraine), Bt. (1908).

Crocker, Sir William Charles, Kt., M.C.

Croft, Sir Bernard Hugh Denman, Bt. (1671).

Croft, Sir John William Graham, Bt. (1818).

Crofton, Sir (Hugh) Patrick Simon, Bt. (1801).

Crofton, Sir Malby Sturges, Bt. (1828).

Crookenden, *Lt.-Gen.* Sir Napier, K.C.B., D.S.O., O.B.E.

Croot, Sir (Horace) John, Kt., C.B.E.

Cross, *Air Chief Marshal* Sir Kenneth Brian Boyd, K.C.B., C.B.E., D.S.O., D.F.C.

Crossland, Sir Leonard, Kt.

Crossley, Sir Christopher John, Bt. (1909).

Crosthwaite, Sir Bertram Maitland, Kt., V.D.

Crosthwaite, Sir (Ponsonby) Moore, K.C.M.G.

Crowe, Sir Colin Tradescant, K.C.M.G.

Crowley, Sir Brian Hurtle, Kt., M.M.

Crowther, Sir William Edward Lodewyk Hamilton, Kt., C.B.E., D.S.O., V.D.

Croysdale, Sir James, Kt.

Crutchley, *Admiral* Sir Victor Alexander Charles, V.C., K.C.B., D.S.C.

Cudmore, *Hon.* Sir Collier Robert, Kt.

Cumings, Sir Charles Cecil George, K.B.E.

Cumming, Sir Duncan Cameron, K.B.E., C.B.

Cumming, Sir Ronald Stuart, Kt., T.D.

Cumming, Sir William Gordon Gordon-, Bt. (1804).

Cunard, Sir Henry Palmes, Bt. (1859).

Cuninghame, Sir John Christopher Foggo Montgomery-, Bt. (N.S. 1672).

Cuninghame, Sir William Alan Fairlie-, Bt., M.C. (S. 1630).

Cunliffe, Sir David Ellis, Bt. (1750).

Cunningham, *General* Sir Alan Gordon, G.C.M.G., K.C.B., D.S.O., M.C.

Cunningham, Sir Charles Craik, K.C.B., K.B.E., C.V.O.

Cunningham, Sir Graham, K.B.E.

Cunningham, Sir Samuel Knox, Bt., Q.C., (1963).

Cunynghame, Sir (Henry) David St. Leger Brooke Selwyn, Bt. (S 1702).

Curlewis, *His Hon.* Sir Adrian Herbert, Kt., C.B.E.

Curran, *Rt. Hon.* Sir Lancelot Ernest, Kt.

Curran, Sir Samuel Crowe, Kt., D.Sc., Ph.D., F.R.S., F.R.S.E.

Currie, Sir George Alexander, Kt.

Currie, Sir James, K.B.E., C.M.G.

Currie, Sir Walter Mordaunt Cyril, Bt. (1847).

Curteis, *Capt.* Sir Gerald, K.C.V.O., R.N.

Curtis, Sir Edward Leo, Kt.

Curtis, Sir George Harold, Kt., C.B.

Curtis, Sir Peter, Bt. (1802).

Cusack, *Hon.* Sir Ralph Vincent, Kt.

Cushion, *Air Vice-Marshal* Sir William Boston, K.B.E., C.B.

Cutforth, *Maj.-Gen.* Sir Lancelot Eric, K.B.E., C.B.

Cuthbert, *Vice-Adm.* Sir John Wilson, K.B.E., C.B.

Cuthbertson, Sir David Paton, Kt., C.B.E., M.D., D.Sc.

Cutler, Sir (Arthur) Roden, V.C., K.C.M.G., K.C.V.O., C.B.E.

Dainton, *Prof.* Sir Frederick Sydney, Kt., Ph.D., Sc.D., F.R.S.

Daldry, Sir Leonard Charles, K.B.E.

Dale, Sir William Leonard, K.C.M.G.

Dalling, Sir Thomas, Kt.

Dalrymple, Sir Hew Fleetwood Hamilton-, Bt. (S 1697).

Dalton, *Maj.-Gen.* Sir Charles James George, Kt., C.B., C.B.E.

Dalton, *Vice-Adm.* Sir Norman Eric, K.C.B., O.B.E.

Daly, *Lt.-Gen.* Sir Thomas Joseph, K.B.E., C.B., D.S.O.

D'Ambrumenil, Sir Philip, Kt.

Danckwerts, *Rt. Hon.* Sir Harold Otto, Kt.

Daniel, *Admiral* Sir Charles Saumarez, K.C.B., C.B.E., D.S.O.

Daniel, Sir Goronwy Hopkin, K.C.V.O., C.B., D.Phil.

Daniell, Sir Peter Averell, Kt., T.D.

Danks, Sir Alan John, K.B.E.

Dannatt, Sir Cecil, Kt., O.B.E., M.C.

Darell, Sir Jeffrey Lionel, Bt., M.C. (1795).

Dargie, Sir William Alexander, Kt., C.B.E.

Darling, Sir Frank Fraser, Kt.

Darling, Sir James Ralph, Kt., C.M.G., O.B.E.

Darling, *General* Sir Kenneth Thomas, G.B.E., K.C.B., D.S.O.

Darlington, *Inst. Rear-Adm.* Sir Charles Roy, K.B.E.

Darvall, Sir Charles Roger, Kt., C.B.E.

Darwin, Sir Robin, Kt., C.B.E., A.R.A.

Dash, Sir Arthur Jules, Kt., C.I.E.

Dash, Sir Roydon Englefield Ashford, Kt., D.F.C.

Dashwood, Sir Francis John Vernon Hereward, Bt., *Premier Baronet of Great Britain* (1707).

Dashwood, Sir Henry George Massy, Bt. (1684).

Datar Singh, *Sardar Bahadur* Sir, Kt.

Davenport, *Lt.-Col.* Sir Walter Henry Bromley-, Kt., T.D.

Davidson, *Hon.* Sir Charles William, K.B.E.

Davidson, *Prof.* Sir (Leybourne) Stanley (Patrick), Kt., M.D., F.R.S.E.

Davie, *Rev.* Sir Arthur Patrick Ferguson-, Bt. (1847).

Davie, Sir Paul Christopher, Kt.

Davies, Sir David Joseph, Kt.

Davies, *Rt. Hon.* Sir (Herbert) Edmund, Kt.

Davies, *Rt. Hon.* Sir (William) Arthian, Kt.

Davis, Sir Charles Sigmund, Kt., C.B.

Davis, Sir Gilbert, Bt. (1946).

Davis, Sir Herbert, Kt., C.B.E.

Davis, *Air Chief Marshal* Sir John Gilbert, G.C.B., O.B.E.

Davis, Sir John Henry Harris, Kt.

Davis, Sir Rupert Charles Hart-, Kt.

Davis, *Admiral* Sir William Wellclose, G.C.B., D.S.O.

Dawnay, *Maj.-Gen.* Sir David, K.C.V.O., C.B., D.S.O.

Dawnay, *Vice-Adm.* Sir Peter, K.C.V.O., C.B., D.S.C.

Dawson, *Cdr.* Sir Hugh Trevor, Bt., C.B.E., R.N. (1920).

†Dawson, Sir Lawrence Savile, Bt. (1929).

Dawson, *Air Chief Marshal* Sir Walter Lloyd, K.C.B., C.B.E., D.S.O.

Day, Sir Albert James Taylor, Kt., C.B.E.

Deacon, Sir George Edward Raven, Kt., C.B.E., F.R.S., F.R.S.E.

Dean, Sir Arthur William Henry, Kt., C.I.E., M.C., E.D.

Dean, Sir John Norman, Kt.

Dean, Sir Maurice Joseph, K.C.B., K.C.M.G.

Dean, Sir Patrick Henry, G.C.M.G.

de Beer, Sir Gavin Rylands, Kt., D.Sc., F.R.S.

Debenham, Sir Gilbert Ridley, Bt. (1931).

De Bunsen, Sir Bernard, Kt., C.M.G.

De Burgh, *General* Sir Eric, K.C.B., D.S.O., O.B.E.

de Freitas, *Rt. Hon.* Sir Geoffrey Stanley, K.C.M.G., M.P.

De Guingand, *Maj.-Gen.* Sir Francis W., K.B.E., C.B., D.S.O.

de Hoghton, Sir (Henry Philip) Anthony (Mary), Bt. (1611).

De la Bère, Sir Rupert, Bt., K.C.V.O. (1953).

Delacombe, *Maj.-Gen.* Sir Rohan, K.C.M.G., K.C.V.O., K.B.E., C.B., D.S.O.

de la Mare, Sir Arthur James, K.C.M.G.

De la Rue, Sir Eric Vincent, Bt. (1898).

De Lestang, Sir Marie Charles Emmanuel Clement Nageon, Kt.

De Lotbinière, *Lt.-Col.* Sir Edmond Joly, Kt.

Delve, Sir Frederick William, Kt., C.B.E.

de Montmorency, Sir Reginald D'Alton Lodge, Bt., (t 1631).

Denholm, Sir John Carmichael, Kt., C.B.E.

Denholm, *Col.* Sir William Lang, Kt., T.D.

Dening, Sir (Maberly) Esler, G.C.M.G., O.B.E.

Denning, *Vice-Adm.* Sir Norman Egbert, K.B.E., C.B.

Denning, *Lt.-Gen.* Sir Reginald Francis Stewart, K.B.E., C.B.

Denny, Sir Alistair Maurice Archibald, Bt., (1913).

Denny, Sir Anthony Coningham de Waltham, Bt.(t 1782).

Denny, Sir (Jonathan) Lionel (Percy), G.B.E., M.C.

Denny, *Admiral* Sir Michael Maynard, G.C.B., C.B.E., D.S.O.

de Normann, Sir Eric, K.B.E., C.B.

Dent, Sir Robert Annesley Wilkinson, Kt., C.B.

Derbyshire, Sir Harold, Kt., M.C., Q.C.

Dering, *Lt.-Col.* Sir Rupert Anthony Yea, Bt. (1627).

Des Forges, Sir Charles Lee, Kt., C.B.E.

De Trafford, *Capt.* Sir Humphrey Edmund, Bt., M.C. (1841).

Deverell, Sir Colville Montgomery, G.B.E., K.C.M.G., C.V.O.

Devitt, Sir Thomas Gordon, Bt. (1916).

Dewey, Sir Anthony Hugh, Bt. (1917).

D'Eyncourt, Sir (Eustace) Gervais Tennyson-, Bt. (1930).

De Zoysa, *Hon.* Sir Cyril, Kt.

de Zulueta, Sir Philip Francis, Kt.

Dhrangadhra, H.H. the Maharaja Raj Saheb of, K.C.I.E.

Dickens, *Air Commodore* Sir Louis Walter, Kt., D.F.C., A.F.C.

Dickson, *Marshal of the Royal Air Force* Sir William Forster, G.C.B., K.B.E., D.S.O., A.F.C.

Dilke, Sir John Fisher Wentworth, Bt. (1862).

Dill, Sir Nicholas Bayard, Kt., C.B.E.

Dillon, Sir Robert William Charlier, Bt. (1801).

Dimsdale, Sir John Holdsworth, Bt. (1902).

Dingle, Sir Philip Burrington, Kt., C.B.E.

Dixie, Sir (Alexander Archibald Douglas) Wolstan, Bt. (1660).

Dixon, Sir Charles William, K.C.M.G., K.C.V.O., O.B.E.

Dixon, *Air Vice-Marshal* Sir (Francis Wilfred) Peter, K.B.E.

Dixon, Sir John, Bt. (1919).

Dixon, *Rt. Hon.* Sir Owen, O.M., G.C.M.G.

Doak, Sir James, Kt.

Dobson, Sir Denis William, K.C.B., O.B.E., Q.C.

Docker, Sir Bernard Dudley Frank, K.B.E.

Dodd, Sir John Samuel, Kt.

Dodds, Sir (Edward) Charles, Bt., M.V.O., D.SC., Ph.D., M.D., F.R.S. (1964).

Dodds, Sir James Leishman, K.C.M.G.

Dods, *Prof.* Sir Lorimer Fenton, Kt., M.V.O.

Dodsworth, Sir John Christopher Smith-, Bt. (1784).

Doig, Sir James Nimmo Crawford, Kt.

Doll, *Prof.* Sir (William) Richard (Shaboe), Kt., O.B.E., F.R.S., D.M., M.D., D.SC.

Domvile, *Admiral* Sir Barry Edward, K.B.E., C.B., C.M.G.

Domville, Sir (Gerald) Guy, Bt. (1814).

Donald, *Air Marshal* Sir Grahame, K.C.B., D.F.C., A.F.C.

Donald, Sir James Bell, Kt.

Donaldson, Sir Dawson, K.C.M.G.

Donaldson, *Hon.* Sir John Francis, Kt.

Donner, Sir Patrick William, Kt.

Dorman, *Maj.* Sir Charles Geoffrey, Bt., M.C. (1923).

Dorman, Sir Maurice Henry, G.C.M.G., G.C.V.O.

Dormer, Sir Cecil Francis Joseph, K.C.M.G., M.V.O.

Dos Santos, Sir Errol Lionel, Kt., C.B.E.

Doubleday, Sir Leslie, Kt.

Dougherty, *Maj.-Gen.* Sir Ivan Noel, Kt., C.B.E., D.S.O., E.D.

Douglas, Sir Sholto Courtenay Mackenzie, Bt., M.C. (1831).

Douglas, *Hon.* Sir William Randolph, Kt.

Dove, Sir Clifford Alfred, Kt., C.B.E., E.R.D.

Dow, Sir Hugh, G.C.I.E., K.C.S.I.

Down, *Lt.-Gen.* Sir Ernest Edward, K.B.E., C.B.

Downer, *Hon.* Sir Alexander Russell, K.B.E.

Dowse, *Maj.-Gen.* Sir Maurice Brian, K.C.V.O., C.B., C.B.E.

Dowty, Sir George Herbert, Kt.

Doyle, *Capt.* Sir John Francis Reginald William Hastings, Bt. (1828).

D'Oyly, *Cdr.* Sir John Rochfort, Bt., R.N. (1663).

Drake, Sir (Arthur) Eric (Courtney), Kt. C.B.E.

Drake, Sir Eugen (John Henry Vanderstegen) Millington-, K.C.M.G.

Drew, Sir Arthur Charles Walter, K.C.B.

Drew, Sir Ferdinand Caire, Kt., C.M.G.

Drew, *Lt.-Gen.* Sir (William) Robert (Macfarlane), K.C.B., C.B.E., Q.H.P.

Dreyer, *Admiral* Sir Desmond Parry, G.C.B., C.B.E., D.S.C.

Dring, *Lt.-Col.* Sir Arthur John, K.B.E., C.I.E.

Driver, Sir Arthur John, Kt.

Driver, *Prof.* Sir Godfrey Rolles, Kt., C.B.E., M.C., F.B.A.

Drucquer, Sir Leonard, Kt.

Druitt, Sir (William Arthur) Harvey, K.C.B.

Drummond, *Lieut.-Gen.* Sir (William) Alexander (Duncan), K.B.E., C.B.

Drummond, Sir William Hugh Dudley Williams-, Bt. (1828).

Drury, Sir Alan Nigel, Kt., C.B.E., M.D., F.R.S.

Dryden, Sir John Stephen Gyles, Bt. (1733 and 1795).

Duckworth, *Maj.* Sir Richard Dyce, Bt. (1909).

Du Cros, Sir Philip Harvey, Bt. (1916).

Dudding, Sir John Scarborough, Kt.

Dudley, Sir Alan Alves, K.B.E., C.M.G.

Duff, Sir (Charles) Michael (Robert Vivian), Bt. (1911).

Duff, Sir (Charles) Patrick, K.C.B., K.C.V.O.

Duffus, *Hon.* Sir Herbert George Holwell, Kt.

Duffus, *Hon.* Sir William Algernon Holwell, Kt.

Dugdale, Sir William Stratford, Bt., M.C., (1936).

du Heaume, Sir Francis Herbert, Kt., C.I.E., O.B.E.

Duke, Sir Charles Beresford, K.C.M.G., C.I.E., O.B.E.

Duke, *Maj.-Gen.* Sir Gerald William, K.B.E., C.B., D.S.O.

Dumas, Sir Lloyd, Kt.

Dumas, Sir Russell John, K.B.E., C.M.G.

Dunbar, Sir Adrian Ivor, Bt., (S 1694).

Dunbar, Sir Archibald Ranulph, Bt., (S 1700).

Dunbar, Sir David Hope-, Bt. (S 1664).

Dunbar, Sir Drummond Cospatrick Ninian, Bt., M.C. (S 1698).

Dunbar, Sir John Greig, Kt.

Dunbar of Hempriggs, Dame Maureen Daisy Helen, Bt. (S 1706).

Duncan, Sir Arthur Bryce, Kt.

Duncan, *Capt.* Sir James Alexander Lawson, Bt. (1957).

Duncan, Sir Val (John Norman Valette), Kt., O.B.E.

Duncombe, Sir Everard Philip Digby Pauncefort-, Bt., D.S.O. (1859).

Dundas, Sir Ambrose Dundas Flux, K.C.I.E., C.S.I.

Dundas, Sir Robert Whyte Melville, Bt. (1821).

Dungarpur, H.H. the Maharawal of, G.C.I.E., K.C.S.I.

Dunk, Sir William Ernest, Kt., C.B.E.

Dunkley, Sir Herbert Francis, Kt.

Dunlop, *Prof.* Sir Derrick Melville, Kt., M.D.

Dunlop, Sir Ernest Edward, Kt., C.M.G., O.B.E.

Dunlop, *Brig.* Sir John Kinninmont, K.B.E., M.C., T.D.

Dunlop, Sir John Wallace, K.B.E.

Dunlop, Sir Thomas, Bt. (1916).

Dunn, *Lt.-Col.* Sir Francis Vivian, K.C.V.O., O.B.E.

Dunn, Sir John Henry, Bt. (1917).

Dunn, *Air Marshal* Sir Patrick Hunter, K.B.E., C.B., D.F.C.

Dunn, *Maj.* Sir Philip Gordon, Bt. (1921).

Dunn, *Hon.* Sir Robin Horace Walford, Kt., M.C.

Dunnett, Sir George Sangster, K.B.E., C.B.

Dunnett, Sir (Ludovic) James, G.C.B., C.M.G.

Dunning, Sir Simon William Patrick, Bt. (1930).

Dunphie, *Maj.-Gen.* Sir Charles Anderson Lane, Kt., C.B., C.B.E., D.S.O.

Duntze, Sir George Edwin Douglas, Bt., C.M.G. (1774).

Dupree, Sir Vernon, Bt. (1921).

Dupuch, Sir (Alfred) Etienne (Jerome), Kt., O.B.E.

Durand, *Rev.* Sir Henry Mortimer Dickon, Bt. (1892).

Durlacher, *Admiral* Sir Laurence George, K.C.B., O.B.E., D.S.C.

Durrant, Sir William Henry Estridge. Bt. (1784).

Duthie, Sir William Smith, Kt., O.B.E.

Duveen, Sir Geoffrey, Kt., R.D.

Dyer, Sir Leonard Schroeder Swinnerton, Bt. (1678).

Dyke, Sir Derek William Hart, Bt. (1677).

Dyson, Sir Cyril Douglas, Kt.

Earle, *Air Chief Marshal* Sir Alfred, G.B.E., C.B.

Earle, Sir Hardman Alexander Mort, Bt. (1869).

East, Sir (Lewis) Ronald, Kt., C.B.E.

Eastick, *Brig.* Sir Thomas Charles, Kt., C.M.G., D.S.O., E.D.

Eastwood, *Maj.* Sir Geoffrey Hugh, K.C.V.O., C.B.E.

Easton, *Air Commodore* Sir James Alfred, K.C.M.G., C.B., F.R.S.

Eaton, *Vice-Adm.* Sir John Willson Musgrave, K.B.E., C.B., D.S.O., D.S.C.

Ebrahim, Sir (Mahomed) Currimbhoy, Bt. (1910).

Eccles, *Prof.* Sir John Carew, Kt., D.Phil., F.R.S.

Echlin, Sir Norman David Fenton, Bt. (I 1721).

Edden, *Vice-Adm.* Sir (William) Kaye, K.B.E., C.B.

Eddie, Sir George Brand, Kt., O.B.E.

Eddis, Sir Basil Eden Garth, Kt.

Eden, Sir John Benedict, Bt., M.P. (1672 and 1776).

Edge, Sir Knowles, Bt. (1937).

Edmenson, Sir Walter Alexander, Kt., C.B.E.

Edmonstone, Sir Archibald Bruce Charles, Bt. (1774).

Edwards, *Lt.-Col.* Sir Bartle Mordaunt Marsham, Kt., C.V.O., M.C.

Edwards, Sir Christopher John Churchill, Bt. (1866).

Edwards, Sir George Robert, Kt., O.M., C.B.E., F.R.S.

Edwards, Sir John Arthur, Kt., C.B.E.

Edwards, Sir John Clive Leighton, Bt. (1921).

Edwards, *Prof.* Sir (John) Goronwy, Kt., D.Litt., F.B.A.

Edwards, Sir Robert Meredydd Wynne-, Kt., C.B.E., D.S.O., M.C.

Edwards, Sir Ronald Stanley, K.B.E.

Egerton, Sir (Philip) John (Caledon) Grey-, Bt. (1617).

Egerton, Sir Seymour John Louis, K.C.V.O.

Eggleston, *Hon.* Sir Richard Moulton, Kt.

Elder, Sir Stewart Duke-, G.C.V.O., M.D., F.R.S.

Eldridge, *Lt.-Gen.* Sir (William) John, K.B.E., C.B., D.S.O., M.C.

Eley, Sir Geoffrey Cecil Ryves, Kt., C.B.E.

Eliott, Sir Arthur Francis Augustus Boswell, Bt. (S 1666).

Elkins, Sir Anthony Joseph, Kt., C.B.E.

Elkins, *Vice-Adm.* Sir Robert Francis, K.C.B., C.V.O., O.B.E.

Ellerman, Sir John Reeves, Bt. (1905).

Elliot, Sir John Blumenfeld, Kt.

Elliott, Sir Claude Aurelius, Kt., O.B.E.

Elliott, Sir Hugh Francis Ivo, Bt., O.B.E. (1917).

Elliott, *Vice-Adm.* Sir Maurice Herbert, K.C.B., C.B.E.

Elliott, Sir Norman Randall, Kt., C.B.E.

Ellis, Sir Charles Drummond, Kt., Ph.D., F.R.S.

Ellis, *Hon.* Sir Kevin, K.B.E.

Ellis, Sir Thomas Hobart, Kt.

Ellwood, *Air Marshal* Sir Aubrey Beauclerk, K.C.B., D.S.C.

Elmhirst, *Air Marshal* Sir Thomas Walker, K.B.E., C.B., A.F.C.

Elphinstone, Sir Howard (Graham), Bt. (1816).

Elphinstone, Sir John, Bt. (S 1701).

Elstub, Sir St. John de Holt, Kt., C.B.E.

Elton, Sir Arthur Hallam Rice, Bt. (1717).

Elworthy, *Marshal of the Royal Air Force* Sir (Samuel) Charles, G.C.B., C.B.E., D.S.O., M.V.O., D.F.C., A.F.C.

Elyan, Sir Isadore Victor, Kt.

Embry, *Air Chief Marshal* Sir Basil Edward, G.C.B. K.B.E., D.S.O., D.F.C., A.F.C.

Emery, Sir (James) Frederick, Kt.

Emmerson, Sir Harold Corti, G.C.B., K.C.V.O.

Empson, Sir Charles, K.C.M.G.

Emson, *Air Marshal* Sir Reginald Herbert, K.B.E., C.B., A.F.C.

Enfield, Sir Ralph Roscoe, Kt., C.B.

Engholm, Sir Basil Charles, K.C.B.

Engineer, Sir Noshirwan Phirozshah, Kt.

Engledow, *Prof.* Sir Frank Leonard, Kt., C.M.G., F.R.S.

Ennor, *Prof.* Sir Arnold Hughes, Kt., C.B.E.

Entwistle, *Maj.* Sir Cyril Fullard. Kt., M.C., Q.C.

Entwistle, Sir (John Nuttall) Maxwell, Kt.

Errington, Sir Eric, Bt., (1963).

Erskine, Sir Derek Quicke, Kt.

Erskine, Sir (Robert) George, Kt., C.B.E.

Erskine, Sir (Thomas) David, Bt. (1821).

Esmonde, Sir Anthony Charles, Bt. (I 1629).

Esplen, Sir William Graham, Bt., (1921).

Eugster, *General* Sir Basil Oscar Paul, K.C.B., K.C.V.O., O.B.E., D.S.O., M.C.

Evans, Sir Anthony Adney, Bt. (1920).

Evans, Sir Arthur Trevor, Kt.

Evans, Sir Athol Donald, K.B.E.

Evans, Sir Bernard, Kt., D.S.O., E.D.

Evans, *Vice-Adm.* Sir Charles Leo Glandore, K.C.B., C.B.E., D.S.O., D.S.C.

Evans, Sir David Lewis, Kt., O.B.E., D.Litt.

Evans, *Air Chief Marshal* Sir Donald Randell, K.B.E., C.B., D.F.C.

Evans, Sir Francis Edward, G.B.E., K.C.M.G.

Evans, *Lt.-Gen.* Sir Geoffrey Charles, K.B.E., C.B., D.S.O.

Evans, Sir Geraint Llewellyn, Kt., C.B.E.

Evans, Sir Ian William Gwynne-, Bt. (1913).

Evans, Sir John Harold, K.B.E., C.B.

Evans, Sir (Robert) Charles, Kt.

Evans, Sir (Sidney) Harold, Bt., C.M.G., O.B.E. (1963).

Evans, Sir Trevor Maldwyn, Kt., C.B.E.

Evans, Sir (William) Vincent (John) K.C.M.G. M.B.E.

Eveleigh, *Hon.* Sir Edward Walter, Kt., E.R.D.

Everard, *Maj.-Gen.* Sir Christopher Earle Welby-, K.B.E. C.B.,

Everard, Sir Nugent Henry, Bt. (1911).

Everson, Sir Frederick Charles, K.C.M.G.

Every, Sir John Simon, Bt. (1641).

Evetts, *Lt.-Gen.* Sir John Fullerton, Kt., C.B., C.B.E., M.C.

Ewart, Sir (William) Ivan (Cecil), Bt., D.S.C. (1887).

Ewbank, *Maj.-Gen.* Sir Robert Withers, K.B.E., C.B., D.S.O.

Ewing, *Prof.* Sir Alexander William Gordon, Kt., Ph.D.

Ewing *Vice-Adm.* Sir (Robert) Alastair, K.B.E., C.B., D.S.C.

Ewing, Sir Ronald Archibald Orr-, Bt. (1886).

Eyre, *Lt.-Col.* Sir Oliver Eyre Crosthwaite-, Kt.

Ezra, Sir Alwyn, Kt.

Fadahunsi, Sir Joseph Odeleye, K.C.M.G.

Fadden, *Rt. Hon.* Sir Arthur William, G.C.M.G.

Fagge, Sir John William Frederick, Bt. (1660).

Fair, *Hon.* Sir Arthur, Kt., M.C.

Fairbairn, Sir William Albert, Bt. (1869).

Fairfax, Sir Vincent Charles, Kt. C.M.G.

Fairfax, Sir Warwick Oswald, Kt.

Fairfield, Sir Ronald McLeod, Kt., C.B.E.

Fairhall, *Hon.* Sir Allen, K.B.E.

Falconer, *Lt.-Col.* Sir George Arthur, K.B.E., C.I.E.

Falk, Sir Roger Salis, Kt., O.B.E.

Falkiner, *Lt.-Col.* Sir Terence Edmond Patrick, Bt. (1 1778).

Falkner, Sir (Donald) Keith, Kt.

Falshaw, Sir Donald, Kt.

Fanshawe, *Maj.-Gen.* Sir Evelyn Dairymple, Kt., C.B., C.B.E.

Faridkot, *Col.* H.H. the Raja of, K.C.S.I.

Farmer, Sir Lovedin George Thomas, Kt.

Farquhar, *Lt.-Col.* Sir Peter (Walter), Bt., D.S.O. (1796).

Farquharson, Sir James Robbie, K.B.E.

Farrer, Sir (Walter) Leslie, K.C.V.O.

Farrington, *Maj.* Sir Henry Francis Colden, Bt. (1818).

Faulkner, Sir Percy, K.B.E., C.B.

Faulks, *Hon.* Sir Neville Major Ginner, Kt., M.B.E., T.D.

Fawcus, Sir (Robert) Peter, K.B.E., C.M.G.

Fayrer, Sir Joseph Herbert Spens, Bt., D.S.C. (1896).

Fedden, Sir Roy, Kt., M.B.E., D.SC.

Feilden, *Maj.-Gen.* Sir Randle Guy, K.C.V.O., C.B., C.B.E.

Feilden, Sir William Morton Buller, Bt. (1846).

Feiling, Sir Keith Grahame, Kt., O.B.E., D.Litt.

Fellowes, Sir William Albemarle, K.C.V.O.

Fenner, Sir Claude Harry, K.B.E., C.M.G.

Fenton, *Col.* Sir William Charles, Kt., M.C.

Ferens, Sir Thomas Robinson, Kt., C.B.E.

Ferguson, *Maj.* Sir John Frederick, Kt., C.B.E.

Ferguson, *Lt.-Col.* Sir Neil Edward Johnson-, Bt., T.D. (1906).

Fergusson, *Brig.* Sir Bernard Edward, G.C.M.G., G.C.V.O., D.S.O., O.B.E.

Fergusson, Sir Ewen MacGregor Field, Kt.

Fergusson of Kilkerran, Sir James, Bt. (S. 1703).

Fergusson, Sir James Herbert Hamilton Colyer-, Bt. (1866).

Ferranti, Sir Vincent Ziani de, Kt., M.C.

Ferrier, Sir Harold Grant, Kt., C.M.G.

Ferris, *Wing-Cdr. Rt. Hon.* Sir Robert Grant Grant-, Kt., M.P.

Festing, *Field Marshal* Sir Francis Wogan, G.C.B., K.B.E., D.S.O.

ffolkes, Sir Robert Francis Alexander, Bt. (1774).

fforde, Sir Arthur Frederic Brownlow, G.B.E.

Fidge, Sir (Harold) Roy, Kt.

Field, Sir Ernest Wensley Lapthorn, Kt., C.B.E.

Field, Sir John Osbaldiston, K.B.E., C.M.G.

Fielden, *Air Vice-Marshal* Sir Edward Hedley, G.C.V.O., C.B., D.F.C., A.F.C.

Fieldhouse, Sir Harold, K.B.E., C.B.

Fiennes, Sir John Saye Wingfield Twisleton-Wykeham-, K.C.B.

Fiennes, Sir Maurice Alberic Twisleton-Wykeham-, Kt.

Fiennes, Sir Ranulph Twisleton-Wykeham-, Bt. (1916).

Figgers, *Col.* Sir John George, K.B.E., C.M.G.

Figgures, Sir Frank Edward, K.C.B., C.M.G.

Findlay, *Lt.-Col.* Sir Roland Lewis, Bt. (1925).

Finlay, *Hon.* Sir George Panton, Kt.

Finlay, Sir Graeme Bell, Bt., E.R.D. (1964).

Finnemore, Sir Donald Leslie, Kt.

Firebrace, *Cdr.* Sir Aylmer Newton George, Kt., C.B.E., R.N.

Fish, Sir (Eric) Wilfred, Kt., C.B.E., M.D., D.SC.

Fisher, *Lt.-Gen.* Sir Bertie Drew, K.C.B., C.M.G., D.S.O.

Fisher, Sir George Read, Kt., C.M.G.

Fisher, *Hon.* Sir Henry Arthur Peers, Kt.

Fisher, Sir John, Kt.

Fisher, Sir Samuel, Kt.

Fisher, Sir Woolf, Kt.

Fison, Sir (Frank Guy) Clavering, Kt.

Fison, Sir Richard Guy, Bt., D.S.C. (1905).

Fitts, Sir Clive Hamilton, Kt., M.D.

Fitzgerald, Sir (Adolf) Alexander, Kt., O.B.E.

Fitzgerald, *Rev.* Sir Edward Thomas, Bt. (1903).

FitzGerald, Sir George Peter Maurice, Bt., M.C., *The Knight of Kerry* (1880).

Fitz-Gerald, Sir Patrick Herbert, Kt., O.B.E.

Fitzgerald, Sir William James, Kt., M.C., Q.C.

FitzHerbert, Sir John Richard Frederick, Bt. (1784).

Fitzmaurice, *Lt.-Col.* Sir Desmond FitzJohn, Kt., C.I.E.

Fitzmaurice, Sir Gerald Gray, G.C.M.G., Q.C.

Fitzpatrick, *General* Sir (Geoffrey Richard) Desmond, G.C.B., D.S.O., M.B.E., M.C.

Flavelle, Sir (Joseph) Ellsworth, Bt. (1917).

Flaxman, *Hon.* Sir Hubert James Marlowe, Kt., C.M.G.

Fleming, *Instr. Rear-Adm.* Sir John, K.B.E., D.S.C.

Flemming, Sir Gilbert Nicolson, K.C.B.

Fletcher, Sir James, Kt.

Fletcher, Sir John Henry Lancelot Aubrey-, Bt. (1782).

Fletcher, *Hon.* Sir Patrick Bisset, K.B.E., C.M.G.

Fletcher, *Air Chief Marshal* Sir Peter Carteret, K.C.B., O.B.E., D.F.C., A.F.C.

Flett, Sir Martin Teall, K.C.B.

Flowers, *Prof.* Sir Brian Hilton, Kt., F.R.S.

Floyd, Sir John Duckett, Bt., T.D. (1816).

Fogarty, *Air Chief-Marshal* Sir Francis Joseph, G.B.E., K.C.B., D.F.C., A.F.C.

Follett, Sir David Henry, Kt., Ph.D.

Follows, Sir (Charles) Geoffry (Shield), Kt., C.M.G.

Fooks, Sir Raymond Hatherell, Kt., C.B.E.

Foot, *Rt. Hon.* Sir Dingle Mackintosh, Kt., Q.C.

Forbes, *Hon.* Sir Alastair Granville, Kt.

Forbes, Sir Archibald Finlayson, G.B.E.

Forbes of Pitsligo, Sir Charles Edward Stuart-, Bt. (S 1626).

Forbes, Sir Douglas Stuart, Kt.

Forbes of Brux, *Hon.* Sir Ewan, Bt. (S 1630).

Forbes, *Hon.* Sir Hugh Henry Valentine, Kt.

Forbes, *Col.* Sir John Stewart, Bt., D.S.O. (1823).

Ford, *Capt.* Sir Aubrey St. Clair-, Bt., D.S.O., R.N. (1793).

Ford, *Prof.* Sir Edward, Kt., O.B.E., M.D.

Ford, *Maj.* Sir Edward William Spencer, K.C.B., K.C.V.O.

Ford, Sir Henry Russell, Bt. (1929).

Ford, Sir Leslie Ewart, Kt., O.B.E.

Ford *Maj.-Gen.* Sir Peter St. Clair-, K.B.E., C.B., D.S.O.

Ford, Sir Sidney William George, Kt., M.B.E.

Fordham, Sir (Alfred) Stanley, K.B.E., C.M.G.

Forget, Sir Joseph Guy, Kt., C.B.E.

Forrest, Sir James Alexander, Kt.

Forsdyke, Sir (Edgar) John, K.C.B.

Forster, Sir Samuel Alexander Sadler, Kt., C.B.E.

Forte, Sir Charles, Kt.

Forwood, Sir Dudley Richard, Bt. (1895).

Foster, Sir (Albert) Ridgeby, Kt.

Foster, Sir John Galway, K.B.E., Q.C., M.P.

Foster, Sir John Gregory, Bt. (1930).

Foster, *Hon.* Sir Peter Harry Batson Woodroffe, Kt., M.B.E., T.D.

Foster, *Air Chief Marshal* Sir Robert Mordaunt, K.C.B., C.B.E., D.F.C.

Foster, Sir Robert Sidney, G.C.M.G., K.C.V.O.

Foulis, Sir Ian Primrose Liston-, Bt. (s 1634).

Fowke, Sir Frederick (Woollaston Rawdon), Bt. (1814).

Fowler, Sir Robert William Doughty, K.C.M.G.

Fox, Sir (Robert) David (John) Scott, K.C.M.G.

Fox, Sir Theodore Fortescue, Kt., M.D., Ll.D.

Foxell, *Rev.* Maurice Frederic, K.C.V.O.

France, Sir Arnold William, K.C.B.

Francis, Sir (Cyril Gerard) Brooke, Kt., Q.C.

Francis, Sir Frank Chalton, K.C.B., F.S.A.

Frank, Sir Robert John, Bt. (1920).

Frankel, Sir Otto Herzberg, Kt., D.S.C., F.R.S.

Franklin, Sir Eric Alexander, Kt., C.B.E.

Fraser, Sir Arthur Ronald, K.B.E., C.M.G.

Fraser, Sir Basil Malcolm, Bt. (1921).

Fraser, Sir Bruce Donald, K.C.B.

Fraser, Sir Douglas Were, Kt., I.S.O.

Fraser, *Air Marshal* Sir (Henry) Paterson, K.B.E., C.B., A.F.C.

Fraser, Sir Hugh, Bt. (1961).

Fraser, Sir Ian, Kt., D.S.O., O.B.E.

Fraser, Sir James David, Bt. (1943).

Fraser, Sir Keith Charles Adolphus, Bt. (1806).

Fraser, Sir (Richard) Michael, Kt., C.B.E.

Fraser, Sir Robert Brown, Kt., O.B.E.

Fraser, Sir (William) Robert, K.C.B., K.B.E.

Frederick, *Maj.* Sir Charles Boscawen, Bt. (1723).

Freeland, *Lt.-Gen.* Sir Ian Henry, G.B.E., K.C.B., D.S.O.

Freeman, Sir John Keith Noel, Bt. (1945).

Freeman, Sir (Nathaniel) Bernard, Kt., C.B.E.

Freeman, Sir Ralph, Kt., C.V.O., C.B.E.

Fressanges, *Air Marshal* Sir Francis Joseph, K.B.E., C.B.

Fretwell, Sir George Herbert, K.B.E., C.B.

Frew, *Air Vice-Marshal* Sir Matthew Brown, K.B.E., C.B., D.S.O., M.C., A.F.C.

Frew, *Eng. Rear-Adm.* Sir Sydney Oswell, K.B.E., C.B.

Frewen, *Admiral* Sir John Byng, G.C.B.

Frome, Sir Norman Frederick, Kt., C.I.E., D.F.C.

Fry, Sir John Nicholas Pease, Bt. (1894).

Fry, Sir Leslie Alfred Charles, K.C.M.G., O.B.E.

Fryars, Sir Robert Furness, Kt.

Fryberg, Sir Abraham, Kt., M.B.E.

Fuchs, Sir Vivian Ernest, Kt., Ph.D.

Fuller, *Maj.* Sir (John) Gerard (Henry Fleetwood), Bt. (1910).

Fung Ping-Fan, *Hon.* Sir Kenneth, Kt., C.B.E.

Furlonge, Sir Geoffrey Warren, K.B.E., C.M.G.

Furness, Sir Christopher, Bt. (1913).

Furse, *Maj.* Sir Ralph Dolignon, K.C.M.G., D.S.O.

Fyffe, *Lt.-Gen.* Sir Richard Alan, K.B.E., C.B., D.S.O., M.C.

Fysh, Sir (Wilmot) Hudson, K.B.E., D.F.C.

Gadsden, Sir Lawrence Percival, Kt.

Gage, Sir Berkeley Everard Foley, K.C.M.G.

Gaggero, Sir George, Kt., O.B.E.

Gairdner, *General* Sir Charles Henry, G.B.E., K.C.M.G., K.C.V.O., C.B.

Gaisford, *Lt.-Col.* Sir Philip, Kt., C.I.E.

Gaitskell, Sir Arthur, Kt., C.M.G.

Gale, *General* Sir Richard Nelson, G.C.B., K.B.E., D.S.O., M.C.

Gallwey, Sir Philip Frankland-Payne-, Bt. (1812).

Galpern, Sir Myer, Kt., M.P.

Galpin, Sir Albert James, K.C.V.O., C.B.E.

Galsworthy, Sir Arthur Norman, K.C.M.G.

Gamage, Sir Leslie Carr, Kt., M.C.

Gamble, Sir David Arthur Josias, Bt. (1897).

Gamble, Sir (Frederick) Herbert K.B.E., C.M.G.

Gammell, *Lt.-Gen.* Sir James Andrew Harcourt, K.C.B., D.S.O., M.C.

Gane, Sir Irving Blanchard, K.C.V.O.

Garbett, Sir Colin Campbell, K.C.I.E., C.S.I., C.M.G.

Gardener, Sir Alfred John, K.C.M.G., C.B.E.

Gardner, Sir Douglas Bruce Bruce-, Bt. (1945).

Gardner, Sir George William Hoggan, K.B.E., C.B.

Garner, Sir Harry Mason, K.B.E., C.B.

Garran, Sir (Isham) Peter, K.C.M.G.

Garrett, *Lt.-Gen.* Sir (Alwyn) Ragnar, K.B.E., C.B.

Garrett, Sir (Joseph) Hugh, K.C.I.E., C.S.I.

Garrett, Sir Ronald Thornbury, Kt.

Garrett, Sir William Herbert, Kt., M.B.E.

Garrow, Sir Nicholas, Kt., O.B.E.

Garthwaite, Sir William Francis Cuthbert, Bt., D.S.C. (1910).

Garvey, Sir Ronald Herbert, K.C.M.G., K.C.V.O., M.B.E.

Garvey, Sir Terence Willcocks, K.C.M.G.

Gascoigne, *Maj.-Gen.* Sir Julian Alvery, K.C.M.G., K.C.V.O., C.B., D.S.O.

Gass, Sir Michael David Irving, K.C.M.G.

Gasson, Sir Lionel Bell, Kt.

Gault, *Brig.* Sir James Frederick, K.C.M.G., M.V.O., O.B.E.

Geddes, Sir (Anthony) Reay (Mackay), K.B.E.

Geddis, *Maj.* Sir William Duncan, Kt.

Gentry, *Maj.-Gen.* Sir William George, K.B.E., C.B., D.S.O.

George, Sir John Clarke, K.B.E.

Georges, Sir James Olva, Kt., O.B.E.

Gerahty, Sir Charles Cyril, Kt., Q.C.

German, Sir Ronald Ernest, K.C.B., C.M.G.

Gethin, *Lt.-Col.* Sir Richard Patrick St. Lawrence, Bt. (1665).

Gibb, *Prof.* Sir Hamilton Alexander Roskeen, Kt., F.B.A.

Gibberd, Sir Frederick, Kt., C.B.E., R.A.

Gibbons, Sir John Edward, Bt. (1752).

Gibbs, Sir Frank Stannard, K.B.E., C.M.G.

Gibbs, *Hon.* Sir Geoffery Cokayne, K.C.M.G.

Gibbs, *Air Marshal* Sir Gerald Ernest, K.B.E., C.I.E., M.C.

Gibbs, *Rt. Hon.* Sir Humphrey Vicary, G.C.V.O., K.C.M.G., O.B.E.

Gibson, Sir Ackroyd Herbert, Bt. (1926).

Gibson, Sir Christopher Herbert, Bt. (1931).

Gibson, *Vice-Adm.* Sir Donald Cameron Ernest Forbes, K.C.B., D.S.C.

Gibson, Sir Donald Edward Evelyn, Kt., C.B.E.

Gibson, Sir Edmund Currey, K.C.I.E.

Gibson, Sir John Hinshelwood, Kt., C.B., T.D., Q.C.

Gibson, *Hon.* Sir Marcus George, Kt.

Gielgud, Sir (Arthur) John, Kt.

Gilbert, Sir Ian Anderson Johnson-, Kt., C.B.E.

Gilbert, *Hon.* Sir (Joseph) Trounsell, Kt., C.B.E., Q.C.

Gilbey, Sir (Walter) Derek, Bt. (1893).

Gilchrist, Sir Andrew Graham, K.C.M.G.

Giles, Sir Alexander Falconer, K.B.E., C.M.G.

Giles, Sir Henry Norman, Kt., O.B.E.

Gill, Sir Archibald Joseph, Kt.

Gillan, *Lt.-Col.* Sir George van Baerle, K.C.I.E.

Gillan, Sir (James) Angus, K.B.E., C.M.G.

Gillett, Sir Edward Bailey, Kt.

Gillett, Sir (Sydney) Harold, Bt., M.C. (1959).

Gilliat, *Lt.-Col.* Sir Martin John, K.C.V.O., M.B.E.

Gillies, Sir Alexander, Kt.

Gillies, Sir William George, Kt., C.B.E., R.A. R.S.A.

Gilmour, Sir John Edward, Bt., D.S.O., T.D., M.P. (1897).

Gilmour, Sir John Little, Bt. (1926).

Gilroy, *His Eminence Cardinal* Norman Thomas, K.B.E.

Gimson, Sir Franklin Charles, K.C.M.G.

Gladstone, Sir (Erskine) William, Bt. (1846).

Gladstone, *Admiral* Sir Gerald Vaughan, G.B.E., K.C.B.

Glanville, Sir William Henry, Kt., C.B., C.B.E., D.SC., Ph.D., F.R.S.

Glass, Sir Leslie Charles, K.C.M.G.

Glen, Sir Alexander, K.B.E., C.B., M.C.

Glen, Sir Alexander Richard, K.B.E., D.S.C.

Glenn, Sir Joseph Robert Archibald, Kt., O.B.E.

Glennie, *Admiral* Sir Irvine Gordon, K.C.B.

Glock, Sir William Frederick, Kt., C.B.E.

Glover, Sir Charles John, Kt.

Glover, *Col.* Sir Douglas, Kt., T.D.

Glover, Sir Gerald Alfred, Kt.

Glubb, *Lt.-Gen.* Sir John Bagot, K.C.B., C.M.G., D.S.O., O.B.E., M.C.

Gluckstein, Sir Louis Halle, G.B.E., T.D., Q.C.

Glyn, Sir Anthony Geoffrey Leo Simon, Bt. (1927).

Glyn, *Col.* Sir Richard Hamilton, Bt., O.B.E., T.D., (1759 and 1800).

Godber, Sir George Edward, G.C.B., D.M.

Goddard, *Air Marshal* Sir (Robert) Victor, K.C.B., C.B.E.

Godfrey, Sir John Albert, Kt.

Godfrey, Sir Walter, K.B.E.

Godfrey, Sir William Maurice, Bt. (I 1785).

Godley, *Brig.* Sir Francis William Crewe Fetherston-, Kt., O.B.E.

Godwin, *Prof.* Sir Harry, Kt., F.R.S.

Goenka, *Rai Bahadur* Sir Badridas, Kt., C.I.E.

Goff, Sir Ernest (William) Davis-, Bt. (1905).

Goff, *Hon.* Sir Reginald William, Kt.

Goldman, Sir Samuel, K.C.B.

Goldney, Sir Henry Hastings, Bt., M.C. (1880).

Goldsmid, Sir Henry Joseph D'Avigdor-, Bt., D.S.O., M.C., M.P. (1934).

Goldsmith, Sir Allen John Bridson, K.C.V.O., F.R.C.S.

Gomes, Sir Stanley Eugene, Kt.

Gonzi, *Most Rev. Monsignor* Michael, K.B.E., D.D. (*Archbishop of Malta*).

Gooch, Sir Robert Douglas, Bt. (1866).

Gooch, *Col.* Sir Robert Eric Sherlock, Bt., D.S.O. (1746).

Goodale, Sir Ernest William, Kt., C.B.E., M.C.

Goodbody, *General* Sir Richard Wakefield, G.C.B., K.B.E., D.S.O.

Goode, Sir William Allmond Codrington, G.C.M.G.

Goodenough, Sir Richard Edmund, Bt. (1943).

Goodeve, Sir Charles Frederick, Kt., O.B.E., V.D., F.R.S.

Goodfellow, Sir William, Kt.

Goodhart, Sir John Gordon, Bt. (1911).

Goodsell, Sir John William, Kt., C.M.G.

Goodson, *Lt.-Col.* Sir Alfred Lassam, Bt. (1922).

Goodwin, Sir Reginald Eustace, Kt., C.B.E.

Goodwin, *Lt.-Gen.* Sir Richard Elton, K.C.B., C.B.E., D.S.O.

Goold, Sir George Leonard, Bt. (1801).

Goonetilleke, Sir Oliver Ernest, G.C.M.G., K.C.V.O., K.B.E.

Gordon, Lord Adam Granville, K.C.V.O., M.B.E.

Gordon, Sir Andrew Cosmo Lewis Duff-, Bt. (1813).

Gordon, Sir Archibald McDonald, Kt., C.M.G.

Gordon, Sir Eyre, Kt., C.S.I., C.I.E.

Gordon, Sir Garnet Hamilton, Kt., C.B.E., Q.C.

Gordon, Sir John Charles, Bt. (S 1706).

Gordon, Sir Lionel Eldred Pottinger Smith-, Bt. (1838).

Gore, *Lt.-Col.* Sir Ralph St. George Brian, Bt. (I 1622).

Goring, Sir William Burton Nigel, Bt. (1627).

Gorman, *Brig.* Sir Eugene, K.B.E., M.C., Q.C.

Goschen, Sir Edward Christian, Bt., D.S.O. (1916).

Gosling, Sir Arthur Hulin, K.B.E., C.B., F.R.S.E.

Gothard, Sir Clifford Frederic, Kt., O.B.E.

Gotz, *Hon.* Sir (Frank) Léon (Aroho), K.C.V.O.

Gough, Sir Arthur Ernest, Kt.

Gould, Sir Robert Macdonald, K.B.E., C.B.

Gould, Sir Ronald, Kt.

Gould, *Hon.* Sir Trevor Jack, Kt.

Goulding, *Hon.* Sir Ernest Irvine, Kt.

Goulding, Sir William Basil, Bt. (1904).

Graaff, Sir de Villiers, Bt., M.B.E. (1911).

Grace, Sir John te Herekiekie, Kt., M.V.O.

Grace, Sir Raymond Eustace, Bt. (1795).

Grade, Sir Lew, Kt.

Graham, *Admiral* Sir Angus Edward Malise Bontine Cunninghame, K.B.E., C.B.

Graham, Sir (Frederick) Fergus, Bt., K.B.E., T.D. (1783).

Graham, Sir George Goldie, Kt.

Graham, Sir John Moodie, Bt. (1964).

Graham, *Hon.* Sir (John) Patrick, Kt.

Graham, Sir John Reginald Noble, Bt., ♥ ℂ, O.B.E. (1906).

Graham, *Maj.-Gen.* Sir Miles William Arthur Peel, K.B.E., C.B., M.C.

Graham, Sir Montrose Stuart, Bt. (1629).

Graham, Sir Norman William, Kt., C.B.

Graham, Sir Richard Bellingham, Bt., O.B.E. (1662).

Grandy, *Marshal of the Royal Air Force* Sir John, G.C.B., K.B.E., D.S.O.

Gransden, Sir Robert, Kt., C.B.E.

Grant, Sir Archibald, Bt. (S 1705).

Grant, *Maj.* Sir Ewan George Macpherson-, Bt. (1838).

Grant, Sir James Monteith, K.C.V.O.

Grant, Sir Kenneth Lindsay, Kt., O.B.E.

Grant, Sir Patrick Alexander Benedict, Bt. (S 1688).

Grantham, Sir Alexander William George Herder, G.C.M.G.

Grantham, *Admiral* Sir Guy, G.C.B., C.B.E., D.S.O.

Grasett, *Lt.-Gen.* Sir (Arthur) Edward, K.B.E., C.B., D.S.O., M.C.

Graves, Sir Hubert Ashton, K.C.M.G., M.C.

Gray, *Prof.* Sir James, Kt., C.B.E., M.C., SC.D., D.SC., LL.D., F.R.S.

Gray, *Vice-Adm.* Sir John Michael Dudgeon, K.B.E., C.B.

Gray, Sir William, Bt. (1917).

Grayson, Sir Ronald Henry Rudyard, Bt. (1922).

Greatbatch, Sir Bruce, Kt., C.M.G., C.V.O., M.B.E.

Greaves, Sir John Bewley, Kt., C.M.G., O.B.E.

Green, Sir (Edward) Stephen (Lycett), Bt., C.B.E. (1886).

Green, Sir George Edward, Kt.

Green, Sir John, Kt.

Green, *Lt.-Gen.* Sir (William) Wyndham, K.B.E., C.B., D.S.O., M.C.

Greenaway, Sir Derek Burdick, Bt. (1933).

Greenaway, Sir Thomas Moore, Kt.

Greene, Sir Hugh Carleton, K.C.M.G., O.B.E.

Greene, Sir Sidney Francis, Kt., C.B.E.

Greenfield, Sir Cornelius Ewen Maclean, K.B.E., C.M.G.

Greenfield, Sir Harry, Kt., C.S.I., C.I.E.

Greenhill, Sir Denis Arthur, K.C.M.G., O.B.E.

Greenwell, Sir Peter McClinbock, Bt. (1906).

Greeson, *Surgeon Vice-Adm.* Sir Clarence Edward, K.B.E., C.B., Q.H.P.

Greeves, *Maj.-Gen.* Sir Stuart, K.B.E., C.B., D.S.O., M.C.

Gregory, *Vice-Adm.* Sir (George) David Archibald, K.B.E., C.B., D.S.O.

Gresley, Sir Nigel, Bt. (1612).

Gresson, *Rt. Hon.* Sir Kenneth Macfarlane, K.B.E.

Gretton, *Vice-Adm.* Sir Peter William, K.C.B., D.S.O., O.B.E., D.S.C.

Grey, Sir Paul Francis, K.C.M.G.

Grey, Sir Robin Edward Dysart, Bt. (1814).

Grierson, Sir Richard Douglas, Bt. (s 1685).

Grieve, Sir (Herbert) Ronald (Robinson), Kt.

Grieve, *Prof.* Sir Robert, Kt.

Griffin, *Vice-Adm.* Sir Anthony Templer Frederick Griffith, K.C.B.

Griffin, Sir Elton Reginald, Kt., C.B.E.

Griffin, Sir Francis Frederick, Kt.

Griffin, Sir John Bowes, Kt., Q.C.

Griffiths, Sir Percival Joseph, K.B.E., C.I.E.

Griffiths, Sir Peter Norton-, Bt. (1922).

Griffiths, *Hon.* Sir (William) Hugh, Kt., M.C.

Grime, Sir Harold Riley, Kt.

Groom, Sir Thomas Reginald, Kt.

Groom, *Air Marshal* Sir Victor Emmanuel, K.C.V.O., K.B.E., C.B., D.F.C.

Grotrian, Sir John (Appelbe) Brent, Bt. (1934).

Grounds, Sir Roy Burman, Kt.

Grove, Sir Walter Philip, Bt. (1874).

Grubb, Sir Kenneth George, K.C.M.G.

Grundy, *Air Marshal* Sir Edouard Michael Fitzfrederick, K.B.E., C.B.

Gubbins, *Maj.-Gen.* Sir Colin McVean, K.C.M.G., D.S.O., M.C.

Guest, *Air Marshal* Sir Charles Edward Neville, K.B.E., C.B.

Guest, *Col. Hon.* Sir Ernest Lucas, K.B.E., C.M.G., C.V.O.

Guinness, Sir Alec, Kt., C.B.E.

Guinness, Sir Kenelm Ernest Lee, Bt. (1867).

Guise, Sir John Grant, Bt. (1783).

Gull, Sir Michael Swinnerton Cameron, Bt. (1872).

Gunn, *Air Marshal* Sir George Roy, K.B.E., C.B.

Gunn, Sir William Archer, K.B.E., C.M.G.

Gunning, Sir Robert Charles, Bt. (1778).

Gunston, *Maj.* Sir Derrick Wellesley, Bt., M.C. (1938).

Gunter, Sir Ronald Vernon, Bt. (1901).

Gutch, Sir John, K.C.M.G., O.B.E.

Guthrie, Sir Giles Connop McEacharn, Bt., O.B.E., D.S.C. (1936).

Guthrie, *Hon.* Sir Rutherford Campbell, Kt., C.M.G.

Guttmann, Sir Ludwig, Kt., C.B.E., M.D.

Gwynne, *Lieut.-Col.* Sir Roland Vaughan, Kt., D.S.O.

Hackett, *General* Sir John Winthrop, G.C.B., C.B.E., D.S.O., M.C.

Hackett, Sir Maurice Frederick, Kt., O.B.E.

Haddow, *Prof.* Sir Alexander, Kt., M.D., Ph.D., D.SC., F.R.S., F.R.S.E.

Haddow, Sir (Thomas) Douglas, K.C.B.

Hadow, Sir Gordon, Kt., C.M.G., O.B.E.

Hadow, Sir Reginald (Michael), K.C.M.G.

Haggerston, Sir (Hugh) Carnaby de Marie, Bt. (1642).

Hague, Sir (Charles) Kenneth (Felix), Kt.

Haines, Sir Cyril Henry, K.B.E.

Hale, Sir Edward, K.B.E., C.B.

Haley, Sir William John, K.C.M.G.

Hall, Sir Arnold Alexander, Kt., F.R.S.

Hall, Sir Douglas Basil, K.C.M.G.

Hall, Sir (Frederick) John (Frank), Bt. (1923).

Hall, Sir John Bernard, Bt. (1919).

Hall, Sir John Hathorn, G.C.M.G., D.S.O., O.B.E., M.C.

Hall, Sir Julian Henry, Bt. (s 1687).

Hall, Sir Noel Frederick, Kt.

Hall, Sir Robert de Zouche, K.C.M.G.

Hall, *Brig.* Sir William Henry, Kt., C.B.E., D.S.O., E.D.

Hallett, *Vice-Adm.* Sir Cecil Charles Hughes-, K.C.B., C.B.E.

Halliday, Sir George Clifton, Kt.

Hallinan, Sir Adrian Lincoln, Kt.

Hallinan, Sir Charles Stuart, Kt., C.B.E.

Hallinan, Sir Eric, Kt.

Hallsworth, Sir Joseph, Kt.

Halsey, *Rev.* Sir John Walter Brooke, Bt. (1920).

Hambling, Sir (Herbert) Hugh, Bt. (1924).

Hamilton, *Capt.* Lord Claud Nigel, G.C.V.O., C.M.G., D.S.O.

Hamilton, Sir Edward Sydney, Bt. (1776 and 1819).

Hamilton, *Admiral* Sir Frederick Hew George Dalrymple-, K.C.B.

Hamilton, Sir Horace Perkins, G.C.B.

Hamilton, *Admiral* Sir John Graham, G.B.E., C.B.

Hamilton, Sir Patrick George, Bt. (1937).

Hamilton, Sir (Robert Charles) Richard Caradoc, Bt. (s 1646).

Hamilton, *Capt.* Sir Robert William Stirling-, Bt., R.N. (s 1673).

Hammett, *Hon.* Sir Clifford James, Kt.

Hammick, Sir Stephen George, Bt. (1834).

Hampshire, Sir (George) Peter, K.C.M.G.

Hancock, *Lt.-Col.* Sir Cyril Percy, K.C.I.E., O.B.E., M.C.

Hancock, Sir Patrick Francis, K.C.M.G.

Hancock, *Air Marshal* Sir Valston Eldridge, K.B.E., C.B., D.F.C.

Hancock, *Prof.* Sir (William) Keith, K.B.E., F.B.A.

Hanham, Sir Henry Phelips, Bt. (1667).

Hankinson, Sir Walter Crossfield, K.C.M.G., O.B.E., M.C.

Hanmer, Sir (Griffin Wyndham) Edward, Bt. (1774).

Hannah, *Air Marshal* Sir Colin Thomas, K.B.E., C.B.

Hanson, Sir Anthony Leslie Oswald, Bt. (1887).

Hanson, Sir (Charles) John, Bt. (1918).

Happell, Sir Arthur Comyn, Kt.

Hardie, Sir Charles Edgar Mathewes, Kt., C.B.E.

Harding, Sir Harold John Boyer, Kt.

Hardinge, Sir Robert, Bt. (1801).

Hardingham, Sir Robert Ernest, Kt., C.M.G., O.B.E.

Hardman, Sir Henry, K.C.B.

Hardman, *Air Chief Marshal* Sir (James) Donald (Innes), G.B.E., K.C.B., D.F.C.

Hardy, *Prof.* Sir Alister Clavering, Kt., D.SC., F.R.S.

Hardy, *General* Sir Campbell Richard, K.C.B., C.B.E., D.S.O., R.M.

Hardy, Sir Edward, Kt.

Hardy, Sir Harry, Kt.

Hardy, Sir James Douglas, Kt., C.B.E.

Hardy, Sir Rupert John, Bt. (1876).

Hare, Sir Ralph Leigh, Bt. (1818).

Harford, Sir James Dundas, K.B.E., C.M.G.

Harford, Sir (John) Timothy, Bt. (1934).

Har Govind Misra, Sir, Kt., O.B.E.

Hargreaves, *His Hon.* Sir Gerald De La Pryme, Kt.

Harington, *General* Sir Charles Henry Pepys, G.C.B., C.B.E., D.S.O., M.C.

Harington, Sir Charles Robert, K.B.E., Ph.D., F.R.S.

Harington, Sir Richard Dundas, Bt. (1611).

Harkness, Sir Douglas Alexander Earsman, K.B.E.

Harley, Sir Stanley Jaffa, Kt.

Harley, Sir Thomas Winlack, Kt., M.B.E., M.C.

Harman, Sir Cecil William Francis Stafford-King-, Bt. (1914).

Harman, Sir (Clement) James, G.B.E.

Harmer, Sir Frederic Evelyn, Kt., C.M.G.

Harmsworth, Sir (Arthur) Geoffrey (Annesley), Bt. (1918).

Harmsworth, Sir Hildebrand Alfred Beresford, Bt. (1922).

Harper, Sir Arthur Grant, K.C.V.O., C.B.E.

Harper, Sir Richard Stephenson, Kt.

Harpham, Sir William, K.B.E., C.M.G.

Harries, *Air Vice-Marshal* Sir Douglas, K.C.B., A.F.C.

Harriman, Sir George William, Kt., C.B.E.

Harris, *Marshal of the Royal Air Force* Sir Arthur Travers, Bt., G.C.B., O.B.E., A.F.C. (1953).

Harris, Sir Charles Felix, Kt., M.D.

Harris, *Prof.* Sir Charles Herbert Stuart-, Kt., C.B.E., M.D.

Harris, Sir Charles Joseph William, K.B.E.

Harris, *Lt.-Gen.* Sir Frederick, K.B.E., C.B., M.C.

Harris, *Lt.-Gen.* Sir Ian Cecil, K.B.E., C.B., D.S.O.

Harris, *Maj.-Gen.* Sir Jack Alexander Sutherland-, K.C.V.O., C.B.

Harris, Sir Jack Wolfred Ashford, Bt. (1932).

Harris, Sir Percy Wyn, K.C.M.G., M.B.E.

Harris, Sir Ronald Montague Joseph, K.C.V.O., C.B.

Harris, Sir William Gordon, K.B.E., C.B.

Harris, Sir William Henry, K.C.V.O., D.Mus.

Harrison, Sir Archibald Frederick, Kt., C.B.E.

Harrison, Sir (Bernard) Guy, Kt.

Harrison, Sir Cyril Ernest, Kt.

Harrison, *Rt. Hon.* Sir Eric John, K.C.M.G., K.C.V.O.

Harrison, Sir Geoffrey Wedgwood, G.C.M.G., K.C.V.O.

Harrison, *Col.* Sir (James) Harwood, Bt., T.D., M.P. (1961).

Harrison, *Maj.-Gen.* Sir James William, K.C.M.G., C.B., C.B.E.

Harrison, Sir Robert Colin, Bt. (1922).

Harrod, Sir (Henry) Roy Forbes, Kt., F.B.A.

Harston, *Maj.* Sir Ernest Sirdefield, Kt., C.B.E.

Hart, Sir Francis Edmund Turton-, K.B.E.

Hart, Sir William Ogden, Kt., C.M.G.

Hartley, *Air Marshal* Sir Christopher Harold, K.C.B., C.B.E., D.F.C., A.F.C.

Hartley, *Brig.-Gen.* Sir Harold, G.C.V.O., C.H., C.B.E., M.C., F.R.S.

Hartnett, Sir Laurence John, Kt., C.B.E.

Hartopp, Sir John Edmund Cradock-, Bt. (1796).

Hartwell, Sir Brodrick William Charles Elwin, Bt. (1805).

Hartwell, Sir Charles Herbert, Kt., C.M.G.

Harvey, *Air Vice-Marshal* Sir Leslie Gordon, K.B.E., C.B.

Harvey, Sir Richard Musgrave, Bt. (1933).

Haskard, Sir Cosmo Dugal Patrick Thomas, K.C.M.G., M.B.E.

Hasluck, *Rt. Hon.* Sir Paul Meernaa Caedwalla, G.C.M.G., G.C.V.O.

Hassan, Sir Joshua Abraham, Kt., C.B.E., M.V.O., Q.C.

Hatty, Sir Cyril James, Kt.

Havelock, Sir Wilfrid Bowen, Kt.

Havers, Sir Cecil Robert, Kt.

Havers, *Air Vice-Marshal* Sir (Ephraim) William, K.B.E., C.B.

Hawker, Sir (Frank) Cyril, Kt.

Hawker, Sir Richard George, Kt.

Hawkey, Sir Roger Pryce, Bt. (1945).

Hawkins, *Admiral* Sir Geoffrey Alan Brooke, K.B.E., C.B., M.V.O., D.S.C.

Hawkins, Sir Humphry Villiers Caesar, Bt. (1778).

Hawkins, *Maj.* Sir Michael Babington Charles, K.C.V.O. M.B.E.

Hawkins, *Vice-Adm.* Sir Raymond Shayle, K.C.B.

Hawley, *Maj.* Sir David Henry, Bt. (1795).

Haworth, Sir (Arthur) Geoffrey, Bt. (1911).

Haworth, *Hon.* Sir William Crawford, Kt.

Hawthorne, *Prof.* Sir William Rede, Kt., C.B.E., SC.D., F.R.S.

Hawton, Sir John Malcolm Kenneth, K.C.B.

Hawtrey, Sir Ralph George, Kt., C.B., F.B.A.

Hay, Sir (Alan) Philip, K.C.V.O., T.D.

Hay, Sir Arthur Thomas Erroll, Bt. (S 1663).

Hay, Sir Frederick Baden-Powell, Bt. (S 1703).

Hay, Sir James Brian Dalrymple-, Bt. (1798).

Hay, Sir James Lawrence, Kt., O.B.E.

Hay, *Lt.-Gen.* Sir Robert, K.C.I.E.

Hayday, Sir Frederick, Kt., C.B.E.

Hayes, *Vice-Adm.* Sir John Osier Chattock, K.C.B., O.B.E.

Hayman, Sir Peter Telford, K.C.M.G., C.V.O., M.B.E.

Haynes, Sir George Ernest, Kt., C.B.E.

Hayter, Sir William Goodenough, K.C.M.G.

Hayward, Sir Alfred, K.B.E.

Hayward, Sir Edward Waterfield, Kt.

Hayward, Sir Isaac James, Kt.

Hayward, Sir Richard Arthur, Kt., C.B.E.

Head, Sir Francis David Somerville, Bt. (1838).

Heading, *Hon.* Sir James Alfred, Kt., C.M.G., D.C.M., M.M.

Heald, *Rt. Hon.* Sir Lionel Frederick, Kt., Q.C.

Healey, *Maj.* Sir Edward Randal Chadwyck-, Bt., M.C. (1919).

Heap, Sir Desmond, Kt.

Heath, *Air Marshal* Sir Maurice Lionel, K.B.E., C.B.

Heathcote, Sir Michael Perryman, Bt. (1733).

Heaton, Sir (John Victor) Peregrine, Bt. (1912).

Hedges, Sir John Francis, Kt., C.B.E.

Heinze, *Prof.* Sir Bernard Thomas, Kt., LL.D.

Hellings, *General* Sir Peter William Cradock, K.C.B., D.S.C., M.C., R.M.

Helmore, Sir James (Reginald Carroll), K.C.B., K.C.M.G.

Helpmann, Sir Robert Murray, Kt., C.B.E.

Henderson, Sir Charles James, K.B.E.

Henderson, Sir Guy Wilmot McLintock, Kt., Q.C.

Henderson, Sir James Thyne, K.B.E., C.M.G.

Henderson, Sir John, Kt.

Henderson, Sir (John James) Craik, Kt.

Henderson, Sir Malcolm Siborne, K.C.M.G.

Henderson, *Admiral* Sir Nigel Stuart, G.B.E. K.C.B.

Hendy, Sir Philip, Kt.

Heneage, *Lt.-Col.* Sir Arthur Pelham, Kt., D.S.O.

Henig, Sir Mark, Kt.

Henley, *Rear-Adm.* Sir Joseph Charles Cameron, K.C.V.O., C.B.

Hennessy, Sir John Wyndham Pope-, Kt., C.B.E., F.B.A., F.S.A.

Hennessy, Sir Patrick, Kt.

Henniker, *Brig.* Sir Mark Chandos Auberon, Bt., C.B.E., D.S.O., M.C. (1813).

Henriques, Sir Cyril George Xavier, Kt.

Henry, Sir James Holmes, Bt., C.M.G., M.C., T.D., Q.C. (1923).

Henry, *Hon.* Sir Trevor Ernest, Kt.

Henty, *Hon.* Sir Norman Henry Denham, K.B.E.

Hepburn, Sir Ninian Buchan Archibald John Buchan-, Bt. (1815).

Herbert, Sir Alan Patrick, Kt., C.H.

Herbert, *Lt.-Gen.* Sir (Edwin) Otway, K.B.E., C.B., D.S.O.

Herchenroder, Sir (Marie Joseph Barnabé) Francis, Kt., Q.C.

Hercus, Sir Charles Ernest, Kt., D.S.O., O.B.E., V.D., M.D.

Herring, *Lt.-Gen. Hon.* Sir Edmund Francis, K.C.M.G., K.B.E., D.S.O., M.C., E.D., Q.C.

Herron, *Hon.* Sir Leslie James, K.B.E., C.M.G.

Hewetson, *General* Sir Reginald Hackett, G.C.B., C.B.E., D.S.O.

Hewett, Sir John George, Bt., M.C. (1813).

Hewitt, Sir Cyrus Lenox Simson, Kt., O.B.E.

Hewitt, *Air Chief Marshal* Sir Edgar Rainey Ludlow-, G.C.B., G.B.E., C.M.G., D.S.O., M.C.

Hewitt, Sir John Francis, K.C.V.O., C.B.E.

Hewitt, Sir Joseph, Bt. (1921).

Hewlett, Sir (Thomas) Clyde, Kt., C.B.E.

Hewson, Sir (Joseph) Bushby, Kt.

Heyes, Sir Tasman Hudson Eastwood, Kt., C.B.E.

Heygate, Sir John Edward Nourse, Bt. (1831).

Heywood, Sir Oliver Kerr, Bt. (1838).

Hezlet, *Vice-Adm.* Sir Arthur Richard, K.B.E., C.B., D.S.O., D.S.C.

Hickinbotham, Sir Tom, K.C.M.G., K.C.V.O., C.I.E., O.B.E.

Hickman, Sir (Alfred) Howard (Whitby), Bt. (1903).

Hicks, Sir (Cedric) Stanton, Kt., M.D., Ph.D.

Hicks, *Col.* Sir Denys Theodore, Kt., O.B.E., T.D.

Hicks, Sir Edwin William, Kt., C.B.E.

Hicks, *Prof.* Sir John Richard, Kt., F.B.A.

Higgs, Sir (John) Michael (Clifford), Kt.

Hildred, Sir William Percival, Kt., C.B., O.B.E.

Hildreth, *Maj.-Gen.* Sir (Harold) John (Crossley), K.B.E.

Hiley, *Hon.* Sir Thomas Alfred, K.B.E.

Hill, *Prof.* Sir Austin Bradford, Kt., C.B.E., Ph.D., D.S.c., F.R.S.

Hill, Sir (George) Cyril Rowley, Bt. (I 1779).

Hill, *Prof.* Sir Ian George Wilson, Kt., C.B.E., T.D., F.R.S.E.

Hill, Sir James, Bt. (1917).

Hill, Sir (James William) Francis, Kt., C.B.E.

Hill, *Prof.* Sir (John) Denis (Nelson), Kt.

Hill, Sir John McGregor, Kt., Ph.D.

Hill, Sir Reginald Herbert, K.B.E., C.B.

Hill, Sir Robert Erskine-, Bt. (1945).

Hillary, Sir Edmund, K.B.E.

Hilton, Sir Derek Percy, Kt., M.B.E.

Himsworth, Sir Harold Percival, K.C.B., M.D., F.R.S.

Hinchcliffe, *Hon.* Sir George Raymond, Kt.

Hinchliffe, Sir (Albert) Henry (Stanley), Kt.

Hinde, *Maj.-Gen.* Sir (William) Robert (Norris), K.B.E., C.B., D.S.O.

Hirst, *Prof.* Sir Edmund Langley, Kt., C.B.E., Ph.D., F.R.S.

Hirst, Sir (Frank) Wyndham, K.B.E.

Hitchman, Sir (Edwin) Alan, K.C.B.

Hoare, Sir Archer, Kt., C.B.E.

Hoare, Sir Frederick Alfred, Bt. (1962).

Hoare, Sir Peter William, Bt. (1786).

Hoare, Sir Samuel, K.B.E., C.B.

Hoare, Sir Timothy Edward Charles, Bt. (I 1784).

Hobart, *Lt.-Cdr.* Sir Robert Hampden, Bt., R.N. (1914).

Hobhouse, Sir Charles Chisholm, Bt., T.D. (1812).

Hochoy, Sir Solomon, G.C.M.G., G.C.V.O., O.B.E.

Hodge, Sir John Rowland, Bt., M.B.E. (1921).

Hodge, Sir Julian Stephen Alfred, Kt.

Hodge, *Prof.* Sir William Vallance Douglas, Kt., SC.D., F.R.S., F.R.S.E.

Hodges, *Air Chief Marshal* Sir Lewis MacDonald, K.C.B., C.B.E., D.S.O., D.F.C.

Hodges, Sir Reginald John, Kt.

Hodgkinson, *Air Marshal* Sir (William) Derek, K.C.B., C.B.E., D.F.C., A.F.C.

Hodson, *Maj.* Sir Edmond Adair, Bt., D.S.O. (I 1789).

Hogan, Sir Michael Joseph Patrick, Kt., C.M.G.

Hogg, *Vice-Adm.* Sir Ian Leslie Trower, K.C.B., D.S.C.

Hogg, Sir John Nicholson, Kt., T.D.

Hogg, *Lieut.-Col.* Sir Kenneth Weir, Bt., O.B.E. (1846).

Hogg, Sir William Lindsay Lindsay-, Bt. (1905).

Holbrook, *Col.* Sir Claude Vivian, Kt., C.B.E.

Holcroft, Sir Reginald Culcheth, Bt. (1921).

Holden, Sir Edward, Bt. (1893).

Holden, Sir George, Bt. (1919).

Holden, Sir James Robert, Kt.

Holder, Sir John Eric Duncan, Bt. (1898).

Holder, *Air Marshal* Sir Paul Davie, K.B.E., C.B., D.S.O., D.F.C., Ph.D.

Holderness, Sir Richard William, Bt. (1920).

Holland, Sir Jim Sothern, Bt. (1917).

Hollings, *Hon.* Sir (Alfred) Kenneth, Kt., M.C.

Hollis, Sir Roger Henry, K.B.E., C.B.

Holman, Sir Adrian, K.B.E., C.M.G., K.C.V.O.

Holmes, Sir Horace Edwin, Kt., D.C.M.

Holmes, Sir Maurice Andrew, Kt.

Holmes, *Maj.-Gen.* Sir Noel Galway, K.B.E., C.B., M.C.

Holmes, Sir Stephen Lewis, K.C.M.G., M.C.

Holroyd, Sir Ronald, Kt., Ph.D., F.R.S.

Holt, Sir James Arthur, Kt.

Holt, Sir John Anthony Langford-, Kt., M.P.

Holt, Sir Stanley Silverwood, Kt.

Holyoake, *Rt. Hon.* Sir Keith Jacka, G.C.M.G., C.H.

Home, *Rt. Hon.* Sir Alexander Frederick Douglas-, K.T., M.P.

Home, Sir David George, Bt. (S 1671).

Hone, Sir Brian William, Kt., O.B.E.

Hone, Sir Evelyn Denison, G.C.M.G., C.V.O., O.B.E.

Hone, *Maj.-Gen.* Sir (Herbert) Ralph, K.C.M.G., K.B.E., M.C., T.D., Q.C.

Honeyman, Sir George Gordon, Kt., C.B.E., Q.C.

Honywood, *Col.* Sir William Wynne, Bt., M.C. (1660).

Hood, *Lt.-Gen.* Sir Alexander, G.B.E., K.C.B., K.C.V.O., M.D.

Hood, Sir Harold Joseph, Bt., T.D. (1922).

Hood, *Col.* Sir Tom Fielden, K.B.E., C.B., T.D.

Hooke, Sir Lionel Alfred George, Kt.

Hooper, Sir Anthony Robin Maurice, Bt. (1962).

Hooper, Sir Leonard James, K.C.M.G., C.B.E.

Hooper, Sir Robin William John, K.C.M.G., D.S.O., D.F.C.

Hope, Sir Archibald Philip, Bt., O.B.E., D.F.C. (S 1628).

Hope, Sir James, Bt., M.M. (1932).

Hope, *Lt.-Col.* Sir Percy Mirehouse, Kt., O.B.E.

Hopkin, Sir (William Aylsham) Bryan, Kt., C.B.E.

Hopkins, *Admiral* Sir Frank Henry Edward, K.C.B., D.S.O., D.S.C.

Hopson, Sir Donald Charles, K.C.M.G., D.S.O., M.C., T.D.

Horlick, *Lt.-Col.* Sir James Nockells, Bt., O.B.E., M.C. (1914).

Hornby, Sir Roger Antony, Kt.

Horne, Sir Alan Edgar, Bt., M.C. (1929).

Hornibrook, Sir Manuel Richard, Kt., O.B.E.

Horobin, Sir Ian Macdonald, Kt.

Horrocks, *Lt.-Gen.* Sir Brian Gwynne, K.C.B., K.B.E., D.S.O., M.C.

Horsfall, Sir (John) Donald, Bt. (1909).

Hort, Sir James Fenton, Bt. (1767).

Horwill, Sir Lionel Clifford, Kt.

Hoskins, Sir Cecil Harold, Kt.

Hoskyns, Sir Benedict Leigh, Bt. (1676).

Hotchin, Sir Claude, Kt., O.B.E.

Houghton, Sir William Frederick, Kt.

Houldsworth, Sir (Harold) Basil, Bt. (1956).

Houldsworth, Sir Reginald Douglas Henry, Bt., O.B.E., T.D. (1887).

Houlton, Sir John Wardle, Kt., C.S.I., C.I.E.

How, Sir Friston Charles, Kt., C.B.

Howard, Sir Douglas Frederick, K.C.M.G., M.C.

Howard, Sir (Hamilton) Edward de Coucey, Bt. (1955).

Howard, Sir John Alfred Golding, Kt.

Howard, *Maj.-Gen.* Hon. Sir Michael Fitzalan-, K.C.V.O., C.B., C.B.E., M.C.

Howard, Sir (Stephen) Gerald, Kt.

Howard, Sir Walter Stewart, Kt., M.B.E.

Howe, Sir (Richard Edward) Geoffrey, Kt., Q.C., M.P.

Howe, Sir Robert George, G.B.E., K.C.M.G.

Howe, Sir Ronald Martin, Kt., C.V.O., M.C.

Howell, Sir Evelyn Berkeley, K.C.I.E., C.S.I.

Howie, Sir James William, Kt. M.D.

Hubble, *Prof.* Sir Douglas Vernon, K.B.E., M.D.

Huddie, Sir David Patrick, Kt.

Hudleston, *Air Chie Marshal* Sir Edmund Cuthbert, G.C.B., C.B.E.

Hudson, Sir Edmund Peder, Kt., F.R.S.E.

Hudson, Sir William, K.B.E., F.R.S.

Hughes, Sir David Collingwood, Bt. (1773).

Hughes, *Air Marshal* Sir (Sidney Weetman) Rochford, K.C.B., C.B.E., A.F.C.

Hughes, Sir Trevor Denby Lloyd-, Kt.

Hugo, *Lt.-Col.* Sir John Mandeville, K.C.V.O., O.B.E.

Hulbert, *Wing-Cdr.* Sir Norman John, Kt.

Hull, Sir Hubert, Kt., C.B.E.

Hull, *Field Marshal* Sir Richard Amyatt, G.C.B., D.S.O.

Hulme, *Hon.* Sir Alan Shallcross, K.B.E.

Hulse, Sir (Hamilton) Westrow, Bt. (1739).

Hulton, Sir Edward George Warris, Kt.

Hulton, Sir Geoffrey Alan, Bt. (1905).

Humphrey, *Air Chief Marshal* Sir Andrew Henry, K.C.B., O.B.E., D.F.C., A.F.C.

Humphreys, Sir Olliver William, Kt., C.B.E.

Humphrys, *Lt.-Col.* Sir Francis Henry, G.C.M.G., G.C.V.O., K.B.E., C.I.E.

Hunt, Sir David Wathen Stather, K.C.M.G., O.B.E.

Hunt, Sir Joseph Anthony, Kt., M.B.E.

Hunt, *General* Sir Peter Mervyn, K.C.B., D.S.O., O.B.E.

Hunter, Sir (Ernest) John, Kt., C.B.E.

Hunting, Sir Percy Llewellyn, Kt.

Hurley, Sir John Garling, Kt., C.B.E.

Hurley, Sir Wilfred Hugh, Kt.

Hurst, Sir Alfred (William), K.B.E., C.B.

Hurst, *His Hon.* Sir (James Henry) Donald, Kt.

Hutchings, Sir Robert Howell, K.C.I.E., C.M.G.

Hutchinson, Sir Arthur Sydney, K.B.E., C.B., C.V.O.

Hutchinson, Sir Herbert John, K.B.E., C.B.

Hutchinson, Sir Joseph Burtt, Kt., C.M.G., SC.D., F.R.S.

Hutchinson, Sir Lewis Bede, K.B.E., C.B.

Hutchison, *Brig.* Sir Eric Alexander Ogilvy, Bt. (1923).

Hutchison, *Lt.-Cdr.* Sir (George) Ian Clark, Kt., R.N.

Hutchison, *Hon.* Sir James Douglas, Kt.

Hutchison, Sir James Riley Holt, Bt., D.S.O., T.D. (1956).

Hutchison, Sir Peter, Bt. (1939).

Hutchison, Sir (William) Kenneth, Kt., C.B.E., F.R.S.

Hutson, Sir Francis Challenor, Kt., C.B.E.

Hutt, Sir (Alexander McDonald) Bruce, K.B.E., C.M.G.

Hutton, Sir Leonard, Kt.

Hutton, Sir Noel Kilpatrick, K.C.B., Q.C.

Hutton, *Lt.-Gen.* Sir Thomas, G.C.I.E., C.B., M.C.

Hutty, Sir Fred Harvey, Kt.

Huxley, Sir Julian Sorell, Kt., D.SC., F.R.S.

Huxley, Sir Leonard George Holden, K.B.E., D.Phil., Ph.D.

Hynes, Sir Lincoln Carruthers, Kt., O.B.E.

Ibadan, The Olubadan of, Kt., O.B.E.

Ife, The Oni of, K.C.M.G., K.B.E.

Igguldsen, Sir Douglas Percy, Kt., C.B.E., D.S.O., T.D.

Iliff, Sir William Angus Boyd, Kt., C.M.G., M.B.E.

Illingworth, *Prof.* Sir Charles Frederick William, Kt., C.B.E.

Ilott, Sir John Moody Albert, Kt.

Imrie, Sir John Dunlop, Kt., C.B.E.

Indore, H.H. *ex*-Maharaja Holkar of, G.C.I.E.

Ingilby, Sir Joslan William Vivian, Bt. (1866).

Inglefield, Sir Gilbert Samuel, G.B.E., T.D.

Inglefield, *Col.* Sir John Frederick Crompton-, Kt., T.D.

Inglis, Sir Claude Cavendish, Kt., C.I.E., F.R.S.

Inglis, *Maj.-Gen.* Sir Drummond, K.B.E., C.B., M.C.

Inglis, *Vice-Adm.* Sir John Gilchrist Thesiger, K.B.E., C.B.

Inglis of Glencorse, Sir Maxwell Ian Hector, Bt. (s 1703).

Ingram, Sir Herbert, Bt. (1893).

Innes of Learney, Sir Thomas, G.C.V.O.

Innes, Sir Walter James, Bt. (s 1628).

Inniss, *Hon.* Sir Clifford de Lisle, Kt.

Iqbal Ahmad, Sir, Kt.

Irish, Sir Ronald Arthur, Kt., O.B.E.

Ironmonger, Sir Charles Ronald, Kt.

Irvine, *Rt. Hon.* Sir Arthur James, Kt., Q.C., M.P.

Irving, *Rear-Adm.* Sir Edmund George, K.B.E., C.B.

Irwin, Sir James Campbell, K O.B.E., E.D.

Isaachsen, Sir Oscar Lionel, Kt.

Isaacson, Sir Robert Spence K.B.E., C.M.G.

Isham, Sir Gyles, Bt. (1627).

Isitt, *Air Vice-Marshal* Sir Leona Monk, K.B.E.

Issigonis, Sir Alec Arnold Co stantine, Kt., C.B.E., F.R.S.

Ismay, Sir George, K.B.E., C.B.

Jack, *Hon.* Sir Alieu Sulayma Kt.

Jack, Sir Daniel Thomson, Kt C.B.E.

Jack, *Hon.* Sir Roy Emile, Kt.

Jackling, Sir Roger Willian K.C.M.G.

Jackman, *Air Marshal* Sir (Harold Douglas, K.B.E., C.B.

Jackson, Sir Donald Edward, Kt.

Jackson, *Col.* Sir Francis Jame Gidlow, Kt., M.C., T.D.

Jackson, Sir George Christophe Mather-, Bt. (1869).

Jackson, Sir Harold Warters, Kt.

Jackson, *General* Sir Henry Chol mondeley, K.C.B., C.M.G., D.S.C

Jackson, Sir Hugh Nicolas, B (1913).

Jackson, Sir John Montrésor, B (1815).

Jackson, *Hon.* Sir Lawrenc Walter, K.C.M.G.

Jackson, Sir Michael Roland, Bt (1902).

Jackson, Sir Richard Leofric, Kt. C.B.E.

Jackson, Sir Robert Gillma Allen, K.C.V.O., C.M.G., O.B.E.

Jackson, *Lt.-Gen.* Sir Willian Godfrey Fothergill, K.C.B. O.B.E., M.C.

Jacob, *Lt.-Gen.* Sir (Edward) Iar (Claud), G.B.E., C.B.

Jacobs, Sir Roland Ellis, Kt.

Jacobs, Sir Wilfred Ebenezer, Kt. O.B.E., Q.C.

Jaffray, Sir William Otho, Bt (1892).

Jakeway, Sir (Francis) Derek K.C.M.G., O.B.E.

James, *Wing-Cdr.* Sir Archibald William Henry, K.B.E., M.C.

James, *Hon.* Sir Arthur Evan, Kt.

James, Sir Gerard Bowes Kingston, Bt. (1823).

James, Sir John Hastings, K.C.V.O. C.B.

James, *Rt. Hon.* Sir (John) Morrice (Cairns), K.C.M.G., C.V.O., M.B.E.

James, *Admiral* Sir William Milbourne, G.C.B.

Janes, Sir Herbert Charles, Kt.

Jansz, Sir Herbert Eric, Kt., C.M.G.

Janvrin, *Vice-Adm.* Sir (Hugh) Richard (Benest), K.C.B., D.S.C.

Jardine, *Maj.* Sir Andrew Rupert John Buchanan-, Bt., M.C. (1885).

Jardine, *Lt.-Col.* Sir Ian Liddell, Bt., O.B.E., M.C. (1916).

Jardine, Sir William Edward, Bt., O.B.E., T.D. (s 1672).

Jarrett, Sir Clifford George, K.B.E., C.B.

Jawara, *Hon.* Sir Dauda Kairaba, Kt.

Jayetileke, *Hon.* Sir Edward George Perera, Kt., Q.C.

Jeans, Sir Alexander Grigor, Kt., T.D.

Jeffcoate, *Prof.* Sir Thomas Norman Arthur, Kt., F.R.C.S.

Jefferson, *Lt.-Col.* Sir John Alexander Dunnington-, Bt., D.S.O. (1958).

Jeffreys, *Prof.* Sir Harold, Kt., D.SC., F.R.S.

Jeffries, Sir Charles Joseph, K.C.M.G., O.B.E.

Jehanghir, Sir Hirjee Cowasjee, Bt. (1908).

Jejeebhoy, Sir Rustom, Bt. (1857).

Jenkin, Sir William Norman Prentice, Kt., C.S.I., C.I.E.

Jenkins, Sir Evan Meredith, G.C.I.E., K.C.S.I.

Jenkins, Sir Owain Trevor, Kt.

Jenkins, Sir (Thomas) Gilmour, K.C.B., K.B.E., M.C.

Jenkins, Sir William, Kt.

Jenkinson, Sir Anthony Banks, Bt. (1661).

Jenks, Sir Richard Atherley, Bt. (1932).

Jennings, Sir Albert Victor, Kt.

Jennings, Sir Raymond Winter, Kt., Q.C.

Jenour, Sir (Arthur) Maynard (Chesterford), Kt., T.D.

Jephcott, Sir Harry, Bt. (1962).

Jerram, *Rear-Adm.* (S.) Sir Rowland Christopher, K.B.E., D.S.O.

Jessel, Sir George, Bt., M.C. (1883).

Jessel, Sir Richard Hugh, Kt.

Joel, *Hon.* Sir Asher Alexander, Kt., O.B.E.

John, *Admiral of the Fleet* Sir Caspar, G.C.B.

John, Sir Rupert Godfrey, Kt.

Johnson, *Hon.* Sir David Powell Croom-, Kt., D.S.C., V.R.D.

Johnson, Sir Frederic Charles, Kt., C.B.

Johnson, *Maj.-Gen.* Sir George Frederick, K.C.V.O., C.B., C.B.E., D.S.O.

Johnson, Sir Henry Cecil, Kt., C.B.E.

Johnson, Sir John Paley, Bt., M.B.E. (1755).

Johnson, Sir Ronald Ernest Charles, Kt., C.B.

Johnson, Sir Victor Philipse Hill, Bt. (1818).

Johnson, Sir William Clarence, Kt., C.M.G., C.B.E.

Johnston, Sir Alexander, G.C.B., K.B.E.

Johnston, Sir Charles Hepburn, G.C.M.G.

Johnston, Sir Gaston, Kt., Q.C.

Johnston, Sir John Baines, K.C.M.G.

Johnston, Sir Thomas Alexander, Bt. (S 1626).

Johnstone, Sir Frederic Allan George, Bt. (S. 1700).

Joint, Sir (Edgar) James, K.C.M.G., O.B.E.

Jolly, *General* Sir Alan, G.C.B., C.B.E., D.S.O.

Jones, *Maj.-Gen.* Sir (Arthur) Guy Salisbury-, G.C.V.O., C.M.G., C.B.E., M.C.

Jones, Sir Arthur Hope-, K.B.E., C.M.G.

Jones, *Prof.* Sir (Bennett) Melvill, Kt., C.B.E., A.F.C., F.R.S.

Jones, Sir Brynmor, Kt., PH.D., SC.D.

Jones, *General* Sir Charles Phibbs, G.C.B., C.B.E., M.C.

Jones, Sir Christopher Lawrence-, Bt. (1831).

Jones, *Air Marshal* Sir Edward Gordon, K.C.B., C.B.E., D.S.O., D.F.C.

Jones, *Rt. Rev.* Edward Michael Gresford, K.C.V.O., D.D.

Jones, Sir Edwin Martin Furnival, Kt., C.B.E.

Jones, Sir Eric Malcolm, K.C.M.G., C.B., C.B.E.

Jones, Sir Eric Newton Griffith-, K.B.E., C.M.G., Q.C.

Jones, *Prof.* Sir Ewart Ray Herbert, Kt., D.SC., PH.D., F.R.S.

Jones, Sir Francis Avery, Kt., C.B.E., F.R.C.P.

Jones, *Rt. Hon.* Sir (Frederick) Elwyn, Kt., Q.C., M.P.

Jones, *Air Marshal* Sir George, K.B.E., C.B., D.F.C.

Jones, Sir (George) Basil Todd-, Kt.

Jones, Sir Glyn Smallwood, G.C.M.G., M.B.E.

Jones, Sir Harry Ernest, Kt., C.B.E.

Jones, *Hon.* Sir Harry Vincent Lloyd-, Kt.

Jones, Sir Henry Frank Harding, K.B.E.

Jones, Sir Hildreth Glyn-, Kt., T.D.

Jones, Sir (John) Henry Morris-, Kt., M.C.

Jones, *Air Marshal* Sir (John) Humphrey Edwardes, K.C.B., C.B.E., D.F.C., A.F.C.

Jones, Sir (John) Kenneth (Trevor), Kt., C.B.E.

Jones, Sir John Prichard-, Bt. (1910).

Jones, *Air Chief Marshal* Sir John Whitworth, G.B.E., K.C.B.

Jones, Sir Owen Haddon Wansbrough-, K.B.E., C.B., PH.D.

Jones, Sir Peter Fawcett Benton, Bt., O.B.E. (1910).

Jones, Sir Philip Frederick, Kt.

Jones, Sir Reginald Watson-, Kt.

Jones, *Air Marshal* Sir (Robert) Owen, K.B.E., C.B., A.F.C.

Jones, Sir Samuel Bankole, Kt.

Jones, Sir Samuel Owen, Kt.

Jones, Sir (William) Emrys, Kt.

Jones, *Hon.* Sir William Lloyd Mars-, Kt., M.B.E.

Jordan, *Air Marshal* Sir Richard Bowen, K.C.B., D.F.C.

Jose, Sir Ivan Bede, Kt., C.B.E., M.C.

Joseph, *Maj.* Sir (Herbert) Leslie, Kt.

Joseph, *Rt. Hon.* Sir Keith Sinjohn, Bt., M.P. (1943).

Joseph, Sir (Samuel) Norman, K.C.V.O., C.B.E.

Joy, Sir George Andrew, K.B.E., C.M.G.

Jude, Sir Norman Lane, Kt.

Jungwirth, Sir William John, Kt., C.M.G.

Kaberry, Sir Donald, Bt., T.D., M.P. (1960).

Kagan, Sir Joseph, Kt.

Kalat, *Maj.* H.H. the Khan of, G.C.I.E.

Karimjee, Sir Tayabali Hassanali Alibhoy, Kt.

Karminski, *Rt. Hon.* Sir Seymour Edward, Kt.

Katsina, The Emir of, K.B.E., C.M.G.

Katz, *Prof.* Sir Bernhard, Kt., F.R.S.

Kaye, Sir John Christopher Lister Lister-, Bt. (1812).

Kaye, Sir Stephen Henry Gordon, Bt. (1923).

Keane, Sir Richard Michael, Bt. (1801).

Keatinge, Sir Edgar Mayne, Kt., C.B.E.

Keay, Sir Lancelot Herman, K.B.E.

Keeling, Sir John Henry, Kt.

Keen, Sir Bernard Augustus, Kt., D.SC., F.R.S.

Keene, Sir Charles Robert, Kt., C.B.E.

Keevil, *Col.* Sir Ambrose, K.B.E., M.C.

Keightley, *General* Sir Charles Frederick, G.C.B., G.B.E., D.S.O.

Keir, Sir David Lindsay, Kt.

Keith, Sir Kenneth Alexander, Kt.

Kellett, Sir Stanley Everard, Bt. (1801).

Kelliher, Sir Henry Joseph, Kt.

Kelly, Sir Arthur John, Kt., C.B.E.

Kelly, Sir Gerald Festus, K.C.V.O., R.A.

Kelly, Sir Robert McErlean, Kt.

Kelly, Sir William Theodore, Kt. O.B.E.

Kemp, Sir Leslie Charles, K.B.E.

Kemsley, *Col.* Sir Colin Norman Thornton-, Kt., O.B.E., T.D.

Kendrew, *Maj.-Gen.* Sir Douglas Anthony, K.C.M.G., C.B., C.B.E., D.S.O.

Kendrick, Sir Thomas Downing, K.C.B., F.B.A., F.S.A.

Kennard, *Lt.-Col.* Sir George Arnold Ford, Bt. (1891).

Kennaway, Sir John Lawrence, Bt. (1791).

Kennedy, Sir Albert Henry, Kt.

Kennedy, Sir James Edward, Bt. (1836).

Kennedy, *Hon.* Sir Robert, Kt.

Kent, Sir Harold Simcox, G.C.B.

Kenyon, Sir Bernard, Kt.

Kerr, Sir Hamilton William, Bt. (1957).

Kerr, *Maj.-Gen.* Sir (Harold) Reginald, K.B.E., C.B., M.C.

Kerr, *Lt.-Col.* Sir Howard, K.C.V.O., C.M.G., D.S.O.

Kerridge, Sir Robert James, Kt.

Keville, Sir (William) Errington, Kt., C.B.E.

Key, Sir Neill Cooper-, Kt.

Keynes, Sir Geoffrey Langdon, Kt., M.D.

Khama, Sir Seretse, K.B.E.

Killick, *Brig.* Sir Alexander Herbert, Kt., C.B.E., D.S.O., M.C.

Killick, Sir John Edward, K.C.M.G.

Kilpatrick, Sir William John, K.B.E.

Kimber, Sir Charles Dixon, Bt. (1904).

Kimmins, *Lt.-Gen.* Sir Brian Charles Hannam, K.B.E., C.B.

Kinahan, *Admiral* Sir Harold Richard George, K.B.E., C.B.

Kinahan, Sir Robert George Caldwell, Kt., E.R.D.

King, Sir Alexander Boyne, Kt., C.B.E.

King, Sir Anthony Highmore, Kt., C.B.E.

King, Sir (Clifford) Robertson, K.B.E.

King, Sir Geoffrey Stuart, K.C.B., K.B.E., M.C.

King, Sir James Granville Le Neve, Bt., T.D. (1888).

King, Sir John Richard Duckworth-, Bt. (1792).

King, Sir Louis, Kt., C.M.G., C.V.O.

King, Sir Peter Alexander, Bt. (1815).

Kingsley, Sir Patrick Graham Toler, K.C.V.O.

Kinloch, Sir Alexander Davenport, Bt. (s 1686).

Kinloch, Sir John, Bt. (1873).

Kipping, Sir Norman Victor, G.C.M.G., K.B.E.

Kirby, Sir Arthur Frank, G.B.E., C.M.G.

Kirby, Sir James Norman, Kt., C.B.E.

Kirby, *Hon.* Sir Richard Clarence, Kt.

Kirkbride, Sir Alec Seath, K.C.M.G., O.B.E., M.C.

Kirkman, *General* Sir Sidney Chevalier, G.C.B., K.B.E., M.C.

Kirkpatrick, Sir Ivone Elliott, Bt. (s 1685).

Kirkwood, Sir Robert Lucien Morrison, Kt.

Kitchen, Sir Geoffrey, Kt., T.D.

Kitson, Sir George Vernon, K.B.E.

Kitto, *Rt. Hon.* Sir Frank Walters, K.B.E.

Kitts, Sir Francis Joseph, Kt.

Kleinwort, Sir Alexander Santiago, Bt. (1909).

Kleinwort, Sir Cyril Hugh, Kt.

Knight, Sir Allan Walton, Kt., C.M.G.

†Knill, Sir Stuart, Bt. (1893).

Knott, *Lt.-Gen.* Sir Harold Edwin, K.C.B., O.B.E., M.D.

Knott, Sir John Laurence, Kt., C.B.E.

Knowles, Sir Francis Gerald William, Bt., F.R.S. (1765).

Knox, Sir Edward Ritchie, Kt., M.C.

Knox, Sir Robert Wilson, Kt.

Knox, Sir (Thomas) Malcolm, Kt.

Koelle, *Vice-Adm.* Sir Harry Philpot, K.C.B.

Kolhapur, *Maj.* H.H. Maharaja of, G.C.S.I.

Kotalawala, *Col. Rt. Hon.* Sir John Lionel, C.H., K.B.E.

Krebs, *Prof.* Sir Hans Adolf, Kt., M.D., F.R.S.

Kwan, Sir Cho-yiu, Kt., C.B.E.

Kyle, *Air Chief Marshal* Sir Wallace Hart, G.C.B., C.B.E., D.S.O., D.F.C.

Labouchere, Sir George Peter, G.B.E., K.C.M.G.

Lacon, Sir George Vere Francis, Bt. (1818).

Lacy, Sir Hugh Maurice Pierce, Bt. (1921).

Laing, Sir (John) Maurice, Kt.

Laing, Sir John William, Kt., C.B.E.

Laing, Sir (William) Kirby, Kt.

Laithwaite, Sir (John) Gilbert, G.C.M.G., K.C.B., K.C.I.E., C.S.I.

Lake, *Capt.* Sir Atwell Henry, Bt., C.B., O.B.E., R.N. (1711).

Lakin, Sir Henry, Bt. (1909).

Lakshmanaswami   Mudaliar, *Diwan Bahadur* Sir Arcot, Kt.

Lala Gujjar Mal, *Rai Bahadur* Sir, Kt.

Lamb, Sir Lionel Henry, K.C.M.G., O.B.E.

Lambart, Sir Oliver Francis, Bt. (1911).

Lambert, Sir Anthony Edward, K.C.M.G.

Lambert, Sir Edward Thomas, K.B.E., C.V.O.

†Lambert, Sir Greville Foley, Bt. (1711).

Lamond, Sir William, Kt.

Lampson, Sir Curtis George, Bt., (1866).

Lancaster, *Vice-Adm.* Sir John Strike, K.B.E., C.B.

Lane, *Hon.* Sir Geoffrey Dawson, Kt., A.F.C.

Lane, Sir William Arbuthnot, Bt., C.B.E. (1913).

Lang, *Lt.-Gen.* Sir Derek Boileau, K.C.B., D.S.O., M.C.

Lang, Sir John Gerald, G.C.B.

Langham, Sir John Charles Patrick, Bt. (1660).

Langker, Sir Erik, Kt., O.B.E.

Langman, Sir John Lyell, Bt. (1906).

Langrishe, Sir Terence Hume, Bt. (I 1777).

Langton, Sir Henry Algernon, Kt.

Lapsley, *Air Marshal* Sir John Hugh, K.B.E., C.B., D.F.C., A.F.C.

Larcom, Sir (Charles) Christopher Royden, Bt. (1868).

Larking, *Lt.-Col.* Sir Charles Gordon, Kt., C.B.E.

Lartigue, Sir Louis Cools-, Kt., O.B.E.

Lascelles, *Rt. Hon.* Sir Alan Frederick, G.C.B., G.C.V.O., C.M.G., M.C.

Lascelles, Sir Francis William, K.C.B., M.C.

Latey, *Hon.* Sir John Brinsmea Kt., M.B.E.

Latham, Sir Joseph, Kt., C.B.E.

Latham, Sir Richard Thomas Pa Bt. (1919).

Lathbury, *General* Sir Gera William, G.C.B., D.S.O., M.B.E

Latimer, Sir Courtenay Robe Kt., C.B.E.

Lauder, *Maj.* Sir George Andre Dick-, Bt. (S 1690).

Laurent, Sir Edgar, Kt., C.M. M.D.

Laurie, *Maj.-Gen.* Sir John En lius, Bt., C.B.E., D.S.O. (1834).

Law, Sir Charles Ewan, Kt.

Law, *Admiral* Sir Horace Roo fort, K.C.B., O.B.E., D.S.C.

Lawes, Sir John Claud Bennet, I (1882).

Lawrence   Sir David Rolan Walter, Bt. (1906).

Lawrence, Sir Frederick, K O.B.E.

Lawrence, Sir John Waldem Bt., O.B.E. (1858).

Lawrence, Sir William, Bt. (1867

Lawson, Sir Henry Brailsfor Kt., M.C.

Lawson, *Lt.-Col.* Sir John Charl Arthur Digby, Bt., D.S.O M.C. (1900).

Lawson, *Hon.* Sir Neil, Kt.

Lawson, *Lt.-Col.* Sir Peter Gra Bt. (1905).

Lawson, Sir Ralph Henry, I (1841).

Lawther, Sir William, Kt.

Lawton, *Hon.* Sir Frederi Horace, Kt.

Lea, Sir Frederick Meacham, K C.B., C.B.E., D.Sc.

Lea, *Lt.-Gen.* Sir George Harr K.C.B., D.S.O., M.B.E.

Lea, Sir Thomas Claude Har Bt. (1892).

Leach, Sir Ronald George, C.B.E.

Leask, *Lt.-Gen.* Sir Henry Lowtl Ewart Clark, K.C.B., D.S. O.B.E.

Leather,   Sir   Edwin   Hartl Cameron, Kt.

Lechmere, Sir Berwick Hung ford, Bt. (1818).

Ledger, Sir Joseph Francis, Kt.

Lee, Sir Arthur James, K.B.E., M

Lee, *Air Chief Marshal* Sir Da John Pryer, G.B.E., C.B.

Lee, Sir (George) Wilton, Kt.

Lee Hau Shik, *Col.* Sir, K.B.E.

Lee, Sir (Henry) Desmond (P chard), Kt.

Leeds, Sir George Graham Mo mer, Bt. (1812).

Lees, *Air Marshal* Sir Alan, K.C C.B.E., D.S.O., A.F.C.

Lees, *Air Marshal* Sir (Rona Beresford, K.C.B., C.B.E., D.F

Lees, Sir Thomas Edward, I (1897).

Lees, Sir Thomas Harcourt Iv Bt. (1804).

Lees, Sir (William) Herewa Clare, Bt. (1937).

Leese, *Lt.-Gen.* Sir Oliver William Hargreaves, Bt., K.C.B., C.B.E., D.S.O. (1908).

Le Fleming, Sir Frank Thomas, Bt. (1705).

Le Gallais, *Hon.* Sir Richard Lyle, Kt.

Legard, Sir Thomas Digby, Bt. (1660).

Leggett, Sir Frederick William, K.B.E., C.B.

Legh, *Major Hon.* Sir Francis Michael, K.C.V.O.

Leigh, Sir John, Bt. (1918).

Leighton, Sir Michael John Bryan, Bt. (1693).

Leith, Sir (Robert) Ian (Algernon) Forbes-, Bt., M.B.E. (1923).

Le Marchant, Sir Denis, Bt. (1841).

Le Masurier, Sir Robert Hugh, Kt., D.S.C.

Lemon, Sir (Richard) Dawnay, Kt., C.B.E.

Lennard, *Lt.-Col.* Sir Stephen Arthur Hallam Farnaby, Bt. (1880).

Lennard, Sir Thomas Richard Fiennes Barrett-, Bt., O.B.E. (1801).

Lennox, *Lt.-Gen.* Sir George Charles Gordon, K.B.E., C.B., C.V.O., D.S.O.

Leon, Sir John Ronald, Bt. (1911).

Le Rougetel, Sir John Helier, K.C.M.G., M.C.

Leslie, Sir (John Randolph) Shane, Bt. (1876).

†Leslie, Sir Percy Theodore, Bt. (S 1625).

Lethbridge, *Capt.* Sir Hector Wroth, Bt. (1804).

Lever, Sir Leslie Maurice, Kt.

Lever, Sir Tresham (Joseph Philip), Bt. (1911).

Levinge, *Maj.* Sir Richard Vere Henry, Bt., M.B.E. (I 1704).

Levy, Sir (Enoch) Bruce, Kt., O.B.E.

Levy, Sir Ewart Maurice, Bt. (1913).

Lewey, Sir Arthur Werner, Kt.

Lewis, Sir Allen Montgomery, Kt., Q.C.

Lewis, *Vice-Adm.* Sir Andrew Mackenzie, K.C.B.

Lewis, *Prof.* Sir Aubrey Julian, Kt., M.D.

Lewis, *Brig.* Sir Clinton Gresham, Kt., O.B.E.

Lewis, Sir Edward Roberts, Kt.

Lewis, Sir Ian Malcolm, Kt.

Lewis, Sir (John) Duncan Orr-, Bt. (1920).

Lewis, Sir John Todd, Kt., O.B.E.

Lewis, Sir William Arthur, Kt.

Lewthwaite, Sir William Anthony, Bt. (1927).

Ley, Sir Gerald Gordon, Bt., T.D. (1905).

Leyland, Sir Vivyan Edward Naylor-, Bt. (1805).

Lidbury, Sir Charles, Kt.

Lidbury, Sir David John, K.C.M.G., C.B., D.S.O.

Lidbury, Sir John Towersey Kt.

Liddle, Sir Donald Ross,, Kt.

Lienhop, *Hon.* Sir John Henry, Kt.

Liesching, Sir Percivale, G.C.M.G., K.C.B., K.C.V.O.

Lighthill, *Prof.* Sir (Michael) James, Kt., F.R.S.

Lighton, Sir Christopher Robert, Bt., M.B.E. (I 1791).

Lim, Sir Han Hoe, Kt., C.B.E.

Lincoln, Sir Anthony Handley, K.C.M.G., C.V.O.

Lindley, Sir Arnold Lewis George, Kt.

Lindo, Sir (Henry) Laurence, Kt., C.M.G.

Lindon, Sir Leonard Charles Edward, Kt.

Lindsay, Sir Ernest Daryl, Kt.

Lindsay, Sir Harvey Kincaid Stewart, Kt.

Lindsay, Sir Martin Alexander, Bt., C.B.E., D.S.O. (1962).

Lindsay, Sir William, Kt., C.B.E.

Lindsay, Sir William O'Brien, K.B.E.

Lindsell, *Lt.-Gen.* Sir Wilfrid Gordon, G.B.E., K.C.B., D.S.O., M.C.

Linstead, Sir Hugh Nicholas, Kt., O.B.E.

Lintott, Sir Henry John Bevis, K.C.M.G.

Lister, Sir (Charles) Percy, Kt.

Lithgow, Sir William James, Bt., (1925).

Little, *Admiral* Sir Charles James Colebrooke, G.C.B., G.B.E.

Little, Sir (Rudolf) Alexander, K.C.B.

Livingston, *Air Marshal* Sir Philip Clermont, K.B.E., C.B., A.F.C.

Llewellyn, Sir David Treharne, Kt.

Llewellyn, *Lt.-Col.* Sir Rhys, Bt. (1922).

Llewellyn, *Col.* Sir (Robert) Godfrey, Bt., C.B., C.B.E., M.C., T.D. (1959).

Llewelyn, Sir Charles Michael Dillwyn-Venables-, Bt., M.V.O. (1890).

Lloyd, *Maj.* Sir (Ernest) Guy (Richard), Bt., D.S.O. (1960).

Lloyd, *Air Chief Marshal* Sir Hugh Pughe, G.B.E., K.C.B., M.C., D.F.C.

Lloyd, Sir John Peter Daniel, Kt.

Lockhart, Sir Allan Robert Eliot, Kt., C.I.E.

Lockhart, Sir Muir Edward Sinclair-, Bt. (S 1636).

Lockhart, *General* Sir Rob (McGregor Macdonald), K.C.B., C.I.E., M.C.

Lockspeiser, Sir Ben, K.C.B., F.R.S.

Lockwood, Sir Joseph Flawith, Kt.

Loder, Sir Giles Rolls, Bt. (1887).

Loder, Sir Louis Francis, Kt., C.B.E.

Loehnis, Sir Clive, K.C.M.G.

Loewen, *General* Sir Charles Falkland, G.C.B., K.B.E., D.S.O.

Logan, Sir Douglas William, Kt., D.Phil.

Lomax, Sir John Garnett, K.B.E., C.M.G., M.C.

Lombe, *Vice-Adm.* Sir Edward Malcolm Evans-, K.C.B.

Long, Sir Bertram, Kt., M.C., T.D.

Long, Sir Ronald, Kt.

Longland, Sir John Laurence, Kt.

Longley, Sir Norman, Kt., C.B.E.

Longworth, Sir Fred, Kt.

Looker, Sir Cecil Thomas, Kt.

Lord, Sir Ackland Archibald, Kt., O.B.E.

Lord, Sir Frank, K.B.E.

Loring, Sir (John) Nigel, K.C.V.O.

Loton, Sir Ernest Thorley, Kt.

Lovell, *Prof.* Sir (Alfred Charles) Bernard, Kt., O.B.E., F.R.S.

Low, Sir Francis, Kt.

Low, Sir James Richard Morrison-, Bt. (1908).

Lowe, Sir David, Kt., C.B.E.

Lowe, *Air Vice-Marshal* Sir Edgar Noel, K.B.E., C.B.

Lowe, Sir (Francis) Gordon, Bt. (1918).

Lowson, Sir Denys Colquhoun Flowerdew, Bt. (1951).

Lowther, *Lt.-Col.* Sir (William) Guy, Bt., O.B.E. (1824).

Loyd, Sir Francis Alfred, K.C.M.G., O.B.E.

Loyd, *General* Sir Henry Charles, G.C.V.O., K.C.B., D.S.O., M.C.

Lubbock, Sir Alan, Kt., F.S.A.

Lucas, *Maj.* Sir Jocelyn Morton, Bt., K.B.E., M.C. (1887).

Luce, Sir William Henry Tucker, G.B.E., K.C.M.G.

Luckhoo, *Hon.* Sir Joseph Alexander, Kt.

Luckhoo, Sir Lionel Alfred, K.C.M.G., C.B.E., Q.C.

Lucy, *Maj.* Sir Brian Fulke Ramsay Fairfax-, Bt. (1836).

Luke, *Hon* Sir Emile Fashole, K.B.E.

Luke, Sir Kenneth George, Kt., C.M.G.

Luke, Sir Stephen Elliot Vyvyan, K.C.M.G.

Lund, Sir Thomas George, Kt., C.B.E.

Lunn, Sir Arnold Henry Moore, Kt.

Lush, Sir Archibald James, Kt.

Lushington, Sir Henry Edmund Castleman, Bt. (1791).

Lusty, Sir Robert Frith, Kt.

Luyt, Sir Richard Edward, G.C.V.O., K.C.M.G., D.C.M.

Lydford, *Air Marshal* Sir Harold Thomas, K.B.E., C.B., A.F.C.

Lyell, Sir Maurice Legat, Kt.

Lyle, Sir Gavin Archibald, Bt. (1929).

Lyle, Sir Ian Duff, Kt., D.S.C.

Lyons, Sir James Reginald, Kt.

Lyons, Sir William, Kt.

Lythgoe, Sir James, Kt., C.B.E.

McAdam, Sir Ian William James, Kt., O.B.E.

Macadam, Sir Ivison Stevenson, Kt., C.V.O., C.B.E., F.R.S.E.

McAdden, Sir Stephen James, Kt., C.B.E., M.P.

McAlpine, Sir Robert Edwin, Kt.

McAlpine, Sir Robin, Kt., C.B.E.

McAlpine, Sir Thomas George Bishop, Bt. (1918).

Macara, Sir (Charles) Douglas, Bt. (1911).

Macartney, Sir John Barrington, Bt. (1 1799).

Macaulay, Sir Hamilton, Kt., C.B.E.

McBride, *Rt. Hon.* Sir Philip Albert Martin, K.C.M.G.

McCall, Sir Alexander, Kt., M.D.

McCall, Sir Charles Patrick Home, Kt., M.B.E., T.D.

McCall, *Admiral* Sir Henry William Urquhart, K.C.V.O., K.B.E., C.B., D.S.O.

MacCallum, Sir Peter, Kt., M.C.

McCance, Sir Andrew, Kt., D.Sc., F.R.S.

McCarthy, Sir Edwin, Kt., C.B.E.

McCarthy, *Rt. Hon.* Sir Thaddeus Pearcey, Kt.

McCaughey, Sir (David) Roy, Kt., C.M.G.

McCauley, *Air Marshal* Sir John Patrick Joseph, K.B.E., C.B.

McConnell, *Cdr.* Sir Robert Melville Terence, Bt., V.R.D. (1900).

McCowan, Sir Hew Cargill, Bt. (1934).

McCullagh, Sir (Joseph) Crawford, Bt. (1935).

McCutcheon, Sir Walter Osborn, Kt.

McDavid, Sir Edwin Frank, Kt., C.M.G., C.B.E.

MacDermot, Sir Dermot Francis, K.C.M.G., C.B.E.

McDonald, *Air Chief Marshal* Sir Arthur William Baynes, K.C.B., A.F.C.

Macdonald, Sir Herbert George de Lome, K.B.E.

Macdonald of Sleat, Sir Ian Godfrey Bosville, Bt. (S 1625).

McDonald, Sir James, K.B.E.

McDonald, *Hon.* Sir John Gladstone Black, Kt.

Macdonald, Sir John Ronald Maxwell-, Bt. (S 1682 and S 1707).

Macdonald, Sir Peter George, Kt.

Macdonald, *Hon.* Sir Thomas Lachlan, K.C.M.G.

McDonald, *Hon.* Sir William John Farquhar, Kt.

MacDonald, *Air Chief Marshal* Sir William Laurence Mary, G.C.B., C.B.E., D.F.C.

MacDougall, Sir (George) Donald (Alastair), Kt. C.B.E., F.B.A.

McDowell, Sir Frank Schofield, Kt.

McDowell, Sir Henry McLorinan, K.B.E.

McEvoy, *Air Chief Marshal* Sir Theodore Newman, K.C.B., C.B.E.

McEwen, *Rt. Hon.* Sir John, G.C.M.G., C.H.

McEwen, Sir Robert Lindley, Bt. (1953).

McEwen, *Hon.* Sir (Alexander) Lyell, K.B.E.

McFadyean, Sir Andrew, Kt.

McFarland, Sir Basil (Alexander Talbot), Bt., C.B.E. (1914).

Macfarlane, Sir George Gray, Kt., C.B.

MacFarquhar, Sir Alexander, K.B.E., C.I.E.

McGeoch, *Vice-Adm.* Sir Ian Lachlan Mackay, K.C.B., D.S.O., D.S.C.

McGlashan, *Rear-Adm.* (E) Sir Alexander Davidson, K.B.E., C.B., D.S.O.

McGovern, Sir Patrick Silvesta, Kt., C.B.E.

McGrath, Sir Charles Gullan, Kt., O.B.E.

MacGregor, Sir Colin Malcolm, Kt.

Macgregor, Sir Edwin Robert, Bt. (1828).

McGregor, *Hon.* Sir George Innes, Kt.

MacGregor of MacGregor, Sir Gregor, Bt. (1795).

McGregor, *Air Marshal* Sir Hector Douglas, K.C.B., C.B.E., D.S.O.

McGregor, Sir James Robert, K.B.E.

McGrigor, *Capt.* Sir Charles Edward, Bt. (1831).

Machtig, Sir Eric Gustav, G.C.M.G., K.C.B., O.B.E.

McIlrath, Sir Martin, Kt.

McIlveen, *Brig.* Sir Arthur William, Kt., M.B.E.

Macintosh, *Prof.* Sir Robert Reynolds, Kt., M.D.

Macintyre, Sir Donald, Kt., C.B.E.

McIntyre, Sir Laurence Rupert, Kt., C.B.E.

Mack, *Hon.* Sir William George Albert, K.B.E.

Mack, Sir (William) Henry (Bradshaw), G.B.E., K.C.M.G.

McKay, Sir Charles Holly, Kt., C.B.E.

Mackay, Sir George Patrick Gordon, Kt., C.B.E.

Mackay, Sir James Mackerron, K.B.E., C.B.

McKay, Sir James Wilson, Kt.

Mackay, Sir William Calder, Kt., O.B.E., M.C.

McKee, *Air Marshal* Sir Andrew, K.C.B., C.B.E., D.S.O., D.F.C., A.F.C.

McKee, *Maj.* Sir William Cecil, Kt., E.R.D.

McKell, *Rt. Hon.* Sir William John, G.C.M.G., Q.C.

MacKenna, *Hon.* Sir Bernard Joseph Maxwell, Kt.

McKenzie, Sir Alexander, K.B.E.

Mackenzie, Sir Alexander Alwyne Brinton Muir-, Bt. (1805).

Mackenzie, Sir (Alexander George Anthony) Allan, Bt. (1890).

Mackenzie, Sir (Edward Montague) Compton, Kt., O.B.E.

Mackenzie, *Vice-Adm.* Sir Hugh Stirling, K.C.B., D.S.O., D.S.C.

Mackenzie, Sir (Lewis) Roderick Kenneth, Bt (S 1703).

Mackenzie, Sir Robert Evelyn Bt. (S 1673).

Mackeson, Sir Rupert Henry, Bt (1954).

McKie, Sir William Neil, Kt., M.V.O., D.MUS.

Mackinlay, Sir George Mason, Kt.

McKinney, Sir William, Kt., C.B.E

McKinnon, Sir James, Kt.

Mackintosh, *Capt.* Sir Kenneth Lachlan, K.C.V.O., R.N. (*ret.*).

McKissock, Sir Wylie, Kt., O.B.E. F.R.C.S.

Macklin, Sir Albert Sortain Romer, Kt.

Mackworth, *Cdr.* Sir David Arthur Geoffrey, Bt. (1776).

Maclaren, Sir Hamish Duncan, K.B.E., C.B., D.F.C.

Maclean, Sir Fitzroy Hew Royle Bt., C.B.E., M.P. (1957).

McLean, Sir Francis Charles, Kt. C.B.E.

MacLean, *Vice-Adm.* Sir Hector Charles Donald, K.B.E., C.B. D.S.C.

McLean, *Lt.-Gen.* Sir Kenneth Graeme, K.C.B., K.B.E.

Maclean, Sir Robert Alexander Kt.

McLeay, *Hon.* Sir John, K.C.M.G., M.M.

Maclehose, Sir Crawford Murray K.C.M.G., M.B.E.

MacLennan, Sir Hector Ross, Kt., M.D.

Maclennan, Sir Ian Morrison Ross, K.C.M.G.

McLennan, Sir Ian Munro, K.B.E.

MacLennan, Sir Robert Laing Kt., C.I.E.

McLeod, Sir Alan Cumbrae Rose, K.C.V.O.

McLeod, Sir Charles Henry, Bt. (1925)

MacLeod, Sir John, Kt., T.D.

McLeod, *General* Sir Roderick William, G.B.E., K.C.B.

McLintock, Sir William Traven. Bt. (1934).

Maclure, *Lt.-Col.* Sir John William Spencer, Bt., O.B.E. (1898).

McMahon, Sir (William) Patrick, Bt. (1817).

McMichael, *Prof.* Sir John, Kt., M.D., F.R.S.

Macmillan, Sir Ernest Campbell, Kt., MUS. DOC.

MacMillan, *General* Sir Gordon Holmes Alexander, K.C.B., K.C.V.O., C.B.E., D.S.O., M.C.

McMullin, *Hon.* Sir Alister Maxwell, K.C.M.G.

Macnab, *Brig.* Sir Geoffrey Alex Colin, K.C.M.G., C.B.

Macnaghten, Sir Antony, Bt. (1836).

McNair, Sir William Lennox, Kt.

McNee, Sir John William, Kt., D.S.O., M.D., D.SC.

McNeice, Sir (Thomas) Percy (Fergus), Kt., C.M.G., O.B.E.

McNeil, Sir Hector, Kt., C.B.E.

McNicoll, *Vice-Adm.* Sir Alan Wedel Ramsay, K.B.E., C.B.,G.M.

McPetrie, Sir James Carnegie, K.C.M.G., O.B.E.

Macpherson, Sir John Stuart, G.C.M.G.

Macready, Sir Nevil John Wilfrid, Bt. (1923).

McRobert, *Col.* Sir George Reid, Kt., C.I.E.

McShine, *Hon.* Sir Arthur Hugh, Kt.

MacTaggart, Sir Andrew McCormick, Kt.

Mactaggart, Sir Ian Auld, Bt. (1938).

MacTaggart, Sir William, Kt., R.S.A., A.R.A.

MacTier, Sir (Reginald) Stewart, Kt., C.B.E.

McTiernan, *Rt. Hon.* Sir Edward Aloysius, K.B.E.

McVeigh, *Rt. Hon.* Sir Herbert Andrew, Kt.

McVey, Sir Daniel, Kt., C.M.G.

McWilliam, Sir John, Kt.

Madden, *Admiral* Sir Charles Edward, Bt., G.C.B. (1919).

Maddex, Sir George Henry, K.B.E.

Maddocks, Sir Kenneth Phipson, K.C.M.G., K.C.V.O.

Maddox, Sir John Kempson, Kt., V.R.D., M.D.

Madgwick, Sir Robert Bowden, Kt., O.B.E.

Madhorao Genesh Deshpande *Rao Bahadur* Sir, K.B.E.

Magill, Sir Ivan Whiteside, K.C.V.O.

Maguire, *Air Marshal* Sir Harold John, K.C.B., D.S.O., O.B.E.

Mahon, Sir George Edward John, Bt. (1819).

Mahon, Sir Gerald MacMahon, Kt.

Maihar ,The Maharaja of, K.C.I.E.

Maini, Sir Amar Nath, Kt., C.B.E.

Mais, *Hon.* Sir Robert Hugh, Bt.

Maitland, *Cdr.* Sir John Francis Whitaker, Kt.

Maitland, Sir Richard John, Bt. (1818).

Major, *Hon.* Sir John Patrick Edward Chandos Henniker-, K.C.M.G., C.V.O., M.C.

Makgill, *Maj.* Sir (John) Donald (Alexander Arthur), Bt. (s 1627).

Makins, Sir (Alfred) John (Ware), Kt.

Makins, Sir Paul Vivian, Bt. (1903).

Malcolm, Sir Michael Albert James, Bt. (s 1665).

Malet, *Col.* Sir Edward William St. Lo, Bt., O.B.E. (1791).

Malik Khizar Hayat Khan Tiwana, *Lt.-Col. Nawab* Sir, K.C.S.I., O.B.E.

Mallabar, Sir John Frederick, Kt.

Mallaby, Sir (Howard) George (Charles), K.C.M.G., O.B.E.

Mallen, Sir Leonard Ross, Kt., O.B.E.

Mallet, Sir (William) Ivo, G.B.E., K.C.M.G.

Mallinson, *Col.* Sir Stuart Sidney, Kt., C.B.E., D.S.O., M.C.

Mallinson, Sir (William) Paul, Bt. (1935).

Mallowan, Sir Max Edgar Lucien, Kt., C.B.E., D.Lit., F.B.A., F.S.A.

Maltby, Sir Thomas Karran, Kt.

Mamo, Sir Anthony Joseph, Kt., O.B.E.

Mance, Sir Henry Stenhouse, Kt.

Mander, Sir Charles Marcus, Bt. (1911).

Mandi, *Col.* H.H. the Raja of, K.C.S.I.

Manifold, *Hon.* Sir (Thomas) Chester, K.B.E.

Manktelow, Sir (Arthur) Richard, K.B.E., C.B.

Mann, Sir Alan Harbury, Kt., M.B.E.

Mann, Sir (Edward) John, Bt. (1905).

Manning, Sir George, Kt., C.M.G.

Mansel, Sir Philip, Bt. (1622).

Mansergh, *Vice-Adm.* Sir (Cecil) Aubrey (Lawson), K.B.E., C.B., D.S.C.

Mansfield, *Hon.* Sir Alan James, K.C.M.G., K.C.V.O.

Mant, Sir Cecil George, Kt., C.B.E.

Manuwa, Sir Samuel Layinka Ayodeji, Kt., C.M.G., O.B.E.

Manzoni, Sir Herbert John Baptista, Kt., C.B.E.

Mappin, Sir Frank Crossley, Bt. (1886).

Mara, *Ratu* Sir Kamisese Kapaiwa Tuimacilai, K.B.E.

Marchant, Sir Herbert Stanley, K.C.M.G., O.B.E.

Marett, Sir Robert Hugh Kirk, K.C.M.G., O.B.E.

Margai, *Hon.* Sir Albert Michael, Kt.

Margetson, *Maj.* Sir Philip Reginald, K.C.V.O., M.C.

Marjoribanks, Sir James Alexander Milne, K.C.M.G.

Markham, Sir Charles John, Bt. (1911).

Markham, Sir (Sydney) Frank, Kt.

Marling, *Lt.-Col.* Sir John Stanley Vincent, Bt., O.B.E. (1882).

Marnham, Sir Ralph, K.C.V.O.

Marr, Sir Leslie Lynn, Bt. (1919).

Marre, Sir Alan Samuel, K.C.B.

Marriott, *Maj.-Gen.* Sir John Charles Oakes, K.C.V.O., C.B., D.S.O., M.C.

Marriott, Sir Ralph George Cavendish Smith-, Bt. (1774).

Marriott, Sir Robert Ecklin, Kt., V.D.

Marsden, Sir John Denton, Bt., (1924).

Marshall, Sir Douglas, Kt.

Marshall, Sir Frank Shaw, Kt.

Marshall, Sir Geoffrey, K.C.V.O., C.B.E., M.D.

Marshall, Sir Hugo Frank, K.B.E., C.M.G.

Marshall, Sir James, Kt.

Marshall, Sir Robert Braithwaite, K.C.B., M.B.E.

Marshall, Sir Sidney Horatio, Kt.

Marshall, Sir Stirrat Andrew William Johnson-, Kt., C.B.E., F.R.I.B.A.

Martell, *Vice-Adm.* Sir Hugh Colenso, K.B.E., C.B.

Martin, Sir David Christie, Kt., C.B.E., Ph.D., F.R.S.E.

Martin, *Admiral* Sir Deric Holland-, G.C.B., D.S.O., D.S.C.

Martin, Sir George William, K.B.E.

Martin, *Air Marshal* Sir Harold Brownlow, K.C.B., D.S.O., D.F.C., A.F.C.

Martin, Sir James, Kt., C.B.E.

Martin, *Prof.* Sir (John) Leslie, Kt., Ph.D.

Martin, Sir John Miller, K.C.M.G., C.B., C.V.O.

Martin, *Prof.* Sir Leslie Harold, Kt., C.B.E.

Martin, *Hon.* Sir Norman (Angus), Kt.

Marwick, Sir Brian Allan, K.B.E., C.M.G.

Mason, Sir Dan Hurdis, Kt., O.B.E., E.R.D.

Mason, *Vice-Adm.* (E.) Sir Frank Trowbridge, K.C.B.

Mason, Sir Frederick Cecil, K.C.V.O., C.M.G.

Mason, Sir Paul, K.C.M.G., K.C.V.O.

Massey, Sir Arthur, Kt., C.B.E.

Massey, *Prof.* Sir Harrie Stewart Wilson, Kt., Ph.D., F.R.S.

Massiah, Sir (Hallam) Grey, K.B.E., M.D.

Masterman, Sir Christopher Hughes, Kt., C.S.I., C.I.E.

Masterman, Sir John Cecil, Kt., O.B.E.

Mather, Sir William Loris, Kt., O.B.E., M.C., T.D.

Matheson, *Major* Sir Torquhil Alexander, Bt. (1882).

Mathias, Sir Richard Hughes, Bt. (1917).

Matters, Sir (Reginald) Francis, Kt., V.R.D., M.D.

Matthew, *Prof.* Sir Robert Hogg, Kt., C.B.E., A.R.S.A.

Matthews, Sir Bryan Harold Cabot, Kt., C.B.E., SC.D., F.R.S.

Matthews, Sir (Harold Lancelot) Roy, Kt., C.B.E.

Matthews, Sir James Henry John, Kt.

Matthews, Sir Stanley, Kt., C.B.E.

Matthews, *Very Rev.* Walter Robert, C.H., K.C.V.O., D.D.

Maufe, Sir Edward Brantwood, Kt., R.A.

Mavor, *Air Marshal* Sir Leslie Deane, K.C.B., A.F.C.

Mawby, Sir Maurice Alan Edgar, Kt., C.B.E.

Maxwell. Sir Alexander Hyslop, K.C.M.G.

Maxwell, Sir Aymer, Bt. (s 1681).

Maxwell, *Maj.-Gen.* Sir Aymer, Kt., C.B.E., M.C.

Maxwell, Sir Patrick Ivor Heron-, Bt. (s 1683).

Maxwell, Sir Robert Hugh, K.B.E.

May, *Surg. Vice-Adm.* Sir (Robert) Cyril, K.B.E., C.B., M.C.

Mayer, Sir Robert, Kt.

Mayo, *Hon.* Sir Herbert, Kt.

Mbanefo, Sir Louis Nwachukwu, Kt.

Mead, Sir Cecil, Kt.

Meade, Sir (Richard) Geoffrey (Austin), K.B.E., C.M.G., C.V.O.

Meagher, Sir Thomas, Kt.

Medawar, Sir Peter Brian, Kt., C.B.E., D.Sc., F.R.S.

Medlicott, *Brig.* Sir Frank, Kt., C.B.E.

Medlycott, Sir (James) Christopher, Bt. (1808).

Meech, Sir John Valentine, K.C.V.O.

Meere, Sir Francis Anthony, Kt., C.B.E.

Megarry, *Hon.* Sir Robert Edgar, Kt., F.B.A.

Megaw, *Rt. Hon.* Sir John, Kt. C.B.E., T.D.

Mehta, Sir Chunilal Baichand, Kt.

Mellor, Sir John Serocold Paget, Bt. (1924).

Melville, Sir Eugene, K.C.M.G.

Melville, Sir Harry Work, K.C.B., Ph.D., D.Sc., F.R.S.

Melville, Sir Leslie Galfreid, K.B.E.

Melville, Sir Ronald Henry, K.C.B.

Mensforth, Sir Eric, Kt., C.B.E.

Menteth, Sir James Wallace Stuart-, Bt. (1838).

Menzies, *Rt. Hon.* Sir Douglas Ian, K.B.E.

Menzies, Sir Laurence James, Kt.

Menzies, *Rt. Hon.* Sir Robert Gordon, K.T., C.H., Q.C., F.R.S.

Meredith, *Air Vice-Marshal* Sir Charles Warburton, K.B.E., C.B., A.F.C.

Merriman, Sir Walter Thomas, Kt.

Merton, *Air Chief Marshal* Sir Walter Hugh, G.B.E., K.C.B.

Messent, Sir Philip Santo, Kt.

Messervy, *General* Sir Frank Walter, K.C.S.I., K.B.E., C.B., D.S.O.

Metcalfe, Sir Ralph Ismay, Kt.

Metcalfe, Sir Theophilus John, Bt. (1802).

Meyer, Sir Anthony John Charles, Bt., M.P. (1910).

Meynell, Sir Francis, Kt.

Meyrick, *Lt.-Col.* Sir George David Elliott Tapps-Gervis-, Bt., M.C. (1791).

Meyrick, *Admiral* Sir Sidney Julius, K.C.B.

Meyrick, *Maj.* Sir Thomas Frederick, Bt. (1880).

Michaelis, *Brig. Hon.* Sir Archie, Kt.

Michelmore, Sir Walter Harold Strachan, Kt., M.B.E.

Michelmore, *Maj.-Gen.* Sir (William) Godwin, K.B.E., C.B., D.S.O., M.C., T.D.

Micklethwait, Sir Robert Gore, Kt., Q.C.

Middlebrook, Sir Harold, Bt. (1930).

Middlemore, Sir William Hawkslow, Bt. (1919).

Middleton, Sir George Humphrey, K.C.M.G.

Middleton, Sir George Proctor, K.C.V.O.

Middleton, Sir Stephen Hugh, Bt. (1662).

Miers, *Rear-Adm.* Sir Anthony Cecil Capel, V℗, C.B.E., C.B., D.S.O.

Miéville, Sir Eric Charles, G.C.I.E., K.C.V.O., C.S.I., C.M.G.

Milbank, *Maj.* Sir Mark Vane, Bt., K.C.V.O., M.C. (1882).

Milburn, Sir John Nigel, Bt. (1905).

†Mildmay, Sir Verus Arundell Maunder St. John-, Bt. (1772).

Miles, *Prof.* Sir (Arnold) Ashley, Kt., C.B.E., M.D., F.R.S.

Miles, Sir Bernard, Kt., C.B.E.

Miles, *Admiral* Sir Geoffrey John Audley, K.C.B., K.C.S.I.

Miles, Sir William Napier Maurice, Bt. (1859).

Millais, Sir Ralph Regnault, Bt. (1885).

Millbourn, Sir (Philip) Eric, Kt., C.M.G.

Miller, *Lt.-Gen.* Sir Euan Alfred Bews, K.C.B., K.B.E., D.S.O., M.C.

Milier, Sir (Ian) Douglas, Kt.

Miller, Sir James, G.B.E.

Miller, *Col.* Sir James MacBride, Kt., M.C., T.D.

Miller, Sir John Francis Compton, Kt., M.B.E., T.D.

Miller, Sir John Holmes, Bt. (1705).

Miller, Sir (Oswald) Bernard, Kt.

Miller, Sir Richard Hope, Kt.

Miller, Sir Stanley Norie-, Bt., M.C. (1936).

Miller of Glenlee, Sir Frederick William Macdonald, Bt. (1788).

Mills, *Vice-Adm.* Sir Charles Piercy, K.C.B., C.B.E., D.S.C.

Mills, *Col.* Sir John Digby, Kt., T.D.

Mills, Sir Peter Frederick Leighton, Bt. (1921).

Milman, Sir Dermot Lionel Kennedy, Bt. (1800).

Milmo, *Hon.* Sir Helenus Patrick Joseph, Kt.

Milne, Sir David, G.C.B.

Milner, Sir (George Edward) Mordaunt, Bt. (1717).

Milton, Sir Frank, Kt.

Milward, Sir Anthony Horace, Kt., C.B.E.

Minter, Sir Frederick Albert, G.C.V.O.

Missenden, Sir Eustace James, Kt., O.B.E.

Mitchell, Sir Godfrey Way, Kt.

Mitchell, Sir Hamilton, K.B.E.

Mitchell, *Col.* Sir Harold Paton, Bt. (1945).

Mitchell, *Prof.* Sir Mark Ledingham, Kt.

Mitchell, Sir (Seton) Steuart Crichton, K.B.E., C.B.

Moberly, Sir Walter (Hamilton), G.B.E., K.C.B., D.S.O., D.Litt.

Mocatta, *Hon.* Sir Alan Abraham, Kt., O.B.E.

Mockett, Sir Vere, Kt., M.B.E.

Moffat, Sir John Smith, Kt., O.B.E.

Mogg, *General* Sir (Herbert) John, K.C.B., C.B.E., D.S.O.

Mohamed, Sir Abdool Razack, Kt.

Moir, Sir Ernest Ian Royds, Bt. (1916).

Molony, Sir Hugh Francis, Bt. (1925).

Molony, Sir Joseph Thomas, K.C.V.O., Q.C.

Monahan, Sir Robert Vincent, Kt.

Moncrieff, *Admiral* Sir Alan Kenneth Scott-, K.C.B., C.B.E., D.S.O.

Moncreiffe, Sir (Rupert) Iain (Kay), Bt. (s 1685).

Monnington, Sir Walter Thomas, Kt., P.R.A.

Monson, Sir (William Bonnar) Leslie, K.C.M.G., C.B.

Montgomery, Sir (Basil Henry) David, Bt. (1801).

Montgomery, Sir Frank Percival, Kt., M.C.

Mookerjee, Sir Birendra Nath, Kt.

Moon, Sir Edward Penderel, Kt., O.B.E.

Moon, Sir John Arthur, Bt. (1887).

Moon, Sir (Peter) Wilfred Giles, Bt. (1855).

Moore, Sir Edward Stanton, Bt., O.B.E. (1923).

Moore, Sir Harold (John de Courcy), Kt.

Moore, *Admiral* Sir Henry Ruthven, G.C.B., C.V.O., D.S.O.

Moore, *General* Sir (James Newton) Rodney, G.C.V.O., K.C.B., C.B.E., D.S.O.

Moore, Sir Norman Winfrid, Bt. (1919).

Moore, Sir William Samson, Bt. (1932).

Mootham, Sir Orby Howell, Kt.

Mordaunt, Sir Nigel John, Bt., M.B.E. (1611).

Mordecai, Sir John Stanley, Kt., C.M.G.

Morgan, Sir (Clifford) Naunton, Kt.

Morgan, Sir David John Hughes-, Bt., M.B.E. (1925).

Morgan, Sir Edward James Ranembe, Kt.

Morgan, Sir Ernest Dunstan, K.B.E.

Morgan, Sir Frank William, Kt., M.C.

Morgan, Sir Morien Bedford, Kt., C.B.

Morgan, *Rear-Adm.* Sir Patrick John, K.C.V.O., C.B., D.S.C.

Morgan, *General* Sir William Duthie, G.C.B., D.S.O., M.C.

Morison, Sir Ronald Peter, Kt., Q.C.

Morland, Sir Oscar Charles, G.B.E., K.C.M.G.

Morley, Sir Alexander Francis, K.C.M.G., C.B.E.

Morley, Sir Godfrey William Rowland, Kt., O.B.E., T.D.

Morren, Sir William Booth Rennie, Kt., C.B.E., M.V.O.

Morris, Sir Cedric Lockwood, Bt. (1806).

Morris, *Air Marshal* Sir Douglas Griffith, K.C.B., C.B.E., D.S.O., D.F.C.

Morris, Sir Geoffrey Newman-Kt., E.D.

Morris, *Hon.* Sir Kenneth James, K.B.E., C.M.G.

Morris, *Air Marshal* Sir Leslie Dalton-, K.B.E., C.B.

Morris, *His Hon.* Sir Owen Temple-, Kt., Q.C.

Morris, Sir Parker, Kt.

Morris, Sir Philip Robert, K.C.M.G., C.B.E.

Morrow, Sir Arthur William, Kt., D.S.O., E.D.

Morshead, Sir Owen Frederick, G.C.V.O., K.C.B., D.S.O., M.C.

Mortimer, *Rev.* Sir Charles Edward, Kt., C.B.E.

Morton, Sir Ralph John, Kt., C.M.G., O.B.E., M.C.

Morton, Sir (William) Wilfred, K.C.B.

Moses, Sir Charles Joseph Alfred, Kt., C.B.E.

Mosley, Sir Oswald Ernald, Bt. (1781).

Moss, Sir Eric de Vere, Kt., C.I.E.

Moss, Sir John Herbert Theodore Edwards-, Bt. (1868).

Mostyn, Sir Jeremy John Antony, Bt. (1670).

Mott, Sir John Harmar, Bt. (1930).

Mott, *Prof.* Sir Nevill Francis, Kt., F.R.S.

Mount, Sir William Malcolm, Bt. (1921).

Mountain, Sir Brian Edward Stanley, Bt. (1922).

Mountford, Sir James Frederick, Kt., D.Litt.

Mowbray, Sir John Robert, Bt. (1880).

Mudaliar, *Diwan Bahadur* Sir Arcot Ramaswami, K.C.S.I.

Mudie, Sir (Robert) Francis, K.C.S.I., K.C.I.E., O.B.E.

Muhamad Noor, *Khan Bahadur* Sir Khaja, Kt., C.B.E.

Muhammad Ahmad Sa'id Khan *Nawab* Sir, G.B.E., K.C.S.I., K.C.I.E.

Muir, Sir David John, Kt., C.M.G.

Muir, Sir Edward Francis, K.C.B.

Muir, Sir Edward Grainger, Kt., F.R.C.S.

Muir, Sir John Harling, Bt. (1892).

Muirhead, Sir John Spencer, Kt., D.S.O., M.C., T.D.

Mulholland, Sir Michael Henry, Bt. (1945).

Mulholland, Sir William Walter, Kt., O.B.E.

Mullens, Sir Harold Hill, Kt.

Mullens, Sir William John Herbert deWette, Kt., D.S.O., T.D.

Mumford, Sir Albert Henry, K.B.E.

Munro, Sir Arthur Herman, Bt. (s 1634).

Munro, *Hon.* Sir Leslie Knox, K.C.M.G., K.C.V.O.

Munro, Sir (Thomas) Torquil (Alfonso), Bt. (1825).

Murdoch, *Air Marshal* Sir Alister Murray, K.B.E., C.B.

Murphy, Sir Alexander Paterson, Kt.

Murphy, Sir Dermod Art Pelly, Kt., C.M.G., O.B.E.

Murphy, Sir (Oswald) Ellis (Joseph), Kt.

Murrant, Sir Ernest Henry, K.C.M.G., M.B.E.

Murray, Sir Alan John Digby, Bt. (s 1628).

Murray, Sir Andrew Hunter Arbuthnot, Kt., O.B.E.

Murray, Sir (Francis) Ralph (Hay), K.C.M.G., C.B.

Murray, *General* Sir Horatius, G.C.B., K.B.E., D.S.O.

Murray, *Hon.* Sir John Murray, Kt.

Murray, Sir (John) Stanley, Kt.

Murray, Sir Kenneth, Kt.

Murray, Sir Robert Alistair, Kt., O.B.E.

Murray, Sir Rowland William Patrick, Bt. (s 1630).

Murray, Sir William Patrick Keith, Bt. (s 1673).

Murrie, Sir William Stuart, G.C.B., K.B.E.

Mursell, Sir Peter, Kt., M.B.E.

Musgrave, Sir Christopher Patrick Charles, Bt. (1611).

Musgrave, Sir (Frank) Cyril, K.C.B.

Musgrave, Sir Richard James, Bt. (I 1782).

Musker, Sir John, Kt.

Muspratt, *General* Sir Sydney Frederick, K.C.B., C.S.I., C.I.E., D.S.O.

Musson, *General* Sir Geoffrey Randolph Dixon, G.C.B., C.B.E., D.S.O.

Musto, Sir Arnold Albert, Kt., C.I.E.

Mutta Venkatasubba Rao, Sir, Kt.

Mya Bu, Sir, Kt.

Mynors, Sir Humphrey Charles Baskerville, Bt. (1964).

Mynors, *Prof.* Sir Roger Aubrey Baskerville, Kt., F.B.A.

Mysore, H.H. the Maharaja of, G.C.B., G.C.S.I.

Nabarro, Sir Gerald David Nunes, Kt., M.P.

Nairac, *Hon.* Sir André Laurence, Kt., C.B.E., Q.C.

Nairn, Sir (Michael) George, Bt. (1904).

Nairn, Sir Robert Arnold Spencer-, Bt. (1933).

Nall, *Lt.-Cdr.* Sir Michael Joseph, Bt., R.N. (1954).

Napier, *Hon.* Sir Albert Edward Alexander, K.C.B., K.C.V.O., Q.C.

Napier, *Hon.* Sir John Mellis, K.C.M.G.

Napier, Sir Joseph William Lennox, Bt., O.B.E. (1867).

Napier, Sir William Archibald, Bt. (s 1627).

Nathan, Sir Maurice Arnold, K.B.E.

Nayudu, *Sri Diwan Bahadur* Sir Madura Balasundram, Kt., C.I.E.

Neale, *Prof.* Sir John Ernest, Kt., F.B.A.

Neame, *Lt.-Gen.* Sir Philip, V.C., K.B.E., C.B., D.S.O.

Neame, Sir Thomas, Kt., M.B.E., F.S.A.

Neave, Sir Arundell Thomas Clifton, Bt. (1795).

Neden, Sir Wilfred John, Kt., C.B., C.B.E.

Negus, Sir Victor Ewings, Kt.

Nelson, *Maj.-Gen.* Sir (Eustace) John (Blois), K.C.V.O., C.B., D.S.O., C.B.E., M.C.

Nelson, *Air Marshal* Sir (Sidney) Richard (Carlyle), K.C.B., O.B.E., M.D.

Nelson, *Maj.* Sir William Vernon Hope, Bt., O.B.E. (1912).

Nepean, *Lt.-Col.* Sir Evan Yorke, Bt. (1802).

Nevill, *Air Vice-Marshal* Sir Arthur de Terrotte, K.B.E., C.B.

Neville, *Lt.-Col.* Sir (James) Edmund (Henderson), Bt., M.C. (1927).

Neville, *Maj.-Gen.* Sir Robert Arthur Ross, K.C.M.G., C.B.E., R.M.

Newbold, Sir Charles Demorée, K.B.E., C.M.G., Q.C.

Newman, Sir Geoffrey Robert, Bt. (1836).

Newman, Sir Gerard Robert Henry Sigismund, Bt. (1912).

Newns, Sir (Alfred) Foley (Francis Polden), K.C.M.G., C.V.O.

Newton, Sir Charles Henry, Kt.

Newton, Sir (Harry) Michael (Rex), Bt. (1900).

Newton, Sir Hubert, Kt.

Newton, Sir Kenneth Garner, Bt., O.B.E., T.D. (1924).

Newton, Sir (Leslie) Gordon, Kt.

Nicholas, Sir Alfred James, Kt., C.B.E.

Nicholas, Sir Herbert Richard, Kt., O.B.E.

Nicholetts, *Air Marshal* Sir Gilbert Edward, K.B.E., C.B., A.F.C.

Nicholls, Sir Harmar, Bt., M.P. (1960).

Nicholls, *Maj.-Gen.* Sir Leslie Burtonshaw, K.C.M.G., C.B., C.B.E.

Nicholson, Sir Arthur William Kt., O.B.E.

Nicholson, *General* Sir Cameron Gordon Graham, G.C.B., K.B.E., D.S.O., M.C.

Nicholson, Sir Godfrey, Bt. (1958).

Nicholson, Sir John Charles, Bt. (1859).

Nicholson Sir John Norris, Bt., K.B.E. C.I.E. (1912).

Nicholson, *Admiral* Sir Randolph Stewart Gresham, K.B.E., C.B., D.S.O., D.S.C.

Nicklin, *Hon.* Sir (George) Francis (Reuben), K.C.M.G., M.M.

Nicoll, Sir John Fearns, K.C.M.G.

Nield, *Hon.* Sir Basil Edward, Kt., C.B.E., Q.C.

Nield, Sir William Alan, K.C.B.

Nightingale, Sir Geoffrey Slingsby, Bt. (1628).

Nihill, *Hon.* Sir (John Harry) Barclay, K.B.E., M.C., Q.C.

Nimmo, Sir Robert, Kt.

Niven, Sir (Cecil) Rex, Kt., C.M.G., M.C.

Nixon. Sir (Charles) Norman, Kt.

Nixon, *Maj.* Sir Christopher John Louis Joseph, Bt., M.C. (1906).

Noad, Sir Kenneth Beeson, Kt., M.D.

Noble, *Cmdr. Rt. Hon.* Sir Allan Herbert Percy, K.C.M.G., D.S.O., D.S.C., R.N.

Noble, Sir Andrew Napier, Bt., K.C.M.G. (1923).

Noble, Sir Marc Brunel, Bt. (1902).

Noble, Sir Peter Scott, Kt.

Noble, Sir (Thomas Alexander) Fraser, Kt., M.B.E.

Nock, Sir Norman Lindfield, Kt.

Norman, Sir Arthur Gordon, K.B.E., D.F.C.

Norman, Sir Charles, Kt., C.B.E.

Norman, Sir Edward James, Kt.

Norman, *Vice-Adm.* Sir (Horace) Geoffrey, K.C.V.O., C.B., C.B.E.

Norman, Sir Mark Annesley, Bt. (1915).

Norman, Sir Robert Wentworth, Kt.

Normand, Sir Charles William Blyth, Kt., C.I.E., D.S.C.

Norrington, Sir Arthur Lionel Pugh, Kt.

Norris, Sir Alfred Henry, K.B.E.

Norris, *Vice-Adm.* Sir Charles Fred Wivell, K.B.E., C.B., D.S.O.

Norris, *Air Chief Marshal* Sir Christopher Neil Foxley-, K.C.B., D.S.O., O.B.E.

Norris, Sir Eric George, K.C.M.G.

Norris, *Maj.-Gen.* Sir Frank Kingsley, K.B.E., C.B., D.S.O., E.D.

North, *Rt. Hon.* Sir Alfred Kingsley, K.B.E.

North, Sir (William) Jonathan (Frederick), Bt. (1920)

Norton, Sir Clifford John, K.C.M.G., C.V.O.

Norton, *Admiral of the Fleet* Sir Peter John Hill-, G.C.B.

Norton, Sir (Walter) Charles, Kt., M.B.E., M.C.

Norwood, Sir Walter Neville, Kt.

Nott, *Cmdr.* Sir James Grenville Pyke-, Kt., C.M.G., R.N.

Nugent, Sir Hugh Charles, Bt. (1 1795).

Nugent, *Maj.* Sir Peter Walter James, Bt. (1831).

Nugent, Sir Robin George Colborne, Bt. (1806).

Nussey, Sir Thomas Moore, Bt. (1909).

Nuttall, Sir Nicholas Keith Lillington, Bt. (1922).

Nutting, Sir Harold Stansmore, Bt. (1903).

Nye, Sir Geoffrey Walter, K.C.M.G., O.B.E.

Nyholm, *Prof.* Sir Ronald Sydney, Kt., D.S.C., PhD., F.R.S.

Oakeley, Sir (Edward) Atholl, Bt. (1790).

Oakes, Sir Christopher, Bt. (1939).

O'Brien, Sir David Edmond, Bt. (1849).

O'Brien, Sir (Frederick) Lucius, Kt.

O'Brien, *Rt. Hon.* Sir Leslie Kenneth G.B.E.

O'Brien, *Admiral* Sir William Donough, K.C.B., D.S.C.

O'Bryan, *Hon.* Sir Norman, Kt.

O'Connell, Sir Morgan Donal Conail, Bt. (1869).

O'Connor, *Lt.-Gen.* Sir Denis Stuart Scott, K.B.E., C.B.

O'Connor, Sir Kenneth Kennedy, K.B.E., M.C., Q.C.

O'Connor, *Hon.* Sir Patrick McCarthy, Kt.

O'Connor, *General* Sir Richard Nugent, K.T., G.C.B., D.S.O., M.C.

Ogden, Sir Alwyne George Neville, K.B.E., C.M.G.

Ogg, Sir William Gammie, Kt.

Ogilvie, Sir Alec Drummond, Kt.

Ogilvy, Sir David John Wilfrid, Bt. (S 1626)

Ohlson, Sir Eric James, Bt. (1920).

Okeover, *Lieut.-Col.* Sir Ian Peter Andrew Monro Walker-, Bt., D.S.O., T.D. (1886).

Oliphant, Sir Marcus Laurence Elwin, K.B.E., F.R.S.

Oliver, Sir (Frederick) Ernest, Kt., C.B.E., T.D.

Oliver, *Admiral* Sir Geoffrey Nigel, G.B.E., K.C.B., D.S.O.

Oliver, *Lt.-Gen.* Sir William Pasfield, G.B.E., K.C.B., K.C.M.G.

O'Loghlen, Sir Coleman Michael, Bt. (1838).

O'Malley, Sir Owen St. Clair, K.C.M.G.

O'Neill, *Hon.* Sir Con Douglas Walter, K.C.M.G.

O'Neill, Sir Matthew John, Kt., C.B.E.

Onslow, *Maj.-Gen.* Sir Denzil Macarthur-, Kt., C.B.E., D.S.O., E.D.

Onslow, Sir Geoffrey Henry Hughes-, K.B.E., D.S.C.

Onslow, Sir John Roger Wilmot, Bt. (1797).

Onslow, *Admiral* Sir Richard George, K.C.B., D.S.O.

Oppenheim, Sir Alexander, K O.B.E., D.SC., F.R.S.E.

Oppenheim, Sir Duncan Morr Kt.

Oppenheimer, Sir Michael Be nard Grenville, Bt. (1921).

Oppenheimer, Sir Philip Jack, K

Opperman, *Hon.* Sir Hube Ferdinand, Kt., O.B.E.

Orde, Sir Charles Willia K.C.M.G.

Orde, Sir John Alexander Cam bell-, Bt. (1790).

Orde, Sir Percy Lancelot, Kt C.I.E.

Organe, *Prof.* Sir Geoffrey Stephe William, Kt., M.D.

Ormerod, *Rt. Hon.* Sir Benjami Kt.

Ormerod, *Maj.* Sir Cyril Berke ley, K.B.E.

Ormond, Sir John Davies Wi der, Kt., B.E.M.

Ormrod, *Hon.* Sir Roger Fra Greenwood, Kt.

Orr, *Rt. Hon.* Sir Alan Stewar Kt., O.B.E.

Orr, Sir Samuel, Kt.

Ortcheson, Sir John, Kt., C.B.E.

Osborn, Sir Danvers Lione Rouse, Bt. (1662).

Osborn, Sir Frederic James, Kt.

Osborne, Sir Basil, Kt., C.B.E.

Osborne, Sir Peter George, B (1 1629).

Osmond, Sir Douglas, Kt., C.B.E.

Oulsnam, Sir (Samuel) Harriso (Yardley), Kt., C.S.I., C.I.E.

Outerbridge, *Col. Hon.* Sir Leonard Cecil, Kt., C.B.E., D.S.O.

Outram, Sir Alan James, B (1859).

Overall, Sir John Wallace, Kt C.B.E., M.C.

Overton, Sir Arnold Edersheim K.C.B., K.C.M.G., M.C.

Overy, Sir Thomas Stuart, Kt.

Owen, Sir Alfred George Beech Kt., C.B.E.

Owen, Sir (Arthur) Douglas K.B.E., C.B.

Owen, Sir Dudley Herber Cunliffe-, Bt. (1920).

Owen, Sir John Arthur, Bt (1813).

Owen, *Rt. Hon.* Sir William Francis Langer, K.B.E.

Owo, The Olowo of, Kt.

Packard, *Lieut.-Gen.* Sir (Charles) Douglas, K.B.E., C.B., D.S.O.

Packer, Sir (Douglas) Frank (Hewson), K.B.E.

Padmore, Sir Thomas, G.C.B.

Pagan, *Brig.* Sir John Ernest. Kt. C.M.G., M.B.E., E.D.

Page, *Prof.* Sir Denys Lionel, Kt. F.B.A.

Page, Sir Harry Robertson, Kt.

Paget, *Capt.* Sir James Francis, Bt., R.N. (1871).

Paget, Sir John Starr, Bt. (1886).

Paine, Sir (Herbert) Kingsley, Kt. C.M.G.

Paley, *Maj.-Gen.* Sir (Alexander George) Victor, K.B.E., C.B. D.S.O.

Palitana, Thakore Saheb of, K.C.S.I., K.C.I.E.

Palmer, Sir Charles Mark, Bt. (1886).

Palmer, Sir Geoffrey Christopher John, Bt. (1669).

Palmer, Sir John Edward Somerset, Bt. (1791).

Palmer, *Brig.* Sir Otho Leslie Prior-, Kt., D.S.O.

Panabokke, Sir Tikiri Banda, Kt.

Panckridge, *Surgeon Vice-Adm.* Sir (William) Robert (Silvester), K.B.E., C.B.

Panna, *Maj.* H.H. Maharaja of, K.C.S.I., K.C.I.E.

Pape, *Hon.* Sir George Augustus, Kt.

Tararajasingam, Sir Sangarapillai, Kt.

Parham, *Admiral* Sir Frederick Robertson, G.B.E., K.C.B., D.S.O.

Paris, Sir Edward Talbot, Kt., C.B., D.SC.

Park, *Hon.* Sir Hugh Eames, Kt.

Park, *Air Chief Marshal* Sir Keith Rodney, G.C.B., K.B.E., M.C., D.F.C.

Parker, Sir Douglas William Leigh, Kt., O.B.E.

Parker, Sir Harold, K.C.B., K.B.E., M.C.

Parker, Sir Karl Theodore, Kt., C.B.E., Ph.D., F.B.A.

Parker, Sir Richard (William) Hyde, Bt. (1681).

Parker, *Vice-Adm.* Sir (Wilfred) John, K.B.E., C.B., D.S.C.

Parker, *Capt.* Sir William Lorenzo, Bt., O.B.E. (1844).

Parkes, Sir Alan Sterling, Kt., C.B.E., Ph.D., D.SC., SC.D., F.R.S.

Parkes, Sir Basil Arthur, Kt., O.B.E.

Parkes, Sir Roderick Wallis, K.C.M.G., O.B.E.

Parkin, Sir Ian, Kt., C.B.E.

Parkinson, Sir Harold, K.B.E.

Parkinson, Sir John, Kt., M.D.

Parkinson, Sir Kenneth Wade, Kt.

Farr, Sir Robert, K.B.E., C.M.G.

Parrott, Sir Cecil Cuthbert, K.C.M.G., O.B.E.

Parry, *Prof.* Sir David Hughes, Kt., Q.C.

Parry, Sir (Frank) Hugh (Nigel), Kt., C.B.E.

Parry, *Admiral* Sir (William) Edward, K.C.B.

Parsons, Sir John Michael, Kt.

Parsons, Sir Maurice Henry, K.C.M.G.

Part, Sir Antony Alexander, Kt., K.C.B., M.B.E.

Partabgarh, H.H. the Maharawab of, K.C.S.I.

Partridge, Sir (Ernest) John, K.B.E.

Paskin, Sir (Jesse) John, K.C.M.G., M.C.

Pasley, Sir Rodney Marshall Sabine, Bt. (1794).

Patch, Sir Edmund Leo Hall-, G.C.M.G.

Patch, *Air Chief Marshal* Sir Hubert Leonard, K.C.B., C.B.E.

Paterson, Sir (Alexander) Swinton, K.B.E., C.M.G.

Paterson, Sir George Mutlow, Kt., O.B.E., Q.C.

Paterson, Sir John Valentine Jardine, Kt.

Patiala, *Lt.-Gen.* H.H. the Maharaja of, G.C.I.E., G.B.E.

Patna, Maharaja of, K.C.I.E.

Paton, *Prof.* Sir George Whitecross, Kt.

Paton, Sir Leonard Cecil, Kt., C.B.E., M.C.

Paton, *Capt.* Sir Stuart Henry, K.C.V.O., C.B.E., R.N. (*ret.*).

Patrick, Sir Paul Joseph, K.C.I.E., C.S.I.

Patron, Sir Joseph, Kt., O.B.E., M.C.

Patterson, Sir John Robert, K.B.E., C.M.G.

Pattinson, *Hon.* Sir Baden, K.B.E.

Paul, Sir John Warburton, G.C.M.G., O.B.E., M.C.

Paul, Sir Brian Kenneth Dean, Bt. (1821).

Paull, Sir Gilbert James, Kt.

Pavlides, Sir Paul George, Kt., C.B.E.

Pawsey, Sir Charles Ridley, Kt., C.S.I., C.I.E., M.C.

Payne, *Hon.* Sir Reginald Withers, Kt.

Payne, Sir Robert Frederick, Kt.

Peake, Sir Francis Harold, Kt.

Leard, *Rear-Adm.* Sir Kenyon Harry Terrell, K.B.E.

Pearson, *Rt. Hon.* Sir Colin Hargreaves, Kt., C.B.E.

Pearson, Sir Francis Fenwick, Bt., M.B.E., (1964).

Pearson, *Hon.* Sir Glen Gardner, Kt.

Pearson, Sir (James) Denning, Kt.

Pearson, Sir (James) Reginald, Kt., O.B.E.

Pearson, Sir Neville, Bt. (1916).

Pearson, *General* Sir Thomas Cecil Hook, K.C.B., C.B.E., D.S.O.

Pease, Sir (Alfred) Vincent, Bt. (1882).

Pease, Sir Richard Thorn, Bt. (1920).

Pechell, *Lt.-Col.* Sir Paul, Bt., M.C. (1797).

Peck, Sir Edward Heywood, K.C.M.G.

Peck, Sir John Howard, K.C.M.G.

Pedder, *Vice-Adm.* Sir Arthur Reid, K.B.E., C.B.

Pedler, Sir Frederick Johnson, Kt.

Peek, Sir Francis Henry Grenville, Bt. (1874).

Peel, *Capt.* Sir (Francis Richard) Jonathan, Kt., C.B.E., M.C.

Peel, Sir John Harold, K.C.V.O.

Peierls, Sir Rudolf Ernst, Kt., C.B.E., D.SC., D.Phil., F.R.S.

Peile, *Vice-Adm.* Sir Lancelot Arthur Babington, K.B.E., C.B., D.S.O., M.V.O.

Peirse, Sir Henry Campbell de la Poer Beresford-, Bt., C.B. (1814).

Pelham, Sir (George) Clinton, K.B.E., C.M.G.

Pelly, *Air Chief Marshal* Sir Claude Bernard Raymond, G.B.E., K.C.B., M.C.

Pelly, Sir Harold Alwyne, Bt., M.C. (1840).

Pelly, Sir Kenneth Raymond, Kt., M.C.

Pendred, *Air Marshal* Sir Lawrence Fleming, K.B.E., C.B., D.F.C.

Penny, Sir James Downing, K.C.I.E., C.S.I.

Pennycuick, *Hon.* Sir John, Kt.

Penrose, Sir Roland Algernon, Kt., C.B.E.

Peppiatt, Sir Kenneth Oswald, K.B.E., M.C.

Percival, Sir Anthony Edward, Kt., C.B.

Peren, *Prof.* Sir Geoffrey Sylvester, K.B.E.

Perkins, *Surgeon Vice-Adm.* Sir Derek Duncombe Steele-, K.C.B., K.C.V.O.

Perkins, Sir (Walter) Robert Dempster, Kt.

Perks, Sir (Robert) Malcolm Mewburn, Bt. (1908).

Perrin, Sir Michael Willcox, Kt., C.B.E.

Perring, Sir Ralph Edgar, Bt. (1963).

Perrott, Sir Donald Cyril Vincent, K.B.E.

Pestell, Sir John Richard, K.C.V.O.

Petch, Sir Louis, K.C.B.

Peters, *Admiral* Sir Arthur Malcolm, K.C.B., D.S.O.

Peters, *Prof.* Sir Rudolph Albert, Kt., M.C., F.R.S.

Petfield, Sir Arthur Henry, Kt.

Petit, Sir Dinshaw Manockjee, Bt. (1890).

Peto, *Brig.* Sir Christopher Henry Maxwell, Bt., D.S.O. (1927).

Peto, *Cdr.* Sir (Henry) (Francis (Morton), Bt., R.N. (1855).

Petrie, Sir Charles Alexander, Bt., C.B.E. (1918).

Petty, *Hon.* Sir Horace Rostill, Kt.

Pevsner, *Prof.* Sir Nikolaus Bernhard Leon, Kt., C.B.E., Ph.D., F.B.A., F.S.A.

Phaltan, *Maj.* the Raja of, K.C.I.E.

Phillimore, *Rt. Hon.* Sir Henry Josceline, Kt., O.B.E.

Phillips, *Maj.-Gen.* Sir Edward, K.B.E., C.B., D.S.O., M.C.

Phillips, Sir (Edward) Charles, Kt., C.B.E.

Phillips, Sir Fred Albert, Kt., C.V.O.

Phillips, Sir Henry Ellis Isidore, Kt., C.M.G., M.B.E.

Phillips, *Hon.* Sir John Raymond, Kt., M.C.

Phillips, Sir Leslie Walter, Kt., C.B.E.

Phillips, Sir Philip David, Kt., C.M.G., M.M., Q.C.

Phillips, Sir Robin Francis, Bt. (1912).

Phillips, *Hon.* Sir Rowland Ricketts, Kt.

Phipps, *Rear-Adm.* Sir Peter, K.B.E., D.S.C., V.R.D.

Pickard, Sir Cyril Stanley, K.C.M.G.

Pickering, *Prof.* Sir George White, Kt., F.R.S.

Pickles, Sir John Sydney, Kt.

Pickthorn, *Rt. Hon.* Sir Kenneth William Murray, Bt., Litt.D. (1959).

Pierre, Sir Joseph Henry, Kt.

Piers, Sir Charles Robert Fitzmaurice, Bt. (1 1661).

Pigot, *Brig.-Gen.* Sir Robert, Bt., D.S.O., M.C. (1764).

Pigott, *Maj.* Sir Berkeley, Bt. (1808).

Pike, Sir Philip Ernest Housden, Kt., Q.C.

Pike, Sir Theodore Ouseley, K.C.M.G.

Pike, *Marshal of the Royal Air Force* Sir Thomas Geoffrey, G.C.B., C.B.E., D.F.C.

Pike, *Lt.-Gen.* Sir William Gregory Huddleston, K.C.B., C.B.E., D.S.O.

Pilcher, Sir John Arthur, K.C.M.G.

Pilditch, Sir Denys, Kt., C.I.E.

Pilditch, Sir Richard Edward, Bt. (1929).

Pile, *General* Sir Frederick Alfred, Bt., G.C.B. D.S.O. M.C. (1900).

Pile, Sir William Denis, K.C.B., M.B.E.

Pilkington, Sir Lionel Alexander Bethune, Kt.

Pilkington, *Capt.* Sir Richard Antony, K.B.E., M.C.

Pilkington, Sir Thomas Henry Milborne - Swinnerton-, Bt. (S 1635).

Pim, *Capt.* Sir Richard Pike, K.B.E., V.R.D., R.N.V.R.

Pinsent, Sir Roy, Bt. (1938).

Piper, *Air Marshal* Sir Thomas William, K.B.E., C.B., A.F.C.

Pirbhai, Sir Eboo, Kt., O.B.E.

Pirie, *Air Chief Marshal* Sir George Clark, K.C.B., K.B.E., M.C., D.F.C.

Pitblado, Sir David Bruce, K.C.B., C.V.O.

Pitman, Sir Hubert Percival Lancaster, Kt., O.B.E.

Pitman, Sir (Isaac) James, K.B.E.

Pitts, Sir Cyril Alfred, Kt.

Pizey, *Admiral* Sir (Charles Thomas) Mark, G.B.E., C.B., D.S.O.

Plant, *Prof.* Sir Arnold, Kt.

Platt, Sir Harry, Bt., M.D. (1958).

Platt, *General* Sir William, G.B.E., K.C.B., D.S.O.

Playfair, Sir Edward Wilder, K.C.B.

Playfair, *Air Marshal* Sir Patrick Henry Lyon, K.B.E., C.B., C.V.O., M.C.

Playford, *Hon.* Sir Thomas, G.C.M.G.

Pleass, Sir Clement John, K.C.M.G., K.C.V.O., K.B.E.

Plimmer, Sir Clifford Ulric, K.B.E.

Plimsoll, Sir James, Kt., C.B.E.

Plowman, *Hon.* Sir (John) Anthony, Kt.

Plummer, Sir (Arthur) Desmond (Herne), Kt., T.D.

Poett, *General* Sir (Joseph Howard) Nigel, K.C.B., D.S.O.

Pole, *Col.* Sir John Gawen Carew, Bt., D.S.O., T.D. (1628).

Pole, Sir Peter Van Notten-, Bt. (1791).

Pollard, Sir Charles Herbert, Kt., C.B.E.

Pollard, *Lt.-Gen.* Sir Reginald George, K.C.V.O., K.B.E., C.B., D.S.O.

Pollen, Sir John Michael Hungerford, Bt. (1795).

Pollock, Sir George, Kt., Q.C.

Pollock, Sir George Frederick, Bt. (1866).

Pollock, Sir George Seymour Montagu-, Bt. (1872).

Pollock, *Admiral* Sir Michael Patrick, G.C.B., M.V.O., D.S.C.

Pollock, Sir Ronald Evelyn, Kt.

Pollock, Sir William Horace Montagu-, K.C.M.G.

Ponsonby, *Col.* Sir Charles Edward, Bt., T.D. (1956).

Poore, Sir Herbert Edward, Bt. (1795).

Pope, Sir George Reginald, Kt.

Pope, Sir Sidney Barton, Kt.

Popper, *Prof.* Sir Karl Raimund, Kt., Ph.D.

Porbandar, *Lt.-Col.* H.H. Maharaja of, K.C.S.I.

Porritt, Sir Arthur Espie, Bt., G.C.M.G., G.C.V.O., C.B.E. (1963).

Portal, Sir Francis Spencer, Bt. (1901).

Portal, *Admiral* Sir Reginald Henry, K.C.B., D.S.C.

Porter, Sir Andrew Marshall Horsbrugh-, Bt., D.S.O. (1902).

Porter, Sir George Swinburne, Bt. (1880).

Porter, *Air Marshal* Sir (Melvin) Kenneth (Drowley), K.C.B., C.B.E.

Porter, *Hon.* Sir Murray Victor, Kt.

Porter, *Rt. Hon.* Sir Robert Wilson, Kt., Q.C.

Pott, Sir Leslie, K.B.E.

Potter, Sir Henry Steven, K.C.M.G.

Potter, *Air Marshal* Sir Patrick Brunton Lee, K.B.E., M.D.

Potter, *Maj.-Gen.* Sir (Wilfrid) John, K.B.E., C.B.

Potter, Sir (William) Ian, Kt.

Pound, Sir Derek Allen, Bt. (1905).

Powell, *Maj.* Sir Richard George Douglas, Bt., M.C. (1897)

Powell, Sir Richard Royle, G.C.B., K.B.E., C.M.G.

Power, Sir John Patrick McLannahan, Bt. (1924).

Power, *Admiral* Sir Manley Laurence, K.C.B., C.B.E., D.S.O.

Powles, Sir Guy Richardson, K.B.E., C.M.G., E.D.

Powlett, *Vice-Adm.* Sir Peveril Barton Reibey Wallop William-, K.C.B., K.C.M.G., C.B.E., D.S.O.

Poynton, Sir (Arthur) Hilton, G.C.M.G.

Prain, Sir Ronald Lindsay, K O.B.E.

Pratt, Sir (Edward) Bernard, I

Prescott, Sir Mark, Bt. (1938).

Prescott, Sir Stanley Lewis, K O.B.E.

Preston, Sir Kenneth Huson, K Preston, *Admiral* Sir Lior George, K.C.B.

Preston, Sir Thomas Hildebran Bt., O.B.E. (1815).

Pretty, *Air Marshal* Sir Wal Philip George, K.B.E., C.B.

Prevost, *Capt.* Sir George Jam Augustine, Bt. (1805).

Price, Sir (Archibald) Grenfe Kt., C.M.G.

Price, Sir Charles Keith Nap Rugge-, Bt. (1804).

Price, Sir (Charles) Roy, K.C.M.

Price, Sir Frank Leslie, Kt.

Price, Sir Robert John Green-, (1874).

Price, Sir Rose Francis, Bt. (181

Prichard, Sir Norman Geor Mollett, Kt.

Prickett, *Air Chief Marshal* Thomas Other, K.C.B., D.S. D.F.C.

Prideaux, Sir Humphrey Pov Treverbian, Kt., O.B.E.

Pridham, *Vice-Adm.* Sir (Arthu Francis, K.B.E., C.B.

Pridie, Sir Eric Denhol K.C.M.G., D.S.O., O.B.E.

Priestley, Sir Gerald Willia K.C.I.E.

Priestley, Sir Raymond Edwar Kt., M.C.

Primrose, Sir John Ure, Bt. (190

Primrose, Sir John Ure, Kt.

Pringle, Sir Stuart Robert, (S 1683).

Prior, Sir Charles Geoffre K.C.I.E.

Pritchard, Sir Asa Hubert, Kt.

Pritchard, *Col.* Sir Derek Wilb ham, Kt.

Pritchard, Sir Edward Ev Evans-, Kt., Ph.D., F.B.A.

Pritchard, Sir Fred Ellis, K M.B.E.

Pritchard, Sir Neil, K.C.M.G.

Proby, *Maj.* Sir Richard Geor Bt., M.C. (1952).

Proctor, Sir George Philip, K.B.

Proctor, Sir (Philip) Denn K.C.B.

Pryke, Sir David Dudley, (1926).

Puckey, Sir Walter Charles, K

Pugh, *His Hon.* Sir (John) Al Kt.

Pugh, *Prof.* Sir William Joh Kt., O.B.E., D.SC., F.R.S.

Pugsley, *Prof.* Sir Alfred Grenvi Kt., O.B.E., D.SC., F.R.S.

Pugsley, Sir Reuben James, K O.B.E.

Purves, Sir Raymond Edgar, F O.B.E.

Puttick, *Lt.-Gen.* Sir Edwa K.C.B., D.S.O.

Pym, *Maj.* Sir Charles Evely Kt., C.B.E.

Pyman, *General* Sir Harold English, G.B.E., K.C.B., D.S.O.

Quartermaine, Sir Allan Stephen, Kt., C.B.E., M.C.

Quénet, *Hon.* Sir Vincent Ernest, Kt.

Quilter, Sir Anthony Raymond Leopold Cuthbert, Bt. (1897).

Raby, Sir Victor Harry, K.B.E., C.B., M.C.

Radcliffe, Sir Joseph Benedict Everard Henry, Bt., M.C. (1813).

Radclyffe, Sir Charles Edward Mott-, Kt.

Radzinowicz, *Prof.* Sir Leon, Kt., LL.D.

Rae, Sir Alexander Montgomery Wilson, K.C.M.G., M.D.

Rae, Sir Robert, Kt., C.B.

Raeburn, Sir Edward Alfred, Bt. (1923).

Raffray, Sir Philippe, Kt., C.B.E., Q.C.

Rahimtoola, Sir Fazil Ibrahim, Kt., C.I.E.

Raikes, *Maj.-Gen.* Sir Geoffrey Taunton, Kt., C.B., D.S.O.

Raikes, Sir (Henry) Victor (Alpin MacKinnon), K.B.E.

Raisman, Sir (Abraham) Jeremy, G.C.M.G., G.C.I.E., K.C.S.I.

Rajapakse, Sir Lalita Abhaya, Kt., Q.C.

Ralli, Sir Godfrey Victor, Bt., T.D. (1912).

Ram Chandra Mardaraj Deo, *Raja Bahadur*, Sir, Kt.

Ramgoolam, *Rt. Hon.* Sir Seewoosagur, Kt.

Ramsay *Maj.-Gen.* Sir Alan Hollick, Kt., C.B., C.B.E., D.S.O.

Ramsay, *Admiral Hon.* Sir Alexander Robert Maule, G.C.V.O., K.C.B., D.S.O.

Ramsay, Sir Alexander William Burnett, Bt. (1806).

Ramsay, Sir Neis Alexander, Bt. (S 1666).

Ramsay, Sir William Clark, Kt., C.B.E.

Ramsden, Sir Geoffrey Charles Frescheville, Kt., C.I.E.

Ramsden, Sir (Geoffrey) William Pennington-, Bt. (1689).

Ramsey, Sir Alfred Ernest, Kt.

Ranasinha, Sir Arthur Godwin, Kt., C.M.G., C.B.E.

Rance, *Maj.-Gen.* Sir Hubert Elvin, G.C.M.G., G.B.E., C.B.

Randall, Sir Alec Walter George, K.C.M.G., O.B.E.

Randall, *Prof.* Sir John Turton, Kt., D.Sc., F.R.S.

Randall, Sir Richard John, Kt.

Rankin, Sir Hugh (Charles Rhys), Bt. (1898).

Rankine, Sir John Dalziel, K.C.M.G., K.C.V.O.

Ransford, *Col.* Sir Alister John, Kt., C.I.E.

Raper, *Vice-Adm.* Sir (Robert) George, K.C.B.

Rapp, Sir Thomas Cecil, K.B.E., C.M.G., M.C.

Rasch, *Maj.* Sir Richard Guy Carne, Bt. (1903).

Rashleigh, Sir Harry Evelyn Battie, Bt. (1831)

Rattigan, Sir Terence Mervyn, Kt., C.B.E.

Rawlinson, Sir Anthony Henry John, Bt. (1891).

Rawlinson, Sir Joseph, Kt., C.B.E.

Rawlinson, *Rt. Hon.* Sir Peter Anthony Grayson, Q.C., M.P.

Rawson, Sir Stanley Walter, Kt.

Raymond, Sir Stanley Edward, Kt.

Rayne, Sir Max, Kt.

Rayner, *Brig.* Sir Ralph Herbert, Kt.

Read, *General* Sir (John) Antony (Jervis), K.C.B., C.B.E., D.S.O., M.C.

Reade, Sir Clyde Nixon, Bt. (1661).

Readhead, Sir James Templeman, Bt. (1922).

Rebbeck, *Rear-Adm.* Sir (Leopold) Edward, K.B.E., C.B.

Reddish, Sir Halford Walter Lupton, Kt.

Redfern, Sir (Arthur) Shuldham, K.C.V.O., C.M.G.

Redgrave, Sir Michael Scudamore, Kt., C.B.E.

Redman, *Lt.-Gen.* Sir Harold, K.C.B., C.B.E.

Redman, Sir (Herbert) Vere, Kt., C.M.G., O.B.E.

Redwood, Sir Thomas Boverton, Bt. (1911).

Reece, Sir Gerald, K.C.M.G., C.B.E.

Reece, Sir (Louis) Alan, Kt., C.M.G.

Reed, Sir Carol, Kt.

Reed, *Hon.* Sir Geoffrey Sandford, Kt.

Reed, *Hon.* Sir Nigel Vernon, Kt., C.B.E.

Reed, Sir Reginald Charles, Kt., C.B.E.

Rees, *Hon.* Sir (Charles William) Stanley, Kt., T.D.

Rees, Sir Hugh Ellis-, K.C.M.G., C.B.

Refshauge, *Maj.-Gen.* Sir William Dudley, Kt., C.B.E.

Reid, Sir Douglas Neilson, Bt. (1922).

Reid, Sir Edward James, Bt., K.B.E. (1897).

Reid, *Air Vice-Marshal* Sir (George) Ranald Macfarlane, K.C.B., D.S.O., M.C.

Reid, *Admiral* Sir (John) Peter (Lorne), G.C.B., C.V.O.

Reid, Sir Norman Robert, Kt.

Reilly, Sir (D'Arcy) Patrick, G.C.M.G., O.B.E.

Reilly, Sir Paul, Kt.

Reiss, Sir John Anthony Ewart, Kt., B.E.M.

Renals, Sir, Stanley, Bt. (1895).

Rendel, Sir George William, K.C.M.G.

Rendell, Sir William, Kt.

Rennie, *Hon.* Sir Alfred Baillie, Kt.

Rennie, Sir Gilbert (McCall), G.B.E., K.C.M.G., M.C.

Rennie, Sir John Ogilvy, K.C.M.G.

Rennie, Sir John Shaw, G.C.M.G., O.B.E.

Renshaw, Sir (Charles) Stephen (Bine), Bt. (1903).

Renton, *Rt. Hon.* Sir David Lockhart-Mure, K.B.E., T.D., Q.C. M.P.

Renwick, Sir Eustace Deuchar, Bt. (1921).

Renwick, Sir John, Kt.

Reynolds, Sir David James, Bt. (1923).

Rhodes, Sir John Christopher Douglas, Bt. (1919).

Ricardo, Sir Harry Ralph, Kt., LL.D., F.R.S.

Rich, Sir Almeric Frederic Conness, Bt. (1791).

Richards, *Hon.* Sir Edward Trenton, Kt., C.B.E.

Richards, Sir Gordon, Kt.

Richardson, *General* Sir Charles Leslie, G.C.B., C.B.E., D.S.O.

Richardson, Sir Egerton Rudolf, Kt., C.M.G.

Richardson, Sir (Horace) Frank, Kt.

Richardson, Sir (John) Eric, Kt.

Richardson, Sir (John) Henry (Swain), Kt.

Richardson, Sir John Samuel, Bt., M.V.O., M.D. (1963).

Richardson, Sir Leslie Lewis, Bt. (1924).

Richardson, Sir Ralph David, Kt.

Richardson, Sir Simon Alasdair Stewart-, Bt. (S 1630).

Richardson, Sir William Robert, Kt.

Richardson, Sir William Wigham, Bt., M.B.E. (1929).

Riches, Sir Derek Martin Hurry, K.C.M.G.

Riches, Sir Eric William, Kt., M.C.

Riches, *General* Sir Ian Hurry, K.C.B., D.S.O.

Richmond, Sir Alan James, Kt.

Richmond, Sir John Christopher Blake, K.C.M.G.

Richmond, Sir John Frederick, Bt. (1929).

Richmond, *Vice-Adm.* Sir Maxwell, K.B.E., C.B., D.S.O.

Richter, *Hon.* Sir Harold, Kt.

Rickett, Sir Denis Hubert Fletcher, K.C.M.G., C.B.

Ricketts, Sir Robert Cornwallis Gerald St. Leger, Bt. (1828).

Ricks, Sir John Plowman, Kt.

Riddell, Sir John Charles Buchanan-, Bt. (S 1628).

Ride, Sir Lindsay Tasman, Kt., C.B.E., E.D.

Rideal, Sir Eric Keightley, Kt., M.B.E., F.R.S., D.Sc.

Ridley, Sir Sidney, Kt.

Rieger, Sir Clarence Oscar Ferrero, Kt., C.B.E.

Rigby, *Lt.-Col.* Sir (Hugh) John (Macbeth), Bt. (1920).

Rigby, *Hon.* Sir Ivo Charles Clayton, Kt.

Rigg, Sir Theodore, K.B.E.

Ripley, Sir Hugh, Bt. (1880).

Risson, *Maj.-Gen.* Sir Robert Joseph Henry, Kt., C.B., C.B.E., D.S.O., E.D.

Ritchie, Sir James Edward Thomson, Bt. (1918).

Ritchie, Sir (John) Douglas, Kt., M.C.

Ritchie, Sir John Neish, Kt., C.B.

Ritchie, *General* Sir Neil Methuen, G.B.E., K.C.B., D.S.O., M.C.

Ritchie, Sir Thomas Malcolm, Kt.

Ritson, Sir Edward Herbert, K.B.E., C.B.

Road, Sir Alfred, Kt., C.B.E.

Robb, Sir (George) Douglas, Kt., C.M.G., M.D.

Roberts, Sir Frank Kenyon, G.C.M.G., G.C.V.O.

Roberts, Sir Gilbert, Kt., F.R.S.

Roberts, Sir Harold Charles West, Kt., C.B.E., M.C.

Roberts, Sir James Denby, Bt. (1909).

Roberts, Sir (James Reginald) Howard, Kt., C.B.E.

Roberts, Sir Leslie, Kt., C.B.E.

Roberts, Sir Norman Stanley, K.B.E., C.M.G.

Roberts, *General* Sir Ouvry Lindfield, G.C.B. K.B.E., D.S.O.

Roberts, Sir Peter Geoffrey, Bt. (1919).

Roberts, *Prof.* Sir Stephen Henry, Kt., C.M.G., D.SC., Litt.D.

Roberts, *Col.* Sir Thomas Langdon Howland, Bt., C.B.E. (1809).

Roberts, Sir Walter St. Clair Howland, K.C.M.G., M.C.

Robertson, *Prof.* Sir Alexander, Kt., C.B.E.

Robertson, Sir James Anderson, Kt., C.B.E.

Robertson, Sir James Wilson, K.T., G.C.M.G., G.C.V.O., K.B.E.

Robieson, Sir William Dunkeld, Kt., LL.D.

Robinson, Sir Albert Edward Phineas, Kt.

Robinson, Sir Dove Myer, Kt.

Robinson, *Hon.* Sir Ernest Stanley, Kt., C.B.E.

Robinson, *Maj.* Sir Frederick Villiers Laud, Bt., M.C. (1660).

Robinson, Sir George Gilmour, Kt.

Robinson, Sir Harold Ernest, Kt.

Robinson, Sir John Beverley, Bt. (1854).

Robinson, Sir John Edgar, Kt.

Robinson, Sir Leslie Harold, K.B.E., C.B.

Robinson, Sir (Montague) Arnet, Kt.

Robinson, Sir Niall Bryan Lynch-, Bt., D.S.C. (1920).

Robinson, Sir Norman de Winton, Kt.

Robinson, Sir Robert, Kt., O.M., D.SC., F.R.S.

Robinson, Sir (Wilfred Henry) Frederick, Bt. (1908).

Robson, Sir Kenneth, Kt., C.B.E., M.D., F.R.C.P.

Robson, Sir Thomas Buston, Kt., M.B.E.

Robson, *Vice-Adm.* Sir (William) Geoffrey (Arthur), K.B.E., C.B., D.S.O., D.S.C.

Roche, Sir Standish O'Grady, Bt., D.S.O. (1938).

Rochfort, *Capt.* Sir Cecil Charles Boyd-, K.C.V.O.

Rodgers, Sir John Charles, Bt., M.P. (1964).

Rodrigo, Sir (Senapathige Theobald) Philip, Kt., O.B.E.

Rodrigues, Sir Alberto Maria, Kt., C.B.E., E.D.

Rogers, Sir Philip, K.C.B., C.M.G.

Rogers, Sir Philip James, Kt., C.B.E.

Roil, Sir Eric, K.C.M.G., C.B.

Roll, *Rev.* Sir James William Cecil, Bt. (1921).

Ronald, Sir Nigel Bruce, K.C.M.G., C.V.O.

Rooney, *Maj.-Gen.* Sir Owen Patrick James, K.B.E., C.B.

Rootes, Sir Reginald Claud, Kt.

Roper, Sir Harold, Kt., C.B.E., M.C.

Ropner, *Col.* Sir Leonard, Bt., M.C., T.D. (1952).

Ropner, Sir Robert Desmond, Kt.

Ropner, Sir Robert Douglas, Bt. (1904).

Rose, Sir Alan Edward Percival, K.C.M.G., Q.C.

Rose, Sir Alec Richard, Kt.

Rose, Sir Francis Cyril, Bt. (1872).

Rose, Sir Hugh, Bt., T.D. (1935).

Rose, Sir Julian Day, Bt. (1909).

Rose, Sir Philip (Humphrey Vivian), Bt. (1874).

Roseveare, Sir Martin Pearson, Kt.

Rosier, *Air Chief Marshal* Sir Frederick Ernest, K.C.B., C.B.E., D.S.O.

Roskill, Sir Ashton Wentworth, Kt., Q.C.

Roskill, *Hon.* Sir Eustace Wentworth, Kt.

Ross, Sir Alexander, Kt.

Ross, Sir Archibald David Manisty, K.C.M.G.

Ross, *Hon.* Sir Dudley Bruce, Kt.

Ross, Sir Henry James, Kt.

Ross, *Prof.* Sir James Paterson, Bt., K.C.V.O. (1960).

Rostron, Sir Frank, Kt., M.B.E.

Rothenstein, Sir John Knewstub Maurice, Kt., C.B.E., Ph.D.

Rous, Sir Stanley Ford, Kt., C.B.E.

Rouse, Sir Anthony Gerald Roderick, K.C.M.G., O.B.E.

Row, *Cdr.* Sir Philip John, K.C.V.O., O.B.E., R.N.

Rowan, Sir (Thomas) Leslie, K.C.B., C.V.O.

Rowe, Sir Michael Edward, Kt., C.B.E., Q.C.

Rowell, Sir Andrew Herrick, Kt.

Rowell, Sir (Herbert Babington) Robin, Kt., C.B.E., A.F.C.

Rowell, *Lt.-Gen.* Sir Sydney Fairbairn, K.B.E., C.B.

Rowlands, *Air Marshal* Sir John Samuel, K.B.E., G.C.

Rowlands, *Surg.-Rear-Adm.* S (Richard) Alun, K.B.E., M.D.

Rowlandson, Sir (Stanley) Graham Kt., M.B.E.

Rowley, Sir Joshua Francis, B (1786).

Rowley, *Lt.-Col.* Sir Willia Joshua, Bt. (1836).

Rowntree, Sir Norman Andre Forster, Kt.

Roxburgh, Sir Ronald Francis, K

Roxburgh, Sir (Thomas) Jam (Young), Kt., C.I.E.

Roy, Sir Asoka Kumar, Kt.

Royden, Sir John Ledward, E (1905).

Royle, Sir Lancelot Carringto K.B.E.

Rucker, Sir Arthur Nev K.C.M.G., C.B., C.B.E.

Ruddle, *Lt.-Col.* Sir (Georg Kenneth (Fordham), Kt., T.D.

Rugg, Sir (Edward) Percy, Kt.

Rumball, *Air Vice-Marshal* S (Campion) Aubrey, K.B.E.

Rumbold, Sir (Horace) Algerno (Fraser), K.C.M.G., C.I.E.

Rumbold, Sir (Horace) Anthon (Claude), Bt., K.C.M.G., K.C.V.* C.B. (1779).

Runciman, *Hon.* Sir James Coch ran Stevenson, Kt.

Rundall, Sir Francis Bria Anthony, G.C.M.G., O.B.E.

Rushton, Sir Reginald Fieldin Kt.

Russell, Sir Charles Ian, B (1916).

Russell, *Rt. Hon.* Sir Charl Ritchie, Kt.

Russell, *Lt.-Gen.* Sir Dudle K.B.E., C.B., D.S.O., M.C.

Russell, Sir (Edward) Lionel, K C.B.E.

Russell, Sir Frederick Stratten, K C.B.E., D.S.C., D.F.C., F.R.S.

Russell, Sir George Michael, B (1812).

Russell, *Admiral* Hon. Sir Gu Herbrand Edward, G.B.* K.C.B., D.S.O.

Russell, Sir John Weir, Kt.

Russell, Sir John Wriothesle G.C.V.O., C.M.G.

Russell, Sir Robert Edwin, K C.S.I., C.I.E.

Russell, Sir Ronald Stanley, K M.P.

Russell, Sir (Sydney) Gordo Kt. C.B.E., M.C.

Russo, Sir Peter George, K C.B.E.

Ryan, Sir Derek Gerald, B (1919).

Rycroft, Sir (Richard) Newto Bt. (1784).

Ryder, Sir Gerard, Kt., C.B.

Rydge, Sir Norman Bede, K C.B.E.

Rylah, *Hon.* Sir Arthur Gordo K.B.E., C.M.G., E.D.

Ryle, *Prof.* Sir Martin, Kt., F.R.S

Rymill, Sir Arthur Campbell, Kt.

Sachs, *Rt. Hon.* Sir Eric, Kt., M.B.E., T.D.

Sainsbury, Sir Robert James, Kt.

Saint, Sir (Sidney) John, Kt., C.M.G., O.B.E.

St. Aubyn, Sir John Molesworth-, Bt., C.B.E. (1689).

St. George, Sir Robert Alan, Bt. (1766).

St. Johnston, *Col.* Sir (Thomas) Eric, Kt., C.B.E.

Salisbury, Sir Edward James, Kt., C.B.E., D.SC., F.R.S.

Salmon, *Rt. Hon.* Sir Cyril Barnet, Kt.

Salmon, *Air Vice-Marshal* Sir (Cyril John) Roderic, K.B.E., C.B.

Salmon, Sir Julian, Kt., C.B.E.

Salmon, Sir Samuel Isidore, Kt.

Salt, Sir David Shirley, Bt. (1869).

Salt, Sir (Thomas) Michael John, Bt. (1899).

Samson, Sir (William) Frederick, Kt.

Samuel, Sir Harold, Kt.

Samuel, Sir Jon Michael Glen, Bt. (1898).

Samuels, Sir Alexander, Kt., C.B.E.

Samuelson, Sir Francis Henry Bernard, Bt. (1884).

Sanders, Sir Harold George, Kt., Ph.D.

Sandars, *Vice-Adm.* Sir (Reginald) Thomas, K.B.E., C.B.

Sanders, *Air Chief Marshal* Sir Arthur Penrose Martyn, G.C.B., K.B.E.

Sanderson, *Air Marshal* Sir (Alfred) Clifford, K.B.E., C.B., D.F.C.

Sanderson, Sir (Frank Philip) Bryan, Bt. (1920).

Sandford, Sir Folliott Herbert, K.B.E., C.M.G.

Sandover, Sir (Alfred) Eric, Kt., M.C.

Sands, *Hon.* Sir Stafford Lofthouse, Kt., C.B.E.

Sarell, Sir Roderick Francis Gisbert, K.C.M.G.

Sargant, Sir (Henry) Edmund, Kt.

Sargent, Sir John Philip, Kt., C.I.E.

Sargent, Sir (Sidney) Donald, K.B.E., C.B.

Saundby, *Air Marshal* Sir Robert Henry Magnus Spencer, K.C.B., K.B.E., M.C., D.F.C., A.F.C.

Saunders, *Air Chief Marshal* Sir Hugh William Lumsden, G.C.B., K.B.E., M.C., D.F.C., M.M.

Saunders, *Prof.* Sir Owen Alfred, Kt., D.SC., F.R.S.

Savage, Sir Alfred William Lungley, K.C.M.G.

Savage, Sir (Edward) Graham, Kt., C.B.

Savill, Sir Eric Humphrey, K.C.V.O., C.B.E., M.C.

Savory, *Lt.-Gen.* Sir Reginald Arthur, K.C.I.E., C.B., D.S.O., M.C.

Sayad Muhammad, *Nawab* Sir Kt.

Sayer, *Vice-Adm.* Sir Guy Bourchier, K.B.E., C.B., D.S.C.

Sayers, *Prof.* Sir Edward George, Kt., C.M.G., M.D.

Sayers, Sir Frederick, Kt., C.I.E.

Scamp, Sir (Athelstan) Jack, Kt.

Scarlett, Sir Peter William Shelley Yorke, K.C.M.G., K.C.V.O.

Scarman, *Hon.* Sir Leslie George, Kt., O.B.E.

Scherger, *Air Chief Marshal* Sir Frederick Rudolph William, K.B.E., C.B., D.S.O., A.F.C.

Schon, Sir Frank, Kt.

Schonland, Sir Basil Ferdinand Jamieson, Kt., C.B.E., Ph.D., F.R.S.

Schreiber, *Lt.-Gen.* Sir Edmond Charles Acton, K.C.B., D.S.O.

Schultz, Sir (Joseph) Leopold, Kt., O.B.E.

Schuster, Sir (Felix) James Moncrieff, Bt., O.B.E. (1906).

Schuster, Sir George Ernest K.C.S.I., K.C.M.G., C.B.E., M.C.

Scicluna, Sir Hannibal Publius, Kt., M.B.E.

Scoones, *General* Sir Geoffry Allen Percival, K.C.B., K.B.E., C.S.I., D.S.O., M.C.

Scoones, *Maj.-Gen.* Sir Reginald Laurence, K.B.E., C.B., D.S.O.

Scopes, Sir Frederick, Kt.

Scopes, Sir Leonard Arthur, K.C.V.O., C.M.G., O.B.E.

Scott, Sir Arleigh Winston, G.C.M.G.

Scott, Sir (Arthur John) Guillum, Kt., T.D.

Scott, Sir (Charles) Hilary, Kt.

Scott, Sir David John Montagu-Douglas-, K.C.M.G., O.B.E.

Scott, *Lt.-Col.* Sir Douglas Winchester, Bt. (1913).

Scott, Sir Edward Arthur Dolman, Bt. (1806).

Scott, Sir Eric, Kt., O.B.E.

Scott, Sir George Edward, Kt., C.B.E.

Scott, Sir (Henry) Maurice, Kt., C.B.E., D.F.C.

Scott, Sir Ian Dixon, K.C.M.G., K.C.V.O., C.I.E.

Scott, *Lt.-Col.* Sir James Walter, Bt. (1962).

Scott, *Col.* Sir Malcolm Stoddart-, Kt., O.B.E., T.D., M.P.

Scott, Sir Oliver Christopher Anderson, Bt. (1909).

Scott, Sir (Robert) Donald, Kt.

Scott, Sir Robert Heatlie, G.C.M.G., C.B.E.

Scott, Sir (Ronald) Bodley, K.C.V.O., D.M.

Scott, Sir Terence Charles Stuart Morrison-, Kt., D.S.C., D.SC.

Scott, Sir Walter, Bt. (1907).

Scott, Sir Walter, Kt., C.M.G.

Scott, *Maj.-Gen.* Sir William Arthur, K.C.M.G., C.B., C.B.E.

Scragg, *Air Vice-Marshal* Sir Colin, K.B.E., C.B., A.F.C.

Scrivenor, Sir Thomas Vaisey, Kt., C.M.G.

Seal, Sir Eric Arthur, K.B.E., C.B.

Seale, Sir John Henry, Bt. (1838).

Sebright, Sir Hugo Giles Edmund, Bt. (1626).

Seddon, Sir Herbert John, Kt., C.M.G., D.M.

Seebohm, Sir Frederic, Kt., T.D.

Seeds, Sir William, K.C.M.G.

Seel, Sir George Frederick, K.C.M.G.

Seely, Sir Victor Basil John, Bt. (1896).

Sekers, Sir Nicholas Thomas, Kt., M.B.E.

Selby, Sir Kenneth, Kt.

Self, Sir (Albert) Henry, K.C.B., K.C.M.G., K.B.E.

Selleck, Sir Francis Palmer, K.B.E., M.C.

Sellers, *Rt. Hon.* Sir Frederic Aked, Kt., M.C.

Sellors, Sir Thomas Holmes, Kt., D.M.

Selway, *Air Marshal* Sir Anthony Dunkerton, K.C.B., D.F.C.

Senior, Sir Edward Walters, Kt., C.M.G.

Serpell, Sir David Radford, K.C.B., C.M.G., O.B.E.

Seton, Sir (Christopher) Bruce, Bt. (S 1663).

Seton, Sir Claud Ramsay Wilmot, Kt., M.C.

Seton, Sir Robert James, Bt. (S 1683).

Seward, Sir Eric John, K.B.E.

Seward, Sir Samuel Conrad, Kt., O.B.E.

Seymour, Sir Horace James, G.C.M.G., C.V.O.

Seymour, *Cdr.* Sir Michael Culme-, Bt., R.N. (1809).

Shakerley, Sir Geoffrey Adam, Bt. (1838).

Shakespeare, *Rt. Hon.* Sir Geoffrey Hithersay, Bt. (1942).

Shankland, Sir Thomas Murray, Kt., C.M.G.

Sharp, Sir Edward Harold Wilfred, Bt. (1922).

Sharp, *Lt.-Gen.* Sir John Aubrey Taylor, K.C.B., M.C.

Sharp, Sir Milton Reginald, Bt. (1920).

Sharpe, Sir Reginald Taaffe, Kt., Q.C.

Shaw, Sir Bernard Vidal, Kt.

Shaw, Sir Evelyn Campbell, K.C.V.O., LL.D.

Shaw, *Cdr.* Sir John James Kenward Best-, Bt., R.N. (1665).

Shaw, Sir John Valentine Wistar, K.C.M.G.

Shaw, Sir Robert, Bt. (1821).

Shaw, *Hon.* Sir Sebag, Kt.

Shearer, Sir Bruce, Kt., C.M.G.

Shearman, Sir Harold Charles, Kt.

Sheehy, *Hon.* Sir Joseph Aloysius, K.B.E.

Sheffield, Sir Robert Arthur, Bt. (1755).

Sheldon, Sir Wilfrid Percy Henry, K.C.V.O.

Shelley, *Brig.* Sir John Frederick, Bt. (1611).

Shepheard, Sir Victor George, K.C.B.

Sheridan, *Hon.* Sir Dermot Joseph, Kt., C.M.G.

Sherlock, Sir Phillip Manderson, Kt., C.B.E.

Shields, Sir Neil Stanley, Kt., M.C.

Shiffner, Sir Henry David, Bt. (1818).

Shires, Sir Frank, Kt.

Shirley, *Air Vice-Marshal* Sir Thomas Ulric Curzon, K.B.E., C.B.

Sholl, *Hon.* Sir Reginald Richard, Kt.

Shone, Sir Robert Minshull, Kt., C.B.E.

Shuckburgh, Sir (Charles Arthur) Evelyn, G.C.M.G., C.B.

Shuckburgh, Sir Charles Gerald Stewkley, Bt. (1660).

Sich, Sir Rupert Leigh, Kt., C.B.

Sie, *Hon.* Sir Banja Tejan-, K.C.M.G.

Sieff. *Hon.* Sir Marcus Joseph, Kt., O.B.E.

Silverstone, Sir Arnold, Kt.

Sim, Sir (George) Alexander (Strachan), Kt.

Sim, Sir Wilfrid Joseph, K.B.E., Q.C.

Simeon, Sir John Edmund Barrington, Bt. (1815).

Simmonds, Sir Oliver Edwin. Kt.

Simpson, *General* Sir Frank Ernest Wallace, G.B.E., K.C.B., D.S.O.

Simpson, Sir James Dyer, Kt.

Simpson, Sir (John) Cyril Finucane, Bt. (1935).

Simpson, Sir John Roughton, Kt., C.B.

Sims, Sir Alfred John, K.C.B., O.B.E.

Sinclair, Sir George Evelyn, Kt., C.M.G., O.B.E., M.P.

Sinclair, *Maj.-Gen.* Sir John Alexander, K.C.M.G., C.B., O.B.E.

Sinclair, Sir John Rollo Norman Blair, Bt. (s 1704).

Sinclair, Sir Kenneth Duncan Leckey, Kt.

Sinclair, *Air Vice-Marshal* Sir Laurence Frank, K.C.B., G.C., C.B.E., D.S.O.

Sinclair, Sir Leonard, Kt.

Sinclair, Sir Ronald Ormiston, K.B.E.

Sinclair, Sir William, Kt., C.B.E.

Sinderson, Sir Harry Chapman, K.B.E., C.M.G., M.V.O., M.D.

Singhania, Sir Padampat, Kt.

Singhateh, *Alhaj'i* Sir Farimang, G.C.M.G.

Sinker, Sir (Algernon) Paul, K.C.M.G., C.B.

Sita Ram, *Rai Bahadur* Sir, Kt.

Sitwell, Sir Sacheverell, Bt. (1808).

Skelhorn, Sir Norman John, K.B.E., Q.C.

Skinner, Sir (Thomas) Gordon, Bt. (1912).

Skipwith, Sir Patrick Alexander D'Estoteville, Bt. (1622).

Skrine, Sir Clarmont Percival, Kt., O.B.E.

Slade, Sir Benjamin Julian Alfred, Bt. (1831).

Slater, *Admiral* Sir Robin (Leonard Francis) Durnford-, K.C.B.

Slattery, *Rear-Adm.* Sir Matthew Sausse, K.B.E., C.B.

Sleigh, Sir Hamilton Morton Howard, Kt.

Sleight, Sir John Frederick, Bt. (1920).

Slesser, *Rt. Hon.* Sir Henry, Kt.

Slessor, *Marshal of the Royal Air Force* Sir John Cotesworth, G.C.B., D.S.O., M.C.

Slimmings, Sir William Kenneth Macleod, Kt., C.B.E.

Sloan, Sir Tennant, K.C.I.E., C.S.I.

Small, Sir Frank Augustus, Kt., C.B.E.

Smallpeice, Sir Basil, K.C.V.O.

Smallwood, *Air Marshal* Sir Denis Graham, K.C.B., C.B.E., D.S.O., D.F.C.

Smart, Sir Eric Fleming, Kt., O.B.E.

Smeeton, *Vice-Adm.* Sir Richard Michael, K.C.B., M.B.E.

Smiley, Sir Hugh Houston, Bt. (1903).

Smirk, *Prof.* Sir Frederick Horace, K.B.E., M.D.

Smith, Sir Alexander Abel, Kt. T.D.

Smith, Sir (Alexander) Rowland, Kt.

Smith, Sir Allan Chalmers, Kt., M.C.

Smith, *Lieut-Gen.* Sir Arthur Francis, K.C.B., K.B.E., D.S.O., M.C.

Smith, Sir Arthur Henry, Kt.

Smith, Sir Bryan Evers Sharwood-, K.C.M.G., K.C.V.O., K.B.E.

Smith, Sir Carl Victor, Kt., C.B.E.

Smith, Sir Cecil Furness-, Kt., Q.C.

Smith, *Maj.-Gen.* Sir Cecil Miller, K.B.E., C.B., M.C.

Smith, Sir Christopher Sydney Winwood, Bt. (1809).

Smith, *Rt. Hon.* Sir Derek Colclough Walker-, Bt., T.D., Q.C., M.P. (1960).

Smith, *Maj.-Gen.* Sir Edmund Hakewill, K.C.V.O., C.B., C.B.E., M.C.

Smith, *Vice-Adm.* Sir (Edward Michael) Conolly Abel, G.C.V.O., C.B.

Smith, Sir (Frank) Ewart, Kt.

Smith, *Vice-Adm.* Sir Geoffrey Thistleton-, K.B.E., C.B., G.M.

Smith, Sir (George) Guy Bracewell, Bt., M.B.E. (1947).

Smith, Sir (Harold) Gengoult, Kt., V.D.

Smith, *Col.* Sir Henry Abel, K.C.M.G., K.C.V.O., D.S.O.

Smith, Sir Henry Martin, Kt., C.B.E.

Smith, Sir Henry Thompson, K.B.E., C.B.

Smith, Sir Henry Wilson, K.C.B., K.B.E.

Smith, Sir Hubert Shirley-, Kt., C.B.E.

Smith, Sir John Hamilton-Spencer-, Bt. (1804).

Smith, Sir John Kenneth Newson-, Bt. (1944).

Smith, Sir Laurence Barton Grafftey-, K.C.M.G., K.B.E.

Smith, Sir Raymond Horace, K.B.E.

Smith, *Col. Rt. Hon.* Sir Reginald Hugh Dorman-, G.B.E.

Smith, Sir Richard Rathborne Vassar-, Bt., T.D. (1917).

Smith, Sir Ross Grey-, Kt.

Smith, *Lt.-Col.* Sir (Thomas) Eustace, Kt., C.B.E., T.D.

Smith, Sir Thomas Gilbert, Bt. (1897).

Smith, *Vice-Adm.* Sir Victor Alfred Trumper K.B.E., C.B., D.S.C.

Smith, Sir (William) Gordon, Bt., V.R.D. (1945).

Smith, Sir William Reardon Reardon-, Bt. (1920).

Smith, Sir (William) Reginald Verdon, Kt.

Smith, Sir (William) Richard Prince-, Bt., (1911).

Smithers, Sir Arthur Tennyson, Kt., C.B.E.

Smithers, *Prof.* Sir David Waldron, Kt., M.D.

Smithers, Sir Peter Henry Berry Otway, Kt., V.R.D., D.Phil.

Smyth, *Brig. Rt. Hon.* Sir John George, Bt., V̶C̶, M.C. (1956).

Smyth, *Capt.* Sir Philip Weyland Bowyer-, Bt., R.N. (1661).

Smythe, Sir Reginald Harry, K.B.E.

Snelling, Sir Arthur Wendell, K.C.M.G., K.C.V.O.

Snelson, Sir Edward Alec Abbott, K.B.E.

Snow, Sir Frederick Sidney, Kt., C.B.E.

Snow, Sir Harold Ernest, Kt., C.B.E.

Soame, Sir Charles Burnett Buckworth-Herne-, Bt. (1697).

Sobha Singh, *Hon. Sardar Bahadur* Sir Sardar, Kt., O.B.E.

Sokhey, *Maj.-Gen.* Sir Sahibsingh, Kt., M.D.

Somerset, Sir Henry Beaufort, Kt., C.B.E.

Somerville, Sir Robert, K.C.V.O.

Sopwith, Sir Charles Ronald, Kt.

Sopwith, Sir Thomas Octave Murdoch, Kt., C.B.E.

Sorley, *Air Marshal* Sir Ralph Squire, K.C.B., O.B.E., D.S.C., D.F.C.

Sorsbie, Sir Malin, Kt., C.B.E.

Southby, *Lt. Col.* Sir (Archibald) Richard (Charles), Bt., O.B.E. (1937).

Southern, Sir Robert, Kt., C.B.E.

Southwell, Sir (Charles Archibald) Philip, Kt., C.B.E., M.C.

Southworth, *Hon.* Sir Frederick, Kt.

Souyave, *Hon.* Sir Louis Georges, Kt.

Soysa, Sir Warusahennedige Abraham Bastian, Kt., C.B.E.

Sparkes, Sir Walter Beresford James Gorden, Kt.

Spearman, Sir Alexander Bowyer, Bt. (1840).

Spearman, Sir Alexander (Cadwallader) Mainwaring, Kt.

Spears, *Maj.-Gen.* Sir Edward (Louis), Bt., K.B.E., C.B., M.C. (1953).

Speed, Sir Robert William Arney, Kt., C.B., Q.C.

Speelman, *Jonkheer* Sir Cornelis Jacob, Bt. (1686).

Speir, Sir Rupert Malise, Kt.

Spence, *Maj.* Sir Basil Hamilton Hebden Neven-, Kt.

Spence, Sir Basil Urwin, Kt., O.M., O.B.E., T.D., R.A.

Spencer, Sir Kelvin Tallent, Kt., C.B.E., M.C.

Spencer, Sir Thomas George, Kt.

Spender, *Hon.* Sir Percy Claude, K.C.V.O., K.B.E., Q.C.

Spicer, *Hon.* Sir John Armstrong, Kt.

Spicer, Sir Peter James, Bt. (1906).

Spotswood, *Air Chief Marshal* Sir Denis Frank, G.C.B., C.B.E., D.S.O., D.F.C.

Springer, Sir Hugh Worrell, K.C.M.G., C.B.E.

Spry, *Brig.* Sir Charles Chambers Fowell, Kt., C.B.E., D.S.O.

Stable, *Rt. Hon.* Sir Wintringham Norton, Kt., M.C.

Stacey, Sir Ernest, Kt.

Stallard, Sir Peter Hyla Gawne, K.C.M.G., C.V.O., M.B.E.

Stamer, Sir (Lovelace) Anthony, Bt. (1809).

Stamp, *Rt. Hon.* Sir (Edward) Blanshard, Kt.

Stanier, *Brig.* Sir Alexander Beville Gibbons, Bt., D.S.O., M.C. (1917).

Stanley, Sir Robert Christopher Stafford, K.B.E., C.M.G.

Stapledon, Sir Robert de Stapeldon, K.C.M.G., C.B.E.

Staples, Sir John Richard, Bt. (I. 1628).

Stapleton, Sir Miles Talbot, Bt. (1679).

Starkey, *Lt.-Col.* Sir William Randle, Bt. (1935).

Starr, Sir Kenneth William, Kt., C.M.G., O.B.E., E.D.

Stedeford, Sir Ivan Arthur Rice, G.B.E.

Stedman, Sir George Foster, K.B.E., C.B., M.C.

Steel, Sir Christopher Eden, G.C.M.G., M.V.O.

Steel, *Maj.* Sir (Fiennes) William Strang, Bt., (1938).

Steel, Sir James, Kt., C.B.E.

Steel, Sir (Joseph) Lincoln (Spedding), Kt.

Steele, *Air-Marshal* Sir Charles Ronald, K.C.B., D.F.C.

Steele, *General* Sir James Stuart, G.C.B., K.B.E., D.S.O., M.C.

Stenhouse, Sir Nicol, Kt.

Stening, *Col.* Sir George Grafton Lees, Kt., E.D.

Stephen, Sir Alexander Murray, Kt., M.C.

Stephen, Sir James Alexander, Bt. (1891).

Stephens, Sir David, K.C.B., C.V.O.

Stephens, Sir (Leon) Edgar, Kt., C.B.E.

Stephenson, *Vice-Adm.* Sir Gilbert Owen, K.B.E., C.B., C.M.G.

Stephenson, *Lt.-Col.* Sir (Henry) Francis (Blake), Bt., O.B.E., T.D. (1936).

Stephenson, Sir Hugh Southern, G.B.E., K.C.M.G., C.I.E., C.V.O.

Stephenson, *Rt. Hon.* Sir John Frederick Eustace, Kt.

Stephenson, Sir Percy, Kt.

Stephenson, Sir William Samuel, Kt., M.C., D.F.C.

Sternberg, Sir Rudy, Kt.

Stevens, *Air Marshal* Sir Alick Charles, K.B.E., C.B.

Stevens, *Hon.* Sir Bertram Sydney Barnsdale, K.C.M.G.

Stevens, *Vice-Adm.* Sir John Felgate, K.B.E., C.B.

Stevens, Sir John Melior, K.C.M.G., D.S.O., O.B.E., T.D.

Stevens, Sir Roger Bentham, G.C.M.G.

Stevenson, *Hon.* Sir (Aubrey) Melford (Steed), Kt.

Stevenson, Sir Matthew, K.C.B., C.M.G.

Stevenson, Sir Ralph (Clarmont) Skrine, G.C.M.G.

Stevenson, Sir William Alfred, K.B.E.

Steward, Sir William Arthur, Kt.

Stewart, Sir Bruce Fraser, Bt. (1920).

Stewart, Sir David James Henderson-, Bt. (1957).

Stewart, Sir Herbert Kay, Kt., C.I.E.

Stewart, Sir Hugh Charlie Godfray, Bt. (1803).

Stewart, Sir Iain Maxwell, Kt.

Stewart, Sir James Watson, Bt. (1920).

Stewart, Sir Jocelyn Harry, Bt. (I 1623).

Stewart, *Maj.-Gen.* Sir Keith Lindsay, K.B.E., C.B., D.S.O.

Stewart, Sir Kenneth Dugald, Bt., G.B.E (1960).

Stewart, Sir Michael Norman Francis, K.C.M.G., O.B.E.

Stewart, Sir Ronald Compton, Bt. (1937).

Stewart, *Lt.-Col.* Sir (Walter) Guy Shaw-, Bt., M.C. (S 1692).

Stirling, Sir Charles Norman, K.C.M.G., K.C.V.O.

Stirling, Sir John, K.T., M.B.E., T.D.

Stirling, *Hon.* Sir (Robert) James (Lindsay), Kt.

Stirling, *General* Sir William Gurdon, G.C.B., C.B.E., D.S.O.

Stoby, Sir Kenneth Sievewright, Kt.

Stockdale, Sir Edmund Villiers Minshull, Bt. (1960).

Stockil, Sir Raymond Osborne, K.B.E.

Stockwell, *General* Sir Hugh Charles, G.C.B., K.B.E., D.S.O.

Stone, Sir (John) Leonard, Kt., O.B.E., Q.C.

Stone, Sir Joseph Ellis, Kt.

†Stonhouse, Sir Philip Allan, Bt. (1628)

Stooke, Sir George Beresford-, K.C.M.G.

Storrar, Sir John, Kt., C.B.E., M.C.

Stott, Sir Philip Sidney, Bt. (1920).

Stourton, Sir Ivo Herbert Evelyn Joseph, Kt., C.M.G., O.B.E.

Stout, Sir (Thomas) Duncan (Macgregor), Kt., C.B.E., D.S.O., E.D.

Stow, Sir Frederic Lawrence Philipson-, Bt. (1907).

Stow, Sir John Montague, G.C.M.G., K.C.V.O.

Stracey, Sir Michael George Motley, Bt. (1818).

Strachan, Sir Andrew Henry, Kt., C.B.E.

Strangman, Sir Thomas Joseph, Kt., Q.C.

Strath, Sir William, K.C.B.

Stratton, Sir (Francis) John, Kt., C.B.E.

Stratton, *Lt.-Gen.* Sir William Henry, K.C.B., C.V.O., C.B.E., D.S.O.

Streat, Sir (Edward) Raymond, K.B.E.

Streatfeild, Sir Geoffrey Hugh Benbow, Kt., M.C.

Street, *Hon.* Sir Kenneth Whistler, K.C.M.G.

Strong, *Maj.-Gen.* Sir Kenneth William Dobson, K.B.E., C.B.

Strong, *Most Rev.* Philip Nigel Warrington, K.B.E., C.M.G., D.D.

Stronge, *Capt. Rt. Hon.* Sir (Charles) Norman (Lockhart), Bt., M.C. (1803).

Strutt, Sir (Henry) Austin, K.C.V.O., C.B.

Stuart, Sir Alexander Moody, Kt., O.B.E., M.C.

Stuart, Sir Campbell, G.C.M.G., K.B.E.

†Stuart, Sir Phillip Luttrell, Bt. (1660).

Stubblefield, Sir (Cyril) James, Kt., D.S.C., Ph.D., F.R.S.

Stucley, Sir Dennis Frederic Bankes, Bt. (1859).

Studd, Sir Eric, Bt., O.B.E. (1929).

Studd, Sir Peter Malden, G.B.E.

Studdy, Sir Henry, Kt., C.B.E.

Studholme, Sir Henry Gray, Bt., C.V.O. (1956).

Style, Sir William Montague, Bt. (1627).

Sugden, *Maj.-Gen.* Sir Henry Haskins Clapham, K.B.E., C.B., D.S.O.

Sugerman, *Hon.* Sir Bernard, Kt.

Suleman Cassum Mitha, *Hon. Sardar Sahib* Sir, Kt., C.I.E.

Sullivan, Sir Richard Benjamin Magniac, Bt. (1804).

Summerhayes, Sir Christopher Henry, K.B.E., C.M.G.

Summers, Sir Geoffrey, Bt., C.B.E. (1952).

Summers, Sir (Gerard) Spencer, Kt.

Summers, Sir Richard Felix, Kt.

Summerscale, Sir John Percival, Kt.

Summerson, Sir John Newenham, Kt., C.B.E., F.B.A., F.S.A.

Summerville, Sir (William) Alan (Thompson), Kt., D.SC.

Sunderland, *Prof.* Sir Sydney, Kt., C.M.G., M.D.

Surridge, Sir (Ernest) Rex (Edward), Kt., C.M.G.

Sutherland, Sir Benjamin Ivan, Bt. (1921).

Sutherland, Sir (Frederick) Neil, Kt., C.B.E.

Sutherland, Sir Gordon Brims Black McIvor, Kt., F.R.S.

Suttie, Sir George Philip Grant-, Bt. (S 1702).

Sutton, Sir (Oliver) Graham, Kt., C.B.E., D.SC., F.R.S.

Sutton, Sir Robert Lexington, Bt. (1772).

Sutton, Sir Stafford William Powell Foster-, K.B.E., C.M.G., Q.C.

Swallow, Sir William, Kt.

Swan, Sir Kenneth Raydon, Kt., O.B.E., Q.C.

Swann, Sir Anthony Charles Christopher, Bt., C.M.G., O.B.E., (1906).

Swanwick, *Hon.* Sir Graham Russell, Kt., M.B.E.

Swaziland, The Ngwenyama of, K.B.E.

Syers, Sir Cecil George Lewis, K.C.M.G., C.V.O.

Syfret, *Admiral* Sir (Edward) Neville, G.C.B., K.B.E.

Sykes, Sir (Benjamin) Hugh, Bt. (1921).

Sykes, Sir Charles, Kt., C.B.E., D.SC., Ph.D., F.R.S.

Sykes, Sir Francis Godfrey, Bt. (1781).

Sykes, Sir (Mark Tatton) Richard, Bt. (1783).

Syme, Sir Colin York, Kt.

Syme, *Prof.* Sir Ronald, Kt., F.B.A.

Symon, Sir Alexander Colin Burlington, K.C.M.G., K.C.V.O., O.B.E.

Symonds, *Air Vice-Marshal* Sir Charles Putnam, K.B.E., C.B.

Symonette, Sir Roland Theodore, Kt.

Synge, Sir Robert Carson, Bt. (1801).

Tailyour, *General* Sir Norman Hastings, K.C.B., D.S.O., R.M.

Tait, Sir James Blair, Kt., Q.C.

Tait, Sir James Sharp, Kt., Ph.D.

Tait, Sir John, Kt.

Tait, *Air Vice-Marshal* Sir Victor Hubert, K.B.E., C.B.

Talbot, *Vice-Adm.* Sir (Arthur Allison) FitzRoy, K.B.E., C.B., D.S.O.

Talbot, *Hon.* Sir Hilary Gwynne, Kt.

Talbot, *Lt.-Gen.* Sir Norman Graham Guy, K.B.E., T.D.

Tallack, Sir Hugh Mackay, Kt.

Tancred, Sir Henry Lawson-, Bt. (1662).

Tang, Sir Shiu-Kin, Kt., C.B.E.

Tange, Sir Arthur Harold, Kt., C.B.E.

Tanner, Sir Edgar Stephen, Kt., C.B.E., E.D.

Tansley, Sir Eric Crawford, Kt., C.M.G.

Tapp, *Maj.-Gen.* Sir Nigel Prior Hanson, K.B.E., C.B., D.S.O.

Tarbat, Sir John Allan, Kt.

Tasker, Sir Theodore James, Kt., C.I.E., O.B.E.

Tate, *Lt.-Col.* Sir Henry, Bt. (1898).

Taylor, Sir Charles Stuart, Kt., M.P.

Taylor, Sir (Eric) Stuart, Bt., O.B.E., M.D. (1917).

Taylor, *Prof.* Sir Geoffrey Ingram, Kt., O.M., F.R.S.

Taylor, Sir George, Kt., D.SC., F.R.S., F.R.S.E.

Taylor, *Maj.-Gen.* Sir (George) Brian (Ogilvie), K.B.E., C.B.

Taylor, *Prof.* Sir Hugh Stott, K.B.E., D.SC., F.R.S.

Taylor, Sir James, Kt., M.B.E., D.SC.

Taylor, Sir John William, K.B.E., C.M.G.

Taylor, Sir Reginald William, Kt., C.M.G.

Taylor, Sir Robert Mackinlay, Kt., C.B.E.

Taylor, Sir William Johnson, Bt., C.B.E. (1963).

Teeling, Sir (Luke) William Burke, Kt.

Temple, *Maj.* Sir Richard Anthony Purbeck, Bt., M.C. (1876).

Templer, *Field Marshal* Sir Gerald Walter Robert, K.G., G.C.B., G.C.M.G., K.B.E., D.S.O.

Tennant, Sir Mark Dalcour, K.C.M.G., C.B.

Tennyson, Sir Charles Bruce Locker, Kt., C.M.G.

Terrell, *Capt.* Sir Thomas Antonio Reginald, Kt.

Terry, *Maj.* Sir Edward Henry Bouhier Imbert-, Bt., M.C. (1917).

Tetley, Sir Herbert, K.B.E., C.B.

Tett, Sir Hugh Charles, Kt.

Tewson, Sir (Harold) Vincent, Kt., C.B.E., M.C.

Thesiger, *Hon.* Sir Gerald Alfred, Kt., M.B.E.

Thiess, Sir Leslie Charles, Kt., C.B.E.

Thomas, *Hon.* Sir (Arwyn) Lynn Ungoed-, Kt.

Thomas, Sir Ben Bowen, Kt.

Thomas, Sir Clement Price-, K.C.V.O.

Thomas, Sir Frederick William, Kt.

Thomas, Sir George Alan, Bt. (1766).

Thomas, Sir (Godfrey) Michael (David), Bt. (1694).

Thomas, *General* Sir (Gwilym) Ivor, G.C.B., K.B.E., D.S.O., M.C.

Thomas, Sir (James William) Tudor, Kt., D.SC., M.D.

Thomas, Sir Leslie Montagu, Kt., M.B.E., T.D.

Thomas, *Lt.-Col.* Sir Regin Aneurin, Kt., C.B.E.

Thomas, Sir Robert Evan, Kt.

Thomas, Sir William Jan Cooper, Bt. (1929).

Thomas, Sir (William) Mich (Marsh), Bt. (1918).

Thompson, Sir Edward Hu Dudley, Kt., M.B.E., T.D.

Thompson, Sir Edward Walt Kt.

Thompson, *Lt.-Gen.* Sir Geoff Stuart, K.B.E., C.B., D.S.O.

Thompson, *Prof.* Sir Harr Warris, Kt., C.B.E., D.SC., F.R.

Thompson, Sir (Humphr Simon Meysey-, Bt. (1874).

Thompson, *Hon.* Sir John, Kt.

Thompson, Sir (Joseph) Herbe Kt., C.I.E.

Thompson, Sir Kenneth Pug Bt. (1963).

Thompson, Sir (Louis) Lio (Harry), Kt., C.B.E.

Thompson, Sir Peile Beaumo Bt. (1890).

Thompson, Sir Richard Hilt Marler, Bt., M.P. (1963).

Thompson, Sir Robert Graing Ker, K.B.E., C.M.G., D.S.O., M

Thompson, Sir (Thomas) Lio Tennyson, Bt. (1806).

Thompson, *Lt.-Gen.* Sir Treff Owen, K.C.S.I., C.B., C.B.E.

Thompstone, Sir Eric Westbur K.B.E., C.M.G., M.C.

Thomson, Sir (Arthur) Lane borough, Kt., C.B., O.B.E., D.

Thomson, *Prof.* Sir Arthur Pe grine, Kt., M.C., M.D.

Thomson, Sir George Paget, K F.R.S.

Thomson, Sir Ivo Wilfrid Hom Bt. (1925).

Thomson, *Hon.* Sir Jam Beveridge, K.B.E.

Thomson, Sir (James) Doug (Wishart), Bt. (1929).

Thomson, Sir John Mackay, K C.B.

Thomson, Sir Ronald (Jordan Kt.

Thomson, *Maj.* Sir William, K O.B.E.

Thorn, Sir Jules, Kt.

Thornley, Sir Colin Hardwic K.C.M.G., C.V.O.

Thornton, Sir (Henry) Gera Kt., D.SC., F.R.S.

Thornton, *Lt.-Gen.* Sir Leona Whitmore, K.C.B., C.B.E.

Thornton, Sir Ronald George, K

Thorold, Sir Anthony Henry, B O.B.E., D.S.C. (1642).

Throckmorton, Sir Robe George Maxwell, Bt. (1642).

Thumboo Chetty, Sir Berna Kt., O.B.E.

Thuraisingham, Sir Ern Emmanuel Clough, Kt., C.B.

Thwin, Sir U, Kt.

Tibbits, Sir Cliff, Kt.

Tickell, *Maj.-Gen.* Sir Eusta Francis, K.B.E., C.B., M.C.

Tippett, Sir Michael Kemp, K C.B.E.

Titman, Sir George Alfred, Kt., C.B.E., M.V.O.

Titterton, *Prof.* Sir Ernest William, Kt., C.M.G.

Tivey, Sir John Proctor, Kt.

Tod, *Air Marshal* Sir John Hunter Hunter-, K.B.E., C.B.

Todd, Sir Geoffrey Sydney, K.C.V.O., O.B.E.

Todd, Sir Herbert John, Kt., C.I.E.

Tollemache, *Maj.-Gen.* Sir Humphry Thomas, Bt., C.B., C.B.E., R.M. (1793).

Tomkins, Sir Edward Emile, K.C.M.G., C.V.O.

Tomlinson, Sir Frank Stanley, K.C.M.G.

Tong, Sir Walter Wharton, Kt.

Tooth, Sir Hugh Vere Huntly Duff Munro-Lucas-, Bt., (1920).

Toothill, Sir John Norman, Kt., C.B.E.

Tory, Sir Geofroy William, K.C.M.G.

Tottenham, Sir (George) Richard (Frederick), Kt., K.C.I.E., C.S.I.

Touche, *Rt. Hon.* Sir Gordon Cosmo, Bt. (1962)

Touche, Sir Norman George, Bt. (1920).

Town, Sir (Hugh) Stuart, Kt.

Townley, Sir John Barton, Kt.

Townend, Sir Harry Douglas, Kt.

Townsend, *Prof.* Sir Sydney Lance, Kt., V.R.D., M.D., F.R.C.S.

Traherne, *Col.* Sir Cennydd George, K.G., T.D.

Travancore, *Maj.-Gen.* H.H. the Maharajah of, G.C.S.I., G.C.I.E.

Treatt, *Hon.* Sir Vernon Haddon, K.B.E., M.M., Q.C.

Tredgold, *Rt. Hon.* Sir Robert Clarkson, K.C.M.G., Q.C.

Trehane, Sir Walter Richard, Kt.

Trelawny, Sir John Barry Salusbury-, Bt. (1628).

Tremayne, *Air Marshal* Sir John Tremayne, K.C.B., C.B.E., D.S.O.

Trench, Sir David Clive Crosbie, G.C.M.G., M.C.

Trend, Sir Burke St. John, G.C.B., C.V.O.

Trevaskis, Sir (Gerald) Kennedy (Nicholas), K.C.M.G.

Trevelyan, Sir George Lowthian, Bt. (1874).

Trevelyan, Sir Willoughby John, Bt. (1662).

Trevor, Sir Cecil Russell, Kt., C.I.E.

Trimmer, Sir George (William Arthur), Kt.

Trinder, Sir (Arnold) Charles, C.B.E.

Tritton, *Maj.* Sir Geoffrey Ernest, Bt., C.B.E. (1905).

Trivedi, Sir Chandulal Madhavlal, K.C.S.I., C.I.E., O.B.E.

Trollope, Sir Anthony Owen Clavering, Bt. (1642).

Troubridge, *Lt.-Cdr.* Sir Peter, Bt., R.N. (1799).

Troup, *Vice-Adm.* Sir James Andrew Gardiner, K.B.E., C.B.

Trout, Sir Herbert Leon, Kt.

Troutbeck, Sir John Monro, G.B.E., K.C.M.G.

Truscott, Sir Denis Henry, G.B.E., T.D.

Truscott, Sir Eric Homewood Stanham, Bt. (1909).

Trusted, Sir Harry Herbert, Kt., Q.C.

Tuck, Sir Bruce Adolph Reginald, Bt. (1910).

Tucker, Sir Henry James, Kt., C.B.E.

Tuite, *Maj.* Sir Dennis George Harmsworth, Bt., M.B.E. (1622).

Tunbridge, *Prof.* Sir Ronald Ernest, Kt., O.B.E., M.D., F.R.C.P.

Tupper, Sir Charles Hibbert, Bt. (1888).

Turbott, Sir Ian Graham, Kt. C.M.G., C.V.O.

Turing, Sir John Leslie, Bt., M.C. (S 1638).

Turnbull, Sir Francis Fearon, K.B.E., C.B., C.I.E.

Turnbull, *Lt.-Col.* Sir Hugh Stephenson, K.C.V.O., K.B.E.

Turnbull, Sir Richard Gordon, G.C.M.G.

Turner, *Rt. Hon.* Sir Alexander Kingcome, Kt.

Turner, *Admiral* Sir Arthur Francis, K.C.B., D.S.C.

Turner, Sir Cedric Oban, Kt., C.B.E.

Turner, *Eng. Vice-Adm.* Sir Frederick Richard Gordon, K.C.B., O.B.E.

Turner, Sir George Wilfred, K.C.B., K.B.E.

Turner, Sir Harvey, Kt., C.B.E.

Turner, Sir Henry Samuel Edwin, Kt.

Turner, Sir Michael William, Kt., C.B.E.

Turner, *Prof.* Sir Ralph Lilley, Kt., M.C., F.B.A.

Turner, *Vice-Adm.* Sir Robert Ross, K.B.E., C.B., D.S.O.

Turner, Sir (Ronald) Mark (Cunliffe), Kt.

Turner, Sir Victor (Alfred Charles), Kt., C.S.I., C.I.E., M.B.E.

Turner, *Lt.-Gen.* Sir William Francis Robert, K.B.E., C.B., D.S.O.

Turton, *Rt. Hon.* Sir Robert Hugh, K.B.E., M.C., M.P.

Tuttle, *Air Marshal* Sir Geoffrey William, K.B.E., C.B., D.F.C.

Tuzo, *Lt.-Gen.* Sir Harry Craufurd, K.C.B., O.B.E., M.C.

Twiss, *Admiral* Sir Frank Roddam, K.C.B., D.S.C.

Tyler, *Maj.-Gen.* Sir Leslie Norman, K.B.E., C.B.

Tymms, Sir Frederick, K.C.I.E., M.C.

Tyndall, *Hon.* Sir Arthur, Kt., C.M.G.

Tyrrell, Sir Murray Louis, K.C.V.O., C.B.E.

Tyrwhitt, Sir Reginald Thomas Newman, Bt. (1919).

Tyson, Sir John (Dawson), K.C.I.E., C.S.I., C.B.E.

Udoma, Sir Ethelbert Udo, Kt.

Unsworth, *Hon.* Sir Edgar Ignatius Godfrey, Kt., C.M.G.

Unwin, Sir Keith, K.B.E., C.M.G.

Upjohn, Sir William George Dismore, Kt., O.B.E., M.D.

Urquhart, Sir Andrew, K.C.M.G., M.B.E.

Urquhart, Sir Robert William, K.B.E., C.M.G.

Urton, Sir William Holmes Lister, Kt., M.B.E., T.D.

Usher, Sir Peter Lionel, Bt. (1899).

Vaghjee, Sir Harilall Ranchhordas, Kt.

Valentine, Sir Alexander Balmain Bruce, Kt.

Vallat, Sir Francis Aimé, K.C.M.G., Q.C.

Van Ryneveld, *General* Sir Pierre, K.B.E., C.B., D.S.O., M.C.

Vasey, Sir Ernest Albert, K.B.E., C.M.G.

Vaughan, Sir (George) Edgar, K.B.E.

Vavasour, *Cdr.* Sir Geoffrey William, Bt., D.S.C., R.N. (1828).

Veale, Sir Douglas, Kt., C.B.E.

Veale, *Hon.* Sir Geoffrey de Paiva, Kt.

Venables, Sir Peter, Kt., Ph.D.

Verdin, *Lt.-Col.* Sir Richard Bertram, K.B.E., O.B.E., T.D.

Vereker, Sir (George) Gordon (Medlicott), K.C.M.G., M.C.

Verity, Sir Edgar William, K.B.E., C.B.

Verner, Sir Edward Derrick Wingfield, Bt. (1846).

Verney, Sir Harry (Calvert Williams), Bt., D.S.O. (1818).

Verney, Sir John, Bt., M.C. (1946).

Vernon, Sir James, Kt., C.B.E.

Vernon, Sir Nigel John Douglas, Bt. (1914).

Vernon, Sir Wilfred Douglas, Kt.

Vesey, *General* Sir Ivo Lucius Beresford, K.C.B., K.B.E., C.M.G., D.S.O.

Vesey, Sir (Nathaniel) Henry (Peniston), Kt., C.B.E.

Vestey, Sir (John) Derek, Bt. (1921).

Vickers, Sir (Charles) Geoffrey, Kt., V.C.

Vickery, Sir Philip Crawford, Kt., C.I.E., O.B.E.

Victoria, Sir (Joseph Aloysius) Donatus, Kt., C.B.E.

Villiers, *Vice-Adm.* Sir (John) Michael, K.C.B., O.B.E.

Vincent, Sir (Harold) Graham, K.C.M.G., C.B., C.V.O.

Vincent, Sir William Percy Maxwell, Bt. (1936).

Vyse, *Lt.-Gen.* Sir Edward Dacre Howard-, K.B.E., C.B., M.C.

Vyvyan, Sir Richard Philip, Bt. (1645).

Wackett, Sir Lawrence James, Kt., D.F.C., A.F.C.

Waddell, Sir Alexander Nicol Anton, K.C.M.G., D.S.C.

Wade, *Col.* Sir George Albert, Kt., M.C.

Wadham, *Prof.* Sir Samuel McMahon, Kt.

Wadley, Sir Douglas, Kt.

Wadsworth, Sir Sidney, Kt.

Waechter, Sir Harry Leonard D'Arcy, Bt. (1911).

Wagner, Sir Anthony Richard, K.C.V.O.

Wake, Sir Hereward, Bt., M.C. (1621).

Wakefield, Sir Edward Humphry Tyrrell, Bt. (1962).

Wakeley, Sir Cecil Pembrey Grey, Bt., K.B.E., C.B., D.S.C. (1952)

Wakely, Sir Clifford Holland, K.B.E.

Wakeman, *Capt.* Sir Offley, Bt., C.B.E. (1828).

Walch, Sir Geoffrey Archer, K.B.E., C.V.O.

Waldock, *Prof.* Sir (Claud) Humphrey (Meredith), Kt., C.M.G., O.B.E., Q.C., D.C.L.

Waldron, Sir John Lovegrove, K.C.V.O.

Walker, Sir Allan Grierson, Kt., Q.C.

Walker, Sir Baldwin Patrick, Bt. (1856).

Walker, Sir (Charles) Michael, K.C.M.G.

Walker, *Vice-Adm.* Sir (Charles) Peter (Graham), K.B.E., C.B., D.S.C.

Walker, Sir Edward Ronald, Kt., C.B.E.

Walker, *Air Chief Marshal* Sir (George) Augustus, G.C.B., C.B.E., D.S.O., D.F.C., A.F.C.

Walker, *Maj.* Sir George Ferdinand Forestier-, Bt. (1835).

Walker, *Admiral* Sir Harold Thomas Coulthard, K.C.B.

Walker, *Maj.* Sir Hugh Ronald, Bt. (1906).

Walker, Sir Hugh Selby Norman-, K.C.M.G., O.B.E.

Walker, Sir James Heron, Bt. (1868).

Walker, Sir John, K.C.M.G., O.B.E.

Walker, *General* Sir Walter Colyear, K.C.B., C.B.E., D.S.O.

Walker, Sir William Giles Newsom, Kt., T.D.

Walkley, Sir William Gaston, Kt., C.B.E.

Wall, Sir (George) Rolande (Percival), Kt., M.C.

Wall, Sir John Edward, Kt., O.B.E.

Wallace, *Hon.* Sir Gordon, Kt.

Wallace, Sir Martin Kelso, Kt.

Waller, *Hon.* Sir George Stanley Kt., O.B.E.

Waller, Sir (John) Keith, Kt. C.B.E.

Waller, Sir John Stanier, Bt. (1815).

Waller, Sir Robert William, Bt. (1780).

Walley, Sir John, K.B.E., C.B.

Wallinger, Sir Geoffrey Arnold, G.B.E., K.C.M.G.

Wallis, Sir Barnes Neville, Kt., C.B.E., F.R.S.

Walmsley, *Air Marshal* Sir Hugh Sydney Porter, K.C.B., K.C.I.E., C.B.E., M.C., D.F.C.

Walsh, *Rt. Hon.* Sir Cyril Ambrose, K.B.E.

Walsh, Sir David Philip, K.B.E., C.B.

Walsh, *Prof.* Sir John Patrick, K.B.E.

Walsham, *Rear-Adm.* Sir John Scarlett Warren, Bt., C.B., O.B.E. (1831).

Walshe, Sir Francis Martin Rouse, Kt., O.B.E., M.D., D.SC., F.R.S.

Walters, Sir Roger Talbot, K.B.E., F.R.I.B.A.

Walton, *Brig.* Sir George Hands, K.B.E., C.B., T.D.

Walton, Sir John Robert, Kt.

Walton, Sir William Turner, Kt., O.M., MUS., DOC.

Wand, *Rt. Rev.* John William Charles, P.C., K.C.V.O., D.D.

Warburg, Sir Siegmund George, Kt.

Ward, *General* Sir (Alfred) Dudley, G.C.B., K.B.E., D.S.O.

Ward, Sir Aubrey Ernest, Kt.

Ward, Sir John Guthrie, G.C.M.G.

Ward, Sir Joseph James Laffey, Bt. (1911).

Ward, *Cdr.* Sir Melvill Wills, Bt., D.S.C., R.N. (1914).

Ward, *Lt.-Gen.* Sir Richard Erskine, K.C.B., D.S.O., M.C.

Ward, Sir Terence George, Kt., C.B.E.

Ward, Sir (Victor) Michael Barrington-, K.C.V.O., C.B.E., D.S.O.

Wardlaw, Sir Henry, Bt. (S 1631).

Wardle, Sir Thomas Edward Jewell, Kt.

Waring, Sir Alfred Harold, Bt. (1935).

Waring, Sir (Arthur) Bertram, Kt.

Waring, Sir Douglas Tremayne, Kt., C.B.E.

Wark, Sir Ian William, Kt., C.M.G. C.B.E., Ph.D., D.SC.

Warmington, *Lt.-Cdr.* Sir Marshall George Clitheroe, Bt., R.N. (1908).

Warner, Sir Edward Courtenay Henry, Bt. (1910).

Warner, Sir Edward Redston, K.C.M.G., O.B.E.

Warner, Sir Frederick Edward, Kt.

Warner, Sir George Redston, K.C.V.O., C.M.G.

Warren, Sir Brian Charles Pennefather, Bt. (1784).

Warren, *Hon.* Sir Edward Emerton, K.C.M.G., K.B.E.

Warren, Sir Mortimer Langton, Kt.

Waterer, Sir (Robert) Bernard, Kt., C.B.

Waterlow, Sir Philip Alexander, Bt. (1873).

Waterlow, Sir Thomas Gordon Bt., C.B.E. (1930).

Waterman, Sir Ewen McIntyre Kt.

Waters, *Maj.* Sir Arnold Horace Santo, Kt., VC, C.B.E., D.S.O. M.C.

Watherston, Sir David Charles K.B.E., C.M.G.

Watkins, *Hon.* Sir Tasker, Kt VC.

Watkinson, Sir (George) Laurence K.B.E., C.B., M.C.

Watson, Sir (David) Ronal Milne-, Bt. (1937).

Watson, *Capt.* Sir Derrick William Inglefield Inglefield-, Bt., T.D (1895).

Watson, *Hon.* Sir (Henry) Keith Kt.

Watson, Sir James Andrew, Bt (1866).

Watson, Sir Michael Milne-, Kt C.B.E.

Watson, Sir Noel Duncan K.C.M.G.

Watson, Sir Norman James, Bt (1912).

Watson, *Vice-Adm.* Sir (Robert Dymock, K.C.B., C.B.E.

Watson, Sir Stephen John, Kt C.B.E., D.S.C., F.R.S.E.

Watson, Sir William, Kt.

Watt, Sir Alan Stewart. Kt., C.B.

Watt, *Brig.* Sir George Steven Harvie-, Bt., T.D., Q.C. (1945)

Watt, Sir Robert Alexand Watson-, Kt., C.B.

Wattie, Sir James, Kt., C.B.E.

Wauchope, Sir Patrick Georg Don-, Bt. (S 1667).

Way, Sir Richard George K chener, K.C.B., C.B.E.

Wayne, *Prof.* Sir Edward Johnso Kt., M.D., Ph.D.

Weatherhead, Sir Arthur Tre ham, Kt., C.M.G.

Weatherstone, Sir Dunca Mackay, Kt., M.C., T.D.

Webb, *Hon.* Sir William Floo K.B.E.

Webber, Sir William Jam Percival, Kt., C.B.E.

Webster, Sir Richard James, K D.S.O.

Webster, Sir Robert Joseph, K C.M.G., C.B.E., M.C.

Webster, *General* Sir Thom Sheridan Riddell-, G.C.B., D.S

Wedderburn, *Cdr.* Sir John Pe Ogilvy-, Bt., R.N. (1803).

Wedderspoon, Sir Thomas Ada Kt.

Wedgwood, Sir John Hamilto Bt., T.D. (1942).

Weedon, *Air Vice-Marshal* Colin Winterbotham, K.B. C.B.

Weeks, Sir Hugh Thomas, K C.M.G.

Weidenfeld, Sir (Arthur) Geor Kt.

Weinstock, Sir Arnold, Kt.

Weipers, *Prof.* Sir William L Kt.

Welby, Sir Oliver Charles Ea Bt. (1801).

Welch, *Lt.-Col.* Sir (George James) Cullum, Bt., O.B.E., M.C. (1957).

Weldon, Sir Thomas Brian, Bt. (I. 1723).

Welensky, *Rt. Hon.* Sir Roy (Roland), K.C.M.G.

Wellington, Sir (Reginald Everard) Lindsay, Kt., C.B.E.

Wells, Sir Charles Maltby, Bt. (1944).

Wells, *Lt.-Gen.* Sir Henry, K.B.E., C.B., D.S.O.

Wells, Sir Henry Weston, Kt., C.B.E.

Wernher, *Maj.-Gen.* Sir Harold Augustus, Bt., G.C.V.O., T.D. (1905).

West, *General* Sir Michael Montgomerie Alston Roberts, G.C.B., D.S.O.

Westall, *General* Sir John Chaddesley, K.C.B., C.B.E., R.M.

Westerman, Sir (Wilfred) Alan, Kt., C.B.E.

Westlake, Sir Charles Redvers, Kt.

Weston, Sir Eric, Kt.

Weston, *Air Vice-Marshal* Sir John Gerard Willsley, K.B.E., C.B.

Westrup, *Prof.* Sir Jack Allan, Kt.

Wetherall, *Lt.-Gen.* Sir (Harry) Edward de Robillard, K.B.E., C.B., D.S.O. M.C.

Wheare, Sir Kenneth Clinton, Kt., C.M.G., F.B.A., D.Litt.

Wheatley, Sir (George) Andrew, Kt., C.B.E.

Wheatley, *Lt.-Col.* Sir Mervyn James, K.B.E.

Wheeler, Sir Charles Reginald, K.B.E.

Wheeler, Sir Charles Thomas, K.C.V.O., C.B.E., R.A.

Wheeler, Sir Frederick Henry, Kt., C.B.E.

Wheeler, *Air Marshal* Sir (Henry) Neil (George), K.C.B., C.B.E., D.S.O., D.F.C., A.F.C.

Wheeler, Sir John Hieron, Bt. (1920).

Wheeler, Sir (Robert Eric) Mortimer, Kt., C.H., C.I.E., M.C., F.R.S., F.B.A., F.S.A.

Wheler, *Capt.* Sir Trevor Wood, Bt. (1660).

Whishaw, Sir Charles Percival Law, Kt.

Whishaw, Sir Ralph, Kt., C.B.E.

Whitaker, *Maj.* Sir James Herbert Ingham, Bt. (1936).

Whitby, Sir Bernard James, Kt.

White, *Hon.* Sir Alfred John, Kt.

White, *Brig.* Sir Bruce Gordon, K.B.E.

White, Sir Dennis Charles, K.B.E., C.M.G.

White, Sir Dick Goldsmith, K.C.M.G., K.B.E.

White, Sir (Eric Henry) Wyndham, K.C.M.G.

White, Sir (Eric) Richard Meadows, Bt. (1937).

White, Sir Ernest Keith, Kt., C.B.E., M.C.

White, Sir Frederick William George, K.B.E., M.D., Ph.D., F.R.S.

White, Sir George Stanley Midelton, Bt. (1904).

White, Sir Harold Leslie, Kt., C.B.E.

White, *Wing-Cdr.* Sir Henry Arthur Dalrymple-, Bt., D.F.C. (1926).

White, *Surgeon Rear-Adm.* Sir Henry Ellis Yeo, K.C.V.O., O.B.E., M.D.

White, Sir John Woolmer, Bt. (1922).

White, Sir Thomas Astley Woollaston, Bt. (1802).

Whitehead, *Hon.* Sir Edgar Cuthbert Fremantle, K.C.M.G., O.B.E.

Whitehead, Sir Rowland John Rathbone, Bt. (1889).

Whiteley, *Capt.* Sir (Herbert) Maurice Huntington-, Bt., R.N. (1918).

Whiteside, Sir Cuthbert William, Kt.

Whitford, *Hon.* Sir John Norman Keates, Kt.

Whitley, *Air Marshal* Sir John René, K.B.E., C.B., D.S.O., A.F.C.

Whitmore, Sir John Henry Douglas, Bt. (1954).

Whitteridge, Sir Gordon Coligny, K.C.M.G., O.B.E.

Whittingham, *Air Marshal* Sir Harold Edward, K.C.B., K.B.E.

Whittington, Sir Richard, K.C.M.G., C.B.E.

Whittle, *Air Commodore* Sir Frank, K.B.E., C.B.

Whittome, Sir Maurice Gordon, Kt., C.B.

Whitworth, *Admiral* Sir William Jock, K.C.B., C.B.E., D.S.O.

Whyatt, Sir John, Kt., Q.C.

Wien, *Hon.* Sir Philip, Kt.

Wigan, Sir Frederick Adair, Bt. (1898).

Wiggin, Sir Charles Richard Henry, Bt., T.D. (1892).

Wigglesworth, *Air Marshal* Sir (Horace Ernest) Philip, K.B.E., C.B., D.S.C.

Wigglesworth, *Prof.* Sir Vincent Brian, Kt., C.B.E., M.D., F.R.S.

Wigram, *Rev.* Sir Clifford Woolmore, Bt. (1805).

Wijeyewardene, *Hon.* Sir (Edwin) Arthur (Lewis), Kt.

Wilbraham, Sir Randle John Baker, Bt. (1776).

Wild, *Rt. Hon.* Sir (Herbert) Richard (Churton), K.C.M.G., E.D.

Wildish, *Eng.-Rear-Adm.* Sir Henry William, K.B.E., C.B.

Wilkinson, Sir Harold, Kt., C.M.G.

Wilkinson, Sir (Leonard) David, Bt., D.S.C., (1941).

Wilkinson, Sir Peter Allix, K.C.M.G., D.S.O., O.B.E.

Wilkinson, Sir (Robert Francis) Martin, Kt.

Wilkinson, Sir Thomas Crowe Spenser-, Kt.

Willan, Sir Harold Curwen, Kt., C.M.G., M.C.

Willert, Sir Arthur, K.B.E.

Williams, Sir Alan Meredith, K.C.M.G.

Williams, Sir Alexander Thomas, K.C.M.G., M.B.E.

Williams, Sir (Arthur) Leonard, G.C.M.G.

Williams, Sir Brandon Meredith Rhys-, Bt., M.P., (1918).

Williams, Sir Charles Henry Trelease, Kt., C.B.E.

Williams, Sir (Daniel) Thomas, Kt., O.B.E.

Williams, Sir Francis John Watkin, Bt., Q.C. (1798).

Williams, Sir Griffith Goodland, K.B.E., C.B.

Williams, Sir Gwilym Tecwyn, Kt., C.B.E.

Williams, *Lt.-Gen.* Sir Harold, K.B.E., C.B.

Williams, Sir Henry Morton Leech, Kt., M.B.E.

Williams, Sir John Francis, Kt.

Williams, *Capt.* Sir John Protheroe, Kt., C.M.G., O.B.E.

Williams, Sir Michael Sanigear, K.C.M.G.

Williams, Sir Osmond, Bt., M.C. (1909).

Williams, Sir Peter Watkin, Kt.

Williams, *Air Marshal* Sir Richard, K.B.E., C.B., D.S.O.

Williams, Sir Robert Ernest, Bt. (1866).

Williams, Sir (Robert) Philip (Nathaniel), Bt. (1915).

Williams, Sir Robin Philip, Bt. (1953).

Williams, Sir Rolf Dudley-, Bt. (1964).

Williams, Sir Roy Ellis Hume-, Bt. (1922).

Williams, Sir Thomas Herbert Parry-, Kt., D.Litt.

Williams, Sir William Emrys, Kt., C.B.E.

Williams, *Lt.-Col.* Sir William Jones, K.C.V.O., O.B.E.

Williamson, Sir George Alexander, Kt.

Williamson, Sir (Nicholas Frederick) Hedworth, Bt. (1642).

Willink, *Rt. Hon.* Sir Henry Urmston, Bt., M.C., Q.C., D.C.L. (1957).

Willis, *Admiral of the Fleet* Sir Algernon Usborne, G.C.B., K.B.E., D.S.O.

Willis, *Hon.* Sir John Ramsay, Kt.

Willis, Sir (Zwinglius) Frank, Kt., C.B.E.

Willison, Sir John Alexander, Kt., O.B.E.

Willmer, *Rt. Hon.* Sir (Henry) Gordon, Kt., O.B.E., T.D.

Willmott, Sir Maurice Gordon, Kt., M.C.

Willoughby, *Maj.-Gen.* Sir John Edward Francis, K.B.E., C.B.

Wills, *Lt.-Col.* Sir (Ernest) Edward de Winton, Bt. (1904).

Wills, Sir John Spencer, Kt.

Wills, Sir John Vernon, Bt. (1923).

Wills, *Brig.* Sir Kenneth Agnew, K.B.E., M.C., E.D.

Wilmot, *Cdr.* Sir John Assheton Eardley-, Bt., M.V.O., D.S.C. R.N. (1821).

Wilmot, Sir Robert Arthur, Bt. (1759).

Wilson, Sir Alan Herries, Kt., F.R.S.

Wilson, Sir (Archibald) Duncan, G.C.M.G.

Wilson, Sir Arton, K.B.E., C.B.

Wilson, Sir Bertram, Kt.

Wilson, Sir Charles Haynes, Kt.

Wilson, Sir Garnet Douglas, Kt.

Wilson, Sir Geoffrey Masterman, K.C.B., C.M.G.

Wilson, Sir George, K.B.E.

Wilson, *Prof.* Sir Graham Selby, Kt., M.D.

Wilson, Sir Horace John, G.C.B., G.C.M.G., C.B.E.

Wilson, Sir Hubert Guy Maryon, Bt. (1661).

Wilson, Sir John Mitchell Harvey, Bt., K.C.V.O. (1920).

Wilson, Sir Keith Cameron, Kt.

Wilson, Sir Leonard, K.C.I.E.

Wilson, Sir (Leslie) Hugh, Kt., O.B.E.

Wilson, Sir Mathew Martin, Bt. (1874).

Wilson, Sir Reginald Holmes, Kt.

Wilson, *Hon.* Sir Robert Christian, Kt., C.M.G.

Wilson, Sir Roland, K.B.E.

Wilson, Sir Roy Mickel, Kt., Q.C.

Wilson, Sir Thomas Douglas, Bt., M.C. (1906).

Wilton, *Lt.-Gen.* Sir John Gordon Noel, K.B.E., C.B., D.S.O.

Windeyer, *Prof.* Sir Brian Wellingham, Kt.

Windeyer, *Rt. Hon.* Sir (William John) Victor, K.B.E., C.B., D.S.O., E.D.

Windham, *Hon.* Sir Ralph, Kt.

Windley, Sir Edward Henry, K.C.M.G., K.C.V.O.

Wingate, *Col.* Sir Ronald Evelyn Leslie, Bt., C.B., C.M.G., C.I.E., O.B.E. (1920).

Winn, *Rt. Hon.* Sir (Charles) Rodger (Noel), Kt., C.B., O.B.E.

Winneke, *Hon.* Sir Henry Arthur, K.C.M.G., O.B.E.

Winnifrith, Sir (Alfred) John (Digby), K.C.B.

Winnington, Sir Francis Salwey William, Bt. (1755).

Winterton, *Maj.-Gen.* Sir (Thomas) John (Willoughby), K.C.B., K.C.M.G., C.B.E.

Wise, Sir John Humphrey K.C.M.G., C.B.E.

Wiseham, *Hon.* Sir Joseph Angus Lucien, Kt.

Wiseman, Sir John William, Bt. (1628).

Witt, Sir John Clermont, Kt.

Wolfenden, Sir John Frederick, Kt., C.B.E.

Wolff, *Hon.* Sir Albert Asher, K.C.M.G.

Wolfson, Sir Isaac, Bt., F.R.S. (1962).

Wollen, Sir (Ernest) Russell (Storey), K.B.E.

Wolseley, Sir Charles Garnet Mark Richard, Bt. (1628).

Wolseley, Sir Garnet, Bt. (1 1745).

Wombwell, Sir (Frederick) Philip (Alfred William), Bt., M.B.E. (1778).

Womersley, Sir Peter John Walter, Bt. (1945).

Wood, Sir Anthony John Page, Bt. (1837).

Wood, Sir David Basil Hill-, Bt. (1921).

Wood, Sir Henry Peart, Kt., C.B.E.

Wood, Sir John Arthur Haigh, Bt., M.C., D.S.C. (1918).

Wood, Sir Kenneth Millns, Kt.

Woodall, *Lt.-Gen.* Sir John Dane, K.C.M.G., K.B.E., C.B., M.C.

Woodhead, Sir John Ackroyd, G.C.I.E., K.C.S.I.

Woodhouse, *Admiral* Sir Charles Henry Lawrence, K.C.B.

Wooding, *Rt. Hon.* Sir Hugh Olliviere Beresford, Kt., C.B.E.

Woodley, Sir (Frederick George) Richard, Kt.

Woodruff, *Prof.* Sir Michael Francis Addison, Kt., D.Sc.

Woods, *Rt. Rev.* Robert Wilmer, K.C.V.O.

Woods, *Admiral* Sir Wilfrid John Wentworth, G.B.E., K.C.B., D.S.O.

Woolley, Sir Charles Campbell, G.B.E., K.C.M.G., M.C.

Woolley, Sir Richard van der Riet, Kt., O.B.E., F.R.S.

Worley, Sir Newnham Arthur, K.B.E., Q.C.

Worsley, *Lt.-Gen.* Sir John Francis, K.B.E., C.B., M.C.

Worsley, *Col.* Sir William Arthington, Bt. (1938).

Wort, Sir Alfred William Ewart, Kt.

Worthington, *Air Vice-Marshal* Sir Geoffrey Luis, K.B.E., C.B.

Wrangham, *Hon.* Sir Geoffrey Walter, Kt.

Wraxall, Sir Morville William Lascelles, Bt. (1813).

Wray, Sir Kenneth Owen Roberts-, G.C.M.G., Q.C.

Wrey, Sir (Castel) Richard Bourchier, Bt. (1628).

Wright, Sir Charles Seymour, K.C.B., O.B.E., M.C.

Wright, Sir Denis Arthur Hepworth, G.C.M.G.

Wright, Sir Michael Robert, G.C.M.G.

Wright, Sir Richard Michael Cory-, Bt. (1903).

Wright, *Admiral* Sir Royston Hollis, G.B.E., K.C.B., D.S.O.

Wrightson, Sir John Garmondsway, Bt. (1900).

Wrigley, Sir John Cromptor, K.B.E., C.B.

Wrisberg, *Lt.-Gen.* Sir Frederick George, K.B.E., C.B.

Wyatt, *Vice-Adm.* Sir (Arthur Guy (Norris), K.B.E., C.B.

Wykeham, *Air Marshal* Sir Peter Guy, K.C.B., D.S.O., O.B.E., D.F.C., A.F.C.

Wylie, Sir Campbell, Kt., E.D Q.C.

Wyndham, Sir Harold Stanley, Kt., C.B.E.

Wynn, *Lt.-Col.* Sir Owen Watkin Williams-, Bt. C.B.E. (1688).

Yarrow, Sir Eric Grant, Bt M.B.E. (1916).

Yates, *Lt.-Gen.* Sir David Pee: K.C.B., C.V.O., D.S.O., O.B.E.

Yates, Sir Thomas, Kt., C.B.E.

Yeabsley, Sir Richard Ernest, Kt C.B.E.

Yeaman, Sir Ian David, Kt.

Yeo, Sir William, Kt., C.B.E.

Yonge, Sir (Charles) Maurice, Kt C.B.E., D.SC., F.R.S., F.R.S.E.

Yorston, Sir (Robert) Keith, Kt C.B.E.

Youens, Sir Peter William, Kt C.M.G., O.B.E.

Young, *Col.* Sir Arthur Edwir K.B.E., C.M.G., C.V.O.

Young, Sir George Samue Knatchbull, Bt. (1813).

Young, Sir James Reid, Kt.

Young, Sir (John) Douglas, Kt.

Young, Sir John William Roe Bt. (1821).

Young, Sir Mark Aitchison G.C.M.G.

Young, Sir Norman Smith, Kt.

Young, Sir Richard Dilworth, Ki

Young, Sir Stephen Stewar Templeton, Bt. (1945).

Young, Sir (Thomas) Eric (Bos well), Kt.

Young, Sir William Neil, Bt (1769).

Younger, *Capt.* Sir James Paton Kt. C.B.E.

Younger, Sir William McEwar Bt., D.S.O. (1964).

Younger, Sir William Robert, Bt (1911).

Yusuf, Sir Mohamad, Kt.

Baronetcies Extinct (Since last issue)—Alison (U.K. 1852); Dalrymple (U.K., 1887); Dundas of Armisto (U.K., 1898); Hart (U.K., 1893); Hornby (U.K., 1899); Moore of Kyleburn (U.K., 1956); Rowland (U.K 1950); Sturdee (U.K.), 1916); Worthington-Evans (U.K., 1916).

Dames Grand Cross and Dames Commanders of the Order of St. Michael and St. George, the Royal Victorian Order and the Order of the British Empire

NOTE.—Dames Grand Cross (G.C.M.G., G.C.V.O. or G.B.E.) and Dames Commanders (D.C.M.G., D.C.V.O. or D.B.E.) are addressed in a manner similar to that of Knights Grand Cross or Knights Commanders, *e.g.* "Miss Florence Smith," after receiving the honour would be addressed as "Dame Florence," and in writing, as "Dame Florence Smith, G. (or D.) C.M.G., G. (or D.) C.V.O., or G. (or D.) B.E." Where such award is made to a lady already in enjoyment of a higher title the appropriate letters are appended to her name, *e.g.* "The Countess of —— G.C.V.O." Peeresses in their own right, and Life Peeresses, are not included in this list. Dames Grand Cross rank after wives of Baronets and before wives of Knights Grand Cross. Dames Commanders rank after the wives of Knights Grand Cross and before the wives of Knights Grand Cross.

DAMES GRAND CROSS AND DAMES COMMANDERS

H.M. Queen Elizabeth The Queen Mother, K.G., K.T., C.I., G.M.V.O.

H.R.H. The Princess Margaret, Countess of Snowdon, C.I., G.C.V.O.

H.R.H. The Duchess of Gloucester, C.I., G.C.V.O., G.B.E.

H.R.H. The Princess Alice, Countess of Athlone, V.A., G.C.V.O., G.B.E.

H.R.H. The Princess Alexandra of Kent, G.C.V.O.

Abbot, Dame Elsie Myrtle, D.B.E.

Abercorn, The Duchess of, D.C.V.O.

Ackroyd, Dame (Dorothy) Elizabeth, D.B.E.

Albemarle, The Countess of, D.B.E.

Alexander of Tunis, The Countess, G.B.E.

Anderson, Dame Judith, D.B.E.

Anderson, Dame Kitty, D.B.E., Ph.D.

Anderson, *Brig.* Hon. Dame Mary Mackenzie, D.B.E.

Ashby, Dame Margery Irene Corbett, D.B.E.

Ashcroft, Dame Peggy (Mrs. Hutchinson), D.B.E.

Ashworth, *Air Commandant* Dame Veronica Margaret, D.B.E., R.R.C.

Baden-Powell, Olave St. Clair, Baroness, G.B.E.

Barker, Dame Sara Elizabeth, D.B.E.

Barnett, *Air Commandant* Dame (Mary) Henrietta, D.B.E.

Berry, Dame Alice Miriam, D.B.E.

Bishop, Dame (Margaret) Joyce, D.B.E.

Bottomley, Dame Bessie Ellen, D.B.E.

Brecknock, The Countess of, D.B.E.

Brookes, Mabel Balcombe, Lady, D.B.E.

Brown, Dame Beryl Paston, D.B.E.

Bryans, Dame Anne Margaret, D.B.E.

Bryce, Dame Isabel Graham, D.B.E.

Buckley, Hon. Dame Ruth Burton, D.B.E.

Buxton, Dame Rita Mary, D.B.E.

Bynoe, Dame Hilda Louisa, D.B.E.

Campbell, Dame Kate Isabel, D.B.E., M.D.

Cartwright, Dame Mary Lucy, D.B.E., ScD., D.Phil., F.R.S.

Cavan, Joan, Countess of, D.B.E.

Cayford, Dame Florence Evelyn, D.B.E.

Cheshire, *Commandant* Dame Mary Kathleen, D.B.E.

Chick, Dame Harriette, D.B.E., D.Sc.

Christie, Dame Agatha Mary Clarissa (Lady Mallowan), D.B.E.

Cockayne, Dame Elizabeth, D.B.E.

Cole, Dame Margaret Isabel, D.B.E.

Coles, Mabel Irene, Lady, D.B.E.

Colvin, *Brig.* Dame Mary Katherine Rosamund, D.B.E., T.D.

Cooper, Dame Gladys Constance (Mrs. Merivale), D.B.E.

Couchman, Dame Elizabeth May Ramsay, D.B.E.

Coulshed, *Brig.* Dame (Mary) Frances, D.B.E., T.D.

Courtney, Dame Kathleen D'Olier, D.B.E.

Cox, Dame Marjorie Sophie, D.B.E.

Cozens, *Brig.* Dame (Florence) Barbara, D.B.E., R.R.C.

Cramer, Mary Terese, Lady, D.B.E.

Cripps, Isobel, Lady, G.B.E.

Crout, Dame Mabel, D.B.E.

Curwen, Dame (Anne) May, D.B.E.

Daly, Dame Mary Dora, D.B.E.

Davenport, Dame Lilian Emily Isabel Jane Bromley-, D.B.E.

Davies, *Commandant* Dame Jean (Mrs. Lancaster), D.B.E.

De La Warr, The Countess, D.B.E.

de Valois, Dame Ninette, D.B.E.

Devonshire, Mary Alice, Duchess of, G.C.V.O., C.B.E.

Doughty, Dame Adelaide Baillieu, D.B.E.

Doyle, *Air Commandant* Dame Jean Lena Annette Conan (Lady Bromet), D.B.E.

Drake, *Brig.* Dame Jean Elizabeth Rivett Rivett-, D.B.E.

Drummond, *Commandant* Dame (Edith) Margaret, D.B.E.

du Maurier, Dame Daphne (Lady Browning), D.B.E.

Elgin & Kincardine, The Countess of, D.B.E.

Evans, Dame Edith Mary (Mrs. Booth), D.B.E.

Evans, Lady Olwen Elizabeth Carey, D.B.E.

Farrer, Hon. Dame Frances Margaret, D.B.E.

Fell, Dame Honor Bridget, D.B.E., F.R.S.

Fonteyn, Dame Margot, D.B.E.

Freyberg, The Dowager Baroness, G.B.E.

Gardiner, Dame Helen Louisa, D.B.E., M.V.O.

Gardner, *Prof.* Dame Helen Louise, D.B.E.

Gibbs, Dame Anstice Rosa, D.C.V.O., C.B.E.

Gibbs, Molly Peel, Lady, D.B.E.

Giles, *Air Commandant* Dame Pauline, D.B.E., R.R.C.

Gillespie, *Brig.* Dame Helen Shiels, D.B.E., R.R.C.

Gillie, Dame (Katharine) Annis Calder (Mrs. Peter Smith), D.B.E.

Godwin, Dame (Beatrice) Anne, D.B.E.

Goodrich, Dame Matilda, D.B.E., R.R.C.

Grafton, The Duchess of, D.C.V.O.

Green, Dame Mary Georgina, D.B.E.

Halifax, Dorothy, Countess of, C.I. D.C.V.O.

Hambleden, Patricia, Viscountess, D.C.V.O.

Hanbury, *Air Commandant* Dame Felicity Hyde, D.B.E.

Hancock, Dame Florence May, D.B.E.

Harlech, Beatrice, Baroness, D.C.V.O.

Hathaway, Dame Sibyl Mary, D.B.E.

Hay, Lady Margaret Katherine, D.C.V.O.

Henderson, *Brig.* Dame Joan Evelyn, D.B.E.

Hepworth, Dame Barbara, D.B.E.

Herring, Mary, Lady, D.B.E.

Hill, *Air-Commandant* Dame Felicity Barbara, D.B.E.

Hillingdon, Edith Mary, Lady, D.B.E.

Holt, Dame Zara Kate, D.B.E.

Humphrys, Gertrude Mary, Lady, D.B.E.

Johnson, *Brig.* Dame (Cecilie) Monica, D.B.E., R.R.C.

Kettlewell, *Commandant* Dame Marion Mildred, D.B.E.

K*

Kilroy, Dame Alix Hester Marie (Lady Meynell), D.B.E.

Lane, *Hon.* Dame Elizabeth Kathleen, D.B.E.

Limerick, Angela, Countess of, G.B.E.

Lloyd, Dame Hilda Nora, D.B.E.

Loughlin, Dame Anne, D.B.E.

Lowrey, *Air Commandant* Dame Alice, D.B.E., R.R.C.

Lyons, Dame Enid Muriel, G.B.E.

Macknight, Dame Ella Annie Noble, D.B.E., M.D.

Macleod of Macleod, Dame Flora, D.B.E.

Manning, Dame (Elizabeth) Leah, D.B.E.

Markova, Dame Alicia, D.B.E.

Marsh, Dame (Edith) Ngaio, D.B.E.

Marsham, Dame Joan (Hon. Mrs. Sydney Marsham), D.B.E.

Maxse, Dame Marjorie, D.B.E.

Menzies, Dame Pattie Maie, G.B.E.

Miles, Dame Margaret, D.B.E.

Millar, *Commandant* Dame (Evelyn Louisa) Elizabeth Hoyer-, D.B.E.

Miller, Dame Mabel Flora Hobart, D.B.E.

Monro, *Hon.* Mary Caroline, Lady, D.B.E.

Morant, Dame Mary Maud (Sister Mary Regis), D.B.E.

Mulholland, *Hon.* Dame Olivia Vernon, D.C.V.O.

Murdoch, Elizabeth Joy, Lady, D.B.E.

Myer, Dame (Margery) Merlyn Baillieu, D.B.E.

Neagle, Dame Anna (Mrs. Wilcox), D.B.E.

Oliver, Beryl, Lady, G.B.E., R.R.C.

Ollorenshaw, Dame Kathleen Mary, D.B.E.

Oudendyk, Dame Margaret, D.B.E.

Parkinson, Dame Nancy Broadfield, D.C.M.G., C.B.E.

Peel, Lady Adelaide Margaret, D.C.V.O.

Pentland, Marjorie Adeline, Baroness, D.B.E.

Pepys, Lady (Mary) Rachel, D.C.V.O.

Perham, Dame Margery Freda, D.C.M.G., C.B.E., D.Litt., F.B.A.

Portland, The Duchess of, D.B.E.

Powell, Dame Muriel Betty, D.B.E.

Railton, *Brig.* Dame Mary, D.B.E.

Railton, Dame Ruth (Mrs. Cecil Harmsworth King), D.B.E.

Rambert, Dame Marie (Mrs. Ashley Dukes), D.B.E.

Rankin, Dame Annabelle Jane Mary, D.B.E.

Rankin, Lady Jean Margaret Florence, D.C.V.O.

Raven, Dame Kathleen Annie (Mrs. J. T. Ingram), D.B.E.

Richmond and Gordon, Hilda Madeleine, Duchess of, D.B.E.

Roberts, Dame Jean, D.B.E.

Robertson, *Commandant* Dame Nancy Margaret, D.B.E.

Robson, Dame Flora McKenzie, D.B.E.

Rosebery, The Countess of, D.B.E.

Rutherford, Dame Margaret Taylor (Mrs. J. B. S. Davis), D.B.E.

Salt, Dame Barbara, D.B.E.

Scarbrough, The Countess of, D.C.V.O.

Scott, Dame Catherine Campbell, D.B.E.

Seymour, Lady Katharine, D.C.V.O.

Shepherd, Dame Margaret Alice, D.B.E.

Smieton, Dame Mary Gullian, D.B.E.

Smith, Dame Enid Mary Russell Russell-, D.B.E.

Smith, *Rt. Hon.* Dame (Margaret) Patricia Hornsby-, D.B.E., M.P.

Snagge, *Air Commandant* Dame Nancy Marion, D.B.E.

Spencer, The Countess, D.C.V.O.

Stephens, *Air Commandant* Dame Anne, D.B.E.

Stevenson, Dame Hilda Mabel D.B.E.

Stewart, Dame Muriel Acadia, D.B.E.

Strickland, Barbara, Lady, D.B.E.

Sutherland, Dame Lucy Stuart, D.B.E., D.Litt.

Tangney, Dame Dorothy Margaret, D.B.E.

Te Ata-I-Rangikaahu, Dame Ariki nui, D.B.E.

Tebbutt, Dame Grace, D.B.E.

Teyte, Dame Maggie (Mrs. Cottingham), D.B.E.

Thorndike, Dame Sybil (Lady Casson), C.H., D.B.E.

Turner, Dame Eva, D.B.E.

Turner, *Brig.* Dame Margot, D.B.E., R.R.C.

Tylecote, Dame Mabel, D.B.E.

Tyrwhitt, *Brigadier* Dame Mary Joan Caroline, D.B.E.

Van Praagh, Dame Margaret (Peggy), D.B.E.

Vaughan, Dame Janet Maria, (Mrs. Gourlay), D.B.E.

Vickers, Dame Joan Helen, D.B.E., M.P.

Wakehurst, Margaret, Lady, D.B.E.

Walwyn, Eileen Mary, Lady, D.B.E.

Ward, Dame Irene Mary Bewick, D.B.E., M.P.

Wedgwood, Dame (Cicely) Veronica, O.M., D.B.E.

Wedgwood, Dame Ivy Evelyn, D.B.E.

Welsh, *Air Chief Commandant* Ruth Mary, Lady, D.B.E.

West, Dame Rebecca (Mrs. Andrews), D.B.E.

Whateley, *Chief Controller* Dame Leslie Violet, D.B.E.

Whyte, *Air Commandant* Dame Roberta Mary, D.B.E., R.R.C.

Williamson, *Air Commandant* Dame Alice Mary, D.B.E., R.R.C., Q.H.N.S.

Winner, Dame Albertine Louise, D.B.E., M.D.

Woollcombe, Dame Jocelyn May, D.B.E.

Wormald, Dame Ethel May, D.B.E.

Yarwood, Dame Elizabeth Ann, D.B.E.

Younghusband, Dame Eileen Louise, D.B.E.

THE VICTORIA CROSS, $V C$

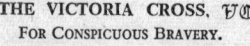

FOR CONSPICUOUS BRAVERY.

The ribbon is *Crimson* for all Services (until 1918 it was *Blue* for Royal Navy).

Instituted on January 29, 1856, the Victoria Cross was awarded retrospectively to 1854, the first being held by Lieut. C. D. Lucas, R.N. for bravery in the Baltic Sea on June 21, 1854, (gazetted Feb. 24, 1857). The first 62 Crosses were presented by Queen Victoria in Hyde Park, London, on June 26, 1857.

The $V C$ is worn before all other decorations, on the left breast, and consists of a cross-pattée of bronze, $1\frac{3}{8}$ inches in diameter, with the Royal Crown surmounted by a lion in the centre, and beneath there is the inscription "For Valour." Holders of the $V C$ receive a tax-free annuity of £100, irrespective of need or other conditions. In 1911, the right to receive the Cross was extendnded to Indian soldiers, and in 1920 a Royal Warrant extended the right to Matrons, Sisters and Nurses, and the Staff of the Nursing Services and other services pertaining to Hospitals and Nursing, and to Civilians of either sex regularly or temporarily under the orders, direction or supervision of the Naval, Military, or Air Forces of the Crown.

Surviving Recipients of the Victoria Cross

Adlam, *Lt.-Col.* T. E. (Bedf. R.), *Gt. War* .. 1916

Agansing Rai, *Havildar* (Gurkha Rifles), *World War* 1944

Ali Haidar, *Sepoy* (Frontier Force Rifles), *World War* 1945

Anderson, *Lt.-Col.* C. G. W., M.C. (Australian M.F.), *World War* 1942

Annand, *Capt.* R. W. (Durham L.I.), *World War* 1940

Axford, *Corpl.* T. L., M.M. (A.I.F.), *Gt. War* 1918

Barrett, *Col.* John C. (R. Leic. R.), *Gt. War* .. 1918
Bassett, *Col.* Cyril R. G. (N.Z.), *Gt. War* .. 1915
Beattie, *Capt.* S. H. (R.N.), *World War*..... 1942
Bent, *R.-S.-M.* S. J. (East Lancs. R.), *Gt. War* 1914
Bhanbhagta Gurung, *Lance-Naik* (2nd Gurkha Rifles), *World War*...................... 1945
Bhandari Ram, *Lance-Naik* (Baluch R.), *World War*................................ 1944
Brereton, *C.-S.-M.* A. (Manitoba R.), *Gt. War*................................ 1918
Burman, *Sergt.* W. F. (Rif. Bgde.), *Gt. War* 1917
Burton, *Corpl.* R. H. (Duke of Wellington's R.), *World War*...................... 1944
Butler, *Pte.* Wm. B. (W. Yorks. R.), *Gt. War* 1917
Cain, *Maj.* R. H. (R. Northumberland Fus.), *World War*........................... 1944
Campbell, *Brigadier* L. M., D.S.O., O.B.E., T.D. (A. & S. Highrs.), *World War* 1943
Carmichael, *Sergt.* J. (N. Staff. R.), *Gt. War* 1917
Carne, *Col.* J. P., D.S.O. (Glos. R.), *Korea*... 1951
Carroll, *Pte.* John (Aus. Inf.), *Gt. War*...... 1918
Cartwright, *Pte.* George (Aust.), *Gt. War*... 1918
Chapman, *Sergt.* E. T. (Monmouthshire R.), *World War*............................ 1945
Cheshire, *Group Capt.* G. L., D.S.O., D.F.C. (R.A.F.), *World War*................... 1944
Christian, *Pte.* H. (K. O. Royal R.), *Gt. War*.. 1915
Cloutman, His Honour Sir Brett M., M.C., Q.C. (R.E.), *Gt. War*.................. 1918
Coltman, *Capt.* William H., D.C.M., M.M. (N. Staff. R.), *Gt. War*.............. 1918
Cooper, *Lt.* E. (K.R.R.C.), *Gt. War*........ 1917
Cruickshank, *Fl. Lt.* J. A. (R.A.F.V.R.), *World War*........................... 1944
Crutchley, *Admiral* Sir Victor Alexander, K.C.B., D.S.C. (R.N.), *Gt. War*.......... 1918
Currie, *Maj.* D. V., C.B.E. (S. Alberta R., Canada), *World War*................... 1944
Cutler, Sir A. R., K.C.M.G., K.C.V.O., C.B.E. (Australia) *World War*................. 1941
Davies, *Sergt.* J. (R. Welch Fus.), *Gt. War*.. 1916
Dean, *Col.* D. J., O.B.E. (R. W. Kent R.), *Gt. War*............................. 1918
De L'Isle, *Maj.* Viscount, K.G., P.C., G.C.M.G., G.C.V.O. (Hon. W. P. Sidney) (Gren. Gds.), *World War*........................... 1944
Dinesen, *Lt.* T. (Roy. Highlanders of Canada), *Gt. War*..................... 1918
Drain, *Sergt.* J. H. C. (R.H.A.), *Gt. War*.... 1914
Dresser, *Pte.* T. (Green Howards), *Gt. War*. 1917
Eardley, *Sergt.* G. H., M.M. (K.S.L.I.), *World War*................................ 1944
Edwards, *Air Commodore* H. I., C.B., D.S.O., O.B.E., D.F.C. (R.A.F.) *World War*...... 1941
Edwards, *Capt.* W. (K.O.Y.L.I.), *Gt. War*.. 1917
Elliott, *Lt.* the Rev. K. (N.Z.M.F.), *World War* 1942
Ervine-Andrews, *Lt.-Col.* H. M. (E. Lancs. R.), *World War*....................... 1940
Foote, *Maj.-Gen.* H. R. B., C.B., D.S.O. (R. Tank R.), *World War*.............. 1942
Foote, *Rev.* J. W. (Canada), *World War* ... 1942
Fraser, *Cdr.* I. E., D.S.C. (R.N.R.), *World War* 1945
Frickleton, *Capt.* Samuel (N.Z.), *Gt. War*... 1917
Fuller, *Sgt.* W. (Welch Regt.), *Gt. War*... 1914
Ganju Lama, *Jemadar*, M.M. (Gurkha Rifles), *World War*....................... 1944
Gardner, *Capt.* P. J., M.C. (R.T.R.), *World War*............................... 1941
Garforth, *Sergt.* C. E. (15th Hrs.), *Gt. War*.. 1914
Geary, *Rev.* B. H., C.F. (E. Surr. R.), *Gt. War* 1915
Ghale, *Subedar* Gaje (Gurkha Rif.), *Wld. War* 1943
Gian Singh, *Jemadar* (Punjab R.), *World War*. 1945
Gordon, *W.O. II* J. H. (Australia), *World War* 1941
Gould, *Lt.* T. W. (R.N.), *World War* 1942

Gourley, *2nd Lt.* C. E., M.M. (R.F.A.), *Gt. War*............................... 1917
Graham, *Lt.-Col.* Sir Reginald, Bt., O.B.E. (M.G.C.), *Gt. War*.................. 1917
Greaves, *Sergt.* Fred. (Sherwood F.), *Gt. War* 1917
Gregg, *Brig.* Hon. Milton F., C.B.E., M.C. (Nova Scotia R.), *Gt. War*............ 1918
Grimshaw, *Lt.-Col.* John (Lanc. Fus.), *Gt. War* 1915
Haine, *Lt.-Col.* R. L. M.C. (H.A.C.), *Gt. War* 1917
Hall, *Sergt.* Arthur (Australia), *Gt. War* .. 1918
Halton, *Pte.* A. (K. O. Royal R.), *Gt. War* .. 1917
Hamilton, *Lt.* I. B. (H.L.I.), *Gt. War* 1917
Harvey, *Brig.* F. M. W., M.C. (Can. Inf.), *Gt. War*............................. 1917
Hinton, *Sergt.* J. D. (N.Z.M.F.), *World War*.. 1941
Holbrook, *Com.* N. D. (R.N.), *Gt. War*.... 1914
Holland, *Capt.* John V. (Leinster R.), *Gt. War* 1916
Hollis, *C.S.M.* S. E. (Green Howards), *World War*................................ 1944
Hulme, *Sergt.* A. C. (N.Z.M.F.), *World War* .. 1941
Hutchinson, *Corpl.* J. (Lanc. Fus.), *Gt. War* ... 1916
Insall, *Group Capt.* Gilbert S. M., M.C. (R.A.F.), *Gt. War*..................... 1915
Inwood, *Corpl.* R. R. (Aust. Imp. Fce.), *Gt. War*............................. 1917
Jackson, *W.O.* N. C. (R.A.F.V.R.), *Wld. War* 1944
James, *Brig.* Manley Angell, D.S.O., M.B.E., M.C. (Glouc. R.), *Gt. War*............ 1918
Jamieson, *Maj.* D. A. (R. Norfolk R.), *World War*............................ 1944
Jefferson, *L.-Corpl.* F. A. (Lancs. Fus.), *Wld. War*................................ 1944
Johnson, *Maj.-Gen.* Dudley G., C.B., D.S.O., M.C. (S. Wales B.), *Gt. War*.......... 1918
Joynt, *Lt.-Col.* W. D. (Aust. I. F.), *Gt. War*.. 1918
Judson, *Capt.* Reginald Stanley, D.C.M., M.M. (Auckland R., N.Z.), *Gt. War*......... 1918
Kamal Ram, *Havildar* (Punjab R.), *Wld. War* 1944
Karanbahadur Rama, *Naik* (Gurkha Rifles), *Gt. War*............................ 1918
Kenna, *Pte.* E. (Australian M.F.), *Wld. War* 1945
Kenneally, *C.-Q.-M.-S.* J. P. (Irish Gds.), *Wld. War*................................ 1943
Kenny, *Pte.* H. E. (Loyal R.), *Gt. War* 1916
Lachiman Gurung, *Rifleman* (Gurkha Rifles), *World War*....................... 1945
Lauder, *Pte.* D. R. (R. Scots Fus.), *Gt. War* 1915
Laurent, *Lt.* H. J. (N.Z. Rif. Bgde.), *Gt. War* 1918
Leak, *Pte.* John (Australia), *Gt. War* 1916
Learoyd, *Wing-Cmdr.* R. A. B. (R.A.F.), *World War*.......................... 1940
Le Patourel, *Col.* H. W. (R. Hampshire R.), *World War*......................... 1942
Lewis, *Pte.* H. W. (Welch R.), *Gt. War*.... 1916
Luke, *Sergt.* F. (R.H.A.), *Gt. War*.......... 1914
McCarthy, *Lt.* L. D. (Aust.), *Gt. War*...... 1918
McNally, *Sergt.* William, M.M. (Green Howards), *Gt. War*.................. 1918
Magennis, *L/S* J. J. (R.N.), *World War*..... 1945
Mahony, *Lt.-Col.* J. K. (Westminster R., Canada), *World War*.................. 1944
Malleson, *Com.* W. St. A. (R.N.), *Gt. War* .. 1915
Martin, *Brig.* C. G., C.B.E., D.S.O. (R.E.), *Gt. War*............................. 1915
Merritt, *Lt.-Col.* C. C. I. (S. Saskatchewan R.), *World War*.................... 1942
Miers, *Rear-Adm.* Sir A. C. C., K.B.E., C.B., D.S.O. (R.N.), *World War*........... 1942
Mitchell, *Lt.-Col.* Coulson N., M.C. (Canad. Engrs.), *Gt. War*................ 1918
Molyneux, *Sergt.* John (R. Fus.), *Gt. War* ... 1917
Moon. *Lt.* Rupert V. (Aust. Inf.), *Gt. War*.. 1917
Moyney, *Sergt.* John (Irish Gds.), *Gt. War*... 1917
Myles, *Capt.* E. K., D.S.O. (Worc. R.), *Gt. War* 1916

Namdeo Jadhao, *Havildar* (Mahratta L. I.), *World War* 1945

Neame, *Lt.-Gen.* Sir Philip, K.B.E., C.B., D.S.O. (R.E.), *Gt. War* 1914

Newman, *Lt.-Col.* A. C., O.B.E., T.D. (Essex R.), *World War* 1942

Nicholls, *L.-Cpl.* H. (G. Gds.), *World War* .. 1940

Norton, *Capt.* G. R., M.M. (S.A.M.F.), *World War* 1944

Parkash Singh, *Capt.* (Punjab R.), *World War* 1943

Payne, *W.O.* K. (Australian Army), *Vietnam* 1969

Pearkes, *Maj.-Gen. Hon.* George Randolph, C.B., D.S.O., M.C. (Can. Ind.), *Gt. War* 1917

Place, *Rear-Adm.* B. C. G., C.B., D.S.C. (R.N.) *World War* 1943

Porteous, *Brig.* P. A. (R.A.), *World War* 1942

Premindra Singh Bhagat, *Capt.* (Corps. of Ind. Engineers), *World War* 1941

Procter, Rev. A. H. (King's R.), *Gt. War* 1915

Rambahadur Limbu, *L/Corpl.* (Gurkha Rifles), *Sarawak* 1965

Ratcliffe, *Pte.* W., M.M. (S. Lanc. R.), *Gt. War* 1917

Rattey, *Sergt.* R. R. (Australia), *World War* . 1945

Reid, *Fl.-Lt.* W. (R.A.F.V.R.), *World War* .. 1943

Roberts, *Maj.-Gen.* F. C., D.S.O., O.B.E., M.C. (Worc. R.), *Gt. War* 1918

Roberts, *Lt.-Com.* P. S. W., D.S.C. (R.N.), *World War* 1942

Roupell, *Brig.* G. R. P., C.B. (E. Surrey R.), *Gt. War* 1915

Rutherford, *Capt.* C. B., M.C., M.M. (Quebec R.), *Gt. War* 1918

Ryder, *Sergt.* Robert (Middx. R.), *Gt. War* 1916

Ryder, *Capt.* R. E. D. (R.N.), *World War* 1942

Sherbrooke, *Rear-Adm.* R. St. V., C.B., D.S.O. (R.N.), *World War* 1942

Simpson, *W.O.* R. S., D.C.M. (Australian Army), *Vietnam* 1969

Smith, *Sergt.* E. A. (Seaforth Highrs. of Canada), *World War* 1944

Smyth, *Brig.* Rt. Hon. Sir J. G., Bt., M.C., (Ludhiana Sikhs), *Gt. War* 1915

Smythe. *Lt.* Q. G. M. (S.A.M.F.), *Wld. War* 1942

Speakman, *Sergt.* W. (Black Watch), *Korea*.. 1951

Stannard, *Capt.* R. B., D.S.O., R.D. (R.N.R.), *World War* 1940

Starcevich, *Pte.* L. T. (Australia), *World War*. 1945

Steele, *Com.* G. C. (R.N.), *Gt. War* 1919

Steele, *Sergt.* T. (Seaforth H.), *Gt. War* 1917

Strachan, *Maj.* H., M.C. (Can. Cav.), *Gt. War* 1917

Tandey, *L/Corpl.* H., D.C.M., M.M. (W. Riding R.), *Gt. War* 1918

Tilston, *Maj.* F. A. (Essex Scottish, Canada), *World War* 1945

Topham, *Corpl.* F. G. (1st Canadian Parachute Bn.), *World War* 1945

Towers, *Pte*.James (Cameronians), *Gt. War* 1918

Towner, *Maj.* Edgar Thomas, M.C. (Aust. M.G.C.), *Gt. War* 1918

Trent, *Group Capt.* L. H., D.F.C. (R.N.Z.A.F.), *World War* 1943

Triquet, *Brig.* P. (R. 22R. of Canada), *World War* 1943

Tulbahadur Pun, *W.O.I.* (Gurkha Rifles), *World War* 1944

Turner, *Lt.-Col.* V. B., C.V.O. (R.B.), *World War* 1942

Umrao Singh, *Havildar* (I.A.), *World War*... 1944

Upham, *Capt.* C. H. (and Bar, 1942), (N.Z.M.F.) *World War* 1941

Veale, *Corpl.* T. W. H. (Devon R.), *Gt. War* 1916

Vickers, *Capt.* Sir C. Geoffrey (Sherwood For.), *Gt. War* 1915

Wakeford, *Maj.* R. (R. Hampshire R.), *World War* 1944

Waters, *Maj.* Sir Arnold, C.B.E., D.S.O., M.C. (R.E.), *Gt. War* 1918

Watkins, *Maj. Hon.* Sir Tasker (Welch R.), *World War* 1944

Welch, *Sgt.* J. (R. Berk. R.), *Gt. War* 1917

West, *Air Commodore* Ferdinand M. F., C.B.E., M.C. (R.A.F.), *Gt. War* 1918

White, *Lt.* Wm. A. (M. Gds Corps), *Gt. War* 1918

Wilson, *Lt.-Col.* E. C. T. (E. Surrey R.), *World War* 1940

Wood, *Pte.* W. (R. Northd. Fus.), *Gt. War*. 1918

Wright, *C.S.M.* P. H. (Coldstream Gds.), *World War* 1943

Zengel. *Sergt.* Raphael L., M.M. (Saskatchewan R.), *Gt. War* 1918

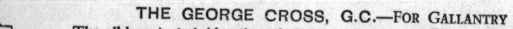

THE GEORGE CROSS, G.C.—FOR GALLANTRY

The ribbon is *dark blue* threaded through a bar adorned with laurel leaves.

INSTITUTED *September 24th, 1940* (with amendments, *November 3, 1942*).

The George Cross is worn before all other decorations (except the V.C.) on the left breast § and consists of a plain silver cross with four equal limbs, the cross having in the centre a circular medallion bearing a design showing St. George and the Dragon. The inscription "For Gallantry" appears round the medallion and in the angle of each limb of the cross is the Royal cypher "G VI" forming a circle concentric with the medallion. The reverse is plain and bears the name of the recipient and the date of the award. The cross is suspended by a ring from a bar adorned with laurel leaves on dark blue ribbon 1½ inches wide.

The cross is intended primarily for civilians and awards to the fighting services are confined to actions for which purely military honours are not normally granted. It is awarded only for acts of the greatest heroism or of the most conspicuous courage in circumstances of extreme danger. From April 1, 1965, holders of the Cross have received a tax-free annuity of £100.

§ When worn by a woman it may be worn on the left shoulder from a ribbon of the same width and colour fashioned into a bow.

Empire Gallantry Medal.—The Royal Warrant which ordained that the grant of the Empire Gallantry Medal should cease authorized holders of that medal to return it to the Central Chancery of the Orders of Knighthood and to receive in exchange the George Cross. A similar provision applied to posthumous awards of the Empire Gallantry Medal made after the outbreak of war in 1939.

THE DISTINGUISHED SERVICE ORDER (1886)—D.S.O.

Ribbon, Red, with Blue Edges.

Bestowed in recognition of especial services in action of commissioned officers in the Navy, Army and Royal Air Force and (1942) Mercantile Marine. The members are Companions only and rank immediately before the 4th Class of the Royal Victorian Order. A Bar may be awarded for any additional act of service.

PRINCIPAL DECORATIONS AND MEDALS (in order of Precedence)

Victoria Cross.—1856.—V.C.
George Cross.—1940.—G.C.
British Orders of Knighthood.
Royal Red Cross.—1883—R.R.C. (Class I.).—For ladies.
Distinguished Service Cross.—1914.—D.S.C.—In substitution for the Conspicuous Service Cross, 1901; is for officers of R.N. below the rank of Captain, and Warrant Officers.
Military Cross.—Dec. 1914.—M.C.—Awarded to Captains, Lieutenants, and Warrant Officers (Cl I. and II.) in the Army and Indian and Colonial Forces.
Distinguished Flying Cross.—1918.—D.F.C.—For bestowal upon Officers and Warrant Officers in the Royal Air Force (and Fleet Air Arm from April 9, 1941) for acts of gallantry when flying in active operations against the enemy.
Air Force Cross.—1918.—A.F.C.—Instituted as preceding but for acts of courage or devotion to duty when flying, although not in active operations against the enemy (extended to Fleet Air Arm since April 9, 1941).
Royal Red Cross (Class II—A.R.R.C.).
Order of British India.
Kaisar-i-Hind Medal.
Order of St. John.
Albert Medal.—1866—A.M.—" For Gallantry in Saving Life at Sea " or " on Land." (Holders receive £100 tax-free annuity).
Union of South Africa Queen's Medal for Bravery, in Gold.
Medal for Distinguished Conduct in the Field.—1854.—D.C.M.—Awarded to warrant officers, non-commissioned officers and men of the Army and R.A.F.
Conspicuous Gallantry Medal.—1874.—C.G.M.—Is bestowed upon warrant officers and men of the R.N. and since 1942 of Mercantile Marine and R.A.F.
The George Medal.—G.M.—Established by King George VI in 1940 is a recognition of acts of gallantry.
The Edward Medal.—1907—In recognition of heroic acts by miners and quarrymen, or of others who have endangered their lives in rescuing those so employed. (Holders receive £100 tax-free annuity).
Royal West African Frontier Force Distinguished Conduct Medal.
King's African Rifles Distinguished Conduct Medal.
Union of South Africa Queen's Medal for Bravery in Silver.
Distinguished Service Medal.—1914.—D.S.M.—For chief petty officers, petty officers, men, and boys of all branches of the Royal Navy, and since 1942 of Mercantile Marine, to non-commissioned officers and men of the Royal Marines, and to all other persons holding corresponding positions in Her Majesty's Service afloat.
Military Medal.—1916.—M.M.—For warrant and non-commissioned officers and men and serving women.
Distinguished Flying Medal.—1918.—D.F.M.—and the Air Force Medal.—A.F.M.—for warrant and non-commissioned officers and men for equivalent services as for D.F.C. and A.F.C. (extended to Fleet Air Arm, April 9, 1941).
Constabulary Medal (Ireland).
Medal for Saving Life at Sea.
Colonial Police Medal for Gallantry.
British Empire Medal.—B.E.M.—(formerly the Medal of the Order of the British Empire, for Meritorious Service; also includes the Medal of the Order awarded before Dec. 29, 1922).
Canada Medal.
Queens' Police (Q.P.M.) and Fire Services Medals for Distinguished Service, (Q.F.S.M.).
Queen's Medal for Chiefs.

War Medals and Stars (in order of date).
Polar Medals (in order of date).
Royal Victorian Medal (Gold, Silver and Bronze).
Imperial Service Medal.
Police Medals for Valuable Service.
Badge of Honour.
Jubilee, Coronation and Durbar Medals.
King George V, King George VI and Queen Elizabeth II.
Long and Faithful Service Medals.
Long Service and Good Conduct Medal.
Naval Long Service and Good Conduct Medal.
Medal for Meritorious Service.
Royal Marine Meritorious Service Medal.
Royal Air Force Meritorious Service Medal.
Royal Air Force Long Service and Good Conduct Medal.
Royal West African Frontier Force Long Service and Good Conduct Medal.
King's African Rifles Long Service and Good Conduct Medal.
Police and Fire Brigade Long Service and Good Conduct Medal.
Colonial Police and Fire Brigades Long Service Medal.
Colonial Prison Service Medal.
Army Emergency Reserve Decoration.
Volunteer Officers' Decoration.—V.D.
Volunteer Long Service Medal.
Volunteer Officers' Decoration (for India and the Colonies).
Volunteer Long Service Medal (for India and the Colonies).
Colonial Auxiliary Forces Long Service Medal.
Medal for Good Shooting (Naval).
Militia Long Service Medal.
Imperial Yeomanry Long Service Medal.
Territorial Decoration.—1908.—T.D.
Efficiency Decoration.—E.D.
Territorial Efficiency Medal.
Efficiency Medal.
Special Reserve Long Service and Good Conduct Medal.
Decoration for Officers, Royal Naval Reserve.—1910.—R.D.
Decoration for Officers, R.N.V.R.—V.R.D.
Royal Naval Reserve Long Service and Good Conduct Medal.
R.N.V.R. Long Service and Good Conduct Medal.
Royal Naval Auxiliary Sick Berth Reserve Long Service and Good Conduct Medal.
Royal Fleet Reserve Long Service and Good Conduct Medal.
Royal Naval Wireless Auxiliary Reserve Long Service and Good Conduct Medal.
Air Efficiency Award.—1942.
The Queen's Medal.—(For Champion Shots in the Army, Territorial Army and R.A.F.)
Cadet Forces Medal.—1950.
Coast Life Saving Corps Long Service Medal.—1911.
Special Constabulary Long Service Medal.
Royal Observer Corps Medal.
Civil Defence Long Service Medal.
Service Medal of the Order of St. John.
Badge of the Order of the League of Mercy.
Voluntary Medical Service Medal.—1932.
Women's Royal Voluntary Service Medal.
Colonial Special Constabulary Medal.
Foreign Orders, Decorations and Medals (in order of date).

THE ORDER OF ST. JOHN (1888)

The Most Venerable Order of the Hospital of St. John of Jerusalem

St. John's Gate, Clerkenwell, E.C.1

Grand Prior, H.R.H. the Duke of Gloucester, K.G.

The Order derives from the ancient Order of Knights Hospitaller founded in Jerusalem after the successful completion of the First Crusade in 1099. Vowed to the relief of sickness and distress without distinction of race, class or creed, the Knights maintained a Hospice for the care of the sick and were an important military body within the Kingdom of Jerusalem. After the loss of the Holy Land the Order became a Sovereign Body in Rhodes and later in Malta. In Britain its properties were sequestrated at the Dissolution of the Monasteries but a branch of the Order was revived in England after the Napoleonic Wars. This was granted a Royal Charter by Queen Victoria in 1888 as a separate, British, Order of St. John. The Queen is the Sovereign Head and since 1888 the Grand Prior has been a member of the Royal Family. The Badge is a white eight-pointed cross, embellished in the four principal angles with a lion and a unicorn; the riband is of black watered silk. The work of the Order consists of the maintenance of two Foundations—The Ophthalmic Hospital in Jerusalem (founded 1882) and The St. John Ambulance Association and Brigade, 1 Grosvenor Crescent, S.W.1, which is concerned with education in First Aid and kindred subjects and provides a body of trained and uniformed volunteers for attendance on the public where the rendering of First Aid may be required.

Lord Prior, The Lord Caccia, G.C.M.G., G.C.V.O.   *Chancellor*, Sir Gilbert Inglefield, G.B.E., T.D.

THE EXECUTIVE

The Crown (the Queen in Council) "makes peace and war, issues charters, increases the peerage, is the fountain of honour, of office, and of justice." The Sovereign entrusts the executive power to Ministers of the Crown, appointed on the advice of the accredited leader of the party in Parliament which enjoys, or can secure, a majority of votes in the House of Commons.

The Cabinet

The Cabinet has no corporate existence, but under the *Ministers of the Crown Act* (1937), provision was made for 17 Ministers of the first rank (Cabinet Ministers) and this number has been increased by later legislation. The *Ministers of the Crown (Parliamentary Secretaries) Act* (1960) laid down an aggregate limit of 33 Parliamentary Secretaries. Parts of these Acts were repealed by the *Ministers of the Crown Act* (1964) which varied the number of Parliamentary Secretaries (other than Treasury Secretaries) to 36.

The Prime Minister

The Prime Minister is appointed by the Sovereign. When a party is in opposition and its leadership becomes vacant it makes its free choice among the various personalities available; but if the party is in office, the Sovereign's choice may anticipate, and in a certain sense forestall, the decision of the party. In 1905 the office of Prime Minister, which had been in existence for nearly 200 years, was officially recognized and its holder was granted a place in the Table of Precedence.

The Leader of the Opposition

In 1937 the office of Leader of the Opposition was similarly recognized and a salary of £2,000 per annum was assigned to the post, thus following a practice which had prevailed in the Dominion of Canada since 1906. In 1957 the salary was increased to £3,000, and in 1965 to £4,500. The present Leader of the Opposition is the Right Hon. Harold Wilson.

LEGISLATION

Legislation is initiated in the Houses of Parliament in the form of Bills. Public Bills are of two kinds, those introduced by the Government of the day, and those introduced by a private member. A Bill (except a Money Bill, which must originate in the House of Commons) can be introduced in either House and when presented receives its *First Reading*, after which it is printed and circulated to members. The next stage is the *Second Reading*, in the debate on which the broad issues raised are discussed. If passed it reaches the *Committee Stage* and is referred to a Committee (of the whole House, Select, or Standing—*see* "Committees," pp. 310–311). Bills of major importance are usually sent to a Committee of the whole House. In committee, a Bill is discussed clause by clause, and is returned to the House with or without amendment. A Private Bill, which is introduced to enable an individual or a body corporate to acquire or vary certain powers, is referred to a *Select Committee*, and if opposed, witnesses may be called and counsel heard by the Committee. The next step is the *Report Stage*, when the Bill is accepted by the House, or sent back to the same, or sent back to another, Committee for further consideration. Finally the Bill receives its *Third Reading* (during which, in the House of Commons, only verbal amendments are permissible) and is sent to the other House. When a Bill has been passed by both Houses it becomes an *Act of Parliament*, on receiving the *Royal Assent*, which is signified by the Sovereign on the Throne, or by Commissioners (normally three Peers), in the Chamber of the House of Lords. The power to withhold assent (colloquially known as the *Royal Veto*) resides in the Sovereign, but has not been exercised in the United Kingdom since 1707, in the reign of Queen Anne.

COUNCILLORS OF STATE

On every occasion that the Sovereign leaves the realm for distant parts of the Commonwealth or a foreign country, it is necessary to appoint Councillors of State under Letters Patent to carry out the chief functions of the monarch, including the holding of Privy Councils and the signature of Acts passed by Parliament. The normal procedure is to appoint as Councillors three or four members of the Royal Family among those remaining in the United Kingdom. For instance, during the Queen's visit to Canada in 1967, the Councillors of State were the Prince of Wales, Queen Elizabeth the Queen Mother, Princess Margaret and the Duke of Gloucester.

In the event of the Sovereign on accession being under the age of eighteen years or at any time unavailable or incapacitated by infirmity of mind or body for the performance of the royal functions, provision is made for a Regency. Since the Prince of Wales attained the age of 18 in November 1966, the provisions of the Regency Act as to age no longer apply in the event of his accession to the throne.

SPEAKERS OF THE COMMONS SINCE 1660

PARLIAMENT OF ENGLAND.

1660	Sir H. Grimston.	1685	Sir John Trevor.
1661	Sir E. Turner.	1688	H. Powle.
1673	Sir J. Charlton.	1694	Paul Foley.
1673	Edwd. Seymour.	1698	Sir T. Lyttelton.
1678	Sir Robt. Sawyer.	1700	Robert Harley
1679	Serjeant William		(*Earl of Oxford*
	Gregory.		*and Mortimer*).
1680	W. Williams.	1702	John Smith.

PARLIAMENT OF GREAT BRITAIN

1708	Sir Richard Onslow (*Lord Onslow*).	1761	Sir John Cust.
		1770	Sir F. Norton.
		1780	C. W. Cornwall.
1710	Wm. Bromley.	1788	Hon. W. Grenville
1713	Sir Th. Hanmer.		(*Lord Grenville*).
1715	Spencer Compton (*Earl of Wilmington*).	1789	Henry Addington (*Viscount Sidmouth*).
1727	Arthur Onslow.		

PARLIAMENT OF UNITED KINGDOM

1801	Sir John Mitford (*Lord Redesdale*).
1802	Charles Abbot (*Lord Colchester*).
1817	Charles M. Sutton (*Viscount Canterbury*).
1835	James Abercromby (*Lord Dunfermline*).
1839	Charles Shaw-Lefevre (*Viscount Eversley*).
1857	J. Evelyn Denison (*Viscount Ossington*).
1872	Sir Henry Brand (*Viscount Hampden*).
1884	Arthur Wellesley Peel (*Viscount Peel*).
1895	William Court Gully (*Viscount Selby*).
1905	James W. Lowther (*Viscount Ullswater*).
1921	John Henry Whitley.
1928	Hon. Edward Algernon FitzRoy.
1943	Col. D. Clifton Brown (*Viscount Ruffside*).
1951	William Shepherd Morrison (*Viscount Dunrossil*).
1959	Sir Harry Hylton-Foster.
1965	Horace Maybray King, ph.d. (*Lord Maybray-King*).
1971	(John) Selwyn (Brooke) Lloyd.

THE HOUSES OF PARLIAMENT

Parliament emerged during the late thirteenth and early fourteenth centuries as a result of diverse forces including the general need for a superior court to deal with legal and administrative problems on a national basis, ambition of the baronage to influence the King's government, and the King's desire to make his government more effective by involving in it all important sections of the community. The nucleus of early Parliaments were the officers of the King's household and the King's judges, who were joined by such ecclesiastical and lay magnates as the King might summon and occasionally by the knights of the shire, burghers and proctors of the lower clergy. The Commons were summoned to all the Parliaments of Edward III and by the end of the reign a "House of Commons" was beginning to appear. The first known Speaker was elected in 1377.

The House of Lords is the ultimate Court of Appeal for all Courts in Great Britain and Northern Ireland, except for criminal cases in Scotland. The Lords surrendered the ancient right of peers to be tried for treason or felony by their peers in 1948. Each House has the right to control its own internal proceedings and to commit for contempt.

The Commons claim exclusive control in respect of national taxation and expenditure and in respect of local rates and charges upon them. Bills such as the Finance Bill, which imposes taxation, and the Consolidated Fund Bills, which authorize expenditure, and are commonly known as Supply Bills, must begin in the Commons and have not been amended by the Lords in any respect in modern times. A bill of which the financial provisions are subsidiary may begin in the Lords; and the Commons may waive their rights in regard to Lords amendments affecting finance.

Normally a bill must be agreed to by both Houses before it receives the Royal Assent, but under the Parliament Acts, 1911 and 1949—(*a*) a bill which the Speaker has certified as a Money Bill, *i.e.* as concerned solely with national taxation, expenditure or borrowing, if not agreed to by the Lords within one month of its being sent to them, receives the Royal Assent and becomes law without their concurrence: (*b*) any other public bill (except one to extend the life of a Parliament) which has been passed by the Commons in two successive sessions and twice rejected by the Lords, receives the Royal Assent and becomes law, provided that one year has elapsed between its Second Reading in the first session and its Third Reading in the second session in the Commons.

The Parliament Act of 1911 also limited the duration of Parliament, if not previously dissolved, to 5 years. The term is reckoned from the date given on the writs for the new Parliament. During the War of 1914–18 the duration of Parliament was extended by successive Acts from 5 to 8 years, but a General Election was held before the end of the term finally prescribed and the Parliament which first met on Jan. 31, 1911, was dissolved on Nov. 25, 1918, fourteen days after the Armistice. At the outbreak of war in 1939 a similar course was followed and Parliament which first met on Nov. 26, 1935, was not dissolved until June 15, 1945.

The longest recorded sitting of the House of Commons is 41 hours 30 minutes (from 4 p.m., Jan. 31 to 9.30 a.m. Feb. 2, 1881), that of the House of Lords is 19 hrs. 16 minutes (from 2.30 p.m. to 9.46 a.m. Feb. 29–Mar. 1, 1968).

Since 1803 reports of the proceedings of Parliament in open session have been published. From 1803–1888 these were known as *Hansard's Parliamentary Debates*, and in 1943 the word " Hansard " was restored to the title page. Copies are obtainable from H.M. Stationery Office and periodical issues are on sale throughout the country.

Payment of Members.—Members of the House of Lords are unpaid. They are entitled to re-imbursement of travelling expenses from their residence to the House in respect of regular attendance and repayment of expenses within a maximum of £6 10s. for each day of such attendance.

Since 1911 Members of the House of Commons have received payments and travelling facilities. Their salary of £400 was increased to £600 in 1937, to £1,000 in 1947, to £1,750 in 1957 and to £3,250 in October 1964; they are entitled to claim income tax relief on expenses incurred in the course of their Parliamentary duties. Since October 1969 Members have been allowed £500 a year for secretarial expenses. The Members' Pensions Act, 1965, introduced the first comprehensive pension scheme providing Members of Parliament and their dependants with a legal right to a pension. Members contribute £150 per annum and the Exchequer an amount equal to the aggregate of the Members' contributions. Members receive pensions from age 65 or on ceasing to be a Member if later, provided they have served for 10 years or more. The pension, £720 per annum for 10 years' service, increases to £1,080 after 15 years' service and by £28·80 for each further year thereafter. Members re-elected at the 1964 General Election would be able to count up 10 years' service before that date on a non-contributory basis. Members also continue to contribute £24 per annum and the Treasury up to £22,000 a year towards a Fund to provide annual or lump sum grants to ex-Members, their widows and children whose incomes are below certain limits. The income of the Fund in 1969–70 was £44,186 and expenditure on grants £30,654. The capital account stood in 1970 at £187,116.

THE HOUSE OF LORDS

The House of Lords consists of some 1,060 Lords Spiritual and Temporal. The Lords Spiritual are the two Archbishops, the Bishops of London, Durham and Winchester, and the 21 senior Bishops from the remaining English sees. The Lords Temporal are: Peers and Peeresses by descent of England, Scotland, Great Britain or the United Kingdom, peers of new creation, Lords of Appeal in Ordinary (who are life peers), Peeresses in their own right, and Life Peers and Life Peeresses created under the Life Peerages Act, 1958. An Irish Peer not in the House of Lords is eligible for election as a member of the House of Commons, and unlike Peers who are members of the House of Lords, to vote in parliamentary elections. Under the Peerage Act, 1963, a person inheriting a peerage may within one year (or one month in the case of a Member of the House of Commons) disclaim the peerage for life. The subsequent descent of the peerage after his death is not affected.

THE HOUSE OF COMMONS

By the *Representation of the People Act* (1885) membership was increased from 658 (at which it had stood since 1801 through the *Act of Union with Ireland*) to 670, and by a similar Act (1918) it was increased to 707. By the *Government of Ireland Act* (1920) and the *Irish Free State Agreement Act* (1922) membership was decreased to 615. Irish

representation being reduced from 105 to 13 members. By the *Representation of the People Act* of 1945 25 new constituencies were created, making the total 640; and by a similar Act of 1948 the total membership was reduced to 625. As the result of Orders in Council made in 1955 under the *House of Commons (Redistribution of Seats) Act*, 1949, the total membership was increased to 630 and under the same Act provision was made in 1970 for further increase to 635.

THE PALACE OF WESTMINSTER

An ordinance issued in the reign of Richard II stated that "Parliament shall be holden or kepid wheresoever it pleaseth the King" and at the present day the Sovereign summons parliament to meet and prescribes the time and place of meeting. The royal palace at Westminster, originally built by Edward the Confessor (Westminster Hall being added by William Rufus) was the normal place of Parliament from about 1340. St. Stephen's Chapel (first mentioned in the reign of John) was used from about 1550 for the meetings of the House of Commons, which had previously been held in the Chapter House or Refectory of Westminster Abbey. The House of Lords met in an apartment of the royal palace.

The disastrous fire of 1834 destroyed the whole palace, except Westminster Hall, and the present Houses of Parliament were erected on the site from the designs of Sir Charles Barry and Augustus Pugin, between the years 1840 and 1867, at a cost of £2,198,000.

The Chamber of the House of Commons was destroyed by enemy action in 1941 and the foundation stone of a new building, from the designs of Sir Giles Gilbert Scott, was laid by the Speaker on May 26, 1948. The new Chamber was used for the first time on Oct. 26, 1950.

The Victoria Tower of the House of Lords is 330 feet high and when Parliament is sitting the Union Jack flies from sunrise to sunset from its flag-staff. The clock tower of the House of Commons is 316 feet high and contains "Big Ben," the 13½-ton hour bell named after Sir Benjamin Hall, First Commissioner of Works when the original bell was cast in 1856. The dials of the clock are 23 feet in diameter, the hands being 9 feet and 14 feet long (including balance piece). The chimes and strike of "Big Ben" have achieved world-wide fame from broadcasting.

A light is displayed in the clock tower from sundown to sunrise during the hours the House is in session.

THE LORD CHANCELLOR

The Lord High Chancellor of Great Britain is (although not addressed as such) the Speaker of the House of Lords. Unlike the Speaker of the House of Commons, he takes part in debates and votes in divisions. He sits on one of the *Woolsacks*, couches covered with red cloth and stuffed with wool. If the Lord Chancellor wishes to address the House in any way except formally as Speaker, he leaves the Woolsack and steps towards his proper place as a peer, below the Royal Dukes.

PRIME MINISTER'S RESIDENCE

Number 10, Downing Street, S.W.1, is the official town residence of the Prime Minister. No. 11 of the Chancellor of the Exchequer and No. 12 is the office of the Government Whips. The street was named after Sir George Downing, Bt., soldier and diplomatist, who was M.P. for Morpeth from 1660 to 1684.

Chequers, a Tudor mansion in the Chilterns, about 3 miles from Princes Risborough, was presented together with a maintenance endowment by Lord and Lady Lee of Fareham in 1917 to serve, from Jan. 1, 1921, as a country residence for the Prime Minister of the day, the Chequers estate of 700 acres being added to the gift by Lord Lee in 1921. The mansion contains a famous collection of Cromwellian portraits and relics.

PRIME MINISTERS

Sir Robert Walpole, *Whig*, April 3, 1721.
Earl of Wilmington, *Whig*, Feb. 16, 1742.
Henry Pelham, *Whig*, Aug. 25, 1743.
Duke of Newcastle, *Whig*, May 18, 1754.
Duke of Devonshire, *Whig*, Nov. 16, 1756.
Duke of Newcastle, *Whig*, July 2, 1757.
Earl of Bute, *Tory*, May 28, 1762.
George Grenville, *Whig*, April 15, 1763.
Marquess of Rockingham, *Whig*, July 10, 1765.
Earl of Chatham, *Whig*, Aug. 2, 1766.
Duke of Grafton, *Whig*, Dec. 1767.
Lord North, *Tory*, Feb. 6, 1770.
Marquess of Rockingham, *Whig*, March 27, 1782.
Earl of Shelburne, *Whig*, July 13, 1782.
Duke of Portland, *Coalition*, April 4, 1783.
William Pitt, *Tory*, Dec. 7, 1783.
Henry Addington, *Tory*, March 21, 1801.
William Pitt, *Tory*, May 16, 1804.
Lord Grenville, *Whig*, Feb. 10, 1806.
Duke of Portland, *Tory*, March 31, 1807.
Spencer Perceval, *Tory*, Dec. 6, 1809.
Earl of Liverpool, *Tory*, June 16, 1812.
George Canning, *Tory*, April 30, 1827.
Viscount Goderich, *Tory*, Sept. 8, 1827.
Duke of Wellington, *Tory*, Jan. 26, 1828.
Earl Grey, *Whig*, Nov. 24, 1830.
Viscount Melbourne, *Whig*, July 13, 1834.
Sir Robert Peel, *Tory*, Dec. 26, 1834.
Viscount Melbourne, *Whig*, March 18, 1835.
Sir Robert Peel, *Tory*, Sept. 6, 1841.
Lord John Russell, *Whig*, July 6, 1846.
Earl of Derby, *Tory*, Feb. 28, 1852.
Earl of Aberdeen, *Peelite*, Dec. 28, 1852.
Viscount Palmerston, *Liberal*, Feb. 10, 1855.
Earl of Derby, *Conservative*, Feb. 25, 1858.
Viscount Palmerston, *Liberal*, June 18, 1859.
Earl Russell, *Liberal*, Nov. 6, 1865.
Earl of Derby, *Conservative*, July 6, 1866.
Benjamin Disraeli, *Conservative*, Feb. 27, 1868.
W. E. Gladstone, *Liberal*, Dec. 9, 1868.
Benjamin Disraeli, *Conservative*, Feb. 21, 1874.
W. E. Gladstone, *Liberal*, April 28, 1880.
Marquess of Salisbury, *Conservative*, June 24, 1885.
W. E. Gladstone, *Liberal*, Feb. 6, 1886.
Marquess of Salisbury, *Conservative*, Aug. 3, 1886.
W. E. Gladstone, *Liberal*, Aug. 18, 1892.
Earl of Rosebery, *Liberal*, March 3, 1894.
Marquess of Salisbury, *Conservative*, July 2, 1895.
A. J. Balfour, *Conservative*, July 12, 1902.
Sir H. Campbell-Bannerman, *Liberal*, Dec. 5, 1905.
H. H. Asquith, *Liberal*, April 8, 1908.
H. H. Asquith, *Coalition*, May 26, 1915.
D. Lloyd-George, *Coalition*, Dec. 7, 1916.
A. Bonar Law, *Conservative*, Oct. 23, 1922.
S. Baldwin, *Conservative*, May 22, 1923.
J. R. MacDonald, *Labour*, Jan. 22, 1924.
S. Baldwin, *Conservative*, Nov. 4, 1924.
J. R. MacDonald, *Labour*, June 8, 1929.
J. R. MacDonald, *Coalition*, Aug. 25, 1931.
S. Baldwin, *Coalition*, June 7, 1935.
N. Chamberlain, *Coalition*, May 28, 1937.
W. S. Churchill, *Coalition*, May 11, 1940.
W. S. Churchill, *Conservative*, May 23, 1945.
C. R. Attlee, *Labour*, July 26, 1945.
Sir W. S. Churchill, *Conservative*, Oct. 26, 1951.
Sir A. Eden, *Conservative*, April 6, 1955.
H. Macmillan, *Conservative*, Jan. 13, 1957.
Sir A. Douglas-Home, *Conservative*, Oct. 19, 1963.
J. H. Wilson, *Labour*, Oct. 16, 1964.
E. R. G. Heath, *Conservative*, June 19, 1970.

OFFICERS OF THE HOUSE OF LORDS

Speaker, The Rt. Hon. Quintin McGarel Hogg, Lord Hailsham of St. Marylebone
(+ £10,500 as Lord Chancellor) £4,000
    Private Secretary to the Lord Chancellor, M. C. Blair.
Lord Chairman of Committees, The Earl of Listowel, P.C., G.C.M.G. £4,875

Clerk of the Parliaments, Sir David Stephens, K.C.B., C.V.O. £14,000
Clerk Assistant, R. W. Perceval £8,700
Reading Clerk and Principal Clerk, Public Bills, P. G. Henderson £6,925
Counsel to Lord Chairman of Committees, T. G. Talbot, C.B., Q.C. £6,925
Principal Clerks, R. P. Cave, M.V.O. (*Judicial Office and Fourth Clerk at the Table*); E. D. Graham (*Private Bills and Committees*) £6,925
Chief Clerks, J. V. D. Webb; J. E. Grey £5,175 to £6,475
Clerk of the Journals, M. A. J. Wheeler-Booth .... £5,175 to £6,475
Senior Clerks, D. Dewar; J. A. Vallance White; J. M. Davies; (*seconded as Secretary to the Leader of the House and the Chief Whip*) P. D. G. Hayter . . £3,425 to £4,575
Clerk of the Records, M. F. Bond, O.B.E., F.S.A. £5,175 to £6,475
Assistant Clerks of the Records, H. S. Cobb, F.S.A.; D. J. Johnson .... £2,602 to £4,310

Accountant, R. W. Hill, O.B.E... £3,425 to £5,375
Assistant Accountant, E. W. Field.
£2,575 to £3,425
Examiner of Private Acts, etc., Miss J. P. Culverwell, M.B.E.
Librarian, C. S. A. Dobson, F.S.A. £5,175 to £6,475
Asst. Librarian, R. H. V. C. Morgan
£4,346 to £6,475
Examiners of Petitions for Private Bills, T. G. Odling; E. D. Graham.
Gentleman-Usher of the Black Rod, Admiral Sir Frank Twiss, K.C.B., D.S.C. £6,925
Yeoman Usher of the Black Rod and Deputy Serjeant-at-Arms, Col. C. L. Sayers, C.B.E.
£3,425 to £4,575
Staff Superintendent, Lt.-Cdr. S. E. Glover, O.B.E., D.S.C.
Shorthand Writer, A. R. Kennedy..... fees
Editor, Official Report (Hansard), W. M. Stuart,
£4,013 to £4,575
    Asst. do., C. W. H. Blogg ... £3,300 to £3,575

OFFICERS OF THE HOUSE OF COMMONS

Speaker, The Rt. Hon. (John) Selwyn (Brooke) Lloyd, C.H., C.B.E., T.D. Q.C., M.P. for Wirral.... £8,500
Chairman of Ways and Means, The Rt. Hon. Sir Robert Grant-Ferris, M.P. for Nantwich £4,875
Deputy Chairman of Ways and Means, Miss Betty Harvie Anderson, O.B.E., T.D., M.P. for Renfrewshire, East £3,750

DEPT. OF THE CLERK OF THE HOUSE

Clerk of the House of Commons, Sir Barnett Cocks, K.C.B., O.B.E. £14,000
Clerk Asst., D. W. S. Lidderdale, C.B. £9,000
Second do., R. D. Barlas, C.B., O.B.E. £9,000
Principal Clerks—
  Public Bills, K. R. Mackenzie, C.B. £6,925
  Journals, S. C. Hawtrey, C.B. £6,925
  Principal Clerk Table Office, C. A. S. S. Gordon, C.B. £6,925
  Private Bills, T. G. Odling £6,925
  Select Committees, D. Scott £6,725
  Clerk of the Overseas Office, M. H. Lawrence £6,725
Clerk of Standing Committees, A. A. Birley . £6,725
Deputy Principal Clerks, E. S. Taylor, PH.D.; F. G. Allen; R. S. Lankester; K. A. Bradshaw; D. A. M. Pring, M.C.; J. H. Willcox; J. P. S. Taylor; C. A. James; H. M. Barclay; M. T. Ryle; D. McW. Millar (*acting*); C. J. Boulton (*acting*); J. F. Sweetman, T.D. (*acting*); A. A. Barrett (*acting*) ..
£5,175 to £6,475
Senior Clerks, D. W. Limon; J. R. Rose; G. S. Ecclestone; C. B. Winnifrith; A. J. Hastings; W. R. McKay; R. J. Willoughby; S. A. L. Panton; R. B. Sands; G. F. Lushington, C.B.E. (*acting*); C. C. Ricketts (*acting*); I. I. Milne, C.M.G., O.B.E. (*acting*); A. S. Martin, C.B.E., (*acting*); G. Cubie ....each £3,425 to £4,575
Examiners of Private Bills, T. G. Odling; E. D. Graham.
Taxing Officer, T. G. Odling.

DEPT. OF THE SPEAKER
Speaker's Secretary, Brig. N. E. V. Short, M.B.E., M.C. .... £3,425 to £4,575

Counsel to the Speaker, Sir Robert Speed, C.B., Q.C. £6,925
Chaplain to the Speaker, The Rev. T. S. Nevill.
Editor, Official Report (Hansard), L. W. Bear
£6,005 to £6,425
Deputy Editor, R. P. Dring £4,975
Shorthand Writer, A. R. Kennedy .... fees
Deliverer of the Vote, P. K. Marsden, O.B.E.
£3,425 to £5,175

DEPT. OF THE SERJEANT AT ARMS
Serjeant at Arms, Rear-Admiral A. H. C. Gordon Lennox, C.B., D.S.O. £6,925
Deputy do., Lt.-Col. P. F. Thorne, C.B.E.
£5,175 to £6,475
Assistant do., Cdr. D. Swanston, D.S.O., D.S.C., R.N. (*ret.*) .... £4,575 to £5,175
Deputy Assistant do., Major G. V. S. Le Fanu
£3,685 to £4,575

DEPT. OF THE LIBRARY
Librarian, D. C. L. Holland £6,925
Deputy Librarian, D. Menhennet, D.Phil.
£5,175 to £6,475
Assistant Librarians, D. J. T. Englefield; E. C. Thompson .... £4,170 to £4,745
Deputy Assistant Librarians, R. F. C. Butcher, V.R.D.; H. J. Palmer; G. F. Lock; M. A. Griffith-Jones; J. B. Poole, Ph.D.
£3,521 to £4,170

ADMINISTRATION DEPT.
Clerk Administrator, H. R. M. Farmer, C.B.
£6,925
Accountant, F. J. Wilkin, O.B.E., D.F.M.
£5,175 to £6,475
Deputy Accountant, G. Powter.. £3,425 to £4,115
Head of Establishments Section, H. McE. Allen .... £4,775 to £5,375

NOTES ON PARLIAMENTARY PROCEDURE

WRITS FOR A NEW PARLIAMENT, ETC.—Writs for a new Parliament are issued, on the Sovereign's warrant, by the Lord Chancellor to Peers individually, but in the case of the Commons to the returning officers of the various constituencies. A Writ of Summons to the House of Lords, before the time when baronies were created by Letters Patent, is held (should the writ be good and the Parliament legally summoned) to create a barony for the recipient and his heirs. The oldest English peerages, the baronies of De Ros and Mowbray, are founded on writs of summons issued in 1264 and 1283 respectively. The right to sit in the House of Lords is determined by the House. A newly-created Peer may not sit or speak in the House of Lords until he has been introduced by two sponsors of his own degree in the Peerage.

VACANT SEATS.—When a vacancy occurs in the House of Commons the Writ for a New Election is generally moved, during a session of Parliament, by the Chief Whip of the party to whom the member whose seat has been vacated belonged. If the House is in recess, the Speaker can issue a writ, should two members certify to him that a seat is vacant. He cannot, however, issue such a writ if the seat has been vacated through the former member's lunacy or his acceptance of the office of Bailiff of the *Chiltern Hundreds*, or Steward of the *Manor of Northstead*, a legal fiction which enables a member to retire from the House, for it has long been established that a member cannot, by his own volition, relieve himself of the responsibilities to his constituents which his membership involves. Until 1926, however, it was necessary for a member to retire from the House on accepting an office of profit under the Crown, which, it may be noted, subjected a private member who accepted ministerial office to the trouble and expense of seeking re-election in his constituency. The Act of 1926, which removed this necessity, retained the Chiltern Hundreds and the Manor of Northstead as offices of profit and thus perpetuated the fiction.

HOURS OF MEETING, ETC.—The House of Lords normally meets during the Session at 2.30 p.m. on Tuesday and Wednesday, and at 3 p.m. on Thursday. The House of Commons meets on Monday, Tuesday, Wednesday and Thursday at 2.30, and on Friday at 11. Morning sittings on Monday and Wednesday were held from February–July, 1967 and occasionally during 1968 and 1969. *Strangers* are present during the debates of both Houses on sufferance, and may be excluded at any time; this applies equally to the *Press Gallery*. Time has modified what was once a rigid exclusion and strangers have in recent years generally been admitted except during the secret sessions of war time. The proceedings are opened by Prayers in both Houses. The *Quorum* of the House of Commons is forty members, including the Speaker, and should a member point out to the Speaker at any time that fewer than forty members are present, the division bells are rung, and if forty members have not appeared within four minutes, the House is said to be *Counted Out*, and the sitting is adjourned. The *Quorum* of the Lords is three.

PROROGATION AND DISSOLUTION.—A session of Parliament is brought to an end by its Prorogation to a certain date, while Parliament itself comes to an end either by Dissolution by the Sovereign or the expiration of the term of 5 years for which it was elected (*see* p. 307).

ELECTION PETITIONS.—The right of a member of the House of Commons to sit in Parliament can be challenged by petition on several grounds, *e.g.*

ineligibility to sit owing to his bribery or co[r]ruption of the electors. Such petitions we[re] originally decided by the House itself, but [as] party feeling was too much inclined to dictate t[he] decision, their trial was in 1868 referred to the Hig[h] Court of Justice.

STANDING ORDERS.—These are rules, which hav[e] from time to time been established by both Hous[es] of Parliament, to regulate the conduct of busines[s]. These orders are not irrevocable, and like t[he] Statutory Laws of England they can be easi[ly] revised, amended or repealed. The custom an[d] precedents of Parliament, which dictate the bu[lk] of Parliamentary procedure, have acquired, [in] seven centuries, prescriptive rights of obedien[ce] as firmly seated as the Common Law. *Sessio[nal] Orders* are applicable only to the session in whic[h] they are passed.

GENERAL PROCEDURE.—There are differences [in] the rules which govern the conduct of debates i[n] the House of Lords and in the House of Common[s]. The Speaker in the Commons is responsible for t[he] preservation of order and discipline in the Hous[e], but the only duty of the Lord Chancellor or t[he] presiding Peer is to put the question. A Pe[er] prefaces his remarks with "My Lords," where[as] a member of the House of Commons address[es] himself to Mr. Speaker.

A member of the House of Commons wishin[g] to speak "rises in his place uncovered." Whe[n] several members rise together the one whom t[he] Speaker calls to continue the debate is described [as] *having caught the Speaker's eye*. In the House [of] Lords in similar circumstances, the House itse[lf] decides who shall speak.

Broadly speaking, a member may not, exce[pt] in Committee, speak more than once to a questio[n] except in explanation or reply, and this privilege [is] granted only to the mover of a motion, or to t[he] Minister or Member in charge of a bill.

A member may address the House from not[es] but must not read his speech, a distinction sometim[es] without a difference. In the Commons membe[rs] must not be mentioned by name; the proceedin[gs] of the other House and matters *sub judice* must n[ot] be discussed; offensive words or epithets must n[ot] be used; a member may not speak after a questio[n] has been put, except on a point of order, and the[n] he must address the Speaker "*seated and covered.*" He must bow to the Speaker on entering and leavin[g] the House.

QUESTION TIME.—After Prayers the first busine[ss] of importance in the House of Commons [is] Question Time, which lasts from 2.45 until 3.3[0]. Two days' notice of questions must be given to t[he] *Clerk of the House of Commons*, the senior offici[al] of the House, who presides over it in the bri[ef] interval between the first assembly of a ne[w] Parliament and the election of a Speaker, and who[se] counterpart in the House of Lords is the *Clerk [of] the Parliaments*. Members of the House may p[ut] an unlimited number of questions to Ministers, b[ut] not more than two demanding an oral answer ma[y] be made in any one day to the same Minister. Su[p]plementary questions may be put either by t[he] member asking the original question, or by oth[er] members, to obtain clarification of a Ministe[r's] answer.

COMMITTEES.—On the Assembly of a ne[w] Parliament, after the election of the Speaker, t[he] House of Commons deals with the subject [of] Committees, which are of three kinds:—*Comm[it]tees of the Whole House, Select Committees* (appointe[d]

for a specific purpose) and the *Standing Committees* which consider public bills and whose composition, though laid down by Standing Orders, is frequently modified by Sessional Orders. When a bill dealing *exclusively* with Scotland or with Wales and Monmouthshire is referred to a Standing Committee, in the first place all Scottish, and in the second, all Welsh members are automatically members thereof.

CLOSURE AND THE GUILLOTINE.—To prevent deliberate waste of Parliamentary time, a procedure known as the *Closure* (colloquially known as "The Gag") was brought into effect on Nov. 10, 1882. A motion may be made *that the question be now put*. If the Speaker decides that the rights of a minority are not being prejudiced and 100 members support the motion, it is put to the vote, and, if carried, the original motion is put to the House, without further debate. The *Guillotine* represents a more rigorous and systematic application of the Closure. Under this system, a bill proceeds in accordance with a rigid time table and discussion is limited to the time allotted to each group of clauses. If the number of amendments put down appears likely to require more time than has been allotted for their discussion, the Speaker selects those which he considers are most important. The guillotine was first put into use on June 17, 1887, after prolonged debates on the Crimes Bill.

THE PREVIOUS QUESTION.—When the House is disinclined to give a decision on a particular question it is possible to avoid the issue by moving the Previous Question, which is done by one of several motions, *e.g.* "That the Question be not now put " or " That the House do now proceed to the Orders of the Day."

MOTION FOR ADJOURNMENT.—Adjournment ends the sitting of either House and takes place either under the provisions of a Standing Order or through an *ad hoc* resolution. In the Commons a method of obtaining immediate discussion of a matter of urgency is by moving the adjournment for the purpose of discussing a specific and important matter that should have urgent consideration. A member may ask leave to make this motion by giving written notice to the Speaker after Question Time and if it obtains the support of 40 members and the Speaker considers the matter of sufficient importance, it is discussed at 7 p.m. on that day. A Committee of the Whole House cannot adjourn but its proceedings may be interrupted by a motion *That the Chairman report Progress*. This brings the Speaker back to the House and the Committee seeks permission to sit on a future date.

PRIVILEGES OF PARLIAMENT.—There are certain rights and jurisdictions peculiar to each House of Parliament, but privileges in their accepted meaning are common to both Houses. The right of imprisoning persons who commit what are in the opinion of the House breaches of privilege is beyond question, and such persons cannot be admitted to bail nor is any Court competent to investigate the causes of commitment. Each House is the sole and absolute judge of its own privileges and where law and privilege have seemed to clash a conflict of jurisdiction has arisen between Parliament and the Courts. Breaches of privilege may be described briefly as disobedience to the orders of either House; assaults or insults to Members or libels on them; and interference with the officers of the House in the carrying out of their duties. The House of Lords may imprison for a period, or may inflict a fine, but the House of Commons only commits generally and the commitment ceases on the prorogation of Parliament. The Bill of Rights established the principle that " freedom of speech and debates and proceedings in Parliament should not be impeached or questioned in any court or place out of parliament." Consequently the House itself is the only authority which can punish a member for intemperance in debate. Freedom from arrest was a much prized privilege, but it applied only to civil arrest for debt (now abolished) and arbitrary arrest by the Government; members are amenable to all other processes of the Law. Freedom from arrest, in the case of members of the House of Commons, applies to the forty days after the prorogation and the forty days before the next meeting of Parliament.

THE SPEAKER.—The *Speaker of the House of Commons* is the spokesman and president of the Chamber. He is elected by the House at the beginning of each Parliament. He was originally a partisan but throughout a century of development between Speaker Onslow (1728) and Speaker Shaw-Lefevre (1839), the theory of the non-partisan Speaker was perfected, and he now neither speaks in debates, nor votes in divisions, except when the voting is equal. His order in the precedence of the Kingdom is high, only the Prime Minister and the Lord President of the Council going before him. He takes precedence of all Peers, except the two Archbishops, and Speakers are almost invariably raised to the Peerage on vacating their office, though Speaker Whitley is believed to have declined the offer of a Viscounty. The Speaker's most severe disciplinary measure against a member is to *Name* him. When a member has been named, *i.e.* contrary to the practice of the House called by surname and not addressed as the " Hon. Member for . . ." (his constituency), the Leader of the House moves that he " be suspended from the service of the House " for (in the case of a first offence) a period of a week. The period of suspension is increased, should the member offend again. Speaker Denison has left it on record that " The House is always kind and indulgent, but it expects its Speakers to be right. If he should be found tripping, his authority must soon be at an end." The Speaker's Deputy is the *Chairman of Committees*, officially the *Chairman of Ways and Means*, who presides in the absence of the Speaker and when the House has resolved itself into Committee by the passage of the motion *that the Speaker do now leave the Chair*. He, like the Speaker, is elected at the beginning of each Parliament, and when he is presiding as chairman of a committee neither speaks in debate nor votes (except when the voting is equal). A *Deputy Chairman of Ways and Means* is also appointed, and several temporary chairmen, who frequently preside either over a Committee of the Whole House or over Standing Committees.

FORFEITED DEPOSITS AT THE GENERAL ELECTION, 1970

Candidates at parliamentary elections who fail to obtain more than one-eighth of the total votes cast in their constituencies forfeit the deposit of £150 which all candidates must lodge.

Deposits forfeited at the 1970 election totalled 406, 169 more than in 1966. Deposits were lost by 182 Liberal candidates (78 more than in 1966), 11 Conservatives, 6 Labour, 58 Communists, 25 Plaid Cymru, 42 Scottish Nationalists and 82 others. In 1950 the record number of 443 deposits was lost.

GOVERNMENT BY PARTY

Towards the close of Charles II's reign the Exclusion Bill debates in Parliament (1679-80) were marked by the rise of two parties in the political life of the nation and they became known as *Whigs* and *Tories*, names given by the opponents to each other but afterwards mutually accepted, to continue as political labels until Whig was changed to *Liberal* and Tory to *Conservative*.

Before the reign of William and Mary the principal Officers of State were chosen by and were responsible to the Sovereign alone and not to Parliament or the nation at large. Such officers acted sometimes in concert with one another, but more often independently, and the fall of one did not, of necessity, involve that of others, although all were liable to be dismissed at any moment.

In 1693 the Earl of Sunderland recommended to William III the advisability of selecting a Ministry from the political party which enjoyed a majority in the House of Commons and the first united Ministry was drawn in 1696 from the Whigs, to which party the King owed his throne, the principal members being Russell (the Admiral), Somers (the Advocate), Lord Wharton and Charles Montague (afterwards Chancellor of the Exchequer). This group became known as the *Junto* and was regarded with suspicion as a novelty in the political life of the nation, being a small section meeting in secret apart from the main body of Ministers. It may be regarded as the forerunner of the *Cabinet* and in course of time it led to the establishment of the principle of joint responsibility of Ministers, so that internal disagreement caused a change of *personnel* or resignation of the whole body of Ministers.

The accession of George I, who was unfamiliar with the English language, led to a disinclination on the part of the Sovereign to preside at meetings of his Ministers and caused the appearance of a *Prime Minister*, a position first acquired by Robert Walpole in 1721 and retained without interruption for 20 years and 326 days.

In 1828 the old party of the Whigs became known as *Liberals*, a name originally given to it by its opponents to imply laxity of principles, but gradually accepted by the party to indicate its claim to be pioneers and champions of political reform and progressive legislation. In 1861 a Liberal Registration Association was founded and Liberal Associations became widespread. As the outcome of a conference at Birmingham in 1877 a National Liberal Federation was formed, with headquarters in London. The Liberal Party was in power for long periods during the second half of the nineteenth century in spite of the set-back during the Home Rule crisis of 1886, which resulted in the secession of the Liberal Unionists, and for several years during the first quarter of the twentieth century, but after a further split into National and Independent Liberals it numbered only 59 in all after the General Election of 1929, with a further fall to 12 (excluding National Liberals) after the 1945 Election. The number is now 6.

Soon after the change from Whig to Liberal the Tory Party became known as *Conservative*, a name traditionally believed to have been invented by John Wilson Croker in 1830 and to have been generally adopted about the time of the passing of the Reform Act of 1832 to indicate that the preservation of national institutions was the leading principle of the party. After the Home Rule crisis of 1886 the dissentient Liberals entered into a compact with the Conservatives, under which the latter undertook not to contest their seats, but a separate *Liberal Unionist* organization was maintained until 1912, when it was united with the Conservatives under the title of National Unionist Association of Conservative and Liberal Unionist Organizations, the members of which became known as *Unionists*.

The Labour Party.—Labour candidates for Parliament made their first appearance at the General Election of 1892, when there were 27 standing as " Labour " or " Liberal-Labour." At the General Election of 1895 the number of successful candidates fell to 12, with a further fall to 11 at the election of 1900.

In 1900 the *Labour Representative Committee* was set up in order to establish a distinct Labour Group in Parliament, with its own whips, its own policy, and a readiness to co-operate with any party which might be engaged in promoting legislation in the direct interest of labour. In 1906 the L.R.C. became known as *The Labour Party*.

Parliamentary Whips

In order to secure the attendance of Members of a particular party in Parliament on all occasions, and particularly on the occasion of an important division, *Whips* (originally known as "Whippers-in ") are appointed for the purpose. The written appeal or circular letter issued by them is also known as a "whip," its urgency being denoted by the number of times it is underlined. Neglect to respond to a three-lined whip, headed " Most important," is tantamount to secession (at any rate temporarily) from the party.

Whips are officially recognized by Parliament and are provided with office accommodation in both Houses. Government Whips receive salaries from public funds, the Parliamentary (Patronage) Secretary to the Treasury (*Chief Whip in the Commons*) receiving £5,625; the Captain of the Gentlemen-at-Arms (*Chief Whip in the Lords*), the Captain of the Yeomen of the Guard (*Assistant do.*) and the first of the Junior Lords of the Treasury (*Deputy Chief Whip in the Commons*), each £3,000 the (Political) Lords in Waiting and the remaining Junior Lords of the Treasury, each £2,000.

The House of Lords

The *Government Whips* are: The Captain of the Honourable Corps of the Gentlemen at Arms (Earl St. Aldwyn), the Captain of the Queen's Bodyguard of the Yeomen of the Guard (Viscount Gosehen) and the (Political) Lords in Waiting.

The *Labour Whips* are: Lord Beswick; Baroness Phillips; Baroness Llewelyn-Davies; Lord Strabolgi.

The *Liberal Whip* is Lord Amulree.

The House of Commons

The *Government Whips* are: The Parliamentary (Patronage) Secretary to the Treasury (*Chief Whip*) and the Junior Lords of the Treasury. *Assistant Whips* are also usually appointed.

The *Labour Whips* are: The Rt. Hon. R. Mellish (*Chief Whip*); W. Harrison (*Deputy Chief Whip*); E. Armstrong; D. R. Coleman; J. I Concannon; J. Dunn; E. A. Fitch; J. Golding J. Hamilton; W. Hamling; J. Harper; E. G. Perry

The *Liberal Whip* is D. M. S. Steel.

x retired 11/71 succeeded by Ld Denham

(July, 1970)

THE CABINET

Prime Minister and First Lord of the Treasury, THE RT. HON. EDWARD RICHARD GEORGE HEATH, M.B.E., M.P., born 1916.

Secretary of State for the Home Department, The Rt. Hon. Reginald Maudling, M.P., *born 1917.* ~~resigned 7/72 succ. by~~ *Robert Carr*

Secretary of State for Foreign and Commonwealth Affairs, The Rt. Hon. Sir Alec Douglas-Home, K.T., M.P., *born 1903.*

Chancellor of the Exchequer, The Rt. Hon. Anthony Perrinott Lysberg Barber, T.D., M.P., born 1920.

Lord High Chancellor, The Rt. Hon. Lord Hailsham of St. Marylebone, born 1907.

Secretary of State for Social Services, The Rt. Hon. Sir Keith Sinjohn Joseph, Bt., M.P., born 1918.

Secretary of State for Defence, The Rt. Hon. Lord Carrington, K.C.M.G., M.C., born 1919.

Secretary of State for Scotland, The Rt. Hon. Gordon Thomas Calthrop Campbell, M.C., M.P., born 1921.

Secretary of State for Employment, The Rt. Hon. Robert Carr, M.P., *born 1916.* MAURICE MACMILLAN

Secretary of State for Education and Science, The Rt. Hon. Margaret Hilda Thatcher, M.P., born 1925.

Secretary of State for Wales, The Rt. Hon. Peter John Mitchell Thomas, Q.C., M.P., born 1920. PETER WALKER

Secretary of State for Trade and Industry and President of the Board of Trade, The Rt. Hon. John Emerson Harding Davies, M.B.E., M.P., born 1916. THE RT. HON. GEOFFREY RIPPON Q.C.

Secretary of State for the Environment, The Rt. Hon. Peter Edward Walker, M.B.E., M.P., *born 1932.*

Lord President of the Council and Leader of the House of Commons, The Rt. Hon. William Stephen Ian Whitelaw, M.C., M.P., born 1918. ROBERT CARR

Lord Privy Seal and Leader of the House of Lords, The Rt. Hon. Earl Jellicoe, D.S.O., M.C., born 1918.

Chancellor of the Duchy of Lancaster, The Rt. Hon. ~~(Aubrey) Geoffrey (Frederick) Rippon, Q.C., M.P., born 1924.~~ JOHN DAVIES

Minister of Agriculture, Fisheries and Food, The Rt. Hon. ~~James Michael Leathes Prior, M.P., born 1927.~~ JOSEPH GODBER

also & deputy chairman of the party

MINISTER OF INDUSTRIAL DEVELOPMENT — CHRIS. CHATAWAY

MINISTER FOR TRADE

MINISTER FOR CONSUMER AFFAIRS

MINISTERS NOT IN THE CABINET

Minister for Trade, The Rt. Hon. ~~Michael Antony Cristobal Noble, M.P., born 1913.~~ SIR GEOFFREY HOWE, Q.C.

Minister for Industry, Sir John Benedict Eden, Bt., M.P., born 1925. MR THOMAS BOARDMAN

Minister for Local Government and Development, (Rodney) Graham Page, M.B.E., M.P., born 1911. ~~the Rt. Hon.~~

Minister for Housing and Construction, The Rt. Hon. Julian Amery, M.P., *born 1919.* PAUL CHANNON

Minister for Transport Industries, The Rt. Hon. John Wynne William Peyton, M.P., born 1919.

Minister for Aerospace, Capt. the Rt. Hon. Frederick Vernon Corfield, M.P., *born 1915.* resigned 10/4/72

Minister for Overseas Development, The Rt. Hon. Richard Frederick Wood, M.P., born 1920.

Minister of Posts and Telecommunications, ~~The Rt. Hon. Christopher John Chataway, M.P., born 1931.~~ Sir John Eden 4/72

Paymaster-General, The Rt. Hon. Viscount Eccles, K.C.V.O., born 1904.

Attorney-General, The Rt. Hon. Sir Peter Anthony Grayson Rawlinson, Q.C., M.P., born 1919.

Lord Advocate, The Rt. Hon. Norman Russell Wylie, V.R.D., Q.C., M.P., born 1923.

Solicitor-General, Sir ~~(Richard Edward) Geoffrey Howe, Q.C., M.P., born 1926.~~ SIR MICHAEL HAVERS QC

Solicitor-General for Scotland, David William Robert Brand, Q.C., born 1923.

Chief Secretary to the Treasury, Maurice Victor Macmillan, M.P., *born 1921.* × MR PATRICK JENKINS

Financial Secretary to the Treasury, ~~(Charles) Patrick (Fleeming) Jenkin, M.P., born 1926.~~ TERENCE HIGGINS

Minister of State (Foreign and Commonwealth Office), The Rt. Hon. Joseph Bradshaw Godber, M.P., *born 1914.* JULIAN AMERY

Ministers of State (Home Office), Richard Christopher Sharples, O.B.E., M.C., M.P., born 1916; The Lord Windlesham, *born 1932.* resigned 4/72 LORD BALNIEL

Minister of State (Scottish Office), The Baroness Tweedsmuir of Belhelvie, born 1915.

Minister of State (Welsh Office), (James) David Gibson-Watt, M.P., born 1918.

Minister of State (Treasury), Terence Langley Higgins, M.P., born 1928.

Minister of State (Health and Social Security), The Lord Aberdare, born 1919.

Minister of State (Department of Employment), ~~Paul Elmore Oliver Bryan, D.S.O., M.C., M.P., born 1913.~~ resigned 4/72

Minister of State (Defence), ~~The Lord Balniel, M.P., born 1927.~~ × IAN GILMOUR

Minister of State (Defence Procurement), I. H. J. L. Gilmour, M.P., born 1926.

Minister without Portfolio, The Rt. Hon. Lord Drumalbyn, born 1908.

PARLIAMENTARY UNDER SECRETARIES, ETC.

Michael Heseltine

Aerospace, D. E. C. Price, M.P. resigned 4/72

Agriculture and Fisheries, ~~J. A. Stodart, M.P.~~ MR PEEL FENNER

Defence, P. M. Kirk, M.P. (*Royal Navy*); G. Johnson Smith, M.P. (*Army*); A. C. F. Lambton, M.P. (*Royal Air Force*).

Education and Science, The Lord Belstead; W. R. van Straubenzee, M.B.E., M.P.

Employment, D. G. Smith, M.P.; D. A. R. Howell, M.P.

Environment, H. P. G. Channon, M.P.; M. R. D. Heseltine, M.P.; E. W. Griffiths, M.P.; The Rev. Lord Sandford, D.S.C.

Foreign and Commonwealth Affairs, The Marquess of Lothian; A. H. F. Royle, M.P.

Health and Social Security, M. J. H. Alison, M.P.; A. P. Dean, M.P.

Home, M. Carlisle, Q.C., M.P.

Overseas Development, J. A. Kershaw, M.C., M.P.

Scottish Office, Hon. A. L. Buchanan-Smith, M.P.; Hon. G. K. H. Younger, T.D. M.P.; H. S. P. Monro, M.P.

Trade and Industry, J. A. Grant, M.P.; The Hon. N. Ridley, M.P. resigned 4/72 LORD LIMERICK

Treasury, The Rt. Hon. F. L. Pym, M.C., M.P. 4/72 *Junior Lords*, B. B. Weatherill, M.P.; W. Clegg, M.P.; V. H. Goodhew, M.P.; P. L. Hawkins, T.D., M.P.

Asst. Whips, T. V. N. Fortescue, M.P.; H. K. Speed, M.P.; H. A. L. Rossi, M.P.

Leader of the Opposition, The Rt. Hon. (James) Harold Wilson, O.B.E., M.P., born 1916.

× P.C. Jan '72

MINISTRIES SINCE 1939

Date	Prime Minister	Exchequer	Lord President	Foreign	Home	Board of Trade*	Lord Chancellor
1939, Sept. 3	N. Chamberlain	Sir J. Simon	Stanhope	Halifax	Sir J. Anderson	O. Stanley	Caldecote
1940, May 11	W. S. Churchill	Sir K. Wood Sir J. Anderson	N. Chamberlain Sir J. Anderson C. R. Attlee	Halifax A. Eden	Sir J. Anderson H. Morrison	Sir A. Duncan O. Lyttelton Sir A. Duncan H. Dalton J. J. Llewellin	Simon
1945, May 23	W. S. Churchill	Sir J. Anderson	Woolton	A. Eden	Sir D. Somervell	O. Lyttelton	Simon
1945, July 26	C. R. Attlee	H. Dalton Sir S. Cripps H. T. N. Gaitskell	H. Morrison Addison	E. Bevin H. Morrison	J. Chuter Ede	Sir S. Cripps J. H. Wilson Sir H. Shawcross	Jowitt
1951, Oct. 26	W. S. Churchill	R. A. Butler	Woolton Salisbury	Sir A. Eden	Sir D. Maxwell Fyfe G. Lloyd-George	G. E. P. Thorneycroft	Simonds Kilmuir
1955, April 7	Sir A. Eden	R. A. Butler H. Macmillan	Salisbury	H. Macmillan J. S. B. Lloyd	G. Lloyd-George	G. E. P. Thorneycroft	Kilmuir
1957, Jan. 13	H. Macmillan	G. E. P. Thorneycroft D. H.-Amory J. S. B. Lloyd R. Maudling	Salisbury Home Hailsham Home Hailsham	J. S. B. Lloyd Home	R. A. Butler H. Brooke	Sir D. Eccles R. Maudling F. J. Erroll	Kilmuir Dilhorne
1963, Oct. 20	Sir A. Douglas-Home	R. Maudling	Hailsham (Q. Hogg)	R. A. Butler	H. Brooke	E. R. G. Heath	Dilhorne
1964, Oct. 16	J. H. Wilson	L. J. Callaghan R. H. Jenkins	H. W. Bowden R. H. S. Crossman T. F. Peart	P. Gordon Walker R. M. M. Stewart G. A. Brown R. M. M. Stewart	Sir F. Soskice R. H. Jenkins L. J. Callaghan	D. P. T. Jay C. A. R. Crosland R. Mason	Gardiner
1970, June 24	E. R. G. Heath	I. N. Macleod A. P. L. Barber	W. S. I. White-law _ROBERT CARR_	Sir A. Douglas-Home	R. Maudling	M. A. C. Noble J. E. H. Davies	Hailsham

* Sec. of State for Trade and Industry, from Oct. 15, 1970.

Date	Health§ (1854)	Agriculture* (1890)	Education† (1857)	Defence	Scotland	Labour**	Works‡
1939, Sept. 3	W. E. Elliot	Sir R. Dorman-Smith	De La Warr	Chatfield	D. J. Colville	E. Brown	H. Ramsbotham
1940, May 11	M. Macdonald, E. Brown, H. U. Willink	R. S. Hudson	H. Ramsbotham, R. A. Butler	W. S. Churchill	E. Brown, T. Johnston	E. Bevin	Tryon, Reith, Portal, D. Sandys
1945, May 23	H. U. Willink	R. S. Hudson	R. K. Law	W. S. Churchill	Rosebery	R. A. Butler	D. Sandys
1945, July 26	A. Bevan, H. A. Marquand	T. Williams	Ellen Wilkinson, G. Tomlinson	C. R. Attlee, A. V. Alexander, E. Shinwell	J. Westwood, A. Woodburn, H. McNeil	G. A. Isaacs, A. Robens	G. Tomlinson, C. W. Key, R. R. Stokes, G. A. Brown
1951, Oct. 26	H. F. C. Crookshank, I. N. Macleod	Sir T. L. Dugdale, D. Heathcoat-Amory	Florence Horsbrugh, Sir D. Eccles	W. S. Churchill, Alexander of Tunis, H. Macmillan	J. G. Stuart	Sir W. T. Monckton	D. M. Eccles, E. N. C. Birch
1955, April 7	I. N. Macleod, R. H. Turton	D. Heathcoat-Amory	Sir D. Eccles	J. S. B. Lloyd, Sir W. T. Monckton, A. H. Head	J. G. Stuart	Sir W. T. Monckton, I. N. Macleod	E. N. C. Birch, P. G. T. Buchan-Hepburn
1957, Jan. 13	D. F. Vosper, D. C. Walker-Smith, J. E. Powell	D. Heathcoat-Amory, J. H. Hare, A. C. J. Soames	Hailsham, G. W. Lloyd, Sir D. Eccles, Sir E. Boyle	D. Sandys, H. A. Watkinson, G. E. P. Thorney-croft	J. S. Maclay, M. A. C. Noble	I. N. Macleod, E. R. G. Heath, J. H. Hare	A. H. E. Molson, Lord John Hope, A. G. F. Rippon
1963, Oct. 20	A. P. L. Barber	A. C. J. Soames	Sir E. Boyle	G. E. P. Thorney-croft	M. A. C. Noble	J. B. Godber	A. G. F. Rippon
1964, Oct. 16	K. Robinson, R. H. S. Crossman	T. F. Peart, C. Hughes	R. M. M. Stewart, C. A. R. Crosland, E. W. Short	D. W. Healey	W. Ross	R. J. Gunter, Mrs. B. A. Castle	C. Pannell, R. E. Prentice, J. E. Silkin
1970, June 24	Sir K. S. Joseph	J. M. L. Prior	Margaret Thatcher	Carrington	G. T. C. Campbell	L. R. Carr [struck through; handwritten: *Maurice Miller*]	J. Amery, P. E. Walker

PRIME MINISTERS.—Sir Robert Walpole, First Lord of the Treasury and Chancellor of the Exchequer from 1721 to 1742, rose to a power no Minister had ever before attained and was the subject of a protest entered in the journal of the House of Lords, the grievance being that the Sovereign should repose confidence in any one Minister to the exclusion of the remainder. He is usually regarded as the first Prime Minister and the eminence he achieved was repeated in the reign of George III, when the illness of the Sovereign necessitated the appearance of a leading and presiding minister, the Prince Regent not taking the Sovereign's place in this respect. After the Regency the Sovereign ceased to preside at Cabinet Meetings and the leading Minister became, in fact, Prime Minister.

* Agriculture, Fisheries and Food since 1970. † Dept. of Education and Science since 1964. § and Social Security (from 1968).
** Employment since 1970. ‡ Public Building and Works 1962–70; absorbed in Department of the Environment, Oct. 15, 1970.

THE PRINCIPAL PARTIES IN PARLIAMENT (1918-1970)

General Election	Conservative	Liberal	Labour
1918	382 (a)	161 (b)	74 (c)
1922	347	118 (d)	142
1923	258	151	191
1924	414	39	150
1929	260	59	287
1931	471	72 (e)	65 (f)
1935	387	54 (g)	166 (h)
1945	189	25 (i)	396 (j)
1950	298 (k)	9	315 (l)
1951	320 (m)	6	296 (l)
1955	344 (m)	6	277 (n)
1959	365 (m)	6	258 (o)
1964	303 (m)	9	317
1966	253 (m)	12	363 (p)
1970	330 (q)	6	287 (r)

NOTES.—(a) Including 48 Non-Coalition Unionists. (b) Including 28 Non-Coalition Liberals. (c) Including 63 Non-Coalition Labour. (d) Liberal National 59; Liberal 59. (e) Liberal National 35 (Simon); Liberal 33 (Samuel); (Lloyd George). (f) National Labour 13 (MacDonald); Labour 52 (Henderson). (g) Liberal National 33; Liberal 21. (h) National Labour 8 Labour 154; I.L.P. 4. (i) Liberal National 13 Liberal 12. (j) Labour 393; I.L.P. 3. (k) Including Nat. Liberal. (l) Irish Nationalists (2) and Speaker make total of 625. (m) Including associates. (n) Sinn Fein (2) and Speaker make total of 630. (o) Independent (1) makes total of 630. (p) Republican Labour (1) makes total of 630. (q) Including Ulster Unionists. (r) Scottish Nationalist (1) Independent (5) and Speaker make total of 630.

PARLIAMENTS SINCE 1852

Assembled	Dissolved	Duration yrs. m. d.	Assembled	Dissolved	Duration yrs. m. d.
Victoria			*George V*		
1852 Nov. 4	1857 March 21	4 4 17	1911 Jan. 31	1918 Nov. 25	7 9 2
1857 April 30	1859 April 23	1 11 23	1910 Feb. 4	1922 Oct. 26	3 8 2
1859 May 31	1865 July 6	6 1 6	1922 Nov. 20	1923 Nov. 16	0 11 2
1866 Feb. 1	1868 Nov. 11	2 9 10	1924 Jan. 8	1924 Oct. 9	0 9
1868 Dec. 10	1874 Jan. 26	5 1 16	1924 Dec. 2	1929 May 10	4 5
1874 March 5	1880 March 25	6 0 20	1929 June 25	1931 Oct. 6	2 3 1
1880 April 29	1885 Nov. 13	5 6 20	1931 Nov. 3	1935 Oct. 25	3 11 2
1886 Jan. 12	1886 June 26	0 5 14	*George V, Edward VIII and George VI*		
1886 Aug. 5	1892 June 28	5 10 24	1935 Nov. 13	1945 June 13	9 5 2
1892 Aug. 4	1895 July 9	2 11 5	*George VI*		
1895 Aug. 15	1900 Sept. 25	5 1 14	1945 Aug. 1	1950 Feb. 3	4 6
			1950 March 1	1951 Oct. 5	1 7
Victoria and Edward VII			*George VI and Elizabeth II*		
1900 Dec. 3	1906 Jan. 8	5 1 6	1951 Oct. 31	1955 May 6	3 6
			Elizabeth II		
Edward VII			1955 June 9	1959 Sept. 18	4 3
1906 Feb. 13	1910 Jan. 15	3 11 2	1959 Oct. 27	1964 Sept. 25	4 10 2
			1964 Nov. 3	1966 March 10	1 4
Edward VII and George V			1966 April 21	1970 May 29	4 1
1910 Feb. 15	1910 Nov. 28	0 9 13	1970 July 2		

MAJORITIES IN THE HOUSE OF COMMONS
(Since the Reform Bill, 1832)

Year	Party	Majority	Year	Party	Majority
1833	Whig	307	1906	Liberal	356
1835	Whig	107	1910 (Jan.)	Liberal	124
1837	Whig	51	1910 (Dec.)	Liberal	126
1841	Conservative	81	1918	Coalition	263
1847	Whig	1	1922	Conservative	79
1852	Liberal	13	1923	No Majority.	
1857	Liberal	79	1924	Conservative	225
1859	Liberal	43	1929	No Majority.	
1865	Liberal	67	1931	National Government	425
1868	Liberal	128	1935	National Government	247
1874	Conservative	46	1945	Labour	146
1880	Liberal	62	1950	Labour	8
1885	Liberal (84) and Irish Nationalist (82)	166	1951	Conservative	16
1886	Unionist	114	1955	Conservative	59
1892	Liberal	40	1959	Conservative	100
1895	Unionist	152	1964	Labour	5
1900	Unionist	134	1966	Labour	99
			1970	Conservative	31

WOMEN MEMBERS OF PARLIAMENT

A movement to grant parliamentary franchise to women was supported in the mid-nineteenth century by Richard Cobden, Benjamin Disraeli and John Stuart Mill, but the vote was not accorded to women until 1918, although they had been included in the County Councils electorate by the Local Government Act of 1888. After a *Speaker's Conference* of all parties, which reported in favour of a limited form of women's suffrage, a clause enfranchising women was carried in both Houses and the *Parliament (Qualification of Women) Act* containing the clause which removed the sex disqualification for membership of the House of Commons and conferred the franchise on women at the age of 30, received the Royal Assent in 1918. A further Act of 1928 granted them the vote on the same terms as men at the age of 21, reduced to 18 1969. At the General Election of 1970, 26 women members (15 Conservative, 10 Labour and one Independent) were returned. At the Dissolution there had been 27.

VOTES CAST AT THE GENERAL ELECTIONS, 1955–70
AND AT BY-ELECTIONS SINCE 1959

General Election, 1955

Conservative and Associate	13,311,938
Labour..........................	12,405,246
Liberal..........................	722,395
Sinn Fein.......................	152,310
Welsh Nationalist................	45,119
Communist.......................	33,144
Scottish Nationalist..............	12,112
Others	78,490

Total.................	26,760,754

General Election, 1959

Conservative and Associate........	13,750,965
Labour..........................	12,195,765
Liberal..........................	1,661,262
Welsh Nationalist................	77,571
Sinn Fein.......................	63,915
Communist.......................	30,897
Scottish Nationalist..............	21,738
Others	61,225

Total.................	27,863,338

By-elections, 1959–64

Labour	856,934
Conservative and Associate	724,861
Liberal..........................	383,006
Independent.....................	30,001
Scottish Nationalist..............	24,948
Communist	5,799
Welsh Nationalist.................	3,711

General Election, 1964

Labour..........................	12,205,581
Conservative and Associate	11,980,783
Liberal..........................	3,101,103
Irish Republican..................	101,628
Welsh Nationalist.................	68,517
Scottish Nationalist..............	63,053
Communist.......................	44,576
Others	90,903

Total.................	27,656,149

By-elections, 1964–66

At 13 by-elections between the General Elections of 1964 and 1966, the following votes were cast:—

Conservative.....................	223,002
Labour...........................	176,793
Liberal..........................	83,832
Independent.....................	2,659
Welsh Nationalist................	1,551

General Election, 1966

Labour...........................	13,064,951
Conservative and Associate.........	11,418,433
Liberal..........................	2,327,533
Scottish Nationalist..............	128,474
Communist.......................	62,112
Plaid Cymru......................	61,071
Others	201,032

Total.................	27,263,606

By-elections, 1966–70

At 38 by-elections between the General Elections of 1966 and 1970, the following votes were cast:

Conservative and Ulster Unionist.....	629,970
Labour...........................	439,358
Liberal..........................	126,301
Independent.....................	57,527
Scottish Nationalist..............	40,737
Plaid Cymru......................	40,518
Communist.......................	4,807

General Election, 1970

Conservative and Ulster Unionist.....	13,144,692
Labour...........................	12,179,166
Liberal..........................	2,117,638
Scottish Nationalist..............	306,796
Plaid Cymru......................	175,016
Communist.......................	38,431
Others	383,068

	28,344,087

By-elections, since June 1970

At 9 by-elections since the General Election of 1970, the following votes have been cast:—

Labour	136,696
Conservative	125,451
Liberal	14,452
Independent......................	7,168

PARLIAMENTARY ASSOCIATIONS

COMMONWEALTH PARLIAMENTARY ASSOCIATION (1911)

The Commonwealth Parliamentary Association consists of 25 main branches in Parliaments of the self-governing countries of the Commonwealth and 6 auxiliary branches. There are also branches in State, Provincial and Territorial Legislatures, as well as in the Parliaments of Northern Ireland, the Isle of Man, and the States of Jersey. In addition, there are 12 affiliated branches in Legislatures of those Commonwealth countries which are not completely self-governing, and 8 subsidiary branches in colonial territories making a total of 88 branches. Commonwealth Parliamentary conferences and general meetings are held every year in different countries of the Commonwealth.

Chairman of the General Council, Senator Hon. Sir Alister McMullin, K.C.M.G. (Australia).

Secretary-General, R. V. Vanderfelt, O.B.E., Houses of Parliament, S.W.1.

Secretary, United Kingdom Branch, P. G. Molloy, M.C., Westminster Hall, Houses of Parliament, S.W.1.

THE INTER-PARLIAMENTARY UNION
Place du Petit-Saconnex, Geneva 19, Switzerland.

The Inter-Parliamentary Union has been in existence since 1889; originally started to popularize the idea of International Arbitration, it achieved its object very substantially in helping to create the Permanent Court of Arbitration by the First Hague Conference and to bring about the convocation of the Second Conference of The Hague. In 1945, the Union resumed work on all questions connected with peace and reconstruction, which have been studied under various aspects.

BRITISH GROUP.

Hon. Presidents, The Lord Chancellor; Mr. Speaker.
President, Rt. Hon. E. R. G. Heath, M.B.E., M.P.
Vice-Presidents, The Marquess of Salisbury, K.G.; The Rt. Hon. Sir Alec Douglas-Home, K.T., M.P.; The Rt. Hon. J. H. Wilson, O.B.E., M.P.; The Lord Butler of Saffron Walden, K.G., P.C., C.H.; The Rt. Hon. R. M. M. Stewart, C.H., M.P.
Chairman, J. Hall, O.B.E., T.D., M.P.
Secretary, Brigadier M. J. A. Paterson, D.S.O.

ALPHABETICAL LIST OF MEMBERS OF THE HOUSE OF COMMONS

(Elected June 18, 1970)

For abbreviations, see page 325. The number before the name of each constituency is for easy reference and corresponds to the number of that constituency given on pp. 325-348

	Maj.
★Abse, L. (b. 1917), Lab., 465Pontypool....	18,533
Adley, R. J. (b. 1935), C. 105Bristol, N.E..	462
★Albu, A. H. (b. 1903), Lab., 216Edmonton	2,145
★Alison, M. J. H. (b. 1926), C., 32Barkston Ash......	11,337
★Allason, J. H. (b. 1912), C., 287Hemel Hempstead....	12,350
★Allaun, F. J. (b. 1913), Lab., 505 Salford, E..	6,270
★Allen, S. S. (b. 1898), Lab., 161Crewe....	3,482
★Amery, Rt. Hon. J. (b. 1919), C., 103 Brighton, Pavilion......	10,594
★Anderson, Miss M. B. H. (b. 1915), C., 477 Renfrewshire, E........	13,101
★Archer, J. H. (b. 1940), C., 380Louth.....	9,256
★Archer, P. K. (b. 1926), Lab., 490Rowley Regis and Tipton......	9,464
★Armstrong, E. (b. 1915), Lab., 198Durham, N.W........	13,655
★Ashley, J. (b. 1922), Lab., 548 Stoke, S.....	7,426
Ashton, J. W. (b. 1933), Lab., 39Bassetlaw	8,261
★Astor, Hon. J. (b. 1923), C., 418Newbury..	11,733
†Atkins, H.E. (b. 1922), C., 535Spelthorne..	9,027
★Atkinson, N. (b. 1923), Lab., 571Tottenham.......	6,392
★Awdry, D. E. (b. 1924), C., 145Chippenham......	10,538
★Bagier, G. A. T. (b. 1924), Lab., 554Sunderland, S........	6,118
†Baker K. W. (b. 1934), C., 503 St.Marylebone.....	6,142
★Baker, W. H. K. (b. 1920), C., 30Banff...	3,451
★Balniel, Lord (b. 1927), C., 294Hertford...	9,570
★Barber, Rt. Hon. A. P. L. (b. 1920), C., 12Altrincham and Sale........	11,233
★Barnes, M. C. J. (b. 1932), Lab., 96Brentford and Chiswick.....	513
★Barnett, J. (b. 1923), Lab., 298Heywood and Royton.....	903
Barnett, N. G. (b. 1928), Lab., 269Greenwich.....	8,521
★Batsford, B. C. C. (b. 1910), C., 200 Ealing, S.......	7,284
★Baxter, W. (b. 1911), Lab., 540Stirling, W..	7,419
★Beamish, Sir T. V. H. (b. 1917), C., 361 Lewes.....	18,688
★Beaney, A. (b. 1905), Lab., 288Hemsworth.	30,479
★Bell, R. M. (b. 1914), C., 113Bucks, S......	23,574
★Benn, Rt. Hon. A. N. Wedgwood (b. 1925), Lab., 108Bristol, S.E.....	5,688
★Bennett, Sir F. M. (b. 1918), C. 568Torquay	18,048
★Bennett, J. (b. 1912), Lab., 245Bridgeton...	7,255
★Bennett, R. F. B. (b. 1911), C., 264Gosport and Fareham.....	17,972
Benyon, W. R. (b. 1930), C., 112Buckingham.....	2,521
★Berry, Hon. A. G. (b. 1925), C., 530Southgate.....	13,574
★Bidwell, S. J. (b. 1917), Lab., 524Southall..	4,223
★Biffen, W. J. (b. 1930), C., 450Oswestry...	9,560
★Bishop, E. S. (b. 1920), Lab., 417Newark..	1,220
★Blaker, P. A. R. (b. 1922), C., 79Blackpool, S........	8,006
★Blenkinsop, A. (b. 1911), Lab., 532South Shields.....	10,231
★Boardman, H. (b. 1907), Lab., 359Leigh..	11,311
★Boardman, T. G. (b. 1919), C., 358Leicester, S.W........	106
★Body, R. (b. 1927), C., 302Holland with Boston.....	9,339
★Booth, A. E. (b. 1928), Lab., 36Barrow in Furness.......	4,864

	Maj.
Boscawen, Hon. R. T. (b. 1923), C. 593 Wells.....	8,77
★Bossom, Hon. Sir C., Bt. (b. 1918), C., 360 Leominster.....	11,16
★Bottomley, Rt. Hon. A. G. (b. 1907), Lab., 402Middlesbrough, E.....	13,95
★Bourke, Sir E. A. H. Legge- (b. 1914), C., 325Isle of Ely.....	9,60
Bowden, A. (b. 1930), C. 102Brighton, Kemptown.....	3,10
★Boyden, H. J. (b. 1910), Lab., 76Bishop Auckland.....	7,48
★Bradley, T. G. (b. 1926), Lab., 355Leicester, N.E......	89
★Braine, B. R. (b. 1914), C., 223Essex, S.E.	17,90
Bray, R. W. T. (b. 1922), C., 487 Rossendale.....	1,88
★Brewis, H. J. (b. 1920), C., 241Galloway..	8,28
★Brinton, Sir E. T. C. (b. 1916), C., 336 Kidderminster.....	9,37
★Broughton, Sir A. D. D. (b. 1902), Lab., 41Batley and Morley.....	7,27
★Brown, Sir E. J. (b. 1913), C., 40Bath....	5,85
★Brown, H. D. (b. 1919), Lab., 255Provan..	13,98
★Brown, R. C. (b. 1921), Lab., 423Newcastle, W.....	9,16
★Brown, R. W. (b. 1921), Lab., 518Shoreditch and Finsbury.....	7,30
★Bryan, P. E. O. (b. 1913), C., 310 Howden.	12,53
★Buchan, N. F. (b. 1922), Lab., 478Renfrewshire, W.....	2,30
★Buchanan, R. (b. 1912), Lab., 258Springburn.....	10,39
★Buck, P. A. F. (b. 1928), C., 153Colchester.	10,23
★Bullus, Sir E. E. (b. 1906), C., 593Wembley, N.....	6,24
★Burden, F. F. A. (b. 1905), C., 244Gillingham.....	7,75
Butler, Hon. A. C. (b. 1931), C., 87Bosworth.....	1,05
★Butler, Mrs. J. S. (b. 1910) Lab., 618Wood Green.....	4,64
★Callaghan, Rt. Hon. L. J. (b. 1912), Lab., 128 Cardiff, S.E.....	5,45
★Campbell, Rt. Hon. G. T. C. (b. 1921), C., 420 Moray and Nairn.....	6,10
Campbell, I. (b. 1926), Lab., 193Dunbartonshire, W.....	6,22
★Cant, R. B. (b. 1915), Lab., 546Stoke, Central.....	7,53
★Carlisle, M. (b. 1929), C., 494Runcorn....	9,06
★Carmichael, N. G. (b. 1921), Lab., 259 Woodside.....	1,3
★Carpenter, Rt. Hon. J. A. Boyd- (b. 1908), C.. 339 Kingston-upon-Thames.....	10,3
★Carr, Rt. Hon. L. R. (b. 1916), C., 407 Mitcham.....	5,2
Carter, R. J. (b. 1935), Lab., 69 Northfield..	1,2
★Cary, Sir R. A., Bt. (b. 1898), C., 394 Withington.....	3,48
★Castle, Rt. Hon. Barbara (b. 1911), Lab., 77Blackburn.....	2,73
★Channon, H. P. G. (b. 1935), C., 528 Southend, W.....	16,88
Chapman, S. B. (b. 1935), C., 67Handsworth.....	1,8
★Chataway, Rt. Hon. C. J. (b. 1931), C., 143Chichester.....	25,54
Churchill, W. S. (b. 1940), C., 550Stretford	4,0
Clark, D. G. (b. 1939), Lab., 154Colne Valley.....	8

Maj.

*Clark, R. Chichester- (b. 1928), U.U., 378 Londonderry............................ 12,135
Clark, W. G. (b. 1917), C., 556Surrey, E.. 24,024
Clarke, K. H. (b. 1940), C., 495Rushcliffe.. 6,168
*Clegg, W. (b. 1920), C., 434North Fylde.. 18,432
Cockeram, E. P. (b. 1924), C., 44Bebington and Airdrie............................. 725
Cocks, M. F. L. (b. 1929), Lab., 107Bristol, S............................... 9,428
Cohen, S. (b. 1927), Lab., 352Leeds, S.E... 5,748
*Coleman, D. R. (b. 1925), Lab., 415Neath. 21,613
*Concannon, J. D. (b. 1930), Lab., 396Mansfield................................. 15,527
*Conlan, B. (b. 1923), Lab., 242Gateshead, E. 13,035
*Cooke, C. Fletcher- (b. 1914), C., 169 Darwen
*Cooke, R. G. (b. 1930), C., 109Bristol, W. 9,094
Coombs, D. M. (b. 1931), C., 75Yardley.. 11,935
Cooper, A. E. (b. 1910), C., 319Ilford, S..... 120
*Corbet, Mrs. F. K. (b. 1900), Lab., 122 Peckham............................... 1,282
*Cordle, J. H. (b. 1912), C., 80Bournemouth, E. and Christchurch..................... 8,839
*Corfield, Rt. Hon. F. V. (b. 1915), C., 261 Gloucestershire, S...................... 20,510
Cormack, P. T. (b. 1939), C., 125Cannock. 8,978
*Costain, A. P. (b. 1910), C., 238Folkestone and Hythe............................. 1,529
Cox, T. M. (b. 1930), Lab., 583Wandsworth, Central............................... 13,259
*Crawshaw, R. (b. 1917), Lab., 373Toxteth.. 2,946
Critchley, J. M. G. (b. 1930), C., 11Aldershot................................. 2,456
*Cronin, J. D. (b. 1916), Lab., 379Loughborough............................ 14,531
*Crosland, Rt. Hon. C. A. R. (b. 1918), Lab., 270Grimsby...................... 534
*Crossman, Rt. Hon. R. H. S. (b. 1907), Lab., 158Coventry, E................... 6,111
*Crouch, D. L. (b. 1919), C., 126Canterbury 12,265
*Crowder, F. P. (b. 1919), C., 493Ruislip-Northwood.......................... 18,050
Cunningham, G. (b. 1931), Lab., 330Islington, S.W.............................. 12,706
Cunningham, J. A. (b. 1939), Lab., 605 Whitehaven............................ 6,275
Curran, C. (b. 1903), C., 575Uxbridge.... 6,556
*Dalkeith, Earl of (b. 1923), C., 212Edinburgh, N.............................. 3,646
*Dalyell, T. (b. 1932), Lab., 602West Lothian 3,878
*Darling, Rt. Hon. G. (b. 1905), Lab., 515 Hillsborough.......................... 13,740
*Davidson, A. (b. 1926), Lab., 9Accrington. 7,330
Davies, D. J. D. (b. 1938), Lab., 377Llanelli 594
*Davies, G. E. (b. 1913), Lab., 479Rhondda, E............................. 23,011
*Davies, I. (b. 1910), Lab., 265Gower...... 12,671
Davies, Rt. Hon. J. E. H. (b. 1916), C., 341 Knutsford............................. 17,050
*Davies, S. O. (b. 1886), Ind. Lab., 400 Merthyr Tydfil........................ 21,582
*Davies, W. R. Rees- (b. 1916), C., 326Isle of Thanet............................. 7,467
*Davis, A. G. F. Hall- (b. 1924), C., 411 Morecambe and Lonsdale............... 11,725
Davis, S. C. (b. 1928), Lab., 272Hackney, Central.............................. 13,526
Davis, T. A. G. (b. 1938), Lab., 111Bromsgrove............................... 8,041
*Davison, J. A. Biggs- (b. 1918), C., 144 Chigwell.............................. 1,868
Deakins, E. P. (b. 1932), Lab., 582Walthamstow, W............................. 8,432
*Dean, A. P. (b. 1924), C., 523Somerset, N.. 4,602
*Deedes, Rt. Hon. W. F. (b. 1913), C., 22 Ashford............................... 10,854
                                      12,612

*de Freitas, Rt. Hon. Sir G. S. (b. 1913), Lab., 335Kettering...................... 4,190
*Delargy, H. J. (b. 1908), Lab., 565Thurrock 11,388
*Dell, Rt. Hon. E. E. (b. 1921), Lab., 62Birkenhead.............................. 5,829
*Dempsey, J. (b. 1917), Lab., 152Coatbridge and Airdrie.......................... 10,543
*Devlin, Miss B. J. (b. 1947), Ind., 406Mid Ulster.............................. 5,929
*Digby, K. S. D. W. (b. 1910), C., 186 Dorset, W............................. 10,545
Dixon, P. J. S. (b. 1928), C., 572Truro.... 8,210
*Doig, P. M. (b. 1911), Lab., 195Dundee, W. 6,822
Dormand, J. D. (b. 1919), Lab., 201Easington 24,961
Douglas, R. G. (b. 1932), Lab., 539Clackmannan and E. Stirling.................. 10,551
*Drayson, G. B. (b. 1913), C., 520Skipton.. 8,806
*Driberg, T. E. N. (b. 1905), Lab., 31Barking 11,788
*du Cann, Rt. Hon. E. D. L. (b. 1924), C., 562Taunton........................... 8,335
Duffy, A. E. P. (b. 1920), Lab., 511Attercliffe 15,496
*Dunn, J. A. (b. 1926), Lab., 371Kirkdale.. 4,063
*Dunnett, J. J. (b. 1922), Lab., 438Nottingham, Central.......................... 3,559
Dykes, H. J. (b. 1939), C., 281Harrow, E.. 4,021
*Eadie, A. (b. 1920), Lab., 405Midlothian... 12,474
*Edelman, M. (b. 1911), Lab., 159Coventry, N.................................. 5,660
*Eden, Sir J. B., Bt. (b. 1925), C., 90Bournemouth, W............................ 14,615
*Edwards, R. J. (b. 1906), Lab., 61Bilston.. 1,000
Edwards, R. N. (b. 1934), C., 455Pembrokeshire........................... 1,231
*Edwards, W. H. (b. 1938), Lab., 399 Merioneth............................. 3,436
*Elliot, Capt. W. (b. 1910), C., 134Carshalton............................ 10,446
*Elliott, R. W. (b. 1920), C., 422Newcastle, N.................................. 3,460
Ellis, R. T. (b. 1924), Lab., 626Wrexham.. 15,440
*Emery, P. F. H. (b. 1926), C., 303Honiton.. 21,555
*English, M. (b. 1930), Lab., 441Nottingham, W................................ 2,252
*Evans, A. T. (b. 1914), Lab., 119Caerphilly 13,467
*Eyre, R. E. (b. 1924), C., 66Hall Green.... 9,389
*Farr, J. A. (b. 1922), C., 278Harborough... 19,205
*Faulds, A. M. W. (b. 1923), Lab., 521 Smethwick............................. 2,109
Fell, A. (b. 1914), C., 628Yarmouth....... 3,157
Fenner, Mrs. P. E. (b. 1922), C., 485 Rochester and Chatham................ 5,341
*Fernyhough, Rt. Hon. E. (b. 1908), Lab., 331Jarrow............................. 11,014
*Ferris, Rt. Hon. Sir R. G. Grant- (b. 1907), C., 414Nantwich...................... 5,273
Fidler, M. M. (b. 1916), C., 116Bury and Radcliffe.............................. 3,204
Finsberg, G. (b. 1926), C., 277Hampstead.. 474
Fisher, Mrs. D. M. G. (b. 1919), Lab., 68 Ladywood............................. 980
*Fisher, N. T. L. (b. 1913), C., 555Surbiton. 6,890
*Fitch, E. A. (b. 1915), Lab., 607Wigan.... 15,220
*Fitt, G. (b. 1926), Repub. Lab., 53Belfast, W.. 3,198
*Fletcher, E. J. (b. 1911), Lab., 167Darlington 3,761
*Fletcher, L. R. (b. 1921), Lab., 320Ilkeston. 17,091
*Foley, M. A. (b. 1925), Lab., 596West Bromwich............................ 4,436
Fookes, Miss J. E. (b. 1936), C., 401Merton and Morden.......................... 3,483
*Foot, M. M. (b. 1913), Lab., 207Ebbw Vale 17,446
*Ford, B. T. (b. 1925), Lab., 92Bradford, N. 1,630
*Forrester, J. S. (b. 1924), Lab., 547Stoke, N. 10,100
*Fortescue, T. V. N. (b. 1916), C., 370Garston 6,925
*Foster, Sir J. G. (b. 1904), C., 435Northwich 4,620

	Maj.
Fowler, C. Brocklebank- (b. 1934), C., 338 King's Lynn	
Fowler, P. N. (b. 1938), C., 440Nottingham, S.	33
Fox, J. M. (b. 1927), C., 517Shipley	3,731
★Fraser, Rt. Hon. H. C. P. J. (b. 1918), C., 536Stafford and Stone	4,777
★Fraser, J. D. (b. 1934), Lab., 343Norwood	9,676
★Freeson, R. (b. 1926), Lab., 608Willesden, E.	631
★Fry, P. D. (b. 1931), C., 592Wellingborough	4,509
★Galbraith, Hon. T. G. D. (b. 1917), C., 251 Hillhead	2,352
★Galpern, Sir M. (b. 1903), Lab., 257Shettleston	7,371
Gardner, E. L. (b. 1912), C., 529South Fylde	9,871
★Gardyne, J. Bruce- (b. 1930), C., 15S. Angus	26,105
★Garrett, W. E. (b. 1920), Lab., 578Wallsend	12,033
Gilbert, J. W. (b. 1927), C., 332Keighley	14,415
★Giles, Rear-Adm. M. C. M. (b. 1914), C., 611Winchester	336
★Gilmour, I. H. J. L. (b. 1926), C., 427 Norfolk, Central	13,476
★Gilmour, Sir J. E., Bt. (b. 1912), C., 233 Fife, E.	13,891
★Ginsburg, D. (b. 1923), Lab., 180Dewsbury	11,863
Glyn, A. J. (b. 1918), C., 612Windsor	4,547
★Godber, Rt. Hon. J. B. (b. 1914), C., 266 Grantham	16,050
★Golding, J. (b. 1931), Lab., 419Newcastle under Lyme	9,774
★Goldsmid, Sir H. J. d'Avigdor-, Bt. (b. 1909), C., 580Walsall, S.	2,106
Goldsmid, Maj.-Gen. J. A. d'Avigdor- (b. 1912), C., 366Lichfield and Tamworth	11,349
★Goodhart, P. C. (b. 1925), C., 45Beckenham.	1,976
★Goodhew, V. H. (b. 1919), C., 500St. Albans	17,732
★Gordon, P. W. Wolrige- (b. 1935), C., 5Aberdeenshire, E.	7,874
Gorst, J. M. (b. 1928), C., 289Hendon, N.	3,489
★Gourlay, H. P. H. (b. 1916), Lab., 340Kirkcaldy	3,179
Gower, H. R. (b. 1916), C., 37Barry	9,793
Grant, G. (b. 1924), Lab., 412Morpeth	8,671
★Grant, J. A. (b. 1925), C., 280Harrow, Cent.	12,311
Grant, J. D. (b. 1932), Lab., 328Islington, E.	3,964
Gray, J. H. N. (b. 1927), C., 323Ross and Cromarty	5,320
Green, A. (b. 1911), C., 473Preston, S.	801
★Grieve, W. P. (b. 1915), C., 522Solihull	1,331
★Griffiths, E. (b. 1929), Lab., 512Brightside.	24,575
★Griffiths, E. W. (b. 1925), C., 117Bury St. Edmunds	15,369
★Griffiths, W. D. (b. 1912), Lab., 390Manchester, Exchange	13,402
★Grimond, Rt. Hon. J. (b. 1913), L., 447 Orkney and Zetland	4,893
Grylls, W. M. J. (b. 1934), C., 139Chertsey	2,532
Gummer, J. S. (b. 1939), C., 364Lewisham, W.	11,586
★Gunter, Rt. Hon. R. l. (b. 1909), Lab., 533 Southwark	760
★Gurden, H. E. (b. 1903), C., 71Selly Oak.	9,794
Hall, J. (b. 1911), C., 627Wycombe	1,523
Hall, Miss J. V. (b. 1935), C., 332Keighley	16,810
★Hamilton, J. (b. 1918), Lab., 88Bothwell	616
★Hamilton, M. A. (b. 1918), C., 507Salisbury	10,711
★Hamilton, W. W. (b. 1917), Lab., 234Fife, W.	9,056
★Hamling, W. (b. 1912), Lab., 620Woolwich. W.	17,092
Hannam, J. G. (b. 1929), C., 225Exeter	618
★Hannan, W. (b. 1906), Lab., 253Maryhill	1,271
	12,287

	Maj.
Hardy, P. (b. 1931), Lab., 489Rother Valley	26,904
★Harper, J. (b. 1915), Lab., 464Pontefract	21,087
★Harrison, A. B. C. (b. 1921), C., 386 Maldon	6,272
★Harrison, Sir J. H., Bt. (b. 1907), C., 226 Eye	8,364
★Harrison, W. (b. 1921), Lab., 576Wakefield	11,684
★Hart, Rt. Hon. Judith (b. 1924), Lab., 345 Lanark	2,473
Haselhurst, A. G. B. (b. 1937), C., 404 Middleton and Prestwich	1,042
★Hastings, S. L. E. (b. 1921), C., 47Mid-Beds.	10,635
★Hattersley, R. S. G. (b. 1932), Lab., 63 Sparkbrook	3,346
Havers, R. M. O. (b. 1923), C., 610 Wimbledon	6,731
★Hawkins, P. L. (b. 1912), C., 430Norfolk, S.W.	5,648
★Hay, J. A. (b. 1919), C., 291Henley	14,142
Hayhoe, B. J. (b. 1925), C., 296Heston and Isleworth	4,599
★Healey, Rt. Hon. D. W. (b. 1917), Lab., 348Leeds, E.	7,715
★Heath, Rt. Hon. E. R. G. (b. 1916), C., 59Bexley	8,058
★Heffer, E. S. (b. 1922), Lab., 374Walton	4,406
★Heseltine, M. R. D. (b. 1933), C., 563 Tavistock	15,449
Hicks, R. A. (b. 1938), C., 82Bodmin	3,920
★Higgins, T. L. (b. 1928), C., 627Worthing	24,062
★Hiley, J. (b. 1902), C., 474Pudsey	5,995
★Hill, J. E. B. (b. 1912), C., 429Norfolk, S.	5,442
Hill, S. J. A. (b. 1924), C., 526Southampton, Test	1,802
★Hilton, W. S. (b. 1926), Lab., 58Bethnal Green	9,905
★Holland, P. W. (b. 1917), C., 132Carlton	12,797
★Holt, Sir J. A. Langford- (b. 1916), C., 519 Shrewsbury	9,206
Holt, Miss M. (b. 1924), C., 472Preston, N.	2,962
★Home, Rt. Hon. Sir A. F. Douglas- (b. 1903), C., 459Kinross and W. Perthshire.	9,764
★Hooson, H. E. (b. 1925), L., 409 Montgomeryshire	2,311
★Hopkins, J. S. R. Scott- (b. 1921), C., 177 Derbyshire, W.	8,716
Horam, J. R. (b. 1939), Lab., 243Gateshead, W.	8,294
★Hordern, P. M. (b. 1929), C., 307Horsham	14,288
★Hornby, R. P. (b. 1922), C. 567Tonbridge.	13,993
★Houghton, Rt. Hon. A. L. N. D. (b. 1898), Lab., 534Sowerby	469
Howe, Sir R. E. G. (b. 1926), C., 276 Reigate	13,029
★Howell, D. A. R. (b. 1936), C., 271Guildford	14,095
★Howell, D. H. (b. 1923), Lab., 72Small Heath	6,871
Howell, R. F. (b. 1923), C., 428Norfolk, North	4,684
★Huckfield, L. J. (b. 1943), Lab., 442Nuneaton	14,108
★Hughes, Rt. Hon. C. (b. 1916), Lab., 13 Anglesey	4,746
Hughes, R. (b. 1932), Lab., 3Aberdeen, N.	17,900
★Hughes, R. J. (b. 1925), Lab., 425Newport.	8,127
Hughes, W. M. (b. 1934), Lab., 197Durham	17,059
★Hunt, J. L. (b. 1929), C., 110Bromley	13,036
★Hunter, A. (b. 1908), Lab., 196Dunfermline	9,446
★Hutchison, A. M. C. (b. 1917), C., 214 Edinburgh, S.	4,780
★Hyslop, R. J. Maxwell- (b. 1931), C., 566 Tiverton	13,866
★Iremonger, T. L. (b. 1916), C., 318Ilford, N.	7,790

Maj.   Maj.

*Irvine, Rt. Hon. Sir A. J. (*b.* 1909), Lab., 368*Edge Hill*...................... 3,948

*Irvine, B. G. (*b.* 1909), C., 498*Rye*.... 23,269

James, D. P. (*b.* 1919), C., 184*Dorset, N.*.. 16,376

Janner, Hon. G. E. (*b.* 1927), Lab., 356 *Leicester, N.W.*..................... 2,642

*Jay, Rt. Hon. D. P. T. (*b.* 1907), Lab., 42*Battersea, N.*..................... 6,694

*Jeger, Mrs. L. M. (*b.* 1915), Lab., 302 *Holborn and St. Pancras, S.*.......... 2,323

*Jenkin, C. P. F. (*b.* 1926), C., 587*Wanstead and Woodford*...................... 11,543

*Jenkins, H. G. (*b.* 1908), Lab., 585*Putney*.. 1,394

*Jenkins, Rt. Hon. R. H. (*b.* 1920), Lab., 74*Stechford*....................... 6,711

*Jennings, J. C. (*b.* 1903), C., 115*Burton*.... 4,365

Jessel, T. F. H. (*b.* 1934), C., 573*Twickenham*............................. 11,621

John, B. T. (*b.* 1934), Lab., 466*Pontypridd*.. 20,209

*Johnson, C. A. (*b.* 1903), Lab., 363*Lewisham, S*....................... 5,552

*Johnson, J. (*b.* 1908), Lab., 315*Hull, W.*.... 9,513

Johnson, W. H. (*b.* 1917), Lab., 174*Derby, S.*................................ 3,149

*Johnston, D. R. (*b.* 1932), L., 322*Inverness*.. 2,674

*Jones, A. A. (*b.* 1915), C., 433*Northants, S.* 7,939

*Jones, D. (*b.* 1908), Lab., 114*Burnley*...... 9,354

*Jones, Rt. Hon. Sir F. E. (*b.* 1909), Lab., 600*West Ham, S.*................. 13,477

Jones, G. G. (*b.* 1942), Lab., 133*Carmarthen* 3,907

*Jones, L. Carter- (*b.* 1920), Lab., 208 *Eccles* 5,455

Jones, S. B. (*b.* 1939), Lab., 236*Flint, E.*.. 4,082

*Jones, T. A. (*b.* 1924), Lab., 480*Rhondda, W.*............................. 15,251

*Jopling, T. M. (*b.* 1930), C., 603*Westmorland*............................ 11,827

*Joseph, Rt. Hon. Sir K. S., Bt. (*b.* 1918), C., 349*Leeds, N.E.*................. 5,067

*Judd, F. A. (*b.* 1935), Lab., 471*Portsmouth, W.*................................ 955

*Kaberry, Sir D., Bt. (*b.* 1907), C., 350 *Leeds, N.W.*...................... 8,432

Kaufman, G. B. (*b.* 1930), Lab., 387*Ardwick* 3,002

*Kelley, R. (*b.* 1904), Lab., 182*Don Valley*.. 23,823

Kellett, Mrs. M. E. (*b.* 1924), C., 347 *Lancaster*.......................... 1,741

*Kerr, R. W. (*b.* 1921), Lab., 231*Feltham*.. 5,555

*Kershaw, J. A. (*b.* 1915), C., 551*Stroud*.... 7,931

Kilfedder, J. A. (*b.* 1928), U.U., 188*Down, N.*................................ 41,433

*Kimball, M. R. (*b.* 1928), C., 240*Gainsborough*............................ 7,709

*King, E. M. (*b.* 1907), C., 185*Dorset, S.*.... 6,864

*King, T. J. (*b.* 1933), C., 97*Bridgwater*.... 8,461

Kinnock, N. G. (*b.* 1942), Lab., 49*Bedwellty* 22,279

Kinsey, J. R. (*b.* 1921), C., 70*Perry Barr*.. 1,266

*Kirk, P. M. (*b.* 1928), C., 409*Saffron Walden*........................... 9,664

*Kitson, T. P. G. (*b.* 1931), C., 482*Richmond, Yorks.*..................... 17,769

*Knight, Mrs. J. C. J. (*b.* 1923), C., 65 *Edgbaston*......................... 10,643

Knox, D. L. (*b.* 1933), C., 354*Leek*...... 1,540

Lambie, D. (*b.* 1925), Lab., 27*Ayrshire, Central*........................... 4,967

*Lambton, A. C. F. (*Visct. Lambton*) (*b.* 1922), C., 57*Berwick-on-Tweed*............ 7,145

Lamond, J. A. (*b.* 1929), Lab., 445*Oldham, E.*................................ 760

*Lane, D. W. S. S. (*b.* 1922), C., 123*Cambridge*............................. 5,061

*Latham, A. C. (*b.* 1930), Lab., 452*Paddington, N.*.......................... 3,055

*Lawson, G. M. (*b.* 1906), Lab., 413*Motherwell*............................. 8,174

*Leadbitter, E. L. (*b.* 1919), Lab., 283*The Hartlepools*...................... 7,516

*Lee, Rt. Hon. F. (*b.* 1906), Lab., 426 *Newton*........................... 9,010

Le Marchant, S. (*b.* 1931), C., 299*High Peak*............................. 1,504

Leonard, R. L. (*b.* 1930), Lab., 486*Romford* 2,760

*Lestor, Miss J. (*b.* 1931), Lab., 224*Eton and Slough*............................ 2,667

*Lever, Rt. Hon. N. H. (*b.* 1914), Lab., 389 *Cheetham*......................... 4,802

*Lewis, A. W. J. (*b.* 1917), Lab., 599*West Ham, S*........................... 10,534

*Lewis, K. (*b.* 1916), C., 497*Rutland and Stamford*.......................... 7,667

*Lewis, R. H. (*b.* 1909), Lab., 131*Carlisle*.. 2,625

*Lipton, M. (*b.* 1900), Lab., 342*Brixton*.... 3,326

*Lloyd, Rt. Hon. G. W. (*b.* 1902), C., 588 *Sutton Coldfield*................... 18,640

*Lloyd, I. S. (*b.* 1921), C., 469*Langstone*.. 17,241

*Lloyd, Rt. Hon. J. S. B. (*b.* 1904), *The Speaker*, 613*Wirral*................ 16,458

*Lomas, K. (*b.* 1922), Lab., 312*Huddersfield, W.*................................ 193

*Longden, G. J. M. (*b.* 1902), C., 295*Herts., S.W.*................................ 8,447

*Loughlin, C. W. (*b.* 1914), Lab., 262*Glos., W.*................................ 1,107

Loveridge, J. W. (*b.* 1925), C., 305*Hornchurch*............................ 5,830

Luce, R. N. (*b.* 1936), C., 20*Arundel and Shoreham*......................... 23,254

*Lyon, A. W. (*b.* 1931), Lab., 630*York*.... 2,197

*Lyons, E. (*b.* 1926), Lab., 91*Bradford, E.*.. 9,138

*Mabon, J. D. (*b.* 1925), Lab., 268*Greenock* 3,234

McAdden, Sir S. J. (*b.* 1907), C., 527 *Southend, E.*....................... 6,960

*MacArthur, I. (*b.* 1925), C., 459*Perth and E. Perthshire*..................... 11,888

McBride, N. (*b.* 1910), Lab., 559*Swansea, E.*................................ 19,992

*McCann, J. (*b.* 1910), Lab., 484*Rochdale*.. 5,171

McCartney, H. (*b.* 1920), Lab., 291*Dunbartonshire, E.*...................... 5,555

McCrindle, R. A. (*b.* 1929), C., 60*Billericay* 3,954

*McElhone, F. P. (*b.* 1929), Lab.,249*Gorbals*. 7,189

McGuire, M. T. F. (*b.* 1926), Lab., 321*Ince* 17,418

*Mackenzie, J. G. (*b.* 1927), Lab., 496*Rutherglen*............................ 3,041

*Mackie, J. (*b.* 1906), Lab., 217*Enfield, E.*.. 4,030

*Mackintosh, J. P. (*b.* 1929), Lab., 56*Berwick and E. Lothian*.................... 641

McLaren, M. J. (*b.* 1914), C., 106*Bristol, N.W.*............................. 1,049

*Maclean, Sir F. H. R., Bt. (*b.* 1911), C., 26*Bute and N. Ayrshire*............ 6,394

*MacLennan, R. A. R. (*b.* 1936), Lab., 120 *Caithness and Sutherland*........... 2,705

McManus, F. (*b.* 1942), Unity, 232*Fermanagh and S. Tyrone*............. 1,447

*McMaster, S. R. (*b.* 1927), U.U., 50*Belfast, E.*................................ 8,519

*Macmilian, M. V. (*b.* 1921), C., 228*Farnham*............................. 14,935

*McMillan, T. (*b.* 1919), Lab., 247*Glasgow, Central*........................... 5,542

*McNamara, J. K. (*b.* 1934), Lab., 314*Hull, N.*................................ 8,390

*Maddan, W. F. M. (*b.* 1920), C., 309*Hove* 18,648

Madel, W. D. (*b.* 1938), C., 48 *Beds., S.*... 4,978

*Maginnis, J. E. (*b.* 1910), U.U., 19*Armagh*. 15,971

*Mahon, S. (*b.* 1914), Lab., 86*Bootle*...... 8,614

*Mallalieu, E. L. (*b.* 1905), Lab., 100*Brigg*.. 3,985

*Mallalieu, J. P. W. (*b.* 1908), Lab., 311 *Huddersfield, E.*................... 4,997

Mann, B. L. H. Douglas- (*b.* 1927), Lab., 333*Kensington, N.*................. 3,383

Maj.

*Marks, K. (b. 1920), Lab., 391Gorton..... 6,085
*Marples, Rt. Hon. A. E. (b. 1907), C., 577Wallasey........................ 3,111
*Marquand, D. I. (b. 1934), Lab., 21Ashfield............................. 17,283
Marsden, F. (b. 1923), Lab., 372Liverpool, Scotland.......................... 5,044
Marshall, Dr. E. I. (b. 1940), Lab., 263Goole........................... 13,333
*Marten, H. N. (b. 1916), C., 29Banbury... 11,546
*Mason, Rt. Hon. R. (b. 1924), Lab., 34Barnsley......................... 24,145
Mather, D. C. M. (b. 1919), C., 222Esher.. 23,278
*Maude, A. E. U. (b. 1912), C., 549Stratford 16,713
*Maudling, Rt. Hon. R. (b. 1917), C., 33Barnet............................ 8,679
*Mawby, R. L. (b. 1922), C., 570Totnes... 15,090
*Mayhew, C. P. (b. 1915), Lab., 619Woolwich, E......................... 9,164
Meacher, M. H. (b. 1939), Lab., 446Oldham, W.............................. 1,675
*Mellish, Rt. Hon. R. J. (b. 1913), Lab., 55Bermondsey...................... 9,736
*Mendelson, J. J. (b. 1917), Lab., 456Penistone........................... 16,718
Meyer, Sir A. J. C., Bt. (b. 1920), C., 237Flint, W.......................... 7,344
*Mikardo, I. (b. 1908), Lab., 468Poplar.... 12,484
*Millan, B. (b. 1927), Lab., 248Craigton... 7,211
*Miller, M. S. (b. 1920), Lab., 252Kelvingrove........................... 832
*Mills, P. M. (b. 1921), C., 569Torrington. 9,873
*Mills, W. S. (b. 1932), U.U., 51Belfast, N. 9,774
*Milne, E. J. (b. 1915), Lab., 81Blyth..... 23,568
*Miscampbell, N. A. (b. 1925), C., 78Blackpool, N......................... 9,236
Mitchell, Lt.-Col. C. C. (b. 1925), C., 6Aberdeenshire, W................. 5,549
*Mitchell, D. B. (b. 1928), C., 38Basingstoke............................. 9,474
†Mitchell, R. C. (b. 1927), Lab., 525Southampton, Itchen.................... 9,675
Moate, R. D. (b. 1938), C., 230Faversham. 3,811
*Molloy, W. J. (b. 1918), Lab., 199Ealing, N. 320
Molyneaux, J. H. (b. 1921), U.U., 17Antrim, S........................ 39,618
Money, E. D. D. (b. 1931), C., 324Ipswich 13
Monks, Mrs. C. M. (b. 1911), C., 147Chorley.......................... 1,677
*Monro, H. S. P. (b. 1922), C., 191Dumfries 9,106
*Montgomery, W. F. (b. 1927), C., 99Brierley Hill...................... 15,237
*More, J. (b. 1907), C., 282Ludlow....... 9,304
*Morgan, D.E. (b. 1932), Lab., 130Cardiganshire............................ 1,263
*Morgan, W. G. O. (b. 1920), C., 171Denbigh......................... 8,709
*Morris, A. (b. 1928), Lab., 395Wythenshawe............................. 5,755
*Morris, C. R. (b. 1926), Lab., 393Openshaw............................. 7,101
*Morris, Rt. Hon. J. (b. 1929), Lab., 1Aberavon........................... 20,895
*Morrison, Hon. C. A. (b. 1932), C., 278Devizes.......................... 8,033
*Moyle, R. D. (b. 1928), Lab., 372Lewisham, N......................... 1,027
Mudd, W. D. (b. 1933), C., 227Falmouth and Camborne.................... 1,523
*Mulley, Rt. Hon. F. W. (b. 1918), Lab., 516Sheffield, Park................ 16,278
Murray, R. K. (b. 1922), Lab., 211Leith.. 1,384
*Murton, H. O. (b. 1914), C., 467Poole.... 13,490
*Nabarro, Sir G. D. N. (b. 1913), C., 622Worcs., S......................... 17,809
Neave, A. M. S. (b. 1916), C., 8Abingdon. 13,073

Maj.

*Nicholls, Sir H., Bt. (b. 1912), C., 460Peterborough...................... 4,56
*Noble, Rt. Hon. M. A. C. (b. 1913), C., 18Argyll........................ 4,48
Normanton, T. (b. 1917), C., 135Cheadle. 1,75
*Nott, J. W. F. (b. 1932), C., 502St. Ives... 8,66
*Ogden, E. (b. 1923), Lab., 376Liverpool, West Derby...................... 5,70
*O'Halloran, M. J. (b. 1928), Lab., 329Islington, N....................... 5,148
*O'Malley, B. K. (b. 1930), Lab., 488Rotherham......................... 12,47
*Onslow, C. G. D. (b. 1926), C., 614Woking.............................. 18,568
Oppenheim, Mrs. S. (b. 1930), C., 260Gloucester......................... 1,06
*Oram, A. E. (b. 1913), Lab., 205East Ham, S............................. 5,23
*Orbach, M. (b. 1902), Lab., 543Stockport, S. 2,06
*Orme, S. (b. 1923), Lab., 506Salford, W... 2,67
*Orr, Capt. L. P. S. (b. 1918), U.U., 189Down, S........................ 13,21
*Osborn, J. H. (b. 1922), C., 513Hallam... 12,25
*Oswald, T. (b. 1904), Lab., 209Edinburgh, Central.......................... 1,56
*Owen, D. A. L. (b. 1938), Lab., 463Plymouth, Sutton.................... 74
Owen, I. W. (b. 1912), C., 542Stockport, N. 87
*Padley, W.E. (b. 1916), Lab., 443Ogmore.. 23,02
*Page, A. J. (b. 1919), C., 282Harrow, W... 13,40
*Page, R. G. (b. 1911), C., 162Crosby..... 5,69
*Paget, R. T. (b. 1908), Lab., 432Northampton.............................. 1,24
Paisley, I. R. K. (b. 1926), Prot. U., 16Antrim, N......................... 2,67
*Palmer, A. M. F. (b. 1912), Lab., 104Bristol, Central........................ 3,24
*Pannell, Rt. Hon. T. C. (b. 1902), Lab., 353Leeds, W...................... 6,86
*Pardoe, J. W. (b. 1934), L., 157Cornwall, N.............................. 63
*Parker, A. D. Dodds- (b. 1909), C., 138Cheltenham........................ 8,6
*Parker, J. (b. 1906), Lab., 166Dagenham.. 19,35
Parkinson, C. E. (b. 1931), C., 218Enfield, W.............................. 8,27
Parry, R. (b. 1933), Lab., 369Liverpool, Exchange.......................... 8,35
*Pavitt, L. A. (b. 1914), Lab., 609Willesden, W............................. 11,75
*Peart, Rt. Hon. T. F. (b. 1914), Lab., 623Workington....................... 9,44
*Peel, W. J. (b. 1912), C., 387Leicester, S.E. 10,69
Pendry, T. (b. 1934), Lab., 537Stalybridge and Hyde......................... 2,84
*Pentland, N. (b. 1912), Lab., 141Chester-le-Street........................... 20,33
*Percival, W. I. (b. 1921), C., 531Southport. 9,14
*Perry, E. G. (b. 1910), Lab., 43Battersea, S. 1,69
*Peyton, Rt. Hon. J. W. W. (b. 1919), C., 629Yeovil.......................... 7,06
*Pike, Miss I. M. P. (b. 1918), C., 397Melton 17,87
*Pink, R. B. (b. 1912), C., 470Portsmouth, S. 10,11
*Pounder, R. J. (b. 1933), U.U., 52Belfast, S. 15,95
*Powell, Rt. Hon. J. E. (b. 1912), C., 617Wolverhampton, S.W............. 14,46
*Prentice, Rt. Hon. R. E. (b. 1923), Lab., 204East Ham, N.................. 3,82
Prescott, J. L. (b. 1938), Lab., 313Hull, E... 22,12
*Price, D. E. C. (b. 1924), C., 206Eastleigh.. 8,05
*Price, J. T. (b. 1902), Lab., 601Westhoughton.............................. 5,82
*Price, W. G. (b. 1934), Lab., 492Rugby.... 2,95
*Prior, Rt. Hon. J. M. L. (b. 1927), C., 381Lowestoft......................... 5,52

Maj.

*Probert, A. R. (b. 1909), Lab., 2Aberdare.. 11,386

Proudfoot, G. W. (b. 1921), C., 101Brighouse and Spenborough............... 59

*Pym, Rt. Hon. F. L. (b. 1922), C., 124 Cambridgeshire...................... 12,271

*Quennell, Miss J. M. (b. 1923), C., 461 Petersfield......................... 20,107

Raison, T. H. F. (b. 1929), C., 24Aylesbury 10,643

*Ramsden, Rt. Hon. J. E. (b. 1923), C., 279 Harrogate.......................... 17,342

Rankin, J. (b. 1890), Lab., 250Govan..... 7,142

*Rawlinson, Rt.Hon.Sir P. A. G. (b. 1919), C., 220Epsom........................ 22,774

Redmond, R. S. (b. 1919), C., 85Bolton, W................................. 1,244

Reed, D. (b. 1945), Lab., 509Sedgefield.... 12,831

Reed, L. D. (b. 1937), C., 84Bolton, E..... 471

*Rees, M. (b. 1920), Lab., 351Leeds, S...... 10,225

Rees, P. W. I. (b. 1926), C., 187Dover..... 1,649

*Renton, Rt. Hon. Sir D. L. M. (b. 1908), 316Huntingdonshire.................. 9,810

*Rhodes, G. W. (b. 1928), Lab., 421Newcastle, E......................... 5,948

*Richard, I. S. (b. 1922), Lab., 35Barons Court............................. 1,105

*Ridley, Hon. N. (b. 1929), C., 148Cirencester and Tewkesbury.............. 14,086

*Ridsdale, J. E. (b. 1915), C., 284Harwich.. 12,831

*Rippon, Rt. Hon. A. G. F. (b. 1924), C., 297Hexham......................... 7,871

*Roberts, A. (b. 1908), Lab., 431Normanton 15,289

*Roberts, Rt. Hon. G. O. (b. 1913), Lab., 118Caernarvon...................... 2,296

Roberts, I.W.P. (b. 1930), C., 156Conway 903

Roberts, M. H. A. (b. 1927), C., 127Cardiff, N................................. 1,776

*Robertson, J. (b. 1913), Lab., 454Paisley... 10,197

Roderick, C. E. (b. 1927), Lab., 95Brecon and Radnor........................ 4,844

*Rodgers, Sir J. C., Bt. (b. 1906), C., 510 Sevenoaks......................... 17,278

*Rodgers, W. T. (b. 1928), Lab., 544 Stockton-on-Tees.................... 4,323

Roper, J. F. H. (b. 1935), Lab., 229Farnworth............................ 8,525

*Rose, P. B. (b. 1935), Lab., 388Blackley.... 2,599

*Ross, Rt. Hon. W. (b. 1911), Lab., 337 Kilmarnock........................ 13,001

*Rossi, H. A. L. (b. 1927), C., 306Hornsey.. 3,789

Rost, P. L. (b. 1930), C., 176Derbyshire, S.E................................ 2,724

*Royle, A. H. R. (b. 1927), C., 481Richmond, Surrey........................ 7,998

*Russell, Sir R. S. (b. 1904), C., 595 Wembley, S......................... 2,242

Sandelson, N. D. (b. 1923), Lab., 286 Hayes and Harlington................ 10,479

*Sandys, Rt. Hon. D. E. (b. 1908), C., 586 Streatham.......................... 5,622

*Scott, Sir M. Stoddart- (b. 1901), C., 483 Ripon............................. 12,064

*Scott, N.P. (b. 1933), C., 453Paddington, S. 2,613

*Sharples, R. C. (b. 1916), C., 557Sutton and Cheam............................. 12,696

*Shaw, M. N. (b. 1920), C., 508Scarborough and Whitby........................ 9,637

*Sheldon, R. E. (b. 1923), Lab., 23Ashtonunder-Lyne........................ 3,954

Shelton, W. J. M. (b. 1929), C., 584Clapham.............................. 3,120

*Shore, Rt. Hon. P. D. (b. 1924), Lab., 538 Stepney........................... 14,071

*Short, Rt. Hon. E. W. (b. 1912), Lab., 420Newcastle, Central................ 9,415

*Short, Mrs. R. (b. 1919), Lab., 616Wolverhampton, N.E..................... 1,893

Maj.

*Silkin, Rt. Hon. J. E. (b. 1923), Lab., 172 Deptford........................... 7,317

*Silkin, Hon. S. C. (b. 1918), Lab., 121 Dulwich........................... 895

*Sillars, J. (b. 1937), Lab., 28Ayrshire, S..... 12,235

*Silverman, J. (b. 1905), Lab., 64Aston..... 3,562

Simeons, C.F.C. (b. 1921), C., 383Luton... 1,349

*Sinclair, Sir G. E. (b. 1912), C., 183Dorking 14,870

Skinner, D. E. (b. 1932), Lab., 83Bolsover.. 20,459

Skeet, T. H. H. (b. 1918), C., 46Bedford... 5,279

*Small, W. W. (b. 1909), Lab., 256Scotstoun 12,005

*Smith, Hon. A. L. Buchanan- (b. 1932), C., 14North Angus and Mearns.......... 9,595

*Smith, Rt. Hon. Sir D. C. Walker-, Bt. (b. 1910), C., 293Herts., E............ 14,067

*Smith, D. G. (b. 1926), C. 589Warwick and Leamington....................... 15,639

Smith, D. G. Stewart- (b. 1933), C., 54 Belper............................. 2,124

*Smith, G. Johnson (b. 1924), C., 203East Grinstead......................... 26,016

Smith, J. (b. 1938), Lab., 346Lanark, N.... 5,019

Smith, Rt. Hon. Dame Patricia Hornsby- (b. 1914), C., 146Chislehurst......... 3,363

Soref, H. B. (b. 1916), C., 448Ormskirk.... 15,031

Spearing, N. J. (b. 1930), Lab., 10Acton... 600

*Speed, H. K. (b. 1934), C., 398Meriden.... 4,724

Spence, J. D. (b. 1920), C., 514Heeley..... 713

*Spriggs, L. (b. 1910), Lab., 510St. Helens.. 15,078

Sproat, I. M. (b. 1938), C., 4Aberdeen, S... 1,089

*Stainton, K. M. (b. 1921), C. 522Sudbury and Woodbridge.................... 12,564

Stallard, A. W. (b. 1921), Lab., 504St. Pancras, N........................ 5,849

Stanbrook, I. R. (b. 1924), C. 449Orpington.............................. 1,322

*Steel, D. M. S. (b. 1938), L., 491Roxburgh, Selkirk and Peebles................. 550

*Stevas, N. A. F. St. John- (b. 1929), C., 136Chelmsford...................... 13,041

Stewart, D. J. (b. 1920), Scot. Nat., 598 Western Isles....................... 726

*Stewart, Rt. Hon. R. M. M. (b. 1906), Lab., 239Fulham...................... 3,505

*Stodart, J. A. (b. 1916), C., 215Edinburgh, W................................. 7,341

Stoddart, D. L. (b. 1926), Lab., 561Swindon 5,576

Stokes, J. H. R. (b. 1917), C., 444Oldbury and Halesowen.................... 2,904

*Stonehouse, Rt. Hon. J. T. (b. 1925), Lab., 591Wednesbury...................... 3,371

Strang, G. S. (b. 1943), Lab., 210Edinburgh, E................................. 5,514

*Strauss, Rt. Hon. G. R. (b. 1901), Lab., 344Vauxhall........................ 5,569

Stuttaford, I. T. (b. 1931), C. 437Norwich, S................................. 826

*Summerskill, Hon. Shirley (b. 1931), Lab., 273Halifax......................... 198

Sutcliffe, J. H. V. (b. 1931), C., 403 Middlesbrough.W................... 388

*Swain, T. H. (b. 1912), Lab., 175Derbyshire, N.E........................ 13,631

*Tapsell, P. H. B. (b. 1930), C., 304Horncastle............................. 10,439

*Taverne, D. (b. 1928), Lab., 367Lincoln... 4,750

*Taylor, Sir C. S. (b. 1910), C., 202Eastbourne............................ 6,988

*Taylor, E. McM. (b. 1937), C., 246Cathcart............................... 4,905

*Taylor, F. H. (b. 1907), C., 392Moss Side... 1,713

Taylor, R. G. (b. 1932), C., 164Croydon, N.W.............................. 4,573

Tebbit, N. B. (b. 1931), C., 219Epping..... 2,575

*Temple, J. M. (b. 1910), C., 140Chester... 7,005

✗ *Deputy Leader of Labour Party.*

	Maj.
★Thatcher, Rt. Hon. Margaret (*b.* 1925), C., 235*Finchley*	11,185
Thomas, J. (*b.* 1933), Lab., 7*Abertillery*	19,341
Thomas, J. S. (*b.* 1925), C., 408*Monmouth*	1,355
★Thomas, Rt. Hon. T. G. (*b.* 1909), Lab., 129*Cardiff, W.*	5,777
Thomas, Rt. Hon. P. J. M. (*b.* 1920), C., 290*Hendon, S.*	6,189
★Thompson, Sir R. H. M., Bt. (*b.* 1912), C., 165*Croydon, S.*	3,703
★Thomson, Rt. Hon. G. M. (*b.* 1921), Lab., 194*Dundee, E.*	2,798
★Thorpe, Rt. Hon. J. J. (*b.* 1929), L., 179*Devon, N.*	369
★Tilney, J. D. R. T. (*b.* 1907), C., 375*Wavertree*	7,477
★Tinn, J. (*b.* 1922), Lab., 150*Cleveland*	5,083
★Tomney, F. (*b.* 1908), Lab., 276*Hammersmith, N.*	6,530
Torney, T. W. (*b.* 1915), Lab., 93*Bradford, S.*	1,976
Trafford, J. A. P. (*b.* 1932), C., 625*The Wrekin*	518
Trew, P. J. E. (*b.* 1932), C., 168*Dartford*	560
★Tuck, R. H. (*b.* 1910), Lab., 590*Watford*	76
Tugendhat, C. S. (*b.* 1937), C., 149*Cities of London and Westminster*	9,040
★Turton, Rt. Hon. Sir R. H. (*b.* 1903), C., 564*Thirsk and Malton*	15,583
Urwin, T. W. (*b.* 1912), Lab., 308*Houghton-le-Spring*	20,974
★van Straubenzee, W. R. (*b.* 1924), C., 615*Wokingham*	20,553
★Varley, E. G. (*b.* 1932), Lab., 142*Chesterfield*	14,169
Vaughan, G. F. (*b.* 1923), C., 475*Reading*	1,154
★Vickers, Dame Joan (*b.* 1907), C., 462*Devonport*	1,372
★Waddington, D. C. (*b.* 1929), C., 416*Nelson and Colne*	1,410
★Wainwright, E. (*b.* 1908), Lab., 170*Dearne Valley*	27,118
★Walden, A. B. (*b.* 1932), Lab., 63*Birmingham, All Saints*	4,279
Walder, A. D. (*b.* 1928), C., 151*Clitheroe*	6,272
★Walker, H. (*b.* 1927), Lab., 181*Doncaster*	3,227
★Walker, Rt. Hon. P. C. Gordon (*b.* 1907), Lab., 365*Leyton*	5,480
★Walker, Rt. Hon. P. E. (*b.* 1931), C., 611*Worcester*	8,442
★Wall, P. H. B. (*b.* 1916), C. 274*Haltemprice*	14,180
★Wallace, G. D. (*b.* 1900), Lab., 436*Norwich, N.*	6,696
★Walters, D. M. (*b.* 1928), C., 597*Westbury*	9,111
★Ward, Dame Irene (*b.* 1895), C., 574*Tynemouth*	6,846

	Maj.
Warren, K. R. (*b.* 1926), C., 285*Hastings*	6,81
★Watkins, D. J. (*b.* 1925), Lab., 155*Consett*	17,07
★Watt, J. D. Gibson- (*b.* 1918), C., 292*Hereford*	7,60
★Weatherill, B. B. (*b.* 1920), C., 163*Croydon, N.E.*	3,97
★Weitzman, D. (*b.* 1898), Lab., 545*Stoke Newington and Hackney, N.*	9,14
★Wellbeloved, J. (*b.* 1926), Lab., 221*Erith and Crayford*	4,85
★Wells, J. J. (*b.* 1925), C., 385*Maidstone*	12,84
★Wells, W. T. (*b.* 1908), Lab., 579*Walsall, N.*	7,41
White, J. (*b.* 1922), Lab., 254*Pollok*	60
White, R. L. (*b.* 1928), C., 267*Gravesend*	1,21
★Whitehead, P. (*b.* 1937), Lab., 173*Derby, N.*	3,47
★Whitelaw, Rt. Hon. W. S. I. (*b.* 1918), C., 457*Penrith and the Border*	13,54
★Whitlock, W. C. (*b.* 1918), Lab., 439*Nottingham, N.*	7,28
★Wiggin, A. W. (*b.* 1937), C., 604*Weston-super-Mare*	19,34
Wilkinson, J. A. D. (*b.* 1940), C., 94*Bradford, W.*	1,53
★Willey, Rt. Hon. F. T. (*b.* 1910), Lab., 553*Sunderland, N.*	9,04
★Williams, A. J. (*b.* 1930), Lab., 560*Swansea, W.*	3,23
★Williams, Sir B. M. Rhys-, Bt. (*b.* 1927), C., 334*Kensington, S.*	14,66
★Williams, Mrs. S. V. T. B. (*b.* 1930), Lab., 300*Hitchin*	3,67
★Williams, W. T. (*b.* 1915), Lab., 588*Warrington*	9,32
Wilson, A. (*b.* 1917), Lab., 275*Hamilton*	8,58
★Wilson, Rt. Hon. J. H. (*b.* 1916), Lab., 317*Huyton*	21,07
★Wilson, P. M. E. D. McNair- (*b.* 1929), C., 424*New Forest*	22,46
★Wilson, R. M. C. McNair- (*b.* 1930), C., 581*Walthamstow, E.*	52
★Wilson, W. (*b.* 1913), Lab., 160*Coventry, S.*	2,19
★Wood, Rt. Hon. R. F. (*b.* 1920), C., 98*Bridlington*	13,50
Woodhouse, Hon. C. M. (*b.* 1917), C., 451*Oxford*	1,88
★Woodnutt, H. F. M. (*b.* 1918), C., 327*Isle of Wight*	17,32
★Woof, R. E. (*b.* 1911), Lab., 80*Blaydon*	11,79
★Worsley, W. M. J. (*b.* 1925), C., 137*Chelsea*	10,11
★Wylie, Rt. Hon. N. R. (*b.* 1923), C., 213*Pentlands*	3,18
★Younger, Hon. G. K. H. (*b.* 1931), C., 25*Ayr*	4,45

SMALL MAJORITIES

E. D. D. Money (*C.*), Ipswich	13
C. Brocklebank-Fowler (*C.*), King's Lynn	33
G. W. Proudfoot (*C.*), Brighouse and Spenborough	59
R. H. Tuck (*Lab.*), Watford	76
T. G. Boardman (*C.*), Leicester, S.W.	106
D. M. Coombs (*C.*), Yardley	120
K. Lomas (*Lab.*), Huddersfield, W.	193
Hon. Shirley Summerskill (*Lab.*), Halifax	198
W. J. Molloy (*Lab.*), Ealing, N.	320
J. W. Gilbert (*Lab.*), Dudley	336
Rt. Hon. J. J. Thorpe (*L.*), Devon, N.	369
J. H. V. Sutcliffe (*C.*), Middlesbrough, W.	388
R. J. Adley (*C.*), Bristol, N.E.	462
Rt. Hon. A. L. N. D. Houghton (*Lab.*), Sowerby	469
L. D. Reed (*C.*), Bolton, E.	471
G. Finsberg (*C.*), Hampstead	474

M. C. J. Barnes (*Lab.*), Brentford and Chiswick	51
J. A. P. Trafford (*C.*), Wrekin	51
R. M. C. McNair-Wilson (*C.*), Walthamstow, E.	52
J. D. Cronin (*Lab.*), Loughborough	53
D. M. S. Steel (*L.*), Roxburgh, Selkirk and Peebles	55
P. J. E. Trew (*C.*), Dartford	56
A. Davidson (*Lab.*), Accrington	59
N. J. Spearing (*Lab.*), Acton	60
J. White (*Lab.*), Pollok	60
Miss J. V. Hall (*C.*), Keighley	61
W. Hambling (*Lab.*), Woolwich, W.	61
J. W. Pardoe (*L.*), Cornwall, N.	63
J. D. Fraser (*Lab.*), Norwood	63
J. P. Mackintosh (*Lab.*), Berwick and E. Lothian	64

THE HOUSE OF COMMONS BY CONSTITUENCIES

The figures following the name of the Constituency denote the total number of *Electors* in the Parliamentary Division at the General Election of 1970.

ABBREVIATIONS.—C. = Conservative; *Comm.* = Communist; *N.I. Lab.* = Northern Ireland Labour; *Ind.* = Independent; *L.* = Liberal; *Lab.* = Labour; *P.C.* = Plaid Cymru; *Scot. Nat.* = Scottish Nationalist; *S.P.G.B.* = Socialist Party of Great Britain; *Repub.* = Republican; *U.U.* = Ulster Unionist.

An asterisk ★ denotes membership of the last House for the same division; † for a different division.

Aberavon (Glamorgan)
E. 62,901
1★Rt. Hon. J. Morris, Lab... 31,314
I. Grist, C............. 10,419
G. Farmer, P.C....... 3,912
J. T. Hart, Comm....... 1,102
Lab. maj............. 20,895
(1966 Lab. maj. 24,394)

Aberdare (Welsh Borough)
E. 49,079
2★A. R. Probert, Lab.... 22,817
G. M. Jones, P.C....... 11,431
D. C. Purnell, C....... 2,484
A. T. M. Wilson, Comm. 1,317
Lab. maj. 11,386
(1966 Lab. maj. 22,118)

Aberdeen (2)
NORTH E. 64,558
3 R. Hughes, Lab........ 27,707
D. J. Williams, C....... 9,807
J. McKenna, Scot. Nat... 3,756
F. McCallum, L......... 2,835
A. J. Ingram, Comm..... 521
Lab. maj............. 17,900
(1966 Lab. maj. 20,031)
SOUTH E. 68,612
4 I. M. Sproat, C......... 23,843
★D. C. Dewar, Lab....... 22,754
K. J. B. S. Macleod, L... 3,135
B. M. Cockie, Scot. Nat.. 2,777
C. maj............... 1,089
(1966 Lab. maj. 1,799)

Aberdeenshire (2)
EAST E. 46,087
5★P. W. Wolrige-Gordon, C. 12,866
A. R. Farquhar, Scot. Nat. 9,377
H. C. Grimes, Lab....... 5,656
G. C. Hoyer-Millar, L.... 3,548
C. maj............... 3,489
(1966 C. Maj. 4,033)
WEST E. 52,458
6 Lt.-Col. C. C. Mitchell, C. 18,396
Hon. Mrs. L. M. Grimond,
L.................. 12,847
W. W. Hay, Lab........ 6,141
J. G. McKinley, Scot.
Nat............... 2,112
C. maj............... 5,549
(1966 L. maj. 1,195)

Abertillery (Monmouthshire)
E. 37,632
7 J. Thomas, Lab........ 22,819
J. E. Rendle, C......... 3,478
D. B. Harries, P.C...... 1,751
Lab. maj............. 19,341
(1966 Lab. maj. 20,202)

Abingdon (Berkshire)
E. 86,319
8★A. M. S. Neave, D.S.O.,
O.B.E., M.C., T.D., C... 36,209
N. H. Price, Lab....... 23,136
S. R. Caradoc-Evans, L. 7,198
C. maj............... 13,073
(1966 C. maj. 3,302)

Accrington (English Borough)
E. 51,444
9★A. Davidson, Lab....... 20,828
Dr. R. C. Webster, T.D.,
C................. 20,234
Lab. maj............. 594
(1966 Lab. maj. 6,822)

Acton (London)
E. 43,861
10 N. J. Spearing, Lab.... 13,960
★K. W. Baker, C....... 13,300
D. A. Scherer, L....... 1,583
M. W. Costin, Comm... 258
Lab. maj............. 660
(March 1968, by-election,
C. maj. 3,720)
(1966 Lab. maj. 4,941)

Aldershot (Hampshire)
E. 85,010
11 J. M. G. Critchley, C... 33,447
R. T. Bogg, Lab........ 18,916
P. Gibbons, L......... 7,551
C. maj............... 14,531
(1966 C. maj. 8,896)

ALL SAINTS—See Birmingham

Altrincham and Sale
(English Borough)
E. 71,125
12★Rt. Hon. A. P. L. Barber,
T.D., C........... 27,904
B. E. Jones, Lab....... 16,671
L. G. Bayley, L........ 7,875
C. maj............... 11,233
(1966 C. maj. 6,837)

Anglesey
E. 41,527
13★Rt. Hon. C. Hughes,
Lab............... 13,966
J. E. Jones, C......... 9,220
J. L. Williams, P.C..... 7,140
G. W. Roddick, L...... 2,013
Lab. maj............. 4,746
(1966 Lab. maj. 5,298)

Angus and Kincardine (2)
NORTH ANGUS AND MEARNS
E. 37,318
14★Hon. A. L. Buchanan-
Smith, C......... 14,687
J. Gourlay, Lab........ 5,092
J. A. McGugan, Scot.
Nat............... 4,677
J. J. Grimond, L....... 3,212
C. maj............... 9,595
(1966 C. maj. 5,530)
SOUTH E. 49,618
15★J. Bruce-Gardyne, C.... 20,439
C. G. M. Slesser, Scot.
Nat............... 8,406
H. Coutts, Lab........ 7,557
C. maj............... 12,033
(1966 C. maj. 13,003)

Antrim (2)
E. 80,506
NORTH
16 I. R. K. Paisley, Prot. U. 24,130
★H. M. Clark, U.U..... 21,451
P. J. McHugh, N.I. Lab. 6,476
A. McDonald, Nat.
Dem.............. 4,312
R. G. Moore, L........ 2,069
Prot. U. maj......... 2,679
(1966 U.U. maj. 22,986)

SOUTH E. 144,734
17 J. H. Molyneaux, U.U... 59,589
T. H. Caldwell, Ind. U. 10,938
D. J. McAllister, Nat.
Dem.............. 6,037
R. A. M. Smith, L..... 913
U.U. maj............ 39,618
(1966 U.U. maj. 18,168)

ARDWICK—See Manchester

Argyll
E. 41,107
18★Rt. Hon. M. A. C. Noble,
C................. 13,521
I. MacCormick, Scot.
Nat............... 9,039
J. McFadden, Lab...... 7,633
C. maj............... 4,482
(1966 C. maj. 3,692)

Armagh
E. 87,868
19★J. E. Maginnis, U.U.... 37,667
H. Lewis, Nat. Unity... 21,696
J. E. Holmes, N.I. Lab.. 8,781
U.U. maj............ 15,971
(1966 U.U. maj. 21,220)

Arundel and Shoreham
(West Sussex) E. 100,941
20★Capt. H. B. Kerby, C... 43,907
B. M. Lyne, Lab....... 16,531
P. F. Bartram, L....... 11,769
C. maj............... 27,376
(By-election, April 1, 1971)
R. N. Luce, C......... 34,482
R. R. Kenward, Lab... 11,228
P. F. Bartram, L....... 7,917
G. Thomas, Ind....... 191
C. Maj.............. 23,254
(1966 C. maj. 18,096)

Ashfield (Nottinghamshire)
E. 68,007
21★D. I. Marquand, Lab.... 32,372
R. N. Kemm, C........ 15,089
Lab. maj............. 17,283
(1966 Lab. maj. 21,486)

Ashford (Kent)
E. 67,362
22★Rt. Hon. W. F. Deedes,
M.C., C........... 26,649
J. M. Bowyer, Lab..... 14,037
F. C. Truman, L....... 7,902
C. maj............... 12,612
(1966 C. maj. 8,113)

L+

Ashton under Lyne
(English Borough)
E. 61,779
23*R. E. Sheldon, Lab.... 23,927
A. d' A. Fearn, C...... 19,973
Lab. maj............. 3,954
(1966 Lab. maj. 7,332)

ASTON—See Birmingham

ATTERCLIFFE—See Sheffield

Aylesbury (Buckinghamshire)
E. 77,818
24 T. H. F. Raison, C..... 31,084
J. E. Mitchell, Lab...... 20,441
P. S. Kinsey, L...... 6,849
C. maj........... 10,643
(1966 C. maj. 3,907)

Ayrshire and Bute (5)
AYR E. 52,105
25*Hon. G. K. H. Younger,
T.D., C............. 22,220
J. M. Craigen, Lab.... 17,770
L. Anderson, Scot. Nat. 2,186
C. maj........... 4,450
(1966 Lab. maj. 484)

BUTE AND NORTH AYRSHIRE
E. 48,111
26*Sir F. H. R. Maclean,
Bt., C.B.E., C....... 18,853
H. G. Millar, Lab...... 12,459
Mrs. M. Macrae, Scot.
Nat............. 3,852
C. maj........... 6,394
(1966 C. maj. 2,656)

CENTRAL E. 58,544
27 D. Lambie, Lab........ 24,536
I. B. Lang, C...... 19,569
Rev. A. Macdonald,
Scot. Nat....... 2,383
T. Menzies, Ind....... 339
Lab. maj........... 4,967
(1966 Lab. maj. 6,398)

SOUTH E. 50,852
28*J. Sillars, Lab.......... 23,910
N. D. Simpson, C..... 11,675
S. H. Purdie, Scot. Nat.. 3,102
Lab. maj........... 12,235
(March 1970, by-election,
Lab. maj. 10,886)
(1966 Lab. maj. 12,053)
See also Kilmarnock

Banbury (Oxfordshire)
E. 89,559
29*H. N. Marten, C........ 36,712
A. C. Booth, Lab...... 25,166
G. J. Fisher, L...... 6,859
C. maj........... 11,546
(1966 C. maj. 4,403)

Banff
E. 31,915
30*W. H. K. Baker, C..... 8,457
H. M. Watt, Scot. Nat.. 5,006
T. R. L. Fraser, L...... 4,589
A. F. Walls, Lab...... 3,795
C. maj........... 3,451
(1966 C. maj. 1,377)

Barking (London)
E. 49,655
31*T. E. N. Driberg, Lab...21,097
G. E. Pattie, C........ 9,309
Lab. maj...........11,788
(1966 Lab. maj. 15,410)

Barkston Ash (Yorks., W. R.)
E. 78,562
32*M. J. H. Alison, C..... 35,198
E. K. Grime, Lab...... 23,861
C. maj........... 11,337
(1966 C. maj. 6,342)

Barnet (London)
E. 72,293
33*Rt. Hon. R. Maudling,
C................. 26,845
Mrs. J. E. M. Baker,
Lab............. 18,166
J. D. O. Henchley, L... 6,329
C. maj........... 8,679
(1966 C. maj. 5,486)

Barnsley (English Borough)
E. 76,211
34*Rt. Hon. R. Mason, Lab. 34,956
R. Godber, C...... 10,811
J. H. Dossett, L...... 8,186
Lab. maj........... 24,145
(1966 Lab. maj. 26,288)

Barons Court (London)
E. 41,534
35*I. S. Richard, Q.C., Lab.. 13,374
R. E. Brum, C...... 12,269
S. H. J. A. Knott, L...... 2,206
Lab. maj........... 1,105
(1966 Lab. maj. 3,470)

Barrow in Furness
(English Borough) E. 54,523
36*A. E. Booth, Lab...... 22,400
H. D. Miller, C........ 17,536
Lab. maj........... 4,864
(1966 Lab. maj. 8,032)

Barry (Glamorgan)
E. 75,551
37*H. R. Gower, C........ 31,957
J. Allison, Lab...... 23,286
E. O. Williams, P.C.... 4,200
C. maj........... 8,671
(1966 C. maj. 1,394)

Basingstoke (Hampshire)
E. 92,492
38*D. B. Mitchell, C...... 35,138
D. V. Carter, Lab...... 25,664
R. A. Musselwhite, L.. 8,183
C. maj........... 9,474
(1966 C. maj. 3,659)

Bassetlaw (Nottinghamshire)
E. 69,531
39*J. W. Ashton, Lab...... 28,959
J. T. Lester, C......... 20,698
M. Haydon-Baillie, L.. 3,125
Lab. maj........... 8,261
(Oct. 1968, by-election,
Lab. maj. 740)
(1966 Lab. maj. 10,428)

Bath (English Borough)
E. 59,518
40*Sir E. J. Brown, M.B.E.,
C................. 22,344
D. W. Young, Lab.... 16,493
R. H. Crowther, L...... 5,967
G. Young, Ind........ 840
C. maj........... 5,851
(1966 C. maj. 800)

Batley and Morley
(English Borough) E. 63,430
41*Sir A. D. D. Broughton,
Lab............. 23,024
D. Thompson, C...... 15,753
P. Wrigley, L...... 6,893
Lab. maj........... 7,271
(1966 Lab. maj. 11,651)

Battersea (2)
NORTH E. 30,357
42*Rt. Hon. D. P. T. Jay,
Lab............. 11,621
A. V. Bradbury, C...... 4,927
Mrs. H. M. G. Small-
bone, L....... 1,012
D. J. Welsh, Comm.... 179
Lab. maj........... 6,694
(1966 Lab. maj. 10,172)

SOUTH E. 34,788
43*E. G. Perry, Lab........ 10,925
I. N. Samuel, O.B.E., C. 9,227
R. A. P. Benad, L...... 1,183
T. Lamb, Nat. Front... 716
Lab. maj........... 1,698
(1966 C. maj. 3,790)

Bebington (English Borough)
E. 82,443
44 E. P. Cockeram, C...... 31,260
*E. Brooks, Lab...... 30,535
C. maj........... 725
(1966 Lab. maj. 2,337)

Beckenham (London)
E. 77,934
45*P. C. Goodhart, C...... 30,763
I. G. Bing, Lab...... 13,031
P. A. Golding, L...... 9,404
C. maj........... 17,732
(1966 C. maj. 13,865)

Bedfordshire (3)
BEDFORD E. 67,844
46 T. H. H. Skeet, C...... 26,330
*B. S. Parkyn, Lab...... 21,051
A. W. Butcher, L...... 4,740
C. maj........... 5,279
(1966 Lab. maj. 378)

MID E. 73,520
47*S. L. E. Hastings, M.C.,
C................. 29,670
D. F. Harrowell, Lab... 19,035
J. P. Christian, L....... 7,799
C. maj........... 10,635
(1966 C. maj. 3,078)

SOUTH E. 101,942
48 W. D. Madel, C...... 38,085
*G. E. Roberts, Lab.... 33,107
G. S. Shocket, L...... 6,956
C. maj........... 4,978
(1966 Lab. maj. 4,230)

Bedwellty (Monmouthshire)
E. 49,521
49 N. G. Kinnock, *Lab.*... 28,078
P. Marland, *C.*...... 5,799
C. M. Davey, *P.C.*.... 3,780
Lab. maj............. 22,279
(1966 Lab. maj. 24,984)

Belfast (4)
EAST E. 59,976
50*S. R. McMaster, *U.U.*... 26,778
D. W. Bleakley, *N.I.*
Lab................ 18,259
U.U. maj............ 8,519
(1966 U.U. maj. 3,633)

NORTH E. 76,375
51*W. S. Mills, *U.U.*..... 28,668
J. Sharkey, *N.I. Lab.*.. 18,894
W. J. Beattie, *Prot. U.*.. 11,173
J. D. McKeague, *Ind. U.* 441
U.U. maj............ 9,774
(1966 U.U. maj. 6,964)

SOUTH E. 57,428
52*R. J. Pounder, *U.U.*... 27,523
J. Coulthard, *N.I. Lab.*.. 11,567
U.U. maj............ 15,956
(1966 U.U. maj. 10,965)

WEST E. 69,245
53*G. Fitt, *Repub. Lab.*... 30,649
B. J. H. McRoberts,
U.U................ 27,451
Repub. Lab. maj...... 3,198
(1966 Repub. Lab. maj.
2,011)

Belper (Derbyshire)
E. 87,100
54 D. G. Stewart-Smith, *C.* 35,757
*Rt. Hon. G. A. Brown,
Lab.*............... 33,633
C. maj............. 2,124
(1966 Lab. maj. 4,274)

Berkshire (4). *See Abingdon,
Newbury, Windsor and Wokingham*

Bermondsey (London)
E. 34,349
55*Rt. Hon. R. J. Mellish,
Lab................ 13,908
G. H. J. Nicholson, *C.*.. 4,172
Lab. maj............ 9,736
(1966 Lab. maj. 12,615)

Berwick and East Lothian
E. 55,726
56*J. P. Mackintosh, *Lab.*... 21,107
J. D. M. Hardie, *C.*..... 20,466
D. R. F. Simpson, *Scot.
Nat.*............... 4,735
Lab. maj............. 641
(1966 Lab. maj. 1,689)

**Berwick upon Tweed
(Northumberland)**
E. 41,974
57*A. C. F. Lambton (*Visct.
Lambton), C.*........ 15,558
R. N. Wareing, *Lab.*.. 8,413
A. J. Beith, *L.*........ 6,741
C. maj.............. 7,145
(1966 C. maj. 4,373)

Bethnal Green (London)
E. 48,096
58*W. S. Hilton, *Lab.*...... 15,483
O. S. Henriques, *C.*.... 5,578
W. O. Smedley, *L.*..... 3,030
Lab. maj............. 9,905
(1966 Lab. maj. 15,253)

Bexley (London)
E. 67,476
59*Rt. Hon. E. R. G.
Heath, *M.B.E., C.*..... 27,075
J. C. Cartwright, *Lab.*.. 19,017
E. P. G. Harrison, *L.*.... 19,017
E. J. R. L. Heath, *Ind.*.. 938
M. P. Coney, *Ind. C.*... 833
C. maj............. 8,058
(1966 C. maj. 2,333)

Billericay (Essex)
E. 124,215
60 R. A. McCrindle, *C.*.... 47,719
*E. Moonman, *Lab.*.... 43,765
Lab. maj............. 3,954
(1966 Lab. maj. 1,642)

Bilston (English Borough)
E. 77,525
61*R. J. Edwards, *Lab.*.... 27,240
C. G. Irving, *C.*...... 26,240
Lab. maj............. 1,000
(1966 Lab. maj. 7,253)

Birkenhead (English Borough)
E. 58,866
62*Rt. Hon. E. E. Dell, *Lab.* 20,980
R. Kris, *C.*........... 15,151
D. T. G. Evans, *L.*..... 4,926
A. B. Williams, *Comm.* 351
Lab. maj............. 5,829
(1966 Lab. maj. 8,750)

Birmingham (13)
ALL SAINTS E. 36,473
63*A. B. Walden, *Lab.*..... 12,041
J. H. Hollingworth, *C.*.. 7,762
D. G. Minnis, *L.*....... 2,271
Lab. maj............. 4,279
(1966 Lab. maj. 4,755)

ASTON E. 47,951
64*J. Silverman, *Lab.*...... 15,456
A. A. Hill, *C.*......... 11,894
C. Jordan, *Brit. Movement*............... 704
Lab. maj............. 3,562
(1966 Lab. maj. 7,400)

EDGBASTON E. 59,141
65*Mrs. J. C. J. Knight,
M.B.E., C............ 23,690
E. J. Sever, *Lab.*...... 13,047
Miss D. C. Howlett,
Ind................ 725
C. maj............. 10,643
(1966 C. maj. 7,534)

HALL GREEN E. 67,189
66*R. E. Eyre, *C.*........ 27,319
T. L. Keene, *Lab.*..... 17,930
C. maj............. 9,389
(1966 C. maj. 3,333)

HANDSWORTH E. 46,872
67 S. B. Chapman, *C.*..... 16,122
Miss S. R. R. Wright,
Lab................ 14,310
C. maj............. 1,812
(1966 C. maj. 1,294)

LADYWOOD E. 18,884
68 Mrs. D. M. G. Fisher,
Lab................ 5,067
*W. L. Lawler, *L.*..... 4,087
C. L. Wade, *C.*....... 2,523
Lab. maj............. 980
(June 1969, by-election,
L. maj. 2,713)
(1966 Lab. maj. 5,315)

NORTHFIELD E. 97,435
69 R. J. Carter, *Lab.*...... 33,364
D. W. Bell, *C.*........ 32,148
D. W. Robinson, *Comm.* 605
Lab. maj............. 1,216
(1966 Lab. maj. 11,902)

PERRY BARR E. 49,752
70 J. R. Kinsey, *C.*....... 18,083
*C. Price, *Lab.*....... 16,817
C. maj............. 1,266
(1966 Lab. maj. 3,665)

SELLY OAK E. 54,986
71*H. E. Gurden, *C.*...... 18,281
M. J. Hartley-Brewer,
Lab................ 16,758
C. maj............. 1,523
(1966 C. maj. 777)

SMALL HEATH E. 39,209
72*D. H. Howell, *Lab.*..... 13,794
N. W. Budgen, *C.*..... 6,923
G. H. Herringshaw, *L.*.. 1,754
Saeeduz Zafar, *Ind.*.... 117
Lab. maj............. 6,871
(1966 Lab. maj. 10,604)

SPARKBROOK E. 43,367
73*R. S. G. Hattersley, *Lab.* 14,773
A. E. J. Mitton, *C.*.... 11,427
J. A. Crofton, *L.*...... 1,813
Lab. maj............. 3,346
(1966 Lab. maj. 6,398)

STECHFORD E. 63,342
74*Rt. Hon. R. H. Jenkins,
Lab................ 22,559
J. B. Stevens, *C.*...... 15,848
D. Hardy, *Ind.*....... 1,438
S. C. Pegg, *Comm.*.... 298
Lab. maj............. 6,711
(1966 Lab. maj. 11,871)

YARDLEY E. 62,836
75 D. M. Coombs, *C.*..... 21,827
*I. L. Evans, *Lab.*.... 21,707
C. maj............. 120
(1966 Lab. maj. 5,759)

Bishop Auckland (Durham)
E. 49,593
76*H. J. Boyden, *Lab.*..... 21,257
T. J. Wiseman, *C.*..... 13,769
Lab. maj............. 7,488
(1966 Lab. maj. 10,079)

Blackburn (English Borough)
E. 56,212
77*Rt. Hon. Barbara Castle,
Lab................ 22,473
Mrs. R. T. Gardner, *C.* 19,737
Lab. maj............. 2,736
(1966 Lab. maj. 7,248)

BLACKLEY—*See Manchester*

Blackpool (2)
NORTH E. 59,180
78*N. A. Miscampbell, *C.*... 22,298
W. Callon, *Lab.*....... 13,062
B. M. Christon, *L.*..... 4,946
C. maj............. 9,236
(1966 C. maj. 5,310)

SOUTH E. 59,230
79*P. A. R. Blaker, C..... 21,273
  P. P. Hall, Lab...... 13,267
  D. Chadwick, L...... 5,730
  C. maj............ 8,006
  (1966 C. maj. 3,398)

Blaydon (Durham)
  E. 55,081
80*R. E. Woof, Lab....... 25,724
  N. H. D'Aguiar, C..... 13,926
  Lab. maj......... 11,798
  (1966 Lab. maj. 14,780)

Blyth (English Borough)
  E. 68,314
81*F. J. Milne, Lab....... 36,118
  E. J. Blackburn, C.... 12,550
  Lab. maj......... 23,568
  (1966 Lab. maj. 26,314)

Bodmin (Cornwall)
  E. 52,092
82 R. A. Hicks, C....... 20,187
  P. A. Tyler, L....... 16,267
  A. F. Long, Lab...... 5,350
  C. maj........... 3,920
  (1966 L. maj. 2,023)

Bolsover (Derbyshire)
  E. 52,882
83 D. E. Skinner, Lab..... 28,830
  I. J. Humphrey, C.... 8,371
  Lab. maj......... 20,459
  (1966 Lab. maj. 24,299)

Bolton (2)
EAST E. 61,675
84 L. D. Reed, C....... 22,769
  *R. L. Howarth, Lab... 22,298
  C. maj........... 471
  (1966 Lab. maj. 8,282)
WEST E. 50,533
85 R. S. Redmond, C.... 19,225
  *G. J. Oakes, Lab..... 17,981
  C. maj........... 1,244
  (1966 Lab. maj. 4,917)

Bootle (English Borough)
  E. 48,830
86*S. Mahon, Lab....... 20,110
  G. Halliwell, C...... 11,496
  Lab. maj......... 8,614
  (1966 Lab. maj. 8,599)

Bosworth (Leicestershire)
  E. 78,838
87 Hon. A. C. Butler, C... 30,732
  *W. L. Wyatt, Lab..... 29,677
  C. maj........... 1,055
  (1966 Lab. maj. 7,773)

Bothwell (Lanarkshire)
  E. 64,610
88*J. Hamilton, Lab...... 26,431
  J. B. Highgate, C...... 15,720
  T. McAlpine, Scot. Nat. 6,157
  Lab. maj......... 10,711
  (1966 Lab. maj. 10,968)

Bournemouth (2)
EAST AND CHRISTCHURCH
  E. 70,830
89*J. H. Cordle, C..... 31,104
  T. C. Bisson, Lab...... 10,594
  G. H. Musgrave, L..... 8,282
  C. Maj........... 20,510
  (1966 C. maj. 14,449)

WEST E. 74,203
90*Sir J. B. Eden, Bt., C.... 28,714
  L. F. Bennett, Lab..... 14,099
  J. F. Mills, L........ 8,303
  C. maj........... 14,615
  (1966 C. maj. 9,406)

Bradford (4)
EAST E. 40,720
91*E. Lyons, Lab......... 17,346
  C. J. Barr, C........ 8,208
  G. Musa, L......... 660
  Lab. maj......... 9,138
  (1966 Lab. maj. 10,344)
NORTH E. 52,702
92*B. T. Ford, Lab....... 20,141
  W. H. P. Laycock, C.... 18,511
  Lab. maj......... 1,630
  (1966 Lab. maj. 4,199)
SOUTH E. 63,880
93 T. W. Torney, Lab..... 20,985
  J. D. W. Bottomley, C. 19,009
  G. Dunkerley, L...... 5,694
  Lab. maj......... 1,976
  (1966 Lab. maj. 7,497)
WEST E. 53,729
94 J. A. D. Wilkinson, C... 20,475
  *C. N. Haseldine, Lab... 18,936
  C. maj........... 1,539
  (1966 Lab. maj. 1,534)

Brecon and Radnor
  E. 52,987
95 C. E. Roderick, Lab..... 18,736
  G. J. J. Neale, C....... 13,892
  G. W. Howells, L...... 8,169
  W. G. Jenkins, P.C.... 2,349
  Lab. maj......... 4,844
  (1966 Lab. maj. 8,379)

Brentford and Chiswick
  (London) E. 37,853
96*M. C. J. Barnes, Lab.... 14,051
  Cmdr. O. C. Wright,
  C................ 13,538
  Lab. maj......... 513
  (1966 Lab. maj. 607)

BRIDGETON—*See* Glasgow

Bridgwater (Somerset)
  E. 66,509
97*T. J. King, C....... 26,685
  R. J. Billington, Lab... 18,224
  P. M. O'Loughlin, L... 6,066
  C. maj............ 8,461
  (March 1970, by-election,
  C. maj. 10,915)
  (1966 C. maj. 2,986)

Bridlington (Yorkshire, E.R.)
  E. 62,108
98*Rt. Hon. R. F. Wood, C. 25,053
  H. A. Clarke, Lab..... 11,546
  T. Silverwood, L...... 6,495
  C. maj........... 13,507
  (1966 C. maj. 10,037)

Brierley Hill (Staffordshire)
  E. 98,287
99*W. F. Montgomery, C... 43,440
  T. S. Pritchard, Lab.... 28,203
  C. maj........... 15,237
  (April 1967, by-election,
  C. maj. 10,220)
  (1966 C. maj. 1,567)

Brigg (Lincolnshire) E. 87,703
100*E. L. Mallalieu, Q.C.,
  Lab.............. 31,434
  Miss A. H. Spokes, C. 27,449
  Lab. maj.......... 3,985
  (1966 Lab. maj. 11,308)

Brighouse and Spenborough
  (English Borough) E. 61,911
101 G. W. Proudfoot, C.... 22,953
  *G. C. Jackson, Lab.... 22,894
  G. H. Manley, L...... 3,781
  C. maj............ 59
  (1966 Lab. maj. 4,524)

Brighton (2)
KEMPTOWN E. 65,980
102 A. Bowden, M.B.E., C... 24,208
  *D. H. Hobden, Lab... 21,105
  O. C. Moxon, L...... 3,833
  C. maj........... 3,103
  (1966 Lab. maj. 831)
PAVILION E. 59,444
103*Rt. Hon. J. Amery, C... 24,365
  F. Tonks, Lab....... 13,771
  G. E. Thomas, Ind.... 1,205
  C. maj........... 10,594
  (March 1969, by-election,
  C. maj. 12,982)
  (1966 C. maj. 6,354)

BRIGHTSIDE—*See* Sheffield

Bristol (6)
CENTRAL E. 36,289
104*A. M. F. Palmer, Lab.. 12,375
  J. R. E. Taylor, C..... 9,130
  A. Rider, L........ 2,569
  Lab. maj......... 3,245
  (1966 Lab. maj. 5,989)
NORTH EAST E. 64,314
105 R. J. Adley, C....... 23,254
  *R. F. H. Dobson, Lab. 22,792
  C. maj........... 462
  (1966 Lab. maj. 3,972)
NORTH WEST E. 65,601
106 M. J. McLaren, C..... 24,124
  *J. Ellis, Lab......... 23,075
  J. Stevens, L....... 3,299
  W. E. Williams, Comm. 227
  C. maj........... 1,049
  (1966 Lab. maj. 669)
SOUTH E. 61,970
107 M. F. L. Cocks, Lab... 24,682
  D. J. F. Hunt, C..... 15,254
  Lab. maj......... 9,428
  (1966 Lab. maj. 13,554)
SOUTH EAST E. 73,627
108*Rt. Hon. A. N. W. Benn,
  Lab.............. 29,176
  N. G. Reece, C....... 23,488
  Lab. maj......... 5,688
  (1966 Lab. maj. 11,416)
WEST E. 50,634
109*R. G. Cooke, C....... 20,110
  D. J. Blackman, Lab... 8,175
  R. G. Stacey, L...... 5,108
  C. maj........... 11,935
  (1966 C. maj. 11,518)

BRIXTON—*See* Lambeth

Bromley (London)
E. 54,793
110*J. L. Hunt, C.......... 22,364
J. F. Spellar, Lab...... 9,328
D. E. A. Crowe, L..... 5,982
C. maj............ 13,036
(1966 C. maj. 9,827)

Bromsgrove (Worcestershire)
E. 84,472
111*J. C. G. Dance, C...... 37,544
T. A. G. Davis, Lab.. 26,670
C. maj............ 10,874
(By-election, May 27, 1971)
T. A. G. Davis, Lab... 29,809
H. D. Miller, C....... 27,941
Lab. maj. 1,868
(1966 C. maj. 3,696)

Buckinghamshire (4)
BUCKINGHAM E. 72,691
112 W. R. Benyon, C...... 28,088
*R. I. Maxwell, M.C.,
Lab................ 25,567
J. M. Cornwall, L...... 5,475
C. maj............. 2,521
(1966 Lab. maj. 2,254)
SOUTH E. 94,399
113*R. M. Bell, Q.C., C..... 40,039
K. Davison, Lab...... 16,465
I. M. Fowler, L...... 11,750
C. maj............. 23,574
(1966 C. maj. 16,992)
See also Aylesbury and Wycombe

Burnley (English Borough)
E. 56,328
114*D. Jones, B.E.M., Lab... 24,200
J. Birch, C........... 14,846
G. Brownbill, L...... 3,446
Lab. maj. 9,354
(1966 Lab. maj. 13,873)

Burton (Staffordshire)
E. 67,180
115*J. C. Jennings, C........ 27,428
R. G. Truman, Lab... 23,063
C. maj............. 4,365
(1966 C. maj. 277)

Bury and Radcliffe
(English Borough) E. 74,954
116 M. M. Fidler, C....... 29,796
D. V. Hunt, Lab...... 26,592
C. maj............. 3,204
(1966 Lab. maj. 4,471)

Bury St. Edmunds (Suffolk)
E. 78,119
117*E. W. Griffiths, C..... 36,688
C. J. V. Seager, Lab... 23,286
C. maj............. 13,402
(1966 C. maj. 4,642)

Bute and North Ayrshire—*See*
Ayrshire and Bute

Caernarvonshire (2)
CAERNARVON E. 41,807
118*Rt. Hon. G. O. Roberts,
Lab................ 13,627
R. Lewis, P.C........ 11,331
Miss K. J. Smith, C.... 6,812
J. A. Williams, L...... 2,195
Lab. maj.......... 2,296
(1966 Lab. maj. 10,678)
See also Conway

Caerphilly (Glamorgan)
E. 52,039
119*A. T. Evans, Lab...... 24,972
P. J. S. Williams, P.C. 11,505
P. N. Price, C........ 3,917
Lab. maj.......... 13,467
(July 1968, by-election,
Lab. maj. 1,874)
(1966 Lab. maj. 21,148)

Caithness and Sutherland
E. 28,940
120*R. A. R. MacLennan,
Lab.............. 8,768
G. Y. Mackie, L...... 6,063
J. M. Young, C....... 5,334
D. G. Barr, *Scot. Nat.*.. 3,690
Lab. maj.......... 2,705
(1966 Lab. maj. 64)

Camberwell (2)
DULWICH E. 66,691
121*Hon. S. C. Silkin, Q.C.,
Lab................ 20,145
P. B. B. Mayhew, C. . 19,250
A. N. H. Blackburn, L 3,301
Lab. maj.......... 895
(1966 Lab. maj. 6,296)
PECKHAM E. 51,089
122*Mrs. F. K. Corbet, Lab. 17,071
I. J. Lawrence, C...... 8,232
Lab. maj.......... 8,839
(1966 Lab. maj. 12,607)

Cambridge (English Borough)
E. 65,905
123*D. W. S. S. Lane, C... 26,252
G. B. Scurfield, Lab...21,191
C. maj............. 5,061
(Sept. 1967, by-election,
C. maj. 5,978)
(1966 Lab. maj. 991)

Cambridgeshire
E. 78,713
124*Rt. Hon. F. L. Pym,
M.C., C............ 32,264
J. N. Hughes, Lab.... 19,993
Mrs. M. M. Brown, L. 6,861
C. maj............. 12,271
(1966 C. maj. 5,167)

Cannock (Staffordshire)
E. 90,556
125 P. T. Cormack, C...... 32,665
*Rt. Hon. Jennie Lee,
Lab................ 31,136
C. maj............. 1,529
(1966 Lab. maj. 11,027)

Canterbury (Kent)
E. 80,774
126*D. L. Crouch, C...... 33,222
H. G. N. Clother, Lab. 15,172
D. C. P. Gracie, L...... 11,553
C. maj............. 18,050
(1966 C. maj. 11,788)

Cardiff (3)
NORTH E. 61,517
127 M. H. A. Roberts, C... 21,983
*E. Rowlands, Lab..... 20,207
H. M. O'Brien, L..... 2,701
B. M. Edwards, P.C... 1,927
C. maj............. 1,776
(1966 Lab. maj. 672)

SOUTH EAST E. 69,567
128*Rt. Hon. L. J. Callaghan,
Lab.............. 26,226
N. Lloyd-Edwards, C. 20,771
R. R. Davies, P.C.... 2,585
G. W. Parsons, *Nat. Front* 982
Lab. maj.......... 5,455
(1966 Lab. maj. 10,837)

WEST E. 61,659
129*Rt. Hon. T. G. Thomas,
Lab.............. 21,655
R. C. Williams, C.... 15,878
D. Hughes, P.C...... 4,378
S. R. C. Wanhill, L... 1,594
Lab. maj.......... 5,777
(1966 Lab. maj. 9,425)

Cardiganshire
E. 40,515
130*D. E. Morgan, Lab..... 11,063
H. C. L. Williams, L.. 9,800
H. W. J. ap Robert,
P.C................ 6,498
D. F. R. George, C... 5,715
Lab. maj. 1,263
(1966 Lab. maj. 523)

Carlisle (English Borough)
E. 52,649
131*R. H. Lewis, Lab...... 21,866
B. A. Marsden, C...... 19,241
Lab. maj.......... 2,625
(1966 Lab. maj. 4,927)

Carlton (Nottinghamshire)
E. 90,106
132*P. W. Holland, C...... 39,840
C. Bennett, Lab...... 27,043
C. maj............. 12,797
(1966 C. maj. 4,046)

Carmarthenshire (2)
CARMARTHEN E. 59,233
133 G. G. Jones, Lab...... 18,719
*G. R. Evans, P.C..... 14,812
H. G. E. Thomas, L... 10,707
L. H. Davies, C....... 4,975
Lab. maj.......... 3,907
(July 1966, by-election,
Plaid Cymru maj. 2,436)
(1966 Lab. maj. 9,233)
See also Llanelli

Carshalton (Surrey)
E. 71,607
134*Capt. W. Elliot, D.S.C.,
R.N., C............ 27,342
G. S. Baker, Lab...... 16,896
J. H. G. Browne, L.... 6,411
C. maj............. 10,446
(1966 C. maj. 5,869)

CATHCART—*See* Glasgow

Cheadle (Cheshire)
E. 107,925
135 T. Normanton, T.D., C. 39,728
*M. P. Winstanley, L.. 37,974
R. Stott, Lab......... 8,062
C. maj............. 1,754
(1966 L. maj. 655)

CHEETHAM—*See* Manchester

Chelmsford (Essex)
E. 88,841
136*N. A. F. St. John-
Stevas, C.......... 36,821
G. Kennedy, Lab..... 23,780
Miss J. Hunt, L....... 5,811
J. D. Steel, Ind...... 350
C. maj............ 13,041
(1966 C. maj. 4,975)

Chelsea (London)
E. 44,260
137*W. M. J. Worsley, C... 15,852
R. J. Madeley, Lab..... 5,737
A. H. S. Beavan, L..... 2,136
N. L. Luard, Ina...... 514
C. maj............ 10,115
(1966 C. maj. 8,703)

Cheltenham (English Borough)
E. 60,571
138*A. D. Dodds-Parker, C. 22,823
L. G. Godwin, Lab..... 14,213
D. G. Aldridge, L...... 8,431
C. maj............ 8,610
(1966 C. maj. 2,915)

Chertsey (Surrey)
E. 68,168
139 W. M. J. Grylls, C.... 27,239
C. P. Slater, Lab..... 15,653
A. F. Cook, L....... 5,239
C. maj............ 11,586
(1966 C. maj. 6,353)

Cheshire (10). *See* Cheadle, Chester (City of), Crewe, Knutsford, Macclesfield, Nantwich, Northwich, Runcorn, Stalybridge and Hyde and Wirral

Chester (City of) (Cheshire)
E. 68,369
140*J. M. Temple, C....... 25,877
J. Crawford, Lab...... 18,872
M. J. G. Tompkins, L. 4,978
C. maj............ 7,005
(1966 C. maj. 2,803)

Chester-le-Street (Durham)
E. 64,216
141*N. Pentland, Lab...... 33,694
D. Ramshaw, C...... 13,363
Lab. maj......... 20,331
(1966 Lab. maj. 22,747)

Chesterfield (English Borough)
E. 71,600
142*E. G. Varley, Lab...... 30,386
J. C. Ramsden, C..... 16,217
T. D. Bamford, L...... 4,891
Lab. maj.......... 14,169
(1966 Lab. maj. 18,099)

Chichester (West Sussex)
E. 87,543
143*Rt.Hon.C.J.Chataway,
C.............. 38,120
N. D. Sandelson, Lab.. 12,574
D. G. Kinsella, L...... 10,506
C. maj............ 25,546
(May 1969, by-election,
C. maj. 26,087)
(1966 C. maj. 17,574)

Chigwell (Essex)
E. 61,468
144*J. A. Biggs-Davison, C. 26,404
W. J. Sheaff, Lab..... 17,972
C. maj........... 8,432
(1966 C. maj. 2,568)

Chippenham (Wiltshire)
E. 63,745
145*D. E. Awdry, T.D., C... 24,371
Mrs. M. E. Wingfield,
L.............. 13,833
J. Eddie, Lab......... 10,807
C. maj........... 10,538
(1966 C. maj. 694)

Chislehurst (Kent)
E. 66,964
146 Rt. Hon. Dame Patricia
Hornsby-Smith, D.B.E.,
C............... 24,650
*A. H. Macdonald,
Lab............ 21,287
R. L. Coverson, L..... 4,268
C. maj........... 3,363
(1966 Lab. maj. 810)

Chorley (Lancashire)
E. 71,869
147 Mrs. C. M. Monks,
O.B.E., C.......... 27,577
D. A. Forwood, Lab... 24,900
G. Payne, L......... 4,428
B. J. A. Elder, Ind..... 264
C. maj........... 1,677
(1966 Lab. maj. 4,744)

**Cirencester and Tewkesbury
(Gloucestershire)** E. 73,266
148*Hon. N. Ridley, C.... 30,217
H. G. Lovell, Lab..... 16,131
D. Robinson, L....... 7,593
C. maj........... 14,086
(1966 C. maj. 7,771)

**Cities of London and
Westminster** E. 59,147
149 C. S. Tugendhat, C..... 19,102
A. M. Dubs, Lab...... 10,062
D. A. Nicholson, L..... 2,708
W. A. Clark, Ind...... 157
L. D. Sutch, Ind...... 142
C. maj........... 9,040
(1966 C. maj. 6,893)

CLACKMANNAN AND EAST STIRLING. *See* Stirling and Clackmannan

CLAPHAM—*See* Wandsworth

Cleveland (Yorkshire, N.R.)
E. 92,978
150*J. Tinn, Lab. 36,213
P. C. Price, ph.D., C... 31,130
Lab. maj......... 5,083
(1966 Lab. maj. 11,880)

Clitheroe (Lancashire)
E. 50,179
151 A. D. Walder, C....... 20,430
K. C. Bodfish, Lab..... 14,158
Mrs. V. I. MacMillan,
L.............. 4,965
C. maj........... 6,272
(1966 C. maj. 2,230)

**Coatbridge and Airdrie
(Scottish Burgh)**
E. 58,674
152*J. Dempsey, Lab....... 26,117
W. J. Rennie, C..... 15,574
W. Brown, Scot. Nat.. 2,667
Nat.............. 2,667
Lab. maj.......... 10,543
(1966 Lab. maj. 11,714)

Colchester (Essex)
E. 75,358
153*P. A. F. Buck, C....... 30,562
J. G. Bartlett, Lab..... 20,325
P. S. Watts, L....... 7,248
C. maj........... 10,237
(1966 C. maj. 1,015)

Colne Valley (Yorkshire, W.R.)
E. 58,952
154 D. G. Clark, Lab...... 18,896
*R. S. Wainwright, L.. 18,040
K. E. Davy, C........ 10,417
Lab. maj......... 856
(1966 L. maj. 2,499)

Consett (Durham)
E. 58,573
155*D. J. Watkins, Lab..... 28,985
N. G. Trotter, C...... 11,914
Lab. maj.......... 17,071
(1966 Lab. maj. 18,895)

Conway (Caernarvonshire)
E. 48,933
156 I. W. P. Roberts, C.... 16,927
*G. E. H. Davies, Lab.. 16,024
D. E. Thomas, P.C.... 4,311
E. L. Morris, L....... 2,626
C. maj........... 903
(1966 Lab. maj. 581)

Cornwall (5)
NORTH E. 48,254
157*J. W. Pardoe, L....... 19,863
S. J. Day, C......... 19,233
E. W. J. Hill, Lab..... 1,741
L. maj........... 630
(1966 L. maj. 1,508)
See also Bodmin, Falmouth and Camborne, St. Ives and Truro

Coventry (3)
EAST E. 87,212
158*Rt. Hon. R. H. S.
Crossman, O.B.E., Lab. 36,275
M. E. Jones, C....... 24,010
J. Hosey, Comm....... 841
Lab. maj.......... 12,265
(1966 Lab. maj. 18,696)
NORTH E. 57,082
159*M. Edelman, Lab...... 24,004
F. A. Tuckman, C.... 18,344
Lab. maj......... 5,660
(1966 Lab. maj. 7,907)
SOUTH E. 78,138
160*W. Wilson, Lab....... 30,010
G. A. Gardiner, C...... 27,816
Lab. maj......... 2,194
(1966 Lab. maj. 5,540)

CRAIGTON—*See* Glasgow

Crewe (Cheshire)
E. 57,819
161*S. S. Allen, Q.C., Lab.. 22,160
A. R. Goodlad, C.... 18,678
Lab. maj........... 3,482
(1966 Lab. maj. 8,711)

Crosby (English Borough)
E. 59,936
162*R. G. Page, M.B.E., B.C... 24,042
P. J. Caswell, Lab..... 18,350
C. maj........... 5,692
(1966 C. maj. 3,306)

Croydon (3)
NORTH EAST E. 59,151
163*B. B. Weatherill, C.... 20,351
G. F. Elliott, Lab........ 16,373
R. J. Mayhew, L....... 4,210
C. maj........... 3,978
(1966 C. maj. 588)
NORTH WEST E. 57,340
164 R. G. Taylor, C...... 19,260
S. J. Boden, Lab....... 14,687
R. E. J. Banks, L....... 4,666
C. maj........... 4,573
(1966 C. maj. 2,696)
SOUTH E. 73,796
165 Sir R. H. M. Thompson,
Bt., C............... 25,986
*D. J. Winnick, Lab.... 22,283
M. R. Lane, L........ 3,673
C. O. Thornton, Ind.. 303
C. maj........... 3,703
(1966 Lab. maj. 81)

Cumberland (3), See Penrith
and the Border, Whitehaven
and Workington

Dagenham (London)
E. 75,479
166*J. Parker, C.B.E., Lab.. 31,335
H. M. McClancy, C.. 11,976
G. C. Wake, Comm.. 982
Lab. maj........... 19,359
(1966 Lab. maj. 24,525)

Darlington (English Borough)
E. 62,986
167*E. J. Fletcher, Lab...... 23,208
A. T. Bourne-Arton,
C............... 19,447
S. Newton, L....... 5,222
Lab. maj........... 3,761
(1966 Lab. maj. 4,363)

Dartford (Kent)
E. 82,239
168 P. J. E. Trew, C...... 27,822
*S. Irving, Lab....... 27,262
J. P. Johnson, L....... 5,453
C. maj........... 560
(1966 Lab. maj. 6,909)

Darwen (Lancashire)
E. 66,968
169*C. Fletcher-Cooke, Q.C.,
C............... 26,728
B. Whittam, Lab...... 17,634
A. Cooper, L....... 6,663
C. maj........... 9,094
(1966 C. maj. 1,735)

Dearne Valley (Yorks., W.R.)
E. 63,409
170*E. Wainwright, Lab.... 33,966
A. B. Cowl, C....... 6,848
P. Hargreaves, L....... 4,426
Lab. maj........... 27,118
(1966 Lab. maj. 30,614)

Denbighshire (2)
DENBIGH E. 61,020
171*W. G. O. Morgan, Q.C.,
C............... 21,246
Mrs. A. C. Roberts,
Lab............... 12,537
I. Hughes-Evans, L.. 8,636
E. G. Matthews, P.C... 5,254
C. maj........... 8,709
(1966 C. maj. 4,657)
See also Wrexham

Deptford (London)
E. 42,868
172*Rt. Hon. J. E. Silkin,
Lab............... 14,672
M. L. Brotherton, C.. 7,355
M. C. Vaux, Nat. Front 1,277
Lab. maj........... 7,317
(1966 Lab. maj. 10,860)

Derby (2)
NORTH E. 57,645
173 P. Whitehead, Lab..... 20,114
J. W. Roberts, C...... 16,635
Lab. maj........... 3,479
(1966 Lab. maj. 8,818)
SOUTH E. 53,348
174 W. H. Johnson, Lab... 19,407
R. Greene, C....... 16,258
Lab. maj........... 3,149
(1966 Lab. maj. 9,576)

Derbyshire (7)
NORTH EAST E. 90,434
175*T. H. Swain, Lab....... 38,181
J. P. Pashley, C...... 24,550
Lab. maj........... 13,631
(1966 Lab. maj. 19,600)
SOUTH EAST E. 82,088
176 P. L. Rost, C........ 32,185
J. Ryman, Lab....... 29,461
C. maj........... 2,724
(1966 Lab. maj. 5,496)
WEST E. 48,086
177*J. S. R. Scott-Hopkins,
C............... 22,692
F. C. Inglis, Lab...... 13,976
C. maj........... 8,716
(Nov. 1967, by-election,
C. maj. 10,623)
(1966 C. maj. 4,592)
See also Belper, Bolsover, High
Peak and Ilkeston

Devizes (Wiltshire)
E. 72,880
178*Hon. C. A. Morrison,
C............... 28,475
R. O. Faulkner, Lab... 20,442
J. D. H. Jones, L....... 6,210
C. maj........... 8,033
(1966 C. maj. 2,597)

DEVONPORT—See Plymouth

Devonshire (6)
NORTH E. 50,795
179*Rt. Hon. J. J. Thorpe,
L............... 18,893
T. C. Keigwin, C..... 18,524
C. J. Mullin, Lab...... 5,268
B. G. Morris, Demo-
cratic Party........ 175
L. maj........... 369
(1966 L. maj. 1,166)
See also Honiton, Tavistock,
Tiverton, Torrington and
Totnes

Dewsbury (English Borough)
E. 60,988
180*D. Ginsburg, Lab...... 22,015
J. M. Stansfield, C.... 17,468
A. Allsopp, L....... 5,688
Lab. maj........... 4,547
(1966 Lab. maj. 10,666)

Doncaster (English Borough)
E. 60,153
181*H. Walker, Lab....... 22,658
P. Davies, C....... 19,431
W. T. W. Blades, L... 2,648
Lab. maj........... 3,227
(1966 Lab. maj. 6,088)

Don Valley (Yorks, W.R.)
E. 84,281
182*R. Kelley, Lab....... 42,496
T. W. G. Jackson, C.. 18,673
Lab. maj........... 23,823
(1966 Lab. maj. 29,235)

Dorking (Surrey)
E. 59,335
183*Sir G. E. Sinclair,
C.M.G., O.B.E., C.... 25,393
W. J. Fahy, Lab....... 10,523
J. A. Baker, L........ 7,103
C. maj........... 14,870
(1966 C. maj. 10,886)

Dorset (3)
NORTH E. 63,041
184 D. P. James, C....... 28,471
P. G. Watkins, L...... 12,095
H. R. White, Lab...... 8,626
C. maj........... 16,376
(1966 C. maj. 5,515)

SOUTH E. 67,503
185*E. M. King, C....... 27,580
R. G. May, Lab...... 20,716
K. N. Scarby, L....... 4,680
C. maj........... 6,864
(1966 C. maj. 1,877)

WEST E. 51,043
186*K. S. D. W. Digby, T.D.
C............... 21,081
G. Sakwa, Lab....... 10,536
A. N. W. Percival, L.. 7,314
C. maj........... 10,545
(1966 C. maj. 5,952)

Dover (Kent)
E. 73,092
187 P. W. I. Rees, Q.C., C. 30,103
*D. H. Ennals, Lab..... 28,454
C. maj........... 1,649
(1966 Lab. maj. 3,216)

Down (2)

NORTH E. 121,330
188 *J. A. Kilfedder, U.U.*... 55,679
K. Young, *N.I. Lab.*... 14,246
R. S. Nixon, *Ind. U.*.. 6,408
J. R. McGladdery, *Ind.* 3,321
Maj. H. Simonds-
Gooding, *L.*........ 1,076
U.U. maj. 41,433
(1966 U.U. maj. 28,124)

SOUTH E. 87,384
189*Capt. L. P. S. Orr, U.U.* 34,894
H.J.Golding,*Nat.Unity* 21,676
J. G. Quinn, *L.*....... 7,747
U.U. maj. 13,218
(1966 U.U. maj. 23,290)

Dudley (English Borough)

E. 82,041
190 *J. W. Gilbert, Lab.*.... 29,499
★W. D. Williams, C.. 29,163
Lab. maj. 336
(March 1968, by-election,
C. maj. 11,656)
(1966 Lab. maj. 10,022)

DULWICH—*See* Camberwell

Dumfries

E. 61,346
191*H. S. P. Monro, C..*... 24,661
R. D. Donnelly, *Lab..* 15,555
J. H. D. Gair, *Scot.*
Nat............... 6,211
C. maj. 9,106
(1966 C. maj. 4,421)

Dunbartonshire (2)

EAST E. 94,516
192 *H. McCartney, Lab..*.. 32,527
J. S. B. Henderson, *C.* 26,972
G.S.Murray, *Scot. Nat.* 8,257
J. G. Brown, *L.*...... 3,460
J. Reid, *Comm.*....... 1,656
Lab. maj. 5,555
(1966 Lab. maj. 9,984)

WEST E. 58,344
193 *I. Campbell, Lab.*..... 23,009
W. Adams, *C.*........ 16,783
R. O. Campbell, *Scot.*
Nat............... 5,414
Lab. maj. 6,226
(1966 Lab. maj. 7,912)

Dundee (2)

EAST E. 62,009
194*Rt. Hon. G. M. Thom-
son, Lab.*........... 22,630
J. A. Stewart, *C.*.... 19,832
I. MacAulay, *Scot.*
Nat............... 4,181
E. G. Macfarlane, *Ind..* 176
Lab. maj. 2,798
(1966 Lab. maj. 5,726)

WEST E. 67,192
195*P. M. Doig, Lab.*..... 26,271
J. B. Armstrong-
Payne, *C.*.......... 19,449
J. A. Shepherd, *Scot.*
Nat............... 4,441
H. McLeavy, *Comm.*.. 809
Lab. maj. 6,822
(1966 Lab. maj. 8,360)

Dunfermline (Scottish Burgh)

E. 51,378
196*A. Hunter, Lab.*...... 21,532
I. C. Kirkwood, *C.*.... 12,086
J. A. Cook, *Scot. Nat.* 3,657
J. Neilson, *Comm.*.... 462
Lab. maj. 9,446
(1966 Lab. maj. 11,263)

Durham (9)

DURHAM E. 69,299
197 *W. M. Hughes, Lab.*.. 33,766
E. Greenwood, *C.*.... 16,707
Lab. maj. 17,059
(1966 Lab. maj. 18,817)

NORTH WEST E. 48,115
198*E. Armstrong, Lab.*.... 24,245
A. E. Page, *C.*....... 10,590
Lab. maj. 13,655
(1966 Lab. maj. 16,190)

See also Bishop Auckland, Blaydon, Chester-le-Street, Consett, Easington, Houghton-le-
Spring and Sedgefield

Ealing (2)

NORTH E. 64,539
199*W. J. Molloy, Lab.*.... 23,459
J. W. Barter, *C.* 23,139
Lab. maj. 320
(1966 Lab. maj. 2,577)

SOUTH E. 53,997
200*B. C. C. Batsford, C..* 19,326
C. Rofe, *Lab.*........ 12,042
G. D. Smith, *L.* 3,784
C. maj. 7,284
(1966 C. maj. 5,083)

Easington (Durham)

E. 60,933
201 *J. D. Dormand, Lab.* .. 33,418
W. M. H. Spicer, *C...* 8,457
Lab. maj. 24,961
(1966 Lab. maj. 24,747)

Eastbourne (East Sussex)

E. 84,610
202*Sir C. S. Taylor, T.D.*
C.................. 30,296
S. Terrell, *Q.C., L.* ... 23,308
C. G. Abley, *Lab.* 8,475
C. maj. 6,988
(1966 C. maj. 9,293)

East Grinstead (East Sussex)

E. 87,050
203*G. Johnson Smith, C...* 38,359
D. C. B. Smithers, *L..* 12,343
A. L. Banks, *Lab.*.... 12,014
C. maj. 26,016
(1966 C. maj. 17,984)

East Ham (2)

NORTH E. 36,896
204*Rt. Hon. R. E. Prentice,*
Lab................ 11,557
D. N. McFarlane, *C..* 7,735
Lab. maj. 3,822
(1966 Lab. maj. 7,182)

SOUTH E. 40,213
205*A. E. Oram, Lab.*..... 13,638
C. M. Jackson, *C.*.... 8,402
Lab. maj. 5,236
(1966 Lab. maj. 10,003)

Eastleigh (Hampshire)

E. 76,167
206*D. E. C. Price, C...*... 30,300
R. T. F. Flach, *Lab...* 22,248
C. J. Clayton, *L.*..... 6,825
C. maj. 8,052
(1966 C. maj. 701)

Ebbw Vale (Monmouthshire)

E. 38,709
207*M. M. Foot, Lab.*..... 21,817
A Donaldson, *L.*..... 4,371
E. S. Jenkins, *C.*..... 2,146
D. J. Baskerville, *P.C.* 1,805
Lab. maj. 17,446
(1966 Lab. maj. 20,584)

Eccles (English Borough)

E. 59,563
208*L. Carter-Jones, Lab...* 23,913
R. Boyson, *C.*....... 18,458
T. E. Keenan, *Comm..* 643
Lab. maj. 5,455
(1966 Lab. maj. 9,257)

EDGBASTON—*See* Birmingham

EDGE HILL—*See* Liverpool

Edinburgh (7)

CENTRAL E. 31,482
209*T. Oswald, Lab.*...... 9,561
M. L. Rifkind, *C.*.... 8,000
Mrs. C. M. Moore,
Scot. Nat. 1,666
A. D. Oliver, *L.*...... 1,486
Lab. maj. 1,561
(1966 Lab. maj. 4,195)

EAST E. 57,804
210 *G. S. Strang, Lab.*..... 22,171
N. Gow, *C.*.......... 16,657
Mrs. H. B. Davidson,
Scot. Nat. 3,502
Mrs. I. Swan, *Comm.*.. 1,474
Lab. maj. 5,514
(1966 Lab. maj. 8,809)

LEITH E. 35,796
211 *R. K. Murray, Q.C.,*
Lab................ 12,066
W. A. Elliott, *C.*..... 10,682
Miss M. G. Thomson,
Scot. Nat. 1,827
Mrs. J. Shein, *L.*..... 1,490
Lab. maj. 1,384
(1966 Lab. maj. 3,964)

NORTH E. 35,264
212*Earl of Dalkeith, V.R.D.,*
C.................. 13,005
R. F. Cook, *Lab.*..... 9,127
C. A. Dow, *L.*....... 2,475
C. maj. 3,878
(1966 C. maj. 3,035)

PENTLANDS E. 61,941
213*Rt. Hon. N. R. Wylie,*
V.R.D., Q.C., C...... 21,829
E. G. F. Stewart, *Lab..* 18,646
D. Clarke, *L.*....... 4,055
A. W. S. Rae, *Scot.*
Nat............... 2,814
C. maj. 3,183
(1966 C. maj. 44)

SOUTH E. 56,141
214*A. M. C. Hutchison, C.* 19,851
J. T. Henderson, *Lab..* 15,071
R. H. Guild, *L.*...... 3,469
D. J. D. Stevenson,
Scot. Nat. 2,861
C. maj. 4,780
(1966 C. maj. 5,333)

WEST *E.* 73,260
215*J. A. Stodart, *C.*...... 26,864
G. Foulkes, *Lab.*...... 19,523
D. C. E. Gorrie, *L.*.... 4,467
Miss M. M. Gibson,
   Scot. Nat......... 3,711
   C. maj............ 7,341
   (1966   C. maj. 4,809)

Edmonton (London)
E. 63,635
216*A. H. Albu, *Lab.*...... 20,626
E. P. Hubbard, *C.*..... 18,481
G. E. Longley, *L.*...... 2,937
   Lab. maj.......... 2,145
   (1966   Lab. maj. 7,725)

Enfield (2)
EAST *E.* 48,553
217*J. Mackie, *Lab.*..... 16,433
Dr. T. Weston, *C.*.... 12,403
A. A. Stowell, *L.*..... 3,373
   Lab. maj.......... 4,030
   (1966   Lab. maj. 7,527)

WEST *E.* 53,358
218*Rt. Hon. I. N. Macleod,
   C.............. 21,858
H. C. King, *Lab.*..... 9,896
J. F. Burnett, *L.*..... 4,820
K. Taylor, *Nat. Front.* 1,175
   C. maj........... 11,962
(By-election, Nov. 19, 1970)
C. E. Parkinson, *C.*..... 15,205
H. C. King, *Lab.*..... 6,926
A. A. Stowell, *L.*..... 3,283
K. Taylor, *Nat. Front.* 1,176
   C. maj........... 8,279
   (1966   C. maj. 10,157)

Epping (Essex)
E. 116,354
219 N. B. Tebbit, *C.*..... 43,615
*A. S. Newens, *Lab.*... 41,040
   C. maj............ 2,575
   (1966   Lab. maj. 7,508)

Epsom (Surrey)
E. 80,471
220*Rt. Hon. Sir P. A. G.
   Rawlinson, Q.C., *C.* .35,541
E. G. Wilson, *Lab.*..... 12,767
P. H. Billenness, *L.*.... 9,563
   C. maj........... 22,774
   (1966   C. maj. 17,593)

Erith and Crayford (London)
221*J. Wellbeloved, *Lab.*.. 23,012
H. J. Jackson, *C.*..... 18,158
   Lab. maj.......... 4,854
   (1966   Lab. maj. 9,210)

Esher (Surrey)
E. 85,333
222 D. C. M. Mather, M.C.,
   C............. 37,727
R. S. Scorer, *Lab.*..... 14,449
G. Kahan, *L.*........ 8,845
   C. maj........... 23,278
   (1966   C. maj. 17,626)

Essex (10)
SOUTH EAST *E.* 100,851
223*B. R. Braine, *C.*..... 41,589
D. W. Edwards, *Lab.*.. 23,684
C. H. Bohling, *L.*..... 6,811
   C. maj........... 17,905
   (1966   C. maj. 5,734)

L*

See also Billericay, Chelmsford,
Chigwell, Colchester, Epping,
Harwich, Maldon, Saffron
Walden and Thurrock

Eton and Slough
(English Borough)
E. 63,461
224*Miss J. Lestor, *Lab.*.... 24,103
N. Lawson, *C.*....... 21,436
P. G. D. Naylor, *L.*.... 3,407
   Lab. maj.......... 2,667
   (1966   Lab. maj. 4,663)

Exeter (English Borough)
E. 59,758
225 J. G. Hannam, *C.*..... 21,680
*Hon. Mrs. G. P. Dunwoody,
   Lab............. 20,409
D. J. Morrish, *L.*..... 6,072
   C. maj............ 1,271
   (1966   Lab. maj. 3,586)

Eye (Suffolk)
E. 64,087
226*Sir J. H. Harrison, Bt.,
   T.D., *C.*.......... 26,099
R. E. Manley, *Lab.*.... 17,735
I. S. T. Senior, *L.*.... 5,962
   C. maj............ 8,364
   (1966   C. maj. 3,613)

Falmouth and Camborne
(Cornwall)
E. 62,353
227 W. D. Mudd, *C.*..... 21,477
*J. E. O. Dunwoody,
   Lab............. 19,954
A. G. S. T. Davey, *L.*.. 5,843
R. G. Jenkin, *Mebyon
   Kernow*........... 960
   C. maj............ 1,523
   (1966   Lab. maj. 3,263)

Farnham (Surrey)
E. 60,365
228*M. V. Macmillan, *C.*.. 25,113
P. M. O. Stonham, *L.*.. 10,178
L. G. R. Pinchen, *Lab.* 8,870
   C. maj........... 14,935
   (1966   C. maj. 8,992)

Farnworth (Lancashire)
E. 70,039
229 J. F. H. Roper, *Lab.*... 29,392
I. A. Johnston, *C.*..... 20,867
   Lab. maj.......... 8,525
   (1966   Lab. maj. 14,686)

Faversham (Kent)
E. 72,090
230 R. D. Moate, *C.*...... 29,914
*T. G. Boston, *Lab.*.... 26,103
   C. maj............ 3,811
   (1966   Lab. maj. 2,489)

Feltham (London)
E. 60,700
231*R. W. Kerr, *Lab.*.... 21,561
Miss B. L. Wallis, *C.*... 16,006
G. R. King, *L.*....... 3,536
   Lab. maj.......... 5,555
   (1966   Lab. maj. 8,457)

Fermanagh and South Tyrone
E. 70,641
232 F. McManus, *Unity*... 32,832
*The   Marquess   of
   Hamilton, *U.U.* ... 31,390
   Unity maj.......... 1,447
   (1966   U.U. maj. 14,707)

Fife (2)
EAST *E.* 53,661
233*Sir J. E. Gilmour, Bt.,
   D.S.O., T.D., *C.*..... 21,619
H. Ewing, *Lab.*...... 9,756
J. Braid, *Scot. Nat.* 4,666
W. R. S. Pickard, *L.*... 3,577
   C. maj........... 11,863
   (1966   C. maj. 10,094)

WEST *E.* 66,545
234*W. W. Hamilton, *Lab.*.. 29,929
J. G. McLaughlan, *C.*.. 12,837
J. Halliday, *Scot. Nat.* . 5,386
A. D. McMillan, *Comm.* 855
   Lab. maj.......... 17,092
   (1966   Lab. maj. 18,823)

Finchley (London)
E. 72,915
235*Rt. Hon. Mrs. Margaret
   Thatcher, *C.*...... 25,480
M. L. Freeman, *Lab.*.. 14,295
G. D. Mitchell, *L.*..... 7,614
   C. maj........... 11,185
   (1966   C. maj. 9,464)

Flintshire (2)
EAST *E.* 65,199
236 S. B. Jones, *Lab.*..... 24,227
R. M. Amyes, *C.*...... 20,145
D. O. Diamond, *L.*.... 5,888
G. Hughes, *P.C.*...... 2,332
   Lab. maj.......... 4,082
   (1966   Lab. maj. 8,482)

WEST *E.* 58,373
237 Sir A. J. C. Meyer, Bt.,
   C.............. 20,999
J. G. Evans, *Lab.*...... 13,655
D. M. Thomas, *L.*..... 7,437
A. O. Jones, *P.C.*..... 3,108
   C. maj............ 7,344
   (1966   C. maj. 3,042)

Folkestone and Hythe (Kent)
E. 61,355
238*A. P. Costain, *C.*...... 27,031
N. A. Hyman, *Lab.*.... 13,772
H. W. Button, *Ind.*.... 1,219
   C. maj........... 13,259
   (1966   C. maj. 7,402)

Fulham (London)
E. 43,289
239*Rt. Hon. R. M. M.
   Stewart, C.H., *Lab.*.. 16,312
Sir I. A. Mactaggart,
   Bt., *C.*........... 12,807
Miss M. P. Arrow-
   smith, *Ind.*........ 421
R. Moody, *Ind.*....... 112
   Lab. maj.......... 3,505
   (1966   Lab. maj. 6,986)

Gainsborough (Lincolnshire)
E. 59,558
240*M. R. Kimball, *C.*..... 22,163
M. P. Tracy, *Lab.*..... 14,454
R. B. Blackmore, *L.*... 7,543
   C. maj............ 7,709
   (1966   C. maj. 3,866)

Galloway
E. 38,925
241*H. J. Brewis, C....... 14,003
A. Donaldson, *Scot.*
Nat.............. 5,723
D. Douglas, *Lab.*...... 5,665
C. B. H. Scott, *L.*..... 2,461
C. maj.......... 8,280
(1966 C. maj. 5,854)

GARSTON—See Liverpool

Gateshead (2)
EAST E. 62,672
242*B. Conlan, *Lab.*....... 28,524
P. R. Wood, C....... 15,489
Lab. maj....... 13,035
(1966 Lab. maj. 15,544)
WEST E. 34,594
243 J. R. Horam, *Lab.*..... 15,622
J. A. O'Sullivan, *C.*... 7,328
Lab. maj....... 8,294
(1966 Lab. maj. 13,503)

Gillingham (English Borough)
E. 60,144
244*F. F. A. Burden, *Lab.*... 25,813
R. E. Bean, *Lab.*..... 18,057
C. maj.......... 7,756
(1966 C. maj. 3,140)

Glamorganshire (7). See Aberavon, Barry, Caerphilly, Gower, Neath, Ogmore and Pontypridd

Glasgow (15)
BRIDGETON E. 31,332
245*J. Bennett, *Lab.*....... 11,056
R. Gavin, C......... 3,801
G. E. J. Wallace, *Scot.*
Nat.............. 1,550
J. T. A. Glass, *Ind.*..... 1,180
Lab. maj....... 7,255
(1966 Lab. maj. 10,600)
CATHCART E. 72,764
246*E. M. Taylor, C....... 29,093
D. C. H. Mackay, *Lab.* 24,188
J. McDonagh, *Ind. Lab.* 419
C. maj.......... 4,905
(1966 C. maj. 1,219)
CENTRAL E. 20,399
247*T. McMillan, *Lab.*..... 7,936
J. G. L. Rennie, C.... 2,394
A. McIntosh, *Scot.*
Nat.............. 1,688
Lab. maj....... 5,542
(1966 Lab. maj. 7,749)
CRAIGTON E. 50,404
248*B. Millan, *Lab.*........ 20,872
W. Wober, C....... 13,661
R. G. Edwards, *Scot.*
Nat.............. 2,946
Lab. maj....... 7,211
(1966 Lab. maj. 9,204)
GORBALS E. 24,901
249*F. P. McElhone, *Lab.*... 10,260
W. Shearer, C....... 3,071
T. Brady, *Scot. Nat.*.... 1,089
J. R. Kay, *Comm.*..... 376
Lab. maj....... 7,189
(By-election, Oct. 1969,
Lab. maj. 4,163)
(1966 Lab. maj. 9,940)

Govan E. 35,538
250*J. Rankin, *Lab.*....... 13,443
G. F. Belton, C....... 6,301
J. M. T. Grieve, *Scot.*
Nat.............. 2,294
T. Biggam, *Comm.*... 326
Lab. maj....... 7,142
(1966 Lab. maj. 10,856)

HILLHEAD E. 34,585
251*Hon. T. G. D. Galbraith, C........... 14,674
J. V. Cable, *Lab.*...... 7,303
Rev. G. Wotherspoon,
Scot. Nat.......... 1,957
C. maj.......... 7,371
(1966 C. maj. 6,515)

KELVINGROVE E. 19,019
252*M. S. Miller, *Lab.*.... 6,106
R. E. Dundas, C....... 5,274
Lab. maj....... 832
(1966 Lab. maj. 2,518)

MARYHILL E. 45,505
253*W. Hannan, *Lab.*..... 18,925
A. K. R. Murchison,
C............... 6,638
A. C. W. Aitken, *Scot.*
Nat.............. 3,273
Lab. maj....... 12,287
(1966 Lab. maj. 13,861)

POLLOK E. 57,991
254 J. White, *Lab.*....... 19,311
*E. Wright, C......... 18,708
G. A. Leslie, *Scot. Nat.* 3,733
Lab. maj....... 603
(March 1967, by-election,
C. maj. 2,201)
(1966 Lab. maj. 1,975)

PROVAN E. 65,716
255*H. D. Brown, *Lab.*..... 25,864
D. D. M. Masterton,
C............... 11,881
W. McRae, *Scot. Nat.* 4,181
J. Jackson, *Comm.*... 601
Lab. maj....... 13,983
(1966 Lab. maj. 15,215)

SCOTSTOUN E. 66,038
256*W. W. Small, *Lab.*.... 26,492
N. J. Mountney, C..... 14,487
A. Mitchell, *Scot. Nat.* 4,313
H. D. Boyd, *Comm.*.. 846
Lab. maj....... 12,005
(1966 Lab. maj. 12,827)

SHETTLESTON E. 47,130
257*Sir M. Galpern, *Lab.*... 17,840
A. N. McCue, C....... 7,969
W. Lindsay, *Scot. Nat.* 3,995
Lab. maj....... 9,871
(1966 Lab. maj. 13,351)

SPRINGBURN E. 38,286
258*R. Buchanan, *Lab.*.... 14,968
J. Sorbie, C......... 4,574
W. Morton, *Scot. Nat.* 3,323
N. McLellan, *Comm.*.. 423
Lab. maj....... 10,394
(1966 Lab. maj. 11,499)

WOODSIDE E. 35,816
259*N. G. Carmichael, *Lab.* 10,785
V. J. MacColl, C...... 9,457
D. R. Rollo, *Scot. Nat.* 1,912
G. R. McKay, *Ind. C.* 614
Lab. maj....... 1,328
(1966 Lab. maj. 2,338)

Gloucester (English Borough)
E. 61,637
260 Mrs. S. Oppenheim, C. 21,838
*Rt. Hon. J. Diamond,
Lab.............. 20,777
J. P. Heppell, *L.*...... 3,935
C. maj.......... 1,061
(1966 Lab. maj. 5,273)

SOUTH E. 88,083
261*Rt. Hon. F. V. Corfield,
C............... 35,045
M. G. Dalling. *Lab.*.... 26,067
A. Lambert, *L.*....... 7,680
C. maj.......... 8,978
(1966 C. maj. 1,424)

WEST E. 64,166
262*C. W. Loughlin, M.B.E.,
Lab.............. 22,637
S. H. A. F. Hopkins, C. 21,530
J. A. Svendsen, *L.*..... 4,932
Lab. maj....... 1,107
(1966 Lab. maj. 7,705)

See also Cirencester and Tewkesbury and Stroud

Goole (Yorks., W.R.)
E. 63,537
263*G. Jeger, *Lab.*....... 26,424
I. R. Bloomer, C....... 17,457
Lab. maj....... 8,967
(By-election, May 27, 1971)
Dr. E. I. Marshall, *Lab.* 24,323
I. R. Bloomer, C....... 10,990
Lab. maj....... 13,333
(1966 Lab. maj. 12,148)

GORBALS—See Glasgow
GORTON—See Manchester

Gosport and Fareham (English Borough)
E. 101,539
264*R. F. B. Bennett, V.R.D.,
C............... 39,234
J. R. Sturges, *Lab.*.... 21,262
P. I. Smith, *L.*....... 11,754
C. maj.......... 17,972
(1966 C. maj. 11,026)

GOVAN—See Glasgow

Gower (Glamorgan)
E. 54,621
265*I. Davies, *Lab.*....... 26,485
M. J. Carter, C....... 9,435
C. G. Davies, P.C....... 5,869
Lab. maj....... 17,050
(1966 Lab. maj. 21,058)

Grantham (Lincolnshire)
E. 74,180
266*Rt. Hon. J. B. Godber,
C............... 33,070
W. F. Higgins, *Lab.*... 23,296
C. maj.......... 9,774
(1966 C. maj. 2,158)

Gravesend (Kent)
E. 84,608
267 R. L. White, C....... 29,924
*A. J. Murray, *Lab.*.... 28,711
M. J. Dunn, *L.*....... 5,234
C. maj.......... 1,213
(1966 Lab. maj. 4,792)

Greenock (Scottish Burgh)
E. 47,740
268*J. D. Mabon, *Lab.*..... 19,334
W. T. C. Riddell, *L.*.. 16,100
A. C. Murray, *Comm.* 559
Lab. maj....... 3,234
(1966 Lab. maj. 11,261)

Greenwich (London)
E. 57,195
269*Rt. Hon. R. W. Marsh,
  Lab............. 20,804
J. S. Thom, C....... 13,195
Mrs. P. M. Wylan, L.. 3,319
  Lab. maj......... 7,609
(By-election, July 8, 1971)
N. G. Barnett, Lab.... 14,671
J. S. Thom, C...... 6,150
R. S. Mallone, F.P.‡ 792
R. Simmerson, Ind... 285
D. Davies, Ind...... 89
  Lab. maj......... 8,521
(1966 Lab. maj. 11,159)

Grimsby (English Borough)
E. 66,015
270*Rt. Hon. C. A. R.
  Crossland, Lab...... 23,571
M. F. Spungin, C... 17,460
D. J. Hardwidge, L.. 3,850
  Lab. maj......... 6,111
(1966 Lab. maj. 8,126)

Guildford (Surrey)
E. 68,606
271*D. A. R. Howell, C.... 27,203
P. B. Smith, Lab...... 13,108
M. J. Walton, L....... 8,822
  C. maj......... 14,095
(1966 C. maj. 8,345)

Hackney, Central (London)
E. 53,325
272 S. C. Davis, Lab...... 17,380
K. S. Lightwood, C... 9,339
A. Qureshi, Ind...... 252
  Lab. maj......... 8,041
(1966 Lab. maj. 14,026)

Halifax (English Borough)
E. 66,586
273*Hon. Shirley Summer-
  skill, Lab...... 24,026
G. A. Turner, C...... 23,828
A.J.W. Graham, I.L.P. 847
  Lab. maj......... 198
(1966 Lab. maj. 5,702)

HALL GREEN—See Birmingham
HALLAM—See Sheffield

Haltemprice (Yorkshire, E.R.)
E. 74,404
274*P. H. B. Wall, M.C.,
  V.R.D., C......... 30,042
C. M. Denton, Lab... 15,862
S. C. Haywood, L... 10,129
  C. maj......... 14,180
(1966 C. maj. 12,549)

Hamilton (Lanarkshire)
E. 60,628
275 A. Wilson, Lab........ 25,431
*Mrs. W. M. Ewing,
  Scot. Nat...... 16,849
J. R. Harper, C...... 5,455
H. C. Taylor, Ind. L.. 295
  Lab. maj......... 8,582
(Nov. 1967, by-election,
Scot. Nat. maj. 1,799)
(1966 Lab. maj. 16,576)

Hammersmith, North (London)
E. 41,677
276*F. Tomney, Lab....... 16,145
B. H. I. H. Stewart, C. 9,615
  Lab. maj......... 6,530
(1966 Lab. maj. 10,665)

‡ Fellowship Party.

Hampshire (6). See Aldershot, Basingstoke, Eastleigh, New Forest, Petersfield and Winchester

Hampstead (London)
E. 72,154
277 G. Finsberg, M.B.E., C.. 21,264
*B. C. G. Whitaker,
  Lab............. 20,790
J. H. R. Calmann, L.. 3,550
  C. maj......... 474
(1966 Lab. maj. 2,253)

HANDSWORTH—See Birmingham

Harborough (Leicestershire)
E. 103,981
278*J. A. Farr, C....... 44,933
J. Marshall, Lab..... 25,728
W. E. Pickard, L..... 9,079
  C. maj......... 19,205
(1966 C. maj. 6,997)

Harrogate (Yorks., W.R.)
E. 62,961
279*Rt. Hon. J. E. Ramsden,
  C......... 26,167
W. Greaves, L........ 8,825
B. Hellowell, Lab..... 8,797
  C. maj......... 17,342
(1966 C. maj. 13,414)

Harrow (3)

CENTRAL E. 46,133
280*J. A. Grant, C....... 16,525
A. R. Judge, Lab..... 12,561
A. H. J. Miller, L..... 3,449
S. G. Carter, Ind..... 358
  C. maj......... 3,964
(1966 C. maj. 1,630)

EAST E. 50,684
281 H. J. Dykes, C....... 19,517
*R. D. Roebuck, Lab.. 15,496
M. D. Colne, L....... 3,185
G. Cramp, Ind....... 72
  C. maj......... 4,021
(1966 Lab. maj. 378)

WEST E. 57,748
282*A. J. Page, C....... 24,867
T. P. C. Daniel, Lab... 11,462
J. F. Smith, L....... 5,440
  C. maj......... 13,405
(1966 C. maj. 10,347)

The Hartlepools (English Borough)
E. 64,831
283*E. L. Leadbitter, Lab... 27,704
R. M. Marshall, C.... 20,188
  Lab. maj......... 7,516
(1966 Lab. maj. 8,652)

Harwich (Essex)
E. 82,580
284*J. E. Ridsdale, C...... 32,754
A. W. Phillips, Lab... 19,923
T. E. Dale, L......... 8,519
  C. maj......... 12,831
(1966 C. and Nat. L. maj. 6,640)

Hastings (English Borough)
E. 53,608
285 K. R. Warren, C...... 20,364
B. Kissen, Lab....... 13,549
Mrs. P. M. Shields, L.. 6,324
  C. maj......... 6,815
(1966 C. maj. 2,340)

Hayes and Harlington (London)
E. 49,886
286*A. M. Skeffington, Lab. 19,192
A. W. Potier, C.......13,728
P. Pink, Comm....... 372
  Lab. maj......... 5,464
(By-election, June 17, 1971)
N. D. Sandelson, Lab.. 15,827
A. W. Potier, C...... 5,348
  Lab. maj......... 10,479
(1966 Lab. maj. 8,824)

HEELEY—See Sheffield

Hemel Hempstead (Hertfordshire)
E. 100,306
287*J. H. Allason, O.B.E., C. 40,417
P. A. Fletcher, Lab... 28,067
J. Wilson, L......... 9,274
  C. maj......... 12,350
(1966 C. maj. 2,038)

Hemsworth (Yorks., W.R.)
E. 69,572
288*A. Beaney, Lab....... 40,013
M. C. Tucker, C...... 9,534
  Lab. maj......... 30,479
(1966 Lab. maj. 34,722)

Hendon (2)

NORTH E. 52,330
289 J. M. Gorst, C....... 18,192
A. A. M. Irvine, Lab.. 15,013
M. G. Cass, L........ 3,704
  C. maj......... 3,179
(1966 C. maj. 600)

SOUTH E. 55,840
290 Rt. Hon. P. J. M.
  Thomas, Q.C., C..... 18,901
Mrs. G. Dimson, Lab.. 12,712
L. Young, L......... 4,981
  C. maj......... 6,189
(1966 C. maj. 4,056)

Henley (Oxon.)
E. 85,299
291*J. A. Hay, C....... 33,452
Miss M. J. Denby, Lab. 19,310
A. W. Giles, L....... 8,907
D. F. B. Brunner, Ind. 960
  C. maj......... 14,142
(1966 C. maj. 5,674)

Herefordshire (2)

HEREFORD E. 56,742
292*J. D. Gibson-Watt,
  M.C., C......... 22,011
G. D. Purnell, Lab... 14,410
T. R. Crowther, L..... 4,953
  C. maj......... 7,601
(1966 C. maj. 2,747)
See also Leominster

Hertfordshire (7)

EAST E. 94,206
293*Rt. Hon. Sir D. C.
  Walker-Smith, Bt.,
  T.D., Q.C., C....... 37,668
M. S. Thomas, Lab.... 23,601
D. Walsh, L......... 7,538
  C. maj......... 14,067
(1966 C. maj. 5,206)

HERTFORD *E.* 88,890
294*Lord Balniel, *C.*...... 36,494
   Mrs. Y. Sieve, *Lab....* 26,924
   J. M. Melling, *L.......* 5,994
   C. maj............. 9,570
   (1966 C. maj. 794)
SOUTH WEST *E.* 86,406
295*G. J. M. Longden,
   M.B.E., *C.*........ 32,661
   B. J. Grocott, *Lab....* 24,214
   J. E. S. Jarrett, *L......* 7,489
   R. W. Skilton, *Ind....* 542
   C. maj............. 8,447
   (1966 C. maj. 3,192)
See also Barnet, Hemel Hempstead, Hitchin, and St. Albans

Heston and Isleworth
(London) *E.* 54,197
296 B. J. Hayhoe, *C.*..... 21,580
   G. J. Samuel, *Lab....* 16,981
   C. maj............. 4,599
   (1966 C. maj. 926)

Hexham (Northumberland)
E. 62,988
297*Rt. Hon. A. G. F.
   Rippon, Q.C., *C.* .. 24,516
   J. E. Miller, *Lab.......* 16,645
   D. V. Cogan, *L.......* 6,021
   C. maj............. 7,871
   (1966 C. maj. 4,784)

Heywood and Royton
(Lancashire)
E. 72,506
298*J. Barnett, *Lab........* 25,081
   I. Macgregor, *C.*..... 24,178
   F. J. Beetham, *L.......* 5,620
   Lab. maj............ 903
   (1966 Lab. maj. 5,653)

High Peak (Derbyshire)
E. 55,656
299 *S. Le Marchant, C.* ... 19,558
   P. M. Jackson, Lab.... 18,054
   D. I. Wrigley, *L.......* 7,119
   C. maj............. 1,504
   (1966 Lab. maj. 814)

HILLHEAD—*See* Glasgow

HILLSBOROUGH—*See* Sheffield

Hitchin (Hertfordshire)
E. 109,704
300*Mrs. S. V. T. B.
   Williams, *Lab......* 40,932
   R. N. Luce, *C.*....... 37,258
   T. N. Willis, *L.*...... 6,148
   Lab. maj............ 3,674
   (1966 Lab. maj. 9,750)

Holborn and St. Pancras South
(London) *E.* 41,893
301*Mrs. L. M. Jeger, *Lab.*.. 12,448
   J. M. E. Byng, *C.* 10,125
   Lab. maj............ 2,323
   (1966 Lab. maj. 5,146)

Holland with Boston
(Lincolnshire)
E. 77,682
302*R. Body, *C.*.......... 33,580
   R. N. H. Sackur, *Lab.*. 24,241
   C. maj............. 9,339
   (1966 C. maj. 316)

Honiton (Devonshire)
E. 72,394
303*P. F. H. Emery, *C.*.... 32,885
   Mrs. B. V. Trethewey,
   L................ 11,330
   M. D. D. Newitt, *Lab.* 11,072
   C. maj............. 21,555
   (March 1967, by-election,
   C. maj. 15,992)
   (1966 C. maj. 13,709)

Horncastle (Lincolnshire)
E. 47,225
304*P. H. B. Tapsell, *C.*.... 19,299
   E. A. Skinns, *Lab....* 8,860
   R. S. Miller, *L.*...... 6,707
   C. maj............. 10,439
   (1966 C. maj. 5,375)

Hornchurch (London)
E. 100,546
305 J. W. Loveridge, *C.*..... 36,124
   *A. L. Williams, *Lab...* 30,294
   B. G. Sell, *L.*....... 6,227
   C. maj............. 5,830
   (1966 Lab. maj. 3,033)

Hornsey (London)
E. 64,993
306*H. A. L. Rossi, *C.*..... 21,434
   Hon. P. A. Wells-
   Pestell, *Lab.......* 17,645
   L. S. Brass, *L.*....... 3,755
   Mrs. M. Morris, *Comm.* 624
   E. S. Grant, *S.P.G.B.*.. 156
   C. maj............. 3,789
   (1966 C. maj. 615)

Horsham (West Sussex)
E. 106,552
307*P. M. Hordern, *C.*...... 41,994
   A. J. Edwards, *Lab....* 27,706
   H. C. A. Gill, *L.*..... 8,574
   C. maj............. 14,288
   (1966 C. maj. 6,041)

Houghton-le-Spring (Durham)
E. 63,011
308*T. W. Urwin, *Lab......* 32,888
   F. H. M. Craig-Cooper,
   C................ 11,914
   Lab. maj............ 20,974
   (1966 Lab. maj. 22,763)

Hove (English Borough)
E. 75,136
309*W. F. M. Madden, *C.*.. 34,287
   D. G. Nicholas, *Lab....* 15,639
   C. maj............. 18,648
   (1966 C. maj. 15,890)

Howden (Yorks, E.R.)
E. 55,071
310*P. E. O. Bryan, D.S.O.,
   M.C., *C.*........... 22,102
   J. W. R. Graham, *Lab.* 9,567
   J. F. Crossley, *L.......* 6,951
   T. Makoni, *Ind......* 154
   C. maj............. 12,535
   (1966 C. maj. 8,280)

Huddersfield (2)
EAST *E.* 54,863
311*J. P. W. Mallalieu, *Lab.* 20,629
   J. G. Holt, *C.*......... 15,632
   G. M. Lee, *L.*........ 4,569
   Mrs. E. Beresford,
   Comm............. 308
   Lab. maj............ 4,997
   (1966 Lab. maj. 10,879)
WEST *E.* 53,470
312*K. Lomas, *Lab........* 16,866
   Hon. R. Storey, *C.*.... 16,673
   W. J. L. Wallace, *L....* 6,128
   R. J. Scott, *Nat. Front.* 1,427
   Lab. maj............ 193
   (1966 Lab. maj. 4,476)

Hull (3)
EAST *E.* 76,241
313 J. L. Prescott, *Lab......* 36,859
   N. S. H. Lamont, *C...* 14,736
   Lab. maj............ 22,123
   (1966 Lab. maj. 23,072)
NORTH *E.* 66,074
314*J. K. McNamara, *Lab.* .. 26,302
   J. E. Townend, *C......* 17,912
   W. A. C. Harvey, *Ind.* .. 1,808
   Lab. maj............ 8,390
   (1966 Lab. maj. 8,769)
WEST *E.* 59,889
315*J. Johnson, *Lab........* 24,050
   T. E. Forrow, *C......* 14,537
   Lab. maj............ 9,513
   (1966 Lab. maj. 12,265)

Huntingdonshire
E. 66,984
316*Rt. Hon. Sir D. L. M.
   Renton, K.B.E., T.D.,
   Q.C., *C.*........... 27,398
   J. P. P. Curran, *Lab...* 17,588
   M. W. B. O'Loughlin,
   L................ 5,082
   C. maj............. 9,810
   (1966 C. and Nat. L. maj.
   5,228)

Huyton (Lancashire)
E. 108,301
317*Rt. Hon. J. H. Wilson,
   O.B.E., *Lab.*........ 45,583
   J. N. M. Entwistle, *C..* 24,509
   J. G. W. Sparrow,
   Dem. Party 1,232
   J. I. Kenny, *Comm....* 890
   Lab. maj............ 21,074
   (1966 Lab. maj. 20,950)

Ilford (2)
NORTH *E.* 70,301
318*T. L. Iremonger, *C....* 25,142
   C. W. Sewell, *Lab....* 17,352
   G. L. P. Wilson, *L.....* 5,425
   C. maj............. 7,790
   (1966 C. maj. 3,344)
SOUTH *E.* 58,617
319 A. E. Cooper, M.B.E., *C.* 18,369
   *A. J. Shaw, *Lab......* 17,087
   G. L. Wilson, *L.......* 3,341
   M. E. L. Skeggs, *Nat.
   Front.*............ 727
   M. J. Marks, *Ind......* 190
   C. maj............. 1,282
   (1966 Lab. maj. 2,520)

Ilkeston (Derbyshire)
E. 74,587
320*L. R. Fletcher, Lab.... 32,961
R. D. Beardsley, C.... 15,870
W. Smit, L........ 6,157
Lab. maj.......... 17,091
(1966 Lab. maj. 20,940)

Ince (Lancashire)
E. 67,067
321*M. T. F. McGuire, Lab. 32,295
A. R. Coupe, C....... 14,877
Lab. maj.......... 17,418
(1966 Lab. maj. 19,840)

Inverness-shire and Ross and Cromarty (3)
INVERNESS E. 54,597
322*D. R. Johnston, L..... 15,052
D. A. Wathen, C..... 12,378
D. Macaulay, Lab..... 9,038
Miss A. C. Cameron,
Scot. Nat......... 2,781
L. maj............ 2,674
(1966 L. maj. 2,395)
ROSS AND CROMARTY E. 27,101
323 J. H. N. Gray, C....... 6,418
*A. R. Mackenzie, L..... 5,617
R. D. Maclean, Lab.... 5,023
G. Nicholson, Scot.
Nat.............. 2,268
C. maj............ 801
(1966 L. maj. 2,044)
See also Western Isles

Ipswich (English Borough)
E. 87,124
324 E. D. D. Money, C..... 27,704
*Rt. Hon. Sir D. M.
Foot, Q.C., Lab..... 27,691
N. S. Lewis, L....... 5,147
D. Brown, Ind....... 2,322
C. maj............ 13
(1966 Lab. maj. 6,873)

Isle of Ely
E. 67,651
325*Sir E. A. H. Legge-
Bourke, K.B.E., C.... 28,972
R. E. O'Hare, Lab..... 19,366
C. maj............ 9,606
(1966 C. maj. 1,754)

Isle of Thanet (Kent)
E. 89,627
326*W. R. Rees-Davies, C. 33,434
L. J. A. Bishop, Lab... 21,709
T. D. Gates, L....... 7,176
I. R. P. Josephs, Ind. . 2,136
C. maj............ 11,725
(1966 C. maj. 4,886)

Isle of Wight
E. 81,135
327*H. F. M. Woodnutt, C. 30,437
K. W. Boulton, Lab... 13,111
S. S. Ross, L....... 12,883
R. W. J. Cowdell,
Vectis Nat.......... 1,607
C. maj............ 17,326
(1966 C. maj. 10,451)

Islington (3)
EAST E. 43,827
328 J. D. Grant, Lab....... 13,980
R. Devonald-Lewis, C. 8,660
Lab. maj.......... 5,320
(1966 Lab. maj. 7,519)
NORTH E. 45,211
329*M. J. O'Halloran, Lab. 13,010
D. A. Pearce, C....... 7,862
B. Green, Nat. Front.. 1,232
Lab. maj.......... 5,148
(By-election, Oct. 1969,
Lab. maj. 1,534)
(1966 Lab. maj. 7,831)
SOUTH WEST E. 43,423
330 G. Cunningham, Lab... 12,876
J. Szemerey, C....... 6,601
A. E. Lomas, Ind. L... 1,161
Mrs. M. Betteridge,
Comm............. 509
Lab. maj.......... 6,275
(1966 Lab. maj. 10,303)

ITCHEN—See Southampton

Jarrow (English Borough)
E. 55,112
331*Rt. Hon. E. Fernyhough,
Lab.............. 25,861
D. J. Robson, C....... 14,847
Lab. maj.......... 11,014
(1966 Lab. maj. 13,557)

Keighley (English Borough)
E. 51,522
332 Miss J. V. Hall, C..... 20,957
*J. Binns, Lab......... 20,341
C. maj............ 616
(1966 Lab. maj. 4,012)

KELVINGROVE—See Glasgow

KEMPTOWN—See Brighton

Kensington (2)
NORTH E. 43,601
333 B. L. H. Douglas-Mann,
Lab............. 13,175
L. Brittan, C........ 9,792
P. D. Spencer, L...... 1,990
Lab. maj.......... 3,383
(1966 Lab. maj. 5,263)
SOUTH E. 57,308
334*Sir B. M. Rhys-
Williams, Bt., C..... 21,591
Mrs. F. M. Bridges,
Lab.............. 6,928
C. maj............ 14,663
(March 1968, by-election,
C. maj. 13,747)
(1966 C. maj. 14,631)

Kent (13). See Ashford, Canterbury, Chislehurst, Dartford,
Dover, Faversham, Folkestone
and Hythe, Gravesend, Isle of
Thanet, Maidstone, Orpington, Sevenoaks, and Tonbridge

Kettering (Northants)
E. 95,564
335*Rt. Hon Sir G. S. de
Freitas, K.C.M.G., Lab. 34,803
J. C. Taylor, C....... 30,613
A. J. W. Haigh, L.... 6,695
Lab. maj.......... 4,190
(1966 Lab. maj. 11,460)

Kidderminster (Worcestershire)
E. 72,886
336*Sir E. T. C. Brinton, C. 27,667
G. F. Smith, Lab. 18,297
H. H. B. Lamb, L..... 7,502
C. maj............ 9,370
(1966 C. maj. 3,177)

Kilmarnock (Ayrshire)
E. 52,573
337*Rt. Hon. W. Ross,
M.B.E., Lab......... 24,477
G. Law, C.......... 11,476
A. MacInnes, Scot. Nat... 2,836
A. J. Wight, L....... 2,459
Lab. maj.......... 13,001
(1966 Lab. maj. 14,087)

King's Lynn (Norfolk)
E. 61,228
338 C. Brocklebank-Fowler,
C............... 23,822
*J. D. Page, Lab....... 23,789
C. maj............ 33
(1966 Lab. maj. 2,019)

Kingston upon Thames (London)
E. 60,119
339*Rt. Hon. J. A. Boyd-
Carpenter, C....... 23,426
R. H. Crockett, Lab... 13,090
S. J. E. Wells, L...... 4,822
C. maj............ 10,336
(1966 C. maj. 7,866)

KINROSS AND WEST PERTHSHIRE—
See Perthshire and Kinross

Kirkcaldy (Scottish Burgh)
E. 57,452
340*H. P. H. Gourlay, Lab. 22,986
A. M. Hogg, C....... 13,193
J. C. Lees, Scot. Nat. .. 4,863
Lab. maj.......... 9,793
(1966 Lab. maj. 12,734)

KIRKDALE—See Liverpool

Knutsford (Cheshire)
E. 74,743
341 Rt. Hon. J. E. H. Davies,
M.B.E., C......... 33,194
A. F. Bennett, Lab.... 11,612
G. Tordoff, L........ 10,684
C. maj............ 21,582
(1966 C. maj. 13,711)

LADYWOOD—See Birmingham

Lambeth (3)
BRIXTON E. 43,506
342*M. Lipton, C.B.E., Lab. 13,053
J. W. Harkess, C...... 9,727
Lab. maj.......... 3,326
(1966 Lab. maj. 6,134)
NORWOOD E. 54,637
343*J. D. Fraser, Lab...... 16,634
P. Temple-Morris, C. 16,003
E. Hawthorne, L...... 2,436
Lab. maj.......... 631
(1966 Lab. maj. 2,273)

VAUXHALL E. 37,843
344*Rt. Hon. G. R. Strauss,
Lab............. 13,046
C. W. Jones, C....... 7,477
Lab. maj.......... 5,569
(1966 Lab. maj. 7,585)

Lanark (Lanarkshire)
E. 85,829
345*Rt. Hon. Judith Hart,
Lab............. 30,194
A. C. S. MacDougall,
C............. 27,721
H. C. D. Rankin, Scot.
Nat............. 7,859
D. McDowall, Comm. 1,273
Lab. maj.......... 2,473
(1966 Lab. maj. 7,740)

Lanarkshire (6)
NORTH E. 55,008
346 J. Smith, Lab........ 21,982
R. B. J. D. Black, C.... 16,963
J. B. Hutchison, Scot.
Nat............. 3,486
Lab. maj.......... 5,019
(1966 Lab. maj. 8,303)
See also Bothwell, Hamilton,
Lanark, Motherwell and
Rutherglen

Lancashire (16). See Chorley,
Clitheroe, Darwen, Farnworth,
Heywood and Royton, Huy-
ton, Ince, Lancaster, Middleton and Prestwich,
Morecambe and Lonsdale,
Newton, North Fylde, Ormskirk, South Fylde, West-
houghton and Widnes

Lancaster (Lancashire)
E. 47,899
347 Mrs. M. E. Kellett, C.. 18,584
*S. Henig, Lab........ 16,843
A. R. C. Paton, L...... 2,436
C. maj............ 1,741
(1966 Lab. maj. 1,811)

LANGSTONE—See Portsmouth

Leeds (6)
EAST E. 77,015
348*Rt. Hon. D. W. Healey,
M.B.E., Lab......... 28,827
P. Crotty, C......... 21,112
Mrs. J. Bellamy, Comm. 513
Lab. maj.......... 7,715
(1966 Lab. maj. 11,277)
NORTH EAST E. 55,924
349*Rt. Hon. Sir K. S.
Joseph, Bt., C....... 20,720
A. J. Patient, Lab..... 15,653
C. maj............ 5,067
(1966 C. maj. 4,962)
NORTH WEST E. 80,742
350*Sir D. Kaberry, Bt.,
T.D., C............ 29,227
K. J. Woolmer, Lab.... 20,795
J. R. Worrall, L...... 6,048
C. maj............ 8,432
(1966 C. maj. 6,124)

SOUTH E. 49,759
351*M. Rees, Lab........ 19,536
G. K. Macpherson, C. 9,311
S. J. Cooksey, L....... 3,810
Lab. maj.......... 10,225
(1966 Lab. maj. 13,358)
SOUTH EAST E. 29,973
352 S. Cohen, Lab....... 10,930
Mrs. M. Sexton, C.... 5,182
E. A. Britten, L....... 1,135
B. Scott, Comm...... 198
Lab. maj.......... 5,748
(1966 Lab. maj. 8,890)
WEST E. 63,829
353*Rt. Hon. T. C. Pannell,
Lab............. 21,618
A. Leitch, C......... 14,749
Mrs. P. A. Armitage,
L............. 5,341
Lav. maj.......... 6,869
(1966 Lab. maj. 10,508)

Leek (Staffordshire)
E. 90,156
354 D. L. Knox, C....... 27,899
*Rt. Hon. H. Davies,
Lab............. 26,359
R. M. Burman, L..... 6,219
C. maj............ 1,540
(1966 Lab. maj. 7,761)

Leicester (4)
NORTH EAST E. 43,562
355*T. G. Bradley, Lab.... 15,016
P. E. F. Heneage, C.... 14,125
D. J. Taylor, Ind...... 1,616
Lab. maj.......... 891
(1966 Lab. maj. 6,238)
NORTH WEST E. 53,417
356 Hon. G. E. Janner, Q.C.,
Lab............. 18,226
S. J. Symington, C.... 15,584
R. J. Rogers, L....... 2,862
R. E. Welford, Ind.... 935
Lab. maj.......... 2,642
(1966 Lab. maj. 7,807)
SOUTH EAST E. 59,171
357*W. J. Peel, C......... 26,483
W. Hilbourne, Lab.... 15,788
C. maj............ 10,695
(1966 C. maj. 7,796)
SOUTH WEST E. 45,087
358*T. G. Boardman, C.... 14,611
C. Grundy, Lab....... 14,505
J. T. Roper, L........ 2,124
J. E. Kyneston, Nat.
Front............. 749
C. maj............ 106
(Nov. 1967, by-election,
C. maj. 3,939)
(1966 Lab. maj. 5,554)

Leicestershire (4). See Bosworth, Harborough, Lough-
borough and Melton

Leigh (English Borough)
E. 64,726
359*H. Boardman, Lab.... 26,625
J. P. McGuire, C...... 15,314
J. Knowles, Ind....... 3,776
Lab. maj.......... 11,311
(1966 Lab. maj. 16,062)

LEITH—See Edinburgh

Leominster (Herefordshire)
E. 41,987
360*Hon. Sir C. Bossom, Bt.,
C............. 17,630
R. J. Pincham, L...... 6,462
M. G. M. Sloman, Lab. 6,321
C. maj............ 11,168
(1966 C. maj. 7,398)

Lewes (East Sussex)
E. 79,471
361*Sir T. V. H. Beamish,
M.C., C........... 33,592
Q. Barry, Lab........ 14,904
M. Holt, L.......... 9,083
C. maj............ 18,688
(1966 C. maj. 12,968)

Lewisham (3)
NORTH E. 52,061
362*R. D. Moyle, Lab..... 18,235
H. R. L. Samuel, C... 17,208
Lab. maj.......... 1,027
(1966 Lab. maj. 2,363)
SOUTH E. 51,656
363*C. A. Johnson, C.B.E.,
Lab............. 19,217
G. L. Dixon, C....... 13,665
Miss D. Hart, Ind..... 821
Lab. maj.......... 5,552
(1966 Lab. maj. 9,918)
WEST E. 57,064
364 J. S. Gummer, C...... 19,676
*J. M. Y. Dickens, Lab. 18,916
C. maj............ 760
(1966 Lab. maj. 2,034)

Leyton (London)
E. 66,970
365*Rt. Hon. P. C. Gordon
Walker, C.H., Lab... 23,386
R. C. Buxton, C...... 17,906
Lab. maj.......... 5,480
(1966 Lab. maj. 8,646)

Lichfield and Tamworth
(Staffordshire) E. 82,720
366 Maj.-Gen. J. A. d'Avig-
dor-Goldsmid, C.B.,
O.B.E., M.C., C...... 31,724
T. J. Pitt, Lab....... 29,298
C. maj............ 1,976
(1966 C. maj. 4,134)

Lincoln (English Borough)
E. 53,243
367*D. Taverne, Q.C., Lab.. 20,090
R. T. Alexander, C... 15,340
G. T. Blades, Ind..... 3,937
Lab. maj.......... 4,750
(1966 Lab. maj. 6,537)

Lincolnshire and Rutland (7).
See Brigg, Gainsborough,
Grantham, Holland with Bos-
ton, Horncastle, Louth and
Rutland and Stamford

Liverpool (9)
EDGE HILL E. 43,805
368*Rt. Hon. Sir A. J.
Irvine, Q.C., Lab.... 14,752
M. Howard, C....... 10,804
Lab. maj.......... 3,948
(1966 Lab. maj. 7,541)

EXCHANGE E. 34,626
369 R. Parry, *Lab.*........ 12,995
    A. G. Phillips, *C.*.... 4,638
    R. O'Hara, *Comm.*.... 775
    Lab. maj......... 8,357
    (1966 Lab. maj. 9,717)

GARSTON E. 76,498
370*T. V. N. Fortescue, C.. 28,381
    C. J. Smith, *Lab.*...... 21,456
    C. maj......... 6,925
    (1966 C. maj. 3,970)

KIRKDALE E. 49,391
371*J. A. Dunn, *Lab.*.... 17,678
    M. P. Tinné, *C.*...... 13,615
    Lab. maj......... 4 063
    (1966 Lab. maj. 6,014)

SCOTLAND E. 29,492
372*W. H. Alldritt, *Lab.*... 11,074
    R. H. Morris, *C.*...... 3,740
    Lab. maj......... 7,334
    (By-election, April 1, 1971)
    F. Marsden, *Lab.*..... 6,795
    G. B. Porter, *C.*...... 1,751
    †P. Mahon, *Ind. Lab.*... 981
    Lab. maj......... 5,044
    (1966 Lab. maj. 9,514)

TOXTETH E. 45,320
373*R. Crawshaw, O.B.E.,
    Lab............. 15,276
    B. M. Keefe, *C.*...... 12,820
    Lab. maj......... 2,456
    (1966 Lab. maj. 3,845)

WALTON E. 54,234
374*E. S. Heffer, *Lab.*...... 20,530
    J. Norton, *C.*...... 16,124
    Lab. maj......... 4,406
    (1966 Lab. maj. 5,333)

WAVERTREE E. 59,661
375*J. D. Tilney, T.D., C.. 19,127
    C. E. Carr, *L.*........ 11,650
    G. Woodburn, *Lab.*.... 10,253
    C. maj......... 7,477
    (1966 C. maj. 5,650)

WEST DERBY E. 61,044
376*E. Ogden, *Lab.*........ 22,324
    M. A. Latham, *C.*.... 16,619
    Lab. maj......... 5,705
    (1966 Lab. maj. 4,838)

Llanelli (Carmarthenshire)
E. 64,948
377 D. J. D. Davies, *Lab.*... 31,398
    C. R. James, *P.C.*.... 8,387
    Miss M. A. Jones, *C.*... 5,777
    D. J. Lewis, *L.*...... 3,834
    R. E. Hitchon, *Comm.* 603
    Lab. maj......... 23,011
    (1966 Lab. maj. 26,531)

Londonderry
E. 91,255
378*R. Chichester-Clark,
    U.U............. 39,141
    E. G. McAteer, *Nat.*
    Unity............ 27,000
    E. J. McCann, *Derry*
    Lab............. 7,565
    U.U. maj......... 12,135
    (1966 U.U. maj. 12,562)

Loughborough (Leicestershire)
E. 64,172
379*J. D. Cronin, *Lab.*.... 22,806
    R. Elton, *C.*........ 22,272
    J. Mokrzycki, *L.*...... 5,185
    Lab. maj......... 534
    (1966 Lab. maj. 6,024)

Louth (Lincolnshire)
E. 67,930
380*J. H. Archer, *C.*...... 25,569
    J. Murray, *Lab.*...... 16,403
    J. Adams, *L.*........ 6,279
    C. maj......... 9,256
    (Dec. 1969, by-election,
    C. maj. 10,727)
    (1966 C. maj. 4,092)

Lowestoft (Suffolk)
E. 72,695
381*Rt. Hon. J. M. L. Prior,
    C................ 28,842
    D. A. Baker, *Lab.*.... 23,319
    D. R. Crome, *L.*.... 4,737
    C. maj......... 5,523
    (1966 C. maj. 358)

Ludlow (Shropshire)
E. 55,331
382*J. E. More, *C.*........ 22,104
    D. Nagington, *Lab.*.... 12,800
    C. R. Oddie, *L.*...... 5,444
    C. maj......... 9,304
    (1966 C. maj. 3,480)

Luton (English Borough)
E. 62,832
383 C. F. C. Simeons, *C.*... 23,308
    *W. Howie, *Lab.*.... 21,959
    A. P. J. Chater, *Comm.* 447
    C. maj......... 1,349
    (1966 Lab. maj. 2,464)

Macclesfield (Cheshire)
E. 73,353
384*Sir A. V. Harvey, C.B.E.,
    C................ 29,023
    B. S. Jeuda, *Lab.*..... 18,571
    R. M. Hammond, *L.* 8,124
    C. maj......... 10,452
    (1966 C. maj. 4,203)
    (By-election pending)

Maidstone (Kent)
E. 85,069
385*J. J. Wells, *C.*........ 31,316
    K. M. Graham, *Lab.*.. 18,473
    S. Blow, *L.*........ 11,167
    C. maj......... 12,843
    (1966 C. maj. 4,994)

Maldon (Essex)
E. 72,829
386*A. B. C. Harrison, *C.*... 29,229
    S. M. A. Haseler, *Lab.*.. 22,957
    J. R. C. Beale, *L.*.... 5,574
    C. maj......... 6,272
    (1966 C. maj. 506)

Manchester (9)
ARDWICK E. 41,004
387 G. B. Kaufman, *Lab.*.. 13,728
    I. K. Paley, *C.*...... 10,726
    Lab. maj......... 3,002
    (1966 Lab. maj. 8,023)

BLACKLEY E. 58,288
388*P. B. Rose, *Lab.*...... 21,437
    A. M. Maguire, Q.C.,
    C................ 18,838
    Lab. maj......... 2,599
    (1966 Lab. maj. 6,300)

CHEETHAM E. 30,614
389*Rt. Hon. N. H. Lever,
    Lab............. 10,912
    T. R. Arnold, *C.*...... 6,110
    Lab. maj......... 4,802
    (1966 Lab. maj. 8,362)

EXCHANGE E. 21,159
390*W. D. Griffiths, *Lab.*.. 8,234
    W. J. Loftus, *C.*.... 3,341
    G. E. Spencer, *Ind.*.... 440
    Lab. maj......... 4,893
    (1966 Lab. maj. 6,664)

GORTON E. 61,885
391*K. Marks, *C.*........ 23,679
    J. A. Kevill, *C.*...... 17,594
    J. M. Ashley, *L.*...... 3,013
    Lab. maj......... 6,085
    (Nov. 1967, by-election,
    Lab. maj. 577)
    (1966 Lab. maj. 8,308)

MOSS SIDE E. 45,843
392*F. H. Taylor, *C.*...... 15,546
    F. Hatton, *Lab.*........ 13,833
    C. maj......... 1,713
    (1966 C. maj. 1,083)

OPENSHAW E. 50,635
393*C. R. Morris, *Lab.*.... 19,397
    B. M. Allanson, *C.*.... 12,296
    B. Panter, *Comm.*.... 552
    Lab. maj......... 7,101
    (1966 Lab. maj. 11,638)

WITHINGTON E. 57,410
394*Sir R. A. Cary, Bt., C.. 18,854
    M. A. Noble, *Lab.*.... 15,305
    J. Clarney, *L.*........ 4,540
    C. maj......... 3,489
    (1966 C. maj. 647)

WYTHENSHAWE E. 78,746
395*A. Morris, *Lab.*........ 30,260
    H. D. Moore, *C.*.... 24,505
    Lab. maj......... 5,755
    (1966 Lab. maj. 8,937)

Mansfield (Nottinghamshire)
E. 67,681
396*J. D. Concannon, *Lab.*.. 30,554
    C. W. H. Morton, *C.*.. 15,027
    F. C. Westacott, *Comm.* 628
    Lab. maj......... 15,527
    (1966 Lab. maj. 18,862)

MARYHILL—*See* Glasgow

Melton (Leicestershire)
E. 91,695
397*Miss I. M. P. Pike, *C.*.. 38,782
    K. Wood, *Lab.*........ 20,907
    J. B. Pick, *L.*........ 9,465
    C. maj......... 17,785
    (1966 C. maj. 7,595)

Meriden (Warwickshire)
E. 100,438
398*H. K. Speed, *C.*...... 40,077
    N. P. Lister, *Lab.*.... 35,353
    C. maj......... 4,724
    (March 1968, by-election,
    C. maj. 15,263)
    (1966 Lab. maj. 4,581)

Merionethshire
E. 26,594
399*W. H. Edwards, *Lab.*... 8,861
    D. W. Wigley, *P.C.*... 5,425
    I. E. Thomas, *L.*...... 5,034
    D. E. H. Edwards, *C.*.. 2,965
    Lab. maj......... 3,436
    (1966 Lab. maj. 1,895)

Merthyr Tydfil
(Welsh Borough)
E. 41,479
400*S. O. Davies, Ind. Lab. 16,701
T. J. Lloyd, O.B.E., Lab. 9,234
E. Jones, C. 3,169
E. C. Rees, P.C. 3,076
Ind. Lab. maj. 7,467
(1966 Lab. maj. 17,655)

Merton and Morden
(London)
E. 50,776
401 *Miss J. E. Fookes, C.*.. 18,727
K. W. May, Lab. 15,244
R. H. Insoll, L. 2,876
C. maj. 3,483
(1966 C. maj. 420)

Middlesbrough (2)
EAST E. 55,561
402*Rt. Hon. A. G. Bottom-
ley, O.B.E., Lab. 23,581
N. N. Laville, C. 9,623
Lab. maj. 13,958
(1966 Lab. maj. 18,984)
WEST E. 59,529
403 J. H. V. Sutcliffe, C. 22,374
*Dr. J. W. Bray, Lab. 21,986
C. maj. 388
(1966 Lab. maj. 3,893)

Middleton and Prestwich
(English Borough)
E. 77,112
404 A. G. B. Haselhurst, C. 25,030
*D. W. Coe, Lab. 23,988
S. Crilly, L. 8,175
C. maj. 1,042
(1966 Lab. maj. 3,817)

Midlothian
E. 77,718
405*A. Eadie, Lab. 30,802
J. L. G. Lamotte, C. 18,328
G. Park, Scot. Nat. 9,047
Lab. maj. 12,474
(1966 Lab. maj. 14,416)

Mid-Ulster
E. 87,473
406*Miss B. J. Devlin, Ind.. 37,739
W. N. J. Thornton,
U.U. 31,810
M. Cunningham, Ind.. 771
P. F. O'Neill, Ind. 198
Ind. maj. 5,929
(April 1969, by-election,
Ind. maj. 4,211)
(1966 U.U. maj. 2,560)

Mitcham (London)
E. 73,040
407*Rt. Hon. L. R. Carr, C. 27,257
R. C. Vincent, Lab. 22,047
S. E. French, Comm. 638
C. maj. 5,210
(1966 C. maj. 528)

Monmouth (Monmouthshire)
E. 76,059
408 J. S. Thomas, C. 28,312
*J. Anderson, Lab. 26,957
D. M. Hando, L. 4,061
S. K. Neale, P.C. 1,501
C. maj. 1,355
(1966 Lab. maj. 2,965)

Monmouthshire (5). *See Abertillery, Bedwellty, Ebbw Vale,
Monmouth and Pontypool*

Montgomeryshire
E. 32,507
409*H. E. Hooson, Q.C., L.. 10,202
D. J. D. Williams, C.. 7,891
D. W. Thomas, Lab.. 5,335
E. G. Millward, P.C... 3,145
L. maj. 2,311
(1966 L. maj. 3,494)

Moray and Nairn
E. 39,569
410*Rt. Hon. G. T. C.
Campbell, M.C., C.... 13,994
T. A. Howe, Scot. Nat. 7,885
P. Talbot, Lab. 6,452
C. maj. 6,109
(1966 C. maj. 3,458)

Morecambe and Lonsdale
(Lancashire) E. 66,672
411*A. G. F. Hall-Davis, C. 27,442
E. Garbutt, Lab. 13,916
A. W. Drury, L. 6,792
C. maj. 13,526
(1966 C. maj. 10,300)

Morpeth (Northumberland)
E. 47,871
412 G. Grant, Lab. 21,826
K. I. Tunnicliffe, C. 9,515
R. McClure, L. 4,825
Lab. maj. 12,311
(1966 Lab. maj. 16,525)

MOSS SIDE—*See Manchester*

Motherwell (Lanarkshire)
E. 53,343
413*G. M. Lawson, Lab.... 20,683
Miss S. S. Bell, C. 12,509
Miss I. Lindsay, Scot.
Nat. 3,861
J. W. Sneddon, Comm. 1,829
Lab. maj. 8,174
(1966 Lab. maj. 9,558)

Nantwich (Cheshire)
E. 57,271
414*Rt. Hon. Sir R. G.
Grant-Ferris, C. 20,397
D. Beetham, Lab.. 15,124
R. N. Cuss, L. 8,595
C. maj. 5,273
(1966 C. maj. 2,233)

Neath (Glamorgan)
E. 53,023
415*D. R. Coleman, Lab.... 28,378
D. H. J. Martin-Jones
C. 6,765
G. John, P.C. 4,012
H. Pearce, Comm.... 579
Lab. maj. 21,613
(1966 Lab. maj. 24,871)

Nelson and Colne
E. 49,278
416*D. C. Waddington, Q.C.,
C. 19,881
E. D. H. Hoyle, Lab.. 18,471
C. maj. 1,410
(June 1968, by-election,
C. maj. 3,522)
(1966 Lab. maj. 4,577)

Newark (Nottinghamshire)
E. 68,387
417*E. S. Bishop, Lab..... 26,455
D. G. Allen, C. 25,235
Lab. maj. 1,220
(1966 Lab. maj. 6,489)

Newbury (Berkshire)
E. 86,352
418*Hon. J. K. Sims, C.... 30,380
T. J. K. Sims, Lab.... 18,647
D. S. C. Clouston, L.. 13,279
C. maj. 11,733
(1966 C. maj. 4,146)

Newcastle under Lyme
(English Borough)
E. 70,215
419*J. Golding, Lab. 22,329
N. R. Winterton, C... 20,223
F. D. Wright, L. 1,954
P. H. Boyle, *Demo-
cratic Party* 1,194
Lab. maj. 2,106
(Oct. 1969, by-election,
Lab. maj. 1,042)
(1966 Lab. maj. 12,051)

Newcastle upon Tyne (4)
CENTRAL E. 31,628
420*Rt. Hon. E. W. Short,
Lab. 13,671
M. St. J. Way, C..... 4,256
D. Lesser, L. 1,433
Lab. maj. 9,415
(1966 Lab. maj. 13,817)
EAST E. 47,340
421*G. W. Rhodes, Lab.... 23,780
P. E. Heselton, C..... 14,832
Lab. maj. 5,948
(1966 Lab. maj. 7,326)
NORTH E. 42,286
422*R. W. Elliott, C....... 15,978
R. G. Eccles, Lab..... 12,518
C. maj. 3,460
(1966 C. maj. 2,693)
WEST E. 74,842
423*R. C. Brown, Lab..... 30,805
C. Lipman, C. 21,644
Lab. maj. 9,161
(1966 Lab. maj. 12,217)

New Forest (Hampshire)
E. 83,865
424*P. M. E. D. McNair-
Wilson, C. 36,041
D. M. Offenbach, Lab. 13,576
P. W. S. Johnson, L... 10,322
C. maj. 22,465
(Nov. 1968, by-election,
C. maj. 19,595)
(1966 C. maj. 13,032)

Newport (Welsh Borough)
E. 72,167
425*R. J. Hughes, Lab..... 30,132
A. D. Arnold, C...... 22,005
A. R. Vickery, P.C... 1,997
Lab. maj. 8,127
(1966 Lab. maj. 10,499)

Newton (Lancashire)
E. 90,146
426*Rt. Hon. F. Lee, Lab... 34,873
J. P. Stanley, C....... 25,863
R. E. Magee, L....... 5,678
Lab. maj. 9,010
(1966 Lab. maj. 15,056)

Norfolk (6)
CENTRAL E. 76,205
427*I. H. J. L. Gilmour, C.. 32,921
C. R. Coyne, Lab..... 19,030
R. Drew, L............ 6,172
 C. maj............ 13,891
 (1966 C. maj. 4,406)

NORTH E. 55,687
428 R. F. Howell, C....... 24,587
*B. Hazell, C.B.E., Lab.. 19,903
 C. maj............ 4,684
 (1966 Lab. maj. 737)

SOUTH E. 55,904
429*J. E. B. Hill, C....... 22,614
C. Shaw, Lab......... 17,172
B. E. Goldstone, L.... 3,811
 C. maj............ 5,442
 (1966 C. maj. 119)

SOUTH WEST E. 48,518
430*P. L. Hawkins, T.D., C. 22,220
L. J. Potter, Lab....... 16,572
 C. maj............ 5,648
 (1966 C. maj. 775)

See also King's Lynn and Yarmouth

Normanton (Yorks, W.R.)
E. 58,393
431*A. Roberts, Lab....... 28,421
D. H. Cargill, C....... 13,132
 Lab. maj.......... 15,289
 (1966 Lab. maj. 20,332)

Northampton (English Borough)
E. 74,983
432*R. T. Paget, Q.C., Lab. 27,424
C.E. Parkinson, C..... 26,183
 Lab. maj.......... 1,241
 (1966 Lab. maj. 7,489)

Northamptonshire (4)
SOUTH E. 73,440
433*A. A. Jones, C....... 29,070
G. J. Roberts, Lab..... 21,131
C. A. P. Smout, L...... 6,626
 C. maj............ 7,939
 (1966 C. maj. 2,691)

See also Kettering, Peterborough and Wellingborough

NORTHFIELD—See Birmingham

North Fylde (Lancashire)
E. 72,008
434*W. Clegg, C........ 33,667
R. W. Hill, Lab...... 15,235
 C. maj............ 18,432
 (1966 C. maj. 10,172)

Northumberland (3). See Berwick upon Tweed, Hexham and Morpeth

Northwich (Cheshire)
E. 50,947
435*Sir J. G. Foster, K.B.E.,
Q.C., C............ 20,366
A. Bates, Lab........ 15,746
T. N. Armstrong, L.... 3,604
 C. maj............ 4,620
 (1966 C. maj. 703)

Norwich (2)
NORTH E. 43,841
436*G. D. Wallace, Lab.... 18,564
A. E. Turner, C....... 11,868
C. C. Fairhead, Ind.... 658
 Lab. maj.......... 6,696
 (1966 Lab. maj. 8,926)

SOUTH E. 46,765
437 I. T. Stuttaford, C..... 17,067
C. F. Ascher, Lab..... 16,241
Mrs. L. Parker, L..... 3,031
 C. maj............ 826
 (1966 Lab. maj. 3,355)

NORWOOD—See Lambeth

Nottingham (4)
CENTRAL E. 52,950
438*J. J. Dunnett, Lab...... 17,638
B. Brook-Partridge,
C............... 14,079
 Lab. maj.......... 3,559
 (1966 Lab. maj. 6,426)

NORTH E. 71,051
439*W. C. Whitlock, Lab... 25,898
W. Derbyshire, C..... 18,616
Mrs. M. V. Edwards,
L............... 3,763
J. H. Peck, Comm..... 741
 Lab. maj.......... 7,282
 (1966 Lab. maj. 11,751)

SOUTH E. 71,566
440 P. N. Fowler, C....... 26,762
*G. H. Perry, Lab..... 23,031
 C. maj............ 3,731
 (1966 Lab. maj. 316)

WEST E. 57,140
441*M. English, Lab....... 21,255
M. W. Suthers, C...... 19,003
 Lab. maj.......... 2,252
 (1966 Lab. maj. 6,548)

Nottinghamshire (6). See Ashfield, Bassetlaw, Carlton, Mansfield, Newark and Rushcliffe

Nuneaton (Warwickshire)
E. 75,561
442*L. J. Huckfield, Lab.... 32,877
Miss S. Lewis-Smith,
C............... 18,769
A. D. N. Harrison, L.. 5,602
 Lab. maj.......... 14,108
 (March 1967, by-election,
 Lab. maj. 4,054)
 (1966 Lab. maj. 11,403)

Ogmore (Glamorgan)
E. 66,099
443*W. E. Padley, Lab..... 33,436
A. F. Gardner, C...... 10,415
E. J. Merriman, P.C... 5,828
 Lab. maj.......... 23,021
 (1966 Lab. maj. 26,673)

Oldbury and Halesowen
E. 77,991
444 J. H. R. Stokes, C..... 29,403
*J. Horner, Lab........ 26,499
 C. maj............ 2,904
 (1966 Lab. maj. 3,470)

Oldham (2)
EAST E. 51,267
445 J. A. Lamond, Lab..... 17,020
H. Holland, C......... 16,260
 Lab. maj.......... 760
 (1966 Lab. maj. 5,635)

WEST E. 50,066
446 M. H. Meacher, Lab... 16,062
*K. B. Campbell, Q.C.,
C............... 14,387
B. M. Lomax, L....... 2,944
 Lab. maj.......... 1,675
 (June 1968, by-election,
 C. maj. 3,311)
 (1966 Lab. maj. 7,572)

OPENSHAW—See Manchester

Orkney and Zetland
E. 25,797
447*Rt. Hon. J. Grimond,
T.D., L.......... 7,896
J. L. Firth, C......... 5,364
W. McP. Reid, Lab... 3,552
 L. maj............ 2,532
 (1966 L. maj. 5,975)

Ormskirk (Lancashire)
E. 91,597
448 H. B. Soref, C........ 40,517
R. M. Kilroy-Silk,
Lab............. 25,486
 C. maj............ 15,031
 (1966 C. maj. 9,780)

Orpington (London)
E. 65,689
449 I. R. Stanbrook, C..... 24,385
*E. R. Lubbock, L.... 23,063
D. I. Grant, Lab...... 4,098
 C. maj............ 1,322
 (1966 L. maj. 1,622)

Oswestry (Shropshire)
E. 55,966
450*W. J. Biffen, C....... 20,361
N. Turner, Lab....... 10,801
E. P. Cadbury, L..... 8,963
 C. maj............ 9,560
 (1966 C. maj. 4,716)

Oxford (English Borough)
E. 71,463
451 Hon. C. M. Woodhouse,
D.S.O., O.B.E., C..... 24,873
*D. E. T. Luard, Lab.. 22,989
P. H. Reeves, L....... 5,103
 C. maj............ 1,884
 (1966 Lab. maj. 2,425)

Oxfordshire (2). See Banbury and Henley

Paddington (2)
NORTH E. 34,045
452*A. C. Latham, Lab..... 11,645
R. S. Price, C........ 8,590
M. R. Uziell-Hamilton, L............. 1,012
 Lab. maj.......... 3,055
 (Oct. 1969, by-election,
 Lab. maj. 517)
 (1966 Lab. maj. 6,464)

SOUTH E. 34,592
453*N. P. *Scott*, M.B.E., C.. 10,526
R. A. Balfe, *Lab*..... 7,913
E. Pemberton, *L*..... 1,367
C. maj............ 2,613
(1966 C. maj. 1,443)

Paisley (Scottish Burgh)
E. 66,126
454*J. *Robertson*, *Lab*.... 25,429
J. C. Workman, *C*.... 15,232
Mrs. M. MacDonald,
Scot. Nat......... 3,432
A. Sked, *L*........... 2,918
Lab. maj........... 10,197
(1966 Lab. maj. 17,268)

PARK—*See* Sheffield

PAVILION—*See* Brighton

PECKHAM—*See* Camberwell

Pembrokeshire
E. 71,075
455 R. N. *Edwards*, C..... 19,120
G. S. D. Parry, *Lab*... 17,889
*D. L. Donnelly, *Demo-
cratic Party*......... 11,824
W. I. Samuel, *P.C*.... 3,681
D. W. Thomas, *L*..... 2,541
C. maj............ 1,231
(1966 Lab. maj. 5,931)

Penistone (Yorks., W.R.)
E. 73,346
456*J. J. *Mendelson*, *Lab*....31,615
A. Pickup, *C*....... 14,897
D. Mirfin, *L*....... 7,347
Lab. maj............ 16,718
(1966 Lab. maj. 19,602)

Penrith and the Border
(Cumberland)
E. 54,593
457*Rt. Hon. W. S. I.
Whitelaw, M.C., C.. 23,800
R. Longworth, *Lab*.. 10,256
W. Jackson, *L*....... 6,316
C. maj............ 13,544
(1966 C. maj. 8,901)

PENTLANDS—*See* Edinburgh

PERRY BAR—*See* Birmingham

Perthshire and Kinross (2)
KINROSS AND WEST E. 34,133
458*Rt. Hon. Sir A. F.
Douglas-Home, K.T.,
C............... 14,434
Mrs. E. Y. Whitley,
Scot. Nat..... 4,670
D. F. Leach, *Lab*..... 3,827
J. M. Calder, *L*....... 2,228
C. maj............ 9,764
(1966 C. maj. 9,582)

PERTH AND EAST E. 57,371
459*I. *MacArthur*, *Lab*.... 21,860
Miss V. A. Friel, *Lab*. 9,972
D. C. Murray, *Scot.
Nat*.............. 7,112
R. A. L. Livsey, *L*...... 3,011
C. maj............ 11,888
(1966 C. maj. 11,218)

Peterborough
(Northamptonshire)
E. 71,687
460*Sir H. *Nicholls*, Bt., C. 30,227
M. J. Ward, *Lab*..... 25,662
C. maj............ 4,565
(1966 C. maj. 3)

Petersfield (Hampshire)
E. 70,116
461*Miss J. M. *Quennell*,
M.B.E., C......... 30,419
K. Horrocks, *Lab*.... 10,307
Mrs. P. Jessel, *L*..... 7,783
Lt.-Col. R. M. Digby,
Ind............. 1,766
C. maj............ 20,107
(1966 C. maj. 13,002)

Plymouth (2)
DEVONPORT E. 59,881
462*Dame Joan *Vickers*,
D.B.E., C........ 21,843
F. K. Taylor, *Lab*.... 20,471
C. maj............ 1,372
(1966 C. maj. 319)

SUTTON E. 80,681
463*D. A. L. *Owen*, *Lab*... 29,383
J. M. Goss, *C*....... 28,636
Lab. maj........... 747
(1966 Lab. maj. 5,222)

POLLOK—*See* Glasgow

Pontefract (English Borough)
E. 60,512
464*J. *Harper*, *Lab*....... 31,774
I. A. Deslandes, *C*..... 10,687
Lab. maj.......... 21,087
(1966 Lab. maj. 23,401)

Pontypool (Monmouthshire)
E. 54,241
465*L. *Abse*, *Lab*....... 27,402
W. M. Bell, *C*....... 8,869
H. Webb, *P.C*....... 2,053
B.Watkinson, *Comm*.. 435
Lab. maj.......... 18,533
(1966 Lab. maj. 20,491)

Pontypridd (Glamorgan)
E. 65,636
466 B. T. *John*, *Lab*....... 28,414
M. C. Withers, *C*.... 8,205
Mrs. M. G. Murphy, *L*. 6,871
D. E. Jones, *P.C*..... 5,059
Lab. maj.......... 20,209
(1966 Lab. maj. 20,515)

Poole (English Borough)
E. 78,422
467*H. O. *Murton*, O.B.E.,
T.D., C 31,100
I. S. Campbell, *Lab*.. 17,610
G. M. Goode, *L*..... 9,846
C. maj............ 13,490
(1966 C. maj. 5,821)

Poplar (London)
E. 42,131
468*I. *Mikardo*, *Lab*....... 16,520
R. C. Denney, *C*..... 4,036
Lab. maj.......... 12,484
(1966 Lab. maj. 17,208)

Portsmouth (3)
LANGSTONE E. 113,552
469*I. S. *Lloyd*, C........ 43,733
R. R. Kenward, *Lab*.. 26,492
R. H. Anstey, *L*...... 10,226
C. maj............ 17,241
(1966 C. maj. 8,249)

SOUTH E. 56,380
470*R. B. *Pink*, C.B.E., V.R.D.,
C................ 23,962
A. F. W. White, *Lab*.. 13,847
C. maj............ 10,115
(1966 C. maj. 7,975)

WEST E. 47,202
471*F. A. *Judd*, *Lab*...... 17,169
Brig. T. H. Clarke,
C.B.E., C......... 16,214
L. B. Gauntlett, *Ind*.. 579
Lab. maj........... 955
(1966 Lab. maj. 1,227)

Preston (2)
NORTH E. 52,023
472 Miss M. *Holt*, C...... 20,102
*R. H. Atkins, *Lab*... 17,140
D. T. Jones, *L*....... 2,458
C. maj............ 2,962
(1966 Lab. maj. 2,418)

SOUTH E. 52,541
473 A. *Green*, C........ 20,480
*P. Mahon, *Lab*...... 19,149
C. maj............ 1,331
(1966 Lab. maj. 2,789)

PROVAN—*See* Glasgow

Pudsey (English Borough)
E. 62,763
474*J. *Hiley*, C......... 24,308
J. Mann, *Lab*........ 18,313
G. V. J. Pratt, *L*...... 6,754
C. maj............ 5,995
(1966 C. maj. 2,372)

PUTNEY—*See* Wandsworth

Reading (English Borough)
E. 63,695
475 G. F. *Vaughan*, C..... 23,598
*J. M. H. Lee, *Lab*..... 22,444
A. Boothroyd, *Demo-
cratic Party*........ 867
C. maj............ 1,154
(1966 Lab. maj. 4,133)

Reigate (Surrey)
E. 72,021
476 Sir R. E. G. *Howe*, Q.C.,
C............... 28,462
M. P. Farley, *Lab*.... 15,433
K. S. Vaus, *L*....... 8,952
C. maj............ 13,029
(1966 C. maj. 7,514)

Renfrewshire (2)
EAST E. 73,978
477*Miss M. B. H. *Ander-
son*, O.B.E., T.D., C.. 29,163
Mrs. J. A. Carnegie,
Lab............. 16,062
Mrs. O. M. Watt, *L*... 7,053
J. M. Buchanan, *Scot.
Nat*.............. 3,733
C. maj............ 13,101
(1966 C. maj. 10,591)

WEST E. 60,654
478*N. F. Buchan, Lab..... 22,999
A. M. Fletcher, C..... 20,699
W. J. Macartney, Scot.
Nat............... 4,195
Lab. maj........... 2,300
(1966 Lab. maj. 3,789)

Rhondda (2)

EAST E. 37,147
479*G. E. Davies, Lab..... 19,602
G. P. James, P.C..... 6,931
R. C. Mullett, C..... 1,359
A. L. Jones, Comm.... 659
Lab. maj........... 12,671
(1966 Lab. maj. 19,218)

WEST E. 31,040
480*T. A. Jones, Lab...... 18,779
H. V. Davies, P.C.... 3,528
J. D. Morgan, C..... 1,610
A. True, Comm...... 1,201
Lab. maj........... 15,251
(March 1967, by-election,
Lab. maj. 2,306)
(1966 Lab. maj. 16,888)

Richmond (London)
E. 57,311
481*A. H. F. Royle, C..... 20,979
A. Palmer, Lab....... 12,981
S. Rundle, L......... 6,934
C. maj........... 7,998
(1966 C. maj. 6,223)

Richmond (Yorkshire, N.R.)
E. 71,299
482*T. P. G. Kitson, C..... 30,471
M. J. Aldrich, Lab.... 12,702
J. R. Smithson, L..... 5,354
C. maj........... 17,769
(1966 C. maj. 13,331)

Ripon (Yorkshire, W.R.)
E. 47,744
483*Sir M. Stoddart-Scott
O.B.E., T.D., M.D., C. 21,211
D. Daniel, Lab....... 9,147
Miss V. S. Craven, L.. 4,583
C. maj........... 12,064
(1966 C. maj. 8,745)

Rochdale (English Borough)
E. 63,879
484*J. McCann, C.B.E., Lab. 19,247
C. Smith, L......... 14,076
M. Andrew, C....... 12,978
Lab. maj........... 5,171
(1966 Lab. maj. 11,242)

Rochester and Chatham
(English Borough)
E. 77,809
485 Mrs. P. E. Fenner, C... 30,263
*Mrs. A. P. Kerr, Lab... 24,922
C. maj........... 5,341
(1966 Lab. maj. 2,246)

Romford (London)
E. 80,148
486 R. L. Leonard, Lab..... 27,899
M. J. Neubert, C..... 25,139
Lab. maj........... 2,760
(1966 Lab. maj. 8,061)

Ross and Cromarty. *See* Inverness-shire and Ross and
Cromarty

Rossendale (English Borough)
E. 50,186
487 R. W. T. Bray, C..... 20,448
Miss B. Boothroyd,
Lab.............. 18,568
C. maj........... 1,880
(1966 Lab. maj. 4,109)

Rotherham (English Borough)
E. 60,802
488*B. K. O'Malley, Lab... 25,246
E. R. Cooke, C..... 12,770
Lab. maj........... 12,476
(1966 Lab. maj. 15,477)

Rother Valley (Yorks, W.R.)
E. 87,932
489 P. Hardy, Lab........ 44,322
R. A. B. Durrant, C.. 17,418
Lab. maj........... 26,904
(1966 Lab. maj. 30,467)

Rowley Regis and Tipton
(English Borough)
E. 64,397
490*P. K. Archer, Q.C., Lab. 25,001
P. M. Smith, C....... 15,537
Lab. maj........... 9,464
(1966 Lab. maj. 13,094)

Roxburgh, Selkirk and Peebles
E. 57,646
491*D. M. S. Steel, L...... 19,524
R. Fairgrieve, C...... 18,974
L. Griffiths, Lab...... 4,454
H. Hastie, Scot. Nat... 3,147
W. R. Cassell, Ind.... 103
L maj........... 550
(1966 L. maj. 2,211)

Rugby (Warwickshire)
E. 58,241
492*W. G. Price, Lab...... 25,041
J. H. P. Griffith, C.... 22,086
A. S. Frost, Ind....... 254
Lab. maj........... 2,955
(1966 Lab. maj. 409)

Ruislip-Northwood
(London)
E. 55,050
493*F. P. Crowder, Q.C., C. 24,247
B. H. Silverman, Lab... 11,541
Miss J. Arram, L...... 4,188
C. maj........... 12,706
(1966 C. maj. 7,276)

Runcorn (Cheshire)
E. 61,753
494*M. Carlisle, Q.C., C.... 25,272
M. J. E. Taylor, Lab.. 16,204
C. K. Sumner, L...... 5,741
C. maj........... 9,068
(1966 C. maj. 5,182)

Rushcliffe (Nottinghamshire)
E. 75,684
495 K. H. Clarke, C....... 30,966
*A. J. Gardner, Lab.... 24,798
P. M. Browne, L...... 4,180
C. maj........... 6,168
(1966 Lab. maj. 380)

Rutherglen (Lanarkshire)
E. 42,967
496*J. G. Mackenzie, Lab.. 17,751
P. C. Hutchison, C.... 14,710
D. N. Livingstone, Ind.
Scot. Nat.......... 1,490
Lab. maj........... 3,041
(1966 Lab. maj. 5,014)

Rutland and Stamford
(Lincolnshire and Rutland)
E. 50,636
497*K. Lewis, C.......... 22,803
H. Toch, Lab........ 15,136
C. maj........... 7,667
(1966 C. maj. 2,287)

Rye (East Sussex)
E. 68,365
498*B. G. Irvine, C........ 32,300
H. A. Fountain, Lab... 9,031
R. K. J. F. Young, L... 8,947
C. maj........... 23,269
(1960 C. maj. 17,099)

Saffron Walden (Essex)
E. 60,392
499*P. M. Kirk, C........ 24,549
K. T. Weetch, Lab... 14,885
F. P. D. Moore, L..... 6,959
C. maj........... 9,664
(1966 C. maj. 3,265)

St. Albans (Hertfordshire)
E. 62,828
500*V. H. Goodhew, C..... 24,503
C. H. Beaumont, Lab. 16,629
C. A. Shaw, L........ 6,439
C. maj........... 7,874
(1966 C. maj. 2,832)

St. Helens (English Borough)
E. 75,190
501*L. Spriggs, Lab....... 31,587
I. D. McGaw, C...... 16,509
Lab. maj........... 15,078
(1966 Lab. maj. 19,549)

St. Ives (Cornwall)
E. 48,811
502*J. W. F. Nott, C...... 18,581
Dr. Maureen E. Castle,
Lab.............. 9,913
H. L. Fry, L......... 7,981
C. maj........... 8,668
(1966 C. and Nat. L. maj.
3,599)

St. Marylebone (London)
E. 47,799
503*Rt. Hon. Q. McG.
Hogg, Q.C., C...... 17,639
K. W. Morrell, Lab... 8,325
M. B. J. Vann, L...... 2,443
C. maj........... 9,314
(By-election, Oct. 22, 1970)
†K. W. Baker, C....... 10,684
K. W. Morrell, Lab... 4,542
M. B. J. Vann, L...... 1,038
M. E. L. Skeggs, Nat.
Front............ 401
J. Papworth, Ind...... 163
C. maj........... 6,142
(1966 C. maj. 8,061)

St. Pancras, North
(London)
E. 50,261
504 *A. W. Stallard, Lab.*... 16,497
C. J. O. Moorhouse,
C................. 10,648
G. McLennan, *Comm.* 670
Lab. maj...... 5,849
(1966 Lab. maj. 10,511)

Salford (2)
EAST E. 45,966
550*F. J. Allaun, Lab.*..... 15,853
J. B. Lack, C....... 9,583
A. F. Bell, L......... 3,000
Lab. maj....... 6,270
(1966 Lab. maj. 9,409)

WEST E. 48,018
506*S. Orme, Lab.*........ 16,986
A. E. Clark, C........ 14,310
Lab. maj...... 2,676
(1966 Lab. maj. 5,980)

Salisbury (Wiltshire)
E. 61,683
507*M. A. Hamilton, C.*.... 26,549
A. Waugh, Lab....... 17,493
C. maj....... 9,056
(1966 C. maj. 4,139)

Scarborough and Whitby
(Yorkshire, N.R.)
E. 73,753
508*M. N. Shaw, C.*....... 26,154
M. F. Pitts, L....... 16,517
Miss J. G. Hewitson,
Lab.......... 9,802
C. maj....... 9,637
(1966 C. maj. 5,542)

SCOTLAND—*See* Liverpool

SCOTSTOUN—*See* Glasgow

Sedgefield (Durham)
509 *D. Reed, Lab.*...... 36,867
A. A. Beck, C....... 24,036
Lab. maj......... 12,831
(1966 Lab. maj. 15,438)

SELLY OAK—*See* Birmingham

Sevenoaks (Kent)
E. 82,165
510*Sir J. C. Rodgers, Bt.,
C.*............ 32,654
J. F. Ovenden, Lab... 15,376
R. F. Webster, L....... 12,290
C. maj......... 17,278
(1966 C. maj. 10,313)

Sheffield (6)
ATTERCLIFFE E. 60,232
511 *A. E. P. Duffy, Lab...* 26,482
Miss P. M. Santhouse,
C................. 10,986
P. H. Sims, Ind....... 581
Lab. maj........... 15,496
(1966 Lab. maj. 22,825)

BRIGHTSIDE E. 53,717
512*E. Griffiths, Lab.*....... 23,941
A. H. Newton, C...... 8,572
G. Ashberry, *Comm.* 605
Lab. maj.......... 15,369
(June 1968, by-election,
Lab. maj. 5,248)
(1966 Lab. maj. 19,177)

HALLAM E. 59,047
513*J. H. Osborn, C.*...... 25,134
A. H. Broadley, Lab.. 12,884
P. Singh, L.......... 2,972
C. maj.......... 12,250
(1966 C. maj. 7,930)

HEELEY E. 81,295
514 *J. D. Spence, C.*...... 27,950
F. O. Hooley, Lab.. 27,237
A. J. Singleton, L..... 4,220
C. maj........... 713
(1966 Lab. maj. 4,729)

HILLSBOROUGH E. 46,718
515*Rt. Hon. G. Darling,
Lab.*.......... 18,775
C. I. Patnick, C....... 11,445
Lab. maj......... 7,330
(1966 Lab. maj. 12,025)

PARK E. 53,208
516*Rt. Hon. F. W. Mulley,
Lab.*.......... 23,302
R. T. Renton, C....... 7,024
C. Morton, *Comm.*.. 637
Lab. maj........... 16,278
(1966 Lab. maj. 19,533)

SHETTLESTON—*See* Glasgow

Shipley (Yorkshire, W.R.)
E. 50,721
517 *J. M. Fox, C.*...... 20,938
N. Free, Lab....... 16,161
A. M. Micklem, L..... 4,468
C. maj............. 4,777
(1966 C. maj. 1,500)

Shoreditch and Finsbury
(London)
E. 44,696
518*R. W. Brown, Lab.*.... 14,474
R. E. Sims, C........ 7,166
Lab. maj.......... 7,308
(1966 Lab. maj. 11,499)

Shrewsbury (Shropshire)
E. 57,847
519*Sir J. A. Langford-Holt,
C.*............ 22,619
P. A. Kent, Lab....... 13,413
I. Brodie, L......... 5,960
C. maj............. 9,206
(1966 C. maj. 2,966)

Shropshire (4). *See* Ludlow,
Oswestry, Shrewsbury and
The Wrekin

Skipton (Yorkshire, W.R.)
E. 51,908
520*G. B. Drayson, T.D., C.* 20,817
K. Targett, Lab....... 12,011
Mrs. J. Y. L. Burns, L. 7,733
C. maj............. 8,806
(1966 C. maj. 4,256)

SMALL HEATH—*See* Birmingham

Smethwick (English Borough)
E. 45,489
521*A. M. W. Faulds, Lab..* 16,077
B. B. Rathbone, C..... 13,968
M. Gupta, L........ 747
Lab. maj........... 2,109
(1966 Lab. maj. 3,490)

Solihull (Warwickshire)
E. 81,013
522*W. P. Grieve, Q.C., C.* 37,756
D. Gray, Lab......... 13,181
R. A. Davis, L....... 7,795
C. maj........... 24,575
(1966 C. maj. 16,248)

Somerset (6)
NORTH E. 85,383
523*A. P. Dean, C.*........ 38,975
J. T. Mitchard, Lab... 28,121
C. maj........... 10,854
(1966 C. maj. 2,298)

See also Bridgwater, Taunton,
Wells, Weston-super-Mare
and Yeovil

Southall (London)
E. 56,289
524*S. J. Bidwell, Lab.*..... 19,389
K. G. Reeves, C....... 15,166
J. S. Shaw, *Nat. Front.* 1,572
Lab. maj.......... 4,223
(1966 Lab. maj. 5,347)

Southampton (2)
ITCHEN E. 81,470
525*Rt. Hon. H. M. King,
D.Phil. (The Speaker) 29,417
E. N. I. Bray, Ind..... 9,581
B. H. Phillips, Ind..... 4,794
The Speaker's maj... 19,836
(By-election, May 27, 1971)
†*R. C. Mitchell, Lab..* 22,575
J. Spicer, C......... 12,900
E. Bray, Ind......... 3,090
J. Cherryson, L....... 2,214
Lab. maj.......... 9,675
(1966 The Speaker's maj.
25,246)

TEST E. 71,189
526 *S. J. A. Hill, C.*...... 24,660
R. C. Mitchell, Lab.. 22,858
J. R. Wallis, L. 4,349
C. maj............. 1,802
(1966 C. maj. 2,440)

Southend (2)
EAST E. 58,057
527*Sir. S. J. McAdden,
C.B.E., C.*........ 24,025
P. R. Clyne, Lab..... 17,065
C. maj............. 6,960
(1966 C. maj. 517)

WEST E. 69,455
528*H. P. G. Channon, C..* 29,304
M. Burstin, Lab....... 12,419
J. Barnett, L......... 7,077
C. maj........... 16,885
(1966 C. maj. 11,857)

South Fylde (Lancashire)
E. 85,808
529 *E. L. Gardner, Q.C., C.* 39,459
D. L. Mahon, Lab..... 13,354
A. Thomson, L....... 9,214
C. maj........... 26,105
(1966 C. maj. 16,324)

Southgate (London)
E. 56,215
530*Hon. A. G. Berry, C...* 22,963
R. B. Bastin, Lab..... 9,389
G. J. Bridge, L....... 5,451
C. maj........... 13,574
(1966 C. maj. 11,428)

Southport (English Borough)
E. 65,139
531**W. I. Percival, Q.C., C.* 22,950
R. C. Fearn, L....... 13,809
B. T. George, *Lab....* 8,950
C. maj............ 9,141
(1966 C. maj. 9,526)

South Shields (English Borough)
E. 75,648
532**A. Blenkinsop, Lab.....* 30,191
J. McKee, C.......... 19,960
Lab. maj......... 10,231
(1966 Lab. maj. 14,489)

Southwark (London)
E. 52,097
533**Rt. Hon. R. J. Gunter,*
Lab............ 16,834
J. Gordon, C........ 7,040
E. Hume, *Comm......* 1,128
Lab. maj.......... 9,794
(1966 Lab. maj. 15,401)

Sowerby (Yorkshire, W.R.)
E. 50,319
534**Rt. Hon. A. L. N. D.*
Houghton, C.H., Lab. 16,583
W. G. Burman, C.... 16,114
D. T. Shutt, L....... 5,137
Lab. maj.......... 469
(1966 Lab. maj. 5,230)

SPARKBROOK—*See* Birmingham

Spelthorne
E. 69,103
535†*H. E. Atkins, C.......* 27,266
P. L. Cheney, *Lab.....* 18,239
R. H. Longland, L..... 4,792
C. maj........... 9,027
(1966 C. maj. 2,487)

SPRINGBURN—*See* Glasgow

Stafford and Stone
(Staffordshire)
E. 75,087
536**Rt. Hon. H. C. P. J.*
Fraser, M.B.E., C.... 30,056
M. J. K. Stanworth,
Lab............... 20,380
W. Williams, *L......* 4,370
C. maj... 5,041
(1966 C. maj. 5,041)

Staffordshire (6). *See* Brierley
Hill, Burton, Cannock, Leek,
Lichfield and Tamworth and
Stafford and Stone

Stalybridge and Hyde
(Cheshire)
E. 64,281
537 T. Pendry, *Lab......* 22,226
Col. J. E. Rogerson, C. 19,377
R. N. Cooke, L....... 5,303
Lab. maj......... 2,849
(1966 Lab. maj. 5,821)

STECHFORD—*See* Birmingham

Stepney (London)
E. 56,846
538**Rt. Hon. P. D. Shore,*
Lab............... 18,993
H. Greenway, C...... 4,922
S. Kaye, *Comm......* 1,468
Lab. maj.......... 14,071
(1966 Lab. maj. 18,049)

Stirling and Clackmannan (2)
CLACKMANNAN AND EAST
E. 62,330
539 R. G. Douglas, *Lab....* 23,729
J. Fairlie, C......... 13,178
I. C. H. Macdonald,
Scot. Nat...... 7,243
R. E. Bell, L........ 2,640
Lab. maj......... 10,551
(1966 Lab. maj. 12,520)

WEST E. 49,281
540**W. Baxter, Lab......* 18,884
J. Glen, C......... 11,465
Dr. R. D. McIntyre,
Scot. Nat...... 8,279
Lab. maj......... 7,419
(1966 Lab. maj. 8,132)

Stirling and Falkirk
(Scottish Burgh) E. 62,425
541**M. MacPherson, M.B.E.,*
Lab............ 22,984
D. R. Anderson, C... 15,754
I. Murray, *Scot. Nat....* 6,571
Lab. maj.......... 7,230
(1966 Lab. maj. 9,420)
(By-election pending)

Stockport (2)
NORTH E. 52,966
542 I. W. Owen, C....... 18,132
**A. Gregory, Lab....* 17,261
S. Collier, L......... 4,022
C. maj......... 871
(1966 Lab. maj. 3,336)

SOUTH E. 49,488
543**M. Orbach, Lab......* 16,747
C. Howson, C....... 14,679
T. G. Jones, L....... 4,613
Lab. maj......... 2,068
(1966 Lab. maj. 4,069)

Stockton on Tees
(English Borough)
E. 56,021
544**W. T. Rodgers, Lab....* 22,283
P. V. Radford, C..... 17,960
E. Jones, *Comm......* 369
Lab. maj......... 4,323
(1966 Lab. maj. 8,701)

**Stoke Newington and
Hackney North**
(London)
E. 65,238
545**D. Weitzman, Q.C.,*
Lab............ 20,446
J. R. Boast, C........ 11,298
M. Goldman, *Comm...* 793
Lab. maj......... 9,148
(1960 Lab. maj. 14,000)

Stoke on Trent (3)
CENTRAL E. 60,394
546**R. B. Cant, Lab......* 18,758
Mrs. E. Ashley, C..... 11,227
Lab. maj......... 7,531
(1966 Lab. maj. 14,138)

NORTH E. 59,308
547**J. S. Forrester, Lab....* 20,642
J. S. Heath, T.D., C.... 10,542
Lab. maj......... 10,100
(1966 Lab. maj. 17,146)

SOUTH E. 68,570
548**J. Ashley, Lab.......* 20,770
R. J. Apps, C........ 13,344
S. J. Lomas, *Comm....* 364
Lab. maj......... 7,426
(1966 Lab. maj. 12,611)

Stratford (Warwickshire)
E. 65,697
549**A. E. U. Maude, T.D.,*
C............... 28,106
P. E. Tombs, *Lab.....* 11,393
D. R. Bruce, L....... 8,895
C. maj........... 16,713
(1966 C. maj. 9,427)

STREATHAM—*See* Wandsworth

Stretford (English Borough)
E. 71,446
550 W. S. Churchill, C.... 28,629
**E. A. Davies, Ph.D.,*
Lab............ 24,614
C. maj........... 4,015
(1966 C. maj. 3,365)

Stroud (Gloucestershire)
E. 66,480
551**I. A. Kershaw, M.C., C.* 27,089
D. Wheatley, *Lab.....* 19,158
D. M. Davies, L....... 6,799
C. maj........... 7,931
(1966 C. maj. 1,545)

Sudbury and Woodbridge
(Suffolk)
E. 78,675
552**K. M. Stainton, C.....* 32,393
B. Orriss, *Lab.......* 19,829
E. M. Wheeler, L..... 7,136
C. maj........... 12,564
(1966 C. maj. 7,009)

Suffolk (4). *See* Bury St.
Edmunds, Eye, Lowestoft and
Sudbury and Woodbridge

Sunderland (2)
NORTH E. 61,360
553**Rt. Hon. F. T. Willey,*
Lab............ 25,779
J. M. Reay-Smith, C.. 16,738
Lab. maj......... 9,041
(1966 Lab. maj. 9,015)

SOUTH E. 68,353
554**G. A. T. Bagier, Lab...* 26,840
D. A. Orde, C........ 20,722
Lab. maj......... 6,118
(1966 Lab. maj. 7,169)

Surbiton (London)
E. 47,950
555**N. T. L. Fisher, M.C.,*
C............... 17,359
R. D. Kerr-Waller,
Lab............ 10,469
C. F. Green, L....... 4,027
E. Scruby, *Ind. C....* 1,706
C. maj........... 6,890
(1966 C. maj. 5,428)

Surrey (10)
EAST E. 79,483
556 W. G. Clark, C.... 35,773
P. W. Meyer, L....... 11,749
M. D. Simmons, *Lab..* 10,186
C. maj........... 24,024
(1966 C. maj. 14,493)

See also **Carshalton, Chertsey, Dorking, Epsom, Esher, Farnham, Guildford, Reigate** and **Woking**

East Sussex (4). *See* **Eastbourne, East Grinstead, Lewes** and **Rye**

West Sussex (3). *See* **Arundel and Shoreham, Chichester** and **Horsham**

SUTTON—*See* Plymouth

Sutton and Cheam
(English Borough)
E. 61,348
557*R. C. Sharples, O.B.E.,
M.C., C............... 23,957
J. Dowsett, *Lab*...... 11,261
N. D. M. McGeorge,
L................. 6,023
C. maj............ 12,696
(1966 C. maj. 9,096)

Sutton Coldfield
(English Borough)
E. 93,328
558*Rt. Hon. G. W. Lloyd,
C................. 36,774
P. M. Tebbutt, *Lab*... 18,134
L. A. King, L........ 9,163
C. maj............ 18,640
(1966 C. maj. 16,093)

Swansea (2)
EAST E. 58,937
559*N. McBride, *Lab*..... 28,183
M. J. Murphy, C...... 8,191
D. R. Evans, *P.C*...... 4,188
W. R. Jones, *Comm*... 563
Lab. maj.......... 19,992
(1966 Lab. maj. 24,049)
WEST E. 65,054
560*A. J. Williams, *Lab*... 24,622
J. E. H. Rees, C..... 21,384
G. ap Gwent, *P.C*..... 3,033
Lab. maj.......... 3,238
(1966 Lab. maj. 6,053)

Swindon (English Borough)
E. 61,814
561 D. L. Stoddart, *Lab*.... 25,731
*C. J. F. Ward, C...... 20,155
Miss J. Gradwell,
Comm............ 456
Lab. maj.......... 5,576
(Oct. 1969 by-election,
C. maj. 477)
(1966 Lab. maj. 10,443)

Taunton (Somerset)
E. 62,277
562*Rt. Hon. E. D. L. du
Cann, C........... 26,158
S. Mama, *Lab*....... 17,823
G. L. O'Donnell, L.... 4,871
C. maj............ 8,335
(1966 C. maj. 3,153)

Tavistock (Devonshire)
E. 60,298
563*M. R. D. Heseltine, C. 25,846
M. E. B. Banks, L...... 10,397
H. M. Luscombe, *Lab*. 8,982
C. maj............ 15,449
(1966 C. maj. 8,183)

TEST—*See* Southampton

Thirsk and Malton
(Yorkshire, N.R.)
E. 64,193
564*Rt. Hon. Sir R. H.
Turton, K.B.E., M.C.,
C................. 30,892
J. R. Bradshaw, *Lab*.. 15,309
C. maj............ 15,583
(1966 C. maj. 9,442)

Thurrock (Essex)
E. 84,951
565*H. J. Delargy, *Lab*.... 30,874
G. F. J. Bright, C..... 19,486
Miss K. J. Fleetwood,
L................. 5,024
Lab. maj.......... 11,388
(1966 Lab. maj. 17,904)

Tiverton (Devonshire)
E. 58,398
566*R. J. Maxwell-Hyslop,
C................. 24,689
R. Hewetson, *Lab*.... 10,823
F. J. Suter, L........ 9,229
C. maj............ 13,866
(1966 C. maj. 9,026)

Tonbridge (Kent)
E. 83,925
567*R. P. Hornby, C..... 31,890
Mrs. M. M. Colquhoun, *Lab*...... 17,897
H. E. Hill, L........ 10,167
C. maj............ 13,993
(1966 C. maj. 6,828)

Torquay (English Borough)
E. 83,249
568*Sir F. M. Bennett, C... 33,996
P. S. T. Bryers, *Lab*... 15,948
K. P. Jenkins, L....... 11,163
C. maj............ 18,048
(1966 C. maj. 12,099)

Torrington (Devonshire)
E. 49,180
569*P. M. Mills, C........ 21,328
L. A. Lacey, L........ 11,455
T. K. Marston, *Lab*... 6,695
C. maj............ 9,873
(1966 C. maj. 3,652)

Totnes (Devonshire)
E. 75,295
570*R. L. Mawby, C...... 31,519
R. Blank, *Lab*....... 16,429
D. C. Penhaligon, L... 9,515
C. maj............ 15,090
(1966 C. maj. 8,723)

Tottenham (London)
E. 51,513
571*N. Atkinson, *Lab*..... 17,367
L. T. Simmonds, C.... 10,975
Lab. maj.......... 6,392
(1966 Lab. maj. 9,889)

TOXTETH—*See* Liverpool

Truro (Cornwall)
E. 66,315
572 P. J. S. Dixon, C..... 24,894
R. C. Cuss, *Lab*..... 16,684
M. Steed, L.......... 8,923
C. maj............ 8,210
(1966 C. maj. 1,608)

Twickenham (London)
E. 74,397
573 T. F. H. Jessel, C...... 28,571
J. H. W. Grant, *Lab*... 16,950
D. K. Rebak, L....... 6,516
R. Franklin, *Ind*...... 462
C. maj............ 11,621
(1966 C. maj. 7,628)

Tynemouth (English Borough)
E. 79,561
574*Dame Irene Ward,
D.B.E., C........... 30,773
J. H. Beecham, *Lab*... 23,927
R. S. Turner, L....... 5,221
C. maj............ 6,846
(1966 C. maj. 3,396)

Uxbridge (London)
E. 63,710
575 C. Curran, C......... 23,414
*J. Ryan, *Lab*....... 19,768
G. R. Goodall, L...... 4,265
C. maj............ 3,646
(1966 Lab. maj. 890)

VAUXHALL—*See* Lambeth

Wakefield (English Borough)
E. 65,224
576*W. Harrison, *Lab*.... 27,352
D. Smith, C......... 15,668
Miss B. N. Seear, L.... 4,071
Lab. maj.......... 11,684
(1966 Lab. maj. 13,608)

Wallasey (English Borough)
E. 72,534
577*Rt. Hon. A. E. Marples,
C................. 24,283
C. J. Wells, *Lab*..... 21,172
D. J. Evans, L....... 5,577
J. D. Hill, *Ind*....... 2,946
C. maj............ 3,111
(1966 C. maj. 589)

Wallsend (English Borough)
E. 86,486
578*W. E. Garrett, *Lab*.... 39,065
E. M. White, C....... 24,650
Lab. maj.......... 14,415
(1966 Lab. maj. 18,539)

Walsall (2)
NORTH E. 72,640
579*W. T. Wells, Q.C., *Lab*. 27,543
A. J. L. Barnes, C..... 20,128
D. J. Brayford, *Comm*. 597
Lab. maj.......... 7,415
(1966 Lab. maj. 13,757)
SOUTH E. 82,284
580*Sir H. J. d'Avigdor-
Goldsmid, Bt., D.S.O.,
M.C., T.D., C....... 35,545
G. S. Rea, *Lab*...... 24,196
C. maj............ 11,349
(1966 C. maj. 3,881)

Walthamstow (2)
EAST E. 43,370
581*R. M. C. McNair-
  Wilson, C.......... 14,260
  J. E. Tomlinson, Lab... 13,732
  D. G. Kirkland, L.... 2,547
  C. maj............ 528
  (March 1969 by-election,
  C. maj. 5,479)
  (1966 Lab. maj. 1,807)
WEST E. 35,380
582 E. P. Deakins, Lab..... 12,472
  *F. J. Sylvester, C..... 7,870
  I. W. Roxbrough, L... 2,564
  Lab. maj.......... 4,602
  (Sept. 1967 by-election,
  C. maj. 62)
  (1966 Lab. maj. 8,725)

WALTON—See Liverpool

Wandsworth (4)
CENTRAL E. 58,756
583 T. M. Cox, Lab...... 19,776
  Mrs. F. P. A. McLaugh-
  lin, C........... 16,830
  Lab. maj.......... 2,946
  (1966 Lab. maj. 5,828)
CLAPHAM E. 53,180
584 W. J. M. Shelton, C... 16,593
  D. T. Pitt, Lab...... 13,473
  E. G. Thwaites, L..... 2,982
  F. E. Simpkins, S.P.
  G.B............. 220
  Lt.-Cmdr. W. G.
  Boaks, D.S.C., Ind... 80
  C. maj............ 3,120
  (1966 Lab. maj. 4,176)
PUTNEY E. 77,134
585*H. G. Jenkins, Lab.... 25,162
  J. Wakeham, C...... 23,768
  G. Broughton, L..... 3,887
  Lab. maj.......... 1,394
  (1966 Lab. maj. 3,487)
STREATHAM E. 53,420
586*Rt. Hon. D. E. Sandys,
  C............... 19,215
  Mrs. A. S. Ward, Lab. 13,593
  D. E. Delaney, L...... 2,680
  C. maj............ 5,622
  (1966 C. maj. 3,367)

Wanstead and Woodford
(London)
E. 48,788
587*C. P. F. Jenkin, C.... 20,065
  A. P. Barker, Lab.... 8,522
  R. H. Hoskins, L..... 4,224
  C. maj........... 11,543
  (1966 C. maj. 10,278)

Warrington (English Borough)
E. 50,307
588*W. T. Williams, Q.C.,
  Lab............. 20 970
  A. B. Gooch, C..... 11,647
  Lab. maj.......... 9,323
  (1966 Lab. maj. 13,012)

Warwick and Leamington
(Warwickshire)
E. 80,862
589*D. G. Smith, C....... 36,994
  J. T. Watkinson, Lab.. 21,355
  C. maj........... 15,639
  (March 1968 by-election,
  C. maj. 21,922)
  (1966 C. maj. 8,697)

Warwickshire (6). See Meriden,
Nuneaton, Rugby, Solihull,
Stratford and Warwick and
Leamington

Watford (English Borough)
E. 57,432
590*R. H. Tuck, Lab..... 19,698
  D. W. Clarke, C..... 19,622
  C. G. Watkins, L.... 3,778
  Lab. maj.......... 76
  (1966 Lab. maj. 3,836)

WAVERTREE—See Liverpool

Wednesbury (English Borough)
E. 65,809
591*Rt. Hon. J. T. Stonehouse,
  Lab 23,998
  D. M. Harman, C... 20,627
  Lab. maj.......... 3,371
  (1966 Lab. maj. 7,828)

Wellingborough
(Northamptonshire)
E. 64,992
592*P. D. Fry, C....... 27,459
  J. H. Mann, Lab..... 25,107
  C. maj............ 2,352
  (Dec. 1969 by-election,
  C. maj. 6,049)
  (1966 Lab. maj. 2,233)

Wells (Somerset)
E. 65,833
593 Hon. R. T. Boscawen,
  M.C., C........... 25,106
  F. R. Thompson, Lab. 16,335
  W. F. J. Pinching, L... 9,174
  C. maj............ 8,771
  (1966 C. maj. 3,539)

Wembley (2)
NORTH E. 47,958
594*Sir E. E. Bullus, C..... 18,345
  K. W. Childerhouse,
  Lab............. 11,916
  J. R. Kingsbury, L.... 4,083
  C. maj............ 6,249
  (1966 C. maj. 4,207)
SOUTH E. 45,127
595*Sir R. S. Russell, C.... 16,578
  M. N. Elliott, Lab.... 14,336
  C. maj............ 2,242
  (1966 C. maj. 1,183)

West Bromwich
(English Borough)
E. 68,855
596*M. A. Foley, Lab.... 23,412
  G. Hawkins, C...... 18,976
  Lab. maj.......... 4,436
  (1966 Lab. maj. 6,874)

Westbury (Wiltshire)
E. 68,097
597*D. M. Walters, M.B.E.,
  C.............. 26,524
  J. McLaren, Lab..... 17,413
  R. G. Otter, L...... 8,781
  C. maj............ 9,111
  (1960 C. maj. 2,797)

WEST DERBY—See Liverpool

Western Isles
(Inverness-shire and Ross and
Cromarty)
E. 23,633
598 D. J. Stewart, Scot.
  Nat............. 6,568
  *M. K. Macmillan, Lab. 5,842
  R. M. Macleod, C..... 2,822
  Scot. Nat. maj...... 726
  (1966 Lab. maj. 5,733)

West Ham (2)
NORTH E. 55,885
599*A. W. J. Lewis, Lab.... 17,664
  W. J. Shearman, C..... 7,130
  B. G. McCarthy, L.... 3,167
  Lab. maj.......... 10,534
  (1966 Lab. maj. 15,896)
SOUTH E. 50,067
600*Rt. Hon. Sir F. E. Jones,
  Q.C., Lab......... 18,899
  B. C. Balcomb, C..... 5,422
  Lab. maj.......... 13,477
  (1966 Lab. maj. 19,492)

Westhoughton (Lancashire)
E. 70,090
601*J. T. Price, Lab..... 29,674
  C. A. Unsworth, C... 23,847
  Lab. maj.......... 5,827
  (1966 Lab. maj. 14,460)

West Lothian
E. 72,894
602*T. Dalyell, Lab...... 29,360
  W. C. Wolfe, Scot.
  Nat............. 15,620
  Earl of Ancram, C..... 10,048
  C. Bett, Comm...... 459
  Lab. maj.......... 13,740
  (1966 Lab. maj. 8,707)

Westmorland
E. 53,724
603*T. M. Jopling, C...... 21,253
  J. G. Pease, L....... 9,426
  R. S. Ward, Lab...... 7,757
  C. maj........... 11,827
  (1966 C. maj. 8,855)

Weston-super-Mare
(Somerset)
E. 79,681
604*A. W. Wiggin, C..... 33,816
  Miss S. R. Palmer, Lab. 14,473
  E. R. F. Deal, L...... 10,120
  C. maj........... 19,343
  (March 1969 by-election,
  C. maj. 20,472)
  (1966 C. maj. 12,393)

Whitehaven (Cumberland)
E. 50,674
605 J. A. Cunningham, Lab. 22,974
  W. G. McKay, C.... 16,418
  Lab. maj.......... 6,556
  (1966 Lab. maj. 8,791)

Widnes (Lancashire)
E. 72,267
606*J. E. MacColl, Lab.... 28,384
  G. H. Pierce, C....... 20,841
  Lab. maj.......... 7,543
  (1966 Lab. maj. 9,378)
  (By-election pending)

Wigan (English Borough)
E. 57,913
607*E. A. Fitch, *Lab*...... 28,102
A. Daniels, *C*...... 12,882
J. Kay *Comm*........ 672
Lab. maj........ 15,220
(1966 Lab. maj. 18,878)

Willesden (2)
EAST E. 57,348
608*R. Freeson, *Lab*...... 20,073
H. W. Cutler, *C*...... 15,564
Lab. maj.......... 4,509
(1966 Lab. maj. 7,006)
WEST E. 55,293
609*L. A. Pavitt, *Lab*...... 21,918
R. F. Dyason, *C*...... 10,163
L. G. Burt, *Comm*.... 515
Lab. maj.......... 11,755
(1966 Lab. maj. 14,582)

Wiltshire (4). *See* Chippenham, Devizes, Salisbury and Westbury

Wimbledon (London)
E. 42,943
610 R. M. O. Havers, Q.C.,
C................ 15,285
R. Holmes, *Lab*...... 8,554
J. R. Macdonald, *L*.... 4,749
C. maj.......... 6,731
(1966 C. maj. 5,674)

Winchester (Hampshire)
E. 61,900
611*Rear-Adm. M. C. M.
Giles, D.S.O., O.B.E.,
G.M., *C*........... 25,249
C. Perry, *Lab*........ 11,773
J. W. Matthew, *L*..... 8,867
C. maj.......... 13,476
(1966 C. maj. 8,677)

Windsor (Berkshire)
E. 78,132
612 A. J. Glyn, E.R.D., *C*... 32,264
T. D. Sullivan, *Lab*.... 16,214
R. J. Trevallion, *L*.... 6,343
C. maj.......... 16,050
(1966 C. maj. 8,330)

Wirral (Cheshire)
E. 95,097
613*Rt. Hon. J. S. B. Lloyd,
C.H., C.B.E., T.D.,
Q.C., *C.* (now *The
Speaker*) 38,655
R. G. Paterson, *Lab*... 22,197
Miss G. Jones, *L*...... 9,276
C. maj.......... 16,458
(1966 C. maj. 9,853)

WITHINGTON—*See* Manchester

Woking (Surrey)
E. 94,508
614*C. G. D. Onslow, *C*... 37,220
R. M. Taylor, *Lab*.... 18,652
P. Wade, *L*........... 9,763
C. maj.......... 18,568
(1966 C. maj. 12,847)

Wokingham (Berkshire)
E. 109,350
615*W. R. van Straubenzee,
M.B.E., *C*...... 43,183
C. A. R. Helm, *Lab*... 22,630
D. H. V. Case, *L*...... 12,704
C. maj.......... 20,553
(1966 C. maj. 9,574)

Wolverhampton (2)
NORTH EAST E. 51,654
616*Mrs. R. Short, *Lab*.... 16,851
G. I. Wright, *C*...... 15,358
Mrs. S. M. Wright,
Nat. Front 1,592
Lab. maj.......... 1,493
(1966 Lab. maj. 8,102)

SOUTH WEST E. 53,888
617*Rt. Hon. J. E. Powell,
M.B.E., *C*........ 26,220
J. A. Bamfield, *Lab*... 11,753
E. Robinson, *L*...... 2,459
P. E. Carter, *Comm*... 189
R. G. P. Menzies, *Ind.* 77
D. P. Dass, *Ind*....... 52
C. maj.......... 14,467
(1966 C. maj. 6,585)

Wood Green (London)
E. 53,897
618*Mrs. J. S. Butler, *Lab*... 18,666
M. P. R. Malynn, *C*... 14,022
Lab. maj.......... 4,644
(1966 Lab. maj. 7,789)

WOODSIDE—*See* Glasgow

Woolwich (2)
EAST E. 49,263
619*C. P. Mayhew, *Lab*... 19,423
J. A. Cope, *C*........ 10,259
Lab. maj.......... 9,164
(1966 Lab. maj. 13,443)
WEST E. 58,048
620*W. Hamling, *Lab*...... 21,036
M. P. Gaffney, *C*...... 20,418
Lab. maj.......... 618
(1966 Lab. maj. 4,088)

Worcester (English Borough)
E. 70,544
621*Rt. Hon. P. E. Walker,
M.B.E., *C*........ 29,717
P. Jones, *Lab*........ 21,275
C. maj.......... 8,442
(1966 C. maj. 3,341)

Worcestershire (3)
SOUTH E. 70,867
622*Sir G. D. N. Nabarro,
C................ 30,648
A. E. Bailey, *Lab*...... 12,839
J. C. Hall, *L*........ 7,262
C. maj.......... 17,809
(1966 C. maj. 11,084)
See also Bromsgrove and Kidderminster

Workington (Cumberland)
E. 52,635
623*Rt. Hon. T. F. Peart,
Lab............ 24,975
M. F. Turner-Bridger,
C................ 15,532
Lab. maj.......... 9,443
(1966 Lab. maj. 10,506)

Worthing (English Borough)
E. 72,267
624*T. L. Higgins, *C*...... 33,051
Mrs. S. M. Bartlett,
Lab............ 8,989
M. J. Rooke, *L*...... 8,336
C. maj.......... 24,062
(1966 C. maj. 19,622)

The Wrekin (Shropshire)
E. 66,433
625 J. A. P. Trafford, *C*.... 26,282
*G. T. Fowler, *Lab*.... 25,764
C. maj.......... 518
(1966 Lab. maj. 846)

Wrexham (Denbighshire)
E. 73,233
626 R. T. Ellis, *Lab*...... 31,089
G. Patterson, *C*...... 15,649
W. McBriar, *L*...... 5,067
C. Golding, *P.C*...... 2,894
Lab. maj.......... 15,440
(1966 Lab. maj. 17,443)

Wycombe (Buckinghamshire)
E. 96,490
627*J. Hall, O.B.E., T.D., *C*. 40,151
B. S. Jones, *Lab*...... 23,341
E. H. Palfrey, *L*...... 8,297
C. maj.......... 16,810
(1966 C. maj. 7,079)

WYTHENSHAWE—*See* Manchester

YARDLEY—*See* Birmingham

Yarmouth (Norfolk)
E. 60,576
628 A. Fell, *C*............ 23,088
*H. Gray, *Lab*........ 19,931
Mrs. J. R. Knott, *L*... 3,523
C. maj.......... 3,157
(1966 Lab. maj. 797)

Yeovil (Somerset)
E. 70,632
629*Rt. Hon. J. W. W.
Peyton, *C*...... 27,689
J. A. Elswood, *Lab*.... 20,621
D. E. Evans, *L*...... 7,418
C. maj.......... 7,068
(1966 C. maj. 2,080)

York (English Borough)
E. 75,215
630*A. W. Lyon, *Lab*...... 29,619
B. Askew, *C*........ 27,422
Lab. maj.......... 2,197
(1966 Lab. maj. 6,100)

Yorkshire, East Riding (3). *See* Bridlington, Haltemprice and Howden

Yorkshire, North Riding (4). *See* Cleveland, Richmond, Scarborough and Whitby and Thirsk and Malton

Yorkshire, West Riding (14). *See* Barkston Ash, Colne Valley, Dearne Valley, Don Valley, Goole, Harrogate, Hemsworth, Normanton, Penistone, Ripon, Rother Valley, Shipley, Skipton and Sowerby

PARLIAMENTARY SUMMARY, LORDS AND COMMONS, 1970–71

Both Houses resumed without ceremony, on *Oct.* 27, the first session of the Parliament which had been opened by the Queen on *July* 2 and suspended for the summer recess on *July* 24 (1970). The Chancellor of the Exchequer set the ball rolling in the Commons with a lengthy statement on fiscal problems which amounted to a " mini-Budget ". Mr. Barber spoke of " fundamental reform of the rôle of Government and public authorities " with the object of concentrating activities and expenditure on tasks they alone could perform, and enabling people to keep more of their earnings. There would be a more selective approach to the social services, spending more on schools and hospitals and payments to those in need, but confining the scope of free or subsidized provision more closely to what was necessary. The Government's aim would be to lessen Government interference, reduce subsidies, and extend opportunities. A thorough review of the functions of Government departments was in hand, and he hoped local authorities would also improve their efficiency. The effect of the policies of recent years was clearly seen in the way the national income had been cut. In 1964 the public sector accounted for 44 per cent. of the gross domestic product: in 1969 it was 50 per cent. This trend was unacceptable.

POLICY CHANGES.—Mr. Barber went on to summarize the main policy changes resulting from the Government's review (figures in terms of 1970 prices and incomes) as follows: on Defence they had found that the long-term costings of the previous administration were considerably above the figures published in their White Paper, but expenditure in 1971–72 would not exceed the figure of £2,327m. stated in it, even after taking account of the added commitments which the present Government would be assuming, which included maintenance of a military presence in South-East Asia and expansion of the Territorial and Army Volunteer Reserve. In 1974–75 defence expenditure would not exceed £2,300m., representing a net saving of £130m. The expansion of overseas aid would be maintained, to reach £340m. in 1974–75. On industrial matters the Government would wind up the Industrial Reorganization Corporation, saving £20m. to £30m. in 1971–72 after meeting commitments, and £40m. a year thereafter. The Regional Employment Premium, costing about £100m. a year, did not justify its cost and would be discontinued after Sept., 1974. Further economies which would be made in expenditure on support for industry would rise to about £70m. in 1974–75. Grants and loans to hotels would be continued only to the existing time-limit; but there would be new assistance to tourism in development areas, and new industrial training projects. The grant to the British Productivity Council would be phased out, and that to the Consumers' Council would be discontinued. Public expenditure on the Research Councils, now running at £110m. a year and rising by 5 per cent. or 6 per cent. a year, would be cut by £2m. in 1971–72, rising to £5m. in 1974–75. Agriculture and the taxpayer would be helped by a new system of import levies, and in the long run they expected to save on the deficiency payments about £150m. by 1974–75, besides the benefit to the Exchequer from the proceeds of the levies. Existing plans for capital expenditure on the national industries had been estimated to require about £1,600m. in 1971–72, rising to £1,900m. by 1974–75, but these estimates now appeared too high by £25m. and £50m. respectively.

SAVINGS AND SUBSIDIES.—By not proceeding with the nationalization of the ports they would save £30m. in 1971–72 and £10m. in 1974–75. Additional savings in the programmes of other nationalized industries which had been examined afresh would amount to £42m. in 1971–72, rising to £73m. in 1974–75. There would also be changes in the subsidy system of rent and rebates to give help where most needed; additional allocation of £110m. between 1971 and 1975 to health services, including hospitals for elderly and handicapped people; charges to be made for admission to national institutions, and for further education; London commuter services grants to be ended by 1973; the passport fee to go up from £2 to £5

which, with other increased charges and consular fees, would bring in an extra £6m. a year; the charge for school meals to be increased in two stages to bring the charge nearer to the actual cost; no more free milk for children over 7; dental treatment charges to be raised to about half actual cost, and spectacle charges to be raised to include dispensing costs; no sickness benefit for the first 3 days' absence from work; additional income supplement of up to £3 a week for poor families; and expenditure on roads and transport to be cut by £13m. in 1971 and 1972, and by £43m. in 1974 and 1975. Mr. Barber's comprehensive recital was completed by his announcement that the rate of Corporation Tax would be reduced from 45 per cent. to 42½ per cent. immediately; and that the standard rate of Income Tax would be reduced by 6d. (2½p) from April 6, 1971. He said he was announcing these changes now so that tax deductions at these new rates could be made from the beginning of the next financial year. The reductions in public expenditure he had announced totalled £330m. in 1971–72, and consequently he felt justified in making this reduction in Income Tax. It would cost about £315m. in the first year and £350m. in a full year. The Chancellor pointed out that this was the first time either tax rate had been reduced for 11 years and he believed the whole House would agree it was right " to take action to break out of the depressing cycle of high taxation and low growth which has bedevilled our country in recent years. These measures are designed to give the nation new impetus, new opportunity and new hope."

CHARGE OF MEANNESS.—Mr. Barber's belief that the whole House would agree with him was soon dispelled by a somewhat acid speech by the former Chancellor, Mr. Roy Jenkins, who described Mr. Barber's statement as " long, complex, at times depressing, at times mean in approach, and at times deliberately vague and difficult to follow." His more specific criticisms opened up a lively debate, but Mr. Barber stood up firmly to the barrage and at times counter-attacked, asserting that Mr. Wilson's statement when he was Prime Minister about the strength of the economy had been " shown to be entirely false "; quoting to a Labour member from Mr. Jenkins's 1969 Budget speech the belief that high direct taxation had disincentive and stifling effects on the economy; and quoting Mr. Wilson to another member on the subject of prescription charges and the hospital building programme. Questioned by Mr. Wilson about the Conservative pledge to abolish Selective Employment Tax, Mr. Barber retorted that this Government had already achieved more than Mr. Wilson's had done in its first 100 days, but they had not promised to abolish SET in their first Budget, although they would certainly abolish it. Replying to other questions the Chancellor said the family income supplement scheme would cost

about £7m. a year; admission charges to museums and galleries would bring in about £1m. in a full year; the further education fees proposed would save £3m. in 1971-72 and £5m. in 1974-75; and the higher prescription charges (for which existing exemptions would remain, except that the age exemption for dental charges would be lowered from 21 to 18) would save £19m. and £35m. in those two financial years, respectively.

Battle was resumed in the following week, when 2 days were devoted to debating a Government motion approving the Chancellor's statement, and an Opposition amendment condemning the Government's policy as being " mean and unfair as between different sections of the community." Opening this debate on *Nov.* 4 the Chancellor said he expected a substantial surplus in the balance of payments in 1971 provided our goods were kept competitive. But they had to build up reserves, and to maintain appropriate repayment of debts inherited from the previous Government, which totalled £1,461m. at June 1970.

" WILD HORSE OF INFLATION."—A two-day debate in the House of Lords was opened on *Nov.* 17 by Lord Beswick (*Lab*) who moved a critical motion regretting that the Chancellor's proposals " run counter to the Government's declared intention to reduce prices." Earl Jellicoe said the Government's strategy was intended to create conditions in which everyone would earn more in real terms. They were determined to " rein the wild horse of inflation." So many peers took part that the House sat until 12.14 a.m. on *Nov.* 18 and resumed the debate the same afternoon. Lord George-Brown, in a maiden speech, said there had to be a climate of expansion. " You cannot deflate yourselves out of a problem. You can only deflate yourselves into a pit. You can only expand yourselves out of it. We are going down, but I do not lay this at the door of this Government." Lord Rhyl retorted that one could not deflate oneself out of a crisis, but could certainly inflate oneself into one. Winding up, the Lord Chancellor said the proposals on school meals would add 250,000 children to the entitlement to means, while reducing the number of subsidized meals. When, he asked, did it become socially just or economically sound to ask other people to pay for your children's meals? The Opposition motion was rejected by 235-98.

Arising out of Mr. Barber's proposals were several Bills needed to put them into effect, one being the Family Income Supplements Bill which, said Sir Keith Joseph, moving its 2nd reading on *Nov.* 10, would bring into benefit nearly 190,000 households, including about 500,000 children. It would channel help to those most in need and provide for the poorest households sums up to £150 a year. An Opposition amendment moved by Mrs. Shirley Williams asserted that the scheme would help only a tiny minority, would extend the complex system of means-testing, and would not encourage employers to improve very low wages. Mr. Enoch Powell (*C*) said the whole purpose of the organization of labour had been to secure for the worker, in cash, a competitive market value for his services, but this was being called in question by the Bill. Mr. Pardoe (*L*) said negative income tax was the only way to solve the problem. The amendment was defeated by 221-188 and the Bill was read a 2nd time. After two days in committee it passed through the remaining stages on *Dec.* 1, moved quickly through the Lords, and received the Royal Assent on *Dec.* 10.

CUT TO AID INVESTMENT.—The Income and

Corporation Taxes Bill, to implement the tax changes proposed by Mr. Barber on *Oct.* 27, had its 2nd reading on *Nov.* 13 on the motion of Mr. Macmillan. He said the corporation tax cut was intended to increase the ability of companies to invest; and after the income tax cut a man earning £5,000 a year would still be paying more tax than his counterparts in France, Germany, Sweden, Canada or the U.S.A. A strong attack on the Bill was launched by Mr. Taverne (*Lab*) who said the corporation tax cut was irrelevant because investment and growth did not depend on the tax rate, but on the confidence of industry in future prospects. The Bill was read a 2nd time without a division. In the committee stage debate on *Nov.* 17 Mr. Pardoe (*L*) moved that the income tax standard rate should be 25 per cent. instead of the 38·75 per cent. proposed in the Bill. He said " incredible " Budget surpluses had been carried in the last few years—that year's was estimated at £2,600m.—but such huge surpluses were no longer justified. Sir Gerald Nabarro (*C*) said no Chancellor ever reduced income tax by more than a few pence at a time because a higher amount would distort the whole economy in the year of the reduction. He hoped further reductions would embrace the principle of taxing earnings less and taxing spending more. The Bill was then read the 3rd time, passed through the Lords, and became law on *Dec.* 17.

REDISTRIBUTION APPROVED.—One of the Government's first actions after the resumption on *Oct.* 27 was to seek to reverse the refusal of the previous Parliament to implement the Boundary Commission's reports on redistribution of seats. The House of Commons (Redistribution of Seats) (No. 2) Bill, 1969, which would have altered or delayed implementation of the proposals, was decisively rejected by the House of Lords (*see* WHITAKER 1970 *and* 1971); and to resolve the stalemate Mr. Callaghan, then Home Secretary, moved (on *Nov.* 12, 1969) that the relevant Orders be *not* approved, although he had been responsible for laying the Orders in the first place. His motions were carried. Now that the Conservatives, who had wished the Orders to be approved, had a majority, they lost no time in dealing with the matter. Mr. Maudling moved on *Oct.* 28 that the four Orders (relating to England, Wales, Scotland, and Northern Ireland, respectively) be approved. He said the Government would carry out the commission's recommendations in full. There was a strong case for accepting the reports of bodies well known to be impartial, and any apparent picking and choosing by a Government was bound to lead to suspicion. The Orders provided for major alterations in 322 of the present 630 constituencies, and minor changes in a further 88; there would be five new constituencies. Unless these Orders were passed now, there could not be a general election in the next 7 or 8 years on anything other than the 1954 boundaries. Mr. Callaghan said this would be the biggest redistribution since 1832; and he still thought it better to await the local government reorganization before altering Parliamentary boundaries. The first three Orders were approved by Government majorities of 69, 71 and 76, and the fourth without a division.

GREENWICH TIME PREFERRED.—The question of Time was debated in the Commons on *Dec.* 2 when Mr. Maudling moved that the British Standard Time Order, 1970, be approved. He said there would be a free vote; and if the House failed to pass the motion there would be reversion to Greenwich Mean Time on *Oct.* 31, 1971. The normal period of Summer Time in 1972 and sub-

squent years would then be from the day following the 3rd Saturday in March to that following the 4th Saturday in October each year, although the Government might vary it by Order in Council if there was substantial public demand. The Home Secretary said that social surveys in winter and spring covering 7,000 people had shown about 50 per cent. favouring BST, about 40 per cent. favouring return to GMT, the rest undecided. He thought difficulties for schools created by BST had been broadly overcome; road casualty figures were open to argument; commercial people thought the coincidence of BST with Central European Time was an advantage; and industry was divided, with 35 per cent. for BST, only 5 per cent. against, and 60 per cent. with no strong views. In Scotland about 61 per cent. wanted GMT, and only 34 per cent. BST. Generally, those opposed to BST were the farming community, the construction industry, and other open-air workers such as postmen. In the debate Scottish members opposed BST which one described as " an abominable system." Mr. D. Stewart, the lone Scottish Nationalist, in a maiden speech, said his constituency (the Western Isles) was more affected than any other; in mid-December it was 10.15 a.m. before people began to see any daylight. But in the division on the motion the M.P. for Orkney and Shetland (Mr. Grimond) voted along with 70 Labour and 10 Conservative members to retain BST. The motion to approve the Order and retain BST was defeated by 366–81 (maj. against 285) and there were loud cheers when the figures were announced. Mr. Maudling was one of many members who abstained from voting.

On *Dec.* 11, a week before Parliament rose for the Christmas recess, Dr. King announced his resignation from the office of Speaker, and from his seat, to take effect on *Dec.* 31. He expressed his gratitude for having been allowed to serve the House in that high office. The Prime Minister expressed the general regret, while recognizing that he had carried the burden for five years. Other tributes were paid by Mr. Wilson and Mr. Thorpe, for the Opposition parties, and Sir Harry Legge-Bourke for the backbenchers. In 1965 Dr. King had succeeded Sir Harry Hylton-Foster, who died suddenly on Sept. 2. When Parliament reassembled on *Oct.* 26, Dr. King's election was proposed by Mr. (now Lord) Shinwell and seconded by Sir W. Anstruther-Gray (now Lord Kilmany). In accepting, Dr. King recalled that he was the first Labour member, first trade unionist, first member of the teaching profession, and first elementary schoolboy to be elected Speaker. Now, five years later, this career was ended and the former elementary schoolboy was retiring with a pension and a peerage—not the customary viscountcy of earlier years but a non-hereditary barony in the post-1964 manner. Mr. Speaker King's Retirement Bill was introduced in the Commons on *Feb.* 15, passed through all stages in both Houses without controversy, and received the Royal Assent on *Mar.* 30. The former Speaker took the title Lord Maybray-King.

NEW SPEAKER OPPOSED.—The first business of the Commons on *Jan.* 12, after a Christmas recess shorter than usual, was to elect the new Speaker, and the name agreed upon was that of Mr. John Selwyn Lloyd, Conservative M.P. for The Wirral since *July*, 1945, who was three years younger than Dr. King. But several M.P.s on both sides objected to the " usual methods " of selecting, rather than electing, a new Speaker; and after Mr. Lloyd had been proposed by Dame Irene Ward (C) and seconded by Mr. Pannell (Lab), Mr. Pardoe (L)

said he did not wish to oppose the nomination, but to express a backbencher's dissatisfaction at the procedure. He thought there should have been a secret ballot. Mr. Maxwell-Hyslop (C) said there were precedents for having a division on the first nomination, without any further name being proposed; but if that were ruled out he nominated Sir Geoffrey de Freitas (Lab). Sir Geoffrey, looking surprised, rose to refuse nomination; but, ignoring this, Mr. W. Hamilton (Lab) seconded his nomination, and went on to speak in protest against alleged lack of consultation with backbenchers. Although he began by saying that he would not say anything reflecting on Mr. Lloyd, and that nobody would deny he had served the country well, he was soon attacking Mr. Lloyd's record. Referring to the Suez conflict in 1956, he said Mr. Lloyd was not only engaged in " that disreputable episode " but he was also engaged in freezing nurses' pay. The rising storm of angry Conservative interruptions, however, dissolved in laughter that followed Mr. Hamilton's concluding words: " I have always been an almost instinctive protector of dumb animals. Mr. Lloyd is no dumb animal, but he will be when he gets the Chair, and I want to protect him from it."

After Mr. Lloyd had briefly submitted himself to the will of the House, Sir Geoffrey said he hoped they would understand his embarrassment. He had not been consulted before his name was proposed, and in fact he would vote for Mr. Lloyd. He hoped his name could be withdrawn; but the Clerk of the House said that as two names had been proposed he must put the question, that Mr. Selwyn Lloyd do take the Chair. There being some cries of " No " a division was called, and the motion was carried by 294–55 (maj. 239). So Mr. Speaker Lloyd, the 152nd Speaker since 1376 and the 40th since 1660, was escorted to the Chair by his two sponsors, making the traditional show of resistance, and thanked the House for " the great honour it has paid me." He added: " My political past had not been altogether free from controversy and I was not surprised that there was some controversy today." He assured those who had voted against the motion that he would have no hard feelings about that in the future. In the absence of the Prime Minister, Mr. Maudling welcomed him for the Government side, and Mr. Wilson and Mr. Thorpe for the Opposition parties. Black Rod summoned the M.P.s to the other House, where the Queen's approval of Mr. Lloyd's election was conveyed by the Lord Chancellor.

(The only previous occasion in this century when a Speaker's nomination was subjected to a division was on *Oct.* 31, 1951, when, after Mr. W. S. Morrison (C) had been nominated, two backbenchers nominated Major J. Milner (Lab), the previous Deputy Speaker. In the division that ensued Mr. Morrison (later Viscount Dunrossil) was elected by 318–251. His opponent went to the House of Lords as Lord Milner of Leeds. He died in 1967, six years after Lord Dunrossil. That had been the first contested election of a Speaker since 1895, when Mr. Gully succeeded Mr. Speaker Peel, defeating Sir Matthew White Ridley by 285–274.)

BUDGET SURPRISES.—The Chancellor of the Exchequer's " mini-Budget " in *Oct.* had given some clues to the direction of his financial planning, particularly in its immediate cut in corporation tax and promise of an income tax cut in *April*, 1971, but few could then have foreseen the wide sweep of the fiscal and social changes which he deployed in his first full Budget on *Mar.* 30. This proved to

be not merely the first Conservative Budget since 1964: it was, according to some commentators, the most purely Conservative Budget within memory. One tax change followed another in steady succession, with the chief surprise saved up to the last in the way beloved of Chancellors; and Mr. Barber's speech, lasting seven minutes under two hours, was rewarded with a standing ovation from his own party, and faint praise and only muted criticism from the Opposition.

Mr. Barber began by saying that the first Budget of a new Parliament should not only fix taxation rates for the coming year: it should also survey economic progress over past years and set the new direction for future years. The first priority was to defeat cost inflation, and their policy in the past months had been to ensure reductions in the level of pay settlements, so as to ensure steadier prices. The policy was succeeding. During 1970 the volume of imports rose fast in proportion to total demand, while the volume of exports rose much less, tending to limit the growth of domestic output. Visible trade was roughly in balance in 1970, and invisibles earned a good surplus; and as the House already knew they ended the year with a record surplus of £630m. on current account. This was because the value of our exports rose by 12 per cent. But the volume rose by less than 4 per cent., while the volume of imports rose by over 6 per cent. However, the current account surplus made possible additions to our overseas assets and reductions in our official liabilities. Consequently the net receipts of foreign exchange, the total currency flow, in 1970 was favourable by nearly £1,300m., nearly twice as much as in 1969.

OVERSEAS DEBTS PAID.—Turning to our overseas debts the Chancellor said that when the Government took office last *June*, short or medium term debt stood at £1,461m., of which £992m. was to the International Monetary Fund and £469m. to other monetary authorities. Members would be glad to know that all the £469m. had now been repaid, and the IMF debt had been reduced by £24m. They were not bound to begin repaying the remaining £968m. until *June* 1971; but he had arranged to repay, in 8 quarterly instalments beginning this month (March), the £551m. that was outstanding in respect of the 1968 drawing. In fact the whole of the first 4 instalments, totalling £285m., would be repaid tomorrow, in one sum, in advance. Thus the total debt of £1,461m. had been reduced to £683m. since the present Government took office. He added that when the Labour Government took office in 1964 the total short and medium term debt was £71m. After dealing with the 1970 figures for central government and public sector transactions, and noting that the Post Office strike had caused a backlog in receipts of £26om., Mr. Barber said there were two special factors which would increase our imports bill: the increased cost of oil because of the Teheran Agreement, and the exceptionally large tonnage of new shipping due to be imported this year.

In the domestic economy much would depend on personal savings, and the extent to which firms passed on in increased prices the higher costs already in the pipeline. Regarding consumer credit, the present hire-purchase arrangements must stay unchanged. But before he came to detailed taxation proposals, the Chancellor went on, he would make an announcement about direct help to those hardest hit by inflation—the old age pensioners. As promised in his party's election manifesto, retirement pensions would be reviewed every two years to ensure that they at least maintained their purchasing power. The Government would now increase the standard pension from £5 to £6 a week for single persons, and from £8·10 to £9·70 for a married couple. Other National Insurance benefits and War pensions would also be improved. These increases would be effective from *Sept.* 20, 1971, and the cost was estimated at about £560m. in a full year. These improvements would involve increases in contributions, and he would also move towards the long-term objective of fully graduated National Insurance contributions.

INCOME TAX CHANGES.—Arising from the pensions increases, he had decided to raise the income tax exemption limits for people of 65 and over; and there would be changes in the level of marginal relief, dependent relative allowance, and investment income age relief. The Finance Bill would also provide for husband and wife, both earning, to be assessed separately for income tax; and to repeal the previous legislation whereby children's investment income was taxed as if it were their parents' income, legislation which he felt was misconceived. These changes would become effective in 1972–73. He estimated the cost of separately assessing husband and wife at £12m. in a full year. He proposed to defer the transitional period for occupational pension schemes to 1980 except for new schemes. The " death in service " benefit would be increased from 2 to 4 years' salary for the maximum lump sum, and rules about retirement annuities would be improved.

On capital gains tax he proposed that the present exemption for small gains (up to £50) be abolished, except in the tax year 1970–71; instead, he would exempt the total disposal proceeds in the tax year (including 1970–71) if they did not exceed £500. This change would take out of liability about one quarter of those now liable to this tax, mostly people of modest means. He would also end the distinction between short-term and long-term gains; from 1971–72 all gains would be subject to long-term tax only. He would abolish the charge to capital gains tax on death, including the death of a life tenant, because he thought that to impose this charge when the estate, including accrued gains, was also being charged with estate duty—which could be up to 80 per cent.—resulted in an excessive burden, especially in the case of small companies. This abolition became effective at once. Estate duty itself was a severe burden and a disincentive to saving, so the starting point for liability would be raised from £10,000 to £12,500, effective in respect of deaths occurring after that day. This would exempt almost one quarter of the estates now liable to duty, and would cost £10m. this year and £20m. in a full year. There would also be help for family businesses.

TAXING SUB-CONTRACTORS.—The Chancellor promised measures in the Finance Bill to prevent " labour only " sub-contractors in the building and construction industry from evading payment of income tax, as some were known to be doing. On personal savings, the stamp duty on mortgages and deeds of covenant would be abolished from Aug. 1, at a cost of £3,500,000 in a full year. Mr. Barber said that in the 6 months to the end of *February* the total invested in National Savings had increased by over £200m., compared with only £4m. in the previous financial year, and he proposed further improvements. Starting in *August* there would be a monthly Premium Bond prize of £50,000, additional to the existing £25,000 weekly prize and the monthly prizes; and the limit on holdings would be raised from 1,250 to 2,000 £1 bonds from *Apr.* 1, 1971. The upper limit on monthly Save As You Earn contracts would go up to £20; a new

issue of British Savings Bonds would go on sale on *May* 3 with the tax-free bonus after 5 years up from £2 to £3 per cent.; and the holdings limit of Decimal savings issue of National Savings certificates would be lifted from £500 to £1,000 from *April* 1. He would appoint an independent committee to examine the whole field of national savings, including the trustee savings banks, and recommend improvements; the chairman would be Sir Harry Page, retiring city treasurer of Manchester.

Then Mr. Barber began to detail his proposals for simplifying business and personal taxation, first announcing a further 2½ per cent. cut in corporation tax, reducing it to 40 per cent., operative for the financial year 1970, and costing £105m. in a full year. He said the present system of personal taxation was cumbersome, complex and absurd. We had two taxes on personal income, ordinary income tax and surtax, with different rates for each, computed and collected separately and at different times. A root-and-branch reform was needed, and he would replace the two taxes with a single, graduated Personal Tax. There would be a basic rate of tax corresponding to the present standard rate less earned income relief, and covering a broad band of income, with higher rates for higher incomes. The present discrimination against investment income discouraged savings, so in future the first slice of such income would be taxed at the earned income rate, with a surcharge on investment income above a certain level. All these changes would require a complete PAYE re-coding, and the new system would operate from *April* 6, 1973. He thought the basic rate might be about 30 per cent. Because surtax would not apply after 1972-73 the Surtax Office would then be abolished, giving substantial saving in staff. There would be an overlap of tax in 1973-74, when some taxpayers would be paying Personal Tax as well as surtax on their previous year's income, but part of the payment could be deferred for a year. This was amended during the committee stage to permit of surtax on 1972-73 income to be paid in 3 annual instalments.

CHILD ALLOWANCE RAISED.—Actually, under the present system, the cut in standard rate of income tax announced in the previous *October* of 6d. (2½p) in the £, with the two-ninths relief, had brought the effective rate of tax down to about 30 per cent. for 1971-72. He now proposed two further changes to give added stimulus to the economy. The first was to help families with children by increasing all child allowances by £40. The second was to reduce the marginal rates on higher incomes so that the top rate would be 75·4 per cent., reached at about £20,500 a year (instead of 91·25 per cent. at £18,500 a year). These changes would take effect for 1971-72, and the PAYE re-coding would be effective in pay packets from July 5, 1971. The cost of improved children's allowances would be £163m. this year, £207m. in a full year; and the relief to higher earned incomes would cost £16m. and £38m. Mr. Barber announced that after 25 years of PAYE it was time to study it afresh, and perhaps to replace it by some better non-cumulative system. The Inland Revenue had begun this study.

Turning to indirect taxation, the Chancellor said that from *April*, 1973, both selective employment tax and purchase tax would be abolished, and replaced by a Value Added tax, which would involve the most fundamental change in indirect taxation since purchase tax was introduced 30 years ago. His party regarded SET as a thoroughly bad tax, unfair and arbitrary, which involved the Government in collecting about £2,000m. with one hand and giving back nearly £1,500m. with the other, but after an interval. This compelled many people not liable to this tax to make a forced loan to the Government. Purchase tax had the great disadvantage that it bore heavily on a limited number of goods but not at all on services. To replace SET and PT by a general employment tax, as had been suggested, would have one conclusive disadvantage: that it would not be rebatable on exports or chargeable on imports, and so would adversely affect our balance of payments. The two taxes at present added £66m. to £70m. a year to our export costs; but their replacement by VAT would permit the removal of the whole tax charge from export prices and its imposition on imports. As VAT would not be introduced until 1973 there would be ample time to decide rates and coverage. Food—except, perhaps, the few items now subject to PT—and newspapers, periodicals and books, and certain small traders, would be exempt from VAT.

CHANCELLOR'S SET TRAP.—Then Mr. Barber, nearing the end of his speech, gently led the House into the sort of trap that all Chancellors enjoy laying. Solemnly, he said " The Government are pledged to abolish SET. I must tell the House that my regret is that this tax, so disliked, but which now yields some £500m. a year, cannot be abolished this year." When the roar from the Labour benches had died away, he quietly added " I have, however, decided that as from the earliest practicable date, July 5, all the rates of SET shall be cut by half." When the cheering from his own side had died down he said that in revenue terms the net cost of the reduction would be £290m. in 1971-72 and £254m. in 1972-73. As in Mr. Jenkins's last Budget in 1970, so now in Mr. Barber's first, there was no mention of any of the favourite taxation change targets of many former Chancellors—tobacco, beer, wines, spirits, petrol, oil or vehicles. He ended with a warning that "All our hopes for the future will be but dust in our mouths if we do not repel the assault on the value of our money." His Budget, he said, would not solve our economic problems. But it did herald a new approach based on the belief that lower and simpler taxation would, over the years ahead, create a new spirit of personal endeavour and achievement which alone could provide our nation with prosperity.

The Leader of the Opposition, as is traditional, then expressed briefly his first impressions of the Budget. But Mr. Wilson was constrained to say at once " I concede the superb form of presentation, which the House enjoyed." He went on that his first impression was that this Budget failed to rise to the occasion. Mr. Barber had offered the family man 12s. a week on child allowances, but that would be eroded by price increases within a few weeks. The change from SET to VAT would mean big increases in the cost of living. He was glad of the £1 increase in pensions, but by next *Sept.* the pension would be little above what it was two years ago. It was the Budget of a Bourbon, a Budget which the country would soon regret. During the debate on the Budget resolutions which occupied three more days almost every proposal was criticized and defended. The plan to prevent income tax evasion by self-employed sub-contractors was set out on *April* 1 by Mr. P. Jenkin, who said the annual loss of tax from this source was about £10m. a year, and in recent years, partly prompted by SET, the practice had grown. In addition to self-employed bricklayers and plasterers with which we had become familiar, we now had to cope with self-employed barrow-boys and hod-carriers, and this was ridiculous. They proposed that in future

any building contractor who paid anyone for sub-contracted work must first deduct 30 per cent. on account of income tax and pay it to the collector of taxes. If the sub-contractor then made a proper tax return, any excess of tax thus paid would be credited against his tax liability, and any over-payment of tax would be repaid.

PERSONAL TAX WELCOMED.—On the last day of the Budget debate, *April 5*, Mr. Powell (C) said he shared in the repudiation of the commonly held opinion that inflation was the product of wage claims which were conceded or of some fault of the system of industrial relations. The Government's ability to prevent inflation depended on its being able to finance its expenditure without the risk of resorting to inflationary expediencies. Mr. Grimond (L) said the recent £10 a week rise to Ford workers was as much as the basic wage for many women in his constituency. He found it incredible that top men in the steel industry took £9,000 a year increase last year when they and others were preaching wage restraint. Mr. Taverne (Lab) said that in principle he welcomed the amalgamation of income tax and surtax and the creation of Personal Tax, and he congratulated the Government on having decided to introduce it. But there was nothing in the Budget as incentive to the lower-paid whose marginal taxation rate was higher than the surtax payer's, and little comfort for the unemployed. Winding up the debate, Mr. Barber said he had been criticized for stimulating demand too much when inflation was so high, but it would be irresponsible to plan for a faster growth of consumer spending than he had done. Nearly £700m. of overseas debt was still outstanding, which was a continuing constraint on the Government's freedom of action. The Government believed one of the main causes of unemployment was cost inflation and the rising cost of labour was causing firms to lay men off. He could not promise unemployment would fall until there was a substantial reduction in the level of pay settlements. The main Budget resolution was carried 301–261.

There was considerable political turbulence throughout this first session of the new Parliament, but nothing aroused more controversy than the Government's proposals for dealing with industrial strife. These were first outlined in a " consultative document " presented to the House on *Nov. 26* by Mr. Carr, who said that in the first 10 months of 1970 there had been 3,491 stoppages of work and the situation, particularly in export industries, was " truly alarming." No Government with any sense of responsibility could refrain from action. That was the view of the public, including a majority of industrial workers, and of Mr. Wilson during the first half of 1969. Unfortunately he was diverted from his course. (The previous Government's White Paper *In Place of Strife* aroused much argument in 1969, and on *June 19* that year Mr. Wilson announced that no Industrial Relations Bill would be introduced. But he had accepted an undertaking by the T.U.C. General Council to intervene in any dispute. *See* WHITAKER 1970.)

ESTABLISHING RIGHTS.—Mr. Carr said the only effective remedy for industrial troubles was to strengthen collective bargaining. Agreements should be binding commitments for both sides of industry. Shop stewards should play a large part in making stable bargains, and their authority and duties should be more clearly integrated into those of their unions. The Government's forthcoming Bill would establish the basic rights and obligations of unions and employers, and would provide a right for anyone to belong or not to belong to a union.

Mrs. Castle, who had sponsored *In Place of Strife* in 1969, led the attack on the proposed legislation, moving an amendment to Mr. Carr's motion (to " take note " of the document) condemning the proposals as being motivated by hostility to unions and expressing determination to reject any legislation based on them. They would reject the Bill " root and branch " as being irrelevant to our industrial problems. Tempers rose as the debate proceeded, but the Speaker kept matters within bounds, and the amendment was defeated by 310–269. The Government motion was carried without a division.

Earlier that day Mr. Heath, answering a question, referred to the threat by militant trade unionists to call a one-day strike for Dec. 8 in protest against the proposed legislation. The Prime Minister said he endorsed the T.U.C.'s condemnation of such action, adding he was sure no-one in the House could tolerate an attempt to dictate to the Government by industrial action against the expressed wishes of the electorate. Mr. Wilson said he supported the T.U.C.'s own methods of dealing with the question of unofficial strikes for political purposes. He asked Mr. Heath how many trades disputes, official and unofficial, had been solved by direct action by the T.U.C. Mr. Heath retorted that the days and the production lost through disputes in the past year had been greater than before, in spite of the T.U.C. The one-day political strike in fact took place on *Dec. 8* but was less widely supported than were two more such strikes against the Government's Bill held on *March 1* and *18*.

INDUSTRIAL RELATIONS BILL.—The Government's Industrial Relations Bill was introduced on *Dec. 1*, and Mr. Carr, moving the second reading on *Dec. 14*, said it contained the most enlightened and comprehensive code of workers' rights in the nation's history. It would increase the strength and size of the unions and their degree of freedom from State interference. New rules were needed on the industrial scene, and the balance between order and chaos must be redressed. The Bill had four principles: freely conducted collective bargaining; orderly principles for peaceful settlement of disputes by negotiation, conciliation and arbitration; free association of workers in unions and of employees in their own associations; and freedom and security for workers with adequate safeguards against unfair industrial practices. The registration of unions was of central importance in the reform of industrial relations law, but they were not stopping workers from associating, whether they chose to register or not. The crucial change in the Bill was that unregistered associations would not be immune from legal action if they induced a breach of contract.

Opposition speakers in the debate described the Bill as " a charter for scab employers " and also " a charter to breakaway unions," and Mrs. Castle accused the Government of " rigging " the industrial courts that the Bill would establish. Mr. Dudley Smith, Under-Secretary for Employment, replied that the fairness of these bodies would be seen when they came to be appointed, and that Mrs. Castle was utterly discredited where industrial relations legislation was concerned.

Resuming the debate next day the Prime Minister said he regretted that Mrs. Castle had tried to undermine the courts before they had even been established, describing them as " Government-dominated." He hoped not to hear that said

about a British court of justice in the House again. To many it must be ironic (he said) that the Labour Party, founded to accelerate the pace of change, should now oppose change which was so obviously needed. Mr. Houghton (*Lab*) said the Opposition were not opposed to change but had their own views on how it should be brought about—by voluntary action and self-discipline instead of statutory discipline. Mr. Wilson said they thought the Bill unworkable, provocative and harmful to industrial relations. There had hardly been a big strike in recent years to which the Bill would be relevant. After further debate the Bill was given a 2nd reading (on *Dec.* 15) by 324 votes to 280 (Govt. maj. 44).

"GUILLOTINE" DEMONSTRATION.—The Industrial Relations Bill entered on its committee stage in the Commons on Jan. 18 and it was soon evident that the battle was to be long and hard. On that day the debate on the first clause (general principles) continued until shortly after midnight, and the resumed debate on *Jan.* 19 kept the House sitting until 7.05 next morning. So it was scarcely surprising that on the third day in committee, *Jan.* 25, the Leader of the House moved a time-table motion (" guillotine ") which would require the committee stage to be completed in 10 or more allotted days, and the report stage and the 3rd reading in a further four days—increased during the subsequent debate to six. Mr. Whitelaw recalled that in the debate on Nov. 25 Mrs. Castle had said, " However long it takes we shall destroy the Bill," which showed that there was no prospect of voluntary co-operation from the Opposition. He had delayed introducing a timetable motion until after the committee stage had begun, but the result had been 20 hours spent on two non-controversial clauses, so the sooner a timetable was introduced the better. The Government believed the passage of the Bill was urgent in the national interest and they had a clear mandate for it. After several M.P.s had spoken there occurred an unprecedented demonstration by some Labour opponents of the motion which halted the business of the House. At 9.45 p.m. about 30 or 40 Labour M.P.s stood up during a speech by Mr. Carr and moved to the centre of the floor, where they lined up facing the Speaker. Amid mounting clamour they remained standing silently after the Speaker had asked them to resume their seats, whereupon Mr. Lloyd suspended the sitting for 15 minutes and left the Chamber. When he returned the recalcitrant members reassembled on the floor and stood silently and, according to one observer, rather sheepishly, apparently not knowing what to do next. The situation was saved by the Government Chief Whip's moving suspension of the standing order that regulates the time of rising of the House, so that the sitting could continue indefinitely. A division was called and Mr. Pym's motion was carried 308–276. The demonstrators then drifted back to their seats, the debate was resumed, the timetable motion was carried 294–252, and the sitting continued until 4.55 a.m.

No part was taken in the demonstration by the Liberal members, who issued a statement that, " having viewed with dismay the chaos " to which both the other parties had brought parliamentary procedures, they had decided to withdraw from the timetable debate and abstain from all votes during the wrangle over the timetable. They also stated that they had intended to vote against the introduction of the guillotine but changed their minds after " the anti-parliamentary demonstration " by Labour members, which they considered " all the more remarkable in view of the Labour Party's previous commitment to introduce similar legislation."

(The guillotine procedure, which dates in its present form from 1887 with later modifications, has been used more than a score of times, and sometimes arouses angry protests from the minority party; but its use may become inevitable when highly controversial legislation is before the House. One notable occasion of its use in recent years was by the Labour Government to secure the passage of the Iron and Steel Nationalization Bill in 1948–49 against strong Conservative opposition.)

ALL-NIGHT WORK.—Through the following days of the committee and report stages the struggle was tenaciously fought, ending with a marathon all-night sitting on *Mar.* 23 which lasted for 21 hours until 12.11 p.m. on *Mar.* 24. During this sitting a record number of 63 divisions were called (the previous record was 43 in one sitting, on the Army Bill of 1907 which abolished flogging of soldiers). The Opposition's intention was to keep the House sitting long enough to prevent the vote on the 3rd reading from being taken that day, and M.P.s had to tramp, more and more wearily, through the lobbies as the night and morning wore on. But the plan was defeated by the Conservative managers, who withdrew 42 amendments, mostly concerned with minor points of wording; and the last division —which gave the Government a majority of 125— was called at 11.30 a.m., and was followed immediately by the 3rd reading debate, the motion for which was carried by 307–269. Up to the completion of the report stage there had been in all 240 divisions and the Government's average majority had been 57, compared with its nominal over-all majority of 27. During the final sitting the Deputy Speaker congratulated the House on its " very good temper."

The 2nd reading of the Bill in the House of Lords was moved on *April* 5 by Lord Drumalbyn, and the House was kept sitting until after midnight. The debate was continued on *April* 6, during which an Opposition motion moved by Lord Delacourt-Smith, that the debate be adjourned until the Government could have free negotiations with both sides of industry to find agreed solutions to industrial relations problems, was rejected by 248–85, and the Bill was read a 2nd time by 224–15. Lord Donovan, chairman of the Commission on Industrial Relations—some of whose recommendations were embodied in the Bill—said there were numerous things in it which the Donovan Commission did not recommend. Because of historical factors workers came to regard the law as their natural enemy and to think that to improve their condition they must rely on their industrial strength. These inherited attitudes remained today in spite of improved conditions, and they were implicit in the banners carried in demonstration marches saying " Kill the Bill " borne by thousands who had never read it.

Peers put down more than 300 amendments for debate during the committee stage which began, after the Easter recess, on *April* 26. Some of these were presented by the Law Lords, aiming to simplify the legal jargon of the Bill.

PROFESSIONAL PROBLEMS.—On the first Opposition amendment the Government had a majority of 97. Proposed by Lord Shackleton, the Labour party leader, it would have altered clause 1 to provide that one of the general principles for promoting good industrial relations should be " orderly and freely conducted collective bargaining on a voluntary basis " rather than " collective bargaining freely and responsibly conducted." He said there

were " grievous anxieties " about the significance
of the policy as set out in the Bill. Earl Jellicoe
replied that the amendment sought to delete the
concept of responsibility at a time when a sense of
responsibility was more than ever needed in
collective bargaining. The debate on clause 1
continued through two more sittings, during which
Lord Platt, an eminent physician, said the Bill was
wholly conceived in terms of industry, but it also
applied to some of the professions. The medical
profession had principles that over-rode those of
manager and worker. The Bill meant adopting
trade union language, methods and practices in his
profession and would lead to lower status and
morale, which could affect recruitment. The
British Medical Association saw itself as a kind of
professional trade union, but he thought it was
misguided in giving acceptance to this Bill. He
wondered whether judges and Law Lords were
going to have an agency shop agreement. Replying, Lord Drumalbyn said the BMA's representations had resulted in provision being made for the
" special register." It was because the Government
recognized the sense of individuality of the professional man that the right *not* to belong to a trade
union was enshrined in the Bill.

There was much debate on *May* 3 on clauses 3
and 4 dealing with the " Code of Practice " provided for in the Bill but not yet available for study.
Lord Drumalbyn said a " consultative draft " of the
code would be published for discussion later. Lord
Shinwell grumbled that when the House should be
debating vital principles the Government were
unable or unwilling to state the contents of the
code. It would not matter " a tinker's cuss " (he
added) whether the Bill were passed or not:
legislation would not prevent turbulence among the
workers until their legitimate claims were understood. The Lord Chancellor said that they had
spent a week reiterating amendments previously
discussed in the Commons. In fact—there being
no time-table or guillotine procedure in the Lords—
the House continued to debate the Bill over many
more weeks, usually on 3 days a week, while keeping abreast of much other legislation, and consequently often sitting late into the night.

PEERS " AT END OF TETHER ".—Matters reached
their peak in May when, after sitting until after
2 a.m. on *May* 10–11 and 11–12, the House settled
down to an all-night stretch on *May* 13. One
subject debated was a provision that dismissal of an
employee should be fair if it was " related to the
conduct of the employee." Lord Beaumont of
Whitley moved an amendment to add " in the
course of his employment " saying it was unfair
that, for example, men could lose their jobs because they were found to be homosexuals, although
they had broken no law. Earl Jellicoe resisted the
amendment, the effect of which (he said) would be
to remove even criminal conduct from the orbit
of unfair dismissal procedure. The Lord Chancellor said that when he used to farm he employed two
cowmen who clashed over a domestic matter.
Although it was not his business he felt he was
entitled to choose which cowman to dismiss, and
his choice had nothing to do with their capabilities
as employees. Lord Hailsham added, amid
laughter, " If I had been the husband of Lady
Chatterley I am bound to say I would have got rid
of my gamekeeper." Lord Beaumont's amendment was defeated. Shortly after 7.30 a.m. on
May 14 Lord Shackleton appealed for a break, saying it was undesirable to overwork the House;
and nearly an hour later he again urged they should
rise, saying the Labour peers were " at the end of
their tether." The sitting was eventually ad-

journed at 8.40 a.m. after sitting continuously for
17 hours 40 minutes. By way of contrast the
House of Commons on *May* 13 twice found themselves without business to keep them going. First
they ran out of questions during Question time
and the sitting was suspended for 7 minutes.
Later, having dealt unexpectedly quickly with two
Bills and some Orders, the House had time for two
" adjournment debates " instead of the usual one,
and rose at 10.30 p.m. The Committee Stage of
the Bill in the Lords occupied a total of more than
150 hours spread over 18 days and was concluded on
June 10, with congratulations being exchanged by
Lord Drumalbyn and Lord Diamond on the dili-
gence, patience and helpfulness shown on both
sides. The draft code of practice, several times referred to and asked for during the committee stage,
was debated in the Lords on *June* 28, when Lord
Drumalbyn said its aim was to give guidance for the
day-to-day conduct of industrial relations. The
Government hoped the consultative document
would be widely discussed, and criticisms and
suggestions would be welcomed so that a revised
version could be laid before Parliament later in the
year. He said the TUC's response to the draft
code had been disappointing. Lord Diamond
gave the document a subdued welcome, describing
it as " paternalistic ", and Lord Byers called it
" wishy-washy " and said it would weaken the
Bill.

BACK TO THE COMMONS.—On the next day the
Lords resumed the battle over the Bill itself on
Report, with further amendments and arguments
which occupied them for 9 more late sittings, but the
Bill was read the 3rd time on *July* 20. On that day
Lord Olivier, making his maiden speech, thanked
the Government for the concession that they had
made in clause 17 to permit the acting profession to
remain a " closed shop " but he hoped a way would
be found of bringing the " ephemeral manager "
inside it. Lady White moved a last-minute
amendment to the same clause, but Lord Drumalbyn resisted this and it was rejected by 102–86. He
said it would still be open to the union and the
ephemeral manager to enter into an agency shop
agreement. Lord Diamond said the Bill would
encourage splinter unions. Lord Beaumont of
Whitley said the Bill was " a good beginning."
The Bishop of Blackburn urged the unions not to
take up a permanent position of obstruction. The
Lord Chancellor said the Bill represented the will of
the electorate and the unions would be both wise
and patriotic to cease from violent diatribes. The
Bill, on which there had been 140 divisions in the
Lords, was then passed, and the 341 amendments
made to it during its passage came up for consideration in the Commons on *July* 28.

Mr. Whitelaw opened the proceedings by moving a timetable motion. He proposed that the
Lords' amendments should be given no more than 5
days' debate, at the end of which all those outstanding (except where privilege was involved)
would be subject to a single vote. There were 9
involving privilege; some might be voted on during
the debates, but any remaining would be voted on
separately at the end of the fifth day. He said this
was a generous allocation of time which compared
favourably with, for example, Mrs. Castle's Transport Bill in 1968, when 250 Lords' amendments
were taken in 3 days. Of the 341 amendments (he
said) 135 had been accepted by the Government or
put down to meet Opposition points, 32 were
purely drafting, and 137 were consequential on
other amendments, leaving only 37 controversial
ones, for which the 5 days provided was the longest
time allowed for consideration of Lords' amend-

ments in the history of Parliament. Mrs. Castle protested that more amendments had been made in the Lords in this Bill than in any Bill since the War, and the Commons were now receiving back virtually a new additional Bill. The Government (she said) were perverting the rights of Parliament. Mr. Nott (C) retorted that Mrs. Castle would have 5 days in which once again to stand on her head. Mr. Carr said there were in fact only 21 basic amendments of a major controversial nature, and 5 days in which to discuss them, by the end of which the Bill would have had 56 days of Parliamentary debate, occupying 481 hours. This would not be called a denial of democracy; the time-table motion was then carried by 308–263 and the House set to work. During the debates Mr. Carr said the object of the Bill and its machinery was to provide an alternative to industrial warfare in solving disputes. Mr. John Fraser (Lab) agreed it was better to have peaceful means of settling disputes, but the Opposition objected to the long and intricate procedure before the Industrial Court as an alternative to striking. Mrs. Castle continued her unremitting opposition throughout the 5 days, and she was still speaking when the " guillotine " fell on the debate at midnight on Aug. 4–5. The remaining Lords' amendments, excluding those involving privilege, were then carried en bloc by 254–217, each of the separate divisions on the 8 remaining amendments involving privilege was carried, and the long and hard-fought struggle reached its end. Later that day, Aug. 5, the Industrial Relations Act received the Royal Assent.

MORE TAX CHANGES.—Sixteen weeks after his Budget the Chancellor of the Exchequer made further changes in taxation and proposed further financial and economic measures on July 19. He said he had been reviewing the economic situation against the background of the two main problems facing the country: unemployment and inflation. Output had increased at a slightly greater rate than the 3 per cent. increase he had forecast in March, as between the first half of 1971 and the first half of 1972, but it had fallen in the first half of 1971 by about one per cent. compared with the first half of 1970. This low level of activity in the economy, and the wage inflation that had been causing employers to lay off labour to cut costs, had resulted in too high a level of unemployment. This might well be higher in the first half of 1972 in the absence of any policy changes. Industrial investment too would be likely to continue downward for a time, without policy changes. There had been a rise in the volume of exports, after a static period since early in 1970, and the current account for 1971 was in surplus at an annual rate of £600m. He had therefore decided to repay to the International Monetary Fund next month, instead of next year, the outstanding £256m. of the 1968 drawing on the Fund. This, with the repayments announced in the Budget, meant that the Government had repaid £1,044m. of the short- and medium-term debt which they had inherited in June 1970, leaving still to be repaid to the IMF only the £417m. debt incurred in 1969–70, which would begin to fall due for repayment in June 1972. Next, Mr. Barber referred to the proposal for price restraint initiated by the Confederation of British Industry and said the chairmen of all the major nationalized industries had agreed to co-operate with it.

He thought it right now to act to provide some further stimulus to demand. First, to encourage industrial investment he proposed to increase from 60 per cent. to 80 per cent. the rate of first year allowance on all capital expenditure on plant and

machinery made between today and Aug. 1, 1973. Second, he would allow from tomorrow free depreciation for immobile plant and machinery in service industries in development areas. These two changes would benefit industry by about £40m. in 1972–73 and £150m. in 1973–74, and the necessary legislation would be in next year's Finance Bill. He had two further proposals for reviving investment. The first was to remove immediately all existing controls on hire purchase, credit sale and rental agreements except those designed to protect the consumer. The other was to reduce immediately the levels of purchase tax by even more than the 10 per cent. permitted by the regulator.

BETTER PRICE PROSPECTS.—So, by an Order under the Purchase Tax Act, 1963, all 4 rates would be reduced by two-elevenths from midnight. This would mean cuts of the 55 per cent. rate to 45 per cent.; the 36⅔ rate to 30 per cent.; the 22 to 18 per cent.; and the 13¾ to 11¼ per cent. The cost of these cuts would be £110m. this year and about £235m. in a full year. This would be the first time the rates had been reduced since 1963, and the biggest reduction since 1953; and it would mean price cuts over a wide range of goods. Added to the tax cuts announced in the Budget and the previous autumn, total reductions in taxation in the current financial year would be about £1,100m. and in 1972–3 over £1,400m. In addition, the new measures announced in the previous week to help the development and intermediate areas meant spending about £100m. more this year and next year. He now expected the increase in national output between the first halves of 1971 and 1972 to be 4–4½ per cent. They had the prospect of a slower rise in prices and a faster growth of demand, and an opportunity to make a decisive breakthrough in the fight against inflation.

A somewhat acrimonious debate followed, which was continued at greater length next day when Mr. Barber moved that the House approve his statement. He recalled that exactly 5 years ago, on July 20, 1966, the Labour Government announced the freeze, with cuts in central and local government and nationalized industry expenditure, a penny more on beer, fourpence on petrol, 10 per cent. on purchase tax, and more restrictions on hire purchase. Opposition speakers had much to say about the rising unemployment figures, " 3 mini-budgets in 9 months " and the cuts in school meals and milk, but the House agreed to the Chancellor's motion.

COMMON MARKET CAMPAIGN.—Statements on the progress of negotiations for Britain's entry into the European Economic Communities (the " Common Market ") were made in Parliament from time to time during the session and gave rise to much questioning and discussion, culminating in the publication by the Government in July of a White Paper entitled *The United Kingdom and the European Communities*. This was debated in both Houses at some length, the debate extending over 3 days in the Lords and 4 in the Commons on motions to " take note " of the White Paper. Opening the debate in the Commons on July 21 the Prime Minister said the reasons that had impelled 2 Conservative governments and one Labour one to apply to join seemed as valid today as when the first application was made 10 years ago. He was sorry about recent Australian criticism of the transitional arrangements negotiated for them, but there was an assurance that if there was any disruptive effect on trade the Community would take action, which was a satisfactory safeguard for Australia. New Zealand was

M+

assured of continuing access to Community markets for 5 years, with a review of the butter situation 3 years after Britain's accession to ensure special arrangements after 1977. It was curious, Mr. Heath remarked, that this feature of the agreement, which the New Zealand Government considered highly satisfactory, had been criticized by Mr. Wilson as " selling New Zealand short." On food prices at home Mr. Heath said the impact would be spread over about 6 years; assuming no change in the present price relativity between world and community prices, the rise in the cost of living after entry would be about ½p. in the £. On the balance of payments costs there would be several effects of our entry, including payments to the Community Budget, changes in agricultural and industrial trade, and the influence on capital movements and invisible trade. The technical problems of making realistic estimates of the effects of our membership were formidable, and it would be a disservice to the House to try to offer detailed calculations of the effects of each of the factors operating on the balance of payments in the first few years after entry. Those, added Mr. Heath, were not his words, but the words of Mr. Wilson in 1967.

ADVANCE TO PEACE.—Turning to long-term safeguards the Prime Minister said the Community had assured us of equitable solutions should an unacceptable situation arise over our budget contribution. On New Zealand there was the review procedure and the promise of special arrangements for butter; on sugar we had an assurance of safeguards for the interests of the producing countries; and on capital movements we had the provisions of the Treaty of Rome. Almost everyone recognized that today neither Britain's membership of the United Nations or the Commonwealth nor our natural relationship with the United States had given us leadership in world affairs. That was also true of our power to influence world trade agreements, and particularly true of our contribution to the relief of world poverty. Now we had an opportunity to join a community which had a better aid record and a lower external tariff than ourselves, and through our membership to develop our resources. But there was another prospect perhaps even more important. World affairs were entering a phase of rapid movement which provided opportunities for statesmanship which could break down many barriers now taken for granted. Britain would be better placed to take her share of that prize once she was a member of the EEC. " Here is a great opportunity for advance to lasting peace in Europe which no MP would wish to see thrown away " Mr. Heath declared.

SELECT COMMITTEE SUGGESTED.—Mr. Wilson followed and set out his and his party's position regarding the Common Market issue. This was at all times, and remained today, that they would support entry given the right terms and the essential safeguards. They had never said that Britain had to accept whatever terms emerged from the negotiations. He doubted the figures in the White Paper of the estimated costs. Mr. Heath had rightly rejected the suggestion of a referendum and, for reasons which he (Mr. Wilson) understood but did not share, the idea of a general election, on the issue. His suggestion was a Select Committee to inquire into the whole subject, with power to call people before it and to sit during the parliamentary recess and produce a report by Sept. 30. Its chairman might be the Speaker, or " some experienced parliamentarian who was above the battle now raging." Mr. Wilson said the terms brought back from Brussels contained no safeguard

for Commonwealth sugar producers; and he would not have recommended a Labour Cabinet to apply for entry except on the basis of assured and continuing access into Britain for New Zealand produce. He and his Government would not have agreed to entry except on the basis of the joint recommendation he and Lord George-Brown had put to their Cabinet in 1967, which was that the transitional period for New Zealand must be for at least a generation. In now opposing the terms arranged by the present Government he had taken exactly the same line as he and his Cabinet took 4 years ago. Mr. Awdry (C) interjected that the very Labour MP who would have led the negotiations if Mr. Wilson had won the last election had said publicly that the terms the present Government had secured would have been acceptable to him and his party. Mr. Wilson retorted that the MP referred to (Mr. George Thomson) was not in the Labour Government at the material time. He was entitled to express a personal view but his negotiating brief was as he (Mr. Wilson) had stated today.

CONFLICTING VIEWS.—Mr. Thorpe, the Liberal party leader, supported the idea of a Select Committee, but he would like to see the issue decided on a free vote in the House. They were entitled to know where the Labour party stood, because it was the one party that had not expressed an opinion. Mr. Wilson's speech on the previous Saturday was " a cause for sadness " because, if he had all those reservations about foreigners, why had he negotiated with them in the first place. Mr. Harold Lever (*Lab*) said he was not suggesting that the Common Market was a new Jerusalem or that Britain would starve to death if she did not go in, but it would benefit us to join. Mr. Rippon (the Government's chief negotiator) said they had broken no promises to Australia, and they had achieved for New Zealand far more than anyone had expected. The Commonwealth sugar producers were satisfied with the safeguards offered, and Lord Campbell of Eskan (*Chairman*, Commonwealth Sugar Exporters) had written to him that he regarded the settlement as satisfactory for the developing countries. Mr. Rippon added that he had Lord Campbell's permission to quote this letter, but this was contradicted by Mr. Wilson, who said that in a telephone call that day from Lord Campbell's office he had been told that Mr. Rippon was not entitled to quote Lord Campbell's letter in the debate. Mr. Rippon repudiated Mr. Wilson's statement. During the next day's debate Mr. Wilson said he had misunderstood the message he had received. He had checked with Lord Campbell, and he now wished to withdraw the words he had used to Mr. Rippon the previous night. Mr. Rippon said he was grateful for " what I take as a handsome apology."

FORMER MINISTER APPROVES.—A notable early speech came from Lord George-Brown in which he attacked Mr. Wilson's speeches both inside and outside Parliament, and firmly commended the White Paper " as I would have done from the Government benches." Recalling that it was Mr. Wilson and he (then Foreign Secretary) who together had visited the capitals of the EEC countries and conducted exhaustive negotiations in 1967, he said there could be no gainsaying that the terms now recommended in the White Paper were in line with the terms the Labour Government had been prepared for; and while the then Cabinet's final position was necessarily reserved all of them would have been bound in honour to recommend the terms, or something not significantly different. These terms were similar to those that Labour had thought right and acceptable, and he saw no reason

why, if they were right then, they became wrong now. Lord Robens of Woldingham in his maiden speech said there was nothing in the Treaty of Rome that would give the National Coal Board or the British Steel Corporation any cause for concern, and entry would open new opportunities for British coal. Lord Stokes said the motor industry accounted for over 10·5 per cent. of our total industrial production, and the European market was 5 times larger than our domestic market. We should not haggle about the terms of entry. If we did not accept them there was no alternative but to go into a state of permanent industrial recession.

Lord Shackleton thought the terms for New Zealand were uniquely favourable, better than he had hoped for. The debate concluded shortly after one a.m. on *July* 28 with the House agreeing to the motion.

———

During the Session, from *Oct.* 27, 1970, to *Aug.* 5, 1971, when both Houses rose for the summer recess, 172 Acts and Measures were debated, passed through all their stages and received the Royal Assent. On *Aug.* 5 the House of Lords adjourned until *Oct.* 11 and the House of Commons until *Oct.* 18.

PUBLIC ACTS OF PARLIAMENT 1970–71

The list commences with notes on seven Public Acts of Parliament which received the Royal Assent before September, 1970. Those Public Acts which follow received the Royal Assent after August, 1970. The date stated after each Act is the date on which it came into operation.

AGRICULTURE ACT 1970 (May 29, 1970) makes provision with respect to agriculture and related matters (for example: marketing of eggs, farm capital grants and smallholdings in England and Wales) and with respect to flood warning systems; and amends the Diseases of Animals Act 1950.

APPROPRIATION (NO. 2) ACT 1970 (July 23, 1970) applies a sum out of the Consolidated Fund to the Service of the year ending March 31, 1971, and appropriates the sums voted for supply services.

INTERNATIONAL MONETARY FUND ACT 1970 (July 23, 1970) enables effect to be given to a proposed increase in the U.K.'s quota to the International Monetary Fund and provides for certain loans to that Fund to be made out of the National Loan Fund instead of the Consolidated Fund.

FIJI INDEPENDENCE ACT 1970 (July 23, 1970) makes provision for, and in connection with, the attainment by Fiji of fully responsible status within the Commonwealth.

NATIONAL INSURANCE (OLD PERSONS AND WIDOWS PENSIONS AND ATTENDANCE ALLOWANCES) ACT 1970 (days to be appointed) provides for retirement pensions and widow's benefit under the National Insurance Act 1965 for or in respect of persons over pensionable age on July 5, 1948; reduces the qualifying age from 50 to 40 for widow's pension under s. 28 of that Act; and for many connected and allied purposes.

EDUCATION (HANDICAPPED CHILDREN) ACT 1970 (July 23, 1970) provides (as respects England and Wales) for discontinuing the classification of handicapped children as unsuitable for education at school, and for connected purposes.

HARBOURS (AMENDMENT) ACT 1970 (July 23, 1970) repeals section 13 (1) of the Harbours Act 1964 and imposes a limit on future loans under section 11 of that Act.

INCOME AND CORPORATION TAXES (No. 2) ACT 1970 (December 17, 1970) fixes the standard rate of income tax for the year 1971–72, alters the marginal relief for persons with small incomes, and reduces the rate of corporation tax for the financial year 1969.

FAMILY INCOME SUPPLEMENTS ACT 1970 (May 3, 1971) provides for the payment of a new benefit for certain families with small incomes; and for connected purposes.

CONTINGENCIES FUND ACT 1970 (January 17, 1971) makes further provision with respect to the Civil Contingencies Fund.

TOWN AND COUNTRY PLANNING (LONDON) (INDEMNITY) ACT 1970 (January 17, 1971) grants an indemnity in respect of the delay in laying before Parliament certain regulations made under section 24 of the London Government Act 1963, and continues in force the provision whereby regulations under that section are subject to annulment in

accordance with the Statutory Instruments Act 1946.

EXPIRING LAWS CONTINUANCE ACT 1970 (December 17, 1970) makes permanent certain expiring laws and continues others.

CONSOLIDATED FUND ACT 1971 (February 17, 1971) applies certain sums out of the Consolidated Fund to the service of the years ending March 31, 1971 and 1972.

TEACHING COUNCIL (SCOTLAND) ACT 1971 (various dates) enables the Secretary of State by regulations to secure the payment of fees to the General Teaching Council for the renewal of registrations in pursuance of section 6 of the Act of 1965, by way of deduction from the salaries of persons employed by education authorities and managers of educational establishments; and provides for connected purposes.

GUARDIANSHIP OF MINORS ACT 1971 (March 17, 1971) consolidates with amendments the enactments relating to the guardianship and custody of minors.

COPYRIGHT (AMENDMENT) ACT 1971 (February 17, 1971) amends the Copyright Act 1956 so as to make provision for the subsequent variation by the Performing Right Tribunal of orders made pursuant to that Act.

AIR CORPORATIONS ACT 1971 (February 17, 1971) raises the limits imposed by the Act of 1967 section 16 (1) on borrowings by an investment in B.O.A.C.

CIVIL AVIATION (DECLARATORY PROVISIONS) ACT 1971 (February 17, 1971) makes declaratory provision with respect to such a particular flight and series of flights as are mentioned in the Civil Aviation (Licensing) Act 1960 section 1 (3) and with respect to the limitations which may be imposed by virtue of the Air Corporations Act 1967, section 3 (5).

LOCAL AUTHORITIES (QUALIFICATION OF MEMBERS) ACT 1971 (February 17, 1971) amends the law relating to the qualification for nomination and election to, and membership of, local authorities in Great Britain. (The Act does not extend to Northern Ireland.)

HOSPITAL ENDOWMENTS (SCOTLAND) ACT 1971 (February 17, 1971) provides for the constitution of a Scottish Hospital Trust; makes provision for transferring endowments to that Trust and for the distribution of the income of those endowments; and for connected purposes.

ROLLS-ROYCE (PURCHASE) ACT 1971 (February 17, 1971) makes provision for and in connection with the acquisition for the benefit of the Crown of any part of the undertaking and assets of Rolls-Royce Ltd. or its subsidiaries, and the carrying on of any undertaking so acquired, and for connected purposes.

VEHICLES (EXCISE) ACT 1971 (various dates)

consolidates certain enactments relating to excise duties on mechanically propelled vehicles and to the licensing and registration of such vehicles with amendments to give effect to the recommendations of the Law Commission and the Scottish Law Commission.

ATOMIC ENERGY AUTHORITY ACT 1971 (day or days to be appointed) provides for the transfer to British Nuclear Fuels Ltd. and The Radiochemical Centre Ltd. of parts of the undertaking of the United Kingdom Atomic Energy Authority and of property, rights, liabilities and obligations appertaining to those parts of the Authority's undertaking, and for various other connected purposes.

HYDROCARBON OIL (CUSTOMS AND EXCISE) ACT 1971 (April 12, 1971) consolidates the enactments relating to the duties of customs and excise on hydrocarbon oil, petrol substitute and power methylated spirits.

MR. SPEAKER KING'S RETIREMENT ACT 1971 (March 30, 1971) settles and secures annuities upon the Right Honourable Horace Maybray King, and after his death upon his wife, Una King, in consideration of his eminent services.

CONSOLIDATED FUND (NO. 2) ACT 1971 (March 30, 1971) applies certain sums out of the Consolidated Fund to the service of the years ending March 31, 1970, 1971 and 1972.

CONSUMER PROTECTION ACT 1971 (April 30, 1971) amends the Act of 1961, section 3.

COAL INDUSTRY ACT 1971 (March 30, 1971) extends the power of the Secretary of State for Trade and Industry to provide grants in connection with pit closures and resulting redundancy payments; gives the National Coal Board power to borrow in foreign currency; and provides for various connected purposes.

INDUSTRY ACT 1971 (April 8, 1971) repeals the Industrial Reorganization Corporation Act 1966 and dissolves the Industrial Reorganization Corporation; terminates the power to make industrial investment schemes under the Industrial Expansion Act 1968 otherwise than for the purpose of revoking or varying any such scheme made before the passing of this Act, and for connected purposes.

LAND COMMISSION (DISSOLUTION) ACT 1971 (July 23, 1970 as regards betterment levy, day to be appointed for other matters) gives effect to the Government decision not to charge betterment levy in respect of any act or event occurring after July 22, 1970; provides for the Land Commission to cease; makes provision for the disposal of land acquired under the Land Commission Act 1967; and provides for connected purposes.

CARRIAGE OF GOODS BY SEA ACT 1971 (day to be appointed) amends the law with respect to the carriage of goods by sea. [It gives the force of law to the Hague Rules of 1924 as amended in 1968.]

MINES MANAGEMENT ACT 1971 (April 8, 1971) amends the law as to the management and control of mines; and for connected purposes.

OIL IN NAVIGABLE WATERS ACT 1971 (various dates) amends the Acts of 1955 and 1963 and the Continental Shelf Act 1964, s. 5; makes further provision for preventing pollution of the sea by oil; and for connected purposes.

ANIMALS ACT 1971 (October 1, 1971) makes new provision with respect to civil liability for damage done by animals and with respect to the protection of livestock from dogs. It replaces the common law rules as to animals *ferae naturae*, *scienter* and cattle trespass and part of the Dogs Act 1906 and imposes on the owners or keepers of many animals a strict liability for any injury or damage done by the animal. It also makes provision for connected purposes.

COURTS ACT 1971 (various dates). This Act abolishes the Assize Courts and quarter sessions and replaces them with a Crown Court to be conducted by Circuit Judges and High Court Judges. Many other local Courts are also abolished, some being merged with the High Court, *e.g.* the Chancery Court of the county palatine of Lancaster and others with the local county courts, *e.g.* the Tolzey and Pie Poudre Courts of the City and County of Bristol. The Act also sets up the consequential amendments to the administration and jurisdiction of the courts and amends the law about courts and court proceedings.

COINAGE ACT 1971 (August 31, 1971) consolidates, so far as they are part of the law of the U.K., the Coinage Acts 1870 to 1946 and certain other enactments relating to coinage, with amendments to give effect to recommendations of the Law Commission and the Scottish Law Commission.

ADMINISTRATION OF ESTATES ACT 1971 (January 1, 1972 except ss. 13 and 14 on May 12, 1971) makes changes in the law relating to reciprocal recognition of grants in England and Wales, Scotland and Northern Ireland, and Commonwealth and Colonial grants, and in the duties of personal representatives in England and Wales; abolishes the rights of preference and retainer where the personal representative has reason to believe the estate is insolvent; and provides for connected purposes.

BETTING, GAMING AND LOTTERIES (AMENDMENT) ACT 1971 (July 1, 1971) amends the provisions of the 1963 Act relating to days on which betting is permitted on tracks.

POWERS OF ATTORNEY ACT 1971 (October 1, 1971) repeals a number of the existing statutory provisions about powers of attorney and replaces them by new provisions facilitating the use of powers of attorney and extending the protection given to people dealing with the donee of such a power.

RENT (SCOTLAND) ACT 1971 (August 12, 1971) consolidates in relation to Scotland various enactments relating to rent including the Rent and Mortgage Interest Restrictions Acts 1920 to 1939, the Rent Act 1965 (except Part III thereof) and Part IV of the Housing (Scotland) Act 1969.

NATIONAL SAVINGS BANK ACT 1971 (June 12, 1971) consolidates certain enactments relating to the National Savings Bank, with amendments to give effect to recommendations of the Law Commission and the Scottish Law Commission.

UNSOLICITED GOODS AND SERVICES ACT 1971 (August 12, 1971) deals with " inertia selling " by allowing a person who receives unsolicited goods to treat them as an unconditional gift unless the sender takes them back within six months or earlier if the recipient gives notice to the sender. The Act makes it a criminal offence to demand payment for unsolicited goods and services and to send unsolicited books, etc., describing or illustrating human sexual techniques.

INTEREST ON DAMAGES (SCOTLAND) ACT 1971 (May 12, 1971) amends the Act of 1958 by extending the power of the courts to order payment of interest on damages.

ATTACHMENT OF EARNINGS ACT 1971 (August 2, 1971) consolidates the enactments relating to the attachment of earnings as a means of enforcing the discharge of monetary obligations.

ARMED FORCES ACT 1971 (various dates) continues the Army Act 1955 and the Air Force Act 1955, limits the duration of the Naval Discipline Act 1957 and amends those Acts and other enactments relating to the armed forces.

WATER RESOURCES ACT 1971 (May 27, 1971) makes further provision with respect to the dis-

charge of water by, or by agreement with, river authorities.

DANGEROUS LITTER ACT 1971 (June 27, 1971) amends the Litter Act 1958 so as to make better provision for the abatement of dangerous litter (*e.g.* the maximum fine has been increased to £100) and to empower local authorities to promote the abatement of litter by means of publicity.

MOTOR VEHICLES (PASSENGER INSURANCE) ACT 1971 (December 1, 1972) requires users of motor vehicles to be covered against any liability which they might incur in respect of the death of or personal injuries to their passengers arising out of the use of motor vehicles on the road and makes void any agreement or arrangement designed to evade the Act.

WELSH NATIONAL OPERA COMPANY ACT 1971 (May 27, 1971) makes further provision for contributions by local authorities in Wales (including Monmouthshire) towards the expenses of the Welsh National Opera Company.

MISUSE OF DRUGS ACT 1971 (various dates) makes new provision with respect to dangerous or otherwise harmful drugs and related matters, *e.g.* by setting up an Advisory Council and dividing drugs into three classes: Class A includes heroin and L.S.D.; Class B includes amphetamine, cannabis and codeine; and Class C includes various appetite suppressants which have a mildly stimulant effect. The maximum penalties for possession are 7 years for Class A drugs, 5 years for Class B and 2 years for Class C whilst those for pushing and other offences are 14 years for Classes A and B and 5 years for Class C. The Home Secretary has been empowered to make regulations to control the supply of drugs.

RATING ACT 1971 (May 27, 1971) extends for any rate period beginning after March 1971 the definitions of agricultural buildings and land (in the General Rate Act 1967, s. 26) for the purposes of derating in England and Wales; and makes similar provision in Scotland by amending the Valuation and Rating (Scotland) Act 1956, s. 7, and enlarging the meaning of " agricultural land and heritages " for 1971–72 and future years. The extension for both England and Scotland relates to such activities as bee-keeping and buildings occupied therefor.

FIRE PRECAUTIONS ACT 1971 (various dates) makes further provision for protection of persons from fire risks. In particular a fire certificate will be required in respect of premises put to certain designated uses. This will not apply to (*inter alia*) any premises consisting of or comprised in a house which is occupied as a single private dwelling.

HIGHWAYS ACT 1971 (various dates) makes further provision with respect to highways, streets and bridges in England and Wales including provisions with respect to means of access to premises from highways, provisions authorizing the provision of picnic sites and public conveniences for the benefit of users of certain highways, and many other provisions affecting the laws of town and country planning and recording public rights of way, and for connected purposes.

EDUCATION (SCOTLAND) ACT 1971 (all except section 4, subsections 1, 2 and 4 on August 1, 1971) re-enacts, with modifications, certain provisions relating to free education; restores the power to charge fees in certain schools to education authorities; makes provision in respect of fees to be charged for outwith-area pupils; and for connected purposes.

LAW REFORM (MISCELLANEOUS PROVISIONS) ACT 1971 (August 1, 1971) extends, in certain cases, the time limit for bringing legal proceedings where damages are claimed which consist of or include damages for personal injuries or in respect of a person's death, and therefore amends the Limitation Act 1963; provides that, in assessing damages for widows in actions arising from the death of their husbands, remarriage and the prospects thereof should not be taken into account; repeals Administration of Justice Act 1965, s. 19 (control of widows' damages where there is also an infant's claim) and for connected purposes.

NULLITY OF MARRIAGE ACT 1971 (August 1, 1971) restates, with alterations, the grounds on which a marriage is void or voidable and the bars to a decree of nullity on the ground that a marriage is voidable; alters the effect of decrees of nullity in respect of voidable marriages and abolishes certain bars to the grant of matrimonial relief.

REDEMPTION OF STANDARD SECURITIES (SCOTLAND) ACT 1971 (July 1, 1971) amends the provisions of the Conveyancing and Feudal Reform (Scotland) Act 1970 relating to the redemption of standard securities; makes provision, as respects Scotland, in relation to the operation of the Companies Act 1948, s. 89; and for connected purposes.

SHIPBUILDING INDUSTRY ACT 1971 (July 1, 1971) amends section 7 of the 1967 Act by raising the limit on the liability which the Secretary of State may assume in respect of guarantees under the section.

WILD CREATURES AND FOREST LAWS ACT 1971 (July 1, 1971) abolishes certain rights of Her Majesty to wild creatures (except royal fish and swans) and certain related rights and franchises; abrogates the forest law (subject to exceptions); repeals enactments relating to those rights and franchises and to forests and the forest law; and for connected purposes.

CRIMINAL DAMAGE ACT 1971 (October 14, 1971) revises the law of England and Wales as to offences of damage to property, and repeals or amends, as respects the U.K., certain enactments relating to such offences.

RURAL WATER SUPPLIES AND SEWERAGE ACT 1971 (July 14, 1971) removes the limit imposed by the Act of 1944, section 1 subs. (5), as amended, on contributions under that section towards the expenses of local authorities in England and Wales.

NATIONAL INSURANCE ACT 1971 (days to be appointed) amends the provisions of the National Insurance Acts 1965 to 1970, the National Insurance (Industrial Injuries) Acts 1965 to 1969 and the Industrial Injuries and Diseases (Old Cases) Acts 1967 and 1969 as to contributions and benefits; makes provision for invalidity benefit for the chronic sick and for a retirement pension and age addition for certain persons over the age of 80; makes new provision in relation to polygamous marriages for the purposes of any of the said Acts or of the Family Allowance Act 1965, and for connected purposes.

ANGUILLA ACT 1971; DIPLOMATIC AND OTHER PRIVILEGES ACT 1971; FRIENDLY SOCIETIES ACT 1971; INVESTMENT AND BUILDING GRANTS ACT 1971; LAND REGISTRATION AND LAND CHARGES ACT 1971; LAW REFORM (JURISDICTION IN DELICT) (SCOTLAND) ACT 1971; LICENSING (ABOLITION OF STATE MANAGEMENT) ACT 1971; MERCHANT SHIPPING (OIL POLLUTION) ACT 1971; MINERAL WORKINGS (OFFSHORE INSTALLATIONS) ACT 1971; PENSION (INCREASE) ACT 1971; POOL COMPETITIONS ACT 1971; PREVENTION OF OIL POLLUTION ACT 1971; RECOGNITION OF DIVORCES AND LEGAL SEPARATIONS ACT 1971; SHERIFF COURTS (SCOTLAND) ACT 1971; STATUTE LAW (REPEALS) ACT 1971; TRIBUNALS AND INQUIRIES ACT 1971; APPROPRIATION ACT 1971; CIVIL AVIATION ACT 1971; EDUCATION (MILK) ACT 1971; FINANCE ACT 1971; HIJACKING ACT 1971; HOUSING ACT 1971; INDUSTRIAL RELATIONS ACT 1971; MEDICINES ACT 1971; MINERAL WORKINGS ACT 1971; SOCIAL SECURITY ACT 1971.

Government and Public Offices

NOTE.—The salaries shown are in most cases those actually received. In certain instances, however, the National Scale without corresponding London weighting is given.

MINISTRY OF AGRICULTURE, FISHERIES AND FOOD
Whitehall Place, S.W.1. †
[01-839-7711]

The Ministry of Agriculture, Fisheries and Food was established in April 1955 and assumed responsibilities previously discharged by the Ministry of Agriculture and Fisheries and the Ministry of Food.

The Ministry has a general responsibility for food supplies, both home produced and imported, and for food manufacture, distribution and storage.

The Ministry provides financial assistance and free technical advice to the agricultural (including horticultural) and fishing industries in England and Wales. Financial assistance under the Agriculture Acts of 1947 to 1967 includes deficiency payments in respect of most of the main agricultural products to ensure a fair return to the producer, and a number of production grants and subsidies to promote improved farming efficiency. Free advice is available on farm management, and the technical aspects of agricultural production, including farm buildings and fixed equipment, land drainage, and crop and animal husbandry.

The Ministry is also responsible for schemes designed to improve the quality of livestock and of other agricultural products through the dissemination of the results of research carried out by the Agricultural Research Council and other institutions and through the control and eradication of animal and plant disease and of pests. It is also concerned with the safety, health, welfare and wages of agricultural workers.

The Ministry is also concerned with agricultural co-operation, the welfare of livestock, food prices and the development of the fishing industry in England and Wales, including the processing and distributive trades, whaling and research.

The Ministry has primary responsibility for administering part of the food and drugs legislation, in particular the composition, labelling and advertising of food; for slaughterhouses and meat inspection, and for the quality and cleanliness of milk; the Ministry maintains relations with Commonwealth and other countries and participates in the work of a number of international bodies, concerned with agriculture, fisheries and food.

The Ministry is also responsible for the Royal Botanic Gardens, Kew.

Minister of Agriculture, Fisheries and Food, THE RT. HON. JAMES MICHAEL LEATHES PRIOR, M.P.
£8,500
Private Sec., D. Evans.
Assistant Private Secs., Mrs. D. F. Robbins; Miss J. E. Wheeler.
Parliamentary Private Secretary, T. M. Jopling, M.P.
Parliamentary Clerk, Miss M. E. Roberts
£2,775 to £3,400
Parliamentary Secretary, I. A. Stodart, M.P... £3,750
Permanent Secretary, Sir Basil Engholm, K.C.B.
£14,000
Private Secretary, G. K. Bruce.
Deputy Secretaries, F. M. Kearns, C.B., M.C.; J. R. Moss (*Group A*); E. W. Maude, C.B. (*Group B*); R. P. Fraser (*Group C*) £9,000
Director General (Agricultural Development and Advisory Service), Sir Emrys Jones........ £9,000
Deputy Directors General, Maj. E. S. Dobb, C.B., T.D.; W. R. Smith £8,300
Liaison Officers, F. K. Abbey, C.B.E.; Sir Richard Boughey, Bt.; J. Brocklebank, C.B.E.; The Lord De Ramsey, T.D.; Lt.-Col. G. W. F. Luttrell, M.C.; Col. N. V. Stopford Sackville, C.B.E., T.D.; Lt.-Col. Sir Richard Verdin, O.B.E., T.D.; S. Williams, C. E. I. Wynne-Finch . .*unpaid*

† *Unless otherwise stated, Divisions of the Ministry are at this address.*

ESTABLISHMENTS DEPARTMENT
Great Westminster House, Horseferry Road, S.W.1.
[01-834-8511]
Under-Secretary (Director of Establishments), J. G. Kelsey............................ £6,750

Personnel Division I
Assistant Secretary, I. P. M. Macdonald
£5,000 to £6,300
Principals, E. A. Airriess; G. Seymour; K. P. Stones
£3,250 to £4,400
Senior Executive Officers, F. C. Coleman; G. A. Millington; A. R. Pierce; J. S. Ransom; G. Reay (*Chief Investigation Officer*); D. A. Stevens
£2,775 to £3,400

Personnel Division II
Assistant Secretary, G. L. Wilde.. £5,000 to £6,300
Resettlement Officer, G. A. Mansfield
£4,695 to £5,240
Principals, A. W. Bunn, I.S.O.; J. H. Maslen; S. L. Palmer .... £3,250 to £4,400
Senior Executive Officers, C. W. Chapman; T. Hetherington; V. A. Hopkins; Mrs. J. I. Leslie; J. Mason.................... £2,775 to £3,400

Office Services Division
Assistant Secretary, B. Dennis (*Office Controller*)
£5,000 to £6,300
Principals, H. M. Allix; H. L. G. Copeman; A. R. Heath .... £3,250 to £4,400
Senior Executive Officers, E. G. Chibnall; Miss D. C. Dixson (*Chief Welfare Officer*); S. O. B. Powell (*Chief Registrar*)...... £2,775 to £3,400

MANAGEMENT SERVICES DIVISIONS I AND II
Great Westminster House, Horseferry Road, S.W.1.
[01-834-8511]
St. Stephen's House, Victoria Embankment, S.W.1.
[01-839-4266]
Under-Secretary, Miss I. O. H. Lepper £6,750
Assistant Secretaries, R. V. Allen; T. P. Marten
£5,000 to £6,300
Principals, K. R. Aunger; J. A. Bamford; R. Dickeson; L. H. Glassberg; J. N. Jotcham; D. W. Peddie; W. E. Rivers....... £3,250 to £4,400
Senior Executive Officers, A. D. Bennett; H. J. Dewar; J. N. Diserens; R. C. Francis; S. Hampson; B. J. Harwood; Miss A. D. Haynes; E. Healds; D. S. Heaps; L. Lewis; N. J. Miller; A. L. Roberts; D. S. Stephenson; R. F. West; P. F. Williams, M.B.E.; L. A. Wilson ...... £2,775 to £3,400

Planning Unit
Assistant Secretary, P. Parkhouse. £5,000 to £6,300
Principal, R. M. Jackson........ £3,250 to £4,400

Administrative Departments
GROUP A
Under-Secretary, J. H. V. Davies £6,750

GENERAL AGRICULTURAL POLICY DIVISIONS I AND II
Assistant Secretaries, N. E. D. Burton; C. H. Shillito
£5,000 to £6,300
Principals, B. H. B. Dickinson; J. M. Lynes; P. N. M. Moore, D.S.O., M.C.; H. S. Newman
£3,250 to £4,400
Senior Executive Officer, G. L. Little
£2,775 to £3,400

Director of Economics and Statistics, L. Napolitan, C.B.
£6,750

ECONOMICS DIVISIONS I AND II
Senior Principal Agricultural Economists, C. W. Capstick; G. Sharp.......... £5,000 to £6,300

Principal Agricultural Economists, A. M. Cowland; Mrs. S. M. Dickinson; J. A. Evans; Miss R. Fennell; K. E. Gubbins; R. E. Mordue

£3,250 to £4,400

Senior Executive Officers, C. Patterson; P. M. Reason, M.B.E.; A. Rigby; B. Vernon

£2,775 to £3,400

STATISTICS DIVISIONS I AND II

Senior Principal Agricultural Economist. E. L. Snowdon.................... £5,000 to £6,300
Chief Statistician, A. H. J. Baines.. £5,000 to £6,300
Statisticians, S. Clayton; D. D. Filtness; J. E. Outlaw; W N. T. Roberts..£3,250 to £4,400
Principal Agricultural Economists, P. A. Power; J. M. Slater................ £3,250 to £4,400
Principals, W. E. N. Charnley; P. G. Horscroft; Miss H. J. Morey; K. T. Wasley

£3,250 to £4,400

Senior Executive Officers L. J. Angel; N. E. Brooker; J. J. O'Neill............... £2,775 to £3,400

Under Secretary, K. Dexter............. £6,750

MEAT DIVISION

Assistant Secretary, E. J. G. Smith £5,000 to £6,300
Principals, J. H. S. Baker; M. E. Blackman; R. G. Butterworth; B.E. Camp.... £3,250 to £4,400
Senior Executive Officer, W. McLaren

£2,775 to £3,400

FATSTOCK DIVISION

Assistant Secretary, M. M. A. Gray

£5,000 to £6,300

Principals, A. J. Burton; C. F. B. Knox; Miss E. J. Marston, M.B.E.; S. Wentworth

£3,250 to £4,400

Senior Executive Officers, A. N. Downing; D. E. Rose .... £2,775 to £3,400
Chief Fatstock Technical Officer, V. G. Clarke, M.B.E.

£4,600 to £5,200

Deputy Chief Fatstock Technical Officer, G. L. Shouler................... £3,250 to £4,400

Under Secretary, B. D. Hayes £6,750

MILK AND MILK PRODUCTS DIVISION

Assistant Secretary, D. F. Williamson

£5,000 to £6,300

Principals, C. J. A. Barnes; B. L. Faux; E. J. Mehew

£3,250 to £4,400

Senior Executive Officers, O. R. Appleby; C. R. Bodrell; N. R. Street....... £2,775 to £3,400

EGGS AND POULTRY DIVISION

Assistant Secretary, G. P. Jupe ..£5,000 to £6,300
Principals, A. R. Cruickshank; G. M. Trevelyan

£3,250 to £4,400

Senior Executive Officer, G. R. Holloway

£2,775 to £3,400

GROUP B

Under Secretary, M. D. M. Franklin....... £6,750

EXTERNAL RELATIONS DIVISIONS I, II, III AND IV

Assistant Secretaries, A. K. H. Atkinson; J. E. Dixon; T. R. M. Sewell; A. V. Vickery £5,000 to £6,300
Principals, Mrs. E. A. Attridge; G. J. L. Avery; M. H. Butcher; R. W. Holmwood; H. R. Neilson; R. J. Packer; Mrs. A. M. Pickering; I. C. Redfern; J. H. H. Vaughan..£3,250 to £4,440
Senior Executive Officers, D. K. Gilbert; B. E. Haines; R. S. Halward.............. £2,775 to £3,400

Under Secretary, M. E. Johnston.......... £6,750

CEREALS DIVISION

Assistant Secretary, K. W. Wilkes

£5,000 to £6,300

Principals, J. S. W. Henshaw; A. Jeffrey-Smith; D. M. L. MacGregor........ £3,250 to £4,400
Senior Executive Officers, V. R. Holmes; R. C. McKinley................ £2,775 to £3,400

SUGAR AND TROPICAL FOODSTUFFS DIVISION

Wellington House, Buckingham Gate, S.W.1

[01-799-6693]

Assistant Secretary, G. E. Myers..£5,000 to £6,300
Principals, H. B. Fawcett; D. A. Hadley; R. J. Hardy; S. T. K. Hester; G. Stapleton

£3,250 to £4,400

Senior Executive Officers, A. B. Cutler; J. A. Young

£2,775 to £3,400

FISHERIES DEPARTMENT

Great Westminster House, Horseferry Road, S.W.1

[01-834-8511]

Fisheries Secretary, J. Graham (*Under Secretary*)

£6,750

Assistant Secretaries, N. J. P. Hutchison; W. R. Small............... £5,000 to £6,300
Principals, K. W. Battrick; G. N. Dixon; E. R. Fiske; D. H. Griffiths; H. Pease; P. Pooley; Miss E. M. Price; L. W. Tolladay

£3,250 to £4,400

Chief Inspector, Sea Fisheries Inspectorate, H. T. Blaney, C.B.E...................... £5,200
Deputy Chief Inspector, Sea Fisheries Inspectorate, P. G. Jeffery.............£3,250 to £4,400

Fisheries Laboratories

Sea Fisheries Laboratory
Pakefield, Lowestoft
[Lowestoft: 4251]

Director of Marine Research (*Chief Scientific Officer*), H. A. Cole, C.M.G................ £6,380
Deputy Director (*Deputy Chief Scientific Officer*), A. J. Lee, D.S.C........... £5,240 to £5,830
Senior Principal Scientific Officers, A. C. Burd; D. H. Cushing; H. W. Hill; F. R. H. Jones; A. Preston; J. E. Shelbourne.........£4,390 to £5,015
Principal Scientific Officers, L. Birkett; R. W. Blacker; G. C. Bolster; D. J. Garrod; D.Harding; M. J. Holden; A. Jamieson; A. R. Margetts; N. T. Mitchell; C. E. Purdom; N. Reynolds; J. W. Talbot; G. C. Trout....£2,820 to £2,930
Senior Executive Officer, G. V. McMorran

£2,775 to £3,400

Shellfish Laboratories
Remembrance Avenue, Burnham-on-Crouch
[Burnham-on-Crouch: 3258]

Senior Principal Scientific Officer (vacant)

£4,390 to £5,015

Principal Scientific Officer, P. C. Wood

£2,820 to £3,902

Castle Bank, Conway
[Conway: 2419]

Principal Scientific Officers, B. T. Hepper; P. R. Walne...............£2,820 to £3,902

Salmon and Freshwater Fisheries Laboratory
Whitehall Place, S.W.1
[01-839-7711]

Chief Salmon and Freshwater Fisheries Officer, I. R. H. Allan (*Senior Principal Scientific Officer*)

£4,390 to £5,015

Principal Scientific Officers, W. G. Hartley; R. Lloyd; J. P. Stevenson; B. Stott; A. Swain

£2,820 to £3,902

Under Secretary, C. D. E. Keeling......... £6,750

DEFENCE, EMERGENCIES AND CROP IMPROVEMENT DIVISION

Great Westminster House, Horseferry Road, S.W.1

[01-834-8511]

Assistant Secretary, W. E. Crump

£5,000 to £6,300

Principals, J. A. Christianson; J. L. Cope; D. Salton

£3,250 to £4,400

Senior Executive Officers, J. S. Bassett; H. G. Lovell; A. G. Robinson.....£2,775 to £3,400

FOOD POLICY DIVISION

Assistant Secretary, Mrs. J. M. Archer
£5,000 to £6,300
Principals, J. R. Catford; G. J. Hill; R. E. Melville; Miss B. M. Shedden ... £3,250 to £4,400
Senior Executive Officers, G. F. Buxton; K. J. Coleman; P. B. C. Stray ... £2,775 to £3,400

FOOD AND DRINK INDUSTRIES DIVISION

Assistant Secretary, Miss M. J. Crighton
£5,000 to £6,300
Principals, Mrs. P. E. Holloway, I.S.O.; J. F. Robinson; E. S. Virgo ... £3,250 to £4,400
Senior Executive Officer, C. J. Young
£2,775 to £3,400

FOOD STANDARDS AND SCIENCE DIVISION

Great Westminster House, Horseferry Road, S.W.1
[01-834-8511]
Assistant Secretary, R. F. Giles ... £5,000 to £6,300
Principals, H. M. Goodall, L. G. Hanson; A. D. McKay ... £3,250 to £4,400
Senior Executive Officers, N. K. S. Baker; B. G. Forrester; A. E. Jefferys; D. L. Orme; S. D. G. Simmons ... £2,775 to £3,400
Chief Scientific Adviser (Food), G. A. H. Elton
£6,380
Senior Principal Scientific Officers, T. J. Coomes; J. F. Hearne ... £4,930 to £5,015
Senior Grade Works Group, J. A. Carr
£3,575 to £4,208
Principal Scientific Officers, L. E. George; R. E. J. Goodman; D. J. McWeeney; D. D. Singer; R. B. Wilson ... £2,820 to £3,902

Under Secretary, G. R. Woodward ... £6,750

HORTICULTURE DIVISIONS I AND II

Great Westminster House, Horseferry Road, S.W.1
[01-834-8511]
Assistant Secretaries, O. A. Robertson; Miss M. E. Vince ... £5,000 to £6,300
Principals, F. S. Anderson; V. T. Humphreys; Miss G. D. McElnea; C. W. Tranter; T. L. W. Windle ... £3,250 to £4,400
Senior Executive Officers; J. N. Jackson; J. A. McCarthy; D. J. Peirce; W. A. Shaw; I. V. Wells ... £2,775 to £3,400

CO-OPERATION AND LABOUR DIVISION

83-91 Artillery Mansions, Victoria Street, S.W.1
[01-839-9030]
Assistant Secretary, J. Stopforth ... £5,000 to £6,300
Principals, J. A. Covell; L. W. Hogg
£3,250 to £4,400
Senior Executive Officers, H. Smeethe; A. D. Thomas
£2,775 to £3,400

GROUP C
Under Secretary, J. B. Foxlee ... £6,750

SAFETY, PESTICIDES AND INFESTATION CONTROL DIVISION

Great Westminster House, Horseferry Road, S.W.1
[01-834-8511]
Hook Rise South, Tolworth, Surbiton, Surrey
[01-337-6611]
Assistant Secretary, D. W. M. Herbert,
£5,000 to £6,300
Principals, V. H. Bath; J. A. Brown; R. C. McIvor ... £3,250 to £4,400
Senior Executive Officers, Miss J. Bailey; W. H. E. Davey; N. J. Pickering ... £2,775 to £3,400

Safety Inspectorate
Chief Inspector, J. C. Weeks ... £4,600 to £5,200
Deputy Chief Inspectors, T. J. Rowe; J. R. Whitaker
£3,250 to £4,400

PEST INFESTATION CONTROL LABORATORY

Hook Rise South, Tolworth, Surbiton, Surrey
[01-337-6611]
Director (Chief Scientific Officer), F. H. Jacob
£6,380
Senior Principal Scientific Officers, E. W. Bentley; J. A. Freeman, O.B.E. ... £4,390 to £5,015
Principal Scientific Officers, G. A. Brett; P. J. Bunyan; R. A. Davis; J. H. Greaves; D. S. Papworth; B. D. Rennison; F. P. Rowe; K. D. Taylor; R. H. Thompson; M. J. Van Den Heuvel; Miss G. C. Williams ... £2,820 to £3,902

London Road, Slough, Bucks.
[75-21295]
Deputy Director (Deputy Chief Scientific Officer), (vacant) ... £5,240 to £5,830
Senior Principal Scientific Officers, W. B. Brown; R. W. Howe ... £4,045 to £4,620
Principal Scientific Officers, C. W. Coombs; C. E. Dyte; A. A. Green, M.B.E.; D. A. Griffiths; S. G. B. Heuser; D. F. Horler; Miss M. B. Hyde; G. E. Woodroffe ... £2,820 to £3,902

FIELD RESEARCH STATION

Tangley Place, Worplesdon, Surrey
[Worplesdon 2581]
Senior Principal Scientific Officer, H. V. Thompson
£4,390 to £5,015
Principal Scientific Officers, H. G. Lloyd; A. R. Mead-Briggs; E. N. Wright ... £2,820 to £3,902

PLANT VARIETY RIGHTS OFFICE AND SEEDS DIVISION

Murray House, Vandon Street, S.W.1
[01-828-611]
83-91 Victoria Street, S.W.1
[01-839-9030]
Controller, L. J. Smith (*Assistant Secretary*)
£5,000 to £6,300
Principal, F. W. Black ... £3,250 to £4,400
Senior Executive Officers, L. Goldthorpe; Miss S. E. Kitchen; Miss E. V. Thornton. £2,775 to £3,400

LAND USE AND LIVESTOCK IMPROVEMENT DIVISION

Great Westminster House, Horseferry Road, S.W.1
[01-834-8511]
Assistant Secretary, M. L. David ... £5,000 to £6,300
Principals, T. Birtwistle; H. J. B. Rice; M. Ring; Mrs. J. J. Tait ... £3,250 to £4,400
Senior Executive Officers, Miss W. H. Burge; Mrs. K. M. Harry; J. Weston ... £2,775 to £3,400

Under Secretary, J. A. K. Christie ... £6,750

LAND IMPROVEMENT DIVISION

Great Westminster House, Horseferry Road, S.W.1
[01-834-8511]
Assistant Secretary, J. M. Grant ... £5,000 to £6,300
Principals, K. W. Boddie; M. Madden
£3,250 to £4,400
Senior Executive Officers, M. J. Griffiths; G. S. Johnson ... £2,775 to £3,400

LAND TENURE DIVISION

Great Westminster House, Horseferry Road, S.W.1
[01-834-8511]
Assistant Secretary, J. A. Barrah ... £5,000 to £6,300
Principal, M. T. Haddon ... £3,250 to £4,400
Senior Executive Officer, G. Belchamber
£2,775 to £3,400
Chief Accountant (Professional), L. C. Bentley
£3,258 to £3,873

LAND DRAINAGE, WATER SUPPLY
AND MACHINERY DIVISION
Great Westminster House, Horseferry Road,
S.W.1
[01-834-8511]
Assistant Secretary, A. Savage .... £5,000 to £6,300
Principals, R. J. Attwell; W. J. Duckham; D. W.
McCall; R. D. Rider........£3,250 to £4,400
Senior Executive Officers, J. L. Bole; J. E. B. Turner
£2,775 to £3,400

Under Secretary, A. C. Sparks............£6,750

ANIMAL HEALTH
DIVISIONS I, II AND III
Hook Rise South, Tolworth, Surbiton, Surrey
[01-337-6611]
Government Buildings, Leatherhead
Road, Chessington, Surrey
[01-397-5266]
Assistant Secretaries, E. H. Doling; A. F. Longworth;
W. E. Mason.............£5,000 to £6,300
Principals, W. T. Barker; K. A. Bird; S. Brookes;
J. Hensley; Mrs. A. G. Hills; L. Hurst; P. W.
Murphy; F. C. Parker; G. M. Pearce; N. W.
Taylor; R. G. Taylor; R. Townsend, D.F.C.
£3,250 to £4,400
Senior Executive Officers, D. Armstrong; R. J. Blake;
R. G. Bruce; C. A. Cockbill; A. Foreman; J. A.
Nisbet; J. H. Seymour; H. A. Straw; R. E. G.
West....................£2,775 to £3,440

Under-Secretary, J. H. Perrin..............£6,750

INFORMATION DIVISION
Chief Information Officer, N. Taylor
£5,000 to £6,300
Principals, T. J. B. Dawes (*Chief Press Officer*); J. A.
Walker....................£3,250 to £4,400
Senior Executive Officers, F. Evershed; R. J. Keil;
Mrs. M. D. White; G. E. Winter
£2,775 to £3,400
Librarian (Grade I), F. C. Hirst ... £3,250 to £4,400
Deputy Librarian (Grade II), E. A. R. Bush
£2,775 to £3,400

REGIONAL ADMINISTRATION
DIVISION
Great Westminster House, Horseferry Road,
S.W.1
[01-834-8511]
Assistant Secretary, W. A. Files ... £5,000 to £6,300
Principals, P. A. Cocking; G. B. Hopley; T. A.
Lambert....................£3,250 to £4,400
Senior Executive Officers, J. A. Davies; A. F. Mitson
£2,775 to £3,400

AGRICULTURAL DEVELOPMENT
AND ADVISORY SERVICE
Agriculture and Science
Chief Agricultural Officer, A. J. Davies.......£6,750
Senior Advisers, P. J. Macfarlan; F. W. Shepherd
£5,640
Senior Scientist, H. C. Gough..............£5,640
Deputy, W. Dermott.........£3,319 to £4,196
Chief Farm Management Adviser, W. H. Helme
£4,695 to £5,240
Director of Experiments, R. Gardner
£4,695 to £5,240
Chief Dairy Husbandry Adviser, J. Gibbons
£4,695 to £5,240
Chief Livestock Husbandry Adviser, W. Longrigg
£4,695 to £5,240
Chief Poultry Husbandry Adviser, J. A. Calvert
£4,695 to £5,240
Chief Mechanisation Adviser, C. Culpin, O.B.E.
£4,695 to £5,240
Regional Agricultural Officers, P. M. Bolam; E. S.
Carter; S. Culpin; H. Edmunds; S. L. Huth-
nance; P. M. T. Jones; J. R. Stubbs; M. Whalley
Taylor, M.B.E...........£4,695 to £5,240
Deputies, E. R. Bullen; J. B. Evans; L. W. Osborne;
Miss B. Thornborrow (+allce.).£3,319 to £4,196
County Agricultural Advisers, Grade I, W. R. B.
Carter; N. E. Chittenden; G. J. Clarke; G. A.

Dowse; M. W. Dymott; E. J. Evans; A. H. Fit-
ton; P. Holmes; R. Hope; J. S. Hopkins; S.
Houghton; G. H. Hughes; R. Hunter-Smith; F.
W. Jameson;I.E.Ketteringham; J. R. Keyworth;
K. Macleod; A. W. Mardon; P. W. Milligan; J.
F. Ormrod; J. Pendlebury; A. W. Prowel; H. E.
Shaw; K. W. Silverthorne, M.B.E.; J. A. M.
Sutherland; W. E. H. Telford; D. L. Torrance;
D. Tudor-Evans; S. E. Turner; T. E. Wathan
£3,319 to £4,196
Grade I Advisers:
Special Duties, R. G. Haines; I. Kinlock; J. A.
Rudderham; A. W. White...£3,319 to £4,196
Crop Husbandry, D. W. Beesley; S. A. Evans;
K. R. Hubbard; R. G. Hughes; H. Jackson; J. J.
North; J. B. Page; E. I. Prytherch
£3,319 to £4,196
Dairy Husbandry, W. H. Alexander, M.B.E.;
J. Beever; H. J. Brooks; W. E. Buck; J. Hutchi-
son; Miss M. Jones; T. I. Jones; Miss K. D.
Maddever, O.B.E.; A. H. Moseley; Miss D. M.
Phillips, O.B.E.; Miss S. H. Read.
£3,319 to £4,196
Entomologists, E. B. Brown; C. A. Collingwood;
B. A. Cooper; R. Gair; B. D. Moreton; L. E.
W. Stone; J. D. Thomas; J. H. White
£3,319 to £4,196
Farm Management, R. S. Boyer; H. V. Dengate;
G. D. Salmon; T. W. D. Theophilus; H. A.
Thomas; W. C. Weston....£3,319 to £4,196
Grassland Husbandry, S. Campbell; J. Davies; T. H.
Davies; R. M. Deakins; G. P. Hughes; C. D.
Price....................£3,319 to £4,196
Horticulture, A. R. Carter; C. I. Chapman; J. B.
Duggan; D. J. Fuller; E. C. Herwin; Miss H. M.
Hughes; W. G. Hume; E. R. Keighley; H. G.
Kingham; P. D. Lees; D. Mellard; A. Moore;
T. W. Pringle; F. A. Roach; L. Roberts; R. C.
Round; C. D. Walker; G. C. Williams
£3,319 to £4,196
Livestock Husbandry, J. E. Campion; E. G. Clifton;
F. K. Deeble; F. J. Fullbrook; E. L. Jones; J. R.
Noble; S. A. C. Oliver; C. G. Pointer; T.
Tweddle................£3,319 to £4,196
Mechanisation Advisers, D. P. Evans; F. L. Gammon;
M. N. S. Henderson; W. S. Shattock; G. P.
Shipway; G. Smith; H. R. Smith; G. B. H. Spear
£3,319 to £4,196
Microbiologists, J. Harrison; J. J. Panes; W. R.
Rosser....................£3,319 to £4,196
Nutrition Chemists, G. Alderman; A. Eden; J. R.
Griffiths; W. Lewis; J. R. Lloyd; N. Trinder
£3,319 to £4,196
Plant Pathologists, W. Campbell; D. L. G. Davies;
H. H. Glasscock; J. E. E. Jenkins; I. F. Storey;
R. E. Taylor; A. G. Walker; H. J. Wilcox
£3,319 to £4,196
Poultry Husbandry, A. E. Beer; F. Carter; R. F.
Hall; C. M. Hann; A. W. Jones; W. J. Lintin;
Capt. M. C. Morgan; E. Owen-Jones; C. T.
Riley; J. Shemtob.........£3,319 to £4,196
Soil Scientists, T. H. Caldwell; L. J. Hooper; R.
C. Little; E. Roberts; R. D. Russell; K. Shaw; J.
Webber; B. Wilkinson......£3,319 to £4,196

HORTICULTURAL MARKETING
INSPECTORS
Chief Horticultural Marketing Inspector, A. F.
Gardner....................£4,600 to £5,200
Deputy Inspectors, R. T. Deakin; W. E. H. Spencer
£3,250 to £4,400

EXPERIMENTAL HUSBANDRY FARMS
Directors, R. Bee; G. P. Chater; P. N. Harvey; P. J.
Jones; S. P. McClean; R. B. Mair; C. H. Mudd;
M. Roberts; F. E. Shotton; J. R. Thompson; R.
Wickens; J. C. Wilcox; J. M. Willcock
£3,319 to £4,196

EXPERIMENTAL HORTICULTURE
STATIONS
Directors, P. G. Allen; G. Baines; A. J. Bedding;
S. P. Craze; H. J. Eaton; W. S. English; J. M. S.
Potter, O.B.E.; F. G. Smith; E. G. Williams
£3,319 to £4,196

ENGINEERS

Chief Engineer, E. A. G. Johnson, C.B.E..... £6,120
Deputy Chief Engineers, G. Cole; K. H. Lambert ....£4,390 to £5,015
Senior Engineers, T. G. Batchelar; C. L. Clayton; R. H. Miers, M.B.E.; K. C. Noble; C. N. Prickett; A. C. Rice, M.B.E.; N. Stathe; B. D. Trafford ....£3,575 to £4,208

LAND

Chief Surveyor, A. J. Langdon............£6,750
Senior Principal Surveyor, J. Keir £5,000 to £5,620
Regional Surveyors, T. D. Cameron; J. H. Dernie; F. G. Eaton-Evans; J. D. Foster; A. C. Middleton; P. G. M. Riding; C. Robinson; H. Walton..................£5,000 to £5,620
Chief Architect and Buildings Officer, W. Magson, M.B.E..................£5,620
Land Commissioners, J. H. Atkinson; J. W. Brierley; A. Brocklehurst; A. J. W. Carlisle; H. Cartwright, T.D.; A. B. Corbin; A. F. Culley; M. C. Damon; W. H. Dempsey; C. Dobson; D. H. Draper; J. H. L. Dunster; F. C. Elliott; N. F. Finn, M.B.E.; D. B. S. Fitch; H. Harland; J. P. Harrison; J. B. Hill; A. P. Hind; J. F. Hoare; E. O. Hughes; P. J. Huguet; T. Jones; W. J. Kinghorn; J. S. Leach; K. S. Lycett; W. V. Machin; W. Metcalfe; B. H. Moore; L. M. Parsons; H. G. Penfold; R. B. Sayce; R. F. Smith; J. P. Smithies; N. E. Stroh; R. J. G. Taylor; J. J. Troon; R. H. Twinch; E. Vaughan; D. C. Wallace; R. H. Watkins; T. H. F. Whitton, T.D.; E. Wightmore; L. J. Williams; P. M. P. Williams; F. J. W. Winship; N. B. Wood; L. Woodhams..................£3,575 to £4,208
Senior Research Officers, Mrs. M. A. Dennis; D. J. Griffiths; Miss J. P. Morgan; Miss J. O'Connor; N. J. Sneesby; J. F. B. Tew.... £2,820 to £3,902

LIME

Chief Technical Officer, G. L. Gray £3,790 to £4,265

PLANT PATHOLOGY LABORATORY
Hatching Green, Harpenden
[Harpenden: 5241]

Director (Deputy Chief Scientific Officer), M. Cohen, Ph.D..................£5,240 to £5,830
Senior Principal Scientific Officers, R. de B. Ashworth; I. W. Prentice (Deputy Director); A. H. Strickland; H. L. G. Stroyan.. £4,390 to £5,015
Principal Scientific Officers, P. Aitkenhead; C. R. B. Baker; J. J. Baker; J. A. R. Bates; K. S. George; K. S. Gostick; Miss M. Gratwick; D. F. Lee; R. A. Lelliott; G. A. Lloyd; Miss F. J. H. Moore; B. A. Rose; J. M. A. Sly; J. F. Southey; G. Stell £2,820 to £3,902

Plant Health and Seeds Inspectors

Chief Inspector, J. P. Cleary.... £4,600 to £5,200
Deputy Chief Inspector, D. Page .. £3,250 to £4,400
Regional Plant Health and Seeds Inspectors, P. R. Boughey; C. Crompton; J. A. Hewitt; A. R. Martin; T. Parish; R. Varley £2,775 to £3,400

VETERINARY
Hook Rise South, Tolworth, Surbiton, Surrey
[01-337-6611]
Government Buildings, Leatherhead
Road, Chessington, Surrey
[01-397-5266]

Chief Veterinary Officer, A. G. Beynon **C.B.** £8,300
Director of Field Service, A. C. L. Brown .. £6,750
Deputy Directors of Field Services, R. V. Blamire; F. J. Hill; R. A. Richards; J. W. Simpson £5,460
Regional Veterinary Officers, J. C. Baird; G. S. Beattie; A. D. Campbell; J. G. Crowhurst; D. B. Davies; J. K. S. Elmslie; R. H. Ewart; A. Kelly; E. Lowes; R. B. T. Munro; J. W. R. Pearce; H. G. Silcock; J. Steele; R. L. Steele; T. W. Stobo; A. M. Taylor; G. B. Taylor; J. Watson; G. Wight; A. Wilson; W. W. Wilson £4,695 to £5,240

Deputy Regional Veterinary Officers, R. A. A. Beament; J. McQ. Brown; J. C. Dring; L. H. Green; A. M. K. McLeod; E. Madden; P. M. Marshall; A. Shaw; R. J. Smith; W. A. Watson .. £4,600
Divisional Veterinary Officers, I. W. Adamson; J. Aitken; J. R. Anderson; N. D. Baird; N. M. Barrie; D. L. Bowen; D. K. Bryson; D. R. P. Buckner; N. M. Burns; G. A. F. Butler; S. R. Campbell; G. S. R. Chalmers; D. Christie; W. A. Clark; D. M. Cochrane; J. Corder; J. G. Cormack; G. J. Crawford; H. Cremlyn-Hughes; D. C. Croft; A. J. Crowley; W. S. Davies; J. I. Davies; D. H. Deans; L. J. R. Devonald; I. B. Dick; T. P. Duffy; F. Dunlop; A. J. Dwyer; W. H. Dymock; H. Edwards; J. Edwardson; T. B. Elphick; A. D. G. Evans; H. T. J. Evans; R. Ford; E. Gallagher; I. G. George; W. G. Gerrand; A. C. Gillespie; H. M. Goalen; R. H. Goodhand; D. K. Gracie; A. M. Grant; J. R. Grey; E. Griffith; J. A. Grisedale; E. W. Hendrie; M. Herlihy; D. M. Hood; D. A. Hughes; R. Hunnam; W. T. Jackson; D. K. Jones; R. G. Jones; W. A. Jones; H. N. Kennedy; E. G. Lamb; G. V. Laugier; H. G. Lloyd; R. D. Locke; A. McAinsh; D. J. Macaulay; M. Macaulay; P. MacGregor; W. J. McIlroy; W. S. Mackay, I.S.O.; R. I. Macrae; R. T. H. Massey; R. C. Matheson; R. Moffat; J. E. Morris; J. H. Ockey; G. Ord; W. G. Parkinson; W. H. G. Rees; N. D. Ritchie; D. Robertson; D. M. Roe; E. W. J. Russell; J. L. Shaw; W. Simpson; A. J. Skea; A. W. Smith; J. G. Souter; A. Steele; E. A. Stewart; John Stewart; J. H. Stewart; A. G. J. Stubbins; G. B. Symons, W. Tait; J. Tarala; J. G. Taylor; D. L. Thomson; R. H. Thoumine; K. M. Tyrrell; C. W. M. Walker; J. M. Ware; A. H. Watson; J. G. Watson; R. H. Wilcox; J. C. Wilson; W. R. Wilson .. £3,302 to £4,213

VETERINARY LABORATORIES
New Haw, Weybridge
[01-29-41111]
Eskgrove, Lasswade, Midlothian
[Lasswade: 2025]

Director, Veterinary Laboratories and Veterinary Investigation Service, A. B. Paterson £6,750
Deputy Directors, Veterinary Laboratory, M. L. Burdin, O.B.E.; E. C. Hulse................£5,640
Senior Research Officers, Grade I, S. F. M. Davies; J. T. Done; T. E. Gibson; L. P. Joyner; S. B. Kendall; M. K. Lloyd; R. McNeil; W. J. B. Morgan; J. G. Ross; G. Slavin; H. N. Spears; D. L. Stewart; P. Stuart........ £4,390 to £5,015
Senior Research Officers, Grade II, W. M. Allen; P. H. Anderson; F. D. Asplin; M. Barr; R. B. A. Carnaghan; Miss S. F. Cartwright; G. A. Cullen; I. Davidson; G. Davies; P. S. Dawson; J. Donnelly; R. H. Duff; J. D. J. Harding; R. A. Huck; P. H. Lamont; R. D. Lapraik; I. W. Lesslie; Miss G. Lewis; A. F. Machin; D. J. MacKinnon; D. A. McMartin; L. M. Markson; J. F. Michel; P. G. Millar; C. B. Ollerenshaw; D. S. P. Patterson; D. H. Roberts; J. H. Rose; N. S. Saba; W. J. Sojka; S. Terlecki; W. V. S. Wijeratne; C. D. Wilson, I.S.O........... £3,302 to £4,213
Deputy Director, Veterinary Investigation Service, A. J. Stevens........................£5,640
Superintending Veterinary Investigation Officers, G. H. Bennett; J. C. Buxton; G. B. S. Heath; L. E. Hughes; W. H. Parker; C. N. Saunders; J. A. J. Venn....................£4,390 to £5,015
Veterinary Investigation Officers, D. R. Allen; N. H. Brooksbank; D. Buntain; F. G. Clegg; D. F. Collings; E. T. Davies; I. H. Fincham; E. A. Gibson; M. Gitter; S. A. Hall; J. F. Harbourne; E. J. Jack; G. F. Kershaw; D. C. Ostler; J. D. Paterson; A. H. Pill; H. E. Roberts; I. G. Shaw; W. B. V. Sinclair; D. M. Thomson; B. M. Williams; A. J. E. Woods.. £3,302 to £4,213
Senior Executive Officer (Laboratory Secretary), G. C. Hampson....................£2,775 to £3,400
Librarian (Grade II), D. E. Gray.. £2,775 to £3,400

REGIONAL ORGANIZATION

Regional Managers, G. H. C. Amos (West Midland); G. W. Ford (East Midland); B. Peart (Yorks. and Lancs.); F. H. Goodwin (Northern); K. Harrison Jones (South Western); R. M. Loosemore (South Eastern); D. M. Sims (Eastern)

(+ *allce.*) £5,000 to £6,300

Regional Officers (*Administration*) (*Assistant Secretaries*), D. F. Mogg (West Midland); B. J. Marshall (East Midland); J. H. Holroyd (Yorks. and Lancs.); H. A. S. Doughty (Northern); A. P. Stevens (South Western); A. J. Hoare (South Eastern); W. H. Pedley (Eastern)

£5,000 to £6,300

Regional Officers (*Agricultural Development and Advisory Service*), W. M. R. Evans (West Midland); H. E. Croxall (East Midland); J. R. Rundle (Yorks. and Lancs.); D. J. Drummond (Northern); F. J. Thomas (South Western); R. G. A. Lofthouse (South Eastern); M. Barker (Eastern)

£5,000 to £6,300

DIVISIONAL OFFICES

Divisional Executive Officers (*Principals*), D. A. Bainton (Beverley); P. B. Barraud (Maidstone); G. Bishop (Gloucester); A. E. Brewer (Alnwick); J. L. Bull (Huntingdon); D. R. Dow (Bury St. Edmunds); P. Ebbage, O.B.E. (Norwich); R. Fancourt (Northampton); J. Farrell, T.D. (Lincoln); H. W. Foot (Chelmsford); E. H. High (Nottingham); F. L. Hobson (March); R. J. Howard, D.S.O. (Truro); G. E. Howell (Shrewsbury); T. Johnston (Guildford); J. Kerr (Durham); E. A. Leslie (Oxford); E. D. O'Brien (Carlisle); A. Pickering (Preston); A. C. Robson (Northallerton); J. E. Simmons (Harrogate); C. D. Spencer (Exeter); C. S. Taylor, M.C. (Taunton); N. F. V. Williams (Winchester); C. N. Withinshaw (Crewe); T. B. Wood (Worcester)

£3,250 to £4,400

Divisional Officers (*Agricultural Development and Advisory Service*), W. T. Baker, T.D. (Guildford); D. C. Barber (Gloucester); G. H. Beard (Taunton); R. E. Blake, D.F.C. (Shrewsbury); W. Bowen-Thomas (Northallerton); V. Cory (Harrogate); J. F. Cottam (Carlisle); T. J. C. David (Durham); C. M. Green (Truro); R. W. Helme (Preston); A. H. Hogg (March); T. T. Hunter (Crewe); D. J. C. Jones (Worcester); J. R. Judson (Alnwick); J. B. Kerr (Northampton); J. G. Loxam (Bury St. Edmunds); K. B. Mosdell (Lincoln); R. Moss (Maidstone); P. A. Naylor (Winchester); T. W. Nicol (Oxford); G. Precious (Norwich); A. K. J. Quinney (Huntingdon); P. L. Rushton (Chelmsford); J. M. Threlkeld (Exeter); J. S. Vaughan (Beverley); G. A. Young (Nottingham)

WELSH DEPARTMENT
Plas Crug, Aberystwyth
[0970–3162]

Under Secretary (*Welsh Secretary*), H. E. Evans

£6,750

Regional Manager, E. G. Griffiths

(+ *allce.*) £5,000 to £6,300

Regional Officer (*Administration*) (*Assistant Secretary*), R. F. Kyle, I.S.O. . . . . £5,000 to £6,300

Regional Officer (*Agricultural Development and Advisory Service*), R. W. Soden, T.D.

£5,000 to £6,300

Senior Principal, J. Medway . . . . . . £4,600 to £5,200

Principals, D. B. L. Davies; D. J. Palmer

£3,250 to £4,400

Senior Executive Officers, R. Davies; W. F. R. Pearson, M.B.E.; J. V. F. Scannell; E. D. Swaffield

£2,775 to £3,400

DIVISIONAL OFFICES

Divisional Executive Officers (*Principals*), A. W. Bridges (Llandrindod Wells); F. Haddon (Ruthin); T. L. Jones (Cardiff); L. G. Keeley (Carmarthen); E. G. Richards (Caernarfon)

£3,250 to £4,400

Divisional Officers (*Agricultural Development and Advisory Service*), D. S. Downey (Llandrindod Wells); J. V. Evans (Ruthin); I. W. Jones (Caernarvon); A. Lloyd Lewis (Cardiff); A. J. B. Ratcliff (Carmarthen)

RESEARCH AND DEVELOPMENT DIVISION
Great Westminster House, Horseferry Road, S.W.1.
[01–834–8511]

Assistant Secretary, W. F. Darke. . £5,000 to £6,300

Principals, V. G. Codd; L. C. Gaskell; P. J. S. Walder. . . . . £3,250 to £4,400

FINANCE DEPARTMENT
Great Westminster House, Horseferry Road, S.W.1.
[01–834–8511]
Wellington House, Buckingham Gate, S.W.1.
[01–799–6693]
Government Buildings, Epsom Road, Guildford, Surrey.
[0483–68121]
Government Buildings, Block C, Tolcarne Drive, Pinner, Middlesex
[01–868–7161]

Principal Finance Officer, H. G. Button. £6,750

Assistant Secretaries, R. J. Bricknell, M.B.E.; C. R. Currie; T. A. Ivey; G. H. B. King

£5,000 to £6,300

Senior Principal, D. Kimber . . . £4,600 to £5,200

Principals, D. A. Atkinson; F. L. Charlton; B. I. Hagel; D. Hall; Miss D. Hastings, M.B.E.; J. W. Hewitt; A. E. Levy; J. Lindsay; H. J. Turner; L. W. Wayne. . . . . £3,250 to £4,400

Chief Accountants (*Professional*), R. W. Meikie; D. P. Scott; J. Thompson. . . £3,250 to £4,400

Senior Executive Officers, C. H. Allen; B. W. Brownsey; R. H. Charles; N. Critchley; F. J. J. Culcheth; W. Edgar; C. V. C. Embury; J. C. Everden; A. J. Gibbins; R. E. Hughes; F. E. Kenny; R. Little; E. H. M. McCarthy; H. Mayor; M. A. Payne; D. Rundle; L. B. Sholl; J. F. Thompson; Miss J. E. Tugwell; H. Waters; H. R. Winter; S. C. Yielding

£2,775 to £3,400

Senior Accountants (*Professional*), R. J. Kent; A. H. McKee; K. V. Stephens

£2,775 to £3,400

LEGAL DEPARTMENT
55 Whitehall, S.W.1.
[01–839–7711]

Legal Adviser and Solicitor, Sir Charles Davis, C.B.

£9,000

Principal Assistant Solicitor, G. F. Aronson . . £6,750

Assistant Solicitors, R. W. Brown; W. D. Curnock; A. Hall-Brown; H. R. Reade; F. A. Richards; H. G. Roberts; W. M. Wadham-Smith

£4,555 to £5,640

Senior Legal Assistants, A. J. Bligh; C. A. Burton; M. G. de Sausmarez; T. B. Foster; J. S. Hunt; G. J. Jenkins; G. W. Jones; J. H. Jordan; N. Monro; A. E. Munir; L. Neville; D. A. Pearson; E. A. Platt, O.B.E.; G. R. J. Robertson; P. Stafford; J. O. Stansfield; J. D. Westlake; W. F. Williams. . . £3,286 to £4,390

Senior Executive Officer, D. R. Lockhart

£2,775 to £3,400

ROYAL BOTANIC GARDENS, KEW

Gardens open daily (except Christmas Day), 10 a.m. to Sunset or 8 p.m. Houses: 1 p.m. to dusk or 4.50 p.m. (weekdays), 1 p.m. to dusk or 5.50 p.m. (Sundays). Museums: 10 a.m. to dusk or 4.50 p.m. (weekdays); 10 a.m. to dusk or 5.50 p.m. (Sundays). Closed on Christmas Day, Boxing Day and Good Friday. Admission 1p. Dogs not admitted. In 1970 there were 1,050,615 visitors to Kew Gardens.

Director of Royal Botanic Gardens, Prof. J. Heslop-Harrison. £6,750

Deputy Director, J. P. M. Brenan . . £5,240 to £5,830

Senior Principal Scientific Officers R. W. G. Dennis; P. S. Green; K. Jones (*Keeper, Jodrell Laboratory*)

£4,390 to £5,015

Principal Scientific Officers, W. D. Clayton; D. M. Dring; L. L. Forman; F. N. Hepper; Miss F. M. Jarrett; C. Jeffrey; E. Launert; R. D. Meikle; R. M. Polhill; D. A. Reid; P. A. Thompson; C. C. Townsend; B. Verdcourt

£2,820 to £3,902

Supervisor of Studies, L. A. Pemberton

£2,775 to £3,400

Librarian, Grade II, R. G. C. Desmond

£2,775 to £3,400

Curator, R. L. Shaw . . . . £3,028 to £3,873
Secretary (Principal), R. W. King, D.F.C.

£3,250 to £4,400

CHAIRMEN OF COUNTY AGRICULTURAL EXECUTIVE COMMITTEES (ENGLAND AND WALES)

J. W. Allen (*Westmorland*); The Lord Barnard, T.D. (*Durham*); T. Brown (*Hunts. and Peterborough*); Sir John Colfox, Bt. (*Dorset*); J. H. Cooke, O.B.E. (*Staffs.*); P. K. Crow (*Salop*); R. J. Cyster (*Sussex East*)); T. D. Dampney, T.D. (*Hants.*); G. T. Davies (*Beds.*); G. T. Davies, O.B.E. (*Caernarvon*); W. Jones Davies (*Radnor*); Maj. J. E. M. Dugdale (*Montgomery*); J. R. Dunstan, O.B.E. (*Cornwall*); J. Gwyn Evans, O.B.E. (*Cardigan*); S. Farrant, M.B.E. (*Berks.*); H. R. Finn, C.B.E. (*Kent*); J. R. C. Gilling (*Somerset*); J. A. I. Hale (*Isles of Scilly*); Maj. B. A. F. Hervey-Bathurst (*Hereford*). Col. R. F. Hesketh, O.B.E. T.D. (*Lancs*); Maj. G. B. Heywood, M.B.E.; (*Glos.*), Lt.-Col. J. H. V. Higgon, O.B.E. (*Pembroke*); J. B. Holliday, O.B.E. (*Cumberland*); J. N. Holmes (*Suffolk*); L. G. F. Horrell, O.B.E. (*Devon*); J. Hughes, O.B.E. (*Worcs.*); C. Jones (*Anglesey*); J. G. Jones (*Merioneth*); K. W. T. Jones, O.B.E. (*Brecon*); J. T. Richardson Jones, O.B.E. (*Denbigh*); The Lord Kenyon (*Flint*); P. Langmead (*Sussex West*)); G. E. Limb (*Notts.*); A. I. May, O.B.E. (*Yorks. (East Riding*)); E. H. Morris (*Cambs. and Isle of Ely*); J. R. D. Morten, O.B.E. (*Derbyshire*); H. D. Petch (*Yorks. (North Riding*)); Col. The Hon. R. G. H. Phillimore O.B.E. (*Oxon.*); P. R. Proctor (*Lincs (Kesteven)*); I. W. Renner, D.F.C. (*Rutland*); G. Richards, O.B.E. (*Glamorgan*); W. J. S. Richards, O.B.E. (*Carmarthen*); J. C. Riddell, O.B.E. (*Northumberland*); D. C. B. Riviere (*Norfolk*); J. L. Roughton, C.B.E. (*Lincs. Lindsey*); P. D. Sapsed (*Herts.*); A. J. Saul (*Lincs. Holland*); J. W. Shirley, O.B.E. (*Bucks.*).; Sir Charles Shuckburgh, Bt. (*Warwicks.*); R. S. Smith (*Northants.*); W. F. Stanley (*Leics.*); R. A. Stark, O.B.E. (*Isle of Wight*); J. M. Stratton (*Wilts.*); J. E. Tabor, O.B.E. (*Essex*); R. E. Thornton (*Surrey*); Lt.-Col. Sir Richard Verdin, O.B.E., T.D. (*Cheshire*); A. Watson (*Yorks. (W. Riding*); K. G. G. Weekes (*Monmouth*).

AGRICULTURAL RESEARCH COUNCIL

160 Great Portland Street, W.1

The Agricultural Research Council was incorporated by Royal Charter on July 23, 1931. The *Science and Technology Act,* 1965, transferred responsibility for the Research Council to the Secretary of State for Education and Science and a new Charter received Royal approval in 1967 The Council is charged with the organization and development of agricultural and food research and may, in particular, establish or develop institutions or departments of institutions and make grants for investigation and research relating to the advance of agriculture. The Council is financed from the Parliamentary vote of the Department of Education and Science.

Council, The Hon. J. J. Astor, M.B.E. (*Chairman*); The Hon. J. Addington; A. G. Beynon; W. A. Biggar, O.B.E., M.C.; Prof. P. W. Brian, SC.D., F.R.S.; Major J. E. M. Dugdale, T.D.; Prof. J. L. Harley, D.PHIL., F.R.S.; Prof. H. Harris, D.PHIL. F.R.S.; W. E. Jones; Prof. Sir Bernard Katz, M.D., PH.D., SC.D., F.R.S.; J. S. Martin; K. S. Mather, C.B.E., D.SC., F.R.S.; Prof. A. Neuberger, C.B.E., M.D., PH.D.; Prof. C. L. Oakley, C.B.E., M.D., D.SC., F.R.S.; Sir John Ritchie, C.B., F.R.S.E.; J. I. Smith; The Visct. Trenchard, M.C.; Prof. A. R. Ubbelohde, C.B.E., D.SC., F.R.S.

Secretary, Sir Ronald Baskett, O.B.E.

Second Secretary, Prof. Helen K. Porter, F.R.S.; F.R.S.E.

Deputy Secretary, W. E. Berry, C.B.E., PH.D.

Assistant Secretaries, D. J. Parkinson, O.B.E.; F. J. S. Culley; G. M. P. Myers.

Scientific Advisers to the Secretary, K. N. Burns; E. Lester; R. Scarisbrick, PH.D.; K. L. Robinson, D.SC.; G. C. Stevenson; C. C. Webster, C.M.G., PH.D.

Senior Principal, J. H. Shimwell.

Principals, L. S. Porter, O.B.E.; M. R. Beauchamp; K. H. J. Clarke; E. E. Croker; F. V. Bird, O.B.E.; T. S. Coltman.

Senior Executive Officers, J. F. Gilliland; Mrs. M. G. Kevis; C. Mason.

For the Research Institutes under the control of the Council, *see Index.*

EXECUTIVE COUNCIL OF THE COMMONWEALTH AGRICULTURAL BUREAUX

Farnham House, Farnham Royal, Bucks.

This Commonwealth organization, governed by an Executive Council composed of nominees of the various Commonwealth Governments, including one for the dependent territories, was set up in 1929 to administer bureaux organized to act as clearing houses of information on research in eight specialized fields of agricultural science, and financed from a common fund provided by the Governments of the Commonwealth and the Republic of Ireland. The Governments of the Commonwealth and Empire instructed it in 1933 to supervise the administration and finances of the Commonwealth (formerly Imperial) Institute of Entomology, the Commonwealth (formerly Imperial) Mycological Institute and the Commonwealth Institute of Biological Control (formerly the Imperial Parasite Service), and in 1937 to organize bureaux for Forestry and Dairy Science. A Commonwealth Bureau of Agricultural Economics has since been established and an International Food Information Service inaugurated. The Annual Reports of the Council are submitted to each of the Governments through their several members on the Council. The bureaux are attached to appropriate research institutions. but are distinct from them.

Chairman, V. Armstrong, PH.D. (*New Zealand*).
Vice-Chairman, E. S. Kapotwe (*Zambia*).
Secretary, Sir Thomas Scrivenor, C.M.G.

Institutes

Commonwealth Institute of Entomology, 56 Queen's Gate, S.W.7. *Director,* R. G. Fennah, SC.D.
Commonwealth Mycological Institute, Ferry Lane, Kew, Surrey. *Director,* A. Johnston.
Commonwealth Institute of Biological Control, Gordon Street, Curepe, Trinidad. *Director,* F. J. Simmonds, PH.D.. D.SC.
Commonwealth Institute of Helminthology, The White House, 103 St. Peter's Street, St. Albans, Herts.— *Director,* Miss S. M. Willmott, PH.D.

Bureaux

Agricultual Economics, Dartington House, Little Clarendon Street, Oxford.—*Director,* J. O. Jones.
Animal Breeding and Genetics, Animal Breeding Research Organization, The King's Buildings, West Mains Road, Edinburgh 9, —*Director,* J. P. Maule.
Animal Health, Central Veterinary Laboratory, New Haw, Weybridge, Surrey.—*Director,* M. R. Dhanda.
Animal Nutrition, Rowett Research Institute, Bucksburn, Aberdeen, Scotland.—*Director,* Miss D. L. Duncan, PH.D.
Dairy Science and Technology, National Institute for Research in Dairying, Shinfield, Reading. —*Director,* E. J. Mann.
Forestry, Commonwealth Forestry Institute. South Parks Road, Oxford.—*Director,* P. G. Beak, M.B.E.

Horticulture and Plantation Crops, East Malling Research Station, nr. Maidstone, Kent.—*Director,* G. E. Tidbury.

Pastures and Field Crops, Hurley, nr. Maidenhead, Berks. *Director,* P. J. Boyle.

Plant Breeding and Genetics, Department of Agricultural Science and Applied Biology, Downing Street Cambridge.—*Director,* R. H. Richens, Ph.D.

Soils, Rothamsted Experimental Station, Harpenden, Herts.—*Director,* W. D. Brind.

AIR REGISTRATION BOARD

Brabazon House, Redhill, Surrey
[Redhill: 65966]

Set up on Feb. 26, 1937, under the *Companies Act,* the Board is an autonomous non-profit making limited company. Delegated to the Board are certain powers relating to the design, construction and maintenance of civil aircraft; investigation by surveyors of aircraft and associated equipment for the purpose of recommending to the Minister concerning issues and renewals of certificates of airworthiness. The Board also conducts technical examinations for licences of aircraft maintenance engineers, flight engineers and commercial pilots.
Chairman, The Lord Kings Norton, Ph.D.
Chief Executive, W. Tye, C.B.E.

AIR TRANSPORT LICENSING BOARD

Gaywood House, Great Peter Street, S.W.1.
[01-222-7231]

Established by the *Civil Aviation (Licensing) Act,* 1960, to license air services (with certain exceptions). The Board considers representations in relation to air transport services by U.K. registered aircraft, or to facilities, tariffs or charges in connection therewith, reporting their conclusions and recommendations to the Board of Trade.
Chairman, J. H. Lawrie £7,000
Deputy Chairman, Sir Algernon Rumbold, K.C.M.G.,
C.I.E. .... *(part-time)* £3,000
Members, Sir Roy Allen, C.B.E.; C. J. Highton;
N. A. Morling; N. C. Pearson, O.B.E.
each 20 gns. per session
Secretary, C. R. F. Lark........ £4,045 to £5,200

COLLEGE OF ARMS OR HERALDS COLLEGE

Queen Victoria Street, E.C.4
[01-248-2762]

The College of Arms is open daily from 10–4 (Saturdays, 10–1, by appointment) when an Officer of Arms is in attendance to deal with enquiries by the public, though such enquiries may also be directed to any of the Officers of Arms, either personally or by letter.

There are 13 officers of the College, 3 Kings of Arms, 6 Heralds and 4 Pursuivants, who specialize in genealogical and heraldic work for their respective clients. The College possesses the finest records on these subjects in the world. It is the official repository of the Arms and pedigrees of English, Northern Irish, and Commonwealth families and their descendants, and its records include official copies of the records of Ulster King of Arms, the originals of which remain in Dublin.

Arms have been and still are granted by Letters Patent from the Kings of Arms under Authority delegated to them by the Sovereign, such authority having been expressly conferred on them since at least the fifteenth century. A right to Arms can only be established by the registration in the official records of the College of Arms of a pedigree showing direct male line descent from an ancestor already appearing therein as being entitled to Arms, or by making application to the College of Arms for a Grant of Arms.
Earl Marshal, His Grace the Duke of Norfolk, K.G., P.C., G.C.V.O., G.B.E. T.D., Royal Victorian Chain.

Kings of Arms

Garter, Sir Anthony Richard Wagner, K.C.V.O., D.Litt., F.S.A.
Clarenceux, John Riddell Bromhead Walker, M.V.O., M.C.
Norroy and Ulster, Richard Preston Graham-Vivian, M.V.O., M.C.

Heralds

Chester, Walter John George Verco, C.V.O. (*Earl Marshal's Secretary*).
Windsor (and Registrar), Alexander Colin Cole, F.S.A.
Richmond, John Philip Brooke Brooke-Little, M.V.O., F.S.A.
Somerset, Lt.-Col. Rodney Onslow Dennys, M.V.O., O.B.E., F.S.A.
York, Conrad Marshall John Fisher Swan, Ph.D.
Lancaster (vacant).

Pursuivants

Portcullis Michael Maclagan, F.S.A.
Bluemantle, Francis Sedley Andrus.
Rouge Croix, David Hubert Boothby Chesshyre.
Rouge Dragon, Theobald David Mathew.

COURT OF THE LORD LYON

H.M. New Register House, Edinburgh
[031-556-7255]

The Scottish Court of Chivalry, including the genealogical jurisdiction of the *Ri-Sennachie* of Scotland's Celtic Kings, adjudicates rights to arms and administration of *The Scottish Public Register of All Arms and Bearings* (under 1672 cap. 47) and *Public Register of All Genealogies.* The Lord Lyon presides and judicially establishes rights to existing arms or succession to Chiefship, or for cadets with scientific "differences" showing position in clan or family. Pedigrees are also established by decrees of Lyon Court, and by Letters Patent. As *Royal Commissioner in Armory,* he grants Patents of Arms (which constitute the grantee and heirs noble in the Noblesse of Scotland) to "virtuous and well-deserving " Scotsmen, and petitioners (personal or corporate) in Her Majesty's overseas realms of Scottish connection, and issues birthbrieves. In Scots Law, Arms are protected by Statute; their usurpation is punishable, and the Registration Fees of Honour on patents and matriculations are payable to H.M. Exchequer.
Lord Lyon King of Arms, Sir James Monteith Grant, K.C.V.O., W.S., F.S.A. *Scot.*

Heralds

Marchmont, Sir Thomas Innes of Learney, G.C.V.O., LL.D., F.S.A. *Scot.,* Advocate.
Rothesay, Lt.-Col. H. A. B. Lawson, C.V.O., F.S.A. *Scot.*
Albany, Sir Iain Moncreiffe of that Ilk, Bt., Ph.D., Advocate.

Pursuivants

Kintyre, Charles Eliot Jauncey of Tullichettle, Q.C. W.S., F.S.A., *Scot.*
Carrick, Malcolm Rognvald Innes of Edingight, W.S., F.S.A., *Scot.*
Unicorn, John Inglis Drever Pottinger.
Falkland Pursuivant Extraordinary, Major David Maitland Maitland-Titterton, T.D.

Lyon Clerk and Keeper of Records, Malcolm Rognvald Innes of Edingight, W.S., F.S.A. *Scot.*
Procurator-Fiscal, Ivor Reginald Guild, W.S.
Herald Painter, Miss M. J. Gordon.
Macer, Thomas C. Gray.

ART GALLERIES, ETC.

ROYAL FINE ART COMMISSION

2 Carlton Gardens, S.W.1
[01-930-3935]

Appointed in May, 1924, "to enquire into such questions of public amenity or of artistic importance as may be referred to them from time to time by any of our Departments of State, and to report

thereon to such Department ; and, furthermore, to give advice on similar questions when so requested by public or quasi-public bodies, where it appears to the said Commission that their assistance would be advantageous." In August, 1933, a Royal Warrant extended the Terms of Reference of the Commission—" so that it shall also be open to the said Commission, if they so desire, to call the attention of any of Our Departments of State, or of the appropriate public or quasi-public bodies, to any project or development which in the opinion of the said Commission may appear to affect amenities of a national or public character"; in May, 1946, a Royal Warrant further extended the Terms of Reference of the Commission as follows :—

We Do give and grant unto you, or any three or more of you, full power to call before you such persons as you shall judge likely to afford you any information upon the subject of this Our Commission; and also to call for, have access to and examine all such books, documents, registers and records as may afford you the fullest information on the subject, and to inquire of and concerning the premises by all other lawful ways and means whatsoever: We Do authorize and empower you, or any three or more of you, to visit and personally inspect such places as you may deem it expedient so to inspect for the more effectual carrying out of the purposes aforesaid:

Chairman, Sir Colin Anderson, K.B.E.

Commissioners Sir Hugh Casson, R.A., F.R.I.B.A.; Miss E. Chesterton; Howard Colvin, C.B.E.; A. W. Cox, F.R.I.B.A.; P. M. Dowson, C.B.E.; Raymond Erith, R.A., F.R.I.B.A.; Sir Ralph Freeman, C.V.O., C.B.E.; Sir Gilbert Inglefield, G.B.E., T.D.; The Lord Llewelyn-Davies, F.R.I.B.A.; Sir Leslie Martin, C.B.E., F.R.I.B.A.,; Prof. Sir Nikolaus Pevsner, C.B.E., Ph.D., F.S.A.; David Piper, C.B.E., F.S.A.; John Piper; A. J. P. Powell, A.R.A., F.R.I.B.A.; (three vacancies)

Secretary, Prof. F. Fielden, F.R.I.B.A.

ROYAL FINE ART COMMISSION FOR SCOTLAND
22 Melville Street,
Edinburgh 3
[031-225-5434]

Commissioners, The Lord Johnston, T.D. (*Chairman*); J. A. Coia, C.B.E., R.S.A., F.R.I.B.A.; Sir Charles Connell; W. A. Fairhurst, C.B.E.; N. Johnston, R.S.A., F.R.I.B.A.; C. L. Matthew, F.R.I.B.A.; Prof. Sir Robert Matthew, C.B.E., A.R.S.A., F.R.I.B.A.; R. Philipson, R.S.A.; A. Reiach, O.B.E., A.R.S.A. F.R.I.B.A.; Mrs. Murray Usher; H. A. Wheeler, A.R.S.A.

Secretary, J. T. Bannatyne, M.B.E.

NATIONAL GALLERY
Trafalgar Square, W.C.2
[01-930-7618-9]

Hours of opening.—Weekdays 10 to 6 (June–Sept. Tuesdays and Thursdays 10 to 9), Sundays and Boxing Day 2 to 6. Closed on Good Friday, Christmas Eve, and Christmas Day.

The National Gallery is the result of a Parliamentary grant of £60,000 in 1824 for the purchase and exhibition of the Angerstein collection of pictures, the present building being opened in 1838 and enlarged in 1876, 1887, 1911, 1928, 1930, 1937 and 1961. Expenses for 1970–71 were estimated at £850,000.

TRUSTEES

Sir John Witt (*Chairman*); Henry Moore, O.M., C.H.; Denis Mahon, C.B.E.; Andrew Forge; John Piper; The Lord Robbins, C.H., C.B. F.S.A.; Sir Edward Playfair, K.C.B.; Dame Veronica Wedgwood, D.B.E.; Miss Mary Woodall, C.B.E., D.Litt, F.S.A.; Sir Gordon Sutherland, F.R.S.; G. W. H. Richardson, M.B.E.

OFFICERS

Director, Martin Davies, C.B.E............£6,925
Keeper, M. V. Levey, M.V.O.....£4,565 to £5,190
Deputy Keeper, C. H. M. Gould £3,960 to £4,565

Assistant Keepers I, A. Braham; A. Smith
£2,368 to £3,826
Scientific Adviser to the Trustees, R. H. G. Thomson
£4,565 to £5,190
Chief Restorer, A. W. Lucas, O.B.E.
£4,565 to £5,190
Building and Security, G. Fox ... £3,425 to £4,575
Finance and Establishments, R. H. Mitchem
£2,950 to £3,975

NATIONAL PORTRAIT GALLERY
St. Martin's Place, Charing Cross Road, W.C.2
[01-930-8511]
Open Monday to Friday 10 to 5. Saturday 10 to 6. Sunday 2 to 6.

The first grant was made in 1856 to form a gallery of the portraits of the most eminent persons in British history, the collections being successively housed in Great George Street, Westminster, in South Kensington, and in Bethnal Green. The present building was opened in 1896, £80,000 being contributed to its cost by Mr. W. H. Alexander; an extension erected at the expense of Lord Duveen was opened in 1933. The amount for salaries and expenses, including a grant of £43,000 for purchase of portraits, was estimated at £164,000 for 1970–71.

Chairman, The Lord Kenyon.

Trustees, The Lord President of the Council; The President of the Royal Academy of Arts; Field-Marshal Sir Gerald Templer, K.G., G.C.B., G.C.M.G., K.B.E., D.S.O.; Lawrence Gowing, C.B.E.; The Duke of Grafton, F.S.A.; J. H. Plumb, Ph.D., Litt.D., F.B.A., F.S.A.; A. D. Powell, C.B.E.; Sir Gyles Isham, Bt., F.S.A.; The Viscount de L'Isle, V.C., K.G., P.C., G.C.M.G., G.C.V.O.; Sir John Summerson, C.B.E., F.B.A., F.S.A.; Dame Helen Gardner, D.B.E., F.B.A., Sir Christopher Cockerell, C.B.E., F.R.S.; The Countess of Longford; Sir Philip Magnus-Allcroft, Bt.; Prof. J. McManners; J. P. Ehrman, F.B.A.

Director, Keeper and Secretary, R. C. Strong, Ph.D., F.S.A....................£5,065
Assistant Keepers (I), J. F. Kerslake, F.S.A.; R. L. Ormond....................£2,193 to £3,651

TATE GALLERY
Millbank, S.W.1
[01-828-1712]

Hours of opening.—Weekdays 10 to 6. Sundays 2 to 6. Closed on Good Friday, Christmas Eve, Christmas Day and Boxing Day.

The Tate Gallery comprises two national art collections: (*a*) British painting, from the 16th century to the present day, including works by Turner, Blake, Constable and the Pre-Raphaelites; (*b*) Modern Foreign Painting, from the Impressionists, and Modern Sculpture, British and foreign. There is an almost continuous programme of temporary exhibitions within the field of the collection. The Gallery was opened in 1897 the cost of erection (£80,000) being defrayed by Sir Henry Tate, who also contributed the nucleus of the present collection. The Turner Wing, built at the expense of Sir Joseph Duveen was opened in 1910. Lord Duveen defrayed the cost of galleries to contain the collection of modern foreign painting, completed in 1926, and a new sculpture hall, completed in 1937. Expenses for 1970–71 were estimated at £593,000.

Director, Sir Norman Reid..............£6,120
Trustees, Sir Robert Sainsbury (*Chairman*); S. de Ferranti; The Lord Harlech, P.C., K.C.M.G.; Dame Barbara Hepworth, D.B.E.; H. Hodgkin; G. A. Jellicoe, C.B.E., F.R.I.B.A.; N. MacDermot, C.B.E., Q.C.; S. Mason, C.B.E.; J. Piper; E. J. Power.
Keeper of the British Collection, M. R. F. Butlin
£4,390 to £5,015
Keeper of the Modern Collection, R. E. Alley
£4,390 to £5,015
Keeper of Exhibitions and Education, M. G. Compton
£4,390 to £5,015
Keeper of Conservation, S. Slabczynski
£4,390 to £5,015

Deputy Keeper, Mrs. J. Jeffreys . . £3,685 to £4,390
Assistant Keepers (Class I), T. Measham; R. E.
Morphet; L. A. Parris; R. Rattenbury; A. Sey-
mour; W. Vaughan . . . . . £2,193 to £3,651
Establishment Officer, M. B. G. Botley
£2,775 to £3,400

WALLACE COLLECTION
Hertford House, Manchester Square, W.1
[01-935-0687]
Admission free. Open on weekdays 10 a.m. to
5 p.m.; Sundays 2 p.m. to 5 p.m. Closed on Good
Friday, Christmas Eve and Christmas Day.
The Wallace Collection was bequeathed to the
nation by the widow of Sir Richard Wallace, Bt.,
K.C.B., M.P., on her death in 1897, and Hertford
House was subsequently acquired by the Govern-
ment. The collection includes pictures, drawings
and miniatures, French furniture, sculpture, bronzes,
porcelain, armour and miscellaneous *objets d'art*.
The total net expenses were estimated at £114,000
in 1970–71.
Director, F. J. B. Watson, C.V.O., F.S.A. . . £5,190
Assistant Directors, R. A. Cecil; A. V. B. Norman,
F.S.A. . . . . £2,175 to £3,826

NATIONAL GALLERIES OF SCOTLAND
Edinburgh
[031-556-8921]
Comprising :—
National Gallery of Scotland, Mound, Edinburgh, 1.
Scottish National Portrait Gallery, Queen Street,
Edinburgh 2.
Scottish National Gallery of Modern Art, Inverleith
House, Royal Botanic Garden, Edinburgh, 4.
Director of the National Galleries of Scotland, T. H.
Scrutton, C.B.E., ... £5,200
Keeper of Paintings, C. E. Thompson
£3,396 to £4,045
Assistant Keeper of Paintings, H. N. A. Brigstock
£2,193 to £3,651
Keeper of Prints and Drawings, K. R. Andrews
£3,396 to £4,045
Keeper, Scottish National Portrait Gallery, Robert E.
Hutchison . . . . £3,396 to £4,045
Assistant Keeper, Scottish National Portrait Gallery,
D. Thomson . . . . £2,193 to £3,651
Keeper, Scottish National Gallery of Modern Art,
W. D. Hall . . (+ allce. £250) £2,193 to £3,651
Secretary Accountant and Establishment Officer, S. M.
Ellis . . . . £2,529 to £3,099

(For other British Art Galleries, *see* Index.)

UNITED KINGDOM ATOMIC ENERGY AUTHORITY
11 Charles II Street, S.W.1
[01-930-6262]
Established by the *Atomic Energy Authority Act,
1954*, the Authority took over, on August 1, 1954,
the control of atomic energy research and develop-
ment. The Minister of Trade and Industry is
responsible to Parliament for general atomic energy
policy and for money provided for the Authority.
Chairman, Sir John Hill, Ph.D. £17,000
Deputy Chairman, Sir Charles Cunningham, K.C.B.,
K.B.E., C.V.O. £13,500
Members (Full-time), Air Chief Marshal Sir Denis
Barnett, G.C.B., C.B.E., D.F.C. (Weapons); R. V.
Moore, G.C., C.B.E. . . . . . each £8,000 to £12,000
(Part-time) The Lord Kearton, O.B.E., F.R.S.;
S. J. Pears; J. L. Williams, C.B.E.; Prof. Sir Brian
Flowers, each £1,000; E. S. Booth, C.B.E.,
F.R.S., Dr. N. L. Franklin, O.B.E. (unpaid).
Secretary, A. M. Allen.

BRITISH AIRPORTS AUTHORITY
2 Buckingham Gate, S.W.1
Set up under the *Airports Authority Act, 1965*, to
manage the three London airports—Heathrow,
Gatwick and Stansted—also Prestwick Airport,
from April 1, 1966 and Edinburgh Airport from
April 1, 1971.
Chairman, P. G. Masefield . . . . . . (part-time) £9,000

BRITISH BROADCASTING CORPORATION
Broadcasting House, W.1
[01-580-4468]
The BBC was incorporated under Royal
Charter as successor to the British Broadcasting
Company, Ltd., whose licence expired Dec. 31,
1926. Its present Charter came into force July 30,
1964, and expires July 31, 1976. The Chairman,
Vice-Chairman and other Governors are appointed
by the Crown. The BBC is financed by revenue
from receiving licences for the Home services
and by a Grant in Aid from Parliament for the
External services. The total number of licences in
force in Feb. 1970 was 18,209,652, of which
15,577,905 were for combined radio and television
licences and 248,948 for combined radio and colour
television services.
Chairman, The Lord Hill of Luton, P.C.
Vice-Chairman, Lady Plowden £2,000
Governors, Lady Avonside, O.B.E. (Scotland), £2,000;
Prof. G. Williams, D.Litt. (Wales), £2,000; The
Lord Dunleath, T.D. (N. Ireland); Sir Ralph
Murray, K.C.M.G., C.B.; Sir Robert Bellinger,
G.B.E.; P. N. Wilson, O.B.E., D.S.C.; T. Jackson;
Dame Mary Georgina Green, D.B.E.;
(each) £1,000
Director-General, C. J. Curran.
Managing Directors, H. Wheldon, O.B.E., M.C.
(Television); I. Trethowan (Radio); G. E. H. Man-
sell (External Broadcasting). Directors, J. Redmond
(Engineering); Hon. K. H. L. Lamb (Public Affairs);
D. F. Attenborough (Programmes, Television);
H. P. Hughes (Finance); P. H. Newby (Pro-
grammes, Radio); M. Tinniswood (Personnel).
Deputy Director of Engineering, D. E. Todd
General Manager, Publications, M. W. Webb.
Legal Adviser, E. C. Robbins, C.B.E.
Controller, Information Services, G. T. M. de M.
Morgan, M.C.
Head of Publicity, G. Campey, O.B.E.
Head of Secretariat, R. D. Pendlebury, M.B.E.
Secretary, C. D. Shaw.

Controllers of Regional Offices
English Regions, P. M. Beech, C.B.E., Broadcasting
Centre, Pebble Mill Road, Birmingham.
Scotland, A. Milne, Broadcasting House, Queen
Margaret Drive, Glasgow, W.2.
Northern Ireland, B. W. Maguire, Broadcasting
House, 25–27 Ormeau Avenue, Belfast.
Wales, J. H. Rowley, C.B.E., Broadcasting House,
Llandaff, Cardiff.

BRITISH EUROPEAN AIRWAYS CORPORATION
Bealine House, Ruislip, Middlesex
[01-845-1234]
Chairman and Chief Executive, H. E. Marlling, C.B.E.,
M.C. £17,000
Deputy Chairman, Sir Kenneth Keith
(part-time) £2,000
Deputy Chief Executive, K. G. Wilkinson.
Executive Board Members, C. A. Herring; Capt. J.
W. G. James, O.B.E.; P. C. F. Lawton, D.F.C.
Personnel Director, R. E. Leach.
Corporate Planning Director, E. E. Pell.
Financial Director, R. A. Spencer.
Director of Medical Services, Dr. J. G. Taylor.
Public Relations Director, W. Simpson, O.B.E., D.F.C.
Secretary and Solicitor, M. J. Lester.

BRITISH OVERSEAS AIRWAYS CORPORATION
Speedbird House, Heathrow Airport,
Hounslow, Middlesex
[01-759-5511]
Established in 1939, British Overseas Airways
Corporation acquired, on April 1, 1940, the air
transport undertakings of Imperial Airways and
British Airways, which had been at the disposal of
the Secretary of State for Air since the outbreak
of war.
B.O.A.C. is the larger of the two Government
Corporations which are charged with the task of

developing and operating British scheduled air transport services under the provisions of the Air Corporations Act 1967. It operates round-the-world services and services to Africa, the Middle and Far East, Australia and New Zealand, and North and South America.

The members of the Corporation are appointed by the President of the Board of Trade.

Chairman, K. Granville, C.B.E.............£17,000
Deputy Chairman, Sir Arthur Norman, K.B.E., D.F.C.
.............£2,000
Managing Director, J. R. Stainton, C.B.E.....£12,000

BRITISH RAILWAYS BOARD
222 Marylebone Road, N.W.1
[01-262-3232]
Chairman, Rt. Hon. R. W. Marsh........£20,000
Deputy Chairman and Chief Executive (Railways),
W. G. Thorpe, C.B.E.............£16,000
Vice-Chairman, J. M. W. Bosworth......£13,000
Full-time Members, A. V. Barker, O.B.E.; Dr. S. Jones, C.B.E.; R. L. E. Lawrence, O.B.E., E.R.D.; D. McKenna, C.B.E.; varying sums between £10,000 and £15,000.
Part-time Members, Sir Frederick Hayday, C.B.E.; D. J. Palmer; The Lord Taylor of Gryfe; H. A. Walker.............£1,000 *each*
Chief Secretary, J. R. Hamilton, M.B.E.

BRITISH STEEL CORPORATION
33 Grosvenor Place, S.W.1
[01-235-1212]
The British Steel Corporation was established under the Iron and Steel Act 1967 which vested in the Corporation the shares of the fourteen major steel companies. The Corporation's main duty is to promote the efficient and economical supply of iron and steel products.
Chairman, The Lord Melchett............£25,000
Deputy Chairman, W. F. Cartwright; Dr. H. M. Finniston, F.R.S.; M. Littman, Q.C.
Members (full-time) T. R. Craig, C.B.E.; The Lord Layton; R. Smith.
Deputy Chairmen and full-time members in salary range £15,000 to £24,000.
Members (part-time), G. R. Chetwynd, C.B.E.; A. Silberston; W. D. Griffiths. *From* £1,000 to £3,750.
Secretary, R. W. Roseveare.

BRITISH TOURIST AUTHORITY
Queen's House, 64 St. James's Street, S.W.1
[01-629-9191]
The functions of the Authority are: (a) to encourage people to visit Great Britain and people living in Great Britain to take their holidays there and (b) to encourage the provision and improvement of tourist amenities and facilities in Great Britain. The authority was created on August 25, 1969, by the *Development of Tourism Act,* 1969, and took over the principal functions of the British Travel Association on January 1, 1970. The Authority operates in close consultation with the Tourist Boards for England, Scotland, Wales and Northern Ireland and all sections of the tourist and holiday industry. The Authority is financed direct by H.M. Government. It consists of a Chairman and 8 members including the Chairmen of the English, Scottish and Welsh Tourist Boards. The Chairman and five ordinary Members are appointed by the Secretary of State, Department of Trade and Industry.
Chairman, Sir Alexander Glen, K.B.E., D.S.C.
Chief Executive, L. J. Lickorish.

BRITISH TRANSPORT DOCKS BOARD
Melbury House, Melbury Terrace,
[01-486-6621]
Constituted under the *Transport Act,* 1962. The Board owns and operates 19 active ports.
Chairman, Sir Humphrey Browne, C.B.E.
(part-time) £9,000
Vice-Chairman, C. R. Cory......(part-time) £2,250

Members, S. Johnson, C.B.E. (*Managing Director*) (£11,000); D. A. Stringer (*Deputy Managing Director*) (£9,000); C. W. Fisher, T.D.; R. F. Pugh (*part-time*) (each £1,500); G. H. Lowthian, C.B.E.; D. F. Martin-Jenkins, T.D. (*part-time*) (each £1,000).
Secretary, K. E. Bantock.

BRITISH WATERWAYS BOARD
Melbury House, Melbury Terrace, N.W.1
[01-262-6711]
Chairman, Sir Frank Price (*part-time*).....£5,250
Vice-Chairman, Sir John Hawton, K.C.B. (*part-time*)
£1,750
Members, B. C. Gillinson; Hon. Alexander Hood; Sir Alex Samuels, C.B.E.; Lt.-Col. R. Seifert*; General Sir Hugh Stockwell, G.C.B., K.B.E., D.S.O.
(*all part-time*) £1,000

* Salary not drawn.
General Manager, D. G. McCance.

CABINET OFFICE
Whitehall, S.W.1
[01-930-5422]
Secretary of the Cabinet, Sir Burke Trend, G.C.B., C.V.O., P.C. 31/1/72.............£15,000
Permanent Secretary, Sir William Nield, K.C.B.
GCMG Jan 72 £14,000
Director General, Central Policy Review Staff, The Lord Rothschild, G.M., Ph.D., SC.D., F.R.S.
£14,000
Chief Scientific Adviser, Sir Alan Cottrell, F.R.S.
£13,000
Deputy Secretaries, Sir Philip Adams, K.C.M.G.; N. F. Cairncross, C.B.; P. W. Carey; Dr. R. Press, CB; C.B.E.; C. R. Ross; Sir Charles Sopwith; P. E. Thornton, C.B. PC.A.U.R.R. 31/1/72 £9,000
Under Secretaries, J. Crocker; P. J. Hudson; J. E. D. Lakin; P. R. Odgers, C.B., M.B.E.; J. A. Thomson; B. G. Tucker, O.B.E.............£6,750
Assistant Secretaries, J. Anson; E. W. Bryant; R. H. F. Croft; B. M. Day (*Establishment Officer*); R. Dronfield; I. T. Lawman; Miss E. M. Llewellyn-Smith; C. C. Lucas; J. F. Mayne; T. D. O'Leary; D. Pilkington, I.S.O.; W. J. L. Plowden; W. C. Rudkin; B. T. W. Stewart;....£5,000 to £6,300
Chief Scientific Officer, Dr. O. Simpson....£6,750
Senior Principal Scientific Officers, Dr. H. H. Atkinson; J. H. Bagley; A. Smith...£4,390 to £5,015
Special Appointments, P. W. Bocock; H. C. G. Hawkins; Mrs. A. H. Jackson; B. Reading.
Central Statistical Office:
Director and Head of the Government Statistical Service, C. A. Moser, C.B.E., F.B.A.....£13,000
Deputy Directors, R. E. Beales, C.B.E........£7,850
Assistant Directors, L. S. Berman; A. J. Boreham; S. F. James.........................£6,750
Chief Statisticians, R. L. Brown; R. E. Fry; R. W. Green; D. Harris; J. Hibbert; Miss R. J. Maurice; S. Rosenbaum; A. A. Sorrell; J. W. S. Walton..........£5,000 to £6,300
Senior Principal Scientific Officer, Dr. J. B. Harding
£4,390 to £5,015
Historical Section:
Chief Historians, Prof. Sir James Butler, M.V.O., O.B.E. (*Military*); Sir Keith Hancock (*Civil*).
C. J. Child (*Departmental Records Officer*)
£4,600 to £5,200
Chief Clerk and Departmental Records Officer, H. L. Theobald. O.B.E.............£3,250 to £4,400

CABLE AND WIRELESS LIMITED
Head Office—Mercury House, Theobald's Road, W.C.1
[01-242-4433]
Chairman, Col. D. McMillan, C.B., O.B.E.
(*part-time*) £7,000
Managing Director, E. G. L. Howitt, O.B.E....£10,000
Directors, W. H. Davies; P. A. McCunn; A. S. Pudner, M.B.E.; R. A. Rice; A. A. Willett (£7,500); R. J. Halsey, C.M.G. (*part-time*) (£2,600); H. E. Matthews, O.B.E. (*part-time*) (£1,975); J. Hodgson (*unpaid*).
Secretary, R. F. Forrest.

CHARITY COMMISSION
Ryder Street, St. James's, S.W.1
[01-930-7621]
Melias Building, Love Lane, Liverpool
[051-207-4441]
Central Register of Charities
St. Alban's House, Haymarket, S.W.1
[01-930-5801]

The Charity Commission was constituted under Act of Parliament in 1853 and reconstituted under the Charities Act, 1900, with the general function of promoting the effective use of charitable monies and a duty to keep a register of charities. The powers of the Commissioners over endowments held for educational purposes are exercised by the Department of Education and Science. The Official Custodian for Charities holds investments for charities and remits the income, free of income tax, to trustees.

Chief Commissioner, T. C. Green, C.B. £6,935
Commissioners, W. E. A. Lewis, O.B.E. (£6,775);
 C. W. E. Shelley............£4,730 to £6,725
Deputy Commissioners, F. H. Pratt; J. P. L. Redfern;
 W. J. Wolfe, O.B.E.; T. Keith
 £5,375 to £6,475
Asst. Commissioners, W. C. Over; D. B. Hodgkinson; C. A. Weston, D.F.C., G.M.; M. B. Tripp; Miss A. M. E. Jacobsen; M. A. Rao; C. A. H. Parsons; F. W. Trinder; R. W. Groves; Miss B. K. Searle; J. Farquharson; J. F. Claricoat; Miss B. R. Heitzman............£3,925 to £5,175
Secretary and Asst. Commissioner, R. S. Morgan
 £4,775 to £5,375
Principals, N. Storr, O.B.E.; R. Booth (*Asst. Commissioner*); I. H. Thomas .... £3,425 to £4,575
Official Custodian for Charities, L. A. Jimenez
 £4,775 to £5,375
Deputy Official Custodian, Miss C. M. Clark
 £3,425 to £4,575
Establishment Officer, H. M. Taylor
 £3,425 to £4,575
Deputy Establishment Officer, Mrs. P. R. Evans
 £2,950 to £3,575
Senior Executive Officers, D. W. Peel; Miss J. A. Stanton; C. E. Plant; G. Duffett; S. H. Way; W. P. Richards; D. McNaught; Miss E. M. M. Thornton; Miss S. M. St. C. Smith; J. Samuels
 £2,950 to £3,575

CHURCH COMMISSIONERS
1 Millbank, Westminster, S.W.1
[01-930-5441]

The Church Commissioners were established on April 1, 1948, by the amalgamation of *Queen Anne's Bounty* (established 1704) and the *Ecclesiastical Commissioners* (established 1836). The Commissioners have three main tasks:—
 (1) the management of their capital assets so that they may earn income;
 (2) the proper distribution of that income; and
 (3) the discharge of a large number of administrative duties conferred on them by Acts of Parliament and Measures of the former Church Assembly.
 The Commissioners' income for the year ended March 31, 1971, was derived from the following sources:—

Stock exchange investments......	£12,692,131
Land and property..............	9,473,826
Mortgages and loans............	1,770,610
Money received for particular beneficiaries..................	1,493,465
	£25,430,032

This income was used as follows:—

Clergy stipends and pensions.....	£18,510,698
Clergy houses (maintenance, outgoings, provision and improvement).........................	3,006,271
Other church property..........	703,195
Other grant schemes............	137,825
Added to capital to improve future income.....................	1,229,520
Administration..................	1,358,044

General reserve (to be used for major schemes)...............	481,479
	£25,430,032

Constitution
The 2 Archbishops, the 41 diocesan Bishops, 5 deans, 10 other clerks and 10 laymen appointed by the Church Assembly; 4 laymen nominated by the Queen; 4 persons nominated by the Archbishop of Canterbury; The Lord Chancellor; The Lord President of the Council; the First Lord of the Treasury; The Chancellor of the Exchequer; The Secretary of State for the Home Dept.; The Speaker of the House of Commons; The Lord Chief Justice; The Master of the Rolls; The Attorney-General; The Solicitor-General; The Lord Mayor and two Aldermen of the City of London; The Lord Mayor of York and one representative from each of the Universities of Oxford and Cambridge.

Church Estates Commissioners:—
First, Sir Ronald Harris, K.C.V.O., C.B.
Second, W. M. J. Worsley, M.P.
Third, Sir Hubert Ashton, K.B.E., M.C.
Secretary, K. S. Ryle, C.B.E., M.C.
Assets Secretary, D. A. Collenette, C.B.E.
Under Secretary General, L. D. Walker, O.B.E.
Assistant Secretaries, K. A. C. Argent (*Pastoral*); L. N. King (*Houses*); E. W. Lyons (*Accountant*); A. I. McDonald (*Investments*); R. K. Pears, D.F.C. (*Estates*); H. M. G. Pryor (*Finance*); D. G. Ward (*Redundant Churches*).
See Houses Officer, E. Denselow.
Development Officer, J. D. M. Barnes.
Assistant Accountant, D. I. Archer.
Deputy to Investments Secretary, I. D. Adam.
Principals, J. M. Davies; D. J. Day; P. Locke; P. T. Rafferty; J. E. Shelley; S. E. Smith; E. W. Turner.
Senior Executive Officers, T. Batchelor; J. R. Beard; Miss E. M. Bollen; C. P. Canton; J. Cheesman; G. Duckworth; D. N. Goodwin; F. R. Neale; L. E. Nelson; F. A. Norman; G. H. Penn; W. J. Pennel; N. H. Rawlings; E. J. Robinson; T. M. Robinson; R. McN. Roxburgh; J. W. Webber.

Legal Department
Legal Adviser, O. H. Woodforde, M.B.E.
Official Solicitor, R. H. Rogers.
Deputy Solicitor, J. W. Cook.
Assistant Solicitor, P. Leslie.
Senior Legal Assistants, A. J. L. Campbell; B. G. Hall; B. J. T. Hanson; R. A. G. Lees; S. J. Palmer.

Architectural Department
Official Architect, R. G. Wood.
Deputy Architect, H. A. Scarth.

Surveyor's Department
Official Surveyor, H. M. Rigby, M.B.E., T.D.
Deputy Surveyor, J. M. N. Barnes.

Agents
Messrs. Clutton, 5 Great College Street, Westminster, S.W.1; Messrs. Smiths Gore, Dean's Court, Minster Precincts, Peterborough; Messrs. Chesterton & Sons, 116 Kensington High Street, W.8.

CIVIL SERVICE DEPARTMENT
Whitehall, S.W.1 (01-839-7733)
The Civil Service Department was set up on November 1, 1968 and took over from the Treasury responsibilities for the management of the Civil Service. The department is headed by the Prime Minister, who is Minister for the Civil Service, and under him the Lord Privy Seal controls the day to day management of the Department. The Civil Service Department's primary functions are the pay and management of the Civil Service and the co-ordination of government policy on pay and pensions throughout the public sector. In particular the Department has central responsibility for personnel management, including training and career management; manpower requirements and the development and dissemination of administrative and managerial techniques. The Civil Service

Commission (which was first constituted by Order in Council in 1855) now forms part of the Department but retains its independence and impartiality in the selection of recruits for posts in the Civil Service.

The Prime Minister.

The Lord Privy Seal.

Parliamentary Secretary, D. A. R. Howell, M.P.

Head of the Home Civil Service and Permanent Secretary to the Civil Service Department, Sir William Armstrong, G.C.B., M.V.O...£15,000

Second Permanent Secretary (vacant).......£14,000

Deputy Secretaries, K. H. Clucas, C.B. (also First Civil Service Commissioner); N. G. Morrison, C.B.; J. J. S. Shaw, C.B.; F. Cooper, C.B., C.M.G...£9,000

Ceremonial Officer, P. S. Milner-Barry, C.B., O.B.E.
£5,000 to £6,300

Central Group

Under Secretary, F. G. Burrett (*Establishment Officer*)
£6,750

Assistant Secretary, J. Blake (*Deputy Establishment Officer*)................£5,000 to £6,300

Director (Statistics), A. R. Smith........£6,750

Assistant Secretary (Planning), N. M. Hale,
£5,000 to £6,300

Head of Information Division, S. J. Cursley
£5,000 to £6,300

Information Adviser to Civil Service Commission, J. T. Hughes, O.B.E.....£5,000 to £6,300

Computers

Under Secretary, S. W. Spain..............£6,750

Assistant Secretary, W. R. Atkinson
£5,000 to £6,300

Deputy Chief Scientific Officer, G. H. Perry
£5,240 to £5,830

Management Services

Under Secretary, J. N. Archer............£6,750

Assistant Secretaries, R. R. Pittam; S. D. Walker; I. H. Wightman; D. M. Dell...£5,000 to £6,300

Chief Scientific Officer (B), E. K. G. James

Manpower

Under Secretary, A. A. Creamer, D.F.C......£6,750

Assistant Secretaries, B. M. Thimont; J. C. Leeming
£5,000 to £6,300

Structure Review

Under Secretary, D. L. Pearson............£6,750

Assistant Secretary, R. H. Bird...£5,000 to £6,300

Machinery of Government

Under Secretary, T. H. Caulcott............£6,750

Assistant Secretaries, N. S. Forward; G. D. Crane; P. Mountfield...........£5,000 to £6,300

Pay

Under Secretary, K. C. Lawrance............£6,750

Assistant Secretaries, P. Mehew; J. B. Pearce; C. R. Walker...................£5,000 to £6,300

Pensions, Conditions, Welfare, etc.

Under Secretary, J. E. Herbecq............£6,750

Assistant Secretaries, P. L. Towers; A. W. Wyatt; K. H. McNeill......£5,000 to £6,300

Director of Catering, F. G. Murray, C.B.E.....£6,035

Management Personnel

Under Secretary, D. R. J. Stephen..........£6,750

Assistant Secretaries, C. F. R. Barclay, C.M.G.; G. W. Watson; Mrs. M. B. Sloman; D. J. Gerhard; D. J. Chapman.....£5,000 to £6,300

Civil Service College
Sunningdale Park

Principal, E. Grebenik...................£9,000

Deputy Principal, J. H. Taylor............£6,750

Assistant Secretary, W. H. Formoy
£5,000 to £6,300

Directors of Studies, B. J. Holland (*Personnel Management*); Dr. H. Parriss (*Public Administration*)
£5,000 to £6,300

Bursar, Air Vice-Marshal R. Deacon-Elliott, C.B., O.B.E., D.F.C...........£3,250 to £4,400

London Centre

Assistant Secretaries, J. B. Bourn; W. C. Knox; G. H. Wollen..................£5,000 to £6,300

Director of Studies, Dr. B. Benjamin (*Statistics*); Dr. C. D. Harbury (*Economics*); Dr. C. S. Smith (*Social Policy and Administration*)
£5,000 to £6,300

Edinburgh Centre

Assistant Secretary, J. B. Hume...£5,000 to £6,300

Medical Advisory Service

Medical Adviser, D. Thompson, C.B., M.D....£7,325

Principal Medical Officers, G. Lorriman, M.B.E., M.D.; P. R. Gilbert, M.D.....................£6,120

Senior Medical Officers, J. W. Parks, M.B.E., M.D.; W. F. Townsend-Coles, M.D.; D. J. Sheehan, M.D.; R. M. Oliver, M.D.............£5,640

Recruitment and Selection

Alencon Link, Basingstoke; Standard House, Northumberland Avenue, S.W.1

Civil Service Commissioners

First Commissioner, K. H. Clucas, C.B....£9,000

Commissioners, S. W. C. Philips, C.B.; K. M. Reader
£6,750

Commissioner, Scientific and Technological Advisor, Dr. F. H. Allen, C.B...................£7,025

Commissioner and Director of Civil Service Selection Board, K. A. G. Murray.................£6,750

General Recruitment Divisions

Assistant Secretary, S. D. Light...£5,000 to £6,300

Science and Technology Divisions

Scientific and Technological Adviser, Dr. F. H. Allen, C.B....................£7,025

Deputy Chief Scientific Officer, J. W. A. Chorley, O.B.E.; C. F. Watkinson....£5,240 to £5,830

Civil Service Selection Board

Director, K. A. G. Murray...............£6,750

Deputy Director, D. G. Daymond
£5,000 to £6,300

Under-Secretary, Miss W. M. Fox..........£6,750

Assistant Director, F. A. K. Harrison
£5,000 to £6,300

Research Division

Head of Division, Dr. E. Anstey..£5,240 to £5,830

COMMONWEALTH DEVELOPMENT CORPORATION
33 Hill Street, W.1
[01-629-8484]

The Corporation was formerly known as the Colonial Development Corporation. The change of name was affected by the Commonwealth Development Act, 1963, which also restored the Corporation's full powers of operation in all those countries which had achieved independence within the Commonwealth since 1948. The Overseas Resources Development Act, 1969, empowered the Corporation, with Ministerial approval, to engage in operations in any country in or out of the Commonwealth. The Corporation is authorized to borrow up to £225,000,000 on long or medium term and £10,000,000 on short term.

Chairman (part-time) The Lord Howick of Glendale, G.C.M.G., K.C.V.O...........£11,900

Deputy Chairman, Sir Eric Griffith-Jones, K.B.E., C.M.G., Q.C.

Members (part-time), Sir Humphrey Browne, C.B.E.; The Lord Campbell of Eskan; J. M. Clay; J. K. Dick; Sir Arthur Gaitskell, C.M.G.; The Lord Greenwood of Rossendale, P.C.; G. F. Smith, C.B.E.; P. P. Streeten; Miss J. Symonds
each £1,000

General Manager, Sir William Rendell.

COMMONWEALTH OFFICE
See FOREIGN AND COMMONWEALTH OFFICE

COMMONWEALTH SECRETARIAT
Marlborough House,
Pall Mall, S.W.1
[01-839-3411]
Secretary-General, A. C. Smith.

COUNTRYSIDE COMMISSION
1 Cambridge Gate, Regent's Park, N.W.1
[01-935-5533]
The Countryside Commission was set up under the Countryside Act, 1968. It has absorbed the National Parks Commission, taking over the duties of that body under the National Parks and Access to the Countryside Act, 1949, and having in addition a wider range of advisory and executive functions relating to the whole of the countryside and coast. Members of the Commission are appointed by the Secretary of State for the Environment and the Secretary of State for Wales acting jointly.

Chairman, J. S. Cripps, C.B.E. £3,000
Deputy Chairman, R. Hubert.
Members, A. Buxton, M.C.; T. Colman; Dr. Margaret Davies; G. Howard; B. Hubbard; S. P. Johnson; Sir Jack Longland; Prof. O. R. McGregor; T. E. Watkins . . . . *unpaid*
Director, R. J. S. Hookway £6,750
Assistant Director (Admin.), R. G. Brown
£5,000 to £6,300
Principals, R. Ditchfield; T. Farmer, M.B.E.; Miss M. B. Jones . . . . £3,250 to £4,400
Principal Planning Officer, A. A. C. Phillips (*acting* (+*allce.*)) £3,575 to £4,208
Senior Planning Officers, P. N. Allen; J. M. Davidson; Miss A. C. Seale . . . . £3,575 to £4,208
Planning Officers, Miss A. B. Batty; K. R. Pennyfather; A. A. Macdonald; A. J. White; R. G. Woolmore; J. A. Zetter . . . . . . £2,583 to £3,396
Senior Executive Officers, E. J. S. Burbidge; W. E. P. Gibbon; T. G. Millar . . . . £2,775 to £3,400
Senior Information Officer R. S. Bush
£2,775 to £3,440

COUNTRYSIDE COMMISSION FOR SCOTLAND
Battleby, Redgarton, Perth
[0738-27921]
Established under the Countryside (Scotland) Act, 1967, with functions for the provision, development and improvement of facilities for the enjoyment of the Scottish countryside, and for the conservation and enhancement of the natural beauty and amenity thereof.
Chairman, Sir John McWilliam.
Members, The Viscount of Arbuthnott, D.S.C.; Mrs. M. Barclay; I. Borthwick; The Marquess of Bute; Mrs. E. Davidson; S. E. A. Landale; D. N. Lowe, O.B.E.; Sir James Mackay, K.B.E., C.B.; Dr. H. S. Mackintosh, C.B.E.; W. H. Murray, O.B.E.; B. K. Parnell; A. C. Trotter, C.B.E.
Director, J. Foster.
Secretary, W. S. Prior.
Asst. Directors, S. R. Mollison (*Planning and Research*); T. Huxley (*Resource Management*); D. Aldridge (*Information and Conservation Education*).

COVENT GARDEN MARKET AUTHORITY
Bedford Chambers, Covent Garden, W.C.2.
[01-240-2311]
The Covent Garden Market Authority is constituted under the Covent Garden Market Acts, 1961 to 1969, the members being appointed by the Ministry of Agriculture, Fisheries and Food. The Authority owns 6½ acres of land at Covent Garden comprising five central market buildings used for wholesale trading in horticultural produce; and other property including five blocks of offices. It is charged with the duty of building a new market on a site of about 60 acres at Nine Elms in the Boroughs of Wandsworth and Lambeth (work on which started in January 1971), and of securing the expeditious and economic development or disposal of its Covent Garden lands.

The Authority is empowered to borrow capital up to £45,000,000.
Chairman, Sir Henry Hardman, K.C.B.
Members, W. M. Balch; R. G. E. Jarvis; J. W. Rodden, C.B.E.; Sir Harold Samuel; Sir Alex Samuels, C.B.E. (*Nominated by the Minister of Transport*); W. J. Tudor.
General Manager, C. M. G. Allen.
Assistant General Manager, L. T. G. Sully, C.B.E.
Secretary, C. H. Bates.

CROWN AGENTS FOR OVERSEA GOVERNMENTS AND ADMINISTRATIONS
4 Millbank, S.W.1
[01-222-7730]
The Crown Agents are the officially appointed business and financial agents of a large number of Governments and public authorities. These include independent Governments such as Bahrain, Brunei, Ceylon, Cyprus, Fiji, Gambia, Guyana, Jamaica, Jordan, Kenya, Libya, Malaysia, Malta, Mauritius, Nigeria, Sierra Leone, Singapore, Tanzania, Trinidad, Uganda, Western Samoa and Zambia and all the territories overseas under British administration or trusteeship. Other authorities for whom they act include the United Nations, many railway, transport, broadcasting, telecommunications and electrical undertakings, port commissions, universities, currency boards and local government authorities, in addition to many development and research bodies. The office is not a Department of the United Kingdom Government, and no vote for it comes before the United Kingdom Parliament. It is self-supporting, its funds being derived from fees charged to its principals from whom instructions are received direct. The Crown Agents do not act for private individuals or commercial concerns.

The work of the Crown Agents' office includes the purchase, inspection, shipment and insurance of engineering plant and equipment and of stores of all kinds; the design of engineering structures; the issue and management of loans and the investment of funds; the payment of salaries to officers on leave; the engagement of staff for certain oversea Government appointments; the booking of passages for Government officers and their families; and many other functions.
Chairman, C. J. Hayes, C.M.G.
Crown Agent, E. A. Morris, C.M.G., O.B.E.
relinquishes off. 31/12/71, no successor as yet 1/2/71

CROWN ESTATE COMMISSIONERS
13/15 Carlton House Terrace, S.W.1.
[01-839-2211]
Mount Lane, Bracknell, Berks.
[0344 20321]
THE CROWN ESTATE (formerly The Crown Lands).—The Land Revenues of the Crown in *England and Wales* have been collected on the public account since 1760, when George III surrendered them and received a fixed annual payment or *Civil List*. At the time of the surrender the gross revenues amounted to about £89,000 and the net return to about £11,000.

In the year ended March 31, 1971, the total Receipts by the Commissioners were £6,500,000. The Expenditure was £2,393,000. The sum of £3,850,000 was paid to the Exchequer in 1970-71 as *Surplus Revenue*, being a net sum from which no deductions have to be made for administration.

The Land Revenues in *Ireland* have been carried to the Consolidated Fund since 1820; from April 1, 1923, as regards Southern Ireland, they have been collected and administered by the Irish Free State (Republic of Ireland).

The Land Revenues in *Scotland* were transferred to the Commissioners in 1833.
First Commissioner and Chairman (part-time), The Earl of Perth, P.C.
Second Commissioner (and Secretary), W. A. Wood, C.B. £9,000
Commissioners (part-time), A. W. H. Allen, C.B.E.; Sir Oliver Chesterton, M.C.; G. K. Denniss; The

Lord Raglan, T.D.; Capt. I. M. Tennant; The
Lord Walston.

Deputy Commissioner, P. S. Bolshaw
£4,390 to £5,640

Assistant Commissioner and Clerk to the Board,
J. Griffiths..............£4,045 to £4,555

Crown Estate Surveyor, E. J. Shaw
£4,390 to £5,015

Deputy Crown Estate Surveyor. N. H. Ash
£3,575 to £4,208

Chief Officer and Establishment Officer, E. F. Richards
£3,258 to £3,873

Accountant and Receiver-General, G. R. Clark
£2,529 to £3,099

Senior Executive Officers, S. A. Allwood; A. Barker;
D. W. Broughton; A. R. Brown; J. S. Hogg;
C. R. Smith; D. T. Hunt (*Edinburgh*)
£2,529 to £3,099

Legal Adviser and Solicitor, J. G. Allan.......£6,750
Senior Legal Assistants, A. W. Robinson; M. A.
Jaffé; J. B. Postgate.........£3,286 to £4,390
Civil Engineer (Marine Survey), J. H. Edwards.
M.B.E.............£3,352 to £4,470
Solicitor, Scotland, D. F. Stewart.
Director of Forestry, R. Lindsay, M.V.O., B.E.M.

Windsor Estate

Surveyor and Deputy Ranger, Maj. A. W. Haig,
M.V.O.

BOARD OF CUSTOMS AND EXCISE
King's Beam House, Mark Lane, E.C.3
[01-626-1515]

Commissioners of Customs were first appointed
in 1671 and housed by the King in London, the
present "Long Room" in the Custom House,
Lower Thames Street, E.C.3, replacing that built
by Charles II and rebuilt after destruction by fire in
1718 and 1814. The Excise Department was
formerly under the Inland Revenue Department,
and was amalgamated with the Customs Department on April 1, 1909.

The Board

Chairman, Sir Louis Petch, K.C.B.........£14,000
Private Sec., C. J. Packman.
Deputy Chairman, R. W. Radford, C.B., M.B.E.
£9,000
*Director of Establishment and Organization and Com-
missioner,* J.M. Woolf £6,750
Commissioners, C. H. Blake, C.B.; E. P. Brown, C.B.;
H. F. Christopherson; C. J. Cross; Mrs. D. C. L.
Johnstone, C.B.E.; E. A. Knight; K. B. Pepper,
C.B. (*Joint Secretaries*) £6,750

Secretaries' Office

Assistan Secretaries, A. R. Ashford, C.M.G.; C.
Bamfield; R. Bamfield; A. H. Barrett; H. J.
Chumas, T.D.; G. B. Diamond; B. M. Field; S. A.
Green; E. N. Griffiths; D. J. Harbour; L. D.
Hawken; J. K. Hulme, O.B.E.; F. J. Kumpf,
I.S.O.; G. G. Leighton-Boyce; J. Midgley; T.
H. Pratt; A. W. Rolfe; C. H. Veale; L. J.
White ....£5,000 to £6,300
Senior Principal, A. C. Ralph, I.S.O.
£4,600 to £5,200
Controller of Valuation Branch, G. Wilson
£5,000 to £6,300
Deputy Controller of Valuation Branch, J. C. Fletcher,
I.S.O..............£4,600 to £5,200
Principals, J. L. Abbott; J. G. Acton; A. Aldous;
Miss E. Armstrong; L. A. Barber, I.S.O.; J.
Barber; F. E. Bartlett; W. A. Bassett; S. Bellew;
H. T. Bigg; Mrs. D. Biggam; R. F. Boyce; J. L.
Broomfield; O. A. Brown, M.M., B.E.M.; P. Cal-
vert; J. Clary; R. Coleman; A. O. Davies; D. K.
Dawson; I. E. De Groot; L. J. Dewing; B. T.
Dobson; E. H. Elliott; E. L. Fletcher; R. A.
Fowkes; Miss O. E. Fuller; F. D. Garnett; C. H.
Gill; W. J. Glover; H. A. C. Griffiths; L. S.
Gross, O.B.E.; B. Halliwell; L. J. Harris; G. S.
Harriss; W. J. Haswell; G. F. Howell; Miss S. A.
Jacobs; M. G. Jeremiah; W. F. Johnson; S. F.
Jordan; H. A. King; V. D. King; L. L. Kirby;

N. S. R. Lindsay; J. R. McCormack; D. M.
McKee; Miss W. M. Maguire; F. G. Marshall;
Miss G. E. Moger, M.B.E.; C. W. Mothersill, I.S.O.;
W. Newman; B. Nicholls; A. G. Northam,
M.B.E.; H. A. O'Neill; P. H. G. Passfield; C. A.
Pilgrim; K. C. Piper; A. Radcliffe; R. J. Rickard;
S. Roberts; R. D. Shearer; B. D. Sheehan; M. N.
Smith; W. A. J. Taft; G. Tiplin; D. Turnell;
A. C. Vince; H. A. Ward; E. G. Webster; G. S.
Welch; H. J. White; J. I. Wilkinson; R. William-
son; E. J. Wiseman............£3,250 to £4,400
Senior Executive Officers, C. A. Bake; Miss E. M.
Baker; R. V. Baker; G. A. Beer; J. A. Bull;
W. R. S. Cerutty; D. J. Clarke; A. W. Cooper;
E. F. J. Corps; Mrs. R. E. Crackett; Miss M. I.
Crane; A. S. Crosbie; J. K. Dornom; T. A. Essam;
Mrs. M. E. Fletcher; J. R. Gilson; R. D. God-
dard; H. W. Goodfellow; W. H. Goodman;
A. R. Gregson; W. R. Grimett; A. H. Hart;
S. Harwood; B. T. Huggett; Miss M. Jackson;
R. L. Jeffrey; H. G. Jones; R. W. Jones; R. L.
Lattimore; L. T. Longdon; T. A. Lonsdale; D. G.
Lovibond; R. T. McGrath; D. E. Maidwell;
R. H. Maury, D.F.C.; D. R. Metcalf; S. G. Mier;
Miss V. B. Mines; A. L. Murphy; P. Nash; G.
Payne; K. W. V. Payne; R. F. Powell; R. M.
Pratt; D. C. Priddon; W. R. H. Prior; E. F.
Reader; W. R. Robinson; L. J. Rose; Miss B. E.
Smith; H. J. Stull; F. Tierney; D. Vandenbergh;
J. E. Wade; W. T. C. Wakefield; Miss D. J.
Welton; W. A. White; G. A. Whittingham;
Miss M. E. Wilkinson......£2,775 to £3,400
Superintendent of Registry, Mrs. J. N. Hopper
£2,775 to £3,400
Principal Information Officer, M. Nockles, O.B.E.
£3,250 to £4,400
Senior Information Officer, T. B. Wynn
£2,775 to £3,400
Chief Welfare Officer, L. A. J. Stribley
£2,775 to £3,400

Departmental Planning Unit

Assistant Secretaries, A. M. Brebner; D. L. Bryers;
A. M. Fraser, T.D.; C. Freedman; A. R. H.
Glover; P. B. Kent; B. H. Knox; J. W. Whitaker
£5,000 to £6,300
Senior Principal, G. M. A. Smith
£4,600 to £5,200
Principals, W. J. Abraham; N. E. Campion; R. A.
B. Crowe; G. Duncan; H. A. Forster; D. J.
Howard; R. J. Petch; R. J. Powell; R. E. Skil-
beck; Mrs. V. P. M. Strachan; M.L. Tomkin-
son; A. Watson; R. Williamson
£3,250 to £4,400
Statistician, M. R. Noyce......£3,250 to £4,400
Librarian, A. J. Card, D.F.C.......£2,775 to £3,400

Solicitor's Office

Solicitor, D. J. Willson, C.B.E., T.D.........£9,000
Principal Assistant Solicitor, G. Krikorian ...£6,750
Assistant Solicitors, W. L. Fearnehough, T.D.; G. F.
Gloak; R. K. F. Hutchings; F. J. de T. Mandley;
E. G. Mosley; W. Rawlinson; J. L. Stewart; P. J.
Sutton............£4,555 to £5,640
Senior Legal Assistants, P. S. Baxter; R. G. R. Cross;
V. E. Eaton; P. J. C. Ellis; J. A. D. Heal; W. S.
Hill; V. E. Jenvey; R. G. C. King; J. N. B. Lainé;
O. W. Levett-Yeats; H. H. Mainprice; C. A.
Ryves; J. Sellers; M. S. Steel, D.F.C.; Miss E. S.
Thomas; F. Townley.......£3,286 to £4,390

Chief Inspector's Office

Chief Inspector. E. P. Brown,C.B............£6,750
Dep. Ch. Insp., F. R. Frost; W. F. Joyce; C. M.
Porter.............£5,990
Principal Inspectors, J. F. Blunt; N. Brazil; W. J.
Campbell, M.B.E.; R. Colling; A. E. Fry; R. Hop-
wood; J. K. Kidson; W. D. Milne; J. D. Price;
S. Sparke, O.B.E.; H. Tennant; G. Tyson
£5,015 to £5,640
Senior Inspectors, G. M. Austin; M. K. Barford;
R. W. H. Baxter; A. R. Reach; H. D. Beale; N.
Brazil; A. J. Brown; V. M. Brown; H. C. Chap-
man; W. R. Chave; G. W. Cox; W. D. Doyle;
E. F. Elfick; J. H. Evans; L. A. Hardham, T.D.;

N. H. Harrild; S. H. P. Holt; S. J. House; J. G. Howells; F. W. Jones; H. C. Kenway, T.D.; C. S. Killingley; G. G. Lawrance; W. H. Leach; W. W. Loudon; D. C. McNeill; T. R. Moore, M.M.; H. Peart; B. S. R. Penney; R. Reeve; H. C. Reid; D. C. Restorick; J. E. Ruberry; L. J. Shew; W. Slatter; D. B. Stanley, I.S.O.; H. F. Stevens; W. Surtees; W. J. Tasker; W. Taylor; F. Turner; W. E. Tyzzer; C. W. Watson; H. J. Webb; C. J. Wilcox; C. B. E. Williams; W. S. Williams; E. F. H. Willis; C. E. Wilson

£4,140 to £4,765

Inspectors, A. S. Ball; J. C. Barnes; W. T. Bate; J. W. H. Berry; C. C. Box; R. J. W. Clarke; N. J. Collinge; J. M. Cutler; F. H. Dare; R. Delahaye; K. H. W. Dorken; S. Earlam; E. H. Elliott; T. A. Forrester; D. S. Frampton; D. G. Furnace; L. S. Gray; D. K. Grindrod; B. Hardern; J. W. Heath; W. C. Hepworth; T. T. Hill; H. J. C. [Holyer; E. J. Hoskin; P. J. Little; D. L. Manson; J. F. Mayes; R. A. Mechem; R. W. Nelson; A. J. Parsons; W. A. R. Phillips; D. G. Pitt; D. J. Pullen; J. B. Randerson; H. B. Rosser; P. H. J. Ryan; J. C. Simons; R. E. Skilbeck, I.S.O.; P. Sutcliffe; J. E. Turnbull; A. P. Wheway; J. N. White; J. R. Williams

£3,258 to £3,873

Accountant and Comptroller-General's Office

Accountant and Comptroller-General, L. E. Dove, C.B.E.........................£6.370

Deputy Accountant-General, R. H. Watson, O.B.E.
£5,000 to £6,300

Assistant Accountants-General, W. M. Cowper; K. J. Macrae, I.S.O.............£4,600 to £5,200

Chief Accountants, S. Best; R. E. Collett; D. W. P. Crooks; R. Dutton; R. S. Graddon; L. Gregory; E. B. W. Johnston.........£3,250 to £4,400

Accountants, H. J. Baker: Miss D. L. Banwell; F. E. Butler; D. L. Carpenter; W. E. Chibbett; E. A. Cooper; Miss M. W. Dobson; T. E. Ellerington; J. T. Hine; A. C. Holdstock, M.B.E.; S. G. Housden; R. A. Huband; P. R. Johnson; M. R. Lacey; A. C. Mundy; P. Russell; A. J. Ryall; J. W. Shirley; R. F. Snowdon; G. Tarrant; B. Wright-Stevens..£2,775 to £3,400

Statistical Office

Controller, J. Mair...............£5,000 to £6,300

Deputy Controller, J. M. Boreham
£4,460 to £5,200

Assistant Controllers, J. C. Lewis, D.S.C.; S. N. Owen
£3,250 to £4,400

Senior Executive Officers, E. J. Catmull; W. S. Criddle; S. H. A. Mills; J. D. Pellett; J. H. Sivyer; E. J. Thompson; W. S. Tough; J. P. Wall; T. G. Wright................£2,775 to £3,400

Stores Branch

Superintendent, W. G. Davis, M.B.E.
£2,775 to £3 400

Collectors of Customs and Excise and Waterguard Superintendents
England and Wales

Birmingham: Higher Collector, K. C. Newnham (c); Senior Assistant Collector, F. Pilkington (e); Assistants, E. Lawton; R. A. Overin; D. A. Pitkeathly (f).

Brighton: N. E. Ellis (e); Assistants, A. E. Buruham; A. Jones; R. G. K. Vincent (f).

Bristol: Higher Collector, W. Wells (c); Senior Assistant, W. A. R. Armstrong (e); Assistant Collectors, C. A. J. Lines; R. Muirhead; A. A. Robinson (f),

Chester: R. Davies (e); Assistant Collectors, S. A. Cheetham; R. J. Heath (f).

Douglas: (Collector-Surveyor): A. Holden (h).

Dover: Higher Collector, T. D. Crellin (c); Senior Assistants, H. L. Ford; J. Henderson (e); Assistants, J. G. Davies; C. R. Lambert; J. H. Martin; V. Smith (f).

Harwich: Higher Collector, S. Cooper (c); Senior Assistant, H. J. Dunhill (e); Assistants, F. J. French, O.B.E., D.F.C., A.F.C.; G. H. Gilbert, D.F.C.; R. J. Whiter (f).

Hull: Higher Collector, S. F. Howard (c); Senior Assistant, G. D. Laws, M.B.E., D.S.C. (e); Assistant Collectors, P. H. Marson; J. Peach; W. M. Pearson; T. Riccalton (f).

Leeds: Higher Collector, S. L. Smith (c); Senior Assistant. J. Lavery (e); Assistants, C. Buist; W. F. Chesterton; J. E. Tate (f).

Liverpool: G. N. Madgen (b); Deputy Collector, P. C. Kerridge, M.C. (c); Senior Assistant Collectors R. A. Ewin; W. F. Egerton; T. Hill; G. A. Hughes (e); Assistant Collectors, F. Coaker; E. Cross; G. H. Dalton; H. P. Langley; L. C. G. Rice (f).

London Airports: Higher Collector, S. G. Allchin, O.B.E. (c); Senior Assistant Collectors, J. D. Adams; E. Kellett (e); Assistant Collectors, L. Battersby; F. E. Booker; R. E. Giles; T. L. McCarthy; F. A. E. Moyce; D. G. Pitt; D. R. R. Robinson (f).

London Port: K. E. Lefever (a); Deputy Collector, W. McKeown, O.B.E. (c); Senior Assistant Collectors, S. R. J. Abraham; D. C. Armstrong; R. Chapman; J. W. Edmondson; G. A. Wagstaffe (e); Assistant Collectors, J. R. Cooper; H. J. Lewis; M. H. Macfarlane; W. R. Maddaford; J. D. Spence; D. Stephenson (f).

London Central: Higher Collector, E. D. Roberts (c); Senior Assistant Collector, J. Hall (e); Assistant Collectors, A. V. Alcock; F. Coggon; D. F. Southorn; F. Veasey (f).

London North: Higher Collector, B. F. Sander, O.B.E. (c); Senior Assistant Collector, C. Rice (e); Assistant Collectors, G. J. Gale; E. Kildruff; H. M. Roe; R. Williams; E. Wright (f).

London South: Higher Collector, R. H. Abbott (c); Senior Assistant Collector, J. T. Hughes (e); Assistant Collectors, R. T. Broyd; G. C. Curtis; D. Tidy (f).

London West: Higher Collector, W. C. V. Tait (c); Senior Assistant Collector, D. Ewings (e); Assistant Collectors, J. E. Buckland; W. G. T. Lampard; F. Lintott; K. P. Wharton (f).

Manchester: Higher Collector, R. F. A. Webber (c); Senior Assistant Collectors, J. M. Carter; P. P. McNamara (e); Assistant Collectors, A. D. Barker; T. V. Dudley; G. Head; W. C. Henderson (f).

Newcastle: Higher Collector, P. J. Muir (c); Senior Assistant, R. V. J. Neeves (e); Assistant Collectors, J. W. Booth; N. Dixon; J. I. S. Downie; R. E. Grinstead (f).

Northampton: Higher Collector, W. S. Stead (c); Senior Assistant Collector, G. W. F. Short (e); Assistant Collectors, R. J. Gadsby; R. S. McGill; K. Taylor (f).

Nottingham: Higher Collector, J. C. Clemett (c); Senior Assistant Collector, F. Clegg (e); Assistant Collectors, J. A. H. Bracken; J. D. Harris, D.F.C. (f).

Plymouth: S. C. Lawrence (e); Assistants, G. W. Cox; B. Mitchell; H. D. Thorne, M.B.E., T.D. (f).

Preston: Higher Collector, E. R. J. Scarrett (c); Senior Assistant Collector. I. Hoile (e); Assistant Collectors, T. Parris; C. Peel; N. Stoddard (f).

Reading: Higher Collector, G. E. A. Rice (c); Senior Assistant Collector, T. C. Gosling (e); Assistant Collectors, S. J. Brownridge; H. J. Gallagher (f).

Southampton: Higher Collector, H. L. Burden (c); Senior Assistant Collectors, M. M. MacLaren; J. S. H. Plummer (e); Assistant Collectors, E. H. Atkins; A. A. Bonynge (f).

South Wales and the Borders: Higher Collector, R. B. Spence (c); Senior Assistant Collector, J. R. Allsopp (e); Assistant Collectors, J. Grice; F. Humphreys; G. D. Jeffers (f).

Scotland

Aberdeen: Higher Collector, W. Welch (c): Senior Assistant Collector, K. W. Thayer (e); Assistants, A. C. Morrow; W. G. Shannon; R. L. Tyler (f).

Edinburgh: Higher Collector, A. A. Brack (c); Senior Assistant Collectors, R. L. Mitchell; D. C. Rose (e); Assistant Collectors, G. M. Allport; R. Bielby; E. R. Gunstone; W. D. Keen, B.E.M.; W. M. Quirk (f).

Glasgow: Higher Collector, R. P. Outhwaite (*c*);
Senior Assistant Collectors, T. J. Gilchrist; J. K.
Lawson (*e*); *Assistant Collectors,* T. J. Chivers;
P. E. J. Dungey; J. M. Kerrigan; J. Kirshaw;
G. G. Shilling (*f*).
Greenock: Higher Collector, W. N. Heasley (*c*);
Senior Assistant Collector, L. Beaty (*c*); *Collectors,*
L. Cairns; S. Thornton; A. E. Thurgood (*f*).

Northern Ireland
Belfast: Higher Collector, T. R. Barber (*c*); *Senior
Assistant Collector,* R. F. Mountjoy (*e*); *Assistant
Collectors,* B. E. Barclay; K. G. Mathews; G. Sayce;
R. F. Stephenson (*f*).
Salaries:
(*a*) £6,370; (*b*) £5,990; (*c*) £5,015 to £5,640;
(*e*) £4,140 to £4,765; (*f*) £3,258 to £3,873;
(*h*) £2,529 to £3,099.

MINISTRY OF DEFENCE
See Armed Forces Section.

DEVELOPMENT COMMISSION
11 Cowley Street, S.W.1
[01-930-7134]
Chairman, The Countess of Albemarle, D.B.E.
Other Commissioners, G. N. Bowman-Shaw; Mrs.
G. Evans; J. P. R. Glyn; Sir Jack Longland; W.
Scholes; W. B. Swan, C.B.E., T.D.; Dr. R. C.
Tress, C.B.E.
Secretary, B. E. Lincoln........£4,390 to £5,640

THE DUCHY OF CORNWALL
10 Buckingham Gate, S.W.1
[Telephone: 01-834-7346]
The Duchy of Cornwall was instituted by
Edward III in 1337 for the support of his eldest
son, Edward, the Black Prince, and since that
date the eldest son of the Sovereign has succeeded
to the Dukedom by inheritance.

The Council
H.R.H. The Prince Philip, Duke of Edinburgh,
K.G., K.T.; The Earl Waldegrave, K.G., T.D. (*Lord
Warden of the Stannaries*); The Lord Ashburton,
K.G., K.C.V.O. (*Receiver General*); The Lord
Clinton; Brig. The Lord Tryon, G.C.V.O., K.C.B.,
D.S.O.; The Lord Franks, P.C., G.C.M.G., K.C.B.
C.B.E., F.B.A.; A. J. L. Lloyd, Q.C. (*Attorney-
General of the Duchy*); F. J. Williams; A. Gray
(*Secretary*).

Other Officers of the Duchy of Cornwall
Auditor, J. H. Bowman.
Solicitor, B. B. D. Stopford, M.V.O.
Asst. Secretary, M. R. E. Ruffer, T.D.
Deputy Receiver, G. A Briggs.
Sheriff (1971-72), Brig. C. T. Edward-Collins.

THE DUCHY OF LANCASTER
Lancaster Place, Strand, W.C.2
[01-836-8277]
The estates and jurisdiction known as the Duchy
and County Palatine of Lancaster have been
attached to the Crown since 1399, when John of
Gaunt's son came to the throne as Henry IV.
As the Lancaster inheritance it goes back to 1265.
Edward III erected Lancashire into a County
Palatine in 1351.
Chancellor of the Duchy of Lancaster, THE RT. HON.
~~(AUBREY) GEOFFREY (FREDERICK) RIPPON~~, Q.C.,
M.P. *JOHN DAVIES* £9,750
Private Secretary, C. C. C. Tickell, M.V.O.
*Attorney-General and Attorney and Serjeant within
the County Palatine of Lancaster,* S. W. Temple-
man, M.B.E., Q.C.
Receiver-General, Brig. The Lord Tryon, G.C.V.O.,
K.C.B., D.S.O.
Vice-Chancellor, T. A. C. Burgess.
Clerk of the Council and Keeper of Records, E. R.
Wheeler, C.V.O., M.B.E.
Solicitor, C. R. Crockett.
Chief Clerk, P. C. Clarke, C.V.O.
Registrar, Lancashire Chancery Court, R. A. For-
rester, C.V.O.

COURT OF CHANCERY OF THE COUNTY PALATINE OF DURHAM
Registrar's Chambers, Saddler Street, Durham
It is uncertain when the existing "Palatine"
privileges were first exercised, but these rights were
recognized by Parliament in 1289 during the
Episcopate of Bishop Bek and as having then
existed "time out of mind" and long prior to the
Norman Conquest. William I, in reorganizing
his Kingdom was, so far as Durham was concerned,
content to confirm the Laws of St. Cuthbert which
previously Guthred, King of Northumbria and
Alfred the Great appear in turn to have confirmed.
Palatine Counties were formed for the protection
and defence of the Border, in this case against the
Scots, and the Lands of the See were far more
extensive than the present County of Durham as
is shown by the Jurisdiction of the present Palatine
Court extending over Norham and Islandshire
(roughly the northern quarter of Northumberland) and Bedlingtonshire. Palatinate rights were
exercised by succeeding Prince Bishops till resumed
by the Crown in 1836; but this Court of co-
ordinate Jurisdiction with the Chancery Division
of the High Court still exists and continues in large
measure to exercise its ancient powers on behalf
of the Crown.
Chancellor, H. E. Francis, Q.C.
Attorney-General (vacant).
Solicitor-General (vacant).
Registrar of Chancery Court, H. Curry, D.F.C.

DEPARTMENT OF EDUCATION AND SCIENCE
Curzon Street, W.1
[01-493-7070]
The Government Department of Education was,
until the establishment of a separate office, a Committee of the Privy Council appointed in 1839 to
supervise the distribution of certain grants which
had been made by Parliament since 1834. The
Act of 1899 established the Board of Education,
with a President and Parliamentary Secretary, and
created a Consultative Committee. The Education Act of 1944 established the Ministry of
Education. In April 1964 the office of the Minister
of Science was combined with the Ministry to form
the Department of Education and Science. The
cost of administration for the financial year 1971-72
was estimated at £9,319,000.
Secretary of State for Education and Science, THE RT.
HON. MRS. MARGARET HILDA THATCHER, M.P.
£8,500
Private Sec., J. A. G. Banks.
Asst. Private Sec., F. W. Clark.
Parliamentary Under-Secretaries of State, The Lord
Belstead; W. R. van Straubenzee, M.B.E., M.P.
£3,750
Permanent Secretary, Sir William Pile, K.C.B.,
M.B.E. £14,000
Deputy Secretaries, T. R. Weaver, C.B.; J. A.
Hudson, C.B.; P. R. Odgers, C.B., M.B.E.; C. W.
Wright, C.B............................£9,000
*Chief Medical Officer (at Dept. of Health and Social
Security),* Sir George Godber, G.C.B., D.M.
*Chief Dental Officer (at Dept. of Health and Social
Security),* Surgeon Rear-Adm. W. Holgate, C.B.,
O.B.E., Q.H.D.S.
Legal Adviser, G. E. Dudman £9,000
Senior Chief Inspector, W. R. Elliott, C.B....£9,000
Chief Architect, W. D. Lacey, C.B.E.........£6,750
Secretary for Welsh Education, L. Jones........£6,750
Under-Secretary for Finance and Accountant General,
J. D. Brierley..........................£6,750
Under-Secretaries, H. T. Bourdillon, C.M.G.; J. P.
Carswell; H. A. Harding, C.M.G.; Miss W. P.
Harte; H. T. Hookway; D. E. Lloyd Jones, M.C.;
E. H. St. G. Moss; E. H. Simpson; P. Sloman; A.
Thomson; R. Toomey................£6,750

Architects and Building Branch
Assistant Secretary, F. A. Harper..£5,000 to £6,300
Principals, C. Booth; D. H. Grattidge; D. H.
Griffiths; S. M. Smith........£3,250 to £4,400

Directing Architects, J. D. Kay; J. L. H. Kitchin
£5,640
Principal Architects, B. H. Cox; K. E. Foster; D. L. Medd, O.B.E.; J. B. Smith, O.B.E.; R. L. Thompson...........................£4,390 to £5,015
Principal Quantity Surveyor, R. C. King
£4,390 to £5,015
Senior Architects, R. Clynes; J. S. B. Coatman; Miss M. B. Crowley, O.B.E.; Miss C. G. Edwards; R. L. Fitzwilliam; W. A. Fletcher; D. H. Griffin; M. S. Hacker; S. C. Halbritter; L. J. P. Halstead; L. S. Holland; G. E. Hughes; F. Jackson; D. S. Pearce; D. H. W. Poole; T. W. Prosser; O. M. Stepan; D. F. Wicks; E. Williamson........................£3,575 to £4,208
Senior Quantity Surveyors, P. F. Bottle; D. W. Carden; B. A. Staples; B. G. Whitehouse
£3,575 to £4,208
Mechanical and Electrical Engineers (Senior Grade), A. Grimshaw; L. E. J. Piper..£3,265 to £3,843
Mechanical Engineer (Senior Grade), G. R. Hammond
£3,265 to £3,843
Architects, R. W. U. Alcock; G. W. Ballard; A. J. Branton; J. R. C. Brooke; A. M. Cutler; A. G. Davidson; I. A. Fraser; G. M. T. Hawkins; G. M. John; H. F. Kendall; P. Marriott; D. S. Nightingale; G. J. Parker; K. F. Routledge; M. V. Sinclair; J. J. Wilson........£2,583 to £3,396
Quantity Surveyors, G. C. Battersby; D. J. Caruth; D. R. H. Drew; A. J. W. Haddon; W. H. Smith.....................£2,583 to £3,396
Senior Executive Officer, N. J. Bennett
£2,775 to £3,400

Arts and Libraries Branch
38, Belgrave Square, S.W.1.
[01-235-4801]
Assistant Secretaries, M. L. Herzig; G. J. Spence
£5,000 to £6,300
Principals, J. C. R. Hudson; Miss M. Nicholls; J. A. Reeve; N. B. W. Thompson
£3,250 to £4,400
Library Advisers, E. M. Broome; A. C. Jones; P. H. Sewell....................£3,258 to £3,873
Senior Executive Officer, G. Etheridge
£2,775 to £3,400

Establishments and Organization Branch
Assistant Secretaries, Miss J. M. Grinham; D. F. E. King; K. R. Rowberry....£5,000 to £6,300
Senior Principals, D. F. Robinson; P. Winter, I.S.O.
£4,600 to £5,200
Principals, W. B. Ashplant; D. M. Basey; E. R. Gibbs; G. Porter............£3,250 to £4,400
Senior Executive Officers, G. J. Aylett; F. W. Beale; R. Bromley; E. J. Brown; R. Burgess; J. E. Clegg; G. L. Emmett; W. H. Miller; R. W. J. Mitchell; Miss J. Reynolds; R. F. Smith; C. Tanner; Miss M. C. Taylor; A. C. G. Wiltshire
£2,775 to £3,400

External Relations and General Branch
Assistant Secretaries, H. Jordan; A. R. M. Maxwell-Hyslop; M. A. Walker......£5,000 to £6,300
Principals, E. Ll. Evans; L. J. Melhuish; H. C. Riddett.......................£3,250 to £4,400
Senior Executive Officers, W. Gamble; W. J. Huntingford; Miss N. E. Jones....£2,775 to £3,400
Senior Catering Adviser, Miss M. J. Warrington
£3,247 to £3,726
Catering Advisers, Miss M. I. Graham; Miss H. J. E. Robertson................£3,099

Information and Library
Information Department
Chief Information Officers, N. F. Cowen (£4,390 to £5,640); E. C. Roberson....£3,728 to £4,200
Principal Information Officers, A. G. Campbell; J. G. Millwood; G. E. Moggridge..£3,258 to £3,873
Senior Information Officers, Mrs. S. F. Brown; M. H. L. Clemans; H. L. Cook; Mrs. S. M. Ellingford; B. H. Hill; L. J. Nichols; Mrs. P. A. O'Brien; Miss G. M. Olds............£2,529 to £3,099

Senior Executive Officer, D. W. Constable
£2,775 to £3,400
Library
Librarian, Miss D. M. Jepson....£2,529 to £3,099

Finance Branch
Assistant Secretary (Deputy Accountant General), H. O. Dovey..............£5,000 to £6,300
Director of Cost Investigation Unit, T. A. J. Warlow
£5,015 to £5,640
Senior Economic Adviser, B. E. Rodmell
£5,000 to £6,300
Assistant Director, T. H. Hopkins £3,962 to £4,675
Senior Principal, J. C. Comper...£4,000 to £5,200
Principals, N. Summers; I. R. M. Thorm; A. W. Thompson.................£3,250 to £4,400
Economic Adviser, D. A. C. Heigham
£3,250 to £4,400
Senior Executive Officers, C. G. Benjamin; Miss K. T. Hosegood, M.B.E. ..£2,775 to £3,400

Further Education Branch
Elizabeth House, York Road, S.E.1
[01-928-9222]
Assistant Secretaries, A. S. Gann; P. S. Litton; D. W. Tanner; G. L. Thornton, C.B.E.
£5,000 to £6,300
Principals, B. L. Baish; D. L. Brazier, D.S.M.; Miss V. D. M. Chapman; M. Cohen; Miss M. d'Armenia; E. B. Granshaw; M. L. James; J. I. Lantry; M. J. F. Rabarts; D. V. Stafford; D. F. H. Taylor
£3,250 to £4,400
Senior Executive Officers, K. E. G. Barber; T. A. Morris...................£2,775 to £3,400

Legal Branch
Assistant Legal Advisers, H. B. C. Horrell; G. R. Hughes..................£4,555 to £5,640
Senior Legal Assistants, E. K. Kitson; G. J. Morgan; A. B. Rabagliati..........£3,286 to £4,390

Medical Branch
Elizabeth House, York Road, S.E.1
[01-928-9222]
Senior Principal Medical Officer, Miss E. E. Simpson, M.D.....................£6,750
Assistant Secretary, Mrs. D. M. White
£5,000 to £6,300
Senior Medical Officers, Miss M. Scott Stevenson; T. K. Whitmore...............£5,640
Medical Officers, R. Burns; Miss S. R. Fine; M. L. Graeme; N. P. Halliday; M. B. Pepper; Miss E. Wales....................£3,552 to £4,875
Dental Officers, W. G. Everett; C. Howard, J. G. Potter................£3,168 to £4,650

Pensions Branch
Mowden Hall, Staindrop Road,
Darlington, Co. Durham
[Darlington: 60155]
Assistant Secretary, S. B. Hallett..£5,000 to £6,300
Principals, K. H. R. Maynard, O.B.E.; R. K. Usher
£3,250 to £4,400
Senior Executive Officers, Miss M. D. Bishop; G. Bleasdale; R. K. Bradley; J. F. Price; K. T. V. Humberstone......£2,775 to £3,400

Planning and Programmes
Assistant Secretary, M. W. Hodges
£5,000 to £6,300
Principals, D. R. Jones; D. McLaughlin; N. Summers................£3,250 to £4,400

Schools Branch
Assistant Secretaries, J. R. Jameson; D. E. Morgan; B. C. Peatey; J. A. Richards..£5,000 to £6,300
Principals, C. A. Clark; D. L. Corder; W. F. Dawson, M.B.E.; R. E. Duff; Miss M. S. Hardwick; J. C. Hedger; N. W. Stuart; J. H. Thompson; L. G. Cook; Miss V. G. Ford; L. G. Gibbs, E.R.D.; H. G. Jenkins; R. Klein; J. R. Middleton................£3,250 to £4,400
Senior Executive Officer, Miss M. J. Bryant
£2,775 to £3,400

Science Branch

Deputy Chief Scientific Officer, J. C. Gray
£5,240 to £5,830

Assistant Secretaries, A. E. Hickinbotham; W. R. Reid (*Sec., Council for Scientific Policy*)
£5,000 to £6,300

Senior Principal Scientific Officers, F. C. Appleyard; R. E. Fairbairn; B. J. Perry.. £4,390 to £5,015
Principal Scientific Officers, C. C. Leamy; D. G. Libby; A. N. McGregor; D. H. May; J. E. Peachey
£2,820 to £3,902

Principals, M. B. Baker; G. F. Hawker; H. G. M. Peters; N. D. Wolf.......... £3,250 to £4,400
Senior Executive Officers, Miss E. Maher; J. H. Player....................£2,775 to £3,400

Special Education Branch
Elizabeth House, York Road, S.E.1
[01-928-9222]

Assistant Secretary, M. A. Walker
£5,000 to £6,300

Principals, Miss N. Bartman; Miss J. A. Gilbey; P. W. Mayer............£3,250 to £4,400
Senior Executive Officers, R. Carpenter, D.S.C.; W. McCoy; G. J. Sheppard.. £2,775 to £3,400

Statistics/ADP Branch

Director of Statistics, K. G. Forecast......... £6,750
Assistant Secretary, W. H. G. Harvey
£5,000 to £6,300

Chief Statisticians, G. M. Goatman; Miss J. R. Weatherburn..............£5,000 to £6,300
Senior Principal Scientific Officer, A. G. Price
£4,390 to £5,015

Principals, J. G. Bagley; R. Griffiths; L. C. Smith
£3,250 to £4,400

Principal Scientific Officer, F. C. Heward
£2,820 to £3,902

Statisticians, C. J. Belliss; H. Collings; A. Eaves; D. Fine; D. B. Halpern; Miss A. E. Rendel; Miss M. Robson; M. Wilson........£3,250 to £4,400
Senior Executive Officers, Miss M. A. Bellamy; A. Chaffer; K. Coombs; R. S. Evans; T. H. Hunt; S. G. Reed; E. A. L. Spackman; G. R. E. Stewart; F. C. Street; L. R. F. Wiggins
£2,775 to £3,400

Teachers Branch I (Supply Salaries and Qualifications)

Assistant Secretaries, S. J. Barker, D.S.C.; D. O'Donovan; V. H. Stevens..........£5,000 to £6,300
Principals, Miss O. R. Arnold; M. A. Barry, E.R.D.; K. C. Humphrey; G. L. Macey; P. Ramsden
£3,250 to £4,400

Senior Executive Officers, J. Blatcher; Miss D. E. Lorenz; G. Mansell; D. G. Smith
£2,775 to £3,400

Teachers Branch II (Training)
Elizabeth House, York Road, S.E.1
[01-928-9222]

Assistant Secretaries, H. C. Rackham; C. Wigfull
£5,000 to £6,300

Senior Principal, J. I. Jones..... £4,600 to £5,200
Principals, W. J. Archibald; R. Dellar; G. Dickson; R. E. Judd; A. Marshall; G. H. Osborne; A. H. Prosser; C. H. Saville...........£3,250 to £4,400
Senior Executive Officers, P. J. Lane; Miss M. E. E. Mills; H. G. Rutherford; F. Sussex; N. E. Worcester...................£2,775 to £3,400
Senior Catering Adviser, Miss F. M. Cowell
£3,247 to £3,726

Universities Branch
Elizabeth House, York Road, S.E.1
[01-928-9222]

Assistant Secretaries, N. T. Hardyman; Miss J. M. Scrimshaw; S. P. Whitley.... £5,000 to £6,300
Principals, E. E. Jenkins; K. W. Morris
£3,250 to £4,400
Senior Executive Officers, Miss I. Buckley; R. G. Manning; Miss B. D. Naylor
£2,775 to £3,400

Awards

Principal, Miss O. Tregurtha.... £3,250 to £4,400
Senior Executive Officers, B. Lowe; G. M. Weaver
£2,775 to £3,400

Computer Board

Senior Principal Scientific Officer, L. F. Rutterford (*Secretary*)................. £4,390 to £5,015

Welsh Education Office
31 Cathedral Road, Cardiff
[0222-42661]

Assistant Secretaries, E. O. Davies; D. A. Routh
£5,000 to £6,300
Principal, Miss H. F. Graham (*a*)
£3,250 to £4,400

(*a*) In London.

National Lending Library for Science and Technology
Walton, Boston Spa, Yorks
[0937-84-2031]

Director, D. J. Urquhart, C.B.E., Ph.D.
£5,240 to £5,830

H.M. Inspectorate (England)

Chief Inspectors, J. M. Birchenough; L. J. Burrows; H. W. French, C.B.E.; A. G. J. Luffman, O.B.E.; Miss M. J. Marshall; R. A. Richardson
£6,120

Divisional Inspectors, R. H. Adams, T.D.; M. J. Beaver; P. M. Burns; H. J. Edwards; H. L. Fenn; F. Makin; C. J. Read; F. C. Ruffett; E. J. Sidebottom...............................£5,435
Staff Inspectors, Miss E. E. Biggs; M. F. Bird; N. Booth; Miss S. J. Browne; Miss K. M. P. Burton; C. W. E. Cave; A. D. Collop; P. D. Dudley; Miss S. M. C. Duncan; W. J. Earl; M. Edmundson; J. L. Gayler; R. P. Greenwood; S. E. Gunn, T.D.; D. M. Hopkinson; E. Houghton; P. H. Hoy; B. W. Kay; T. C. Keay; A. G. King; J. G. Lavender; W. G. Lewis; R. C. Lyness; Miss E. McDougall; J. Maitland-Edwards; G. W. Milburn; R. Money; J. W. Morris; R. W. Morris; J. H. Mundy; D. B. Nield; G. S. V. Petter; P. Phillips; Miss E. G. Pollard; D. I. R. Porter; R. R. Roberts; C. W. Rowland; H. Sagar; P. Samuel; R. Sibson; E. Sims; J. L. Smedley; G. Snowball; M. E. Sprinks; L. A. Stockdale; E. W. Sudale; N. Thomas; G. R. A. Titcomb; Miss K. M. Tobin; D. G. Toose; R. A. Wake; W. M. White; E. Whiteley; E. Wilkinson; C. L. Williams
£5,435

H.M. Inspectors, Miss K. Addison; O. P. Alexander; T. W. F. Allan; J. P. Allen; Mrs. H. G. Alston; T. I. Ambrose; P. T. Armitstead; R. Arnold; F. A. Arrowsmith; B. C. Arthur; Miss P. M. Ash; A. Ashbrook; K. L. Ashurst; P. F. Atherton; Miss J. L. Atkin; M. F. Atkins; A. B. Baddeley; D. Baillie; R. C. Baker; D. Bamber; Miss C. H. Barker; G. Barratt; D. A. Barton Wood; Miss N. B. Batley; W. K. Beal; A. Bell; Mrs. J. Bell; G. Benfield; T. H. Bennetts; D. B. F. Billimore; Miss G. M. Bishop; R. W. Blake; H. H. Blisset; G. E. Bone; Mrs. J. W. Bonnard; P. R. Booth; Miss J. M. Bosdét; Mrs. B. K. Bottomley; D. M. W. Boulton; G. J. Boyden; H. A. Boyer; D. M. Brancher; R. S. Breckon; J. K. Brierley; W. H. Briggs; J. Broadbent; Miss M. I. Brogden; Mrs. B. M. Brook; D. G. Buckland; K. R. Bull; T. A. Burdett; K. R. Burford; P. J. Burn; Miss A. Burns; J. W. Butler; I. B. Butterworth; P. Cadenhead; Mrs. D. M. Caffery; W. F. Campbell; Mrs. E. Cave; R. B. Chalmers; M. G. C. Channon; Miss J. Chreeson; J. T. G. Chugg; Miss G. D. Clark; A. G. Clegg; Miss M. I. Clough; E. W. Clubb; Miss R. D. Coburn; Miss C. Collingwood; P. Collister; R. M. Cooper; E. C. Cordell; Miss N. K. Cornforth; T. C. Cradock; J. Creedy; Miss S. Crisp; C. J. Crumpler; Mrs W. M. Curzon; Miss D. Dain; J. D. Dale; Mrs. R. D. Dale; J. Dalglish; D. M. Davies; I. Davies; Miss I. E. Davies; J. A. Davies, D.F.C.; N. Davis; Mrs. O. H. Davis; Miss M. B. Davison; J. E. B. Dawson, O.B.E.; J. R. Deans; Mrs. E. V. de Bray; D. A. Denegri; Mrs. K. V. Dewar; T. Dickinson; Miss G. J. Diment; Mrs. H. W. Doubleday; R. C. Dove; F. J. Downs

S. R. G. Downs; W. Drabble; Mrs. B. J. Dutton; W. M. Dutton; F. Edwards; Miss P. I. Edwin; K. T. Elsdon; G. W. Elsmore; D. W. Emery; P. Enticknap; Miss G. L. O. Evans; L. Evans; Miss V. J. Evans; J. A. Everson; E. Fanthorpe; V. A. Farthing; J. Featherstone; Miss R. R. Feldmeier; J. R. Fish; C. D. Flanagan; T. J. Fletcher; P. H. Forrest; W. S. Fowler; Miss J. M. Francis; W. H. Francis; Miss M. G. Fraser; J. A. Fuller; H. E. Gardiner; Mrs. M. Gaskell; B. Gay; G. D. Gibbs; A. Gibson; Miss P. M. Giles; M. S. Girling; D. J. Gold; D. R. T. Goodwin; Miss M. I. Gordon; P. Gordon; J. G. Goulding; J. F. Graber; Miss S. Gracey; J. Graham; W. Graham; Miss S. E. Grant; E. A. Greatwood; F. H. Green; R. E. Greenway; J. W. Gregory; W. A. Grier; R. M. Griffith; N. M. Griffiths; R. M. Griffiths; L. S. Grimsdale; P. C. Haeffner; Miss D. Haigh; A. A. Haimes; B. J. Hall; W. G. Hamflett; J. Hampson; G. Hankin; E. Harcourt-Parsons; G. B. Harrison; Miss K. Harrison; D. F. Harrop; K. N. Hastings; B. W. V. Hawes; F. W. Hawkins; B. P. Hayes; G. M. Hearnshaw; R. Heworth; R. Hiley; Miss A. A. Hill; Miss B. E. Hill; J. A. Hill; D. Hilton; M. W. Himsworth; Miss M. E. Hodkinson; L. Holdsworth; D. Hollingsworth; Mrs. M. I. Holmes; F. R. Holterman; R. O. Hopkins; T. Howarth; J. S. Hudson; Miss A. M. Hughes; R. A. J. Hughes; Miss M. Hulme; W. E. Husband; K. B. Hutton; A. J. Hymans; E. S. Ingiedew; K. M. Jack; A. Jackson; L. Jackson; K. Jary; W. F. J. Jeff; T. O. R. A. Jeffrey; J. C. Jennings; D. W. John; W. T. John; Miss S. H. Johns; Miss E. M. Johnson; Miss M. Knox Johnston; Miss D. M. Jones; H. Jones; H. C. H. Jones; H. R. Jones; J. L. Kay; G. S. Keeney; Miss M. Kellett; L. P. Kelley; R. A. Kelly; F. R. Kitchen; Miss A. A. Knowles; L. S. Laid; D. G. Lambert; B. M. Lane; Miss A. A. E. M. Leevers; A. J. Legge; J. R. Lewis; Miss M. D. Lewis; Miss M. K. Lightowler; Miss B. M. Lockwood; Mrs. R. Lockwood; Eric Lord; E. Lord; G. A. Lucas; B. W. Lucke; D. W. McAllister; Miss M. T. McBride; E. McDonald; Mrs. J. E. McDonald; J. McGinn; Mrs. J. C. McGinty; F. O. Machin; Miss E. McKaig; G. W. S. Mackay; Miss E. M. Mackinlay; H. J. J. Malcolm; Miss K. L. Malcolm; Miss J. L. Maltby; W. J. A. Mann; D. J. Marjoram; D. T. E. Marjoram; H. E. S. Marks; Miss R. J. Marlor; P. F. Marlow; Mrs. G. D. Marshall; T. W. Martin; C. H. Maude; F. G. Mee; Miss B. E. Megson; C. M. Melanefy; R. F. Mildon; A. Monkman; Miss S. I. J. Moore; Miss P. M. W. Morecombe; J. O'C. Morgan; D. A. Morris; R. C. Morton; Miss N. R. Mulcahy; A. M. Munday; G. P. Murgett; Miss P. W. Myers; G. J. Neal; G. F. Neesnam; A. W. Newton; Miss N. Newton-Smith; C. A. Norman; E. Norris; Miss K. M. O'Leary; P. J. Oliver; Miss M. Osborn; J. Ounsted; A. Owen; I. P. Owen; J. A. Page; K. Parker; J. B. Parnaby; Mrs. B. Parr; F. Parrott; W. H. Parry; C. P. Parsons; Miss J. Paterson; Mrs. R. W. Peacocke; G. T. Peaker; Miss I. Perlmutter; Mrs. P. Perry; K. Pinder; P. J. Pitman; Miss E. M. Potts; J. W. Powell, T.D.; D. R. Prestwich; H. A. Price; R. M. Prideaux; B. H. Procter; Miss R. C. Ramirez; P. B. Rattenbury; Miss B. E. Rawlins; Miss M. Rayment; D. Raymond; D. Ll. Rees; J. Reynolds; J. D. Richards; C. D. Roberts; J. R. Roberts; I. A. Robertson, D.F.C.; Miss E. M. Robinson; N. H. Roche; G. R. Romans; R. Roundhill; D. H. Rutt; I. P. Salisbury; M. V. Salter; K. J. Sargent; Miss E. M. Saunders; Miss H. M. Sebestyen; C. H. Selby; E. L. Sewell; J. H. Shackley; D. R. Shannon; B. E. Shaw; J. R. Shirtcliff; T. A. G. Silk; P. J. Silvester; R. H. D. Sinclair; P. Singh; J. G. Slater; P. F. Smart; P. R. Smith; R. T. Smith; W. H. Snowdon; Mrs. M. H. Somers; L. Speak; J. F. Spencer; M. E. Sprakes; J. W. Stephens; B. C. G. Stevens; L. W. Stewart; R. W. Stockdale; H. C. Story; C. E. Strafford; R. Summersby; Miss J. Sumner Smith; F. Sutcliffe; E. F. A.

Suttle; G. H. Swinden; D. F. Symes; C. J. Symonds; B. Taylor; W. W. Taylor; J. D. Thomas; R. V. Thomas; Miss A. D. Thompson; W. H. Thomson, D.S.C.; R. J. Todd; G. E. Trodd; F. A. Tucker; T. N. Tunnard; A. F. Tuberfield; M. J. Tyerman; A. Urie; G. W. Verow; W. H. Wainwright; A. Walmsley; F. Walsh; Miss P. Walters; R. E. Ward; Miss J. R. Warner; R. K. Warren; E. R. Wastnedge; D. H. Watts; Miss O. C. Weilenbeck; E. H. Wells; P. E. Weston; J. B. Whinnerah; C. G. White; Miss S. Whitworth; A. Wigglesworth; M. R. Wigram; I. G. E. Wilding; A. J. Wiles; J. Wilkinson; G. M. Willan, D.F.C.; D. G. Williams; H. G. Williams; R. C. Williams; P. G. Willmore; Miss D. E. Wiseman; D. C. Wollman; Miss M. S. Wood; J. T. Woodend; Miss B. Wooldridge; E. H. Wright; J. L. Wright; M. Wylie; J. R. Yorke-Radleigh; F. P. Young; T. R. Young

£2,997 to £4,570

H.M. Inspectorate (Wales)

Chief Inspector, W. Ll. Lloyd, C.B. £6,120
Staff Inspectors. E. O. Davies; T. I. Davies; G. Gratton; I. R. Lloyd; G. A. V. Morgan; M. D. Owen; P. E. Owen; W. J. Thomas; P. C. Webb
£5,435
H.M. Inspectors, Miss M. Anthony: G. Bowen; E. Ll. Davies; Miss E. M. Davies, O.B.E.; Miss E. C. Edwards; T. R. Edwards; G. Evans; K. M. Evans; L. M. Evans; N. B. Evans; R. W. Evans; Miss W. M. Hopkins-Jones; Miss J. E. Hughes; E. H. Hutton; R. L. James; T. W. John; D. B. Jones; G. L. Jones; Miss G. Jones; L. Jones; R. E. Jones; C. Reid; D. A. Thomas; Glyndwr Thomas; G. Thomas, O.B.E.; P. Thomas; R. Thomas; T. H. Thomas; W. E. Thomas; G. Warren; Miss E. N. Williams; M. J. F. Wynn
£2,997 to £4,570

ELECTRICITY AUTHORITIES
THE ELECTRICITY COUNCIL
30 Millbank, S.W.1

Chairman, Sir Norman Elliott, C.B.E. £20,000
Deputy-Chairmen, N. F. Marsh, C.B.E (£16,000),
Sir Alan Wilson, F.R.S. (*part-time*) £2,000
Members, P. A. Lingard; R. D. V. Roberts, C.B.E.
(*each*) £10,000 to £15,000
The Lord Douglass of Cleveland (*part-time*)
£1,000
Members from the Central Electricity Generating Board,
F. E. Bonner; Sir Stanley Brown, C.B.E.; O. Francis, C.B.
Secretary, J. A. Wedgwood.

CENTRAL ELECTRICITY GENERATING BOARD
Sudbury House, 15 Newgate Street, E.C.1
[01-248-1202]

Chairman, Sir Stanley Brown, C.B.E. £19,000
Deputy Chairman, O. Francis, C.B. £15,000
Members, E. S. Booth, C.B.E.; F. E. Bonner; D. Clark; A. E. Hawkins, *each* £8,000 to £15,000
(*part-time*) The Lord Holford, R.A.; P. T. Menzies; The Lord Wright of Ashton-under-Lyne, C.B.E.
each £1,000
Secretary, E. J. Turner.

ELECTRICITY BOARDS
The 12 Area Electricity Boards
(The Chairmen of Area Boards receive a salary of £10,000 to £15,000).

London, 46-47 New Broad Street, E.C.2. *Chairman*, W. D. D. Fenton, C.B.E. *Sec.*, S. M. Gore.
South Eastern, Queen's Gardens, Hove, 3, Sussex. *Chairman*, E. Sinnott. *Sec.* G. Wray, O.B.E.
Southern, Southern Electricity House, Littlewick Green, Maidenhead, Berks. *Chairman*, R. R. B. Brown, C.B.E. *Sec.*, C. M. de L. Byrde.
South Western, Electricity House, Colston Avenue, Bristol 1. *Chairman*, A. N. Irens, C.B.E. *Sec.*, D. S. Bentham.

X *A.E. HAWKINS Deputy Chairman (31/72)*
until 1/7/72 when he becomes Chairman

Eastern, Wherstead, nr. Ipswich, Suffolk. *Chairman*, H. D. B. Wood, O.B.E.   *Sec.*, M. R. Hyde.

East Midlands, P. O. Box 4, North P.D.O., 398 Coppice Road, Arnold, Nottingham. *Chairman*, P. Sydney.   *Sec.*, T. F. C. Walker.

Midlands, Mucklow Hill, Halesowen, nr., Birmingham. *Chairman*, E. Bates.   *Sec.*, C. Wickstead.

South Wales, St. Mellons, Cardiff, *Chairman*, W. E. Richardson,   *Sec.*, R. G. Williams.

Merseyside and North Wales, Sealand Road, Chester. *Chairman*, D. G. Dodds.   *Sec.*, M. M. Parker.

Yorkshire, Scarcroft, Leeds. *Chairman*, A. Bond. *Sec.*, E. K. Richmond, T.D.

North Eastern, Carliol House, Newcastle upon Tyne 1. *Chairman*, A. H. Norris.   *Sec.*, J. E. Hayes.

North Western, Cheetwood Road, Manchester 8, *Chairman*, R. F. Richardson, M.B.E.   *Sec.*, G. H. Richardson.

NORTH OF SCOTLAND HYDRO-ELECTRIC BOARD
16 Rothesay Terrace, Edinburgh 3
[031-225-1361]

Chairman, Rt. Hon. T. Fraser (*part-time*). . . . £7,000
Deputy Chairman, I. A. D. Millar, M.C. (*part-time*)
£3,700
Members (*part-time*), D. D. S. Graib (*Chairman of Consultative Council*) (£2,100); N. Hogg, C.B.E. C. L. C. Allan (*unpaid*); The Lord Tayside, O.B.E.; Col. H. A. C. Mackenzie, C.B.E., M.C.; A. Wallace. . . . .*each* £1,000
Member (*full-time*) *and General Manager*, K. R. Vernon.
Secretary and Solicitor H. W. Simpson.

SOUTH OF SCOTLAND ELECTRICITY BOARD
Inverlair Avenue, Glasgow, S.4
[041-637-7177]

Chairman, C. L. C. Allan. £14,000
Deputy-Chairman, A. Christianson, C.B.E., M.C.
£11,000
Part-time Members, J. Ballantyne; Sir John Dunbar; T. Fulton (*Chairman of Consultative Council*) (£2,100); C. H. Martineau; C. H. Offord, C.B.E.; W. Ure, M.B.E. (*each* £1,000); Rt. Hon. T. Fraser (*unpaid*).
Secretary, D. M. McGrouther.

DEPARTMENT OF EMPLOYMENT
8 St. James's Square, S.W.1
[01-930-6200]

The Department of Employment is generally responsible for the efficient use of Britain's manpower resources. It provides a free service, through a national network of employment exchanges, for employers seeking labour and for workers who are unemployed or wish to change their jobs. The exchanges also act as agencies for other Government Departments in such matters as the payment of unemployment benefit and the issue of passports.

In Government Training Centres, courses are provided to help persons in need of training and retraining, and to reduce shortages of skilled labour. Through its 25 Industrial Rehabilitation Units, the department helps disabled and handicapped men and women to regain working fitness. It is also responsible for the central, and some local, administration of the Youth Employment Service; the promotion of safety, health and welfare amongst workpeople in factories, offices, shops and railway premises; the enforcement of statutory minimum wages, holidays and hours of work laid down by Wages Councils; and the collection and publication of statistics about manpower, wages, hours of work, and the index of retail prices. The Department is also responsible for the administration of the *Redundancy Payments Act*, 1965 and 1969 and the *Industrial Training Act*, 1964.

The department, through its advisory and conciliation services, assists in the prevention or settlement of industrial disputes and the promotion of good management/employee practices, and increased security at work. Its activities overseas include the maintenance of labour attachés in certain foreign countries and liaison with the International Labour Organisation.

Secretary of State for Employment, THE RT. HON. ROBERT CARR, M.P. £8,500
Private Secretary, D. B. Smith.
Assistant Private Secretaries, P. J. H. Edwards; P. Syson.
Parliamentary Private Secretary, D. W. S. S. Lane, M.P.
Minister of State, PAUL ELMORE OLIVER BRYAN, D.S.O., M.C., M.P. £5,625
Parliamentary Secretary, D. G. Smith, M.P. . . . £3,750
Permanent Secretary, Sir Denis Barnes, K.C.B.
all Treasury £14,000
Deputy Secretaries, R. R. D. McIntosh, C.B.; K. Barnes, C.B.; J. H. Locke. £9,000
Solicitor, F. D. Lawton. £9,000

Industrial Relations
Under-Secretary, J. L. Edwards. £6,750
Assistant Secretaries, A. W. Brown; D. P. Buckley; M. A. Simons. . . . . £5,000 to £6,300
Chief Conciliation Officer, A. S. Kerr
£5,015 to £5,640

Incomes Division
Under-Secretary, D. J. Derx. £6,750
Assistant Secretaries, L. J. Gosse; D. J. Hodgkins; J. R. Lloyd-Davies, C.M.G.; W. R. B. Robinson
£5,000 to £6,300
Chief Wages Inspector, I. Prost. . . £4,600 to £5,200
Secretary of Wages Councils, Miss Y. M. Simmons
£3,750 to £4,400

Manpower and Productivity Services Division
Under-Secretary, D. G. Cox. £6,750
Assistant Secretary, W. H. Marsh, O.B.E.
£5,000 to £6,300
Grade I Officer, Miss M. Towy Evans, O.B.E.
£4,600 to £5,200

Overseas Division
Under-Secretary, A. M. Morgan, C.M.G. £6,750
Assistant Secretaries, Miss B. Green; D. J. Sullivan
£5,000 to £6,300

Research and Planning Division
Assistant Secretary, G. A. Brand. . £5,000 to £6,300

Employment General Division
Under-Secretary, F. Pickford. £6,750
Assistant Secretaries, N. Covington; D. Pointon
£5,000 to £6,300

Employment Services Division
Under-Secretary, C. J. Maston, C.B., C.B.E. . . . £6,750
Assistant Secretaries, E. Betterton; R. M. Walker; L. G. Morgan. . . . . £5,000 to £6,300
H.M. Inspector of Schools, E. Lord £3,461 to £5,215
Economic Policy (Manpower) Division
Under-Secretary, I. F. Hudson. £6,750
Assistant Secretary, R. M. Hobsbaum
£5,000 to £6,300
Senior Economic Adviser, F. J. Bayliss
£5,000 to £6,300

Establishments Division
Director of Establishments, R. F. Keith, O.B.E. . £6,750
Assistant Secretaries, P. C. D. Archer, O.B.E.; A. H. Dangerfield, O.B.E.; Mrs. D. M. Kent; D. G. Storer. . . . . £5,000 to £6,300
Chief Inspector, E. W. Fawcett. . . £4,600 to £5,200
Chief Information Officers, B. Ingham (£5,000 to £6,300); N. Gaffin. . . . . £4,600 to £5,200

Finance Division
Accountant-General, A. F. A. Sutherland. £6,750
Director of Accounts and Audit, A. R. Cooke
£4,600 to £5,200
Assistant Accountants-General, F. Bailey; C. Broadbent; S. H. N. Hinton; G. F. Lloyd; M. Sheinfeld . . . . £5,000 to £5,200
Regional Finance Officers, W. H. Clayton (*Wales and South Western*); E. G. Thomas (*Midlands*); F. J. C. B. Macmillan (*London and South Eastern*); L. Reason (*Eastern and Southern*); A. G. Read, O.B.E. (*North Western*); G. L. Brook (*Scotland*);

W. H. Simons (*Yorkshire and Humberside and Northern*)................£3,750 to £4,400

Safety, Health and Welfare Division
Under-Secretary, C. H. Sisson £6,750
Assistant Secretaries, J. L. B. Garcia; Miss M. F. Gracey; M. W. Smart; M. Wake
£5,000 to £6,300

H.M. Factory Inspectorate
Chief Inspector of Factories, B. H. Harvey....£6,750
Deputy Chief Inspectors of Factories, C. F. Carr; C. Mainwaring; W. S. Moore; Miss L. A. Pitton...............................£5,990
Senior Electrical Inspector, G. L. Leighton
£4,390 to £5,015
Senior Chemical Inspector, K. L. Goodall
£4,390 to £5,015
Senior Engineering Inspector, W. Lister
£4,390 to £5,015
Senior Civil Engineering Inspector, G. Baker
£4,390 to £5,015
Superintending Inspectors, J. R. Bloor (*London and Home Counties (West)*); T. K. Cross (*London and Home Counties (East)*); J. A. Davis (*Midlands (Nottingham)*); A. Gow (*Scotland*); A. W. Grimsey (*Midlands (Birmingham)*); J. L. Hobson (*North Western (Manchester)*); V. B. Jones (*Wales and South Western*); L. Livesey (*West Riding and North Lincs.*); J. Nixon (*North Western (Liverpool)*); C. R. Noble (*Northern*); A. D. Sill (*London and Home Counties (North)*)....£4,092 to £5,018
Industrial Health and Safety Centre, 97 Horseferry Road, Westminster, S.W.1.—A permanent exhibition of methods, arrangements and appliances for promoting the safety, health and welfare of industrial workers.
Director, R. G. Seconde (+ allce.) £2,570 to £3,873

Medical Services Division
Chief Medical Adviser, T. A. Lloyd Davies, Q.H.P.
£6,120
Senior Medical Advisers, A. H. Baynes; W. D. Buchanan; M. H. P. Sayers (*Glasgow*); R. Owen
£5,640
Medical Inspectors, E. S. Blackadder (*Scotland*); M. S. Catton (*London and Home Counties (East)*); H. J. Davies (*Cardiff*); L. E. Evinton (*Nottingham*); M. Greenberg (*Headquarters*); M. D. Kipling (*Birmingham*); R. Morley (*Newcastle*); G. L. Ritchie, O.B.E. (*Wolverhampton*); G. F. Smith (*Bristol*); J. B. L. Tombleson (*Manchester*); D. G. Trott (*London and Home Counties (North)*); A. Watt (*Liverpool*); G. J. S. West (*Leeds and Sheffield*); R. Whitelaw (*Glasgow*)
£3,552 to £4,875

Government Wool Disinfecting Station
Manager, S. Gibbon.............£2,465 to £2,889

Solicitor's Division
Solicitor, F. D. Lawton...........£8,050
Principal Assistant Solicitor, D. E. Belham...£6,150
Assistant Solicitors, J. B. H. Billam, D.F.C.; D. Bowden-Dan; D. M. D. D. Grazebrook; G. E. McClelland...............£4,555 to £5,640
Senior Legal Assistants, C. D. R. Barker; K. Halil; C. N. L'Angellier; R. Mollart; H. T. Morgan; Miss V. Rice-Pyle..........£3,286 to £4,390

Statistics Division
Director of Statistics, A. R. Thatcher........£6,750
Deputy Director, R. Turner......£4,390 to £5,640
Chief Statisticians, R. Ash; F. G. Forsyth
£4,390 to £5,640
Grade I. Miss M. A. Barkess.....£4,600 to £5,200

Training Division
Under-Secretary, D. R. F. Turner........£6,750
Assistant Secretaries, J. Wild; B. A. Smith; D. W. J. Orchard; C. A. Larsen.......£5,000 to £6,300
Chief Adviser on Industrial Training, E. R. L. Lewis
£5,500

Regional Organization
Northern Region
Controller, E. Robbie.........£5,000 to £6,300
Deputy Controller, A. Grant.....£4,600 to £5,200
Yorkshire and Humberside Region
Controller, A. A. G. McNaughton
£5,000 to £6,300
Deputy Controller, A. J. Dechant .£4,600 to £5,200
Eastern and Southern Region
Controller, J. H. Devey, O.B.E....£5,000 to £6,300
Deputy Controller, D. A. Savage £4,600 to £5,200
London and South Eastern Region
Controller, K. D. Jones, C.B.E....£5,000 to £6,600
Deputy Controllers, J. A. Potter; J. A. Tannahill
£4,600 to £5,200
South Western Region
Controller, W. D. Scott.........£5,000 to £6,300
Deputy Controller, D. A. Holland
£4,600 to £5,200
Wales
Controller, A. E. L. Winter......£5,000 to £6,300
Deputy Controller, L. R. Frost....£4,600 to £5,200
Midland Region
Controller, A. Y. W. Cowie.....£5,000 to £6,300
Deputy Controller, G. C. H. Breden
£4,600 to £5,200
North Western Region
Controller, J. C. Healey.........£5,000 to £6,300
Deputy Controller, R. C. Stephenson
£4,600 to £5,200
Scotland
Controller, W. A. Treganowan, C.B.E.......£6,600
Deputy Controller, J. S. P. McKenzie
£5,000 to £6,300

INDEPENDENT OFFICES
The Industrial Court
1 Abbey Garden, Great College Street
Westminster, S.W.1
[01-030-4571]
The Industrial Court was set up by the Industrial Courts Act, 1919. Under this and other Acts the Secretary of State for Employment may refer trade disputes and certain other matters to the Court for settlement.
President, Sir Roy Wilson, Q.C..........£10,950
Independent Members, A. Ll. Armitage; Sir Daniel Jack, C.B.E.; D. Karmel, C.B.E., Q.C.; Prof. J. C. Wood, C.B.E.
Representative Members, J. G. Bothwell, O.B.E.; H. Briggs, C.B.E; S. M. Caffyn, C.B.E.; Sir Andrew Crichton; The Lord Douglass of Cleveland; Sir Sydney Ford, M.B.E.; C. Henniker-Heaton, C.B.E.; A. J. Hubbard; Sir Norman Longley, C.B.E.; Miss B. L. Napier; H. Norton, O.B.E.; J. M. Prain, D.S.O., O.B.E., T.D.; J. Rhodes; S. A. Robinson; Sir Jack Scamp; Brigadier J. J. Sloan, C.B.E., M.C.; P. E. Trench, C.B.E., F. I. Tuckwell, C.B.E.; The Lord Wright of Ashton-under-Lyme, C.B.E.
Secretary, O. Killick............£2,570 to £3,186

The Industrial Tribunals
Established under the Industrial Training Act 1964.
Central Office (England and Wales)
93 Ebury Bridge Road, S.W.1
President, Sir Diarmaid Conroy, C.M.G., O.B.E., T.D., Q.C.
Secretary, K. C. Ashfold ......£2,570 to £3,186
Central Office (Scotland)
St Andrew House, West Nile Street, Glasgow, C.1
President, R. Reid, Q.C.
Secretary, B. M. Sheridan.......£2,570 to £3,186

Committee on Safety and Health at Work
Chairman, The Lord Robens of Woldingham, P.C.

Office of the Umpire
6 Grosvenor Gardens, S.W.1
[01–730–9236]

Independent statutory authority—appointed by the Crown to decide appeals under Reinstatement in Civil Employment Act and National Service Acts.

Umpire, D. W. E. Neligan, O.B.E. .... *fees*
Deputy Umpire, S. I. W. Price .... *fees*

DEPARTMENT OF THE ENVIRONMENT
2 Marsham Street, London
[01–212–3434]

The Department was formed in November 1970, by merging the Ministries of Housing and Local Government, Public Building and Works and Transport. Under the Secretary of State for the Environment are the Ministers for Local Government and Development, Housing and Construction and Transport Industries.

The Department is responsible for housing policy, planning legislation, supervision of local authorities, government policy on transport, the sponsorship of the construction industry, the programming, design and construction of building for central government, the Post Office and the Armed Forces. Its functions also include management of the Royal Parks, preservation of ancient monuments and historic buildings and protection of the coast and countryside, the control of air and water pollution and noise, and research related to the above topics.

Secretary of State for the Environment, THE RT. HON. PETER EDWARD WALKER, M.B.E., M.P. £8,500
Private Secretary, J. P. G. Rowcliffe.
Assistant Private Secretaries, P. Fletcher; J. Hobson.
Parliamentary Private Secretary, The Hon. Anthony Berry, M.P.
Minister for Local Government and Development, R. GRAHAM PAGE, M.B.E., M.P.
£7,625 to £8,500
Private Secretary, J. M. Hope.
Assistant Private Secretary, J. S. Stevens.
Parliamentary Private Secretary, H. O. Murton, O.B.E., T.D., M.P.
Minister for Housing and Construction, THE RT. HON. JULIAN AMERY, M.P. ...... £7,625 to £8,500
Private Secretary, D. C. Pickup.
Assistant Private Secretaries, J. Hale; J. Winder.
Parliamentary Private Secretary, W. S. Churchill, M.P.
Minister for Transport Industries, THE RT. HON. JOHN WYNNE WILLIAM PEYTON, M.P.
£7,625 to £8,500
Private Secretary, J. R. Coates.
Assistant Private Secretaries, J. S. Gill; L. F. Thomas.
Parliamentary Private Secretary, P. M. E. D. McNair-Wilson, M.P.
Parliamentary Under-Secretaries of State:—
H. P. G. Channon, M.P. (Housing and Construction); E. W. Griffiths, M.P. (Transport Industries); M. R. D. Heseltine, M.P. (Local Government and Development); The Lord Sandford, D.S.C. (Local Government and Development) £3,750
Permanent Secretary, Sir David Serpell, K.C.B., C.M.G., O.B.E. £14,000
Private Secretary, J. W. Baker.
Assistant Private Secretary, Miss J. Cornell.
Director-General of Organization and Establishments, I. P. Bancroft, C.B. £9,000

Senior Staff Management
Director (Under Secretary), J. H. Street, C.B. ... £6,750
Assistant Secretary, R. A. Isaacson
£5,000 to £6,300

Personnel Management
Director (Under Secretary), T. H. Shearer ... £6,750
Assistant Secretaries, W. J. S. Batho; G. T. Bright; P. D. Davies; L. R. Mustill, M.B.E.; J. W. T. Pritchard .... £5,000 to £6,300

Manpower Resources
Director (Under Secretary), J. H. P. Draper. £6,750
Assistant Secretaries, E. F. J. Bignell; E. S. Foster; M. J. Hislop .... £5,000 to £6,300

Management Services
Director, D. Bishop, M.C. £6,750
Assistant Secretaries, Miss J. M. Foster; R. C. Geall; M. Mendoza .... £5,000 to £6,300
Chief Librarian, W. Pearson, M.B.E.
£3,458 to £4,070

Organization Development
Assistant Secretaries, J. A. L. Gunn; M. Mendoza
£5,000 to £6,300

Information
Director, H. L. James £6,750
Chief Information Officers, K. D. McDowell; L. E. E. Jeanes; J. P. Morris; W. S. G. Smele
£4,390 to £5,640

Research Services
Director General of Research, D. J. Lyons £9,000
Director of Research Requirements, W. J. Reiners
£6,750
Chief Scientific Officer, L. B. Mullett £6,750
Deputy Chief Scientific Officer, A. P. Goode
£5,240 to £5,790
Assistant Secretary, J. A. Fowles .. £5,000 to £6,300
Director Building Research Station, J. B. Dick
£5,640 to £10,950
Director Fire Research Station, D. I. Lawson
£5,640 to £10,950
Director Forest Products Research Laboratory, T. A. Oxley .... £5,640 to £10,950
Director Hydraulics Research Station, R. C. H. Russell .... £5,640 to £10,950
Director Road Research Laboratory, A. Silverleaf
£5,640 to £10,950
Director Water Pollution Research Laboratory, Dr. A. L. Downing .... £5,640 to £10,950

Resource Allocation and Central Economic Services
Director General Economics and Resources, J. A. Jukes C.B. £10,950

Economics A
Director, H. Cole £6,100
Senior Economic Adviser, P. T. McIntosh
£5,000 to £6,300

Economics B
Director, I. C. R. Byatt £6,100
Chief Statistician, B. C. Brown .. £5,000 to £6,300
Senior Economic Advisers, A. E. Holmans; D. F. Hagger .... £5,000 to £6,300
Assistant Secretary, G. P. Jefferies £5,000 to £6,300

Economics C
Director, E. H. M. Price £6,100

Statistics
Director, A. H. Watson, C.B.E. £6,100
Chief Statisticians, K. Glover; H. Palca; J. A. Rushbrook .... £5,000 to £6,300

Strategic Planning
Under Secretary, J. R. Madge £6,750
Assistant Secretary, P. C. McQuail
£5,000 to £6,300

Finance Organization
Principal Finance Officer (Central Services), G. C. Wardale £6,750
Principal Finance Officer (Housing and Construction), Mrs. J. Toohey £6,750
Assistant Secretary, G. May ...... £5,000 to £6,300
Director of Contracts, I. C. Fletcher £6,750
Assistant Secretaries, R. F. Halse; J. H. Lewis
£5,000 to £6,300
Principal Finance Officer (Local Government and Development), J. D. W. Janes. £6,750
Assistant Secretaries, M. S. Albu; H. H. Browne; P. H. Elsley; C. E. Seward; R. D. Widdas
£5,000 to £6,300
Principal Finance Officer (Transport Industries), G. C. Wardale £6,750
Assistant Secretaries, A. J. Rosenfeld; P. R. Sheaf
£5,000 to £6,300
Comptroller of Accounts, C. R. Bossom, O.B.E.
£5,990

Jan'72 SIR KCB

LOCAL GOVERNMENT AND DEVELOPMENT

Secretary, J. D. Jones, C.B..............£13,000
Sir T. A. Jukes
Deputy Secretary Local Government, R. C. Chilver, C.B................£9,000
Director (*Chief Scientific Officer*) *Central Unit on Environmental Pollution*, Dr. M. W. Holdgate
£6,750

Assistant Secretary, M. McF. Davis
£5,000 to £6,300
Under Secretary—*Local Government A*, J. E. Beddoe, C.B................£6,750
Assistant Secretaries, A. G. Rayner; J. R. Niven; R. G. Adams; H. Pryce...£5,000 to £6,300
Under Secretary—*Local Government B*, H. L. Jenkyns
£6,750
Assistant Secretaries, W. M. Schwab; W. Dawson; A. Leavett; A. L. Vincent...£5,000 to £6,300
Under Secretary—*Local Government C*, C. J. Pearce
£6,750
Assistant Secretaries, J. E. Hannigan; D. C. Milefanti
CO 6/7/72 £5,000 to £6,300
Chief Planner, W. Burns, C.B.E., D.SC.....£9,000
Deputy Chief Planner—*Planning Services A* (vacant).
Assistant Secretaries, L. M. Dunstan; R. T. Scowen
£5,000 to £6,300
Deputy Chief Planner—*Planning Services B*, J. T. Wilkinson......................£6,120
Deputy Chief Planner—*Planning Services C*, P. L. Joseph..........................£6,120
Deputy Secretary—*Planning*, R. N. Heaton, C.B. *retd* £9,000
J. Garlick 8/7/72
Under Secretary—*Planning A*, D. Caplan...£6,750
Assistant Secretaries, K. F. J. Ennals; A. Flexman
£5,000 to £6,300
Under Secretary—*Planning C*, P. D. Coates..£6,750
Assistant Secretaries, L. Goodman; V. D. Lipman; B. Taylor...............£5,000 to £6,300
Under Secretary—*Planning D*, J. W. Vernon, C.M.G.
£6,750.
Assistant Secretaries, D. J. King; K. P. Leary; L. Mann..................£5,000 to £6,300
Under Secretary—*Planning E*, J. Rogerson..£6,750
Assistant Secretaries, K. W. S. MacKenzie, C.M.G.; H. F. Ellis Rees............£5,000 to £6,300
Under Secretary—*Planning G*, J. Catlow.....£6,750
Assistant Secretaries, M. W. Bennitt; Mrs. J. Bridgeman; P. L. Daniel.......£5,000 to £6,300
Deputy Secretary, *Planning*, R. Brain, C.B...£9,000
Under Secretary—*Planning B*, G. W. Moseley
£6,750
Assistant Secretaries, W. Deakin; F. W. Girling; J. D. Higham, C.M.G........£5,000 to £6,300
Under Secretary—*Planning South-East*, A. Sylvester-Evans............................£6,750
Assistant Secretaries, P. Critchley; A. G. Semple; J. M. Hawksworth.......£5,000 to £6,300

MECHANICAL ENGINEERING AND VEHICLE INSPECTION DIVISIONS

Chief Mechanical Engineer, H. Perring......£7,800
Assistant Chief Engineer (*Vehicle Inspection*), J. W. Furness...............£4,875 to £5,640
Assistant Chief Engineer (*Mechanical*), C. C. Toyne
£4,875 to £5,640

URBAN AND REGIONAL PROFESSIONAL GROUP

Deputy Chief Engineer, J. S. Berry.....£6,120
Senior Principal Scientific Officer, R. Spence
£4,390 to £5,015
Assistant Chief Engineer, D. Greenwood
£4,875 to £5,640
Senior Economic Adviser, P. R. Smethurst
£5,000 to £6,300

PASSENGER TRANSPORT AND URBAN PLANNING GROUP

Assistant Secretaries, J. H. H. Baxter; D. G. Burr; N. E. Godfrey; C. N. Tebay..£5,000 to £6,300
Adviser on Bus Management and Operations, A. F. Neale.

LONDON GROUP

Under Secretary, J. Garlick. *Deputy Sec. Local Gov.*...£6,750
Assistant Secretaries, G. H. Chipperfield; P. F. Grant; K. Peter.............£5,000 to £6,300
Assistant Chief Engineer, G. E. Rowland
£4,875 to £5,640

ROAD SAFETY AND VEHICLE GROUP

Under Secretary, L. E. Dale..............£6,750
Assistant Secretaries, W. H. Alexander, S. T. Garrish; P. N. Gerosa; D. Holmes; P. A. Waller
£5,000 to £6,300

HIGHWAYS

Director General Highways, Sir William Harris, K.B.E., C.B................£10,950
Chief Highways Engineer, A. D. Holland, T.D.
£7,800
Deputy Directors General, M. Milne; L. S. Mills, C.B.
£7,250 to £7,800
Deputy Chief Highways Engineer, L. R. Greenway, O.B.E.......................£6,120
Assistant Chief Engineers, R. P. Sleep; J. Ford; K. Sriskandan; J. T. Duff; G. D. Spearing; G. H. Oversby-Powell...£4,875 to £5,640
Chief Quantity Surveyor, G. A. Hughes......£5,015
Under Secretary, D. C. Haslegrove..........£6,750
Assistant Secretaries, G. Cockerham; W. W. Scott
£5,000 to £6,300
Deputy Chief Engineer, F. J. Best..........£6,120

PLANNING AND ECONOMICS

Director, D. McKean....................£6,750
Senior Economic Adviser, G. A. C. Searle
£5,000 to £6,300
Assistant Secretary, J. A. Dole....£5,000 to £6,300
Assistant Chief Engineer, K. C. Westhorp
£4,875 to £5,640

ADMINISTRATION SERVICES

Director, W. J. Sharp...................£6,750
Assistant Secretaries, J. M. Entwistle; L. E. Henderson; J. Lane.............£5,000 to £6,300

PROFESSIONAL SERVICES

Solicitor and Legal Adviser, K. A. T. Davey..£9,000
Principal Assistant Solicitor, G. E. Gammie..£6,750
Chief Alkali Inspector, F. E. Ireland........£6,380
Chief Inspector of Audit, S. V. Collins, C.B...£6,750
Deputy Chief Inspector of Audit, L. Tovell....£6,370
Director General of Water Engineering, W. J. Glenn, C.B................£9,000
Deputy Chief Engineers, T. P. Hughes; H. S. Tricker..........................£6,120
Chief Housing and Planning Inspector, C. F. Allan
£6,750
Deputy Chief Housing and Planning Inspector, R. F. F. Williams, G.M...........£6,120

COUNTRYSIDE COMMISSION
See p. 375

WATER RESOURCES BOARD
See p. 436

CHAIRMEN, ECONOMIC PLANNING BOARDS

N. H. Calvert (*Northern, Newcastle upon Tyne*); P. J. Harrop (*Yorkshire and Humberside, Leeds*); J. W. Farnsworth (*East Midlands, Nottingham*); D. J. King (*East Anglia*); J. Catlow (*South-East*); A. W. J. Scoble (*South-West, Bristol*); A. Emanuel, C.M.G. (*West Midlands, Birmingham*); W. R. Corrie (*North-West, Manchester*)
each £5,000 to £6,300

PRINCIPAL REGIONAL HOUSING AND PLANNING OFFICERS

G. J. Shoebridge (*West Midlands, Birmingham*); S. H. Godsell (*South-West, Bristol*); G. M. Wedd (*Yorkshire and Humberside, Leeds*); J. Stobart (*North-West, Manchester*); (vacant) (*Northern, Newcastle upon Tyne*); (vacant) (*East Midlands, Nottingham*)............each £5,000 to £6,300

HOUSING, CONSTRUCTION AND TRANSPORT INDUSTRIES

Secretary, I. V. Pugh, C.B....................£13,000
Deputy Secretaries, W. P. D. Skillington, C.B.; W. L. Wilson, C.B., O.B.E.; C. P. Scott-Malden, C.B..................................£9,000

Housing A

Under Secretary, F. J. Ward............£6,750
Assistant Secretaries, A. MacC. Armstrong; T. M. Heiser; H. W. Marshall; W. O. Ulrich
£5,000 to £6,300

Housing B

Under Secretary (vacant)............£6,750
Assistant Secretaries, N. Hamilton; T. L. Jones; Mrs. D. M. O'Brien; J. H. Ward
£5,000 to £6,300

NEW TOWNS

Under Secretary, S. W. Gilbert............£6,750
Assistant Secretaries, J. Delafons; A. J. Fairclough; J. C. H. Marlow; J. Palmer..£5,000 to £6,300

HOME ESTATE MANAGEMENT

Director, E. Vickers....................£6,750
Assistant Directors, W. S. Bryant, M.B.E.; D. W. Cain; G. R. Inkpen............£5,640
Assistant Secretary, R. G. S. Johnston
£5,000 to £6,300

SUPPLIES DIVISION

Controller of Supplies, H. Leadbeater.....£6,750
Assistant Controllers, A. E. Davies; A. D. Ormond; R. H. Salter..............£5,000 to £6,300

ANCIENT MONUMENTS AND SPECIAL SERVICES

Director, H. H. Hobbs, C.B............£6,750
Assistant Secretaries, R. W. Barrow, C.V.O.; A. W. Cunliffe, M.B.E........£5,000 to £6,300
Assistant Director, G. A. H. Pearce £5,000 to £6,300
Chief Inspector of Ancient Monuments, (vacant)
£5,200
Bailiff of Royal Parks, Major I. K. C. Hobkirk, M.V.O., M.C.

HOME REGIONAL SERVICES

Director, A. J. Isaac....................£6,750
Assistant Secretaries, R. P. Cooke, C.B., T.D.; H. A. Cridland..............£5,000 to £6,300

SCOTTISH SERVICES

Director, P. H. Ogle-Skan, T.D............£6,750
Assistant Secretary, M. D. King..£5,000 to £6,300
Assistant Director, R. A. S. Jamieson, O.B.E.
£5,640

REGIONAL DIRECTORS (WORKS)

C. E. Bedford (*London*); N. E. Higgitt (*Eastern*); N. P. Walsh (*Midland*); R. G. Wilson, M.B.E. (*North Eastern*); S. Ashburner (*North Western*); A. W. T. Ellis (*South Eastern*); F. S. Butler (*South Western*); L. C. Chapman (*Southern*).
£5,990 to £6,120

WALES

Director, G. G. Walters, C.B.E............£6,750

ESTATE MANAGEMENT OVERSEAS

Director, B. Roberts....................£6,750

POST OFFICE SERVICES

Director, F. Walley....................£6,750
Assistant Secretary, D. J. Crouch. £5,000 to £6,300
Assistant Director, J. O. Stevens..........£6,120

DEFENCE SERVICES 1

Director (*Under Secretary*), E. H. A. Stretton. £6,750
Assistant Secretaries, G. M. Patrick; R. J. Smith
£5,000 to £6,300
Director B, K. W. Dando..............£5,640

DEFENCE SERVICES 2

Director, M. J. Cotton..................£6,750
Assistant Secretaries, P. Jenkins; S. J. Vincent
£5,000 to £6,300
Directors A and B, R. Campbell; G. F. Woodward
£5,640 to £6,120

SOCIAL AND RESEARCH SERVICES

Director, J. C. Knight..................£6,750
Assistant Secretary, D. W. Royle £5,000 to £6,300

DIRECTORATE OF DEVELOPMENT

Director General of Development, J. T. Redpath, C.B. M.B.E............£9,000

HOUSING DEVELOPMENT

Directors A, A. A. Bellamy; C. E. D. Wooster
Directors B, A. D. H. Embling; T. O'Toole

BUILDING DEVELOPMENT

Director, G. H. Wigglesworth............£6,750
Assistant Director, W. J. Appleton; L. J. F. Stone
£5,640

CIVIL ENGINEERING DEVELOPMENT

Director, L. R. Creasy, O.B.E............£6,750
Assistant Director, F. R. Martin............£5,640

ENGINEERING SERVICES DEVELOPMENT

Director, M. Woolfson..................£6,750
Assistant Directors, H. P. Johnson; E. G. Mallalieu
£5,640

QUANTITY SURVEYING DEVELOPMENT

Director, R. C. Miller, C.B.E............£6,750
Assistant Directors, H. P. Golds; K. C. Linsdell
£5,640

CONSTRUCTION INDUSTRY

Director, J. H. S. Burgess..............£6,750
Assistant Secretaries, T. W. Hall; O. H. Lawn
£5,000 to £6,300
Assistant Director, R. R. Lack...£5,000 to £6,300

TRANSPORT INDUSTRIES

Deputy Secretary, T. L. Beagley............£9,000

PORTS

Under Secretary, J. E. Sanderson............£6,750
Assistant Secretary, D. C. Fagan £5,000 to £6,300

RAILWAYS

Under Secretary, J. M. Moore, D.S.C............£6,750
Assistant Secretaries, A. C. Lyall; J. Peeler
£5,000 to £6,300
Chief Inspecting Officer, Col. J. R. H. Robertson
£6,120

NATIONALIZED TRANSPORT

Under Secretary, R. D. Poland..............£6,750
Assistant Secretaries, A. F. Parr; P. H. Lawrence; J. A. L. Barber..............£5,000 to £6,300
Assistant Chief Engineer, Brig. J. Constant (*ret.*)
£4,875 to £5,640

INTERNATIONAL TRANSPORT AND DEFENCE

Under Secretary, B. P. H. Dickinson............£6,750
Assistant Secretaries, G. G. D. Hill, C.M.G.; A. S. Robertson..................£5,000 to £6,300

FREIGHT TRANSPORT

Under Secretary, S. M. A. Banister............£6,750
Assistant Secretaries, R. J. E. Dawson; Miss S. W. Fogarty..............£5,000 to £6,300
Senior Principal Scientific Officer, E. J. Wilson
£4,390 to £5,015

CENTRALIZED LICENSING

Under Secretary, E. S. Ainley.............£6,750
Assistant Secretaries, Miss E. P. Kruse; S. Emm,
C.B.E.; W. L. W. Isdale......£5,000 to £6,300

EXCHEQUER AND AUDIT DEPARTMENT
Audit House, Victoria Embankment, E.C.4
[01-353-8901]

This is the Department of the Comptroller and
Auditor General, an office created by the Act 29
& 30 Vict. c. 39 (1866) to replace, with extended
powers, the separate offices of Comptroller
General of the Receipt and Issue of the Exchequer
and of the Commissioners for Auditing the Public
Accounts. This officer is appointed by Letters
Patent under the Great Seal, and is irremovable
except upon an address from the two Houses of
Parliament. In his capacity as Comptroller
General of the Receipt and Issue of the Exchequer,
he authorizes all issues from the Consolidated and
National Loans Funds after satisfying himself that
Parliament has given authority for them. He
examines the accounts of the Consolidated and
National Loans Funds and makes an annual report
on them to Parliament. In his capacity of Auditor
General of Public Accounts, he is charged with the
duty of examining on behalf of the House of
Commons the accounts of expenditure out of
funds provided by Parliament, the accounts of the
receipt of revenue, and generally all other public
accounts, including the accounts of Government
stores and of trading services conducted by Government Departments. The results of his examination
of those accounts are reported to the House of
Commons.

Comptroller and Auditor General, Sir David Pitblado,
K.C.B., C.V.O.........................£14,000
Secretary, A. R. Siyth, C.B., O.B.E.........£6,750
Deputy Secretary, H. A. Long, C.B.E........£6 600
Director of Establishments and Accounts, W. H.
Nichols...............£5,000 to £6,300
Directors of Audit, D. V. Boyd; R. A. Cheeseman;
C. H. Davies; R. C. Hooper; G. P. Morrell;
E. J. Lowe, O.B.E.; J. French; J. F. T. Cheetham;
D. F. Smith..............£5,000 to £6,300
Deputy Directors of Audit, R. H. Plaister; T. N.
Finch; Miss W. M. Cragg, I.S.O., M.B.E.; P. G.
Spary; H. R. Francis; J. H. D. Sant; S. L. Teas-
dale; P. R. Billett; J. C. McDowell; F. T.
Womack; F. W. Eele; R. Stewart; R. Thomas;
M. F. Hughes; H. Solomon; F. J. E. Blanks;
E. K. Williams; D. K. Clark; G. N. Debenham
£4,600 to £5,200

EXPORT CREDITS GUARANTEE DEPARTMENT
Aldermanbury House, Aldermanbury, E.C.2
[01-606-6699]

The Export Guarantees Acts, 1968 and 1970,
empower the Department of Trade and Industry
to give guarantees to United Kingdom exporters
for the purpose of encouraging export trade. The
power is administered by the Export Credits Guarantee Department. Commercial guarantees, under
Section 1 of the Acts, are given after consultation
with an Advisory Council set up for the purpose.

Export Guarantees Advisory Council
Chairman, Sir Frederick Seebohm, T.D.
Deputy Chairman, E. I. N. Warburton. C.B.E.
Other Members, Sir Walter Barrie; E. Kaye, C.B.E.;
A. E. F. Lovick; Sir Hector McNeil, C.B.E.; J. R.
Milbourn; Sir Leslie Robinson; D. G. Scholey;
J. A. R. Staniforth, C.B.E.; K. Taylor.

Officers
Secretary, R. Fell, C.B.E.............£9,000
Under-Secretaries, K. W. Cotterill; S. D. Wilks
£6,925
Assistant Secretaries, V. I. Chapman; J. Gill;
R. T. Kemp; W. H. Paxman; J. M. Reynolds;
E. T. Walton; D. A. Ward....£5,175 to £6,475
Senior Principals, Mrs. M. E. Belsham; C. C. Birch,
M.B.E.; W. B. Davies; J. A. Dyer; L. Elmes;
M. W. Gentle; K. C. Harrison; W. H. Johnson,
D.F.C., D.F.M.; E. G. Lowton; V. E. Young
£4,775 to £5,375

Chief Executive Officers, A. E. J. Berry; B. G.
Blackburn; Miss J. D. Bolwell; G. E. J. Breach;
L. M. Broad; G. Bromley; J. Caldwell; L. H.
Clarke; J. W. Coggins; T. H. Collinson; J. A.
Crossen; J. Cunningham; Mrs. E. Davidson;
A. Dawson; J. L. Drinkwater; P. C. B. Duncan;
J. E. Elliott; A. C. Elston; G. W. Ethail; F. H.
Fishpool; D. H. J. Furbank; C. W. Gentry;
M. J. C. Glaze; J. H. Hall; L. Halligan; L. C.
Harmer; G. H. Harvey; C. E. Henderson;
P. Henley; N. J. A. Hooker; E. J. Jackson; D. M.
Jaffray; H. K. Jones; Miss J. U. Kilsby; J. Lake;
N. F. Lowe; H. B. Lynch; G. J. Macmahone,
C.B., C.M.G.; F. C. Mann; R. F. L. Martin;
R. Mathrani; R. A. Napier-Andrews; W. H.
Neuff, O.B.E.; E. Panton; R. K. Pearson; W. J. C.
Pinnell; C. P. Rawlings, C.B.E.; Miss K. M.
Sleven, O.B.E.; A. J. Somerville; J. G. Sorbie;
G. P. Stay; M. G. Stephens; H. L. H. Stevens,
M.B.E.; D. H. Twyford; R. A. Wild
£3,425 to £4.575
Principal Information Officer, P. A. D. Jones, O.B.E.
£4,975
Senior Executive Officers, Miss A. F. Bannatyne;
H. R. Barber; J. A. H. Bayliss; Miss D. Bell;
G. C. Bird; J. Bolsover; Miss D. E. Brandel;
A. J. Bray; L. D. N. Charman; Miss B. K.
Cleaver; P. G. Coles; Miss L. A. Connor; D. R.
Coombe; A. J. Croft; H. C. Cunningham;
A. R. Currie; B. J. Davison; T. W. Denyer;
K. Dixey; Miss M. E. Duck; B. J. Duffield;
A. J. Dunstan; C. L. W. Durning; V. C. Earl;
T. W. Ebers; J. C. Edmondson; P. A. F. Field;
R. D. Foister; A. P. Fowell; J. F. Gaynor;
F. W. R. Gore; R. E. Gove; L. M. Haines;
P. Handovsky; C. W. Hanny; H. Harris; Miss
O. K. R. Hender; Miss E. M. I. Heslop; J. H.
Hibbert; H. F. Kinshelwood; R. C. Hirschfeld;
Miss V. Horigan; Miss B. M. Howard; Miss S. J.
Hunt; K. F. Jackson; I. Jennings; R. E. Johnson;
A. L. Jolley; F. Jones; R. W. Lane; F. H. Light;
J. R. Llewelyn; K. G. Lockwood; M. J. Long;
E. S. Lowe; W. A. Mann; R. C. Milsted;
C. A. E. Nelson; B. Oattes; J. W. Pannell;
O. H. Pettafer; R. A. Phelps; P. G. Plows;
A. C. Polti; C. G. Purdy; R. F. Reville; Mrs.
B. G. Reynolds; Miss J. A. Roffey; C. F.
Russell; C. Rylance; T. Sanderson; E. G.
Sandys; A. J. Saunders; J. K. Sedman; D. W.
Shannon; P. W. Shaw; B. M. Sidwell; R. W.
Smeatham; W. E. Smith; Miss E. Thornhill;
D. L. Townley; F. W. Vernau; J. F. Vose;
H. Watson; D. E. Wiltshire; C. R. Wright;
T. D. Wright; J. R. G. Wythers, B.E.M.
£2,950 to £3.575

Regional Organization
J. V. Baker; D. A. Green; D. G. Hake; C. J. A.
Link (£2,950 to £3,575); A. E. Beedle; B. T.
Clark; W. Ford; R. H. K. Hughes; K. I. Humph-
rey; F. Wilmot.............£2,775 to £3,400
Head of New York Office, J. Dorrian, D.F.M.
£3,425 to £4.575

FOREIGN AND COMMONWEALTH OFFICE
(See also Overseas Development Administration)

On the recommendations of the Committee on
Representational Services Overseas appointed by
the Prime Minister under the Chairmanship of
Lord Plowden in 1962, H.M. Diplomatic Service
was created on Jan. 1, 1965, by the amalgamation of
the Foreign Service, the Commonwealth Service,
and the Trade Commission Service, and is now
responsible for the manning of the overseas posts of
these three former services. On Aug. 1, 1966, the
Colonial Office was merged into the Commonwealth Relations Office to form the Commonwealth Office. The Foreign Office and
Commonwealth Office combined on Oct. 1, 1968.

Downing Street, S.W.1
[01-930-8440, 01-930-2323]
Secretary of State, The RT. HON. SIR ALEXANDER
FREDERICK DOUGLAS-HOME, K.T., M.P.   £8,500

Private Secretary, J. A. N. Graham *CMG* 6/72
$£5,175$ to $£6,475$
Assistant Private Secretaries, N. J. Barrington; P. H. Grattan; Miss J. A. Holden; P. J. McCormick . . . . $£3,425$ to $£4,575$
Parliamentary Private Secretary, M. J. McLaren, M.P.
Minister of State, THE RT. HON. JOSEPH BRADSHAW Julian AMERY GODBER, M.P. . . . . . LORD BALNIEL $£5,525$
Parliamentary Under-Secretaries of State, The Marquess of Lothian; A. H. R. Royle, M.P.; J. A. Kershaw, M.C., M.P. . . . . $£3,750$
Permanent Under-Secretary of State and Head of the Diplomatic Service, Sir Denis Greenhill, K.C.M.G., GCMG O.B.E. $£15,000$
Jul 72 *Private Secretary*, T. L. A. Daunt.
Deputy Under-Secretaries, J. R. A. Bottomley, C.M.G.; Sir Thomas Brimelow, K.C.M.G., O.B.E.; Sir Stewart Crawford, K.C.M.G., C.V.O., (*Deputy to the Permanent Under-Secretary of State*); C. M. Le Quesne, C.M.G.; Sir Leslie Monson, K.C.M.G., GCMG C.B.; The Hon. Sir Con O'Neill, K.C.M.G.; Sir John Rennie, K.C.M.G.; Sir Stanley Tomlinson, JAN 72 K.C.M.G.; J. O. Wright, C.M.G., D.S.C. (*Chief Clerk*) . . . . $£9,000$

Assistant Under-Secretaries, D. L. Cole, C.M.G., M.C. (*Deputy Chief Clerk*); S. J. G. Fingland, C.M.G.; H. A. A. Hankey, C.M.G., C.V.O.; D. G. Holland (*Chief Economic Adviser*); H. B. C. Keeble, C.M.G.; A. D. Parsons, C.M.G., M.V.O., M.C.; G. F. N. Reddaway, C.B.E.; C. M. Rose, C.M.G.; C. P. Scott, C.M.G., O.B.E.; D. A. Scott, C.M.G.; H. Smedley, C.M.G., M.B.E.; J. A. Turpin, C.M.G.; C. D. Wiggin, C.M.G., D.F.C., A.F.C.; K. M. Wilford, C.M.G. . . . . $£6,925$
Home Inspector, A. T. Lamb, M.B.E., D.F.C.
$£5,175$ to $£6,475$
Inspectors, T. W. Aston, C.M.G.; D. J. Brown, M.B.E.; M. Brown, O.B.E.; J. H. Lewen; R. S. Swan, M.B.E.; K. C. Thom . . . . $£5,175$ to $£6,475$
Commercial Inspectors, C. G. Cruickshank; C. B. Heathcote-Smith, C.B.E. . . . . $£5,175$ to $£6,475$
Legal Adviser, Sir Vincent Evans, K.C.M.G., M.B.E.
$£10,950$
Second Legal Adviser, J. L. Simpson, C.M.G., T.D.
$£9,000$
Deputy Legal Advisers, A. R. Rushford, C.M.G.; I. M. Sinclair . . . . $£6,925$
Legal Counsellors, F. Burrows; H. G. Darwin; P. R. N. Fifoot; D. G. Gordon-Smith, C.M.G.; H. Steel, O.B.E.; A. D. Watts . $£4,730$ to $£5,815$
Historical Adviser, R. d'O. Butler, C.M.G. . . $£3,489$
Director (Economic) and Head of Economists Dept., J. K. Wright . . . . $£5,175$ to $£6,475$
Overseas Labour Adviser, G. Foggon, C.M.G. O.B.E.
$£6,505$
Overseas Police Adviser, M. J. Macoun, C.M.G., O.B.E.
$£5,175$ to $£5,795$
Director of Communications, R. W. Snelling, £6,753
Deputy Director of Communications, D. Bayley
$£6,200$
Establishment Officer, N. Walton, O.B.E.
$£5,000$ to $£6,300$
Signals Department (Government Communications Headquarters)
Priors Road, Cheltenham, Gloucestershire [0242–21491]
Director, Sir Leonard Hooper, K.C.M.G., C.B.E.
$£9,000$
Principal Establishment Officer, J. A. F. Somerville, C.B.E. . . . . $£6,750$

Heads of Departments
($£5,175$ to $£6,475$: Assistant Heads of Dept., $£3,425$ to $£4,575$: except where stated)
Accommodation and Services Dept., D. G. Crawford; *Deputy Head*, W. Sharpe, O.B.E.; *Assts.*, J. A. Stockwell, M.B.E.; E. G. Andrews.
Arabian Dept., A. A. Acland; *Asst.*, D. G. Allen.
Arms Control and Disarmament Research Unit. Director, M. F. Cullis, C.V.O. *Asst.* Maj.-Gen. R. E. Lloyd, C.B. C.B.E., D.S.O., (*ret.*)
Atlantic and Indian Ocean Dept., I. B. Watt, C.M.G.; *Asst.*, R. C. Cox, M.B.E.

Aviation and Telecommunications Dept., R. Hanbury-Tenison; *Asst.*, R. I. T. Cromartie.
Caribbean Dept., C. S. Roberts; *Assts.*, J. H. Fawcett; D. M. Kerr, O.B.E.
Central and Southern African Dept., W. Wilson; *Senior Desk Officers*, J. E. C. Macrae; A. B. Moore, M.B.E.
Claims Dept., W. F. Morris; *Asst.*, Sir Alexander Morley, K.C.M.G., C.B.E.
Commodities Dept., H. E. J. Hale, O.B.E.; *Asst.*, J. Dodds.
Commonwealth Co-ordination Dept., Miss L. E. T. Storar; *Asst.*, P. D. McEntee, O.B.E.
Communications Dept., B. A. Flack; *Deputy Head of Dept.*, A. Routledge; *Assistants*, B. C. Harries; A. D. Morgan.
Computer Services Branch, J. L. Stevenson; *Asst.* J. J. Sinclair, O.B.E.
Consular Dept., Dr. C. G. Thornton, C.B.E., M.V.O.; *Assts.*, W. R. Loveridge; B. Rose.
Cultural Exchange Dept., E. V. Vines, O.B.E.; *Asst.*, K. Kirby, O.B.E.
Cultural Relations Dept., C. C. B. Stewart, C.M.G.; *Assts.*, R. C. Shawyer; C. Spearman.
$£3,383$ to $£3,998$
Defence Dept., R. M. Tesh, C.M.G.; *Assts.*, B. O. White; T. E. F. Pooley.
Dependent Territories General Dept., J. D. B. Shaw, M.V.O.; *Asst.*, P. Scanlon.
Disarmament Dept., D. M. Summerhayes; *Asst.*, D. L. Benest.
East African Dept., E. G. Le Tocq; *Asst.* E. H. M. Counsell, C.B.E.
Eastern European and Soviet Dept., J. L. Bullard.
European Communities Information Unit, W. J. Adams; *Asst.*, S. A. Budd.
European Integration Dept., N. Statham, C.M.G., C.V.O.; *Assts.*, W. K. Slatcher; M. R. Morland.
Export Promotion Dept., D. T. West; *Asst.*, W. J. Cheesman.
Far Eastern Dept., J. A. L. Morgan; *Asst.* R. B. Crowson.
Finance Dept., A. H. Hughes, O.B.E.; *Assistants*, E. N. Smith D. W. T. Smithies, O.B.E.; Mrs. B. M. Sherstone, M.B.E.; E. G. White.
Financial Policy and Aid Dept., P. H. R. Marshall; *Assistants*, Miss C. E. Pestell; J. W. R. Shakespeare, M.V.O.
Guidance and Information Policy Dept., D. N. Brinson M.C.; *Assts.*, C. F. Hill; N. W. H. Gaydon, O.B.E.; P. R. Metcalfe.
Hong Kong Dept., E. O. Laird, C.M.G., M.B.E.
India Office Library and Records. Librarian and Keeper. S. C. Sutton, C.B.E., F.S.A.; *Deputy Librarian and Deputy Keeper*, Miss J. C. Lancaster, F.S.A.
$£3,860$ to $£4,515$
Asst. Keepers (Grade I), Miss J. R. Watson; M. J. C. O'Keefe; Miss O. M. Lloyd; Mrs. M. Archer; M. I. Moir.
Information Administration Dept., R. A. Fyjis-Walker; *Asst.*, M. F. Chapman.
Information Research Dept., T. C. Barker; *Assistants*, H. H. Tucker, O.B.E.; J. G. McMinnies.
Latin America Dept., J. M. Hunter, M.C.; *Asst.*; J. A. Robson.
Library and Records Dept., B. Cheeseman, O.B.E. ($£5,175$ to $£6,475$); *Assistants*, Miss E. C. Blayney; J. S. Dixon, O.B.E.; E. L. Blundell, M.B.E.
Marine and Transport Dept., H. A. Dudgeon; *Asst.*, D. A. Campbell.
Migration and Visa Dept., H. J. Downing; *Asst.*, T. G. Streeton, M.B.E.
Nationality and Treaty Dept., H. V. Richardson, O.B.E.; *Assts.*, R. R. G. B. Smedley; C. O. Adams, O.B.E.
Near Eastern Dept., R. M. Evans; *Assts.*, P. M. Laver; S. L. Egerton.
News Dept., J. H. G. Leahy; *Deputy Head*, Miss E. M. Booker, M.B.E.
North African Dept., R. C. Hope-Jones, C.M.G.; *Asst.*, J. C. Kay.
North America Dept., H. T. A. Overton; *Asst.*, C. D. Lush.

Oil Dept., G. B. Chalmers; *Asst.*, P. G. P. D. Fullerton.

Pacific Dependent Territories Dept., Miss E. J. Emery; *Asst.*, J. D. Massingham.

Permanent Under-Secretary's Dept., K. G. Ritchie, C.M.G.; *Deputy Head*, A. D. S. Goodall; *Asst.*, A. H. Wyatt.

Personnel Operations Dept., D. M. Day; *Deputy Head*, J. C. Thomas; *Assistants*, S. J. Barrett; A. Rendall, O.B.E.

Personnel Policy Dept., N. Aspin, C.M.G.; *Asst.*, J. S. Whitehead.

Personnel Services Dept., E. Youde, C.M.G., M.B.E.; *Assts.*, W. R. Bickford, M.B.E.; R. H. Davies, M.B.E., D.F.C.

Planning Staff, P. Cradock, C.M.G.

Protocol and Conference Dept., A. L. Mayall, C.M.G., C.V.O. (*H.M. Vice-Marshal of the Diplomatic Corps*); G. M. F. Stow; G. G. Collins (*Assistant Marshals of the Diplomatic Corps*). £3,425 to £4,575; *Assts.*, C. D. Smith; Miss S. M. Strachan, M.B.E.

Research Dept., E. E. Orchard, C.B.E. (*Director*).

Rhodesia Economic Dept., J. M. Dutton; *Asst.*, D. G. Reid.

Rhodesia Political Dept., P. R. A. Mansfield; *Assts.*, A. K. Mason; B. G. Cartledge.

Science and Technology Dept., R. Arculus, C.M.G.; *Assistants*, J. B. Ure, M.V.O.; M. J. Newington.

Security Dept., P. C. H. Holmer; *Assistants*, T. Empson; J. C. Strong.

South Asian Dept., I. J. M. Sutherland; *Asst.*, H. C. Byatt.

South-East Asian Dept., D. McD. Gordon, C.M.G.; *Assistants*, J. W. D. Margetson; A. B. P. Smart.

Southern European Dept., R. L. Secondé, C.V.O., C.M.G.; *Assts.*, W. J. A. Wilberforce; D. C. Thomas.

South-West Pacific Dept., J. K. Hickman; *Assts.*, W. A. Ward; D. F. B. Le Breton.

Trade Policy Dept., G. L. Simmons, M.V.O.; *Asst.*, K. F. X. Burns.

Training Dept., *Head of Dept. and Director of Language Dept.*, A. C. Goodison; *Asst.*, Mrs. M. E. Barraclough, O.B.E.

United Nations (Economic and Social) Dept., T. W. Keeble; *Asst.*, K. G. MacInnes.

United Nations (Political) Dept., R. J. Stratton, *Assts.*, Mrs. M. B. Chitty; I. C. L. Alexander, O.B.E.

West African Dept., Hon. R. J. McM. Wilson, C.M.G.; *Asst.*, J. de C. Ling.

West Indian Dept., R. N. Posnett, O.B.E.; *Assts.*, A. McM. Webster; J. W. Maslen.

Western European Dept., C. M. James; *Assistants*, P. W. Unwin; W. K. K. White.

Western Organizations Dept., The Lord Bridges; *Assts.*, R. Q. Braithwaite; N. A. I. French, M.V.O.

Passport Office
Clive House, Petty France, S.W.1
[01-222-8010]

Chief Passport Officer, M. G. Dixon, O.B.E.
£5,000 to £6,300

Deputy Chief Passport Officer, R. P. B. Cave, O.B.E.
£4,600 to £5,200

Liverpool Branch Office
India Buildings, Water Street, Liverpool 2
[051-236-9411]

Officer in Charge, Miss V. M. Brady
£3,250 to £4,400

Glasgow Branch Office
Empire House, 131 West Nile Street, Glasgow, C.1
[041-332-0271]

Officer in Charge, Miss S. C. Small
£2,775 to £3,400

Newport Branch Office
Olympia House, Dock Street, Newport, Mon.
[0633-52431]

Officer in Charge, D. Carlyle.... £2,775 to £3,400

Peterborough Branch Office
Westwood, Peterborough
[0733-263636]

Officer in Charge, R. W. Dennis. £2,775 to £3,400

Belfast Agency
30 Victoria Street, Belfast 1
[OBE-2-32371]

Officer in Charge, Mrs. M. T. Haughey.

Corps of Queen's Messengers
Superintendent of the Queen's Messenger Service, Capt. J. G. Canning.

Queen's Diplomatic Service Messengers, R. A. Perryman; T. D. Nettleton; Wing-Cdr. J. C. Norris, D.F.C.; Col. J. H. Wakefield; Lt.-Col. A. F. Rowe; Lt.-Col. H. S. Stansfield; Lt.-Col. R. K. Constantine; Lt.-Col. C. F. Bagot, O.B.E.; Lt.-Col. J. M. B. Poyntz, O.B.E.; Maj. M. P. D. Cruickshank; Sq.-Ldr. A. P. Hollick; J. D. Blake, M.B.E., T.D.; Maj. H. S. Lyons, M.B.E.; A. P. H. Lousada; Lt.-Col. P. H. Huth, D.S.O., M.C.; Lt.-Col. A. I. G. Ramsey; Wing-Cdr. T. Stevenson, A.F.C.; Sq.-Ldr. S. G. R. White; Wing-Cdr. J. M. Morgan, D.F.C.; Capt. D. V. Walmsley; Maj. W. R. A. Catcheside; J. H. Kidner; R. C. H. Risley; J. O. Hollis; Flt-Lt. P. C. Stevens, D.F.C.; Lt.-Col. B. A. A. Plummer; Maj. P. Sherston-Baker, M.C.; Maj. C. M. Tuffill; Maj. J. K. Nairne; Lt.-Col. B. A. Hannaford; F. N. Cory-Wright; Group Capt. S. P. Coulson, D.S.O., D.F.C.; Sqn.-Ldr. L. V. Davies, D.F.M.; E. W. J. Eyers; Maj. A. W. Gay; J. A. Golding, C.V.O.; Maj. L. A. Smeeton; Maj. K. H. M. O'Kelly; Sq.-Ldr. J. N. Yates; Lt.-Col. H. Forwood; Lt.-Cdr. W. L. Irving; P. L. Burkinshaw, O.B.E.; Maj. D. B. Metcalfe; Lt.-Col. C. R. Sims-Reeve; Wing Cdr. K. Smith, D.F.C.; G. Whitfield; R. J. Angel; L. C. Bazalgetbi.

India Office Library and Records
Orbit House, 197 Blackfriars Road, S.E.1
The Record Office has the custody of the archives of the East India Company (1600–1858), the Board of Control (1784–1858), the India Office (1858–1947) and the Burma Office (1937–1947).
Keeper, S. C. Sutton, C.B.E.

FORESTRY COMMISSION
25 Savile Row, W.1
[01-734-0221]

The Forestry Commissioners are charged with the general duty of promoting the interests of forestry, the development of afforestation, the production and supply of timber and the maintenance of reserves of growing trees in Great Britain. Including the former Crown Woods, transferred to it in 1924, the Commission has acquired about 2,900,000 acres of land (70 per cent. being plantable), of which 1,700,000 acres are under plantations. Under various grant schemes, financial assistance is given to private owners and local authorities in respect of approved works of afforestation.
Chairman, The Lord Taylor of Gryfe (*part-time*)
£5,500

Director-General and Deputy Chairman, J. A. Dickson, C.B. £9,000

Head of Forest and Estate Management, G. G. Stewart
£6,750

Head of Administration and Finance, P. Nicholls
£6,750

Head of Harvesting and Marketing, Dr. F. C. Hummel
£6,750

Senior Officer, Scotland (25 Drumsheugh Gardens, Edinburgh), E. S. M. Davies £5,640

Senior Officer, Wales (Churchill House, Cardiff), J. W. L. Zehetmayer £5,640

NATIONAL FREIGHT CORPORATION
Argosy House, 215 Great Portland Street, W.1
[01-636-8688]

The National Freight Corporation is a statutory corporation set up under the Transport Act, 1968, to provide integrated road and rail freight services in Great Britain and in so doing to make the maximum economic use of rail, with due regard to the needs of the person for whom the goods are being carried, and the requirements of the goods themselves. On January 1, 1969, it inherited the securities, rights and liabilities of the Road Haulage and Shipping Subsidiaries of the Transport Holding Company. It also acquired from the British Rail-

ways Board, National Carriers Ltd. and a 51 per cent. interest in Freightliners Ltd. (formerly the "Sundries" and "Freightliner" Divisions respectively of the Railways Board).
Chairman, D. E. A. Pettit.............£17,000
Members, Rt. Hon. F. Cousins; Sir Andrew Chrichton; F. Lane, B.E.M.; F. S. Law; R. L. E. Lawrence, O.B.E., E.R.D.; Sir Robert MacLean
each (*part-time*) £1,000
Comptroller, H. E. Osborn, C.B.E.
Secretary, L. Mapleston.

FREIGHT INTEGRATION COUNCIL
2 Marsham Street, S.W.1
[01-212-8168]
Chairman, A. G. B. Burney.............£3,000
Members, Sir Sidney Greene, C.B.E.; A. H. Kitson Col. F. T. Davies; J. A. McMullen; Rt. Hon. R. W. Marsh; D. E. A. Pettit.
Secretary, I. Yass.

REGISTRY OF FRIENDLY SOCIETIES (CENTRAL OFFICE) AND OFFICE OF THE INDUSTRIAL ASSURANCE COMMISSIONER
17 North Audley Street, W.1
[01-629-7001]
A Barrister was appointed in 1828 to certify the Rules of Savings Banks, and in 1829 to certify those of Friendly Societies. In 1846 he was constituted Registrar of Friendly Societies. By the Friendly Societies Act, 1875, the Central Office of the Registry of Friendly Societies was created consisting of the Chief Registrar and the Assistant Registrars for England. It exercises numerous and important functions under the Friendly Societies Acts, the Industrial and Provident Societies Acts, the Building Societies Acts, the Trade Union Acts, the Trustee Savings Banks and Post Office Savings Bank Acts, the Loan Societies Act, the Shop Clubs Acts and the Superannuation and other Trust Funds (Validation) Act. Under the Industrial Assurance Acts and the Insurance Companies Acts, the Chief Registrar is charged with various powers and duties in relation to Industrial Assurance Companies and Collecting Societies, and in that capacity is styled the Industrial Assurance Commissioner.
Chief Registrar and Industrial Assurance Commissioner, S. D. Musson, C.B., M.B.E............£9,000
Private Sec., Miss M. E. Blake.
Assistant Registrar and Deputy Industrial Assurance Commissioner, K. Brading, M.B.E........£6,295
Asst. Registrar, A. Vollmar.....£4,730 to £5,815
Executive Registrar, A. A. C. Soper, I.S.O. (*also Establishment Officer*)........£4,220 to £4,730
Senior Legal Assistants, J. E. Gower, M.C.; M. J. Pearce...................£3,461 to £4,565
Registration Branch (*Head*), J.W.D. Goss, £3,433 to £4,048; (*Assist. Head*), I. D. Christie
£2,704 to £3,274
Returns and Statistics Branch (*Head*), J. A. Walter, £3,433 to £4,048; (*Assist. Head*), E. S. Burgess
£2,704 to £3,274
Establishment and Records Branch (*Head*), L. G. Hill
£2,704 to £3,274
Investigations Branch (*Head*), A. G. Kilbey
£2,704 to £3,274
Disputes Branch (*Head*), E. C. Jones
£2,704 to £3,274
Registry of Friendly Societies, Scotland
19 Heriot Row, Edinburgh, 3
[031-556-4371]
Assistant Registrar, J. Craig, O.B.E., W.S.

GAMING BOARD FOR GREAT BRITAIN
Berkshire House, 168-173 High Holborn, W.C.1
[01-240-0821]
Established on October 25, 1968, to maintain a broad oversight of developments in gaming in Great Britain, to check prospective gaming licensees management and staff, and to advise the Home Secretary on making regulations which may be needed for the further control of gaming.

Chairman, Sir Stanley Raymond.........£7,000
Members, Sir Ranulph Bacon; M. Cohen; Hon. R. Stanley; K. A. Usherwood, C.B.E.
Secretary, T. A. Critchley.

THE GAS COUNCIL
59 Bryanston Street, W.1
[01-723-7030]
Chairman, Sir Henry Jones, K.B.E.
(*plus allowances* £1,000) £20,000
Deputy Chairman, A. F. Hetherington, D.S.C.
(*plus allowances* £500) £16,000
Members, J. A. Buckley; C. E. Mills; D. E. Rooke, C.B.E.; and the Chairmen of the 12 Area Gas Boards.
Secretary, T. E. D. Mason.

Chairmen of Area Gas Boards
(The Chairmen of Area Boards receive a salary of £9,900 to £11,000.)
Scottish, Granton House, 340 West Granton Road, Edinburgh 5.
Chairman, R. W. Parker, C.B.E. *Sec.*, A. T. Herd, O.B.E.
Northern, G.P.O. Box 1G.B., Newcastle-upon-Tyne 1.
Chairman, L. J. Clark, B.E.M. *Sec.*, A. G. Doxford.
North Western, Welman House, Altrincham, Cheshire.
Chairman, W. Hodkinson, O.B.E. *Sec.*, J. Wadsworth.
North Eastern, New York Road, Leeds 2.
Chairman, Dr. A. E. Haffner. *Sec.*, C. W. A. Hunt.
East Midlands, P.O. Box 145, De Montfort Street, Leicester.
Chairman, K. L. Pearce. *Sec.*, W. Burnstone.
West Midlands, 5 Wharf Lane, Solihull, Warwickshire.
Chairman, D. Beavis. *Sec.*, J. Swan.
Wales, Snelling House, Bute Terrace, Cardiff.
Chairman, P. E. Gallaher. *Sec.*, C. B. Mawer.
Eastern, Star House, Potters Bar, Herts.
Chairman, R. H. Sandford Smith. *Sec.*, R. R. Hardwicke.
North Thames, 30 Kensington Church Street, W.8.
Chairman, G. E. Cooper. *Sec.*, J. S. Barnes.
South Eastern, Katherine Street, Croydon, Surrey.
Chairman, R. N. Bruce, O.B.E. *Sec.*, G. L. May.
Southern, 164 Above Bar, Southampton, Hants.
Chairman, Wilfrid Bailey. *Sec.*, L. Bean, C.M.G., M.B.E.
South Western, 9a Quiet Street, Bath.
Chairman, E. H. Harman, O.B.E. *Sec.*, R. G. Laycock.

THE GOVERNMENT ACTUARY
Caxton House East, Tothill Street, S.W.1
[01-222-4234]
Government Actuary, Sir Herbert Tetley, K.B.E., C.B.
£10,950
Directing Actuaries, P. R. Cox, C.B. (*Deputy Government Actuary*); C. E. Clarke, C.B.E........£6,750
Principal Actuaries, J. R. Ford, O.B.E.; E. A. Johnston; L. V. Martin; G. G. Newton; C. M. Stewart...................£5,000 to £6,300
Actuaries, E. A. Drake; J. L. Field; R. T. Foster; R. C. Gilder; C. A. Harris; D. H. Loades; W. M. Low; D. F. Renn; J. R. Watts
£3,258 to £4,175

THE GOVERNMENT CHEMIST
See under DEPARTMENT OF TRADE AND INDUSTRY

GOVERNMENT HOSPITALITY FUND
2 Carlton Gardens, S.W.1
[01-839-6272]
Instituted in 1908 for the purpose of organizing official hospitality on a regular basis, with a view to the promotion of international goodwill.
Minister in Charge, RT. HON. JULIAN AMERY, M.P.
Secretary, W. J. M. Paterson, C.M.G.

GOVERNMENT SOCIAL SURVEY DEPARTMENT
See OFFICE OF POPULATION CENSUSES AND SURVEYS.

DEPARTMENT OF HEALTH AND SOCIAL SECURITY
Alexander Fleming House, Elephant and Castle, S.E.1.

[01-407-5522]

The Department of Health and Social Security was created on November 1, 1968, from the Ministry of Health and Ministry of Social Security. The new Department performs the functions of the two former Ministries.

The Department is responsible for the administration of the National Health Service in England and for the welfare services run by local authorities in England for the elderly, infirm, handicapped and other persons in need. It has functions relating to food hygiene and welfare foods. The Department is also concerned with the medical and surgical treatment of war pensioners in England, the Channel Isles, Isle of Man or living in the Irish Republic, and is responsible for the ambulance and first aid services in emergency, under the Civil Defence Act, 1948. The Department represents the United Kingdom on the World Health Organization of the United Nations. Responsibility for the administration of the Health Services in Wales was transferred to the Welsh Office on April 1, 1969. The Department is responsible for the social security services in England, Scotland and Wales. These services comprise schemes for war pensions, national insurance, family allowances and supplementary benefits. Within the Department, the Supplementary Benefits Commission is responsible, subject to regulations made by the Secretary of State for Social Services, for guiding the scheme of supplementary benefits.

Secretary of State for Social Services, The RT. HON. SIR KEITH SINJOHN JOSEPH, BT., M.P... £8,500
Private Secretary, R. G. Wendt
£3,795 to £4,945
Assistant Private Secretaries, D. Brereton; Miss M. L. Purvis.
Parliamentary Private Secretary, D. B. Mitchell, M.P.
Minister of State, THE LORD ABERDARE..... £5,625
Parliamentary Under-Secretaries of State, M. J. H. Alison, M.P. (*Health*); A. P. Dean, M.P. (*Social Security*)... £3,750
Chairman, Supplementary Benefits Commission, The Lord Collison, C.B.F....................... £5,500
Deputy Chairman, Prof. R. M. Titmuss, C.B.E.
Members, Mrs. C. M. Carmichael; K. J. Griffin, O.B.E.; S. C. Hamburger, C.B.E.; Prof. D. C. Marsh; Mrs. B. N. Rodgers; M. R. F. Simson, O.B.E.
Permanent Secretary, Sir Philip Rogers, K.C.B., C.M.G. £14,000
Private Secretary, Miss H. M. Knight.
Second Permanent Secretary, Miss M. Riddelsdell, C.B.E. £13,000
Private Secretary, R. A. Wallace.
Deputy Secretaries, A. R. W. Bavin, C.B.; M. M. V. Custance, C.B.; L. Errington, C.B.; R. Gedling, C.B.; N. Jordan Moss, C.M.G.; F. W. Mottershead, C.B..... S. P. O S M R A N...... £9,000
Chief Medical Officer, Sir George Godber, K.C.B., D.M., F.R.C.P....................... £13,000
Librarian, Miss B. W. C. Samman
£3,258 to £3,873

Establishments and Personnel Division
Principal Establishments Officer and Director of Personnel, R. S. Swift, C.B................ £6,750
Assistant Secretaries, Miss J. A. Bates; R. L. Briggs; E. Halliday; E. L. Wallis..... £5,000 to £6,300

Manpower and Management Division
Under Secretary, T. C. Stephens........... £6,750
Assistant Secretaries, G. G. Beltram; D. C. Jones; R. S. Matthews; J. H. C. Nightingall
£5,000 to £6,300

Management Services Division
Under Secretary, K. R. Stowe........... £6,750
Deputy Chief Scientific Officer, E. J. C. Fowell
£5,240 to £5,830
Assistant Secretaries, L. G. S. Mason, O.B.E.; D. W. Polley; D. White; W. G. Wilson, O.B.E.
£5,000 to £6,300

Statistics and Research Division
Director of Statistics and Research, W. Rudoe £6,750
Deputy Chief Scientific Officer, A. G. McDonald
£5,240 to £5,830
Assistant Secretaries, J. B. Cornish; P. G. Perry
£5,000 to £6,300
Chief Statisticians, D. Evans; K. M. Francis, O.B.E.; F. E. Whitehead........... £5,000 to £6,300

International Relations Division
Under Secretary, G. D. Caldwell......... £6,750
Assistant Secretaries, F. B. Hindmarsh; H. N. Roffey, C.M.G...................... £5,000 to £6,300

Information Division
Director of Information, A. P. G. Brown
(+allce. £500) £4,390 to £5,640
Deputy Directors, Chief Information Officers, I. M. Gillis (*News*); J. M. Bolitho (*Publicity*)
£4,045 to £4,555

Economic Advisers Office
Chief Economic Adviser, J. L. Nicholson.... £6,750
Senior Economic Adviser, J. D. Pole
£5,000 to £6,300

Solicitors Division
Solicitor, W. H. M. Clifford, C.B.E........ £9,000
Principal Assistant Solicitors, G. H. Brinkworth, C.B.E.; H. W. Hornsby; M. W. M. Osmond
£6,750

Office of the Chief Insurance Officer
Chief Insurance Officer, Mrs. E. M. Kemp-Jones, C.B.E................................ £6,370

Insurance Division A
Under Secretary, G. D. Caldwell.......... £6,750
Assistant Secretaries, I. G. Gilbert; J. W. Stackpoole
£5,000 to £6,300

Insurance Division B
Under Secretary, A. G. Beard............ £6,750
Assistant Secretaries, H. S. McPherson; P. R. Oglesby; C. M. Regan...... £5,000 to £6,300

Insurance Division C
Under Secretary, K. R. Malcolm, C.B.E.... £6,750
Assistant Secretaries, J. Cartmell, C.B.E.; Mrs. M. E. Parsons; E. T. Randall...... £5,000 to £6,300

Insurance Division D
Under Secretary, S. B. Kibbey........... £6,750
Assistant Secretaries, M. J. A. Partridge; E. L. Trew
£5,000 to £6,300

Insurance Division K
Under Secretary, J. A. Atkinson, D.F.C...... £6,750
Assistant Secretaries, H. Archer, D.F.C.; M. P. Fennell
£5,000 to £6,300

War Pensions and Industrial Injuries
Under Secretary, R. Windsor............. £6,750
Assistant Secretaries, F. K. Forrester, M.B.E.; D. C. Ward; R. Windsor......£5,000 to £6,300

Registrar of Non-Participating Employments
Registrar, I. G. Gilbert................. £6,750

Supplementary Benefits—Division 1
Under Secretary, H. A. Turner........... £6,750
Assistant Secretaries, R. D. F. Whitelaw; R. W. L. Wilding.................. £5,000 to £6,300

Supplementary Benefits—Division 2
Under Secretary, A. J. G. Crockes........ £6,750
Assistant Secretaries, J. S. Campbell-Dick; Miss G. M. Jones, C.B.E........... £5,000 to £6,300

Accountant General (Finance Division) [Social Security]
Accountant General (Social Security), D. Overend, C.B. £6,750
Directors of Accounts, F. D. S. Waterton; W. L. Williams...................£5,000 to £6,300
Assistant Secretaries, L. J. Hayward; M. E. H. Platt
£5,000 to £6,300

Accountant General Division [Health]
Accountant General (Health), H. C. Salter, D.F.C.
£6,750
Assistant Secretaries, S. Bayfield; H. W. Seabourn; C. G. Taylor...............£5,000 to £6,300

Finance Policy Division [Health]
Under Secretary for Finance (Health), C. L. Bourton
£6,750
Assistant Secretaries, B. H. Betts; F. L. Wormald
£5,000 to £6,300

Executive Councils Division
Under Secretary, P. Benner £6,750
Assistant Secretaries, B. J. Ellis; W. H. Hornby; N. Illingworth; Mrs. M. A. J. Pearson; W. O. Roberts...................£5,000 to £6,300

Remuneration and Staffing Division 1
Under Secretary, J. T. Woodlock..........£6,750
Assistant Secretaries, T. A. Howell; R. B. Mayoh; W. O. Paget............£5,000 to £6,300

Remuneration and Staffing Division 2
Under Secretary, E. B. S. Alton, M.B.E., M.C. £6,750
Assistant Secretaries, C. W. R. Benwell; Miss B. Hirst; S. I. Smith; Mrs. P. M. Williamson
£5,000 to £6,300

Supply Division
Controller of Supply, F. J. Aldridge........£6,750
Directors of Supply, S. M. Davies, C.M.G.; N. Hollens; G. E. John...........£5,000 to £6,300
Director of Scientific and Technical Services, G. E. Gale
£5,640
Assistant Secretary, G. G. Hulme £5,000 to £6,300

Local Authority—Social Services Division 1
Under Secretary, J. E. Pater, C.B. £6,750
Assistant Secretaries, G. M. Bebb; Mrs. P. A. Lee; R. T. P. Pronger............£5,000 to £6,300

Local Authority—Social Services Division 2
Under Secretary, G. J. Otton..............£6,750
Assistant Secretaries, R. S. King; M. G. Russell; E. W. Whittemore, M.M.......£5,000 to £6,300

Social Work Services Division
Director of Social Work Services, Miss J. D. Cooper, C.B. 6/72
£5,990
Deputy Director of Social Work Services, Miss A. M. Sheridan..................£5,340
Assistant Directors, Miss E. L. Hope Murray; Mrs. B. J. Kahan; E. C. Morris; Mrs. D. Ottley
£4,765
Principal Social Work Service Officers, E. Glithero; Miss P. E. Harwood; Miss E. C. N. Winnicott
£4,296

Medicines and Food Division
Under Secretary, Mrs. J. A. Hauff..........£6,750
Senior Principal Medical Officer, D. Mansel-Jones
£6,750
Principal Medical Officers, F. A. Fairweather; J. A. Holgate..............................£6,120
Assistant Secretaries, R. E. Tringham; R. F. Tyas; T. B. Williamson.........£5,000 to £6,300

Community Health Services Division
Under Secretary, A. J. Collier.............£6,750
Assistant Secretaries, E. L. Mayston; P. V. Muston; B. R. Rayner............£5,000 to £6,300

Health Services Superannuation Division
Under Secretary, Mrs. J. A. Hauff..........£6,750
Assistant Secretary, C. K. Whitaker
£5,000 to £6,300

Health Services Organization Division
Under Secretary, J. P. Dodds..............£6,750
Assistant Secretaries, J. P. Cashman; T. E. Nodder
£5,000 to £6,300

Hospital Division 1
Under Secretary, L. H. Brandes............£6,750
Assistant Secretaries, B. O. B. Gidden; M. J. Hewitt; Mrs. V. J. M. Poole; J. C. C. Smith
£5,000 to £6,300

Hospital Division 2
Under Secretary, Miss M. M. Hedley.......£6,750
Assistant Secretaries, W. F. Farrant; K. J. Moyes, M.B.E.; M. M. Rossington, C.B.E.
£5,000 to £6,300

Hospital Division 3
Under Secretary, J. S. Orme, C.B., O.B.E....£6,750
Assistant Secretaries, R. B. Hodgetts; E. L. McMillan, C.B.E., A.F.C.; A. F. Taggart; F. D. K. Williams
£5,000 to £6,300

Hospital Building Division
Under Secretary, D. Somerville, C.B........£6,750
Assistant Secretaries, J. R. Brough; N. E. Clarke; C. P. Goodale; W. J. Littlewood; M. Nelson
£5,000 to £6,300

Hospital Catering Division
Chief Adviser on Catering and Dietetics, Miss E. Washington, O.B.E. ....£3,646 to £4,215
Deputy Chief Adviser, A. R. Horton
£2,860 to £3,441

Hospital Domestic Management Division
Chief Adviser, I. W. Little......£2,894 to £3,543

Architectural Division
Chief Architect, R. H. Goodman..........£6,750
Assistant Chief Architects, M. J. Bench; W. J. H. Dungey; R. F. Radford..............£5,640

Quantity Surveying Division
Chief Quantity Surveyor, L. McL. Watson...£6,120
Deputy Chief Quantity Surveyor, R. T. V. Amery
£4,390 to £5,015
Superintending Quantity Surveyors, W. V. F. Buckle; A. P. R. Pell-Hiley; D. A. Turner
£4,390 to £5,015

Engineering Division
Chief Engineer, J. Bolton................£6,750
Assistant Chief Engineers, G. Copple; M. Drury; R. Manser.........................£5,640

Medical Division (Community Medical Services)
Deputy Chief Medical Officer, R. M. Shaw...£7,800
Senior Principal Medical Officer, T. E. A. Carr
£6,750
Principal Medical Officers, G. M. Fleming; E. Ring; A. T. Roden; J. M. Ross, C.B.E.; J. E. Struthers; G. Wynne Griffith.....................£6,120

Medical Division (Hospital Medical Services)
Deputy Chief Medical Officer, H. Yellowlees £7,800
Senior Principal Medical Officers, A. J. P. Oldham
£6,750
Principal Medical Officers, H. M. Archibald; J. Brothwood; D. H. D. Burbridge, O.B.E.; A. B. Harrington; W. Lees; P. Seelig; R. Wilkins
£6,120

Medical Division (Special and Hospital Medical Services)
Deputy Chief Medical Officer, R. H. L. Cohen
£7,800
Senior Principal Medical Officer, D. Mansel Jones
£6,750
Principal Medical Officers, W. T. C. Berry; C. Dennis; F. A. Fairweather; T. J. Geffen; R. Goulding; J. A. Holgate; D. S. McKenzie; J. M. G. Wilson
£6,120

Medical Division (Social Security)
Deputy Chief Medical Adviser, J. A. G. Carmichael
£6,750
Principal Medical Officers, R. T. Fletcher, M.B.E.; M. R. Hayes; R. M. McGowan; E. G. Wright, O.B.E.............................£6,120

x retiring end of '72 succeeded by Prof. Dennis Lees.

3/72

1972]   **HEA** *Government and Public Offices* **HEA**   393

Dental Division
Chief Dental Officer, G. D. Gibb.........£6,750
Deputy Chief Dental Officer, M. A. Freeman
            £5,830
Senior Dental Officers, R. A. Campbell, E.D.; H. A. Dixey; I. C. S. Fraser; H. M. Hughes; R. Middleton; G. B. Roberts; J. Rogers, D.F.M.; J. H. Whittle.........................£5,360

Nursing Division
Chief Nursing Officer, Dame Kathleen Raven, D.B.E.
            £5,640
Deputy Chief Nursing Officers, Miss A. M. Lamb; Miss D. M. White, O.B.E.; Miss J. G. Whitehead
        £4,073 to £4,630

Pharmaceutical Division
Chief Pharmacist, T. D. Whittet.........£5,640
Deputy Chief Pharmacists, E. Fawcitt, I.S.O.; A. G. Fishburn.........................£5,640
Pharmacists Senior Grade, R. Baker; H. Glynn; S. F. Hall; W. P. Jones; Miss C. E. Mozley-Stark, M.B.E.................£3,575 to £4,208
Senior Principal Scientific Officers, C. A. Johnson; G. R. Kitteringham.........£4,390 to £5,015

Blackpool Central Office
Controller, V. W. B. Slater...............£6,750

Newcastle upon Tyne Central Office
Controller, J. H. McCarthy, C.B.........£6,750

NATIONAL INSURANCE ADVISORY COMMITTEE
10 John Adam Street, W.C.2
[01–930–9066]

The National Insurance Advisory Committee was appointed on Oct. 28, 1947, under the National Insurance Act, 1946 to give advice and assistance to the Secretary of State in connection with the discharge of his functions under the Act, and to perform any other duties allotted to it under the Act. These other duties include the consideration of preliminary drafts of regulations to be made under the National Insurance Acts, and of representations received thereon. When the regulations are laid before Parliament, the Committee's Report in the preliminary draft is laid with them, together with a statement by the Secretary of State showing what amendments to the preliminary draft have been made, what effect has been given to the Committee's recommendations, and, if effect has not been given to any recommendation, the reasons for not adopting it. The Secretary of State may also refer to the Committee for consideration and advice any questions relating to the operation of the acts including questions as to the advisability of amending the Acts).

Chairman, The Lord Evans of Hungershall. ✗
Members, W. C. Anderson, C.B.E.; Prof. J. A. Faris; Mrs. I. M. Howell, C.B.E.; L. E. Kenyon, C.B.E.; Miss A. M. Patrick; S. A. Robinson; D. H. Roper, O.B.E.; Prof. R. M. Titmuss, C.B.E.; N. C. Turner, C.B.E.
Secretary, C. Emerson.

INDUSTRIAL INJURIES ADVISORY COUNCIL
10 John Adam Street, W.C.2
[01–930–9066]

The Industrial Injuries Advisory Council, established under the National Insurance (Industrial Injuries) Act, 1946, considers and advises the Secretary of State for Social Services on the regulations proposed under the Act, and on other questions which the Secretary of State refers to it.

Chairman, Sir Harry Crane, O.B.E.
Members, W. C. Anderson, C.B.E.; P. L. Bidstrup; S. Chapman, C.B.E.; J. S. Grant; Prof. R. E. Lane, C.B.E.; T. A. E. Layborn, C.B.E.; Prof. C. R. Lowe; G. H. Lowthian, C.B.E.; J. Ll. McQuitty, Q.C.; A. Martin; J. G. C. Milligan; I. G. Reid; Alice M. Stewart; M. Vines.
Secretary A. C. Palmer.

NATIONAL INSURANCE AND INDUSTRIAL INJURIES JOINT AUTHORITIES
10 John Adam Street, W.C.2
[01–930–9066]

Members, The Secretary of State for Social Services; the Minister of Health and Social Services for Northern Ireland.
Deputies for the Secretary of State for Social Services, Sir Philip Rogers, K.C.B., C.M.G.; G. D. Caldwell; for the Minister of Health and Social Services for Northern Ireland, N. Dugdale; C. G. Oakes.
Joint Financial Advisers, Sir Herbert Tetley, K.B.E., C.B.; D. Overend, C.B.; J. E. Aiken.
Secretary, D. J. Carter, I.S.O.

PNEUMOCONIOSIS, BYSSINOSIS AND MISCELLANEOUS DISEASES BENEFIT SCHEME (1966) AND WORKMEN'S COMPENSATION (SUPPLEMENTATION) SCHEME (1966)
Norcross, Blackpool, Lancs.
[Blackpool: 52311]
Chairman, D. M. Campbell, Q.C.
Deputy Chairman J. R. Pickering.
Members, A. J. Collins; J. C. Hobbs; A. J. Lewis; T. Parry; R. Pilkington, O.B.E.; J. C. Robinson.
Secretary, F. Briers.

OFFICE OF THE CHIEF INSURANCE OFFICER FOR NATIONAL INSURANCE
Penderel House, 287 High Holborn, W.C.1
[01–242–9020]
Chief Insurance Officer, Mrs. E. M. Kemp-Jones, C.B.E.
          £5,725
Deputy Chief Insurance Officer, E. F. Hannam
        £3,236 to £3,976

OFFICE OF THE REGISTRAR OF NON-PARTICIPATING EMPLOYMENTS
Penderel House, 287 High Holborn, W.C.1
[01–242–9020]
Registrar, I. G. Gilbert.........£4,045 to £5,200
Deputy Registrar, W. G. Pye....£3,258 to £3,873

NATIONAL HEALTH SERVICE REGIONAL HOSPITAL BOARDS
England and Wales are divided into 15 hospital regions, each with its own Hospital Board which administers the hospital and specialist services in the area. The Hospital Boards do not, however, administer Teaching Hospitals, which have their own Boards of Governors.

The Chairmen and members of Hospital Boards and Boards of Governors are appointed by the Secretary of State in accordance with the third schedule to the National Health Service Act, 1946.

Areas
Newcastle, Benfield Road, Walker Gate, Newcastle upon Tyne 6. *Chairman,* Col. W. A. Lee, O.B.E., T.D. *Secretary,* R. Dobbin, O.B.E.
Leeds, Park Parade, Harrogate, Yorks. *Chairman,* L. E. Laycock, C.B.E. *Secretary,* W. Bowring.
Sheffield, Fulwood House, Old Fulwood Road, Sheffield, 10. *Chairman,* S. P. King, O.B.E. *Secretary,* W. M. Naylor.
East Anglian (Cambridge), Union Lane, Chesterton, Cambridge. *Chairman,* Sir Stephen Lycett Green, Bt., C.B.E. *Secretary,* K. V. F. Morton, C.I.E., O.B.E.
North West Metropolitan, 40 Eastbourne Terrace, W.2. *Chairman,* Sir Maurice Hackett, O.B.E. *Secretary,* G. H. Weston.
North East Metropolitan, 40 Eastbourne Terrace, W.2. *Chairman,* Sir Graham Rowlandson, M.B.E. *Secretary,* C. Phipps.
South East Metropolitan, Randolph House, 46–48 Wellesley Road, Croydon. *Chairman* J. C. Donne. *Secretary,* H. N. Lamb.
South West Metropolitan, 40 Eastbourne Terrace, W.2. *Chairman,* Sir Desmond Bonham-Carter, T.D. *Secretary,* E. G. Braithwaite.

Oxford, Old Road, Headington, Oxford. *Chairman,* Dame Isabel Graham-Bryce, D.B.E. *Secretary,* D. Norton.

South Western, 27 Tyndalls Park Road, Bristol 8. *Chairman,* W. J. English, M.B.E. *Secretary,* H. W. White, O.B.E.

Wales, Temple of Peace and Health, Cathays Park, Cardiff. *Chairman,* G. Prys-Davies. *Secretary,* A. E. Newell, O.B.E.

Birmingham, Arthur Thomson House, 146-150 Hagley Road, Birmingham 16. *Chairman,* D. A. Perris, M.B.E. *Secretary,* F. S. Adams, O.B.E.

Manchester, Gateway House, Piccadilly South, Manchester 1. *Chairman,* T. Hourigan. *Secretary,* F. Pethybridge.

Liverpool, Wilberforce House, The Strand, Liverpool 2. *Chairman,* D. A. Solomon, M.B.E. *Secretary,* J. D. Shepherd.

Wessex, Highcroft, Romsey Road, Winchester, Hants. *Chairman,* P. G. Templeman, C.B.E. *Secretary,* J. T. Shaw.

DEPARTMENT OF HEALTH FOR SCOTLAND
See Scottish Office

HERRING INDUSTRY BOARD
1 Glenfinlas Street, Edinburgh 3
[031-225-4241]
Chairman, G. W. Middleton, C.B.E.
(part-time) £3,350
Members, W. J. L. Dean, O.B.E. (part-time) £2,800 in respect of this and other appointments in White Fish Authority; E. H. M. Clutterbuck; Admiral Sir Deric Holland-Martin, G.C.B., D.S.O., D.S.C. (part-time)..........................£1,000
Secretary-Manager, A. Fairley.

HIGHLANDS AND ISLANDS DEVELOPMENT BOARD
Bridge House, Bank Street, Inverness.
The Board, a grant-aided body, responsible to the Secretary of State for Scotland, has two broad objectives. These are (1) to assist the people of the Highlands and Islands to improve their economic and social conditions; (2) to enable the Highlands and Islands to play a more effective part in the economic and social development of the nation. To this end the Board will concert, promote, assist or undertake measures for the economic and social development of the seven Highland counties.
Chairman, Sir Andrew Gilchrist, K.C.M.G.
Secretary, R. A. Fasken.

HISTORIC BUILDINGS COUNCILS
Under the *Historic Buildings and Ancient Monuments Act,* 1953, as since amended, these councils advise the Secretary of State for the Environment and the Secretaries of State for Scotland and Wales on the exercise of the powers contained in the Act to make grants and loans towards the repair or maintenance of buildings of outstanding historic or architectural interest, their contents and adjoining land, and, where necessary, to acquire such buildings or to assist the National Trusts or local authorities to acquire them. In 1971-72, £1,000,000 is available for repair and maintenance grants in England. Over the three-year period, April 1, 1970-March 31, 1973, £410,000 is available for allocation as repair and maintenance grants in Scotland, and £193,000 in Wales.

England
Queen Anne's Mansions, Queen Anne's Gate, S.W.1.
Chairman. The Lord Halles, P.C., G.B.E., C.H.
Members, J. M. Brandon-Jones; H. M. Colvin, C.B.E., F.S.A.; J. Cornforth; T. E. N. Driberg, M.P.; R. S. Dutton, F.S.A.; The Lord Faringdon; The Duke of Grafton, F.S.A.; Sir Francis Hill, C.B.E.; S. J. Garton, O.B.E., F.S.A.; The Lord

Holford, R.A.; Mrs. M. E. Kaines-Thomas, D.Litt. F.S.A.; Sir Nikolaus Pevsner, C.B.E., Ph.D., F.S.A. F.B.A.; The Rt. Hon. J. E. Ramsden, M.P. J. Smith; Sir John Summerson, C.B.E., F.S.A., F.B.A. H. W. K. Wontner, C.V.O.
Secretary, I. M. Glennie.

Wales
Welsh Office, Summit House, Windsor Place, Cardiff
Chairman, Maj. H. J. Lloyd-Johnes, T.D., F.S.A.
Members, The Marquess of Anglesey, F.S.A. W. Edwards, M.P.; J. Eynon, F.R.I.B.A.; J. D. K Lloyd, O.B.E., F.S.A.; Prof. Glanmor Williams D.Litt.
Secretary, W. G. M. Jones.

Scotland
Argyle House, Edinburgh 3
Chairman, The Lord Stratheden and Campbell C.B.E.
Members, Miss B. Harvie Anderson, O.B.E., T.D. M.P.; R. G. Cant; J. D. Dunbar Nasmith J. F. A. Gibson; W. A. P. Jack, F.R.I.B.A.; M. Liddell, M.B.E.; Sir Robert Matthew, C.B.E. D. C. Scott-Moncrieff, C.V.O., W.S.; J. F. Smith Rt. Hon. A. Woodburn.
Secretary, T. Rarity.

HISTORICAL MANUSCRIPTS COMMISSION
See Record Office

ROYAL COMMISSION ON HISTORICAL MONUMENTS (ENGLAND)
Fielden House, Great College Street, S.W.1
[01-930-9652]
The Royal Commission on Historical Monuments (England) was appointed in 1908 to survey and publish in inventory form an account of every building, earthwork or stone construction up to the year 1714. The terminal date was extended after the late war to 1850. The Commission has published up to present date inventories covering nin counties, three cities, Roman York and Roma London. It is a purely recording body and thoug the Commissioners may recommend that certai structures should be preserved, they have no powe to implement their recommendations. The Commission is also responsible for the direction of th National Monuments Record, created in 1964 which includes the National Buildings Record begun in 1941, of which the Commissioners are th managing trustees.
Chairman, The Marquess of Salisbury, K.G., P.C., F.S.A
Commissioners, Sir John Summerson, C.B.E., F.B.A F.S.A.; C. A. Ralegh Radford, D.Litt., F.B.A F.S.A.; F. Wormald, C.B.E., Litt.D., F.B.A., F.S.A. H. M. Colvin, C.B.E., F.S.A.; D. B. Harden, C.B.E. Ph.D., F.S.A.; W. A. Pantin, F.B.A., F.S.A.; A. Taylor, C.B.E., F.S.A.; Prof. W. F. Grimes, C.B.E D.Litt., F.S.A.; Prof. S. S. Frere, F.S.A.; M. W Barley, F.S.A.; Prof. R. J. C. Atkinson, F.S.A. Prof. H. C. Darby, O.B.E., Ph.D., Litt.D., F.B.A. J. N. L. Myres, F.S.A., F.B.A.; Sir John Betjeman C.B.E.; and the Lords Lieutenant of the counties a the time of survey.
Secretary, A. R. Dufty, C.B.E., F.S.A........£4,70.

ROYAL COMMISSION ON ANCIENT MONUMENTS IN WALES AND MONMOUTHSHIRE
Edleston House, Queens Road, Aberystwyth
[Aberystwyth: 2256]
The Commission was appointed in 1908 to mak an inventory of the Ancient and Historical Monuments in Wales and Monmouthshire. The Commission now includes the National Monument Record for Wales and Monmouthshire.
Chairman, Prof. W. F. Grimes, C.B.E., D.Litt., F.B.A. F.S.A.

Commissioners, Prof. R. J. C. Atkinson, F.S.A.; Prof. I. Ll. Foster, F.S.A.; Prof. E. M. Jope, F.S.A.; J. D. K. Lloyd, O.B.E., F.S.A.; H. N. Savory, D.Phil., F.S.A.; A. J. Taylor, C.B.E., F.S.A.; Prof. D. Prys-Thomas; Prof. Glanmor Williams, Litt.D.; Prof. J. G. Williams; R. B. Wood-Jones, D.Phil., F.S.A.

Secretary, A. H. A. Hogg, F.S.A.

ROYAL COMMISSION ON ANCIENT AND HISTORICAL MONUMENTS OF SCOTLAND
52–54 Melville Street, Edinburgh 3
[031–225–5994]

The Commission was appointed in 1908 to make an inventory of the Ancient and Historical Monuments of Scotland from the earliest times to 1707, and to specify those that seem most worthy of preservation. The terms of reference were extended by Royal Warrant dated Jan. 1, 1948, to cover the period since 1707 at the Commissioners' discretion. On April 1, 1966, the Scottish National Building Record was transferred to the Commission. It has been extended in scope, and the name has been changed to the National Monuments Record of Scotland.

Chairman, The Earl of Wemyss and March, K.T., Ll.D.

Commissioners, Prof. S. A. Piggott, D.Litt., F.R.S.E., F.B.A., F.S.A.; Mrs. A. I. Dunlop, O.B.E., Ph.D., D.Litt., Ll.D.; A. Graham, F.S.A.; Prof. K. H. Jackson, Litt.D., D.Litt., D.Litt.Celt., F.B.A.; Prof. G. Donaldson, Ph.D., D.Litt.; Prof. P. J. Nuttgens, Ph.D.; Prof. A. A. M. Duncan.

Secretary, K. A. Steer, Ph.D., F.R.S.E., F.S.A...£5,000

ANCIENT MONUMENTS BOARDS
England
Sanctuary Buildings, S.W.1

Chairman, Sir Edward Muir, K.C.B., F.S.A.

Members, Prof. E. Birley, M.B.E., D.Phil., F.B.A., F.S.A.; R. L. S. Bruce-Mitford, D.Litt., F.S.A.; Prof. J. G. D. Clark, C.B.E., Sc.D., Ph.D., F.B.A., F.S.A.; A. R. Dufty, C.B.E., F.S.A.; B. M. Feilden, O.B.E., F.R.I.B.A., F.S.A.; Sir David Follett, Ph.D.; Prof. S. S. Frere, F.S.A.; Prof. W. F. Grimes, C.B.E., D.Litt., F.S.A.; D. B. Harden, C.B.E., Ph.D., F.S.A.; J. N. L. Myres, F.B.A., F.S.A.; Prof. S. A. Piggott, D.Litt., F.R.S.E., F.B.A., F.S.A., F.S.A.Scot.; Sir John Pope-Hennessy, C.B.E., F.B.A., F.S.A.; C. A. Ralegh Radford, D.Litt., F.B.A., F.S.A.; J. K. S. St. Joseph, O.B.E., Ph.D., F.S.A.; Marshall Sisson, C.B.E., R.A, F.R.I.B.A., F.S.A.

Secretary, R. Tatton-Brown, O.B.E.

Wales
Government Buildings, St. Agnes Road, Gabalfa, Cardiff

Chairman, J. D. K. Lloyd, O.B.E., F.S.A.

Members, Prof. R. J. C. Atkinson, F.S.A.; Prof. A. H. Dodd, D.Litt.; Prof. Sir Goronwy Edwards, D.Litt., F.S.A., F.B.A.; C. A. Gresham D.Litt., F.S.A.; Prof. W. F. Grimes, C.B.E., D.Litt. F.S.A.; A. H. A. Hogg, F.S.A.; C. N. Johns, F.S.A.; E. D. Jones, C.B.E., F.S.A.; L. Jones; C. A. Ralegh Radford, F.S.A., F.B.A.; D. M. Rees, F.S.A.; H. N. Savory, D.Phil., F.S.A.

Secretary, T. F. Lucas.

Scotland
Argyle House, Edinburgh 3

Chairman, Prof. E. L. G. Stones, Ph.D., F.S.A.

Members, The Earl of Haddington, K.T., M.C., F.S.A.Scot.; Prof. S. G. E. Lytbe, F.S.A.Scot.; Prof. J. Donaldson, Ph.D., D.Litt.; J. D. Dunbar-Nasmith; B. R. S. Megaw, F.R.S.E., F.S.A., F.S.A.Scot.; C. A. Ralegh Radford, F.B.A., F.S.A., F.S.A.Scot.; Miss A. S. Robertson, D.Litt., F.S.A., F.S.A.Scot.; Prof. W. J. Smith, M.C., F.R.I.B.A., F.S.A.; K. A. Steer, Ph.D., F.R.S.E., F.S.A., F.S.A. Scot.; R. B. K. Stevenson, F.S.A., F.S.A.Scot.

Secretary, A. M. Thomson.

HOME OFFICE
Whitehall, S.W.1
[01–930–8100]

The Home Office deals with such internal affairs of England and Wales as are not assigned to other Departments. The Home Secretary is the channel of communication between Her Majesty the Queen and Her subjects, and between the U.K. Government and the Governments of Northern Ireland, the Channel Islands and the Isle of Man. The chief matters with which the Home Office is concerned are—maintenance of law and order; efficiency of the police service; control and administration of the prison service; treatment of offenders; efficiency of the probation and after-care services; organization of magistrates' courts; legislation on criminal justice; supervision of the fire service; civil defence; control of Commonwealth citizens and aliens and the naturalization of aliens; community relations; the law relating to parliamentary and local government elections. In addition, many other subjects are dealt with, including explosives, firearms, dangerous drugs, poisons, vivisection, liquor licensing, shops, public safety, entertainments, by-laws on good rule and government and other subjects, cremations and burials, betting and gaming; addresses and petitions to the Queen, ceremonials and formal business connected with honours.

Secretary of State for the Home Department, THE RT. HON. REGINALD MAUDLING, M.P......£8,500

Private Secretary, G. L. Angel.

Assistant Private Secretaries, J. G. Pilling; D. Roberts.

Parliamentary Private Secretary, Hon. Sir Clive Bossom, Bt., M.P.

Parliamentary Clerk, D. S. J. Evans.

Ministers of State, ~~RICHARD CHRISTOPHER SHARPLES,~~ *resigns 4/2* O.B.E., M.C., M.P.; THE LORD WINDLESHAM
£5,625

Parliamentary Under-Secretary of State, M. Carlisle, Q.C., M.P...............................£3,750

Permanent Under-Secretary of State, Sir Philip Allen, G.C.B.....................................£15,000

Deputy Under-Secretaries of State, W. R. Cox, C.B. (*Director-General of the Prison Service*); F. L. T. Graham-Harrison, C.B.; J. H. Waddell, C.B.
£9,000

Director-General of Research and Chief Scientist, C. J. Stephens....................£7,525

Chief Medical Officer, Sir George Godber, G.C.B., D.M. F.R.C.P.

Economic Adviser, G. J. Wasserman.
£3,425 to £4,575

Honorary Catering Adviser, Sir Norman Joseph, K.C.V.O., C.B.E.

Community Programmes Department
Kingsgate House, 66–74 Victoria Street, S.W.1
[01–828–4366]

Assistant Under-Secretary of State, A. R. Isserlis
£6,925

Assistant Secretaries, A. J. Langdon; D. A. C. Morrison................£5,175 to £6,475

Principals, R. A. Birch; D. L. Bird; R. J. Fries
£3,425 to £4,575

Senior Executive Officers, J. A. Lomas; Miss D. H. Judd, M.B.E..............£2,950 to £3,575

Criminal Department
Assistant Under-Secretary of State, H. B. Wilson
£6,925

Assistant Secretaries, A. D. Gordon-Brown; R. L. Jones; M. J. Moriarty; R. W. Mott; C. H. Prior; J. H. Walker..........£5,175 to £6,475

Adviser on Magistrates' Courts, H. H. Cooper £3,677

Principals, A. E. Corben; Miss J. M. F. Cousins; J. C. Hindley; G. T. L. Hubert; N. F. Law; R. A. McDowall; S. G. Norris; Miss K. A. O'Neill, O.B.E.; Miss M. M. Peck; A. R. Rawsthorne; E. A. Slater; Miss C. E. Soret; D. B. Staines; Q. J. Thomas; C. J. Train
£3,425 to £4,755

Senior Executive Officers, B. F. Jones; Miss M. Norman; Miss B. Scobie; Miss M. V. Wakefield-Richmond...............£2,950 to £3,575

Deputy 7/72

Establishment and Organization Department

Assistant Under-Secretary of State (Principal Establishment and Organization Officer), A. R. Bunker, C.B. £6,925
Assistant Secretaries, J. H. J. Beck; P. A. McIlvenna, M.B.E.; N. S. Ross; R. W. G. Smith; P. L. Taylor .... £5,175 to £6,475
Senior Principals, T. J. Kempton; E. A. Sedgley
£4,775 to £5,375
Principals, S. R. Cameron; Miss E. M. Chadwell; R. F. Elliott; R. G. Fouracre; J. Hay; F. H. Keens; I. D. King; D. S. McCutcheon; L. G. Madin; R. G. Oram; G. W. Penn; J. F. Rogers; I. R. Thomas; J. R. Troop; F. B. Warner; Miss M. L. O. Williams, M.B.E. .... £3,425 to £4,575
Governor II, J. Williams .... £3,821 to £4,327
Principal Psychologist, J. H. Fitch. £2,995 to £4,077
Head of Work Study, A. D. Jackson
£3,425 to £4,575
Senior Executive Officers, C. Archer; J. Blythin; K. J. Bradley; B. G. Chaplin; D. L. Cole; M. E. Dewberry; G. E. Dunkley; J. A. Gibbs; R. M. Hoare; J. T. Horrocks; W. C. J. Horwood; W. A. Jones; D. Mannings; B. Morgan; N. L. Morgan; H. G. Pearson; J. Pitty; Mrs. M. E. W. Pusovnik; J. Roy; E. J. White £2,950 to £3,575

Public Relations Branch
Chief Information Officer, K. D. McDowall.

Finance Department

Horseferry House, Dean Ryle Street, S.W.1
[01-834-6655]
Tolworth Tower, Surbiton, Surrey
[01-399-5191]
Assistant Under-Secretary of State (Principal Finance Officer), G. H. McConnell, C.B. £6,875
Assistant Secretaries, L. W. Goringe, O.B.E.; D. A. Peach .... £5,175 to £6,475
Senior Principal, L. C. Sones. .... £4,775 to £5,375
Principals, J. A. Atfield; A. J. Bellett; J. F. Boxell; M. A. Christian; L. H. Foss; B. C. Holmes; A. H. Stringer; P. H. L. Trodden
£3,425 to £4,575
Senior Executive Officers, A. E. Coleshill; H. W. Gillies; H. A. Pendlebury; R. E. Wiscombe
£2,950 to £3,575

Fire Department

Ruskin Avenue, Kew, Surrey
[01-876-0444]
Assistant Under-Secretary of State, I. Roy £6,925
Assistant Secretaries, J. McIntyre; G. P. Renton; G. T. Rudd; D. R. Sands. ... £5,175 to 6,475
Principals, H. E. Lewis; D. G. McMurray; H. V. H. Marks; G.T. Newton; J. G. Quarrell; P. M. Scott; F. W. Stacey; A. H. Turney; C. F. Whitfield
£3,425 to £4,575
Senior Executive Officers, R. Atwell, M.B.E.; Miss L. P. Beevor; Miss G. M. Benn, M.B.E.; R. Kendall; W. E. Kocher; S. R. Mann; G. A. Rouse; G. Terry; R. C. Yeates
£2,950 to £3,575

Explosives Branch
Chief Inspector, E. G. Whitbread. £5,815
Second Inspector, R. T. Eaton. £4,565
Inspectors, F. W. Ireland; G. J. Jeacocke; C. Johnstone; J. G. N. Poyntz; M. G. L. Sewell; F. E. Tate .... £3,567 to £4,184

Fire Service Inspectorate
Chief Inspector, Sir Henry Martin Smith, C.B.E.
£6,600
Inspectors (Grade I), C. Bidgood, O.B.E.; L. O. Clarke, O.B.E.; A. J. Frame, M.B.E.; E. T. Hayward, O.B.E.; D. G. M. Middleton; G. R. H. Payne, O.B.E., B.E.M.; P. G. Robinson; P. S. Wilson-Dickson, M.B.E. .... £4,881 to £5,499
Inspector (Grade II), W. J. Carvin
£3,905 to £4,290
Engineering Inspector F. C. A. Shirling
£3,305 to £3,950

Fire Service Staff College
Wotton House, Abinger Common, Dorking, Surrey
Commandant, E. A. R. Hibbit, M.B.E. (acting)
£4,881 to £5,499
Fire Service Technical College
Moreton-in-Marsh, Gloucestershire
Commandant, H. Judge. .... £4,881 to £5,499
Senior Executive Officer, C. J. Titchener
£2,950 to £3,575
Programmed Learning Unit
Fire Service Technical College, Moreton-in-Marsh, Gloucestershire

General Department

Assistant Under-Secretary of State, K. P. Witney
£6,925
Assistant Secretaries, Capt. N. F. Carrington, D.S.C., R.N.(ret.); G. I. de Deney; K. Eddy; D. Heaton
£5,175 to £6,475
Principals, Miss M. A. Clayton; Miss M. D. Cook; J. V. Dance; M. E. Head; G. P. Pratt; C. L. Scoble; J. Stephens; W. J. Stephens
£3,425 to £4,575
Senior Executive Officers, W. G. Feakins; J. H. Howard; B. Lockett; L. R. Jacobs; Miss M. R. Simmons; Miss A. Turner; J. D. Webb
£2,950 to £3,575

Immigration and Nationality Department

Princeton House, 271/277 High Holborn, W.C.1
[01-242-8811]
Assistant Under-Secretary of State, T. FitzGerald
£6,925
Assistant Secretaries, W. J. Bohan; G. Emerson; W. M. Lee; R. F. D. Shuffrey £5,175 to £6,475
Senior Principal, J. Hamilton. .... £4,775 to £5,375
Principals, Miss K. N. Coates, O.B.E.; S. J. Gregory; J. C. H. Holden; Miss P. G. W. Hunt; J. E. Johnson; W. Middlemass; R. M. Whitfield; J. V. Wingfield. .... £3,425 to 4,575
Senior Executive Officers, C. J. Abbott; P. D. Brown; E. A. Gray; J. A. Green; N. C. L. Hackney; S. D. Holdershaw; F. Janaway; Miss M. E. Millson; R. K. Prescott; R. B. Prosser; A. R. Ralf; D. J. H. Walker; C. F. Woodiss
£2,950 to £3,575

Immigration Branch
Chief Inspector, A. J. Clarke. .... £5,175 to £6,475
Deputy Chief Inspector, H. J. G. Richards
£4,775 to £5,375
Assistant Chief Inspectors, S. A. Bennett; T. W. E. Roche; J. H. B. Sanders. .... £3,425 to £4,575
Inspectors, C. J. Allen; A. J. Arthy; H. Brown; C. P. Ennis; J. R. Garstang; D. C. W. Hogg; A. A. Holton; A. S. McCallum; L. J. Perry; H. G. Pickering; G. A. Reid; T. Russell; P. J. Saunders; B. J. Smith; R. G. Smith; E. L. Ward
£2,782 to £3,276

Legal Adviser's Branch

Legal Adviser, Sir Kenneth Jones, C.B.E. £9,000
Principal Assistant Legal Adviser, G. V. Hart. £6,925
Assistant Legal Advisers, P. Harvey; J. D. Semken, M.C.; H. W. Wollaston. .... £4,730 to £5,815
Senior Legal Assistants, A. H. Hammond; J. Nursaw; J. Pakenham-Walsh; Miss B. R. Pugh
£3,461 to £4,565

Northern Ireland Department

Assistant Under-Secretary of State, P. J. Woodfield, C.B.E. £6,925
Assistant Secretaries, J. T. A. Howard-Drake; E. J. Lindley. .... £5,175 to £6,475
Chief Executive Officers, J. F. Halliday; Miss B. M. Latimer; P. Leyshon; A. P. Pemberton
£3,425 to £4,575

Police Department

Horseferry House, Dean Ryle Street, S.W.1
[01-834-6655]
Assistant Under-Secretaries of State, J. B. Howard; T. G. Weiler; R. J. Whittick; E. D. Wright
£6,925

Forensic Science Adviser, E. G. Davies
　　　　　　　　£5,415 to £6,005
Assistant Secretaries, A. S. Baker, O.B.E., D.F.C.;
G. H. Baker, D.S.C.; J. F. D. Buttery; E. R.
Cowlyn; D. H. J. Hilary; J. Trevelyan
　　　　　　　　£5,175 to £6,475
Principals, M. J. Addison; S. S. Bampton; V. G.
Barry, D.F.C.; B. O. Bubbear; J. E. Clark; J. M.
Clift; W. O. Fortune; Miss M. Hornsby; J. A.
Howard; K. E. Hughes; E. Hutchings; S. C.
Jackson; J. P. Jarvis; F. A. V. Jenkins; R. O.
Lane, D.F.C.; L. A. Scudder; H. S. Seaford; Miss
P. J. Stacey; E. Todd, C.B.E.; Mrs. P. D. White
　　　　　　　　£3,425 to £4,595
Senior Executive Officers, D. A. Birks; M. K.
Brenchley; J. W. Clark; W. F. Delamare; Miss
B. O. Lloyd; D. McQueen; J. J. G. Warnick;
F. J. Woodland.......£2,950 to £3,575
Principal Warning Officers, W. J. Carney; G. A.
Potter.......£3,425 to £4,575
Assistant Chief Training Officer, Lt.-Col. G. W.
Laverick.......£2,846 to £3,288
Sector Controllers, P. Buswell; R. F. Cooke; R. F.
Cumings; G. C. Perkins......£2,950 to £3,575
H.M. Chief Inspector of Constabulary, J. A. McKay,
C.B.E.......£8,112
H.M. Inspectors, R. G. Fenwick; N. Galbraith;
J. T. Manuel C.B.E.; S. E. Peck, B.E.M.; A. U. R.
Scroggie, O.B.E.; F. E. Williamson......£7,314

Police Research Services Group
Director, S. E. Bailey...........£3,720 to £4,140

Police Scientific Development Branch
Director, G. Phillips...........£5,415 to £6,605
Principal Scientific Officers, A. T. Burrows, M.B.E.;
A. Gansen; G. N. Marriott; P. L. Parsons.
　　　　　　　　£2,995 to £4,077
Senior Engineer, D. E. Foott......£3,440 to £4,018

Police Management and Planning Group
Head of Group (Economic Adviser), G. J. Wasserman
　　　　　　　　£3,725 to £4,875
Economic Adviser, G. H. Phillips...£3,425 to £4,485
Senior Assistant Auditor, G. F. S. McMillan
　　　　　　　　£3,425 to £4,575

Police National Computer Unit
Tintagel House, Albert Embankment, S.E.1
[01-230-1212]
Assistant Secretary, J. P. Miller
　　　　　　　　£5,175 to £6,475
Senior Principals, G. W. A. Duguid; H. Eccles
　　　　　　　　£4,775 to £5,375
Principals, G. F. Atherton; A. G. Bailey; G. M.
Cole; G. C. Maxted; E. E. Quinney
　　　　　　　　£3,425 to £4,575
Principal Scientific Officer, J. R. Lowe
　　　　　　　　£2,995 to £4,077
Senior Executive Officers, G. H. Basson; R. G.
Boughey; E. J. M. Brown; M. A. Button;
C. A. Carter; J Clarke; W. S. Cowie; J. McA.
Cox; G. B. Dorow; D. K. Dunkin; T. Egan;
K. Gadson; R. M. Gregory; D. A. Quarmby;
H. Randall; K. M. Shewry; P. J. A. Somerville;
B. G. Stocking...........£2,950 to £3,575
Senior Communications Officers, J. H. Kitsell; J. N.
Warley...........£2,705 to £3,275
Senior Scientific Officer, I. Clark..£2,368 to £2,878

Home Office and Metropolitan Police Joint ADP Unit*
Tintagel House, Albert Embankment, S.E.1
[01-230-1212]
Senior Principal, M. D. Hutton...£4,725 to £5,375
Principals, P. G. V. Pike; K. E. Salmon; R. V.
Robinson; R. G. Urquhart; T. O. Youlten
　　　　　　　　£3,425 to £4,575
Senior Executive Officers, J. Bedson; H. L. Bowker;
T. Clark; F. R. Hayhurst; A. F. G. Hitchman;
J. E. G. King; D. C. Moulton; K. G. Pleant;
J. K. Richards; B. Rollins; J. Smedley; H.
Warland; F. M. Wormley...£2,950 to £3,575

ADP Central Services Unit*
Senior Executive Officer, Mrs. B. Simmonds
　　　　　　　　£2,950 to £3,575
Directorate of Telecommunications
60 Rochester Row, S.W.1
[01-828-9848]
Director of Telecommunications, W. P. Nicol. £5,835
Deputy Directors, R. J. P. Hayes; N. Morley;
E. W. F. Yirrell...........£4,775 to £5,375
Principal, W. Heggie...........£3,425 to £4,575
Senior Executive Officers, F. J. Atkins; D. E. N. Boon;
R. F. J. Heath...........£2,950 to £3,575
Chief Wireless Engineers, E. W. Crompton; J.
O'Connor, M.V.O.; P. P. H. Smith; J. P. Tither-
adge...........£3,750 to £4,383
Chief Communications Officer, R. E. Glaysher
　　　　　　　　£3,435 to £4,050

Supply and Transport Branch
Crown House, 52 Elizabeth Street,
Corby, Northants.
[Corby 2101] *4/72*
Director, G. F. Gartan. *I.S.O.*...£4,600 to £5,200
Senior Executive Officers, J. D. Lodder; L. W. Moore
　　　　　　　　£2,950 to £3,575

Police College
Bramshill House, Basingstoke, Hampshire
Commandant, J. C. Alderson.......£6,190
Deputy Commandant, Brig. C. H. A. Olivier, C.B.E.
　　　　　　　　£4,731
Director of General Studies, P. J. Stead, O.B.E.
　　　　　　　　£3,539
Senior Executive Officer, P. N. Neighbour
　　　　　　　　£2,950 to £3,575

Civil Defence Training School
The Hawkhills, Easingwold, Yorks.
Commandant, E. Bunting.......£3,043 to £3,532

Prison Department
89 Eccleston Square, S.W.1
[01-828-9848]
Director-General of the Prison Service, W. R. Cox,
C.B.......£9,000
Controller (Administration), B. C. Cubbon
　　　　　　　　£6,925
Controller (Operations), A. Bainton. *C.B.E.* £7,6,530
Controller (Planning and Development), M. S. Gale,
M.C.......£6,370
Chief Inspector of the Prison Service, S. G. Clarke
　　　　　　　　£6,370
Director of Prison Medical Services, I. G. W. Picker-
ing, V.R.D., M.D.......£6,750
Assistant Secretaries, A. J. E. Brennan; K. H. Daw-
son; D. E. R. Faulkner; W. N. Hyde; Miss G. M.
B. Owen...........£4,515 to £5,765
Assistant Controllers, G. W. Fowler; D. G. Hew-
lings, D.F.C., A.F.C.......£5,640
Assistant Directors, F. C. Foster, O.B.E.; J. L. Gilder;
Mrs. J. E. Kelley; H. G. Reeve £5,450
Senior Principals, V. G. Gotts; F. C. Millward
　　　　　　　　£4,775 to £5,375
Governors I, G. G. S. Chambers; K. Gibson; R. A.
B. A. Howden; N. C. Honey £4,965
Principals, D. V. Bailey; E. W. Durndell; Mrs.
H. E. Forbes; B. L. H. Ford; Miss M. I. F. Green;
A. K. Guymer; A. H. Hewins; P. W. Jamieson,
A.F.C.; R. G. Jones; L. Lerego; A. Marshall;
D. Polley; Maj. L. Snowden, M.B.E.; C. H.
Taylor; J. D. F. Turnham; E. C. Walduck;
G. W. Waring.......£3,425 to £4,575
Governors II, T. R. Carnegie; B. A. Emes
　　　　　　　　£3,821 to £4,327
Chief Psychologist, A. Straker.....£4,390 to £5,015
Chief Education Officer, A. S. Baxendale.....£4,765
Police Adviser, Cdr. J. T. R. Barnett
　　　　　　　　£3,560 to £3,980
Assistant Police Adviser, Det. Chief Supt. P. A.
Pinfold.......£3,075 to £3,295
Chaplain General, Rev. Canon L. L. Rees..£3,280
Senior Executive Officers, C. Barlow; M. A. Blackler;
B. Chesover; I. M. Clark; B. Ferguson; G. C.
High; J. B. Irving; A. Jenkinson; J. E. A.
Munford; Mrs. N. Needler; A. G. Pridmore;
J. F. Theobald; D. A. R. Wood
　　　　　　　　£2,950 to £3,575

---

*Automatic Data Processing

Catering Adviser. F. G. T. Belcham £2,654 to £3,224

Organizer of Physical Education, I. T. Copeland £2,765 to £3,201

Directorate of Industries and Supply
Tolworth Tower, Tolworth, Surbiton, Surrey [01-399-5491]

Director, K. J. Neale, O.B.E. £6,530

Planning and Services Manager, J. F. Quirk £5,090 to £6,390

Commercial Manager, R. D. S. Swann. £5,630

General Products Manager, I. E. Scarlett £3,665 to £4,298

Clothing and Textiles Manager, K. A. W. Channon £3,665 to £4,298

Chief Farms and Garden Manager, P. D. Stevens £3,409 to £4,286

Production Services Manager, A. D. Jackson £3,348 to £3,963

Accountant, G. S. West £3,348 to £3,963

Principals, O. Allen; W. R. Dalingwater; D. B. D. Petrie; P. R. Wall £3,340 to £4,490

Senior Executive Officers, P. F. Hewett; H. A. Layton; J. H. Treacy; D. C. Twine £2,865 to £3,490

Chief Architect's Branch and Directorate of Works
30 Orange Street, W.C.2 [01-930-8499]

Chief Architect and Director of Works, A. C. Hopkinson, C.B.E. £5,815

Deputy Chief Architect and Deputy Director of Works, A, Ball £4,785 to £5,410

Superintending Architects, R. H. Clare; N. E. Hill £4,565 to £5,190

Senior Architects, M. A. Brooks; J. A. Burrell; J. H. Cooper; R. A. Greaves; A. H. Millington £3,750 to £4,383

Superintending Grade Engineer, G. McLean £4,565 to £5,190

Senior Engineers, D. H. Harris; A. F. Lane; J. B. Lievens; S. B. Nash; B. R. Redd; R. J. Scott; V. A. C. Trigwell £3,750 to £4,383

Superintending Grade Quantity Surveyor, R. G. Read, O.B.E. £4,565 to £5,190

Senior Quantity Surveyors, P. W. H. Davis; R. D. Evernden; P. A. G. Walker £3,750 to £4,383

Senior Surveyor, L. O. Lee £3,750 to £4,383

Senior Structural Engineer, R. W. T. Haines £3,750 to £4,383

Regional Offices

Birmingham
Regional Director, E. A. Towndrow £5,640
Deputy Regional Directors, W. B. Gibbs (Administration) (£3,250 to £4,400); D. T. Cross (Operations) £3,646 to £4,152

Bristol
Regional Director, T. W. H. Hayes £5,640
Deputy Regional Directors, G. C. Woods (Administration) (£3,250 to £4,400); F. M. Liesching (Operations) £3,646 to £4,152

Manchester
Regional Director, A. Gould £5,640
Deputy Regional Directors, D. L. Tacey (Administration) (£3,250 to £4,400); S. E. Henderson Smith; M. S. Winston (Operations) £3,646 to £4,152

Redhill
Regional Director, A. D. W. Sanderson £5,640
Deputy Regional Directors, R. U. Hampton (Administration) (£3,250 to £4,400); M. Bryan; A. R. Moreton (Operations) £3,646 to £4,152

PRISONS
Governors
Albany, I.O.W., G. Footer £4,790
Appleton Thorn, Lancs., A. C. Kearns £2,860 to £3,293
Ashwell, Rutland, F. Palmer £2,860 to £3,293
Askham Grange, Yorks., Miss M. Morgan £2,860 to £3,293
Aylesbury, R. A. Attrill £3,646 to £4,152
Bedford, R. W. Downton £2,860 to £3,293
Bela River, Westmorland, P. O. E. Randell £2,860 to £3,293

Birmingham, E. E. Gregory £4,790
Blundeston, Suffolk, J. M. Crawford £3,646 to £4,152
Bristol, A. B. Hughes £3,646 to £4,152
Brixton, S.W.2, L. R. Ogier £4,790
Camp Hill, I.O.W., P. E. Marshall £3,646 to £4,152
Canterbury, M. J. Terry £2,860 to £3,293
Cardiff, T. Ryan £2,860 to £3,293
Chelmsford, G. E. Griffiths £3,646 to £4,152
Coldingley, Surrey, C. P. Honey £3,646 to £4,152
Dartmoor, N. H. Golding £4,790
Dorchester, J. S. McCarthy £2,860 to £3,293
Drake Hall, Staffs., J. W. N. Brown £2,860 to £3,293
Durham, L. W. F. Steinhausen £4,790
Eastchurch, Kent, R. C. Townsend £3,646 to £4,152
Exeter, P. A. M. Heald £3,646 to £4,152
Ford, Sussex, L. V. D. Dewar £3,646 to £4,152
Gartree, Leics., R. E. Adams £3,646 to £4,152
Gloucester, J. H. Absalom £2,860 to £3,293
Grendon and Spring Hill, Bucks., W. J. Gray (Medical Superintendent) £6,750
Haverigg, Cumberland, W. E. Cowper-Johnson
Holloway, N.7, Mrs. D. M. Wing £3,646 to £4,152
Hull, E. R. Cooper £3,646 to £4,152
Kingston, Portsmouth, F. S. Richardson £2,860 to £3,293
Kirkham, Lancs., N. Clay £3,646 to £4,152
Lancaster, A. W. Driscoll £2,860 to £3,293
Leeds, D. W. Fisher £4,790
Leicester, B. D. Wigginton £3,646 to £4,152
Lewes, F. V. Elvy, O.B.E. £3,646 to £4,152
Leyhill, Glos., A. B. Roberton £3,646 to £4,152
Lincoln, S. Mitchell £3,646 to £4,152
Liverpool, G. F. Bride £4,790
Long Lartin, Worcs., W. Perrie £4,790
Maidstone, G. Lister £3,646 to £4,152
Manchester, Capt. W. I. Davies £4,790
Moor Court, Staffs., Miss O. J. Prichard-Carr £2,860 to £3,293
Northeye, Sussex, D. A. Ward £2,840 to £3,293
Northallerton, E. S. Nash £2,860 to £3,293
Norwich, P. L. James £2,860 to £3,293
Nottingham, W. S. Smith, D.S.C. £2,860 to £3,293
Oxford, D. O'C. Grubb £2,860 to £3,293
Parkhurst, I.O.W., M. D. Macleod £4,790
Pentonville, N.7, A. C. Miller, M.B.E., T.D. £4,790
Preston, Maj. G. Nash £3,646 to £4,152
Ranby Camp, G. R. Feather £2,860 to £3,293
Reading, L. A. Portch £2,860 to £3,293
Shepton Mallet, G. J. Burford £2,860 to £3,293
Shrewsbury, R. B. Nix £2,860 to £3,293
Stafford, K. F. Watson £4,790
Styal, Cheshire, Miss I. M. McWilliam £3,646 to £4,152
Sudbury, C. M. Miles £3,646 to £4,152
Swansea, N. F. Low £2,860 to £3,293
Thorp Arch, Yorks, R. J. Spencer £2,860 to £3,293
The Verne, Dorset, E. A. Esquillant £3,646 to £4,152
Wakefield, J. R. Watson £4,790
Wakefield Staff College, W. J. Booth £4,790
Wandsworth, S.W.18, R. S. Llewellyn £4,790
Winchester, R. F. Owens £3,646 to £4,152
Wormwood Scrubs, W.12, L. J. F. Wheeler £4,790

BORSTALS
Governors
Bullwood Hall, Essex, Miss O. Parry £2,860 to £3,293
Dover, E. A. Stratford £3,646 to £4,152
East Sutton Park, Kent, Miss M. Farmery £2,860 to £3,293
Everthorpe, Yorks., R. K. Lawson £3,646 to £4,152
Feltham, Middx., R. M. Dauncey £3,646 to £4,152
Finnamore, Middx., M. P. Goodall £2,301 to £2,656
Gaynes Hall, Hunts., C. M. D. Burnett, M.B.E. £2,860 to £3,293
Guys Marsh, Dorset, B. A. Marchant £2,860 to £3,293

Hatfield, Yorks., J. W. Green.... £2,860 to £3,293
Hewell Grange, Worcs., D. Atkinson
£2,860 to 3,293
Hindley, Lancs., M. H. P. Coombs
£3,646 to £4,152
Hollesley Bay Colony, Suffolk, D. W. Higman
£3,646 to £4,152
Huntercombe, Oxon., A. F. H. Arnold
£2,860 to £3,293
Lowdham Grange, Notts., B. J. Chilvers
£3,646 to £4,152
Morton Hall, Lincs., D. E. Preston, M.B.E.
£2,860 to £3,293
North Sea Camp, Lincs., D. A. Guild, D.S.M.
£2,860 to £3,293
Onley, Warwicks., L. C. Oxford ..£2,860 to £3,293
Pollington, Yorks., J. E. Wood ...£2,860 to £3,293
Portland, Dorset, H. H. Harrison..£3,646 to £4,152
Rochester, D. F. Dennis..........£3,646 to £4,152
Stoke Heath, Salop, S. A. Bester. £3,646 to £4,152
Usk, Mon., G. J. Dadds.........£2,860 to £3,293
Wellingborough, W. Fingland....£2,860 to £3,293
Wetherby, Yorks., P. R. D. Meech
£2,860 to £3,293

REMAND CENTRES
Governors

Ashford, Middx., W. A. Brister ..£3,646 to £4,152
Brockhill, Worcs., D. St. L. Simon
£2,860 to £3,293
Low Newton, Co. Durham, W. A. Holman
£2,301 to £2,656
Pucklechurch, Bristol, R. J. Kenduck
£2,301 to £2,656
Risley, Lancs, Maj. M. Oldfield, M.C.   £4,790
Thorp Arch, Yorks., C. D. Sherwood
£2,301 to £2,656

DETENTION CENTRES
Wardens

Aldington, Kent, E. Sumner......£2,820 to £3,293
Blantyre House, Kent, C. J. Knight, D.S.M.
£2,860 to £3,293
Buckley Hall, Lancs., W. L. Killip, B.E.M.
£2,860 to £3,293
Campsfield House, Oxford, R. Croxford
£2,301 to £2,656
Eastwood Park, Glos., H. J. W.White
£2,301 to 2,656
Erlestoke House, Wilts., K. Whetton
£2,860 to £3,293
Foston Hall, Derby, W. P. MacG. Cargill
£2,301 to £2,656
Haslar, Hants, A. R. Parsons....£2,860 to £3,293
Kirklevington, Yorks., W. A. Williamson
£2,301 to £2,656
Latchmere House, Surrey, L. E. Davies
£2,301 to £2,656
Medomsley, Co. Durham, M. J. Brown
£2,860 to £3,293
New Hall, Yorks., J. D. O. Lewis £2,860 to £3,293
Send, Surrey, R. Green.........£2,301 to £2,656
Swinfen Hall, Staffs., E. Owens..£2,860 to £3,293
Werrington House, Staffs., P. C. Pye
£2,860 to £3,293
Whatton, Notts., W. B. Ritson...£2,860 to £3,293

Probation and After-Care Department
Romney House, Marsham Street, S.W.1
[01-799-3488]

Assistant Under-Secretary of State, H. W. Stotesbury.
£6,925
Assistant Secretaries, P. Beedle; A. W. Glanville;
E. N. Kent................£5,175 to £6,475
Adviser in After Care, A. Hague, R.D....£5,210
Principals, N. W. R. Baker; P. E. Baker; Miss P.
M. Strong; M. G. Thompson; R. J. H. West;
A. P. Wilson; W. J. Wright..£3,425 to £4,575
Senior Executive Officers, P. A. Chadwell; H. L. J.
Gonsalves; Miss J. M. Jeffery; B. G. Meilton;
J. A. Peacock; K. W. Rowe...£2,950 to £3,575

Principal Probation Inspector, J. MacRae, O.B.E., D.F.C.
£6,475
Deputy Principal Probation Inspector, M. H. Hogan
£4,815
Director of Training, Miss M. Irvine
£4,775 to £5,375
Superintending Inspectors, R. F. Lampard; R. W.
Spiers; C. T. Swann.........£4,220 to £4,730
Senior Inspectors, Miss M. E. P. Corner, M.B.E.;
Miss M. D. Samuels.........£3,075 to £4,318
Inspectors, J. D. Benwell; R. A. Betteridge; J. J.
Dand; G. E. Davies; R. O. Davies; D. F.
Duchemin; J. C. Flatt; M. J. Hensman; Miss
M. H. Johnson; Miss M. J. McCarthy; H. M.
Morton; G. L. Orton; Miss M. G. Packer;
P. G. Parker; K. G. W. Parris; D. N. Rogers;
F. N. Stephens; Miss F. M. Stone; Mrs. M.
Stuart.....................£2,923 to £4,166

Drugs Branch

Chief Inspector, C. G. Jeffery ....£4,775 to £5,375
Deputy Chief Inspector, H. B. Spear
£3,425 to £4,575
Principals, E. C. Huggett; F. Stewart; D. G. Turner
£3,425 to £4,575
Senior Executive Officer, H. R. Emery
£2,950 to £3,575

Cruelty to Animal Acts Inspectorate

Chief Inspector, R. S. Vine...............£6,295
Superintending Inspectors, Group Capt. J. R. Cellars,
A.F.C.; R. C. Macpherson, M.B.E.........£6,815
Inspectors, Mrs. R. M. Collister, M.D.; M. G.
Jackson-Smyth; H. L. Jenkins, M.D.; J. D. Laws;
R. Mitchell; J. D. Rankin, Ph.D.; M.A.Richards;
C. E. Stuart; W. D. Tavernor; A. G. Warren
£3,727 to £5,050

Programme Analysis Review Unit
Romney House, Marsham Street, S.W.1.
[01-799-3488]
Assistant Secretary, A. S. Pratley..£5,175 to £6,475
Principal, M. Youngs..........£3,425 to £4,575

Research and Statistics Department
Romney House, Marsham Street, S.W.1
[01-799-3488]

Director of Research and Statistics, T. S. Lodge, C.B.E.
£6,925
Head of Research Unit, Miss S. V. Cunliffe
£4,565 to £5,815
Deputy Head of Research Unit, W. H. Hammond,
Ph.D....................£2,995 to £4,077
Principals, Miss W. M. Goode, C.B.E.; D. E. Luke
£3,425 to £4,575
Senior Research Officers, Miss E. K. C. Banks, Ph.D.;
I. J. Croft; L. Davidoff; P. J. Didcott (Edinburgh);
M. S. Folkard, Ph.D. (Manchester); Miss N. M.
Goodman; Miss J. W. Mott; Mrs. F. H. Simon;
I. A. C. Sinclair...........£2,995 to £4,077
Senior Executive Officer, J. E. Plant
£2,950 to £3,575

Tolworth Tower, Surbiton, Surrey
[01-399-5191]
Chief Statistician, Mrs. E. H. Gibson
£4,480 to £5,720
Statisticians, C. M. Glennie, Ph.D.; Mrs. E. Oatham;
A. D. Weatherhead.........£3,250 to £4,400
Principals, S. Klein; R. T. Tudor £3,425 to £4,575
Senior Executive Officers, K. Luff; A. Williamson
£2,950 to £3,575

Scientific Advisory Branch
Horseferry House, Dean Ryle Street, S.W.1
[01-834-6655]
Director, J. D. Culshaw........£5,415 to £5,995
Senior Principal Scientific Officer, F. H. Pavry
£4,570 to £5,190
Principal Scientific Officers, J. C. Cotterill; Mrs.
J. M. Hogg; J. A. Miles; A. N. Rapsey; A. M.
Western..................£2,995 to £4,077

Women's Royal Voluntary Service
17 Old Park Lane, W.1
[01-499-6040]
Chairman, Mrs. C. Clode, C.B.E.
Social Services Administrator, Miss A. C. Johnston, C.B.E.
Chief Administrator (Regions), Miss K. M. Halpin, C.B.E.

HORSERACE TOTALISATOR BOARD
Tote House, 8–12 New Bridge Street, E.C.4.
[01-353-1066]
Established by the Betting Levy Act, 1961, as successor in title to the Racecourse Betting Control Board established by the Racecourse Betting Act, 1928.

Its function is to operate totalisators on approved horse racecourses in Great Britain, and thus to provide moneys for the improvement of breeds of horses, the sport of horse racing and the advancement and encouragement of veterinary science and education, by means of an annual levy paid to the Horserace Betting Levy Board established under the same Act in 1961.

Members
Chairman, A. W. Taylor, C.B............ £6,900
Apptd. by the Home Secretary: The Lord Oakshott, M.B.E.; R. A. Withers.
Director-General, D. D. Bartlett.

INDEPENDENT TELEVISION AUTHORITY
70 Brompton Road, S.W.3.
[01-584-7011]
The Independent Television Authority was created in August, 1954, to provide public television services of information, education and entertainment. The Television Act was renewed in 1964 for a further 12 years. The Chairman and Members of the Authority are appointed by the Minister of Posts and Telecommunications. The programmes transmitted from the Authority's 45 stations are provided by 15 independent programme contractors whose revenue derives from the sale, subject to controls exercised by the Authority, of advertising time. The contractors pay a rent to the Authority, to meet the ITA's own requirements and a levy based on net advertising revenue to the Exchequer.
Chairman, The Lord Aylestone, P.C., C.B.E. £6,000
Deputy Chairman, Sir Ronald Gould £2,000
Members, T. F. Carbery; T. G. Davies, C.B.E.; Sir Frederick Hayday, C.B.E.; S. Keynes; The Baroness Macleod of Borve; H. McMillan; Prof. J. M. Meek, D.Eng.; A. W. Page; The Baroness Sharp, G.B.E........................ £1,000
Director-General, B. W. M. Young.
Deputy Directors General, B. C. Sendall, C.B.E. (*Programme Services*); A. W. Pragnell, O.B.E., D.F.C. (*Administrative Services*).
Director of Engineering, H. Steele.
Director of Finance, A. S. Curbishley, O.B.E.   ✗
Secretary, B. Rook.

CENTRAL OFFICE OF INFORMATION
Hercules Road, Westminster Bridge Road, S.E.1
[01-928-2345]
The Central Office of Information is a common service department which produces information and publicity material, and supplies publicity services, for other Government departments which require them. In the United Kingdom it conducts Government display press, television and poster advertising (except for the National Savings Committee), produces and distributes booklets, leaflets, films, television material, exhibitions, photographs and other visual material; and distributes departmental press notices. For the overseas departments it supplies British Information posts overseas with press, radio and television material, booklets, magazines, reference services, films, exhibitions, photographs, display and reading room material; manages schemes for promoting the overseas sale of British books, periodicals and newspapers; arranges tours in the United Kingdom for official visitors from

overseas; and provides exhibition stands at trade fairs (for the Board of Trade). Administratively, the Central Office of Information is responsible to Treasury ministers, while the ministers whose departments it serves are responsible for the policy expressed in its work.
Director-General, Sir Fife Clark, C.B.E...... £9,000
Private Secretary, Miss E. M. Butler, M.B.E.
Controllers, F. D. Bickerton, C.B.E. (*Home*); D. F. Kerr, C.V.O., O.B.E. (*Overseas*).......... £6,555
Assistant Controller (Overseas), R. Dean, C.B.
                                  £4,220 to £4,730
Senior Information Officer, Miss G. R. Hembry
                                  £2,704 to £3,274

Advertising Division
Director, O. G. Thetford....... £4,220 to £4,730
Principal Information Officers, J. Bessant; D. G. Marsh; Mrs. E. J. Rodnight; Miss V. E. Thorne
                                  £3,433 to £4,048
Senior Information Officers, M. J. C. Brodie; B. F. C. Crampin; J. C. Danckwerts; A. H. C. Royou; G. W. Tavender .... £2,704 to £3,274
Senior Executive Officer, D. F. Parsons
                                  £2,950 to £3,575

Establishment and Organization Division
Atlantic House, Holborn Viaduct, E.C.1
[01-248-5744]
Director, R. W. Kingsbury, O.B.E. (*Establishment Officer*) .... £5,175 to £6,475
Principals, E. Bridger; W. F. Garnett; C. T. Sawyer; A. Youngs................... £3,425 to £4,575
Senior Executive Officers, M. Collins; W. J. Colwill; R. K. Evans; I. L. Margetts; D. C. Marquet; D. P. Morgan; Miss J. M. Reid; J. G. Rowbotham.................... £2,950 to £3,575

Exhibitions Division
St. Christopher House Annexe,
Sumner Street, S.E.1
[01-928-2371]
Director, R. A. Fleming....... £4,575 to £5,815
Chief Information Officers, N. Bicknell; S. Hart-Still
                                  £3,730 to £4,220
Principal Information Officers, N. J. Holland; R. J. Reeves; H. H. Rossney; A. V. Whitehead; D. Wilkes.................. £3,433 to £4,048
Senior Information Officers, G. W. Bennett; H. O. Bryant, O.B.E.; A. J. Chard; P. R. Daniell; A. D. Estill; W. H. Farrow; A. E. Humphries; H. Jennings-Bateman; E. J. Lewington; F. Lightfoot, M.B.E.; P. J. London; A. S. McConnell; K. S. McDowall; A. McMillan; T. J. Marsh; J. C. Martin; L. A. Miller; B. H. Reynolds; M. A. Richardson; C. W. Tosdevin; R. J. Vallance; P. G. Velarde; Miss E. B. Woolgar
                                  £2,704 to £3,274
Senior Executive Officer, H. Cook
                                  £2,950 to £3,575

Films and Television Division
Director, H. J. Bewg........... £4,565 to £5,815
Chief Information Officer, Miss D. V. F. Cockburn
                                  £4,220 to £4,730
Principal Information Officers, J. Baird; Mrs. R. Brownrigg; J. A. Leys; D. B. Mayne, M.B.E.; A. C. White................ £3,433 to £4,048
Principal, G. W. M. Pearson..... £3,425 to £4,575
Senior Information Officers, J. J. N. Barran; A. S. P. B. Dann; Mrs. P. Davidson; R. A. P. Duval; W. J. G. Evans; J. B. Frankfort; Miss W. M. Habberfield; J. Harris; A. Hinton; Miss A. B. I. James; Miss E. V. Moynihan; Mrs. M. G. Reynolds; E. H. J. Runkel; A. W. Thomson; Miss A. A. Wiersma; N. B. Wilkinson; Miss J. G. Willett; G. A. Woodford
                                  £2,704 to £3,274

Finance and Accounts Division
Director, G. E. Iles.............. £5,175 to £6,475

Finance Branch
Principal, D. J. Etheridge....... £3,425 to £4,575
Senior Executive Officers, R. W. Clarke; J. F. Hinds; E. W. Whyman.............. £2,950 to £3,575

Accounts Branch
Sutherland House, Brighton Road,
Sutton, Surrey
[01-642-6022]

Principal, D. Hall, D.F.M. . . . . £3,340 to £4,490
Senior Executive Officer, K. R. Stephens
£2,865 to £3,490

Overseas Press Services Division
Director, H. J. Watters . . . . £4,565 to £5,815
Chief Information Officers, J. K. Holroyd; G. Holt
£4,225 to £4,730
Principal Information Officers, J. C. B. Hannah;
R. C. Herbert; D. W. James; D. J. Payton-
Smith; D. A. Smith; K. W. Sutton; E. Turnbull
£3,433 to £4,048
Senior Information Officers, Mrs. A. A. Beattie; J. D.
Beaumont; A. G. Bourne; P. T. Brazier; N. H.
Browne; Miss R. Clifford, M.B.E.; R. E. Collins;
R. M. Douglas; G. L. Duffus; J. Ensoll; N. D.
Evans; A. J. Forrest; B. C. Freestone; G. P. H.
Garton; J. A. K. Goldthorpe; L. A. J. Hawkings;
D. W. MacRow; Miss E. C. C. Mayson; J. H.
Neil; F. R. Pickering, M.B.E.; G. L. Strickland;
R. W. Tindall; Miss B. H. Turner; Miss P. J.
Tyler; J. F. F. Webb . . . . £2,704 to £3,274

Photographs Division
Director, E. R. I. Allan, O.B.E. . . . . £4,220 to £4,730
Principal Information Officer, R. E. Hicks
£3,433 to £4,048
Senior Information Officers, J. A. Bond; Miss H. R.
Dunt; F. J. S. Mitchell-Hedges
£2,704 to £3,274
Senior Executive Officer, K. F. G. Fogwill
£2,950 to £3,575

Publications Division
Director, E. R. Kelly . . . . £4,220 to £4,730
Principal Information Officers, J. C. Bayliss, O.B.E.;
J. L. Bishop; F. V. Ellis; W. J. Masters, O.B.E.
£3,433 to £4,048
Senior Information Officers, A. M. Clark; Miss
M. M. Foster; H. P. Jolowicz; Miss B. M.
Kirby; H. D. Liversidge; Miss M. E. J. Orna;
Miss J. Penfold; R. T. Ronan; E. H. Sired;
L. C. K. Vaughan-Jones . . . . £2,704 to £3,274

Radio Division
Director, J. P. Langston, O.B.E. . . . £4,565 to £5,825
Principal Information Officer, R. J. Hall
£3,433 to £4,048
Senior Information Officers, C. G. Cave, M.B.E.;
F. N. Hunter; P. D. Wallace . £2,704 to £3,274

Reference Division
Director, A. E. Bevens . . . . £4,220 to £4,730
Principal Information Officers, E. G. Farmer; H.
Witheford . . . . £3,433 to £4,048
Senior Information Officers, Mrs. J. Bonnor; J. F.
Langley; Mrs. D. L. Long (*part-time*); C. E. F.
Manning; K. G. Mather; J. H. D. Page; Miss
H. M. Taylor . . . . £2,704 to £3,274
Senior Executive Officer, R. F. Stapley
£2,950 to £3,575

Tours and Production Services Division
Director, R. G. Biggs, O.B.E. . . . . . £4,565 to £5,815
Principal Information Officers, R. Blundell, D.F.C.;
C. H. Bourchier; J. B. Crompton; D. N.
Steward . . . . £3,433 to £4,048
Senior Information Officers, S. C. Bignell, M.B.E.;
Miss B. M. E. Breden; C. J. Davies; K. Dear;
H. Edwards; A. E. Gatland; S. S. Hordern;
C. M. Hull; D. A. Loxley; G. R. Parsons;
E. W. Taylor; N. J. A. Throckmorton; C. A.
Willson . . . . £2,704 to £3,274
Senior Executive Officers, A. H. Kemp; A. H. Robin-
son . . . . £2,950 to £3,575

Regional Unit
Principal Information Officer, J. J. N. Parker
£3,433 to £4,048

News Distribution Service
Duty Officers, H. R. G. Burton; H. P. Smithson.

Regional Offices
Northern—Wellbar House, Gallowgate,
Newcastle upon Tyne
Chief Regional Officer, A. A. McLoughlin
£4,045 to £4,555
Senior Information Officer, L. W. Mandy, M.B.E.
£2,529 to £3,099

East and West Ridings—City House,
New Station Street, Leeds
Chief Regional Officer, D. de M. Guilfoyle, O.B.E.
£4,045 to £4,555
Senior Information Officer, C. E. Dove
£2,529 to £3,099

North Midland—Cranbrook House,
Cranbook Street, Nottingham
Chief Regional Officer, T. Cooban
£4,045 to £4,555
Senior Information Officer, P. D. Yorke
£2,529 to £3,099

Eastern—Block A, Government Buildings, Brooklands
Avenue, Cambridge
Chief Regional Officer, P. L. K. Schwabé, M.V.O.
£3,258 to £3,873
Senior Information Officer, O. J. B. Prince-White
£2,529 to £3,099

London and South Eastern—
St. Christopher House Annexe,
Sumner Street, S.E.1
Chief Regional Officer, E. A. Hunt
£4,270 to £4,730
Senior Information Officer, A. J. Goodson
£2,704 to £3,274
Southern—Market Place House, Reading
Chief Regional Officer, P. T. Ede . £3,258 to £3,873
Senior Information Officer, A. S. Poole
£2,529 to £3,099

South Western—The Pithay, Bristol, 1
Chief Regional Officer, W. J. D. Irving, M.V.O.
£3,258 to £3,873
Senior Information Officer, F. Barrett
£2,529 to £3,099

Midland—Five Ways House,
Islington Row, Birmingham, 15
Chief Regional Officer, D. C. Boyd
£4,045 to £4,555
Senior Information Officer, A. Thompson
£2,529 to £3,099

North Western—Sunley Building,
Piccadilly Plaza, Manchester
Chief Regional Officer, H. V. Tillotson, M.V.O.
£4,045 to £4,555
Senior Information Officer, H. Cope
£2,529 to £3,099

BOARD OF INLAND REVENUE
Somerset House, W.C.2
[01-836-2407]

The Board of Inland Revenue was constituted
under the Inland Revenue Board Act, 1849, by the
consolidation of the Board of Excise and the Board
of Stamps and Taxes. In 1909 the administration
of excise duties was transferred to the Board of
Customs. The Board of Inland Revenue is
responsible for the management and collection of
income tax, surtax, profits tax, capital gains tax,
corporation tax, estate duty, stamp duties and other
direct taxes, and for the valuation of freehold and
leasehold property for Inland Revenue taxation,
for certain purposes on behalf of other Government Departments and public authorities and, in
England and Wales, for local authority rating. The
Board is also responsible for the management and
collection of tithe redemption annuities, and for
administering the Scheme of compensation for
War Damage (except to highways) under the War
Damage Act, 1943. Salaries and expenses of
the Board for 1971–72 were estimated at
£125,210,000.

The Board *GCB 6/72*
Chairman, Sir Arnold France, K.C.B. £14,000
Private Secretary, M. A. Johns.

Deputy Chairmen, A. Lord; N. C. Price, C.B.;
£9,000

Other Members, Sir Leonard Barford; A. H. Dalton; J. M. Green; W. H. B. Johnson; J. A. Johnstone; D. A. Smith; J. Webb; Miss G. E. M. Wolters
£6,750

Establishments Division
Personnel Group
Director of Personnel, J. Webb.............£6,750
Assistant Secretaries, J. M. Crawley; B. T. Houghton; E. J. King............£5,000 to £6,300
Principals, R. A. Baldwin; P. Beever; J. B. Berry; S. Brown; *R. S. Hayward (*Chief Welfare Officer*); W. J. Maddren; D. W. Mason; I. R. Spence*; G. A. Spencer........£3,250 to £4,400
Senior Executive Officers, C. G. Baseley; R. J. Ewens; E. M. Hayes; J. B. E. Leighton
£2,775 to £3,400

Manpower and Organization Group
Director of Manpower and Organization, J. M. Green
£6,750
Assistant Secretaries, A. M. W. Battishill; J. B. Sweeting; G. D. Wroe........£5,000 to £6,300
Principals, J. P. B. Bryce; *G. W. Hopkinson; C. E. Howick; D. B. Willis...£3,250 to £4,400
Management Services (A.D.P.)
Senior Principal, S. G. Day......£4,600 to £5,200
Principals, H. R. Brockwell; H. R. Game; G. I. Harding; R. E. M. Kirkman..£3,250 to £4,400
Senior Executive Officers, R. C. Fullbrook; A. R. J. Green; R. C. Lincoln; E. F. Smith; D. R. Webb-Bourne.............£2,775 to £3,400
Management Services (General)
Senior Management Services Officers (Principals), F. W. J. Boggiss; R. W. S. Haines; J. W. Waters
£3,250 to £4,400
Management Services Officers (Senior Executive Officers), A. O. H. Blair; J. D. J. Bonfield; G. Britton; D. B. Duff; G. A. A. Elmer; P. Harrison; R. G. Lusk; B. O'Connor; K. Pryce; J. M. Stuart; F. P. Sturges......£2,775 to £3,400
Controller of Office Services (Senior Principal), R. O. Burnett............£4,600 to £5,200
Principal, S. E. S. Whitby (*Accommodation Officer*)
£3,250 to £4,400
Senior Executive Officers, A. S. Bridle; J. B. Clifton; A. L. Cowden, M.B.E.; N. Cumming; S. Richardson....................£2,775 to £3,400

Stamps and Taxes Division
Assistant Secretaries, R. F. Bailey; L. J. H. Beighton; W. E. Bruce; M. H. Collins; P. D. Hall; F. B. Harrison; G. B. N. Hartog; D. Hopkins; A. J. G. Isaac; E. A. Knight; Miss A. H. McNicol; T. J. Painter; F. I. Robertson; J. P. Strudwick, C.B.E.; J. D. Taylor-Thompson; D. B. Vernon N. Wainwright..........£5,000 to £6,300
Senior Economic Adviser, E. B. Butler
£5,000 to £6,300
Principals, J. D. Benson; P. Bhose; R. J. Bitton; *F. Cuerden; P. W. Davenport; C. L. Deller; D. G. Draper; M. J. G. Elliott; R. Ellis; C. G. Field; S. G. Hammond; G. M. Kirby; P. Lewis; E. McGivern; J. Marshall; S. C. T. Matheson; A. G. Morgan; F. W. Newcombe; D. Y. Pitts; *J. E. Redman; D. J. Ritchie; A. F. Royle, O.B.E. (*Press Officer*); J. B. Shepherd; C. Stewart; B. J. Thomas; J. D. Thomas; E. V. Wigglesworth
£3,250 to £4,400
Statistician, W. Gonzalez........£3,250 to £4,400
Senior Executive Officer, R. F. Knight
£2,775 to £3,400

Statistics and Intelligence Division
Somerset House, W.C.2
Director, G. Paine................£6,750
Chief Statistician, M. M. Erritt; J. R. L. Schneider
£5,000 to £6,300
Statisticians, A. T. Dunn; F. R. L'Aiguille; R. V. S. Quinn....................£3,250 to £4,400
Principals, *W. G. Meadows; *E. B. Paterson; *A. G. Solly ....£3,250 to £4,400

* Temporary

Assessments Division
Barrington Road, Worthing, Sussex
Controller, H. Leigh............£4,600 to £6,500
Principals, R. Heeley; D. H. Pooley
£3,250 to £4,400

Office of the Controller of Stamps
Bush House, South-West Wing, Strand, W.C.2 and Barrington Road, Worthing, Sussex
Controller, A. A. E. E. Ettinghausen........£5,470
Principals, A. Blaney; J. A. Cargill
£3,250 to £4,400

Director of Stamping
Avon House, 275 Borough High Street, S.E.1
Director, J. Green, I.S.O..........£3,250 to £4,400

Estate Duty Office
Minford House, Rockley Road,
West Kensington, W.14
Controller of Death Duties, E. W. C. Lewis, C.B.
£6,750
Deputy Controllers of Death Duties, W. J. G. Allen; H. W. Hewitt, I.S.O...........£6,300
Asst. Controllers of Death Duties, K. W. Chetwood; R. R. Greenfield; C. D. Harding; R. K. Johns; D. J. Lawday; D. H. McCartie; E. J. Mann; C. A. Robertson; J. B. Wells £5,335
Chief Examiners, J. D. Armour; W. J. Atkinson; T. E. Austen; J. A. Banks; G. A. Beasley; J. W. Bogle; H. Booth, M.B.E.; J. Bugden; *E. C. Burden; W. G. Cannon; C. G. Carter; W. G. Carter; *A. Cherne; Miss M. Clark; J. G. Colebrook, M.B.E.; S. Collingwood; M. F. B. Couzens, O.B.E.; E. N. Crowther; J. F. Cunningham; W. E. Dallas; G. F. Dawe; J. F. Daykin; P. H. Fletcher; A. B. Gardner; B. E. Glaze; N. B. Gudgin; W. Hall; R. Horrex; C. D. Hughes; F. Irwin; J. F. Johnson; Miss M. M. Jones; J. G. Kingsley; K. S. Lake; K. J. Lees; *F. W. Leigh; A. D. Mitchner; P. H. Moss; S. Noden; E. W. J. Panting; A. R. Payne; R. T. Peak; J. Pearce; N. L. Pearce; E. G. Peel; C. M. Phillips; D. F. Reading; E. O. Rice; W. K. Sisman; P. B. Smallwood; F. E. Spurrell; R. A. Suckling; E. Sykes; G. Thompson; F. H. Thornton; R. F. J. Thornton; P. Vernon, O.B.E.
£3,250 to £4,499
Senior Executive Officer, W. Hardman, M.B.E.
£2,775 to £3,400

Solicitor's Office
Somerset House, W.C.2
Solicitor, E. G. R. Moses................£7,100
Principal Assistant Solicitors, R. S. Boyd; J. S. Clarke, M.C.; J. W. Weston........£6,125
Assistant Solicitors, K. G. Blake, C.B.E.; Mrs. A. Boyd; P. Carter; J. C. Doggett; J. F. Easton; M. C. Furey; D. M. Hatton; E. O. Jackson; H. G. Kingston; R. J. Lloyd; R. K. Miller; A. K. Tavaré ....£5,200 to £6,300
Senior Legal Assistants, A. L. L. Alexander; C. J. C. Baron; J. G. H. Bates; D. S. Blair; R. T. Brand; K. O. Butterfield; B. R. D. Clarke; R. P. Gibbons; Miss A. Joslin; D. MacDonagh; A. A. MacKeith; R. L. M. Parsey; N. R. Phillips; Mrs. E. K. Picard; M. J. Rawlinson; P. Towle; B. J. Walker; A. Wheaten; J. T. Woodhouse
£3,750 to £5,000
Principal, E. Davidson........£3,250 to £4,400
Senior Executive Officers, I. P. Dunkley; A. E. Meek
£2,775 to £3,400

Superannuation Funds Office
42–46 Weston Street, S.E.1
Controller, D. S. Kirtley........£5,000 to £6,300
Assistant Controllers, Miss D. Bickmore; R. V. Binding; H. H. Jago; R. C. Tebboth
£4,600 to £5,200
Principals, Miss M. I. Fetherston; J. N. Gosling; W. T. Lyons; K. J. Style; B. S. Taylor; R. A. White....................£3,250 to £4,400

* Temporary

Surtax Office
Lynwood Road, Thames Ditton, Surrey
Companies Division
Apex Tower, Malden Road, New Malden, Surrey
Office of the Inspector of Foreign Dividends
New Malden House, Blagdon Road, New Malden, Surrey
Controller of Surtax and Inspector of Foreign Dividends, H. H. Leedale, C.B.E. ... £6,490
Deputy Controller of Surtax and Deputy Inspector of Foreign Dividends, G. Briddon £5,000 to £6,300
Assistant Controllers of Surtax, W. H. S. Howell, I.S.O.; E. A. Rapsey; J. Richardson; W. M. Stewart; R. A. J. Webber ... £4,600 to £5,200
Assistant Inspector of Foreign Dividends, N. W. Sydee

£4,600 to £5,200

Principals, H. Booth; S. J. C. Boucher; A. W. Coates; W. H. Day; H. B. Every; R. K. Ewan; R. A. Forth; B. E. Greville; R. G. Hughes; J. G. Hull; W. J. Hunt; L. S. Jowsey; G. S. Lancaster; B. Lyons; A. McKenzie; G. E. P. Matthews; W. J. Moore; G. H. Pentelow; M. W. Potter; C. W. Price; M. L. Reardon; D. V. Roberts; C. A. Thorpe; A. E. Wadey; P. L. Wolsey ... £3,250 to £4,400

Tithe Redemption Office
Barrington Road, Worthing, Sussex
Controller, G. F. K. Grant, I.S.O. £4,600 to £5,200
Deputy Controller, E. L. Cannon

£3,250 to £4,400

Accountant and Comptroller-General's Office
Bush House, South-West Wing, Strand, W.C.2
Accountant and Comptroller-Gen., F. H. Brooman

£6,600

Deputy do., J. F. Hill ... £5,000 to £6,300
Assistant Accountants and Comptrollers-General, S. G. Ash, M.B.E.; L. C. Gilbertson; W. Holmes; G. B. Walker, I.S.O.; E. E. Wheeler £4,600 to £5,200

General Accounting and Collection of Taxes Division
Principal Collectors, R. G. Balls; F. E. Bance; J. A. Bolton; J. L. Cridge; F. C. Cullington; V. G. Ellen; K. L. Fickling; D. C. Geddes; H. G. Grimshaw; J. G. C. Hopkins; W. A. Impey; E. G. Lewin; G. R. Lister; W. J. Millan; A. J. Morrison; R. A. Newbery; B. H. Reynolds; W. H. J. Sharp; A. L. Smith ... £3,250 to £4,400

Audit Division
Principals, A. E. Bleksley, I.S.O.; P. D. Connell; G. Edmiston ... £3,250 to £4,400

Office of the Chief Inspector of Taxes
Somerset House W.C.2
Chief Inspector, Sir Leonard Barford ... £9,000
Deputy Chief Inspectors, E. V. Adams; E. Bramley, C.B.E.; E. V. Symons ... £6,750
Senior Principal Inspectors, G. L. Ayres; N. E. Beck; J. F. Boyd; E. W. Boyles; J. T. Cannon; O. P. Davies; F. S. Dodd; F. B. Gibson; C. H. Godden; V. H. T. Grout, C.B.E.; R. A. Hogg; K. A. Job; D. A. Jones; R. Kingsbury; R. E. Kirby; A. W. Mason; L. L. Milner, C.B.E.; D. H. Moorcraft; W. A. T. Morton; W. A. Perry; R. W. Rae; R. D. Rawson, M.B.E.; A. B. Scott, V.R.D.; F. Seale; K. C. Southall; L. S. Stratford; P. R. Sweetman; I. R. E. Symons; F. J. Taylor-Gooby; I. D. Thomson; P. Tillson; C. G. Ware; J. H. Williams; P. E. Woodcock ... £6,490
Principal Inspectors (at Head Office), J. N. Allen; F. W. Bailey, O.B.E.; J. F. S. Banks; A. J. Baynes; T. Bingham; R. A. Blythe; A. D. M. Brown; R. T. W. Butter; F. Carr; R. C. H. Crozier; W. Dermit; M. Eastham; W. T. C. Edwards; G. R. Evans; G. Galey; E. T. Griffiths, I.S.O.; W. S. Grimshaw; D. G. Hackston; N. Hannah; H. C. Hart; I. N. Hunter; F. D. Johns; R. F. Jones; N. Kinder; A. G. King; N. J. Knights; J. E. Lawrance; J. Livesey; F. T. J. Magee; J. Moule; P. L. O'Leary. P. G. Pearce; D. B. Rogers; T. Scott; K. A. Skinner; I. R. R. H. Sturtevant; J. P.

Tomlinson; T. W. M. Tuite; P. Tyrer; J. K. Ward; H. A. White; W. B. Wilkinson; A. S. Wray ... £5,000 to £6,300
Senior Inspectors (at Head Office), J. B. Anderson; A. R. Arnold; A. Ashton; D. D. Bottomley; T. Boyle; K. R. Brown; A. R. Brunsdon; A. W. Bryant; E. J. Burnett, I.S.O.; B. S. Caley; C. Cherry; G. Citrine; J. P. Conn; E. A. Crossland, I.S.O.; T. M. Ditchfield; F. W. F. Dobby; L. F. Dray; J. Dunn; E. Earnshaw; J. G. Ellis; R. J. Fairlie; G. Findley; T. C. Forsyth; J. P. G. Fysh; P. G. Gill; W. C. Gladstone; M. L. Gordon; K. J. Griffin; J. F. Hall; G. F. Hamilton; D. Hanson; K. D. Hill; J. A. P. Hoadley; J. J. H. Hopkins; G. M. Howell; E. Howie; S. R. Hunt; H. R. Ingram; P. B. G. Jones; B. J. Lane; H. G. A. Last; L. C. L. Lavender; S. R. Lock; D. M. Loudon; A. McIsaac; I. A. MacLean; Miss. V. Marston; Miss P.Millen; L. Morawetz; L. T. W. Morley; R. Morton; I. S. Murdoch; J. P. Murphy; R. C. Murgatroyd; M. D. E. Newstead; W. Northend; F. A. O'Leary; W. A. Page; J. D. Pay; J. H. W. Phillips; J. K. Phillips; R. Quinlan; W. Ralph; W. S. Rankin; R. F. Ratcliff; J. E. L. Ratty; H. T. Reed; J. A. Rignell; J. D. Robertson; D. A. Rolfe; D. B. B. Rouse; W. Sanderson; R. A. Savours; J. M. Sentinella; F. H. Shea; N. T. Shepherd; Miss D. M. Sirett; R. Smith; G. A. Spencer; G. E. Stoker; P. G. Suddaby; L. G. Taylor; D. L. Walker; Miss K. B. Walker; J. C. Watkis; J. S. Wilson; S. J. Wood; K. Yates ... £4,025 to £5,200
Principal Inspectors (Scotland), J. H. Gardner; A. D. R. Maclean; J. H. B. Wilson

£5,000 to £6,300

Senior Inspector (Scotland), A. O. Brown

£4,025 to £5,200

Principal Inspector (Northern Ireland), L. N. Mathers, O.B.E. ... £5,000 to £5,200
Principal Accountants, E. Lawson; A Wilson

£4,503 to £5,390

Chief Accountants, A. E. Allchurch; J. M. Fulton; R. Halsall; W. E. Haslam; W. A. Heslop; C. U. Mack; S. R. F. Porter; G. A. Reed; W. H. Simon; R. J. Ward; N. J. Wykes; A. B. Yewdall

£3,250 to £4,400

Valuation Office
New Court, Carey Street, W.C.2
Chief Valuer, Sir Douglas Iggulden, C.B.E., D.S.O., T.D. ... £9,000
Deputy Chief Valuers, H. C. Grenyer; W. A. Hobbs, C.B.E. ... £6,750
Assistant Chief Valuers, T. Broad, C.B.E.; R. J. Cowling; H. S. Ford; D. F. Mills; E. M. Neville, C.B.E.; W. P. Rees, M.C.; C. H. Tinsley

£6,440

Superintending Valuers (at Head Office), N. I. Behr; J. J. Claringbull; W. J. Dawkins, T.D.; J. B. Hyne; J. Newton; D. C. Papworth; E. Passingham; R. F. S. Port; H. D. C. Radford; G. Williams ... £5,620 to £6,075
First Class Valuers (at Head Office), J. V. C. Anthony; R. M. Barraball; G. I. Coe; G. Crawshaw; R. G. Edwards; A. B. Fallows; M. C. Fuller-Hall, O.B.E.; K. G. Goodman; D. J. Goodwin; J. F. Parker; R. V. Payne; T. H. Pursey; D. Record; E. H. Robinson; M. F. Robinson; G. M. Scudamore; W. A. Stewart-Jones; D. F. Taylor; K. C. Walter; F. J. West

£4,823 to £5,455

Principal, D. W. G. Bragg, O.B.E.

£3,250 to £4,400

Senior Executive Officers, L. N. Fletcher; A. H. Haggart; W. C. Hughes; D. McCluskey

£2,775 to £3,400

INLAND REVENUE (SCOTLAND)
Comptroller of Stamps and Taxes
16 Waterloo Place, Edinburgh 1
Comptroller, D. Glass ... £5,150 to £6,450
Deputy Comptroller, L. J. E. Hatchett

£3,358 to £4,508

Principal, D. M. Watson ...... £3,250 to £4,400
Principal Collector, B. Etty ...... £3,250 to £4,400

Estate Duty Office
P.O. Box 94, Waterloo Place, Edinburgh 1
Registrar of Death Duties, R. L. Balfour £6,300
Deputy Registrar of Death Duties, I. W. Grant
£5,335
Chief Examiners, J. B. Donald; G. T. Graham, D.S.C.; J. W. Grant; E. G. Lucas; J. B. M. Mc-Kean; A. M. McPake; J. A. Taylor; V. D. E. Webb .... £3,250 to £4,499

Solicitor's Office
16 Waterloo Place, Edinburgh 1
Solicitor, J. K. W. Dunn £6,380
Senior Legal Assistants, G. K. Petrie-Hay; W. W. C. Pollock .... £3,750 to £5,000

Valuation Office, Scotland
43 Rose Street, Edinburgh 2
Chief Valuer for Scotland, M. L. Barclay, I.S.O.
£6,490
Assistant Chief Valuers, J. Beggs; W. L. Chesser, M.C., T.D. .... £5,620 to £6,075
First Class Valuers (at Head Office), M. A. Newbury; J. D. Sutherland; W. D. Sutherland
£4,823 to £5,445

SPECIAL COMMISSIONERS OF INCOME TAX
Turnstile House, High Holborn, W.C.1
[01–836–2407]
The Special Commissioners are an independent body appointed by the Treasury to hear appeals against surtax, and in some cases income tax, assessments.
Presiding Special Commissioner, R. A. Furtado, C.B.
£7,125
Special Commissioners, W. E. Bradley; G. R. East, C.M.G.; J. B. Hodgson; B. James; J. G. Lewis; N. F. Rowe; H. G. Watson £6,490
Clerk to Special Commissioners of Income Tax, C. H. Windeatt .... £3,250 to £4,400

H.M. LAND REGISTRY
Lincoln's Inn Fields, W.C.2
[01–405–3488]
The registration of title to land was first introduced in England and Wales by the Land Registry Act, 1862. Many changes have been made to the original system by subsequent legislation and H.M. Land Registry operates today under the Land Registration Acts, 1925 to 1966. The object of registering title to land is for dealings with it to be made more simple and economical. This is achieved by maintaining a register of land owners whose title is guaranteed by the State and by providing simple forms for the transfer, mortgage and other dealings with real property. Under the Land Registration Act 1966, the voluntary first registration of land in non-compulsory areas was severely curtailed in order to facilitate an accelerated programme for the extension of the compulsory system to cover all the built-up areas of the country within a few years. The intention is that registration of title shall ultimately be universal throughout England and Wales. Nevertheless, a great deal of land was formerly registered voluntarily in non-compulsory areas and it is still possible to register building estates, upon certain conditions, throughout the country. A great deal of land in non-compulsory areas is therefore already registered. H.M. Land Registry is administered under the Lord Chancellor by the Chief Land Registrar and the work is decentralized to a number of regional offices. The Chief Land Registrar is also responsible for the Land Charges Department and the Agricultural Credits Department.

Headquarters Office
Chief Land Registrar, T. B. F. Ruoff, C.B., C.B.E.
£8,050
Deputy Chief Land Registrar, S. L. Whiteley £6,510
Chief Assistant (Establishment Officer), K. E. Aris
£5,910
Land Registrar, R. B. Roper .... £4,555 to £5,640

Assistant Land Registrar, Mrs. A. B. Macfarlane
£3,286 to £4,390
Controllers, H. R. Goose (*North*); B. M. White (*South*) .... £5,015 to £5,640
Senior Principal (Management Services), J. L. Memory
£4,045 to £4,556
Principals, P. Gittings; J. C. Poynter; L. A. Jenks; T. Chipperfield; G. H. Fisher; R. B. Parker; A. Whittle; C. E. McLeish; B. J. Moulden
£3,258 to £3,873

Establishment and Accounts
Deputy Establishment Officer, G. E. Marriott, O.B.E.
£4,045 to £4,556
Finance Officer, J. H. Haynes .... £3,258 to £3,873

Land Charges and Agricultural Credits Department
Kidbrooke, S.E.3
[01–856–5677]
Superintendent, S. A. Durrant, M.B.E.
£2,529 to £3,099

Tunbridge Wells District Land Registry
Curtis House, Tunbridge Wells, Kent
[Tunbridge Wells 26141]
District Land Registrar, D. P. Chivers
£4,555 to £5,640
Land Registrar, P. Kendall ...... £4,555 to £5,640
Assistant Land Registrars, E. D. Wetton, C.B.E.; Miss M. Gray; J. S. R. Bevington; D. G. Thomas; A. Gould; R. H. Ellis . £3,286 to £4,390
Area Manager, J. C. Eames, M.B.E. £4,045 to £4,556

Lytham District Land Registry
Birkenhead House, Lytham St Annes, Lancs.
[Lytham: 7541]
District Land Registrar, C. N. T. Waterer
£4,555 to £5,640
Land Registrar, R. E. Shorrocks . £4,555 to £5,640
Assistant Land Registrars, A. P. Roberts; B. E. Berry; K. J. Charles; F. G. D. Emler; L. D. Jefferies; J. B. Rhodes. .... £3,286 to £4,390
Area Manager, P. J. Dix .... £4,045 to £4,556

Nottingham District Land Registry
Chalfont Drive, Nottingham
[Nottingham: 291111]
District Land Registrar, A. G. W. James
£4,555 to £5,640
Assistant Land Registrars, N. U. A. Hogg; Miss C. M. Bannister; J. A. Hicks; D. L. Groom; F. G. Adamson .... £3,286 to £4,390
Area Manager, R. Palmer .... £4,045 to £4,556

Harrow District Land Registry
Lyon Road, Harrow, Middlesex
[01–427–8811]
District Land Registrar, C. C. Scarth
£4,555 to £5,640
Assistant Land Registrars, Miss J. E. Bagshaw; A. D. Dewar; Miss A. M. Phillips; P. A. Meehan
£3,286 to £4,390
Area Manager, A. G. Caudle. ... £4,045 to £4,556

Gloucester District Land Registry
Twyver House, Bruton Way,
Gloucester
[Gloucester: 28666]
District Land Registrar, C. W. K. Donaldson
£4,555 to £5,640
Assistant Land Registrars, A. O. Viney; B. D. A. McCaully; F. Quickfall ..... £3,286 to £4,390
Area Manager, H. J. Wiles ...... £3,258 to £3,873

Stevenage District Land Registry
Brickdale House, Danestrete, Stevenage, Herts.
[Stevenage: 4488]
District Land Registrar, C. W. Furneaux
£4,555 to £5,640
Assistant Land Registrars, M. H. Baines; D. M. T. Mullett; H. S. Early .... £3,286 to £4,390
Area Manager, A. C. Forrester. . £3,258 to £3,873

Durham District Land Registry
Aykley Heads, Durham
[Durham 61361]
District Land Registrar, Miss M. M. F. G. Walker
£4,555 to £5,640

Assistant Land Registrars, E. J. Pryer; P. H. Curnow
£3,286 to £4,390
Area Manager, F. E. J. Allen.....£3,258 to £3,873

Croydon District Land Registry
Sunley House, Bedford Park, Croydon
[01-686-8833]

District Land Registrar, S. Jacey..£4,555 to £5,640
Land Registrar, U. Davidson.... £4,555 to £5,640
Assistant Land Registrars, G. A. Weddell; R. G. Glenister; A. E. Farwell.....£3,286 to £4,390
Area Manager, A. M. Wallace...£4,045 to £4,556

Plymouth District Land Registry
Railway Offices, North Road, Plymouth, Devon
[Plymouth 69381]

District Land Registrar, W. D. Hosking
£4,555 to £5,640
Assistant Land Registrar, E. G. Thomas
£3,286 to £4,390
Area Manager, E. W. Hannam..£3,258 to £3,873

H.M. Land Registry, Swansea
37, The Kingsway, Swansea, Glam.
[Swansea 50971]

Assistant Land Registrar, J. L. Inskipp
£3,286 to £4,390
Office Manager, H. Walter......£2,529 to £3,099

LAW OFFICERS' DEPARTMENT
Royal Courts of Justice, W.C.2
[01-405-7641]

The Law Officers of the Crown for England and Wales (the Attorney-General and the Solicitor-General) represent the Crown in courts of justice, advise Government departments and represent them in court. The Attorney-General has also certain administrative functions, including supervision of the Director of Public Prosecutions.

Attorney-General, THE RT. HON SIR PETER ANTHONY GRAYSON RAWLINSON, Q.C., M.P.
£13,000
Parliamentary Private Secretary, D. C. Waddington, M.P.   *SIR MICHAEL HAVERS Q.C.*
Solicitor-General, SIR (RICHARD EDWARD) GEOFFREY HOWE, Q.C., M.P....................£9,000
Parliamentary Private Secretary, K. H. Clarke, M.P.
Legal Secretary, T. C. Hetherington, C.B.E., T.D.
£3,650 to £4,500
Asst. Legal Sec., H. J. Davies, V.R.D.
£3,650 to £4,500

LIBRARIES
BRITISH MUSEUM
See under MUSEUMS

NATIONAL LIBRARY OF SCOTLAND
George IV Bridge, Edinburgh 1
[031-225-4104]

Open free. Reading Room, weekdays, 9.30 a.m. to 8.30 p.m.   Saturdays 9.30 to 1.   Map Room, weekdays, 9.30 to 5 p.m.; Saturdays, 9.30 to 1.   Exhibition, weekdays, 9.30 a.m. to 5 p.m. Saturdays, 9.30 to 1; Sundays, 2 to 5.   During Edinburgh International Festival open till 8.30 p.m. on weekdays.   (Sundays, 2 to 5.)

The Library, which had been founded as the Advocates' Library in 1682, became the National Library of Scotland by Act of Parliament in 1925. It continues to share the rights conferred by successive Copyright Acts since 1710.   Its collections of printed books and MSS., augmented by purchase and gift, are very large and it has an unrivalled Scottish collection.   The present building was opened by H.M. the Queen in 1956.

The Reading Room is for reference and research which cannot conveniently be pursued elsewhere. Admission is by ticket issued to an approved applicant.

Chairman of the Trustees, The Earl of Crawford and Balcarres, K.T., G.B.E.
Librarian and Secretary to the Trustees, E. F. D. Roberts, Ph.D....................£5,640
Secretary of the Library, M. A. Pegg, Ph.D.
(+allce. £250) £2,193 to £3,651

Keepers of Printed Books, D. M. Lloyd (£4,390 to £5,015); J. H. Loudon; J. R. Seaton
£3,685 to £4,390
Assistant Keepers, First Class, M. A. Begg; T. A. F. Cherry; R. Donaldson, Ph.D.; Isabel B. Henderson, Ph.D.; L. J. G. Heywood; Alexia F. Howe; Ann Young................ £2,193 to £3,651
Senior Research Assistants, Margaret E. Cramb; Ruth I. Hope; J. B. McKeeman.....£2,529 to £3,099
Keeper of Manuscripts, W. Park, O.B.E.
£3,685 to £4,390
Deputy Keeper, J. S. Ritchie (+allce. £250)
£2,193 to £3,651
Assistant Keepers, First Class, A. S. Bell; P. M. Cadell; I. C. Cunningham; T. I. Rae, Ph.D.; S. M. Simpson; Elspeth D. Yeo
£2,193 to £3,651

THE NATIONAL LIBRARY OF WALES
LLYFRGELL GENEDLAETHOL CYMRU
Aberystwyth

Readers' room open on weekdays, 9.30 a.m. to 6 p.m. (Saturdays, 5 p.m.); closed on Sundays. Admission by Reader's Ticket.

Founded by Royal Charter, 1907, and maintained by annual grant from the Treasury.   One of the six libraries entitled to most privileges under Copyright Act.   Contains nearly 2,000,000 printed books, 30,000 manuscripts, 3,500,000 deeds and documents, and numerous maps, prints and drawings.   Specializes in manuscripts and books relating to Wales and the Celtic peoples.   Repository for pre-1858 Welsh probate records.   Approved by the Master of the Rolls as a repository for manorial records and tithe documents, and by the Lord Chancellor for certain legal records.   Bureau of the Regional Libraries Scheme for Wales and Monmouthshire.

Librarian, D. Jenkins.

NATIONAL CENTRAL LIBRARY
Store Street, W.C.1
[01-636-0755]

Incorporated by Royal Charter and maintained by annual grants from the Department of Education and Science, Municipal and County Authorities, University and special libraries, adult education bodies, and public Trusts.

The Library is the national centre for the loan of books (other than fiction and students' text-books) and periodicals to readers in all parts of the British Isles, through their public, university, or other library; and also to and from foreign libraries through their national centres.   It is able to draw on over 21,000,000 books in nearly all the principal British libraries.   Other work undertaken by the Library includes loans to organized classes of adult students; and the recording of duplicates and discarded books and periodicals and their distribution to appropriate libraries at home and abroad; also the establishment of a catalogue of Slavonic books and periodicals in British libraries and the production of the British Union Catalogue of Periodicals. The Library's own stock for loan comprises about 650,000 volumes.

Applications to borrow books must be made through the reader's library and not directly to the National Central Library.

Librarian and Secretary to the Trustees, M. B. Line.
Deputy Librarian, I. P. Gibb.

NATIONAL LENDING LIBRARY
FOR SCIENCE AND TECHNOLOGY
Boston Spa, Yorkshire.

Officially opened on November 5, 1962, the library provides a postal loan service to organizations, including industrial companies, learned societies and educational establishments.   Individuals can borrow through the public library system.   It has a stock of about 900,000 volumes and 36,000 current periodicals.   Part of the initial stock was drawn

from the library of the Science Museum, London.
Gross total annual expenditure £1,331,000.
Director, D. J. Urquhart, C.B.E., Ph.D.

NATIONAL REFERENCE LIBRARY OF SCIENCE AND INVENTION
See under British Museum

SCOTTISH CENTRAL LIBRARY
Lawnmarket, Edinburgh, 1
Carries out in Scotland functions similar to those of the National Central Library, i.e. acts as a clearing-house for inter-library lending, and maintains a Union Catalogue and other records of books held by Scottish libraries. Its own stock of 40,000 books is freely available to all. Photo-copying facilities. *Applications to borrow books must be made through the reader's library.*
Librarian and Secretary to the Trustees, M. C. Pottinger, D.S.C.
Deputy Librarian, Miss C. E. G. Wright.

LOCAL GOVERNMENT. *See* DEPARTMENT OF THE ENVIRONMENT

LONDON TRANSPORT EXECUTIVE
55 Broadway, S.W.1
[01-222-5600]
The Greater London Council is responsible for the overall policy and financial control of London Transport, but the Executive is wholly responsible for the day-to-day management and operation.
Chairman, Sir Richard Way, K.C.B., C.B.E. .£17,000
Deputy Chairman and Managing Director (Buses), R. Bennett.........................£13,500
Managing Director (Railways), R. M. Robbins
£11,500
Members, H. J. H. C. Hildreth; J. E. Mortimer; K. G. Shave (*each* £8,500 to £10,000); S. J. Barton; L. W. Robson (*part-time*)..*each* £1,000
Secretary, W. E. G. Hewings.

LORD ADVOCATE'S DEPARTMENT
3 Dean's Yard, Westminster, S.W.1.
The Law Officers for Scotland are the Lord Advocate and the Solicitor-General for Scotland. The Lord Advocate's Department is responsible for drafting Scottish legislation, for providing legal advice to other departments on Scottish questions and for assistance to the Law Officers for Scotland in certain of their legal duties.
Lord Advocate, The Rt. Hon. Norman Russell Wylie, V.R.D., Q.C., M.P..............£8,000
Solicitor-General for Scotland, D. W. R. Brand, Q.C.
£5,625
Legal Secretary and First Parliamentary Draftsman, G. I. Mitchell, C.B....................£9,000
Deputy Legal Secretary and Parliamentary Draftsman, J. M. Moran........................£6,750
Asst. Legal Secs. and Parlty. Draftsmen. A. C. B. Reid; J. F. Wallace........£5,015 to £6,120
Junior Legal Secs. and Parlty. Draftsmen. N. I. Adamson; Miss M. S. Christie; W. C. Galbraith
£3,286 to £4,390

LORD GREAT CHAMBERLAIN'S OFFICE
House of Lords, S.W.1
[01-930-6240]
The Lord Great Chamberlain is a Great Officer of State, the office being hereditary since the grant of Henry 1 to the family of De Vere, Earls of Oxford.
Lord Great Chamberlain, The Marquess of Cholmondeley, M.C.
Secretary to the Lord Great Chamberlain, Admiral Sir Frank Twiss, K.C.B., D.S.C.
Clerks to the Lord Great Chamberlain, Lady Elizabeth Montgomerie; Miss L. K. Willis Fleming.

LORD PRIVY SEAL
House of Lords
Lord Privy Seal and Leader of the House of Lords, THE EARL JELLICOE, P.C., D.S.O., M.C.
Private Secretary, B. T. Gilmore.

OFFICE OF MANPOWER ECONOMICS
New Court, 48 Carey Street, W.C.2.
[01-405-5944]
The intention to set up the Office of Manpower Economics was announced in the House of Commons on November 2, 1970, by the Secretary of State for Employment and the Director was appointed in January 1971. The Office, an independent non-statutory body, is responsible first for providing a common secretariat for three review bodies advising on sectors of public service pay for which no negotiating machinery is appropriate; secondly, for servicing any *ad hoc* enquiries in the field of pay problems that may be established from time to time; and thirdly, for carrying out, either at the request of Ministers or with their approval, research in the pay and manpower fields.
Director, J. H. Galbraith.
Assistant Secretary, H. J. Gummer.
Senior Consultant, R. W. Williams.
Senior Economic and Industrial Relations Adviser, G. Roberts.
Chief Statistician, R. F. Burch.

MEDICAL RESEARCH COUNCIL
20 Park Crescent, W.1
[01-636-5422]
The Council, formerly the Medical Research Committee established in 1913 under the National Health Insurance Act, was incorporated under its present title by Royal Charter on April 1, 1920; a revised charter was issued in 1966. It is responsible to the Secretary of State for Education and Science.
The Council's constitution enables it to pursue an independent policy for the advancement of knowledge in the medical sciences and to initiate and encourage research both in this country and abroad: it is advised by three Research Boards and a number of expert Committees covering particular fields. The Council supports research by employing its own scientific staff in the National Institute for Medical Research, the Clinical Research Centre, and other research establishments (listed below); by financing projects in university and other departments through various schemes of research grants; and by the award of fellowships and scholarships for training in research methods. The Council is supported by a Parliamentary grant-in-aid but is also in a position to receive funds from private sources.
Members, The Duke of Northumberland, K.G., T.D., F.R.S. (*Chairman*); J. A. B. Gray, Sc.D. (*Secretary*); Prof. D. A. K. Black, M.D.; J. P. Bull, M.D.; Prof. W. R. S. Doll, O.B.E., D.SC., F.R.S.; L. A. Pavitt, M.P.; Prof. W. S. Peart, M.D., F.R.S.; Prof. D. A. Pond, M.D.; Prof. R. R. Porter, Ph.D., F.R.S.; T. Symington, M.D., F.R.S.E.; Prof. P. M. B. Walker, Ph.D.; Prof. R. E. O. Williams, M.D.
Second Secretary, S. G. Owen.
Administrative Secretary, J. G. Duncan.

Research Programme Division A
Principal Medical Officer, Joan Faulkner.
Senior Medical Officers, R. C. Norton; H. W. Bunjé, M.D.; M. Ashley-Miller.
Medical Officers, D. G. Berry; E. M. B. Clements; Elizabeth Neale; R. J. Wrighton.
Principal Scientific Officers, G. M. A. Gray, Ph.D., J. C. Stewart, Ph.D.

Research Programme Division B
Principal Medical Officer, M. P. W. Godfrey.
Senior Medical Officers, P. J. Chapman; Sheila Howarth; Katherine Lévy.
Medical Officers, June Hill; Barbara Rashbass; Martha Robson.
Principal Scientific Officer, J. H. Morris, Ph.D.

Tropical Medical Section
Medical Officer, A. M. Baker.

Universities, Grants and Training Awards Division
Head of Division, B. S. Lush, M.D.
Deputy Head, D. J. Cawthron.
Scientific Administrative Officers, J. S. Gordon; D. R. James, Ph.D.; Daphne Self, Ph.D.; Sheila Wright.

Administrative Division
Assistant Secretaries, A. E. Turner; G. M. Levack, O.B.E.; F. Rushton.

Secretariat
Head of Department, C. A. Kirkman.

Headquarters Establishment and O. & M.
Head of Section, D. Noble.

National Institute for Medical Research
Mill Hill, N.W.7
[01-959-3666]
Director, A. S. V. Burgen, M.D., F.R.S.

Clinical Research Centre
Watford Road, Harrow, Middlesex
[01-864-5311]
Director, G. M. Bull, M.D.

Research Units
Air Pollution Unit, St. Bartholomew's Hospital Medical College, Charterhouse Square, E.C.1. *Director*, Prof. P. J. Lawther.
Biophysics Unit, 26 Drury Lane W.C.2. *Directors*, Prof. M. H. F. Wilkins, C.B.E., Ph.D., F.R.S.; Prof. Jean Hanson, Ph.D., F.R.S.
Blood Group Reference Laboratory (administered for Dept. of Health and Social Security), Gatliff Road, S.W.1. *Director*, K. L. G. Goldsmith, Ph.D.
Blood Group Unit, Lister Institute of Preventive Medicine, Chelsea Bridge Road, S.W.1. *Director*, R. R. Race, C.B.E., Ph.D., F.R.S.
Blood Pressure Unit, Western Infirmary, Glasgow, W.1. *Director*, A. F. Lever.
Brain Metabolism Unit, Dept. of Pharmacology, The University, 1 George Square, Edinburgh. *Director*, G. W. Ashcroft.
Cardiovascular Unit, Royal Postgraduate Medical School, Ducane Road, W.12. *Director*, Prof. J. P. Shillingford, M.D.
Child Nutrition Unit, Mulago Hospital, Kampala, Uganda. *Director*, R. G. Whitehead, Ph.D.
Department of Clinical Research, University College Hospital Medical School, W.C.1. *Director*, E. E. Pochin, C.B.E., M.D.
Common Cold Unit (Clinical Research Centre), Harvard Hospital, Salisbury. *Head of Division*, D. A. J. Tyrrell, M.D., F.R.S.
M.R.C. Computer Unit (London), 242 Pentonville Road, N.1. *Director*, C. C. Spicer.
Cyclotron Unit, Hammersmith Hospital, Ducane Road, W.12. *Director*, D. D. Vonberg.
Demyelinating Diseases Unit, Newcastle General Hospital, Westgate Road, Newcastle-upon-Tyne. *Hon. Director*, Prof. E. J. Field, M.D., Ph.D.
Dental Unit, Dental School, Lower Maudlin Street, Bristol 1. *Hon. Director*, Prof. A. I. Darling, D.D.Sc.
Dental Epidemiology Unit, Dental School, London Hospital Medical College, Turner Street, E.1. *Hon. Director*, Prof. G. L. Slack, O.B.E., T.D.
Clinical Endocrinology Unit, 2 Forrest Road, Edinburgh 1. *Director*, J. A. Loraine, D.Sc.
Unit for the Study of Environmental Factors in Mental and Physical Illness, London School of Economics and Political Science, 20 Hanway Place, W.1. *Director*, J. W. B. Douglas.
Epidemiology and Medical Care Unit, Northwick Park Hospital, Harrow, Middx. *Director*, T. W. Meade.
Epidemiology Unit (Jamaica), University of the West Indies, Mona, Kingston, Jamaica. *Director*, A. Davis, M.D.

Epidemiology Unit (South Wales), 4 Richmond Road, Cardiff. *Director*, A. L. Cochrane, C.B.E.
Medical Research Council Laboratories, Gambia, Fajara, nr. Bathurst, Gambia, W. Africa. *Director*, I. A. McGregor, C.B.E.
Gastroenterology Unit, Central Middlesex Hospital Park Royal, N.W.10. *Director*, E. N. Rowlands, M.D.
Clinical Genetics Unit, Institute of Child Health, 30 Guildford Street, W.C.1. *Director*, C. O. Carter, D.M.
Experimental Genetics Unit, Dept. of Animal Genetics, University College, Wolfson House, N.W.1. *Hon. Director*, Prof. H. Grüneberg, M.D., D.Sc., F.R.S.
Human Biochemical Genetics Unit, Galton Laboratory University College, Wolfson House, N.W.1. *Hon. Director*, Prof. H. Harris, M.D., F.R.S.
Molecular Genetics Unit, University Dept. of Molecular Biology, King's Buildings, West Mains Road, Edinburgh. *Hon Director*, Prof. W. Hayes, D.Sc., F.R.S.
Population Genetics Unit, Old Road, Headington, Oxford. *Director*, A. C. Stevenson, M.D.
Experimental Haematology Unit, St. Mary's Hospital Medical School, W.2. *Director*, Prof. P. L. Mollison, M.D., F.R.S.
Abnormal Haemoglobin Unit, University Dept. of Biochemistry, Tennis Court Road, Cambridge. *Hon. Director*, Prof. H. Lehmann, M.D., Sc.D.
Hearing and Balance Unit, Institute of Neurology, The National Hospital, Queen Square, W.C.1. *Director*, J. D. Hood, D.Sc.
Immunochemistry Unit, University Department of Biochemistry, South Parks Road, Oxford. *Hon. Director*, Prof. R. R. Porter, Ph.D., F.R.S.
Cellular Immunology Unit, Sir William Dunn School of Pathology, Oxford. *Hon. Director*, Prof. J. L. Gowans, D.Phil., F.R.S.
Industrial Injuries and Burns Unit, Birmingham Accident Hospital, Bath Row, Birmingham 15. *Director*, J. P. Bull, M.D.
Laboratory Animals Centre, M.R.C. Laboratories, Woodmansterne Road, Carshalton, Surrey. *Director*, J. Bleby.
Unit for Metabolic Studies in Psychiatry, University Dept. of Psychiatry, Middlewood Hospital, Sheffield. *Hon. Director*, Prof. F. A. Jenner, Ph.D.
Metabolic Reactions Unit, Imperial College of Science and Technology, S.W.7. *Hon. Director*, Prof. Sir Ernst Chain, D.Phil., Ph.D., F.R.S.
Microbial Systematics Unit, Adrian Building, University Road, Leicester. *Director*, P. H. A. Sneath, M.D.
Mineral Metabolism Unit, The General Infirmary, Leeds 1. *Director*, Prof. B. E. C. Nordin, M.D., Ph.D.
Laboratory of Molecular Biology, University Postgraduate Medical School, Hills Road, Cambridge. *Chairman of Board*, M. F. Perutz, C.B.E., Ph.D., F.R.S.
Molecular Pharmacology Unit, Medical School, Hills Road, Cambridge. *Hon. Director*, Prof. A. S. V. Burgen, M.D., F.R.S.
Unit on Neural Mechanisms of Behaviour, Department of Psychology, University College, Gower Street, W.C.1. *Director*, I. S. Russell, Ph.D.
Neuroendocrinology Unit, University Dept. of Human Anatomy, South Parks Road. Oxford. *Hon Director*, Prof. G. W. Harris, C.B.E., M.D., D.M., Sc.D., F.R.S.
Neuropharmacology Unit, Dept. of Pharmacology (Pre-Clinical), The Medical School, Birmingham 15. *Hon. Director*, Prof. P. B. Bradley, D.Sc.
Neuropsychiatry Unit, M.R.C. Laboratories, Woodmansterne Road, Carshalton, Surrey. *Director*, D. Richter, Ph.D.
Dunn Nutritional Laboratory, Milton Road, Cambridge. *Director*, E. H. Kodicek, M.D., Ph.D.
Unit for Research for Physical Aids for the Disabled, Princess Margaret Rose Orthopædic Hospital, Fairmilehead, Edinburgh 10. *Hon. Director*, D. C. Simpson, M.B.E., Ph.D., F.R.S.E.
Environmental Physiology Unit, London School of

Hygiene and Tropical Medicine, Keppel Street, W.C.1. *Director,* Prof. J. S. Weiner, Ph.D.

Pneumoconiosis Unit, Llandough Hospital, Penarth, Glam. *Director,* J. C. Gilson, C.B.E.

Powered Limbs Unit, West Hendon Hospital, Goldsmith Av nue, The Hyde, N.W.9. *Director,* A. B. Kinnier Wilson.

Neurological Prostheses Unit, Institute of Psychiatry, de Crespigny Park, Denmark Hill, S.E.5. *Hon. Director,* Prof. G. S. Brindley, M.D., F.R.S.

Unit for Epidemiological Studies in Psychiatry, University Department of Psychiatry, Royal Edinburgh Hospital, Morningside Park, Edinburgh, 10. *Hon. Director,* N. Kreitman, M.D.

Clinical Psychiatry Unit, Graylingwell Hospital, Chichester. *Director,* P. Sainsbury, M.D.

Social Psychiatry Unit, Institute of Psychiatry, de Crespigny Park, S.E.5. *Director,* Prof. J. K. Wing, M.D., Ph.D.

Applied Psychology Unit, 15 Chaucer Road, Cambridge. *Director,* D. E. Broadbent, Sc.D., F.R.S.

Developmental Psychology Unit, Drayton House, Gordon Street, W.C.1. *Director,* N. O'Connor, Ph.D.

Clinical and Population Cytogenetics Unit, Western General Hospital, Crewe Road, Edinburgh 4 and Derbyshire House, St. Chad's Street, W.C.1. *Director,* H. J. Evans, Ph.D.

Environmental Radiation Unit, University Dept. of Medical Physics, The General Infirmary, Leeds 1. *Hon. Director,* Prof. F. W. Spiers, C.B.E., D.Sc.

Radiobiology Unit, Harwell, Berks. *Director,* R. H. Mole.

Experimental Radiopathology Unit, Hammersmith Hospital, Ducane Road, W.12. *Director,* Miss T. Alper, D.Sc.

Reproduction and Growth Unit, Princess Mary Maternity Hospital, Newcastle-upon-Tyne. *Director,* Prof. A. M. Thomson.

Rheumatism Unit, Canadian Red Cross Memorial Hospital, Taplow, Maidenhead, Berks. *Director,* Prof. E. G. L. Bywaters.

Unit on the Experimental Pathology of Skin, The Medical School, The University, Birmingham 15. *Director,* C. N. D. Cruickshank, M.D.

Social Medicine Unit, London School of Hygiene, and Tropical Medicine, Keppel Street, W.C.1. *Hon. Director,* Prof. J. N. Morris, D.Sc.

Medical Sociology Unit, Centre for Social Studies, Westburn Road, Aberdeen. *Hon. Director,* Prof. R. Illsley, Ph.D.

Speech and Communication Unit, University of Edinburgh, 31 Buccleuch Place, Edinburgh 8. *Director,* Prof. R. C. Oldfield.

Toxicology Unit, M.R.C. Laboratories, Woodmansterne Road, Carshalton. *Director,* J. M. Barnes, C.B.E.

Trachoma Unit, Lister Institute of Preventive Medicine, Chelsea Bridge Road, S.W.1. and M.R.C. Laboratories, Fajara, Bathurst, Gambia. *Hon. Director,* Prof. L. H. Collier, M.D., D.Sc.

Tuberculosis and Chest Diseases Unit, Brompton Hospital, Fulham Road, S.W.3. *Director,* W. Fox, M.D.

Unit for Laboratory Studies of Tuberculosis, Royal Postgraduate Medical School, Ducane Road, W.12. *Hon. Director,* Prof. D. A. Mitchison.

Virology Unit, Institute of Virology, Church Street, Glasgow, W.1. *Hon. Director,* Prof. J. H. Subak-Sharpe, Ph.D.

Vision Unit, School of Biological Sciences, University of Sussex, Falmer, Brighton, Sussex. *Director,* H. J. A. Dartnall, D.Sc.

Biochemical Parasitology Unit, Molteno Institute of Biology and Parasitology, Downing Street, Cambridge. *Director,* B. A. Newton, Ph.D.

Leukemia Unit, Royal Postgraduate Medical School, Ducane Road, W.12. *Hon. Director,* D. A. G. Galton, M.D.

Statistical Research and Services Unit, University College Hospital Medical School, W.C.1. *Director,* I. Sutherland, D.Phil.

Social and Applied Psychology Unit, Department of Psychology, the University, Sheffield. *Hon. Director,* Prof. H. Kay, Ph.D.

Lipid Metabolism Unit, Hammersmith Hospital, Ducane Road, W.12. *Director,* N. B. Myant, D.M.

Cell Mutation Unit, School of Biological Sciences, University of Sussex, Falmer, Brighton. *Director,* B. A. Bridges, Ph.D.

Unit on Development and Integration of Behaviour, Sub-Dept. of Animal Behaviour, Madingley, Cambridge. *Director,* Prof. R. A. Hinde, D.Phil., Sc.D.

Biological Research Board
Chairman, Prof. P. M. B. Walker, Ph.D.

Clinical Research Board
(Appointed in consultation with the Department of Health and Social Security and the Scottish Home and Health Department).
Chairman, Prof. D. A. K. Black, M.D.

Tropical Medicine Research Board
(Appointment in consultation with the Ministry of Overseas Development)
Chairman, G. M. Bull, M.D.

METRICATION BOARD
22 Kingsway, W.C.2
[01-242-6828] *LORD ORR-EWI
41*
Chairman, ~~The Lord Ritchie-Calder,~~ C.B.E.
Members, M. A. Abrams, Ph.D.; G. Bowen, C.B., C.M.G., *(Director);* H. J. Cruickshank, C.B.E.; D. H. Darbishire; A. G. Dawtry, C.B.E., T.D.; J. M. Ferguson; P. Hanley; E. F. Knight; Prof. M. L. McGlasham; Sir Thomas Padmore, G.C.B.; F. L. Ralphs, Ph.D.; Mrs. A. Stanley.
Secretary, F. H. Whitaker, C.M.G., O.B.E.

METROPOLITAN WATER BOARD
New River Head, Rosebery Avenue, E.C.1
[01-837-3300]

The Board serves an area of about 540 sq. miles. The charges are levied on net annual value at such rate not exceeding 10 per cent., as the Board may fix, the charge for 1971–72 being 4¼ per cent. on net annual value. The Capital Debt on March 31, 1971, amounted to £71,286,151. The supply for the year 1970–71 was 147,807,000,000 gallons (representing 660,000,000 tons), a daily average of 405 million gallons.
Chairman of the Metropolitan Water Board, Sir Samuel Salmon.
Clerk of the Board and Chief Executive Officer, H. Pitchforth.

THE ROYAL MINT
Tower Hill, E.C.3
[01-488-3424]
Master Worker and Warden, The Chancellor of the Exchequer *(ex officio).*
Deputy Master and Comptroller, and ex officio Engraver of H.M. Seals, H. Glover.
Secretary and Establishment Officer, J. E. Lucas
£4,390 to £5,640
Director of Marketing and Sales, A. J. Dowling, O.B.E., D.F.C. . . . . £4,390 to £5,040
Principals, F. Corneli; B. W. Tucker
£2,820 to £3,902
Superintendent, Operative Department, A. R. Fisher
£4,390 to £5,015
Senior Grade Engineers, E. M. Phillips; M. R. Tidmarsh . . . . £3,265 to £3,843
Chemist and Assayer, E. G. V. Newman, O.B.E.
£4,390 to £5,015
Chief Engraver, W. J. Newman, M.V.O.
£2,861 to £3,170

Llantrisant, S. Wales
[0443-87-2311]
Director of Production, R. A. Yates £5,640
Senior Grade Engineer, E. J. Howlett
£3,265 to £3,843
Chief Administrative Officer, R. F. Liggins
£2,820 to £3,902

*Deputy Chairman
Baroness White*

MONOPOLIES COMMISSION
New Court, 48 Carey Street, W.C.2.
[01-405-9722]

The Monopolies and Restrictive Practices Commission, which was set up under the Monopolies and Restrictive Practices (Inquiry and Control) Act, 1948, was reconstituted on Oct. 31, 1956, as the Monopolies Commission in accordance with a provision of the Restrictive Trade Practices Act, 1956. It was again reconstituted and enlarged under the Monopolies and Mergers Act, 1965. The Commission has the duty of investigating and reporting on the existence, in industries referred to it by the Department of Employment and Productivity, of monopoly, restrictive practices affecting exports and other arrangements not registrable under Part I of the Restrictive Trade Practices Act, 1956, and, where so required by the Department, to report on the effect of such arrangements on the public interest. Under the 1965 Act this duty is extended to monopoly in the supply of services and to the merger of two or more enterprises, one at least carried on in the United Kingdom or under the control of a body incorporated in the United Kingdom.

Chairman, Sir Ashton Roskill, Q.C. £12,500
Deputy Chairman, Sir Alexander Johnston, G.C.B.,
   K.B.E. (*part-time*) £2,500
Members, Prof. T. Barna, Ph.D.; T. P. Bowman; B. Boxall, C.B.E.; Sir Roger Falk, O.B.E.; J. Gratwick; Prof. H. L. A. Hart; D. A. H. Johnston; K. A. Noble; R. G. Opie; E. L. Richards, C.B.E., M.C., T.D.; G. B. Richardson; L. Robertson, C.B.E.; S. A. Robinson; L. H. Williams; Prof. B. S. Yamey . . . . each £1,950
Secretary, E. L. Phillips, C.M.G.

MUSEUMS

STANDING COMMISSION ON MUSEUMS AND GALLERIES
2 Carlton Gardens, S.W.1
[01-930-0995]

First appointed Feb. 11, 1931. The functions of the Commission are:—(1) To advise generally on questions relevant to the most effective development of the National Institutions as a whole and on any specific questions which may be referred to them from time to time; (2) to promote cooperation between the National Institutions themselves and between the National and Provincial Institutions; (3) to stimulate the generosity and direct the efforts of those who aspire to become public benefactors.

Chairman, The Earl of Rosse, M.B.E., F.S.A.
Members, J. D. Cowen, M.C., T.D., F.S.A.; Sir Trenchard Cox, C.B.E., F.R.S.A., F.S.A.; The Earl of Cranbrook, C.B.E.; The Earl of Crawford and Balcarres, K.T., G.B.E.; Prof. I. L. Foster, F.S.A.; The Earl of Halsbury, F.R.S.; Sir Gilbert Laithwaite, G.C.M.G., K.C.B., K.C.I.E, C.S.I.; Sir Edward Muir, K.C.B., F.S.A.; The Viscount Norwich; P. F. Scott; Dame Mary Smieton, D.B.E.; F. J. Stott; Sir John Witt, F.S.A.
Secretary, Mrs. B. Granger-Taylor.

THE BRITISH MUSEUM
Bloomsbury, W.C.1
[01-636-1555]

Exhibitions.—Manuscripts, Printed Books, Prints and Drawings; Egyptian, Assyrian, Greek and Roman, Romano-British, Prehistoric, Mediæval European and Oriental Antiquities; Coins and Medals; Ethnography. Main Entrance, Great Russell Street W.C.1; North Entrance, Montague Place, W.C.1. Open weekdays (including Bank Holidays) 10 to 5 and Sundays 2.30 to 6. Closed on Good Friday, Christmas Eve, Christmas Day and Boxing Day. The ethnographical collections re displayed in newly opened galleries at 6 Burlington Gardens, W.1. Opening times as above.

Reading-room open daily to readers, from 9 to 5, Tues.—Thurs., 9 p.m.), and Newspaper Room, at Colindale), from 10 to 5 throughout the year,

except Good Friday, Christmas Eve, Christmas and Boxing Day and Sundays. Closed for cleaning the week beginning with first Monday in May. Long-period tickets of admission for purposes of research and reference which cannot be carried on elsewhere, are granted on written application beforehand to the Director. The applicant should state abode, business or profession and full particulars of purpose, and should send a recommendation from a person of recognized position.

The British Museum may be said to date from 1753, when Parliament granted funds to purchase the collections of Sir Hans Sloane and the Harleian manuscripts, and for their proper housing and maintenance. The building (Montague House) was opened in 1759. The present buildings were erected between 1823 and the present day, and the original collection has increased to its present dimensions by gifts and purchases, and by the operation of the Copyright Acts. The administrative expenses were estimated at £3,833,000 in 1971–72, and were met by a vote under " Museums, Galleries and the Arts," Class VIII of the Civil Estimates. The constitution of the British Museum was revised under the terms of the *British Museum Act,* 1963.

BOARD OF TRUSTEES

Appointed by the Sovereign: The Marquess of Cambridge, G.C.V.O. *Appointed by the Prime Minister:* The Lord Trevelyan, G.C.M.G., C.I.E., O.B.E. (*Chairman*); The Lord Annan, O.B.E.; Prof. Misha Black, O.B.E.; The Viscount Boyd of Merton, P.C., C.H.; The Lord Boyle of Handsworth, P.C.; The Earl of Crawford and Balcarres, K.T., G.B.E.; Prof. H. J. Emeléus, C.B.E., D.SC., F.R.S.; The Lord Fletcher, P.C., Ll.D.; L. C. B. Gower, M.B.E., F.B.A.; C. D. Hamilton, D.S.O.; The Lord Holford, R.A., F.R.I.B.A.; A. N. L. Munby, T.D., Litt.D.; Sir Ronald Nyholm, D.SC., Ph.D., F.R.S.; Dame Mary Smieton, D.B.E.; Sir Richard Thompson, Bt., M.P.
Nominated by the Royal Society, Royal Academy, British Academy and Society of Antiquaries of London: T. E. Allibone, C.B.E., D.SC., Ph.D., F.R.S. (*Royal Society*); J. Fitton, R.A. (*Royal Academy*); Sir Mortimer Wheeler, C.H., C.I.E., M.C., D.Lit., F.B.A., F.S.A. (*British Academy*); Prof. F. Wormald, C.B.E., Litt.D., F.B.A., F.S.A. (*Society of Antiquaries of London*).
Appointed by the Trustees of the British Museum: Sir Eric Ashby, D.SC., F.R.S.; Mrs. E. M. Chilver; The Lord Clark, C.H., K.C.B., F.B.A.; Miss Kathleen Kenyon, C.B.E., D.Lit., L.H.D., F.B.A., F.S.A.; Prof. Stuart Piggott, F.S.A.

OFFICERS

Director and Principal Librarian, Sir John Wolfenden,
   C.B.E. £9,650
Assistant Director, Maysie F. Webb
   . . . . £5,240 to £5,640
Secretary, B. P. C. Bridgewater
   . . . . £4,565 to £5,190
Assistant Secretary, A. N. E. D. Schofield
   . . . . £2,368 to £3,826
Administrative Assistant, Barbara J. Youngman
   . . . . £2,368 to £3,826
Publications Officer, H. Jacob . . . . £2,368 to £3,826
Exhibitions Officer, Margaret Hall
   . . . . £2,368 to £3,826
Principal, J. F. W. Ryde . . . . £3,425 to £4,575
Senior Executive Officers, H. E. Cole; G. E. Cooper; D. A. Thomas . . . . £2,950 to £3,575
Guide Lecturers, O. E. Holloway; K. P. Whitehorn
   . . . . £2,704 to £3,274
Principal Keeper of Printed Books, K. B. Gardner
   . . . . £5,240 to £5,640
Keepers, J. L. Wood; R. J. Fulford
   . . . . £4,565 to £5,190
Deputy Keepers, A. H. King; G. H. Spinney; H. M. Nixon; R. F. L. Bancroft; R. S. Pine-Coffin; P. R. Harris; Helen M. Wallis; P. J. Fairs
   . . . . £3,860 to £4,565
Assistant Keepers, G. A. F. Scheele; ★ Annie O'Donovan; Audrey C. Broadhurst; G. D.

Painter; E. J. Miller; A. F. Allison; *H. G. Whitehead; *F. J. Hill; Anna E. C. Simoni; L. J. Thomas; G. J. R. Arnold; T. T. Tuckey-Smith; D. E. Rhodes; O. W. Neighbour; P. A. H. Brown; I. R. Willison; P. C. Meade; R. J. Roberts; M. G. Atkins; Hanna M. Swiderska; D. B. Chrastek; G. B. Morris; Cynthia M. Howard; D. L. Paisey; D. T. Rodger; J. A. Mackay; R. A. Christophers; B. G. F. Holt; J. R. Barr; L. L. Dethan; Miss J. M. Bellord; Miss E. P. McLaren; D. N. Jervis; Sarah J. Tyacke.

Superintendent, Newspaper Library (Colindale), P. E. Allen.

Keeper of Manuscripts and Egerton Librarian, T. C. Skeat................£4.565 to £5,190
Deputy Keepers, C. E. Wright; G. R. C. Davis; L. J. Gorton.................£3,860 to £4,565
Assistant Keepers, *Pamela J. Willetts; J. P. Hudson; D. H. Turner; M. A. F. Borrie; T. A. J. Burnett; T. S. Pattie; Janet M. Backhouse; Anita J. Stratford; Ann Payne; H. M. T. Cobbe; W. H. Kelliher; Patricia M. Higgins.

Keeper of Oriental Printed Books and Manuscripts, M. Lings.................£4,565 to £5,190
Assistant Keepers, J. Rosenwasser; Albertine Gaur; C. E. Marrison; H. G. H. Nelson; J. P. Losty; A. P. Waley.

Keeper of Prints and Drawings, E. F. Croft-Murray, C.B.E.....................£4,565 to £5,190
Deputy Keeper, J. A. G. Gere... £3,860 to £4,565
Assistant Keepers, P. H. Hulton; J. K. Rowlands; J. A. R. Wilton.

Keeper of Coins and Medals, G. K. Jenkins
£4,565 to £5,190
Deputy Keeper, R. A. G. Carson £3,860 to £4,565
Assistant Keepers, J. P. C. Kent; Marion M. Archibald; N. M. Lowick; M. J. Price.

Keeper of Egyptian Antiquities, I. E. S. Edwards, C.B.E.....................£4,565 to £5,190
Assistant Keepers, *T. G. H. James; A. F. Shore.

Keeper of Western Asiatic Antiquities, R. D. Barnett
£4,565 to £5,190
Deputy Keeper, E. Sollberger... £3,860 to £4,565
Assistant Keeper, T. C. Mitchell.

Keeper of Greek and Roman Antiquities, D. E. L. Haynes...................£4,565 to £5,190
Deputy Keeper, R. A. Higgins... £3,860 to £4,565
Assistant Keepers, Ann Birchall; B. F. Cook.

Keeper of Mediæval and Later Antiquities, R. L. S. Bruce-Mitford...............£4,565 to £5,190
Deputy Keeper, G. H. Tait...... £3,860 to £4,565
Assistant Keepers, J. Cherry; Leslie E. Webster; R. M. Camber.

Keeper of Prehistoric and Romano-British Antiquities, J. W. Brailsford............£4,565 to £5,190
Assistant Keepers, G. de G. Sieveking; K. S. Painter; I. H. Longworth.

Keeper of Oriental Antiquities, D. E. Barrett
£4,565 to £5,190
Deputy Keeper, R. H. Pinder-Wilson
£3,860 to £4,565
Assistant Keepers, W. Zwaif; L. R. H. Smith; Jessica M. Rawson; R. Whitfield.

Keeper of Ethnography. W. B. Fagg, C.M.G.
£4,565 to £5,190
Deputy Keeper, B. A. L. Cranstone
£3,860 to £4,565
Assistant Keepers, Elizabeth M. Carmichael; Sheila G. Weir; J. W. Picton.

Keeper of Laboratory, A. E. A. Werner
£4,565 to £5,190
Principal Scientific Officers, A. D. Baynes-Cope; H. Barker.................£2,995 to £4,077

National Reference Library of Science and Invention

Holborn Division, 25 Southampton Buildings, W.C.2
[01-405-8721]

Bayswater Division, 10 Porchester Gardens, W.2.
[01-727-3022]

This Library is part of the Department of Printed Books of the British Museum, though it operates in two separately housed divisions. The Holborn Division incorporates the former Patent Office Library, which was transferred to the British Museum on April 1, 1966. Its stock of nearly half a million volumes of modern scientific and technical literature is primarily related to industrial and technological innovation. Most is on open-access and it includes some 18,000 periodicals and the only comprehensive collection in Britain of patent literature. The Bayswater Division contains over 10,000 current periodicals and is particularly rich in literature related to the life sciences.

Opening Hours; Holborn Division Mon. to Fri., 9.30 a.m.–9 p.m. (Foreign Patents Annexe, 9.30 a.m.–5.30 p.m.), Saturdays, 10 a.m.–1 p.m. (Foreign Patents Annexe closed). Bayswater Division, Mon. to Fri. 9.30 a.m.–5.30 p.m. No admission ticket is required. Closed on Sundays and public holidays.

Keeper, M. W. Hill...........£4,565 to £5,190
Deputy Keeper, S. P. Cooper.... £3,860 to £4,565
Assistant Keepers, *A. Sandison; G. J. Sassoon; Susan Lammle; J. R. Lansley; R. H. De Vere; P. J. Gazder; Amelia D. Crews; D. R. Jamieson; *C. D. M. Johnston; Margaret Graham; J. R. Chiswell; R. R. O. Skelton; D. T. Worthy; E. J. Copley; Jane Britton; L. J. A. Leigh; Miss A. Clarke; Mrs. H. E. Kempson.
    * Receives an allowance.

THE BRITISH MUSEUM (NATURAL HISTORY)
Cromwell Road S.W.7
[01-589-6323]

Open free on week-days (except Good Friday, Christmas Eve, Christmas Day and Boxing Day) 10 to 6, and on Sundays from 2.30 to 6.

The Natural History Museum originates from the natural history departments of the British Museum, Bloomsbury. During the 19th century the natural history collections grew so extensively that it became necessary to find new quarters for them and in 1881 they were moved to South Kensington. The British Museum Act, 1963, made the Natural History Museum completely independent with its own body of Trustees. The five departments are shown below. The Zoological Museum, Tring, bequeathed by the second Lord Rothschild, has formed part of the Museum since 1938. Research workers are admitted to the libraries and study collections by Student's Ticket, applications for which should be made in writing to the Director. Official Guide Lecturers conduct visitors round some of the exhibition galleries at 3 p.m. on week-days free of charge, and their services are available at other times for special parties (also free of charge) by arrangement with the Director.

The administrative expenses were estimated at £1,424,000 in 1971–72.

Board of Trustees

Director, G. F. Claringbull, Ph.D..........£6,925
Deputy Director, R. H. Hedley, D.SC.
£5,415 to £6,005
Secretary, A. P. Coleman *(Establishment Officer)*
£4,775 to £5,375

Office Manager, B. Johnston ..... £3,425 to £4,575
Librarian, M. J. Rowlands ..... £2,995 to £4,077
Education Officer, F. H. Brightman
£2,995 to £4,077
Exhibition Officer, M. G. Belcher
£3,433 to £4,048

Department of Zoology

Keeper, J. G. Sheals, Ph.D....... £4,565 to £5,190
Deputy Keeper, G. B. Corbet, Ph.D.
£4,565 to £5,190
Senior Principal Scientific Officers, P. H. Greenwood, D.Sc.; N. B. Marshall, Sc.D., F.R.S.; D. W. Snow, D.Phil.; C. A. Wright, D.Sc... £4,565 to £5,190
Principal Scientific Officers, Miss A. M. Clark; I. C. J. Galbraith; Miss A. G. C. Grandison; J. F. Peake; R. W. Sims; P. J. P. Whitehead
£2,995 to £4,077
Chief Experimental Officers, R. P. D. Goodwin; S. Prudhoe.................. £3,433 to £4,048

Department of Entomology

Keeper, P. Freeman, D.Sc.........£5,415 to £6,005
Deputy Keepers, Miss T. R. Clay, D.Sc.; D. R. Ragge, Ph.D.............£4,565 to £5,190
Senior Principal Officers, V. F. Eastop, Ph.D.; P. F. Mattingly, D.Sc.; H. Oldroyd. £4,565 to £5,190
Principal Scientific Officers, J. P. Doncaster, C.B.E.; W. J. Knight, Ph.D.; L. A. Mound; I. W. B. Nye, Ph.D.; J. F. Perkins, Agr.D.; R. D. Pope; K. S. O. Sattler, Ph.D.; A. Watson; P. E. S. Whalley; I. H. H. Yarrow, Ph.D.
£2,995 to £4,077

Department of Palaeontology

Keeper, H. W. Ball, Ph.D.........£4,565 to £5,190
Deputy Keepers, C. G. Adams, Ph.D.; G. F. Elliott, D.Sc................£4,565 to £5,190
Principal Scientific Officers, R. H. Bate, Ph.D.; A. J. Charig, Ph.D.; M. K. Howarth, Ph.D.; R. P. S. Jefferies, Ph.D.; R. S. Miles, D.Sc.; C. Patterson, Ph.D.; J. M. Pettitt, Ph.D.; A. J. Sutcliffe, Ph.D............£2,995 to £4,077
(*Sub-Department of Physical Anthropology*)
Principal Scientific Officer, D. R. Brothwell
£2,995 to £4,077

Department of Mineralogy

Keeper, A. A. Moss, Ph.D........£5,415 to £6,005
Deputy Keeper, J. D. H. Wiseman, Ph.D.
£4,565 to £5,190
Principal Scientific Officers, A C. S. Bishop, Ph.D.; R. J. Davis, D.Phil.; P. G. Embrey; P. M. Game
£2,995 to £4,077

Department of Botany

Keeper, R. Ross...........£5,415 to £6,005
Deputy Keeper, A. Melderis, Ph.D. £4,565 to £5,190
Senior Principal Scientific Officer, W. T. Stearn, D.Sc.
£4,565 to £5,190
Principal Scientific Officers, J. F. M. Cannon; P. W. James; J. Lewis; N. K. B. Robson, Ph.D.
£2,995 to £4,077

MUSEUM OF LONDON

This museum, which will amalgamate the London and Guildhall Museums under a Board of 18 Governors, appointed (6 each) by the Government, the Corporation of London and the Greater London Council, was approved by Act of Parliament in 1965. When amalgamation takes place, the Museum will be controlled by the Board of Governors and financed in equal shares by the three authorities. It will eventually be housed in a new building to be erected in the City at the west end of London Wall. Meanwhile its two constituent parts will continue to be housed in their present buildings.

THE LONDON MUSEUM
Kensington Palace, W.8.
[01-937-9816]

The collections illustrate the history of London from the earliest times to the present and include archæological remains, topographical pictures and models, costumes, and royal relics. Originally housed at Kensington Palace, the collections were transferred to Lancaster House in 1914, where they remained till 1950, when most of Lancaster House was converted for use solely as a centre for government hospitality and conferences, and the museum was again granted temporary accommodation at Kensington Palace by King George VI. In 1956 the State Apartments at Kensington Palace were reopened to the public under the administrative control of the London Museum. The Apartments contain pictures from the royal collections, royal costumes, and furniture formerly belonging to Queen Mary.
Director, J. T. Hayes, Ph.D., F.S.A.
Assistant Keepers, First Class, B. W. Spencer, F.S.A.; C. E. Sorensen.

THE GUILDHALL MUSEUM
Gillett House, 55 Basinghall Street E.C.2
[01-606-3030]

The collection contains archæological remains excavated from within the boundaries of the City of London, and other material illustrating the history of the City. It is specially strong on the Roman and mediæval periods, including the splendid marble statuary and other finds from the Temple of Mithras.
Director, M. Hebditch.
Assistant Director, R. Merrifield, F.S.A.

THE SCIENCE MUSEUM
South Kensington, S.W.7
[01-589-6371]

Open on weekdays 10 to 6; Sundays 2.30 to 6. Closed on Good Friday, Christmas Eve, Christmas Day and Boxing Day.
For Science Museum Library, see below.
The Science Museum, which is the National Museum of Science and Industry, was instituted in 1853 under the Science and Art Department as a part of the South Kensington Museum, and opened in 1857; to it were added in 1883 the Collections of the Patent Museum. In 1909 the administration of the Science Collections was separated from that of the Art Collections, which were transferred to the Victoria and Albert Museum. The Collections in the Science Museum illustrate the development of science and engineering and related industries.
The administrative expenses of the Museum and Library were estimated at £825,000 for 1971-72.
Director and Secretary, Sir David Follett.... £6,925
Museum Superintendent, V. C. Clark
£3,425 to £4,575

Department of Physics

Keeper, V. K. Chew...........£4,565 to £5,190
Assistant Keepers (First Class), A. B. Sahiar; D. Vaughan...................£2,368 to £3,826

Department of Chemistry

Keeper, F. Greenaway...........£4,565 to £5,190
Deputy Keeper, D. B. Thomas... £2,618 to £4,076
Assistant Keeper (First Class), L. R. Day
£2,368 to £3,826

Department of Land Transport, Aeronautics and Circulation Collections

Keeper, W. Winton...........£4,565 to £5,190
Deputy Keepers, P. L. Sumner; T. M. Simmons; W. J. Tuck...............£2,618 to £4,076

Department of Electrical Engineering, Communications and Agriculture

Keeper, D. Chilton............£4,565 to £5,190
Assistant Keepers (First Class), Mrs. L. A. West; W. K. E. Geddes; B. P. Bowers
£2,368 to £3,826

Department of Water Transport and Mining

Keeper, G. R. M. Garratt....£4,565 to £5,190
Assistant Keeper (First Class), B. W. Bathe
£2,368 to £3,826

Department of Mechanical and Civil Engineering
Keeper, K. R. Gilbert.........£4,565 to £5,190
Deputy Keeper, G. B. L. Wilson. £2,618 to £4,076
Assistant Keeper (First Class), R. J. Law
£2,368 to £3,826

Department of Astronomy and Geophysics
Keeper, J. Wartnaby.........£4,565 to £5,190
Deputy Keeper, A. G. Thoday... £2,618 to £4,076
Assistant Keeper (First Class), C. St. C. B. Davison
£2,368 to £3,826

Department of Museum Services
Keeper, Miss M. K. Weston..... £4,565 to £5,190
Deputy Keeper G. W. B. Lacey. £2,618 to £4,076
Assistant Keeper (First Class), M. R. Preston; J. T.
Van Riemsdijk.............£2,368 to £3,826

Library
SCIENCE MUSEUM LIBRARY, South Kensington,
S.W.7.—A national library especially devoted
to pure and applied science, 417,000 volumes,
10,800 periodicals and transactions of learned
societies, about 5,300 current. Bibliographies sup-
plied.—Open on weekdays 10 to 5.30. Closed on
Sundays and Bank Holiday weekends. Photo-
copying service.
Keeper, J. A. Chaidecott........£4,565 to £5,190
Deputy Keeper, Miss H. J. Parker £2,618 to £4,076
Assistant Keepers (First Class), Miss H. D. Phippen;
H. Woolfe.................£2,368 to £3,826

THE VICTORIA AND ALBERT MUSEUM
South Kensington, S.W.7
[01-589-6371]
Hours 10 to 6 (weekdays and Bank Holidays);
Sundays, 2.30 to 6. Closed Good Friday, Christmas Eve, Christmas Day and Boxing Day. The
National Art Library is open on weekdays from
10 to 5.45 and the Print Room from 10 to 4.45.
Is a museum of all branches of fine and applied art,
under the Department of Education and Science,
and descends direct from the Museum of Manufactures (later called Museum of Ornamental Art)
opened in Marlborough House in 1852. The
Museum was moved in 1857 to become part of the
collective South Kensington Museum. It was renamed the Victoria and Albert Museum in 1899.
The branch museum at Bethnal Green was opened
in 1872 and the building is the most important
surviving example of the type of glass and iron
construction used by Paxton for the Great Exhibition
of 1851. The Victoria and Albert Museum
also administers the Wellington Museum (Apsley
House); Ham House, Richmond and Osterley Park,
Middlesex. Administrative expenses of the
Museum were estimated at £1,340,000 for 1970–71.
Director and Secretary, Sir John Pope-Hennessy,
C.B.E............................£6,875
Assistant Director (Works), Miss E. M. Aslin.

Department of Architecture and Sculpture
Keeper, T. W. L. Hodgkinson, C.B.E.
£4,565 to £5,190
Deputy Keeper, J. G. Beckwith.. £2,368 to £3,826†
Assistant Keeper, I, C. H. F. Avery
£2,368 to £3,826†

Department of Ceramics
Keeper, R. J. Charleston........£4,565 to £5,190
Deputy Keeper, J. V G. Mallet (also Sec. to Advisory
Council) ....£2,368 to £3,826†
Assistant Keeper, D. M. Archer. £2,368 to £3,826†

Department of Circulation
Keeper, H. G. Wakefield.......£4,565 to £5,190
Deputy Keeper, C. Hogben .... £2,368 to £3,826†
Assistant Keeper I, Mrs. B. J. Morris (Officer-in-
Charge, Bethnal Green Museum) £2,368 to £3,826

Library
Keeper, J. P. Harthan...........£4,565 to £5,190
Assistant Keepers I, R. C. Kennedy; A. P. Burton;
C. H. Gibbs-Smith (Keeper Emeritus)
£2,368 to £3,826

Department of Metalwork
Keeper, B. W. Robinson.......£4,565 to £5,190
Deputy Keeper, C. Blair.......£2,368 to £3,826†
Assistant Keepers I, R. W. Lightbown; Mrs. S. J.
Bury.....................£2,368 to £3,826

Department of Public Relations
Keeper II, J. A. C. Dempsey.... £3,810 to £4,515
Deputy Keeper, T. M. MacRobert
£2,368 to £3,826†

Department of Education Services
Assistant Keeper I, Mrs. M. Mainstone
£2,368 to £3,826

Department of Prints and Drawings
Keeper, A. G. Reynolds........£4,565 to £5,190
Deputy Keepers, J. H. Mayne; B. E. Reade; P. W.
Ward-Jackson..............£2,368 to £3,826†
Assistant Keeper I, C. M. Kauffmann
£2,368 to £3,826

Department of Textiles
Keeper, G. F. Wingfield Digby. £4,565 to £5,190
Deputy Keeper, D. King....... £2,368 to £3,826†
Assistant Keeper I, Miss N. K. A. Rothstein
£2,368 to £3,826

Department of Furniture and Woodwork
Keeper, P. K. Thornton........£4,565 to £5,190
Assistant Keepers I, D. J. V. FitzGerald; S. S. Jervis
£2,368 to £3,826

Oriental Department
Keeper, J. C. Irwin............£4,515 to £5,190
Indian Section
Assistant Keepers I, J. J. Lowry; R. W. Skelton
£2,368 to £3,826
Far Eastern Section
Keeper II, J. G. Ayers..........£3,860 to £4,565

**Department of Conservation and Technical
Services**
Keeper, N. S. Brommelle......£4,565 to £5,190
Assistant Keeper, J. F. Physick.. £2,368 to £3,826

Secretariat
Museum Superintendent, W. G. Easeman, T.D.
† Plus Allce. £250.

BETHNAL GREEN MUSEUM
Cambridge Heath Road, Bethnal Green, E.2.
A branch of the Victoria and Albert Museum,
opened in 1872. 18th–20th century costumes,
Spitalfields silks, dolls, toys, dolls' houses, model
theatres, 19th century Continental decorative arts,
Rodin sculpture, British ceramics and domestic
silver.
Officer-in-Charge, Mrs. B. J. Morris
£2,368 to £3,826

THE COMMONWEALTH INSTITUTE
Kensington High Street, W.8
[01-602-3252]
The management of the Institute is vested in a
Board of Governors of which Lord Garner,
G.C.M.G. is the Chairman and Sir Evelyn Hone,
G.C.M.G., C.V.O., O.B.E., Vice-Chairman. Membership of the Board consists of the High Commissions
in London of the Commonwealth Governments
and of representatives of Commonwealth, educa-
tional, cultural and commercial interests as appointed
by the Minister.
Exhibition Galleries open weekdays, 10 a.m. to
5.30 p.m.; Sundays, 2.30 p.m. to 6 p.m. Admis-
sion free. Cinema. Closed Good Fridays,
Christmas Eve, Christmas Day and Boxing Day,
Director, J. K. Thompson, C.M.G...........£6,475
Establishment and Finance Officer, E. E. Crowhurst
£3,925 to £4,575
Curator, Exhibition Galleries, J. H. Swain
£3,925 to £4,575
Curator, Art Gallery, D. G. Bowen, F.R.S.A.
£2,950 to £3,575
Librarian, A. J. Horne.........£2,950 to £3,575

Public Relations Officer, J. R. Turner
£2,950 to £3,575

Senior Education Officers, A. J. Spicer, O.B.E.; J. F. Callander (*Conferences and Talks*)
£2,950 to £3,575

IMPERIAL WAR MUSEUM
Lambeth Road, S.E.1

[01–735 8922]

Open free daily (except Good Friday, Christmas Eve, Christmas Day and Boxing Day) 10 a.m.–6 p.m. Reference Depts. open Tuesday–Friday (except on public holidays), 10 a.m.–5 p.m.

The Museum was founded in 1917, and established by Act of Parliament in 1920 to record all aspects of the First World War. In 1939 its terms of reference were enlarged to cover the Second World War, and in 1953 they were again extended to cover all operations involving British or Commonwealth troops since August 1914. The Museum was opened in its present home, formerly Bethlem Hospital, in 1936. Displayed in the public galleries are weapons and equipment of all kinds, including aircraft, armoured fighting vehicles and field guns, as well as models, decorations, uniforms, posters, photographs and paintings. The Art collection comprises over 9,000 paintings, drawings and pieces of sculpture, which constitute a unique eyewitness record of wartime scenes and personalities. The Photographic Library contains over 3,000,000 prints, and the Printed Books and Documents sections hold more than 100,000 printed and manuscript works in many languages. The Film Library holds about 30,000,000 feet of film. Administrative expenses of the Museum, 1971–72, £351,000.

Director, A. N. Frankland, D.F.C., D.Phil. £5,065
Deputy Director, C. H. Roads, Ph.D.
£4,170 to £4,745
Assistant Director and Keeper of Art Department, J. C. Darracott . . . . £3,521 to £4,170
Keepers, P. J. Simkins (*Exhibits*); D. G. Lance (*Libraries and Archives*); C. Dowling, D.Phil. (*Education and Publications*), G. T. C. Coultass (*Film*) . . . . £2,318 to £3,776
Secretary, J. J. Chadwick . . . . . . £2,318 to £3,776
Establishment and Finance Officer, J. F. Golding
£2,654 to £3,224

NATIONAL MARITIME MUSEUM
Greenwich, S.E.10

[01–858–4422]

Open weekdays 10 till 6; Sundays 2.30 to 6. Closed on Good Friday, Christmas Eve, Christmas Day and Boxing Day.

Reading Room open on weekdays 10 to 5; tickets of admission on written application to the Director.

The National Maritime Museum was established by Act of Parliament in 1934, for the illustration of the maritime history, archæology and art of Great Britain. The Museum, which has absorbed the Royal Naval Museum and the Painted Hall Collections, is in two groups of buildings, in Greenwich Park, the Main Buildings, centred round the Queen's House (built by Inigo Jones, 1617–35) and the Old Royal Observatory, including the Wren Flamsteed House, to the south. The collections include paintings; ship-models; ships' lines; prints and drawings; maps, atlases and charts; navigational instruments; relics; books and MSS. The amount for salaries and expenses, including a Grant-in-Aid, was estimated at £417,000 for 1971–72.

Director and Accounting Officer, B. J. Greenhill, C.M.G.
£5,640
Keeper, D. W. Waters £5,015
Secretary, D. V. Proctor . . . . £2,193 to £3,651
Deputy Keepers, B. T. Carter; Dr. A. P. McGowan; J. Munday . . . . £3,685 to £4,390
Assistant Keepers (First Class), P. G. W. Annis; E. H. H. Archibald; H. D. Howse, M.B.E., D.S.C.;

A. W. H. Pearsall; Dr. M. W. B. Sanderson; Mrs. A. M. Shirley; A. N. Stimson
£2,193 to £3,651
Administration Officer, L. A. Young.

(For other Museums in England—*see* Index).

THE NATIONAL MUSEUM OF WALES
AMGUEDDFA GENEDLAETHOL CYMRU
Cardiff

Open on weekdays, 10 a.m. to 5 p.m. (April to Sept., 10 a.m. to 6 p.m.). Sundays 2.30 to 5 p.m. Founded by Royal Charter, 1907. and maintained principally by annual grant from the Government and partly by Museum rate from the Cardiff City Council. The collections consist of: (Geology), Collections of geological specimens (rocks, minerals and fossils) from all parts of Wales with comparative material from other regions. Relief maps, models and photographs illustrating the structure and scenery of Wales. (Botany), the Welsh National Herbarium, illustrating especially the flora of Wales and comprising the Griffith, D. A. Jones, Vachell, Salter, Shoolbred, Wheldon and other herbaria, and display collections illustrating general and forest botany and the ecology of Welsh plants. (Zoology), Collections of skins, British mammals and birds, eggs of British birds, extensive entomological collections, Melvill-Tomlin collection of molluscs, spirit collections, chiefly of Welsh interest. (Archæology), Welsh prehistoric, Roman and mediæval antiquities, casts of pre-Norman monuments of Wales, important numismatic collection. (Industry), The history and development of industry in Wales, illustrated by models, dioramas, original objects and machines. (Art), The works of Richard Wilson, Augustus John, O.M., and Sir Frank Brangwyn, are well represented; the Gwendoline and Margaret Davies Bequests of works of the 19th-century French School, the British School and Old Masters, Pyke Thompson collection of watercolour drawings, and a general collection of paintings in oil; sculpture, including many works by Sir W. Goscombe John, R.A., Swansea and Nantgarw porcelain, the De Winton collection of Continental porcelain and the Jackson collection of silver, etc.

President, The Earl of Plymouth, F.R.S.A.
Vice-President, A. B. Oldfield-Davies, C.B.E.
Director, G. O. Jones, Ph.D., D.SC.
Secretary, R. J. H. Lloyd, T.D.
Keepers (*Geology*), D. A. Bassett, Ph.D; (*Botany*), S. G. Harrison; (*Zoology*), J. A. Bateman; (*Archæology*), H. N. Savory, D.Phil., F.S.A.; (*Industry*), D. Morgan Rees, F.S.A.; (*Art*), R. L. Charles, M.C.

Welsh Folk Museum
Amgueddfa Werin Cymru
St. Fagans

The museum is situated 4 miles west of Cardiff. Open weekdays (except Monday) 11 a.m. to 7 p.m. April to September, and 11 a.m. to 5 p.m. October to March (admission 10p). Open Sundays from 2.30 p.m. The museum was made possible by the gift of St. Fagans Castle and its grounds by the Earl of Plymouth in 1947. The rooms of the Castle contain period furniture; the gardens are maintained. A woollen factory from Brecknockshire, a tannery from Radnorshire, a 16th-century barn from Flintshire, four farmhouses, an 18th century cockpit from Denbigh, a turnpike house, a cottage and an 18th-century chapel have been re-erected and other typical Welsh buildings are being re-erected in an area adjoining the Castle to picture the Welsh way of life and to show the rural crafts of the past. A Gallery of Material Culture illustrating domestic and social life in Wales is open and a further new museum building is in course of construction.

Curator, T. M. Owen, F.S.A.
Keepers (*Material Culture*), J. G. Jenkins, F.S.A.; (*Oral Tradition and Dialects*), V. H. Phillips.

Legionary Museum of Caerleon
Caerleon, Mon.

Open on weekdays (April–September) 11 a.m. to 5 p.m. (Sundays, 2.30 p.m. to 5 p.m.), and at other times on application to the Caretaker (admission 5p).

Contains material found on the site of the Roman fortress of Isca and its suburbs.

Turner House Art Gallery
Penarth, Nr. Cardiff

Open weekdays, 11 a.m.–12.45 p.m. and 2 p.m. to 5 p.m. Sundays, 2 p.m. to 5 p.m. Closed Mondays, except Bank Holidays.

ROYAL SCOTTISH MUSEUM
Chambers Street, Edinburgh, 1
[031–225–7534]

Open free, Mon.–Sat., 10 a.m. to 5 p.m.; and Sun. 2 to 5 p.m.
Director, W. I. R. Finlay, C.B.E. £4,500
Keeper, Department of Art and Archæology, C. Aldred
..............................£3,234 to £3,850
Keeper, Department of Technology, A. G. Thomson, Ph.D..............£3,234 to £3,850
Keeper, Department of Natural History, A. R. Waterston, O.B.E...........£3,234 to £3,850
Keeper, Department of Geology, C. D. Waterston, Ph.D..............£3,234 to £3,850
Assistant Keepers (First Class), A. S. Clarke, Ph.D.; R. Oddy; H. G. Macpherson, Ph.D.; E. C. Pelham-Clinton; J. D. Storer; H. O. A. F. Fernandez; Miss J. M. Scarce; I. H. J. Lyster; Miss D. Idiens..............£1,925 to £3,205

NATIONAL MUSEUM OF ANTIQUITIES OF SCOTLAND
Queen Street, Edinburgh, 2
[031–556–8921]

Founded in 1781 by the Society of Antiquaries of Scotland, and transferred to the Nation in 1858. Open free. Weekdays, 10 a.m. to 5 p.m.; Sundays, 2–5 p.m. Annexe at 18 Shandwick Place (closed on Sundays).
Keeper, R. B. K. Stevenson..............£5,015
Deputy Keeper, S. Maxwell.
Assistant Keepers, A. Fenton; Miss J. Close-Brooks.
Senior Scientific Officer, Dr. H. McKerrell.

NATIONAL BUS COMPANY
25 New Street Square, E.C.4
[01–583–9177]

The National Bus Company is a statutory body under the provisions of the Transport Act, 1968. It controls more than 50 operating companies covering almost every part of England and Wales outside London and the municipal undertakings. The N.B.C. bus and coach fleets total some 22,000 vehicles and it employs a staff of over 80,000.
Chairman, A. N. Todd..........(*part-time*) £7,750
Members (part-time), W. Alker; A. P. de Boer; Sir William Hart, C.M.G.; J. Lancaster; M. W. Rosser; F. A. S. Wood (*each* £1,000); W. M. Little.
Chief Executive, T. W. H. Gailey........£13,500

NATIONAL COAL BOARD
Hobart House, Grosvenor Place, S.W.1
[01–235–2020]

The National Coal Board was constituted in 1946. It took over the mines on January 1, 1947.
Chairman, D. J. Ezra, M.B.E..............£20,000
Deputy Chairman, W. V. Sheppard, C.B.E..£16,000
Members, J. Brass, C.B.E.; D. M. Clement, C.B.E.; L. Grainger; W. L. Miron, C.B.E., T.D.; G. C. Shepherd; N. Siddall.......£9,900 to £11,975
Part-time Members, H. J. Marsh, C.B.E.; J. A. Peel; J. A. Wellings, C.B.E..............£1,000
Secretary, K. S. Jefferies.

NATIONAL DEBT OFFICE
and Office for Payment of Government Life Annuities
Bank Buildings, 19 Old Jewry, E.C.2
Secretary to the National Debt Commissioners and Comptroller-General, I. de L. Radice, C.B.
..............................£6,925
Asst. Comptroller, F. D. Ashby..£4,220 to £4,730
Chief Executive Officer, S. J. Payne
..............................£3,433 to £4,048
Senior Executive Officers, W. G. Stevens; G. F. W. Berry; L. A. S. Swift; E. T. Taylor
..............................£2,704 to £3,224
Brokers, Messrs. Mullens & Co..........£2,000

NATIONAL DOCK LABOUR BOARD
22–26 Albert Embankment, S.E.1

The National Dock Labour Board administers the scheme for giving permanent employment to dock workers under the *Dock Workers (Regulation of Employment) (Amendment) Scheme*, 1967.
Chairman, P. G. H. Lewison.
General Manager and Secretary, J. H. C. Pape.

NATIONAL ECONOMIC DEVELOPMENT OFFICE
Millbank Tower, Millbank, S.W.1
[01–834–3811]
Council

Government Members, The Chancellor of the Exchequer (*Chairman*); the Secretary of State for Employment; the Secretary of State for Trade and Industry and the President of the Board of Trade. *Management Members*, W. O. Campbell Adamson; M. J. S. Clapham; The Lord Netherthorpe; Sir John Partridge, K.B.E.; G. Richardson, M.B.E.; *Trade Union Members*, A. W. Allen; The Lord Cooper of Stockton Heath; V. Feather, C.B.E.; Sir Sidney Greene, C.B.E.; J. L. Jones, C.B.E.; H. Scanlon. *Nationalized Industries*, The Lord Melchett. *Independent Member*, Prof. W.G. McClelland. *National Economic Development Office*, Sir Frank Figgures, K.C.B., C.M.G. (*Director-General*).

Secretary, E. A. Ferguson.
Industrial Director, T. C. Fraser.
Industrial Advisers and Assistant Industrial Directors, J. M. Beales; J. R. S. Homan; P. F. D. Wallis; H. R. Windle.
Economic Director, D. K. Stout.

NATIONAL GALLERIES
See ART GALLERIES

NATIONAL HEALTH SERVICE
See HEALTH SERVICE
(under Ministry of Health)

NATIONAL PORTS COUNCIL
17 North Audley Street, W.1
[01–493–7911]

The Council was established by the *Harbours Act* 1964 with the principal duties of formulating and keeping under review a national plan for the development of harbours in Great Britain, encouraging the efficient functioning of harbour authorities, and giving advice to the Minister of Transport on matters relating to port improvement, maintenance and management. The Council also has research and training functions and is empowered to consider and determine appeals against ship, passenger and goods dues imposed by statutory harbour authorities.
Chairman, P. Chappell.
Deputy Chairman, J. L. Jones, M.B.E.
Members, J. Morris Gifford (*Director-General*); F. B. Bolton, M.C.; F. D. P. Braun; A. G. P. Burney, O.B.E.; Sir William Lithgow, Bt.; D. E. A. Pettit; L. J. Reynolds; A. W. Suddaby, C.B.E.
Joint Secretaries, R. C. Livesey (*Asst.-Director General*); K. A. Heathcote.

DEPARTMENT FOR NATIONAL SAVINGS
Blythe Road, W.14.
[01-603-2000]

The Department for National Savings was established as a Government Department when the former Post Office Savings Department became separated from the Post Office on October 1, 1969. The Department operates the National Savings Bank and maintains the records of holdings of National Savings Certificates, Save As You Earn contracts, Premium Savings Bonds, British Savings Bonds (and their forerunners Defence and National Development Bonds) and Government stock on the National Savings Stock Register.

Director of Savings, A. Currall, C.B., C.M.G.. £9,000
Deputy Directors, J. Littlewood..(£6,750); R. G. Armstrong, M.C., T.D. (*Controller (National Savings Bank)*)...£6,530
Assistant Directors, Miss B. K. Billot; J. Higson
£5,000 to £6,300
Establishment Officer, C. W. Hand
£5,000 to £6,300
Controllers, G. W. Mantle; H. R. West, O.B.E.; J. P. Wilde, O.B.E.; J. W. King (*Publicity*)
£5,000 to £6,300
Finance Officer, L. W. Sturt.....£5,000 to £6,300
Senior Principals, R. H. Dryden; H. G. D. Gabriel, M.B.E...........................£4,600 to £5,200
Principals, A. G. Craner, I.S.O.; M. Marshall; B. C. Smith, M.B.E.; A. K. Grant; K. G. Taylor, I.S.O., E.R.D.; T. A. Martin; S. A. Ingham; A. Green; S. J. Allison; M. Morris; D. M. Jones; J. A. Cuthbertson; J. R. Acland; C. M. Roberts; C. F. H. Taylor; A. Watson; K. J. Thomas; Miss J. M. J. Wedge; J. Saynor; R. J. F. Lindsay; C. L. Dann; T. Wilson; Miss C. N. Lall, M.B.E.; J. Stamp; G. R. Wilson; R. S. Robinson; S. W. Shepherd.............£3,250 to £4,400
Commissioner (*Department for National Savings, Headquarters*), R. J. Heathorn..£3,250 to £4,400
Principal Information Officers, P. G. Hutchings; R. C. Davy.....................£3,250 to £4,400

THE NATIONAL SAVINGS COMMITTEE
Alexandra House, Kingsway, W.C.2
[01-836-1599]

President, The Lord Thomas D.F.C.
Chairman, Sir Robert Bellinger, G.B.E.
Vice-Presidents, Sir Harold Parkinson, K.B.E.; Sir Kenneth Stewart, Bt., G.B.E.; E. A. G. Caröe, C.B.E.
Vice-Chairmen, The Rt. Hon. G. Woodcock, C.B.E.; Sir Alfred Owen, C.B.E.; J. Anstey, C.B.E., T.D.; General Sir Geoffrey Musson, G.C.B., C.B.E., D.S.O.; V. G. H. Feather, C.B.E.

OFFICERS
Secretary and Chief Commissioner, K. T. Pinch
£5,000 to £6,300
Commissioners, S. Burke; K. G. Burton; D. J. Creswell, M.B.E.; J. N. G. Davies; F. Dyer; A. W. W. Fairley; J. Gilmour; K. J. Griffin; K. Nicholas; R. Rees, M.B.E.; J. K. Roberts; J. C. Timms, O.B.E. ....£3,250 to £4,400

NATIONAL SAVINGS COMMITTEE FOR SCOTLAND
22 Melville Street, Edinburgh 2
[031-225-5486]

President, The Lord Erskine of Rerrick, G.B.E.
Chairman, The Hon. Lord Birsay, C.B.E., T.D.
Secretary, A. M. Swanson, O.B.E. £4,600 to £5,200
Deputy Secretary, R. F. Johnson, I.S.O.
£3,250 to £4,400

NATURAL ENVIRONMENT RESEARCH COUNCIL
Alhambra House, 27/33 Charing Cross Road, W.C.2
[01-930-9232]

The Natural Environment Research Council was established by Royal Charter on June 1, 1965, under the Science and Technology Act, 1965, to encourage, plan and conduct research in those sciences, both physical and biological, which relate to man's natural environment.

The component establishments of the Council are as shown below. It is also responsible for supporting: the Marine Biological Association, the Scottish Marine Biological Association, the Freshwater Biological Association, the Fisheries Helminthology Unit and the Marine Invertebrate Biology Unit. These bodies have their own governing boards or advisory committees.

In addition the Council advises the Ministry of Agriculture, Fisheries and Food and the Department of Agriculture and Fisheries for Scotland on the research programmes of their fisheries laboratories. Much of the Council's activities is related to university research in the environmental sciences, which it supports by post-graduate training awards, research grants and fellowships.

Chairman, Prof. F. H. Stewart, F.R.S., F.R.S.E.
Secretary, R. J. H. Beverton, C.B.E.
Deputy Secretaries, P. H. Cooper (*Administration*); D. J. Maclean (*Scientific*).

Institute of Geological Sciences
Exhibition Road, South Kensington, S.W.7.
[01-589-3444]

The Geological Museum, Exhibition Road, South Kensington, S.W.7. Open weekdays, 10 to 6; Sundays 2.30 to 6. Closed on Good Friday, Christmas Eve, Christmas Day and Boxing Day.
Director, K. C. Dunham, D.SC., F.R.S., F.R.S.E.

National Institute of Oceanography
Wormley, Godalming, Surrey
[042879-2122]

Whale Research Unit, British Museum of Natural History, Cromwell Road, S.W.7.
Director, H. Charnock.

The Nature Conservancy
19 Belgrave Square, S.W.1
[01-235-3241]

Director, M. E. D. Poore, Ph.D.

Institute of Hydrology
Howbery Park, Wallingford, Berks.
[04913-2265]

Director, J. S. G. McCulloch, Ph.D.

British Antarctic Survey
30 Gillingham Street, S.W.1
[01-834-3687]

Director, Sir Vivian Fuchs, Ph.D.

Institute of Coastal Oceanography and Tides
(formerly the Liverpool Tidal Institute)
The Observatory, Bidston, Birkenhead
[051-652-2396]

Director, J. R. Rossiter, D.SC.

Culture Centre of Algae and Protozoa
36 Storeys Way, Cambridge
[0223-61378]

Director, E. A. George.

Research Vessels Unit
No. 1 Dock, Barry, Glamorgan
[04462-7745X]

Director, Capt. D. M. H. Stobie, D.S.C., R.N.(*ret.*).

Institution of Tree Biology
King's Building, Mayfield Road, Edinburgh 9
[031-667-1011]

Director, F. T. Last, D.SC.

Unit of Coastal Sedimentation
Beadon Road, Taunton, Sussex
[0823-82691]

Officer-in-Charge, R. L. Cloet, Ph.D.

Institute of Marine Environmental Research
13-14 St. James Terrace, Plymouth
[0752-20681]

Director, R. S. Glover.

Seals Research Unit
c/o Fisheries Laboratory, Lowestoft, Suffolk
[0502-4251]
Officer-in-Charge, W. N. Bonner.

ORDNANCE SURVEY
Romsey Road, Maybush, Southampton
[Southampton 75555]
Director-General, Maj.-Gen. B. St.G. Irwin.
Directors:
  Field Survey, Brig. J. Kelsey, C.B.E.
  Map Publication, Brig. E. P. J. Williams.
  Establishment and Finance, A. R. Atherton
  £4,390 to £5,640
Deputy Directors:
  Field Survey, Col. D. V. Hutchinson.
  Planning and Development, Col. R. C. Gardiner-
  Hill, O.B.E.
  Map Production, Col. G. A. Hardy.
  Establishments, R. W. Gough, O.B.E.
  £4,045 to £4,555
Assistant Directors:
  Geodetic Services, Lt.-Col. M. J. K. Davies.
  Topographic Surveys, Lt.-Col. E. W. Barton.
  Cartography, Lt.-Col. J. S. Coulson.
  Reproduction, A. C. Marles... £4,228 to £4,344
  Publication, Miss B. D. Drewitt
  £3,258 to £3,873
  Training and Information, W. A. Seymour
  £4,228 to £4,344
Personnel, A. St. J. Perkins ...... £3,258 to £3,873
Office Services, F. Judd, B.E.M.... £3,258 to £3,873
Finance, A. E. Rich .... £3,258 to £3,873

OVERSEAS AUDIT DEPARTMENT
Queen Anne's Chambers, 41 Tothill Street,
S.W.1
[01-930-8307]
The Accounts of most of the dependent terri-
tories overseas are audited on behalf of the Secretary
of State for Foreign and Commonwealth Affairs by
Audit Officers acting under the supervision of the
Director General of the Overseas Audit Service.
The cost of this audit is borne by the territories
affected.
Director General of the Overseas Audit Service, F. E. L.
  Carter, C.B.E. £6,400
Assistant Director, G. C. Jarvis, O.B.E. £4,170

OVERSEAS DEVELOPMENT ADMINISTRATION
Eland House, Stag Place, Victoria, S.W.1
[01-834-2377]
The development work of the Foreign and
Commonwealth Office is the charge of a Minister
for Overseas Development, who has, by delegation
from the Secretary of State full charge of the
functional wing knows as the Overseas Develop-
ment Administration of the Foreign and Common-
wealth Office. It is staffed by the officers of the
former Ministry of Overseas Development, which
was dissolved in November, 1970.
Minister for Overseas Development, THE RT. HON.
  RICHARD FREDERICK WOOD, M.P........£8,500
Parliamentary Private Secretary, Hon. John Astor,
  M.P.
Parliamentary Under-Secretary of State, J. A. Ker-
  shaw, M.C., M.P. £3,750
Private Secretary, Miss M. Norman, M.B.E.
Secretary (Overseas Development Administration), Sir
  Michael Walker, K.C.M.G. £14,000
Deputy Secretaries, R. B. M. King, C.B., M.C.;
  W. A. C. Mathieson, C.B., C.M.G., M.B.E. £9,000
Under-Secretaries, R. H. Belcher, C.M.G.; N. Leach,
  C.M.G.; J. Mark, M.B.E.; L. C. J. Martin; M. G.
  Smith; A. R. Thomas, C.M.G.; D. Williams,
  C.V.O. £6,750
Director-General of Economic Planning, R. S. Porter,
  O.B.E. £7,800
Deputy-Director-General of Economic Planning. J. K.
  Wright £6,750

Director, Statistics Division, K. V. Henderson
  £6,120
Director of Geographical Division, Economic Planning,
  D. J. Ovens.......................... £6,120
Director of International Economics Division, Dr. J. M.
  Healey.............................. £6,120
Director of Population Bureau, Dr. D. Wolfers £5,390

Advisory and Specialist Staff
Land Tenure Adviser, J. C. D. Lawrance, O.B.E.
  £4,390 to £5,015
Chief National Resources Adviser, A. R. Melville,
  C.M.G................... £5,240 to £5,830
Agricultural Adviser, D. C. P. Evans
  £4,390 to £5,015
Assistant Agricultural Adviser, K. Wilson-Jones
  £2,820 to £3,902
Agricultural Research Adviser, Dr. R. K. Cunning-
  ham .... £4,390 to £5,015
Animal Health Adviser, A. L. C. Thorne, C.B.E.
  £5,240 to £5,830
Deputy Animal Health Adviser, J. Davie
  £4,390 to £5,015
Co-operatives Adviser, B. J. Youngjohns
  £4,390 to £5,015
Chief Education Adviser, J. E. C. Thornton, O.B.E.
  £5,240 to £5,830
Education Advisers, Miss J. H. Deas (£5,435); Sir
  Norman Alexander, C.B.E. (part-time)... £3,968
Education Adviser (Technical), Dr. G. E. Watts,
  C.B.E..................... £4,390 to £5,015
Assistant Education Adviser (Technical), J. W. Gailer
  £2,820 to £3,902
Assistant Education Adviser, W. A. Dodd.... £3,526
Engineering Adviser, B. M. U. Bennell
  £4,390 to £5,015
Deputy Engineering Adviser, M. W. Todd, M.B.E.
  £4,390 to £5,015
Fisheries Adviser, Dr. D. N. F. Hall
  £4,390 to £5,015
Forestry Adviser, J. Wyatt-Smith £5,240 to £5,830
Overseas Labour Adviser, G. Foggon, C.M.G., O.B.E.
  £5,240 to £5,830
Assistant Labour Adviser, D. I. Goodwin.... £3,995
Consultant on Water Development, D. S. Ferguson
  (part-time).......................... £1,440
Medical Adviser, Dr. J. M. Liston, C.M.G.... £7,350
Deputy Medical Advisers, Dr. P. W. Dill-Russell,
  C.B.E.; Dr. W. J. M. Evans, C.B.E.
  £5,240 to £5,830
Nursing Adviser, Miss G. B. Schofield, O.B.E.
  £4,740
Marketing Adviser, H. C. Biggs £4,390 to £5,015
Social Development Adviser, A. R. G. Prosser, C.M.G.
  M.B.E..................... £4,390 to £5,015
Police Training Adviser, M. J. Macoun, C.M.G., O.B.E.
  £4,505 to £5,190
Deputy Police Training Adviser, L. A. Hicks
  £2,995 to £4,077
**Head of British Development Division, Caribbean*
  (Bridgetown), W. L. Bell, C.M.G., M.B.E.... £5,640
Head of Middle East Development Division (Beirut),
  J. C. Rowley.......................... £5,640
Assistant Secretaries, K. G. Ashton; R. L. Baxter;
  R. A. Browning; J. L. F. Buist; E. C. Burr;
  M. L. Cahill; W. T. A. Cox; K. H. Critchley;
  J. H. Francis, C.B.E.; I. H. Harris; N. B. J.
  Huijsman; A. G. Hurrell; C. R. O. Jones;
  J. M. Kisch, C.M.G.; D. M. Kitching; W. G.
  Lamarque, M.B.E.; A. A. W. Landymore, C.B.E.;
  M. P. J. Lynch; L. W. Norwood; D. L. Pearson;
  A. J. Peckham; R. E. Radford; C. R. A. Rae;
  J. E. Rednall; B. E. Rolfe; D. M. Smith;
  W. J. Smith; W. D. Sweaney, C.M.G. (Establish-
  ment Officer); A. M. Turner... £4,390 to £5,640
Head of Information Department, R. T. G. Miles
  £4,390 to £5,640
Chief Statistician, H. A. Fell..... £4,390 to £5,640
**Statisticians,* R. M. Allen; B. J. Moore
  £2,820 to £3,902
Senior Economic Advisers, *R. M. Ainscow; *G. A.
  Bridger; Dr. B. E. Cracknell; J. B. Wilmshurst
  £4,390 to £5,640

Economic Advisers, ★G. A. Beattie; ★J. C. H. Morris; ★C. H. Smee; ★D. C. Stafford; J. N. Stevens; ★J. T. Winpenny............£2,820 to £3,902
Senior Principal Scientific Officer, D. C. Mandeville, O.B.E.............£4,390 to £5,015
Principals, B. D. Barber; A. D. Beaty; E. A. Bennett; W. T. Birrell; J. Blades; H. H. Bracken, C.B.E.; F. N. Brockett; ★J. R. V. A. Bromage, C.B.E.; S. A. Bunce; J. A. Burgess, O.B.E.; D. E. B. Carr; R. O. Carter; Miss R. M. B. Chevailler; D. H. Christie; B. Cook; D. Cooper; L. E. Dawes; R. F. R. Deare; A. J. A. Douglas, C.M.G., O.B.E.; P. C. Duff; J. C. Edwards; M. de N. Ensor, O.B.E.; ★F. W. Essex; J. A. L. Faint; A. S. Fair; F. W. Foreman; D. S. Foster; K. W. G. Frost; Hon. D. C. Geddes; S. A. Gibbins, M.B.E.; D. E. Glason; D. W. Goodman, M.B.E.; Miss S. K. L. Guiton; ★C. J. Hall, M.B.E.; Hon. C. A. Hankey, O.B.E.; ★C. M. H. Harrison; W. Hobman; F. J. Holloway; A. W. Horner, C.M.G., T.D.; J. W. Howard; ★H. E. O. Hughes, C.B.E.; ★P. H. Johnston, C.M.G.; B. T. Jordan; J. V. Kirby; K. D. Law; ★S. C. Lawrence, C.M.G., O.B.E.; A. N. MacCleary; P. S. McLean, O.B.E.; Miss M. P. Maguire; W. D. Maniece; R. G. M. Manning; B. G. Meara; B. A. Mitchell; H. A. Moisley; S. J. Moore; W. D. J. Morgan; ★C. N. F. Odgers, O.B.E.; K. O. H. Osborne; P. G. Ottewill, G.M., A.F.C.; ★N. F. Page, C.B.E.; D. G. Perrin; D. A. Pott, O.B.E.; R. M. Prideaux; A. G. Ridley, M.V.O.; A. K. Robertson; Mrs. M. C. Rosser; A. K. Russell, D.Phil.; D. J. Scanlan, M.V.O., O.B.E.; J. M. Scoular; F. E. Sitch; D. F. Smith; G. F. H. Stapley; A. H. Tansley; D. A. T. Thain, M.B.E.; A. M. Trick; S. Wellington; J. L. West; J. E. Whitelegg; T. J. Wilshire; K. J. Windsor; K. A. F. Woolverton; R. W. Wootton; T. D. Wright, M.V.O.; Miss E. M. Young
............£2,820 to £3,902
Appointments Officers, H. L. Adams, C.M.G., T.D.; F. K. Boyle; A. B. Cozens, O.B.E.; Sir George Duntze, Bt., C.M.G.; ★W. A. R. Gorman, O.B.E., M.C.; F. L. Greenland; J. F. Hayley; ★G. C. M. Heathcote; H. Holmes; ★A. G. Simpson; ★M. F. G. Wentworth, C.M.G., O.B.E.
............£2,820 to £3,526
Senior Executive Officers, Miss J. W. Balls, M.B.E.; E. T. Barnes; D. H. Braun; Miss M. Bristow; L. L. Brooks; E. A. Byron; D. G. Camps; E. Eames; K. C. Elkins; C. E. Eyles; Miss M. Fairlie, M.B.E.; C. R. V. Farran; H. J. Finch; C. T. R. Gordon; J. R. Hards; A. H. Harrison; T. N. Jenkins; R. O. Kiernan; Miss M. J. Kinchington; L. A. Lampard; Miss B. E. Langley; L. J. McCarthy; J. M. McDonough; C. A. Maher; K. H. R. Mundy; Miss D. Nicholls; S. C. Pennock; R. S. Ridgwell; Miss L. H. R. Roberts; Miss E. F. Saracco; E. Scott; P. J. Shaw; G. H. Sinclair; I. F. Stickels; W. J. C. Tomlinson; R. J. Walsgrove; Miss E. M. Ware; A. F. Watkins; P. J. Watson; D. M. Whitecross; G. A. Williams; P. M. Wilson £4,045 to £4,555

Centre for Overseas Pest Research
College House, Wright's Lane, W.8
[01-937-6084]
Director, P. T. Haskell, Ph.D..... £5,240 to £5,830

Council for Technical Education and Training for Overseas Countries
29 Bressendon Place, S.W.1
[01-828-3665]
Secretary, H. M. Collins, O.B.E............£4,390

Directorate of Overseas (Geodetic and Topographic) Surveys
Kingston Road, Tolworth, Surbiton, Surrey
[01-337-8661]
Director, D. E. Warren........ £5,240 to £5,830

Inter-University Council for Higher Education Overseas
90/91 Tottenham Court Road, W.1
[01-580-6572]
Director, R. C. Griffiths................£6,750

Overseas Services Resettlement Bureau
Eland House, Stag Place, S.W.1
[01-828-4366]
Director and Head of Bureau, Sir Edwin Arrowsmith, K.C.M.G............£3,873

Tropical Products Institute
56/62 Gray's Inn Road, W.C.1
[01-242-5412]
Director, P. C. Spensley, D.Phil. . £5,240 to £5,830
★Temporary.

OVERSEAS TERRITORIES INCOME TAX OFFICE
26 Grosvenor Gardens, S.W.1

The Official Representative acts as agent in the United Kingdom for some 30 Overseas Governments in relation to the income tax liability of certain companies and pensioners resident in the United Kingdom and in dealing with general enquiries regarding overseas tax. He also runs a Training School for overseas tax officials.
Official Representative, J. E. Comben, O.B.E. . £5,200

OFFICE OF THE PARLIAMENTARY COMMISSIONER FOR ADMINISTRATION
Church House, Great Smith Street, S.W.1
[01-222-5852]

The Parliamentary Commissioner for Administration was appointed by the *Parliamentary Commissioner Act, 1967,* for the investigation of administrative action taken on behalf of the Crown. He is appointed by Letters Patent under the Great Seal, and is irremovable except upon an Address from the two Houses of Parliament. His function is to investigate complaints referred to him by Members of the House of Commons from members of the public who claim to have sustained injustice in consequence of maladministration in connection with actions taken by or on behalf of Government Departments but not other public bodies. Under the Act, the Commissioner is required to report the results of an investigation to the Member of the House. He is also required to report to Parliament on the performance of his functions and he may make special reports to Parliament upon cases of maladministration where it appears to him that an injustice has not been or will not be remedied.
Parliamentary Commissioner, Sir Alan Marre, K.C.B.
............£14,000
Secretary, E. L. Sykes, C.M.G............£6,750
Directors, R. A. Best; Miss J. Horsham; T. W. Jones, O.B.E............£5,000 to £6,300
Establishment Officer, D. G. Plaister, O.B.E.
............£4,600 to £5,200
Chief Executive Officers, S. J. T. Beck; H. Billing; K. H. Green; I. R. W. Hargest; E. L. P. Smith; A. Thompson; H. L. Woodward
............£3,250 to £4,400

PARLIAMENTARY COUNSEL
36 Whitehall, S.W.1 [01-930-1234]
First Counsel, Sir John Fiennes, K.C.B......£14,000
Second Counsel, S. M. Krusin, C.B........£10,950
Counsel, Mrs. E. A. Eadie, C.B.E.; G. J. Engle; F. B. Humphrey; H. P. Rowe, C.B.; B. A. Russell-Davis; T. R. F. Skemp; A. N. Stainton, C.B.; C. H. de Waal............£7,625 to £9,000
Deputy Counsel, G. J. Carter; P. Graham...£6,925

PAROLE BOARD
Romney House, Marsham Street, S.W.1
[01-799-3488]
The Board was constituted under section 59 of the Criminal Justice Act, 1967 and the Members were appointed on November 7, 1967.
The function of the Board is to advise the Secretary of State for the Home Department with respect to: (1) Release on licence under section 60 (i) or 61 and recall under section 62 of the Criminal Justice Act, 1967 of persons whose cases have been referred to the Board by the Secretary of State; (2) The conditions of such licences, and the variation and cancellation of such conditions; and (3) any other matter so referred which is connected with release

on licence or recall of persons to whom section 60 or 61 of the Act applies.

Chairman, The Lord Hunt, C.B.E., D.S.O.

Vice-Chairman, Mr. Justice Waller, O.B.E.

Members, R. H. Beeson, O.B.E.; Miss E. M. Blackford; Prof. G. J. Borrie; J. Bradley; S. Brown, Q.C.; His Hon. Judge B. D. Bush; R. Calderwood; W. G. Curson; His Hon. Judge R. David, Q.C.; A. A. Dumont; S. R. Eshelby, M.B.E.; R. D. Fairn; B. Glen; Mrs. M. Innes; E. Jacoby, M.D.; Mrs. M. C. Jay; G. Jones; Mrs. S. Komrower; Mr. Justice Geoffrey Lane; J. W. Marsh; N. J. de V. Mather; M. A. Partridge, D.M.; Hon. Mrs. L. Price; H. R. Rollin, M.D.; Prof. G. Rose; Mr. Justice Shaw; H. A. Skinner, Q.C.; J. C. S. Thomas; A. F. Wilcox; J. E. H. Williams; A. Worthy, O.B.E.

Secretary, H. L. J. Gonsalves... £2,775 to £3,400

PATENT OFFICE
(and Industrial Property and Copyright Department,
Department of Trade and Industry)
25 Southampton Buildings, W.C.2
[01-405-8721]
Sale Branch: Orpington, Kent

The duties of the Department consist in the administration of the Patent Acts, the Registered Designs Act and the Trade Marks Act and in dealing with questions relating to the Copyright Acts. The Department also provides information service about patent specifications published during the last 50 years. In 1970 the Office sealed 40,004 patents and registered 5,135 designs and 9,372 trade marks.

Comptroller-General, E. Armitage........£7,325
Assistant Comptrollers, J. Field............£6,345
    W. Wallace, C.M.G.; J. D. Fergusson....£6,145
Superintending Examiners, J. E. Mirams; K. M. Smith; H. S. Walton; D. G. Gay; H. W. Brace; N. W. P. Wallace; R. E. Branton; R. Bowen; A. L. Pheasey; F. C. Strachan.........£5,915
Principal Examiners, P. J. Hutchings; R. C. Hocking; C. L. Smith, O.B.E.; M. R. G. de Bray; J. Rowbotham; W. H. Blair; J. R. Osborn; W. E. Tomkin; K. H. Aldcroft; J. W. Johns; R. W. Haward; O. O. Thorp; J. H. Callow; E. A. McMillan; A. E. Bishop; W. J. Cluff; W. A. Burnett; R. E. Dalley; C. W. Smith; J. A. Watkinson; T. H. Mobbs; E. W. E. Butcher; G. E. Craven; G. A. C. Ashcroft; E. C. Tee; C. Littler; M. D. Moore; K. F. Sloman; H. F. Viney; James Harrison; A. H. W. Kennard; A. G. Edwards; D. C. Snow; J. C. Keeping; E. C. Goodanew; J. R. Mends; W. Anderton; D. J. H. Day; I. J. G. Davis; D. S. G. Collins; D. A. Cowlett; J. G. Clark; B. P. Scanlan; H. C. Bailey; G. O. Byfleet; A. K. Jones; J. K. Signournay; L. F. Oliver; A. F. C. Miller; D. Muir; R. E. Bridges; C. W. Hackett; F. J. Kearley; F. E. Wastell; C. G. Harrison; V. S. Dodd; A. G. Lilleker; N. A. Robertson; D. C. L. Blake; D. L. T. Cadman; D. F. Carter; G. E. K. Askew; R. H. R. Barber; L. L. Bow; N. B. Dean; K. P. Jessop......£4,910 to £5,365
Assistant Registrar, Trade Marks, R. L. Moorby
    £5,140 to £5,765
Senior Principals, J. W. Bennetto; Miss B. Belson, M.B.E...............£4,170 to £4,680
Senior Examiner, Information Retrieval Services, A. McDowell...............£2,926 to £4,513

Manchester Office
Baskerville House, Browncross Street, Salford
[061-832-9571]
Keeper, W. E. Edwards, M.B.E....£2,529 to £3,099

PAYMASTER GENERAL
Department of Education and Science,
38 Belgrave Square, S.W.1
[01-235-4801]
Paymaster General, THE VISCOUNT ECCLES, P.C., K.C.V.O...............£7,625
Private Secretary, Mrs. C. M. Chattaway.

Paymaster General's Office
Russell Way, Crawley, Sussex
[0293-27833]

The Paymaster General's Office was formed by the consolidation in 1835 of various separate pay departments then existing. some of which dated back at least to the Restoration of 1660. Its function is that of paying agent for Government Departments, other than the Revenue Departments. Most of its payments are made through banks, to whose accounts the necessary transfers are made at the Bank of England. The payment of many types of public service pensions is an important feature of its work. The expenses of the office were estimated at £1,372,000 for 1971–72.

Assistant Paymaster General, F. J. Clay, O.B.E.
    £5,000 to £6,300
Dep. Asst. Paymaster Gen., D. M. Wheble
    £4,600 to £5,200
Principals, N. C. Norfolk, I.S.O.; F. T. Simmons; E. F. Webster, M.B.E...........£3,250 to £4,400
Senior Executive Officers, L. A. Andrews; Miss H. M. Bottrill, M.B.E.; D. J. P. Dutton; R. A. Heavens, M.B.E.; Miss K. M. Kennerell; A. J. Kennett; A. Lawrence; H. C. Leng; B. J. McCarthy; I. J. Pells; Miss M. Pollard; H. T. Reading; G. F. Tidy; G. T. Wheway
    £2,775 to £3,400

POLITICAL HONOURS SCRUTINY COMMITTEE
Civil Service Department, Whitehall, S.W.1
[01-839-7733]
Chairman, The Lord Crathorne, P.C., T.D.
Members, The Lord Rea, P.C., O.B.E.; The Baroness Summerskill. P.C., C.H.
Secretary, P. S. Milner-Barry, C.B., O.B.E.

OFFICE OF POPULATION CENSUSES AND SURVEYS
Somerset House, W.C.2
[01-836-2407]
Hours of public access, Mon.–Fri., 9.30 a.m.– 4.30 p.m. Saturday, 9.30 a.m.–12.30 p.m.
Atlantic House, Holborn Viaduct, E.C.1
[01-583-8931]
Registrar General, M. Reed, C.B...........£7,975
Deputy Director, P. Redfern...............£6,925
Assistant Secretaries, T. E. H. Hodgson, C.B. (*Establishment Officer*); F. A. Rooke-Matthews
    £5,000 to £6,300
Chief Statisticians, A. M. Adelstein (*Medical*), £6,120; H. J. M. Jones (*Census*); Miss J. H. Thompson (*Population*)......£5,000 to £6,300
Head of Social Survey Division, C. G. Thomas
    £5,000 to £6,300
Adviser on Survey Research, L. Moss
    £5,300 to £6,600
Statisticians (*Medical*), P. M. Lambert; Mrs. J. A. C. Weatherall; W. A. Wilson...£3,552 to £4,875
Chief Social Survey Officers, P. C. Gray; W. F. F. Kemsley; Miss R. Morton-Williams
    £4,600 to £5,200
Statisticians (*Census*), N. H. W. Davis; C. A. Myers; D. Newman...............£3,250 to £4,400
Statisticians (*Population*), O. Adegboyega; J. Craig; D. L. Pearce; D. Ramprakash £3,250 to £4,400
Senior Principal, D. J. Smale......£4,600 to £5,200
Principals, G. F. P. Boston; T. E. Broughton; A. A. Cushion; L. M. Feery; Miss A. B. Graham; V. M. Harris; I. Hutchinson; C. F. James; J. R. Jeffrey...............£3,250 to £4,400
Principal Social Survey Officers, Miss J. A. Atkinson; R. M. Blunden; Miss A. I. Harris; Mrs. E. A. Hunt; D. F. O. Stuart........£3,250 to £4,400
Senior Social Survey Officers, R. Barnes; Mrs. M. R. Bone; M. R. Bradley; Miss J. A. Higgins; S. R. Parker; Mrs. I. Rauta; R. K. Thomas; Miss J. E. Todd; D. W. Walker...£2,775 to £3,400
Senior Executive Officers, N. W. Brown; R. J. Deacon; G. A. Fielden; R. K. Freeman; A. L. Gay; E. Graver; I. M. Golds; R. P. Hackett, M.B.E.; F. J. Harvey; K. R. Hedderly; J. P.

Hisley; E. A. Hunter; J. J. Huttly; F. G. Johnson;
E. T. Jones; J. F. Kempf; Miss R. M. Loy;
J. A. McNiven, M.B.E.; M. E. M. Mumford;
M. L. Pennington; T. A. Russell; R. Schueller;
E. E. Simpson; D. F. Stobart; S. C. Stracey;
Miss M. M. Turvey; W. Williams

£2,775 to £3,400

PORT OF LONDON AUTHORITY
Head Office, Trinity Square, E.C.3
[01-481-2000]

The Port of London Act, 1968, consolidated and brought up to date the Port of London legislation.

Under the Harbour Revision Order, 1967, the Board was reduced to not fewer than 15 and not more than 16 members as from October 1, 1967. The members are appointed by the Secretary of State for the Environment after consultation with interested organizations as follows: National Ports Council (2 members). The Chamber of Shipping of the United Kingdom and the London General Shipowners' Society (3). The London Chamber of Commerce and the British Shippers' Council (3). The London Wharfingers' Association (1). The Association of Master Lightermen and Barge Owners in London (1). The Greater London Council (1). The Corporation of the City of London (1). The Corporation of Trinity House (1). Persons representative of organized labour (2). The sixteenth member is the Director-General who is co-opted by the Board.

The working of the Port for the year ended Dec. 31, 1970, showed a deficit of £1,807,000.
Chairman, The Lord Aldington, P.C., K.C.M.G., C.B.E., D.S.O., T.D.
Vice-Chairman, Sir Andrew Crichton.

Board of Management
Director-General, J. Lunch, V.R.D.
Assistant Directors-General, W. Bowey; N. N. B. Ordman.
Solicitor, I. Hughes.
Director of Personnel, P. G. Hutchon.
Director of Engineering, J. F. Stanbury.
Director of Upper Docks, J. H. Gabony.
Director of Tilbury Docks, R. H. Butler.
Financial Controller, J. D. Presland.

THE POST OFFICE
23, Howland Street, W.1
[01-631-2345]

By the Post Office Act, 1969, the Post Office became a public corporation on October 1, 1969 and ceased to be a Government department.
Chairman, A.W. C. Ryland, C.B............£20,000
Deputy Chairman, Whitney Straight, C.B.E., M.C., D.F.C.......................*(part-time)* £8,000
Members:—
  Managing Director, Telecommunications, E. Fennessy, C.B.E.
  Managing Director, Posts, ~~Brig. K. S. Holmes, C.B.,~~ *R. CURRALL from 1/8*
  C.B.E.
  Member for Technology, Prof. J. H. H. Merriman, C.B., O.B.E.
  Member for Industrial Relations, Sir Richard Hayward, C.B.E.
  Member for Data Processing, F. J. M. Laver, C.B.E.
  Member for Giro, G. H. Vieler.
  Member for Finance and Corporate Planning, ~~A. S. Ashton.~~ *A. G. HERRON 19/8/71*
Salary range for Members...... £10,000 to £12,500

MINISTRY OF POSTS AND TELE-COMMUNICATIONS
Waterloo Bridge House, Waterloo Road, S.E.1
[01-928-7878]

Minister of Posts and Telecommunications, THE RT. HON. ~~CHRISTOPHER JOHN CHATAWAY, M.P.~~ *Sir John Eden* X £8,500
Private Secretary, Miss J. M. Goose.
Assistant Private Secretary, J. Ellis.
Parliamentary Private Secretary, T. J. King, M.P.
Parliamentary Clerk, Miss M. E. Martin.

Deputy Secretary, F. Wood, C.B........£9,000 *SIR KBE 6/72*
Under Secretaries, H. A. Daniels *(Administration and Radio Dept.)*; B. Gottlieb, C.B. *(Posts and Telecommunications Dept.)*; D. G. C. Lawrence, O.B.E. *(Broadcasting Dept.)*............*each* £6,750
Assistant Secretaries, D. E. Baptiste; D. M. Elliott; Miss S. P. M. Fisher; N. M. Johnson; J. L. Judd; C. E. Lovell; A. G. Manzie; T. U. Meyer

£5,000 to £6,300
Principals, A. D. Carter; R. L. Collins; A. Fortnam; P. W. E. Fryer; Mrs. J. M. Goodman; H. C. Greenwood; A. R. Marsh; K. H. Maunder; A. A. Mead; Miss S. R. Muir; P. Neale; J. M. Norman; E. W. Pearcey; R. J. Roscoe; I. H. Slee; R. W. Story, D.F.C.; Mrs. M. A. G. Veal; J. Woods; N. M. K. Worman £3,250 to £4,400
Director of Radio Technology, C. F. Sowton, O.B.E.
£5,640
Superintending Engineer, T. Kilvington
£4,390 to £5,015
Chief Information Officer, P. L. Marshall
£4,600 to £5,200
Senior Information Officer, Miss J. O' M. Ince
£2,775 to £3,400
Senior Grade Engineers, D. B. Balchin; R. A. Dilworth; P. N. Parker, M.B.E.
£3,265 to £3,843

PRIVY COUNCIL OFFICE
Whitehall, S.W.1

Lord President of the Council (and Leader of the House of Commons), RT. HON. WILLIAM STEPHEN IAN WHITELAW, M.C., M.P................£8,500
  Private Secretary, P. L. P. Davies.
  Assistant Private Secretary, Miss F. A. Yonge.
  Parliamentary Private Secretary, W. M. J. Worsley, M.P.
Clerk of the Council, Sir Godfrey Agnew, K.C.V.O.
£6,875
Deputy Clerk of the Council, N. E. Leigh, C.V.O.
£4,515 to £5,765
Senior Clerk, J. K. Dixon, M.B.E.
£2,752 to £3,356

PUBLIC HEALTH LABORATORY SERVICE
24 Park Crescent, W.1
[01-636-2223]

The Service was originally set up in 1939 as an emergency service to augment the existing public health resources of England and Wales in combating outbreaks of infectious diseases such as might arise from enemy action or abnormal conditions in time of war. In 1945 the Government decided to retain the Service on a permanent footing, and statutory authority for doing so was included in the National Health Service Act, 1946, the Minister of Health being empowered to provide a Bacteriological Service in England and Wales for the control of the spread of infectious diseases. The Service was administered by the Medical Research Council, as agents of the Ministry of Health until August 1, 1961, when, under the provision of the Public Health Laboratory Service Act, 1960, a new Public Health Laboratory Service Board was established as a statutory body capable of acting in its own right as agent for the Department of Health and Social Security.
Members of the Board: E. T. C. Spooner, C.M.G., M.D, *(Chairman)*; F. A. Adams, C.B.; R. C. Bryant, C.B.; Prof. A. C. Cunliffe, M.D.; J. B. M. Davies, M.D.; G. D. Duncan A. J. Essex-Cater; Prof. K. Mc-Carthy, M.D.; R. M. Shaw, C.B.; Prof. R. A. Shooter, M.D.; C. E. G. Smith, C.B., M.D.; C. C. Stevens, O.B.E.; J. F. Warin, O.B.E., M.D.; G. I. Watson, O.B.E., M.D.; Prof. P. Wildy, F.R.S.E.
Director, Sir James Howie, M.D.
Deputy Director, J. C. Kelsey, M.D.
Secretary, J. D. Whittaker, M.B.E.

CENTRAL PUBLIC HEALTH LABORATORY,
LONDON, N.W.9
Director, J. C. Kelsey, M.D.

X Special Adviser
ROBIN HUTTON 7/72

REFERENCE LABORATORIES
(With names of Directors)

Cross-Infection Reference (incorporating Streptococcus and Staphylococcus Reference) M. T. Parker. M.D.
Disinfection Reference, J. C. Kelsey, M.D.
Dysentery Reference, Vacant
Enteric Reference, E. S. Anderson, M.D., F.R.S.
Leptospirosis Reference (London School of Hygiene and Tropical Medicine), L. H. Turner, M.B.E., M.D.
Mycological Reference (London School of Hygiene and Tropical Medicine (vacant).
Mycoplasm Reference, B. E. Andrews.
Salmonella Reference, B. Rowe
Tuberculosis Reference, University Hospital of Wales, Cardiff.   J. Marks, M.D.
Venereal Diseases Reference, London Hospital, E.1. A. E. Wilkinson *(part-time).*
Virus Reference, Mrs. M. S. Pereira

SPECIAL LABORATORIES
(With name of Director)

Computer Trials, S. P. Lapage.
Epidemiology Research Laboratory, T. M. Pollock.
Epidemiology Research Unit, Cirencester, R. E. Hope-Simpson, O.B.E. *(part-time).*
Food Hygiene, Miss B. C. Hobbs, D.Sc.
National Collection of Type Cultures, S. P. Lapage.
Standards Laboratory for Serological Reagents, Mrs. C. M. P. Bradstreet.

CONSTITUENT PUBLIC HEALTH LABORATORIES
(With name of Director)

Bath, P. G. Mann, M.D.; *Bedford,* W. F. Lane; *Birmingham,* J. G. P. Hutchinson, M.D.; *Bradford,* H. G. M. Smith, Ph.D.; *Brighton,* J. E. Jameson; *Bristol,* H. R. Cayton; *Cambridge,* G. R. E. Naylor, M.D.; *Cardiff,* C. H. L. Howells, M.D. *Carlisle,* D. G. Davies, M.D.; *Carmarthen,* H. D. S. Morgan; *Chelmsford,* R. Pilsworth, M.D.; *Chester,* Miss P. M. Poole, M.D.; *Conway,* A. J. Kingsley Smith; *Coventry,* J. E. M. Whitehead; *Derby,* B. W. Barton; *Dorchester,* G. H. Tee, Ph.D.; *Epsom,* D. R. Gamble; *Exeter,* B. Moore, M.D.; *Gloucester,* A. E. Wright, T.D., M.D.; *Guildford,* Miss J. M. Davies, M.D.; *Hereford,* D. R. Christie; *Hull,* J. H. McCoy; *Ipswich,* P. K. Fraser, M.D.; *Leeds,* G. B. Ludlam, M.D.; *Leicester,* N. S. Mair; *Lincoln,* (vacant); *Liverpool,* G. C. Turner, M.D.; *London,* C. E. D. Taylor, M.D. (Central Middlesex Hospital); D. G. Fleck, M.D. (St. George's Hospital, Tooting Grove); B. T. Thom (Whipps Cross Hospital); *Luton,* A. T. Willis, M.D.; *Maidstone,* A. L. Furniss, M.D.; *Manchester,* J. O'H. Tobin; *Newcastle,* J. H. Hale, O.B.E., M.D.; *Newport (Mon.),* R. D. Gray, M.D.; *Northallerton,* (vacant); *Northampton,* L. Hoyle; *Norwich,* Miss L. M. Dowsett, M.D.; *Nottingham,* E. R. Mitchell; *Oxford* (vacant); *Peterborough,* E. J. G. Glencross; *Plymouth,* P. D. Meers, M.D.; *Poole,* W. L. Hooper *(acting); Portsmouth,* D. J. H. Payne; *Preston,* L. Robertson; *Reading,* J. V. Dadswell; *Salisbury,* P. J. Wormald, M.D.; *Sheffield,* E. H. Gillespie; *Shrewsbury,* A. C. Jones; *Southampton,* J. M. Graham; *Southend,* J. A. Rycroft; *Stafford,* P. Cavanagh, M.D.; *Sunderland,* P. B. Crone, M.D.; *Swansea,* W. Kwantes; *Taunton,* J. V. S. Pether; *Truro,* G. I. Barrow, M.D.; *Wakefield,* L. A. Little; *Watford,* B. R. Eaton; *Winchester,* M. H. Hughes, D.M.; *Wolverhampton,* I. A. Harper *(Hon.); Worcester,* R. J. Henderson, M.D.

PUBLIC RECORD OFFICE
See RECORD OFFICES

PUBLIC TRUSTEE OFFICE
Sardinia Street, Kingsway, W.C.2
[01-405-4300]
This is a Government Office (opened in 1908) by means of which the State acts as executor and trustee under a will, or as trustee under a settlement, and in other capacities of a like nature. The value of the trusts accepted up to March 31, 1971, was £732,000,000.

The facts of any trust, new or old, in which it is desired that the Public Trustee should act may be brought to his notice by letter or by personal interview. The appointment is effected in the same way as a private trustee, or by an Order of the Court. He can act solely or jointly with others.

In the case of a will, all that the testator need say is, "I appoint the Public Trustee executor and trustee of this my Will"; or the appointment may be a joint one with others. Executors who have obtained probate can transfer their duties to him under an Order of the Court. He can also act as administrator with, or without, the will annexed.

Strict secrecy is observed in all matters dealt with in the Department. Accounts in simple form are furnished to the beneficiaries as required. An interview with the Public Trustee or with any of his senior officers can be arranged at any time. A pamphlet giving particulars and details of the fees can be obtained free of cost from the Office of the Public Trustee, Kingsway, W.C.2.

Public Trustee, C. A. J. N. O'Sullivan......£8,475
Assistant Public Trustee, W. Ross Taylor...£6,925
Chief Administrative Officers, H. H. W. Duffy; D. A. Wakeford; R. O. A. Wertheim
£4,730 to £5,815
Acceptance Officer and Officer in Charge of Legality of Investments, B. W. James.....£3,461 to £4,565
Trust Officers, J. G. Allen; R. C. Annis; J. A. Boland; V. J. Burt; A. P. Carlton Smith; J. S. Chapman; K. H. Mackinder; J. Radford; J. C. Rowe; F. Wheatley; S. A. Williams
£3,461 to £4,565
Senior Legal Assistant, S. J. Dunn £3,461 to £4,565
Establishment Officer, L. A. Widden
£4,220 to £4,730
Deputy Establishment Officer, G. Davison
£2,704 to £3,274
Training Officer, E. N. T. Platt..£2,704 to £3,274
Chief Accountant, H. T. Bowden £4,220 to £4,730
Asst. Chief Accountants, P. Habgood; R. R. Smith
£3,433 to £4,048
Accountants, F. A. Boocock; R. A. Cunningham; J. E. Duffy; A. A. Philpott; Miss J. E. Randles
£2,704 to £3,274
Income Tax Officer, M. J. Blyth £2,704 to £3,274
Capital Gains Tax Officer, R. L. Mew
£2,704 to £3,274
Chief Investment Managers, F. R. Lee, O.B.E.; A. C. B. Urwin............£4,220 to £4,730
Senior Investment Manager, F. A. Beecham
£5,433 to £4,048
Investment Managers, I. L. Brydon; A. L. Childs; T. H. Nicholls; K. Stilliard...£3,433 to £4,048
Securities Officer, E. C. Brannon..£2,704 to £3,274
Chief Property Adviser, S. Vidler, O.B.E.
£3,750 to £4,383
Senior Property Advisers, D. E. Fewings; R. Myers
£2,758 to £3,571

PUBLIC WORKS LOAN BOARD
19 Old Jewry, E.C.2
[01-606-6234]
The Board is an independent statutory body, consisting of 12 unpaid Commissioners appointed by the Crown to hold office for 4 years; 3 Commissioners retire each year and may be reappointed.

The functions of the Commissioners, derived chiefly from the Public Works Loans Act, 1875, and the National Loans Act, 1968, are to consider applications for loans by Local Authorities and other prescribed bodies, and, when loans are approved, to collect the repayments.

Funds for loans are authorised from time to time by Parliament and are drawn from the National Loans Fund. Rates of interest on the Board's loans and fees to cover management expenses are fixed by the Treasury.

During the year ended March 31, 1971, estimated gross issues from the National Loans Fund for advance by the Public Works Loan Board amounted to £855,000,000.

Chairman, J. Binns, C.B.E................*unpaid*
Deputy Chairman, Sir Bernard Waley-Cohen, Bt.
....*unpaid*

Other Commissioners, E. Geddes; J. E. A. R.
Guinness; F. Haywood, C.B.E.; H. F. Jones;
A. W. Medd; T. N. Ritchie, T.D.; W. A. Shail;
A. G. Tritton; R. W. Wallis; The Lord Ward-
ington................................*unpaid*
Secretary, I. de L. Radice, C.B. (*Secretary to National
Debt Commissioners—q.v.*).
Asst. Secretary and Establishment Officer, H. W.
Darvill...................£4,045 to £4,555
Senior Executive Officers, E. D. Cronin; P. A. Good-
win.....................£2,529 to £3,099

RACE RELATIONS BOARD
5 Lower Belgrave Street, S.W.1.
[01-730-6291]

Chairman, Sir Geoffrey Wilson, K.C.B., C.M.G.
£8,500
Members, L. T. Blakeman, C.B.E.; M. R. Malik;
Miss A. Patrick; T. S. Roberts; Mota Singh;
Miss E. Steel; Mrs. L. Townsend; Sir Roy
Wilson, Q.C........................£1,000
Chief Officer, J. G. Lyttle.......£5,175 to £6,475
Chief Conciliation Officer, T. Connelly
£4,775 to £5,375
Principal Conciliation Officers, P. Cowling; C. H.
Fudge; P. W. Philpott.......£3,795 to £4,575

RECORD OFFICES, ETC.
THE PUBLIC RECORD OFFICE
Chancery Lane, W.C.2
[01-405-0741]

National Records since the Norman Conquest
brought together from Courts of Law and Government Departments. Search rooms open daily from
9.30 to 5; Saturdays, 9.30 to 1. The Museum (open
Monday to Friday, 1 to 4 p.m., and to organized
parties at other times by arrangement) contains
Domesday Book (2 vols.), made by order of William
the Conqueror in 1085, and *Domesday Chest;
the Gunpowder Plot* papers (1605); bull of Pope
Clement VIII, confirming Henry VIII as *Fidei
Defensor* (1524); the Log Book of H.M.S. *Victory*
at Trafalgar (1805); and many other documents of
national interest.

Keeper of Public Records, J. R. Ede.........£6,925
Deputy Keeper, N. J. Williams..£4,565 to £5,190
Records Administration Officer, A. W. Mabbs
£4,565 to £5,190
Establishment Officer, F. T. Williams, D.F.M.
£3,433 to £4,048
Principal Assistant Keepers, Miss P. M. Barnes;
L. Bell; E. W. Denham; Miss D. H. Gifford;
R. F. Hunnisett; M. Roper; E. K. Timings
£3,860 to £4,565
Assistant Keepers, First Class, C. D. Chalmers;
J. H. Collingridge, C.B.E.; N. E. Evans; Mrs.
J. M. Hoare; A. A. H. Knightbridge; C. A. F.
Meekings; R. F. Monger, M.B.E.; P. A. Penfold;
J. L. Walford...............£2,368 to £3,826
Inspecting Officers, R. L. Anslow; J. D. Cantwell;
J. A. Gavin; A. J. W. McDonald; N. D. Robert-
son; J. G. Wickham.........£2,704 to £3,274

ADVISORY COUNCIL ON PUBLIC
RECORDS
Public Record Office, Chancery Lane, W.C.2
Created by the Public Records Act, 1958, to advise
the Lord Chancellor, as minister responsible for
public records, on matters concerning public records
in general and, in particular, on those aspects of the
work of the Public Record Office which affect
members of the public who make use of its facilities.
Chairman, The Master of the Rolls.
Members, Sir Roy Allen, C.B.E., F.B.A.; The Rt. Hon.
Lord Justice Buckley, M.B.E.; Alan Bullock,
F.B.A.; Prof. Sir Herbert Butterfield, F.B.A.;
The Lord Caccia, G.C.M.G., G.C.V.O.; Prof. A. G.
Dickens, F.B.A.; P. C. Goodhart, M.P.; Prof.
P. N. S. Mansergh, O.B.E.; D. L. Marquand,

M.P.; Dame Mary Smieton, D.B.E.; G. D. Squibb
Q.C.; Sir John Summerson, C.B.E., F.B.A.
Secretary, N. G. C. Cox.

HOUSE OF LORDS RECORD OFFICE
House of Lords, S.W.1
[01-930-6240]

Until 1497 the records of Parliament were
normally transmitted at the end of a session to
Chancery, and are now therefore preserved in the
Public Record Office. Since 1497, however, the
records of Parliament have been kept within the
Palace of Westminster. They are in the custody
of the Clerk of the Parliaments, who in 1946
established a record department to supervise their
preservation and their production to students.
The Search Room of this office is open to the
public throughout the year, Mondays to Fridays
inclusive, from 10 to 5. The records preserved
number some 2,000,000 documents, and include
Acts of Parliament from 1497, Journals of the House
of Lords from 1510, Minutes and Committee proceedings from 1610, and Papers laid before Parliament, from 1531. Amongst the records are the
Petition of Right, the Death Warrant of Charles I,
the Declaration of Breda and the Bill of Rights.
The House of Lords Record Office also has charge
of the Journals of the House of Commons (from
1547), and other surviving records of the Commons
(from 1572), which include plans and annexed
documents relating to Private Bill legislation from
1818. The records of both Houses are preserved
in the Victoria Tower at the Houses of Parliament
Clerk of the Records, M. F. Bond, O.B.E., F.S.A.
£4,170 to £5,325
Assistant Clerks of the Records, H. S. Cobb, F.S.A.;
D. J. Johnson................£2,318 to £3,776

ROYAL COMMISSION ON
HISTORICAL MANUSCRIPTS
Quality House, Quality Court, Chancery Lane,
W.C.2
[01-242-2981]

National Register of Archives, [01-242-3205]
The Historical Manuscripts Commission was
first appointed by Royal Warrant in 1869, and was
empowered to make enquiry into the place of
deposit of collections of manuscripts and papers of
historical interest and with the consent of the
owners to publish their contents. The Commission
was reconstituted by Royal Warrant in 1959, with
wider terms of reference, including the preservation
of records and assistance to other bodies working in
the same field. The Master of the Rolls, who is the
Chairman of the Commission, now exercises
through the Commission his responsibility under
the Law of Property (Amendment) Act 1924, and
the Tithe Act, 1936, for manorial and tithe documents. The Commission has published over 200
volumes of printed reports upon manuscripts of
historical import, and under its authority is compiled
the *National Register of Archives,* which now contains over 15,000 typed reports upon privately-
owned records, with extensive indexes, and may be
consulted by historical researchers. At present a
grant-in-aid is made through the Commission to
the *Records Preservation Section* of the British
Records Association. The Commission undertakes
to advise owners upon the preservation and use of
their manuscripts and records.
Chairman, The Master of the Rolls.
Commissioners, The Marquess of Salisbury, K.G.,
P.C.; Prof. E. F. Jacob, D.Phil., F.B.A., F.S.A.; Prof.
Sir J. G. Edwards, D.Litt., F.B.A.; Prof. G. R.
Potter, Ph.D., F.S.A.; Dame Veronica Wedgwood,
O.M., D.B.E., Ll.D.; Sir David L. Evans, O.B.E.,
D.Litt.; Sir James Fergusson of Kilkerran, Bt.,
Ll.D.; The Very Rev. S. J. A. Evans, F.S.A.; Sir
John Summerson, C.B.E., F.B.A., F.S.A.; Sir Edgar
Stephens, C.B.E., F.S.A.; Sir Robert Somerville,
K.C.V.O., F.S.A.; Prof. J. C. Beckett; The Lord
Kenyon, F.S.A.; The Lord Fletcher, P.C. Ll.D.,
F.S.A.; Prof. A. Goodwin; The Hon. Nicholas
Ridley, M.P.

Secretary, R. H. Ellis, F.S.A.
Assistant Secretary, H. M. G. Baillie, M.B.E., F.S.A.
Registrar, *National Register of Archives*, Miss F. Ranger.

SCOTTISH RECORD OFFICE

H.M. General Register House, Edinburgh 1
[031-556-6585]

The Scottish Record Office has a continuous history from the 13th century. Its present home, the General Register House, was founded in 1774 and built to designs by Robert Adam, later modified by Robert Reid. Here are preserved, in accordance with the Treaty of Union, the older public records of Scotland and many collections of local and church records and family muniments. Search Rooms open daily from 9 to 4.45; Saturdays, 9 to 12.30 (Historical Search Room only). Certain groups of records, mainly the more modern records of courts and government departments and the plans collection, are preserved in the Scottish Record Office's auxiliary repository at the West Register House in Charlotte Square—the former St. George's Church which was designed by Robert Reid. The West Register House Search Room opens daily from 9 to 4.45 (Mondays to Fridays). Permanent and special exhibitions of documents are mounted in the Museum at the West Register House, which is open to the public on weekdays during Search Room hours.
Keeper of the Records of Scotland, J. Imrie
£5,015 to £5,640
Curator of Historical Records (Deputy Keeper), A. Anderson, O.B.E......... £3685, to £4,390

DEPARTMENT OF THE REGISTERS OF SCOTLAND

Register House, Edinburgh
[031-556-2561]

The Registers of Scotland consist of:—
(1) General Register of Sasines; (2) Register of Deeds in the Books of Council and Session; (3) Register of Protests; (4) Register of English and Irish Judgments; (5) Register of Service of Heirs; (6) Register of the Great Seal; (7) Register of the Quarter Seal; (8) Register of the Prince's Seal; (9) Register of Crown Grants; (10) Register of Sheriffs' Commissions; (11) Register of the Cachet Seal; (12) Register of Inhibitions and Adjudications; (13) Register of Entails; (14) Register of Hornings.

The largest of these is the General Register of Sasines, which forms the chief security in Scotland of the rights of land and other heritable (or real) property.
Keeper of the Registers of Scotland, G. Black, O.B.E.
£5,015 to £5,640
Deputy Keeper, W. P. Armit.... £4,045 to £4,555
Assistant Keepers, D. R. Peatie; J. D. Robertson; J. F. Stewart; D. Williamson. £3,258 to £3,873
Accountant, J. Carmichael...... £2,771 to £3,341
Senior Examiners, W. A. J. Cunningham; A. Farquharson; A. R. Fullerton; J. Galloway; J. D. Morton; W. S. Morwood; W. S. Penman; D. Sharp; J. Spence; J. Thomson
£2,528 to £3,099

CORPORATION OF LONDON RECORDS OFFICE

Guildhall, E.C.2
[01-606-3030]

Contains the municipal archives of the City of London which are regarded as the most complete collection of ancient municipal records in existence. Includes charters of William the Conqueror, Henry II, and later Kings and Queens to 1957; ancient custumals: Liber Horn, Dunthorne, Custumarum, Ordinacionum, Memorandorum and Albus, Liber de Antiquis Legibus, and collections of Statutes; continuous series of judicial rolls and books from 1252 and Council minutes from 1275; records of the Old Bailey and Guildhall Sessions from 1603, and financial records from

the 16th century, together with the records of London Bridge from the 12th century and numerous subsidiary series and miscellanea of historical interest. A Guide was published in 1951. Readers' Room open Monday to Friday, 9.30 A.M. to 5 P.M.; Saturday, by appointment only.
Keeper of the City Records, The Town Clerk.
Deputy Keeper, Miss B. R. Masters.
Assistant Keeper, J. R. Sewell.

OFFICE OF THE REGISTRAR OF RESTRICTIVE TRADING AGREEMENTS

Chancery House, 53 Chancery Lane, W.C.2
[01-242-2858]
Registrar, Sir Rupert Sich, C.B............ £9,000
Principal Assistant Registrar, P. Harris..... £6,750

Restrictive Trade Practices Acts, 1956 and 1968
Registration Division
Assistant Registrar, W. A. N. Alstead
£4,555 to £5,640
Senior Legal Assistants, M. N. Ben-Levi, M.C.; Lt.-Col. M. J. D. Drummond; P. A. Featherstone-Witty..................... £3,286 to £4,390
Legal Assistants, A. F. Lobo; Miss M. C. Robertson
£1,946 to £3,048

Proceedings Division
Assistant Registrar, E. G. Marriott
£5,000 to £6,300
Principal, Mrs. R. M. J. Esdale.. £3,250 to £4,400
Senior Executive Officers, V. A. Frost; Miss H. M. Sparks; L. F. Tivey......... £2,775 to £3,400

Services Branch
Establishment Officer (Senior Executive Officer), R. J. Heasman.................. £2,775 to £3,400

Scotland
9 Hope Street, Edinburgh, 2
[031-225-3185]
Head of the Scottish Section (Senior Executive Officer)
A. Purves .... £2,775 to £3,400

Northern Ireland
64 Chichester Street, Belfast 1.

THE CONVENTION OF THE ROYAL BURGHS OF SCOTLAND

Agents' Chambers, 51 Castle Street, Edinburgh 2.
Instituted about 1150, and extended in 1405 and 1487; Annual General Convention meets in Edinburgh; Committees meet in Edinburgh City Chambers.—Preses, The Lord Provost of Edinburgh; Chaplain, The Very Rev. A. N. Davidson, M.A.; Standing Counsel, I. MacDonald, M.C., Q.C.; Engineer, W. P. Haldane, M.B.E.; Convention Officer, W. R. H. Thomson, B.E.M. (City Chambers, Edinburgh); Parly. Agents, Beveridge & Co.; Agent, Clerk, and Treasurer, J. Gibson Kerr, C.B.E., W.S., F.R.S.E., 51 Castle Street, Edinburgh 2.

ROYAL COMMISSION FOR THE EXHIBITION OF 1851

1 Lowther Gardens, Exhibition Road, S.W.7
[01-589-3665]
Incorporated by Supplemental Charter as a permanent Commission after winding up the affairs of the Great Exhibition of 1851. It has for its object the promotion of scientific and artistic education by means of funds derived from its Kensington Estate, purchased with the surplus left over from the Great Exhibition.
President, H.R.H. The Duke of Edinburgh, K.G., P.C., K.T., O.M., G.B.E.
Chairman, Board of Management, Marshal of the Royal Air Force, Sir Charles Elworthy, G.C.B., C.B.E., D.S.O., M.V.O., D.F.C., A.F.C.
Secretary to Commissioners, C. A. H. James.

SCIENCE RESEARCH COUNCIL
State House, High Holborn, W.C.1
[01-242-1262]

Chairman, Prof. Sir Brian Flowers, F.R.S.
Members of the Council, A. H. Chilver, Ph.D., D.Sc.;
D. S. Davies, D.Phil.; E. Eastwood, C.B.E., Ph.D.,
F.R.S.; Prof. H. Ford, F.R.S.; Prof. J. C. Gunn,
F.R.S.E; Prof. F. Hoyle, F.R.S.; Prof. H. L. Korn-
berg, F.R.S.; Prof. P. T. Mathews, F.R.S.; J. W.
Menter, Ph.D., Sc.D., F.R.S.; Prof. E. W. J.
Mitchell; D. L. Nicholson; Prof. Sir Ronald
Nyholm, D.Sc., Ph.D., F.R.S.; E. J. Richards, O.B.E.,
D.Sc.; Prof. P. A. Sheppard, C.B.E., F.R.S.; Prof.
M. M. Swann, F.R.S.
Secretary, W. L. Francis, C.B.E., Ph.D.

SCOTTISH OFFICE
Dover House, Whitehall, S.W.1
[01-930-6151]

Secretary of State for Scotland, THE RT. HON.
GORDON THOMAS CALTHROP CAMPBELL, M.C.,
M.P................................£8,500
Private Secretary, H. Robertson, M.B.E. A.W. Russell
Assistant Private Secretary, G. A. D. Philip.
Parliamentary Private Secretary, J. Bruce-Gardyne,
M.P.
Ministry of State, THE BARONESS TWEEDSMUIR OF
BELHELVIE..........................£5,625
Private Secretary, H. W. Bradford.
Parliamentary Under-Secretaries of State, The
Hon. A. L. Buchanan-Smith, M.P. (*Home Affairs
and Agriculture*); The Hon. G. K. H. Younger,
T.D., M.P. (*Development*); H. S. P. Monro, M.P.
(*Health and Education*)................£3,750
Permanent Under-Secretary of State, Sir Douglas
Haddow, K.C.B........................£14,000
Private Secretary, Miss N. C. Telfer, M.V.O.
Assistant Under-Secretary of State, J. S. Scott Whyte
£6,750
Liaison Staff:
Assistant Secretary, T. V. Hughson
£5,000 to £6,300
Principals, G. A. M. McIntosh; Miss W. J.
Strongman; C. T. Hole....£3,250 to £4,400

St. Andrew's House, Edinburgh 1
[031-556-8501]

REGIONAL DEVELOPMENT DIVISION
Assistant Under-Secretary of State, J. H. McGuinness,
C.B................................£6,750
Assistant Secretaries, R. F. Butler; J. B. Fleming;
G. F. Hendry; T. L. Lister....£5,000 to £6,300
Principals, D. H. Collier; D. Connelly; I. R.
Duncan, O.B.E.; D. J. Essery; L. Jobson; K. J.
MacKenzie; G. S. Murray....£3,250 to £4,400
Senior Executive Officer, W. A. McKenzie
£2,775 to £3,400
Senior Economic Adviser, R. G. L. McCrone, Ph.D.
£5,000 to £6,300
Economic Adviser, P. M. Scola ...£3,250 to £4,400

CENTRAL SERVICES
Establishment Division
Director of Establishments, J. A. Ford, M.C...£6,750
Assistant Secretaries, J. Inglis; I. D. Penman; C. D.
Smith..............................£5,000 to £6,300
Principals, R. Barrie; I. M. L. Batts; D. H. Bayes;
T. Collinson; J. N. Davison; Miss I. W. Inglis;
D. S. MacKenzie; Miss A. Murdison; J. Petti-
grew; J. W. Sinclair; W. A. Smith; D. C.
Thompson; A. Woodburn....£3,250 to £4,400
Senior Executive Officers, J. Blaikie; P. Charles;
T. Cooper; M. A. Duffy; Miss M. B. Farquhar;
H. J. Graham; S. R. Hook; I. F. Hunter; G.
Leadbetter; I. J. MacKenzie; W. R. McKie;
R. P. Macnab; J. G. Milne, M.B.E.; A. New-
bigging; R. Patton; R. C. Sinclair; R. J. T. S.
Walker; C. Wilkinson....£2,775 to £3,400
Librarian, A. G. Brown......£2,775 to £3,400
Computer Service
Broomhouse Drive, Edinburgh 11
[031-443 4040]

Manager (Senior Principal), J. S. Robertson
£4,600 to £5,200
Deputy Manager (Principal), D. Miller
£3,250 to £4,400
Senior Executive Officers, H. J. Boatwright; I. Bowie;
G. E. Brewerton; J. B. Currie; J. Duffy;
F. Ibbotson; R. T. McGeorge; H. Mackay;
A. B. Patton; G. A. Paul; J. S. Wheeler
£2,775 to £3,400
Statistical Services
Chief Statistician, W. J. Fearnley £5,000 to £6,300
Finance
Under Secretary, R. A. Dingwall-Smith....£6,750
Administrative Adviser, J. Macpherson
£5,000 to £6,300
Principal, A. D. F. Findlay......£3,250 to £4,400
Solicitor's Office
(*For the Scottish Department and certain U.K. services,
including H.M. Treasury, in Scotland*).
Solicitor, R. W. Deans..................£7,800
Principal Assistant Solicitor, J. A. Beaton....£6,750
Assistant Solicitors, J. B. Allan; *A. G. Brand, M.B.E.;
D. Cunningham; R. A. Lawrie; A. A. McMillan;
E. S. Robertson; *A. J. F. Tannock, M.C.;
J. E. Taylor; C. J. Workman, T.D.
£5,200 to £6,300
* Seconded to Scottish Law Commission

Scottish Information Office
(*for the Scottish Departments and certain
U.K. services*)
St. Andrew's House, Edinburgh, 1
[031-556-8501]
Director, C. McGregor, M.B.E. ...£5,000 to £6,300

DEPARTMENT OF AGRICULTURE AND FISHERIES FOR SCOTLAND
St. Andrew's House, Edinburgh, 1
[031-556-8501]
Dover House, Whitehall, London, S.W.1
[01-930-6151] 6/72

Secretary, W. G. Pottinger, C.V.O..........£9,000
Fisheries Secretary, E. L. Gillett..........£6,750
Under-Secretaries, W. I. McIndoe; J. I. Smith £6,750
Assistant Secretaries, W. Baird; A. T. Brooke;
J. Cormack; J. S. Gibson; Miss I. F. Haddow;
J. Lawless; D. A. Leitch; H. G. Robertson;
N. J. Steele; S. H. Wright....£5,000 to £6,300
Principals, T. M. Brown; J. Cruickshank; W. Din-
nie; J. W. Dougal; J. A. Downie; D. A. Flett;
J. Glendinning, M.B.E.; B. Gordon; J. R. Gordon;
L. P. Hamilton; J. I. McBeath; L. D. M. Mac-
kenzie; A. J. Monk; G. B. Robinson; Miss J. L.
Ross; A. B. Scott; J. Smith; T. G. Strong;
D. C. Todd; R. M. Williamson
£3,250 to £4,400
Senior Executive Officers, R. W. Alexander; Miss
E. A. Buglass; J. Coltherd; W. G. Dalgleish;
D. J. Davidson; Miss M. I. Davis; J. A. C. Fair-
bairn; P. Gowans; T. E. H. Hartland; T. John-
son; G. G. Lyall; A. I. Macdonald; T. D.
Mackenzie; J. A. M. MacLeod; Miss E. V.
Ramsay; Miss M. F. M. Roy; T. Spence;
A. Walker..................£2,775 to £3,400
Chief Civil Engineer, J. Storry..........£5,620
Chief Agricultural Economist, O. J. Beilby
£5,000 to £6,300
Chief Fatstock Officer, A. Scott...£3,250 to £4,400
Chief Inspector, W. O. Kinghorn..........£6,300
Deputy Chief Inspectors, G. S. Lawrie; J. L. Mac-
Kenzie (*General Duties*); D. C. Collie (*Livestock*)
£5,000 to £5,620
Chief Lands Officer, J. S. Weddell..........£6,300
Divisional Lands Officers, A. H. Boggan; J. White,
M.B.E.....................£5,000 to £5,620
Chief Marketing Officer, A. M. N. Steward
£3,250 to £4,400
Chief Surveyor, A. Malcolm..........£6,300
Deputy Chief Surveyor, J. G. Cullen
£5,000 to £5,620
Technical Development Officer, C. Mackay
£5,830

* H. Robertson being promoted
to Scottish Education Dept.

Royal Botanic Garden
Inverleith Row, Edinburgh 3
[031-552-5532]
Regius Keeper, D. M. Henderson, F.R.S.E.
£5,830 to £6,380
Senior Principal Scientific Officer, B. L. Burtt, F.R.S.E.
£5,000 to £5,620

Agricultural Scientific Services
East Craigs, Corstorphine, Edinburgh, 12.
[031-334-3361]
Director, D. W. Williams, Ph.D.
£5,830 to £6,380
Deputy Director, J. R. Thomson
£5,000 to £5,620
Senior Principal Scientific Officer, J. M. Todd
£5,000 to £5,620

Fisheries Research Services
Marine Laboratory, Victoria Road, Torry,
Aberdeen.
[0224-53281]
Director, B. B. Parrish, F.R.S.E. £6,600
Deputy Director, J. H. Fraser, D.Sc., Ph.D., F.R.S.E.
£5,830 to £6,380
Senior Principal Scientific Officers, B. B. Rae, Ph.D.;
A. Saville; T. H. Simpson, Ph.D., F.R.S.E.; J. H.
Steele, D.Sc., F.R.S.E.; H. J. Thomas, Ph.D., F.R.S.E.
£5,000 to £5,620

Freshwater Fisheries Laboratory,
Faskally, Pitlochry, Perthshire
[Pitlochry: 329]
Senior Principal Scientific Officers, K. A. Pyefinch,
F.R.S.E.; T. A. Stuart, D.Sc., F.R.S.E.
£5,600 to £5,620

Sea Fisheries Inspectorate
Chief Inspector of Sea Fisheries, J. M. Steven, £5,200
Inspector of Salmon Fisheries, S. D. Sedgwick
£3,048 to £3,902
Marine Superintendent, Captain F. C. Chisholm
£4,282 to £4,577

Crofters Commission
9 Ardross Terrace, Inverness
[0463-32711]
Chairman, J. S. Grant, C.B.E. £6,750
Members (part-time), N. A. MacAskill (£3,335);
R. H. W. Bruce, C.B.E.; A. Fraser, Ph.D.; A.
Gillespie, M.B.E.; G. McIver, O.B.E.; J. M.
Macmillan £1,670
Secretary and Solicitor, D. J. MacCuish
£5,000 to £6,300
Assistant Secretary, D. F. Campbell
£3,250 to £4,400
Chief Technical Officer, A. McArthur
£5,000 to £5,620

Red Deer Commission
Elm Park, Island Bank Road, Inverness
[0463-31751]
Chairman, The Viscount of Arbuthnott, D.S.C.
£2,500
Secretary, J. Dooner .... £2,775 to £3,400

SCOTTISH EDUCATION DEPARTMENT
St. Andrew's House, Edinburgh 1
[031-556-8501]
Dover House, Whitehall,
London, S.W.1
[01-930-6151]
Secretary, Sir Norman Graham, C.B. £9,000
Under-Secretaries, J. M. Fearn; I. M. Robertson,
M.V.O. £6,750
Assistant Secretaries, S. C. Aldridge; Miss P. A. Cox;
G. M. Fair; W. A. M. Good; I. D. Hamilton;
J. Kidd; J. F. McClellan; T. H. McLean; P. C.
Rendle .... £5,000 to £6,300
Principals, B. J. Bennett; A. W. Brodie; N. G.
Campbell; R. J. W. Clark; Miss E. C. G. Craghill;
T. Drummond; A. C. Easson; J. J. Farrell;
I. G. F. Gray; R. R. Hillhouse; J. Leithead; D. G.
McCulloch; Miss M. Maclean; A. J. C. Mitchell;
H. Morison; Miss C. M. Steele; W. A. P.
Weatherston; A. C. Wilson . £3,250 to £4,400
Senior Executive Officers, G. H. J. Bell; W. A. Bruce;

Miss W. S. Duguid; T. B. Haig; J. Loudfoot;
H. M. McGilvray; G. G. McHaffie; R. Naylor;
Miss A. C. C. Smart; M. T. A. Vance; G. H.
Walker; J. P. Wallace; L. C. Watterson; N.
Wood .... £2,775 to £3,400

H.M. Inspectors of Schools
Senior Chief Inspector, J. Bennett, M.B.E. £6,750
Chief Inspectors, A. D. Chirnside; J. P. Forsyth;
J. Shanks, C.B.E.; J. Gilbert, Ph.D.; N. Fullwood;
J. F. McGarrity; W. Mitchell £6,000
Inspectors, R. Allan; W. Anderson; M. T. J.
Axford; W. F. L. Bigwood; Miss C. L. Boyle;
G. J. Brown; J. R. M. M. Brown; T. Brown;
W. C. Brown; E. D. Brunjes; J. Bryce;
J. W. Burdin; J. B. Caird; Miss C. S. Cameron;
Miss G. C. Campbell; L. Clark; A. Cochrane;
G. A. B. Craig; T. Crippin; J. Cumming;
W. Cunningham; A. H. B. Davidson; J. Deans;
D. W. Duncan; A. H. Ferguson; J. A. Ferguson;
W. K. Ferguson; A. W. Finlayson; A. K. Forbes;
Miss M. K. G. Fraser; T. N. Gallacher; A. R.
Gallon; A. Garden; W. A. Gatherer, Ph.D.;
G. P. D. Gordon; D. S. Graham; Miss M. J.
Hay; J. Howgego; J. Inglis; R. D. Jackson; A.
Jamieson; A. W. Jeffrey; R. S. Johnston; E. S.
Kelly; W. F. Kerr, M.B.E.; J. Kiely; I. Lawson;
Miss M. M. Lawson; J. C. Leitch; J. McAlpine;
D. McCalman; S. E. McClelland, Ph.D.; J. F.
MacDonald; G. M. McGavin; Miss E. M. H.
McGill; Miss M. C. McKellar; J. Mackinnon;
H. M. MacLaren; M. Macleod; D. R. McNicoll;
A. A. McPherson; H. L. Martin; D. G. Marwick;
A. Milne; S. Milne, Ph.D.; W. A. Milne;
H. Morris; J. G. Morris; G. C. Morrison;
R. Morrison; Miss W. Morrison; Miss E. R.
Mowat; G. S. Mutch; B. Nickerson, Ph.D.;
W. Nicol; A. Nisbet; J. Nisbet; I. P. Pascoe;
L. Pendleton; D. S. Petrie; Mrs. J. G. Pillans;
Miss A. H. M. Prain; R. B. Prescott; J. Rankin;
J. C. Rankine; J. J. Reid; W. R. Ritchie;
J. Robertson, Ph.D.; J. N. Robertson; Miss
H. J. S. Sandison; M. G. Scott; G. M. Sinclair,
Ph.D.; S. T. S. Skillen; J. A. Sloggie; H. Smith;
H. F. Smith; J. Stark, Ph.D.; E. F. Thompkins;
Miss E. M. W. Thomson; J. H. Thomson;
S. Thornton, Ph.D.; H. Walker; P. D. B. Walker;
G. Wallis; D. M. Whyte; T. F. Williamson;
D. B. Young; R. W. J. Young, Ph.D.
£3,461 to £5,215

Social Work Services Group
York Buildings, Queen Street, Edinburgh
[031-556-2491]
The Social Work Services Group, which is
attached to the Scottish Education Department,
administers the provisions of the Social Work
(Scotland) Act, 1968.
Under-Secretary, J. A. M. Mitchell, C.V.O., M.C.
£6,750
Assistant Secretaries, F. H. Cowley; G. J. Murray;
A. F. Reid .... £5,000 to £6,300
Principals, D. A. Bennet; R. J. Edie; Mrs. E. M. A.
McGregor; K. B. T. Mackenzie; A. M. Mac-
pherson; D. Stevenson ...... £3,250 to £4,400
Senior Executive Officer, Miss J. M. Lawson
£2,775 to £3,400
Chief Adviser on Social Work in Scotland, Miss B.
Jones £6,600
Deputy Chief Adviser on Social Work in Scotland,
Miss M. M. McInnes ...... £5,000 to £6,300
Senior Advisers on Social Work in Scotland, D. Colvin;
Miss B. E. Drake; R. Percival; Miss P. M.
Hammond .... £4,600 to £5,620

SCOTTISH HOME AND HEALTH
DEPARTMENT
St. Andrew's House, Edinburgh 1
[031-556-8501]
Dover House, Whitehall, London,
S.W.1
[01-930-6151]
Secretary, Sir Ronald Johnson, C.B. £9,000
Under-Secretaries, E. U. E. Elliott-Binns; W. K.
Fraser; J. Hogarth £6,750

H. Robertson from Scottish Office
1/72

Assistant Secretaries, D. J. Cowperthwaite; J. E. Fraser; W. Hutchison; W. P. Lawrie; Miss M. K. Macdonald; A. H. M. Mitchell; A. T. F. Ogilvie (*Finance Officer*); G. Robertson; I. L. Sharp; N. E. Sharp; J. Scrimgeour (*Director of Scottish Prison Service*); V. C. Stewart; J. Walker; I. M. Wilson.....................£5,000 to £6,300

Principals, G. P. H. Aitken; G. Aithie; G. F. Belfourd; R. M. Bell; Brig. A. I. Buchanan-Dunlop, C.B.E., D.S.O.; R. D. M. Calder; J. P. Fraser; F. A. Hamilton; T. B. Hamilton; J. J. Haughney; A. W. M. Heggie; F. J. Hope, M.B.E., D.F.C.; J. J. Hunter, D.F.C.; R. J. Inglis; D. Jones; R. W. Macintosh; P. Mackay; Miss M. A. McPherson; Miss L. R. Maddock; W. R. Miller; H. H. Mills; K. W. Moore; G. Murray; D. M. W. Napier; F. H. Orr; G. Paterson; E. Redmond; G. H. Rigg; F. H. Roberts; A. D. Robertson; I. S. Scott; W. J. A. Scott; J. E. Smith; A. M. Stephen; W. A. Strain; Miss B. S. Thomson; J. E. Tinkler; G. R. Wilson £3,250 to £4,400

Senior Executive Officers, R. C. Allan; D. C. Anderson; C. Barbour; J. Borthwick; Miss M. H. B. Brown; J. S. Burnett; D. Clark; J. S. Dick; C. S. Donaldson; G. B. Downie; C. S. W. Forbes; E. E. Hancock; J. M. Haynes; W. W. Howitt; Miss D. Jones; W. Liddle; J. Linn; J. S. C. Little; W. H. McCulloch; A. Macdonald; A. Macdonald; N. S. McIntyre; T. M. McNair; I. A. Macpherson; J. G. Middlemiss; T. A. Murray; R. N. Roberts; D. D. Rose; R. M. Russell; G. Scott; A. Simmen; G. G. Stewart; R. S. Stewart; W. H. Stewart; J. Taylor; A. Walker; R. W. Williamson; Miss M. J. Yeats
£2,775 to £3,700

Counsel to the Secretary of State for Scotland, under Private Legislation Procedure (Scotland) Act, 1936 (2 Parliament Square, Edinburgh), *Counsel* (2 vacancies).

Medical Staff

Chief Medical Officer, J. H. F. Brotherston, M.D., F.R.S.E...................£7,800
Deputy Chief Medical Officer, J. Smith, O.B.E.
£6,750
Principal Medical Officers, W. A. Cramond, O.B.E.; M. A. Heasman; I. M. Macgregor; W. K. Henderson; G. D. Forwell; J. K. Hunter, O.B.E.; Elspeth M. Warwick...................£6,490
Senior Medical Officers, A. Laurie; R. M. Gordon; I. S. Macdonald; J. B. Barr, M.B.E.; G. A. Scott; D. M. Pendreigh; D. W. A. McCreadie; R. A. W. Ratcliff; J. Watson...................£6,300
Medical Officers, J. A. Ward; J. T. Baldwin, O.B.E.; Margaret H. Bell; J. W. Galloway; J. H. Grant; J. L. Tester; D. A. Player; W. T. Thom, O.B.E.; J. D. Donnelly; H. Miller; A. Yarrow; L. F. Howitt; K. T. Gruer; N. McNeil; A. D. McIntyre; A. E. Bell...........£4,031 to £5,490
Regional Medical Officers, D. E. Walker; R. I. T. Dunnachie; J. H. Leckie; J. W. Gibb; F. B. Davidson; J. W. Logan; D. B. N. Morrison; A. F. Nelson; R. C. Nimmo-Smith; A. C. McBlane; I. G. Coun; J. A. Morton; W. M. Reid
£4,031 to £5,490
Chief Dental Officer, J. L. Trainer.....£5,830
Senior Dental Officer, A. Pacitti..........£5,360
Dental Officers, R. A. Morrison; A. B. Potts; A. Boyd; C. G. Chester.....£3,480 to £4,650
Chief Nursing Officer, Dame Muriel Powell, D.B.E.
£4,073 to £4,630

Miscellaneous Appointments

H.M. Chief Inspector of Constabulary for Scotland, St. Andrew's House, Edinburgh 1, D. Gray, O.B.E.
£7,713
H.M. Inspector of Constabulary, W. MacG. Smith, O.B.E...................£7,314
Commandant, Scottish Police College, Col. R. C. Robertson-Macleod, D.S.O., M.C., T.D....£5,153
H.M. Inspector of Fire Services, J. Jackson, O.B.E.
£4,881 to £5,499
Commandant, Scottish Fire Service Training School, J. Hartil...................£2,775 to £3,400

Senior Principal Scientific Officer, Scientific and Technical Services, W. F. Gunn £5,000 to £5,620
Chief Food and Dairy Officer, M. E. M. Anderson
£3,319 to £4,196
Chief Pharmacist, R. Higson.....£3,575 to £4,208
Chief Communications Officer, J. E. Young, O.B.E.
£3 099 to £4,226
Educationist, S. C. Mitchell.....£2,997 to £4,570

Prisons Division
Broomhouse Drive, Edinburgh 11
[031-443-4040]
Director of Scottish Prison Service, J. Scrimgeour
£5,000 to £6,300
Chief Inspector of Scottish Prison Service, J. Oliver
£6,300
Inspector of Scottish Prison Service, J. McIntyre
£5,415

Prison Governors
Aberdeen, D. M. Maciver.....£3,125 to £3,664
Edinburgh, J. H. A. Frisby.....£4,112 to £4,726
Glasgow (Barlinnie), D. Mackenzie, I.S.O....£5,415
Greenock, Lady Martha Bruce, O.B.E., T.D.
£3,125 to £3,664
Perth, R. F. Hendry.............£4,112 to £4,726
Peterhead, A. Angus...................£5,415
Polmont Borstal Institution, C. W. Hills
£4,112 to £4,726

Mental Welfare Commission for Scotland
12 Melville Street, Edinburgh, 3
Commissioners, R. H. McDonald, M.C., Q.C. (*Chairman*), £1,000; Mrs. Joan Wolrige-Gordon; Prof.W.M.Millar,C.B.E.,M.D.; Lt.-Col. R. C. M. Monteith, M.C., T.D.; R. W. Paterson; J. F. A. Gibson; Dr. E. J. C. Hewitt............£241·50
Medical Commissioners, Anne N. M. Brittain; J. M. Loughran...................£6,300
Medical Officers, Elizabeth M. Whiteside; R. M. Young; Iole L'E. K. McLean. £4,031 to £5,490
Secretary, J. S. Dick........£2,529 to £3,099

Regional Hospital Boards
Northern, Reay House, Old Edinburgh Road, Inverness, *Chairman,* Dr. J. A. MacLean. *Secretary,* R. R. W. Stewart.
North-Eastern, 1 Albyn Place, Aberdeen. *Chairman,* W. M. Farquharson-Lang, C.B.E. *Secretary,* A. R. Batchelor.
Eastern, Vernonholme, Riverside Drive, Dundee. *Chairman,* J. Knox. *Secretary,* J. K. Johnston, O.B.E.
South-Eastern, 11 Drumsheugh Gardens, Edinburgh. *Chairman,* Mrs. R. T. Nealon. *Secretary,* W. L. Douglas.
Western, 351 Sauchiehall Street, Glasgow, C.2. *Chairman,* S. Stevenson. *Secretary,* R. D. R. Gardner.

SCOTTISH DEVELOPMENT DEPARTMENT
St. Andrew's House, Edinburgh, 1
[031-556-9501]
Dover House, Whitehall, London, S.W.1
[01-930-8501]
Secretary, A. B. Hume, C.B..................£9,000
Under Secretaries, J. B. Beaumont; R. D. M. Bell, C.B.; T. R. H. Godden; K. Newis, C.B., C.V.O.
£6,750
Assistant Secretaries, A. C. Cowan, C.B.E.; R. D. Cramond; F. Dawson; W. W. Gauld; C. Gilbraith; F. M. M. Gray; J. Keeley; H. F. G. Kelly; J. Kerr; D. G. Mackay; J. M. Ross; J. A. Scott, M.V.O.; J. E. Stark £5,000 to £6,300
Senior Principal, F. B. Drysdale. £4,600 to £5,200
Principals, R. M. Alexander; G. B. Baird; H. R. M. Beattie; J. A. Cowell, O.B.E.; A. J. Crawford; B. J. Fiddes; H. C. Fraser; Mrs. K. S. Gillender; A. Gow; A. Heyworth; K. Mackay; P. McKinlay; H. McNamara; J. B. More; R. Mowat; A. S. Neilson; I. Nicholson; M. H. Orde, O.B.E.; T. Rarity; Miss S. D. Riddell; R. E. S. Robinson; J. Rodger; A. W. Russell; N. J. Shanks; R. E.

Smith; A. M. Thomson; J. M. Thomson;
J. Torrance, I.S.O. . . . . £3,250 to £4,400
Director, Road Safety Advisory Unit, Lt. Col. D.
Birrell. . . . . £3,250 to £4,400
Senior Executive Officers, D. Bannatyne; Miss F. J.
Christie; P. W. Daley; R. Earle; L. J. Fothering-
ham; T. G. Gass; Miss A. M. Hamilton; G.
Hardie; Miss M. E. Hay; J. M. Howieson;
R. M. Laidlaw; G. K. Lambie; G. P. S. Mac-
Arthur; G. P. McConnell; G. L. McLaughlan;
N. S. Macleod; G. Mason; T. J. Muirhead; S. G.
Patterson; Miss M. A. Potter; G. T. Reed;
W. M. Robertson; A. W. Russell; D. Stott;
J. Thompson; B. A. F. Vincent
£2,775 to £3,400

Professional Staff
Chief Engineer, J. W. Shiell. £6,750
Deputy Chief Engineer, S. C. Agnew. £6,300
Assistant Chief Engineer, A. Wotherspoon
£5,000 to £5,620
Senior Engineering Inspectors, J. G. Munro; E. H.
Nicoll £5,535
Chief Architect, B. P. Beckett. £6,750
Deputy Chief Architect, D. I. Black £6,300
Superintending Architects, Miss M. J. Blanco White;
J. H. Fullarton; I. S. Gavin; A. M. Graham;
R. S. Morton; J. N. Pollock . £5,000 to £5,620
Chief Planning Officer, W. D. C. Lyddon . . . £6,750
Deputy Chief Planning Officer, A. S. Hood . . £6,300
Regional Planning Officers, W. Amcotts; H. Irving;
G. A. Lyall; R. G. H. Turnbull
£5,000 to £5,620
Chief Quantity Surveyor, B. E. Drake. £6,300
Deputy Chief Quantity Surveyor, T. Wilson
£5,000 to £5,620
Chief Road Engineer, G. F. Norris. £6,750
Deputy Chief Road Engineer, R. A. H. Allen
£5,492 to £6,300
Assistant Chief Road Engineer, W. Henderson, M.B.E.
£5,492 to £6,300
Superintending Engineers, D. M. Beaton; J. R. A.
Griffith. . . . . £5,000 to £5,620
Chief Chemical Inspector, Dr. E. A. B. Birse, O.B.E.
£5,620
Chief Estate Officer, P. H. Miller £5,000 to £5,620

GENERAL REGISTER OFFICE (Scotland)
New Register House, Edinburgh 2
[031–556–3952]
Registrar General, A. L. Rennie.
£4,390 to £5,640
Deputy Registrar General, R. MacLeod
£4,045 to £4,555
Senior Statistician, H. B. Lawson £4,045 to £4,555
Statistician, J. Travers. . . . . . £2,820 to £3,902
Principals, D. J. Baird; J. Boyd; A. R. Clark;
J. A. Hamilton . . . . £3,258 to £3,873
Senior Executive Officers, W. Anderson; G. F. Baird;
R. A. DeMellow; J. Duncan; A. M. Dunlop;
A. R. Irons; Mrs. J. H. B. Walker
£2,529 to £3,099

**OFFICE OF THE NATIONAL
INSURANCE COMMISSIONER**
6 Grosvenor Gardens, S.W.1
[01–730–9236]

23 Melville Street, Edinburgh 3
[031–225–2201]
7 Park Place, Cardiff
[0222–32623]

The Commissioner is the final Statutory
Authority to decide claims under the Family
Allowances Acts, the National Insurance Acts and
the National Insurance (Industrial Injuries) Acts.
Chief Commissioner, Sir Robert Micklethwait, Q.C.
Commissioners, H. A. Shewan, O.B.E., Q.C.; D. W. E.
Neligan, O.B.E.; D. Reith, Q.C.; H. B. Magnus,
Q.C.; J. S. Watson, M.B.E., Q.C.; R. S. Lazarus,
Q.C.; E. R. Bowen, Q.C.; R. J. A. Temple, C.B.E.
Q.C.; ~~M. STRADDERS, Q.C. 11/971~~
Senior Legal Assistant, Mrs. C. R. Corbett.

Legal Assistants, D. E. Buckley; Mrs. M. V. Steel.
Secretary, D. H. Alexander.

HER MAJESTY'S STATIONERY OFFICE
Atlantic House, Holborn Viaduct, E.C.1
[01–248–9876]
Sovereign House, St. George's Street, Norwich
[0603–22211]
Bookshops in London:—
Retail.—49 High Holborn, W.C.1.
*Wholesale and post orders.—*P.O. Box 569, S.E.1.

H. M. Stationery Office was established in 1786
and is the British Government's central organization for the supply of printing, binding, office
supplies, automatic data processing equipment and
office machinery of all kinds, and published books
and periodicals, for the Public Service at home and
abroad; it also undertakes duplicating, distributing
and computer bureau services for government
departments. The Stationery Office is the pub-
lisher for the government, and has bookshops for
the sale of government publications in London,
Edinburgh, Cardiff, Manchester, Bristol, Birmingham and Belfast; leading booksellers in the larger
towns act as agents; and there are wholesale departments in London, Edinburgh and Belfast from
which booksellers may obtain supplies. It is also
the agent for the sale of publications of the United
Nations and its specialized agencies and for certain
other international organizations. The Controller
of the Stationery Office is under Letters Patent the
Queen's Printer of Acts of Parliament and in him is
vested the *Copyright in all British Government
documents.*

Government publications are of a wide and varied
range and over 6,500 publications are produced
each year. They include the *London Gazette,* which
has been issued since 1665, and *Hansard,* the ver-
batim report of the proceedings in both Houses of
Parliament, available on the morning following the
debate. The Stationery Office has in stock some
90,000 titles and its subscriptions and standing order
lists contain about 220,000 names. The annual
sales total about 30,000,000 copies.

The aggregate net estimate for the department
for 1970–71 was £43,988,000 (an increase of
£5,842,000 on the same estimate for 1969–70).

Generally the department obtains its supplies
from commercial sources by competitive tender.
For printing and binding, however, the Stationery
Office has its own printing works and binderies
which produce about one-third of the total requirement, including telephone directories, pension
allowance books, national savings certificates and
stamps, postal orders, premium bonds, National
Insurance stamps, road fund licences, television and
wireless licences.

The staff employed on April 1, 1970, was 7,716,
including 1,868 in warehouses and 2,809 at printing
works; the total space occupied was 2,470,000
square feet, including 1,250,000 sq. ft. for warehouse
space and 720,000 sq. ft. for the printing works.
Controller, C. H. Baylis, C.B. £9,000
Deputy Controller, W. Donaldson, C.B. £6,750
Assistant Controllers, J. P. Turner, O.B.E.; J. J. Cherns
£6,370
*Head of Production (Printing Works and Reprographic
Divisions),* D. E. Masson, O.B.E.
£5,620 to £6,300
Head of Management Services, D. C. Dashfield, O.B.E.,
M.V.O. . . . . £5,620 to £6,300
Head of Publishing and Distribution, N. G. Thomp-
son, O.B.E. . . . . £5,620 to £6,300
Head of Planning Unit, A. S. Borrie
£5,620 to £6,300
Adviser on Typography, Ruari McLean.

Printing Works Division
Director, J. Brookes, O.B.E. . . . . . £4,600 to £5,200
Deputy Directors, E. J. Deller; J. H. Hynes, O.B.E.
£3,250 to £4,400
Assistant Directors, A. H. Redway; K. J. Baxter;
G. C. Beard; E. H. Scarborough
£2,775 to £3,400

Senior Works Managers, K. A. Allen; R. H. Gowen;
C. J. Errington; F. A. G. Lonon
£3,250 to £4,400
Works Managers, J. W. H. Elvin; E. Warburton
£2,755 to £3,400
Deputy Senior Works Managers, W. D. Bissett;
K. P. Sandford; A. A. Smith; F. J. Beesley;
F. L. Pymm; A. J. B. Baptie; M. Warner; A. S.
Brown; C. T. Goddard...... £2,775 to £3,400
Chief Engineer, R. Miller......... £3,575 to £4,208

Reprographic Division
Director, D. A. Jamieson........ £3,250 to £4,400
Deputy Director, E. G. N. Calver £2,775 to £3,400
Assistant Director, J. W. Brunton £2,775 to £3,400

Technical Development Division
Director, J. McCausland, O.B.E...£4,600 to £5,200
Deputy Director, A. H. Phillips.. £3,250 to £4,400
Assistant Directors, W. J. Scott; E. J. Cletheroe;
N. Frost..................£2,775 to £3,400
Co-ordinator, Reproduction Services Section, A. W.
Martyn..................£3,250 to £4,400
Deputy Co-ordinator, G. J. York £2,775 to £3,400
Head of Laboratory, J. S. Pugh...£3,250 to £4,400
Deputy Heads of Laboratory, W. J. R. Howell;
T. James; J. A. Harris........ £2,775 to £3,400

Printing and Binding Division
Director, G. D. Macaulay....... £4,600 to £5,200
Deputy Directors, A. S. Powis; R. H. Sloane, M.B.E.
£3,250 to £4,400
Assistant Directors, B. Currie; G. J. Hillier; K. E.
Hutchings, B.E.M.; C. E. Whitehouse
£2,775 to £3,400

Industrial Relations Division
Director, G. Lambsdale.................£5,000
Deputy Director, N. M. Turns.... £3,250 to £4,400
Assistant Directors, R. A. Youl; D. D. Hinnigan;
E. B. McKendrick.......... £2,775 to £3,400

Establishments Division
Director, C. W. Blundell, O.B.E.. £4,600 to £5,200
Deputy Directors, R. F. Norris; G. Furn; A. M.
Foote....................£3,250 to £4,400
Assistant Directors, W. S. Porter; F. R. Payne; T. S.
Harris, M.B.E.; R. A. Dunn; F. G. Gibbs; J. R.
Wilson...................£2,775 to £3,400
Chief Welfare Officer, J. L. A. G. Jones
£2,775 to £3,400

Finance Division
Director, R. H. Chisholm....... £4,600 to £5,200
Deputy Directors, P. N. Reynolds; P. W. Bucker-
field....................£3,250 to £4,400
Assistant Directors, A. J. Curtis; E. J. Woods; R. E.
H. Mills; Miss F. V. Page.... £2,775 to £3,400
Chief Accountant, C. G. Wood... £3,250 to £4,400
Chief Examiner, Printers' and Binders' Accounts, S. R.
Hays....................£2,775 to £3,400

Computer Bureau
Director, N. H. Kelly........... £4,600 to £5,200
Deputy Directors, V. H. Morley; D. C. Anderson
£3,250 to £4,400
Assistant Directors, Miss E. A. Beech; W. A. Beard;
P. Jefford; H. J. D. Magee.... £2,775 to £3,400
Managers, Bureau Systems, A. L. T. Skedd; A. C.
Withall; M. Bickers; D. J. Balls
£2,775 to £3,400
Managers, Operations, A. M. MacKillop; J. K.
Mitchelmore..............£2,775 to £3,400

Computer Procurement Division
Director, R. E. Pysden........ £3,775 to £4,600
Deputy Directors, A. W. Symons; H. Wild
£3,250 to £4,400
Assistant Directors, J. Holden; W. F. Papworth;
N. W. J. Seago; F. J. Wilson; R. J. Craig
£2,775 to £3,400

Supplies Division
Director, H. V. Roe, O.B.E. ....£4,600 to £5,200
Deputy Director, B. C. E. Lee....£3,250 to £4,400
Assistant Directors, G. F. C. Clarke; D. N. Roberts;
F. E. Ashman; C. G. Lloyd; E. L. Franklin
£2,775 to £3,400
Manager, Office Machinery Technical Service, K. L.
Beak....................£2,583 to £3,396

Publications Division
Director, J. P. Morgan.......... £4,600 to £5,200
Deputy Directors, H. W. Leader; J. Carpenter
£3,250 to £4,400
Assistant Directors, R. C. Barnard; L. B. Mills;
R. Brearley; E. S. Brooks; A. J. Woolway
£2,775 to £3,400

Management Services Unit
Director, D. W. Ray........... £3,250 to £4,400
Assistant Director, D. A. Prutton. £2,775 to £3,400
Chief Work Study Officer, D. S. Henshall
£2,775 to £3,400

Inspection, Transport and Warehouses Division
Director, F. E. Davey.......... £4,600 to £5,200
Deputy Director, A. E. J. Brunwin
£3,250 to £4,400
Assistant Director, A. H. MacDonald
£2,775 to £3,400

REGIONAL OFFICES AND BOOKSHOPS
Scotland
Government Buildings, Bankhead Avenue,
Edinburgh 11.
Bookshop: 13a Castle Street, Edinburgh 2.
Director, G. L. Birch.......... £3,250 to £4,400
Deputy Director, C. E. Harrold.. £2,775 to £3,400

Wales
Bookshop: 109 St. Mary Street, Cardiff.
Chief Officer, A. Mackenzie.

Northern Ireland
12 Linenhall Street, Belfast 2
Retail and Trade Bookshop: 7-11 Linenhall Street,
Belfast 2.
Director, R. O. Stonehouse..... £3,250 to £4,400

Manchester
Broadway, Chadderton, Lancs.
Bookshop: Brazennose House, Brazennose Street,
Manchester 2.
Director, C. P. Bradshaw...... £3,250 to £4,400
Deputy Director, Miss E. M. Coyle
£2,775 to £3,400
Assistant Director, C. E. S. Robbs £2,775 to £3,400

Bristol
Ashton Vale Road, Bristol 3
Bookshop: 50 Fairfax Street, Bristol 1.
Director, S. A. Cowie........ £2,775 to £3,400

Birmingham
Bookshop: 258 Broad Street,
Birmingham 1

STATUTE LAW COMMITTEE
House of Lords, S.W.1
President, The Lord Chancellor.
Vice-Chairman, Mr. Justice Scarman, O.B.E.

Members, The Attorney-General; the Lord Advo-
cate; Sir Philip Allen, K.C.B.; C. H. Baylis, C.B.;
Sir Barnett Cocks, K.C.B., O.B.E.; The Viscount
Colville of Culross; Sir Dennis Dobson, K.C.B.,
O.B.E.; Sir Harvey Druitt, K.C.B.; Sir John Fiennes,
K.C.B.; The Lord Fletcher, P.C.; C.Fletcher Cooke,
Q.C., M.P.; Sir Douglas Haddow, K.C.B.; The
Lord Kilbrandon, P.C.; The Lord MacDermott,
P.C.; G. I. Mitchell, C.B.; Sir David Pitblado,
K.C.B., C.V.O.; H. W. Pritchard, C.B.E.; The Lord
Reid, P.C.; C.H.; Sir David Serpell, K.C.B., C.M.G.;
Sir David Stephens, K.C.B., C.V.O.; Sir Robert
Speed, C.B., Q.C.; T. G. Talbot, C.B., Q.C.; Sir
Burke Trend, G.C.B., C.V.O.; The Lord Wilber-
force, P.C., C.M.G., O.B.E.
Secretary, R. W. Perceval, T.D.

Statutory Publications Office
Queen Anne's Chambers, 41 Tothill Street, S.W.1
[01-930-7363]
Editor, A. B. Lyons............ £3,175 to £3,900
Assistant Editor, S. G. G. Edgar, C.B.E.
£2,306 to £3,050

SUGAR BOARD
52, Mark Lane, E.C.3
[01-480-6221]

The Sugar Board was constituted under the Sugar Act, 1956, on October 15, 1956. The Board buys the sugar which the United Kingdom has contracted to buy under the Commonwealth Sugar Agreement at prices negotiated triennially by the Government and resells the sugar commercially at world prices. The Board also provides temporary finance for the British Sugar Corporation and receives from or pays to the Corporation any surplus or deficit arising on the production and refining of home grown beet sugar. The Board, in turn, balances its accounts, taking one year with another, by receiving a surcharge or making a distribution payment, on all imported and home produced sugar.

Chairman, R. G. R. Wall, C.B............£9,900
Vice-Chairman, Sir Leonard Cooke, O.B.E....£2,300
Members (part-time), P. G. Smith; N. Vinson; Sir John Wall, O.B.E.........................£1,003
Secretary and Joint General Manager, A. V. Parsons, M.B.E.
Joint General Manager R. Holland, B.E.M.
Finance Officer, G. Keddie, M.B.E.

THAMES CONSERVANCY
Burdett House,
15 Buckingham Street, W.C.2
[01-839-2441]

The conservation of the River Thames was originally granted to twelve Conservators in 1857. In 1909 the Port of London Authority took over all rights, powers and duties of the Conservators in respect of the river below Teddington. The Conservators of the River Thames under the Thames Conservancy Acts and Orders, 1932 to 1966, now have jurisdiction over the River Thames from Cricklade in Wiltshire to a point about 265 yards below Teddington Lock, and are constituted the Drainage Board of the Thames Catchment Area for the purposes of the Land Drainage Acts, 1930 and 1961. The principal duties of the Conservators as a Navigation Authority are the maintenance and improvement of the navigation, and the registration and regulation of craft. The Conservators exercise jurisdiction for the prevention of pollution over the Thames Catchment Area (both surface and underground water), and over the fisheries in the River Thames from Cricklade to Teddington.

The Conservators also exercise the new water resources functions of River Authorities under the Water Resources Act, 1963, in respect of both surface and underground water in the Thames Catchment Area and underground water in London (the London "Excluded" Area), including the prevention of pollution.

The Conservators' income is obtainable by precept from the Councils of the various counties, county boroughs and London boroughs within the Thames Catchment Area, from the Greater London Council, licence fees and charges for water abstracted. In addition, the Conservators derive income from various navigation tolls, fees, licences and rents.

Chairman, The Lord Nugent of Guildford, P.C.
Vice-Chairman, Sir Aubrey Ward.
Secretary and Chief Administrative Officer, R. P Owen.
Chief Engineer, E. J. Brettell.
Treasurer and Accountant, E. J. Gilliland.

NATIONAL THEATRE BOARD
10a Aquinas Street, S.E.1
[01-928-2033]

Appointed by the Chancellor of the Exchequer to administer the National Theatre.
Chairman, Sir Max Rayne.
Members, H. Beaumont; A. R. M. Carr; A. Francis, O.B.E.; V. Mishcon; J. C. Mortimer, Q.C.; H. H.

Sebag-Montefiore; Prof. T. J. B. Spencer; S. Sutton.
Director of the National Theatre, The Lord Olivier.
Secretary, K. Rae.

DEPARTMENT OF TRADE AND INDUSTRY
1 Victoria Street, S.W.1.*
[01-222 7877] *PETER WALKER*

Secretary of State for Trade and Industry and President of the Board of Trade, THE RT. HON. ~~JOHN EMERSON HARDING DAVIES,~~ M.B.E., M.P. £8,500
Principal Private Secretary, E. Wright.
Assistant Private Secretaries, Miss P. D. Baxter; J. R. R. Ebsworth; P. H. Twyman.
Parliamentary Private Secretary, M. N. Shaw, M.P.
Minister for Trade, THE RT. HON. ~~MICHAEL ANTONY CRISTOBAL NOBLE,~~ M.P................£8,500
Parliamentary Private Secretary, D. A. Walder, M.P.
Minister for Aerospace, THE RT. HON. FREDERICK VICTOR CORFIELD, M.P. ~~4/72~~ £8,500
Parliamentary Private Secretary, P. W. Holland, M.P. *THOMAS BOARDMAN*
Ministry for Industry, SIR JOHN BENEDICT EDEN, Bt., M.P................................£7,625
Parliamentary Private Secretary, R. J. Pounder, M.P.
× *Parliamentary Under-Secretary of State for Trade,* J. A. Grant, M.P.....................£3,750
Parliamentary Under-Secretary of State for Aerospace, D. E. C. Price, M.P.................£3,750
Parliamentary Under-Secretary of State for Industry, Hon. Nicholas Ridley, M.P. ~~...........~~ £3,750
Permanent Secretary, Sir Antony Part, K.C.B., M.B.E. £14,000

Secretary (Trade), Sir Max Brown, K.C.B., C.M.G. £13,000
Secretary (Industry), Sir Robert Marshall, K.C.B., M.B.E. £13,000
Deputy Secretaries, R. H. W. Bullock, C.B.; G. R. Denman, C.M.G.; R. R. Goodison, C.B.; J. A. Hamilton, M.B.E.; D. F. Hubback, C.B.; W. Hughes, C.B.; J. Leckie, C.B. (*Principal Establishment and Finance Officer*); A. D. Peck, C.B., M.B.E.; J. L. Rampton, C.B.; F. R. P. Vinter, C.B...£9,000
Chief Economic Adviser, F. J. Atkinson, C.B...£9,000
Economic Advisers (part-time) Civil Aviation, Prof. A. C. L. Day (£2,334); Prof. J. B. Heath £2,062
Chief Scientist, Dr. I. Maddock, C.B., O.B.E., F.R.S. *D. RIPPENGAL 9/22* £9,000
Solicitor, ~~Sir Gerard Ryder,~~ C.B. *HALES* £9,000
Director of Statistics, J. Stafford, C.B........£9,000
Chief Scientific Adviser (Energy) and Chief Inspector of Nuclear Installations, E. C. Williams, C.B...£9,000

TRADE GROUP
Europe, Industry and Technology Division *on 72*
Under Secretary, W. P. Shovelton, C.M.G. £6,750
Assistant Secretaries, J. F. J. Jardine; C. L. Silver £5,000 to £6,300

Commercial Relations and Exports Divisions
Division 1
Under Secretary, M. P. Lam...........£6,750
Assistant Secretaries, Miss K. E. Boyes; R. W. Gray; O. H. Kemmis............£5,000 to £6,300

Division 2
Under Secretary, C. W. Sanders, C.B.........£6,750
Assistant Secretaries, A. F. Toms; Miss M. J. Lackey, O.B.E. (*see also Division 3*).....£5,000 to £6,300

Division 3
Under Secretary, P. S. Preston............£6,750
Assistant Secretaries, G. A. Barry; G. C. Dick; J. R. D. Gildea; Miss M. J. Lackey, O.B.E. (*see also Division 2*)..............£5,000 to £6,300

Division 4
Under Secretary, B. E. Bellamy, C.B.........£6,750
* Unless otherwise stated, Divisions of the Ministry are at this address.

Assistant Secretaries, J. W. McMeekin; T. H. Sinclair; H. W. Woodruff, C.M.G. £5,000 to £6,300
Division 5
Under Secretary, S. L. Edwards, C.M.G. £6,750
Assistant Secretaries, L. C. W. Figg; W. Nicoll
£5,000 to £6,300

Export Planning and Development Division
Under Secretary, J. R. Cross, C.M.G. £6,750
Assistant Secretaries, W. A. Newsome; C. B. Nixon
£5,000 to £6,300
Hillgate House, 26 Old Bailey, E.C.4
[01-248 5757]
Director (*Fairs and Promotions Branch*), W. T. Pearce
£5,000 to £6,300
Norman Shaw North Building,
Victoria Embankment, S.W.1
[01-930 4349]
Controller (*Export Licensing Branch*), D. A. Whitby
£3,250 to £4,400

Export Services Division
Export House, 50 Ludgate Hill, E.C.4
[01-248 5757]
Under Secretary, R. B. Tippetts. £6,750
Co-ordination of Export Services:
Director, G. Booth, C.M.G. .... £5,000 to £6,300
General Export Services Branch:
Director, N. S. Belam. ...... £5,000 to £6,300
Field Force Branch and Special Services:
Director, D. N. Royce. ...... £5,000 to £6,300
Export Data Branch:
Director, G. McMahon. ...... £4,600 to £5,200

Overseas Projects and Technology Division
Under Secretary, K. Taylor. £6,750
Assistant Secretaries, A. H. K. Slater; N. E. Robins;
L. C. Watson ..... £5,000 to £6,300

Regional Industrial Development Division
Under Secretary, P. le Cheminant. £6,750
Assistant Secretaries, Miss B. M. Eyles; C. A. Gay;
L. Lightman; M. H. M. Reid; E. J. D. Warne
£5,000 to £6,300

Regional Organization
Office for Scotland
314 St. Vincent Street, Glasgow, C3
[041-248 3320]
Director for Scotland, P. J. L. Homan. £6,750
Office for Wales
Government Buildings, Gabalfa, Cardiff
[Cardiff 62131]
Director for Wales, I. Gray. ... £5,000 to £6,300
Northern Region
Wellbar House, Gallowgate, Newcastle upon Tyne
[Newcastle upon Tyne 27575]
Regional Director, R. Wood. ... £5,000 to £6,300
North Western Region
Sunley Building, Piccadilly Plaza, Manchester
[061-236 2171]
Regional Director, E. Atherton. £5,000 to £6,300
Yorkshire and Humberside Region
City House, New Station Street, Leeds
[Leeds 38232]
Regional Director, Dr. L. Bovey. £5,240 to £5,830
East Midlands Region
Cranbrook House, Cranbrook Street, Nottingham
[Nottingham 46121]
Regional Director, E. T. Watson. £5,000 to £6,300
West Midlands Region
Five Ways House, Islington Row, Birmingham
[021-643 8191]
Regional Director, R. L. Sutton. £5,000 to £6,300
Eastern Region
Cromwell House, Dean Stanley Street, S.W.1
[01-828 6271]
Regional Director, F. Lacey. £5,000 to £6,300
London and South-East Region
Cromwell House, Dean Stanley Street, S.W.1
[01-828 4355]
Regional Director, P. B. Hunt. ... £5,000 to £6,300

O*

South Western Region
The Pithay, Bristol
[Bristol 21071]
Regional Director, L. I. Macbeth £5,000 to £6,300

Investment Grants Division
Sanctuary Bldgs., 16-20 Great Smith Street, S.W.1
[01-222 7877]
Under Secretary, C. G. Thorley. £6,750
Assistant Secretaries, Mrs. E. L. K. Sinclair; R. G. Stuart. .... £5,000 to £6,300

Civil Aviation Division 1
Shell Mex House, Strand, W.C.2
[01-836 1207]
Under Secretary (vacant). £6,750
Assistant Secretaries, R. Colegate; G. C. Lowe;
T. Sharp. .... £5,000 to £6,300

Civil Aviation Division 2
Shell Mex House, W.C.2
[01-836 1207]
Under Secretary, R. E. M. Le Goy £6,750
Assistant Secretaries, W. J. Coe; A. P. Gardner;
G. Lanchin. .... £5,000 to £6,300
Director (*Operational Services Overseas*), A. M. Raffael. .... £5,000 to £6,300

Directorate General of Safety and Operations
Shell Mex House, Strand, W.C.2
[01-816 1207]
Director General, Group Capt. J. B. Veal, C.B.E., A.F.C. £6,750
Directors, G. C. Chouffot, M.B.E. (*Flight Operations*)
£6,600; J. R. Neill (*Flight Safety*); R. Broadbent,
D.F.C. (*Training and Licensing*); M. H. Vivian
(*Advanced Aircraft Operations*); K. A. Wood (*All Weather Operations*); D. F. Peel (*Aerodromes (Technical)*); R. W. N. B. Gilling (*Administration Safety and Operations*) .... £5,000 to £6,300

Civil Aviation Division 3
The Adelphi, John Adam Street, W.C.2
[01-836 1207]
Under Secretary, J. E. Barnes. £6,750
Assistant Secretaries, A. V. Davies, M.B.E.; P. A. Robinson; D. C. Smith. .... £5,000 to £6,300

Controllerate of National Air Traffic Services
The Adelphi, John Adam Street, W.C.2
[01-836 1207]
Controller, G. W. Stallibrass, O.B.E. £7,800
Deputy Controller, Air Vice-Marshal E. D. Crew, D.S.O., D.F.C.
Hillingdon House, Uxbridge, Middlesex
[89-31581]
Joint Field Commander, W. C. Woodruff. £6,750
Director, A. Field, O.B.E. .... £5,000 to £6,300
19-29 Woburn Place, W.C.1
[01-837 3366]
Director General of Telecommunications, T. J. McWiggan £6,750
Director of Communications and Navigation, J. F. Montgomerie. £6,300
Director of Air Traffic Services, R. E. Cox. ... £6,300
Director of Staff Management, W. H. Garnett, O.B.E.
£6,300
1-6 Tavistock Square, W.C.1
[01-837 3366]
Chief Air Traffic Control Officer, C. A. M. Kyrke-Smith, O.B.E. .... £5,000 to £6,300
The Adelphi, John Adam Street, W.C.2
[01-836 1207]
Director of Control Operations, Air Commodore W. Harbison, C.B.E., A.F.C.
Director of Control (*Plans*), A. P. J. Flynn
£5,000 to £6,300
Director of Administration, Air Traffic Control, S. R. Walton. .... £5,000 to £6,300
Director of Finance, Air Traffic Control, J. S. Norman
£5,000 to £6,300
Director of Control, Linesman-Mediator, D. G. Terrington. £6,300

Scientific Adviser's Division (Civil Aviation)
Shell Mex House, Strand, W.C.2
[01-836 1207]

Scientific Adviser, D. E. Morris............£7,350
Directors, O. B. St. John (*Technical Research and Development*); K. H. Treweek (*Operational Research and Analysis*).........£5,240 to £5,830

Shipping Policy Division
The Adelphi, John Adam Street, W.C.2
[01-836 1207]

Under Secretary, G. R. W. Brigstocke.....£6,750
Assistant Secretaries, C. M. Drukker; J. K. T. Frost; K.W. McQueen, O.B.E......£5,000 to £6,300

× Marine Division
Sunley House, 90-93 High Holborn, W.C.1
[01-405 6911]

Under Secretary, R. F. Prosser, M.C.......£6,750
Assistant Secretaries, D. N. Byrne; A. Eales-Johnson, M.B.E.; E. R. Hargreaves; W. J. Madigan, O.B.E.; M. J. Service....................£5,000 to £6,300
Director of Sea Transport, K. A. B Sampson, O.B.E. £5,620 to £6,300
Chief Nautical Surveyor, Capt. A. C. Manson
£5,640
Engineer Surveyor in Chief, G. Victory......£5,640
Chief Ship Surveyor, D. R. Murray Smith..£5,640

Accidents Investigation Branch
Shell Mex House, Strand, W.C.2
[01-836 1207]

Chief Inspector, Capt. V. A. M. Hunt, C.B.E. £6,600

CENTRAL GROUP
Central Secretariat
Under Secretary, A. M. Houghton.........£6,750
Assistant Secretaries, S. Abramson; R. Jardine
£5,000 to £6,300

Information Division
Chief Information Officers, D. C. Moon; N. Shepherd....................£4,390 to £5,640

Solicitor's Department
Kingsgate House, 66-74 Victoria Street, S.W.1
[01-828 1299]

Solicitor, Sir Gerard Ryder, C.B............£9,000
Principal Assistant Solicitor, J. A. E. Davies.. £6,750
Assistant Solicitors, H. C. Cotman, C.B.E., M.C.; F. A. Bayly; J. B. Evans; D. A. Grant, M.C.; C. A. Shewell; J. A. Trapnell; M. J. Kerry; F. J. Stone; L. V. Wellard....£4,555 to £5,640
Shell Mex House, Strand, W.C.1
[01-836 1207]

Principal Assistant Solicitor, A. W. G. Kean.. £6,750
Assistant Solicitor, T. D. Salmon..£4,555 to £5,640

Industrial and Commercial Policy Divisions
Division 1 (Insurance and Companies Department), Sanctuary Bldgs., 16-20 Great Smith Street, S.W.1
[01-222 7877]

Under Secretaries, P. A. R. Brown; C. W. Jardine, C.B....................£6,750
Assistant Secretaries, C. J. Homewood; J. H. Macphail; J. B. Smith; D. Steel...£5,000 to £6,300
Inspector General of Companies, Companies Liquidation and Bankruptcy, C. A. Taylor.......£6,600
Registrar of Companies, R. W. Westley
£4,600 to £5,200

Division 2
Under Secretary, R. Goldsmith...........£6,750
Assistant Secretaries, Miss S. M. Cohen; Mrs. P. B. M. James; A. J. Lippitt; D. Simpson
£5,000 to £6,300
Assistant Director, R. G. Fall, O.B.E.
£4,390 to £5,015

Division 3
Under Secretary, C. E. Coffin............£6,750
Assistant Secretaries, R. M. Allott; A. Dunning; S. W. T. Mitchelmore....£5,000 to £6,300

Standards Weights and Measures Division
Abell House, John Islip Street, S.W.1
[01-834 4422]

Adviser on Standards and Head of Division, Dr. E. N. Eden...................£6,750

Assistant Secretaries, J. E. M. Beale; G. T. Rogers
£5,000 to £6,300
Directing Engineer, J. D. Platt..............£5,640
Deputy Chief Scientific Officers, D. E. Fox; E. E. Williams, O.B.E............£5,240 to £5,830
26 Chapter Street, S.W.1
[01-834 7032]
Controller, S. Abbott, O.B.E.....£3,575 to £4,208

Tariff Division
Brunswick House, 2 Central Buildings, Matthew Parker Street, S.W.1.
[01-222 7877]

Under Secretary, D. Carter, C.B............£6,750
Assistant Secretaries, D. P. Brearley; J. Whaley
£5,000 to £6,300

Economics and Statistics Divisions
Chief Economic Adviser, F. J. Atkinson, C.B... £9,000
Director of Statistics, J. Stafford, C.B.....£9,000

Division 1
Head of Division, T. A. Kennedy.........£6,750
Deputy Director, J. D. Gribbin...£5,000 to £6,300
Senior Economic Advisers, R. O. Goss; R. S. Howard
£5,000 to £6,300

Division 2
Thames House South, Millbank, S.W.1
[01-222 7000]

Head of Division, C. I. K. Forster, C.B.E.....£6,750
Chief Statisticians, G. W. Clarke; H. R. Fisher, O.B.E.; F. W. Hutber.......£5,000 to £6,300
Senior Economic Advisers, B. D. Cullen; N. J. Cunningham......£5,000 to £6,300

Division 3
Head of Division, G. Penrice...........£6,750
Assistant Secretary, K. G. H. Binning
£5,000 to £6,300
Chief Statistician, J. D. Wells....£5,000 to £6,300
Senior Economic Adviser, D. A. W. Broyd
£5,000 to £6,300

Division 4
Dean Bradley House, 52 Horseferry Road, S.W.1
[01-799 5688]

Head of Division, T. S. Pilling.............£6,750
Chief Statisticians, M. J. G. M. Lockyer; M. L. M. Neifield.................£5,000 to £6,300
Senior Economic Adviser, P. J. Goate
£5,000 to £6,300

Division 5
Head of Division, T. Paterson.............£6,750
Chief Statisticians, B. A. Wainewright; W. A. Wessell..................£5,000 to £6,300

Division 6
Head of Division, A. G. Carruthers........£6,750
Chief Statisticians, Mrs. J. G. Cox; B. F. Middleton; H. C. Stanton........£5,000 to £6,300

Business Statistics Office
Lime Grove, Ruislip, Middlesex
[01-866 0085/9]

Director, M. C. Fessey.................£6,750
Chief Statisticians, H. E. Browning; Dr. B. Mitchell
£5,000 to £6,300
Assistant Secretary, J. A. Tiffin...£5,000 to £6,300
Senior Principal, R. F. L. Sims...£4,600 to £5,200

Finance and Economic Appraisal Division
Abell House, John Islip Street, S.W.1
[01-834 4422]

Under Secretary, H. Scholes............£6,750
Assistant Secretaries, Mrs. E. C. Jones; W. M. Knighton; Miss A. E. Mueller; J. E. Sellars
£5,000 to £6,300
Pembroke House, 40-56 City Road, E.C.1
[01-253 9933]
Director, Accounts Branch, R. F. Fenn
£5,000 to £6,300

Accountancy Services Division
Hillgate House, 26 Old Bailey, E.C.4
[01-248 5757]

Senior Director, H. A. Parfitt, O.B.E.........£6,370
Directors, N. A. Atley; A. R. Shove, O.B.E.
£5,015 to £5,640

The Adelphi, John Adam Street, W.C.2
[01-836 1207]
Director (Civil Aviation) Branch, H. J. Holdsworth
£5,640

Establishment Divisions
Personnel
Under Secretary, D. N. Charlish.........£6,750
Assistant Secretaries, J. Banfield; J. Fish; N. E. Martin
£5,000 to £6,300
Principal Medical Officer, Dr. G. Bennett...£6,120
Organization
Under Secretary, K. J. Willoughby.........£6,750
Assistant Secretaries, R. L. Davies; R. E. Dearing;
F. T. Jones.................£5,000 to £6,300
Reorganization
Under Secretary, G. Parker, C.B.........£6,750
Assistant Secretaries, R. C. M. Cooper; W. Hancox;
G. R. Smith...............£5,000 to £6,300

INDUSTRY GROUP
Electronics and Computers Division
Dean Bradley House, 52 Horseferry Road, S.W.1
[01-799 5688]
Under Secretary, F. W. Glaves Smith.....£6,750
Assistant Secretaries, G. H. Gillings; I. T. Manley
£5,000 to £6,300
Deputy Chief Scientific Officer, E. S. Mallett
£5,240 to £5,830

**Machine Tools and Manufacturing Machinery
Division**
Abell House, John Islip Street, S.W.1
[01-834 4422]
Under Secretary, L. J. T. Clifton.........£6,750
Chief Scientific Officer (B), Dr. C. Timms...£6,380
Directing Engineers, S. Bentall; A. J. Havelock
£5,640

Systems and Automation Division
52 Horseferry Road, S.W.1 [01-799 5688]
Chief Scientific Officer (A), J. W. de L. Nichols
£6,750
Deputy Chief Scientific Officers, D. Harrison; B. W.
Oakley.................£5,240 to £5,830

Shipbuilding Policy Division
Thames House South, Millbank, S.W.1
[01-222 7000]
Under Secretary, E. V. Marchant.........£6,750
Assistant Secretaries, M. B. Casey; A. J. Suich
£5,000 to £6,300
Deputy Chief Scientific Officer, D. Neville-Jones
£5,240 to £5,830

Iron and Steel Division
Thames House South, Millbank S.W.1
[01-222 7000]
Under Secretary, W. R. G. Bell.........£6,750
Assistant Secretaries, A. Blackshaw; J. R. Jenkins;
J. C. Y. de Pauley............£5,000 to £6,300

Research Division
Abell House, John Islip Street, S.W.1
[01-834 4422]
Chief Scientific Officer (A), J. Knox.........£6,750
Assistant Secretary, P. F. G. Twinn £5,000 to £6,300
Deputy Chief Scientific Officers, E. Barlow Wright;
C. G. Giles, O.B.E.; Dr. A. B. Hammond; M. O.
Robins.................£5,240 to £5,830

Industrial Research Review Division
Millbank Tower, Millbank, S.W.1.
[01-834 2255]
Under Secretary, C. E. H. Tuck.........£6,750
Assistant Secretary, K. W. N. George
£5,000 to £6,300

Energy Technology Division
Thames House South, Millbank S.W.1
[01-222 7000]
Chief Scientific Officer (B), L. H. Leighton....£6,380
Deputy Chief Scientific Officer, Dr. S. Masterman,
O.B.E.................£5,240 to £5,830

Mines and Quarries Inspectorate
Thames House South, Millbank, S.W.1
[01-222 700]
Chief Inspector, J. W. Calder, O.B.E.........£7,800

Fuel and Nationalized Industry Policy Division
Thames House South, Millbank, S.W.1
[01-222 7000]
Under Secretary, D. le B. Jones.........£6,750
Assistant Secretaries, J. Caines; W. E. Fitzsimmons;
Miss J. A. M. Oliver........£5,000 to £6,300
Deputy Chief Scientific Officer, Dr. R. G. S. Skipper
£5,240 to £5,830

Coal Division
Thames House South, Millbank, S.W.1
[01-222 7000]
Under Secretary, W. K. Ward.........£6,750
Assistant Secretaries, J. F. Gwynn; P. S. Ross; R.
Wakefield...............£5,000 to £6,300

Gas Division
Thames House South, Millbank, S.W.1
[01-222 7000]
Under Secretary, Mrs. J. M. Spencer, C.B., C.B.E.
£6,750
Assistant Secretaries, G. G. Campbell; J. W. Farrell;
A. B. Powell, C.M.G........£5,000 to £6,300
Gas Standards Branch, Government Buildings,
Saffron Road, Wigston, Leicester
Controller, M. W. Jones, O.B.E.........£5,640
Deputy Controller, G. R. Boreham £4,390 to £5,015

Electricity Division
Thames House South, Millbank S.W.1
[01-222 7000]
Under Secretary, M. R. Garner.........£6,750
Assistant Secretaries, A. C. Campbell; P. G. M.
Clark; J. H. Thomas........£5,000 to £6,300

Nuclear Installations Inspectorate
Thames House South, Millbank, S.W.1
[01-222 7000]
Chief Inspector, E. C. Williams, C.B........£9,000
Deputy Chief Inspector, T. Griffiths.........£6,750

Atomic Energy Division
Millbank Tower, Millbank, S.W.1
[01-834 2225]
Under Secretary, J. G. Liverman, O.B.E.......£6,750
Assistant Secretaries, P. J. Kelly; G. W. Thynne
£5,000 to £6,300

Petroleum Division
Thames House South, Millbank, S.W.1
[01-222 7000]
Under Secretary, J. A. Beckett, C.B., C.M.G...£6,750
Assistant Secretaries, D. Eagers; A. R. D. Murray;
S. Stewart, M.C.; A. Warrington £5,000 to £6,300

Chemicals and Textiles Division
Millbank Tower, Millbank, S.W.1.
[01-834 2255]
Under Secretary, P. W. Ridley, C.B.E........£6,750
Assistant Secretaries, D. M. J. Gwinnell; J. H.
McEnery; Miss Y. Lovat-Williams; Miss L.
Lowne.................£5,000 to £6,300

**Minerals, Metals and Electrical Engineering
Division**
Thames House South, Millbank, S.W.1
[01-222 7000]
Under Secretary, D. C. Clark.........£6,750
Assistant Secretaries, F. A. Carter; M. S. Morris
£5,000 to £6,300
Deputy Chief Scientific Officer, J. A. Roberts
£5,240 to £5,830

**Vehicles and Mechanical Engineering Products
Division**
Abell House, John Islip Street, S.W.1
[01-834 4422]
Under Secretary, E. W. G. Haynes, C.B........£6,750
Assistant Secretaries, J. Darragh; S. J. Irwin
£5,000 to £6,300
Deputy Chief Scientific Officer, S. A. Hunwicks,
O.B.E.................£5,240 to £5,830

Safety and Health Division
Thames House South, Millbank, S.W.1
Assistant Secretary, J. R. Wilson £5,000 to £6,300

**Paper, Printing, Publishing, Services
and Distribution Division**
Millbank Tower, Millbank, S.W.1
[01-834 2255]
Under Secretary, H. Bailey, C.M.G.........£6,750

Assistant Secretaries, E. Y. Bannard; H. F. Heinemann; E. Wagstaff............£5,000 to £6,300

AIR 1 DIVISION
Horse Guards Avenue, S.W.1
[01-930 7022]

Under Secretary, L. Williams.............£6,750
Assistant Secretaries, J. A. Battersby; G. F. Kear;
S. G. McKay, C.B.E.........£5,000 to £6,300

AIR 2 DIVISION
Horse Guards Avenue, S.W.1
[01-930 7022]

Under Secretary, W. G. Downey, C.B.......£6,750
Assistant Secretary, M. J. Treble..£5,000 to £6,300
Senior Economic Adviser, D. R. M. Sawers
£5,000 to £6,300

AEROSPACE (ASSESSMENT AND RESEARCH) DIVISION
Abell House, John Islip Street, S.W.1
[01-834 4422]

Director General, H. G. R. Robinson, O.B.E. £6,750
Deputy Chief Scientific Officer, Dr. D. Cameron
£5,240 to £5,830

CONCORDE DIVISION
St. Giles Court, 1–13 St. Giles High Street, W.C.2
[01-636 3644]

Director General, T. P. Jones..............£6,750
Assistant Secretary, C. B. Benjamin
£5,000 to £6,300
Deputy Chief Scientific Officer, J. D. Hayhurst, O.B.E.
£5,240 to £5,830

SPACE DIVISION
Prospect House, 100 New Oxford Street, W.C.1
[01-636 3644]

Under Secretary, A. Goodson.............£6,750
Assistant Secretary, R. A. Neate..£5,000 to £6,300
Deputy Chief Scientific Officer, D. Cavanagh
£5,240 to £5,830

INDUSTRIAL RESEARCH ESTABLISHMENTS
Laboratory of the Government Chemist
Cornwall House, Stamford Street, S.E.1
[01-928 7900]

Government Chemist, Dr. H. Egan.........£6,750

National Engineering Laboratory
East Kilbride, Glasgow
[East Kilbride 20222]

Director, R. H. Weir, C.B................£7,350

National Physical Laboratory
Teddington, Middlesex
[01-977 3222]

Director, Dr. J. V. Dunworth, C.B., C.B.E.... £9,000

Safety in Mines Research Establishment
Central Laboratories, off Broad Lane, Sheffield 3
[Sheffield 78141]

Director, Dr. C. A. A. Wass.............£6,750

Torry Research Station
P.O. Box 31, 135 Abbey Road, Aberdeen
[Aberdeen 54171]

Director, Dr. G. H. O. Burgess..£5,240 to £5,830

Warren Spring Laboratory
Stevenage, Herts.
[Stevenage 3388]

Director, Dr. A. J. Robinson.............£6,750

Local Employment Acts Financial Advisory Committee
2 Bunhill Row, E.C.1
[01-638 1744]

Chairman, Sir William Lawson, C.B.E.
Members, S. Douglas; N. S. Huntly; E. E. Tait,
O.B.E.; W. T. Welch; D. J. Young, C.B.E.
Secretary, A. J. Mills.

THE TRANSPORT HOLDING COMPANY
Argosy House, 215 Great Portland Street, W.1
[01-636-8688]

The Transport Holding Company is a statutory company established under the Transport Act, 1962. Until January 1, 1969, it owned and managed all the transport investments of the former British Transport Commission except those trans-

ferred to the British Railways Board, London Transport Board, British Transport Docks Board and the British Waterways Board.

As a result of the Transport Act, 1968, its shareholdings in bus companies vested in either the National Bus Company or the Scottish Transport Group, and those in the road haulage and shipping companies vested in the National Freight Corporation. The Transport Holding Company's remaining shareholdings are chiefly in companies engaged in travel and tourism, *e.g.* Thos. Cook & Son Ltd.

Chairman, B. Whyte.
Directors, R. C. Clifford-Turner; Sir Harry Crane, O.B.E.; J. A. R. Falconer; T. R. Grieve, C.B.E., M.C.; B. H. Harbour, C.B.E.; F. L. Perkins, D.S.C.
Comptroller, H. E. Osborn, C.B.E.
Secretary, L. H. Mapleston.

THE TREASURY
Great George Street, S.W.1
[01-930 1234]

The office of the Lord High Treasurer has been continuously in commission for well over 200 years. The Lords Commissioners of H.M. Treasury consist of the First Lord of the Treasury (who is also the Prime Minister), the Chancellor of the Exchequer and five Junior Lords. This Board of Commissioners is assisted at present by a Chief Secretary, a Parliamentary Secretary who is the Chief Whip, a Financial Secretary and a Minister of State, who are also members of the Government, and the Permanent Secretary. The Prime Minister and First Lord is not concerned in the day-to-day aspects of Treasury business. The Junior Lords are Government Whips in the House of Commons. The management of the Treasury devolves upon the Chancellor of the Exchequer, and, under him, on the Chief Secretary, the Financial Secretary and the Minister of State. The Chief Secretary, with the assistance of the Minister of State, is responsible for the control of public expenditure. The Financial Secretary is concerned with matters of home and overseas finance and discharges the traditional responsibility of the Treasury for the largely formal procedures of voting of funds by Parliament. All ministers are concerned in tax matters.

Prime Minister and First Lord of the Treasury, THE RT. HON. EDWARD RICHARD GEORGE HEATH, M.B.E., M.P....................£14,000
Principal Private Secretary, R. T. Armstrong.
Private Secretaries, P. J. S. Moon (*Overseas Affairs*); P. L. Gregson (*Parliamentary Affairs*); C. W. Roberts (*Home Affairs*); A. J. C. Simcock (*Home Affairs*).
Secretary for Appointments, Sir John Hewitt, K.C.V.O., C.B.E.
Political Secretary, The Hon. D. R. Hurd.
Chief Press Secretary, D. J. D. Maitland, C.M.G., O.B.E. £6,925
Press Secretary, T. D. McCaffrey *HR HAYLES*
£5,175 to £6,475
Chief Press Officer, G. Holt, C.B.E.
£5,175 to £6,475
Assistant Private Secretaries, Miss D. R. Edmunds, M.B.E.; Miss J. M. Porter, M.B.E.; D. Pragnell.
Parliamentary Private Secretary, T. P. G. Kitson, M.P.

Lords Commissioners of the Treasury
The Prime Minister (*First Lord*); The Chancellor of the Exchequer.

Junior Lords of the Treasury
B. B. Weatherill, M.P.; W. Clegg, M.P.; V. H. Goodhew, M.P.; P. L. Hawkins, T.D., M.P.
each £3,000

Chancellor of the Exchequer, THE RT. HON. ANTHONY PERRINOTT LYSBERG BARBER, T.D., M.P. £8,500
Principal Private Secretary, W. S. Ryrie.
Private Secretaries, P. E. Middleton; N. A. Nagler.

CORPORATION OF TRINITY HOUSE
Trinity House, Tower Hill, E.C.3
[01-480-6601]

Trinity House, the first General Lighthouse and Pilotage Authority in the Kingdom, was a body of importance when Henry VIII granted the institution its first charter in 1514, *inter alia* " for the relief, increase and augmentation of the Shipping of this Realm of England." Since that period the duty of erecting and maintaining lighthouses and other marks and signs of the sea has by Royal Charter and Acts of Parliament been entrusted to the Corporation of Trinity House, and until 1874 Masters of the Navy were examined by the Elder Brethren of the Corporation. In the present day, the principal duty of the Corporation of Trinity House, as a Public Department, is the administration of the Lighthouse, &c., Service of England and Wales with certain statutory jurisdiction in regard to lighthouses and other seamarks in Scotland, Ireland, the Channel Islands and Gibraltar, while the Corporation is also the chief Pilotage Authority in the United Kingdom, and in its capacity as a private corporation or guild it administers certain Charitable Trusts specifically dedicated to the relief of aged and distressed master mariners, their widows and spinster daughters. The Corporation controls nearly 90 lighthouses and over 30 lightships, and maintains a fleet of lighthouse tenders and a fleet of pilot vessels. The Active Elder Brethren of the Corporation also sit with the Judges of the Admiralty Division of the High Court of Justice to act as Nautical Assessors in Marine Causes tried in that Court. The Lighthouse Service of Trinity House is maintained out of the General Lighthouse Fund, this fund being provided by means of special dues called Light Dues levied on shipping using the ports of the United Kingdom. The accounts are submitted annually to Parliament.

Elder Brethren
Master, H.R.H. the Duke of Edinburgh, K.G.
Deputy Master, Captain Sir George Barnard.
Elder Brethren, H.R.H. The Duke of Windsor; K.G.; H.R.H. The Duke of Gloucester, K.G.; Capt. W. R. Chaplin, C.B.E.; Capt. W. E. Crumplin; Capt. Sir Gerald Curteis, K.C.V.O., R.N. (ret.); Commodore R. L. F. Hubbard, C.B.E., R.D., R.N.R.(ret.); Capt. C. St. G. Glasson; Commodore T. L. Owen, O.B.E., R.D., R.N.R. (ret.); Capt. G. C. H. Noakes, R.D., R.N.R. (ret.); Admiral of the Fleet the Earl Mountbatten of Burma, K.G., P.C., G.C.B., O.M., G.C.S.I., G.C.I.E., G.C.V.O., D.S.O.; Capt. D. Dunn; Capt. G. P. McCraith; Capt. R. J. Galpin, R.D., R.N.R.(ret.); The Earl of Avon, K.G., P.C., M.C.; Capt. R. N. Mayo; Capt. D. S. Tibbits, D.S.C., R.N.(ret.); Capt. D. A. G. Dickens; Capt. J. E. Bury; The Duke of Norfolk, K.G., P.C., G.C.V.O., G.B.E.; Sir Donald Anderson; Capt. J. A. N. Bezant, D.S.C., R.D., R.N.R.(ret.); Capt. F. W. White, O.B.E.; Capt. D. J. Cloke; The Rt. Hon. J. H. Wilson, O.B.E., M.P.; Capt. M. B. Wingate; Capt. A. J. Newport.

Officers
Secretary, L. N. Potter.
Deputy Secretary, S. W. Heesom.

COMMISSIONERS OF NORTHERN LIGHTHOUSES
28 North Bridge, Edinburgh 1
[031-226-7051]

The Commissioners of Northern Lighthouses are the General Lighthouse Authority for Scotland and the Isle of Man. The present Board owes its origin to an Act of Parliament passed in 1786 which authorized the erection of 4 lighthouses; 19 Commissioners were appointed to carry out the Act. At the present time the Commissioners operate under the Merchant Shipping Act, 1894 and are 23 in number.

The Commissioners control 66 Major manned Lighthouses, 1 manned Lightvessel, 21 Major unmanned Lighthouses, 87 Minor Lights and many Lighted and Unlighted Buoys. They have a fleet of 4 Motor Vessels.

Commissioners
The Lord Advocate, the Solicitor General, the Lord Provost and Senior Bailie of Edinburgh, the Lord Provost and Senior Bailie of Glasgow, the Lord Provosts of Aberdeen and Dundee, and the Provosts of Inverness, Campbeltown and Greenock, the Sheriffs of the Lothians and Peebles; Lanark; Renfrew and Argyll; Inverness, Moray, Nairn, and Ross and Cromarty; Aberdeen, Kincardine and Banff; Ayr and Bute; Fife and Kinross; Perth and Angus; Caithness, Sutherland, Orkney and Zetland; Dumfries and Galloway; Roxburgh, Berwick and Selkirk; and Stirling, Dunbarton and Clackmannan.

Officers
General Manager, W. Alastair Robertson, D.S.C.
Assistant General Manager, P. H. Hyslop, D.S.C.
Secretary, A. R. Malcolm.

CLYDE PORT AUTHORITY
16 Robertson Street, Glasgow C.2
Chairman, A. G. McCrae.
General Manager, J. P. Davidson.
Secretary and Solicitor, J. B. Maxwell.

UNIVERSITY GRANTS COMMITTEE
14 Park Crescent, W.1
[01-636-7799]

The Committee was appointed by the Chancellor of the Exchequer in July, 1919, and its present terms of reference are as follows:

" To inquire into the financial needs of university education in Great Britain; to advise the Government as to the application of any grants made by Parliament towards meeting them; to collect, examine, and make available information relating to university education throughout the United Kingdom; and to assist, in consultation with the universities and other bodies concerned, the preparation and execution of such plans for the development of the universities as may from time to time be required in order to ensure that they are fully adequate to national needs."

Chairman, Sir Kenneth Berrill, K.C.B......£13,000
Deputy Chairman, Sir Robert Aitken, M.D., D.Phil.
               fees
Other Members, Prof. G. A. Barnard; Prof. C. E. H. Bawn, C.B.E., F.R.S.; Prof. J. Black, Ph.D.; G. S. Bosworth, C.B.E.; Miss E. J. Bradbury, C.B.E.; S. L. Bragg; Prof. A. J. Brown, D.Phil.; C. C. Butler, Ph.D., F.R.S.; D. Cook; Ph.D.; Prof. R. C. Cross; Prof. J. Cruickshank; Prof. A. Davies; Prof. J. Diamond, C.B.E.; Mrs. J. Floud; H. R. Galleymore; Prof. N. C. Hunt, Ph.D.; Prof. D. Lewis, D.SC., F.R.S.; Prof. P. G. Stein, Ph.D.; Prof. Sir Charles Stuart-Harris, C.B.E., M.D.
Secretary, L. R. Fletcher, C.B............£9,000
Under Secretaries, G. K. Caston; E. H. St. G. Moss
               £6,750
Assist. Secretaries, L. P. Angell; D. W. MacDowall; A. E. L. Parnis; Miss M. L. Senior
          £5,000 to £6,300
Principals, Mrs. E. W. Cahan; A. A. Croxford (*Statistician*); A. P. J. Edwards; C. Graham; A. C. Locke; N. P. Thomas; J. C. Walne; Mrs. D. R. Williams............£3,250 to £4,400
Directing Architect, S. Meyrick............£5,640
Superintending Quantity Surveyor, P. E. Bathurst
          £4,390 to £5,015

COMMONWEALTH WAR GRAVES COMMISSION
32 Grosvenor Gardens, S.W.1
[01-730-0751]

The Commonwealth War Graves Commission (formerly Imperial War Graves Commission) was founded by Royal Charter in 1917. It is responsible for the commemoration of 1,695,000 members of the forces of the Commonwealth who fell in the

two world wars. More than one million graves are
maintained in 23,630 cemeteries throughout the
world. Nearly three-quarters of a million men and
women who have no known grave or who were
cremated are commemorated by name on memorials built by the Commission.

The funds of the Commission are derived from
the seven Governments participating in its work—
The United Kingdom, Canada, Australia, New
Zealand, South Africa, India and Pakistan.

President, H.R.H. The Duke of Kent, G.C.M.G.,
G.C.V.O.
Chairman: The Secretary of State for Defence.
Vice-Chairman, Air Chief Marshal Sir Walter
Cheshire, G.B.E., K.C.B.
Members, The Minister for Housing and Construc-
tion; The High Commissioners for Canada,
the Commonwealth of Australia, New Zealand,
India and Pakistan; the Ambassador for the
Republic of South Africa; Sir Robert Black,
G.C.M.G., O.B.E.; V. Wylie; Col. Sir Richard
Glyn, Bt., O.B.E., T.D.; Miss Joan Woodgate,
C.B.E., R.R.C.; Sir John Winnifrith, K.C.B.;
Admiral Sir Frank Twiss, K.C.B., D.S.C.; E. L.
Gardner, Q.C., M.P.; G. D. Wallace, M.P.; General
Sir Noel Thomas, K.C.B., D.S.O., M.C.
Director-General, W. J. Chalmers, C.B.E.
Director of External Relations and Records, P. H. M.
Swan.
Director of Finance and Establishments, A. K. Pallot,
C.M.G.
Director of Works, Brigadier K. F. Daniell, C.B.E.
Legal Adviser and Solicitor, H. L. Simmons.
Chief Horticultural Officer, W. F. W. Harding,
O.B.E.
Honorary Artistic Adviser, The Lord Holford, R.A.,
F.R.I.B.A.
Hon. Consulting Engineer, P. A. Scott.
Hon. Botanical Adviser, Sir George Taylor, D.Sc.,
F.R.S., F.R.S.E.
Hon. Literary Adviser, Professor Edmund Blunden,
C.B.E., M.C.

Imperial War Graves Endowment Fund

Trustees, A. H. Carnwath; Air Chief Marshal Sir
Walter Cheshire, G.B.E., K.C.B.; Sir John Hogg,
T.D.
Hon. Secretary to the Trustees, W. J. Chalmers, C.B.E.

WATER RESOURCES BOARD
Reading Bridge House, Reading, Berks.
[Reading: 57551]

Established on July 1, 1964 under the Water
Resources Act, 1963 and charged with the duty of
building up comprehensive information about water
resources and demands in England and Wales,
working out action needed to augment resources,
securing the promotion of schemes to meet growing
demands and commissioning and supervising research. In carrying out its tasks the Board advises
the Secretary of State for the Environment and
the Secretary of State for Wales on national policy
for water and also advises the 29 river authorities
established under the Act with respect to the performance of their water resources functions. In
addition the Board has close liaison with all major
abstractors and users of water. With one exception,
Chairman and members serve part-time.
Chairman, Sir William Goode, G.C.M.G.
Deputy Chairman, A G. McLellan. C.B.E.
Members, R. A. Banks, C.B.E.; D. A. Bassett;
Lt.-Col. the Hon. P. E. Brassey; F. W. W.
Pemberton, C.B.E.; Sir Norman Rowntree (*full-
time Director*)
Secretary, D. G. Jones.

WELSH OFFICE
Gwydyr House, Whitehall, S.W.1
[01-930-3151]

Secretary of State, THE RT. HON. PETER JOHN
MITCHELL THOMAS, Q.C., M.P. £8,500
Private Secretary, L. M. Lloyd, M.B.E.

Parliamentary Private Secretary, L. W. P. Roberts
M.P.
Minister of State, (JAMES) DAVID GIBSON-WATT,
M.C., M.P. £5,625
Private Secretary, G. C. G. Craig.
Permanent Secretary, H. W. Evans. £9,000
Assistant Secretary, S. T. Charles . £5,000 to £6,300
Principal, H. K. Trimnell. . . . . . . £3,250 to £4,400

Cathays Park, Cardiff
[0222–28066]

Under Secretaries, J. H. Clement; L. Jones; D. G.
McPherson; O. H. Morris, C.M.G.; J. W. M.
Siberry. £6,750
Assistant Secretaries, J. A. Annand; I. Davey;
E. O. Davies; I. S. Dewar; B. H. Evans; R. Hall-
Williams; P. J. Hosegood; J. E. King; A. Owen,
M.C.; R. A. Owen; L. Pritchard; P. I. Wolf
£5,000 to £6,300
Assistant Secretary (Finance Officer), W. B. Jones
£5,000 to £6,300
Senior Economic Adviser, O. T. Hooker
£5,000 to £6,300
Principals, M. E. Bevan; J. E. Booker; F. E. Brewer;
G. G. Elliott; M. G. Evans; W. J. Griffiths;
S. H. Hindley, M.B.E.; Mrs. E. O. James;
G. M. Jenkins; A. H. H. Jones; R. H. Jones,
C.V.O.; H. E. Leonard; J. C. Lewis; P. E. Love-
luck; D. Morgan; G. H. Nowell, M.B.E.; R. D.
Potter; O. Rees; F. D. Riddett, I.S.O.; T. Roberts;
H. I. W. Sparkes; J. G. Stephens; J. Taffinder;
D. J. Tallis; R. Thomas. . . . £3,250 to £4,400
Statistician, D. A. Jones. . . . . . £3,250 to £4,400
Head of Road Safety Unit, G. G. Gates, M.B.E.
£3,250 to £4,400

Architectural Staff
Chief Architect, G. J. Kelly. £5,640
Architects (Senior Grade), H. O. M. Coleman; J. R.
Coward; J. T. Darch; C. Eyres; J. L. Grove;
S. C. Halbritter; G. N. Harding; D. C. Long;
E. T. Williams. . . . . £3,575 to £4,208
Quantity Surveyors (Senior Grade), T. A. Campden;
A. D. Hill; I. Smith. . . . . . £3,575 to £4,208

Engineering Staff
Chief Engineer, R. S. Offord. . . . £4,920 to £5,640
Engineering Inspectors, J. L. Arnold; H. Cronshaw;
G. M. Jones; A. S. R. Mutch. £3,352 to £4,470
Engineer (Senior Grade), J. Jarvis. £3,575 to £4,208

Engineering Staff (Roads)
Director of Highways, D. A. R. Hall. £6,120
Deputy Chief Road Engineer, G. F. Leadbeter, O.B.E.
£4,390 to £5,015
Senior Engineers, P. I. Adams; L. P. Cole, M.B.E.;
J. E. Morgan; W. H. Prosser; O. J. Watt
£3,575 to £4,208

Health Staff
Chief Medical Officer, R. T. Bevan, M.D. . . . £6,510
Senior Medical Officers, T. J. M. Gregg, O.B.E.;
A. G. Jones; W. C. D. Lovett, O.B.E. . . . £5,640
Medical Officers, R. Buntwal; E. J. S. Evans; G. M.
Evans; R. Y. Forbes; Mrs. M. M. G. Gray;
A. J. R. Hudson; Mrs. M. W. Jenkins; G. A. L.
Jones; H. A. Mullen, T.D., Q.H.P.; P. R. E.
Williams. . . . . £3,552 to £4,875
Dental Officers, T. W. Beer; G. Morris; T. A.
Williams. . . . . £3,480 to £4,647
Nursing Officers, E. E. Beckerton; Miss I. John
£3,268 to £4,311

Planning Staff
Chief Planner, G. H. C. Cooper. £5,640
Senior Research Officers, D. T. M. Davies; C. G.
Parry. . . . . £2,820 to £3,902
Senior Planning Officers, G. Fairhurst; W. L. Hulley,
O.B.E.; I. N. Jones. . . . . £3,575 to £4,208
Senior Estate Officer, W. Bradley £3,575 to £4,208
Principal Scientific Officer, T. M. Thomas
£2,820 to £3,902
Senior Housing and Planning Inspectors, R. W. Deans,
G.M.; M. R. Mullins, M.B.E.; L. G. H. Parnell;
S. Roberton; J. W. Tester. . . . £3,660 to £4,390

Legal Staff

Legal Adviser, G. Davies .... £4,555 to £5,640
Assistant Legal Adviser, A. Howe £4,555 to £5,640

Information Staff

Director, Information Division, J. E. B. Evans
£4,390 to £5,640

Social Work Service

Principal Social Work Service Officer, R. L. Jones
£3,997 to £5,002
Social Work Service Officers, B. F. Brien; H. J. Devey; Miss J. C. M. Jones; L. Pugh; G. W. Smith .... £2,748 to £3,991

WHITE FISH AUTHORITY

Lincoln's Inn Chambers, 2/3 Cursitor Street, E.C.4
[01–242–9441]

Chairman, Sir Charles Hardie, C.B.E. (*part-time*)
£4,375
Deputy-Chairman, Sir Matthew Campbell, K.B.E., C.B., F.R.S.E. .... (*part-time*) £3,000
Members (*part-time*), W. J. L. Dean, O.B.E. (£2,500); Sir Frederick Brundrett, K.C.B., K.B.E., D.Sc.; D. Basnett; Admiral Sir Deric Holland-Martin, G.C.B., D.S.O., D.S.C. £1,000
Chief Executive, C. I. Meek, C.M.G.

COMMISSIONS, ETC.

COMMISSION ON THE CONSTITUTION
GKN House, 22 Kingsway, W.C.2
[01–242–6828]

Appointed on April 15, 1969, " to examine the present functions of the central legislature and government in relation to the several countries, nations and regions of the United Kingdom; to consider, having regard to developments in local government organization and in the administrative and other relationships between the various parts of the United Kingdom, and to the interests of the prosperity and good government of Our people under the Crown, whether any changes are desirable in those functions or otherwise in present constitutional and economic relationships; to consider, also, whether any changes are desirable in the constitutional and economic relationships between the United Kingdom and the Channel Islands and the Isle of Man."

Chairman, The Lord Crowther.
Members, D. Basnett; A. T. Davies, Q.C.; The Lord Foot; Sir Mark Henig; Rt. Hon. A. L. N. D. Houghton, C.H., M.P.; N. C. Hunt, Ph.D.; The Lord Kilbrandon, P.C.; The Very Rev. J. B. Longmuir, T.D., D.D.; Prof. F. H. Newark, C.B.E.; Prof. A. T. Peacock, D.S.C.; Rt. Hon. Sir David Renton, K.B.E., T.D., Q.C., M.P.; Sir James Steel, C.B.E.; Prof. H. Street, Ph.D., F.B.A.; Sir Ben Bowen Thomas; Mrs. M. S. Trenaman.
Secretary, R. J. Guppy, C.B.

COMMISSION ON INDUSTRIAL RELATIONS
22, Kingsway, W.C.2
[01–242–6828]

Chairman, L. F. Neal £15,000
Deputy Chairman, C. F. Heron £11,000
Members, L. T. Blakeman, C.B.E. (£6,500); J. R. Edwards, C.B.E. (*part-time*).
Secretary, N. Singleton, C.B.

COMMUNITY RELATIONS COMMISSION
Russell Square House
10–12, Russell Square, W.C.1
[01–636–8412]

Established on November 26, 1968, under the Race Relations Act, 1968, to help people of different races and cultures to live and work together in harmony.
Chairman, Hon. Mark Bonham-Carter. REV. A. JOWETT
Deputy Chairmen, J. Burgh; D. T. Pitt.
Members, Miss J. Barrow; The Lord Campbell of Eskan; P. C. Chitnis; Sir Ronald Gould; B. Lyons, C.B.E.; B. J. Pechies; A. F. A. Sayeed; The Baroness Serota; Prof. R. M. Titmuss, C.B.E.
Chief Officer, Miss N. Peppard.

FOREIGN COMPENSATION COMMISSION
Alexandra House, Kingsway, W.C.2
The Commission was set up by the *Foreign Compensation Act*, 1950, to distribute funds paid by foreign governments as compensation for expropriated British property and other losses sustained by British nationals. The *Foreign Compensation Act*, 1962, provided, *inter alia*, for the payment out of moneys provided by Parliament of additional compensation in respect of claims arising in connection with certain events in Egypt. The Foreign Compensation Act, 1969, provided, *inter alia*, for the payment by the Board of Trade to the Commission for distribution of moneys held by the Custodian of Enemy Property being former property of a Baltic State or ceded territory. The Commission has completed the final distribution of the funds contributed by Yugoslavia, Czechoslovakia, Bulgaria, Poland, Rumania and Hungary. The Commission has registered certain British claims in Czechoslovakia and also in the Baltic States and territories annexed by the Soviet Union. The U.S.S.R. Distribution Order in respect of British owned property affected by nationalization or expropriation of bank balances, government and municipal bonds and debts held by or owing to British nationals at the material time, and unredeemed Lena and Tetiuhe State Notes irrespective of the nationality of the holders, came into operation on June 16, 1969, and the Commission is engaged in determining claims thereunder. The £27,500,000 compensation paid by the Government of the United Arab Republic under the financial agreement of Feb. 28, 1959, has been fully distributed, and claims under the Egypt Order are now being paid from funds provided by Parliament.
Chairman, C. Montgomery White, Q.C.
Vice-Chairman, Sir Ralph Windham.
Commissioners, Sir James Henry, Bt., C.M.G., M.C., T.D.; D. Eifion Evans, Q.C.; Sir Daniel Crawshaw.
Legal Officer, J. R. Whimster.
Chief Examiner, Miss H. M. Walsh, O.B.E.
Registrar, W. H. Pridmore.

ROYAL COMMISSION ON ENVIRONMENTAL POLLUTION
Great George Street, S.W.1
[01–930–3324]

Set up on Feb. 20, 1970, " to advise on matters, both national and international, concerning the pollution of the environment; on the adequacy of research in this field; and the future possibilities of danger to the environment".

Chairman, Sir Eric Ashby, D.Sc., F.R.S.
Members, Prof. W. Beckerman; A. L. O. Buxton, M.C.; Sir Frank Fraser Darling, D.Sc., F.R.S.E.; N. A. Iliff, C.B.E.; The Rt. Rev. the Dean of Windsor; Sir John Winnifrith, K.C.B.; Prof. V. C. Wynne-Edwards, D.Sc., F.R.S., F.R.S.E.; The Lord Zuckerman, O.M., K.C.B., M.D. D.Sc., F.R.S.
Secretary, Miss D. M. Wilde.

CRIMINAL INJURIES COMPENSATION BOARD
10-12 Russell Square, W.C.1
[01-636-2812]

The Board was constituted in 1964 to administer the Government scheme for the compensation of victims of crimes of violence, which came into operation on August 1, 1964.

Chairman, His Hon. Sir Walker Kelly Carter, Q.C.; *Members,* D. A. Barker, Q.C.; W. O. Carter; J. Law, Q.C.; Sir Ronald Long; D. G. A. Lowe, Q.C.; R. H. McDonald, Q.C.; Sir Ronald Morison, Q.C.; M. Ogden, Q.C.

Secretary, D. H. Harrison.

THE BRITISH COUNCIL
65 Davies Street, W.1

The British Council was established in 1934. Its Royal Charter (1940) defines its aims as the promotion of a wider knowledge of Britain and English abroad, and the development of closer cultural relations with other countries. Most of its funds are provided by Parliament: the gross budget for 1971–72 is £16,014,000, and it administers a further sum, estimated for 1971–72 at £8,196,000, as agent for Government Departments and international organizations. *Ld Ballantrae* 10/7
Chairman, Sir Leslie Rowan, K.C.B., C.V.O.
Director-General, The Hon. Sir John Henniker, K.C.M.G., C.V.O., M.C. *from 1/7/72 DR F J LLEWELLYN*

THE NATIONAL TRUST
40-42 Queen Anne's Gate, Westminster, S.W.1

The National Trust was founded in 1895 by Miss Octavia Hill, Sir Robert Hunter and Canon Rawnsley, their object being to preserve as much as possible of the history and beauty of their country for its people. It has since become an organization incorporated by Act of Parliament to ensure the preservation of lands and buildings of historic interest or natural beauty for public access and benefit. It is independent of the State and relies mainly on the voluntary support of private individuals for working funds. As a charity, however, it is allowed certain tax exemptions. A further, and more recently instituted, branch of the Trust's work is the acquisition and preservation, with the co-operation of the Royal Horticultural Society, of gardens of national importance. It also has under its care bird sanctuaries and nature reserves, together with several hundred farms.

The National Trust now administers more than 400,000 acres of land in England, Wales and Northern Ireland; and in this area are over 1,000 properties. These properties have come into its hands mainly by gift or bequest; but since 1946 certain land and buildings accepted by the Treasury in lieu of death duties have been handed over to the Trust, the Treasury recompensing itself from the National Land Fund. Properties acquired by the National Trust include the Ashridge Estate (Bucks. and Herts.); Cliveden (Bucks.); West Wycombe Park and village (Bucks.); Wicken Fen (Cambs.); Lyme Park (Cheshire); Cotehele House (Cornwall); Pentire Head (Cornwall); St. Michael's Mount (Cornwall); Trerice (Cornwall); Dovedale (Derbys. and Staffs.); Arlington Court Estate (Devon); Hatfield Forest (Essex); Chedworth Roman Villa (Glos.); Hidcote Manor Gdn. (Glos.); Knole (Kent); over 70,000 acres in the Lake District, including the Buttermere Valley, Monk Coniston Estate, Scafell Pike and Troutbeck Park Farm; Tattershall Castle (Lincs.); Osterley Park (Middx.); Blickling Hall Estate (Norfolk); Farne Islands (Northumberland); Clumber Park (Notts.); Holnicote Estate (Somerset); Montacute House (Somerset); Flatford Mill (Suffolk); Box Hill (Surrey); Ham House (Surrey); Bodiam Castle (Sussex); Petworth House (Sussex); Charlecote Park (Warwicks.); Lacock Abbey and village (Wilts.); Stourhead Estate (Wilts.); Derwent Estate (Yorks. and Derbys.); Hardwick Hall (Derbys.); Bodnant Gardens (N. Wales); Powis Castle (Mont.); Castlecoole (N. Ireland); Hanbury Hall (Warwicks.); Lanhydrock (Cornwall); Tintinhull House (Somerset); Nymans Gardens (Sussex); Sheffield Park Gardens (Sussex); Uppark (Sussex); Nostell Priory (Yorks.); Staunton Harold Church (Leics.); Penard Cliff (Glam); Blundell's Old School (Devon); Castleward (N. Ireland).

Recent acquisitions include more than 130 coastal properties obtained as a result of the Trust's campaign to save the coastline. Since 1965 the campaign has raised £1,650,000 and brought 170 miles of coast under the Trust's protection.

THE NATIONAL TRUST FOR SCOTLAND
5 Charlotte Square, Edinburgh 2

The National Trust for Scotland was founded in 1931, and its objects are similar to those of the National Trust. Like that organization, it is incorporated by Act of Parliament, is dependent for finance upon legacies, donations and the subscriptions of its members, is recognized as a charity for tax exemption purposes, and enjoys certain privileges under various Finance Acts regarding death duties.

The Trust administers about 60 major properties covering over 80,000 acres. Great houses in its care include:— The Binns, West Lothian; Brodick Castle, Isle of Arran; Crathes Castle, Kincardineshire; Culzean Castle, Ayrshire; Falkland Palace, Fife; Hill of Tarvit and Kellie Castle, Fife, and Leith Hall and Craigievar Castle, Aberdeenshire.

In the Trust's care are also several noteworthy gardens. Some are associated with the great houses, others are:— Inverewe, in Wester Ross; the re-created 17th century garden of Pitmedden in Aberdeenshire; and Threave in Kirkcudbrightshire, where a School of Practical Gardening is run; and Branklyn Gardens, Perth.

Among the mountainous country owned by the Trust is the Pass of Glencoe and the mountain group " The Five Sisters of Kintail " and the estate of Torridon in Wester Ross.

Islands in the Trust's care include the St. Kilda group, and the Fair Isle. At Bannockburn, Killiecrankie, Glenfinnan and Culloden, the Trust owns sites associated with Scottish history.

Among smaller properties are houses associated with famous Scots:— the birthplaces of Barrie in Kirriemuir, Carlyle in Ecclefechan, and Hugh Miller in Cromarty; and Burns' Bachelors' Club, Tarbolton and Souter Johnnie's House, Kirkoswald in Ayrshire.

At Culross in Fife, and at Dunkeld, Perthshire, the restoration of attractive groups of houses led to the creation of a special fund under which such properties are bought, restored and sold. Under this scheme over 100 properties in the coastal burghs of East Fife and elsewhere have been and are being restored.

THE PILGRIM TRUST
Millbank House, 2 Great Peter Street, S.W.1

Trustees, Richard Fleming, M.C. (*Chairman*); The Lord Franks, P.C., G.C.M.G., K.C.B., C.B.E.; The Earl of Crawford and Balcarres, K.T., G.B.E.; W. F. Oakeshott; The Lord Harlech, P.C., K.C.M.G.; The Hon. Sir Henry Fisher; The Lord Boyle of Handsworth, P.C.

Secretary, Sir Edward Ford, K.C.B., K.C.V.O.

The Pilgrim Trust was founded in 1930 by the late Edward S. Harkness of New York, who placed in the hands of British trustees £2,000,000 for the benefit of Great Britain. Since then the

Trust has been able to make substantial grants for the repair of ancient buildings, the preservation of the countryside, the support of learned societies, the preservation of historical records, the purchase of works of art and the assistance of social welfare schemes.

Since its foundation the Trust has made grants amounting to over £6,143,200 and in 1970 the Trustees voted sums totalling £373,045. These grants were made under the following three heads:—Preservation, £156,820, Art and Learning, £153,625. Social Welfare, £62,000.

In 1970, two of the larger grants made by Trustees were a further £23,000 to the York Minster Fund (to which they had already contributed £50,000 in 1967), and £15,000 for the renovation of the Royal Albert Hall, London. Other grants included £10,000 to the National Trust for Scotland towards the purchase of Kellie Castle, Fife; £10,000 each to the Royal School of Church Music and to the Friends of Lancing Chapel for the completion of the Chapel; £5,000 each to The Birmingham Repertory Theatre, the Leeds Theatre Trust and the Bristol Old Vic Trust Ltd.; £15,000 for the repair of the archives of the Court of Arches in Lambeth Palace Library; £5,000 each to Girton College, Cambridge and to the United World College of the Atlantic; £6,000 to provide a pit lift in the rebuilt Concert Hall at Aldeburgh; £7,500 to the National Old People's Welfare Council; £5,000 to the Samaritans and £4,500 to the North Kensington Neighbourhood Law Centre; and £5,000 to the Upper Avon Navigation Trust Ltd. for the provision of a lock between Bidford and Stratford-upon-Avon.

BRITISH STANDARDS INSTITUTION
British Standards House, 2 Park Street, W.1

The British Standards Institution is the recognized authority in the U.K. for the preparation and publication of national standards for industrial and consumer products. The Institution originated in 1901, when the Institutions of Civil, Mechanical and Electrical Engineers, together with the Iron and Steel Institute and the Institution of Naval Architects, formed a joint Engineering Standards Committee—which subsequently became the British Engineering Standards Association. A Royal Charter was granted in 1929 and with the extension of the scope of the organization to include the building, chemical and textile industries its title was later changed to " British Standards Institution ".

The Institution, in consultation with the interests concerned, now prepares standards relating to nearly every sector of the nation's industry and trade. There are over 5,000 British Standards covering specifications of quality, construction dimensions, performance or safety; methods of test and analysis; glossaries of terms; and codes of practice. About 500 new and revised British Standards are published each year.

The Institution represents the U.K. in the International Organization for Standardization (ISO), the International Electrotechnical Commission (IEC) and other international bodies concerned with harmonizing standards.

British Standards are issued for voluntary adoption though in a number of cases compliance with a British Standard is required by legislation. The Institution operates certification schemes under which industrial and consumer products are certified as complying with the relevant British Standard and manufacturers satisfying the requirements of such schemes may use the Institution's registered certification mark (known as the " Kitemark "). Other testing and certification services, together with information services, are available to industry,

including help in meeting technical requirements in export markets.

The Institution is financed by voluntary subscriptions, an annual Government grant, the sale of its publications and fees for testing and certification. There are more than 14,000 subscribing members of B.S.I., including public authorities, trade and technical bodies, professional institutions, manufacturers, distributors and large scale purchasers.

Chairman of the Executive Board, E. W. Greensmith.
Director General, G. B. R. Feilden, C.B.E., F.R.S.
Director General International, H. A. R. Binney, C.B.

HOUSING CORPORATION
Sloane Square House, S.W.1
[01-730-9991]

Set up on Sept. 1, 1964 to promote the growth of housing societies and, through them, to stimulate the building of new houses and flats for letting at cost-rents or for co-ownership. The societies are expected to raise about two-thirds of the money from building societies or other financial institutions. The remainder comes from the Housing Corporation lending on second mortgage. £100,000,000 is being made available for this purpose by the Government to the Corporation. Loans are repayable over 40 years.

Chairman, H. Ashworth.
Members, D. H. D. Alexander, O.B.E., T.D.; H. Campbell; E. Clark; Mrs. P. Crabbe; W. S. Jones, C.B.E.; A. Meikle, C.B.E.; L. E. Waddilove, O.B.E.
General Manager, R. L. Thomas.
Secretary, R. Vipond, D.F.C.

COUNCIL OF INDUSTRIAL DESIGN
28 Haymarket, S.W.1
[01-839-8000]

The Council of Industrial Design, with its Scottish Committee, was set up in December, 1944, by the President of the Board of Trade, " to promote . . . the improvement of design in the products of British Industry." For manufacturers, the Council provides advice on the application of design policy, and recommends designers from its Designer Selection Service. For retailers, it provides courses for buyers and salesmen on design appreciation, and organizes exhibitions in retail stores. For the public it provides selective exhibitions of well designed goods.

The Council has a Design Centre for British Industries at 28 Haymarket, S.W.1. and a Scottish Design Centre at 72 St. Vincent Street, Glasgow, C.2.

The Council maintains a selective, pictorial and sample record of well designed goods in current production known as *Design Index*, which is available for consultation at the Design Centre. The Council also maintains a photograph library and slide loan service, press and information services and a lecture panel, and publishes a monthly journal *Design*.

Chairman, Sir Duncan Oppenheim.
Chairman of Scottish Committee, M. J. G. Wylie.
Director, Sir Paul Reilly.
Chief Executive, Scottish Committee, R. G. Clark.

BRITISH NATIONAL EXPORT COUNCIL
6-14 Dean Farrar Street, S.W.1
[01-930-3121]

The British National Export Council was founded in 1964 to satisfy a common desire of the Government and existing national organizations to revise and improve collective arrangements for encouraging British exports. Initially BNEC took under its wing the Export Council for Europe, formed in 1960, the Council for Middle East Trade (1963) and elements of the Western Hemi-

sphere Export Council which had gone out of existence some few months earlier.

The British National Export Council is an independent and non-political organization whose principal task is to influence the successful promotion at home of British exports. Sponsored by the Department of Trade and Industry, the Association of British Chambers of Commerce, the Confedera-

export activities, stimulating sales of capital and consumer goods and advanced technology in all actual and potential markets. The chairmen of these area committees serve on the central Council together with leading exporters and senior Government officials. Each area body has a chairman who is personally appointed by the Minister for Trade of the Department of Trade and Industry on the recommendation of the Chairman of the British

THE BANK OF ENGLAND
Threadneedle Street, E.C.2

The Bank of England was incorporated in 1694 under Royal Charter. It is the banker of the Government on whose behalf it manages the Note Issue, and also manages the National Debt and administers the Exchange Control regulations. As central reserve bank of the country, the Bank keeps the accounts of British banks, who maintain with it a proportion of their cash resources, and of most overseas central banks; but it has gradually withdrawn from new commercial business.

Governor, The Rt. Hon. Sir Leslie Kenneth O'Brien, G.B.E. (*1976).
Deputy Governor, Jasper Quintus Hollom (*1975).
Directors, George Adrian Hayhurst Cadbury (*1974); Jack Gale Wilmot Davies, O.B.E. (*1972); Leopold David de Rothschild (*1975); Sir Val Duncan, O.B.E. (*1973); John Standish Fforde (*1974); Sir Sidney Francis Greene, C.B.E. (*1974); William Johnston Keswick (*1975); Sir (John) Maurice Laing (*1972); Christopher

William McMahon (*1973); Christopher Jeremy Morse (*1973); The Lord Nelson of Stafford (*1975); The Lord Pilkington (*1972); Gordon William Humphreys Richardson, M.B.E. (*1975); The Lord Robens of Woldingham, P.C. (*1974); Sir Eric Roll, K.C.M.G., C.B. (*1973); Sir John Melior Stevens, K.C.M.G., D.S.O., O.B.E., T.D. (*1972).

* Date of Retirement.

Chief Cashier, J. B. Page.
Chief Accountant, R. C. Balfour, M.B.E.
Chief of the Overseas Dept., R. P. Fenton, C.M.G.
Chief of the Economic Intelligence Dept., M. J. Thornton, M.C.
Secretary, P. A. S. Taylor.
Chief of Establishments, K. J. S. Andrews, M.B.E.
Chief of Management Services, R. E. Heasman.
Advisers to the Governors, E. P. Haslam; J. A. Kirbyshire; R. G. Raw.
General Manager, Printing Works, G. C. Fortin. retires 1/4/72 succeeded by M. J.S. CUBBAGE

THE LONDON CLEARING BANKS

COMMITTEE OF LONDON CLEARING BANKERS
(1821), 10 Lombard Street, E.C.3.

The Committee consists of the Chairmen of the six Clearing Banks (Barclays, Coutts, Lloyds, Midland, National Westminster, and Williams & Glyns) and meets regularly to discuss matters of common interest. It is the body through which the Bank of England communicates official policy to the banks and through which the banks may present their views to the Bank of England and the Treasury. The Committee controls the London Bankers' Clearing House.
Secretary, R. K. C. Giddings, M.C.
Deputy Secretaries, L. M. Mears; M. C. Swift, M.C.
Asst. Secretaries, G. B. Scrine; M. N. Karmel; Miss V. A. Novarra.

INTER-BANK COMPUTER BUREAU
10 Lombard Street, E.C.3.

The Inter-Bank Computer Bureau forms part of the money transfer service operated by the Clearing Banks, the Scottish Banks and the Bank of England, its main function being the inter-change of Standing Orders between the Banks. The Bureau also processes data relating to Bank Giro Credits and Debits originated under the Direct Debiting scheme, through the medium of magnetic or punched paper tape, on behalf of customers of the Banks.
Chief Manager, D. J. Pyne.

BANKERS' CLEARING HOUSE
10 Lombard Street, E.C.3.

This is the organization through which the Clearing Banks and the Bank of England exchange

cheques drawn on each other and settle their indebtedness to one another. The clearing system came into being in London during the second half of the eighteenth century, and has served as a pattern for the Clearing Houses that have been established since throughout the world.

To obtain payment for any cheque received from a customer for his credit, a banker must present it for payment to the bank on which it is drawn, and the Bankers' Clearing House affords a quick and efficient means of doing this. On an average day 3,000,000 cheques with a total value of £3,000 million, are exchanged and paid for by the six Clearing Banks and the Bank of England on behalf of their branches throughout England and Wales which number over 10,000.

At present two cheque clearings are operated each business day. The Town Clearing, which takes place from 2.30 p.m. until 3.45 p.m., enables cheques of £5,000 and over to be cleared the same day, provided that such cheques are drawn on, and paid into, a Town Clearing branch. There are over ninety branches of the Clearing Banks so designated within a half-mile radius of the Clearing House.

The General Clearing, which takes place each morning, handles all cheques, drawn on branches of the member banks, which cannot be passed through the Town Clearing or cleared under local arrangements. Since April, 1960, a Credit Clearing has been operated through which the member banks exchange credit items in respect of monetary transfers between their customers. The daily

X Deputy Gov. now 11/4/73
D.C. Ingram

average for this Clearing, including work passed
hrough the Inter-Bank Computer Bureau, is
800,000 items with a total value of £55 million.

At the end of the day each member bank works
out the net balance resulting from its transactions
in that day's Town Clearing, the previous day's

General Clearing and Credit Clearing, and such
differences as need to be adjusted. This net balance
is either credited to or deducted from the bank's
own account at the Bank of England.
Chief Inspector, K. L. Tibbatts.
Deputy Inspector, S. C. Veal.

PRINCIPAL BANKS OPERATING IN THE BRITISH COMMONWEALTH

* *Clearing Bankers.*   ‡ *Army Agents.*

London Banking Hours are 9.30 a.m. to 3.30 p.m. (Saturdays, *closed*). In addition, most branches open on
one evening a week from 4.30 p.m. to 6.00 p.m.   *Scotland.*—Banking hours in Scotland are: Mon.-Wed.,
9.30–12.30; 1.30–3.30; Thursday, 9.30–12.30; 1.30–3.30; 4.30–6 p.m.; Fri. 9.30–3.30; Saturday, *Closed.*

ALEXANDERS DISCOUNT CO., LTD. (1810), 24
Lombard St., E.C.3.—Capital, authorized
£4,000,000. Issued £200,000 in £2 (fully-
paid 6 p.c.) Cumulative Preference Shares,
£3,300,000 £1 Ordinary Shares, fully paid;
Reserves £3,143,293; Loans, £219,548,011;
Deposits, etc., £13,366,453; Dividend, 1970,
6 p.c. on Cumulative Preference Shares; 15 p.c. on
Ordinary Shares.

ALLEN HARVEY & ROSS LIMITED (1888), 45
Cornhill, E.C.3.—(1971) Issued Capital,
£1,862,000; Reserves, £2,484,000; Deposits,
etc., £157,540,000.

THE AMERICAN EXPRESS INTERNATIONAL BANKING
CORPORATION. The Subsidiary of American
Express Co., New York (1868), 65 Broadway,
New York, U.S.A.; 25 Abchurch Lane, E.C.4.—
Capital, $6,000,000 (Shares fully paid).

ANGLO-ISRAEL BANK LTD. (affiliated to the Bank
Leumi Le-Israel B.M.), Bow Bells House,
11 Bread Street, E.C.4.—Capital: Authorized,
£1,500,000; Issued and fully paid, £1,500,000
Ordinary Shares £1 each; Reserves, £930,000.

ANGLO-PORTUGUESE BANK, LTD. (1929), 7–9 Bishopsgate, E.C.2.—Capital, £2,500,000. Issued
and fully paid, £2,000,000; Reserve £3,000,000;
Deposits, 31/1/71, £53,738,237.

AUSTRALIA AND NEW ZEALAND BANKING GROUP
LIMITED, *Head Office*, 71 Cornhill, E.C.3.—
Capital Authorized, £35,000,000; issued and
paid up, £32,130,000; 30/9/70; Reserves,
£28,859,000; Total assets, £1,773,902,000.

AUSTRALIA AND NEW ZEALAND SAVINGS BANK
LIMITED, *Head Office*, 351 Collins Street, Melbourne; Capital Authorized, $A14,000,000; Is-
sued and Paid up, $A5,000,000; Reserve Fund at
30/6/70, $A10,700,000. Total Assets at 30/9/70,
$A728,819,000.

A.N.Z. SAVINGS BANK (NEW ZEALAND) LIMITED,
Regd. Office, 196 Featherston Street, Wellington,
New Zealand. Capital Authorized, Issued and
Paid up, $NZ500,000; Deposits, etc., at
30/9/70, $NZ86,465,108; Reserve Fund,
$NZ680,000; Total Assets at 30/9/70,
$NZ89,797,121.

BANCO DE BILBAO (1857), *Bilbao*, Spain (Bilbao
House, New Broad St., E.C.2. and 40 King Street,
W.C.2; 74 Commercial Street, E.1 and 32 Cran-
bourn Street, W.C.2.)—Capital Subscribed and
paid-up, *Pesetas* 3,119.854,000; Reserve Fund,
Pesetas 6,086,785,715; Deposits, *Pesetas*
119,461,829,906 (434 Branches in Spain, Canary
Islands, France and London).

BANGKOK BANK LTD. (1941), *Bangkok*, Thailand
(59–67 Gresham Street, E.C.2.)—(31/12/70)
Capital issued and paid-up, *Baht* 300,000,000;
Reserve, *Baht* 267,900,000; Undivided Profit,
Baht 30,689,500; Deposits, etc., *Baht*
11,197,432,352.

BANKERS TRUST COMPANY, 16 Wall St., *New York*
(9 Queen Victoria Street, E.C.4 and 32–34
Grosvenor Square, W.1).—Capital stock (par
value $10 per share), $90,886,000.

BANK OF ADELAIDE (1865), *Adelaide*, South Australia
(11 Leadenhall St., E.C.3). Capital, Authorized
$A50,000,000; issued $A21,003.125 (Shares in
units of $A1 each, fully paid); Reserve Fund,
$A9,881,625. (171 Offices.)

BANK OF AMERICA NATIONAL TRUST AND SAVINGS
ASSOCIATION, *San Francisco, California, U.S.A.*
(27–29 Walbrook, E.C.4 and 29 Davies St.,
W.1).—Capital Funds, $1,137,731,000; Loan
Reserves, $276,001,000; Total Deposits,
$22,171,463,000.

BANK OF BERMUDA, LTD. (1889), *Hamilton*, Ber-
muda (*London Agents*, Bank of Bermuda (Europe)
Ltd.)—Capital paid up BD$3,600,000; Reserves,
BD$7,629,442; Resources 31/12/70,
BD$313,282,329; Dividend, 1970, BD$0·49 per
share.

BANK OF N. T. BUTTERFIELD & SON, LTD., *Hamilton*,
Bermuda. Established 1858. (*Representative
Office*, 10 Old Jewry, E.C.2.) Capital, fully paid,
BD$2,400,000. Reserves and Undivided Profits
31/12/70, BD$6,007,406. Total Resources,
BD$222,312,613.

BANK OF ENGLAND. *See* p. 440.

BANK OF INDIA, LTD. (1906), *Bombay* (Kent House,
11–16 Telegraph Street, E.C.2).—Capital paid
up, *Rs.* 4,05,00,000 (7,10,000 shares *Rs.* 100.,
Rs. 50 paid; 1,00,000 shares *Rs.* 50); Reserve
Fund, *Rs.* 6,52,00,000 (250 Branches).

BANK OF IRELAND (1783), College Green, *Dublin*
(*London Agents*, Bank of England; Coutts & Co.,
Brown, Shipley & Co. Ltd.).—Capital (Author-
ized), £11,500,000; (Issued and Fully Paid),
£11,235,608. Reserves, £9,808,087 (150
Branches and Sub-Branches).

BANK OF LONDON AND MONTREAL, LTD. (1958),
P.O. BOX N 1262, Nassau, Bahama Islands. A
wholly-owned subsidiary of the Bank of London
& South America Ltd. Capital (Authorized),
$Bah.30,000,000; (Paid up), $Bah 21,450,000.
(52 Branches and Agencies.)

BANK OF LONDON & SOUTH AMERICA, LTD. (1862),
40–66 Queen Victoria Street, E.C.4.—Authorized Capital, £30,000,000; Paid-up Capital,
£25,701,919. Reserve, £16,409,000. Deposits,
etc., 31/12/70, £700,177,000. Dividend, 1970,
9·83 p.c. (93 Branches and Agencies.)

BANK OF MONTREAL (1817), *Montreal*, Canada
(47 Threadneedle St., E.C.2, and 9 Waterloo
Place, S.W.1).—Capital, authorized, $100,000,000;
fully paid $68,000,000. Rest, $234,000,000;
Deposits, 31/3/71, $8,501,000,000; Dividend,
1970, 75 cents per share. (Over 1,000 Branches
and Agencies.)

BANK OF NEW SOUTH WALES (1817) AND BANK OF NEW SOUTH WALES SAVINGS BANK LTD. (1955), Head Office, *Sydney*, N.S.W. (29 Threadneedle St., E.C.2, 9–15 Sackville Street, W.1. and 14 Kingsway, W.C.2.—At 30/9/70: Capital, authorized and paid up, $A80,009,684; Reserve Fund $A60,199,600; Aggregate Assets, $3,390,654,412; Dividend, 1970, 10 p.c. (1,214 Branches and Agencies.)

BANK OF NEW ZEALAND, Incorporated in New Zealand in 1861. (1 Queen Victoria St., E.C.4.) 31/3/71: Capital Authorized, $NZ14,062,500; Paid up, $NZ12,656,250; Capital Reserve, $NZ15,595,000; Deposits $NZ583,024,352; Total Assets, $NZ700,209,117; (422 Branches and Agencies in New Zealand; also Branches in Melbourne, Sydney, Fiji and London).

BANK OF NOVA SCOTIA (1832). *Halifax*, N.S.; Executive Offices, *Toronto*, Ontario, Canada (Regional Office, 19/23 Knightsbridge, S.W.1.)— Capital, Authorized, $50,000,000; Paid-up $33,750,000 ($2 Shares); Reserve Fund, $175,875,000; Total Assets, $6,369,464,601; (873 Branches and Sub-Branches in Canada, Caribbean, etc.)

BANK OF SCOTLAND (1695), The Mound, *Edinburgh*; (30 Bishopsgate, E.C.2; 16/18 and 198 Piccadilly, W.1; 57–60 Haymarket, S.W.1; 332 Oxford St., W.1 and 140 Kensington High St., W.8.)— Capital £12,900,000. Reserve Fund and Balance carried forward, £29,318,092. Deposits and Credit Balances, 28/2/71, £476,731,888. (671 Branches and Sub-Branches.)

BANQUE BELGE LTD. (1934), 4 Bishopsgate, E.C.2.— Capital: Subscribed, £3,400,000; Paid-up, £1,800,000.

BANQUE CANADIENNE NATIONALE, *Montreal*, Canada (Bank of Hochelaga and Banque Nationale amalgamated).—Capital (issued), $12,000,000; Reserve, $54,000,000; Assets, $1,908,000,000. (539 Offices in Canada.)

★BARCLAYS BANK LIMITED (1896), Head Office, 54 Lombard St., E.C.3; *Chief Foreign Branch*, 152 Upper Thames St., E.C.4; *City Office*, 170 Fenchurch St., E.C.3—Capital Authorized, £110,000,000. Capital Issued £83,445,377; Reserves, £337,178,000; Deposits, £3,129,276,000. Dividend, 1970: Ord. Stock, 16 p.c., Staff Stock, 20 p.c. Over 3,200 branches in England and Wales. Subsidiary Companies: BARCLAYS BANK D.C.O.; BARCLAYS OVERSEAS DEVELOPMENT CORPORATION LTD.; NATIONAL BANK DEVELOPMENT and INVESTMENT CORPORATION LTD., BARCLAYS BANK (LONDON AND INTERNATIONAL) LTD.; BARCLAYS BANK S.A.; BARCLAYS BANK OF CALIFORNIA; BARCLAYS BANK EXPORT AND FINANCE COMPANY LTD.; BARCLAYS BANK FINANCE CO. (JERSEY) LTD.; BARCLAY TRUST CHANNEL ISLANDS LTD.; BARCLAYS BANK OF NIGERIA LTD; BARCLAYS BANK TRUST COMPANY LTD.; BARCLAYS FINANCE COMPANY (GUERNSEY) LTD.; BARCLAYS GRIFFIN LIFE ASSURANCE COMPANY LTD.; BARCLAYS UNICORN LTD.; BARCLAYS INSURANCE SERVICES COMPANY LTD.; UNION REGISTRAR SERVICES LTD.; DILLON WALKER AND COMPANY LTD.; CREDIT CONGOLAIS S.C.A.R.L.; Barclays Bank Ltd. is closely associated with the BANK OF SCOTLAND, UNITED DOMINIONS TRUST LTD., and BARIC COMPUTING SERVICES CO. LTD.; in the Bahamas with BANK OF LONDON AND MONTREAL LTD.; in Belgium and Luxemburg with SOCIÉTÉ FINANCIÈRE EUROPÉENNE and BANQUE DÉ BRUXELLES S.A.; in Spain with BANCO DEL DESARROLLO ECONOMICO ESPANOL (BANDESCO).

BARCLAYS BANK D.C.O., 54 Lombard St., E.C.3.— Authorized Capital, £50,000,000; Issued Capital, £40,000,000; Reserves, £111,019,000; Deposits, 31/3/71, £2,062,817,000. (1,646 Branches, Sub-Branches and Agencies.)

BARING BROTHERS & CO., LTD. (1763), 8 Bishopsgate, E.C.2, and Liverpool. — Capital, Authorized, issued and fully paid, £4,300,000; Reserve, £5,000,000; Deposits, 31/12/70, £131,457,496.

WM. BRANDT'S SONS & CO. LTD. (1805), 36 Fenchurch Street, E.C.3.—Capital Authorized, £3,000,000; Issued and Fully Paid, £3,000,000.

BRITISH AND FRENCH BANK LTD., *Head Office*: 9–13 King William St., E.C.4. Capital authorized and fully paid, £3,000,000. (Subsidiary of the BANQUE NATIONALE DE PARIS.)

BRITISH BANK FOR FOREIGN TRADE, LTD. (1911), 1 Crown Court, Cheapside, E.C.2.—Subscribed Capital, £700,000; 7,000,000 Shares of 2s. each fully paid.

BRITISH BANK OF COMMERCE LTD. (1936), 145–165 West Regent Street, Glasgow C.2.—Capital, fully-paid, £3,133,750; Reserves, £2,617,805; Deposits, 31/3/71, £12,886,987. Dividend, 1970–71, 12 p.c. (84 representative offices.)

BRITISH BANK OF THE MIDDLE EAST (1889), 20 Abchurch Lane, E.C.4.—Capital, authorized £5,000,000; issued and fully paid, £3,500,000 (£1 shares): 31/12/70: Revenue Reserves, £6,468,498; Deposits, £312,975,498; Dividend, 1970, Nil.

BROWN, SHIPLEY & CO. LTD. (1810), Founders Court, Lothbury, E.C.2.—Capital, Authorized, £3,500,000; Issued, £3,500,000; Reserve £1,000,000.

BUNGE & CO., LIMITED (1905), Bunge House, St. Mary Axe, E.C.3.—Capital subscribed and paid up £1,000,000.

CANADIAN IMPERIAL BANK OF COMMERCE (1961), *Toronto*, Ontario, Canada (2 Lombard St., E.C.3). —Capital Authorized $125,000,000 (62,500,000 shares of $2); Paid up $69,680,000. Reserve Fund, $332,337,131; Total Assets, $11,050,582,874; Dividend 1970, 34 p.c. (1,562 Branches in Canada and elsewhere.)

CATER RYDER & CO. LTD. (1960), 1 King William Street, E.C.4.—Capital authorized, £5,500,000; issued and fully paid, £5,469,000. Reserve £2,500,000. Deposits, etc., 31/5/71, £244,159,229; Dividend 1970–71 (11 mnths.), 15 p.c.

CENTRAL BANK OF INDIA (1911), Bombay. 31/12/69: Paid-up capital (wholly owned by Central Government of India), Rs.4,75,14,600; Reserve Fund and other reserves, Rs.7,88,34,762; Deposit and other accounts, Rs.5,00,74,94,463. (504 branches, etc.)

CHARTERED BANK (1853), 38 Bishopsgate, E.C.2.— Capital, Authorized, £15,000,000 (divided into 15,000,000 shares of £1 each); Issued and converted into stock, £9,680,000; Reserve Fund, £22,000,000; Deposits, 31/12/70, £674,692,757. (171 Branches.)

CHARTERHOUSE JAPHET LIMITED (1880), 1 Paternoster Row, E.C.4.—Capital, authorized and paid-up, £2,000,000.

THE CHASE MANHATTAN BANK, N.A. *New York*, U.S.A. (Woolgate House, Coleman Street, E.C.2. and 1 Mount Street, W.1.)—Capital, $398,488,937; Surplus and Undivided Profits, $639,749,085; Deposits $18,988,656,704. (150 branches in New York and Branches and affiliated Banks in 54 overseas countries.)

CLIVE DISCOUNT COMPANY, LTD. (1965), 1 Royal Exchange Avenue, E.C.3.—Capital, Authorized, issued and fully paid, £3,100,000.

CLYDESDALE BANK, LTD (1838), St. Vincent Place, Glasgow, C.1 (Aberdeen, Chief Office, 5 Castle St.) Chief London Office, 30 Lombard St., E.C.3. *Affiliated to* Midland Bank, Ltd.—Authorized Capital, £10,419,000; Paid-up Capital, £6,419,000; Reserve Fund, £21,802,000; Deposits, 31/12/70, £267,153,000. (362 Branches.)

COMMERCIAL BANK OF AUSTRALIA, LTD. (1866), Collins St., *Melbourne* (12 Old Jewry, E.C.2).—Paid-up Capital; $A24,421,662 ($A20 Preference, fully paid; $A1 Ordinary, fully paid); Deposits, etc., 30/6/70, $A749,689,595; Reserve Funds $A21,300,000. (870 Branches and Agencies.)

COMMERCIAL BANK OF THE NEAR EAST, LTD. (1922), Bankside House, 107–112 Leadenhall Street, E.C.3.—Capital, fully paid, £200,000; Reserve Fund, £395,000. Deposits, 31/12/70, £14,648,318.

COMMERCIAL BANKING CO., OF SYDNEY, LTD. (1834), 343 George St., *Sydney*, N.S.W. (27–32 Old Jewry, E.C.2).—Authorized Capital, $A30,000,000 (Shares of $A1 each); Issued and paid-up $A22,125,000 ($A1 shares); Reserve Fund, $A24,200,000. (601 Branches in Australia.)

COMMONWEALTH SAVINGS BANK OF AUSTRALIA, *Sydney*, N.S.W. (8 Old Jewry, E.C.2 and 48 Aldwych, W.C.2.) Owned and guaranteed by the Government of the Commonwealth. Deposits, etc.,30/6/70, $A2,958,742,250; Reserve Fund, $A38,872,282. (8,631 Branches and Agencies.)

COMMONWEALTH TRADING BANK OF AUSTRALIA (1953), *Sydney*, N.S.W. (8 Old Jewry, E.C.2; Australia House, Strand, W.C.2).—Owned and guaranteed by the Government of the Commonwealth. 30/6/70: Deposits, etc., $A1,692,722,520; Reserve Fund, $A19,277,543. (1,123 Branches and Agencies.)

CONTINENTAL ILLINOIS NATIONAL BANK AND TRUST COMPANY OF CHICAGO, *Chicago*,. Ill., U.S.A. (58–60 Moorgate, E.C.2 and 47 Berkeley Square, W.1).—31/12/69. Capital Stock, $168,643,000; Surplus, $275,906,000; Undivided Profits, $47,296,000; Reserves $123,788,000. (21 Branches, etc.)

CO-OPERATIVE BANK (Co-operative Wholesale Society Ltd.) (1872), New Century House, *Manchester* (and 110 Leman St., E.1).—Capital, paid up, £31,525,915. (33 Branches.)

COPLEYS BANK, LTD. (1916), Ludgate House, 107–11 Fleet Street, E.C.4.—Capital authorized, £1,000,000; paid up, £380,000.

*COUTTS & CO. (1692), 440 Strand, W.C.2; 15 Lombard St., E.C.3; 1 Old Park Lane, W.1; 16 Cavendish Square, W.1.; 1 Cadogan Place, Sloane Street, S.W.1.; 10 Mount Street, W.1.; 188 Fleet Street, E.C.4; Royex House, Aldermanbury Square, E.C.2; and 15 High Street, Windsor.—Capital issued and paid up, £1,000,000; Reserves, £5,836,585; Deposits, etc., 31/12/70, £307,183,112. (*A subsidiary of* National Westminster Bank, Ltd.) *Main Subsidiary:* COUTTS FINANCE CO.

CREDIT LYONNAIS (1863), 19 Boulevard des Italiens, *Paris* (40 Lombard St., E.C.3.; 18 Regent St., S.W.1; 19 Old Brompton Road, S.W.7).—Capital, Frs. 480,000,000; Reserve Fund, Frs. 389,345,725. (1,950 Branches throughout the world.)

DISCOUNT BANK (OVERSEAS) LTD., 63–66 Hatton Garden, E.C.1; 89 Duke Street, W.1.

EASTERN BANK LTD. Merged on July 1, 1971, with THE CHARTERED BANK (*see p.* 442.)

FIRST NATIONAL CITY BANK OF NEW YORK (1812), 399 Park Avenue, *New York* 10022 (34 Moorgate, E.C.2 and 17 Bruton St., Berkeley Sq., W.1). 31/12/69: Capital, $366,273,000; 4 p.c. Convertible Capital Notes $258,383,000; Deposits, $19,141,963,000; Surplus, Undivided Profits and unallocated Reserve for Contingencies, $812,885,000. (187 Branches in New York, 641 Branches [including affiliates] in 83 countries.)

FLEMING (ROBERT) & CO. LTD. (1932), 8 Crosby Square, E.C.3.

ANTONY GIBBS & SONS, LTD. (1808), 22 Bishopsgate, E.C.2.

GILLETT BROTHERS DISCOUNT CO., LTD. (1867), 65 Cornhill, E.C.3. Issued Capital, £2,000,000; Reserve, £1,000,000; Deposits, 31/1/71, £144,319,280. Dividend, 1971, 15 p.c.

*‡GLYN, MILLS & CO. (1753), incorporating CHILD & CO. and HOLT & CO., See WILLIAMS AND GLYNS BANK LIMITED.

GUINNESS MAHON & CO. LTD. (1836), 3 Gracechurch Street, E.C.3.

GUINNESS & MAHON LTD. (1836), 17 College Green, *Dublin* 2 (affiliated to Guinness Mahon & Co. Ltd., London).

HAMBROS BANK, LTD. (1839). *Head Office*, 41 Bishopsgate, E.C.2; *West End Office*, 67 Pall Mall, S.W.1; *Holborn Office*, 1 Charterhouse St., E.C.1.—Authorized Capital, £12,500,000; Paid-up Capital, £12,500,000; Reserve £35,525,000; Deposits, 31/3/71, £516,938,000. Hambros Bank Ltd. is a wholly-owned subsidiary of Hambros Ltd., the dividend of which for 1970–71 was 30 p.c. on £10 and 25p fully-paid shares; 6 p.c. on "A" shares.

HARRODS (KNIGHTSBRIDGE) LIMITED, (1889), 87-135 Brompton Rd., S.W.1.

HELBERT, WAGG & CO., LTD. See J. HENRY SCHRODER WAGG & CO. LIMITED.

HILL, SAMUEL GROUP LTD. (1831), 100 Wood Street, E.C.2.—(31/3/71): Capital, authorized and issued, £11,643,000 (shares of £1 each); Reserves, £13,100,000; Current Deposit and other accounts, £494,830,000; Dividend, 1970–71, 15 p.c.

C. HOARE & CO. (1672), 37 Fleet St., E.C.4, and Aldford House, Park Lane, W.1.—Capital and Reserve Fund, £1,000,000; Deposits, 5/4/71, £25,699,920.

HONGKONG AND SHANGHAI BANKING CORPORATION (1865), *Hong Kong* (9 Gracechurch St., E.C.3.)—Capital, authorized $HK500,000,000; Issued and fully paid $HK420,841,575 ($HK25 Shares); Reserve Funds, $HK 270,000,000; Deposits, etc., 31/12/70, $HK10,220,196,215.

IONIAN BANK, LTD. (1839), 64 Coleman Street, E.C.2.—Capital, Authorized, £2,500,000; Issued and fully paid, £1,600,000; Reserve Fund, £725,000; Deposits, £25,900,606.

ISLE OF MAN BANK LTD. (1865). (A Member Bank of the National Westminster Group), *Douglas, I.O.M.* (*London Agents*, National Westminster Bank Ltd.).—Issued Capital, £750,000 in 750,000 shares of £1 each, fully paid, converted into stock; Reserve Fund £450,000; Deposits, 31/12/70, £21,732,602. (19 Branches.)

S. JAPHET & CO. LTD., *see* CHARTERHOUSE JAPHET LIMITED.

LEOPOLD JOSEPH & SONS LTD. (1919) 31–45 Gresham Street, E.C.2.—Capital, authorized, £1,000,000; issued and paid up, £654,500.

JESSEL, TOYNBEE & CO. LTD. (1922), 30 Cornhill, E.C.3.—Capital authorized, £2,000,000; paid up, £1,700,000.

KEYSER ULLMANN LIMITED (1966). Amalgamation of Ullmann & Co. Ltd. (1932) and A. Keyser & Co. Ltd. (Estd. 1868, Inc. 1946). Regd. Office. 31 Throgmorton Street, E.C.2.

KING AND SHAXSON, LTD. (1866), 52 Cornhill, E.C.3. Capital authorized £2,500,000; issued and fully paid, £2,200,000; General Reserve, £1,200,000.

KLEINWORT, BENSON LIMITED (1830), 20 Fenchurch St., E.C.3 and at Sheffield, Geneva, Brussels and New York.

LAZARD BROTHERS & CO., LTD. (1870), 11 Old Broad St., E.C.2. Capital authorized and paid up, £3,375,000.

*‡LLOYDS BANK, LIMITED (1865), Head Office, 71 Lombard St., E.C.3; Branches Stock Office, 111 Old Broad Street, E.C.2; Overseas Department 6 Eastcheap, E.C.3; Executor and Trustee Department, 34 Threadneedle St., E.C.2: Principal London Offices:—City Office, 72 Lombard St., E.C.3; 39 Threadneedle St., E.C.2; 6 Pall Mall, S.W.1 (Cox's & King's Branch); 16 St. James's St., S.W.1; Law Courts, 222 Strand, W.C.2.— Capital authorized, £74,000,000; issued £64,883,008; Reserves, £200,113,000; Current, Deposit and Other Accounts, 31/12/70, £2,147,673,000; Dividend 1970, interim 6 p.c.; 2nd interim, 8 p.c. Over 2,300 Offices.
The LLOYDS BANK GROUP, in addition to LLOYDS BANK LIMITED, comprises LLOYDS & BOLSA INTERNATIONAL BANK LIMITED, LLOYDS ASSOCIATED BANKING COMPANY LIMITED, LEWIS'S BANK LIMITED, THE NATIONAL BANK OF NEW ZEALAND LIMITED, EXPORTERS' REFINANCE CORPORATION LIMITED, LLOYDS ASSOCIATED AIR LEASING LIMITED, LLOYDS BANK EXECUTOR AND TRUSTEE COMPANY (CHANNEL ISLANDS) LIMITED, LLOYDS BANK PROPERTY COMPANY LIMITED and LLOYDS BANK UNIT TRUST MANAGERS LIMITED. LLOYDS BANK LIMITED is closely associated with NATIONAL AND COMMERCIAL BANKING GROUP LIMITED, NATIONAL AND GRINDLAYS HOLDINGS LIMITED, YORKSHIRE BANK LIMITED, INTERCONTINENTAL BANKING SERVICES LIMITED AND LLOYDS & SCOTTISH LIMITED.

LLOYDS AND BOLSA INTERNATIONAL BANK LIMITED (1971), 40–66 Queen Victoria Street, E.C.4.— Authorized Capital, £50,000,000; Paid-up Capital, £39,801,919. Branches in Birmingham, Bradford, Manchester, Paris and New York. Wholly owns Bank of London & South America Limited, Lloyds Bank Europe Limited and Bank of London & Montreal Limited. (See separate entries.)

LLOYDS BANK EUROPE LIMITED (1911), 100 Pall Mall, S.W.1.—Capital £25,375,000 (£1 Shares, fully paid). (21 Branches in U.K., Belgium, France, Germany, Monaco, Netherlands and Switzerland.) (Wholly owned subsidiary of Lloyds and Bolsa International Bank Limited, see above.)

MANUFACTURERS HANOVER TRUST COMPANY (1961), New York, U.S.A. (6 Lombard Street, E.C.3 and 88 Brook Street, W.1).—Capital, $210,000,000; Surplus, $290,000,000.

MARTINS BANK LTD. (1831). Merged 15/12/69 with BARCLAYS BANK LIMITED, q.v.

MERCANTILE BANK LTD. (1892), 1 Queen's Road Central, Hong Kong (15 Gracechurch Street, E.C.3).—Issued Capital, £2,940,000 (2,940,000 Ordinary Shares, £1 each fully paid); Reserve Fund, £2,400,000; Deposits, £94.754,427. Share capital acquired in 1959 by Hongkong and Shanghai Banking Corporation. (52 Branches and Agencies.)

*MIDLAND BANK, LTD. (1836), Head Office, Poultry. E.C.2; Principal City Branches, Poultry and Princes St., E.C.2; 5 Threadneedle St., E.C.2; Overseas Branch, 60 Gracechurch Street, E.C.3 —Authorized Capital, £80,000,000; Issued Capital, £64,697,467 (Shares of £1 each, fully paid); Reserve Fund, £145,386,000; Deposits, 31/12/70, £2,248,085,000; Dividend, 1970, 16 p.c. (2,663 offices in England and Wales). Affiliations: CLYDESDALE BANK LTD., UNITED NORTHERN BANK LTD., MIDLAND BANK EXECUTOR AND TRUSTEE CO., LTD., MIDLAND BANK EXECUTOR AND TRUSTEE CO. (CHANNEL ISLANDS), LTD.; NORTHERN BANK LTD.; NORTHERN BANK TRUSTEE CO. LTD.; MIDLAND BANK FINANCE CORPORATION LTD.; MIDLAND BANK FINANCE CORPORATION (JERSEY) LIMITED; MIDLAND BANK FINANCE CORPORATION (GUERNSEY) LTD.; NORTHERN BANK FINANCE CORPORATION LTD.; CLYDESDALE BANK FINANCE CORPORATION LTD.; CLYDESDALE BANK INS. SERVICES LTD.; FORWARD TRUST LTD.; FORWARD TRUST (FINANCE) LTD.; FORWARD TRUST (NORTHERN IRELAND) LTD.; FORWARD LEASING LTD.

MIDLAND BANK EXECUTOR AND TRUSTEE CO., LTD. (1909). Head Office, 6 Threadneedle Street, E.C.2. Affiliated to Midland Bank, Ltd. Subscribed Capital, £1,000,000; Paid-up Capital, £250,000 (200,000 Shares of £5, £1 5s. paid); Reserve Fund, £250,000. (41 offices.)

SAMUEL MONTAGU & CO. LTD. (1853), 114 Old Broad St., E.C.2. Capital, authorized and paid up, 9,000,000; Reserves, £3,433,000; Current Deposits, etc., £301,733,000.

MONTREAL CITY AND DISTRICT SAVINGS BANK (1846), Montreal, Canada (London Agents, Bank of Montreal).—Capital (paid up), $2,000,000; Reserve Fund $18,500,000. (81 Branches in Montreal and District.)

MORGAN GRENFELL & CO. LIMITED (1838), 23 Great Winchester St., E.C.2.; Private limited Coy. (1934).—Authorized Capital, £4,500,000; issued and fully paid, £4,105,000.

MORGAN GUARANTY TRUST COMPANY OF NEW YORK (1959), 23 Wall Street, New York, U.S.A. (33 Lombard Street, E.C.3 and 31 Berkeley Sq., W.1).—Capital, $228,085,000 (9,123,400 shares —$25 par); Surplus Fund, £336,500,000.

MUNSTER AND LEINSTER BANK, LTD. (1885), South Mall, Cork, Eire. A member of Allied Irish Banks Group. (London Agents, National Westminster Bank, Ltd.).—Capital authorized, £7,500,000 (7,500,000 Shares of £1 each); paid up, £1,937,500; Reserve Fund £3,759,375; Deposits, 31/12/69, £200,236,881.

NATIONAL AND COMMERCIAL BANKING GROUP LIMITED. Registered Office: 36 St. Andrew Square, Edinburgh. London Office, 3 Bishopsgate, E.C.2.—(30/9/70): Capital authorized, £30,000,000; issued, £28,995,000; Reserves, £70,725,000; Deposit and current accounts, £1,042,154,000: Ordinary dividend: interim 7½ p.c.; final 8 p.c. (Approximately 1,000 offices). Owns (inter alia) all capital of THE ROYAL BANK OF SCOTLAND LIMITED and WILLIAMS & GLYN'S BANK LIMITED.

NATIONAL AND GRINDLAYS BANK LIMITED, 23 Fenchurch Street, E.C.3.—(31/12/70) Capital authorized, issued and paid up, £11,250,000 (Shares of £1 each); Reserve Funds, £26,829,000 Deposits, 31/12/70, £817,150,000. Dividend 1970, 19 p.c. (160 Branches.)

NATIONAL BANK, LTD. (1835), 13–17 Old Broad St., E.C.2.—Capital, Authorized, £7,500,000 (10s. Shares); Issued, £3,000,000; Capital Reserves, £3,124,000; Deposits, 30/9/68, £49,091,224; Dividend, 1968, 9 p.c. gross.

NATIONAL BANK OF AUSTRALASIA, LTD., THE (1858), Collins St., *Melbourne* (6–8 Tokenhouse Yard, E.C.2).—Capital paid up $A25,222,592; Reserve Fund, $A26,500,000; Deposits, 30/9/70, $A1,098,643,803. Dividend, 1970, 12 p.c. (975 Branches and Agencies in Australia.) The NATIONAL BANK SAVINGS BANK LIMITED, (Collins, Street, Melbourne) a wholly owned subsidiary of The National Bank of Australasia Limited was incorporated on May 16, 1962, with Capital, Authorized, $A20,000,000; paid-up, $A2,000,000.

NATIONAL BANK OF MALTA LTD. (*Incorporating* ANGLO-MALTESE BANK and BANK OF MALTA), 45 Kingsway, Valletta, Malta. With which is affiliated Sciclunas Bank, Malta. Authorized Capital, £2,000,000; Paid-up Capital £1,000,000. (Branches in important centres of Malta and Gozo.)

NATIONAL BANK OF NEW ZEALAND, LTD. (1872), 8 Moorgate, E.C.2.—Capital (Authorized, £6,000,000), Issued and fully-paid, £3,500,000; Reserve Fund, £3,705,925. (219 Branches and Agencies.)

NATIONAL DISCOUNT CO., LTD. Merged on June 16, 1970, with GERRARD & REID, LTD., under the name of GERRARD & NATIONAL DISCOUNT CO. LTD.

★NATIONAL WESTMINSTER BANK LIMITED, *Head Office:* 41 Lothbury, E.C.2. Est. 1968 to merge the businesses of National Provincial, Westminster and District Banks: Balance Sheet at December 31, 1970, showed total assets, £3,640,519,000; Deposits, current and other accounts, £3,212,345,000. Over 3,600 Branches. *Principal subsidiary companies:* CENTRE-FILE LTD.; COUNTY BANK LTD.; COUTTS & CO. (*q.v.*) and its subsidiary (Coutts Finance Co.); CREDIT FACTORING LTD.; ISLE OF MAN BANK LTD. and its subsidiary (Isle of Man and National Westminster Trust Co. Ltd.); LOMBARD BANKING LTD. and its subsidiaries (including Lombank Ltd. and Lombard Australia Ltd.); NATIONAL WESTMINSTER BANK FINANCE (C.I.) LTD.; NATIONAL WESTMINSTER GUERNSEY TRUST CO. LTD.; NATIONAL WESTMINSTER JERSEY TRUST CO. LTD.; NORTH CENTRAL FINANCE LTD. and its subsidiaries (Consumer Credit Corporation Ltd, North Central Finance (London) Ltd., North Central Finance (Southern Counties) Ltd., North Central Finance (Stanton) Ltd.); ULSTER BANK LTD. and its subsidiaries (Ulster Merchant Bank Ltd., Ulster Merchant Finance (Dublin) Ltd., Ulster Merchant Finance Ltd.; Ulster Bank Trust Co.; Ulster Bank Dublin Trust Co.); WESTMINSTER FOREIGN BANK LTD.

NETHERLANDS BANK OF SOUTH AFRICA LIMITED, *Head Office*, Johannesburg, S. Africa (37 Lombard Street, E.C.3; 71 Haymarket, S.W.1).—Capital, issued and fully paid, R12,555,625 (shares of R1 each); Reserves, R20,038,000. Current, deposit and other accounts, 30/9/70, R484,141,000. Dividend, 1969–70, 16½ p.c.

NORTHERN BANK LTD. (1824), *Belfast (Affiliated with* Midland Bank Ltd.).—Capital, £6,000,000 (£1 Shares); Capital paid up, £6,000,000; Reserve Fund, £12,815,000; Deposits, 31/12/70, £172,305,000; Dividend, 1970, 6 per cent. on capital of £3,500,000; 6½ per cent. on capital of £6,000,000. (160 Branches and 116 Sub-Branches.)

OTTOMAN BANK (1863), Bankalar Caddesi, Karakoy, *Istanbul*, Turkey (23 Fenchurch Street, E.C.3). —Capital, £10,000,000 (£20 Shares, £10 paid); Statutory Reserve, £1,250,000.

PROVINCIAL BANK OF CANADA (1900) (BANQUE PROVINCIALE DU CANADA), 221 St. James St. West, *Montreal.*—Capital $9,000,000 ($2 Shares, fully paid); Reserve Fund, $21,200,000; Deposits, 31/10/69, $795,447,221. Regular dividend, 1969, 22·5 p.c.; Special, 10 p.c. (219 Branches and 69 Agencies.)

PROVINCIAL BANK OF IRELAND LTD. (1825), 5 College St., Dublin (*London Agents,* Barclays Bank, Ltd.) (A member of the Allied Irish Banks Group.) Capital, £4,080,000; Issued, 1,130,000 Ordinary Shares of £1; Reserve Fund, £1,600,000; Deposits, 31/3/71, £121,166,857. (149 Branches and Sub-Branches.)

GERALD QUIN, COPE & CO. (1892), 7 Birchin Lane, E.C.3.

RELIANCE BANK, LTD. (1900), 101 Queen Victoria St., E.C.4.—Capital, £60,000; Reserve Fund, £407,413; Deposits, 31/3/71, £5,115,490.

RESERVE BANK OF NEW ZEALAND (1934), *Wellington, N.Z. Branches at Christchurch and Auckland, N.Z.* (*London Agents, Bank of England*). *Owned by the New Zealand Government.*—Reserve Funds, $NZ20,897,000; Total Assets, 31/3/70, $NZ.445,678,000.

N. M. ROTHSCHILD & SONS LTD. (1804), New Court, St. Swithin's Lane, E.C.4.—Capital issued and paid up £10,000,000.

ROYAL BANK OF CANADA (1869), *Montreal* (6 Lothbury, E.C.2, and 2 Cockspur St., S.W.1). —Capital, $100,000,000 ($2 Shares); Paid-up. $66,528,000; Rest Account, $323,000,000; Undivided Profits, $1,497,387; Assets, $11,368,623,053; Deposits, 31/10/70, $10,303,211,520; Dividend, 1970, $0·86 per share. (1,312 Branches.)

ROYAL BANK OF SCOTLAND LIMITED. *Registered Office:* 42 St. Andrew Square, Edinburgh. (30/9/70.—Capital, authorized and issued, £15,000,000; Reserves, £37,751,800; Deposit and current accounts, £518,089,876. Approximately 650 Branches in Scotland and in London. Owns all capital of NATIONAL COMMERCIAL & GLYNS LIMITED, R B DEVELOPMENT LIMITED and LOGANAIR LIMITED. Also owns 49.3 p.c. of the capital of LLOYDS & SCOTTISH LIMITED. A member of the NATIONAL AND COMMERCIAL BANKING GROUP.

DAVID SASSOON AND CO., LIMITED (1960), 11/12 St. Swithin's Lane, E.C.4.—Capital authorized, issued and paid up, £500,000.

E. D. SASSOON BANKING CO., LIMITED (1967), Winchester House, 100 Old Broad Street, E.C.2. —Capital, authorized, issued and paid up, £2,000,000. *Subsidiary,* E. D. SASSOON BANKING INTERNATIONAL, LIMITED, Sassoon Building, Parliament Street, Nassau, Bahamas. Capital $Bah.2,857,000.

J. HENRY SCHRODER WAGG & CO. LIMITED (1804), 120 Cheapside, E.C.2.—Capital, Authorized, £7,500,000; issued and paid up, £7,500,000.

SCOTTISH CO-OPERATIVE WHOLESALE SOCIETY LTD. (1868), 11 Laidlaw Street, *Glasgow*, C.5.

SINGER AND FRIEDLANDER LTD. (1907), 20 Cannon Street, E.C.4.—Capital, Authorized and issued, £5,000,000. (5,000,000 Ordinary shares of £1 each.)

SLATER, WALKER, LIMITED, 30 St. Paul's Churchyard, E.C.4. Capital, Authorized £6,000,000; Issued and paid up, £6,000,000.

SMITH ST. AUBYN & CO. LTD. (1801), White Lion Court, Cornhill, E.C.3.—Capital authorized, £2,500,000; issued, £2,070,000; General Reserves, £1,500,000; Deposits and Contingency Reserve, 5/4/71, £11,439,059.

SOCIÉTÉ GÉNÉRALE (1864), 29 Boulevard Haussmann, *Paris* (105–108 Old Broad St., E.C.2 and 28–32 Fountain Street, Manchester).—Subscribed Capital authorized, issued and paid up, *Francs* 400,000,000. Reserve Funds, *Francs* 310,000,000. (1,900 Branches.)

STANDARD BANK, LTD., THE (1862), 10 Clements Lane, E.C.4.—Authorized Capital, £40,000,000; Issued Capital, £26,808,075; Reserve Fund, £39,306,168. (Over 1,200 offices.) A member of THE STANDARD AND CHARTERED BANKING GROUP LIMITED.

STATE BANK OF INDIA (1955), *Bombay, Calcutta, Madras, New Delhi, Ahmedabad, Hyderabad* and *Kanpur* (Clements House, Gresham Street, E.C.2).—Capital, Authorized, *Rs.* 20,00,00,000; Paid up, *Rs.* 5,62,50,000; Reserve, *Rs.* 15,61,00,000.

GEORGE STEUART & CO. LTD., *Colombo,* Ceylon (*London Correspondents,* Coutts & Co.).

SWISS BANK CORPORATION (1872), *Basle* (99 Gresham Street, E.C.2.—Capital and Reserves, *Swiss Francs* 1,240,200,000; Dividend, 1970, 16 p.c. (112 Branches, etc.)

TAGLIAFERRO BANK LIMITED (1812), *Malta* (*London Agents,* Westminster Bank Ltd., Midland Bank Ltd., Lloyds Bank Ltd.)

TORONTO-DOMINION BANK, *Toronto,* Ontario, Canada (an amalgamation (1955) of The Bank of Toronto (1856) and The Dominion Bank (1871)) (62 Cornhill, E.C.3 and 103 Mount Street, W.1).—Capital (paid-up), $30,000,000; Rest Account, $117,500,000; Undivided Profits, $1,764,945. (760 Branches in Canada.)

ULSTER BANK, LTD. (1836), *Head Office,* Waring St., *Belfast.* (A member of the National West-minster Group).—Capital, £3,000,000 (£1 Shares); Issued and fully paid, £2,250,000; Reserve Fund £6,800,000; Share Premium Account, £250,000; Deposits, 31/12/69, £108,287,868; Dividend, 1969, 14 p.c. (131 Offices and 99 Sub-Offices.)

UNION BANK OF INDIA LTD. (1919), 66–80 Apollo Street, *Bombay* 1. Acquired July 18, 1969, by the Government of India. Capital: Authorized, *Rs.*20,000,000. Issued and paid-up *Rs.*12,500,000; Deposits, 31/12/70, *Rs.*1,740,000,000. (374 branches.)

UNION DISCOUNT COMPANY OF LONDON, LTD. (1885), 39 Cornhill, E.C.3.—Capital Issued, £7,500,000 in units of £1 each fully paid; Reserves and carry forward, £5,556,689; Deposits, other liabilities and reserve for contingencies, £428,893,254; Dividend, 1970, 18½p.c.

UNITED COMMERCIAL BANK LTD., 10 Brabourne Road, *Calcutta.*—Capital, paid-up (Shares of *Rs.* 100, *Rs.* 50 paid). *Rs.* 2,80,00,000 Reserves *Rs.* 4,38,00,000. (Over 350 Branches.)

WARBURG (S. G.) & CO. LTD. (Incorporating Seligman Brothers), 30 Gresham Street, E.C.2.—Capital, authorized, £12,500,000; issued and paid-up, £10,000,000.

WESTMINSTER FOREIGN BANK, LTD. (1913), 41 Lothbury, E.C.2.

★WILLIAMS & GLYNS BANK, LTD., *Registered Office,* 20 Birchin Lane, E.C.3. Established to merge the businesses of WILLIAMS DEACON'S, GLYN, MILLS and NATIONAL BANKS (326 branches). Capital authorized and issued, £13,500,000; Reserves, £28,777,000; Deposit and current accounts, £462,863,000. (318 branches in England and Wales.)
Owns all the capital of WILLIAMS, GLYN & CO.; WILLIAMS & GLYN'S TRUST CO. LTD; WILLIAMS & GLYN'S REGISTRARS LTD.; WILLIAMS & GLYN'S BANK INVESTMENTS (JERSEY) LTD.; WILLIAMS & GLYN'S BANK EXECUTOR & TRUSTEE COMPANY (CHANNEL ISLANDS) LTD.; ST. MARGARET'S TRUST LTD.

YORKSHIRE BANK LIMITED (1911), 56–58 Cheapside, E.C.2 (2 Infirmary Street, *Leeds*). Capital, £5,000,000 (Capital paid up, £5,000,000, £1 Shares fully paid); Reserves, £17,099,326; Deposits, 31/12/70, £146,117,431. (186 Branches.)

PREMIUM SAVINGS BONDS

One of the most popular forms of saving in the United Kingdom is through Premium Savings Bonds. These bonds are a United Kingdom Government security and were first introduced on November 1, 1956. Instead of earning interest, however, each bond offers to its holder the chance of winning a money prize in a prize draw. Bonds are issued in values ranging from £1 to £500 and each £1 buys one bond, which has one chance in the prize draw.

Bonds are sold only to individuals, not to groups or corporate bodies. No more than 2,000 bonds can be held by any one person. The bonds are sold at Post Offices, Banks, Trustee Savings Banks and through certain National Savings Groups. Holders may redeem bonds at any time by completing a form which is available at Post Offices and Banks.

Prizes are paid from a fund formed by the interest, at present 4¾ per cent. *per annum,* on each bond eligible for the draw. A bond becomes eligible for the draw three clear calendar months following the month of purchase and goes into every subsequent draw whether or not it has won a prize until the end of the month in which it is repaid. Bonds belonging to a deceased bondholder will remain eligible for all Prize Draws held in the month of death and in the following 12 calendar months. provided they have not been repaid earlier. They will then become ineligible for all further draws. These terms also apply to bonds purchased before August 1, 1960 (Series "A"). Prizes range in value from £5,000 to £25 every month with a single prize of £50,000 each month and one of £25,000 each week, the winning numbers being selected by the electronic random number indicator equipment—usually called "ERNIE". Winning numbers are printed monthly in the *London Gazette.*

It is estimated that by the end of May, 1971, bonds to the value of £1,341,447,851 had been sold. Of these £506,334,460 had been cashed, leaving £835,113,391 still invested. After the draw in May, 1971, 7,420,827 prizes, totalling £274,849,300 had been distributed since the inception of the Premium Savings Bond Scheme.

NATIONAL SAVINGS CERTIFICATES

The amount, including accrued interest, remaining to the credit of investors in National Savings Certificates on March 31, 1971, was approximately £2,507,524,000. In 1970–71 £244,283,000 was subscribed and £231,309,000 (excluding interest) was repaid.

Note.—Certificates may be bought in denominations of 1, 2, 3, 4, 5, 10, 20, 50, 100 and 200 £1 units.

Issue and Maximum Holding	Unit Cost *s. d.*	Value after Years	Value after £ p	Interest per Unit
1st (1916–22).........	15 6	10	1·30	After 10 years, $^5/_{12}$p per completed month*.
2nd (1922–23)........	16 0	10	1·30	
3rd (1923–32) & Conversion (1932)....	16 0	22	1·65	After 22 years, $^5/_{12}$p per completed month*.
4th (1932–33)........	16 0	20	1·45	After 20 years, $1^1/_{24}$p per completed three months*.
5th (1933–35)........	16 0	21	1·45	After 21 years, $1^1/_{24}$p per 3 months*.
6th (1935–39)........	15 0	22	1·35	After 22 years, $1\frac{1}{4}$p per 3 months*.
7th (1939–47)........ (Maximum holding 1st–7th combined, 500)	15 0	22	$1·37\frac{1}{2}$	After 22 years, $1\frac{1}{4}$p per 3 months and a bonus of $2\frac{1}{2}$p at the end of 29th year.
		29	1·75	After 29 years, $2^1/_{12}$p per 4 months; after 30 years, $2\frac{1}{2}$p per 4 months; and a bonus of $1\frac{1}{4}$p at the end of the 35th year.†
		30	$1·81\frac{1}{4}$	
		35	2·20	
£1 (1943–47) (250)...	20 0	22	1·35	After 22 years, $1\frac{1}{2}$p per 4 months and a bonus of 5p at the end of the 29th year.
		29	$1·66\frac{1}{4}$	After 29 years, $2\frac{1}{4}$p per 4 months; after 30 years, $2\frac{1}{2}$p per 4 months; and a bonus of $4\frac{1}{2}$p at the end of the 33rd year.†
		33	2·00	
8th (1947–51) (1,000) .	10 0	20	0·90	After 20 years, $^5/_6$p per 4 months; after 22 years, $1\frac{1}{4}$p per 4 months; after 24 years, $1\frac{3}{8}$p per 4 months. Then $1\frac{1}{2}$p per 4 months till end of 29th year, when $4\frac{1}{2}$p bonus added.†
		22	0·95	
		25	$1·07\frac{1}{2}$	
		29	1·30	
9th (1951–56) (1,400)	15 0	10	$1·01\frac{1}{4}$	After 10 years, $1\frac{1}{4}$p per 4 months; $2\frac{1}{2}$p bonus at end of 17th year. After 17 years $1\frac{3}{8}$p per 4 months; $2\frac{1}{2}$p bonus at end of 22nd year.†
		17	1·30	
		22	$1·57\frac{1}{2}$	
10th (1956–63) (1,200)	15 0	7	1·00	After 7 years, $1\frac{1}{4}$p per 4 months and a bonus of $2\frac{1}{2}$p at end of the 15th year.
		15	$1·32\frac{1}{2}$	After 15 years, $1\frac{3}{8}$p per 4 months; after 16 years, 2p per 4 months; and a bonus of $4\frac{1}{2}$p at the end of the 19th year.†
		19	1·60	
11th (1963–66) (600)..	20 0	6	1·25	4th to 6th years, $1\frac{3}{8}$p per 4 months; and bonus of $1\frac{3}{8}$p at end of 6th year. After 6th year, $1\frac{3}{8}$p per 4 months and bonus of 5p at end of 12th year.†
		12	1·60	
12th (1966–70) (1,500)	20 0	5	1·25	After 1 year, $2\frac{1}{2}$p added; $1\frac{1}{4}$p per 4 months in 2nd year; $2^1/_{12}$p per 4 months in 3rd, 4th and 5th years. After 5 years, $1\frac{1}{2}$p per 4 months and bonus of 7p at end of 9th year.†
		9	1·50	
Decimal (1970–).... (1,000)	£1·00	4	1·25	After 1 year, 3p added; $1\frac{1}{2}$p per 4 months in 2nd year; $2\frac{1}{2}$p per 4 months in 3rd year; 3p per 4 months in 4th year; and bonus of 1p at end of 4th year.†

May be held from date of issue: * until further notice; † as announced by the Treasury.

BRITISH SAVINGS BONDS

7% British Savings Bonds (2nd Issue) are a guaranteed state security. They cost £5 each and may be held up to a maximum of £10,000. Bonds acquired by inheritance do not count towards this limit. They may be held by individuals solely or jointly; by trustees; by charitable, friendly and provident societies; by clubs and funds, by corporate bodies generally. Interest is earned at the rate of 7% a year, provided they are held for a minimum period of 6 months. The interest which is payable half yearly is taxable but tax is not deducted at source. The value of British Savings Bonds remains constant and they may be encashed at par on one month's notice. They will be redeemable at the rate of £103 for £100 of Bonds on the next interest date after 5 years have passed from the purchase date. The £3 capital bonus is exempt from United Kingdom Income Tax (and from Surtax, Corporation Tax and Capital Gains Tax). British Savings Bonds may be bought at any Post Office transacting Savings Bank business, Trustee Savings and other Banks.

GOVERNMENT STOCKS AND BONDS

Government Stocks and Bonds on the National Savings Stock Register can be bought and sold at low rates of commission through the Department for National Savings, Bonds and Stock Office, Lytham St. Annes, Lancashire, or a Trustee Savings Bank. Prices are those current on the Stock Exchange at the time of the transaction. Application forms and information leaflets with a list of the Stocks and Bonds are available at Post Offices transacting Savings Bank business and at Trustee Savings Banks. The amount standing to the credit of holders in the Department for National Savings section of the National Savings Stock Register as at March 31, 1971 was £790,318,045.

SAVE AS YOU EARN

The " Save As You Earn " Service was brought into operation on October 1, 1969. Any individual aged 16 or over may participate by agreeing to save a fixed monthly amount in whole pounds up to a maximum of £20 for a period of five years. Savings may be contributed by deduc-

tion from pay, by standing order on a bank or National Giro or by cash payments at most post offices. A bonus equal to one year's savings, free of income tax, surtax and capital gains tax, will be paid in return for regular monthly savings over five years. Alternatively, and without making any further payments, if the savings are left invested for a further two years a double bonus equal to two years' savings is payable.

Savers who wish to stop payments can withdraw the total sum saved. Compound interest is added to such withdrawals at the following rates: 2½% tax free on amounts withdrawn after the first year but before the end of the fifth year; 4½% tax free where payments cease but the savings are left invested for the remainder of the full five years. Savings withdrawn in a first year are repaid without interest. A saver may miss payments on six occasions during the period of the contract and still qualify for a bonus, if all such missed payments are made up in the months immediately following the fifth anniversary of the starting date. The bonus date will be deferred by one month in respect of each missed payment.

By the end of May, 1971, 257,397 SAYE contracts had been registered in the Department for National Savings, with a total monthly commitment to save of £1,690,661. The total payments received since October 1, 1969 amounted to £22,490,356.

SAVINGS BANKS

National Savings Bank.—On Dec. 31, 1970. there were approximately 21 million active accounts with the sum of £1,443,057,444 due to depositors

in Ordinary accounts and £309,081,639 in Investment accounts. Interest on National Savings Bank Ordinary deposits is allowed at 3½ per cent. per annum, from Jan. 1, 1971, *on accounts remaining open at Dec. 31, 1971.* A higher rate of interest is paid on deposits in National Savings Bank Investment accounts (the current rate can be ascertained at any Savings Bank Post Office). To open an Investment account a depositor must have at least £50 in an Ordinary account. A depositor may have more than one account in either series but both types of account are subject to an aggregate limit of £10,000 with certain exceptions.

On Dec. 31, 1970, the average amount held in Ordinary accounts was £69·35; in Investment accounts, approximately £479.

Trustee Savings Banks were started in the early years of the 19th century by public-spirited men who recognized the importance of individual thrift to the well-being of the community.

On Nov. 20. 1970, there were 12,806,373 active accounts in the Trustee Savings Banks. The total assets of the Banks amounted to £2,805,518,886 which comprised £2,538,572,484 due to depositors in the Ordinary, Current and Special Investment Departments, £197,497,913 Stocks and Bonds held for depositors, £6,630,871 in respect of Save As You Earn contributions and £47,587,450 representing the accumulated surplus of the individual Trustee Savings Banks throughout the country. Information about these banks and their offices, numbering 1,505 (principal and subordinate) in November, 1970, can be obtained from the *Trustee Savings Banks Association*, Knighton House, Mortimer Street, W.1. *Chairman*, E. A. G. Caröe, C.B.E. *Secretary*, J. F. D. Miller.

HOLIDAY STATISTICS

	1951	1961	1966	1967	1968	1969
Holidays* taken by Great Britain residents (millions)						
In Great Britain	25	30	31	30	30	30½
Abroad	1½	4	5½	5	5	5¾
TOTAL	26½	34	36½	35	35	36¼
Holiday visits to Western European Countries by U.K. residents (percentages)						
France	..	..	13·1	13·7	10·7	12·5
Western Germany	..	..	3·7	3·9	3·6	3·9
Italy	..	..	14·1	11·4	9·3	9·4
Belgium and Luxemburg	..	..	4·3	4·6	4·3	3·8
Netherlands	..	..	3·3	3·3	3·6	3·9
Austria	..	..	5·6	5·5	5·3	4·2
Switzerland	..	..	5·6	5·0	4·2	4·3
Spain	..	..	19·3	21·4	27·0	29·8
Irish Republic	..	..	23·5	24·2	25·0	20·4
Rest of Western Europe	..	..	7·5	7·0	7·0	7·6
All Western European countries—(percentages)	..	..	100	100	100	100
—(thousands)	..	..	4,700	4,698	4,489	4,785
TOTAL holiday visits abroad by U.K. residents† (thousands)	..	..	5,058	5,127	4,969	5,346

* A holiday is defined as four or more nights away from home.   † Including cruises.

Law Courts and Offices

LAW SITTINGS (1972)—*Hilary*, Jan. 11 to March 29; *Easter*, April 11 to May 19; *Trinity*, May 30 to July 31; *Michaelmas*, Oct. 2 to Dec. 23.

THE JUDICIAL COMMITTEE

The Judicial Committee of the Privy Council consists of the Lord Chancellor, Lord President, ex-Lords President, the Lords of Appeal in Ordinary (*see* below) and such other members of the Privy Council as shall from time to time hold or have held "high judicial office." Among the last are included Viscount Radcliffe, Lord Morton of Henryton, Lord MacDermott, Lord Tucker, Lord Cohen, Lord Pearce, Lord Devlin, Sir John Beaumont, Sir Gordon Willmer, and certain judges from the Commonwealth.

Office—Downing Street, S.W.1.
Registrar of the Privy Council, E. R. Mills.
Chief Clerk (Judicial), D. G. Brown.

THE HOUSE OF LORDS

The Supreme Judicial Authority for Great Britain and Northern Ireland is the House of Lords, which is the ultimate Court of Appeal from all the Courts in Great Britain and Northern Ireland (except criminal courts in Scotland).

The Lord High Chancellor—
The Rt. Hon. the Lord Hailsham of St. Marylebone (*born* 1907, *apptd.* 1970), (£10,500 as Judge and £4,000 as Speaker of the House of Lords) £14,500.
Lords of Appeal in Ordinary (each £15,500)

	Apptd.
Rt. Hon. Lord Reid, C.H., *born* 1890......	1948
Rt. Hon. Lord Morris of Borth-y-Gest, C.B.E., M.C., *born* 1896................	1960
Rt. Hon. Lord Donovan, *born* 1898	1964
Rt. Hon. Lord Wilberforce, C.M.G., O.B.E. *born* 1907................	1964
Rt. Hon. Lord Pearson, C.B.E., *born* 1899...	1965
Rt. Hon. Lord Diplock, *born* 1907........	1968
Rt. Hon. Viscount Dilhorne, *born* 1905...	1969
Rt. Hon. Lord Cross of Chelsea, *born* 1904..	1971
Rt. Hon. Lord Simon of Glaisdale, *born* 1911	1971
Rt. Hon. Lord Kilbrandon, *born* 1906......	1971

Registrar: The Clerk of the Parliaments, Sir David Stephens, K.C.B., C.V.O.

SUPREME COURT OF JUDICATURE
COURT OF APPEAL

Ex officio Judges.—The Lord High Chancellor, the Lord Chief Justice of England, the Master of the Rolls, and the President of the Probate, Divorce and Admiralty Division.

The Master of the Rolls (£15,500)
The Rt. Hon. Lord Denning (*born* 1899, *apptd.* 1962).
Clerk, C. L. King.
Lords Justices of Appeal (each £14,000)— Apptd.

	Apptd.
Rt. Hon. Sir William Arthian Davies, *born* 1901................	1961
Rt. Hon. Sir Charles Ritchie Russell, *born* 1908................	1962
Rt. Hon. Sir Cyril Barnet Salmon, *born* 1903	1964
Rt. Hon. Sir Eric Sachs, M.B.E., T.D., *born* 1898................	1966
Rt. Hon. Sir (Herbert) Edmund Davies, *born* 1906................	1966
Rt. Hon. Sir Henry Josceline Phillimore, O.B.E., *born* 1910................	1968

Rt. Hon. Sir Seymour Edward Karminski, *born* 1902............	1969
Rt. Hon. Sir John Megaw, C.B.E., T.D., *born* 1909............	1969
Rt. Hon. Sir Denys Burton Buckley, M.B.E., *born* 1906............	1970
Rt. Hon. Sir David Arnold Scott Cairns, *born* 1902............	1970
Rt. Hon. Sir (Edward) Blanshard Stamp, *born* 1905............	1971
Rt. Hon. Sir John Frederick Eustace Stephenson, *born* 1910............	1971
Rt. Hon. Sir Alan Stewart Orr, O.B.E., *born* 1911............	1971

HIGH COURT OF JUSTICE
Chancery Division
President, The Lord High Chancellor

Judges (each £14,000)—	Apptd.
Hon. Sir John Pennycuick (*Vice-Chancellor*), *born* 1899....	1960
Hon. Sir (John) Anthony Plowman, *born* 1905....	1961
Hon. Sir (Arwyn) Lynn Ungoed-Thomas, *born* 1904....	1962
Hon. Sir Reginald William Goff, *born* 1907	1966
Hon. Sir Robert Edgar Megarry, *born* 1910	1967
Hon. Sir (John) Patrick Graham, *born* 1906	1969
Hon. Sir Peter Harry Batson Woodroffe Foster, M.B.E., T.D., *born* 1912	1969
Hon. Sir John Norman Keates Whitford, *born* 1913....	1970
Hon. Sir John Anson Brightman, *born* 1911	1970
Hon. Sir Edward Irving Goulding, *born* 1910	1971

Queen's Bench Division
The Lord Chief Justice of England (£16,750)

The Rt. Hon. The LORD WIDGERY, O.B.E., T.D. (*born* 1911, *apptd.* 1971)
Secretary, S. E. S. Bolton; *Clerk*, A. E. Shelton.

Judges (each £14,000)—	Apptd.
Hon. Sir John Percy Ashworth, M.B.E., *born* 1906....	1954
Hon. Sir George Raymond Hinchcliffe, *born* 1900....	1957
Hon. Sir (Aubrey) Melford (Steed) Stevenson, *born* 1902....	1957
Hon. Sir Gerald Alfred Thesiger, M.B.E., *born* 1902....	1958
Hon. Sir Basil Edward Nield, C.B.E., *born* 1903....	1960
Hon. Sir Geoffrey de Paiva Veale, *born* 1906	1961
Hon. Sir Frederick Horace Lawton, *born* 1911	1961
Hon. Sir Bernard Joseph Maxwell MacKenna, *born* 1906....	1961
Hon Sir Alan Abraham Mocatta, O.B.E., *born* 1907....	1961
Hon. Sir John Thompson, *born* 1907.......	1961
Hon. Sir Daniel James Brabin, M.C., *born* 1913....	1962
Hon. Sir Eustace Wentworth Roskill, *born* 1911....	1962
Hon. Sir Helenus Patrick Joseph Milmo, *born* 1908....	1964
Hon. Sir Joseph Donaldson Cantley, O.B.E., *born* 1910....	1965
Hon. Sir Patrick Reginald Evelyn Browne, O.B.E., T.D., *born* 1907	1965

Hon. Sir George Stanley Waller, O.B.E., born 1911 ... 1965
Hon. Sir Arthur Evan James, *born* 1916 1965
Hon. Sir Ralph Vincent Cusack, *born* 1916. 1966
Hon. Sir Stephen Chapman, *born* 1907..... 1966
Hon. Sir John Ramsay Willis, *born* 1908... 1966
Hon. Sir Graham Russell Swanwick, M.B.E., born 1906 ... 1966
Hon. Sir Patrick McCarthy O'Connor, born 1914 ... 1966
Hon. Sir John Francis Donaldson, *born* 1920 1966
Hon. Sir Henry Vivian Brandon, M.C., *born* 1920 ... 1966
Hon. Sir Geoffrey Dawson Lane, A.F.C., born 1918 ... 1966
Hon. Sir (John) Robertson (Dunn) Crichton, born 1912 ... 1967
Hon. Sir Samuel Burgess Ridgway Cooke, born 1912 ... 1967
Hon. Sir Bernard Caulfield, *born* 1914 1968
Hon. Sir Nigel Cyprian Bridge, *born* 1917.. 1968
Hon. Sir Sebag Shaw, *born* 1906 1968
Hon. Sir Hilary Gwynne Talbot, *born* 1912 1968
Hon. Sir Edward Walter Eveleigh, E.R.D., born 1917 ... 1968
Hon. Sir William Lloyd Mars-Jones, M.B.E., born 1915 ... 1969
Hon. Sir George Joseph Bean, O.B.E., *born* 1915 ... 1969
Hon. Sir Ralph Kilner Brown, O.B.E., T.D., born 1909 ... 1970
Hon. Sir Phillip Wien, *born* 1913 1970
Hon. Sir Peter Henry Rowley Bristow, *born* 1913 ... 1970
Hon. Sir Hugh Harry Valentine Forbes, *born* 1917 ... 1970
Hon. Sir Desmond James Conrad Ackner, born 1920 ... 1971
Hon. Sir William Hugh Griffiths, M.C., *born* 1923 ... 1971
Hon. Sir Robert Hugh Mais, *born* 1907 1971
Hon. Sir Neil Lawson, *born* 1908 1971
Hon. Sir David Powell Croom-Johnson, D.S.C., V.R.D., *born* 1914 ... 1971
Hon. Sir John Raymond Phillips, M.C., *born* 1915 ... 1971

Court of Appeal (Criminal Division)
Judges, The Lord Chief Justice of England, The Master of the Rolls, Lord Justices of Appeal and all the Judges of the Queen's Bench Division.

Family Division
President (£15,000)
Rt. Hon. Sir George Gillespie Baker, O.B.E. (*born* 1910, *apptd.* 1971).
Sec., Miss M. E. Manisty, M.B.E.; *Clerk*, B. H. Erhard.

Judges (each £14,000)—   Apptd.
Hon. Sir Geoffrey Walter Wrangham, *born* 1900 ... 1958
Hon. Sir Harry Vincent Lloyd-Jones, *born* 1901 ... 1960
Hon. Sir Leslie George Scarman, O.B.E., born 1911 ... 1961
Hon. Sir Roger Fray Greenwood Ormrod, born 1911 ... 1961
Hon. Sir Charles William Stanley Rees, T.D., born 1907 ... 1962
Hon. Sir Reginald Withers Payne, *born* 1904 1962
Hon. Sir Neville Major Ginner Faulks, M.B.E., T.D., *born* 1908 ... 1963
Hon. Sir (Robert) James Lindsay Stirling, born 1907 ... 1964
Hon. Sir (James) Roualeyn Cumming-Bruce, *born* 1912 ... 1964

Hon. Sir John Brinsmead Latey, M.B.E., *born* 1914 ... 1965
Hon. Sir Hugh Eames Park, *born* 1910..... 1965
Hon. Dame Elizabeth Kathleen Lane, D.B.E., born 1905 ... 1965
Hon. Sir Robin Horace Walford Dunn, M.C., *born* 1918 ... 1969
Hon. Sir William Arthur Bagnall, M.B.E., born 1917 ... 1970
Hon. Sir (Alfred) Kenneth Hollings, M.C., born 1918 ... 1971
Hon. Sir Tasker Watkins, *V.C.*, *born* 1918.. 1971
Judge Advocate of the Fleet, Hon. E. E. S. Montagu, C.B.E., Q.C.
Queen's Proctor, Sir Harvey Druitt, K.C.B.

LORD CHANCELLOR'S OFFICE
House of Lords, S.W.1
Clerk of the Crown in Chancery and Permanent Secretary to the Lord Chancellor, Sir Denis Dobson, K.C.B., O.B.E., Q.C............£14,000
Private Sec. to the Lord Chancellor and Assistant Sergeant-at-Arms, M. C. Blair, £3,711 to £4,815
Deputy Clerk of the Crown in Chancery, H. Boggis-Rolfe, C.B., C.B.E............£9,000
Deputy Secretary, ~~S. P. Osmond~~, C.B. £9,000
Principal Assistant Solicitors, W/T. C. Skyrme, C.B., C.B.E., T.D.; J. W. Bourne............£6,925
Principal Establishment and Finance Officer, J. A. Bergin............£6,925
Assistant Secretaries, N. Digney; R. H. Stone; W. N. Hanna, M.V.O.; M. C. Priss; Miss J. M. Brewster.............£4,565 to £5,815
Principals, T. E. Radice; J. A. Church; C. J. Smitten, M.B.E.; J. H. J. Hunt, M.V.O.; G. Davies; A. C. Draycott; A. Davis.........£3,425 to £4,575
Senior Executive Officers, Miss A. Barry, M.B.E.; R. B. Rowe; Miss D. M. P. Malley, M.B.E.; Miss M. F. Taylor.........£2,704 to £3,274
Secretary for Ecclesiastical Patronage (also *Prime Minister's Appointments Secretary*) Sir John Hewitt, K.C.V.O., C.B.E.............£4,515 to £5,765
Assistant Secretary for Ecclesiastical Patronage, Col. W. A. Salmon, O.B.E. ....£2,795 to £3,582
Secretary of Commissions of the Peace, W. T. C. Skyrme, C.B., C.B.E., T.D.
Deputy Secretary of Commissions of the Peace, A. M. F. Webb, C.M.G. .....£4,730 to £5,815
Assistant Secretaries of Commissions of the Peace H. G. Croly, C.B.E. (£3,998) D. J. Williams £3,411 to £4,515
Assistant Solicitors, R. C. L. Gregory; K. M. Newman; R. E. K. Thesiger, O.B.E.; A. D. M. Oulton; R. H. Widdows. £4,730 to £5,815
Senior Legal Assistants, D. R. Wells; C. B. O'Beirne, O.B.E.; D. S. Gordon; T. S. Legg; M. C. Blair; M. D. Huebner; R. J. Holmes £3,461 to £4,565

SUPREME COURT OFFICES, ETC.
Conveyancing Counsel of the Supreme Court
E. J. T. G. Bagshawe; E. G. Wright; W. S. Wigglesworth.

Examiners of the Court
(Empowered to take Examination of Witnesses in all Divisions of the High Court)
J. E. Previté; K. S. Lewis, T.D.; M. Singh; L. S. Barlow; B. E. D. Cuddon; M. F. Meredith-Hardy.

Official Referees of the Supreme Court
Courts, Victory House, Kingsway, W.C.2
His Honour Sir Walker Kelly Carter, Q.C.; His Honour Norman Grantham Lewis Richards, O.B.E., Q.C.; His Honour William Walter Stabb Q.C............each £8,300

Official Solicitor's Department
Room 213B—Royal Courts of Justice, W.C.2
Official Solicitor to the Supreme Court, N. H. Turner
£6,925
Asst. Do., T. W. Swift......£4,730 to £5,815
Assistant Solicitor, R. S. Dhondy £4,730 to £5,815
Senior Legal Assts., R. Andreae; D. C. Relf; D. H. S.
  Venables................£3,461 to £4,615
Legal Assts., H. J. Baker; W. H. McBryde
£2,121 to £3,223
Chief Clerk, C. W. Vickery, O.B.E.
£3,407 to £3,680
Principal Clerks, K. A. Scollay, O.B.E.; B. C. Harris;
  R. F. Dunn; S. J. Rist; F. R. Blott; I. D. Abbott;
  L. E. Harris; J. A. P. Morris; L. A. Richardson;
  H. M. Lewis...............£2,956 to £3,274

Supreme Court Pay Office
Royal Courts of Justice, W.C.2
Accountant-General, Sir Denis Dobson, K.C.B., O.B.E.,
  Q.C.
Chief Accountant, T. C. Spicer ..£3,425 to £4,575
Senior Executive Officers, W. P. Coult; D. E. Banks;
  D. A. Dant; T. C. Weidner...£2,704 to £3,274

Central Office of the Supreme Court
Royal Courts of Justice, W.C.2
*Senior Master of the Supreme Court (Q.B.D.), and
  Queen's Remembrancer*, W. R. Lawrence. £7,850
Masters of the Supreme Court (Q.B.D.), I. H. Jacob;
  J. Ritchie, M.B.E.; J. B. Elton; J. R. Bickford-
  Smith; D. J. Hyamson; I. S. Warren; C. W. S.
  Lubbock...............£5,780 to £6,650
Chief Clerk (Central Office), H. B. Hinton, I.S.O.
£3,407 to £3,680
Chief Clerk to the Q.B. Judges in Chambers, R. C.
  Newman ....£3,407 to £3,680
Action Department*
Chief Clerk, W. E. Garrod......£2,956 to £3,274
Filing Department*
Chief Clerk, F. Simmons........£2,424 to £2,938
*Masters' Secretary's Department and Queen's
  Remembrancer's Department**
Chief Clerk (Secretary to the Masters), J. F. Mason
£2,956 to £3,274
Crown Office and Associates' Dept.
Head Clerk (Crown Office), W. N. Last
£2,956 to £3,274
Chief Associate, B. M. Spicer....£2,956 to £3,274
Criminal Appeals Office
(Royal Courts of Justice, W.C.2)
Registrar, D. R. Thompson £7,280
Assistant Registrars, W. H. Greenwood; M. W.
  Palmer; B. D. J. Walsh......£4,730 to £5,815
Deputy Assistant Registrars, P. C. Kratz; M. S. Faiz;
  E. G. Blandford, C.B.E.; C. E. S. Horsford;
  G. A. Whiteley; G. B. Davies; G. Hoffman
£3,451 to £4,555
Head Clerk, C. R. Hunt........£2,956 to £3,274
Courts-Martial Appeals Office
(Royal Courts of Justice, W.C.2)
Registrar, D. R. Thompson.
Assistant Registrar, W. H. Greenwood.
* Office hours, 10 to 4.30; (1 Aug. to 31 Aug.,
10 to 2.30.) Saturdays, closed.

Supreme Court Taxing Office
Chief Master, Paul Adams, C.B., T.D.......£7,850
Masters of the Supreme Court, Graham John Graham-
  Green, T.D.; Leonard Humphrey Razzall;
  Edwin James Thomas Matthews; Frederic
  Thomas Horne; Michael Arthur Clews; Frederic
  George Berkeley ....£5,780 to £6,850
Chief Clerk, E. W. Pinder......£3,037 to £3,355
Principal Clerks, A. G. Warren; E. P. A. Jack;
  H. J. C. Rainbird; A. J. Hancock; G. H. R.

Scales; V. C. Farrance, M.B.E.; J. Price; R. W.
E. Ranger; E. W. Guest.....£2,956 to £3,274

CHANCERY DIVISION
Chancery Judges' Chambers
Royal Courts of Justice, W.C.2
Chief Master (attached to all the Judges), Robert
  Edward Ball, M.B.E...................£7,850
Chief Clerk and Secretary to Chief Master, W. J.
  Barnes...................£2,850 to £3,144

GROUP A
At Chambers.—Masters of the Supreme Court, A to F,
  Thomas Lutwyche Dinwiddy; *G to N*, Donald
  Charles Smith; *O to Z*, Edmund Rawlings
  Heward..................£5,780 to £6,850

GROUP B
At Chambers.—Masters of the Supreme Court, A to F,
  Peter Athol Taylor; *G. to N*, Richard Wake-
  ford, T.C.; *O to Z*, Richard Chamberlain, T.D.
£5,780 to £6,850
Principal Clerks, C. L. R. Dalley; C. A. C.
  Partridge; R. G. Moore; D. F. J. Emery;
  W. E. Loveday; D. F. James; A. T. D. Higgs;
  A. T. Cole ....£2,769 to £3,063

Chancery Registrars' Office
Royal Courts of Justice, W.C.2
Chief Registrar, C. M. Kidd, £5,875; *Registrars*,
  P. Halliday; H. J. Wilson; D. G. Leach; M. S.
  Edwards; H. W. Nichols.....£4,595 to £5,485
Senior Assistant Registrars, L. F. Manning; A. W.
  Hancock; R. S. Stevens; R. F. Russell
£3,222 to £4,239
Assistant Registrars, D. G. Pullen; J. T. Glover
£2,066 to £3,068
Chief Clerk and Secretary to Chief Registrar, J. M.
  Jones.
Petition and Entry Clerk, E. P. N. Andrews.

Companies Court
Thomas More Building,
Royal Courts of Justice, W.C.2
Judges, The Hon. Mr. Justice Pennycuick; The Hon.
  Mr. Justice Plowman; The Hon. Mr. Justice
  Megarry; The Hon. Mr. Justice Brightman.
Registrar, A. F. M. Berkeley.
Chief Clerk, J. G. Usher, O.B.E... £3,407 to £3,680
Principal Clerk, C. F. Pryke.....£2,956 to £3,254
Senior Official Receiver, Companies Department,
  C. A. Taylor.........................£4,175

Bankruptcy (High Court) Department
Thomas More Building, Royal
Courts of Justice, Strand, W.C.2
Judges, The Hon. Mr. Justice Ungoed-Thomas; The
  Hon. Mr. Justice Goff; The Hon. Mr. Justice
  Foster; The Hon. Mr. Justice Goulding.
Chief Registrar, A. F. M. Berkeley.........£7,850
Registrars, G. M. Parbury; R. H. Hunt
£5,780 to £6,850
Principal Clerk, J. J. Cummings. .£2,956 to £3,274
Official Receivers' Department
Senior Official Receiver, W. Whitehead, O.B.E.
£4,305 to £4,855
Official Receiver, N. Sadler.....£3,805 to £4,515
Assistant do., R. L. Lockhead; F. Dirs; R. B. Wood;
  G. B. Gillvray; D. A. Thorne
£3,128 to £3,773

FAMILY DIVISION
PRINCIPAL REGISTRY
Somerset House, W.C.2
Senior Registrar, Sir John F. Compton Miller,
  M.B.E., T.D............................£7,850
Registrars, D. A. Newton; R. L. Bayne-Powell;
  W. D. S. Caird; D. R. L. Holloway; L. I.
  Stranger-Jones; C. Kenworthy; B. Garland; Mrs.
  A. E. O. Sloss; B. P. Tickle....£6,300 to £6,850

Secretary, C. F. Turner........£3,425 to £4,575
Establishment Officer, Miss J. J. Learmonth
£3,425 to £4,575
Clerk of the Rules and Orders (Royal Courts of Justice), W. G. Mason......£3,425 to £4,575
Principals, W. J. Pickering; B. W. Campbell
£3,425 to £4,575
Senior Executive Officers, Miss K. W. Simes; R. S. G. Norman; Mrs. M. G. Cooper; Miss I. L. Murray; Mrs. P. M. Fern; Mrs. I. L. L. Brooker; L. T. Hyder; G. A. Wood; W. I. Martyn
£2,950 to £3,575

DISTRICT PROBATE REGISTRIES
Birmingham and *Coventry*, F. R. E. Jones.
Brighton and *Maidstone*, E. E. Hosking.
Bristol, *Exeter* and *Bodmin*, T. B. Williams.
Ipswich, *Norwich* and *Peterborough*, R. C. Robinson.
Leeds, *Hull* and *York*, H. Wilkinson.
Liverpool and *Lancaster*, G. Wentworth.
Llandaff, *Bangor* and *Carmarthen*, A. Crawshaw.
Manchester, D. H. Colgate.
Newcastle, *Carlisle* and *Middlesbrough*, H. M. Hall.
Nottingham, *Leicester* and *Lincoln*, C. S. Fisher.
Oxford and *Gloucester*, Miss M. L. Farmborough.
Sheffield, *Chester* and *Stoke on Trent*, H. W. Jackson.
Winchester, J. D. Drayson.

Admiralty Registry and Marshal's Office
Royal Courts of Justice, W.C.2
Registrar, K. C. McGuffie ..... £5,780 to £6,850
Marshal and Chief Clerk, P. V. Gray
£2,931 to £3,384

COURT OF PROTECTION
25 Store Street, W.C.1
Master, J. A. Armstrong, O.B.E., T.D........£7,850
Deputy Master, P. W. E. Currie, M.C.
£4,595 to £5,485
Assistant Masters, D. G. Hunt, I.S.O.; R. A. G. Whiteman; H. Rowland; H. F. Compton
£3,579 to £4,580
Chief Clerk, N. F. Chidley.....£3,407 to £3,680
Registrar and Assistant Chief Clerk, A. M. Creasy
£3,106 to £3,424
Principal Clerks, R. H. Penfold; G. R. Isard; E. R. Taylor; A. P. Bloomfield.....£2,956 to £3,274

OFFICE OF THE LORD CHANCELLOR'S VISITORS
25 Store Street, W.C.1
Legal Visitor, I. G. H. Campbell, T.D., Q.C. . £5,900
Medical Visitors, G. Somerville, M.D.; Prof. E. W. Anderson, M.D.; Prof. D. Curran, C.B.E., F.R.C.P.
£5,900

RESTRICTIVE PRACTICES COURT
Royal Courts of Justice, W.C.2
Judicial Members, Mr. Justice Mocatta (President); Mr. Justice Cumming-Bruce; Mr. Justice Bagnall; Lord Justice McVeigh; Lord Kissen.
Lay Members, P. A. Delafield; Prof. A. J. Youngson, D.Litt.; A. I. Mackenzie; A. M. Knox; N. C. Pearson, O.B.E., T.D.; W. L. Heywood, C.B.E.; W. R. Booth; N. L. Salmon.
Clerk of the Court, Mr. Registrar Berkeley.

LAW COMMISSION
England and Wales
Conquest House, 37–38 John Street,
Theobald's Road, W.C.1
Set up on June 16, 1965, under the Law Commissions Act, 1965, to make proposals to the Government for the examination of the Law and for its revision where it is unsuited for modern require-

ments, obscure, or otherwise unsatisfactory. It recommends to the Lord Chancellor programmes for the examination of different branches of the law and suggests whether the examination should be carried out by the Commission itself or by some other body. The Commission is also responsible for the preparation of Consolidation and Statute Law Revision Bills.
Chairman, The Hon. Mr. Justice Scarman, O.B.E.
Members, C. Bicknell, O.B.E.; L. C. B. Gower; W. D. T. Hodgson, Q.C.; N. S. Marsh, Q.C.
Secretary, J. M. Cartwright Sharp.

COUNTY COURTS
In 1970 the total number of proceedings in County Courts of England and Wales (including the Mayor's and City of London Court) was 1,822,740 (as against 1,664,702 for the year 1969). The number of debtors imprisoned under the *Debtors Act*, was 2,364 (1969) and 2,252 (1970).

Circuit Court Judges (each £6,550)
The figures in parentheses indicate the number of the County Court Circuit in which the Judges sit.
Addleshaw, John Lawrence (10), Cheshire.
Bailey, Desmond Patrick (8), Manchester.
Barr, Reginald Alfred (34), Brentford.
Baxter, Herbert James, O.B.E. (37), West London.
Bell, Philip Ingress, T.D., Q.C. (4), Blackburn.
Beresford, Eric George Harold (46), Willesden.
Blomefield, Peregrine Maitland (44), Westminster.
Booth, James (12), Bradford, etc.
Boughey, John Fenton Coplestone- (46), Willesden.
Braithwaite, Bernard Richard (39), Shoreditch.
Brown, Harold John, M.C., Q.C. (50), Sussex.
Buckee, Henry Thomas, D.S.O. (62), Southend, etc.
Bulger, Anthony Clare (24), Cheltenham.
Burrell, John Glyn, Q.C. (28), Shropshire, etc.
Bush, Brian Drex (25), Staffs. and Worcs.
Chope, Robert Charles (59), Cornwall.
Clover, Robert Gordon, Q.C. (36), Oxford.
Cohen, Clifford Theodore, M.C., T.D., (11), Stockton-on-Tees.
Corcoran, Percy John (45), Wandsworth.
Corley, Michael Early Ferrand (33), Suffolk.
Cunliffe, Christopher Joseph (51), Sussex.
Cunliffe, Thomas Alfred (7), Birkenhead.
Curtis, Phillip (3), Cumberland
Davison, William Norris (23), Coventry.
De Cunha, John Wilfrid (7), Birkenhead.
Dewar, Thomas (41), Clerkenwell.
Dow, Ronald Graham (41), Clerkenwell.
Drabble, John Frederick, Q.C. (33), Suffolk.
Duveen, Claude Henry, M.B.E., Q.C. (61), Reading.
Edmondson, Anthony Arnold (7), Birkenhead.
Evans, David Meurig (29), Caernarvonshire.
Everett, Richard Marvin Hale, Q.C. (44), Westminster.
Fife, Ian Braham, M.C., T.D. (65), Bromley.
Figgis, Arthur Lenox (44), Westminster.
Finlay, Bernard, Q.C. (44), Westminster.
Forrest, Gilbert Alexander (39), Shoreditch.
Francis, William Norman (30), Glamorgan.
Freeman, Richard Gavin (58), Ilford.
Gage, Conolly Hugh (35), Cambridge.
Garrard, Henry John (26), Salop and Staffs.
Gerrard, Basil Harding (9), South Lancs.
Glazebrook, Francis Kirkland (63), Kent.
Goodall, Anthony Charles, M.C. (40), Bow.
Grant, Hubert Brian (38), Edmonton.
Green, Geoffrey (22), Worcs.
Harding, Rowe (31), Swansea, etc.
Harington, John Charcles Dundas, Q.C. (25), Staffs. and Worcs.
Hartley, Gilbert Hillard (14), Leeds, etc.
Heald, Thomas Routledge (18), Nottingham.
Hillard, Richard Arthur Loraine, M.B.E. (54), Bristol.

Hinchcliffe, Frank Philip Rideal, Q.C. (44), Westminster.
Honig, Frederick (47), Southwark.
Jellinek, Lionel, M.C. (60), Surrey.
Jones, Ewan Perrins Wallis- (27), Cardiff.
Jones, John Edward (6), Liverpool.
Jones, Thomas Elder- (52), Somerset and Wilts.
Lee, Arthur Michael, D.S.C., Q.C. (53), Hampshire.
Leech, Robert Radcliffe (3), Cumberland.
Lermon, Norman, Q.C. (44), Westminster.
Leslie, Gilbert Frank (42), Bloomsbury and Marylebone.
Lewis, Bernard (34), Brentford.
Lewis, Edward Daly (17), Lincolnshire.
Llewellyn, John Charles (42), Bloomsbury and Marylebone.
Llewellyn, John Desmond Seys (10), Cheshire.
Lloyd, Ifor Bowen, Q.C. (45), Wandsworth.
Lovegrove, Geoffrey David, Q.C. (44), Westminster.
McDonnell, Denis Lane, O.B.E. (47), Southwark.
McIntyre, Frederick Donald Livingstone, Q.C. (34), Brentford and Uxbridge.
McKee, Dermot St. Oswald (14), Yorks.
McLellan, Eric Burns (41), Clerkenwell.
MacManus, John Leslie Edward, T.D., Q.C. (44), Westminster.
Moylan, John David Fitzgerald (45), Wandsworth.
Nance, Francis James (6), Liverpool.
Nevin, Thomas Richard, T.D. (16), Hull.
Nicklin, Robert Shenstone (21), Birmingham.
Noakes, Sidney Henry (56), Croydon.
Olson, Sven Olaf (44), Westminster.
Ould, Ernest (13), Sheffield.
Parnall, Robert Boyd Cochrane (44), Westminster.
Paterson, Frank David (6), Liverpool.
Paton, Douglas Shaw Forrester-, Q.C. (2), Durham.
Peck, David Edward (48), Lambeth.
Pennant, David Edward Thornton (55), Bournemouth and Dorset.
Perks, John Clifford, MC., T.D. (46), Willesden.
Perrett, John (26), Salop and Staffs.
Potter, Douglas Charles Loftus (64), Kingston-upon-Thames.
Pratt, Hugh Macdonald (57), Devon.
Prestt, Arthur Miller, Q.C. (10), Cheshire.
Raleigh, Nigel Hugh Curtis- (42), Bloomsbury and Marylebone.
Ranking, Robert Duncan (40), Bow.
Reeve, Charles Trevor, Q.C. (47), Southwark.
Robson, Denis Hicks, Q.C. (20), Leicester, etc.
Ross, James, Q.C. (18), Nottingham.
Rowland, Miss Deborah Molly (44), Westminster.
Russell, Henry Stanway (54), Bristol.
Ruttle, Henry Samuel Jacob (44), Westminster.
Saul, Bazil Sylvester Wingate- (48), Lambeth.
Sheldon, John Gervaise Kensington (48), Lambeth.
Slack, George Granville (56), Croydon.
Smith, Gerard Gustave Lind- (23), Warwickshire.
Smith, Stuart Hayne Granville, O.B.E. (38), Edmonton, etc.
Stansfield, James Warden (9), South Lancs., etc.
Steel, Edward (8), Manchester and Leigh.
Stinson, David John (35), Cambridge, etc.
Stockdale, Frank Alleyne (58), Ilford.
Suddards, Henry Gaunt (12), Bradford.
Sumner, William Donald Massey, O.B.E., Q.C. (49), Kent.
Sunderland, George Frederick Irvon (21), Birmingham.
Trotter, Richard Stanley (6), Liverpool.
Vick, Richard William (60), Guildford
Wilkes, Lyall (1), Newcastle, etc.
Willis, John Brooke (19), Derby, etc.
Willis, Roger Blenkiron, T.D. (39), Shoreditch.
Wingate, William Granville, Q.C. (50), Sussex.

P+

Youds, Edward Ernest (5), Burnley.
Zigmond, Joseph (5), Bolton and Burnley.

CENTRAL CRIMINAL COURT
Old Bailey, E.C.4

Judges, The Lord Mayor, the Lord Chancellor, the Lord Chief Justice, the Judges of the Queen's Bench Division of the High Court; the Aldermen, Recorder, and Common Serjeant, of the City of London, the additional Judges appointed under the *City of London (Courts) Act,* 1964 (at present His Hon. Bernard Benjamin Gillis, Q.C.; His Hon. Myer Alan Barry King-Hamilton, Q.C.; His Hon. Edward Clarke, Q.C.; His Hon. Norman John Lee Brodrick, Q.C.; His Hon. Travers Christmas Humphreys, Q.C.; His Hon. Alexander David Karmel, Q.C.; His Hon. Neil Nairn McKinnon, Q.C.; His Hon. Peter Stanley Price, Q.C.; His Hon. Edward Davis Sutcliffe, Q.C.; His Hon. Derek Aldwin Grant, Q.C.; His Hon. Michael Victor Argyle, M.C., Q.C.; His Hon. Edward James Patrick Cussen) and such other persons as may be appointed by Royal Commission.

Clerk of the Court, Leslie Balfour Boyd.

Deputies, D. G. Blackaller; J. D. Stutfield; P. J. Morrish; R. V. Grobler.

Secondary and Under Sheriff (1970–71), Ralph Mordaunt Snagge, M.B.E., T.D., 78 Cranmer Court, S.W.3.

COURTS SERVICE

Following the coming into operation of the Courts Act, 1971, the High Court and the newly created Crown Courts are organized into six Circuits.

The places described in the following list as first-tier centres will deal with both civil and criminal cases and will be served by High Court and Circuit Judges. Second-tier centres will deal with criminal cases only but will be served by both High Court and Circuit Judges. Third-tier centres will deal with criminal cases only and will be served only by Circuit Judges.

Midland and Oxford Circuit.

First-tier—Birmingham, Lincoln, Nottingham, Stafford, Warwick. Second-tier—Leicester, Northampton, Oxford, Shrewsbury, Worcester. Third-tier—Coventry, Derby, Dudley, Grimsby, Hereford, Huntingdon, Stoke-on-Trent, Walsall, Warley, West Bromwich, Wolverhampton.

Peterborough will replace Huntingdon as a third-tier centre as soon as suitable court accommodation can be provided there.

Circuit Administrator, F. D. Howarth, Calthorpe House, Hagley Road, Birmingham 15 . . . £7,000

Deputy Circuit Administrator, W. Lewis, T.D.

Courts Administrators, Birmingham Group, F. Cox; *Stafford Group,* S. C. Redhead.

North Eastern Circuit.

First-tier—Leeds, Newcastle upon Tyne, Sheffield, York. Second-tier—Durham, Teesside. Third-tier—Beverley, Bradford, Doncaster, Huddersfield, Kingston-upon-Hull, Wakefield.

Beverley will cease to be a third-tier centre as soon as additional court accommodation can be made available at Kingston-upon-Hull.

Circuit Administrator, P. D. Robinson, 1 Tranquility, Crossgates, Leeds £6,750

Deputy Circuit Administrator, B. Cooke.

Courts Administrator, Leeds Group, A. H. Page.

Northern Circuit.

First-tier—Carlisle, Liverpool, Manchester, Preston. Third-tier—Barrow-in-Furness, Birkenhead, Burnley, Kendal, Lancaster.

Circuit Administrator, T. A. Whittington, Aldine House, West Riverside, New Barley St., Salford, Lancs..................................£7,000

Deputy Circuit Administrator, E. T. Connolly.

Courts Administrators, Manchester Group, G. W. Jackson; *Liverpool Group*, Miss M. Williams; *Preston Group*, G. Davies.

South Eastern Circuit.

First-tier—London, Norwich. Second-tier—Chelmsford, Ipswich, Lewes, Maidstone, Reading, St. Albans. Third-tier—Aylesbury, Bedford, Brighton, Bury St. Edmunds, Cambridge, Canterbury, Chichester, Guildford, Kings Lynn, Southend.

Circuit Administrator, Sir Maurice Holmes, Thanet House, 231/2 Strand, W.C.2..............£8,000

Deputy Circuit Administrator, G. H. O. Briegel.

Courts Administrators, Chelmsford Group, W. J. Piper; *Maidstone Group*, J. E. Greenwood; *Norwich Group*, F. G. Fuller; *Kingston Group*, A. G. Keats.

Wales and Chester Circuit.

First-tier—Caernarvon, Cardiff, Chester, Mold, Swansea. Second-tier—Carmarthen, Newport, Welshpool. Third-tier—Dolgellau, Haverfordwest, Knutsford, Merthyr Tydfil.

Circuit Administrator, D. W. Jones-Williams, O.B.E., M.C., T.D., Churchill House, Churchill Way, Cardiff................................£6,750

Deputy Circuit Administrator, L. R. Beckett.

Courts Administrators, Chester Group, S. W. L. James; *Swansea Group*, E. H. Thomas.

Western Circuit.

First-tier—Bodmin, Bristol, Exeter, Winchester. Second-tier—Dorchester, Gloucester, Plymouth. Third-tier—Barnstaple, Bournemouth, Poole, Devizes, Newport (I.O.W.), Portsmouth, Salisbury, Southampton, Swindon, Taunton.

Circuit Administrator, I. E. Ashworth, Bridge House, Clifton, Bristol........................£6,750

Deputy Circuit Administrator, B. Sayer.

Courts Administrators, Bristol Group, A. C. E. Cook, I.S.O.; *Exeter Group*, R. A. J. Barker; *Winchester Group*, J. K. W. Phipps.

RECORDERS

(The Recorder of London is addressed as " Right Worshipful " and, when sitting as a Commissioner in the Central Criminal Court, as "My Lord." Others as " The Worshipful " and " Your Worship.")

Abingdon, Patrick William Medd, O.B.E. (1964).

Andover, James Peter Comyn, Q.C. (1964).

Banbury, Richard Michael Arthur Chetwynd Talbot (1955).

Barnstaple, Cyril Michael Lavington, M.B.E. (1964).

Barrow-in-Furness, Thomas Patrick Russell (1971).

Bath, Jeremy Nicolas Hutchinson, Q.C. (1962).

Bedford, Hon. Samuel Charles Silkin, Q.C., M.P. (1966).

Birkenhead, William Thomas Williams, Q.C., M.P. (1969).

Birmingham, Joseph Marie Davies, Q.C. (1970).

Blackburn, David Bruce McNeill, Q.C. (1969).

Blackpool, Cecil Montacute Clothier, Q.C. (1965).

Bolton, Griffith Winston Guthrie-Jones, Q.C. (1968).

Bournemouth, John Hampden Inskip, Q.C. (1970).

Bradford, Cyril Douglas Chapman, Q.C. (1969).

Bridgwater, Leslie Herrick Collins, O.B.E. (1962).

Brighton, Charles John Addison Doughty, Q.C. (1955).

Bristol, Sir Joseph Thomas Molony, K.C.V.O., Q.C. (1964).

Burnley, Miss Rose Heilbron. Q.C. (1956).

Burton-on-Trent, Oliver Bury Popplewell, Q.C. (1970).

Bury St. Edmunds, Robert Ives (1963).

Cambridge, Thomas Michael Eastham, Q.C. (1971).

Canterbury, Francis Brooks Purchas, Q.C. (1969).

Cardiff, Alun Talfan Davies, Q.C. (1969).

Carlisle, Albert Michael Maguire, M.C., M.M., Q.C. (1970).

Chester, Sir Francis John Watkin Williams, Bt., Q.C. (1958).

Colchester, Frederick Petre Crowder, Q.C., M.P. (1967).

Coventry, Christopher James Saunders French, Q.C. (1971).

Deal, Ian Percival, Q.C., M.P. (1971).

Derby, Alfred William Michael Davies, Q.C. (1965).

Devizes, Desmond Harvey Weight Vowden, Q.C. (1971).

Doncaster, Harold Snowden Pears (1968).

Dover, John Huxley Buzzard (1968).

Dudley, Gilbert Griffiths (1944).

*Durham, James Kenneth Hope, C.B.E.

Exeter, Milson George Polson, Q.C. (1966).

Folkestone, Francis Irwin (1971).

Gloucester, Charles Lawson, Q.C. (1968).

Grantham, Robert Davison Lymbery, Q.C. (1965).

Gravesend, Fredman Ashe Lincoln, Q.C. (1967).

Great Grimsby, William Arnold Sime, M.B.E., Q.C. (1963).

Guildford, Rt. Hon. Sir David Lockhart-Mure Renton, K.B.E., T.D., Q.C., M.P. (1968).

Halifax, John Anthony Cotton (1971).

*Hartlepool, Leslie Othen Williams (1949).

Hastings, Edward Michael Ogden, Q.C. (1971).

Hereford, Gordon Slynn, Q.C. (1971).

Huddersfield, Derek Joshua Clarkson, Q.C. (1971).

Hull, Charles Raymond Dean, Q.C. (1970).

Ipswich, William McLaren Howard, Q.C. (1968).

King's Lynn, William Thomas Wells, Q.C., M.P. (1965).

Leeds, Henry Cooper Scott, Q.C. (1970).

Leicester, Henry Albert Skinner, Q.C. (1966).

Lichfield, Cuthbert George Heron (1968).

Lincoln, Douglas Gordon Arthur Lowe, Q.C. (1964).

Liverpool (*Crown Court*), Judge Rudolph Lyons, Q.C. (1970).

London, Sir Carl Douglas Aarvold, O.B.E., T.D. (1964).

Maidstone, John Douglas May, Q.C. (1971).

Manchester (*Crown Court*), Judge William Gerard Morris (1967).

Margate, Leslie Kenneth Edward Boreham, Q.C. (1968).

Merthyr Tydfil, Philip Loscombe Wintringham Owen, T.D., Q.C. (1971).

Newark, Guy Holford Dixon (1964).

Newbury, Edward Terrell, O.B.E., Q.C. (1935).

Newcastle under Lyme, William Field Hunt (1945).

Newcastle upon Tyne, Roderick Philip Smith, Q.C. (1970).

Northampton, William Percival Grieve, Q.C., M.P. (1965).

Norwich, Robert Michael Oldfield Havers, Q.C., M.P. (1968).

Nottingham, Matthew Anthony Leonard Cripps, C.B.E., D.S.O., T.D., Q.C. (1961).

Oldham, Richard Martin Bingham, T.D., Q.C. (1960).

Oxford, Edward Brian Gibbens, Q.C. (1965).

Penzance, Charles Fiennes Ingle (1964).

Plymouth, Edgar Stewart Fay, Q.C. (1964).

Pontefract, Denis Thelwall Lloyd (1971).

Poole, Malcolm McGougan (1954).

Portsmouth, Cyril Lewis Hawser, Q.C. (1969).
*Preston, William Harrison Openshaw (1958).
Reading, Michael Thomas Ben Underhill (1970).
Rochester, Geoffrey Hollis Crispin, Q.C. (1968).
Rotherham, Richard Hampton Hutchinson (1971).
Salford, Godfrey Heilpern, Q.C. (1964).
Salisbury, Henry Edward Lewis McCreery, Q.C. (1969).
Scarborough, Joseph Stanley Snowden (1951).
Sheffield, John Francis Scott Cobb, Q.C. (1970).
Shrewsbury, Douglas Patrick Draycott, Q.C.(1966).
Southampton, Raymond Stock, Q.C. (1966).
Southend, Malcolm John Morris, Q.C. (1966).
Stoke on Trent, George Kenneth Mynett, Q.C. (1961).
Sunderland, Geoffrey Baker, Q.C. (1971).
Swansea, Hugh Emlyn Hooson, Q.C., M.P. (1971).
Swindon, John Anthony Sanderson Hall, D.F.C., Q.C. (1971).
Teesside, Peter Murray Taylor, Q.C. (1970).
Walsall, Edmund Harry Paul Garmondsway Wrightson, Q.C. (1965).
Warley, Francis Walter Ibbetson Barnes (1964).
*Wells, William Mack Huntley.
West Bromwich, Stephen Brown, Q.C. (1965).
Wigan, Harry Sibson Leslie Rigg, Q.C. (1964).
Winchester, James Roland Blake Fox-Andrews, Q.C. (1971).
Windsor, New, Francis Alfred Blennerhassett, Q.C. (1965).
Wolverhampton, Kenneth George Illtyd Jones, Q.C. (1966).
Worcester, Hon. Thomas Gabriel Roche, Q.C. (1959).
Yarmouth, Great, Sir Harold Felix Cassel, Bt., Q.C. (1968).
York, Harry Graham Bennett, Q.C. (1968).
*Boroughs having no Quarter Sessions.

METROPOLITAN STIPENDIARY MAGISTRATES
(Under the Administration of Justice Act, 1964).

Bow Street, Covent Garden, W.C.2.
Chief Metropolitan Stipendiary Magistrate,
Sir Frank Milton.....................£7,850
Magistrates, Kenneth James Priestley Barraclough, C.B.E., T.D.; Evelyn Charles Sadwith Russell; David Fairbairn................each £6,850
Principal Chief Clerk and Establishment Officer,
A. V. E. J. Mindham..................£5,781
Chief Clerks, R. Hines; Miss P. M. Austin
£4,365 to £4,929 or £5,121

Clerkenwell, King's Cross Road, W.C.1.
Magistrates, John Denis Purcell; Christopher Gerald Lea, M.C.; David Prys Jones.........each £6,850
Senior Chief Clerk, D. V. Wainwright.....£5,121
Chief Clerk, S. G. Clixby.......£4,365 to £4,929

Great Marlborough Street, W.1.
Magistrates, Edward George Haydon Robey; St. John Bernard Vyvyan Harmsworth; John Robert Thomas Hooper................each £6,850
Senior Chief Clerk, P. J. Calnan...........£5,121
Chief Clerk, A. L. Gooch......£4,365 to £4,929

Greenwich (Blackheath Road, S.E.10) and Woolwich (Market Street, S.E.18).
Magistrates, Kenneth Harington; Albert William Clark................each £6,850
Senior Chief Clerk, G. Crankshaw. £5,120
Chief Clerk, G. T. Edwards ....£4,365 to £4,929

Marylebone, 181 Marylebone Road, N.W.1.
Magistrates, John Constantine Phipps; David Mure Wacher; Anthony Patrick Babington; Rupert Rawden Rawden-Smith..........each £6,850
Chief Clerks, C. E. Reston; M. B. Geidt....£5,121

North London, Stoke Newington Road, N.16
Magistrates, William Henry Hughes; David Armand Hopkin..................each £6,850
Chief Clerk: J. A. Bradbury....£4,365 to £4,929
Old Street, E.C.1
Magistrates, Neil Martin McElligott; Ian Graeme McLean.....................each £6,850
Senior Chief Clerk, J. T. Taylor, M.C.......£5,121

South Central Petty Sessional Division

Camberwell Green Magistrates' Court, D'Eynsford Road, S.E.5.
Magistrates, Clive Stuart Saxon Burt, Q.C.; Maurice Juniper Guymer; Edgar Leonard Bradley
each £6,050
Senior Chief Clerk, F. A. Green...........£5,121
Chief Clerk, I. Fowler.........£4,365 to £4,929
Tower Bridge Magistrates' Court, Tooley Street, S.E.1
Magistrates, Nigel Francis Maltby Robinson; Charles Richard Beddington......each £6,850
Chief Clerk, C. E. Hollingdale....£4,365 to £4,929
Lambeth Magistrates' Court, Renfrew Road, S.E.11
Magistrate, Herbert Christopher Beaumont, M.B.E.
£6,850
Chief Clerk, J. A. Patron........£4,365 to £4,929
Thames, Aylward Street, Stepney, E.1.
Magistrates, Tobias Springer; Eric John Ronald Crowther........................each £6,850
Senior Chief Clerk, A. L. Gooch. £5,121
Wells Street, 59–65 Wells Street, W.1
Magistrates, Christopher Besley; Richard Kenneth Cooke; David Fairbairn; Peter Walter Goldstone; William Edward Charles Robins
each £6,850
Chief Clerks, G. D. Shaw; E. L. Yabsley
£4,365 to £4,929
West London, Southcombe Street, W. Kensington, W.14
Magistrates, Alan Leslie Stevenson; Nina Lowry
each £6,850
Senior Chief Clerk, K. Edwards...........£5,121
South Western, Lavender Hill, S.W.11
Magistrates, Lancelot Elliot Barker; Donaldson Loudon; Edgar Dennis Smith .....each £6,850
Senior Chief Clerk, J. V. Hayward.........£5,121
Chief Clerk, J. S. L. Pulford.....£4,365 to £4,929

JUVENILE COURTS
Office: 163A Seymour Place, W.1
Senior Chief Clerk, L. Goodman...........£5,250
Chief Clerk, R. N. W. Harbord
£4,365 to £4,929
Juvenile Courts, in separate buildings from Magistrates' Courts, are held at 58B Bow Road, E.3; 4 Kimpton Road, Camberwell Green, S.E.5; 7 Blackheath Road, Greenwich, S.E.10; Anchor Mission, 272 Garratt Lane, Wandsworth, S.W.18; 163A Seymour Place, W.1.

STIPENDIARY MAGISTRATES

Birmingham, John Frederic Milward (1951).
Cardiff, John Cleverdon Rutter (1966).
Kingston upon Hull, Dennis Neil O'Sullivan (1952).
Leeds, John Hugh Edward Randolph (1965).
Liverpool, Leslie Mervyn Pugh (1965).
Manchester, John Bamber (1965).
Merthyr Tydfil, David Powys Rowland (1961).
Pontypridd, Philip Guy Dudley Sixsmith (1966).
Salford, Leslie Walsh (1951).
Stoke-on-Trent, Geoffrey Arthur John Smallwood (1960).
Wolverhampton, Howard William Maitland Coley (1961).

CITY OF LONDON JUSTICE ROOMS
MANSION HOUSE JUSTICE ROOM.
Chief Magistrate, The Lord Mayor.
Chief Clerk, J. H. Tratt.....................£5,580
Deputy Chief Clerk, C. F. Grimwood.......£4,185

GUILDHALL JUSTICE ROOM
Chief Clerk, A. G. J. Chandler.............£5,580
Deputy Chief Clerk, F. A. Treeby..........£4,185

DIRECTOR OF PUBLIC PROSECUTIONS
12 Buckingham Gate, S.W.1.

Director, Sir Norman Skelhorn, K.B.E., Q.C.,£10,950
Deputy Director, R. L. D. Thomas........£6,920
Assistant Directors, E. G. MacDermott; M. J. Jardine; J. M. Evelyn; O. Nugent
£5,015 to £6,100
Assistant Solicitors, M. D. Hutchison; P. M. J. Palmes; P. R. Barnes; J. Wood
£4,370 to £5,815
Senior Legal Assistants, A. G. Flavell; J. E. Leck; T. J. Taylor; C. J. I. Bourke; J. M. Walker; K. M. Horn; D. G. Williams; K. Dowling; C. H. Cossham; A. H. Whitfield; A. R. H. Thomas; J. P. Smith; Mrs. M. Phillips; R. D. Maitland; G. D. Grant-Whyte; W. H. Walker
£3,461 to £4,565
Legal Assistants, T. Waring; Miss V. Snook; P. G. Spencer; C. J. Cleugh; Miss D. Shammah; T. R. Pogson; G. O. N. Emanuel; W. A. H. a'Beckett Terrell; M. D. Kew; Mrs. R. Wright; N. Lumley; M. K. Martyn-Woodnutt; I. D. Davies; M. O'Byrne; M. Bibby; G. Adams
£2,121 to £3,273
Establishment Officer, K. Dowling.
Senior Executive Officers, H. Smethurst; W. J. Adams; K. J. Winfield (*Deputy Establishment Officer*)
£2,950 to £3,575

OFFICE OF THE JUDGE ADVOCATE GENERAL OF THE FORCES
(*Lord Chancellor's Establishment; Joint Service for the Army and the Royal Air Force*)
6 Spring Gardens, Cockspur Street, S.W.1

Judge Advocate General, B. A. C. Duncan, C.B.E.
£8,400
Vice Judge Advocate General, F. H. Dean....£6,750
Assistant Judge Advocates General, E. H. V. Harington; J. G. Morgan-Owen, M.B.E.; N. B. Birrell; W. E. Stubbs, M.B.E. (£5,615 to £5,640); B. R. Allen; G. H. L. Rhodes, T.D.; J. Stuart-Smith; G. Ll. Chapman.....£4,390 to £5,015
Deputy Judge Advocates, J. F. X. McEvoy; C. G. Gould; J. E. Pullinger; G. E. Empson; G. R. Canner; A. R. W. Hancox...£3,286 to £4,390
Legal Assistant, G. D. Lindley.
Registrar, M. R. Cockrem.

METROPOLITAN POLICE OFFICE
New Scotland Yard, Broadway, S.W.1
[01-230 1212]

Commissioner, Sir John Waldron, K.C.V.O.,£14,000
Deputy Commissioner R. Mark...........£8,112

"A" Department
Administration and Operations
Assistant Commissioner, J. Starritt.........£7,314
Deputy Assistant Commissioners, J. H. Gerrard, M.C.; H. J. E. Hunt, O.B.E.........£5,106 to £5,850
Principal, G. E. Stonely.........£3,425 to £4,575
Commanders, H. Hodgson; E. O. Howells; I. E. King; E. T. Matthews; V. J. H. Rignell
£4,212 to £4,680
Commander of Women Police, Mrs. S. C. Becke
£3,792 to £4,212

Senior Executive Officers, W. T. Davis; C. R. A. Messenger.................£2,950 to £3,575

"B" Department
Traffic
Assistant Commissioner, C. P. J. Woods.....£7,314
Deputy Assistant Commissioners, P. J. H. Candy; S. Hebbes.................£5,106 to £5,800
Senior Principal, D. Meyler, D.S.C.
£4,775 to £5,375
Principals, P. A. Barwood; S. H. Carter; R. V. Clark; J. C. Cutts; G. H. T. Shrimpton, C.B.E., T.D.....................£3,425 to £4,575
Commanders, H. Crowden; J. Renton
£4,212 to £4,680
Senior Executive Officers, R. S. Ainsworth; G. W. Barns; E. C. Cox; M. E. B. Keller; S. G. Monk; H. D. Moore; G. T. Smith; K. J. Tetley; K. H. Varney.................£2,950 to £3,575

"C" Department
Criminal Investigation
Assistant Commissioner, P. E. Brodie, O.B.E...£7,314
Deputy Assistant Commissioners, R. C. Chitty; B. N. Halliday; H. W. Hudson, O.B.E.; F. G. D. Smith, C.V.O., D.F.C.; I. Forbes (*National Co-ordinator, Regional Crime Squad, seconded to Home Office*)......................£5,106 to £5,850
Commanders, E. R. Bond; S. Coates; J. W. D. Crane; A. Cunningham; D. C. Dilley; K. Drury; V. S. Gilbert; R. Huntley, B.E.M.; G. J. Kelland; W. C. Marchant; J. E. O'Connell; R. A. Peat; W. H. Virgo; H. D. Walton; J. S. Wilson, O.B.E.; A. H. Wise; R. Yorke..£4,212 to £4,680
Senior Executive Officer, K. Jones £2,950 to £3,575

"D" Department
Personnel and Training
Assistant Commissioner, J. M. Hill, C.B.E., D.F.C.
£7,314
Deputy Assistant Commissioners, P. V. Collier; R. J. Mastel, C.B.E.........£5,106 to £5,850
Principals, R. G. Giddings; G. A. Perry; F. C. B. Varney.................£3,425 to £4,575
Commanders, R. Butler; N. J. H. Darke; A. Lowndes, B.E.M.; D. McIver; E. L. Williams
£4,212 to £4,680
Senior Executive Officers, O. A. Collier; J. H. Mailing; S. H. Scard.........£2,950 to £3,575
Welfare Officer, Capt. J. S. Dalglish, C.V.O., C.B.E., R.N.(ret.).................£2,950 to £3,575
Director of Catering, Col. R. R. Owens, O.B.E.
£4,775 to £5,375
Deputy Director, A. F. Taylor...£3,925 to £4,575

Metropolitan Police Cadet Corps
Commandant, B. Dix...........£4,212 to £4,680
Director of Academic Training, K. H. Patterson, V.R.D.
£2,950 to £4,115

Medical and Dental Branch
Chief Surgeon, R. W. Nevin, T.D.
Consulting Physician and Deputy to Chief Surgeon, Sir John Richardson, Bt., M.V.O.
Medical Officer, E. C. A. Bott.
Chief Dental Surgeon, (vacant).

Public Relations Department
Public Relations Officer, G. D. Gregory, O.B.E., D.S.C.
£4,565 to £5,815
Public Information Officers, J. S. Courtney; E. Wright.....................£3,425 to £4,575
Senior Information Officers, J. H. V. Bradley; M. C. Johnson; R. A. A. Moore.....£2,950 to £3,575
Senior Executive Officers, C. J. Boorman; M. G. Down; A. J. James; M. Ferry, T.D.; T. Gibson
£2,950 to £3,575

Inspectorate
Deputy Assistant Commissioner, C. P. Attwood, O.B.E. . . . . £5,106 to £5,850

Management Services
Director, R. A. Root . . . . £5,175 to £6,475
Senior Principal Scientific Officer and Deputy Director,
N. E. Hand, Ph.D. . . . . £4,565 to £5,190
Principal Scientific Officer, D. Porch
£2,995 to £4,087

DIRECTORATE OF ADMINISTRATION AND FINANCE
Receiver, K. A. L. Parker, C.B. £8,250

"E" Department
Establishments and Secretariat
Secretary, G. S. Downes . . . . £5,175 to £6,475
Senior Principals, J. E. Mitchell, D.F.C.; J. W. Syms
£4,775 to £5,375
Principals, M. Lee; E. Tyler . . . . . £3,425 to £4,575
Senior Executive Officers, E. R. Bright; A. Hartley;
F. E. Heron; R. B. Jones; M. W. Maidenent;
C. E. D. Reeves; L. G. Spencer; J. E. Tubb
£2,950 to £3,575

General Registry
Senior Executive Officer, R. W. Coysh, M.B.E.
£2,950 to £3,575

"F" Department
Finance
Director of Finance, J. Last . . . . £5,175 to £6,475
Senior Principal, B. G. David . . . . £4,775 to £5,375
Principals, J. L. Davies; C. N. Hill; S. A. Mudd;
F. A. W. Pilborough. . . . . £3,425 to £4,575
Senior Executive Officers, R. W. Barker; R. F.
Gridley; D. C. T. Humphries; N. A. E. Rex;
R. C. H. Taylor . . . . £2,950 to £3,575

"G" Department
Administration
Director of Administration, P. J. G. Buckley
£5,175 to £6,475
Senior Principals, R. H. Beaver; A. R. Pike, O.B.E.;
F. R. Pollard, O.B.E. . . . . £4,775 to £5,375
Principals, J. J. Dolan; H. E. W. Hodson; L. Joughin,
M.C. . . . . £3,425 to £4,575
Senior Executive Officers, D. M. Davis; C. E. Ford;
J. R. Hamilton; J. S. Johnstone; R. J. Nicholls;
R. P. Sargent; R. F. Spain. . . . . £2,950 to £3,575
Superintendent of Printing, H. T. Hudson
£2,950 to £3,575
Senior Accident Claims Officer, A. Morley
£3,300 to £4,115

Architect and Surveyor's Department
Chief Architect and Surveyor, J. I. Elliott. £5,815
Deputy Chief Architect and Surveyor, G. B. Townsend
£4,565 to £5,190
Architects, Superintending Grade, S. J. Hanchet;
G. B. Vint. . . . . £4,565 to £5,190
Senior Surveyors, A. H. Bailey; J. W. Burton; H. R.
Ewence, O.B.E.; D. N. Fogden. . £3,750 to £4,383
Senior Architects, C. A. Legerton; C. G. Liardet;
A. E. Matcham; I. G. Mowat; P. Silsby
£3,750 to £4,383
Senior Public Health Engineer, C. L. Langshaw, O.B.E.
£3,750 to £4,383

Engineering Department
Chief Engineer, B. France £5,815
Deputy Chief Engineers, R. H. Campin; T. R.
Jones . . . . £3,992 to £4,625
Senior Engineers, E. Blade; J. L. Breese; D. Hale;
I. O. Levy; G. A. Smith, M.B.E.
£3,750 to £4,383

"L" Department
Solicitors
Solicitor, E. O. Lane, D.F.C., A.F.C. £7,725
Deputy Solicitor, R. E. T. Birch. £6,925

Assistant Solicitors, G. E. Clark; J. B. Egan; R. L.
Kiley; R. G. Mays; D. M. O'Shea; W. H. S.
Relton; A. H. Simpson; D. W. Warran; M. H.
Wilmot; C. N. Winston . . . . . . £4,730 to £5,815
Senior Legal Assistants, D. M. Barlow; R. P. Coupland;
H. J. Drake; W. S. Frost; I. G. F. Graham;
H. B. Hargrave; M. R. Holmes; R. E. Marsh;
J. O'Keefe; C. S. Porteous; J. M. Tuff; R. B.
Vince; H. M. Weston. . . . . . . £3,461 to £4,565
Legal Assistants, T. G. Cowling; J. F. Crocker; R.W.
Davies; D. E. Dracup; P. L. Draddy; B. Hall;
S. M. Howard; Miss P. Iremonger; G. B. Isted;
J. R. McCann; P. A. Shawdon; R. N. Short;
R. M. D. Thorne; R. Wait-Brown; D. E. B.
Waters; Miss M. E. Wilkie; A. G. I. Wontner;
Miss M. Wood; H. A. Youngerwood
£2,121 to £3,223
Senior Chief Managing Clerks, W. McCrorie; E.
Worboys; J. P. Worboys, M.B.E.
£3,925 to £4,575
Chief Managing Clerks, W. E. Ball; G. Davies; P.
Stenning; K. Stokes; C. W. White
£2,950 to £3,575

Metropolitan Police Laboratory
Director, R. L. Williams, D.Phil., D.Sc.
£5,415 to £6,005
Deputy Director, T. H. Jones . . . . £4,565 to £5,190
Senior Principal Scientific Officers, B. J. Culliford;
Miss M. Pereira. . . . . £4,565 to £5,190
Principal Scientific Officers, C. F. M. Fryd; D. Neylan
£2,995 to £4,077

Special Assistant to Commissioner
*General Secretary of the Association of Chief Police
Officers for England and Wales,* F. W. C. Pennington, O.B.E. . . . . £3,925 to £4,575

Metropolitan Special Constabulary
Chief Commandant, A. A. Hammond.

CITY OF LONDON POLICE
26 Old Jewry, E.C.2
Commissioner, C. J. Page
Assistant Commissioner, (vacant)
£5,340 to £6,087
Commanders, A. McGregor (*C.I.D.*); W. Stapleton
(*Operations*) . . . . £4,212 to £4,680
Chief Superintendents, W. Burley (*Administration*);
K. Short (*Traffic and Communications*); B. Rowland ("*B*" *Divn.*); J. Stimson ("*C*" *Divn.*); A.
Francis ("*D*" *Divn.*); P. Coppack (*C.I.D.*); G.
Lee (*C.I.D.*). . . . . £3,612 to £3,972

City of London Special Constabulary.
Commandant, H. E. Wright.
Chief Staff Officer, J. Oakley.

INDUSTRIAL AND OTHER TRIBUNALS
Compensation (Defence) Act 1939
SHIPPING CLAIMS TRIBUNAL.
President, The Rt. Hon. Sir Gordon Willmer, O.B.E.,
T.D.
Registrar, K. C. McGuffie, The Admiralty Registrar,
Admiralty Registry, Royal Courts of Justice,
W.C.2.

Lands Tribunal
3 Hanover Square, W.1
President, Sir Michael Rowe, C.B.E., Q.C.
Members, H. P. Hobbs; J. R. Laird; R. C. G.
Fennell; R. C. Walmsley; J. S. Daniel, Q.C.;
J. H. Emlyn Jones, M.B.E.; E. C. Strathon.
Registrar, J. H. Ayers.

Patents and Registered Designs Appeal Tribunal
Room 169, Royal Courts of Justice, W.C.2
Judges, The Hon. Mr. Justice Graham; The Hon.
Mr. Justice Whitford.
Registrar, C. L. R. Dalley.

Performing Right Tribunal.
Room 105, 25 Southampton Buildings, W.C.2
Chairman, H. E. Francis, Q.C.
Secretary, D. Daley.

Transport Tribunal
Watergate House, 15 York Buildings.
Adelphi, W.C.2
President, G. D. Squibb, Q.C.
Registrar and Secretary, E. F. Callow, M.B.E.

Board of Referees Income Tax Act, 1952
Room 552, Royal Courts of Justice, W.C.2.
Registrar, F. H. Cowper.

Parliamentary and Local Government Election
Petitions Office.
Room 120, Royal Courts of Justice, W.C.2
Prescribed Officer, W. R. Lawrence.

Pensions Appeal Tribunals.
Staffordshire House, Store St., W.C.1
President, Sir Stafford Foster-Sutton, K.B.E., C.M.G., Q.C.
Secretary, E. D. Fagg..........£2,950 to £3,575

Benefices Act, 1898.
Room 120, Royal Courts of Justice, W.C.2
Registrar of the Court, J. R. Bickford Smith.

Immigration Appeals Act, 1969
Office of Immigration Appeals
231 Strand, W.C.2
Chief Adjudicator, J. Bennett.

Immigration Appeals Tribunal
Thanet House, 231 Strand, W.C.2
President, Sir Derek Hilton, M.B.E.
Vice-President, P. N. Dalton.
Secretary to the Appellate Authorities, R. S. Weekes.

UNITED KINGDOM DEFENCE

Government defence policy was stated in 1970 (*Cmnd.* 4521) to be based on three main objectives, (1) to enable Britain to resume, within her resources, a proper share of the responsibility for the preservation of peace and stability in the world; (2) to improve the capabilities of the Armed Forces, to overcome their manpower difficulties, and to enhance their role in the community; (3) to establish and maintain a sound financial basis on which to develop and carry out defence policy and plans in the years ahead.

COMBAT FORCES.—The combat forces consist of the following six elements:

(1) **The Nuclear Strategic Force** of four Polaris-carrying submarines—*Renown, Repulse, Resolution* and *Revenge*. The force is manned by 3,000 servicemen and 3,800 civilians and is estimated to be maintained at a cost of £34m. in 1971–72.

(2) **Royal Navy General Purpose Combat Forces** are composed of (a) amphibious forces, including a Commando Brigade Headquarters and four Royal Marine Commandos; (b) aircraft carriers; (c) submarines; (d) cruisers; (e) destroyers and frigates; (f) mines countermeasures forces; and (g) support and other ships. These forces are manned by 39,200 servicemen and 10,800 civilians and are estimated to be maintained at a cost of £301m. in 1971–72.

(3) **European Theatre Ground Forces** are (a) the British Army of the Rhine (BAOR), consisting of one corps of three divisional headquarters, five armoured brigades and one mechanized brigade, with corps troops including an armoured reconnaissance force and two artillery brigades; (b) the Berlin Brigade which fulfils Britain's commitment to the security of the Western Sector of Berlin; (c) forces in the United Kingdom which are (i) The majority of the field force headquarters and units stationed in the United Kingdom in Army Strategic Command, which includes the land elements of the United Kingdom Mobile Force (UKMF), a division of three air-portable brigades with additional logistic support together with one parachute force of two battalions; (ii) the British contribution to Allied Command Europe Mobile Force (Land); and (iii) a Special Air Service Regiment. All of these have primary roles in support of NATO and in addition Army Strategic Command supports those forces based outside Europe to meet Commonwealth and treaty obligations. These forces are manned by 95,900 servicemen and 32,200 civilians and are estimated to be maintained at a cost of £363m. in 1971–72.

(4) **Other Army Combat Forces** are (a) in the Far East (excluding Hong Kong), a battalion group in Singapore, including an artillery battery, an engineer troop and an Army Aviation detachment; a Gurkha battalion in Brunei (dispositions from Jan. 1, 1972); (b) in Hong Kong, a garrison consisting of five infantry battalions (including three Gurkha battalions), an artillery regiment and supporting units; (c) in the Persian Gulf, infantry and engineers stationed at Bahrain and Sharjah; (d) in the Mediterranean, at Gibraltar one infantry battalion plus a company group, with engineer support; in Cyprus, one infantry battalion, an airportable armoured reconnaissance squadron and logistic support to the United Nations Force; a garrison of an armoured car squadron and an infantry battalion in the Sovereign Base Areas; in Malta, one infantry battalion; (e) in the Caribbean, an infantry company group at British Honduras and a force of Royal Engineers with supporting elements in Anguilla. These forces are manned by 24,100 servicemen and 12,100 civilians and maintained at an estimated cost of £54m. in 1971–72.

(5) **Royal Air Force General Purpose Combat Forces** consist of all the R.A.F. front-line formations and units except those designated Air Mobility Forces (*i.e.* transport and tanker forces) and are deployed within (a) Strike Command (four groups —bomber, fighter, maritime and signals), responsible for the Military Air Traffic Organization and with the majority of its aircraft committed to NATO; (b) Air Support Command, providing offensive support aircraft for support of the Army in the field and forming the offensive air element in UKMF (*Harriers* of this Command are assigned to SACEUR); (c) R.A.F. Commands Overseas, which are (i) Royal Air Force Germany (tactical force assigned to SACEUR as part of 2 Tactical Allied Air Force); (ii) Far East Air Force, including units of the Royal Australian Air Force and Royal New Zealand Air Force (long-range maritime reconnaissance, transport aircraft and helicopters); (iii) Air Force Gulf, of *Hunters, Shackletons* and supporting aircraft; (iv) Near East Air Force, at Cyprus, a force of *Vulcans* (declared to CENTO), *Lightnings, Bloodhound* and light anti-aircraft guns for air defence, and transport aircraft; at Malta reconnaissance aircraft for SACEUR and CENTO. These forces are manned by 50,000 servicemen and 15,400 civilians and are maintained at an estimated cost of £379m. in 1971–72.

(6) **Air Mobility Forces** are the strategic transport squadrons equipped with VC10, *Comet, Belfast* and *Britannia* aircraft and the tactical force with *Hercules, Argosy, Andover, Wessex* and *Whirlwind* aircraft. These forces are manned by 16,700 servicemen and 3,600 civilians and are maintained at an estimated cost of £112m. in 1971–72.

Details of ships of H.M. Fleet appear on p. 462.

MINISTRY OF DEFENCE
Main Building
Whitehall, S.W.1
[01–930 7022]

On April 1, 1964 a unified Ministry of Defence was created which absorbed the four separate departments which had previously been responsible for defence matters, namely the Admiralty, the War Office, the Air Ministry and the Ministry of Defence. This Department is now responsible for the formulation of defence policy and the control and administration of the armed forces.

The Ministry is broadly organized into central staffs, who are concerned with general defence policy and strategy, and staffs, under the Admiralty Board, the Army Board and the Air Force Board of the Defence Council, who are responsible for the control and administration of the three Services. The Minister in charge of the department is the Secretary of State for Defence and he is assisted by two Ministers of State and by one Parliamentary Under-Secretary of State for each Service.

Secretary of State for Defence, THE LORD CARRINGTON, P.C., K.C.M.G., M.C. £8,500
  Private Secretary, R. J. Andrew.
  Assistant Private Secretaries, A. W. Stephens; R. C. Mottram; G. W. Fuller; K. R. May.
Minister of State for Defence, THE LORD BALNIEL, P.C. M.P... *Hugh Gilmour* £7,625
  Private Secretary, K. P. Jeffs.
  Assistant Private Secretaries, D. R. Marsh; A. R. Brown.
  Parliamentary Private Secretary, A. W. Wiggin, M.P.
Minister of State for Defence Procurement, I. H. J. Gilmour, M.P. £7,625
  Private Secretary, D. C. M. Duffus.
Parliamentary Under-Secretary of State for Defence for the Royal Navy, P. M. Kirk, M.P. £3,750
Parliamentary Under-Secretary of State for Defence for the Army, G. Johnson Smith, M.P. £3,750
Parliamentary Under-Secretary of State for Defence for the Royal Air Force, A. C. F. Lambton, M.P. £3,750

Chief of the Defence Staff, Admiral of the Fleet Sir Peter Hill-Norton, G.C.B.
Chief of the Naval Staff and First Sea Lord, Admiral Sir Michael Pollock, G.C.B., M.V.O., D.S.C.
Chief of the General Staff, General Sir Michael Carver, G.C.B., C.B.E., D.S.O., M.C., A.D.C. (Gen.).
Chief of the Air Staff, Air Chief Marshal Sir Dennis Spotswood, G.C.B., C.B.E., D.S.O., D.F.C.

Permanent Under-Secretary of State, Sir James Dunnett, G.C.B., C.M.G. £14 000
  Private Secretary, M. Gainsborough
Chief Executive, Procurement Executive, D. G. Rayner.
  Private Secretary, J. McClelland.
Secretary, Procurement Executive, Sir Michael Cary, K.C.B. £14,000
  Private Secretary, M. R. Pack.
Second Permanent Under-Secretaries of State, Sir Arthur Drew, K.C.B. (*Administration*); Sir Martin Flett, K.C.B. (*Equipment*) £13,000
Vice Chief of Defence Staff, Air Marshal Sir John Barraclough, K.C.B., C.B.E., D.F.C., A.F.C.
Director-General of Intelligence (Ministry of Defence), Air Marshal Sir Harold Maguire, K.C.B., D.S.O., O.B.E. (ret.) £7,900
Deputy Chief of the Defence Staff (Intelligence), Vice-Admiral L. E. S. H. Le Bailly, C.B., O.B.E.
Deputy Chief of the Defence Staff (Operational Requirements), Vice-Admiral I. S. McIntosh, C.B., D.S.O., M.B.E., D.S.C.

Chief of Personnel and Logistics, Air Chief Marshal Sir Christopher Foxley-Norris, K.C.B., D.S.O., O.B.E.
Assistant Chief of Personnel and Logistics, Rear Admiral J. D. Trythall, C.B., O.B.E.
Assistant Chiefs of the Defence Staff, (vacant) (*Operations*); Maj.-Gen. D. W. Fraser, O.B.E. (*Policy*); Maj.-Gen. Sir John Anderson, K.B.E. (*Signals*).

Chief of Naval Personnel and Second Sea Lord, Vice-Admiral L. D. Empson, C.B.
Chief of Fleet Support, Vice-Admiral C. F. A. Trewby.
Vice-Chief of Naval Staff, Vice-Admiral T. T. Lewin, M.V.O., D.S.C.

Adjutant-General, General Sir John Mogg, K.C.B., C.B.E., D.S.O., A.D.C. (Gen.).
Quarter-Master-General, General Sir Antony Read, K.C.B., C.B.E., D.S.O., M.C., A.D.C. (Gen.).
Vice-Chief of the General Staff, Lieutenant General Sir Cecil Blacker, K.C.B., O.B.E., M.C.

Air Member for Personnel, Air Chief Marshal Sir Lewis Hodges, K.C.B., C.B.E., D.S.O., D.F.C.
Air Member for Supply and Organization, Air Marshal Sir Neil Wheeler, K.C.B., C.B.E., D.S.O., D.F.C., A.F.C.
Vice-Chief of the Air Staff, Air Marshal Sir Denis Smallwood, K.C.B., C.B.E., D.S.O., D.F.C.
Chief Scientist (Royal Air Force), J. E. Henderson £6,750

Defence Services Secretary, Major-General C. Blair, O.B.E., M.C.
Naval Secretary, Rear-Admiral I. G. Raikes, C.B.E., D.S.C.
Military Secretary, General Sir Thomas Pearson, K.C.B., C.B.E., D.S.O.
Air Secretary, Air Marshal Sir Gareth Clayton, K.C.B., D.F.C.
Chief Scientific Adviser, Prof. H. Bondi, F.R.S. £14,000
Director-General of Supply Co-ordination, Maj.-Gen. I. H. Lyall Grant, M.C.(ret.) £6,750
Director, Women's Royal Naval Service, Commandant Daphne M. Blundell, Hon.A.D.C.
Director, Women's Royal Army Corps, Brig. Sheila A. E. Heaney, M.B.E., T.D., Hon.A.D.C.
Director, Women's Royal Air Force, Air Commodore Philippa F. Marshall, C.B., O.B.E., Hon.A.D.C.
Chaplain of the Fleet, The Ven. A. W. M. Weekes, C.B., Q.H.C.
Chaplain-General to the Forces, The Ven. J. R. Youens, C.B., O.B.E., M.C., Q.H.C.
Chaplain-in-Chief, R.A.F., The Ven. L. J. Ashton, C.B., Q.H.C.
Matron-in-Chief, Queen Alexandra's Royal Naval Nursing Service, Miss C. Thompson, R.R.C., Q.H.N.S.
Matron-in-Chief and Director of Army Nursing Services, Brig. Barbara Gordon, C.B., R.R.C., Q.H.N.S.
Matron-in-Chief, Princess Mary's R.A.F. Nursing Service, Air Commandant Ann McDonald, A.R.R.C., Q.H.N.S.
Chief Executive, Royal Dockyards, L. W. Norfolk, O.B.E., T.D. £11,000
Commandant, Royal College of Defence Studies, General Sir Mervyn Butler, K.C.B., C.B.E., D.S.O., M.C.
Deputy Under-Secretaries of State, S. Redman, C.B.; J. M. Wilson, C.B.; I. Montgomery, C.B.; E. H. Gwynn, C.B.; R. C. Kent, C.B.; H. W. Cauthery, C.B.; P. D. Nairne, C.B., M.C. £9,000

Director of Dockyard Manpower and Productivity, S. T. Flannery..................£6,750
Director of Dockyard Production and Support, Rear-Admiral H. C. Hogger, C.B., D.S.C. *(ret.)* .£6,750
Deputy Chief Adviser (Projects and Nuclear), V. H. B. Macklen..................£7,350
Director of Armament Supplies (Naval), K. A. Haddacks, M.B.E...................£6,750
Assistant Under-Secretaries of State, J. M. Addis; H. C. Budden; A. Campbell, C.M.G.; E. G. Cass, O.B.E.; T. A. G. Charlton, C.B.; L. H. Curzon, C.B.; G. C. B. Dodds; G. R. R. East; P. T. E. England; D. M. Evans; H. P. Hall, C.M.G., M.B.E.; A. D. Harvey; R. Haynes; F. C. Herd; A. P. Hockaday, C.M.G.; H. O. Hooper, C.B., C.M.G.; T. C. G. James, C.M.G.; E. Jones; W. Marshall; R. J. Penney; E. K. Stopford, C.B.; C. Wallworth..................£6,750
Director-General of Supplies and Transport (Naval), E. J. Braybrook..................£6,960
Director-General of Defence Accounts, L. R. Palmer, C.B.E...................£6,750
Comptroller of Defence Lands and Claims, E. H. Palmer. C.B. *6.1.72*...................£6,750
General Managers of H.M. Dockyards, W. R. N. Hughes *(Chatham)*; Capt. H. G. Southwood, C.B.E., D.S.C., R.N.*(retd.) (Devonport)*; H. J. Fulthorpe *(Portsmouth)*; H. R. P. Chatten *(Rosyth)*..................£6,750
Asst. Chief Scientific Advisers, I. L. Davies *(Projects)*; P. R. Wallis *(Research)*; J. W. Gibson *(Studies)*..................£6,750
Chief Scientific Officers, D. Cardwell; F. H. East; G. L. Hutchinson; E. Lee; W. B. H. Lord; H. W. Pout, O.B.E.; A. W. Ross, O.B.E.; D. Stewart-Watson, C.B., O.B.E. £7,350
S. Bolshaw; G. N. Gadsby; R. J. C. Harris; M. H. Oliver; A. Stratton..................£6,750

Procurement Executive Controllers and Directing Staff

Controller Guided Weapons and Electronic Systems, E. C. Cornford, C.B. ..W.V.S.CHANLEY £6,000 *9/12*
Controller Aircraft, Air Chief Marshal Sir Peter Fletcher, K.C.B., O.B.E., D.F.C., A.F.C.
Controller Personnel, W. Geraghty, C.B.....£9,000
Controller of the Navy, Vice-Admiral Sir Anthony Griffin, K.C.B.   E.C.CORNFORD *10/12*
Controller Policy, G. Leitch, C.B., O.B.E. £9,000
Controller Research and Development Establishments and Research, Sir George MacFarlane, C.B...................£10,950
Master-General of the Ordnance, General Sir Noel Thomas, K.C.B., D.S.O., M.C.
Head of Defence Sales, H. J. L. Suffield....£12,500
Assistant Under-Secretary Sales, R. Anderson £6,750
Military Deputy to Head of Defence Sales, Rear-Admiral H. C. N. Goodhart.
Assistant Under Secretary Operational Requirements, E. Broadbent, C.M.G...................£6,750
Assistant Under Secretary International and Industrial Policy, G. H. Green..................£6,750
Director General Defence Contracts, E. F. Hedger, O.B.E...................£6,750
Director General Quality Assurance, H. E. Drew, C.B...................£7,000
Assistant Under Secretary Personnel, G. Wheeler, C.B...................£6,750
Assistant Under Secretary Management Services, D. A. Lovelock..................£6,750
Assistant Under Secretary Finance, N. V. Meeres, C.B...................£6,750
Controller of Royal Ordnance Factories, S. C. Bacon, C.B...................£8,095
Deputy Controllers of Royal Ordnance Factories, D. A. Hutton-Williams, M.B.E.; J. Cook......£6,750

Assistant Under Secretary Ordnance, F.W. Armstrong, M.V.O...................£6,750
Deputy Master General of the Ordnance, Major General A. E. Walkling, O.B.E.
Director General Fighting Vehicles and Engineer Equipment, Major General A. G. Lewis, C.B.E.
Director General Weapons (Army), Major General H. Knutton.
Assistant Under Secretary Material (Naval), A. R. M. Jaffray..................£6,750
Director General Ships, Vice-Admiral Sir George Raper, C.B.   CB6/72
Deputy Director-General, Ships, S. J. Palmer, O.B.E...................£8,725
Director of Naval Ship Production, J. R. F. Moss, O.B.E...................£8,300
Director of Warship Design, N. Hancock....£8,300
Director of Engineering (Ships), Rear-Admiral L. D. Dymoke.
Deputy Director, Naval Engineering (Construction), H. R. Mason..................£6,750
Deputy Director, Naval Construction (A), M. K. Purvis..................£6,750
Deputy Director, Naval Construction (B), J. E. S. Vincent..................£6,750
Deputy Director Design Electrical, P. Smith ..£6,750
Director General Weapons (Navy), Rear-Admiral P. A. Watson, M.V.O.
Director of Weapons Production and Superintendent Production Pool (Naval), J. I. G Evans....£6,750
Deputy Controller Polaris, Rear-Admiral C. W. H. Shepherd, C.B.E.
Director Project Team (Submarines), H. J. Tabb..................£8,300
Vice-Controller Aircraft, L. F. Nicholson, C.B. £7,800
Deputy Controllers Aircraft, Rear-Admiral P. H. C. Illingworth, C.B.; R. P. Probert........£7,800
Assistant Under Secretary Aircraft, J. R. Christie..................£6,750
Deputy Controller Guided Weapons, W. J. Charnley..................£7,800
Deputy Controller Electronics, C. P. Fogg....£7,800
Deputy Controller Equipment, Air Vice-Marshal S. H. Bonser, C.B., M.B.E.
Assistant Under Secretary Guided Weapon and Electronic Systems, T. M. Wilson..................£6,750
Deputy Controllers Research and Development Establishments and Research, N. Coles; B. W. Lythall, C.B.; Dr. W. H. Penley, C.B., C.B.E......£9,000
Assistant Under Secretary Research and Development Establishments and Research, H. L. Lawrence-Wilson..................£6,750
Director, National Gas Turbine Establishment, I. M. Davidson..................£6,750
Director, Royal Aircraft Establishment, Sir Morien Morgan, C.B...................£9,000
Director, Royal Radar Establishment, E. V. D. Glazier, C.B...................£7,800
Director General Telecommunications, R. E. Sainsbury..................£6,750

Meteorological Office
London Road, Bracknell, Berks.
[Bracknell: 20242]

The Meteorological Office is the State Meteorological Service. It forms part of the Ministry of Defence, the Director General being ultimately responsible to the Secretary of State for Defence.

Except for the common services provided by other government departments as part of their normal functions, the cost of the Meteorological Office is borne by Defence Votes.

Of the expenditure chargeable to Defence Votes

about £7,200,000 represents expenditure associated with staff and £3,300,000 on stores, communications and miscellaneous services. About £2,400,000 is recovered from outside bodies in respect of special services rendered, sales of meteorological equipment, etc.

Director General, B. J. Mason, D.SC., F.R.S. £8,300
Director of Services, P. J. Meade, O.B.E..... £6,750

THE ROYAL NAVY

THE QUEEN

Admirals of the Fleet

H.R.H. the Duke of Windsor, K.G., K.T., K.P., *born* June 23, 1894 ....Jan. 21, 1936
The Lord Fraser of North Cape, G.C.B., K.B.E., *born* Feb. 5, 1888 ....Oct. 22, 1948
Sir Algernon U. Willis, G.C.B., K.B.E., D.S.O., *born* May 17. 1889 ....Mar. 20, 1949
H.R.H. the Prince Philip, Duke of Edinburgh, K.G., P.C., K.T., O.M., G.B.E., *born* June 10, 1921...Jan. 15, 1953
Sir George E. Creasy, G.C.B., C.B.E., D.S.O., M.V.O., *born* Oct. 13, 1895...................April 22, 1955
The Earl Mountbatten of Burma, K.G., P.C., G.C.B., O.M., G.C.S.I., G.C.I.E., G.C.V.O., D.S.O., *born*
June 25, 1900..Oct. 21, 1956
Sir Caspar John, G.C.B., *born* March 22, 1903..May 22, 1962
Sir Varyl C. Begg, G.C.B., D.S.O., D.S.C., *born* Oct. 1, 1908 (*Governor and Commander-in-Chief,
Gibraltar*)..Aug. 12, 1968
Sir Peter Hill-Norton, G.C.B., *born* Feb. 8, 1915 (*Chief of the Defence Staff*)..............March 12, 1971

Admirals

Sir Horace R. Law, K.C.B., O.B.E., D.S.C. (*Commander-in-Chief, Naval Home Command*) (*First and Principal Naval Aide-de-Camp*).

Sir Michael Pollock, G.C.B., M.V.O., D.S.C. (*Chief of Naval Staff and First Sea Lord*).

Sir Edward Ashmore, K.C.B., D.S.C. (*C.-in-C., Western Fleet, Allied C.-in-C. Channel and C.-in-C. Eastern Atlantic Area*).

Sir Andrew Lewis, K.C.B.

Vice-Admirals

Sir Anthony Griffin, K.C.B. (*Controller of the Navy*).

Sir George Raper, K.C.B. (*Director-General, Ships*).

Sir Eric Bradbury, K.B.E., C.B., Q.H.P. (*Medical Director-General*).

P. W. B. Ashmore, C.B., M.V.O., D.S.C. (*Chief of Allied Staff, NATO Naval HQ, Southern Europe*).

D. B. H. Wildish, C.B. (*Director-General, Personnel Services and Training*).

J. E. L. Martin, C.B., D.S.C. (*Deputy Supreme Allied Commander, Atlantic*).

L. D. Empson, C.B. (*Second Sea Lord*).

L. E. S. H. Le Bailly, C.B., O.B.E. (*Deputy Chief of Defence Staff (Intelligence)*).

M. F. Fell, C.B., D.S.O., D.S.C. (*Flag Officer, Naval Air Command*).

J. C. Y. Roxburgh, C.B., C.B.E., D.S.O., D.S.C.

T. T. Lewin, M.V.O., D.S.C. (*Vice-Chief of Naval Staff*).

I. S. McIntosh, C.B., D.S.O., M.B.E., D.S.C. (*Deputy Chief of Defence Staff (Operational Requirements)*).

J. R. McKaig, C.B.E. (*Flag Officer, Plymouth*).

G. F. A. Trewby (*Chief of Fleet Support*).

Rear-Admirals

W. T. C. Ridley, C.B., O.B.E.
D. A. Dunbar-Nasmith, C.B.,

D.S.C. (*Flag Officer, Scotland and Northern Ireland*).

P. H. C. Illingworth, C.B. (*Deputy Controller of Aircraft, Royal Navy*).

I. D. McLaughlan, C.B., D.S.C. (*Admiral Commanding Reserves*).

J. D. Trythall, C.B., O.B.E. (*Assistant Chief of Personnel and Logistics*).

A. M. Power, M.B.E. (*Flag Officer, Flotillas, Western Fleet*).

E. F. Gueritz, C.B., O.B.E., D.S.C. (*Commandant, Joint Warfare Establishment*).

R. D. Roberts, C.B. (*Rear-Admiral (Engineering) to Flag Officer, Naval Air Command*).

E. G. N. Mansfield (*Flag Officer, Sea Training*).

J. A. R. Troup, D.S.C. (*Commander, Far East Fleet*).

I. Easton, D.S.C. (*Flag Officer, Admiralty Interview Board*).

A. R. B. Sturdee, C.B., D.S.C. (*Flag Officer, Gibraltar*).

J. E. Pope (*Chief of Staff to Commander-in-Chief, Western Fleet*).

C. C. H. Dunlop, C.B.E. (*Flag Officer, Medway, and Admiral Superintendent, H.M. Dockyard, Chatham*).

N. S. Hepburn, C.B., C.B.E., Q.H.P. (*Medical Officer-in-Charge, R.N. H., Haslar*).

J. Watt, Q.H.S. (*Medical Officer-in-Charge, Institute of Naval Medicine*).

R. P. Phillips, O.B.E., Q.H.S. (*Medical Officer-in-Charge, R.N. H., Plymouth*).

B. J. Morgan (*Director of the Naval Education Service*).

C. W. H. Shepherd, C.B.E. (*Assistant Controller (Polaris)*).

I. G. Raikes, C.B.E., D.S.C. (*Naval Secretary*).

J. P. K. Harkness, C.B. (*Director-General, Naval Manpower*).

J. E. Dyer-Smith (*Director-General, Aircraft (Naval)*).

P. White, C.B.E. (*Port Admiral, Rosyth*).

J. A. Templeton-Cotill (*Flag Officer Malta and NATO Commander South-East Area Mediterranean*).

R. J. Trowbridge (*Flag Officer, Royal Yachts*).

D. Williams (*Flag Officer Second-in-Command, Far East Fleet*).

A. C. W. Wilson (*Defence Adviser, Canberra*).

P. R. C. Higham (*Assistant Chief of Naval Staff (Operational Requirements)*).

M. N. Lucey, D.S.C.

H. C. N. Goodhart (*Military Deputy to Head of Defence Sales*).

J. D. Treacher (*Flag Officer, Carriers and Amphibious Ships*).

P. A. Watson, M.V.O. (*Director-General, Weapons (Naval)*).

L. D. Dymoke (*Director of Engineering (Ships)*).

G. P. D. Hall, D.S.C. (*Hydrographer of the Navy*).

P. G. LaNiece, C.B.E. (*Flag Officer Spithead and Admiral Superintendent H.M. Dockyard, Portsmouth*).

H. D. Nixon, M.V.O. (*Senior Naval Member, Ordnance Board*).

A. S. Morton (*Senior Naval Member, Royal College of Defence Studies*).

H. C. Leach (*Assistant Chief of Naval Staff (Policy)*).

G. C. Mitchell (*Assistant Chief of Staff (Logistics)*).

P. M. Austin (*Assistant Chief of Naval Staff (Operations and Air)*).

I. J. Lees-Spalding (*Chief Staff Officer (Technical) to Commander-in-Chief Western Fleet and Inspector-General Fleet Maintenance*).

W. D. S. Scott (*Commander British Navy Staff Washington and U.K. National Liaison Representative to Supreme Allied Commander Atlantic*).

D. G. Spickernell (*Deputy Director, Quality Assurance*).

A. J. Miller.

J. Hunter O.B.E. (*Director, Naval Dental Services*).

E.W. Ellis, C.B.E. (*Admiral President, Royal Naval College, Greenwich*).

L. R. Lygo

J. H. F. Eberle (*Director-General, Fleet Services*).

P*

HER MAJESTY'S FLEET

Type/Class	Operational, preparing for service or engaged on trials and training	Reserve or undergoing long refit, conversion, etc.
Aircraft Carriers	Ark Royal, Eagle	
Commando Ships	Albion, Bulwark	Hermes
Submarines (24)		(11)
Polaris Submarines	Renown, Resolution, Revenge	Repulse
Fleet Submarines	Dreadnought, Churchill, Conqueror*, Courageous*	Valiant, Warspite
OBERON Class	Oberon, Orpheus, Osiris, Ocelot, Otus, Opossum, Opportune, Onyx	Odin, Olympus, Onslaught, Oracle, Otter
PORPOISE Class	Porpoise, Rorqual, Finwhale, Grampus, Sea Lion, Walrus	Narwhal, Cachalot
A Class	Aeneas, Alliance, Auriga	Andrew
Assault Ships	Fearless, Intrepid	
Cruisers	Blake	Lion, Tiger
Guided Missile Destroyers (7)	Devonshire, London, Fife, Glamorgan, Antrim, Norfolk, Bristol*	Kent, Hampshire
Other Destroyers		
CA Class	Cavalier, Caprice	
Battle Class		Matapan
General Purpose Frigates (25)		(6)
LEANDER Class	Dido, Aurora, Argonaut, Andromeda, Jupiter, Charybdis, Achilles, Arethusa, Cleopatra, Phoebe, Minerva, Sirius, Juno, Danae, Hermione, Bacchante, Scylla, Diomede*, Euryalus, Penelope, Naiad	Leander, Ajax, Galatea
Tribal Class	Ashanti, Gurkha, Tartar, Zulu	Mohawk, Eskimo, Nubian
Anti-Aircraft Frigates (4)		
Type 41	Puma, Lynx, Leopard, Jaguar	
Aircraft Direction Frigates (3)		
Type 61	Lincoln, Salisbury, Llandaff	Chichester
Anti-Submarine Frigates (19)		(7)
WHITBY Class	Scarborough, Tenby, Eastbourne	Whitby, Torquay
ROTHESAY Class	Falmouth, Londonderry, Plymouth, Yarmouth, Lowestoft, Rothesay, Berwick	Brighton, Rhyl
BLACKWOOD Class		
Type 14	Palliser, Dundas, Hardy, Exmouth, Keppel	Russell, Duncan, Malcolm
Type 15	Undaunted, Rapid, Grenville, Ulster	
Fleet Maintenance Ships	Triumph	Hartland Point, Berry Head
Submarine Depot Ship		Forth
MCM Support Ship	Abdiel	
Diving Trials Ship	Reclaim	
Mine Countermeasures Forces	(49)	(8)
Royal Yacht/Hospital Ship	Britannia	
Ice Patrol Ship	Endurance	

* Under construction on March 31, 1971 and due to be accepted into service during the year. At that date 3 more Fleet submarines, 1 Type 42 destroyer, 2 more LEANDER Class frigates, 4 Type 21 frigates and 1 minehunter were also under construction.

In addition the following were operational in 1971: Accommodation Ships, 2; Survey Ships and Vessels, 13; Mooring, Salvage and Boom Vessels, 21; Fast Training and Patrol Boats, 5; and Seaward Defence Boats, 2.

ROYAL MARINES

The Corps of Royal Marines (instituted 1664) is trained for service on sea and land. The primary duty of the Royal Marines is the provision of four commandos, of which one is at present serving abroad. They also serve at sea in H.M. Ships and provide landing-craft crews, special boat sections (frogmen) and other detachments for amphibious operations. One commando unit also specializes in mountain and arctic warfare. The Royal Marines Band Service provides bands for the Royal Navy and Royal Marines. Estimated strength of the Royal Marines in 1971–1972, 8,000 all ranks.

The Royal Marines Reserve consists of nearly 1,000 volunteers belonging to five main units centred on London, Bristol, Liverpool, Newcastle and Glasgow. These reservists are in continuous training for their primary task of reinforcing the regular Corps, and exercise regularly with Royal Marines Commandos in the United Kingdom and Far East.

Commandant-General, Royal Marines, Lieut.-Gen. B. I. S. Gourlay, O.B.E., M.C.

Major-Generals, P. R. Kay, M.B.E. (*Chief of Staff*); R. B. Loudoun, O.B.E. (*Training Group*); P. J. F. Whiteley, O.B.E. (*Commando Forces*).

THE ARMY
THE QUEEN
Field Marshals

H.R.H. the Duke of Windsor, K.G., K.T., K.P., *born June 23, 1894*.....................Jan. 21, 1936

The Viscount Montgomery of Alamein, K.G., G.C.B., D.S.O., *born Nov. 17, 1887*.............Sept. 1, 1944

Sir Claude J. E. Auchinleck, G.C.B., G.C.I.E., C.S.I., D.S.O. O.B.E., Col. 1 Punjab R. and Indian Grenadiers, *born June 21, 1884*.......................June 1, 1946

H.R.H. the Prince Philip, Duke of Edinburgh, K.G., P.C., K.T., O.M., G.B.E., Field-Marshal, Australian Military Forces, Col.-in-Chief, Q.R.I.H., D.E.R.R., Q. O. Hldrs., Corps of Royal Electrical and Mechanical Engineers, A.C.F., The Royal Canadian Regt., Royal Capadian Army Cadets, Royal Corps of Australian Electrical and Mechanical Engineers and Australian Cadet Corps, Col. W. G., Hon. Col., O.T.C., *born June 10, 1921*.......................Jan. 15, 1953

The Lord Harding of Petherton, G.C.B., C.B.E., D.S.O., M.C., *born Feb. 10, 1896*.............Jan. 21, 1953

H.R.H. the Duke of Gloucester, K.G., P.C., K.T., K.P., G.M.B., G.C.M.G., G.C.V.O., Col.-in-Chief Royal Irish Rangers, Glosters, Gordons, Royal Corps of Transport, Royal Canadian Army Service Corps, Royal Winnipeg Rifles, Royal Australian Armoured Corps, Royal Australian Army Service Corps, Royal New Zealand Army Service Corps and Ceylon Light Infantry, Dep. Col.-in-Chief, R.G.J., Col. S.G. (*Hon. Col., R.A. (T. & A.V.R.) and O.T.C.*) (*Personal A.D.C. to the Queen*), *born March 31, 1900*.......................March 31, 1955

Sir Gerald W. R. Templer, K.G., G.C.B., G.C.M.G., K.B.E., D.S.O., Col. R. H. G., Hon. Col. N.I.M., *born Sept. 11, 1898*.......................Nov. 27, 1956

Sir Francis W. Festing, G.C.B., K.B.E., D.S.O., *born Aug. 28, 1902*.......................Sept. 1, 1960

Sir Richard A. Hull, G.C.B., D.S.O. (*Constable of the Royal Palace and Fortress of London*), *born May 7, 1907*.......................Feb. 8, 1965

Sir A. James H. Cassels, G.C.B., K.B.E., D.S.O., *born Feb. 28, 1907*.......................Feb. 29, 1968

Sir Geoffrey H. Baker, G.C.B., C.M.G., C.B.E., M.C., Col. Comdt. R.A. and R.H.A. (*Master-Gunner, St. James's Park*), *born June 20, 1912*.......................March 31, 1971

Generals

Sir Michael Carver, G.C.B., C.B.E., D.S.O., M.C., A.D.C. (*Gen.*), Col. Comdt. R.T.R. & R.E.M.E. (*Chief of the General Staff*).

Sir Desmond Fitzpatrick, G.C.B., D.S.O., M.B.E., M.C., A.D.C. (*Gen.*), Deputy Col. R.H.G./D., Col. Comdt. R.A.C. (*Deputy to SACEUR*).

Sir John Mogg, K.C.B., C.B.E., D.S.O., A.D.C. (*Gen.*), Col. Comdt. R.G.J. and A.A.C. (*Adjutant-General*).

Sir Antony Read, K.C.B., C.B.E., D.S.O., M.C., A.D.C. (*Gen.*), Col. Comdt. The Light Div. A.C.C. and S.A.S.C. (*Quarter-Master-General*).

Sir Walter Walker, K.C.B., C.B.E., D.S.O., Col. 7 G.R. (*C.-in-C., Allied Forces, N. Europe*).

Sir Victor FitzGeorge-Balfour, K.C.B., C.B.E., D.S.O., M.C. (*U.K. Military Representative, HQ, NATO*).

Sir Peter Hunt, K.C.B., D.S.O., O.B.E., Col. Q. O. Hldrs. and 10 G.R. (*C.-in-C., B.A.O.R.*).

Sir Basil Eugster, K.C.B., K.C.V.O., C.B.E., D.S.O., M.C., Col. I.G. (*C.-in-C., United Kingdom Land Forces*).

Sir Noel Thomas, K.C.B., D.S.O., M.C., Col. Comdt. R.E. and R.P.C. (*Master-General, Ordnance*).

Sir Thomas Pearson, K.C.B., C.B.E., D.S.O. (*Military Secretary*).

Sir Mervyn Butler, K.C.B., C.B.E., D.S.O., M.C., Col. Comdt. Para. (*Commandant, Royal College of Defence Studies*).

Lieutenant-Generals

Sir Napier Crookenden, K.C.B., D.S.O., O.B.E., Col. Comdt.

Prince of Wales Div. (*G.O.C.-in-C., Western Command*)

Sir Norman Talbot, K.B.E., T.D., M.D., Q.H.S. (*Director General, Army Medical Services*).

Sir Cecil Blacker, K.C.B., O.B.E., M.C., Col. Comdt. R.M.P. and A.P.T.C. (*Vice-Chief General Staff*).

Sir Henry Leask, K.C.B., D.S.O., O.B.E., Col. Comdt., Scottish Div. (*Governor of Edinburgh Castle*).

Sir Richard Ward, K.C.B., D.S.O., M.C., Col. Comdt. R.T.R. (*Commander, British Forces, Hong Kong*).

Sir John Sharp, K.C.B., M.C. (*G.O.C., 1st British Corps*).

Sir William Jackson, K.C.B., O.B.E., M.C., Col. Comdt. R.E. (*G.O.C.-in-C., Northern Command*).

Sir Harry Tuzo, K.C.B., O.B.E., M.C. (*G.O.C. and Director of Operations, Northern Ireland*).

F. D. King, C.B., M.B.E. (*G.O.C., Army Strategic Command*).

Major-Generals

Sir John Willoughby, K.B.E., C.B.

P. T. Tower, C.B., D.S.O., M.B.E., Col. Comdt., R.A. (*Commandant, R.M.A., Sandhurst*).

A. G. Patterson, C.B., D.S.O., O.B.E., M.C., Col. 6 G.R. (*Director of Army Training*).

P. R. C. Hobart, C.B., D.S.O., O.B.E., M.C., Col. Comdt., R.T.R. (*Director, Royal Armoured Corps*).

J. H. Gibbon, C.B., O.B.E.

R. E. Coaker, C.B.E., M.C., Col. 17/21 L. (*Director of Military Operations*).

D. G. T. Horsford, C.B.E., D.S.O.

J. D. Lunt, C.B.E. (*Vice-Adjutant-General*).

F. J. C. Bowes-Lyon, C.B., O.B.E., M.C. (*G.O.C., London District*).

D. L. Lloyd Owen, C.B., D.S.O., O.B.E., M.C. (*President, Regular Commissions Board*).

R. B. Penfold, C.B., M.V.O. (*G.O.C., S.E. Dist.*).

Sir John Anderson, K.B.E., Col. Comdt, R. Signals (*Assistant Chief of Defence Staff (Signals)*).

G. T. A. Armitage, C.B.E. (*G.O.C., Northumbrian District*).

J. C. Cowley, C.B. (*Paymaster-in-Chief*).

C. Blair, O.B.E., M.C. (*Defence Services Secretary*).

A. M. Taylor, M.C. (*Commandant, Staff College, Camberley*).

J. H. S. Read, O.B.E. (*Director, International Military Staff, NATO*).

T. D. H. McMeekin, O.B.E. (*Commandant, National Defence College*).

J. M. Spencer-Smith, C.B., O.B.E., M.C. (*Director of Manning (Army)*).

R. L. Clutterbuck, C.B., O.B.E. (*Chief Army Instructor, Royal College of Defence Studies*).

J. M. D. Ward-Harrison, O.B.E., M.C. (*Chief of Staff, Northern Command*).

C. W. Dunbar, C.B.E., Col. R.H.F. (*Director of Infantry*).

I. G. Gill, O.B.E., M.C. (*Assistant Chief of General Staff (Operational Requirements)*).

W. B. Thomas, C.B., D.S.O., M.C., E.D. (*Commander, Far East Land Forces*).

M. S. Hancock, M.B.E., Col. Comdt., R. Signals (*Vice-Quartermaster-General*).

The Earl Cathcart, D.S.O., M.C. (*G.O.C., Berlin*).

S. M. O'. H. Abraham, M.C. (*Chief Joint Service Liaison Officer, B.A.O.R.*).

J. P. Baird, M.D., Q.H.P. (*Commandant, Royal Army Medical College*).

R. J. Gray, Q.H.S. (*Deputy Director of Medical Services, Southern Command*).

N. C. Rogers, Q.H.S. (*Director of Army Surgery*).

M. W. Holme, C.B.E., M.C., Deputy Col. R. Anglian (*G.O.C., Near East Land Forces*).

P. H. Girling, O.B.E. (*Director of Electrical and Mechanical Engineering*).

A. E. Walkling, O.B.E. (*Deputy Master-General of the Ordnance*).

B. St. G. Irwin (*Director-General, Ordnance Survey*).

J. B. Dye, C.B.E., M.C. (*Director, Volunteers, Territorials and Cadets*).

D. W. Fraser, O.B.E. (*Assistant Chief of Defence Staff (Policy)*).

R. C. Gibbs, C.B.E., D.S.O., M.C.

D. A. H. Toler, O.B.E., M.C. (*G.O.C.. East Midland District*).

J. W. Harman, O.B.E., M.C.(*G.O.C., No. 1 Div.*)

M. Janes, M.B.E. (*Director, Royal Artillery*).

E. J. Younson, O.B.E. (*Vice-President, Ordnance Board*).

J. D. Goddard, M.C.

G. C. A. Gilbert, M.C. (*G.O.C., No. 3 Div.*).

H. R. S. Pain, M.C. (*G.O.C., No. 2 Div.*).

J. K. I. Douglas-Withers, C.B.E., M.C.

D. R. Horsfield, O.B.E. (*Chief Staff Officer, H.Q., B.A.O.R.*).

N. St. G. Gribbon, O.B.E. (*Asst. Chief of Staff (Intelligence) SHAPE*).

A. E. Younger, D.S.O., O.B.E. (*Chief of Staff, Allied Forces, Northern Europe*).

A. J. Wilson, C.B.E., M.C. (*G.O.C., North West District*).

F. W. J. Cowtan, C.B.E., M.C. (*Director, Royal Military College of Sciences*).

R. J. Mitchell, O.B.E., Q.H.P. (*Director of Medical Services, B.A.O.R.*).

J. H. Robertson, Q.H.D.S. (*Director of Army Dental Services*).

H. H. Evans (*Director of Army Education*).

J. McGhie, M.D., Q.H.P. (*Director of Army Psychiatry*).

D. R. Carroll, O.B.E. (*Chief Engineer, B.A.O.R.*).

R. J. D. E. Buckland, M.B.E. (*Chief of Staff, Army Strategic Command*).

A. J. Woodrow, M.B.E. (*G.O.C., Wales*).

P. J. Howard-Dobson, Col. The Queen's Own Hussars.

D. J. Willison, O.B.E., M.C. (*Director, Service Intelligence*).

A. G. Lewis, C.B.E. (*Director-General, Fighting Vehicles and Engineering Equipment*).

L. T. H. Phelps, O.B.E. (*Director, Ordnance Services*).

R. B. Darkin, C.B.E. (*Command Base Organization, R.A.O.C.*).

R. M. Somerville, O.B.E. (*G.O.C. Yorkshire District*).

C. E. Page, M.B.E. (*Director, Combat Development*).

J. M. Strawson, O.B.E. (*Chief of Staff, SHAPE*).

D. G. House, C.B.E., M.C. (*Chief of Staff, B.A.O.R.*).

J. H. S. Majury, O.B.E., Col' Comdt., King's Div. (*G.O.C.. West Midland District*).

G. V. Hayward (*Comdt., Technical Group, R.E.M.E.*).

F. G. Caldwell, O.B.E., M.C. (*Engineer-in-Chief*).

H. Knutton (*Director-General of Weapons (Army)*).

D. W. Scott-Barrett, M.B.E., M.C. (*G.O.C., Eastern District*).

W.N.R. Scotter, O.B.E., M.C. (*Chief of Staff, Southern Command*).

A. H. Farrar-Hockley, D.S.O. M.B.E., M.C. (*G.O.C., No. 4 Div.*).

H. C. Jeffrey (*Director of Army Pathology*).

J. Irvine, O.B.E., M.D. (*Deputy Director-General of Army Medical Services*).

W. Bate, O.B.E. (*Director of Movements*).

R. S. Marshall (*Director of Army Legal Services*).

T. A. Richardson, M.B.E. (*Director of Army Aviation*).

V. H. J. Carpenter M.B.E., (*Transport Officer-in-Chief*).

G. de E. Collin, M.C.

R. C. Ford, C.B.E. (*Commander, Land Forces, Northern Ireland*).

R. W. T. Britten (*Deputy Quartermaster-General*).

P. L. de C. Martin, C.B.E.

J. M. Sawers (*Signal Officer-in-Command*).

W. G. H. Beach (*Director of Army Staff Duties*).

E. J. S. Burnett (*Deputy Commander, Land Forces, Hong Kong*).

H. P. Cunningham (*G.O.C., South West District*).

CONSTITUTION OF THE BRITISH ARMY

The Regular Forces include the following Arms, Branches and Corps. Soldiers' Records Offices are shown at the end of each group; the records of officers are maintained at the Ministry of Defence.

Household Cavalry.—The Life Guards; The Blues and Royals (Royal Horse Guards and 1st Dragoons). *Records*, Horse Guards, London, S.W.1.

Royal Armoured Corps—Cavalry Regiments: 1st The Queen's Dragoon Guards; The Royal Scots Dragoon Guards (Carabiniers and Greys); 4th/7th Royal Dragoon Guards; 5th Royal Inniskilling Dragoon Guards; The Queen's Own Hussars; The Queen's Royal Irish Hussars; 9th/12th Royal Lancers (Prince of Wales's); The Royal Hussars (Prince of Wales's Own), 13/18th Royal Hussars (Queen Mary's Own); 14th/20th King's Hussars; 15th/19th The King's Royal Hussars; 16/5th The Queen's Royal Lancers; 17th/21st Lancers; Royal Tank Regiment comprising four regular regiments. *Records*, Friern Barnet Lane, Whetstone, N.20.

Artillery.—The Royal Regiment of Artillery. *Records*, Foots Cray, Sidcup, Kent.

Engineers.—The Corps of Royal Engineers. *Records*, Ditchling Road, Brighton.

Signals.—The Royal Corps of Signals. *Records*, Balmore House, Caversham, Reading.

Infantry—The Brigades/Regiments of Infantry of the Line have now been reformed into Divisions as follows:—

The Guards Division—Grenadier, Coldstream. Scots, Irish and Welsh Guards. Divisional HQ: HQ Household Division, Horse Guards, S.W.1. *Depôt*: Pirbright Camp, Brookwood, Surrey. *Records:* Each Regiment of Foot Guards has its own Record Office in Birdcage Walk, S.W.1.

The Scottish Division—The Royal Scots (The Royal Regiment); The Royal Highland Fusiliers (Princess Margaret's Own Glasgow and Ayrshire Regiment); The King's Own Scottish Borderers; The Black Watch (Royal Highland Regiment); Queen's Own Highlanders (Seaforth and Camerons); The Gordon Highlanders; The Argyll and Sutherland Highlanders (Princess Louise's). *Divisional HQ*, The Castle, Edinburgh. *Depôts*, Scottish Infantry Depôt, Glencorse, Milton Bridge, Midlothian; Scottish Infantry Depôt, Gordon Barracks, Bridge of Don, Aberdeen. *Records*, Infantry and General Service Corps Record Office, York.

The Queen's Division—The Queen's Regiment, The Royal Regiment of Fusiliers, The Royal Anglian Regiment. *Divisional HQ*, 4 Napier Road, Colchester, Essex. *Depôt*, Bassingbourne Barracks, Royston, Herts. *Records*, Infantry Record Office, Exeter, Devon.

The King's Division—The King's Own Royal Border Regiment, The King's Regiment; The Prince of Wales's Own Regiment of Yorkshire; The Green Howards (Alexandra, Princess of Wales's

Own Yorkshire Regiment); The Royal Irish Rangers (27th (Inniskilling) 83rd and 87th); The Queen's Lancashire Regiment; The Duke of Wellington's Regiment (West Riding); The York and Lancaster Regiment. *Divisional HQ*, Imphal Barracks, York. *Depôts*, The King's Division Depôt (Lancashire), Fulwood Barracks, Preston, Lancs. The King's Division Depôt (Yorkshire), Queen Elizabeth Barracks, Strensall, Yorks. The King's Division Depôt (Royal Irish Rangers), St. Patrick's Barracks, Ballymena, Northern Ireland. *Records*, Infantry and General Service Corps Record Office, York.

The Prince of Wales's Division—The Devonshire and Dorset Regiment; The Cheshire Regiment; The Royal Welch Fusiliers, The Royal Regiment of Wales (24th/41st Foot); The Worcestershire and Sherwood Foresters Regiment; The Gloucestershire Regiment; The Royal Hampshire Regiment; The Staffordshire Regiment (The Prince of Wales's); The Duke of Edinburgh's Royal Regiment (Berkshire and Wiltshire). *Divisional HQ*, Whittington Barracks, Lichfield, Staffs. *Depôts*, Wessex Depôt, The Prince of Wales's Division, Wyvern Barracks, Exeter, Devon; Mercian Depôt, The Prince of Wales's Division, Whittington Barracks, Lichfield, Staffs; Welsh Depôt, The Prince of Wales's Division, Cwrt-y-Gollen, Crickhowell, Breconshire. *Records*, Infantry and General Service Corps Record Office, York.

The Light Division—The Light Infantry; The Royal Green Jackets. *Depôts*, The Light Infantry Depôt, Sir John Moore Barracks, Copthorne, Shrewsbury, Salop. The Rifle Depôt, Peninsula Barracks, Winchester, Hants. *Records*, Infantry Record Office, Exeter.

The Parachute Regiment—*Depôt*, Browning Barracks, Aldershot, Hants. *Records*, Infantry Record Office, Exeter.

The Brigade of Gurkhas—2nd King Edward VII's Own Gurkha Rifles (The Sirmoor Rifles);

6th Queen Elizabeth's Own Gurkha Rifles; 7th Duke of Edinburgh's Own Gurkha Rifles; 10th Princess Mary's Own Gurkha Rifles. *Brigade HQ*, Victoria Barracks, Hong Kong. *Depôt*, Training Depôt, Brigade of Gurkhas, c/o GPO Sungei Patan, Malaysia. *Records*, The Brigade of Gurkha Record Office, c/o GPO Singapore.

The Special Air Service Regiment—*Regimental HQ*, Duke of York's Headquarters, Sloane Square, S.W.3. *Depôt*, Bradbury Lines, Hereford. *Records*, Infantry Record Office, Exeter, Devon.

Royal Corps of Transport, Army Catering Corps. *Records*, Ore Place, Hastings.

Royal Army Medical Corps, Royal Army Dental Corps, Queen Alexandra's Royal Army Nursing Corps, and Women's Royal Army Corps. *Records*, Lower Barracks, Winchester.

Royal Army Ordnance Corps, Royal Electrical and Mechanical Engineers. *Records*, Glen Parva Barracks, Saffron Road, South Wigston, Leicester.

Small Arms School Corps. *Records*, Higher Barracks, Exeter.

General Service Corps. *Records*, Cavalry Barracks, Fulford Road, York.

Army Air Corps, Royal Military Police, Royal Army Pay Corps, Royal Army Veterinary Corps, Royal Army Educational Corps, Royal Pioneer Corps, Intelligence Corps, and other ancillary corps not listed above. *Records*, Higher Barracks, Exeter, Devon.

The Territorial and Army Volunteer Reserve (T & AVR) came into being on April, 1, 1967, replacing the Army Emergency Reserve and the Territorial Army. Its main function is to reinforce the Regular Army in times of national emergency.

The Establishment is approximately 74,000 and the T & AVR is designed to provide a reserve of highly trained and well equipped units and individuals.

THE ROYAL AIR FORCE
THE QUEEN
Marshals of the Royal Air Force

H.R.H. the Duke of Windsor, K.G., K.T., K.P., *born* June 23, 1894........................ Jan. 21, 1936
Sir Arthur T. Harris, Bt., G.C.B., O.B.E., A.F.C., *born* April 13, 1892 .... Jan. 1, 1946
Sir John C. Slessor, G.C.B., D.S.O., M.C., *born* June 3, 1897............................ June 8, 1950
H.R.H. the Prince Philip, Duke of Edinburgh, K.G., P.C., K.T., O.M., G.B.E. (*Air Commodore-in-Chief, Air Training Corps, Marshal of the R.A.A.F.*) *born* June 10, 1921 .... Jan. 15, 1953
Sir William F. Dickson, G.C.B., G.C.V.O., K.B.E., D.S.O., A.F.C., *born* Sept. 24, 1898 .... June 1, 1954
Sir Dermot A. Boyle, G.C.B., K.C.V.O., K.B.E., A.F.C., *born* Oct. 2, 1904 .... Jan. 1, 1958
H.R.H. the Duke of Gloucester, K.G., P.C., K.T., K.P., G.M.B., G.C.M.G., G.C.V.O. (*Personal Aide-de-Camp to the Queen*), *born* March 31, 1900 .... June 12, 1958
Sir Thomas G. Pike, G.C.B., C.B.E., D.F.C., *born* June 29, 1906........................ April 6, 1962
Sir Charles Elworthy, G.C.B., C.B.E., D.S.O., M.V.O., D.F.C., A.F.C. (*Governor and Constable of Windsor Castle*), *born* March 23, 1911.. April 1, 1967
Sir John Grandy, G.C.B., K.B.E., D.S.O., *born* Feb. 8, 1913.............................. April 1, 1971

Air Chief Marshals

Sir Brian Burnett, G.C.B., D.F.C., A.F.C., A.D.C. (*C.-in-C., Far East Command*).

Sir Denis Spotswood, G.C.B., C.B.E., D.S.O., D.F.C. A.D.C. (*Chief of Air Staff*).

Sir Frederick Rosier, K.C.B., C.B.E., D.S.O. (*Deputy C.-in-C., Allied Forces, Central Europe*).

Sir Christopher Foxley-Norris, K.C.B., D.S.O., O.B.E. (*Chief of Personnel and Logistics*).

Sir Andrew Humphrey, K.C.B., O.B.E., D.F.C., A.F.C. (*A.O.C.-in-C., Strike Command*).

Sir Lewis Hodges, K.C.B., C.B.E., D.S.O., D.F.C. (*Air Member for Personnel*).

Sir Peter Fletcher, K.C.B., O.B.E., D.F.C., A.F.C. (*Controller of Aircraft, Aviation Supply*).

Air Marshals

Sir Neil Wheeler, K.C.B., C.B.E., D.S.O., D.F.C., A.F.C. (*Air Member for Supply and Organization*).

Sir Denis Smallwood, K.C.B., C.B.E., D.S.O., D.F.C. (*Vice-Chief of Air Staff*).

Sir Gareth Clayton, K.C.B., D.F.C. (*Air Secretary*).

Sir John Lapsley, K.B.E., C.B., D.F.C., A.F.C. (*Head, British Defence Staff and Defence Attaché, Washington*).

Sir Leslie Mavor, K.C.B., A.F.C. (*A.O.C.-in-C., Training Command*).

Sir John Barraclough, K.C.B., C.B.E., D.F.C., A.F.C. (*Vice-Chief of the Defence Staff*).

Sir Robert Craven, K.B.E., C.B., D.F.C. (*A.O.C., No. 18 Maritime Group*).

T. N. Stack, C.B., C.V.O., C.B.E., A.F.C. (*U.K. Member, Permanent Military Deputies Group, Cento*).

Sir Harold Martin, K.C.B., D.S.O. D.F.C., A.F.C. (*C.-in-C., R.A.F., Germany*).

Sir Derek Hodgkinson, K.C.B., C.B.E., D.F.C., A.F.C. (*A.O.C.-in-C., Near East Air Force*).

Sir Harry Burton, K.C.B., C.B.E., D.S.O. (*A.O.C.-in-C., Air Support Command*).

Sir John Hunter-Tod, K.B.E., C.B. (*Director-General of Engineering*).

E. S. Sidey, C.B., Q.H.S. (*Director-General of Medical Services*).

A. W. Heward, C.B., O.B.E., D.F.C., A.F.C. (*Chief of Staff, Strike Command*).

Sir John Rowlands, K.B.E., G.C. (*A.O.C.-in-C., Maintenance Command*).

Air Vice-Marshals

P. de L. Le Cheminant, C.B., D.F.C. (*Assistant Chief of Air Staff (Policy)*).

F. D. Hughes, C.B.E., D.S.O., D.F.C., A.F.C. (*Commandant, R.A.F. College, Cranwell*).

D. Crowley-Milling, C.B.E., D.S.O., D.F.C. (*A.O.C., No. 38 Group*).

R. G. Knott, C.B., D.S.O., D.F.C., A.F.C. (*A.O.A., Air Support Command*).

B. P. Young, C.B.E. (*Commandant-General, R.A.F. Regiment*).

L. W. G. Gill, D.S.O. (*Director-General of R.A.F. Manning*).

R. L. Wade, C.B., D.F.C. (*Deputy C.-in-C., R.A.F., Germany*).

B. P. T. Horsley, C.B.E., M.V.O., A.F.C. (*A.O.C., No. 1 (Bomber) Group*).

F. R. Bird, C.B., D.S.O., D.F.C., A.F.C. (*Assistant Chief of Staff (ADP) SHAPE*).

N. Cameron, C.B., C.B.E., D.S.O., D.F.C. (*S.A.S.O., Air Support Command*).

N. M. Maynard, C.B., C.B.E., D.F.C., A.F.C. (*Commander, Far East Air Force*).

C. M. Clementi, C.B.E. (*Senior R.A.F. Instructor, Royal College of Defence Studies*).

J. F. Powell, O.B.E. (*Director of Educational Services*).

K. C. Giddings, O.B.E., D.F.C., A.F.C. (*Chief of Staff No. 18 (Maritime) Group*).

J. A. C. Aiken, C.B. (*Director-General of R.A.F. Training*).

A. McK. S. Steedman, C.B.E. D.F.C. (*S.A.S.O., Strike Command*).

C. N. S. Pringle, C.B.E. (*A.O. Engineering, Strike Command*).

C. H. Beamish, C.B., Q.H.D.S. (*Director, R.A.F. Dental Services*).

The Ven. L. J. Ashton, C.B., Q.H.C. (*Chaplain-in-Chief*).

A. H. W. Ball, C.B., D.S.O., D.F.C. (*Director-General of R.A.F. Organization*).

E. D. Crew, D.S.O., D.F.C. (*Deputy Controller, National Air Traffic Control Services*).

D. E. Hawkins, C.B., C.B.E., D.F.C. (*Director-General of R.A.F. Personal Services*).

S. H. Bonser, C.B., M.B.E. (*Deputy Controller of Equipment, Aviation Supply*).

P. C. Cleaver, C.B., O.B.E. (*A.O. Engineering, Air Support Command*).

M. M. Gardham, C.B.E (*A.O.A., Training Command*).

R. C. Jackson, C.B., Q.H.P. (*Consultant Adviser, C.M.E.*).

H. A. C. Bird-Wilson, C.B.E., D.S.O., D.F.C., A.F.C. (*A.O.C., No. 23 (Training) Group*).

J. C. T. Downey, D.F.C., A.F.C. (*Commander Southern Maritime Air Region*).

I. G. Broom, C.B.E., D.S.O., D.F.C., A.F.C. (*A.O.C., No. 11 (Fighter) Group*).

D. C. Lowe, C.B., D.F.C., A.F.C. (*Assistant Chief of Air Staff (Operational Requirements)*).

R. T. Morison, C.B.E. (*President, Ordnance Board*).

R. E. W. Harland (*A.O.C. No. 24 (Training) Group*).

P. G. D. Farr, C.B., O.B.E., D.F.C. (*A.O.A., Strike Command*).

I. R. Campbell, C.B.E., A.F.C. (*Director of Management and Support Intelligence*).

R. G. Wakeford, M.V.O., O.B.E., A.F.C. (*Commander Northern Maritime Air Region*).

G. H. Dhenin, A.F.C., G.M., Q.H.P. (*P.M.O., Strike Command*).

H. L. Roxburgh, C.B.E., Q.H.S. (*Consultant Adviser, I.A.M.*).

E. Plumtree, O.B.E., D.F.C. (*A.O.C., No. 22 (Training) Group*).

M. J. Beetham, C.B.E., D.F.C., A.F.C. (*Commandant, R.A.F. Staff College*).

D. G. Evans, C.B.E. (*Assistant Chief of Air Staff (Operations)*).

H. Durkin (*A.O.C. No. 90 (Signals) Group*).

F. S. R. Johnson, O.B.E. (*Director-General of Supply*).

R. J. A. Morris, O.B.E., Q.H.S. (*Deputy Director-General of Medical Services*).

A. Sidney-Wilmot, O.B.E. (*Director of Legal Services*).

F. B. Sowrey, C.B., O.B.E., A.F.C. (*S.A.S.O., Training Command*).

J. T. Lawrence, C.B.E., A.F.C.

R. W. G. Freer, C.B.E. (*S.A.S.O., Near East Air Force*).

E. D. Hills, C.B.E. (*S.A.S.O., Maintenance Command*).

E. L. Frith (*A.O.A., Maintenance Command*).

M. W. L. White (*P.M.O., Training Command*).

E. B. Bright, A.F.C., Q.H.P.

P. J. O'Connor.

ROYAL OBSERVER CORPS
Bentley Priory, Stanmore, Middlesex

Established 1925, the Royal Observer Corps is a uniformed voluntary civilian organization originally set up to identify and track the movement of aircraft in war. In 1955 the Corps assumed the modern role of detecting nuclear bursts and monitoring radioactive fall-out in support of the United Kingdom Warning and Monitoring Organization. The Corps is affiliated to the Royal Air Force and is administered by Strike Command.

Air Commodore-in-Chief, H.M. THE QUEEN.

Commandant, Air Commodore E. B. Sismore, D.S.O., D.F.C., A.F.C.

THE UNION JACK SERVICES CLUBS

Patron: H.R.H. the Duke of Gloucester, K.G.
President: Major-Gen. Sir Julian Gascoigne, K.C.M.G., K.C.V.O., C.B., D.S.O.
Comptroller: Col. C. A. la T. Leatham.
Secretary: Lt.-Cdr. H. Cole, R.N.

THE UNION JACK CLUB
Exton Street, Waterloo, S.E.1
[Tel.: 01-928 6401]

These Clubs, which comprise the Union Jack Club and the Union Jack Families and Women's Services Clubs, were founded to provide residential accommodation for service and ex-service men and women and their families. All serving men and women below commissioned rank are automatically members, and honorary membership is extended to the Forces of other Powers visiting England.

At present the Clubs, which are one of our great National Institutions, are being rebuilt on the Waterloo Road site of the Union Jack Club and completion is expected in 1974. The new premises will provide the most modern standards of accommodation and up-to-date facilities for its members.

During the period of rebuilding, the Exton Street premises of the present Union Jack Families Club will be available, together with the main Club Annexe, to male members only, priority being given to serving members.

SERVICE PAY AND PENSIONS

The military salary was introduced on April 1, 1970, having been devised with the aid of job evaluation techniques and comparisons with civilian earnings, and became fully effective from April 1, 1971. The next regular review of pay of the Armed Forces should be made before April 1, 1972, and in the meantime the Government has approved an interim general increase in pay of 7 per cent. of the current rates effective from Aug. 1, 1971. The details of Service Pay which follow include this increase and are subject to alteration at April 1, 1972, in the light of fresh recommendations which may be made before then by the Armed Forces Pay Review Body. The pay of Senior Officers (above Brigadier or equivalent ranks) was increased from Jan. 1, 1971, and was not affected by the interim general increase in August, 1971. Senior Officers' scales will in future be reviewed by a separate board.

Pay of the Women's Services was increased by 7 per cent. on Aug. 1, 1971, maintaining the relativity of 87 per cent. of equivalent men's rates.

Rates of retired pay and pensions were also increased by 7 per cent. from August 1, 1971, except for senior officers whose retired pay was increased on Jan. 1, 1971.

ROYAL NAVY AND ROYAL MARINES
Normal rates

Rank (and equivalent rank, R.M.)	Pay	
	Daily	Annual
	£	£
Cadet R.N.	2·68	978
Midshipman R.N.	3·96	1,445
Acting Sub-Lieutenant R.N.	4·71	1,719
Sub-Lieutenant R.N.	5·40	1,971
Lieutenant R.N.	6·58	2,402
After 1 year in the rank	6·74	2,460
After 2 years in the rank	6·90	2,519
After 3 years in the rank	7·06	2,577
After 4 years in the rank	7·17	2,617
After 5 years in the rank	7·33	2,675
After 6 years in the rank	7·49	2,734
After 7 years in the rank	7·60	2,774
Lieutenant R.M.	5·40	1,971
After 1 year in the rank	6·58	2,402
After 2 years in the rank	6·74	2,460
After 3 years in the rank	6·90	2,519
After 4 years in the rank	7·06	2,577
After 5 years in the rank	7·17	2,617
After 6 years in the rank	7·33	2,675
After 7 years in the rank	7·49	2,734
Lieutenant-Commander	8·56	3,124
After 1 year in the rank	8·72	3,183
After 2 years in the rank	8·88	3,241
After 3 years in the rank	8·99	3,281
After 4 years in the rank	9·15	3,340
After 6 years in the rank	9·31	3,398
After 8 years in the rank	9·47	3,457
After 10 years in the rank	9·58	3,497
After 12 years in the rank	9·74	3,555
Commander R.N.	11·24	4,103
After 2 years in rank or with 19 years' service	11·50	4,198
After 4 years in rank or with 21 years' service	11·81	4,311
After 6 years in rank or with 21 years' service	12·07	4,406
After 8 years in rank or with 25 years' service	12·37	4,515
Captain R.N.	13·61	4,968
After 2 years in rank	14·03	5,121
After 4 years in rank	14·46	5,278
Captain R.N. with 6 years seniority/Colonel R.M.	16·81	6,136
Rear Admiral/Major-General R.M.†	19·85	7,245
Vice Admiral/Lieutenant-General R.M.†	25·35	9,253
Admiral/General R.M.‡	34·25	12,501
Admiral of the Fleet‡	38·35	13,998

ARMY
Officers

Rank	Pay	
	Daily	Annual
	£	£
Second-Lieutenant	4·71	1,719
Lieutenant	5·40	1,971
After 1 year in the rank	5·56	2,029
After 2 years in the rank	5·73	2,091
After 3 years in the rank	5·89	2,150
After 4 years in the rank	5·99	2,186
Captain	6·58	2,402
After 1 year in the rank	6·74	2,460
After 2 years in the rank	6·90	2,519
After 3 years in the rank	7·06	2,577
After 4 years in the rank	7·17	2,617
After 5 years in the rank	7·33	2,675
After 6 years in the rank	7·49	2,734
After 7 years in the rank	7·60	2,774
After 8 years in the rank	7·76	2,832
After 10 years in the rank	7·92	2,891
After 12 years in the rank	8·08	2,949
After 14 years in the rank	8·18	2,986
After 16 years in the rank	8·35	3,048
Major	8·56	3,124
After 1 year in the rank	8·72	3,183
After 2 years in the rank	8·88	3,241
After 3 years in the rank	8·99	3,281
After 4 years in the rank	9·15	3,340
After 6 years in the rank	9·31	3,398
After 8 years in the rank	9·47	3,457
After 10 years in the rank	9·58	3,497
After 12 years in the rank	9·74	3,555
Lieutenant-Colonel—Special List	11·05	4,035
Lieutenant-Colonel	11·24	4,103
After 2 years in the rank or 19 years' service	11·50	4,198
After 4 years in the rank or 21 years' service	11·81	4,311
After 6 years in the rank or 23 years' service	12·07	4,406
After 8 years in the rank or 25 years' service	12·37	4,515
Colonel	13·60	4,968
After 2 years in the rank	14·03	5,121
After 4 years in the rank	14·46	5,278
After 6 years in the rank	14·89	5,435
After 8 years in the rank	15·37	5,610
Brigadier	16·81	6,136
Major-General†	19·85	7,245
Lieutenant-General†	25·35	9,253
General‡	34·25	12,501
Field-Marshal‡	38·35	13,998

† W.e.f. Jan. 1, 1971.
‡ W.e.f. July 1, 1971.

ROYAL AIR FORCE
Officers. Basic Pay

Rank * In this rank	Daily	Annual	Rank * In this rank	Daily	Annual
	£	£		£	£
Acting Pilot Officer............	3·96	1,445	After 12 years* in rank or 18 years' service†............	8·08	2,959
After 6 months* (aircrew officers only)............	4·07	1,486	After 14 years* in rank or 20 years' service†............	8·18	2,986
After 1 year* (other officers) .	4·07	1,486	After 16 years* in rank or 22 years' service †............	8·35	3,048
Pilot Officer.................	4·71	1,719	Squadron Leader.............	8·56	3,124
Flying Officer................	5·40	1,971	After 1 year*.............	8·72	3,183
After 1 year* or 3 years' service.................	5·56	2,209	After 2 years*.............	8·88	3,241
After 2 years* or 4 years' service.................	5·73	2,091	After 3 years*.............	8·99	3,281
After 3 years* or 5 years' service.................	5·89	2,150	After 4 years*.............	9·15	3,340
After 4 years* or 6 years' service	5·99	2,186	After 6 years*.............	9·31	3,398
			After 8 years*.............	9·47	3,457
Flight Lieutenant.............	6·58	2,402	After 10 years*.............	9·58	3,497
After 1 year* in rank or 7 years' service.............	6·74	2,460	After 12 years*.............	9·74	3,555
After 2 years* in rank or 8 years' service.............	6·90	2,519	Wing Commander.............	11·24	4,103
After 3 years* in rank or 9 years' service.............	7·06	2,577	After 2 years* or 19 years' commissioned service.....	11·50	4,198
After 4 years* in rank or 10 years' service.............	7·17	2,617	After 4 years* or 21 years' commissioned service.....	11·81	4,311
After 5 years* in rank or 11 years' service.............	7·33	2,675	After 6 years* or 23 years' commissioned service.....	12·07	4,406
After 6 years* in rank or 12 years' service.............	7·49	2,734	After 8 years* or 25 years' commissioned service.....	12·37	4,515
After 7 years* in rank or 13 years' service†............	7·60	2,774	Group Captain................	13·61	4,968
After 8 years* in rank or 14 years' service†............	7·76	2,832	After 2 years in the rank...	14·03	5,121
			After 4 years in the rank...	14·46	5,278
After 10 years* in rank or 16 years' service†............	7·92	2,891	After 6 years in the rank...	14·89	5,435
			After 8 years in the rank...	15·37	5,610
			Air Commodore..............	16·81	6,136
			Air Vice-Marshal‡...........	19·85	7,245
			Air-Marshal‡................	25·35	9,253
			Air Chief Marshal§..........	24·25	12,501
			Marshal of the Royal Air Force§	38·35	13,998

† These increments apply to all ground branch officers; but in the G.D. (Flying) branch only to those officers who have been designated specialist aircrew.   ‡W.e.f. Jan. 1, 1971.   §W.e.f. July 1, 1971.

ROYAL NAVY SEAMAN BRANCH, AND ROYAL MARINES (All Branches). Daily Rates

Rating/Rank	4 years Scale A			7 years Scale B			9 years Scale C		
Scale	III	II	I	III	II	I	III	II	I
	£	£	£	£	£	£	£	£	£
Ordinary Rating.................	—	2·68	2·94	—	2·89	3·15	—	3·22	3·48
Able Rating....................	3·26	3·48	3·68	3·47	3·69	3·90	3·80	4·02	4·23
Leading Rating.................	4·07	4·28	4·44	4·28	4·49	4·65	4·61	4·82	4·98
Petty Officer..................	—	—	—	5·03	5·13	5·24	5·36	5·46	5·57
Chief Petty Officer (incl. Artisans)....	—	—	—	5·45	5·56	5·67	5·78	5·89	6·00
Fleet Chief Petty Officer...........	—	—	—	—	—	6·04	—	—	6·37

	7-yr. Rate	9-yr. Rate	Mechanicians (*contd.*)	7-yr. Rate	9-yr. Rate
Artificer (Daily Rate)	£	£		£	£
Artificer 3rd Class (Leading Rating)	4·28	4·61	Mechanician Acting 4th Class (Acting Leading Rating)............	4·44	4·77
Artificer Acting 2nd Class (Petty Officer)...................	5·29	5·62	Mechanician 4th Class (Leading Rating)...................	4·81	5·14
Artificer 2nd Class (Petty Officer)...	5·56	5·89	Mechanician 3rd Class (Petty Officer)...................	5·24	5·57
Artificer 1st Class (Chief Petty Officer)...................	5·78	6·11	Mechanician 2nd Class (Petty Officer)...................	5·51	5·84
After 2 years.................	5·99	6·32	Mechanician 1st Class (C.P.O.)...	5·78	6·11
After 4 years.................	6·10	6·43	After 2 years.................	5·99	6·32
After 6 years.................	6·15	6·48	After 4 years.................	6·10	6·43
Chief Artificer................	6·31	6·64	After 6 years.................	6·15	6·48
Fleet Chief Artificer...........	6·47	6·80	Chief Mechanician..............	6·31	6·64
			Fleet Chief Technician..........	6·47	6·80
Mechanicians (Daily rates)	£	£			
Mechanician 5th Class (Able Rating)	3·90	4·23			

ARMY
Other Ranks. Daily Rates

Rank	Scale A★	Scale B★	Scale C★
	£	£	£
Band I			
Warrant Officer:—			
Class I	5·51	5·72	6·05
Class II	5·24	5·45	5·78
Staff-Sergeant	4·92	5·13	5·46
Sergeant	4·60	4·81	5·14
Corporal:—			
Class I	4·12	4·33	4·66
Class II	3·96	4·17	4·50
Lance-Corporal:—			
Class I	3·64	3·85	4·18
Class II	3·42	3·63	3·96
Class III	3·26	3·47	3·80
Private:—			
Class I	3·26	3·47	3·80
Class II	3·10	3·31	3·64
Class III	2·94	3·15	3·48
Class IV	2·68	2·89	3·22
Band II			
Warrant Officer:—			
Class I	5·83	6·04	6·37
Class II	5·56	5·77	6·10
Staff Sergeant	5·24	5·45	5·78
Sergeant	4·92	5·13	5·46
Corporal:—			
Class I	4·44	4·65	4·98
Class II	4·28	4·49	4·82
Lance-Corporal:—			
Class I	3·96	4·17	4·50
Class II	3·74	3·95	4·28
Class III	3·58	3·79	4·12
Private:—			
Class I	3·58	3·79	4·12
Class II	3·42	3·63	3·96
Class III	3·26	3·47	3·80
Band III			
Warrant Officer:—			
Class I	6·26	6·47	6·80
Class II	5·99	6·20	6·53
Staff Sergeant	5·67	5·88	6·21
Sergeant	5·35	5·56	5·89
Corporal	4·87	5·08	5·41
Lance-Corporal	4·39	4·60	4·93
Private	4·01	4·22	4·55

★ SCALES.—A=Less than 6 years; B=6 years but less than 9 years; C=9 years or more.

Army length of service increments

Rank	Total increment after completion of the number of years reckonable man's service stated				
	9	12	15	18	22
	£	£	£	£	£
Warrant Officer I..	0·11	0·37	0·48	0·64	0·75
Warrant Officer II.	0·11	0·37	0·48	0·64	0·75
Staff Sergeant	0·11	0·37	0·48	0·64	0·64
Sergeant	0·11	0·37	0·48	0·59	0·59
Corporal	0·11	0·27	0·27	0·27	0·27
Lance-Corporal ...	0·11	0·16	0·16	0·16	0·16
Private	0·11	0·16	0·16	0·16	0·16

ROYAL AIR FORCE
Pay★—Daily Rates

Rank	A★	B★	C★
Aircrew	£	£	£
(i) *Pilots, Navigators, Air Electronics Operators and Air Engineers (A):*			
Band III			
Sergeant	5·35	5·36	5·89
Flight Sergeant	5·78	5·99	6·32
Master Aircrew	6·26	6·47	6·80
(Aircrew Cadet, £2·68; £2·89; £3·22; £4·39; after 12 months, £4·60; £4·93).			
(ii) *Air Signallers, Air Engineers, Radio Observers and Air Quartermasters:*			
Band II			
Sergeant	4·92	5·13	5·46
Flight Sergeant	5·35	5·56	5·89
Master Aircrew	5·83	6·04	6·37
(Aircrew Cadet, £2·68; £2·89; £3·22; after 12 months, £3·85; £4·06; £4·39. (ALM Cadet, £4·39; £4·60; £4·93))			

Ground Tradesmen
Band I

	A★	B★	C★
Aircraftman	2·68	2·89	3·22
Leading Aircraftman.........	2·94	3·15	3·48
Senior Aircraftman..........	3·26	3·47	3·80
Junior Technician...........	3·64	3·85	4·18
Corporal...................	4·07	4·28	4·61
Sergeant...................	4·60	4·81	5·14
Chief Technician............	4·82	5·03	5·36
Flight Sergeant.............	5·03	5·24	5·57
Warrant Officer............	5·51	5·27	6·05

Band II

	A★	B★	C★
Aircraft	2·68	2·89	3·22
Leading Aircraftman.........	3·26	3·47	3·80
Senior Aircraftman..........	3·58	3·79	4·12
Junior Technician...........	3·96	4·17	4·50
Corporal...................	4·39	4·60	4·93
Sergeant...................	4·92	5·13	5·46
Chief Technician............	5·14	5·35	5·68
Flight Sergeant.............	5·35	5·56	5·89
Warrant Officer............	5·83	6·04	6·37

Band III

	A★	B★	C★
Aircraftman	2·68	2·89	3·22
Leading Aircraftman.........	3·69	3·90	4·23
Senior Aircraftman..........	4·01	4·22	4·55
Junior Technician...........	4·39	4·60	4·93
Corporal...................	4·87	5·08	5·41
Sergeant...................	5·35	5·56	5·89
Chief Technician............	5·57	5·78	6·11
Flight Sergeant.............	5·78	5·99	6·32
Warrant Officer............	6·26	6·47	6·80

★ SCALES.—A, not less than 5 years; B, less than 9 years but not less than 5 years; C, not less than 9 years.

Officer Cadets
Army Officer Cadets.—Cadet at Officer Cadet Schools and Arms Schools, basic pay daily, £2·68.
Cadet at R.A.F. College or R.M.A..........£2·68
 after 1 year's service.....................£3·10
 after 2 years' service.....................£3·53

Length of service increments (Airmen)

	Total after 12 years' service	Total after 17 years' service	Total after 22 years' service
	p	p	p
Ldg. or Senr. Air-craftman, Jr. Technician..	11	16	16
Corporal...........	21	27	27
Sergeant..........	43	54	59
Chief Technician....	43	59	64
Flight Sergeant......	64	70	75
Warrant Officer.....	64	70	75

Officers of W.R.N.S.

Rank	Daily	Annual
	£	£
Probationary Third Officer....	4·07	1,486
Third Officer...............	4·28	1,562
After 2 years★.............	4·71	1,719
After 3 years★.............	4·82	1,759
After 4 years★.............	4·98	1,818
After 5 years★.............	5·08	1,854
Second Officer.............	5·73	2,091
After 1 year★.............	5·83	2,128
After 2 years★.............	5·99	2,186
After 3 years★.............	6·10	2,227
After 4 years★.............	6·21	2,267
After 5 years★.............	6·37	2,325
After 6 years★.............	6·47	2,362
After 8 years★.............	6·58	2,402
After 10 years★............	6·74	2,460
After 12 years★............	6·85	2,500
First Officer...............	7·44	2,716
After 1 year★.............	7·54	2,752
After 2 years★.............	7·70	2,811
After 3 years★.............	7·81	2,851
After 4 years.............	7·92	2,891
After 6 years★.............	8·08	2,949
After 8 years★.............	8·18	2,986
After 10 years★............	8·35	3,048
After 12 years★............	8·45	3,084
Chief Officer...............	9·74	3,555
After 2 years★ or 19 years' commissioned service.....	9·95	3,362
After 4 years★ or 21 years' commissioned service.....	10·22	3,730
After 6 years★ or 23 years' commissioned service.....	10·49	3,829
After 8 years★ or 25 years' commissioned service.....	10·75	3,924
Superintendent..............	11·88	4,336
After 2 years★.............	12·25	4,471
After 4 years★.............	12·68	4,628
After 6 years★.............	13·05	4,763
After 8 years★.............	13·48	4,920
Director, W.R.N.S...........	14·82	5,409

Officers of W.R.A.C., and non-nursing officers of Q.A.R.A.N.C.

Rank	Daily	Annual
	£	£
Second-Lieutenant..........	4·07	1,486
Lieutenant.................	4·71	1,719
After 1 year★.............	4·82	1,759
After 2 years★.............	4·98	1,818
After 3 years★.............	5·08	1,854
Captain...................	5·73	2,091
After 1 year★.............	5·83	2,128
After 2 years★.............	5·99	2,186
After 3 years★.............	6·10	2,227
After 4 years★.............	6·21	2,267
After 5 years★.............	6·37	2,325
After 6 years★.............	6·47	2,362

W.R.A.C.—*continued*

Rank	Daily	Annual
	£	£
Captain (*continued*)		
After 8 years★.............	6·58	2,402
After 10 years★............	6·74	2,460
After 12 years★............	6·85	2,500
After 14 years★............	7·01	2,559
After 16 years★............	7·11	2,595
Major.....................	7·44	2,716
After 1 year★.............	7·54	2,752
After 2 years.............	7·70	2,811
After 3 years★.............	7·81	2,851
After 4 years★.............	7·92	2,891
After 6 years★.............	8·08	2,949
After 8 years★.............	8·18	2,986
After 10 years★............	8·35	3,048
After 12 years★............	8·45	3,084
Lieutenant-Colonel	9·74	3,555
After 2 years★ or 19 yrs'. commissioned service......	9·95	3,632
After 4 years★ or 21 yrs'. commissioned service......	10·22	3,730
After 6 years★ or 23 yrs'. commissioned service......	10·49	3,829
After 8 years★ or 25 yrs'. commissioned service....	10·75	3,924
Colonel....................	11·88	4,336
After 2 years★.............	12·25	4,471
After 4 years★.............	12·68	4,628
After 6 years★.............	13·05	4,763
After 8 years★.............	13·48	4,920
Brigadier..................	14·82	5,409

Officers of W.R.A.F.

Rank	Daily	Annual
	£	£
Acting Pilot Officer...........	3·42	1,248
After 1 year................	3·53	1,288
Pilot Officer................	4·07	1,486
Flying Officer...............	4·71	1,719
After 1 year★ or 3 yrs'. commissioned service.....	4·82	1,759
After 2 years★ or 4 yrs'. commissioned service.....	4·98	1,818
After 3 years★ or 5 yrs'. commissioned service.....	5·08	1,854
Flight Lieutenant.............	5·73	2,091
After 1 year★ or 7 yrs'. commissioned service.....	5·83	2,128
After 2 years★ or 8 yrs'. commissioned service.....	5·99	2,186
After 3 years★ or 9 yrs'. commissioned service.....	6·10	2,227
After 4 years★ or 10 yrs'. commissioned service.....	6·21	2,267
After 5 years★ or 11 yrs'. commissioned service.....	6·37	2,325
After 6 years★ or 12 yrs'. commissioned service.....	6·47	2,362
After 8 years★ or 14 yrs'. commissioned service.....	6·58	2,402
After 10 years★ or 16 yrs'. commissioned service.....	6·74	2,460
After 12 years★ or 18 yrs'. commissioned service.....	6·85	2,500
After 14 years★ or 20 yrs'. commissioned service.....	7·01	2,559
After 16 years★ or 22 yrs'. commissioned service.....	7·11	2,595
Squadron Leader.............	7·44	2,716
After 1 year★...............	7·54	2,752

★ In the rank.

W.R.A.F.—*continued*

Rank	Daily	Annual
	£	£
Squadron Leader (*continued*)		
After 2 years★............	7·70	2,811
After 3 years★............	7·81	2,851
After 4 years★............	7·92	2,891
After 6 years★............	8·08	2,949
After 8 years★............	8·18	2,986
After 10 years★...........	8·35	3,048
After 12 years...........	8·45	3,084
Wing Commander...........	9·74	3,555
After 2 years★ or 19 yrs'. commissioned service.....	9·95	3,632
After 4 years★ or 21 yrs'. commissioned service.....	10·22	3,730
After 6 years★ or 23 yrs'. commissioned service.....	10·49	3,829
After 8 years★ or 25 yrs'. commissioned service.....	10·75	3,924
Group Captain.............	11·88	4,336
After 2 years★............	12·25	4,471
After 4 years★............	12·68	4,628
After 6 years★............	13·05	4,763
After 8 years★............	13·48	4,920
Air Commodore.............	14·82	5,409

★ In the rank.   † plus £1·44 per day Education Grant.

W.R.N.S. Ratings and Naval Nurses

Daily Rates	Band 1	Band 2	Band 3
	£	£	£
Wren..............	2·30	2·30	2·30
Wren (Able Rating):—			
Scale II.............	2·57	2·84	3·21
Scale I..............	2·94	3·21	3·58
Leading Rating:—			
Scale II.............	3·26	3·53	3·90
Scale I..............	3·58	3·85	4·22
Petty Officer Wren:—			
Scale II.............	3·91	4·18	4·55
Scale I..............	4·07	4·34	4·71
Chief Wren:—			
Scale II.............	4·28	4·55	4·92
Scale I..............	4·44	4·71	5·08
Fleet Chief Wren:—			
Scale I..............	4·76	5·03	5·40

Length of Service Pay.—Totals, after 3 years' service, 21p daily, all ranks, rising by 3-yearly increments to the following totals: Ordinary Rating, 37p; Able Rating 75p; Leading Rating 96p; Petty Officer/C.P.O./Fleet C.P.O., £1·12 after 18 years' service.

W.R.A.C./Q.A.R.A.N.C.

Rank	Band 1	Band 2	Band 3
Daily Rates	£	£	£
Warrant Officer, Class I	4·76	5·03	5·40
Class II..............	4·55	4·82	5·19
Staff-Sergeant.........	4·28	4·55	4·92
Sergeant..............	4·01	4·28	4·65
Corporal			
Class I	3·58	3·85	
Class II..............	3·42	3·69	
L/Corporal			3·80
Class I..............	3·16	3·43	
Class II..............	2·94	3·21	
Class III.............	2·84	3·11	
Private...............			3·48
Class I..............	2·84	3·11	
Class II..............	2·68	2·95	
Class III.............	2·57		
Class IV.............	2·30		

Sergeants and above in Band 2 whose trade classification is lower than Class I and Corporals whose trade classification is lower than Class II shall be paid £0·11 or £0·05 a day respectively less than the rates shown.

Sergeants and above in Band 3 whose trade classification is other than the highest in their trade shall be paid £0·11 a day less than the rates shown.

Length of service increments.—All ranks: after 3 years' service, 21p daily; after 6 years', 37p; after 9 years', 59p; after 12 years', 75p; Corporals and above, after 15 years' service, 96p; Sergeants and above, after 18 years' service, £1·12; Warrant Officers, after 22 years' service, £1·23 daily.

W.R.A.F. Airwomen

AIRCREW.—Daily rates of basic pay for Air Quartermasters: Cadet, £2·30 & £3·80; Sergeant, £4·28; Flight-Sergeant, £4·66; Master Aircrew, £5·03.

	Band 1	Band 2	Band 3
	£	£	£
Aircraftwoman........	2·30	2·30	2·30
Leading Aircraftwoman	2·57	2·84	3·21
Senior Aircraftwoman..	2·84	3·11	3·48
Junior Technician......	3·16	3·43	3·80
Corporal..............	3·53	3·80	4·22
Sergeant..............	4·01	4·28	4·65
Chief Technician.......	4·17	4·44	4·81
Flight-Sergeant........	4·39	4·66	5·03
Warrant Officer........	4·76	5·03	5·40

Q.A.R.N.N.S., Q.A.R.A.N.C., AND P.M.R.A.F.N.S.

Rank	Daily	Annual
Nursing Sister/Lieutenant/Flying Officer....................	£4·71 to £5·08	£1,719 to £1,854
Senior Nursing Sister/Captain/Flight Officer.................	£5·73 to £6·47	£2,091 to £2,362
Superintending Sister/Matron/Major/Squadron Officer.........	£7·44 to £8·45	£2,716 to £3,084
Principal Matron/Lieut.-Colonel/Wing Officer.................	£9·74 to £10·75	£3,555 to £3,924
Colonel/Group Officer............	£11·88 to £13·48	£4,336 to £4,920
Matron-in-Chief/Brigadier/Air Commandant..................	£14·82	£5,409

CHARGES FOR MARRIED QUARTERS

Officers★			Other Ranks	
	Weekly	Annual	Daily	Weekly
Type V.........	£0·77	£281·05		
IV.........	0·89	324·85	Type A........... £0·33 (£0·22)	£2·31 (£1·54)
III.........	0·97	354·05	B........... 0·47 (£0·31)	3·29 (£2·17)
II.........	1·13	412·45	C........... 0·52 (£0·35)	3·64 (£2·45)
I.........	1·25	456·25	D/WO........ 0·58 (£0·39)	4·06 (£2·73)

★ Each including garage charge, £25·55 p.a.   *Sub-standard Married Quarters.*—Charges for sub-standard quarters, other ranks, are shown in *italic* figures above; for officers, 3 bedrooms or less, £0·47 daily (£171·55); 4 bedrooms or more, £0·55 daily (£200·75), excluding garage charges, £25·55 p.a.

RETIREMENT BENEFITS (MEN)
Officers and Men—All Services

£ per annum

Years of reckonable service over age 21	Capt. §	Major	Lt.-Col.	Col.	Brigadier	Maj.-Gen.	Lt.-Gen.	General	Field Marshal‡
	£ a year	£ a year	£ a year	£ a year	£ a year	£ a year	£ a year	£ a year	£ a year
16★	835	925	1,175	—	—	—	—	—	—
17	870	970	1,245	—	—	—	—	—	—
18	910	1,025	1,300	1,670	—	—	—	—	—
19	945	1,065	1,365	1,740	—	—	—	—	—
20	980	1,105	1,420	1,790	—	—	—	—	—
21	1,000	1,155	1,470	1,855	—	—	—	—	—
22	1,035	1,200	1,515	1,920	2,210	—	—	—	—
23	1,065	1,230	1,575	1,980	2,275	—	—	—	—
24	1,080	1,275	1,615	2,050	2,340	2,505	—	—	—
25	1,095	1,305	1,665	2,105	2,400	2,600	—	—	—
26	1,105	1,340	1,710	2,165	2,460	2,695	—	—	—
27	1,120	1,370	1,755	2,225	2,530	2,795	3,495	—	—
28	1,145	1,405	1,800	2,280	2,595	2,890	3,635	—	—
29	1,155	1,440	1,840	2,340	2,655	2,985	3,770	—	—
30	1,175	1,475	1,885	2,390	2,720	3,080	3,910	5,365	—
31	1,195	1,505	1,925	2,445	2,780	3,170	4,040	5,555	—
32	1,215	1,525	1,965	2,495	2,850	3,265	4,180	5,755	—
33	1,235	1,550	2,000	2,550	2,900	3,365	4,320	5,945	—
34†	1,245	1,575	2,045	2,605	2,955	3,455	4,445	6,150	7,000

★ Minimum rates.   † Maximum rates.   ‡ " Half-pay ".   § and below.

NOTES:—The above rates apply to all officers serving on permanent regular commissions except in the case of R.N. Special Duties List Officers and of Lieutenant-Colonels (Quarter-master) and equivalent ranks in the other services who receive a lead of £135 over the Major's scale above. Rates shown are for compulsory retirement; there will be a reduction in certain circumstances for voluntary retirement. Terminal grants continue to be three times the rate of retired pay.

OFFICERS' GRATUITIES (All Services).—Rate of gratuity for an officer retiring compulsorily for age or non-employment, or voluntarily, before becoming eligible for retired pay and who has at least 10 years' qualifying service:
For the first 10 years' qualifying service, £1,840.
For each further year's qualifying service, £370.
Standard rate of Short Service gratuity for each year of service, £275.

Ratings, Soldiers and Airmen—Basic Weekly Rates of Pension

Rank (and equivalents R.N. and R.A.F.)	For each of first 22 years	For each additional year	Rank (and equivalents R.N. and R.A.F.)	For each of first 22 years	For each additional year
	£	£		£	£
Below Corporal	0·24	0·48	Staff Sergeant	0·41	0·82
Corporal	0·30	0·60	Warrant Officer Class II	0·44	0·88
Sergeant	0·36	0·72	Warrant Officer Class I	0·45	0·90

EXAMPLES OF PENSIONS AND APPROXIMATE TERMINAL GRANTS.—PRIVATE, with 22 years' service: Pension, £5·28; Grant, £823; with 37 years' service: Pension, £12·48; Grant, £1,946. SERGEANT, with 22 years' service: Pension, £7·92; Grant, £1,235; with 37 years' service: Pension, £18·72; Grant, £2,920. WARRANT OFFICER, CLASS I, with 22 years' service: Pension, £9·90; Grant, £1,544; with 37 years' service: Pension, £23·40; Grant, £3,650. GRATUITIES.—Rate of gratuity payable to ratings, soldiers and airmen who leave the service with at least 12 years qualifying service, £275; 13 yrs., £335; 14 yrs., £405; 15 yrs., £490; 16 yrs., £590; 17 yrs., £685; 18 yrs., £785; 19 yrs., £890; 20 yrs., £1,000; 21 yrs., £1,125.

RETIREMENT BENEFITS (WOMEN)

OFFICERS' GRATUITIES.—For the first 10 years' qualifying service, £1,600; for each further year's qualifying service an addition of £322.

OFFICERS' RETIRED PAY.—*Minimum after* 16 *years' reckonable service:* Captain and below, £726·50 per annum; Major, £804·75; Lt.-Colonel, £1,022·25. *Maximum after* 34 *years' reckonable service:* Captain and below, £1,083·25 per annum; Major, £1,370·25; Lt.-Colonel, £1,779·25. These rates are subject to a deduction for voluntary retirement in certain circumstances. Terminal grants are three times the annual rate of pension.

OTHER RANKS' GRATUITIES.—Rate of gratuity to women who leave the Service with at least 12 years' reckonable service, £239; 13 yrs., £291; 14yrs., £352; 15 yrs., £426; 16 yrs, £513; 17 yrs, £596; 18 yrs., £683; 19 yrs., £774; 20 yrs., £870; 21 yrs., £979.

OTHER RANKS' PENSIONS

Rank (and equivalents, W.R.N.S. and W.R.A.F.)	For each of first 22 years	For each additional year
	£	£
Below Corporal	0·21	0·42
Corporal	0·27	0·54
Sergeant	0·32	0·64
Staff-Sergeant	0·36	0·72
Warrant Officer, Class II	0·39	0·78
Warrant Officer, Class I	0·40	0·80

Terminal grants are three times the annual rate of pension.

The Church of England

Province of Canterbury

CANTERBURY. £7,500.

100th *Archbishop and Primate of All England*, Rt. Hon. and Most Rev. Arthur Michael Ramsey, D.D. (Lambeth Palace, S.E.1.), *cons.* 1952, *trs.* 1956 and 1961. [Signs Michael Cantuar:]...1961
Assistant Bishops, Rt. Rev. Kenneth Charles Harman Warner, D.D. (*cons.* 1947) 1962
Rt. Rev. Norman Harry Clarke, M.A. (*cons.* 1950)..1962

Bishops Suffragan.

Dover, Rt. Rev. Anthony Paul Tremlett, M.A. (Upway, St. Martin's Hill, Canterbury)...1964
Croydon, Rt. Rev. John Taylor Hughes, M.A. (26 Birdhurst Rise, South Croydon).........1956
Maidstone, Rt. Rev. Geoffrey Lewis Tiarks, M.A. (Lambeth Palace, S.E.1.)................1969

Dean (£2,400).

Very Rev. Ian Hugh White-Thomson, M.A....1963
Canons Residentiary (£1,500)
H. M. Waddams, M.A. |Archdn. Prichard..1968
 1962| J. Robinson, M.Th.,
Archdn. Nott....1965| B.D...............1968
Organist, Allan Wicks, M.A., F.R.C.O.......1961

Archdeacons.

Canterbury, Ven. M. J. Nott, B.D., A.K.C......1968
Croydon, The Bishop of Croydon...........1968
Maidstone, Ven. T. E. Prichard, M.A........1968
Benefited Clergy, 239; *Curates, &c.*, 76.
Vicar-General of Province and Diocese, Sir Harold Kent, G.C.B.
Commissary of Diocese, J. H. F. Newey, Q.C., M.A., LL.B.....................................1971
Registrar of the Province and Archbishop's Legal Sec., D. M. M. Carey, M.A., 1 The Sanctuary, S.W.1.
Registrar of the Diocese of Canterbury, D. M. M. Carey, M.A., 9 The Precincts, Canterbury.

LONDON. £5,500.

114th *Bishop*, Rt. Hon. and Rt. Rev. Robert Wright Stopford, C.B.E., D.D., D.C.L, *cons.* 1955, *trs.* 1956 and 1961 (Fulham Palace, S.W.6) [Signs Robert Londin:].........................1961

Bishops Suffragan.

Kensington, Rt. Rev. Ronald Cedric Osbourne Goodchild, M.A. (19 Campden Hill Square, W.8) 1964
Willesden, Rt. Rev. Graham Douglas Leonard, M.A. (2 Church Road, Highgate, N.6) 1964
Stepney, Rt. Rev. Ernest Urban Trevor Huddleston, M.A. (400 Commercial Road, E.1.) (*cons.* 1962)..............................1968
Edmonton, Rt. Rev. Alan Francis Bright Rogers, M.A. (14 Manor Mansions, Belsize Grove, N.W.3) (*cons.* 1959).............................1970
Fulham (for North and Central Europe), Rt. Rev. John Richard Satterthwaite, B.A...........1970
Assistant Bishops, Rt. Rev. Cyril Kenneth Sansbury D.D. (*cons.* 1961) 1966; Rt. Rev. Cecil John Patterson, C.M.G., C.B.E., D.D. (*cons.* 1942), 1969; Rt. Rev. Ian Wotton Allnutt Shevill, M.A., Th.D. (*cons.* 1953)............................1971

Dean of St. Paul's (£2,800).

Very Rev. Martin Gloster Sullivan, M.A., The Deanery, Dean's Court, E.C.4...........1967

Canons Residentiary (each £1,700).

L. J. Collins, M.A....1948 | D. Webster, M.A.,
Archdn. Wood- | 1969
house........ 1968| B. C. Pawley, M.A. 1970
Organist, C. H. Dearnley, M.A., B.Mus., F.R.C.O.1968

Receiver of St. Paul's, E. T. Floyd Ewin, O.B.E., M.V.O., M.A.

Archdeacons.

London, Ven. S. M. F. Woodhouse, M.A.......1967
Middlesex, Ven. J. R. G. Eastaugh, B.A.......1966
Hampstead, Ven. H. A. S. Pink, M.A...........1964
Hackney, Ven. G. B. Timms, M.A..............1971
Benefited Clergy, 515; *Curates, &c.*, 460.
Chancellor and Commissary of the Dean and Chapter
 G. H. Newsom, Q.C., M.A....................1971
Registrar, D. W. Faull, 1 The Sanctuary, S.W.1 1969
Chapter Clerk, R. M. Hollis.

Westminster. £3,000.

The Collegiate Church of St. Peter—(*A Royal Peculiar*)
Dean, Very Rev. Eric Symes Abbott, K.C.V.O., M.A., D.D......................................1959
 Canons Residentiary (£1,200 to £1,400)
Archd. Carpenter..1951| R. C. D. Jasper, M.A., D.D.
M. A. C. Warren, M.A. | 1968
 D.D. (*Sub-Dean*).1963| D. L. Edwards, M.A. 1970
Archdeacon, Ven. E. F. Carpenter, Ph.D., M.A., D.D......................................1963
Chapter Clerk, Registrar, and Receiver General, W. R. J. Pullen, M.V.O., 11.B.............1963
Precentor, Rev. R. Simpson, M.A.............1963
Organist, D. Guest, M.A., Mus.B., F.R.C.M., A.R.C.O. 1963
Legal Secretary, J. S. Widdows, M.B.E.........1963

WINCHESTER. £3,500.

93rd *Bishop*, Rt. Rev. Sherard Falkner Allison, D.D., LL.D., (*cons.* 1951). (Wolvesey, Winchester) [Signs Falkner Winton:].................1961

Bishop Suffragan.

Southampton (vacant).
Assistant Bishop, Rt. Rev. Nigel Edmund Cornwall, C.B.E., M.A. (*cons.* 1949)...................1963

Dean (£2,400).

Very Rev. Michael Staffurth Stancliffe, M.A...1969

Dean of Jersey, Very Rev. Thomas Ashworth Goss, M.A......................................1971
Dean of Guernsey, Very Rev. Frederick Walter Cogman, A.K.C., B.D...................1966

Canons Residentiary (£1,500).

E. A. de Mendieta,| F. Bussby, M.B.E., M.A.,
 Ph.D........ 1962| M.Litt., B.D......1967
Bp. Cornwall ....1963| A. G. Wedderspoon,
 | M.A., B.D.....1970
Precentor, Rev. Canon H. C. A. Gaunt, M.A....1967
Organist, Martin Neary, F.R.C.O.............1972

Archdeacons.

Winchester, Ven. J. R. Beynon..............1962
Basingstoke, Ven. G. G. Finch, M.A..........1971
Benefited Clergy, 289; *Curates, &c.*, 70.
Chancellor, Prof. A. Phillips, O.B.E., M.A., Ph.D. .1964
Registrar, D. L. R. Thomas, Winchester.......1964
Legal Secretary, D. M. M. Carey, 1 The Sanctuary, S.W.1.

BATH AND WELLS. £3,000.

73rd *Bishop*, Rt. Rev. Edward Barry Henderson, D.S.C., D.D., *cons.* 1955. (The Palace, Wells.) [Signs Edward Bath: et Well:]............1960

Bishop Suffragan.

Taunton, Rt. Rev. Francis Horner West, M.A..1962
Assistant Bishop, Rt. Rev. Douglas John Wilson, M.A. (*cons.* 1938).....................1956

Dean (£2,400)

Very Rev. Irven David Edwards, M.A.........1963

Canons Residentiary of Wells (each £1,500).

Bp. Wilson.......1956 | Archd. Lance.....1963
D. S. Bailey, Ph.D., | P. M. Martin, M.A..1970
D.Litt. 1962
Organist, A. Crossland.....................1970

Archdeacons

Bath, Ven. T. G. A. Baker, M.A..............1971
Taunton, Ven. A. Hopley.....................1971
Wells, Ven. J. du B. Lance, M.A., M.A..........1963
Beneficed Clergy, 490; Curates, &c., 70.
Chancellor, G. H. Newsom, Q.C................1970
Registrar, Sec. & Chapt. Clerk, C. W. Harris, Wells.

BIRMINGHAM. £3,000.

5th Bishop, Rt. Rev. Laurence Ambrose Brown, M.A. (*cons.* 1960) (Bishop's Croft, Harborne, Birmingham 17) [Signs Laurence Birmingham] 1969

Bishop Suffragan.

Aston, Rt. Rev. David Brownfield Porter, M.A. (259 Bristol Road, Birmingham 5).........1962

Provost.

Rt. Rev. George Sinker, M.A..................1962

Archdeacons.

Aston, Ven. F. F. G. Warman, M.A.............1965
Birmingham, Ven. V. S. Nicholls.............1967
Beneficed Clergy 168; *Curates, &c.,* 94.
Organist, R. Massey, B.Mus., F.R.C.O........1968
Chancellor, F. J. Aglionby.....................1970
Registrar and Legal Secretary, R. L. Ekin, B.A. (85 Cornwall Street, Birmingham 3).

BRISTOL. £3,000.

52nd Bishop, Rt. Rev. Oliver Stratford Tomkins, D.D. (Bishop's House, Clifton Hill, Bristol 8) [Signs Oliver Bristol].................1959

Bishop Suffragan.

Malmesbury, Rt. Rev. Clifford Leofric Purdy Bishop, B.A. (15 Henleaze Road, Bristol)....1962

Dean.

Very Rev. Douglas Ernest William Harrison, M.A., D.Litt.............................1957

Canons Residentiary.

Bishop of Malmesbury | C. H. Shells, M.A...1971
1962 |
E. M. Pilkington, M.A. | P. E. Coleman, LL.B.,
1967 | A.K.C..........1971

Organist, Clifford Harker, B.Mus., F.R.C.O., A.R.C.M.
1949

Archdeacons.

Bristol, Ven. L. A. Williams, M.A.............1967
Swindon, Ven. F. S. Temple, M.A.............1970
Beneficed Clergy, 142; *Curates, &c.,* 69.
Chancellor, D. C. Calcutt, LL.B., Mus.B. 1971
Registrar and Sec., J. L. Press, M.A...........1949

CHELMSFORD. £3,100.

6th Bishop, Rt. Rev. Albert John Trillo, A.K.C., B.D., M.Th. (*cons.* 1963) (Bishopscourt, Chelmsford) [Signs John Chelmsford]............1971

Bishops Suffragan.

Colchester, Rt. Rev. Roderic Norman Coote, D.D. (Bishop's House, 32 Inglis Road, Colchester) (*cons.* 1951) 1966
Barking, Rt. Rev. William Frank Percival Chadwick, M.A. (West Dene, Whitehall Lane, Buckhurst Hill).............................1959
Bradwell, Rt. Rev. William Neville Welch, M.A. (222 Springfield Road, Chelmsford)......1968
Provost, Very Rev. Hilary Martin Connop Price, M.A..1967
Organist, J. W. Jordan, M.A., Mus.B., F.R.C.O..1966

Archdeacons.

Southend, The Bishop of Bradwell............1953
West Ham, Ven. A. J. Adams, B.A. 1971
Colchester, The Bishop of Colchester.........1969
Beneficed Clergy, 498; *Curates, &c.,* 142.

Chancellor, Miss S. M. Cameron, M.A........1970
Diocesan Registrar, D. W. Faull, 1 The Sanctuary,
S.W.1....................................1963

CHICHESTER. £3,000.

98th Bishop, Rt. Rev. Roger Plumpton Wilson, D.D. (*cons.* 1949, *trans.* 1958) (The Palace, Chichester) [Signs Roger Cicestr.]...........1958

Bishops Suffragan.

Lewes, Rt. Rev. James Herbert Lloyd Morrell, F.K.C. (83 Davigdor Road, Hove).........1959
Horsham, Rt. Rev. Simon Wilton Phipps, M.C., M.A. (The Old Rectory, Worth, Crawley).....1968
Assistant Bishop, Rt. Rev. Richard Ambrose Reeves, M.A. (*cons.* 1949).......................1966

Dean

Very Rev. John Walter Atherton Hussey, M.A. 1955

Canons Residentiary

Archd. Mason....1949 | A. K. Walker, B.Sc.,
V. K. Lippiett, M.A.1964 | Ph.D. 1971
Organist, J. A. Birch, F.R.C.O...............1958

Archdeacons.

Chichester, Ven. L. Mason, M.A..............1946
Hastings, Ven. G. Mayfield, M.A..............1956
Lewes, Ven. D. H. Booth, M.B.E., M.A........1959
Beneficed Clergy, 298; *Curates, &c.,* 98.
Chancellor, B. T. Buckle, M.A................1960
Legal Secretary to the Bishop, and Diocesan Registrar, C. L. Hodgetts, LL.B.

COVENTRY. £3,000.

5th Bishop, Rt. Rev. Cuthbert Killick Norman Bardsley, C.B.E., D.D. (The Bishop's House, 23 Davenport Road, Coventry.) [Signs Cuthbert Coventry.]...............................1956
Assistant Bishop, Rt. Rev. John David McKie, M.A. *cons.* 1946).........................1960
Provost, Very Rev. Harold Claude Noel Williams, B.A..1958
Organist, D. F. Lepine, M.A., F.R.C.O.........1961

Canons Residentiary

J. W. Poole, M.A..1963 | G. P. A. Spink....1970
A. H. Dammers, M.A.
1965 |

Archdeacons.

Coventry, Ven. E. A. Buchan, B.A.............1965
Warwick, Ven. J. H. Proctor, M.A.............1958
Beneficed Clergy, 165, *Curates, &c.,* 42.
Chancellor, His Hon. Conolly Hugh Gage, M.A. 1948
Registrar, S. L. Penn, Coventry 1957

DERBY. £3,000.

4th Bishop, Rt. Rev. Cyril William Johnston Bowles, M.A.(Bishop's House, Turnditch, Derby) [Signs Cyril Derby.] 1969

Bishop Suffragan.

Repton, Rt. Rev. William Warren Hunt, M.A..1965
Assistant Bishop, Rt. Rev. Thomas Richards Parfitt, M.A. (*cons.* 1952).......................1962
Provost, Very Rev. Ronald Alfred Beddoes, M.A.
1953

Canons Residentiary.

Archd. Richardson. 1955 |P. W. Miller.......1966

Archdeacons.

Derby, Ven. J. F. Richardson, M.A.............1952
Chesterfield, Ven. T. W. I. Cleasby, M.A.......1963
Organist, W. M. Ross, Mus. Bac., F.R.C.O......1958
Beneficed Clergy, 207; *Curates, &c.,* 52.
Chancellor, A. W. M. Davies, Q.C.............1971
Registrar, J. R. S. Grimwood-Taylor, Derby.

ELY. £3,000.

65th Bishop, Rt. Rev. Edward James Keymer Roberts, D.D. (*cons.* 1956, *trans.* 1962 and 1964) (The Bishop's House, Ely) [Edward Elien:]..1964

Bishop Suffragan.

Huntingdon, Rt. Rev. Robert Arnold Schürhoff Martineau, M.A..........................1966
Assistant Bishop, Rt. Rev. Gordon John Walsh D.D. (*cons.* 1927)............................1942

Dean (£2,400).

Very Rev. Michael Sausmarez Carey, M.A....1970

Canons Residentiary (each £1,500).

Bp. of Huntingdon.1966	G. Youell 1970
P. C. Moore, M.A., D.Phil.	G. C. Stead, M.A...1971
1967	

Organist, A. W. Wills, MUS. DOC., F.R.C.O.....1959

Archdeacons.

Ely, Ven. J. S. Long, M.A....................1970
Wisbech, Ven. B. G. B. Fox, M.C............1965
Huntingdon, Ven. D. F. Page, M.A............1965
Beneficed Clergy, 250; *Curates*, &c., 85.
Chancellor, R. M. O. Havers, Q.C., M.P........1970
Registrar, J. B. Green, M.A.
Legal Secretary, D. M. Moir Carey, M.A., 1 The Sanctuary, S.W.1.

EXETER. £3,000.

67th Bishop, Rt. Rev. Robert Cecil Mortimer, D.D. (The Palace, Exeter). [Signs Robert Exon:].1949

Bishops Suffragan.

Crediton, Rt. Rev. Wilfrid Arthur Edmund Westall, B.A. (The Close, Exeter) 1954
Plymouth, Rt. Rev. Wilfrid Guy Sanderson, M.A. (Coltsfoot, Yeoland Lane, Yelverton).......1962

Dean (£2,400).

Very Rev. Marcus Knight, B.D. 1960

Canons Residentiary

H. Balmforth, M.A. 1956	Archd. Ward 1970
Archd. Newhouse. 1966	F. G. Rice........1970

Organist, L. F. Dakers, MUS.BAC., F.R.C.O....1957
Chapter Clerk, J. F. Eden, B.A................1966

Archdeacons.

Barnstaple, Ven. R. G. Herniman, B.A........1970
Totnes, Ven. R. J. D. Newhouse, M.A.......1966
Plymouth, Ven. F. A. J. Matthews, M.A.......1962
Exeter, Ven. A. F. Ward, B.A.................1970
Beneficed Clergy, 406 ; *Curates*, &c., 69
Chancellor, D. Calcutt, M.A., LL.B., MUS.B. 1971
Registrar and Secretary, J. F. G. Michelmore, 18 Cathedral Yard, Exeter.

GLOUCESTER. £3,000.

36th Bishop, Rt. Rev. Basil Tudor Guy, M.A. (*cons.* 1957) (Palace House, Gloucester) [Signs Basil Gloucestr:]...........................1962

Bishop Suffragan.

Tewkesbury, Rt. Rev. Forbes Trevor Horan, M.A. 1960

Dean (£2,455).

Very Rev. Seiriol John Arthur Evans, C.B.E., M.A., F.S.A.....................................1953

Canons Residentiary (£1,533).

W. T. Wardle, M.A.	D. D. Thomas, M.A.
1948	1968
C. F. Pare, M.A....1963	W. R. Houghton, M.A.
D. A. R. Keen, M.A.,	1968
F.S.A..........1965	T. E. Evans, M.A...1969

Organist, J.D. Sanders, M.A., MUS.B., F.R.C.O., A.R.C.M. 1967

Archdeacons.

Gloucester, Ven. W. T. Wardle, M.A. 1948
Cheltenham, Ven. G. F. Hutchins, M.A......1965
Beneficed Clergy, 228 ; *Curates*, &c., 59.
Chancellor & Vicar-Gen., Rev. E. Garth Moore, M.A..1957
Registrar, J. Martin, 34 Brunswick Road, Gloucester 1957

Legal Sec., D. M. Moir Carey, M.A., 1 The Sanctuary, Westminster, S.W.1.
Diocesan Sec., P. J. Davies, Church House, College Green, Gloucester.

GUILDFORD. £3,000.

5th Bishop, Rt. Rev. George Edmund Reindorp, D.D. (Willow Grange, Stringer's Common, Guildford) [Signs George Guildford].......1961

Bishop Suffragan

Dorking, Rt. Rev. Kenneth Dawson Evans, M.A. (13 Pilgrim's Way, Guildford)............1968
Assistant Bishops, Rt. Rev. St. John Surridge Pike, D.D. (*cons.* 1958) 1963
Rt. Rev. Lucian Charles Usher-Wilson, C.B.E., M.A., (*cons.* 1936).......................1964
Dean, Very Rev. Antony Cyprian Bridge....1968

Canons Residentiary

C. T. Chapman, Ph.D.	L. E. Tanner, M.A..1971
1961	

Organist, B. Rose.............................1960

Archdeacons.

Surrey, Ven. J. M. Evans, M.A. 1968
Dorking, Ven. W. H. S. Purcell, M.A.........1968
Beneficed Clergy, 153 ; *Curates*, &c., 73.
Chancellor, M. B. Goodman, M.A.
Legal Sec., R. M. Hollis, M.A.
Registrar of Diocese, R. M. Hollis, M.A.
Registrar of the Archdeaconries, R. M. Hollis, M.A.

HEREFORD. £3,000.

102nd Bishop, Rt. Rev. Mark Allin Hodson, B.A. (The Palace, Hereford), *cons.* 1956 [Signs Mark Hereford]..................................1961
Assistant Bishop, Right Rev. William Arthur Partridge, B.A. (*cons.* 1953).................1963

Dean (£2,400).

Very Reverend Norman Stanley Rathbone, M.A. 1968

Canons Residentiary (£1,500).

E. W. Eyden, B.A., B.D.	J. M. Irvine, M.A...1965
1964	Archd. Lewis.....1970

Organist, Richard Lloyd, MUS.B., F.R.C.O......1966

Archdeacons.

Hereford, Ven. J. W. Lewis, M.A.............1970
Ludlow, Ven. A. H. Woodhouse, D.S.C., M.A. 1970
Beneficed Clergy, 226 ; *Curates*, &c., 27.
Chancellor, Rev. K. J. T. Elphinstone........1952
Registrar, Philip Gwynne James, 5 St. Peter Street, Hereford.

LEICESTER. £3,200.

3rd Bishop, Rt. Rev. Ronald Ralph Williams, D.D. (Bishop's Lodge, Leicester.) [Signs Ronald Leicester]..................................1953
Assistant Bishops, Rt. Rev. James Lawrence Cecil Horstead, C.M.G., C.B.E., D.D. (*cons.* 1936).1961
Rt. Rev. Thomas Geoffrey Stuart Smith, M.A. (*cons.* 1947)................................1966
Provost, Very Rev. John Chester Hughes, M.A. 1963

Canons Residentiary

D. W. Gundry, B.D.,	Rt. Rev. J. E. L. Mort,
M.Th...........1963	C.B.E., M.A.....1970
F. L. Godfrey, M.A. 1968	

Organist, Peter White, M.A., MUS.B., F.R.C.O....1968

Archdeacons.

Leicester, Ven. R. B. Cole...................1963
Loughborough, Ven. H. Lockley, Ph.D.........1963
Beneficed Clergy, 220 ; *Curates*, &c., 45.
Chancellor, R. A. Forrester, M.A.............1953
Registrar, R. J. Moore, 5 Bowling Green Street, Leicester.

LICHFIELD. £3,000.

95th Bishop, Right Rev. Arthur Stretton Reeve, D.D. (22 The Close, Lichfield.) [Signs Stretton Lichfield]..................................1953

Bishops Suffragan.

Shrewsbury, Rt. Rev. Francis William Cocks, C.B., M.A. (Athlone, London Road, Shrewsbury).1970
Stafford, Rt. Rev. Richard George Clitherow, M.A. (Eversly, Bramshall Road, Uttoxeter).....1958

Dean (£2,400).
Rt. Rev. George Edward Holderness, M.A. ..1969
    Canons Residentiary (each £1,500).

Archd. Stratton.....1960	D. A. Hodges, M.A.
D. K. Robertson, B.A.	1965
1960	

Organist, R. G. Greening, M.A., B.Mus., F.R.C.O. 1959

Archdeacons.

Stafford, Ven. B. Stratton, M.A.............1959
Salop, Ven. S. D. Austerberry...............1959
Stoke on Trent, Ven. C. W. Borrett, M.A......1971
  Beneficed Clergy, 424; Curates, &c., 122.
Chancellor, His Hon. C. H. Gage............1954
Diocesan Registrar and Bishop's Sec., M. B. S. Exham.

LINCOLN. £3,000.

68th Bishop, Rt. Rev. Kenneth Riches, D.D. (cons. 1952, trans. 1956) (Bishop's House, Eastgate, Lincoln). [Signs Kenneth Lincoln :].......1956

Bishops Suffragan.

Grimsby, Rt. Rev. Gerald Fitzmaurice Colin, M.A. 1966
Grantham, Rt. Rev. Ross Sydney Hook, M.C., M.A. 1965
Assistant Bishops, Rt. Rev. Anthony Otter, M.A. (cons. 1949).........................1965
  Rt. Rev. Kenneth Healey, M.A. (cons. 1958).1965
  Rt. Rev. George William Clarkson, M.A. (cons. 1954) 1968

Dean (£2,700)
Very Rev. the Hon. Oliver William Twisleton-Wykeham-Fiennes, M.A. 1968
    Canons Residentiary (£1,800).

P. B. G. Binnall, M.A.,	D. C. Rutter, M.A. 1965
F.S.A. 1962	V. A. de Waal, M.A.
	1969

Organist, Philip Marshall, Mus.Doc., F.R.C.O....1966

Archdeacons.

Stow, Ven. S. Harvie Clark, M.A...........1967
Lincoln, Ven. A. C. Smith, V.R.D., M.A......1960
Lindsey (vacant).
  Beneficed Clergy, 350; Curates, &c., 110.
Chancellor, M. B. Goodman, M.A............1971
Registrar, H. J. J. Griffith, 2 Bank Street, Lincoln.

NORWICH. £3,000.

69th Bishop (and 110th of East Anglia, Rt. Rev. Maurice Arthur Ponsonby Wood, M.A. (Bishop's House, Norwich) [Signs Maurice Norvic]..1971

Bishops Suffragan.

Lynn, Rt. Rev. William Somers Llewellyn, M.A. 1963
Thetford, Rt. Rev. Eric William Bradley Cordingly, M.B.E. 1963

Dean
Very Rev. Alan Brunskill Webster, M.A., B.D. 1970

Canons Residentiary.

A. G. G. Thurlow, M.A.,	M. Kaye, M.A.....1967
F.S.A. 1964	M. A. Mann......1969

Organist, M. B. Nicholas, M.A., F.R.C.O.......1971

Archdeacons.

Norfolk, The Bishop of Thetford............1962
Norwich, Ven. W. A. Aitken, M.A............1961
Lynn, The Bishop of Lynn..................1961
  Beneficed Clergy, 388; Curates, &c., 30.
Chancellor, J. H. Ellison, M.A..............1955
Registrar & Sec., B. O. L. Prior.

OXFORD. £3,000.

39th Bishop, Rt. Rev. Kenneth John Woollcombe, M.A. (Bishop's House, Cuddesdon, Oxford) [Signs Kenneth Oxon]...................1971

Bishops Suffragan.

Reading, Rt. Rev. Eric Henry Knell, M.A. (Well House, Upper Basildon, Reading).........1955
Dorchester, Rt. Rev. David Goodwin Loveday, M.A. (Wardington, Banbury)............1957
Buckingham, Rt. Rev. George Chistopher Cutts Pepys, M.A..............................1964
Assistant Bishops, Rt. Rev. Robert Milton Hay, M.A., B.D (cons. 1944)...................1969
  Rt. Rev. David Goodwin Loveday, M.A. (cons. 1957)................................1971

Dean of Christ Church (£3,000).
Very Rev. Henry Chadwick, D.D...........1969
    Canons Residentiary (£1,500).
The Canons of Christ Church (with the exception of the Archdeacon of Oxford) are Professors in the University of Oxford.

V. A. Demant, D.D....1949	W. R. F. Browning,
Archd. Witton-Davies	M.A., B.D. (Canon of
1956	the Cathedral Church)
S. L. Greenslade, D.D.	1965
1959	J. Macquarrie, D.Lit.
	1969
	M. F. Wiles, M.A.1970

Organist, S. Preston, M.A., B.Mus.............1970

Archdeacons.

Oxford, Ven. C. Witton-Davies, M.A.........1956
Berks., Ven. E. Wild, M.A..................1967
Bucks., Ven. D. I. T. Eastman, M.C., M.A.....1970
  Beneficed Clergy. 385; Curates, &c., 467.
Chancellor, P. T. S. Boydell...............1958
Registrar and Legal Sec., F. E. Robson........1969

Windsor. £3,250.

(The Queen's Free Chapel of St. George within Her Castle of Windsor—A Royal Peculiar)
Dean, Rt. Rev. William Launcelot Scott Fleming, D.D...................................1971

    Canons Residentiary (each £1,800).

G. B. Bentley, M.A. 1957	S. E. Verney. M.A..1970
J. A. Fisher, M.A...1958	

Organist, S. S. Campbell, D.Mus., F.R.C.O.....1961
Chapter Clerk, Mrs. V. Hamer..............1970

PETERBOROUGH, £3,000.

34th Bishop, Rt. Rev. Cyril Eastaugh, M.C., M.A. (The Palace, Peterborough) [Signs Cyril Petriburg] (cons. 1949)......................1961
Assistant Bishops, Rt. Rev. Archibald Rollo Graham-Campbell, C.B.E., M.A. (cons. 1948) 1965
  Rt. Rev. George Frederick Townley, M.A. (cons. 1957)...............................1970

Dean (£2,400)
Very Rev. Richard Shuttleworth Wingfield-Digby, M.A............................1966
    Canons Residentiary (each £1,500)
Archd. Towndrow.1966 | A. S. Gribble, M.A. .1967
Master of the Music, W. S. Vann, D.Mus., F.R.C.O. 1953

Archdeacons

Northampton, Ven. B. R. Marsh, B.A.........1964
Oakham, Ven. F. N. Towndrow, M.A.........1967
  Beneficed Clergy, 250; Curates, &c., 30.
Chancellor, T. R. Fitzwalter Butler, O.B.E. ...1962
Registrar, E. T. Channell, 37 Priestgate, Peterborough.

PORTSMOUTH. £3,000.

5th Bishop, Rt. Rev. John Henry Lawrence Phillips, D.D. (Bishopswood, Fareham, Hants.) [Signs John Portsmouth].........................1960
Assistant Bishop, Rt. Rev. Laurence Henry Woolmer, M.A. (*cons.* 1949)...............1968
Provost, Very Rev. Eric Noel Porter Goff, M.A. 1939
Organist, C. Gower, M.A., F.R.C.O.

Canons Residentiary.

T. C. Heritage, M.A.	J. R. G. Ragg, M.A.
1964	1968
F. C. Carpenter, M.A.	E. S. C. Lowman..1971
1968	

Archdeacons.

Portsmouth, Ven. C. Prior, C.B., M.A.........1969
I. of Wight, Ven. R. V. Scruby, M.A.........1965
Beneficed Clergy, 119; *Curates, &c.,* 62.
Chancellor, B. T. Buckle, M.A................1971
Registrar and Legal Sec., T. B. Birkett, 132 High Street, Portsmouth.....................1957

ROCHESTER. £3,000.

104th Bishop, Rt. Rev. Richard David Say, D.D. (Bishopscourt, Rochester). [Signs David Roffen:]
Bishop Suffragan. [1961
Tonbridge, Rt. Rev. Henry David Halsey, B.A. 1968
Assistant Bishop, Rt. Rev. John Keith Russell, M.A. (*cons.* 1955)..............................1965

Dean (£2,400).

Rt. Rev. Stanley Woodley Betts, C.B.E., M.A...1966
Canons Residentiary.

F. H. Gripper, M.A.1965	Archd. Stewart-Smith
P. A. Welsby, M.A.,	1969
Ph.D...........1966	

Organist, R. J. Ashfield, D.MUS., F.R.C.O.......1956

Archdeacons.

Tonbridge, Ven. E. E. Maples Earle, M.A. 1952
Bromley, Ven. H. W. Cragg, M.A.............1969
Rochester, Ven. D. C. Stewart-Smith, M.A.....1969

Beneficed Clergy, 220 : *Curates, &c.,* 124.
Chancellor, M. B. Goodman, M.A..............1971
Registrars, H. S. Wharton (1949) and O.R. Woodfield (1955), Rochester.
Sec. D. W. Faull, 1 The Sanctuary, S.W.1....1963

ST. ALBANS. £3,730.

7th Bishop, Rt. Rev. Robert Alexander Kennedy Runcie, M.C., M.A. (Abbey Gate House, St. Albans) [Signs Robert St. Albans]........1970

Bishops Suffragan.

Bedford, Rt. Rev. John Tyrell Holmes Hare, M.A. (168 Kimbolton Road, Bedford).........1968
Hertford, Rt. Rev. Hubert Victor Whitsey, M.A. 1971

Dean (£2,400)

Very Rev. Noel Martin Kennaby, M.A.......1964
Organist, P. Hurford, M.A., MUS.B., F.R.C.O., A.R.C.M. [1958

Archdeacons.

St. Albans, Ven. B. C. Snell, M.A............1962
Bedford, The Bishop of Bedford.............1962
Beneficed Clergy, 265 ; *Curates, &c.,* 154
Chancellor, G. H. Newsom, Q.C., M.A..........1958
Joint Registrars and Legal Secs., D. W. Faull (1963) and P. F. B. Beesley (1969), 1 The Sanctuary, S.W.1.

ST. EDMUNDSBURY AND IPSWICH. £3,000.

6th Bishop, Rt. Rev. Leslie Wilfrid Brown, C.B.E. D.D. (Bishop's House, Ipswich), *cons.* 1953, *trans.* 1966 [Signs Leslie St. Edm. & Ipswich]....1966

Bishop Suffragan.

Dunwich, Rt. Rev. David Rokeby Maddock, M.A. 1967

Provost, Very Rev. John Albert Henry Waddington, M.B.E., T.D., M.A................1958
Canons Residentiary.
C. Rhodes, M.A.....1964J. H. Churchill, M.A. 1967

Archdeacons.

Ipswich, Ven. C. G. Hooper, M.A............1963
Suffolk, Ven. P. H. T. Hartley, M.A..........1970
Sudbury, Ven. K. Child, B.A................1970
Organist, T. F. H. Oxley, M.A., B.MUS., F.R.C.O.1957
Beneficed Clergy, 245 ; *Curates, &c.,* 25.
Chancellor, R. M. O. Havers, Q.C., M.P.........1966
Registrar, G. P. V. Creagh, M.A., 80 Guildhall Street, Bury St. Edmunds.

SALISBURY. £3,000.

74th Bishop, Right Rev. Joseph Edward Fison, D.D. (South Canonry, The Close, Salisbury.) [Signs Joseph Sarum.]........................1963

Bishop Suffragan.

Sherborne, Rt. Rev. Victor Joseph Pike, C.B., C.B.E., D.D. (69 The Close, Salisbury)...........1960
Assistant Bishop, Rt. Rev. Angus Campbell MacInnes, C.M.G., D.D. (*cons.* 1953)...........1968
Dean (£3,015).
Very Rev. William Fenton Morley, M.A., B.D..1971
Canons Residentiary (£1,945).

| Archd. Wingfield- | C. V. Taylor, M.A..1969 |
| Digby........1968 | |

Organist, R. G. Seal, M.A., F.R.C.O...........1968

Archdeacons.

Wilts, Ven. C. A. Plaxton, M.A..............1951
Dorset, Ven. E. L. Seager, M.A..............1956
Sherborne, Ven. E. J. G. Ward, M.V.O., M.A.....1967
Sarum, Ven. S. B. Wingfield-Digby, M.B.E., M.A. 1968
Beneficed Clergy, 300 ; *Curates, &c.,* 47.
Chancellor of the Diocese, J. H. Ellison, M.A.....1955
Registrar and Legal Secretary, Alan M. Barker, B.A., Bishop's Walk, The Close, Salisbury.

SOUTHWARK. £3,000.

6th Bishop, Rt. Rev. Arthur Mervyn Stockwood, D.D. (Bishop's House, 38 Tooting Bec Gardens, S.W.16) [Signs Mervyn Southwark].......1959
Assistant Bishops, Rt. Rev. Edward Lawrence Barham, M.A. (6 Malcolm Road, S.W.19)(*cons.* 1964)...............................1967
Rt. Rev. John Boys, M.A., L.Th. (41 Elm Bank Gardens, Barnes, S.W.13) (*cons.* 1948) ...1968
Rt. Rev. John Arthur Thomas Robinson, M.A., PH.D., B.D. (*cons.* 1959)................1969

Bishops Suffragan

Kingston on Thames, Rt. Rev. Hugh William Montefiore, M.A., B.D. (23 Bellevue Road, Wandsworth Common, S.W.17).......1970
Woolwich, Rt. Rev. David Stuart Sheppard, M.A. (12 Asylum Road, S.E.15).............1969
Provost, Very Rev. Harold Edward Frankham 1970

Canons Residentiary.

I. G. Davies, B.A., B.D.	E. A. James, A.K.C., B.D.
1957	1966
F. Colquhoun, M.A.	P. F. Miller, M.A...1969
1961	P. H. Penwarden, M.A.
D. M. P. Tasker, B.A.	1971
1961	

Organist, E. H. Warrell, A.R.C.O., A.R.C.M....1968

Archdeacons.

Southwark, Ven. R. V. Bazire..............1966
Lewisham, Ven. W. S. Hayman, M.A.........1960
Kingston, Ven. P. D. Robb, M.A.............1953
Beneficed Clergy, 315; *Curates, &c.,* 338.
Chancellor, Rev. E. Garth Moore, M.A........1948
Secretary and Registrar, D. W. Faull, 1 The Sanctuary, S.W.1.............................1963

TRURO. £3,000.

10th Bishop, Rt. Rev. John Maurice Key, D.D. (Lis Escop, Truro) (*cons.* 1947, *trans.* 1960) [Signs Maurice Truron:].......................1960

Assistant Bishop, Rt. Rev. William Quinlan Lash, M.A. (*cons.* 1947)....................1962

Dean

Very Rev. Henry Morgan Lloyd, D.S.O., O.B.E., M.A...........................1960

Canons Residentiary.

J. A. Simcock......1952| Archd. Young...1965
H. A. Blair, M.A., B.D..1960|

Organist, J. Winter.......................1971

Archdeacons.

Cornwall, Ven. P. C. Young, B.Litt., M.A......1965
Bodmin, Ven. C. J. E. Meyer, M.A............1969
Beneficed Clergy, 180; *Curates, &c.*, 19.

Chancellor, P. T. S. Boydell.................1957
Registrar and Secretary, R. W. Money, 2 Princes Street, Truro.

WORCESTER. £3,000

110th Bishop, Rt. Rev. Robert Wilmer Woods, K.C.V.O., M.A.|(The Bishop's House, Hartlebury Castle, Kidderminster) [Signs Robin Worcester] 1970

Assistant Bishop (£1,500), Rt. Rev. David Howard Nicholas Allenby, M.A. (*cons.* 1962)........1968
Dean (£2,400).

Very Rev. Eric Waldram Kemp, D.D..........1969
Canons (£1,500).

G. C. B. Davies, D.D. |W. E. Purcell, M.A.1966
1963 |E. S. Turnbull, M.A.
Archd. Eliot.........1965| 1971
Organist, C. J. Robinson, M.A., B.Mus., F.R.C.O..1963
Archdeacons.

Dudley, Ven. J. C. Williams, B.A............1968
Worcester, Ven. P. C. Eliot, M.A............1961
Beneficed Clergy, 175; *Curates, &c.*, 106.

Chancellor, P. T. S. Boydell...............1959
Registrar, J. A. Dale, Diocesan Registry, Worcester.

Probince of York

YORK. £6,000.

93rd Archbishop and Primate of England, Right Hon. and Most Rev. Frederick Donald Coggan, D.D., *cons.* 1956, *trs.* 1961. (Bishopthorpe, York.) [Signs Donald Ebor:]..................1961

Assistant Bishop, Rt. Rev. George Eyles Irwin Cockin, B.A. (*cons.* 1959)...............1969
Bishops Suffragan.

Selby (vacant).

Whitby, Rt. Rev. John Yates, M.A. 1971
Hull, Rt. Rev. Hubert Lawrence Higgs, M.A. (Hullen House, Woodfield Lane, Hessle)...1965
Dean (£2,600)

Very Rev. Alan Richardson, M.A., D.D.......1964
Canons Residentiary (£1,650)

R. E. Cant, M.A....1957 | D. G. Galliford, M.A.
I. P. Burbridge, M.A. | 1970
1966

Organist, Francis Jackson, MUS.D., F.R.C.O.....1946
Archdeacons.

York, Ven. C. R. Forder, M.A..............1957
East Riding, Ven. D. G. Snelgrove, M.A. 1970
Cleveland, Ven. S. F. Linsley 1965
Beneficed Clergy, 321; *Curates, &c.*, 76.

Official Principal and Auditor of the Chancery Court, W. S. Wigglesworth, Q.C., D.C.L.
Chancellor of the Diocese, Rev. K. J. T. Elphinstone, M.A.......................1971
Vicar-General of the Province and Official Principal of the Consistory Court, W. S. Wigglesworth, Q.C., D.C.L.
Registrar and Secretary, G. P. Knowles, M.A., LL.B. 1968

DURHAM. £4,500.

90th Bishop, Rt. Rev. Ian Thomas Ramsey, M.A., D.D. (Auckland Castle, Bishop Auckland). [Signs Ian Dunelm]...................1966

Assistant Bishop, Rt. Rev. Kenneth John Fraser Skelton, M.A. (*cons.* 1962)................1970

Bishop Suffragan.

Jarrow, Rt. Rev. Alexander Kenneth Hamilton, M.A.........................1965

Dean (£3,300).

Very Rev. John Herbert Severn Wild, M.A., D.D. 1951

Canons Residentiary (£1,500).

H. E. W. Turner, D.D.|D. R. Jones, M.A. ..1964
1950|Archd. Perry......1970
Archd. Stranks....1954|
A. H. Couratin, M.A.|C. H. G. Hopkins, B.A.
1962| 1970

Organist, C. W. Eden, MUS.B., A.R.C.O.......1936

Archdeacons.

Durham, Ven. M. C. Perry, M.A............1970
Auckland, Ven. C. J. Stranks, M.A..........1958
Beneficed Clergy, 250; *Curates*, *&c.*, 100

Chancellor, Rev. E. Garth Moore, M.A.......1954
Registrar (1948) and Legal Secretary (1929), H. C. Ferens, M.A. (The College, Durham).

BLACKBURN. £3,000.

4th Bishop, Rt. Rev. Charles Robert Claxton, D.D., *cons.* 1946, *trans.* 1960 (Bishop's House, Blackburn) [Signs Charles Blackburn]..........1960

Bishops Suffragan.

Lancaster, Rt. Rev. Anthony Leigh Egerton Hoskyns-Abrahall (Pedders Wood, Scorton)1955
Burnley, Rt. Rev. Richard Charles Challinor Watson, M.A. (Palace House, Burnley)......1970
Provost, Very Rev. Norman Robinson, B.SC...1961

Canons Residentiary.

T. A. Rockley, B.A....1964| G. A. Williams M.A.
C. W. D. Carroll, M.A.| 1965
1964| J. W. Dixon, M.A.1965

Archdeacons

Lancaster, Ven. G. Gower-Jones, M.A........1966
Blackburn, Ven. H. N. Hodd, M.A...........1962
Organist, J. Bertalot, M.A., F.R.C.O., A.R.C.M...1964
Beneficed Clergy, 267; *Curates, &c.*, 51.

Chancellor, R. A. Forrester, M.A............1949
Registrar, Leslie Ranson, LL.B.,............1954

BRADFORD. £3,000.

Bishop (vacant).

Provost, Very Rev. William Hugh Alan Cooper, M.A.......................1962
Organist, K. V. Rhodes. B.MUS., F.R.C.O.......1964

Archdeacons.

Bradford, Ven. W. Johnston, M.A. 1965
Craven, Ven. A. Sephton, M.A..............1956
Beneficed Clergy, 136; *Curates, &c.*, 34.

Chancellor, H. C. Scott, Q.C., M.A..........1957
Registrar and Secretary, H. Firth, Martins Bank Chambers, Tyrrel Street, Bradford.

CARLISLE. £3,200.

63rd Bishop, Rt. Rev. Sydney Cyril Bulley, M.A. (Rose Castle, Dalston, Carlisle), *cons.* 1959 [Signs Cyril Carliol] 1967

Bishop Suffragan.

Penrith, Rt. Rev. William Edward Augustus Pugh, M.A......................1970

Dean (£3,300).

Very Rev. Lionel Meiring Spafford du Toit, M.A. 1960

Canons Residentiary (about £1,500).
C. E. Nurse, M.A...1958 | Archd. Bradford...1966
| W. A. Batty, M.A..1968
Organist, R. A. Seivewright, M.A. A.R.C.O....1960

Archdeacons
Carlisle, Ven. R. B. Bradford, B.A. 1971
West Cumberland, Ven. A. G. Hardie, M.A....1971
Westmorland and Furness, Ven. W. F. Ewbank, M.A.,
B.D.......................................1971
Beneficed Clergy, 229.
Chancellor, His Hon. D. J. Stinson, M.A......1971
Registrar and Sec., I. S. Sutcliffe, M.A., LL.B., Carlisle
1964

CHESTER. £3,000.
37th Bishop, Rt. Rev. Gerald Alexander Ellison,
D.D. (Bishop's House, Chester.) cons. 1950
[Signs Gerald Cestr:]....................1955
Bishops Suffragan.
Stockport, Rt. Rev. Rupert Gordon Strutt, B.D.1965
Birkenhead, Rt. Rev. Eric Arthur John Mercer
1965

Dean (£2,460).
Very Rev. George William Outram Addleshaw,
M.A., B.D., F.S.A........................1963
Canons Residentiary (£1,560).
C. E. Jarman........1943 | Archd. Fisher...1965
B. A. Hardy, M.A....1946 |
Organist, R. A. Fisher........................1967

Archdeacons
Chester, Ven. L. G. Fisher, A.L.C.D...........1965
Macclesfield, Ven. F. H. House, O.B.E., M.A.....1967
Beneficed Clergy, 290; *Curates, &c.*, 78.
Chancellor, Rev. K. J. T. Elphinstone, M.A......1950
Legal Secretaries, Gamon & Co., 2 White Friars,
Chester.

LIVERPOOL. £3,730.
5th Bishop, Rt. Rev. Stuart Yarworth Blanch, M.A.
(Bishop's Lodge, Woolton Park, Liverpool)
[Signs Stuart Liverpool]..................1966
Bishop Suffragan.
Warrington, Rt. Rev. John Monier Bickersteth,
M.A.......................................1970
Asst. Bishop, Rt. Rev. William Scott Baker, M.A.
(cons. 1943)..............................1968
Dean (£2,900).
Very Rev. Edward Henry Patey, M.A........1964
Canons Residentiary
C. B. Naylor, M.A...1956 | L. F. Hopkins, M.A., B.D.
H. Ellis, M.A........1962 | 1964
| Archd. Corbett...1971
Organist, Noel Rawsthorne, F.R.C.O..........1955

Archdeacons
Liverpool, Ven. C. E. Corbett, M.A............1971
Warrington, Ven. J. A. Lawton, M.A...........1970
Beneficed Clergy, 227; *Curates, &c.*, 103.
Chancellor, His Hon. E. Steel, LL.B............1957
Joint Registrars, E. C. Arden and R. H. Arden,
1 Hanover Street, Liverpool, 1.

MANCHESTER. £3,000.
8th Bishop, Rt. Rev. Patrick Campbell Rodger,
M.A., (Bishopscourt, Bury New Road, Man-
chester 7), [Signs Patrick Manchester] 1970
Bishops Suffragan.
Hulme, Rt. Rev. Kenneth Venner Ramsey, B.D.
(Westholme, 22 Pine Road, Didsbury, Man-
chester 20)...............................1953
Middleton, Rt. Rev. Edward Ralph Wickham, B.D.
(1 Portland Road, Eccles, Manchester) 1959
Dean (£2,750) Very Rev. Alfred Jowett, M.A..1964
Canons Residentiary (£1,800).
Archd. Price........1966 | M. M. Hennell, M.A. 1970
F. S. Wright, M.A....1966 | G. O. Morgan, B.Sc.1971
Organist, D. E. Cantrell, M.A., B.Mus., F.R.C.O...1961

Archdeacons.
Manchester, Ven. S. H. Price, M.A...........1966
Rochdale, Ven. A. H. Ballard, M.A...........1966
Beneficed Clergy, 363; *Curates, &c.*, 120.
Chancellor, His Hon. E. Steel, LL.B...........1971
Registrar and Bishop's Secretary, L. H. Orford, M.A.,
LL.B., 90 Deansgate, Manchester...........1933

NEWCASTLE. £3,000.
8th Bishop, Rt. Rev. Hugh Edward Ashdown, D.D.
(The Bishop's House, Gosforth, Newcastle upon
Tyne, 3) [Signs Hugh Newcastle]........1957
Assistant Bishop, Rt. Rev. John Alexander Rams-
botham, D.D. (cons. 1950)..................1968
Provost, Very Rev. Conrad Clifton Wolters, M.A.
1962

Canons Residentiary.
Archd. Unwin....1963 | D. E. F. Ogden, B.A.1966
A. Wilson, M.A....1964 | R. G. Cornwell, M.A.
| 1968
Organist, Russell A. Missin, F.R.C.O..........1967
Archdeacons
Northumberland, Ven. C. P. Unwin, T.D., M.A...1963
Lindisfarne, Ven. M. H. Bates, M.A...........1970
Beneficed Clergy, 154; *Curates, &c.*, 68.
Chancellor, A. J. Blackett-Ord, M.A............1971
Registrar and Sec., Ian Dickinson, Cross House,
Westgate Road, Newcastle upon Tyne.

RIPON. £3,000.
9th Bishop Rt. Rev. John Richard Humpidge
Moorman, D.D., Litt.D. (Bishop Mount, Ripon.)
[Signs John Ripon]......................1959
Bishop Suffragan.
Knaresborough, Rt. Rev. John Howard Cruse, M.A.
1965

Dean (£2,440)
Very Rev. Frederick Edwin Le Grice, M.A....1968
Canons Residentiary (each £1,500)
Archd. Turnbull.....1962 | R. Emmerson, B.D.,
J. G. B. Ashworth, M.A.1965 | A.K.C.........1966
Organist, Ronald Perrin, F.R.C.O.............1966

Archdeacons
Leeds, Ven. A. C. Page, M.A.................1969
Richmond, Ven. J. W. Turnbull, B.A..........1962
Beneficed Clergy, 172; *Curates, &c.*, 58
Chancellor, H. C. Scott, Q.C., M.A............1957
Registrar and Secretary, J. R. Balmforth, M.A.,
Phoenix House, South Parade, Leeds.

SHEFFIELD. £3,000.
4th Bishop, Rt. Rev. William Gordon Fallows, M.A.
(Bishopscroft, Snaithing Lane, Sheffield 10) (cons.
1968) [Signs Gordon Sheffield]............1971
Asst. Bishop, Rt. Rev. George Vincent Gerard,
C.B.E., M.C., M.A. (cons. 1938)............1947
Provost, Very Rev. Ivan Delacherois Neill, C.B.,
O.B.E., M.A..............................1966

Archdeacons
Sheffield, Ven. H. Johnson, M.A..............1963
Doncaster, Ven. E. J. G. Rogers, B.A..........1967
Organist, G. Matthews, B.Mus., F.R.C.O.......1967
Beneficed Clergy, 161; *Curates, &c.*, 112.
Chancellor, G. B. Graham, Q.C................1971
Registrar and Legal Sec., V. H. Sandford, M.A., 30
Bank Street, Sheffield.

SODOR AND MAN. £3,000.
76th Bishop, Rt. Rev. George Eric Gordon, M.A.
(Bishop's Court, Kirk Michael, Isle of Man)
[Signs Eric Sodor and Man]...............1966
Archdeacon, Ven. E. B. Glass, M.A............1964
Beneficed Clergy, 27; *Curates, &c.* 14.
Vicar-General and Registrar, Frank Barnes Johnson,
M.B.E., M.A., 24 Athol Street, Douglas.
Secretary and Deputy, P. W. S. Farrant.

SOUTHWELL. £3,870.

7th Bishop, Rt. Rev. John Denis Wakeling, M.C., M.A. (Bishop's Manor, Southwell) [Signs Denis Southwell]....................1970

Bishop Suffragan.

Sherwood, Rt. Rev. Kenneth George Thompson, M.A. (Kneesall Vicarage, Newark)........1965
Asst. Bishop, Rt. Rev. Wilfrid Lewis Mark Way, M.A. (cons. 1952)........................1960
Provost, Very Rev. John Francis Isaac Pratt, M.A. 1970

Canons Residentiary

E. E. Roberts.....1969	C. S. Bayes, B.A...1970
H. A. Kirton, M.A..1970	

Organist, K. B. Beard.........................1959

Archdeacons

Newark, Ven. B. W. Woodhams, B.A. 1965
Nottingham, Ven. M. R. W. Brown, M.A....1960
Beneficed Clergy, 170 ; Curates, &c., 45.
Chancellor, B. T. Buckle, M.A...............1959
Registrar, P. H. Mellors....................1970

WAKEFIELD. £3,000.

8th Bishop, Rt. Rev. Eric Treacy, M.B.E. (Bishop's Lodge, Woodthorpe, Wakefield) (cons. 1961) [Signs Eric Wakefield]..................1968

Bishop Suffragan

Pontefract, Rt. Rev. Thomas Richard Hare, M.A. 1971
Asst. Bishops, Rt. Rev. Kenneth Graham Bevan (cons. 1940)........................1968
Rt. Rev. Victor George Shearburn, M.A. (cons. 1955).........................1967
Provost, Very Rev. Philip Norris Pare, M.A. ...1961

Archdeacons

Pontefract, Ven. E. C. Henderson, B.D........1968
Halifax, Ven. J. F. Lister, M.A.............1961

Organist, J. L. Bielby, M.A., F.R.C.O., MUS.B. ...1971
Beneficed Clergy, 212; Curates, &c., 44.
Chancellor, G. B. Graham, Q.C., LL.B.........1959
Registrar and Sec., C. E. Coles, M.A., Burton Street, Wakefield........................1963

The General Synod of the Church of England, Church House, Dean's Yard, S.W.1.—Presidents, The Archbishop of Canterbury; The Archbishop of York; Sec.-Gen., Sir John Guillum Scott, T.D., D.C.L. THE HOUSE OF BISHOPS.—Chairman, The Archbishop of Canterbury; Vice-Chairman, The Archbishop of York. THE HOUSE OF CLERGY.—Chairman, Rev. Preb. H. Riley; Vice-Chairman, The Dean of Chester. THE HOUSE OF LAITY.—Chairman, Prof. J. N. D. Anderson; Vice-Chairman, O. W. H. Clark.

THE CHURCH IN WALES

BANGOR. £2,100.

78th Bishop and 7th Archbishop of Wales, Rt. Rev. Gwllym Owen Williams, D.D., b. 1913. (Ty'r Esgob, Bangor, Caerns.), cons. 1957, elected Archbishop of Wales, 1971.

LLANDAFF. £2,675.

Bishop (vacant).

MONMOUTH. £2,940.

5th Bishop of Monmouth, Rt. Rev. Eryl Stephen Thomas, M.A., b. 1910 (Bishopstow, Stow Hill, Newport, Mon.).......................1968

ST. ASAPH. £2,100.

73rd Bishop, Rt. Rev. Harold John Charles, M.A., b. 1914 (The Palace, St. Asaph)...........1971

ST. DAVID'S. £2,675.

123rd Bishop, Rt. Rev. Eric Matthias Roberts, M.A., b. 1914 (The Palace, Abergwili, Carmarthen). 1971

SWANSEA AND BRECON £2,805

5th Bishop, Rt. Rev. John James Absalom Thomas, D.D., b. 1908 (Ely Tower, Brecon).........1958

BISHOPS ABROAD

CANADA

Acting Primate

The Archbishop of Algoma.

Sees.	Apptd.	Clgy.

Province of Canada.
The Most Rev. Archbishop.

Fredericton, Alexander Henry O'Neil b. 1907 (cons. 1957), Archbishop and Metropolitan........................1963 86

The Rt. Rev. Bishops.

Fredericton (see above).		
Montreal, R. K. Maguire, b. 1923.......1963		113
Newfoundland, R. L. Seaborn, b. 1911 (cons. 1958).........................1966		94
Nova Scotia, W. W. Davis, b. 1908 (cons. 1958).........................1963		123
Quebec, T. J. Matthews, b. 1907.......1971		50

Province of Rupert's Land.
The Most Rev. Archbishop.

Qu' Appelle, George Frederic Clarence Jackson, b. 1907 (Archbishop and Metropolitan) 1970.....................1960 63

The Rt. Rev. Bishops.

Arctic, D. B. Marsh, b. 1903...........1950		24
Athabasca, R. J. Pierce, b. 1909........1950		19
Brandon, T. W. Wilkinson, b. 1904......1969		36
Calgary, M. L. Goodman, b. 1917.......1967		61
Edmonton, W. G. Burch, b. 1911 (cons. 1960)........................1960		49
Keewatin, H. V. Stiff, b. 1916..........1969		19
Rupert's Land, B. Valentine, b. 1927 (cons. 1969).........................1970		63

Sees.	The Rt. Rev. Bishops.	Apptd.	Clgy.
Saskatchewan, H. V. R. Short 1970			30
Saskatoon, D. A. Ford...............1970			28

Province of Ontario.
The Most Rev. Archbishop.

Algoma, William Lockridge Wright, b. 1904 (cons. 1944), Archbishop and Metropolitan........................1955 79

The Rt. Rev. Bishops

Huron, C. J. Queen (cons. 1967)........1970		216
Bp. Suff., H. F. Appleyard.		
Moosonee, J. A. Watton, b. 1915........1963		29
Bp. Suff. (James Bay), N. R. Clarke.		
Niagara, W. E. Bagnall, b. 1903........1949		148
Asst. Bp., J. C. Bothwell............1971		
Ontario, J. B. Creggan..............1970		61
Ottawa, W. J. Robinson..............1970		85
Toronto, G. B. Snell (cons. 1956)........1966		327
Bps. Suff., H. R. Hunt; L. S. Garnsworthy.		

Province of British Columbia.
The Most Rev. Archbishop.

(vacant).

The Rt. Rev. Bishops

British Columbia, F. R. Gartrell, b. 1914...1970		55
Caledonia, D. W. Hambidge, b. 1927...1969		19
Cariboo, R. S. Dean, b. 1915 1957		14
Kootenay, E. W. Scott, b. 1919.........1966		31
New Westminster, T. D. Somerville, b. 1915 (cons. 1969)........................1971		85
Yukon, J. T. Frame, b. 1934.............1968		12

AUSTRALIA
Primate of Australia.
The Most Rev. Frank Woods, Archbishop of Melbourne, *b.* 1907, *cons.* 1952, *trs.* 1957. Elected Primate of Australia, 1971.

Sees.	Apptd.	Clgy.
Province of New South Wales.		
Archbishop and Metropolitan.		
Sydney, The Most Rev. Marcus Lawrence Loane, *b.* 1911 (*cons.* 1958)..........1966		302
Bps. Coadj., F. O. Hulme-Moir, *b.* 1910 (*cons.* 1953) (1964); A. J. Dain, *b.* 1912 (1964); H. G. S. Begbie, *b.* 1905 (1967); G. R. Delbridge, *b.* 1917 (1969).		
The Rt. Rev. Bishops.		
Armidale, R. C. Kerle, *b.* 1915 (*cons.* 1956)1965		43
Bathurst, E. K. Leslie, *b.* 1911..........1958		43
Canberra and Goulburn, (vacant)		63
Asst. Bp., C. A. Warren, *b.* 1924......1965		
Grafton, R. G. Arthur, *b.* 1909 (*cons.* 1956)........................1961		41
Newcastle, J. A. G. Housden, *b.* 1904 (*cons.* 1947).................1958		85
Asst. Bp., L. Stibbard, *b.* 1929.......1964		
Riverina (vacant).		
Province of Victoria.		
Archbishop and Metropolitan.		
Melbourne (*see* above).		319
Bps. Coadj., R. W. Dunn, *b.* 1914 (1969); J. A. Grant, *b.* 1931 (1970); C. B. Muston (*b.* 1927)..............1971		
The Rt. Rev. Bishops.		
Ballarat, W. A. Hardie, *b.* 1904........1960		60
Bendigo, R. E. Richards, *b.* 1908.......1957		31
Gippsland, D. A. Garnsey, *b.* 1909 1959		37
St. Arnaud. A. E. Winter, *b.* 1903......1951		26
Wangaratta, K. Rayner, *b.* 1929........1969		34
Province of Queensland		
Archbishop and Metropolitan.		
Brisbane The Most Rev. Felix Raymond Arnott, *b.* 1911 (*cons.* 1963) 1970		
Bp. Coadj., W. J. Hudson, *b.* 1904 (*cons.* 1950).................1960		
The Rt. Rev. Bishops.		
Carpentaria, E. E. Hawkey, *b.* 1909......1968		14
New Guinea, G. D. Hand, *b.* 1918 (*cons.* 1950)....................1963		16
Asst. Bps., G. Ambo (1960); B. S. Meredith, *b.* 1927 (1967); H. T. A. Kendall, *b.* 1905 (1968).		
N. Queensland (vacant)		30
Northern Territory, K. B. Mason, *b.* 1927 1968		
Rockhampton, D. N. Shearman, *b.* 1926..1964		
Province of Western Australia.		
Archbishop and Metropolitan.		
Perth, The Most Rev. Geoffrey Tremayne Sambell, *b.* 1914 (*cons.* 1962)......1969		125
Aux. Bps., T. B. Macdonald, O.B.E., (1964); A. C. Holland (1970).		
The Rt. Rev. Bishops.		
Bunbury, R. G. Hawkins, *b.* 1911 1957		34
Coadj. Bp., W. S. Bastian..........1968		
Kalgoorlie, D. W. Bryant...........1967		
N.W. Australia, H. A. J. Witt, *b.* 1920...1965		13
Extra-Provincial Dioceses.		
The Rt. Rev. Bishops.		
Adelaide, T. T. Reed, *b.* 1902.........1957		126
Murray, R. G. Porter, *b.* 1924.........1970		
Tasmania, R. E. Davies, *b.* 1913 (*cons.* 1960).....................1963		78
Willochra, S. B. Rosier, *b.* 1928 (*cons.* 1967)........................1970		19

PROVINCE OF NEW ZEALAND		
Archbishop and Primate.		
(Vacant).		
Sees.	Apptd.	Clgy.
The Rt. Rev. Bishops.		
Auckland, E. A. Gowing, *b.* 1913......1960		112
Asst. Bp., G. R. Monteith, *b.* 1904....1965		
Christchurch, W. A. Pyatt...........1966		112
Dunedin, W. W. Robinson, *b.* 1919....1969		42
Melanesia, J. W. Chisholm (*cons.* 1964)..1967		75
Asst. Bps., D. Tuti (1963); L. Alufurai, O.B.E. (1963)		
Nelson, P. E. Sutton, *b.* 1923..........1965		32
Polynesia, J. T. Holland, *b.* 1912 (*cons.* 1951)........................1969		
Bp. Suff. (*Naku' alofa*), F. T. Halapua, *b.* 1910......................1967		
Waiapu, P. A. Reeves, *b.* 1932........1971		65
Bp. Suff. (*Aoteroa*), M. A. Bennett, *b.* 1916.......................1968		
Waikato, A. H. Johnston, *b.* 1912 (*cons.* 1953)........................1970		42
Wellington, H. W. Baines, *b.* 1905 (*cons.* 1949)........................1960		116
Asst. Bp., G. M. McKenzie, O.B.E.....1962		
PROVINCE OF SOUTH AFRICA		
Archbishop and Metropolitan.		
Cape Town, The Most Rev. Robert Selby Taylor, *b.* 1909 (*cons.* 1941) 1964		141
Bp. Suff., S. W. Wade, *b.* 1909......1970		
The Rt. Rev. Bishops.		
Bloemfontein, F. A. Amoore, *b.* 1913....1967		
Damaraland, C. O'B. Winter, *b.* 1932...1968		23
George, P. H. F. Barron, *b.* 1911 (*cons.* 1964)......................1966		26
Grahamstown, B. B. Burnett, *b.* 1917 (*cons.* 1957).....................1969		
Johannesburg, L. E. Stradling, *b.* 1908 (*cons.* 1945)....................1961		140
Bp. Suff., J. S. Carter, *b.* 1927.....1968		
Asst. Bp., S. C. Pickard, C.B.E., *b.* 1910 (*cons.* 1958).................1968		
Kimberley & Kuruman, P. W. Wheeldon, O.B.E., *b.* 1913 (*cons.* 1954) 1967		
Lebombo, D. P. Cabral, *b.* 1924 (*cons.* 1967) 1968		
Lesotho, J. A. Arrowsmith Maund, *b.* 1909......................1950		36
Bp. Suff., F. Makhetha, *b.* 1916......1967		
Natal, T. G. V. Inman, *b.* 1904 1951		96
Bp. Suff., K. B. Hallowes, *b.* 1913....1969		
Port Elizabeth, P. W. R. Russell, *b.* 1919 (*cons.* 1966)..................1970		
Pretoria, E. G. Knapp-Fisher, *b.* 1915 ...1960		48
St. Helena, E. M. H. Capper, *b.* 1905....1967		4
St. John's, J. L. Schuster, *b.* 1912 1956		106
Bp. Suff., E. A. Sobukwe, *b.* 1908.....1969		
Swaziland, A. G. W. Hunter, *b.* 1916...1968		
Zululand, A. H. Zulu, *b.* 1905 (*cons.* 1961).1967		65
PROVINCE OF THE WEST INDIES		
Archbishop of West Indies		
Guyana, The Most Rev. Alan John Knight, C.M.G., *Archbp. & Metropolitan,* *b.* 1902 (*cons.* 1937) 1950		52
Bp. Suff. (*Stabroek*), P. E. R. Elder, *b.* 1923............................1966		
The Rt. Rev. Bishops		
Antigua, O. U. Lindsay.............1970		28
Barbados, E. L. Evans, *b.* 1904 (*cons.* 1957).1960		59
Honduras, (vacant)		9
Jamaica, J. C. E. Swaby, C.B.E., *b.* 1905 (*cons.* 1968)...................1968		
Bp. Suff. (*Kingston*), J. T. Clark......1966		

Sees.	Apptd.	Clgy.
Nassau and the Bahamas, B. Markham, *b.*		
1907....................1962	30	
Bp. Suff. (*New Providence*), M. H.		
Eldon....................1971		
Trinidad, C. O. Abdulah..........1970	40	
Bp. Suff., G. Marshall, M.B.E.........1966		
Windward Islds., E. C. M. Woodroffe..1969	22	

PROVINCE OF WEST AFRICA
Archbishop
Sierra Leone, The Most Rev. Moses Nathanial ChristopherOmobialaScott, C.B.E., *b.* 1911 (*cons.* 1961) *elected Archbp. of West Africa* 1969   42

The Rt. Rev. Bishops

Accra, I. S. M. LeMaire (*cons.* 1963).....1968	59	
Asst. Bps. K. A. Nelson (1966); J. B. Arthur (1966)		
Benin, A. Iwe........................1962	49	
Ekiti, J. A. Adetiloye................1970	37	
Enugu, G. N. Otubelu, *b.* 1927........1969		
Gambia and Rio Pongas (vacant)	6	
Ibadan, T. O. Olufosoye, *b.* 1918 (*cons.* 1965) 1970	116	
Asst. Bps., I. G. A. Jadesimi 1967		
Lagos, S. I. Kale, M.B.E................1963	94	
Asst. Bps., J. S. Adeniyi............1970		
The Niger, L. M. Uzodike (*cons.* 1961)..1969	87	
Niger Delta, A. A. Fubura............1971	62	
Asst. Bp., H. A. I. Afonya............1957		
Northern Nigeria, F. O. Segun..........1970	30	
Ondo, E. O. Idowu...................1971	65	
Owerri, B. C. Nwankiti (*cons.* 1968)....1969		

PROVINCE OF CENTRAL AFRICA
Archbishop
Southern Malawi, The Most Rev. Donald Seymour Arden, *b.* 1916 (*cons.* 1961) .1971
The Rt. Rev. Bishops
Central Zambia, J. Cunningham, *b.* 1922.1971
Lake Malawi, J. Mtekateka, *b.* 1903 (*cons.* 1965) 1971
Lusaka, F. Mataka, *b.* 1909 (*cons.* 1964)..1970
Mashonaland, J. P. Burrough, M.B.E., *b.* 1916........................1968
Matabeleland, S. M. Wood, *b.* 1919.....1971
Northern Zambia, J. Mabula, *b.* 1922....1971

PROVINCE OF KENYA
Archbishop
Nairobi, The Most Rev. Festo Habakkak Olang' (*cons.* 1965).................1970   27

The Rt. Rev. Bishops

Maseno North, J. Mundia 1970		
Maseno South, E. Agola (*cons.* 1965) 1970		
Mombasa, P. Mwang'ombe, *b.* 1918....1964	27	
Mount Kenya, O. Kariuki (*cons.* 1955)...1961	44	
Nakuru, N. Langford-Smith (*cons.* 1960).1961	42	
Asst. Bp., M. Kuria................1970		

PROVINCE OF TANZANIA
Archbishop
Dar es Salaam, The Most Rev. John Sepeku, *b.* 1907 (*cons.* 1963)..........1965

The Rt. Rev. Bishops
Central Tanganyika, Y. Medinda, *b.* 1926 (*cons.* 1964)....................1971
Masasi, H. G. Chisonga................1968
Morogoro, G. Chitemo................1965
Ruvuma, M. Ngahyoma...............1971

Sees.	Apptd.	Clgy.
South West Tanganyika, J. R. W. Poole-Hughes, *b.* 1916...................1962		
Asst. Bps., J. Mlele..............1965		
Victoria Nyanza, M. L. Wiggins (*cons.* 1959).........................1963		
Western Tanganyika, M. Kahurananga, *b.* 1921 (*cons.* 1962)................1969		
Zanzibar and Tanga, J. Jumaa..........1968		

PROVINCE OF UGANDA, RWANDA AND BURUNDI
Archbishop
Ruwenzori, The Most Rev. Erica Sabiti (*cons.* 1960)........................1961

Bishops
Ankole, A. Batungura.................1970
Burundi, Y. Nkunzumwami, (*cons.* 1965) .1966
Kigezi, R. E. Lyth...................1967
Madi and West Nile, S. G. Wani (*cons.* 1964)........................1969
Mbale, E. K. Masaba, M.B.E...........1964
Namirembe, D. K. Nsubuga (*cons.* 1964) .1965
Northern Uganda, J. Luwum...........1969
Rwanda, A. Sebununguri (*cons.* 1965)...1966
Soroti, A. Maraka....................1965
West Buganda, S. S. Tomusange (*cons.* 1952)........................1965

UNDER THE ARCHBISHOP OF CANTERBURY
The Rt. Rev. Bishops
Antananarivo, J. Marcel (*cons.* 1956).....1969
Argentina and E. S. America with the Falkland Is. C. J. Tucker, *b.* 1911.........1963
Bermuda, E. J. Trapp, *b.* 1910 (*cons.* 1947).1969
Chile, Bolivia and Peru (vacant)
  Asst. Bps., C. F. Bazley (1969); G. E. D. Pytches........................1971
Diego Suarez, G. Josoa (*cons.* 1957) 1969
Gibraltar, J. R. Satterthwaite, *b.* 1925....1970
Hong Kong, J. G. H. Baker, *b.* 1910.....1966
Kuching, B. Temengong...............1968
Mauritius, E. E. Curtis 1966
Paraguay, and North Argentina, J. W. H. Flagg.......................1969
  Asst. Bp., D. Leake.................1969
Sabah (vacant).
Seoul, P. Lee 1965
Singapore, Chiu Ban It................1966
Taejon, C. R. Rutt (*cons.* 1967)........1968
Tamatave, J. Seth (*cons.* 1963).........1968
West Malaysia, R. P. Koh, *b.* 1908 (*cons.* 1958)..........................1970
★ Shortly to become part of a new Province.

UNDER THE ARCHBISHOP IN JERUSALEM
Archbishop in Jerusalem, The Most Rev. George Appleton, M.B.E., *b.* 1902 (*cons.* 1961)....................1969
  Asst. Bp., A. K. Cragg, *b.* 1913.......1970

Bishops
Iran, H. B. Dehqani-Tafti............1961
Jordan, Lebanon and Syria, N. A. Cuba'in .1958
Sudan, O. C. Allison, C.B.E., *b.* 1908 (*cons.* 1948)........................1953
  Asst. Bps., E. J. Ngalamu (1963); Y. K. Dotiro (1963); B. T. Shukai (1970); B. W. Yugusuk.................1970

CHURCH OF ENGLAND ARCHBISHOPS AND BISHOPS WHO HAVE RESIGNED THEIR SEES OR SUFFRAGAN BISHOPRICS

	Cons.	Res.
G. F. Allen, *b.* 1902; *Derby*	1947	1968
D. H. N. Allenby, *b.* 1909; *Kuching*	1962	1969
W. L. Anderson, *b.* 1892; *Salisbury*	1937	1962
J. Armstrong, *b.* 1935; *Bermuda*	1963	1968
M. Armstrong, *b.* 1906; *Jarrow*	1958	1964
C. A. W. Aylen, *b.* 1882; *St. Helena*	1930	1939
W. S. Baker, *b.* 1902; *Zanzibar*	1943	1968
W. F. Barfoot, *b.* 1893; *Rupertsland*	1941	1958
F. R. Barry, *b.* 1890; *Southwell*	1941	1963
L. J. Beecher, *b.* 1906; *Nairobi*	1950	1970
S. W. Betts, *b.* 1912; *Maidstone*	1956	1966
K. G. Bevan, *b.* 1898; *E. Szechwan*	1940	1950
D. B. Blackwood, *b.* 1884; *Gippsland*	1942	1955
T. Bloomer, *b.* 1895; *Carlisle*	1946	1966
J. Boys, *b.* 1900; *Kimberley and Kuruman*	1948	1960
P. J. Brazier, *b.* 1903; *Ruanda-Urundi*	1951	1964
G. H. Brooks, *b.* 1905; *Honduras*	1950	1968
H. J. Buxton, *b.* 1880; *Gibraltar*	1933	1947
H. J. Carpenter, *b.* 1901; *Oxford*	1955	1970
P Carrington, *b.* 1892; *Quebec*	1935	1960
T. H. Cashmore, *b.* 1892; *Dunwich*	1955	1967
S. G. Caulton, *b.* 1895; *Melanesia*	1947	1953
F. N. Chamberlain, *b.* 1900; *Trinidad*	1957	1961
L. M. Charles-Edwards, *b.* 1902; *Worcester*	1956	1970
G. A. Chase, *b.* 1886; *Ripon*	1946	1959
N. H. Clarke, *b.* 1892; *Plymouth*	1950	1962
G. W. Clarkson, *b.* 1897; *Pontefract*	1954	1961
K. J. Clements, *b.* 1905; *Canberra and Goulburn*	1949	1971
G. E. I. Cockin, *b.* 1908; *Owerri*	1959	1969
W. R. Coleman, *b.* 1917; *Kootenay*	1961	1968
N. E. Cornwall, *b.* 1900; *Borneo*	1950	1963
G. F. Cranswick, *b.* 1894; *Tasmania*	1944	1960
D. H. Crick, *b.* 1885; *Chester*	1934	1955
C. E. Crowther, *b.* 1929; *Kimberley and Kuruman*	1965	1967
B. M. Dale, *b.* 1905; *Jamaica*	1950	1955
J. C. S. Daly, *b.* 1903; *Taejon*	1935	1967
J. H. Dickinson, *b.* 1901; *Melanesia*	1932	1937
J. H. Dixon, *b.* 1888; *Montreal*	1943	1962
Lord Fisher of Lambeth, *b.* 1887; *Canterbury*	1932	1961
W. L. S. Fleming, *b.* 1906; *Norwich*	1949	1971
R. Foskett, *b.* 1909; *Penrith*	1967	1970
J. Frewer, *b.* 1883; *N.W. Australia*	1929	1965
G. V. Gerard, *b.* 1898; *Waiapu*	1938	1944
W. P. Gilpin, *b.* 1902; *Kingston upon Thames*	1952	1970
H. R. Gough, *b.* 1905; *Sydney*	1948	1966
G. P. Gower, *b.* 1899; *New Westminster*	1951	1971
A. R. Graham-Campbell, *b.* 1903; *Colombo*	1948	1964
T. Greenwood, *b.* 1907; *Yukon*	1952	1961
W. D. L. Greer, *b.* 1902; *Manchester*	1947	1970
E. M. Gresford-Jones, *b.* 1901; *St. Albans*	1942	1969
R. O. Hall, *b.* 1895; *Hong Kong*	1932	1965
M. H. Harland, *b.* 1896; *Durham*	1942	1966
R. M. Hay, *b.* 1884; *Buckingham*	1944	1960
K Healey, *b.* 1899; *Grimsby*	1958	1965
G. E Holderness, *b.* 1913; *Burnley*	1955	1969
J. L. C. Horstead, *b.* 1898; *Sierra Leone*	1936	1961
F. Houghton, *b.* 1891; *E. Szechwan*	1937	1940
K. W. Howell, *b.* 1909; *Chile, Bolivia and Peru*	1963	1972
W. J. Hughes, *b.* 1894; *Trinidad*	1944	1970
L. S. Hunter, *b.* 1890; *Sheffield*	1939	1962
F. M. Jackson, *b.* 1902; *Trinidad*	1946	1949
T. S. Jones, *b.* 1872; *Hulme*	1930	1945
D. R. Knowles, *b.* 1898; *Antigua*	1953	1969
K. E. N. Lamplugh, *b.* 1901; *Southampton*	1951	1971

	Cons.	Res.
L. H. Lang, *b.* 1889; *Woolwich*	1936	1947
B. Lasbrey; *Niger*	1922	1945
W. Q. Lash, *b.* 1904; *Bombay*	1947	1961
T. Longworth, *b.* 1891; *Hereford*	1939	1961
D. G. Loveday, *b.* 1896; *Dorchester*	1957	1971
F. E. Lunt, *b.* 1900; *Stepney*	1957	1968
A. C. MacInnes, *b.* 1901; *Jerusalem*	1953	1968
G. L. G. Mandeville, *b.* 1894; *Barbados*	1951	1960
H. H. Marsh, *b.* 1899; *Yukon*	1962	1968
C. A. Martin, *b.* 1895; *Liverpool*	1944	1965
H. D. Martin, *b.* 1889; *Saskatchewan*	1939	1959
S. J. Matthews, *b.* 1900; *Carpentaria*	1960	1968
J. A. Meaden; *Newfoundland*	1956	1965
R. H. Moberly, *b.* 1884; *Stepney*	1936	1952
R. W. H. Moline, *b.* 1889; *Perth*	1947	1962
E. R. Morgan, *b.* 1888; *Truro*	1943	1959
A. H. Morris, *b.* 1898; *St. E. and Ipswich*	1949	1965
J. E. L. Mort, *b.* 1915; *N. Nigeria*	1952	1969
J. S. Moyes, *b.* 1884; *Armidale*	1929	1964
S. C. Neill, *b.* 1901; *Tinnevelly*	1939	1945
R. S. M. O'Ferrall, *b.* 1890; *Madagascar*	1926	1940
A. Otter, *b.* 1896; *Grantham*	1949	1965
T. R. Parfitt, *b.* 1911; *Madagascar*	1952	1961
C. G. St. M. Parker, *b.* 1900; *Bradford*	1954	1971
W. A. Parker, *b.* 1897; *Shrewsbury*	1959	1969
C. J. Patterson, *b.* 1908; *Niger*	1942	1969
B. W. Peacey, *b.* 1889; *Lebombo*	1929	1935
S. C. Pickard, *b.* 1910; *Lebombo*	1958	1968
H. G. Pigott, *b.* 1894; *Windward Islands*	1962	1969
St. J. S. Pike, *b.* 1909; *Gambia*	1958	1963
J. A. Ramsbotham, *b.* 1906; *Wakefield*	1950	1967
R. A. Reeves, *b.* 1899; *Johannesburg*	1949	1961
C. L. Riley, *b.* 1888; *Bendigo*	1938	1956
C. J. G. Robinson, *b.* 1903; *Bombay*	1947	1970
J. A. T. Robinson, *b.* 1919; *Woolwich*	1959	1969
R. R. Roseveare, *b.* 1902; *Accra*	1956	1968
J. K. Russell, *b.* 1916; *N. Uganda*	1955	1964
C. K. Sansbury, *b.* 1905; *Singapore*	1961	1966
D. N. Sargent, *b.* 1907; *Selby*	1962	1971
C. J. G. Saunders, *b.* 1888; *Lucknow*	1928	1938
D. H. Saunders-Davies, *b.* 1894; *Stockport*	1951	1965
G. D. Savage, *b.* 1915; *Southwell*	1960	1970
V. G. Shearburn, *b.* 1901; *Rangoon*	1955	1966
I. W. A. Shevill, *b.* 1917; *N. Queensland*	1953	1970
G. Sinker, *b.* 1900; *Nagpur*	1949	1954
K. J. F. Skelton, *b.* 1918; *Matabeleland*	1962	1970
G. D'O. Snow, *b.* 1903; *Whitby*	1961	1971
A. H. Sovereign, *b.* 1881; *Athabasca*	1932	1950
R. W. Stannard, *b.* 1895; *Woolwich*	1947	1959
A. Stanway, *b.* 1908; *Cent. Tanganyika*	1951	1971
C. E. Storrs, *b.* 1889; *Grafton*	1946	1955
C. E. Stuart, *b.* 1893; *Uganda*	1932	1952
W. J. Thompson, *b.* 1885; *Iran*	1935	1960
F. O. Thorne, *b.* 1892; *Nyasaland*	1936	1961
J. G. Tiarks, *b.* 1903; *Chelmsford*	1962	1971
G. W. R. Tobias, *b.* 1888; *Damaraland*	1939	1949
G. F. Townley, *b.* 1891; *Hull*	1957	1965
L. C. Usher-Wilson, *b.* 1903; *Mbale*	1936	1961
B. N. Y. Vaughan, *b.* 1917; *Honduras*	1961	1971
G. J. Walsh, *b.* 1880; *Hokkaido*	1927	1945
J. W. C. Wand, *b.* 1885; *London*	1934	1954
G. H. Warde, *b.* 1889; *Lewes*	1946	1959
A. K. Warren, *b.* 1900; *Christchurch*	1951	1966
R. H. Waterman, *b.* 1897; *Nova Scotia*	1948	1963
W. L. M. Way, *b.* 1905; *Masasi*	1952	1959
J. Wellington, *b.* 1890; *Shantung*	1940	1950
G. A. West, *b.* 1893; *Rangoon*	1935	1954
R. B. White, *b.* 1896; *Tonbridge*	1959	1967
A. L. E. Williams, *b.* 1892; *Bermuda*	1956	1962
F. R. Willis, *b.* 1900; *Delhi*	1951	1966
D. J. Wilson, *b.* 1903; *Trinidad*	1938	1956
L. H. Woolmer, *b.* 1906; *Lahore*	1949	1968

ECCLESIASTICAL COURTS

Judge, The Rt. Worshipful Walter Somerville Wigglesworth, Q.C., D.C.L.
[Judge of the Provincial Courts of Canterbury and York under " The Ecclesiastical Jurisdiction Measure, 1963."]

Court of Arches

Registry, 1 The Sanctuary, Westminster, S.W.1
Dean, The Rt. Worshipful Walter Somerville Wigglesworth, Q.C., D.C.L.
Registrar, D. M. M. Carey.

Court of Faculties

[Registry and Office for Marriage Licences (Special and Ordinary). Appointment of Notaries Public, &c., 1, The Sanctuary, Westminster, S.W.1 Office hours, 10 to 4; Saturdays, 10 to 12.]
Master, The Rt. Worshipful Walter Somerville Wigglesworth, Q.C., D.C.L.
Registrar, D. M. M. Carey.

Vicar General's Office,

for granting Marriage Licences for Churches in the Province of Canterbury, and COURT OF PECULIARS; 1 The Sanctuary, Westminster, S.W.1. Office hours, 10 to 4; Saturdays, 10 to 12. Closed on Sundays, Good Friday, Christmas Day, and Bank Holidays.
Vicar General & Chancellor, Sir Harold Kent, G.C.B.
Registrar, D. M. M. Carey.
Apparitor General, M. Saunders.
OFFICE OF THE VICAR GENERAL OF THE PROVINCE OF YORK.
Vicar General & Chancellor, The Rt. Worshipful Walter Somerville Wigglesworth, Q.C., D.C.L.
Registrar, G. P. Knowles.

Chancery Court of York.

Official Principal, The Rt. Worshipful Walter Somerville Wigglesworth, Q.C., D.C.L.
Registrar, G. P. Knowles.

THE CHURCH OF SCOTLAND
Church Office, 121 George Street, Edinburgh 2.

THE CHURCH OF SCOTLAND is Presbyterian in constitution, and is governed by Kirk Sessions, Presbyteries, Synods, and the General Assembly, which consists of both clerical and lay representatives from each of the Presbyteries. It is presided over by a Moderator (chosen annually by the Assembly), to whom Her Majesty the Queen has granted precedence in Scotland, during his term of office, next after the Lord Chancellor of Great Britain. The Sovereign, if not present in person, is represented by a Lord High Commissioner (appointed each year by the Crown), who receives up to £7,500 towards his expenses. The country, for Church purposes, is divided into 12 Synods and 59 Presbyteries, and there are about 2,000 ministers and licentiates engaged in ministerial and other work. There are now 63 Presbyteries in all, including: (1) The Presbytery of England and (2) the Presbyteries of (a) Northern Europe. (b) Southern Europe, (c) Spain and Portugal. The figures at Dec. 31, 1968, were:—

Congregations, 2,115: total membership 1,201,933. In 21 Overseas Mission fields, there are 220 European missionaries (and in addition many missionaries' wives, most of whom are doing mission work in the various fields).
LORD HIGH COMMISSIONER (1971–72), The Lord Clydesmuir, C.B., M.B.E., T.D.
MODERATOR OF THE ASSEMBLY (1971–72), Right Rev. A. Herron, M.A., B.D., LL.B.
Principal Clerk, Very Rev. J. B. Longmuir, T.D., D.D., M.A., B.L.
Deputy Clerk, Rev. A. G. McGillivray, M.A., B.D.
Procurator, W. R. Grieve, Q.C.
Law Agent and Solicitor of the Church, R. A. Paterson, M.A., LL.B.
Parliamentary Solicitor, Colin McCulloch (London).
General Treasurer, W. G. P. Colledge, C.A.

Other Presbyterian Churches

(1) *The Presbyterian Church in Ireland.*—The largest of the Presbyterian churches in Ireland consists of 22 presbyteries, 477 ministers, 566 congregations, with 142,498 communicants, 131,504 families and 7,501 Sabbath-school teachers. During the 12 months ended Dec. 31, 1969, this branch contributed by congregational effort £290,293 for religious, charitable, and missionary purposes. The total income for the period raised by congregations for all purposes was £2,148,328—Moderator (1971–72), Rt. Rev. F. R. Gibson; *General Sec.,* Rev. A. J. Weir, M.SC., B.D., Church House, Belfast, 1.

(2) *The Presbyterian Church of England* has 14 presbyteries, 308 congregations, 23 preaching stations, 59,473 members, and 8,512 office-bearers. It has a Theological College (Westminster College, Cambridge), and supports 21 missionaries abroad, including 10 women. In 1970 the amount raised for all purposes was £1,088,641.
Moderator (1971–72), Rt. Rev. A. L. Macarthur, M.A., M.Litt.; *General Sec.,* Rt. Rev. A. L. Macarthur, M.A., M.Litt., Church House, 86 Tavistock Place, W.C.1.

THE EPISCOPAL CHURCH IN SCOTLAND

Sees.	THE RT. REV. BISHOPS.	Cons.	Clgy.	Stipd.
Aberdeen and Orkney, Edward				
Frederick Easson, D.D., *b.* 1905	1956.	32	£*1,600	
Argyll and the Isles, Richard				
Knyvet Wimbush, M.A., *b.*				
1909	1963.	12	*1,900	
Brechin, John Chappell Sprott,				
D.D., M.A., *b.* 1903	1959.	21	*1,485	
Edinburgh, Kenneth Moir				
Carey, D.D., M.A., *b.* 1908	1961	.76	*2,578	

Sees.	THE RT. REV. BISHOPS.	Cons.	Clgy.	Stipd.
Glasgow and Galloway, Francis				
Hamilton Moncreiff, M.A.				
(*Most Rev. Primus,* 1962). *b.*				
1907	1952.	.71	£*2,250	
Moray, Ross and Caithness, George				
Minshull Sessford, M.A., *b.* 1931				
	1970.	.18	*1,950	
St. Andrews, Dunkeld and				
Dunblane, Michael Geoffrey				
Hare-Duke, M.A., *b.* 1925	1969.	.37	*1,800	

* With residence.

Registrar of the Episcopal Synod, I. R. Guild, W.S., 16 Charlotte Square, Edinburgh, 2.
Churches, Mission Stations, &c., 348. Clergy, 312. Communicants, 48,967.

THE CHURCH OF IRELAND

Sees	ARCHBISHOPS	Appointed	Clergy
Armagh*	Most Rev. George Otto Simms, D.D., Ph.D., *b.* 1910 (*cons.* 1952)	1969	63
Dublin	Most Rev. Alan Alexander Buchanan, M.A., D.D., *b.* 1907 (*cons.* 1958)	1970	97

	BISHOPS		
Meath	Most Rev. Robert Bonsall Pike, M.A., D.D., *b.* 1905	1959	23
Cashel	Rt. Rev. John Ward Armstrong, B.D., *b.* 1915	1969	13
Clogher	Rt. Rev. Richard Patrick Crossland Hanson, M.A., D.D., *b.* 1916	1970	41
Connor	Rt. Rev. Arthur Hamilton Butler, M.B.E., D.D., *b.* 1912 (*cons.* 1958)	1970	126
Cork, Cloyne & Ross	Rt. Rev. Richard Gordon Perdue, D.D., *b.* 1910 (*cons.* 1954)	1957	44
Derry & Raphoe	Rt. Rev. Cuthbert Irvine Peacocke, M.A., *b.* 1903	1970	73
Down & Dromore	Rt. Rev. George Alderson Quin, M.A.	1970	118
Killaloe	Rt. Rev. Henry Arthur Stanistreet, D.D., *b.* 1901	1957	20
Kilmore	Rt. Rev. Edward Francis Butler Moore, D.D., Ph.D., *b.* 1906	1958	39
Limerick	Rt. Rev. Donald Arthur Richard Caird, B.D., *b.* 1925	1970	16
Ossory	Rt. Rev. Henry Robert McAdoo, Ph.D., D.D., *b.* 1916	1962	47
Tuam	Rt. Rev. John Coote Duggan, B.D.	1970	16

* *Primate.*

St. Patrick's National Cathedral, Dublin. *Dean and Ordinary*, Very Rev. V. G. B. Griffin, Ph.D., B.A.

Chief Officer and Secretary to the Representative Church Body, D. W. Pratt, Church of Ireland House, Upper Rathmines, Dublin 6.

THE METHODIST CHURCH

Under the general designation of Methodists are included all those religious bodies which owe their existence, directly or indirectly, to the efforts of the Revd. John Wesley (*born* June 17, 1703; *died* March 2, 1791) and his brother, Revd. Charles Wesley (*born* Dec. 18, 1707; *died* March 29, 1788).

On September 20, 1932, the separate Methodist Churches were united and became "The Methodist Church." (*see* below).

The Methodist Church is governed primarily by the Conference, secondarily by the District Synods (held in September and May), consisting of all the ministers and of selected laymen in each district, over which a chairman is appointed by the Conference; and thirdly by circuit quarterly meeting of the ministers and lay officers of each circuit. The authority of both Synods and Quarterly Meetings is subordinate to the Conference, which has the supreme legislative and judicial power in Methodism.

President of the Conference (July, 1971–72), Rev. K. L. Waights.

Vice-President of the Conference (July, 1971–72), J. W. Kellaway.

Secretary of the Conference, Rev. K. G. Greet, D.D., 1 Central Buildings, Westminster, S.W.1.

President Designate (1972–73), Rev. H. O. Morton, M.A.

Vice-President Designate (1972–73), Dr. H. Souster.

Statistics.—In 1969 in association with the Conference in Great Britain (at home and in overseas Districts) there were 4,167 Ministers, 20,244 Local Preachers, 759,128 Members and Probationers, and 9,948 Churches.

The *World Methodist Council*, founded 1881, re-organized 1951, associates Methodism throughout the world in 82 countries.

The Methodist Church was founded in 1739 by the two brothers Wesley and rapidly spread throughout the British Isles and to America before 1770. The Methodist Church in Great Britain was united in 1932 by the fusion of the Wesleyan Methodist Church which was the original section, the Primitive Methodist Church, which arose through the evangelists Hugh Bourne and William

Clowes in 1810, and the United Methodist Church, itself a fusion in 1907 of the Methodist New Connexion which dated from 1797, the Bible Christian Methodist Church, which dated from 1815 and the United Methodist Free Churches which originated in controversies in 1828 and 1849. The United Methodist Church of America was formed by a union of United Methodist denominations with the United Evangelical Brethren.

Methodist Church in Ireland

The Methodist Church in Ireland has 231 Ministers, 311 Lay Preachers, 28,089 Adult and 19,124 Junior Members.

President (1971–72), Rev. C. H. Bain, B.D.

Secretary, Rev. H. Sloan, 3 Upper Malone Road, Belfast, 9.

The United Church of Canada

The United Church of Canada is the result of the union (1925) of Methodist, Presbyterian and Congregational Churches in Canada. *Sec. of General Council*, Rev. Ernest E. Long, B.A., D.D., LL.D., The United Church House, 85 St. Clair E., Toronto.

Independent Methodists

Independent Methodists.—This body is Congregational in its organization, with an unpaid Ministry. Its first Conference was held in 1805. In 1971 there were in Great Britain 208 Ministers, 6,449 Members, 142 Chapels and 6,563 Sunday School scholars. *Secretary*, D. S. Downing, 55 Toothill Road, Loughborough, Leics.

Wesleyan Reform Union

This Union is Methodist in doctrine, Congregational in government, with, if any church desires it, a paid ministry. It is the remnant of the original Reformers expelled from Wesleyan Methodism in 1849. The adherents are mainly in the Midland and Northern counties. In 1971 there were in Great Britain 24 Ministers, 248 Lay Preachers, 4,696 Members, 154 Chapels and 5,574 Sunday scholars.—*President* (1971–72), R. Sowerby, Barnsley, Yorks. *General Secretary and Connexional Editor*, Rev. A. Halladay, Wesleyan Reform Church House, 123 Queen Street, Sheffield 1.

THE CALVINISTIC METHODIST CHURCH OF WALES

The Calvinistic Methodist or Presbyterian Church of Wales is the only Church of purely Welsh origin, and embraces a very large section of the Welsh-speaking population. Its form of

government being Presbyterian, it is a constituent of the Pan-Presbyterian Council or Alliance. It is also a member of the British Council of Churches and the World Council of Churches. It has

a mission in India.

In 1970 the body numbered—chapels and other buildings, 1,328; ministers in pastoral charge, 346; elders, 6,328; communicants 108,064; Sunday-school scholars 46,675. Contributions for various religious purposes (including the ministry), £1,190,771.

One of the features of the Welsh churches is the Sunday-school, which is attended by adults as well as children.

The *Eastern Association* which now includes nine of the English Presbyteries, was formed in 1947.

Moderator of General Assembly (1971–72), Rev. T. B. Phillips, B.A., B.D., Colwyn Bay.

Moderator of Associations (1971–1972) *South Wales*, Rev. V. Thomas, B.A., Bow Street, Cardiganshire; *North Wales*, R. G. Pritchard, Abergele; *The East*, Rev. J. H. Hughes, B.A., Pontypridd.

Chief Secretary, Rev. W. D. Jones, B.A., 32 Carstairs Road, Liverpool 6.

THE INDEPENDENTS AND THE BAPTISTS

The INDEPENDENTS, or CONGREGATIONALISTS, are the most ancient community of Dissenters. In 1831 the majority of their churches united to form the Congregational Union of England and Wales, incorporated in 1902, and in 1920 nine provinces were formed, each with a Moderator. There are 31 county and other Associations in England and Wales, with 2,386 churches and preaching stations with 1,683 ministers and 181,101 members. The Congregational Church in England and Wales was formed in 1966. *President of the Congregational Church of England and Wales* (1971–72), Rev. C. S. Duthie, M.A., D.D. *Minister Secretary*, Rev. J. Huxtable, M.A., Livingstone House, 11 Carteret Street, S.W.1.

THE CONGREGATIONAL UNION OF SCOTLAND. In 1795 James and Robert Haldane left the Church of Scotland and the churches which they founded formed the *Congregational Union* in 1812, which in 1896 united with the *Evangelical Union* (founded in 1843 by James Morison). There are 119 Churches of the *Congregational Union of Scotland* with a membership of 25,284. Of the 138 Ministers, 89 are Pastors. *President*, J. K. Melville. *Secretary*, Rev. R. Waters, 215 West George Street, Glasgow, C.2.

The BAPTISTS have over 31,000,000 members in all countries. In Britain they are for the most part grouped in associations of churches, and the majority of these belong to the Baptist Union, which was formed in 1812–13. In the British Isles there were, in 1970, 2,090 pastors and deaconesses. The members numbered 269,315, young people (14–20), 54,341, juveniles (under 14) 197,326. *President of the Baptist Union of Great Britain and Ireland* (1971–72), Dr. G. Henton Davies. *Secretary*, Rev. D. S. Russell. *Office*, 4 Southampton Row, W.C.1.

THE JEWS

It is estimated that about 450,000 Jews are resident in the British Isles, some 280,000 being domiciled in Greater London.

The *Board of Deputies of British Jews*, established in 1760, is the representative body of British Jewry and is recognized by H.M. Government. The basis of representation is mainly synagogal, but secular organizations are also represented. It is a deliberative body and its objects are to watch over the interests of British Jewry, to protect Jews against any disability which they may suffer by reason of their creed and to take such action as may be conducive to their welfare.

President (Woburn House, Upper Woburn Place, W.C.1), M. M. Fidler, M.P.

Secretary, A. I. Marks.

CHIEF RABBI—The Very Rev. I. Jakobovits, Ph.D. *Executive Director* Rabbi M. Rose, *Office*, Adler House, Tavistock Square, W.C.1.

The *Beth Din* (Court of Judgment) is a rabbinic body consisting of *Dayanim* (Assessors) and the Chief Rabbi, who is President of the Court. The Court arbitrates when requested in cases between Jew and Jew and gives decisions on religious questions. The decisions are based on Jewish Law and practice and do not conflict with the law of the land. The *Beth Din* also deals with matters concerning dietary laws and marriages and divorces, according to Jewish Law.

Dayanim. L. Grossnass; A. Rapoport; Dr. M. Lew; M. Swift.

Clerk to the Court, Marcus Carr, Adler House, Tavistock Square, W.C.1

OTHER RELIGIOUS DENOMINATIONS

The General Assembly of Unitarian and Free Christian Churches has about 226 ministers, 330 chapels and other places of worship in Great Britain and Ireland. *Gen. Sec.*, Rev. B. L. Golland, Essex Hall, Essex Street, W.C.2.

The Salvation Army, first known as the Christian Mission, was founded by William Booth, in the East End of London in 1865. In 1878 it took its present name and adopted a quasi-military method of government. Since then it has become established in over 70 countries of the world. The head of the denomination, known as the General, is elected by a High Council, consisting of all the Commissioners of the Army. In 1969 there were, in Great Britain, 1,035 Corps (Churches), 2,728 Officers engaged in evangelistic work and 53,353 Local Officers (lay workers). The latest statistics for the world (1970) are 16,044 Corps and 25,069 Officers. *General*, Erik Wickberg.

International Headquarters:—101 Queen Victoria Street, E.C.4.

The Brethren number about 80,000, of whom five-eighths belong to the "Open" body.

The Society of Friends (Quakers) consists of 20,752 members in Great Britain, and has 435 places of worship (*Recording Clerk*, Arthur J. White).

The total number in the world is about 197,000 (121,000 are in U.S.A. and Canada). *Central Offices* (*Great Britain*), Friends House, Euston Road, N.W.1. (*Ireland*), 6 Eustace Street, Dublin.

The First Church of Christ, Scientist, in Boston, Massachusetts, U.S.A. (District Manager, Committees on Publication for Great Britain and Ireland, Ingersoll House, 9 Kingsway, W.C.2), has 315 branch churches and societies in Great Britain and Ireland.

The Moravian Church, 5 Muswell Hill, N.10, has in the U.K. 40 congregations and preaching stations, with 2,838 communicants.

The Free Church of England (otherwise called The Reformed Episcopal Church) has 33 churches in England. *Gen. Sec.*, Rt. Rev. W. C. Watkins, 16 Waldron Road, Broadstairs, Kent.

The Seventh Day Adventists (*Hdqrs.*, Stanborough Park, Watford, Herts.), have 138 organized churches, 49 companies and 12,145 members in the British Isles.

At Woking, Surrey, is the Shah Jehan Mosque for Moslems, the first in Great Britain, built in 1889. There are also Mosques at Southfields, S.W.18, Commercial Road, E.1, Birmingham, Manchester, Cardiff, Newcastle upon Tyne, South Shields, Coventry and Glasgow.

THE ROMAN CATHOLIC CHURCH

HIS HOLINESS POPE PAUL VI (Giovanni Battista Montini), Roman Pontiff, *born* in Concesio, Italy, September 26, 1897; *ordained priest* May 29, 1920; nominated *Archbishop* of Milan, November 1, 1954; *Cardinal*, December 15, 1958; *elected Pope* June 21, 1963; *crowned* June 30, 1963.

THE SACRED COLLEGE OF CARDINALS, when complete, consisted of six Cardinal Bishops, fifty Cardinal Priests and fourteen Cardinal Deacons. This number was fixed by Pope Sixtus V in 1586. Pope John XXIII created 52 new Cardinals. The present Pope created 27 new Cardinals on Feb. 22, 1965, 27 on June 26, 1967, and a further 33 on Apr. 28, 1969. In July 1971 there were 123 Cardinals. The Cardinals are advisers and assistants of the Sovereign Pontiff and form the supreme council or Senate of the Church. On the death of the Pope they elect his successor. The assembly of the Cardinals at the Vatican for the election of a new Pope is known as the Conclave in which, in complete seclusion, the Cardinals elect by secret ballot; a two-thirds majority is necessary before the vote can be accepted as final. When a Cardinal receives the necessary votes the Dean of the Sacred College formally asks him if he will accept election and the name by which he wishes to be known. On his acceptance of the office the Conclave is dissolved and the First Cardinal Deacon announces the election to the assembled crowd in St. Peter's Square. On the first Sunday or Holyday following the election the new Pope is crowned with the tiara, the triple crown, the symbol of his supreme spiritual authority. A new pontificate is dated from the coronation.

FORMS OF ADDRESS: *Cardinal*, " His Eminence Cardinal ... " (if an Archbishop, " His Eminence the Cardinal Archbishop of ... "); *Archbishop*, " The Most Rev. Archbishop of ... "; *Bishop*, " The Rt. Rev. the Bishop of ... "

ENGLAND AND WALES

Apostolic Delegate to Gt. Britain and Gibraltar, The Most Rev. Domenico Enrici

The Most Revd. Archbishops CONS. CLERGY*

Westminster, H.E. Cardinal John Heenan (1963)..................................1951	956
Auxil., Basil Christopher Butler....1966	
Auxil., Victor Guazzelli.............1970	
Auxil., Gerald Mahon 1970	
Birmingham, George Dwyer (1966)....1959	636
Auxil. Joseph Cleary...............1966	
Auxil. Anthony Emery...............1968	
Cardiff, John A. Murphy (1961) 1948	187
Auxil. Daniel Mullins..............1970	
Liverpool, Andrew Beck (1964).......1948	664
Auxil. Augustine Harris............1966	
Auxil. Joseph Gray................1969	
Southwark, Cyril Cowderoy 1949	556

The Rt. Revd. Bishops

Arundel and Brighton, Michael Bowen (1971).............................1970	366
Brentwood, Patrick Casey (1970)......1966	207
Clifton, Joseph Rudderham 1949	275
Hexham and Newcastle, James Cunningham (1958)....................1957	398
Auxil., H. Lindsay................1970	
Lancaster, Brian C. Foley 1962	273
Auxil., Thomas Pearson 1949	
Leeds, Gordon Wheeler 1964	372
Auxil. Gerald Moverley............1968	
Menevia (Wales), John E. Petit......1947	195
Auxil.. Langton Fox 1965	
Middlesbrough, John McClean........1967	234
Northampton, Charles Grant.........1961	269
Auxil. Alan Clark 1969	
Nottingham, Edward Ellis...........1944	299
Plymouth, Cyril Restieaux..........1955	228
Portsmouth, Derek Worlock..........1965	309
Salford, Thomas Holland, D.S.C. (1964).1961	527
Auxil. Geoffrey Burke.............1967	
Shrewsbury. William Eric Grasar.....1962	245

SCOTLAND

The Most Revd. Archbishops

St. Andrews & Edinburgh, H.E. Cardinal Gordon Gray...........................1951	262
Auxil., James Monaghan..........1970	
Glasgow, James D. Scanlan (1964) 1946	393
Auxil., James Ward...............1960	

The Rt. Revd. Bishops

Aberdeen, Michael Foylan 1965	75
Argyll & Isles, Colin MacPherson 1969	35
Dunkeld, William Hart..............1955	107
Galloway, Joseph McGee.............1952	86

Motherwell, Francis Thomson........1965	193
Paisley, Stephen McGill (1969).......1960	105

NORTHERN IRELAND†

The Most Revd. Archbishop

CONS. CLERGY.

Armagh, H.E. Cardinal William Conway (1963)...............................1958	275

The Rt. Revd. Bishops

Clogher, Patrick Mulligan 1969	147
Derry, Neil Farren 1939	149
Down & Connor, William Philbin 1962	341
Dromore, Eugene O'Doherty.........1944	81
Kilmore. Austin Quinn..............1950	139

BRITISH COMMONWEALTH

Europe

CONS.

The Most Revd. Archbishop

Malta, Michael Gonzi, K.B.E. (1943)	1924

The Rt. Revd. Bishops

Gozo, Joseph Pace.................	1944
Gibraltar, John F. Healy, C.B.E.............	1956

America

Pro-Nuncio to Canada, Most Rev. Guido Del Mestri (*Archbishop* of *Tuscamia*).

The Most Revd. Archbishops CONS.

Edmonton, Anthony Jordan (1964).........	1945
Halifax, James Martin Hayes (1967).........	1965
Kingston, Joseph L. Wilhelm (1967)	1963
Moncton, Norbert Robichaud.........	1942
Montreal, Paul Gregoire................	1968
Ottawa, Joseph A. Plourde (1967)	1964
Port of Spain, Anthony Pantin.............	1967
Quebec, H.E. Cardinal Maurice L. Roy, O.B.E. (1947)..............................	1946
Regina, Michael C. O'Neill.............	1948
Rimouski, Abp. Louis Levesque (1967)	1944
St. Boniface, Maurice Baudoux (1955).......	1948
*St. John's,Newfoundland,*Patrick Skinner(1951)	1950
Sherbrooke, John Fortier (1968).........	1962
Toronto, H.E. Cardinal James McGuigan (1934)................................	1930
Coadj-Abp., Philip F. Pocock (1961)	1951
Vancouver, B.C., James F. Carney (1969)...	1966
Winnipeg, Cardinal George Flahiff (1961)	1961
Winnipeg (Byzantine Rite), Maxim Hermaniuk (1956)......................	1951

* In addition there are 73 priests serving as regular chaplains in H.M. Forces. The Right Rev. Gerard Tickle, *Bp.* of *Bela,* was appointed Bishop-in-Ordinary to H.M. Forces in 1963.

† There is one hierarchy for the whole of Ireland. Several of the Dioceses listed above have territory partly in the Republic of Ireland and partly in Northern Ireland.

CONS.

The Rt. Revd. Bishops

Alexandria, Adolphe Proulx............	1967
Amos, Gaston Hains (1969)............	1964
Antigonish, William Power..	1960
Bahamas, Leonard Hagarty............	1950
Bathurst in Canada, Edgar Godin	1969
Belize, Robert Hodapp................	1958
Bermuda Islands, Bernard Murphy....	1967
Calgary, Paul J. O'Byrne............	1968
Castries, B.W.I., Charles Gachet......	1957
Charlottetown, Francis John Spence....	1970
Chicoutimi, Mario Paré......	1956
Churchill, Omer Robidoux............	1970
Edmundston, Fernand Lacroix........	1970
Edmonton (Byzantine Rite), Nicholas Savaryn (1943).........................	1956
Fort William, Norman Gallagher......	1970
Gaspé, Giles Ouellet..................	1968
Georgetown, Richard Guilly, O.B.E. (1956)..	1954
Gravelbourg, Aimé Decosse...........	1953
Grouard, Henry Routhier, (1953)......	1945
Gulf of St. Lawrence, Gerard Couturier......	1957
Hamilton, Joseph Ryan...............	1937
Harbour Grace-Grand Falls, John M. O'Neill.	1940
Hearst, Jacques Landriault (1964)......	1962
Hull, Paul Charbonneau (1963)........	1961
James Bay, Justin A. Driscoll........	1970
Joliette, René Audet (1968)...........	1963
Kamloops, B.C., Michael A. Harrington..	1952
Keewatin, Paul Dumouchel...........	1955
Kingston (Jamaica), Samuel Carter (1970)	1966
Labrador, Henri Legare.............	1968
London, Gerald Carter (1964)........	1962
Mackenzie, Paul Piché (1967)........	1959
Moononee, Jules Leguerrier (1967)......	1964
Mont Laurier, Joseph Ouellette (1957)..	1965
Montego Bay, Edgerton Clarke........	1967
Nelson, William Doyle..............	1958
Nicolet, Albert Martin...............	1950
Pembroke, William Smith............	1945
Peterboro', Anthony Marrocco (1968)......	1956
Prince Albert, Lawrence Morin (1959).......	1955
Prince George, Fergus J. O'Grady...........	1956
Roseau (Dominica), Arnold Boghaert......	1957
St. Anne de la Pocatière, Charles Lévesque (1968)	1965
St. Catharines, Thomas J. McCarthy (1958)..	1955
St. George's, N.F., Richard McGrath......	1970
St. George's (Grenada), Patrick Webster	1969
St. Hyacinthe, Albert Sanschagrin......	1967
St. Jean de Quebec, Gerard Coderre (1955)....	1951
St. Jerome, Emil Frenette.............	1951
St. John in Canada, Joseph MacNeill......	1969
St. Paul in Alberta, Edward Gagnon......	1969
Saskatoon, James P. Mahoney........	1967
Saskatoon (Byzantine Rite), Andrew Roborecki (1956).....................	1948
Sault Ste. Marie, Alexander Carter (1958)..	1957
Timmins, Maxim Tessier (1955)........	1951
Toronto (Byzantine Rite), Isidore Borecky (1956)............................	1948
Trois Rivières, Georges L. Pelletier (1947)..	1943
Valleyfield, Guy Belanger............	1969
Victoria, B.C., Remi De Roo........	1962
Whitehorse, J. Mulvihill, O.M.I........	1965
Yarmouth, Austin Burke............	1968

Africa

EAST AFRICA: *Pro-Nuncio to Uganda*, Most Rev. Luigi Bellotti; *Pro-Nuncio to Malawi and Zambia*, Most Rev. Luciano Angeloni; *Pro-Nuncio to Kenya*, Most Rev. Pierluigi Satorelli; *Pro-nuncio to Tanzania*, Franco Brambilla.

WEST CENTRAL AFRICA: Most Rev. Amelio Poggio.

WEST AFRICA: Most Rev. John Mariani.

CONS.

The Most Revd. Archbishops

Blantyre, James Coina (1967)............	1965
Cape Coast, John Kodwo Amissah (1960) ..	1957
Dar-es-Salaam, H.E. Cardinal Laurence Rugambwa (1969)..................	1952
Freetown and Bo, Thomas Brosnahan........	1953
Kaduna, John McCarthy (1959)...........	1954
Kampala, Emmanuel Nsubuga 1967)......	1966
Kasama, Clement Chabukasansha (1967).....	1963
Lagos, John Aggey (1966)	1957
Lusaka, Emmanuel Milingo.............	1969
Nairobi, John McCarthy (1953).........	1946
Onitsha, Francis Aringe (1967)........	1965
Salisbury, Francis Markall............	1956
Tabora, Mark Mihayo................	1960

The Rt. Revd. Bishops

Accra, Joseph Bowers	1953
Arua, Angelo Tarantino...............	1959
Arusha, Denis Durning...............	1963
Baifra, Andrea Loucher...............	1968
Bathurst in Gambia, Michael Molony, C.B.E..	1959
Benin City, Patrick J. Kelly (1950)........	1940
Botswana, Urban Murphy, C.P.........	1966
Buea, Guilo Peeters	1962
Bukoba, Gervasio Nkalanga	1969
Bulawayo. Adolf Schmitt (1953)........	1951
Calabar, Brian Usanga (1970).........	1969
Chikwawa, Franz Vroemen, S.M.M.......	1965
Chipata, Medardo Mazombwe	1970
Dedza, Cornelius Citsulo (1959)........	1957
Dodoma, Anthony Pesce (1953)........	1951
Eldoret, Joseph Njenga	1970
Enugu, Godfrey Okoye (1970).........	1961
Fort Portal, Vincent McCauley	1961
Gulu, Cipriano Kihangire (1969).......	1963
Gwelo, Louis Haene (1955)...........	1950
Hoima, Edward Barhgarate	1969
Ibadan, Richard Finn	1959
Ijebu-Ode, Antonio Sansusi	1969
Ikotepene, Dominie Ekandem (1954)......	1963
Ilorin, William Mahony	1969
Iringa, Mario Mgulunde	1970
Jinja, Joseph Willigers	1967
Jos, John Redington	1954
Kabale, Barnabas Halem' Imana	1969
Kanema, Joseph Ganda	1970
Keta, Antony Konings	1954
Kigoma, Alphonse Nsabi	1969
Kisii, Tiberio Mugendi	1969
Kisumu, John de Reeper (1965)........	1964
Kitui, William Dunne...............	1964
Kumasi, Peter Sapong	1970
Lilongwe, Joseph Fady (1959)..........	1951
Lira, Caesar Asili (1968).............	1969
Livingstone, Phelim O'Shea (1959)	1950
Lodwar, John Mahon (Pref.-Ap.)	
Lokoja, A. Delisle C.S.Sp.............	1964
Machakos, Raphael Ndingi	1969
Mahenge, Nikasius Kipengele	1970
Maiduguri, Timothy Cotter, O.S.A.	1966
Makeni, Augusto Azzolini	1962
Makurdi, Donal Murray, C.S.Sp.......	1968
Mansa, René Pailloux (1968)	1961
Marsabit, Charles Cavallero	1964
Masaka, Adrian Ddungu	1962
Mbala, Adolf Furstenberg (1968).......	1959
Mbarara, John Kakubi	1969
Mbeya, James Sangu	1966
Mbulu, Patrick Winters (1953)	1952
Meru, Laurence Bessone	1954
Mombasa, Eugene Butler	1957
Monze, James Corboy	1962
Minna, Edmund Fitzgibbon (Pref.-Ap.)	
Morogoro, Adrian MKoba.............	1967
Moroto, Sisto Mazgoldi (1967)........	1966
Moshi, Joseph Sipendi................	1967

CONS.

Musoma, John Rudin.................... 1957
Mwanza, Renatus Lwamosa
Mzuzu, Jean Jobidon.................... 1961
Nachingwea, Arnold Coty 1963
Nakuru, Desmond Newman (*Ap.-Admin.*)...
Navrongo, Gerard Bertrand (1957) 1948
Ndanda, Victor Haelg (1961)............ 1949
Ndola, Nicola Agnozzi O.F.M. Conv. (1966) . 1962
Nyeri, *Kenya*, Caesar Gatimu (1964) 1961
Ngong, Colin Davies (*Pref.-Ap.*) ....
Njombe, Bruno Zwissler (*Ap. Admin.*)......
Ogoja, Thomas McGettrick.............. 1955
Ondo, William Field.... 1958
Oweri, Mark Unegbu.................... 1970
Oyo, Owen McCoy 1963
Port Harcourt (vacant)
Port Louis, Jean Margéot................ 1969
Port Victoria, Marcel Maradan, C.B.E........ 1937
Qacha's Nek, Joseph des Rosiers, O.M.I. (1951) 1948
Rulenge, Christopher Mwoleka.......... 1969
Same, Henry Winkelmolen (*Pref.-Ap.*).
Sekondi-Takoradi, Amihere Essuah (1969)..... 1962
Shinyanga, Edward McGurkin............ 1956
Sokoto, Michael Dempsey, O.P........... 1967
Solwezi, Rupert Hillerich (*Pref.-Ap.*) ....
Songea, James Komba (1969)............. 1962
Sumbawanga, Charles Msakila (1970) 1958
Tamale, Gabriel Champagne............. 1957
Tanga, Maura Komba.................. 1970
Tororo, James Odongo 1969
Umtali, Daniel Lamont 1957
Umuahia, Antony Nwedo, O.B.E. 1959
Wa, Peter P. Dery 1960
Wankie, Ignatius Vega 1963
Warri, Luca Nwaezeapu................ 1964
Yola, Patrick Sheehan 1970
Zanzibar and Pemba, Adrian Mkoba (*Ap. Admin.*) (1969)..................... 1967
Zomba, Matthias Chimole 1970

Asia

Pro-Nuncio to India, Most Rev. Maria Giuseppi Lemieux...................... 1969
Pro-Nuncio to Pakistan, Most Rev. Giuseppe Uhac............................ 1970
Apostolic Delegate to Ceylon, Most Rev. Luciano Storio..................... 1969

The Most Revd. Archbishops

Agra, Domenic Athaide.................. 1956
Bangalore, Duraisamy Lourdusamy (1968).... 1962
Bhopal, Eugene D'Souza (1963).......... 1951
Bombay, H. E. Cardinal Valerian Gracias (1950) 1945
Calcutta, Lorenzo Picachy 1969
Changanacherry, Anthony Padiyara (1970)... 1955
Colombo, H.E. Cardinal Thomas Cooray (1947)............................ 1946
Dacca, Theotonius Ganguly (1968)........ 1960
Delhi, Angelo Fernandes (1967)......... 1959
Ernakulam, H.E. Cardinal Joseph Parecattil (1956)........................ 1953
Hyderabad (*India*), Joseph Mark Gopu (1953).. 1948
Karachi, Joseph Cordeiro................ 1958
Madhurai, Justin Diraviam.............. 1967
Madras and Mylapore, Arulappa Rayappa.... 1965
Malacca–Singapore, Michel Olcomendy (1953) 1947
Nagpur, Leonard Raymond (1964) 1947
Pondicherry, Ambrose Rayappan (1955)..... 1953
Ranchi, Pio Kerketta (1961) 1961
Trivanarum (*Syro-Malankara Rite*), Gregorios Thangalathil (1955) 1953
Verapoly (vacant)

The Rt. Revd. Bishops

Ahmedabad, Edwin Pinto................ 1949
Ajmer and Jaipur, Leo D'Mello.......... 1949
Allahabad, Alfred Ferrandez (1970) 1967
Alleppey, Michael Arattukulam........... 1954

CONS.

Amravati, Joseph A. Rosario 1955
Arabia, Irzio Magliancani O.F.M. 1950
Banaras, Patrick D'Souza 1970
Baroda, Ignatius de Souza 1966
Belgaum, Ignazio Lobo 1968
Bellary, Ambrose Yednapally, O.F.M. 1964
Bhagalpur, Urban McGarry 1965
Calicut, Aldo Patroni................... 1948
Chikmagalur, Alphonse Matthias 1964
Chilaw, Edmund Peiris.................. 1940
Chittagong, Joachim Rozario 1968
Cochin, Alexander Edezhath 1952
Coimbatore, Savari Muthu Muthappa........ 1950
Cuttack, Paolo Gonzalez................. 1950
Cyprus, Elias Farah..................... 1954
Darjeeling, Enrico Benjamin.............. 1962
Dibrugarh, Robert Kerketta 1970
Dinajpur, Michael Rozario 1968
Dumka, Leone Tigga.................... 1962
Galle, Antonio De Sacrum (1965) 1963
Gauhati-Shillong, Alberto D'Rosario (1969) . 1964
Guntur, Ignatius Mummadi............... 1943
Hong Kong, Francis Hsu Kan Ping (1969)... 1967
Hyderabad in Pakistan, Paul Bonaventura (*Admin., Apost.*)
Indore, Francis Simons.................. 1952
Jabalpur, Leonard de Souza (1966) 1964
Jaffna, Emile Pillai (1950)................ 1949
Jalpaiguri, Francis Ekka 1968
Jameshedpur, Joseph Rodericks 1970
Jhansi, John Mudartha (1967) 1963
Jullundur, Alban Swarbrick (*Pref.-Ap.*).......
Kandy, Leo Nanayakkara............ [*Ap.*] 1959
Kashmir and Jammu, John Boerkamp (*Pref.-Khulna*, Michael D'Rozario............... 1970
Kota Kinabalu, James Buis, C.B.E., V.A......... 1952
Kothamangalam, Matthew Potanamuzhi..... 1956
Kottar, Marianus Arokiasamy 1970
Kottayam, Thomas Tharayil (1951).......... 1945
Krishnagar (vacant)
Kuala Lumpur, Dominic Vendargon....... 1955
Kuching, Charles Reiterer, V.A. (1968)....... 1967
Kumbakonam, Daniel Arulswami........... 1955
Kurnool, Joseph Rayappa 1967
Lahore, Felice Raeymaekers (1967).......... 1963
Lucknow (vacant)
Lyallpur, Francis Cialeo (1960)............. 1939
Mangalore, Salvador D'Souza 1965
Meerut, *Archbishop* Joseph B. Evangelisti(1956) 1952
Miri, Anthony Galvin, V.A. 1960
Mysore, Matthias Fernandes 1964
Multan, Ernest Boland, O.P. 1966
Nellore, Shoury Thumma (1970) 1967
Ootacamund (vacant)
Palai, Sebastian Vayalil.................. 1950
Patna, Augustine Wildermuth............. 1947
Penang, Gregorio Yong Sooi Nghean 1968
Poona, William Gomes (1967)............. 1961
Quilon, Jerome Fernandez................ 1937
Raigarh-Ambikapur (vacant)
Raipur, John Weidner, S.A.C. [P.A.]
Rawalpindi, Nicholas Hettinga............. 1947
Salem, Lurdu Selvanden................. 1949
Sambalpur, Herman Westermann.... 1951
Silchar, Denzil de Souza 1969
Simla, Edward Cleary (Apost. Admin.)
Tanjore, Arokiaswami R. Sundaram........ 1953
Tellicherry, Sebastian Valloppilly.......... 1956
Tezpur, Joseph Mittathani................ 1969
Tiruchirapally, James Fernando (1970) 1953
Tiruvalla, Cheriyan Polachirakal (1955) 1954
Trichur, Joseph Kundukulam............. 1970
Trincomalee, Ignatius Glennie 1947
Trivandrum (*Latin Rite*), Peter Pereira (1966) . 1955
Tuticorin (vacant)
Vellore (vacant)

CONS.

Vijayapuram, Juan Abasolo y Leuce......... 1950
Vijayavada, Ambrogio De Battista......... 1952
Visakhapatnam, Ignatio Gopu (1966) 1962
Warangal, Alfonso Beretta (1951) 1953

Australia
Apostolic Delegate to Australia, Papua and New
Guinea, Most Rev. Gino Paro........... 1969

The Most Revd. Archbishops
Adelaide, Matthew Boevich. 1940
Brisbane, Patrick O'Donnell (1965) 1949
Canberra–Goulbourn, Thomas Cahill (1967).. 1949
Hobart, Guilford Young (1955)............ 1948
Melbourne, James Knox (1967) 1953
Perth, Lancelot Goody (1969)............. 1954
Sydney, James Freeman (1971)............ 1957

The Rt. Revd. Bishops
Armidale (vacant).
Australia (Byzantine Rite), John Prasko..... 1958
Ballarat, James O'Collins (1941) 1930
Bathurst, Albert Thomas 1963
Broome, John Jobst (1966)............... 1959
Bunbury, Myles McKeon (1969)........... 1962
Cairns, John Aherne 1967
Darwin, John O'Loughlin................ 1949
Geraldton, Francis Thomas............... 1962
Lismore, Patrick Farrelly (1949).......... 1931
Maitland, John Toohey (1956) 1948
Port Pirie, Bryan Gallagher.............. 1952
Rockhampton, Francis Rush (1961) 1961
Sale, Arthur Francis Fox (1968).......... 1957
Sandhurst, Bernard Stewart (1950)........ 1947
Toowoomba, William Brennan............. 1953
Townsville, Anthony Faulkner............ 1967
Wagga-Wagga, Francis Patrick Carroll (1968) 1967
Wilcannia-Forbes, Douglas J. Warren (1967).. 1964
Wollongong, Thomas McCabe (1939) 1951

CONS.

New Zealand
Apostolic Delegate to New Zealand and the
Pacific Islands, Most Rev. Raimondo
Etteldorf (1968).

The Most Revd. Archbishop
Wellington, H.E. Cardinal Peter McKeefry
(1954)................................. 1947

The Rt. Revd. Bishops
Auckland, Archbishop James Liston, C.M.G.(1953)

1920
Christchurch, Brian Patrick Ashby......... 1964
Dunedin, John Kavanagh (1957)........... 1949
Rarotonga, Henry M. de Cocq (1966) 1964

Oceania
The Most Revd. Archbishops
Madang, Adolf Noser (1966)............... 1947
Port Moresby, Virgil Copas (1966) 1960
Rabaul, John Hohne (1966)............... 1963
Suva, George Pearce (1957)............... 1956
Tonga and Niue Islands, John Rodgers (1966). 1954

The Rt. Revd. Bishops
Aitape, Kevin Rowell.................... 1969
Apia, Pio Taofinu'u 1956
Bereina, Eugene Klein (1966)............. 1960
Bougainville, Leo Lemay (1966)........... 1960
Daru, Gerard Deschamps................. 1966
Gizo, John Crawford (1966).............. 1960
Goroka, John Cahill 1969
Honiara, Daniel Stuyvemberg (1966)....... 1957
Kavieng, Alfred Stemper (1966)........... 1957
Lae, Enrico van Lieshout 1966
Mendi, Firmin Schmitt.................. 1966
Mount Hagen, George Bernarding (1966).... 1960
Port Vila, Louis Julliard (1966).......... 1962
Sideia, Desmond Moore.................. 1970
Taiohae (vacant)
Tarawa, Pierre Guichet (1966)............ 1961
Vanimo, Pascal Sweeney................. 1966
Wewak, Leo Arkfield (1966).............. 1948

LONDON CATHEDRALS, CHURCHES, ETC.

ST. PAUL'S CATHEDRAL, City of London, E.C.4 (1675–1710), cost £747,660. The cross on the dome is 365 ft. above the ground level, the inner cupola 218 ft. above the floor. "Great Paul," in S.W. tower, weighs 17 tons. Organ by Father Smith (enlarged by Willis) in case carved by Grinling Gibbons (who also carved the choir stalls). The choir and high altar were restored in 1958 after war damage and the North Transept in 1962. The American War Memorial Chapel was consecrated in November, 1958. The Chapel of the Most Excellent Order of the British Empire in the Crypt of the Cathedral was dedicated on May 20, 1960. Nave and transepts free; Fees to the following parts (on weekdays only, 11 a.m. to 3.30 p.m. and—during Summer Time only—4.45 p.m. to 6.30 p.m.); Crypt, 10p library, whispering gallery, stone gallery and ball, 15p: total, 25p. Service on Sundays at 8, *10.30, *3.15 and *6.30. Weekdays at 8, *10, *4. Also Fridays, *12.30 p.m. short mid-day service. (*Services are choral.)

WESTMINSTER ABBEY, S.W.1 (built A.D. 1050–1760).—Open on weekdays 8 a.m. to 6 p.m. (8 p.m., Weds.). Admission to Royal Chapels by fee of 15p. (children 5p) (weekdays) except on Fridays (open free). Transepts and Nave open on Sundays only between services. Holy Communion at 8; matins at 10.30; Holy Communion at 11.30. Evensong at 3. Evening service with Sermon at 6.30; Daily—Holy Communion at 8 a.m.; Westminster School Service at 9 a.m.; matins 9.20 a.m. (choral Tuesdays and Fridays); evensong (choral), 5.0 p.m. (Saturday, 3 p.m.). Chapel of Henry VII, Chapter House and Cloisters; King Edward the Confessor's shrine, A.D. 1269, tombs of kings (Edward I, Edward III, Henry V, Mary Queen of Scots, Queen Elizabeth I), and many other monuments and objects of interest, including the grave of "An Unknown Warrior" and St. George's Chapel at the W. end of Nave (1920), and Poets' Corner. The Coronation Chair encloses the "Stone of Scone" brought from Scotland by Edward I in 1297.

SOUTHWARK CATHEDRAL, south side of the Thames, near London Bridge, S.E.1.—Mainly 13th century, but the nave is largely rebuilt. Known as St. Mary Overie before 1540. Open 7.30 a.m. to 6.30 p.m., free. Sunday services, Holy Communion. 8.30 and 11 a.m., Morning Prayer, 10 a.m., Evening Prayer, 3 p.m., Discussion, 6.30 p.m. Weekdays: Matins, 7.40 a.m.; Evensong, 5.30 p.m. (choral except Thursdays and Saturdays) (5 p.m. on Saturdays). Holy Communion, 8 a.m., also 5.30 p.m.. Thursdays and 1.10 p.m. Fridays. The tomb of John Gower (1330–1408) is between the Bunyan and Chaucer memorial windows, in the N. aisle; Shakespeare effigy backed by view of Southwark and Globe Theatre in S. aisle; the altar screen (erected 1520) has been restored; the tomb of Bishop Andrewes (died 1626) is near screen. The Early English Lady Chapel (behind the choir), restored 1930, is the scene of the Consistory Courts of the reign of Mary (Gardiner and Bonner); and is still used for this purpose. John Harvard, after whom Harvard University is named, was baptized here in 1607.

TEMPLE CHURCH. The Temple, E.C.4.—The nave formed one of five remaining round churches in England, the others being at Cambridge, Northampton, Little Maplestead (Essex), and Ludlow Castle. Rebuilding of the church was completed in 1958. Sunday morning services, open to the public, 11.15 a.m., except in August and September. *Master of the Temple*, Very Rev. R. L. P. Milburn, M.A. *Reader*, Rev. W. D. Kennedy-Bell, M.A.

Church of Scotland

CROWN COURT CHURCH, Russell Street, Covent Garden, W.C.2.—Sundays, 11.15 and 6.30. *Minister*, Rev. J. M. Scott, M.A., B.D., F.S.A.Scot.

ST. COLUMBA'S, Pont Street, S.W.1. Sundays, 11 and 6.30. *Minister*, Rev. J. F. McLuskey, M.C., D.D.

Congregational

CITY TEMPLE, Holborn Viaduct, E.C.1.—Sundays 11 and 6.30. *Minister*, Rev. K. Slack, M.B.E., B.A., LL.D.

WESTMINSTER CHAPEL, Buckingham Gate, S.W.1. —Sundays, 11 and 6.30. *Minister*, Rev. J. G. Owen, B.A., B.D.

Methodist

WESLEY'S CHAPEL, City Road, E.C.1. Contains many personal possessions of John and Charles Wesley and other great founders of Methodism. As the "Mother Church of Methodism" visitors attend from all parts of the world.—Sunday morning at 11; evening at 6.30. Thursday, 7.30 a.m., Holy Communion. Thursday lunch time, 1.15—1.45. John Wesley's tomb in graveyard behind chapel. In front is Wesley's House and Museum. *Minister*, Rev. C. M. Morris, 49 City Road, E.C.1.

CENTRAL HALL, Westminster, S.W.1.—Sunday Services, 11 a.m. and 6.30 p.m. *Minister*, Rev.

M. Barnett, M.A., B.D., Ph.D.

KINGSWAY HALL, Kingsway and Great Queen Street, W.C.2.—Sundays at 10, 11, and 6.30. *Minister*, Rev. the Lord Soper, M.A., Ph.D.

Baptist

BLOOMSBURY CENTRAL BAPTIST CHURCH, Junction of Shaftesbury Avenue and New Oxford Street, W.C.2.—Sundays, 11 and 6.30. *Minister*, Rev. H. Howard Williams, Ph.D.

Society of Friends

FRIENDS' HOUSE, Euston Road, N.W.1.

Roman Catholic

WESTMINSTER CATHEDRAL, Ashley Place, Westminster, S.W.1 (close to Victoria Station), built 1895–1903 from the designs of J. F. Bentley (the campanile is 283 feet high—open to public by lift, 10p).—*Sundays.* Masses, 6, 7, 8, 9, 10.30 (High), 12 noon, 5.30 p.m. and 7 p.m.; Solemn Vespers and Benediction, 3.30. *Weekdays.* Masses, 6.30, 7, 7.30, 8.30, 9, 10.30 (High), 12.30 and 6 p.m. Morning Office, 10.5, Vespers and Benediction, 5 p.m. *Holy days of obligation.* Low Masses, 6, 6.30, 7, 7.30, 8, 8.30, 9, 10.30 (High), 11.50, 12.30, 6 and 8 p.m. Cathedral open 6 a.m. to 9 p.m.

THE ORATORY, Brompton, S.W. 7.—Sundays: Masses, 6.15, 7, 8, 9, 10, 11; (High Mass); 12.30 (with Sermon), 4.30, 7; Vespers and Benediction 3.30. Weekdays: Masses, 6.30, 7, 7.30, 8, 10; 12.30, 6 p.m. (no 12.30 on Sats.). Service Thurs. 8 p.m. Holy days: Masses 6.15, 7, 8, 9, 10, 11, 12.15, 1.15 and 8 p.m.; 6 p.m. (High Mass), on the eve; Vespers and Benediction, 5.30 p.m.

CHIEF LEISURE ACTIVITIES IN THE UNITED KINGDOM

Figures in the following section are drawn from a survey on *Planning for Leisure*, leisure time being defined as " the period when a person was not in paid employment or travelling to or from such employment; or for housewives or mothers when not engaged in domestic duties and caring for the essential needs of their families. The survey was conducted between Sept. 1965 and March 1966, on a total sample of 2,824 males and 3,451 females. *Figures are in respect of the percentage of leisre time devoted to the activity cited, when this was the chief pursuit.*

MALE LEISURE ACTIVITIES.—Males of all ages in the sample were found to spend 23 per cent. of their leisure periods in watching television; 12 per cent. in gardening; 11 per cent. in taking part in physical recreation including dancing and 3 per cent. in watching sport, etc. Seven per cent. of leisure time was spent on excursions, 5 per cent. on reading, 5 per cent. on non-physical games or club activities, 5 per cent. on walking or park visits. Decorating and house or vehicle maintenance took up 8 per cent. of leisure periods and crafts and hobbies 4 per cent. Drinking occupied 3 per cent. and visiting or entertaining also took 3 per cent.

The highest percentage shown for any single activity were: television watching, 34 per cent. among married men with children in the age group 46–60 and 29 per cent. in the age group 31–45; participation in sport, 27 per cent. in each of the age groups 15–18 and 19–22; gardening took up to 20 per cent. of leisure time for men over 60,

15 or 16 per cent. for men of 46–60, 8 per cent. for married men of 23–30 with children. Chief leisure pursuits of single men in the age group 19–22 years were cited as sport, excursions, crafts and hobbies and house or vehicle maintenance or decorating.

FEMALE LEISURE ACTIVITIES.—Females of all ages in the sample were found to spend 23 per cent. of their leisure periods in watching television: 17 per cent. in crafts and hobbies, mainly knitting; 9 per cent. in social activities (visiting or entertaining); 9 per cent. in reading. Gardening occupied 7 per cent. of female leisure time and excursions accounted for 7 per cent. 4 per cent. of leisure time was spent in non-physical games or club activities and 4 per cent in taking part in physical recreation including dancing. One per cent. of leisure periods was devoted respectively to decorating, drinking and cinema or theatre-going

The highest percentages shown for any single activity were: television, 29 per cent. among married women aged 61 or over (married women with children, 24 per cent.); participation in sport, 28 per cent. among single women of 19–30 years of age (girls of 15–18, 24 per cent.); crafts and hobbies (mainly knitting), 24 per cent. among married women of 23–30 with children. Chief leisure pursuits of single women of 19–22 were cited as sport, crafts and hobbies (including knitting) 13 per cent., television, 10 per cent. and cinema and theatre-going, excursions, and visiting or entertaining, each 7 per cent.

NATIONAL INSURANCE AND RELATED CASH BENEFITS

For Combined Contributions, see p. 499.

The State insurance and assistance schemes in force from July 5, 1948, comprised schemes of national insurance and industrial injuries insurance, national assistance and non-contributory old age pensions, and family allowances. The Ministry of Social Security Act, 1966, introduced a scheme of non-contributory benefits in place of national assistance and non-contributory old age pensions, and provided for the establishment of a new Ministry of Social Security (now the Department of Health and Social Security), with overall responsibility for the existing insurance schemes and family allowances scheme and the new scheme of non-contributory benefits, in place of the Ministry of Pensions and National Insurance and the National Assistance Board, which were abolished.

Acts consolidating the provisions of the National Insurance, Industrial Injuries, Family Allowances and National Health Service Contributions Acts passed since 1946 were brought into effect on September 6, 1965, and the Statute Law Revision (Consequential Repeals) Act, 1965, which repealed the provisions of the old Acts came into effect on the same date.

NATIONAL INSURANCE

The National Insurance Scheme operates under the National Insurance Act, 1965, as amended by the National Insurance Acts, 1966 and 1967, the Family Allowances and National Insurance Acts, 1967 and 1968, the Public Expenditure and Receipts Act, 1968, the National Insurance Acts, 1969 and 1971, the National Insurance (Old Persons' and Widows' Pensions and Attendance Allowance) Act, 1970, the Social Security Act, 1971, and Regulations made under those Acts.

The scheme provides, in return for regular weekly flat-rate contributions, weekly flat-rate cash benefits as stated below. For employees over 18 earning over £9 a week and their employers there are additional contributions graduated according to earnings, with related graduated additions to retirement pensions for employees or their widows.

The National Insurance Act, 1966, provides for the payment to persons over 18 of earnings-related short-term benefits supplementing unemployment and sickness benefit and widow's allowance.

The National Insurance Act, 1971, increased retirement pensions and other insurance benefits, together with graduated and some flat-rate contributions, from the week beginning September 20, 1971.

The 1971 Act also made a number of selective changes, notably affecting the chronic sick and persons aged over 80, following on those made in the 1970 Act.

INSURED PERSONS AND CONTRIBUTIONS

Subject to certain statutory exceptions, every person living in Great Britain who is over school leaving age and under pension age becomes insured under the Acts.

There are three classes of insured persons namely:—

  (*a*) Class 1. Employed persons, i.e. persons who work for an employer under a contract of service or are paid apprentices.
  (*b*) Class 2. Self-employed persons, i.e. persons gainfully occupied but not working under the control of an employer.
  (*c*) Class 3. Non-employed persons, i.e. persons who are not gainfully occupied.

The estimated number of persons in respect of whom flat-rate contributions were paid or excused in 1968 was as follows: employed, 23·32 million; self-employed, 1·52 million; non-employed, 0·28 million.

National Insurance contributions are payable by insured persons, by employers of employed persons (*see* p. 499), and out of moneys provided by Parliament.

The ordinary flat-rate contributions are usually paid by means of stamps on a single insurance card; the stamp also covers the National Health Service contribution; in the case of employed persons the Industrial Injuries contribution; the Selective Employment Tax payable by all employers; and, in the case of employees aged 18 and over, the employer's contribution to the Redundancy Fund (see p. 499).

Since September 20, 1971, employed persons over age 18 earning more than £9 in any week unless contracted out in part as members of approved occupational pension schemes, and their employers, have each paid, in addition to the flat-rate contribution covering earnings up to £9 a week, a graduated contribution of 4·75 per cent. of earnings over £9 and up to £18 a week, and 4·35 per cent on earnings over £18 and up to £42. Employed persons over age 18 who are contracted out, and their employers, have each paid a graduated contribution of 0·05 per cent. on earnings between £9 and £18 a week, and 4·35 per cent. on earnings between £18 and £42. People in class 1 who are contracted out pay a higher flat-rate contribution (*see* pp. 495, 499).

Regulations made under the Acts give married women and widows, upon certain conditions, the choice whether to pay the National Insurance flat-rate contribution or not.

Men aged 70 and over and women aged 65 and over in classes (1) and (2) pay no National Insurance contribution. Men aged 65 to 70 and women aged 60 to 65 in these classes, with certain exceptions, are liable to pay contributions, including any graduated contributions, if they have not retired from regular employment. Normally no contributions are payable by men over 65 or women over 60 in class (3).

Regulations state the cases in which insured persons may be excepted from paying National Insurance contributions, and the conditions upon which contributions are credited to persons who are excepted.

The yearly Exchequer Supplement to flat-rate contributions is equal to one-quarter of the national insurance portion of the contributions paid by employers and employed persons (excluding graduated contributions and the extra flat-rate contributions paid by employed persons who are in part contracted out of the graduated scheme and their employers) and one-third of the national insurance portion of self-employed and non-employed contributions. To maintain the Exchequer proportion of the total contribution income of the scheme at its present level of about 18 per cent., the Exchequer also makes a special additional payment each year: this is to be £135 million a year for 1971–72 and 1972–73 and £185 million a year thereafter.

BENEFITS

The Acts give the following benefits:—
  Unemployment benefit.
  Sickness benefit.
  Invalidity pension and allowance.

Maternity benefits, including maternity grant and maternity allowance.

Widow's benefits, including widow's allowance, widowed mother's allowance and widow's pension.

Child's special allowance.

Guardian's allowance.

Retirement pension.

Death grant.

The benefits available to the various classes of insured persons are as follows:

Employed persons.... All benefits.

Self-employed persons. All benefits *except* unemployment benefit.

Non-employed persons All benefits *except* unemployment, sickness and invalidity benefits and maternity allowance.

There is one system of adjudication on all claims for benefit under the Acts; with certain exceptions, questions as to the right to benefit are decided by independent statutory authorities, consisting of insurance officers, local tribunals and the Chief National Insurance Commissioner and National Insurance Commissioners.

UNEMPLOYMENT BENEFIT

The *standard weekly rates of flat-rate benefit are as follows:*

	£
Man, single woman or widow over 18....	6·00
Married woman over 18: ordinary rate....	4·20
Person under 18: ordinary rate...........	3·30
Increase of benefit for only child or elder or eldest child (where payable)............	1·85
Increase of benefit for second child (where payable) in addition to family allowances	0·95
Increase of benefit for each additional child (where payable) in addition to family allowances	0·85
Increase of benefit for wife or other adult dependant (where payable).............	3·70

Normal Contribution Conditions.—The claimant must have paid 26 Class 1 flat-rate contributions since he last became insured, and, to be entitled to benefit at the standard rate during a benefit year, must have paid or had credited 50 Class 1 flat-rate contributions during the preceding contribution year.

Waiting Period.—Under the Social Security Act, 1971, benefit is not payable for the first three days of a spell of unemployment.

Duration of Benefit.—Benefit is payable in a period of interruption of employment for up to 312 days (a year).

Requalification for Benefit.—A person who has exhausted benefit requalifies therefor when he has paid 13 Class 1 flat-rate contributions.

Disqualifications.—There are disqualifications for receiving benefit, e.g. for a period not exceeding six weeks if a person has lost his employment through his misconduct, or has voluntarily left his employment without just cause, or has, without good cause, refused an offer of suitable employment or training.

Earnings-related Supplement.—Until May 1973 the supplement payable to claimants over 18 and under minimum pension age who are entitled to flat-rate unemployment benefit is one third of the amount by which average weekly earnings exceed £9, subject to a maximum supplement of £7 (payable where average earnings are £30 a week or more) and a maximum total benefit, including increases for dependants, of 85 per cent. of earnings. Average weekly earnings will normally be taken as one-fiftieth of total earnings in the previous income tax year. The supplement starts from the thirteenth day of a period of interruption of employment and lasts for up to a maximum of six months. Periods of unemployment or sickness not separated by more than 13 weeks are treated as one period of interruption of employment. Where employment is suspended but not terminated by the employer, e.g. short-time working or lay-off, the supplement is not payable for the first six days (except Sundays and holidays) in any continuous period of suspension.

Numbers Unemployed.—During the year 1970 the average number of persons registered as unemployed in Great Britain was 603,400. In November, 1969, 279,400 persons were receiving unemployment benefit.

SICKNESS BENEFIT

Standard Rates of flat-rate Benefit.—Same as for unemployment benefit.

Normal Contribution Conditions.—Same as for unemployment benefit, except that Class 2 as well as Class 1 flat-rate contributions and credits are counted.

Waiting Period.—Same as for unemployment benefit.

Duration of Benefit.—A person who has paid 156 Class 1 flat-rate or Class 2 contributions receives sickness benefit for 168 days and thereafter invalidity benefit of unlimited duration (*see* below). If he has paid less than 156 such contributions, sickness benefit is limited to 312 days (one year); but he will requalify for benefit when he has paid contributions for 13 weeks.

Disqualifications.—Regulations provide for disqualifying a person for receiving sickness benefit for a period not exceeding six weeks if he has become incapable of work through his own misconduct, or if he fails without good cause to attend for or submit himself to prescribed medical or other examination or treatment, or if he acts in a way which would retard his recovery.

Earnings-related Supplement.—The supplement and the rules as to duration are the same as for the supplement to unemployment benefit.

Number of Claims.—During 1969, about 11·4 million new claims for sickness benefit were received.

INVALIDITY BENEFIT

Under the National Insurance Act, 1971, after a person who has paid 156 Class 1 flat-rate or Class 2 contributions has qualified for sickness benefit for 168 days in a period of interruption of employment, sickness benefit is replaced by an *invalidity pension* of £6·00 (£3·70 for a wife) unless the claimant is over pension age and has retired from regular employment. In addition an *invalidity allowance* is payable if incapacity for work begins more than five years before pension age. The allowance varies in amount from 30p to £1·00 a week according to the age on falling sick, and if still in payment at pension age will continue as an addition to retirement pension. The increases of benefit for children of an invalidity pensioner are at the higher rate, viz., £2·95 for the first child, £2·05 for a second child and £1·95 for any other child, in addition to family allowances. The dependent wife of an invalidity pensioner residing with him is subject to the same tapered earnings rule as applies to retirement pensioners which begins to operate when her earnings exceed £9·50.

MATERNITY BENEFITS

Maternity Grant.—A cash grant of £25 is payable on the mother's own insurance or on her husband's, whether she is confined at home or in hospital. Extra grants are payable, in certain circumstances, if more than one child is born. The normal contribution conditions for this grant are (i) that the mother or her husband has paid not less than 26 flat-rate contributions of any class since his or her entry into insurance, and (ii) that not less than 26 flat-rate contributions of any class have been paid by or credited to that person during the previous contribution year, or the mother has satisfied the contribution conditions for a maternity allowance at the standard rate or at a reduced rate.

Maternity Allowance.—A woman who is gainfully occupied receives in addition a maternity allowance of £6·00 a week normally for 18 weeks beginning eleven weeks before the expected week of confinement, provided that she abstains from work. The rate of allowance is increased where the woman has dependants. The normal contribution conditions for this benefit are (i) that the claimant has paid or had credited 50 Class 1 or 2 flat-rate contributions during the 52 weeks ending 13 weeks before the expected week of confinement; and (ii) that in the same 52 weeks at least 26 Class 1 or 2 flat-rate contributions have been paid.

During the year ended March 31, 1969, maternity grants were paid for about 877,000 births; in addition, about 243,000 women received weekly maternity allowances.

WIDOW'S BENEFITS

This benefit in any of its three forms is payable to the widow of any class of insured person. The normal contribution conditions to be satisfied by the husband are (a) that he had paid not less than 156 flat-rate contributions of any class since his last entry into insurance (104 if he was married before July 5, 1948, and insured from before September 30, 1946), and (b) that the yearly average of the flat-rate contributions paid by or credited to him since his insurance started was not less than 50.

Widow's Allowance.—A woman who at her husband's death is under 60 (or over 60, if he had not retired), receives (during the first 26 weeks of widowhood) a cash allowance usually of £8·40 a week with increases of £2·95 for the first or only child, £2·05 for the second child and £1·95 for each other child, in addition to family allowances. Women widowed on or after October 5, 1966, before the husband's retirement, also receive a supplement to widow's allowance amounting to one-third of the husband's average weekly earnings between £9 and £30 (reckoned in the same way as for earnings-related supplements to unemployment and sickness benefit (see p. 493).

Widowed Mother's Allowance.—When the 26 weeks of widow's allowance have elapsed, a widow who is left with one or more dependent children receives a cash allowance usually of £8·95 a week as long as she has a child of qualifying age, and in addition £2·05 a week for the second child and £1·95 for each additional child, as well as family allowances. A widowed mother's personal allowance, usually £6·00 a week, is payable to widows who, when their widow's or widowed mother's allowance ends, have living with them a child under 19, who has left school and is not an apprentice.

Widow's Pension.—A widow receives this pension usually of £6·00 a week (i) when widow's allowance ends, if she was over 50 at the time of her husband's death and had been married for not less than three years; or (ii) when her widowed mother's allowance or widowed mother's personal allowance ends, if she is then over 50 (40 if widowed before February 4, 1957) and not less than three years have elapsed since marriage.

Flat-rate widow's pensions on a graduated scale were introduced in April 1971 for women who are widowed between the ages of 40 and 50. Starting at £1·80 for those aged 40, the pension rises 42p a year to the full rate at 50.

Widow's benefit of any form ceases upon re-marriage.

If a woman who was married before July 5, 1948, to a man insured under the old scheme immediately before that date does not qualify for widow's benefit, she may qualify for a widow's basic pension, usually, since September 1971, of £1·80 a week.

At the end of 1969, about 553,000 widows were receiving widowed mother's allowance, widow's pension or widow's basic pension.

CHILD'S SPECIAL ALLOWANCE

A woman whose marriage has been dissolved or annulled and who has not re-married is paid a special allowance on the ex-husband's death. The normal condition is that she has a child to whose maintenance he was contributing, or had been liable to contribute, at least 25p a week in cash or its equivalent. The allowance is £2·95 a week for the first or only child, £2·05 for the second child and £1·95 for each other child, in addition to family allowances. The contribution conditions for the allowance are substantially the same as for widow's benefit.

GUARDIAN'S ALLOWANCE

Where the parents of a child are dead, and one at least of them was an insured person, any person who has the child in his family receives a guardian's allowance of £2·95 a week while the child is of qualifying age. At the end of 1969 about 5,000 allowances were being paid.

RETIREMENT PENSIONS

A flat-rate retirement pension is payable for life to an insured person who (a) is over pension age (65 for a man and 60 for a woman), (b) has retired from regular employment, and (c) has paid the prescribed number of flat-rate contributions. Men aged 70 and over and women aged 65 and over are not required to satisfy condition (b).

The standard flat-rate pension for an insured person or widow is £6·00 a week, plus £3·70 for a dependent wife who is not qualified for a pension, plus £2·95 for the first or only child, £2·05 for the second child and £1·95 for each other child, in addition to family allowances. As to the age addition payable at age 80, see p. 498.

Where the insured person postpones retirement beyond minimum pension age, the weekly rate of pension is increased, when he or she finally retires or reaches the age of 70 (65 for women), in respect of flat-rate contributions paid as an employed or self-employed person during the five years after reaching minimum pension age. The increment to pension is now 6p for every 9 contributions.

A man aged 65 to 70 (or a woman aged 60 to 65) who has qualified for pension will have it reduced by 5p for each 10p of net earnings in excess of £9.50 and a further 5p for each 10p of net earnings in excess of £11·50. The same earnings rule applies to the dependent wife of a retirement pensioner who is residing with him.

The Normal Contribution Conditions for the flat-rate pension are (a) that 156 flat-rate contributions of any class have been paid (104 if insurance began before September 30, 1946), and (b) that the yearly average of flat-rate contributions paid or credited is not less than 50.

Special Provisions as to Women.—Subject to certain conditions, a married woman over the age of 60 or a woman on marriage after that age receives by virtue of her husband's insurance a retirement pension of £3·70 a week when he retires at 65 or after or reaches 70. A retirement pension payable to a woman by virtue of her husband's insurance is increased by 3p during his lifetime and 6p on widowhood for every 12 (from October, 1967, 9) contributions paid by the husband as an employed or self-employed person while he is over 65 and under 70 and she is over 60, and her pension in widowhood is increased by 3p for every 12 of these contributions paid by him on or after December 25, 1961, while she is under 60 (from October, 1967, 9). A widow who qualifies for retirement pension on her own insurance can receive, in addition to any increments she may earn by deferring her own retirement and paying contributions beyond age 60, half of all the 6p increments which her husband earned by deferring retirement and paying contributions on or after December 25, 1961.

Unemployment and sickness benefit is payable to men between 65 and 70 and women between 60 and 65 who have not retired from regular employment at the same rate as the retirement pension they would have been entitled to had they retired from regular employment.

At the end of 1969 retirement pensions, or contributory old age pensions under the old Acts, were being paid to approximately 7,130,000 persons, about 157,000 more than a year earlier.

THE GRADUATED PENSION SCHEME

Since April, 1961, when the graduated pension scheme came into operation, National Insurance contributions and retirement pensions have been graduated, within specified limits, according to earnings. The scheme does not apply to employed persons under 18, or to self-employed or non-employed persons (*see* p. 499).

Graduated Contributions.—Employed persons over 18 (including men over 65 and under 70, and women over 60 and under 65, who have not retired), unless contracted out in part as members of occupational pension schemes satisfying certain conditions, and their employers, each pay, in addition to the weekly flat-rate contribution covering earnings up to £9 a week, a graduated contribution of 4·75 per cent. on all earnings over £9 and up to £18 a week; plus, since September 20, 1971, 4·35 per cent. on earnings between £18 and £42 (*see* p. 499).

The flat-rate contribution, which includes the separate National Health Service and Industrial Injuries contributions, the Selective Employment Tax (employer only) and the employer's contribution to the Redundancy Fund, is £3·03 for an employed man (of which the employee pays £0·88 and the employer £2·15) and £2·15 for an employed woman (of which the employee pays £0·75 and the employer £1·40 (*see* p. 499).

The graduated contribution is the same for men and women. Employed married women, and widows receiving certain benefits, are still able to choose not to pay the flat-rate contribution other than the 4p Industrial Injuries contribution), but they pay their share of the graduated contribution on their earnings over £9 a week.

The graduated contributions are in general payable on the gross earnings (including overtime pay, bonus, etc.) received in each week (or month, etc.) taken separately, and not on the cumulative total over the year.

Contracted-out employees over age 18 (whatever their earnings) and their employers pay flat-rate contributions which are higher than those payable

by or for employees who are not contracted out (*see* p. 499). Since September 20, 1971, they have also each been liable for graduated contributions of about 0·05 per cent. of earnings between £9 and £18 a week and 4·35 per cent. of earnings between £18 and £42 (*see* p. 499).

The flat-rate contributions are usually paid by means of a combined weekly stamp. The graduated contributions are collected through the P.A.Y.E. system, in association with income tax.

The graduated pension.—The graduated addition to the flat-rate retirement pension for each contributor is at the rate of 2½p a week for each unit of graduated contributions paid by him or her since the start of the scheme (half a unit or more counts as a whole unit). A unit of contributions is £7·50 for men, and £9 for women, of graduated contributions paid by the employee. A widow gets a graduated addition to her flat-rate retirement pension equal to half of any graduated addition earned by her late husband, plus any addition earned by her own graduated contributions.

Graduated additions are subject to the usual condition of retirement. Persons who defer retirement will continue to pay graduated contributions until they retire or reach 70 (65 for women) whether retired or not, when they will qualify for graduated additions to pension in respect of graduated contributions they have paid. In addition, half of the graduated additions they have forgone by deferring retirement will be treated as extra graduated contributions paid by them and will count towards further graduated pension.

Contracting out.—Adult employees who have retirement pension rights in an occupational pension scheme can be contracted out of part of the graduated pensions scheme if the following conditions are satisfied:

(1) the occupational scheme is financially sound;
(2) it provides the employees contracted out with retirement pension rights at least equal to the maximum graduated pension that could have been earned in the State scheme for a corresponding period of service up to age 65 (women 60);
(3) pension rights at least up to this amount are preserved should the employee change his job.

To be contracted out, an employee must be in an employment covered by a Certificate of Non-participation issued to his employer by the Registrar of Non-participating Employments.

A leaflet R1, which explains the arrangements for contracting out and for modifying schemes for the purpose of satisfying the contracting out conditions, can be obtained from the Registrar of Non-participating Employments, 287 High Holborn, London, W.C.1.

DEATH GRANT

A death grant is payable on the death of an insured person or of his wife, child or widow or, if the insured person is a woman, of her husband, child or widower, and also in respect of the deaths of certain handicapped persons on the insurance of close relatives. The normal grant is for an adult £30, a child aged 6–17 £22 10s., a child aged 3–5 £15, a child under 3 £9. For the deaths of people who on July 5, 1948, were between 55 and 65 (men) or between 50 and 60 (women) the grant is £15.

The normal contribution conditions for death grant are that (*a*) not less than 26 flat-rate contributions of any class have been paid by or credited to the deceased or the person by virtue of whose insurance the grant is claimed since July 5, 1948, and (*b*) either not less than 45 such contributions have been paid by him or credited to him in the previous

contribution year, or the yearly average of the contributions paid or credited since July 5, 1948 (or 16th birthday if later) is not less than 45. No grant is payable for deaths of persons already over pension age on July 5, 1948. For deaths in 1968 about 485,000 grants were awarded.

The grant is paid to the deceased person's executors or administrators, if any; otherwise it is paid to the person who meets the funeral expenses or to the next of kin.

FINANCE

Under the National Insurance Acts two funds are set up, viz. the National Insurance Fund, and the National Insurance (Reserve) Fund. The income from contributions, Exchequer grants and interest from both funds are paid into the National Insurance Fund, and payments are made out of the Fund to meet the cost of benefits and administration. Under the National Health Service Contributions Act, provision is made for separate National Health Service contributions to be collected in conjunction with the National Insurance contributions, in place of payments formerly made from the Fund towards the cost of the National Health Service. (*See* p. 499.)

Approximate receipts and payments of the National Insurance Fund for the year ended March 31, 1970, were as follows:—

Receipts	£'000
Balance, April 1, 1969	244,043
Flat-rate contributions from employers and insured persons	1,416,220
Exchequer contribution	353,522
Graduated contributions	541,167
Income from investments	15,235
Transfer from the Reserve Fund of income from investments, etc.	38,571
Other receipts	131
	2,608,889

Payments		£'000
Benefit:—	£'000	
Unemployment benefit..	127,117	
Sickness benefit	382,680	
Maternity benefit	38,000	
Widow's benefit	162,000	
Guardian's allowance	600	
Child's special allowance	60	
Retirement pension	1,626,895	
Death grant	11,896	
		2,349,248 (a)
Administration expenses		85,473
Other payments		20,452
Balance, March 31, 1970		153,716
		2,608,889

(*a*) Including estimated amounts of earnings-related supplement as follows: unemployment benefit £21 million; sickness benefit £59·25 million; widow's benefit £5·8 million; graduated retirement benefit £10 million.

Payments exceeded receipts during the year by £90 million. Compared with 1968–69, receipts, excluding the transfer from the Reserve Fund in that year, increased by £128 million and payments by £147 million.

The balance in the Reserve Fund at March 31, 1970, was £924·5 million.

INDUSTRIAL INJURIES INSURANCE

The National Insurance (Industrial Injuries) Act, 1946, substituted for the Workmen's Compensation Acts, 1925 to 1945, a system of insurance against personal injury caused by accident arising out of and in the course of a person's employment and

against prescribed diseases and injuries due to the nature of a person's employment. The scheme, which insures against personal injury caused and prescribed diseases and injuries developed on or after July 5, 1948, now operates under the National Insurance (Industrial Injuries) Act, 1965, as amended by the National Insurance Act, 1966, the National Insurance (Industrial Injuries) (Amendment) Act, 1967, the National Insurance Act, 1967, the Family Allowances and National Insurance Acts, 1967 and 1968, the National Insurance Acts, 1969 and 1971, the Social Security Act, 1971, and Regulations made under those Acts. The National Insurance Act, 1971, provided for increases in the rates of benefit and in amounts of contribution, with effect from the week beginning September 20, 1971.

The Workmen's Compensation Acts continue to apply, subject to certain amendments, to cases arising before the Industrial Injuries scheme started. Statutory schemes have also been made providing for the payment of allowances supplementing workmen's compensation in certain circumstances, and for the payment of benefits in certain cases where neither workmen's compensation nor Industrial Injuries benefits are payable.

INSURED PERSONS

The persons covered by the Industrial Injuries scheme correspond closely to the class of " employed persons " under the National Insurance scheme (excluding members of the Forces), and numbered in 1968 23.2 million, of whom more than one-third were women.

CONTRIBUTIONS

Contributions are payable by insured persons and their employers, unless exempted, and the Exchequer contributes an amount equal to one-fifth of the combined contributions of insured persons and employers.

The normal weekly rates of contributions payable by insured persons and employers respectively are 5p and 6p for men over 18, 4p and 5p for women over 18, 3p and 3p for boys under 18, and 2p and 3p for girls under 18. Normally contributions are paid by means of stamps on a single insurance card, the same stamp also covering the flat-rate National Insurance and the National Health Service contributions, etc. (*see* p. 499).

There are no contribution conditions for the payment of benefits. Persons employed in insurable employment are covered from the time of starting work, but if employed while at school age pay no contributions.

BENEFITS

Injury Benefit is payable for not more than the first 26 weeks of incapacity. Under the Social Security Act, 1971, no payment is made for the first three days of a period of interruption of employment during the injury benefit period. Benefit is payable to persons over 18 and to juveniles with dependant's allowances, at the weekly rate of £8·75 (days being paid for at one sixth of the weekly rate) *plus* £3·70 for a wife or other adult dependant, *plus* £1·85 for the first or only child, 95p for the second child, and 85p for each other child, in addition to family allowances. Other juveniles receive lower rates. Where a claimant who is entitled to sickness benefit under the National Insurance scheme draws injury benefit instead, any earnings-related supplement to sickness benefit to which he is entitled will be paid with the injury benefit (*see* p. 493).

Disablement Benefit is payable if at or after the end of the injury benefit period the insured person suffers from loss of physical or mental faculty such that the resulting disablement is assessed

at not less than one per cent. (In cases of pneumoconiosis and byssinosis disablement benefit is paid from the start without a period of injury benefit.) The amount of disablement benefit varies according to the degree of disablement (in the form of a percentage) assessed by a medical board or medical appeal tribunal. In cases of disablement of less than 20 per cent., except in pneumoconiosis or byssinosis cases, benefit normally takes the form of a *gratuity* paid according to a prescribed scale, but not exceeding £660. Where the degree of disablement is 20 per cent. or more, or if it is due to pneumoconiosis or byssinosis, the benefit is a weekly *pension* payable either for a limited period or for life, according to the following scale:

Degree of disablement	Weekly Rate £
100 per cent.	10·00
90 ,, ,,	9·00
80 ,, ,,	8·00
70 ,, ,,	7·00
60 ,, ,,	6·00
50 ,, ,,	5·00
40 ,, ,,	4·00
30 ,, ,,	3·00
20 ,, ,,	2·00

These are basic rates applicable to adults and to juveniles entitled to an increase for a child or adult dependant; other juveniles receive lower rates.

Basic rates of pension are not related to the pensioner's loss of earning power, and are payable whether he is in work or not. Upon prescribed conditions, however, pension is supplemented for unemployability and in cases of special hardship. There is provision also for increases of pension during approved hospital treatment or if the pensioner requires constant attendance or if his disablement is exceptionally severe. Increases normally of £3·70 for an adult dependant and of £1·85 for the first and only child, £0·95 for the second child, and £0·85 for each other child are payable (in addition to family allowances). If the beneficiary is entitled to an unemployability supplement the increases for children are £2·95, £2·05 and £1·95 respectively. Subject to certain exceptions, a pensioner who is not in receipt of unemployability supplement can draw other national insurance benefits in full in addition to disablement pension.

Death Benefit, in the form of a pension, a gratuity or a weekly allowance for a limited period, available for widows and other dependants in fatal cases, depends in amount upon their relationship to the deceased and their circumstances at the time of death and not upon the deceased's earnings. A widow who was living with her husband at the time of his death receives a pension of £8·40 a week for the first 26 weeks *plus* any earnings-related supplement she would have received if she had been entitled to national insurance widow's allowance (*see* p. 494), and thereafter a pension of £6·55 or less a week according to circumstances, *plus* £2·95 for the first or only child, £2·05 for the second child and £1·95 for each other child, in addition to family allowances.

Regulations impose certain obligations on claimants and beneficiaries and on employers, including, in the case of the former, that of submitting to medical examination and treatment and attending courses of vocational training or rehabilitation approved by the Department of Employment.

Industrial Diseases, etc.—The Industrial Injuries Act extends insurance to prescribed industrial diseases and prescribed personal injuries not caused by accident, which are due to the nature of an insured person's employment and developed on or after July 5, 1948.

Determination of Questions and Claims.—Provision is made for the determination of certain questions (*e.g.* as to insurability and liability to contribute) by the Secretary of State for Social Services, and of "disablement questions" by a medical board (or a single doctor) or medical appeal tribunal or, on appeal on a point of law, by the National Insurance Commissioners, subject to leave. Claims for benefit and certain questions arising in connection with a claim for or award of benefit (e.g. whether the accident arose out of and in the course of the employment) are determined by an insurance officer appointed by the Secretary of State, or a local appeal tribunal consisting of a chairman appointed by the Secretary of State and equal numbers of members representing employers and insured persons, or, on appeal, by the Commissioners.

Over 900,000 new claims for injury benefit are made each year. The number of disablement pensions in payment at September 30, 1968, was 203,700, of which 45,300 were in respect of pneumoconiosis. During the year ended September 30, 1968, the number of special hardship allowances in payment increased from 137,500 to 142,200. The annual number of awards of death benefit is about 1,500; at the end of 1968 about 26,900 widows' pensions and 13,010 allowances to dependent children were in payment.

FINANCE

Contributions from employers, insured persons and the Exchequer are paid into, and benefits and administrative expenses are paid out of, a fund established under the Industrial Injuries Act, viz., the Industrial Injuries Fund.

Receipts, 1969–70	£'000
Balance, April 1, 1969	343,505
Contributions from employers and insured persons	86,593
Exchequer contribution	17,200
Income from investments	16,021
Other receipts	17
	463,337

Payments, 1969–70		£'000
Benefit:—		
Injury		33,381
Disablement		60,579
Death		8,500
Other benefits		2,919
		105,380
Administration expenses		11,932
Other payments		325
Balance, March 31, 1970		345,699
		463,337

SUPPLEMENTARY BENEFITS

The Ministry of Social Security Act, 1966, as amended by the Social Security Act, 1971, introduced a scheme of non-contributory benefits termed supplementary allowances and pensions in place of national assistance and of non-contributory old age pensions, and vested responsibility for these supplementary benefits in a new Ministry of Social Security (now the Department of Health and Social Security). A Supplementary Benefits Commission within the Department is now responsible, subject to Regulations made by the Secretary of State for Social Services, for operating the scheme of supplementary benefits.

The supplementary pension may be claimed by persons over pension age and the supplementary allowance by persons aged 16 or over but under

pension age, who are not in full-time work. The benefit payable is the amount, assessed under the provisions of the Act, by which the claimant's income requirements exceed his resources. The scale of *normal* income requirements (exclusive of rent) since the week beginning September 20, 1971, is as follows:

	Ordinary	Blind persons
	£	£
Married couple	9·45	10·70 (a)
Single householder	5·80	
Other persons:—		
Aged 21 or over	4·60	7·05
Aged 18-20	4·05	5·05
Aged 16-17	3·60	4·40
Aged 13-15	3·00	3·00
Aged 11-12	2·45	2·45
Aged 5-10	2·00	2·00
Aged under 5	1·70	1·70

(a) £11·50 when both are blind.

For long-term cases, in place of discretionary additions under national assistance to meet small special needs, there is an addition of 50p a week to the income requirements. It applies to those over pension age who claim supplementary pensions (with certain exceptions), and also to those below pension age, other than the unemployed, after they have been in receipt of an allowance for two years. The addition is 75p if the claimant or a dependant of the claimant is aged 80 or over.

The amount to be added for rent if the claimant (or his wife or her husband) is the householder is normally his net rent and rates in full; and in the case of the non-householder aged 18 or over, 65p a week.

The rules for the computation of resources contain provisions for the treatment of capital and earnings and for certain disregards.

Persons registering for employment as a condition of receiving a supplementary allowance will not generally receive more than is required to bring their total income to what it would be if they were in full-time work in their normal occupation (the "wagestop").

Individual awards of benefit are determined by the Commission; a claimant who is dissatisfied with the amount assessed has a right of appeal to an independent Appeal Tribunal.

The Commission may vary an assessment if there are exceptional circumstances but, in the case of a claim to supplementary pension, may not reduce it. The Commission also has powers, similar to those in the national assistance scheme, to award lump-sum payments to meet non-recurring exceptional requirements, and to meet charges for appliances or services supplied under the National Health Service, *e.g.* for glasses, dentures or dental treatment, and prescriptions.

The number of supplementary benefits in payment in November 1969 was: pensions 1,875,000; allowances 813,000.

At the end of November, 1969, about 228,000 recipients were registered at the Employment Exchange; most of the rest were old, sick or otherwise out of the employment field. At the same date, 98 per cent. of those with pensions and 35 per cent. of those with allowances were receiving the long-term addition. In 1969 assistance amounting to £2,376,000 was given to meet charges under the National Health Service for spectacles, dentures and dental treatment.

OLD PERSONS' PENSIONS

The National Insurance Acts of 1970 and 1971 provide, subject to a residence test, a non-contributory retirement pension of £3·60 a week (£2·20

for a married woman) for persons who were over pensionable age on July 5, 1948, and for others when they reach 80 if they are not already getting a national insurance retirement or old persons' pension or if they are getting a national insurance pension at less than these rates. Persons who are entitled to national insurance retirement or old persons' pension receive an *age addition* of 25p per week to their pension if they are aged 80 or over.

ATTENDANCE ALLOWANCES

The Acts of 1970 and 1971 provide for the payment of a constant attendance allowance of £4·80 a week (less for younger children) to the severely disabled, as determined by an Attendance Allowance Board. The allowance, which became payable from December 6, 1971, is treated as an additional requirement under the supplementary benefits scheme.

FAMILY ALLOWANCES

The scheme provides for a payment out of moneys provided by Parliament of a weekly allowance for each child in a family other than the elder or eldest. The scheme now operates under the Family Allowances Act, 1965, as amended by the Family Allowances and National Insurance Acts, 1967 and 1968. From October 8, 1968, under the Family Allowances and National Insurance Act, 1968, the allowance was increased to 90p for second children and £1.00 for subsequent children, and consequential reductions were made in dependency benefit for second and subsequent children under the National Insurance Acts and the Industrial Injuries Acts.

The Ministry of Social Security Act, 1966, transferred the administration of the family allowances scheme from the Ministry of Pensions and National Insurance to the new Ministry of Social Security (now the Department of Health and Social Security). The allowance is payable (through the Post Office) while a child is of school age or, if handicapped, under 16, and up to 19 if he or she is undergoing full-time instruction in a school or is an apprentice. Claim forms for allowances can be obtained at any local Social Security Office. Claims are decided by the National Insurance adjudication authorities.

At the end of 1969, allowances were in payment for over 4 million families (comprising about 11 million children). The cost of family allowances in the financial year 1968–69 was about £297 million, as compared with about £160 million in 1967–68.

FAMILY INCOME SUPPLEMENTS

From August 3, 1971, under the Family Income Supplements Act, 1970, and regulations made thereunder, a new benefit of up to £4·00 a week, met out of Exchequer funds, became payable to families with at least one dependent child under 16 (or over 16 if still at school) whose total family income is below the "prescribed amount" if the head of the family (in the case of a couple, the man) is engaged, and normally engaged, in remunerative full-time work (i.e., 30 or more hours a week). The "prescribed amount" is £18 if there is one child in the family and rises by £2 for each additional child. "Total income" includes gross earnings, family allowances and a wife's earnings. The supplement is one-half of the amount by which the family's total income falls below the "prescribed amount": odd amounts are rounded up to the next 10p above, and the minimum amount payable is 20p a week. Claim forms can be obtained at a Social Security Office or a Post Office. Claims are decided by the Supplementary Benefits Commission but there is an appeal to an independent Appeal Tribunal.

COMBINED WEEKLY FLAT-RATE CONTRIBUTIONS

From September 20, 1971, the main combined weekly flat-rate contributions for National Insurance, the National Health Service and, in the case of employed persons, Industrial Injuries Insurance, paid by means of stamps on a single insurance card, were as follows:—

	Employees contracted out			Employees not contracted out			Self-employed persons	Non-employed persons
	Employee	Employer	Total	Employee	Employer	Total		
	£	£	£	£	£	£	£	£
Men 18 and over......	1·00	1·007	2·007	0·88	0·887	1·767	1·50	1·20
Women 18 and over ..	0·83	0·851	1·681	0·75	0·771	1·521	1·25	0·94
Boys under 18........ }	FLAT-RATE		{	0·57	0·62	1·19	0·85	0·68
Girls under 18........ }	CONTRIBUTIONS		{	0·48	0·53	1·01	0·73	0·55

All employers now pay with National Insurance contributions the Selective Employment Tax (£1·20 a week for each man employed, £0·60 for each woman, £0·60 for each boy under 18, and £0·40 for each girl under 18). Employers of persons aged 18 and over pay a further £0·063 for men and £0·029 for women in the combined contribution as a contribution to the Redundancy Fund under the Redundancy Payments Act. Further details of the various contributions including the special rates for certain employed married women, widows and people over pension age are obtainable at local Social Security Offices.

Distribution of Combined Weekly Flat-rate Contributions

	Employed Person				Employer			
	Men	Women	Boys	Girls	Men	Women	Boys	Girls
National Insurance:	£	£	£	£	£	£	£	£
Employees:								
Contracted out.......	0·792	0·665			0·864	0·718		
Not contracted out....	0·672	0·585	0·461	0·381	0·744	0·638	0·507	0·417
Industrial Injuries Insurance	0·05	0·04	0·03	0·02	0·06	0·05	0·03	0·03
National Health Service....	0·158	0·125	0·079	0·079	0·083	0·083	0·083	0·083

	Self-employed Person				Non-employed Person			
	Men	Women	Boys	Girls	Men	Women	Boys	Girls
	£	£	£	£	£	£	£	£
National Insurance........	1·333	1·117	0·762	0 642	1·033	0·807	0·592	0·462
National Health Service....	0·167	0·133	0·088	0·088	0·167	0·133	0·088	0·088

GRADUATED NATIONAL INSURANCE CONTRIBUTIONS (see p. 495)

Employed men and women aged 18 or over who are not in part contracted out of the graduated pension scheme pay in addition to the ordinary flat-rate contribution a weekly graduated contribution (collected in association with P.A.Y.E. income tax). This amounts to approximately 4·75 per cent of that part of their pay between £9 and £18 a week plus 4·35 per cent. of pay between £18 and £42 a week. The employer pays the same amount. Contracted-out persons aged 18 or over and their employers each pay about 0·05 per cent of earnings between £9 and £18 a week and 4·35 per cent. of earnings between £18 and £42 a week.

Examples of the weekly graduated contributions payable by weekly paid employees are given below:

Total Weekly Pay	If not contracted out	If contracted out
£	£	£
10...	0·06	
20...	0·54	0·15
30...	0·97	
42 or over..	1·47	1·08

Fuller details are given in leaflets available at local Social Security Offices.

NATIONAL HEALTH SERVICE

The National Health Service came into being on July 5, 1948, as a result of the *National Health Service Act*, 1946. The Act places a duty on the Secretary of State for Social Services to promote the establishment in England of a comprehensive Health Service designed to secure improvement in the mental and physical health of the people and the prevention, diagnosis and treatment of illness. The Secretary of State for Wales administers the National Health Service in Wales. There are separate Acts for Scotland and Northern Ireland, where the Health Services are run on very similar lines. The Secretaries of State are responsible to Parliament for seeing that Health Services of all kinds of the highest possible quality are available to all who need them. They are advised by the Central Health Services Council (and certain Standing Advisory Committees dealing with special subjects), appointed after consultation with the various interested bodies.

The National Health Service which covers a comprehensive range of hospital, specialist, practitioner (medical, dental, ophthalmic), pharmaceutical, appliance and local authority health and social services, is available to every man, woman and child in the country. Everyone normally resident in the country is entitled to use the Service as a whole or any complete part of it. No insurance qualification is necessary. Most of the cost of running the service is met from the Consolidated Fund—that is, from taxes. Other sources of finance are: (1) the weekly National Health Service contributions (since September, 1957), which are estimated to produce about £208,000,000, approximately 11·1 per cent. of the total cost of the Service in 1971–72. (For convenience these are collected with the National Insurance contribution in a single combined weekly stamp); (ii) local taxation, which with Consolidated Fund grants pays for 88·2 per cent. of the cost of local health and welfare services; (iii) partial charges to patients for drugs and dressings, spectacles, dentures and dental treatment and amenity beds in hospital. The cost of the Health and Welfare Services in England and Wales rose from £860,000,000 in 1960–61 to an estimated total of £2,197,000,000 in 1971–72. In Scotland the National Health Service vote totalled £228,367,000 in 1971–72 compared with a revised estimate of £194,903,000 in 1970–71.

THE HEALTH SERVICES
Family Doctor Service

In England and Wales the Family Doctor Service is organized by 134 Executive Councils which also organize the General Dental, Pharmaceutical and Ophthalmic Eye Services for their areas. With few exceptions there is an Executive Council for each county and county borough area; members, who serve voluntarily, are appointed by local doctors, dentists, pharmacists and opticians (15), the Local Health Authority (8) and the Secretary of State for Social Services (7). Any doctor may take part in the Family Doctor Scheme, provided the area in which he wishes to practise has not already an adequate number of doctors, and about 20,000 general practitioners do so. They may at the same time have private fee-paying patients. Family doctors are paid for their Health Service work in accordance with a scheme of remuneration which includes *inter alia* a basic practice allowance, capitation fees, reimbursement of certain practice expenses and payments for " out of hours " work.

Everyone aged 16 or over can choose his doctor (parents or guardians choose for children under 16) and the doctor is also free to accept a person or not as he chooses. A person may change his doctor if he wishes, either at once if he has changed his address or obtained permission of the doctor on whose list he is, or by informing the local Executive Council (in which case 14 days must elapse before the other doctor can accept him). When people are away from home they can still use the Family Doctor Service if they ask to be treated as " temporary residents", and in an emergency, if a person's own doctor is not available, any doctor in the service will give treatment and advice.

Patients are treated either in the doctor's surgery or, when necessary, at home. Doctors may prescribe for their patients all drugs and medicines which are medically necessary for their treatment and also a certain number of surgical appliances (the more elaborate being provided through the hospitals).

Drugs, Medicines and Appliances.—The number of chemists (including drug stores and appliance suppliers) in England and Wales, within the National Health Service at December 31, 1970, was 13,018. 295,458,000 prescriptions were dispensed in 1970.

Dental Service

Dentists, like doctors, may take part in the Service and may also have private patients. About 10,400 of the dentists available for general practice

have joined the National Health Service. They are responsible to the Executive Councils in whose areas they provide services.

Patients are free to go to any dentist taking part in the Service and willing to accept them, and cannot register with any particular dentist. Dentists receive payment for items of treatment for individual patients, instead of the capitation fee received by doctors. There is no need for the patient to obtain a recommendation before seeking dental treatment. The dentist is able to carry out at once all normal conservative treatment (*e.g.* fillings), provision of dentures in some cases, emergency treatment and ordinary denture repairs; he seeks prior approval from the Dental Estimates Board before undertaking treatment when it involves the extraction of teeth and the provision of dentures (in some cases); extensive and prolonged treatment of the gums; inlays and crowns (in some cases); special appliances and oral surgery and certain other items.

A dentist may, with the approval of the Dental Estimates Board, charge his patient a prescribed sum for such types of treatment as crowns, inlays or metal dentures where these are not clinically necessary, if the patient wishes to have them. Where a denture supplied under the Service has to be replaced because of loss or damage the whole or part of the cost may be charged to the patient if he has been careless. In May, 1951, charges were introduced for dentures; these were increased in May, 1961, to £2 5s.–£2 15s.for the supply of one denture or up to £5 for a set. In June, 1952, a charge of £1, or the full cost of any treatment if less than £1, was introduced. This charge was increased to £1 10s. from May 1, 1968. From Aug. 11, 1969, the charge for a set of dentures was increased to £6 5s., with proportionate increases for partial dentures. From April 1, 1971, the system of charges was changed so that patients became liable for half the cost of treatment, including the supply of dentures, if required, up to a maximum charge of £10 for one course of treatment, unless they were exempt from charges or entitled to remission on income grounds. No charge is made for clinical examination of a patient's mouth. Expectant mothers or mothers who have had a child during the preceding twelve months, children under 16, or 16 or over, but still in full-time attendance at school, do not pay charges. Other patients between 16 and 20 years of age pay half the cost for dentures only.

General Ophthalmic Service

General Ophthalmic Services, which are administered by Executive Councils, form part of the ophthalmic services available under the National Health Service and provide for the testing of sight and supply of glasses to meet more normal needs only. Diagnosis and specialist treatment of eye conditions is available through the Hospital Eye Service as well as the provision of glasses of a special type. Testing of sight may be carried out by any ophthalmic medical practitioner or ophthalmic optician, and glasses supplied by any ophthalmic optician or dispensing optician taking part in the Services. On the first occasion a person wishes to use the Services he must obtain a medical recommendation from his doctor that his sight needs testing. No further recommendation is required subsequently and the Services may be used direct.

Sight testing is free. The charges for lenses broadly cover the cost of the lenses and the opticians dispensing fee. They range from £1.20 per lens to a maximum of £3.50 per lens. The cost of the frame must also be paid. Children up to the age of 16 or older children attending full-time school may be supplied free of charge with standard lenses in children's standard frames. Additionally, school-children aged 10 years or over may be supplied with standard lenses without charge if any other type of NHS frame is used. The charge for the frame must then be paid.

Hospitals and Specialists

On July 5, 1948, ownership of 2,688 out of 3,040 voluntary and municipal hospitals in England and Wales was vested in the Minister of Health (now Secretary of State for Social Services). The Minister has a duty to provide hospital accommodation and specialist services to such an extent as he considers necessary to meet all reasonable requirements for the treatment of the acutely ill, maternity cases, the chronic sick and those suffering from tuberculosis or infectious diseases as well as the mentally disordered. Convalescent treatment is also provided for those who need it and surgical and medical appliances are supplied in appropriate cases.

In the main, this part of the Service is organized by 15 Hospital Boards (*see* pp. 393-4); in all of these regions there is a University having a teaching hospital or medical school. Hospitals are administered on behalf of the Boards by about 300 Hospital Management Committees. The only hospitals in the Service outside the Regional Boards' immediate responsibility are the teaching hospitals which provide facilities for undergraduate and postgraduate medical or dental education and which are administered by Boards of Governors. There are 25 Boards of Governors in London and 9 in the rest of the country.

Specialists and consultants who take part in the Service (and nearly all of them do so) hold hospital appointments on a whole or part-time basis. Those who have part-time appointments can engage in private practice including the treatment of their private patients in NHS hospitals.

In a number of hospitals accommodation is available for the treatment of private in-patients who undertake to pay full hospital maintenance costs and (usually) separate medical fees to a specialist as well. The amount of these fees is a matter for agreement between doctor and patient. Hospital charges for private patients are determined annually, on a national basis for class of hospital, by the Secretary of State in accordance with the Health Services and Public Health Act, 1968. These charges are revised annually from April 1 each year to reflect the average cost, for class of hospital, which it is estimated will be incurred during the current financial year in the treatment of in-patients.

For in-patients paying specialists' fees separately, the hospital daily charges from April 1, 1971 for accommodation and services in each class of hospital are as follows:—

	Single room	Other
Long stay hospitals*	£ 6.10	£ 5.60
Psychiatric hospitals*	£ 3.60	£ 3.20
Acute and other hospitals*	£10.10	£ 9.20
London teaching hospitals	£14.60	£13.30
Private teaching hospitals and university hospitals	£12.00	£11.00

* other than teaching or university hospitals.

Certain hospitals have accommodation in single rooms or small wards which, if not required for patients who need privacy for medical reasons, may be made available to patients who desire it as an amenity. Amenity bed charges are at present £1.50 per day in single rooms and 75p per day in small wards. In such cases the patients are treated in every other respect as National Health patients.

With certain exceptions, hospital out-patients have to pay fixed charges for dentures and glasses. The charge for glasses will be related to the type of lens prescribed; and for dentures to the type of denture provided, subject to a maximum charge of £10.00.

Local Authority Health and Welfare Services

Local authorities are responsible for the organization, management and administration of the personal social services and each authority has a Social Services Committee responsible for the social services functions placed upon them by the Local Authority Social Services Act, 1970 and a Director of Social Services. The " personal social services " are broadly speaking as follows: The services for children, including the care of children and young persons received into care, the provision of treatment for young offenders and adoption; family services, including the day care of pre-school children in day nurseries and by child minders, the care of unsupported mothers both in the community and in mother and baby homes, and the home help service; services for the elderly, including residential accommodation; temporary accommodation for the homeless; welfare services for the disabled and physically handicapped; welfare services for the mentally disordered, including day centres; clubs, adult training centres, workshops and residential accommodation.

EDUCATION DIRECTORY

THE UNIVERSITY OF OXFORD

FULL TERMS, 1972

Hilary, Jan. 16 to March 11
Trinity, April 23 to June 17
Michaelmas, Oct. 15 to Dec. 9

NUMBER OF UNDERGRADUATES IN RESIDENCE
Michaelmas Term, 1970, 11,071

UNIVERSITY OFFICES, &c.   Elect.

Chancellor, Rt. Hon. Harold Macmillan,
Balliol............................... 1960
High Steward, The Lord Wilberforce, P.C.,
C.M.G., O.B.E., M.A., All Souls 1967
Vice-Chancellor, A. L. C. Bullock, M.A.,
D.Litt., Master of St. Catherine's......... 1969
Proctors, H. Davies, M.A., D.Phil., Christ
Church; P. G. H. Sandars, M.A., D.Phil.,
Balliol............................... 1971
Assessor, A. Jones, M.A., St. Cross.......... 1971
Assessor of the Chancellor's Court, Sir Humph-
rey Waldock, C.M.G., O.B.E., Q.C., D.C.L.,
All Souls.............................. 1947
Public Orator, C. G. Hardie, M.A., Magdalen. 1967
Bodley's Librarian, R. Shackleton, M.A.,
D.Litt., Brasenose..................... 1966
Keeper of Archives, T. H. Aston, M.A., Corpus
Christi............................... 1969
Keeper of the Ashmolean Museum, R. W.
Hamilton, M.A., Magdalen.............. 1962
Keeper of the Dept. of Western Art, K. J.
Garlick, M.A., Balliol.................. 1968
Keeper of Dept. of Antiquities, R. W.
Hamilton, M.A., Magdalen.............. 1957
Keeper of Dept. of Eastern Art, J. C. Harle, M.A.,
D.Phil., Christ Church 1967
Keeper of Heberden Coin Room, C. H. V.
Sutherland, C.B.E., M.A., D.Litt., Ch. Ch ... 1957
Curator of the Museum of History of Science,
F. R. Maddison, M.A., Linacre 1965
Registrar of the University, Sir Folliott Sand-
ford, K.B.E., C.M.G., M.A. New College.... 1958
Secretary for Administration, B. G. Campbell,
M.A., Merton......................... 1961
Deputy do., A. L. Fleet, M.A., Pembroke.... 1963
Senior Assistant Registrars, C. H. Paterson,
M.A., Corpus (1971); Miss E. R. M. Noyce,
M.A., Linacre (1969); A. J. Dorey, M.A.,
D.Phil., Pembroke (1969); A. Ostler, B.C.L.,
M.A., Queen's......................... 1970
Assistant Registrars, R. A. Malyn, M.A., St.
Peter's (1961); H. P. Ruglys, M.A., Hert-
ford (1966); G. P. Collyer, M.A., St.
Catherine's (1966); P. S. Crane, M.A., Jesus
(1966); J. P. W. Roper, M.A., Lincoln
(1967); P. Garnham, M.A. Worcester, (1967);
Miss M. E. Grinyer, M.A., St. Hilda's
(1968); Miss A. M. Barr (1969); J. D.
Brown................................ 1971
Secretary of Faculties, H. W. Deane, M.A..... 1971
Secretary to the Curators of the University
Chest, J. K. Batey, M.A., Christ Church.... 1964
Chief Accountant, H. Barrett, M.A., Balliol.. 1961
Registrar of the Chancellor's Court, F. R.
Williamson, M.A., Pembroke............. 1964
University Counsel, F. H. B. W. Layfield, M.A.,
Corpus............................... 1971
Clerk of the Schools, G. A. Barnes.......... 1971
Land Agent to the University, J. R. Mills, M.A.,
Pembroke............................. 1961
Surveyor to the University, J. Lankester, M.A.,
Univ................................. 1956

Director, Department of Educational Studies,
A. D. C. Peterson, O.B.E., M.A., Balliol.... 1957
SECRETARY TO DELEGATES OF:—
Examination of Schools, J. M. Todd, M.A.,
Queen's.
Local Exams., J. R. Cummings, B.Litt.,
M.A., B.N.C.
Science Area, G. E. S. Turner, M.A., St.
Catherine's.
University Press, C. H. Roberts, M.A., St.
John's.
SECRETARY OF:—
Accommodation Committee, A. W. Davies,
M.A., Magdalen
Committee for Appointments, T. Snow, M.A.,
New College.
The Rhodes Trustees, E. T. Williams, C.B.,
C.B.E., D.S.O., M.A., Balliol.

HEBDOMADAL COUNCIL

Ex-Officio Members, the Chancellor; the Vice-
Chancellor; the Principal of Jesus; Dr. R. N.
Franklin; the Proctors; the Assessor.

Elected by the Congregation—
The Provost of Oriel; the Provost of Queen's; the
President of Magdalen; the President of Corpus
Christi; the Dean of Christ Church; the Principal
of Linacre; the Principal of St. Hugh's; the
Principal of St. Anne's; J. H. C. Thompson, M.A.,
D.Phil.; E. T. Williams, C.B., C.B.E., D.S.O., M.A.;
M. G. Brock, M.A.; R. A. Fletcher, M.A., D.Phil.;
R. P. H. Gasser, M.A., D.Phil.; M. Shock, M.A.;
Miss E. A. O. Whiteman, M.A., D.Phil.; Prof.
J. Harley, M.A., D.Phil.; A. H. Cooke, M.A.,
D.Phil.; R. J. Elliott, M.A., D.Phil.

Oxford Colleges and Halls
(With dates of foundation)

All Souls (1438), J. H. A. Sparrow, M.A., Warden
(1952).
Balliol (1263), J. E. C. Hill, M.A., D.Litt., Master
(1965).
Brasenose (1509) Sir Noel Hall, M.A., Principal (1960).
Christ Church (1546), Very Rev. H. Chadwick, D.D.,
Dean (1969).
Corpus Christi (1517), G. D. G. Hall, M.A., President
(1969).
Exeter (1314), Sir Kenneth Wheare, C.M.G., M.A.,
D.Litt., F.B.A., Rector (1956).
Hertford (1874), Principal (vacant).
Jesus (1571), H. J. Habakkuk, M.A., Principal (1967).
Keble (1868), Rev. D. E. Nineham, B.D., M.A.,
Warden (1969).
Linacre (1962), J. B. Bamborough, M.A., Principal
(1962).
Lincoln (1427), W. F. Oakeshott, M.A., F.S.A.,
Rector (1953).
Magdalen (1458), J. H. E. Griffiths, O.B.E., M.A.,
D.Phil., President (1968).
Merton (1264), R. E. Richards, M.A., D.Phil., D.Sc.,
Warden (1969).
New College (1379), Sir William Hayter, K.C.M.G.,
M.A., Warden (1958).
Nuffield (1937), D. N. Chester, M.A., Warden (1954).
Oriel (1326), K. C. Turpin, M.A., B.Litt., Provost
(1957).
Pembroke (1624), Sir George Pickering, D.M., F.R.S.,
Master (1969).
Queen's (1340), The Lord Blake, M.A., Provost (1969).
St. Antony's (1950), A. R. M. Carr, M.A., Warden
(1968).
St. Catherine's (1962), A. L. C. Bullock, M.A.,
D.Litt., Master (1962).
St. Cross (1965), W. E. van Heyningen, M.A., Ph.D.,
D.Sc., Master (1965).

St. Edmund Hall (1270), Rev. Canon J. N. D. Kelly, D.D., *Principal* (1951).

St. John's (1555), R. W. Southern, M.A., (*President*) (1969). [(1969)

St. Peter's (1929) Sir Alec Cairncross, K.C.M.G. *Master*

Trinity (1554), A. G. Ogston, M.A., D.SC., F.R.S., *President* (1970).

University (1249), The Lord Redcliffe-Maud, G.C.B., C.B.E., *Master* (1963).

Wadham (1612), S. N. Hampshire, M.A., *Warden* (1970).

Wolfson (1965), Sir Isaiah Berlin, O.M., C.B.E., M.A., *President* (1966).

Worcester (1714), The Lord Franks, P.C., G.C.M.G., K.C.B., C.B.E., M.A., *Provost* (1962).

Campion Hall, Rev. E. J. Yarnold, M.A., *Master* (1965).

St. Benet's Hall, Rev. C. L. J. Forbes, M.A., *Master* (1964).

Mansfield (1886), Rev. G. B. Caird, D.Phil., D.D., *Principal* (1970).

Regent's Park, Rev. B. R. White, M.A., D.Phil., *Principal* (1971).

Greyfriars Hall, Very Rev. P. E. L. Peacock, M.A., D.Mus., *Warden* (1953).

Lady Margaret Hall (1878), Mrs. E. M. Chilver, M.A. *Principal* (1971).

St. Anne's (1952) (Originally *Society of Oxford Home-Students* (1879)), Mrs. N. K. Trenaman, M.A., *Principal* (1966).

St. Hilda's (1893) Mrs. M. L. S. Bennett, M.A., *Principal* (1965).

St. Hugh's (1886), Miss K. M. Kenyon, C.B.E., M.A., D.Litt., F.B.A., *Principal* (1962).

Somerville (1879), Mrs. B. Craig, M.A., *Principal* (1967).

UNIVERSITY PROFESSORS

	Elect.
American History (Harmsworth), W. E. Leuchtenberg, M.A., *Queen's*	1971
American History and Institutions (Rhodes), H. G. Nicholas, M.A., *New College*	1969
Anatomy (Lee's), G. W. Harris, C.B.E., D.M., F.R.S., *Hertford*	1962
Anæsthetics (Nuffield), A. C. Smith, M.A., *Pemb.*	1965
Anglo-Saxon, A. Campbell, B.Litt., M.A., *Pembroke*	1963
Animal Behaviour, N. Tinbergen, M.A., D.Phil., F.R.S., *Wolfson*	1966
Anthropology, Social, M. Freedman, M.A., *All Souls*	1970
Arabic (Laudian), A. F. L. Beeston, M.A., D.Phil., *St. John's*	1955
Archæology, European, C. F. C. Hawkes, M.A., *Keble*	1946
Archæology (Lincoln), C. M. Robertson, M.A., *Linc.*	1961
Archæology of the Roman Empire, S. S. Frere, M.A., *All Souls*	1966
Armenian Studies (Gulbenkian), C. J. F. Dowsett, M.A., *Pembroke*	1965
Astronomy (Savilian), D. E. Blackwell, M.A., *New Coll.*	1960
Biochemistry (Whitley), R. R. Porter, M.A., *Trinity*	1967
Biomathematics, M. S. Bartlett, M.A.	1967
Botany (Sherardian), F. R. Whatley, M.A., *Magdalen*	1971
Byzantine and Modern Greek Lang. and Lit. (Bywater and Sotheby), K. Mitsakis, *Exeter*	1968
Celtic, I. Ll. Foster, M.A., *Jesus*	1947
Chemical Crystallography, H. M. Powell, B.SC., M.A., *Hertford*	1964
Chemical Crystallography (Royal Society's Wolfson Research Professor), Mrs. D. M. Hodglein, B.SC., M.A., *Somerville*	1960

	Elect.
Chemical Microbiology (Iveagh), J. Mandelstam, M.A., *Linacre*	1966
Chemical Pathology, E. P. Abraham, M.A., D.Phil, *Lincoln*	1964
Chemistry, Inorganic, J. S. Anderson, M.A., *St. Catherine's*	1963
Chemistry (Lee's), Sir Frederick Dainton, Ph.D., SC.D., F.R.S., *Exeter*	1970
Chemistry (Waynflete), Sir Ewart Jones, M.A., F.R.S., *Magd.*	1955
Chemistry, Sir Harold Thompson, C.B.E., M.A., D.SC., *St. John's*	1964
Chinese (vacant).	
Civil Law (Regius), A. M. Honoré, D.C.L., *All Souls*	1971
Clinical Neurology, W. B. Matthews, D.M., *St. Edmund Hall*	1970
Comparative Philology, Mrs. A. E. Davies, M.A., *Somerville*	1971
Comparative Slavonic Philology, R. Auty, M.A., *Brasenose*	1965
Computation, C. Strachey, M.A., *Wolfson*	1971
Divinity (Regius), Rev. Canon M. F. Wiles, D.D., *Ch. Ch.*	1970
Divinity (Lady Margaret), Rev. Canon J. Macquarrie, M.A., *Ch. Ch.*	1970
Eastern Religions and Ethics (Spalding), R. C. Zaehner, M.A., *All Souls*	1952
Ecclesiastical History (Regius), Rev. Canon S. L. Greenslade, D.D., *Ch. Ch.*	1960
Economic History (Chichele), P. Mathias, M.A., *All Souls*	1968
Economics, Applied, J. A. C. Brown, M.A., *Merton*	1970
Economics, J. A. Mirrlees, M.A., *Nuffield*	1968
Economics of Underdeveloped Countries, I. M. D. Little, M.A., D.Phil., *Nuffield*	1971
Egyptology, Rev. J. W. B. Barns, M.A., D.Phil., *Queen's*	1965
Engineering Science, D. W. Holder, M.A., F.R.S., *B.N.C.*	1961
Engineering, Structural (Stewarts and Lloyds), W. S. Hemp, M.A., *Keble*	1965
English Language, E. J. Dobson, M.A., D.Phil., *Jesus*	1961
English Language and Literature (Merton), N. Davis, M.A., *Merton*	1959
English Literature (Merton), Dame Helen Gardner, D.B.E., M.A., D.Litt., F.B.A., *St. Hilda's*	1966
English Literature (Goldsmiths'), R. Ellmann, *New*	1970
Exegesis (Ireland), Rev. G. D. Kilpatrick, D.D., *Queen's*	1949
Experimental Philosophy (Lee's), B. Bleaney, C.B.E., M.A., D.Phil., F.R.S., *Wadham*	1957
Fine Art (Slade), R. Rosenblum	1971
Forest Science, J. L. Harley, M.A., D.Phil., *St. John's*	1969
French (Foch), J. J. Seznec, M.A., F.B.A., Ph.D., *All Souls*	1950
French Literature, I. D. MacFarlane, M.A.	1971
Genetics, W. F. Bodmer, M.A., *Keble*	1970
Geography, J. Gottmann, M.A., *Hertford*	1968
Geology, E. A. Vincent, M.A., *University*	1966
Geometry (Savilian), I. M. James, M.A., D.Phil., F.R.S., *St. John's*	1970
George Eastman Visiting, H. L. Teuber, M.A., *Balliol*	1971
German Language and Literature (Taylor), S. S. Prawer, M.A., D.Litt., *Queen's*	1969
Government and Public Administration (Gladstone), M. Beloff, B.Litt., M.A., *All Souls*	1957
Greek (Regius), P. H. J. Lloyd-Jones, M.A., *Ch. Ch.*	1960

Elect.

Hebrew (Regius), W. D. McHardy, M.A., D.Phil., *St. John's*...... 1960

History, Ancient (Camden), P. A Brunt, *Brasenose*........ 1970

History, Ancient (Wykeham), A. Andrewes, M.A., *New Coll*.......... 1953

History of Art, F. J. H. Haskell, M.A., *Trinity*. 1967

History of the British Commonwealth (Beit), R. E. Robinson, M.A., *Balliol*...... 1971

History of Latin America (vacant).

History of Philosophy, J. L. Ackrill, M.A., *B.N.C.*......... 1966

History of War (Chichele), N. H. Gibbs, M.A., D.Phil., *All Souls*....... 1953

Icelandic Literature and Antiquities (Vigfusson), E. O. G. Turville-Petre, B.Litt., M.A., *Ch. Ch*........ 1953

International Relations (Montague Burton), Hon. A. F. Buchan, C.B.E., M.A., *Balliol*... 1972

Interpretation of Holy Scripture, Rev. H. F. D. Sparks, D.D., F.B.A., *Oriel*...... 1952

Italian (Serena), C. Grayson, M.A., *Magdalen*. 1958

Jurisprudence, R. M. Dworkin, M.A., *University*....... 1969

Latin (Corpus), R. G. M. Nisbet, M.A., *Corpus* 1970

Law (Comparative), J. K. B. M. Nicholas, M.A., *Brasenose*...... 1971

Law (English), H. W. R. Wade, Q.C., D.C.L., *St. John's*......... 1961

Law (English) (Vinerian), A. R. N. Cross, D.C.L., *All Souls*........ 1964

Logic (Wykeham), Sir Alfred Ayer, M.A., F.B.A., *New Coll*....... 1959

Mathematics, J. F. C. Kingman, M.A., *St. Cross*........ 1969

Mathematics (Rouse Ball), C. A. Coulson, M.A., F.R.S., *Wadham*....... 1952

Mathematics (Theory of Plasma), L. C. Woods, M.A., D.Phil., D.Sc., *Balliol*........ 1970

Medicine (Regius), Sir William Doll, O.B.E., M.D., D.Sc., F.R.S., *Christchurch*...... 1969

Medicine, Clinical (Nuffield), P. B. Beeson, D.M., *Magd*....... 1965

Metallurgy (Wolfson), P. B. Hirsch, M.A., D.Phil., F.R.S., *St. Edmund Hall*...... 1966

Metallurgy, Physical, J. W. Christian, M.A., D.Phil., *St. Edmund Hall*...... 1967

Metaphysical Philosophy (Waynflete), P. F. Strawson, M.A., *Magd*...... 1968

Modern History (Chichele), G. Barraclough, M.A., *All Souls*........ 1970

Modern History (Regius), H. R. Trevor-Roper, M.A., *Oriel*....... 1957

Modern History, R. B. Wernham, M.A., *Worcester*........ 1951

Molecular Biophysics, D. C. Phillips, M.A., *Corpus Christi*...... 1966

Moral and Pastoral Theology (Regius) (vacant).

Moral Philosophy (White's), R. M. Hare, M.A., *Corpus Christi*...... 1966

Music, J. W. Kerman, M.A., *Wadham*...... 1971

Natural Philosophy (Sedleian), A. E. Green, M.A., *Queen's*....... 1968

Neurophysiology, C. G. Phillips, M.A., B.Sc., D.M., F.R.S., *Trin*. 1966

Numerical Analysis (and Director of Computing Laboratory), L. Fox, M.A., D.Phil., D.Sc., *Balliol*........ 1964

Nuclear Structure, K. W. Allen, M.A., *Balliol* 1963

Obstetrics and Gynæcology (Nuffield), J. A. Stallworthy, M.A., *Queen's*....... 1967

Orthopædic Surgery (Nuffield), R. B. Duthie, M.A., *Worcester*....... 1966

Pathology, H. Harris, M.A., D.Phil., F.R.S., *Lincoln*........ 1963

Elect.

Pathology (Royal Society's), J. L. Gowans, M.A., D.Phil., *St. Catherine's*...... 1962

Pharmacology, W. D. M. Paton,, C.B.E., D.M., F.R.S., *New Coll*....... 1959

Philosophy of the Christian Religion (Nolloth), B. G. Mitchell, M.A., *Oriel*...... 1967

Physics, N. Kurti, M.A., *B.N.C.* 1967

Physics (Wykeham), Sir Rudolf Peierls, C.B.E., M.A., *New College*....... 1963

Physics, Elementary Particle, D. H. Perkins, M.A., F.R.S.......... 1965

Physics, Experimental, D. H. Wilkinson, M.A., F.R.S., *Ch. Ch*........ 1959

Physics, Theoretical (Royal Society's), R. H. Dalitz, M.A., *All Souls*........ 1963

Physiology (Waynflete), D. Whitteridge, B.Sc., D.M., F.R.S. *Magd*........ 1968

Poetry, R. B. Fuller, C.B.E., M.A., *New College* 1968

Political Economy (Drummond), R. C. O. Matthews, M.A., *All Souls*........ 1965

Psychiatry (Handley) M. G. Gelder, D.M., *Merton*......... 1969

Psychology, L. Weiskrantz, M.A., *Magdalen*.. 1967

Psychology (Watts), J. S. Bruner, M.A., *Wolfson* 1972

Public International Law (Chichele), Sir Humphrey Waldock, C.M.G., O.B.E., Q.C., D.C.L., *All Souls*....... 1947

Pure Mathematics (Waynflete), G. Higman, M.A., D.Phil., F.R.S., *Magdalen*...... 1960

Race Relations (Rhodes), K. Kirkwood, M.A., *St. Ant*...... 1954

Romance Languages, S. Ullmann, M.A., *Trinity* 1968

Rural Economy (Sibthorpian), J. H. Burnett, M.A., D.Phil., *St. John's*....... 1970

Russian, J. L. I. Fennell, M.A., *New Coll*..... 1966

Russian and Balkan History, D. Obolensky, M.A., *Ch. Ch*....... 1961

Sanskrit (Boden), T. Burrow, M.A., F.B.A., *Balliol*....... 1944

Social and Political Theory (Chichele), J. P. Plamenatz, M.A., *Nuffield*....... 1967

Spanish Studies (King Alfonso XIII), P. E. Russell, M.A., *Exeter*....... 1953

Surgery (Nuffield), P. R. Allison, D.M., *Balliol* 1954

Zoology (Entomology) (Hope), G. C. Varley, M.A., *Jesus*....... 1948

Zoology (Linacre), J. W. S. Pringle M.B.E., M.A., D.Sc., F.R.S., *Merton*....... 1961

THE UNIVERSITY OF CAMBRIDGE
FULL TERMS, 1972

Lent, Jan. 11 to Mar. 10; *Easter*, Apr. 18 to June 9; *Michaelmas*, Oct. 3 to Dec. 3.

NUMBER OF UNDERGRADUATES IN RESIDENCE

1970–71: *Men*, 7,346; *Women*, 1,091.

Chancellor, The Lord Adrian, O.M., M.D., F.R.S., *Trin*........ 1967

Vice-Chancellor, Prof. W. A. Deer, Ph.D., F.R.S., Master of *Trinity Hall*....... 1971

High Steward, The Lord Devlin, P.C., M.A., F.B.A., *Chr*....... 1966

Deputy High Steward, Rt. Hon. J. S. B. Lloyd, C.H., C.B.E., Q.C., M.P., M.A., *Magd*....... 1971

Commissary, The Lord Morris of Borth-y-Gest, P.C., C.B.E., M.C., Q.C., *Tr. H*....... 1968

Orator, L. P. Wilkinson, M.A., *King's*...... 1958

†*Registrary*, R. E. Macpherson, M.A., *King's* 1969

†*Deputy Registrary*, F. Wild, M.A., Ph.D., *Down*...... 1966

Librarian, E. B. Ceadel, M.A., *Corp*........ 1967

Treasurer, T. C. Gardner, C.B.E., M.A., *Univ*. 1969

Deputy Treasurer, A. B. Shone, M.A., *Selw*... 1969

† Correspondence for the *Registrary* and *Deputy Registrary* should be sent to the *University Registry*, The Old Schools, Cambridge.

Secretary General of the Faculties, W. J. Sartain, M.A., *Selw*.................................... 1961

Deputy Secretary General of the Faculties, L. M. Harvey, M.A., *Chur*............... 1963

Esquire Bedells, P. T. Sinker, M.A., *Cla*..... 1960

P. C. Melville, M.A., *Selw*.................. 1968

Proctors, H. R. Beck, M.A., *Pemb*.; A. J. F. Metherell, Ph.D., *Chr*.................... 1971

Organist, D. V. Willcocks, M.C., M.A., MUS.B., F.R.C.O., *King's*........................ 1958

Director, Dept. of Applied Economics, Hon. W. A. H. Godley, M.A., *King's*......... 1970

Director of the Observatories, Prof. R. O. Redman, M.A., Ph.D., F.R.S., *Joh*........ 1947

Director of the Fitzwilliam Museum, D. T. Piper, C.B.E., M.A., F.S.A., *Chr*........... 1967

Director of the Museum of Zoology, K. A. Joysey, M.A., *Fitzw*...................... 1970

Director, University Computing Service, D. F. Hartley, M.A., Ph.D., *Darw*............. 1970

Director in Industrial Co-operation, *Wolfson Cambridge Industrial Unit*, D. B. Welbourn, M.A., *Selw*............................. 1971

Curator of the Museum of Archæology and Ethnology, P. W. Gathercole, M.A., *Pet*.... 1970

Curator of the Museum of Classical Archæology, Prof. R. M. Cook, M.A., *Cla*........... 1962

Curators of the Sedgwick Museum of Geology, C. L. Forbes, M.A., Ph.D., *Cla*........... 1967

R. B. Rickards, M.A., *Emm*................ 1968

Curator of the Whipple Museum of the History of Science, D. Bryden.................... 1970

Director of the Botanic Garden, J. S. L. Gilmour, M.A., *Cla*........................... 1950

Representative on General Medical Council, W. S. Lewin, M.A., *Darw*............... 1971

SECRETARY TO:—

Local Examinations Syndicate, T. S. Wyatt, M.A., M.Litt., *Sid.*, Syndicate Buildings... 1961

Board of Extra-mural Studies, J.M.Y. Andrew, M.A., *Cath.*, Stuart House............. 1967

Highest Grade Schools Examination Syndicate, H. F. King, M.A., M.SC., *Emm.*, 10 Trumpington Street........................ 1969

Appointments Board, W. P. Kirkman, M.A., *Univ.*, 6 Chaucer Road.................. 1968

Women's Appointments Board, Miss J. F. Holgate, M.A., *Newn.*, 6 Chaucer Road.. 1966

University Library, A. Tillotson, M.A., *Univ.* 1949

University Press, T. C. Gardner, C.B.E., M.A., *Univ*................................... 1970

COUNCIL OF THE SENATE
(Secretary, The Registrary)

Ex officio Members, The Chancellor; Vice-Chancellor.

Heads of Colleges, The Master of *Magdalene*; The Master of *Pembroke*; The Master of *Trinity*; The President of *New Hall*.

Professors and Readers, Prof. C. Parry, LL.D., *Down*; J. R. Pole, M.A., *Chur.*; D. E. C. Yall, M.A., LL.B., *Chr.*; Prof. O. L. Zangwill, M.A., *King's*.

Elected as Members of the Regent House, P. W. Avery, M.A., *King's*; R. W. M. Dias, M.A., LL.B., *Magd.*; D. Harrison, M.A., Ph.D., *Selw.*; H. P. F. Swinnerton-Dyer, M.A., F.R.S., *Trin.*; B. M. Herbertson, M.A., *Fitzw.*; C. M. P. Johnson, M.A., Ph.D., *Joh.*; A. M. M. McFarquhar, M.A., Ph.D., *Down* (one vacancy).

Cambridge Colleges
(With dates of foundation)

Christ's (1505), The Lord Todd, M.A., F.R.S., *Master* (1963).

Churchill (1960), Prof. Sir William Hawthorne, C.B.E., M.A., F.R.S., *Master* (1968).

Clare (1326), Sir Eric Ashby, M.A., F.R.S., *Master* (1958).

Clare Hall (1966), Prof. A. B. Pippard, SC.D., F.R.S., *President* (1966).

Corpus Christi (1352), Sir Duncan Wilson, G.C.M.G., *Master* (1971).

Darwin (1964), Prof. F. G. Young, M.A., F.R.S., *Master* (1964).

Downing (1800), Prof. W. K. C. Guthrie, Litt.D., F.B.A., *Master* (1957).

Emmanuel (1584), Sir Gordon Sutherland, SC.D., F.R.S., *Master* (1964)

Fitzwilliam (1966), E. Miller, M.A., F.R. Hist.S., *Master* (1971).

Gonville & Caius (1348), N. J. T. M. Needham, SC.D., F.R.S., *Master* (1966).

Jesus (1496), Prof. Sir Denys Page, Litt.D., F.B.A., *Master* (1959).

King's (1441), E. R. Leach, M.A., *Provost* (1966).

Magdalene (1542), W. Hamilton, M.A. *Master* (1966).

Pembroke (1347), W. A. Camps, M.A., *Master* (1970).

Peterhouse (1284), J. C. Burkill, SC.D., F.R.S., *Master* (1968).

Queens' (1448), D. W. Bowett, M.A., LL.B., *President* (1970).

St. Catharine's (1473), Prof. E. E. Rich, Litt.D., *Master* (1957).

St. Edmund's House (1896), Very Rev. Canon G. D. Sweeney, M.A., *Master* (1964).

St. John's (1511), Prof. P. N. S. Mansergh, O.B.E., Litt.D., *Master* (1969).

Selwyn (1882), Rev. Prof. W. O. Chadwick, D.D., F.B.A., *Master* (1956).

Sidney Sussex (1596), Prof. J. W. Linnett, Ph.D., F.R.S., *Master* (1970).

Trinity (1546), The Lord Butler of Saffron Walden, K.G., P.C., C.H., M.A., HON.LL.D., *Master* (1965).

Trinity Hall (1350), Prof. W. A. Deer, Ph.D., F.R.S., *Master* (1966).

University (1965), J. S. Morrison, M.A., *President* (1966).

COLLEGES FOR WOMEN

Girton (1869), Miss M. C. Bradbrook, Litt.D., *Mistress* (1968).

Newnham (1871), Miss R. L. Cohen, C.B.E., M.A., *Principal* (1954).

Hughes Hall (formerly Cambridge T.C (1885), post-graduate students in training for teaching) Miss M. A. Wileman, M.A., *Principal* (1953).

New Hall (1954), Miss A. R. Murray, M.A., D.Phil., *President*.

Lucy Cavendish Collegiate Society (1965) (for women research students and other graduates), Mrs. C. K. Bertram M.A., Ph.D., *President* (1970).

UNIVERSITY PROFESSORS	Elect.
Aeronautical Engineering (Francis Mond), W. A. Mair, C.B.E., M.A., *Down*........	1952
Agriculture (Drapers), J. W. L. Beament, SC.D., F.R.S., *Qu*.............................	1969
American History and Institutions (Pitt), H. F. May, M.A., Ph.D., *Pemb*. (for 1971–72)	
Anatomy, R. J. Harrison, M.D., *Down*......	1968
Ancient History, M. I. Finley, M.A., *Jes*.....	1970
Ancient Philosophy (Laurence), W. K. C. Guthrie, Litt.D., F.B.A., *Down*...........	1952
Anglo-Saxon (Elrington and Bosworth), P. A. M. Clemoes, Ph.D., *Emm*...........	1969

Elect.

Animal Embryology (Charles Darwin), C. R. Austin, M.A., *Fitzw* 1967

Animal Pathology, W. I. B. Beveridge, M.A., *Jes* 1947

Applied Mathematics, G. K. Batchelor, Ph.D., F.R.S. *Trin* 1964

Applied Thermodynamics (Hopkinson and Imperial Chemical Industries), Sir William Hawthorne, C.B.E., M.A., F.R.S., *Chur* 1951

Arabic (Sir T. Adams's), R. B. Serjeant, Ph.D., *Trin* 1970

Archæology (Disney), J. G. D. Clark, C.B.E., Sc.D., F.B.A., *Pet* 1952

Architecture, Sir Leslie Martin, M.A., F.R.I.B.A., *Jes* 1956

Astronomy and Experimental Philosophy (Plumian), F. Hoyle, M.A., F.R.S., *Joh* 1958

Astronomy and Geometry (Lowndean), J. F. Adams, M.A., Ph.D., F.R.S., *Trin* 1970

Astrophysics, R. O. Redman, M.A., Ph.D., F.R.S., *Joh* 1947

Biochemistry (Sir William Dunn), F. G. Young, M.A., F.R.S., *Darw* 1949

Biology (Quick), R. R. A. Coombs, Sc.D., F.R.S., *Corp* 1966

Biophysics (John Humphrey Plummer), A. L. Hodgkin, Sc.D., F.R.S., *Trin* 1970

Botany, P. W. Brian, Sc.D., F.R.S., *Qu* 1968

Chemical Engineering (Shell), P. V. Danckwerts, G.C., M.B.E., M.A., F.R.S., *Pemb* 1959

Chemical Microbiology, E. F. Gale, Sc.D., F.R.S., *Joh* 1960

Chemistry (1968), A. D. Buckingham, Ph.D., *Pemb* 1969

Chemistry (1970), J. Lewis, M.A., *Sid* 1970

Chinese, D. C. Twitchett, M.A., Ph.D., *Cath* 1968

Civil Law (Regius), P. G. Stein, M.A., Ll.B., *Qu* 1968

Classical Archæology (Laurence), R. M. Cook, M.A., *Cla* 1962

Clinical Biochemistry, H. Lehmann, Sc.D., *Chr.* 1967

Comparative Law, C. J. Hamson, M.A., LL.M., *Trin* 1953

Comparative Philology, W. S. Allen, M.A., Ph.D., *Trin* 1955

Comparative Physiology, J. A. Ramsay, M.B.E., M.A., Ph.D., F.R.S., *Qu* 1969

Computer Technology, M. V. Wilkes, M.A., Ph.D., F.R.S., *Joh* 1965

Criminology (Wolfson), Sir Leon Radzinowicz, Ll.D., *Trin* 1959

Divinity (Ely), Rev. G. C. Stead, M.A., *King's* 1971
  ,,   *(Lady Margaret's),* Rev. C. F. D. Moule, M.A., F.B.A., *Cla* 1951
  ,,   *(Norris-Hulse),* D. M. MacKinnon, M.A., *Corp* 1960
  ,,   *(Regius)* Rev. Canon G. W. H. Lampe, M.C., D.D., *Cai* 1971

Ecclesiastical History (Dixie), Rev. E. G. Rupp, D.D., F.B.A., *Emm* 1968

Economic History, D. C. Coleman, B.Sc., Ph.D. 1971

Economics (1951), The Lord Kahn, C.B.E., M.A., F.B.A., *King's* 1951

Economics (1965), R. R. Neild, M.A., *Trin* 1971

Economics (1966), N. Kaldor, M.A., F.B.A., *King's* 1966

Economics and Statistics, D. G. Champernowne, M.A., *Trin* 1970

Education, P. H. Hirst, M.A., *Univ* 1971

Egyptology (Herbert Thompson), Rev. J. M. Plumley, M.A., *Selw* 1957

Electrical Engineering, P. S. Brandon, M.A., *Jes* 1971

Elect.

Engineering, J. F. Coales, O.B.E., M.A., F.R.S., *Clare Hall* (1965); A. H. W. Beck, M.A., *Corp* (1966); J. H. Horlock, M.A., Ph.D., *Joh.* (1967); P. McG. Ross, M.A., *Univ.* (1970); J. Heyman, M.A., Ph.D., *Pet.* (1971); *(Rank)* (vacant).

English, Miss M. C. Bradbrook, Litt.D., *Girton* (1966); G. G. Hough, Litt.D., *Darw.* 1966

English Constitutional History, Prof. G. R. Elton, Litt.D., F.B.A., *Cla* 1967

English Law (Rouse Ball), G. Ll. Williams, Q.C., Ll.D., F.B.A., *Jes* 1968

English Literature (King Edward VII), L. C. Knights, M.A., Ph.D., *Qu* 1964

Experimental Psychology, O. L. Zangwill, M.A., *King's* 1952

Finance and Accounting (P. D. Leake), J. R. N. Stone, C.B.E., Sc.D., F.B.A., *King's* 1955

Fine Art (Slade), G. H. Hamilton 1971

French (Drapers), Ll. J. Austin, M.A., F.B.A., *Jes* 1967

French Literature, J. B. M. Barrère, M.A., *Joh.* 1954

Genetics (Arthur Balfour), J. M. Thoday, Sc.D., F.R.S., *Emm* 1959

Geography, H. C. Darby, O.B.E., Litt.D., F.B.A., *King's* 1966

Geology (Woodwardian), H. B. Whittington, M.A., F.R.S., *Sid* 1966

Geophysics, Sir Edward Bullard, Sc.D., F.R.S., *Chur* 1964

German (Schröder), L. W. Forster, M.A., *Selw.* 1961

Greek (Regius), Sir Denys Page, Litt.D., F.B.A., *Jes* 1950

Hæmatological Medicine (Leukaemia Research Fund), F. G. J. Hayhoe, M.D., *Darw* 1968

Hebrew (Regius), Rev. J. A. Emerton, M.A., B.D., *Joh.* 1968

Histology, C. C. D. Shute, M.D., *Chr* 1969

History of International Relations, F. H. Hinsley, O.B.E., M.A., *Joh* 1969

History of the British Commonwealth (Smuts), E. T. Stokes, M.A., Ph.D., *Cath* 1970

Imperial and Naval History (Vere Harmsworth), J. A. Gallagher, M.A. *Trin* 1970

Industrial Relations (Montague Burton), H. A. F. Turner, M.A., *Chur* 1964

International Law, C. Parry, Ll.D., *Down* 1969

International Law (Whewell), R. Y. Jennings, Q.C., M.A., Ll.B., *Jes* 1955

Italian, U. Limentani, M.A., *Magd* 1962

Land Economy, D. R. Denman, M.A., *Pemb* .. 1968

Latin (Kennedy), C. O. Brink, M.A., F.B.A., *Cai* 1954

Latin-American Studies (Simón Bolívar), S. Villalobos, *Qu* 1971

Laws of England (Downing), S. A. de Smith, M.A., *Fitzw* 1970

Mathematical Physics, J. C. Polkinghorne, M.A., Ph.D., *Trin* 1968

Mathematical Statistics, D. G. Kendall, M.A., F.R.S., *Chur* 1962

Mathematics, H. P. F. Swinnerton-Dyer, M.A., F.R.S., *Trin* 1971

Mathematics (Lucasian), Sir James Lighthill, B.A., F.R.S., F.B.A., *Trin* 1969

Mathematics (Rouse Ball), J. G. Thompson, *Chur* 1971

Mathematics for Operational Research (Churchill), P. Whittle, M.A., *Chur* 1967

Mechanics, E. W. Parkes, M.A., Ph.D., *Cai* .. 1965

Medicine, I. H. Mills, M.D., *Chur* 1963

Medieval and Renaissance English, J. A. W. Bennett, M.A., *Magd* 1964

Elect.

Medieval Ecclesiastical History, W. Ullmann, Litt.D., *Trin.* 1966

Medieval History, C. R. Cheney, M.A., F.B.A., *Corp.* 1955

Metallurgy (Goldsmiths'), R. W. K. Honeycombe, Ph.D., *Tr. H.* 1966

Mineralogy and Petrology, W. A. Deer, Ph.D., F.R.S., *Tr. H.* 1961

Modern English History, J. H. Plumb, Litt.D., F.B.A., F.S.A., *Chr.* 1966

Modern History, C. H. Wilson, M.A., F.B.A., *Jes.* 1963

Modern History (Regius), Rev. W. O. Chadwick, D.D., F.B.A., *Selw.* 1968

Modern Languages, D. H. Green, M.A., *Trin.* .. 1966

Music, R. K. Orr, MUS.D., *Joh.* 1965

Mycology, S. D. Garrett, SC.D., *Magd.* 1971

Natural Philosophy (Jacksonian), O. R. Frisch, O.B.E., M.A., F.R.S., *Trin.* 1947

Organic Chemistry (1702) (vacant).

Numismatics, P. Grierson, Litt.D., F.B.A., *Cai.* 1971

Organic Chemistry (1969), A. R. Battersby, M.A., F.R.S., *Cath.* 1969

Pathology, R. I. N. Greaves, M.D., *Cai.* 1962

Pharmacology (Sheild) (vacant).

Philosophy, Miss G. E. M. Anscombe, M.A., *New H.* 1970

Philosophy (Knightbridge), B. A. O. Williams, M.A., *King's* 1967

Physic (Regius), J. S. Mitchell, C.B.E., M.D., F.R.S., *Joh.* 1957

Physical Chemistry, J. W. Linnett, Ph.D., F.R.S., *Sid.* 1965

Physics (Cavendish), A. B. Pippard, F.R.S., *Cl. H.* 1971

Physics (John Humphrey Plummer) (vacant).

Physiology, Sir Bryan Matthews, C.B.E., SC.D., F.R.S., *King's* 1952

Physiology of Reproduction (Mary Marshall and Arthur Walton), T. R. R. Mann, C.B.E., SC.D., F.R.S., *Trinity Hall* 1967

Political Economy, W. B. Reddaway, M.A., *Cla.* 1969

Political Science, W. B. Gallie, M.A., *Pet.* 1967

Pure Mathematics (Sadleirian), J. W. S. Cassels, Ph.D., F.R.S., *Trin.* 1967

Radio Astronomy, Sir Martin Ryle, M.A., F.R.S., *Trin.* 1959

Radio Astronomy (1971), A. Hewish, M.A., Ph.D., F.R.S., *Chur.* 1971

Sanskrit, J. Brough, M.A., F.B.A., *Joh.* 1967

Slavonic Studies, L. R. Lewitter, M.A., Ph.D., *Christ's* 1968

Social Anthropology (William Wyse), M. Fortes, M.A., F.B.A., *King's* 1950

Sociology, J. A. Barnes, D.S.C., M.A., *Chur.*. . 1969

Spanish, E. M. Wilson, M.A., Ph.D., F.B.A., *Emm.* 1953

Surgery, R. Y. Calne, M.A., F.R.C.S., *Tr. H.*. . 1965

Theoretical Astronomy, R. A. Lyttelton, M.A., Ph.D., F.R.S., *Joh.* 1969

Theoretical Physics (Visiting), P. W. Anderson, M.A., *Jes.* 1967

Tropical Botany, E. J. H. Corner, M.A., F.R.S., *Sid.* 1966

Veterinary Clinical Studies, A. T. Phillipson, M.A., Ph.D., *Chur.* 1963

Zoology, T. Weis-Fogh, M.A., *Christ's* 1966

THE UNIVERSITY OF DURHAM
(Founded 1832; re-organized 1908, 1937 and 1963)
Old Shire Hall, Durham

Undergraduates (1970–71), 3,384.

Chancellor, Rt. Hon. Malcolm J. MacDonald, O.M.

Vice-Chancellor and Warden, Sir Derman Christopherson, O.B.E., D.Phil., D.C.L., Ll.D., D.SC., F.R.S.

Pro-Vice-Chancellor, L. Slater

Second Pro-Vice-Chancellor, Prof. W. K. R. Musgrave, Ph.D., D.SC.

Registrar and Secretary, I. E. Graham, M.A.

Professor of Education, Prof. H. S. N. McFarland, M.A., B.Ed.

Director of Institute of Education, J. J. Grant, C.B.E., M.A., Ed.B., D.C.L.

Colleges

University, L. Slater, M.A., *Master.*

Hatfield, T. Whitworth, M.A., D.Phil., *Master.*

Grey, S. Holgate, M.A., Ph.D., *Master.*

Van Mildert, W. A. Prowse, O.B.E., T.D., B.SC., Ph.D., *Master.*

St. Chad's, Rev. J. C. Fenton, M.A., B.D., *Principal.*

St John's, Rev. J. C. P. Cockerton, M.A., *Principal.*

St. Mary's, Mrs. M. Holdsworth, M.A., *Principal.*

St. Aidan's, Miss I. Hindmarsh, M.A., *Principal.*

Trevelyan, Joan Constance Bernard, M.A., B.D., *Principal.*

Bede, K. G. Collier, M.A., *Principal.*

**St. Hild's*, Nina Mary Elizabeth Joachim, M.A., *Principal.*

**Neville's Cross*, R. G. Emmett, B.SC., M.A., Ph.D., *Principal.*

St. Cuthbert's Society, Prof. J. L. Brooks, M.A., *Principal.*

The Graduate Society, Prof. W. B. Fisher, B.A., *Principal.*

Ushaw, Rt. Rev. Mgr. P. Loftus, B.C.L., *President.*

* Halls of Residence.

THE UNIVERSITY OF LONDON, 1836
Senate House, W.C.1

Internal Students (1969–70), 38,551. Registered External Students, 35,198.

Visitor, H.M. the Queen in Council.

Chancellor, H.M. Queen Elizabeth the Queen Mother.

Vice-Chancellor, Prof. Sir Brian Windeyer, M.B., B.S., LL.D., D.SC., F.R.C.P., F.R.C.S.

Chairman of the Court, Hon. Sir Leslie Scarman, O.B.E., M.A., Ll.D.

Chairman of Convocation, Sir Charles Harris, M.D., F.R.C.P., F.R.C.S.

Principal, Sir Douglas Logan, M.A., D.Phil., D.C.L., Ll.D. (1947).

THE COURT

Ex Officio, The Chancellor, The Vice-Chancellor, The Chairman of Convocation.

Appointed by the Senate, Sir John Hackett, G.C.B., C.B.E., D.S.O., M.C., Ll.D.; F. Hartley, C.B.E., Ph.D.; Prof. C. T. Ingold, C.M.G., D.SC.; Sir Harry Melville, K.C.B., F.R.S.; Prof. C. H. Philips, Ph.D., D.Litt.; Sir Bernard Waley-Cohen, Bt., M.A., Ll.D. *By Her Majesty in Council*, M. Clapham, M.A.; P. Parker, M.V.O., M.A.; Rt. Hon. A. G. F. Rippon, Q.C., M.P.; The Lord Shawcross, P.C., Q.C.; *By the I.L.E.A.*, Sir Reginald Goodwin, C.B.E.; Sir Desmond Plummer, T.D.; *Home Counties and Outer London Boroughs Member*, T. I. Smith, O.B.E., M.A.; *Co-opted Member*, Hon. Sir Leslie Scarman, O.B.E., M.A., Ll.D.

THE SENATE

Ex Officio, The Chancellor, The Vice-Chancellor, The Chairman of Convocation, The Principal.

Heads of the following Schools—University College, King's College, Bedford College, Birkbeck College, Imperial College of Science and Technology, London School of Economics and Political Science, Queen Mary College, Royal Holloway College, School of Oriental and African Studies, Westfield College. *Appointed by Convocation*—*(Arts)* H. A. L. Cockerell, O.B.E.; The Lord Fletcher, P.C.; V. I. Gaster, O.B.E.; Miss M. C.

Grobel; Mrs. J. Russell-Gebbett; (*Economics*),
J. B. Bonham; (*Engineering*), F. E. A. Manning,
C.B.E., M.C., T.D.; J. Gratwick; (*Laws*), S. R.
Speller, O.B.E.; (*Medicine*), Prof. J. P. Quilliam;
N. A. Thorne; (*Music*), C. P. J. Steinitz; (*Science*),
J. S. Cook; Mrs. M. F. Church; M. V. Hoare;
W. C. Peck; J. H. Pryor; (*Theology*), Rev. G.
Huelin. *Appointed by the Faculties*—(*Arts*), Prof.
R. Browning; Prof. R. Quirk; Prof. A. Carey
Taylor; Prof. F. M. L. Thompson; (*Economics*),
Prof. F. J. Fisher; (*Engineering*), Prof. H. Billett;
Prof. A. D. Young, O.B.E.; (*Laws*), Prof. F. R.
Crane; (*Medicine*), M. I. A. Hunter; Prof. A.
Kekwick; Prof. L. B. Strang; S. F. Taylor;
(*Music*), B. L. Trowell; (*Science*), Prof. C. T.
Ingold; Prof. J. F. Kirkaldy; Prof. A. Maccoll;
Prof. B. C. L. Weedon; (*Theology*), Rev. Prof.
P. R. Ackroyd. *Appointed by General Medical
Schools*, J. C. Houston; Frances V. Gardner.
By King's College Theological Dept., Rev. Canon
S. H. Evans. *By University College*, Sir Bernard
Waley-Cohen, Bt. *Director of British Post-
Graduate Medical Federation*, Prof. G. Smart.
Co-opted Members, H. L. Elvin; M. R. Gavin,
C.B.E.; F. Hartley; H. B. May.

Principal Officers

Clerk of the Court, J. R. Stewart, C.B.E., M.A.
Clerk of the Senate, L. L. Pownall, M.A., Ph.D.
Registrars: (*Academic*) M. A. Baatz, M.A.;
(*External*), P. F. Vowles, M.A.
*Secretary to University Entrance and School Examina-
tions Council*, A. R. Stephenson, M.A.
*Director of the University Library and Goldsmiths'
Librarian*, D. T. Richnell, B.A., F.L.A.
Director, Careers Advisory Service, E. H. K. Dibden,
B.SC., M.A.
Secretary to the Athlone Press, A. M. Wood, M.SC.,
M.A.

University Institutes

Courtauld Institute of Art, 20 Portman Square, W.1,
Prof. Sir Anthony Blunt, K.C.V.O., D.Litt., F.B.A.,
Dir.
Institute of Advanced Legal Studies, 25 Russell
Square, W.C.1, Prof. J. N. D. Anderson, O.B.E.,
M.A., LL.D., *Dir.*
Institute of Archæology, 31–34 Gordon Square,
W.C.1, Prof. W. F. Grimes, C.B.E., D.Litt.,
F.S.A., *Dir.*
Institute of Classical Studies 31–34 Gordon Square,
W.C.1, Prof. E. W. Handley, M.A., *Dir.*
Institute of Commonwealth Studies, 27 Russell Square,
W.C.1, Prof. W. H. Morris-Jones, B.SC.(Econ.),
Dir.
Institute of Computer Science, 44 Gordon Square,
W.C.1, Prof. R. A. Buckingham, Ph.D., *Dir.*
Institute of Education, Malet Street, W.C.1, H. L.
Elvin, M.A., *Dir.*
Institute of Germanic Studies, 29 Russell Square,
W.C.1, Prof. W. D. Robson-Scott, M.A., D.Phil.,
Hon. *Dir.*
Institute of Historical Research, Senate House, W.C.1
Prof. A. G. Dickens, M.A., D.Lit., F.B.A., F.S.A.,
Dir.
Institute of Latin American Studies, 31 Tavistock
Square, W.C.1, Prof. R. A. Humphreys, O.B.E.,
Ph.D., D. Litt., *Dir.*
School of Slavonic and E. European Studies, University
of London, Senate House, W.C.1, G. H. Bolso-
ver, C.B.E., Ph.D., *Dir.*
Institute of United States Studies, 31 Tavistock Square,
W.C.1, Prof. E. Wright, M.A., *Dir.*
Warburg Institute, Woburn Square. W.C.1, Prof.
E. H. J. Gombrich, C.B.E., D.Litt., Litt.D., F.B.A.,
F.S.A., *Dir.*
British Institute in Paris, 6 Rue de la Sorbonne,
Paris Ve., Prof. F. H. Scarfe, O.B.E., M.A., M.Litt.,
Dir.

Schools of the University★

Bedford College, Inner Circle, Regent's Park, N.W.1,
Prof. J. N. Black, M.A., D.Phil., *Principal* (1971).
Birkbeck College, Malet Street, W.C.1, R. C. Tress,
C.B.E., B.SC. (Econ.), D.SC., *Master* (1968).
Chelsea College of Science and Technology, Manresa
Road, S.W.3, M. R. Gavin, M.B.E., D.SC., *Principal*
(1965).
Imperial College of Science and Technology, Prince
Consort Road, S.W.7, The Lord Penney, O.M.,
K.B.E., Ph.D., D.SC., F.R.S., *Rector* (1967).
King's College, Strand, W.C.2, Sir John Hackett,
G.C.B., C.B.E., D.S.O., M.C., M.A., LL.D., *Principal*
(1968).
London School of Economics and Political Science,
Houghton Street, Aldwych, W.C.2, Sir Walter
Adams, C.M.G., O.B.E., B.A., LL.D., *Director* (1967).
Queen Elizabeth College, Campden Hill Road, W.8,
K. G. Denbigh, D.SC., F.R.S., *Principal* (1966).
Queen Mary College, Mile End Road, E.1, Sir Harry
Melville, K.C.B., Ph.D., D.SC., F.R.S., *Principal* (1967).
Royal Holloway College, Englefield Green, Surrey,
Miss E. Marjorie Williamson, M.SC., Ph.D.,
Principal (1962).
School of Oriental and African Studies, University of
London, W.C.1, Prof. C. H. Philips, M.A., Ph.D.,
D.Litt., *Dir.* (1957).
School of Pharmacy, Brunswick Square, W.C.1, F.
Hartley, C.B.E., B.SC., Ph.D., *Dean* (1962).
University College, Gower Street, W.C.1, The Lord
Annan, O.B.E., M.A., D.Litt., *Provost* (1966).
Westfield College, Kidderpore Avenue, Hampstead,
N.W.3, B. Thwaites, M.A., Ph.D. *Principal* (1966).
Wye College, nr. Ashford, Kent, H. S. Darling,
C.B.E., B.SC., M.Agric., Ph.D. (1968).
King's College Theological Department, Rev. Canon
S. H. Evans, B.D., M.A., *Dean* (1956).
New College, 527 Finchley Road, N.W.3, Rev.
C. S. Duthie, D.D., *Principal* (1964).
Richmond College, Richmond, Surrey, Rev. A. R.
George, B.D., M.A., *Principal* (1968).
Heythrop College, 11 Cavendish Square, W.1, Rev.
F. C. Copleston, S.J., M.A., D.Phil., *Principal* (1971).
Lister Institute of Preventive Medicine, Chelsea Bridge
Road, S.W.1, Prof. Sir Ashley Miles, C.B.E., M.A.,
M.D., F.R.C.P., F.R.S., *Director* (1952).
★ For Medical Schools, Training Colleges and
Veterinary Colleges, *see under* Professional Educa-
tion.

THE UNIVERSITY OF MANCHESTER
Oxford Road, Manchester
(Founded 1851; re-organized 1880 and 1903).
Full-time Students (1970–71), *Men*, 8,593; *Women*,
3,206.
Chancellor, The Duke of Devonshire, P.C., M.C.
(1965).
Vice-Chancellor, Prof. A. L. Armitage, M.A., LL.D.
(1970).
Registrar, V. Knowles, M.A. (1951).

MANCHESTER INSTITUTE OF SCIENCE
AND TECHNOLOGY (1824)
Sackville Street, Manchester
Full-time Students (1970–71), (*Men*) 3,026; (*Women*)
305.
Principal, The Lord Bowden, M.A., Ph.D. (1964).
Secretary and Registrar, J. Burgess, M.A.

THE UNIVERSITY OF NEWCASTLE
(Founded 1852; re-organized 1908, 1937 and 1963)
Newcastle upon Tyne.
Students (1970–71), 5,905.
Chancellor, The Duke of Northumberland, K.G., T.D.,
F.R.S. (1964)

Vice-Chancellor, H. Miller, M.D., F.R.C.P.
Pro-Vice-Chancellors, Prof. S. R. Dennison, C.B.E., M.A.; Prof. M. McG. Cooper, C.B.E.
Registrar, E. M. Bettenson, M.A.

THE UNIVERSITY OF BIRMINGHAM, 1900
Birmingham 15
Full-time Students (1970–71), 6,657
Chancellor, The Earl of Avon, K.G., P.C., M.C. (1945)
Vice-Chancellor and Principal, R. B. Hunter, M.B.E. F.R.C.P. (1968).
Secretary, H. Harris, B.Sc.(Econ.), Ll.B.
Registrar, W. R. G. Lewis.

THE UNIVERSITY OF LIVERPOOL, 1903
Liverpool
Students (1970), 6,679.
Chancellor (vacant).
Vice-Chancellor, T. C. Thomas (1970).
Treasurer, H. B. Chrimes, M.A.
Registrar, H. H. Burchnall, M.A. (1962).

THE UNIVERSITY OF LEEDS, 1904
Full-time Students (1971), 9,126.
Chancellor, H.R.H. the Duchess of Kent (1966).
Vice-Chancellor, The Lord Boyle of Handsworth, P.C. (1970).
Registrar, J. MacGregor, Ph.D. (1971)
Bursar, E. Williamson, T.D. (1956).

THE UNIVERSITY OF SHEFFIELD, 1905
Sheffield
Full-time Students (1970–71)—Men, 4,096; Women, 1,648.
Chancellor, The Lord Butler of Saffron Walden, K.G., P.C., C.H., M.A., Ll.D. (1959).
Vice-Chancellor, Prof. H. N. Robson, M.B., F.R.C.P. (1966).
Registrar, A. M. Currie, B.A., B.Litt. (1965).

THE UNIVERSITY OF BRISTOL, 1909
Bristol 2
Full-time Students (1970)—Men, 3,964; Women, 2,274.
Chancellor, Prof. Dorothy Hodgkin, O.M., Ph.D., D.Sc., F.R.S. (1971).
Vice-Chancellor, A. W. Merrison, B.Sc., Ph.D., F.R.S. (1967).
Registrar and Secretary, H. C. Butterfield, M.A. (1950).

THE UNIVERSITY OF READING, 1926
Whiteknights, Reading
Number of Students (1970), 4,930.
Chancellor, The Lord Sherfield, G.C.B., G.C.M.G. (1970).
Vice-Chancellor, H. R. Pitt, Ph.D., F.R.S. (1964).
Registrar, J. F. Johnson, B.A. (1955).

THE UNIVERSITY OF NOTTINGHAM, 1948
University Park, Nottingham
Undergraduates (1970–71), 4,268.
Chancellor, The Duke of Portland, K.G., T.D. (1955).
Vice-Chancellor, W. J. H. Butterfield, O.B.E., M.D., D.M., F.R.C.P. (1970).
Registrar, A. Plumb, M.A. (1958).

THE UNIVERSITY OF SOUTHAMPTON, 1952
Students (1970–71), Men, 3,130; Women, 1,290.
Chancellor, The Lord Murray of Newhaven, K.C.B., Ll.D. (1964).
Vice-Chancellor, L. C. B. Gower, M.B.E., Ll.D., F.B.A. (1971).
Secretary and Registrar, R. M. Urquhart, O.B.E., M.A. (1966).
Academic Registrar, D. A. Schofield, M.A. (1969).

THE UNIVERSITY OF HULL, 1954
Full-time Students (1970–71)—Men, 2,450; Women, 1,508.
Chancellor, The Lord Cohen of Birkenhead, M.D., D.Sc., Ll.D., F.R.C.P. (1970).
Vice-Chancellor, Sir Brynmor Jones, Ph.D., Sc.D., F.R.I.C. (1956).
Registrar, W. D. Craig (1954).

THE UNIVERSITY OF EXETER, 1955
Full-time students (1971–72), 3,500.
Chancellor (vacant).
Vice-Chancellor, F. J. Llewellyn, Ph.D., D.Sc., Ll.D.
Secretary, Roderick Ross, M.A. (Admin.).
Academic Registrar, A. G. Bartlett, M.A.

THE UNIVERSITY OF LEICESTER, 1957
Full-time Students (1971–72), 3,630.
Chancellor, Prof. A. L. Hodgkin, F.R.S. (1971).
Vice-Chancellor, Sir Thomas Noble, M.B.E., M.A. (1962).
Registrar, H. B. Martin, B.Com. (1947).

THE UNIVERSITY OF SUSSEX, 1961
Brighton
Full-time Students (1970–71), 3,785.
Chancellor, The Lord Shawcross, P.C., Q.C., Ll.D.
Vice-Chancellor, Prof. A. Briggs, B.Sc.(Econ.), M.A.
Registrar and Secretary, A. E. Shields, M.B.E., M.A.

THE UNIVERSITY OF KEELE, 1962
Keele, Staffordshire.
Undergraduates (1970–71), 1,758.
Chancellor, H.R.H. the Princess Margaret, Countess of Snowdon, C.I., G.C.V.O. (1962).
Vice-Chancellor, Prof. W. A. C. Stewart, M.A., Ph.D.
Registrar, J. F. N. Hodgkinson, M.A.

THE UNIVERSITY OF EAST ANGLIA, 1963
Earlham Hall, Norwich.
Students (1971), 2,951.
Chancellor, The Lord Franks, P.C., G.C.M.G., K.C.B., C.B.E., M.A., F.B.A. (1965).
Vice-Chancellor, F. Thistlethwaite, M.A., F.R.Hist.S.
Registrar and Secretary, G. A. Chadwick, B.Sc.

THE UNIVERSITY OF YORK, 1963
Heslington, York
Undergraduates (1970), 1,990.
Chancellor, The Lord Clark, C.H., K.C.B., D.Litt., F.B.A. (1969).
Pro-Chancellors, The Rt. Hon. and Most Rev. the Archbishop of York; R. S. Butterfield, O.B.E., M.C.; A. S. Rymer, O.B.E.
Vice-Chancellor, The Lord James of Rusholme, M.A., D.Phil., Ll.D.
Registrar, J. P. West-Taylor, M.A.

THE UNIVERSITY OF LANCASTER, 1964
Bailrigg, Lancaster
Undergraduates (1971–72), 2,425.
Chancellor, H.R.H. the Princess Alexandra, G.C.V.O.
Vice-Chancellor, C. F. Carter, M.A., D.Econ.Sc., F.B.A.
Secretary, A. S. Jeffreys, B.A., B.Litt.

THE UNIVERSITY OF ESSEX, 1964
Wivenhoe Park, Colchester
Students (1971–72), 2,040.
Chancellor, The Lord Butler of Saffron Walden, K.G., P.C., C.H., M.A., Ll.D.
Pro-Chancellor, Col. Sir John Ruggles-Brise, Bt., C.B., O.B.E., T.D.
Vice-Chancellor, A. E. Sloman, M.A., D.Phil.
Registrar, D. W. Girvan, M.A., Ll.B.

THE UNIVERSITY OF WARWICK, 1965
Coventry, Warwickshire
Students (1970–71), 2,178.
Chancellor, The Viscount Radcliffe, P.C., G.B.E.

Pro-Chancellor, The Lord Goodman.
Vice-Chancellor, J. B. Butterworth, M.A.
Registrar, D. W. Dykes, M.A., F.R.Hist.S.
ASS. VICE-CHANCELLOR SIR WALTER COUTTS

UNIVERSITY OF KENT AT CANTERBURY, 1965
Canterbury, Kent

Students (1970–71), 2,378.
Chancellor, Rt. Hon. J. Grimond, T.D., M.P. (1970).
Vice-Chancellor, G. Templeman, M.A., Ph.D., F.S.A.
Registrar, E. Fox, M.A.

LOUGHBOROUGH UNIVERSITY OF TECHNOLOGY, 1966

Students (1970–71), 2,760.
Chancellor, The Lord Pilkington.
Vice-Chancellor, E. J. Richards O.B.E., D.SC., M.A.
Registrar, F. L. Roberts, B.A.

THE UNIVERSITY OF ASTON IN BIRMINGHAM, 1966
Gosta Green, Birmingham 4

Full-time Students (1970–71), 3,240.
Chancellor, The Lord Nelson of Stafford, M.A.
Vice-Chancellor, J. A. Pope, D.SC., Ph.D.
Secretary, R. J. Rackham, M.A.

THE CITY UNIVERSITY, 1966
St. John Street, E.C.1

Students (1970–71), 2,607.
Chancellor, The Lord Mayor of London.
Vice-Chancellor, Sir James Tait, LL.D., Ph.D.
Registrar, L. A. Fairbairn, B.SC., Ph.D.

BRUNEL UNIVERSITY, 1966
Uxbridge, Middlesex

Students (1970–71), 2,343.
Chancellor, The Earl of Halsbury, F.R.S.
Vice-Chancellor, S. L. Bragg.
Academic Registrar, E. R. Chandler.

UNIVERSITY OF BATH, 1966
Claverton Down, Bath, Som.

Undergraduates (1970–71), 1,905.
Chancellor, The Lord Hinton of Bankside, K.B.E., M.A., F.R.S.
Vice-Chancellor, L. Rotherham, C.B.E., D.SC., F.R.S.
Registrar, G. S. Horner, M.A.

UNIVERSITY OF BRADFORD, 1966
Bradford, 7 Yorks.

Undergraduates (1970–71), Men, 2,430; Women, 543.
Chancellor, Rt. Hon. J. H. Wilson, O.B.E., M.P., M.A.(Oxon.).
Vice-Chancellor and Principal, E. G. Edwards, Ph.D., B.SC.
Registrar, D. H. McWilliam, B.A.

UNIVERSITY OF SURREY 1966
Guildford, Surrey

Undergraduates (1970–71), 2,043.
Chancellor, The Lord Robens of Woldingham, P.C.
Vice-Chancellor, D. M. A. Leggett, M.A., D.SC., Ph.D.
Registrar, A. E. Johnston, C.B.E., B.SC.

UNIVERSITY OF SALFORD, 1967

Undergraduates (1970–71), 3,001.
Chancellor, H.R.H. the Prince Philip, Duke of Edinburgh, K.G., P.C., K.T.
Vice-Chancellor, C. Whitworth, M.SC., Ph.D., D.SC.
Registrar, S. R. Bosworth.

ROYAL COLLEGE OF ART, 1837
Kensington Gore, S.W.7

Under Royal Charter (1967) the Royal College of Art grants the degrees of Doctor, Master and Bachelor of Art or Design (RCA).
Students (1971), 573 (all postgraduate).
Provost, Sir Colin Anderson.
Rector and Vice-Provost, The Viscount Esher, C.B.E., D.Litt.
Registrar, B. Cooper, B.A.

CRANFIELD INSTITUTE OF TECHNOLOGY 1969
Cranfield, Bedford.

Under Royal Charter (1969) the Cranfield Institute of Technology grants the degrees of Doctor and Master in applied science, engineering, technology and management.
Students (1970), 400 (all postgraduate); 2,500 short course.
Chancellor, The Lord Kings Norton, Ph.D., D.I.C., D.SC.
Vice-Chancellor, A. H. Chilver, D.SC., Ph.D., M.A.
Secretary and Registrar, L. Wilson, M.A.

THE OPEN UNIVERSITY (1969)
Walton Hall, nr. Bletchley, Bucks.

Students (1971), 25,000.
Tuition by correspondence packages, special radio and television programmes, summer schools at regional centres and a locally-based tutorial and counselling service. Under Royal Charter the University awards degrees of B.A., B.Phil., M.Phil., Ph.D., D.SC. and D.Litt. There are six faculties—arts, educational studies, mathematics, science, social sciences and technology.
Chancellor, The Lord Crowther, M.A., LL.D., D.SC. (ECON.)
Vice-Chancellor, W. Perry, O.B.E., M.D., D.SC.
Registrar, D. J. Clinch.

THE UNIVERSITY OF WALES, 1893
University Registry, Cardiff

Chancellor, H.R.H. the Prince Philip, Duke of Edinburgh, K.G., P.C., K.T., (1948).
Pro-Chancellor, The Lord Morris of Borth-y-Gest, P.C., C.B.E., M.C., LL.D. (1956).
Vice-Chancellor, Sir Charles Evans, D.SC., F.R.C.S. (1971).
Registrar, J. Gareth Thomas, M.A. (1962).

COLLEGES
(with number of undergraduates, 1970–71)

Aberystwyth (2,579).—*Princ.*, Sir Goronwy Daniel, K.C.V.O., C.B., D.Phil. (1969).
Bangor, N. Wales (2,461).—*Princ.*, Sir Charles Evans, M.A., D.SC., F.R.C.S. (1958).
Cardiff, Institute of Science and Technology (1,929).—*Princ.*, A. F. Trotman-Dickenson, M.A., Ph.D., D.SC. (1968).
Cardiff, National School of Medicine (355).—J. P. D. Mounsey, M.A., M.D., F.R.C.P. (1969).
Cardiff (S. Wales and Monmouthshire) (3,586).—*Princ.*, C. W. L. Bevan, C.B.E., Ph.D. (1966).
Lampeter (St. David's College) (328), Rev. Canon J. R. Lloyd Thomas, M.A. (1953).
Swansea (3,525).—*Princ.*, F. Llewellyn-Jones, C.B.E., M.A., D.Phil., D.SC. (1965).

SCOTLAND

UNIVERSITY OF ST. ANDREWS, 1411

Students (1970–71), Men, 1,530; Women, 1,055.
Chancellor, The Duke of Hamilton, P.C., K.T., G.C.V.O., A.F.C. (1948).

Principal and Vice-Chancellor, J. S. Watson, M.A., D.Litt., F.R.Hist.S., F.R.S.E. (1966).
Rector, J. Cleese, M.A., Ll.D. (1971).
Registrar and Secretary, A. N. Mitchell, O.B.E., M.A. (1961).

UNIVERSITY OF GLASGOW, 1451
Gilmorehill, Glasgow

Students (1970–71), Men, 6,247; Women, 3,020
Chancellor (vacant).
Vice-Chancellor, Sir Charles Wilson, M.A., Ll.D. (1961).
Rector, The Very Rev. The Lord MacLeod of Fuinary, M.C., D.D. (1968).
Secretary to the University Court and Registrar, Robert T. Hutcheson, O.B.E., M.A., Ph.D. (1942).

UNIVERSITY OF ABERDEEN, 1494

Undergraduates (1971), 4,941.
Chancellor, The Lord Polwarth, T.D., Ll.D.
Rector, Rt. Hon. J. Grimond, T.D., M.P. (Jan., 1970– Dec. 1972).
Principal, E. M. Wright, M.A., D.Phil., Ll.D., F.R.S.E. (1962).
Vice-Principal, Prof. W. S. Watt, M.A.
Secretary, T. B. Skinner, M.A.

UNIVERSITY OF EDINBURGH, 1583
Old College, South Bridge, Edinburgh 8

Students (1970–71), 10,429.
Chancellor, H.R.H. the Prince Philip, Duke of Edinburgh, K.G., P.C., K.T., (1952).
Rector, K. Allsop (1968).
Vice-Chancellor and Principal, Prof. M. M. Swann, M.A., Ph.D., F.R.S., F.R.S.E. (1965).
Secretary, C. H. Stewart, O.B.E., M.A., Ll.B. (1948).

UNIVERSITY OF STRATHCLYDE, 1964
George Street, Glasgow C.1.

Full-time students (1970–71), 5,181.
Chancellor, The Lord Todd, D.Sc., D.Phil., F.R.S. (1964).
Principal, Sir Samuel Curran, Ph.D., D.Sc., F.R.S. (1959).
Registrar, G. P. Richardson, M.A. (1966).

HERIOT-WATT UNIVERSITY, 1966
Edinburgh 1

Students (1970–71), 2,551.
Chancellor, Rt. Hon. Sir Alexander Douglas-Home, K.T., M.P. (1966).
Principal and Vice-Chancellor, R. A. Smith, C.B.E., M.A., Ph.D., F.R.S., F.R.S.E. (1968).
Secretary, D. I. Cameron (1966).

UNIVERSITY OF DUNDEE, 1967

Full-time students (1970–71), 2,531.
Chancellor, H.M. Queen Elizabeth the Queen Mother.
Principal and Vice-Chancellor, J. Drever, M.A., F.R.S.E.
Rector, Peter Ustinov, Ll.D., F.R.S.A. (1968).
Secretary, R. N. M. Robertson, M.A., Ll.B.

UNIVERSITY OF STIRLING, 1967

Undergraduates (1970–71), 1,062.
Chancellor, The Lord Robbins, C.H., C.B., F.B.A. (1967).
Vice-Chancellor, T. L. Cottrell, D.Sc. (1965).
Secretary, Sir Derek Lang, K.C.B., D.S.O., M.C. (1970).

NORTHERN IRELAND

THE QUEEN'S UNIVERSITY OF BELFAST, 1908

Full-time Students (1967–68), 5,523.
Chancellor, Sir Eric Ashby, D.Sc., Sc.D., F.R.S., (1970).

President and Vice-Chancellor, F. A. Vick, O.B.E. B.Sc., Ph.D.
Secretary, G. R. Cowie, M.A., Ll.B. (1948).
Secretary to the Academic Council, D. G. Neill, M.A., (1966).

NEW UNIVERSITY OF ULSTER, 1965
Coleraine, Co. Londonderry
(First students admitted, 1968).

Undergraduates (1970–71), 1,200.
Chancellor, The Duke of Abercorn.
Vice-Chancellor, N. A Burges, M.Sc., Ph.D. (1966).
Registrar and Secretary, W. T. Ewing, M.A., Ll.B. (1966)

THE ASSOCIATION OF COMMONWEALTH UNIVERSITIES
36 Gordon Square, W.C.1

The Association holds quinquennial Congresses of the Universities of the Commonwealth and other meetings in the intervening years, publishes the *Commonwealth Universities Yearbook*, etc., acts as a general information centre on universities in U.K. and Commonwealth countries and provides an advisory service for the filling of university teaching staff appointments overseas. It also supplies the secretariat for the Commonwealth Scholarship Commission in the United Kingdom, for the Marshall Aid Commemoration Commission and for the Kennedy Memorial Trust.
Secretary-General, Sir Hugh Springer, K.C.M.G., C.B.E., D.Sc.Soc.

REPUBLIC OF IRELAND

UNIVERSITY OF DUBLIN TRINITY COLLEGE, 1591

Undergraduates (1971–72), 3,750.
Chancellor, F. H. Boland, Ll.D. (1964).
Provost, A. J. McConnell, Sc.D. (1952).
Registrar, D. I. D. Howie, Ph.D. (1966).

NATIONAL UNIVERSITY OF IRELAND, DUBLIN, 1908
49 Merrion Square, Dublin

Chancellor, Eamonn de Valéra, Ph.D., Ll.D., Sc.D., F.R.S. (1921).
Vice-Chancellor, M. D. McCarthy, M.A., Ph.D., D.Sc.
Registrar, Séamus Wilmot, B.A., B.Comm., Ll.D.

CONSTITUENT COLLEGES
Univ. Coll., Dublin, J. J. Hogan, M.A., D.Litt., President (1964).
Univ. Coll., Cork, M. D. McCarthy, M.A., Ph.D., D.Sc., President (1967).
Univ. Coll., Galway, M. O. Tnúthail, D.Sc., President (1960).

RECOGNIZED COLLEGE
St. Patrick's Coll. Maynooth, Right Rev. Mgr. J. Newman, M.A., D.Ph., President (1967).

ADULT EDUCATION

Adult Education is carried on in the United Kingdom by universities and university colleges (pp. 502–511), local education authorities (pp. 514–517) and by a wide variety of voluntary organizations.

The Universities Council for Adult Education, consisting of two representatives from each university was constituted in 1946 for interchange of ideas and formulation of common policy on extra-mural education.—Hon. Secretary, F. W. Jessup, M.A., Ll.B., F.S.A., Rewley House, Wellington Square, Oxford.

The National Institute of Adult Education (England and Wales), 35 Queen Anne Street, W.1 (Sec.,

A. K. Stock), and the Scottish Institute of Adult Education, Education Offices, Alloa, Clackmannan, exist to provide a means of consultation and co-operation between the various forces in adult education.

COUNCIL FOR
NATIONAL ACADEMIC AWARDS
3 Devonshire Street, W.1

Established in 1964 with powers to award degrees and other academic distinctions, comparable in standard with awards granted and conferred by universities, to students who pursue their higher education in establishments for further education which do not have the power to award their own degrees. The Council awards first degrees of B.A. and B.SC. and has established a structure of higher degrees, including M.A. and M.SC. for postgraduate courses of study; M.Phil. and Ph.D. for research work. The Council has taken over the Diploma in Technology and the work of the College of Technologists.

President, H.R.H. the Duke of Edinburgh, K.G., K.T.
Chairman, M. Clapham.
Vice-Chairman and Chief Officer, F. R. Hornby, M.B.E.

Registrar and Secretary, F. G. Hanrott.

UNIVERSITY DEPARTMENTS OF
EXTRA-MURAL STUDIES AND
ADULT EDUCATION

OXFORD, Department for External Studies, Rewley House, Wellington Square, Oxford.—*Dir.*, F. W. Jessup.
CAMBRIDGE, Board of Extra-Mural Studies, Stuart House, Mill Lane, Cambridge.—*Sec.*, J. M. Y. Andrew.
DURHAM, Department of Extra-Mural Studies, 32 Old Elvet, Durham.—*Dir.*, J. F. Dixon.
LONDON, Department of Extra-Mural Studies, University of London, 7 Ridgmount Street, W.C.1.—*Dir.*, W. Burmeister.
BIRMINGHAM, Department of Extramural Studies, P.O. Box 363, University of Birmingham, Birmingham, 15.—*Dir.*, A. M. Parker.
BRISTOL, Department of Extra-Mural Studies, The University, Bristol.—*Dir.*, Prof. G. Cunliffe.
EXETER, Department of Extra-Mural Studies, The University, Exeter.—*Head*, Prof. T. F. Daveney.
HULL, Department of Adult Education, the University, Hull.—*Dir.*, Prof. W. E. Styler.
KEELE, Department of Adult Education, The University, Keele, Staffs.—*Dir.*, Prof. R. Shaw.
LEEDS, Department of Adult Education and Extra-Mural Studies, The University, Leeds, 2.—*Head of Dept.*, Prof. N. A. Jepson.
LEICESTER, Department of Adult Education, The University, Leicester.—*Head of Dept.*, Prof. H. A. Jones.
LIVERPOOL, Institute of Extension Studies, 1 Abercromby Square, Liverpool.—*Dir.*, Prof. T. Kelly, Ph.D.
MANCHESTER, Department of Extra-Mural Studies, The University, Manchester, 13.—*Dir.*, Prof. E. G. Wedell.
NEWCASTLE, Department of Adult Education, The University, Newcastle upon Tyne.—*Dir.*, E. W. Hughes.
NOTTINGHAM, Department of Adult Education, 14-22 Shakespeare Street, Nottingham.—*Dir.*, Prof. H. C. Wiltshire.
READING, The University, Whiteknights, Reading. *Registrar*, J. F. Johnson.
SHEFFIELD, Department of Extramural Studies, The University, Sheffield.—*Dir.*, Prof. M. Bruce.

SOUTHAMPTON, Department of Extra-Mural Studies, University of Southampton.—*Dir.*, P. E. Fordham.
WALES, The University Extension Board, University Registry, Cathays Park, Cardiff.—*Sec.*, J. Gareth Thomas.
ABERYSTWYTH, University College, Aberystwyth.—*Dir.*, A. D. Rees.
BANGOR, University College, Bangor.—*Dir.*, A. Llywelyn-Williams.
CARDIFF, University College Cardiff, Department of Extra-Mural Studies, 38-40 Park Place, Cathays Park, Cardiff.—*Dir.*, J. S. Davies.
SWANSEA, University College Swansea.—*Dir.*, I. M. Williams.
ABERDEEN, Department of Extra-Mural Studies, The University, Aberdeen.—*Dir.*, K. A. Wood.
DUNDEE, Department of Extra-Mural Education, The University, Dundee.—*Dir.*, A. G. Robertson.
EDINBURGH, Department of Educational Studies, 11 Buccleuch Place, Edinburgh.—*Dir. of Extra-Mural Studies*, J. Lowe, Ph.D.
GLASGOW, Department of Extra-Mural and Adult Education, 57-9 Oakfield Avenue, Glasgow, W.2.—*Dir.*, N. Dees.
ST. ANDREWS, Department of Extra-Mural Education, University of St. Andrews, 3 St. Mary's Place.—*Dir.*, J. C. Geddes.
BELFAST, Queen's University, Department of Extra-Mural Studies and Adult Education.—*Dir.*, E. C. Read.

RESIDENTIAL COLLEGES FOR
ADULT EDUCATION
(Offering courses for a year or longer)

England

CLIFF COLLEGE, Calver, Sheffield. Residential Methodist Lay Training College open to all denominations (Men and Women).—*Principal*, Rev. H. A. G. Belben.
CO-OPERATIVE COLLEGE, Stanford Hall, Loughborough, Leics. (Men and Women).—*Principal*, R. L. Marshall, O.B.E.
FIRCROFT COLLEGE, Selly Oak, Birmingham 29 (Men) (50).—*Principal*, A. J. Corfield.
HILLCROFT RESIDENTIAL COLLEGE FOR WOMEN, Surbiton, Surrey(75).—*Principal*, Mrs. J. Cockerill.
PLATER COLLEGE, Boars Hill, Oxford (Men and Women).—*Principal*, J. R. Kirwan.
RUSKIN COLLEGE, Oxford (Men and Women)(165). *Principal*, H. D. Hughes.
WOODBROOKE, 1046 Bristol Road, Selly Oak, Birmingham 29. Quaker centre for religious, social and international studies (Men and Women). Shorter Courses also available.—*Warden* (vacant).

Wales

COLEG HARLECH, Harlech, Merioneth (Men and Women) (125).—*Warden*, I. W. Hughes.

Scotland

NEWBATTLE ABBEY COLLEGE, Dalkeith, Midlothian (Men and Women)—*Warden*, C. L. Rigg.

Residential Colleges
(Offering shorter Courses)

ATTINGHAM PARK, nr. Shrewsbury (Shropshire Adult College).—*Warden*, G. Toms.
AVONCROFT RESIDENTIAL COLLEGE FOR SHORT-TERM ADULT EDUCATION COURSES, Stoke Prior, nr. Bromsgrove, Worcs.—*Principal*, B. G. Foord.
BELSTEAD HOUSE, nr. Ipswich, Suffolk.—*Warden*, G. E. Curtis.
BURTON MANOR, Neston, Wirral, Cheshire.—*Warden*, John Newton.

DEBDEN HOUSE, Debden Green, Loughton, Essex (Newham Education Cttee.).—*Warden*, L. Halcrow, M.A.

DENMAN COLLEGE, Marcham, Abingdon, Berks. (N.F.W.I.).—*Warden*, Miss H. Anderson.

DILLINGTON HOUSE, Ilminster, Somerset.—*Warden*, Instr. Capt. G. M. Hines R.N. (*ret.*).

DUNFORD HOUSE, Midhurst, Sussex (Y.M.C.A. Adult Education and Training Centre).—*Principal*, Rev. P. G. Hayman.

GRANTLEY HALL, Ripon, Yorks.—*Warden*, Dr. H. C. Strick.

HOLLY ROYDE COLLEGE (Of Manchester University Extra-Mural Dept.), 56–62 Palatine Road, West Didsbury, Manchester 20.—*Warden*, D. Garside.

HORNCASTLE RESIDENTIAL COLLEGE, Horncastle, Lincs.—*Warden*, S. L. Josephs.

HUNTERCOMBE MANOR, Taplow, Maidenhead, Berks. (Buckinghamshire Education Cttee.).—*Warden*, G. F. Thomas.

KINGSGATE COLLEGE, Broadstairs, Kent (Y.M.C.A. College for Adults).—*Principal*, E. F. Bellchambers.

KNUSTON HALL, Irchester, Wellingborough, Northants.—*Warden*, Miss E. Smith.

MISSENDEN ABBEY, Great Missenden, Bucks.—*Warden*, M. Lloyd.

MOOR PARK COLLEGE, Farnham, Surrey.—*Warden*, F. S. Grimwood, D.Phil.

ROFFEY PARK INSTITUTE, Management College, Horsham, Sussex.—*Director*, W. J. Giles.

UNIVERSITY COLLEGE, Cambridge. Offers 10 places each term to managers (incl. women) in industry, commerce or public services on a 2-month course in preparation for further responsibilities.—*Tutor*, P. J. Alexander.

URCHFONT MANOR, Devizes, Wilts.—*Warden*, A. T. C. Slee, Ph.D.

WANSFELL COLLEGE, Theydon Bois, Epping.—*Principal*, A. Kingsbury.

WEDGWOOD MEMORIAL COLLEGE, Barlaston, nr. Stoke-on-Trent—*Warden*, W. E. Lloyd.

WESTHAM HOUSE, Barford, nr. Warwick.—*Principal*, F. Owen, T.D.

PRINCIPAL UNIVERSITY SETTLEMENTS AND ADULT EDUCATION CENTRES

BEDFORD INSTITUTE ASSOCIATION, 128A Hoxton Street, N.1. (5 Friends' centres at Barking, Bethnal Green, Clerkenwell, Hoxton, Islington, Walthamstow).—*Gen. Sec.*, Miss M. Osmond.

BERNHARD BARON ST. GEORGE'S JEWISH SETTLEMENT, Henriques Street, E.1.—*Warden*, L. Rogers.

BIRMINGHAM SETTLEMENT, 318 Summer Lane, Birmingham, 1944.—*Warden and Dir.*, P. D. Houghton.

BLACKFRIARS SETTLEMENT (formerly Women's University Settlement), 44 Nelson Square, S.E.1.—*Warden*, A. Markham.

BOSTON, Department of Adult Education, University of Nottingham, Pilgrim College.—*Warden and Resident Tutor*, A. Champion.

BRADFORD, LEEDS UNIVERSITY ADULT EDUCATION CENTRE, 10 Mornington Villas, Manningham Lane, Bradford 8. (Dept. of Adult Education and Extra-Mural Studies, University of Leeds).

BRISTOL, The Folk House, 40 Park Street.—*Warden*, Miss E. Curzon.

BRISTOL (Headquarters, 43 Ducie Road, Barton Hill).—*Warden*, Mrs. M. N. Maddock.

CAMBRIDGE HOUSE, 131–139 Camberwell Road, S.E.5.—*Head*, Rev. P. Bibby.

CITY LITERARY INSTITUTE, Stukeley Street, Drury Lane, W.C.2.—*Principal*, R. J. South, Ph.D.

DOCKLAND SETTLEMENTS, branches at Isle of Dogs, E.14; Bristol; Rotherhithe, S.E.16; Dagenham, Essex; Stratford, E.15; Hainault Estate, Essex; School of Adventure, Ross-shire; Holiday Home, Herne Bay, Kent.—*Gen. Sec.*, R. W. Logan-Hunt, 164 Romford Road, Stratford, E.15.

EDINBURGH UNIVERSITY SETTLEMENT, 32 Lothian Street, Edinburgh.—*Dir.*, J. R. Waddington; *Adult Education Centre*, Kirk o' Field College, Morton House, Blackfriars Street, Edinburgh, 1.—*Sec.*, Miss E. Wood.

GOLDSMITHS' COLLEGE, New Cross, S.E.14.—*Principal, Dept. of Adult Studies*, P. A. Baynes.

LEEDS, Swarthmore Educational Centre, 3–5 Woodhouse Square, Leeds 3.—*Warden*, B. J. W. Thompson.

LEICESTER, Vaughan College.—*Warden*, D. J. Rice.

LIVERPOOL UNIVERSITY SETTLEMENT, Nile Street.—*Warden*, G. C. P. Riches.

LIVERPOOL, Victoria Settlement, 294 Netherfield Road, N., Liverpool 5.—*Warden*, Miss D. M. Bouckley.

LOUGHBOROUGH, Quest House, Loughborough Technical College, Radmoor.—*Wardens*, D. H. Bodger, Dept. of Adult Education, University of Nottingham; M. F. Somerton, W.E.A. (East Midlands).

MANSFIELD HOUSE, Fairbairn Hall, E.13.—*Warden*, Rev. Canon E. A. Shipman.

MORLEY COLLEGE, 61 Westminster Bridge Road, S.E.1.—*Principal*, B. Till.

PRESBYTERIAN SETTLEMENT AND TRAINING CENTRE, c/o St. Mildred's House, Roserton Street, E.14.

ROBERT BROWNING SETTLEMENT, Browning Street, Walworth, S.E.17.—*Warden*, Rev. H. Rathbone Dunnico, LL.D.

ROLAND HOUSE RESIDENTIAL SCOUT CENTRE AND SCOUT HALL, 29 Stepney Green, E.1.—*Warden*, P. W. Grinstead.

ST. MARGARET'S HOUSE SETTLEMENT, 21 Old Ford Road, Bethnal Green, E.2.—*Warden*, Miss T. J. Fleming.

SPENNYMOOR SETTLEMENT, King Street, Spennymoor, Co. Durham.

TEESSIDE: MIDDLESBROUGH SETTLEMENT COMMUNITY CENTRE, 132–134 Newport Road, Middlesbrough—*Warden*, E. Delves.

TEESSIDE: UNIVERSITY ADULT EDUCATION CENTRE, 37 Harrow Road, Middlesbrough (Department of Adult Education and Extra-mural Studies, University of Leeds).—*Warden*, J. W. Saunders.

TOYNBEE HALL, THE UNIVERSITIES' SETTLEMENT IN EAST LONDON, 28 Commercial Street, Whitechapel, E.1.—*Warden*, W. Birmingham.

WORKING MEN'S COLLEGE, Crowndale Road, N.W.1.—*Principal*, L. P. Thompson-McCausland, C.M.G.; *Warden*, W. J. Evans.

YORK EDUCATIONAL SETTLEMENT, 128 Holgate Hill.—*Wardens*, A. J. Peacock; M. Peacock.

EDUCATIONAL TRUSTS

BOEKE TRUST, care of Messrs. Cadbury Brothers, Bournville, Birmingham. (Applications by individuals for financial assistance not considered.)—*Sec.*, G. O. Jones.

CARNEGIE TRUST FOR THE UNIVERSITIES OF SCOTLAND, The Merchants' Hall, Hanover Street, Edinburgh.—*Sec. and Treasurer*, A. E. Ritchie.

CASSEL EDUCATIONAL TRUST, 21 Hassocks Road, Hurstpierpoint, Sussex.—*Sec.*, D. Hardman.

DARTINGTON HALL TRUST, Totnes, Devon.—*Chairman*, L. K. Elmhirst.

EDUCATION SERVICES, 19 Norham Road, Oxford.—*Hon. Sec.*, Mrs. R. W. Bellerby.

GILCHRIST EDUCATIONAL TRUST, 1 York Street, W.1.—*Sec.*, S. J. Worsley, D.S.O., M.C., LL.D.

HARKNESS FELLOWSHIPS OF THE COMMONWEALTH FUND OF NEW YORK, Harkness House, 38 Upper Brook Street, W.1.—*Dir.*, R. L. Johnston, Ph.D.

KING GEORGE'S JUBILEE TRUST, 166 Piccadilly, W.1.—*Sec.*, D. S. Miller, C.B.E.

LEVERHULME TRUST FUND (1925), 21–23 New Fetter Lane, E.C.4.—Annual income, about £1,000,000. Awards to institutions, at home and overseas, mainly in the form of fellowships, studentships and scholarships for research and education. Awards to individuals are also made on the recommendation of a Research Awards Advisory Committee under four specific schemes. *Dir.*, Lord Murray of Newhaven, K.C.B.; *Sec.*, Miss J. Bennett.

LORD KITCHENER NATIONAL MEMORIAL FUND, Finsbury Barracks, City Road, E.C.1.—*Sec.*, C. R. Allison. Awards annually for university courses 30 to 40 scholarships established to reward long and distinguished service, and especially war service, in H.M. Armed Forces. Competition is open to (*a*) sons of members or ex-members (men or women) of the British Navy, Army or Air Force, aged over 17 and under 20 on 1st January of year of competing, and (*b*) male applicants aged under 30, who have done regular or national service. *No awards are made in respect of postgraduate studies.* Application forms, available after Nov. 1, are returnable by Jan. 28.

MITCHELL CITY OF LONDON CHARITY AND EDUCATIONAL FOUNDATION, Bedford Chambers, Covent Garden, W.C.2.—*Clerk*, A. E. L. Cox.

NUFFIELD FOUNDATION, Nuffield Lodge, Regent's Park, N.W.1.—*Dir.*, C. C. Butler, F.R.S.

ROYAL COMMISSION FOR THE EXHIBITION OF 1851, 1 Lowther Gardens, Exhibition Road, S.W.7.—*Sec.*, C. A. H. James.

SIR RICHARD STAPLEY EDUCATIONAL TRUST, 121 Gloucester Place, Portman Square, W.1.—*Sec.*, R. Groves.

TRUSTEES OF THE LONDON PAROCHIAL CHARITIES, 10 Fleet Street, E.C.4. Income 1970, £620,017. Grants made for the maintenance of City Churches and for the welfare of the poorer classes of the Metropolitan Police District of London.

THOMAS WALL TRUST, 1 York Street, W.1. *Sec.*, Miss B. S. Salmon.

LOCAL EDUCATION AUTHORITIES

English and Welsh Counties

ANGLESEY, Shire Hall, Llangefni.—*Director* D. G. Hopkin.

BEDFORDSHIRE, County Hall, Bedford.—*Director*, P. Shallard, O.B.E.

BERKSHIRE, County Hall, Reading.—*Director*, T. D. W. Whitfield, T.D.

BRECKNOCKSHIRE, Watton Mount, Brecon.—*Chief Education Officer*, D. Williams.

BUCKINGHAMSHIRE, County Offices, Aylesbury.—*Chief Education Officer*, R. P. Harding.

CAERNARVONSHIRE, 4 Castle Street, Caernarvon.—*Director*, M. Williams.

CAMBRIDGESHIRE AND ISLE OF ELY, Shire Hall, Cambridge.—*Chief Education Officer*, G. D. Edwards.

CARDIGANSHIRE, County Office, Marine Terrace, Aberystwyth.—*Director*, J. H. Jones, Ph.D.

CARMARTHENSHIRE, County Hall, Carmarthen.—*Director*, I. Howells.

CHESHIRE, County Hall, Chester.—*Director*, J. Tomlinson.

CORNWALL, County Hall, Truro.—*Secretary*, J. G. Harries, M.B.E.

CUMBERLAND, 5 Portland Square, Carlisle.—*Director*, G. S. Bessey, C.B.E.

DENBIGHSHIRE, Ruthin.—*Director*, D. W. E. Erasmus.

DERBYSHIRE, County Offices, Matlock.—*Director*, H. K. Fowler.

DEVON, County Hall, Exeter.—*Chief Education Officer*, D. Cook, Ph.D.

DORSET, County Hall, Dorchester.—*County Education Officer*, J. R. Bradshaw.

DURHAM, County Hall, Durham.—*Director* G. H. Metcalfe.

ESSEX, County Hall, County Gardens, Chelmsford.—*Chief Education Officer*, D. N. Bungey.

FLINTSHIRE, Shire Hall, Mold.—*Director*, J. H. Davies.

GLAMORGAN, County Hall, Cardiff.—*Director*, B. Jones.

GLOUCESTERSHIRE, Shire Hall, Gloucester.—*Chief Education Officer*, C. P. Milroy.

HAMPSHIRE, The Castle, Winchester.— *County Education Officer*, R. M. Marsh.

HEREFORDSHIRE, County Offices, Bath Street, Hereford.—*Director*, M. L. Edge.

HERTFORDSHIRE, County Hall, Hertford.—*County Education Officer*, S. T. Broad.

HUNTINGDONSHIRE AND PETERBOROUGH, Gazeley House, Huntingdon.—*Director*, I. C. Currey.

ISLE OF WIGHT, County Hall, Newport.—*County Education Officer*, H. W. Barrett.

KENT, Springfield, Maidstone.—*County Education Officer*, J. Haynes.

LANCASHIRE, County Hall, Preston.—*Chief Education Officer*, J. S. B. Boyce, T.D.

LEICESTERSHIRE, County Hall, Glenfield, Leicester.—*Director*, A. N. Fairbairn, M.C.

LINCOLNSHIRE (Holland), Boston.—*County Education Officer*, A. W. Newsom.

LINCOLNSHIRE (Kesteven), Sleaford.—*Director*, G. R. Scott.

LINCOLNSHIRE (Lindsey), Lincoln.—*Director*, G. V. Cooke.

LONDON. *See* p. 515.

MERIONETH, County Offices, Penarlag, Dolgellau.—*Director*, W. E. Jones.

MONMOUTHSHIRE, County Hall, Newport, Mon.—*Director*, T. M. Morgan.

MONTGOMERYSHIRE, County Offices, Newtown.—*Director*, T. A. V. Evans.

NORFOLK, County Hall, Norwich.—*Chief Education Officer*, F. L. Ralphs, Ph.D.

NORTHAMPTONSHIRE, County Hall, Northampton.—*Chief Education Officer*, G. E. Churchill.

NORTHUMBERLAND, Eldon House, Regent Centre, Gosforth, Newcastle upon Tyne.—*Director*, M. Trollope.

NOTTINGHAMSHIRE, County Hall, West Bridgford.—*Director*, W. G. Lawson.

OXFORDSHIRE, County Offices, New Road, Oxford.—*Director*, E. J. Dorrell.

PEMBROKESHIRE, County Offices, Haverfordwest.—*Director*, W. Davies.

RADNORSHIRE, County Hall, Llandrindod Wells.—*Chief Education Officer*, R. W. Bevan.

RUTLAND, County Offices, Oakham.—*Chief Education Officer*, J. A. Simmonds.

SHROPSHIRE, Shirehall, Shrewsbury.—*Chief Education Officer*, J. Boyers.

SOMERSET, County Hall, Taunton.—*Chief Education Officer*, R. M. Parker, O.B.E.

STAFFORDSHIRE, Earl Street, Stafford.—*Director*, N. E. Browning, M.B.E.

SUFFOLK (East), Rope Walk, Ipswich.—*Chief Education Officer*, J. H. Aldam, M.C.

SUFFOLK (West), 5–6 St. Mary's Square, Bury St. Edmunds.—*Chief Education Officer*, F. J. Hill.

SURREY, County Hall, Kingston on Thames.—*Chief Education Officer*, J. W. Henry.

SUSSEX (East), County Hall, Lewes.—*Chief Education Officer*, J. R. Jones.

SUSSEX (West), County Hall, Chichester.—*Chief Education Officer*, C. W. W. Read, Ph.D.

WARWICKSHIRE, 22 Northgate Street, Warwick.—*County Education Officer* (vacant).

WESTMORLAND County Hall, Kendal.—*Director*, K. G. Greenwood.

WILTSHIRE, County Hall. Trowbridge.—*Chief Education Officer*, J. H. Bradley.

WORCESTERSHIRE, 17 Castle Street, Worcester.—*County Education Officer*, J. C. Brooke.

YORKSHIRE, E.R., County Hall, Beverley.—*Chief Education Officer*, J. Bower.

YORKSHIRE, N.R., County Hall, Northallerton.—*Director*, G. A. Winter.

YORKSHIRE, W. R., County Education Office, Bond Street, Wakefield.—*Chief Education Officer*, Sir Alexander Clegg.

London

INNER LONDON EDUCATION AUTHORITY—*Education Officer* (vacant).

Education Officers

BARKING, Civic Centre, Dagenham.—J. L. Haselden.

Barnet, Town Hall, Friern Barnet, N.11.—J. Dawkins.

BEXLEY, Town Hall, Crayford.—S. Semple, Ph.D.

BRENT, Town Hall, Forty Lane, Wembley.—F. W. Wyeth.

BROMLEY, Sunnymead, Bromley Lane, Chislehurst.—D. R. Barraclough.

CROYDON, Taberner House, Park Lane.—K. J. Revell.

EALING, 22–24 Uxbridge Road, W.5. (vacant).

ENFIELD, Church Street, Edmonton, N.9.—D. B. Denny.

HARINGEY, Somerset Road, Tottenham, N.17.—(*Director*), P. J. Glover, C.B., C.B.E.

HARROW, Hanover House, Lyon Road.—(*Director of Education*), R. S. Ball.

HAVERING, Upminster Court, 133 Hall Lane, Upminster, Essex.—D. H. Wilcockson.

HILLINGDON, Council Offices, 265 High Street, Uxbridge, Middx.—Miss C. A. Pratt.

HOUNSLOW, 88 Lampton Road.—(*Director of Education*), P. J. Lee.

KINGSTON UPON THAMES, Tolworth Tower, Surbiton, Surrey.—J. S. Bishop.

MERTON, Station House, London Road, Morden, Surrey.—R. Greenwood.

NEWHAM, 29 Broadway, Stratford, E.15.—R. Openshaw.

REDBRIDGE, Lynton House, High Road, Ilford, Essex.—J. E. Fordham.

RICHMOND UPON THAMES, Regal House, Twickenham, Middx.—W. R. Wainwright.

SUTTON, The Grove, Carshalton, Surrey.—H. M. Evans.

WALTHAM FOREST, Municipal Offices, Leyton, E.10.—W. E. D. Stephens, Ph.D.

English and Welsh County Boroughs

BARNSLEY.—*Director*, H. A. Redburn, O.B.E., T.D.

BARROW IN FURNESS, John Whinnerah Institute, Abbey Road.—*Chief Education Officer*, B. L. Blake.

BATH, Guildhall.—*Director*, E. F. Warren.

BIRKENHEAD, Cleveland Street.—*Director*, R. E. Price.

BIRMINGHAM, Margaret Street, Birmingham 3.—*Chief Education Officer*, K. Brooksbank, D.S.C.

BLACKBURN, Town Hall.—*Director*, G. Mayall.

BLACKPOOL, 3 Caunce Street.—*Chief Education Officer*, R. E. Hodd.

BOLTON, Victoria House, Civic Centre.—*Chief Education Officer*, W. T. Selley.

BOOTLE, Balliol House, The Stanley Precinct.—*Director*, W. R. J. Coe.

BOURNEMOUTH, Portman House, Richmond Hill.—*Director*, W. R. Smedley.

BRADFORD, City Hall.—*Director*, F. J. Adams.

BRIGHTON, 54 Old Steine.—*Director*, K. A. Antcliffe.

BRISTOL, The Council House, College Green.—*Chief Education Officer*, H. S. Thompson, M.B.E.

BURNLEY, 14 Nicholas Street.—*Director*, R. O. Beeston.

BURTON UPON TRENT, Guild Street.—*Director*, G. S. Bull.

BURY, Town Hall.—*Director*, J. Ashworth.

CANTERBURY, 78–79 London Road.—*Chief Education Officer*, N. Polmear.

CARDIFF, Magne House, Kingsway.—*Director*, A. J. Mackay.

CARLISLE, Civic Centre.—*Director*, L. Charnley.

CHESTER, Mezzanine Floor, Public Market.—*Director*, L. E. Griffiths.

COVENTRY, Council Offices, Earl Street.—*Director*, R. Aitken.

DARLINGTON, Town Hall.—*Chief Education Officer*, L. G. Reedman.

DERBY, Becket Street.—*Director*, C. Middleton.

DEWSBURY, Halifax Road.—*Chief Education Officer*, J. Clitheroe.

DONCASTER, Princegate.—*Chief Education Officer*, M. J. Pass.

DUDLEY, 23 St. James's Road.—*Chief Education Officer*, H. W. C. Eisel.

EASTBOURNE, Grove Road.—*Chief Education Officer*, C. L. Smith, D.Phil.

EXETER, 32 St. David's Hill.—*Director* S. Nielsen.

GATESHEAD, Prince Consort Road South.—*Director*, Miss M. A. Sproat.

GLOUCESTER, Belsize House, Brunswick Square.—*Education Officer*, R. Turner.

GRIMSBY, Eleanor Street.—*Director*, W. P. Knight.

HALIFAX, West House.—*Chief Education Officer*, L. T. Jackson.

HARTLEPOOL, Park Road.—*Director*, A. D. Jackson.

HASTINGS, 20 Wellington Square.—*Chief Education Officer*, M. O. Palmer.

HUDDERSFIELD, Civic Centre.—*Chief Education Officer*, H. Gray.

IPSWICH, 17 Tower Street.—*Chief Education Officer*, A. Owen.

KINGSTON UPON HULL, Guildhall, Hull.—*Chief Education Officer*, S. W. Hobson.

LEEDS, Municipal Buildings, Calverley Street.—*Director*, J. H. Taylor.

LEICESTER, Newarke Street.—*Director*, E. Thomas, Ph.D.

LINCOLN, 4 Lindum Road.—*Chief Education Officer*, F. A. Stuart.

LIVERPOOL, 14 Sir Thomas Street.—*Education Officer*, C. P. R. Clarke.

LUTON, 35 Old Bedford Road.—*Director*, F. D. Bailey.

MANCHESTER, Cumberland House, Crown Square.—*Chief Education Officer*, D. A. Fiske.

MERTHYR TYDFIL, Pontmorlais.—*Director*, J. Beale.

NEWCASTLE UPON TYNE, Civic Centre, Barras Bridge.—*Director*, J. F. Chadderton.

NEWPORT, Mon., Educ. Dept., Civic Centre.—*Chief Education Officer*, E. H. Loudon.

NORTHAMPTON, Springfield, Cliftonville.—*Chief Education Officer*, M. J. Henley.

NORWICH, Education Office, City Hall.—*Director*, C. Harrison, Ph.D.

NOTTINGHAM, Exchange Buildings.—*Director*, W. G. Jackson.

OLDHAM, Union Street West.—*Director*, G. R. Pritchett.

OXFORD, Education Office, City Chambers, Queen Street.—*Chief Education Officer*, J. Garne, M.C.

PLYMOUTH, Municipal Offices.—*Director*, J. F. Chadderton.

PORTSMOUTH, 17–18 Western Parade, Southsea.—*Chief Education Officer*, W. G. Lumb.

PRESTON, Municipal Building.—*Chief Education Officer*, W. R. Tuson.

READING, Blagrave Street.—*Chief Education Officer*, W. L. Thomas.

ROCHDALE, Fleece Street.—*Chief Education Officer*, F. H. Pedley.

ROTHERHAM, Wellgate.—*Director*, L. G. Taylor.

ST. HELEN'S, Century House.—*Director*, W. H. Cubitt.

SALFORD, Chapel Street, Salford, 3.—*Director*, J. A. Barnes.

SHEFFIELD, Leopold Street.—*Director*, G. M. A. Harrison.

SOLIHULL, The Council House.—*Director*, D. B. Love.

SOUTHAMPTON, Civic Centre.—*Chief Education Officer*, D. P. J. Browning.

SOUTHEND ON SEA, Civic Centre.—*Chief Education Officer*, D. B. Bartlett.

SOUTHPORT, Pavilion Buildings, Lord Street.—*Chief Education Officer*, K. Robinson.

SOUTH SHIELDS, Westoe Hall.—*Director*, G. Denton.

STOCKPORT, Town Hall.—*Director*, C. G. Davey.

STOKE ON TRENT, Town Hall, Hanley.—*Chief Education Officer*, H. Dibden.

SUNDERLAND, Town Hall.—*Director*, J. Bridge, G.C., G.M.

SWANSEA, The Guildhall.—*Director*, L. J. Drew.

TEESSIDE, Woodlands Road, Middlesbrough.—*Director*, E. D. Mason.

TORBAY, Oldway, Paignton.—*Director*, K. W. Baddeley.

TYNEMOUTH, The Chase, North Shields.—*Chief Education Officer*, G. Wilson.

WAKEFIELD, King Street.—*Director*, M. Gray.

WALLASEY, Town Hall.—*Director*, K. A. Rowland.

WALSALL, Darwall Street.—*Director*, R. D. Nixon.

WARLEY, Flash Road, Oldbury.—*Chief Education Officer*, H. N. Atherton.

WARRINGTON, Sankey Street.—*Chief Education Officer*, C. J. Ross.

WEST BROMWICH, Highfields.—*Chief Education Officer*, M. J. Gifford.

WIGAN, Town Hall.—*Director*, K. Crawford.

WOLVERHAMPTON, St. John's Square.—*Director*, D. Grayson.

WORCESTER, 5–6 Barbourne Terrace.—*Director*, T. A. Ireland.

YARMOUTH, 22 Euston Road.—*Chief Education Officer*, D. G. Farrow, O.B.E.

YORK, 5 St. Leonard's Place.—*Chief Education Officer*, J. Threlfall.

Channel Islands. etc.

JERSEY, Pier Road, St. Helier.—*Director*, H. C. A. Wimberley.

GUERNSEY, La Couperderle, St. Peter Port.—*Director*, L. K. Redford.

ISLE OF MAN, Strand Street, Douglas.—*Director*, F. Bickerstaff.

ISLES OF SCILLY, Town Hall, St. Mary's.—*Clerk*, R. Phillips.

Scotland

ABERDEEN (City), St. Nicholas House, Broad Street.—*Director*, J. R. Clark, C.B.E.

ABERDEENSHIRE, 22 Union Terrace, Aberdeen.—*Director*, J. A. D. Michie.

ANGUS, County Buildings, Forfar.—*Director*, A. McLellan.

ARGYLL (County), Education Offices, Dunoon.—*Director*, T. G. Henderson.

AYRSHIRE, County Buildings, Ayr.—*Director*, J. I. Wallace.

BANFF (County), Earlsmount, Keith.—*Director*, J. K. Purves.

BERWICK (County), Education Office, Southfield, Duns.—*Director*, R. D. Birch.

BUTE (County), County Offices, Rothesay.—*Director*, J. E. Harrison.

CAITHNESS, Education Office, Rhind House, Wick.—*Director*, H. R. Stewart.

CLACKMANNAN (County), Education Offices, Glebe Terrace, Alloa.—*Director*, T. E. M. Landsborough.

DUMFRIESSHIRE, Huntingdon, 27 Moffat Road, Dumfries.—*Director*, J. L. Brown.

DUNBARTON, County Offices, Dumbarton.—*Director*, A. B. Cameron.

DUNDEE, 14 City Square.—*Director*, J. Carson.

EAST LOTHIAN, Education Offices, Haddington.—*Director*, Dr. J. Meiklejohn.

EDINBURGH, St. Giles Street, Edinburgh.—*Director*, G. Reith, C.B.E., Ph.D.

ELGIN. *See* MORAY AND NAIRN.

FIFE, County Offices, Wemyssfield, Kirkcaldy.—*Director*, I. S. Flett.

GLASGOW, Education Offices, 129 Bath Street and 25 Bothwell Street, Glasgow, C.2.—*Director*, J. T. Bain.

INVERNESS (County), County Buildings, Inverness.—*Director*, R. J. Macdonald.

KINCARDINESHIRE, Education Office, Stonehaven.—*Director*, B. B. Smith.

KINROSS. *See* PERTHSHIRE

STEWARTRY OF KIRKCUDBRIGHT, Castle-Douglas.—*Director*, D. J. Baillie.

LANARKSHIRE, County Buildings, Hamilton.—*Director*, J. S. McEwan.

MIDLOTHIAN, County Buildings, George IV Bridge, Edinburgh, 3.—*Director*, T. Henderson.

MORAY AND NAIRN, Academy Street, Elgin.—*Director*, W. F. Lindsay.

ORKNEY (County), Albert Street, Kirkwall.—*Director*, A. Bain.

PEEBLES (County), County Buildings, Peebles.—*Director*, A. H. R. Calderwood.

PERTHSHIRE and KINROSS-SHIRE, County Offices, York Place, Perth.—*Director*, L. B. Young.

RENFREWSHIRE, 16 Glasgow Road, Paisley—*Director*, H. Fairlie.

ROSS and CROMARTY, County Buildings, Dingwall.—*Director*, R. M. Inglis.

ROXBURGH (County), Newtown St. Boswells.—*Director*, C. Melville.

SELKIRK, County Offices, Melrose Road, Galashiels.—*Director*, D. G. Robertson.

STIRLING (County), Spittal Street.—*Director*, J. S. Meldrum.

SUTHERLAND (County), Education Office, Brora.—*Director*, J. McLellan.

WEST LOTHIAN, Linlithgow.—*Director*, A. Sinclair.

WIGTOWNSHIRE, 10 Market Street, Stranraer.—*Director*, D. G. Gunn.

ZETLAND (County), Brentham Place, Lerwick.—*Director*, J. H. Spence.

Northern Ireland

ANTRIM COUNTY, Education Office, County Hall, Galgorm Road, Ballymena—*Director* R. J. Dickson, Ph.D.

ARMAGH COUNTY, Education Office, 8 Beresford Row, Armagh.—*Director*, W. J. Dickson.

BELFAST (County Borough), Education Office, 40 Academy Street, Belfast, 1.—*Director*, W. C. H. Eakin.

DOWN COUNTY, Education Office, 18 Windsor Avenue, Belfast 9.—*Director*, F. H. Ebbitt.

FERMANAGH COUNTY, Education Office, East Bridge Street, Enniskillen.—*Chief Education Officer,* J. Malone.

LONDONDERRY COUNTY, Education Office, County Hall, Coleraine.—*Director,* R. B. Hunter, O.B.E.

LONDONDERRY (City), Education Office, Brooke Park, Londonderry.—*Director,* H. M. D. McWilliam, M.B.E., T.D.

TYRONE COUNTY, Education Office, Omagh.—*Director of Education,* A. Gibson.

PROFESSIONAL EDUCATION

NOTE.—References to university courses in the sections following cover *first* degrees; the considerable facilities available at universities for postgraduate study or research are not treated.

ACCOUNTANCY

Degrees.—Under a scheme arranged by the Joint Standing Committee on Degree Studies and the Accountancy Profession (details from the Secretary to the Joint Standing Committee, Institute of Chartered Accountants in England and Wales), it is possible to obtain in a specified period both a university or C.N.A.A. degree and certain exemptions from the examinations of the six accountancy bodies participating in the scheme. The participating universities and colleges in the United Kingdom are:

Universities: Aston in Birmingham, Bath, Belfast, Birmingham, Bradford, Bristol, Edinburgh, Glasgow, Heriot-Watt, Hull, Kent at Canterbury, Lancaster, Leeds, Liverpool, London (London School of Economics and Political Science), Manchester (Institute of Science and Technology), Newcastle upon Tyne, Nottingham, Sheffield, Southampton, Strathclyde, Wales (University Colleges at Aberystwyth and Cardiff; and Institute of Science and Technology).

Colleges providing courses for C.N.A.A. degrees, are the following Polytechnics: Central London, Hatfield, Kingston, Lanchester, City of Leicester, Newcastle upon Tyne, North-East London, Portsmouth, Sheffield, Thames and Wolverhampton; and Dundee College of Technology, Ealing Technical College, Enfield College of Technology and Hendon College of Technology.

Professional Bodies.—The main bodies granting membership on examination after a period of practical work are:

INSTITUTE OF CHARTERED ACCOUNTANTS IN ENGLAND AND WALES, Chartered Accountants' Hall Moorgate Place, E.C.2.

INSTITUTE OF CHARTERED ACCOUNTANTS OF SCOTLAND, 27 Queen Street, Edinburgh, 2, and 213 St. Vincent Street, Glasgow C.2.

ASSOCIATION OF CERTIFIED AND CORPORATE ACCOUNTANTS, 22 Bedford Square, W.C.1.

INSTITUTE OF MUNICIPAL TREASURERS AND ACCOUNTANTS, 1 Buckingham Place, S.W.1.

INSTITUTE OF COST AND WORKS ACCOUNTANTS, 63 Portland Place. W.1.

ACTUARIES

Two professional organizations grant qualifications after examination:

INSTITUTE OF ACTUARIES, Staple Inn Hall, High Holborn, W.C.1.

FACULTY OF ACTUARIES IN SCOTLAND, *Hall and Library,* 23 St. Andrew Square, Edinburgh.

AERONAUTICS
and Aeronautical Engineering

Degrees in *Aeronautical Engineering* are granted by Bath University of Technology and by the Universities of Belfast, Bristol, Cambridge (*Aeronautics*), the City University, the Universities of Glasgow, London (Imperial College of Science and Techno-

logy; Queen Mary College), Loughborough, Manchester, Salford and Southampton; and in *Air Transport Engineering* by the City University. Courses leading to degrees granted by the Council for National Academic Awards are provided by Hatfield Polytechnic and Kingston Polytechnic.

COLLEGE OF AERONAUTICAL AND AUTOMOBILE ENGINEERING, 102 Sydney Street, Chelsea, S.W.3, and Redhill Aerodrome, Surrey.

COLLEGE OF AIR TRAINING, Hamble, Southampton.

CRANFIELD INSTITUTE OF TECHNOLOGY, Cranfield, Bedford.

AGRICULTURE

Degrees in *Agriculture* or *Agricultural Science(s)* are granted by the Universities of Aberdeen, Belfast, Cambridge, Edinburgh, Glasgow, Leeds, London (Wye College), Newcastle upon Tyne, Nottingham, Oxford, Reading and Wales (University Colleges of Aberystwyth and Bangor); and in *Horticulture* by Bath, London (Wye College), Nottingham, Reading and (provisional) Strathclyde. Other schools of agriculture are:

ABERDEEN (North of Scotland College of Agriculture, 581 King Street).—*Sec.,* H. Munro.

CIRENCESTER, Royal Agricultural College.—*Principal,* G. R. Dickson, Ph.D.

EDINBURGH SCHOOL OF AGRICULTURE, THE, West Mains Road, Edinburgh, 9.—*Principal,* Prof. N. F. Robertson, B.SC., Ph.D.

HARPER ADAMS AGRICULTURAL COLLEGE, Newport, Salop.—*Principal,* R. Kenney. B.SC.

SEALE-HAYNE AGRICULTURAL COLLEGE, Newton Abbot, S. Devon.—*Principal,* G. J. Dowrick, B.SC., Ph.D.

SHUTTLEWORTH AGRICULTURAL COLLEGE, Old Warden Park, Biggleswade, Bedfordshire.—*Principal,* J. E. Scott, B.SC., M.S.

WEST OF SCOTLAND AGRICULTURAL COLLEGE, 6 Blythswood Square, Glasgow, and Auchincruive, Ayr.—*Principal,* Prof. J. S. Hall, B.SC.

There are in addition over twenty county Agricultural Institutes giving a one-year course.

ARBITRATION

THE INSTITUTE OF ARBITRATORS, 16 Park Crescent, W.1, conducts examinations and maintains a Register of Fellows and Associates.—*Secretary,* G. Darling.

ARCHÆOLOGY

Degrees in Archæology (sometimes in combination with another subject) are granted by the Universities of Belfast, Birmingham, Cambridge, Edinburgh, Exeter, Glasgow, Liverpool, London (Institute of Archæology, Bedford and University Colleges), Manchester, Nottingham, Reading, Sheffield, Southampton, Wales (University Colleges of Cardiff and Bangor).

ARCHITECTURE

The Board of Education of THE ROYAL INSTITUTE OF BRITISH ARCHITECTS, 66 Portland Place, W.1, sets standards and guides the whole system of architectural education throughout the United Kingdom. Courses at the following Schools are recognized by the R.I.B.A. They are visited regularly by the R.I.B.A. Visiting Board to ensure that they meet the minimum standards for exemption from the R.I.B.A.'s own examinations.

UNIVERSITY SCHOOLS

(Subject to exceptions noted below, courses are full-time for five years, leading to a degree or diploma; number of students and name of Head of School or Department of Architecture are included).

BELFAST: Queen's University (157).—Prof. J. A. Potter.

R+

BATH: University School of Architecture and Building Technology, Claverton Down (104).—Prof. K. Panter (6-yr. composite course).

BRISTOL: University Dept. of Architecture (153).—Prof. A. D. Jones.

CAMBRIDGE: University School of Architecture (189).—Prof. Sir Leslie Martin, Ph.D.

CARDIFF: The Welsh School of Architecture, University of Wales, Institute of Science and Technology (173).—Prof. D-P. Thomas.

EDINBURGH: University of Edinburgh, Dept. of Architecture (128).—Prof. G. B. Oddie.
— Heriot Watt University (joint course with Edinburgh College of Art), Lauriston Place (202).—Prof. R. Cowan.

GLASGOW: University of Strathclyde School of Architecture (201).—Prof. T. A. Markus.

LIVERPOOL: University of Liverpool School of Architecture (220).—Prof. R. Gardner-Medwin.

LONDON: School of Environmental Studies, University College London (190).—*Bartlett Professor of Architecture*, N. Watson.

MANCHESTER: University of Manchester School of Architecture (184).—Prof. N. L. Hanson.

NEWCASTLE UPON TYNE: University School of Architecture (165).—Prof. D. Wise.

NOTTINGHAM: University Dept. of Architecture and Civic Planning (94).—Prof. J. N. Tarn.

SHEFFIELD: University Dept. of Architecture (187).—Prof. J. Needham.

NON-UNIVERSITY SCHOOLS

(Subject to the exceptions listed below, courses are full-time and lead to a diploma. Number of students and name of Head of School are shown.)

ABERDEEN: Scott Sutherland School of Architecture, Robert Gordon's Institute of Technology (200).—S. Wilkinson (C.N.A.A. degree).

BIRMINGHAM: School of Architecture, Birmingham Polytechnic, New Corporation Street (223).—Prof. D. Hinton (five-year sandwich course).

BRIGHTON: School of Architecture, Brighton Polytechnic, 62 Grand Parade (156).—J. P. Lomax, Ph.D.

CANTERBURY: School of Architecture, Canterbury College of Art, St. Peter's Street (119).—R. W. Paine.

DUNDEE: School of Architecture and Town Planning, Duncan of Jordanstone College of Art, Perth Road (185).—J. Paul.

GLASGOW: The Macintosh School of Architecture, Glasgow University School of Art, 167 Renfrew Street* (307).—Prof. J. H. W. Voelcker.

HULL: School of Architecture, Regional College of Art, Anlaby Road (92).—A. Arschavir.

KINGSTON UPON THAMES: Polytechnic School of Architecture and Civic Design, Knight's Park (230).—D. Berry.

LEEDS: School of Architecture, Leeds Polytechnic, 43A Woodhouse Lane (210).—J. M. Jenkins.

LEICESTER: Polytechnic School of Architecture, 1 Newarke Street (232).—R. Howrie, M.B.E.

LONDON: Architectural Association School of Architecture, 36 Bedford Square, W.C.1. (381).—M. Lloyd.
Department of Architecture, Brixton School of Building, Ferndale Road, S.W.4.* (121).—A. Reed.
School of Architecture, Surveying and Town Planning, The Polytechnic, Regent Street, W.1 (192).—D. J. Oakley.
Dept. of Architecture, Surveying, Building and Interior Design, Northern Polytechnic, Holloway, N.7 (186).—C. G. Bath. (C.N.A.A. degree).
Dept. of Architecture, Hammersmith College of Art and Building, Lime Grove, W.12 (172)—P. Nightingale.

MANCHESTER: Polytechnic School of Architecture, Dept. of Environmental Design, Cavendish Street (6-yr. composite course) (134).—M. H. Darke.

OXFORD: Polytechnic School of Architecture, College of Technology, Headington Road (260).—R. Cave.

PORTSMOUTH: Polytechnic School of Architecture, Portsmouth College of Technology, High Street (198).—G. H. Broadbent.

* Recognized for exemption from the R.I.B.A. Intermediate Examination only.

ART

Degrees in *Art* or *History of Art* (sometimes in combination with another subject) are granted by the Universities of Bristol, Cambridge, East Anglia, Edinburgh, Essex, Exeter, Glasgow, Leeds, London (Courtauld Institute of Art; Birkbeck, University and Westfield Colleges), Manchester, Newcastle upon Tyne, Nottingham, Reading, Sussex and Wales (University College, Aberystwyth). The degrees in *Art*, granted by the Royal College of Art are higher degrees.

Among the many non-degree qualifications in art are the Diploma in Art and Design and the Art Teachers' Diploma, for which courses are provided by many colleges of art.

THE NATIONAL COUNCIL FOR DIPLOMAS IN ART AND DESIGN (16 Park Crescent, W.1) was set up in March, 1961, as an independent body to administer the award of diplomas available to students in Colleges of art and design who successfully complete courses approved by the Council.
Chairman, S. C. Mason, C.B.E.
Chief Officer, E. E. Pullee, C.B.E.

LONDON.—Royal Academy Schools of Painting and Sculpture, Burlington Gardens, W.1. (65).—*Keeper*, Peter Greenham, B.A.; *Secretary*, S. C. Hutchison; *Curator*, W. Woodington; *Registrar*, K. J. Tanner.

LONDON.—The Slade School of Fine Art, University College, W.C.1, provides courses in Drawing, Painting and Sculpture, Etching, Engraving, Lithography, Silk Screen Printing and Stage Design. Facilities available for the Study of Film.—*Slade Professor*, Sir William Coldstream, C.B.E.; *Sec.*, I. E. T. Jenkin, M.A.

LONDON.—Royal Drawing Society, 17 Carlton House Terrace, S.W.1.—*Pres.*, R. R. Tomlinson, O.B.E., A.R.C.A., R.B.A.; *Sec.*, W. Manston.

LONDON.—Royal College of Art, see p. 510.

OXFORD, The Ruskin School of Drawing and Fine Art, at The Ashmolean Museum (90 students).—*Principal*, P. Morsberger (Ruskin Master of Drawing). Courses in Drawing, Painting and Design. The University awards a Certificate in Fine Art.

GLASGOW, School of Art, 167 Renfrew Street.—*Chairman*, R. W. Begg; *Director*, H. J. Barnes, C.B.E.; *Sec. & Treas.*, F. W. Kean.

ASTRONOMY

Degrees in *Astronomy* are granted by the Universities of Glasgow, London (University College), Newcastle upon Tyne, and St. Andrews; and in *Astrophysics* by the Universities of Edinburgh and London (Queen Mary College).

BANKING

Professional organizations granting qualifications after examination:—

THE INSTITUTE OF BANKERS, 10 Lombard Street, E.C.3.

THE INSTITUTE OF BANKERS IN SCOTLAND, 62 George Street, Edinburgh.

BIOLOGY, CHEMISTRY, PHYSICS

Degrees are granted by Universities and by the Council for National Academic Awards. Technical College courses lead to diplomas and to National Certificates. Professional qualifications are awarded by:—

THE INSTITUTE OF BIOLOGY, 41 Queen's Gate, S.W.7.—*Gen. Sec.*, D. J. B. Copp.

THE INSTITUTE OF PHYSICS AND THE PHYSICAL SOCIETY, 47 Belgrave Square, S.W.1.

THE ROYAL INSTITUTE OF CHEMISTRY, 30 Russell Square, W.C.1.—*President*, Sir Ewart Jones, F.R.S.; *Sec. and Registrar*, R. E. Parker, PH.D.

BREWING

FULL-TIME COURSES for brewers are conducted *for those in possession of an approved University Degree in Science (with Chemistry as a main subject)*, at The British School of Malting and Brewing, University of *Birmingham*, and at Heriot-Watt University, *Edinburgh*. The latter also offers a three-year undergraduate course.

Professional qualifications are awarded after examination by:—

THE INSTITUTE OF BREWING, 33 Clarges Street, W.1; *Sec.*, Capt. S. Le H. Lombard-Hobson, C.V.O., O.B.E., R.N.

BUILDING

Degrees in *Building* or *Building Technology* are granted by the following Universities: Aston in Birmingham, Bath, Brunel (provisional), Heriot-Watt, Liverpool, London (University College: *Architecture, Planning, Building and Environmental Studies*), Manchester (Manchester Institute of Science and Technology), Salford and Wales (Institute of Science and Technology). Courses leading to degrees in Building granted by the Council for National Academic Awards are provided by Brighton Polytechnic (*Building Technology and Management*), Lanchester Polytechnic, Leeds Polytechnic, and the Polytechnic of the South Bank.

Ordinary and Higher National Diplomas and certificates in Building are awarded by Technical Colleges in agreement with the Department of Education and Science, the Scottish Education Department and The Institute of Building.

Examinations are conducted by:—

THE INSTITUTE OF BUILDING, Englemere, King's Ride, Ascot, Berks.

THE INSTITUTE OF CLERKS OF WORKS OF GREAT BRITAIN, Sardinia House, 52 Lincoln's Inn Fields, W.C.2.—*Sec.* R. G. Staples.

THE INSTITUTION OF MUNICIPAL ENGINEERS, 25 Eccleston Square, S.W.1 (Building Inspector's Ordinary and Higher Certificate).

BUSINESS, MANAGEMENT AND ADMINISTRATION

Degrees in *Business Studies* are granted by the Universities of Aston, Bath (provisional), Bradford (*Economics and Business Management*), Belfast (*Business Administration*), Salford (*Business Operation and Control*), Sheffield (*Engineering with Business Studies*), Strathclyde (School of Business and Administration), Wales (University College, Aberystwyth) (*Economics and Business*); in *Administration* by the Universities of Aston in Birmingham (*Administrative Science*), and Strathclyde; in *Management Sciences* by the City University (provisional) (*Systems and Management*), Loughborough University of Technology, and the Universities of Manchester (Institute of Science and Technology) and Warwick; and in *Commerce* by the following universities: Birmingham, Edinburgh, Heriot-

Watts, Leeds, Liverpool and Strathclyde. These subjects also form part of degree courses in other universities.

Courses leading to degrees in *Business Studies* granted by the Council for National Academic Awards are provided by Brighton Polytechnic, Bristol Polytechnic, City of London Polytechnic, Dundee College of Technology, Ealing Technical College, Enfield College of Technology, Hatfield Polytechnic, Hendon College of Technology, Kingston Polytechnic, Lanchester Polytechnic, Leeds Polytechnic, City of Leicester Polytechnic, Manchester Polytechnic, Newcastle upon Tyne Polytechnic, North East London Polytechnic, N. Staffordshire Polytechnic, The Polytechnic of Central London, Portsmouth Polytechnic, Sheffield Polytechnic, Thames Polytechnic, Trent Polytechnic and Wolverhampton Polytechnic.

The Thames Polytechnic also provides courses for the C.N.A.A. degree in *International Marketing*; and City of Leicester and Sheffield Polytechnics courses for C.N.A.A. degree in *Public Administration.*

Professional bodies conducting training and/or examinations in Administration and Management include:

ROYAL INSTITUTE OF PUBLIC ADMINISTRATION, 24 Park Crescent, W.1.

THE INSTITUTE OF GENERAL MANAGERS, 90 Buckingham Palace Road, S.W.1.

THE INSTITUTE OF HOSPITAL ADMINISTRATORS, 75 Portland Place, W.1.

THE INSTITUTE OF PERSONNEL MANAGEMENT, 5 Winsley Street, W.1.

INSTITUTION OF WORKS MANAGERS, 34 Bloomsbury Way, W.C.1.

INSTITUTE OF HOUSING MANAGERS, Victoria House, Southampton Row, W.C.1.

INSTITUTE OF OFFICE MANAGEMENT, 167 Victoria Street, S.W.1.

ADMINISTRATIVE STAFF COLLEGE, Greenlands, Henley-on-Thames, Oxon.—*Princ.*, J. P. Martin-Bates (1961).

LONDON GRADUATE SCHOOL OF BUSINESS STUDIES, Sussex Place, Regent's Park, N.W.1.—*Princ.*, A. F. Earle, B.SC., PH.D.

Courses of advanced training in most branches of commerce, including preparation for examinations of the recognized professional organizations as well as for the National Certificate in Business Studies are available at the Polytechnics and other institutions listed by cities on pp. 534-5.

Throughout the country commercial education at a lower level is provided at *Evening Institutes*, particulars of which may be obtained from the Local Education Authority.

There are also numbers of well-established private schools awarding certificates which are widely accepted.

Institutions awarding Professional Qualifications in Commerce:—

A. GENERAL

THE ROYAL SOCIETY OF ARTS (Examinations Dept.), 18 Adam Street, Adelphi, W.C.2.

THE LONDON CHAMBER OF COMMERCE, 69 Cannon Street, E.C.4.

THE SCOTTISH COUNCIL FOR COMMERCIAL, ADMINISTRATIVE AND PROFESSIONAL EDUCATION, 22 Great King Street, Edinburgh 3.

THE EAST MIDLAND EDUCATIONAL UNION, Robins Wood House, Aspley, Nottingham.

THE NORTHERN COUNTIES TECHNICAL EXAMINATIONS COUNCIL, 5 Grosvenor Villas, Grosvenor Road, Newcastle upon Tyne, 2.

THE UNION OF EDUCATIONAL INSTITUTIONS, Norfolk House, Smallbrook Ringway, Birmingham 5.

THE UNION OF LANCASHIRE AND CHESHIRE INSTITUTES, 36 Granby Road, Manchester 1.

THE YORKSHIRE COUNCIL FOR FURTHER EDUCATION, Bowling Green Terrace, Leeds.

WELSH JOINT EDUCATION COMMITTEE, 25 Western Avenue, Cardiff.

B. SPECIALIZED

THE CHARTERED INSTITUTE OF SECRETARIES, 16 Park Crescent, W.1.

CRIPPLEGATE SECRETARIAL COLLEGE, Wilson Street, E.C.2.

THE FACULTY OF SECRETARIES, 51 Tormead Road, Guildford, Surrey.

THE INSTITUTE OF EXPORT, Export House, 14 Hallam Street, W.1.

THE INSTITUTE OF CHARTERED SHIPBROKERS, 25 Bury Street, E.C.3.

INSTITUTE OF MARKETING, Marketing House, Richbell Place, Lamb's Conduit Street, W.C.1.

THE INSTITUTE OF TRANSPORT, 80 Portland Place, W.1.

THE ADVERTISING ASSOCIATION, 1 Bell Yard, W.C.2.

INSTITUTE OF PRACTITIONERS IN ADVERTISING, 44 Belgrave Square, S.W.1.

INSTITUTE OF PURCHASING AND SUPPLY, York House, Westminster Bridge Road, S.E.1.

INSTITUTE OF PERSONNEL MANAGEMENT, 5 Winsley Street, W.1.

COMPUTER SCIENCE

Degrees in *Computer/Computing Science(s)* are granted by Brunel, City and Heriot-Watt Universities and by the Universities of Bradford, Essex, Glasgow, Lancaster, Leeds (provisional) (*Computational Science*), London (Queen Mary College), Loughborough, Manchester (*also* Institute of Science and Technology: *Computation*), Newcastle upon Tyne, St. Andrews (*Computational Science*), Strathclyde and Wales (University College, Swansea: *Computer Technology*). These subjects also form part of degree courses, often as Mathematics and Computer Science, at many other universities and colleges.

Courses leading to degrees in *Computer Science* granted by the Council for National Academic Awards are provided by Brighton Polytechnic, Polytechnic of Central London (*Applied Computing*), Hatfield Polytechnic, Kingston Polytechnic, Leeds Polytechnic (*Operational Research with Computing*), City of Leicester Polytechnic and North Staffordshire Polytechnic, Paisley College of Technology (*Computing with Operational Research*); Portsmouth Polytechnic, Teesside Polytechnic and Wolverhampton Polytechnic; and in *Computer Systems Engineering* by Lanchester Polytechnic.

DANCING

THE ROYAL ACADEMY OF DANCING (incorporated by Royal Charter), 6 Addison Road, W.14 (trains students of exceptional promise in Ballet, 3 years' teachers' course and conducts examinations).—*Dir.*, Miss L. Charlesworth, C.B.E.

THE ROYAL BALLET SCHOOL, 155 Talgarth Road, W.14. and White Lodge, Richmond Park.—*Director*, M. Wood.

IMPERIAL SOCIETY OF TEACHERS OF DANCING (1904), 70 Gloucester Place, W.1.—*Gen. Sec.*, P. J. Pearson.

LONDON COLLEGE OF DANCE AND DRAMA, 100 Marylebone Lane, W.1.

DEFENCE
Royal Naval Colleges

ROYAL NAVAL COLLEGE, Greenwich, S.E.10.

President, Rear-Admiral E. W. Ellis, C.B.E.
Secretary, C. W. Coffin.

ROYAL NAVAL STAFF COLLEGE, Greenwich, S.E.10.

Director, Capt. A. J. Cooke.

INSTITUTE OF NAVAL MEDICINE, Alverstoke, Hants.

Medical Officer in Charge and Dean of Naval Medicine, Surgeon Rear Adm. J. Watt, Q.H.S., M.S., F.R.C.S.

BRITANNIA ROYAL NAVAL COLLEGE, Dartmouth (2141)

Captain, Capt. A. G. Tait., D.S.C.
Commander, Cdr. D. E. Macey.
Dir. of Studies, H. C. Stewart, M.B.E., M.A.
Captain's Secretary, Lt.-Cdr. D. M. Dow.

ROYAL NAVAL ENGINEERING COLLEGE, H.M.S. *Thunderer*, Manadon, Plymouth (500)

Captain, Capt. C. P. H. Gibbons.
Commander, Cdr. G. A. F. Hitchens.
Dir. of Engineering, Cdr. A. J. R. Smith.
Dean, Instr. Capt. H. J. Hair.

JOINT MARITIME OPERATIONAL TRAINING STAFF, Royal Air Force. Turnhouse, Edinburgh

Director, R.N., Capt. J. A. G. Evans.
Director, R.A.F., Gp. Capt. D. R. Locke, O.B.E.
Deputy Directors, Cdr. A. G. Claridge; Wing Cdr. C. P. Donovan.

Military Colleges

STAFF COLLEGE, CAMBERLEY

Officers who graduate at the college have the letters *p.s.c.* after their names in Service Lists.

Commandant, Maj.-Gen. P. J. Howard-Dobson.
Deputy Commandant, Brig. D. A. D. J. Bethell.

ROYAL MILITARY ACADEMY SANDHURST, Camberley, Surrey.

The Royal Military Academy, Woolwich, founded in 1741, and the Royal Military College, Sandhurst, founded in 1799, were amalgamated in 1946 under the above title.

The Academy trains officer cadets for regular commissions in the Army. Length of course, 2 years. Entrance from school, from Welbeck College, or from the ranks of the Regular Army.

Commandant, Maj.-Gen. J. W. Harman, O.B.E., M.C. (Feb., 1972)

ROYAL MILITARY COLLEGE OF SCIENCE, Shrivenham, nr. Swindon, Wilts.

The College was founded at Woolwich in 1864 and transferred to Shrivenham in 1946. Officer (and a few civilian) students are prepared for degrees in Applied Science and Engineering, of the Council for National Academic Awards; Staff Officers for the Home and Commonwealth armies take postgraduate courses in science and technology and officers of the three Services take more advanced courses.

Commandant, Maj.-Gen. F. W. J. Cowtan, M.B.E., M.C.
Dean, F. J. M. Farley, Sc.D., Ph.D.
Registrar, H. A. Shaw, C.B.E.

ARMOUR SCHOOL
R.A.C. CENTRE
Bovington Camp, nr. Wareham, Dorset.
Commandant and Chief Instructor, Col. A. A. V. Cockle.

WELBECK COLLEGE
Worksop, Notts.
Headmaster D. A. Rickards, C.B.E., M.A.
Bursar, Col. W. R. Potter, M.B.E., T.D.

INSTITUTE OF ARMY EDUCATION
Court Road, S.E.9 (90)
Commandant, R. V. M. Benn, O.B.E.

Royal Air Force Colleges
ROYAL AIR FORCE STAFF COLLEGE
Bracknell, Berks.
Commandant, Air Vice-Marshal M. J. Beetham, C.B.E., D.F.C., A.F.C. (1970).

ROYAL AIR FORCE COLLEGE
Cranwell
Founded in 1920, the College provides permanent officers for the General Duties, Engineer, Secretarial and R.A.F. Regiment Branches of the Royal Air Force. It also provides engineering training for all officers of the Engineer Branch.
Air Officer Commanding and Commandant, Air Vice-Marshal F. D. Hughes, C.B.E., D.S.O., D.F.C., A.F.C.
Director of Studies, Air Cdre. C. E. P. Suttle, O.B.E., B.SC.(Eng.).

ROYAL AIR FORCE SCHOOL OF EDUCATION
Upwood, Huntingdon
Commanding Officer, Gp. Capt. J. Walsh, B.E.M.

DENTISTRY
Degrees in Dentistry are granted by the Universities of Belfast, Birmingham, Bristol, Dundee, Edinburgh, Glasgow, Leeds, Liverpool, London (Guy's Hospital Dental School, King's College Hospital Medical School, London Hospital Medical College, Royal Dental Hospital School of Dental Surgery, University College Hospital Medical School), Manchester, Newcastle upon Tyne, Sheffield, Wales (University College, Cardiff, and Welsh National School of Medicine).

Any person is entitled to be registered in the Dentists Register if he holds the degree or diploma in dental surgery of a University in the United Kingdom or Republic of Ireland or the diploma of any of the Licensing Authorities (The Royal College of Surgeons of England, of Edinburgh and in Ireland, and the Royal College of Physicians and Surgeons of Glasgow).

DIETETICS
Courses leading to *degrees* in *Dietetics* granted by the Council for National Academic Awards are provided by Leeds Polytechnic. The professional association which exercises general supervision over training is the British Dietetic Association, 251 Brompton Road, S.W.3. Membership is open to dietitians holding a recognized qualification who may also become State Registered Dietitians through the Council for Professions Supplementary to Medicine (*q.v.*).

DOMESTIC SCIENCE AND CATERING
(*See also* DIETETICS, FOOD, HOTELKEEPING and INSTITUTIONAL MANAGEMENT).
Degrees are granted by the Universities of Bristol (*Domestic Science*), London (Queen Elizabeth College: *Food and Management Science*), Strathclyde (*Hotel and Catering Management*) and Surrey (*Home Economics*; and *Hotel and Catering Administration*).
Courses leading to degrees in *Catering Studies*

granted by the Council for National Academic Awards are provided by Huddersfield Polytechnic.
In addition to Colleges listed below, the Colleges of Education marked with an asterisk on pp. 532-4 offer specialist courses in Home Economics:
BATH (Coll. of Education (Home Economics), Sion Hill Place).
CARDIFF (Coll. of Domestic Arts of S. Wales and Monmouthshire, Llandaff).
LEEDS (Yorkshire Coll. of Education and Home Economics, Calverley Street); (Leeds Polytechnic).
LIVERPOOL (F.L.Calder College of Education for Domestic Science, Dowsefield Lane).
LEICESTERSHIRE (Coll. of Domestic Science, Knighton Fields).
LONDON (Battersea Coll. of Education, Manor House, 58 North Side, Clapham Common, S.W.4.).
SEAFORD, Sussex (Seaford Coll. of Education, Cricketfield Road).
SHREWSBURY (Radbrook College).

DRAMA
Degrees in Drama are granted by the Universities of Birmingham, Bristol, Hull and Manchester. Drama also forms part of degree courses in other universities.
The chief training institutions in Drama are:—
GUILDHALL SCHOOL OF MUSIC AND DRAMA (*see* p. 529).
ROYAL ACADEMY OF DRAMATIC ART (founded by Sir Herbert Beerbohm Tree, 1904) 62-64 Gower Street, W.C.1.—*Principal,* H. P. Cruttwell.
BRITISH DRAMA LEAGUE, 9 Fitzroy Square, W.1.
CENTRAL SCHOOL OF SPEECH AND DRAMA, Embassy Theatre, Swiss Cottage, N.W.3.
LONDON ACADEMY OF MUSIC AND DRAMATIC ART (L.A.M.D.A.), Tower House, 226 Cromwell Road, S.W.5.—*Principal,* N. Ayrton.
ROSE BRUFORD COLLEGE OF SPEECH AND DRAMA, Lamorbey Park, Sidcup, Kent.—*Principal,* J. N. Benedetti.

ENGINEERING
Degrees in *General Engineering* or *Engineering Science* are granted by the Universities of Cambridge, Durham, Exeter, Lancaster, Leicester, Loughborough, Oxford, Reading, and Warwick. Courses leading to *degrees* in *Engineering* granted by the Council for National Academic Awards are provided by Enfield College of Technology, Kingston Polytechnic; Lanchester Polytechnic; Sheffield Polytechnic and Thames Polytechnic; also by the Royal Air Force College, Cranwell (R.A.F. personnel only) and Royal Military College of Science. The fourteen member institutions of The Council of Engineering Institutions, 2 Little Smith Street, S.W.1, are the principal qualifying Societies (*see below*).

Aeronautical Engineering
See main heading:
AERONAUTICS AND AERONAUTICAL ENGINEERING
Agricultural Engineering
Degrees are granted by the University of Newcastle upon Tyne. Courses leading to degrees granted by the Council for National Academic Awards are provided by National College of Agricultural Engineering, Silsoe, Beds.

Chemical Engineering
Degrees are granted by the Universities of Aston in Birmingham, Bath, Birmingham, Bradford, Cambridge, Edinburgh, Exeter, Heriot-Watt, Leeds, London (Imperial College of Science and

Technology; University College) Loughborough, Manchester (Manchester Institute of Science and Technology), Newcastle upon Tyne, Nottingham, Salford, Sheffield, Strathclyde, Surrey, Wales (University College, Swansea). Courses leading to degrees of the University of London are provided by North-East London Polytechnic, and the Polytechnic of the South Bank. Courses leading to degrees granted by the Council for National Academic Awards are provided by Glamorgan Polytechnic and Teesside Polytechnic.

Civil, Electrical & Mechanical Engineering

Degrees in *Civil, Electrical and Mechanical Engineering* are granted by Aberdeen, Aston in Birmingham, Bath (*E. & M.*), Belfast, Birmingham, Bradford, Bristol, Brunel (*E. & M.*), Cambridge, City, Dundee, Edinburgh, Glasgow, Heriot-Watt, Leeds, Liverpool, London (Imperial College of Science and Technology, King's College, Queen Mary College, University College), Loughborough, Manchester, *also* Manchester Institute of Science and Technology, Newcastle upon Tyne, Nottingham, Reading (*E. & M.*), Salford, Sheffield, Southampton, Strathclyde, Surrey, Sussex (*E. & M.*), Wales (University Colleges at Cardiff and Swansea; Institute of Science and Technology, Cardiff).

Some 30 polytechnics or colleges of technology provide courses (in one or more of civil, electrical and mechanical engineering) leading to external degrees of the University of London or to degrees granted by the Council for National Academic Awards.

Electronic Engineering & Electronics

Degrees in *Electronic Engineering* or *Electronics* or *Electrical and Electronic Engineering* are granted by the following universities: Bath, Belfast, Birmingham, Bradford, Brunel, City, Dundee, Edinburgh, Essex, Glasgow, Heriot-Watt, Hull, Kent at Canterbury, Leeds, Liverpool, London (Chelsea College of Science and Technology, King's, Queen Mary and University Colleges), Loughborough, Manchester (*also* Manchester Institute of Science and Technology), Nottingham, Salford, Sheffield, Southampton, Surrey, Sussex, Wales (University Colleges of Bangor and Cardiff; Institute of Science and Technology).

Courses leading to degrees in *Electronic Engineering* granted by the Council for National Academic Awards are provided by Bolton Institute of Technology, Brighton Polytechnic, North Staffordshire Polytechnic and Robert Gordon's Institute of Technology; and in *Physical Electronics* by Newcastle upon Tyne Polytechnic; in the *Physics and Technology of Electronics* by the Polytechnic of North London.

Marine Engineering and Naval Architecture

Degrees in *Marine Engineering* and *Naval Architecture* are granted by the University of Newcastle upon Tyne; in *Mechanical Engineering* (*Naval Architecture*) by the University of London (University College); in *Mechanical Engineering* (*Marine Engineering*) by the University of Surrey; in *Naval Architecture* by Glasgow and Strathclyde; and in *Ship Science* by the University of Southampton. Courses leading to degrees in *Marine Engineering* of the University of Newcastle upon Tyne are also provided by Sunderland Polytechnic.

Production Engineering

Degrees are granted by the following Universities: Aston in Birmingham, Bath, Birmingham, Brunel, City (*Automation Engineering*), Loughborough, Nottingham, Strathclyde and Wales (Institute of Science and Technology). Courses leading to degrees granted by the Council for

National Academic Awards are provided by Lanchester Polytechnic, Leeds Polytechnic and Trent Polytechnic.

Structural Engineering

Degrees are granted by the Universities of Bath, Cambridge, Sheffield and Wales (University College, Cardiff (*Civil and Structural Engineering*; Swansea). Courses leading to degrees granted by the Council for National Academic Awards are provided by the Polytechnic of the South Bank.

Qualifying Engineering Institutions

ROYAL AERONAUTICAL SOCIETY, 4 Hamilton Place, W.1.

INSTITUTION OF CHEMICAL ENGINEERS, 16 Belgrave Square, S.W.1.

INSTITUTION OF CIVIL ENGINEERS, Great George Street, S.W.1.

INSTITUTION OF ELECTRICAL ENGINEERS, Savoy Place, Victoria Embankment, W.C.2.

INSTITUTION OF ELECTRONIC AND RADIO ENGINEERS, 9 Bedford Square, W.C.1.

INSTITUTION OF GAS ENGINEERS, 17 Grosvenor Crescent, S.W.1.

INSTITUTE OF MARINE ENGINEERS, 76 Mark Lane, E.C.3.

INSTITUTION OF MECHANICAL ENGINEERS, 1 Birdcage Walk, S.W.1.

INSTITUTION OF MINING ENGINEERS, 3 Grosvenor Crescent, S.W.1.

INSTITUTION OF MINING AND METALLURGY, 44 Portland Place, W.1.

INSTITUTION OF MUNICIPAL ENGINEERS, 25 Eccleston Square, S.W.1.

INSTITUTION OF PRODUCTION ENGINEERS, 10 Chesterfield Street, W.1.

INSTITUTION OF STRUCTURAL ENGINEERS, 11 Upper Belgrave Street, S.W.1.

ROYAL INSTITUTION OF NAVAL ARCHITECTS, 10 Upper Belgrave Street, S.W.1.

ESTATE MANAGEMENT AND SURVEYING

Degrees are granted by the Universities of Cambridge (*Land Economy*) and Reading (*Estate Management*). Courses for the Reading degree are provided by the College of Estate Management and Bristol Polytechnic.

Degrees in *Surveying* and another subject are granted by the University of Newcastle upon Tyne and in *Quantity Surveying* by the University of Reading. The Council for National Academic Awards grants degrees in *Land Surveying Sciences* with courses at North-East London Polytechnic; in *Quantity Surveying* with courses at Leeds Polytechnic, Polytechnic of the South Bank, Thames Polytechnic and Trent Polytechnic; in *Estate Management* with courses at the Polytechnic of the South Bank and Thames Polytechnic; in *Urban Estate Surveying* with courses at Trent Polytechnic; and in *Urban Land Economics* with courses at Sheffield Polytechnic.

Qualifying professional bodies include:

THE INCORPORATED SOCIETY OF VALUERS AND AUCTIONEERS, 3 Cadogan Gate, S.W.1.

RATING AND VALUATION ASSOCIATION, 29 Belgrave Square, S.W.1.

THE INCORPORATED ASSOCIATION OF ARCHITECTS AND SURVEYORS, 29 Belgrave Square, S.W.1.

THE ROYAL INSTITUTE OF BRITISH ARCHITECTS, 66 Portland Place, W.1.

THE ROYAL INSTITUTION OF CHARTERED SURVEYORS, 12 Great George Street, S.W.1.

THE INSTITUTE OF QUANTITY SURVEYORS, 98 Gloucester Place, W.1.

THE FACULTY OF ARCHITECTS AND SURVEYORS, 68 Gloucester Place, W.1.

FOOD AND NUTRITION SCIENCE
(*See also* Dietetics, Domestic Science, and Hotelkeeping)

Degrees in *Food Science* are granted by the Universities of Belfast, Leeds, London (Queen Elizabeth College: *Food Science and Management Science*), Nottingham, Reading (also *Food Technology*), and Strathclyde; and in *Nutrition* by the Universities of London (Queen Elizabeth College), Nottingham and Surrey.

Courses leading to degrees in *Food Science* granted by the Council for National Academic Awards are provided by the Polytechnic of the South Bank.

Scientific and professional bodies include:
NUTRITION SOCIETY, Chandos House, 2 Queen Anne Street, W.1.
SOCIETY OF CHEMICAL INDUSTRY, 14 Belgrave Square, S.W.1.
INSTITUTE OF FOOD SCIENCE AND TECHNOLOGY OF THE U.K., 41 Queen's Gate, S.W.7.

FORESTRY
Degrees in Forestry are granted by the Universities of Aberdeen, Edinburgh, Oxford and Wales (University College, Bangor).

Professional Organizations
THE COMMONWEALTH FORESTRY ASSOCIATION, Royal Commonwealth Society, Northumberland Avenue, W.C.2.
THE ROYAL FORESTRY SOCIETY OF ENGLAND, WALES AND NORTHERN IRELAND, 102 High Street, Tring, Herts.
THE ROYAL SCOTTISH FORESTRY SOCIETY, 26 Rutland Square, Edinburgh.
THE SOCIETY OF FORESTERS OF GREAT BRITAIN, 18 Northumberland Avenue, W.C.2.

FUEL TECHNOLOGY
Degrees in *Fuel and Combustion Science* and in *Fuel and Combustion Engineering* are granted by the University of Leeds; and in *Oil Technology* by London (Imperial College of Science and Technology).

Courses leading to certificates and qualification by professional bodies are available at many Technical Colleges.

The principal professional bodies are:—
THE INSTITUTION OF GAS ENGINEERS, 17 Grosvenor Crescent, S.W.1.
THE INSTITUTE OF FUEL, 18 Devonshire Street, Portland Place, W.1.
THE INSTITUTE OF PETROLEUM, 26 Portland Place, W.1.

GEOLOGY
Degrees in *Geology* or *Applied Geology* are granted by the Universities of Aberdeen, Belfast, Birmingham, Bristol, Cambridge, Dundee, Durham, Edinburgh, Exeter, Glasgow, Hull, Keele, Leeds, Leicester, Liverpool, London (Bedford College, Birkbeck College, Chelsea College of Science and Technology, Imperial College of Science and Technology, King's College, Queen Mary College, University College), Manchester, Newcastle upon Tyne, Nottingham, Oxford, Reading, St. Andrews, Sheffield, Southampton, Strathclyde, Wales (University Colleges at Aberystwyth, Cardiff and Swansea). Courses leading to external degrees in *Geology* of the University of London are provided by the City of London Polytechnic, Derby and District College of Technology, and Plymouth Polytechnic.

Courses leading to degrees in *Engineering Geology* granted by the Council for National Academic Awards are provided by Portsmouth Polytechnic.

HOTELKEEPING
Degrees are granted by the Universities of Strathclyde (*Hotel and Catering Management*) and Surrey (*Hotel and Catering Administration*).

Three-year courses leading to a Higher National Diploma in Hotelkeeping and Catering are available at the following centres:—Barnet (Hendon Coll. of Technology); Birmingham Coll. of Food and Domestic Arts; Blackpool College of Technology and Art; Bournemouth College of Technology; Brighton Polytechnic; S. Devon Technical College; Ealing Technical College; N. Gloucestershire Technical College; Huddersfield Polytechnic; Westminster Technical College; Manchester (Hollings College); Oxford Polytechnic; and in Wales at Llandrillo Technical College.

Two-year full-time courses leading to an Ordinary National Diploma are available at all the above centres and at 32 other colleges in England and Wales.

Details of the diploma conditions are obtainable from H.M. Stationery Office. (*See also* DOMESTIC SCIENCE AND CATERING).

INSTITUTIONAL MANAGEMENT
Three-year sandwich courses leading to a Higher National Diploma in Institutional Management are available at the following centres in England and Wales:
CARDIFF.—Llandaff College of Education and Home Economics.
GLOUCESTER.—Gloucestershire College of Education.
LEEDS.—Leeds Polytechnic.
LONDON.—Northern Polytechnic.
MANCHESTER.—Elizabeth Gaskell College of Education.
NEWCASTLE UPON TYNE.—Newcastle College of Further Education.
OXFORD.—Oxford Polytechnic.
SHEFFIELD.—Sheffield Polytechnic.
SHREWSBURY.—Radbrook College.

Two-year full-time courses leading to an Ordinary National Diploma are available at the Birmingham, Leeds, Manchester and Newcastle centres mentioned above and at 23 other centres in England and Wales.

Qualifying professional bodies in the two subjects above are:
INSTITUTIONAL MANAGEMENT ASSOCIATION, Swinton House, 324 Gray's Inn Road, W.C.1 (awards certificates in Institutional Management).
HOTEL AND CATERING INSTITUTE, 191 Trinity Road, Tooting, S.W.17.
THE BRITISH HOTELS AND RESTAURANTS ASSOCIATION, 20 Upper Brook Street, W.1.
CATERERS' ASSOCIATION OF GREAT BRITAIN (1917), Victoria House, Vernon Place, Southampton Row, W.C.1.
NATIONAL CATERERS' FEDERATION, 156 Camden High Street, N.W.1.
INDUSTRIAL CATERING ASSOCIATION, 53–54 King William Street, E.C.4.

INSURANCE
Organizations conducting examinations and awarding diplomas:—
THE CHARTERED INSURANCE INSTITUTE, 20 Aldermanbury, E.C.2.
THE ASSOCIATION OF AVERAGE ADJUSTERS, 12 Great James Street, W.C.1.
THE CHARTERED INSTITUTE OF LOSS ADJUSTERS, 2–3 Broad Street Place, E.C.2.

JOURNALISM

Courses for working journalists are available at 8 centres. One-year full-time courses are also available for selected students leaving school. Particulars of all these courses are available from the Secretary of the National Council for Training of Journalists, Harp House, 179 High Street, Epping, Essex.

Short courses for experienced newspapermen and periodical and public relations journalists are also arranged by the National Council.

LANGUAGES

Degrees in a very wide range of languages (including Oriental and African languages) are granted by universities. Degrees in *Linguistics* are awarded by the University of Reading, in *Language* by the University of York, and in *Languages (Interpreting and Translating)* by Heriot-Watt University. These subjects also form part of degree courses at many other universities.

Courses leading to external degrees of the University of London in *French* and in *German* are provided by the Polytechnic of North London and Manchester Polytechnic. Courses leading to degrees in *Languages* granted by the Council for National Academic Awards are provided by Cambridgeshire College of Arts and Technology, Polytechnic of Central London, Ealing Technical College, Lanchester Polytechnic, Leeds Polytechnic, Liverpool Polytechnic and the Polytechnic of the South Bank; and in *French Studies, Latin American Studies, Russian and Soviet Studies* and *Spanish* by Portsmouth Polytechnic.

LAW

Degrees in Law are granted by the Universities of Aberdeen, Belfast, Birmingham, Bristol, Cambridge, Dundee, Durham, Edinburgh, Exeter, Glasgow, Hull, Keele, Kent at Canterbury, Leeds, Leicester, Liverpool, London (King's College; London School of Economics and Political Science; Queen Mary College; University College), Manchester, Newcastle upon Tyne, Nottingham, Oxford, Sheffield, Southampton, Strathclyde, Sussex, Wales (University Colleges at Aberystwyth and Cardiff, Institute of Science and Technology) and Warwick.

Courses leading to external degrees in Law of the University of London are provided by Birmingham Polytechnic, Polytechnic of Central London, City of Leicester Polytechnic, Leeds Polytechnic, Liverpool Polytechnic, Mid-Essex Technical College, North London, and Trent Polytechnic. Courses leading to degrees in Law granted by the Council for National Academic Awards are provided by Bristol Polytechnic, City of London Polytechnic, Ealing Technical College, Kingston Polytechnic, Lanchester Polytechnic, Manchester Polytechnic, Newcastle upon Tyne Polytechnic and Trent Polytechnic.

Qualifications for Barrister are obtainable only at one of the Inns of Court or Faculty of Advocates; for Solicitor, from the Law Society or its equivalent in Scotland or Ireland.

THE INNS OF COURT
THE SENATE OF THE FOUR INNS OF COURT
5 Essex Court, Temple, E.C.4

Established in 1966 to represent the common view of the Inns, and to exercise jurisdiction in matters of legal education, discipline, professional planning and public relations.

President, Rt. Hon. Lord Justice Buckley, M.B.E.
Vice-President, J. L. Arnold, Q.C.
Hon. Treasurer, M. Morris, Q.C.
Secretary, Miss N. Gow.

THE INNER TEMPLE, E.C.4
Treasurer (1971), Hon. Sir Cecil Havers.
Sub-Treasurer, Cdr. R. S. Flynn, R.N.
Asst. Sub-Treasurer, Miss J. Morris.

THE MIDDLE TEMPLE, E.C.4
Treasurer (1971), Sir Robert Micklethwait, Q.C.
Under-Treasurer, J. B. Morison.
Asst. Under-Treasurer, H. W. Challoner.

LINCOLN'S INN, W.C.2
Treasurer (1971), C. Montgomery White, Q.C.
Master of the Library, Rt. Hon. Sir Charles Russell.
Under-Treasurer and Steward, Col. E. R. Bridges, O.B.E.
Deputy do., F. C. Coales.

GRAY'S INN, W.C.1
Treasurer (till Dec. 31, 1971), Sir Humphrey Waldock, C.M.G., O.B.E., Q.C.
Master of Library, Rt. Hon. Sir Frederic Sellers, M.C.
Under-Treasurer, Oswald Terry.
Deputy do., C. R. G. Hughes.

COUNCIL OF LEGAL EDUCATION
(4 Gray's Inn Place, W.C.1.)

Established by the four Inns of Court to superintend the Education and Examination of Students for the English Bar.

Chairman, Sir George Coldstream, K.C.B., K.C.V.O., Q.C.
Vice-Chairman, Rt. Hon. Sir David Renton, K.B.E., T.D., Q.C., M.P.
Chairman, Board of Studies, R. L. A. Goff, Q.C.
Chairman of the Finance Committee, Sir George Coldstream, K.C.B., K.C.V.O., Q.C.
Inns of Court School of Law, Dean of Faculty, C. A. Morrison.
Sub-Dean, V. W. Taylor.

FACULTY OF ADVOCATES
(Advocates' Library, Edinburgh)

Application for admission as an Advocate of the Scottish Bar is made by Petition to the Court of Session. The candidate is remitted for examination to the Faculty of Advocates. Enquiries should be addressed to The Clerk of Faculty.

Dean of Faculty, R. S. Johnston, Q.C.
Vice-Dean, D. M. Ross, Q.C.
Treasurer, D. A. O. Edward.
Clerk of Faculty, J. M. Pinkerton.
Keeper of the Library, A. J. Mackenzie Stuart, Q.C.
Agent, P. J. Oliphant.

NORTHERN IRELAND

Admission to the Bar of Northern Ireland is controlled by the Honourable Society of the Inn of Court of Northern Ireland (established Jan. 11, 1926), Royal Courts of Justice (Ulster), Belfast.

Treasurer, Rt. Hon. Lord MacDermott.
Under-Treasurer and Librarian, J. A. L. McLean.

THE LAW SOCIETY
(113 Chancery Lane, W.C.2)

The Society controls the education and examination of articled clerks, and the admission of solicitors in England and Wales. Number of members, 21,842.

President of the Society (1971–72), W. O. Carter.
Vice-President (1971–72), Sir Desmond Heap.
Secretary-General, H. Horsfall Turner.
Secretaries, J. F. Warren (*Legal Education*); A. F. S. Pollock (*Contentious Business*); P. A. Leach (*Professional Purposes*); J. R. Bonham (*Non-Contentious Business*); P. G. W. Sims (*Law Reform*); S. J. Saunders (*Finance*).

THE COLLEGE OF LAW (incorporating The Law Society's School of Law), Braboeuf Manor, St. Catherine's, Guildford, Surrey (and at 33–35 Lancaster Gate, W.2 and 27 Chancery Lane), provides courses for The Law Society, Bar and London ll.b. examinations.

LAW SOCIETY OF SCOTLAND
Law Society's Hall, 26–27 Drumsheugh Gardens, Edinburgh

The Society comprises all practising solicitors in Scotland. It controls the examination of legal apprentices and the admission of solicitors in Scotland and acts as registrar of solicitors under the Solicitors (Scotland) Acts, 1933 to 1965.

The Law Society of Scotland administers the Legal Aid and Advice Scheme set up under the Legal Aid (Scotland) Act, 1967.

Secretary, R. B. Laurie, O.B.E., W.S.

LIBRARIANSHIP AND ARCHIVE ADMINISTRATION

Degrees are granted by Loughborough University of Technology (*Library Studies*), and the University of Wales (Aberystwyth) (*Librarianship*) (jointly with the College of Librarianship, Wales), and by the University of Strathclyde (*Librarianship*). Courses leading to degrees in *Librarianship* granted by the Council for National Academic Awards are provided by Birmingham Polytechnic, Leeds Polytechnic, Manchester Polytechnic, The Polytechnic of North London, N.W.5, and Newcastle upon Tyne Polytechnic; and in *Information Science* are provided by Leeds Polytechnic.

Post-graduate courses are available at the Universities of London (*Dir.*, Prof. A. Brown), Sheffield (*Dir.*, Prof. W. L. Saunders), Strathclyde (*Dir.*, Prof. W. Tyler), and at Queen's University, Belfast (*Dir.*, P. Havard-Williams) where a non-graduate diploma course is also available.

The Library Association, 7 Ridgmount Street, W.C.1, maintains the professional register of Chartered Librarians (Fellows and Associates), for which examinations are held twice yearly.

Schools of Librarianship conducting full-time courses of instruction in preparation for the examinations of the Library Association: Robert Gordon's Institute of Technology, Aberdeen; College of Librarianship, Wales, Llanbadarn, Aberystwyth; Birmingham Polytechnic, Birmingham 4; Brighton Polytechnic, Brighton 7; Ealing Technical College, W.5; Leeds Polytechnic; Polytechnic of North London, N.W.5; Loughborough Technical College, Leics.; Manchester Polytechnic; The Polytechnic, Education Precinct, St. Mary's Place, Newcastle upon Tyne.

Archive Administration

The University of London offers a Postgraduate Diploma in Archive Administration, intended primarily for candidates hoping to obtain appointments in local record offices and similar institutions. The full-time course lasts one year, and a first or second class honours degree in an arts subject is required. Information may be obtained from the Director, School of Librarianship, Archives and Information Studies, University College London, Gower Street, W.C.1. The University of Liverpool (Department of History) offers a rather similar Diploma in the Study of Records and the Administration of Archives, and the University College of Wales, Aberystwyth, offers a post graduate Diploma in Palæography and Archive Administration. The I.L.E.A. provides a course of palæography and one also in archive repair work each year.

MATHEMATICS
Degrees in *Mathematics* and/or *Applied Mathematics* are granted by all universities. Courses leading to external degrees in *Mathematics* of the University of London are provided by City of London Polytechnic, Derby and District College of Technology, North-East London Polytechnic, Plymouth Polytechnic, Polytechnic of Central London, Polytechnic of North London, and Portsmouth Polytechnic.

Courses leading to degrees in *Mathematics* granted by the Council for National Academic Awards are provided by Brighton Polytechnic, Enfield College of Technology (*Mathematics for Business*), Glamorgan Polytechnic (*Mathematics; Mathematics and Computer Science*); Hatfield Polytechnic, Kingston Polytechnic, Lanchester Polytechnic, City of Leicester Polytechnic, Newcastle upon Tyne Polytechnic, North-East London Polytechnic, Polytechnic of North London (*Mathematics and Computing*), Portsmouth Polytechnic, Teesside Polytechnic, Thames Polytechnic, and Wolverhampton Polytechnic.

MEDICINE
Degrees in *Medicine and Surgery* are granted by the Universities of Aberdeen, Belfast, Birmingham, Bristol, Cambridge, Dundee, Edinburgh, Glasgow, Leeds, Leicester (from 1975), Liverpool, London (*see Teaching Hospitals, below*), Manchester, Newcastle upon Tyne, Nottingham, Oxford, Sheffield, Southampton, Wales (University College, Cardiff, and Welsh National School of Medicine).

TEACHING HOSPITALS IN LONDON
Under the National Health Service (Designation of Teaching Hospitals) Order, 1957, and subsequent amendments, the following were designated Teaching Hospitals for the *University of London*.

CHARING CROSS HOSPITAL, Agar Street, Strand W.C.2.—Number of beds, 255; In-patients, 1970, 6,573; New out-patients, 1970, 9,985, 47 house appointments open annually in Group. *House Governor and Secretary,* Frank Hart. *Medical School,* Adelphi, John Adam Street, W.C.2. *Dean,* S. J. R. Reynolds, M.A., M.B., B.Ch. *Secretary,* B. S. Drewe, E.R.D., T.D., LL.B., M.A. Charing Cross Hospital Group: Fulham (409 beds); Kingsbury Maternity (56 beds); West London (217 beds).

GUY'S HOSPITAL, St. Thomas Street, S.E.1.— number of beds, 1,562 (in Group); In-patients 1970, 27,542; New out-patients, 1970, 57,233; Accident and Emergency Dept. attendances 1970, 103,018. *Chairman of Board of Governors,* The Lord Robens of Woldingham, P.C.; *Clerk to the Governors,* A. H. Burfoot; *Superintendent,* P. J. Helliwell. *Medical School, Dean,* J. C. Houston, M.D., F.R.C.P.; *Sub-Dean,* Prof. J. R. Trounce, M.D., F.R.C.P. *Dean of Dental Studies,* Prof. R. D. Emslie, B.D.S., F.D.S. *Secretary,* D. G. Bompas, C.M.G. Guy's Hospital Group, New Cross Hospital, Avonley Road, S.E.14; St. Olave's Hospital, Lower Road, Rotherhithe, S.E.16; Evelina Hospital for Sick Children, Southwark Bridge Road, S.E.1; Dunoran Home, Park Farm Road, Bickley, Kent; Public Health Centre, Grange Road, S.E.1; Southwark Chest Clinic, Walworth Road, S.E.17.

KING'S COLLEGE HOSPITAL, Denmark Hill. S.E.5.— Number of beds, 658; In-patients, 1970, 20,240; Casualty attendances, 1970, 90,946. *Chairman, Board of Governors,* The Marquess of Normanby, M.B.E. *House Governor and Secretary,* J. D. Banks, M.A. *Medical School. Dean,* D. I. Williams, M.B., B.S., F.R.C.P. *Sub-Dean, Director of Dental Studies,* Prof. R. Cocker, F.D.S.R.C.S. *Secretary,*

R*

W. F. Gunn, LL.B. King's College Hospital Group. Dulwich Hospital, East Dulwich Grove (356 beds); St. Giles Hospital, St. Giles Road, S.E.5 (300 beds); St. Francis Hospital, Constance Road, S.E.22 (416 beds); Belgrave Hospital for Children, Clapham Road (53 beds). *Annexe*, Camberley (40 beds). The Group complement of 1,823 beds includes 50 for private patients.

THE LONDON HOSPITAL, Whitechapel, E.1.—Number of beds, 1,400; In-patients, 1970, 29,326; New out-patients, 1970, 62,112; Accident and emergency attendances, 1970, 73,175. *House Governor*, Hon. J. L. Scarlett; *Deputy House Governor*, M. J. Fairey. Medical College and Dental School, Turner Street, E.1. *Dean*, J. R. Ellis, M.B.E., M.D., F.R.C.P. *Dean of Dental Studies*, Prof. R. Duckworth, M.D., B.D.S., F.D.S. *Secretary*, H. P. Laird. The London Hospital Group: Queen Mary's Maternity Home, Hampstead, N.W.3; Mile End Hospital, E.1; St. Clement's Hospital, E.3. *Annexes* at Banstead, Hayes and Reigate.

THE MIDDLESEX HOSPITAL, Mortimer Street, W.1.—Number of beds in Group, 1,073; In-patients, 1970, 22,483; New out-patients, 1970, 43,475; Total out-patients, 1970, 205,889. *Chairman, Board of Governors*, The Lord Cobbold, K.G., P.C., G.C.V.O. *Secretary-Superintendent*, G. K. Buckley. Medical School. *Dean*, Prof. E. W. Walls, M.D., F.R.S.(Ed.). *Secretary*, G. Clark. Middlesex Hospital Group; St. Luke's-Woodside Hospital, N.10; Hospital for Women, Soho Square, W.1; Recovery Geriatric Unit, Highgate, N.6; Convalescent Home, Clacton-on-Sea.

ROYAL DENTAL HOSPITAL OF LONDON, Leicester Square, W.C.2.—New out-patients, 1970, 23,560; total attendances, 138,057. House appointments open twice yearly, 16. *Hospital Secretary*, Miss L. J. M. Brace. School of Dental Surgery: Scholarships and Prizes open, 1; value £100. *Dean*, Prof. R. B. Lucas, M.D., M.R.C.P. *Secretary*, K. R. McK. Biggs, B.A.

ROYAL FREE HOSPITAL, Gray's Inn Road, W.C.1.—Number of beds, 1,063 (in Group); In-patients, 1970, 21,516; New out-patients, 1970, 35,647; Casualty attendances, 1970, 70,118. *Chairman, Board of Governors* Dame Anne Bryans, D.B.E. *Secretary to the Board of Governors*, W. E. Bardgett. School of Medicine, Hunter Street, W.C.1. *Dean*, Miss F. Gardner, M.D., F.R.C.P. *Secretary*, C. C. Moore. Royal Free Hospital Group: Lawn Road, New End, and Hampstead General Hospitals, N.W.3; Liverpool Road, N.1 and Coppetts Wood Hospital, N.10.

ST. BARTHOLOMEW'S HOSPITAL, Smithfield, E.C.1. Number of beds, 817; In-patients, 1970, 18,159; New out-patients, 1970 (including Accident and Emergency), 70,982; 43 resident appointments open annually. *Chairman, Board of Governors*, R. E. Brook, C.M.G., O.B.E. *Clerk*, J. W. Gooddy. Medical College. *Dean*, J. S. Malpas; *Secretary*, C. E. Morris.

ST. GEORGE'S HOSPITAL, Hyde Park Corner, S.W.1. —Number of beds, 903 (in group); In-patients 1970, 24,598. Clinic attendances, 1970, 379,029, Casualty Dept., 1970, 81,238. 55 resident appointments open annually. *House Governor and Secretary*, R. Ellis. Medical School. *Dean*, R. D. Lowe, Ph.D., M.R.C.P. *Secretary*, R. W. Pembleton. St. George's Hospital Group. St. George's Hospital (293 beds); Atkinson Morley's Hospital, Wimbledon (160 beds); St. George's Hospital, S.W.17 (450 beds); Royal Dental Hospital (*q.v.*).

ST. MARY'S HOSPITAL, Praed Street, W.2.—Number of beds, 1,327 (in Group); In-patients, 1970, 31,323; New out-patients,1970, 73,138. *House Governor and Secretary to the Board of Governors*, A. Powditch, M.C. Medical School, Norfolk Place, W.2. Scholarships and Prizes: Entrance, 1 of £100 and 2 of £40 p.a. for 5 years; University, for Clinical students, 1 of £100, 1 of £50 p.a. and 1 of £40 a year for 3 years. *Dean*, Prof. R. E. O. Williams, M.D., F.R.C.P. *Secretary* J. E. Stevenson, LL.B. St. Mary's Hospital Group: Paddington Green Children's Hospital, W.2; Princess Louise Hospital, Kensington, St. Quintin Avenue, W.10; Samaritan Hospital for Women, N.W.1; St. Luke's Hospital, Bayswater, W.2; St. Mary's Hospital, Harrow Road, W.9; Western Ophthalmic Hospital, N.W.1; Chepstow Lodge Pre-Convalescent Annexe, Chepstow Place, W.2; Joyce Grove Convalescent Home, Nettlebed, Oxon.

ST. THOMAS' HOSPITAL, S.E.1.—Number of beds, 1,479 (in Group); In-patients, 1970, 31,781; New out-patients 1970, 103,767. The Hospital, which was founded in Southwark, was rebuilt on its present site in 1868-71. The main hospital buildings were extensively damaged during the war of 1939-45 and a comprehensive reconstruction scheme is in progress. *Treasurer and Chairman, Board of Governors*, J. F. Prideaux, O.B.E.; *Clerk of the Governors*, B. A. McSwiney. Medical School. Albert Embankment, S.E.1. *Dean*, Prof. P. Rhodes, F.R.C.S., F.R.C.O.G. *Secretary*, V. H. Warren, St. Thomas' Hospital Group; Lambeth Hospital, S.E.11; Grosvenor Hospital, S.W.1; Royal Waterloo Hospital, S.E.1; South Western Hospital, S.W.9.

UNIVERSITY COLLEGE HOSPITAL, Gower Street, W.C.1.—Number of beds, 1,146; In-patients. 1970, 23,779; New out-patients, 1970, 107,665. *Chairman, Board of Governors*, Sir Desmond Bonham-Carter, T.D. *Administrator and Secretary*, O. R. Cross. Medical School. University Street, W.C.1. *Dean*, B. J. Harries, F.R.C.S.; *Secretary*, D. H. Lloyd Morgan. University College Hospital Group: St. Pancras Hospital, N.W.1; Hospital for Tropical Diseases, N.W.1.; Thomas Barlow Home, Highgate, N.6; National Temperance Hospital, Hampstead Road, N.W.1.

WESTMINSTER HOSPITAL, Dean Ryle Street, Horseferry Road, S.W.1. Number of beds, 429; In-patients, 1970, 12,155; New out-patients, 1970, 39,433. *House Governor and Secretary*, R. P. MacMahon, M.A. Medical School. *Dean*, Dr. J. B. Wyman, M.B.E. *Secretary*, Capt. A. D. Robin, D.S.C., R.N. (*ret.*). Westminster Hospital Group: Queen Mary's Hospital, Roehampton (439 beds); Westminster Children's Hospital (106 beds), Vincent Square, S.W.1; The Gordon Hospital (111 beds), Vauxhall Bridge Road, S.W.1; All Saints Hospital (52 beds), Austral Street, S.E.11.

Postgraduate Teaching Hospitals

HAMMERSMITH HOSPITAL, W.12; St. Mark's Hospital for Diseases of the Rectum and Colon, E.C.1. HOSPITAL FOR SICK CHILDREN, W.C.1; Queen Elizabeth Hospital for Children, E.2. (Country Branches, Banstead and Tadworth, Surrey). NATIONAL HOSPITAL, Queen Square, W.C.1; Maida Vale Hospital for Nervous Diseases, W.9. ROYAL NATIONAL THROAT, NOSE AND EAR HOSPITAL, Gray's Inn Road, W.C.1 and Golden Sq., W.1. MOORFIELDS EYE HOSPITAL, City Road, E.C.1 and High Holborn, W.C.1. BETHLEM ROYAL HOSPITAL AND MAUDSLEY HOSPITAL, Beckenham, Kent and Denmark Hill, S.E.5. ST. JOHN'S HOSPITAL FOR DISEASES OF THE SKIN, Lisle Street, W.C.2 and

Homerton, E.9. BROMPTON HOSPITAL, S.W.3; Brompton Hospital, Frimley, Surrey; London Chest Hospital, E.2. ROYAL NATIONAL ORTHOPÆDIC HOSPITAL, Gt. Portland Street, W.1. and Stanmore. NATIONAL HEART HOSPITAL, W.1. ST. PETER'S HOSPITAL, W.C.2. ROYAL MARSDEN HOSPITAL, S.W.3. Royal Marsden Hospital, Sutton, Surrey. QUEEN CHARLOTTE'S MATERNITY HOSPITAL, W.6; Chelsea Hospital for Women, S.W.3. EASTMAN DENTAL HOSPITAL, W.C.1.

POSTGRADUATE MEDICAL SCHOOLS OF THE UNIVERSITY OF LONDON

London School of Hygiene and Tropical Medicine, Keppel Street, W.C.1.   C. E. Gordon Smith, C.B., *Dean.*

British Postgraduate Medical Federation (University of London), 33 Millman Street, W.C.1. G. A. Smart, B.SC., M.D., F.R.C.P., *Director.*
Comprises:—
ROYAL POSTGRADUATE MEDICAL SCHOOL, Du Cane Road, Shepherd's Bush, W.12.   S. Taylor, M.A., D.M., M.Ch., F.R.C.S., *Dean.*
INSTITUTE OF BASIC MEDICAL SCIENCES, Royal College of Surgeons, Lincoln's Inn Fields, W.C.2. H. Hanley, M.D., F.R.C.S., *Dean.*
INSTITUTE OF CANCER RESEARCH, Royal Cancer Hospital, 34 Sumner Place, S.W.7. H. E. M. Kay, M.D., F.R.C.P., F.R.C.Path., *Director.*
INSTITUTE OF CARDIOLOGY, 35 Wimpole Street, W.1.   R. S. O. Rees, M.A., M.B., B.Chir., *Dean.*
INSTITUTE OF CHILD HEALTH, 30 Guilford Street, W.C.1.   G. H. Newns, M.D., F.R.C.P., *Dean.*
INSTITUTE OF DENTAL SURGERY, Eastman Dental Hospital, Gray's Inn Road, W.C.1.   Prof. I. R. H. Kramer, M.D.S., F.D.S.R.C.S., F.R.C.Path., *Dean.*
INSTITUTE OF DERMATOLOGY, St. John's Hospital for Diseases of the Skin, Lisle Street, W.C.2. R. H. Meara, M.A., M.B., B.Chir., F.R.C.P.
INSTITUTE OF DISEASES OF THE CHEST, Brompton Hospital, S.W.3.   J. Smart, M.A., M.D., F.R.C.P., *Dean.*
INSTITUTE OF LARYNGOLOGY AND OTOLOGY, Royal National Throat, Nose and Ear Hospital, 330–332 Gray's Inn Road, W.C.1.   R. F. McNab Jones, M.B., B.S., F.R.C.S., *Dean.*
INSTITUTE OF NEUROLOGY, National Hospital, Queen Square, W.C.1.   R. E. Kelly, M.D., F.R.C.P., *Dean.*
INSTITUTE OF OBSTETRICS AND GYNÆCOLOGY, Chelsea Hospital for Women, Dovehouse Street, S.W.3.   R. B. K. Rickford, M.D., F.R.C.S., F.R.C.O.G., *Dean.*
INSTITUTE OF OPHTHALMOLOGY, Judd Street, W.C.1. A. G. Cross, M.D., F.R.C.S., *Dean.*
INSTITUTE OF ORTHOPÆDICS, Royal National Orthopædic Hospital, 234 Great Portland Street, W.1.   P. D. Byers, M.D., *Dean.*
INSTITUTE OF PSYCHIATRY, De Crespigny Park, Denmark Hill, S.E.5.   J. L. T. Birley, D.M., F.R.C.P., *Dean.*
INSTITUTE OF UROLOGY, 10 Henrietta Street, W.C.2. D. Innes Williams, M.D., M.Chir., F.R.C.S., *Dean.*

ROYAL ARMY MEDICAL COLLEGE, Millbank, S.W.1. —*Commandant*, Maj.-Gen. J. P. Baird, Q.H.P., M.D., F.R.C.P.

LIVERPOOL SCHOOL OF TROPICAL MEDICINE, Pembroke Place, Liverpool 3.—*Dean*, Prof. B. G. Maegraith, C.M.G.

OTHER TEACHING HOSPITALS

Under the National Health Service Designation of Teaching Hospitals Order, 1959, the following have been designated teaching hospitals in the 10 university medical centres outside London:

University of Newcastle.—Includes, Royal Victoria Infirmary and Country Branch, Wylam; Princess Mary Maternity Hospital; Babies' Hospital; Dental Hospital; Newcastle General Hospital; Hunter's Moor Hospital; Ponteland Hospital; Walker Park Hospital; Rye Hill Hospital; and hospitals at Gosport, Lemington and Throckley.

University of Leeds.—United Leeds Hospitals: General Infirmary, Leeds: Hospital for Women, Leeds; Maternity Hospital, Leeds; Leeds Dental Hospital; The Ida and Robert Arthington Branch Hospital, Leeds 16; Leeds (St. James's), University Hospital; Chapel Allerton Hospital; Cookridge Hospital.

University of Sheffield.—United Sheffield Hospitals: Royal Infirmary, Sheffield; Royal Hospital, Sheffield and Annexe; Jessop Hospital for Women, Sheffield, including Firth Auxiliary Hospital, Sheffield; Children's Hospital, Sheffield and Annexes; Edgar Allen Physical Treatment Centre; Charles Clifford Dental Hospital; Hallamshire Hospital Out-patients Dept.

University of Cambridge.—United Cambridge Hospitals: Addenbrooke's Hospital, Cambridge; Maternity Hospital, Cambridge; Brookfields Hospital, Cambridge; Chesterton Hospital, Cambridge.

University of Oxford.—United Oxford Hospitals: Radcliffe Infirmary, Churchill Hospital; Cowley Road Hospital; Slade Hospital. *Chairman of Board of Governors*, E. W. Towler. **Medical School:** *Regius Professor of Medicine*, Sir Richard Doll, O.B.E., D.M., M.D., D.SC.   *Director of Clinical Studies*, M. S. Dunnill, M.A., M.D.   *Director of Post-Graduate Medical Education and Training* (vacant).   *Pre-Clinical Adviser*, R. V. Coxon, D.Phil., M.D.   *Secretary of the Medical School*, P. H. Brown, M.A.

University of Bristol.—United Bristol Hospitals: Bristol Royal Hospital (including Bristol Royal Infirmary and Bristol General Hospital); Bristol Maternity Hospital; Bristol Royal Hospital for Sick Children; Bristol Eye Hospital; Bristol Homœopathic Hospital; Bristol Dental Hospital; Southmead Hospital.

University of Wales.—The University Hospital of Wales Group (University Hospital of Wales; Cardiff Royal Infirmary, Llandough Hospital, the Maternity Hospital, the Royal Hamadryad Hospital; St. David's Hospital, Cardiff; Whitchurch Hospital; Lansdowne Hospital; Prince of Wales (Orthopædic) Hospital, Rhyd-Lafar; Cefn Mably and Glan Ely Hospitals and Sully (Chest Diseases) Hospital; Velindre Hospital).

University of Birmingham.—United Birmingham Hospitals: Queen Elizabeth Hospital; General Hospital; Children's Hospital; Midland Nerve Hospital, Birmingham; Birmingham Dental Hospital; Birmingham and Midland Hospitals for Women; Birmingham Maternity Hospital.

University of Manchester.—United Manchester Hospitals: Manchester Royal Infirmary and Annexes; St. Mary's Hospitals for Women and Children, Manchester; Manchester Royal Eye Hospital; Dental Hospital of Manchester; Manchester Foot Hospital; University Hospital of South Manchester.

University of Liverpool.—United Liverpool Hospitals: Liverpool Royal Infirmary; Royal Southern Hospital; Royal Northern Hospital; Women's Hospital, Liverpool; Liverpool Maternity Hospital; Royal Liverpool Children's Hospitals; Liverpool

Ear, Nose and Throat Infirmary; St. Paul's Eye Hospital, Liverpool; Liverpool Dental Hospital.

Licensing Corporations granting Diplomas

THE ROYAL COLLEGE OF PHYSICIANS OF LONDON AND THE ROYAL COLLEGE OF SURGEONS OF ENGLAND, Examining Board in England, Examination Hall, Queen Square, W.C.1.

THE SOCIETY OF APOTHECARIES, Black Friars Lane, E.C.4.

ROYAL COLLEGE OF OBSTETRICIANS AND GYNÆCOLOGISTS, Sussex Place, Regent's Park, N.W.1.

THE ROYAL COLLEGE OF PHYSICIANS AND THE ROYAL COLLEGE OF SURGEONS, Edinburgh.

THE ROYAL COLLEGE OF PHYSICIANS AND SURGEONS OF GLASGOW.

THE SCOTTISH CONJOINT BOARD, 18 Nicolson Street, Edinburgh 8, and 242 St. Vincent Street, Glasgow, C.2.

PROFESSIONS SUPPLEMENTARY TO MEDICINE

The standard of professional education in chiropody, dietetics, medical laboratory technology, occupational therapy, orthoptics, physiotherapy, radiography and remedial gymnastics is the responsibility of eight professional boards, which also publish an annual register of qualified practitioners. The work of the Boards is co-ordinated and supervised by The Council for Professions Supplementary to Medicine (York House, Westminster Bridge Road, S.E.1).

CHIROPODY

Professional qualifications are granted by the Society of Chiropodists, 8 Wimpole Street, W.1, to students who have passed the qualifying examinations after attending a course of full-time training for three years at one of the six recognized schools in England and Wales and two in Scotland. Qualifications granted by the Society are approved by the Chiropodists Board for the purpose of State Registration, which is a condition of employment within the National Health Service.

DIETETICS

(See main heading, p. 520)

MEDICAL LABORATORY TECHNOLOGY

Courses in technical institutions and training in medical laboratories are approved for progress to the professional examinations and qualifications of the Institute of Medical Laboratory Technology, 12 Queen Anne Street, W.1.

OCCUPATIONAL THERAPY

Professional qualifications are awarded after examination by the Association of Occupational Therapists, 251 Brompton Road, S.W.3 which recognizes 9 training schools in England and Wales. Training courses leading to the qualification awarded by the Scottish Association of Occupational Therapists are available in Edinburgh and Glasgow.

ORTHOPTICS

Orthoptists undertake the diagnosis and treatment of all types of squint and other anomalies of binocular vision, under the direction of an ophthalmic surgeon or a recognized ophthalmic medical practitioner. The training and qualification of Orthoptists are the responsibility of the British Orthoptic Council. Training consists of a two-years and three months' course at one of 11 approved Orthoptic Schools in England and Wales and 1 in Scotland.

The Professional Association is the British Orthoptic Society and the recognized qualifying body, The British Orthoptic Council, Tavistock House (North), Tavistock Square, W.C.1.

(See also under Optics.)

PHYSIOTHERAPY

Examinations leading to qualification are conducted by the Chartered Society of Physiotherapy, 14 Bedford Row, W.C.1. Full-time 3-yr. courses are available at 39 recognized schools in Great Britain.

RADIOGRAPHY AND RADIOTHERAPY

Examinations leading to qualification are conducted by The Society of Radiographers, 14 Upper Wimpole Street, W.1.

There are recognized training centres in radiography and radiotherapy at 49 cities and towns in England and Wales, 4 in Scotland and 2 in Northern Ireland.

In London courses are available at the London Teaching Hospitals listed on pp. 525-7; and at Hammersmith, Lambeth and Royal Northern Hospitals, at Oldchurch County Hospital, Romford, Essex and at Woolwich.

REMEDIAL GYMNASTICS

Examinations leading to qualification are conducted by the Society of Remedial Gymnasts, c/o Northampton Town F.C., County Ground, Abington, Northampton. The recognized training centre is the School of Remedial Gymnastics and Recreational Therapy, Pinderfields Hospital, Wakefield, Yorks.

METALLURGY

Degrees in *Metallurgy* and/or *Metallurgical Engineering* are granted by the following universities: Aston in Birmingham, Birmingham, Brunel, Cambridge, Leeds, Liverpool, London (Imperial College of Science and Technology), Loughborough, Manchester, *also* Manchester Institute of Science and Technology, Newcastle upon Tyne, Nottingham, Oxford, Salford, Sheffield, Strathclyde, Surrey, Wales (University Colleges at Cardiff and Swansea).

Courses leading to degrees in *Metallurgy/Metallurgy and Materials* granted by the Council for National Academic Awards are provided by the City of London Polytechnic, Lanchester Polytechnic and Sheffield Polytechnic.

THE INSTITUTION OF METALLURGISTS, 17 Belgrave Square, S.W.1, is a qualifying body.

MINING AND MINING ENGINEERING

Degrees in *Mining* or *Mining Engineering* are granted by the following universities: Birmingham (*Minerals Engineering*), Leeds, London (Imperial College of Science and Technology), Newcastle upon Tyne, Nottingham, Strathclyde, Wales (University College, Cardiff: *Mineral Exploitation*). Courses in Metalliferous Mining are available at the School of Metalliferous Mining, Camborne, Cornwall. Courses of study in preparation for certificates of competence in Mining and Mining Engineering awarded by the Board for Mining Examinations and the Institution of Mining Engineers are available at these universities together with most Technical Colleges in mining districts.

Miscellaneous Authorities

MINING QUALIFICATIONS BOARD, Ministry of Technology, Millbank Tower, Millbank, S.W.1.

THE INSTITUTION OF MINING ENGINEERS, 3 Grosvenor Crescent, S.W.1.

COUNCIL OF ENGINEERING INSTITUTIONS, 2 Little Smith Street, S.W.1.

MUSIC

Degrees in Music are granted by the Universities of Aberdeen, Belfast, Birmingham, Bristol, Cambridge, Durham, East Anglia, Edinburgh, Exeter, Glasgow, Hull, Leeds, Liverpool, London

(King's College, Royal Holloway College; *also* Goldsmiths' College, Royal Academy of Music, Royal College of Music, and Trinity College of Music), Manchester, Newcastle upon Tyne, Nottingham, Oxford, Reading, Sheffield, Southampton, Surrey, Sussex, Wales (University Colleges at Aberystwyth, Bangor and Cardiff), and York. Courses leading to degrees in Music granted by the Council for National Academic Awards are provided by Huddersfield Polytechnic and North-East Essex Technical College.

ASSOCIATED BOARD OF THE ROYAL SCHOOLS OF MUSIC, 14 Bedford Square, W.C.1.

Instituted in 1889 to conduct the local examinations in music of the Royal Academy of Music and the Royal College of Music, which were joined in 1947 by the Royal Manchester College of Music and the Royal Scottish Academy of Music, Glasgow.

Secretary, W. Cole, M.V.O., D.Mus., F.R.A.M., F.R.C.M., F.R.C.O.

ROYAL ACADEMY OF MUSIC (1822)
Marylebone Road, N.W.1

A complete training is offered to students of both sexes intending to take up music as a profession. Scholarships are offered for competition in March. The particulars are available in January. All students must take the full curriculum. No. of Students, 720. Examinations for Licentiates (L.R.A.M.) are held three times a year.

Principal, A. Lewis, C.B.E., M.A., MUS.B.
Administrator, G. J. C. Hambling, D.S.C.
Warden, D. Gaye, M.A.

ROYAL COLLEGE OF MUSIC (1883)
Prince Consort Road, South Kensington, S.W.7

A.R.C.M., G.R.C.M. and M.MUS.R.C.M. awarded by examination. No. of Students 700.

Director, Sir Keith Falkner, F.R.C.M.
Registrar, J. R. Stainer, B.A., MUS.B., F.R.C.M., F.R.C.O.
Bursar, Capt. J. Shrimpton, C.B.E., R.N.

GUILDHALL SCHOOL OF MUSIC AND DRAMA (1880)
John Carpenter Street, E.C.4

Full-time and part-time courses in Music, Speech and Drama. Awards Diplomas of Graduateship (G.G.S.M.), Associateship (A.G.S.M.) and Licentiateship (L.G.S.M.). The Diploma of Graduateship (G.G.S.M.) confers graduate addition to salary.

Principal, A. Percival, MUS.B.
Director of Drama, P. A. Bucknell.
Gen. Administrator, John Isard.

TRINITY COLLEGE OF MUSIC (1872)
Mandeville Place, W.1

Complete training in music for teachers and performers. Courses lead to the university degree of B.Mus., the Graduate Diploma in Music (approved for Graduate equivalent status), the Teacher's Diploma in Music and the Performer's Diploma in Music.

Principal, M. Foggin, F.R.A.M.
Dir. of Studies. C. Cork, B.Mus.
Secretary and Dir. of Examinations, E. Heberden, M.A.

LONDON COLLEGE OF MUSIC
Great Marlborough Street, W.1 (500)

Complete training in music and courses in speech. Awards diplomas of Graduateship (G.L.C.M.) and Licentiateship (L.L.C.M.). Courses recognized by the Dept. of Education and Science and Burnham Committee.

Director, W. S. L. Webber, D.Mus., F.R.C.M., F.R.C.O.
Secretary, K. R. Beard.

ROYAL COLLEGE OF ORGANISTS (1864)
Kensington Gore, S.W.7

For the promotion of the highest standard in organ playing and choir-training. Awards Diplomas of Associateship (A.R.C.O.) and Fellowship (F.R.C.O.); Diploma in choir-training (CHM).

Hon. Sec., Sir John Dykes Bower, C.V.O., M.A., D.Mus.

BIRMINGHAM POLYTECHNIC
BIRMINGHAM SCHOOL OF MUSIC
27 Dale End, Birmingham 4

Principal, G. Clinton, F.R.C.M., D.D.

TONIC SOL-FA COLLEGE OF MUSIC (1863)
Curwen College, 18 Holwood Road, Bromley, Kent

International teaching and examining body for dual notation. Awards Associateship (A.T.S.C.), Licentiateship (L.T.S.C.), Fellowship (F.T.S.C.) and Dip. Mus. Ed.

Principal, Rev. P. Faunch, D.D.

ROYAL SCHOOL OF CHURCH MUSIC
Addington Palace, Croydon, Surrey

Founded (1927) for the advancement of good music in the Church

Director, Gerald H. Knight, C.B.E., D.Mus.
Secretary, V. E. Waterhouse.

ROYAL MANCHESTER COLLEGE OF MUSIC
Devas Street, Oxford Road, Manchester, 15 (332).

Awards diplomas of Graduateship and Associateship.

NORTHERN SCHOOL OF MUSIC
99 Oxford Road, Manchester, 1 (900)

Principal, Miss I. Carroll, O.B.E., M.A.

ROYAL MILITARY SCHOOL OF MUSIC
Kneller Hall, Twickenham (42)

Commandant, Col. F. J. Jefferson.
Director of Music and Chief Instructor, Lt.-Col. R. B. Bashford, M.B.E.

ROYAL MARINES SCHOOL OF MUSIC
Deal, Kent (250)

Commandant, Col. F. H. Bristowe.
Principal Director of Music, Royal Marines, Maj. P. J. Neville, M.V.O., A.R.A.M., R.M.
(Eleven Bands in commission in 1971.)

ROYAL SCOTTISH ACADEMY OF MUSIC AND DRAMA
St. George's Place, Glasgow C.2 (900)

Curriculum provides for all branches of study necessary for entry into the professions of music and drama. Special Diploma Courses for those who wish to teach music and drama in schools.

Principal, K. Barritt, D.MUS., F.R.A.M., F.R.C.O.

NAUTICAL STUDIES

Degrees.—The University of Wales grants a degree in *Maritime Studies* (courses at Institute of Science and Technology) and the University of Southampton grants a degree in *Nautical Studies*. Courses leading to degrees in *Nautical Studies* granted by the Council for National Academic Awards are provided by Liverpool Polytechnic, Plymouth Polytechnic and Sunderland Polytechnic; and in *Maritime Studies* by City of London Polytechnic.

Merchant Navy Training Schools

For Officers

H.M.S. CONWAY (1859) Merchant Navy Cadet School, Llanfairpwll, Anglesey (210). *Headmaster*, B. E. Lord.

MERCHANT NAVY COLLEGE, Greenhithe, Kent.—*Principal*, Capt. K. E. Ballard.

UNIVERSITY OF SOUTHAMPTON (School of Navigation), Warsash, Southampton (1935). *Director*, Capt. H. Stewart, M.B.E.

For Seamen

INDEFATIGABLE AND NATIONAL SEA TRAINING SCHOOL, Plas Llanfair, Anglesey, N. Wales (140). *Capt. Supt.*, Capt. W. Wade. *Sec.* R. N. Hatfield, Room 22, Oriel Chambers, 14 Water Street, Liverpool 2.

NATIONAL SEA TRAINING SCHOOL, Denton, Gravesend, Kent. *Princ.*, Capt. P. H. Adlam; *Secretary*, G. R. Browne, M.B.E., 146–150 Minories, E.C.3.

NURSING

Courses leading to *degrees* or other qualifications in Nursing are provided by the Universities of Manchester and Wales (Welsh National School of Medicine); Edinburgh, Liverpool, the University of London a B.A. (*Nursing/Sociology*); and the University of Surrey a B.SC. in *Human Biology* with a nursing option.

Three-year courses for State Registration in general, sick children's, mental and mental deficiency nursing. Two-year course for State enrolment. Training schools in many parts of Great Britain.

Diplomas or certificates are granted by the following Universities: Aston in Birmingham (*Nursing Administration*); Edinburgh (*Nursing Studies*); London (*Nursing*); (for Sister Tutors), Queen Elizabeth College; Manchester (*Community Nursing*).

THE ROYAL COLLEGE OF NURSING
AND NATIONAL COUNCIL OF NURSES OF
THE UNITED KINGDOM
1A Henrietta Place, W.1

The Royal College of Nursing provides education at post-registration level in hospital, occupational health and community health fields. Full-time courses are held in preparation for senior posts in administration and teaching as well as training courses for health visitors, occupational health nurses, ward sisters, clinical teachers and teachers of pupil nurses.

Director of Education, Miss J. B. Rule.

CENTRAL MIDWIVES BOARD
39 Harrington Gardens, S.W.7

Chairman, H. G. E. Arthure, C.B.E., F.R.C.S., F.R.C.O.G.
Secretary, R. J. Fenney, M.B.E., B.A. (Admin.).

CENTRAL MIDWIVES BOARD
for Scotland
24 Dublin Street, Edinburgh 1

Chairman, G. D. Matthew, M.D., F.R.C.O.G., F.R.C.S.E.
Secretary, Miss D. S. Young, M.A.

OPTICS

Degrees in *Ophthalmic Optics* are granted by the following Universities: Aston in Birmingham, Bradford, City, Manchester (Manchester Institute of Science and Technology), and Wales (Institute of Science and Technology). Courses leading to degrees in *Ophthalmic Optics* granted by the Council for National Academic Awards are provided by the Glasgow College of Technology.

Examining bodies granting qualifications as an ophthalmic or dispensing optician:—

THE BRITISH OPTICAL ASSOCIATION, 65 Brook Street, W.1.

THE WORSHIPFUL COMPANY OF SPECTACLE MAKERS, Apothecaries Hall, Black Friars Lane, E.C.4.

THE ASSOCIATION OF DISPENSING OPTICIANS, 22 Nottingham Place, W.1 (training institution; qualification as dispensing optician).

THE SCOTTISH ASSOCIATION OF OPTICIANS, 116 West Regent Street, Glasgow C.2 (qualification as ophthalmic optician).

OSTEOPATHY

LONDON COLLEGE OF OSTEOPATHY, 24–25 Dorset Square, N.W.1.—*Sec.*, A. F. Lockwood.

PATENT AGENCY

The Register of Patent Agents is kept, under the authority of the Board of Trade, by the Chartered Institute of Patent Agents. Qualification is by examination; Intermediate and Final Examinations are held each year. Details can be obtained from the Institute.

CHARTERED INSTITUTE OF PATENT AGENTS, Staple Inn Buildings, W.C.1.—*Sec. and Registrar*, P. E. Lincroft, M.B.E.

PHARMACY

Degrees in Pharmacy are granted by the Universities of Aston in Birmingham, Bath, Belfast, Bradford, Heriot-Watt, London (Chelsea College and The School of Pharmacy), Manchester, Nottingham, Strathclyde, Wales (Institute of Science and Technology).

Courses leading to degrees in Pharmacy granted by the Council for National Academic Awards are provided by Brighton Polytechnic, City of Leicester Polytechnic, Liverpool Polytechnic, Portsmouth Polytechnic, Robert Gordon's Institute of Technology (Aberdeen), and Sunderland Polytechnic.

Further information may be obtained from The Registrar, The Pharmaceutical Society of Great Britain, 17 Bloomsbury Square, W.C.1.

PHOTOGRAPHY

Courses leading to *Degrees* in *Photographic Arts* and in *Photographic Technology* granted by the Council for National Academic Awards are provided by The Polytechnic of Central London.

INSTITUTE OF INCORPORATED PHOTOGRAPHERS (1901) (*formerly* BRITISH PHOTOGRAPHERS), Amwell End, Ware, Herts.—*Gen. Sec.*, E. I. N. Waughray.

Professional qualifying examinations in Commercial and Industrial, Scientific and Technical, Medical, Portrait, Illustrative, Advertising and Editorial Photography, for Associateships; general vocational examinations in photography leading to Licentiateships.

PHYSICAL EDUCATION

CENTRAL COUNCIL OF PHYSICAL RECREATION (26 Park Crescent, W.1).—*President*, H.R.H. the Prince Philip, Duke of Edinburgh, K.G., K.T.; *Secretary*, W. Winterbottom, O.B.E. Brings together about 300 national organizations in England, Wales and N. Ireland concerned with outdoor and indoor physical recreation; advises local authorities, youth organizations and industry, arranges training for coaches and leaders, administers National Sports Centres at Bisham Abbey, Berks.; Lilleshall Hall, Salop; Crystal Palace, London; also The National Mountaineering Centre, Plas y Brenin, N. Wales; The National Sailing Centre, Cowes, Isle of Wight; National Sports Centre for Wales, Cardiff; National Water Sports Centre, Holme Pierrepont, Notts.

Training Colleges
M.=For Men; *W.*=For Women

BEDFORD (College of Physical Education, Lansdowne Road, Bedford). *W.* (450).—*Principal,* Mrs. P. A. Bowen-West.

BIRMINGHAM UNIVERSITY. *M.* & *W.* (60).—*Director,* W. J. Slater.

CHESTER (Chester College), *see* p. 532.

DARTFORD Kent (Dartford College of Education), *see* p. 532.

DOVER (Nonington College of Physical Education, Dover). *M.* & *W.* (330).—*Principal,* Miss E. M. Hinks.

EASTBOURNE (Chelsea College of Physical Education, Denton Road). *W.* (550).—*Principal,* Miss A. J. Bambra.

EDINBURGH (Dunfermline College of Physical Education, Cramond). *W.* (430). *Principal,* Miss M. P. Abbott.

EXETER (St. Luke's College). *See* p. 532.

LIVERPOOL (I. M. Marsh College of Physical Education, Barkhill Road, Liverpool, 17). Lancashire Education Committee. *W.* (482).—*Principal,* Miss M. I. Jamieson.

LONDON (I.L.E.A. Coll. of Physical Education, 16 Paddington Street, W.1). Courses for serving teachers only. *M.* & *W.*—*Principal,* P. C. McIntosh.

LOUGHBOROUGH, Leics. (Loughborough T.C.). *See* p. 533.

SUTTON COLDFIELD, Warwickshire (Anstey College of Physical Education, Chester Road), Staffordshire Education Committee. *W.* (192).—*Principal,* Miss I. Webb.

WENTWORTH WOODHOUSE, Yorks. (Lady Mabel College of Education), *see* p. 534.

YORK (St. John's College). *M.* & *W.*—*see* p. 534.

PRINTING
Courses leading to *Degrees* in *Printing Technology* granted by the Council for National Academic Awards are provided by Watford College of Technology.

Courses in technical and general, design and administrative aspects of printing are available at technical colleges throughout the United Kingdom. Details can be obtained from the Institute of Printing and the British Federation of Master Printers (*see below*).

In addition to the examining and organizing bodies listed below, examinations are held by various independent regional examining boards in further education.

INSTITUTE OF PRINTING (1961), 10–11 Bedford Row, W.C.1.

JOINT COMMITTEE (AND SCOTTISH JOINT COMMITTEE) FOR NATIONAL CERTIFICATES IN PRINTING.

BRITISH FEDERATION OF MASTER PRINTERS, 11 Bedford Row, W.C.1.

CITY AND GUILDS OF LONDON INSTITUTE, 76 Portland Place, W.1.

PRINTING INK AND ROLLER MAKING TECHNICAL TRAINING BOARD, Burley House, Theobalds Road, W.C.1.

NATIONAL COUNCIL FOR DIPLOMAS IN ART AND DESIGN, 16 Park Crescent, W.1.

PSYCHIATRIC SOCIAL WORK
Courses suitable for those wishing to train as psychiatric social workers are provided (1 year except where otherwise indicated) by the Universities of Aberdeen (2 years); Belfast; Birmingham (1 year); Bradford (4 years); Bristol; Edinburgh; Exeter (2 years); Keele (4 years); Glasgow; Leeds; Liverpool (1 or 2 years); London (London School of Economics and Political Science); Manchester;

Newcastle upon Tyne; St. Andrews; Southampton; Sussex (2 years); Wales (University College, Cardiff); York (2 years); and by Hatfield and Lanchester Polytechnics (4 years).

SOCIAL WORK
Degrees in *Social Studies* or in *Social Sciences* are granted by most universities. Courses leading to degrees in *Social Science* or *Social Sciences* granted by the Council for National Academic Awards are provided by Enfield College of Technology, Hatfield Polytechnic, Kingston Polytechnic, Lanchester Polytechnic, Manchester Polytechnic and the Polytechnic of the South Bank.

The following are among the associations awarding professional qualifications and/or providing training:—

THE BRITISH ASSOCIATION OF SOCIAL WORKERS, The Oxford House, Derbyshire Street, E.2.

THE NATIONAL ASSOCIATION FOR MENTAL HEALTH, 39 Queen Anne Street, W.1.—*Gen. Sec.,* Miss Mary Applebey, O.B.E.

THE INSTITUTE OF HOUSING MANAGERS, Victoria House, Southampton Row, W.C.1.—*Sec.,* H. Key.

JOSEPHINE BUTLER MEMORIAL COLLEGE, 34 Alexandra Drive, Liverpool, 17.

SPEECH THERAPY
The University of Newcastle upon Tyne awards a B.SC. in Speech.

The Directory of qualified Speech Therapists is published by the College of Speech Therapists, 47 St. John's Wood High Street, N.W.8. Courses leading to the Diploma of Licentiateship of The College of Speech Therapists are available at:

THE CENTRAL SCHOOL OF SPEECH AND DRAMA (Department of Speech Therapy), Embassy Theatre, Swiss Cottage, N.W.3.

THE KINGDON-WARD SCHOOL OF SPEECH THERAPY, 26 Lower Sloane Street, S.W.1.

THE OLDREY-FLEMING SCHOOL OF SPEECH THERAPY, 84a Heath Street, Hampstead, N.W.3.

THE WEST END HOSPITAL SPEECH THERAPY TRAINING SCHOOL, 59 Portland Place, W.1.

THE BIRMINGHAM SCHOOL OF SPEECH THERAPY, Matthew Boulton Technical College, Sherlock Street, Birmingham 5.

ELIZABETH GASKELL COLLEGE, SCHOOL OF SPEECH THERAPY, Hathersage Road, Manchester 13.

LEEDS COLLEGE OF TECHNOLOGY, School of Speech Therapy, Calverley Street, Leeds 1.

CITY OF LEICESTER COLLEGE OF EDUCATION, Dept. of Speech Therapy, Pelham House, 100 Welford Road, Leicester.

THE EDINBURGH SCHOOL OF SPEECH THERAPY, 7 Buccleuch Place, Edinburgh 8.

JORDANHILL COLLEGE OF EDUCATION, School of Speech Therapy, 76 Southbrae Drive, Glasgow, W.3.

SURVEYING, *see* ESTATE MANAGEMENT AND SURVEYING

TEACHING
Following a recommendation of the Robbins Committee, *degrees* in *Education* (B.Ed.) are granted by most universities (to selected students training to become teachers at colleges of education associated with the Universities usually through their Institutes or Schools of Education). Graduates in other subjects may take at many universities a one-year course leading to a postgraduate diploma or certificate in education.

Courses leading to a degree in *Sociology of Education* granted by the Council for National Academic Awards are provided by Enfield College of Technology.

COLLEGES OF EDUCATION

(With number of students and name of Principal; Colleges marked ★ below offer specialist courses in Home Economics; for Colleges of Physical Education, *see* p. 531.)

M.=For Men; W.=For Women; L.E.A.=Local Education Authority; C. of E.=Church of England; R.C.=Roman Catholic.

ABERDEEN (Aberdeen College, Hilton Place). *M. & W.* (1,800).—J. Scotland.

ABINGDON, Berks. (Culham College). C. of E. *M. & W.* (590).—J. F. Wyatt.

ALNWICK (Alnwick College). L.E.A. *W.* Mature Course (2-yr. and 3-yr.) *M. & W.* (400).—Miss L. K. Hollamby.

ALSAGER (Alsager College). L.E.A. *M. & W.* (1,550).—R. Wesley.

AMBLESIDE, Westmorland (Charlotte Mason College). *M. & W.* (300).—S. W. Percival.

AYR (Craigie College of Education). *M. & W.* (900).—Miss E. M. Rennie.

BANGOR Caernarvonshire (St. Mary's College, Bangor). Church in Wales. *W.* (400).—F. E. Clegg.

„ ★(Normal College, Bangor). L.E.A. *M. & W.* (820).—J. A. Davies.

BARNSLEY, Yorks. (Wentworth Castle College). L.E.A. *W.* (300).—J. G. Minton.

BARRY, S. Wales (Glamorgan College). L.E.A. *M. & W.* (750).—E. D. Lewis, D.SC.

BATH, Somerset (Newton Park College). L.E.A. *M. & W.* (655).—N. P. Payne.

BEDFORD (Bedford College, Polhill Avenue). L.E.A. *M. & W.* (660).—H. H. Humphrey.

BINGLEY, YORKS. L.E.A. *M. & W.* (900).—E. T. Butcher.

BIRMINGHAM (Bordesley College). L.E.A. *W.* (Day College) (450).—Mrs. R. M. D. Roe.

„ (City of Birmingham College). L.E.A. *M. & W.* (1,150).—Miss M. M. Rigg.

„ (Newman College). R.C. *M. & W.* (720)—S. Quinlan.

„ (St. Peter's College, Saltley). C. of E. *M. & W.* (650).—Rev. C. Buckmaster.

„ (Westhill College, Selly Oak). *M. & W.* (500).—Rev. R. T. Newman.

BISHOP'S STORTFORD, Herts (Hockerill College). *M. & W.* (500). C. of E.—Miss J. A. Hall.

BLETCHLEY, Bucks. (Milton Keynes College). L.E.A. *M. & W.* (320).—K. W. S. Garwood, ph.d.

BOGNOR REGIS, Sussex (Bognor Regis College, Upper Bognor Road). L.E.A. *M. & W.* (660).—J. P. Parry.

BOLTON (Bolton College of Education (Technical), Chadwick Street). L.E.A. *M. & W.* (450).—*Director*, V. J. Sparrow.

BRADFORD (Margaret McMillan College). L.E.A. *M. & W.* (750).—Miss M. R. Goodison.

BRENTWOOD, Essex (Brentwood College, Sawyers Hall Lane). L.E.A. *M. & W.* (800).—C. Crane.

BRIGHTON (Brighton College, Falmer). L.E.A. *M. & W.* (1,200).—A. Steward.

BRISTOL (The College of St. Matthias, Fishponds). C. of E. *M. & W.* (800).—R. A. Adcock.

„ (Redland College, Redland Hill). L.E.A. *M. & W.* (820).—J. W. P. Taylor.

BROMSGROVE, Worcs. (Shenstone New College, Burcot Lane). L.E.A. *M. & W.* (850).—D. Brailsford.

CAERLEON (Monmouthshire College). L.E.A. *M. & W.* (750).—H. Edwards.

CAMBRIDGE (Homerton College). *W.* (680).—Miss A. C. Shrubsole.

CANTERBURY (Christ Church College). C. of E. *M. & W.* (720).—Rev. F. Mason.

CARDIFF (City of Cardiff College, Cyncoed). *M. & W.* (1,050).—L. G. Bewsher.

CARMARTHEN (Trinity College). Church in Wales. *Bilingual. M. & W.* (730).—Rev. Canon D. G. Childs.

CHALFONT ST. GILES, Bucks (Newland Park College). L.E.A. *M. & W.* (586).—A. H. Ensor.

CHELTENHAM, Glos. (St. Mary's College). *W.* (700). C. of E.—Miss G. M. Owen, Ph.D.

„ (St. Paul's College). *M.* (720). C. of E.—E. L. Bradby.

CHESTER (Chester College). *M. & W.* (900). C. of E.—M. V. J. Seaborne.

CHICHESTER, Sussex (Bishop Otter College). *M. & W.* (700). C. of E.—G. P. McGregor.

CHORLEY, Lancs. (Chorley College, Union Street). L.E.A. *M. & W.* (1,080).—L. Kenworthy.

CLACTON-ON-SEA, Essex★ (St. Osyth's College, Marine Parade). L.E.A. *M. & W.* (800).—Miss J. G. Pilmer.

COVENTRY, Warwicks (Coventry College). L.E.A. *M. & W.* (1,350).—Miss J. D. Browne.

CREWE (Crewe College). L.E.A. *M. & W.* (900).—Miss B. P. R. Ward.

DARLINGTON (Darlington College). Voluntary. *M. & W.* (450).—J. A. Huitson.

„ (Middleton St. George College). L.E.A. *M. & W.* (720)—E. L. Black.

DARTFORD, Kent (Dartford College of Education) (I.L.E.A.). *M. & W.* (520).—*Principal*, Mrs. M. J. Chamberlain.

DERBY (Bishop Lonsdale College, Western Road, Mickleover). *M. & W.* (770). C. of E.—N. Evans.

DONCASTER (Doncaster College, High Melton Hall), L.E.A. *M. & W.* (750).—D. C. A. Bradshaw.

„ (Scawsby College), L.E.A. *M. & W.* (360).—H. F. Mathews.

DUDLEY, Worcs. (Dudley College, Castle View). L.E.A. *M. & W.* (860).—D. Broadhurst.

DUNDEE (Dundee College, Park Place). *M. & W.* (1,250).

DURHAM (Neville's Cross College). L.E.A. *M. & W.* (650).—R. Emmett.

„ (St. Hild's College). *W.* (410). C. of E.—Miss N. M. E. Joachim.

„ (The Venerable Bede). *M.* (725). C. of E.—K. G. Collier.

EASTBOURNE, Sussex (Eastbourne College, Darley Road). L.E.A. *M. & W.* (700).—Miss T. S. Hichens.

EDINBURGH (Craiglockhart College). R. C. *W.* (370).—Mother Veronica Blount.

„ (Moray House College). *M. & W.* (2,650).—D. M. McIntosh, C.B.E., LL.D., F.R.S.E.

ENFIELD (Trent Park College). L.E.A. *M. & W.* (930).—T. R. Theakston.

EXETER (St. Luke's College). *M. & W.* (1,260). C. of E.—J. C. Dancy.

EXMOUTH, Devon (Rolle College). L.E.A. *M. & W.* (860).—Miss D. E. L. Spicer.

FALKIRK, Stirlingshire (Callendar Park College). *M. & W.* (800).—C. E. Brown.

GLASGOW (Jordanhill College). *M. & W.* (3,500).—Sir Henry Wood, C.B.E.

„ (Notre Dame College, Bearsden). R.C. *M. & W.* (1,500).

GLOUCESTER★ (Gloucestershire College). L.E.A. *W.* (600).—Miss N. E. Bradshaw.

HAMILTON (Hamilton College, Bothwell Road). *M. & W.* (950).—G. Paton.

HEREFORD (County College). L.E.A. *M. & W.* (650).—Miss M. E. Hipwell.

HERTFORD (Balls Park College) L.E.A. *M.* & *W.* (630).—P. E. Sangster.

HUDDERSFIELD (College of Education, Technical). L.E.A. *M.* & *W.* (650).—A. MacLennan, C.B.E.

ILKLEY, Yorks.★ (Ilkley College). L.E.A. *W.* (450) —Miss C. M. Harding.

KINGSTON ON THAMES, Surrey (Gipsy Hill College, Kenry House, Kingston Hill). L.E.A. *M.* & *W.* (785) —Miss F. D. Batstone.

KINSTON UPON HULL (Endsleigh College). R. C. *M.* (Day) & *W.*(645).—Sister Mary Aquin Delany.

,, (Kingston upon Hull College, Cottingham Road). L.E.A. *M.* & *W.* (825).—Dr. C. Bibby.

LANCASTER (St. Martin's College). C. of E. *M.* & *W.* (730).—H. M. Pollard, Ph.D.

LEEDS (City of Leeds and Carnegie College, Beckett Park). L.E.A. *M.* & *W.* (1,400). — L. Connell, Ph.D.

,, (James Graham College, Chapel Lane, Farnley). L.E.A. *M.* & *W.* (Day students only (422).—Miss J. Harland.

,, (Trinity College). R.C. *W.* (900).—Sister Augusta Maria; *and* (All Saints' College). R.C. *M.*—A. M. Kean.

LEICESTER (City of Leicester College, Scraptoft). L.E.A. *M.* & *W.* (1,150).—B. A. Fisher, Ph.D.

LINCOLN (Bishop Grosseteste College). *M.* & *W.* (650). C. of E.—Miss J. E. Skinner.

LIVERPOOL (City of Liverpool, C. F. Mott College, Prescot). L.E.A. *M.* & *W.* (1,200).—R. J. A. F. Clarke.

,, (S. Katharine's College). *M.* & *W.* (750). C. of E.—G. L. Barnard, Ph.D.

,, (Notre Dame College, Mount Pleasant). *W.* (810). R.C.—Miss A. Rawcliffe.

LONDON (Avery Hill College, Eltham, S.E.9). L.E.A. *M.* & *W.* (1,200; Annexe, 300).— Mrs. K. E. Jones.

,, (Borough Road College, Isleworth, Middx.). *M.* & *W.* (1,000).—K. E. Priestley.

,, ★(College of All Saints, N.17). C. of E. *M.* & *W.*(690).—G.E. Cunliffe.

,, (North-Western Polytechnic, Kentish Town, N.W.5). L.E.A. *M.* & *W.* (360) (Day College.—G. W. Pollard.

,, (Philippa Fawcett College, Leigham Court Road, S.W.16). L.E.A. *M.* & *W.* (660). —Mrs. R. O. Brown.

,, (College of S. Mark and S. John, King's Road, Chelsea, S.W.10). *M.* & *W.* (650), C. of E.—Rev. W. H. Mawson.

,, ★(Digby Stuart College, Roehampton, S.W. 15). *W.*(840). R.C.—Sister D. Bell.

,, (Froebel Institute College, Grove House, Roehampton Lane, S.W.15). *M.* & *W.* (640).—Miss P. Steele.

,, (Furzedown College, Welham Road, S.W.17). L.E.A. *M.* & *W.* (780).—Miss M. E. Garvie.

,, (Garnett College (Technical), Downshire House, Roehampton Lane, S.W.15.) L.E.A. *M.* & *W.* (500).—E. J. Brent.

,, (Goldsmiths' College, Dept. of Arts, Science and Educ., New Cross. S.E.14). London Univ. *M.* & *W.* (1,900).—Sir Ross Chesterman.

,, (Maria Assumpta College, 23 Kensington Square, W.8). *W.* (420). R.C.—Sister Augustine Mary.

,, (Maria Grey College, 300 St. Margaret's Road, Twickenham). L.E.A. *M.* & *W.* (950).—Mrs. K. M. Saunders.

,, Polytechnic of North London, Pr. of Wales Road, N.W.5. L.E.A. Day College. *M.* & *W.* (360).—*Head, Dept. of Teaching Studies,* S. Jones.

LONDON (Rachel McMillan College, Deptford, S.E.8). *W.*(550).—Miss E. M. Puddephat.

,, (St. Gabriel's College, Cormont Road, Camberwell, S.E.5). *W.* (400). C. of E.— Miss E. Blackburn.

,, (St. Mary's College, Strawberry Hill, Twickenham). *M.* & *W.* (1,200). R.C.—Very Rev. T. P. Cashin.

,, Shoreditch College, Cooper's Hill, Englefield Green, Surrey). I.L.E.A. *M.* & *W.* (710).—J. N. Smith.

,, ★(Sidney Webb Day College, 9-12 Barrett Street, W.1). L.E.A. *M.* & *W.* (500).—Miss R. Beresford.

,, (Southlands College, 65 Wimbledon Parkside, S.W.19). *M.* & *W.* (830). Methodist.— Miss M. P. Callard.

,, (Stockwell College, Bromley, Kent). L.E.A. *M.* & *W.* (1,130).—Miss R. F. Carr.

,, (Whitelands College, West Hill, Putney. S.W.15). C. of E. *M.* & *W.* (870).—R. F. Knight.

LOUGHBOROUGH, Leics. (Loughborough College). L.E.A. *M.* & *W.* (1,230).—J. W. S. Hardie.

MADELEY, Staffs. ★(College, Madeley, nr. Crewe). L.E.A. *M.* & *W.* (1,260).—E. Johnson.

MANCHESTER (Manchester College, Long Millgate). L.E.A. *M.* & *W.* (875).—Miss M. A. Mycock.

,, (Didsbury College, Wilmslow Road, Didsbury). *M.* & *W.* (1,550).—F. Gorner.

,, ★(Elizabeth Gaskell College). L.E.A. *M.* & *W.* (920).—Miss M. Allen.

MATLOCK, Derbyshire. L.E.A. *M.* & *W.* (785). —R. Clayton.

MIDDLETON, Manchester (De la Salle College). *M.* (800). R.C.—The Rev. Brother Augustine.

NEWCASTLE UPON TYNE (Newcastle upon Tyne College). L.E.A. *M.* & *W.* (750).—N. G. Dearden.

,, ★(Northern Counties College, Coach Lane). L.E.A. *M.* & *W.* (960).—P. T. Underdown, Ph.D

,, (St. Mary's College). *M.* & *W.* (800). R.C.—Sister P. M. Baker.

,, (Northumberland College, Ponteland). L.E.A. *M.* & *W.* (900).—Miss E. M. Churchill.

NORWICH (Keswick Hall). *M.*&*W.* (700). C. of E.—Rev. Canon J. Gibbs.

NOTTINGHAM (Nottingham College, Clifton). L.E.A. *M.* & *W.* (1,275).—K. A. Baird.

,, ★(Mary Ward College, Keyworth). R.C. *W.* (540).—Sister Mary Barry.

ORMSKIRK, Lancs. (Edge Hill College, St. Helens Road). L.E.A. *M.* & *W.* (1,100).—P. K. C. Millins.

OXFORD (Westminster College, North Hinksey). *M.* & *W.* (670). Methodist.—D. W. Crompton. (*See also* WHEATLEY).

PLYMOUTH, Devon (College of S. Mark and S. John, Albert Road, Devonport). C. of E. *M.* & *W.* (75).

PORTSMOUTH (City of Portsmouth College, Milton). L.E.A. *M.* & *W.* (970).—Mrs. D. J. Williams.

POULTON-LE-FYLDE, Nr. Blackpool, Lancs. (College of Educ.). L.E.A. *M.* & *W.* and Mature Course. (500).—Miss M. H. Wilson.

PRESTWICH, Lancs. (Sedgley Park College). *W.* (550). R.C.—Madame P. Grogan.

READING, Berks. (Berkshire College) L.E.A. *M.* & *W.* (1,250).—J. F. Porter.

RETFORD, Notts (Eaton Hall College). L.E.A. *M.* & *W.* (650).—E. L. Ableson.

RIPON, Yorks. (Ripon, Wakefield and Bradford Diocesan College). *M.*&*W.* (570). C. of E.—Miss M. D. Gage.

RUGBY, Warwicks. (St. Paul's College, Newbold Revel, Stretton-under-Fosse). *W.* (540). R.C. —Sister Christina.

SAFFRON WALDEN, Essex (British and Foreign School Society). *W.* (350).—Miss G. P. Collins.

SALISBURY, Wilts. (College of Sarum St. Michael). C. of E. *W.* (480).—Miss A. M. D. Ashley.

SCARBOROUGH, Yorks. (North Riding College). L.E.A. *M. & W.* (360).—Miss E. L. Madge.

SHEFFIELD (Sheffield City College, Collegiate Crescent). *M. & W.* (1,360).—H. J. Peake, PH.D.
„ *(Totley-Thornbridge College, Totley). L.E.A. *M. & W.* (930).—J. Banfield.

SOUTHAMPTON (La Sainte Union College, The Avenue). *M. & W.* (750). R.C.—Miss M. E. Ward.

STOKE ROCHFORD, Lincs. (Kesteven College). L.E.A. *M. & W.* (720).—S. R. Dawes.

SUNDERLAND (Sunderland College). L.E.A. *M. & W.* (750).—H. Armstrong-James.

SWANSEA (Swansea College, Townhill Road, Cockett). L.E.A. *M. & W.* (780).—Miss M. R. Smith.

WAKEFIELD, Yorks. (Bretton Hall College). L.E.A. *M. & W.* (620).—A. S. Davies.

WARRINGTON, Lancs. (Padgate College, Fearnhead). L.E.A. *M. & W.* (1,050).—J. L. Dobson, PH.D.

WATFORD, Herts. (Wall Hall College, Aldenham). L.E.A. *M. & W.* (720).—Miss A. K. Davies.

WENTWORTH WOODHOUSE, Yorks. (Lady Mabel College of Education). *W.* (356).—*Principal,* Miss E. H. Casson.

WEST WICKHAM, Kent (Coloma Coll., Wickham Court). *M. & W.* (700). R.C.—Sister Mary More.

WEYMOUTH, Dorset. (Weymouth College, Dorchester Road; Annexe at Poole). L.E.A. *M. & W.* (800).—Miss N. M. O'Sullivan.

WHEATLEY, Oxon. (Lady Spencer-Churchill College). L.E.A. *W.* (550).—Lady Linstead, D.Phil.

WINCHESTER, Hants. (King Alfred's College). *M. & W.* (995). C. of E.—M. Rose.

WOLVERHAMPTON (Day College, Walsall Street). L.E.A. *M. & W.* (490).—R. H. Durham.
„ (Technical Teachers' College, Compton Road West). L.E.A. *M. & W.* (330).—F. Elliott.

WORCESTER* (Worcester College, Henwick Grove). L.E.A. *M. & W.* (1,200).—E. G. Peirson, C.B.E.

WREXHAM (Cartrefle College). L.E.A. *M. & W.* (750).—Miss M. Taylor.

YORK.—(St. John's College). *M. & W.* (950). C. of E.—J. V. Barnett.

For Teachers of the Deaf

DEPARTMENT OF AUDIOLOGY AND EDUCATION OF THE DEAF, Manchester University. *M. & W.* (100).—*Head of Dept.,* Prof. I. G. Taylor, M.D.

For Teachers of the Blind

THE COLLEGE OF THE TEACHERS OF THE BLIND *Hon Registrar,* B. Hechle, Royal School for the Blind, Church Road North, Wavertree, Liverpool 15. Award certificates after examination to social welfare officers, school teachers and craft instructors of the Blind (700).
Courses of training are also available at:
THE NORTH REGIONAL ASSOCIATION FOR THE BLIND. *M. & W.* (40), Headingley Castle, 72 Headingley Lane, Leeds 6.

NOTE.—Birmingham University offers a one-year postgraduate course of training for teachers of blind or partially-sighted children and a number of

other universities offer post-graduate training in special teaching of, for example, subnormal children or deaf children.

TECHNICAL EDUCATION

Almost all universities award degrees in one or more technologies. Details are given under individual subject headings.
(*See also:* AERONAUTICS; BUILDING; COMPUTER SCIENCE; ENGINEERING; FUEL TECHNOLOGY; MINING; OPTICS; PATENT AGENCY; PRINTING AND TEXTILES.)

Regional Advisory Councils

Set up in 1947 (i) to bring education and industry together to find out the needs of young workers and advise on the provision required, and (ii) to secure reasonable economy of provision. They also have certain responsibilities in connection with the procedure for the approval by the Department of Education and Science of advanced courses, and issue handbooks, etc., giving, for the guidance of students and teachers, information about the facilities available within a region or district for various types of training (*e.g.* electrical engineering, textiles, building and chemistry). There are ten Regional Advisory Councils, in England and Wales:—

REGION 1 (LONDON AND HOME COUNTIES).— Regional Advisory Council for Technological Education, Tavistock House South, Tavistock Square, W.C.1.

REGION 2 (SOUTHERN).—Regional Council for Further Education, 9 Bath Road, Reading.

3 (SOUTH-WEST).—Regional Council for Further Education, Kent House, 37-38 Fore Street, Taunton.

4 (WEST MIDLANDS).—Advisory Council for Further Education, Pitman Buildings, 161 Corporation Street, Birmingham, 4.

5 (EAST MIDLANDS).—Regional Advisory Council for the Organization of Further Education, Robins Wood House, Robins Wood Road, Aspley, Nottingham.

6 (EAST ANGLIA).—Regional Advisory Council for Further Education, County Hall, Martineau Lane, Norwich.

7 (YORKSHIRE).—Council for Further Education, Bowling Green Terrace, Jack Lane, Leeds 11.

8 (NORTH-WEST).—Regional Advisory Council for Further Education, 36 Granby Row, Manchester, 1.

9 (NORTHERN).—Advisory Council for Further Education, 5 Grosvenor Villas, Grosvenor Road, Newcastle upon Tyne, 2.

10 (WALES).—Welsh Joint Education Committee, 245 Western Avenue, Cardiff.

CITY AND GUILDS OF LONDON INSTITUTE, 76 Portland Place, W.1.—*Dir. Gen.,* C. R. English.

Technical Colleges

Nearly all technical colleges in England and Wales are maintained or assisted by local education authorities. There are about 550 colleges, many of which provide a substantial amount of higher education (including some full-time and sandwich courses) as well as less advanced courses. Future development of such courses in higher education will be mainly concentrated in some 30 institutions, known as Polytechnics.
Twenty-eight Polytechnics have now been formally established. These are:
CITY OF BIRMINGHAM POLYTECHNIC, Franchise Street, Perry Barr, Birmingham.—*Dir.,* S. W. Smethurst.
BRIGHTON POLYTECHNIC, Moulsecoomb, Brighton. —*Dir.,* G. R. Hall.

BRISTOL POLYTECHNIC, Ashley Down Road, Bristol.—*Dir.*, R. W. Bolland.

GLAMORGAN POLYTECHNIC, Llantwit Road, Treforest, Pontypridd, Glamorgan.—*Princ.*, D. P. Evans, C.B.E.

HATFIELD POLYTECHNIC, Hatfield, Herts.—*Dir.*, N. Lindop.

HUDDERSFIELD POLYTECHNIC, Queensgate, Huddersfield.—*Dir.*, K. J. Durrands.

KINGSTON POLYTECHNIC, Penrhyn Road, Kingston upon Thames.—*Dir.*, L. E. Lawley.

LANCHESTER POLYTECHNIC, Priory Street, Coventry.—*Dir.*, Sir Alan Richmond, Ph.D.

LEEDS POLYTECHNIC, Calverley Street, Leeds, 1.—*Dir.*, P. J. Nuttgens.

CITY OF LEICESTER POLYTECHNIC, P.O. Box 143, Leicester.—*Dir.*, R. E. Wood.

LIVERPOOL POLYTECHNIC, Clarence Street, Liverpool.—*Rector*, G. Bulmer.

LONDON:

CITY OF LONDON POLYTECHNIC, 117–119 Houndsditch, E.C.3.—*Prov.*, A. Suddaby.

NORTH-EAST LONDON POLYTECHNIC, Romford Road, E.15.—*Dir.*, G. S. Brosan, T.D.

POLYTECHNIC OF CENTRAL LONDON, 309 Regent Street, W.1.—*Dir.*, C. Adamson, D.SC.

POLYTECHNIC OF NORTH LONDON, Holloway, N.7.—*Dir.*, T. G. Miller, T.D.

POLYTECHNIC OF THE SOUTH BANK, Borough Road, S.E.1.—*Dir.*, V. Pereira Mendoza.

THAMES POLYTECHNIC, Wellington Street, S.E.18.—*Dir.*, D. E. R. Godfrey.

MANCHESTER POLYTECHNIC, Lower Ormond Street, All Saints, Manchester.—*Dir.*, A. M. Smith.

NEWCASTLE UPON TYNE POLYTECHNIC, Ellison Building, Ellison Place, Newcastle upon Tyne.—*Dir.*, G. S. Bosworth, C.B.E.

NORTH STAFFORDSHIRE POLYTECHNIC, Beaconside, Stafford.—*Dir.*, J. F. Dickenson.

OXFORD POLYTECHNIC, Gipsy Lane, Headington, Oxford.—*Dir.*, B. B. Lloyd.

PLYMOUTH POLYTECHNIC, Tavistock Road, Plymouth.—*Dir.*, E. Bailey.

PORTSMOUTH POLYTECHNIC, Ravelin House, Alexandra Road, Portsmouth.—*Pres.*, W. Davey.

SHEFFIELD POLYTECHNIC, Pond Street, Sheffield.—*Dir.*, G. Tolley, Ph.D.

SUNDERLAND POLYTECHNIC, Chester Road, Sunderland.—*Rector*, M. Hutton, Ph.D.

TEESSIDE POLYTECHNIC, Borough Road, Middlesbrough.—*Dir.*, S. Houghton.

TRENT POLYTECHNIC, Burton Street, Nottingham.—*Dir.*, R. Hedley.

THE POLYTECHNIC—WOLVERHAMPTON, Wulfruna Street, Wolverhampton.—*Dir.*, R. Scott.

Two further Polytechnics remain to be established, a proposed polytechnic in central Lancashire based on the Harris College, Preston and part of the work of Blackburn College of Technology and Design; and The Middlesex Polytechnic based on Enfield College of Technology, Hendon College of Technology and Hornsey College of Art.

In addition to these colleges, there are 7,968 Evening Institutes and similar types of establishment providing a wide variety of non-vocational classes for adults.

Scottish Technical Colleges

Technical education is available at approximately 100 day-course schools and colleges in Scotland, including those which specialize in a particular subject. The following are among those recognized by the Scottish Education Department as " central institutions " (colleges for higher technical learning); other Scottish central institutions appear under Agriculture, Art, Domestic Science and Music.

ABERDEEN: ROBERT GORDON'S INSTITUTE OF TECHNOLOGY, Aberdeen.—*Director*, P. Clarke, Ph.D.

DUNDEE INSTITUTE OF ART AND TECHNOLOGY, 40 Bell Street, Dundee.—*Princ.* (*Technical*), H. G. Cuming, Ph.D.

GALASHIELS: SCOTTISH COLLEGE OF TEXTILES, Galashiels, Selkirkshire.—*Princ.*, J. G. Martindale, Ph.D.

LEITH NAUTICAL COLLEGE, 59 Commercial Street, Leith, Edinburgh.—*Princ.*, E. T. Morgan.

PAISLEY COLLEGE OF TECHNOLOGY, High Street, Paisley.—*Princ.*, E. Kerr, Ph.D.

Northern Ireland

BELFAST (College of Technology).—*Princ.*, W. F. K. Kerr, Ph.D.

LONDONDERRY (Technical and Teacher Training Coll.).—*Princ.*, T. Williams.

Industrial Training Boards

Established under the Industrial Training Act, 1964.

AGRICULTURAL, HORTICULTURAL AND FORESTRY, Bourne House, 32–34 Beckenham Road, Beckenham, Kent.—*Sec.*, R. F. B. Eager.

AIR TRANSPORT AND TRAVEL INDUSTRY, Staines House, 158–162 High Street, Staines, Middx.—*Sec.*, R. N. Boyd, C.B.E., E.D.

CARPET, Evelyn House, 32 Alderley Road, Wilmslow, Cheshire.—*Sec.*, D. Borthwick.

CERAMICS, GLASS AND MINERAL PRODUCTS, Bovis House, Northolt Road, Harrow, Middx.—*Sec.*, H. B. Chubb, O.B.E.

CHEMICAL AND ALLIED PRODUCTS, Staines House, 158–162 High Street, Staines, Middx.—*Sec.*, E. G. J. Willing.

CLOTHING AND ALLIED PRODUCTS, Tower House, Merrion Way, Leeds.—*Sec.*, K. F. Swinfen.

CONSTRUCTION, Radnor House, London Road, Norbury, S.W.16.—*Sec.*, G. R. Gardner.

COTTON AND ALLIED TEXTILES, Sunlight House, Quay Street, Manchester 3.—*Sec.*, N. T. Hunt.

DISTRIBUTIVE INDUSTRY, MacLaren House, Talbot Road, Stretford, Manchester.—*Sec.*, H. A. Whitehead, M.B.E.

ELECTRICITY SUPPLY, 30 Millbank, S.W.1.—*Sec.*, M. Skinner.

ENGINEERING, St. Martin's House, 140 Tottenham Court Road, W.1.—*Sec.*, H. M. Lang.

FOOD, DRINK AND TOBACCO, Leon House, High Street, Croydon.—*Sec.*, J. T. Newton.

FOOTWEAR, LEATHER AND FUR SKIN, Maney Building, 29 Birmingham Road, Sutton Coldfield, Warwicks.—*Sec.*, C. J. Bailey.

FOUNDRY INDUSTRY TRAINING COMMITTEE, 50–54 Charlotte Street, W.1.—*Sec.*, L. A. Rice.

FURNITURE AND TIMBER, 31 Octagon Parade, High Wycombe, Bucks.—*Secretaries*, P. J. D. Nesbitt. Hawes (*Training*); H. A. d'Avray (*Administration*).

GAS, 5 Grosvenor Crescent, S.W.1.—*Sec.*, J. H. Evans.

HOTEL AND CATERING Ramsey House, Central Square, Wembley, Middx.—*Sec.*, J. Crabtree.

IRON AND STEEL, 4 Little Essex Street, W.C.2.—*Dir.*, R. Duncan.

KNITTING, LACE AND NET, 4 Hamilton Road, Sherwood Rise, Nottingham.—*Sec.*, A. B. Ross.

MAN-MADE FIBRES PRODUCING, 8th floor, Bowater House East, 68 Knightsbridge, S.W.1.—*Sec.*, E. Lord, O.B.E.

PAPER AND PAPER PRODUCTS, Star House, Potters Bar, Herts.—*Sec.*, O. T. P. Carne.

PETROLEUM, York House, Empire Way, Wembley, Middx.—*Sec.*, J. A. Bey.

PRINTING AND PUBLISHING, Merit House, Edgware Road, Colindale, N.W.9.—*Sec.*, G. F. Reid.

ROAD TRANSPORT, Capitol House, Empire Way, Wembley, Middx.—*Dir. Gen.*, T. E. Tindall.

RUBBER AND PLASTICS PROCESSING, 950 Great West Road, Brentford, Middx.—*Sec.*, S. K. Hardy.

SHIPBUILDING, Raeburn House, Northolt Road, South Harrow, Middx.—*Sec.,* D. O. Savill.

WATER SUPPLY, 104A Park Street, W.1.—*Sec.,* A. R. Porter.

WOOL, JUTE AND FLAX, 55 Well Street, Bradford 1. —*Sec.,* F. Bingham.

LOCAL GOVERNMENT TRAINING BOARD, Alembic House, 93 Albert Embankment, S.E.1.—*Dir.,* D. Lofts.

Industrial Training Foundation
18 Thurloe Place, S.W.7

Formed in 1964 with the support of the Ministry of Labour (now Department of Employment and Productivity) and the Department of Education and Science to assist in implementing the Industrial Training Act, 1964.

It provides a service for all industries and all categories of employees through its six regional offices. A Training Officer and Advisory Service assists individual firms in the development of training programmes and makes available the part-time services of qualified training officers. This service also provides assistance in maintaining training records required by Industrial Training Boards and advice on dealing with questionnaires and grant claims.

The main activities of the ITF are: assessment of training needs; provision of training for apprentices, operators, supervisors, instructors and salesmen. There is a personal tutorial service for management. The Foundation operates training schemes to the requirements of individual firms or on a group basis.

A further activity of the ITF under its training officer service is the operation of the Engineering Industries Group Apprenticeship Scheme (EIGA) formed in 1953, which serves 1,000 firms throughout the country and provides 3,000 training places.

TEXTILES
Degrees in *Textiles* or *Fibre Science* are awarded by the Universities of Bradford, Leeds, Manchester (Manchester Institute of Science and Technology) and Strathclyde. Courses leading to degrees in *Textile Marketing* granted by the Council for National Academic Awards are provided by Huddersfield Polytechnic; and in *Textile Technology* by the City of Leicester Polytechnic.

THE TEXTILE INSTITUTE, 10 Blackfriars Street, Manchester, is an examining body.—*Gen. Sec.,* D. B. Moore, M.A.

THEOLOGY
The degree of B.D. granted by the Universities of Aberdeen, Belfast, Birmingham, Cambridge, Durham, Edinburgh, Glasgow, Hull, Leeds, London (King's College; New College; Richmond College), Manchester, Nottingham, Oxford, St. Andrews and Wales. At most of these the degree is open to graduates.

Theological Colleges
Church of England and Church in Wales
BANGOR (Church Hostel) (30).—*Warden,* Rev. B. Evans.

BIRMINGHAM (Queen's Coll., Somerset Road, Edgbaston) (75).—*Princ.,* Rev. Canon J. S. Habgood, Ph.D. (Ecumenical College).

BRAMCOTE, Notts. (St. John's College) (78).—*Princ.,* Rev. Canon E. M. B. Green.

CAMBRIDGE (Ridley Hall) (50).—*Princ.,* Rev. F. H. Palmer.

„   (Westcott House, Jesus Lane) (45).—*Princ.,* Rev. Canon P. K. Walker.

CANTERBURY (St. Augustine's College—King's College, London) (60)—*Warden,* Rev. A. E. Harvey.

CHICHESTER (50).—*Princ.,* Rev. Canon A. B. Wilkinson, Ph.D.

CLIFTON, BRISTOL (Tyndale Hall) (50).—*Princ.,* Rev. J. I. Packer.

CLIFTON THEOLOGICAL COLLEGE, Stoke Bishop, Bristol, 9 (63).—*Princ.,* Rev. J. C. F. O'Byrne.

CUDDESDON, Oxon. (54).—*Princ.,* Rev., J. L. Houlden.

DURHAM. *See* University of Durham—St. Chad's; St. John's.

HAWARDEN, Flints. (St. Deiniol's Residential Library, Gladstone Memorial) (12).—*Warden,* Rev. J. S. Lawton, B.D., D.Phil.

KELHAM (House of the Sacred Mission).—*Warden,* Rev. H. Greenwood.

LAMPETER (St. David's College), *see* University of Wales.

LINCOLN (Theological College) (65).—*Warden,* Rev. Canon A. A. K. Graham.

LLANDAFF, Cardiff (St. Michael's) (57).—*Warden,* Rev. Canon O. G. Rees.

LONDON (King's College, W.C.2).—*See* University of London.

MIRFIELD (College of the Resurrection) (50).— *Princ.,* Rev. W. Wheeldon.

OAK HILL (Southgate, N.14) (78).—*Princ.,* Rev. D. H. Wheaton, M.A., B.D.

OXFORD (Ripon Hall) (46).—*Princ.,* Rev. A. O. Dyson, D.Phil.

„   (St. Stephen's House) (45).—*Princ.,* Rev. D. W. Allen.

„   (Wycliffe Hall) (50).—*Princ.,* Rev. J. P. Hickinbotham.

SALISBURY (100).—*Princ.,* Rev. Canon H. Wilson. (Incorporating Wells Theological College from Oct. 1, 1971.)

Church of Scotland
ABERDEEN (Christ's Coll.).—*Master,* Rev. Prof. J. S. McEwen, D.D.

EDINBURGH (New Coll., Univ. of Edinburgh) (196). —*Princ.,* Rev. J. McIntyre, D.D., D.Litt.

GLASGOW (Trinity Coll.) (70).—*Princ.,* Rev. Prof. J. Mauchline, D.D.

ST. ANDREWS (College of St. Mary, University of St. Andrews).

Scottish Episcopal Church
EDINBURGH (24).—*Princ.,* Rev. Canon A. I. M. Haggart, LL.D.

Presbyterian
BELFAST (Presbyterian Coll.).—*Princ.,* Very Rev. J. L. M. Haire, D.D.

CAMBRIDGE (Westminster Coll., Presbyterian Church of England) (30).—*Princ.,* Rev. A. G. MacLeod.

Presbyterian Church of Wales
ABERYSTWYTH (United Theological Coll.) (31).— *Princ.,* Rev. Prof. S. I. Enoch.

Methodist
BELFAST (Edgehill Coll.) (25).—*Princ.,* Rev. R. Greenwood.

BRISTOL (Wesley Coll., Westbury-on-Trym) (58).—*Princ.,* Rev. R. E. Davies.

CAMBRIDGE (Wesley House) (20).—*Princ.,* Rev. Prof. E. G. Rupp, D.D., F.B.A.

MANCHESTER (Hartley Victoria College, Alexandra Road South) (102).—*Princ.,* Rev. P. Scott, D.Theol.

RICHMOND.—*See* University of London.

Congregational
BANGOR (Bala-Bangor Independent Coll.)—*Princ.,* R. T. Jones, D.Phil., D.D.

CAMBRIDGE (Cheshunt College, with Westminster Presbyterian College, Madingley Road, Cambridge) (7).—*Pres.,* Rev. J. E. Newport.

EDINBURGH (Scottish Congregational College, Hope Terrace) (10).—*Princ.*, Rev. J. Wood.
LONDON (New College) (19).—*See* Universities.
MANCHESTER (Congregational College) (36).—*Princ.*, Rev. E. Jones, Ph.D.
OXFORD (Mansfield College) (97).—*Princ.*, Rev. G. B. Caird, D.Phil., D.D.
SWANSEA (19).—*Princ.*, Prof. W. T. Pennar Davies, Ph.D.

Roman Catholic
(Colleges for the Diocesan Clergy)

ABERYSTWYTH (St. Mary's College (for late vocations, secular and regular)) (30).—*Prior*, Very Rev. P. L. Geary, O.Carm.
GLASGOW (St. Peter's Coll., Cardross, Dunbartonshire) (33).—*Rector*, Very Rev. M. J. Connolly, D.D., Ph.D.
KIRKBY LONSDALE (viâ Carnforth, Lancs.) (St. Michael's Minor Seminary, Underley Hall) (150).—*Rector* Rt. Rev. Mgr. B. Kershaw.
OSCOTT COLL., Sutton Coldfield, Warwicks. (110).—*Rector*, Rt. Rev. Mgr. F. G. Thomas.
OSTERLEY, Middlesex (Campion House, 112 Thornbury Road) (165).—*Superior*, Rev. F. J. O'Callaghan, S.J.
UP HOLLAND, nr. Wigan, Lancs. (St. Joseph's Diocesan College) (200).—*Rector*, Rt. Rev. Mgr. S. F. Breen.
USHAW (Durham) (270).—*Pres.*, Rt. Revd. Mgr. P. Loftus.
WARE (Old Hall Green) (122).—*Pres.*, Rt. Rev. Bishop B. C. Butler, O.S.B.
WONERSH, Guildford (St. John's) (114).—*Rector*, Very Rev. J. P. McConnon.

Baptist

BANGOR (North Wales Baptist Coll.) (22).—*Princ.*, Rev. G. R. M. Lloyd.
BRISTOL (40).—*Pres.*, Rev. L. G. Champion.
CARDIFF (S. Wales Baptist Coll.) (16).—*Princ.*, D. G. Davies.
GLASGOW (The Baptist Theological College of Scotland, 31 Oakfield Avenue, Glasgow, W.2) (20).—*Princ.*, Rev. R. E. O. White.
LONDON (Spurgeon's Coll., South Norwood Hill, S.E.25) (62).—*Princ.*, Rev. G. R. Beasley-Murray, Ph.D., D.D.

MANCHESTER (Northern Baptist College, Brighton Grove, Rusholme) (affiliated to Manchester Univ.) (60).—*Princ.*, Rev. M. H. Taylor.
OXFORD (Regent's Park Baptist Coll.) (48).—*Princ.*, Rev. G. Henton Davies, D.D.

Unitarian

MANCHESTER (Unitarian College, Victoria Park) (14).—*Princ.*, Rev. F. Kenworthy.

Interdenominational—Unitarian

OXFORD (Manchester Coll.).—*Princ.*, Rev. H. L. Short.

Jewish

JEWS' COLLEGE (and Institute for the Training of Teachers), Montagu Place, W.1.—*Princ.*, Rabbi N. L. Rabbinovitch.
LEO BAECK COLLEGE, 33 Seymour Place, W.1.—*Hon. Dir. of Studies*, Rabbi H. Gryn.

TOWN AND COUNTRY PLANNING

Degrees are granted by Heriot-Watt University (*Town Planning*), and by the Universities of Aston in Birmingham (*Town Planning*), London (University College; *Architecture, Planning, Building and Environmental Studies*), Manchester (*Town and Country Planning*), Newcastle upon Tyne (*Town and Country Planning*), Reading (*Scientific Bases of Planning*), and Wales (Institute of Science and Technology: *Town Planning Studies*). Courses leading to degrees in *Town Planning* granted by the Council for National Academic Awards are provided by the Polytechnic of the South Bank; and in *Urban and Regional Planning* with courses at Lanchester Polytechnic.
The TOWN PLANNING INSTITUTE, 26 Portland Place, W.1, conducts examinations in town planning.

VETERINARY STUDIES

Admission to the Register of Veterinary Surgeons under the Veterinary Surgeons Act, 1966, may be obtained by holders of veterinary degrees of the universities of Bristol, Cambridge, Edinburgh, Glasgow, Liverpool and London (Royal Veterinary College).

PUBLIC SCHOOLS

With a few exceptions the schools in the list following are members of the Association of Governing Bodies of Public Schools (G.B.A.). Other schools in membership of G.B.A. but not of the Headmasters' Conference are:—

Ackworth, Pontefract, Yorks.
Adams' Grammar Sch., Newport, Salop.
Austin Friars Sch., Carlisle.
Bearwood College, Wokingham.
Belmont Abbey Sch., Hereford.
†Canon Slade Gr. Sch., Bolton.
Cathedral Sch., Bristol.
Cheadle Hulme Sch., Cheshire.
Churchers, Petersfield, Hants.
Colston's Boys' Sch., Bristol.
Cranbrook School, Kent.
Dollar Academy, Clackmannan.
Duke of York's R.M. Sch., Dover.
Dundee High School.
†Frensham Heights Sch., Farnham, Surrey.
Friends' Sch., Great Ayton, N. Yorks.
Friends' Sch., Saffron Walden.
Grenville Coll., Bideford, Devon.
Hardye's Sch., Dorchester.
King's School, Gloucester.
Langley School, Norwich.
Melville College.
Millfield School, Somerset.
Morrison's Academy, Crieff.
Newcastle High Sch., Staffs.

Oswestry School, Salop.
Pangbourne College, Berks.
Rannoch School, Perthshire.
Rishworth Sch., nr. Halifax, Yorks.
Redrice Sch., nr. Andover, Hants.
Royal Lancaster Grammar Sch.
Royal Wolverhampton School.
Ruthin School, Denbighshire.
St. Augustine's Coll., Ramsgate, Kent.
St. Bartholomew's Sch., Newbury.
St. Bede's Coll., Manchester.
St. Boniface's Coll., Plymouth.
St. Brendan's Coll., Bristol.
St. John's Coll., Southsea, Hants.
St. Peter's Sch., Bournemouth.
Scarborough College.
Shebbear Coll., Beaworthy, Devon.
Shiplake Coll., Henley, Oxon.
†Sidcot Sch., Winscombe, Som.
Truro Cathedral School.
Wakefield Grammar School.
†Wells Cathedral School.
Woodbridge School, Suffolk.
Worth Sch., Crawley, Sussex.

† Co-educational School.

HEADMASTERS' CONFERENCE SCHOOLS

THE HEADMASTERS' CONFERENCE.—*Chairman* (1971), A. R. D. Wright (*Shrewsbury School*); *Sec.*, R. St. J. Pitts-Tucker, 29 Gordon Square, W.C.1.; *Deputy Sec.*, B. C. Harvey. The annual meetings are, as a rule, held at the end of September.

In considering applications for election to membership the Committee will have regard to the scheme or other instrument under which the school is administered (taking particularly into consideration the degree of independence enjoyed by the Headmaster and the Governing Body); the number of boys over thirteen years of age in the school; the number of boys in proportion to the size of the school who are in the sixth form, *i.e.* engaged on studies at the Advanced Level of the General Certificate of Education.

Name of School	F'ded.	No. of Boys	Annual Fees D=Day Boys	Headmaster (*With date of Appointment*)
England and Wales				
Abbotsholme, Uttoxeter, Staffs........	1889	222	£792 D£528	S. D. Snell (1967)
Abingdon, Berks...................	1256	610	£564......D£225	W. E. K. Anderson (1970)
Aldenham, Elstree, Herts...........	1597	340	£699......D£390	P. Griffin, M.B.E. (1962)
Alleyn's School, Dulwich, S.E.22.....	1619	800	..........D£243	J. L. Fanner (1967)
Allhallows, Rousdon, Dorset........	1515	281†	£711. D£321–378	G. E. Hewan (1965)
Ampleforth College (*R.C.*), York.....	1802	700	£711............	Rev. N. P. Barry, O.S.B. (1964)
Archbishop Holgate's Grammar, York.	1546	850	£285........Dnil	D. A. Frith (1959)
Ardingly Coll., Haywards Heath, Sussex*	1858	320	£741............	C. H. Bulteel, M.C. (1962)
Arnold School, Blackpool...........	1896	685	£425......D£195	O. C. Wigmore (1966)
Ashville College, Harrogate.........	1877	420	£420......D£180	G. R. Southam (1958)
Bablake, Coventry................	1344	840	..........D£168	E. H. Burrough, T.D. (1962)
Banbury Sch., Oxon	1967	2250	..........Dnil	H. G. Judge, Ph.D. (1967)
Bancroft's, Woodford Green, Essex ...	1737	480	£491......D£201	I. M. Richardson (1965)
Barnard Castle, Co. Durham.........	1883	484	£453......D£183	S. D. Woods (1965)
Bedales, Petersfield, Hants..........	1893	400†	£774......D£414	T. W. Slack (1962)
Bedford School...................	1552	967	£654......D£333	W. M. Brown (1955)
Bedford Modern School.............	1566	1030	£471......D£186	B. H. Kemball-Cook (1965)
Berkhamsted, Herts...............	1541	760	£600......D£300	B. H. Garnons-Williams (1953)
Birkenhead, Cheshire..............	1860	640	£453......D£213	J. A. Gwilliam (1963)
Bishop's Stortford Coll., Herts.......	1868	322	£765......D£453	G. C. Greetham (1971)
Bloxham School, Banbury, Oxon* ...	1860	310	£705......D£393	D. R. G. Seymour (1965)
Blundell's, Tiverton..............	1604	400	£705......D£390	A. C. S. Gimson, M.B.E., M.C. (1971)
Bolton..........................	1524	1030	..........D£205	C. D. A. Baggley (1966)
Bootham, York...................	1823	260	£666......	A. F. Lindley (1961)
Bradfield College, Berks...........	1850	435	£801......	A. O. H. Quick (1971)
Bradford Gr., Yorks...............	1548	1090	..........D£185	K. D. Robinson (1963)
Brentwood Sch., Essex.............	1557	890	£497......D£215	R. Sale (1966)
Brighton College, Sussex...........	1845	350	£625......D£459	W. S. Blackshaw (1971)
Bristol Grammar..................	1532	1207	..........D£153	J. Mackay, D.Phil. (1960)
Bromsgrove, Worcs...............	1553	310	£648......D£462	Rev. J. N. F. Earle (1971)
Bryanston School, Blandford........	1928	450	£732......	F. G. R. Fisher (1959)
Bury Grammar, Lancs.............	1600	700	..........D£165	W. J. H. Robson (1969)
Canford Wimborne, Dorset.........	1923	450	£732......D£444	I. A. Wallace (1961)
Carmel College, Wallingford, Berks...	1948	350	£765......D£291	D. M. Stamler (1962)
Caterham, Surrey.................	1811	470	£486......D£191	T. R. Leathem (1950)
Charterhouse, Godalming...........	1611	653	£795......D£600	A. O. Van Oss (1965)
Cheltenham College...............	1841	430	£780......D£465	D. Ashcroft, T.D. (1959)
Chigwell, Essex..................	1629	380	£600......D£300	B. J. Wilson (1971)
Christ Coll., Brecon..............	1541	240	£609......D£426	J. Sharp, D.Phil. (1962)
Christ's Hospital, Horsham.........	1553	820	(various)........	D. H. Newsome (1970)
City of London, E.C.4.............	1442	780	..........D£340	J. A. Boyes (1965)
Claysmore, Iwerne Minster, Blandford	1896	163	£675......D£360	R. McIsaac (1966)
Clifton College, Bristol............	1862	615	£753......D£411	S. J. McWatters (1963)
Cranleigh, Surrey................	1863	490	£840......D£540	M. van Hasselt (1970)
Culford Sch., Bury St. Edmunds......	1881	450	£513......D£228	D. Robson (1971)
Dame Allan's School, Newcastle on Tyne	1705	450	..........D£185	F. Wilkinson (1970)
Dauntsey's, Devizes...............	1543	421	£588......D£234	G. E. King-Reynolds (1969)
Dean Close, Cheltenham...........	1884	355†	£783......D£480	C. G. Turner (1968)
Denstone Coll., Uttoxeter, Staffs.* ...	1868	322	£649......D£433	D. Maland (1969)
Douai (*R.C.*), Woolhampton........	1615	260	£540......	Rev. F. A. Tierney, O.S.B. (1952)
Dover College, Kent..............	1871	325	£699......D£399	T. H. Cobb (1958)
Downside (*R.C.*), Stratton-on-the-Fosse, Som..........................	1607	573	£777......D£389	Rev. C. A. P. Watkin, F.S.A. (1962)
Dulwich College, S.E.21...........	1619	1360	£636......D£345	C. W. Lloyd (*Master*) (1967)
Durham.........................	1414	240	£705......D£399	W. B. Cook (1967) (1970)
Eastbourne College, Sussex.........	1867	470	£760......D£510	J. McG. K. Kendall-Carpenter

† Pupils.   * a Woodard Corporation school.

Name of School	F'ded.	No of Boys	Annual Fees D=Day Boys	Headmaster (With date of Appointment)
Ellesmere Coll., Shropshire*	1879	340	£750.....D £500	D. J. Skipper (1969)
Eltham College, S.E.9	1842	450	£564.....D £204	C. Porteous (1959)
Epsom College, Surrey	1853	550	£723.....D £480	O. J. T. Rowe (1970)
Eton College, Windsor	1440	1200	£861..........	M. W. McCrum (1970)
Exeter, Devon	1633	485	£498.....D £210	R. M. Hone (1966)
Felsted, Dunmow, Essex	1564	461	£660.....D £357	A. F. Eggleston, O.B.E. (1968)
Forest Sch., Snaresbrook, E.17	1834	518	£418.....D £324	D. A. Foxall (1960)
Framlingham Coll., Suffolk	1864	485	£470.....D £190	L. I. Rimmer (1971)
Giggleswick, Settle, Yorks	1512	370	£615.....D £330	R. A. C. Meredith (1970)
Gresham's, Holt, Norfolk	1555	448	£774.....D £474	L. Bruce Lockhart (1955)
Haberdashers' Aske's, Elstree, Herts	1690	1124	£600.D £240–300	T. W. Taylor, Ph.D. (1946)
Haileybury, Herts	1862	585	£660.....D £438	W. Stewart, M.C. (*Master*) (1963)
Harrow, Middlesex	1571	734	£759.....D £380	B. M. S. Hoban (1971)
Hemel Hempstead Sch., Herts.	1931	740†	.........Dnil	J. S. Robinson (1951)
Hereford, Cathedral Sch	1381	362	£375.....D £180	D. M. Richards (1968)
Highgate, N.6.	1565	680	£666.....D £336	A. J. F. Doulton, O.B.E., T.D.
High Wycombe (Royal Gr.)	1562	1060	£363.........Dnil	M. P. Smith (1965) [(1955)
Hulme Gr. Sch., Oldham	1611	710	.........D £165	S. W. Johnson (1965)
Hurstpierpoint College, Sussex*	1849	335	£657.....D £486	R. N. P. Griffiths (1964)
Hymers Coll., Hull	1893	650	.........D £210	J. Ashurst (1971)
Ipswich, Suffolk	1400	170	£639–660 D £387–408	P. H. F. Mermagen, T.D. (1950)
John Lyon School, Harrow	1868	430	.........D £252	G. V. Surtees (1968)
Kelly College, Tavistock	1867	223	£660.....D £390	J. T. Melvin, T.D. (1959)
Kent College, Canterbury	1885	395	£501.....D £234	D. E. Norfolk (1960)
Kimbolton, Hunts.	1600	440	£526.....D £217	C. H. Lewis, M.B.E. (1947)
King Edward VI Grammar, Stourbridge, Worcs.	1552	630	.........Dnil	R. L. Chambers (1951)
King Edward VII School, Lytham	1908	650	.........D £147	C. J. Lipscomb (1966)
King Edward's, Bath, Som.	1552	450	.........D £170	B. H. Holbeche (1961)
King Edward's, Birmingham	1552	700	.........D £135	Rev. Canon R. G. Lunt, M.C. (*Chief Master*) (1952)
King Henry VIII, Coventry	1545	850	.........D £174	H. Walker (1950)
King's Coll., Taunton*	1522	366	£720.....D £408	J. M. Batten (1969)
King's College Sch., Wimbledon, S.W.19	1829	560	£615.....D £375	F. H. Shaw, M.B.E., T.D. (1960)
King's Sch., Bruton	1519	255	£660.....D £360	R. C. Davey (1957)
King's Sch., Canterbury	600	600	£702.....D £375	Rev. Canon J. P. Newell (1962)
King's Sch., Chester	1541	525	.........D £206	A. R. Munday (1964)
King's Sch., Ely	970	402	£687.....D £406	H. Ward (1970)
King's Sch., Macclesfield	1502	1200	.........D £216	A. H. Cooper (1966)
King's Sch., Rochester	604	482	£603.....D £327	Rev. Canon D. R. Vicary (1957)
King's Sch., Worcester	1541	656	£498.....D £322	D. M. Annett (1959)
Kingston Grammar, Kingston upon Thames	1561	560	.........D £180	J. A. Strover (1970)
Kingswood Sch., Bath	1748	430	£681.....D £417	L. J. Campbell (1970)
Lancing College, Sussex*	1848	420	£780.....D £465	I. D. S. Beer (1969)
Latymer Upper, Hammersmith, W.6.	1624	1100	.........D £210	M. L. R. Isaac (1971)
Leeds Gr. Sch., Leeds 6	1552	1000	.........D £180	A. H. Aldous (1970)
Leighton Park Sch., Reading	1890	312	£666.....D £444	W. H. Spray (1971)
The Leys Sch., Cambridge	1875	475	£759.....D £483	W. A. Barker (1958)
Liverpool College, Liverpool 18	1840	805	£543.....D £333	M. F. Robins (1970)
Llandovery Coll.	1848	242†	£600.....D £300	R. G. Jones (1967)
Lord Wandsworth Coll., Long Sutton, Hants.	1912	300	£690.....D £396	C. A. N. Henderson (1968)
Loughborough Grammar	1496	760	£418.....D £163	N. S. Walter (1959)
Magdalen Coll. Sch., Oxford	1478	470	£549.....D £227	*Master* (vacant)
Malvern Coll., Worcs.	1865	585	£726.....D £468	M. J. W. Rogers (1971)
Manchester Gr. Sch.	1515	1440	.........D £191	P. G. Mason, M.B.E. (*High Master*) (1962)
Manchester, Wm. Hulme's Gr.	1887	800	.........D £201	J. G. Bird, M.B.E., T.D. (1947)
(Sir Roger) Manwood's, Sandwich, Kent.	1563	340	£315.........Dnil	J. F. Spalding (1960)
Marlborough Coll., Wilts.	1843	840†	£768..........	J. C. Dancy (*Master*) (1961)
Merchant Taylors', Northwood	1561	663	£670.....D £450	B. Rees (1965)
Merchant Taylors', Crosby, Lancs.	1620	762	£471.....D £192	Rev. H. M. Luft (1964)
Mill Hill, N.W.7.	1807	452	£702.....D £411	M. Hart (1967)
Monkton Combe, Bath	1868	312	£678.....D £456	R. J. Knight (1968)
Monmouth	1615	450	£459.....D £204	R. F. Glover, T.D. (1959)

† Pupil.   ★ a Woodard Corporation school.

Name of School	F'ded.	No. of Boys	Annual Fees D=Day Boys	Headmaster (With date of Appointment)
Mount St. Mary's Coll., Spinkhill Derbyshire (R.C.)	1842	350	£495.....D£231	Rev. A. A. Nye, S.J. (1968)
Newcastle on Tyne (Royal Gr. Sch.)	1525	850	.........D£192	W. D. Haden, T.D. (1960)
Norwich Sch.	1240	670	£453.....D£192	S. M. Andrews (1967)
Nottingham High Sch.	1513	950	.........D£300	D. T. Witcombe (1970)
Oakham, Rutland	1584	710†	£630.....D£340	J. D. Buchanan, M.B.E. (1958)
Oratory, Woodcote, Reading	1859	210	£720.....D£405	W. W. Wilson (1967)
Oundle, Peterborough, Northants	1556	720	£798	B. M. W. Trapnell, Ph.D.
Perse Sch. for Boys, Cambridge	1015	630	£458.....D£198	A. E. Melville (1969) [(1968)
Plymouth College	1877	615	£414.....D£180	C. M. Meade-King (1955)
Pocklington Sch., E. Yorks.	1514	607	£405.....D£171	G. L. Willatt (1966)
Portsmouth Gr. Sch.	1732	725	.........D£204	C. Macdonald (1965)
Prior Park Coll., Bath	1924	240	£534	Rev. J. J. Cowley (1969)
Queen Elizabeth's Gr., Blackburn	1509	900	.........D£195	D. J. Coulson (1965)
Queen Elizabeth Gr. Sch., Wakefield	1591	725	£414.....D£174	J. K. Dudley (1964)
Queen Elizabeth's Hospital, Bristol	1586	400	£420.....D£230	H. G. Edwards, M.B.E. (1967)
Queen Mary's Grammar, Walsall, Staffs.	1554	620	..........Dnil	S. L. Darby (1955)
Queen's College, Taunton, Som.	1843	372	£528.....D£285	S. J. Haynes (1953)
Radley Coll., Abingdon	1847	498	£780	D. R. W. Silk (*Warden*) (1968)
Ratcliffe Coll. (R.C.), Leicester	1847	325	£609	Very Rev. J. F. Morris (1963)
Reed's, Cobham, Surrey	1813	310	£570.....D£360	R. N. Exton (1964)
Rendcomb College, Cirencester, Glos.	1920	160	£435	R. M. A. Medill (1971)
Repton Sch., Derby	1557	486	£795.....D£510	J. F. Gammell, M.C. (1968)
Rossall, Fleetwood, Lancs.	1844	516	£708.....D£432	R. W. Ellis (1967)
Royal Grammar, Lancaster	1469	775	£261.....Dnil	J. L. Spencer, T.D. (1961)
Royal Masonic School, Bushey	1857	440	.........Dnil	H. G. Mullens, T.D. (1957)
Rugby, Warwickshire	1567	700	£780.....D£375	J. S. Woodhouse (1967)
Rydal, Colwyn Bay, Denbighshire	1885	280	£621	P. F. Watkinson (1968)
St. Albans, Herts.	948	650	.........D£210	F. I. Kilvington (1964)
St. Bees, Cumberland	1583	230	£717.....D£360	G. W. Lees (1963)
St. Benedict's, Ealing, W.5 (R.C.)	1902	565	.....D£282–318	Rev. G. G. Brown, O.S.B.
St. Dunstan's, Catford, S.E.6.	1446	840	.........D£240	R. R. Pedley (1967) [(1969)
St. Edmund's, Canterbury	1749	350	£648.....D£405	F. R. Rawes, M.B.E. (1964)
St. Edmund's Coll., Ware, Herts.	1568	350	£624.....D£321	Rev. M. Garvey (1968)
St. Edward's, Oxford	1863	515	£801.....D£575	C. H. Christie (*Warden*) (1971)
St. George's College, Weybridge (R.C.)	1869	567	£615.....D£333	Rev. B. P. Murtough (1958)
St. John's, Leatherhead	1851	345	£720.....D£504	E. J. Hartwell (1970)
St. Lawrence Coll., Ramsgate	1879	370	£684.....D£421	P. H. Harris (1969)
St. Paul's, Lonsdale Road, Barnes, S.W.13 }	1509	670	£627.....D£387	T. E. B. Howarth, M.C., T.D. (*High Master*) (1962)
St. Peter's, York	627	390	£645.....D£300	P. D. R. Gardiner (1967)
Sedbergh, Yorks.	1525	435	£750.....D£375	G. M. C. Thorneley (1954)
Sevenoaks School, Kent	1418	830	£693.....D£345	A. R. Tammadge (1971)
Sherborne, Dorset	1550	609	£798.....D£480	D. A. Emms (1970)
Shrewsbury School	1552	600	£750.....D£350	A. R. D. Wright (1963)
Silcoates School, Wakefield, Yorks.	1820	290	£486.....D£267	R. J. M. Evans, Ph.D. (1960)
Solihull, Warwicks.	1560	910	£555.....D£285	B. H. McGowan (1964)
Stamford, Lincs.	1532	770	£497.....D£201	H. A. Stavely (1968)
Stockport Sch., Cheshire	..	..	..	L. H. Shave (1968)
Stockport Gr. Sch.	..	500	.........D£183	F. W. Scott (1962)
Stonyhurst Coll (R.C.), nr. Whalley, Lancs.	1593	500	£744	Rev. G. H. Earle, S.J. (1963)
Stowe, Bucks.	1923	600	£771	R. Q. Drayson, D.S.C. (1964)
Sutton Valence, Kent	1576	350	£660.....D£405	M. R. Ricketts (1967)
Taunton, Somerset	1847	537	£666.....D£384	N. S. Roberts (1970)
Tettenhall College, Staffs.	1863	353	£480–600 D£306–381	W. J. Dale (1968)
Tonbridge, Kent	1553	557	£741.....D£450	R. M. Ogilvie (1970)
Trent College, Long Eaton, Derbyshire	1866	380	£648.....D£336	A. J. Maltby (1968)
Trinity Sch., Croydon	1596	690	.........D£120	O. C. Berthoud (1952)
Truro, Cornwall	1879	600	£471.....D£204	D. W. Burrell (1959)
(Sir William) Turner's Sch., Redcar, Yorks.	1602	890	£395.......Dnil	S. G. Barker (1953)
University Coll. Sch., Frognal, N.W.3	1830	500	.........D£345	C. D. Black-Hawkins (1956)
Uppingham, Rutland	1584	613	£696.....D£464	J. C. Royds (1965)
Warwick	914	100c	£495–534 D£246–279	P. W. Martin, T.D. (1962)
Wellingborough, Northants	1595	252	£648.....D£390	J. G. Sugden (1965) [(1966)
Wellington Coll., Crowthorne, Berks.	1859	680	£777–789.D£510	Hon. F. F. Fisher, M.C. (*Master*)

† Pupils.

Name of School	F'ded.	No. of Boys	Annual Fees D=Day Boys	Headmaster (With date of Appointment)
Wellington Sch., Somerset..........	1842	454	£480.....D £213	J. C. Stredder (1957)
West Buckland Sch., Barnstaple......	1858	250	£570.....D £243	Rev. G. Ridding (1968)
Westminster, Dean's Yard, S.W.1.....	1560	472	£780.....D £450	J. M. Rae, Ph.D. (1970)
Whitgift, Croydon..................	1596	800	.........D £198	D. A. Raeburn (1970)
William Ellis Sch., Highgate, N.W.5..	1862	650	.............Dnil	S. L. Baxter (1954)
Winchester College.................	1382	530	£867............	J. L. Thorn (1968)
Wolverhampton Gr. Sch., Staffs.....	1512	610	.............Dnil	E. R. Taylor (1956)
Woodhouse Grove Sch., Bradford....	1812	368	£444.....D £186	F. C. Pritchard, Ph.D. (1950)
Worcester College for the Blind......	1866	70	£930............	R. C. Fletcher (1959)
Worcester (Royal Gr.)..............	1291	760	£300.........Dnil	A. G. K. Brown (1950)
Worksop College, Notts*............	1895	396	£780.....D £540	C. H. D. Everett (1970)
Worth School, Crawley, Sussex......	1933	381	£720............	Rev. J. H. D. Gaisford, O.S.B. (1959)
Wrekin Coll., Wellington, Salop.....	1880	380	£681............	G. C. L. Hadden (1971)
Wycliffe Coll., Stonehouse, Glos......	1882	280	£627.....D £330	R. D. H. Roberts (1967)
Scotland				
Daniel Stewart's Coll., Edinburgh 7...	1855	965	£489.....D £189	B. T. Bellis (1965)
The Edinburgh Academy, Edinburgh 3	1824	560	£622.....D £330	H. H. Mills, M.C., Ph.D. (Rector) (1962)
Fettes College, Edinburgh 4.........	1870	450	£750............	A. Chenevix-Trench (1971)
George Heriot's, Edinburgh 3........	1628	1500	.....D £102–108	A. S. McDonald (1970)
George Watson's Coll., Edinburgh....	1723	1500	£489.....D £189	R. W. Young (1958)
Glasgow Academy, Glasgow, W.2.....	1846	940	£486–546 D £144–246	B. M. Holden (Rector) (1959)
Gordonstoun, Elgin, Morayshire......	1934	406†	£858.....D £330	J. W. R. Kempe (1969)
Hutchesons' Gr. Sch., Beaton Road, Glasgow, S.1......................	1641	830	.........D £124	P. Whyte (1966)
Kelvinside Academy, Glasgow........	1878	650	.........D £198	C. J. R. Mair (1958)
Loretto Sch., Musselburgh, Midlothian	1827	240	£510............	R. B. Bruce Lockhart (1960)
Melville College, Edinburgh 3........	1832	589	£429.D £156–195	G. R. B. Sherriff (1962)
Merchiston Castle, Edinburgh 13......	1833	320	£675............	D. J. Forbes (1969)
Robert Gordon's Coll., Aberdeen.....	1729	1216	£390.....D £102	J. Marshall (1960)
Royal High Sch., Edinburgh 1........	1519	1250	.............Dnil	B. T. Ruthven (1965)
Strathallan, Forgandenny, Perthshire..	1912	364	£684............	A. D. D. McCallum, T.D. (1970)
Trinity Coll., Glenalmond, Perthshire.	1847	360	£750............	D. J. Graham-Campbell (Warden) (1964)
Northern Ireland				
Campbell Coll., Belfast..............	1894	485	£514.....D £224	R. M. Morgan (1971) [(1954)
Portora Royal, Enniskillen..........	1608	367	£514.....D £154	Rev. P. H. Rogers, M.B.E.
Royal Belfast Academical Instn.......	1810	1040	.........D £142	S. V. Peskett (Principal) (1959)
Isle of Man				
King William's College..............	1668	365	£699.....D £360	G. R. Rees-Jones (Principal) (1958)
Channel Islands				
Elizabeth Coll. Guernsey.............	1563	620	£440.....D £150	R. A. Wheadon (1972)
Victoria Coll. Jersey................	1852	410	£465.....D £150	M. H. Devenport (1967)
Republic of Ireland				
St. Columba's College, Rathfarnham..	1843	160	£540............	Rev. F. M. Argyle (Warden) [(1949)

* a Woodard Corporation school.

SOCIETY OF HEADMASTERS OF INDEPENDENT SCHOOLS (1961)
Hon. Secretary, S. M. Mischler, M.B.E., Cathedral School, Truro, Cornwall.

Name of School	F'ded.	No. of Boys	Annual Fees D=Day Boys	Headmaster (With date of Appointment)
Austin Friars', Carlisle (R.C.).........	1951	320	£519.....D £246	Rev. B. O'Connor, O.S.A. (1966)
Bearwood Coll., Wokingham, Berks..	1827	310	£715.....D £366	P. M. Cunningham (1963)
Belmont Abbey, Hereford (R.C.).....	1926	280	£585.....D £230	Rev. J. M. Jabalé, O.S.B. (1969)
Bembridge, Isle of Wight............	1919	270	£570.....D £300	P. G. Rendall (1959)
Bentham Grammar, Bentham, Lancs..	1726	406†	£489.....D £216	E. W. T. Kaye (1967)
Churcher's College, Petersfield, Hants..	1722	440	£372.........Dnil	D. Goodfield (1966)
Cotton College, Oakamoor, Staffs.....	1762	200	£420............	Rev. Mgr. T. J. Gavin (1967)
Frensham Heights, Farnham, Surrey...	1925	260†	£800.....D £400	M. Bridgeland (1971)
Grenville College, Bideford, Devon*..	1954	287	£660.....D £312	J. R. Crabbe, O.B.E. (1964)
Keil Sch., Dumbarton...............	1915	183	£585.....D £324	E. S. Jeffs (1962)
Kingham Hill School, Oxford........	1886	210	£570............	E. C. Cooper (1954)

Name of School	F'ded	No. of Boys	Annual Fees D=Day Boys	Headmaster (With date of Appointment)
King's School, Gloucester............	1541	350	£564–594 D£300–330	A. P. David (1969)
Milton Abbey Schl., nr. Blandford, D'set	1954	250	£723.........	W. M. T. Holland (1969)
Oswestry, Shropshire................	1407	270	£503.....D£200	P. G. A. Gem (1966)
Pangbourne College, Berks..........	1917	280	£747.....D£399	P. D. C. Points (1969)
Rannoch School, Perthshire.........	1959	225	£585–645....	P. J. MacLellan (1967)
Rishworth, Nr. Halifax, Yorks.......	1724	350	£525.....D£255	Rev. J. Williams (1968)
Royal Wolverhampton School, Staffs.	1850	300	£570.....D£372	P. G. C. Howard (1961)
Ruthin School, Denbighshire........	1574	150	£594.....D£279	A. S. Hill (1967)
Ryde School, Isle of Wight..........	1921	300	£591.....D£255	K. N. Symons (1966)
Scarborough College, Yorks.........	1898	300	£543.....D£243	D. K. Crews, M.B.E., T.D. (1959)
Seaford College, Petworth, Sussex....	1884	350	£630..........	Rev. C. E. Johnson (1944)
Shebbear College, Beaworthy, Devon.	1841	310	£504.....D£225	G. W. Kingsnorth (1964)
Sidcot School, Winscombe, Somerset..	1808	300†	£654.....D£218	R. N. Brayshaw (1957)
Truro Cathedral, Cornwall..........	1549	209	£490.....D£265	S. M. Mischler, M.B.E. (1937)
Wells Cathedral, Somerset..........	1180	470†	£498–573 D£249–276	A. K. Quilter (1964)

† Pupils. * a Woodard Corporation school. NOTE.—The Headmasters of Abbotsholme School, Bedale's School, Carmel College, Prior Park College, Reed's School, Rendcomb College, St. George's College, Weybridge and Tettenhall College are also members of the Society. Details of these schools are included in the list of Headmasters' Conference schools.

PUBLIC SCHOOLS OVERSEAS

NOTE.—Headmasters of Schools marked (*) are Members of the *Headmasters' Conference*; marked (†) of the *Headmasters' Conference of Australia*.

Name of School	F'ded	No. of Boys	Annual Fees D=Day Boys	Headmaster (With date of Appointment)
South America				
*Markham Coll., Lima, Peru.........	1946	900	.........D£180	R. C. Pinchbeck (1966)
*Queen's Coll., Georgetown, Guyana..	1844	762	...........Dnil	D. Hetram (1963)
*St. George's Coll., Quilmes, Argentine	1898	284	$8,360....D$4,600	C. G. Graham (1968)
India				
*Mayo College, Ajmer..............	1875	670	Rs.3,000 ..DRs.300	S. R. Das (1969)
*Cathedral and John Connon Sch., Bombay	1860	1562	.....DRs.1,020	K. K. Jacob (1969)
*St. Joseph's Coll., Darjeeling.......	1887	472	Rs. 3,330 DRs. 720	Rev. H. Nunn, S.J. (1970)
*St. Paul's, Darjeeling..............	1823	360	Rs.4,000......	D. S. Gibbs (Rector) (1964)
*Doon School, Chand Bagh, Dehra Dun.	1935	515	Rs.3,000	Lt.-Col. E. J. Simeon (1971)
*Scindia Sch., Gwalior.............	1897	662	Rs.2,850...DRs.75	S. P. Sahi (Principal) (1968)
Canada				
*Ashbury Coll., Ottawa............	1891	290	$3,050....D$1,550	W. A. Joyce, D.S.O., E.D. (1966)
Hillfield College, Hamilton, Ont.....	1901	320	....D$1,000–1,400	M. B. Wansbrough (1969)
*Lakefield College Sch., Ontario......	1879	216	$3,200....D$1,850	J. T. M. Guest (1971)
Lower Canada Coll., Montreal......	1909	570	.......D$1,530	G. H. Merrill (1968)
Ridley Coll., St. Catharines, Ont.....	1889	450	$3,100 ...D$1,250	E. V. B. Pilgrim (1962)
*St. Andrew's Coll., Aurora, Ont.....	1899	320	$3,550...D$1,700	J. R. Coulter (1958)
*Trinity Coll. Sch., Port Hope, Ont...	1865	340	$3,400....D$1,550	A. C. Scott (1962)
*Upper Canada Coll., Toronto.......	1829	840	$3,200....D$1,550	P. T. Johnson (Principal) (1965)
Australia				
N.S.W.:—				
*†Armidale Sch., Armidale...........	1894	355	$A1,380..D$A435	A. H. Cash (1962)
†Barker Coll., Hornsby............	1890	920	$A1,350..D$A630	T. J. McCaskill (1963)
*†Sydney C. of E. Gr. Sch., North Sydney	1889	1170	$A1,545..D$A735	B. H. Travers, O.B.E. (1959)
*†Cranbrook Sch. Sydney...........	1918	600	$A1,635–1695 D$A735–795	M. Bishop (1963)
*†The King's Sch., Parramatta.......	1831	906	$A1,395–1,605 D$A630–840	Rev. S. W. Kurrle (1965)
†Knox Gr. Sch., Wahroonga........	1924	1300	$A1,200. D$A600	I. W. Paterson, Ph.D. (1969)
†Newington Coll., Stanmore........	1863	823	$A1,485 ..D$A795	(vacant)
†St. Aloysius Coll. (R.C.), Sydney....	1879	978	......D$A330–390	Rev. T. F. O'Donovan, S.J. (1968)
†St. Ignatius Coll. (R.C.), Riverview, Lane Cove, N.S.W. 2066.......	1880	714	$A1,350..D$A540	Rev. G. F. Jordan, S.J. (1968)
†St. Joseph's Coll. (R.C.), Hunter's Hill	1881	830	$A1,035.......	Rev. Br. A. Dwyer (1970)
*Scots Coll., Sydney...............	1893	1182	$A1,635..D$A765	G. Wilson, M.C. (1966)
*†Sydney Gr. Sch., Sydney..........	1857	1113	$A1,623–1683 D$A738–798	A. M. MacKerras (1969)
†Trinity Gr. Sch., Sydney...........	1913	1072	$A1,518..D$A690	J. W. Hogg (1944)

School	F'ded.	No. of Boys	Annual Fees D = Day Boys	Headmaster (With date of appointment)
Victoria:—				
†Ballarat Coll.	1864	400	$A1,400–1,600 D$A500–700	R. M. Horner (1967)
†Carey Baptist Gr. Sch., Kew	1923	1270	.........D$A750	G. L. Cramer (1965)
†Caulfield Gr. Sch.	1881	987	$A1,110 D$A459–711	B. C. Lumsden (1965)
*†Geelong Coll., Geelong	1861	771	$A1,972..D$A852	P. N. Thwaites (1960)
*†Geelong C. of E. Gr. Sch., Corio	1857	1057	$A2,286..D$A885	T. R. Garnett (1961)
*†Haileybury Coll., E. Brighton	1892	1442	$A1,953..D$A858	D. M. Bradshaw (1954)
†Ivanhoe Gr. Sch.	1915	728	$A1,665..D$A720	V. R. C. Brown (1948)
*†Melbourne, C. of E. Gr. Sch.	1858	1570	$A1,950..D$A960	N. A. H. Creese (1970)
*†Scotch Coll.. Hawthorn, Melbourne	1851	1593	$A1,779–1,800 D$A678–840	C. O. Healey, O.B.E., T.D. (1964)
†Trinity Gr. Sch., Kew	1902	966	$A1,801..D$A796	J. J. Leppitt (1959)
†Wesley Coll., Melbourne	1865	1138	$A2,070 D$A765–900	T. H. Coates, O.B.E., Ph.D.(1957)
†Xavier Coll. (R.C.), Melbourne	1878	735	$A1,290..D$A585	Rev. J. G. Hawkins, S.J. (1968)
Queensland:—				
†All Souls' Sch., Charters Towers	1920	307	$A930...D$A150	M. A. P. Mattingley (1958)
†Brisbane Boys' Coll., Toowong	1902	710	$A1,047..D$A357	A. J. Birtles (1956)
*Brisbane C. of E. Grammar Sch.	1912	1417	$A1,149..D$A435	Hon. C. D. Fisher (1970)
†Brisbane Grammar Sch.	1868	1236	$A1,119..D$A399	M. A. Howell (1965)
†The Southport Sch.	1901	640	$A1,050..D$A450	C. G. Pearce (1951)
†Toowoomba Gr. Sch.	1876	483	$A972...D$A270	W. M. Dent (1970)
South Australia:—				
†Sacred Heart College, Somerton Park	1902	846	$A780...D$A222	Br. C. Pratt (1969)
*†St. Peter's Coll., Adelaide	1847	1038	$A1,500..D$A690	Rev. J. S. C. Miller (1961)
*†Prince Alfred Coll., Adelaide	1869	975	$A1,350..D$A585	G. B. Bean (1970)
†Pulteney Grammar Sch., Adelaide	1847	847	.........D$A519	Rev. Canon W. R. Ray, O.B.E.
*Scotch Coll., Mitcham	1919	630	$A1,440..D$A660	P. A. V. Roff (1970) [(1947)
Western Australia:—				
*†Christ Church Gr. Sch., Claremont	1910	871	$A1,422..D$A747	P. M. Moyes (1951)
†Guildford C. of E. Gr. Sch.	1896	532	$A1,356..D$A711	D. A. L. Davies (1957)
*Hale School, Wembley Downs	1858	800	$A1,500..D$A750	K. G. Tregonning (1967)
†Scotch Coll., Swanbourne	1897	840	$A1,485..D$A714	D. H. Prest (1969)
†Wesley Coll., Perth	1923	770	$A1,425..D$A705	C. A. Hamer (1965)
Tasmania:—				
†Launceston Church Gr. Sch.	1846	381	$A1,567–1,752 D$A290–615	R. P. Hutchings (1971)
†Hutchins Sch., Hobart	1846	540	$A1,128–1,437 D$A330–639	D. R. Lawrence (1964)
†Scotch College, Launceston	1900	313	$A1,047–1,248 D$A94–200	J. T. Sykes (1966)
New Zealand				
*Auckland Gr. Sch.	1869	1236	$NZ420.....Dnil	W. H. Cooper, C.B.E. (1954)
*King's Coll., Otahuhu	1896	600	$NZ870.D$NZ378	G. N. T. Greenbank, O.B.E. [(1946)
Canterbury:—				
*Christchurch Boys' High	1881	1086	$NZ480......Dnil	C. F. S. Caldwell (1959)
*Christ's Coll., Christchurch	1850	593	$NZ1,005D$NZ474	A. M. Brough (1970)
*St. Andrew's Coll., Christchurch	1916	710	$NZ996 D$NZ426	I. T. Galloway, C.B.E., E.D.
*Timaru High Sch.	1880	743	$NZ420......Dnil	R. J. Welch (1965) [(1962)
Nelson College, Nelson	1856	920	$NZ510......Dnil	E. J. Brewster (1969)
New Plymouth Boys' High School	1881	980	$NZ465......Dnil	W. E. Alexander (1967)
*Waitaki Boys' High Sch., Oamaru	1883	900	$NZ460......Dnil	J. H. Donaldson (1961)
*Wanganui Collegiate	1852	508	$NZ1030D $NZ415	T. U. Wells (1960)
Wellington Coll., Wellington	1876	1060	$NZ519......Dnil	S. H. W. Hill (1963)
South Africa				
*St. Andrew's Sch., Bloemfontein	1863	300	R.680....DR.280	B. C. Thiel (1968) [(1964)
*St. Andrew's Coll., Grahamstown	1855	475	R.1,050...DR.468	Rev. Canon J. W. Aubrey
*Diocesan Coll., Rondebosch	1849	400	R.904....DR.484	A. W. H. Mallett (1964)
*St. John's Coll., Johannesburg	1898	754	R.1,124...DR.580	J. J. Breitenbach (1971)
Hilton College, Natal	1872	375	R.1,060............	R. G. Slater (1967)
*Michaelhouse, Balgowan, Natal	1896	430	R.1,180............	R. F. Pennington (1969)
Rhodesia				
*Falcon College, Essexvale	1954	350	$780............	D. E. Turner (1962)
*Peterhouse, Marandellas	1954	380	$840............	B. R. Fieldsend (1968)
*St. George's College, Salisbury	1896	694	$564–600 D$204–240	Rev. J. Brogan, S.J. (1968)
Hong Kong				
St. Stephen's College	1903	270	$HK4,500$HK1,700	Rev. R. B. Handforth (1965)
Kenya				
*Alliance High Schl., Kikuyu	1926	564	EAs625..........	A. C. E. Sanders (1970)
*Nairobi School	1931	760	EAs3,240–7,680 DEAs1,170	F. W. Dollimore (1969)

School	F'ded.	No. of Boys	Annual Fees See note (a) D=Day Boys	Headmaster See notes (b) and (c)
*Lenaha Sch., Nairobi	1949	625	EAs. 2,700 DEAs. 1,000	T. W. Brown, V.R.D. (1965)
West Indies				
*Harrison College, Barbados........	1729	666	............D$14	A. G. Williams (1965)
*Lodge School, St. John, Barbados...	1721	498	$1,560	P. McD. Crichlow (1965)
*Munro College, Jamaica	1856	425	$480.......D$120	R. B. D. Roper (1954)
Wolmer's Sch., Jamaica	1729	701	...........D$165	D. L. Bogle (1966)
Malta				
*St. Edward's College, Cottonera ..	1929	275	£.330	Rev. B. Rickett (1967)

PRINCIPAL GIRLS' SCHOOLS

NOTES:—(a) "Annual Fees" represent average amount payable annually, *exclusive* of fees for optional subjects. (b) "Headmistress." In certain schools other titles prevail, e.g., St. Paul's, "High Mistress." (c) Headmaster.

School	F'ded.	No. of Girls	Annual Fees See note (a) D=Day Girls	Headmistress See notes (b) and (c)
Abbey Sch., Malvern Wells	1880	260	£645............	J. F. Jones (1963)
Abbey Sch., Reading................	1887	670	......D £183–192	S. M. Hardcastle (1960)
Abbots Hill, Hemel Hempstead......	1912	105	£720....D £360	Mrs. J. E. Anderson (1966)
The Alice Ottley Sch., Worcester.....	1883	600	£570.D £165–300	E. D. Millest (1964)
All Hallows, Ditchingham, Bungay, Suffolk	1864	157	£480......D £255	D. M. Forster (1968)
Ashford, Middlesex, St. David's.......	1716	230	£453.....D £288	J. D. Alderson (1954)
Ashford Sch. for Girls, Kent.........	1910	747	£549.....D £276	M. Nightingale (1955)
Ashstead, Surrey, Parsons Mead Sch...	1897	353	£633 D £177–318	M. E. Long (1969)
Badminton Sch., Bristol.............	1858	245	£696.....D £354	M. F. C. Harvey (1969)
Bath, Royal Sch. for Daughters of Officers of the Army..............	1864	325	£600.....D £300	M. Campbell (1968)
Bedford High Sch...................	1882	625	£483–540 D £213–270	E. K. Wallen (1965)
Bedford, Dame Alice Harpur School ..	1882	860	£436.....D £175	S. M. Morse (1970)
Benenden, Kent....................	1924	330	£750...........	E. B. Clarke (1954)
Berkhampsted, Herts...............	1888	495	£507.....D £237	M. R. C. Bateman (1971)
Bilston Girls' High, Staffs..........	1919	400	............Dnil	H. E. Mottershead (1961)
Bishop's Stortford, Herts. & Essex H.S.	1909	600	............Dnil	J. Hammersley (1965)
Blackpool, Elmslie Girls' Sch.........	1918	462	......D £195	E. L. Oldham (1952)
Bolton, Lancs.....................	1877	723	......D £204	M. D. Higginson (1952)
Bradford Girls' Gr. Sch.............	1875	605	......D £158	M. M. Black (1955)
Brentwood, Ursuline Convent High (R.C.)	1900	759	£456.....D £210	Sister Mary Gabriel (1969)
Bridlington High Sch...............	1905	550	£285.......Dnil	D. I. Matthews (1956)
Bruton School for Girls, Som........	1900	621	£486.....D £216	D. F. Cumberlege (1964)
Burgess Hill, Sussex (P.N.E.U.).....	1906	220	£510.....D £195	Mrs. D. E. Harford (1971)
Bury St. Edmunds, East Anglian Sch...	1935	245	£606.....D £312	M. Tuck (1949)
Casterton Sch., Kirkby Lonsdale, Westmorland..........................	1823	330	£585.....D £315	R. Willson (1963)
Charters Towers, Bexhill on Sea, Sussex	1929	260	£600...........	E. M. McGarry (1946)
Chatham, Grammar Sch. for Girls.....	1907	560	............Dnil	H. Evans (1962)
Chelmsford County High Sch........	1907	673	............Dnil	P. Pattison (1961)
Cheltenham Ladies' College.........	1853	841	£702.....D £405	M. G. Hampshire (*Princ.*) (1964)
Chester, Ursuline Convent Sch. (R.C.).	1850	538	......D £158	Sister Mary Paul Flood, O.S.U) (1951)
Christ's Hospital, Hertford..........	1552	300	Various.........	E. M. Tucker (1971)
Church Education Corporation (35 Denison House, Westminster, S.W.1):				
Bedgebury Park, Goudhurst, Kent..	1920	180	£615............	J. M. Nixon (1964)
Uplands, Sandecotes, Parkstone.....	1903	150	£585.....D £255	M. P. Poots (1971)
Church Schools Company (29 Euston Road, N.W.1):				
Eothen, Caterham, Surrey..........	1892	251	......D £156–300	J. Harrison (1955)
Guildford High Sch................	1888	502	......D £180–270	M. J. Harley-Mason (1969)
Hull High Sch., Tranby Croft......	1890	441	£366–384 D £180–284	H. W. Thompson (1956)
Southampton (Atherley Sch.).......	1926	294	......D £180–270	U. V. Laidlaw (1950)
Sunderland Church High Sch.......	1884	348	......D £159–225	J. L. Wisbach (1957)
Surbiton High Sch................	1884	461	......D £180–270	E. M. Kobrak (1964)
York College.....................	1908	353	......D £180–270	M. G. Drury (1966)
Clevedon, St. Brandon's Sch........	1831	290	£597.....D £279	(c) P. Searle (1971)
Clifton High Sch. for Girls..........	1877	740	£597.....D £261	P. M. Stringer (1965)

School	F'ded.	No. of Girls	Annual Fees (See note (a)) D=Day Girls	Headmistress See notes (b) and (c)
Cobham Hall, Kent.................	1962	275	£720.....D £375	D. B. Hancock (1961)
Colston's, Bristol..................	1891	645	.........D £225	A. M. S. Dunn (1954)
Commonweal Lodge, Purley, Surrey..	1916	200	......D £75–315	J. M. Blunden (1966)
Cranborne Close Sch., Tisbury, Wilts..	1946	160	£705.....D £379	(c) M. D. Neal (1969)
Croft House Sch., Shillingstone, Dorset	1941	185	£594.....D £279	Mrs. E. H. Warley (1971)
Croham Hurst, South Croydon, Surrey	1899	430	.........D £375	D. J. Seward (1970)
Derby High Sch....................	1892	350	.........D £222	D. M. Hatch (1957)
Dolgellau, Dr. Williams' Sch........	1878	230	£600.....D £270	N. Lloyd-Jones (1969)
Doncaster, Grammar School for Girls .	1905	400	.........D nil	H. V. Mellor (1949)
Downe Hse., Cold Ash, Newbury, Berks.	1907	270	£660...........	Mrs. L.Wilson (1967)
Durham High Sch..................	1884	365	.........D £240	C. I. Salter (1958)
Edgbaston High, Birmingham........	1876	881	.........D £236	V. R. Belton (1967)
Edgbaston C. of E. Coll............	1886	475	....D £135–225	M. E. Joice (1967)
Edgehill Coll., Bideford, N. Devon...	1884	560	£444.....D £195	A. M. Shaw (1955)
Ely High School..................	1905	384	.........D nil	E. Moody (1966)
Exeter, Maynard's Girls' Sch........	1658	548	..........£168	J. M. Bradley (1963)
Farnborough Hill, Hants............	1889	500	£510.....D £255	Sr. M. Dawson (1971)
Farringtons, Chislehurst, Kent......	1911	352	£615.....D £417	J. M. Smith (1968)
Felixstowe College, Suffolk..........	1929	320	£627.....D £314	E. M. Manners, T.D. (1967)
Girls' Public Day School Trust (26 Queen Anne's Gate, Westminster, S.W.1):				
Bath High.......................	1875	586	£417.....D £192	J. Chapman (1969)
Birkenhead High..................	1901	795	.........D £192	F. Kellett (1971)
Blackheath High..................	1880	528	.........D £201	F. M. Abraham (1962)
Brighton and Hove High..........	1876	580	£456.....D £192	J. P. Turner (1969)
Bromley High....................	1883	698	.........D £201	P. M. F. Reid (1971)
Croydon High....................	1874	1101	.........D £201	E. B. J. Cameron (1960)
Ipswich High....................	1878	559	.........D £192	P. M. Hayworth (1971)
Liverpool (Belvedere).............	1880	562	.........D £192	M. C. L. Ward (1962)
Newcastle (Central) High..........	1895	719	.........D £192	C. Russell (1962)
Norwich High....................	1875	661	.........D £192	D. F. Bartholomew (1954)
Nottingham High.................	1875	895	.........D £192	L. L. Lewenz (1967)
Notting Hill and Ealing High......	1873	591	.........D £201	J. M. S. Hendry (1960)
Oxford High.....................	1875	518	£432.....D £192	Mrs. H. M. Warnock (1966)
Portsmouth High.................	1882	562	.........D £192	M. L. Clarke (1968)
Putney High.....................	1893	647	.........D £201	R. Smith (1963)
Sheffield High...................	1878	591	.........D £192	M. C. Lutz (1959)
Shrewsbury High.................	1885	560	.........D £192	M. Crane (1963)
South Hampstead High............	1876	581	.........D £201	Mrs. S. Wiltshire (1969)
Streatham Hill and Clapham High..	1887	460	.........D £201	I. A. Wulff (1963)
Sutton High......................	1884	898	.........D £201	J. R. Glover (1959)
Sydenham High...................	1887	572	.........D £201	M. I. J. Hamilton (1966)
Wimbledon High.................	1880	612	.........D £201	Mrs. A. A. Piper (1962)
Godolphin, Salisbury..............	1726	300	£657.....D £339	V. M. Fraser (1968)
Gravesend Sch....................	1914	520	.............D nil	Mrs. M. Dell (1971)
Gt. Crosby, Lancs. Seafield Gr. Sch., Sacred Heart of Mary (R.C.)......	1908	658	.........D £141	Sr. S. Murphy (1971)
Greenacre, Banstead, Surrey........	1933	310	£600....D £300	G. W. Steele (1962)
Harrogate College, Harrogate.......	1893	433	£678.....D £336	M. W. S. Todd (1952)
Haslemere, Royal Naval Sch........	1840	260	£605....D £309	D. M. Otter (1970)
Hawnes, Haynes Park, Beds.........	1929	210	£540..........	E. M. J. Webber (1971)
Headington Sch., Oxford...........	1915	498	£612–654	
			D £114–330	P. A. Dunn (1959)
Hollington Park, St. Leonards, Sussex..	1860	160	£150–180........	A. M. Amos (1960)
Howells', Denbigh.................	1859	395	£681....D £339	J. Sadler (1968)
Howell's, Llandaff.................	1860	535	£410....D £174	M. Ll. Lewis (1941)
Hulme Gr. Sch., Oldham...........	1887	403	.........D £165	E. M. Crabtree (1968)
Hunmanby Hall, Yorks.............	1928	312	£627.....D £321	M Bray 1967)
Ipswich, Northgate Gr.............	1906	600	.........D nil	E. J. Atkinson (1957)
King Edward VI High Sch., B'ham...	1883	520	.........D £135	J. R. F. Wilks (1965)
King's High Sch., Warwick.........	1879	616	.........D £174	M. Leahy (1970)
Lady Eleanor Holles, Hampton, Middx.	1710	720	.........D £276	R. Garwood-Scott (1950)
Leamington, Kingsley Sch..........	1884	376	£444–507	
			D £153–273	N. K. Jones (1961)
Leeds Girls' High.................	1876	809	.........D £155	A. A. Jackson (1970)
Lillesden Sch., Hawkhurst, Kent.....	1901	140	£591.....D £330	D. M. Mills (1965)
Lincoln, Christ's Hosp. Girls' High Sch.	1893	570	.........D nil	Mrs. S. M. Wood (1970)
Liverpool, Huyton College..........	1894	355	£732.....D £432	Mrs. E. Rees (1971)
Liverpool (Everton Valley), Notre Dame Collegiate (R.C.).................	1869	596	.........D £149	[(1966) Sr. Marie Philippa, S.N.D.
Liverpool (Woolton), Notre Dame High Sch. (R.C.)...............	1852	917	.........D nil	M. M. Taylor, S.N.D. (1970)

School	F'ded.	No. of Girls	Annual Fees See note (a) D=Day Girls	Headmistress See note (b) and (c)
London*:				
C. E. Brooke Sch., Langton Rd., S.W.9	1898	360	............Dnil	C. F. A. Frazer (1970)
Burlington Wood Lane, W.12......	1699	550	............Dnil	Mrs. E. Moore (1967)
Camden, Sandall Rd., N.W.5......	1871	700	............Dnil	A. M. Dennis (1969)
Channing Sch., Highgate, N.6.....	1885	360	......D £168–351	E. M. Saunders (1964)
City of London, Barbican, E.C.2....	1894	470	........D £276	G. M. Colton (1949)
Godolphin and Latymer, W.6.......	1905	660	............Dnil	M. C. Gray (1963)
Haberdashers' Aske's Acton, W.3...	1690	720	.........Various	J. C. Gillett (1969)
Haberdashers' Aske's, Hatcham, S.E.14	1690	570	............Dnil	J. A. Kirby (1958)
Francis Holland, Clarence Gate, N.W.1.	1878	320	........D £327	Mrs. H. Brigstocke (1965)
Francis Holland, Graham Terr., S.W.1	1881	276	..D £198–327	R. Colvile (1965)
James Allen's Girls', Dulwich, S.E.22	1741	530	........D £240	I. Prissian (1969)
Lady Margaret, Parsons Green, S.W.6	1917	400	............Dnil	A. E. Cavendish (1971)
Mary Datchelor, Camberwell Green, S.E.5............................	1877	640	............Dnil	E. B. Godwin (1968)
North London Collegiate, Canons, Edgware.........................	1850	850	........D £180	M. M. N. McLaughlan (1965)
Prendergast Grammar, Catford, S.E.6	1890	600	............Dnil	C. M. Johnson (1957)
Queen's College, Harley Street, W.1.	1848	270	........D £285	S. C. P. Fierz (1964)
St. Angela's, Ursuline Convent Sch., Forest Gate, E.7 (R.C.)...........	1862	912	............Dnil	M. M. Mylod, o.s.u. (1967)
St. Paul's Girls' Sch., Brook Green, W.	1904	516	........D £324	Mrs. A. Munro, c.b.e. (1964)
St. Saviour's and St. Olave's Gr., New Kent Rd., S.E.1	1903	500	............Dnil	E. M. Wilson (1959)
Loughborough High Sch., Leicestershire	1850	550	£342.....D £147	P. J. Hadley (1963)
Loughton High Sch.	1906	650	............Dnil	M. E. Heald (1945)
Lowther College, nr. Rhyl..........	1900	240	£657.....D £315	G. E. Kelly (1963)
Luckley-Oakfield, Wokingham, Berks.	1894	170	£525.....D £255	R. A. Cooper (1971)
Malvern Girls' College..............	1893	465	£675.....D £345	Miss V. M. H. Owen (1968)
Manchester High Sch. for Girls......	1874	950	........D £172	K. L. Cottrell (1959)
Manchester, Withington Girls' Sch...	1890	550	........D £154	M. Hulme (1961)
Merchant Taylors', Gt. Crosby.......	1888	439	........D £183	M. E. Walsh (1963)
Monmouth Sch. for Girls............	1892	460	£429.....D £168	A. Page (1960)
Newcastle upon Tyne Church High Sch.	1885	600	..D £180–210	M. B. Lewis (1965)
Northampton High Sch..............	1878	760	........D £147	S. J. Lightburne (1964)
North Foreland Lodge, Sherfield-on-Loddon, Hants....................	1909	150	£696...........	D. R. K. Irvine (1967)
Northwood Coll., Northwood, Middx.	1878	460	£477–531 D £135–276	M. D. Hillyer-Cole (1966)
Norwich, Blyth.....................	1889	†900	............Dnil	Mrs. V. M. Glauert (1965)
Oakdene, Beaconsfield..............	1911	376	£540.....D £315	A. J. Havard (1959)
Orme Girls' Sch.,Newcastle under Lyme	1876	635	............Dnil	Mrs. W. M. G. Barlow (1969)
Overstone Sch., Northampton........	1929	175	£585...........	(c) J. W. Airs (1968)
Palmer's Girls' School, Grays, Essex...	1700	560	............Dnil	K. W. H. Jackson (1962)
Pate's Gr. Sch., Cheltenham........	1905	765	............Dnil	M. M. Moon (1971)
Penrhos Coll., Colwyn Bay..........	1880	300	£693–726.......	M. Waddington (1966)
Perse Sch. for Girls, Cambridge.....	1881	580	........D £176	C. M. Bedson (1967)
Plymouth, Notre Dame High (R.C.)..	1860	430	........D £164	Sister V. Henderson (1968)
Polam Hall, Darlington.............	1848	395	£543–594 D £123–282	Mrs. K. M. Davies (1963)
Preston, Winckley Sq. Convent (R.C.)	1875	649	........D £155	Sr. C. Walsh (1968)
Princess Helena Coll., Temple Dinsley, Hitchin. Herts....................	1820	130	£585.....D £315	(c) D. Clarke, ph.d. (1971)
Prior's Field, Godalming, Surrey.....	1902	200	£690...........	Mrs. F. M. Hiles (1964)
Queen Anne's, Caversham..........	1894	325	£597...........	M. J. Challis (1958)
Queen Ethelburga's, Harrogate‡.....	1912	200	£660...........	D. Tweed (1966)
Queen Margaret's, Escrick Park, York‡	1901	260	£600...........	B. D. Snape (1960)
Queen Mary, Lytham...............	1930	830	........D £147	J. Charlton (1970)
Queen's Sch., Chester..............	1878	583	........D £165	E. N. MacLean (1947)
Queenswood, Hatfield, Herts........	1894	426	£735...........	A. E. M. Essame (1943)
Redland High Sch., Bristol.........	1882	577	........D £149	W. Hume (1970)
Red Maid's, Bristol................	1634	306	£324.....D £177	D. D. Dakin (1960)
Rochester Gr. Sch., Kent...........	1888	624	............Dnil	N. C. Day (1962)
Roedean, Brighton.................	1885	405	£732...........	(c) J. M. Hunt (1971)
Rosemead, Littlehampton...........	1919	230	£600...........	Mrs. N. R. Tobenhouse (1969)
Royal Masonic Sch.,Rickmansworth Pk.	1788	350	Nil...........	Mrs. U. J. Campbell (1959)
Runton Hill, W. Runton, Norfolk....	1911	140	£570...........	(c) K. Fisher (1971)
Rye St. Antony, Oxford............	1930	166	£510.....D £240	J. B. King (1930)
St. Albans High School, Herts.......	1907	520	....D £156–285	M. E. Denham (1966)
St. Audries, West Quantoxhead, Som..	1906	182	£612.....D £267	L. M. Ayres (1967)

* See also: Girls' Public Day School Trust, and Church Schools Company. † Pupils.
‡ a Woodard Corporation school.

School	F'ded.	No. of Girls	Annual Fees See note (a) D = Day Girls	Headmistress See notes (b) and (c)
St. Catherine's, Bramley, Guildford...	1885	300	£600.....D £336	B. Platt (1970)
St. Clare, Polwithen, Penzance‡.......	1885	210	£537.....D £279	M. M. Coney (1969)
St. Dominic's High Sch., Stoke-on-Trent (R.C.)	1857	700	.........D £156	Sr. Mary Edward (1970)
St. Elphin's, Darley Dale, Matlock....	1844	420	£507.....D £264	P. M. Robinson (1958)
St. Felix, Southwold, Suffolk.........	1897	399	£600.....D £285	M. Oakeley (1958)
St. Helen and St. Katharine, Abingdon.	1903	420	£414.....D £165	F. P. B. Hayward (1968)
St. Helen's, Northwood...............	1899	607	£552-609 D £195-315	J. D. Leader (1966)
St. James's School, West Malvern.....	1896	206	£250.....D £135	R. R. Braithwaite (1969)
St. Joseph's Coll., Bradford (R.C.)....	1908	1050	£423.....D £159	Sr. Wilfrid, C.P. (1965)
St. Margaret's, Bushey, Herts........	1749	344	£606.....D £276	B. Scatchard (1965)
St. Mary & St. Anne, Abbots Bromley‡	1874	491	£600.....D £315	M. E. Roch (1953)
St. Mary Sch., Baldslow, St. Leonard's.	1913	211	£420.....D £195	Sr. B. Allen (1958)
St. Mary's, Calne, Wilts.............	1873	221	£636.....D £306	E. M. Gibbins (1947)
St. Mary's Convent, Cambridge (R.C.)	1908	600	£360.....D £180	Sr. M. Christopher (1949)
St. Mary's Sch., Gerrard's Cross, Bucks.	1872	200	.....D £225-315	(c) Rev. V. J. Bailey (1969)
St. Mary's Sch., Wantage, Berks......	1873	240	£615.............	Sr. Anne Julian, C.S.M.V. (1967)
S. Michael's, Burton Park, Petworth‡.	1844	260	£696.............	P. M. Lancaster (1962)
St. Stephen's College, Broadstairs.....	1867	175	£390-615 D £90-345	J. Selby-Lowndes (1968)
St. Swithin's, Winchester.............	1884	435	£648 .....D £342	P. M. C. Evans (1963)
Salford, Adelphi House (R.C.)........	1852	700	.........D £168	Sr. Mary Gray (1967)
Sheffield, Notre Dame High (R.C.)....	1885	780	.........D £155	Sr. Helen Mary, S.N.D. (1965)
Sherborne Sch. for Girls, Dorset.....	1899	435	£645.....D £321	D. Reader Harris (1950)
Southend-on-Sea High Sch............	1913	730	.........D nil	M. R. Haine (1969)
Stamford High Sch., Lincs...........	1876	748	£431.....D £168	M. L. Medcalf (1968)
Stonar, Atworth, Melksham, Wilts....	1923	330	£639.....D £294	F. D. Denmark (1962)
Stover Sch., Newton Abbot..........	1932	110	£507.....D £264	C. A. Smith (1969)
Talbot Heath Sch., Bournemouth......	1886	565	£388.....D £154	A. L. Macpherson, Ph.D. (1956)
Teesside High Sch. for Girls, Eaglescliffe	1970	500	.........D £219	M. E. Hardwick (1971)
Tormead, Cranley Road, Guildford...	1905	430	£540.....D £270	M. C. Shackleton (1959)
Truro High Sch.....................	1880	503	£525.....D £213	E. J. Davis (1971)
Tudor Hall, Wykham Park, Banbury..	1850	145	£705.............	M. R. Blyth (1969)
Upper Chine, Shanklin, I.O.W.	1799	302	£525.....D £270	P. M. Gifford (1955)
Wadhurst College...................	1930	250	£549.....D £363	R. G. Barclay (1969)
Walsall, Queen Mary's High Sch......	1893	572	.........D nil	Mrs. B. E. Richardson (1968)
Walthamstow Hall, Sevenoaks, Kent..	1838	562	£400.....D £173	E. B. Davies, M.B.E. (1970)
Watford Gr. Sch., Herts.............	1704	827	.........D nil	J. Tennet (1957)
Wentworth Milton Mt., Bournemouth	1899	260	£492.....D £240	N. A. E. Hibbert (1961)
Westcliff-on-Sea High Sch............	1926	840	.........D nil	J. K. Raeburn (1952)
Westonbirt, Tetbury, Glos...........	1928	310	£750.....D £375	M. Newton (1965)
Westwood House, Peterborough......	1936	350	£495.....D £255	Mrs. G. J. Bowis (1960)
Wheelwright Grammar Sch.,Dewsbury	1888	355	.........D nil	D. M. Levitt (1963)
Wigan Girls' High Sch., Lancs........	1887	630	.........D nil	(c) J. Robinson (1971)
Wycombe Abbey, Bucks..............	1896	415	£780.............	P. A. Fisher (1962)
Wyggeston Girls' Sch., Leicester......	1878	615	.........D nil	M. E. Pedley (1948)
York, The Mount School.............	1831	250	£648.............	J. Blake (1960)

Scotland

School	F'ded.	No. of Girls	Annual Fees	Headmistress
Craigholme, Glasgow................	1894	600	.....D £102-129	G. MacLean (1962)
George Watson's Ladies, Edinburgh...	1871	980	.........D £189	H. Fleming (1958)
High School, Glasgow...............	1878	610	.........D £45	H. E. Jamieson (1969)
Hutcheson's Girls' Gr. Sch., Glasgow..	1876	895	.........D £124	I. G. McIver (1948)
James Gillespie's, Edinburgh.........	1803	790	.........D nil	M. G. McIver (1967)
Laurel Bank, Glasgow...............	1903	600	.....D £106-147	A. J. B. Sloan (1968)
Mary Erskine, Edinburgh............	1894	970	.........D £138	J. Thow (1967)
Morrison's Academy Crieff...........	1860	477	£450 .....D £153	M. Baillie (1965)
Park Sch., 25 Lynedoch Ter., Glasgow...	1879	495	.....D £134-182	J. Lightwood (1962)
St. Bride's, Helensburgh.............	1895	413	£435-450 D £110-158	R. D. Smith (1953)
St. Columba's, Kilmacolm...........	1897	526	.....D £138-192	E. M. Clark (1966)
St. Denis', Edinburgh	1858	455	£585.....D £255	Mrs. N. E. Law (1971)
St. George's, Garscube Terr., Edinburgh	1888	650	£534-585 D £234-285	Mrs. J. O. Lindsay (1960)
St. Leonards, St. Andrews, Fife.......	1877	439	£672.....D £270	M. Hamilton (1970)

Channel Islands, etc.

School	F'ded.	No. of Girls	Annual Fees	Headmistress
Buchan Sch., Castletown, I.O.M......	1875	229	£486.....D £234	Mrs. J. M. Watkin (1961)
Jersey College for Girls, Jersey.......	1888	520	.........D £150	E. M. Farewell (1960)
Châtelard Sch., Les Avants, Montreux, Switzerland..................	1927	210	Sw. Frs.7,575-10,500	J. M. Blacklock (1960)

‡ a Woodard Corporation school.

THE ROYAL HOUSE

(1970) Oct. 3. The Queen was present at luncheon given by Prime Minister at Chequers for President Nixon. **7.** The Prince of Wales left Heathrow Airport to visit Fiji, the Gilbert and Ellice Islands, Bermuda and Barbados; he returned on Oct. 26. **16.** Queen Elizabeth the Queen Mother visited Fettes College on occasion of its centenary celebrations.

Nov. 2. Princess Alexandra and Mr. Angus Ogilvy left Gatwick Airport for the Argentine; they returned on Nov. 10. **4.** The Queen was present at service in Westminster Abbey on occasion of inauguration of General Synod of Church of England; Her Majesty later addressed the Synod. It was announced that Order of the Bath would in future admit women members. **5.** Princess Margaret visited Sunderland and opened new town hall and civic centre. **8.** The Queen and the Duke of Edinburgh laid a wreath at Cenotaph on Remembrance Day. **9.** Queen Elizabeth the Queen Mother, accompanied by Princess Margaret and Lord Snowdon, was present at variety performance at Palladium Theatre in aid of Variety Artistes' Benevolent Fund.

Dec. 23. The Queen and the Duke of Edinburgh arrived at Windsor Castle to spend Christmas with other members of Royal Family. **30.** Her Majesty and the Duke of Edinburgh, with Queen Elizabeth the Queen Mother, arrived at Sandringham.

(1971) Jan. 1. New Year's Honours List was published naming three new life peers. **20.** The Queen visited Stirling. **Feb. 2.** The Duke of Edinburgh left R.A.F. Marham to join *Britannia* for two-month tour of Pacific Islands and Australia; on following day Princess Alexandra and Earl Mountbatten left Heathrow Airport for Panama to join His Royal Highness on *Britannia*. **4.** The Queen arrived at Buckingham Palace from Sandringham. **5.** Prince of Wales visited Chester. **10.** Her Majesty visited Star and Garter Home for Disabled Sailors, Soldiers and Airmen at Richmond upon Thames. **17.** The Queen visited the Central Criminal Court. **26.** Her Majesty visited Harrow School on occasion of quater-centenary of school's foundation.

March 2. Prince of Wales was admitted to freedom of City of London at the Guildhall. **3.** The Duchess of Kent opened the Arkwright School at Irchester, Northants. **7.** Queen Elizabeth the Queen Mother visited Eton College and opened restored school library; on following day she attended Royal Film Performance in London with Princess Margaret and Prince William of Gloucester. **8.** Prince of Wales arrived at R.A.F. College, Cranwell, for five-month flying course. **22.** The Duchess of Kent opened Sheppey School, Isle of Sheppey. **23.** Princess Anne visited Manchester. **29.** The Queen and Queen Elizabeth the Queen Mother were present at Royal Albert Hall grand centenary concert. **31.** Princess Margaret and Lord Snowdon left Heathrow Airport to visit Paris; they returned on April 2.

April 2. Princess Anne opened new St. Pancras Library and Shaw Theatre. **5.** The Queen and the Duke of Edinburgh arrived at Windsor Castle. **7.** The Queen and the Duke visited Birmingham. **8.** Her Majesty distributed Royal Maundy money outside Tewkesbury Abbey. **13.** Princess Alexandra and Mr. Angus Ogilvy left Heathrow Airport for New Zealand.

THE ROYAL VISIT TO BRITISH COLUMBIA. **May. 3.** The Queen and the Duke of Edinburgh, with Princess Anne, left Heathrow Airport for British Columbia; they subsequently arrived in Vancouver and then boarded *Britannia* for crossing to Victoria, where their tour of the province officially began. **11.** The royal party returned to Victoria and attended state banquet at Government House; on following day they left Vancouver by air for London, where they arrived early on May 13.

May 4. Queen Elizabeth the Queen Mother visited Cheltenham. **10.** It was announced that the Queen, the Duke of Edinburgh and Princess Anne would visit Turkey in October. **11.** Princess Margaret carried out engagements in East Riding of Yorkshire. **23.** The Queen and the Duke of Edinburgh, with the Prince of Wales, visited Eton College. **24.** Her Majesty and other members of the Royal Family attended Chelsea Flower Show. **26.** Princess Anne visited Wolverhampton, Sutton Coldfield and Birmingham. **27.** It was announced that Mr. Lester Pearson, former Prime Minister of Canada, Sir George Edwards, chairman of British Aircraft Corporation and Sir Isaiah Berlin, the philosopher, had been appointed members of Order of Merit. **28.** Her Majesty visited Maldon, Essex, on occasion of octocentenary celebrations of granting of town's charter, and Wixoe to inaugurate Essex River Authority's Ely Ouse Scheme.

June 1. Princess Anne visited borough of Weymouth and Melcombe Regis on occasion of its 400th anniversary celebrations. **2.** The Queen and the Duke of Edinburgh, with other members of Royal Family, watched the Derby. **3.** Princess Anne left Heathrow Airport to visit Norway; she returned four days later. **8.** Queen Elizabeth the Queen Mother visited Derby; on following day she visited Manchester. **10.** The Queen launched guided missile destroyer, the *Sheffield*, during visit to Barrow-in-Furness. **12.** The Queen's Birthday Honours List was published naming only one new life peer, Major Chichester-Clark, former Prime Minister of Northern Ireland. **14.** The Queen and the Duke of Edinburgh, with Princess Anne, arrived at Windsor Castle. **15, 16, 17 and 18.** Her Majesty, with the Duke of Edinburgh, was present at Ascot Races. **21.** The Queen arrived at Buckingham Palace and later watched Test match between England and Pakistan at Lord's; on following day Her Majesty and the Duke of Edinburgh attended Royal Tournament at Earls Court. **24.** Her Majesty visited Manchester and Liverpool, where she declared second Mersey Tunnel open. **25.** Princess Anne visited Hull. **28.** The Queen and the Duke of Edinburgh visited York in celebration of city's 1,900th anniversary, and later travelled to Holyroodhouse. Princess Anne visited Durham and Newcastle upon Tyne. **29.** Her Majesty and the Duke of Edinburgh, with Princess Anne, visited Dunbartonshire.

July 1. Princess Anne visited Fife, and on following day opened Erskine Bridge over River Clyde. **2.** Princess Alexandra presented trophies at Wimbledon Lawn Tennis Championships. **5.** Her Majesty and the Duke of Edinburgh, with Princess Anne, arrived at Buckingham Palace. **6.** Princess Margaret visited North Riding of Yorkshire. **21.** The Queen and the Duke of Edinburgh, and Princess Margaret, attended Royal International Horse Show at Empire Pool, Wembley. **22.** Her Majesty was present at Test match between England and India at Lord's. **23.** Princess Alexandra opened Brixton extension of Victoria Underground Line. **28.** The Prince of Wales made 1,200 feet parachute jump into the English Channel as part of his R.A.F. training.

Aug. 2. A 21st birthday party for Princess Anne was held aboard *Britannia* in Portsmouth. **6.** The Duke of Edinburgh, with the Prince of Wales and Princess Anne, was at Hamble to welcome Chay

THE ROYAL VISIT TO BRITISH COLUMBIA

The Queen is seen with a group of Indian people at Kamloops in British Columbia during the Royal tour of the province in May.

THE QUEEN OPENS THE NEW MERSEY TUNNEL

The Queen is seen walking along the approach road to the second Mersey Tunnel, which she opened in Liverpool on June 24.

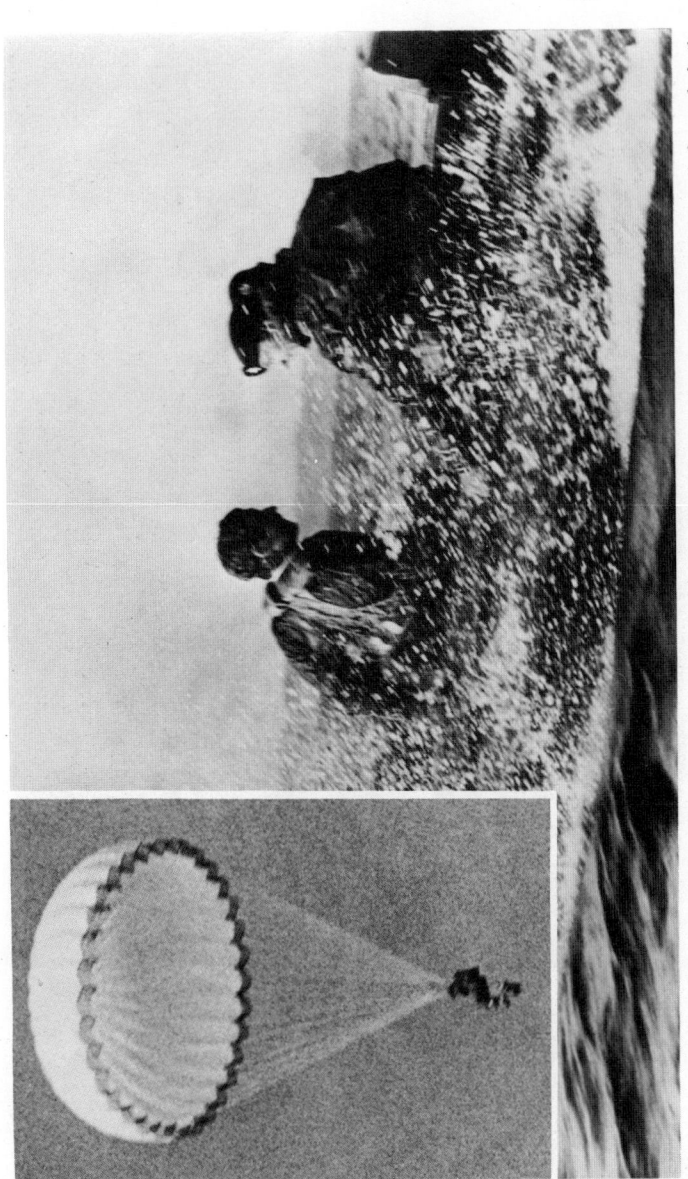

A ROYAL PARACHUTIST

The Prince of Wales is shown making a 1,200 foot parachute jump into the English Channel on July 28, as part of his R.A.F. training, and afterwards, in the rubber dinghy by which he was picked up.

GENERAL DE GAULLE

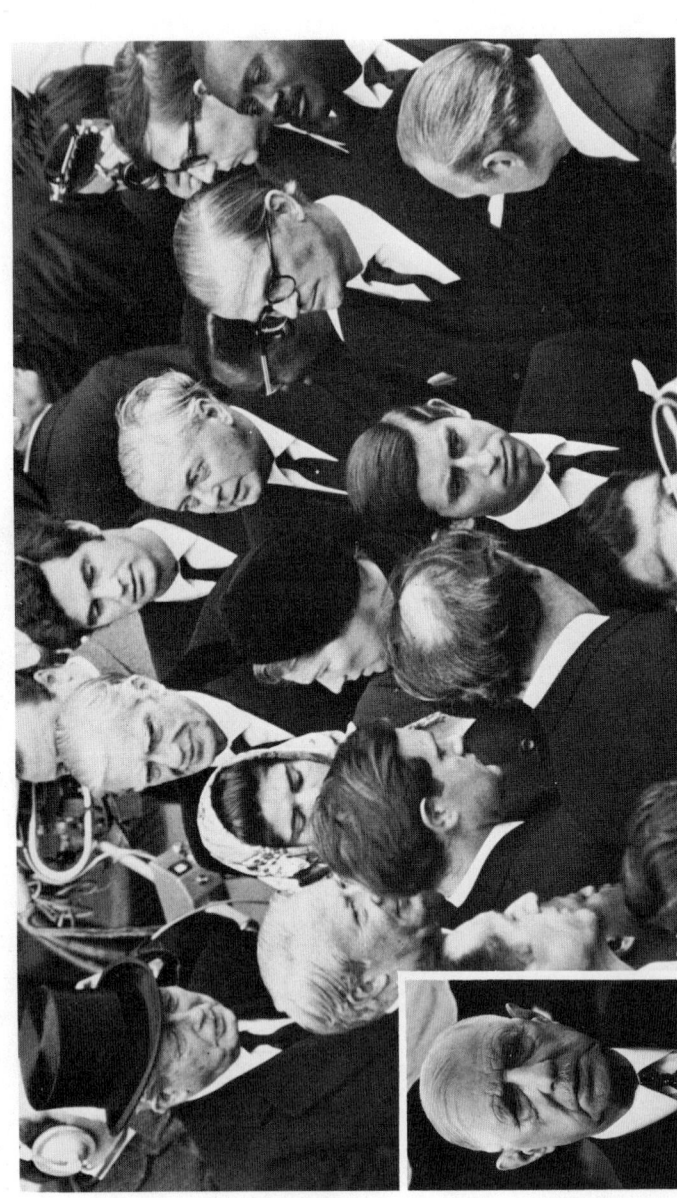

General Charles de Gaulle, French war leader and former President of the French Republic, was buried on November 12, 1970, in the village of Colombey-les-Deux Églises, three days after his death at the age of 79. On the same day, the Prince of Wales, Mr. Heath, the Earl of Avon, Mr. Macmillan and Mr. Wilson are seen leaving Notre Dame Cathedral in Paris after attending a requiem mass.

NORTHERN IRELAND

Northern Ireland was troubled during the year by increasingly violent disturbances. British troops are shown facing stone-throwing rioters in the Bogside area of Londonderry.

THE IBROX PARK DISASTER

The steps leading from the terrace at Ibrox Park, Glasgow, where sixty-six spectators were crushed to death when a barrier collapsed at the end of the Rangers *v.* Celtic football match on January 2.

A bitter civil war erupted in East Pakistan in March after the province had declared its independence.
A few of the thousands of refugees who flocked to India are seen (*above*) preparing to board a bus to take
them to the border.   Dwellings (*below*) completely destroyed by the cyclone and vast tidal wave which
swept the Ganges Delta in November 1970, killing thousands of people in the coastal region of East
Pakistan.

THE LUNAR ROVER

The rover vehicle, in which the *Apollo 15* astronauts travelled on the Moon in July and August, is shown standing on the lunar surface.

THE POST OFFICE STRIKE

A woman outside a post office displaying a " closed " notice during the strike by postal and telephone workers, which began on January 20 and lasted for nearly seven weeks. Some post offices remained open for the payment of pensions.

THE COMMON MARKET

Mr. Geoffrey Rippon, Chancellor of the Duchy of Lancaster, is seen holding the White Paper on the terms negotiated for British entry into the Common Market during his talks with the member countries in Luxemburg in June.

THE DECIMAL COINS

On February 15, decimal currency became the official currency of the United Kingdom. The illustration shows the six coins involved in the changeover—the new halfpenny, the new penny, and the two, five, ten and fifty new pence pieces.

HONOURED IN 1971

Among those honoured in 1971 were Agatha Christie, the writer, who was appointed a D.B.E., Sir Arthur Bliss, Master of the Queen's Music (*top right*), who was made a Companion of Honour, Mr. Terence Rattigan, the playwright (*bottom left*), and Mr. Charles Clore, the financier, who both received knighthoods.

THE DEATHS OF FAMOUS MEN

Two British war leaders (*above*), *Marshal of the Royal Air Force* Viscount Portal of Hungerford, who died at the age of 77 on April 22, and *Field-Marshal* Viscount Slim, also remembered as Governor-General of Australia, who died on December 14, 1970, aged 79.　Two other famous men to die during the year were Lord Goddard, Lord Chief Justice of England from 1946 to 1958 (*bottom right*), who died at the age of 94 on May 29, and Igor Stravinsky, the composer, who died on April 6, aged 88.

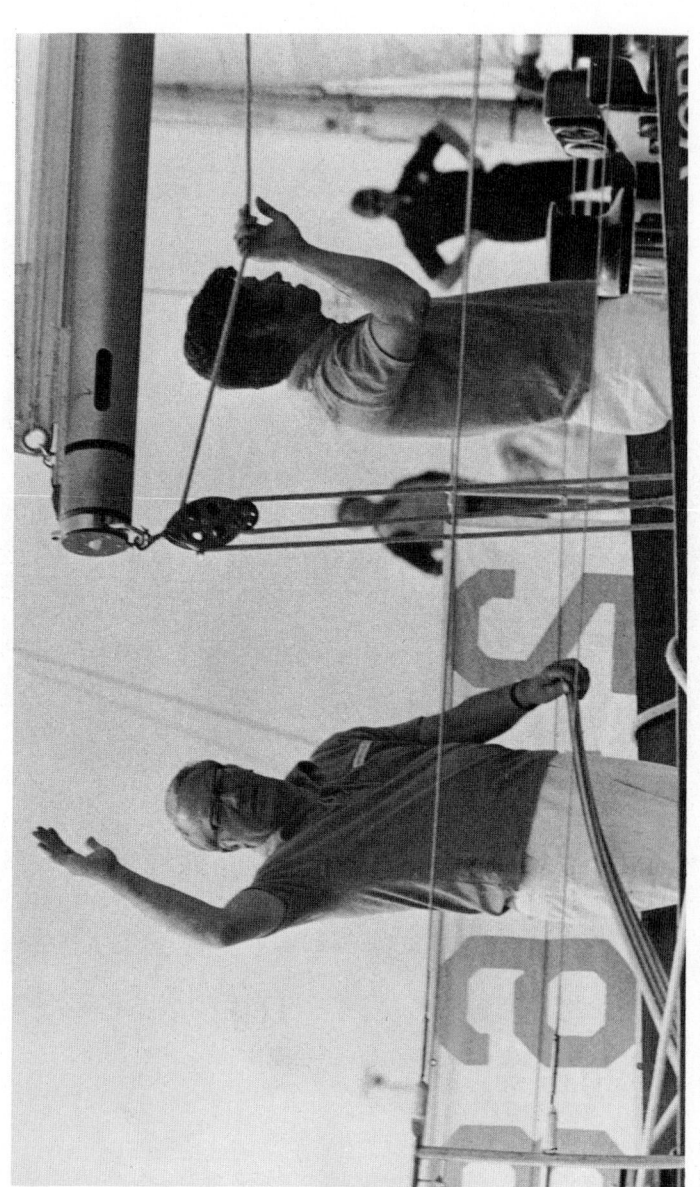

The Prime Minister led the British team to victory in the Admiral's Cup yachting series in July and August. Mr. Heath is seen at the helm of his yacht *Morning Cloud*.

THE WALKER CUP

The victorious Great Britain and Ireland amateur golf team are seen at St. Andrews in May with the Walker Cup. Led by M. F. Bonallack, they defeated

The England cricket team regained the Ashes during their tour of Australia in the winter, winning the Test series by two matches to nil. The M.C.C. touring party was: B. L. d'Oliveira, K. Shuttleworth, G. G. A. Saulez (Scorer), D. Wilson, P. Lever. *Middle row*—A. P. E. Knott, K. W. R. Fletcher, B. W. Luckhurst, D. L. Underwood, J. H. Hampshire, R. W. Taylor, A. Ward. *Front row*—B. W. Thomas (physiotherapist), J. A. Snow, M. C. Cowdrey (vice-captain), R. Illingworth (captain), J. H. Edrich, G. Boycott, D. G. Clark (manager).

THE BRITISH LIONS

The British Lions rugby union team which returned to England in August as the first British team to win an international series in New Zealand. The team was captained by John Dawes; Dr. D. W. C. Smith was manager and Carwyn James coach.

Blyth on his return from east to west circumnavigation of world in yacht *British Steel*. **9.** Her Majesty and the Duke of Edinburgh with the Prince of Wales, the Princess Anne, the Prince Andrew and the Prince Edward embarked in *Britannia* from Southampton and sailed for Aberdeen. **15.** Princess Anne celebrated her 21st birthday; with the royal party she left *Britannia* at Thurso and drove to lunch with the Queen Mother at the Castle of Mey. **16.** The royal party left *Britannia* at Aberdeen and drove to Balmoral. **20.** The Prince of Wales was presented with his pilot's wings at annual passing-out parade at Cranwell.

Sept. 5. Princess Anne won the individual championship at the three-day European Horse Trials at Burghley, Lincs. **23.** Princess Margaret and the Earl of Snowdon left for Canada to preside at opening of new art gallery in Winnipeg.

BRITISH POLITICS

(1970) Oct. 8. Conservative Party conference at Blackpool carried by large majority motion supporting Government's Common Market policy. **9.** It was stated that more than £105,000,000 would be distributed among 163 local education authorities to spend on new schools or extensions to existing ones. **13.** Chairman of Gas Council confirmed that most, if not all, area boards were planning price increases. **15.** White Paper on reorganization of central government machinery was published— Ministry of Technology was merged with Board of Trade in new Department of Trade and Industry, the Ministries of Housing and Local Government, Transport, and Public Building and Works were all integrated in new Department of Environment, and Ministry of Overseas Development was transferred to Foreign and Commonwealth Office; a new temporary Ministry of Aviation Supply was set up; Mr. John Davies, Minister of Technology, was appointed Secretary of State for Trade and Industry and President of the Board of Trade, and Mr. Peter Walker, Minister of Housing and Local Government, was appointed Secretary of State for the Environment; the Cabinet was reduced in size from 18 to 17 members. **22.** In by-election at St. Marylebone, Conservatives held seat with reduced majority of 6,142, compared with 9,134 at General Election. **26.** Mr. Gromyko, Soviet Foreign Minister, arrived in London for talks with British Ministers. **27.** Mr. Barber, Chancellor of the Exchequer, announced wide-ranging changes including standard rate of income tax to be cut by 2½p from April 6, 1971, corporation tax to be cut from 45 to 42½ per cent., charges for school meals to be raised in two stages from 9 p to actual running cost of about 14 p, free milk to children over age of seven to be discontinued, charges for dental treatment to be related to about half the cost, prescription charges to be increased from 12½p to 20p per item, fee for passports to be raised from £2 to £5, and charges for admission to national museums and galleries to be introduced; it was also announced that Industrial Reorganization Corporation would be wound up. **28.** Family Income Supplements Bill was published introducing income supplement for poor families of maximum of £3 a week. Defence White Paper was published outlining plans for British " East of Suez " force of about 4,500 and retention of four or five Gurkha battalions. Commons reversed Labour Government's decision to reject Boundary Commission's proposals for fairer constituencies. **29.** Bank lending capacity was cut by £103,000,000. Prices and Incomes Board report was published recommending reduction in number of independent television companies and mergers of companies. Government

approved rise of 16 per cent. in price of industrial coal, adding more than £50,000,000 to cost of producing electricity.

Nov. 2. Mr. Carr, Secretary of State for Employment and Productivity, told Commons that Prices and Incomes Board was to be wound up in about six months and that Government was to set up three new review bodies for salaries in public sector, backed by new Office of Manpower Economics. **3.** Mr. Walker, Secretary of State for Environment, announced that Government would be introducing countrywide system of rent rebates and allowances for everyone in need, including private tenants. Mrs. Golda Meir, Prime Minister of Israel, arrived in London for talks with British Ministers. **11.** Government made extra £42,000,000 available to Rolls-Royce to rescue firm from financial crisis. **17.** Government announced that nearly 1,000,000 public service pensioners, including ex-members of the armed forces, were to receive increases the following September, at cost of about £50,000,000 a year. **19.** Conservatives held Enfield West in by-election with majority of 8,279, compared with 11,962 at General Election. **20.** Agreement was reached on rises of 15 per cent. from Dec. 13 for 250,000 ancillary workers in National Health Service. **25.** It was announced that Lord Hall had been dismissed as Chairman of the Post Office Corporation; thousands of Post Office workers subsequently staged strikes in protest. **26.** Commons rejected Opposition motion criticizing Government's trade union reform proposals by 310 votes to 269.

Dec. 2. Commons voted by 366 to 81 to end British Standard Time as from following year. Mrs. Thatcher, Secretary of State for Education and Science, announced £38,500,000 plan under which 460 of worst and oldest primary schools in England and Wales would be improved or replaced. **3.** Government's Industrial Relations Bill was published, including proposal to enable industrial relations court to award £100,000 compensations against an offending union with more than 100,000 members. **8.** Prime Minister announced that High Court judges, senior civil servants and chiefs of nationalized industry boards had volunteered to forgo for six months salary increases due to them on Jan. 1. Mr. Maudling, Home Secretary, told Commons that licensing laws of England and Wales were to be reviewed by independent committee of inquiry; Mr. Campbell, Secretary of State for Scotland, also announced formation of separate and parallel committee to examine licensing system in Scotland. **10.** Dr. Horace King announced his decision to retire as Speaker of the House of Commons. **15.** Industrial Relations Bill was given second reading in Commons by 324 votes to 280. **18.** Department of Trade and Industry issued summary of report by Roskill Commission in which it recommended that London's third airport should be sited at Cublington, Buckinghamshire; Commission's full report was later published on Jan. 21, 1971.

(1971) Jan. 4. Lord Robens said he was resigning as chairman of National Coal Board. **6.** Prime Minister left London by air to visit Cyprus, Pakistan, India and Malaysia *en route* to Commonwealth Heads of Government conference in Singapore. **12.** Mr. Selwyn Lloyd was elected Speaker of House of Commons; his nomination was approved by 294 votes to 55. Lord Carrington, Secretary of State for Defence, told Lords that Territorial and Army Volunteer Reserve was to be expanded by 10,500 men. **13.** White Paper was published announcing £36,000,000 scheme to establish a national libraries organization, the

T +

British Library; involving building of new library for reference and research next door to British Museum. **14.** It was stated that Britain achieved visible trade surplus of £56,000,000 in December. **18.** Mr. Maudling had talks with Major Chichester-Clark, Prime Minister of Northern Ireland, at Home Office on measures for stamping out new wave of violence in Northern Ireland. **25.** The sitting of House of Commons was suspended for fifteen minutes after demonstration on floor of the House by some 40 Labour M.P.s in protest at Government guillotine on Industrial Relations Bill, then being debated.

Feb. 4. It was stated that Rolls-Royce had gone into voluntary liquidation and that assets of aero-engine and marine and industrial gas turbine engine divisions of the company would be nationalized by Government. **13 and 14.** Prime Minister and other senior Ministers had talks with Major Chichester-Clark at Chequers. **15.** Nation changed officially to decimal currency and three new coins—½ p, 1 p and 2 p—came into use; charges for first and second-class mail were raised to 3 p and 2½ p respectively. Mr. Chataway, Minister of Posts and Tele-communications, announced in Commons an increase of £1 in television licence fee to take effect on July 1 and £10,000,000 reduction in annual levy on advertising revenue paid by Independent Television. **17.** Lord Carrington said defence spending in next financial year would total £2,545,000,000. **24.** Immigration Bill was published establishing single code of permanent legislation on immigrant control, under which Commonwealth and alien entrants would be treated alike. **March 5.** Central Electricity Generating Board said that wholesale electricity prices would rise by 9 per cent. during following twelve months. **9.** Agreement was reached for pay increases of 8½ per cent. to about 330,000 nurses and midwives. **10.** Sir Keith Joseph, Secretary of State for Social Services, announced that committee to study allegations of abuse of social security benefits had been set up by the Government. **11.** Mr. Heath and other Ministers had talks with T.U.C. leaders at 10 Downing Street. **16.** Major Chichester-Clark had urgent talks with Prime Minister, Mr. Maudling and Lord Carrington in London. **24.** Sir Keith Joseph announced that maximum payment under new family income supplement scheme was to be increased from £3 to £4 a week and income level below which family could qualify was to be increased by £3 a week. **25.** Mr. George Woodcock resigned as chairman of Commission on Industrial Relations; he was later succeeded by Mr. Len Neal. **29.** Social Security Bill was published under which supplementary benefits paid to families of men on strike would be cut by £3·35 a week. White Paper was published detailing plan for ultimate total of sixty local commercial radio stations. **30.** In Budget statement, Mr. Barber announced sweeping changes in tax system and net reduction in revenue of £546,000,000 in 1971–72 and about £680,000,000 in full year; main proposals were—selective employment tax to be halved, and both S.E.T. and purchase tax to be abolished from April, 1973, and replaced by value added tax; child allowances to be increased by £40 a year for each child; old age pensions for single persons to be raised from £5 to £6 and for married couples from £8·10 to £9·70; estate duty liability to be raised to £12,500; corporation tax to be reduced by 2½ per cent. to 40 per cent.; income tax and surtax to be replaced by single graduated tax from April, 1973; earned income relief for those earning more than £4,005 a year to be raised to 15 per cent.; income tax exemption limits for old persons to be raised; higher tax on short-term gains to be abolished and all gains

subjected to long-term tax; and stamp duty on mortgages to be abolished. **31.** Sir Keith Joseph announced increased social service benefits to favour very old and chronic sick and consequently higher national insurance contributions from workers and employers, with top contribution rise for worker of 65 p.

April 1. In by-election at Arundel and Shoreham, Conservatives retained seat with majority of 23,254 compared with 27,376 at General Election; in by-election at Liverpool, Scotland, Labour held seat with majority of 5,044 compared with 7,334 at General Election. Bank rate was cut by one per cent. to six per cent. Prime Minister and other Ministers had talks with Mr. Brian Faulkner, new Prime Minister of Northern Ireland, in London. **2.** Fourteen per cent. increase in steel prices announced by British Steel Corporation was immediately halved on Government orders. **7.** List of five new life barons and three new life baronesses, including the widow of Mr. Iain Macleod, was announced from 10 Downing Street. It was stated that Ministry of Aviation Supply was being abolished on May 1. **9.** Coal price increases averaging between 7 and 8 per cent. were approved by Government. It was confirmed that Mr. Derek Ezra had been appointed chairman of National Coal Board in succession to Lord Robens. **19.** It was disclosed that 814,189 people were unemployed, the highest figure since May, 1940. **22.** Mr. William Ryland was appointed chairman of Post Office Corporation. **25.** Decennial census was taken in United Kingdom. **26.** Mr. Davies, Secretary of State for Trade and Industry, announced in Commons that Government had decided to site third London airport at Foulness, Essex. **27.** Prices and Incomes Board report was published stating that domestic coal users were heavily subsidizing industrial customers under terms of National Coal Board's present pricing policies.

May 6. Prime Minister had talks with Herr Brandt, West German Chancellor, in London. Mrs. Thatcher announced that students were to receive an extra £76,000,000 in grants over next three years. **7.** It was announced that National Coal Board made profit of about £500,000 in financial year ended last March. Bill was published under which public service pensioners would receive increases of at least 18 per cent. from Sept. 1. **11.** It was stated that British National Export Council was to be wound up and replaced by new organization, the British Export Board. **18.** White Paper was published proposing adult admission fee of 10p to national museums and galleries. **19.** The Queen sent message to Commons requesting it to consider increasing provision for Civil List. **27.** In by-elections at Itchen division of Southampton and Goole, Labour retained both seats; at Bromsgrove, Labour won seat from Conservatives, turning Conservative majority of 10,874 at General Election into their own majority of 1,868.

June 7. It was announced that 200,000 civil servants in clerical grades would receive pay increases of between 10 and 13 per cent., back-dated to Jan. 1. **10.** It was stated that Decimal Currency Board was to be wound up on Sept. 30. Government announced pay deal giving 100,000 senior civil servants pay rises of between 7 and 15 per cent. **14.** Government decided to withhold aid requested by Upper Clyde Shipbuilders and to let company go into liquidation, but also to do all it could to help preserve in new groupings as much of the shipyard capacity involved as could be deemed viable. **17.** In by-election at Hayes and Harlington, Labour held seat with greatly increased majority of 10,479, compared with 5,464 at General Election. **25.** Mrs Thatcher announced that Government was

to inject £132,000,000 into its programme to get rid of 6,000 slum primary schools.

July 7. White Paper was published on terms negotiated for British entry into Common Market. **8.** In by-election at Greenwich, Labour held seat with majority of 8,521 compared with 7,609 at General Election. **15.** Decimal Currency Board announced that old pennies and three-penny bits would cease to be legal tender at end of August. **19.** Mr. Barber announced immediate cuts of two elevenths in purchase tax and removal of all hire-purchase and rental controls in statement designed to cut unemployment and stimulate the economy. **20.** Ten per cent. pay increase, back dated to April 1, was awarded to 350,000 teachers under Pearson arbitration tribunal's recommendations. **29.** Mr. Davies announced in Commons that two of the three Upper Clyde Shipyards were to be closed and sold off, and 400 workers made redundant immediately, and that efforts were being made to launch new company backed by Government and private capital to continue shipbuilding at remaining yard; on following day workers began occupying yards.

Aug. 3. It was announced that Armed Forces were to get interim seven per cent. pay rise. **4.** It was announced in Commons that further £300,000,000 of credit was to be made available to help British shipyards, increasing total available to £1,000,000,000. **5.** Mr. Heath had talks with Mr. Faulkner, Northern Ireland Prime Minister, in London. Government stated that British Gas Corporation was to be set up in 1973 to replace area gas boards and the Gas Council. **15.** Britain signed treaty of friendship with newly independent Bahrain. **16.** Mr. Heath called emergency Cabinet meeting in consequence of President Nixon's financial and economic measures announced earlier in day. **18.** Provisional results of 1971 Census showed population increase of more than 2,500,000 in United Kingdom since 1961; total figure being 55,346,551; population in London and other big cities showed considerable decrease. **19.** Mr. Lynch, Prime Minister of Republic of Ireland, sent telegram to Mr. Heath saying that he would support policy of passive resistance by Opposition Groups in Northern Ireland unless political solution was achieved; in reply Mr. Heath said that Mr. Lynch's telegram was unjustified in content and unacceptable in its attempt to interfere in affairs of United Kingdom. Lord Carrington, replying to complaints of B.B.C. reports from Northern Ireland, said that on occasions " the B.B.C.'s reporting falls below the standard of fairness and accuracy which we are entitled to expect." **21.** At request of Army, Government agreed to set up inquiry into allegations of brutality against detained persons in Northern Ireland. **23.** London foreign currency market re-opened after week's closure; pound was left to " float ", and rose by three per cent. above its old par value.

Sept. 2. Bank rate was reduced from 6 to 5 per cent. **6.** Mr. Heath and Mr. Lynch met for talks at Chequers; talks continued on following day, but ended in near deadlock. **9.** Government agreed to recall Parliament for two days at end of month for debates on situation in Northern Ireland. **10.** Bank of England, on authority of the Government, freed banks from direct controls over amount of money they might lend and borrowers to whom they might lend it. **14.** White Paper was published outlining scheme to come into operation by Sept. 1975, whereby all but self-employed or financially independent persons would have basic flat rate pension together with occupational pension related to earnings. **15.** Mrs Thatcher announced that more than 500 old primary schools would be

replaced or improved in 1973, at estimated cost of £44,000,000. **16.** In Stirling and Falkirk by-election, Labour retained seat with majority of 4,488 over Scottish Nationalist candidate; Conservative candidate was at bottom of poll. **23.** Two-day debate on Northern Ireland ended in Commons; Opposition back-benchers forced division against advice of their leaders; Government had majority of 203–74. Labour retained seat in Widnes by-election with majority increased from 5,118 at General Election to 12,661. Unemployment figures for month showed increase of 24,931, to total of 929,121. **24.** Following upon disclosures made by Russian KGB agent who had defected, Government expelled 90 Russian diplomats and officials for spying, forbade return of 15 others temporarily out of the country and put limit on number of Soviet officials to be stationed in London. **27.** Mr. Heath, Mr. Faulkner and Mr. Lynch began talks at Chequers on situation in Northern Ireland; they concluded discussions on following day, issuing statement condemning violence; British Government spokesman said that talks had been satisfactory. **30.** Conservatives held seat in Macclesfield by-election with majority reduced from 10,452 at General Election to 1,079; Liberal and two Independent candidates forfeited their deposits.

NORTHERN IRELAND

(1970) Oct. 21. Northern Ireland Government announced that it was to spend £293,000,000 in attempt to solve country's housing problems. **31.** Three soldiers were injured, one seriously, when seven bombs exploded in Belfast. **Nov. 16.** Two men were murdered on street in Belfast suburb by gunman. **Dec. 8.** Northern Ireland Government declared state of emergency because of overtime ban and work-to-rule by power station workers.

(1971) Jan. 18. Mr. F. McManus, Unity M.P. for Fermanagh and South Tyrone, was jailed for six months at Enniskillen for his part in civil rights march there on Nov. 28. **24.** Ten policemen were injured in Belfast when about 500 rioters attacked a police station. **Feb. 5.** Violent riots in Belfast caused deaths of one soldier and five civilians. **8.** A soldier was shot in head when two army vehicles were machine-gunned and bombed in Belfast; he later died. **9.** Two engineers and three construction workers travelling to television relay station at Brougher Mountain, Co. Tyrone were killed instantly when their vehicle broke trip wire across track which set off bomb. **26.** Two policemen were killed and three seriously injured by machine-gun fire as they helped to keep rival Protestant and Roman Catholic crowds apart in west Belfast. **March 4.** Mr. Maudling, Home Secretary, arrived in Belfast at start of his three-day visit to Northern Ireland. **6.** Man was shot dead when troops fired on rioters in Falls Road area of Belfast; two days later in the same district another man was killed during a gun battle. **10.** Three young soldiers, two of them teenaged brothers, all in civilian clothes, were shot dead in ambush at Ligoniel, a north suburb of Belfast; two days later British Government announced that no more soldiers under age of 18 were to be sent to Northern Ireland and those already there would be replaced. **20.** Major Chichester-Clark announced his resignation as Prime Minister of Northern Ireland; three days later he was succeeded by Mr. Brian Faulkner. **April 11.** Twelve soldiers were injured in fierce rioting in Londonderry. **May 16.** One man was killed and two soldiers wounded in gun battle in Belfast. **25.** Soldier was killed and about twenty people injured when bomb was thrown into entrance of a combined police and army post in

Belfast. **July 8.** Troops shot dead a youth during bitter rioting in Londonderry; earlier they had shot suspected gunman who later died in hospital. **12.** Soldier was shot dead by a sniper in Belfast; two days later another soldier was shot dead in ambush on outskirts of the city.

Aug. 7. In Belfast, investigations began after soldier had shot dead civilian van driver; on following night, three soldiers were injured and youth shot dead during serious rioting in city for second night in succession. **9.** Severe rioting flared up in Belfast, which was the worst affected, Londonderry and Newry with announcement that more than 300 arrests had been made under new emergency powers of internment taken by Northern Ireland Government; it was reported that at least eleven people were killed as troops fought with terrorists armed with automatic weapons and petrol and gelignite bombs; violence continued on following day in Londonderry and Belfast and it was reported death toll had risen to at least seventeen during two days with nearly 100 people having been injured and about 300 houses wrecked by fire in Belfast. **11.** Troops killed five terrorists in gun battles in Belfast as rioting continued in the city, as well as in Londonderry; on following day it was reported that at least 5,000 Roman Catholics had left Ulster for camps in Irish Republic and that about 2,000 Protestants were homeless. **13.** Gunman was shot dead by troops in Londonderry. **15.** Policeman was seized by I.R.A. men in Londonderry and beaten unconscious. Nine Northern Ireland Opposition M.P.s called for campaign of civil disobedience. **18.** Man was shot dead by troops at Strabane after civil rights meeting which had been addressed by Miss Bernadette Devlin; two Northern Ireland Opposition M.P.s were arrested in Londonderry. **22.** Bomb wrecked front gates of Crumlin Road jail, Belfast, injuring two prison officers and two prisoners. **23.** Republic of Ireland Ministers met representatives of Opposition in Northern Ireland, and it was stated that regular consultations could take place between them. Soldier on observation post duty in Belfast was killed by sniper. **25.** Gelignite bomb exploded at headquarters of Belfast electricity board; an employee was killed and 35 others, many of them girl clerks and typists, injured. **29.** Two British soldiers who had accidentally crossed Eire border were detained, and corporal who went to their assistance was shot dead by I.R.A. men. **Sept. 2.** Forty persons were injured in Belfast when four bombs exploded in the shopping and commercial area within 15 minutes. **3.** Eighteen-month girl was killed in Belfast by sniper's bullet aimed at British soldier. **6.** During gun-battle between troops and I.R.A. in Londonderry, girl of 14 was killed. **14.** Two British soldiers were killed by I.R.A., one in Londonderry, and one in ambush at Dungannon, and on Sept. 17 a soldier was shot dead in an ambush in Belfast. **23.** Man and woman died following explosion in Republican stronghold of Belfast. **29.** Two persons were killed and 17 injured after bomb exploded in crowded Belfast public-house.

LOCAL AFFAIRS

(1970) Oct. 12. London boroughs were given permission by Ministry of Housing and Local Government to suspend part of their smoke-control orders because of shortage of smokeless fuel. **Nov. 4.** Mr. Walker, Secretary of State for Environment, said that Government had decided that Thames flood barrier should be at Silvertown in Woolwich Reach, as recommended by GLC. **26.** Rent increases averaging £1·50 and spread over three years until Oct. 1973, were announced by GLC's housing committee.

(1971) Jan. 4. It was stated that Mr. Walker had approved building of £30,000,000 marina under cliffs at Black Rock, Brighton. **19.** Mr. Maudling, Home Secretary, stated that state-owned public houses at Carlisle, Gretna Green and Cromarty Firth were to be wound up or sold to private enterprise. **Feb. 16.** Government published proposals for reorganization of local government in England into six new metropolitan county councils, 38 county councils and about 300 district councils. **March 19.** Plans for £1,300,000 extension to Tate Gallery were made public. **April 28.** It was announced that Government had decided that Llantrisant in south-east Wales should become a new town. **May 4.** Labour party made sweeping gains in Scottish municipal elections, mainly at expense of Scottish Nationalists, and regained control in Glasgow and Dundee; the party also claimed net gain of some 600 seats in the urban and rural district council elections held in England and Wales during week commencing May 10. **13.** Voting took place in 374 English and Welsh boroughs and resulted in Labour gains of over 1,200 seats and Conservative losses of over 1,000; voting also took place in 32 London Boroughs and resulted in Labour controlling 21 boroughs, 17 of which they won from Conservatives. **26.** It was announced that Government had approved building of £20,000,000 Humber Bridge. **Sept. 29.** Sir Edward Howard was elected Lord Mayor of London.

ACCIDENTS

(1970) Oct. 15. Fifty men were killed when span of West Gate bridge being built at Melbourne collapsed into River Yarra. **23.** A number of sailors were killed after two Liberian oil tankers, *Allegro* and *Pacific Glory*, collided six miles off St. Catherine's Point, Isle of Wight, and later caught fire and went aground. **Nov. 1.** A dance hall at St. Laurent du Pont, near Grenoble caught fire, 142 people, mostly young, were killed. **12.** Five men were killed in mid-air collision between two Wessex helicopters above R.A.F. Odiham, Hampshire. **12 and 13.** In worst disaster of its kind in present century, thousands of people lost their lives in coastal region of East Pakistan when Ganges Delta was swept by cyclone and vast tidal wave; large areas were devastated, thousands made homeless, and practically all survivors were reduced to destitution by the damage and losses to agricultural crops and livestock. **20.** Three men and a woman were killed when R.A.F. Whirlwind rescue helicopter on training flight exploded and crashed near Patrick Brompton, North Riding.

(1971) Jan. 2. Sixty-six spectators were crushed to death and over 100 injured when barrier collapsed at Rangers *v.* Celtic football match at Ibrox Park, Glasgow. **11.** Eight men were reported missing after explosion ripped apart Panamanian tanker *Texaco Caribbean* as she was in collision with Peruvian ship, *Paracas*, six miles off Folkestone; on following day it was believed that West German freighter *Brandenburg* hit bow section of *Texaco Caribbean* and sank; seven people were killed and fourteen reported missing. **20.** Four of R.A.F.'s Red Arrows aerobatic team were killed in mid-air crash over R.A.F. base at Kemble, Glos. **Feb. 6.** A number of people were killed and many injured when Italian town of Tuscania was devastated in succession of nine earthquakes. **9.** Earthquake struck Los Angeles and 350-mile area of southern California; a number of people were killed and many injured. **22.** It was stated that at least 75 people had died and about 500 been injured after more than fifty tornadoes had devastated U.S. States of Louisiana and Mississippi. **March 2.**

Three R.A.F. pilots were killed when two planes collided in mid-air and crashed near Cliffe, Yorks. **19.** Many people were killed when landslide engulfed small Peruvian mining town of Chungar, in the Andes. **23.** Three women and a man were killed in explosion at explosives factory at South Normanton, Derbys. **April 6.** Six miners died and 24 were injured when methane gas and blinding dust burst from seam at Cynheidre Colliery in Carmarthenshire. **25.** Three members of rowing eight were drowned in a weir after their boat sank on River Thames at Penton Hook, near Chertsey. **12.** Earthquake struck region round Burdur in south-west Turkey killing a number of people. **20.** Three Press photographers in Royal Navy helicopter died as it plunged into the sea off Portland Bill. **22.** Earthquake struck province of Bingol in Eastern Turkey, killing hundreds of people and leaving thousands homeless. **23.** Seventy-eight people, 72 of them British holidaymakers, were killed when their jet plane crashed at Rijeka airport in Yugoslavia. **June 18.** Small craft taking part in Navy sailing race from Plymouth to Fowey, Cornwall, were overwhelmed by rough seas and three of boats capsized; one man was drowned and second died later in hospital. **July 1.** Submarine *Artemis* sank at her moorings at Haslar Creek, Gosport, with three men trapped in forward compartment; they later escaped safely. **2.** Two children were killed and thirty children and adults injured when coach of school seaside excursion train was derailed and overturned at Waverton, near Chester. **8 and 9.** Earthquake shook most of Chile and shattered towns and cities along thousand-mile stretch of country; a number of people were killed and injured and thousands made homeless. **30.** All 162 people aboard Japanese All-Nippon Airways Boeing 727 were killed as plane broke up in flames after colliding with Japanese Air Force jet fighter in mountainous area near town of Shizu-kuishi in northern Japan; it was world's worst air disaster. **Aug. 11.** Four people lost their lives when hotel annexe collapsed at Benalmadena in Spain; three British boys were dug out alive from rubble. **28.** Greek ferry, sailing from Patras to Ancona, was swept by fire off Brindisi; 25 persons lost their lives. **Sept. 6.** Chartered B.A.C. 1-11 aircraft crashed on *autobahn* shortly after taking-off from Hamburg; 21 persons out of 121 passengers and crew were killed. **13.** Ten persons were killed and more than 60 injured in series of accidents during fog on M6 motorway near Lancashire-Cheshire border. **17.** Five seamen died in fire aboard a Fleetwood trawler in Irish Sea. **29.** Explosion on submarine *Alliance* at Portland caused death of a sailor and injuries to 14 others.

CRIMES, TRIALS, Etc.

(1970) Oct. 6. Two brothers, Nizamodeen and Arthur Hosein, were found guilty at Central Criminal Court of murder of Mrs. Muriel McKay, whose body was never found, and were sentenced to life imprisonment; they were also convicted on other charges including kidnapping of Mrs. McKay and demanding £1,000,000 in ransom money from her husband. **Nov. 11.** John McVicar, who escaped from special maximum security block at Durham prison in Oct. 1968 while serving 23-year sentence, was recaptured at flat in Blackheath, south London.

(1971) Jan. 12. Two bombs exploded at the home of Mr. Carr, Secretary of State for Employment and Productivity, at Hadley Green, Herts.; the house and a car were damaged but no one was hurt. **Feb. 17.** James Anthony Roche was sentenced at Central Criminal Court to 18 months' imprisonment for throwing two CS gas grenades into House of Commons in July, 1970 and conspiring to do so.

March 24. Sidney Sporle, former Mayor of Battersea and former chairman of Wandsworth Borough housing committee, was found guilty at Central Criminal Court on seven charges of corruption involving council housing contracts and was sentenced to six years' imprisonment (reduced to four years on appeal). **26.** Armed gang ambushed armoured security van at Croydon and escaped with £458,240. **May 10.** At Liverpool Stipendiary court, Lustre Fibres Ltd. was fined £46,250 for exporting goods to Rhodesia. **28.** Five members of crew of trawler, *Mary Craig*, were sentenced in High Court at Aberdeen to imprisonment after being found guilty of piracy. **June 23.** Nicholas Anthony Prager was jailed for twelve years at Leeds Assizes on two charges of spying for Czechoslovakia while serving as R.A.F. technician in 1961. **27.** A detective was shot and critically wounded in Reading; he died on July 23. **July 21.** Verdict of murder by person or persons unknown was returned by jury at inquest on nine people who died in fire at New Langham Hotel annexe in Bayswater, London on May 11. **27.** At Hertford Assizes, 19-year-old gunman was sentenced to life imprisonment for attempting to murder two policemen by shooting at them during ten-day rampage across country in stolen cars. **31.** A bomb damaged unoccupied London flat of Mr. Davies, Secretary of State for Trade and Industry. **Aug. 23.** Blackpool police head, Supt. Richardson, died after being shot in stomach while grappling with gunman; he was leading chase of 5 men after jeweller's shop had been robbed; two constables were wounded by shots. **24.** Three London men were charged at Blackpool with robbery at a jeweller's shop, and a fourth man was later arrested in Worcestershire. **Sept. 2.** Two paintings by Guardi were stolen from Kenwood House. **24.** A painting by Saftleven was stolen from Buckingham Palace, valued at £2,000.

LABOUR

(1970) Oct. 5. Daily newspaper deliveries in London area, which had been seriously curtailed since Sept. 20, began to return to normal following settlement of pay dispute involving packers and drivers employed by wholesale distributors. Further 30,000 employees throughout country joined strike by local authority manual workers. **20.** Farmworkers in England and Wales were given £1·65 a week wage increase by Agricultural Wages Board and the 43-hour week cut by one hour. **24.** Troops moved into Tower Hamlets in East London to move mounting pile of rubbish left uncollected because of local authority manual workers' strike.

Nov. 2. Unofficial strike by miners in support of extra pay spread as pits in South Wales and Scotland joined those already on strike in Yorkshire, bringing total number of men involved to more than 48,000 at fifty pits; by Nov. 9 strike had spread further to involve 95,000 men at 119 pits. **5.** Strike by local authority manual workers ended when unions accepted £2·50 pay rise for men and £2·12½ for women. **15.** Collapse of unofficial miners' strike began with decisions for return to work by more than 40,000 men; on Nov. 23 South Wales and Yorkshire miners returned to work. **24.** Agreement was reached on 10 per cent. average rises for 98,000 provincial busmen. **25.** Unions representing 50,000 manual workers in gas industry rejected offer by Gas Council of increase of £1·50 a week in basic pay. **26.** It was stated that members of National Union of Mineworkers had decided in secret ballot to accept pay rises of between £2·37½ and £3 a week. It was declared that working days lost through strikes in 1970—8,828,000 by end of October—already exceeded those for any other year since general strike of 1926.

Dec. 4. British Leyland announced that 5,000 workers would be made redundant and two factories closed in its Austin-Morris car division. **7.** Official overtime ban and work-to-rule by 125,000 power station workers began to cause blackouts throughout the country. **8.** Several hundred thousand workers staged unofficial one-day strike against Industrial Relations Bill; no national newspapers appeared. **12.** Government declared state of emergency to deal with effects of work-to-rule by power station workers; use of electricity for advertising and display, including shop windows, and floodlights was prohibited; on Dec. 14 unions called off work-to-rule and over-time ban and agreed to refer dispute to court of inquiry, and on Dec. 16 Government lifted its emergency order. **23.** London editorial staff of *Daily Mail* and *Daily Sketch* staged 10-hour un-official strike in dispute over future of house agree-ments and consequently *Daily Mail* was not pub-lished in London and production of *Daily Sketch* was disrupted. **31.** Editorial staffs of *Daily Mirror* and *Sun* went on unofficial strike over new house agreements and both papers were produced by editorial executives.

(1971) Jan. 1. New Year's Day absenteeism caused widespread disruption in factories; about 40,000 trade unionists crippled much of industry in Midlands with demonstration against Industrial Relations Bill. **12.** Industry was affected by national demonstration called by T.U.C. in protest at Industrial Relations Bill. **14.** British Airline Pilots' Association agreed to accept B.O.A.C.'s offer of £9,000 a year for all senior captains for all types of aircraft thus ending dispute which had grounded Corporation's fleet of *Boeing 747* jumbo jets. **15.** Leaders of Union of Post Office Workers ordered all-out strike by Britain's post and telephone workers in support of their 15 per cent. pay claim after rejecting Post Office Corporation's " final offer " of 8 per cent.; strike began officially at midnight on Jan. 19. **26.** Out-going B.E.A. flights were halted by strike of 3,000 engineering and maintenance workers in protest at dismissal of 28 Heathrow staff who were work-ing-to-rule in support of pay claim; three days later they voted to end strike and returned to work. **29.** Conveners of fifteen unions representing 50,000 workers at 21 Ford Motor Company plants recom-mended all-out strike from Feb. 1 in protest at 10 per cent. pay rise offered by management in reply to unions' claim for rises of 50 per cent. to give parity with Midland car workers; on Feb. 1 the Company's entire manufacturing capacity was stopped when about 45,000 workers responded to unofficial strike call.

Feb. 10. Report of Wilberforce court of inquiry into power station workers' dispute was published; its main recommendations were an increase of £2 a week for 122,000 workers, with additional 67½p a week for 43,000 skilled men, higher shift allowances and extra three days holiday a year. **25.** It was stated that about 100,000 policemen, ranging from constable to chief inspector, had been awarded pay increases varying from 11 to 22 per cent.

March 1. About 1,200,000 engineering and other workers took part in one-day strike called by Engineering Union against Industrial Relations Bill; no national morning newspapers or London evening newspapers were published and several provincial newspapers failed to appear because of the stoppage. **4.** Peace formula to end Post Office strike by giving wage increases at end of inquiry into efficiency of Post Office staff and management was agreed after more than thirteen hours of talks at Department of Employment; workers subse-quently voted to end strike by large majority and

returned to work on March 8. **8.** Associated News-papers announced that production of *Daily Sketch* as separate newspaper would cease not later than mid-May and its title would be merged with *Daily Mail*. It was stated that Rolls-Royce was to make 4,300 employees redundant in the Derby, Glasgow and Barnoldswick areas. **11.** It was stated that British Steel Corporation was to close five plants by end of year, making 2,600 people redundant in Manchester, South Wales, Rotherham and Corby. Civil Service unions accepted pay increases of up to 13 per cent. for 140,000 members. **18.** Special T.U.C. conference at Croydon defeated call for General Council to organize further industrial action against Industrial Relations Bill, as about 1,250,000 workers held one-day strike against Bill; no national morning or London evening newspapers were published.

April 1. Executive of Associated Society of Locomotive Engineers and Firemen decided to order work-to-rule in support of pay claim of 15 per cent. following rejection of British Rail's offer of 9⅜ per cent.; work-to-rule began at mid-night on April 4 and caused widespread disruption of services, London and South-East being the worst affected areas. **2.** Seventy-one per cent. of Ford workers voted to call off their strike and accept Company's offer of 33 per cent. pay rises over two years with guarantee of no strikes for that period; on April 5, workers returned to all Ford plants except Swansea and Halewood, where men voted to continue strike, but on following day strikers at Swansea decided to resume work and on April 7, workers at Halewood followed suit. **14.** Rail work-to-rule was called off when A.S.L.E.F. executive voted to accept British Rail's offer of 8½ to 11 per cent. pay rises. **21.** British Steel Cor-poration announced plans to dismiss 7,255 workers and close ten plants in next 18 months and gave warnings of further redundancies.   Port of London Authority announced that 3,000 of its employees would lose their jobs by 1975 under streamlining plan. **28.** It was stated that total of 9,502,000 working days had been lost through strikes in first three months of 1971.

May 5. Committee of inquiry into Post Office pay dispute recommended 9 per cent. overall pay rise backdated to Jan. 1 for postal workers.

June 1. About 12,000 British Steel Corporation blastfurnacemen began official strike in support of 35 per cent., or £10 a week, pay claim, but it was called off three days later. **30.** One-day strike by about 70,000 teachers in protest against way their salary claim was being handled affected thousands of schoolchildren. **July 28.** *The Times* newspaper was not published owing to industrial dispute in machine room.

Aug. 2. Swan Hunter shipbuilding group shut its five Tyneside yards, laying off 7,700 men, after 2,800 ancillary workers went on unofficial strike over pay dispute. **24.** Nine Lucas factories in Birmingham were brought to standstill by strike of 300 maintenance engineers; 13,000 workers were made idle.

Sept. 7. T.U.C., meeting at Blackpool, carried two resolutions, one " instructing " unions to boycott new register of trade unions and employers' associations, and the other " strongly advising " deregistration. **8.** T.U.C. voted almost unani-mously against entry into Common Market on terms negotiated by Government. **15.** Dispute caused loss of nearly 4,000,000 copies of national and London evening newspapers. **16.** Newspaper Publishers Association told members of National Graphical Association that further interruptions of production would lead to dismissal. **22.** After four days during which no national newspapers

were issued, employers agreed to pay rises of 5 per cent. on earnings, or 10 per cent. on basic rates, whichever was the greater, over 15 months. On following day, production of several newspapers was again delayed by chapel meetings during working hours.

LEGAL

(1970) Nov. 11. Government published Courts Bill abolishing assizes and quarter sessions and replacing them with system of Crown courts empowered to sit anywhere in England and Wales. **Dec. 1.** Nine national newspaper proprietors were granted High Court order restraining executive of Society of Graphical and Allied Trades, Division A, from " doing any further act " to call the newspapers' employees out on one-day strike on Dec. 8 in protest against Government's proposed industrial relations legislation. **21.** Church of Scientology lost its libel action in High Court against Mr. G. Johnson Smith, Conservative M.P. for East Grinstead, and it was ordered to pay costs.

(1971) Jan. 8. Immigration Appeals Tribunal recommended dismissal of appeal by Rudi Dutschke, former West German student leader, against refusal of Home Secretary to extend his stay in Britain. **18.** It was stated that Lord Parker was to retire as Lord Chief Justice and be succeeded by Sir John Widgery, a Lord Justice of Appeal. **Feb. 24.** Criminal Damage Bill was published under which life imprisonment would be maximum sentence for vandals. **March 25.** Report of Crowther Committee on Consumer Credit was published, recommending sweeping changes in laws of hire purchase and consumer credit. **Sept. 28.** Justice Roskill was appointed Lord Justice of Appeal upon resignation of Lord Justice Atkinson.

SPORT

(1970) Oct. 3. Tony Densham driving a Dragster broke British land speed record with average of 207·6 m.p.h.

(1971) Jan. 15. South Africa and Rhodesia were excluded from Davis Cup lawn tennis championship. **27.** Ove Andersson of Sweden and David Stone, his English co-driver, won Monte Carlo Rally. **Feb. 17.** England beat Australia in final Test match at Sydney to win series 2–0 and regain Ashes. **March 10.** It was stated that the Test and County Cricket Board had agreed to proposals for sponsored one-day League Cup competition and a county championship of twenty matches to begin in 1972. **29.** It was stated that Rhodesia had received and accepted an official invitation to take part in 1972 Olympic Games. **31.** It was announced that Cricket Council was to receive £75,054 compensation from Government for cancellation of 1970 South African cricket tour. **April 22.** Mr. Vorster, Prime Minister of South Africa, announced certain concessions towards limited multi-racial sport in his country. **May 8.** Arsenal, who had won League Championship only a few days before, beat Liverpool in F.A. Cup Final at Wembley Stadium, to become only second team in twentieth century to win League and Cup in same season. **27.** At St. Andrews, Great Britain and Ireland won Walker Cup amateur golf trophy from U.S.A. for first time since 1938 and for only second time in history of event. **June 10.** It was announced that Government was to establish independent Sports Council to replace advisory Sports Council. Football Association ordered Leeds United to close their ground for three weeks from Aug. 14 because of rioting by their fans at home league match on April 17, and Liverpool were fined £7,500 for failing to give satisfactory explanation for fielding weakened team in league

match on April 26; on July 16, F.A. ordered Manchester United to close their ground from Aug. 14 to 28 inclusive, and to pay costs for alleged misconduct following finding of flick knife on pitch during league match last season. **Aug. 11.** The British team, led by Prime Minister, won Admiral's Cup for yachting. **14.** British Lions rugby team, by drawing last Test at Auckland, became first British team to win series in New Zealand. **15.** Jackie Stewart of Scotland won world racing drivers' championship for 1971. **24.** India, by defeating England in third Test at The Oval, won series, and won a Test match in England for first time. **27.** Stewards of Jockey Club disqualified *Rock Roi*, winner of Ascot Gold Cup more than two months earlier because test had found trace of oxyphenbutazone; stewards fined the trainer, Peter Walwyn, £100, but acquitted him and his head lad of any corrupt practice or intent. **Sept. 8.** Australian Cricket Board of Control cancelled South African tour of Australia due to begin in following month.

TRANSPORT

(1970) Oct. 21. New independent airline, Caledonian-BUA, was formed when Caledonian Airways signed contracts for take-over of BUA. **27.** It was announced in Chancellor of Exchequer's statement that grants to London area commuter services would be eliminated by 1973; on following day it was stated that rail fares in London and Home Counties would rise by 30p in the £ over next two years. **29.** Rise of £1·65 a week in basic pay was agreed for 65,000 provincial municipal busworkers. **Nov. 6.** Government agreed to underground link between central London and Heathrow Airport, but decided to give no grant towards the scheme; work began on April 28, 1971. **24.** Government announced that new independent Civil Aviation Authority would be set up to control civil aviation and an Airways Board would run B.O.A.C. and B.E.A. **25.** It was stated that fares on British Rail's Southern Region would go up by as much as 30p in the £ in March 1971 in one step instead of being spread over two years as originally forecast. **Dec. 2.** Mr. Corfield, Minister of Aviation Supply, announced in Commons that Government had decided that it could not support either British Aircraft Corporation 311 airbus or its European counterpart.

(1971) Jan. 20. Board of Skyways Coach Air announced that Transport Holding Company, managers of Government's 50 per cent. interest in Skyways, had appointed receiver; on Feb. 5 it was stated that executives and staff of Skyways had raised more than £500,000 to revive the firm. **March 1.** British Railways Board announced that passengers in London and South-East were to pay up to 33 per cent. more in fares from March 28; Inter-City fares were to be increased by up to 20 per cent. from April 25, and in London Midland Region local fares outside London would go up by 15 per cent. from March 28. **2.** It was stated that taxi fares in London were to rise by approximately 25 per cent. **April 6.** Appointment of Mr. Richard Marsh as next chairman of British Railways Board was confirmed. **May 11.** It was stated that Government had decided to establish new National Railway Museum at York. **14.** Big increases in cost of food and drink on British Rail trains were announced, to come into force on May 23. **July 7.** National Bus Company reported loss of £8,100,000 in 1970. **27.** Government said that there should be no new runways at Heathrow, Gatwick, Luton and Stansted and that Stansted might be closed when Foulness became London's third airport. **Aug. 18.** It was announced that

work on new Underground Fleet Line would begin within few weeks and that Government was making 75 per cent. grant towards cost of first stage. **Sept. 23.** It was announced that all domestic air fares would rise by 5 per cent. from Nov. 1.

BRITISH COMMONWEALTH
(*See also* under Africa)

(1970) Oct. 1. Indian state of Uttar Pradesh was brought under President's rule direct from New Delhi as result of political crisis. **10.** Terrorists in Canada, who already held Mr. James Cross, British trade commissioner, kidnapped Mr. Pierre Laporte, Quebec Minister of Labour, from his Montreal home. Fiji Islands became independent. **16.** Canadian Government assumed emergency powers, outlawed extremist Quebec Liberation Front (F.L.Q.) and ordered arrest of more than 250 of its members and supporters. **17.** The body of Mr. Laporte was found in boot of car near Montreal's St. Hubert Airport; he had been shot dead. **Nov. 10.** President Kaunda of Zambia announced series of sweeping nationalization and economic reform measures. **Dec. 3.** Mr. Cross was released in Montreal by his F.L.Q. kidnappers who were allowed to fly to Cuba. **15.** Supreme Court in New Delhi declared illegal and unconstitutional Indian Government's action in stripping former princes of titles, privy purses and other privileges in Sept. 1970. **16.** Mr Trudeau, Prime Minister of Canada, had talks with Mr. Heath in Ottawa. **27.** Mrs. Gandhi, Indian Prime Minister, dissolved Parliament and decided to hold General Elections.

(1971) Jan. 5. Tun Abdul Razak, Prime Minister of Malaysia, declared his country a disaster area following severe floods. **14.** Commonwealth Heads of Government Conference opened in Singapore. **March 5.** It was reported that 3,000 people had died in East Pakistan during several days of rioting; thousands of demonstrators called for total independence of the province. **10.** Mr. William McMahon succeeded Mr. John Gorton as Prime Minister of Australia. **11.** Mrs. Gandhi's ruling Congress Party won an absolute majority in Indian General Election. **26.** Civil war broke out in East Pakistan following declaration of independence by the province, but by April 18 Pakistan Army had defeated secessionists; many thousands of civilians fled to India, causing serious relief and administrative problems for the Indian authorities, which were aggravated by outbreaks of cholera among refugees which claimed several thousand lives. **April 9.** Ceylon Government imposed 24-hour curfew and brought in laws carrying death penalty and confiscation of property for aiding insurgents who had terrorised the island for five days. **May 13.** Indian Government announced that all general insurance companies would be nationalized. President's rule was declared in western Indian state of Gujarat following breakdown in state's government. **June 12, 13 and 14.** General elections held in Malta resulted in victory for Labour Party led by Mr. Dom Mintoff, who subsequently became Prime Minister in succession to Dr. Borg Olivier.

Aug. 12. Mr. Gorton, former Australian Prime Minister, was dismissed from his post as Minister for Defence in consequence of articles which he had written for Sunday newspaper. **13.** N.A.T.O. announced that it was moving its Mediterranean naval headquarters from Malta at request of Mr. Mintoff. **Sept. 1.** State of Qatar declared itself independent.

U.S.A.

(1970) Oct. 12. President Nixon announced speed-up in rate of withdrawal of U.S. troops from Vietnam; a further 40,000 men would be repatriated by end of year. **22.** The President had talks with Mr. Gromyko, the Russian Foreign Minister, at White House. **Nov. 3.** In Congressional elections, Democrats won 21 of 35 Senate seats contested and Republicans 11; Democrats also made net gain of nine seats for new House of Representatives. **30.** Mr. Laird, U.S. Defence Secretary, said that U.S.A. would keep its military strength in Western Europe at present level until 1972, subject to Congressional authorization. **Dec. 14.** President Nixon announced resignation of Mr. David Kennedy as U.S. Treasury Secretary and his replacement by Mr. John Connally. **17.** Mr. Heath arrived in Washington for two days of talks with President Nixon. **29.** U.S. Senate approved President's request for supplementary military aid funds to supply Cambodia with £106,000,000 worth of arms and to grant Israel £208,000,000 credit to buy Phantom jets and other weapons.

(1971) Jan. 22. President Nixon delivered State of the Union message in which he described " a new American revolution—a peaceful revolution in which power was turned back to the people." **25.** Charles Manson, hippie leader, and two of his girl followers were found guilty in Los Angeles of murder of Sharon Tate, the actress, and six others, and another girl follower was found guilty of two murders; on March 29 all four were sentenced to death. **29.** The President presented to Congress Budget with deficit of $11,600,000,000. **31.** Three-man *Apollo 14* spacecraft was launched from Cape Kennedy on journey to the Moon; subsequently two of the astronauts carried out various tasks on Moon's surface before *Apollo 14* returned to earth, splashing down safely in South Pacific on Feb. 9. **March 24.** Both Houses of Congress rejected President Nixon's request for continued federal subsidy for America's supersonic transport airliner. **29.** Lieut. William Calley was found guilty at Fort Benning, Georgia, of murdering South Vietnamese civilians during massacre at village of My Lai in South Vietnam in March, 1968; two days later, he was sentenced to life imprisonment, but on April 1, President Nixon ordered that he be removed from military prison and confined instead to officers' quarters until review of his case was completed; on Aug. 20 the sentence was reduced to 20 years. **April 7.** President announced withdrawal of another 100,000 U.S. troops from Vietnam by Dec. 1. **May 3.** Anti-Vietnam War demonstrators failed in their efforts to bring Washington to standstill and 7,000 were arrested; on following day more than 1,000 were arrested. **8.** U.S. spacecraft *Mariner 8*, designed to orbit Mars, plunged into Atlantic only ten minutes after perfect launch from Cape Kennedy; on May 30, *Mariner 9* was launched from Cape Kennedy on voyage to Mars. **June 10.** President Nixon issued list of goods that U.S. businessmen could export to China, thus ending strict embargo on trade between two countries. **July 15.** U.S. bank-rate was raised from 4¾ to 5 per cent. **26.** *Apollo 15* spacecraft, with three men on board, was launched from Cape Kennedy on journey to the Moon; subsequently two of the astronauts carried out exploration programme on lunar surface with aid of a rover vehicle before *Apollo 15* returned to earth, splashing down in Pacific Ocean on Aug. 7. **28.** U.S. Government reported massive Budget deficit during fiscal year ending on June 30, amounting to $23,242,000,000, second largest since the war. **Aug. 2.** U.S. Senate voted to approve new loans of $250,000,000 to Lockheed Aircraft Corporation for its Tri-Star airliner programme, upon which jobs of many British Rolls-Royce workers depended.

15. President Nixon proclaimed national emergency and commenced series of financial and economic measures; he suspended U.S. agreement to exchange dollars into gold, imposed 90-day freeze on wages and prices and 10 per cent. surcharge on most imports and ordered 10 per cent. cut in foreign economic aid and heavy cuts in Federal aid at home; cuts were also to be made in income tax. **19.** U.S. Government refused to exempt Rolls-Royce RB-211 engines from 10 per cent. import surcharge. **Sept. 9.** U.S. Government Emergency Loan Guarantee Board approved loan guarantees up to $250,000,000 to Lockheed. **13.** Several hundred police and troops, with helicopters dropping tear gas, stormed Attica State Prison, New York, after rioting had taken place in the prison for some days; 37 persons were killed, including nine prison officers who had been held as hostages.

FRANCE

(1970) Oct. 21. It was stated that France had agreed to end sale to South Africa of arms suitable for use against insurgents. **Nov. 9.** General Charles de Gaulle, former President of France, died suddenly at his home in village of Colombey-les-Deux-Eglises; three days later he was buried without ceremony at family tomb in village while world leaders attended a requiem mass at Notre Dame Cathedral in Paris. **Dec. 15.** At ceremony in Paris the Place de l'Etoile was renamed the Place Charles de Gaulle. **(1971) Jan. 25.** Herr Brandt, West German Chancellor, arrived in Paris for two days of talks with President Pompidou. **May 13.** France raised bank rate from $6\frac{1}{2}$ to $6\frac{3}{4}$ per cent. **19.** Mr. Heath arrived in Paris for two days of talks with President Pompidou on Britain's proposed entry into the Common Market. **Aug. 18.** Following upon President Nixon's currency moves, President Pompidou said that there would be no change in fixed exchange value of franc and called for two-tier foreign exchange market.

U.S.S.R.

(1970) Oct. 6. President Pompidou of France arrived in Moscow on one-week official visit and began talks with Soviet leaders. **21.** Russians seized two U.S. generals whose plane strayed across border from Turkey and held them incommunicado; they were finally released on Nov. 10. **Nov. 17.** Russian unmanned spacecraft *Luna 17* landed on the Moon and self-propelled vehicle left the craft to begin carrying out investigation of Moon's surface. **(1971) Jan. 26.** It was disclosed that Russian *Venus-7* automatic spacecraft had sent back signals to earth after landing on Venus. **April 19.** Russians launched unmanned space station *Salyut* into earth orbit and four days later they launched *Soyuz 10* spacecraft, with three men on board, also into earth orbit; on April 24 the two craft linked up and on following day *Soyuz 10* returned to earth. **May 19.** Russia launched unmanned spacecraft towards Mars to carry out scientific research around the planet; another was launched on May 28. **June 6.** Russia launched three-man *Soyuz 11* spacecraft into earth orbit and on following day it linked with orbiting space station *Salyut* and crew went aboard; after their record-breaking flight the cosmonauts returned to earth in *Soyuz 11* on June 30 but when craft was opened after landing in Kazakhstan they were found to be dead. **Sept. 28.** It was reported that new automatic space station, *Luna 19*, had been launched towards Moon.

AFRICA

(1970) Oct. 5. Anwar Sadat, acting President of Egypt since death of President Nasser, was unani-
T*

mously nominated to succeed to the presidency; on Oct. 16 it was stated that his nomination had been approved by 90·04 per cent. of the electorate. **(1971) Jan. 15.** Aswan High Dam was officially inaugurated by President Sadat and President Podgorny of the Soviet Union. **24.** After trial lasting seven days, 92 people were sentenced to death in Guinea, all accused of being involved in invasion of capital of Conakry in Nov. 1970; a further 66 were sentenced to life imprisonment; on following day 58 of the condemned people were hanged. **25.** Troops led by Maj.-Gen. Idi Amin, former Commander-in-Chief, seized control of Uganda in twelve hours of fighting, ousting President Obote, who was on his way home from Commonwealth Conference in Singapore; on following day Maj.-Gen. Amin declared himself new head of state and on Feb. 2 he announced dissolution of Uganda Parliament and appointed himself absolute ruler. **Feb. 24.** President Boumédienne of Algeria announced that he was taking 51 per cent. controlling interest in all French oil companies operating in the country. **March 28.** Guinean troops entered Sierra Leone at request of Mr. Siaka Stevens, the Prime Minister, to help prevent overthrow of Government following two attempted *coups* by Sierra Leone Army; on April 19, Sierra Leone was declared a republic. **July 10.** Moroccan Army launched counter *coup* after rebel soldiers had attempted to overthrow King Hassan of Morocco. **19.** Left-wing *coup* took place in Sudan under leadership of Major Hashem el Atta and held power for three days when they were dislodged; General al Nemery was restored to power and leaders of the *coup* were arrested; four of them, including Major el Atta, were executed on July 23 and others later. **Aug. 16.** President Banda of Malawi arrived in Pretoria for first State visit to Republic of South Africa by a black African head of State.

OTHER COUNTRIES

(1970) Oct. 2. President Nixon arrived in Madrid from Belgrade on European tour; on following day he flew to London for talks with Mr. Heath at Chequers and then on to Dublin; he returned to Washington on Oct. 5. **7.** Left-wing General Juan Torres took over presidency of Bolivia following three days of political upheaval. **9.** Cambodia became a republic, taking the name of Khmer. **22.** State of emergency was declared in Chile after gunmen tried to assassinate Army Commander-in-Chief. **23.** Mr. Charles Haughey, former Irish Republic Minister for Finance, was acquitted in Dublin of illegally importing guns and ammunition into Eire. **Nov. 13.** General Hafez el Assad became new military ruler of Syria in bloodless *coup*. **21. and 22.** U.S. planes carried out large-scale bombing raids into North Vietnam. **27.** A man was prevented from attacking the Pope with dagger shortly after His Holiness had arrived at Manila airport for visit to Philippines. **Dec. 4.** Republic of Ireland Government said that it believed armed conspiracy existed to kidnap prominent persons, organize bank raids and perhaps attempt murder, and that it would be forced to intern people without trial unless threat was removed. **14.** Spanish Government declared state of emergency for six months throughout country following several weeks of widespread unrest. **16.** It was stated that a number of people had been killed and many injured in riots in northern Baltic coast area of Poland in protest at greatly increased food prices. **20.** Mr. Wladyslaw Gomúlka ceased to be First Secretary of Polish Communist Party and was replaced by Mr. Edward Gierek. **(1971) Jan. 7.** U.S. military command said that

4,204 U.S. servicemen were killed and 29,734 wounded on battlefields of Indo-China in 1970. **8.** Armed guerrillas kidnapped Mr. Geoffrey Jackson, British Ambassador in Uruguay, as he was being driven to British Embassy in Montevideo. **Feb. 4.** It was stated that 30,000 U.S. and South Vietnamese troops, supported by large-scale air strikes into Laos, had massed on borders of South Vietnam and Laos; on Feb. 8 large South Vietnamese forces crossed border to strike Communist supply bases and staging areas. **7.** In Switzerland, women were granted Federal vote, and right to stand for Parliament, in referendum of all-male electorate. **March 12.** Turkish Government resigned after Army commanders threatened to take over country unless new administration was formed immediately; on March 19 Mr. Nihat Erim became Prime Minister in succession to Mr. Demirel. **22.** Military junta deposed President Levingston of Argentina. **23.** About 80,000 farmers demonstrated in Brussels against Common Market agricultural policy; one was killed and many injured in violent clashes with police. **25.** South Vietnam troops were withdrawn from Laos. **April 5.** Herr Brandt, West German Chancellor, had two days of talks with Mr. Heath in Bonn. **20.** A Royal Navy survey launch was towed away from moorings in fishing village of Baltimore, Co. Cork, and blown up and sunk in I.R.A. terrorist raid. **22.** It was an-

nounced that Dr. François Duvalier, President of Haiti, had died and been succeeded by his son, Jean-Claude. **May 3.** In East Germany, Herr Walter Ulbricht resigned as First Secretary of Central Committee of German Socialist Unity Party and was succeeded by Herr Erich Honecker. **9.** West German Cabinet agreed to let Deutsche Mark float, but not to revalue it formally against U.S. dollar and Dutch Government followed suit with the guilder; Switzerland revalued Swiss franc by 7 per cent. and Austria revalued schilling by 5·05 per cent. **23.** Mr. Stanley Sylvester, British Consul in Rosario, Argentina, was kidnapped by armed terrorists outside his home; he was freed on May 30. **June 22.** In Luxemburg, Mr. Rippon, Britain's chief negotiator, and members of Common Market brought their talks on terms for British entry into the Market to a satisfactory conclusion. **July 5.** President Pompidou of France began two-day visit to West Germany for talks with Herr Brandt. **Aug. 22.** After three days' fighting, army forces in Bolivia overthrew left-wing Government of President Torres. **Sept. 9.** Mr. Geoffrey Jackson, British ambassador in Uruguay, who had been kidnapped by left-wing guerillas in January, was released in suburb of Montevideo. **16.** Bombs were thrown on site of Tokyo's second international airport by demonstrators protesting against its construction; three policemen were killed.

OBITUARY, OCT. 1, 1970—SEPT. 30, 1971

Albery, Sir Bronson James, distinguished theatre director, aged 90—*July* 21.

Armstrong, Louis, famous jazz musician, aged 71—*July* 6.

Astor of Hever, *Col.* John Jacob Astor, 1st Baron, chief proprietor of *Times* newspaper, 1922–66, aged 85—*July* 19.

Bentley, Walter Owen, car designer, aged 83—*Aug.* 13.

Bernal, *Prof.* John Desmond, F.R.S., physicist, aged 70—*Sept.* 15.

Board, Lillian, athlete, aged 22—*Dec.* 26, 1970.

Bowra, Sir Cecil Maurice, F.B.A., Warden of Wadham College, Oxford, 1938–70, aged 73—*July* 4.

Boyd-Orr, John Boyd Orr, C.H., D.S.O., M.C., M.D., F.R.S., 1st Baron, leading authority on nutrition, aged 90—*June* 25.

Braddock, Elizabeth Margaret, Labour M.P. for Liverpool Exchange from 1945–70, aged 71—*Nov.* 13, 1970.

Bragg, *Prof.* Sir William Lawrence, C.H., O.B.E., M.C., F.R.S., eminent physicist, aged 81—*July* 1.

Brown, Jackie, former world flyweight boxing champion, aged 61—*March* 14.

Cardenas, *Gen.* Lazaro, former President of Mexico, aged 75—*Oct.* 19, 1970.

Charteris, Hugo Francis Guy, M.C., writer, aged 48—*Dec.* 20, 1970.

Clark, *Prof.* Sir Wilfrid Edward Le Gros, F.R.S., D.SC., outstanding anatomist, aged 76—*June* 28.

Constantine, Learie Nicholas Constantine, M.B.E., Baron, famous West Indian cricketer, aged 69—*July* 1.

Cumming, *Brig.* Arthur Edward, 𝒱.𝒞., O.B.E., M.C., aged 74—*April* 10.

Daladier, Edouard, former French Prime Minister, aged 86—*Oct.* 10, 1970.

Dance, James, Conservative M.P. for Bromsgrove since 1955, aged 63—*March* 16.

Daniels, Bebe, actress, aged 70—*March* 16.

de Gaulle, *Général* Charles André Joseph Marie, President of the French Republic, 1959–69, aged 79—*Nov.* 9, 1970.

Dewey, Thomas Edmund, Republican candidate

for Presidency of U.S.A. in 1944 and 1948, aged 68—*March* 16.

Davidson, John Colin Campbell Davidson, P.C., G.C.V.O., C.H., C.B., 1st Visct., former Conservative Minister, aged 81—*Dec.* 11, 1970.

Dorrell, *Lt.-Col.* G. T., 𝒱.𝒞., M.B.E., aged 90—*Jan.* 7.

Emery, *Prof.* Walter Bryan, C.B.E., F.B.A., F.S.A., eminent Egyptologist, aged 67—*March* 11.

Engelhard, Charles William, U.S. industrialist and racehorse owner, aged 54—*March* 2.

Ervine, St. John Greer, dramatist and novelist, aged 87—*Jan.* 24.

Falls, *Capt.* Cyril Bentham, C.B.E., military historian, aged 83—*April* 23.

Fleming, Peter, O.B.E., author and traveller, aged 64—*Aug.* 18.

Goddard, Rayner Goddard, P.C., G.C.B., Baron, Lord Chief Justice of England, 1946–58, aged 94—*May* 29.

Godfrey, *Admiral* John Henry, C.B., wartime Director of Naval Intelligence, aged 83—*Aug.* 29.

Guthrie, Sir William Tyrone, theatrical producer and director, aged 70—*May* 15.

Harman, *Rt. Hon.* Sir Charles Eustace, a Lord Justice of Appeal, 1959–70, aged 75—*Nov.* 14, 1970.

Holmes, Percy, Yorkshire and England cricketer, aged 84—*Sept.* 3.

Hunter, Norman Charles, playwright and novelist, aged 62—*April* 19.

Hutchinson, Arthur Stuart Menteth, novelist, aged 91—*March* 13.

Jeger, George, Labour M.P. for Goole since 1950, aged 67—*Jan.* 6.

Kerby, *Capt.* Henry Briton, Conservative M.P. for Arundel and Shoreham since 1954, aged 56—*Jan.* 4.

Knox, Edmund George Valpy, former Editor of *Punch*, aged 89—*Jan.* 2.

Lee, *Rt. Hon.* Sir Frank Godbould, G.C.M.G., K.C.B., Master of Corpus Christi College, Cambridge since 1962, aged 67—*April* 28.

Le Fanu, *Admiral of the Fleet* Sir Michael, G.C.B., D.S.C., Chief of Naval Staff and First Sea Lord, 1968–70, aged 57—*Nov.* 28, 1970.

Lemass, Seán Francis, former Prime Minister of Republic of Ireland, aged 71—*May* 11.

Leslie, Sir Shane, Bt., man of letters, aged 85—*Aug.* 13.

Lewis, Ted (" Kid "), former world welterweight boxing champion, aged 75—*Oct.* 20, 1970.

Liston, Charles " Sonny ", former world heavyweight boxing champion, aged 38—*Jan.* 3.

Lloyd, Harold, film comedian, aged 77—*March* 8.

Longmore, *Air Chief Marshal* Sir Arthur Murray, G.C.B., D.S.O., pioneer of naval aviation, aged 85 —*Dec.* 10, 1970.

Lonsdale, *Prof.* Dame Kathleen, D.B.E., D.SC., F.R.S., first woman president of British Association, aged 68—*April* 1.

Luce, *Admiral* Sir John David, G.C.B., D.S.O., O.B.E., Chief of Naval Staff and First Sea Lord, 1963–66, aged 64—*Jan.* 6.

MacColl, James Eugene, Labour M.P. for Widnes since 1950, aged 62—*June* 16.

McCorquodale of Newton, Malcolm Stewart McCorquodale, P.C., K.C.V.O., first and last Baron, former junior Minister, aged 70—*Sept.* 25.

Mackail, Denis George, novelist and biographer, aged 79—*Aug.* 4.

MacPherson, Malcolm, M.B.E., Labour M.P. for Stirling and Falkirk Burghs since 1948, aged 66—*May* 24.

Malvern, Godfrey Martin Huggins, P.C., C.H., K.C.M.G., 1st Visct., Prime Minister of Federation of Rhodesia and Nyasaland, 1953–56, aged 87—*May* 8.

Martin, Reginald James, banker and journalist and special contributor to *Whitaker's Almanack*, 1946–1966, aged 78—*Nov.* 2, 1970.

McCracken, Esther Helen, dramatist, aged 69—*Aug.* 9.

Mikkelsen, *Capt.* Ejnar, famous Danish Arctic explorer, aged 90.

Mills, *Air Chief Marshal* Sir George Holroyd, G.C.B., D.F.C., Gentleman Usher of the Black Rod, House of Lords, 1963–70, aged 69—*April* 14.

Montgomery Campbell, *Rt. Rev.* and *Rt. Hon.* Henry Colville, K.C.V.O., M.C., D.D., Bishop of London, 1956–61, aged 83—*Dec.* 26, 1970.

Mottram, Ralph Hale, author, aged 87—*April* 15.

Nash, Ogden, U.S. author, aged 68—*May* 19.

Newsom, Sir John Hubert, C.B.E., eminent educationist, aged 60—*May* 23.

Niemeyer, Sir Otto Ernst, G.B.E., K.C.B., former Director of Bank of England, aged 87—*Feb.* 6.

Niebuhr, *Rev. Prof.* Reinhold, D.D., U.S. theologian, aged 78—*May* 31.

Peter, ex-King of Yugoslavia, aged 47—*Nov.*, 1970.

Portal of Hungerford, *Marshal of the Royal Air Force* Charles Frederick Algernon Portal, K.G., G.C.B., O.M., D.S.O., M.C., 1st and last Visct., Chief of the Air Staff, 1940–45, aged 77—*April* 22.

Postgate, Raymond William, writer, aged 74—*March* 29.

Rawsthorne, Alan, C.B.E., composer, aged 66—*July* 24.

Reith, John Charles Walsham Reith, P.C., K.T., G.C.V.O., G.B.E., C.B., T.D., 1st Baron, creator of British broadcasting and first Director-General of B.B.C., aged 81—*June* 16.

Rennie, Michael, film actor, aged 62—*June* 10.

Rodriguez, Pedro, Mexican racing driver (*accidentally killed*), aged 31—*July* 11.

Ross, Sir William David, K.B.E., D.Litt., former Vice-Chancellor of Oxford University, aged 94—*May* 5.

Saint-Denis, Michel Jacques, Consultant Director of Royal Shakespeare Theatre Company since 1966, aged 73—*July* 31.

Scott, Cyril, musical composer, librettist, and author, aged 91—*Dec.* 31, 1970.

Segrave, Edmond, Editor of *The Bookseller* since 1933, aged 66—*March* 28.

Selborne, Roundell Cecil Palmer, P.C., C.H., 3rd Earl of, former Minister and Conservative M.P., aged 84—*Sept.* 3.

Simonds, Gavin Turnbull Simonds, P.C., 1st and last Visct., Lord Chancellor, 1951–54, aged 89—*June* 28.

Skeffington, Arthur Massey, Labour M.P. for Hayes and Harlington since 1953, aged 61—*Feb.* 18.

Slim, *Field-Marshal* William Joseph Slim, K.G., G.C.B., G.C.M.G., G.C.V.O., G.B.E., D.S.O., M.C., 1st Visct., commander of 14th Army in Burma during Second World War, aged 79—*Dec.* 14, 1970.

Smith, Sir Frank Edwin Newson-, Bt., Lord Mayor of London, 1943–44, aged 92—*April* 23.

Smith, Stevie, author and poet, aged 68—*March* 7.

Soulbury, Herwald Ramsbotham, P.C., G.C.M.G., G.C.V.O., O.B.E., M.C., 1st Visct., former junior Minister and Governor-General of Ceylon, aged 83—*Jan.* 30.

Stopford, *Gen.* Sir Montagu George North, G.C.B., K.B.E., D.S.O., M.C., aged 78—*March* 10.

Stravinsky, Igor, famous composer, aged 88—*April* 6.

Stuart of Findhorn, James Gray Stuart, P.C., C.H., M.V.O., M.C., 1st Visct., former Conservative M.P. and Secretary of State for Scotland, aged 74—*Feb.* 20.

Swanborough, Stella Isaacs, G.B.E., Baroness, (Dowager Marchioness of Reading), founder and chairman of Women's Royal Voluntary Service, aged 77—*May* 22.

Terriss, Ellaline (Lady Hicks), actress, aged 100—*June* 16.

Tovey, *Admiral of the Fleet* John Cronyn Tovey, G.C.B., K.B.E., D.S.O., 1st and last Baron, aged 85—*Jan.* 12.

Trevethin and Oaksey, Geoffrey Lawrence, P.C., D.S.O., T.D., Lord, former Lord of Appeal and president of Nuremburg War Criminals Tribunal, aged 90—*Aug.* 28.

Tubman, *Hon.* William Vacanararat Shadrach, G.C.B., G.C.M.G., President of Liberia since 1944, aged 75—*July* 23.

Upjohn, Gerald Ritchie Upjohn, P.C., C.B.E., Baron, a Lord of Appeal in Ordinary since 1963, aged 67—*Jan.* 27.

Wakehurst, John de Vere Loder, K.G., K.C.M.G., 2nd Baron, Governor of Northern Ireland, 1952–64, aged 75—*Oct.* 30, 1970.

Wayne, Naunton, actor, aged 69—*Nov.* 17, 1970.

Webster, Sir David Lumsden, K.C.V.O., General Administrator of Royal Opera House, Covent Garden, 1946–70, aged 67—*May* 11.

Weir, Sir John, G.C.V.O., Royal Victorian Chain, Physician to the Queen, 1952–68, aged 91—*April* 17.

White, *Col.* Archie Cecil Thomas, *V.C.*, M.C., aged 80—*May* 20.

Whitehead, Sir Edgar Cuthbert Fremantle, K.C.M.G., O.B.E., former Prime Minister of Southern Rhodesia, aged 66—*Sept.* 22.

Wilkinson, Norman, C.B.E., marine artist, aged 92—*May* 30.

Woodward, Sir Ernest Llewellyn, F.B.A., distinguished historian, aged 80—*March* 11.

Wymark, Patrick Carl, actor, aged 44—*Oct.* 20, 1970.

THE CENTENARIES OF 1972

THE CENTENARIES OF 1972

The tangled history of the *Alabama* claim, which had troubled relations between Britain and the United States since the American Civil War, was at last brought to an end in 1872. Under the terms of the Washington Treaty of 1871, an arbitration tribunal had been set up at Geneva to settle the claim, but there was further delay before arbitration could proceed. This arose from the inclusion in the U.S. case of " indirect claims ", which, if they had been upheld, would have made Britain financially responsible for the prolongation of the Civil War. In the event the indirect claims were withdrawn, and in September the arbitrators made an award against Britain of £3,229,166 in respect of damage done by the *Alabama*, the *Florida* and the *Shenandoah*.

At home the Ballot Act was at last passed though not without further contention between the Commons and the Lords, who had thrown out a similar Bill the previous year. The Act as passed was a temporary one and it was not until 1918 that its provisions were made permanent.

The only other legislation of note was a Licensing Act, which was far from popular, but the undoubted decline in fortunes of Mr. Gladstone's Ministry during the year can be attributed more to a series of administrative blunders and scandals which beset it. Mr. Lowe's Budget, however, was less controversial than that of 1871; the income tax was reduced from sixpence to fourpence in the pound, but there were few other significant changes.

The Home Rule movement in Ireland received considerable impetus from by-election victories in Kerry and Galway. In the latter case, however, Judge Keogh unseated the successful Home Rule candidate on petition, stating in his judgment that there had been undue clerical influence. This in turn roused strong feeling in Ireland, though attempts in the House of Commons to have the Judge removed were not successful.

The civil action of the Tichborne claimant, which had been in progress for ten months, came to a sudden end in March when the jury stopped the case and the claimant was committed for trial on charges of perjury.

In February the Viceroy of India, the Earl of Mayo, while on an official visit to the Andaman Islands, the site of the Indian penal settlement, was fatally stabbed by a convict.

By the New Year the Prince of Wales was well on the road to recovery after his dangerous illness of December, 1871, and on February 27th the Queen, with the Prince and Princess of Wales, drove through crowded streets from Buckingham Palace to St. Paul's to attend a thanksgiving service for the Prince's recovery. Two days later as the Queen was returning from a drive and was about to alight from her carriage at the garden entrance of Buckingham Palace, a youth of seventeen named Arthur O'Connor pointed a pistol at her. He was seized by John Brown, the Queen's personal attendant, and the pistol was found to be unloaded. It was supposed that O'Connor was of weak intellect and, when brought to trial, he received a comparatively light sentence.

These two occurrences aroused general sympathy with the Queen, and when on March 19 Sir Charles Dilke brought forward a motion in the Commons calling for retrenchment in the Civil List, it was rejected, after noisy demonstrations against its supporters, by 276 votes to 2. The Queen's other appearances during the year were restricted, though she carried out a review of troops at Aldershot on July 5 and she paid an inaugural visit in May to the Albert Hall which had been completed and opened

in 1871. But suggestions that she should visit Ireland or that the Prince of Wales should take up residence there were rejected, though her second son, the Duke of Edinburgh, went to Ireland in June and opened the Dublin Exhibition of Arts.

On Sept. 23 the death occurred, at the age of 65, of the Queen's half-sister, Princess Feodore of Hohenlohe, daughter of the Duchess of Kent by her previous marriage to the Prince of Leiningen.

In January the Metropolitan Board of Works took formal possession of Hampstead Heath, which, with the help of a public subscription, had been purchased from the Maryon Wilson family for £55,045. In Leeds Roundhay Park was officially opened to the public by Prince Arthur (later the Duke of Connaught) on September 19. In November the new Guildhall Library in the City of London was opened.

Developments in communications during the year included the arrival in Stamboul in January of the first train to connect Asiatic Turkey with Europe, and the opening of direct telegraphic communication between England and Australia, which was marked by a banquet at the Cannon Street Hotel in November.

One of the worst eruptions of Mount Vesuvius to be recorded took place between April 26 and May 1; many lives were lost. Spain continued to be in a state approximating to civil war; a Carlist insurrection spread to most parts of the country in April and May, there was an unsuccessful attempt to assassinate King Amadeo in Madrid in July and a Republican rising took place in Ferrol in October.

General Grant was re-elected President of the United States, securing an overwhelming majority over the Democratic and Liberal Republican candidate, Horace Greeley, Editor of the New York *Tribune*.

Publications in 1872 included George Eliot's *Middlemarch*, which had begun to appear in parts in 1871, Thomas Hardy's *Under the Greenwood Tree*, Kingsley's *Collected Poems*, Tennyson's *Gareth and Lynette*, Oliver Wendell Holmes' *The Poet at the Breakfast Table*, John Morley's *Voltaire*, Bagehot's *Physics and Politics*, and the first volume of John Forster's *Life of Dickens*. H. M. Stanley's book *How I Found Livingstone* had great popular success.

Finally, two passages from " Remarkable Occurrences of 1872 ", printed in *Whitaker's Almanack* for 1873, seem to strike a note familiar to modern ears, though the first may perhaps have been somewhat exaggerated!

" During the month [July, 1872] strikes were nearly universal in all branches of trade, causing much commercial disturbance ".

" Sept. 9. Great meeting in Trafalgar Square, respecting the high price of provisions".

CENTENARIES OF 1972

The following is a list of the principal centenaries which will be commemorated in 1972.

Died 1872

Feb. 8.	Earl of Mayo. Governor-General of India (assassinated).	
March 10.	Giuseppe Mazzini. Italian nationalist leader.	
April 1.	Frederick Denison Maurice. Theologian.	
April 19.	Richard Westmacott. Sculptor.	
June 1.	Charles Lever. Irish novelist.	
Sept. 23.	Princess Feodore of Hohenlohe. Half-sister of Queen Victoria.	
Oct. 23.	Théophile Gautier. French critic.	
Dec. 15.	Viscountess Beaconsfield. Wife of Benjamin Disraeli.	

Born 1872

Jan. 16.	Gordon Craig. Stage designer.
Jan. 29.	Sir William Rothenstein. Painter.
Feb. 5.	Sir William Nicholson. Artist.
Feb. 20.	Earl Beauchamp. Liberal politician.
Feb. 28.	Viscount Hailsham. Lord Chancellor.
March 10.	Serge Diaghilev. Producer of Russian ballet.
March 16.	Josiah Wedgwood (Lord Wedgwood). Labour politician.
March 31.	Arthur Griffith. Irish political leader.
April 9.	Léon Blum. French politician.
April 25.	C. B. Fry. Cricketer and all-round sportsman.
May 12.	Eleanor Rathbone. Social reformer.
May 18.	Bertrand Russell (Earl Russell). Social reformer.
May 31.	Sir Charles Harington. General.
May 31.	W. Heath Robinson. Humorous artist.
July 4.	Calvin Coolidge. President of U.S.A.
July 5.	Edouard Herriot. French politician.
July 12.	Earl of Birkenhead (F. E. Smith). Lord Chancellor.
July 16.	Roald Amundsen. Norwegian explorer.
July 18.	J. L. Hammond. Historian.
Aug. 3.	King Haakon of Norway.
Aug. 15.	Lord Rushcliffe (Sir Henry Betterton). Conservative politician.
Aug. 24.	Aubrey Beardsley. Illustrator.
Sept. 10.	K. S. Ranjitsinhji (The Jam Saheb of Nawanagar). Cricketer.
Sept. 23.	Lord Bradbury. Permanent Secretary of the Treasury.
Sept. 25.	Joseph Herman Hertz. Chief Rabbi.
Sept. 25.	Sir Charles B. Cochran. Impresario.
Oct. 4.	Lord Keyes. Admiral of the Fleet.
Dec. 2.	Dame Irene Vanbrugh. Actress.

Died 1772

March 29.	Emmanuel Swedenborg. Philosopher.

Born 1772

April 19.	David Ricardo. Economist.
Oct. 25.	Samuel Taylor Coleridge. Poet.

Died 1672

Aug. 19.	John de Witt. Netherlands statesman.

Born 1672

(exact date unknown)	Sir Richard Steele. Essayist.
May 1	Joseph Addison. Man of letters.

1572

Aug. 24.	Massacre of St. Bartholomew.

CENTENARIES OF 1973

The following is a list of the principal centenaries which will be commemorated in 1973.

Died 1873

Jan. 9.	Napoleon III, ex-Emperor of the French.
Jan. 18.	Lord Lytton. Novelist.
April 20.	Sir William Tite. Architect.
April 27.	William Charles Macready. Actor.
May 1.	David Livingstone. Explorer.
May 9.	John Stuart Mill. Economist and man of letters.
July 19.	Samuel Wilberforce. Bishop.
Oct. 1.	Edwin Landseer. Painter.
Oct. 27.	Sir Henry Holland. Physician.

Born 1873

Jan. 5.	Visct. Southwood. Newspaper proprietor.
Jan. 28.	M. A. Noble. Australian cricketer.
Jan. 28.	Charles Sims. Painter.
Feb. 1.	Dame Clara Butt. Singer.
Feb. 3.	Lord Trenchard. "Father" of the Royal Air Force.
Feb. 15.	Fedor Ivanovich Chaliapin. Singer.
Feb. 28.	Visct. Simon. Lawyer and politician.
March 7.	J. D. Beresford. Novelist.
March 9.	Dame Lilian Braithwaite. Actress.
March 17.	Margaret Bondfield. First woman Cabinet Minister in Britain.
March 26.	Sir Gerald du Maurier. Actor.
April 2.	Serge Rachmaninoff. Composer and pianist.
April 19.	Sydney F. Barnes. Cricketer.
April 25.	Walter de la Mare. Poet and novelist.
May 26.	Sir Cuthbert Whitaker. Editor of *Whitaker's Almanack*.
June 7.	Sir Landon Ronald. Musician.
July 20.	Alberto Santos-Dumont. Aviator.
Aug. 11.	Bertram Mills. Circus proprietor.
Aug. 21.	Omar Ramsden. Goldsmith.
Sept. 9.	Max Reinhardt. Producer.
Sept. 13.	Sir John Clapham. Economic historian.
Sept. 27.	Lord Chatfield. Admiral of the Fleet.
Oct. 1.	Sir Pelham Warner. Cricketer.
Nov. 22.	Leopold Amery. Politician.
Dec. 17.	Ford Madox Ford. Author.

Died 1773

March 24.	Earl of Chesterfield. Politician and man of letters.

Born 1773

Oct. 23.	Francis Jeffrey (Lord Jeffrey). Critic.

Died 1673

March 15.	Salvator Rosa. Painter.

Born 1573

July 15.	Inigo Jones. Architect.
Oct. 7.	William Laud. Archbishop.

Born 1473

Feb. 19.	Nicolaus Copernicus. Astronomer.

THE PERIODS OF ENGLISH ARCHITECTURE

Date		Style
I.	Before 55 B.C.	Ancient British.
II.	55 B.C. to A.D. 420.	Roman Period.
III.	A.D. 449 to Norman Conquest (1066).	Anglo-Saxon.
IV.	1066–1189 (*i.e.* to end 12th cent.).	Norman.
V.	1189–1307 (*i.e.* 13th cent.).	Early English (Lancet, or Geometrical).
VI.	1307–1377 (*i.e.* 14th cent.).	Decorated (or Curvilinear).
VII.	1377–1485 (*i.e.* 15th cent.).	Perpendicular (or Rectilinear).
VIII.	1485–1558 (*i.e.* first half 16th cent.).	Tudor.
IX.	A.D. 1558–1625. Early Renaissance	{ Elizabeth (A.D. 1558–1603). { Jacobean (A.D. 1603–1625).
X.	A.D. 1625–1830. Late Renaissance	{ Stuart (A.D. 1625–1702). { Queen Anne and Georgian (A.D. 1702–1803).
XI.	Modern Architecture (The Age of Revivals) } 19th cent.	{ William IV. (A.D. 1830–1837). { Victoria (A.D. 1837–1901).
XII.	Recent Architecture. 20th cent.	{ Edward VII. (A.D. 1901–1910). { George V. (A.D. 1910–1935). { Edward VIII. (A.D. 1936). { George VI. (A.D. 1936–1952).

NAUTICAL MEASURES

Distance is measured in nautical (or sea) miles. The nautical mile is traditionally defined as the length of a minute of arc of a great circle of the earth; but as this length varies in different latitudes (owing to the fact that the earth is not a perfect sphere), 6,080 feet, a "rounded off value" of the mean length, has been adopted in British practice as the standard length of the nautical mile. On this basis 33 nautical miles exactly equal 38 statute miles; the statute (land) mile contains 5,280 feet. A *cable*, as a measure used by seamen, is 600 feet (100 fathoms) approximately one-tenth of a nautical mile. *Soundings at sea* are recorded in fathoms (6 feet).

6 feet= 1 fathom.
100 fathoms = 1 cable length.
10 cables= 1 nautical mile.

Note.—Some other countries, including the United States in 1954, have adopted the nautical mile of 1,852 metres as recommended by the International Hydrographic Bureau in 1929.

Speed is measured in *nautical miles per hour*, called *knots*. A knot is a measure of speed and is not used to express distance. A ship moving at the rate of 30 nautical miles per hour is said to be "doing 30 knots" and as the nautical mile is longer than the land or statute mile this represents a land speed of over 34½ miles per hour. In 1945 the *Royal Air Force* adopted the knot and the nautical mile as the standard measurements for speed and distance.

Knots	m.p.h.	Knots	m.p.h.	Knots	m.p.h.
1	1.1515	15	17.2727	29	33.3939
2	2.3030	16	18.4242	30	34.5454
3	3.4545	17	19.5757	31	35.6969
4	4.6060	18	20.7272	32	36.8484
5	5.7575	19	21.8787	33	38.0000
6	6.9090	20	23.0303	34	39.1515
7	8.0606	21	24.1818	35	40.3030
8	9.2121	22	25.3333	36	41.4545
9	10.3636	23	26.4848	37	42.6060
10	11.5151	24	27.6363	38	43.7575
11	12.6666	25	28.7878	39	44.9090
12	13.8180	26	29.9393	40	46.0606
13	14.9696	27	31.0908	41	47.2121
14	16.1212	28	32.2424	42	48.3636

Gross tonnage.—The total volume of all the enclosed spaces of a vessel, the unit of measurement being a ton of 100 cubic feet.

Net tonnage.—The gross tonnage less certain deductions for crew space, engine room, water ballast and other spaces not used for passengers or cargo.

BRITISH FORCES BROADCASTING SERVICE
King's Building, Dean Stanley Street, S.W.1

The Service came into existence during the early part of the Second World War to entertain, inform and to maintain the morale of the Serviceman in the field. No exact date can be given for the inception of the Service because, in answer to the need, special broadcasting for the Services overseas began in many different places almost simultaneously during 1942. The first mobile transmitters were provided by the then War Office in 1943 and these were sent with specially selected staff to North Africa. From 1943 onwards a whole network of Forces Broadcasting Stations grew up covering the Mediterranean area, the Persian Gulf, India, Ceylon and Germany.

After the war the Service continued to entertain and inform Servicemen wherever they might be stationed overseas and the network was extended from Germany and the Mediterranean to the Far East.

In 1960 the War Office called on the help of the BBC to reorganize B.F.B.S. and as a result, a Head Office was created in London and a Director appointed. The Head Office now produces between 30 and 35 hours a week of programmes of entertainment and information and these are recorded, dubbed and flown out to the B.F.B.S. stations abroad. The number of these stations has diminished in recent years with the withdrawal of British Forces overseas but there are still stations in Germany, Gibraltar, Malta, Cyprus and Singapore, with a Gurkha commitment in Hong Kong. Each of these stations broadcasts for 14 or more hours a day. Much of their output is produced locally and the task of the stations is to reflect the life of the Serviceman and his family in their surroundings overseas, drawing them in to take part in quizzes, discussions, interviews, etc. Through the programmes produced in Head Office and by relays of BBC news and current affairs the B.F.B.S. stations overseas create for the Serviceman a strong link with home, and keep him abreast of the changes that are going on while he is away.

There is also a section of B.F.B.S. whose function it is to engage artists and produce live entertainment shows which each year tour the Commands overseas. Many of the great names in the entertainment world have entertained the Services in this way.

B.F.B.S. is organized to serve all three Services. Its staff are all civilian, professional broadcasters and engineers, and many of the household names of radio and television at home have had their initial training through Forces broadcasting. The Service is administered by the Army on behalf of the other two Services and is financed from the Treasury through the Ministry of Defence.

Director, I. J. Woolf.

BANK HOLIDAYS, 1972–74

	ENGLAND, WALES, NORTHERN IRELAND, THE CHANNEL ISLANDS				SCOTLAND		
	Easter Monday	Spring Holiday	Autumn Bank Holiday	Boxing Day	New Year's Day	Spring Holiday	Autumn Bank Holiday
1972	April 3	May 29	August 28	December 26	Jan. 1	May 1	August 7
1973	April 23	May 28	August 27	December 26	Jan. 1	May 7	August 6
1974	April 15	May 27	August 26	December 26	Jan. 1	May 6	August 5

New Year's Day and *Liberation Day* (May 9) are bank and public holidays in the Channel Islands. Banks are also closed on *Good Friday* and *Christmas Day* and on *Saturdays*.

RADIO AND TELEVISION SETS: GRAMOPHONES AND RECORDS
United Kingdom Production and Licences Current

ITEM	1966	1967	1968	1969	1970
Radios and Radiograms					
Production..................thousands	—	1,530	1,736	1,420	1,303
Home Sales.................thousands	—	1,583	1,638	1,276	1,282
Value.....................£ million	—	18·4	21·1	17·4	18·6
Export Sales................thousands	—	32	35	131	128
Value...................£ thousand	—	439	464	1,480	1,407
Television Sets					
Production..................millions	—	1·3	2·0	1·9	2·2
Home Sales.................millions	—	1·35	1·87	1·83	2·14
Value.....................£ million	—	56·5	91·3	88·1	133·0
Export Sales................thousands	—	43·6	57·3	53·9	71·6
Value.....................£ million	—	1·6	2·3	2·4	3·4
Broadcasting Licences Current					
Radio only*.................thousands	2,513	2,583	2,502	2,375	2,074
Monochrome television.......thousands	13,919	14,910	15,431	15,612	15,660
Colour television.............thousands	—	—	75	197	528
Record Players					
Sales.....................thousand units	—	412·6	533·1	467·8	560·5
Value.....................£ million	—	5·2	6·8	6·3	7·7
Home Sales...............thousand units	—	398·4	509·2	444·5	544·9
Value.....................£ million	—	5·0	6·5	6·0	7·5
Export sales................thousand units	—	14·2	23·9	23·2	15·6
Value...................£ thousand	—	156·8	279·4	292·5	228·7
Gramophone Records					
Production (all types)..........millions	84·9	89·8	98·6	106·4	112·9
78 r.p.m....................thousands	400	308	206	173	106
45 r.p.m....................millions	51·2	51·6	49·2	46·6	47·0
33⅓ r.p.m..................millions	33·3	38·0	49·2	59·6	65·9
Sales:—					
Manufacturers' total (excl. P.T.)					
£ million	25·1	27·9	30·1	32·4	39·3
Manufacturers' export sales...£ million	3·7	3·9	5·0	5·7	6·5
Cinema Statistics					
Admissions: weekly averages......millions	5·6	5·17	4·70	4·24	3·82
Gross box-office receipts: weekly averages					
£ million	1·20	1·14	1·14	1·13	1·16

★ Sound licences abolished Feb. 1, 1971.

UNITED KINGDOM FOOD IMPORTS, 1967–70

ITEM	Monthly Averages—'000 tons			
	1967	1968	1969	1970
Meat*....................................	60·2	60·8	69·0	57·7
Bacon...................................	33·5	33·8	32·2	31·5
Canned meat............................	14·8	14·3	12·6	14·1
Butter..................................	40·3	37·2	34·8	33·3
Cheese..................................	13·1	14·8	12·8	12·9
Eggs in shell, million dozen..........	2·23	1·70	1·46	1·42
Wheat..................................	313·8	336·2	388·5	404·2
Barley..................................	18·2	5·9	53·4	99·3
Maize...................................	305·0	310·4	258·3	255·8
Flour...................................	7·7	6·2	6·5	6·8
Oranges.................................	33·8	33·9	34·6	37·8
Bananas.................................	29·0	28·4	29·3	27·5
Apples..................................	23·8	24·6	23·8	21·2
Dried Fruit..............................	11·1	11·5	11·2	11·5
Tinned or bottled fruit..................	28·9	30·7	34·3	34·6
Tomatoes................................	13·0	14·0	13·2	13·5
Unrefined sugar.........................	175·3	163·2	171·4	150·8
Coffee..................................	6·7	7·8	8·6	8·2
Raw cocoa..............................	7·3	6·3	8·4	6·7
Tea and maté...........................	20·3	22·1	17·4	20·9
Oilcake and meal........................	78·1	81·1	76·7	81·1
Margarine and shortenings..............	15·6	16·0	14·8	15·8
Oilseeds and nuts.......................	57·4	55·7	55·9	54·0
Whale and fish oils......................	23·5	18·5	16·4	14·4
Vegetable oil............................	33·4	39·7	42·8	46·2

*Beef, veal, mutton, lamb, pork and offal: fresh, salted, chilled and frozen.

AGRICULTURE

Agricultural Holdings

In 1875 there were 550,796 agricultural holdings in Great Britain, with a crop and grass acreage (excluding holdings of rough grazing only) of 31,448,000 acres—England and Wales, 470,000 (26,837,000 acres); Scotland 80,796 (4,611,000 acres). Figures at the 1966 census were Great Britain, 366,742 holdings totalling 28,635,000 acres; England and Wales 312,182 (24,326,000 acres); Scotland, 54,560 (4,309,000 acres). The numbers of holdings by size of farm in 1966 was:—

Size of Holding	England and Wales	Scotland	Great Britain
Under 5 acres.......	63,546	10,784	74,330
5 to 20† acres.......	70,024	17,527	..
20† to 50 acres......	52,713	4,115	..
50 to 100 acres......	51,757	7,645	59,402
100 to 300 acres.....	58,418	11,452	69,870
300 to 500 acres.....	10,331	2,205	12,536
500 to 1,000 acres....	4,460	775	5,235
Over 1,000 acres....	933	57	990
TOTAL NUMBER	312,182	54,560	366,742

† Scotland—30 acres

NOTE.—A *farm* may consist of more than one *holding*. There are about 220,000 full-time farmers in the United Kingdom (Great Britain, 196,000).

About 200,000 holdings, 50 per cent. of all holdings in the United Kingdom, are on average 16 acres per holding and have a standard labour requirement of under 275 standard man-days*. These are very small holdings occupying about 10 per cent. of the U.K. crop and grass acreage and supplying about 8 per cent. of total agricultural output.

* 8 hrs. manual work for an adult male worker under average conditions: 275 smds = a year's work for one man.

Holdings by Farm Product

The following figures relate to the United Kingdom, except that figures for sugar beet and wheat exclude Northern Ireland where sugar beet is not produced and wheat only to a negligible extent. Breeding sheep figures exclude N. Ireland; Scottish element of the figures is for breeding ewes. Acreages are for the stated crop only; animal numbers for the stated kind only.

	1969		1970	
	No. of Holdings	Average Acreage	No. of Holdings	Average Acreage
Wheat.....	46,100	44.6	48,400	51.5
Barley.....	110,300	54.0	102,100	54.3
Oats......	72,800	13.0	66,100	14.1
Potatoes...	85,100	7.2	82,900	8.0
Sugar Beet.	21,800	20.9	20,800	22.3
		Average Herd		Average Herd
Dairy Cows	117,900	28	109,600	30
Beef Cows.	102,400	12	102,000	13
Breeding Pigs.....	70,700	13	65,900	14
		Average Flock		Average Flock
Breeding Sheep...	90,100	134	80,700	144
Broilers....	3,500	10,700	2,900	16,900
Laying Fowl....	157,200	341	136,600	404

United Kingdom
Crop Acreage and Production

Commodity	Acreage (thousand acres)		Estimated harvest (thousand tons)	
	June, 1969	June, 1970	1969	1970
Wheat.........	2,059	2,527	3,311	4,108
Barley.........	5,962	5,560	8,527	7,378
Oats..........	945	942	1,287	1,214
Mixed Corn....	156	186	216	253
Rye...........	9	12	11	13
Potatoes.......	614	674	6,117	7,364
Sugar Beet	457	469	5,939	6,311
Fodder Crops:				
Beans.........	220	191	232	157
Turnips and Swedes......	261	248	5,461	5,561
Mangolds......	26	25	611	571
Other fodder crops.......	292	269	4,184	3,730
Hops..........	17	17	10	12
Mustard.......	23	16	—	—
Fruit..........	215	759	—	—
Vegetables....	453	—	—	—
Flowers, etc....	5	—	—	—
Temporary Grassland....	5,738	5,804	†4,572	†4,213
Permanent Grassland....	12,348	12,285	†3,958	†3,640
TOTAL ARABLE LAND.......	17,943	17,988		

† Hay only.

Livestock

Livestock in U.K.	June, 1970 thousands	June, 1971 thousands
Cattle: total..............	12,585	12,836
Cows and heifers in milk .	3,949	4,004
Cows in calf but not in milk	597	570
Heifers in calf with first calf	863	831
Sheep.....................	26,080	26,061
Pigs......................	8,088	8,789
Poultry...................	143,430	

Production and Finance, 1970–71

Agricultural production in 1970–71 was higher than in 1969–70. Production of sheep, alone of the major commodities, has continued to decline and the guaranteed price was increased to 22·3p per lb. for fat sheep, an increase of about 2·8p, at the 1971 Annual Review of Prices.

Aggregate net income continued to show a rising trend in money terms though some decline in real terms. When account is taken of the continuing fall in the total number of farms, however, there does not appear to have been a corresponding decline in real net income per farm, taking the industry as a whole. Net costs have risen since 1970 by £217 million for all products and for produce to which the guaranteed prices apply by £141 million. These are by far the largest cost increases that have been recorded for the purposes of an Annual Review.

About a third of the total increase is accounted for by higher feeding-stuffs prices. Machinery, labour and fertilizers also showed large increases. The index of net product was expected to rise by 4 points from 106 in 1969–70 to 110 in 1970–71.

Because of unfavourable spring-sowing conditions, the cereals acreage harvested in 1970 was only marginally higher than the low level of 1969, and total production of cereals was less than in

1969–70 by about 500,000 tons. The 1970 plantings of potatoes (669,000 acres) were above target and yields were very high, giving a surplus over the requirement for human consumption. The 1971 target has been set at 640,000 acres. The beef herd expanded more than in any other year and the dairy herd, providing about two-thirds of the calves for beef, declined marginally. The sheep breeding flock again declined in numbers but home-fed supplies of mutton and lamb were expected to exceed those of 1969–70. The upward trend in the pig breeding herd continued with a 7 per cent. increase in numbers in the year to December, 1970, bacon production being estimated at 256,000 tons in 1970–71, an increase of 10 per cent. over 1969–70.

Farming Income.—Farming net income increased by £79 million in 1969–70 over 1968–69 and the forecast for 1970–71 showed a further increase of £15 million to £589 million, a total sustained by increases in the guarantees announced in October, 1970. When adjusted to a normal weather basis, income showed an increase for 1970–71 of £34 million.

Agricultural Support.—The cost to the Exchequer of agricultural support in 1970–71 was estimated at £269 million, about £8 million less than the outturn for 1969–70 and substantially less than the estimate for 1970–71 as adjusted. The estimate for 1971–72 is £297 million, the main increase being for pigs and cereals. Additional cost of bacon stabilization arrangements for 1971–72 is estimated at £15.5 million (1970–71, £22 million).

Crop Prices, 1970–71
Guaranteed prices for the 1970 and 1971 Harvests

Commodity	1970	1971
	revised	
Wheat, millable; average price per cwt. (a).........	£1.56	£1.63
Barley, price per cwt. (a) (b)	1.40	1.45
Oats, price per cwt. (b).....	1.39	1.44
Rye, millable, price per cwt.	1.08	1.08
Potatoes, standard ware. average per ton........ .	15.875	16.55
Sugar Beet, 16 per cent. sugar content, per ton...	6.95	7.60

(a) Subject to target indicator price arrangements.
(b) Merchantable grain only.

Livestock Prices, 1971–72

A list of Guaranteed Prices in 1971–72 of Livestock and Livestock products. Changes from final Guaranteed Prices in 1970–71 are indicated where applicable.

FAT CATTLE.—Steers, heifers and special young cows, per live cwt., gross weight, including quality premiums (+ £1.225) £12.35

FAT SHEEP AND LAMBS.—1st grade, average of shorn and unshorn, and including any headage payments or other bonuses: per lb. estimated dressed carcase weight.... 22.3p
(+2.8p)

FAT PIGS.—Clean pigs in quality premium range. Per score dead weight, including quality premiums............(+ 7p) 2.93*

Livestock Products

MILK.—Average wholesale price, plus production bonus and quality premiums, per gallon.....................(2.5p) 22.1p

HEN EGGS.—Sold through packing stations, guaranteed average support price for 1st quality eggs, average per dozen†... 16.5p
(− 0.5p)

DUCK EGGS.—Sold through packing stations, guaranteed average support price for 1st quality eggs, average per doz.... 15.5p
(− 0.3p)

WOOL.—Average per lb. greasy for fleece wool, inclusive of increase in marketing cost.........................(+ 0.5p) 22.7p

★ Price shown is related to a standard feed price. Adjustments are made to take account of changes in the price of feed over the year: fat pig price, 1971–1972 is related to a feed price of £2.20 per cwt.

† Subject to a standard quality arrangement with an upper limit of 651 million dozen, varying the basic subsidy. The former lower limit of 480 million dozen was discontinued for 1971–72.

Estimated Gross Value of Agricultural Output of the United Kingdom
(£ million)

Commodity	1967–68	1968–69	1969–70
Grain...........	239.3	219.1	234.9
Potatoes...........	84.9	80.2	111.9
Sugar Beet.........	42.3	43.0	40.7
Hops.............	7.0	6.5	7.2
Other farm crops....	8.4	9.8	8.2
Fatstock...........	605.1	613.5	656.8
Milk and milk products...........	443.4	447.0	458.0
Eggs...............	178.8	198.9	199.6
Poultry...........	100.9	111.4	119.3
Wool.............	15.9	14.7	13.5
Other livestock products...........	2.1	2.5	3.1
Fruit...............	41.2	47.8	49.0
Vegetables	110.1	120.3	126.7
Flowers............	43.5	46.5	50.5
Sundry output......	30.9	27.4	35.0
TOTAL........	1,939.4	1,983.5	2,141.9

Farming Net Income, 1962–71 (U.K.)

The following table shows the aggregate farming net income in each year since 1961–62, compared with the three-year moving average of actual net income. Figures allow for depreciation. Net income is defined as the reward for the manual and managerial labour of the farmer and his wife and for the use of the occupier's investment. Figures given are assessed from the statistics of income and expenditure for all farms in the United Kingdom. £'000,000

Year to May 30	Actual	Three-year average
1961/62.................	424.0	418.5
1962/63.................	445.0	425.0
1963/64.................	406.5	442.0
1964/65.................	474.0	447.0
1965/66.................	461.0	472.5
1966/67.................	483.0	486.0
1967/68.................	514.5	492.5
1968/69.................	479.5	518.5
1969/70.................	561.5	..
New Basis		
1968/69.................	495	
1969/70.................	574	..
1970/71 (forecast)........	589	..

Adjusted to normal weather conditions net income for 1969–70 and 1970–71 are respectively £566m. and £600m.

Agricultural Workers

In June, 1971, there were 424,700 persons employed in agriculture in the United Kingdom (males, 314,400; females 115,000), compared with 430,000 persons employed in June, 1970 (women, 106,400). Of the total in 1971, 27,100 (women,

7,000) were employed in Northern Ireland. In Great Britain there were 323,600 regular agricultural workers (men, 255,400; women, 68,200), including regular part-time workers, and in Northern Ireland, 16,800 (women 5,100).

The Crops of 1971

The following table shows the condition of the principal crops in Great Britain on September 2, compared with the previous five years and with the 10-year averages (1960–69) at the same date:—

	Wheat	Barley	Oats	Potatoes	Sugar Beet	Grass
1967....	94	93	95	92	94	96
1968....	91	88	93	93	99	99
1969....	95	92	94	92	92	95
1970....	94	83	88	90	89	88
1971....	93	93	95	94	94	97
10-year averages	94	92	92	92	94	95

FISHERIES

Quantity and Value of Fish of British taking landed in Great Britain during 1970*

Kind of Fish	Weight and Value	
	Cwt.	£
Cod................	6,774,024	32,307,529
Haddock...........	3,467,569	13,605,155
Hake...............	52,821	777,703
Plaice..............	865,692	6,215,998
Skate and Ray......	172,924	1,021,780
Whiting............	587,498	1,674,309
Herring.............	2,780,358	4,553,157
Mackerel...........	86,062	241,071
Other..............	3,130,466	8,809,911
Total Wet Fish......	17,917,404	69,206,613
Shell Fish..........	1,042,631	6,278,987
Grand Total, All Fish.	18,960,035	75,485,600

* In 1970 there were 17,080 fishermen regularly and 3,823 partially employed in commercial fishing.

THE POST OFFICE

Crown services for the conveyance of Government letters and despatches by posts or stages were set up under a Master of the Posts about 1516. Public correspondence was officially accepted for the first time for conveyance by these services at fixed postage rates in 1635, but they were still under direct Crown control. In 1657 a Post Office was created under a Postmaster-General by Oliver Cromwell, and responsibility for the carrying of all letters was thus transferred to Parliament, Charles II ratified this arrangement by statute in 1660.

A Money Order Office was inaugurated in 1792, uniform Penny Post in 1840, the Book Post in 1848, the Post Office Savings Bank in 1861, Post Office Telegraphs in 1870, Postal Orders and the Post Office Telephone Service in 1881 and the Parcel Post in 1883.

The Post Office also acts as agent for many Government Departments in the collection and payment of money.

The financial arrangements brought into effect by the Post Office Act, 1961, separated Post Office finances from the Exchequer and established the Post Office Fund on April 1, 1961.

By the Post Office Act 1969, the Post Office was formally set up as a public corporation, and ceased to be a Government Department run by civil servants. It is now headed by a chairman and board of control, appointed by and responsible to the Minister of Posts and Telecommunications.

POST OFFICE FINANCIAL RESULTS   £ million

	1969–70			1970–71		
	Posts	Telecommunications	DPS*	Posts	Telecommunications	DPS*
INCOME						
Main Services...................	319·4	636·7	5·3	294·9	753·3	10·1
Giro and Remittance Services.....	14·3	—	—	13·5	—	—
Agency Services.................	57·8	15·1	—	54·3	16·1	—
Miscellaneous...................	14·1	0·4	—	16·7	2·9	—
Total Income...................	405·6	652·2	5·3	379·4	772·3	10·1
EXPENDITURE						
Operating......................	354·5	136·2	2·8	356·6	146·9	6·2
Plant Maintenance, etc..........	5·2	91·9	—	5·9	109·9	—
Purchase and Supplies Dept.......	1·4	13·3	—	1·7	15·8	—
Motor Transport.................	10·7	13·0	—	10·9	14·7	—
Accommodation.................	15·3	30·2	0·5	16·7	34·4	0·8
Administration..................	13·2	29·0	0·9	15·7	34·4	1·3
Use of other business service......	1·7	5·6	0·2	3·5	12·0	0·2
Incidental expenses..............	7·4	10·1	—	7·8	11·2	—
Interest payable.................	13·5	97·6	0·5	18·4	117·0	0·9
Depreciation....................	7·4	131·6	0·7	9·2	157·2	1·1
Payment to other administrations..		32·4			29·2	
	430·3	590·9	5·6	446·4	682·7	10·5
PROFIT or LOSS (—)...............	−24·8	61·3	−0·3	−72·6**	93·5**	−0·4

* Data Processing Service.   ** After allowing for exceptional and prior year items of (−) £5·6m. (Posts) and (+) £3·9m. (Telecommunications); total profit (1970–71), £20·5m. (1969–70, £36·2m.)

FUEL AND POWER

ELECTRICITY PRODUCTION
England and Wales

In the year ended March 31, 1970, the electricity industry sold 174,254 million units to all consumers, an increase of 3·6 per cent. over 1969–70. Average price per unit to consumers was 0·797p compared with 0·789p in 1969–70. At the end of the year there were 18,508,000 consumers, 1·3 per cent. more than at March 31, 1970.

72,572 million units were supplied to industry (an increase of 2·5 per cent.), 66,134 million to domestic users (4·9 per cent. more) and 26,262 million to commercial users (4·3 per cent. more). 15,484 million units were sold on off-peak tariffs, an increase of 16·5 per cent. over 1969–70.

On March 31, 1971, the Central Electricity Generating Board had 187 power stations (1970, *193*) with a maximum output capacity of 49,281 *MW*, an increase in capacity of 5·2 per cent. over 1970. Additional output capacity in 1970–71 was 3,533 *MW*. C.E.G.B. power stations supplied 186,158 million kWh in 1970–71, 3·0 per cent. more than in 1969–70. Maximum simultaneous demand met during the year was 38,619 *MW* (1969–70, *38,153*).

Lines owned or operated by the Generating Board during the year totalled 11,010 miles (1969–70, *10,660*) and the number of substations rose from 921 to 945.

The industry employed 188,235 persons at March 31, 1971, 8,727 less than in 1969–70.

The following results are those of the Electricity Council and Area Boards in England and Wales, the figures being rounded off.

Electricity Industry Finance 1970–71

	£ million	
	1969–70	1970–71
Revenue		
Sales of Electricity..........	1,328·0	1,388·4
Other....................	21·3	23·6
TOTAL	1,349·3	1,412·0
Expenditure		
Generation and purchases...	552·2	677·3
Main transmission and Distribution..................	72·4	78·0
Consumer Service..........	24·2	27·4
Administration, Collection of Accounts, etc............	73·8	82·7
Rates....................	40·6	44·2
Depreciation..............	260·7	276·0
Other....................	19·3	21·7
TOTAL	1,043·2	1,207·3
Operating Profit	306·1	204·7
Deduct Interest payable......	241·6	260·5
NET PROFIT/*Loss*	64·5	55·8

COAL PRODUCTION

Year	Saleable Mined Coal	Open Cast Coal	Total
1964–65..	183,662,000	7,040,000	192,501,000
1965–66 .	174,066,000	7,123,000	182,744,000
1966–67..	164,559,000	7,125,000	172,969,000
1967–68..	162,700,000	7,084,000	170,850,000
1968–69..	153,007,000	6,574,000	160,595,000
1969–70..	139,777,000	6,571,000	147,385,000
1970–71..	133,315,000	8,331,000	141,646,000

Coal Distribution.—Of the 148,286,000 tons consumed at home in 1970–71, Industry used 18,452,000 tons, domestic users 18,407,000 tons (incl. miners' coal), electricity generating stations 73,511,000 tons, gas works 3,472,000 tons, coke ovens 24,666,000 tons, and colliery consumption 1,763,000 tons.

National Coal Board Finance

	£ million	
	1969–70†	1970–71†
Income		
From Sales (Net)............	781·2	863·6
Principal Items:—		
Coal....................	684·2	757·0
Coke...................	49·9	55·3
Gas, Benzole, Tar, etc.,..	10·9	10·4
Processed Fuel...........	17·6	20·4
Other Receipts............	27·2	24·8
NET INCOME..........	819·3	899·5
Expenditure		
Wages, Salaries, etc..........	452·0	476·5
Open-Cast Contractors' payments..................	25·4	33·5
Materials, Stores, Power......	195·1	217·0
Other....................	138·0	138·4
TOTAL EXPENDITURE......	810·5	865·4
PROFIT.....................	8·8	34·1
Less Interest Payable, etc....	35·1	33·6
SURPLUS or *DEFICIENCY*...	26·3	0·5

† April to March.

GAS PRODUCTION
1970–71

Gas made at gasworks: (Million therms)		Gas Bought: (Million therms)	
Coal Gas....	238	Refinery gas.	134
Water and.. other gases.	32	L.P.G......... Coke Oven gas	206 279
Oil gas......	1,208	Natural gas, etc.........	2,487
Total......	1,478	Total gas available....	6,740

Consumption of coal in the production of gas fell from 21·8 million tons in 1963–64 to 3·4 million tons in 1970–71.

Total oil used for all purposes in 1970–71 was 2·7 million tons, compared with 4·6 million tons in 1968–69.

Gas Industry Finance

	£ million	
	1969–70	1968–69
Gross Revenue		
Sales—Gas.................	498·1	537·0
By-Products...........	40·9	29·9
Appliances...........	61·5	63·2
Other Revenue..............	58·9	65·4
TOTAL REVENUE.........	659·4	695·9
Gross Expenditure		
Process Materials:		
Coal and Coke..............	40·5	26·0
Oil......................	40·0	25·3
Natural Gas	44·3	66·1
Other	27·3	21·8
Payments to employees.......	145·7	162·7
Cost of Appliances...........	46·5	46·8
Depreciation................	66·5	79·6
Interest....................	88·0	106·7
Rates	9·5	10·4
Other materials and services	137·4	148·1
TOTAL EXPENDITURE........	645·7	693·5
SURPLUS or *DEFICIENCY*....	13·7	2·0

PETROLEUM CONSUMPTION, 1970

Institute of Petroleum statistics show that the inland oil consumption of the United Kingdom (excluding bunker fuel deliveries for ships engaged in the foreign trade) reached a new record level in 1970: total U.K. consumption amounted to 95,336,808 tons—an increase of 6·7 per cent. over the 89,342,950 tons used during 1969. More than half of 1970's inland demand was for gas oil, diesel oil (other than for road transport) and fuel oils. Deliveries of this group of products were 14·1 per cent. higher than in 1969 and amounted to 49,893,116 tons. This figure does not include the further 5,933,171 tons of fuel oil used in the refineries themselves.

Motor spirit accounted for 14,009,898 tons of total consumption compared with 13,231,476 tons in 1969. As in earlier years, by far the largest dealer demand was for the Four Star Grade, which amounted to 7,307,607 tons (or more than half of all motor spirit deliveries). Nevertheless, in terms of a percentage increase, by far the most pronounced growth in requirements was for brands in the Three Star grade. Demand here soared from 1,606,085 tons in 1969 to 2,312,659 tons in 1970.

Heavier commercial road transport use of derv (diesel-engined road vehicle) fuel brought a rise in demand for this product of 3·4 per cent., deliveries totalling 4,955,070 tons. Aviation fuels supplied increased by almost 4·0 per cent. representing 3,426,005 tons, of which 3,202,369 tons comprised aviation turbine fuel other than wide-cut.

Estimated end use of the 14,010,000 tons of *motor spirit* supplied by the industry in 1970 was: cars and motor cycles 11,250,000 tons; public service vehicles and taxis, 75,000 tons; goods vehicles 2,454,000 tons; Services and other Government uses, 173,000; and miscellaneous uses, 58,000. Of 4,955,000 tons of *derv fuel*, 973,000 tons was estimated to have been used by public service vehicles, 3,865,000 tons by goods vehicles and 117,000 tons by the petroleum industry itself (81,000) and miscellaneous users.

FUEL AND POWER MEASURES

British Thermal Unit (B. Th. U.) = The amount of heat required to raise 1 lb of water through 1 degree Fahrenheit at or near 39·1 degrees F. 1 B.Th.U. = 1·055 06kJ.

Unit of electricity (kilowatt-hour) = Output of 1,000 watts for one hour. 1 k.w.h. = 3,413 B.Th.U.

Therm = 100,000 B.TH.U. = 29·3 k.w.h. = 105·506 MJ.

Atmosphere = pressure of 14·223 lb. per sq. in. = 1 kilogram per sq. cm.

Petroleum

Barrel = 35 Imperial gallons = 42 U.S. gallons.
Petroleum products are commonly quoted in metric tonnes, the conversion to barrels varying slightly according to the specific gravity of the product, e.g. the metric tonne in the major oil producing states (U.S.A.), Venezuela, Persian Gulf, Saudi-Arabia, Iraq, etc.) varies from 7·0 barrels per metric tonne to 7·7 barrels, and in the smaller oil producing states (e.g., Albania) is as low as 6·7 barrels per tonne. Crude petroleum in the United Kingdom, 7·355 barrels per metric tonne (2,205 lbs.); 7·472 barrels per long ton (2,240 lbs.).

POLICE

Strength of the Police Force (Men and Women).

Year	England & Wales	Scotland
1966	86,505	10,196
1967	90,640	10,247
1968	90,782	10,296
1969	91,762	10,308
1970	93,748	10,459

The Police of England and Wales are administered by the Home Office, those of Scotland by the Scottish Home and Health Department and those of Northern Ireland by the Ministry of Home Affairs.

In 1970 there were 3,612 women police in England and Wales; in Scotland there were 382.

On Dec. 31, 1970, the number of special constables enrolled in England and Wales was: Men, 29,138; Women, 1,869; Scotland (March 31, 1971), Men, 4,316; Women, 118.

On Dec. 31, 1970, the Metropolitan Police had a total strength of 21,056, including 615 women; City Police, 760, including 19 women.

BRITISH TRANSPORT DOCKS BOARD, 1969–70

Traffic

Traffic through the Board's ports in 1970 totalled 86,159,000 tons (1969, *78,773*), consisting of ('ooo tons): ores 9,437; timber, 1,475; coal, 8,208; petroleum, 50,654; manufactured goods and other commodities, 16,385. Net registered tonnage of shipping entering and leaving the ports in 1970 totalled 112,943,000 tons (1969, *108,773,000*). Passengers in transit through the Board's ports in 1970 numbered 2,610,000 (1969, *2,705,000*).

Finance

Finance. — Operating receipts totalled £33,629,000 (1969, *£29,630,000*) and working expenses, £29,165,000 (*£25,756,000*). Interest charges, £5,462,000 (1969, *£3,712,000*); Deficit (after historic depreciation, £998,000 (1969, Surplus, *£162,000*); Reserve for additional depreciation, £835,000 (*£602,000*); Exceptional profits, £203,000 (1969, *Nil*); Net deficit, 1970, £1,630,000 (1969, deficit, *£440,000*).

U.K. OFFICIAL RESERVES

£ million

End of	Gold	IMF Special Drawing Rights	Convertible Currencies	TOTAL
1965	809	—	264	1,073
1966	693	—	414	1,107
1967	538	—	585	1,123
1968	614	—	395	1,089
1969, Mar.	615	—	415	1,029
June	614	—	404	1,018
Sept.	608	—	406	1,014
Dec.	613	—	440	1,053
1970, Mar.	612	127	390	1,129
June	612	119	432	1,163
Sept.	606	112	393	1,111
Dec.	562	111	505	1,178
1971, Mar.	468	201	713	1,382

WORLD TRADE

(Value in million U.S. $)

Countries	Exports (f.o.b.)			Imports (c.i.f.)		
	1968	1969	1970	1968	1969	1970
World Total (a)	212,300	234,100	278,200	224,400	255,300	291,900
North America	47,380	51,910	59,520	47,630	52,400	56,740
Canada *(e)*	12,602	13,812	16,187	11,431	13,071	13,349
U.S.A.	34,199	37,462	42,593	33,066	35,863	39,768
Latin America	12,200	13,350	14,580	12,260	13,350	15,140
Argentina..................	1,368	1,612	1,773	1,169	1,576	..
Brazil.....................	1,881	2,311	2,738	2,129	2,263	2,849
Chile......................	941	369	..	743	907	..
Colombia..................	558	608	..	643	686	..
Mexico....................	1,258	1,430	1,373	1,962	2,078	2,461
Peru......................	865	864	1,039	628	603	618
Venezuela.................	2,857	2,893	2,637	1,515	1,564	..
Western Europe:—						
Austria....................	1,989	2,412	2,857	2,496	2,825	3,549
Belgium–Luxemburg........	8,164	10,065	11,609	8,333	9,989	11,344
Denmark..................	2,640	3,021	3,356	3,237	3,813	4,404
Finland...................	1,637	1,987	2,306	1,598	2,025	2,636
France....................	12,672	14,876	17,742	13,927	17,219	18,780
Germany..................	24,842	29,052	34,189	20,150	24,926	29,814
Greece....................	468	554	643	1,394	1,594	1,958
Italy......................	10,186	11,729	13,210	10,286	12,450	14,939
Netherlands...............	8,342	9,965	11,766	9,292	10,994	13,393
Norway...................	1,938	2,204	2,457	2,706	2,942	3,702
Portugal..................	762	853	950	1,178	1,296	1,582
Spain *(b)*	1,589	1,900	2,387	3,502	4,202	4,715
Sweden...................	4,940	5,695	6,782	5,126	5,909	7,005
Switzerland...............	3,066	4,625	5,128	4,513	5,285	6,480
Turkey....................	496	537	589	770	754	886
Yugoslavia................	1,264	1,474	1,679	1,797	2,134	2,874
European Common Market	64,210	75,690	88,520	61,990	75,580	88,270
EFTA	31,070	35,700	40,240	37,660	41,410	47,800
Sterling Area:—						
Australia..................	3,402	4,043	4,622	3,858	4,003	4,479
Ceylon....................	342	322	340	365	427	389
Hong Kong................	1,744	2,178	2,514	2,058	2,457	2,905
India	1,754	1,834	2,026	2,510	2,044	2,095
Irish Republic.............	800	892	1,035	1,192	1,417	1,569
Malaysia *(f)*	1,390	1,711	1,757	1,205	1,240	1,468
New Zealand..............	1,031	1,211	1,225	895	1,003	1,245
Nigeria...................	591	905	1,240	539	696	1,059
Pakistan..................	720	682	716	996	1,015	1,089
Singapore.................	1,271	1,549	1,554	1,661	2,040	2,461
United Kingdom...........	14,838	16,894	19,351	18,409	19,336	21,724
South Africa *(c)*	2,109	2,140	2,148	2,636	2,983	3,556
Jamaica...................	224	256	..	384	442	..
Trinidad and Tobago........	472	468	482	427	479	543
Eastern Europe:—						
Bulgaria..................	1,615	1,794	2,009	1,782	1,749	1,815
Czechoslovakia............	3,005	3,320	3,958	3,077	3,294	3,698
Germany, East............	3,791	4,153	4,581	3,393	4,105	4,847
Hungary..................	1,790	2,084	2,317	1,803	1,928	2,506
Poland....................	2,858	3,142	3,547	2,853	3,210	3,607
Rumania..................	1,469	1,633	1,851	1,609	1,741	1,960
U.S.S.R..................	10,634	11,655	12,800	9,410	10,327	11,739
Africa (g)						
Morocco..................	453	485	488	563	560	686
Tunisia...................	158	166	181	217	265	305
U.A.R....................	622	745	762	666	639	770
Asia:—						
Indonesia..................	689	800	811	722	782	..
Iraq......................	1,041	1,042	1,099	404	440	509
Israel.....................	603	684	731	1,061	1,281	1,410
Japan.....................	12,973	15,991	19,318	12,988	15,024	18,811
Korea, S..................	455	623	834	1,463	1,823	1,984
Philippines................	946	965	1,067	1,280	1,254	1,210

(a) World total exclusive of China (Mainland), U.S.S.R., and Eastern European countries not mentioned for which data are not reported currently. *(b)* Including Canary Islands. *(c)* Including S.W. Africa. *(e)* Imports (f.o.b.). *(f)* Malaya, Sabah and Sarawak; including inter-state trade. *(g)* Excluding South Africa *(see above)*.

BRITAIN'S OVERSEAS TRADE

Section and Division	Imports		Exports	
	1969	1970	1969	1970
	£'000	£'000	£'000	£'000
0. Food and Live Animals—				
Live animals (excluding zoo animals, dogs and cats)	53,865	56,488	28,841	32,629
Meat and meat preparations	432,497	438,201	15,849	21,260
Dairy products and eggs	184,050	185,524	13,630	14,441
Fish (not of British taking) and fish preparations	69,960	74,247	14,127	20,839
Cereals and cereal preparations	251,907	281,428	25,735	33,721
Fruit and vegetables	358,295	379,908	17,776	22,179
Sugar, sugar preparations and honey	112,514	117,479	27,982	30,734
Coffee, tea, cocoa, spices and manufactures thereof	182,657	209,690	20,736	41,568
Feeding stuff for animals (not including unmilled cereals)	81,383	88,219	9,469	11,418
Miscellaneous food preparations	23,143	31,421	17,327	20,545
1. Beverages and Tobacco—				
Beverages	69,201	79,049	190,034	224,911
Tobacco and tobacco manufactures	114,550	110,348	34,853	40,097
2. Crude Materials, Inedible, Except Fuels—				
Hides, skins and furskins, undressed	78,147	70,161	9,719	53,061
Oil seeds, oil nuts and oil kernels	38,509	41,745	407	1,126
Crude rubber (including synthetic and reclaimed)	60,878	57,693	19,114	23,105
Wood, lumber and cork	217,518	238,818	882	2,109
Pulp and waste paper	165,445	197,948	2,300	2,987
Textile fibres (not manufactured into yarn, thread and fabrics) and their waste, old clothing and other textile articles; rags.	210,873	183,940	99,021	96 377
Crude fertilizers and crude minerals (excluding coal, petroleum and precious stones)	63.109	65,340	36,923	47,820
Metalliferous ores and metal scrap	291,214	346,575	17,958	26,394
Crude animal and vegetable materials, not elsewhere specified	55,437	60,936	5,072	10,552
3. Mineral Fuels, Lubricants and Related Materials—				
Coal, coke and briquettes	1,252	3,416	25,062	29,081
Petroleum and Petroleum products	889,581	925,375	145,693	176,341
Gas, natural and manufactured	18,057	15,311	676	1,435
Electric energy	1,376	1,640	4	4
4. Animal and Vegetable Oils and Fats—				
Animal oils and fats	16,104	23,420	1,790	2,316
Fixed vegetable oils and fats	50,404	68,133	2,024	1,792
Animal and vegetable oils and fats, processed, and waxes of animal or vegetable origin	6,628	9,123	4,506	5,176
5. Chemicals—				
Chemical elements and compounds	202,282	237,807	166,493	210,340
Mineral tar and crude chemicals from coal, petroleum and natural gas	4,945	5,509	3,858	3,483
Dyeing, tanning and colouring materials.	27,817	33,389	76,235	81,477
Medicinal and pharmaceutical products..	25,453	33,724	117,692	139,751
Essential oils and perfume materials; toilet, polishing and cleansing preparations...	21,987	23,210	60,685	67,021
Fertilizers, manufactured	24,237	23,088	5,375	4,785
Explosives and pyrotechnic products	1,114	1,035	12,042	10,997
Plastic materials, regenerated cellulose and artificial resins	92,727	110,863	128,381	143,747
Chemical materials and products, not elsewhere specified	62,467	74,168	114,276	124,499
6. Manufactured Goods classified chiefly by Material—				
Leather, leather manufactures, not elsewhere specified, and dressed furskins...	37,419	32,484	45,784	50,651
Rubber manufactures, not elsewhere specified	24,647	27,619	72,432	92,667

BRITAIN'S OVERSEAS TRADE—*continued*

Section and Division	Imports 1969	Imports 1970	Exports 1969	Exports 1970
	£'000	£'000	£'000	£'000
Manufactured Goods classified chiefly by Material—*contd.*				
Wood and cork manufactures (excluding furniture)	90,108	108,530	7,156	11,197
Paper, paperboard and manufactures thereof	203,636	231,145	78,596	89,228
Textile yarn, fabrics, made-up articles and related products	238,670	256,394	347,136	396,832
Non-metallic mineral manufactures, not elsewhere specified	386,881	382,338	454,148	390,318
Iron and steel	173,887	222,475	284.999	347,887
Non-ferrous metals	608,880	608,677	312,046	350,571
Manufactures of metal, not elsewhere specified	75,835	97,037	214,568	260,449
7. *Machinery and Transport Equipment*—				
Machinery other than electric	681,080	855,737	1,417,538	1,642,376
Electrical machinery, apparatus and appliances	266,336	342,236	465,642	579,052
Transport equipment	371,711	298,525	1,071,176	1,079,789
8. *Miscellaneous Manufactured Articles*—				
Sanitary, plumbing, heating and lighting fixtures and fittings	7,608	10,016	17,299	20,809
Furniture	13,488	15,618	23,213	25,328
Travel goods, handbags and similar articles	5,300	5,735	4,142	4,435
Clothing, knitted or crocheted articles including elastic or rubberized fabric and articles of fur	124,513	129,431	107,510	123,116
Footwear, gaiters and the like	35,501	40,574	33,528	35,511
Professional, scientific and controlling instruments; photographic and optical goods, watches and clocks	115,279	141,508	179,091	208,591
Miscellaneous manufactured articles not elsewhere specified	212,864	231,033	271,206	313,064
9. *Unclassified*—				
Post parcels and Animals, not elsewhere specified (including zoo animals, dogs and cats), etc	79,918	109,985	159,593	260,758
TOTAL	8,315,141	9,051,466	7,039,346	8,062,750

CAR PRODUCTION IN MAIN PRODUCING COUNTRIES   (thousands)

	1960	1961	1962	1963	1964	1965	1966	1967	1968	1969
United Kingdom	1,353	1,004	1,249	1,608	1,868	1,722	1,604	1,552	1,816	1,717
France	1,175	1,064	1,340	1,521	1,390	1,423	1,786	1,777	1,833	2,168
W. Germany	1,817	1,904	2,109	2,414	2,650	2,734	2,830	2,296	2,862	3,313
Italy	596	694	878	1,105	1,029	1,104	1,282	1,439	1,545	1,477
Sweden	108	110	129	146	162	182	173	194	223	243
Japan	165	250	269	408	580	696	878	1,376	2,056	2,611
USA (Factory sales)	6,675	5,543	6,933	7,638	7,752	9,306	8,598	7,437	8,849	8,224
Canada	326	328	429	534	561	711	702	721	901	1,035
Total	12,215	10,897	13,336	15,374	15,992	17,878	17,853	16,792	20,085	20,788
UK % of total	11	9	9	10	12	10	9	9	9	8

Over the ten-year period production by the above eight countries has increased by just over 70 per cent. In 1969, the USA proportion of combined production was 38 per cent. West Germany has been the second largest producer throughout the period, with the third position taken over by Japan. Japan has by far enjoyed the fastest rate of growth, rising from seventh position in the table to third.

BRITISH MOTOR VEHICLE PRODUCTION AND EXPORTS

Year	Weeks	Passenger Cars (including taxis) For Export	Passenger Cars (including taxis) Total	Passenger Cars (including taxis) Weekly average	Commercial Road Vehicles For Export	Commercial Road Vehicles Total	Commercial Road Vehicles Weekly average
1967	..52..	563,740	1,552,013	29,846	139,414	385,106	7,406
1968	..52..	802,773	1,815,936	34,922	149,855	409,186	7,869
1969	..53..	824,315	1,717,073	32,398	192,778	465,776	8,788
1970	..52..	722,857	1,640,066	31,557	190,125	457,532	8,799
1971 1st Qtr.	..13..	202,868	432,417	33,263	48,325	109,687	8,437

SALES OF BRITISH CARS, 1971

Top-ten in Car Sales.—Figures issued by the Society of Motor Manufacturers and Traders show that in the first half of 1971 sales of various makes (with Jan.-June, 1970, in *italics*) were: *Austin-Morris* 1100/1300, 73,941 (*73,108*); *Mini*, 49,594 (*39,931*); *Vauxhall Viva*, 48,067 (*42,136*); *Ford Escort*, 38,673 (*51,993*); *Cortina*, 37,062 (*73,357*); *Hillman Avenger*, 33,740 (*27,056*); *Austin Maxi*/1600, 23,253 (*21,518*); *Austin Morris* 1800/3 litre, 21,776 (*17,213*); *Hillman Hunter/GT Minx*, 20,500 (*15,282*); *Vauxhall Victor*, 19,459 (*13,120*).

UNITED KINGDOM AIR TRANSPORT
OPERATING STATISTICS OF U.K. AIRLINES SCHEDULED SERVICES

	Aircraft Miles Flown	Passengers Carried	Passenger Miles	Available Seat Miles	Freight Carried (excluding mail)	Non-scheduled Capacity " Sold "
	thousands	thousands	millions	millions	Short tons	Short ton miles (thousands)
1966.....	143,749	12,059	8,295	13,750	359,925	587,962
1967.....	152,598	12,318	8,742	14,979	319,461	596,562
1968.....	154,040	12,205	8,764	15,608	304,452	664,579
1969.....	168,030	13,222	10,088	17,551	312,739	807,789
1970.....	182,148	13,874	10,832	19,313	267,362	1,132,379

ACTIVITY AT AIRPORTS

Year	Aircraft Movements		Passengers Handled*	Freight Handled†	Mail Handled†
	Total	Air Transport		Metric Tons	
All United Kingdom Airports					
1966....................	1,093,258	556,236	23,356,260	517,195·3	40,328·4
1967....................	1,213,270	565,803	24,743,985	488,425·8	38,053·0
1968....................	1,279,423	560,251	25,601,747	524,484·3	39,621·6
1969....................	1,399,147	591,366	28,931,115	585,436·1	43,841·2
1970....................	1,468,346	606,708	32,410,633	579,643·8	49,078·5
London Airports:					
1966....................	320,205	243,106	13,600,918	248,243·0	26,524·3
1967	342,909	258,614	14,610,520	267,684·0	27,263·8
1968....................	363,206	269,866	15,576,834	314,772·9	29,664·9
1969....................	394,073	290,886	17,557,763	375,410·7	33,112·0
1970....................	413,841	306,832	19,828,304	376,462·5	37,210·3
London Airports, 1970					
Heathrow..............	270,286	246,021	15,607,610	335,670·1	36,496·5
Gatwick...............	92,185	53,615	3,702,872	30,831·1	713·6
Stansted...............	44,486	6,164	515,187	9,961·3	0·2
Westland Heliport.......	6,884	1,032	2,635	—	—

*Terminal and transit passengers on air transport movements only.
† Commercial freight on air transport movements only.

UNITED KINGDOM PASSENGER MOVEMENT BY AIR

	1967	1968	1969	1970
Europe and the Mediterranean				
France......................	2,182,000	1,880,000	2,156,000	2,365,000
Belgium.....................	718,000	731,000	735,000	818,000
Netherlands.................	982,000	1,037,000	1,166,000	1,306,000
Germany....................	1,008,000	1,175,000	1,398,000	1,874,000
Italy........................	918,000	952,000	1,131,000	1,430,000
Spain.......................	1,676,000	2,256,000	3,065,000	3,472,000
Switzerland.................	682,000	774,000	880,000	1,053,000
Scandinavia.................	505,000	579,000	662,000	756,000
Middle East countries........	248,000	339,000	371,000	437,000
Other countries.............	1,124,000	1,239,000	1,508,000	1,783,000
Total....................	10,044,000	10,962,000	13,071,000	15,294,000
Rest of World				
United States...............	1,463,200	1,639,600	2,019,800	2,511,200
Canada.....................	558,900	640,000	795,400	904,300
Australia and New Zealand........	62,200	69,800	92,300	113,400
South Africa................	77,600	91,900	110,300	143,100
E. & W. Africa..............	166,600	179,500	203,000	223,200
West Indies and Bermuda........	124,400	132,600	153,700	159,900
India, Pakistan, Ceylon............	142,600	152,600	161,000	162,100
Other countries.............	275,000	342,300	398,900	498,000
Total....................	2,864,400	3,249,300	3,934,300	4,715,100

BRITISH OVERSEAS AIRWAYS CORPORATION

Operating Accounts, 1969–70 and 1970–71

	1969–70	1970–71
Revenue		
Scheduled Services:		
Passenger....................................	£142,490,000	£144,425,000
Excess baggage.............................	2,289,000	2,205,000
Mail..	17,459,000	16,996,000
Diplomatic bags............................	121,000	160,000
Commercial freight.........................	28,952,000	27,536,000
Contract services..........................	1,142,000	..
Non-Scheduled Services.........................	5,520,000	4,210,000
TOTAL...................	£197,973,000	£195,532,000
Expenditure		
Aircraft standing charges....................	15,402,000	19,349,000
Aircraft maintenance........................	25,668,000	29,903,000
Flying operations...........................	43,016,000	46,836,000
Technical training, etc.....................	3,933,000	4,388,000
Charter of aircraft and crews...............	228,000	196,000
Passenger service...........................	18,457,000	21,210,000
Station and traffic costs...................	15,506,000	19,937,000
Sales, advertising and publicity............	24,862,000	29,585,000
Commission on traffic revenue...............	11,385,000	11,678,000
Central administration......................	7,419,000	9,398,000
Integrated data processing development......	499,000	267,000
TOTAL...................	£166,862,000	£189,628,000
OPERATING SURPLUS...................	£31,111,000	£5,904,000

Aircraft Types

The operational fleet of British Overseas Airways Corporation: Boeing 707-436, 18; Vickers VC 10, 11; Super VC10, 16; Boeing 707-336 C, 6 passenger; 3 freighter; Boeing 707-336B, 2; Boeing 747, 6.

BRITISH EUROPEAN AIRWAYS

B.E.A. was formed on August 1, 1946, and from that time has been responsible for operating the great majority of British scheduled passenger, mail and freight air services between Britain and the continent of Europe and within the British Isles. B.E.A. and its associated companies now serves 101 destinations in 35 European and Near Eastern countries and currently carries over 8 million passengers in a year.

Operating Accounts, 1969–70 and 1970–71

	1969–70	1970–71
Revenue		
Passenger Traffic............................	£104,077,000	£111,903,000
Excess Baggage..............................	859,000	888,000
Mail..	3,007,000	2,951,000
Cargo.......................................	10,556,000	9,501,000
Non-scheduled services......................	3,548,000	3,581,000
Commissions.................................	3,255,000	3,420,000
Other revenue...............................	736,000	1,106,000
TOTAL...................	£126,038,000	£133,350,000
Expenditure		
Aircraft standing charges...................	£13,004,000	£11,661,000
Aircraft maintenance........................	21,379,000	26,642,000
Flying operations...........................	27,688,000	31,946,000
Cabin services..............................	7,263,000	8,796,000
Passenger, cargo and aircraft handling......	19,040,000	23,330,000
Sales and publicity.........................	20,560,000	22,869,000
Head Office administration and centralized services.	5,500,000	7,847,000
Aircraft introductory costs written off.....	584,000	1,037,000
TOTAL...................	£115,018,000	£134,128,000
Operating surplus/*deficit*	£11,020,000	£778,000

Aircraft Types

The following types of aircraft were in service with B.E.A. (and its wholly-owned subsidiaries) in June, 1971: *Trident IC*, 21; *Trident II*, 15; *Trident III*, 6 (and 20 on order); *BAC Super 1-11*, 18; *Comet IVB*, 1; Vanguard *V. 951*, 5; *V. 953*, 8; *Merchantman*, 6; *Viscount 800*, 24; *Heron*, 2; S61N Helicopter, 3.

AERODROMES AND AIRPORTS

There are 169 aerodromes in Great Britain, Northern Ireland, the Isle of Man and the Channel Islands which are either State owned or licensed for use by civil aircraft. A number of unlicensed airfields not included in this list are also available for private use by permission of the owner or controlling authority.

> S= Aerodrome owned and operated by the State.
> BAA= Aerodrome operated by the British Airports Authority.
> M= Aerodrome owned or operated by Municipal Authority.
> J= Military airfield available for civil use by prior permission.
> H= Licensed helicopter station.

Those aerodromes which are designated as Customs airports are printed in bold type. Customs facilities are available at certain other aerodromes by special arrangement.

ENGLAND AND WALES (128)

Abingdon, Berks. J
Andover, Hants. J
Ashford, Kent.
Barrow (Walney Island), Lancs.
Bembridge, I.O.W.
Benson, Oxon. J
Bicester, Oxon. J
Biggin Hill, Kent.
Binbrook, Lincolnshire, J
Birmingham, Warwicks. M
Bitteswell, Warwicks.
Blackbushe, Hants.
Blackpool, Lancs. M
Bournemouth (Hurn), Hants. M
Bristol (Lulsgate). M
Cambridge.
Carlisle, Cumberland.
Chichester (Goodwood), Sussex.
Chivenor, Devon. J
Church Fenton, Yorks. J
Colerne, Wilts. J
Coltishall, Norfolk. J
Compton Abbas, Dorsetshire.
Cosford, Shropshire. J
Coventry, Warwicks. M
Cranfield, Beds.
Cranwell, Lincs. J
Crowland, Lincs.
Culdrose, Cornwall. J
Denham, Bucks.
Dishforth, Yorks. J
Doncaster, Yorks.
Dunkeswell, Devon.
East Midlands, Leics. M
Elstree, Herts.
Elvington, Yorks. J
Exeter, Devon.
Fair Oaks, Surrey.
Fairford, Glos. J
Glamorgan (Rhoose). M
Gloucester/Cheltenham (Staverton). M
Great Yarmouth (North Denes), Norfolk.
Grindale Field, Yorks.
Halfpenny Green, Staffs.
Halton, Bucks. J
Hamble, Hants.
Hatfield, Herts.
Hawarden, Flintshire.
Hucknall, Notts.
Ipswich, Suffolk.
Kemble, Glos. J
Land's End (St. Just).
Lashenden, Headcorn, Kent.
Leavesden, Herts.
Leconfield, Yorks. J
Leeds and Bradford, Yorks. M
Leeming, Yorks. J
Lee-on-Solent, Hants. J

Leicester East, Leics.
Lindholme. Yorks. J
Linton-on-Ouse, Yorks. J
Little Rissington, Gloucs. J
Liverpool, Lancs. M
London (Gatwick). BAA
London (Heathrow) BAA
London (Westland Heliport). H
Luton, Beds. M
Lydd, Kent.
Lyneham, Wilts. J
Manby, Lincs. J
Manchester. M
Manchester (Barton).
Manston, Kent. J
Nether Thorpe, Notts.
Newcastle (Woolsington), Northumberland. M
Newton, Notts. J
Northampton (Sywell), Northants.
Northolt, Mddx. J
Norwich, Norfolk. M
Nottingham, Notts.
Oakington, Cambs. J
Odiham, Hants. J.
Old Sarum, Wilts. J
Ouston, Northumberland. J
Oxford (Kidlington), Oxfordshire.
Paull, Yorks.
Penzance Heliport, Cornwall. H
Pickering, Yorks.
Plymouth (Roborough), Devon.
Portland Air Station, Dorset. JH
Portsmouth, Hants. M
Rochester, Kent.
St. Mawgan, Cornwall. J
Sandown (Isle of Wight).
Scilly Isles (St. Mary's).
Shawbury, Shropshire. J
Sherburn-in-Elmet, Yorks.
Shobdon, Herefordshire.
Shoreham, Sussex. M
Sibson Peterborough), Cambs.
Skegness (Ingoldmells), Lincs.
Southampton, Hants.
Southend, Essex. M
Southport (Birkdale Sands), Lancs) M
Stansted, Essex. BAA
Stapleford Tawney, Essex.
Strubby, Lincs. J
Sunderland, Co. Durham. M
Swansea, Glam. M
Teesside, Co. Durham. M
Ternhill, Shropshire. J
Thorney Island, Hants. J
Thruxton, Hants.
Topcliffe, Yorks. J
Upavon, Wilts. J

Valley, Anglesey. J
Waddington, Lincs. J
Warton, Lancs.
Wattisham, Suffolk. J
Weston-super-Mare, Somerset.
White Waltham, Berks. J
Wittering, Sussex. J
Woodford, Cheshire.
Woodvale, Lancs. J
Wroughton, Wilts. J
Wycombe Air Park (Booker), Bucks.
Yeovil, Somerset.
Yeovilton, Somerset. J

SCOTLAND (31)

Aberdeen (Dyce). S
Barra, Hebrides.
Benbecula, Hebrides. S
Coll, Inner Hebrides. M
Dounreay (Thurso).
Dundee (Riverside Park), Angus. M
Eday. M
Edinburgh (Turnhouse). BAA
Glasgow. M
Glenforsa (Mull). M
Glenrothes. M
Inverness (Dalcross). S
Islay (Port Ellen). S
Kinloss. J
Kirkwall. S
Leuchars. J
Lossiemouth. J
Machrihanish, Kintyre. J
North Connel (Oban), Argyll. M
North Ronaldsay, Orkneys. M
Papa Westray, Orkneys. M
Perth (Scone).
Prestwick. BAA
Sanday, Orkneys. M
Stornoway, Hebrides. S
Stronsay, Orkneys. M
Sumburgh, Shetlands. S
Tiree. S
Unst. M.
Westray, Orkneys. M
Wick. S

NORTHERN IRELAND (5)

Belfast (Aldergrove) S
Belfast (Sydenham).
Enniskillen (St. Angelo). M
Londonderry (Eglinton).
Newtownards.

ISLE OF MAN (2)

Jurby.
Ronaldsway.

CHANNEL ISLANDS (3)

Alderney.
Guernsey.
Jersey.

ROADS

On April 1, 1971, the total mileage of public roads in Great Britain, including green lanes, was 209,925, of which 159,455 were in England, 29,493 in Scotland and 20,977 in Wales. There were 9,075 miles of Trunk Roads and 20,304 miles of Principal Roads. There were 744 miles of Trunk and Principal Road Motorway. The remaining 180,546 miles were classified and unclassified.

Highway Authorities.—The Secretary of State for the Environment became the highway authority for trunk roads on the formation of the Department of the Environment in October, 1970. The Secretary of State took over these functions from the former Minister of Transport. The Minister of Transport had become the highway authority for some 8,190 miles of roads in Great Britain under the Trunk Roads Acts of 1936 and 1946, whose provisions for England and Wales were consolidated in the Highways Act 1959. These roads, which now also comprise most of the motorway system, are known as trunk roads and are intended to form the national system of routes for through traffic. The Secretary of State is responsible for the maintenance and improvement of the trunk roads in England. In Scotland (since April, 1956) and in Wales and Monmouthshire (since April, 1965) these duties are the responsibility of the Secretaries of State. The highway powers and responsibilities of local authorities in England and Wales are contained in the Highways Act, 1959. County borough councils are responsible for all highways in their areas other than trunk roads; county councils are the highway authorities for all highways other than trunk roads in rural districts, and for all county roads in the urban areas within their jurisdiction for which the borough or district council is not the highway authority; non-county boroughs or district councils with population over 20,000 may " claim " the right to maintain county roads in their area (at the county council's expense) and they thus become the highway authorities for them; all non-county boroughs and district councils are the highway authorities for all the roads in their area other than trunk roads and " unclaimed " county roads. In Greater London the most important non-trunk roads are metropolitan roads, which are the responsibility of the Greater London Council. Other roads are the responsibility of the Common Council of the City of London and the London Borough Councils. In Scotland provisions similar to those in Wales and England (outside London) exist under separate legislation.

Under the present system of highway grants, the Secretary of State pays specific Capital grants at the rate of 75 per cent. to local highway authorities for the construction and improvement of roads classified as " principal roads " (these are the main roads other than trunk roads, and are roughly equivalent in mileage to the former Class I roads or non-trunk " A " roads). Other local authority expenditure on highways is assisted, along with other rate borne expenditure, through the general non-specific support grant.

Motorways

The network in England and Wales is based on six main routes—London–Yorkshire (M1), Medway Towns (M2), London–South Wales (M4), Birmingham–Bristol–Exeter (M5), Birmingham–Carlisle (M6) and Lancashire–Yorkshire (M62). From the junction of the M5 and M6 in the Birmingham area an eastward extension of M6, part of the Midland Links Motorway, will connect with the existing M1 near Rugby. Other motorways in use or under construction include M3 London–Basingstoke, M18 Rotherham–Goole,

M40 London–Oxford, M53 Mid-Wirral, M56 North Chesire, M73 Maryville, (M74)–Mollisburn (A80), M74 Draffen–Stonehouse (A74)—Glasgow, M9 Edinburgh–Stirling and M90 Inverkeithing–Perth.

Motorway schemes in various stages of preparation are London–Cambridge (M11), London–Crawley (M23), North and South Orbital (M25), South Coast (M27), Birmingham–Nottingham (M42), Stoke–Derby (M64), M80 Glasgow–Stirling, M90/M85 Perth By-Pass and M876 Dennyloanhead–Kincardine Bridge. Motorways by-pass Darlington, Doncaster, Baldock and Stevenage on A1, Maidstone on A20. At the end of 1971 almost 920 miles of motorway were open to traffic in England and Wales and about 160 were under construction. 195 miles of M1 and 140 miles of M4 were in use. The M6 which runs from Carlisle, together with the M5 provide 285 continuous miles of motorway from Carlisle to near Bristol. A continuous 50 miles of motorway is in use from Preston to Huddersfield.

Motor Vehicles.—The number of vehicles in Great Britain with current licences in 1970 totalled 14,950,200; Cars 11,515,100; Motor Cycles, Scooters and Mopeds 1,048,500; Public Transport Vehicles 103,000; Goods Vehicles 1,616,400; Agricultural Tractors 434,100. There were 134,800 vehicles exempt from licensing.

Driving Tests.—The number of driving tests conducted in Great Britain in the year 1970 was 1,710,098, of which 919,600 or 53·8 per cent. resulted in failure. The comparable figure for 1969 was 1,710,091, with 912,310 failures, representing 53·4 per cent. of the total.

Expenditure on roads in Great Britain rose from £610,900,000 in 1969/70 to £738,997,000 in 1970/71. The expenditure during 1970/71 may be broken down as follows: New Construction and Improvement, £491,336,000 (Trunk roads, £267,764,000; Principal roads, £172,376,000; Other roads, £51,196,000); Maintenance, £161,569,000 (Trunk roads, £23,137,000; Principal roads, £33,859,000; Other roads, £104,573,000); Cleansing, Watering and Snow-Clearing, £33,812,000 (Other roads, £24,485,000); Administration £52,280,000 (Non-trunk roads £46,104,000). In addition to the 1970/71 total of expenditure on roads, the cost of road lighting was £40,499,000, and of car parks £31,604,000 (gross).

Expenditure on new construction and improvement of trunk roads in England during 1970/71 was £230,854,000. In Scotland and Wales, the figures were £22,177 and £14,733 respectively. Grants made to local highway authorities for the improvement of principal roads in the same financial year were: England, £96,207,000; Scotland, £12,769,000; Wales £3,672,000.

Road Casualties, 1955–1970

In 1970 there were 72 vehicles for every mile of road, or one vehicle for every 24 yards. Twenty road users were killed and 975 injured on an average day.

Year	Killed	Injured	Year	Killed	Injured
1955	5,526	262,396	1963	6,922	349,257
1956	5,367	262,593	1964	7,820	377,679
1957	5,550	268,308	1965	7,952	389,985
1958	5,970	293,797	1966	7,985	384,472
1959	6,520	326,933	1967	7,319	362,659
1960	6,970	340,581	1968	6,810	342,398
1961	6,908	342,859	1969	7,383	345,811
1962	6,709	334,987	1970	7,501	355,852

BRITISH RAILWAYS IN 1970

The British Railways Board was set up, along with our other separate nationalized transport undertakings, by the terms of the Transport Act, 1962. This Act dissolved the British Transport Commission and shared its assets between the new bodies which assumed their responsibilities on January 1, 1963. Under the Act the finances of the railways were reconstructed and previous restrictions were modified to give them greater commercial freedom than they had enjoyed in the past.

For the purposes of management and operation the railways are divided into Regions. They cover the following areas:

1. London Midland Region—bounded by a line joining Carlisle, Oldham, Nottingham, Bedford, London, Banbury, Kidderminster, Aberystwyth.
2. Western Region—west of a line joining Yeovil, Westbury, Reading, London and the southern border of the L.M. Region.
3. Southern Region—south of a line joining Dorchester, Salisbury, London and the Thames.
4. Eastern Region—east of a line joining London, Peterborough, Sheffield, Bradford and Carlisle.
5. Scottish Region—north of a line joining Carlisle and Berwick.

Financial Results, 1970.—The balance sheet for 1970 showed a profit of £9,500,000, compared with a profit of £14,700,000 for 1969 while the railway working profit (before taking interest charges or revenue from other activities into account) was £47,400,000, compared with £48,500,000 for the previous year.

Railways	£ million 1970
Gross receipts:	
Passenger (including Grants)....	289·4
Freight (including parcels and mails)......................	270·6
Miscellaneous..................	11·4
TOTAL................	571·4
Working expenses:	
Train services................	265·1
Terminal traffic..............	91·9
Miscellaneous traffic expenses...	6·2
Track and signalling..........	88·5
General expenses..............	80·2
TOTAL....................	532·0
Railway net income....................	39·5
Net income from Operational Property (Letting), Advertising and Catering....	7·9
OPERATING PROFIT...............	47·4

OPERATING STATISTICS

At the end of 1970, British Railways had 31,281 miles of standard gauge lines and sidings in use, representing 11,799 miles of route of which 1,969 miles were electrified. Standard rail on main lines has a weight of 109 lbs. per yard. British Railways had 4,449 locomotives (diesel and diesel electric, 4,126 and electric, 323); 3,621 diesel multiple-unit vehicles, 7,358 electric multiple-unit vehicles and 7,669 locomotive-hauled passenger carriages with a capacity of 1,154,587 seats or berths in 1970. Loaded train miles run in passenger service totalled 195,879,000. 823,867,000 passenger journeys were made during the year, including 297,454,000 made by holders of season tickets. The average distance of each passenger journey on ordinary fare was 26·09 miles: and on season ticket, 17·35 miles. Passenger stations in use in 1970 numbered 2,423 and freight stations 646.

Freight.—There were 370,917 freight-vehicles and 6,508 other vehicles in the non-passenger-carrying stock. 112.521,000 tons of coal and coke were carried in 1970, 39,531,000 tons of iron and steel and 46,940,000 tons of other traffic. Loaded train miles run in freight service totalled 62,714,000.

Staff and Wages

On Dec. 31, 1970, British Railways employed a total staff of 213,236, compared with 215,791 on Dec. 31, 1969. Average weekly earnings of selected grades at May 4, 1970 (with numbers of staff) were: Male Clerks (23,089) £28·32; Train Drivers (21,820) £32·12; Senior Railmen (7,009) £29·11; Trackmen (12,100) £27·49.

Casualties in Train Accidents

(includes British Railways, London Transport and other railways).

	Average 1966–70	1970
Fatal Accidents.......	36	19
Passengers killed......	19	2
Passengers seriously injured...............	33	8
Railwaymen killed....	6	7
Railwaymen seriously injured.............	14	8
Other persons killed...	11	10
Other persons seriously injured.............	11	6
Passengers carried per passenger killed.....	71 200,000	690,500,000
Passenger miles run per passenger killed....1,128,100,000		11,072,000,000

RAILWAY ACCIDENTS IN WHICH 20 PERSONS AND OVER WERE KILLED IN THE UNITED KINGDOM SINCE 1945

Year	Date	Name of Accident	Railway	Number Killed	Cause
1945	Sept. 30	Bourne End	L.M. & S.	43	Points at excessive speed.
1946	Jan. 1	Lichfield (T.V.)	L.M. & S.	20	Point mechanism jammed.
1947	Oct. 24	South Croydon	S.R.	32	Collision in fog.
1947	Oct. 26	Goswick	L. & N.E.	28	Derailment.
1948	Apl. 17	Winsford	L.M. Region	24	Collision.
1952	Oct. 8	Harrow	L.M. Region	112	Collision.
1957	Dec. 4	Lewisham	S. Region	90	Collision in fog.
1967	Nov. 5	Hither Green	S. Region	49	Track failure

BRITISH RAILWAY FARES, 1953–1971

The following table shows rail fares for 12 specimen journeys in 1953, in years from 1958 when a change was made, and the fares current in October, 1971. The fares are 3rd or 2nd class ordinary returns. In 1957 the 3rd class was renamed 2nd.

LONDON TO:—	JANUARY 1953	1958	1960	1961	1962	1964	OCTOBER 1966	1967	1968	1969	1970	1971 £
	s. d.	s. d.	s. d.	s. d.	s. d.	s. d.	s. d.	s. d.	s. d.	s. d.	s. d.	£
Birmingham (New St.)	32 6	37 6	42 0	47 0	51 0	55 6	60 6	61 0	64 0	68 0	76 0	4·50
Bournemouth	31 6	36 0	41 0	45 0	50 0	54 0	58 6	58 6	60 0	60 0	72 0	5·00
Brighton	15 0	17 0	19 6	21 6	23 6	25 6	28 0	28 0	30 0	30 0	34 0	2·00
Bristol	34 6	39 4	45 0	50 0	55 0	59 0	64 0	64 0	65 0	65 0	70 0	4·10
Edinburgh (Waverley)	114 8	131 0	142 0	142 0	142 0	162 0	178 0	198 0	208 0	208 0	228 0	12·90
Glasgow (via Carlisle)	117 4	134 0	144 0	144 0	144 0	168 0	190 0	202 0	208 0	208 0	228 0	12·90
Liverpool	56 8	64 8	73 0	81 0	89 0	97 0	105 6	105 6	116 0	120 0	132 0	7·80
Manchester	53 8	61 4	69 0	77 0	85 0	92 0	100 0	100 0	110 0	116 0	128 0	7·55
Norwich	33 8	38 4	44 0	46 0	53 0	57 0	62 6	62 6	66 0	70 0	76 0	4·40
Oxford	18 8	21 4	24 0	27 0	29 6	32 0	35 0	35 0	35 0	36 0	39 0	2·25
Sheffield	46 6	53 0	60 0	67 0	73 0	79 6	86 6	86 6	88 0	90 0	98 0	5·90
York	55 2	63 0	71 0	79 0	87 0	94 6	102 6	102 6	110 0	114 0	122 0	7·10

LONDON SUBURBAN RAIL AND COACH FARES
London Underground Railway Return Fares

Specimen Journey	JANUARY 1957	1958	1959	1960	1963	1964	OCTOBER 1965	1967	1968	1969	1970	1971 £
	s. d.	s. d.	s. d.	s. d.	s. d.	s. d.	s. d.	s. d.	s. d.	s. d.	s. d.	£
Tottenham Court Rd.-Morden	2 10	3 0	3 4	3 6	4 0	4 8	5 0	5 6	5 6	6 0	8 0	0·40
Liverpool Street-Ealing Broadway	3 0	3 4	3 8	3 10	4 4	5 0	5 4	5 10	6 0	7 0	8 0	0·40
Tower Hill-Putney Br.	2 8	2 8	2 8	2 10	3 4	3 10	4 0	4 6	4 6	5 0	6 0	0·30
Piccadilly Circus-Cockfosters	3 4	3 8	3 10	4 0	4 8	5 4	5 4	6 2	6 6	7 0	8 0	0·40

The fare for each of the above journeys rose by 2d. between January and June, 1962.

Southern Region of British Railways 2nd Class Return Fares

Specimen Journey	JANUARY 1953	1958	1960	1961	1962	1964	OCTOBER 1965	1967	1968	1969	1970	1971 £
	s. d.	s. d.	s. d.	s. d.	s. d.	s. d.	s. d.	s. d.	s. d.	s. d.	s. d.	£
Charing Cross-Orpington	4 2	4 8	5 4	5 10	6 6	7 0	7 0	7 0	7 8	7 8	7 2	0·44
Waterloo-Esher*	4 2	5 0	5 8	6 4	7 0	7 6	7 6	7 6	8 2	8 2	8 10	0·52
Victoria-Sanderstead	3 10	4 4	5 0	5 6	6 0	6 6	6 6	6 6	7 4	7 2	8 0	0·48
Charing Cross-Bexleyheath	3 10	4 4	5 0	5 6	6 0	6 6	6 6	6 6	7 4	7 2	6 10	0·40

* This return fare also rose by 4d. in 1957.

Green Line Coach Return Fares

Specimen Journey	JANUARY 1953	1956	1958	1960	1963	1964	OCTOBER 1965	1967	1968	1969	1970	1971 £
	s. d.	s. d.	s. d.	s. d.	s. d.	s. d.	s. d.	s. d.	s. d.	s. d.	s. d.	£
Hyde Park Corner-Bromley South Station	3 6	4 0	4 4	4 8	5 4	6 0	6 4	6 10	7 0	8 0	8 0	0·50
Marble Arch-Purley	3 10	4 4	4 8	5 0	5 8	6 4	6 8	7 2	7 6	8 0	8 0	0·50
Marble Arch-Enfield Town	3 0	3 6	3 10	4 0	4 8	5 4	5 8	6 2	6 6	7 0	7 2	0·40
Aldgate-Romford Market Place	3 4	3 10	4 2	4 4	5 0	5 8	6 0	6 6	7 0	7 0	8 0	0·50

The fare for each of the above journeys rose by 2d. between January and June, 1962.

PRINCIPAL SHIPPING LINES
LONDON OFFICES OR AGENCIES

AMERICAN PRESIDENT LINES, LTD., 107 Leadenhall Street, E.C.3.

ANCHOR LINE. LTD., 52 Leadenhall Street, E.C.3.

BANK LINE, LTD., 21 Bury Street, E.C.3.

BELFAST STEAMSHIP CO., LTD. (Agents: Coast Lines, Ltd., *see below*).

BEN LINE STEAMERS, LTD., THE (*Loading Brokers and Passenger Agents*, Killick Martin & Co., Ltd., Dunster House, 20 Mark Lane, E.C.3).

BERGEN LINE (Bergen Steamship Co. Ltd.), 21–24 Cockspur Street, S.W.1.

BIBBY LINE, LTD. (Agents: Alexr. Howden & Co., Ltd., 112–113 Fenchurch Street, E.C.3).

BLUE FUNNEL LINE, 16 St. Helen's Place, E.C.3 (*Head Office*, India Buildings, Liverpool, 2).

BLUE STAR LINE LTD., Albion House, 34–5 Leadenhall Street, E.C.3.

BOOTH STEAMSHIP CO., LTD., 3 Lower Regent Street, S.W.1.

BOWRING STEAMSHIP CO., LTD., Tower Place, E.C.3.

BRITISH & IRISH S. P. CO., LTD. (Agents: Coast Lines, *see below*).

BRITISH INDIA STEAM NAVIGATION CO., LTD., P. & O. Building, Leadenhall Street, E.C.3.

BP TANKER CO. LTD., Britannic House, Moor Lane, E.C.2.

BROCKLEBANK LINE (T. & J. Brocklebank Ltd.). London Agents: Gosman & Smith, Ltd., Berth 36, Tilbury Docks.

BROCKLEBANK'S WELL LINE, Gosman & Smith, Ltd., Berth 36, Tilbury Docks.

BURNS AND LAIRD LINES LTD. (Agents: Coast Lines Ltd., *see below*).

CANADIAN PACIFIC RAILWAY COMPANY, Trafalgar Square, W.C.2.

CLAN LINE STEAMERS, LTD., THE; *Managers*, CAYZER, IRVINE & CO., LTD., 2 and 4 St. Mary Axe, E.C.3.

COAST LINES, LTD., 35 Crutched Friars, E.C.3; 288 The Highway, E.1.

CUNARD STEAM-SHIP CO., LTD., 15 Regent Street, S.W.1.

DONALDSON LINE, LTD., 110 Fenchurch Street, E.C.3.

ELDER DEMPSTER LINES, LTD. (Agents: Killick, Martin & Co. Ltd., Dunster House, 20 Mark Lane, E.C.3).

ELLERMAN LINES LTD., 12-20 Camomile Street, E.C.3.

ELLERMAN & PAPAYANNI LINES, LTD., 12–20 Camomile Street, E.C.3.

ELLERMAN'S WILSON LINE, LTD.: Agents: Mariner House, Pepys Street, E.C.3.

(WM.) FRANCE, FENWICK & CO., LTD., 23 Rood Lane, E.C.3.

FRENCH LINE, Compagnie Générale Transatlantique, Ltd., 20 Cockspur Street, S.W.1.

FURNESS, WITHY & CO., LTD., Furness House, 56 Leadenhall Street, E.C.3.

FYFFES LINE, 15 Stratton Street, W.1.

GENERAL STEAM NAVIGATION CO. LTD., Three Quays, Tower Hill, E.C.3.

GLEN LINE LTD., 16 St. Helen's Place, E.C.3.

HARRISON LINE: THOS. & JAS. HARRISON, LTD., Fountain House, Fenchurch Street, E.C.3. *Head Office*, Mersey Chambers, Liverpool, 2.

HENDERSON LINE, LTD., Dunster House, 20 Mark Lane, E.C.3.

HOLLAND-AMERICA LINE (LONDON), LTD., 52 Haymarket, S.W.1.

HOULDER BROTHERS & CO., LTD., 53 Leadenhall Street, E.C.3.

MACANDREWS & CO., LTD., Plantation House, Mincing Lane, E.C.3.

MAERSK LINE, 3–6 Bury Court, E.C.3.

MOSS HUTCHISON LINE, LTD., Three Quays, Tower Hill, E.C.3.

NEDLLOYD LINES, 22 Billiter Street, E.C.3.

NEW ZEALAND SHIPPING CO., LTD., P. & O. Building, Leadenhall Street, E.C.3.

NIPPON YUSEN KAISHA, 104–5 Leadenhall Street, E.C.3.

OLSEN, FRED, LTD., 33–34 Bury Street, E.C.3.

ORANJE LINE (Agents: Holland–America Line (London) Ltd. (*see above*).

PACIFIC STEAM NAVIGATION CO., THE, *Head Office*, Pacific Building, James Street, Liverpool 2.

P. & O. S. N. COMPANY, Leadenhall Street, E.C.3; 14 Cockspur Street, S.W.1.

PORT LINE LTD., Cleveland House, St. James's Square, S.W.1.

PRINCE LINE, LTD., 56 Leadenhall Street, E.C.3.

ROYAL MAIL LINES, LTD., 56 Leadenhall Street, E.C.3 and 10 Haymarket, S.W.1.

SCOTTISH SHIRE LINE, THE, Cayzer House, 2–4 St. Mary Axe, E.C.3.

SHAW SAVILL LINE, 14–19 Leadenhall Street, E.C.3 and 10 Haymarket, S.W.1.

SHELL TANKERS (U.K.) LTD., Shell Centre, S.E.1.

SMITH, SIR W. R., & SONS, LTD., 18 London Street, E.C.3.

SUN LINE/OCEANIC SHIPPING CO.: *Agents*, Holland-America Line (London) Ltd. (*See above*.)

SWEDISH LLOYD, LTD., Marlow House, Lloyds Avenue, E.C.3.

TOR LINE, LTD., 34 Panton Street, S.W.1.

TYNE-TEES STEAM SHIPPING CO. LTD. (*Agents*: Coast Lines Ltd., *see above*.)

UNION-CASTLE MAIL STEAMSHIP CO., LTD., *Head Office*, Cayzer House, 2–4 St. Mary Axe, E.C.3.

UNITED STATES LINES, 58 St. James's Street; *Freight*, 110 Bishopsgate, E.C.2.

HISTORIC ATLANTIC PASSAGES

Year	Days	Ship	Tons	Year	Days	Ship	Tons
1862a	9	Scotia	3,871	1932c	4d. 15h. 56m.	Europa	51,656
1869a	8	City of Brussels	3,081	1933c	4d. 17h. 43m.	Bremen	51,650
1882a	7	Alaska	6,400	1934d	4d. 6h. 58m.	Emp. of Britain	42,348
1889a	6	City of Paris	10,669	1935f	4d. 3h. 2m.	Normandie	80,000
1894a	5½	Lucania	12,950	1936f	4d. 0h. 27m.	Queen Mary	81,237
1897b	6	Kaiser Wilhelm	14,349	1936g	3d. 23h. 57m.	Queen Mary	81,237
1903c	5½	Deutschland	16,502	1937f	3d. 23h. 2m.	Normandie	80,000
1909a	4d. 10h. 41m.	Mauretania	30,696	1938f	3d. 21h. 45m.	Queen Mary	81,237
1924e	5d. 1h. 49m.	Mauretania	30,696	1938g	3d. 20h. 42m.	Queen Mary	81,237
1929c	4d. 18h. 17m.	Bremen	51,650	1952f	3d. 12h. 12m.	United States	51,500
1930c	4d. 17h. 6m.	Europa	51,656	1952g	3d. 10h. 40m.	United States	51,500

a From Queenstown; *b* from Southampton; *c* from Cherbourg; *d* Quebec to Cherbourg; *e* to Cherbourg; Bishop Rock to Ambrose Light (2,907 miles); *g* Ambrose Light to Bishop Rock (2,938 miles).

MERCHANT SHIPPING

Foreign Trade Movements

Total net tonnage of 92,644 vessels entering United Kingdom ports in 1970 was 166,564,000 tons (with cargo, 137,888,000 tons; in ballast 28,676,000 tons) compared with 158,397,000 tons in 1969. Net tonnage of 59,962 vessels clearing United Kingdom ports in 1970 was 165,759,000 tons (with cargo, 74,207,000 tons; in ballast, 91,552,000 tons) compared with 154,446,000 tons cleared in 1969. The following table shows foreign trade entrances and clearances *with cargo* in 1962–1970:—

Year	Entered				Cleared			
	Number of vessels	Total	Common-wealth‡	Foreign	Number of vessels	Total	Common-wealth‡	Foreign
		'ooo tons net				'ooo tons net		
1962.....	55,529	95,434	46,789	48,645	47,243	56,318	32,590	23,727
1963.....	57,063	98,089	48,060	50,029	50,435	58,409	32,375	26,034
1964.....	62,960	103,858	49,675	54,183	52,847	57,827	31,525	26,303
1965.....	64,462	108,233	49,381	58,852	52,667	57,767	31,222	26,545
1966.....	63,807	108,294	43,384	64,910	51,645	58,298	28,404	29,895
1967.....	72,157	118,727	48,092	70,635	54,309	62,766	32,327	30,439
1968.....	75,242	122,670	48,653	74,017	57,572	66,818	33,142	33,676
1969.....	74,573	130,496	52,210	78,286	59,191	70,733	34,429	36,304
1970.....	72,626	137,888	54,454	83,434	59,962	74,207	35,438	38,789

‡ Commonwealth and Irish Republic; including (1970) 22,030 vessels registered in the United Kingdom (50,088,000 net tons) entering; 19,948 U.K. vessels (32,239,000 net tons) clearing.

Foreign Trade Movement by Flags, 1970

Flag	Entered‡	Cleared‡	Flag	Entered‡	Cleared‡
	'ooo tons	'ooo tons		'ooo tons	'ooo tons
Commonwealth........	54,454	35,418	Norwegian..........	15,184	5,569
Belgian.............	2,585	2,488	Panamanian.........	2,278	735
Danish.............	3,463	2,413	Polish..............	334	175
Finnish.............	1,377	501	Spanish.............	830	713
French.............	6,590	3,811	Swedish.............	5,997	3,285
German.............	8,435	6,280	U.S.A..............	2,971	2,906
Greek.............	4,153	1,393	U.S.S.R...........	1,290	289
Italian.............	1,766	280	Yugoslav...........	391	102
Liberian.............	14,663	1,367	Other Flags........	3,573	1,577
Netherlands.........	7,554	4,905	*Total Foreign*......	83,434	38,789

‡ Net tonnage with cargo: vessels with mail only are excluded.

Principal British Seaports in 1970

The grand total values of trade passing through United Kingdom seaports, airports and land boundary in in 1970 are: Imports, £9,017,845,238; Exports and Re-exports, £8,024,173,925.

Port	Value of Trade			Volume of Trade‡	
	Imports	Exports§	Total	Arrived	Departed
	£	£	£	tons	tons
LONDON............	1,933,972,644	2,032,831,988	3,966,804,632	42,720,091	42,123,530
Liverpool............	1,024,547,514	1,195,043,785	2,219,591,299	21,795,428	21,196,724
Harwich............	444,096,685	507,277,342	951,374,027	*9,093,437	*9,234,778
Hull............	448,007,982	430,886,746	878,894,728	6,001,144	5,982,837
Southampton........	392,564,521	322,929,147	715,491,668	25,425,382	25,622,106
Felixstowe..........	298,645,344	301,518,836	600,164,180	*3,049,042	*2,981,404
Dover.............	259,376,279	235,031,561	494,407,840	*13,766,427	*13,863,132
Manchester.........	285,136,472	159,170,983	444,307,455	5,424,705	4,855,899
Middlesbrough.......	150,979,413	127,863,921	278,843,334	8,769,928	8,861,617
Immingham.........	165,718,187	108,320,234	274,038,421	‡9,864,983	‡9,875,890
Bristol............	227,686,213	42,495,085	270,181,298	4,389,570	4,470,842
Glasgow............	123,777,282	139,469,194	263,246,476	4,865,452	4,869,114
Milford Haven......	184,508,296	45,155,551	229,663,847	18,236,342	18,858,916
Swansea............	110,863,254	76,329,843	187,193,097	4,507,957	4,461,106
Belfast............	121,895,601	27,425,941	149,321,542	10,141,714	9,817,222

The value of trade passing through United Kingdom *Airports* rose further in 1970, a large proportion passing through London Airport, figures for which are shown in parentheses: Imports £1,271,784,990 (£927,361,620); Exports and Re-exports, £1,143,207,164 (£876,306,880); Total £2,414,992,454 (£1,803,668,500).

* Excluding coastwise tonnages.

† *Net* registered tonnage of vessels that arrived and departed with cargoes and in ballast, foreign and coastwise, during 1970. ‡ Including Grimsby tonnages. § Includes re-exports.

MERCHANT SHIPPING
MERCHANT FLEETS OF THE WORLD
Source: Lloyd's Register of Shipping

Flag	1955 No.	1955 Tons Gross	1960 No.	1960 Tons Gross	1965 No.	1965 Tons Gross	1970 No.	1970 Tons Gross
United Kingdom	5,632	19,356,660	5,246	21,130,874	4,437	21,530,264	3,822	25,824,820
Australia	374	612,430	330	619,996	306	726,099	344	1,074,112
Canada	1,095	1,521,015	1,085	1,578,077	1,154	1,829,741	1,266	2,399,949
Cyprus	9	6,005	2	991	9	46,454	207	1,138,229
India	221	569,718	257	848,916	354	1,522,603	399	2,401,656
Other Commonwealth Countries	914	1,164,628	976	1,648,799	1,034	2,362,445	1,331	3,437,745
Total British Commonwealth	8,245	23,230,456	7,896	25,837,653	7,294	28,018,596	7,369	36,276,511
Argentina	364	1,043,056	355	1,041,507	323	1,288,656	327	1,265,510
Belgium	193	497,536	206	728,981	220	831,976	230	1,062,152
Brazil	396	892,823	423	1,054,733	397	1,252,968	422	1,721,608
China (Taiwan)		not recorded	68	281,662	128	638,274	274	1,166,230
Denmark	680	1,651,686	868	2,269,847	923	2,561,599	1,210	3,314,320
Finland	346	739,573	334	714,483	420	1,009,486	388	1,397,232
France	1,220	3,924,478	1,456	4,808,728	1,558	5,198,435	1,420	6,457,900
Germany (West)	1,885	2,644,130	2,449	4,536,591	2,525	5,279,493	2,868	7,881,000
Greece	350	1,245,288	747	4,529,234	1,377	7,137,244	1,850	10,951,993
Italy	1,149	3,910,658	1,312	5,122,240	1,413	5,701,342	1,639	7,447,610
Japan	1,770	3,735,318	3,124	6,931,436	5,836	11,971,157	8,402	27,003,704
Liberia	436	3,996,904	977	8,882,240	1,887	17,539,462	1,869	33,296,644
Netherlands	1,716	3,695,610	1,891	4,884,049	1,847	4,891,041	1,598	5,206,663
Norway	2,351	7,249,087	2,725	11,203,246	2,742	15,641,498	2,808	19,346,911
Panama	555	3,922,539	607	4,235,983	692	4,405,407	886	5,645,877
Poland	147	316,065	262	619,144	390	1,039,966	516	1,580,298
Russia (U.S.S.R.)*	1,158	2,505,850	1,138	3,429,472	1,845	8,237,847	5,924	14,831,775
Spain	1,225	1,383,239	1,453	1,800,721	1,814	2,132,002	2,234	3,440,952
Sweden	1,217	2,807,166	1,211	3,746,866	1,123	4,290,103	995	4,920,704
United States of America†	4,537	26,422,683	4,059	24,837,069	3,416	21,527,349	2,983	18,463,207
Yugoslavia	166	300,412	237	661,061	353	990,846	348	1,515,563
Other Countries	2,386	4,465,132	2,573	5,212,554	3,942	8,745,757	5,884	13,295,500
WORLD TOTAL	32,492	100,568,779	36,311	129,769,500	41,865	160,391,504	52,444	227,489,864

* Information incomplete. † Including ships of the United States Reserve Fleet.

TONNAGE CLASSED WITH LLOYD'S REGISTER.

At July 1970, 84 per cent of the tonnage in the British Commonwealth was classed by Lloyd's Register. Of the total tonnage owned in the world, 73,351,951 tons were classed with that Society.

MERCHANT SHIPPING

STEAMSHIPS AND MOTORSHIPS LAUNCHED IN THE WORLD* DURING 1970

Source: *Lloyd's Register of Shipping*

Country of Build	Steamships No.	Steamships Tons Gross	Motorships No.	Motorships Tons Gross	Total No.	Total Tons Gross
United Kingdom	2	253,077	128	984,057	130	1,237,134
Australia	1	34,025	15	19,475	16	53,500
Canada			17	32,838	17	32,838
India			6	28,716	6	28,716
Other Commonwealth			29	8,434	29	8,434
Argentina			8	17,920	8	17,920
Belgium			13	155,312	13	155,312
Brazil			16	100,411	16	100,411
†Bulgaria			14	52,588	14	52,588
China (Taiwan)			23	90,743	23	90,743
Denmark	3	363,611	45	150,053	48	513,664
Egypt (U.A.R.)			5	8,695	5	8,695
Finland			37	221,761	37	221,761
France	8	582,436	121	377,774	129	960,210
Germany (East)			104	333,744	104	333,744
Germany (West)	11	728,888	183	958,599	194	1,687,487
Greece			19	72,725	19	72,725
Hungary			5	7,020	5	7,020
Irish Republic	6	431,467	45	166,412	51	597,879
Italy	43	4,444,693	970	6,031,111	1,013	10,475,804
Japan	3	260,919	106	199,584	109	460,503
Netherlands	2	219,270	109	419,500	111	638,770
Norway			4	27,892	4	27,892
Peru			98	35,493	98	35,493
Poland			52	463,442	52	463,442
Portugal			14	15,425 }	15	15,924
Angola			1	499 }		
Spain			156	925,697	156	925,697
Sweden	11	1,171,168	27	540,022	38	1,711,190
Turkey			12	10,921	12	10,921
U.S.A.	11	283,285	150	54,792	161	338,077
Yugoslavia			24	393,424	24	393,424
Other Countries			54	11,595	54	11,595
WORLD TOTAL	101	8,772,839	2,599	12,916,674	2,700	21,689,513

For Registration in	Total Steamships and Motorships No.	Total Steamships and Motorships Tons Gross
United Kingdom	184	2,703,133
Australia	18	85,396
Bahamas	4	55,904
Bermuda	5	311,885
Canada	18	33,138
India	15	161,936
Other Commonwealth	21	33,852
Belgium	8	84,583
Brazil	20	140,485
Bulgaria	5	31,752
China (Taiwan)	34	222,423
Denmark	48	61,966
Finland	9	44,626
France	52	809,243
Germany (West)	205	1,253,888
Greece	97	1,471,232
Italy	42	512,121
Japan	791	4,116,552
Korea (South)	9	88,620
Liberia	115	4,275,956
Mexico	40	34,499
Netherlands	37	265,548
Norway	122	2,189,599
Panama	21	51,987
Peru	101	63,885
Poland	21	185,913
Portugal	16	37,264
Russia (U.S.S.R.)	128	700,484
Spain	89	477,117
Sweden	24	366,956
Turkey	18	67,358
U.S.A.	143	381,202
Other Countries	240	369,010
WORLD TOTAL	2,700	21,689,513

Tonnage launched to Lloyd's Register Class.—Of the world tonnage launched during 1970, 26·3 per cent. (5,700,150 tons) was to Lloyd's Register Class. This figure includes 1,051,567 tons (85·0 per cent.) of the tonnage built in British yards.
† Information incomplete.
* Excluding China and U.S.S.R.

U+

THE LARGEST SHIPS AFLOAT
As recorded by Lloyd's Register at July 1971

NAME	Propulsion	Flag	Tons Gross	Length Overall	Breadth Extreme	Draught Summer	Year Built	Owners
Oil Tankers, etc.*								
Nisseki Maru...	Tb	Japan	185,000	1133·6	178·8	88·6	1971	Tokyo Tanker K.K.
Universe Iran...	Tb	Liberia	149,623	1132·8	175·2	81·4	1969	Bantry Transportation Co.
Universe Japan...	Tb	Liberia	149,623	1132·8	175·2	81·4	1969	Bantry Transportation Co.
Universe Korea...	Tb	Liberia	149,623	1132·8	175·2	81·4	1969	Bantry Transportation Co.
Universe Portugal...	Tb	Liberia	149,623	1132·8	175·2	81·4	1968	Bantry Transportation Co.
Universe Ireland...	Tb	Liberia	149,609	1132·8	175·2	81·4	1968	Bantry Transportation Co.
Universe Kuwait...	Tb	Liberia	149,609	1132·8	175·2	81·4	1968	Bantry Transportation Co.
Berge King...	Oe	Norway	140,012	1125·0	170·1	70·9	1970	Sig. Bergesen d.y. & Co.
Berge Queen...	Oe	Norway	139,999	1125·0	170·1	70·9	1971	Sig. Bergesen d.y. & Co.
T. G. Shaughnessy...	Oe	Bermuda	133,701	1109·3	170·2	67·5	1971	Canadian Pacific (Bermuda) Ltd.
Port Hawkesbury...	Oe	Bermuda	133,699	1109·3	170·2	67·5	1970	Canadian Pacific (Bermuda) Ltd.
Okinoshima Maru...	Tb	Japan	130,841	1107·3	176·0	64·8	1970	Idemitsu Tanker K.K.
Terukuni Maru...	Tb	Japan	129,319	1103·8	179·0	62·8	1971	Terukuni Kaiun K.K.
†Hoegh Hill...	Tb	Norway	128,980	1027·0	170·6	67·0	1970	Leif Hoegh & Co. A/S
Jalinga...	Tb	Norway	128,431	1109·3	170·2	67·6	1970	A/S Kosmos
Jamunda...	Tb	Norway	128,431	1109·3	170·2	67·6	1971	A/S Kosmos
Esso Europoort...	Tb	Netherlands	127,176	1141·1	170·2	65·5	1970	Esso Tankvaart Nederlandse Antilles N.V.
Esso Nederland...	Tb	Netherlands	127,176	1141·1	170·2	65·5	1970	Esso Tankvaart Nederlandse Antilles N.V.
Esso Cambria...	Tb	Great Britain	127,158	1141·1	170·2	65·5	1969	Esso Petroleum Co. Ltd.
Esso Scotia...	Tb	Great Britain	127,158	1141·1	170·2	65·4	1969	Esso Petroleum Co. Ltd.
Passenger Liners								
France...	Tb	France	66,348	1035·2	110·9	34·4	1961	Cie. Générale Transatlantique
Queen Elizabeth 2...	Tb	Great Britain	65,863	963·0	105·2	32·6	1969	Cunard Line Ltd.
Raffaello...	Tb	Italy	45,933	904·6	101·8	30·6	1965	"Italia" Soc. per Azioni di Nav.
Michelangelo...	Tb	Italy	45,911	904·9	101·8	30·6	1965	"Italia" Soc. per Azioni di Nav.
Canberra...	Tb	Great Britain	44,807	818·5	102·5	32·7	1961	P. & O. Steam Nav. Co.
Oriana...	Tb	Great Britain	41,910	804·0	97·2	32·0	1960	P. & O. Steam Nav. Co.
United States...	Tb	U.S.A.	38,216	990·0	101·6	31·0	1952	United States Lines Co.
Rotterdam...	Tb	Netherlands	37,783	748·6	94·2	29·7	1959	N.V. Nederl.-Amerika Stoomv. Maats.
Nieuw Amsterdam...	Tb	Netherlands	36,982	758·5	88·3	31·5	1938	N.V. Nederl.-Amerika Stoomv. Maats.
Windsor Castle...	Tb	Great Britain	36,123	783·1	92·5	32·1	1960	Union Castle Mail S.S. Co. Ltd.

* All oil tankers unless otherwise stated.　　† Ore/oil carrier.　　Tb = Turbine engines.　　Oe = Oil engines.

THE UNITED KINGDOM

Area.—The land area of the United Kingdom (England, Wales, Scotland and N. Ireland) is 93,026 sq. miles or 59,537,000 acres. The area of inland water* in the United Kingdom is 1,190 sq. miles. Total 94,216 sq. miles.

	Land Area		Inland water*	Total
	Sq. miles	'ooo acres	Sq. miles	Sq. miles
England............................	50,053	32,034	280	50,334
Wales...............................	7,969	5,100	48	8,016
Scotland...........................	29,798	19,071	616	30,414
Northern Ireland..................	5,206	3,332	246	5,452

* Excluding tidal water.

POPULATION: CENSUS RESULTS, 1801–1971   Thousands

	United Kingdom			England and Wales			Scotland			Northern Ireland†		
	Total	Males	Females	Total	Males	Females	Total	Males	Females	Total	Males	Females
1801	11,944	5,692	6,252	8,893	4,255	4,638	1,608	739	869	1,443	698	745
1811	13,368	6,368	7,000	10,165	4,874	5,291	1,806	826	980	1,397	668	729
1821	15,472	7,498	7,974	12,000	5,850	6,150	2,092	983	1,109	1,380	665	715
1831	17,835	8,647	9,188	13,897	6,771	7,126	2,364	1,114	1,250	1,574	762	812
1841	20,183	9,819	10,364	15,914	7,778	8,137	2,620	1,242	1,378	1,649	800	849
1851	22,259	10,855	11,404	17,928	8,781	9,146	2,889	1,375	1,513	1,443	698	745
1861	24,525	11,894	12,631	20,066	9,776	10,290	3,062	1,450	1,612	1,396	668	728
1871	27,431	13,309	14,122	22,712	11,059	11,653	3,360	1,603	1,757	1,359	647	712
1881	31,015	15,060	15,955	25,974	12,640	13,335	3,736	1,799	1,936	1,305	621	684
1891	34,264	16,593	17,671	29,003	14,060	14,942	4,026	1,943	2,083	1,236	590	646
1901	38,237	18,492	19,745	32,528	15,729	16,799	4,472	2,174	2,298	1,237	590	647
1911	42,082	20,357	21,725	36,070	17,446	18,625	4,761	2,309	2,452	1,251	603	648
1921	44,027	21,033	22,994	37,887	18,075	19,811	4,882	2,348	2,535	1,258	610	648
1931	46,038	22,060	23,979	39,952	19,133	20,819	4,843	2,326	2,517	1,243	601	642
1951	50,225	24,118	26,107	43,758	21,016	22,742	5,096	2,434	2,662	1,371	668	703
1961	52,676	25,478	27,198	46,072	22,299	23,773	5,178	2,484	2,694	1,425	695	731
1971	55,347	26,872	28,475	48,594	23,608	24,986	5,228	2,515	2,713	1,525	748	777

NOTES.—1. Before 1801 there existed no official return of the population of either England or Scotland. Estimates of the population of England at various periods, calculated from the number of baptisms, burials and marriages, are: in 1570, 4,160,221; 1600, 4,811,718; 1630, 5,600,517; 1670, 5,773,646; 1700, 6,045,008; 1750, 6,517,035.

2. The last official Census of Population in respect of England and Wales, Scotland, Northern Ireland, the Isle of Man and Guernsey, was taken on the night of April 25, 1971, and in respect of Jersey on April 4, 1971. Preliminary figures, reported in August, 1971, appear in the table above, rounded to the nearest 1,000. The exact figures from the preliminary reports appear in the main articles in this edition on England, Wales, Scotland, N. Ireland, and in County and municipal directories.

3.†All figures refer to the area which is now Northern Ireland. Figures for N. Ireland in 1921 and 1931 are estimates based on the Censuses held in 1926 and 1937.

ISLANDS.—*The figures given above do not include islands of the British seas.* Populations of these islands at census years since 1900 were:—

	ISLE OF MAN			JERSEY			GUERNSEY		
	Total	Male	Female	Total	Male	Female	Total	Male	Female
1901............	54,752	25,496	29,256	52,576	23,940	28,636	43,042	21,140	21,902
1911............	52,016	23,937	28,079	51,898	24,014	27,884	45,001	22,215	22,786
1921............	60,284	27,329	32,955	49,701	22,438	27,263	40,529	19,303	21,226
1931............	49,308	22,443	26,865	50,462	23,424	27,038	42,743	20,675	22,068
1951............	55,123	25,749	29,464	57,296	27,282	30,014	45,747	22,094	23,380
1961............	48,151	22,060	26,091	57,200	27,200	30,000	47,198	22,890	24,288
1971............	49,743	23,007	26,736	72,532	35,423	37,109	52,708	25,382	27,326

INCREASE OF THE PEOPLE

In England and Wales during the 19th Century, intercensal increases in the population ranged from 18·06 per cent. to 11·65 per cent., an average of 14 per cent. every ten years; there was an average proportion of 1,050 females to 1,000 males. Between the censuses of 1961 and 1971 the increase was 5·3 per cent. The proportion of 1,088 females to 1,000 males in 1931 declined to 1,082 in 1951, to 1,066 in 1961, and further to 1,058 in 1971.

Estimates of the future total population of the United Kingdom, based on the mid-1967 annual estimate, have been prepared by the Government Actuary in consultation with the Registrars-General. It is assumed in their projections below that, at ages under 40 for males and 50 for females,

death rates will decline steadily until after 40 years they are at one-half or less of the present rates. Above these ages the assumed rates of decline become progressively smaller as age advances until they vanish at ages over 90. Annual live births are assumed to reach 993,000 in 1976, 1,020,000 in 1981 and 1,165,000 in 2001. The ratio of male to female births is taken as 1·06 (N. Ireland 1·07) throughout and a net outward migration of 30,000 persons per year is assumed for all future years.

Estimated Future Population of the U. K.
Thousands

1972...56,336	1975....57,167	1991....62,343
1973...56,606	1976....57,453	2001....66,509
1974...56,886	1981....58,903	

THE ANNUAL ESTIMATES OF POPULATION

Since 1948, estimates of the total population and of populations of counties and other local authority areas at June 30 each year have been prepared by the Registrars-General and published by Her Majesty's Stationery Office. The following table shows the estimated home population of the United Kingdom at June 30, 1970. and its distribution. Populations at the 1971 Census (April 25, 1971) for the counties and other administrative areas will be found on pp. 631 *et seq.*

thousands

Age Groups	United Kingdom			England and Wales		Scotland		Northern Ireland	
	Total	Males	Females	Males	Females	Males	Females	Males	Females
Total, all ages..	55,710·7	27,072·9	28,637·8	23,830·9	25,156·8	2,497·0	2,702·0	745·0	779·0
Under 5.........	4,617·6	2,368·3	2,249·3	2,054·7	1,953·1	231·3	218·6	82·3	77·6
5–9.............	4,698·4	2,408·7	2,289·7	2,084·3	1,981·8	243·6	231·8	80·9	76·0
10–14...........	4,082·4	2,093·6	1,988·8	1,798·0	1,707·5	223·6	212·7	72·0	68·6
15–19...........	3,822·3	1,939·9	1,882·4	1,678·1	1,629·3	196·5	191·0	65·3	62·1
20–24...........	4,311·9	2,167·7	2,144·2	1,908·3	1,885·0	202·3	202·3	57·1	56·9
25–29...........	3,597·5	1,812·1	1,785·4	1,605·8	1,575·1	160·0	162·6	46·3	47·7
30–34...........	3,339·0	1,696·4	1,642·6	1,511·3	1,450·0	143·1	149·5	42·0	43·1
35–39...........	3,270·9	1,669·9	1,601·0	1,488·2	1,410·9	141·4	148·3	40·3	41·8
40–44...........	3,356·6	1,689·5	1,667·1	1,502·1	1,468·3	146·7	155·3	40·7	43·5
45–49...........	3,676·5	1,827·5	1,849·1	1,629·5	1,637·3	155·9	167·0	42·1	44·8
50–54...........	3,191·9	1,559·4	1,632·4	1,387·1	1,441·5	134·0	150·1	38·3	40·8
55–59...........	3,428·6	1,636·5	1,792·1	1,451·7	1,584·0	146·9	166·5	37·9	41·6
60–64...........	3,172·5	1,479·4	1,693·2	1,313·9	1,498·7	132·5	156·3	33·0	38·2
65–69...........	2,661·3	1,171·0	1,490·3	1,040·0	1,318·5	105·0	138·3	26·0	33·5
70–74...........	1,948·3	784·2	1,200·1	663·6	1,064·1	65·4	108·4	19·2	27·5
75–79...........	1,325·5	453·9	871·6	403·1	777·6	39·1	75·9	11·7	18·1
80–84...........	772·8	235·4	537·4	209·0	482·7	19·9	43·7	6·5	11·0
85 and over......	436·9	115·6	321·3	102·2	291·4	10·0	23·6	3·4	6·1

Excluding H.M. forces overseas.

LIVE BIRTHS, MARRIAGES AND DEATHS IN THE UNITED KINGDOM

Year	Live Births	Rate per 1,000	Marriages	Rate per 1,000	Deaths	Rate per 1,000	
						Males	Females
1938	735,573	15·5	409,101	17·2	559,598	12·6	11·0
1960	918,000	17·5	393,598	15·0	603,328	12·1	10·9
1961	944,000	17·8	397,101	15·1	631,788	12·6	11·4
1962	976,000	18·3	397,818	14·9	636,051	12·6	11·3
1963	990,000	18·5	401,137	14·9	654,288	12·8	11·6
1964	1,015,000	18·7	410,163	15·2	611,130	12·0	10·7
1965	998,000	18·3	422,054	15·5	627,798	12·2	10·9
1966	980,000	17·8	437,083	16·0	643,754	12·4	11·2
1967	962,000	17·5	439,092	15·9	616,600	11·8	10·6
1968	947,000	17·1	462,758	16·7	656,000	12·4	11·3
1969	920,900	16·6	451,310	16·3	659,536	12·5	11·3
1970	904,000	16·2	479,700	16·8	655,400	11·8	

DIVORCE STATISTICS

England and Wales

	1967	1968	1969
Dissolution			
Petitions filed.....	49,969	54,036	60,134
By husbands....	18,651	20,130	22,270
By wives.......	13,318	33,906	37,864
Grounds:—			
Adultery.......	23,655	26,011	29,891
Desertion.......	10,584	11,147	11,490
Cruelty.........	11,516	12,753	14,538
Several.........	3,964	3,836	3,950
Lunacy.........	68	63	56
Presumed death.	72	109	75
Rape, etc.......	120	117	134
Decrees ab. granted	42,378	45,036	50,063
Nullity of Marriage			
Petitions filed.....	987	971	1,082
Decrees ab. granted	715	758	1,247
Judicial Separations...	127	105	116

Scotland

	1967	1968	1969
Divorce			
Actions completed.	3,101	4,953	4,421
By husbands......	1,047	1,518	1,324
By wives.........	2,054	3,435	3,101
On grounds of—			
Adultery, etc....	1,276	1,939	1,679
Desertion.......	857	1,267	1,122
Insanity........	5	11	3
Cruelty, etc.....	963	1,736	1,617
Divorces granted..	2,963	1,736	4,215
Actions completed	2	5	4
Separation granted	2	5	3

Northern Ireland

Divorce............	272	298	298
Nullity of marriage	9	8	8
Judicial separation .	..	1	1

CAUSES OF DEATH IN ENGLAND AND WALES, 1969 AND 1970
(*Eighth Revision, International Classification of Diseases*, 1968—abbreviated)

Causes of Death	1969	1970	Causes of Death	1969	1970
Natural Causes			**Natural Causes**		
Enteritis & other diarrhœal diseases.....	730	586	Heart disease (other forms)............	30,693	29,375
Tuberculosis:—			Subarachnoid hæmorrhage...........	3,996	4,158
Respiratory.......	1,092	913	Cerebral hæmorrhage	19,413	18,225
Other...........	748	693	Cerebral embolism & thrombosis........	32,987	31,232
Meningococcal infections............	117	143	Other cerebrovascular disease...........	23,332	25,677
Viral encephalitis.....	90	77	Arteriosclerosis......	11,468	11,178
Infectious hepatitis...	208	186	Aortic aneurysm (non-syphilitic)........	4,418	4,620
Other viral diseases...	216	217	Other diseases of arteries, arterioles and		
Syphilitic disease.....	226	193	capillaries.........	3,372	3,309
Malignant neoplasms:			Venous thrombosis & embolism.........	5,779	6,239
Buccal cavity and pharynx........	1,630	1,665	Other diseases of circulatory system....	388	362
Oesophagus.......	2,891	2,992	Acute bronchitis & bronchiolitis.......	2,840	2,401
Stomach..........	12,711	12,738	Influenza............	4,734	7,250
Intestines except rectum..........	10,114	10,306	Pneumonia	41,081	42,679
Rectum and recto-sigmoid junction....	5,883	5,837	Bronchitis, emphysema.............	32,630	28,938
Larynx...........	726	760	Asthma.............	1,327	1,244
Trachea, bronchus and lung........	29,768	30,281	Pneumoconiosis......	582	579
Bone..............	486	518	Other diseases of respiratory system.....	2,962	3,058
Skin..............	997	966	Ulcer of stomach....	2,263	2,069
Breast............	10,698	10,751	Ulcer of duodenum...	1,894	1,696
Cervix uteri.......	2,417	2,343	Appendicitis........	375	327
Uterus, other......	1,584	1,508	Intestinal obstruction and hernia........	2,506	2,426
Prostate..........	4,000	3,905	Cirrhosis of liver.....	1,578	1,393
Pancreas..........	4,984	5,020	Other diseases of digestive system.....	5,477	5,491
Ovary, fallopian tube, etc.......	3,548	3,653	Nephritis & nephrosis.	2,441	2,335
Bladder...........	3,764	3,828	Infections of kidney...	2,571	2,293
Other sites........	11,598	11,820	Hyperplasia of prostate.............	1,454	1,276
Leukæmia.........	3,051	2,985	Other genito-urinary diseases...........	1,361	1,473
Lymphosarcoma&reticulum cell sarcoma.	1,308	1,337	Pregnancy, childbirth & abortion........	155	147
Other neoplasms of lymphatic and hæmatopoietic tissue..	2,546	2,519	Toxæmias of pregnancy, etc........	24	24
Benign and other neoplasms...........	1,331	1,353	Hæmorrhage of pregnancy and childbirth	12	12
Diabetes mellitus.....	4,720	4,684	Abortion...........	35	32
Other endocrine and metabolic diseases..	1,932	1,884	Complications of pregnancy	84	79
Deficiency anæmias...	718	730	Skin diseases........	341	360
Other anæmias......	933	957	Rheumatoid arthritis	1,016	969
Other diseases of the blood, etc........	227	233	Other arthritis and spondylitis........	488	529
Psychoses...........	1,116	1,145	Spina bifida........	499	554
Neuroses, personality disorders, etc......	170	120	Congenital anomalies of heart.........	1,719	1,782
Meningitis..........	382	399	Other congenital anomalies of circulatory system............	363	324
Multiple sclerosis.....	884	826	Nervous and other congenital anomalies	1,884	1,790
Epilepsy............	631	619	Perinatal mortality (various causes)....	6,639	6,697
Otitis media and mastoiditis...........	136	108	Senility............	3,146	2,798
Paralysis agitans.....	1,794	1,755	Other natural causes..	2,246	2,409
Other diseases of nervous system and sense organs.......	2,511	2,474			
Chronic rheumatic heart disease.......	7,512	7,254	**TOTAL (natural causes)**	556,078	552,514
Hypertensive heart disease...........	8,492	7,763			
Other hypertensive disease...........	2,457	2,340			
Acute myocardial infarction...........	97,628	97,307			
Other ischæmic heart disease............	41,800	42,014			

Cause of Death	1969	1970	Cause of Death	1969	1970
Deaths by Violence:—			Industrial.........	781	787
Motor and road accidents.........	6,700	6,869	Suffocation.........	842	797
Other transport accidents.........	448	358	All other accidents.	505	571
Poisoning.........	917	951	Suicide............	4,326	3,939
Falls............	5,768	5,633	Homicide..........	320	350
Burning..........	745	792	Other violent deaths..	1,398	1,137
Drowning & submersion.........	523	486	**TOTAL (by violence)**	**23,300**	**22,699**
Shooting.........	27	29	TOTAL, ALL CAUSES...	579,378	575,213

CRIMINAL STATISTICS
ENGLAND AND WALES

In 1970 the total number of persons found guilty of offences of all kinds was 1,674,056 of whom 322,898 (males, 280,217; females, 42,681) were found guilty of indictable offences, 1,351,158 of non-indictable offences. The most numerous offences in 1969 and 1970 are listed below. In addition 55,686 persons (44,486 under 17 years) were cautioned by the police in 1970 for indictable offences and 29,766 (8,992 juveniles) for non-indictable (other than motoring) offences.

Ages of Offenders.—The 37,159 persons found guilty of indictable offences by the *higher courts* in 1970 included 1,485 persons under 17 years of age 10,451 persons aged 17 and under 21, and 25,583 persons aged 21 and over. In *magistrates' courts*, of 285,379 persons convicted of indictable offences in 1970, 23,861 were under 14 yers of age, 49,051 were aged 14 and under 17, 66,475 persons were aged 17 and under 21 and 145,992 were aged 21 years and over.

Persons Found Guilty of Indictable Offences in 1970

Age group and sex		Violence against the person	Sexual offences	Burglary and robbery	Theft and unauthorized-taking	Handling stolen goods	Fraud	Other offences	Total
Under 14	M	289	145	9,568	9,721	1,247	87	367	21,424
	F	26	1	389	1,867	142	18	18	2,461
14 and under 17.......	M	2,332	722	16,144	22,602	2,519	304	533	45,156
	F	180	1	536	4,104	392	85	58	5,356
17 and under 21.......	M	6,066	1,187	18,213	37,148	3,733	1,681	1,614	69,642
	F	232	4	520	5,281	507	426	314	7,284
21 and under 30.......	M	7,568	1,698	16,229	38,010	5,954	3,968	2,999	76,426
	F	395	11	364	7,387	575	655	691	10,078
30 and over..........	M	5,883	2,871	8,510	35,832	6,807	4,433	3,233	67,569
	F	472	16	205	14,550	799	649	811	17,502
All ages...........	M	23,138	6,623	68,664	143,313	20,260	10,473	8,746	280,217
	F	1,305	33	2,014	33,189	2,415	1,833	1,892	42,681
TOTALS, 1970.........		23,443	6,656	70,678	176,502	22,675	12,306	10,638	322,898
1969.........		*20,855*	*6,497*	*69,424*	*167,440*	*19,378*	*11,415*	*9,061*	*304,070*

Persons Found Guilty

	1969	1970
Motoring...............	946,853	970,598
Highways Acts..........	20,983	20,576
Intoxicating Liquor Laws	84,828	86,764
Revenue Offences*......	81,399	91,359
Railway Offences.......	16,693	17,446
Local and Other Regulations†.........	4,338	4,590
Disorderly Behaviour.....	10,186	9,870
Betting and Gaming......	2,392	1,868
Assaults................	11,997	11,828
Education Acts.........	3,144	3,145
Malicious Damage.......	17,889	19,827
Offences by Prostitutes....	2,318	2,347
Vagrancy Acts...........	4,819	5,190
Wireless Telegraphy Acts	37,727	40,274
Cruelty to a child........	343	242
Other Offences..........	56,739	65,234
TOTAL...............	1,302,658	1,351,158

* Mainly failure to take out licences for dogs or motor vehicles.

† Excluding disorderly behaviour.

Murder

The Murder (Abolition of Death Penalty) Act, 1965, came into force on November 9, 1965, and was made permanent from December 17, 1969. Its main provisions are as follows.

Section 1(1) abolishes the death penalty for murder and provides that a person aged 18 or over convicted of murder shall be sentenced to imprisonment for life. Section 1 (2) provides that on sentencing any person convicted of murder to imprisonment for life the Court may at the same time declare the period which it recommends to the Secretary of State as the minimum period which in its view should elapse before the Secretary of State orders the release of that person on licence. Section 61 (1) of the Criminal Justice Act, 1967, provides that no person convicted of murder shall be released by the Secretary of State on licence unless the Secretary of State has before such release consulted the Lord Chief Justice and the trial judge, if available.

The number of victims of murder known to the police in 1970 was 138, compared with 154 in 1967, 148 in 1968 and 119 in 1969. These figures repre-

sent rather less than 3 victims per million of the home population of England and Wales.

A further 48 cases in 1970 were recorded in 1971 as other than murder: manslaughter, 36; infanticide, 2; in 10 cases the courts found that no murder had been committed (self defence, 3 and accident, 7).

Of 294 persons committed for trial for murder in 1970, 2 were found unfit to plead and 2 not guilty by reason of insanity. Ninety-seven persons were convicted of murder, 145 were convicted of manslaughter and 8 persons were convicted of a lesser offence. 35 persons were acquitted. In the cases of 5 persons committed for trial for murder, proceedings were pending at the time of report.

Statistics of murder in England and Wales from 1969 distinguish between " abnormal " murders where the suspects were found insane or committed suicide and " normal " murders, although in some instances the offender may have had a history of mental illness. In 94 cases in 1970 involving 97 victims there were 135 " normal " suspects; in 4 cases involving 4 victims, 4 " abnormal " suspects were found insane and in 17 cases involving 19 victims, 17 " abnormal " suspects committed suicide. Incidents involving 18 victims had not been cleared up at the time of report.

In the 138 cases of murder known to the police

the method of murder was classified as follows: Sharp instrument, 53; blunt instrument, 26; hitting, kicking, etc., 10; strangulation or asphyxiation, 28; shooting, 16; other methods, 5.

Estimated motives for 97 " normal " murders in 1970 were recorded as follows: Rage or quarrel, 35; jealousy or revenge, 17; sexual, 12; theft or gain, 20; other motives, 9; apparently motiveless or not known, 4. The relationship of the victim to the suspected murderer in 120 murders cleared up was: son or daughter, 8 (3 " abnormal " suspects committed suicide); spouse or co-habitant, 23 (10 suspects committed suicide); other relative, 5; lover, etc., 10; other associate, 48; stranger, 25; not known, 1.

Magistrates' Courts
Non-Criminal Proceedings

In 1970, 49,302 orders were made in magistrates' courts in respect of 53,012 applications, mainly in separation, maintenance and child welfare cases; Affiliation orders, 7,902; Maintenance orders 1,547; Matrimonial orders, 20,934; Guardianship of infants, 5,427; Committals to approved schools, 6,609; to care of fit persons, 4,197; Supervision orders, 2,821; Parental control of children orders, 45.

SCOTLAND
Persons proceeded against

Indictable Offences	Average 1935–39	1967	1968	1969	1970
Crimes					
Against the person...................	2,545	3,706	3,819	3,576	3,488
Against property:—					
with violence......................	3,473	12,683	12,273	13,171	14,837
without violence..................	12,186	20,986	21,246	22,924	24,934
Malicious injuries to property...........	3,639	567	585	788	818
Forgery, etc........................	79	268	248	360	302
Other Crimes.......................	406	795	925	966	1,318
Total........................	22,328	39,005	39,096	41,775	45,697
Miscellaneous Offences					
Breach of Peace....................	20,706	38,557	41,249	41,663	44,039
Against Intoxicating Liquor Laws.........	16,953	14,872	15,078	14,142	14,372
Against Police Acts, etc...............	11,048	21,258	14,124	14,815	16,271
Against Road Acts, etc...............	43,905	82,089	77,302	80,697	*80,512
Other (including war legislation)........	15,790	19,471	18,623	21,689	21,874
Total........................	108,402	176,247	166,376	173,006	177,068
TOTAL, ALL CRIMES AND OFFENCES...........	130,730	215,252	205,472	214,781	222,765

*Vehicle licences in force in the September quarter, excluding trade licences and Service vehicles, 1,123,500.

NOTE.—The figures show the number of *persons* proceeded against, not the number of *crimes and offences*. Where, therefore, any person is charged at the same time with several offences, one of these has to be selected for tabulation. The rule followed is to select that offence for which the proceedings were carried to the furthest stage. If there were several convictions or findings of guilt, the offence selected is that for which the heaviest punishment was awarded. If the final result of proceedings on two or more charges is the same, the most serious offence appears in the tables.

Cases of Murder.—In 1970, 29 cases of murder were known to the police. 6 of the 29 victims were under 10 years of age (one boy and one girl aged two years, one girl aged 1 year, and two were new-born female infants). Two of the victims were over 60.

Eighteen persons were prosecuted in respect of 13 of these cases of murder. Fifteen were sentenced to life imprisonment, two (aged under 18) were ordered to be detained during Her Majesty's Pleasure and one was acquitted on account of insanity, and committed to a mental hospital. In one case the suspect committed suicide. At the end of 1970 proceedings were pending in 11 cases. Four cases were unsolved.

Juvenile Crime.—In 1970, 29,496 juveniles were proceeded against for crimes and offences of all kinds. Of these 1,741 were acquitted or the

charge against them was withdrawn. In 4,931 cases the charge was proved and an order made without a finding of guilt, 1,415 young persons being discharged absolutely and 3,513 placed on probation. Three were found to be mentally ill. In 22,180 cases where charges were proved and an order made with a finding of guilt, 7,822 juveniles were admonished, etc., and 150 were cautioned (with or without surety). 1,171 juveniles were committed to approved schools, 542 to remand homes, 316 for Borstal training, 374 to detention centres and 37 to the care of fit persons. Sixteen were placed on probation. 10,936 offenders were fined, and in 733 cases fines were imposed on the parent or guardian of the offender. 644 juveniles were discharged without trial. Eighty cases were disposed of in other ways and 3 offenders were recalled from licence.

POST WAR BUILDING PROGRESS

New Houses and Flats

Of the 134,874 new dwellings completed by local authorities in England and Wales in 1970, 53·3 per cent. were flats. 37·2 per cent. of the new dwellings had 3 bedrooms, 30·5 per cent. had 2 bedrooms, 28·6 per cent. had 1 bedroom and 3·7 per cent. 4 or more bedrooms.

Cost.—The average tender price for a traditional three-bedroom house at the beginning of 1956 was £1,448 (or 31s. 6½d. per square foot), with a smaller average floor area of 918 square feet. Since 1968, the classification of dwellings has been based on designed bedspaces. In 1969, the average tender price for all types of 5 bedspace homes, the nearest equivalent to a 3-bedroom house was £3,159 or 63s. 6½d. per sq. ft., providing an average floor area per house of 964 sq. ft.

Conversions and Improvements

In 1970, applications for grants under the Housing Acts for the improvement or conversion of 156,557 houses were approved, including applications made by local authorities for the conversion of 2,668 dwellings, for improvements to 30,745 dwellings and for provision of standard amenities in 8,547 dwellings. Applications by private persons and housing associations were approved for 11,719 conversions, improvements in 42,266 dwellings and provision of standard amenities in 60,612 dwellings.

Slum Clearance and Repair

In 1970, 67,804 houses were demolished or closed in England and Wales, including 52,538 in scheduled clearance areas, and 169,598 persons were moved to other housing in consequence. At the end of 1970, a total of 10,855 unfit houses were retained in temporary occupation. As a result of informal action by local authorities, 36,224 unfit dwellings were made fit; in formal proceedings under the Health and Housing Acts, a further 14,785 dwellings were made fit by their owners or by local authorities in default of action by the owners.

Permanent Houses and Flats completed

Year	For Local Authorities‡	For Private Owners	Other†	TOTAL
England and Wales				
1945–63 .	2,321,097	1,545,545	132,029	4,098,671
1964....	119,468	210,432	6,605	336,505
1965....	133,024	206,246	7,911	347,181
1966....	142,430	197,502	9,548	349,480
1967....	159,347	192,940	10,611	362,898
1968....	148,049	213,273	10,404	371,726
1969....	139,850	173,377	10,938	324,165
1970....	134,874	162,084	10,308	307,266
1971*...	30,808	38,064	3,579	72,451
Scotland				
1945–63 .	418,968	61,794	11,081	491,843
1964....	29,156	7,662	353	37,171
1965....	26,584	7,553	979	35,116
1966....	27,515	7,870	644	36,029
1967....	33,222	7,498	738	41,458
1968....	32,011	8,720	1,258	41,989
1969....	33,932	8,326	370	43,628
1970....	34,401	8,220	546	43,167
1971*...	7,087	2,467	129	9,683
Northern Ireland				
1945–63 .	68,314	41,169	2,878	112,361
1964....	6,130	3,170	216	9,516
1965....	5,349	3,363	225	8,937
1966....	6,926	3,275	299	10,500
1967....	7,180	3,770	149	11,099
1968....	7,924	4,075	121	12,120
1969....	7,176	4,213	142	11,531
1970....	7,692	4,038	104	11,834
1971*...	2,839	1,135	66	4,040
United Kingdom				
1945–71*	4,091,353	3,227,781	222,231	7,541,365

† Incl. certain housing associations and accommodation for families of police, prison staff, H.M. Forces, etc.

* To March 31, 1971, only.   ‡ and New Towns.

Cost of the Housing Programme, 1945–70
England and Wales

The following table shows the Exchequer contributions in the post-war period towards the construction of new permanent houses and flats under the Housing Acts and the conversion or improvement of existing houses under the Housing (Financial Provisions) Act, 1958, the Housing and House Purchase Act, 1959 and the Housing Act, 1969.

Year	Construction of new permanent houses				Conversions and improvements	
	Under pre-war legislation	Under post-war legislation	Capital grants for post-war houses*	Total	By local authorities	By private owners
	£	£	£	£	£	£
1945–56 ..	136,221,770	147,104,543	25,596,386	309,103,061	64,260	257,283
1956–57 ..	11,095,451	39,240,028	9,250	50,344,729	55,440	491,101
1957–58 ..	11,045,881	41,966,550	4,500	53,016,931	83,753	856,137
1958–59 ..	10,991,878	46,701,859	10,847	57,704,584	139,852	1,480,958
1959–60 ..	10,886,112	49,199,125	450	60,085,687	218,230	1,811,420
1960–61 ..	10,834,182	50,155,200	—	60,989,412	253,888	2,142,805
1961–62 ..	10,848,030	52,797,973	—	63,646,003	534,719	3,260,681
1962–63 ..	10,810,853	56,878,090	—	67,688,943	748,205	4,332,663
1963–64 ..	9,399,575	58,565,945	—	67,965,520	1,128,423	6,117,489
1964–65 ..	9,330,758	63,627,922	—	72,958,680	1,277,895	6,579,216
1965–66 ..	9,000,058	68,669,426	—	77,669,484	1,428,142	7,232,031
1966–67 ..	8,435,684	73,948,538	—	82,384,222	1,673,969	8,315,816
1967–68 ..	7,957,517	86,534,205	—	94,131,722	2,004,022	9,282,543
1968–69 ..	7,137,904	99,975,821	—	107,113,725	2,644,402	10,511,646
1969–70 ..	6,631,149	118,868,682	—	125,499,831	3,072,452	11,510,031

* Houses constructed by new tradition methods (Housing Act, 1946).

PROGRESS OF THE NEW TOWNS (To March 31, 1971)‡

Town	New Industries Number of firms	New Industries Numbers employed	New shops	New houses and flats	Actual Expenditure for all purposes§ £
Basildon	147	21,977	368	18,663	91,525,000
Bracknell	35	8,808	180	8,926	45,272,000
Crawley	90	17,552	291	14,685	36,482,000
Harlow	113	17,040	341	21,410	70,430,000
Hatfield	19	1,385	103	4,402	11,956,000
Hemel Hempstead	70	13,196	304	13,824	44,752,000
Milton Keynes	2	115	—	36	9,240,000
Stevenage	73	18,233	346	17,923	65,074,000
Welwyn Garden City	21	3,624	133	6,549	18,155,000
Aycliffe	—*	*	92	6,142	17,416,000
Corby	24	3,611	207	7,611	26,791,000
Peterlee	29	3,557	157	6,939	23,986,000
Redditch	113	3,330	9	2,122	30,573,000
Runcorn	42	1,461	16	2,360	30,053,000
Skelmersdale	56	6,655	61	5,010	41,342,000
Telford†	44	2,119	18	2,462	33,601,000
Washington	69	2,419	16	2,237	21,081,000
Cwmbran	57	1,434	199	7,929	2,962,000
Cumbernauld	37	4,577	60	9,120	51,667,000
East Kilbride	93	11,548	180	18,508	69,051,000
Glenrothes	36	5,264	83	7,999	32,482,000
Livingston	15	2,255	35	4,626	33,518,000
Irvine	6	233	4	541	5,634,000
§ Total	1,197	150,663	3,203	190,110	£828,520,000

* Industry already exists in the trading estate at Aycliffe.   † Dawley New Town Designated Area extended and renamed Telford.   ‡ By Development Corporations or on Corporation Land.
§ Expenditure total includes smaller amounts in respect of Northampton (£6,130,000), Peterborough (£7,324,000), Warrington (£1,873,000) and Newtown (£150,000).

IMMIGRATION CONTROL STATISTICS

Figures in the table below relate to those Commonwealth citizens (including British protected persons) whose entry to the United Kingdom is subject to control.   Persons born in the United Kingdom and citizens of the United Kingdom and Colonies holding U.K. passports, as defined in s. 1 of the Commonwealth Immigrants Act, and foreign nationals, are excluded.   There is no control over travel from Ireland.

Territory issuing passport	Admitted 1969	Admitted 1970	Embarked 1969	Embarked 1970	Net Balance 1969	Net Balance 1970
Associated (W. Indies) States	1,973	2,017	962	997	+ 1,011	+ 1,020
Australia	89,815	106,866	92,392	116,739	− 2,577	− 9,873
Barbados	3,574	4,554	4,009	4,461	− 435	+ 93
Canada	211,132	244,054	229,151	260,956	−18,019	−16,902
Ceylon	6,655	6,593	5,474	5,372	+ 1,181	+ 1,221
Cyprus	10,677	10,043	11,166	10,615	− 489	− 572
Gambia	318	342	323	311	− 5	+ 31
Ghana	6,380	7,692	5,845	6,366	+ 535	+ 1,326
Gibraltar	2,162	2,683	2,265	2,964	− 103	− 281
Guyana	4,240	5,064	3,552	4,211	+ 688	+ 853
Hong Kong	7,441	7,516	5,651	5,542	+ 1,790	+ 1,974
India	59,319	65,815	46,981	57,399	+12,338	+ 8,416
Jamaica	16,241	18,544	17,603	19,815	− 1,362	− 1,271
Kenya	4,040	4,722	3,902	3,931	+ 138	+ 791
Malawi	402	394	220	247	+ 182	+ 147
Malaysia	8,437	11,156	6,802	8,098	+ 1,635	+ 3,058
Malta	10,012	11,355	10,171	11,918	− 159	− 563
Mauritius	4,483	6,508	3,140	4,510	+ 1,343	+ 1,998
New Zealand	21,755	26,371	25,153	31,303	− 3,398	− 4,932
Nigeria	9,288	12,673	10,087	13,865	− 799	− 1,192
Pakistan	40,729	43,139	27,917	33,251	+12,812	+ 9,888
Sierra Leone	1,866	1,914	1,402	1,939	+ 464	− 25
Singapore	3,311	4,477	2,731	4,141	+ 580	+ 336
Tanzania	3,016	3,372	2,692	2,696	+ 324	+ 676
Trinidad & Tobago	6,196	7,419	5,410	6,365	+ 786	+ 1,054
Uganda	2,542	3,060	2,287	2,529	+ 255	+ 531
Zambia	1,286	1,392	1,091	1,159	+ 195	+ 233
United Kingdom passport holders from East Africa	12,950	14,177	3,270	3,170	+ 9,680	+11,007
All other territories	11,717	12,347	10,937	14,182	+ 780	− 1,845
TOTAL	561,957	646,259	542,586	639,052	+19,371	+ 7,207

U*

EMPLOYMENT

Distribution of total manpower in Great Britain

The total working population of Great Britain in December, 1970, was 25,048,000 (males, 16,074,000; females, 8,973,000), compared with 25,209,000 in December, 1969. Included in the total were 24,072,000 in civil employment (employers and self-employed, 1,744,000); 604,000 persons wholly unemployed; and 371,000 in H.M. Forces and Women's Services. For National Government figures, *see also* p. 608 for Agriculture, *see* pp. 581–2.

Numbers in Civil Employment.★
(Standard Industrial Classification, 1968.)

Production Industries		Bricks, Pottery, Glass, Cement, etc....	329,000
Mining and Quarrying..............	412,700	Timber, Furniture, etc...............	295,000
Food, Drink, Tobacco...............	857,000	Paper, Printing and Publishing........	628,700
Coal and Petroleum Products........	62,100	Other Manufacturing Industries.......	346,700
Chemicals and Allied Industries.......	461,300	Construction......................	1,300,900
Metal Manufacture..................	558,500	Gas, Electricity and Water..........	376,700
Mechanical Engineering.............	1,149,200		
Instrument Engineering..............	151,300	**Other Industries and Services**	
Electrical Engineering...............	881,500	Transport and Communications......	1,567,000
Shipbuilding and Marine Engineering.	200,300	Distributive Trades.................	2,651,000
Vehicles...........................	810,000	Insurance, Banking, Business Services..	954,000
Metal Goods.......................	608,200	Professional and Scientific Services....	2,818,000
Textiles...........................	658,400	Catering, hotels, etc.	569,000
Leather, Leather Goods and Fur.......	51,900	Miscellaneous Services..............	1,240,000
Clothing and Footwear..............	489,700	Public Administration and Defence....	1,391,000

★ In June, 1971; *italic* figures are the latest available for the industry group, *i.e.* 1970 (June).

UNEMPLOYMENT

Annual average numbers registered as unemployed, 1967–70; June and August figures for 1971

	Great Britain						United Kingdom Total
	Wholly Unemployed		Temporarily Stopped		Total	Percentage†	
	Males	Females	Males	Females			
1967...............	420,700	100,200	30,500	8,000	559,500	2·4	599,100
1968...............	460,700	88,800	13,100	1,600	564,100	2·4	601,300
1969...............	461,900	81,900	14,000	1,500	559,300	2·4	597,100
1970...............	495,300	86,900	18,700	2,400	603,400	2·6	639,900
1971 (June 14)	589,100	98,100	33,700	3,400	724,400	3·2	762,100
(Aug. 9)........	—	—	—	—	858,900	3·7	904,200

† Registered unemployed as percentage of total number of employees.

STOPPAGES OF WORK, 1959–1970

Year	Number of Stoppages Beginning in Year	Number of Workers★ Involved in Stoppages			Aggregate Number of Working Days Lost in Stoppages		
		Beginning in Year Directly	Indirectly	In Progress in Year	Beginning in Year (a)	(b)	In Progress in Year
		'000	'000	'000	'000	'000	'000
1959	2,093	522	123	646	5,257	5,280	5,270†
1960	2,832	698	116	819	3,001	3,049	3,024
1961	2,686	673	98	779	2,998	3,038	3,046
1962	2,449	4,297	123	4,423	5,757	5,778	5,798†
1963	2,068	455	135	593	1,731	1,997	1,755
1964	2,524	700	172	883	2,011	2,030	2,277
1965	2,354	673	195	876	2,906	2,932	2,925
1966	1,937	414	116	544	2,372	2,395	2,398
1967	2,116	552	180	734	2,765	2,783	2,787
1968	2,378	2,073	182	2,258	4,672	4,719	4,690†
1969	3,116	1,426	228	1,665	6,799	6,925	6,846
1970	3,906	1,460	333	1,801	10,854	10,908	10,980

(a) Including days lost in the year in which the stoppages began.
(b) Including days lost both in the year in which the stoppages began and also in the following year.
★ Workers involved in more than one stoppage in any year are counted more than once in the year's total. Workers involved in a stoppage beginning in the year and continuing into another are counted in both years in the column showing the number of workers involved in stoppages in progress.
† In 1959 about 3½ million days were lost through a single stoppage in the printing industry; in 1962 about 3,785,000 days were lost through two national one-day stoppages of engineering and shipbuilding workers and a stoppage in the railway industry; and in 1968 about 1½ million days were lost as a result of a one-day national stoppage in the engineering industry. In 1970 there were 267 stoppages which caused a loss of 5,000 or more working days, compared with 169 in 1969.

STOPPAGES OF WORK: INDUSTRIAL ANALYSIS, 1969 AND 1970

Industry Group (Standard Industrial Classification 1968)	1969 (Jan.–Dec.) No. of Stoppages Beginning in Period	Stoppages in Progress No. of Workers Involved†	No. of Working Days Lost†	1970 (Jan.–Dec.) No. of Stoppages Beginning in Period	Stoppages in Progress No. of Workers Involved†	No. of Working Days Lost
Agriculture, forestry, fishing	6	1,900	62,000	4	1,400	33,000
Coal mining	186	145,100	1,039,000	160	117,500	1,090,000
All other mining and quarrying	7	600	2,000	5	200	1,000
Grain milling	—	—	—	6	1,100	6,000
Bread, flour, biscuits, etc.	115	34,500	161,000	11	6,200	135,000
All other food industries				82	34,800	263,000
Drink				49	10,500	43,000
Tobacco						
Coal and petroleum products	—	—	—	13	4,300	11,000
Chemicals, dyestuffs, plastics	52	17,200	52,000	61	23,100	132,000
Pharmaceutical, toilet preps.				9	3,600	34,000
Paints, soap, etc.				14	5,200	8,000
Iron and steel	220	86,300	570,000	251	63,100	443,000
Other metal manufacture	116	22,200	95,000	75	18,600	178,000
Mechanical engineering	635	258,900	1,950,000	522	152,200	876,000
Instrument engineering				37	11,300	79,000
Electrical engineering				287	125,700	713,000
Shipbuilding; marine engineering	89	52,200	192,000	121	40,200	410,000
Motor vehicles	276	276,000	1,636,000	336	271,400	1,105,000
Aerospace equipment	88	54,000	181,000	73	48,800	304,000
All other vehicles	10	4,500	27,000	42	22,400	138,000
Other metal goods	10	4,500	27,000	177	36,600	295,000
Cotton flax and man-made fibres	72	18,300	120,000	29	12,000	55,000
Woollen and worsted				7	900	3,000
Hosiery; other knitted goods				18	5,700	24,000
Other textile industries				42	15,900	109,000
Clothing (excl. footwear)	24	10,000	19,000	22	28,500	187,000
Footwear				5	1,500	5,000
Bricks, fireclay, etc.	53	9,200	35,000	15	5,700	15,000
Pottery				2	400	16,000
Glass				19	12,900	361,000
Cement, building materials				44	5,800	34,000
Furniture, bedding and upholstery	39	7,000	33,000	18	2,100	4,000
Timber and manufactures				35	3,400	30,000
Paper, board, cartons, etc.	54	18,800	81,000	42	9,200	37,000
Printing, publishing, etc.				33	30,100	120,000
Other manufacturing industries	86	28,900	90,000	91	49,600	324,000
Construction	285	44,000	278,000	337	50,800	242,000
Gas, electricity, water	31	10,900	18,000	20	3,000	21,000
Railways	172	201,200	363,000	29	14,400	53,000
Road passenger transport				106	75,100	380,000
Road haulage contracting				150	15,900	87,000
Sea transport				5	1,700	8,000
Port, canal transport	368	194,600	424,000	259	197,900	727,000
Other transport, etc.	172	201,200	363,000	35	41,700	58,000
Distributive trades	42	3,900	18,000	83	10,500	40,000
Insurance, banking, finance	80	160,000	329,000	8	9,100	271,000
Professional, scientific services				24	88,200	350,000
Miscellaneous sces. (entertainment, sport, catering, etc.)	21	7,000	16,000	28	2,900	24,000
Public administration (incl. Defence)	—	—	—	66	106,700	1,100,000
	*3,116	1,665,000	6,846,000	*3,906	1,800,700	10,980,000

* Some stoppages of work involved workers in more than one industry group, but have each been counted as only one stoppage in the total for all industries taken together. † Figures rounded to nearest 100 workers and 1,000 hours; sums may not agree with totals shown.

Stoppages of work in 1971 (Jan.–Aug.).—A total of 11,661,000 working days were lost in 1,542 stoppages in progress in the first 8 months of 1971, involving 828,300 workers. Causes of stoppages beginning in this period were—Claims for increased wages, 627 stoppages involving 379,200 workers; Other wage disputes, 199 involving 87,500 workers; Hours of work disputes, 17 involving 2,200 workers; Employment of particular classes or persons, 379 involving 76,900 workers; Other disputes concerning working arrangements, rules and discipline, 233 involving 43,500 workers; Disputes concerning trade union status, 66 involving, 23,300, workers; Stoppages in sympathy with other disputes, 27 involving 19,700 workers. Total number of workers directly involved, 632,300.

STAFFING OF PUBLIC DEPARTMENTS, 1971–72

The Estimates for 1971–72 provided for the employment of 788,667 industrial and non-industrial personnel by public departments, at a total cost for salaries, etc. of £1,313,384,000, allowing for expected changes in staff numbers up to March 1, 1972. The comparable figures for 1970–71 are: Staff, numbers, 801,426; Cost, £1,266,752,000. Provision for casual staff employed in 1971–72 was £6,200,000 (1970–71, £4,630,000).

The following table shows the estimated strength of each department at April 1, 1971, excluding casual staff and excluding a total of 85,562 staff locally engaged abroad. Cash provision for casual staff, employers' National Insurance and other contributions and fees is included in the final column.

It should be noted that these estimates apply to the *United Kingdom* and include classes of staff who do not appear as employed in National Government Service in employment statistics based on the Standard Industrial Classification.

Department	Non-industrial Staff		Industrial Staff		Total provision for salaries, etc.
	Numbers	Salaries, etc.	Numbers	Salaries, etc.	
		£'000		£'000	£'000
Agriculture, Fisheries and Food	14,950	25,174	1,180	1,114	33,444
Aviation Supply	16,970	31,938	11,275	12,553	55,073
British Museum	1,565	2,483	105	118	3,069
British Museum (Natural History)	605	1,092	..	..	1,239
Cabinet Office	585	1,334	..	..	1,538
Civil Service Dept	2,175	4,600	150	115	6,035
County Courts	5,700	7,794	..	..	8,877
Customs and Excise	18,100	30,798	..	..	37,911
Defence	112,000	175,129	141,660	143,013	457,570
Education and Science	4,165	8,137	155	157	9,479
Employment	31,375	43,826	1,245	1,088	52,220
Environment	39,095	69,848	32,495	33,610	168,672
Exchequer and Audit	580	1,373	..	..	1,513
Exports Credits Guarantee	1,570	2,704	..	..	3,047
Foreign and Commonwealth:—					
Diplomatic Service	10,380	20,505	255	239	44,733
Overseas Development	2,520	4,559	50	55	5,422
Health and Social Security	72,080	92,258	205	217	107,827
Home Office	21,730	32,901	4,370	4,382	55,528
Information	1,435	2,715	60	62	3,181
Inland Revenue	70,185	94,717	25	24	108,223
Land Registry	4,100	5,007	6	8	5,774
National Savings	15,025	15,802	150	153	18,718
Ordnance Survey	4,225	5,826	460	415	7,251
Population Censuses Office	2,080	3,007	14	20	3,716
Public Trustee Office	565	919	..	..	1,061
Scottish Courts Service	525	797	..	..	922
Scottish Office	8,365	14,162	1,070	876	17,910
Stationery Office	3,530	4,981	4,315	6,125	13,813
Supreme Court	2,085	5,182	..	12	5,844
Trade and Industry	24,750	46,321	1,675	1,791	54,374
Treasury, etc.	1,985	3,593	3	3	4,432
Treasury Solicitor	530	1,319	..	..	1,454
Welsh Office	910	1,841	..	..	2,014
Other Departments	4,655	7,886	1,078	1,147	11,500
Estimated Totals, 1971–72	501,095	770,528	202,010	207,309	1,313,384
Totals, 1970–71	*495,282*	*747,731*	*211,367*	*189,563*	*1,266,752*

STRENGTH OF THE CIVIL SERVICE, 1902–1970

Thousands

Year (April 1)	Non-Industrial Staff	Year (April 1)	Non-Industrial Staff
1902	50	1927	108
1910	55	1928	106
1914	70	1929	109
1918	221	1930	111
1919	194	1931	118
1920	161	1932	119
1921	158	1933	118
1922	133	1934	117
1923	124	1935	128
1924	115	1936	133
1925	114	1937	142
1926	110	1938	152

Year (April 1)	Non-Industrial	Industrial	Total	Year (April 1)	Non-Industrial	Industrial	Total
1939	163	184	347	1957	381	314	696
1944	505	658	1,164	1958	375	289	664
1945	499	615	1,114	1959	375	271	647
1946	452	366	819	1960	380	263	643
1947	457	326	784	1961	387	256	643
1948	445	317	761	1962	394	253	647
1949	458	326	784	1963	410	252	662
1950	433	313	746	1964	414	244	658
1951	425	316	740	1965	420	235	655
1952	429	333	762	1966	430	232	662
1953	414	341	756	1967	451	229	680
1954	405	347	751	1968	471	222	693
1955	386	334	719	1969	470	214	684
1956	384	328	711	1970	493	208	701

UNITED KINGDOM REVENUE AND EXPENDITURE
(Exchequer Account)

Year	Revenue	Expenditure	Surplus
	£	£	£
1959-60	5,874,100,000	5,526,200,000	347,900,000
1960-61	6,207,500,000	6,053,100,000	154,400,000
1961-62	6,969,800,000	6,544,500,000	425,300,000
1962-63	7,186,700,000	6,857,000,000	329,700,000
1963-64	7,287,500,000	7,197,600,000	89,900,000
1964-65	8,157,100,000	7,712,900,000	444,200,000
1965-66	9,144,400,000	8,455,700,000	688,700,000
1966-67	10,278,900,000	9,541,400,000	737,500,000
1967-68	11,855,100,000	11,525,100,000	330,000,000

Consolidated Fund: New Presentation

£ million

Year ending March 31:—	1968	1969	1970	1971 Provisional	1972 Budget Estimates
REVENUE					
Inland Revenue	5,765·1	6,531·5	7,476·1	8,185·0	9,120·0
Customs and Excise	3,721·3	4,600·5	4,952·5	4,720·0	5,359·0
Motor vehicle duties	269·0	393·1	416·7	423·0	440·0
Selective Employment Tax★	1,063·8	1,362·7	1,888·1	1,985·0	1,298·0
Miscellaneous receipts	408·1	475·6	533·2	528·0	545·0
Total revenue	11,227·3	13,363·4	15,266·6	15,841·0	16,762·0
EXPENDITURE					
Supply services†	9,975·9	10,809·8	12·016·5	13,450·0	13,871·0
Debt interest‡	668·5	552·5	512·8	327·0	225·0
Payments to Northern Ireland	194·3	223·6	251·9	277·0	320·0
Other expenditure	32·6	29·1	41·0	30·0	30·0
Total expenditure	10,871·3	11,615·0	12,822·2	14,084·0	14,446·0
Surplus transferred to National Loans Fund	356·0	1,748·4	2,444·4	1,757·0	2,316·0

★ Actual receipts in the year are shown gross, and payments of refunds and premiums are included in expenditure on Supply Services.   † The total of the Supply Estimates shown by classes in the following pages, together with Consolidated Fund Standing Services. (*See* p. 613.)   ‡ Payment to National Loans Fund representing its payments for the service of the national debt less its receipts of interest on loans outstanding, etc.

UNITED KINGDOM REVENUE, 1968-69 to 1971-72
Figures for 1968-69 and 1969-70 show Payments to Consolidated Fund.

Year ending March 31:—	1969	1970	1971 Provisional	1972 Budget Estimate
	£	£	£	£
INLAND REVENUE	6,531,508,000	7,476,062,000	8,185,000,000	9,120,000,000
Income Tax	4,337,198,000	4,899,862,000	5,725,000,000	6,491,000,000
Surtax	224,200,000	255,400,000	240,000,000	360,000,000
Corporation Tax	1,345,800,000	1,686,500,000	1,600,000,000	1,620,000,000
Capital Gains Tax	46,800,000	126,800,000	140,000,000	165,000,000
Death Duties	379,200,000	365,500,000	360,000,000	375,000,000
Stamp Duties	124,100,000	120,200,000	115,000,000	108,000,000
Other	74,210,000	21,800,000	5,000,000	1,000,000
CUSTOMS AND EXCISE	4,600,561,000	4,952,467,000	4,720,000,000	5,359,000,000
MOTOR VEHICLE DUTIES	393,087,000	416,749,000	423,000,000	440,000,000
SELECTIVE EMPLOYMENT TAX§	1,362,703,860	1,888,078,462	1,985,000,000	1,298,000,000
BROADCASTING LICENCES	84,700,000	101,200,000	101,000,000	120,000,000
INTEREST and DIVIDENDS	91,977,479	92,350,480	97,000,000	105,000,000
OTHER REVENUE	433,921,415	526,651,983	330,000,000	320,000,000
TOTAL REVENUE	13,498,458,853	15,453,558,925	15,841,000,000	16,762,000,000

§ Estimated refunds of S.E.T. deductible from gross figures shown: 1968-69, £726m. (6·7%); 1969-70 £1,088m. (9·1%); 1970-71, £1,201m. (8·8%); 1971-72, £1,183m. (8·4%).

UNITED KINGDOM EXPENDITURE

THE SUPPLY *Estimates.*—The original Supply Estimates for 1971–72 showed United Kingdom Expenditure at £14,149,300,000, compared with a net total estimate for 1970–71 of £13,633,300,000. The 1971–72 Budget reduced the original Supply Estimates by £278m.—additional provision for increased Social Security Benefits (£93m.) and Agricultural Support (£47m.) being offset by reduction in Selective Employment Tax refunds to the private sector, public corporations and local authorities (£367m.) and reduced tax payable in respect of public service employees (£51m.). The *Defence Budget* is included in the Supply Estimates and consists of Class XII together with Defence expenditure falling in Classes IV and VI (*see* p. 612).

SUPPLY ESTIMATES

Figures for 1970–71 are Net Total Estimates, *i.e.* including Supplementary Estimates.

Class I: Government and Finance

	1970–71	1971–72
House of Lords	£554,000	£603,000
House of Commons‡	4,051,000	4,211,000
Treasury and Subordinate Departments	5,149,000	8,583,000
Civil Service Dept.	7,305,000	8,588,000
Cabinet Office	1,571,000	1,629,000
Privy Council Office	83,000	95,000
Customs and Excise	40,815,000	43,360,000
Inland Revenue	121,213,000	125,210,000
Corporation Tax: Transitional Relief	35,000,000	22,000,000
Exchequer and Audit Department	1,344,000	1,385,000
Royal Commissions, etc	626,000	666,000
Office of Parliamentary Commissioner	151,000	152,000
TOTAL	£217,862,000	£216,482,000

Class II: Commonwealth and Foreign

	1970–71	1971–72
Diplomatic Service	£53,440,000	£49,302,000
Foreign and Commonwealth Services	30,366,000	23,969,000
British Council	8,786,000	9,117,000
Overseas Development Administration	3,789,000	3,857,000
Overseas Aid:—		
International	188,699,000	191,407,000
General Services	31,502,900	32,704,000
Commonwealth War Graves Commission	1,840,000	2,110,000
TOTAL	£318,442,900	£312,466,000

Class III: Home and Justice

	1970–71	1971–72
Home Office	£42,087,000	£48,522,000
Scottish Home and Health Dept.	3,902,000	4,132,000
Civil Defence:—		
England and Wales	3,544,000	4,584,000
Scotland	591,000	532,000
Police:—		
England and Wales	155,904,000	171,644,000
Scotland	15,171,000	15,958,000
Prisons:—		
England and Wales	53,231,000	59,002,000
Scotland	5,944,000	7,339,000
Supreme Court	1,644,000	2,108,000
County Courts	2,580,000	2,009,000
Legal Aid Fund	13,351,000	15,219,000

‡ Including Members' Salaries, £2,455,000 (1970–71, £2,418,000) Travelling Allowances, £308,000 (1970–71, £259,000).

Home and Justice—*continued*

	1969–70	1970–71
Law Charges	£1,653,000	£1,655,000
do and Courts of Law, Scotland	1,135,000	1,178,000
Supreme Court, N. Ireland	154,000	161,000
TOTAL	£300,911,000	£334,043,000

Class IV: Trade, Industry and Employment

Token estimates in respect of Export Credits and Purchase of U.S. Aircraft omitted.

	1970–71	1971–72
Dept. of Trade and Industry	£48,381,500	£49,034,000
do. Civil Aviation and Shipping	29,102,000	27,098,000
do. Export Promotion	7,197,000	8,207,000
do. Development of Tourism, etc.	10,858,000	14,414,000
do. Industrial Sces.	138,784,000	114,500,000
Promotion of Local Employment	72,015,000	78,414,000
Investment Grants	600,000,000	620,000,000
Atomic Energy	41,341,000	42,809,000
Dept. of Employment	84,062,000	81,189,000
do. Selective Employment Payments	1,056,000,000	1,039,000,000
Ministry of Posts and Telecommunications§	206,578,000	224,759,000
Aviation Supply	325,369,000	291,091,000
do. Special Materials	23,940,000	19,886,000
do. Purchasing (Repayment) Services	1,000	4,700,000
TOTAL	£2,648,516,500	£2,615,104,000

§ Vote includes Broadcasting, 1971–72: B.B.C. Home Services, £111,700,000; B.B.C. External Broadcasting Services, £12,938,000.

Class V: Agriculture

	1970–71	1971–72
Ministry of Agriculture, Fisheries and Food	£39,436,000	£40,951,000
Dept. of Agriculture and Fisheries for Scotland	19,293,000	19,885,000
Grants and Subsidies:—		
England and Wales	126,433,000	127,103,000
Scotland	33,269,000	34,525,000
Price Guarantees:—		
England and Wales	125,949,000	107,979,000
Scotland	15,735,000	11,380,000
Agriculture and Food Services	73,979,000	70,944,000
Fishery Grants and Services	7,835,000	8,073,000

Class V—*continued*

	1970–71	1971–72
Fisheries (Scotland) and Herring Industry...	£3,771,000	£3,306,000
Forestry Commission	16,240,000	16,000,000
	£462,600,000	£440,881,000

Class VI: Environmental Services

	1970–71	1971–72
Dept. of the Environment...........	£82,334,000	£85,220,000
do. Research......	7,031,000	8,225,000
Scottish Office (Central Services)....	3,086,000	3,612,000
Scottish Development Dept...........	37,506,000	40,992,000
Welsh Office........	17,820,000	19,142,000
Civil Accommodation Services:—		
United Kingdom..	111,335,300	124,830,000
Overseas..........	9,500,000	11,000,000
Defence Accommodation Services, etc.	159,460,000	179,900,000
Housing:—		
England..........	194,834,000	230,665,000
Scotland..........	45,520,000	50,091,000
Wales.............	10,037,000	11,967,000
Transport Industries..	154,106,943	144,302,000
Transport Services...	37,898,057	35,995,000
Roads, etc., England.	358,065,000	327,052,000
Roads and Transport Sces. (Scotland)..	44,310,000	50,124,000
do. Wales.........	21,161,000	23,747,000
Local Government and Development....	213,910,860	216,903,000
Rate Support Grants:—		
England and Wales.	1,883,388,000	2,032,599,000
Scotland..........	222,522,000	252,082,000
TOTAL.....	£3,613,825,800	£3,848,448,000

Class VII: Social Services

	1970–71	1971–72
Dept. of Health and Social Security...	£81,414,000	£84,433,000
Misc. Health and Welfare Services, England........	68,066,000	44,950,000
National Health Sce.:— England		
Hospital Services	969,618,000	1,077,725,000
Exec. Cncls. Serv.	363,523,000	353,499,000
Scotland..........	194,903,000	206,246,000
Wales.............	89,352,000	91,017,000
National Insurance...	426,500,000	420,400,000
Family Allowances...	344,960,000	343,950,000
Non-contributory Benefits........	541,500,000	639,000,000
War Pensions, etc.*..	128,850,000	124,380,000
Social Work, Scotland	1,895,000	2,016,000
TOTAL.....	£3,210,585,000	£3,387,618,000

Totals include nominal net estimates in respect of N.H.S. Superannuation.

* Includes average of 82,000 pensions, etc. in respect of 1914–18 War (1971–72, £19,000,000; 1970–71, 92,000 pensions, etc., £21,400,000) and 36,000 widows' and dependants' pensions, etc. (1971–72, £13,800,000; 1970–71, 39,000 pensions, etc., £14,700,000). 291,000 pensions, etc. in respect of 1939–45 War, and later service were current in 1971–72 (£63,300,000); 1970–71, 295,000 pensions (£64,400,000); and 95,000 widows' and dependants' pensions, etc. (1971–72, £27,700,000; 1970–71, 97,000 pensions, etc., £27,800,000).

Class VIII: Education and Science

	1970–71	1971–72
Dept. of Education and Science.......	£70,016,149	£73,500,000
Scottish Education Dept.............	39,228,500	42,131,000
Universities and Colleges, etc., Great Britain...........	309,361,000	326,551,000
Social Science Research Council....	3,264,000	4,141,000
Science Research Council..........	50,426,000	55,733,000
Natural Environment Research Council .	13,893,000	15,888,000
Medical Research Council..........	20,998,000	23,015,000
Agricultural Research Council..........	16,926,000	18,704,000
British Museum (Natural History)..	1,357,000	1,424,000
Grants for Science....	1,603,000	2,029,000
TOTAL......	£528,999,649	£564,324,000

Class IX: Museums, Galleries and the Arts

	1970–71	1971–72
British Museum.....	£3,538,000	£3,833,000
Science Museum.....	785,000	825,000
Victoria and Albert Museum..........	1,442,000	1,544,000
Imperial War Museum	321,000	351,000
London Museum.....	142,000	157,000
National Gallery.....	834,000	850,000
National Maritime Museum..........	364,000	398,000
National Portrait Gallery...........	174,000	193,000
Tate Gallery........	593,000	634,000
Wallace Collection...	108,000	114,000
Royal Scottish Museum..........	326,500	363,000
National Galleries of Scotland..........	303,000	314,000
National Library of Scotland..........	299,000	314,000
National Museum of Antiquities of Scotland..............	105,000	104,000
National Library and Nat. Museum of Wales............	955,000	1,117,000
Arts Council and other Grants for the Arts.	10,996,000	14,014,000
TOTAL........	£21,285,500	£25,125,000

Class X: Other Public Departments and Common Government Services

	1970–71	1971–72
Charity Commission.	£634,000	£628,000
Crown Estate Office .	306,000	311,000
Friendly Societies' Registry........	216,000	222,000
Registrar of Restrictive Trading Agreements.....	161,000	174,000
Ordnance Survey....	6,177,000	5,985,000
Public Record Office.	378,000	386,000
Scottish Record Office	169,000	177,000
Office of Population Censuses........	3,232,000	9,951,000

Class X—*continued*

	1970–71	1971–72
Registrar General, Scotland........	£319,000	£1,572,000
Decimal Currency Bd.	183,000	75,000
Dept. for Natl. Savings	18,113,000	18,299,000
Rates on Government Property........	43,480,000	50,047,000
Stationery and Printing	47,754,000	53,756,000
Central Office of Information.....	14,118,000	14,344,000
Government Actuary	79,000	85,000
Governmt. Hospitality	170,000	169,000
Civil Superannuation, etc............	79,874,000	83,680,000
TOTAL.......	£215,376,000	£239,867,000

(Totals include token estimates for the Royal Mint, National Debt Office, Public Works Loan Commission, Public Trustee, Land Registry, etc.)

Class XI: Miscellaneous

	1970–71	1971–72
Pensions (Overseas Services).............	£16,089,100	£25,328,000
Royal Irish Constabulary Pensions........	883,000	800,000
Irish Land Purchase Services..............	513,000	475,000
Development Fund....	2,876,000	3,000,000
Secret Service.......	10,250,000	10,750,000
Miscellaneous Expenses★	462,000	489,000
TOTAL..........	£31,166,100	£40,844,000

★ Includes grants to Commonwealth Parliamentary Association, £84,000 (£76,000); Inter-Parliamentary Union (British Group), £29,000 (£28,000); History of Parliament Trust, £43,000

(£27,000); various expenses in connection with Honours and Dignities of the Lord Chamberlain's Office, Central Chancery, Lyon Court and Garter King of Arms, £65,000 (£60,040); expenses of Sheriffs in connection with Judges on Circuit, £245,000 (£204,000); and other smaller charges.

Class XII and the Defence Budget

	1970–71	1971–72
Pay, Allowances, etc.:—		
Royal Navy and Royal Marines..	£141,250,000	£163,570,000
Army............	261,440,000	315,410,000
Royal Air Force...	188,380,000	221,400,000
Retired Pay (all services)............	128,670,000	131,600,000
Defence Administrative Services......	303,846,000	234,260,000
Ministry of Defence, Pay of Civilians...	408,750,000	419,400,000
Defence Equipment and Stores........	626,693,000	628,200,000
Royal Ordnance Factories.............	3,800,000	4,300,000
Defence Purchasing (Repayment) Services	1,000	6,000,000
TOTAL of CLASS	£2,062,830,000	£2,124,140,000

	1970–71	1971–72
Dept. of Trade and Industry........	£4,500,000	£4,900,000
Ministry of Aviation Supply.....	203,898,010	216,056,000
Dept. of the Environment....	185,390,000	205,958,000
TOTAL DEFENCE BUDGET...	£2,456,617,010	£2,545,054,000

ACTIVE STRENGTHS OF THE DEFENCE FORCES

thousands

	1 April 1970				1 January 1971 (actual)				1 April 1972 (forecast)			
	Royal Navy	Army	R.A.F.	Total	Royal Navy	Army	R.A.F.	Total	Royal Navy	Army	R.A.F.	Total
Male:												
Officers......	10·9	18·9	19·5	49·3	10·7	18·6	19·0	48·3	10·2	17·6	18·9	46·7
Servicemen...	71·9	149·7	87·9	309·5	69·7	149·6	87·2	306·5	68·1	145·5	83·9	297·5
Female.........	3·3	5·3	5·6	14·2	3·3	5·5	5·8	14·6	3·2	5·2	6·0	14·4
TOTALS..	86·0	174·0	113·0	373·0	83·8	173·6	111·9	369·3	81·5	168·3	108·8	358·6

In addition to the above, 16,300 persons, enlisted into the Defence Forces outside the United Kingdom (Royal Navy, 1,500; Army, 14,200; Royal Air Force, 600), were on the strength on January 1, 1971.

Reserve Forces.—Total strength of the Tri-Service reserve forces (all ranks) on January 1, 1971, was 411,800 (male, 407,200; female 4,600), consisting of the Regular Reserves (male, 347,700; female, 1,900) and Volunteer Reserves and Auxiliary Forces (male, 59,500; female, 2,700). Estimated cost of the reserve forces during 1971–72 is £34,000,000 (Army Reserves, £28m.).

Royal Navy and Royal Marines reserves consisted of: Regular Reserves, male, 24,100: female, 100; Volunteer Reserves, male, 7,500; female, 900. There were 21,900 Sea Cadets on Jan. 1, 1971.

Army Reserves consisted of: Regular Reserves, male 291,400; female, 1,200; T. & A.V.R., male 47,700; female, 1,700. The Ulster Defence Regiment (formed April 1, 1970) had a strength of 4,000. There were 71,100 Army Cadets on Jan. 1, 1971.

Royal Air Force Reserves consisted of : Regular Reserves, male, 32,200; female, 600; Volunteer Reserves, male, 300; female, 100. There were 43,000 Air Training Corps Cadets on Jan. 1, 1971.

THE NATIONAL LOANS FUND

Under the National Loans Act, 1968, effective from April 1, 1968, most of the Government's domestic lending and the whole of the Government's borrowing transactions are removed from the Consolidated Fund and brought to account in The National Loans Fund. Revenue from taxation and miscellaneous receipts, including interest and dividends on loans made from Votes, continue to be paid into the Consolidated Fund. After ordinary expenditure on Supply Services (details of which appear under Supply Estimates in the preceding pages) and on Consolidated Fund Standing Services (*e.g.* payment in respect of interest, etc. on the National Debt, The Civil List, Annuities, Pensions for Political, Civil and Judicial Services. Parliamentary and Judicial Salaries and Allowances) the surplus on the Consolidated Fund is payable into the National Loans Fund.

The table following shows issues in 1970–71 and in 1971–72 from the National Loans Fund to nationalized industries. Loans to other public corporations were estimated for 1971–72 at £157,200,000 (1970–71, *£151,000,000*) and to local and harbour authorities £884,800,000 (*£686,900,000*). Including loans within Central Government (£31,000,000), total issues from the National Loans Fund were estimated at £2,052,300,000 for 1971–72 (1970–71 *£1,557,200,000*).

£ million

	Current Statutory Limit	Increase Permissible by Order	Loans Outstanding March 31, 1971	Loans 1970–71 Provisional	Loans 1971–72 Budget Estimate
The Post Office	2,300	500	2,257	253	274
National Coal Board	900	50	659	−31	32
Electricity Council and Boards	4,400	..	4,052	187	176
North of Scotland Hydroelectric Board }	700	100	664	14	8
South of Scotland Electricity Board }				42	44
Gas Council and Area Boards	2,100	300	1,686	133	300
British Steel Corporation	500	150	366	43	289
British Overseas Airways Corporation	250	130	118	−17	..
British European Airways Corporation	200	30	151	41	37
British Airports Authority	70	..	58	..	5
British Railways Board	550	150	395	15	41
British Transport Docks Board	160	..	118	7	11
British Waterways Board	12	..	8	..	1
Transport Holding Company	100	..	2	..	..
National Freight Corporation	200	100	135	15	10
National Bus Company	130	..	100	2	4
Scottish Transport Group	50	..	23	..	..
TOTAL	12,622	1,510	10,592	704	982

Other National Loans Fund advances outstanding on March 31, 1970 are shown on pp. 614–5.

THE NATIONAL DEBT

On March 31, 1971, the National Debt was approximately £33,420,000,000, of which £29,607,000,000 was internal debt, £1,664,000,000 external debt payable in sterling, and £2,149,000,000 external debt payable in other currencies (*provisional figures*). The list which follows shows the distribution under these heads. Amounts shown are those outstanding on March 31, 1969 and March 31, 1970 (in millions of £).

Internal Debt

MARKETABLE SECURITIES

£ million

	1969	1970
Final Redemption Date up to 5 years		
3% B.O.A.C. Stock, 1960–70	1	1
3% Savings Bonds, 1960–70	1,018	758
6½% Treasury Stock, 1971	568	568
5% Conversion Stock, 1971	409	409
6¾% Exchequer Loan, 1971	700	900
4% Victory Bonds	30	24
6% Conversion Stock, 1971	301	301
5¼% Conversion Stock, 1974	299	299
Brit. Transport 3% Stock, 1967–72	13	13
6¼% Exchequer Loan, 1972	915	915
6¾% Exchequer Stock, 1973	700	700
Brit. Transport 3% Stock, 1968–73	136	136
Redemption 5–15 years		
3% Savings Bonds, 1965–75	1,073	1,073
6½% Treasury Loan, 1976	300	300
2½% B.O.A.C. Stock, 1971–76	2	2
Brit. Transport 4% Stock, 1972–77	242	242
4½% B.E.A. Stock, 1972–77	10	10
5% Exchequer Loan, 1976–78	400	400
4% B.O.A.C. Stock, 1974–80	14	14
3½% Treasury Stock, 1977–80	262	262
5¼% Funding Loan, 1978–80	400	400
3½% Treasury Stock, 1979–81	483	483
2½% B.O.A.C. Stock, 1977–82	5	5
8½% Treasury Load, 1980–82	..	861
3% B.O.A.C. Stock, 1980–83	16	16
3% B.E.A. Stock, 1980–83	6	6
5½% Funding Stock, 1982–84	500	500
Redemption over 15 years		
6½% Funding Loan, 1985–87	559	559
Brit. Transport 3% Stock, 1978–88	1,052	1,052
5% Treasury Stock, 1986–89	602	602
4% Funding Loan, 1960–90	86	70
5¾% Funding Loan, 1987–91	400	400
6% Funding Loan, 1993	600	600

	£ million 1969	1970
9% Treasury Loan, 1994	400	400
8¾% Treasury Loan, 1994	400	400
6¾% Treasury Loan, 1995–98	1,000	1,000
3½% Funding Stock, 1999–2004	443	443
5½% Treasury Stock, 2008–12	1,000	1,000
2½% Treasury Stock, 1986–2016	78	78
Undated		
4% Consolidated Loan	372	371
3½% War Loan	1,909	1,909
3½% Conversion Loan	419	398
3% Treasury Stock, 1966 or after	58	58
2¾% Annuities	2	2
2½% Annuities	21	21
2½% Consols	276	276
[illegible]½% Treasury Stock, 1975 or after	482	482
Total Marketable Securities	19,229	19,720
OTHER INTERNAL DEBT		
Terminable Annuities due to National Debt Commissioners	474	390
Life Annuities	4	4
Debt to Bank of England	11	11
National Savings Securities:—		
National Savings Certificates	2,016	1,926
Defence Bonds	185	84
National Development Bonds	578	418
British Savings Bonds	146	322
Premium Savings Bonds	715	766
National Savings Stamps and Gift Tokens	36	38
Save as you earn	..	..
Tax Reserve Certificates	344	292
Floating Debt:—		
Treasury Bills	5,741	4,561
Ways and Means Advances	338	428
Total Internal Debt	29,817	28,964

External Debt

PAYABLE IN STERLING	£ million	
Interest-free notes: I.M.F. and International Development Association	1,860	1,861
Bk. of England—Treasury Liability	28	—
Government of Portugal	22	17
Miscellaneous Sterling Loan Agreements	4	4
External (sterling debt)	1,914	1,882
Total Payable in Sterling	31,731	31,748
PAYABLE IN OTHER CURRENCIES		
United States Loans	1,822	1,780
Government of Canada	369	361
Debt created on liquidation of European Payments Union:—		
Federal Republic of Germany	25	18
Deutsche Bundesbank Credit	21	23
B.I.S. Credit	16	,,
Total Payable in other Currencies	2,253	2,234
Total National Debt	33,984	33,079

Loans Guaranteed

The Nominal Net Liability of the State on March 31, 1970, in respect of loans guaranteed by the British Government was:—

Sudan Loans, £74,300; Northern Ireland 4½% Bonds, £4,405,955; Northern Ireland 2¾% Stock, £3,793,569; Northern Ireland 3% Stock, £9,871,801; Ulster Savings Certificates, £12,663; certain liabilities in external currencies; Malawi, £108,819; 3 per cent. Redemption Stock (1986–96) to provide compensation in respect of *Tithe Rent Charge*, £35,028,601; General Practice Finance Guaranteed 8 per cent. Stock, 1978–83, £2,000,000; General Practice Finance 9% Stock, 1976–79, £2,500,000; and liabilities in external currencies in respect of U.S. loans to the Central African Power Corporation, the East African Common Services Organization, Kenya, Malta, Mauritius, Nigeria, Rhodesia, Singapore, Swaziland, Trinidad and Tobago, Uganda and Zambia.

Cost of the Debt, 1969–70

The total cost of the service of the National Debt in 1969–70 was £1,448,052,743. This cost comprised interest on the National Debt of £1,411,612,388, management charges of £9,357,223 and expenses totalling £37,083,132 (of which £32,837,025 was paid as prizes on Premium Savings Bonds). This cost was met from interest on loans repayable to the National Loans Fund (£888,269,145), profits of the Issue Department of the Bank of England (£56,685,759), a payment from the Consolidated Fund (£512,828,003) and miscellaneous receipts (£269,836).

Repayments 1969–70

Reductions in the Debt are by means of Sinking Funds, including the Terminable Annuities, the capital value of which is deducted from the Debt upon the expiry of the term for which the annuities are payable. Exchequer issues to the National Debt Commissioners in 1969–70 were:—

Repayment of Life Annuities (Principal)	£432,149
For 3½% Conversion Loan	8,277,773
For 4% Funding Loan, 1960–90	15,051,175
For 4% Victory Bonds	18,920,510
Total Sinking Funds	£42,681,607

National Loans Fund Assets, 1970

National Loans Fund assets on March 31, 1970, were summarized as follows:

Advances Outstanding*	£15,895,071,755
Exchange Equalization Account—sterling capital	100,000,000
Subscriptions and contributions:—	
International Monetary Fund	1,016,666,667
European Fund	3,207,083
Other assets	17,394,962

*Advances Outstanding

The Post Office	£1,921,102,000
National Coal Board	713,150,000
Electricity Council	3,163,360,000
North of Scotland Hydro-Electric Board	169,519,667
South of Scotland Electricity Bd.	349,100,000
Gas Council	1,127,340,000
British Steel Corporation	321,746,517
British Overseas Airways Corpn.	16,909,090
British European Airways Corpn.	102,985,056
British Airports Authority	58,585,000
British Railways Board	350,000,000
British Transport Docks Board	109,942,881
British Waterways Board	6,700,000
Transport Holding Company	200,503,436
Total	£8,620,943,647
Loans to other Public Corporations:	
New Towns—Development Corporations and Commission	737,420,876
Scottish Special Housing Association	144,154,637
Housing Corporation	47,113,613
Covent Garden Market Authy.	7,673,600
Sugar Board	4,271,000
Industrial Reorganization Corpn.	43,987,500
Total	£984,621,226

Loans to Local and Harbour Authorities: £

Local Authorities	5,629,123,020
Harbour Authorities	59,400,856

Total ... £5,688,523,876

Loans to the Private Sector:

Shipbuilding Industry Board	13,055,000
Shipowners (Ship Credit Scheme)	28,891,085
Housing Associations	24,091,541
Building Societies	57,799,886

Total ... £123,837,512

Loans within the Central Government:

Purchases of United States military aircraft	203,047,124
Married quarters for Armed Forces	88,754,377
Town and Country Planning compensation	23,649,834
Redundancy Fund	3,790,000
Land Commission	8,574,000
Northern Ireland Exchequer	149,263,378
Irish Land Purchase Annuities	66,781

Total ... £477,145,494

Consolidated Fund Assets

International Subscriptions which constitute assets†	£219,386,773
Amounts due from Overseas Governments*	92,736,192
Loans Made from Votes	1,265,690,834
Additional Assets (revenue collected but not yet paid over; Civil Contingencies Fund advances outstanding; B.O.A.C. and I.R.C. public dividend capital)	942,724,054

TOTAL ASSETS EVALUATED £2,520,537,853

† International Bank (I.B.R.D.), £108,333,333; International Finance Corporation, £6,000,000; International Development Association, £102,553,440; and Asian Development Bank, £2,500,000.

* Advances to allied governments (China, Czechoslovakia and Poland) arising during 1939–45, outstanding on March 31, 1970, totalled £79,484,793. Other advances outstanding were from Austria (£1,783,981), Jordan (£404,917); and Southern Rhodesia (in respect of payments made under guarantee to I.B.R.D.) (£11,062,501).

Other Assets

The principal assets not currently evaluated are: Bank of England capital stock, £14,553,000; British Sugar Corporation shares, £1,125,000; Rumanian 4% Consolidated Bonds, 1922, £4,000,000; Fairfields (Glasgow) Ltd., stock, £940,000; I. C. Holdings Ltd. shares, £3,500,000; Upper Clyde Shipbuilders Ltd. shares, £875,000; Beagle Aircraft Ltd. shares, £1,000,000; British Petroleum Co. stock, £174,462,538; Dividend, 1969–70, £34,645,234; Cable and Wireless Shares, £30,000,000; Dividend, £1,800,000; Suez Finance Company Shares, Frs. 04,559,100. Dividends and interest received on the shares 1969–70 was £458,067. Other receipts by the Treasury in 1969–70 were: Bank of England (in lieu of dividend, £1,746,360); British Sugar Corporation (dividends), £63,492.

National Debt Funds, 1970

The National Fund.—Established in 1927 by a gift from an anonymous donor of approximately £500,000. The audited balance sheet, as at March 31, 1970, shows the following net additions during the year:—Net revenue, £280,133; net profits on investments realized, £50,616. The value of the Fund (investments at middle market prices) on March 31, 1970, was £5,046,504.

The Elsie Mackay Fund.—The sum of £527,809 was set aside in 1929 by Lord and Lady Inchcape in memory of their daughter, to accumulate for not more than 50 years and then to be applied to reduction of the National Debt. The fund was valued on March 31, 1970, at £2,373,457.

The John Buchanan Fund.—Established in 1932 under the will of Dr. John Buchanan who died in 1930 and left the residue of his estate, subject to certain annuities, to be accumulated for fifty years beginning two years after his death and then to be applied in reduction of the National Debt. The fund was valued on March 31, 1970, at £61,229.

THE NATIONAL DEBT 1900–1971

War years are indicated by italic figures.   £million

Mar. 31		Mar. 31		Mar. 31		Mar. 31	
1900	638·9	*1943*	15,822·6	1952	25,890·5	1962	28,674·4
1915	1,161·9	*1944*	18,562·2	1953	26,051·2	1963	29,847·6
1919	7,481·0	*1945*	21,365·9	1954	26,583·0	1964	30,226·3
1920	7,875·6	1946	23,636·5	1955	26,933·7	1965	30,440·6
1930	7,596·2	1947	25,630·7	1956	27,038·9	1966	31,340·7
1939	7,130·8	1948	25,620·8	1957	27,007·5	1967	31,985·6
1940	7,899·2	1949	25,167·6	1958	27,232·0	1968	34,193·9
1941	10,366·4	1950	25,802·3	1959	27,376·3	1969	33,984·0
1942	13,041·1	1951	25,921·6	1960	27,732·6	1970	33,079·1
				1961	28,251·7	1971	33,420·0

THE BANK RATE, 1960–1971

1960	per cent.	1961	per cent.	1964	per cent.	1967	per cent.	1969	per cent.
21 Jan.	5	2 Nov.	6	27 Feb.	5	16 Mar.	6	27 Feb.	8
23 June	6	8 Mar.	5½	23 Nov.	7	4 May	5½	1970	
27 Oct.	5½	1962		1965		19 Oct.	6	5 Mar.	7½
8 Dec.	5	22 Mar.	5	3 June	6	9 Nov.	6½	15 April	7
1961		26 April	4½	1966		18 Nov.	8	1971	
26 July	7	1963		14 July	7	1968		1 April	6
5 Oct.	6½	3 Jan.	4	1967		21 Mar.	7½	2 Sept.	5
				26 Jan.	6½	19 Sept.	7		

UNITED KINGDOM GROSS NATIONAL PRODUCT

£ million

	1960	1961	1962	1963	1964	1965	1966	1967	1968	1969	1970
Expenditure											
Consumer's expenditure.	16,933	17,835	18,924	20,127	21,519	22,943	24,315	25,447	27,236	28,799	31,238
Public authorities' current expenditure on goods and services....	4,252	4,593	4,924	5,187	5,516	6,047	6,577	7,282	7,739	8,130	9,055
Gross domestic fixed capital formation	4,120	4,619	4,731	4,912	5,863	6,315	6,718	7,261	7,884	8,121	8,886
Value of physical increase in stocks and work in progress............	589	317	53	191	637	392	266	215	211	374	454
Total domestic expenditure at market prices..	25,894	27,364	28,632	30,417	33,535	35,697	37,876	40,205	43,070	45,424	49,633
Exports and property income from abroad...	6,309	6,587	6,840	7,225	7,687	8,309	8,742	8,932	10,774	12,168	13,775
less Imports and property income paid abroad...	− 6,483	− 6,480	− 6,607	− 6,964	− 7,896	− 8,177	− 8,456	− 8,899	− 10,823	− 11,496	− 12,979
less Taxes on expenditure	− 3,391	− 3,643	− 3,896	− 4,047	− 4,458	− 4,986	− 5,611	− 5,996	− 6,939	− 7,860	− 8,458
Subsidies..............	487	586	600	560	509	564	560	801	893	841	848
Gross national product at factor cost	22,816	24,414	25,569	27,191	29,377	31,407	33,111	34,943	36,975	39,077	42,819
Factor incomes											
Income from employment	15,174	16,407	17,306	18,190	19,702	21,261	22,746	23,686	25,305	27,182	30,487
Income from self-employment★..............	1,997	2,101	2,141	2,201	2,321	2,515	2,665	2,821	3,017	3,165	3,345
Gross trading profits of companies★†	3,736	3,643	3,595	4,103	4,590	4,761	4,442	4,608	5,017	4,961	5,028
Gross trading surplus of public corporations★..	534	639	745	840	924	988	1,042	1,132	1,363	1,452	1,379
Gross trading surplus of other public enterprises★..............	179	96	71	78	91	96	87	88	108	114	112
Rent‡...............	1,262	1,358	1,476	1,581	1,722	1,892	2,060	2,231	2,429	2,692	2,988
Total domestic income before providing for depreciation and stock appreciation	22,882	24,244	25,334	27,003	29,350	31,513	33,042	34,566	37,239	39,566	43,339
less Stock appreciation	− 138	− 174	− 147	− 202	− 298	− 330	− 348	− 180	− 638	− 828	− 976
Residual error........	− 161	90	48	− 8	− 68	− 211	− 11	172	33	− 162	− 56
Gross domestic product at factor cost§	22,583	24,160	25,235	26,793	28,984	30,972	32,718	34,558	36,634	38,576	42,307
Net property income from abroad	233	254	334	398	393	435	393	385	341	501	512
Gross national product.	22,816	24,414	25,569	27,191	29,377	31,407	33,111	34,943	36,975	39,077	42,819
less Capital consumption	− 1,933	− 2,065	− 2,197	− 2,318	− 2,492	− 2,697	− 2,937	− 3,121	− 3,384	− 3,723	− 4,132
National Income	20,883	22,349	23,372	24,873	26,885	28,710	30,174	31,822	33,591	35,354	38,687

★ Before providing for depreciation and stock appreciation.
† Selective employment tax is included on a cash basis and refunds or premiums are allowed for when they are received.
‡ Before providing for depreciation.
§ Equals total final expenditure on goods and services at market prices less imports of goods and services less taxes on expenditure plus subsidies.

INCOME FROM EMPLOYMENT, 1968–69
(including offices and Occupational Pensions)

£ million

Item	England and Wales	Scotland	Northern Ireland	United Kingdom
Charged by P.A.Y.E.............	21,202	1,756	386	23,350
Other Income...................	1,177	97	21	1,295
Deductions...................	1,113	61	16	1,190
Net True Income..............	21,272	1,792	391	23,455
Actual Income................	21,059	1,770	384	23,213

AVERAGE EARNINGS IN GREAT BRITAIN, 1966–1970

Figures shown are for men of 21 years and over; women, 18 years and over
(Based on Standard Industrial Classification, 1968; SIC 1958 figures in *italic* type).

Year*	Manual Workers (All Industries)				Administrative, Technical and Clerical Employees		Clerical Employees only‡	
	Men		Women		Average Earnings†		Average Earnings†	
	Hours	Wages	Hours	Wages	Men	Women	Men	Women
		£ s. d.		£ s. d.	£ s. d.	£ s. d.	£ s. d.	£ s. d.
1966........	46·0	20 6 0	38·1	10 1 0	26 13 9	14 4 11	16 18 1	12 17 5
1967........	46·2	21 8 0	38·2	10 11 0	27 18 1	14 18 0	17 5 7	13 6 8
1968........	46·4	23 0 0	38·3	11 6 0	29 15 5	15 15 2	18 12 5	14 8 0
1969........	46·5	24 17 0	38·1	12 2 0	32 1 4	17 0 11	20 9 2	15 9 6
1970........	45·7	28 1 0	37·9	14 0 0	36 2 5	19 11 10	22 11 6	17 9 10

*Average in October of each year.   † Monthly-paid and weekly-paid combined on weekly basis.
‡ In the public sector, insurance and banking.

DISTRIBUTION OF PERSONAL INCOMES

Tables showing estimated distribution of personal incomes in the United Kingdom by ranges of income in 1968–69. Tax figures include both income tax and surtax.

Before Taxation

Range of Income	Number of Incomes	Income Before Tax	Tax	Income After Tax
Incomes before tax				
£275.............	263,000	£75,700,000	£100,000	£75,600,000
300.............	1,181,000	413,900,000	8,400,000	405,500,000
400.............	1,387,000	624,700,000	29,800,000	594,900,000
500.............	1,511,000	829,700,000	59,600,000	770,100,000
600.............	1,428,000	926,700,000	75,400,000	851,300,000
700.............	1,477,000	1,106,900,000	105,200,000	1,001,700,000
800.............	1,469,000	1,247,600,000	134,000,000	1,113,600,000
900.............	1,396,000	1,325,700,000	154,200,000	1,171,500,000
1,000.............	3,484,000	3,906,000,000	470,300,000	3,435,700,000
1,250.............	3,001,000	4,099,600,000	534,500,000	3,565,100,000
1,500.............	3,573,000	6,108,800,000	917,200,000	5,191,600,000
2,000.............	1,304,000	3,054,700,000	605,100,000	2,449,600,000
3,000.............	437,000	1,626,600,000	435,100,000	1,191,500,000
5,000.............	173,000	1,144,200,000	415,300,000	728,900,000
10,000.............	37,000	488,200,000	261,100,000	227,100,000
20,000 and over.....	7,000	220,600,000	164,900,000	55,700,000
TOTAL.......	22,128,000	£27,199,600,000	£4,370,200,000	£22,829,400,000

After Taxation

Range of Net Income	Number of Incomes	Total Income Before Tax	Income Tax and Surtax	Net Income After Tax
Income after tax				
£275.............	294,000	£84,900,000	£200,000	£84,700,000
300.............	1,349,000	486,000,000	12,200,000	473,800,000
400.............	1,802,000	865,200,000	53,900,000	811,300,000
500.............	1,724,000	1,035,200,000	89,900,000	945,300,000
600.............	1,801,000	1,304,700,000	133,900,000	1,170,800,000
700.............	1,847,000	1,569,300,000	187,400,000	1,381,900,000
800.............	1,672,000	1,626,800,000	207,300,000	1,419,500,000
900.............	1,651,000	1,797,600,000	230,000,000	1,567,600,000
1,000.............	3,873,000	4,983,600,000	638,100,000	4,345,500 000
1,250.............	2,903,000	4,609,500,000	638,600,000	3,970,900,000
1,500.............	2,229,000	4,476,900,000	736,400,000	3,740,500,000
2,000.............	669,000	2,086,900,000	506,200,000	1,580,700,000
3,000.............	247,000	1,395,200,000	471,000,000	924,200,000
5,000.............	66,500	832,500,000	426,300,000	406,200,000
10,000 and over.....	500	45,300,000	38,800,000	6,500,000
TOTAL.........	22,128,000	£27,199,600,000	£4,370,200,000	£22,829,400,000

PERSONAL EXPENDITURE

A table showing personal expenditure on consumer goods and services with totals of consumers' expenditure in U.K. and abroad: (a) in 1960 and 1970 at current market prices; and (b) in 1970 at 1963 prices.

Heads of Expenditure	£ million (a) 1960	£ million (a) 1970	£ million (b) 1970	Heads of Expenditure	£ million (a) 1960	£ million (b) 1970	£ million (b) 1970
Household Food	4,228	6,363	4,984	Recreational Goods	585	1,181	807
Bread and Cereals	558	829	603	Books	53	93	62
Meat and Bacon	1,140	1,788	1,311	Newspapers	134	268	143
Fish	153	219	157	Magazines	56	102	61
Oils and Fats	220	266	249	Other	342	718	541
Sugar, Preserves and				Chemists' Goods	247	455	337
Confectionery	413	605	457	Other Goods	233	381	257
Dairy Products	640	908	745	Private Motoring	1,022	2,659	2,063
Fruit	260	364	303	Vehicles, New and Used	568	980	839
Potatoes and Vegetables	437	775	644	Running Costs	454	1,679	1,224
Beverages	270	398	342	Travel	572	1,025	719
Other manufactured food	137	211	173	Railway	145	232	163
Alcoholic Drink	962	2,178	1,548	Bus, Coach	312	439	274
Beer	566	1,258	892	Other	115	354	282
Wines, Spirits, Cider, etc.	396	920	656	Communication Services	140	319	240
Tobacco	1,140	1,720	1,248	Postal	72	109	76
Cigarettes	1,002	1,504	1,092	Telephone and Telegraph	68	210	164
Other	138	216	156	Entertainments	285	566	420
Housing	1,660	3,904	2,641	Cinema	67	61	33
Rent, Rates and Water	1,367	3,192	2,113	Other	218	505	387
Maintenance, Repairs, etc.	293	712	528	Domestic Service	103	158	104
Fuel and Light	751	1,489	1,274	Catering (meals and accommodation)	906	1,594	
Coal and Coke	323	357	235	Wages, salaries, etc. paid by			
Electricity	236	660	560	private non-profit making			2,826
Gas	136	385	400	bodies	137	406	
Other	56	87	79	Insurance	166	429	
Durable Household Goods	832	1,287	1,007	Other Services	684	1,564	
Furniture and Floor Coverings	410	626	467	Expenditure not included above	46	35	27
Radio and Electrical Goods	422	661	540	*Deduct Expenditure by Foreign*			
Other Household Goods	536	910	712	*Tourists, etc. in U.K.*	−225	−517	−356
Textiles, Soft Furnishings	160	273	200				
Hardware	191	376	292				
Matches, Soap and other				Personal Expenditure:—			
Cleaning Materials	185	261	220	in the United Kingdom	16,674	30,740	23,053
Clothing	1,664	2,634	2,195	abroad	259	498	343
Footwear	293	451	375				
Other Clothing:							
Men's and Boy's Wear	457	717	581				
Women's, Girl's and Infant's Wear	914	1,466	1,239	Total	16,933	31,238	23,396

UNITED KINGDOM PERSONAL INCOME AND EXPENDITURE   £ million

	1960	1967	1968	1969	1970
Income before tax					
Wages and salaries	13,735	21,120	22,480	24,215	27,080
Pay in cash and kind of H.M. Forces	393	524	541	543	653
Employers' contributions:					
National insurance, etc.	425	966	1,099	1,141	1,355
Other	621	1,076	1,185	1,283	1,399
Total income from employment	15,174	23,686	25,305	27,182	30,487
Professional persons*	355	514	553	569	602
Farmers*	500	664	672	720	778
Other sole traders and partnerships	1,142	1,643	1,792	1,876	1,965
Total income from self-employment*	1,997	2,821	3,017	3,165	3,345
Rent, dividends and net interest and Other Receipts	2,399	3,999	4,241	4,504	4,644

£ million

Income before Tax—contd.	1960	1967	1968	1969	1970
Current transfers to charities from companies..........	17	32	34	35	36
National insurance benefits and other current grants from public authorities..........	1,569	3,199	3,689	3,944	4,321
Total personal income*†.......	21,156	33,737	36,286	38,830	42,833
Expenditure					
Consumers' expenditure.......	16,933	25,447	27,236	28,799	31,238
Transfers abroad (net).........	—13	43	60	55	45
Taxes paid abroad...........	12	20	22	22	24
United Kingdom taxes on income:					
Payments..................	1,991	4,115	4,592	5,211	5,981
Additions to tax reserves....	95	83	148	101	102
National insurance, etc. contributions..............	913	1,909	2,165	2,244	2,655
Total current expenditure......	19,931	31,617	34,223	36,432	40,045
Balance: saving before providing for depreciation and stock appreciation but after providing for additions to tax reserves†.............	1,225	2,120	2,063	2,398	2,788
Total......................	21,156	33,737	36,286	38,830	42,833

* Before providing for depreciation and stock appreciation.
† Total personal income *less* United Kingdom taxes on income, national insurance, etc. contributions, transfers abroad (net) and taxes paid abroad equals personal disposable income. Estimates of personal disposable income and saving before providing for additions to tax reserves are as follows (£ million):

	1960	1967	1968	1969	1970
Personal disposable income......	18,253	27,650	29,447	31,298	34,128
Saving (and percentage)..........	1,320(7·2)	2,203(8·0)	2,211(7·5)	2,499(8·0)	2,890(8·5)

UNITED KINGDOM COMPANIES: NET TRADING PROFITS* £ million

	1960	1966	1967	1968	1969
Forestry and fishing..................	—1	1	5	5	10
Mining and quarrying.................	13	23	26	24	24
Manufacturing:					
Food, drink and tobacco..............	293	352	379	399	372
Coal and petroleum products.........	26	39	36	48	7
Chemicals and allied industries.........	180	192	216	257	234
Metal manufacture....................	201	160	144	95	70
Mechanical engineering	201	246	237	290	307
Instrument engineering...............	25	29	57	31	46
Electrical engineering................	122	157	174	240	204¦
Shipbuilding and marine engineering...	12	2	4	15	12
Vehicles............................	135	82	133	167	65
Metal goods not elsewhere specified....	99	117	115	120	130
Textiles............................	126	111	116	187	168
Leather, leather goods and fur.........	9	8	8	13	13
Clothing and footwear...............	53	46	43	56	52
Bricks, pottery, glass, cement, etc.......	74	63	71	87	85
Timber, furniture, etc................	20	20	21	37	36
Paper, printing and publishing.........	135	141	150	188	174
Other manufacturing industries........	43	54	61	63	48
Total.........................	1,754	1,819	1,945	2,293	2,023
Construction........................	85	126	114	118	136
Gas, electricity and water.............	13	11	10	9	10
Transport and communication...........	37	8	59	93	110
Distributive trades...................	496	610	606	687	725
Insurance, banking and finance†	553	940	994	1,174	1,288
Other services......................	156	160	183	196	183
Adjustments........................	—583	—1,088	—1,021	—1,410	—1,476
Total.......................	2,523	2,610	2,921	3,189	3,033

* Net profits are equal to gross profits *less* the statutory depreciation allowances granted for purposes of tax assessment.   † Including net receipts of interest.

UNITED KINGDOM COMPANIES: INCOME AND INTEREST £ million

	1960	1967	1968	1969	1970
Income					
Income arising in the United Kingdom:					
Gross trading profits*	3,736	4,608	5,017	4,961	5,028
Rent and non-trading income	843	1,485	1,708	1,910	2,128
Total	4,579	6,093	6,725	6,871	7,156
Income from abroad†	949	1,401	1,702	2,008	2,137
Total	5,528	7,494	8,427	8,879	9,293
Allocation of interest					
Dividends and interest:					
Payments:					
Debenture and loan interest	107	384	436	487	549
Dividends on preference shares	112	112	98	94	81
Dividends on ordinary shares	1,040	1,605	1,645	1,765	1,701
Co-operative society dividends and interest	58	41	37	32	31
Interest on building society shares and deposits	132	392	467	581	679
Other interest paid by banks, etc.	134	323	417	486	484
Total	1,583	2,857	3,100	3,445	3,525
Additions to dividend reserves	63	1	114	−87	10
Current transfers to charities	17	32	34	35	36
Profits due abroad net of United Kingdom tax†	179	222	336	290	340
United Kingdom taxes on income‡:					
Payments on profits due abroad	91	143	131	166	270
Payments on other income	612	820	903	938	1,172
Additions to reserves on profits due abroad	40	18	138	93	−36
Additions to reserves on other income	277	285	467	525	142
Taxes paid abroad	369	548	710	795	912
Balance: undistributed income after taxation*	2,297	2,568	2,494	2,679	2,922
Total	5,528	7,494	8,427	8,879	9,293

* Before providing for depreciation and stock appreciation. Including United Kingdom branches and subsidiaries of non-resident parent companies. Selective employment tax is included on a cash basis and refunds or premiums are allowed for when they are received.
† After deducting depreciation allowances but before providing for stock appreciation.
‡ Total United Kingdom taxes on the total income of companies, including tax on distributions made by companies is as follows (£ million):

	1960	1967	1968	1969	1970
Accruals	1,550	2,189	2,647	2,749	2,638
Payments	1,216	1,886	1,995	2,167	2,528

COMPANIES

(Registered by the Dept. of Trade and Industry *Registrar of Companies*, Companies House, 55–71 City Road, E.C.1. The *Registry of Business Names* is also located at Companies House.)

During 1970, 29,837 new companies having a share capital were registered in Great Britain (England and Wales, 28,755; Scotland, 1,082), with nominal capital of £239,822. There were 16,639 public and 542,858 private companies, making a total of 559,497 companies on the Registers at the end of 1970. The number of public companies with a share capital was 10,270.

TAXATION REFORM: UNIFIED TAXATION

In his Budget Speech on March 30, 1971 the Chancellor of the Exchequer announced a radical reform of Income Tax and Surtax to operate from April, 1973. The delay in bringing these reforms into effect is designed to permit during 1972/73 a complete P.A.Y.E. recoding and time also for the changes to be debated both inside and outside Parliament.

The changes proposed are:
1. The abolition of the two tier (income tax and surtax) system and its replacement by a single graduated tax.

2. The abolition of the earned income relief. The distinction between earned and unearned income is to be retained, however, as the latter will be subject to a special investment income surcharge.

3. The existing pattern of personal reliefs is to be retained at approximately the present level. To compensate for the loss of earned income relief, however, the personal allowance for a single person is to be increased from £325 to £420; the other allowances are to be similarly increased. In contrast to the present system, reliefs will be given as deductions from income and not in terms of tax. It is important, however, to appreciate that although the 1971 Finance Act gives the allowances which are to apply from April 1973 these are in fact only provisional and are subject to adjustment before they commence to operate.

4. The provisional basic rate of Income Tax to be levied for the tax year commencing April 5, 1973, will be 30 per cent. (*i.e.* approximately the 1971/72, rate of 38·75 per cent. less the two-ninths earned income allowance).

No indication has been given of the level at which the proposed investment surcharge is to operate or of the scale of this charge. Similarly no details are given of the new graduated rates of tax which are to replace surtax on the higher levels of income.

Persons already subject to Surtax will be faced with a double liability in the year 1973/74 since the surtax payment for the year 1972/73 will be due on January 1, 1974 at a time when they may already (under P.A.Y.E.) be subject to both the basic and higher rates for the year 1973/74. Although the Chancellor considered that those affected were being given ample warning to enable them to meet this contingency, the 1971 Finance Act provides that where the 1972/73 Surtax attributable to income, other than that taxed by deduction at source, (*i.e.* principally dividend income) exceeds £100, one-third of the tax so payable may be deferred until January 1, 1975 and one third until January 1, 1976.

Although, as already stated, the 1971 Finance Act only gives a provisional basic rate and provisional allowances for the tax year 1973/74, it outlines in some detail the manner in which the new system is to operate. In general, personal and other reliefs are to be given in whatever way results in the greatest reduction in tax liability. In contrast, however, for investment surcharge purposes personal reliefs will be set first against earned income and then against the slice of investment income not subject to the surcharge (*i.e.* below the threshold from which the surcharge is to apply).

It is important also to note that deductions from earned income under P.A.Y.E. will extend to the full graduated rates and not merely the basic rate. These rates will also be applied in assessing business profits, income from property, etc. However, the basic rate of 30 per cent. only will be deducted by companies paying dividends and interest, and where an individual receiving income taxed only at this rate is subject also to the investment surcharge or, by reason of the size of his income at rates in excess of 30 per cent., a separate assessment will be made on him after the end of the tax year and the additional tax will be due on July 5 in the following tax year or one month after the assessment is made, if later.

It will be seen from these brief notes that the changes proposed are mainly of a technical and administrative nature. It is hoped that substantial administrative savings will result; in particular the abolition of Surtax in its present form, which

should enable the existing Surtax assessing machinery to be dismantled, is expected to release a substantial number of officers to local tax offices where in future all tax assessments will be made.

Although the reforms proposed are not apparently designed to shift the incidence of taxation the opportunity may be taken to narrow differences in the taxation of earned and unearned income which in recent years have tended to widen; such a move, however, is bound to give rise to political controversy.

The Chancellor also announced the publication of Green Papers dealing with changes in the taxation of company profits and proposals for a Value Added Tax.

Corporation Tax Reform

The Company Tax changes proposed in the Green Paper have two principal aims. They are designed to remove the discrimination against distributed profits in the present system which it is argued "distorts the working of market forces and so tends towards the misallocation of scarce investment resources". Secondly, in considering which of three alternative systems to adopt it is clear that an important factor will be the importance of our conforming with Common Market practice.

The Paper considers briefly a return to the system which prevailed prior to 1965 with profits subject to a single rate of corporation tax and dividends paid less income tax retained by the company. This scheme is not looked on with much favour.

The two schemes considered seriously are broadly similar in character. They are the "two rate system" and the "imputation system". Under the first system corporation tax is paid at a lower rate on distributed profits but income tax is also deducted from dividends as an advance on the shareholder's eventual liability thereon. The imputation system achieves much the same object but with a single corporation tax rate part of which is allowed as a credit against the shareholder's personal tax liability. On balance, for domestic reasons the Paper appears to favour the two rate system but there are many important technical complications and clearly the final decision must take account of the representations from interested parties which the Chancellor has invited.

Value Added Tax

The proposed Value Added Tax to come into effect in April, 1973, is designed to replace both the Selective Employment Tax (cut by 50 per cent. in the 1971 Budget) and Purchase Tax. In contrast to these selective taxes VAT is to be a broadly based tax covering a wide range of goods and services.

The Government favours the invoice system as most suitable for use in this country. Under this system a person supplying goods or services in the home market would be required to account for tax thereon being in general tax on his output less a credit for the tax on goods and services supplied to him. The Green Paper mentions probable exemptions which include food, housing, banking, life assurance and publishing. Although these areas of the economy may appear to benefit from exemption it should be appreciated that goods and services supplied to such industries would remain subject to tax. Against this, an industry with a zero rating (principally exporters) will be able to obtain full credit and possibly repayment of the tax invoiced to them by their suppliers.

Undoubtedly an all-embracing tax of this type will present many complex problems.

LOCAL GOVERNMENT IN THE UNITED KINGDOM

ENGLAND AND WALES

Local government is carried on by directly elected councils whose powers and duties are defined by statute, under the general supervision of various departments of the central government. Departments principally concerned are the Department of the Environment and the Departments of Health and Social Security, and Education and Science; and, in matters affecting law and order, police, fire services, care of children, civil defence preparations, etc., the Home Office. Supervision is by means of inspections and enquiries, issue of Regulations and Orders, approval of bye-laws, loan sanctions for capital expenditure, examination of accounts and the administration of government grants.

County Councils.—Constituted by the Local Government Act, 1888, they were made responsible for administrative duties which were previously performed by the justices of the peace in quarter sessions. In the main their functions relate to the more important services. In most cases the area of the administrative county is that of the geographical county, excluding county boroughs. Lincolnshire, Suffolk, Sussex and Yorkshire are exceptions, being divided into parts, each with a separate council, for administrative convenience. Councils consist of a chairman, aldermen and councillors. The chairman, who may receive remuneration, is elected annually by the council, either from among the aldermen or councillors or from persons eligible for election as aldermen or councillors. The aldermen form a quarter of the council; they are elected by the councillors from among themselves or persons eligible to be councillors and hold office for six years, half retiring every three years. Councillors are elected by local government electors for three years. Excluding Greater London there are 58 county councils in England and Wales (see pp. 631-3; Wales, pp. 675-6).

County Borough Councils.—Boroughs with populations of 50,000 or more in 1888 and some ancient counties of cities were constituted by the Local Government Act, 1888, as county boroughs; their councils were given the same powers and duties as county councils, but they are also governed by the general law affecting boroughs and have the same constitution. Until 1926 other boroughs reaching 50,000 population could seek county borough status, but the figure was then raised to 75,000. The Local Government Act, 1958, again raised the figure (to 100,000), and placed a 15-year prohibition on Private Bills for this purpose. (Although important, level of population is only one factor in the attainment of county borough status.) There are 83 county borough councils in England and Wales (see pp. 657-68; Wales, 675-6).

The district councils within a county are borough councils (other than county borough councils), urban district councils and rural district councils.

Borough Councils.—Constituted in their present form by the Municipal Corporations Act, 1882. Urban or Rural district councils may by royal charter be incorporated as boroughs. Borough councils consist of a mayor, aldermen and councillors. The mayor, who presides at council meetings and may be paid, and the aldermen are elected and hold office for the same terms as chairmen and aldermen of county councils (see above). Councillors are elected by the burgesses (local government electors of the borough) for a term of three years, one-third of the council retiring each year. The lists on pp. 671-3 indicate how the political parties were represented on the councils of the more important boroughs in 1970. Excluding the London boroughs there are 259 non-county boroughs in England and Wales (see pp. 664-9; Wales, p. 675).

Urban and Rural District Councils.—The Public Health Act, 1875, consolidated legislation on public health and conferred various powers and duties on local sanitary authorities and these bodies were reconstituted by the Local Government Act, 1894, as urban and rural district councils. They are corporate bodies and have a common seal. District councils consist of a chairman, elected annually by the council, and councillors elected for a term of three years. The chairman may receive an allowance. An important part of their responsibility is in the local administration of the Public Health Acts and Housing Acts. Urban district councils are also highway authorities. Both types of authority levy rates; they may raise loans for various purposes and make bye-laws with the sanction of the central Government. There are 522 urban district councils (see pp. 668-70 and 675) and 469 rural district councils in England and Wales.

Parish Councils and Parish Meetings.—Local government responsibility is for the area of the *civil* parish in rural areas and for purely secular matters. Parish meetings consist of all the local government electors of the parish under a chairman chosen by the meeting and must be held at least twice a year where there is no parish council. Parish councils consist of a chairman and a number of councillors which may vary from five to twenty-one, elected for three years. Parishes with a population of more than 300 must have a parish council. A parish meeting must be held annually and is presided over by the chairman of the parish council. Rates to meet the expenses of the parish council are levied by the rural district council.

London.—The Greater London Area embraces the old counties of London and Middlesex (except Potter's Bar, Staines and Sunbury-on-Thames) and parts of the neighbouring counties of Essex, Herts., Kent and Surrey and the whole of the county boroughs of Croydon, East Ham and West Ham.

For those functions which need to be considered for the whole of the Area, the Greater London Council (see pp. 634-6) is responsible; such functions as traffic, major roads and overall planning. All other matters are the concern of the 32 London borough councils (12 inner and 20 outer; see p. 642); the City of London, besides retaining its previous functions, has the powers of a London borough.

Local Government Reorganization.—In February, 1971, the Government published a White Paper (*Cmnd.* 4584) setting out proposals for the reorganization of local government in England outside Greater London. The White Paper proposed that the existing structure of local government should be replaced by a new pattern of local government based everywhere on two levels of executive authorities. It was intended to introduce legislation to give effect to these proposals in the 1971-72 session of Parliament. The new local authorities would come into full effect in 1974.

Local Government Elections

Generally speaking, all British subjects or citizens of the Republic of Ireland of 18 years or over, resident on the qualifying date in the area for which the election is being held are entitled to vote at local government elections. A register of electors is prepared and published annually by local electoral registration officers. The number of local government electors on the February, 1970, registers for England and Wales was: County Boroughs, 10,005,469; Non-county Boroughs and urban districts including Greater London and the City of London, 17,217,349; and rural districts, 7,308,450. The total electorate of Greater London was 5,514,120 and the City of London, 3,501.

Ordinary county council elections are held triennially in April and elections for other authorities annually or triennially in May.

Voting takes place at polling stations arranged by the local authority and under the supervision of a presiding officer specially appointed for the purpose. Candidates, who are subject to various statutory qualifications and disqualifications designed to secure that they are suitable persons to hold office, must be nominated by two electors and, except in rural district, rural borough, or parish council elections, must secure the assent of eight other electors to the nomination. County council elections are based on divisions of the county regulated by the Home Secretary, each of which returns a single member; most boroughs, including county and London boroughs, are divided into wards, each electing its own members; other authorities may be so divided or may remain as single units, depending upon their size.

Local Government Services

Local authorities must in their areas provide the services and carry out the functions required by various Acts of Parliament. They may provide additional services under general permissive legislation or under " local " Acts of Parliament which they have promoted as Private Bills. The nature of the duties imposed on local authorities and the scope of the services which they provide vary according to the type of authority. The only all-purpose council is that of the county borough. In the counties functions are divided between the county council and the borough and district councils and there is considerable delegation of functions by the county council to these other authorities, *e.g.* in education and planning matters. Principal subjects of local government administration are:—

Public health services (prevention of epidemics, abatement of sanitary nuisances, etc.) under the Public Health Act, 1936; local health services under the National Health Service; Care of deprived children; Welfare services for the aged and infirm and for the handicapped, under the National Assistance Act, 1948 and the chronically Sick and Disabled Persons Acts, 1970.

Housing; Land drainage; Water supply; Sewerage; Refuse collection and disposal; Baths and washhouses; Cemeteries.

Town and country planning; Parks and recreation grounds; Smallholdings and allotments.

Roads and bridges; Road safety; Street lighting; Harbours, docks and piers; Passenger transport.

Education; Public libraries, museums and art galleries; Municipal entertainments; Civic restaurants; Information centres.

Police; Fire services; Civil defence services.

Food and drugs inspection; Weights and measures.

Local Government Committees and Staff

Detailed administration of local government services is commonly carried out by committees, matters of policy being decided by the council as a whole; the appointment of certain committees is made compulsory by Act of Parliament. Committees may be executive or advisory; they may be constituted on a permanent basis as Standing Committees or as Special Committees set up for a limited period to deal with a particular subject; their powers and duties are laid down in the Standing Orders of the Council (subject in some cases to special statutory provisions). Where services such as water supply and sewerage are shared between two or more authorities, Joint Committees or Boards of representatives of the authorities concerned are set up to administer the services.

The executive policy of the local authority is carried out by a salaried staff varying in number according to the type of authority. The chief official is, in boroughs, the Town Clerk, and elsewhere the Clerk of the Council, and these appointments, together with those of certain other executive officers, are compulsory. Appointments of staff (including professional, technical and clerical classes, and manual workers) are made to a set establishment.

Local Government Finance

Local government is financed from various sources. (1) *Rates.*—Levied by county borough, borough and district councils and in London by the City Corporation and the London boroughs. Sums required by the Greater London Council and by county councils are included in the rates levied by London and non-county borough and district councils. Rates are levied by a poundage tax on the rateable value of property in the area of the rating authority. Under the General Rate Act, 1967, rating authorities are required to charge a lower rate in the pound on dwellings than on property generally in their area. Differentials of 5d., 10d., 1s. 3d., 1s. 8d. and 9½p. in the pound respectively were prescribed for the years 1967–68 to 1971–72. New valuation lists, prepared by valuation officers of the Board of Inland Revenue, came into force on April 1, 1963. All rateable property is rated on the basis of 1963 values until the next revision of the lists, due in 1973. Agricultural land and buildings are exempt from rates. Under the General Rate Act, 1967, local authorities may decide to charge half rates on empty property; otherwise empty property is not rateable. The General Rate Act also makes provision for rate rebates for domestic ratepayers with small incomes. (2) *Government Grants.*—From 1948–49 to 1958–59, the Exchequer made annual equalization grants to counties and county boroughs whose rateable value was below the average rateable value per head of weighted population in England and Wales to bring their respective rateable values up to the average level. Equalization grants replaced the former " block " grants paid to local authorities until 1948, which included an element of compensation for loss of revenue through de-rating. Percentage grants covered an agreed proportion of expenditure on approved services such as education, health, police and fire services. Special grants were also made.

The Local Government Act, 1958, provided for a new general grant, payable from 1959–60 onwards, in replacement of a number of specific grants, of which the largest were for the education, local health, fire and child care services. It also provided for the replacement of the equalization grant, payable under the 1948 Act, by a rate-deficiency grant based on rate products instead of rateable values, and payable to county districts as well as counties and county boroughs.

The Local Government Act, 1966, provides rate support grant, to be paid to local authorities from 1967–68 in place of the general grant and rate-deficiency grant. The aggregate of Exchequer grants on revenue account is estimated in advance for a period of not less than two years, though not necessarily at the same level for each year of the period, and it may subsequently be increased if there is an unforeseen increase in the level of prices, costs and remuneration. From the aggregate is deducted the estimated amount of the specific grants for the year in aid of revenue expenditure and the balance is the rate support grant. This is then divided into three parts known as the needs, resources and domestic elements.

The *needs element* is broadly similar to the general grant, though covering a wider field. It is distributed to county and county borough councils, the Common Council of the City of London, London Borough Councils and the Council of the Isles of Scilly by reference to population, the numbers of pupils and students at different stages of education and on other objective factors which are readily ascertainable and afford a fair and reasonable measure of the relative needs of each authority. The *resources element* is payable to any local authority whose rate resources per head of population fall below the national average. The *domestic element* is payable to all rating authorities and reimburses them for the cost of charging a lower rate in the pound on dwelling houses, as required by the General Rate Act, 1967.

(3) *Loans.*—Local authorities may raise loans on the security of the rates, normally with the prior approval of the appropriate Government department for key areas of expenditure, *e.g.* housing, education, police. Certain associated items are entirely free from control. In the remaining, locally determined sector, individual authorities or groups of authorities are given a block allocation within which they are free to decide which projects to undertake. On March 31, 1969, there were outstanding loans in England and Wales to the amount of £12,136,854,000; against this total the sum of £33,991,000 stood at the credit of various sinking funds.

Income of Local Authorities, 1968–69

Revenue from:—

Rates	£1,398,033,000
Government Grants	1,712,912,000
Private Improvements	12,833,000
Housing (Rents, etc.)	525,692,000
Town and Country Planning	11,403,000
Small Holdings and Allotments	3,784,000
Trading Services:—	
Water Supply	110,540,000
Passenger Transport	97,516,000
Harbours, Docks, Piers, etc.	68,053,000
Other	62,157,000
Miscellaneous Income	437,341,000
Total	**£4,450,264,000**

Capital Receipts:—

Loans	£1,341,711,000
Government Grants	85,695,000
Repayment of Advances	94,839,000
Sales and other sources	66,609,000
Total	**£1,588,854,000**
Total Receipts	**£6,039,118,000**

Expenditure

1968–69

Education	£1,644,189,000
Libraries and Museums	50,019,000
Local Health Services (N.H.S.)	152,053,000
Public Health Services:	
Sewers and Sewage Disposal	106,699,000
House and Trade Refuse	82,128,000
Baths and Washhouses	23,745,000
Parks, Pleasure Grounds, etc.	55,943,000
Other	39,779,000
Care of the Aged, Handicapped and Homeless	92,682,000
Protection of Children	50,996,000
Housing	699,772,000
Town and Country Planning	44,839,000
Allotments and Small Holdings	5,073,000
Land Drainage, etc.	26,150,000
Highways and Bridges	242,112,000
Private Street Works	13,418,000
Public Footway Lighting	29,386,000

Fire Service	£59,471,000
Police	263,903,000
Administration of Justice	32,871,000
Civil Defence	9,179,000
Trading Services:—	
Water Supply	120,085,000
Passenger Transport	102,499,000
Harbours, Docks and Piers	72,566,000
Other Trading Services	73,085,000
Other Works and Purposes	84,740,000
Unallotted	153,908,000
Total	**£4,322,290,000**
Capital Expenditure	1,597,220,000
Total Expenditure	**£5,919,510,000**

Rates and Rateable Values.—In 1968–69, the latest year for which final figures were available, a total of £1,450,847,000 was collected from local government rates in England and Wales, the average rate per £ being 150p, on a total valuation of £2,313,678,000. Provisional figures for 1970–71 show a total receipt from rates of £1,754,000,000 on a value of £2,440,549,000—average rate per £ levied, 172p. Exchequer Grants in respect of rate rebates are treated as rate income and included in the total receipts.

Average Rates.—In 1971–72 average rates levied in England and Wales were: County Boroughs, 86·3p; Inner London Boroughs, 81·1p; Outer London Boroughs, 80·6p. Non-County Boroughs, 87·8p; Urban Districts, 86p; Rural Districts, 74·2p.

Product of 1p Rate and amount raised per Head of Population in 1971–72

	Product of 1p Rate (Net)	Rates Raised per Head, 1971–72†
	£	£
Westminster	1,090,000	325·94
Birmingham	519,500	44·08
Camden	343,000	118·36
Manchester	276,000	45·95
Liverpool	262,190	37·93
Kensington and Chelsea	253,800	77·88
Sheffield	239,791	40·50
Ealing	236,000	56·91
Croydon	232,800	47·39
Bristol	225,600	47·62
Leeds	224,500	37·67
Barnet	221,000	43·83
Teesside	212,145	46·17
Brent	202,250	47·20
Lambeth	195,720	43·32
Islington	195,600	65·99
Enfield	189,000	48·35

† Includes domestic element of rate support grant.

In the City of London the product of a 1p rate is £499,000. £8,136·42 is raised per head in 1971–72.

The figures above are from the *Annual Return of Rates* issued by The Institute of Municipal Treasurers and Accountants (Incorporated).

SCOTLAND

Scotland is divided for local government purposes into counties, burghs and districts, and local authorities are similar to those in England and Wales.

County Councils.—First constituted in 1889, they are responsible for local government of the geographical area of the county excluding for most purposes the large burghs. For certain purposes the counties of Perth and Kinross, and Moray and Nairn are combined. County councils include repre-

sentatives from the landward areas and from all the burghs which are within the county for any purpose, town councils electing representatives from among their own members. Councillors are elected triennially. The chairman of the county council is the Convener of the County. There are 33 county councils in Scotland (*see* pp. 679–80).

Town Councils.—The town Councils of the counties of cities (Edinburgh, Glasgow, Aberdeen and Dundee) are all-purpose authorities similar to the county borough councils in England and Wales and are presided over by the Lord Provost. Town councils consist of a provost (chairman), bailies and councillors. The provost and bailies (the equivalent of aldermen in England) are elected by the councillors from among themselves and hold office for three years; they are the magistrates of the burgh.

Large burghs, other than the counties of cities, are independent for all purposes except that for valuation, electoral registration, education and police, they are included in the county; small burghs are within the county not only for these purposes but also for such purposes as classified roads, planning, etc.

There are 201 town councils in Scotland (counties of cities, 4; other large burghs, 21; small burghs, 176). (*See* pp. 680–1; 685–6.)

District Councils.—Outside the burghs the county council is responsible for most local government functions but district councils have statutory functions with regard to recreation grounds, rights of way, allotments, bus shelters and other local matters. Two counties—Kinross and Nairn—are not divided into districts. District councils consist of elected members and the county councillors for

the district *ex officio*. There are 196 district councils in Scotland.

Local Government Electors—In Scotland there are 1,241,213 electors in counties of cities, 662,594 in other large burghs, 732,090 in small burghs and 1,049,576 in landward areas—Total 3,685,413.

Rates and Rateable Values.—In 1968–69, the latest year for which final figures were available a total of £165,840,000 was received from local government rates in Scotland, the average rate per £ being the equivalent of 112p on a total valuation of £148,144,000. Provisional figures for 1970–71 show a total receipt from rates of £213,135,000 on a value of £154,905,000—average rate per £ levied (equivalent of) 137½p.

NORTHERN IRELAND

The structure of local government in Northern Ireland is similar to that of England and Wales. Types of local authority are: county councils, 6; county boroughs, 1; non-county boroughs or municipal councils, 9; urban district councils. 26; and rural district councils, 26. (*See* p. 691.) In addition there are three development commissions two of which exercise municipal functions.

Electors.—The register published on Feb. 15, 1971, contained the names of 1,031,604 local government electors. Of this total, 257,508 related to the County Borough of Belfast and 33,307 to Londonderry. A new electoral register will be published on Feb. 15, 1971.

Local Government Debts.—The total amount of outstanding loans and capitalized annuities in Northern Ireland on March 31, 1970, was £284,216,859 (excluding Hospitals).

RIVER AUTHORITIES (ENGLAND AND WALES)

The Water Resources Act, 1963, established for England and Wales the 29 river authorities listed below. River Authorities have functions and duties in relation to land drainage, prevention of pollution and the regulation and improvement of fisheries, taken over from the former River Boards. They have the added responsibility, under the Act, of developing conservation schemes to provide the extra water required by water undertakings and industry. Much of the revenue required for water conservation is obtained through River Authorities' Charging Schemes introduced on April 1, 1969. A river authority derives its other income from precepts on the general rates of those counties and county boroughs within the river authority area. In the list below, the name of the Clerk or Chief Officer of the Authority is added to its address.

River Authorities

AVON AND DORSET, 3 St. Stephen's Road, Bournemouth, Hants.—A. S. Wisdom.
BRISTOL AVON, Green Park Road, Bath, Som.—G. M. Yates.
CORNWALL, St. John's, Western Road, Launceston.—J. H. Morgan.
CUMBERLAND, 256 London Road, Carlisle.—R. Birkett.
DEE AND CLWYD, 2 Vicar's Lane, Chester.—H. H. Crann.
DEVON, County Hall, Exeter.—A. G. C. Williams.
EAST SUFFOLK AND NORFOLK, The Cedars, Albemarle Road, Norwich.—S. V. Ellis.
ESSEX, Rivers House, Springfield Road, Chelmsford.—G. L. Sturgess.
GLAMORGAN, Tremains House, Coychurch Road, Bridgend.—T. D. Lynch.
GREAT OUSE, Great Ouse House, Clarendon Road, Cambridge.—J. S. Bissett.

GWYNEDD, Highfield, Caernarvon.—M. G. Crewe.
HAMPSHIRE, The Castle, Winchester.—A. H. M. Smyth.
ISLE OF WIGHT, County Hall, Newport.—L. H. Baines.
KENT, Rivers House, London Road, Maidstone.—A. G. Stirk.
LANCASHIRE, 48 West Cliff, Preston.—H. Holmes.
LINCOLNSHIRE, 50 Wide Bargate, Boston.—G. E. Phillippo, M.B.E.
MERSEY AND WEAVER, Liverpool Road, Great Sankey, Warrington.—R. E. Woodward, M.B.E.
NORTHUMBRIAN, 110 Osborne Road, Newcastle upon Tyne, 2.—N. H. Thomas.
SEVERN, Portland House, Church Street, Malvern, Worcs.—J. G. M. Rimmer.
SOMERSET, 12 King Square, Bridgwater.—T. J. M. Barrington
SOUTH WEST WALES, Penyfai House, Penyfai Lane, Llanelli.—E. A. Griffiths.
SUSSEX, 137/139 Preston Road, Brighton 6.—B. R. Thorpe.
TRENT, 206 Derby Road, Nottingham.—I. R. Drummond.
USK, The Croft, Goldcroft Common, Caerleon, Newport, Mon.—W. J. R. Howells.
WELLAND AND NENE, North Street, Oundle, Nr. Peterborough.—D. S. Akroyd.
WYE, 4 St. John Street, Hereford.—J. A. Weston.
YORKSHIRE OUSE AND HULL, 21 Park Sq. South, Leeds 1.—D. C. North.

Catchment Boards

THAMES CONSERVANCY, 15 Buckingham Street, W.C.2.—R. Penrhyn Owen.
LEE CONSERVANCY CATCHMENT BOARD, Brettenham House, Lancaster Place, W.C.2.—J. L. Spiller, D.F.C.

THE NATIONAL PARKS

The ten National Parks described below in their order of designation have been established in England and Wales. These areas are not public property and visitors are not free to wander over private land within the Park boundaries. They have been marked out for special care aimed at two prime purposes: to preserve and enhance their natural beauty, and to promote their enjoyment by the public.

Peak District National Park (542 sq. miles).—Mainly in Derbyshire but extending into Staffordshire, Cheshire, the West Riding of Yorkshire and the City of Sheffield. In the south and east are limestone uplands, and finely wooded dales with swift, clear rivers and unspoilt stone villages. Northwards, moorlands, edged by gritstone crags, attract hill walkers and climbers. There are information centres at Bakewell, Edale, Castleton and at Buxton (just outside the Park) and an information caravan tours the Park.

Lake District National Park (866 sq. miles).—In Cumberland, Lancashire and Westmorland. Spectacular mountain scenery with wooded lower slopes enhanced by lakes and tarns. The area includes England's highest mountains (Scafell Pike, Helvellyn and Skiddaw) and largest lakes. Walking and rock-climbing are the principal recreations, but there are fishing, swimming, sailing, boating and winter sports as well. There are information centres at Keswick, Ambleside and Windermere and two information vans tour the Park. At Brockhole is a National Park centre.

Snowdonia National Park (845 sq. miles).—In Caernarvonshire and Merioneth and a small section of Denbighshire in North Wales. A wild mountainous region, traversed by high passes, offering some of the finest rock-climbing and mountain walking for both beginner and expert. The main valleys, often finely wooded, hold lakes (or llyns) and are watered by rivers with cascading falls. There are information centres at Bala, Blaenau Ffestiniog, Dolgellau, Llanberis and Llanrwst and an information van tours the park.

Dartmoor National Park (365 sq. miles).—In Devon, the highest area of high moorland in southern England, famous for its granite " tors " often weathered into strange shapes. Fine hanging oak woods adorn the river valleys which lead up into the Moor. The Park is rich in prehistoric relics and offers fine walking and riding. An information van is sited at Two Bridges during the summer months.

Pembrokeshire Coast National Park (225 sq. miles).—A spectacular section of Britain's coastline, where rocky cliffs alternate with bays and sandy coves. In the north is Mynydd Presely, abounding in prehistoric relics. The Park includes the fine estuary of Milford Haven, Tenby, the Cathedral of St. David's, and Carew and other Norman castles. There are information centres at Tenby, St. David's, Pembroke and Haverfordwest. A countryside unit is open at Broad Haven.

North York Moors National Park (553 sq. miles).—In the North Riding of Yorkshire, the Park stretches from the Hambleton Hills in the west to the coastline above Scarborough. On the coast sheltered bays and sandy beaches alternate with headlands harbouring villages such as Staithes and Robin Hood's Bay. The heart of the Park offers tracts of open moorland, intersected by beautiful wooded valleys. Mount Grace Priory and the abbeys of Rievaulx and Byland are within the Park.

Yorkshire Dales National Park (680 sq. miles).—An area of upland moors, cut by deep valleys, in the North and West Ridings of Yorkshire, the Park includes some of the finest limestone scenery in Britain: Kilnsey Crag in Wharfedale, Gordale Scar, and Malham Cove in Malhamdale. In the Park

also are Swaledale and Wensleydale, the three peaks of Ingleborough, Whernside and Pen-y-Ghent, and many relics of the past such as the Roman fort at Bainbridge and Bolton Abbey in Wharfedale. There are information centres at Clapham and Aysgarth and an information van tours the West Riding area of the Park.

Exmoor National Park (265 sq. miles).—Mainly in Somerset but extending into Devon, this is a moorland plateau seamed with finely wooded combes. The well-known coastline between Minehead and Combe Martin Bay is exceptionally beautiful. In the east are the Brendon Hills. There are information centres at Combe Martin, Minehead and at the Lyn and Exmoor Museum, Lynton.

Northumberland National Park (398 sq. miles).—A region of hills and moorland, stretching from Hadrian's Roman Wall in the south to the Cheviot Hills on the Scottish Border. The area is rich in historic interest. There are information centres at Byrness, Ingram and Once Brewed and an information van tours the Park.

Brecon Beacons National Park (519 sq. miles).—The most recent National Park, established in 1957, is centred on " The Beacons " with its three peaks: Corn Du, Cribyn and Pen y Fan, rising to nearly 3,000 feet. Bounded in the east by the Black Mountains in Monmouthshire, its western boundary rests on the Black Mountain in Carmarthenshire. The Usk valley, Llangorse Lake, Brecon Cathedral, Carreg Cennen Castle and Llanthony Abbey are all within the Park. There are information centres at Brecon, Abergavenny, Llandovery, a mountain centre near Libanus, and a van tours the Park.

AREAS OF OUTSTANDING BEAUTY

Generally these are smaller in extent than the National Parks. No special arrangements for their administration are laid down and there is no special provision for the development of facilities for open-air recreation. The 27 areas so far designated are:—

Anglesey (83 sq. miles).—Except for breaks around the urban areas and in the vicinity of Wylfa, the designated area extends along the entire coastline with its many isolated stretches. The rugged cliffs, sandy bays, small coves and miles of soft dunes are famed for their beauty, as also are the Menai Straits, separating the island from the mainland.

Cannock Chase (26 sq. miles).—This is an area of high heathland in Staffordshire, relieved by varied scenery in which parklands adjoin farms, woodlands and pleasant villages. Deer continue to roam over the Chase.

Chichester Harbour (29 sq. miles).—Well known for its small boating and sailing facilities, the area extends from Hayling Island in the west to Appledram in the east and contains the whole of Thorney Island.

Chilterns (309 sq. miles).—The well-known chalk downlands from Goring in South Oxfordshire northeastwards through Buckinghamshire, Hertfordshire and Bedfordshire to Dunstable and Luton, including the outlying group of hills beyond Luton. Contains several National Trust properties and Whipsnade Zoo.

Cornwall (360 sq. miles).—Comprising a number of separate areas including Bodmin Moor and some of the finest and best-known coastal scenery in Britain. Most of the Land's End peninsula; the

coast between St. Michaels Mount and St. Austell with Falmouth omitted; the Fowey Estuary and Rame Head are all included: in north Cornwall most of the coast to Bedruthan Steps, north of Newquay, and between Perranporth and Godrevy Towans.

Cotswolds (582 sq. miles).—Contains the great limestone escarpment overlooking the Vales of Gloucester and Evesham. The remainder is high undulating country and narrow wooded valleys traversed by shallow rapid streams. Noted for its beautiful villages.

Dedham Vale (22 sq. miles).—This, the smallest area so far designated, is the flat land of water meadows with hedges and woodland where John Constable (1776–1837) painted during most of his life. Flatford Mill, Willy Lott's Cottage and the church of Stoke-by-Nayland still stand.

East Devon (103 sq. miles).—The area comprises the fine stretch of coastline between Orcombe Rocks, near Exmouth, and the Dorset area near Lyme Regis, with Sidmouth, Beer and Seaton omitted. Inland Gittisham Hill, East Hill and Woodbury and Aylebeare Commons are all included.

North Devon (66 sq. miles).—Comprising three sections of fine coastline—the whole of the Hartland peninsula; from Bideford Bar to the western limits of Ilfracombe, and from east of Ilfracombe to the boundary of the Exmoor National Park. Clovelly, Braunton Burrows, Woolacombe and Combe Martin are all included.

South Devon (128 sq. miles).—It includes the magnificent coast between Bolt Head and Bolt Tail, a National Trust property; Salcombe, Slapton Sands and Dartmouth, and the four estuaries and valleys of the Yealm, Erme, Avon and Dart.

Dorset (400 sq. miles).—Takes in the whole of the coastline between Lyme Regis and Poole, with the Isle of Portland and Weymouth omitted, and stretches inland to include the Purbeck Hills and the downs, heaths and wooded valleys of the Hardy country.

Forest of Bowland (310 sq. miles).—A fine tract of high open moorland running westward from near Settle and Bolton by Bowland in the Pennines, to Caton and Scorton in Central Lancashire. A small outlying area east of the River Ribble includes Pendle Hill and Pendleton Moor.

Gower (73 sq. miles).—Partly in the county of Glamorgan and partly in Swansea, South Wales, the area is known for its beautiful coastline, its rocky limestone cliffs, sandy bays and coves and for its wooded ravines stretching inland.

East Hampshire (151 sq. miles).—The area stretches from the outskirts of Winchester to the Hampshire/Sussex border at a distance of about 10 miles inland from the south coast.

South Hampshire Coast (30 sq. miles).—14 miles of coastline on the northern shores of the Solent, between Hurst Castle and Calshot Castle, southeast of Fawley, with the central part of the area extending inland up the Beaulieu River for about six miles, including a beautiful part of the New Forest. Along much of the coast woods of oak and Scots pine stretch down to the water's edge, while at the western end are some attractive salt marshes.

Kent Downs (326 sq. miles).—Running from the Surrey border near Westerham (its boundary adjoining that of the Surrey Hills area), about 60 miles to the coast near Dover and Folkestone, with a coastal outlier at South Foreland and a narrow strip

of the old sea cliff escarpment west of Hythe overlooking Romney Marsh. Pleasant pastoral scenery, picturesque villages, ancient churches and castles, with the Downs rising to 600 feet.

Lleyn (60 sq. miles).—An isolated peninsula in North Wales of unique character, still largely unspoilt by the hand of man.

Malvern Hills (40 sq. miles).—The area embodies the whole range of the Malvern Hills in the counties of Gloucester, Hereford and Worcester. Such well-known features as the Worcestershire Beacon, North Hill, the Herefordshire Beacon, and Midsummer Hill, a National Trust property, are within the area.

Norfolk Coast (174 sq. miles).—With coastal scenery ranging from salt marsh and mudflats, sand-dunes and shingle ridges to sea cliffs, this area includes six miles of the south-east coast of the Wash, an almost continuous coastal strip three to five miles in depth from Hunstanton to Bacton, with a further small strip between Sea Palling and Winterton-on-Sea. The area, which is rich in wild-life, also includes part of the Sandringham Estate.

Northumberland Coast (50 sq. miles).—Low cliffs and rocky headlands with active fishing villages comprise this area which stretches from just south of Berwick to Amble. It includes Holy Island, with the oldest monastic ruins in the country; the Farne Islands, and the great castles of Bamburgh, Dunstanburgh and Warkworth.

Quantock Hills (38 sq. miles).—The main feature of this area in Somerset is the range of red sandstone hills rising to a height of 1,260 feet at Will's Neck above Crow Combe.

Shropshire Hills (300 sq. miles).—This area includes the fine landscape around Church Stretton, with Caer Caradoc, the Long Mynd, the Stiperstones, and the long ridge of Wenlock Edge from which it extends north-east to the Wrekin and the Ercall.

Solway Coast (41 sq. miles).—A stretch of beautiful coastline from above Maryport to the estuaries of the Rivers Eden and Esk (with Silloth omitted) backed by the Solway Plain and noted for its historic and scientific interests.

Suffolk Coast and Heaths (151 sq. miles).—Takes in 38 miles of coastline and parts of the Stour and Orwell estuaries, while the Deben, Alde and Blyth flow through it. With heath, woodland, marsh and beaches, the scenery is attractively varied and the area important to ornithologists.

Surrey Hills (160 sq. miles).—The Hog's Back and the ridge of the North Downs from Guildford to Titsey in the east are within this area, as are Leith Hill, Hindhead Common, the Devil's Punch Bowl; the well-known villages of Abinger, Shere, Hambledon and Chiddingfold; Box Hill and Frensham Ponds.

Sussex Downs (379 sq. miles).—The area includes the chalk escarpment of the South Downs from Beachy Head to the West Sussex/Hampshire border, with such well-known features as Firle Beacon and Chanctonbury Ring, and stretches down to the coast between Eastbourne and Seaford. In the west the boundary adjoins the East Hampshire and Surrey Hills areas.

Isle of Wight (73 sq. miles).—A number of separate areas comprising unspoiled stretches of coastline, the Yar Valley, the high downland behind Ventnor and the fine chalk downland ridge east of Newport to Culver Cliff and Foreland.

BRITISH ISLES

SHETLAND IS.
Lerwick

ORKNEY IS.
Kirkwall
PENTLAND FIRTH

Stornoway

MORAY FIRTH

Inverness

HEBRIDES

SCOTLAND
Aberdeen

Perth Dundee

Oban
Stirling
FIRTH OF FORTH

Glasgow Edinburgh
Ayr
FIRTH OF CLYDE

*NORTH
SEA*

Newcastle
Carlisle

**NORTHERN
IRELAND** Belfast

SOLWAY FIRTH

ENGLAND

York

ISLE OF MAN
IRISH SEA
Bradford Leeds Hull

**REPUBLIC OF
IRELAND**

Liverpool Manchester
Sheffield
Dublin Stoke
ANGLESEY Nottingham
THE WASH

Leicester
Birmingham Coventry Norwich
Cambridge

WALES
Stratford

Oxford

Swansea
Cardiff Bristol
BRISTOL CHANNEL
LONDON
Canterbury
Winchester
Southampton Portsmouth Calais
Exeter
ISLE OF WIGHT
Plymouth

ATLANTIC

OCEAN

Cork

ENGLISH CHANNEL

SCILLY IS

0 50 100 MILES

CHANNEL IS.

FRANCE

THE KINGDOM OF ENGLAND

Position and Extent.—The Kingdom of England occupies the southern portion of the island of Great Britain and lies between 55° 46′ and 49° 57′ 30″ N. latitude (from the mouth of the Tweed to the Lizard), and between 1° 46′ E. and 5° 43′ W. (from Lowestoft to Land's End). England is bounded on the north by the summit of the Cheviot Hills, which form a natural boundary with the Kingdom of Scotland; on the south by the English Channel; on the east by the Straits of Dover (Pas de Calais) and the North Sea; and on the West by the Atlantic Ocean, Wales and the Irish Sea. It has a total area of 50,333 sq. miles (land, 50,053; inland water 280) and a population (1971 Census, preliminary) of 45,870,062.

Relief.—There is a natural orographic division into the hilly districts of the north, west and south-west, and the undulating downs and low-lying plains of the east and south-east. In the extreme north the *Cheviot Hills* run from east to west, culminating in the Cheviot, 2,676 feet above mean sea level. Divided from the Cheviots by the Tyne Gap is the *Pennine Chain*, running N. by W. to S. by E., with its highest point in Cross Fell, 2,930 feet above mean sea level. West of the Pennines are the *Cumbrian Mountains*, which contain in *Scafell Pike* (3,210 feet) the highest land in England, and east of the Pennines are the *Yorkshire Moors*, their highest point being Urra Moor (1,489 feet). South of the Pennines are the *Peak of Derbyshire* (2,088 feet) and *Dartmoor* (High Willhays, 2,039 feet). In the western county of Shropshire are the isolated Wrekin (1,335 feet), Longmynd (1,696 feet), and Brown Clee (1,792 feet); in Herefordshire the Black Mountain (2,310 feet), in Worcestershire the Malvern Hills (1,395 feet), in Monmouthshire (now usually grouped with Wales) the Sugar Loaf (1,955 feet) and Coity (1,905 feet), and the Cotswold Hills of Gloucestershire contain Cleeve Cloud (about 1,100 feet).

Hydrography.—The *Thames* is the longest and most important river of England, with a total length of 210 miles from its source in the Cotswold Hills to its outflow into the North Sea, and is navigable by ocean-going steamers to London Bridge. The Thames is tidal to Teddington (69 miles from its mouth) and forms county boundaries almost throughout its course; on its banks are situated London, the capital of the British Commonwealth; Windsor Castle, the home of the Sovereign, Eton College, the first of the public schools, and Oxford, the oldest university in the kingdom. The *Severn* is the longest river in Great Britain, rising in the north-eastern slopes of Plinlimmon (Wales) and entering England in Shropshire, with a total length of 220 miles from its source to its outflow into the Bristol Channel, where it receives on the left the Bristol Avon, and on the right the Wye, its other tributaries being the Vyrnwy, Tern, Stour, Teme and Upper (or Warwickshire) Avon. The Severn is tidal below Gloucester, and a high bore or tidal wave sometimes reverses the flow as high as Tewkesbury (13½ miles above Gloucester). The scenery of the greater part of the river is very picturesque and beautiful, and the Severn is a noted salmon river, some of its tributaries being famous for trout. Navigation is assisted by the Gloucester and Berkeley Ship Canal (16⅜ miles), which admits vessels of 350 tons to Gloucester. The *Severn Tunnel*, begun in 1873 and completed in 1886 (at a cost of £2,000,000) after many difficulties from flooding, is 4 miles 628 yards in length of which 2¼ miles are under the river). A road bridge over the Severn estuary, between Haysgate, Mon., and Almondsbury, Glos., with a centre span of 3,240 ft. was opened by Her Majesty the Queen on September 8, 1966. Of the remaining English rivers those flowing into the North Sea are the Tyne, Wear, Tees, Ouse and Trent from the Pennine Range, the Great Ouse (160 miles) from the Central Plain, and the Orwell and Stour from the hills of East Anglia. Flowing into the English Channel are the Sussex Ouse from the Weald, the Itchen from the Hampshire Hills, and the Axe, Teign, Dart, Tamar and Exe from the Devonian Hills; and flowing into the Irish Sea are the Mersey, Ribble and Eden from the western slopes of the Pennines and the Derwent from the Cumbrian Mountains. The *English Lakes* are noteworthy rather for their picturesque scenery and poetic associations than for their size. These lie mainly in Cumberland, but partly in Westmorland and Lancashire, the largest being Windermere (10 miles long), Ullswater and Derwentwater.

Islands.—The *Isle of Wight* is separated from Hampshire by the Solent; total area 147 sq. miles, population (1971 Census, prelim.) 109,284. The climate is mild and healthy, and many watering places have grown up during the last century. Capital, Newport, at the head of the estuary of the Medina, Cowes (at the mouth) being the chief port; other centres are Ryde, Sandown, Shanklin, Ventnor, Freshwater, Yarmouth, Totland Bay, Seaview and Bembridge. The *Scilly Islands*, 25 miles from Land's End, consist of about 40 islands, with a total area of about 4,000 acres, only St. Mary's, Tresco, St. Martin's, St. Agnes and Bryher being inhabited (population, 1971, 2,428). The capital is Hugh Town, in St. Mary's. The climate is unusually mild, and vegetation luxuriant, semi-tropical plants flourishing in the open. *Lundy* (=Island) 11 miles N.W. of Hartland Point, Devon, is about 2 miles long and about ½ mile broad (average), with a total area of about 1,050 acres (mainly picturesque), and a population of about 20; it became the property of the National Trust in 1969 and has 3 lighthouses (one disused).

Climate.—The *mean annual air temperature* reduced to sea-level varies from 52° F. at Penzance and the Scilly Islands to 48° F. near Berwick-on-Tweed. In January the south and west are warmer than the east, the mean temperature reduced to sea-level being less than 40° F. over the eastern half of the country. In July the warmest districts are more definitely in the south and inland, the range being from 63° F. around London to less than 59° F. in the extreme north. The decrease of mean temperature with height is about 1° F. per 300 ft. The coldest month of the year is January and the warmest July. Sea temperature reaches its maximum rather later than air temperature. The average annual *rainfall* decreases from west to east, owing to the preponderance of south-west winds, and also increases with altitude. The annual average, 1916–1950, varies from about 20 in. in the neighbourhood of the Thames Estuary and locally in Cambridgeshire to more than 100 in. over the mountains of the Lake District. Rather more rain falls in the summer half-year in parts of the east, but in the west much more falls in the winter half-year. The months of least rain are March to June and the wettest months October to January. The mean annual number of hours of bright *sunshine* varies from 1,750 hours along the south-east coast to less than 1,300 hours in the neighbourhood of the Pennine range. June is the sunniest month, followed by May, July and August in that order.

x +

EARLY INHABITANTS

Prehistoric Man.—Palæolithic and Neolithic remains are abundantly found throughout England. The Neolithic period is held to have merged into the Bronze Age about 2000 to 1500 B.C., and a date between these years has been given to *Stonehenge* (10 miles N. of Salisbury, Wiltshire) which consists of two circles of menhirs (the largest monolith being 22½ feet in height). The village of *Avebury* and its surroundings were scheduled in 1937, and in 1943 about 1,000 acres of Avebury were purchased by the National Trust, thus preserving the Circle of megalithic monuments, the Avenue, Silbury Hill, etc., relics of Stone Age culture of 1900–1800 B.C., which make this one of the most important archæological sites in Europe. The *Devil's Arrows*, near Boroughbridge, Yorkshire, are regarded as the finest remaining megalithic monoliths in northern Europe; the tallest arrow is 30 ft. 6 in. high and its greatest circumference is 16 ft. In the latter part of the Bronze Age the *Goidels*, a people of Celtic race, and in the Iron Age other Celtic races of *Brythons* and *Belgae*, invaded the country and brought with them Celtic civilization and dialects, place names in England bearing witness to the spread of the invasion over the whole kingdom.

The Roman Conquest.—Julius Cæsar raided Britain in 55 B.C. and 54 B.C. The Emperor Claudius, nearly 100 years later (A.D. 42), dispatched Aulus Plautius, with a well-equipped force of 40,000 all arms, and himself followed with reinforcements in the same year.

The British leader from A.D. 48–51 was *Caratacus* (Caractacus), who was finally captured and sent to Rome. By A.D. 70 the conquest of South Britain was completed a great revolt under *Boadicea*, Queen of the Iceni, being crushed in A.D. 61. In A.D. 122, the Emperor Hadrian visited Britain and built a continuous rampart, since known as *Hadrian's Wall*, from Wallsend to Bowness (Tyne to Solway). The work was entrusted by the Emperor Hadrian to Aulus Platorius Nepos, legate of Britain from 122 to 126, and it is now regarded as "the greatest and most impressive relic of the Roman frontier system in Europe."

The Romans administered Britain as a Province under a Governor, with a well-defined system of local government, each Roman municipality ruling itself and the surrounding territory. Colchester, Lincoln, York, Gloucester and St. Albans stand on the sites of five Roman municipalities, while London was the centre of the road system and the seat of the financial officials of the Province of Britain. Well-preserved Roman towns have been uncovered at (or near) *Silchester* (Calleva Atrebatum), 10 miles south of Reading, *Wroxeter* (Viroconium), near Shrewsbury, and *St. Albans* (Verulamium) in Hertfordshire.

Four main groups of roads radiated from London, and a fifth (the Fosse) ran obliquely from Ermine Street (at Lincoln), through Leicester, Cirencester and Bath to Exeter. Of the four groups radiating from London one ran S.E. to Canterbury and the coast of Kent, a second to Silchester and thence to parts of Western Britain and South Wales, a third (now known as *Watling Street*) ran through Verulamium to Chester, with various branches, and the fourth reached Colchester, Lincoln, York and the eastern counties.

Christianity reached the Roman province of Britain from Gaul in the 3rd century (or possibly earlier), *Alban*, "the protomartyr of Britain,"
being put to death as a Christian during the persecution of Diocletian (June 22, 303), at his native town Verulamium. The Bishops of Londinium, Eboracum (York), and Lindum (Lincoln) attended the Council of Arles in 314.

The Roman garrison of Britain was much harassed in the 4th century by Saxon pirates, who invaded the eastern areas. A system of coast defence was organized from the Wash to Southampton Water, with forts at Brancaster, Burgh Castle (Yarmouth), Walton (Felixstowe), Bradwell, Reculver, Richborough, Dover, Stutfall, Pevensey and Porchester (Portsmouth). About A.D. 350 incursions in the north of Irish (Scoti) and Picts became most formidable, and towards the end of the 4th century many troops were removed from Britain for service in other parts of the Roman Empire. Early in the 5th century Gaul was taken from the Romans by Teutonic invaders and Britain was cut off from Rome. The last Roman garrison was withdrawn from Britain in A.D. 442 and the S.E. portion was conquered by the Saxons.

The Latin-speaking Celts of England were replaced by their heathen and Teutonic conquerors, to the submergence of the Christian religion and the loss of Latin speech. According to legend, the British King *Vortigern* called in the Saxons to defend him against the Picts, the Saxon chieftains being *Hengist* and *Horsa*, who landed at Ebbsfleet, Kent, and established themselves in the Isle of Thanet. Bede, a Northumbrian monk, author of the Ecclesiastical History at the opening of the 8th century, described these settlers as Jutes, and there are traces of differences in Kentish customs from those of other Anglo-Saxon kingdoms.

Anglo-Saxons and Normans.—What happened in Britain during the 150 years which elapsed between the final break with Rome and the coming of St. Augustine is shrouded in the deepest mystery. The Jutes, the Saxons and the Angles (whose gods Twi, Woden, Thunor and Frigg are commemorated in "Tuesday, Wednesday, Thursday and Friday") were converted to Christianity by a mission under Augustine (dispatched by Pope Gregory in 597), which established Archbishoprics at Canterbury and York, and England appears to have been again converted by the end of the 7th century. In the 8th century Offa, King of Mercia, is stated to have built a wall and rampart, afterwards known as *Offa's Dike*, from the mouth of the Dee to that of the Wye, as a protection against the Welsh.

The greatest of the English kingdoms was *Wessex*, with its capital at Winchester, and the greatest of the Wessex kings was *Alfred the Great* (871–899), who resisted the incursions of the Northmen (Danes) and fixed a limit to their advance by the Treaty of Wedmore (878). In the 10th century the Kings of Wessex recovered the whole of England from the Danes, but subsequent rulers were unable to resist the invaders, and England paid tribute (*Danegelt*) for many years, and was ruled by Danish Kings from 1016 to 1042, when Edward the Confessor was recalled from exile. In 1066 Harold (brother-in-law of Edward and son of Earl Godwin of Wessex) was chosen King of England, but after defeating (at Stamford Bridge, Yorkshire, Sept. 25) an invading army under Harald Hadraada, King of Norway (aided by the outlawed Earl Tostig, of Northumbria, younger son of Earl Godwin), he was himself defeated at the *Battle of Hastings* on Oct. 14, 1066, and the Norman Conquest secured the throne of England for Duke William of Normandy.

AREA AND POPULATION OF ENGLISH COUNTIES

County or Shire and Administrative Headquarters	Acreage 1967	Population of Counties, 1971 Census (prelim.)		Rateable Value, April, 1970 (c) £	Average Rates, 1970–71 p
		Administrative (a)	Geographical (b)		
Bedfordshire (Bedford)............	305,089	302,315	463,493	15,003,100	182
Berkshire (Reading)...............	463,830	501,434	633,457	23,539,900	167
Buckinghamshire (Aylesbury)	477,750	586,211	586,211	34,575,700	160
Cambridgeshire and Isle of Ely (Cambridge).......................	531,555	302,507	302,507	13,057,600	181
Cheshire (Chester).................	649,682	1,105,496	1,542,624	48,100,700	181
Cornwall (Truro).................	880,290	379,892	379,892	12,954,400	163
Cumberland (The Courts, Carlisle)...	973,143	220,512	292,009	7,891,400	178
Derbyshire (Matlock).............	638,300	664,991	884,339	23,923,000	163
Devonshire (The Castle, Exeter)......	1,658,288	452,445	896,245	15,937,600	147
Dorset (Dorchester)...............	625,761	361,213	361,213	16,046,100	173
Durham (Durham)................	649,502	813,454	1,408,103	25,314,200	172
Essex (Chelmsford)...............	907,855	1,191,238	1,353,564	55,183,300	181
Gloucestershire (Gloucester).......	805,669	554,117	1,069,454	21,162,000	177
Hampshire (The Castle, Winchester)..	962,159	996,381	1,561,605	43,812,300	157
Herefordshire (Hereford)..........	539,121	138,425	138,425	4,906,400	172
Hertfordshire (Hertford)..........	403,798	922,188	922,188	57,281,000	168
Huntingdonshire and Peterborough (Huntingdon)...................	310,864	202,337	202,337	7,990,500	196
Kent (Maidstone).................	921,689	1,362,873	1,396,030	57,259,700	175
Lancashire (Preston)..............	1,201,798	2,505,299	5,106,123	88,923,300	174
Leicestershire (Grey Friars, Leicester)..	533,545	487,664	771,213	19,214,000	173
Lincolnshire:—					
Holland (Boston)..............	267,850	105,643	105,643	3,387,800	174
Kesteven (Sleaford)............	461,082	158,008	232,215	4,925,800	167
Lindsey (Lincoln)..............	975,099	374,841	470,526	17,664,000	166
Greater London (County Hall, S.E.1)	394,487	7,379,014	7,379,014	673,855,500	166
Norfolk (Martineau Lane, Norwich)..	1,314,363	444,587	616,427	14,462,600	155
Northamptonshire (Northampton)....	584,998	341,235	467,843	13,446,900	177
Northumberland (Newcastle on Tyne)	1,292,031	503,961	794,975	17,311,100	179
Nottinghamshire (West Bridgford)...	539,297	674,882	974,640	25,643,800	151
Oxfordshire (Oxford)..............	479,186	272,250	380,814	10,213,800	172
Rutland (Catmose, Oakham)........	97,273	27,463	27,463	961,100	142
Shropshire (Shrewsbury)..........	862,488	336,934	336,934	12,686,200	168
Somerset (Taunton)..............	1,032,059	597,429	681,974	22,027,600	170
Staffordshire (Stafford)...........	740,404	735,948	1,856,890	26,181,400	177
Suffolk:—					
East Suffolk (Ipswich)...........	557,356	257,710	380,524	8,850,900	171
West Suffolk (Bury St. Edmunds)..	390,918	164,201	164,201	5,289,600	178
Surrey (Kingston on Thames)........	415,877	999,588	999,588	57,493,600	168
Sussex:—					
East Sussex (Lewes)..............	527,168	441,567	750,312	23,860,200	163
West Sussex (Chichester)..........	405,352	491,020	491,020	28,555,700	153
Warwickshire (Warwick)..........	623,674	624,626	2,079,799	25,407,000	177
Westmorland (Kendal).............	504,917	72,724	72,724	2,680,600	161
Wight, Isle of (Newport, I. of W.)...	94,141	109,284	109,284	4,307,800	168
Wiltshire (Trowbridge)............	860,104	486,048	486,048	19,504,600	169
Worcestershire (Worcester).........	449,936	455,772	692,605	18,333,100	182
Yorkshire:—					
East Riding (Beverley)...........	750,362	257,093	542,565	8,702,700	146
North Riding (Northallerton)......	1,361,795	328,986	724,463	10,666,500	167
West Riding (Wakefield).........	1,791,036	1,792,020	3,780,539	54,207,300	163

(a) Administrative Counties, excluding County Boroughs; (b) Geographical Counties, including County Boroughs; (c) includes value of property occupied by the Crown for public purposes upon which contributions in lieu of rates are paid.

Lords Lieutenant of Counties.—The actual words used in the Letters Patent relative to these appointments are " Her Majesty's Lieutenant of and in the County of ... " and this is the official title whether the individual appointed be a Peer or a Commoner. In documents of the highest formality the proper term is therefore " Her Majesty's Lieutenant." In less formal and informal documents and colloquially, the style " Lord Lieutenant " has been applied to H.M. Lieutenants, Peers and Commoners alike, for a great many years. The duties of the Lord Lieutenant are to advise the Lord Chancellor as to the appointment of magistrates to the county bench, to appoint Deputy Lieutenants and to raise the militia, if need be, in time of riot or invasion. The Lord Lieutenant is usually a peer or a baronet and a large landowner and is often appointed *custos rotulorum* (keeper of the records).

ENGLISH COUNTIES AND SHIRES
LORDS LIEUTENANT, HIGH SHERIFFS AND CHAIRMEN OF COUNTY COUNCILS

County or Shire	Lord Lieutenant	★High Sheriff, 1971-72	Chairman of C.C.
(1) Bedford	Maj. Simon Whitbread.	B. S. Porter, T.D.	L. G. Bowles.
(2) Berks	Maj. the Hon. D. J. Smith, C.B.E.	M. G. T. Webster.	R. H. C. Seymour.
(3) Bucks	Maj. J. D. Young.	Maj. L. S. Marler, O.B.E., T.D.	Sir Aubrey Ward.
(4) Cambridge and Isle of Ely	Col. G. T. Hurrell, O.B.E.	Col. D. R. B. Kaye, D.S.O.	T. H. Ellingham, O.B.E.
(5) Cheshire	The Viscount Leverhulme, T.D.	C. T. Ockleston, T.D.	H. J. S. Dewes, C.B.E., T.D.
(6) Cornwall	Col. Sir John C. Pole, Bt., D.S.O., T.D.	Brig. C. Edward-Collins.	K. G. Foster, C.B.E.
(7) Cumberland	J. C. Wade, O.B.E.	W. S. Trimble.	J. Westoll.
(8) Derby	Col. Sir Ian Walker-Okeover, Bt., D.S.O., T.D.	G. Kenning, D.F.C., T.D.	J. W. Trippett.
(9) Devon	The Lord Roborough.	J. H. Cornish-Bowden.	Col. J. E. Palmer, T.D.
(10) Dorset	Col. J. W. Weld, O.B.E., T.D.	Maj. N. D. Martin.	Lt.-Col. G. W. Mansell, C.B.E.
(11) Durham	The Lord Barnard, T.D.	R. S. Pease.	J. W. Clark, B.E.M.
(12) Essex	Col. Sir John Ruggles-Brise, Bt., C.B., O.B.E., T.D.	A. J. V. Arthur, M.B.E.	Mrs. F. L. Coker.
(13) Gloucester	The Duke of Beaufort, K.G., P.C., G.C.V.O.	Maj. G. T. St. J. Sanders, T.D.	Maj. P. D. Birchall.
(14) Hampshire	The Lord Ashburton, K.G., K.C.V.O.	Lt.-Col. F. W. McClenaghan.	Brig. Sir Richard Calthorpe, Bt., C.B.E.
(15) Isle of Wight			Maj. S. C. Selwyn, M.B.E., E.R.D.
(16) Hereford	Col. J. F. Maclean.	N. D. O. Capper.	W. D. Porter.
(17) Hertford	Maj.-Gen. Sir George Burns, K.C.V.O., C.B., D.S.O., O.B.E., M.C.	Lt.-Col. J. C. Thomson, M.B.E., T.D.	Mrs. I. D. Paterson.
(18) Huntingdon and Peterborough	The Lord Hemingford.	R. M. Maris.	J. R. Horrell, T.D.
(19) Kent	The Lord Cornwallis, K.C.V.O., K.B.E., M.C.	Col. Sir Derek Greenaway, Bt., T.D.	J. A. Hill, T.D.
(20) Lancashire	The Lord Clitheroe, P.C.	S. P. E. C. W. Towneley.	H. Lumby, C.B.E.
(21) Leicester	Col. R. A. St. G. Martin, O.B.E.	A. S. Clowes.	Col. P. H. Lloyd, C.B.E., T.D.
Lincoln:			
(22) Lindsey			T. W. Scholey.
(23) Kesteven	The Earl of Ancaster, K.C.V.O., T.D.	Maj. R. C. Bellamy, T.D.	J. H. Lewis.
(24) Holland			H. E. Chappell.
(25) Greater London	Fd.-Marshal Sir Gerald Templer, K.G., G.C.B., G.C.M.G., K.B.E., D.S.O.	W. W. Harris, O.B.E.	R. Mitchell.
(26) Norfolk	Col. Sir Edmund Bacon, Bt., K.G., K.B.E., T.D.	E. D. Mackintosh, C.B.E.	W. J. Hayden.
(27) Northampton	Lt.-Col. J. Chandos-Pole, O.B.E.	Capt. J. L. Lowther.	Mrs. D. P. Oxenham.
(28) Northumberland	The Duke of Northumberland, K.G., T.D., F.R.S.	Hon. P. J. W. Fairfax.	The Visct. Ridley, T.D.
(29) Nottingham	Rear-Adm. R. St. V. Sherbrooke, V.C., C.B., D.S.O.	Lt.-Cdr. Sir Michael Nall, Bt.	Mrs. E. A. Yates.
(30) Oxford	Col. J. Thomson, T.D.	Maj.-Gen. Sir Randle Feilden, K.C.V.O., C.B., C.B.E.	Viscountess Parker.
(31) Rutland	Col. T. C. S. Haywood, O.B.E.	J. G. C. Gore-Brown.	The Earl of Gainsborough.
(32) Salop	Lt.-Col. A. Heywood-Lonsdale, C.B.E., M.C.	J. S. E. Rocke.	Sir Leonard Dyer, Bt.
(33) Somerset	Col. C. T. Mitford-Slade.	H. W. F. Hoskyns, M.B.E.	G. C. Wyndham.
(34) Stafford	A. Bryan.	R. S. A. Hardy.	F. J. Oxford.
(35) Suffolk, E.	Cdr. the Earl of Stradbroke, R.N. (ret.)	Sir Joshua Rowley, Bt.	Hon. C. B. A. Bernard, C.B.E.
(36) Suffolk, W.			Sir Joshua Rowley, Bt.
(37) Surrey	The Earl of Munster, P.C., K.B.E.	P. S. Henman.	J. H. S. Eve.
(38) Sussex, E.	The Duke of Norfolk, K.G., P.C., G.C.V.O., G.B.E.	J. R. Greenwood.	A. B. Haworth-Booth.
(39) Sussex, W.			Sir Peter Mursell, M.B.E.
(40) Warwick	C. M. T. Smyth-Ryland.	Capt. Sir William Dugdale, Bt., M.C.	M. H. Warriner, M.B.E.
(41) Westmorland	Lt.-Cdr. P. N. Wilson, O.B.E., D.S.C., R.N.V.R.	J. A. Cropper.	P. G. Thomson, C.B.E.
(42) Wilts	The Lord Margadale, T.D.	Maj. the Hon. J. I. Morrison, T.D.	Sir Henry Langton, D.S.O., D.F.C.
(43) Worcester	The Viscount Cobham, K.G., P.C., G.C.M.G., T.D.	H. B. Huntington-Whiteley.	Sir Michael Higgs.
(44) Yorks.—E.R.	The Earl of Halifax.	Brig. R. Heathcoat-Amory, M.C.	The Earl of Halifax.
(45) Yorks.—N.R.	The Marquess of Normanby, M.B.E.	Maj. W. Warde-Aldam (Hallamshire).	J. T. Fletcher, C.B.E.
(46) Yorks.—W.R.	Brig. K. Hargreaves, C.B.E., T.D.		Maj. T. H. Ives, C.B.E.

★ High Sheriffs are nominated by the Queen on November 12 and come into office after Hilary Term.

NOTE.—The office of Chairman of Quarter Sessions was abolished by the Courts Act, 1971, s. 44, effective from Jan. 1. 1971. Jurisdiction of courts of quarter session passed to The Crown Court on that date.

ENGLISH COUNTIES AND SHIRES

CLERKS OF COUNTY COUNCILS, COUNTY TREASURERS, CHIEF CONSTABLES AND M.O.H.

Clerk of the Council	County Treasurer	Chief Constable‡	Medical Officer
(1) G. O. Brewis.	R. E. Brooks.	A. Armstrong.	M. C. Macleod, M.D.
(2) E. R. Davies.	M. C. Beasley.	(Thames Valley Constabulary)	D. E. Cullington.
(3) R. E. Millard.	J. R. Worboys.	(Thames Valley Constabulary)	J. J. A. Reid, T.D., M.D.
(4) W. L. Hann.	M. T. Aves.	F. Drayton-Porter.	P. A. Tyser, M.D.
(5) J. K. Boynton, M.C.	R. H. A. Chisholm, C.B.E.	H. Watson, C.B.E., Q.P.M.	B. G. Gretton-Watson.
(6) A. L. Dennis.	K. Hyde.	Lt.-Col. R. B. Greenwood, C.B.E.	H. Binysh, M.D.
(7) T. J. R. Whitfield.	S. Litchfield.	W. T. Cavey, Q.P.M.	J. L. Leiper, M.B.E., T.D.
(8) H. Crossley.	H. F. Full.	W. Stansfield, M.C.	A. H. Snaith.
(9) H. G. Godsall.	O. A. Sanders.	Lt.-Col. R. B. Greenwood, C.B.E.	J. Lyons.
(10) K. A. Abel.	T. J. J. Emmings.	A. Hambleton, O.B.E., M.C., Q.P.M.	G. F. Wilson. M.D.
(11) J. T. Brockbank.	J. B. Cadigan.	A. G. Puckering, Q.P.M.	S. Ludkin, M.D.
(12) J. S. Mills, M.C.	J. R. Green.	J. C. Nightingale, C.B.E., B.E.M. Q.P.M.	J. A. C. Franklin.
(13) D. G. Rogers.	J. V. Miller.	E. P. B. White, O.B.E., Q.P.M.	A. Withnell, M.D.
(14) A. H. M. Smyth.	B. Dufton.	} Sir Douglas Osmond, C.B.E., Q.P.M.	I. A. MacDougall, O.B.E.
(15) L. H. Baines.	A. W. White.		} R. K. Machell.
(16) F. D. V. Cant.	A. B. Turner.	(West Mercia Authority).	P. J. C. Walker.
(17) F. P. Boyce.	J. Alexander.	R. N. Buxton, B.E.M., Q.P.M.	G. W. Knight, M.D.
(18) E. P. Smith.	E. N. Leafe.	F. Drayton-Porter.	G. Nisbet.
(19) J. E. Greenwood, M.C., T.D.	J. L. Hampshire.	Sir Dawnay Lemon, C.B.E., Q.P.M.	A. Elliott, M.D.
(20) Sir Charles McCall, M.B.E., T.D.	J. Conway.	W. J. H. Palfrey, C.B.E.	C. H. T. Wade, M.D.
(21) J. A. Chatterton.	J. S. Blackburn.	J. A. Taylor, C.B.E., Q.P.M.	A. R. Buchan, M.D.
(22) W. E. Lane.	B. Fieldhouse.		C. D. Cormac.
(23) R. A. Pearson.	G. R. Prentice.	} G. W. R. Terry.	E. W. G. Birch, D.F.M.
(24) G. E. Edmondson-Jones.	J. Mitchell.		J. Fielding, M.D.
(25) A. W. Petersen, C.B., M.V.O.	W. L. Abernethy.	(Metropolitan Police Area).	†A. B. Stewart, M.D.
(26) R. A. Beckett.	B. Taylor, M.C.	F. P. C. Garland, C.V.O.	A. G. Scott.
(27) O. M. Jones, M.C.	H. G. Lloyd.	J. A. H. Gott, O.B.E., G.M., Q.P.M.	W. J. McQuillan.
(28) C. W. Hurley, O.B.E., T.D.	W. H. Foakes.	C. H. Cooksley.	J. B. Tilley, O.B.E., M.D.
(29) A. R. Davis.	W. H. Lake.	R. S. Fletcher, Q.P.M.	H. L. Lockett.
(30) G. G. Burkitt.	W. H. P. Davison.	(Thames Valley Constabulary)	M. J. Pleydell, M.C., M.D.
(31) A. Bond, O.B.E.	I. Evans.	J. A. Taylor, C.B.E., Q.P.M.	R. A. Matthews.
(32) W. N. P. Jones.	L. Copplestone.	(West Mercia Authority)	P. C. Moore.
(33) E. S. Rickards.	W. Hollinrake.	K. W. L. Steele, O.B.E.	A. P. Jones.
(34) T. H. Evans, C.B.E.	E. H. Bugg.	A. M. Rees, O.B.E., Q.P.M.	G. Ramage, M.D.
(35) C. W. Smith.	F. Wroe.	} A. Burns, D.S.O., Q.P.M.	{ S. T. G. Gray.
(36) A. F. Skinner, O.B.E.	E. T. Knott.		{ D. A. McCracken, M.D.
(37) W. W. Ruff.	B. J. Gooby.	P. J. Matthews, Q.P.M.	J. Drummond, V.R.D.
(38) J. Atkinson.	T. Abell.	} T. C. Williams, C.B.E., Q.P.M.	{ J. A. G. Watson.
(39) G. C. Godber, C.B.E.	C. W. Mallinson.		{ T. McL. Galloway, M.D.
(40) D. G. Fuller.	J. K. B. Howell.	R. B. Matthews, C.B.E., Q.P.M.	G. H. Taylor, M.D.
(41) K. S. Himsworth, C.B.E.	L. Farnham.	W. T. Cavey, Q.P.M.	H. P. Ferrer.
(42) R. P. Harries.	R. L. W. Moon.	G. R. Glendinning, O.B.E.	C. D. L. Lycett, M.D.
(43) W. R. Scurfield.	T. H. Bradley.	(West Mercia Authority)	J. D. Willins.
(44) R. A. Whitley.	N. Hewitt.		{ W. Ferguson.
(45) R. A. Wotherspoon.	K. R. Hounsome.	} H. H. Salisbury.	{ J. T. A. George, M.D.
(46) P. J. Butcher.	E. A. Lund.	R. Gregory, Q.P.M.	R.W. Elliott, M.D.

The office of Clerk of the Peace was abolished by the Courts Act, 1971, effective from Jan. 1, 1972.

† Medical Adviser to the Greater London Council.

‡ *Thames Valley Constabulary*—D. Houldsworth (*Chief Constable*); *West Mercia Authority*—Sir John Willison, O.B.E., Q.P.M. (*Chief Constable*).

GREATER LONDON COUNCIL

The Greater London Council and 32 London Borough Councils were constituted under the London Government Act, 1963. They replaced, on April 1, 1965, the London County Council, the Middlesex County Council, the County Borough Councils of Croydon, East Ham and West Ham, 28 metropolitan borough, 39 non-county borough and 15 urban district councils. The boundaries and constitution of the Corporation of the City of London were not affected.

Under the Act, Greater London became for the first time a clearly defined local government area with a population of 7,379,014 (1971 Census preliminary) and an area of 610 square miles, including, in addition to the former counties of London and the greater part of Middlesex, parts of Metropolitan Essex, Kent, Surrey and Hertfordshire.

The Greater London Council consists of 100 councillors and 16 aldermen. Elections are held every third year. For the first three elections in April 1964, 1967, and 1970, the electoral areas were the 32 London Boroughs, each returning two, three or four councillors according to the size of the electorate. Aldermen, who are chosen by the councillors, hold office for six years, half their number retiring every third year. The Chairman, Vice-Chairman and Deputy Chairman are elected annually by the councillors and aldermen. The political head of the administration is the Leader of the Council, elected by the majority party. The Council meets fortnightly at 2.30 p.m. on Tuesdays except in holiday periods. Of the 13 standing and 2 special committees, one meets fortnightly, 10 monthly and the others as required.

Greater London Council
(Elected April 13, 1970)

Chairman (1971–72), R. Mitchell.
Vice-Chairman (1971–72), G. F. Everitt.
Deputy-Chairman (1971–72), H. G. Lamborn.
Leader of the Council, Sir Desmond Plummer, T.D.
Leader of the Opposition, Sir Reginald Goodwin, C.B.E.

†Abbott, F. L. (C.).............*Alderman till 1976*
*Andrews, J. W. (Lab.).........*Greenwich*
*Aplin, G. W. (C.).............*Croydon*
*Bains, L. A. (C.).............*Haringey*
Banks, A. L. (Lab.)...........*Hammersmith*
Bastin, R. B. (Lab.)..........*Lewisham*
*Bell, E. P. (Lab.)............*Newham*
Bell, W. (C.).................*Kensington and Chelsea*
Bendall, V. W. H. (C.)........*Croydon*
*Bennett, F.E., C.B.E. (C.)....*Alderman till 1976*
*Berney, A. A. (C.)............*Brent*
*Black, P. B. (C.).............*Barnet*
Bolton, S. C. (C.)............*Merton*
Bondy, L. (Lab.)..............*Islington*
Bonham, Mrs. I. (Lab.)........*Hammersmith*
*Boyce, S., O.B.E. (Lab.)......*Newham*
*Bramall, E. A. (Lab.).........*Tower Hamlets*
*Branagan, J. P. (Lab.)........*Tower Hamlets*
*Brew, R. M. (C.)..............*Alderman till 1973*
*Brown, B. J. (C.).............*Hillingdon*
*Bryant, R. C. Beecher- (C.)...*Bromley*
Carr, E. G., B.E.M. (Lab.)....*Alderman till 1973*
Chalkley, D. (Lab.)...........*Lewisham*
Chaplin, Mrs. I. (Lab.).......*Hackney*
*Chorley, A. F. J., M.B.E. (Lab.)..*Alderman till 1976*
Clack, W. S. (C.).............*Harrow*
*Cockell, Mrs. A. Forbes- (C.)..*Brent*
*Cockell, S. Forbes- (C.)......*Kensington and Chelsea*
Collins, R. (Lab.)............*Camden*
Cox, J. R. W. (C.)............*Hillingdon*
*Crane, R. J. (Lab.)...........*Barking*
Crofton, Sir Malby, Bt. (C.)..*Lambeth*
*Cutler, H. W., O.B.E. (C.)....*Harrow*
*Dartmouth, Countess of (C.)...*Richmond upon Thames*
*Denington, Mrs. E. J., C.B.E. (Lab.)................*Islington*
Dimson, Mrs. G. F. (Lab.).....*Wandsworth*
Dobson, J. C. (C.)............*Ealing*
*Edwards, A. F. G. (Lab.)......*Newham*
Edwards, A. G. (Lab.).........*Hammersmith*
*Everitt, G. F. (C.)...........*Sutton*
*Farmer, T. (C.)...............*Alderman till 1973*
Farrow, M. (C.)...............*Ealing*
*Fielding, D.M. (C.)...........*Bexley*
Francis, F. (Lab.)............*Southwark*
*Freeman, L., O.B.E. (C.)......*Alderman till 1976*

†Gaffney, M. P. (C.)..........*Cities of London and Westminster*
*Gardener, G. Chase (C.).......*Hounslow*
Gardner, Mrs. T. (C.).........*Havering*
Garside, Mrs. M. E. (Lab.)....*Greenwich*
Geddes, Hon. Mrs. J. (C.).....*Lambeth*
*Gilbey, A. R. D., C.B.E. (C.)..*Haringey*
*Gluckstein, Sir Louis, G.B.E., T.D., Q.C. (C.)...............*Alderman till 1973*
*Goodwin, Sir Reginald, C.B.E. (Lab.) ....*Southwark*
Grant, A. (Lab.)..............*Lewisham*
Grieves, Mrs. A. Ll. (Lab.)...*Lambeth*
Hammond, J. (C.)..............*Redbridge*
*Hardy, A. (C.)................*Brent*
Harrington, I. (Lab.).........*Alderman till 1973*
*Harris, D. (C.)...............*Bromley*
Henry, J. C. (Lab.)...........*Lewisham*
†Hichisson, A. J. (C.)........*Alderman till 1976*
*Hillman, E. S. (Lab.)........*Hackney*
*Hinds, Rev. Canon H.W. (Lab.)..*Southwark*
Hudson, T. C. (C.)............*Enfield*
*Jardine, Lt.-Col. A. (C.).....*Hounslow*
Jenkins, Mrs. M. (Lab.).......*Wandsworth*
*Jessel, T. F. H., M.P. (C.) ..*Richmond upon Thames*
Kazantzis, A. (Lab.)..........*Camden*
*Lamborn, H. G. (Lab.)........*Southwark*
*Langton, V. R. M. (C.).......*Bexley*
*Leach, A. H. C. (C.)..........*Sutton*
*Livingston, W. W. (C.).......*Lambeth*
*Malynn, M. P. R. (C.)........*Haringey*
*Marks, R. (C.)................*Barnet*
*Mason, J. (C.)................*Bexley*
*Middleton, Mrs. P. A. (Lab.)..*Greenwich*
*Mitchell, R. (C.).............*Redbridge*
*Mitcheson, T. B. (C.).........*Enfield*
*Montefiore, H. H. Sebag- (C.)..*Cities of London and Westminster*
*Morgan, Miss G. E. (C.).......*Croydon*
*Mote, H. T. (C.)..............*Harrow*
*Munday, N. S. (C.)...........*Waltham Forest*
O'Connor, L. P. (Lab.)........*Camden*
*Partridge, B. Brook- (C.).....*Havering*
Patterson, Dr. M. (C.)........*Ealing*
*Peacock, A. S. (C.)...........*Barnet*
*Pitt. Dr. D. T. (Lab.)........*Hackney*
*Plummer, Sir Desmond, T.D. (C.)..*Cities of London and Westminster*
Ponsonby, T. (Lab.)...........*Alderman till 1976*
Pratt, C. H. E. (C.)..........*Bromley*
Prichard, Sir Norman (Lab.)...*Wandsworth*
*Ripley, S. W. L. (C.).........*Kingston upon Thames*
Roberts, Miss S. (C.).........*Havering*

*Rowlandson, Sir Graham, M.B.E.
(C.)......................*Enfield*
Samuels, J. S. (*Lab.*)..........*Wandsworth*
Scorgie, M. (*C.*)..............*Cities of London and Westminster*
*Scott, Miss J. L. (*C.*)..........*Barnet*
*Seaton, G. J. D. (*C.*)...........*Kingston upon Thames*
*Smith, F. W. (*C.*)...........*Alderman till 1973*
*Stephenson, M. (*C.*)..........*Alderman till 1973*
*Stewart, S. J. (*C.*)..............*Croydon*
*Taylor, Mrs. R. G. N., O.B.E.
(C.)......................*Brent*
*Thorne, N. G., T.D. (*C.*).......*Redbridge*
†Townsend, Mrs. L. M. (*C.*).....*Alderman till 1976*
Tremlett, G. (*C.*)..............*Hillingdon*
*Udal, J. (*C.*).................*Alderman till 1973*
*Usher, D. C. L., C.B.E. (*C.*).....*Hounslow*

†Vaughan, G. F., M.P. (*C.*).......*Alderman till 1976*
*Vigars, R. L. (*C.*)..............*Kensington and Chelsea*
*Walker, F. W. (*C.*)...........*Merton*
Ward, J. B. (*Lab.*)............*Barking*
Watts, W. (*Lab.*)............*Alderman till 1973*
*Webb, G. A. (*C.*)............*Waltham Forest*
*Wicks, A. E. (*Lab.*)...........*Islington*
Williams, D. (*C.*)............*Waltham Forest*
Young, Sir George, Bt. (*C.*)....*Ealing*
Party Representation: *Conservative,* 76; *Labour,* 40.

*Denotes members of last Council for same division, or Aldermen retaining office. † Denotes members of last Council for different divisions, or Councillors who were Aldermen in last Council, or Aldermen who were Councillors.

CHIEF OFFICERS OF THE GREATER LONDON COUNCIL

Director-General and Clerk to the Council, A. W. Peterson, C.B., M.V.O.............£15,000
Controller of Services, A. Morrison......£10,600
Director of Secretariat, J. N. Dennis.......£7,700
Architect to the Council (and Superintending Architect of Metropolitan Buildings), Sir Roger Walters, K.B.E................................£11,500
Director of Establishments, D. S. Mitchell.. £10,600
Joint Directors of Planning and Transportation, P. F. Stott (£11,500); B. J. Collins, C.B.E.... £10,600
Traffic Commissioner and Director of Development, D. Dennington.....................£10,600
Solicitor and Parliamentary Officer, H. F. W. Wilson £10,600
Treasurer to the Council, W. L. Abernethy.£11,500

Chief Officer of the London Fire Brigade, J. Milner, Q.F.S.M. (*with residence*)...................£9,000
Director of Housing, C. J. A. Whitehouse, O.B.E. £10,600
Director of Mechanical and Electrical Services, C. A. Belcher...............................£9,300
Director of Public Health Engineering, S. H. Dainty £9,300
Director of Supplies, S. Swallow...........£9,300
Medical Adviser, A. B. Stewart, M.D........£7,700
Valuer and Estates Surveyor, K. H. Blessley, M.B.E. £10,600
Chief Officer of the Parks Department, J. C. Kennedy £7,300
Education Officer, Inner London Education Authority, Sir William Houghton...............£12,100

G.L.C. Services

The services provided by the G.L.C. include planning, roads, traffic management and control, fire and ambulance services, refuse disposal, housing, parks, licensing, main drainage and sewage disposal. For many of these services it shares responsibility with the London Borough Councils and the City Corporation.

Education.—The local education authority for an area corresponding with the area of the twelve inner London boroughs and the City of London is the Inner London Education Authority, a special committee of the G.L.C. consisting of the members of the Council elected for the inner London boroughs together with a representative of each inner London Borough Council and of the Common Council. The Council charges to the rating authorities in the Inner London Education Area the expenditure of the I.L.E.A., the amount being determined by the Authority. This unique arrangement preserves the continuity of the service which has developed since 1870 as a unity without regard to local boundary divisions.

The total number of pupils on the rolls of the Authority's nursery, primary and secondary schools (including special schools for handicapped children) is 425,716. There are 29 nursery, 745 county (including 3 at Children's homes), 354 voluntary and 97 special schools, staffed by the equivalent of 21,844 full-time teachers. Vocational instruction, cultural studies and recreational activities for persons over compulsory school age are arranged at the various establishments for further education. The Authority maintains 22 technical and commercial colleges and 5 schools of art and makes grants to 13 polytechnics and other institutions. There are 3 general and commercial colleges and 13 colleges for further education. Non-vocational classes are offered at 32 evening and literary institutes, 4 recreational institutes and 41 youth centres, including 2 drama centres. Nine colleges for the training of teachers are also managed by the Authority. The 20 outer London Borough Councils are the education authorities for their Boroughs.

Housing.—The Council shares with the London Borough Councils responsibility for housing in London and it accommodates 15,000 families a year, more than 5,000 of them in expanding towns many miles from London. The G.L.C. has more than 209,000 homes, 44,000 homes having been transferred to the London Borough Councils on April 1, 1971.

Planning and Transportation.—The Council as planning authority for Greater London as a whole has prepared a strategic development plan which lays down basic planning policies and principles for the whole area, including proposals for a future road system. This Greater London Development Plan has been submitted to the Secretary of State for the Environment for approval, and is the subject of a public enquiry. Since the submission of the plan, the Transport (London) Act, 1969, has given the G.L.C. responsibility for preparing more detailed transport plans and, through a London Transport Executive appointed by the Council, for London Transport policies and finance. It is thus now able to consider and co-ordinate priorities for investment in all forms of transport in London.

Within the framework of the Development plan, the London Borough Councils and the City Corporation will prepare their own detailed local development plans. Town planning control of private development proposals is mainly the concern of the London Boroughs but the G.L.C. has some responsibilities in this field. As planner and developer the Council is involved in many major schemes. Notable examples are the Thamesmead project and the Covent Garden area.

The Council is responsible for the construction,

improvement and maintenance of metropolitan roads. As the traffic authority for all roads in Greater London it prepares or approves schemes for one-way working, traffic signals, clearways, waiting and loading restrictions and speed limits and makes the orders which enforce them. It maintains the Thames tunnels, the Woolwich Free Ferry, and maintains all but four of the Thames bridges (London, Tower, Blackfriars and Southwark, which are maintained by the Corporation of London).

The Transport (London) Act, 1969, gives the Council the primary responsibility for overall transport planning, including the fullest possible integration of all forms of public transport, traffic measures and the development of the most important roads, in close association with land use planning.

Expanding towns.—An important aspect of the Council's policy is the decentralization of population and industry to towns expanding under agreements with the G.L.C. made under the Town Development Act, 1952. The Council has such agreements with 30 towns and is negotiating with several other towns which wish to expand.

Parks.—The Council maintains some 5,530 acres of parks and open spaces. The London Borough Councils and the City Corporation between them provide a further 33,000 acres. Over 1,500 open-air entertainments are arranged in G.L.C. parks each summer and almost all games and sports are provided for. At Crystal Palace, in addition to the Council's 70 acre park is the Crystal Palace National Sports Centre, owned by the Council and managed by the Central Council of Physical Recreation.

Other features of the G.L.C.'s administration include its responsibility for the Royal Festival Hall, Queen Elizabeth Hall and Purcell Room and the Hayward Gallery; the maintenance of the Iveagh Bequest, Ken Wood, several other buildings of historic interest and two museums. The Greater London Record Office and Library house official records and other manuscripts, books, maps, drawings and photographs relating to London and are open to the public for reference purposes. The Research and Intelligence unit is concerned with information and research on any matters concerning Greater London. The results of its work will be available to government departments, local authorities and the public.

Main drainage and sewage purification.—The Council provides the main drainage service for about seven million people in the 625 square miles of the Greater London sewerage area, dealing with some 570,000,000 gallons of sewage a day. The sewage is carried by gravity and by pumping through over 680 miles of main sewers to 15 sewage treatment works, including the three largest in Western Europe (the Beckton (Newham), Crossness (Bexley) and Mogden (Hounslow) Works), where it is treated and the residual sludge removed for disposal.

Refuse disposal.—The Council has been responsible since April 1, 1965, for the disposal of refuse throughout Greater London—some 2,750,000 tons of refuse being handled each year. It operates twenty-nine transfer stations (where refuse is transferred into bulk carrying vehicles, barges or railway wagons); fourteen incinerators and a pulverization plant. Refuse is used for infilling at thirty land reclamation sites. The Boroughs continue to be responsible for refuse collection.

Land drainage, pollution and flood prevention.—The Council is the land drainage authority for an area of 416 square miles, known as the London Excluded Area. Within this area the Council is responsible for improvement, maintenance and prevention of flooding on all main metropolitan watercourses; for other metropolitan watercourses the Council shares the responsibility with the London Borough Councils concerned. Pollution prevention is exercised over all watercourses in the area, except the tidal Thames itself and the tidal stretches of its tributaries. The Council is responsible for flood prevention along 120 miles of river bank of the Thames and its tidal tributaries.

Licensing.—The Council licenses triennially 8,000 premises for the storage of petroleum and annually 1,875 premises, including 65 theatres and 259 cinemas, where entertainment is regularly provided. In addition, it issues some 1,300 occasional entertainment licences each year. It is also responsible for the licensing and registration of motor vehicles and the licensing of drivers. Records are kept of 3,500,000 drivers and 2,500,000 vehicles. During the year 1969–70 1,200,000 driving licences and 2,000,000 vehicle licences were issued by the Council (a further 1,200,000 vehicle licences being issued at Greater London Post Offices). Revenue from these vehicle and driving licences, which was collected on behalf of the Ministry of Transport, amounted to £69,000,000.

Fire and Ambulance Services.—The Council runs both the fire and ambulance services for its whole area. *The London Ambulance Service.*—With a fleet of nearly 1,000 vehicles, based at 76 stations and manned by 2,500 operational and control staff, the London Ambulance Service has about a sixth of the total ambulance resources of England and Wales. Including help given by the hospital car service as agents, more than 3,000,000 patients are carried each year.

The London Fire Brigade set up on April 1, 1965, under the London Government Act, 1963, consists of the Brigades of the former counties of London and Middlesex (excluding the districts of Staines, Sunbury and Potters Bar), the former county boroughs of East Ham, West Ham and Croydon and of parts of Essex, Herts., Kent and Surrey. *Headquarters*, Albert Embankment, S.E.1.

The Brigade is organized in 3 Commands (Eastern, Northern and Southern) and 11 Divisions. It has 115 land and 2 river stations. Whole-time authorized establishment, 5,467. There are 548 land appliances and 2 fire boats in commission. Fire calls (estimated), 65,000 per annum.

Chief Officer, J. Milner, Q.F.S.M.

Deputy Chief Fire Officer, F. S. Mummery, C.B.E.

Assistant Chief Officers, J. K. H. Cunningham; O.B.E.; H. F. Chisnall; F. R. Trust, M.B.E.; R. S. Watts, M.B.E. (*Northern Command*); A. G. W. Sellwood, M.B.E. (*Eastern Command*); R. R. Lloyd, O.B.E. (*Southern Command*).

Finance.—The gross revenue expenditure of the G.L.C. in 1971–72 was estimated at over £265,000,000, and that of the I.L.E.A. £175,000,000, making a total of more than £440,000,000. Of this 50 per cent. (£221,000,000) will be met from rates, 36 per cent. (£157,000,000) from income from services, rents, etc., and the balance (£62,000,000) from Government grants. The amount raised by rates varies for different areas according to the services provided. Capital expenditure of the G.L.C. and the I.L.E.A., mainly met by borrowing, will amount to about £220,000,000. More than half of this will be used for housing and loans for house purchase.

THE CORPORATION OF LONDON

The City of London is the historic centre at the heart of London known as "the square mile" around which the vast metropolis has grown over the centuries. The City's population is 4,234 (1971 Census, preliminary). The civic government is carried on by the Corporation of London through the Court of Common Council, a body consisting of the Lord Mayor, 25 other Aldermen and 159 Common Councilmen. The legal title of the Corporation is "the Mayor and Commonalty and Citizens of the City of London."

The City is the financial and business centre of London and includes the head offices of the principal banks, insurance companies and mercantile houses, in addition to buildings ranging from the historic interest of the Roman Wall and the 15th century Guildhall, to the massive splendour of St. Paul's Cathedral and the architectural beauty of Wren's spires.

The City of London was described by Tacitus in A.D. 61 as " a busy emporium for trade and traders ". Under the Romans it became an important administrative centre and hub of the road system. Little is known of London in Saxon times when it formed part of the kingdom of the East Saxons. In 886 Alfred recovered London from the Danes and reconstituted it a burgh under his son-in-law. In 1066 the citizens submitted to William the Conqueror who in 1067 granted them a charter, which is still preserved, establishing them in the rights and privileges they had hitherto enjoyed. The mayoralty was established on the recognition of the corporate unity of the citizens by Prince John in 1191, the first Mayor being Henry Fitz Ailwyn, who filled the office for 21 years and was succeeded by Fitz Alan (1212–15). A new charter was granted by King John in 1215, directing the Mayor to be chosen annually, which has ever since been done, though in early times the same individual often held the office more than once. A familiar instance is that of "Whittington, thrice Lord Mayor of London" (in reality four times, A.D. 1397, 1398, 1406, 1419); and many modern cases have occurred. The earliest instance of the phrase " Lord Mayor " in English is in 1414. It is used more generally in the latter part of the 15th century and becomes invariable from 1535 onwards. At Michaelmas the Liverymen in Common Hall choose two Aldermen who have served the office of Sheriff for presentation to the Court of Aldermen, and one is chosen to be Lord Mayor for the ensuing mayoral year. The Lord Mayor is presented to the Lord Chief Justice at the Royal Courts of Justice on the second Saturday in November to make the final declaration of office, having been sworn in at Guildhall on the preceding day. The procession to the Royal Courts of Justice is popularly known as the *Lord Mayor's Show.*

Aldermen are mentioned in the 11th century and their office is of Saxon origin. They were elected annually between 1377 and 1394, when a charter of Richard II. directed them to be chosen for life. The *Common Council*, elected annually on December 17, was, at an early date, substituted for a popular assembly called the *Folkmote.* At first only two representatives were sent from each ward, but the number has since been greatly increased.

Sheriffs were Saxon officers; their predecessors were the *wic-reeves* and *portreeves* of London and Middlesex. At first they were officers of the Crown, and were named by the Barons of the Exchequer; but Henry I. (in 1132) gave the citizens permission to choose their own Sheriffs, and the annual election of Sheriffs became fully operative under King John's charter of 1199. The citizens lost this privilege, as far as the election of Sheriff of Middlesex is concerned, by the Local Government Act, 1888; but the Liverymen continue, as heretofore, to choose two Sheriffs of the City of London, who are appointed on Midsummer Day, and take office at Michaelmas.

Officers.—The Recorder was first appointed in 1298. The office of Chamberlain is an ancient one, the first contemporary record of which is 1276. The Town Clerk (or Common Clerk) is mentioned in 1274 and the Common Serjeant in 1291.

Activities.—The work is assigned to a number of committees which present reports to the Court of Common Council. These Committees are:— City Lands and Bridge House Estates, Coal, Corn and Rates Finance, Planning and Communications, Central Markets, Billingsgate and Leadenhall Markets, Spitalfields Market, Police, Port and City of London Health, Library (Library, Records, Art Gallery and Museum), City of London Education, Music (Guildhall School of Music and Drama), General Purposes, Establishment, Housing, Gresham (City side), Epping Forest and Open Spaces, West Ham Park, Policy and Parliamentary, Privileges, Welfare, Guildhall Reconstruction, Barbican, Central Criminal Court (Extension) and Licensing Planning.

The Honourable the *Irish Society,* which manages the Corporation's Estates in Ulster, consists of a Governor and 5 other Aldermen, the Recorder, and 19 Common Councilmen, of whom one is elected Deputy Governor.

The City's *Estate,* in the possession of which the Corporation of London differs from other municipalities, is managed by the City Lands and Bridge House Estates Committee, the Chairmanship of which carries with it the title of " Chief Commoner."

The Right Honourable the Lord Mayor 1970–1971*

Sir Peter Malden Studd, G.B.E., D.S.C., born 1916; Alderman of Cripplegate, 1960; Sheriff of London, 1967; Lord Mayor, 1970 .... £18,750
Private Secretary, Rear-Adm. P. N. Howes, C.B., D.S.C., R.N.(ret.).

The Aldermen

Aldermen.	Ward	Born.	C.C.	Ald.	Shff.	Lord Mayor
Sir Denys Lowson, Bt.	Bridge Without	1906	1940	1942	1939	1950
Sir Denis Henry Truscott, G.B.E., T.D.	Dowgate	1908	1938	1947	1951	1957
Sir Bernard Nathaniel Waley-Cohen, Bt.	Portsoken	1914	....	1949	1955	1960
Sir Ralph Edgar Perring, Bt.	Langbourn	1905	1948	1951	1958	1962
Sir James Miller, G.B.E., D.S.C.	Bishopsgate	1905	....	1957	1956	1964
Sir Robert (Ian) Bellinger, G.B.E., D.S.C.	Cheap	1910	1953	1958	1962	1966
Sir Gilbert (Samuel) Inglefield, G.B.E., T.D., D.S.C.	Aldersgate	1909	....	1959	1963	1967
Sir (Arnold) Charles Trinder, G.B.E., D.S.C.	Aldgate	1906	1951	1959	1964	1968

X*

Aldermen	Ward	Born.	C.C.	Ald.	Shff.	Lord Mayor
Lt.-Col. Sir Ian (Frank) Bowater, G.B.E., D.S.O., T.D.	Coleman Street	1904	....	1960	1965	1969
Sir Peter Malden Studd, G.B.E., D.Sc.	Cripplegate	1916	....	1960	1967	1970
All the above have passed the Civic Chair.						
Sir Edward Howard, Bt.	Cornhill	1915	1951	1963	1966	*19.71*
Lt.-Col. Godfrey Sturdy Incledon-Webber, T.D., D.S.C.	Farringdon Within	1904	....	1963	1968	....
The Lord Mais, O.B.E., E.R.D., T.D.	Walbrook	1911	....	1963	1969	....
Hugh Walter Kingwell Wontner, C.V.O.	Broad Street	1908	....	1963	1970	....
Alan Pearce Greenaway	Lime Street	1913	1952	1965	1962	..
Henry Murray Fox	Bread Street	1912	1962	1966	1971	....
George Boughen Graham, Q.C.	Queenhithe	1920	1960	1966	....	....
Lindsay Roberts Ring	Vintry	1914	1964	1968	1967	....
Lt.-Cdr. Robin Danvers Penrose Gillett, R.D.	Bassishaw	1925	1965	1969	....	....
Stanley Alfred Field	Candlewick	1913	....	1969	....	....
Gp. Capt. Hon. Peter Beckford Rutgers Vanneck, O.B.E., A.F.C., A.D.C.	Cordwainer	1922	....	1969	....	....
Kenneth Russell Cork	Tower	1913	1951	1970	....	....
Alan Seymour Lamboll	Castle Baynard	1923	1949	1970	....	....
Sir Charles Gundry Alexander, Bt	Bridge	1923	1969	1970	....	....
Michael Herbert Hinton	Billingsgate	1934	1970	1971	....	....
Peter Drury Gadsden	Farringdon Wt	1929	1969	1971	....	....

★The Lord Mayor for 1971-72 was elected on Michaelmas Day. *See* Events of the Year.

The Sheriffs 1971–1972

Alderman Henry Murray Fox (*see above*) and Neville Rayner (*see below*), *elected June 24; assumed office September 28, 1971.*

THE COMMON COUNCIL OF LONDON

Amies, T. H. C. (1961).........*Bridge*
Angell, O. D. (1964)............*Bishopsgate*
Artaud, H. F. J. (1963)........*Cornhill*
Arthur, B. G., C.B.E. (1954)....*Walbrook*
Baker, C. W. (1957).........*Cripplegate Wt.*
Ballard, K. A., M.C. (1969)......*Castle Baynard*
Balls, H. D. (1970).........*Cripplegate Wn.*
Barratt, *Deputy* T. E. C., C.B.E. (1944).............*Candlewick*
Batty, J. G. (1968).........*Portsoken*
Baylis, C. E. (1968).........*Tower*
Beck, R. T. (1963).............*Farringdon Wn.*
Beer, *Deputy* G. Allison- (1942) ..*Cordwainer*
Betty, Capt. F. A. K., O.B.E., V.R.D., R.N.R. (1967).........*Broad St.*
Blankley, W. H. R. (1946)......*Lime St.*
Bowen, I., C.M.G. (1971).........*Broad St.*
Brewer, H. G. (1970).........*Langbourn*
Brighton, A. G. (1966)...........*Portsoken*
Brookhouse, *Lt.-Col.* H., M.V.O. (1947)............*Dowgate*
Brooks, W. I. B. (1967)............*Cripplegate*
Bull, P. A. (1968)...........*Cheap*
Burrow, G. W. (1965)...........*Lime Street*
Burston, N. B. (1961)............*Portsoken*
Champness, P. H. (1966).........*Walbrook*
Charvet, R. C. L., R.D. (1970)....*Aldgate*
Chubb, S. J. (1966).........*Cripplegate Wn.*
Clack, D. R. (1967)..........*Bridge*
Clackson, *Deputy* D. L., M.B.E. (1951)............*Farrington Wt.*
Cleary, F. E., M.B.E. (1959)......*Coleman St.*
Clements, G. E. I. (1960)......*Farringdon Wt.*
Cohen, S. E., C.B.E. (1951)......*Farringdon Wt.*
Cole, A. C. (1964).............*Castle Baynard*
Collens, *Deputy* F. J., T.D. (1946) *Castle Baynard*
Collett, *Deputy* Sir Kingsley, C.B.E. (1945)................*Bridge.*
Cope, Dr. J. (1963)............*Farringdon Wt.*
Coulson, *Deputy* A. G. (1961)....*Broad St.*
Coward, C. R. (1966)...........*Cripplegate Wt.*
Cresswell, P. H. (1958)............*Aldgate*
Dean, H. R. (1958)...........*Cordwainer*
Deith, R. C. (1944).............*Farringdon Wn.*
Denny, A. M. (1971)...........*Billingsgate*

Dewhirst, W. (1971)..............*Cripplegate Wn.*
Donaldson, Lady (1966)...........*Farringdon Wt.*
Duckworth, *Deputy* H. (1960)....*Lime St.*
Duffett, E. G., T.D. (1966).......*Aldgate*
Dyer, C. F. W., E.R.D. (1966).....*Aldgate*
Dyter, P. J. (1959) ....*Queenhithe*
Ebbisham, The Lord, T.D. (1947)....*Candlewick*
Ercolani, V. A. (1968)...........*Broad St.*
Eskenzi, A. N. (1971)...........*Farringdon Wn.*
Evans, *Deputy* D. I., T.D. (1952)....*Vintry*
Ewin, E. T. Floyd-, M.V.O., O.B.E. (1963) ....*Castle Baynard*
Fairweather, C. H. F. (1958)....*Queenhithe*
Fell, *Deputy* C. A. (1947).........*Langbourn*
Fish, H. I. (1950)...............*Farringdon Wt.*
Fisher, D. G. (1958).............*Cornhill*
Fordham, W. E. (1966)............*Aldgate*
Frankenberg, J. (1964)...........*Portsoken*
Game, *Deputy* D. S. (1950)......*Farringdon Wt.*
Gapp, J. G. (1956)...............*Cheap*
Gardener, C. J. (1964)...........*Broad St.*
Gass, G. J. (1967)............*Coleman St.*
Gold, R. (1965)............*Castle Baynard*
Goodinge, A. W. (1966)..........*Aldersgate*
Gorman, *Deputy* R. W. (1956)....*Aldersgate*
Graham, J. (1969).............*Candlewick*
Hall, N. L., M.B.E. (1952)......*Farringdon Wt.*
Harding, N. H. (1970).........*Farringdon Wn.*
Harries, W. G. A. (1965)........*Langbourn*
Harris, *Deputy* W. H. Wylie (1957)*Farringdon Wn.*
Harrowing, *Deputy* T. C. (1940) . *Bishopsgate*
Hart, M. G. (1970)..............*Bridge*
Hatfield, A. F. R. (1968).........*Bishopsgate*
Hayman, L. C. R. (1954).........*Aldersgate*
Hayward, *Deputy* R. J., C.B.E. (1943)..........*Walbrook*
Hedderwick, R. A. R. (1968)....*Walbrook*
Henderson, J. S. (1962)...........*Cripplegate Wn.*
Hill, E. W. F., T.D. (1962)......*Tower*
Hoare, J. E. (1966)...........*Bishopsgate*
Horlock, H. W. S. (1969)......*Farringdon Wn.*
Hornby, Sir Antony (1971)......*Broad St.*
Hunt, W. G. G. (1962)...........*Cripplegate Wt.*
Jones, *Lt.-Col.* O. Campbell-, T.D. (1961)...................*Dowgate*

Keith, J. M., T.D. (1962) . . . . *Candlewick*
Lascelles, J. C., D.F.C. (1970) . . . . . *Billingsgate*
Last, A. W. (1948) . . . . *Bridge*
Lewis, *Deputy* C. F., C.B.E. (1936) . *Coleman St.*
Ley, A. H. (1964) . . . . *Bishopsgate*
Liss, H. (1965) . . . . *Aldersgate*
Longman, M. H. (1967) . . . . *Langbourn*
Lovely, *Deputy* P. T. (1949) . . . . . . *Tower*
Lowrie, W. E. (1952) . . . . *Farringdon Wn.*
Luckin, I. F. (1964) . . . . *Candlewick*
Luke, A. L. (1968) . . . . *Bishopsgate*
McAuley, C. (1957) . . . . *Bread St.*
Mills, A. P. (1969) . . . . *Bassishaw*
Mills, *Deputy* D. G. (1954) . . . . . . *Billingsgate*
Monkhouse, F. J. (1952) . . . . *Cheap*
Morgan, B. L., C.B.E. (1963) . . . . *Bishopsgate*
Mount, H. W. (1968) . . . . *Cornhill*
Murkin, C. H. (1969) . . . . *Vintry*
Oram, M. H., T.D. (1963) . . . . *Cordwainer*
Osborn, A. J. (1947) . . . . *Broad St.*
Park, J. W. (1966) . . . . *Tower*
Parker, *Deputy* E. A. (1952) . . . . . *Cripplegate Wt.*
Parkin, A. M. (1961) . . . . *Cheap*
Peacock, R. W. (1956) . . . . *Vintry*
Perkins, *Deputy* G. K. (1957) . . . . . *Aldgate*
Pike, *Deputy* H. T. (1946) . . . . *Cornhill*
Prince, *Deputy* L. B. (1950) . . . . . . *Bishopsgate*
Pritchard, F. S. (1961) . . . . *Walbrook*
Pryke, Sir David, Bt. (1960) . . . . . . *Queenhithe*
Quekett, Lt.-Col. D. A. F., E.R.D.
  (1965) . . . . *Cornhill*
Rawson, C. S. P. (1963) . . . . *Bread St.*
Rayleigh, R. (1966) . . . . *Portsoken*
Rayner, N. (1960) . . . . *Farringdon Wt.*
Reed, J. L., M.B.E. (1967) . . . . *Farringdon Wn.*
Renton, P. I. (1971) . . . . *Coleman St.*
Rodgers, C. (1969) . . . . *Farringdon Wt.*
Roney, E. R. (1965) . . . . *Bishopsgate*
Rowlandson, Sir Graham, M.B.E.
  (1961) . . . . *Coleman St.*

Rutherford, A. J. B., C.B.E. (1950) *Tower*
Samuels, *Deputy* W. (1950) . . . . . . *Portsoken*
Sheppard, S., O.B.E., (1957) . . . . . . *Billingsgate*
Shill, Lt.-Col. C. G. S. (1956) . . . *Castle Baynard*
Shillingford, R. G., M.B.E. (1961) . *Vintry*
Shindler, A. B. (1966) . . . . *Billingsgate*
Skilbeck, *Deputy* C. (1948) . . . . . . *Queenhithe*
Smith, F. S., T.D. (1958) . . . . *Cordwainer*
Smith, L. J. W. (1958) . . . . *Cripplegate Wt.*
Smith, *Deputy* Sir John Newson-,
  Bt. (1945) . . . . *Bassishaw*
Smith, P. A. Revell- (1959) . . . . . *Vintry*
Spurrier, H. J. (1971) . . . . *Dowgate*
Stanham, *Deputy* A. F. G. (1943) . . *Dowgate*
Steiner, F. N. (1962) . . . . *Bread St.*
Stevenson, J. L. (1970) . . . . *Coleman St.*
Stitcher, G. M. (1966) . . . . *Farringdon Wt.*
Stunt, F. F. (1967) . . . . *Farringdon Wn.*
Sudbury, Col. F. A., O.B.E., E.R.D.
  (1963) . . . . *Tower*
Sunderland, O. (1968) . . . . *Billingsgate*
Tallon, C. R. (1962) . . . . *Dowgate*
Theobald, G. P. (1968) . . . . *Queenhithe*
Titchener, H. B. (1966) . . . . *Cripplegate*
Traill, A. T. (1970) . . . . *Langbourn*
Tremellen, N. C. (1951) . . . . *Langbourn*
Trentman, G. D. (1941) . . . . *Bread St.*
Vine, G. M., C.B.E. (1955) . . . . *Farringdon Wt.*
Walker, *Deputy* S.R., C.B.E. (1937) *Bread Street*
Ward, Maj. B. M., M.V.O. (1963) *Bridge*
Wells, *Deputy* Maj. S. W., M.B.E.
  (1949) . . . . *Cripplegate Wn.*
Wharton, W. H. (1966) . . . . *Lime St.*
Wilkins, *Deputy* E. F., C.B.E. (1946) *Cheap*
Willard, R. H. (1970) . . . . *Bishopsgate*
Wilson, A. B. (1960) . . . . *Aldersgate*
Wilson, E. S. (1971) . . . . *Aldersgate*
Wingfield, E. H. (1943) . . . . *Cordwainer*
Wixley, G. R. A., O.B.E. (1964) . . . *Bassishaw*
Yates, J. T., M.B.E. (1959) . . . . *Cheap*
Young, *Deputy* D. S. (1939) . . . . . . *Farringdon Wn.*

Deputies.—In the preceding list each Common Councilman so described serves as *Deputy* to the Alderman of his Ward.

OFFICERS OF THE CITY OF LONDON

		Elect.
Recorder, His Hon. Sir Carl Douglas Aarvold, O.B.E., T.D.	£10,500	1964
Chamberlain, Charles Richard Whittington, M.C.	9,225	1964
Town Clerk, Edward Henry Nichols, T.D.	10,620	1954
Common Serjeant, John Mervyn Guthrie Griffith-Jones, M.C.	9,500	1964
Assistant Judge of the Mayor's and City of London Court, Col. G. Rogers, T.D.	8,000	1969
Commissioner of the City Police, J. Page, Q.P.M.	8,112	1971
Comptroller and City Solicitor, Sir Desmond Heap.	9,000	1947
Remembrancer, Geoffrey Arden Peacock.	7,863	1968
Secondary and Under Sheriff and High Bailiff of Southwark, R. M. Snagge, M.B.E., T.D.	3,150	1969
Medical Officer for the Port and City of London, W. G. Swann, M.D.,	8,358	1963
Coroner, D. M. Paul	920	1966
Clerk of the Peace, Leslie Boyd	1,000	1955
Surveyor, Robert Scott Walker	8,358	1954
Engineer, H. K. King, C.B.E.	8,358	1964
City Architect, E. G. Chandler	8,358	1961
Swordbearer, Brig. R. H. S. Popham, O.B.E.	2,949	1961
Common Cryer and Serjeant-at-Arms, Lt.-Col. St. J. C. Brooke-Johnson	2,364	1970

		Elect.
Marshal, Lt.-Col. P. M. Milo	2,460	1969
Head Master of City of London School, J. A. Boyes.	5,601	1964
Head Master of City of London Freemen's School, M. J. Kemp	3,905	1963
Head Mistress, City of London School for Girls, Miss G. M. Colton	3,970	1949
Director, Guildhall Museum, M. G. Hebditch.	3,798	1971
Principal, Guildhall School of Music and Drama, A. D. Percival	6,402	1965
Librarian and Curator and Director of the Art Gallery, W. G. Thompson.	6,234	1966
Deputy-Keeper of the Records, Miss B. R. Masters, F.S.A.	3,579	1970
Registrar of Mayor's and City of London Court and Clerk of the Seal, A. M. Myers.	5,750	1963
Deputy Town Clerk, S. J. Clayton.	6,579	1969
Deputy Comptroller and City Solicitor, S. F. Heather.	5,814	1968
Principal Clerk, Chamberlain's Dept., J. P. Griggs, M.C.	4,602	1971
Market Superintendents:—		
Central, D. J. Noakes.	4,119	1967
Billingsgate and Leadenhall, C. A. Wiard, M.B.E.	4,995	1956
Spitalfields, C. A. Lodemore.	4,119	1967
Supt. Engineer, Tower Bridge, H. H. Buckley.	4,332	1969

EXPENDITURE AND INCOME ON RATE ACCOUNTS, 1970-1971

The Rateable Value of the City on April 1, 1971, was £49,413,021; rate levied, 1971-72, 78p. On the POOR RATE ACCOUNT, expenditure under G.L.C. Precept, etc., was £19,171,968. Greater London Equalization Scheme, £3,536,630, and other other heads £194,876 (Credit). Exchequer Grant, £89,780.

Services	Expenditure (including Debt Charges)	Income (other than Exchequer Grants)	Exchequer Grants	Net Expenditure falling upon Rates
	£	£	£	£
GENERAL RATE—				
Library, Museum and Art Gallery.....	570,191	14,856	—	555,335
Local Health Authority Services......	60,295	9,459	1,371	49,465
Public Health (inc. Port Health Services)	1,386,392	104,778	129,400	1,152,214
Town and Country Planning.........	3,421,634	2,301,262	165,000	955,372
Highways and Bridges, Lighting, etc...	1,421,344	140,233	—	1,254,820
City Police..................	3,384,816	230,922	1,041,029	2,112,865
Administration of Justice.............	815,419	65,097	88,212	662,110
Housing...................	3,226,157	797,758	140,502	2,287,897
Spitalfields Market...............	452,985	365,428	—	87,557
Other Services..................	1,454,426	967,616	4,756	482,054
TOTAL.......	£16,193,659	£4,997,409	£1,596,561	£9,599,689

THE CITY GUILDS (LIVERY COMPANIES)

The Livery Companies of the City of London derive their name from the assumption by their members in the 14th century.

The order of precedence (according to 2nd Report of Municipal Corporations' Commissioners, 1837), omitting extinct companies, is given in parentheses after the name of each Company There are 84 Guilds in existence.

About 10,000 Liverymen of the Guilds are entitled to vote at elections in *Common Hall*.

MERCERS (1). *Hall*, Ironmonger Lane, E.C.2. *Livery*, 209.—*Clerk*, G. E. Logsdon, C.B.E., T.D.; *Master*, Lt.-Col. H. R. G. Howard.

GROCERS (2). *Hall*, Princes Street, E.C.2. *Livery*, 254.—*Clerk*, A. S. Cox; *Master*, A. D. W. Hunter.

DRAPERS (3). *Hall*, Throgmorton Street, E.C.2. *Livery*, 210.—*Clerk*, H. Farmar; *Master*, Maj-Gen. H. A. Borradaile, C.B., D.S.O.

FISHMONGERS (4). *Hall*, London Bridge, E.C.4. *Livery*, 285.—*Clerk*, Cdr. O. S. M. Bayley, R.N.; *Prime Warden*, Col. C. F. H. Gough, M.C., T.D.

GOLDSMITHS (5). *Hall*, Foster Lane, E.C.2. *Livery*, 240.—*Clerk*, W. A. Prideaux, M.C.; *Prime Warden*, The Viscount Amory, K.G., P.C., G.C.M.G.

SKINNERS (6 and 7). *Hall*, 8 Dowgate Hill, E.C.4. *Livery*, 297.—*Clerk*, M. H. Glover; *Master*, Hon. L. H. L. Cohen.

MERCHANT TAYLORS (6 and 7). *Hall*, 30 Threadneedle Street, E.C.2. *Livery*, 330.—*Clerk*, J. M. Woolley, M.B.E., T.D.; *Master*, H. Boggis-Rolfe, C.B., C.B.E.

HABERDASHERS (8). *Hall*, Staining Lane, E.C.2. *Livery*, 314.—*Clerk*, Cdr. W. R. Miller, R.N.; *Master*, G. T. Bentley.

SALTERS (9). *Livery*, 150.—*Clerk*, W. R. Nichols, T.D., 36 Portland Place, W.1.; *Master*, H. Smith.

IRONMONGERS (10). *Hall*, Shaftesbury Place, Aldersgate, E.C.1. *Livery*, 33.—*Clerk*, J. M. Adams Beck; *Master*, T. R. Twallin.

VINTNERS (11). *Hall*, Upper Thames Street, E.C.4. *Livery*, 326.—*Clerk*, Cdr. R. D. Ross, R.N.; *Master*, S. Dow.

CLOTHWORKERS (12). *Hall*, Dunster Court, Mincing Lane, E.C.3. *Livery*, 180.—*Clerk*, E. J. Reed; *Master*, G. C. Oliver.

The above are the Twelve "Great" London Companies in order of Civic precedence.

AIR PILOTS AND AIR NAVIGATORS, GUILD OF (81). *Grand Master*, H.R.H. the Prince Philip, Duke of Edinburgh, K.G.; *Clerk*, W. E. B. Griffiths, C.B.E., c/o Royal Aeronautical Society, Alitalia House, 251/9 Regent Street, W.1.; *Master*, A. P. W. Cane.

APOTHECARIES, SOCIETY OF (58). *Hall*, Black Friars Lane, E.C.4. *Livery*, 675.—*Clerk*, E. Busby, M.B.E.; *Master*, Sir John Richardson, Bt., M.V.O., M.D., F.R.C.P., F.R.C.S.

ARMOURERS AND BRASIERS (22). *Hall*, 81 Coleman Street, E.C.2. *Livery*, 120.—*Clerk*, Col. G. C. Chatfeild-Roberts, T.D.; *Master*, R. C. Pontifex.

BAKERS (19). *Hall*, Harp Lane, Lower Thames Street, E.C.3. *Livery*, 260.—*Clerk*, H. M. Collinson; *Master*, T. V. Liddle.

BARBERS (17). *Livery*, 160.—*Clerk*, N. L. Hall, M.B.E., 48 West Smithfield, E.C.1.; *Master*, W. T. Kenny.

BASKETMAKERS (52). *Livery*, 350.—*Clerk*, B. Stroulger, Battlebridge House, 87–95 Tooley Street, S.E.1.; *Prime Warden*, C. A. Rust.

BLACKSMITHS (40). *Livery*, 201.—*Clerk*, J. Green, 201 Bishopsgate, E.C.2.; *Prime Warden*, A. Truelove.

BOWYERS (38). *Livery*, 48.—*Clerk*, M. J. Smyth, Provincial House, 98–106 Cannon Street, E.C.4; *Master*, Col. N. Ireland-Smith, C.B.E. (1970-1972).

BREWERS (14). *Hall*, Aldermanbury Square, E.C.2. *Livery*, 32.—*Clerk*, R. C. Stanley-Baker; *Master*, R. D. Wise.

BRODERERS (48). *Livery*, 106.—*Clerk*, S. G. B. Underwood, 80 Bishopsgate, E.C.2; *Master*, A. Aldington.

BUTCHERS (24). *Hall*, Bartholomew Close, E.C.1. *Livery*, 387.—*Clerk*, W. M. Collins; *Master*, H. B. Swain.

CARMEN (77). *Livery*, 423.—*Clerk*, U. J. Burke, The Rectory, St. Mary-at-Hill, E.C.3; *Master*, Rev. W. H. Dormor.

CARPENTERS (26). *Hall*, Throgmorton Avenue, E.C.2. *Livery*, 150.—*Clerk*, Capt. G. B. Barstow, R.N.; *Master*, V. J. G. Stavridi.

CITY OF LONDON SOLICITORS (79). *Livery*, 450.—*Clerk*, K. S. G. Hinde, 27 Leadenhall Street, E.C.3.; *Master*, L. A. D. Martin.

CLOCKMAKERS (61). *Livery*, 248.—*Clerk*, R. C. Pennefather, M.B.E., 116 Cannon Street, E.C.4; *Master*, G. M. Vine, C.B.E.

COACHMAKERS (72). *Livery*, 356.—*Clerk*, R. J. D. Smith, 9 Lincoln's Inn Fields, W.C.2; *Master*, G. McGregor-Craig.

COOKS (35). *Livery*, 75.—*Clerk*, C. E. Messent, 83 Clarence Street, Kingston upon Thames; *Master*, J. H. Balls.

COOPERS (36). *Livery*, 230.—*Clerk*, R. R. Watson, 13 Devonshire Square, E.C.2; *Master*, D. G. Baker.

CORDWAINERS (27). *Livery*, 126.—*Clerk*, E. J. Mander, 7 New Square, Lincoln's Inn, W.C.2; *Master*, R. B. Skinner.

CURRIERS (29). *Livery*, 65.—*Clerk*, I. R. McNeil, 43 Church Road, Hove; *Master*, Sir Oliver Chesterton, M.C.

CUTLERS (18). *Hall*, 4 Warwick Lane, E.C.4. *Livery*, 95.—*Clerk*, G. H. Mitchell; *Master*, E. L. Northover, M.B.E.

DISTILLERS (69). *Livery*, 150.—*Clerk*, H. B. Dehn, Compter House, Wood Street, E.C.2; *Master*, W. R. Guillet.

DYERS (13). *Hall*, 10 Dowgate Hill, E.C.4. *Livery*, 110.—*Clerk*, D. R. B. Park; *Prime Warden*, Hon. S. R. Cawley.

FAN MAKERS (76). *Livery*, 163.—*Clerk*, E. J. H. Geffen, Africa House, 64–78 Kingsway, W.C.2; *Master*, W. E. Arnold.

FARMERS (80). *Office*, 15 Eastcheap, E.C.3. *Livery*, 245.—*Clerk*, O. Sunderland; *Master*, F. H. Garner.

FARRIERS (55). *Livery*, 288.—*Clerk*, M. J. Burke, Moor House, London Wall, E.C.2; *Master*, Sir Hugh Linstead, O.B.E.

FELTMAKERS (63). *Livery*, 350.—*Clerk*, E. J. P. Elliott, 53 Davies Street, Berkeley Square, W.1; *Master*, E. G. Embleton.

FLETCHERS (39). *Livery*, 69.—*Clerk*, F. N. Steiner, Compter House, 4–9 Wood Street, E.C.2; *Master*, J. H. Page, O.B.E.

FOUNDERS (33). *Hall*, 13 St. Swithin's Lane, E.C.4. *Livery*, 143.—*Clerk*, H. W. Wiley; *Master*, Capt. W. Gregson, C.B.E.

FRAMEWORK KNITTERS (64). *Livery*, 225.—*Clerk*, H. C. Weale, St. Saviour's School, New Kent Road, S.E.1; *Master*, R. P. Guild.

FRUITERERS (45). *Livery*, 220.—*Clerk*, D. L. Hohnen, 199 Piccadilly, W.1; *Master*, R. W. Manners.

FURNITURE MAKERS (83). *Livery*, 156.—*Clerk*, G. Benbow. c/o J. Ward & Co., Robertsbridge, Sussex; *Master*, J. Beresford, C.B.E.

GARDENERS (66). *Livery*, 215.—*Clerk*, J. G. Fleming, Saddlers Hall, Gutter Lane, E.C.2; *Master*, J. L. Stevenson.

GIRDLERS (23). *Hall*, Basinghall Avenue, E.C.2. *Livery*, 80.—*Clerk*, J. A. M. Rutherford; *Master*, B. J. Gardner.

GLASS-SELLERS (71). *Livery*, 160.—*Hon. Clerk*, H. K. S. Clark, 6 Eldon Street, E.C.2; *Master*, Lt.-Col. R. S. Williams-Thomas, D.S.O., T.D.

GLAZIERS (53). *Livery*, 250.—*Clerk*, R. C. Pennefather, M.B.E., 116 Cannon Street, E.C.4; *Master*, D. S. Pierson.

GLOVERS (62). *Livery*, 180.—*Clerk*, H. M. Collinson, Bakers Hall, Harp Lane, Lower Thames Street, E.C.3; *Master*, E. A. Copeland.

GOLD AND SILVER WYREDRAWERS (74). *Livery*, 296.—*Clerk*, P. H. Cresswell, 9 The Crescent, E.C.3; *Master*, A. G. Johnson.

GUNMAKERS (73). *Livery*, 84.—*Clerk*, F. B. Brandt, 12 Devonshire Square, E.C.3; *Master*, T. G. Austin.

HORNERS (54). *Livery*, 440.—*Clerk*, G. S. Wood, 1 College Hill, E.C.4.; *Master*, Sir James Miller, G.B.E., D.SC.

INNHOLDERS (32). *Hall*, College Street, Dowgate Hill, E.C.4. *Livery*, 107.—*Clerk*, J. H. Bentley, O.B.E.; *Master*, A. J. Evans, D.F.C.

JOINERS (41). *Livery*, 44.—*Clerk*, B. J. Turner, 14 Parkway, N.14; *Master*, D. S. Batfield.

LEATHERSELLERS (15). *Hall*, 15 St. Helens Place, E.C.3. *Livery*, 150.—*Clerk*, J. Hingtson; *Master*, L. A. Powell.

LORINERS (57). *Livery*, 268.—*Clerk*, D. B. Morris, Africa House, 64–78 Kingsway, W.C.2; *Master*, G. A. Davies.

MASONS (30). *Livery*, 92.—*Clerk*, H. J. Maddocks, 9 New Square, W.C.2; *Master*, A. F. Phillpotts.

MASTER MARINERS, HONOURABLE COMPANY OF (78). H.Q.S. *Wellington*, Temple Stairs, W.C.2 *Livery*, 300.—*Clerk*, D. H. W. Field; *Admiral*, H.R.H. the Prince Philip, Duke of Edinburgh, K.G.; *Master*, Cdre. A. Henney, O.B.E.

MUSICIANS (50). *Livery*, 220.—*Clerk*, W. R. I. Crewdson, 4 St. Paul's Churchyard, E.C.4; *Master*, Prof. Sir Jack Westrup, D.Mus., F.B.A.

NEEDLEMAKERS (65). *Livery*, 230.—*Clerk*, R. H. Lane, 3–4 Clements Inn, Strand, W.C.2; *Master*, P. F. Allday.

PAINTER STAINERS (28). *Hall*, 9 Little Trinity Lane, E.C.4. *Livery*, 300.—*Clerk*, A. H. Pangborn; *Master*, R. H. Willard.

PATTENMAKERS (70). *Livery*, 141.—*Clerk*, A. N. Eskenzi, 18 Bride Lane, E.C.4; *Master*, W. M. Pybus.

PAVIORS (56). *Livery*, 225.—*Clerk*, F. A. Barragan, 130 Mount Street, W.1; *Master*, Sir Frank Lord, K.B.E.

PEWTERERS (16). *Hall*, Oat Lane, E.C.2. *Livery*, 100.—*Clerk*, C. G. Grant; *Master*, D. H. Gaydon.

PLAISTERERS (46). *Livery*, 154.—*Clerk*, H. Mott, 73 Southampton Row, W.C.1; *Master*, W. J. Bell.

PLAYING CARD MAKERS (75). *Livery*, 150.—*Clerk*, K. King, 21A Northampton Square, E.C.1; *Master*, Col. J. Reading, M.B.E., E.R.D.

PLUMBERS (31). *Livery*, 240.—*Clerk*, A. J. Young, 10 Staple Inn, Holborn, W.C.1; *Master*, H. E. Baker.

POULTERS (34). *Livery*, 160.—*Clerk*, I. G. Williamson, 22 St. Andrew Street, E.C.4; *Master*, D. S. Game.

SADDLERS (25). *Hall*, Gutter Lane, Cheapside, E.C.2. *Livery*, 90.—*Clerk*, Maj. A. D. H. Jones, R.M.(ret.).; *Master*, J. O. Terry F.R.C.P.

SCIENTIFIC INSTRUMENT MAKERS (84). *Livery*, 149. —*Clerk*, H. Mott, 73 Southampton Row, W.C.1; *Master*, C. C. Hanrott.

SCRIVENERS (44). *Livery*, 124.—*Clerk*, H. S. S. Trotter, D.F.C., 2 Seaforth Place, S.W.1; *Master*, J. Jenkins.

SHIPWRIGHTS (59). *Livery*, 500.—*Hon. Clerk*, D. Walker, 14–20 St. Mary Axe, E.C.3; *Permanent Master*, H.R.H. the Prince Philip, Duke of Edinburgh, K.G.; *Prime Warden*, The Viscount Leathers.

SPECTACLEMAKERS (60). *Livery*, 200.—*Clerk*, C. J. Eldridge, Apothecaries' Hall, E.C.4; *Master*, O. R. M. Sebag-Montefiore.

STATIONERS AND NEWSPAPER MAKERS (47). *Hall*, Stationers' Hall, E.C.4. *Livery*, 380.—*Clerk*, G. St. P. Wells; *Master*, P. Unwin.

TALLOWCHANDLERS (21). *Hall*, 4 Dowgate Hill, E.C.4. *Livery*, 140.—*Clerk*, R. H. Monier-Williams; *Master*, His Hon. Cdr. L. K. A. Block, D.S.C.

TIN PLATE WORKERS (67). *Livery*, 181.—*Clerk*, H. B. Dehn, Compter House, Wood Street, E.C.2; *Master*, A. J. Balcombe, T.D.

TOBACCO PIPE MAKERS AND TOBACCO BLENDERS (82). *Livery*, 200.—*Clerk*, W. M. Wilson,

38 Finsbury Square, E.C.2; *Master*, F. Spellacy, B.E.M.

TURNERS (51). *Livery*, 160.—*Clerk*, A. T. Reed, Provincial House, 98–106 Cannon Street, E.C.4; *Master*, H. E. Senior.

TYLERS AND BRICKLAYERS (37). *Livery*, 95.—*Clerk*, J. C. Peck, 6 Bedford Row, W.C.1; *Master*, F. A. G. Rider.

UPHOLDERS (49). *Livery*, 193.—*Clerk*, U. J. Burke, 36 St. Andrew's Hill, E.C.4.; *Master*, F. W. Mosey.

WAXCHANDLERS (20). *Hall*, Gresham Street, E.C.2. *Livery*, 70.—*Clerk*, T. Wood; *Master*, H. T. Pike.

WEAVERS (42). *Livery*, 125.—*Clerk*, R. S. Ouvry, 53 Romney Street, S.W.1: *Upper Bailiff*, C. J. Maples.

WHEELWRIGHTS (68). *Livery*, 280.—*Clerk* (vacant), 15 Eastcheap, E.C.3; *Master*, D. T. Russell.

WOOLMEN (43). *Livery*, 117.—*Clerk*, P. P. D.

Harper, 3 Albany Court Yard, W.1; *Master*, F. Brame.

PARISH CLERKS (*No livery*) (*Members*, 65).—*Clerk*, R. H. Adams, T.D., 108 Dulwich Village, S.E.21; *Master*, R. G. Ellen.

WATERMEN AND LIGHTERMEN (*No livery*).—*Hall*, 18 St. Mary-at-Hill, E.C.3.—*Clerk*, B. G. Wilson; *Master*, R. V. Sargent.

LAUNDERERS (*No livery*).—*Clerk*, D. K. Rollit, O.B.E., 5 Oak Road, Rochford, Essex; *Master*, A. R. L. Oliver.

BUILDERS MERCHANTS OF THE CITY OF LONDON (*No livery*) (*Members*, 120).—*Clerk*, V. J. Fanstone, O.B.E., 34–35 Farringdon Street, E.C.4; *Master*, A. G. P. Lincoln, M.C., T.D.

NOTE.—In certain companies the election of Master or Prime Warden for the year does not take place till the autumn. In such cases the Master or Prime Warden for 1970–71 is given.

LONDON BOROUGHS

City or Borough, ★ Inner London Borough	Municipal Offices	Population, 1971 Census (prelim.)	Rateable Value, April 1, 1971	Rate Levied 1971–72 ∅	Town Clerk	Mayor or Lord Mayor
			£	p		
CITY OF WESTMINSTER ★	City Hall, Victoria St., S.W.1.	225,632	112,416,973	72	A. G. Dawtry, C.B.E., T.D.	J. Wells (*Lord Mayor*).
Barking.........	†Barking.	166,499	10,234,455	97½	K. Lauder.	M. J. Spencer.
Barnet.........	†The Burroughs, Hendon, N.W.4.	303,578	23,000,954	69	R. H. Williams.	K. W. Hughes.
Bexley.........	†Erith, Kent. [Middx.	216,172	11,541,470	87½	C. G. Dennis.	K. J. Smith.
Brent............	†Forty Lane, Wembley.	278,541	20,955,035	69½	R. S. Forster.	H. V. Drury.
Bromley........	†Bromley, Kent.	304,357	17,443,482	79½	P. J. Bunting.	A. T. Johnson.
Camden★......	†Euston Rd., N.W.1.	200,784	35,475,707	86½	B. H. Wilson, C.B.E.	A. E. Skinner.
Croydon........	†Taberner House, Park Lane, Croydon.	331,851	22,705,525	71½	A. Blakemore.	R. G. Willis.
Ealing.........	†Ealing, W.5.	299,450	24,643,752	71	P. J. Coomber.	K. H. Acock.
Enfield.........	‡Enfield.	266,788	18,802,528	72½	C. E. C. R. Platten.	W. J. Watson.
Greenwich★....	†Wellington St., Woolwich, S.E.18.	216,441	12,646,090	81	R. L. Doble.	Mrs. M. I. Kingwell.
Hackney★......	†Mare Street, E.8.	216,659	15,048,551	87	L. G. Huddy.	Miss L. Karpin.
Hammersmith★..	†King St., W.6.	184,935	14,039,329	79	C. Randall.	T. Morris.
Haringey.......	‡Civic Centre, High Road, N.22.	236,956	13,816,991	84½	B. Cooper.	Mrs. B. S. Remington.
Harrow.........	¶Harrow Weald Lodge, Uxbridge Rd., Harrow.	202,718	12,328,273	72½	S. Lancaster.	Mrs. M. M. Haslam.
Havering.......	†Main Road, Romford, Essex. [Hayes, Middx.	246,778	13,003,973	82	J. E. Symons.	F. J. Coffin.
Hillingdon.....	†Wood End, Green Road,	234,718	18,512,633	70½	G. Hooper.	O. Garvin, M.B.E.
Hounslow.......	†Treaty Rd., Hounslow.	206,182	17,455,761	77½	D. Mathieson.	F. W. Powe.
Islington★......	†Upper St., N.1.	199,129	20,431,251	80	F. L. Croft.	E. C. Gough.
Kensington and Chelsea (Royal Borough)★....	†Kensington, W.8.	184,392	26,427,037	68½	L. E. Holmes.	Mrs. W. Gumbel.
Kingston upon Thames......	Guildhall, Kingston upon Thames	140,210	10,656,109	75½	J. N. Martin.	J. Harrison.
Lambeth★......	†Brixton Hill, S.W.2.	302,616	20,644,636	76	F. D. Ward.	G. W. M. West.
Lewisham★.....	†Catford, S.E.6.	264,800	12,684,000	62½	J. H. French.	P. Goirin.
Merton.........	†Broadway, S.W.19.	176,524	11,731,061	82½	S. Astin.	J. L. Coombes.
Newham........	†East Ham, E.6.	235,700	14,859,038	96	G. E. Smith.	E. C. S. Kebbell.
Redbridge......	†High Rd., Ilford, Essex.	238,614	13,301,883	94½	A. McC. Findlay.	C. Loveless.
Richmond upon Thames......	§Twickenham, Middx.	173,592	11,485,477	83½	A.W.B. Goode, M.C.	Mrs. H.A.M. Champion.
Southwark★....	†Peckham Rd., S.E.5.	259,982	18,937,421	97½	S. T. Evans.	Mrs. M. V. Goldwin.
Sutton.........	§3 Throwley Rd., Sutton, Surrey.	168,775	10,543,411	85	T. M. H. Scott.	E. W. Harding.
Tower Hamlets★.	†Cambridge Heath Rd., E.2.	164,948	14,970,633	100	J. Wolkind.	W. Harris.
Waltham Forest.	†Walthamstow, E.17	233,528	12,472,615	85	Miss E. A. Cann.	G. R. Smith.
Wandsworth★..	†Wandsworth, S.W.18.	298,931	16,425,179	69	N. B. White.	J. A. Golding.

† Town Hall. ‡ Civic Centre. § Municipal Offices. ¶ Harrow: Town Clerk's Office. Borough Architect, Cottesmore, Uxbridge Road, Stanmore and (Housing Section), 15-21 Headstone Drive, Wealdstone. Treasurer, Education, Health and Information, Hanover House, Lyon Road, Harrow. *Engineer and Surveyor*, Woodlands, Clamp Hill, Stanmore, Middx.
∅ Mixed hereditaments, 4½ *p* less; Domestic properties, 9½ *p* less.

Public and Private Buildings in London

ADELPHI, Strand, W.C.2.—Adelphi Terrace and district commemorate the four architect brothers, James, John, Robert and William ADAM, who laid out the district (formerly Durham House) at the close of the 18th century. Four of the streets in the Adelphi were formerly called James, John, Robert, and William Streets to commemorate these founders of the Adam style of architecture and internal decoration. They are now Adam Street, John Adam Street, Robert Street and Durham House Street. Extensive rebuilding took place between the two World Wars, and there are now few 18th-century houses left in the district. In the neighbourhood of the Adelphi was York House, built by the Duke of Buckingham in 1625 (the Water Gate of which still stands in Embankment Gardens), the commemorative streets being *Charles* Street, *Villiers* Street. *Duke* Street, *Of* Lane, *Buckingham* Street (Of Lane is now " York Buildings").

AUSTRALIA HOUSE, Strand, W.C.2.—A handsome and imposing building, erected 1911–14 by the Commonwealth of Australia as the offices of the High Commissioner for the Commonwealth. NEW SOUTH WALES, QUEENSLAND, VICTORIA and WESTERN AUSTRALIA have separate offices in the Strand; TASMANIA at Golden Cross House, Charing Cross, and SOUTH AUSTRALIA at S.A. House, 50 Strand, W.C.2.

BALTIC EXCHANGE, St. Mary Axe, E.C.3.—The world market for the chartering of cargo ships. The present Exchange was built in 1903 and the new wing opened by Her Majesty the Queen on Nov. 21, 1956.

BANK OF ENGLAND, Threadneedle Street. E.C.2. (Not open to sightseers.)—The Bank of England, founded in 1694, has always been closely connected with the Government. The present building, completed in 1940 to the designs of Sir Herbert Baker, incorporates features reminiscent of the earlier architects, Sampson (1734), Sir Robert Taylor (1765) and Sir John Soane (1788). A Bank picquet is mounted every evening by the Brigade of Guards.

BRIDGES.—The bridges over the Thames (from East to West) are the *Tower Bridge* (built by the Corporation of London and opened in 1894), with its bascules, affording a fine view of the Pool and of the metropolis; *London Bridge* (opened after rebuilding in 1831, and until 1750 the only bridge over the Thames in London), with the London Monument (*q.v.*) and Fishmongers' Hall; *Southwark Bridge* (opened in 1819, and rebuilt by the Corporation of London, 1922); *Blackfriars Bridge* (opened in 1869 and widened by the Corporation of London in 1909); width, 105 ft.; *Waterloo Bridge* (Rennie), opened in 1817, length, 1,242 ft. 6 in.; width 79 ft. 9 in.) commanding a fine view of western London (rebuilt by L.C.C. and re-opened 1944); *Hungerford Bridge* (railway bridge with a footbridge); *Westminster Bridge* (built in 1750 and then presenting a view that inspired Wordsworth's sonnet; rebuilt and re-opened in 1862; width, 84 ft.) with Thornycroft's *Boadicea* at the north-eastern end; this bridge leads from Westminster Abbey and the Houses of Parliament to the County Hall (*q.v.*) and St. Thomas's Hospital; *Lambeth Bridge* (rebuilt by L.C.C. and opened in 1932) leading from Lambeth Palace to Millbank; *Vauxhall Bridge* (rebuilt in 1906) leading to Kennington Oval; *Chelsea Bridge*, leading from Chelsea Hospital to Battersea Park (reconstructed and widened 1937); and *Albert Bridge* (1873); *Battersea Bridge* (opened in 1890); *Wandsworth Bridge* (opened in 1873; rebuilt and re-opened in 1940); *Putney Bridge* (opened in 1886 and widened in 1933

where the Oxford and Cambridge Boat Race is started for Mortlake; *Hammersmith Bridge* (rebuilt 1887); *Barnes Bridge* (for pedestrians only, 1933); *Chiswick Bridge* (opened in 1933); *King Edward VII Bridge, Kew* (rebuilt in 1902, opened 1903, leading to the Royal Botanic Gardens, Kew; *Twickenham Lock Bridge*; *Twickenham Bridge* (opened 1933); *Richmond Bridge* (opened in 1777); *Kingston Bridge* and *Hampton Court Bridge* (rebuilt, 1933).

BUCKINGHAM PALACE, St. James's Park, S.W.1. (Not open to the public.)—Was purchased by King George III in 1762 from the heir of the Duke of Buckingham, and was altered by Nash for King George IV. The London home of the Sovereign since Queen Victoria's accession in 1837. Re-fronted in stone (part of the Queen Victoria Memorial) by Sir Aston Webb in 1913.

The Queen's Gallery, containing a changing selection of the finest pictures and works of art from all parts of the royal collection, was opened to the public on July 25, 1962. Open: Tues.-Sat., 11–5 p.m.; Sundays, 2–5 p.m. Admission 15p; *Children*, 5p, entering from Buckingham Palace Road.

The Royal Mews is open to visitors on Wednesdays and Thursdays throughout the year (except in Ascot Week), 2–4 p.m. The following charges, the net proceeds of which are devoted to charities, are payable on admission: *Adults*, 15p; *Children*, 5p.

CANADA HOUSE, Trafalgar Square, S.W.1.—A conspicuous building on the Western side of the Square, housing the Office of the High Commissioner for Canada in the United Kingdom. Designed by Sir Robert Smirke in 1820, it was renovated and embellished when acquired from the Union Club in 1924. Further major alterations have been completed to incorporate the former Royal College of Physicians building, also designed by Sir Robert Smirke, which was acquired in 1964. The renovated building was re-opened in March, 1967. The exteriors of the two buildings were originally designed to create the appearance of a single building by presenting a common façade facing Trafalgar Square. Certain interior features of the original building are preserved and the spacious, richly furnished room now occupied by the High Commissioner is much admired. Surrounded by Offices of Canadian Banks, Steamship, Railway and other Companies, the Canadian Building is one of London's landmarks. It was opened by King George V. in June, 1925.

CANONBURY TOWER, Canonbury, N.1.—The largest remaining part of a 16th-century house originally built by the Priors of St. Bartholomew, and since 1952 used as the headquarters of a non-professional theatre company. Contains the " Spencer " and " Compton " oak-panelled rooms. Other relics of Canonbury House can be seen nearby.

CARLYLE'S HOUSE, 24 Cheyne Row, Chelsea, S.W.3. The home of Thomas Carlyle for 47 years until his death in 1881, and containing much of his furniture, etc. Now the property of the National Trust. Open daily, except Tuesdays, 10–1, 2–6, or dusk, if earlier. Sundays, 2–6. Closed Good Friday, Christmas and Boxing Days. Admission, 15p; Children and Students, 7½p.

CATHOLIC CENTRAL LIBRARY, St. Francis Friary, 47 Francis Street, S.W.1.—Founded as a private library in 1914, it was taken over in 1959 by the Franciscan Friars of the Atonement. Stock of 50,000 volumes for lending and reference on many aspects of religion (devotional, Church history, doctrine, etc.), sociology, fine arts, literature,

history, travel, biography and fiction. Books are sent by post when required. Hours of opening: Mon.–Fri. 10.30–6.30; Sat. 10.30–4.30.

CEMETERIES.—In *Kensal Green Cemetery*, North Kensington, W.10 (70 acres), are tombs of W. M. Thackeray, Anthony Trollope, Sydney Smith, Shirley Brooks, Wilkie Collins, Tom Hood, W. Mulready, George Cruikshank, John Leech, Leigh Hunt, Brunel (" Great Eastern "), Ross (Arctic), Charles Kemble and Charles Mathews (Actors). In *Highgate Cemetery*, N.6, are the tombs of George Eliot, Herbert Spencer, Michael Faraday, Karl Marx and G. J. Holyoake. In *Abney Park Cemetery*, Stoke Newington, N.16, are the tomb of General Booth, founder of the Salvation Army, and memorials to many Nonconformist Divines. In the *South Metropolitan Cemetery*, Norwood, S.E.27, are the tombs of C. H. Spurgeon, Lord Alverstone, Douglas Jerrold, John Belcher, R.A., Theodore Watts-Dunton, Dr. Moffat (Missionary), Sir H. Bessemer, Sir H. Maxim, Sir J. Barnby, Sir A. Manns, and J. Whitaker, F.S.A. (*Whitaker's Almanack*). In the churchyard of the former *Marylebone Chapel* are buried Allan Ramsay (poet), Hoyle (whist), Ferguson (astronomer), Charles Wesley (hymn writer) and his son Samuel Wesley (musician). The chapel itself was demolished in 1949. CREMATORIA.—*Ilford* (City of London); *Norwood*; *Hendon*; *Streatham Park*; *Finchley* (St. Marylebone) and *Golder's Green* (12 acres), near Hampstead Heath, with " Garden of Rest " and memorials to famous men and women.

CENOTAPH, Whitehall, S.W.1.—(Literally " empty tomb "). Monument erected " To the Glorious Dead," as a memorial to all ranks of the Sea, Land and Air Forces who gave their lives in the service of the Empire during the First World War. Erected as a temporary memorial in 1919 and replaced by a permanent structure in 1920. Unveiled by King George V on Armistice Day, 1920. An additional inscription was added after the 1939–45 War, to commemorate those who gave their lives in that conflict.

CHARTERHOUSE, Charterhouse Square, E.C.1. (*Master*, Rev. T. S. Nevill; *Registrar and Clerk to the Governors*, N. Long-Brown), a Carthusian monastery until 1538, purchased from the Earl of Suffolk in 1611 by Thomas Sutton as a home for aged "Brothers" and a School (at Godalming since 1872). The buildings are partly 14th (but mainly 16th) century. They suffered much damage during the 1939–45 War but are now restored and can accommodate nearly 40 " Brothers." Visitors must apply to the Registrar for permission to see the Hall, etc. (Charge for admission, 25p. per person). Roger Williams, the founder and governor of Rhode Island, U.S.A., was on June 25, 1621, elected a scholar of Sutton's Hospital. Other famous Carthusians are John Wesley; the poets Crashaw and Lovelace; Addison and Steele; Sir William Blackstone and Thackeray, who described " Greyfriars School " (Charterhouse) in " The Newcomes."

CHELSEA PHYSIC GARDEN, Royal Hospital Road, S.W.3.—A garden of general botanical research, established in latter part of 17th century by the Society of Apothecaries, occupies site presented in 1722 by Sir Hans Sloane. Transferred in 1899 to the Trustees of the London Parochial Charities. Tickets of admission for *bona fide* students and teachers obtainable from the Clerk to the Trustees, 10 Fleet Street, E.C.4.

CHELSEA ROYAL HOSPITAL (founded by Charles II, in 1682, and built by Wren; opened in 1692), Royal Hospital Road, Chelsea, S.W.3, for old and disabled soldiers. Great Hall, Chapel, Museum open daily 10 to 12 and 2 to 5, and on Sunday afternoons. Council Chamber open on Sundays, 11.45 to 12 and 2 to 4 p.m. The exten-

sive grounds include the former Ranelagh Gardens. *Governor*, General Sir Charles Jones, G.C.B., C.B.E., M.C.; *Lieut-Governor and Secretary*, Major-Gen. Sir Nigel Tapp, K.B.E., C.B., D.S.O.

CITY BUSINESS LIBRARY (formerly Guildhall Commercial Library), 55 Basinghall Street, E.C.2. Open, Mon.–Fri. 9.30–5.30.

COLLEGE OF ARMS OR HERALDS' COLLEGE, Queen Victoria Street, E.C.4.—Her Majesty's Officers of Arms (Kings, Heralds and Pursuivants of Arms) were incorporated by Richard III., and granted Derby House on the site of the present College building by Philip and Mary. The building now in use was built after the Fire of London. The powers vested by the Crown in the Earl Marshal (The Duke of Norfolk) with regard to State ceremonial are largely exercised through the College, which is the official repository of English coats of arms and pedigrees. Enquiry may be made to the Officer on duty in the Public Office, Mon.–Fri. between 10 a.m. and 4 p.m.

COMMONWEALTH INSTITUTE, Kensington High Street, W.8.—A permanent exhibition opened on Nov. 6, 1962, by Her Majesty the Queen, replacing the former Imperial Institute opened in 1893 in S. Kensington. An interesting feature of the building is its paraboloid copper-sheathed roof. The Institute contains, in 60,000 square feet arranged in 3 galleries, a visual representation of the history and geography of the Commonwealth countries and dependencies: on the ground floor, exhibits of Canada, Australia, New Zealand, India, Pakistan and Ceylon; on the middle gallery, the African territories; and on the upper gallery, the other territories of the Commonwealth. Art gallery; Cinema, showing documentary films daily.

Open, week-days, 10–5.30; Sundays, 2.30–6. Admission free. Closed Good Friday, Christmas Eve and Christmas Day.

COUNTY HALL, Westminster Bridge, S.E.1.— The Headquarters of the Greater London Council (*see* pp. 634–6) built on the Pedlar's Acre, Bishop's Acre, Four Acres and Float Mead, Lambeth, from the designs of Ralph Knott, with a river façade of 750 ft. The foundation stone was laid by King George V on March 9, 1912, and the ceremonial opening took place on July 17, 1922, although the main building was not completed until 1933. The building of the North and South blocks on a site to the East of the main building started in the early 1930's. They were occupied in 1939 but not finally completed until 1963. The main building contains, in addition to office accommodation, the council chamber, a conference hall, committee rooms; education and members' libraries and the county record office. The Council, when in session, meets in public in the council chamber fortnightly on Tuesday afternoons at 2.30 p.m. The times for public inspection of the building are, on Saturdays and Bank Holidays (except Christmas Day) from 10.30–1; 1.30–4 p.m. Admission free.

CUSTOM HOUSE, Lower Thames Street, E.C.3.— Built early in 19th century, with a wide quay on Thames. The *Long Room* is about 190 ft. long.

DICKENS HOUSE, 48 Doughty Street, W.C.1.— In this house Charles Dickens lived from 1837 to 1839, and here he completed *Pickwick Papers*. It is the headquarters of The Dickens Fellowship and contains many relics of the novelist. It is open to the public daily, 10 to 5 (Sundays and Bank Holidays excepted); admission 15p; students, 10p; Children, 5p.

DR. JOHNSON'S HOUSE, Gough Square, Fleet Street, E.C.4.—A tall late 17th-century house in which Samuel Johnson (and his wife) lived. His *Dictionary* was compiled here. The house is furnished with 18th century pieces and there is an

excellent collection of Johnsoniana. Open daily (except Sundays and Bank Holidays) from 10.30 to 5 (Winter, 4.30). Admission 10p; Students, 5p.

ELY PLACE, Holborn Circus, E.C.1.—The site of the London house of former Bishops of Ely, Ely Place is a private street whose affairs are administered by Commissioners under a special Act of Parliament. The 14th-century chapel, now St. Etheldreda's (R.C.) Church, is open daily until dusk.

FULHAM PALACE, Bishop's Avenue, Fulham, S.W.6.—The courtyard is 16th century, remainder 18th and 19th century. Residence of the Bishop of London. Grounds of about 9 acres.

GEFFRYE MUSEUM, Kingsland Road, E.2.—Open on Tuesdays to Saturdays 10 to 5, Sundays 2 to 5. Closed on Christmas Day and on Mondays except Bank Holidays. Admission free.

The Museum is housed in a building erected originally as almshouses in 1715. It was eventually purchased by the London County Council and opened as a museum in 1914. The exhibits are shown in a series of period rooms dating from 1600 to the present day, each containing furniture and domestic equipment of a middle-class English home. An 18th century woodworker's shop and an openhearth kitchen are also shown. Temporary exhibitions and occasional recitals are held in the Lecture Hall. There is a reference library of books on furniture, social history and art. Special arrangements for children visiting the Museum in school parties and in their leisure time. *Curator*, J. Daniels.

GEORGE INN, Southwark.—Near London Bridge Station. Given to National Trust in 1937. Last galleried inn in London, built in 1677.

GUILDHALL, King Street, City, E.C.2.—Scene of civic government for the City for more than a thousand years. Built, 1411-1425, damaged in the Great Fire, 1666, and by incendiary bombs, 1940. The main hall and crypt (the most extensive mediæval crypt in London) have been restored. Events in Guildhall include the annual election of Lord Mayor, election of Sheriffs, receptions in honour of Sovereigns and Heads of State, and the fortnightly meetings of the Court of Common Council (*see* "Corporation of London"). Open free; weekdays, 10-5; Sundays (May to Sept.) 2-5. *Keeper of the Guildhall*, W. Parker.

The Library, Museum and Art Gallery adjoining mainly escaped damage, and are open to the public, Mon. to Sat., 10-5, Admission free. The Library contains Plans of London, 1570; Deed of Sale with Shakespeare's signature; first, second and fourth folios of Shakespeare's plays, etc. (*see also* City Business Library).

The Guildhall Museum, Bassishaw Highwalk, London Wall, E.C.2, contains Roman and mediæval archæological exhibits and mementos of civic life in the City. Mon.–Sat., 10 a.m.–5 p.m. Closed on Bank Holidays.

HONOURABLE ARTILLERY COMPANY'S HEADQUARTERS, City Road, E.C.1.—The H.A.C. (*Sec.*, Lt.-Col. P. Massey, M.C.) received its charter of incorporation from Henry VIII. in 1537, and has occupied its present ground since 1641. The Armoury House dates from 1735. Four of its members who emigrated in the 17th century, founded in 1638 the Ancient and Honorable Artillery Company of Massachusetts. The H.A.C. is the senior regiment of the Territorial Army Volunteer Reserves, and maintains a Headquarters with an Officer Training Wing, and Artillery and Infantry components.

HORNIMAN MUSEUM AND LIBRARY, London Road, Forest Hill, S.E.23. Open daily except Mondays and Bank Holidays, 10.30 to 6, Sundays 2 to 6. Admission free. The Museum was presented in 1901 to the London County Council by the founder, Mr. F. J. Horniman, M.P. The Museum has three main departments, anthropology, musical instruments and natural history. In the anthropology department the large collections include exhibits illustrating man's progress in the arts and crafts from prehistoric times. The natural history department includes an aquarium. Reference library. Schools Service. Free concerts and lectures (autumn to spring). *Curator*, D. M. Boston.

HORSE GUARDS, Whitehall, S.W.1.—Archway and offices built about 1753. The mounting of the guard (Life Guards, or the Blues and Royals at 11 a.m. (10 a.m. on Sundays) and the dismounting at 4 p.m. are picturesque ceremonies. Only those on the Lord Chamberlain's list may drive through the gates and archway into *Horse Guards' Parade* (230,000 sq. ft.), where the Colour is "trooped" on the Queen's Official Birthday. (Trafalgar Square is 168,850 sq. ft. (the island site, 102,050 sq. ft.); Parliament Square, 136,900 sq. ft.; Leicester Square, 100,000 sq. ft.)

HOUSES OF PARLIAMENT, Westminster, S.W.1.—After its destruction by fire in 1834, the Palace of Westminster was re-built in 1840-68 from the designs of Sir Charles Barry and Augustus Welby Pugin, at a cost of over £2,000,000.—Open (free) to visitors on Saturdays, on Easter Monday and Tuesday, Spring and late summer Bank Holiday Mondays and Tuesdays; Mon., Tues. and Thurs. in August and Thurs. in September, if neither House be sitting. Admission at the Sovereign's Entrance, House of Lords, on the above-mentioned days, from 10 a.m. to 4.30 p.m. Closed to visitors on Christmas Day, Boxing Day and Good Friday and the Saturday preceding the State Opening of Parliament. Admission to the Strangers' Gallery of the House of Lords as arranged by a Peer or by queue viâ the St. Stephen's Entrance. Admission to the Strangers' Gallery of the House of Commons, during session, by Member's order, or order obtained on personal application at the Admission Order Office in St. Stephen's Hall after the House meets. The present House of Commons was used for the first time on October 26, 1950, the original Chamber having been destroyed by bombs in 1941. The Victoria Tower (House of Lords) is about 330 ft. high, and when Parliament is sitting the Union Jack flies by day from its flagstaff. The Clock Tower of the House of Commons is about 320 ft. high and contains "Big Ben," the Hour Bell, named after Sir Benjamin Hall, First Commissioner of Works when the original bell was cast in 1856. This bell which weighed 16 tons 11 cwt., was found cracked in 1857. The present bell (13½ tons) is a recasting of the original and was first brought into use in July, 1859. A light is displayed from this tower at night when Parliament is sitting.

INNS OF COURT.—The *Inner* and *Middle Temple*, S. of Fleet Street, E.C.4, and N. of Victoria Embankment, to which the gardens extend, have occupied (since early 14th century) the site of the buildings of the Order of Knights Templars. *Inner Temple Hall* is open to the public on Monday–Friday, 10-11.30 a.m. and 2.30-4 p.m., except during Vacations. *Temple Church*, restored in 1958 after severe damage by bombing, is open on weekdays 10-5 p.m. and the public are admitted to Sunday services. *Middle Temple Hall* (sixteenth century) is open to the public when not in use, Monday–Friday, 10-12 and 3-4.30 p.m.; Saturday, 10-4.30. Closed 1-2 p.m. and Sundays. In Middle Temple Gardens (not open to the public) Shakespeare (Henry VI, Part I) places the incident which led to the "Wars of the Roses" (1455-85). *Lincoln's Inn*, from Chancery Lane to Lincoln's Inn Fields, W.C.2, occupies the site of the palace of a

former Bishop of Chichester and of a Black Friars monastery. The records show the Society as being in existence in 1422. The new Hall and Library Buildings are modern, although the Library is first mentioned in 1474, and the old Hall early 16th century, the Chapel (Inigo Jones) early 17th century. *Lincoln's Inn Fields* (7 acres); the Square contains many fine old houses with handsome interiors. *Gray's Inn*, Holborn/Gray's Inn Road, W.C.1. Early 14th century. Hall (16th cent.); Chapel (Services 11.15 a.m. during Law Dining Terms only). Holy Communion 1st Sunday in every month except Aug.–Sept. Public welcome. Library (30,000 vols. mss. and printed books) may be viewed by appointment. Gardens open to the public from 12 noon to 2 p.m. (May–July), 9.30 a.m.–5 p.m. (Aug.–Sept.). The Inn, although badly damaged during the last war has been completely restored to its former beauty with gracious red brick buildings overlooking grass covered squares and gardens. Strong Elizabethan associations. No other " Inns " are active, but what remains of *Staple Inn* is worth visiting as a relic of Elizabethan London; though heavy damage was done by a flying-bomb, it retains a picturesque gabled front on Holborn (opposite Gray's Inn Road). *Clement's Inn* (near St. Clement Danes' Church), *Clifford's Inn*, Fleet Street, and *Thavies Inn*, Holborn Circus, are all rebuilt. *Serjeant's Inn*, Fleet Street (damaged by bombing) and another (demolished 1910) of the same name in Chancery Lane, were composed of Serjeants-at-Law, the last of whom died in 1922.

JEWISH MUSEUM, Woburn House, Upper Woburn Place, W.C.1.—Opened in 1932, the Museum contains a comprehensive collection of Jewish antiquities, liturgical paraphernalia and " Anglo-Judaica." Open free (Mon.–Thurs.), 2.30–5; (Fri. and Sun.), 10.30–12.45. Closed on Saturdays, Jewish Holy days and Bank Holidays. Conducted tours of parties by arrangement with the Secretary/Curator.

KEATS HOUSE AND MUSEUM, Keats Grove, Hampstead, N.W.3.—In two houses here, now made into one, John Keats lived at various times between 1818 and 1820. The house and the museum are open free, weekdays, 10 a.m. to 6 p.m. The Keats Memorial Library (5,000 volumes) in the adjoining Branch Library is open free on weekdays 9.30–8 p.m.; Saturday, 9.30–5 p.m.

KENSINGTON PALACE, W.8.—Built by Christopher Wren for King William III (1689–94), and continued as a royal residence until 1760. The birthplace of Queen Victoria in 1819. State apartments, re-opened to the public in 1956 under administrative control of the London Museum, contain pictures from the royal collections, royal costumes and furniture formerly belonging to Queen Mary. *Hours of Opening:* (March 1–Sept. 30) 10 a.m.–6 p.m.; Sundays, 2–6 p.m.; (Oct. 1–Feb. 28) 10–5; Sundays, 2–5 p.m. *Kensington Gardens* (*q.v.*) adjoin.

LAMBETH PALACE, S.E.1.—The official residence of the Archbishop of Canterbury, on south bank of Thames; the oldest part is 13th century, the house itself is early 19th century. For leave to visit the historical portions, applications should be made by letter to the Archbishop's Chaplain.

LIVERY COMPANIES' HALLS.—The Principal Companies (*see* pp. 640–642) have magnificent halls, but admission to view them has generally to be arranged beforehand. Among the finest or more interesting may be mentioned the following: Goldsmiths' Hall, Foster Lane. The present hall was completed in 1835, and contains some magnificent rooms. Exhibitions of plate have been shown here periodically in recent years. Fishmongers' Hall, London Bridge (built 1831–3), now

admirably restored after severe bomb damage, also contains fine rooms. Apothecaries' Hall, Black Friars Lane, was rebuilt in 1670, after the Great Fire, and has library, hall and kitchen which are good examples of this period, together with a pleasant courtyard. Vintners' Hall, Upper Thames Street, was also rebuilt after the Great Fire, and its hall has very fine late 17th century panelling. The Watermen and Lightermen's Company is not, strictly speaking, a Livery Company, but its hall, in St. Mary at Hill, is a good example of a smaller 18th century building, with pilastered façade. It was completed in 1780. Stationers' Hall, in Stationers' Hall Court, behind Ludgate Hill, another post-Fire Hall, standing in its own court, has a particularly finely carved screen. Barbers' Hall, Monkwell Street, with a Hall attributed to Inigo Jones, was completely destroyed by bombing, but is to be rebuilt. The new hall is to be built some 30 ft. from the old site to enable one of the bastions and part of the wall of the Roman fort to remain exposed to view. Mercers' Hall, Ironmonger Lane, built to replace the hall destroyed by bombing, was opened in 1958.

LLOYD'S, Lime Street, E.C.3.—Housed in the Royal Exchange for 150 years and in Leadenhall Street from 1928–1957. The present building was opened by H.M. Queen Elizabeth the Queen Mother on Nov. 14, 1957. The underwriting space has an area of 44,250 sq. ft.

LORD'S CRICKET GROUND, St. John's Wood Road, N.W.8.—The headquarters (since 1814) of the Marylebone Cricket Club, the premier cricket club in England, the scene of some of the principal matches of the season and Middlesex County headquarters. Tennis court in building behind members' pavilion.

The Cricket Memorial Gallery, a museum of cricket, open to the public on match days, until close of play, and on other days by prior arrangement. Adults, 10p, children, 5p. In winter, admission is by prior arrangement.

MANSION HOUSE, City, E.C.4.—(Reconstructed 1930–31.) The official residence of the Lord Mayor; the Egyptian Hall and Ballroom are the chief attractions. Admission by order from the Lord Mayor's Secretary.

MARKETS.—The London markets (administered by the Corporation of the City of London) provide foodstuffs for 8,500,000 to 9,000,000 people. The dead meat market at Smithfield is the largest in the world, the supplies marketed amounting to nearly 500,000 tons annually. *Central Meat, Fish, Fruit, Vegetable, and Poultry Markets*, Smithfield; *Leadenhall Market* (Meat and Poultry); *Billingsgate* (Fish), Thames Street; *Spitalfields*, E.1 (Vegetables, Fruit, etc.), enlarged 1928, and opened by the late Queen Mary; *London Fruit Exchange*, Brushfield Street (built by Corporation of London 1928–29) faces Spitalfields Market. Other markets are—*Covent Garden*, W.C.2 (established under a charter of Charles II, in 1661) and *Borough Market*, S.E.1, for vegetables, fruit. flowers, etc.

MARLBOROUGH HOUSE, Pall Mall, S.W.1.—The London home of Queen Mary until her death in 1953. Built by Wren for the great Duke of Marlborough and completed in 1711, the house finally reverted to the Crown in 1835. Prince Leopold lived there until 1831, and Queen Adelaide from 1837 until her death in 1849. In 1863 it became the London house of the Prince of Wales. The Queen's Chapel, Marlborough Gate, begun in 1623 from the designs of Inigo Jones for the Infanta Maria of Spain, and completed for Queen Henrietta Maria, is open to the public for services during part of the year. In 1959 Marlborough House was given by the Queen as a Commonwealth centre for Govern-

ment conferences and it was opened as such in March, 1962. It is open to the public at certain times when conferences are not taking place.

LONDON MONUMENT, (commonly called "The Monument"), Monument Street, E.C.3.—Built from designs of Wren, 1671–77, to commemorate the *Great Fire of London*, which broke out in Pudding Lane, Sept. 2, 1666. The fluted Doric column is 120 ft. high (the moulded cylinder above the balcony supporting a flaming vase of gilt bronze is 42 ft. in addition), and is based on a square plinth 40 ft. high, with fine carvings on W. face (making a total height of 202 ft.). Splendid views of London from gallery at top of column (311 steps). Admission (until 20 minutes before closing time) 5p; children, 2½p, Monday to Saturday, 9 a.m. to 6 p.m. (Oct.–March to 4 p.m.). Sundays—May to Sept. 2–6 p.m. Closed Christmas Day, Boxing Day and Good Friday.

MONUMENTS.—VICTORIA MEMORIAL in front of Buckingham Palace; ALBERT MEMORIAL, South Kensington; AIR, Victoria Embankment; BEACONSFIELD, Parliament Square; BEATTY, JELLICOE and CUNNINGHAM, Trafalgar Square; BELGIAN, Victoria Embankment; BOADICEA (or "Boudicca"), Queen of the Iceni, E. Anglia, Westminster Bridge; BURNS, Embankment Gardens; BURGHERS OF CALAIS (replica of Rodin's statue), Victoria Tower Gardens, Westminster; CAVALRY, Hyde Park; CAVELL, St. Martin's Place; CENOTAPH, Whitehall; CHARLES I. (erected Jan. 29, 1675), Trafalgar Square; CHARLES II. (Grinling Gibbons), inside the Royal Exchange; CLEOPATRA'S NEEDLE (68½ ft. high, erected 1878), Thames Embankment (the Sphinx, W. of pedestal, and the surrounding stonework, bear scars from an air raid); CAPTAIN COOK (Brock), The Mall; CRIMEAN, Broad Sanctuary; OLIVER CROMWELL (Thornycroft), outside Westminster Hall; DUKE OF CAMBRIDGE, Whitehall; DUKE OF YORK (124 ft.), St. James's Park; EDWARD VII. (Mackennal), Waterloo Place. ELIZABETH I (1586, oldest outdoor statue in London), Fleet Street; EROS (Shaftesbury Memorial) (Gilbert), Piccadilly Circus; MARECHAL FOCH, Grosvenor Gardens; GEORGE III., Cockspur Street; GEORGE IV. (Chantrey), riding without stirrups, Trafalgar Square; GEORGE V., Abingdon Street; GEORGE VI., Carlton Gardens; GLADSTONE, facing Australia House, Strand; GUARDS' (Crimea), Waterloo Place; (Great War), Horse Guards' Parade; HAIG (Hardiman), Whitehall; IRVING (Brock), N. side of National Portrait Gallery; JAMES II., Trafalgar Square; KITCHENER, Horse Guards' Parade; ABRAHAM LINCOLN (St. Gaudens), Parliament Square; LONDON TROOPS, Royal Exchange; MARY, QUEEN OF SCOTS, Fleet Street; MILTON, St. Giles, Cripplegate; MONUMENT, THE (*see above*); NELSON (170ft. 1½ in.), Trafalgar Square, with Landseer's lions (cast from guns recovered from the wreck of the *Royal George*); FLORENCE NIGHTINGALE, Waterloo Place; "PETER PAN" (Frampton), Kensington Gardens; PRINCE CONSORT, Holborn Circus; RALEIGH, Whitehall; RICHARD COEUR DE LION (Marochetti), Old Palace Yard; ROBERTS, Horse Guards' Parade; FRANKLIN D. ROOSEVELT, Grosvenor Square; ROYAL ARTILLERY (South Africa), The Mall; (Great War), Hyde Park Corner; ROYAL MARINES, The Mall; CAPTAIN SCOTT, Waterloo Place; SHACKLETON, Kensington Gore; SHAKESPEARE (Fontana), Leicester Square; CAPTAIN JOHN SMITH, Cheapside; SMUTS (Epstein), Parliament Square; TRENCHARD, Victoria Embankment; GEORGE WASHINGTON (Houdon copy), Trafalgar Square; WELLINGTON, Hyde Park Corner; WELLINGTON (Chantrey) riding without stirrups, Royal Exchange; JOHN WESLEY, City Road; WOLSELEY, Horse Guards' Parade.

PERCIVAL DAVID FOUNDATION OF CHINESE ART, 53 Gordon Square, W.C.1.—Set up in 1951 to promote the study and teaching of the art and culture of China and the surrounding regions, and provide facilities necessary to that end. The Foundation contains the collection of Chinese ceramics formed by Sir Percival David and his important library of books on Chinese art. To these was added a gift from the Hon. Mountstuart Elphinstone of part of his collection of Chinese monochrome porcelains. The galleries were opened to the public in 1952. The Foundation is administered on behalf of the University of London by the School of Oriental and African Studies. *Hours of opening:* Galleries, Mon. 2 to 5 p.m.; Tues. to Fri. 10.30 a.m. to 5 p.m.; Sat. 10.30 a.m. to 1 p.m.; Library, Mon. 2.30 to 4.30 p.m.; Tues. to Fri. 10.30 a.m. to 12.30 p.m.; 1.30 to 4.30 p.m. *Head of the Foundation*, Prof. W. Watson.

PORT OF LONDON.—The Port of London comprises the tidal portion of the River Thames from Teddington to the sea, a distance of 94 miles and three dock systems covering an area of 4,816 acres, of which 644 acres are water. The governing body is the Port of London Authority, whose Head Offices in Trinity Square, E.C.3, were designed by Sir Edwin Cooper. Particulars of the docks are as follows:—*India & Millwall Docks, E.14.*—Area 454 acres including 127 acres water. Principal commodities handled are sugar, grain, hardwood, fruit, plywood, wood pulp and wine in bulk. *Royal Victoria & Albert & King George V Docks, E.16.*—Area, 1,055 acres including 230 acres water—have special facilities for handling frozen and chilled meat, grain, tobacco and bananas. Large quantities of wool, fruit, dairy produce and general cargo are also dealt with. *Tilbury Docks, Essex.*—Area 1,057 acres, including 155 acres water. These docks are 26 miles below London Bridge and are used principally by vessels plying on the Australian, North American, Indian, other Eastern routes, West Africa and the Continent. Tilbury Passenger Landing Stage provides accommodation for liners at all states of the tide and adjoins Tilbury Riverside Station.

A development and extension scheme at Tilbury has added nearly 2 miles of deepwater quays, to provide 13 new berths, of which 6 are for container traffic and 3 for packaged timber. Also included are a freight-liner rail container terminal and a riverside grain terminal which can accommodate vessels up to 65,000 tons deadweight and provide a rated maximum discharge of 2,000 tons per hour. Cost of this development (including Grain Terminal) was estimated at about £35 million.

The St. Katharine Docks were sold to the G.L.C. in 1969 and the London Docks were closed on May 31, 1969. Surrey Commercial Docks were closed in 1970.

PRINCE HENRY'S ROOM, 17 Fleet Street, E.C.4.—Early 17th century timber-framed house containing fine room on first floor with panelling and moulded plaster ceiling. Open Mon. to Fri. 1.45 p.m. to 5 p.m.; Sat. to 4.30 p.m. Closed Christmas Day and Good Friday. Available occasionally for evening lettings to societies, etc. on application to The Town Clerk, Guildhall, E.C.2.

ROMAN LONDON.—Though visible remains are very few, almost every excavation for the foundations of new buildings in the City reveals Roman remains. Sections of the City wall, often however merely a mediæval re-build on the Roman foundations, are the most striking remains still to be seen. Fragments may be seen near the White Tower in the Tower of London, Trinity Square, No. 1 Crutched Friars, All Hallows, London Wall—its semi-circular vestry being built on the remains

of a round bastion—St. Alphage, London Wall, recently restored by the Corporation of London and showing a striking succession of building and repairs from Roman till later mediæval times, St. Giles, Cripplegate and, by permission only, the great bastion beneath the pavement of the yard of the G.P.O. in Giltspur Street. Recent excavations in the Cripplegate area have revealed that a fort was built in this area and later incorporated in the town wall in this north-west corner of the City. Evidence from these excavations proves that the fort was not built until about A.D. 100–120, and the date of the town wall must therefore be considerably later. Remains of a bath building are preserved beneath the Coal Exchange in Lower Thames Street and other foundations may be seen in the Crypt of All Hallows Barking by the Tower. The governmental headquarters of the town was a great basilica, more than 400 ft. long from east to west, the massive walls of which have been encountered, extending from Leadenhall Market across Gracechurch Street as far as St. Michael's, Cornhill. Excavations during the past few years have shown that buildings over the river front were erected on huge oaken piles and a framework of timber for a considerable distance both east and west of the present London Bridge. The " Roman Bath," in Strand Lane, which is not now held by most authorities to be of Roman origin, is maintained by the G.L.C. on behalf of the National Trust, and is open to the public on weekdays from 10 a.m. to 12.30 p.m. (*Admission*, 10p). Excavations since 1948 on a bombed site in Walbrook, on the banks of the old Wall Brook, produced interesting discoveries, including a Temple of Mithras, from which the splendid marble statues have been placed in Guildhall Museum, now in the Royal Exchange, where many other relics from the Roman City may be seen.

ROYAL EXCHANGE, E.C.3 (founded by Sir Thomas Gresham, 1566, opened as " The Bourse " and proclaimed " The Royal Exchange " by Queen Elizabeth I., 1571, rebuilt 1667–69 and 1842–44).—Open to the public, free. Statues of Queen Elizabeth I., Charles II., Queen Victoria, Sir Thomas Gresham and others; mural paintings in the ambulatory by Leighton, Abbey, Brangwyn, Wyllie and others. The carillon of the Royal Exchange (reinstated 1950) plays English, Scottish, Irish, Welsh, Canadian and Australian melodies at 9 a.m., 12 noon and 3 and 6 p.m. With the exception of the courtyard and ambulatory (now used for exhibitions, art displays, etc.) and the shops the whole of the building is occupied by departments of the Guardian Royal Exchange Assurance Group (which has had its head office there since 1720) and is administered by the Gresham Committee (*Clerk*, Mercers' Hall, Ironmonger Lane, E.C.2).

ROYAL GEOGRAPHICAL SOCIETY, Kensington Gore, S.W.7.—Map Room open to public, *free*.

ST. JAMES'S PALACE, in Pall Mall, S.W.1.—(Not open to the public.) Built by Henry VIII.; the Gatehouse and Presence Chamber remain, and part of the Chapel Royal, which in 1955 was reopened to the public for services during part of the year. A royal residence from 1697 to 1762. Representatives of Foreign Powers are still accredited " to the Court of St. James's " and (by the permission of the Crown) the Conference of the Allies (1921) and later conferences have been held here.

ST. JOHN'S GATE, Clerkenwell, E.C.1.—Now the Chancery of the Order of St. John of Jerusalem, and formerly the gate of the Priory of that Order, of which the gate house (early 16th century) and crypt of Church (12th century) alone survive. The gatehouse may be inspected on application to the Secretary at the Chancery.

SIR JOHN SOANE'S MUSEUM, 13 Lincoln's Inn Fields, W.C.2. The house and galleries, built 1812–24, are the work of the founder, Sir John Soane (1753–1837) and contain his collections, arranged as he left them, in pursuance of an Act procured by him in 1833. Exhibits include the Sarcophagus of Seti I. (*c.* 1290 B.C.), classical vases and marbles, Hogarth's *Rake's Progress* and *Election* series, paintings by Canaletto, Reynolds, Turner, Lawrence, etc., and sculpture by Chantrey, Flaxman, etc. Soane's library of 8,000 vols. and a collection of 20,000 architectural drawings are available for study. Open Tues.–Sat. inclusive, 10 a.m. to 5 p.m. Closed Bank Holidays and in August. *Curator*, Sir John Summerson, C.B.E., F.B.A. *Inspectress*, Miss D. Stroud, M.B.E., F.S.A.

SOMERSET HOUSE, Strand, W.C.2, and Victoria Embankment, W.C.2.—The beautiful river façade (600 ft. long) was built at the close of the 18th century from the designs of Sir W. Chambers; the remainder of the building is early 19th century. Somerset House was the property of Lord Protector Somerset, at whose attainder in 1552 the palace passed to the Crown, and it was a royal residence until about the close of the 17th century. The building is now occupied by the *Board of Inland Revenue* and other branches of the Civil Service and by the *Principal Probate Registry*.

STOCK EXCHANGE, E.C.2.—The foundation stone of the present building was laid in 1801, but the building was almost entirely reconstructed in 1854 from the designs of Thomas Allason. The Stock Exchange is being rebuilt as a large tower block 331 feet high and a new trading Floor to the west of the block. Completion is planned for 1972.

The Stock Exchange provides a market for the purchase and sale of about 9,200 securities quoted in the Stock Exchange Daily Official List and valued at over £121,113,000,000 and also securities listed on other Exchanges. At present the members of the Stock Exchange, who consist of brokers (agents for clients) and jobbers (dealers in specific securities) number about 3,400. Visitors' Gallery open between 10 a.m. and 3.15 p.m. from Monday to Friday. Admission free and without ticket. Film show.

THAMES EMBANKMENTS.—The Victoria Embankment, on the N. side (from Westminster to Blackfriars), was constructed by Sir J. W. Bazalgette for the Metropolitan Board of Works, 1864–70 (the seats, of which the supports of some are a kneeling camel, laden with spicery, and of others a winged sphinx, were presented by the Grocers' Company, and by Rt. Hon. W. H. Smith, M.P., in 1874); the Albert Embankment on the S. side (from Westminster Bridge to Vauxhall), 1866–69; the Chelsea Embankment, 1871–74. The total cost exceeded £2,000,000. Sir J. W. Bazalgette (1819–91) also inaugurated the London main drainage system, 1858–65. A medallion has been placed on a pier of the Victoria Embankment to commemorate the engineer of the Thames waterside improvements (" Flumini vincula posuit "). The headquarters of the G.L.C. include an embankment on the Surrey side.

THAMES TUNNELS.—The *Rotherhithe Tunnel*, constructed by the L.C.C. and opened in 1908, connects Commercial Road E.14, with Lower Road, Rotherhithe; the total length is 1 mile 332 yards, of which 474 yards are under the river. The cost of the tunnel and its approaches was £1,506,914. The first *Blackwall Tunnel* (foot passengers and vehicles) was constructed by the L.C.C. and opened in 1897, connecting East India Dock Road, Poplar, with Blackwall Lane, East Greenwich. The cost of the tunnel with its approaches was about £1,323,663. A second

tunnel (for southbound vehicles only) was opened in August, 1967, at a cost of about £9,000,000 and the old tunnel was improved at a cost of about £1,100,000 and made one-way northbound. Both tunnels are for vehicles only. The relative lengths of the tunnels measured from East India Dock Road to the Gate House on the south side are 6,215 ft. (old tunnel) and 6,152 feet. *Greenwich Tunnel* (foot passengers only), constructed by the L.C.C. and opened in 1902, connects the Isle of Dogs, Poplar, with Greenwich. The length of the subway is 406 yards, and the cost was about £180,000. The *Woolwich Tunnel* (foot passengers only), constructed by the L.C.C. and opened in 1912, connects North and South Woolwich below the passenger and vehicular ferry from North Woolwich Station, E.16, to High Street, Woolwich, S.E.18. The length of the subway is 552 yards, and its cost was about £86,000. The *Thames Tunnel* (1,300 feet) was opened in 1843 to connect Wapping (N.) with Rotherhithe (S.). In 1866 it was closed to the public, and purchased by the East London Railway Company. The *Tower Subway* for foot passengers was opened in 1870, and has long been closed.

TOWER HILL, E.C.1 and E.C.3, was formerly the place of execution for condemned prisoners from the Tower, the site of the scaffold being marked in the gardens of Trinity Square.

TOWER OF LONDON, E.C.3.—Admission to a general view of the Tower, the White Tower (Armouries), the Beauchamp and Bloody Towers and the Chapels Royal—20p; children, 5p (Oct.–March, 10p & 5p); to the Jewel House, 10p, children 5p. On Sundays throughout the year the public is admitted to Holy Communion, 9.15 a.m. and Morning Service, 11 a.m. Open on weekdays, March 1 to October 31, 9.30–5; Nov. 1–Feb. 28, 9.30–4; Sundays, 2 p.m. to 5 p.m., Mar. 1.–Oct. 31. only; Tower closed Christmas Eve, Christmas Day, Boxing Day and Good Friday. CONSTABLE, Field-Marshal Sir Richard Hull, G.C.B., D.S.O.; LIEUTENANT, Lieut.-General Sir Richard E. Goodwin, K.C.B., C.B.E., D.S.O.; RESIDENT GOVERNOR AND KEEPER OF THE JEWEL HOUSE, Maj.-Gen. W. D. M. Raeburn, C.B., D.S.O., M.B.E.; MASTER OF THE ARMOURIES, A. R. Dufty, F.S.A.; CHAPLAIN AT THE CHAPEL ROYAL OF ST. PETER AD VINCULA, Rev. J. G. Nicholls.

The White Tower is the oldest and central building in Her Majesty's Royal Palace and Fortress of the Tower of London. It was built at the order of William I. and constructed by Gundulph, Bishop of Rochester, in the years 1078–98. The Inner Wall, with thirteen towers, was constructed by Henry III. in the 12th century. The Moat was extended and completed by Richard I. and the Wharf first mentioned in 1228. The Outer Wall was completed in the reign of Edward I. and now incorporates 6 towers and 2 bastions. The last Monarch to reside in the Tower of London was James I. The Crown Jewels came to the Tower in the reign of Henry III. All coinage used in Great Britain was minted in the Outer Ward of the Tower of London until 1810 when the Royal Mint was formed. The Tower of London has had a military garrison since 1078. The Chapel Royal of St. John the Evangelist, within the White Tower (1080–1088) is the oldest Norman church in London.

WELLINGTON MUSEUM, Apsley House, Hyde Park Corner, W.1.—Admission on weekdays and Bank Holidays, 10 to 6; Sundays, 2.30 to 6. Closed Good Friday, Christmas Day and Boxing Day. Adults, 5p, Children, 2½p. Organized School parties admitted free. Apsley House was designed by Robert Adam for Lord Bathurst and built 1771–8. It was bought in 1817 by the Duke of Wellington,

who in 1828–29 employed Benjamin Wyatt to enlarge it. face it with Bath stone and add the Corinthian portico. The museum contains many fine paintings, services of porcelain and silver plate and personal relics of the 1st Duke of Wellington (1769–1852) and was given to the Nation by the present Duke. It was first opened to the public in 1952, under the administration of the Victoria and Albert Museum.

WESTMINSTER HALL, S.W.1 (built by William Rufus, A.D. 1097–99 and altered by Richard II., 1377–99), adjacent to and incorporated in the Houses of Parliament—Westminster Hall is part of the old Palace of Westminster and survived the fire, which destroyed most of the remainder of the Palace (Oct. 16, 1834) and the bombs of 1941. The Hall is about 240 ft. long, 69 ft. wide, and 90 ft. high. The hammer beam roof of carved oak, dating from 1396–98, is one of the principal attractions. King Charles I. was tried in the Hall. Extensive repairs to the Hall have recently been carried out. Admission: During sessions—Mon. to Thurs., 10 a.m. until 1.30 p.m., provided neither House is sitting. Sat. 10 a.m.–5 p.m. During Recess—Mon. to Fri., except Good Friday, Christmas Day and Boxing Day, 10 a.m.–4 p.m.; Sat., 10 a.m.–5 p.m.

WHITECHAPEL ART GALLERY, High Street, E.1. Charitable institution founded in 1901 for the organization of temporary exhibitions of the Fine Arts and Architecture. There is no permanent collection. Open: Tuesdays to Saturdays, 11–6; Sundays 2–6, closed Mondays. Admission Free. *Director*, M. Glazebrook.

PARKS, SPACES AND GARDENS

The principal Parks and Open Spaces in the Metropolitan area are maintained as under:—

By the Crown

BUSHY PARK (1,099 acres), see p. 651.

GREEN PARK (49 acres), W.1.—Between Piccadilly and St. James's Park with *Constitution Hill*, leading to Hyde Park Corner.

GREENWICH PARK (196½ acres), S.E.10, see p. 651.

HAMPTON COURT GARDENS (54 acres).

HAMPTON COURT GREEN (17 acres).

HAMPTON COURT PARK (622 acres).

HYDE PARK (341 acres).—From Park Lane, W.1, to Kensington Gardens, W.2, containing the Serpentine. Fine gateway at Hyde Park Corner, with Apsley House, the Achilles Statue, Rotten Row and the Ladies' Mile. To the north-east is the *Marble Arch*, originally erected by George IV. at the entrance to Buckingham Palace and re-erected in present position in 1851.

KENSINGTON GARDENS (275 acres), W.2.—From western boundary of Hyde Park to Kensington Palace, containing the Albert Memorial.

KEW, ROYAL BOTANIC GARDENS (300 acres).—Accessible by railway and omnibus. Open daily, except Christmas Day, from 10 a.m. The closing hour varies from 4 p.m. in mid-winter to 8 p.m. in mid-summer. Admission, 1p. Museums open 10 a.m.; Glasshouses, 1 p.m. to dusk or 4.50 p.m. (week-days); 1 p.m. to dusk or 5.50 p.m. (Sundays). Dogs not admitted.

REGENT'S PARK and PRIMROSE HILL (464 acres), N.W.1.—From Marylebone Road to Primrose Hill surrounded by the Outer Circle and divided by the *Broad Walk* leading to Zoological Gardens.

RICHMOND PARK (2,469 acres).

ST. JAMES'S PARK (93 acres), S.W.1.—From Whitehall to Buckingham Palace. Ornamental lake of 12 acres. The original suspension bridge built in 1857 was replaced in 1957. The *Mall* leads from the Admiralty Arch to the Queen Victoria Memorial and Buckingham Palace. *Birdcage*

Walk from Storey's Gate, past Wellington Barracks, to Buckingham Palace.

By the Corporation of London

BURNHAM BEECHES and FLEET WOOD (490 acres), *see* col. 2.

COULSDON COMMON, Surrey (111 acres).

EPPING FOREST (6,000 acres), *see* p. 651.

FARTHINGDOWN, Surrey (121 acres).

HIGHGATE WOOD (70 acres).

KENLEY COMMON, Surrey (80 acres).

QUEEN'S PARK, Kilburn (30 acres).

RIDDLESDOWN, Surrey (87 acres).

SPRING PARK, West Wickham (51 acres).

WEST HAM PARK (77 acres).

WEST WICKHAM COMMON, Kent (25 acres).

with smaller open spaces within the City of London, including FINSBURY CIRCUS GARDENS.

By the Greater London Council

(On April 1, 1971, administration of 126 parks and open spaces formerly controlled by the G.L.C. was assumed by the London Borough Councils.)

ALEXANDRA PARK and PALACE (208 acres), with roller skating and ski slope.

AVERY HILL (87 acres), S.E.9, with Winter Garden.

BATTERSEA PARK (200 acres), S.W.8 to S.W.11, with Festival gardens, concert pavilion, zoo and lake.

BLACKHEATH (271 acres), S.E.3.—*Morden College*, founded in 1695 as a home for " decayed Turkey merchants," is near the S.E. corner. The building was designed by Wren and its Chapel doors have carvings attributed to Grinling Gibbons. Concerts and poetry recitals are held at Rangers House, an early 18th Century mansion.

BOSTALL HEATH AND WOODS (159 acres), S.E.2.

CRYSTAL PALACE (199 acres), S.E.19, with motor-racing circuit; concert bowl; ski slope and National Recreation Centre. Zoo.

DULWICH PARK (72 acres), with lake, S.E.21.

FINSBURY PARK (115 acres), N.4.

GOLDER'S HILL (36 acres), adjoining West Heath, Hampstead.

HACKNEY MARSH (343 acres), E.5, E.9 and E.10. 112 football pitches.

HAINAULT FOREST (1,108 acres), Hainault, Essex, has two 18-hole public golf courses.

HAMPSTEAD HEATH and Extension (294 acres), N.W.3.

HERNE HILL STADIUM (9 acres), with cycle racing and athletics track.

HOLLAND PARK (55 acres), W.8. Open air theatre and concerts; floodlit gardens; King George VI Memorial Youth Hostel and Restaurant Belvedere.

HORNIMAN GARDENS (21 acres), S.E.23. Adjoining Horniman Museum.

KEN WOOD (200 acres), the northern part of Hampstead Heath. Part purchased in 1922 by public subscription. Opened and dedicated by King George V., July 18, 1925. Open air symphony concerts each summer. The Iveagh Bequest, in an 18th-century Mansion (open to the public), includes a fine Adam library and valuable art treasures. Recitals and poetry readings in the Orangery each summer. Ladies' swimming bath.

KING GEORGE'S FIELD (16 acres), E.3, with East London Stadium.

LESNES ABBEY WOODS (215 acres), Erith.—Ruins of an Augustinian abbey.

MARBLE HILL (66 acres).—Twickenham, Middlesex.—A beautiful park, running down to the riverside, on the left bank of the Thames; includes a mansion (open to the public), formerly the residence of Mrs. Fitzherbert, morganatic wife of George IV.

OXLEAS WOOD (213 acres), S.E.9.

PARLIAMENT HILL (271 acres)—part of Hampstead Heath. Lido and swimming bath. Important cross-country events are held here.

PARSLOES PARK (118 acres), Becontree, Essex.

TRENT PARK (600 acres), Cockfosters, Enfield. Country park with nature trail, riding school, picnic sites, fishing, etc.

VICTORIA PARK (217 acres), E.9. Lido.

WORMWOOD SCRUBS (193 acres), Hammersmith, W.12 and N.W.10. West London Stadium.

EXHIBITIONS ETC., IN LONDON

MADAME TUSSAUD'S EXHIBITION, Marylebone Road, N.W.1. Oct.–Mar., Weekdays, 10–5.30; Saturdays and Sundays, 10–6.30; April–Sept., daily 10–6.30. Admission, 50p, children under fourteen, 25p. Royal ticket, 70p, children, 35p. Includes:—

LONDON PLANETARIUM, Marylebone Road, N.W.1. Presentations hourly from 11 a.m. daily incl. Sundays. Admission, 25p; children (5–13 yrs.), 15p.

ROYAL HORTICULTURAL SOCIETY, Vincent Square, S.W.1, holds regular exhibitions at its Halls in Greycoat Street and in Vincent Square, S.W.1, and the Chelsea Flower Show at the Royal Hospital Grounds, Chelsea (May).

ZOOLOGICAL GARDENS, Regent's Park, N.W.1. — Opened 1828. Admission: (Mar.–Oct.) Monday to Saturday, 9–5; Sundays and Bank Holidays, 9–7; (Nov.–Feb.), 10–5. Mondays throughout the year (except Bank Holidays), Adults, 35p; Children under 14, 20p; all other days, Adults, 45p; Children, 25p. Additional charge for admission to the Aquarium and the Children's Zoo. Special rates for parties.

WHIPSNADE ZOOLOGICAL PARK, Whipsnade Park, nr. Dunstable, Beds. (34 miles from London, 8½ miles from Luton and 3 miles from Dunstable). Opened 1931. Admission on Sundays and week-days, from 10 a.m. to 7 p.m., or sunset, whichever is the earlier. Adults, 40p; Children under 14, 20p. Cars admitted at extra charge. Special rates for parties.

MUSIC

ROYAL OPERA HOUSE, Covent Garden, W.C.2. —Opera and Ballet throughout the year. The (third) Covent Garden Theatre was opened May 15, 1858 (the first was opened Dec. 7, 1732). *General Administrator*, J. Tooley.

ROYAL ALBERT HALL, Kensington, S.W.7— Regular seasons of Promenade Concerts. Also used for public meetings, concerts and other entertainments. The elliptical hall, one of the largest in the world, was completed in 1871.

ROYAL FESTIVAL HALL, South Bank, S.E.1.— Opened for the Festival of Britain, 1951, and administered by Greater London Council. Concerts and regular ballet seasons. Queen Elizabeth Hall and Purcell Room opened 1967. *Director, South Bank Concert Halls*, J. Denison, C.B.E.

KNELLER HALL, Twickenham.—Royal Military School of Music. The full band of 250 instrumentalists holds concerts in the grounds on Wednesdays throughout the summer season, commencing at 8 p.m. Members of the public are welcome to attend; admission, 10p. Season tickets available.

ENVIRONS OF LONDON

BARNET AND HADLEY GREEN.—Scene of Battle, A.D. 1471. Hadley Woods.

BURNHAM BEECHES and FLEET WOOD, Bucks.— Magnificent wooded scenery (425 acres), purchased by the Corporation of London for the benefit of the public in 1879; Fleet Wood (65 acres) presented in 1921. During summer omnibus runs

daily, Sundays included, from Slough Station (Western Region), passing within 250 yards of "Gray's Elegy" Church. *See* "Stoke Poges."

BUSHY PARK (1,099 acres).—Adjoining Hampton Court, contains many fine trees and avenue of horse-chestnuts enclosed in a fourfold avenue of limes, planted by King William III. "Chestnut Sunday" (when the trees are in full bloom with their "candles") is usually about May 1 to 15.

CHEQUERS, a country residence for Prime Ministers, was presented to the Nation (with an endowment to maintain the estate, etc.) by Lord and Lady Lee of Fareham, as the official country residence for the Prime Minister of the day, and the gift was approved by Parliament in the *Chequers Estate Act, 1917*. In 1921 the Chequers Estate of 700 acres was added to the gift by Lord Lee. Chequers is a mansion in Tudor style in the Chilterns, about 3 miles from Princes Risborough, Bucks, and contains a collection of Cromwellian portraits and relics.

DARWIN AND DOWN HOUSE, Downe, Farnborough, Kent.—Where Charles Darwin thought and worked for 40 years and died in 1882. Maintained by the Royal College of Surgeons. Open daily (except Fridays and Christmas Day 10 to 5 (Nov.–March, 11 to 5). Admission, 25p; Children, 10p.

DORNEYWOOD, country house in 215 acres, near Burnham Beeches, Bucks., was presented to the nation by Lord Courtauld-Thomson (died 1954) as an official residence for any Minister of the Crown chosen by the Prime Minister during office. Administered by the National Trust. Open to the public on Saturdays only (August and Sept., 2–6 p.m.) Admission 10p, Children, 5p.

DULWICH, S.E.21 (5 miles from London), contains *Dulwich College* (founded by Edward Alleyn in 1619), the *Horniman Museum* and *Dulwich Park* (72 acres). The *Dulwich Picture Gallery*, built by Sir John Soane to house the collection bequeathed by the artist, Sir Francis Bourgeois, was damaged by enemy action in the Second World War. The pictures, however, were saved, and the gallery has been rebuilt with the aid of a grant from the Pilgrim Trust. It was reopened by Queen Elizabeth the Queen Mother on April 27, 1953. In *Dulwich Village* the rural characteristics of the pre-suburban period are preserved.

ELTHAM, Kent (10 miles from London by Southern Region). Remains of 13th–15th century Eltham Palace, the birthplace of John of Eltham (1316), son of Edward II. The hall, built by Edward IV., contains fine hammer-beam roof of chestnut. In the churchyard of St. John the Baptist is the tomb of Thomas Doggett, the comedian and founder of the Thames Watermen's championship (Doggett's Coat and Badge).

EPPING FOREST (6,000 acres, originally purchased by the Corporation of London for £250,000 and thrown open to the public in 1882; the present forest is 12 miles long by 1 to 2 miles wide, about one-tenth of its original area). LOUGHTON, BUCKHURST HILL, CHINGFORD, HIGH BEECH (London Transport and Eastern Region). Beautiful forest scenery.

ETON COLLEGE.—22 miles from London. The most famous of English schools, founded by Henry VI in 1440, the scholars numbering 1,195 in July, 1970. Buildings date from 1442.

GREENWICH, S.E.10.—*Greenwich Hospital* (since 1873, the Royal Naval College) was built by Charles II, from designs by Inigo Jones, and by Queen Anne and William III, from designs by Wren, on the site of an ancient royal palace, and of the more recent *Placentia*, an enlarged edition of the palace, constructed by Humphrey, Duke of Gloucester (1391–1447), son of Henry IV. Henry

VIII, Queen Mary I and Queen Elizabeth I were born in the Royal Palace (which reverted to the Crown in 1447) and King Edward VI died there. In the principal quadrangle is a marble statue of George II, by Rysbraeck. (For *National Maritime Museum*, see Index.) *Painted Hall* and *Chapel* open daily except Thursdays from 2.30 p.m.to 5 p.m. (closed on Sundays, Oct.–April inclusive). Visitors are also admitted to Morning Service in the Chapel at 11 a.m., summer and winter, except during College vacations. *Greenwich Park* (196½ acres) was enclosed by Humphrey, Duke of Gloucester, and laid out by Charles II, from the designs of Le Nôtre. On a hill in Greenwich Park is the former Royal Observatory (founded 1675). Part of its buildings at Greenwich have been taken over by the Maritime Museum and named *Flamsteed House*, after John Flamsteed (1646–1719), first Astronomer Royal. The parish church of Greenwich (*St. Alfege*) was rebuilt by Hawksmoor (Wren's pupil) in 1728, and restored after severe damage during the Second World War. General Wolfe (Heights of Abraham) and Tallis ("the father of Church Music") are buried in the church. Henry VIII was christened in the former church. *Charlton House*: built in the early 17th century (1607–1612) for Adam Newton, tutor to Prince Henry, brother to Charles I. The house is largely in the Jacobean style of architecture. *Cutty Sark*, the last of the famous tea clippers, which has been preserved as a memorial to ships and men of a past era. The ship is fully restored and re-rigged, with a museum of sail on board. Open to visitors: weekdays, 11 to 5 (Summer, 6 p.m.); Sundays and Boxing Day, 2.30 to 5. The yacht *Gipsy Moth IV* in which Sir Francis Chichester sailed single-handed round the world, 1966–67, is preserved alongside *Cutty Sark*.

HAM HOUSE, Richmond.—A notable example of 17th-century domestic architecture, long the home of the Tollemache family (Earls of Dysart). The contents, described as "probably the finest and most varied collection of Charles II.'s reign to survive," were purchased for the Victoria and Albert Museum which now administers the house. Ham House may be seen on Tues.–Sun. inclusive and on Bank Holidays, 2–6 p.m., March–Sept., 12–4 p.m., Oct.–Feb. Closed Mon. (except Bank Holidays), Christmas Day and Good Friday. Admission, 10p; Children 5p.

HAMPTON COURT.—Sixteenth-century Palace built by Cardinal Wolsey, with additions by Sir Christopher Wren for William and Mary, 15 miles from London. Fine view of river. Beautiful gardens with maze and prolific grape vine (planted in 1769). Old Royal Apartments and collection of pictures. Tennis Court, built by King Henry VIII in 1530. The Palace is *closed* on Christmas Day, Boxing Day and Good Friday. Comprehensive ticket for all parts of the Palace open to the public, 20p; Children under 15, 5p. Individual tickets for Vine (1p) and Maze (2p) also available. Admission, Oct.–March, when the Tudor Tennis Court and the Banqueting House are closed, Adults, 10p; Children, 5p. Refreshments can be obtained in the Tilt Yard gardens during the summer season. *Bushy Park* adjoins the Lion Gates of Hampton Court Palace.

Grace and Favour Residences.—Hampton Court contains a total of 57 residences occupied by favour of Her Majesty the Queen. The Minister of Public Building and Works reported in Parliament on April 17, 1962, that, of 140 grace and favour residences, the remainder were situated at Windsor Castle (46), Kensington Palace (16), St. James's Palace (8), Marlborough House Mews (9), Bushy Park (2), Kew Palace (1) and Hyde Park (1).

HARROW-ON-THE-HILL.—10 miles by Metropolitan and other railways. Large public school founded by John Lyon in 1571. The "Fourth Form Room" dates from 1608.

HUGHENDEN MANOR, High Wycombe, Bucks.— The home of Disraeli from 1847 till his death and contains much of his furniture, books, etc. Conveyed to the National Trust in 1947. Open daily including Sundays and Bank Holidays, 2-6 or till dusk. Saturdays and Sundays, 12.30 to 6. Closed Tuesdays and all January, Good Friday and Christmas Day. Admission (non-members), 20p; Children, 10p.

JORDANS AND CHALFONT ST. GILES, near Beaconsfield, Bucks, contain the Old _Quaker Meeting House_ (1688) at Jordans, in the burial ground of which lies William Penn (Pennsylvania); a barn built out of the timbers of the _Mayflower_ by the 17th-century owner of Jordans (Gardener). At Chalfont St. Giles is the cottage where Milton lived during the Great Plague (1665-1666).

KEW, Surrey, was a favourite home of the early Hanoverian monarchs. Kew House, the residence of Frederick, Prince of Wales, and later of his son, George III, was pulled down in 1803, but the earlier Dutch House, now known as Kew Palace, survives. It was built in 1631 and acquired by George III as an annexe to Kew House in 1781. The famous Kew Gardens (_see_ p. 649) were originally laid out as a private garden for Kew House for George III's mother in 1759 and were much enlarged in the nineteenth century, notably by the inclusion of the grounds of the former Richmond Lodge.

MARBLE HILL HOUSE, Twickenham, Middlesex. —Example of the English Palladian style. Reopened 1966, after restoration work on the elevations of the house, entrance hall, main staircase and first floor rooms. The Great Room and mahogany staircase are noteworthy. Open Tues. to Sat., 10-5; Sunday, 2-5; and on Bank Holiday Mondays. Closed Xmas Eve and Xmas Day. Admission, 10p.

NATIONAL ARMY MUSEUM, Royal Hospital Road, S.W.3. Established by Royal Charter (1960). Official Museum for British Army, Honourable East India Company, Indian Services and Colonial Forces. British Army section in new building at Chelsea. Indian Army room remains open at R.M.A. Sandhurst, Camberley, Surrey.

OSTERLEY PARK, Isleworth.—House and park of 300 acres given to the National Trust by the Earl of Jersey in 1949. Part of the Elizabethan house, built in 1577 for Sir Thomas Gresham, remains, but it was largely remodelled by Robert Adam, and the staterooms are among the best examples of Adam decoration. Open daily, except Mondays, (April-Sept.) 2-6 p.m.; (Oct.-Mar.) 12 noon-4 p.m. Closed Monday (except Bank Holidays), Christmas Day, Boxing Day and Good Friday. Admission 5p., children 2½p.

RICHMOND, Surrey, contains the red brick gateway of _Richmond Palace_ (Henry VII, 1485-1509) and buildings of the Jacobean, Queen Anne, and early Georgian periods, including _White Lodge_ in Richmond Park, the former home of Queen Mary's mother (the Duke of Windsor was born there, June 23, 1894). The _Star and Garter_ Home for Disabled Soldiers, Sailors, and Airmen (the Women's Memorial of the Great War) was opened by Queen Mary in 1924. _Richmond Park_ (2,469 acres) contains herds of fallow and red deer. From the _Terrace Gardens_, Richmond Hill, can be obtained a wonderful view of the Valley of the Thames.

RUNNIMEDE.—A meadow of about 100 acres, on S. bank of Thames (part of the Crown Lands),

between Windsor and Staines. From June 15-23, 1215, the hostile Barons encamped on this meadow during negotiations with King John, who rode over each day from Windsor. The 48 "Articles of the Barons" were accepted by the King on June 15, and were subsequently embodied in 1 charter, since known as _Magna Carta_, of which several copies were sealed on June 19. About half a mile N.E. of the meadow is _Magna Carta Island_ (claimed as the actual site of the sealing), presented to the National Trust in 1930 by Lady Fairhaven and her sons.

A memorial at _Cooper's Hill_, near Runnimede, to members of the Commonwealth air forces who lost their lives in the Second World War while serving from bases in the United Kingdom and north-western Europe and have no known grave, was unveiled by the Queen on October 17, 1953. Her Majesty on May 14, 1965, unveiled a memorial to the late President of the United States, John F. Kennedy, on ground nearby.

ST. ALBANS.—A city in Hertfordshire, on the river Ver, 22 miles N.W. of London. The abbey church, built partly of materials from the old Roman city of Verulamium by Paul of Caen, was consecrated in 1115. Parts still remain of the Norman structure. The city was the scene of the overthrow of Henry VI in 1455, and of the Earl of Warwick in 1461. The site of the pre-Roman city of King Tasciovanus and the remains of the ancient City of Verulamium, with well preserved theatre and many other features, excavated in recent years. St. Michael's Church, thought to contain the burial place of Sir Francis Bacon.

STOKE POGES (2 miles from Slough station, Western Region) contains the 14th-century Church with the Churchyard of Gray's "Elegy" and "Ode on a Distant Prospect of Eton College." The poet was buried in the church in 1771.

SYON HOUSE, Brentford.—The summer home of the Duke of Northumberland. The House is built on the remains of the Nunnery of Syon, founded by the order of Henry V in 1415. At the Dissolution of the Monasteries the estate reverted to the Crown. In 1594 it was granted to the 9th Earl of Northumberland, who altered and improved the property. In the eight years, 1762-1770, the interior was transformed and furnished by Robert Adam. The lion on the river front stood originally on Northumberland House in the Strand, which was demolished in 1874. Open Easter to Sept.

WALTHAM ABBEY (or WALTHAM HOLY CROSS), 13 miles from London (Eastern Region).—The Abbey ruins, Harold's Bridge (11th century), the Nave of the former cruciform Abbey Church (the oldest Norman building in England (consecrated May 3, 1060) and the traditional burial place of King Harold II (1066), and a Lady Chapel of Edward II, with crypt below. New evidence of the position and style of several buildings, which once stood on the site of the Augustinian monastery, were revealed by the prolonged drought in the summer of 1933. At Waltham Cross, 1 mile from the Abbey, is one of the crosses (partly restored) erected by Edward I to mark a resting place of the corpse of Queen Eleanor on its way to Westminster Abbey. (Ten crosses were erected, but only those at Geddington, Northampton and Waltham remain; "Charing" Cross originally stood near the spot now occupied by the statue of Charles I at Whitehall.)

WINDSOR CASTLE (begun by William the Conqueror, A.D. 1066-87).—22 miles from London, by Western and Southern Regions. The Castle Precincts are open daily, free of charge, from 10 a.m. to sunset. When the Court is not in

residence, the *State Apartments* of Windsor Castle are open to the public, during Her Majesty's pleasure, on every weekday and on certain Sunday afternoons during the summer months. When the State Apartments are open, the charges for admission are for Adults, 15p and for Children, 5p. By the Queen's command, the net proceeds go to charities. An authorized guide book can be obtained at the office, price 10p. The hours of admission to the State Apartments are: May–Sept., 11–5; Mar. and April, 11–4; Oct. 11–4; Sundays, May–Sept., 1.30–5; Oct. 1.30–4; closed Nov.–March). *Queen Mary's Doll's House*, the *Exhibition of Dolls* and the *Old Master Drawings* can be seen on the same days and hours as the State Apartments, admission 5p. each person to each. When the State Apartments are closed, Queen Mary's Doll's House and the Exhibition of Old Master Drawings remain open to the public. The *Albert Memorial Chapel* is open throughout the year from 10–1; 2–4 closed on Sundays; the *Round Tower* or *Keep* is open from April 1 to Sept. 30 (except when the Royal Standard is flying) the same days and hours as the State Apartments. Admission free. By permission of the Dean and Chapter, *St. George's Chapel* may be viewed on Mon.–Thurs., between 11 a.m. and 3.45 p.m.; Fridays, 1 p.m. to 3.45 p.m.; Sundays, 2.30 to 3.45 p.m. Admission, except at service times: 15p, children 5p. The chapel is usually closed during January. The Daily Services in the Chapel are open to the public. The *Curfew Tower* may be seen under the guidance of the Keeper to whom application must be made at the entrance (admission 5p).

The *Royal Mausoleum*, Frogmore Gardens, Home Park, is open annually on two days in early May, usually the first Wednesday and Thursday in the month, in conjunction with the opening of Frogmore Gardens in aid of the National Garden Scheme, 10 a.m.-dusk. Also open on the Wednesday nearest to May 24 (Queen Victoria's birthday) from 11 a.m. to 4 p.m. Admission free.

HOUSES OPEN TO THE PUBLIC

Times of summer opening and admission fees shown are those which obtained in 1971, and are subject to modification. Space permits only a selection of some of the more noteworthy houses in England which are open to the public. A fuller description of some houses in or near London will be found in the preceding section.

ADLINGTON HALL, Cheshire.—Sun. and Bank Holidays (Sats., July and August), 2.30–6. Admission, 20p.

ALNWICK CASTLE, Northumberland. Seat of the Duke of Northumberland.—May–Sept., Sun.–Thurs., 1–5. Admission, 20p.

ALTHORP, nr. Northampton. Seat of Earl Spencer.—May, Sun. only, June–Sept., Sun., Tues., Thurs. and Bank Holidays (also Easter Sun. and Mon.) 2.30–6. Admission, 20p.

*ANGLESEY ABBEY, Cambs.—Easter to first week in Oct., Wed., Thurs., Sat., Sun., and Bank Holidays, 2–6. Admission 25p.

*ANTONY HOUSE, Cornwall.—Tues., Wed., Thurs. and Bank Holidays, 2–6. Admission 25p.

*ARLINGTON COURT, nr. Barnstaple.—April-mid-Oct., daily, 11–1, 2–6. Admission, 35p.

ARRETON MANOR, Isle of Wight.—Daily, 10–6 (Sun., 2.30–6.30). Admission, 15p.

ARUNDEL CASTLE, Sussex. Seat of the Duke of Norfolk—Mid-April to mid-June, Mon.–Thurs.; mid-June to end of Sept., Mon.–Fri. (and some Suns. in August), 1–4.30. Admission, 25p.

*ASCOTT, Wing, Bucks.—Including Anthony de Rothschild collection of pictures. April–Sept. Wed., Sat. and Bank Holidays (also some Suns. in July and August), 2–6. Admission 25p.

AUDLEY END, Saffron Walden.—April–early Oct., daily, except Mon. (but including Bank Holidays), 11.30–5.30. Admission, 15p.

AVEBURY MANOR, Wiltshire. (Adjoining the famous Avebury stone circle, which is also on public view).—May–August, daily except Tues., 2–6; April and Sept., Sat., Sun. and Bank Holidays, 10–6. Admission, 20p.

BELVOIR CASTLE, nr. Grantham. Seat of the Duke of Rutland.—Easter–Sept., Wed., Thurs., Sat., 12–6; Bank Holidays and day following, 11–7; Sundays, 2–7. Admission, 25p.

BERKELEY CASTLE, Glos.—Easter–Sept., daily, except Mon., (but including Bank Holidays), 2–5.30; Bank Holidays, 11–5.30. Admission, 20p.

BLENHEIM PALACE, Woodstock. Seat of the Duke of Marlborough and birthplace of Sir Winston Churchill.—April–third week in July and third week in Sept. till end of Oct., Mon.–Thurs. (open Easter week-end except Good Friday, but closed Spring Bank Holiday); third week in July–third

week in Sept., daily except Fri., 1–6. Admission 30p.

*BLICKLING HALL, Norfolk.—Easter–first week in Oct., Wed, Thurs., Sat., Sun. and Bank Holidays, 2–6. Admission, 25p.

*BUCKLAND ABBEY, Tavistock.—Including Drake relics. Easter–Sept. 30, weekdays and Bank Holidays, 11–6. Sun. 2–6. Admission, 10p.

CASTLE ASHBY, nr. Northampton. A home of the Marquess of Northampton.—Thurs., Sat. and Bank Holidays; also Easter week-end. Sundays in June, July and August, 2–5.30. Admission, 30 p.

CASTLE HOWARD, Yorkshire.—Tues., Wed., Thurs., Sat., Sun., 1.30–5; Bank Holidays, 11.30–5.30. Admission, 40p.

*CHARLECOTE PARK, Warwicks. Associations with Shakespeare.—Daily, except Mon., but incl. Bank Holidays, 11.15–5.45. Admission, 20p.

*CHARTWELL, Kent.—Home of the late Sir Winston Churchill. Sat., Sun and Bank Holidays, 11–6; Wed. and Thurs., 2–6. Admission, 30p.

CHATSWORTH, Derbyshire. Seat of the Duke of Devonshire.—Wed., Thurs. and Fri., 11.30–4; Sat. and Sun., 2–5.30; Bank Holidays and Tuesdays after Bank Holidays, 11.30–5.30. Admission, 30p.

*CLAYDON HOUSE, Bucks.—Daily except Mondays, but including Bank Holiday, 2–6. Admission, 25 p.

*CLIVEDEN, Bucks.—Wed., Sat. and Sun, 2.30–5.30. Admission, 5p.

*COMPTON CASTLE, nr. Paignton.—Fortified manor house. Mon., Wed. and Thurs., 10.30–12.30, 2–5. Admission, 20 p.

COMPTON WYNYATES, Warwickshire. A home of the Marquess of Northampton.—Wed., Sat. and Bank Holidays. Sundays (June–August only), (also Easter week-end), 2–5.30. Admission, 40p.

CORSHAM COURT, Wilts.—April to mid-July, and mid-Sept. to Oct., Wed., Thurs., Sun. and Bank Holidays; mid-July to mid-Sept., daily except Mon. and Fri., 11–12.30, 2–6. Admission, 17½p.

*COTEHELE, nr. Calstock, Cornwall.—Daily except Mon. (but including Bank Holidays), 11–1, 2–6. Admission 30 p.

*DYRHAM PARK, Glos.—Wed.–Sun., 2–6; Bank Holidays, 12–6 (Oct., Wed, Sat. and Sun., 2–6). Admission, 25p.

EYE MANOR, Hertfordshire.—Mon., Wed., Thurs. and Sat. (and Tues. after Bank Holidays)

* Property of the National Trust.

(mid-July–mid-Sept., daily), 2.30–5.30. Admission, 20 p.

GAWSWORTH HALL, Cheshire.—Sun., Wed., Sat. and Bank Holidays, 2–6. Admission, 20p.

HADDON HALL, Derbyshire.—Tues.–Sat. and Bank Holidays, 11–6; Sun. preceding Bank Holidays, 2–6. Admission, 25p.

*HARDWICK HALL, Derbyshire.—Wed., Thurs., Sat., Sun. and Bank Holidays, 2–6. Admission 30p.

HAREWOOD HOUSE, Yorks. Seat of the Earl of Harewood.—Easter–Sept., daily. Oct., Sundays only, 11–6. Admission, 20p.

HATFIELD HOUSE, Hertfordshire. Seat of the Marquess of Salisbury.—April, weekdays (and Easter Sun. and Mon.). May–first week in Oct., daily except Mon. (but including Bank Holidays). Weekdays, 12–5. Sun., 2.30–5.30. Admission, 18p.

HEDINGHAM CASTLE, Essex.—May–Sept., Tues., Thurs. and Sat., 2–6. Bank Holidays (incl. Easter Monday), 10–6. Admission, 12½p.

HOLKER HALL, Lancashire.—Easter–second week in Oct., daily except Sat., 10.30–6. Admission, 25 p.

KNEBWORTH HOUSE, Herts.—April, Sat., Sun. and Bank Holidays; May–Sept., daily, except Mon. (and Tues. after Bank Holidays) (but including Bank Holidays), 2.30–5.30. Admission 25 p.

*KNOLE, Sevenoaks.—Wed.–Sat. and Bank Holidays, 10–12, 2–5. Admission, 30p. (Fridays, 40p.).

*LACOCK ABBEY, Wilts.—House: Wed., Thurs., Sat. and Bank Holidays, 2–6. Admission, 15p. Monastic remains: Daily except Friday, 2–6. Admission, 15p.

*LITTLE MORETON HALL, Cheshire. Famous example of "black and white" timbering.—Daily except Tuesday and Good Friday, 2–6. Admission, 20 p.

LONGLEAT HOUSE, Wilts. Seat of the Marquess of Bath.—Daily, 10–6. Admission, 30p.

LUTON HOO, Beds.—Easter–Sept., Mon., Wed., Thurs. and Sat., 11–6; Sundays, 2–6. Admission, 25p.

*MELFORD HALL, Suffolk.—April–Sept., Sun., Wed., Thurs. and Bank Holidays, 2.30–6. Admission, 20 p.

MILTON MANOR HOUSE, nr. Abingdon.—May–Sept., Sat., Sun. and Bank Holidays (also Easter Sun. and Mon.). 2–6; Admission, 25p.

*MONTACUTE HOUSE, Yeovil.—Daily, except Mon. and Tues. (but including Bank Holidays), 12.30–6 (Oct., Sun., Wed. and Sat., 2–6). Admission, 25p. (Friday, 50p.).

OSBORNE HOUSE, Isle of Wight. State and Private Apartments are shown, including the room in which Queen Victoria died.—Mon.–Fri., 11–5.30. Admission, 20p.

*OXBURGH HALL, Norfolk.—Sun, Wed., Thurs. Sat. and Bank Holidays, 2–6. Admission, 20 p.

PARHAM, Pulborough, Sussex.—Sun., Wed., Thurs. and Bank Holidays, 2–5.30. Admission, 25p. (last Sunday of each month, 40p.).

*PAYCOCKE'S, Coggeshall, Essex. Tudor woolmerchant's town house.—Easter–Sept., Wed., Thurs., Sun. and Bank Holidays, 2–5.30. Admission, 15p.

*PECKOVER HOUSE, Wisbech, Cambs.—Sun., Wed., Thurs., Sat. and Bank Holidays, 2–6 (Oct., 2–5). Admission, 15p.

PENSHURST PLACE, Kent. Seat of Visct. De L'Isle, ℣℃.—April, Sat. and Sun; May–Sept., Wed., Thurs., Sat., Sun. and Bank Holidays (also Tues., June–mid-Sept.), 2–6 (July–Sept., 12.30–6, Bank Holidays, 11.30–6). Admission, 30p.

*PETWORTH HOUSE, Sussex.—Wed., Thurs., Sat. and Bank Holidays, 2–6. Admission, 25p. First and third Tuesday in each month, 35p.

POWDERHAM CASTLE, Devonshire. Seat of the Earl of Devon.—June to first week in Sept., daily, except Sat., 2–6. Admission, 20 p.

RABY CASTLE, Co. Durham.—Easter week-end and May, Sun. and Spring Holiday week-end; June–Sept., Sun., Wed., Sat. and Bank Holidays (daily, Aug. to first week in Sept., except Fri.), 2–5. Admission, 20 p.

RAGLEY HALL, Warwickshire. Seat of the Marquess of Hertford.—Easter–Sept., Sun., Tues., Wed., Thurs., Sat. and Bank Holidays, 2–6. Admission, 25 p.

*ST. MICHAEL'S MOUNT. Situated on island off Marazion, Cornwall.—Wed. and Fri. Also Mon. from June–Sept., 10.30–4.30. Closed Good Friday. Admission, Wed. and Fri., 10p., Mon., 15p.

*SALTRAM HOUSE, nr. Plymouth.—Easter–mid-Oct., daily, 2–6. Admission, 35p. (Tues. and Fri., 50p.)

SHERBORNE CASTLE, Dorset.—Sun., Thurs., Sat. and Bank Holidays, 2–6. Admission 25p.

*SISSINGHURST CASTLE, Kent.—Daily, 10–7. Admission, 20p.

SKIPTON CASTLE, Yorkshire.—Weekdays, 10 a.m. till sunset, Sundays from 2 p.m. Admission, 10p.

*SNOWSHILL MANOR, nr. Broadway.—May–Sept., Sun., Wed., Thurs., Sat. and Bank Holidays (April and Oct., Sat., Sun. and Easter Monday only), 11–1, 2–6. Admission, 25p.

STANFORD HALL, Rugby.—Thurs., Sat. and Sun., 2.30–6. Bank Holidays and Tues. after Bank Holidays, 12–6. Admission, 18p.

STOKESAY CASTLE, Salop.—Daily, except Tuesdays, 9–6. Admission, 15p.

*STOURHEAD, Wiltshire.—Wed., Thurs., Sat. Sun. and Bank Holidays (Oct., Wed., Sat. and Sun. only), 2–6. Admission, 15p.

SULGRAVE MANOR, Northamptonshire. Former home of members of the Washington family.—Daily, except Weds., 10.30–1, 2–5.30 (closes at 4 p.m., Oct.). Admission, 15p.

TATTON PARK, Cheshire.—Daily, except Mondays, but including Bank Holidays, 2–5.15 (2–5.45, first week in May–first week in Sept.). Admission, 10p.

*UPPARK, nr. Petersfield.—Wed., Thurs., Sun. and Bank Holidays, 2–6. Admission, 25p.

*THE VYNE, Basingstoke.—April–Sept., Wed. and Bank Holidays, 11–1, 2–6; Sun. and Thurs., 2–6. Admission, 20p.

*WADDESDON MANOR, Bucks.—Wed.–Sun., 2–6. Bank Holidays, 11–6. Admission, 30p. (Fri. 50p.)

WARWICK CASTLE. Seat of the Earl of Warwick. —Daily, 10–5.30. Admission, 40p.

WESTON PARK, Salop. Seat of the Earl of Bradford.—Daily, except Mon. and Tues. (but including Bank Holidays), 2–6, (Sun. and Bank Holidays), 1.30–6. Admission, 30p.

WILTON HOUSE, Wilts. Seat of the Earl of Pembroke.—April–Sept., Tues.–Sat., and Bank Holidays, 11–5.30. Sun., 2–5.30. Admission, 30p.

WOBURN ABBEY (and Zoo Park). Seat of the Duke of Bedford.—Daily, 11.30–6 (Sun., 11.30–7). Admission, various.

* Property of the National Trust.

MUSEUMS AND ART GALLERIES OUTSIDE LONDON

BIRMINGHAM.—*City Museum and Art Gallery.* The art collection contains outstanding examples by British and European masters from 14th to 20th centuries, with particularly strong Pre-Raphaelite and Burne-Jones collections, sculpture, prints, drawings and watercolours, British and European gold, silver and jewellery, pottery and porcelain, furniture, toys, textiles and costume. Open, free, Weekdays, 10–6; Sundays 2–5.30. Closed Christmas Day, Boxing Day and Good Friday.

Museum of Science and Industry, Newhall Street. Founded 1950, the first provincial museum of its kind devoted to the history of science from the Industrial Revolution to the present. Many working machines under steam, gas, etc. Open, free, Weekdays, 10–5; Saturdays, 10–5.30; Sundays, 2–5.30. Open to 9 on first Wednesday evening of each month. Other Birmingham museums are: *Aston Hall, Blakesley Hall, Cannon Hill Museum, Sarehole Mill* and *Weoley Castle.*

BOWES MUSEUM, Barnard Castle. Important paintings of Italian, Dutch, French and Spanish schools. Fine porcelain and pottery, tapestries and furniture. Open, weekdays, May–Sept., 10–5.30; March, April and October, 10–5; Nov.–Feb., 10–4. Sundays, 2–5 (Summer); 2–4 (Winter). Admission, 10p.

BRADFORD.—*Cartwright Hall* contains Italian Old Masters, British paintings, drawings and watercolours from the 18th century onwards. Chinese ceramics. *Bolling Hall* is a furnished Period house *circa* 1400 to *circa* 1800. Open all week; (May–Aug.), 10–8; (April and Sept.), 10–7; (Oct.–Mar.), 10–5. *Bradford Industrial Museum*, Moorside Mills, Eccleshill, illustrates local industries, particularly wool textiles.

BRIGHTON.—The Royal Pavilion. Palace of George IV. Annual Regency Exhibition, early July to end of Sept. Open daily, 10–5 (10–8 during Regency Exhibition). Closed on Christmas Day and Boxing Day.

Art Gallery and Museum. Housed in buildings which were once part of Stables of Royal Pavilion. Open 10–7 (Saturdays, 10–5; Sundays, 2–5).

Preston Manor, Preston Park. (Thomas-Stanford: Macquoid bequests of English period furniture, furnishings, china and silver). Open weekdays 10–5, Sundays, 2–5. Admission 10p; Children 2½p. Gardens open, free

The Grange, Rottingdean. Includes Sussex Room, Kipling Room and Museum of Children's Toys. Open, free, 10–7; Saturdays, 10–5; Sundays, 2–6 (winter, 2–5).

BRISTOL.—*City Art Gallery.* Collection of Old Masters, 19th cent. and modern paintings, English watercolours, Chinese ceramics, glass, English silver, glass, porcelain and delftware, English and foreign embroideries. Open weekdays, 10–5.30. *Red Lodge*, Park Row. Furnished in style of 17th and very early 18th centuries. Open weekdays, 1–5. *Georgian House*, Great George Street. Furnished in style of period. Open weekdays, 11–5.

CAMBRIDGE.—Fitzwilliam Museum. The Fine Art collections of the University, and one of the most important museums outside London. The chief collections, largely due to private benefaction, comprise Egyptian, Greek and Roman antiquities, coins and medals, mediæval manuscripts, paintings and drawings, prints, pottery and porcelain, textiles, arms and armour, mediæval and renaissance objects of art, and a library. Open, free, weekdays 10–5; Sundays, 2.15–5. Closed Christmas Day, Boxing Day and Good Friday.

CANTERBURY.—Royal Museum. Collections include archæology, geology and natural history.

Much Roman material from post-war excavations of Canterbury. Open free weekdays, 9.30–5.30.

CARISBROOKE.—Castle Museum. Former home in Carisbrooke Castle of Governor of Isle of Wight. Collections cover archæology and history of Isle of Wight, and personal relics of Charles I, who was imprisoned in Castle from 1647 to 1648. Open, March–April and Oct. 9.30–5.30 (Sundays, 2–5.30); May–Sept. 9.30–7 (Sundays, 2–7); Nov.–Feb. 10–4.30. (Sundays, 2–4.30). Admission to Castle and Museum, 15p. (in winter, 10p.).

COLCHESTER.—Colchester and Essex Museum, The Castle. The Norman Castle contains local archæological antiquities, especially the extensive finds from Roman Colchester. The *Holly Trees Mansion* (1718) covers the activities of social life of the 18th and 19th centuries. *Natural History Museum*, All Saints Church. Natural history of Essex. Open, weekdays, 10–5 (branches closed 1–2 p.m.); Sundays, 2.30–5 (April–Sept.). Weekdays: admission to all museums free; Sundays, Adults, 10p.; Children free.

DERBY.—Museum and Art Gallery, Strand. Important collections of works by Joseph Wright of Derby, A.R.A., 1734–1797; Derby porcelain. Unique exhibit illustrating the history of the Midland Railway including a working model layout. Open, weekdays, 10–6 (Saturdays, 10–5); Sundays, 2.30–4.30 (art gallery only).

GUILDFORD.—Guildford Museum and Muniment Room, Castle Arch. Local museum for archæology and history of Surrey based on collections of the Surrey Archæological Society. Record Office for Borough records, Guildford Diocese parish records, and private records of West Surrey. Open every day except Sunday, 11–5.

HULL.—Ferens Art Gallery. Collection of foreign paintings includes works by Hals, Canaletto and Guardi; British 18th and 19th century works, especially sea-pieces and pictures by the Hull marine painters, but the bulk of the collection is 20th century, including paintings or sculpture by most of the best known modern British painters. Open weekdays, 10–5.30; Sundays, 2.30–4.30.

HUNTINGDON.—*Cromwell Museum.* Housed in the only remaining portion of the 12th-century Hospital of St. John. Portraits of Cromwell, his family and Parliamentary notables (by Walker, Lely etc.); as well as reproductions and engravings covering the whole Puritan field. Unique collection of Cromwelliana—objects, documents, armour, coins and medals. Open free, Sundays 2 to 4, Tuesday to Saturday 11 to 1; 2 to 5. Closed Mondays, Christmas Day and Good Friday.

IPSWICH.—*Ipswich Museum.* Archæology, geology and natural history of Suffolk and general collections. Open weekdays, 10–5, Sundays, 3–5. Admission free. Closed Good Friday and Christmas Day. *Christchurch Mansion.* Started in 1548 on site of Augustinian Priory. Domestic nature of house is retained and collections include furniture, etc., from Suffolk houses, portraits of Suffolk families and pictures by local artists: Gainsborough, Constable, Steer, etc. Porcelain and glass. Open weekdays, 10–5; Sundays, 3–5. Admission free. Closed Good Friday and Christmas Day.

LEEDS.—*City Art Gallery.* Important collection of early English watercolours. British and European painting, modern sculpture, Chinese ceramics etc. Print Room and Art library contains study collection of drawings and prints. Open weekdays, 10.30–6.30, Sundays, 2.30–5. (Print Room and Art library 9–9, closed Sundays). *Temple Newsam House.* Tudor/Jacobean house altered in mid-18th cent. to make suite of state rooms. Collection of English furniture mostly of 17th and

18th cents., silver, European porcelain and pottery, pictures, etc. Open daily, 10.30–6.15 or dusk; Weds. (May–Sept.), 10.30–8.30. Admission 10p; Children (with adults), 5p. *Lotherton Hall*, Gascoigne art collection, park and gardens, opened 1969. Open daily, 10.30–6.15 (or dusk in winter); Thursdays (May–Sept.), 10.30–8.30. Admission to Hall, 10p; children (with adult), 5p.

LEICESTER.—*Museum and Art Gallery*, New Walk (1849). 18th and 19th Century paintings, including the Ellesmere Collection of drawings and German expressionist painting; oriental ceramics; library and study collections in biology, geology and mineralogy. Open, Oct.–Mar., 10–5; April and Sept., 10–6; May–Aug. and Saturdays, 10–7; Sundays, 2–5. *Newarke Houses*, The Newarke. Social history of Leicestershire from mediæval times; costume; local clocks; knitting machinery. *Jewry Wall*, St. Nicholas Circle. Archæological collection with emphasis on Roman Leicester. Remains of Roman Baths adjoin. Open weekdays, 10.30–7; Saturdays, 9.30–7; Sundays, 2–5. *Belgrave Hall*, Thurcaston Road. A Queen Anne house with collection of furniture and garden of note. Open as for Museum and Art Gallery. *Magazine Gateway*, Museum of Royal Leicestershire Regiment in a 14th Century gateway. *Guildhall*, Guildhall Lane, 14th Century timber-framed building. Closed on Sundays. *Railway Museum*, Stoneygate. Four locomotives and local railway material. Open Thurs., Fri., 2–5, Sat., Sun., 11–5. *Museum of Technology*, Corporation Road, Abbey Lane. Road transport collection and industries of East Midlands.

LEWES.—*Barbican House*, near Castle (Sussex Archæological Trust). Large prehistoric and Roman collections relating to Sussex; Sussex pottery, mediæval and Saxon antiquities; pictures and prints relating to the county, etc. Open weekdays, 10–6 (or dusk).

Anne of Cleves' House, Southover. Open weekdays (Feb.–Nov.), 10.30–1; 2–5.30. Admission, 15p; Children, 5p.

LINCOLN.—*Usher Gallery*. Collection of watches, miniatures, porcelain, silver, etc., Peter de Wint collection of oils and watercolours, Tennyson collection of manuscripts, etc. associated with Alfred, Lord Tennyson, collection of pictures relating to the city of Lincoln and small general collection of works of art. Open weekdays, 10–5.30; Sundays, 2.30–5. Admission free. *City and County Museum*. In the Greyfriars, a 13th-cent. Franciscan building. Collections include armour, local archæology with special emphasis on Romano-British collections from the city and county. Open weekdays, 10–5.30; Sundays, 2.30–5. Admission free.

LIVERPOOL.—*Walker Art Gallery*. One of the few Galleries outside London where a representative collection of European painting from the 14th century to the present day can be seen. Particularly strong in early Italian and Northern painting, Pre-Raphaelite and Academic 19th century paintings. Open, weekdays, 10–5; Sundays, 2–5. Closed on Good Friday, Christmas Day and Boxing Day. *Sudley Art Gallery & Museum* (Emma Holt Bequest), Mossley Hill Road. Collection of 18th and 19th-century paintings, mainly English, including Reynolds, Gainsborough and Romney, Wilkie, Mulready and Holman Hunt. Open as for Walker Art Gallery. *City Museum*. New Galleries now open include; Archæology, Ethnography, Applied Arts, Pottery, Geology, Zoology, Shipping, Local History displays including Watch-making and Craft shops, Aquarium, Planetarium. Open weekdays, 10–5; Sunday, 2–5. Closed Christmas Day, Boxing Day and Good Friday.

MANCHESTER.—City Art Galleries. Comprising: *City Art Gallery*, Mosley Street, Manchester 2; *Annexe*, Princess Street, and five branches: *Heaton Hall; Platt Hall (Gallery of English Costume); Wythenshawe Hall; Queen's Park Art Gallery; Fletcher Moss Museum*. The City Art Gallery (architect, Sir Charles Barry) was built for the Royal Manchester Institution and opened in 1829; it was presented to the city in 1882. Principal collection of paintings is at the City Art Gallery; ceramics at Annexe; costume at Platt Hall; watercolours at Fletcher Moss Museum; furniture at Heaton Hall and Wythenshawe Hall; Rutherston Loan Collection, Queen's Park Art Gallery. *Hours of opening*—City Art Gallery: weekdays 10–6, Sundays 2.30–5. Other galleries: weekdays 10–8 (May–Aug.); 10–4 (Nov.–Feb.); 10–6 (other months). Sunday opening at 2 p.m. Admission free except to certain temporary exhibitions. Closed Good Friday and Christmas Day.

Whitworth Art Gallery, University of Manchester.—Founded 1889 through bequest of Sir Joseph Whitworth (1803–1887). Important collections of: English watercolours; Old Master prints and drawings; textiles, including notable examples of Coptic cloths; and contemporary works of art. Hours of opening: daily, 10–5 p.m., except Sundays; Thursdays to 9 p.m.

NEWCASTLE UPON TYNE.—*Laing Art Gallery and Museum*, Higham Place. British oil paintings and watercolours from 17th century to the present day; etchings and engravings; Japanese prints; sculpture; Egyptian, Greek and Roman antiquities; pottery and porcelain; glass; silver; wrought ironwork; European and Oriental arms and armour; costumes; textiles; and exhibits illustrative of the artistic industries of Tyneside. Open, weekdays, 10–6; Tues. and Thurs., 10–8; Sundays, 2.30–5.30. *Museum of Science and Engineering*, Exhibition Park, Great North Road. Open, Summer, weekdays, 10–6; Tues. and Thurs., 10–8; Sundays, 2.30–5.30; Winter, weekdays, 10–4.30; Sundays, 1.30–4.30. Admission 5p; Children, 2p. Educational parties free, by arrangement. *Plummer Tower Museum*, furnished in 18th century style. Open, weekdays, 10–1, 2.30–6. *John G. Joicey Museum*, City Road. Local historical exhibits; furniture and armour. Open weekdays, 10–1; 2–6.

NORWICH.—*Castle Museum*. Exhibits illustrating art, local archæology and natural history. Open, weekdays 10–5; Sundays 2.30–5. *Strangers' Hall* (Museum of Domestic Life, Charing Cross). Late mediæval mansion furnished as a museum of urban domestic life, 16th–19th centuries, with displays of costume, transport, shop signs and toys. Open, weekdays, 10–5. *Bridewell Museum*, Bridewell Alley. Exhibits illustrating transport, crafts and industries of Norwich, Norfolk and North Suffolk. Open, weekdays, 10–5. *St. Peter Hungate Church Museum*, Princes Street. Fifteenth century church used for display of church art and antiquities Open, weekdays, 10–5.

NOTTINGHAM.—*City Art Gallery and Museum*, housed in Nottingham Castle. English and Netherlands paintings and drawings 17th–20th centuries; special collections Bonington and Paul Sandby. English mediæval alabasters; English ceramics and silver; glass; metalwork; furniture; 17th and 18th-century carriages; costume, embroidery and lace, 16th–19th centuries; ethnography; local archæology; the regimental collection of the Sherwood Foresters. Open, Summer, 10–6.45; (Fri. 5.45; Sun., 2–4.45); Winter, 10 till dusk (Sun. 2–4.45).

Natural History Museum (1867) housed in Wollaton Hall. Botanical, zoological and geological material; extensive British and foreign herbaria;

Crowfoot collection of exotic butterflies; Pearson collection of European butterflies; Fowler collection of British coleoptera; Hollier collection of Wenlock Limestone fossils; Carrington series of Mountain Limestone fossils. Formal gardens, deer park and lake. Open, Summer 10–7 (Sun. 2.30–5.30); Winter, 10 till dusk (Sun. the three hours before dusk).

Newstead Abbey, 9 miles N. of Nottingham. Originally a Priory founded *c.* 1170, later property of Byron family, 1540–1817. Collections associated with poet Byron include Roe–Byron collection of Mss., books and pictures; Fraser collection of furniture and paintings; Gatty collection of furniture; Munster collection of paintings and engravings. Extensive grounds. Abbey open Good Friday to end of September. Monday to Saturday conducted tours at 2, 3, 4 and 5 p.m. On Sundays and Bank Holidays except Good Friday the Abbey is open from 2 to 6.30 p.m. Admission 10p; children, 5p. Gardens open all year, daily 10 till dusk. Admission 10p; children, 5p.

OXFORD, Ashmolean Museum.—Department of Western Art, Department of Antiquities, Heberden Coin Room, Department of Eastern Art, Cast Gallery. Open weekdays, 10–4, Sundays, 2–4 (Heberden Coin Room, weekdays, 10–12.30 and 2–4; Cast Gallery closed from 1 p.m. Saturdays and all day Sunday).

PLYMOUTH.—*City Museum and Art Gallery*, Drake Circus. Collection of ceramics, including Cookworthy's Plymouth and Bristol hard paste porcelain, collections of paintings, drawings and prints, archæological and natural history collection. Temporary exhibitions arranged. Open weekdays, 10–6 (Fridays, 10–8), Sundays 3–5. Admission free. *Elizabethan House*, 32 New Street. Restored Elizabethan house, furnished according to period. Open 10–1, 2.15–6 (till dusk in winter). Admission free. *See also* Buckland Abbey, p. 653.

PORT SUNLIGHT, Cheshire. *Lady Lever Art Gallery*. Paintings and watercolour drawings, mainly of British School, antique, renaissance and British sculpture, English furniture, mainly 18th cent., Chinese pottery and porcelain, and important collection of old Wedgwood. Open weekdays 10–5, Sundays 2–5.

SHEFFIELD.—*City Museum, Weston Park*. Founded in 1875, the present building was erected in 1937 and extended in 1965. Seven galleries are normally open to the public, and the reference library and students' collections may be consulted on request. The exhibits cover a wide range of subjects, and include the Bateman Collection of antiquities from the Bronze Age barrows of the Peak District. The cutlery and Old Sheffield

Plate collections are considered to be the finest of their kind in the world. Open, weekdays, Sept.–May, 10–5; June–Aug. 10–8.30; Sundays 2–5 (Closed Christmas Eve and Christmas Day). *Abbeydale Industrial Hamlet*, Abbeydale Road South. A late 18th and early 19th century scytheworks with associated housing. Open, weekdays, 11–5; Sundays, 2–5 (closes at 8 p.m. each day during summer). *Shepherd Wheel*, Whiteley Wood. A cutler's water-driven grinding wheel and associated machinery. *Graves Art Gallery* (opened 1934) and *Mappin Art Gallery* (rebuilt 1965). Collections of English watercolours, including works by Constable, Cotman, Cozens, Gainsborough, Girtin and Turner. Oil paintings: English portraits from the 17th to the 20th century; English landscape of the 18th and 19th century, including examples by Constable, Turner and Wilson. Examples by Corot, Cézanne and French 19th century landscapists. Small representative selection of Dutch 17th century art, with examples by Hobbema and Van Goyen. Twentieth century British art is represented by works of Sickert, Paul Nash, Gilman, Gore, Beran, Gwen John, Matthew Smith, Stanley Spencer, Lowry, and others. Frequent loan exhibitions. *Graves Art Gallery:* weekdays, 10–8; Sundays, 2–5. *Mappin Art Gallery*, weekdays 10–5; Sundays, 2–5 (later opening in summer).

SOUTHAMPTON.—*Southampton Art Gallery*. British painting from 18th cent., particularly 20th cent. artists; work of some 14th to 17th cent. Italian, Flemish, Dutch and French painters; a few late 19th and early 20th cent. French paintings and sculpture. Frequent temporary exhibitions. Open weekdays, 10–7; Sundays, 2–5. (Closed Christmas Day and Good Friday). Admission free.

YORK.—*Castle Museum*. Folk museum of Yorkshire life of the past four centuries. Open weekdays, 9.30–7.30; Sundays, 10–7.30; Closes 4.30, Oct.–Mar. Admission, 20p; children, 10p.

Yorkshire Museum and Gardens, Museum Street. Roman and mediæval antiquities, and architecture, ceramics and natural history. Open, weekdays, 10–5 or dusk if earlier; Sundays, 1–5. Gardens open weekdays, 8 till dusk; Sundays 10 till dusk. Admission free.

Art Gallery, Exhibition Square. European paintings, 14th–20th century; watercolours and prints of Yorkshire; modern English stoneware pottery. Open weekdays, 10–5; Sundays, 2.30–5 (summer months, 2.30–8). Admission free.

Railway Museum, Queen Street. Contains 12 locomotives, including "Stirling Single, No. 1" and "Gladstone" and exhibits of railway equipment. Open, weekdays, 10–5. Adults, 10p; children, 5p.

THE PRINCIPAL ENGLISH CITIES

BIRMINGHAM

BIRMINGHAM (Warwickshire) is the second largest City in Britain and the chief centre of the hardware trade. The municipal area is about 80 sq. miles, with a population (1971 Census, preliminary) of 1,013,366. It is estimated that over 1,500 distinct trades are carried on in the city, the chief industries being the manufacture of buttons, bedsteads, plastic goods, chocolate, chemicals, electro-plate, guns, machine tools, glass, motor-cars and motor cycles, motor tyres, nuts and bolts, pens and nibs, tubes, paint and enamels, tools, toys, electrical apparatus, wire, jewellery and brass working, etc.

Water is supplied by the City Corporation, which also owns the airport, markets, restaurants and Municipal Bank. The first section of Birmingham's Queen Elizabeth Hospital, erected at Edgbaston at a cost of approximately £1,000,000, is claimed to be the finest of its type in Europe. A

new maternity hospital adjoining was opened in 1969. The construction of an inner ring road round the centre was completed in 1971, hotel accommodation has been increased and there have been many improvements in the shopping centre including the redevelopment of the old market centre in the Bull Ring at a cost of £8,000,000. A complex of buildings in course of erection near the Town Hall includes a School of Music, Central Library, a shopping precinct and Corporation offices. A new television centre is also being built and the City's new repertory theatre was expected to be opened in October, 1971.

The principal buildings are the Town Hall, built in 1832–1834; the Council House and Corporation Museum and Art Gallery (1878); Victoria Law Courts (1891); the University (1909); the Central Library; the 13th century Church of St. Martin (rebuilt 1873); the Cathedral (formerly St.

Philip's Church); the Roman Catholic Cathedral of St. Chad (Pugin) and the Methodist Central Hall. Birmingham was incorporated as a borough in 1838, and was created a city in 1889; it is governed by a Lord Mayor and City Council of 39 Aldermen and 117 Councillors. The generally accepted derivation of "Birmingham" is the *ham* or dwelling-place of the *ing* or the family of *Beorma* presumed to have been a Saxon. Between the 11th and 16th centuries the de Berminghams were Lords of the Manor.

The Lord Mayor (1971–72), V. E. Turton.
Stipendiary Magistrate, J. F. Milward (1951).
Town Clerk, T. H. Parkinson (1960).

BRADFORD

BRADFORD (Yorkshire, West Riding), 192 miles N.N.W. of London and 8 miles W. of Leeds, is a centre of the woollen and worsted trade. The municipal area is 25,504 acres (about 40 square miles), with a population (1971 Census, preliminary) 293,756.

The principal textile industries are worsteds, woollens, silks and cottons, and there are also important engineering, iron and printing works and quarries of freestone.

The chief public buildings, in addition to the 15th century Cathedral (formerly the Parish Church) and Bolling Hall (14th century), are the City Hall (1873), the tower of which contains a clock with dials, chimes and a carillon, Cartwright Hall (1904) commemorating the inventor of the power loom, the Windsor Baths and the Queen's Hall (1905), Grammar School (Charter 1662), St. George's Hall (Concert Hall, 1853), Technical College (1882), the Mechanics' Institute (1832), Wool Exchange (1867), Kirkgate Market Hall (1872), Britannia House (1933) and Bradford University. A new Central Library, planned on the "subject department" principle was opened in 1967.

The Saxon township was created a parliamentary borough in 1832, a borough in 1847, a county borough in 1889, and a city in 1897. The office of Lord Mayor was created in 1907. The Council consists of a Lord Mayor, 19 Aldermen and 57 Councillors.

The Lord Mayor (1971–72), H. Moran.
Town Clerk, G. C. Moore (1969).

BRISTOL

BRISTOL, situated on the borders of Gloucestershire and Somerset, is a City and County of itself, and is 119 miles W. of London. The present municipal area is 27,068 acres (1971 Census, preliminary) of 425,303.

Among the various industries are aircraft and aero-engine construction, general and nuclear engineering, boot and shoe manufacture, chocolate and cocoa, tobacco, paper bags, cardboard and allied products, printing, chemical industry and shipbuilding and repairing. The principal imports are grain, flour and other cereal products, cocoa, tea, coffee, molasses, feeding stuffs, fruit, provisions, frozen meat, metals, ores, phosphates, paper, petroleum and chemicals, fertilizers, timber, tobacco, wood pulp and other goods, and the chief exports are metals and machinery, chemicals, unmanufactured clay, motor vehicles and parts, coke, carbon black, petroleum, electrical apparatus, tea, wines and spirits and manufactured goods.

The chief buildings, in addition to the 12th century Cathedral (with later additions), with Norman Chapter House and gateway, the 14th century Church of St. Mary, Redcliffe (described by Queen Elizabeth I as "the fairest, goodliest, and most famous parish church in England"), and

Wesley's Chapel, Broadmead, are the Merchant Venturers' Almshouses, the Council House (opened by H.M. the Queen in April, 1956), Guildhall, Exchange (erected from the designs of John Wood in 1743), City Museum and Art Gallery, Central Library, Cabot Tower, the University and Clifton College, Red Lodge (Tudor), Georgian House, and Blaise Castle and Mansion with Folk Museum. The *Clifton Suspension Bridge*, with a span of 702 feet over the Avon, was projected by Brunel in 1836 but was not completed until 1864.

Bristol was a Royal Borough before the Norman Conquest. In 1373 it received from Edward III a charter granting it county status and in 1899 its Mayor became a Lord Mayor. The Corporation includes 28 Aldermen and 84 Councillors. The earliest forms of the name are *Brigstowe* and *Bristow*.

The Lord Mayor (1971–72), Mrs. H. Bloom.
Sheriff (1971–72), R. V. Cooke, F.R.C.S.
Town Clerk, W. J. Hutchinson.

CAMBRIDGE

CAMBRIDGE, a settlement far older than its ancient University, lies on the Cam or Granta, 51 miles north of London and 65 miles south-west of Norwich. It has an area of 10,060 acres and a population (1971 Census, preliminary) of 98,519.

The city is a parliamentary borough, county town and regional headquarters. Its industries, which include radio and electronics, flour milling, cement making and the manufacture of scientific instruments are extensive but nowhere obtrusive. Among its open spaces are Jesus Green, Sheep's Green, Coe Fen, Parker's Piece, Christ's Pieces, the University Botanic Garden, and the Backs, or lawns and gardens through which the Cam winds behind the principal line of college buildings. East of the Cam, King's Parade, upon which stand Great St. Mary's Church, Gibbs' Senate House and King's College Chapel with Wilkins' screen, joins Trumpington Street to form one of the most beautiful thoroughfares in Europe.

University and College buildings provide the outstanding features of Cambridge architecture but several churches (especially St. Benet's, the oldest building in the City, and St. Sepulchre's, the Round Church) also make notable contributions. The modern Guildhall (1939) stands on a site of which at least part has held municipal buildings since 1224.

The City Council consists of a Mayor, 14 Aldermen and 42 Councillors. Four of the Councillors are elected by the Colleges and Halls and two by Grace of the Senate of the University. Two of the Aldermen are elected by the Council from the University and College representatives.

Mayor (1971–72), Mrs. J. A. C. Barker.
Town Clerk, J. W. Elven (1966).

CANTERBURY

CANTERBURY, the Metropolitan City of the Anglican Communion, has an unbroken history going back to prehistoric times. It was the Roman Durovernum and the Saxon Cantwaraburg (stronghold of the men of Kent). Here in 597 St. Augustine began the re-conversion of the English to Christianity, when Ethelbert, King of Kent, was baptized. In 1170 the rivalry of Church and State culminated in the murder in Canterbury Cathedral, by Henry II.'s knights, of Archbishop Thomas Becket, whose shrine became a great centre of pilgrimage as described by Chaucer in his *Canterbury Tales*. After the Reformation pilgrimages ceased, but the prosperity of the City was strengthened by an influx of Huguenot refugees, who introduced weaving. In the first Elizabethan

era Christopher Marlowe, the poetic genius and precursor of Shakespeare, was born and reared in Canterbury, and there are literary associations also with Defoe, Dickens and Barham, author of the *Ingoldsby Legends*, and Somerset Maugham.

The Cathedral, with its glorious architecture ranging from the eleventh to the fifteenth centuries, is world-famous. Modern pilgrims are attracted particularly to the Martyrdom, the Black Prince's Tomb and other historic monuments, the Warriors' Chapel and the many examples of mediæval stained glass.

Of the Benedictine St. Augustine's Abbey, burial place of the Jutish Kings of Kent (whose capital Canterbury was) only extensive ruins remain. St. Martin's Church, on the eastern outskirts of the City, is stated by Bede to have been the place of worship of Queen Bertha, the Christian wife of King Ethelbert, before the advent of St. Augustine.

The mediæval City Walls are built on Roman foundations and the fourteenth century West Gate is one of the finest buildings of its kind in the country.

The University of Kent at Canterbury admitted its first students in 1965.

The city is a county borough and county of itself, with an area of 4,810 acres and a population (1971 Census, preliminary) of 33,157. Before the institution of the Mayoralty in 1448 it was governed by bailiffs and earlier still by prefects or provosts.

Mayor (1971–72), Col. J. Tilleard, T.D.
Sheriff (1971–72), Mrs. M. R. Keith-Lucas.
Town Clerk, J. Boyle.

COVENTRY

COVENTRY (Warwickshire) is a city and a county borough, 92 miles N.W. of London, and an important industrial centre. It has a population (1971 Census preliminary) of 334,839.

Coventry owes its beginnings to Leofric, Earl of Mercia and his wife Godiva in 1043, when they founded a Benedictine Monastery. The beautiful guildhall of St. Mary dates from the 14th century, three of its churches date from the 14th and 15th centuries. Sixteenth century almshouses may still be seen. Coventry's first cathedral was destroyed at the Reformation, its second in the 1940 blitz (its walls remain) and the great new cathedral designed by Sir Basil Spence, consecrated in 1962, now draws innumerable visitors.

Post-war public buildings include the Art Gallery and Museum, Lanchester Polytechnic, the Civic Theatre and new swimming baths. The city centre has been redeveloped.

Coventry returns three M.P.'s. It is governed by a Lord Mayor and a Council of 72. Coventry produces cars, agricultural machinery, machine tools (the world's largest machine tool organization); the telecommunication industry has become the largest employer of industrial labour.

Lord Mayor (1971–72), T. Meffen.
Town Clerk, J. D. Hender.

KINGSTON UPON HULL

HULL (officially " Kingston upon Hull ") is situated in the East Riding of Yorkshire, at the junction of the River Hull with the Humber, 22 miles from the North Sea and 205 miles N. of London. The municipal area is 17,537 acres, with a population (1971 Census, preliminary) of 285,472.

Hull is one of the great seaports of the United Kingdom. It has docks covering a water area of over 200 acres, well equipped for the rapid handling of cargoes of every kind, and its many industries include oil-extracting, saw-milling, flour-milling, engineering and chemical industries. It also claims to be the premier distant-water fishing port.

The City, restored after very heavy air raid damage during World War II, is well laid out with fine thoroughfares. It has good office and administrative buildings, its municipal centre being the Guildhall, its educational centre the University of Hull and its religious centre the Parish Church of the Holy Trinity, 272 feet in length.

Kingston upon Hull was so named by Edward I. City status was accorded in 1897 and the office of Mayor raised to the dignity of Lord Mayor in 1914. The Lord Mayor presides over a Council of 21 Aldermen and 63 Councillors, representing the 21 wards of the City.

The Lord Mayor (1971–72), J. Campbell.
Sheriff (1971–72), D. Robinson.
Stipendiary Magistrate, D. N. O'Sullivan (1952).
Town Clerk, J. H. W. Glen.

LEEDS

LEEDS (Yorkshire, West Riding) is a junction for road, rail and canal services and an important commercial centre, situated in the lower Aire Valley, 195 miles by road N.N.W. of London.

Leeds has a wide variety of manufacturing industries, notably cloth and ready-made clothing, heavy and light engineering, leather and chemical products.

The municipal area is 40,619 acres, the population (1971 Census, preliminary) is 494,971.

The principal buildings are the Civic Hall (1933), the Town Hall (1858), the Municipal Buildings and Art Gallery (1884), the Corn Exchange (1863) and the University. The Parish Church (St. Peter's) was rebuilt in 1841; the 17th century St. John's Church has a fine interior with a famous English renaissance screen; the last remaining 18th century church is Holy Trinity, Boar Lane (1727). Kirkstall Abbey (about 3 miles from the centre of the city), founded by Henry de Lacy in 1152, is one of the most complete examples of Cistercian houses now remaining. Temple Newsam, birthplace of Lord Darnley, was acquired by the Corporation in 1922. The present house, a stately building in red brick, was largely re-built by Sir Arthur Ingram in about 1620. Adel Church, about 5 miles from the centre of the city, is a fine Norman structure.

Leeds was first incorporated by Charles I in 1626, made a county borough in 1889, and created a city in 1893. The Lord Mayor presides over a Council of 30 Aldermen and 90 Councillors. The earliest forms of the name are *Loidis* or *Ledes*, the origin of which is obscure.

The Lord Mayor (1971–72), J. T. V. Watson.
Stipendiary Magistrate, J. H. E. Randolph (1965).
Town Clerk, N. C. Haslegrave (1964).

LEICESTER

LEICESTER is situated geographically in the centre of England, 100 miles north of London. The City dates back to pre-Roman times and was one of the five Danish *Burhs*. In 1589 Queen Elizabeth I granted a Charter to the City and the ancient title was confirmed by Letters Patent in 1919. The title of Lord Mayor was conferred upon the Chief Magistrate in 1928. Leicester has an area of 18,141 acres and a population (1971 Census, preliminary) of 283,549

The principal industries of the city are hosiery, boots and shoes, and light engineering. The growth of Leicester as a hosiery centre increased rapidly from the introduction there of the first stocking frame in 1670; in 1833 there were 14,000 knitting frames in the city, which to-day has some of the largest hosiery factories in the world. Hosiery produced includes stockings and every kind of woollen and cotton underwear, outerwear, fabrics and gloves, much of which is exported. Leicester is also a centre for the ancillary industries.

Engineering, developed partly for the supply of

machinery to the hosiery and boot and shoe industries, has become one of the foremost industries in the city. Printing and the manufacture of motor tyres and cellulose goods are also carried on.

The principal buildings in the city are the Town Hall; the University; Leicester Polytechnic; De Montfort Hall, one of the finest concert halls in the provinces, with accommodation for over 3,000 persons, and the Museum and Art Gallery. The ancient Churches of St. Martin (now Leicester Cathedral) St. Nicholas, St. Margaret, All Saints, St. Mary de Castro, and buildings such as the Guildhall, the 14th century Newarke Gate, the Castle and the Jewry Wall Roman site still exist. Leicester has a large number of parks and open spaces.

The Lord Mayor (1971–72), P. C. Watts.
Town Clerk, R. R. Thornton.

LIVERPOOL

LIVERPOOL (Lancashire), on the right bank of the river Mersey, 3 miles from the Irish Sea and 194 miles N.W. of London, is one of the greatest trading centres of the world and the principal port in the United Kingdom for the Atlantic trade. The municipal area is 27,819 acres (which includes 2,840 acres in the bed of the river Mersey) (about 43 square miles, excluding the bed of the river), with a population (1971 Census, preliminary) of 606,834. Quays on both sides of the river are about 38 miles long, and the Gladstone Dock can accommodate the largest vessels afloat. Net tonnage of ships entering and leaving the port annually exceeds 62,000,000 tons. The main imports are petroleum, grain, ores, non-ferrous metals, sugar, wood, oil, fruit and cotton. A new dock system at Crosby was in course of construction in 1971.

The Corporation owns large industrial estates at Speke, Kirkby and Aintree, on which many modern factories have been built. These three estates have provided work for some 65,000 people. In 1943 a lease for 99 years was taken of the Elizabethan mansion at *Speke Hall* at a nominal rent.

The principal buildings are the Anglican Cathedral, erected from the designs of Sir Giles Gilbert Scott and consecrated in 1924; when completed this will be the largest ecclesiastical building in England; the Metropolitan Cathedral of Christ the King, designed by Sir Frederick Gibberd and consecrated in 1967; St. George's Hall, erected 1838–1854, and regarded as one of the finest modern examples of classical architecture; the Town Hall, erected 1754 from the designs of Wood; the Walker Art Gallery; Victoria Building of Liverpool University; the Royal Infirmary; the Municipal Offices; and the Philharmonic Hall.

Constructed between 1925 and 1934, the *Mersey Tunnel* connecting Liverpool and Birkenhead was opened to traffic on July 18, 1934, the total cost being estimated at £6,077,800. More than 17,000,000 vehicles pass through the Mersey Tunnel annually. A second tunnel between Liverpool and Wallasey was opened by the Queen on June 24, 1971.

Liverpool was incorporated as a borough early in the 13th century and was created a city in 1880. The Corporation consists of a Lord Mayor and a City Council of 40 Aldermen and 120 Councillors.
The Lord Mayor (1971–72), C. Cowlin.
Stipendiary Magistrate, Leslie Mervyn Pugh (1965).
Town Clerk, S. Holmes (1967).

MANCHESTER

MANCHESTER (Lancashire) (the *Mancunium* of the Romans, who occupied it in A.D. 78) is 189 miles N.W. of London. The municipal area is 27,255 acres (about 43 square miles) and the population (1971 Census, preliminary), 541,468.

Manchester is a commercial rather than an industrial centre, the industries being largely in the neighbouring towns. Within 25 miles radius, lives a population of 4,500,000 engaged in engineering, chemical, clothing, food processing and textile industries and in providing the packing, transport, banking, insurance and other distributive facilities for those industries. The city is connected with the sea by the Manchester Ship Canal, opened in 1894, 35½ miles long, and accommodating ships up to 15,000 tons. Manchester Airport handles approximately 1,500,000 passengers yearly.

The principal buildings are the Town Hall, erected in 1877 from the designs of Alfred Waterhouse, R.A., together with a large extension; the Royal Exchange, built in 1869 and enlarged in 1921: the Central Library (1934) : the Art Gallery; Heaton Hall; the Gallery of English Costume; the 17th century Chetham Library; the Rylands Library (1899), which includes the Althorp collection; the University (Owens College); the University Institute of Science and Technology; the 15th-century Cathedral (formerly the parish church) and the Free Trade Hall. Manchester is one of the principal centres of political, literary and scientific advancement, and the Hallé Concerts have placed the city in the forefront of musical development.

The town received a charter of incorporation in 1838 and was created a city in 1853. The City Council consists of 33 Aldermen and 99 Councillors.

The Lord Mayor (1971–72), D. J. Edwards.
Stipendiary Magistrate, J. Bamber (1965).
Town Clerk, G. C. Ogden, C.B.E. (1966).

NEWCASTLE UPON TYNE

NEWCASTLE UPON TYNE (Northumberland) a City and County on the north bank of the River Tyne, 8 miles from the North Sea and 272 miles N. of London, has an area of 11,401 acres and a population (1971 Census, preliminary) of 222,153. A Cathedral and University City, it is the administrative, commercial and cultural centre for north-east England and the principal port. It is an important manufacturing centre with a wide variety of industries.

The principal buildings include the Castle Keep (12th century), Black Gate (13th century), West Walls (13th century), St. Nicholas's Cathedral (15th century, fine lantern tower), St. Andrew's Church (12th–14th century), St. John's (14th–15th century), All Saints (Georgian masterpiece), St. Mary's Roman Catholic Cathedral (1844), Trinity House (17th century), Sandhill (16th century houses), Guildhall (Georgian), Grey Street (1834–39), Central Station (1846–50), Laing Art Gallery (1904), University of Newcastle Physics Building (1962), Civic Centre (1963) and Central Library (1969). Open spaces include the Town Moor (927 acres) and Jesmond Dene. Seven bridges span the Tyne at Newcastle.

The City derives its name from the "new castle" (1080) erected as a defence against the Scots. In 1400 it was made a County, and in 1882 a City. The City Corporation comprises a Lord Mayor (1906), 19 Aldermen and 57 Councillors.
Lord Mayor (1971–72), Mrs. M. E. Graham, M.B.E.
Town Clerk, F. Ireland.

NORWICH

NORWICH (Norfolk) is an ancient City and County 110 miles N.E. of London. It grew from an early Anglo-Saxon settlement near the confluence of the Rivers Yare and Wensum, and now serves as provincial capital for the predominantly agricultural region of East Anglia. The name is

thought to relate to the most northerly of a group of Anglo-Saxon villages or "wics". The present City comprises an area of 9,655 acres, with a population (1971 Census, preliminary) of 121,688.

Norwich serves its surrounding area as a market town and commercial centre, banking and insurance being prominent among the City's businesses. Continuously from the fourteenth century, however (when Flemish immigrants helped to establish Norwich as the centre of the woollen industry until the Industrial Revolution) it has combined industry with commerce, and manufactures of a wide variety are now produced in the City. The biggest single industry is the manufacture of shoes and other principal trades are engineering, printing, and the production of chemicals, clothing, confectionery and other foodstuffs. Norwich is accessible to seagoing vessels by means of the River Yare, entered at Great Yarmouth, 20 miles to the east.

Among many historic buildings are the Cathedral (completed in the twelfth century and surmounted by a fifteenth century spire 315 feet in height), the Keep of the Norman Castle (now serving as a museum and also housing the Colman Collection of works by the Norwich School of painters), the fifteenth century flint-walled Guildhall, some thirty mediæval parish churches, St. Andrew's and Blackfriars' Halls, the Tudor houses preserved in Elm Hill and the Georgian Assembly House. The administrative centre of the City is the City Hall, built in 1938. A new central library, opened in 1963, is adjacent to the City Hall. The University of East Anglia has been established in Norwich and received its first students in 1963. The buildings of the University occupy a spacious site at Earlham on the City's western boundary.

The City's first known Charter was granted in 1158 by Henry II and its privileges and form of self government were prescribed successively by later Charters until the enactment of the Municipal Corporations Act, 1835. The City Council consists of the Lord Mayor, 16 Aldermen and 48 Councillors.

The Lord Mayor (1971–72), D. M. Pratt.
Sheriff (1971–72), L. G. Richards.
Town Clerk, G. G. Tilsley.

NOTTINGHAM

NOTTINGHAM (Nottinghamshire) stands on the River Trent, 124 miles N.N.W. of London in one of the most valuable coalfields of the country with excellent railway, water (being connected by canal with the Atlantic and the North Sea), and road facilities. The municipal area is 18,364 acres and population (1971 Census, preliminary) of 299,758.

The principal industries are hosiery, lace, bleaching, dyeing and spinning, tanning, engineering and cycle works, brewing, the manufacture of tobacco, chemicals, furniture, typewriters and mechanical products.

The chief buildings are the 17th century Nottingham Castle (restored in 1878, and now the City Museum and Gallery of Art), Wollaton Hall (1580–88) owned by the Corporation and now a Natural History Museum, St. Mary's, St. Peter's, and St. Nicholas's Churches, the Roman Catholic Cathedral (Pugin, 1842–4), the Council House (1929), the Guildhall and Court House (1888), Shire Hall, Albert Hall, the University and Newstead Abbey, home of Lord Byron.

Snotingaham or *Notingham*, "the village or home of the sons of Snot" (the Wise), is the Anglo-Saxon name for the Celtic *Tuigogobauc*, "Cave Homes.' The City possesses a Charter of Henry II, and was created a City in 1897. The Corporation consists of 18 Aldermen and 54 Councillors (including the Lord Mayor).

Y +

The Lord Mayor (1971–72), E. Want.
Town Clerk, P. M. Vine.

OXFORD

OXFORD is a University City, an important industrial centre, and a county, assize, and market town.

It has been a City from time immemorial and a County Borough since 1889. It has an area of 8,785 acres and a population (1971 Census, preliminary) of 108,564. Oxford is a parliamentary constituency returning one member and is governed by a Council of 68 members of whom 8 are, by special enactment, elected by the University.

Industry played a minor part in Oxford until the motor industry was established in 1912. To-day this and the adjoining pressed steel works employ about 15,000.

It is for its architecture that Oxford is of most interest to the visitor, its oldest specimens being the reputed Saxon tower of St. Michael's church, the remains of the Norman castle and city walls and the Norman church at Iffley. It is chiefly famous however, for its Gothic buildings, such as the Divinity Schools, the Old Library at Merton College, William of Wykeham's New College, Magdalen College and Christ Church and many other college buildings. Later centuries are not represented by so many examples, but mention can be made of the exquisite Laudian quadrangle at St. John's College, the Renaissance Sheldonian Theatre by Wren, Trinity College Chapel, and All Saints Church; Hawksmoor's mock-Gothic at All Souls College, and the superb example of eighteenth century architecture afforded by Queen's College. In addition to individual buildings, High Street and Radcliffe Square, just off it, both form architectural compositions of great beauty. Most of the Colleges have gardens, those of Magdalen, New College, St. John's (designed by "Capability" Brown) and Worcester being the largest.

The visitor will always find some of the college chapels, halls and gardens open for public inspection between 10 a.m. and 5 p.m.

Lord Mayor (1971–72), T. J. Meadows.
Town Clerk, A. T. Brown (1966).

PLYMOUTH

PLYMOUTH is situated on the borders of Devon and Cornwall at the confluence of the Rivers Tamar and Plym, 210 miles from London, with an area of 19,936 acres and a population (1971 Census, preliminary) of 239,314.

Following extensive war damage, the city centre comprising a large shopping centre, municipal offices, law courts and public buildings, has been re-built. The main employment is provided by H.M. Dockyard. Many new industrial firms have become established in the post-war period. In conjunction with the Cornwall County Council, the Tamar Bridge was constructed linking the City by road with Cornwall.

Parliament in 1439 passed the Plymouth Act of Incorporation and Plymouth is therefore the first creation of a Municipal Corporation in England by statute. The Lord Mayor presides over a Council consisting of 22 Aldermen and 66 Councillors.

The Lord Mayor (1971–72), Mrs. D. F. W. Innes.
Town Clerk, H. R. Haydon.

PORTSMOUTH

PORTSMOUTH, a city, county and parliamentary borough, with an area of 14½ sq. miles, occupies Portsea Island, Hampshire, with boundaries extending to the mainland. Portsmouth is 70 miles by road from London (90 minutes by electric train). It has a population (1971 Census, preliminary) of 196,973.

Industries include the Royal Dockyard, the principal centre of employment with a labour force exceeding 20,000, which with the naval station, occupies the south-western part of the Island. The holiday and tourist industry, centred on the coast at the resort area of Southsea, caters annually for 150,000 visitors and 800,000 day trippers. Other industries are shipbuilding and maintenance, aircraft engineering and the manufacture of corsets, cardboard boxes, confectionery, baby products, refrigerators and brushes. The commercial port (the Camber) and the airport are owned and run by the City Corporation.

Among many tourist attractions are Lord Nelson's flagship, H.M.S. *Victory*; Charles Dickens' birthplace at 393 Commercial Road, now a Dickens museum; Southsea Castle, now a museum of military history, and the Round Tower and Point Battery, which for hundreds of years have guarded the entrance to Portsmouth Harbour. Southsea is particularly noted for its panoramic views of the busy shipping lanes of the Solent and Spithead.

Lord Mayor (1971–72), A. D. Derby.
Town Clerk, J. R. Haslegrave, O.B.E., T.D.

SHEFFIELD

SHEFFIELD (Yorkshire, West Riding), the centre of the special steel and cutlery trades, is situated 159 miles N.N.W. of London, at the junction of the Sheaf, Porter, Rivelin and Loxley with the river Don. The City is set in a beautiful countryside, its residential suburbs penetrating the Peak District of Derbyshire.

Sheffield has an area of 45,363 acres (nearly 71 square miles), including 3,666 acres of publicly owned parks and woodland, and a population (1971 Census, preliminary) of 519,703. Though its cutlery, silverware and plate have long been famous, Sheffield has other and now more important industries—special and alloy steels, engineering and tools in great variety. Refractory materials, silver refining, brush making, the manufacture of confectionery, canning, typefounding and the making of snuff are other contrasting industries in Sheffield. Research in glass, metallurgy, radiotherapy and other fields is carried on.

The parish church of St. Peter and St. Paul, founded in the twelfth century, became the Cathedral Church of the Diocese of Sheffield in 1914. Parts of the present building date from about 1435. The principal modern buildings are the Town Hall (1897 and 1923), the Cutlers' Hall (1832), the University (1905 and recent extensions, including 19-storey Arts Tower), City Hall (1932), Central Library and Graves Art Gallery (1934), City Museum (1937), Castle Market Building (1959), the rebuilt Mappin Art Gallery and the Crucible Theatre, which replaces the Sheffield Playhouse.

Sheffield was created a borough on Aug. 24, 1843, a county borough in 1888 and a city in 1893, the Mayor becoming a Lord Mayor in 1897. The Corporation consists of 27 Aldermen and 81 Councillors.

The Lord Mayor (1971–72), H. Hebblethwaite.
Master Cutler (1971–72), (348th Master of the Company of Cutlers in Hallamshire), A. Carr.
Town Clerk, D. B. Harrison.

SOUTHAMPTON

SOUTHAMPTON is Britain's premier passenger port. As the majority of ocean travellers to this country arrive at Southampton, the City is recognized as " The Gateway to Britain ". The first Charter was granted by Henry II and Southampton was created a county of itself in 1447. In February, 1964, Her Majesty the Queen granted city status by Royal Charter. The City has an area of 12,071 acres excluding tidal waters and a population (1971 Census, preliminary) 214,826. The University of Southampton (1952) had 4,420 students in 1970–71.

The Civic Centre, completed in 1939, comprises four blocks, municipal offices and law courts, guildhall, library and art galleries. The tower, which is a notable land-mark for shipping using Southampton Water and which can be seen for many miles from vantage points in the surrounding countryside, incorporates a clock and bells. Public open spaces total over 1,000 acres in extent and comprise 9 per cent. of the city's area. The Sports Centre is 267 acres in extent. The Common covers an area of 328 acres in the central district of the city and is mostly natural parkland.

The City Council consists of 18 aldermen and 54 councillors.

Mayor (1971–72), J. Barr.
Town Clerk, G. Guest (1968).

STOKE-ON-TRENT

STOKE-ON-TRENT (Staffordshire), familiarly known as The Potteries, stands on the River Trent 157 miles N. of London. The present municipal area is 22,916 acres (36 square miles), with a population (1971 Census, preliminary) of 265,153. The City is the main centre of employment for the half-million population of North Staffordshire. It is the largest clayware producer in the world (chinaware, earthenware, sanitary goods, refractories, bricks and tiles) and has a large coal mining output drawn from one of the richest coalfields in Western Europe, with proved reserves exceeding one thousand million tons. The City has iron works, steelworks, foundries, chemical works, engineering plants, rubber works, paper mills, and a very wide range of manufactures including textiles, furniture, electrical goods, vehicle components, toys, machinery, plastic materials, metal stampings, glass and glazes.

Extensive reconstruction has been carried on since 1930. A unique feature of the city is that it has six " centres " and more shops and public halls than other areas of comparable size. The City was formed by the federation in 1910 of the separate municipal authorities of Tunstall, Burslem, Hanley, Stoke-upon-Trent, Fenton, and Longton, all of which are now combined in the present City of Stoke-on-Trent. Each of the six areas still has its own public buildings and amenities, but all civic administration is controlled by the City Council.

The City has 72 Councillors and 24 Aldermen, and elects 3 Members of Parliament.

The Lord Mayor (1971–72), F. A. Cholerton.
Town Clerk, L. K. Robinson.

STRATFORD UPON AVON

STRATFORD UPON AVON (a municipal borough in Warwickshire, on the banks of the River Avon) had a population of 19,449 at the Census of 1971 (preliminary). As the birthplace of Shakespeare the borough is visited annually by travellers from all parts.

Shakespeare's Birthplace. Half timbered house preserved by Shakespeare Birthplace Trust. Contains period furniture and a collection of rare books, mss. and objects of Shakespearian interest. Garden contains the new Shakespeare centre. *King Edward VI School.* Founded by the mediæval Guild of the Holy Cross of Stratford, and re-endowed by King Edward VI. Here Shakespeare acquired his " small Latin and less Greek." *Anne Hathaway's Cottage.* At Shottery, one mile from the centre of the town, is the thatched farmstead, the early home of Shakespeare's wife. Anne

Hathaway. A fine specimen of domestic architecture. *Shakespeare Memorial.* Mainly due to munificence of C. E. Flower (1830–92) and his wife Group comprises *Library*, with 10,000 volumes of Shakespeare editions and dramatic literature. *Gallery* of pictures. *Gardens. Royal Shakespeare Theatre* burnt down in 1926, rebuilt 1932, with 1,300 seats, chiefly by American generosity. The Shakespeare Festival takes place from spring to autumn each year at this theatre.

Mayor (1971–72), P. B. P. Sainsbury.
Town Clerk, T. Cox.

WINCHESTER

WINCHESTER, the ancient capital of England, is situated on the River Itchen 65 miles S.W. of London and 12 miles north of Southampton. The City has an area of 3,890 acres and a population (1971 Census, preliminary) of 31,041.

Occupation of the city area can be traced back to 1800 B.C. but organized settlements appeared later. Saxon history is somewhat obscure but Winchester became the capital of Wessex and in the 9th century capital of all England. Alfred the Great made Winchester a centre of education. William the Conqueror marched straight from his victory at Hastings to Winchester where he established a new Palace, his Treasury and his capital. Here he compiled Domesday Book as the returns came in from the shires. Winchester remained the capital for many years, but its decline as a capital began with the civil war between Stephen and Matilda; and by 1338 it had lost its favourable position.

Winchester is rich in architecture of all types but the Cathedral takes first place. The longest Gothic cathedral in the world, it was built in 1079–1093 and exhibits splendid examples of Norman, Early English and Perpendicular styles. Winchester College, founded in 1382, is one of the most famous public schools, the original building (of 1393) remaining almost unaltered. St. Cross Hospital, the third great mediæval foundation in Winchester, lies 1 mile south of the City. Founded in 1136 by Bishop Henry de Blois, the Almhouses were re-established in 1445 by Cardinal Henry Beaufort. The Chapel and dwellings are of great architectural interest, and visitors may still receive the "Wayfarer's Dole" of bread and ale.

It is not certain when Winchester was first designated a city but it is probable that the term was applied between 650 and 700. Winchester is one of the oldest corporations in the country; the first written record of a Mayor occurs in 1200.

Mayor (1971–72), Mrs. A. E. E. Cleary.
Town Clerk, R. H. McCall, O.B.E.

YORK

YORK is a county borough, an archiepiscopal seat, the county town of Yorkshire and a county in its own right, standing at the junction of the three Ridings. York has an area of 7,295 acres, and a population (1971 Census, preliminary) of 104,513. The City returns one member to Parliament and is governed by a Lord Mayor, 13 Aldermen and 39 Councillors.

The recorded history of York dates from A.D. 71, when the Roman Ninth Legion established a base which later became the fortress of Eboracum. By the 14th century the city had become prosperous and was used as the chief base against the Scots. It became a great mercantile centre, chiefly owing to its control of the wool trade, but under the Tudors its fortunes declined, though Henry VIII made it the headquarters of the Council of the North, so preserving its status as the Northern capital.

With its development as a railway centre in the 19th century the commercial life of York expanded and it is now a flourishing modern city. The principal industries are the manufacture of chocolate, railway coaches, scientific instruments, glass containers and sugar. The City is also an important tourist centre.

It is rich in examples of architecture of all periods, but its finest features are the Minster with its stained glass, and the mediæval city walls and gateways, guildhalls and churches. Other notable examples of domestic architecture are the Georgian mansions of The Mount, Micklegate and Bootham. Its museums are world-famous, and its Art Gallery contains an important collection of paintings from the 14th to the 20th century. The University of York was opened in 1963 at Heslington on the City's eastern boundary.

Rt. Hon. Lord Mayor (1971–72), R. Scruton.
Sheriff (1971–72), W. Ward.
Town Clerk, H. J. Evans.

FREEMEN'S GUILDS

London.—Guild of Freemen of the City of London, 4 Dowgate Hill, E.C.4. *Clerk*, D. Reid.

Berwick upon Tweed.—Freemen's Guild of Berwick upon Tweed. *Sec.*, W. Herriott, 7 Percy Terrace.

Chester.—Freemen and Guilds of the City of Chester. *Hon. Sec.*, D. W. White, The Guildhall, Chester.

Coventry.—City of Coventry Freemen's Guild. *Clerk.*—N. R. Davies, 67 Woodfield Road, Earlsdon.

Grimsby.—Enrolled Freemen of Grimsby. *Clerk*,

W. J. Savage, St. Mary's Chambers, Grimsby.

Lincoln.—Lincoln Freemen's Committee. *Clerk*, E. Mason, St. Swithin's Square, Lincoln.

Newcastle upon Tyne.—Freemen of Newcastle upon Tyne. *Secretary*, R. F. Walker, 3 Ellison Place, Newcastle upon Tyne.

Oxford.—Oxford Freemen's Committee. *Chairman*, T. E. Eeley, 126 High Street, Oxford.

Shrewsbury.—Association of Shrewsbury Freemen. *President*, M. Peele, Dogpole, Shrewsbury.

York.—Guild of Freemen of the City of York. *Hon. Clerk*, L. Buckle, 187 Tadcaster Road, York.

BANK HOLIDAYS, 1972–74

	ENGLAND, WALES, NORTHERN IRELAND, THE CHANNEL ISLANDS.				SCOTLAND		
	Easter Monday	Spring Holiday	Autumn Bank Holiday	Boxing Day	New Year's Day	Spring Holiday	Autumn Bank Holiday
1972	April 3	May 29	August 28	December 26	Jan. 1	May 1	August 7
1973	April 23	May 28	August 27	December 26	Jan. 1	May 7	August 6
1974	April 15	May 27	August 26	December 26	Jan. 1	May 6	August 5

New Year's Day and *Liberation Day* (May 9) are bank and public holidays in the Channel Islands. Banks are also closed on *Good Friday* and *Christmas Day* and on *Saturdays*.

MUNICIPAL DIRECTORY OF ENGLAND

A list of CITIES (in SMALL CAPITALS) and Boroughs (in ordinary type): the County Boroughs are distinguished by having § prefixed. The figures in parentheses show the date of the first recorded Charter of Incorporation. For London Boroughs, *see* p. 642; for Urban Districts, *see* pp. 668–70.

CITIES and Boroughs	Population, 1971 Census (prelim.)	Rateable Value 1971 £	† Rate Levied 1971–72 p	Town Clerk	Mayor, 1971–72 ★Lord Mayor
Abingdon, Berks. (1556)	18,596	838,214	84½	E. W. J. Nicholson.	Dr. J. Harcourt-Norris.
Accrington, Lancs. (1878)	36,838	1,165,333	88½	N. D. MacGregor.	C. G. Smith.
Aldeburgh, East Suffolk (1529)	2,793	130,819	85½	D. J. Owen.	F. S. Wightman.
Aldershot, Hants (1922)	33,311	1,748,946	80	H. B. Sales.	E. J. Hicks.
Altrincham, Cheshire (1937)	40,752	1,947,597	95	E. G. Thomas.	J. B. Dunn.
Andover, Hants (1175)	25,538	1,287,011	86	J. Whatley.	G. Finch.
Appleby, Westmorland (1179)	1,946	75,112	84	F. Flynn.	Rev. A. G. W. Dixon.
Arundel, West Sussex (1586)	2,382	125,762	73	G. Campbell.	W. H. K. Fox.
Ashton (Lyne), Lancs. (1847)	48,865	1,729,615	88½	G. A. Malone.	J. Peace.
Aylesbury, Bucks. (1916)	41,288	2,601,785	78	R. D. W. Maxwell.	Mrs. Z. A. P. Williams.
Bacup, Lancs. (1882)	15,102	373,690	92½	W. A. Duggleby.	A. Howarth.
Banbury, Oxon. (1554)	29,216	1,656,415	84½	J. S. T. Williams.	R. L. Keys.
§Barnsley, Yorks.—W.R. (1869)	75,330	2,461,401	77	A. Bleasby.	B. Varley.
Barnstaple, Devon (930)	17,342	835,493	77½	R. P. Crompton.	G. Casey.
§Barrow-in-Furness, Lancs. (1867)	63,998	2,226,940	81½	A. M. Woll.	E. Marston.
Basingstoke, Hants (1392)	52,502	2,883,277	87	R. J. Purvis.	J. Eddie.
§BATH, Somerset (1590)	84,545	3,755,520	90	N. J. L. Pearce.	Mrs. M. M. Grosvenor.
Batley, Yorks.—W.R. (1868)	42,004	1,048,776	88½	E. S. Dixon.	R. Ineson.
Bebington, Cheshire (1937)	61,488	2,955,937	90	G. Chappell, O.B.E.	Mrs. H. G. Hebron.
Beccles, East Suffolk (1584)	8,015	284,800	91½	F. W. Leah.	R. D. Marshall.
Bedford (1166)	73,064	4,462,101	90	G. F. Simmonds.	Mrs. W. M. Fowler.
Berwick upon Tweed, Northumberland (1302)	11,644	434,709	85	J. Healy.	D. L. Dawson.
Beverley, Yorks.—E.R. (1573)	17,124	624,781	74½	E. Bailey.	K. Jackson.
Bewdley, Worcs. (1462)‡	7,212	225,863	93½	W. O. E. Bryan.	Mrs. E. M. Wormald.
Bexhill, East Sussex (1902)	32,849	1,989,421	86	R. S. Robinson.	W. G. Sansom.
§Birkenhead, Cheshire (1877)	137,738	5,351,094	85	I. G. Holt.	K. W. Porter.
BIRMINGHAM (1838)	1,013,366	54,506,515	96	T. H. Parkinson.	★V. E. Turton.
§Blackburn, Lancs. (1851)	101,672	3,690,681	104½	B. Scholes.	J. Simpson.
§Blackpool, Lancs. (1876)	151,311	8,610,324	69½	R. O. F. Hickman.	H. S. A. Ward.
Blandford Forum, Dorset (1605)	3,643	171,698	82	C. K. Lavington.	A. W. G. Adams.
Blyth, Northumberland (1922)	34,617	1,020,603	91½	E. W. Carter.	F. N. Smith.
Bodmin, Cornwall (1798)	9,204	271,470	75	I. Whiting.	Mrs. M. Kendall.
§Bolton, Lancs. (1838)	153,977	5,839,830	91½	R. Calderwood.	A. Townend.
§Bootle, Lancs. (1868)	74,208	3,446,194	91½	A. J. E. Taylor, O.B.E.	G. Halliwell.
Boston, Lincs.—Holland (1545)	25,995	1,146,896	85½	R. E. Coley.	N. McClement.
§Bournemouth, Hants. (1890)	153,425	10,808,695	75	J. M. Bowen.	R. A. Judd..
Brackley, Northants (1260)	4,615	161,083	75	J. M. Wild.	J. F. Yates.
§BRADFORD, Yorks. (1847)	293,756	10,618,715	90½	G. C. Moore.	★H. Moran.
Bridgwater, Somerset (1200)	26,598	1,212,324	88	J. L. Turner.	Mrs. I. A. Y. Tester.
Bridlington, Yorks.—E.R. (1899)	26,729	1,096,430	83½	S. Briggs.	M. Y. Richardson.
Bridport, Dorset (1253)	6,362	304,173	81½	E. Andrews.	P. C. Norfolk.
Brighouse, Yorks.—W.R.	34,111	997,216	83½	J. R. Liddle.	S. Firth.
§Brighton, East Sussex (1854)	166,081	12,628,182	67½	W. O. Dodd.	S. W. Theobald.
§BRISTOL (1188)	425,303	23,519,346	94½	W. J. Hutchinson.	★Mrs. H. Bloom.
Buckingham (1554)	5,075	260,612	81½	A. Archdeacon.	Mrs. E. D. Embleton.
§Burnley, Lancs. (1861)	76,483	2,634,430	89½	C. V. Thornley, O.B.E.	D. Parkinson.
§Burton upon Trent (1878)	50,175	2,471,935	100	F. N. Brammer.	E. W. Plant.
§Bury, Lancs. (1876)	67,776	2,279,247	82½	J. A. McDonald.	J. Skellern.
Bury St. Edmunds, W. Suffolk (1606)	25,629	1,337,026	93	R. R. Hiles.	A. G. T. Shearing.
Buxton, Derbys. (1917)	20,316	688,453	92	G. D. Jones.	W. C. Poulter.
Calne, Wilts. (1565)	9,685	354,517	84	L. Cave.	D. V. Law.
CAMBRIDGE (1207)	98,519	6,247,061	87	J. W. Elven.	Mrs. J. A. C. Barker.
§CANTERBURY, Kent (1448)	33,157	1,750,494	87½	J. Boyle.	J. Tilleard.
§CARLISLE, Cumberland (1158)	71,497	3,013,651	83½	W. Hirst.	H. Fawcett.
Castleford, Yorks.—W.R. (1955)	38,220	1,222,895	95	E. Hutchinson.	Mrs. W. McLoughlin.
Chard, Somerset (1570)	7,905	297,075	87½	G. T. Leeson.	G. F. Quick.
Chatham, Kent (1891)	56,921	2,228,025	91	R. Hill.	V. S. Bruce.
Chelmsford, Essex (1888)	58,125	3,748,038	80	B. A. Francis.	J. H. C. Roots.
Cheltenham, Glos. (1876)	69,734	3,888,800	91½	A. A. Crabtree.	C. Irving.
§CHESTER (1506)	62,696	3,754,183	87½	D. M. Kermode.	L. Edwards.
Chesterfield, Derbys. (1598)	70,153	3,401,460	86½	R. A. Kennedy.	B. C. Willett.
CHICHESTER, West Sussex	20,547	1,325,857	89½	G. G. Heather.	J. M. Gilbert.

† Full rate levied. Mixed hereditaments, 4½p less; Dwelling-houses, 9½p less.

Cities and Boroughs	Population, 1971 Census (prelim.)	Rateable Value 1971 £	†Rate Levied 1971-72 p	Town Clerk	Mayor, 1971-72 *Lord Mayor
Chippenham, Wilts. (1554)	18,662	824,607	86½	P. R. Morris.	L. A. Doggett, M.B.E.
Chipping Norton, Oxon. (1606)	4,763	176,068	87	E. F. Cunningham.	D. Hunt.
Chorley, Lancs. (1881)	31,609	1,083,155	82½	R. Potter.	H. V. Davies.
Christchurch, Hants (1886)	31,373	2,001,262	77	J. Macfadyen, D.F.C.	W. J. Bentley.
Cleethorpes, Lincs.—Lindsey (1936)	35,785	1,149,260	81½	G. Sutcliffe.	A. W. Cox.
Clitheroe, Lancs. (1147)	13,191	557,020	90½	J. Cowdall.	S. J. Moore.
Colchester, Essex (1189)	76,145	3,326,993	89½	N. Catchpole.	Mrs. A. M. Smith.
Colne, Lancs. (1895)	18,873	556,958	88½	A. Haigh.	Mrs. M. Craddock.
Congleton, Cheshire (1272)	20,324	790,391	83½	H. Lawton.	F. Bowers.
§Coventry (1345)	334,839	14,871,764	95	J. D. Hender.	*T. Meffen.
Crewe, Cheshire (1877)	51,302	2,117,249	99½	A. Brook.	S. S. Bayman.
Crosby, Lancs. (1937)	57,405	2,081,287	95½	H. O. Roberts, O.B.E.	F. L. Prichard.
§Darlington, Co. Durham (1867)	85,889	4,115,000	80½	C. N. S. Nicholson.	Mrs. N. Cottam.
Dartford, Kent (1933)	45,670	2,014,142	87½	A. F. Hargraves.	A. W. May.
Dartmouth, Devon (1341)	5,695	233,856	72½	S. J. Woolnough.	F. C. Mullett.
Darwen, Lancs. (1878)	28,880	955,695	96½	J. C. Fielding.	H. W. Lees.
Daventry, Northants (1595)	11,813	641,053	90½	D. B. Adnitt.	J. Meers.
Deal, Kent (1699)	25,415	866,841	89	R. Purnell, D.F.M.	D. W. Yates-Mercer.
§Derby (1154)	219,348	10,508,006	82	N. S. Fisher.	J. J. Carty.
Devizes, Wilts. (1605)	10,170	451,654	77½	J. J. Diver.	J. A. G. Peare.
§Dewsbury, Yorks.—W.R. (1862)	51,310	1,719,229	94	A. N. James.	A. Ramsden.
§Doncaster, Yorks.—W.R. (1194)	82,505	4,618,892	91	V. Douglas Knox, D.F.C.	W. Clarke.
Dorchester, Dorset (1324)	13,737	766,969	72½	R. W. Broom, B.E.M.	H. Durrant.
Dover, Kent (1278)	34,322	1,385,583	87½	I. G. Gill.	R. G. Lock.
Droitwich, Worcs. (1215)	12,766	546,382	96½	R. W. Russell.	D. Platts.
§Dudley‡ (1865)	185,535	8,481,062	70	P. D. Wadsworth.	K. C. Rogers.
Dukinfield, Cheshire (1899)	17,294	592,758	86½	D. W. Yates.	E. Ollerenshaw.
Dunstable, Beds. (1864)	31,790	2,817,536	83½	L. V. Rallison.	E. L. Royce.
Durham (1602)	24,744	1,323,196	91	D. B. Martin-Jones.	T. W. Leonard.
§Eastbourne, East Sussex (1883)	70,495	4,106,154	80½	F. H. Busby.	J. W. Robinson.
Eastleigh, Hants (1936)	45,320	2,177,801	78	D. A. Tranah.	F. J. Heal.
East Retford, Notts. (1246)	18,402	582,720	73	K. D. Hanna.	G. B. Ostick.
Eccles, Lancs. (1892)	39,413	1,520,018	97½	N. Mitchell.	R. Rhodes.
Ellesmere Port, Cheshire (1955)	61,556	4,811,482	83	R. J. Bernie.	R. Cresswell.
Ely, see Urban Districts List.					
Epsom and Ewell, Surrey (1937)	72,054	4,234,506	87	E. Moore.	Mrs. D. J. Fender.
Evesham, Worcs. (1604)	13,847	629,015	83½	N. F. Davies.	H. A. H. Millward.
§Exeter (1156)	95,598	5,863,247	82½	A. E. Bennett.	H. S. Sargent.
Eye, East Suffolk (1206)	1,659	76,028	73½	S. T. Andrew.	M. J. Harber.
Falmouth, Cornwall (1661)	17,883	830,008	85½	D. Hall.	C. Madden.
Farnworth, Lancs. (1939)	26,841	782,074	92½	T. Hitchen.	W. Hardman.
Faversham, Kent (1252)	14,807	602,995	93½	R. Lawrie.	R. W. Barnicott.
Fleetwood, Lancs. (1933)	28,584	1,029,788	82½	J. R. Barnes.	H. Chippendale.
Folkestone, Kent (1313)	43,760	2,282,884	96	N. C. Scragg.	J. M. Jacques.
§Gateshead, Co. Durham (1835)	94,457	3,801,931	94½	C. D. Jackson.	W. Collins.
Gillingham, Kent (1903)	86,714	3,202,097	72	G. C. Jones.	J. N. Forster.
Glastonbury, Somerset (1705)	6,571	278,820	82½	G. H. Harland.	Mrs. S. E. Openshaw.
Glossop, Derbys. (1866)	24,147	636,128	93	D. G. Hodgkinson.	Mrs. D. E. Singleton.
§Gloucester (1483)	90,134	3,762,327	80	D. Hall.	H. Worrall.
Godalming, Surrey (1575)	18,634	963,168	85	R. C. Hodgins.	H. Denningberg.
Goole, Yorks.—W.R. (1933)	18,066	514,908	83	Miss M. H. Sindell.	T. A. Jaques.
Gosport, Hants (1922)	75,947	3,111,360	79	E. Addenbrooke, O.B.E.	R. A. Kirkin.
Grantham, Lincs.—Kesteven (1463)	27,913	1,127,727	79½	K. R. Cann.	W. C. Bradley.
Gravesend, Kent (1562)	54,044	2,112,856	88	J. V. Lovell.	R. Farthing.
§Grimsby, Lincs.—Lindsey (1201)	95,685	4,518,505	84½	F. W. Ward.	Mrs. L. Trayer.
Guildford, Surrey (1257)	56,887	4,590,061	76	H. C. Weller.	R. F. Sparrow.
Halesowen, Worcs. (1936)	52,933	2,506,898	87½	J. B. McCooke.	A. Brown.
§Halifax, Yorks.—W.R. (1848)	91,171	2,887,719	84½	R. de Z. Hall.	G. H. Smith.
Harrogate, Yorks.—W.R.	62,290	2,757,239	81	J. N. Knox.	R. G. Welch.
§Hartlepool, Co. Durham (1201)	96,898	4,343,621	80	E. J. Waggott, O.B.E.	J. W. Pounder, M.B.E.
Harwich, Essex (1603)	14,892	553,887	89½	T. B. A. Moonlight.	A. J. Thorn. [T.D.
Haslingden, Lancs. (1891)	14,953	442,915	95	R. B. McMillan.	T. B. Fisher.
§Hastings, East Sussex (1588)	72,169	3,283,061	87	D. J. Taylor.	H. F. Paine.
Hedon, Yorks.—E.R. (1154)	2,600	62,477	81½	G. Baslington.	P. A. Garvey.
Helston, Cornwall (1201)	9,827	301,382	71½	E. R. Crawshaw.	W. H. Scott.
Hemel Hempstead, Herts. (1898)	69,371	4,720,898	80	C. W. G. T. Kirk, O.B.E.	P. G. Wood.
Henley, Oxon. (1526)	11,402	587,502	83½	A. Ford.	A. C. Lane.

† Full rate levied. Mixed hereditaments, 4½p less; Dwelling-houses, 9½p less. ‡ Geographically Dudley is in Worcestershire, but areas added to the County Borough in 1966 lie in Staffordshire. For some purposes the whole area is in Staffordshire.

Cities and Boroughs	Population, 1971 Census (prelim.)	Rateable Value 1971 £	† Rate Levied 1971–72 p	Town Clerk	Mayor, 1971–72 ★Lord Mayor
Hereford (1189)	46,503	2,307,681	88½	H. G. Culliss.	M. H. Thomas.
Hertford (1555)..................	20,379	1,271,470	78	A. I. Clough.	Mrs. I. O. Sandford.
Heywood, Lancs. (1881)...........	30,418	879,175	93	W. R. Parker.	A. J. Ryan.
Higham Ferrers, Northants. (1251)..	4,700	194,698	86	G. H. Crapper.	Mrs. G. M. Murdin.
High Wycombe, Bucks. (1237)......	59,298	4,267,843	79	N. M. Fowler.	A. W. Goodearl.
Honiton, Devon (1846)............	5,058	251,007	67	A. D. Johnson.	S. J. Stone.
Hove, East Sussex (1898)..........	72,659	6,462,756	76	J. E. Stevens.	S. Howard, M.B.E.
§Huddersfield, Yorks.—W.R. (1868)..	130,964	4,737,178	87½	E. V. Hartley.	Mrs. E. M. Whitteron.
HULL, see KINGSTON UPON HULL					
Huntingdon and Godmanchester.....	16,540	827,068	91½	F. J. E. Dyer.	M. E. Collinson.
Hyde, Cheshire (1881).............	37,075	1,361,354	88½	C. E. Spence.	J. Baldwin.
Hythe, Kent (1575)...............	11,949	568,374	85	J. Nowell.	C. T. Sanford.
Ilkeston, Derbys. (1887)..........	34,123	1,208,880	81½	J. Yates.	Mrs. M. A. R. Boyd.
§Ipswich, East Suffolk (1200).......	122,814	5,775,921	78½	J. C. Nelson.	C. G. Skinner.
Jarrow, Co. Durham (1875).........	28,779	1,092,589	91½	Miss E. V. Wayper.	D. Dixon.
Keighley, Yorks.—W.R. (1882)......	55,263	1,819,910	87½	J. A. Caesar.	S. Bancroft.
Kendal, Westmorland (1575)........	21,572	893,515	83½	N. C. Bizley.	K. O'Loughlin.
Kettering, Northants (1938)........	42,628	1,794,436	90½	D. D. Price.	P. J. Leonard.
Kidderminster, Worcs. (1636).......	47,255	2,322,268	98½	J. L. Evans.	R. C. Reid-Jones.
King's Lynn, Norfolk (1204)........	30,102	1,952,908	87½	J. R. Davison.	Mrs. N. Lumb.
§KINGSTON UPON HULL (1440).......	285,472	9,935,986	105½	J. H. W. Glen.	★J. Campbell.
LANCASTER (1193).................	49,525	1,845,208	89½	J. D. Waddell.	Mrs. W. Sweeney.
Launceston, Cornwall (1199)........	4,725	204,520	86½	C. W. Parsons.	J. Hughes.
Leamington Spa, Warwicks. (1875)..	44,989	2,187,903	82	J. N. Stothert.	S. W. T. Birch, T.D.
§LEEDS, Yorks.—W.R. (1626).......	494,971	23,265,000	88½	N. C. Haslegrave.	★J. T. V. Watson.
§LEICESTER (1589).................	283,549	15,676,819	76½	R. R. Thornton.	★P. C. Watts.
Leigh, Lancs. (1899)..............	46,117	1,525,709	88½	C. Sarginson.	H. Davies.
Leominster, Hereford (1554)........	7,071	267,238	79½	K. Downs.	A. E. Bengry.
Lewes, East Sussex (1881)..........	14,015	890,743	85½	N. C. Walsh.	J. E. Tilbury.
Lichfield, Staffs. (1594)..........	22,672	931,572	94½	K. D. Brownlow.	Mrs. M. E. Halfpenny.
§LINCOLN (Lindsey) (1154).........	74,207	2,950,909	100	J. S. Horsnell.	★F. Blackbourn.
Liskeard, Cornwall (1240).........	5,255	188,488	90	H. J. Timbrell.	W. E. Hambly.
§LIVERPOOL (1207)................	606,834	27,727,863	101	S. Holmes.	★C. Cowlin.
Loughborough, Leics. (1888)........	45,863	2,278,196	85	A. Usher.	V. B. Wilson.
Louth, Lincs.—Lindsey (1551)......	11,746	451,162	84½	M. B. Mehta.	R. Wilkinson.
Lowestoft, East Suffolk (1885)......	52,182	2,118,015	93½	P. A. Taylor.	J. E. Scarles.
§Luton, Beds. (1876)...............	161,178	10,649,735	69	J. V. Cowan.	J. Cussen.
Lydd, Kent (1885)................	4,301	377,958	79½	C. L. Winkfield.	A. E. Burrage.
Lyme Regis, Dorset (1284).........	3,394	164,982	79½	H. Williams.	V. J. Homyer.
Lymington, Hants (1150)...........	35,644	1,906,774	79	A. L. Slater.	Mrs. I. L. Nedderman.
Lytham St. Annes, Lancs. (1922).....	40,089	2,356,769	79½	R. A. Cork.	A. W. Jealous.
Macclesfield, Cheshire (1261).......	44,240	1,768,824	94½	W. Isaac.	Mrs. L. Davenport.
Maidenhead, Berks. (1582).........	45,306	2,833,601	79	S. Platt.	Mrs. J. K. Fotherby.
Maidstone, Kent (1549)............	70,918	3,451,346	94	T. Scholes, M.C.	E. G. J. Flood.
Maldon, Essex (1171)..............	13,840	593,743	89	K. C. Robertson.	C. Dowsett.
Malmesbury, Wilts. (1885).........	2,526	98,114	85½	J. Bailey.	E. J. Wakefield.
§MANCHESTER (1838)...............	541,468	28,524,685	102	G. C. Ogden, C.B.E.	★D. J. Edwards.
Mansfield, Notts. (1891)..........	57,598	2,260,478	83	S. W. R. Christmas.	E. Groves, M.B.E.
Margate, Kent (1857).............	50,145	2,541,364	99½	V. H. Mellor.	H. Anish.
Marlborough, Wilts. (1575)........	6,031	239,473	82½	R. Betteley.	D. H. Chandler.
Middleton, Lancs. (1886)..........	53,415	1,707,652	88	J. M. Russum.	J. Aspinall.
Morecambe and Heysham,Lancs.(1902)	41,863	1,810,109	99½	C. E. Bottomley.	T. Standidge.
Morley, Yorks.—W.R. (1885)........	44,340	1,173,767	82	A. C. C. Furniss.	R. B. Senior.
Morpeth, Northumberland (1662).....	14,055	534,495	99	M. Cole.	Miss I. Smail.
Mossley, Lancs. (1885)............	10,055	310,708	87½	M. A. Thomas.	H. Bentley.
Nelson, Lancs. (1890).............	31,225	895,800	89½	C. A. Simmonds.	A. F. Evans.
Newark, Notts. (1549).............	24,631	929,245	78½	G. Goodall.	R. H. Lamb.
Newbury, Berks. (1506)............	23,696	1,301,355	82½	L. Southern.	P. W. G. Burgess, O.B.E.
Newcastle under Lyme, Staffs.) (1173)	76,970	2,674,430	87	C. J. Morton.	W. Nixon.
§NEWCASTLE UPON TYNE (1175)......	222,153	12,958,399	105	F. Ireland.	★Mrs. M. E. Graham,
Newport, Isle of Wight............	22,286	901,766	80	W. R. Wilks.	P. Bryan. [M.B.E.
New Romney, Kent (1563)..........	3,414	143,088	94½	D. E. Collins.	C. W. Poll.
§Northampton (1189).............	126,608	6,087,241	87	A. C. Parkhouse.	C. E. Stopford.
§NORWICH (1194)	121,688	6,632,393	81½	G. G. Tilsley.	★D. M. Pratt.
§NOTTINGHAM (1155)...............	299,758	16,122,456	70	P. M. Vine.	★E. Want.
Nuneaton, Warwicks. (1907)........	66,979	2,546,338	87½	P. C. Eccles.	S. T. S. Walters.
Okehampton, Devon (1272).........	3,908	133,463	70	A. E. F. Dear.	H. R. Horne, B.E.M.
§Oldham, Lancs. (1849)............	105,705	3,567,228	104½	E. Haines, O.B.E.	F. Baxter.

† Full rate levied.   Mixed hereditaments, 4½p less; Dwelling-houses, 9½p less.

Cities and Boroughs	Population, 1971 Census (prelim.)	Rateable Value 1971 £	† Rate Levied 1971-72 p	Town Clerk	Mayor, 1971-72 *Lord Mayor
Ossett, Yorks.—W.R. (1890)	17,181	477,410	83½	F. L. Ronan.	J. Spurr.
§Oxford	108,564	7,361,472	87½	A. T. Brown.	*T. J. Meadows.
Penryn, Cornwall (1275)	5,082	165,343	71½	E. G. Dawkins.	Mrs. E. V. Grevatte-
Penzance, Cornwall (1614)	19,352	761,341	73½	H. O. Wheale.	W. J. Turney. [Ball.
Peterborough (1874)	70,021	3,252,511	99	C. P. Clarke.	D. W. Bracey.
§Plymouth (1493)	239,314	11,198,478	70	H. R. Haydon.	*Mrs. D. F. W. Innes.
Pontefract, Yorks.—W.R. (1194)	31,335	957,746	90	L. A. Tawn.	B. Wood.
Poole, Dorset (1248)	106,697	6,306,632	83	J. G. Hillier.	B. A. Greenwood.
§Portsmouth (1194)	196,973	10,309,169	96½	J. R. Haslegrave, O.B.E.	*A. D. Darby.
Preston, Lancs. (1179)	97,365	4,804,306	84	W. E. E. Lockley. [T.D.	T. Dewhurst.
Prestwich, Lancs. (1939)	32,838	1,168,612	84½	C. A. Cross.	S. Clynes.
Pudsey, Yorks.—W.R. (1899)	38,127	1,212,540	77½	L. Wilby.	O. L. Walker.
Queenborough-in-Sheppey, Kent	31,541	1,229,152	100	D. A. Clarke.	W. G. Baxter.
Radcliffe, Lancs. (1935)	29,320	968,854	86½	H. A. Fox.	R. Morris.
Ramsgate, Kent (1884)	39,482	1,555,826	92	K. F. Speakman.	L. T. J. Corbitt.
Rawtenstall, Lancs. (1891)	21,404	627,594	104½	W. B. Wolfe.	T. Dugdale.
§Reading, Berks. (1253)	132,023	7,878,854	75	W. H. Tee.	W. Badnall.
Reigate, Surrey (1863)	56,088	3,328,101	79	C. W. Brightwell.	E. A. C. Pearce.
Richmond, Yorks.—N.R. (1093)	7,245	233,975	94½	M. F. Tooze.	Mrs. K. M. Carr.
Ripon, Yorks.—W.R. (886)	10,987	365,496	85½	J. A. Berry.	N. W. Pollard.
§Rochdale, Lancs. (1856)	91,344	3,004,581	101½	K. B. Moore.	J. F. Grant.
Rochester, Kent (1189)	55,460	2,357,672	88½	J. A. McGhee.	B. E. Wildish.
Romsey, Hants (1607)	10,057	442,645	80	S. L. Flood.	Miss L. R. Jackson.
§Rotherham, Yorks.—W.R. (1871)	84,646	3,780,594	94½	L. I. Frost.	J. S. Crowther.
Rugby, Warwicks. (1932)	59,372	2,536,955	80½	J. S. Watling.	Mrs. P. M. Hill.
Ryde, Isle of Wight (1868)	23,171	915,003	81	K. L. Heath.	J. Langdon.
Rye, East Sussex (1289)	4,434	212,021	90	J. D. Smith.	Mrs. E. Philpott.
Saffron Walden, Essex (1513)	9,945	548,183	75	J. H. Macklin.	D. M. Miller. [M.B.E.
St Albans, Herts. (1553)	52,057	3,478,058	81½	Miss B. V. Entwistle.	Sqn. Ldr. I. A. Parry,
St. Austell with Fowey, Cornwall (1968)	32,252	1,252,205	82	D. W. Cross.	H. C. Orchard.
§St. Helens, Lancs. (1868)	104,173	4,021,959	48	T. Taylor, M.C.	C. Martin.
St. Ives, Cornwall (1639)	9,710	460,545	78½	W. Rainey-Edwards.	T. K. Slocombe.
Sale, Cheshire (1935)	55,623	2,167,824	90	B. Finch.	P. W. Croft.
§Salford, Lancs. (1835)	130,641	5,252,529	94½	R. C. Rees.	R. Evans.
Salisbury, Wilts. (1227)	35,271	1,935,447	90½	F. W. Colquhoun.	G. T. Burden.
Saltash, Cornwall	9,923	328,790	80	A. G. Bellingham.	A. V. Harding.
Sandwich, Kent (1226)	4,467	360,555	75½	B. Roberts.	Mrs. C. J. Maughan.
Scarborough, Yorks.—N.R. (1181)	44,370	2,144,657	93½	W. G. Morgan.	P. Jaconelli.
Scunthorpe, Lincs.—Lindsey (1936)	70,880	5,646,956	77½	T. M. Lister.	O. Duffelen.
Shaftesbury, Dorset (1604)	3,976	163,983	76	S. F. Esland.	Miss M. L. B. Young,
					[O.B.E.
§Sheffield, Yorks. (1843)	519,703	24,605,110	92½	D. B. Harrison.	*H. Hebblethwaite.
Shrewsbury, Salop (1189)	56,140	3,018,070	88½	N. R. Cave.	Mrs. E. M. Parsonage.
Slough, Bucks. (1938)	86,757	8,072,776	80	N. T. Berry.	Mrs. N. B. Denman.
§Solihull, Warwicks. (1954)	106,968	5,629,393	74½	D. W. Chapman.	T. W. Clark.
§Southampton (1447)	214,826	12,182,682	83½	G. Guest.	J. Barr.
§Southend, Essex (1892)	162,326	8,954,615	79½	F. G. Laws.	H. C. G. Hill.
Southport, Lancs. (1867)	84,349	4,305,987	65	P. P. Bayley-Brown.	A. V. F. Langfeld.
§South Shields, Co. Durham (1550)	100,513	3,443,821	79½	R. S. Young.	H. Marshall.
Southwold, East Suffolk (1489)	1,992	117,335	79½	H. Townsend.	R. J. Pizzey, T.D.
Spenborough, Yorks.—W.R. (1955)	40,693	1,150,609	85	K. H. Chorlton.	R. Sewell.
Stafford (1206)	54,890	2,632,640	86½	D. E. Almond.	Miss E. S. Kidman.
Stalybridge, Cheshire (1857)	22,782	751,698	90½	D. Leeming.	G. Rayner.
Stamford, Lincs.—Kesteven (1461)	14,485	533,212	78½	H. Bedford.	E. H. Steele.
§Stockport, Cheshire (1220)	139,633	5,928,539	85½	D. W. Hay.	C. Orford.
§Stoke on Trent, Staffs. (1910)	265,153	10,374,464	90	L. K. Robinson.	*F. A. Cholerton.
Stourbridge, Worcs. (1914)	54,331	2,390,534	89½	M. Duffell.	J. A. H. Edmonds.
Stratford upon Avon, Warwicks. (1553)	19,449	1,206,967	73½	T. Cox.	P. B. P. Sainsbury.
Stretford, Lancs. (1933)	54,011	3,637,991	89½	W. G. Hatton.	C. Warbrick.
Sudbury, West Suffolk (1554)	8,183	318,923	83	G. C. Mountstephen.	W. R. Barker.
§Sunderland, Co. Durham (1634)	216,892	8,387,580	77	J. J. Gardner.	W. S. Martin.
Sutton Coldfield, Warwicks. (1528)	83,130	4,161,266	89½	J. P. Holden.	Mrs. E. E. Dunnett.
Swindon, Wilts. (1900)	90,830	4,218,213	89	D. M. John, O.B.E.	A. N. Palmer.
Swinton and Pendlebury, Lancs. (1934)	40,124	1,665,914	88	D. Cudworth.	J. Birmingham.
Tamworth, Staffs. (1560)	40,245	1,549,861	93½	H. B. Leake.	G. E. Perkins.
Taunton, Somerset (1627)	37,373	1,741,957	92½	K. A. Horne.	C. S. Williams.
§Teesside (1968)	395,477	20,871,514	93	E. C. Parr.	R. Hall. [yen
Tenterden, Kent	5,922	235,001	85½	C. A. Saunders.	Mrs. M. M. G. MacFad-

† Full rate levied.   Mixed hereditaments, 4½p less; Dwelling-houses, 9½p less.

CITIES and Boroughs	Population, 1971 Census (prelim.)	Rateable Value 1971 £	† Rate Levied 1971–72 p	Town Clerk	Mayor, 1971–72 *Lord Mayor
Tewkesbury, Glos. (1574)	8,742	304,186	87½	K. E. Smale.	L. A. Webber.
Thetford, Norfolk (1573)	13,706	662,562	80½	W. E. Clarke.	J. T. Mayes.
Tiverton, Devon (1615)	15,548	611,408	77	R. C. Greensmith.	F. H. Shapland.
Todmorden, Yorks.—W.R. (1896)	15,150	376,815	88½	J. D. Moys.	F. W. Mills, D.F.C.
§Torbay, Devon (1968)	108,888	5,581,364	80	L. Wormersley.	Miss A. G. Illingworth.
Torrington, Devon (1554)	3,536	120,401	79½	A. W. G. Fitt.	H. Pollard.
Totnes, Devon (1206)	5,771	234,183	87½	W. Holt.	S. R. Williams.
TRURO, Cornwall (1589)	14,830	795,774	75	T. H. Johnson.	A. D. Barber.
Tunbridge Wells, Kent (1889)	44,506	2,267,764	92½	M. J. H. Girling.	J. W. Lawrence.
§Tynemouth, Northumberland (1849)	68,861	2,895,000	80	E. B. Lincoln.	A. A. Chambers.
§WAKEFIELD, Yorks.—W.R. (1848)	59,650	2,619,552	73½	A. I. Wylie.	A. E. Lofthouse.
§Wallasey, Cheshire (1910)	97,061	3,854,733	87	A. G. Harrison, D.S.C.	H. T. K. Morris.
Wallingford, Berks. (1155)	6,184	342,916	87	B. R. Brewster.	G. A. Bradburn.
Wallsend, Northumberland (1901)	45,793	1,762,000	92½	J. Stoker.	J. B. Wood.
§Walsall, Staffs. (1159)	184,606	8,062,009	81	J. A. Galloway.	S. Wright.
Wareham, Dorset (1211)	4,379	188,054	73½	F. R. Shutte.	E. E. Mole.
§Warley, Worcs. (1966)	163,388	8,012,426	81	K. Pearce.	C. Lee.
§Warrington, Lancs. (1847)	68,262	3,402,742	81½	J. P. Aspden.	H. Whitehead.
Warwick (1545)	18,289	1,049,046	83½	H. B. Dolphin, M.C., T.D.	L. T. Howlett.
Watford, Herts (1922)	78,117	6,263,761	77½	G. H. Hall.	Mrs. H. M. Dodd.
Wells, Somerset (1201)	8,586	383,964	80½	D. M. Cursley.	G. R. Stiles.
§West Bromwich, Staffs. (1882)	166,626	8,286,303	85	J. M. Day.	J. A. Williams.
Weston-super-Mare, Somerset (1937)	50,794	2,286,579	97½	R. G. Lickfold.	G. W. Couch.
Weymouth and Melcombe Regis, Dorset (1280)	42,332	1,991,456	83	E. J. Jones.	A. D. W. Biles.
Whitehaven, Cumberland (1894)	26,720	1,086,983	91½	G. E. E. Lyon.	J. M. Ruddy.
Whitley Bay, Northumberland (1954)	37,775	1,542,896	93½	F. S. Watson.	H. S. Botham.
Widnes, Lancs. (1892)	56,709	2,300,944	91½	F. Howarth.	K. Mason.
§Wigan, Lancs. (1246)	81,258	3,430,186	93½	J. H. Craik.	J. Harte.
Wilton, Wilts. (1100)	3,815	178,344	70	G. L. Lush.	B. J. Egland.
WINCHESTER, Hants (1155)	31,041	1,830,662	82½	R. H. McCall, O.B.E.	Mrs. A. E. E. Cleary.
Windsor, Berks. (1277)	30,065	1,563,025	84	G. N. Waldram.	F. Burton.
Wisbech, Cambs. (1549)	17,002	980,000	91	W. G. E. Lewis.	A. W. Burton.
Wokingham, Berks. (1583)	21,058	1,178,436	85	L. G. Smalley.	R. Child.
§Wolverhampton, Staffs. (1848)	268,847	14,040,640	74	(vacant).	F. V. Law.
Woodstock, Oxon. (1543)	1,940	80,449	84	M. E. Sawyer.	A. A. England.
§WORCESTER (1189)	73,445	3,497,423	80	B. Webster, M.C.	J. W. Blackman.
Workington, Cumberland (1888)	28,414	1,192,952	90½	G. McK. Porter.	J. Sinclair.
Worksop, Notts. (1931)	36,034	1,450,878	81	R. C. Pharaoh.	R. Babbitt.
Worthing, West Sussex (1890)	88,120	6,054,187	89	T. Foord.	S. M. Knight.
§Yarmouth, Norfolk (1208)	50,152	2,514,798	84½	K. C. Bibby-Cheshire.	A. W. Harvey.
Yeovil, Somerset (1854)	25,492	1,427,915	90½	T. S. Jewels.	P. R. Unwin.
§YORK (c. 1160)	104,513	4,192,035	85½	H. J. Evans.	★R. Scruton.

† Full rate levied. Mixed hereditaments, 4½p less; Dwelling-houses, 9½p less.

URBAN DISTRICTS

A list of Urban Districts in England with a population exceeding 20,000.

URBAN DISTRICTS	Population, 1971 Census (prelim.)	Rateable Value 1971 £	† Rate Levied 1971–72 p	Clerk	Chairman of Council, 1971–72
Aireborough, Yorks.—W.R.	29,477	997,115	83½	J. Rawnsley.	H. W. Freeman.
Aldridge–Brownhills, Staffs.	88,475	3,158,920	81½	H. G. G. Nichols.	R. Arkell.
Alfreton, Derbys.	21,670	680,087	84½	S. Beedham.	T. G. England.
Arnold, Notts.	33,254	1,318,792	73	D. O. Pepper.	M. S. Hall.
Ashford, Kent	35,560	1,591,322	80½	G. H. Redfern.	Mrs. P. F. Ruffle.
Ashington, Northumberland	25,645	826,098	91½	R. R. Nuttall.	J. Murphy.
Ashton-in-Makerfield, Lancs.	26,271	713,431	83½	J. C. Taylor.	S. M. Lea.
Atherton, Lancs.	21,758	584,349	79	K. Hanney, D.F.C.	F. Fildes.
Banstead, Surrey	44,986	2,498,417	81	I. B. Brown.	R. F. A. Hutchinson.
Basildon, Essex	129,073	6,222,828	88	D. H. Taylor.	J. E. Morgan.
Bedlingtonshire, Northumberland	28,167	1,234,779	88½	J. W. Firth.	J. Caine.
Bedworth, Warwicks.	40,535	1,345,958	84	B. E. Walters.	A. Walker.

† Full rate levied. Mixed hereditaments, 4½p less; Dwelling houses, 9½p less.

URBAN DISTRICTS	Population, 1971 Census (prelim.)	Rateable Value 1971 £	† Rate levied 1971–72 p	Clerk	Chairman of Council, 1971–72
Beeston and Stapleford, Notts........	63,498	2,857,574	76½	H. D. Jeffries.	G. E. Mee.
Benfleet, Essex....................	47,924	1,744,674	83½	A. R. Neighbour.	Mrs. J. A. Selby.
Bentley with Arksey, Yorks.—W.R....	22,888	601,275	81½	R. E. Cadwallader.	G. Gallimore.
Bingley, Yorks.—W.R...............	26,540	880,055	93½	J. H. Carr.	A. G. Raistrick.
Bishop Auckland, Co. Durham........	33,292	1,139,872	89½	J. R. Passey.	W. Ruddock.
Bishop's Stortford, Herts...........	22,084	1,202,064	85	A. N. Bullough.	Mrs. V. Sparrow.
Blaydon, Co. Durham...............	32,018	936,313	88½	N. Graham.	Mrs. E. Ainsworth.
Bletchley, Bucks...................	30,608	1,703,076	74½	J. F. Smithie, O.B.E.	C. E. Bowden.
Bognor Regis, West Sussex..........	34,389	2,321,720	90	R. J. M. Sheppard.	D. W. Hansford.
Boldon, Co. Durham................	23,904	719,563	81½	R. I. McClean.	R. H. Burdsall.
Braintree and Bocking, Essex........	24,839	1,230,658	82	P. W. Cotton.	G. A. Warne.
Bredbury and Romiley, Cheshire......	28,472	1,084,014	92½	D. W. Tattersall.	G. A. Young.
Brentwood, Essex..................	57,976	2,796,529	85½	C. Booth.	L. B. Wickes.
Broadstairs and St. Peter's, Kent.....	19,996	994,388	85	K. G. Denne.	B. R. White, B.E.M.
Bromsgrove, Worcs.................	40,669	1,603,376	82½	G. A. Hall, D.F.C.	B. P. Cranmore.
Bushey, Herts.....................	23,729	1,495,704	75½	C. G. Everatt.	G. C. Dalby.
Camborne–Redruth, Cornwall........	42,029	1,336,287	73½	F. J. Pearson.	K. Bowden.
Cannock, Staffs....................	55,873	1,813,884	90	B. E. Rastall.	W. Holston.
Canvey Island, Essex...............	26,462	997,742	83½	J. Rumble.	W. H. Ashworth.
Carlton, Notts.....................	45,211	1,712,727	73½	E. Jones.	H. N. Noble.
Caterham and Warlingham, Surrey ...	35,781	1,675,547	80½	B. J. Smerdon.	I. C. R. Bews.
Chadderton, Lancs.................	32,406	1,379,782	89½	P. W. Musther.	T. K. Ogden.
Cheadle and Gatley, Cheshire	60,648	2,691,451	87½	R. Roberts.	R. G. Crook.
Chertsey, Surrey...................	44,886	2,089,561	83½	L. W. Way.	G. T. Tollett.
Chesham, Bucks...................	20,416	1,009,891	79	G. H. Malin.	Mrs. K. L. Harries.
Cheshunt, Herts...................	44,947	2,294,448	83½	H. F. Bishop.	H. J. Collins.
Chester le Street, Co Durham........	20,531	667,117	88	T. D. Gibbs.	Mrs. D. H. Riddell.
Chigwell, Essex...................	53,620	3,172,209	80½	B. R. Ostler.	D. W. James. [O.B.E.
Clacton, Essex....................	37,942	1,974,315	93½	C. H. Ramsden.	J. E. Webster.
Coalville, Leics...................	28,334	1,095,340	82	N. Marson.	G. A. Peacey.
Colne Valley, Yorks.—W.R..........	21,188	507,244	89½	W. Pogson.	J. Buckley.
Consett, Co. Durham...............	35,391	1,737,324	87	J. Quinn.	J. K. Sessford.
Corby, Northants..................	47,716	3,142,753	95	G. B. Blackall.	J. R. Carr.
Crawley, West Sussex..............	67,571	4,402,723	81	R. W. J. Tridgell.	E. H. Wignall.
Crook and Willington, Co. Durham...	21,485	520,548	86½	R. Fawcett.	Mrs. T. E. Moralee.
Cuckfield, East Sussex.............	25,888	1,550,095	84	D. M. Balmford.	Miss C. C. Bolding.
Dawley, Shropshire................	25,935	898,989	79	A. G. Matthews, M.B.E.	D. L. Chilton.
Dearne, Yorks.—W.R...............	25,029	625,371	81½	G. F. Fox.	Mrs. A. M. Taylor.
Denton, Lancs.....................	38,107	1,272,728	81½	M. Batley.	F. Adshead.
Dorking, Surrey...................	22,354	1,224,532	82½	F. G. Sutherland, M.B.E.	I. H. Fraser.
Droylsden, Lancs..................	24,134	673,918	95½	C. Jefferson.	E. Torr.
Egham, Surrey	30,510	1,812,010	86	D. Brunton.	Mrs. E. Collins.
‡Ely..............................	9,969	497,294	85½	P. H. Brown.	H. R. Halls.
Esher, Surrey.....................	64,186	4,399,278	82	A. E. Gilbert.	A. E. A. Charlton.
Exmouth, Devon...................	25,815	1,194,299	74½	R. S. Bagshaw.	Mrs. M. J. Palmer.
Failsworth, Lancs..................	23,233	783,109	79½	R. N. L. Hamm.	J. E. Mitchell.
Fareham, Hants....................	80,296	3,381,835	82	L. E. Page.	N. G. Robinson.
Farnborough, Hants................	41,233	1,848,169	84	A. R. O'Dowd-Booth.	G. I. Lewis.
Farnham, Surrey..................	31,175	1,943,480	78	A. J. A. Mason.	A. G. Hurdle.
Felling, Co. Durham...............	38,595	1,143,625	96½	J. Myrddin-Baker.	J. R. Foster.
Fleet, Hants......................	21,362	875,812	80	E. Robinson.	J. D. Scott-Curtis.
Formby, Lancs....................	23,501	919,244	78	J. Breese.	J. Morrison.
Frimley and Camberley, Surrey	44,784	2,531,227	88½	D. J. L. Horn.	I. Goodchild.
Fulwood, Lancs....................	21,741	759,995	75½	A. R. Jameson.	Mrs. N. M. Howard.
Garforth, Yorks.—W.R..............	25,296	593,035	76½	C. V. MacDonald.	E. Wilson.
Golborne, Lancs...................	28,178	907,943	74½	T. J. Robson.	J. E. Hilton.
Gosforth, Northumberland..........	26,826	1,148,504	87½	L. Weddle.	Mrs. A. C. Forsyth.
Haltemprice, Yorks.—E.R...........	52,239	1,864,652	59½	W. J. H. Thomas.	C. Boyce.
Harlow, Essex.....................	77,666	4,741,934	84½	D. F. Bull.	Mrs. E. I. V. Morris.
Harpenden, Herts..................	24,161	1,420,000	74½	D. G. Best.	Mrs. W. M. M. Wyborn.
Havant and Waterloo, Hants........	108,999	4,435,495	92	B. R. W. Gofton, V.R.D.	Mrs. M. E. Weekes.
Hazel Grove and Bramhall, Cheshire..	39,534	2,054,173	87	D. W. West.	J. T. Fletcher.
Heanor, Derbys....................	24,352	551,900	76	J. R. Barlow.	S. Mellors.
Hebburn, Co. Durham..............	25,117	1,117,133	96	W. Kinghorn.	C. Bonnar.
Herne Bay, Kent..................	23,597	1,014,708	101½	G. A. Bagnall.	C. E. Taber.
Hinckley, Leics...................	47,982	1,935,133	80	J. Hilton.	F. W. Dagley.
Hindley, Lancs....................	24,307	657,430	84½	J. Marsden.	J. Whittle.
Hitchin, Herts....................	28,680	1,801,008	75	W. Wilson.	Mrs. B. F. Wearmouth.

† Full rate levied.   Mixed hereditaments, 4½p less; Dwelling houses, 9½p less.
‡ Ely is a city, administered by an Urban District Council.

Y*

Urban Districts	Population, 1971 Census (prelim.)	Rateable Value 1971 £	† Rate Levied 1971–72 p	Clerk	Chairman of Council, 1971–72
Hoddesdon, Herts	26,071	1,650,981	77½	C. Campbell.	J. S. Hastings.
Horsham, West Sussex	26,378	1,751,444	76	S. A. Stray.	A. H. Windrum.
Houghton-le-Spring, Co. Durham	32,666	826,965	88	R. J. Sutherland.	E. Bramfitt.
Hoylake, Cheshire	32,196	1,380,876	93½	H. R. Keighley.	W. Whitehurst.
Hucknall, Notts	26,349	862,076	69½	H. Sharp.	S. Grainger.
Huyton with Roby, Lancs	66,629	1,891,716	81	D. Willgoose.	W. Peters.
Irlam, Lancs	20,571	1,172,605	90½	R. Warburton.	C. A. Borrino.
Kenilworth, Warwicks	20,121	888,952	79	C. Riley.	R. Stansfield.
Kidsgrove, Staffs	22,036	607,137	81½	B. V. Taylor.	J. J. Beech.
Kingswood, Glos	30,269	1,082,113	83½	F. Edmonds.	J. H. Murphy.
Kirkby, Lancs	59,759	2,435,260	102½	W. Byron.	J. J. Chambers.
Kirkby in Ashfield, Notts	23,638	626,125	65	J. A. Green.	A. Mead, B.E.M.
Leatherhead, Surrey	40,112	2,403,038	80½	L. A. Stray.	S. J. Taylor, M.B.E.
Leighton–Linslade, Beds	20,326	1,083,422	88½	R. C. Cranmer.	H. E. Mason.
Letchworth, Herts	30,884	2,586,005	80	M. Kelly.	C. W. Sax.
Leyland, Lancs	23,391	868,326	80½	W. C. F. Godsell.	B. Pickup.
Litherland, Lancs	23,670	724,337	75½	W. I. Murray.	W. Gregg.
Longbenton, Northumberland	48,970	1,588,516	87½	G. Harrison.	F. J. Murray.
Long Eaton, Derbys	33,694	1,356,267	80	G. F. Clegg.	T. G. Taylor.
Malvern, Worcs	29,004	1,128,699	85½	L. J. Martin.	Mrs. D. A. Taylor.
Mangotsfield, Glos	23,269	847,558	82½	A. Lloyd Jones.	W. G. Dixon.
Mansfield Woodhouse, Notts	24,787	649,954	69½	C. J. R. Johnson.	D. F. Haynes.
Marple, Cheshire	23,217	834,897	89½	K. Turner.	J. Brady.
Matlock, Derbys	19,575	707,941	82	J. O. Hunt.	H. A. Briddon.
Newburn, Northumberland	39,379	1,296,865	93½	C. H. Walker.	V. A. Waddington.
Newton-le-Willows, Lancs	22,380	746,829	77½	J. Roberts.	E. Kershaw.
Northfleet, Kent	26,679	1,478,239	80½	D. F. Bunkall.	L. Curd.
Ormskirk, Lancs	27,618	1,099,170	81½	G. Williams.	T. Leyland.
Potters Bar, Herts	24,583	1,559,164	86	A. C. Bonser.	M. J. Watts.
Rayleigh, Essex	26,265	1,092,647	83½	C. E. Fitzgerald.	R. W. C. Offwood.
Redditch, Worcs	40,775	1,768,156	90½	P. G. Rust.	Mrs. P. K. Wilson.
Rickmansworth, Herts	29,510	2,353,282	75½	J. J. B. Dutfield.	R. E. Groves.
Rothwell, Yorks.—W.R.	28,353	904,275	79½	A. T. S. Robertson.	W. H. Banks.
Rugeley, Staffs	22,234	878,014	86	M. J. Freeman.	J. E. McGinty.
Runcorn, Cheshire	35,953	1,906,300	83½	T. J. Lewis, O.B.E.	S. Williams.
Seaham, Co. Durham	23,410	611,907	86	W. W. Hay.	E. Watson.
Seaton Valley, Northumberland	32,011	1,009,705	88½	P. W. Ferry.	J. W. Patterson, M.B.E.
Shipley, Yorks.—W.R.	28,444	99,708	91½	E. Pears, M.B.E.	Mrs. J. B. Evans.
Sittingbourne and Milton, Kent	30,861	1,535,498	83½	D. Allen.	H. I. Price.
Skelmersdale with Holland, Lancs	30,522	1,196,894	84½	(vacant).	P. Bond.
Staines, Surrey	56,386	3,812,648	74½	F. Entwistle.	E. Westbrook.
Stanley, Co. Durham	41,940	1,036,245	92	R. Collicott.	J. T. S. Graham.
Stevenage, Herts	66,918	4,339,629	77½	E. J. Bowers.	M. Cotter.
Sunbury-on-Thames, Surrey	40,035	2,547,806	78½	E. J. Robinson.	P. C. Williamson.
Sutton-in-Ashfield, Notts	40,725	1,285,843	86½	W. Laughton, M.B.E.	T. H. May.
Swadlincote, Derbys	20,235	622,615	81½	J. A. Rigg.	G. C. Holmes, M.B.E.
Thornton Cleveleys, Lancs	26,869	1,472,637	81½	W. F. Dolman.	Mrs. I. Cass.
Thurrock, Essex	124,682	8,986,032	79	G. W. Plater.	M. B. Jones.
Tonbridge, Kent	31,006	1,302,132	92½	W. E. Battersby.	R. D. Large.
Turton, Lancs	21,500	708,592	76	H. Lewis.	K. C. Richardson.
Tyldesley, Lancs	21,163	547,720	82½	R. Wood.	S. Little.
Urmston, Lancs	44,523	3,113,817	80	A. Bancroft.	F. H. Eadie.
Walton and Weybridge, Surrey	51,004	3,677,577	79	E. G. Hubbard.	Mrs. E. M. Hart.
Walton le Dale, Lancs	26,841	885,006	74½	F. W. Roscoe.	R. Welham.
Washington, Co. Durham	24,105	769,743	85	J. Reay.	P. Walmsley.
Wellingborough, Northants	37,589	1,717,945	87	W. G. Palmer, M.B.E.	F. W. Grundy.
Welwyn Garden City, Herts	40,369	3,606,433	66½	L. J. Slocombe.	J. McKnight.
West Bridgford, Notts	28,496	1,365,160	77	R. M. Hughes.	J. D. Dady.
Whickham, Co. Durham	28,704	892,244	89½	J. D. Mitchinson.	G. M. Hunter.
Whitefield, Lancs	21,841	699,402	86½	F. H. Buckley.	H. Donn.
Whitstable, Kent	25,404	990,339	96½	G. P. Young.	Mrs. C. J. Grundon.
Wigston, Leics	30,230	1,380,897	74	L. Brookes.	W. L. Boulter.
Wilmslow, Cheshire	28,982	1,445,675	90½	J. H. Morris.	J. Millett.
Winsford, Cheshire	24,791	983,942	91½	N. F. E. Browning,	J. Wilkinson.
Wirral, Cheshire	26,834	1,092,902	90½	J. Platt. [O.B.E.	L. I. Sissons.
Woking, Surrey	75,771	4,150,952	87½	M. Shawcross.	D. A. Boorman.
Worsley, Lancs	49,573	1,591,806	85½	R. E. Huband, O.B.E.	C. Mullineux.

† Full rate levied. Mixed hereditaments, 4½p less; Dwelling-houses, 9p½ less.

PARTY REPRESENTATION IN GREATER LONDON BOROUGHS

(Results of elections, May 13, 1971)

Barking............*Lab.* 53, *Ind.* 4.
Barnet............*C.* 50, *Lab.* 19, *Lib.* 1.
Bexley............*Lab.* 32, *C.* 28.
Brent............*Lab.* 38, *C.* 27.
Bromley............*C.* 48, *Lab.* 13, *Lib.* 4.
Camden............*Lab.* 54, *C.* 16.
Croydon............*C.* 34, *Lab.* 27, *Ind.* 4.
Ealing............*Lab.* 40, *C.* 25.
Enfield............*C.* 37, *Lab.* 28.
Greenwich............*Lab.* 55, *C.* 10.
Hackney............*Lab.* 60, *C.* 5.
Hammersmith............*Lab.* 63, *C.* 7.
Haringey............*Lab.* 41, *C.* 24.
Harrow............*Lab.* 27, *C.* 26, *Lib.* 2, *Ind.* 1.
Havering............*Lab.* 30, *C.* 17, *Ind.* 12.
Hillingdon............*Lab.* 34, *C.* 31.
Hounslow............*Lab.* 47, *C.* 18.
Islington............*Lab.* 60, *C.* 5.
Kensington and
Chelsea............*C.* 43, *Lab.* 22.
Kingston............*C.* 44, *Lab.* 21.
Lambeth............*Lab.* 51, *C.* 14.
Lewisham............*Lab.* 56, *C.* 4.
Merton............*Lab.* 30, *C.* 24, *Ind.* 4.
Newham............*Lab.* 58, *Ind.* 7.
Redbridge............*C.* 46, *Lab.* 18.
Richmond............*C.* 41, *Lab.* 14, *Lib.* 3.
Southwark............*Lab.* 63, *C.* 2.
Sutton............*C.* 29, *Lab.* 21, *Ind.* 5.
Tower Hamlets.....*Lab.* 70.
Waltham Forest......*Lab.* 43, *C.* 13.
Wandsworth......*Lab.* 53, *C.* 12.
Westminster......*C.* 39, *Lab.* 26.

PARTY REPRESENTATION IN ENGLISH CITIES AND BOROUGHS

The representation of parties in English cities and boroughs after the municipal elections of May 1971, was as follows: (*C.*=Conservative; *Comm.*=Communist; *Ind.*=Independent, including Ratepayers' Association, etc.; *Lab.*=Labour; *Lib.*=Liberal; *P.C.*=Plaid Cymru). Later changes consequent upon aldermanic elections and by-elections are not included.

Abingdon.........*C.* 17, *Lab.* 5, *Ind.* 2.
Accrington.........*Lab.* 20, *C.* 14, *Lib.* 2.
Aldeburgh.........*Ind.* 16.
Aldershot ....*C.* 25, *Lib.* 4, *Ind.* 3, *Lab.* 3.
Altrincham ....*C.* 17, *Lab.* 8, *Lib.* 6, *Ind.* 1.
Andover.............*C.* 7, *Ind.* 4, *Lab.* 2, *Lib.* 1.
Appleby.............*Ind.* 16.
Arundel.............*Ind.* 14, *C.* 1, *Lab.* 1.
Ashton under Lyne...*C.* 23, *Lab.* 21.
Aylesbury.........*C.* 14, *Lab.* 9, *Lib.* 1.
Bacup.............*C.* 14, *Lab.* 6, *Lib.* 4.
Banbury.........*C.* 15, *Lab.* 9.
Barnsley.............*Lab.* 30, *Ind.* 5, *Lib.* 5.
Barnstaple.........*Lib.* 11, *Ind.* 10, *Lab.* 2, *C.* 1.
Barrow in Furness...*Lab.* 24, *C.* 7, *Ind.* 1.
Basingstoke.........*C.* 15, *Lab.* 9.
Bath............*C.* 27, *Lab.* 19, *Lib.* 10, *Ind.* 4.
Batley.............*Lab.* 14, *C.* 7, *Lib.* 7, *Ind.* 4.
Bebington.........*C.* 28, *Lab.* 12.
Beccles.............*C.* 8, *Lab.* 7, *Ind.* 1.
Bedford Town.......*C.* 20, *Lab.* 8.
Berwick-on-Tweed.*Ind.* 21, *Lab.* 3.
Beverley............*Ind.* 16, *Lib.* 6, *Lab.* 2.
Bewdley............*Ind.* 6, *C.* 5, *Lab.* 1.
Bexhill............*C.* 14, *Ind.* 6, *Lab.* 4.
Bideford.............*Ind.* 13, *Lab.* 2, *Lib.* 1.
Birkenhead.........*Lab.* 32, *C.* 28, *Lib.* 4.
Birmingham......*C.* 81, *Lab.* 67, *Lib.* 8.
Blackburn.........*Lab.* 29, *C.* 22, *Lib.* 3, *Ind.* 2.
Blackpool.........*C.* 49, *Lab.* 10, *Lib.* 4, *Ind.* 3.
Blandford.........*Ind.* 15, *Lab.* 1.
Blyth.............*Lab.* 32, *Ind.* 7, *Lib.* 1.
Bodmin.............*Ind.* 16.
Bolton.........*C.* 54, *Lab.* 38.
Bootle.............*Lab.* 28, *C.* 27, *Ind.* 1.
Boston.............*C.* 12, *Lab.* 6, *Ind.* 5, *Lib.* 5.
Bournemouth......*C.* 58, *Lab.* 5, *Ind.* 1.
Brackley.............*Ind.* 14, *C.* 1, *Lab.* 1.
Bradford.........*C.* 48, *Lab.* 26, *Lib.* 2.
Bridgwater.........*Lab.* 20, *C.* 4.
Bridlington.........*Ind.* 21, *Lib.* 2, *C.* 1.
Bridport.............*Ind.* 12, *C.* 7, *Lab.* 3, *Lib.* 1.
Brighouse.........*C.* 22, *Lab.* 10.
Brighton.........*C.* 56, *Lab.* 20.
Bristol.............*Ind.* 61, *Lab.* 51.
Buckingham.......*Ind.* 11, *Lab.* 3, *C.* 2.
Burnley.........*Lab.* 26, *C.* 16, *Lib.* 6.
Burton on Trent....*C.* 17, *Lab.* 13, *Ind.* 2.
Bury.............*C.* 30, *Lab.* 18.
Bury St. Edmunds...*C.* 16, *Ind.* 10, *Lab.* 6.
Buxton.............*Lab.* 11, *C.* 10, *Ind.* 2, *Lib.* 1.
Calne.............*Lib.* 5, *C.* 4, *Lab.* 4, *Ind.* 3.
Cambridge.........*C.* 30, *Lab.* 16, *Ind.* 8, *Lib.* 2.
Canterbury.........*C.* 12, *Lib.* 6, *Lab.* 5, *Ind.* 1.
Carlisle............*C.* 25, *Lab.* 15.
Castleford.........*Lab.* 35, *C.* 4, *Ind.* 1.
Chard.............*C.* 10, *Lab.* 5, *Ind.* 1.
Chatham.........*C.* 16, *Lab.* 8.
Chelmsford.........*C.* 27, *Lab.* 5.
Cheltenham.........*C.* 22, *Lab.* 11, *Lib.* 4, *Ind.* 3.
Chester.............*C.* 37, *Lab.* 16, *Ind.* 3.
Chesterfield.......*Lab.* 24, *C.* 20, *Ind.* 4.
Chichester.........*Ind.* 10, *Lib.* 8, *Lab.* 4, *C.* 2.
Chippenham.........*C.* 11, *Lab.* 6, *Ind.* 4, *Lib.* 3.
Chipping Norton...*C.* 10, *Lab.* 4, *Ind.* 2.
Chorley.........*C.* 22, *Lab.* 10.
Christchurch.........*C.* 16, *Ind.* 5, *Lab.* 2.
Cleethorpes.........*C.* 11, *Lab.* 4, *Ind.* 3, *Lib.* 2.
Clitheroe.........*C.* 13, *Lab.* 2, *Ind.* 1.
Colchester.........*C.* 23, *Lab.* 12, *Lib.* 1.
Colne.............*C.* 11, *Lab.* 10, *Lib.* 2, *Ind.* 1.
Congleton.........*C.* 13, *Lab.* 12, *Ind.* 3.
Coventry.........*C.* 42, *Lab.* 30.
Crewe.............*Lab.* 23, *Ind.* 9.
Crosby.............*C.* 22, *Ind.* 10, *Lab.* 8.
Darlington.........*Lab.* 23, *C.* 12, *Lib.* 6, *Ind.* 3.
Dartford.............*Lab.* 19, *C.* 13.
Dartmouth.........*Ind.* 16.
Darwen.............*C.* 8, *Lab.* 7, *Lib.* 7, *Ind.* 2.
Daventry.........*Lab.* 11, *Ind.* 5.
Deal.............*C.* 23, *Lab.* 9.
Derby.............*C.* 39, *Lab.* 33.
Devizes.............*C.* 13, *Ind.* 6, *Lib.* 3, *Lab.* 2.
Dewsbury.........*Lab.* 21, *C.* 10, *Ind.* 3, *Lib.* 2.
Doncaster.........*Lab.* 25, *C.* 22, *Ind.* 1.
Dorchester.........*Ind.* 16, *Lab.* 6, *Lib.* 2.
Dover.............*C.* 15, *Lab.* 9.
Droitwich.........*C.* 11, *Ind.* 5.
Dudley.............*Lab.* 32, *C.* 28.
Dukinfield.........*Lab.* 16, *C.* 5, *Lib.* 2, *Ind.* 1.
Dunstable.........*C.* 18, *Lab.* 5, *Ind.* 1.
Durham.............*Ind.* 19, *Lab.* 9.
Eastbourne.........*C.* 26, *Lib.* 8, *Lab.* 5, *Ind.* 1.
Eastleigh.........*Lab.* 14, *C.* 11, *Lib.* 3.
East Retford.......*C.* 13, *Lab.* 7, *Ind.* 3, *Lib.* 1.
Eccles.............*Lab.* 18, *C.* 10, *Lib.* 4.
Ellesmere Port ....*Lab.* 18, *C.* 11, *Ind.* 3.
Epsom and Ewell...*Lab.* 36, *Lab.* 4.
Evesham.............*Ind.* 19, *Lab.* 1.
Exeter.............*C.* 39, *Lab.* 19, *Lib.* 8, *Ind.* 2.
Eye ....*Ind.* 16.
Falmouth.........*Lab.* 8, *C.* 4, *Ind.* 4.
Farnworth.........*Lab.* 21, *C.* 3.
Faversham.........*C.* 9, *Lab.* 4, *Ind.* 2.

Fleetwood.........*C.* 19, *Lab.* 4, *Ind.* 1.
Folkestone.........*C.* 28, *Lab.* 8.
Gateshead.........*Lab.* 35, *Ind.* 13.
Gillingham.........*C.* 26, *Lab.* 6.
Glastonbury.........*C.* 13, *Ind.* 1, *Lib.* 1, *Lab.* 1.
Glossop.........*C.* 9, *Ind.* 6, *Lab.* 6, *Lib.* 3.
Gloucester.........*C.* 28, *Lab.* 16.
Godalming.........*C.* 16, *Lib.* 5, *Lab.* 3.
Goole.............*Ind.* 13, *Lab.* 8, *C.* 3.
Gosport.........*C.* 24, *Lab.* 11, *Ind.* 8.
Grantham.........*Lab.* 13, *C.* 9, *Ind.* 2.
Gravesend.........*C.* 20, *Lab.* 12.
Grimsby.........*C.* 28, *Lab.* 27, *Lib.* 1.
Guildford.........*C.* 23, *Lab.* 7, *Lib.* 2.
Halesowen.........*C.* 17, *Lab.* 7, *Lib.* 7, *Ind.* 1.
Halifax.........*C.* 33, *Lab.* 17, *Lib.* 9, *Ind.* 1.
Harrogate.........*C.* 21, *Lib.* 15.
Hartlepool.........*C.* 30, *Lab.* 30.
Harwich.........*Ind.* 9, *C.* 3, *Lab.* 3, *Lib.* 1.
Haslingden.........*C.* 13, *Lab.* 7, *Lib.* 3, *Ind.* 1.
Hastings.........*C.* 28, *Lab.* 7, *Lib.* 4, *Ind.* 1.
Hedon.............*Ind.* 12.
Helston.........*Ind.* 16.
Hemel Hempstead.*C.* 18, *Lab.* 18.
Henley.........*Ind.* 12, *Lab.* 2, *C.* 1, *Lib.* 1.
Hereford.........*C.* 12, *Lab.* 5, *Lib.* 5, *Ind.* 2.
Hertford.........*C.* 18, *Ind.* 1, *Lab.* 1.
Heywood.........*C.* 15, *Lab.* 13, *Lib.* 8.
Higham Ferrers...*C.* 7, *Lab.* 7, *Ind.* 2.
High Wycombe....*C.* 19, *Lab.* 11, *Ind.* 2.
Honiton.........*Ind.* 24.
Hove.........*C.* 37, *Ind.* 2, *Lab.* 1.
Huddersfield.........*C.* 35, *Lab.* 17, *Lib.* 7, *Ind.* 1.
Hull.............*Lab.* 46, *C.* 37, *Ind.* 1.
Huntingdon and
  Godmanchester...*C.* 11, *Lab.* 9, *Ind.* 4.
Hyde.........*C.* 12, *Lab.* 8, *Ind.* 2, *Lib.* 2.
Hythe.........*C.* 13, *Lab.* 3.
Ilkeston.........*Lab.* 12, *C.* 5, *Lib.* 5, *Ind.* 1.
Ipswich.........*C.* 35, *Lab.* 20, *Lib.* 1.
Jarrow.........*Lab.* 22, *C.* 6.
Keighley.........*C.* 26, *Lab.* 14.
Kendal.........*Ind.* 21, *Lab.* 3.
Kettering.........*Lab.* 16, *C.* 11, *Lib.* 7, *Ind.* 2.
Kidderminster.....*C.* 13, *Lab.* 9, *Lib.* 5.
King's Lynn.........*C.* 14, *Lab.* 9, *Lib.* 1.
Lancaster.........*C.* 18, *Lab.* 16, *Ind.* 2.
Launceston.........*Ind.* 15, *Lab.* 1.
Leamington Spa....*C.* 25, *Lab.* 7.
Leeds.............*C.* 71, *Lab.* 45, *Lib.* 4.
Leicester.........*C.* 39, *Lab.* 25.
Leigh.........*Lab.* 22, *C.* 8, *Lib.* 2.
Leominster.........*C.* 12, *Ind.* 2, *Lib.* 2.
Lewes.........*C.* 12, *Lab.* 11, *Ind.* 1.
Lichfield.........*C.* 9, *Ind.* 9, *Lab.* 6.
Lincoln.........*Lab.* 22, *C.* 15, *Ind.* 6.
Liskeard.........*Ind.* 15, *Lab.* 1.
Liverpool.........*C.* 82, *Lab.* 67, *Lib.* 7, *Ind.* 4.
Loughborough.....*C.* 14, *Lab.* 8, *Lib.* 6.
Louth.........*C.* 14, *Ind.* 7, *Lab.* 2.
Lowestoft.........*Lab.* 20, *C.* 14, *Ind.* 4, *Lib.* 1.
Luton.........*C.* 28, *Lab.* 20.
Lydd.............*Ind.* 16.
Lyme Regis......*Ind.* 16.
Lymington.........*Ind.* 20, *C.* 15, *Lib.* 1.
Lytham St. Annes..*C.* 28, *Lib.* 2, *Ind.* 1, *Lab.* 1.
Macclesfield.........*C.* 30, *Lab.* 16, *Ind.* 2.
Maidenhead.........*C.* 18, *Lab.* 1, *Lib.* 1.
Maidstone.........*C.* 17, *Lib.* 8, *Lab.* 7.
Maldon.........*C.* 11, *Lab.* 9.
Malmesbury.........*Ind.* 16.
Manchester.........*Lab.* 81, *C.* 68.
Mansfield.........*Lab.* 13, *C.* 11.
Margate.........*C.* 29, *Ind.* 5, *Lab.* 5, *Lib.* 1.
Marlborough.........*Ind.* 11, *C.* 5.
Middleton.........*Lab.* 17, *C.* 15, *Lib.* 2, *Ind.* 1.

Morecambe and
  Heysham.........*C.* 20, *Ind.* 10, *Lab.* 5, *Lib.* 1.
Morley.........*Ind.* 26, *Lab.* 14, *C.* 4.
Morpeth.........*Ind.* 15, *Lab.* 1.
Mossley.........*Lib.* 11, *C.* 9, *Lab.* 4.
Nelson.........*Lab.* 29, *C.* 3.
Newark.........*C.* 14, *Lab.* 7, *Ind.* 2.
Newbury.........*C.* 9, *Lib.* 7, *Ind.* 5, *Lab.* 3.
Newcastle (Lyme)..*Lab.* 26, *C.* 17, *Lib.* 3, *Ind.* 2.
Newcastle (Tyne)...*C.* 44, *Lab.* 32.
Newport (I.O.W.)..*Lab.* 10, *C.* 9, *Lib.* 5.
New Romney.....*Ind.* 16.
Northampton.........*C.* 31, *Lab.* 17.
Norwich.........*Lab.* 44, *C.* 20.
Nottingham.........*C.* 38, *Lab.* 33, *Ind.* 1.
Nuneaton.........*Lab.* 16, *C.* 14, *Ind.* 1.
Okehampton.......*Ind.* 16.
Oldham.........*Lab.* 28, *C.* 23, *Lib.* 1.
Ossett.........*Ind.* 6, *Lab.* 6, *C.* 2, *Lib.* 2.
Oxford.........*C.* 36, *Lab.* 22, *Ind.* 8, *Lib.* 2.
Penryn.........*Ind.* 11, *Lab.* 5.
Penzance.........*Ind.* 31, *Lib.* 1.
Peterborough.....*C.* 21, *Lab.* 15.
Plymouth.........*C.* 58, *Lab.* 30.
Pontefract.........*Lab.* 19, *C.* 5.
Poole.........*C.* 25, *Lab.* 9, *Ind.* 3, *Lib.* 3.
Portsmouth.........*C.* 46, *Lab.* 18.
Preston.........*C.* 26, *Lab.* 20, *Ind.* 2.
Prestwich.........*C.* 17, *Lab.* 4, *Ind.* 3.
Pudsey.........*C.* 22, *Lab.* 5, *Lib.* 5.
Queenborough ....*C.* 20, *Lab.* 13, *Ind.* 3.
Radcliffe.........*C.* 17, *Lab.* 17, *Ind.* 2.
Ramsgate.........*C.* 18, *Lab.* 10, *Ind.* 4.
Rawtenstall.........*C.* 13, *Lab.* 10, *Lib.* 1.
Reading.........*C.* 31, *Lab.* 17, *Lib.* 4.
Reigate.........*C.* 20, *Lab.* 8.
Richmond (Yorks).*Ind.* 16.
Ripon.........*C.* 8, *Ind.* 5, *Lab.* 3.
Rochdale.........*Lab.* 22, *C.* 14, *Lib.* 11, *Ind.* 1.
Rochester.........*C.* 17, *Lab.* 7, *Ind.* 3.
Romsey.........*C.* 10, *Lib.* 4, *Ind.* 2.
Rotherham.........*Lab.* 38, *C.* 5, *Ind.* 1.
Rugby.........*C.* 18, *Lab.* 11, *Ind.* 4, *Lib.* 3.
Ryde.........*Ind.* 28.
Rye.........*Ind.* 16.
Saffron Walden....*C.* 8, *Lab.* 6, *Ind.* 1, *Lib.* 1.
St. Albans.........*C.* 22, *Lib.* 4, *Lab.* 2.
St.Austell and Fowey *Ind.* 32.
St. Helens.........*Lab.* 29, *C.* 6, *Lib.* 5.
St. Ives (Cornwall).*Ind.* 11, *Lib.* 4, *Lab.* 1.
St. Ives (Hunts.)....*Ind.* 16.
Sale.........*C.* 18, *Lab.* 9, *Lib.* 5.
Salford.........*C.* 31, *Lab.* 29, *Lib.* 3, *Ind.* 1.
Salisbury.........*C.* 20, *Lab.* 7, *Ind.* 5.
Saltash.........*Ind.* 16.
Sandwich.........*C.* 9, *Ind.* 3, *Lab.* 3, *Lib.* 1.
Scarborough.........*C.* 18, *Lab.* 3, *Lib.* 2, *Ind.* 1.
Scunthorpe.........*Lab.* 31, *C.* 9.
Shaftesbury.........*Ind.* 13, *Lib.* 3.
Sheffield.........*Lab.* 80, *C.* 27, *Lib.* 1.
Shrewsbury.........*C.* 23, *Lab.* 16, *Lib.* 5.
Slough.........*C.* 26, *Lab.* 16, *Ind.* 1, *Lib.* 1.
Solihull.........*Ind.* 25, *C.* 12, *Lab.* 2, *Lib.* 1.
Southampton.........*C.* 47, *Lab.* 25.
Southend.........*C.* 51, *Lab.* 9, *Lib.* 4.
Southport.........*C.* 46, *Lib.* 10, *Lab.* 5.
South Shields......*Ind.* 30, *Lab.* 30.
Southwold.........*Ind.* 16.
Spenborough.........*C.* 26, *Lab.* 13, *Lib.* 1.
Stafford.........*Ind.* 24, *Lab.* 12.
Stalybridge.........*C.* 15, *Lab.* 12, *Lib.* 5.
Stamford.........*C.* 19, *Lab.* 4, *Ind.* 1.
Stockport.........*C.* 39, *Lab.* 31, *Ind.* 1, *Lib.* 1.
Stoke on Trent.....*Lab.* 64, *C.* 19, *Ind.* 13.
Stourbridge.........*C.* 22, *Lab.* 7, *Ind.* 3.
Stratford
  upon Avon......*Ind.* 23, *Lib.* 4, *Lab.* 1.

Stretford	C. 18, Lab. 14.	Warley	C. 32, Lab. 26, Ind. 1, Lib. 1.
Sudbury	Lab. 6, C. 5, Ind. 5.	Warrington	Lab. 23, C. 13.
Sunderland	C. 47, Lab. 39, Ind. 2.	Warwick	C. 16, Lab. 6, Ind. 2.
Sutton Coldfield	C. 32, Lib. 6, Ind. 2.	Watford	C. 26, Lab. 17, Lib. 1.
Swindon	Lab. 24, C. 21, Ind. 3.	Wells	C. 6, Ind. 6, Lib. 3, Lab. 1.
Swinton and Pendlebury	Lab. 15, C. 12, Lib. 1.	West Bromwich	C. 31, Lab. 28, Ind. 1.
		Weston-s-Mare	C. 24, Lab. 7, Ind. 1.
Tamworth	Lab. 20, Ind. 11, C. 1.	Weymouth	Lab. 18, C. 17, Ind. 4, Lib. 1.
Taunton	C. 15, Lab. 9, Ind. 4.	Whitehaven	Lab. 18, C. 6.
Teesside	C. 53, Lab. 46, Ind. 5.	Whitley Bay	C. 17, Ind. 7, Lab. 7, Lib. 1.
Tenterden	Ind. 16.	Widnes	C. 18, Lab. 14.
Tewkesbury	Lib. 6, C. 5, Ind. 4, Lab. 1.	Wigan	Lab. 42, C. 14.
Thetford	C. 6, Lab. 6, Ind. 4.	Wilton	Ind. 14, Lab. 1, Lib. 1.
Tiverton	Ind. 14, Lab. 5, Lib. 5.	Winchester	C. 12, Ind. 5, Lab. 5, Lib. 2.
Todmorden	Lab. 10, Ind. 9, C. 5.	Windsor	C. 29, Lab. 10.
Torbay	C. 38, Ind. 5, Lab. 3, Lib. 2.	Wisbech	C. 20, Lab. 8, Ind. 2, Lib. 2.
Torrington	Ind. 16.	Wokingham	C. 16, Ind. 7, Lab. 1.
Totnes	Ind. 10, Lib. 4, Lab. 2.	Wolverhampton	C. 47, Lab. 33.
Truro	Ind. 23, Lib. 1.	Woodstock	Ind. 16.
Tunbridge Wells	C. 27, Lab. 5.	Worcester	C. 28, Lab. 17, Ind. 3.
Tynemouth	Ind. 26, Lab. 10.	Workington	Lab. 22, C. 6, Ind. 4.
Wakefield	Lab. 26, C. 16, Ind. 2.	Worksop	Lab. 17, C. 4, Ind. 3.
Wallasey	C. 33, Lab. 24, Lib. 5, Ind. 2.	Worthing	C. 34, Ind. 6.
Wallingford	C. 5, Ind. 4, Lib. 4, Lab. 3.	Yarmouth	C. 25, Lab. 20, Lib. 3.
Wallsend	Lab. 32, Lib. 2. C. 1, Ind. 1.	Yeovil	C. 13, Lab. 7, Lib. 3, Ind. 1.
Walsall	C. 26, Lab. 21, Ind. 13.	York	C. 35, Lab. 17.
Wareham	Ind. 16.		

Welsh Cities and Boroughs

Abergavenny	C. 11, Lab. 5.	Llandovery	Ind. 16.
Aberystwyth	Ind. 13, Lab. 11.	Llanelli	Lab. 22, Ind. 1, Lib. 1.
Bangor	Ind. 15, Lab. 11, C. 1.	Llanidloes	Ind. 9, Lab. 5, P.C. 2.
Barry	Lab. 17, C. 10.	Merthyr Tydfil	Lab. 29, Ind. 3.
Beaumaris	Ind. 16.	Monmouth	C. 11, Lab. 3, Lib. 1, P.C. 1.
Brecon	Ind. 7, C. 6, Lab. 3.	Montgomery	Ind. 8.
Caernarvon	Ind. 23, Lab. 1.	Neath	Lab. 15, Ind. 8, Comm. 1.
Cardiff	C. 53, Lab. 22, P.C. 1.	Newport	Lab. 29, C. 21, Ind. 2.
Cardigan	Ind. 16.	Pembroke	Ind. 24.
Carmarthen	Ind. 14, Lab. 9, P.C. 2.	Port Talbot	Lab. 28, Ind. 4.
Colwyn Bay	Ind. 15, C. 5, Lib. 5, Lab. 2.	Pwllheli	Ind. 16.
Conway	Ind. 14, Lab. 3, C. 2. Lib. 1.	Rhondda	Lab. 40, Comm. 2, Ind. 2.
Cowbridge	Ind. 16.	Ruthin	Ind. 16.
Denbigh	Ind. 16.	Swansea	Lab. 44, C. 11, Ind. 5.
Flint	Lab. 13, C. 8, Ind. 3.	Tenby	Ind. 15.
Haverfordwest	Ind. 16.	Welshpool	Ind. 13, Lab. 3. [P.C. 1.
Kidwelly	Ind. 9, Lab. 6, P.C. 1.	Wrexham	Lab. 15, Ind. 9, C. 7, Lib. 4.
Lampeter	Ind. 16.		

PATRON SAINTS

St. George, *Patron Saint of England.*—St. George is believed to have been born in Cappadocia, of Christian parents, in the latter part of the 3rd century and to have served with distinction as a soldier under the Emperor Diocletian, including a visit to England on a military mission. When the persecution of Christians was ordered, St. George sought a personal interview to remonstrate with the Emperor and after a profession of faith resigned his military commission. Arrest and torture followed and he was martyred at Nicomedia on April 23, 303, a day ordered to be kept in remembrance as a national festival by the Council of Oxford in 1222, although it was not until the reign of Edward III that he was made patron saint of England. His connection with a dragon seems to date from the close of the 6th century and to be due to the transfer of his remains from Nicomedia to Lydda, close to the scene of the legendary exploit of Perseus in rescuing Andromeda and slaying the sea monster, credit for which became attached to the Christian martyr.

St. David, *Patron Saint of Wales.*—St. David is believed to have been born near the beginning and to have died towards the end of the 6th century. St. David was an eloquent preacher and became Primate of South Wales while Bishop of Caerleon on Usk, but he afterwards moved the seat of the Primacy from Caerleon to Menevia, now St. David's.

At the request of Henry I he was canonized in the early part of the 12th century and became the tutelary saint of Wales, his annual festival being observed on March 1.

St. Andrew, *Patron Saint of Scotland.*—St. Andrew, one of the Christian Apostles and brother of Simon Peter was born at Bethsaida on the Lake of Galilee and lived at Capernaum. He preached the Gospel in Asia Minor and in Scythia along the shores of the Black Sea and became the patron saint of Russia. It is believed that he suffered crucifixion at Patras in Achaea, on a *crux decussata* (now known as St. Andrew's Cross) and that his relics were removed from Patras to Constantinople and thence to St. Andrews, probably in the 8th century, since which time he has been the patron saint of Scotland. The festival of St. Andrew is held on November 30, a church festival indicated in the calendar by red letters.

St. Patrick, *Patron Saint of Ireland.*—St. Patrick was born in England about 389 and was carried off to Ireland as a slave about sixteen years later, escaping to Gaul at the age of 22. He was ordained deacon at Auxerre and having been consecrated Bishop in 432 was despatched to Wicklow to reorganize the Christian communities in Ireland. He founded the see of Armagh and introduced Latin into Ireland as the language of the Church. He died in 461 and his festival is celebrated on March 17.

THE PRINCIPALITY OF WALES AND MONMOUTHSHIRE

Position and Extent.—Wales and Monmouthshire occupy the extreme west of the central southern portion of the island of Great Britain, with a total area of 8,017 sq. miles (5,130,880 acres); they are bounded on the N. by the Irish Sea, on the S. by the Bristol Channel, on the E. by the English counties of Cheshire, Salop, and Hereford, and on the W. by St. George's Channel. Across the Menai Straits is the Welsh island-county of *Anglesey* or *Môn* (276 sq. miles), communication with which is facilitated by the Menai Suspension Bridge (1,000 ft. long), built by Telford in 1826 (freed from toll as from Jan. 1, 1941) and by the tubular railway bridge (1,100 ft. long) of the former L.M. & S. Railway, built by Stephenson in 1850. Holyhead harbour, on Holy Isle (N.W. of Anglesey), provides accommodation for a fast steam packet service to Dun Laoghaire and Dublin (70 miles).

Population.—The population at the Census of 1971 was 2,723,596 (inclusive of Monmouthshire) (preliminary figures), compared with 2,644,023 at the 1961 Census.

Relief.—Wales is mostly mountainous, the chief systems being those of North Wales (Snowdon 3,560 ft., Carnedd Llywelyn 3,484 ft., Carnedd Dafydd 3,426 ft.); Berwyn (Aran-mawddwy 2,970 ft.); Powys (Plinlimmon 2,468 ft., Drygan Fawr 2,115 ft., Radnor 2,163 ft.); and the Black Mountain, Brecknock Beacons and Black Forest ranges (Carmarthen Van 2,632 ft., Brecon Beacon 2,906 ft., Pen-y-gader fawr 2,660 ft.).

Hydrography.—The principal river of those rising in Wales is the *Severn* (*see* England), which flows from the slopes of Plinlimmon to the English border, dividing Montgomeryshire on its way. The *Wye* (130 miles) also rises in the slopes of Plinlimmon, and flows between Radnor and Brecon on its course to England. The *Usk* (56 miles) flows into the Bristol Channel, through Monmouthshire. The *Dee* (70 miles) rises in Bala Lake and flows through the Vale of Llangollen, where an aqueduct (built by Telford in 1805) carries the Pontcysyllte branch of the Shropshire Union Canal across the valley. The estuary of the Dee is the navigable portion, 14 miles in length and about 5 miles in breadth, and the tide rushes in with dangerous speed over the " Sands of Dee." The *Towy* (68 miles), *Teifi* (50 miles), *Taff* (40 miles), *Dovey* (30 miles), *Taf* (25 miles), and *Conway* (24 miles), the last named broad and navigable, are wholly Welsh rivers.

The largest natural lake in Wales is *Bala* (Llyn Tegid) in Merionethshire, 4 miles long and about 1 mile wide; *Lake Vyrnwy* is an artificial reservoir, about the size of Bala, and forms the water supply of Liverpool, and Birmingham is supplied from a chain of reservoirs in the Elan and Claerwen valleys.

The Welsh Language.—Statistics published on Sept. 11, 1962, show that only 656,000 persons (of three years and over) in Wales and Monmouthshire were able to speak Welsh at the time of the 1961 Census, compared with 715,000. at the 1951 Census. One per cent. of the population could speak Welsh only, compared with 4 per cent. in 1931. The proportion of people speaking Welsh fell from 28·9 per cent. in 1951 to 26 per cent. in 1961. As in 1951, the Western Counties, Anglesey, Caernarvon, Merioneth (75.9 per cent.), Cardigan and Carmarthen had the highest proportion of Welsh speakers.

Flag.—A red dragon on a green and white field (per fess argent and vert a dragon passant gules). The flag was augmented in 1953 by a royal badge on a shield encircled with a riband bearing the words *Ddraig Goch Ddyry Cychwyn* and imperially crowned. Only the unaugmented flag is flown on Government offices in Wales and, where appropriate, in London. Both flags continue to be used elsewhere.

EARLY HISTORY

Celts and Romans.—The earliest inhabitants of whom there is any record appear to have been subdued or exterminated by the *Goidels* (a people of Celtic race) in the Bronze Age, and a further invasion of Celtic *Brythons* and *Belgae* followed in the ensuing Iron Age. The *Roman* conquest of South Britain and Wales was for some time successfully opposed by *Caratacus* (Caractacus or Caradog), Chieftain of the Catuvellauni and son of *Cunobelinus* (Cymbeline) King of the Trinobantes. In A.D. 78 the conquest of Wales was completed under Julius Frontinus, and communications were opened up by the construction of military roads from Chester to Caerleon-on-Usk and Caerwent, and from Chester to Conway (and thence to Carmarthen and Neath). *Christianity* was introduced (during the Roman occupation) in the 4th century.

The Anglo-Saxon Attacks.—The Anglo-Saxon invaders of South Britain drove the Celtic Goidels and Brythons into the mountain fastnesses of Wales, and into Strathclyde (Cumberland and S.W. Scotland) and Cornwall, giving them the name of *Waelisc*, or Welsh (=Foreign). The West Saxons' victory of Deorham (577) isolated Wales from Cornwall and the battle of Chester (613) cut off communication with Strathclyde. In the 8th century the boundaries of the Welsh were further restricted by the annexations of Offa, King of Mercia, and counter-attacks were largely prevented by the construction of an artificial boundary from the Dee to the Wye (Offa's Dike). In the 9th century Rhodri Mawr united the country against further incursions of the Saxons by land and against the raids of Norse and Danish pirates by sea, but at his death his three provinces of *Gwynedd* (N.), *Powys* (Mid.) and *Dehenbarth* (S.) were divided among his three sons—Anarawd, Mervyn and Cadell—the son of the last named being Howel Dda, who codified the laws of the country, while Llewelyn ap Sitsyhlt (husband of the heiress of Gwynedd) again united the provinces and reigned as Prince from 1018 to 1023.

The Norman Conquest.—After the Norman conquest of England, William I. created Palatine counties along the Welsh frontier, and Robert FitzHamon, the Norman Earl of Gloucester, raided South Wales and erected fortresses from the Wye to Milford Haven. Henry I. introduced Flemish settlers into South Wales, but after his death the Welsh rose under the leadership of Griffith ap Rhys and routed the Norman-Flemish forces at the fords of the Teifi (Cardigan) in 1136. From the early years of the 13th century the house of Gwynedd, in the north, gained an ascendancy over the whole of Wales, and Llywelyn ap Iorwerth was in constant strife with England for recognition as an independent sovereign. Llywelyn ap Grufydd (grandson of Llywelyn ap Iorwerth), the last native prince, was killed in 1282 during hostilities between the Welsh and English. On Feb. 7, 1301, Edward of Caernarvon, son of Edward I., was created *Prince of Wales*.

The Welsh are a distinct nationality, with a language and literature of their own, and the national bardic festival (Eisteddfod), instituted by Prince Rhys ap Griffith in 1176, is annually maintained. These *Eisteddfodau* (sessions) form part of the *Gorsedd* (assembly), which is believed to date from the time of Prydian, a ruling prince in an age many centuries before the Christian era.

County or Shire with Administrative Headquarters (a), (b), (c) See notes, p. 631	Acreage 1967	Population of Counties		Rateable Value 1970 (a)	Average Rates, 1970–71
		Administrative (a)	Geographical (b)		
				£	p‡
(1) Anglesey (Llangefni)................	176,694	59,705	59,705	1,521,000	219
(2) Brecknockshire (Brecon)............	469,281	53,234	53,234	1,402,400	197
(3) Caernarvonshire (Caernarvon).......	364,108	122,852	122,852	3,844,700	218
(4) Cardiganshire (Aberystwyth)........	443,189	54,844	54,844	1,404,600	193
(5) Carmarthenshire (Carmarthen)......	588,472	162,313	162,313	4,772,000	208
(6) Denbighshire (Ruthin).............	427,977	184,824	184,824	6,206,700	200
(7) Flintshire (Mold).................	163,707	175,396	175,396	7,805,200	188
(8) Glamorgan (Cardiff)...............	523,270	749,372	1,255,374	24,828,900	218
(9) Merioneth (Dolgellau).............	422,372	35,277	35,277	1,229,200	200
(10) Monmouthshire (Newport)..........	346,749	349,411	461,459	11,556,900	200
(11) Montgomeryshire (Welshpool)......	510,110	42,761	42,761	964,900	183
(12) Pembrokeshire (Haverfordwest)....	393,007	97,295	97,295	4,321,100	181
(13) Radnorshire (Llandrindod Wells)...	301,165	18,262	18,262	585,300	196

‡ Decimal equivalent of 1970–71 average rates.

MUNICIPAL DIRECTORY OF WALES AND MONMOUTH
County Boroughs are prefixed by the sign §.

CITIES and BOROUGHS (with year of incorporation) and *Urban Districts* (over 20,000 population)	Population, 1971 Census (prelim.)	Rateable Value 1971 £	★ Rate Levied 1971–72 p	Town Clerk (or Clerk U.D.C.)	Mayor, 1971–72 ★Lord Mayor †Chairman U.D.C.
Aberdare, Glam.	37,760	880,778	134½	D. G. James.	†W. S. Jones.
Abergavenny, Mon. (1542).	9,388	347,740	115½	G. Cummings.	T. L. Morgan.
Abertillery, Mon...	21,140	408,284	111½	H. A. Lewis.	†S. R. Harris.
Aberystwyth, Cards...	10,680	476,751	96	J. K. Harris.	S. J. Lewis.
BANGOR, Caerns...................	14,526	605,336	96	E. J. Lloyd.	V. Lewis.
Barry, Glam. (1939).	41,578	1,425,541	100½	J. C. Colley.	Mrs. Q. Mitchell.
Beaumaris, Anglesey (1294).	2,096	76,066	99½	G. Roberts.	H. D. P. Raban.
Bedwelty, Mon.	25,326	607,361	113½	J. E. Rogers.	†W. E. Park.
Brecon (1412).	6,283	221,259	108	E. F. Jones.	W. R. R. Elliott.
Caernarvon (Royal Borough) (1284) ..	9,253	310,692	96½	J. O. Smith, O.B.E.	R. T. C. Williams.
Caerphilly, Glam...................	40,689	1,071,500	112½	M. O. Rawlins.	†D. Thomas.
§CARDIFF, Glam. (1608).	278,221	14,209,335	89	S. Ll. Jones.	★H. F. Jones, O.B.E.
Cardigan (1230).	3,800	132,028	87½	R. A. Davies.	Miss S. R. Owen.
Carmarthen (1313).	13,072	654,983	105½	V. M. Williams.	R. B. Evans.
Colwyn Bay, Denbighs. (1934).	25,535	1,136,878	102	G. Edwards.	A. J. Hislop.
Conway, Caerns. (1284).	12,158	435,481	88½	E. C. Holmes.	R. Jones.
Cwmbran, Mon.	31,614	1,110,926	107	A. S. Challoner.	†O. E. James, M.B.E.
Denbigh (1290).	8,100	280,113	88	W. T. Williams.	E. Cunnah.
Ebbw Vale, Mon.	26,049	1,409,311	116½	S. Sami.	†B. J. Scully.
Flint (1284).	14,660	503,671	107½	L. E. W. Beesley.	E. Joyce.
Gelligaer, Glam.	33,670	727,606	120½	D. W. C. Morgan.	†B. Harris.
Haverfordwest, Pembroke (1479).	9,101	432,710	93	R. I. Rees.	D. J. Evans.
Lampeter, Cards. (1884).	2,189	82,086	92½	D. Ll. Evans.	A. E. Young.
Llandovery, Carmarthen. (1485).	1,999	49,812	95	I. A. Pugh.	E. H. Griffiths.
Llanelli, Carmarthen. (1913).	26,320	1,083,012	99½	S. Samuel, O.B.E.	C. R. Edwards.
Llanidloes, Mont. (1280).	2,333	59,681	77	G. Edwards.	D. M. Jones.
Llwchwr, Glam.	26,845	1,005,131	113½	R. D. Davies.	†D. R. James.
Maesteg, Glam.	20,970	445,649	107½	T. King-Davies.	†D. Jones.
§Merthyr Tydfil, Glam. (1905).	55,215	1,463,807	122	S. Jones.	G. M. Donovan.
Monmouth (1447).	6,545	222,959	101½	D. G. Allen.	R. Bishop.
Montgomery (1885).	968	17,222	78½	N. O. Davies.	R. I. Bainbridge.
Mountain Ash, Glam.	27,806	499,606	105½	G. W. Hosgood.	†H. Phillips.
Neath, Glam.	28,568	1,106,433	115½	F. A. Rennison.	G. Hemming.
§Newport, Mon. (1623).	112,048	5,675,874	94	J. R. Long.	S. M. Watson, B.E.M.
Ogmore and Garw, Glam.	19,415	381,018	100½	R. Hunter.	†R. Cornelius.
Pembroke (1100).	14,092	390,918	95	R. D. Lowless, M.B.E.	C. E. Nicholls.
Penarth, Glam.	23,965	852,276	107½	P. Metcalf. [T.D.	†T. T. G. Llewellyn.
Pontypool, Mon.	37,014	1,205,464	113½	H. Cook.	†J. W. Haycock.
Pontypridd, Glam.	34,465	1,198,086	115	G. Hockin.	†Mrs. M. G. Murphy.
Port Talbot, Glam. (1921).	50,658	4,338,648	115½	W. E. Griffiths.	†D. M. John.
Pwllheli, Caerns. (1355).	3,832	122,180	89½	C. C. Davies.	G. Roberts.
Rhondda, Glam. (1955).	88,924	1,680,466	121½	W. N. Thomas.	B. J. Jones.
Rhyl, Flint.	21,715	1,305,117	96½	F. J. K. Davies.	†D. Roberts.
§Swansea, Glam. (1169).	172,566	7,746,685	87½	I. J. Watkins.	A. J. K. Hare.
Tenby, Pembroke (1402).	4,985	273,440	85	W. I. Samuel.	H. H. B. Lee.
Welshpool, Mont.	6,705	228,790	87½	K. A. S. Fletcher.	Mrs. K. E. Silver.
Wrexham, Denbighs. (1157).	38,955	1,405,000	97	J. P. Hughes.	G. H. Parry.

★Full rate levied. Mixed hereditaments, 4½p less; Dwelling-houses, 9½p less.

LORDS LIEUTENANT, HIGH SHERIFFS AND CHAIRMEN OF COUNTY COUNCILS

County or Shire	Lord Lieutenant	High Sheriff (1971–72)	Chairman of C.C.
(1) Anglesey.....	Sir R. H. D. Williams-Bulkeley, Bt.	Capt. E. Hewitt, R.D.	H. Jones, M.B.E.
(2) Brecon	Capt. N. G. Garnons-Williams, M.B.E., R.N.(ret.).	The Lady Brecon, C.B.E.	J. T. H. Davies.
(3) Caernarvon...	Sir Michael Duff, Bt.	Maj. J. R. E. Harden, D.S.O., M.C.	O. G. Roberts.
(4) Cardigan.....	Capt. J. H. Lewes, O.B.E., R.N. (ret.).	Mrs. G. M. Fraser.	H. H. Roberts.
(5) Carmarthen..	Col. C. W. Nevill, O.B.E., T.D.	Mrs. J. R. Thomas.	D. G. J. Jones.
(6) Denbigh......	Col. Sir (Owen) Watkin Williams-Wynn, Bt., C.B.E.	Lt.-Cdr. A. F. W. Boumphrey, D.S.C.	E. McMahon.
(7) Flint.........	Brig. H. S. K. Mainwaring, C.B., C.B.E., D.S.O., T.D. [T.D.	Maj. B. H. P. Heaton, M.B.E.	H. O. Roberts.
(8) Glamorgan...	Col. Sir Cennydd Traherne, K.G.,	C. P. M. Methuen-Campbell.	P. Squire, O.B.E.
(9) Merioneth....	Col. J. F. Williams-Wynne, D.S.O.	H. F. Shuker.	J. Jones.
(10) Monmouth...	Col. E. R. Hill, D.S.O.	G. R. Jones, M.D.	A. E. Smith.
(11) Montgomery..	Col. J. L. Corbett-Winder, O.B.E., M.C.	C. E. V. Owen.	S. G. Pritchard.
(12) Pembroke....	Hon. R. H. Phillips, M.B.E.	H. G. Partridge.	O. G. John, O.B.E.
(13) Radnor.......	Brig. Sir C. M. Dillwyn-Venables-Llewelyn, Bt., M.V.O.	Lt.-Col. J. A. T. Barstow, D.S.O., T.D.	R. P. L. Hughes.

WELSH COUNTY OFFICIALS

County, etc.	Clerk of the Council	County Treasurer	Chief Constable	Medical Officer
(1) Anglesey.....	I. Davies.	I. L. Pugh.	(See Caernarvon) (b)	G. Crompton.
(2) Brecon	T. F. G. Young.	H. W. Davies.	(See Cardigan) (a)	R. G. Evans.
(3) Caernarvon...	J. E. Owen Jones, C.B.E.	E. E. Wigley.	P. A. Myers.	C. T. Baynes, M.D.
(4) Cardigan.....	J. E. R. Carson.	R. Jones.	⎫ J. R. Jones, C.V.O.	I. M. Watkin, Ph.D.
(5) Carmarthen..	W. S. Thomas.	D. M. Mason.	⎬	D. G. G. Jones.
(6) Denbigh......	D. E. A. Jones.	E. Hughes.	⎭ (See Caernarvon) (b)	M. T. Islwyn Jones, M.D.
(7) Flint.........	T. M. H. Rees.	S. Elmitt, O.B.E.		G. W. Roberts.
(8) Glamorgan...	T. V. Walters.	B. A. Greenway.	T. G. Morris (c)	W. E. Thomas, Q.H.P.
(9) Merioneth....	E. J. Lloyd-Jones.	A. A. Hemphill.	(See Caernarvon) (b).	E. F. W. Richards.
(10) Monmouth...	K. H. Walker.	M. Morgan.	W. Farley, M.C.	A. J. Essex-Cater.
(11) Montgomery..	R. T. D. Williams.	F. A. Humphreys.	(See Cardigan) (a).	E. S. Lovgreen.
(12) Pembroke....	H. L. Underwood.	E. C. Essex.	(See Cardigan) (a).	D. J. Davies, M.B.E., M.D.
(13) Radnor......	D. C. S. Lane.	C. Roberts.	(See Cardigan) (a).	F. J. H. Crawford, M.D.

(a) Dyfed Powys Constabulary; (b) Gwynedd Police Authority; (c) South Wales Police Force.

CARDIFF

CARDIFF (Glamorgan), at the mouth of the rivers Taff (Caer Taff), Rhymney and Ely, was declared to be the capital of Wales on Dec. 20, 1955. The port of the South Wales coalfields, it has an area of 22,736 acres and a population (1971 Census, preliminary) of 278,221. Within the City there is a great variety of industry including iron and steel works, rolling mills and foundries, patent fuel works, engine wagon works, motor vehicle factories, flour mills, breweries, jam, vinegar and ice factories, enamel-ware and hollow-ware, paint works, furniture and bedding, clothing and footwear, sweets and confectionery, tobacco, electrical goods and appliances, food products and building materials.

The principal buildings are Cardiff Castle, built in the 11th century, Llandaff Cathedral, the National Museum of Wales, Public Library, the University College of South Wales and Monmouthshire, the Registry of the University of Wales, the Institute of Science and Technology, City Hall, Law Courts, Glamorgan County Hall, Offices of Government Departments, and "The Temple of Peace and Health." The City returns 3 members to Parliament.

Rt. Hon. Lord Mayor (1971–73), H. F. Jones.

Stipendiary Magistrate, J. C. Rutter (1966).
Town Clerk, S. Lloyd Jones.

SWANSEA

SWANSEA (in Welsh, Abertawe), a seaport of Glamorgan, is a City (1969) and a County Borough, at the mouth of the River Tawe. The trade of the port includes coal, patent fuel, ores, and the import and export of oil. There is also a large ship-repairing industry. The municipal airport is situated at Fairwood Common, Gower, a few miles away from the City. The municipal area is 24,241 acres, with a population (1971 Census, preliminary) of 172,566.

The principal buildings are the Norman Castle (rebuilt in 1330), the Royal Institution of South Wales, founded in 1835 (containing Museum and Library), the University College at Singleton and the Guildhall, containing Brangwyn panels. Swansea was chartered by the Earl of Warwick, *circa* 1158–1184, and further charters were granted by King John, Henry III., Edward II., Edward III., and James II., 2 from Cromwell and 1 Lord Marcher. The City returns 2 members to Parliament.

Mayor (1971–72), A. J. K. Hare.
Town Clerk, I. J. Watkins.

Position and Extent.—The Kingdom of Scotland occupies the northern portion of the main island of Great Britain and includes the Inner and Outer Hebrides, and the Orkney, Shetland, and many other islands. The Kingdom lies between 60° 51′ 30″ and 54° 38′ N. latitude and between 1° 45′ 32″ and 6° 14′ W. longitude, its southern neighbour being the Kingdom of England, with the Atlantic Ocean on the N. and W., and the North Sea on the E. The greatest length of the mainland (Cape Wrath to the Mull of Galloway) is 274 miles, and the greatest breadth (Buchan Ness to Applecross) is 154 miles. The total area of the Kingdom is 29,798 square miles (or 19,068,724 acres) exclusive of inland water, tidal water and foreshore. The population (1971 Census, prelim.) was 5,227,706, an increase of 48,362 or 0·09 per cent. annually since the census of 1961. The average density of the population in 1971 was 175 persons per square mile, compared with 171 persons per square mile in 1951.

Land's End to John o' Groats.—The customary measurement of the Island of Great Britain is from the site of John o' Groat's house, near Duncansby Head, Caithness (at the N.E. extremity of the island) to Land's End, Cornwall (at the S.W. extremity), a total distance of 603 miles in a straight line and (approximately) 900 by road. But the site of the house of John de Groot (with its 8 doors and octagonal table, to solve the question of precedence between John and his 7 brothers) is about 4 miles S.W. of Duncansby Head, while Dunnet Head (also in Caithness) extends farther N. than Duncansby. John de Groot is believed to have obtained permission to settle in Caithness (from the Netherlands) in the reign of James IV (1488–1513).

Relief.—There are three natural orographic divisions of Scotland. The *Southern Uplands* have their highest points in Merrick (2,764 feet), Rinns of Kells (2,668 feet), and Cairnsmuir of Carsphairn (2,612 feet), in Kirkcudbright; Hartfell (2,651 feet) in Dumfries; and Broad Law (2,754 feet) in Peebles. The *Central Lowlands* include the valleys of the Tay, Forth and Clyde, and the cities of Edinburgh, the capital of the Kingdom, and Glasgow, its principal seaport. The heather-clad *Northern Highlands* extend almost from the extreme north of the mainland to the central lowlands, and are divided into a northern and southern system by the *Great Glen*; they contain, in the central Grampian Hills, Ben Nevis (4,406 feet), the highest point in the British Isles, and Ben Muich Dhui (4,296 feet). The *Cheviot Hills* form a natural boundary between Scotland and England, their highest point being The Cheviot (2,676 feet).

Hydrography.—The principal river of Scotland is the *Clyde* (106 miles), one of the most important rivers in the world, with the greatest commercial estuary in Scotland. The Clyde is formed by the junction of Daer and Portrail water, and flows through the city and port of Glasgow to the Firth of Clyde. During its course it passes over the picturesque *Falls of Clyde,* Bonnington Linn (30 feet), Corra Linn (84 feet), Dundaff Linn (10 feet), and Stonebyres Linn (80 feet), above and below Lanark. The *Tweed* (96 miles) has important woollen industries in its valley. The *Tay,* noted for its salmon, and the longest river in Scotland (117 miles), flows into the North Sea, with Dundee (the centre of the jute industry) on the estuary, which is spanned by the *Tay Bridge* (10,289 ft.), opened in 1887, and the *Tay Road Bridge* (7,365 ft.), opened by H.M. Queen Elizabeth the Queen Mother on Aug. 18, 1966. The *Dee* (90 miles), a noted salmon river, flows through scenery of unequalled beauty to the North Sea at Aberdeen. The *Spey* (110 miles), the swiftest flowing river in the British Isles, and

also noted for its salmon and its scenery, flows into the Moray Firth. The *Forth* (66 miles), navigable to Stirling, is spanned by the *Forth (Railway) Bridge* (1890), constructed at a cost of £3,000,000, with a length of 5,330 ft., and the *Forth (Road) Bridge,* with a total length of 6,156 ft. (over water) and a single span of 3,300 ft. The latter was completed in 1964 at a cost of £20,000,000.

The waterfall, *Eas-Coul-Aulin* in Sutherland with a total height of 658 ft. and the *Falls of Glomach* in Ross-shire, with a drop of 370 feet, are the highest in the British Isles; the *Grey Mare's Tail* (Dumfriesshire) is 200 feet.

The *lochs* are the principal hydrographic feature of the Kingdom, both on the mainland and in many of the Islands. The largest in the Kingdom and in Great Britain is *Loch Lomond* (24 miles long), with Lochs Awe, Tay, Rannoch and Ericht in the Grampian valleys; *Loch Ness* (24 miles long and 800 feet deep), with Lochs Oich and Lochy, in the Great Glen; and Lochs Shin (20 miles) and Maree in the northern Highlands.

Climate.—The general climatic values for Scotland are given below, together with the corresponding values for England and Wales within brackets—mean air temperature reduced to sea level 47·1° F. (49·7); *rainfall,* 50·3 inches (35·4); number of days with rain 217 (188); mean hours per day of bright sunshine, 3·36 (3·96).

Gaelic Language.—The preliminary report on the 1961 Census of Scotland showed that 76,587 persons were Gaelic speakers, compared with 95,447 in 1951. 1,079 persons spoke Gaelic only and not English (compared with 2,178 in 1951). The majority of Gaelic speakers lived in the counties of Ross and Cromarty (38·29 per cent.) and Inverness (24·44 per cent.). 75,508 persons spoke both Gaelic and English, compared with 93,269 in 1951.

Commerce.—The principal exports are machinery, ships and vehicles, iron and steel manufactures, non-ferrous metals, woollen and worsted yarns and products, food and drink and textile materials. Whisky continues to be the leading export to dollar countries.

THE SCOTTISH ISLANDS

The preliminary report on the 1971 Census of Scotland showed a continued decline in the population of the islands. The populations at April 25, 1971, with 1961 populations in parenthesis, are: Islay, 3,825 (1961, 3,871); Mull (including Iona, etc.), 1,560 (1,635); Coll and Tiree, 1,021 (1,173); Harris, 2,879 (3,418); Skye 7,372 (7,772); Barra, 1,087 (1,564); North Uist, 1,732 (1,982); South Uist, 3,781 (4,000).

Orkney.—About 6 miles N. of the Caithness coast, separated from the mainland by the *Pentland Firth,* is the island county of Orkney, a group of 90 islands and islets ("holms" and "skerries"), of which one-third are inhabited. The total area of the group is 375½ square miles, with a population (1971 Census, preliminary) of 17,075 (1961, 18,888). 1971 populations of the islands (with 1961 figures in italic are: Eday, 179 (202); Hoy and Walls, 531 (699); Mainland, 6,502 (7,764); N. Ronaldsay, 134 (166); Rousay, 256 (350); Sanday, 592 (682); Shapinsay, 346 (432); S. Ronaldsay, 990 (1,275); Stronsay, 440 (497); Westray, 841 (1,015). Kirkwall (4,618), in *Mainland* (Pomona), the largest island of the group, is the capital of the county. Many of the Orkney (and Shetland) Islands contain *brochs* (Pictish towers) and other Pictish and Scandinavian remains. *Scapa Flow,* between *Mainland* and *Hoy,* was the war station of the Grand Fleet from 1914–19 and the scene of the scuttling of the surrendered German High Seas Fleet (June 21, 1919).

Zetland.—About 50 miles N. of Orkney (with

the detached *Fair Isle* at 25 miles N.) is the island county of *Zetland* or *Shetland*, a group of about 100 islands and islets, of which one-fifth are inhabited. The total area of the group is 551 square miles, with a population (1971 Census, prelim.) of 17,298 (1961, 17,978). Lerwick (6,107), in *Mainland* (the largest and principal island), is the capital of the county. *Fair Isle*, the southernmost of the group, is famous for handknitted hosiery, and *Unst* (with Fair Isle, 1,129) for the finest of the Shetland woollen work for which the county is famous. *Muckle Flugga*, about 1 mile N. of Unst, is the most northerly of the group and of the British Isles (60° 51′ 30″ N. lat.).

Western Islands.—Off the W. coast, at varying distances, and extending from Sutherland to Argyll, are over 500 islands and islets, of which 102 are inhabited. The total area of these Western Islands is 2,812 square miles, but owing to the mountainous surface [of the land only about 300 square miles are under cultivation. *The Hebrides.*—Until the closing years of the 13th century "The Hebrides" included other Scottish islands in the Firth of Clyde, the peninsula of Kintyre (Argyllshire), the Isle of Man, and the (Irish) Isle of Rathlin. The origin of the name is stated to be the Greek *Eboudai*, latinized as *Hebudes* by Pliny, and corrupted to its present form. The Norwegian name *Sudreyjar* (Southern Islands) was latinized as *Sodorenses*, a name that survives in the Anglican bishopric of "Sodor and Man." The *Inner Hebrides* include the island of *Skye* (643 square miles—capital, Portree, famous as a refuge of Prince Charlie after his defeat at Culloden, Inverness-shire, in 1746), which contains the *Cuillins* (Sgurr Alasdair 3,309 feet), *Red Hills* (Ben Caillich, 2,403 feet), and many other picturesque mountains; *Mull* (367 square miles), containing *Ben More* (3,169 feet), *Ben Buy* (2,354 feet), and *Ben Creach* (2,289 feet); *Jura* (160 square miles), with a chain of hills culminating in the *Paps of Jura* (Beinn-an-Oir, 2,571 feet and Beinn Chaolais, 2,407 feet); *Islay* (235 square miles), and many smaller islands. The *Outer Hebrides*, separated from the mainland by the *Minch*, include *Lewis with Harris* (770 square miles), celebrated for its homespun "Tweeds," *North Uist*, *South Uist*, *Barra* and other islands. Thirteen miles W. of *Stornoway* (the largest town of Lewis and of the Hebrides) are the "Druidical" remains of *Callanish*, a well-preserved series of monolithic circles, cruciform in general arrangement, but usually regarded as a heathen monument of the remote Stone Age.

EARLY HISTORY

Prehistoric Man.—The *Picts*, believed to be of non-Aryan origin, and stated to have been named *Picti* by the Romans on account of the tribal habit of painting the body, seem to have inhabited the whole of North Britain and to have spread over the north of Ireland. *Picts' Houses* are most frequent in the northern counties of Caithness and Sutherland and in the Orkney Islands. Celtic *Goidels*, *Brythons* and *Belgae* arrived from Belgic Gaul during the latter part of the Bronze Age and in the early Iron Age, and except in the extreme north of the mainland and in the islands the civilization and speech of the people were definitely Celtic at the time of the Roman Invasion of Britain.

The Roman Invasion.—In A.D. 80 Julius Agricola extended the Roman conquests in Britain by advancing into *Caledonia* as far as the "*Grampian*" Hills, but after a victory at *Mons Graupius* (since corrupted to "Grampius") he was recalled, and no further advance was made for about 60 years, when the Roman frontier was carried to the isthmus between the Forth and Clyde and marked by the *Wall of Pius*, towards which ran military roads from the Cheviots. The Roman occupation of Southern Caledonia was not so effective as that of South Britain, and before the close of the second century the northern limit of Roman Britain had receded to *Hadrian's Wall* (Tyne to Solway Firth).

The Scots.—During the later years of the Roman occupation the garrison was continually harassed by Pictish tribes north of the Wall, aided by Scots (the Gaelic tribe then dominant in Ireland), and when the garrison was withdrawn these *Picts* and *Scots* were the principal enemies of the Celtic Brythons, who are believed to have called in the Saxons to protect them from the invasions of their neighbours. A relic of the struggle between Pict and Brython is still to be seen in the *Catrail*, or Picts' Work Dyke, of Roxburgh (from Torwoodlee, near Galashiels, to Peel Fell in the Cheviots). *Christianity* was introduced into Southern Caledonia about 380 by missionaries from Romanized Britain, who penetrated to the northern districts and islands. After the withdrawal (or absorption) of the Roman garrison of Britain there were many years of tribal warfare between the Picts and Scots, the Brythonic *Waelisc* (Welsh) of Strathclyde (South-west Scotland and Cumberland), and the Anglo-Saxons of the Lothians. The Waelisc were isolated from their kinsmen in Wales by the victory of the West Saxons at Chester (613), and towards the close of the 9th century the Scots under *Kenneth Macalpine* became the dominant power in Caledonia. In the reign of Malcolm I (943–954) the Brythons or Waelisc (Welsh) of Strathclyde were brought into subjection, the lowland kingdom of the English (Lothian) being conquered by Malcolm II (1005–1034). From the close of the 11th century until the middle of the 16th there were constant wars between Scotland and England, the outstanding figures in the struggle being *William Wallace*, who defeated the English at Stirling Bridge (1297), and *Robert Bruce*, who won the victory of Bannockburn (1314). James IV and many of his nobles fell at the disastrous battle of *Flodden* (1513), and in 1603 James VI, the Stuart King of Scotland and the heir to the Tudor line of England (his mother, Mary Queen of Scots, was the great-granddaughter of Henry VII), succeeded Queen Elizabeth I on the throne, his successors reigning as Sovereigns of Great Britain. After the abdication (by flight) of James VII and II, the crown devolved upon William III (grandson of Charles I) and Mary (daughter of James VII and II) and, their issue failing, upon Anne (second daughter of James VII and II). Anne's children died young, and the throne devolved upon George I (great-grandson of James VI and I) In 1689 Graham of Claverhouse "roused the Highlands" on behalf of James VII and II, but died after a military success at Killiecrankie. In 1715, armed risings led to the indecisive battle of Sheriffmuir, but the movement died down until 1745, when Prince Charles Edward defeated the Royalist troops under Sir John Cope at Prestonpans and advanced to Derby in England (1746). From Derby, the adherents of "James VIII and III" (the title claimed for his father by Prince Charles Edward) fell back on the defensive, and the *Jacobite* movement was finally crushed by the Royalist troops under the Duke of Cumberland at *Culloden* (April 16, 1746).

The Hebrides did not become part of the Kingdom of Scotland until 1266, when they were ceded to Alexander III by Magnus of Norway. Orkney and Shetland fell to the Scottish Crown as a pledge for the unpaid dowry of Margaret of Denmark, wife of James III, in 1468, the Danish suzerainty being formally relinquished in 1590.

Scotland is represented in Parliament by 71 members.

AREA AND POPULATION OF SCOTTISH COUNTIES, ETC.

Counties and Headquarters	Acres	Population Estimated 1970	Rateable Value 1970–71	County Rate 1970–71	Lord Lieutenant
			£	p *	
(1) ‡Aberdeen (Aberdeen)....	1,252,267	137,881	2,011,141	106	Sir Ian Forbes-Leith, Bt., M.B.E.
(2) ‡Angus (Forfar).........	546,861	97,312	738,487	97¼	The Earl of Dalhousie, K.T., G.B.E., M.C.
(3) Argyll (Lochgilphead).....	1,990,521	59,909	840,800	106	Maj. The Lord Maclean, K.T., K.B.E.
(4) Ayr (Ayr)...............	724,234	361,074	3,481,988	90	Sir James Fergusson of Kilkerran, Bt.
(5) Banff (Banff)...........	403,054	43,501	401,183	104	Col. T. R. Gordon-Duff, M.C.
(6) Berwick (Duns).........	292,535	20,750	343,400	71	Lt.-Col. W. B. Swan, C.B.E.
(7) Bute (Rothesay).........	139,711	13,237	138,965	78	The Marquess of Bute.
(8) Caithness (Wick)........	438,833	27,754	215,578	126½	J. Sinclair, M.B.E.
(9) Clackmannan (Alloa)....	34,937	45,553	678,694	167	The Earl of Mar and Kellie.
(10) Dumfries (Dumfries)	688,112	88,215	975,716	80	K. M. McCall.
(11) Dunbarton (Dumbarton)..	154,362	237,518	1,900,000	98	Maj. R. Arbuthnott, M.B.E., T.D.
(12) East Lothian (Haddington).	170,971	55,891	751,040	104	The Earl of Wemyss and March, K.T.
(13) Fife (Cupar)...........	322,878	326,989	3,161,332	78¼	Sir John McWilliam.
(14) Inverness (Inverness).....	2,695,094	89,545	1,064,593	110	Lt.-Col. D. H. Cameron of Lochiel, C.V.O., T.D.
(15) Kincardine (Stonehaven)...	242,460	26,050	369,099	85	G. A. M. Saunders.
(16) Kinross (Kinross).........	52,392	6,422	159,961	92½	Lt.-Col. R. C. Stewart, T.D.
(17) Kirkcudbright (Kirkcudbright).........	574,024	27,450	446,700	70	Col. The Earl of Galloway.
(18) ‡Lanark (Hamilton)......	535,862	627,217	7,480,189	107½	Lt.-Col. The Lord Clydesmuir, C.B., M.B.E., T.D.
(19) ‡Midlothian (Edinburgh)..	201,046	142,209	2,251,883	100	Sir Maxwell Inglis of Glencorse, Bt.
(20) Moray (Elgin)...........	304,931	51,485	614,340	80	Capt. I. M. Tennant.
(21) Nairn (Nairn)...........	104,251	11,049	63,690	86¼	The Earl of Leven and Melville.
(22) Orkney (Kirkwall)........	240,848	17,075	108,784	85¼	Col. H. W. Scarth.
(23) Peebles (Peebles)..........	222,240	13,675	204,741	115	Sir Robert Scott, G.C.M.G., C.B.E.
(24) Perth (Perth).............	1,595,804	127,138	1,436,370	100	(vacant).
(25) Renfrew (Paisley)........	143,829	362,144	3,597,143	91¼	The Viscount Muirshiel, P.C., C.H., C.M.G.
(26) Ross and Cromarty (Dingwall)........	1,977,254	58,267	606,067	105	Capt. A. F. Matheson, R.N. [(ret.)].
(27) Roxburgh (Newtown St. Boswells)..............	425,564	41,942	349,410	85	The Duke of Buccleuch and Queensbury, P.C., K.T., G.C.V.O., T.D.
(28) Selkirk (Selkirk)..........	171,209	20,868	59,316	111½	Vice-Adm. Sir Conolly Abel Smith, G.C.V.O., C.B.
(29) Stirling (Stirling)........	288,349	208,956	2,306,953	124	The Visct. Younger of Leckie, O.B.E., T.D.
(30) Sutherland (Golspie)......	1,297,913	13,053	203,835	91¼	Lord Migdale.
(31) West Lothian (Linlithgow).	76,859	108,474	1,449,228	157	The Marquess of Linlithgow, M.C. [M.B.E.]
(32) Wigtown (Stranraer)......	311,984	27,335	270,423	86	The Earl of Stair, C.V.O., C.B.E.
(33) Zetland (Lerwick)........	352,337	17,298	71,229	125	R. H. W. Bruce, C.B.E.

‡ The Cities of Edinburgh, Glasgow, Dundee and Aberdeen are each a County of a City, and the Lord Provost of each is entitled, by virtue of his office, to be appointed Lord Lieutenant; population estimates given above exclude the four cities.   * Decimal equivalent of rate levied.

THE ARMS OF SCOTLAND

ARMS.—*Or*, a lion rampant *gules*, armed and langued *azure*, within a double-tressure flory counter-flory of the second.   CREST.—An imperial crown *proper*, surmounted by a lion sejant-guardant *gules* crowned *or*, holding in his dexter paw a naked sword and in the sinister a sceptre both *proper*.   SUPPORTERS.—Two unicorns *argent*, armed, tufted and unguled *or*, crowned with imperial and gorged with eastern crowns, chains reflexed over the backs *or*; the dexter supporting a banner charged with the arms of Scotland, the sinister supporting a similar banner *azure*, thereon a saltire *argent*.   MOTTOES.—Over the arms, " In Defens " ; under the arms " Nemo me impune lacessit."

CONVENERS AND COUNTY OFFICIALS

Convener	County Clerk	Clerk of the Peace
(1) M. Mackie C.B.E.	J. L. Russell.	J. M. Melvin.
(2) C. W. Renilson.	I. A. MacKnight.	A. G. M. Whitson.
(3) J. G. Mathieson, C.B.E., M.C.	A. D. Jackson.	J. Harvey, W.S.
(4) W. Paterson.	J. Hair.	H. G. McFadzean.
(5) J. A. S. McPherson.	F. G. Armstrong.	J. D. G. McLeod.
(6) Maj. J. M. Askew.	K. H. Candlish.	G S. Morrison.
(7) J. McMillan.	W. C. Morrison.	W. Skelton.
(8) A. Rugg.	R. H. Stevenson.	R. H. Stevenson.
(9) F. J. Dawson.	A. Stewart.	E. D. MacKenzie
(10) Maj. F. Moffat, M.C.	L. T. Carnegie.	J. B. McGowan.
(11) J. McL. Williamson.	J. F. Miller.	D. McIntosh.
(12) J. B. Miller.	A. Harkess.	T. I. McIntyre.
(13) Sir David Erskine, Bt.	J. Dunlop.	C. D. Pagan.
(14) Maj. A. J. Macdonald.	R. Wallace, C.B.E.	G. H. Munro.
(15) G. A. M. Saunders.	J. Slevin.	F. W. Robertson, M.B.E.
(16) R. C. Stewart, T.D.	H. R. W. Gardner, W.S.	H. R. W. Gardner, W.S.
(17) Col. G. G. M. Batchelor.	R. C. Monteath, C.B.E.	J. D. Sturrock.
(18) J. Aiton.	I. V. Paterson, C.B.E.	J. W. Jackson.
(19) J. Kelly.	A. A. L. Evans.	J. McBoyle, C.B.E.
(20) Brig. J. A. Grant-Peterkin, D.S.O.	A. Thomson.	G. M. Spence.
(21) The Earl of Leven and Melville.	C. Paterson.	G. S. Storm.
(22) J. D. Brown.	D. M. Wood.	C. E. S. Walls.
(23) Maj. D. J. Anderson, M.C.	W. Geddes, M.B.E.	R. W. Goodburn.
(24) I. A. D. Millar, M.C.	A. L. Bushnell, C.B.E.	H. Cruickshank.
(25) J. W. Macfarlane, Ph.D., F.R.S.E.	C. Ross.	J. J. Jack.
(26) The Earl of Cromartie, M.C., T.D.	K. J. Clark.	L. Rapin.
(27) The Duke of Roxburghe.	J. Kyle.	R. B. Anderson, W.S.
(28) Sir William Strang Steel, Bt.	W. T. Dundas, T.D.	A. T. Little.
(29) A. K. Davidson, C.B.E.	J. D. Kennedy.	J. Muirhead.
(30) D. McBain.	J. B. Rodger.	D. Macdonald.
(31) P. Walker.	J. Calder.	J. T. Kidd, O.B.E., T.D., W.S.
(32) J. F. Niven, C.B.E.	D. R. Wilson.	S. Thomson.
(33) E. Thomason.	I. R. Clark.	Mrs. C. Johnson.

CHIEF CONSTABLES.—*Aberdeen, Banff, Moray, Kincardine and Nairn*, T. W. Chasser, C.V.O.; *Angus*, J. Farquharson; *Argyll*, K. MacKinnon, M.B.E.; *Ayr*, Q. Wilson; *Berwick, Roxburgh and Selkirk*, T. McCallum, O.B.E.; *Caithness, Orkney and Zetland*, R. F. P. McNeill; *Dunbarton*, W. Kerr, O.B.E., Q.P.M.; *Dumfries, Kirkcudbright and Wigtown*, A. Campbell; *Fife*, R. F. Murison, Q.P.M.; *Inverness*, A. L. Mclure; *Lanark*, J. K. McLellan; *Midlothian, East Lothian, West Lothian and Peebles*, J. H. Orr; *Perth and Kinross*, D. A. MacInnes, Q.P.M.; *Renfrew and Bute*, D. Williamson, O.B.E., Q.P.M.; *Ross and Cromarty*, K. Ross; *Stirling and Clackmannan*, E. Frizzell; *Sutherland*, K. Ross.

PRINCIPAL SCOTTISH CITIES

EDINBURGH

EDINBURGH, the Capital of Scotland, has a municipal area of 34,781 acres, and a population (1971 Census, preliminary) of 448,895. The city is built on a group of hills and contains in Princes Street one of the most beautiful thoroughfares in the world. The principal buildings are the Castle, which includes St. Margaret's Chapel, the oldest building in Edinburgh, and near it, the Scottish National War Memorial; the Palace of Holyroodhouse; Parliament House, the present seat of the judicature; the University; St. Giles' Church (restored 1879–83); St. Mary's (Scottish Episcopal) Cathedral (Sir Gilbert Scott); the General Register House (Robert Adam); the National and the Signet Libraries; the National Gallery; the Royal Scottish Academy; and the National Portrait Gallery. The city is governed by a town council of 71 Members and sends 7 Members to Parliament.

Rt. Hon. Lord Provost, Sir James McKay.
Town Clerk, W. Borland.
City Chamberlain, A. L. Imrie, C.B.E.

GLASGOW

GLASGOW, a Royal Burgh, City and County of a City, and the principal commercial centre in Scotland, has a municipal area of 39,725 acres and a population (1971 Census, preliminary) of 897,848. The city occupies the north and south banks of the Clyde, one of the chief commercial estuaries in the world. The principal industries are iron and steel works, ship-building, chemicals, leather, woollens, carpets, muslin-weaving, distilling, tobacco, cotton-mills and furniture. The chief buildings are the Early English former Cathedral, the University (Sir Gilbert Scott), the City Chambers, the Royal Western and Victoria Infirmaries, Kelvingrove Art Gallery and the Mitchell Library. The city is governed by a town council of 113 Members, and sends 15 Members to Parliament.

Rt. Hon. Lord Provost, Sir Donald Liddle.
Town Clerk, J. F. Falconer, M.B.E.
City Chamberlain, L. Boyle, Ph.D.

ABERDEEN

ABERDEEN, a City and a Royal, Municipal and Parliamentary Burgh, 126 miles N.E. of Edinburgh, received its charter as a Royal Burgh from William the Lion in 1179. The municipal area is 12,439 acres, with a population (1971 Census, preliminary) of 178,441. The chief industries are tourist traffic, quarrying and granite working, white fish, salmon and herring fisheries, engineering, chemicals, plastics, ship-building, paper-making, clothing manufacture, woollen and linen manufacture. Aberdeen is famous for its many beautiful buildings, including Marischal College, reputed to

be the most imposing white granite building in the world, King's College (1494), St. Machar Church (1378), the Auld Brig o'Balgownie (1320) and the Municipal Buildings. There is a sea beach promenade which stretches for fully two and a half miles along golden sands, and at Hazlehead an open public park of 800 acres, of which 200 are wooded, with one of the finest public golf courses in Scotland and a zoo. The climate is bracing and healthy. The city is governed by a Town Council of 37 Members, and sends 2 Members to Parliament.

The Lord Provost (1971–74), J. F. Smith.
Town Clerk, J. F. Watt.
City Chamberlain, W. G. A. McInnes.

DUNDEE

DUNDEE, a City and Royal Burgh, on the North bank of the River Tay, 42 miles N. of Edinburgh, has a municipal area of 12,229 acres, and a population (1971 Census, preliminary) of 182,467. Principal buildings are the University, the Institute of Art and Technology, High School, Albert Institute and the Caird Hall Buildings. There is a magnificent public park of 400 acres at Camperdown and other parks of 646 acres and an observatory at Balgay Park. The principal industries are jute manufacture in all its branches, and various forms of linen weaving, the making of preserves, ship-building, engineering, dyeing, fruit, etc., canning, watch and clock making. The city is governed by a Town Council of 37 members and sends 2 Members to Parliament.

The Lord Provost (1970–73), W. K. Fitzgerald.
Town Clerk, G. S. Watson.
City Chamberlain, J. C. Milne.

CHIEFS OF CLANS AND NAMES IN SCOTLAND

The following list of Chiefs comprises the persons officially recognized as such by inheritance of the ancestral arms " without brisur or mark of cadency " under the Act 1672 c. 47, and/or relative supporters, under decree of the Lyon Court. It does not include selfstyled, or Society-selected " chiefs ", but the hereditary Heads of Families who conform to the evidence that " clan and family mean exactly the same thing "; and the definitions of Sir George Mackenzie of Rosehaugh, Lord Advocate to Charles II, that the undifferenced arms denote the " Chief for so we call the Representative of the Family . . . and in the Erse (Gaelic) with us the Chief of the Family is called the Head of the Clan,"—and the unanimous opinions of the Law Lords in *Seaforth* v. *Allangrange,* 1921, to the same effect that the undifferenced shield of arms denotes the Chief of the Clan; which in this hereditary familial sense of parental organization or *kin,* is denoted by the determination of armorial succession by decree of the Court of the Lord Lyon. These organizations were termed " Names " in the Lowlands, where all members bore the same basic surname, and " Clans " in the Border and Highland areas where surnames were a later development and evolved from complicated genealogical descriptions, the " clan name " being normally that of the chief.

THE ROYAL HOUSE: H.M. The Queen.

ARBUTHNOTT: Viscount of Arbuthnott, D.S.C., Arbuthnott House, Laurencekirk, Kincardineshire.

BARCLAY: Peter C. Barclay of that Ilk, Gatemans, Stratford St. Mary, Colchester, Essex.

BORTHWICK: Maj. J.H.S. Borthwick of Borthwick, T.D., Crookston, Midlothian.

BRODIE: Ninian Brodie of Brodie, Brodie Castle, Forres.

BRUCE: Earl of Elgin and Kincardine, Culross Abbey House, Culross by Dunfermline, Fife.

BUCHAN: David S. Buchan of Auchmacoy, Auchmacoy, Ellon, Aberdeenshire.

BURNETT: J. C. A. Burnett of Leys, Crathes Castle, Kincardineshire.

CAMERON: Col. Donald Cameron of Lochiel, C.V.O., T.D., Achnacarry, Spean Bridge, Inverness.

CAMPBELL: Duke of Argyll, T.D., Inverary, Argyll.

CARNEGIE: Earl of Southesk, K.C.V.O., Kinnaird Castle, Brechin.

CHISHOLM: Alastair Chisholm of Chisholm (*The Chisholm*), Silver Willows, Bury St. Edmunds.

CLAN CHATTAN: K. A. Mackintosh of Clan Chattan, Maxwell Park, Gwelo, Rhodesia.

COCHRANE: Earl of Dundonald, Lochnell Castle, Ledaig, Argyllshire.

COLQUHOUN: Sir Ivar Colquhoun of Luss, Bt., Rossdhu, Luss, Dunbartonshire.

DARROCH: Lt.-Col. D. Darroch of Gourock, Swanston Cottage, Edinburgh.

DRUMMOND: Earl of Perth, P.C., Stobhall, Perth.

DUNBAR: Sir Adrian I. Dunbar of Mochrum, Bt., Mochrum Park, Wigtownshire.

DUNDAS: Ian H. Dundas of that Ilk and Inchgarvie, Moreson, Starke Road, Bergvliet, Cape Town, S. Africa.

ELIOTT: Sir Arthur Eliott of Stobs, Bt., Redheugh, Newcastleton, Roxburghshire.

ERSKINE: Earl of Mar and Kellie, Claremount House, Alloa.

FARQUHARSON: Capt. A. A. C. Farquharson of Invercauld, M.C., Invercauld, Braemar.

FERGUSSON: Sir James Fergusson of Kilkerran, Bt., Kilkerran, Maybole, Ayrshire.

FORBES: Lord Forbes, K.B.E., Balforbes, Alford, Aberdeenshire.

FRASER: Lord Saltoun, M.C., Cairnbulg Castle, Fraserburgh, Aberdeenshire.

FRASER (OF LOVAT)*: Lord Lovat, D.S.O., M.C., T.D., Beaufort Castle, Beauly, Inverness-shire.

GORDON: Marquess of Huntly, Aboyne Castle, Aberdeenshire.

GRAHAM: Duke of Montrose, Auchmar, Drymen, Stirlingshire.

GRANT: Lord Strathspey, c/o National Bank Ltd., 15 Whitehall, S.W.1.

HAIG: Earl Haig, O.B.E., Bemersyde, Melrose, Roxburgh.

HAY: Countess of Erroll, crim on mogate, Lon may, Aberdeenshire.

KEITH: The Countess of Kintore, Keith Hall, Inverurie, Aberdeenshire.

KENNEDY: Marquess of Ailsa, O.B.E., Cassillis House, Maybole, Ayrshire.

KERR: Marquess of Lothian, Monteviot, Ancrum, Roxburgh.

KINCAID: A. C. Kincaid of Kincaid, Murarashi, Kenya.

LAMONT: Noel B. Lamont of that Ilk, 63 Patrick Street, Blacktown, Sydney, N.S.W.

LESLIE: Earl of Rothes, Strawberry House, Chiswick Mall, W.4.

LINDSAY: Earl of Crawford and Balcarres, K.T., G.B.E., Balcarres, Colinsburgh, Fife.

McBAIN: H. M. McBain of McBain, Kinchyle House, P.O. Box 2, Hubbard Woods, Illinois, 60093, U.S.A.

MALCOLM (MACCALLUM): Col. George Malcolm of Poltalloch, Duntrune Castle, Argyll.

MACDONALD: Lord Macdonald (*The Macdonald of Macdonald*), Ostaig House, Skye.

MACDONALD OF CLANRANALD*: Ranald A. Macdonald of Clanranald, 38 Compton Road, W.1.

MACDONALD OF SLEAT (CLAN HUSTEAIN)*: Sir Ian Bosville-Macdonald of Sleat, Bt., Thorpe Hall, Rudston, Driffield, Yorks.

MACDONELL OF GLENGARRY*: Air Cdre. Aeneas R. MacDonell of Glengarry, C.B., D.F.C., Rockwood, Fairwarp, Uckfield, Sussex.

MACDOUGALL: Madame Coline MacDougall of MacDougall, Dunollie, Argyll.

MACGREGOR: Sir Gregor MacGregor of MacGregor, Bt., Edinchip, Lochearnhead.

MACKAY: Lord Reay, 11 Wilton Crescent, S.W.1.

MACKINNON: The Mackinnon of Mackinnon, Field End, Nailsbourne, nr. Taunton, Somerset.

MACKINTOSH: The Mackintosh of Mackintosh, Moy Hall, Inverness.

MACLACHLAN: Madam Marjorie MacLachlan of MacLachlan, Castle Lachlan, Argyll.

MACLAREN: Donald MacLaren of MacLaren and Achleskine, 65 Ashley Gardens, S.W.1.

MACLEAN: The Lord Maclean, K.T., K.B.E., Duart Castle, Mull.

MACLEOD: Dame Flora Macleod of Macleod, D.B.E., Dunvegan Castle, Skye.

MACMILLAN: Gen. Sir Gordon MacMillan of MacMillan, K.C.B., K.C.V.O., C.B.E., D.S.O., M.C., Langbank, Renfrewshire.

MACNAB: J. C. Macnab of Macnab (*The Macnab*), Kinnell House, Killin, Perthshire.

MACNAGHTEN: Sir Antony Macnaghten of Macnaghten and Dundarave, Bt., Dundarave, Bushmills, Co. Antrim.

MACNEIL OF BARRA: Ian R. Macneil of Barra (*The Macneil of Barra*), Kismull Castle, Barra.

MACPHERSON: William A. Macpherson of Cluny, Newtown of Blairgowrie, Perthshire.

MACTHOMAS: Andrew P. C. MacThomas of Finegand in Glenshee, Perthshire.

MAITLAND: Earl of Lauderdale, Thirlestane Castle, Berwickshire.

MAR: Earl of Mar, Fernleigh, Haddington, E. Lothian.

MARJORIBANKS: William Marjoribanks of that Ilk, Pitmedden Udny, Aberdeenshire.

MATHESON: Col. B. H. Matheson of that Ilk, M.C., United Service Club, Pall Mall, S.W.1.

MENZIES: David R. Menzies of Menzies, Mundena, Walebing, 6510, Western Australia.

MONCREIFFE: Sir Iain Moncreiffe of that Ilk, Bt., Easter Moncreiffe, Bridge of Earn, Perthshire.

MONTGOMERIE: Earl of Eglinton and Winton, Skelmorlie Castle, Ayrshire.

MORRISON: John Morrison of Ruchdi, Ruchdi, by Lochmaddy, N. Uist.

MUNRO: Patrick G. Munro of Foulis, T.D., Foulis Castle, Ross.

MURRAY: Duke of Atholl, Blair Castle, Blair Atholl, Perthshire.

NICOLSON OF SCORRYBRECK: Norman A. Nicolson of Scorrybreck, Campbell Town, Tasmania.

OGILVY: Earl of Airlie, Airlie Castle, Kirriemuir, Angus.

RAMSAY: Earl of Dalhousie, K.T., G.B.E., M.C., Brechin Castle, Angus.

RATTRAY: James S. Rattray of Rattray, Craighall, Rattray, Perthshire.

ROBERTSON: Langton Robertson of Struan (*Struan-Robertson*), 7 Washington Drive, Devon Pen, P.O. Box 337, Halfway Tree P.O., Kingston 10, Jamaica.

ROSE: Miss Elizabeth Rose of Kilravock, Kilravock Castle, Nairn.

ROSS: David C. Ross of that Ilk and Shandwick, 18A Esher Avenue, Walton-on-Thames, Surrey.

RUTHVEN: Earl of Gowrie, Dunlewy House. Gweedore, Co. Donegal.

SINCLAIR: Earl of Caithness, Girnigoe Castle, Caithness.

SWINTON: W. F. H. Swinton of that Ilk, 11729, 97 Street, Edmonton, Alta., Canada.

URQUHART: W. F. Urquhart of that Ilk, 507 Jefferson Park Avenue, New Orleans, U.S.A.

WALLACE, Lt.-Col. M. R. Wallace of that Ilk, Corsee, Nairn.

WEMYSS: Michael Wemyss of that Ilk, Wemyss Castle, Fife.

Only chiefs of *whole* Names or Clans are included (except certain special instances (marked *), who though not chiefs of a " whole name ", were, or are, for some reason, *e.g.* the Macdonald forfeiture, independent). Under decision (*Campbell-Gray*, 1950) that a bearer of a "double or triple-barrelled " surname cannot be held chief of a part of such, several others cannot be included in the list at present.

PRECEDENCE IN SCOTLAND

The Sovereign.

The Prince Philip, Duke of Edinburgh.

The Lord High Commissioner to the General Assembly (while that Assembly *is sitting*).

The Duke of Rothesay (eldest son of the Sovereign). H.R.H. Prince Andrew. H.R.H. Prince Edward.

The Duke of Gloucester, the Duke of Windsor, Uncles of the Sovereign, Nephews of the Sovereign.

Lords Lieutenant of Counties, Lord Provosts of Counties of Cities, and Sheriffs Principal (successively — within their own localities and during holding of office).

Lord Chancellor of Great Britain.

Moderator of the General Assembly of the Church of Scotland

The Prime Minister.

Keepers of the Great Seal and of the Privy Seal (successively —if Peers).

Hereditary Lord High Constable of Scotland. Hereditary Master of the Household.

Dukes (successively) of England, Scotland, Great Britain and United Kingdom (including Ireland since date of Union).

Eldest sons of Royal Dukes.

Marquesses, in same order as Dukes.

Dukes' eldest sons.

Earls, in order as Dukes.

Younger sons of Dukes of Blood Royal.

Marquesses' eldest sons.

Dukes' younger sons.

Keepers of the Great Seal and of the Privy Seal (successively —if not Peers).

Lord Justice General.

Lord Clerk Register.

Lord Advocate.

Lord Justice Clerk.

Viscounts, in order as Dukes.

Earls' eldest sons.

Marquesses' younger sons.

Lord-Barons, in order as Dukes.

Viscounts' eldest sons.

Earls' younger sons.

Lord-Barons' eldest sons.

Knights of the Garter.

Privy Councillors not included in above ranks.

Senators of Coll. of Justice (Lords of Session).

Viscounts' younger sons.

Lord-Barons' younger sons.

Sons of Life Peers.

Baronets.

Knights of the Thistle.

Knights of other Orders as in England.

Solicitor-General for Scotland.

Lord Lyon King of Arms.

Sheriffs Principal (except as shown in column 1).

Knights Bachelor.

Sheriffs Substitute.

Companions of Orders as in England.

Commanders of Royal Victorian and British Empire Orders.

Eldest sons of younger sons of Peers.

| Companions of Distinguished Service Order.
Members (Class 4) Royal Victorian Order.
Officers of British Empire Order.
Baronets' eldest sons. | Knights' eldest sons successively (from Garter to Bachelor).
Members of Class 5 of Royal Victorian Order.
Members of British Empire Order. | Baronets' younger sons.
Knights' younger sons.
Queen's Counsel.
Barons-feudal.
Esquires.
Gentlemen. |

SCOTTISH LAW COURTS AND OFFICES
COURT OF SESSION (Established 1532).

Lord President, Lord Clyde (Rt. Hon. James Latham McDiarmid Clyde).

INNER HOUSE.—First Division.
The Lord President	£11,500
Lord Migdale, J. F. Gordon Thomson	9,500
Lord Cameron, Sir John Cameron, D.S.C.	9,500
Lord Johnston, Douglas Harold Johnston, T.D.	9,500

Second Division.
Lord Justice Clerk, Lord Grant, Rt. Hon. William Grant, T.D.	£11,250
Lord Wheatley, Rt. Hon. John Wheatley	9,500
Lord Milligan, Rt. Hon. William Rankine Milligan	9,500
Lord Walker, James Walker	9,500

OUTER HOUSE.
Lord Hunter, John Oswald Mair Hunter	£9,500
Lord Kissen, Manuel Kissen	9,500
Lord Fraser, Walter Ian Reid Fraser	9,500

Lord Avonside, Rt. Hon. Ian Hamilton Shearer	£9,500
Lord Leechman, James Leechman	9,500
Lord Thomson, Alexander Thomson	9,500
Lord Robertson, Ian Macdonald Robertson, M.B.E., T.D.	9,500
Lord Stott, Rt. Hon. George Gordon Stott	9,500
Lord Emslie, George Carlyle Emslie, M.B.E.	9,500
Alastair McPherson Johnston, T.D.	9,500

Principal Clerk of Session, George MacDonald, O.B.E.	£5,240
Deputy Principal Clerk, George H. Robertson (+allce.)	£3,250 to £4,400
Depute Clerks, Inner House H. G. Manson; T. I. McWhannell	£2,775 to £3,400
Depute Clerks, Outer House, D. Scott; J. Watson; A. S. Rodger; P. Whitten; H. C. Macpherson; E. Smith; A. Wylie; R. Sibbald; V. A. Woods	£2,775 to £3,400

*Appointed Lord Ordinary with effect from Oct. 1, 1971; title to be announced.

NOTE.—The word "Lord" prefixed to the names of Judges of the Court of Session, or to titles different from their names, is strictly an official honour and may be compared with the terms "Hon. Mr. Justice" and "Lord Chief Justice" in England.

The same judges constitute the High Court of Justiciary, the supreme criminal court of Scotland. When presiding in this court the Lord President is known as Lord Justice General.

Lord Advocate's Department
See Index.

Crown Office,
9 Parliament Square, Edinburgh, 1.
Crown Agent, Stanley Bowen ... £6,750
Principal Assistant, W. G. Chalmers, M.C. £5,015 to £5,640
Senior Legal Assistant, I. Dean ... £3,286 to £4,390
Legal Assistant, J. D. Allan ... £1,946 to £3,048

Justiciary Office,
2 Parliament Square, Edinburgh, 1
Clerk of Justiciary, O. J. Brown ... £3,488 to £4,103
Deputes and Assistants, R. Johnston; W. Howard; G. Paton ... £2,529 to £3,059

Exchequer,
102 George Street, Edinburgh, 2.
Queen's and Lord Treasurer's Remembrancer, J. B. I. McTavish ... £4,860
Chief Clerk, D. E. D. Robertson £3,258 to £3,873
Senior Executive Officers, A. J. Ware; R. G. B. Wilkie ... £2,529 to £3,099

Companies Registration Office
102 George Street, Edinburgh 2.
Registrar (and Keeper, Edinburgh Gazette Office), J. B. I. McTavish.

Sheriff Court of Chancery.
Sheriff Court, Edinburgh 21 York Place, Edinburgh
Sheriff of Chancery, S. Shaw, Q.C.
Sheriff Clerk of Chancery, William George Purves, W.S.
Sheriff Clerk Depute, J. D. Crerar, W.S.

H.M. Commissary Office,
16 North Bank Street, Edinburgh.
Commissary Clerk, R. D. Gould.
Deputy do., Alexander E. McRae.

Crown Estate Commissioners
2 St. Andrew Square, Edinburgh 2.
Crown Estate Receiver, D. T. Hunt.

SCOTTISH LAND COURT
1 Grosvenor Crescent, Edinburgh.
Members, The Hon. Lord Birsay, C.B.E., T.D. (*Chairman*); C. M. S. Grant; G. F. Ross; John McVicar.
Principal Clerk, T. MacD. Wilson.
Depute Clerks of Court and Senior Legal Assessors, S. Forrest; D. H. Cameron.
Deputy Clerks of Court and Legal Assessors, R. Bland; J. G. Riddoch.
Clerk of Accounts and Establishment, R. Landels.

SCOTTISH LAW COMMISSION
Old College, South Bridge, Edinburgh 8
[031-667-3437/8]
Chairman, The Hon. Lord Hunter.
Commissioners, Ewan Stewart, Q.C. (*full-time*); Prof. A. E. Anton; Prof. J. M. Halliday, C.B.E.; Prof. T. B. Smith, Q.C., D.C.L., Ll.D., F.B.A. (*part-time*).
Secretary, A. G. Brand, M.B.E.
Asst. Secretary, H. D. Glover.
Chief Clerk, Miss M. H. McNeilage.

STIPENDIARY MAGISTRATES (GLASGOW)
Court Chambers
Central, Thomas Joseph McLauchlan (1966).
Marine, James Robertson (1965).
Govan, Robert John Boyd (1970).

SHERIFFS, SHERIFFS SUBSTITUTE, SHERIFF CLERKS AND PROCURATORS FISCAL OF COUNTIES IN SCOTLAND

SHERIFFS	SHERIFFS SUBSTITUTE	SHERIFF CLERKS	PROCURATORS
Caithness, Sutherland, Orkney and Zetland.— Frederick William Fitzgerald O'Brien, Q.C., 12 Boswall Road, Edinburgh, 5.	Wick, E. Stewart............ Kirkwall, A. A. Macdonald.... Lerwick, A. A. Macdonald..... Dornoch, Dingwall and Tain, Capt. W. R. M. Murdoch C.B.E., D.S.C., V.R.D.	A. McFadzean.... Miss N. Mackenzie Mrs. C. F. Johnson D. MacDonald...	C. J. H. Campbell. F. McGinn. J. M. Goodlad. T. F. Aitchison.

Inverness, Moray, Nairn and Ross & Cromarty.—
Douglas Mason Campbell, Q.C., 10 Forres Street, Edinburgh 3.
	Fort William, R. A. Inglis.....
	Inverness, D. A. Donald.......
	Elgin & Nairn, M. Layden.....
	Portree, R. A. Inglis...........
	Lochmaddy and Stornoway, H. R. McLean............
		}G. Proctor......{
		}R. J. Macdonald.{ W. J. Cruikshank
		G. Proctor
		}T. D. McIntosh.{
			J. M. Hogg.
			W. M. Paterson.
			J. T. MacDougall.
			D. Macmillan.
			D. S. Shaw.
			C. S. Mackenzie, Jr.

Aberdeen, Kincardine & Banff.— Frederick William Fitzgerald O'Brien, Q.C., 12 Boswall Road, Edinburgh.	Aberdeen & Stonehaven, A. M. G. Russell, Q.C.; M. J. A. Rose, D.F.C. Peterhead & Banff, T. M. Croan.	}W. D. McInnes.{ Miss L.E. Cameron W. D. McInnes. G. Gordon.......	M. T. MacNeill. D. W. M. MacKay. W. A. Brown.
Perth & Angus.— Miss Margaret Henderson Kidd, Q.C., 5 India Street, Edinburgh 3.	Perth & Dunblane, H. F. Ford.. Dundee, J. B. W. Christie (and Perth); G. L. Cox (and Perth).. Forfar, Arbroath, and Perth, S. O. Kermack.	A. A. Steele..... }M. Hardy.....{	R. L. J. Miln. C. G. Hogg. E. W. Lockhart.
Fife and Kinross.— John Adam Lillie, Q.C., 85 Great King Street, Edinburgh 3.	Cupar, R. R. Kydd........... Kirkcaldy, J. Allan........... Dunfermline, J. S. Mowat..... Kinross, R. H. Kydd..........	}J. A. C. Weir....{ H. R. W. Gardner	J. W. Gibb. E. G. Smith. J. H. Douglas. J. H. Douglas.
Stirling, Dunbarton and Clackmannan.— Robert Richardson Taylor, Q.C., Ph.D., 51 Northumberland Street, Edinburgh.	Alloa, A. B. Wilkinson....... Stirling, A. B. Wilkinson..... Dumbarton, J. C. M. Jardine; M. Stone. Falkirk, R. R. Kerr..........	D. G. MacGregor J. A. Johnston.... T. R. Marshall.... J. A. Johnston....	G. Summerfield. W. Hawthorn, I.S.O. W. F. Irvine. D. B. MacFarlane.
Renfrew and Argyll.— William Robertson Grieve, V.R.D., Q.C., 20 Belgrave Crescent, Edinburgh 4.	Paisley, A. K. F. Hunter; W. C. Henderson; H. R. MacLean; H. Lyons (Dunoon) Greenock, J. B. Patrick........ Campbeltown, Dunoon and Oban, D. J. McDiarmid.	}A. McDougall....{ }J. McGhie......{	J. Skeen. W. Macnab. A. I. B. Stewart. D. S. Thaw. G. H. Pagan.
The Lothians and Peebles.— Gerald Paisley Sinclair Shaw, Q.C., Sheriffs Chambers, Lawnmarket, Edinburgh 1.	Edinburgh, J. A. Smith; V. D. B. Skae; K. W. B. Middleton; N. Macvicar, Q.C.; J. A. Dick, Q.C. Haddington, K. W. B. Middleton Linlithgow, W. T. Hook. Peebles, Miss I. L. Sinclair, Q.C. (Edinburgh and Selkirk).	R. D. Gould..... J. G. C. Bone.... J. F. Mackenzie... R. D. Gould.....	N. Milne. P. K. Morrison. P. F. Hamilton. E. Laverock.
Lanark.— Sir Allan Grierson Walker, Q.C., Sheriff's Chambers, County Buildings, Glasgow, C.1.	Glasgow, Lord Wilson of Langside, P.C., Q.C.; W. J. Bryden, C.B.E.; H. W. Pirie; F. Middleton; M. G. Gillies, T.D., Q.C.; J. Bayne; T. A. U. Wood; S. E. Bell; C. H. Johnston, Q.C.; W. O. Pattullo; J. I. Smith; A. C. Horsfall; P. G. B. McNeill; J. M. Peterson; N. D. MacLeod. Airdrie, J. J. Maguire...... Lanark, M. G. Gillies, T.D., Q.C.. Hamilton, I. A. Dickson; P. Thomson; N. E. D. Thomson	}W.R.Docherty, O.B.E.{ C. M. Anderson..	H. Herron. J. Farrell. T. J. Cochrane. D. B. Copeland.
Roxburgh, Berwick and Selkirk.—Hon. H. S. Keith, Q.C., 33 Heriot Row, Edinburgh.	Jedburgh & Duns, J. V. Paterson. Hawick, J. V. Paterson....... Selkirk, Miss I. L. Sinclair, Q.C..	J. F. McNish (Duns); H.W.Miller, V.R.D.	}C. B. Allan.{
Ayr and Bute.—Robert Howat McDonald, M.C., Q.C., 5 Doune Terrace, Edinburgh 3.	Ayr, G. S. Reid; D. M. K. Grant Kilmarnock, R. N. Levitt, M.B.E., T.D.; D. M. K. Grant....... Rothesay, H. Lyons........	H. M. Barron.... R. R. Dale	R. J. Cruickshank. J. M. Tudhope.
Dumfries & Galloway.— P. Maxwell, Q.C., 46 Heriot Row, Edinburgh.	Dumfries, C. G. B. Nicholson.. Kirkcudbright, Wigtown, Stranraer, N. J. G. Ramsay......	J. G. Cleaver.... W. B. Davidson.. A. Hogg..........	D. S. Thaw. I. G. Pirie. W. M. Morton.

SCOTTISH BURGH DIRECTORY

Burghs of population less than 3,000 are excluded, except where they are the headquarters of the county administration—
Duns, Kinross, Kirkcudbright and Lochgilphead.

Burgh (*Royal Burgh)	Population 1971 Census (prelim.)	Rateable Value £	Rate levied‡ p	Town Clerk	Provost †Lord Provost
ABERDEEN★	178,441	6,056,756	142½	J. F. Watt.	†J. F. Smith.
Airdrie, Lanarkshire	37,908	1,016,100	175	J. Taylor.	W. G. Ferguson.
Alloa, Clackmannan	14,213	476,442	167	P. W. Buchanan.	G. Robertson.
Alva, Clackmannan	4,245	165,094	131½	I. A. Grant.	J. M. Glass.
Annan,★ Dumfries-shire	6,148	147,370	129	G. Gilchrist.	W. Graham.
Arbroath,★ Angus	22,786	560,000	128½	R. Robertson.	R. R. Spink, O.B.E.
Ardrossan, Ayrshire	10,649	263,021	121½	W. M. Cumming.	J. McManus.
Armadale, West Lothian	7,188	154,433	175	I. E. Hoey.	F. Fagan.
Ayr★	47,756	2,633,219	109	D. C. Richmond	D. C. McLean.
Banff★	3,789	109,416	115	P. B. Regan.	A. W. Gordon.
Barrhead, Renfrewshire	18,420	446,378	133	A. Douglas.	J. McGuire.
Bathgate, West Lothian	14,357	748,637	151	G. Brown.	J. Hardy.
Bearsden, Dunbartonshire	24,812	820,131	106	D. L. Cuthbert.	W. H. Cumming.
Bishopbriggs, Lanarkshire	21,442	567,603	119	D. Blane.	J. Proctor, M.C.
Blairgowrie and Rattray, Perthshire	5,638	147,191	143	A. D. Paterson.	J. Drennan-Smith.
Bo'ness, West Lothian	12,956	351,609	157	A. E. O'Neill.	C. Snedden.
Bonnyrigg and Lasswade, Midlothian	7,151	165,483	122	E. H. Thomson.	W. J. Scott.
Brechin,★ Angus	6,740	170,000	97½	R. Thom.	A. Buchan.
Bridge of Allan, Stirlingshire	4,284	126,000	90	H. H. Christie.	R. W. M'Alley.
Buckhaven and Methil, Fife	18,553	404,091	123	D. S. Davidson.	T. Hogg.
Buckie, Banffshire	8,044	165,204	102½	J. A. Riddell.	E. Douglas.
Burntisland,★ Fife	5,741	152,582	115	Mrs. A. M. Hadden.	S. S. Bolam.
Campbeltown,★ Argyllshire	6,066	139,000	90	W. Wilson.	D. McKinven.
Carnoustie, Angus	6,325	145,774	118½	J. A. McAdam.	A. R. Winter.
Castle Douglas, Kirkcudbrightshire	3,373	98,553	97	J. K. Welsh.	D. K. Whitelaw.
Clydebank, Dunbartonshire	48,600	1,354,891	205	R. A. Nixon.	R. Fleming.
Coatbridge, Lanarkshire	52,344	1 302,778	182	(vacant).	R. M. Arthur.
Cockenzie and Port Seton, E. Lothian	3,608	76,318	124	T. M. Walker.	J. Marshall.
Cowdenbeath, Fife	10,531	277,131	135	J. C. L. Gibson.	R. Smith.
Crieff, Perthshire	5,467	159,929	118	W. T. Martin.	J. Rae.
Cumbernauld, Dunbartonshire	31,957	858,036	126	R. Kyle, M.B.E.	G. S. Murray.
Cumnock and Holmhead, Ayrshire	5,719	145,674	127	R. D. Hunter.	D. B. Lorimer.
Cupar,★ Fife	6,745	247,758	122½	F. M. Coutts.	A. M. Scott.
Dalbeattie, Kirkcudbrightshire	3,475	78,902	110½	R. Johnston.	J. F. Charters.
Dalkeith, Midlothian	9,676	265,905	120	T. E. G. Sinclair.	D. R. Smith.
Darvel, Ayrshire	3,232	77,289	97	J. C. Leith.	J. Anderson.
Denny and Dunipace, Stirlingshire	9,933	197,607	141	A. Duncan.	A. F. Hendry.
Dingwall,★ Ross and Cromarty	4,156	101,000	110	T. K. Marshall.	R. Macleod.
Dumbarton★	25,406	806,315	166½	L. MacKinnon.	I. Campbell.
Dumfries★	29,139	833,845	130	G. D. Grant.	E. Robertson, O.B.E.
Dunbar★, East Lothian	4,607	130,684	130	S. W. Brown.	R. H. James.
Dunblane, Perthshire	4,528	108,000	89	A. C. Sheddon.	Mrs. S. Maclachlan.
DUNDEE★	182,467	6,163,640	126½	G. S. Watson.	†W. K. Fitzgerald.
Dunfermline,★ Fife	50,099	1,503,232	122½	J. Douglas, O.B.E.	J. Crawford.
Dunoon, Argyllshire	9,680	259,049	145	D. W. Anderson.	J. M. J. Dickson.
Duns, Berwickshire	1,811	51,566	120	W. Renton, M.B.E.	T. Lennie.
East Kilbride, Lanarkshire	63,328	1,999,000	142	W. G. McNay.	W. M. Niven.
EDINBURGH★	448,895	18,688,948	125	W. Borland	†Sir James McKay.
ELGIN★	16,499	441,509	139	H. G. Tait.	†G. Edgar.
Falkirk, Stirlingshire	37,399	2,506,000	103	J. G. Morris.	W. Fenney.
Forfar,★ Angus	10,632	295,836	122½	T. G. Milne.	Mrs. M. G. Thorpe.
Forres,★ Moray	4,799	112,000	83	A. Macdonald, M.B.E.	A. H. Forbes.
Fort William, Inverness	4,301	110,243	111½	M. J. Cross.	Rev. Canon G. K. B. Henderson.
Fraserburgh, Aberdeenshire	10,752	282,701	83	J. M. Boyle.	A. W. Noble.
Galashiels, Selkirk	12,551	352,298	161	G. Knox.	W. Pate.
Galston, Ayrshire	4,252	71,511	94	J. Winning.	A. Lundie.
Girvan, Ayrshire	7,407	196,088	110	J. H. Cunningham.	J. Miller.
GLASGOW★	897,848	32,861,024	159	J. F. Falconer, M.B.E.	†Sir Donald Liddle.
Gourock, Renfrewshire	11,024	257,664	124	S. R. Cumming.	R. Williamson.
Grangemouth, Stirlingshire	24,674	2,036,929	113½	W. B. Johnston.	W. Ure, M.B.E.
Greenock, Renfrewshire	68,970	1,680,411	145	J. D. Smith.	W. Riddell.
Haddington,★ East Lothian	6,595	234,991	105	J. McVie.	A. F. Spowage.
Hamilton, Lanarkshire	46,329	1,398,711	121½	F. C. Marks.	A. S. Reid.
Hawick, Roxburghshire	16,449	401,802	150½	W. C. Hogg.	D. Atkinson.
Helensburgh, Dunbartonshire	12,954	423,392	105	R. Mackay.	N. M. Glen.
Huntly, Aberdeenshire	3,790	90,094	112½	J. A. Christie.	W. Watson.

‡ Last full rate levied at the time of going to press (usually 1970–71; dwelling houses 3s. 4d. *less* = 17p). Water rates are excluded from rate figures.

Burgh (★Royal Burgh)	Population 1971 Census (prelim.)	Rateable Value £	Rate levied‡ p	Town Clerk	Provost †Lord Provost
Inverkeithing,★ Fife	5,923	130,671	148	Mrs. J. Ossowski.	R. MacShimi-Sim.
Inverness★	34,655	1,106,310	121	J. R. Hill.	W. A. Smith.
Inverurie,★ Aberdeenshire	5,503	130,229	74	G. D. Kellas.	A. McNab.
Irvine,★ Ayrshire	23,160	501,642	111½	R. M. Whyte, M.B.E.	J. Hunter.
Jedburgh,★ Roxburghshire	3,910	91,284	118	L. S. Prentice.	G. Yellowlees.
Johnstone, Renfrewshire	22,779	482,663	136	R. S. Macrae.	A. C. Ferguson.
Keith, Banffshire	4,243	12,901	125	W. A. H. Johnston.	I. Robertson.
Kelso, Roxburghshire	4,915	138,428	117	M. D. Carlaw, M.B.E.	J. T. Stewart.
Kilmarnock, Ayrshire	49,057	1,424,299	156	J. C. W. Nicol.	J. Mackie.
Kilsyth, Stirlingshire	10,242	207,567	133	A. D. Mathie.	R. Meechan.
Kilwinning, Ayrshire	8,369	284,446	..	D. J. M. Bolton; K. F. Barclay.	K. Cox.
Kinross,★	2,455	75,361	137	W. Shand.	T. McBain.
Kirkcaldy,★ Fife	50,490	1,718,550	136	C. D. Chapman.	H. A. Nicholson.
Kirkcudbright★	2,574	72,371	90	A. C. Watson.	W. W. Holroyd.
Kirkintilloch, Dunbartonshire	25,393	606,115	134	A. Macleod.	W. Leslie.
Kirkwall,★ Orkney	4,638	87,623	123	A. R. Buchan.	G. W. Leitch.
Kirriemuir, Angus	4,222	160,000	127	W. G. R. Smith.	A. P. Fairlie.
Lanark★	8,668	274,000	114	J. G. Good.	A. W. Yuill.
Largs, Ayrshire	9,592	285,712	123	J. G. Young.	D. Doris.
Lerwick, Zetland	6,255	94,269	152	R. L. C. Manson.	W. A. Smith, B.E.M.
Leslie, Fife	3,370	78,261	116	W. Bow.	J. B. Ramsay.
Leven, Fife	9,560	284,667	136	J. L. D. M. Urquhart.	G. S. Barron.
Linlithgow,★ West Lothian	5,726	186,207	164	I. Cameron.	F. Byrne.
Loanhead, Midlothian	6,025	125,560	117	W. H. Harper.	A. B. Raeburn.
Lochgelly, Fife	8,042	160,210	122	G. Johnston.	A. D. Morris.
Lochgilphead, Argyllshire	1,234	29,427	113	J. King.	W. A. MacDonald.
Lossiemouth and Branderburgh, Moray.	5,849	105,000	105	W. Gilmour.	D. Freeman.
Macduff, Banffshire	3,771	74,000	111	Miss E. L. Innes.	R. Henry.
Maybole, Ayrshire	4,551	83,276	127	J. R. Boyd.	W. Cuthbert.
Milngavie, Dunbartonshire	10,749	344,865	144	A. R. Rae.	J. G. Breckenridge.
Monifieth, Angus	6,251	253,000	112½	I. M. Allan.	A. C. Wart.
Montrose,★ Angus	10,178	260,790	115	J. R. Richardson.	Miss M. M. Mitchell.
Motherwell and Wishaw, Lanarkshire	74,649	3,228,110	155	A. McIntosh.	H. B. Sneddon.
Musselburgh, Midlothian	16,790	465,576	135½	D. Taylor, M.B.E.	W. Caird.
Nairn★	8,083	201,887	146	G. S. Storm.	A. M. Duncan.
Newmilns and Greenholm, Ayrshire.	3,441	122,000	120	G. Mair.	W. Dempster.
Newport-on-Tay, Fife	3,738	95,212	107	A. Gilruth.	R. Webster.
North Berwick,★ East Lothian	4,392	318,290	95	R. S. Wotherspoon.	J. B. Macnair.
Oban, Argyllshire	6,517	188,732	134	A. MacInnes.	I. Jackson.
Paisley, Renfrewshire	95,403	2,737,252	144	J. Aitken.	J. S. Smart.
Peebles★	5,934	174,666	170½	E. Laverock.	A. Melrose.
Penicuik, Midlothian	10,216	256,171	112	Col. J. J. Lamb, O.B.E., T.D., W.S.	M. Gray.
PERTH★	42,905	1,321,066	126½	A. H. Martin.	†D. K. Thomson, M.B.E., [T.D.
Peterhead, Aberdeenshire	14,353	318,607	86	A. Craig.	T. J. Smith.
Port Glasgow, Renfrewshire	22,549	476,355	176	J. Wooler, D.F.C.	A. MacLean.
Prestonpans, East Lothian	3,213	62,414	129	R. S. Wilson.	R. B. Henderson.
Prestwick, Ayrshire	13,541	351,186	112	W. A. Morton.	F. Horton, M.B.E.
Queensferry,★ West Lothian	5,221	128,600	112½	W. G. Moodie.	J. Milne.
Renfrew★	18,686	931,700	141	H. D-M. McCutcheon.	R. N. W. Mitchell.
Rothesay,★ Bute	6,456	205,110	139	A. M. Matheson.	R. MacLean.
Rutherglen,★ Lanarkshire	25,071	681,954	132	R. N. O'Sullivan.	J. Hutchison.
St. Andrews,★ Fife	10,477	480,000	104	N. C. H. Mackenzie.	D. Niven.
Saltcoats, Ayrshire	14,992	287,536	133½	W. F. McAllum.	Mrs. N. Lambie.
Selkirk★	5,753	140,411	161	J. C. Robertson.	L. G. W. Thomson.
Stevenston, Ayrshire	12,111	207,581	135	J. Campbell.	A. Lambie.
Stewarton, Ayrshire	4,550	81,023	109	J. Hamilton.	A. MacDougall.
Stirling★	29,949	962,953	160	D. M. Bowie.	R. D. McIntyre.
Stonehaven, Kincardineshire	4,796	110,441	111	I. B. Robertson.	J. H. Stewart.
Stornoway, Ross and Cromarty	5,279	141,839	164	M. Macleod.	A. Matheson.
Stranraer,★ Wigtownshire	9,945	252,519	119	E. J. Hendry.	J. J. Wales.
Thurso, Caithness	9,122	149,629	138	J. S. Campbell.	T. W. Pollok.
Tillicoultry, Clackmannan	4,078	98,962	129	J. C. Donaldson.	H. McV. Jones.
Tranent, East Lothian	6,338	149,619	109	R. M. Sorbie.	G. F. McNeill.
Troon, Ayrshire	11,376	307,999	110½	D. P. Hepburn.	A. D. Paton.
Whitburn, West Lothian	10,260	210,000	157	R. Mickel.	J. Boyle.
Wick,★ Caithness	7,706	126,429	114	A. Lindsay.	W. G. Mowat.

‡ Last full rate levied at the time of going to press (usually 1970–71; dwelling houses 3s. 4d. *less* = 17p). Water rates are excluded from rate figures.

NEW TOWNS IN GREAT BRITAIN

(Populations shown as at 1971 Census are preliminary figures; *see also* Municipal Directories)

Commission for the New Towns, Glen House, Stag Place, S.W.1.—The Commission was established on October 1, 1961, under the New Towns Act, 1959, to take over new towns in England and Wales from development corporations whose purposes have been achieved or substantially achieved. In each town, the management of residential property is conducted by a local committee appointed by the Commission in accordance with the New Towns Act, 1965 and administration of all property is carried out through the Commission's local staff.

Chairman, C. D. Pilcher, C.B.E.

Deputy Chairman, Mrs. B. F. R. Paterson.

Members, W. A. J. Chapman; S. R. Collingwood; G. D. Hitchcock; R. May, O.B.E.; P. G. Grimshaw; J. D. Russell.

Secretary, F. Schaffer.

CRAWLEY, Sussex.—*Chairman,* R. May, O.B.E. *Manager,* R. M. Clarke, M.C. *Offices,* Broadfield, Crawley, Sussex. Area, 6,047 acres. Population (Census, 1971), 67,571. Estimated eventual population, 120,000.

HATFIELD, Herts.—*Chairman,* W. A. J. Chapman, Ph.D. *Manager,* M. W. Biggs, C.B.E. *Offices:* Church Road, Welwyn Garden City, Herts. Area: 2,340 acres. Population (estimated, 1971), 26,500. Estimated eventual population: 29,000.

HEMEL HEMPSTEAD, Herts.—*Chairman,* G. D. Hitchcock. *Manager,* Brig. J. R. Blomfield, O.B.E., M.C. *Offices,* Swan Court, Waterhouse Street, Hemel Hempstead, Herts. Area, 5,910 acres. Population (Census, 1971), 69,371. Estimated eventual population, 80,000.

WELWYN GARDEN CITY, Herts. *Chairman,* S. R. Collingwood. *Manager,* M. W. Biggs, C.B.E. *Offices:* Church Road, Welwyn Garden City, Herts. Area: 4,317 acres. Population (Census, 1971): 40,369. Estimated eventual population: 50,000.

Development Corporations

AYCLIFFE, Co. Durham.—Formed 1947. *Chairman* (vacant). *General Manager,* A. V. Williams, C.B.E. *Offices,* Churchill House, Newton Aycliffe, nr. Darlington, Co. Durham. Area, 2,508 acres. Population (estimated, 1971), 23,588. Estimated eventual population, 45,000.

BASILDON, Essex.—Formed 1949. *Chairman,* A. O. Keiting. *General Manager,* R. C. C. Boniface. *Offices,* Gifford House, Basildon, Essex. Area, 7,818 acres. Population (Census, 1971), 129,073. Estimated eventual population, 140,000.

BRACKNELL, Berks.—Formed 1949. *Chairman,* J. Hughes. *General Manager,* J. V. Rowley. *Offices,* Farley Hall, Bracknell, Berks. Area, 3,303 acres. Population (estimated, 1971), 38,000. Estimated eventual population, 60,000.

CORBY, Northants.—Formed 1950. *Chairman,* Sir Henry Chisholm, C.B.E. *General Manager,* Brig. H. G. W. Hamilton, C.B.E. *Offices,* Spencer House, Corporation Street, Corby, Northants. Area, 4,423 acres. Population (Census, 1971), 47,716. Estimated eventual population, 82,000.

CWMBRAN, Mon.—Formed 1949. *Chairman,* The Lord Raglan. *General Manager,* J.E. McComb, C.B.E., D.F.C. *Offices,* Victoria Street, Cwmbran, Mon. Area, 3,157 acres. Population (Census, 1971), 31,614. Estimated eventual population, 55,000.

HARLOW, Essex.—Formed 1947. *Chairman,* Sir John Newsom, C.B.E., LL.D. *General Manager,* B. H. Harvey, O.B.E. *Offices,* Gate House, The High, Harlow, Essex. Area 6,305 acres. Population (Census, 1970), 77,666. Estimated eventual population, 90,000

MILTON KEYNES, Bucks.—Formed 1967. *Chairman,* The Lord Campbell of Eskan. *General Manager,* F. Ll. Roche. *Offices,* Wavendon Tower, Wavendon, near Bletchley, Bucks. Area 22,000 acres (9,000 hectares). Population (Census, 1970), 70,021. Estimated eventual population, 250,000.

PETERBOROUGH.—Formed 1968. *Chairman,* C. T. Higgins; *General Manager,* W. Thomas. *Offices,* Peterscourt, Peterborough. Area, 15,940 acres. Population (estimated, 1970), 88,000. Estimated eventual population, 188,000.

PETERLEE, Co. Durham.—Formed 1948. *Chairman,* R. D. Appleton, T.D. *General Manager,* A. V. Williams, C.B.E. *Offices,* Shotton Hall, Peterlee, Co. Durham. Area, 2,785 acres. Population (estimated, 1971), 25,000. Estimated eventual population, 30,000.

REDDITCH, Worcs.—Formed 1964. *Chairman,* Sir Edward Walter Thompson; *General Manager,* A. M. Grier, C.M.G. *Offices,* Holmwood, Plymouth Road, Redditch, Worcs. Area 7,200 acres. Population (Census 1971), 40,775. Estimated eventual population, 70,000.

RUNCORN, Cheshire.—Formed 1964. *Chairman,* V. A. Arnold, C.B.E., M.C., T.D. *General Manager,* D. F. Banwell. *Offices,* Chapel Street, Runcorn, Cheshire. Area, 7,234 acres. Population (Census, 1971), 35,953. Eventual population 90/100,000.

SKELMERSDALE, Lancs.—Formed 1962. *Chairman,* G. H. Heywood; *General Manager,* R. W. Phelps. *Offices,* High Street, Skelmersdale, Lancs. Area, 4,100 acres. Population (Census 1971) 30,522 Estimated eventual population 80,000.

STEVENAGE, Herts.—Formed 1946. *Chairman,* Mrs. E. Denington. *General Manager,* J. A. Balchin. *Offices,* Swingate House, Stevenage, Herts. Area 6,256 acres. Population (Census, 1971), 66,918.

TELFORD, Shropshire.—Formed 1963. *Chairman* (vacant). *General Manager,* E. Thomas. *Offices,* Priorslee Hall, Telford, Salop. Area, 19,243 acres. Population (estimated, 1970), 75,000. Estimated eventual population, 222,000.

WASHINGTON, Co. Durham.—Formed 1964. *Chairman,* Sir James Steel, C.B.E. *General Manager,* W. S. Holley. *Offices,* Usworth Hall, Washington. Area 5,300 acres. Population (Census, 1971) 24,105 estimated population 1995, 80,000.

Scotland

CUMBERNAULD, Dunbartonshire.—Formed 1956. *Chairman,* Dame Jean Roberts, D.B.E. *General Manager,* Brig. C. H. Cowan. *Headquarters,* Cumbernauld House, Cumbernauld. Population (Census, 1971), 31,787. Estimated eventual population, 70,000.

EAST KILBRIDE, Lanarkshire.—Formed 1947. *Chairman,* G. Wallace. *General Manager,* G. B. Young. *Offices,* Norfolk House, East Kilbride, Lanarkshire. Population (Census, 1971), 63,505 Estimated eventual population, 100,000.

GLENROTHES, Fife.—Formed 1948. *Chairman,* R. R. TAYLOR, C.B.E. *General Manager,* Brig. R. S. Doyle, C.B.E. *Offices,* Glenrothes. Population (Census, 1970), 27,137. Estimated eventual population, 70,000.

IRVINE, Ayrshire. Designated, 1966. *Chairman,* A. W. Hardie. *General Manager,* D. Kirby, M.V.O., M.B.E. *Offices,* Perceton House, Irvine. Population (Census, 1971), 23,011. Estimated eventual population, 120,000.

LIVINGSTON, West Lothian. Designated, 1962. *Chairman,* W. Taylor. *Offices,* Livingston, W. Lothian.—Population (1971), 14,000. Estimated population (1985), 70,000 (rising to 100,000).

Northern Ireland

(For geographical and historical notes on Ireland, see Index)

A preliminary report on the 1971 Census of Population showed a total of 1,525,187 for Northern Ireland (males, 748,420; females, 776, 767) compared with a total population of 1,484,755 at the Census of 1961. In 1961 the number of persons in the various religious denominations, (expressed as percentages of the total population) were: Roman Catholic, 34·9; Presbyterian, 29; Church of Ireland, 24·2; Methodist, 5; others 4·9; not stated, 2. Northern Ireland has a total area of 5,452 sq. miles (land, 5,206 sq. miles; inland water and tideways, 246 sq. miles) with a density of population of 293 persons per sq. mile in 1971.

Constitution and Government.—Under the Government of Ireland Act, 1920, a separate Parliament and Executive Government were established for Northern Ireland. Under the Constitution certain legislative and fiscal powers are reserved to the Parliament of the United Kingdom.

The Northern Ireland Parliament consists of a *House of Commons* of 52 elected members (who receive an allowance) and a *Senate* of 2 *ex officio* Senators and 24 Senators elected by the members of the House of Commons on the proportional representation system. The state of the parties in July 1970, was: Unionists 34, Nationalists 6, Independent Unionists 3, Northern Ireland Labour 2, Republican Labour 2, Independent 4; Protestant Unionist 2. Northern Ireland continues under the Act of 1920 to return 12 members to the House of Commons at Westminster.

The *Executive* power is vested in the Governor on behalf of Her Majesty the Queen; he holds office for 6 years, and is advised by 12 Ministers responsible to Parliament.

Governor, His Excellency the LORD GREY OF NAUNTON, G.C.M.G., K.C.V.O., O.B.E., *born* April 15, 1910; *appointed Governor,* Dec. 3, 1968 (Goverment House, Hillsborough, Northern Ireland) .. £4,000 *plus allowances.*

Private Secretary and Principal A.D.C., Maj. R. Stephens, C.V.O., E.R.D.
Asst. Private Secretary, Miss H. Strange.

The Privy Council

Senator J. L. O. Andrews (1957); Sir Anthony Babington, Q.C. (1926); R. J. Bailie, M.P.; D. W. Bleakley; R. H. Bradford, M.P.; Capt. J.W. Brooke, M.P.; The Viscount Brookeborough, K.G., C.B.E.,M.C. (1933); W. Craig, M.P. (1963); Sir Lancelot Curran (*Lord Justice*) (1957); J. Dobson, M.P. (1969); A. B. D. Faulkner, M.P. (1959); W. K. Fitzsimmons, M.P. (1965); Senator Col. the Lord Glentoran, H.M.L. (1953); Mr. Justice E. W. Jones (1965); B. Kelly, Q.C., M.P. (1969); H. V. Kirk, M.P. (1962); Capt. W. J. Long, M.P. (1966); Sir Robert Lowry (*Lord Chief Justice*) (1964); R. W. B. McConnell (1964); The Lord MacDermott, M.C. (1940); Sir Herbert McVeigh (*Lord Justice*) (1965); N. O. Minford, M.P.; W. J. Morgan (1961); The Lord Moyola; Ivan Neill, M.P.(1950);P. R. H. O'Neill, M.P.; The Lord O'Neill of the Maine (1956); Sir Robert Porter, Q.C., M.P.; The Lord Rathcavan (1922); R. Simpson, M.P. (1969); Capt. Sir Norman Stronge, Bt. M.C., H.M.L. (1946); J. D. Taylor, M.P.; Judge W. W. B. Topping (1967); J. E. Warnock, Q.C. (1944); H. W. West, M.P. (1960).

Clerk of the Privy Council, Sir Harold Black, Stormont Castle, Belfast 4.

The Senate

Rt. Hon. J. L. O. Andrews (*U.*); J. E. N. Barnhill (*U.*); Rt. Hon. the Lord Mayor of Belfast (*U.*); W. M. Cameron, M.B.E. (*U.*); Lt.-Col. J. G. Cunningham, O.B.E. (*U.*); J. C. Drennan, C.B.E.(*U.*); N. Elder (*U.*); A. D. Gibson (*U.*); Col. the Lord Glentoran, P.C., H.M.L. (*U.*); J. S. Johnston (*U.*); N. Kennedy (*Lab.*); S. Kingham (*U.*); J. G. Lennon (*N.*); D. A. McClelland (*U.*); H. I. McClure (*U.*); C. McCullough (*U.*); P. F. McGill (*N.*); D. R. McGladdery (*U.*); P. F. Mallon (*N.*); P. J. O'Hare; W. Stewart (*U.*); Mrs. E. A. Taggart, O.B.E. (*U.*); P. G. Wilson (*SDLP*); Maj. W. Wilson (*U.*); C. J. Wilton (*Ind.*).

The House of Commons

Belfast (16 Members).—D. Boal (*U.*); R. H. Bradford (*U.*); T. H. Caldwell (*I.U.*); J. Cardwell (*U.*); P. J. Devlin (*Lab.*); G. Fitt (*SDLP*); Rt. Hon. W. K. Fitzsimmons (*U.*); R.L. Hall-Thompson (*U.*); P. Kennedy (*Rep. Lab.*); J. W. Kennedy (*U.*); Rt. Hon. H. V. Kirk (*U.*); J. D. Laird (*U.*); J. McQuade (*U.*); Rt. Hon. I. Neill (*U.*); W. Scott (*U.*); F. V. Simpson (*Lab.*).

Antrim (9 Members).—Rt. Hon. R. J. Baillie

(*U.*); Rt. Hon. W. Craig (*U.*); Mrs. A. L. Dickson (*U.*); Rev. W. J. Beattie (*P.U.*); W. B. McIvor (*U.*); Rt. Hon. N. O. Minford (*U.*); Rt. Hon. P. R. H. O'Neill (*U.*); Rev. I. R. K. Paisley (*P.U.*); Rt. Hon. R. Simpson (*U.*).

Armagh (4 Members).—Capt. R. J. Mitchell (*U.*); P. M. O'Hanlon (*SDLP*); J. M. Stronge (*U.*); H. Whitten (*U.*).

Down (10 Members.—R. J. Babington (*U.*); Rt. Hon. J. Dobson (*U.*); Rt. Hon. A. B. D. Faulkner (*U.*); M. J. Keogh (*N.*); Rt. Hon. J. W. B. Kelly, Q.C. (*U.*); Capt. Rt. Hon. W. J. Long (*U.*); S. Magowan (*U.*); R. D. McConnell (*I.U.*); J. O'Reilly (*N.*); Rt. Hon. Sir Robert Porter Q.C. (*U.*).

Fermanagh (3 Members).—Capt. Rt. Hon. J. Brooke (*U.*); J. Carron (*N.*); Rt. Hon. H. W. West (*U.*).

Londonderry City (1 Member).—A. W. Anderson (*U.*).

Londonderry County (4 Members).—J. Burns (*U.*); I. A. Cooper (*Ind.*); J. Hume (*Ind.*); The Lord Moyola, P.C. (*U.*).

Tyrone (5 Members).—W. S. Fyffe (*U.*); T. C. Gormley (*N.*); Rt. Hon. J. D. Taylor (*U.*); R. H. O'Connor (*N.*); J. A. Currie (*SDLP*)

Ind.=Independent; *Lab.*=Labour; *N.*=Nationalist; *Rep. Lab.*=Republican Labour; *U.*=Unionist; *I.U.*=Independent Unionist; *P.U.*=Protestant Unionist; *SDLP*=Social Democratic and Labour Party.

Officers of Parliament

Speaker of the Senate, Col. the Lord Glentoran, P.C., H.M.L.

Speaker of the House of Commons, Maj. Rt. Hon. Ivan Neill.

Chairman of Ways and Means and Deputy Speaker, W. Scott.

Deputy Chairman, F. V. Simpson.

Serjeant-at-Arms, Brig. J. Y. Calwell, C.B.E., M.V.O.

Black Rod and Deputy Serjeant-at-Arms, Capt. J. C. Cattwright, D.S.O., R.N.

Clerk of Parliaments, R. H. A. Blackburn.

Clerk Assistant, J. A. D. Kennedy.

Librarian, T. Hamilton.

Editor of Official Report, J. F. Burns.

The Cabinet

Prime Minister and Minister of Home Affairs, Rt. Hon. A. B. D. Faulkner, M.P. (*b.* Feb. 18, 1921), appointed 1971 .... £5,750

Minister of Finance, Rt. Hon. H. V. Kirk, M.P.
Health and Social Services Rt. Hon. W. K. Fitz-simmons, M.P.
Education, Rt. Hon. W J. Long, M.P.
Agriculture, Rt. Hon. H. W. West, M.P.
Commerce, Rt. Hon. R. J. Bailie, M.P.
Development, Rt. Hon. R. H. Bradford, M.P.
Minister in the Senate, Rt. Hon. J. L. O. Andrews.
Community Relations, Rt. Hon. D. W. Bleakley, M.P.
Leader of the House of Commons and Minister of State (Development), Rt. Hon. N. O. Minford, M.P.
Minister of State (Home Affairs), Rt. Hon. J. D. Taylor, M.P.
Minister of State (Finance) and Chief Whip, Capt. Rt. Hon. J. W. Brooke, M.P.
Ministers, each £4,250; Ministers of State, £3,500; and Expenses, £300.

PARLIAMENTARY SECRETARIES
Prime Minister's Department, Senator D. R. McGladdery.
Ministry of Health and Social Services, J. Burns, M.P.
Asst. Parlity. Sec., Ministry of Finance, S. Magowan, M.P.
Parliamentary Secretaries, each £2,500.

PRIME MINISTER'S DEPT. AND CABINET OFFICE
Secretary, Sir Harold Black.
Deputy Secretary, K. P. Bloomfield.
Private Secretaries to the Prime Minister, R. Ramsay (*Principal*); B. R. Cummings.
Security Adviser to the Prime Minister, W. F. Stout, C.B.
Dir. of Information, W. E. Montgomery, M.B.E.
Deputy Director of Information, T. M. Roberts.
Liaison Officer, Home Office, London, R. McClelland.

Government Offices
MINISTRY OF FINANCE *KBE 6/72*
Permanent Secretary, D. C. B. Holden, C.B., E.R.D.
Second Secretary, R. H. Kidd.
First Parliamentary Draftsman, W. A. Leitch, C.B.
Second Parliamentary Draftsman, S. F. R. Martin.
Director of Law Reform, A. G. Donaldson.
Director of Establishments, K. R. Shimeld.
Senior Asst. Secretaries, J. Reid, O.B.E.; H. Love.
Asst. Secretaries, C. F. Darling; S. H. Jamieson; R. M. McDonald; J. P. McGrath.
Registrar-General, J. Y. Malley, D.S.O., D.F.C.

MINISTRY OF HOME AFFAIRS
Permanent Secretary, J. G. Hill.
Senr. Asst. Secretary, D. W. Lowry.
Asst. Secretaries, G. Buchanan; J. H. Parkes; W. G Robinson.
Attorney-General, Rt. Hon. B. Kelly, Q.C., M.P.
Chief Crown Solicitor, T. H. Goligher.

MINISTRY OF HEALTH AND SOCIAL SERVICES
Permanent Secretary, N. Dugdale.
Deputy Secretaries, W. H. G. Quigley; J. E. Aiken.

Senior Asst. Secretary, D. W. Lowry.
Asst. Secretaries, J. H. Copeland; W. N. Drummond; W. S. Long; C. G. Oakes; S. H. O'Fee; S. E. Taylor; N. I. Kells; L. R. Kelly; F. A. Elliott; J. H. Scott.
Chief Medical Officer, F. D. Beddard.

MINISTRY OF EDUCATION *6/72*
Permanent Secretary, P. Shea, O.B.E.
Senior Asst. Secretaries, G. Dent; J. Finney.
Asst. Secretaries, A. Howard; T. R. Meharg; E. J. Kirkpatrick.

MINISTRY OF AGRICULTURE
Permanent Secretary, J. A. Young, C.B.
Deputy Secretary, W. G. Malcolm, M.B.E.
Senior Asst. Secretary, A. E. W. Steen.
Asst. Secretaries, A. McKelvie; H. S. Oliver; J. M. C. Parke; R. Shaw; J. Eaton, O.B.E.
Chief Scientific Officer, W. O. Brown.

MINISTRY OF COMMERCE
(64 Chichester Street, Belfast)
Permanent Secretary, A. C. Brooke.
Senior Asst. Secretary, F. T. Mais.
Asst. Secretaries, J. H. Armstrong; W. McC. Taylor; K. Darwin.
Director of Industrial and Forensic Science, A. J. Howard.
Financial Controller, J. E. Hawkins.
Registrar of Friendly Societies and Industrial Assurance Commissioner, E. Simpson.
Registrar of Joint Stock Companies and of Business Names, S. D. Solomen.

MINISTRY OF DEVELOPMENT
Permanent Secretary, J. A. Oliver, C.B.
Senior Asst. Secretaries, J. F. Irvine; C. D. Hoey; L. V. D. Calvert; P. A. Sythes.
Asst. Secretaries, J. A. D. Higgins; T. J. McCormick; D. J. Perham.

MINISTRY OF COMMUNITY RELATIONS
Secretary, W. Slinger.

EXCHEQUER AND AUDIT DEPARTMENT
(Arnotts Building, Belfast, 2)
Comptroller and Auditor-General, H. A. Lowry.
Chief Auditor, J. W. Acheson, O.B.E.

SUPPLEMENTARY BENEFITS COMMISSION
(Ormeau Avenue, Belfast, 2).
Chairman, T. J. Rainsford, M.B.E.

ROYAL ULSTER CONSTABULARY
(Knock Road, Belfast 5)
Chief Constable, R. Shillington, C.B.E.
Deputy Chief Constable, J. B. Flanaggan, O.B.E.

NORTHERN IRELAND AGENT IN LONDON
11 Berkeley Street, W.1.
Agent, Sir Harry Jones, C.B.E.

U.K. REPRESENTATIVE IN N. IRELAND
Representative, Howard Frank Trayton Smith, C.M.G. (1971), Lanside, Craigavad Holywood, Co. Down.

THE JUDICATURE

SUPREME COURT OF JUDICATURE, THE ROYAL COURTS OF JUSTICE (ULSTER), BELFAST.
The Rt. Hon. Sir Robert Lowry, Lord Chief Justice of Northern Ireland £13,250
The Rt. Hon. Lord Justice (Sir Lancelot E.) Curran; Rt. Hon. Lord Justice (Sir Herbert Andrew) McVeigh; Rt. Hon. Mr. Justice (Edward Warburton) Jones; The Hon. Mr. Justice (Ambrose Joseph) McGonigal; The Hon. Mr. Justice (Maurice White) Gibson; The Hon. Mr. Justice (Turlough) O'Donnell; each £11,750.

Secretariat
Permanent Secretary to Supreme Court and Clerk of the Crown for Northern Ireland, J. A. L. McLean.

Asst. Secretary to the Supreme Court and Private Secretary to the Lord Chief Justice, J. W. Wilson.

Registrar's Department
Registrar, D. S. Stephens.
Asst. Registrar, V. A. Care.
Deputy Asst. Registrar, Miss M. Cullen.

Chief Clerk's Department
Chief Clerk (and Registrar in Lunacy), J. K. Davis, O.B.E.
Asst. Chief Clerk and Asst. Registrar in Lunacy, R. L. G. Davison.
Bankruptcy and Chancery Registrar's Department
Registrar, J. M. Hunter.
Deputy Asst. Registrar, V. G. Bridges.

Recorders

Belfast, Rt. Hon. W. W. B. Topping, Q.C..£8,350
Londonderry, D. J. Little, Q.C.............£7,850

Chairmen of Quarter Sessions

Antrim, The Recorder of Belfast.
Armagh and Fermanagh, R. H. Conaghan, Q.C.
　　　　　　　　　　　　　　　　£7,850
Down, J. A. Brown, Q.C.................£7,850
Londonderry, The Recorder of Londonderry.
Tyrone, W. Johnson, Q.C.................£7,850

FINANCE

The greater part of the taxation in Northern Ireland is imposed and collected by the United Kingdom Government. After deducting the cost of collection, certain services reserved to the United Kingdom Parliament, and the Imperial Contribution, the balance is paid over to Northern Ireland's Exchequer. The Contribution so made by Northern Ireland to the cost of United Kingdom services, *i.e.* Navy, Army and Air Force, National Debt, etc. for the period from 1921 to March 31, 1971, amounted to £459,874,344. The United Kingdom contribution has been provisionally fixed at £1,000,000 for 1970–71 and £1,000,000 for 1971–72.

Estimated Public Income..........£422,900,000
Estimated Public Expenditure (in-
　cluding Imperial contribution)....£422,783,900

EXTERNAL TRADE†

	£'000		
	1967	1968	1969
Total Imports..	551,709	659,596	727,915
Total Exports..	507,040	596,071	668,619

† Including cross-Channel trade with Great Britain.

PRODUCTION

Industries.—The total value of the industrial production of Northern Ireland in 1969 was approximately £1,194,000,000, and employment on industrial production was given to about 220,000 persons. The products of the engineering, ship-building and aircraft industries which employed 48,000 persons, were valued at £143,000,000. The textile industries, employing 44,000 persons, produced yarns, fabrics, household textiles, handkerchiefs, carpets, hosiery, ropes and a wide variety of other products valued at approximately £177,000,000. The food, drink and tobacco industries, giving employment to 28,000 persons, produced goods valued at £524,000,000 and clothing to the value of £48,000,000 was manufactured in 1969, of which £17,000,000 represented shirts and collars, which are manufactured principally in Londonderry. Other industries of importance to the economy of Northern Ireland are synthetic rubber and products, cardboard boxes and packing cases, furniture and building materials and mineral oil refining.

Minerals.—2,160 persons were employed in mining and quarrying operations in Northern Ireland in 1970, and the minerals raised were valued at £4,978,000.

Fisheries.—The total value of sea and freshwater fish caught in 1969 was £1,613,000.

COMMUNICATIONS

Seaports.—The net tonnage of shipping using the principal ports in 1970 was about 22,000,000 tons. *Belfast.*—Nightly passenger and freight services operate to Heysham and Liverpool. Regular vehicle ferry services are maintained to Ardrossan, Preston and Liverpool and freight services operate to the major ports in Great Britain and to foreign ports. *Larne.*—A frequent passenger, vehicle ferry and general cargo service to

Stranraer, a regular vehicle ferry service to Preston and a cargo service to Ardrossan are operated. *Londonderry.*—A container service operates to Preston. Shipping services also operate from Coleraine, Newry and Warrenpoint to Liverpool, Preston and Garston.

Road and Rail Transport.—The reorganization of public transport in Northern Ireland was completed by the Transport Act (N.I.), 1967, which provided for the abolition of the Ulster Transport Authority and the establishment of the Northern Ireland Transport Holding Company. The Holding Company took over the assets of the Authority and is responsible for the supervision of the subsidiary companies, Ulsterbus Ltd. which operates the public road passenger services and Northern Ireland Railways Co. Ltd. which provides the railway services. A few privately operated bus services are provided in rural areas under licence. The Belfast Corporation provides omnibus services in the Belfast area. Road freight services are provided by a large number of hauliers operating competitively under licence.

Air Transport.—Passenger and freight services operate between Belfast Airport and airports throughout Great Britain. A limited number of services is also operated to North America. In 1970 over one million passengers, 26,000 metric tons of freight, including mail, were carried. In 1971 the main runway at Belfast Airport was in course of extension to 9,100 ft. (completion, 1972).

FLAG.—The national flag is that of the United Kingdom and there is a second flag authorized by the Government which may be flown by any citizen of Northern Ireland—a red St. George's Cross on a white field bearing in centre a white six-point star surmounted by a crown; and in the star the red hand of Ulster.

BELFAST

BELFAST, a City, the seat of Government of Northern Ireland, situated at the mouth of the River Lagan at its entrance to Belfast Lough, has a municipal area of 16,017 acres, exclusive of tidal water (2,034) and a population (1971) of 383,600. The city received its first charter of incorporation in 1613 and has since grown, owing to its easy access by sea to Scottish coal and iron, to be a great industrial centre. The chief industries are ship-building and the manufacture of aircraft, machinery, textiles, ropes and tobacco. Belfast is an important seaport with extensive docks.

The principal buildings are of a relatively recent date and include the Parliament Buildings at Stormont, the City Hall, the Law Courts, the Public Library and the Museum and Art Gallery. The Queen's University (previously Queen's College) was chartered in 1908.

The city returns 16 members to the Parliament of Northern Ireland and 4 members to the House of Commons at Westminster. Belfast was created a city in 1888 and the title of Lord Mayor was conferred in 1892.

Lord Mayor (1971–72), J. F. Cairns.
Town Clerk, D. Jamison.

LONDONDERRY

LONDONDERRY, a City situated on the River Foyle, has a population (estimated, 1970) of 56,000 and was reputedly founded in 546 by St. Columba. Londonderry (formerly *Derry*) has important associations with the City of London. The Irish Society, under its royal charter of 1613, fortified the city and was for long closely associated with its administration. On April 2, 1969, the Corporation of Londonderry and Londonderry R.D.C. were

dissolved and replaced by the Londonderry Development Commission.

Famous for the great siege of 1688–89, when for 105 days the town held out against the forces of James II until relieved by sea, Londonderry was an important naval base throughout the Second World War. Interesting buildings are the Protestant Cathedral of St. Columb's (1633) and the Guildhall reconstructed in 1912 and containing a number of beautiful stained glass windows, many of which were presented by the livery companies of London. The famous Walls are still intact and form a circuit of almost a mile around the old city. The manu-facture of shirts and collars is the staple industry. Other industries include motor and mechanical engineering and fancy box making. New industries established in Londonderry in the post-war period include the manufacture of synthetic fibre and rubber, tyre cord and light engineering. A large part of Ulster's agricultural export trade passes through the port.

Chairman, Londonderry Development Commission B. Morton.

General Manager, G. J. Bryan, C.M.G., C.V.O., O.B.E. M.C.

COUNTIES OF NORTHERN IRELAND

Counties and *County Boroughs*	Area* sq. miles	Population 1966‡	Lord Lieutenant	High Sheriff, 1971–2
(1) Antrim............	1,099	313,991	Capt. R. A. F. Dobbs. [P.C.	C. H. G. Kinahan.
Belfast County Borough.......	25	398,405	Col. the Lord Glentoran,	F. W. Watson, O.B.E., M.C.
(2) Armagh..........	489	125,164	Capt. Rt. Hon. Sir Norman Stronge, Bt., M.C., M.P.	Maj. G. A. N. Boyne.
(3) Down.............	952	286,631	The Earl of Clanwilliam.	Capt. J. C. Brownlow.
(4) Fermanagh.......	657	49,886	J. J. Maguire, O.B.E.	Maj-Gen. T. P. D. Scott.
(5) Londonderry†	810	118,964	J. C. Drennan, C.B.E.	W. Bristow Stevenson.
Londonderry City	3·4	55,694	Col. Sir Basil McFarland, Bt., C.B.E.	T. F. Cooke.
(6) Tyrone...........	1,218	136,040	The Duke of Abercorn.	Capt. J. R. McAusland.

*Excluding tidal waters and large lakes. † Excluding the City of Londonderry. ‡ Census of 1966. Chairmen of County Councils.—*Antrim,* W. M. Cameron, M.B.E.; *Armagh,* A. D. Gibson, O.B.E.; *Down,* G. C. Bell; *Fermanagh,* Capt. Hon. J. W. Brooke; *Londonderry,* Lt.-Col. D. J. Christie, C.B.E., E.R.D.; *Tyrone,* J. P. Duff, C.B.E.

MUNICIPAL DIRECTORY OF NORTHERN IRELAND

CITIES, Boroughs and *Urban Districts*	Population 1970 Estimated	Rateable Value	Rate* levied 1971–2	Town Clerk (or Clerk, U.D.C.)	Mayor, 1971–72 †Chairman, U.D.C.
		£			
Armagh...................	12,300	117,007	275	D. J. Ryan.	† A. Briggs.
Ballymena.................	17,580	200,674	260	J. S. McIlroy.	J. B. Millar.
Bangor...................	30,600	491,941	228½	R. Wolsey.	R. Topping
BELFAST..................	383,600	5,710,832	216	D. Jamison.	J. F. Cairns. [O.B.E.
Carrickfergus.............	14,200	140,901	209	D. Barry.	T. J. Patterson.
Coleraine.................	14,340	194,424	260½	W. E. Henry, M.B.E.	C. H. Hamill.
Craigavon................	11,400	99,842	242½	E. E. H. Cage.	†S. J. McMahon, C.B.E.
Larne....................	18,100	193,850	236	R. Lyttle, M.C.	A. Marrs.
Lisburn..................	25,800	252,651	230½	M. S. Fielding.	H. G. Bass.
LONDONDERRY‡...........	56,000	462,941	239½	*See above.*	
Lurgan...................	23,340	192,524	273	J. N. T. McGaffin.	W. J. Gordon.
Newry...................	12,000	119,418	277	G. Cronin M.B.E.	†P. McMahon.
Newtownabbey	55,400	539,386	192½	A. R. Martin	A. W. McGowan
Newtownards..............	14,500	156,701	241½	W. C. Scott.	J. D. Beckett.
Omagh...................	10,940	113,160	209½	J. McGale	†N. R. J. Wilson, M.B.E.
Portadown.................	21,800	231,327	252½	K. Jones, M.B.E.	A. T. Newell.

* Full rate levied. Mixed hereditaments, 14p less; Dwelling-houses, 28½p less.
‡City Corporation dissolved, 1969 (*see* notes above).

THE ISLE OF MAN (MONA)

An island in the Irish Sea, in lat. 54° 3′–54° 25′ N., and long. 4° 18′–4° 47′ W., nearly equidistant from England, Scotland, and Ireland. The total land area is 141,263 acres (227 sq. miles), of which 78,142 acres are under cultivation. A preliminary report on the 1971 Census showed a total population of 49,743 (males, 23,007; females, 26,736). In 1970 the births numbered 840 and the deaths 909. 165 persons were returned at the Census of 1961 as able to speak the Manx language, compared with 4,657 in 1901 and 355 in 1951. The Island's main industry is catering for holidaymakers (numbering about 500,000 in the year) from all parts of the British Isles. Some agricultural produce is exported.

Government.—The Isle of Man is governed by a Legislature, called the Tynwald, consisting of two branches—the Legislative Council and the House of Keys. The Council consists of the Lieutenant-Governor, the Bishop of Sodor and Man, the First

Deemster, the Attorney-General and 7 members appointed by the House of Keys. The House of Keys (possibly from the Scandinavian *keise*=chosen) is one of the most ancient legislative assemblies in the world. It consists of 24 members, elected by the adult male and female population, 13 from the six *sheadings*, 7 from Douglas, 2 from Ramsey, and 1 each from Castletown and Peel. Bills after having passed both Houses are signed by the members, and then sent for the Royal Assent. After receiving the Royal Assent, a Bill does not become law unless promulgated within the ensuing twelve months, and on the first "Tynwald Day" (July 5) following it is announced in the English and Manx languages on the Tynwald Hill. On the promulgation taking place a certificate thereof is signed by the Lieutenant-Governor and the Speaker of the House of Keys.

Finance.—An annual contribution of 5 per cent. of the net "Common Purse" Receipts is made to the United Kingdom Government. In 1921 Tynwald accepted liability for the redemption of £250,000 War Stock, and in 1927 liability for a further sum of £500,000 of War Stock was accepted in final settlement of all responsibility to the Imperial Government in respect of the cost of the War (1914–18). The Isle of Man has made, in all, free gifts of £1,250,000 to the British Government and has lent £1,000,000 free of interest, £500,000 of the latter being converted into a free gift on June 15, 1948; of the balance of £500,000, a sum of £250,000 was repaid by the Treasury in October, 1961.

The chief source of revenue is found in the customs duties, the only direct taxation being income tax. Income tax ranges from 10p in the £, on the first £250 of taxable income, the standard rate being 21 in the £. There are no surtax or death duties, surtax having been abolished from April 6, 1961. There are 34 primary, 4 secondary schools, a college of further education and a domestic science college, in addition to King William's College and the Buchan School for Girls; the net expenditure on public education in 1970–71 was £1,302,000.

CAPITAL, Ψ Douglas. Population (1966), 19,518. ΨCastletown (2,378) is the ancient capital; the other towns are ΨPeel (2,739), and ΨRamsey (3,880).

FLAG.—Three legs in white and gold armed conjoined on a red ground.

Lieutenant-Governor, His Excellency Sir Peter Stallard, K.C.M.G., C.V.O., M.B.E. (1966) (*plus allowance, tax free* £3,000)............£4,400
Government Secretary, W. B. Kennaugh...£3,163
Government Treasurer, W. Dawson.......£3,413
First Deemster, His Hon. G. E. Moore (*plus allee.* £100 *as Deputy Governor*)..............4,225
Second Deemster, His Hon. R. K. Eason......3,850
Attorney-General, D. D. Lay. 3.850
High Bailiff, H. W. Callow..............£3,146
Speaker, House of Keys, H. C. Kerruish, O.B.E.
Judge of Appeal, R. M. Bingham, O.B.E., T.D., Q.C.

THE CHANNEL ISLANDS

Situated off the north-west coast of France (at distances of from ten to thirty miles), are the only portions of the *Dukedom of Normandy* now belonging to the Crown, to which they have been attached ever since the Conquest. They consist of Jersey (28,717 acres), Guernsey (15,654 acres), Alderney (1,962 acres), Brechou (74), Great Sark (1,035), Little Sark (239), Herm (320), Jethou (44), and Lihou (38), a total of 48,083 acres, or 75 square miles. In 1971 the population of Jersey was 72,532, and of Guernsey, etc. 52,708 (Guernsey, 50,436; Alderney, 1,660; Sark, 582).

The climate is mild, and the soil exceptionally productive. The land under cultivation is about 38,765 vergées (2¼ vergées=1 acre) in Jersey, and about 16,500 vergées (2½ vergées=1 acre) in Guernsey, the principal product of the soil of Jersey being potatoes, tomatoes and flowers, and of Guernsey, tomatoes, flowers and fern. The famous Jersey and Guernsey breed of cows have earned a well-deserved celebrity. The Lieutenant-Governors and Commanders-in-Chief of Jersey and Guernsey are the Personal Representatives of the Sovereign and the channel of communication between H.M. Government and the Insular Governments. The Bailiffs of Jersey and Guernsey, appointed by the Crown, are Presidents both of the Assembly of the States (the Insular Legislature) and of the Royal Courts respectively.

The official language is English and a Norman-French *patois* is also in use (except in Alderney). The principal imports are coal and coke, building material and groceries and provisions, and the chief exports potatoes, tomatoes, grapes, flowers, granite and cattle. The chief town of Jersey is ΨSt. Helier on the south coast; the principal town of Guernsey is Ψ St. Peter Port, on the east coast, and of Alderney is St. Anne's.

JERSEY

Lieutenant-Governor and Commander-in-Chief of Jersey, His Excellency Air Chief Marshal Sir John Gilbert Davis, G.C.B., O.B.E. (1969) £4,640

Secretary and A.D.C., Lt.-Comdr. O. M. B. de Las Casas, O.B.E., R.N.(*ret.*).
Bailiff of Jersey, Sir Robert Le Masurier, D.S.C.
Dean of Jersey, Very Rev. T. A. Goss.
Attorney-General and Receiver-General, P. L. Crill.
Solicitor-General, V. A. Tomes.
States Treasurer, J. Clennett.

Year to Dec. 31:	1969	1970
Revenue.........	£13,071,992	£17,061,724
Expenditure.........	10,143,901	15,949,624
Public Debt.........	5,115,048	4,599,599

The standard rate of Income Tax is 4s. in the £. No super tax or death duties are levied.

FLAG.—White, bearing a red diagonal cross.

GUERNSEY AND DEPENDENCIES

Lieutenant-Governor and Commander-in-Chief of Guernsey, His Excellency Vice-Adm. Sir Charles Piercy Mills, K.C.B., C.B.E., D.S.C. (1969). £4,640
Secretary and A.D.C., Capt. M. H. T. Mellish, O.B.E., E.R.D.
Bailiff of Guernsey, Sir William Arnold, C.B.E.
Dean of Guernsey, Very Rev. F. W. Cogman.
Deputy Bailiff, J. H. Loveridge, C.B.E.
Attorney-General, E. P. Shanks.
Solicitor General, C. K. Frossard.
States Supervisor, L. A. Guillemette, O.B.E.
Receiver General, R. H. Collenette.

	1969	1970
Revenue............	£6,071,232	£7,627,237
Expenditure.........	4,829,498	5,432,895
Net Funded Debt.....	3,221,058	—
Note and Coin issue ..	1,490,301	2,657,102

ALDERNEY
President of the States, G. W. Baron.
Clerk to the States, P. W. Radice.
Clerk to the Court. G. M. P. Crombie.

SARK
La Dame de Serq, Dame Sibyl Hathaway, D.B.E.
Deputy Seigneur, B. S. Allen, M.B.E.
Seneschal, B. G. Jones.
FLAG.—White, bearing a red cross of St. George.

The Commonwealth

The Commonwealth is a free association of the 32 sovereign independent states listed below together with their dependencies (mostly small islands which are dependencies of Britain, Australia or New Zealand) and the Associated States of the Eastern Caribbean.

UNITED KINGDOM	MALAWI
CANADA	MALAYSIA
AUSTRALIA	MALTA G.C.
NEW ZEALAND	MAURITIUS
BARBADOS	NAURU
BOTSWANA	NIGERIA
CEYLON	PAKISTAN
CYPRUS	SIERRA LEONE
FIJI	SINGAPORE
GAMBIA	SWAZILAND
GHANA	TANZANIA
GUYANA	TRINIDAD AND TOBAGO
INDIA	UGANDA
JAMAICA	ZAMBIA
KENYA	TONGA
LESOTHO	WESTERN SAMOA

AREA AND POPULATION.—The total area of the British Commonwealth is estimated to be about 14 million square miles. Details of the areas and populations of the Member States and dependencies appear in the following pages and are also tabulated on pp. 199–203. The total population of the Commonwealth is estimated to be approaching 900,000,000.

GOVERNMENT.—Most members of the Commonwealth are parliamentary democracies, their laws being made with the consent of a freely elected parliament after discussion in that parliament, the executive government holding office by virtue of majority in parliament. However, Nigeria (1966) has suspended its constitution and is under military rule: the Constitution granted to Lesotho on independence in 1966 was suspended in January, 1970; Pakistan is governed by a martial law administration; and in January, 1971, Uganda came under military rule and was without a Parliament in August, 1971.

Queen Elizabeth II is recognized as Queen and Head of State in the following Member countries of the Commonwealth: Britain, Canada, Australia, New Zealand, Ceylon, Jamaica, Trinidad and Tobago, Malta, Fiji, Barbados and Mauritius. In each of these countries (except Britain) Her Majesty is personally represented by a Governor-General, who in many respects holds the same position in relation to the administration of public affairs as is held by the Sovereign in Britain (with the exception of certain constitutional functions which are performed by Her Majesty personally). The Governor-General is appointed by the Queen on the recommendation of the Government of the country concerned and is wholly independent of the British Government; in many cases he is a national of the country in which he holds office.

India, Pakistan, Ghana, Nigeria, Cyprus, Uganda, Tanzania, Kenya, Malawi, Zambia, Singapore, The Gambia, Guyana, Nauru, Sierra Leone and Botswana are Republics with Presidents as Head of State; Malaysia has one of the State Rulers as elected Monarch (*Yang Di-Pertuan Agong*) and Head of State; Lesotho, Tonga and Swaziland are monarchies which have their own Kings. Western Samoa has a Head of State whose functions are analogous to those of a constitutional monarch. All Members of the Commonwealth accept the Queen as the symbol of the free association of the Member Nations of the Commonwealth and as such, Head of the Commonwealth.

The status of member nations was defined by the Imperial Conference of 1926 and given legal substance by the *Statute of Westminster*, 1931, in which the Commonwealth nations were described as " autonomous communities within the British Empire, equal in status, in no way subordinate one to another, but united by a common allegiance to the Crown and freely associated as members of the British Commonwealth of Nations." (Modifications were subsequently made for the Republics and the Monarchies of which Her Majesty is not sovereign.) Other parts of the Commonwealth, such as the Dependent Territories and Associated States, are regarded as forming part of the Commonwealth by virtue of their relationship with Member states of the Commonwealth.

CONSULTATION.—The most important means of consultation between Governments are Prime Ministers' Meetings. These Meetings, which replaced the more formal pre-war Imperial Conferences, have been held at frequent intervals since 1944. They are a useful means whereby Commonwealth Heads of Government consult together on major issues of international affairs and other matters which affect them all. It is not their practice to pass Resolutions or seek to formulate common and binding policies on international issues; but they have on occasion made general statements of principle to which they all subscribe—such as the Commonwealth Declaration agreed at Singapore in January, 1971—and of policies of individual Governments are clearly often influenced by the information and ideas exchanged at these meetings. In addition to meetings of Prime Ministers, there are annual meetings of Finance Ministers, as well as less frequent meetings between Ministers or officials responsible for subjects such as Trade, Education, Medicine and Law.

A Commonwealth Secretariat was established in 1965, staffed from Commonwealth countries (*see* p. 375).

RHODESIA.—Southern Rhodesia was united with Northern Rhodesia and Nyasaland in a federation which lasted from 1953 until 1963, since when Nyasaland (as Malawi, 1964) and Northern Rhodesia (as Zambia, 1964) have become independent. Southern Rhodesia made a unilateral declaration of independence on Nov. 11, 1965. Its constitutional status in 1971 remained as set out in the Southern Rhodesia Act, 1965.

CITIZENSHIP AND NATIONALITY.—Each member of the Commonwealth of Nations defines the citizenship and nationality of its own people and determines the status of other Commonwealth nationals within its own boundaries. In most cases, though not in all, they possess a common status as British subjects (or Commonwealth citizens). Even where there is no such provision for a common status, the Members of the Commonwealth differentiate, in greater or less degree, as regards the grant of privileges, between citizens of the Commonwealth and aliens. The Republic of Ireland, which in 1949 ceased to be a member of the Commonwealth, is not regarded by the other Commonwealth nations as a foreign country or her citizens as foreigners.

THE JUDICIARY.—The Supreme Judicial Authority of dependencies in the Commonwealth is the Judicial Committee of the Privy Council, before which appeals may be brought (in the form of a petition to the Crown) from Consular Courts and Courts of Vice-Admiralty, and also from the Courts of certain members of the Commonwealth (Commonwealth of Australia (*inter se* matters

only), Australian States, New Zealand, Ceylon, Jamaica, Trinidad and Tobago, Malaysia, Singapore, Malta G.C., The Gambia, Barbados, Botswana and Mauritius). The Committee consists of such members of the Privy Council as have held or are holding high judicial office, provision being made for the inclusion of judges of certain Commonwealth countries from whose courts appeals lie to the Judicial Committee and of which H.M. the Queen is Head of State. The Supreme Judicial Authority for Great Britain and Northern Ireland is the House of Lords.

DEFENCE.—Each of the independent members of the Commonwealth is completely responsible for its own defence and all are members of the United Nations. The United Kingdom and Canada belong to N.A.T.O.; the United Kingdom and Pakistan are in C.E.N.T.O.; the United Kingdom, Australia, New Zealand and Pakistan are members of S.E.A.T.O.; Australia and New Zealand are signatories of the Pacific Security Treaty. The United Kingdom has defence agreements with Malta and Mauritius, and is a signatory to the Treaty of Guarantee of Cyprus. It is also a partner in joint defence arrangements with Malaysia and Singapore.

THE ASSOCIATED STATES.—Early in 1967 the former colonies of Antigua, Dominica, Grenada, St. Kitts–Nevis–Anguilla and St. Lucia became " non-dependent " States in association with Great Britain. Legal effect was given to this status by the West Indies Act, 1967. In October, 1969, St. Vincent also became an Associated State. The main features of the association are that each State is responsible for its own internal affairs, may amend its own Constitution and may sever the association by unilateral declaration, subject to the observance of procedures contained in the Constitution of each State. Her Majesty's Government retains responsibility for the external affairs and defence of each territory.

OVERSEAS DEPENDENCIES.—The United Kingdom, Australia and New Zealand have dependencies for which they are independently responsible. (*See* following sections.)

Colony (or *Settlement):* a territory belonging by settlement, conquest or annexation to the British Crown.

Protectorate: a territory not formally annexed, but in respect of which, by treaty, grant, usage, sufferance, and other lawful means, Her Majesty has power and jurisdiction.

Protected State: a territory under a ruler which enjoys Her Majesty's protection, over whose foreign affairs she exercises control but in respect of whose internal affairs she does not exercise jurisdiction.

Condominium: a territory for which responsibility is shared by two administering powers.

Leased Territories: this term applies only to that part of the mainland of China which was in 1898 leased to Great Britain for 99 years and is administered by the Government of Hong Kong.

Other Commonwealth Dependencies.—Australia is responsible for the Trust Territory of Papua and New Guinea. In addition Australia and New Zealand administer a number of island territories and extensive Antarctic areas.

DEVELOPMENT AND FINANCE.—Complete financial autonomy is enjoyed by all members of the Commonwealth. In some countries, customs tariffs are lower for merchandise of Commonwealth origin than for imports from foreign countries. The British Government provides guarantees for the capital issues made by dependent territories and also provides budgetary assistance in many cases as well as direct loans and grants to assist development.

Under the Colonial Development and Welfare Act, 1940, annual sums of £5,000,000 were made available for developments and £500,000 for research for a ten-year period. Succeeding Acts increased the total sum to be made available and extended the period to be covered. In 1965 the Act was extended for a final 5 years. It authorized Exchequer Loans towards the cost of approved development programmes amounting to £125,000,000 and a ceiling of £390,000,000 for development and welfare assistance in the period 1941–1970. Thereafter the development needs of the remaining dependencies have been dealt with under the provisions of the Overseas Aid Act, 1966.

COMMONWEALTH COUNTRIES NOW MEMBER STATES

1931   Canada; Australia; New Zealand
In 1931 the Statute of Westminster clarified the legal position of Canada, Australia and New Zealand which had long been self-governing and independent states.

1947   India (Republic, 1950)
      Pakistan (Republic, 1956)
1948   Ceylon (Republic, 1970)
1957   Ghana, *formerly* Gold Coast (Republic, 1960)
      Malaya (an elective monarchy, now MALAYSIA; *see* Sabah and Sarawak, 1963)
      Cyprus (Republic, 1960; Cwlth. Member, 1961)
1960   Nigeria (Republic, 1963)
1961   Sierra Leone (Republic, 1971)
      Tanganyika (Republic, 1962; united 1964 with Zanzibar as TANZANIA)
1962   Jamaica; Trinidad and Tobago; Uganda
1963   Zanzibar; Kenya (Republic, 1964)
      Sabah   } in Federation of Malaysia (an
      Sarawak } elective monarchy)
      Singapore, as State in Federation of Malaysia, seceded as Republic, 1965
1964   Malawi (*formerly* Nyasaland Protectorate; Republic, 1966); Malta
      Zambia (Republic; *formerly* Northern Rhodesia)
1965   Gambia (The) (Republic, 1970)
      Guyana, *formerly* British Guiana (Republic, 1970)
      Botswana (Republic; *formerly* Bechuanaland Protectorate)
      Lesotho (Monarchy; *formerly* Basutoland)
      Barbados
1968   Mauritius; Nauru (Special Membership)
      Swaziland
1970   Fiji; Tonga

Associated States

From the dates shown, the following are fully self-governing states within the Commonwealth. The United Kingdom continues to be responsible for their defence and external relations:—

      Antigua (Feb. 27, 1967); Dominica (March 1 1967); Grenada (March 3, 1967); St. Christopher, Nevis and Anguilla (Feb. 27, 1967); St. Lucia (March 1, 1967); St. Vincent (Oct. 27, 1969).

Countries which have left the Commonwealth

1948   Burma; Palestine (mandate ended; State of Israel constituted May 15)
1949   Eire or Republic of Ireland
1956   Sudan
1960   British Somaliland (joined Italian Somaliland as SOMALI REPUBLIC).
1961   South Africa (on becoming a republic).
      Southern Cameroons (joined French Cameroons as CAMEROON REPUBLIC).
1963   Maldive Islands (ceased to be a protected state).
1967   Yemen P.D.R. (*formerly* Aden).

Canada

AREA AND POPULATION

Provinces or Territories and Capitals (with official contractions)	Area (English Sq. Miles). Land and Water	Population	
		Census, 1966	Estimated (April 1, 1970)
Alberta, *Alta.* (Edmonton)..................	255,285	1,463,203	1,593,000
British Columbia, *B.C.* (Victoria).............	366,255	1,873,674	2,128,000
Manitoba, *Man.* (Winnipeg)................	251,000	963,000	981,000
New Brunswick, *N.B.* (Fredericton)..........	28,354	616,788	623,000
Newfoundland, *Nfld.* (St. John's)...........	156,185	493,396	517,000
Nova Scotia, *N.S.* (Halifax).................	21,425	756,039	765,000
Ontario, *Ont.* (Toronto)....................	412,582	6,960,870	7,611,000
Prince Edward Island, *P.E.I.* (Charlottetown)....	2,184	107,535	109,000
Quebec, *P.Q.* (Quebec).....................	594,860	5,780,845	6,005,000
Saskatchewan, *Sask.* (Regina)................	251,700	955,344	943,000
Yukon Territory (Whitehorse)...............	207,076	14,382	16,000
Northwest Territories (Yellowknife)..........	1,304,903	28,738	33,000
Total.............	3,851,809	20,014,880	21,324,000

Land Area, 3,560,238 square miles; Water Area, 391,571 square miles. (For areas of individual provinces, excluding freshwater areas, *see* p. 200.)

Of the total immigration of 161,531 in 1969 31,977 were from the United Kingdom, 10,383 from Italy, 22,785 from the United States and 96,386 from some 160 other countries, including Ireland (1,235).

Increase of the People

Census Year	Population			Decennial Increase	Immigrants during Census Year
	Males	Females	Total		
1891..........	2,460,471	2,372,768	4,833,239	508,429	82,165
1901..........	2,751,708	2,619,607	5,371,315	538,076	55,747
1911..........	3,821,995	3,384,648	7,206,643	1,835,328	331,288
1921..........	4,529,643	4,258,306	8,787,949	1,581,306	91,728
1931..........	5,374,541	5,002,245	10,376,786	1,588,837	27,530
1941..........	5,900,536	5,606,119	11,506,655	1,129,869	9,329
1951..........	7,088,873	6,920,556	14,009,429	2,502,774	194,391
1956..........	8,151,879	7,928,912	16,080,791	..	164,857
1961..........	9,218,893	9,019,354	18,238,247	4,228,818	71,689
1966..........	10,054,344	9,960,536	20,014,880	..	194,743

Origins	1951	1961	Religions	1951	1961
British Races	6,709,685	7,996,669	Roman Catholic.......	6,069,496	8,342,826
English	3,630,344	4,195,175	United Church of Canada	2,867,271	2,128,000
Scottish	1,547,470	1,902,302	Anglican Church of Canada	2,060,720	2,409,068
Irish.................	1,439,635	1,753,351	Presbyterian............	781,747	818,558
Other	92,236	145,841	Baptist	519,585	593,553
European Races	6,872,889	9,657,195	Lutheran	444,923	662,744
French	4,319,167	5,540,346	Jewish	204,836	254,368
Austrian	32,231	106,535	Ukrainian (Greek) Catholic..	191,051	189,653
Belgian	35,148	61,382	Greek Orthodox.......	172,271	239,766
Czech and Slovak......	63,959	73,061	Mennonite	125,938	152,452
Finnish	43,745	59,436	Pentecostal	95,131	143,877
German	619,995	1,049,599	Salvation Army	70,275	92,054
Hungarian	60,460	126,220	Mormon	32,888	50,016
Italian	152,245	450,351	Church of Christ, Disciples................	14,920	19,512
Jewish	181,670	173,344	Christian Science	20,795	19,466
Netherlands..........	264,267	429,679	Adventist	21,398	25,999
Polish	219,845	323,517	Confucian and Buddhist..	13,975	16,700
Rumanian	23,601	43,805	Others	302,209	543,627
Russian	91,279	119,168			
Scandinavian..........	283,024	386,534	Totals	14,009,429	18,238,247
Ukrainian	395,043	473,337			
Other	87,210	240,881			
Asiatic Races..........	72,827	121,753			
Chinese	32,528	58,197			
Japanese	21,663	29,157			
Other	18,636	34,399	Indian population (1951) 155,874; (1961), 208,286. Eskimo population (1951) 9,733; (1961), 11,835.		
Indian and Eskimo	165,607	220,121			
All other	188,421	242,509			
Totals	14,009,429	18,238,247			

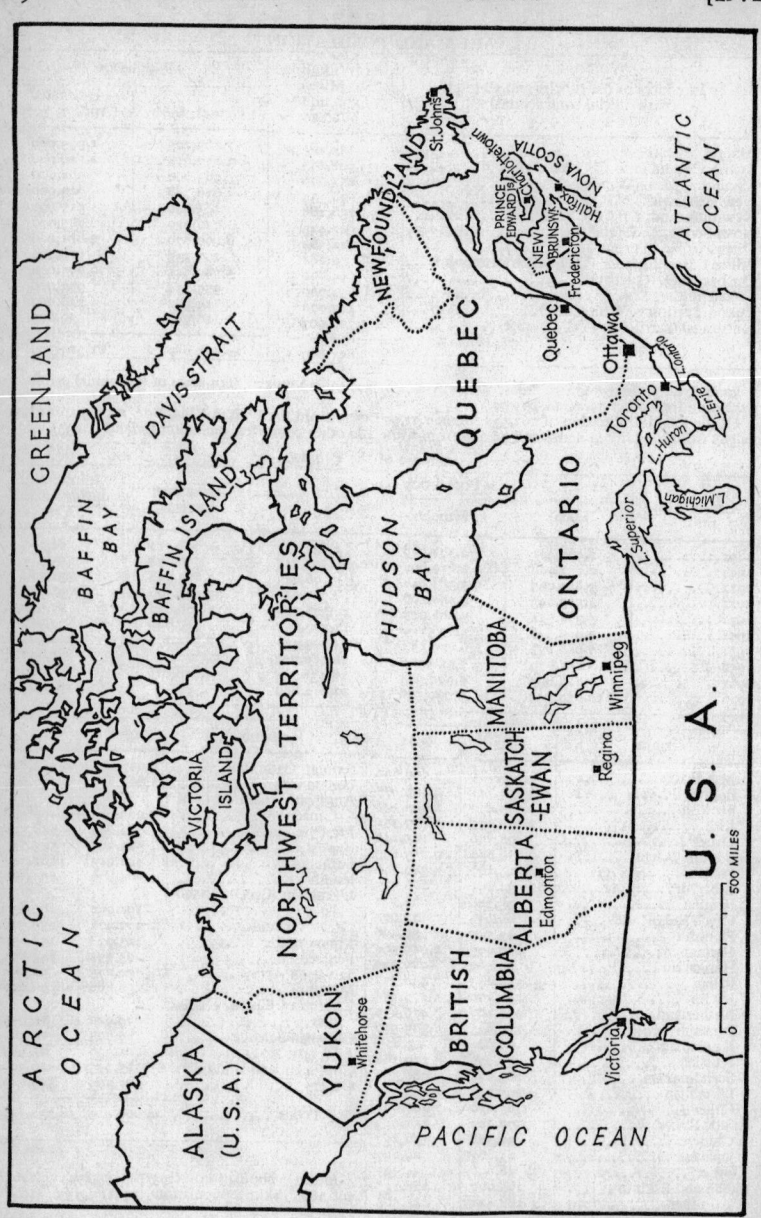

PHYSIOGRAPHY

Canada was originally discovered by Cabot in 1497, but its history dates only from 1534, when the French took possession of the country. The first permanent settlement at Port Royal (now Annapolis), Nova Scotia, was founded in 1605, and Quebec was founded in 1608. In 1759 Quebec was captured by the British forces under General Wolfe, and in 1763 the whole territory of Canada became a possession of Great Britain by the Treaty of Paris of that year. Nova Scotia was ceded in 1713 by the Treaty of Utrecht, the Provinces of New Brunswick and Prince Edward Island being subsequently formed out of it. British Columbia was formed into a Crown colony in 1858, having previously been a part of the Hudson Bay Territory, and was united to Vancouver Island in 1866.

Canada occupies the whole of the northern part of the North American Continent (with the exception of Alaska), from 49° North latitude to the North Pole, and from the Pacific to the Atlantic Ocean. In Eastern Canada, the southernmost point is Middle Island in Lake Erie, at 41° 41′.

Relief.—The relief of Canada is dominated by the mountain ranges running north and south on the west side of the Continent, by the Pre-Cambrian shield on the east, with, in between, the northern extension of the North American Plain. From the physiographic point of view Canada has six main divisions. These are: (1) Appalachian–Acadian Region, (2) the Canadian Shield, (3) the St. Lawrence–Great Lakes Lowland, (4) the Interior Plains, (5) the Cordilleran Region and (6) the Arctic Archipelago. The first region occupies all that part of Canada lying southeast of the St. Lawrence. In general, the relief is an alternation of highlands and lowlands, and is hilly rather than mountainous. The lowlands area seldom rises over 600 feet above sea level. The great Canadian Shield comprises more than half the area. The interior as a whole is an undulating, low plateau (general level 1,000 to 1,500 feet), with the more rugged relief lying along the border between Northern Quebec and Labrador. Throughout the whole area water or muskeg-filled depressions separate irregular hills and ridges, 150 to 200 feet in elevation. Newfoundland, an outlying portion of the shield, consists of glaciated, low rolling terrain broken here and there by mountains. The flat relief of the St. Lawrence–Great Lakes lowland varies from 500 feet in the east to 1,700 feet south of Georgian Bay. The whole area in the western part slopes gently to the Great Lakes. The most striking relief is provided by the eastward facing scarp of the Niagara escarpment (elevation 250 to 300 feet). The interior plains, comprising the Prairie Provinces, slope eastward and northward a few feet per mile. The descent from west to east is made from 5,000 feet to less than 1,000 feet in three distinct levels, with each new level being marked by an eastward facing *coteau* or scarp. Horizontal strata and peneplanation make for slight relief of the level to rolling type. Five fairly well-developed topographic divisions mark out the Cordilleran region of western Canada. These are: (1) coastal ranges, largely above 5,000 feet with deep fiords and glaciated valleys, (2) the interior plateau, around 3,500 feet and comparatively level, (3) the Selkirk ranges, largely above 5,000 feet, (4) the Rocky Mountains with their chain of 10,000 to 12,000-feet peaks, and (5) the Peace River or Tramontane region with its rolling diversified country. The Arctic Archipelago, with its plateau-like character has an elevation between 500 and 1,000 feet, though in Baffin Land and Ellesmere Island the mountain ranges rise to 8,500 and 9,500 feet. Two tremendous waterway systems, the St. Lawrence and the Mackenzie, providing thousands of miles of water highway, occupy a broad area of lowland with their dominant axis following the edge of the shield.

Climate.—The climate of the eastern and central portions presents greater extremes than in corresponding latitudes in Europe, but in the southwestern portion of the Prairie Region and the southern portions of the Pacific slope the climate is milder. Spring, summer, and autumn are of about seven to eight months' duration, and the winter four to five months.

GOVERNMENT

The Constitution of Canada has its source in the British North America Act of 1867 which formed a Dominion, under the name of Canada, of the four provinces: Ontario, Quebec, New Brunswick and Nova Scotia; to this Federation the other Provinces have subsequently been admitted. Under this Act Canada came into being on July 1, 1867 (Dominion Day), and under the Statute of Westminster, which received the royal assent on Dec. 11, 1931, Canada and the Provinces were exempted (in common with other self-governing Dominions of the Commonwealth of Nations) from the operation of the Colonial Laws Validity Act, the Statute of Westminster having removed all limitations with regard to the legislative autonomy of the Dominions. Provinces admitted since 1867 are: Manitoba (1870), British Columbia (1871), Prince Edward Island (1873), Alberta and Saskatchewan (1905) and Newfoundland (1949).

The Executive power is vested in a Governor-General appointed by the Sovereign on the advice of the Canadian Ministry, and aided by a Privy Council.

FLAG.—Red maple leaf with 11 points on white square, flanked by vertical red bars one half the width of the square.

GOVERNOR GENERAL AND STAFF

Governor-General and Commander-in-Chief, His Excellency the Right Hon. ROLAND MICHENER, C.D. born April 19, 1900, assumed office April 17, 1967.
Secretary to the Governor-General, E. U. Butler.
Assistant Secretary, Brig.-Gen. L.-F. Trudeau, D.S.O., O.B.E., C.D.
Deputy Asst. Secretary and Registrar of the Order of Canada, R. de C. Nantel, C.D.
Comptroller of the Household, Capt. (S.) D. C. McKinnon, C.D.
Attaché, P. McKellar.
Aides-de Camp, Capt. (S) P. M. Goineau; Capt. (A) J. M. P. Bourget; Capt. (L) J. A. Lemay.

THE CANADIAN MINISTRY
THE FEDERAL CABINET

Prime Minister, Rt. Hon. Pierre Elliott Trudeau.
Government Leader in the Senate, Hon. Paul Martin.
External Affairs, Hon. Mitchell Sharp.
Solicitor-General, Hon. Jean-Pierre Goyer.
Public Works, Hon. Arthur Laing.

Manpower and Immigration, Hon. Otto E. Lang (and Canadian Wheat Board).
President of the Treasury Board, Hon. Charles M. Drury.
Finance and Receiver-General, Hon. Edgar J. Benson.
National Defence, Hon. Donald S. Macdonald.
Industry, Trade and Commerce, Hon. Jean-Luc Pépin.

Regional Economic Expansion, Hon. Jean Marchand.
Energy, Mines and Resources, Hon. John J. Greene.
National Revenue, Hon. Herbert Gray.
Justice and Attorney-General, Hon. John N. Turner.
Indian Affairs and Northern Development, Hon.
Jean Chrétien.
Labour, Hon. Bryce S. Mackasey.
President of Queen's Privy Council, Hon. Allan J.
MacEachen.
National Health and Welfare, Hon. John C. Munro.
Secretary of State, Hon. Gérard Pelletier.
Fisheries and Forestry, Hon. Jack Davis.
Agriculture, Hon. Horace A. Olson.
Veterans Affairs, Hon. Jean-Eudes Dubé.
Consumer and Corporate Affairs, Hon. Ronald
Basford.
Supply and Services, Hon. James A. Richardson.
Transport, Hon. Donald C. Jamieson.
Communications and Postmaster-General, Hon.
Robert Stanbury.
Ministers without Portfolio, Hon. Robert K. Andras;
Hon. Joseph Jean-Pierre Coté; Hon. Martin
O'Connell; Hon. Joseph Julien (*Post Office*).
Minister of State for Science and Technology, Hon.
Alistair Gillespie.
Leader of the Opposition, Hon. Robert L. Stanfield,
$15,000.

The Prime Minister receives remuneration of
$25,000; other ministers, each $15,000; without
Portfolio, $7,500. In every case—including the
Prime Minister's—a sessional allowance of
$12,000 *per annum* is paid to a Minister of the
Crown as a member of either the Senate or
the House of Commons in Canada. A motor
vehicle allowance of $2,000 is paid to each Minister
of the Crown and to the Leader of the Opposition
in the House of Commons; these allowances are not
taxable. Senators receive an annual expense
allowance of $3,000 and Members of Parliament
receive an expense allowance of $6,000, neither of
which is subject to income tax.

CANADIAN HIGH COMMISSION

Canada House, Trafalgar Square, London, W.C.2.—
[01-930-9741]
High Commissioner, His Excellency Charles Stewart
Almon Ritchie (1967). × *J. H. WARREN*
Deputy High Commissioner, R. L. Rogers.
Minister, C. J. Van Tighem (*Commercial*).
Minister-Counsellor, R. M. Tait (*Economic*).
Counsellors, I. R. Smyth (*Commercial*); F. M. Meech
(*Administration*); A. D. Small; D. R. Hill; M.
André Potvin; J. W. Graham; D. M. Miller;
I. C. Clark (*Information*); G. E. Blackstock (*Commercial*); K. D. Taylor (*Commercial*); A. de W.
Mathewson; W. L. Haney (*Nat. Research Council*);
Dr. G. Schonning (*Labour*); N. A. Smith (*Nat.
Research Council*); Dr. W. Petrie (*Defence Research*); J. L. Orr (*Scientific*); E. W. Greenwood
(*Defence Research*); O. W. Bennett (*Defence
Production*).
1st Secretaries, T. D. McGhee (*Commercial*); T. A.
Charles (*Commercial*); J. C. Bradford (*Commercial*).
Commander, Defence Liaison Staff, Brig.-Gen.
D. W. Cunnington, G.M.

BRITISH HIGH COMMISSION

80 Elgin Street, Ottawa 4

High Commissioner, His Excellency Sir Peter Telford
Hayman, K.C.M.G., C.V.O., M.B.E. £14,000
Deputy High Commissioner and Minister (Commercial), G. S. Whitehead, C.M.G., M.V.O.
Counsellors, The Viscount Dunrossil (*Head of
Chancery*); B. E. P. MacTavish (*Commercial*);
P. R. Noakes, O.B.E. (*Information*); D. F. Downing
(*Scientific*); J. A. Cayton, O.B.E. (*Cultural Affairs*);

Air Cdre. H. E. C. Boxer, C.B., O.B.E. (*Defence
Equipment*).
Defence Adviser, Cdr. H. H. Cook, R.N.
Air Adviser, Gp. Capt. Groocock, A.F.C.
Naval Adviser, Capt. H. D. S. Waite, R.N.
Military Adviser, Col. K. Neely, M.B.E.
1st Secretaries, D. J. Wyatt; J. R. S. Guinness (*Commercial*); E. T. Davies; D. A. MacLeod; B. Coleman (*Information*); J. S. Clayden (*Admin.*); R. C.
Carroll (*Commercial*); B. Coleman (*Information*);
D. K. Urquhart (*Defence Equipment*); A. H.
Dartnall (*Information*).
British Council Representative, F. D. Hughes, O.B.E.

THE LEGISLATURE

Parliament consists of a Senate and a House of
Commons. The *Senate* consists of 102 members,
nominated by the Governor-General (age limit
75). They are distributed between the various
provinces thus: 24 each for *Ontario,* and *Quebec,* 10
each for *Nova Scotia* and *New Brunswick,* 6 each for
Newfoundland, British Columbia, Manitoba, Alberta,
and *Saskatchewan* and 4 for *Prince Edward Island;*
each Senator must be at least thirty years
old, a resident in the province for which he is
appointed, a natural-born or naturalized subject
of the Queen, and the owner of a property qualification amounting to $4,000. The Speaker of the
Senate is chosen by the Government of the day.
The *House of Commons* is elected every five years at
longest.

The House of Commons has 264 members.
Representation by provinces is at present as follows:
Newfoundland 7, Prince Edward Island 4, Nova
Scotia 11, New Brunswick 10, Quebec 74, Ontario
88, Manitoba 13, Saskatchewan 13, Alberta 19,
British Columbia 23, Yukon 1, Northwest Territories 1.

The Senate.

Speaker of the Senate, Hon. Jean-Paul Deschatelet (*with Member's annual indemnity $12,000, residence allowance $3,000, expense allowance $3,000, motor-car allowance $1,000 and Salary $9,000*).....	$28,000
Clerk of the Senate & Clerk of the Parliaments, Robert Fortier..............	29,000

The House of Commons.

Speaker of the House of Commons, Hon. Lucien Lamoureux (*with Member's annual indemnity $12,000, expense allowance $6,000, car allowance $1,000, residence allowance $3,000 and salary $9,000*)....................	31,000
Deputy Speaker, H. Faulkner (*with Member's annual indemnity $12,000, expense allowance $6,000, residence allowance, $1,500 and salary $6,000*)............	25,500
Clerk of the House of Commons, Alistair Fraser.................	29,000

THE JUDICATURE

The Judicature is administered by judges
following the Civil Law in Quebec Province and
Common Law in other Provinces. All Superior
and County Court Judges are appointed by the
Governor-General, the others by the Lieutenant-
Governors of the Provinces, until age 70, except
present incumbents who may remain until age 75.
Each Province has its Court of Appeal and the
highest court is the Supreme Court of Canada,
composed of a Chief Justice and eight puisne judges,
which holds three sessions each year. There is only
one other Dominion Court, the Federal Court of
Canada which has both a trial and an appeal
division and which replaces the Exchequer Court
with expanded jurisdiction.

Chief Justice of Canada, Rt. Hon. Gerald
  Fauteux.................... $42,000
  Supreme Court of Canada.
Chief Justice of Canada, Rt. Hon. Joseph
  H. G. Fauteux.................... $40,000
Puisne Judges, Hon. D. C. Abbott, P.C.;
  Hon. R. Martland; Hon. W. Judson;
  Hon. R. A. Ritchie; Hon. E. M. Hall;
  Hon. W. F. Spence; Hon. L-P. Pigeon;
  Hon. B. Laskin ....each $37,000
  Federal Court of Canada
Chief Justice, Hon. W. R. Jackett, P.C..... $34,000
Associate Chief Justice, Hon. C. Noel.
Court of Appeal Judges, Hon. J. Dumoulin;
  Hon. A. L. Thurlow.
Trial Division Judges, Hon. A. A. Cattanach; Hon. H. F. Gibson; Hon. A. A.
  M. Walsh; Hon. R. Kerr; Hon. L.
  Pratte..........................each $30,000

NATIONAL DEFENCE

On Aug. 1, 1964, the Headquarters of the Royal
Canadian Navy, the Canadian Army and the Royal
Canadian Air Force were integrated to form a single
Canadian Forces Headquarters (C.F.H.Q.) under a
single Chief of Defence Staff. The role of C.F.H.Q.
is to provide military advice to the Minister of
National Defence and to control and administer the
Canadian Forces, which are organized in seven
major commands: *Mobile Command* (units for support of the United Nations or other peacekeeping
operations; ground forces, with tactical air support,
for the protection of Canadian territory; combat
forces in Canada for support of overseas commitments); *Maritime Command* (all sea and air forces on
the Atlantic and Pacific coasts for defence of
Canada against attack by sea, provision of antisubmarine defence in support of N.A.T.O., conduct of search and rescue operations and sea transport in support of Mobile Command; No. 1 Air
Division (the Canadian contribution to strike reconnaissance forces available to the Supreme Allied
Commander Europe (SACEUR); *Air Defence
Command* (participates with U.S.A. in air defence of
North America through NORAD; *Air Transport
Command* (air transport for all Canadian forces;
search and rescue operations in Ontario and Quebec); *Training Command; Canadian Forces Communications System.* In addition there is a *Reserve
and Survival Organization* (aid to the civil power,
emergency forces for national survival). Armed
Forces expenditure in each of the three years to
1972 was estimated at $1,800 m.
Chief of Defence Staff, Lt.-Gen. F. Sharp.

In October, 1969, the total strength of the
Canadian Armed Forces was 95,019—Royal
Canadian Navy, 17,555; Canadian Army, 36,255;
Royal Canadian Air Force, 42,100.

EDUCATION AND LANGUAGE

Education is under the control of the Provincial
Governments, the cost of the publicly controlled
schools being met by local taxation, aided by
provincial grants. There were (1968–69) 16,532
publicly controlled schools with 5,318,760 pupils.
In addition there were 144,111 pupils in 1,190
private elementary, secondary and commercial
schools. There are special schools for Indians with
29,472 pupils (1968–69). In 1968–69, there were
nearly 110 universities and colleges with a full-time
university grade enrolment of 270,093. Sixty-four
of the total were degree-granting institutions.

Canada has two official languages, English and
French. At the 1961 census 67·4 per cent. of
the total population gave English and 19·1 per
cent. gave French as their native tongue. Some
2,231,172 (or 12·2 per cent.) are bilingual.

VITAL STATISTICS
BIRTHS, DEATHS AND MARRIAGES, 1968

Province	Births	Deaths	Marriages
Alberta............	30,149	9,963	13,640
British Columbia....	33,687	16,828	16,914
Manitoba...........	17,424	7,878	8,291
New Brunswick.....	11,607	4,995	5,389
Newfoundland......	12,820	3,123	4,242
Nova Scotia.......	13,774	6,610	6,284
Ontario...........	126,257	55,552	62,109
P.E.I.............	2,105	990	750
Quebec...........	96,622	39,537	46,004
Saskatchewan......	18,197	7,498	7,747
Yukon.............	370	84	170
N. W. Territories....	1,298	228	226
	364,310	153,196	171,766

Canada's Birth Rate per 1,000 population (1968)
17·6; Death Rate 7·4; Marriage Rate 8·3; Divorces
(1968) 10,750.

REVENUE AND EXPENDITURE

Year ended March 31	Total Revenue	Total Expenditure
	$	$
1966	7,695,820,204	7,734,795,525
1967	8,358,178,383	8,779,680,996
1968	9,029,305,904	9,824,080,573
1969	10,191,135,794	10,767,248,637

DEBT

Year ended March 31	Gross Public Debt	Net Public Debt
1965	$26,573,425,709	$15,504,472,544
1966	27,428,940,350	15,543,447,865
1967	30,340,137,314	15,964,950,478
1968	32,924,170,009	16,759,725,147
1969	35,919,260,883	17,335,837,990

Banking.—There were 10 chartered banks on
April 30, 1970, with assets of $42,863,048,000.
Deposits were $39,056,136,000 of which
$15,815,467,000 were personal savings.

TRADE

Total trade of Canada in 1969 was valued at
$14,441,556,000 (exports) and $14,201,627,000
(imports). Value of trade with Canada's largest
trading partners in 1969 was as follows:

Country	Imports	Exports
	$	$
United Kingdom	790,974,000	1,096,480,000
Australia.........	96,285,000	163,258,000
Belgolux C'tries..	60,936,000	116,232,000
Brazil..........	42,128,000	50,246,000
France..........	153,712,000	124,708,000
W. Germany....	354,714,000	277,382,000
Hong Kong.....	72,942,000	17,678,000
India...........	40,905,000	95,552,000
Italy...........	141,117,000	133,671,000
Jamaica........	45,978,000	40,481,000
Japan..........	495,704,000	624,837,000
Mexico.........	64,067,000	72,872,000
Netherlands.....	78,679,000	184,966,000
Norway........	44,895,000	103,645,000
South Africa....	45,944,000	78,513,000
Spain..........	28,714,000	55,908,000
Sweden........	84,505,000	41,278,000
Switzerland.....	83,926,000	34,239,000
United States....	10,312,631,000	10,215,400,000
Venezuela......	345,596,000	92,902,000

Board of Trade figures of Canada's trade with the United Kingdom are:

	1969	1970
Imports from U.K..	£300,633,000	£288,123,000
Exports to U.K.....	504,858,000	682,732,000

CANADIAN PRODUCTION

Agriculture.—About 8 per cent. of the total land area of Canada is classified as farm land and approximately half of this is under cultivation, the remainder being woodland or suitable only for grazing purposes. Three-quarters of the land at present cultivated is found in the prairie region of Western Canada. The cash benefits for the sale of farm products in 1969 were $4,195,593,000. Livestock and poultry contributed $2,948,036,000; field crops (1968) $2,278,534,000 and dairy products (1969) $676,948,000.

Canadian grain crops (in thousands of bushels):

ALL CANADA	1967	1968	1969
Wheat.......	592,920	649,844	684,276
Oats.........	304,178	362,576	371,387
Barley.......	248,662	325,373	378,383
Rye.........	11,984	13,049	16,493
Flaxseed......	9,378	18,166	30,748

Livestock.—On June 1, 1969, the livestock included 341,300 horses, 12,467,000 cattle, 883,000 sheep, 5,792,000 hogs and 71,744,000 poultry. The total milk production in 1969 was 18,698,085,000 lb.; butter, 355,585,000 lb.; factory cheese, 206,576,000 lb.; concentrated milk products, 820,282,000 lb.; ice cream mix, 29,071,000 gallons.

Fur Production.—There were 2,585 fur farms in Canada in 1968-69 producing 1,688,969 pelts valued at $22,925,933, mink contributing 99 per cent. of the total. Wild life pelts totalled 3,920,332 with a value of $18,663,153.

Fisheries.—The total value of the fish marketed in 1967 was $330,222,000.

Forestry.—About 57 per cent. of the total land area is in forests, with almost 1,710,788 sq. miles capable of producing merchantable timber. The value of forest products in 1967 was: newsprint $998,019,000; lumber $803,262,000; paper (other than newsprint) $544,707,000; pulp (exports only) $627,874,000.

Minerals.—Canada was, in 1969, the world's greatest producer of nickel and zinc, and ranked second in asbestos, molybdenum, silver, sulphur, titanium oxide, and uranium. The value of the principal minerals produced in 1969 was: crude petroleum $1,010,230,132; copper $574,193,275; nickel $482,412,858; iron ore $431,930,310; zinc $364,390,237; natural gas $263,564,593; asbestos $196,759,000; cement $171,257,887; Natural gas by product $135,566,258; sand and gravel $130,650,000; lead $95,391,671; gold $94,331,773.

COMMUNICATIONS

Railways.—The total first main track mileage of railways in operation on Dec. 31, 1968, was 43,168 miles, the capital of the railways being $5,301,133,608; operating revenues $1,528,962,071; and operating expenses $1,437,735,624. In 1968 the passengers carried on railways numbered 24,603,604, and revenue freight 242,653,709 tons.

Shipping.—The registered shipping on Dec. 31 1967, including inland vessels, was 26,451 vessels with gross tonnage 3,668,429.

Canals.—In 1968 the number of vessel passages through 11 Canadian canal systems was 20,378 and the registered net tonnage was 79,385,174. The St. Lawrence Canals and the Welland Canal carried 33,611,648 and 42,613,881, or 96 per cent. of the total.

Civil Aviation.—The number of revenue-producing passengers carried in 1968 (all carriers) was 9,305,328. Revenue cargo was 194,196 tons.

Motor Vehicles.—Total motor vehicle registrations numbered 7,877,547 in 1968.

Post.—There were 10,450 post offices on March 31, 1969, and 5,561 rural and urban mail routes serving 697,808 households and businesses. Total postal revenue was $374,902,000 in the fiscal year 1968-69; total expenditure $463,089,000.

YUKON TERRITORY

The Yukon Act, 1952, as amended, provides for the administration of the Territory by a Commissioner acting under instructions from time to time given by the Governor in Council or the Minister of Indian Affairs and Northern Development. Legislative powers, analogous to those of a provincial government, are exercised by the Commissioner in Council. The Council comprises seven members elected from electoral districts in the Territory. The area of the Territory is 207,076 square miles with a population (April 1, 1970) of 16,000. Mining is the chief industry, though trapping remains important and there is considerable timber production. Mining production, including asbestos, copper, silver, lead, zinc, and gold, was valued at $37,655,800 in 1969.

SEAT OF GOVERNMENT, Whitehorse. Pop. (1966) 4,771.

Commissioner, J. Smith.

NORTHWEST TERRITORIES

Area 1,304,903 square miles; population (estimated, April 1, 1970) 33,000.

The Northwest Territories are subdivided into the districts of Mackenzie, Keewatin and Franklin.

The chief industry of the Northwest Territories is mining, with a total value of $116,456,132 in 1969. Zinc and lead contributed 84 per cent. of the total. Gold, silver and crude petroleum are the next most valuable minerals.

SEAT OF GOVERNMENT.—On May 1, 1967, the territorial government was moved from Ottawa to Yellowknife, and all meetings of the Council are held there.

Commissioner, S. M. Hodgson.

PROVINCES OF CANADA

ALBERTA

Area and Population.—The Province of Alberta has an area of 255,285 square miles, including about 6,485 square miles of water, with a population (estimated April, 1971) of 1,628,000.

Government.—The Government is vested in a Lieutenant-Governor and Legislative Assembly composed of 65 members, elected for five years, representing 65 electoral districts in the Province.

At a provincial election held in August, 1971, the Progressive Conservative Party took 48 seats, Social Credit Party (in office for the past 36 years), 26, and the New Democratic Party, one seat.

Lieut.-Governor, His Honour J. W. Grant MacEwan (1966) ....*special allowance*

Executive

Premier, and President of Council, Hon. Peter Lougheed........................ $18,000

The outgoing Social Credit government had been organized in 14 Ministries (Health and Environment, Social Development, Municipal Affairs, Attorney General, Public Works, Agriculture, Lands and Forests, Education, Highways and Transport, Labour and Telephones, Industry and Tourism, Provincial Treasurer, Mines and Minerals, Culture Youth and Recreation) and there were two Ministries without Portfolio. (*Details of Mr. Lougheed's Ministry were not available at the time of going to press.*)
Ministers, each $15,000; *without Portfolio*, each $4,800.

Speaker of the Legislative Assembly, Hon. A. J. Dixon $12,000
Deputy Speaker, A. H. Cooper 9,600
Leader of the Opposition, P. Lougheed 10,800
Clerk of the Executive Council and Clerk of the Legislative Assembly, W. H. MacDonald.

The Judicature.
The Supreme Court of Alberta.
Appellate Division, Hon. S. B. Smith (*C.J.*) $30,000
Judges, Hons. J. M. Cairns; C. W. Clement; H. G. Johnson; E. W. S. Kane; N. D. McDermid; G. H. Allen each 26,000
Trial Division, Hon. J. V. H. Milvain (*C.J.*) 30,000
Judges, Hons. N. Primrose; P. Greschuk; H. W. Riley; M. E. Manning; W. J. C. Kirby; A. M. Dechene; M. B. O'Byrne; W. S. Sinclair; H. J. MacDonald; S. S. Lieberman; A. J. Cullen 26,000

London Office, Dept. of Industry and Tourism, 37 Hill Street, W.1.
Production.—The mining, manufacturing and construction industries have increased in economic impact so much more forcibly, that agriculture is no longer of prime importance in Alberta.
The net value of production by industries (estimated 1971) is: mining $1,270,000,000; manufacturing $650,000,000; construction $790,000,000; agriculture $625,000,000; electric power $107,000,000; forestry $7,000,000; trapping $1,900,000; fisheries $1,100,000. Total $3,452,000,000.
Mining (1970 estimates):—Crude oil $991,300,000; natural gas $243,900,000; natural gas by-products $144,000,000; sulphur $27,400,000; cement $19,730,000; coal $26,710,000.
Manufacturing.—The gross value of output in 1969 was $1,815,492,000. Number of industrial establishments 1,977 total employees 51,650, salaries and wages $323,208,498. The leading industries are meat packing, oil refining, dairy and poultry products, iron and steel products, industrial chemicals and plastics, flour and feed milling, timber products, pulp and paper mills, printing and publishing, and brewing and distilling.
Finance.—Net Funded Debt, Mar. 31, 1970, $37,320,713. Revenue, March 31, 1970, $933,160,911; Expenditure, March 31, 1970, $962,059,843.
CAPITAL.—Edmonton. Population (1971), 435,000. Other centres are Calgary (398,000), Lethbridge (40,856), Medicine Hat (25,813) and Red Deer (27,000).

BRITISH COLUMBIA

Area and Population.—British Columbia has a total area estimated at 366,255 square miles, with a population of 1,873,674 at the census of June 1, 1966; estimated, Dec. 31, 1970, 2,187,000.

Government.—The Government consists of a Lieutenant-Governor and an Executive Council together with a Legislative Assembly of 55 members.
Lieut.-Governor, Col. the Hon. J. R. Nicholson, P.C., O.B.E., Q.C.

Executive Council
Premier, President of the Council and Minister of Finance, Hon. W. A. C. Bennett, P.C. $23,000
Provincial Secretary and Minister of Highways, Hon. W. D. Black 20,000
Attorney-General and Minister of Labour, Hon. L. R. Peterson, Q.C. 20,000
Lands, Forests and Water Resources, Hon. R. G. Williston 20,000
Agriculture, Hon. C. M. Shelford 20,000
Mines and Petroleum Resources and Commercial Transport, Hon. F. X. Richter.. 20,000
Education, Hon. D. L. Brothers, Q.C. 20,000
Industrial Development, Trade and Commerce, Hon. W. McT. Skillings 20,000
Municipal Affairs and Social Welfare, Hon. D. R. J. Campbell 20,000
Health Services and Hospital Insurance, Hon. R. R. Loffmark 20,000
Public Works, Hon. W. N. Chant 20,000
Recreation, Conservation and Travel Industry, Hon. W. K. Kiernan 20,000
Rehabilitation and Social Improvement, Hon. P. A. Gaglardi 20,000
Ministers without Portfolio, Hon. Isabel P. Dawson; Hon. Patricia P. Jordan; Hon. Grace M. McCarthy .... each 6,500

Speaker, Legislative Assembly, Hon. W. H. Murray $9,000

The Judicature.
Court of Appeal—Chief Justice of British Columbia, Hon. H. W. Davey $30,000
Justices of Appeal, Hons. C. W. Tysoe; E. B. Bull; H. A. Maclean; M. M. McFarlane; A. E. Branca; A. B. Robertson; N. T. Nemetz; J. D. Taggart..... 26,000
Supreme Court—Chief Justice, Hon. J. O. Wilson.............................. 30,000
Puisne Judges, Hons. J. G. Ruttan; D. R. Verchere; R. A. B. Wootton; F. C. Munroe; J. S. Aikins; V. L. Dryer; G. F. T. Gregory; J. G. Gould; T. A. Dohm; J. A. Macdonald; P. D. Seaton; W. R. McIntyre; W. K. Smith; G. G. S. Rae; A. B. Macfarlane; E. E. Hinkson each 26,000
Deputy Judge, Exchequer Court, F. A. Sheppard.
Deputy District Judge in Admiralty, Hon. C. W. Tysoe.

Agent-General in London, Rear Adm. M. G. Stirling, British Columbia House, 1 Regent Street, S.W.1.
Finances—Estimated current Revenue for 1971-72, $1,301,232,415. Estimated current expenditure, including all capital expenditure, $1,165,460,000 There is no direct debt.
Production and Industry.—The production levels of the four leading industries were estimated for 1970 as follows: forestry $1,762,000,000; minerals, $485,234,000; agriculture $205,050,000; fisheries $123,300,000. Manufacturing activity is based largely on the processing of products of the four main basic industries. The principal manufacturing centres are Vancouver, New Westminster, Victoria,

North Vancouver and Port Moody. Forestry and forest-based industries form the most important economic activity, accounting for approximately 40 per cent. of total production. British Columbia is the leading province of Canada in the quantity and value of its timber and sawmill products. Mining, the second most important economic activity, is based on copper, zinc, lead, iron concentrates, molybdenum, natural gas, crude petroleum, asbestos and nickel. Molybdenum production is approximately 90 per cent. of the Canadian total. The most important agricultural products are livestock, eggs and poultry, fruits and dairy products. Salmon accounts for approximately 80 per cent. of the value of fisheries. Other species include halibut, herring, soles, cod, flounder, perch, tuna and shellfish. The climate is healthy, quite moderate on the coast and continental east of the coast mountains. The economy is dependent upon markets outside the province for the disposal of most of the products of her industry. Canadian and world markets receive forestry, mineral, fishing and agricultural products.

Transport.—The province has deep water harbours which are well serviced by railways and modern paved highways. Vancouver is the base for regular scheduled air routes to other parts of Canada, the United States, Europe, Mexico, South America, Hawaii, Australia, and Japan.

Principal Cities.—CAPITAL, Ψ VICTORIA. Metropolitan population (1966 census) 173,455. Ψ Vancouver (founded in 1886), the largest city in the Province, metropolitan population (1966 census) 892,286, is the western terminus of the Canadian Pacific Railway and the Canadian National Railways (the C.N.R. also has a terminus at Prince Rupert) and the southern terminus of the Pacific Great Eastern Railway, and possesses one of the finest natural harbours in the world. Other towns and cities are Prince George 24,471), Kamloops (22,078) and Kelowna (17,006).

MANITOBA

Area and Population.—Manitoba, originally the Red River settlement, is the central province of Canada. The Province has a considerable area of prairie land but is also a land of wide diversity combining 400 miles of sea-coast, large lakes and rivers covering an area of 39,225 square miles and Precambrian rock which covers about three-fifths of the Province. The total area is 251,000 square miles with a population, estimated, 1970, of 981,000.

Government.—The Government is administered by a Lieutenant-Governor, assisted by an Executive Council of 13 Ministers, who are members of the Legislative Assembly of 57 members. Each member of the Legislative Assembly receives an annual sessional indemnity of $7,200.

At the General Election held on June 25, 1969, the Progressive Conservative Party led by the Premier, Mr. Walter Weir, was defeated, the New Democratic Party led by Mr. Schreyer gaining 16 seats in the Legislature. Mr. Schreyer formed a ministry on July 9, 1969 (*see below*). Two by-elections held in April, 1971, were won by the N.D.P. Standing in the House on June 1, 1971, was: N.D.P. 31; Conservative 21; Liberal, 3; Social Credit, 1; Independent, 1, when a Liberal Democrat joined the N.D.P. caucus.

Lieut.-Governor, His Honour W. J. McKeag (1970).

Executive

Premier, President of the Council, Minister of Dominion-Provincial Relations, Hon. Edward Richard Schreyer............ $23,800

Minister of Finance, Hon. Saul M. Cherniack, Q.C.
Labour, Hon. A. R. (Russ) Paulley.
Attorney-General, Hon. Alvin H. Mackling.
Health and Social Development, Hon. René E. Toupin.
Agriculture and Co-operative Development, Hon. Samuel Uskiw.
Mines, Resources and Environmental Management and Commissioner of Northern Affairs, Hon. Sydney Green.
Tourism, Recreation and Cultural Affairs, Hon. Peter Burtniak.
Youth and Education, Hon. Saul A. Miller.
Public Works and Highways, Hon. J. P. Borowski.
Municipal Affairs, Hon. Howard Pawley.
Industry and Commerce, Hon. Leonard Evans.
Consumer and Corporate Affairs and Internal Services, Hon. Ben Hanuschak.
Without Portfolio, Hon. Russell Doern.
Ministers each $22,800

Speaker of the Legislative Assembly, Hon. B. Hanuschap.

The Judicature

Court of Appeal:—
Chief Justice of Manitoba, Hon. Samuel Freedman........................ $30,000
Puisne Judges, Hons. R. D. Guy; A. M. Monnin; R. G. B. Dickson; G. C. Hall........................each 26,000

Queen's Bench:—
Chief Justice, Q.B.D., Hon. G. E. Tritschler..................... 30,000
Puisne Judges, Hons. F. M. Bastin; I. Nitikman; L. Deniset; J. E. Wilson; R. Matas; J. M. Hunt; J. R. Solomon each 26,000

Finance.—The revenue of the provincial government, 1970–71, was $448,868,819 and the expenditure $448,043,500.

Agriculture and Live Stock.—The total land area in Manitoba is 135,536,000 acres, of which 7,461,000 acres were under field crops in June 1970. The gross value of agricultural production in 1970 was estimated at $471,000,000, of which field crops represented $247,000,000 and livestock $221,000,000. Farm animals in June, 1970, numbered 1,120,000 cattle, 884,000 pigs, 47,000 sheep, 30,000 horses and 6,340,000 poultry.

Manufactures.—The gross annual value of manufactured products is estimated at $1,215,000,000. Manufacturing enterprises employed about 50,200 persons. The chief manufacturing centres are Winnipeg, St. Boniface, St. James-Assiniboia, Brandon and Selkirk. The largest manufacturing industry is the food and beverage industry, followed by the metal fabricating and clothing industries.

CAPITAL.—Winnipeg, population (estimated, 1970), 249,886 (Greater Winnipeg, 535,000). Other centres are Brandon (35,500), Thompson (23,000) and Portage la Prairie (13,200).

NEW BRUNSWICK

Area and Population.—New Brunswick is situated between 45°–48° N. lat. and 63° 47′–69° W. long. and comprises an area of 27,085 square miles with an estimated population (1970) of 623,000. It was first colonized by British subjects in 1761, and in 1783 by inhabitants of New England, who had been dispossessed of their property in consequence of their loyalty to the British Crown.

Government.—The Government is administered by a Lieutenant-Governor, assisted by an Executive Council, and a Legislative Assembly of 58 members elected by the people. At the General Election

of October 26, 1970, 32 Conservative and 26 Liberal members were returned.

Lieutenant-Governor, His Honour W. S. Bird (1967)......................... $18,000

Executive.

Premier, Hon. Richard B. Hatfield....... $20,000
Justice, Hon. J. B. M. Baxter.
Finance, Hon. J. M. Simard.
Public Works and Highways, Hon. J. S. Brooks.
Economic Growth, Agriculture and Rural Development, Hon. A. E. Stairs.
Health and Welfare, Hon. P. S. Creughan.
Education, Hon. J. L. McGuigan.
National Resources, Hon. W. G. Bishop.
Labour and Provincial Secretary, Hon. R. E. Logan.
Chairman, New Brunswick Electric Power Commission, Hon. G. E. McInerney.
Municipal Affairs, Hon. J. P. LeBlanc.
Fisheries, Hon. E. W. N. Cockburn.
Tourism, Hon. J. C. Van Horne.
Youth, Hon. B. Robertson.
Ministers, each $12,000.

Speaker of the House, Hon. L. Garvey.... $9,000

The Judicature.
Court of Appeal.

Chief Justice, Hon. G. F. G. Bridges..... $30,000
Judges of Appeal, Hons. R. V. Limerick;
C. J. A Hughes; J. H. Bugold....each 26,000

Queen's Bench Division.

Chief Justice, Q.B.D., Hon. A. J. Cormier. 30,000
Judges, Hons. A. M. Robichaud; J. A. Pichette; D. Dickson; J. P. Barry; J. McL. Prescott.................each 26,000

Finance.—The estimated revenue for the year ending March 31, 1971, is $481,279,000 and ordinary expenditure, $512,769,000.

Manufactures.—Forest products: pulp, paper and timber form the major manufactured group, followed by foods, oil refining, shipbuilding and general manufacturing including electronics, cooking and heating equipment, chemicals and fertilizers and diversified other products. Saint John is the principal manufacturing centre. Total value of manufactured products was $672,800,000 in 1970.

Agriculture and Livestock.—The total land area is 17,582,720 acres of which about 85 per cent. is forested. The Province is the largest potato-producing area of Canada, grown chiefly in the upper Saint John River Valley. Dairy farming is next in importance with some mixed garden production. The livestock in 1970 included 112,000 cattle, 14,000 sheep, 53,000 hogs and 1,374,000 poultry. Farm income was $61,505,000 (gross) in 1970.

Fishing.—The chief commercial fish are lobsters, sardines, herring, cod, haddock and salmon with an estimated market value of $73,000,000 in 1970.

Minerals.—Extensive zinc, lead and copper deposits are now being mined in the north-eastern part of the Province with a smelter having recently come into operation. Total mineral production is valued at about $101,000,000 annually. Coal continues to be mined on a decreasing scale with lesser amounts of non-metallic minerals.

Principal Cities.—CAPITAL Ψ Fredericton: population (1966), 22,460. Ψ Saint John (pop. 91,198) is one of the principal winter ports of Canada and is connected by C.P.R. and Canadian National Railways with Montreal; Moncton (45,847); Bathurst (15,256); Edmundston (12,517).

NEWFOUNDLAND

Area and Population.—The Island of Newfoundland is situated between 46° 37′–51° 37′ N. latitude and 52° 44′–59° 30′ W. longitude, on the north-east side of the Gulf of St. Lawrence, and is separated from the North American Continent by the Straits of Belle Isle on the N.W. and by Cabot Strait on the S.W. The island is about 317 miles long and 316 miles broad and is triangular in shape, with Cape Bauld (N.), Cape Race (S.E.) and Cape Ray (S.W.) at the angles. It comprises an area of 156,185 sq. miles (inclusive of Labrador) with a population (April 1, 1970) of 517,000.

Government.—On March 31, 1949, the island, with its dependency of Labrador, became the 10th Province of the Dominion of Canada. The Government is administered by a Lieutenant-Governor, aided by an Executive Council and a Legislative Assembly of 42 members.

Lieutenant-Governor, Hon. E. John A. Harnum (April 2, 1969).............. $9,000

Executive.

Premier, Hon. J. R. Smallwood, D.C.L., LL.D.
President of the Council and Minister of Justice, Hon. L. R. Curtis, Q.C.
Minister of Labour, Hon. W. J. Keough.
Public Works, Hon. J. R. Chalker.
Education and Youth, Hon. F. W. Rowe.
Provincial Affairs, Hon. G. A. Frecker.
Finance, Hon. E. S. Jones.
Health, Hon. E. M. Roberts.
Fisheries, Hon. A. J. Maloney.
Labrador Affairs, Hon. E. W. Winsor.
Mines, Agriculture and Resources, Hon. W. R. Callahan.
Highways, Hon. H. G. Starkes.
Community and Social Development, Hon. W. N. Rowe.
Social Services and Rehabilitation, Hon. S. A. Neary.
Supply and Services, Hon. J. A. Nolan.
Municipal Affairs and Housing, Hon. E. N. Dawe.
Ministers without Portfolio, Hons. P. J. Lewis; G. I. Hill.

Clerk of the Executive Council, J. G. Channing.

The Legislature.

A General Election was held on Sept. 8, 1966. The present state of parties is: *Liberal*, 38; *Progressive Conservative*, 4.

Speaker of the House of Assembly, Hon. G. W. Clarke.

Finance.—The estimated net general revenue in the fiscal year ending March 31, 1969, was $194,670,000 and the net general expenditure $224,560,000.

Production and Industry.—With the exception of Gander, Bishop's Falls, Badger, Millertown, Buchans, Howley, Deer Lake and that portion of the West Coast between St. George's and Port aux Basques the inhabitants are chiefly located on the coast-line of the shore and bays. In 1965 there were fourteen mines in operation, of which five were iron, five base metal and four non-metallic mineral mines. There were also eight establishments mining structural materials such as sand and gravel, stone, cement and clay. Five pulp and paper mills are in operation. The value in 1969 of mineral products was $239,093,692, including iron ore, $178,992,960. Copper, asbestos, zinc and lead contributed an additional $46,758,991. Mining was the largest primary industry in the Province and contributes over 32 per cent. of total production by value.

Railways.—The main line of the railway extends from St. John's on the east coast to Port aux Basques on the west coast—a distance of 547 miles—with branches connecting with the ports of Argentia,

Carbonear, Bonavista and Lewisporte, a total mileage of 705. There are also 230 miles of private line. Communication between various points on the coast and between Port aux Basques and North Sydney, Nova Scotia, is maintained by a fleet of 20 motor vessels and 5 steam vessels, operated by the Railway.

Principal Cities.—The Capital, Ψ ST. JOHN'S (population, 1966 Census, Greater St. John's 90,838), contains two cathedrals, several banks and numerous public buildings. The second city of Newfoundland is Corner Brook (27,116).

LABRADOR

Labrador, the most northerly district in the Province of Newfoundland, forms the most easterly part of the North American continent, and extends from Blanc Sablon, at the north-east entrance to the Straits of Belle Isle, on the south, to Cape Chidley, at the eastern entrance to Hudson's Straits on the north. The territory under the jurisdiction of Newfoundland has an area estimated at 112,826 square miles, with a population (1966) of 21,157. Labrador is noted for its cod fisheries and also possesses valuable salmon, herring, trout and seal fisheries. Newfoundland (Labrador) supplies more iron ore than any other province in Canada and the huge hydro-electric plant on the Churchill River will be the largest in the world with a 5,250,000 kW. capacity when completed.

NOVA SCOTIA

Area and Population.—Nova Scotia is a peninsula between 43° 25'-47° N. lat and 59° 40'-66° 25' W. long., and is connected with New Brunswick by a low fertile isthmus about thirteen miles wide. It comprises an area (with Cape Breton Island) of 21,068 square miles (325 miles of which consists of lakes, rivers and inlets of the sea); total population (estimated, 1970), 765,000.

Government.—The Government is administered by a Lieutenant-Governor, aided by an Executive Council and a Legislative Assembly of 46 members.

Lieutenant-Governor, Hon. V. de B. Oland,
E.D. (1963) $18,000

Executive

Premier, Hon. G. I. Smith $18,500
Works and Lands and Forests, Hon. G. A. Snow.
Attorney-General and Minister of Public Health, Hon. R. A. Donahoe, Q.C.
Trade, Industry and Labour, Hon. T. J. McKeogh, M.D.
Fisheries, Hon. J. M. Harding, Q.C.
Mines and Public Welfare, Hon. P. Gaum.
Finance and Economics, Hon. W. S. K. Jones, Q.C.
Highways, Hon. I. W. Akerley.
Education, Hon. G. J. Doucet.
Provincial Secretary, Hon. E. D. Haliburton.
Municipal Affairs and Agriculture and Marketing, Hon. H. Veniot, A.C.
Minister without Portfolio, Hon. D. R. MacLeod.
Ministers, each $16,500; *without Portfolio*, $3,750.

The Judicature
Supreme Court—Appeal Division

Chief Justice, Hon. A. H. McKinnon $32,000
Judges, Hons. T. H. Coffin; A. G. Cooper
each 28,000

Trial Division

Chief Justice, Hon. G. S. Cowan 32,000
Judges, Hons. F. W. Bissett; J. L. Dubinsky; G. S. Hart; D. J. Gillis;
one vacancy .... each 28,000

Finance.—The revenue in 1967–68 was estimated at $215,247,260 and the expenditure $207,115,910; the funded debt (March 31, 1968) was $580,136,000.

Agriculture and Live Stock.—According to the 1966 census Nova Scotia has a total land area of 13,275,000 acres, of which 1,851,895 acres are held as farm land. At the same census, the total number of occupied farms was listed at 9,621. Of the total area in farm land, 314,143 acres are devoted to the production of principal field crops.

The Annapolis Valley section of Nova Scotia is famous for its fruit production, with an average crop of 3,000,000 bushels annually.

The number of live stock is estimated (1968) as follows: horses, 5,500; cattle and calves, 146,000; sheep and lambs, 38,000; hogs, 65,000; poultry, 2,793,000.

Manufactures.—The value of manufacturing shipments in 1967 exceeded $598,155,000. Petroleum refining, fish products, primary steel, pulp and paper mills, and shipbuilding are the major industries in terms of output. The principal industrial centres are Sydney, Halifax, Trenton, Amherst, Truro and Yarmouth.

Fisheries.—The total landed value of the fisheries in 1968 was $54,600,000, including lobsters, $10,944,000; scallops, $11,861,000; cod, $7,364,000; haddock, $6,356,000; and swordfish, $3,728,000.

Minerals.—3,134,310 tons of coal were produced in 1968. Gypsum production was 4,201,395 tons, barite totalled 123,041 tons, salt output was 503,287 tons, anhydrite 269,961 tons and limestone 435,575 tons. Silver production exceeded 375,000 oz.; production of lead was 5,306,000 lb. and of zinc 450,000 lb. Cement production began in 1965, and reached 231,000 tons in 1968. Metallurgical grade limestone and dolomite totalled 530,000 tons and salt production reached a record of 494,000 tons. Preliminary figures show the total value of mineral output at just over $58,000,000 in 1968.

Principal Cities.—CAPITAL, Ψ HALIFAX, population of Metropolitan area (1966) 198,193, one of the terminals of the Canadian National Railway, with a magnificent harbour, is one of the principal winter ports of Canada, and the *entrepôt* of a large trade with the West Indies, South America and Europe. One of the largest bridges in the British Commonwealth spans the harbour and connects the city of Dartmouth and surrounding area with the city of Halifax. A shipyard for the building of large ocean-going steamers, with a dry dock, is one of the leading industries; other cities and towns are Sydney, Glace Bay and New Waterford (*see below*), Truro (13,226), Amherst (10,551), New Glasgow (10,489) and Yarmouth (8,319).

CAPE BRETON ISLAND.

Cape Breton Island, formerly a distinct Colony, was incorporated with Nova Scotia in 1819. It contains an area of 3,975 sq. miles, population (1966) 166,943. The chief city, Sydney (pop. 33,007), on the eastern coast, has valuable collieries in the neighbourhood and is the site of the third largest steel works in Canada. Glace Bay and New Waterford, also coal mining centres, have populations of 23,516 and 9,725 respectively. The Canadian National Railway provides service to the island. A large rail-highway causeway joins the island to the mainland.

ONTARIO

Area and Population.—The Province of Ontario contains a total area of 412,582 sq. miles, with a population (estimated June, 1970) of 7,788,000.

Government.—The Government is vested in a Lieutenant-Governor and a Legislative Assembly of 117 members elected for five years. The state of the parties in July, 1971, was 68 Progressive Conservatives, 26 Liberals, 21 New Democratic Party, 1 Independent and 1 Liberal–Labour.

Lieutenant-Governor, Hon. William Ross
Macdonald, P.C., Q.C. (1968) $20,000

Executive Council

Prime Minister and President of the Council,
Hon. William G. Davis..............$16,000
Public Works, J. A. C. Auld.
Health, Hon. A. B. Lawrence.
Social and Family Services, Hon. T. L. Wells.
Financial and Commercial Affairs, Hon. A. A.
Wishart.
Correctional Services, Hon. C. J. S. Apps.
Agriculture and Food, Hon. W. A. Stewart.
Treasurer of Ontario and Minister of Economics, Hon.
W. D. McKeogh.
Highways and Transport, Hon. C. S. MacNaughton.
Tourism and Information, Hon. F. Guindon.
Education, Hon. R. S. Welch.
University Affairs, Hon. J. H. White.
Energy and Resources Management, Hon. G. A. Kerr.
Trade and Development, Hon. A. Grossman.
Justice, Hon. A. F. Lawrence.
Lands and Forests, Hon. R. Brunelle.
Labour, Hon. R. G. Carton.
Provincial Secretary and Minister of Citizenship, Hon.
J. Yaremko.
Municipal Affairs, Hon. D. A. Bales.
Mines and Northern Affairs, Hon. L. E. Bernier.
Revenue, Hon. E. A. Winkler.
Ministers Without Portfolio, Hons. E. A. Dunlop;
R. T. Potter; J. W. Snow.
   Departmental Ministers, each $12,000; Without
Portfolio, $2,500.

Secretary to the Cabinet, C. E. Brannan.
Speaker, Legislative Assembly, Hon. F. M. Cass, Q.C.
$3,000

Chief Justice of Ontario, Hon. G. A. Gale.
Chief Justice of the High Court, Hon. D. C. Wells.

AGENT-GENERAL IN LONDON A. A. Rowan-Legg,
13 Charles II Street, S W.1.
   Livestock.—In 1969 the numbers of livestock
included—horses, 70,000; cattle, 3,820,000; sheep
and lambs, 262,000; pigs, 2,010,000, and poultry,
3,040,000.
   Forestry.—Productive forested lands cover
150,000 sq. miles or about 40 per cent. of the land
area of the Province. Pulp and paper is one of the
most important manufacturing industries.
   Manufacture and Minerals.—Ontario is the chief
manufacturing province of Canada and leads the
other Provinces in mineral production.
   CAPITAL.—Ψ Toronto (population, estimated
June 1, 1970: Metropolitan area, 2,366,000), has a
wide range of manufacturing and service industries
and is a centre of education. Other major urban
areas are: Ottawa, the national capital; Ψ Hamilton
(484,000), with iron and steel industry, metal
fabrication, machinery, electrical and chemical
industries; London (228,000), a business, educational
and manufacturing centre; Ψ Windsor (226,000);
Kitchener (210,000) and Sudbury (124,000).

FEDERAL CAPITAL

OTTAWA, the Federal Capital, 111 miles west of
Montreal and 247 miles north-east of Toronto, is a
city on the south bank of the Ottawa river. The
city was chosen as the Capital of the Province
of Canada in 1857 and was later selected
as the site of the Dominion capital. Ottawa contains the Parliamentary Buildings, the Public
Archives, Royal Mint, National Museum, National
Art Gallery and the Dominion Observatory.
   A National Arts Centre opened on June 2, 1969,
near the Parliament buildings. Facilities provided
on 6½ acres of terraced land include an opera house
with seating for 2,300, a theatre (800 seats) and an experimental studio (300 seats) and a hall (100 seats).
   Manufacturing is also carried on, food produc-

tion, printing and publishing being of greatest
importance. Ottawa is connected with Lake Ontario by the Rideau Canal. Its population was
290,741 at the Census of 1966; Metropolitan
Ottawa (estimated, 1970), 536,000.

PRINCE EDWARD ISLAND

   Area and Population.—Prince Edward Island lies
in the southern part of the Gulf of St. Lawrence,
between 46°-47° N. lat. and 62°-64° 30′ W. long.
It is about 130 miles in length, and from 4 to 34
miles in breadth; its area is 2,184 square miles
(rather larger than that of the English county of
Norfolk), and its population (estimated, 1970)
109,000.
   Government.—The Government is vested in a
Lieut.-Governor and an Executive Council, and
Legislative Assembly of 32 members elected for a
term of 5 years, 16 as Councillors and 16 as As-
semblymen. Party representation following the
election of 1970 is: Liberal, 27; Conservative, 5.
Lieutenant-Governor, His Honour J. George
McKay (1969)..................... $16,000

Executive

Premier and Minister of Development, Hon.
A. B. Campbell....................   9,000
Health and Welfare, Hon. J. H. Maloney.
Education and Justice and President of the Executive
Council, Hon. G. L. Bennett.
Tourist Development, Hon. M. L. Bonnell, M.D.
Fisheries, Labor, Industry and Commerce, Hon. B. L.
Stewart.
Highways and Public Works, Hon. G. L. Ferguson.
Agriculture and Forestry, Hon. D. J. MacDonald.
Finance and Provincial Secretary, Hon. T. E. Hickey.
Community Services, Hon. R. C. Schurman.
Without Portfolio, Hon. R. E. Campbell.
   Ministers, each $6,000; without Portfolio, $3,600
(plus expenses)

Speaker of the Legislative Assembly, Hon.
C. A. Miller....................... $1,000

Supreme Court

Chief Justice, C. St. C. Trainor.......... $32,000
Assistant Judges, Hon. G. J. Tweedy; Hon.
R. R. Bell; Hon. J. P. Nicholson...each   28,000
   Finance.—The estimated revenue in 1970-71 was
$81,252,458 and the expenditure was $81,201,434.
   Education.—A university and a college of applied
arts and technology were established in 1969,
estimated enrollment for 1971-72 being 1,800-2,000
and 600 students respectively.
   CAPITAL, Ψ Charlottetown (pop. 18,500), on the
shore of Hillsborough Bay, which forms a good
harbour.

QUEBEC

   Area and Population.—The Province of Quebec
contains an area estimated at 594,860 square miles,
with a population (April, 1970), of 6,005,000.
Immigration in 1969 reached a total of 28,230.
   Government.—The Government of the Province
is vested in a Lieutenant-Governor, a Council of
Ministers and a National Assembly of 108 members
elected for five years. There are at present 72
Liberals, 17 Union Nationale, 12 Social Credit Rally
and 7 Parti Quebecois.
Lieut.-Governor, The Hon. Hugues Lapointe, Q.C.
(Feb. 22, 1966).

Executive

Prime Minister, President of the Executive Council and
Minister of Intergovernmental Affairs, Robert
Bourassa.
Minister of Education, Guy St.-Pierre.
Labour and Manpower, Jean Cournoyer.
Social Affairs, Claude Castonguay.
Justice, Jérôme Choquette.
Municipal Affairs, Maurice Tessier.

Financial Institutions, William Tetley.
Industry and Commerce, Gérard-D. Lévesque.
Equipment, Bernard Pinard.
Transportation, Georges Tremblay.
Communications and Civil Service, Jean-Paul L'Allier.
Tourism, Fish and Game, Claire Kirkland-Casgrain.
Lands and Forests, Kewin Drummond.
Revenue, Gérald Harvey.
Cultural Affairs and Immigration, François Cloutier.
Agriculture and Colonization, Normand Toupin.
Natural Resources, Gilles Massé.
Finance, Raymond Garneau.
Solicitor-General, Roy Fournier.
(and 5 Ministers without Portfolio).
AGENT-GENERAL IN LONDON.—Hon. Guy Roberge, 12 Upper Grosvenor Street. W.1.

The Judicature
Queen's Bench (*Montreal*):—
Chief Justice, Hon. L. Tremblay.
Puisne Judges (Montreal); Hons. P. C. Casey; G. Miller Hyde; G. E. Rinfret; G. R. W. Owen; G. H. Montgomery; E. Salvas.
Puisne Judges (Quebec).—Hons. R. Brossard; A. Taschereau; F. Choquette; A. Rivard; J. Turgeon.
Superior Court:—
Chief Justice, Hon. Frédéric Dorion.

Finance.—The revenue for the year 1969–70 was $3,003,992,453; ordinary expenditure amounted to $2,979,884,982. The net bonded debt (March 31, 1970) was $2,105,539,969.

Production and Industry.—The principal manufacturing centres are Montreal, Montreal East, Quebec, Trois-Rivières, Sherbrooke, Shawinigan Drummondville and Lachine. Forest lands cover 378,125 sq. miles, of which 220,625 sq. miles are productive, 137,578 sq. miles with merchantable softwood, mixed wood and hardwood, and 80,547 sq. miles with young growth. Forest products in 1970 included: wood pulp, 6,523,000 tons; paper and paperboard, 5,786,000 tons.
Total value of shipments in the manufacturing industries in 1970 was $12,898,000,000. Value of 1968 shipments in the chief industries: Food and beverages, $2,097,973,000; Paper and allied industries, $1,190,747,000; Primary metal industries, $870,292,000; Textiles, $822,728,000; Clothing $823,716,000.

Agriculture and Fisheries.—In 1970 total farm receipts were: Crops, $55,694,000; Livestock and livestock products, $566,772,000; Other farm receipts, $39,786,000. 257,214,000 lb. of fish to the value of $10,799,000 were landed in 1970.

Mineral Production.—Minerals to the value of $798,565,390 were mined during 1970, compared with $728,783,871 in 1969. Distribution of the 1970 total was: copper, $201,542,000; iron ore, $131,319,000; zinc, $63,073,100; gold, $25,045,140; asbestos, $165,454,000.

Miscellaneous Statistics.—2,253,656 motor vehicles were registered in 1969, including 1,818,468 passenger vehicles. Quebec has 16 television and 60 radio broadcasting stations and 14 daily newspapers are published in the Province. In 1969, 1,156,000 households had at least one telephone. The average annual income per head in 1970 was estimated at $2,797. Total personal incomes, $16,803,000,000.

Principal Cities.—CAPITAL, Ψ Quebec (population, estimated, 1970, 193,984), historic city visited annually by thousands of tourists, and one of the great seaport towns of Canada; and Ψ Montreal (municipal population, 1,466,500; with suburbs, of Montreal Island, 2,225,420), the commercial metropolis, and the principal centre of the Canadian grain export trade. Other important cities are Laval (237,918); Verdun (91,051) and Sherbrooke (81,881).

SASKATCHEWAN

Area and Population.—The Province of Saskatchewan lies between Manitoba on the east and Alberta on the west and has an area of 251,700 square miles (of which the land area is 220,182 sq. miles), with a population (estimated, 1970) of 943,000. Saskatchewan extends along the Canada–U.S.A. boundary for 393 miles and northwards for 761 miles. Its northern width is 276 miles.

Government.—The Government is vested in the Lieutenant-Governor, with a Legislative Assembly of 60 members. There is an Executive Council of 10 members. The Legislative Assembly is elected for 5 years and the state of the parties in July, 1971, was: N.D.P., 45; Liberals, 15.

Lieut.-Governor, His Honour Stephen Worobetz, M.C., M.D. (1970) $9,000
Executive Council.
Premier and President of the Council, Provincial Treasurer and Minister of Industry and Commerce, Hon. A. Blakeney................... $18,500
Attorney-General, Deputy Premier and Provincial Secretary, Hon. R. Romanow.
Agriculture, Hon. J. R. Messer.
Public Health, Hon. W. E. Smishek.
Municipal Affairs and Public Works, Hon. E. I. Wood.
Labour and Welfare, Hon. G. T. Snyder.
Mineral Resources and Indian and Metis, Hon. G. R. Bowerman.
Highways and Telephones, Hon. N. E. Byers.
Education, Hon. G. MacMurchy.
Natural Resources, Co-operation and Co-operative Development, Hon. E. Kramer.
Ministers, each $13,500.

AGENT-GENERAL IN LONDON.—F. H. Larson, 28 Chester Street, S.W.1.
The Judicature
Chief Justice of Saskatchewan, Hon. E. M. Culliton............................ $31,000
Judges of Appeal, Hons. M. J. Woods; R. L. Brownridge; P. H. Maguire; R. N. Hall ....each 27,000
Chief Justice, Queen's Bench, Hon. A. H. Bence............................... 31,000
Puisne Judges, Hons. A. L. Sirois; C. S. Davis; D. C. Disbery; M. A. MacPherson; F. W. Johnson; R. A. MacDonald; W. A. Tucker................... each 27,000

Finance.—Estimated revenue year ending March 31, 1971, is $394,684,800; expenditure, $405,081,640. Net assets, 1970, $54,710,925.

Agriculture.—In an average crop year, Saskatchewan produces some 60 per cent. of Canada's wheat. Wheat production in 1970 was 210,000,000 bushels. Cash income from the sale of farm products in 1970 was estimated at $728,000,000. Livestock population in June, 1970, included 2,386,000 cattle and calves, 985,000 hogs and 102,000 sheep. Income from livestock sales was $196,371,000. Forest products were estimated at $50,867,000 for 1970.

Industries.—In 1970 net value of commodity production was estimated at $1,259,000,000. Value of factory shipments (preliminary) $573,500,000; private and public investment $886,300,000 and retail trade was estimated at $1,016,000,000.

Mineral production for 1970 was estimated at $392,500,000; oil accounted for $201,200,000 and metallic minerals some $37,200,000. Potash production increased to $116,400,000.

CAPITAL.—Regina. Population (estimated 1970), 145,500. Other cities: Saskatoon (131,000), Moose Jaw (33,500) and Prince Albert (28,000).

The Commonwealth of Australia

AREA AND POPULATION

States and Capitals	Area (English Sq. Miles)	Population		
		Census June 30, 1961	Census June 30, 1966	Estimated Dec. 31, 1970
States				
New South Wales (Sydney)..........	309,433	3,918,501	4,237,901	4,623,900
Queensland (Brisbane)..............	667,000	1,527,514	1,674,324	1,820,000
South Australia (Adelaide)...........	380,070	971,487	1,094,984	1,177,800
Tasmania (Hobart).................	26,383	350,340	371,436	395,600
Victoria (Melbourne)...............	87,884	2,930,366	3,220,217	3,480,800
Western Australia (Perth)...........	975,920	746,750	848,100	1,001,300
Territories				
Australian Capital Territory (Canberra)	939	58,828	96,032	139,800
Northern Territory (Darwin).........	520,280	44,481	56,504	74,100
Total.....................	2,967,909	10,548,267	11,599,498	12,713,400

Increase of the People

Year	Increase			Decrease			Net Increase†	Marriages*
	Births*	‡Overseas Arrivals	Total	Deaths*	Overseas Departures	Total		
1965	222,854	525,136	747,990	99,715	420,280	519,995	225,000	93,546
1966	222,626	557,591	780,217	103,929	470,665	574,594	205,000	96,046
1967	229,296	637,170	866,466	102,703	545,261	647,964	218,500	100,000
1968	240,906	771,792	1,012,698	109,547	658,739	768,288	244,400	106,345
1969	250,176	898,858	1,149,034	106,496	769,812	876,308	272,700	112 470
1970	257,516	1,026,675	1,284,191	113,048	903,801	1,016,849	267,300	116,066

* Figures for years before 1967 exclude full-blood Aborigines.
‡ Including the following arrivals under the Commonwealth Government's various schemes for assisted immigration: 1966, 89,743; 1967, 82,247; 1968, 105,102; 1969, 125,958; 1970, 134,428.
† = natural increase (excess of births over deaths), net overseas migration gain; adjusted to make the series of increases agree with total inter-censal increase shown by 1966 census.

Inter-Censal Increases, 1933-1966

Year of Census	Population at Census*			Inter-Censal Increase	Net Immigration during Period
	Males	Females	Total		
1933	3,367,111	3,262,728	6,629,839	1,194,105	1921-1933 .. 282,975
1947	3,797,370	3,781,988	7,579,358	949,519	1933-1947 .. 41,106
1954	4,546,118	4,440,412	8,986,530	1,407,172	1947-1954 .. 639,028
1961	5,333,185	5,215,082	10,548,267	1,561,737	1954-1961 .. 584,754
1966	5,841,588	5,757,910	11,599,498	1,051,231	1961-1966 .. 395,485

* Excludes full-blood Aborigines before 1961.   Inter-censal increase figure for 1954–61 excludes full-blood Aborigines.

Races and Religions

Races	1961	1966	Religions	1961	1966
European...........	10,418,761	11,453,374	Church of England....	3,668,940	3,877,473
Chinese.............	23,568	26,723	Roman Catholics*.....	2,619,984	3,036,130
Japanese............	2,671	818	Methodists............	1,076,395	1,124,310
Indians and Cingalese.	4,956	6,000	Presbyterians..........	976,721	1,043,570
Aborigines..........	79,253	80,207	Other Christians.......	932,101	1,123,555
			Hebrews..............	59,329	63,271
Other Races.........	19,058	32,286	Other‡	1,214,797	1,331,189

* Including Catholics, so described, 1,480,335 in 1961 and 1,932,161 in 1966.
† Including 1,102,929 and 1 138,900 who did not state their religion at the 1961 and 1966 Census respectively.

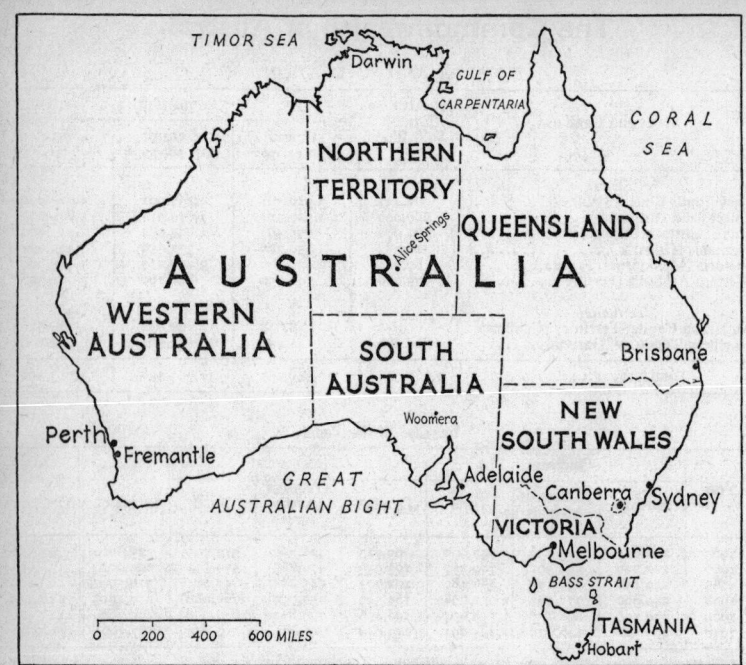

PHYSICAL FEATURES

Australia was separated from the other great land surfaces at a remote period, and exhibits therefore some very archaic types of fauna and flora. It may be regarded as the largest island or the smallest continent, being surrounded by the following waters:—*North*, the Timor and Arafura Seas and Torres Strait; *East*, Pacific Ocean; *South*, Bass Strait (which separates Tasmania from the Continent) and Southern Ocean; and *West*, Indian Ocean. The total area of the mainland is 2,941,526 square miles, the island of Tasmania having an area of 26,383 square miles, and making a total area for the Commonwealth of 2,967,909 square miles. The coastline of Australia is approximately 12,000 miles (including Tasmania, 900 miles), and its geographical position is between 10° 41′–39° 8′ (43° 39′, including Tasmania) South latitude and 113° 9′–153° 39′ East longitude; the greatest length East to West is 2,500 miles, and from North to South 2,000 miles (2,300 miles, including Tasmania). Nearest distances from England *via* Cape of Good Hope are East Coast 12,400 and West Coast, 10,800 miles.

From a physical standpoint the continent of Australia is divisible into an eastern and a western area, the former containing a regular coast-line with a good harbourage, roadsteads, rivers, and inland waterways, and a greater development of fauna and flora; the latter a broken coast-line with estuaries rather than rivers, and but little inland water communication. The whole continent is, roughly speaking, a vast, irregular, and undulating plateau, part of which is below the level of the sea, surrounded by a mountainous coast-line, with frequent intervals of low and sandy shore on the north, west and south. The Great Barrier Reef extends parallel with the East coast of Queensland for 1,200 miles, at a distance of about 60 miles from the mainland. A large part of the interior, particularly in the west, consists of sandy and stony desert, covered with spinifex, and containing numerous salt-marshes, though reaches of grass-land occur here and there. The geological formation of Australia is remarkable for its simplicity and regularity; the *strike* of the rocks is, with a single exception, coincident with the direction of the mountain-chains, from N. to S.; and the tertiary formation to be found in the N., S., and W. develops in the S.E. into a gigantic tertiary plain, watered by the Darling and the Murray Rivers. Nearly all round the coast, however, and in eastern and south-eastern Australia, stretching far inland from the coastal range, is a fertile area devoted partly to agriculture, partly to dairying, while the inland districts particularly are admirably adapted to the rearing of sheep. The most extensive mountain system takes its rise near the S.E. point, and includes a number of ranges known by different names in different places, none of them being of any great height. The highest peak, Mount Kosciusko, in New South Wales, reaches an elevation of more than 7,300 feet. The principal rivers are the Murray, which debouches on the south coast, after receiving the waters of its tributaries the Murrumbidgee, Lachlan, and Darling, in the S.E. part of the continent: on the east coast, the Hawkesbury, Hunter, Clarence, Richmond, Brisbane, Mary, Burnett, Fitzroy, and Burdekin; on the west, the Swan, Murchison, Gascoyne, Ashburton, Fortescue,

De Grey, and Fitzroy; on the north, the Drysdale, Ord, Victoria and Daly; and the Roper, Flinders, and Mitchell, which debouch into the Gulf of Carpentaria. The scarcity of the natural water supply in the interior has, however, been mitigated by successful borings and by the construction of large dams. The work of conserving the vast quantities of water which run to waste in the wet season is being vigorously prosecuted by a system of locks and weirs on some of the rivers. A major development is the use of the waters of the Snowy River in south-eastern New South Wales for hydro-electricity generation and irrigation.

Significant mineral resources comprise bauxite, coal, copper, gold, gypsum, ilmenite, iron ore, lead, limestone, manganese, nickel, pyrite, rutile, silver, tin, tungsten, uranium, zinc and zircon. Recently, geological exploration has significantly increased the mineral resources of the nation and the pace of exploration activity is increasing.

Australia now has four commercial oilfields, Gippsland, offshore Victoria; Moonie and Alton in Queensland, and Barrow Island, Western Australia, together capable of producing 60 per cent. of the nation's requirements. The largest deposits are in the Gippsland Basin where crude oil production began in the latter months of 1969.

Production from natural gas deposits in Queensland, South Australia and offshore Victoria began during 1969. Other natural gas reserves have been discovered in Western Australia and the Northern Territory.

Climate.—The seasons are: summer, December to February; autumn, March to May; winter, June to August; spring, September to November. Australia is less subject to extremes of climate than are regions of similar size in low parts of the world, though the climate varies considerably from the tropical to the alpine.

GOVERNMENT

The Commonwealth of Australia was constituted by an Act of the Imperial Parliament dated July 9, 1900, and was inaugurated Jan. 1, 1901. The Government is that of a Federal Commonwealth within the British Commonwealth of Nations, the executive power being vested in the Sovereign (through the Governor-General), assisted by a Federal Ministry of twenty-seven Ministers of State. Under the Constitution the Federal Government has acquired and may acquire certain defined powers as surrendered by the States, residuary legislative power remaining with the States. Trade and customs passed under Federal control immediately on the establishment of the Commonwealth; posts, telegraphs and telephones, naval and military defence, lighthouses and quarantine on proclaimed dates. The Federal Government also controls such matters as social services, patents and copyrights, naturalization, navigation, &c. The right of a State to legislate is not abrogated except in connection with matters exclusively under Federal control, but where a State law is inconsistent with a law of the Commonwealth the latter prevails to the extent of the inconsistency.

FLAG.—The British Blue Ensign, consisting of a blue flag, with the Union Jack occupying the upper quarter next the staff, differenced by a large white star (representing the six States of Australia and the Territories of the Commonwealth) in the centre of the lower quarter next the staff and pointing direct to the centre of the St. George's Cross in the Union Jack and five white stars, representing the Southern Cross, in the fly.

AUSTRALIA DAY.—January 26.

GOVERNOR-GENERAL AND STAFF

Governor-General, His Excellency the Rt. Hon. Sir Paul Meernaa Caedwalla Hasluck, G.C.M.G., G.C.V.O., *born* April 1, 1905, *assumed office* May 1, 1969.

Official Secretary, Sir Murray Tyrrell, K.C.V.O., C.B.E.

Comptroller, W. H. J. Perring.

THE COMMONWEALTH MINISTRY

The amount estimated to be spent on Ministers' salaries under the Ministers of State Act during 1970–71 was $A362,000.

Prime Minister, Rt. Hon. W. McMahon, M.P.

Deputy Prime Minister and Minister for Trade and Industry, Rt. Hon. J. D. Anthony, M.P.

Defence, Hon. D. E. Fairbairn, D.F.C., M.P.

Primary Industry, Hon. I. McC. Sinclair, M.P.

Supply, Hon. R. V. Garland, M.P.

National Development and Leader of the House, Hon. R. W. C. Swartz, M.B.E., E.D., M.P.

Treasurer, Hon. B. M. Snedden, Q.C., M.P.

Attorney-General, Senator Hon. I. J. Greenwood, Q.C.

Education and Science, Hon. M. Fraser.

Postmaster-General and Vice-President of the Executive Council, Hon. Sir Alan Hulme, K.B.E., M.P.

Foreign Affairs, Hon. N. H. Bowen, Q.C., M.P.

Shipping and Transport, Hon. P. J. Nixon, M.P.

Labour and National Service, Hon. P. R. Lynch, M.P.

The above form the Cabinet.

External Territories, Hon. C. E. Barnes, M.P.

Immigration, Hon. A. J. Forbes, M.P.

Social Services, Hon. W. C. Wentworth, M.P.

Works and Minister in Charge of Tourist Activities, Senator Hon. R. C. Wright.

Civil Aviation, Senator Hon. R. C. Cotton.

Customs and Excise and Minister assisting the Minister for National Development, Hon. D. L. Chipp, M.P.

Air, Senator Hon. T. C. Drake-Brockman, D.F.C.

The Army, and Minister assisting the Treasurer, Hon. A. S. Peacock, M.P.

Repatriation, Hon. R. McN. Holten, M.P.

Health and Leader of the Government in the Senate, Senator Hon. Sir Kenneth Anderson.

Navy, Hon. M. G. Mackay, M.P.

Interior, Hon. R. J. Hunt, M.P.

Housing, Hon. M. K. Cairns, M.P.

Environment, Aborigines and the Arts, Hon. P. Howson, M.P.

AUSTRALIAN HIGH COMMISSION
Australia House, Strand, London, W.C.2.
[01-836-2435]

High Commissioner, His Excellency the Hon. Sir Alexander Downer, K.B.E. (1964).

Deputy High Commissioners, R. W. Boswell, O.B.E.; W. B. Pritchett.

Official Secretary, W. R. Cumming, C.V.O.

Head, Joint Services Staff and R.A.A.F. Attaché, Air Vice-Marshal F. Headlam, C.B., C.B.E.

Special Commercial Adviser, F. P. Donovan.

Economic Adviser (Treasury), I. Castles.

Migration Adviser, R. E. Armstrong, O.B.E.

Inter-Services Technical Officer, Air Cdre. G. D. Marshall, O.B.E., A.F.C.

Trade Commissioners, D. R. Cristofani (*Marketing*); K. H. Jarvie (*Publicity*); E. L. Jenkins (*Agriculture*); E. B. Waldron (*Minerals*); W. B. Nicholson (*Transport*).

BRITISH HIGH COMMISSION
Commonwealth Avenue, Canberra

High Commissioner, His Excellency the Rt. Hon. Sir Morrice James, K.C.M.G., C.V.O., M.B.E. (1971) £14,000

Deputy High Commissioners, H. D. V. Pakenham, C.B.E. (*Sydney*); R. W. B. Carter, C.M.G. (*Melbourne*); F. S. Fielding, O.B.E. (*Brisbane*);

A. H. Birch, C.M.G., O.B.E. (*Perth*); H. O'Brien (*Adelaide*).

Minister, D. P. Aiers.

Defence Adviser and Head of British Defence Liaison Staff, Rear-Adm. A. C. W. Wilson.

Counsellors, P. Lloyd, C.B.E. (*Technology*); T. Jones, O.B.E.; L. Bevan (*Commercial*); R. Hickling (*Information*).

First Secretaries, R. A. Neilson, M.V.O.; R. Elphick O.B.E. (*Agric. and Food*); T. F. W. Knapp; W. Francis; R. S. Edwards; P. W. M. Vereker.

Naval Adviser, Capt. V. C. Merry, D.S.C., R.N.

Military Adviser, Col. P. A. Lowe.

Air Adviser, Group Capt. J. Fennell, M.B.E., A.F.C.

Cultural Attaché and British Council Representative, E. R. H. Paget, O.B.E., 18 Greenoaks Avenue, Edgecliff, Sydney.

THE LEGISLATURE

The Parliament of the Commonwealth of Australia consists of the Queen, a Senate and a House of Representatives. The Constitution provides that the number of members of the House of Representatives shall be, as nearly as practicable, twice the number of Senators. An Act, assented to on May 18, 1948, provided for an increase in the number of members of the Senate from thirty-six to sixty, and as a result the number of members of the House of Representatives was increased from 74 to 123. There are now 125 members in the House of Representatives, including one member each for the Northern Territory and the Australian Capital Territory. Members of the Senate are elected for six years by universal suffrage, half the members retiring every third year and each of the six States returning an equal number. The House of Representatives, similarly elected for a maximum of three years, contains members proportionate to the population, with a minimum of five members for each State. The state of parties in the House of Representatives in June. 1971, was Liberal 46, Country Party 20, Labour 59. Members of both Houses received $A9,500 per annum, with allowances and free air and rail travel on parliamentary business.

President of the Senate, Senator Hon. Sir Alister McMullin, K.C.M.G.

Clerk of the Senate, J. R. Odgers, C.B.E.

Speaker, House of Representatives, Hon. Sir William Aston, K.C.M.G., M.P.

Clerk of the House, A. G. Turner, C.B.E.

THE JUDICATURE

HIGH COURT OF AUSTRALIA

There is a Federal High Court with a Chief Justice and 6 Justices having original and appellate jurisdiction. The principal seat of the Court is at Melbourne, Victoria.

Chief Justice, Rt. Hon. Sir Garfield Edward John Barwick, G.C.M.G. $A30,000

Justices, Rt. Hon. Sir Edward Aloysius McTiernan, K.B.E.; Rt. Hon. Sir Douglas Ian Menzies, K.B.E.; Rt. Hon. Sir (William John) Victor Windeyer, K.B.E., C.B., D.S.O., E.D.; Rt. Hon. Sir William Owen, K.B.E.; Rt. Hon. Sir Cyril Ambrose Walsh, K.B.E.; Hon. Sir Harry Talbot Gibbs, K.B.E....... $A27,000

Principal Registrar, A. N. Gamble.

COMMONWEALTH INDUSTRIAL COURT

Chief Judge, Hon. Sir John Spicer $A24,000

Judges, Hons. E. A. Dunphy; P. E. Joske, C.M.G.; Sir Richard Eggleston; R. A. Smithers; J. R. Kerr, C.M.G.; J. A. Nimmo, C.M.G.

each $A22,000

COMMONWEALTH CONCILIATION AND ARBITRATION COMMISSION

President, Hon. Sir Richard Kirby..... $A24,000

Deputy Presidents, Hons. F. H. Gallagher; J. C. Moore; L. H. Williams; A. P. Aird; R. J. A. Frank; J. Robinson; P. A. Coldham

each $A22,000

FEDERAL COURT OF BANKRUPTCY

Judge, Hon. C. A. Sweeney........... $A22,000

SUPREME COURT OF THE AUSTRALIAN CAPITAL TERRITORY

Judges, Hons. R. W. Fox; E. A. Dunphy; P. E. Joske, C.M.G.; Sir Richard Eggleston; R. A. Smithers; J. R. Kerr, C.M.G.; H. T. Gibbs; J. A. Nimmo, C.B.E.

SUPREME COURT OF THE NORTHERN TERRITORY

Judge, Hon. R. A. Blackburn.

Additional Judges, Hons. E. A. Dunphy; P. E. Joske, C.M.G.; R. A. Smithers; C. A. Sweeney; J. A. Nimmo, C.B.E.

DEFENCE

Subject to the authority of Cabinet the Minister and Department of Defence are responsible for the formulation and general application of a unified defence policy relating to the Defence Forces and their requirements. Separate Ministers and Departments of the Navy, Army and Air are responsible for the administration of their respective Services in accordance with defence policy. The Minister and Department of Supply are responsible for the supply, manufacture and overhaul of services and goods, including munitions, for the Defence Forces and for defence research and development, in accordance with approved policy.

Royal Australian Navy

Under the Naval Defence Acts, 1910–68, the naval forces of the Commonwealth are administered by a Naval Board of Administration responsible to the Minister of State for the Navy.

The Royal Australian Navy consists of an Anti-Submarine Warfare support carrier, a troop-transport, 7 destroyers, 7 destroyer escorts, 4 submarines, a destroyer tender, a fleet oiler, 20 patrol boats, 1 survey ship, 1 coastal survey ship, 2 oceanographic research ships, 4 minesweepers and 2 minehunters. There are 7 air squadrons including Iroquois, Wessex and Scout helicopters and Skyhawk, Macchi, Tracker and Dakota aircraft.

The strength of the Royal Australian Navy on May 31, 1971, was 2,120 officers and 15,257 sailors.

Army

Under the Minister for the Army, the Military Board is charged with the control and administration of all matters relating to the Australian Military Forces. Command and control is exercised through the framework of Army Headquarters and Commands geographically related to States—Northern Command, Eastern Command, Southern Command, Central Command, Western Command, Tasmania Command, Northern Territory Command and Papua New Guinea Command.

Since 1957, the basis of the readiness of the Army has been with emphasis on South-East Asia as an area of primary strategic importance to Australia. The strength of the Regular Army, including National Servicemen, was approximately 44,000 at the end of April, 1971. The field force organization has been expanded with emphasis on a substantial increase in the combat element and high priority logistic units. The aim has been to give greater flexibility in deployment to meet the present requirement for "cold" and limited warfare with light, airportable formations.

Compulsory selective service to increase the numbers in the Regular Army applies to young men in their 21st year. The number inducted at

present is 8,400 a year. Recruits serve two years full time, followed by three years in the Reserve. They are liable for overseas service.

A volunteer Regular Army Emergency Reserve of approximately 700 former Regular Army members has been formed and can be called out when the Governor-General considers it desirable.

The strength of the Citizen Military Forces was approximately 30,000 and the strength of the Army cadets 40,325. In addition, the Pacific Islands Regiment has two battalions and supporting units; total strength, about 2,600.

Currently about 7,400 Australian Army personnel are serving overseas in Singapore and Vietnam.

Air

The total strength of the R.A.A.F. on June 1, 1971, was 22,562. There were 16 flying squadrons, 5 maintenance squadrons, 18 training units, 3 aircraft depots, one airfield construction squadron, 4 control and reporting units, 5 auxiliary squadrons, 6 university squadrons and 7 A.T.C. squadrons. Four flying squadrons, one maintenance squadron and supporting personnel were serving outside Australia in the South-East Asian theatre.

COMMONWEALTH FINANCE

Revenue and expenditure of the consolidated fund balanced at $A6,978,750,000 in 1969-70, compared with $A6,085,765,000 in 1968-69. Gross Loan Fund expenditure on works totalled $A143,538,000 in 1969-70(1968-69, $A140,595,000).

The unit of Australian currency is the $A. Rates of exchange in June, 1971, were $A2·1429=£1 (buying) and $A2·1514 (selling).

DEBT

The total of the Commonwealth Debt on December 31, 1970, was $A4,691,047,000. Adding the indebtedness of the States, viz. $A9,476,719,000, the "face" or "book" value of Australian government securities on issue amounted (December 31, 1970) to $A14,167,766,000.

The Debt per head of population at Dec. 31, 1970, was $A1,114·40.

SOCIAL WELFARE

With the exception of repatriation and a few minor benefits, Commonwealth social and health benefits are financed through the National Welfare Fund (see table below). The rates and conditions, at June 30, 1971, of the major benefits are as follows:

Age and invalid pensions.—Subject to a means test the maximum weekly amounts payable are: standard rate, $A16; married rate (both pensioners, $A14·25 each.) There are additional allowances in respect of a dependent spouse, dependent children, etc. *Age pensions* are payable to men aged 65 years and over and to women 60 years and over; *invalid pensions* are payable to persons 85 per cent. permanently unfit for work, or permanently blind, and who are aged 16 years and over.

Widows pensions—subject to a means test, the maximum weekly rates are: Class "A" (a widow maintaining one or more children), $A16 with a mother's allowance of from $A4 to $A6 and an additional allowance for each child; Class "B" (a widow without dependent children and aged 50 years or over) $A14·25; Class "C" (temporary pensions for other widows in necessitous circumstances) $A14·25. Supplementary assistance of up to $A2 a week may also be paid.

Maternity allowance—payable to all mothers, irrespective of means, in respect of every child born (alive or dead). The rates range from $A30 to $A35 according to the number of other children aged under 16 years in the family. An extra $A10 is paid for each additional child in a multiple birth.

Child endowment—is paid, without means test, at the following weekly rates—for children under 16 years; $A0·50 for the first or only child in a family; $A1·00 for the second child; $A1·50 for the third and then by cumulative increases of $A0·25 making $A1·75 for the fourth child, $A2 for the fifth and so on. For each dependent full-time student child, aged 16 to 21 years, in a family the rate is $A1·50. $A1·50 is also paid for each child under 16 years, or eligible student child, in an approved institution.

Unemployment, Sickness and Special benefits are payable, subject to a means test on income only, to males between the ages of 16 and 65 years and females between the ages of 16 and 60 years who have suffered loss of income through unemployment or sickness (other than tuberculosis for which a special allowance is paid). The weekly rates are: $A10 for an adult or married minor; $A6 for persons aged 18 to 21 years and $A4·50 for persons aged 16 to 18 years. Additional allowances are paid for a dependent spouse and for dependent children under 16 years.

Hospital benefits.—Contributions to registered hospital benefits funds range from 35c. to 95c. per week for a single person and from 70c. to $1.90 per week for a married contributor. Total Commonwealth and fund benefits range from $A10.40 to $A26.00 per day. From July 1, 1970, $A2.00 per day is payable by the Commonwealth to hospitals for patients hospitalized free of charge whether or not the patient is insured. $A2 per day is payable for each qualified patient in an approved nursing home, whether the patient is insured or not, and $A5 per day for persons covered by the pensioner medical service. From Jan. 1, 1969, a supplementary benefit of $A3 a day is payable for nursing home patients who are medically classified as in need of and receiving intensive care.

Medical benefits.—Contributions to registered medical benefits funds range from 28c. to 38c. per week for a single person and from 40c. to 60c. per week for a married contributor. The level of benefits has been set by the Commonweath so that a contributor is required to pay 80c. of the "most common fee" charged for a general practitioner consultation, and up to $A5.00 for operations where "the most common fee" is charged.

Pensioners' medical service—provides free medical service and pharmaceutical benefits to eligible pensioners and their dependants.

Pharmaceutical benefits—a comprehensive range of drugs and medicinal preparations is available. In general, a fee of 50c. is charged for each prescription.

Tuberculosis campaign—this provides for diagnosis, treatment, after-care and allowances to sufferers and their dependants. The Commonwealth Government meets approved additional maintenance costs and provides all capital money required.

Free hospital and medical benefits insurance is provided, under certain conditions, for low income families; recipients of unemployment and sickness benefits; and for migrants during the first two months following their arrival in Australia.

Repatriation Benefits

War pensions are payable without a means test, to ex-service men and women who have incurred incapacity as a result of war service, and to their dependants. The maximum weekly amounts payable are: *Special rate,* $A39; *Intermediate rate,* $A28·50; *General rate,* $A12.

Service pensions are paid, subject to a means test, to ex-service men and women who are aged 60 and 55 years respectively; permanently unemployable; or suffering from tuberculosis; and to their dependants. The maximum weekly amounts payable are: *standard rate*, \$A16; *married rate* (both pensioners), \$A14·25 each.

Expenditure on repatriation benefits during 1969–70 was: war pensions, \$A183,086,000; service pensions, \$A39,912,000; medical treatment, \$68,395,000; other benefits, \$A5,311,000.

National Welfare Fund Expenditure

Service	1968–69	1969–70
	\$A'000	\$A'000
Age and Invalid Pensions	558,587	641,982
Child Endowment	193,263	220,143
Commonwealth Rehabilitation Service	2,260	2,758
Funeral Benefits	1,571	1,512
Maternity Allowances	7,960	8,000
Unemployment, Sickness, Special Benefits	16,830	18,592
Widows' Pensions	69,080	81,753
Other Welfare	1,806	3,646
Hospital Benefits	85,942	111,376
Medical Benefits	66,468	76,093
Milk for Children	10,053	10,051
Pharmaceutical Benefits	118,373	136,718
Tuberculosis Campaign	12,381	11,326
Miscellaneous health services	4,700	5,440
Rental Rebates	60	74
Home Savings Grants	13,015	12,336
Total	1,162,350	1,341,800

CONSOLIDATED REVENUE FUNDS

State, etc.	1969–70		
	Rev. \$A,000 omitted	Exp. \$A,000 omitted	Surplus(+) or Deficit(−)
N.S.W.	1,076,381	1,080,782	− 4,401
Victoria	726,900	742,282	− 15,382
Queensland	441,074	444,618	− 3,544
S. Australia	323,824	320,904	+ 2,920
W. Australia	318,189	318,901	− 712
Tasmania	123,719	120,904	+ 2,815
Total Six States	3,010,086	3,028,390	− 18,304
Commonwealth	6,978,750	6,978,750	..
Grand Total (a)	8,688,716	8,707,020	− 18,304

(a) To avoid duplication in aggregating particulars for the Commonwealth and States, the grand totals exclude payments by the Commonwealth to the States included in State consolidated revenue funds in respect of interest on States' debts, special grants, financial assistance, grants to Universities, tuberculosis capital expenditure and National Welfare Fund payments, and payments by the States to the Commonwealth in respect of Commonwealth Pay-roll tax.

BANKING

The average Australian liabilities and assets (excluding shareholders' funds, interbranch accounts and contingencies) of the 7 major trading banks operating in the Commonwealth in March, 1971, were: Liabilities in Australia, \$A7,703,558,000 (1970, \$A7,406,265,000); Assets in Australia,

\$A7,838,897,000 (1970, \$A7,415,022,000). Total amount on deposit in savings banks in Australia in March, 1971, was \$A7,427,271,000 or \$A580·51 per head of population (1970, \$A6,955,168,000 or \$A555·42 per head).

PRODUCTION AND INDUSTRY
(Commonwealth)

The estimated net values of production:—

	1968–69 (\$A)	1969–70 (\$A)
Agricultural	1,212,721,000	1,008,741,000
Pastoral	1,194,994,000	1,204,444,000
Dairying, etc. (a)	465,514,000	518,905,000
Forests and Fisheries	170,230,000	177,051,000
Mining	701,627,000	..
Manufacturing	..	..

(a) Includes poultry, bee-farming, trapping.

PRIMARY PRODUCTION

Years	Wool (million lb.)	Wheat (million bushels)	Butter (million lb.)
1966–67	1,762	467	489
1967–68	1,770	277	432
1968–69	1,948	544	439
1969–70	2,036	388	494
†1970–71	1,934	284	..

† Estimated.

Agriculture and Livestock.—The total area of rural holdings in 1969–70 was 1,222,387,146 acres. The principal crops were:—

Crop	Acreage	Bushels
Wheat*	23,440,290	387,512,341
Oats	3,396,082	68,722,656
Barley	3,758,876	74,900,875
Maize	191,258	6,797,450
Hay	3,192,293 Tons	5,733.457
Sugar-cane†	525,816 Tons	15,535,017

* Wheat estimate (1970–71) 284,000,000 bushels.
† Cut for crushing.

Livestock (in thousands)

	1966	1967	1968	1969	1970
Sheep	157,563	164,237	166,912	174,602	180,080
Cattle	17,936	18,270	19,218	20,606	22,162
Pigs	1,747	1,804	2,056	2,253	2,398
Horses	n.r.	479	..	..	456

In 1969–70 Australia produced 2,035,739,000 lb. of wool (in the grease), estimated value, \$A735,233,000; 494,206,000 lb. of butter; 168,206,000 lb. of cheese; and 53,572 tons (cured weight) of bacon and hams. The total meat production (beef, veal, mutton, lamb and pig meat) in terms of fresh meat was 1,909,023 tons.

Mines and Minerals.—In 1969–70 the mine production of gold was 656,775 fine oz. and of black coal 47,720,000 tons. Smelter and refinery production of principal metals in 1969–70 was: pig iron, 5,899,269 tons; ingot steel, 6,769,316 tons; copper (refined), 103,485 tons; blister copper, 108,508 tons; lead (incl. bullion), 355,446 tons; tin, 4,637 tons; zinc, 257,676 tons; silver, 10,240,516 fine oz. Value added by the mining industry in 1968–69 was estimated at \$A279,200,000.

Manufactures.—In 1968–69 there were in Australia 38,834 industrial establishments, employing 1,320,167 persons; wages paid amounted to \$A3,996·9m.; value of materials, fuel, etc. used \$A12,003·2m.; value added by manufacture \$A7,589·0m.; and value of total output \$A19,349·7m.

Trade Unions.—On December 31, 1970, there were 305 separate trade unions in Australia with a total membership of 2,314,600.

TOTAL EXTERNAL TRADE
(including Bullion and Specie.)

Years	Imports $A	Exports $A
1965–66	2,939,492,000	2,720,953,000
1966–67	3,045,341,000	3,023,925,000
1967–68	3,264,473,000	3,044,675,000
1968–69	3,468,505,000	3,374,263,000
1969–70	3,881,227,000	4,131,543,000

Country	Imports from	Exports to
	1969–70	
United Kingdom .	$A845,344,000	$A488,230,000
Canada	151,031,000	112,773,000
Ceylon	11,321,000	14,718,000
India	31,839,000	40,237,000
Pakistan	18,953,000	16,394,000
Malaysia	34,922,000	68,525,000
New Zealand	86,435,000	198,872,000
Hong Kong	54,022,000	84,718,000
Belgium and Luxemburg .	29,120,000	42,863,000
China (mainland) .	32,082,000	125,815,000
France	70,059,000	114,640,000
Germany (Fed. Rep.)	258,275,000	115,557,000
Indonesia	48,882,000	35,266,000
Iran	12,770,000	14,794,000
Italy	77,378,000	105,961,000
Japan	481,203,000	1,021,446,000
Netherlands	59,981,000	71,542,000
Norway	10,226,000	6,201,000
Papua N. Guinea .	21,631,000	147,298,000
Poland	2,981,000	20,108,000
Saudi Arabia	42,099,000	10,385,000
South Africa	21,631,000	64,860,000
Sweden	59,136,000	9,635,000
Switzerland	59,004,000	3,456,000
U.S.A.	965,245,000	556,431,000
U.S.S.R.	3,475,000	51,438,000

IMPORTS FROM ALL COUNTRIES, 1969–70

	$A'000
Live animals	4,355
Meat and meat preparations	2,288
Dairy products and eggs	5,757
Fish	33,368
Cereals	4,747
Fruit and vegetables	23,855
Sugar	3,004
Coffee, tea, cocoa, spices, etc.	51,396
Feeding-stuff for animals	6,882
Miscellaneous preparations chiefly for food	4,199
Beverages	16,469
Tobacco	31,975
Hides and skins	1,664
Oil-seeds, etc.	9,897
Crude rubber	30,111
Wood, timber and cork	53,077
Pulp and waste paper	36,550
Textile fibres	33,853
Crude fertilizers and minerals	60,989
Metalliferous ores and metal scrap	7,877
Crude animal and vegetable materials	13,265
Coal and coke	804
Petroleum and products	254,390
Petroleum gases	45
Oils and fats	15,644
Chemical elements and compounds	117,454
Mineral tar, etc.	2,162
Dyeing, tanning and colouring materials	22,364

	$A'000
Medicinal and pharmaceutical products.	51,220
Essential oils and perfume materials	16,505
Fertilizers, manufactured	7,209
Explosives	4,922
Plastic materials, etc.	91,161
Chemical materials and products	49,726
Leather	7,332
Rubber manufactures	41,995
Wood and cork manufactures	15,391
Paper, paperboard and manufactures	107,799
Textile yarn and fabrics	287,324
Non-metallic mineral manufactures	78,267
Iron and steel	95,286
Non-ferrous metals	24,515
Manufactures of metal	94,650
Machinery (except electric)	708,828
Electrical machinery, apparatus and appliances	251,367
Transport equipment	567,496
Sanitary, plumbing, heating and lighting fixtures and fittings	5,664
Furniture	5,463
Travel goods etc.	5,740
Clothing and clothing accessories	34,385
Footwear	15,481
Scientific instruments	120,711
Miscellaneous manufactured articles	162,218
Commodities and transactions of merchandise trade, not elsewhere classified	123,611
Commodities and transactions not included in merchandise trade	58,604

MAJOR EXPORTS 1969–70

Meat and meat preparations	$A417,909,000
Dairy products and eggs	102,254,000
Fish and fish preparations	39,107,000
Cereal grains and cereal preparations	431,792,000
Fruit and vegetables	94,102,000
Sugar, sugar preparations and honey	121,848,000
Hides, skins and fur skins, undressed	89,922,000
Textile fibres and their waste	768,802,000
Metalliferous ores and scrap	506,567,000
Coal, coke and briquettes	172,414,000
Petroleum and petroleum products.	27,722,000
Animal oils and fats	24,836,000
Chemical elements and compounds	94,155,000
Chemical materials and products, n.e.s.	23,537,000
Non-metallic mineral manufactures, n.e.s.	27,042,000
Iron and steel	135,707,000
Non-ferrous metals	284,112,000
Manufactures of metal, n.e.s.	42,466,000
Machinery (except electric)	89,804,000
Electrical machinery, apparatus and appliances	36,927,000
Transport equipment	153,071,000
Miscellaneous manufactured articles, not elsewhere specified	23,765,000
Commodities and transactions of merchandise trade, not elsewhere classified	286,267,000

FOOD EXPORTS TO BRITAIN, 1969–70

Butter	$A36,441,000
Cheese	5,719,000
Eggs	1,180,000
Meats:—	
Bovine animals	15,712,000
Sheep, lambs and goats	11,931,000
Preserved in airtight containers.	3,388,000
Milk and Cream	1,599,000
Dried fruit—grapes	6,042,000
Fruit (preserved in airtight containers)	24,996,000

Flour (wheaten), plain white.....	466,000
Wheat........................	51,354,000
Sugar-cane	30,726,000

AUSTRALIA'S TRADE WITH U.K.
1968–70
Value of Merchandise

Year	From U.K.	To U.K.
1967–68........	$A718,355,000	$A415,004,000
1968–69........	741,526,000	416,392,000
1969–70........	837,284,000	482,111,000

COMMUNICATIONS
Railways.—Total length of Commonwealth-owned and State-owned railways open for general traffic at June 30, 1970 and gross earnings during 1969–70:

State-owned	Route miles	Gross Earnings
New South Wales.....	6,061	$A247,288,000 (a)
Victoria.............	4,166	105,045,000 (a)
Queensland..........	5,813	108,831,000
South Australia......	2,444	33,340,000 (a)
Western Australia....	3,828	56,044,000
Tasmania...........	500	6,920,000
Commonwealth-owned		
Trans-Australian.....	1,108	17,389,000
Central Australia.....	818	7,510,000
Northern Territory...	317	2,478,000
Capital Territory.....	5	271,000
Total...........	25,060	$A585,116,000

(a) Excludes certain government subsidies aggregating $A17,883,000.

The Indian–Pacific 4 ft 8½ in. gauge railway now links Perth (Western Australia) and Sydney (New South Wales), a distance of 2,461 miles. Passenger service on this railway commenced on Feb. 23, 1970. All mainland capital cities, except Adelaide and Darwin, are now linked by standard gauge system.

The gross earnings of all Government lines in 1969–70 were $A585,116,000, working expenses $A565,967,000, and net earnings $A22,150,000. In 1969–70 passenger journeys numbered 450,122,000 and 32,351,000 tons of goods and livestock were carried. There are 270 miles of electrified line in New South Wales and 262 miles in Victoria.

Tramways and Omnibuses.—The total route mileage on June 30, 1970, under Government and semi-Government control was 163 for trams and 7,198 for omnibuses.

Shipping.—The entrances and clearances (one entrance and one clearance per voyage, irrespective of the number of ports visited) of vessels engaged in overseas trade at the various Australian ports in 1969–70 were: entered 4,969 (44,484,747 tons); cleared 5,053 (44,573,307 tons).

The total, including local shipping, entering the ports of the capital cities during 1969–70 was: Sydney, 3,818 vessels of 18,513,000 tons; Melbourne, 2,854 (13,714,000); Brisbane, 1,621 (7,684,000); Adelaide, 1,372 (5,226,000); Fremantle, 1,243 (8,099,000); Hobart, 643 (1,763,000 tons). At June 30, 1970, the Australian trading fleet vessels 200 tons gross and over comprised 143 vessels with a total 1,149,437 tons gross. Of these, 129 vessels totalling 1,041,286 tons gross were coastal trading vessels.

Posts and Telegraphs.—In the year ended June 30, 1970, there were 7,153 post offices dealing with 2,270,936,000 letters, 417,068,000 packets and newspapers, 13,104,000 registered articles and 23,682,000 parcels. 20,508,000 internal telegrams were despatched and 2,648,000 international telegrams received and despatched. At June 30, 1970, there were 6,128 telephone exchanges with 2,703,668 services and 3,913,167 instruments.

Broadcasting and Television.—On June 30, 1970, the Australian Broadcasting Commission operated 90 stations, including 18 short-wave stations in Australia. Privately owned commercial broadcasting stations totalled 114. On June 30, 1970, there were in force in Australia 2,670,393 listeners' licences, including 2,274,860 combined broadcast and television receiving licences. On June 30, 1970, 86 television stations were in operation, 23 in the various State capitals (including Canberra), and 63 in country areas. Television licences in force at June 30, 1970, numbered 2,757,974 (including combined licences, as above).

Motor Vehicles.—At June 30, 1970, there were 4,860,877 motor vehicles registered in Australia. These comprised 3,779,743 cars and station wagons, 122,400 motor cycles, and 958,734 commercial vehicles; revenue derived from motor registration fees and motor tax, &c. in 1969–70 was $A244,528,000.

Civil Aviation.—At June 30, 1970, there were 499 recognized landing grounds, including 381 licensed public aerodromes, in the various States and Territories, and 10 flying boat bases and alighting areas. Aircraft on the Australian Register at June 30, 1970. numbered 3,729. Mileage flown on regular internal air services in 1969–70 was 66,241,000 and on overseas services owned by Australia, 37,537,000.

CAPITAL
Canberra is the fast-growing national capital of the Australian Commonwealth. It is situated in the Australian Capital Territory which was acquired from New South Wales in 1911. The A.C.T. has an area of 939 sq. miles (including Jervis Bay) and is 150 miles (by air) from Sydney. On Dec. 31, 1970, the population was 139,800. Canberra is the seat of the federal government which moved from Melbourne in 1927. Apart from Parliament House, the city also contains other National Institutions, such as the Australian War Memorial, National Library, Royal Australian Mint and the Australian National University. Most Commonwealth departments now have their headquarters in Canberra. An artificial lake is a central feature of this planned city, based on Walter Burley Griffin's design. Canberra is well served with road, rail and air links to the State capitals.

THE NORTHERN TERRITORY
The Northern Territory has a total area of 520,280 square miles, and lies between 129°–138° East longitude and 11°–26° South latitude. The administration was taken over by the Commonwealth on January 1, 1911, from the government of the State of South Australia. The headquarters of the Administrator are at Darwin. Under the provisions of the Northern Territory (Administration) Act a Legislative Council has been established. The Council, which has power to make ordinances for the peace, order and good government of the Territory (subject to the assent of the Administrator), consists of six official members and eleven elected members. The President of the Council is chosen from the elected members.

The population of the Northern Territory (including Aborigines) at Dec. 31, 1970, was estimated to be 74,100. The number of Aborigines at the Census of 1966 was 21,119.

Beef cattle raising is the chief pastoral activity, and the staple industry of the Territory. On March 31, 1970, there were 1,179,000 cattle, 41,000 horses and 8,000 sheep in the Territory. The northern part of the Territory is capable under improved pastures of carrying successfully and profitably a great expansion of the beef cattle industry. Export abattoirs established at Darwin and Katherine in 1963 have created stable markets for

pastoralists. A cold store has been constructed in Darwin. Hides and skins exported from the Northern Territory during the year ended June 30, 1970, were as follows: Cattle hides, wet, salted, 2,400,000 lb.; bovine hides 31,000 lb. and reptile skins (no.) 975.

Agriculture in the Northern Territory hitherto has been confined to small farm settlements in the Darwin, Katherine, Daly River, Alice Springs, Adelaide River and Pine Creek areas. Principal crops grown in the Territory are grain sorghum, vegetables and fruit (pineapples, paw-paws, bananas and citrus). However, extensive experiments are being carried out, particularly in the area between Darwin and Katherine to determine what crops can be successfully grown in the Northern Territory on a commercial scale. Experimental work on pastures is also being undertaken.

The mineral industry has always contributed largely to the income of the Northern Territory and the value of mineral production exceeds that of the beef cattle industry. The principal minerals produced are manganese, copper, iron-hematite, gold, uranium and bismuth. Large-scale production of bauxite was expected to commence in 1971–72. In 1969–70, the total value of minerals produced (excluding uranium) was $A38,637,000.

Tourism is an important industry and there were more than 70,000 visitors to the Territory in 1969–70. The industry is estimated to be worth $A19,000,000 a year and is expanding by more than 12 per cent annually.

The chief rivers of the Territory are Victoria, Adelaide, Daly, Roper, South Alligator, McArthur, Liverpool, and Goyder. The first six are navigable, from 40 to 100 miles from their entrance, for boats drawing 4 feet. A limited amount of pearling is carried on from Darwin. The mother of pearl shell is of good quality.

The railway extends from Darwin to Larrimah (316 miles) and Alice Springs is connected by rail with Adelaide. A good bitumen road (the Stuart Highway) links Darwin with Alice Springs (956 miles) and another bitumen road, the Barkly Highway, runs from this road near Tennant Creek to Mt. Isa in Queensland (403 miles). The Commonwealth Government's programme for reconstructing nine other roads (1,600 miles, costing $30,200,000) in the Northern Territory, to such a standard as will facilitate the movement of beef cattle by large road trains, was nearing completion in 1971. Further major road works have been approved.

Regular shipping services operate to Darwin from the Eastern States and Western Australia and oversea ships call frequently to discharge general cargoes and petroleum products and to load export cargoes. There is also a service from Brisbane to Gulf of Carpentaria ports. During 1969–70, 906 vessels entered Darwin and 1,531,639 tons of cargo were handled. The cargo included 1,087,398 tons of iron ore which were exported through Darwin to Japan by two mining companies.

There are regular air services between Darwin and the capital cities and two airlines operate internal services.

ΨDarwin (estimated population of the urban area at June 30, 1970, 32,943) occupies an elevated site 97 ft. above sea level, overlooking Port Darwin. Alice Springs is situated in the MacDonnell Ranges Climate of the Northern Territory ranges from dry in the south to wet-monsoonal in the north.

Administrator of the Northern Territory (Darwin), F. C. Chaney, C.B.E., A.F.C.

Judges of the Supreme Court, Hons. R. A. Blackburn, O.B.E.; E. A. Dunphy; P. E. Joske, C.M.G.; R. A.

Smithers; J. A. Nimmo, C.B.E.; C. A. Sweeney; J. R. Kerr, C.M.G.

TERRITORY OF PAPUA NEW GUINEA

The Papua and New Guinea Act, 1949, which came into force on July 1, 1949, approved the placing of the Territory of New Guinea under the Trusteeship system of the United Nations and the agreement by which Australia became the sole administering authority. It provides for the Government of the Territory of Papua and the Territory of New Guinea in the Administrative Union. (The name Papua New Guinea is now used officially.)

In 1968 membership of the House of Assembly was increased to 94 members. The number of open electorates was increased to 69 and 15 electorates were created for candidates having prescribed minimum educational qualifications. There are 10 official members appointed by the Governor-General on the nomination of the Administrator.

The House of Assembly elects its own Speaker and a Nominations Committee to select 15 elected members as nominees for Ministerial office. The Australian Minister for External Territories, after receiving the recommendation of the Administrator, may then appoint from this list, 7 Ministerial members and 8 Assistant Ministerial Members. The Ministerial Members are responsible in the House for the functions of seven departments within the Administration while the Assistant Ministerial Members have more limited functions. The Ministerial members have seats on the Administrator's Executive Council which also includes 3 official members and an additional member of the House of Assembly nominated by the Administrator. The Council advises on the more important Departmental questions referred to it by Ministerial members and is consulted on all significant policy issues including the annual Territory budget.

The Territory of Papua, which was placed under the authority of the Commonwealth of Australia in 1906, comprises the south eastern portion of the island of New Guinea, together with the Trobriands, Woodlark, D'Entrecasteaux and Louisiade groups of islands and is separated from Australia by Torres Strait. The Territory lies wholly within the Tropics, between the 141st and the 155th meridians of east longitude and the 5th and 12th parallels of south latitude. The total area is 86,100 sq. miles, of which 83,325 are on the mainland. The non-indigenous population of Papua New Guinea at June 30, 1970, was 48,960; the indigenous population was 2,473,930, of whom nearly 950,000 live in the Highlands Districts of the Territory. Owing to heavy rainfall Papua is well watered in most parts and possesses a large number of streams. The best-known rivers are the Fly (730 miles long, including its tributary, the Strickland, and navigable by vessels with a draught of up to 8 ft. for about 500 miles) and the Purai. The climate is favourable to the cultivation of tropical products.

The Trust Territory includes (1) *North-Eastern New Guinea*, the northern section of east New Guinea between 2° 35'–8° S. lat., and 141°–148° E. long., with a total area of 60,095 sq. miles. This includes adjacent islands (Manam, Karkar, Long, Bagabag, Schouten and D'Urville or Kairiru Island). The chief centres are Lae, Bulolo, Finschhafen, Wau, Madang, Wewak, Goroka and Mount Hagen; (2) *Bismarck Archipelago*, including New Britain, New Ireland, and islands adjacent to both; (3) *Admiralty Islands* (chief town, Lorengau, in Manus Island); and (4) the two northernmost *Solomon Islands* (Bougainville and Buka with

adjacent islands). The estimated area of the islands is 23,065 square miles, making a total area for the territory of 92,160 square miles.

The principal river in N.E. New Guinea is the Sepik, 690 miles long, and navigable for about 300 miles by vessels with a draught of up to 13 ft.

The most important road linking Lae with the populous and developing highlands has recently been improved. Other major roads are between Lae and Wau and Oro Bay (being extended beyond Kokoda), and in the hinterlands of Port Moresby, Rabaul, Madang and Wewak.

Trans-Australian Airlines and Ansett-A.N.A. operate regular air services from Australia to Port Moresby. Internal scheduled and charter services are provided by T.A.A., Ansett Mandated Airlines, Papuan Air Lines and other companies. There are regular services to the British Solomon Islands and to West Irian. Qantas calls at Port Moresby on its Far East Service linking Australia with Manila and Hong Kong.

Several shipping companies operate regular cargo and passenger services between the Territory and Australia, Europe and the Far East. In 1968–69 oversea shipping entries at the eight main Territory ports totalled 1,542 ships, and over a million tons of cargo were handled through these ports.

The climate is hot and moist along the coast, becoming cooler and dryer as the higher altitudes are reached. It is suitable for the growth of all tropical products. The main products are copra, coconut oil, desiccated coconut, cocoa, coffee, rubber and timber; tea, oil palm, pyrethrum, passion fruit, timber and plywood are expected to increase in importance. The local fishing industry is also becoming a significant export income earner. The mining of gold has declined considerably, but copper mines are being established on Bougainville and are expected to provide one of the largest sources of income for the territory.

OVERSEAS TRADE
(Papua New Guinea)

	1968–69 $A'000	1969–70* $A'000
Total imports............	150,455	214,161
Total exports.............	75,244	93,745
Imports from U.K........	8,574	12,312
Exports to U.K..........	18,769	15,614

* Preliminary.

PUBLIC FINANCE
(Papua New Guinea)

	1969–70 $A'000	1970–71* $A'000
Grants from Australia.....	97,271	70,750 (a)
Local Revenue...........	62,924	73,700
Loans...................	25,620	41,200
Total Receipts .	185,815	185,650

* Estimated.

(a) In addition, Australia provides $A29,250,000 for salaries of overseas officers of the Papua New Guinea Public Service; this amount is not included in the Administration budget.

ECONOMIC AID FROM AUSTRALIA

	1967–70 $A'000	1970–71* $A'000
Grants to Administration..	97,271	70,750
Other Economic Aid(b)....	18,476	55,021
Total Aid from Australia ..	115,747	125,771

* Estimated.

(b) Includes loans from Australia and expenditures of an economic nature by Australian Government Departments.

SEAT OF ADMINISTRATION.—Administrative Headquarters of the Territory of Papua New Guinea is ꟼ Port Moresby, the principal port and town of Papua, with a non-indigenous population (estimated, 1970) of 13,590. ꟼ Rabaul (in New Britain), is the largest port in the Territory and second town, while ꟼ Lae (in Morobe District) is the third port and town, being the outlet for the Morobe plywood and gold mining district and for the Highlands region, and one of the principal air centres in the Territory.

Administrator, L. W. Johnson (1970).

Port Moresby is 1,800 miles from Sydney.

NORFOLK ISLAND

This island is about 1,035 miles from Sydney and 400 miles north of New Zealand. It is about five miles in length by three in breadth, and was discovered by Capt. Cook in 1774. Its area is 8,528 acres and circumference 20 miles. The climate is mild, with a mean temperature of 68° and an annual rainfall of 53 inches. The descendants of the mutineers of the *Bounty* were brought here from Pitcairn Island in 1856. The island is a popular tourist resort, and a large proportion of the population depends on tourism and its ancillaries for employment. Resident population (1970), 1,240.

Seat of Government and Administration Offices, Kingston. The Norfolk Island Council advises the Administrator on policy and the control of public finance.

An airfield was constructed in 1943, and bi-weekly air services operate from Australia and New Zealand.

Administrator, Air Cdre. R. N. Dalkin, D.F.C. (R.A.A.F., ret.).

Deputy Administrator and Official Secretary, G. Hitch.

COCOS (KEELING) ISLANDS

The Cocos (Keeling) Islands were declared a British possession in 1857. In 1878 they were placed under the control of the Governor of Ceylon and were later annexed to the Straits Settlements and incorporated with Singapore. On Nov. 23 1955, their administration was transferred to the Commonwealth of Australia. They are two separate atolls comprising some 27 small coral islands with a total area of about 5½ square miles, situated in the Indian Ocean in latitude 12° 5′ South and longitude 96° 53′ East. The main islands are West Island (the largest, about 6 miles from north to south) on which are the aerodrome and the administrative centre, and most of the European community; Home Island, the headquarters of the Clunies Ross Estate; Direction Island, on which is situated the Department of Civil Aviation's marine base; and Horsburgh. North Keeling Island, which forms part of the Territory, lies about 15 miles to the north of the group and has no inhabitants. The climate is equable and pleasant, being usually under the influence of the south-east trade winds for about three-quarters of the year. A fortnightly air charter service operates between Perth and the Cocos Islands. Population (estimated, 1970), 611.

Official Representative, C. W. Suthern.

CHRISTMAS ISLAND

Until the end of 1957 a part of the then Colony of Singapore, Christmas Island was administered as a separate colony until October 1, 1958, when it became Australian territory by Order in Council. It is situated in the Indian Ocean about 224 miles S. of Java Head and 520 miles E. of the Cocos (Keeling) Islds. Area, 52 sq. miles. Population (estimated, June 30, 1970), 3,361. The island is densely wooded and contains extensive deposits of phosphate of lime.

Administrator, J. G. White.

THE ANTARCTIC CONTINENT

The area of the Antarctic Continent is estimated at approximately 5,750,000 square miles. The greater part of the coastline has been charted, but considerable portions of the interior have not been visited, or at best have been seen only from the air. The question of territorial rights is complicated and there is no general international agreement thereon.

The *Australian Antarctic Territory* was established by an Order in Council, dated February 7, 1933, which placed under the government of the Commonwealth of Australia all the islands and territories, other than Adélie Land, which are situated south of the latitude 60°S. and lying between 160° E. longitude and 45° E. longitude. The Order came into force on August 24, 1936, after the passage of the Australian Antarctic Territory Acceptance Act, 1933. The boundaries of Terre Adélie were definitely fixed by a French Decree of April 1, 1938, as the islands and territories south of 60° S. latitude lying between 136° E. longitude and 142° E. longitude. The Australian Antarctic Territory Act, 1954 declared that the laws in force in the Australian Capital Territory are, so far as they are applicable, in force in the Australian Antarctic Territory.

On February 13, 1954, the Australian National Antarctic Research Expeditions (ANARE) established a station on MacRobertson Land at latitude 67° 36′ S. and longitude 62° 53′ E. The station was named Mawson in honour of the late Sir Douglas Mawson and was the first permanent Australian station to be set up on the Antarctic continent. Scientific Research conducted at Mawson includes Upper Atmosphere Physics, Meteorology, Earth Sciences, Biology and Medical Science. Mawson is also the centre for coastal and inland exploration.

A second Australian scientific research station was established on the coast of Princess Elizabeth Land on January 13, 1957, at latitude 68° 34′ S. and longitude 77° 57′ E. The station was named in honour of Captain John King Davis, second in command of two of Mawson's expeditions and master of several famous Antarctic ships The station was temporarily closed on Jan. 25, 1965 and reopened on Feb. 15, 1969. Scientific programmes carried out at Davis include meteorology, biology, upper atmosphere physics, with field investigations in glaciology and geology. In February, 1959, the Australian Government accepted from the United States Government custody of Wilkes Station on the Budd Coast, Wilkes Land in about 66° 15′ S. and longitude 110° 33′ E. The station was closed in February 1969, and activities were transferred to Casey station. Casey station was named in honour of Lord Casey, former Governor-General of Australia, in recognition of his long association with Australia's Antarctic effort. The station, at 66° 17′ S., 110° 32′ E., is of advanced design and scientific programmes carried out there include upper atmosphere physics, cosmic ray physics, geophysics, meteorology with field programmes in glaciology, geology, etc.

Since 1948 ANARE has also operated a station on Macquarie Island, a dependency of Tasmania, situated at 54° 28′ S. and 158° 57′ E., about 900 miles north of the Antarctic Continent.

On December 1, 1959, Australia signed the Antarctic Treaty with Argentine, Belgium, Chile, France, Japan, New Zealand, Norway, South Africa, the United Kingdom, the United States and U.S.S.R., all countries which have been active in Antarctic operations and research. The Treaty reserves the Antarctic area south of 60° S. latitude for peaceful purposes, provides for international co-operation in scientific investigation and research, and preserves, for the duration of the Treaty, the *status quo* with regard to territorial sovereignty, rights and claims. The Treaty came into force on June 23, 1961, and has been acceded to by another four nations not actively engaged in the area.

For other Commonwealth dependencies in the Antarctic *see* New Zealand, p. 735.

STATES OF THE COMMONWEALTH OF AUSTRALIA

NEW SOUTH WALES

The State of New South Wales is situated entirely between the 28th and 38th parallels of S. lat. and 141st and 154th meridians of E. long., and comprises an area of 309,433 square miles (exclusive of 939 square miles of Australian Commonwealth Territory which lies within its borders).

POPULATION.—The estimated population at December 31, 1970, was: Males. 2,320,600; Females, 2,303,306. Total, 4,623,900.

Births, Deaths and Marriages.

Year	Births	Deaths	Marriages
1967	78,841	39,613	37 077
1968	81,696	41,803	39,213
1969	86,036	40,665	41,285
1970	88,448	43,601	42,928

Vital Statistics.—Annual rate per 1,000 of mean population in 1970 :—Births, 19.70; Deaths, 9.53; Marriages, 9.38. Deaths under 1 year per 1,000 live births, 19.71.

Religions.

The members of the Church of England in New South Wales, according to the Census of 1966, number 1,622,066. Roman Catholic (including "Catholic") 1,174,779, Presbyterian 353,084, Methodist 305,733, Congregational 23,017, Baptist 55,774, Orthodox 96,606, Lutheran 30,019, Salvation Army 17,368, and Hebrew 25,913. The religion of 382,447 persons was not stated in the census schedules.

PHYSIOGRAPHY.

Natural features divide the State into four strips of territory extending from north to south, viz., the Coastal Divisions: the Tablelands, which form the Great Dividing Range between the coastal districts and the plains; the Western Slopes of the Dividing Range; and the Western Plains. The highest points are Mounts Kosciusko, 7,328 feet, and Townsend, 7,266 feet. The coastal district is well watered by numerous rivers flowing from the ranges into fertile flats which form their lower basins. The western portion of the State is watered by the rivers of the Murray-Darling system and immense reservoirs have been constructed for irrigation purposes, and there are many artesian bores. The Darling, 1,702 miles, and the Murrumbidgee, 981 miles, are both tributaries of the Murray, part of which forms the boundary between the States of New South Wales and Victoria. Other inland rivers are: Lachlan, Bogan, Macquarie, Castlereagh, Namoi and Gwydir.

Climate.—New South Wales is situated entirely in the Temperate Zone. The climate is equable and very healthy. At the capital (Sydney) the average mean shade temperature is 64°. The mean (shade) temperature ranges for the various divisions of the State are as follows: coastal, 59° in the south to 67° in the north; northern and central tableland, 53° to 61°; southern tableland, 44° to 58°;

and for the rest of the State (western slope, central plains, Riverina and western), 59° in the south to 68° in the north.

GOVERNMENT.

New South Wales was first colonized as a British possession in 1788, and after progressive settlement a partly elective legislature was established in 1843. In 1855 Responsible Government was granted, the present Constitution being founded on the Constitution Act of 1902. New South Wales federated with the other States of Australia in 1901. The executive authority of the State is vested in a Governor (appointed by the Crown), assisted by a Council of Ministers.

GOVERNOR.

Governor of New South Wales, His Excellency Sir (Arthur) Roden Cutler, V.C., K.C.M.G. K.C.V.O., C.B.E., assumed office Jan. 20, 1966
                                           $A23,000

Lieutenant-Governor, Hon. Sir Kenneth Whistler Street, K.C.M.G. (1950).

THE MINISTRY.
(March 11, 1971)

Premier and Treasurer, Hon. R. W. Askin, M.L.A.

Deputy Premier and Minister for Education and for Science, Hon. C. B. Cutler, E.D., M.L.A.

Chief Secretary and Minister for Tourism and Sport, Hon. E. A. Willis, M.L.A.

Decentralization and Development and Vice-President of the Executive Council, Hon. J. B. M. Fuller, M.L.C.

Public Works, Hon. D. Hughes, M.L.A.

Attorney-General, Hon. K. M. McCaw, M.L.A.

Local Government and for Highways, Hon. P. H. Morton, M.L.A.

Transport, Hon. M. A. Morris, M.L.A.

Lands, Hon. T. L. Lewis, M.L.A.

Environment Control, Hon. J. G. Beale, M.L.A.

Agriculture, Hon. G. R. Crawford, D.C.M., M.L.A.

Housing and for Co-operative Societies, Hon. S. T. Stephens, M.L.A.

Justice, Hon. J. C. Maddison, M.L.A.

Health, Hon. A. H. Jago, M.L.A.

Mines and for Conservation, Hon. W. C. Fife, M.L.A.

Cultural Activities and Asst. Treasurer, G. F. Ferudenstein, M.L.A.

Child Welfare and for Social Welfare, Hon. I. L. Waddy, O.B.E., D.F.C., M.L.A.

Labour and Industry, Hon. F. H. Hewitt, M.L.C.

The annual salaries of Ministers are: Premier, $A18,215; Deputy Premier, $A16,075; other Ministers $A15,040 each. Ministers also receive an expense allowance (Premier, $A4,700, Deputy Premier $A2,115, and other Ministers $A1,880 each) and the Leader and Deputy Leader of the Government in the Legislative Council further special allowances of $A1,410 and $A355 per annum respectively. In addition, Ministers who are members of the Legislative Assembly receive an electoral allowance (ranging from $A1,945 to $A2,880 according to the location of the electorate).

N.S.W. GOVERNMENT OFFICES IN LONDON,
56–57 Strand, W.C.2.

Agent-General, Sir John Pagan, C.M.G., M.B.E., E.D. (1970).

THE LEGISLATURE.

The Legislature consists of the Sovereign and the two Houses of Parliament (the Legislative Council and the Legislative Assembly). The *Legislative Council* consists of 60 members, elected jointly by both Houses of Parliament. Membership is for 12 years, 15 members retiring in rotation triennially. The *Legislative Assembly* consists of 96 members. The Women's Legal Status Act, 1918, removed disqualification regarding the election of women to be members of the Legislative Assembly. Natural-born or naturalized persons 21 years of age, who have resided 6 months in the Commonwealth, 3 months in the State and 1 month in the electoral district are entitled to the franchise. Voting is compulsory. At the State General Elections in February, 1961, there were 2,496,867 persons enrolled. In contested elections 2,291,484 persons voted, representing 93 per cent. of the persons enrolled.

President of the Legislative Council, Hon. Sir Harry Budd............(incl. allce.) $A10,575

Chairman of Committees, Legislative Council, Hon. T. S. McKay
                            (incl. allce.)   7,050

Speaker, Legislative Assembly, Hon. Sir Kevin Ellis, K.B.E.........(incl. allce.)   14,100

Chairman of Committees, Legislative Assembly, L. A. Punch....(incl. allce)   10,010

Leader of Opposition, Legislative Assembly, P. D. Hills..............(incl. allce.)   15,510

(Office-holders above who are members of the Legislative Assembly also receive an electoral allowance, ranging from $A1,945 to $A2,880 according to the location of the electorate.)

THE JUDICATURE.

The judicial system includes a Supreme Court (with the Chief Justice, eight Judges of Appeal, and 25 Puisne Judges), Land and Valuation Court, Industrial Commission, District Courts, Workers' Compensation Commission, Courts of Quarter Sessions, Petty Sessions and Children's Courts.

Supreme Court

Chief Justice, Hon. Sir Leslie James Herron, K.B.E. C.M.G. (+allce. $A1,150).......$A25,917

Judges of Appeal, Hon. Sir Bernard Sugerman (*President, Court of Appeal*) ($A24,539+allce. $A875); Hon. C. McLelland; Hon. K. S. Jacobs; Hon. K. W. Asprey; Hon. J. D. Holmes; Hon. A. F. Mason, C.B.E.; Hon. J. K. Manning; Hon. A. R. Moffitt (+allce. $A875)..............................   23,824

Puisne Judges, Hon. J. H. McClemens; Hon. R. Le G. Brereton; Hon. H. Maguire; Hon. F. G. Myers; Hon. M. F. Hardie; Hon. W. H. Collins; Hon. R. Else-Mitchell; Hon. B. P. Macfarlan, O.B.E.; Hon. J. F. Nagle; Hon. R. L. Taylor; Hon. D. M. Selby, E.D.; Hon. C. E. Begg; Hon. P. H. Allen; Hon. J. O'Brien; Hon. S. Isaacs; Hon. N. A. Jenkyn; Hon. L. W. Street; Hon. J. A. Lee; Hon. R. G. Reynolds; Hon. M. M. Helsham; Hon. C. L. D. Meares; Hon. P. B. Toose, C.B.E.; Hon. R. M. Hope; Hon. G. Carmichael; Hon. J. P. Slattery (+allce. $A875).............   23,824

Crown Employees Appeal Board

Chairman, Hon. W. B. Perrignon (+allce. $A875)..............................   23,824

Industrial Commission

President, Hon. A. C. Beattie (+allce. $A875)..............................   24,539

Members, R. C. Cook; J. J. McKeon; J. A. Kelleher; W. B. Perrignon; J. A. Sheehy; W. S. Sheldon; J. F. Sheppard; J. J. Cahill (+ allce. $A875) ....each   24,539

Land and Valuation Court Judges, Hons. Mr. Justice Hardie; Mr. Justice Else-Mitchell.

Workers' Compensation Commission, Chairman, His Honour A. T. Conybeare (+allce. $A875)........................   21,439

District Court, Chairman, His Honour J. H. Staunton (+allce. $A875).............   21,439

EDUCATION.

Education.—Education is compulsory between the ages of 6 and 15 years. It is non-sectarian and free at all state schools. The enrolment in August 1970 in 2,415 state schools was 760,092. In addition to the state schools there were, in 1970, 790 private colleges and schools, with an enrolment of 221,533 scholars. The five universities had an enrolment of 45,885 students (28,458 full-time, 13,560 part-time and 3,867 external students) in 1970; 16,571 at Sydney (incorporated 1850), 16,629 at the University of New South Wales (1948), 5,337 at New England (1954), 4,229 at Macquarie (1964) and 3,079 at Newcastle (1965). The State expenditure on Education was $A344,131,000 in the year 1969–1970. Students attending the State agricultural colleges numbered 2,548 in 1970.

FINANCE.

Year ended June 30th	Revenue*	Expenditure*
	$A	$A
1967	830,685,000	833,832,000
1968	888,077,000	887,618,000
1969	966,743,000	970,330,000
1970	1,076,380,000	1,080,782,000

* Excluding the self-balancing Road Transport and Traffic Fund.

The Public Debt of New South Wales at June 30, 1970, was $A3,078,539,000, of which an amount of $A190,538,000 was repayable in London (interest $A8,951,000), $A55,345,000 was repayable in New York (interest $A2,894,000), $A3,158,000 was repayable in Canada (interest $A182,000), $A3,233,000 was repayable in Switzerland (interest $A145,000), $A2,049,000 was repayable in the Netherlands (interest $A102,000) and $A2,824,216,000 was held in Australia, with an annual interest bill of $A143,776,000.

Banking, etc.—There were (Jan. 1971) 11 trading banks with deposits of $A3,195,538,000. Savings bank deposits amounted to $A2,459,772,000, representing $A532 per head of the population. The amount assured in New South Wales in *Life Assurance Societies* in 1969 was $A4,621,200,000 ordinary, $A621,300,000 superannuation and $A430,200,000 industrial. The membership of *Friendly Societies* was 136,037, and the funds at June 30, 1969, were $A30,200,000. Members of *Trade Unions* at Dec. 31, 1969, numbered 797,162, the funds of 176 Unions being $A11,216,000. Balances outstanding on *Instalment Credit* for retail sales on June 30, 1970, were $A741,000,000.

PRODUCTION AND INDUSTRY.

Value of Production.—In 1968–69 the net value of production of the primary industry was $A1,157,602,000. The values for the principal primary industries (in 1969–70) were: pastoral $A373,033,000, agricultural $A312,670,000, dairying and farmyard $A161,123,000. Net value of mining and quarrying in 1968–69 was $A239,505,000.

Agriculture.—During the year to Mar. 31, 1970, 14,302,000 acres were under crops.

The total area under wheat was 8,824,736 acres, of which 8,622,652 acres were harvested for grain, and 95,585 acres for hay. The production of wheat was 162,786,000 bushels of grain and 149,810 tons of hay. Other important crops in 1969–70 were 4,006,000 bushels of maize, 19,238,000 bushels of oats, 239,531 tons of rice, besides other kinds of grain, 142,047 tons of potatoes, and 27,334 cwt. of dried leaf tobacco. Sugar-cane to the extent of 835,232 tons was crushed; while 3,820,697

bushels of bananas were obtained; almost every kind of fruit and vegetable is grown. There were 25,442 acres of vineyards, of which 20,087 acres were bearing.

Land Tenure.—The total extent of land alienated and in process of alienation from the Crown on June 30, 1970, was 66,483,000 acres, while the area of land under lease, etc., from the Crown was 107,792,000 acres, and the balance 23,762,000 acres, consisted of reserve and other lands neither alienated nor leased; the total area of the State, exclusive of the Australian Capital Territory, is 198,037,000 acres.

Pastoral, etc.—The country is admirably adapted for sheep-farming, the principal breed of sheep being the celebrated merino, which was introduced in 1797. On Mar. 31, 1969, there were 5,637,039 cattle, 72,283,564 sheep and lambs, and 707,831 pigs. In 1969–70, 749,839,000 lb. (stated as in the grease) of wool were produced, 63.881,000 lb. of butter, 17,291,000 lb. of cheese, and 35,721,000 lb. of bacon and ham.

Forests.—The estimated forest area is 32,390,000 acres (U.N. classification), of which State forests cover 7,069,000 acres and 1,033,000 have been set aside as timber reserves.

Mining Industry.—The principal minerals are coal, lead, zinc, rutile, zircon, copper and tin. The total value of minerals won in 1968 was $A300,015,000; the value of output of the coal-mining industry was $A144,899,000 and of the silver–lead–zinc industry, $A99,765,000 (1969–70). The mining industry gave employment to 25,284 miners during 1969–70. In 1969–70, 34,952,000 tons of coal were produced.

Factories.—In 1968–69 there were 14,805 manufacturing establishments (the sharp fall in the number of factories in 1968–69 was due to a substantial change in the scope of the manufacturing census). The number of persons employed in June, 1969, was 532,448. The value added to materials in manufacturing establishments was $A3,125,600,000. Large iron and steel works with subsidiary factories are in operation at Newcastle and Port Kembla in proximity to the coalfields. Products of the regions include iron and steel of various grades, pipes, boilers, steel wire and wire netting, copper wire, copper and brass cables and tin-plate. The production (1969–70) of pig-iron was 4,307,000 tons, and of steel ingots 5,691,000 tons.

OVERSEAS TRADE.

Year ended June 30	Oversea Imports $A (f.o.b.)	Oversea Exports $A (f.o.b.)
1967	1,323,597,000	878,446,000
1968	1,405,331,000	943,182,000
1969	1,500,534,000	1,010,488,000
1970	1,707,445,000	1,158,603,000

The chief exports in 1969–70 were wool, wheat, coal, iron and steel, meat etc., machinery and copper and copper base alloys. Chief imports were machinery, motor vehicles, textiles, crude petroleum, chemicals, paper products, iron and steel, medical instruments, etc., foodstuffs, plastic materials, pharmaceuticals and printed matter.

TRANSPORT AND COMMUNICATIONS.

Shipping.—Excluding coastal trade, 4,041 vessels entered ports of N.S.W. during the year ended June 30, 1969, the net tonnage being 24,456,000. The shipping entries at Sydney, including coastal, were 3,896 vessels of 16,244,000 net tonnage.

Roads and Bridges.—There are 129,700 miles of roads and streets in New South Wales, including

26,400 miles of natural surface and cleared only. The total expenditure by the Government and the local councils on roads, bridges, &c., in 1968-69 was $193,004,000. Sydney Harbour bridge which was completed and opened for traffic in March, 1932, carries eight lanes of roadway with a total width of 84 ft., two footways each 10 ft. wide, and two lines of railway. At mean high water there is a headway of 172½ ft.

Motor Vehicles.—At Dec. 31, 1970, there were 1,764,295 registered motor vehicles (cars, 1,146,507).

Railways.—The railways of New South Wales are controlled by the State, which also operates omnibus services. At June 30, 1970, the mileage of the State railways open for traffic was 6,061, revenue in the year 1969-70 being $A250,488,000.

Aviation.—Sydney is the principal oversea terminal in Australia. Traffic movements at Sydney airport in 1969-70 were: passengers 4,214,322 (3,390,322 domestic, 824,000 international); freight, 76,290 short tons (48,962 domestic, 21,328 international); aircraft, 87,750 (75,179 domestic, 12,571 international).

Posts, Telegraphs and Telephones.—The postal, telegraphic, telephonic and radio services are administered by the Commonwealth Government. At June 30, 1970, there were 2,285 post offices in New South Wales. The postal matter carried during 1969-70 included 758,173,000 letters and registered articles and 173,283,000 newspapers and parcels posted for delivery in Australia. The overseas mails consisted of 51,592,000 registered articles and letters and 13,617,000 newspapers and parcels despatched, 80,262,000 registered articles and letters and 33,667,000 newspapers and parcels received. During the year 7,014,000 telegrams were despatched to places within Australia and 1,339,000 cablegrams to places outside Australia. Transit time between Sydney and London is approximately 2½ days for airborne mail and between 4 and 6 weeks for seaborne mail. The telephone services in operation numbered 1,050,477.

Radio and Television.—In June, 1970, there were 21 National Broadcasting Stations in New South Wales and 38 commercial stations operating under licence. The number of broadcast listeners' licences was 959,776. At June 30, 1970, there were 29 television stations (14 national, 15 commercial) in operation and the number of viewers' annual licences was 931,478.

TOWNS.

Ψ SYDNEY, the chief city and capital and the largest city in Australia, stands on the shores of Port Jackson, with a water frontage of 152 miles; the depth of water at the Heads is not less than 80 ft. and at the wharves up to 40 ft. There are extensive facilities for handling cargo, and for storing and loading grain in bulk or bags; also for replenishing coal and oil bunkers. For 13 miles Sydney Harbour extends inland, the finest harbour in the world, and is surrounded by scenery of surpassing beauty. The principal wharves are situated in close proximity to the business centre of the city. The total area of water in the harbour is 13,600 acres, or about 21 square miles, of which approximately one-half has a depth of not less than 30 ft.: the rise and fall of the tide is from 3 to 6 ft.

The parks in or adjacent to the metropolitan area include the Royal National Park which measures about 36,700 acres, Kuring-gai Chase 35,300 acres, Lane Cove River Park 1,000 acres and Centennial Park 490 acres.

The Sydney Statistical Division embraces an area of approximately 1,573 square miles, with a population of 2,780,310 (at June 30, 1970). The Newcastle and Wollongong Statistical Districts contain populations of 346,970 and 203,110 respectively.

The population of principal municipalities located outside the boundaries of these statistical areas are: Broken Hill 30,620, Wagga Wagga 28,330, Albury 27,330, Tamworth 23,850, Orange 22,860, Goulburn 21,540, Lismore 20,540, Bathurst 17,550, Blue Mountains 16,980 (part not included in Sydney Statistical Division) and Dubbo 16,640.

DEPENDENCY OF NEW SOUTH WALES.

LORD HOWE ISLAND (436 miles north-east of Sydney). Lat. 31° 33' 4" S., Long. 159° 4' 26" E. Area 4,088 acres. Pop. June 30, 1970, 280. The island is of volcanic origin and Mount Gower reaches an altitude of 2,840 ft. The affairs of the Island and the supervision of the Kentia palm seed industry are controlled by an elected Island Committee and a Board at Sydney. *Office,* Chief Secretary's Department, Sydney.

QUEENSLAND

This State, situated in lat. 10° 40'-29° S. and long. 138°-153° 30' E., comprises the whole northeastern portion of the Australian continent.

Queensland possesses an area of 667,000 square miles (*i.e.*, equal to more than 5½ times the area of the British Isles).

POPULATION.—At Dec. 31, 1970, the population numbered 1,820,000 persons.

Births, Deaths and Marriages

Year	Births	Deaths	Marriages
1968	35,190	16,078	14,860
1969	36,576	15,786	15,669
1970	37,530	17,055	16,082

Vital Statistics:—Annual rate per 1,000 of mean population in 1970: Births, 20·8; Deaths, 9·5; Marriages 8·9. Deaths under 1 year, 17·9 per 1,000 live births.

Religions.

At the Census of 1966 there were 522,540 Church of England, 425,669 Roman Catholics (including Catholics undefined), 188,492 Presbyterians, 179,591 Methodists, 40,237 Lutherans, 26,032 Baptists, 13,896 Orthodox, 9,949 Congregationalists, 66,063 other Christians, and 1,629 Hebrews.

PHYSIOGRAPHY.

The Great Dividing Range on the eastern coast of the continent produces a similar formation to that of New South Wales, the eastern side having a narrow slope to the coast and the western a long and gradual slope to the central plains, where the Selwyn and Kirby Ranges divide the land into a northern and southern watershed. The Brisbane, Burnett, Fitzroy and Burdekin rise in the eastern ranges and flow into the Pacific, the Flinders, Mitchell, and Leichhardt into the Gulf of Carpentaria, and the Barcoo and Warrego rise in the central ranges and flow southwards.

Climate.—At Brisbane the mean temperature for 1970 was 69·3°, the maximum and minimum shade temperatures being 94·7° and 37·9°; mean barometer, 30·04 inches. The coastal regions are warm and moist, but the rainfall decreases away from the coast and is scanty in the far west. The rainfall in Brisbane during 1970 was 56·68 inches, compared with average rainfall of 43·0 inches.

GOVERNMENT.

Queensland was constituted a separate colony with Responsible Government in 1859, having previously formed part of New South Wales. The executive authority is vested in a Governor (appointed by the Crown), aided by an Executive Council of 14 members.

GOVERNOR.

Governor of Queensland, Hon. Sir Alan James Mansfield, K.C.M.G., K.C.V.O., *appointed* March 21, 1966.................... $A26,500

EXECUTIVE COUNCIL.

(H.E. the Governor presides.)
Premier and Minister for State Development, Hon. J. Bjelke-Petersen............. $A15,795
Deputy Premier and Treasurer, Hon. Sir Gordon Chalk, K.B.E. 13,540
Mines and Main Roads, Hon. R. E. Camm.
Minister for Justice and Attorney-General, Hon. P. R. Delamothe, O.B.E.
Education and Cultural Activities, Hon. A. R. Fletcher.
Primary Industries, Hon. J. A. Row.
Health, Hon. S. D. Tooth.
Labour and Tourism, Hon. J. D. Herbert.
Transport, Hon. W. E. Knox.
Industrial Development, Hon. F. A. Campbell.
Lands, Hon. V. B. Sullivan.
Works and Housing, Hon. A. M. Hodges.
Conservation, Marine and Aboriginal Affairs, Hon. N. T. E. Hewitt.
Local Government and Electricity, Hon. W. A. R. Rae.

Ministers, each $A12,415.

AGENT-GENERAL IN LONDON.

Agent-General for Queensland, C. H. Curtis, 392–393 Strand, W.C.2.

THE LEGISLATURE.

Parliament consists of a *Legislative Assembly* of 78 members, elected by universal adult suffrage. Members of the Assembly receive $A7,560 per annum and an electorate allowance ranging from $A1,245 to $A2,970 p.a. The Assembly, as elected on May 17, 1969, was composed of: Country Party, 26. Australian Labour Party 31, Liberal Party 19, Democratic Labour Party 1, North Queensland Labour Party 1. The Country and Liberal parties form a coalition government.

Speaker, Hon. D. E. Nicholson.......	$A10,380
Chairman of Committees. K. W. Hooper	8,465
Clerk of Parliament, C. George.......	13,240

THE JUDICATURE.

There is a Supreme Court, with a Chief Justice, a Senior Puisne Judge and 12 Puisne Judges: District Courts, with 12 Judges; an Industrial Court, with a Supreme Court Judge as President; a Land Appeal Court and a Medical Assessment Tribunal, each presided over by a Judge of the Supreme Court; a Local Government Court, pre-sided over by a District Court Judge; and the Industrial Conciliation and Arbitration Commis-sion consisting of 5 members; and Inferior Courts at all the principal towns, presided over by Stipendiary Magistrates.

Chief Justice, Supreme Court, Hon. Mostyn Hanger	$A24,800
Senior Puisne Judge, Hon. C. G. Wanstall	17,700
Puisne Judges, Hons. N. S. Stable; R. W. Skerman; G. L. Hart; G. A. G. Lucas; J. A. Douglas; D. M. Campbell (Central Judge); B. M. Hoare; W. B. Campbell; R. H. Matthews; J. P. G. Kneipp (Northern Judge); D. G. Andrews; E. S. Williams ....each	22,200

EDUCATION.

Education is compulsory between the ages of 6 and 15, and is free in state primary and secondary schools. On Aug. 1, 1970, there were 1,236 state schools, including 227 providing secon-dary education, in operation, with 12,251 teachers and an enrolment of 297,889 children, and 334 pri-vate and 8 grammar schools, with an enrolment of 89,856. In 1970, tertiary level course enrolments at colleges of advanced education, technical colleges, and government teachers' colleges were 5,373 full-time and 1,878 part-time. Sub-tertiary level course enrolments at these establishments and rural training schools numbered 1,585 full-time and 25,536 part-time, including correspondence and apprenticeship students. The state-aided Univer-sities had an enrolment of 8,313 full-time students. State expenditure on education in 1969–70 was $A118,091,000.

PRODUCTION AND INDUSTRY.

The gross value of primary production (excluding mining) in 1969–70 was $A741,866,000 (agriculture $A315,530,000, dairying $A70,959,000, pastoral $A301,577,000, poultry and bee-keeping $A25,376,000 forestry $A18,162,000 fisheries $A8,034,000, hunting and trapping $A2,229,000. Net value of manufacturing in 1968–69 $A663,000,000.

Land Tenure.—Of the total area of 426,880,000 acres 57,551,000 acres were alienated or in process of alienation at Dec. 31, 1970, and 347,571,000 acres were held under Crown leases.

Agriculture and Livestock.—The total area under crop in 1969–70 was 5,364,733 acres. The most important crop was sugar-cane, under which there were 640,521 acres, producing 2,081,000 tons of raw sugar, 1,504,049 acres were under wheat (yielding 14,898,292 bushels), 108,679 under maize (2,713,425 bushels), 371,234 under sorghum (6,789,303 bushels), and 416,819 under barley (7,586,610 bushels). The livestock on March 31, 1970, included 7,514,917 cattle, 706,563 being dairy cattle, 16,445,833 sheep, 172,768 horses, and 479,586 pigs.

Forestry.—At June 30, 1970, 7,500,000 acres were permanently dedicated State forests and 1,699,000 acres were timber reserves. Total Aus-tralian grown timber processed amounted to 406,000,000 super feet.

Minerals.—There are rich deposits of bauxite, copper, lead, silver, uranium and zinc, and deposits of gold, tin, limestone, ironstone, wolfram and mineral sands. Coal is mined in the Ipswich (near Brisbane) and some northern districts, and there is extensive production by open-cut method in Central Queensland. Commercial production of oil began at Moonie in South Queensland in 1964 and at Alton nearby in 1966. The output in 1970 included gold, $A2,403,000; coal, $A54,617,765; copper $A128,862,410; tin $A3,617,048; silver $A19,610,014; lead $A41,372,256; zinc $A26,355,056.

Factories.—In 1968–69, 4,314 factories employed 116,448 persons. Value of production (value added to raw materials) was $A663,000,000. Much pro-duction was the processing of primary products, e.g. sugar, meat, butter, flour, timber, minerals and fruit. Included in other factory production were the products from engineering, railway, metal, chemical fertilizer works, cement, paper and woollen mills and oil refineries.

FINANCE.

Receipts and Expenditure of the Consolidated Revenue Fund and Debt of Queensland for three years ended June 30:—

Year	Revenue	Expenditure	Debt (Gross)[1]
	$A	$A	$A
1968...	376,986,968	376,016,940	1,077,655,597
1969...	387,866,245	388,777 359	1,148,819,719
1970...	441,074,095	444,618,034	1,222,707,176

[1]At par rates of exchange.

Banking.—Advances made by Trading Banks (including the Commonwealth Trading Bank of Australia) at June 30, 1970, totalled $A580,339,000. The deposits at the same date amounted to $A917,254,000. Depositors' balances in Queensland savings banks at June 30, 1970, $A875,580,000, averaged $A487 for each inhabitant. There were 2,010,835, operative accounts.

COMMUNICATIONS.

Road and Rail.—The State is served by 5,814 miles of railways, practically all of 3 ft. 6 in. gauge. During 1969-70, 28,515,000 passengers and 14,439,000 tons of goods and livestock were carried. At June 30, 1970, there were 79,058 miles of formed roads and 40,167 miles of unconstructed roads in the State, and 688,675 motor vehicles were on the register.

Aviation.—Regular services operate between Brisbane, the main Queensland coastal and inland towns and the southern capitals. Brisbane is also a port of call on several international services.

Radio and Television.—On June 30, 1970, 18 national and 25 commercial sound broadcasting and 8 national and 10 commercial television stations were operating in Queensland.

OVERSEAS TRADE.

Year	Imports	Exports
1967–68	$A227,021,903	$A562,938,460
1968–69	288,599,689	677,458,758
1969–70	294,113,000	773,519,000

The chief overseas exports are minerals, meat, sugar, wool, alumina, wheat and hides.

TOWNS.

CAPITAL, Ψ BRISBANE, is situated on the Brisbane River, which is navigable by large vessels to the city, over 10 miles from Moreton Bay. The population of the Brisbane Statistical Division at June 30, 1970, was 853,000. This area includes the cities of Brisbane (703,000), Ipswich (59,300) and Redcliffe (32,200). Of the 957 square miles in the Division, 385 square miles are under the control of the Brisbane City Council, presided over by a Lord Mayor

Other cities and towns with population over 10,000 at June 30, 1970, are: Ψ Townsville, 69,000, Gold Coast, 63,400; Toowoomba, 60,250; Ψ Rockhampton, 48,100; Ψ Cairns, 28,300; Ψ Bundaberg, 27,750; Mount Isa, 21,000; Ψ Maryborough, 20,100; Ψ Mackay, 20,000.

Transmission of mails from London to Brisbane, by air, 3 days; by sea 5 to 6 weeks.

SOUTH AUSTRALIA

The State of South Australia is situated between 26° and 38° S. lat. and 129° and 141° E. long., the total area being 380,070 sq. miles.

POPULATION.—At Dec. 31, 1970, the population was estimated to be 1,177,800.

Births, Deaths and Marriages

Year	Births	Deaths	Marriages
1967	20,386	9,071	9,434
1968	21,207	9,916	9,652
1969	21,077	9,337	10,599
1970	22,617	10,138	10,864

Before 1967, registrations of vital events of full-blood Aborigines, where identified, have been excluded.

Religions.

Religion is free and receives no State aid. At the Census, 1966, the persons belonging to the principal religious denominations were as follows: Church of England, 286,154; Methodists, 227,483; Congregationalists, 18,288; Baptists, 22,235; Lutherans, 59,281; Roman Catholics, 220,576; Presbyterians, 42,687; Churches of Christ, 25,344; and Orthodox, 27,753.

PHYSIOGRAPHY.

The most important physical features of South Australia are broad plains, divided longitudinally by four great secondary features, which form barriers to east–west movement, and which have thus largely determined the direction of roads and railways, the sites of towns and villages and the manner of distribution of the population. These four barriers are Spencer Gulf, Gulf St. Vincent, the Mt. Lofty–Flinders Ranges and the River Murray. The long, deeply-indented coast-line, which provides a few major, and a multitude of lesser harbours, trends generally south-eastward. Pleasant weather conditions and good rainfall are experienced in most coastal areas.

The north-western portion of the State is mostly desert, while north of latitude 32°S. the country is unpromising by comparison with the fertile land which surrounds the hill country of the east. The Murray, which flows for some 400 miles through the south-eastern corner, is the only river of importance.

The lack of rivers and fresh-water lakes in the settled areas has necessitated the building of a number of reservoirs, which have been supplemented since 1941 by the construction of pipelines from the River Murray.

Climate.—The mean annual temperature at Adelaide is 63°, the winter temperature (June–August) averaging 54°, and the summer (November–March) 71°. During the summer months the maximum temperature at times exceeds 100°, but is associated with a relatively low humidity. The average annual rainfall at Adelaide, derived from over 100 years' record is 21 inches. This total is rather higher than the approximate average annual rainfall over the whole of the agricultural areas. In the Mount Lofty Ranges the mean yearly rainfall in places exceeds 40 inches, while in Adelaide the precipitation has fallen as low as 10.11 inches.

GOVERNMENT.

South Australia was proclaimed a British Province in 1836, and in 1851 a partially elective legislature was established. The present Constitution rests upon a Law of Oct. 24, 1856, the executive authority being vested in a Governor appointed by the Crown, aided by a Council of 10 Ministers.

GOVERNOR.

Governor of South Australia, His Excellency Maj-Gen. Sir James William Harrison, K.C.M.G., C.B., C.B.E. (1968) $A15,000
Lieut.-Governor, Hon. Sir (John) Mellis Napier, K.C.M.G. (1942).

THE MINISTRY.

($A131,650 was voted in 1969–70 as salaries and allowances to Ministers.)
Premier, Treasurer, Minister of Development and Mines, Hon. D. A. Dunstan, Q.C., M.P.
Deputy Premier and Minister of Works and Marine, Hon. J. D. Corcoran, M.P.
Chief Secretary and Minister of Health, Hon. A. J. Shard, M.L.C.
Education, Hon. H. R. Hudson, M.P.
Attorney-General, Minister of Social Welfare and of Aboriginal Affairs, Hon. L. J. King, Q.C., M.P.

Roads and Transport and Minister of Local Government,
Hon. G. T. Virgo, M.P.
Agriculture and Minister of Forests, Hon. T. M. Casey,
M.L.C.
Conservation and Minister Assisting the Premier, Hon.
G. R. Broomhill, M.P.
Labour and Industry, Hon. D. H. McKee, M.P.
Lands, Repatriation and Irrigation, Hon. A. F. Knee-
bone, M.L.C.

AGENT-GENERAL IN LONDON.

*Agent-General and Trade Commissioner for South
Australia,* R. C. Taylor, South Australia House,
50 Strand, W.C.2.

THE LEGISLATURE.

Parliament consists of a *Legislative Council* of
20 members elected for 6 years, one-half retiring
every 3 years; and a *House of Assembly* of 47
members, elected for a maximum duration of 3
years. Election is by ballot, with universal adult
suffrage for the House of Assembly for all British
subjects, male and female, subject to some residential qualifications; there are certain property or war
service qualifications for electors to the Legislative
Council, who numbered 261,565 in 1970, those for
the Assembly numbering 635,533.

The elections to the House of Assembly in May,
1970, returned 27 Labour members and 20 Liberals,
and a Labour administration was subsequently
formed.

President of the Legislative Council, Hon.
Sir Lyell McEwin, K.B.E. $A12,500
Speaker of the House of Assembly, Hon.
R. E. Hurst 11,700
Leader of the Opposition, R. S. Hall.

THE JUDICATURE.

Law and Justice.—The Supreme Court is pre-
sided over by the Chief Justice and seven Puisne
Judges; there are Courts of Vice-Admiralty and
Insolvency, as well as Local and District Criminal
Courts with stipendiary magistrates, and Magis-
trates' Courts.

Chief Justice and Judge of Vice-Admiralty,
Hon. J. J. Bray $A19,400
Judges Hon. Sir Reginald Chamberlain;
Hon. D. S. Hogarth; Hon. C. H.
Bright; Hon. Roma F. Mitchell, C.B.E.;
Hon. G. H. Walters; Hon. H. E. Zell-
ing; Hon. W. A. N. Wells 17,500

EDUCATION.

Public Education (Primary, Secondary and Technical) is provided by the State, and controlled by a
responsible Minister; it is secular, compulsory,
and free. In 1970 there were 651 State schools,
with 228,788 students. The Government grants
Exhibitions and Scholarships, carrying the holders
to higher schools and the University. Private
schools number 170 with 37,106 students.

There are two universities: the University of
Adelaide, founded in 1874, and the Flinders
University of South Australia, opened in 1966, with
a total enrolment of 7,036 full-time students in 1970.
A State Institute of Technology has also been established, and there are technical schools at 9 country
centres and technical colleges at 4 and also special
trade schools for apprentices and domestic art
centres. The public library, museum, art gallery
and local institutes are supported or assisted by the
State

FINANCE

Banking.—There are 8 trading banks in Adelaide
including the Commonwealth Trading Bank
and the State Bank of South Australia, having total
average deposits of $A420,266,000 in December
quarter, 1970. The nine savings banks had deposits
of $A757,370,000 at December 31, 1970.

Revenue and Expenditure
(For years ended June 30)

Year	Revenue	Expenditure	Debt
	$A	$A	$A
1967...	258,823,000	258,717,000	1,013,060,000
1968...	274,544,000	277,404,000	1,074,959,000
1969...	298,335,000	297,895,000	1,143,954,000
1970...	338,498,000	335,578,000	1,210,489,000

PRODUCTION AND INDUSTRY.

The gross value of primary production in 1969–70
was: crops $A185,593,000, pastoral $A148,939,000,
dairying $A45,415,000, poultry $10,952,000,
and other primary $A19,358.

Land Tenure.—Of the total area of the State
(243,000,000 acres), 16,600,000 acres have been
sold or are in the process of alienation by the
Crown under systems of deferred payment;
127,000,000 acres are held under pastoral leases and
22,900,000 under other miscellaneous leases.

Agriculture.—The total area cultivated in 1969–70
was 13,822,000 acres—under wheat 3,209,700
acres, oats 371,600, barley 1,383,600. Wheat
harvest 1969–70, 59,158,600 bushels; barley,
30,453,600 bushels. Oranges, lemons, apples,
apricots, peaches, and all stone fruits and olives are
successfully grown, and fruit drying is profitable.
In 1969–70, there were 65,000 acres of vines with a
production of 43,754,000 gallons of wine and
6,458 tons of currants and raisins. Considerable
quantities of fruits (fresh and dried), wine and
brandy, are annually sent to overseas countries,
principally the United Kingdom, and to other
Australian States. Some areas of the State, particularly near Adelaide, are also very suitable for growing all kinds of root crops and vegetables.

Livestock (March 31, 1970).—There were
19,747,000 sheep, 1,026,000 cattle, 351,000 pigs.
Wool production (1969–70), 274,540,000 lb.

Minerals.—Iron, pyrite, gypsum, salt, coal, limestone, clay, &c., are found. The total mineral output was valued at $A98,526,000 in 1969, including
iron ore valued by the South Australian Director
of Mines at $A61,159,000.

Manufactures.—In 1968–69 there were 3,224
factories, employing 118,319 hands, the value of
production being $A639,800,000.

Transport and Communications.—There were (June,
1970) 3,817 miles of railway in South Australia,
171 miles of tram and bus routes and 75,291 miles
of roads, including roads and tracks outside local
government areas. There are a number of excellent harbours, of which Port Adelaide is the most
important. The number of vessels (exceeding
200 net tons) entering South Australia from overseas and interstate during 1968–69 was 1,747 with
net tonnage of 10,005,872. The total value of
shipping at South Australian ports during 1968–69
was 12,744,585 net tons involving 3,030 recorded
entries of vessels. The countries of registration
of vessels entered were: Australia, 1,745; United
Kingdom, 356; Japan, 92; Norway, 110; Sweden
98; New Zealand, 103; Netherlands, 82; all other
countries, 440. Cargo loaded for overseas was
3,376,966 tons weight and 151,537 tons measure,
and cargo discharged from overseas was 2,603,664
tons weight and 407,929 tons measure. There are
888 post offices in the State.

Civil Aviation.—There are 30 Government and
licensed airports; the largest of these, Adelaide airport, recorded 1,022,085 passenger movements
during 1969–70.

Motor Vehicles.—The registrations on Dec. 31,
1970, were 482,306, equal to 1 per 2·44 persons.

Wireless and Television (1970)—Broadcasting stations 16; listeners' licences 307,229. Television stations 8; viewers' licences 296,742.

OVERSEAS TRADE

Year	Imports	Exports
	$A	$A
1966–67	196,771,000	325,170,000
1967–68	215,619,000	282,767,000
1968–69	231,956,000	300,934,000
1969–70	201,223,000	417,030,000

The principal exports are wool, wheat, barley, fruit, lead and lead alloys, and ores and concentrates of iron, lead and zinc.

TOWNS

Ψ ADELAIDE, the chief city and capital, estimated population (June 30, 1970), 757,900, inclusive of suburbs. Other centres (with 1970 populations) are: Whyalla (30,500); Mt. Gambier (17,650); Ψ Port Pirie (15,850); Ψ Port Augusta (11,400); and Ψ Port Lincoln (9,800).

Transit.—Transmission of mails from London to Adelaide, approximately 29 days by sea and 2 days by air.

TASMANIA

Tasmania is an island in the Southern Ocean off the south-eastern extremity of Australia, from which it is separated by Bass Strait, about 140 miles wide, in which are situated the Furneaux Group and King Island, included within the State. It lies between 40° 40'–43° 39' S. lat. and 144° 31'–148° 18' E. long., and contains an area of 26,383 square miles.

POPULATION.—At June 30, 1970, the estimated population numbered 392,458; estimated Dec. 31, 1970, 395,573.

Year	Births	Deaths	Marriages
1967	7,547	3,228	3,213
1968	8,317	3,284	3,426
1969	8,445	3,309	3,532
1970	8,185	3,174	3,535

Vital Statistics.—The birth rate in 1970 was 20·83, death rate 8·08, marriage rate 9·00 per 1,000. Infant mortality (1970) 14·3 per 1,000 births.

Religions.

In 1966 there were 166,028 members of the Church of England, 71,089 Roman Catholics, 43,084 Methodists, 17,498 Presbyterians, 4,530 Congregationalists and Independents, and 7,759 Baptists.

PHYSIOGRAPHY.

The surface of the country is generally hilly and timbered, with mountains from 1,500 to 5,300 ft. in height, and expanses of level, open plains. There are numerous rivers, the Gordon, Derwent and Tamar being the largest. The climate is fine and salubrious, and well suited to European constitutions; the hot winds of Australia do not often reach the island. At Hobart the mean maximum temperature ranges from 53·5° in winter to 69·8° in summer, the minimum from 40·7° to 51·5°. The western side of the island is very wet, the eastern side being much drier; the average rainfall varies from 20 inches to 140 inches in different parts.

GOVERNMENT

The island was first settled by a British party from New South Wales in 1803, becoming a separate colony in 1825. In 1851 a partly elective legislature was inaugurated, and in 1856 responsible government was established. In 1901 Tasmania became a State of the Australian Commonwealth. The State executive authority is vested in a Governor (appointed by the Crown), but is exercised by Cabinet Ministers responsible to the Legislature, of which they are members.

GOVERNOR.

Governor of Tasmania, His Excellency Lieut.-Gen. Sir Edric Montague Bastyan, K.C.M.G., K.C.V.O., K.B.E., C.B., *b.* April 5, 1903; *assumed office* Dec. 2, 1968.

THE MINISTRY.

Premier, Treasurer and Minister in charge of Hydro-Electric Commission, Hon. W. A. Bethune, M.H.A.
Deputy Premier, Chief Secretary and Minister for Tourism, Hon. K. O. Lyons, M.H.A.
Minister for Education, Hon. R. Mather, M.H.A.
Agriculture and Forests, Hon. E. C. Beattie, M.H.A.
Attorney-General, Minister for Police and Licensing, Hon. E. M. Bingham, M.H.A.
Land, Works and Local Government, Hon. W. G. Barker, M.H.A.
Transport, Racing and Gaming and Mines, Hon. L. H. Bessell, M.H.A.
Housing, Industrial Development and Sea Fisheries, Hon. D. F. Clark, M.H.A.
Health and Road Safety, Hon. N. D. Abbott, M.H.A.

AGENT-GENERAL IN LONDON.

Agent-General for Tasmania, Hon. R. R. Neville, 458–9 Strand, Charing Cross, W.C.2.

THE LEGISLATURE.

Parliament consists of two Houses, a *Legislative Council* of 19 members, elected for six years (3 retiring annually, in rotation, except in every sixth year, when four retire) and a *House of Assembly* of 35 members, elected by proportional representation for five years in five 7-member constituencies, the electors for both Houses being all adult Tasmanians who have resided continuously in the State for 6 months. The term of the House of Assembly is reduced to 3 years after the expiry of the present term in 1974.

At the election held on May 10, 1969, the Labour Party lost its majority in the House of Assembly and the longest period of continuous government by a single party in any Australian state ended after 35 years. A Liberal-Centre Party coalition was formed by Mr. Bethune on May 27, 1969. The composition of the House of Assembly in May, 1969, was: Labour, 17, Liberal, 17 and Centre Party, 1.

President of the Legislative Council, Hon. W. J. T. Davis.

Clerk of the Council, G. W. Brimage.
Speaker of the House of Assembly, Hon. C. R. Ingamells.

Clerk of the House, B. G. Murphy.

THE JUDICATURE.

The Supreme Court of Tasmania, with civil, criminal, ecclesiastical, admiralty and matrimonial jurisdiction, was established by Royal Charter on October 13, 1823.

Chief Justice, Hon. Sir Stanley Charles Burbury, K.B.E.

Puisne Judges, Hon. G. H. Crawford; Hon. F. M. Neasey; Hon. D. M. Chambers; Hon. R. R. Nettlefold.

Local Courts established under the Local Courts Acts, 1896, are held before Commissioners who are legal practitioners, with a jurisdiction up to $A1,500 in the case of liquidated claims ($A1,000, unliquidated claims). Courts of General Sessions, constituted

by a chairman who is a Justice of the Peace and at least one other Justice, are established in the municipalities for the recovery of debts and demands not exceeding $A100. Courts of Petty Sessions are established under the Justices Act, 1959, constituted by Police Magistrates sitting alone, or any two or more justices. A single justice may hear and determine certain matters.

EDUCATION.

Government schools are of three main types: primary, secondary and matriculation schools. On Aug. 1, 1970, there were 79,499 scholars enrolled in 283 Government schools. There were also 65 independent schools with an enrolment of 14,623. The University of Tasmania at Hobart, established 1890, had 2,255 full-time students and 864 part-time (including external) students in 1970.

FINANCE.

Revenue and expenditure of the Consolidated Revenue Fund and debt of Tasmania at current rates of exchange (June 30) was:—

Year	Revenue $A	Expenditure $A	Debt $A
1966–67	92,676,009	93,248,028	535,606,361
1967–68	100,562,811	102,413,435	568,295,999
1968–69	107,845,604	111,540,383	606,671,386
1969–70	123,818,530	121,003,534	643,811,341

Banking.—The average weekly deposits of cheque-paying banks during December, 1970, were $A136,983,000; the savings bank deposits, Dec., 1970, were $A206,774,000.

PRODUCTION AND INDUSTRY

The net values of production in 1969–70 for the following were: agriculture, $A22·6 m.; pastoral, $A19·3 m, dairying, $A20 m.; forestry, $A13·6 m.; and other primary industries, $A6·8 m. Total value added in manufacturing in 1968–69 was $A204·4 m.

Agriculture and livestock.—Of the total area of the State (16,885,000 acres) there were in 1969–70, 427,356 acres of crops. The principal crops are potatoes, apples and other fruit, hay, hops, oats, green peas, turnips (for stock feed), barley and wheat. The livestock included (March 31, 1970) 646,000 cattle, 4,560,000 sheep and 111,000 pigs. The wool production (1969–70) was 48,195,000 lb.

Electrical Energy.—Tasmania, the smallest Australian state, ranks third as a producer of electrical energy—most of it derived from water power, with an output of 5,139,653,000 kWh in 1969–70. By reason of its low-cost electrical energy, Tasmania has the Commonwealth's only plants producing ferro-manganese, newsprint and calcium carbide and it is the source of the bulk of Australian requirements of electrolytic zinc, aluminium and fine papers. The Hydro-Electric Commission has nearly completed a network of ten stations on north-western rivers, and a hydro station is being constructed in the south-west. Two stations (one thermal and one hydro) were completed in 1970 and one hydro station in 1971. Present and planned future output: 1972, 1,322,400 kW; 1975, 1,545,000 kW.

Forestry.—State forest areas in 1969–70 occupied 2,783,217 acres. The quantity of timber (excluding firewood) of various species cut in 1969–70 was 754,903,000 true super feet, including 318,286,000 true super feet for wood-pulp.

Minerals.—The chief ores mined are those con-

taining copper, zinc, tin, silver, iron, and lead. The gross value of output in all mines and quarries in 1968–69 was $A57,782,000.

Manufactures.—The chief manufactures for export are: refined metals, preserved fruit and vegetables, butter, woollen manufactures, paper, confectionery, wood chips and sawn timber. The value added in 1968–69 was $A204,400,000. 32,465 persons, including working proprietors, were employed and salaries and wages paid totalled $A96·1 m.

COMMUNICATIONS

Road and Rail.—Tasmania is served by a 3 foot 6 inch gauge Government railway system of 500 route miles. An additional 83 route miles of the same gauge is privately operated. During 1969–70 the Government system carried 907,000 passengers and 1,258,000 tons of goods and livestock. At June 30, 1970 there were 13,688 miles of road normally open to traffic. Of this total 3,875 miles were sealed. Motor vehicles on the register at June 30, 1970, were: cars and station wagons, 119,274; commercial vehicles, 34,519 and motor cycles, 3,116.

Aviation.—Regular services operate between Tasmania and the other Australian States. During 1969–70 509,000 passengers were carried on these services. The main cities and towns in the State are served by regular internal services.

OVERSEAS TRADE

Year	Imports	Exports
	$A'000	$A'000
1967–68	45,024	76,888
1968–69	37,509	102,061
1969–70	46,998	143,470

The principal overseas exports in 1969–70 were: ores and concentrates, refined metals, fresh fruit, greasy wool, meat and butter.

TOWNS

CAPITAL, ΨHOBART, founded 1804. Population (June 30, 1970), 127,260.

Other towns (with population at June 30, 1970) are ΨLaunceston (62,500), ΨDevonport (17,120), Burnie-Somerset (19,710), Ulverstone (7,580) and New Norfolk (6,350).

Transmission of mails from London to Hobart, 28 days by sea; 2 days by air.

VICTORIA

The State of Victoria comprises the south-east corner of Australia, at that part where its mainland territory projects farthest into the southern latitudes; it lies between 34°–39° S. latitude and 141°–150 °E. longitude. Its extreme length from east to west is about 493 miles, its greatest breadth is about 290 miles, and its extent of coast-line is about 980 geographical miles, including the length around Port Phillip Bay, Western Port and Corner Inlet, the entire area being 87,884 square miles.

Population.—The population at Dec. 31, 1970, was 3,480,800 (1,747,000 males and 1,733,800 females).

Births, Deaths and Marriages.

Year	Births	Deaths	Marriages
1967	65,485	28,373	28,004
1968	70,228	29,967	29,724
1969	71,035	28,976	30,860
1970	73,019	30,335	31,729

Vital Statistics.—Annual rate per 1,000 of population in 1970: Births, 21·17; Deaths, 8·79; Marriages, 9·20. Deaths under 1 year per 1,000 births, 14·5.

Religions.

Members of the Church of England at the date of the census in 1966 numbered 923,078, Roman Catholics 889,495, Presbyterians 387,108, Methodists 279,300, Orthodox 100,387, Baptists 41,419, Churches of Christ 39,263, Lutheran 37,637 and Hebrew 31,058. The number of persons who did not state their religion was 333,734.

PHYSIOGRAPHY.

The *Australian Alps* and the *Great Dividing Range* pass through the centre of the State, and divide it into a northern and southern watershed, the latter sloping down to the ocean and containing, especially in the south-east, well-wooded valleys. The length of the Murray River, which forms part of the northern boundary of Victoria, is about 1,200 miles along the Victorian bank. Melbourne, the capital city, stands upon the Yarra-Yarra, which rises in the southern slopes of the Dividing Range.

Climate.—The climate of Victoria is characterized by warm summers, rather cold winters, and rain in all months with a maximum in winter or spring. Prevailing winds are southerly from November to February inclusive, with a moderate percentage of northerlies often associated with high temperatures. Northerly or westerly winds predominate from March to October inclusive. Rain on an average falls in Melbourne on 143 days per year, the annual average being 25·79 inches.

GOVERNMENT.

Victoria was originally known as the Port Phillip District of New South Wales and was created a separate colony in 1851, with a partially elective legislature. In 1855 Responsible Government was conferred. The executive authority is vested in a Governor, appointed by the Crown, aided by an Executive Council of Ministers.

Governor of the State of Victoria, His Excellency Maj.-Gen. Sir Rohan Delacombe, K.C.M.G., K.C.V.O., K.B.E., C.B., D.S.O., *born* Oct. 25, 1906, *assumed office* May 8, 1963.................. $A20,500

Lieutenant-Governor, Lieut.-General Hon. Sir Edmund Herring, K.C.M.G., K.B.E., D.S.O., M.C., E.D., Q.C.

THE MINISTRY.

Premier and Treasurer, Hon. Sir Henry Bolte, K.C.M.G.

Chief Secretary, Hon. R. J. Hamer, E.D.

Agriculture, Hon. G. L. Chandler, C.M.G.

Local Government, Hon. A. J. Hunt.

Attorney-General, Hon. G. O. Reid, Q.C.

Education, Hon. L. H. S. Thompson.

Housing, Forests and Aboriginal Affairs, Hon. E. R. Meagher, M.B.E., J.P.

Fuel and Power, and Mines, Hon. J. C. M. Balfour.

Health, Hon. J. F. Rossiter.

Transport, Hon. V. F. Wilcox.

State Development, Tourism and Immigration, Hon. V. O. Dickie.

Lands, Soldier Settlement and Conservation, Hon. W. A. Borthwick.

Labour and Industry and Assistant Minister of Education, Hon. J. A. Rafferty.

Public Works, Hon. Murray Byrne.

Water Supply, Hon. R.C. Dunstan, D.S.O.

Social Welfare, Hon. I. W. Smith.

AGENT-GENERAL IN LONDON.

Agent-General for Victoria, Hon. Sir Murray Porter, Victoria House, Melbourne Place, Strand, W.C.2.

THE LEGISLATURE.

Parliament consists of a *Legislative Council* of 36 members, elected for the 18 Provinces for 6 years, one-half retiring every 3 years; and a *Legislative Assembly* of 73 members, elected for a maximum duration of 3 years. Voting is compulsory. The electors on the rolls at June 30, 1970, numbered 1,852,023.

President of the Legislative Council, Hon. R. W. Garrett, A.F.C................. $A11,875

Speaker of the Legislative Assembly, Hon. V. Christie......................... 11,875

THE JUDICATURE

There are Magistrates' Courts, a County Court and a Supreme Court with a Chief Justice and 16 Puisne Judges.

Supreme Court.

Chief Justice, Hon. Sir Henry Winneke, K.C.M.G., O.B.E. (1964).............. $A24,800

Puisne Judges, Hon. T. W. Smith; Hon. Sir George Pape; Hon. Sir Alexander Adam; Hon. D. M. Little; Hon. U. G. Gowans; Hon. O. J. Gillard; Hon. J. E. Starke; Hon. E. H. E. Barber; Hon. M. V. McInerney; Hon. G. H. Lush; Hon. C. I. Menhennitt; Hon. H. R. Newton; Hon. F. Nelson; Hon. K. V. Anderson; Hon. W. C. Crockett Hon. N. M. Stephen ....each   22,000

County Court

Chairman of County Court Judges, Hon. G. L. Dethridge.................... 17,950

Judges, Their Honours J. G. Norris; B. J. Dunn; T. G. Rapke; H. Frederico; N. Vickery; D. Corson; A. Adams; J. X. O'Driscoll; J. Forrest; C. Harris; E. E. Hewitt; G. Just; R. J. Leckie; I. F. C. Franich; T. B. Shillito; J. P. Somerville; W. J. Martin; I. Gray; A. J. Southwell; J. O'Shea; J. G. Gorman each   16,450

Masters of the Supreme Court, C. P. Jacobs, M.B.E.; S. H. Collie; E. N. Bergere; G. S. Brett......................each   13,300

Crown Law Department

Solicitor-General, B. L. Murray, Q.C..... 22,200

Secretary to the Law Department, R. Glenister........................... 14,900

Crown Solicitor, J. Downey............ 16,350

EDUCATION.

Primary Education is compulsory, secular and free between the ages of 6 and 15. At Aug. 3, 1970, there were 1,823 Primary Schools attended by 355,848 pupils, 52 Primary-Secondary Schools with 14,885 pupils, and 246 Secondary Schools (excluding Junior Technical Schools) with an enrolment of 156,911. There were also 94 Government Junior Technical Schools with 57,796 pupils. In addition there are various Senior Colleges and Colleges of Advanced Education.

At Aug. 3, 1970, 191,028 pupils attended 581 non-Government schools, 487 of which were Roman-Catholic.

There are three State-aided Universities—Melbourne, Monash and La Trobe. Enrolments for 1970 at Melbourne were 14,726, at Monash 10,384 and at La Trobe 2,519.

PRODUCTION AND INDUSTRY.

The gross value of primary production in 1969–70 was $A1,079,409,000, agricultural $A319,699,000, pastoral $A385,025,000, dairying $A224,141,000, poultry and bee-keeping $A49,325,000, trapping $A3,078,000, forestry $A30,010,000, mining and quarries $A62,500,000, fisheries $A5,631,000. The net value of production of primary industries was

$A792,220,000. Wool, wheat, flour, butter, live stock, fruits, milk and cream, meats, poultry and eggs are staple products.

Agriculture.—Of the 8,058,000 acres under cultivation in 1969–70, 3,340,000 were wheat crops including hay and 884,000 oats for grain, 1,200,000 acres were cut for hay, and 1,745,000 acres were lying fallow. In 1969–70 7,251,000 gallons of wine were produced.

Live Stock.—There were on rural holdings in March, 1970, 33,157,000 sheep, 4,462,000 cattle, and 495,000 pigs. The quantity of wool produced in 1968–69 was 364,347,000 lb., valued at $A155,547,000 (preliminary figures).

Minerals.—Production of gold in 1968 was 11,210 fine oz. Other minerals raised consisted principally of coal (black and brown), limestone, kaolin, fireclay, white clay and gypsum. Production of brown coal in 1968 amounted to 22,970,653 tons.

FINANCE.

Year	Revenue	Expenditure	Debt
	$A	$A	$A
1967–68	601,328,373	604,122,006	1,998,611,000
1968–69	664,183,442	666,644,486	2,130,294,000
1969–70	726,899,896	742,281,898	2,254,361,000

Banking, etc.—State Savings Bank deposits at June 30, 1970, amounted to $A1,163,381,000; in addition, deposits in the Commonwealth Savings Bank (in the State of Victoria) amounted to $A536,971,000, and in other savings banks $A686,409,000.

Insurance (other than Life).—There were 274 companies or other bodies transacting business in Victoria during the year 1969–70. Total revenue amounted to $A290,627,000, made up of premium income $A275,014,000 and other income $A15,614,000. Expenditure totalled $A271,667,000, comprising claims $A185,219,000, commission and agents' charges $A26,982,000 and other expenditure $A59,467,000.

Secondary Industry.—In 1967–68 there were 316,108 males and 133,837 females (including working proprietors) employed in Victoria factories. Salaries and wages paid totalled $A1,244,216,000. The total cost of materials used, containers, tools replaced and repairs to plant was $A2,956,509,000, and of power, fuel and light, lubricants and water $A143,086,000. Gross value of output was $A5,351,311,000 and added value (net value of production) $A2,394,801,000. Principal factory products are motor vehicles and light engineering products, foodstuffs, chemicals, textiles, clothing, paper and rubber products.

TRANSPORT.

Victoria State Railways.—At June 30, 1970, there were 4,166 miles of railway open for traffic. The revenue and expenditure for the year ended June 30, 1970, were $A105,044,755 and $A118,558,104 respectively. Total traffic mileage was 20,543,327 and passenger journeys numbered 144,308,547. The tonnage of goods and live stock carried was 11,835,141.

Shipping.—During the year ended June 30, 1969, 3,618 vessels with net tonnage 17,944,435 entered Victorian ports and 3,591 vessels with total net tonnage of 17,768,772 were cleared.

Motor Vehicle Registrations.—The number of vehicles on the register at Dec. 31, 1970, was: cars and stationwagons, 1,098,140; utilities and vans, 131,273; trucks and omnibuses, 102,290, and motor cycles, 24,847.

OVERSEAS TRADE.

The export trade (excluding inter-state trade) consists largely of agricultural and pastoral products. The principal overseas imports of the State are aircraft and parts, apparel and textiles, manufactured fibres, machines and machinery, motor vehicles and tractors, metals and metal manufactures, rubber and rubber manufactures, crude petroleum, paper drugs and chemicals, synthetic resins and foodstuffs of vegetable origin.

Year	Imports	Exports
	$A	$A
1965–66	1,017,360,000	763,963,000
1966–67	1,072,514,000	801,187,000
1967–68	1,130,741,000	685,755,000
1968–69	1,182,747,000	707,579,000
1969–70	1,347,053,000	912,596,000

CITIES, TOWNS AND BOROUGHS.

ΨMELBOURNE, the capital city, which is an archiepiscopal see, was originally laid out in the year 1837 with wisdom and foresight; its wide streets, park lands, public gardens, university, public library, museum, art gallery and large churches are the principal features of the city. At the Census of June 30, 1966, the Melbourne Metropolitan Area had a population of 2,110,168. Other cities and towns are ΨGeelong, 105,059; Ballarat, 56,290; Bendigo, 42,208; Moe-Yallourn, 23,198; Shepparton, 17,506; ΨWarrnambool, 17,499; Wangaratta, 15,175; Traralgon, 14,079.

WESTERN AUSTRALIA

Includes all that portion of the continent west of 129° E. long., the most westerly point being in 113° 9′ E. long., and from 13° 44′ to 35° 8′ S. lat. Its extreme length is 1,480 miles, and 1,000 miles from east to west; total area 975,920 sq. miles.

POPULATION.—At December 31, 1970, the population was estimated at 1,001,315 (males, 509,033; females, 492,282). The figures include full-blood Aborigines.

Year	Births	Deaths	Marriages
1966	17,007	6,772	7,001
1967	18,023	6,779	7,430
1968	19,541	7,468	8,086
1969	20,754	7,350	8,993
1970	21,618	7,543	9,227

Religions.—Census of 1966—Church of England 316,153, Roman Catholics 213,659, Methodists 80,840, and Presbyterians 44,055.

Physical Features.—Large areas of the State, for some hundreds of miles inland, are hilly and even mountainous, although the altitude, so far as ascertained, rises nowhere above that of Mount Meharry (4,082 ft.) in the north-west division or that of Bluff Knoll (3,640 ft.) in the Stirling Range in the south-west. The coastal regions are undulating, with an interior slope to the unsettled central portion of Australia. The Darling and Hamersley ranges of the west have a seaward slope to the Indian Ocean, into which flow many streams, notably the Preston, Collie, Murray, Swan, Murchison, Gascoyne, Ashburton, Fortescue and De Grey. In the north the Fitzroy flows from the King Leopold ranges into the Indian Ocean, and the Drysdale and Ord into the Timor Sea. The greater portion of the State may be described as an im-

mense tableland, with an average elevation of 1,000 to 1,500 ft. above sea-level, the surface of which varies from stretches of clay soils to the sand dunes of the far interior. The climate is one of the most temperate in the world. The total rainfall at Perth during 1970 was 35·76 inches, the average for the previous 94 years 34·77. Of the total area two-thirds is suitable for pastoral purposes.

GOVERNMENT.

Western Australia was first settled by the British in 1829, and in 1870 it was granted a partially elective legislature. In 1890 Responsible Government was granted, and the Administration vested in a Governor, a Legislative Council, and a Legislative Assembly. The present constitution rests upon the Constitution Act, 1889, the Constitution Acts Amendment Act, 1899, and amending Acts. The Executive is vested in a Governor appointed by the Crown and aided by a Council of responsible Ministers.

The Legislative Assembly (elected Feb., 1971) is composed of Australian Labor Party 26, Liberal Party 17, Country Party 8.

GOVERNOR

Governor of Western Australia, His Excellency Major-General Sir Douglas Anthony Kendrew, K.C.M.G., C.B., C.B.E., D.S.O., *appointed* 1963 .... $A17,000
Lieut.-Governor, Hon. Sir Albert Asher Wolff, K.C.M.G., *appointed* 1968.

EXECUTIVE COUNCIL

Premier and Minister for Education, Environmental Protection and Cultural Affairs, Hon. J. T. Tonkin, M.L.A. $A17,200
Deputy Premier and Minister for Industrial Development and Decentralisation, and Town Planning, Hon. H. E. Graham, M.L.A. $A13,800
Treasurer and Minister for Forests and Tourism, Hon. T. D. Evans, M.L.A.
Minister for Community Welfare and Leader of the Government in the Legislative Council, Hon. W. F. Willesee, M.L.C. $A13,800
Police and Transport, Hon. J. Dolan, M.L.C.
Mines and the North-West, Hon. D. G. May, M.L.A.
Works, Water Supplies and Electricity, Hon. C. J. Jamieson, M.L.A.
Lands, Agriculture and Immigration, Hon. H.D. Evans, M.L.A.
Prices Control, Consumer Protection, Health and Fisheries and Fauna, Hon. R. Davies, M.L.A.
Housing and Labour, Hon. A. D. Taylor, M.L.A.
Attorney-General and Minister for Railways, Hon. R. E. Bertram, M.L.A.
Local Government and Chief Secretary, Hon. R. H. C. Stubbs, M.L.C.
Ministers, each $A12,200, unless shown otherwise above.

AGENT-GENERAL IN LONDON.

Offices, Western Australia House, 115 Strand, London, W.C.2.
Agent-General, Hon. W. S. Bovell £3,500

THE LEGISLATURE.

Parliament consists of a *Legislative Council* and a *Legislative Assembly*, elected by adult suffrage subject to qualifications of residence and registration. The qualifying age for electors for both the Legislative Council and Legislative Assembly was lowered in 1970 from 21 to 18 years. There are 30 members in the Legislative Council, two from each Province, for a period of 6 years, one member from each Province retiring triennially. The Legislative Assembly is composed of 51 members, who are elected for a term of 3 years.

President of the Legislative Council, Hon. L. C. Diver, M.L.C. $A9,800
Speaker of the Legislative Assembly, Hon. J. M. Toms, ... $A9,800

THE JUDICATURE

Chief Justice, Hon. Sir Lawrence Jackson, K.C.M.G. $A21,000
Senior Puisne Judge, Hon. J. E. Virtue 19,800
Puisne Judges, Hons. R. V. Nevile; J. Hale; F. T. P. Burt; J. M. Lavan; J. L. C. Wickham .... each 19,200

EDUCATION.

Education.—In 1970 there were 589 government schools and 196 non-government schools (excluding kindergartens) with 174,024 and 41,558 pupils respectively. The total amount expended on education (from State Revenue) during the year ended June 30, 1970, was $A68,663,556, including grants of $A5,064,861 to the University of Western Australia (4,966 full-time students in 1970).

PRODUCTION AND INDUSTRY

The gross value of primary production (excluding mining and quarrying) in 1969–70 was: agricultural $A155,937,604; pastoral $A176,386,814; dairying $A25,927,033; poultry farming $A13,873,867; bee-keeping $A658,557; trapping $A1,098,386; forestry $A13,631,997; fishing and whaling $A19,659,550.

Crops and Livestock.—Of the total area under crop (9,675,648 acres), 6,788,177 acres were under wheat for grain, the 1969–70 production being 66,700,000 bushels. On March 31, 1970, the livestock included 1,681,090 cattle, 33,633,957 sheep, and 250,051 pigs. In 1969–70 there were 6,651 acres of vineyards and 23,470 acres of orchards. The wool clip in 1969–70 was 316,322,000 lb. in the grease.

Manufacturing Industries.—During the year ended June 30, 1969, a total of 2,774 manufacturing establishments operated in the State. The total number of persons employed (including working proprietors) by these establishments at the end of June, 1969, was 63,796. (Figures not comparable with previous years owing to reclassification of manufacturing establishments.)

Forestry.—The forests contain some of the finest hardwoods in the world. The total quantity of timber sawn and hewn during 1969–70 was 216,428,991 superficial feet.

Minerals.—The State has large deposits of a wide range of minerals, many of which are being mined or are under development for production. The ex-mine value of all minerals produced during 1968–69 was $A244,993,000. The principal minerals produced during 1968–69 were: iron ore 23,457,000 tons ($A150,426,000); crude oil 11,649,000 barrels ($A33,549,000); gold 641,804 fine ounces ($A18,890,000); nickel concentrates 51,140 tons ($A5,334,000); ilmenite concentrates 638,533 tons ($A5,334,000); coal 1,103,000 tons ($A4,853,000); bauxite 2,075,000 tons; tin concentrates 899 tons ($A1,733,000); zircon concentrates 51,785 tons ($A1,194,000) and manganese ore 163,169 tons ($A1,159,000). Significant quantities of copper ores and concentrates, salt, monazite concentrates, talc, limestone, clays, gypsum and stone for construction were also produced. Extensive exploration is being undertaken in the State for many minerals including petroleum and nickel.

Communications.—On June 30, 1970, there were 3,828 miles of State government railway open for general and passenger traffic; and 454 miles of the Commonwealth line (Kalgoorlie–Port Pirie junction). In the year ended June 30, 1969, 3,170 vessels

(net tonnage 20,479,121) entered Western Australian ports and 3,162 (net tonnage 20,441,133) cleared. The total length of roads at June 30, 1969 was 95,824 miles. The number of registered motor vehicles on June 30, 1970, was 430,369 (316,401 motor cars and station wagons, 102,291 utilities, vans, trucks and omnibuses and 11,677 motor cycles and motor scooters).

FINANCE

Total revenue of Western Australia in 1969–70 was $A318,188,779, compared with $A275,081,341 in 1968–69. Expenditure in 1969–70 totalled $A318,900,637 (1968–69, $A276,136,959). The net public debt of the State at June 30, 1970 was $A886,596,676 (1969, $A837,328,617).

TRADE

Year	Imports	Exports
	$A	$A
1965–66	578,744,158	434,023,439
1966–67	634,242,049	537,354,970
1967–68	734,031,213	599,764,941
1968–69	765,845,661	696,257,549
1969–70	882,487,348	824,887,727

The principal exports in 1969–70 were gold bullion ($A13,873,874), wool ($A137,795,208), wheat ($A86,592,636), wheat flour ($A2,257,054), hides and skins ($A7,967,722), oats ($A914,675), timber ($A5,665,788), beef ($A21,290,887), mutton and lamb ($A11,271,345), live animals ($A3,936,197), rock lobster tails ($A15,694,681), apples ($A4,955,006); silver bullion ($A3,944,633), ilmenite ores and concentrates ($A6,067,688), manganese ores and concentrates ($A3,086,228), iron ore ($A233,580,062), barley ($A4,651,726), petroleum and petroleum products ($A49,767,006), iron and steel ($A34,305,555), machines and machinery ($A13,723,893); transport equipment ($A15,180,138); chemical elements and compounds ($A40,999,765); metal waste and scrap ($A5,684,765) and tallow ($A2,983,456).

TOWNS

CAPITAL, Ψ PERTH. Population (estimated, June 30, 1970) of Perth Statistical Division, including the port of Fremantle, 663,000.

Perth, the capital, stands on the right bank of the Swan River estuary, 12 miles from Fremantle. Other towns are Ψ Fremantle (33,300), Kalgoorlie —Boulder and environs (21,700), Ψ Bunbury (17,600); Ψ Geraldton (14,900); Ψ Albany (12,700).

BRITISH COMMERCIAL REPRESENTATIVES IN THE COMMONWEALTH

CANADA.—*Ottawa* (80 Elgin Street), G. S. Whitehead, C.M.G., M.V.O.
Montreal (635 Dorchester Boulevard W.), P. H. Scott.
Toronto (200 University Avenue), R. McC. Samples, D.S.O., C.M.G., O.B.E.
Vancouver (602 W. Hastings Street), C. C. Clemens, M.C.
Winnipeg (333 Broadway Avenue), G. S. McWilliam, O.B.E.
Regina (815 Avord Tower, 2002 Victoria Ave.), J. R. Bolton, O.B.E.
Edmonton (10025 Jasper Avenue), G. Miles, O.B.E.
Atlantic Provinces (1645 Granville Street, Halifax, N.-S.), T. W. Robinson.
Quebec (100 D'Youville Square), R. H. Link, O.B.E.

AUSTRALIA.—*Canberra* (Commonwealth Avenue), H. B. C. Keeble, C.M.G.
Sydney (Gold Fields House, Sydney Cove), R. E. Gamble, O.B.E.
Melbourne (The Colonial Mutual Life Building, 330 Collins Street), R. W. B. Carter, C.M.G.
Brisbane (M. L. C. Building), F. S. Fielding, O.B.E.
Perth (84 St. George's Terrace), A. H. Birch, *Adelaide* (15 Franklin Street), R. E. Jones. [C.M.G.

NEW ZEALAND.—*Wellington* (P.O. Box 369, Customhouse Quay), R. A. Daniell, C.B.E.
Auckland (Norwich Union Building, Queen Street), C. E. Dymond, C.B.E.
Christchurch (B.N.Z. House, Cathedral Square), W. J. Rumble.

BARBADOS.—*Bridgetown* (Roebuck Street, P.O. Box 676c), J. A. B. Stewart.

CEYLON.—*Colombo* (P.O. Box 1433, Galle Road, Kollupitya), J. W. Nicholas.

GAMBIA.—*Bathurst* (78 Wellington Street, P.O. Box 507), S. A. Downton.

GHANA.—*Accra* (Barclays Bank Building, High Street, P.O. Box 296), L. Reid.

GUYANA.—*Georgetown* (44 Main Street, P.O. Box 625), E. G. Wickens.

HONG KONG.—(P.O. Box 528, 707 Shell House), J. K. Blackwell, C.B.E.

INDIA.—*Delhi* (Chanakyapuri, New Delhi), E. F. G. Maynard.
Calcutta (1 Ho Chi Minh Sarani), F. S. Miles.
Madras (150A Mount Road), V. C. Martin.
Bombay (Mercantile Bank Building), M. H. G. Rogers.

JAMAICA.—*Kingston* (Barclay's Bank Building), E. M. Smith, B.E.M.

KENYA.—*Nairobi* (Commercial Dept., Bruce House, Standard St., P.O. Box 30133), J. H. Symons.

LESOTHO.—*Maseru* (P.O. Box 521), M. F. Chapman.

MALAWI.—*Blantyre* (Victoria Avenue, P.O. Box 479), R. S. Howe.

MALAYSIA.—*Kuala Lumpur* (Wisma Damansara Jalan Semantan), H. C. White, M.B.E.
Kuching (P.O. Box 1745, Jalan Tunku Abdul Rahman), L. S. Price.

MALTA.—*Floriana* (7 St. Anne St.), R. K. Robertson.

MAURITIUS.—*Port Louis* (P.O. Box 586), Cerne House, Chaussée Street), A. H. G. Amy.

PAKISTAN.—*Karachi* (Finlay House), A. J. Brown.
Lahore (4 Race Course Road), P. R. Oliver, C.M.G.
Dacca (P.O. Box 90, Dilkusha), A. J. Collins.

SIERRA LEONE.—*Freetown* (Leone House, Westmorland Street), S. I. Levene.

SINGAPORE.—(Phoenix Park, Tanglin Road), G. F. Finlayson.

SWAZILAND.—*Mbabane* (Alister Miller Street), A. G. Elgar, O.B.E.

TANZANIA.—*Dar es Salaam* (Independence Avenue P.O. Box 9112), R. T. White.

TRINIDAD AND TOBAGO.—*Port of Spain* (P.O. Box 778, 90 Independence Square), B. A. F. Pennock, O.B.E.

UGANDA.—*Kampala* (P.O. Box 7070), R. W. Howell.

New Zealand
AREA AND POPULATION

Islands	Area (English Sq. Miles)	Population Census, Mar. 22, 1966	Census Mar. 23, 1971†§
(a) *Exclusive of Island Territories:*			
North Island..	44,281	1,893,326	2,050,208
South Island..	58,093	783,593	810,267
Stewart Island...	670	332*	420*
Chatham Islands.......................................	372	520*	735*
Minor Islands:			
Inhabited—			
Kermadec Islands................................	13	9*	9*
Campbell Island..................................	44	10*	10*
Uninhabited—			
Three Kings	3	..	..
Snares...	1	..	..
Solander..	½	..	..
Antipodes...	24	..	..
Bounty..	½	..	..
Auckland..	234	..	..
Total exclusive of Island Territories.............	103,736	2,676,919	2,860,475
(b) *Island Territories:*			
Tokelau Islands.......................................	..	1,861	1,687‡
Niue Island..	..	5,157	5,184§
Total, inclusive of Island Territories............	103,939	2,704,456	2,867,346
(c) Cook Islands¶.......................................	..	..	21,260‖
Ross Dependency.......................................	175,000	262	..

* Included in North Island and South Island totals.   § Provisional figures.
† Excluding 1,753 members of the Armed Forces overseas.
‡ Sept. 25, 1970.   § Dec. 31, 1970.   ‖ Dec. 31, 1969.
¶ The Cook Islands have had complete internal self-government since Aug. 4, 1965, but Cook Islanders remain New Zealand citizens.
Maori Population included in the totals for New Zealand proper—1966 Census, 201,159 (males 102,107; females 99,052): estimated Dec. 31, 1970, 232,022 (males 117,433; females 114,589).

Increase of the People.

Year	Increase			Decrease			Net Increase	Marriages
	Births	Arrivals	Total	Deaths	Departures	Total		
1967	61,169	468,372	529,541	23,007	471,854	494,861	34,680	23,515
1968	62,284	486,416	548,700	24,464	494,228	518,692	30,008	24,057
1969	62,564	501,667	564,231	24,161	508,235	532,396	31,835	24,971
1970	62,207	554,025	616,232	24,840	542,864	567,704	48,528	25,953

Birth rate (1970) 22·02; death rate 8·79; marriage rate 9·19; infant mortality 16·72 per 1,000.

Inter-censal Increases.

Year	Results of Census			Numerical Increase	Net Passenger Arrivals over inter-censal periods
	Males	Females	Total		
*1956	1,093,211	1,080,851	2,174,062	234,590	+27,486
*1961	1,213,376	1,201,608	2,414,984	240,922	+68,726
*1966	1,343,743	1,333,176	2,676,919	261,935	+48,660
*†1971	1,429,895	1,430,580	2,860,475	183,556	..

* Excluding 2,559 members of the Armed Forces overseas at the time of the 1961 census, 1,936 at the 1966 census and 1,753 (provisional) at the 1971 census.   † Provisional figures.

Races and Religions.

Races	1961	1966	Religions	1961	1966
				Per cent.	Per cent.
Europeans..............	2,216,886	2,426,352	Church of England......	34·6	33·7
Maoris.................	167,086	201,159	Presbyterians...........	22·3	21·8
Chinese................	8,524	10,283	Roman Catholics.......	15·1	15·9
Polynesians (other than			Methodists.............	7·2	7·0
N. Z. Maoris).......	14,340	26,271	Baptists...............	1·7	1·7
Other races............	8,148	12,854			

PHYSIOGRAPHY

New Zealand consists of a number of islands of varying size in the South Pacific Ocean, and has also administrative responsibility for a large tract in the Antarctic Ocean. The two larger and most important islands, the North and South Islands of New Zealand, are separated by only a relatively narrow strait. The remaining islands are very much smaller and, in general, are widely dispersed over a considerable expanse of ocean. The boundaries, inclusive of the most outlying islands and dependencies, range from 8° South latitude to south of 60° South latitude, and from 160° East longitude to 150° West longitude.

Geographical Features.—The two principal islands have a total length of 1,040 miles, and a combined area of 102,374 square miles. A large proportion of the surface is mountainous in character. The principal range is that of the Southern Alps, extending over the entire length of the South Island and having its culminating point in Mount Cook (12,349 ft.). The North Island mountains include several volcanoes, two of which are active, others being dormant or extinct. Mt. Ruapehu (9,175 ft.) and Mt. Ngauruhoe (7,515 ft.) are the most important. Of the numerous glaciers in the South Island, the Tasman (18 miles long by 1¼ wide), the Franz Josef and the Fox are the best known. The North Island is noted for its hot springs and geysers. For the most part the rivers are too short and rapid for use in navigation. The more important include the Waikato (270 miles in length); Wanganui (180), and Clutha (210). Lakes (Taupo, 234 sq. miles in area; Wakatipu, 113; and Te Anau 133) are abundant, many of them of great beauty.

Climate.—New Zealand has a moist-temperate marine climate, but with abundant sunshine. A very important feature is the small annual range of temperature which permits of some growth of vegetation, including pasture, all the year round. Very little snow falls on the low levels even in the South Island. The mean temperature ranges from 59° F. in the North to about 49° F. in the South. Rainfall over the more settled areas in the North Island ranges from 35 to 70 inches and in the South Island from 25 to 45 inches. The total range is from approximately 13 to over 250 inches. The number of rainy days is generally in the neighbourhood of 160 to 180 in the North Island and between 110 and 140 in the South, except in the southern portion of the west coast. The amount of sunshine is generally over 2,000 hours per annum and range between 1,600 to 2,500 hours.

GOVERNMENT

The west coast of the South Island of New Zealand was discovered by Abel Janszoon Tasman, the navigator (voyaging under the direction of the Netherlands' East India Company), on December 13, 1642.

The islands were visited, and charted, in 1769 by Captain Cook, who returned to them in 1773, 1774 and 1777. From 1800 onwards sealers and whalers settled along the coasts, and trade in timber and flax followed. Christianity was introduced in 1814, and in 1832 a British Resident was appointed. In 1840 British sovereignty was proclaimed, and on May 3, 1841, New Zealand was, by letters patent, created a separate colony distinct from New South Wales. Organized colonization on a large scale commenced in 1840 with the New Zealand Company's settlement at Wellington. On Sept. 26, 1907, the designation was changed to *The Dominion of New Zealand.* The Constitution rests upon the Imperial Act of 1852, and on the New Zealand Constitution (Amendment) Act of Dec. 10, 1947. The Statute of Westminster was formally adopted by New Zealand in 1947. The executive authority is entrusted to a Governor-General appointed by the Crown and aided by an Executive Council, within a Legislature consisting of one chamber, the House of Representatives.

FLAG: Blue ground, with Union Jack in top left quarter, four five-pointed red stars with white borders on the fly. On June 20, 1968, a new naval ensign bearing the Southern Cross was adopted, replacing the British white ensign.

Governor General and Staff

Governor-General and Commander-in-Chief of New Zealand (1967–72), His Excellency Sir Arthur Espie Porritt, Bt., G.C.M.G., G.C.V.O., C.B.E., born 1900 .... $NZ 31,500.
Official Secretary, D. C. Williams, C.V.O.
Comptroller, Col. H. N. Hoare, M.V.O.
Assistant Official Secretary, P. J. H. Purvis, M.V.O.
Aides-de-Camp, Lieut. N. E. Hodge, R.N.; Capt. B. M. de L. Cazenove, Coldstream Guards.
Lady-in-Waiting, Miss Caroline Moore.
(Sir Arthur Porritt retires in Sept. 1972 and will be succeeded by Sir (Edward) Denis Blundell, K.B.E.)

THE EXECUTIVE COUNCIL.

His Excellency the GOVERNOR-GENERAL. *Norman Kirk 14/72*
Prime Minister and Minister of Foreign Affairs, Rt. Hon. Sir Keith Holyoake, G.C.M.G., C.H.
Deputy Prime Minister, Minister of Overseas Trade, Labour and Immigration, Rt. Hon. J. R. Marshall.
Industries, Commerce and Mines, Hon. N. L. Shelton.
Education, and Science, Hon. B. E. Talboys.
Works and Electricity, Hon. P. B. Allen.
Transport, Railways and Civil Aviation, Hon. J. B. Gordon.
Finance, Hon. R. D. Muldoon. *Wallee Rowling 14/72*
Defence and Police, Hon. D. S. Thomson, M.C., E.D.
Agriculture, Hon. D. J. Carter.
Lands, Forests, Maori Affairs and Island Affairs, Hon. D. MacIntyre, D.S.O., O.B.E., E.D.
Internal Affairs, Civil Defence and Local Government, Hon. D. C. Seath.
Housing, Hon. J. Rae.
Attorney-General, Justice and Associate Minister of Labour and Immigration, Hon. D. J. Riddiford.

Health, Social Security, and Minister for the Welfare of Women and Children, Hon. D. N. McKay.
Postmaster-General and Marine, Hon. A. McCready.
Customs and Associate Minister of Industries and Commerce, Hon. L. R. Adams-Schneider.
Tourism and Broadcasting, Hon. H. J. Walker.
Associate Minister of Finance, Hon. H. E. L. Pickering.

Members of the Executive Council travelling within the country on public service are entitled to an allowance not exceeding $14·00 *per diem* when so engaged, but not during attendance at a session of the General Assembly. The Prime Minister receives $17,000 per annum with a tax-free allowance of $4,000 for expenses of his office and the Ministerial residence. The salary of each Minister holding a portfolio is $11,250 with tax-free expense allowance of $1,500 and that of each Minister without portfolio $8,650, with $1,275 tax-free expense allowance.

NEW ZEALAND REPRESENTATIVES OVERSEAS.
High Commissioners
Australia, A. J. Yendell.
Canada, D. J. Eyre.
Fiji, Sir John Grace, M.V.O.
India, Ceylon and Nepal, B. S. Lendrum.
Malaysia, R. L. Hutchens, D.S.O.
Singapore, H. H. Francis.

NEW ZEALAND HIGH COMMISSION
New Zealand House, Haymarket, S.W.1.
[01-930 8422]
High Commissioner, His Excellency Sir (Edward) Denis Blundell, K.B.E.
Deputy High Commissioner, R. M. Miller.
Ministers, N. V. Farrell; A. E. Monaghan (*Commercial*).
Counsellor, E. Farnon (*Economic*).
Head, N.Z. Defence Liaison Staff, Cdre. E. C. Thorne.
1st Secretaries, J. D. L. Richards; C. J. McKenzie; J. D. Kerr (*Commercial*).
2nd Secretaries, A. C. Doyle; N. W. Bridge; A. M. Bisley; G. A. Cheyne (*Commercial*); A. C. Davies (*Commercial*).

OVERSEAS REPRESENTATIVES IN N.Z.
High Commissioners
Australia, Dame Annabelle Rankin, D.B.E.
Canada, J. A. Dougan, M.C.
India, P. S. Naskar.
Singapore, K. M. Byrne.

BRITISH HIGH COMMISSION
Customhouse Quay (P.O. Box 1812), Wellington, C.1.
High Commissioner, His Excellency Sir Arthur Norman Galsworthy, K.C.M.G. (1969)... £9,000
Minister (Commercial and Economic), R. A. Daniell, C.B.E.
1st Secretary, D. Tonkin (*Head of Chancery*).
Defence Adviser, Capt. I. Campbell, R.N.
Asst. do., Sqn.-Ldr. E. H. Hunter.
1st Secretaries, J. L. McGrath, O.B.E. (*Agriculture and Food*); A. C. McCarthy (*Commercial*); A. K. Goldsmith (*Information*).
2nd Secretaries, A. Lovell; E. Bennett (*Commercial*); I. W. Mackley.

British Council Representative, J. H. Grimes.

Ambassadors
Austria, F. Pein.
Belgium, André Domus.
Brazil, Senhora M. Guedes Nogueira
Burma, U. Nyo Tun.
China, Konsin C. Shah.
Denmark, P. A. von der Hude.

France, Christian de Nicolay.
German Federal Republic, Kurt Luedde-Neurath.
Greece, B. L. Tsamissis.
Indonesia, Air V/M Sukirno
Italy, Giulio Carnevali.
Japan, K. Yoshida.
Korea, Cheong Sik Min.
Laos, O. Souvannavong.
Netherlands, H. C. Jorissen.
Sweden, C. G. Beve.
Switzerland, M. Corti.
Thailand, P. Bunchoem.
United States, M. Franzheim.
U.S.S.R., A. I. Ivantsov.

THE LEGISLATURE
Parliament consists of a House of Representatives consisting of 84 members elected for 3 years. The General Election of November, 1969, returned 45 National Party members and 39 Labour. Labour won an additional seat from National at a by-election in February, 1970. Four of the members are Maoris elected by the Maori electors. Women have been entitled to vote since 1893, and to be elected Members of the House of Representatives since the passing of the Women's Parliamentary Rights Act, 1919. There are at present 4 women members. Members of the House receive $NZ6,100 *per annum*, with an allowance of $NZ1,250 *per annum* for expenses, depending on the size of electorate. The Leader of the Opposition receives $NZ10,500 *per annum* and $NZ1,500 *per annum* for expenses, plus travelling allowance of $NZ1,275.
Speaker of the House of Representatives, Hon. Sir Roy Jack (*plus expense allowance of $NZ1,300 per annum and residential quarters in Parliament House*) $NZ10,000
Parliamentary Commissioner, Sir Guy Powles, K.B.E., C.M.G., E.D.

THE JUDICATURE
The judicial system comprises a Supreme Court and a Court of Appeal; also Magistrates' Courts having both civil and criminal jurisdiction.
Chief Justice, Rt. Hon. Sir Richard Wild, K.C.M.G., E.D. $NZ16,845
Court of Appeal, Rt. Hon. Sir Alfred North, K.B.E. (*President*) 16,060
Judges, Rt. Hon. Sir Alexander Turner; Rt. Hon. Sir Thaddeus McCarthy . . . 15,275
Supreme Court Puisne Judges, Hons. Sir Trevor Henry; A. L. Haslam; I. H. Macarthur; C. P. Richmond; A. O. Woodhouse; A. C. Perry; J. N. Wilson; L. F. Moller; G. D. Speight; C. M. Roper; J. C. White; D. S. Beattie; J. P. Quilliam; D. W. McMullin 15,275
Supreme Court Administrative Divn., Rt. Hon. Sir Richard Wild (*Chief Justice*); Hons. A. O. Woodhouse; J. N. Wilson; G. D. Speight.
Judge, Court of Arbitration, Judge A. P. Blair 15,275
Judge, Compensation Court, Judge J. B. Thomson 15,275

POLICE
On March 31, 1971, the strength of the Police Force was 3,214 of all ranks, equivalent to 1 for every 890 of the population. The total cost of police protection in 1970-71 was $NZ18,811,000.

DEFENCE
A unified Ministry of Defence was set up on Jan. 1, 1964. The Ministry is responsible, under the Minister of Defence, for the whole field of

national defence. The former Navy, Army and Air Departments have been abolished, but the three Armed Services retain their separate identities within the Ministry. Defence expenditure in 1969–70 amounted to $NZ89,721,000.

Navy.

The Royal New Zealand Navy was greatly expanded during the Second World War and a number of small vessels were built in New Zealand. The naval forces include the Women's Royal New Zealand Naval Service, and Volunteer Reserve forces in four divisions. The strength is 4 frigates, 1 survey ship, 1 Antarctic support ship and 2 minesweepers. Active naval personnel number 318 officers and 2,571 ratings. A cruiser or a frigate is normally attached to the Far East Station.

Army.

The New Zealand Army consists of the Regular Force, the Territorial Force, the Army Reserve and the Cadet Corps. The strength of the Regular Force at March 31, 1969, was 5,730 and of the Territorial Force 11,217.

In 1962 selective national service was introduced to build the Territorial Force up to 10,000. The Army is now organized on the basis of one integrated Regular/Territorial Brigade Group, with its own logistic support and reserves. In addition, a regular force battalion is stationed as part of the Commonwealth Far East strategic reserve in Malaysia. An infantry company has been withdrawn from this battalion for deployment in South Vietnam.

Air.

The Royal New Zealand Air Force was constituted as a separate defence service in 1937. The Air Force now consists of the Regular Air Force, the Air Force Reserve, the Women's Royal New Zealand Air Force and the Air Training Corps. One Air Force transport unit is based outside New Zealand in Singapore. The strength of the Regular Force at March 31, 1969, was 4,498.

FINANCE.

Into the Consolidated Revenue Account (New Zealand's main public account) are paid the proceeds of income tax, social security income tax, sales tax, customs and excise duties and other taxes. Revenue from taxation is also paid into the National Roads Fund principally from a tax on motor spirits and registration and licence fees for motor vehicles. Figures of the Consolidated Revenue Account shown in this table are quoted on a gross basis, *i.e.* credits have not been deducted from departmental expenditure, but have been included as receipts

Year ended March 31	Revenue	Expenditure
	$NZ	$NZ
1968	1,096,696,000	1,095,318,000
1969	1,154,609,477	1,146,929,939
1970	1,282,506,344	1,275,137,231
1971	1,566,180,566	1,560,852,048*

* Includes $NZ833,282,942 for the social services, incl. education and health, $NZ118,631,217 for development of primary and secondary industries, $NZ204,133,000 for debt services and $NZ109,075,098 for defence.

Revenue from taxation in 1970–71 amounted to $NZ1,444,992,229, of which $NZ1,363,035,637 represented receipts into the Consolidated Revenue Account, and $NZ81,956,592 receipts into the National Roads Fund.

2 A*

DEBT.

The gross *Public Debt* amounted on March 31, 1971, to $NZ3,006,962,491, ot which $NZ397,816,000 was domiciled in London and $NZ104,092,000 in the U.S.A.; $NZ74,526,000 represented World Bank loans.

CURRENCY.

On July 10, 1967, New Zealand changed to decimal currency. The basic unit is the N.Z. dollar, divisible into 100 cents. On Nov. 21, 1967, New Zealand devalued its currency by 19·45 per cent. in relation to the U.S. dollar, bringing the N.Z. dollar to parity with the Australian dollar. At IMF par value the $NZ became worth £0·4667 sterling.

BANKING.

There are five trading banks (with numerous branches) doing business, two of which are predominantly New Zealand banks. Of these the Bank of New Zealand is owned by the State. At Mar. 31, 1971, assets of all trading banks in respect of New Zealand business amounted to $NZ1,017,700,000; liabilities, $NZ1,062,600,000; and the value of notes in circulation amounted to $NZ193,800,000. The Reserve Bank of New Zealand commenced business on August 1, 1934. The note-issuing powers of other banks have since been withdrawn and the Reserve Bank notes are legal tender. New Zealand's official overseas reserves at March 31, 1971, amounted to $NZ372,500,000, of which $NZ172,400,000 represented assets of the New Zealand banking system. Trading banks' advances, including discounts on Mar. 25, 1971, totalled $NZ801,400,000 compared with $NZ685,800,000 in the previous year. Deposits with trading banks on Mar. 31, 1971, amounted to $NZ956,100,000 (1970, $NZ907,000,000).

Post-office and trustee savings banks had, at the close of the year 1970–71, nearly 4 million accounts having $NZ1,418,304,000 to their credit. Private savings banks have been operated by the trading banks since Oct. 1964. and at March 31, 1971, deposits totalled $NZ352,467,000.

EDUCATION.

Schools are free and attendance is compulsory between the ages of 6 and 15. There are opportunities for apt pupils to proceed to university. In 1969 there were 2,237 public primary schools, with 461,305 scholars; there were also 344 registered private primary schools with 52,407 scholars. The secondary education of boys and girls in the cities and large towns is carried on in 204 state secondary schools, 66 state secondary departments of district high schools and 115 private secondary schools. The total number of pupils receiving full-time secondary education in July 1969 was 155,873 and in addition there were 84,812 students attending technical classes and 14,165 receiving part-time tuition from the Technical Correspondence School. The university system consists of the University of Auckland, the University of Waikato, Massey University of Manawatu, Victoria University of Wellington, the University of Canterbury and the University of Otago. The Lincoln university college of agriculture is associated with the University of Canterbury. The university system is co-ordinated by the University Grants Committee. The Universities had a total of 31,542 students in 1969.

The total expenditure on education out of public funds in 1969–70 was $NZ209,064,524.

PRODUCTION AND INDUSTRY
Gross Farming Income

	1968–69	1969–70
	$NZ(000)	$NZ(000)
Wool..................	155,800	139,400
Mutton and Lamb.......	168,500	197,400
Beef..................	141,800	199,000
Dairying................	237,500	216,200
Pigs...................	21,400	26,100
Grain and Field Crops, Poultry and Bees....	160,600	146,400
All Farm Produce........	885,600	924,500

Industrial Production

	1967–68 $NZ	1968–69 $NZ
Value of Production	2,538,349,000	2,790,448,000

Net Output (Net Value Added), consisting only of the rewards to the factors of production, *i.e.* salaries and wages, interest on borrowed capital, and proprietors' surplus, in 1968–69 amounted to $NZ814,263,000, compared with $NZ756,657,000 in the previous year.

Agricultural and Pastoral Production

	1968–69	1969–70
Wheat......bushels	16,779,000	10,221,000
Wool.......lb.	732,000,000	723,000,000
Butter.......lb.	663,000,000	612,000,000
Cheese ......tons	95,400	99,500
Stock slaughtered—	1968–69	1969–70
Lambs.....No.	26,857,000	27,538,000
Sheep.....No.	9,602,000	9,846,000
Cattle.....No.	1,694,000	1,848,000
Calves.....No.	1,357,000	1,310,000
Pigs......No.	790,000	829,000

Agriculture and Forestry.—The total area of New Zealand (excluding its Island Territories) is 66,390,700 acres; of this, approximately 42,893,000 acres are occupied land, 22,708,000 acres being under cultivation. The output of sawn timber for 1969–70 was 765,012,000 board ft., of which 567,712,000 board ft. represented exotic varieties, mainly pine.

Livestock.—Livestock on farms at Jan. 31, 1970, included 3,729,284 dairy cattle (of which 2,304,252 were dairy cows in milk during season), 4,811,791 beef cattle (of which 1,486,324 were beef breeding cows), and 553,388 pigs. At June 30, 1970, sheep numbered 60,276,111, including 42,911,581 breeding ewes.

Manufactures.—Statistics of factory production show (1968–69) 10,501 factories in operation, employing 229,074 persons. Salaries and wages amounted to $NZ527,805,000; cost of materials used, $NZ1,662,326,000. Total value of production, $NZ2,790,448,000.

Minerals.—Coal output in 1969 was 2,326,607 tons. Gold-mining was formerly an important industry, but production has declined greatly in recent years. Gold produced in 1969 was 10,400 oz. Other minerals produced on a relatively small scale are copper, silver, iron ore, manganese ore, zinc, lead, cadmium, tungsten and asbestos. Valuable deposits of natural gas have been discovered in Taranaki, and this has been piped to some main North Island centres. New Zealand has large resources of potential iron ore in the black sands of many of its beaches and steelworks have been built near Auckland to utilize such deposits.

TRADE.

Provisional figures of New Zealand's trade during the year ended June, 1970, were: Imports (c.i.f.) $NZ1,006,000,000, compared with $NZ852,887,000 in 1968–69; Exports, (f.o.b.) $NZ1,087,000,000, compared with $NZ 989,097,000 in 1968–69.

Trade with U.K.

	1969	1970
Imports from U.K..	£120,230,000	£129,285,000
Exports to U K.....	216,159,000	203,558,000

(Board of Trade Totals)

New Zealand produce exported to the U.K. in the 12 months ending June, 1970, was valued at $NZ383,106,002 and included butter, valued at $NZ98,661,915, cheese ($NZ32,999,959); meat ($NZ66,439,474); dried and condensed milk ($NZ6,149,110); wool ($NZ40,813,747); and fruit ($NZ6,527,997).

Railways.—In March, 1970, there were 3,063 route miles of Government railway in operation. The number of passengers carried on Government lines in 1969–70, including season-ticket holders, was 21,031,000. Goods railed amounted to 11,593,000 tons. Railway total revenue and expenditure were $NZ99,729,000 and $NZ94,121,000 in 1969–70.

Motor Vehicles.—On March 31, 1971, there were 1,239,670 motor vehicles licensed, including 918,700 cars, and 53,206 motor cycles and power cycles. The number of persons per passenger car was 3·1.

Shipping.—During 1970 the vessels entered from overseas ports numbered 3,757 (net tonnage 17,258,000) and those cleared for overseas 3,749 (net tonnage 17,272,000).

Post Office Statistics.—During 1969–70 internal postal services handled 595,361,000 items, including 288,604,000 letters and 291,049,000 items of printed matter. Overseas mails included 1,696,836 lb. of airmail received and 1,062,931 lb. despatched. Telephones totalled 1,202,590 in 1970.

Civil Aviation.—In 1969–70 domestic scheduled services flew 11,797,000 miles and carried 1,478,800 passengers. Freight carried amounted to 67,100 tons. In 1969–70 international services to and from New Zealand carried 487,200 passengers, 11,263 tons of freight and 1,337 tons of mail.

CAPITAL, Ψ Wellington, in the North Island (pop. April 1, 1970, Wellington-Hutt urban area, 301,300).

Other large centres: Ψ Auckland, 603,500; Ψ Christchurch, 260,200; Ψ Dunedin, 110,100; Palmerston North, 52,700; Hamilton, 71,900; Ψ Wanganui, 38,800; Ψ New Plymouth, 36,700; Ψ Napier, 41,500; Hastings, 41,000; Rotorua, 37,300; Ψ Tauranga, 35,300.

NATIONAL DAY (Waitangi Day).—February 6.

THE ISLANDS OF NEW ZEALAND.

In addition to North, South, Stewart and Chatham Islands:—

The Three Kings (discovered by Tasman on the Feast of the Epiphany), in 34° 9′ S. lat. and 172° 8′ 8″ E. long. (uninhabited). *Auckland Islands,* about 290 miles south of Bluff Harbour, in 50° 32′ S. lat. and 166° 13′ E. long. The islands contain several good harbours, but are uninhabited. *Campbell Island* (used as a weather station). *Antipodes Group* (40° 41′ 15 S. lat. and 178° 43′ E. long.) uninhabited. *Bounty Islands* (47° 4′ 43 S. lat., 170° 0′ 30 E. long.). *Snares Islands and Solander* (uninhabited).

The Kermadec Group (population 10 in 1966) between 29° 10′ to 31° 30′ S. lat., and 177° 45′ to 179° W. long., includes Raoul or Sunday, Macaulay, Curtis Islands, L'Esperance, and some islets.

Cook and other Islands, included in the boundaries of New Zealand since June, 1901, consist of the

islands of Rarotonga (9,971), Aitutaki (2,579), Mangaia (2,002), Atiu (1,327), Mauke (671), Matiaro (293), Manuae (15), Takutea (uninhabited), Palmerston (86), Penrhyn or Tongareva (545), Manihiki (584), Rakahanga (323), Pukapuka or Danger (684), Nassau (68). The population figures for individual islands are at the Census of 1966, the total for the Group being 19,777. Niue, which is geographically part of Cook Islands, but which is administered separately, had a population (estimated Mar., 1970) of 5,302. The chief exports of the Cook Islands are fruit juice, clothing, copra, tomatoes, citrus fruit and pearl shell. The trade is chiefly with New Zealand, Australia, Japan, the U.K. and the U.S.A. The exports in 1967 were valued at $NZ1,777,369; imports at $NZ 2,991.307 for Cook Islands, and at $NZ125,867 and $NZ598,156 for Niue Island.

The High Commissioner of the Cook Islands is employed in a dual role, since he represents both the Queen and the New Zealand Government. Since Aug. 4, 1965, the Islands have enjoyed complete internal self-government, executive power being in the hands of a Cabinet consisting of the Premier and five other ministers. The new Constitution Act was passed by the New Zealand Parliament in November 1964, but did not come into force until

it had been endorsed by the 22-member Legislative Assembly of the Cook Islands, elected in April 1965.

The New Zealand citizenship of the Cook Islanders is embodied in the Constitution, and assurances have been given that the changed status of the Islands will in no way affect the consideration of subsidies or the right of free entry into New Zealand for exports from the group.

A Resident Commissioner is also stationed at Niue and is assisted in the executive government of that island by the Niue Island Assembly.

Tokelau (or *Union) Islands*.—A group of atolls (Fakaofo, Nukunono and Atafu) (population 1,745 in Sept. 1969), proclaimed part of New Zealand as from Jan. 1, 1948.

THE ROSS DEPENDENCY.

The *Ross Dependency*, placed under the jurisdiction of New Zealand by Order in Council dated July 30, 1923, and defined as all the islands and territories between 160° E. and 150° W. longitude which are situated south of the 60° S. parallel. The Ross Dependency includes Edward VII Land and portions of Victoria Land. For some years there have been permanent bases in the area, staffed by survey and scientific personnel.

Barbados

Barbados, the most easterly of the West India islands, is situated in latitude 13° 14′ N. and longitude 59° 37′ W. The island has a total area of 166 square miles, the land rising in a series of tablelands marked by terraces to the highest point, Mt. Hillaby (1,104 ft.). It is nearly 21 miles long by 14 miles broad. Some 46 acres are covered by forest and 68,875 acres are cultivated. *Climate.*—Barbados has a pleasant climate with annual average temperature 26·5° C. (79·8° F.) and rainfall varying from a yearly average of 75 inches in the high central district to 50 inches in some of the low-lying coastal areas. *Population.*—Since the Census held in 1960, the population has risen from 232,820 to an estimated total of 253,633 on Dec. 31, 1969.

CAPITAL.—Ψ Bridgetown (population, estimated 1969, 12,430). Populations of other administrative areas (parishes) in 1960 were: Christ Church (36,520); St. Philip (18,770); St. George (18,520); St. James (14,960); St. Peter (11,920) and St. John (11,920). Bridgetown, the only port of entry, has a deep-water harbour with berths for 8 ships, opened in 1961. Oil is pumped ashore at one installation on the West Coast. *FLAG.*—Three vertical stripes, dark blue, gold and dark blue, with trident device on gold stripe. *NATIONAL DAY.*—Nov. 30 (Independence Day).

Government.—Barbados was first settled by the British in 1627 and was a Crown Colony from 1652 until it became an independent state within the Commonwealth on November 30, 1966. The Legislature consists of the Governor-General, a Senate and a House of Assembly. The Senate comprises 21 members appointed by the Governor-General, of whom 12 are appointed on the advice of the Prime Minister, 2 on the advice of the Leader of the Opposition and 7 by the Governor-General at his discretion to represent religious, economic or social interests in the Island or such other interests as the Governor-General considers ought to be represented. The House of Assembly comprises 24 members elected every five years by adult suffrage. In 1963 the voting age was reduced to 18. In June, 1971, seats in the House of Representatives were held as follows: Democratic Labour Party, 15; Barbados Labour Party, 7; Barbados National Party, 1; Independent, 1.

Governor-General, Sir Winston Scott, G.C.M.G. (1967) (+ *duty allowance* $12,000) $26,400

CABINET

Premier and Minister of Finance and External Affairs, Rt. Hon. E. W. Barrow.
Deputy Prime Minister and Minister of State for Caribbean and Latin American Affairs, Hon. J. C. Tudor, C.M.G.
Health and Social Welfare, Hon. C. E. Talma.
Labour, National Insurance and Housing, Hon. N. W. Boxhill.
Trade, Tourism, Community Development and Youth Affairs, Hon. K. N. R. Husbands.
Agriculture, Science and Technology, Hon. A. da C. Edwards.
Education, Senator L. E. Sandiford.
Communications and Works, Hon. G. G. Fergusson.
Home Affairs, Senator P. M. Greaves.
Attorney-General, Senator F. G. Smith, Q.C.

President of the Senate, Senator Sir Stanley Robinson, C.B.E.
Speaker, House of Assembly, Sir Theodore Brancker, Q.C.

BARBADOS HIGH COMMISSION
6 Upper Belgrave Street, S.W.1
High Commissioner, His Excellency Waldo Emerson Waldron-Ramsey (1971).

BRITISH HIGH COMMISSION
147–9 Roebuck Street (P.O. Box 676C)
Bridgetown
High Commissioner, His Excellency David Arthur Roberts (1971)...................... £5,765
Deputy High Commissioner, J. A. B. Stewart (*Head of Chancery*).

JUDICATURE

There is a Supreme Court of Judicature consisting of a High Court and a Court of Appeal. In certain cases a further appeal lies to the Judicial Committee of H.M. Privy Council. The Chief Justice is appointed by the Governor-General on the recommendation of the Prime Minister in consultation with the Leader of the Opposition. Puisne Judges are appointed by the Governor-General, on the advice of the Judicial and Legal Service Commission.

Chief Justice, Hon. Sir William Douglas.... $21,600
Puisne Judges, A. J. H. Hanschell, C.M.G.; D. H. L. Ward; D. Williams.

Education.—Primary and secondary education is free in Government-aided schools.

Communications.—Barbados has some 800 miles of roads, of which about 720 miles are asphalted. There is an international airport at Seawell, 12 miles from Bridgetown, and frequent scheduled services connect Barbados with the major world air routes. There are a television service, a radio broadcasting service operated by the Caribbean Broadcasting Corporation, and a wired broadcasting service operated by a local subsidiary of Rediffusion Ltd.

Production, etc.—The principal *exports* are sugar, molasses, rum, margarine, lard and laundry soap, and the *imports* meat, rice, salted fish, dairy products, flour, corn meal, lumber, textiles, animal foods and chemical fertilizers. The tourist industry is an important source of revenue.

TRADE

Goods to the value of $68,824,293 were exported in 1969, including sugar ($22,131,204), molasses $2,800,664, and rum $2,938,376.

	1969–70	1970–71
Total imports	$194,589,761	$235,005,185
Total exports........	68,824,293	78,033,285

Trade with U.K.

	1969	1970
Imports from U.K...	£9,283,000	£11,973,000
Exports to U.K.....	6,680,000	6,836,000

FINANCE

	1970–71	1971–72
Revenue...........	$76,818,283	$97,442,000
Expenditure........	88,959,379	98,959,000
Public Debt, April 1, 1970		54,862,000

Botswana

Botswana (formerly the British Protectorate of Bechuanaland) lies between latitudes 18° and 26° S. and longitudes 20° and 28° W. and is bounded by the Cape and Transvaal Provinces of South Africa on the south and east, by Rhodesia, the Zambesi and Chobe (Linyanti) Rivers on the north and north-east and by South West Africa on the west. Botswana extends some 500 miles by 550 miles, with a total area of 220,000 square miles. The climate of the country is generally sub-tropical, but varies considerably with latitude and altitude. A plateau at a height of about 4,000 feet divides Botswana into two main topographical regions. To the east of the plateau streams flow into the Marico, Notwani and Limpopo Rivers; to the west lies a flat region comprising the Kgalagadi Desert, the Okavango Swamps and the Northern State Lands area. The Kgalagadi Desert is a level tract closely covered with thorn bush and grass, extending 300 miles to the west and bounded by the Makgadikgadi salt pans and the Boteti River in the north. Its rainfall varies from 20 inches in the east to 9 inches in the south-west. The Okavango Swamps, 6,500 square miles in area, lie in the remote north-western corner of Botswana, and, apart from the Limpopo and Chobe Rivers, are the only source of permanent surface water in the country. North of the Boteti River and the Makgadikgadi depression the Kgalagadi Desert gives way to forest and dense bush of the Northern State Lands. Large areas of the country support only herds of game. Elephant numbers have been estimated at 10,000.

Population.—Botswana has a population estimated Jan. 31, 1969, at 611,000. The annual increase is believed to be about 3 per cent. The eight principal Botswana tribes (with population in 1964) are Bakgatla (32,118), Bakwena (73,088), Bangwaketse (71,289), Bamalete (13,861), Bamangwato (199,782), Barolong (10,662), Batawana (42,347) and Batlowka (3,735). The non-African population at the Census of 1964 numbered only 7,830. CAPITAL.—Gaborone, estimated population, 18,000. Other business centres are Francistown (11,000) and Lobatse (8,000). The four largest towns are Serowe (37,000), Kanye (37,000), Molepolole (32,000) and Mochudi (19,000). FLAG.—Horizontal bands of blue, white, blue, with a black stripe on the white band.

Government.—On September 30, 1966, Bechuanaland became a Republic within the Commonwealth under the name Botswana. The President of Botswana is Head of State and appoints as Vice-President a member of the National Assembly who is his principal assistant and leader of Government business in the National Assembly. The Assembly consists of the President, 31 members elected on a basis of universal adult suffrage, 4 specially elected members, the Attorney-General (non-voting) and the Speaker. There is also a House of Chiefs. 28 seats in the House of Assembly were won by the Bechuanaland Democratic Party at the first General Election in 1965 and its leader, Sir Seretse Khama, became the country's first Prime Minister and subsequently President. He was re-elected at a General Election in 1969 with a slightly reduced majority. Botswana is a member of the United Nations and of the Organization for African Unity.

PRESIDENT AND CABINET

President, Sir Seretse Khama, K.B.E., *assumed office*, Sept. 30, 1966.
Vice-President and Minister of Finance and Development Planning, Dr. Q. K. J. Masire.
Minister of Education, B. C. Thema, M.B.E.
Works and Communications, J. G. Haskins, O.B.E.
Minister of State, E. S. Masisi.
Commerce, Industry and Water Affairs, M. K. Segokgo.
Agriculture, A. M. Dambe, B.E.M.
Health, Labour and Home Affairs, M. P. K. Nwako.
Local Government and Lands, E. M. K. Kgabo.

Assistant Ministers

State, K. P. Morake.
Finance and Development Planning, B. K. Kgari.

BOTSWANA HIGH COMMISSION

3 Buckingham Gate (6th Floor), S.W.1
High Commissioner, Her Excellency Miss G. K. T. Chiepe, M.B.E. (1970).

BRITISH HIGH COMMISSION

Private Bag 23, Gaborone
High Commissioner, His Excellency George David Anderson, C.M.G. (1967)...............£5,765

Chief Justice of Botswana, Hon. Mr. Justice J. R. Dendy Young.
Attorney-General, M. D. Mokama.

The country is essentially pastoral, although sorghum, maize, beans, pumpkins, melons and some cotton are sown. Cattle thrive, in spite of the drought of 1965, during which some 200,000

died. In 1969 they numbered more than 1,300,000.

Schemes for improvements in agriculture, medical services, education and communications, and schemes for combating soil erosion, investigating mineral resources, improving water supplies, irrigation dams, tribal granaries and roads and for improving living conditions are being carried out.

Education.—In 1969, there were 314 primary schools with enrolment of 82,377 and 10 secondary schools with enrolment of 3,049. There were also three teacher training establishments with enrolment of 359. The principal languages in use in the country are English and Setswana.

Communications.—The railway from Kimberley to Vryburg and Mafeking traverses Botswana on its way to Rhodesia and Zambia. There are telegraph and telephone lines from Cape Province through from Mafeking, *via* Gaborone and Francistown to Bulawayo and Salisbury.

FINANCE

	1968-69	1969-70
Estimated Revenue ...	R16,053,000	R21,404,000
Estimated Expenditure	15,903,000	20,394,000

Rand 1 = 11s. 8d. sterling.

TRADE

	1967	1968
Imports*	R19,975,281	R23,230,752
Exports	9,218,503	8,597,897

* Estimated

Trade with U.K.

	1969	1970
Imports from U.K. .	£346,000	£426,000
Exports to U.K.	835,000	3,153,000

SRI LANKA ~~Ceylon~~ *becoming "a free & sovereign & independent republic 22/5/72*

AREA AND POPULATION

Ceylon is an island in the Indian Ocean, off the southern tip of the peninsula of India and separated from it by a narrow strip of shallow water, the Palk Strait. Situated between 5° 55'- 9° 50' N. latitude and 79° 42'-81° 52' E. longitude, it has an area of 25,332 square miles, including 333 square miles of inland water. Its greatest length is from north to south, 270 miles; and its greatest width 140 miles, no point in Ceylon being more than 80 miles from the sea.

At the Census of 1963, the population was 10,582,064; (estimated, 1969, 12,240,000).

Races and Religions

The races of Ceylon are low-country Sinhalese, Kandyan Sinhalese, Ceylon Tamils, Indian Tamils, Ceylon Moors, Indian Moors, Burghers and Eurasians, Malays and Veddahs. Generally Sinhalese who trace their descent to a low-country district are classified as low-country Sinhalese, others as Kandyan Sinhalese. The Western and Southern Provinces, the Southern (Chilaw) District and the Western parts of Puttalam District are low-country areas; the Central and North Central Provinces, Uva, Sabaragamuwa, Kurunegala and the Sinhalese divisions of the districts of Batticaloa, Trincomalee and Vavuniya are regarded as Kandyan districts. At the 1953 Census 42·3 per cent. of the population were low-country Sinhalese, 28·8 per cent. Kandyan Sinhalese. The religion of the great majority of inhabitants is Buddhism, introduced from India, according to ancient Sinhalese chronicles, in 300 B.C. Next to Buddhism, Hinduism has a large following

PHYSIOGRAPHY

Ceylon is a compact area, except for the Island of Mannar and an almost detached portion in the north, the Jaffna Peninsula and its satellite islands of Delft, Kayts, etc. The relief of the island includes a mountainous area in the south-central region of 3,000 to 7,000 feet above sea level, surrounded by an upland belt of about 1,000 to 3,000 feet and a narrow coastal plain broadening out to a vast tract in the north. The coastal plain continues for a distance out to sea as a continental shelf and a coral reef, for the most part submerged, lies close to the coast. On the Central Ridge of the hill country are some of the highest peaks in Ceylon, Pidurutalagala (8,281 ft.), Kirigalpotta (7,857 ft.) and Totapolakanda (7,741 ft.) and the high plains Nuwara Eliya (over 6,000 ft.), Elk Plains (6,000 ft.) and Horton Plains (over 7,000 ft.). The other principal peaks are Adam's Peak (7,360 ft.), Namunukula (6,679 ft.), Knuckles (6,112 ft.) and Haycock (2,167 ft.). The Peninsula of Jaffna and the Island of Mannar are featureless level stretches.

The Mahaveli-ganga, 206 miles long, is the largest river of Ceylon. Rising on the western side of the central hilly ridge, it flows north and east to empty into the Koddiyar Bay on the east coast. Other rivers are the Kelaniganga (90 miles), Aruvi-aru (104), Kala-oya (97), Yam-oya (94) and Deduru-oya (87). Waterfalls girdle the central mountainous massif and offer some of the best scenic features in the island; Dunhinda (Badulla), Diyaluma (Koslanda), Elgin (Hatton Plateau) and Perawella are among the outstanding falls. Forests, jungle and scrub cover the greater part of the island, often being intermingled. The forests, of varying species, extend from fairly near the coast right into the hill country. In areas over 2,000 feet above sea level grasslands (*patanas* or *talawas*) are found. Their total area is some 250 square miles, principally in the Province of Uva.

Climate.—The climate of Ceylon is warm throughout the year, with a high relative humidity. Temperatures average 80° F. during the year in the lowlands, falling off in the hills to 60° F. at elevations over 6,000 ft. Day humidity is over 70 per cent. and night humidity over 85 per cent. Temperature ranges vary little between wet and dry seasons. In the hilly areas morning mists sometimes occur. Traces of ground frost appear occasionally at night, at the highest levels, and disappear at sunrise. Thunderstorms occasionally give hail, but snow is completely absent. Rainfall is generally heavy, with marked regional variations; the heaviest falls (200-250 inches) are recorded on the south-west slopes of the central hills. Some depressional or cyclonic activity occurs generally during October to December.

GOVERNMENT

Early in the sixteenth century the Portuguese landed in Ceylon and founded settlements, eventually conquering much of the country. Portuguese rule in Ceylon lasted 150 years during which the Roman Catholic religion was established among the Sinhalese inhabitants and to some extent Portuguese modes of living adopted. In 1658, following a twenty-year period of decline, Portuguese rule gave place to that of the Dutch East India Company which was to exploit Ceylon with varying fortunes until 1796.

The Maritime Provinces of Ceylon were ceded by the Dutch to the British on February 16, 1798, becoming a British Crown Colony in 1802 under the terms of the Treaty of Amiens. With the annexation of the Kingdom of Kandy in 1815. all Ceylon came under British rule.

On February 4, 1948, Ceylon became a self-governing state and a member of the British Commonwealth

of Nations under the *Ceylon Independence Act* 1947. The Parliament of Ceylon consists of (*a*) The Queen (represented by the Governor-General) and (*b*) two houses, namely, the Senate and the House of Representatives. The Executive consists of the Prime Minister and a Cabinet chosen from the party which has the majority in the House of Representatives. A committee was appointed by the House of Representatives in July, 1970, to draft a republican constitution for Ceylon.

CAPITAL.— Ψ Colombo, population (estimated 1970), 551,200. Other principal towns are Ψ Jaffna (99,800), Kandy (75,900), Ψ Galle (71,700), Negombo (51,600) and Trincomalee (38,800).
Colombo is distant from London 5,495 miles; transit 17 days; by air 13½ hours.
NATIONAL DAY.—February 4.
FLAG.—Yellow lion of Kandy on a maroon ground; Sinhalese pinnacle at the corners; yellow border; two vertical stripes at the staff side.

Governor-General

Governor-General, His Excellency WILLIAM GOPALLAWA, M.B.E., *b.* 1897 (March 2, 1962)........ £8,000

CABINET

Prime Minister and Minister of Defence and External Affairs, Planning and Employment, Hon. Sirimavo R. D. Bandaranaike.
Irrigation, Power and Highways, Hon. Maitripala Senanayake.
Foreign and Internal Trade, Hon. T. B. Illangaratne.
Education, Hon. Badiudin Mahmud.
Shipping and Tourism, Hon. P. B. G. Kalugalle.
Labour, Hon. M. P. De Z. Siriwardene.
Public Administration, Local Government and Home Affairs, Hon. Felix R. D. Bandaranaike.
Industries and Scientific Affairs, Hon. T. B. Subasinghe.
Finance, Hon. Dr. N. M. Perera.
Communications, Hon. Leslie S. Goonewardene.
Plantation Industry and Constitutional Affairs, Hon. Dr. Colvin R. de Silva.
Justice, Hon. J. M. Jayamanne.
Agriculture and Lands, Hon. H. S. R. B. Kobbe-kaduwa.
Fisheries, Hon. George Rajapakse.
Housing and Construction, Hon. Pieter G. B. Keuneman.
Posts and Telecommunications, Hon. Chelliah Kumarasurier.
Health, Hon. W. P. G. Ariyadasa.
Information and Broadcasting, Hon. R. S. Perera.
Social Services, Hon. T. B. Tennekoon.
Cultural Affairs, Hon. S. S. Kulatilake.
Parliamentary Affairs and Chief Government Whip, and Minister of Sport, Hon. K. B. Ratnayake.
Leader of the House, Hon. Maitripala Senanayake.
The Prime Minister and other members of the Cabinet receive remuneration of *Rs.*18,000 yearly.

CEYLON HIGH COMMISSION
13 Hyde Park Gardens, W.2

High Commissioner His Excellency Tilak E. Gooneratne (1970).

BRITISH HIGH COMMISSION
Galle Road, Kollupitiya (P.O. Box 1433), Colombo 3

High Commissioner, His Excellency Angus Mackay Mackintosh, C.M.G. (1969)............. £6,875
Deputy High Commissioner, J. W. Nicholas (*and Commercial Counsellor*).
British Council Representative, W. R. McAlpine, O.B.E. (*Counsellor*). There are British Council libraries at *Colombo* and *Kandy*.
Defence Adviser, Wing-Cdr. R. M. Robson.

THE LEGISLATURE

Parliament consists of the House of Representatives and the Senate. The House of Representatives is composed of 157 members, of whom 151 are elected by universal suffrage and 6 nominated. The Senate consists of 30 members, 15 of whom are elected by the House of Representatives and 15

appointed by the Governor-General. One-third of the Senators retire every second year
President of the Senate, Senator Hon. A. Ratnayake.
Speaker of the House of Representatives, Hon. Stanley Tillakaratne.

THE JUDICATURE

The Judicial System includes a Supreme Court composed of a Chief Justice and eleven Puisne Judges, Court of Criminal Appeal, District Courts, Magistrates' Courts, Courts of Requests, Municipal Magistrates' Courts and Rural Courts. Trial by jury obtains in the Supreme Court.

PRODUCTION

Agriculture.—The staple products of the island are agricultural. The areas under cultivation in 1969 in acres were: Paddy, 979,000; tea, 596,514; replanted tea, 33,429; rubber, 569,528; coconuts, 1·15 million; areca nuts, cinnamon, tobacco, and cocoa, 160,000 acres. Production in 1969 was: tea, 484 million lbs.; rubber, 333 million lbs.; paddy 65·9 million bushels and coconuts 2,601 million nuts. The livestock in 1968 included 1,659,603 cattle, 783,238 buffaloes, 24,891 sheep, 584,432 goats, 124,377 pigs, 6,747,873, poultry and 39,896, ducks.
Industry.—Factories are established for the manufacture or processing of ceramic ware, vegetable oils and by-products, paper, tanning and leather goods, plywood, cement, chemicals, sugar, salt, textiles, ilmenite, tiles, tyres, fertilizers and hardware and there is a petroleum refinery.

FINANCE

	1968–69	1969–70*
Revenue....	Rs.2,497 million	Rs.2,528 million
Expenditure*	Rs.3,445 million	Rs.3,899 million
Net Public Debt		
(Sept. 30)	Rs.6,239 million	—

* Revised estimates.

BANKING

In 1969 there were 12 commercial banks doing business in the Island with total deposits (31 December, 1969) of Rs.1,917 million. The Ceylon Savings Bank had deposits (Dec. 1969) of Rs.98·8 million and the Post Office Savings Bank had deposits (Dec. 1969) of Rs.489·7 million.

TRADE

In 1969, 39·28 per cent. of Ceylon's import trade was with Commonwealth countries (U.K., 17·42 per cent.) and 60·52 with other countries; 36·87 per cent. of Ceylon's exports went to Commonwealth countries (U.K., 20·19 per cent.) and 63·06 to other countries.

	1968	1969
Total imports	Rs.2,173,089,271	Rs.2,543,455,206
Total exports	1,975,134,685	1,875,219,855

Trade with U. K.

	1969	1970
Imports from U.K.....	£29,094,000	£18,508,000
Exports to U.K.......	33,101,000	36,558,000

COMMUNICATIONS

There are 13,315 miles of motorable roads in Ceylon. In September, 1969, there were 167,572 motor vehicles on register—86,197 private cars and cabs, 9,557 buses and private coaches, 30,812 lorries, 18,687 motor cycles, 12,838 tractors, 4,119 other vehicles registered as lorries.

In 1968, 2,891 ocean-going merchant vessels of a total net register tonnage of 9,485,780 entered the port of Colombo

In 1968 there were 2,361 Money Order Offices, 1,320 Telegraph Offices and 33,409 Telephones. There were 41 Telex subscribers in 1968.

A commercial wireless telegraph station has a range of 500 miles by day and about 1,000 to 2,000 miles by night and handles ship-to-shore traffic.

Since 1965 Air Ceylon has been chartering a VC-10 aircraft from B.O.A.C. for operation on a weekly service on the route: London—Rome—Karachi—Colombo—Kuala Lumpur—Singapore. Air Ceylon's regional services are operated direct to Madras four times weekly. Services between Jaffna and Tiruchirapalli operate thrice weekly and two services a week are operated to Bombay. A *Trident* service was introduced in 1969 and covers Karachi, Bombay, Madras, Colombo, Bangkok, Kuala Lumpur and Singapore. There are internal services linking Colombo with Trincomalee, Jaffna, Tiruchirapalli, Batticoloa and Gal Oya.

Cyprus

Area, Climate and Population.—Cyprus with an area of 3,572 square miles, is the third largest island in the Mediterranean Sea, exceeded in size by Sicily and Sardinia. Its greatest length is 140 miles and greatest breadth 60 miles. It is situated at the extreme north-east corner of the Mediterranean in latitude 35° N. and longitude 33° 30′ E. It is about 40 miles distant from the nearest point of Asia Minor, 60 miles from Syria and 240 miles from Port Said. The main topographical features of Cyprus are: (*a*) A narrow limestone range of mountains extending in an unbroken chain for nearly 100 miles along the north coast, at an average height of 2,000 feet; (*b*) A broad central plain, running for some 60 miles from west to east; (*c*) An extensive igneous massif rising to over 6,000 feet in the west of the island; and (*d*) Narrow coastal plains between the mountains and the sea. The rivers are little more than mountain torrents. There is no permanent stream of any volume.

Cyprus has a somewhat intense Mediterranean climate (with a hot dry summer and a variable warm winter). There are two contrasted seasons, winter and summer, while the intermediate ones are short and transitional. The winter is generally sunny with frequent cold spells between the beginning of December and end of February. The mean temperatures of the coldest month range from 35° to 50° F.

The rainy season lasts from October to April with average total rainfall of about 20 inches.

The summers are hot, dry and almost cloudless. July and August are the warmest months, with mean temperatures ranging from 80°–85° F in the lowlands, to 70° in the mountains. At the end of 1970 the estimated population was 633,000. There are two major communities, Greek Cypriots (78 per cent.) and Turkish Cypriots (18·2 per cent.); and minorities of Armenians, Maronites and others. The population increases on the average at about 1 per cent. annually. Birth rate is moderately high (21·3 per thousand) and the death rate (6·8 per thousand) is one of the lowest in the world. Infant mortality rate is about 25·7 per thousand.

CAPITAL.—Nicosia, near the centre of the island, with a population of 115,000 (including suburbs); the other principal towns are ΨLimassol (population 51,500), ΨFamagusta (42,500), ΨLarnaca (21,400), Paphos (11,800) and Kyrenia (4,900). Nicosia is distant from London 2,028 miles by air.

FLAG.—Gold map of Cyprus on a white ground, surmounting crossed olive branches (green).

President, Archbishop Makarios, *elected* Dec. 14, 1959; *assumed office* Aug. 16, 1960; *re-elected* Feb. 25, 1968.

CABINET

A joint Greek–Turkish Cabinet was formed in 1960, but the three Turkish members ceased to attend, following events in Dec. 1963, and their Ministries were taken over by Greek Ministers.

CYPRUS HIGH COMMISSION
93 Park Street, W.1
High Commissioner, His Excellency Costas Ashiotis, M.B.E.

BRITISH HIGH COMMISSION
Alexander Pallis Street (P.O. Box 1978)
Nicosia
High Commissioner, His Excellency Robert Humphrey Gordon Edmonds (1971) £6,875
British Council Representative, J. M. E. Toor, M.B.E., P.O. Box 1995, 17–19 Archbishop Makarios III Avenue, Nicosia.

GOVERNMENT

Cyprus was formally annexed to Great Britain on Nov. 5, 1914, on the outbreak of war with Turkey. From 1925 to 1960 it was a Crown Colony administered by a Governor, assisted by an Executive Council and also for a time by a partly-elected Legislative Council. A state of emergency was declared in November, 1955, and Archbishop Makarios was deported. Further proposals for a workable constitution made in 1956 and a seven-year-plan for the government of Cyprus in association with Greece and Turkey were rejected by the Greek Government and Greek Cypriots. Archbishop Makarios was released in March, 1957, but was not allowed to return immediately to Cyprus. Following a meeting at Zürich between the Prime Ministers of Greece and Turkey, a conference was held in London and an agreement was signed on February 19, 1959, between the United Kingdom, Greece, Turkey and the Greek and Turkish Cypriots which provided that Cyprus would be a Republic.

Constitution.—Under the Cyprus Act, 1960, the island became an independent sovereign republic on August 16, 1960. The constitution provides for a Greek Cypriot President and a Turkish Cypriot Vice-President elected for a five-year term by the Greek and Turkish communities respectively. The House of Representatives, elected for five years by universal suffrage of each community separately, consists of 35 Greek and 15 Turkish members. The 1960 Constitution proved unworkable in practice and led to the intercommunal troubles. Talks were in progress between Greeks and Turks in 1971 on a new Constitution for the island.

A General Election was held for the 35 Greek Cypriot seats on July 5, 1970, resulting in the following state of parties: *Unified Party,* 15; *Akel* (Communist), 9; *Progressive Front,* 7; *Democratic Centre Union,* 2; and *Independents,* 2. On the same day elections were held in the Turkish sector to elect 15

members for Turkish Cypriot national seats and 15 Turkish communal seats which together form a temporary chamber in the Turkish Cypriot sector first set up in December, 1967, but which is not recognized by the Cyprus Government.

British Sovereign Areas.—The United Kingdom retained full sovereignty and jurisdiction over two areas—Akrotiri–Episkopi–Paramali and Dhekelia–Pergamos–Ayios Nicolaos–Xylophagou—and use of roads and other facilities. The British Administrator of these areas is appointed by the Queen and is responsible to the Secretary of State for Defence.

Production and Industries.—About 36 per cent. of those gainfully employed take part in agriculture, the chief agricultural products being:—cereals, vine products, potatoes, carobs, carrots, citrus and other fresh and dried fruit, tobacco and legumes. Various kinds of livestock are raised, principally sheep, goats, pigs and poultry. The value of agricultural and livestock exports in 1970 was about £23,427,000. Mining is an important industry in Cyprus; the value of minerals exported in 1969 was £13,114,044. The principal minerals are cupreous and copper concentrates, copper and iron pyrites, and asbestos. There is no heavy industry, but a wide variety of light manufacturing industries. Tourism is becoming an increasingly important source of revenue. Long-stay visitors to the island in 1970 numbered 126,580.

Communications.— Ψ Famagusta is the main seaport. In 1970, 2,625 steam and motor ships (4,666,824 net tons) and 275 sailing vessels (31,836 tons) engaged in the foreign trade. Air passenger traffic in, out and through Nicosia airport in 1970 totalled 349,314 persons (1969, 332,853).

FINANCE

	1968	1969
Ordinary Revenue....	£30,963,578	£35,726,061
Ordinary Expenditure.	25,738,782	27,881,153
Public Debt..........	14,071,145	12,148,651

TRADE

	1969	1970
Imports..............	£84,607,763	£98,229,000
Exports..............	40,902,699	45,189,000
Imports from U.K....	£25,641,000	£26,088,000
Exports to U.K......	18,943,000	20,432,000

Fiji

This is a group of 322 islands (of which only 106 are inhabited) in the South Pacific Ocean, about 1,100 miles north of New Zealand. The gross area of the group, which extends 300 miles from east to west, and 300 north to south, between 15′ 45′—21° 10′ S. lat. and 176° E.—178° W. long. is 7,083 square miles. Many of the islands are of volcanic origin, with lofty mountains, and well wooded. The principal are Viti Levu, Vanua Levu, Taveuni and Kandavu. The climate is oceanic. Shade temperatures seldom rise above 93°F. or fall below 60°F. except in the mountains. On the windward sides of the larger islands rainfall is copious and vegetation luxuriant; on the leeward (or dry) sides the vegetation is sparse and scattered. The chief products are sugar cane, coconuts, gold, rice, bananas, pineapples, yams, and dalo or taro (colocasia).

The population (census 1966) was 476,727 (240,960 Indians, 202,176 Fijians, 9,687 part Europeans, 6,590 Europeans, 12,165 other Pacific races, and 5,149 Chinese): estimated (Dec., 1970), 524,457.

CAPITAL.— Ψ Suva, in the island of Viti Levu.   Population (1966 Census), 54,157.

Government.—Fiji was a British colony from 1874 until October 10, 1970, when it became an independent state and a member of the Commonwealth. Under the Constitution there is a Governor-General appointed by the Queen. An elected House of Representatives (52 members) consists of 12 Fijians, 12 Indians and 3 General members elected on Communal rolls; and 10 Fijians, 10 Indians and 5 General members elected on National rolls, in which members of all races vote on the same register. General members are in the main representatives of the European and Chinese communities.

There is a Senate of 22 members, 8 appointed by the Great Council of Chiefs, 7 by the Prime Minister, 6 by the Leader of the Opposition and one by the Council of Rotuma, an island dependency 400 miles from Suva, discovered in 1879 and annexed in 1881.

Governor-General, His Excellency Sir Robert Sidney Foster, K.C.M.G., K.C.V.O. (1968).

CABINET

Prime Minister, Hon. Ratu Sir Kamisese Mara, K.B.E.
Attorney-General, Hon. J. N. Falvey, O.B.E.
Minister of Finance, Hon. W. M. Barrett.
Fijian Affairs and Local Government, Hon. Ratu G. K. Cakobau, O.B.E.
Labour, Hon. Ratu Sir Etuate Cakobau, K.B.E., M.C., E.D.
Commerce, Industry and Co-operatives, Hon. Vijay R. Singh.
Social Services, Hon. J. Mavoa.
Communications, Works and Tourism, Hon. C. A. Stinson, O.B.E.
Natural Resources, Hon. D. W. Brown, M.B.E.
Home Affairs, Lands and Mineral Development, Hon. P. K. Ganilau, C.M.G., C.V.O., D.S.O., O.B.E.
Youth, Sport and Rural Development, Hon. J. B. Naisara.

Asst. Minister, Social Services, Hon. K. S. Reddy.
Secretary to the Cabinet, R. T. Sanders.

Speaker, House of Representatives, R. G. Q. Kermode.
Deputy Speaker, Hon. R. D. Patel.
Chairman of the Senate, Hon. R. L. Munro, C.B.E.

Fijian High Commissioner in London, His Excellency, Josua Rasilau Rabukawaqa, M.V.O., M.B.E.

BRITISH HIGH COMMISSION
Suva

High Commissioner, His Excellency John Robert Williams (1970) £5,765

JUDICIARY

Chief Justice of Fiji, Sir Clifford Hammett.. $8,004
Puisne Judge, M. Tikaram 7,008

FINANCE

	1969	1970
Public Income......	$37,565,000	$42,089,091
Public Expenditure..	34,423,000	39,853,684
Public Debt (Dec. 31)	35,789,128	40,184,961

TRADE

	1969	1970
Total Imports......	$77,888,000	$88,540,000
Total Exports......	53,227,000	58,939,000
Imports from U.K....	£5,836,000	£6,083,000
Exports to U.K.....	11,727,000	10,206,000

Currency.—Currency is the *Fiji dollar.* Exchange rate: $2.09 = £100 sterling.

The principal exports are sugar, coconut oil, gold, oil seed cake and meal, lumber, bananas, copra, molasses, copper ore, manganese ore, biscuits, fish and unmanufactured tobacco. The chief imports are machinery, electrical goods, foodstuffs, all types of fabrics, petroleum products, motor

vehicles and miscellaneous manufactured articles. The tourist trade continues to expand.

Communications.—Fiji is approximately 11,000 miles from the United Kingdom; transit time from London *viâ* Panama Canal about 28–30 days. Air connections are provided between the United Kingdom and Fiji *viâ* Canada, United States of America, Mexico and the Caribbean, Japan and U.S.S.R., and the Middle East either through New Zealand and Australia or through New Caledonia and Singapore. The following trunk route operators provide services through Nadi Airport; Qantas, Pan American, British Overseas Airways, Air New Zealand, U.T.A., Air India, CP Air and American Airlines. Flights connecting with Fiji operate to Auckland, Sydney–Perth and Darwin and points beyond; Honolulu, San Francisco or Los Angeles or Vancouver and points beyond; Tahiti and points beyond; Pago Pago; Noumea and points beyond. Fiji is one of the main aerial crossroads in the Pacific.

Air Pacific Ltd. (previously Fiji Airways Ltd.) is based at Nausori Airport near Suva and with HS.748, DC3 and DH *Heron* aircraft operates scheduled domestic services within the Fiji islands and from Suva provides connection to Nadi, Labasa, Savusavu and Matei, and there are regional services to Tonga, Western Samoa, Papua, New Guinea (Port Moresby) *viâ* the New Hebrides (Vila and Santo); the Solomon Islands (Honiara) and the Republic of Nauru *viâ* Funafuti and Tarawa in the Gilbert and Ellice Islands and the island of Nauru. Fiji Air Services Ltd. operates Charter flights within the Fiji group of islands and provides services to the island of Ovalau and to airstrips on Viti Levu at Koreleva and Natadola.

The Gambia

The West African river Gambia was discovered by the Portuguese in 1447; and in 1588, the year of the Spanish Armada, Queen Elizabeth I, being then at war with Spain and Portugal, gave a charter to a British Company to trade with the Gambia, and as early as 1618 an effort to do so was made, but it was not successful. In 1686 a fort was built upon a rocky island, and, in honour of the new King, was named Fort James; but the English merchants had formidable rivals in the Portuguese and French, and it was not until 1783 that the river was recognized, by the *Treaty of Versailles*, as British. The Colony had no regular political institutions until 1807, when it was put under the Government of Sierra Leone. The Colony of the Gambia was created in 1843, and was constituted a separate government in 1888. It consists of a narrow strip of land, estimated at 4,003 sq. miles, lying on both sides of the River Gambia to a distance of about 300 miles, mainly between 13° 15′–13° 45′ N. and 13° 45′–13° 65′ W. The river is navigable to ocean-going vessels for 150 miles and to river steamers up to 300 miles from its mouth. The capital and chief port, Bathurst, is situated on the island of Banjal at the mouth of the River. The total population of the country was 315,486 at the 1963 Census (estimated, 1970, 374,000). The climate of Bathurst is extremely pleasant except during the rainy season from June to October, when it sometimes becomes uncomfortably warm. Rainfall 30–60 inches a year.

CAPITAL.— Ψ Bathurst. Population (1963 census), 27,809.

FLAG.—Horizontal stripes of red, blue and green, separated by narrow white stripes.

Government.—On February 18, 1965, the Gambia became an independent monarchy within the Commonwealth, with the Queen as Head of State. On April 24, 1970, following a referendum, the constitution was changed to that of a Republic (within the Commonwealth) with an executive President. The House of Representatives, which elects its own Speaker, consists of 32 elected members, 4 elected Head Chiefs, 3 nominated members and the Attorney General (who is also a nominated member with voting rights). The Vice-President, who is the Government leader in the House, and other Ministers are appointed by the President. The latter's tenure of office is co-terminous with the life of a Parliament.

PRESIDENT AND CABINET

President, Sir Dawda Jawara.
Vice-President and Minister of Finance and Trade, Hon. S. M. Dibba.
External Affairs, Hon. A. D. Camera.
Local Government, Lands and Mines, Alhaji Hon. Yaya Ceesay.
Works and Communications, Alhaji Hon. K. Singaleh.
Education. Health and Social Welfare, Alhaji Hon. I. M. Carba-Jahumpa.
Agriculture and Natural Resources, Hon. H. O. Semega-Janneh.
Minister of State, President's Office, Alhaji Hon. A. B. N'jie.
Attorney-General, Alhaji M. L. Saho.

―――

Chief Justice, Hon. P. R. Bridges, C.M.G.

―――

Speaker, Hon. Alhaji Sir Alieu Sulayman Jack.

GAMBIA HIGH COMMISSION
28 Kensington Court, W.8
High Commissioner, His Excellency Bocar Ousman Semega-Janneh, M.B.E. (1971).
BRITISH HIGH COMMISSION
78 Wellington Street, Bathurst
High Commissioner (vacant).

Communications.—Bathurst is 2,600 miles from London. There is one direct air service weekly *viâ* Las Palmas and three weekly, changing at Dakar. There is no regular passenger or mails service by sea. Ocean-going vessels entering the ports in 1970 totalled 279 (net tonnage 669,209). There is an international aerodrome at Yundum 17 miles from Bathurst. Internal communication is by road and river. There are 794 miles of motor road, including 180 miles of bituminous surface roads, 330 miles of gravel roads and 284 miles of Commissioners' roads. There are eight Government wireless stations and a V.H.F. telephone service linking Bathurst with the principal towns in the provinces. In 1962 a broadcasting service was started.

Education.—There are 95 primary schools and 21 secondary schools, with a total enrolment of 22,318 pupils, including 6,506 girls. There are 136 students, including 29 females, at the Uundum Teacher Training College. A Vocational and Training Centre operates in Bathurst, with courses in Carpentry and Joinery, Mechanical Engineering, Craft Practice, Masonry, Clerical Studies, Motor Mechanics, Welding and Fitting. Government Expenditure on education in 1969–70 was about £524,700.

Production.—Most of the population is engaged in agriculture, the chief product being ground-nuts which is the single important cash crop. Other crops are rice, millet and various kinds of fruit and

vegetables. Fishing and livestock production are considerable. No minerals are at present being exploited and there are practically no manufactures other than ground-nut processing.

FINANCE

	1969/70 (Actual)		1970/71 (Revised Estimate)	
	Re-current £'000	Develop-ment £'000	Re-current £'000	Develop-ment £'000
Revenue.....	3,524	597	5,087	703
Expenditure..	3,634	581	4,661	833

The Government financial year begins on July 1.

Currency.—Decimal currency was introduced in the Gambia on July, 1, 1971. The new unit is the *dalasi* of 100 *butbut*, equal to 4 shillings of the previous currency.

TRADE

	1968–69	1969–70
Total imports.......	£9,331,000	£7,123,000
Total exports.......	7,381,300	6,557,000

	1969	1970
Imports from U.K....	£2,521,000	£2,110,000
Exports to U.K.......	2,024,000	4,139,000

The chief exports are ground-nut products, which account for 95 per cent. of total exports, the main markets being Italy, the United Kingdom, W. Germany, Switzerland and the Netherlands. Other exports are palm kernels, dried fish and hides. Foodstuff imports include rice, sugar, flour and kola nuts. Manufactured goods of all kinds are imported, the chief being textiles and apparel, vehicles, machinery, metal goods and petroleum products.

Ghana

Ghana (formerly the British Colony of the Gold Coast) is situated on the Gulf of Guinea, between 3° 07′ W. long. and 1° 14′ E. long. (about 334 miles), and extends 441 miles north from Cape Three Points (4° 45′ N.) to 11° 11′ N. It is bounded on the north by the Republic of Upper Volta, on the west by the Republic of Ivory Coast, on the east by the Republic of Togo, and on the south by the Atlantic Ocean. Although a tropical country, Ghana is cooler than many countries within similar latitudes.

Area and Population.—Ghana has a total area of 92,100 sq. miles with a total population (Census of 1970, preliminary) of 8,545,561, some 27 per cent. more than the population at the Census of 1960. Almost all Ghanaians are Sudanese Negroes, although Hamitic strains are common in Northern Ghana.

CAPITAL.— Ψ ACCRA. Population of the Capital District (including Accra Tema City Council area, and Accra Rural area) (estimated, 1970), 633,800. Other towns are Kumasi, Tamale, Sekondi-Takoradi, Cape Coast, Sunyani, Ho, Koforidua, Tarkwa and Winneba. Accra is 3,920 miles by sea from Liverpool, transit 12 to 30 days.

FLAG.—Equal horizontal bands of red over yellow over green; five-point black star on yellow stripe.
INDEPENDENCE DAY—March 6.

GOVERNMENT

The Gold Coast region of West Africa was first visited by European traders in the fifteenth century. The Gold Coast Colony, Ashanti, the Northern Territories and Trans-Volta-Togoland, the constituent parts of the new State, came under British administration at various times, the original Gold Coast Colony, the coastal and Southern areas, being first constituted in 1874; Ashanti in 1901; and the Northern Territories Protectorate in 1902. The territory of Trans-Volta-Togoland, part of Togo, a former German colony, was mandated to Britain by the League of Nations after the First World War, and remained under British administration as a United Nations Trusteeship after the Second World War. After a plebiscite in May, 1956, under the auspices of the United Nations, the territory was integrated with the Gold Coast Colony.

The former Gold Coast Colony and associated territories became the independent state of Ghana and a member of the British Commonwealth on March 6, 1957, under the *Ghana Independence Act*, 1957, and adopted a Republican constitution on July 1, 1960.

On Feb. 24, 1966, the Army seized power and Dr. Nkrumah and his ministers were dismissed.

Ghana was administered until October 1, 1969, by a National Liberation Council of four representatives each from the Army and the police, during which time a Constitution for the Second Republic of Ghana was evolved and brought into force by a 150 member Constituent Assembly on Aug. 22, 1969. The new Constitution provides for a President, a Council of State, a 140-member National Assembly and a Judiciary.

General elections were held on August 29, 1969, in which Dr K. A. Busia's Progress Party won 105 seats and Mr. K. A. Gbedemah's National Alliance of Liberals 29, the remaining 6 seats being won by minority parties. Dr. Busia was appointed Prime Minister on Sept. 3, 1969, and the N.L.C. formally handed over to the civilian government on October 1, 1969.

President, Edward Akufo-Addo, *born* 1906, *elected and assumed office,* Aug. 31, 1970.

The Council of State, appointed to aid and counsel the President, consists of the Prime Minister, the Speaker of the National Assembly, the President of the National House of Chiefs and the Leader of the Parliamentary Opposition (*ex officio*), and normally 8 other members appointed by the President.

Cabinet

Prime Minister, Dr. Kofi A. Busia.
Minister for Parliamentary Affairs, J. K. Lamptey.
Foreign Affairs, W. O. Atta.
Trade, Industries and Tourism, R. A. Quarshie.
Health, S. D. Dombo.
Education and Sports, R. R. Amponsah.
Justice (and Attorney-General), V. Owusu.
Finance, J. H. Mensah.
Works and Housing, S. W. Awuku Danko.
Land and Mineral Resources, T. D. Brodie-Mends.
Transport and Communications, J. Kaloe.
Internal Affairs, N. Y. B. Adade.
Labour and Co-operatives, Dr. D. G. Bruce-Konuah.
Minister of State, K. G. Osei-Bonsu (*State Protocol*).
Rural Development and Social Welfare, A. A. Munu-fie.
Agriculture, K. Safo Adu.
Defence, B. K. Adama.
Ministers are assisted by 27 Ministerial Secretaries.

Chief Executives of Regional Administrations

Greater Accra, A. S. O. Mensah.
Eastern Region, M. K. Owusu.
Western, A. E. Chinbuah.
Central, J. A. Annobil.
Ashanti, H. R. Annan.

Brong-Ahafo, A. A. Owusu.
Northern, J. A. Braimah.
Upper, I. Salifu.
Volta, A. S. Kpodonu.

GHANA HIGH COMMISSION
13 Belgrave Square, S.W.1
High Commissioner, His Excellency A. B. Attafua
(1970).

BRITISH HIGH COMMISSION
P.O. Box 296, High Street, Accra
High Commissioner, His Excellency Henry Sydney
Herbert Stanley, C.M.G. (1970) £6,875
Counsellors, R. M. Blaikley (*Head of Chancery*);
L. Reid (*Economic and Commercial*).

British Council Representative, H. C. Burrow, O.B.E.,
P.O. Box 771, Liberty Avenue, Accra, and an
office in *Kumasi.*

JUDICIARY

Jurisdiction in all matters civil and criminal is
vested in the Judiciary under a Chief Justice.
Superior courts are the Supreme Court of Ghana,
Court of Appeal and High Court of Justice.
Inferior courts are the Circuit Courts and District
Courts.

PRODUCTION, ETC.

Agriculture.—Agriculture forms the basis of
Ghana's economy, employing 70 per cent. of the
working population. Crops of the *Forest Zone*
include cocoa, which is the largest single source of
revenue, rice and a variety of other foodstuff crops
grown on mixed-crop farms. Fruits such as
avocado pears, oranges and pineapples are grown.
Cassava is the most important crop of the *Coastal
Savannas Zone,* which consists of the Accra Plains
(1,400 sq. miles) and Ho-Keta Plains (2,600 sq.
miles) of the lower Volta area. Fishing is important
in coastal areas and in the Volta itself. Production
of pulses such as groundnuts, tiger nuts and cowpeas
is widespread. Near the Togo border oil palms,
yams, maize, cassava, fruit and vegetables are produced. Livestock is raised in the uncultivated
areas. The *Northern Savanna Zone* is Ghana's
principal cattle rearing area and other livestock production there is important for home consumption.
Corn and millet crops are produced in the far north
and maize, yams, rice and groundnut crops in more
southerly parts of the Zone.

A State Farms Corporation, established in 1963
to further larger scale farming enterprise, had in 1971
more than 100 farms in various parts of the country
and operates from eight regional centres.

Fisheries.—Some 150,000 of the country's
population are engaged in fisheries which now produce about 65,000 tons annually. Ghana's estimated annual requirement is at least 200,000 tons
and there are considerable imports of fish products.
About 80 per cent of home supply is obtained from
sea fisheries, but production from the Volta Lake
and other inland fisheries is increasing rapidly
thanks to greatly increased fish population.

Mineral Production.—The area within a 60
mile radius of Dunkwa produces 90 per cent. of
Ghana's mineral exports. Manganese production
(from Nsuta) ranks among the world's highest and
gold, industrial diamonds and bauxite are also produced. Some 30,000 persons are employed by
the mining companies.

Manufacturers.—Examples of the small-scale traditional industries are tailoring, goldsmithing and
carpentry. Priority has been given in recent years
to the establishment of a number of "Pioneer
Industries" including sawmill furniture, prefabricated doors, boatbuilding, refrigerator assembly,
food processing (biscuits, edible oils, confectionery,
brewing, etc.), clothing, footwear, printing and
other light industries. A modern industrial complex is growing in the Accra-Tema area.

Volta River Project.—The Volta River is
formed at the confluence of the Black and White
Voltas, both of which rise in the neighbouring
republic of Upper Volta. With its tributaries
the Volta drains an area of 150,000 sq. miles of
which 61,000 sq. miles lie in Ghana. The Volta
Dam at Akosombo was inaugurated in January,
1966, to generate hydro-electric power for the
processing of bauxite and feed a power transmission
network for the Accra-Kumasi-Takoradi area.
When completely filled the lake raised by the Volta
Dam will have a maximum area of 3,275 sq. miles,
a length of 250 miles and a shore line of 4,500 miles.
A water transport service from Akosombo to the
farthest points reached is planned.

Power output from Akosombo is planned to
reach 768 megawatts, 22 times the country's 1959
generating capacity. Smaller dams with 150 MW.
and 93 MW. capacity are to be built at Kpong
rapids and at Bui in the Northern Region. Planned
aluminium output in Ghana by 1973 is 145,000 tons
(1969, 103,000 tons).

COMMUNICATIONS

There are four aerodromes in Ghana, situated at
Accra, Takoradi, Kumasi and Tamale. Accra Airport is an international airport and is the terminus
for services from the United Kingdom, the Northern, Ashanti and Western Regions.

Railway communications consist of a main line
running from Takoradi to Kumasi thence to Accra,
a distance of 357 miles. From Huni Valley on the
Kumasi line north of Takoradi a line runs to
Kotoku on the railway about 17 miles north of
Accra. Branch lines run to Sekondi, Prestea, Kade,
Awaso and Tema. Total railway mileage open to
traffic in 1971 was 792. There are 20,245 miles of
motorable roads of which 2,051 are bitumen.

Takoradi Harbour consists of two breakwaters
enclosing a water area of 220 acres. Seven quay
berths are situated on the lee breakwater—five are
used for the handling of general cargo, one is
leased specially for manganese exports and one is
used for shallow draft colliers. Tema Harbour—
Africa's largest artificial harbour and a prospective
major port of the South Atlantic—was opened in
1962. There are 10 berths for larger ocean going
vessels and the harbour also has the largest dry dock
on the West African coast. An oil berth has also
been built to serve the Ghaip refinery which has
been constructed at Tema.

TRADE

	1969	1970
Total imports..	N₵354,000,000	N₵394,000,000
Total exports...	369,000,000	435,000,000

Trade with U.K.

	1969	1970
Imports from U.K..	£36,746,000	£38,380,000
Exports to U.K.....	43,304,000	38,948,000

FINANCE

	1969–70	1970–71
	N₵'000	N₵'000
Ordinary Revenue..........	360,600	373,300
Recurrent Expenditure......	311,000	324,400

Financial year is from July 1–June 30.
Currency of Ghana is the *New Cedi* (N₵) (of
100 *New Pesewas*), equivalent to 8s. 2d. sterling.
Estimated surplus on current account in 1970–71
is N₵48·9 m. (1969–70, N₵49·6m.). Develop-

National Redemption Council. Mr. J. F. ANSAH

ment expenditure in 1970–71 is estimated at NC̸137·5m. (1969–70, NC̸90m.), giving a net deficit of NC̸88·6m. (1969–70, NC̸40·4m.), to be met from foreign aid (NC̸50m.), social security receipts (NC̸20m.) and borrowing (NC̸10m.), total NC̸80m. Service of the external debt for 1970–71 is estimated to cost NC̸57·9m., leaving an overall deficit of NC̸66·5m. (1969–70, NC̸7·3m.).

Guyana

GUYANA, the former colony of British Guiana, which includes the Counties of Demerara, Essequibo and Berbice, is situated on the north-east coast of South America and has a total area of 83,000 square miles with a seaboard of about 270 miles. The population at December 31, 1970, was estimated at 714,233. There are about 31,460 aboriginal Indians. The territory is bounded on the south by Brazil, on the east by Surinam, on the west by Venezuela, and on the north and N.E. by the Atlantic. The coastland is very like the Netherlands, below the level of the sea, and intersected with canals constructed by its former Dutch owners. At the junction of the Guyana–Venezuela–Brazil boundaries is Mt. Roraima, a flat topped mountain 9,000 feet above sea-level. There are many beautiful waterfalls in Guyana: on the Potaro River (a tributary of the Essequibo) is the *Kaieteur Fall*, with a clear drop of 741 feet and a total fall of 822 feet, and on the Essequibo, the *Horse Shoe Falls* (discovered in 1934); a fall, with a drop of some 500 feet, discovered in 1934 on the Ipobe River, a tributary of the Kuribrong, has been named the *Marina Fall*, and other falls were discovered in 1938 on the Kamarang River, 80 miles north-east of Mt. Roraima.

The seasons are divided into dry and wet, the two dry seasons lasting from the middle of February to the end of April, and from the middle of August to the end of November. The climate on the coast is pleasant and healthy for the greater part of the year. In the Aug.–Oct. period it is hot. The mean temperature is 80·3°, its extremes during 86 years ranging between 68° and 96°, but these are very rare, the usual extremes being 70° and 90°. In the interior the mean temperature is higher—82·6°, its extremes ranging from 66° to 103°. The yearly rainfall is subject to marked variation, its mean on the coast lands averaging about 90 inches with an average of 58 inches on the savannahs. The daily average sunshine is nearly 7 hours and, except when rain is falling, dull and cloudy weather is rarely experienced.

Government.—Guyana became independent on May 26, 1966, with a Governor-General appointed by the Queen. It became a Cooperative Republic on Feb. 23, 1970, and Mr. Arthur Chung was elected first President on March 17, 1970, for a term of six years. The electoral system is a Proportional Representation or "single list " system, each voter casting his vote for a party list of candidates. The Prime Minister and Cabinet are responsible collectively to a National Assembly of 53 members elected by secret ballot; the voting age is 21. Elections to the National Assembly are held every five years; the last election was in December, 1968.

An important feature of the Constitution is its provision for the appointment of an *Ombudsman.* The life of the existing Assembly, presided over by a Speaker, who may or may not be a Member of the Assembly, is four years, but future Assemblies will continue for up to five years from the date of the first meeting after the dissolution of the previous Assembly. The Attorney-General and the Ministers of Works, Hydraulics and Supply; Mines and Forests; and Health are members of the Cabinet but not elected members of the National Assembly.

CAPITAL.—Ψ Georgetown. Estimated population, including environs, 168,000. Other towns are: Linden (Mackenzie) (population 20,000); Ψ New Amsterdam (population 15,000). FLAG.—Red triangle with black border, pointing from hoist to fly, on a yellow triangle with white border, all on a green field. *President*, His Excellency Arthur Chung, *elected for a six-year term*, March 17, 1970.

CABINET

Prime Minister, L. F. S. Burnham.
Minister of Agriculture and Deputy Prime Minister, Dr. P. A. Reid.
Finance, H. D. Hoyte.
Communications, M. Kasim.
Education, Information and Culture, Miss S. Field-Ridley.
Health, Dr. S. E. Talbot.
Home Affairs, O. Clark.
Housing and Reconstruction, D. A. Singh.
Local Government, V. Mingo.
Labour and Social Security, W. G. Carrington.
Trade, B. Ramsaroop.
Works, Hydraulics and Supply, H. Green.
Attorney-General and Minister of State, S. S. Ramphal., C.M.G., Q.C.
Mines and Forests, H. Jack.

GUYANA HIGH COMMISSION
28 Cockspur Street, S.W.1
High Commissioner, His Excellency John Carter.

BRITISH HIGH COMMISSION
44 Main Street (P.O. Box 625),
Georgetown
High Commissioner, His Excellency William Stanley Bates, C.M.G. (1970) £5,765
Deputy High Commissioner, R. M. James.

British Council Representative, J. M. G. Halsted, 125 Carmichael Street, Georgetown.

JUDICATURE

The Supreme Court of Judicature consists of a Court of Appeal and a High Court. There are also Courts of Summary Jurisdiction. The Court of Appeal consists of the Chancellor, as President, the Chief Justice and such number of Justices of Appeal as may be prescribed by Parliament. This Court came into operation on June 30, 1966. *Chancellor and President of the Court of Appeal*, Hon. E. V. Luckhoo.

Chief Justice, Hon. Harold Bollers.

Justices of Appeal, Hons. G. L. B. Persaud; P. A. Cummings; V. E. Crane.

The High Court consists of the Chief Justice, as President, and nine Puisne Judges. It is a court with unlimited jurisdiction in civil matters and exercises exclusive jurisdiction in probate, divorce and admiralty, and certain other matters. It also sits as a Full Court of the High Court of the Supreme Court of Judicature comprising not less than 2 Puisne Judges and then its jurisdiction is almost entirely appellate.

Chief Justice and President of the High Court, Hon. Harold Bollers.

Puisne Judges, Hons. Akbar Khan; D. Jhappan; C. J. E. Fung-a-Fatt; H. L. Mitchell; F. Vieira; K. M. George; R. M. Morris; J. Gonsalves-Sabhola; L. F. Collins; K. Massiah. *Ombudsman*, G. A. S. Van Sertima.

Production, etc.—Much of the country is forest. The cultivated portion (about 600,000 acres, of which 107,182 are under sugar-cane and 316,950 in rice) is largely confined to the narrow coastal alluvial belt. There are extensive deposits of gold, diamonds, manganese, bauxite and mica.

Communications.—There were 13,540 telephones in use in 1969; the Georgetown Automatic Exchange had 5,080 direct extension lines involving 11,060 stations. 17 sub-automatic and 3 manual exchanges provided an additional 1,527 lines with 3,605 telephone stations. 39 land-line telegraph stations are maintained at coastal post offices and telegraph stations in the interior, providing communications with the coast. In Georgetown a central radio station, operated by the Guyana Telecommunication Corporation, provides radio-telephone communication with 5 branch offices, 16 stations operated by other Government departments, and 48 by private concerns. Overseas telephone, telex and telegraph services are provided by Cable and Wireless (W.I.) Ltd. in association with the Guyana Telecommunications Corporation. At the end of 1970, there were 48 district post offices at which all classes of postal business were transacted. There are two broadcasting stations operated on a commercial basis. There are 40 miles of railway, and the Guyana Airways Corporation (Government) provides internal and coastal air-services.

Education.—In August, 1970, there were 389 primary schools with an enrolment of 163,122 pupils, 31 government secondary schools, 13 government-aided schools and about 50 private secondary schools—a total of 30,000 pupils in secondary schools. Reforms proposed in 1968 include (i) new education legislation; (ii) the abolition of the All-Age School System; (iii) that primary school instruction should start at 5 years 9 months and end at 16; (iv) introduction of the multilateral type of secondary education; (v) full scale curriculum reforms; (vi) the establishment of a Teachers' Service

Commission, a National Educational Council and a National Advisory Board on Technical Education. There are three institutions for the training of teachers. A total of 654 teachers graduated from these institutions in 1969–70. There are two government vocational schools, the Government Technical Institute and the Carnegie School of Home Economics with an enrolment of 2,639 pupils. There are 5,490 teachers in the primary schools and 868 in the government and aided secondary schools. There are 1,112 students in the University of Guyana. In 1970, 96 students graduated. Of the total Primary School age children (5–14), 69·6 per cent. are in Government and Aided Primary Schools.

Current expenditure on Education amounted to 16·6 per cent. of Government total current expenditure while 6·4 per cent. of the total capital expenditure was allocated to education.

FINANCE

	1969	1970
	G$'000,000	
Current revenue......	G$111,967	G$127,501
Current expenditure...	110,515	124,622
Capital receipts.......	34,610	43,203
Capital expenditure....	44,265	51,486
Public debt...........	230,719	233,600

TRADE

	1969	1970
Total imports.....	G$235,832,000	G$268,240,000
Total exports......	242,015,000	267,975,000

Trade with U.K.

	1969	1970
Imports from U.K....	£13,163,000	£14,903,000
Exports to U.K.......	13,182,000	12,550,000

The leading exports are sugar, rum, molasses, diamonds, gold, timber, balata, bauxite, rice, alumina and manganese.

India

AREA AND POPULATION.—The land area of the Republic of India is 1,261,816 sq. miles, and the population, at the census of 1961, was 439,072,582. The estimated population at June 30, 1969, was 536,984,000.

FLAG.—The National Flag is a horizontal tricolour with bands of deep saffron, white and dark green in equal proportions. On the centre of the white band appears an Asoka wheel in navy blue.

CAPITAL.—Delhi (3,780,423, including Delhi, New Delhi and Cantonment).

NATIONAL DAY—January 26 (Republic Day).

President of the Republic of India, Varaha Venkata Giri, *born 1894, assumed office Aug. 24, 1969.*
Vice-President, G. S. Pathak.

GOVERNMENT OF INDIA (May 2, 1971)

Ministers

Prime Minister and Minister of Atomic Energy, Home Affairs, Information and Broadcasting, Mrs. Indira Gandhi.
External Affairs, Swaran Singh.
Minister of Food and Agriculture, Fakhruddin Ali Ahmed.
Finance, Y. B. Chavan.
Railways, K. Hanumanthaiya
Defence, Jagjivan Ram.
Parliamentary Affairs and Shipping and Transport, Raj Bahadur.
Tourism and Civil Aviation, Dr. Karan Singh.
Industrial Development, Moinul Haq Chaudhuri.
Education and Social Welfare, Siddartha Shankar Ray.
Law and Justice, H. R. Gokhale.
Steel and Mines, S. Mohan Kumaramangalam.
Health and Family Planning, Uma Shankar Dikshit.
Planning (and Dept. of Science and Technology), C. Subramaniam.

Ministers of State

Irrigation and Power, Dr. K. L. Rao.
Foreign Trade, L. N. Mishra.
Labour and Rehabilitation, R. K. Khadilkar.
Company Affairs, K. V. Raghunath Reddy.
Supply, D. R. Chavan.
Petroleum and Chemicals, P. C. Sethi.
Communications, H. N. Bahuguna.
Works and Housing, I. K. Gujral.
Agriculture, Prof. Sher Singh.
Law and Justice, Niti Raj Singh Chaudhury.
Parliamentary Affairs and Shipping and Transport, Om Mehta.
Home Affairs and Department of Personnel, Ram Niwas Mirdha.
Home Affairs, K. C. Pant (Will also assist Prime Minister in Parliamentary work relating to Departments of Atomic Energy and Electronics).
Information and Broadcasting, Mrs. Nandini Satpathy.
Defence (Defence Production), V. C. Shukla.

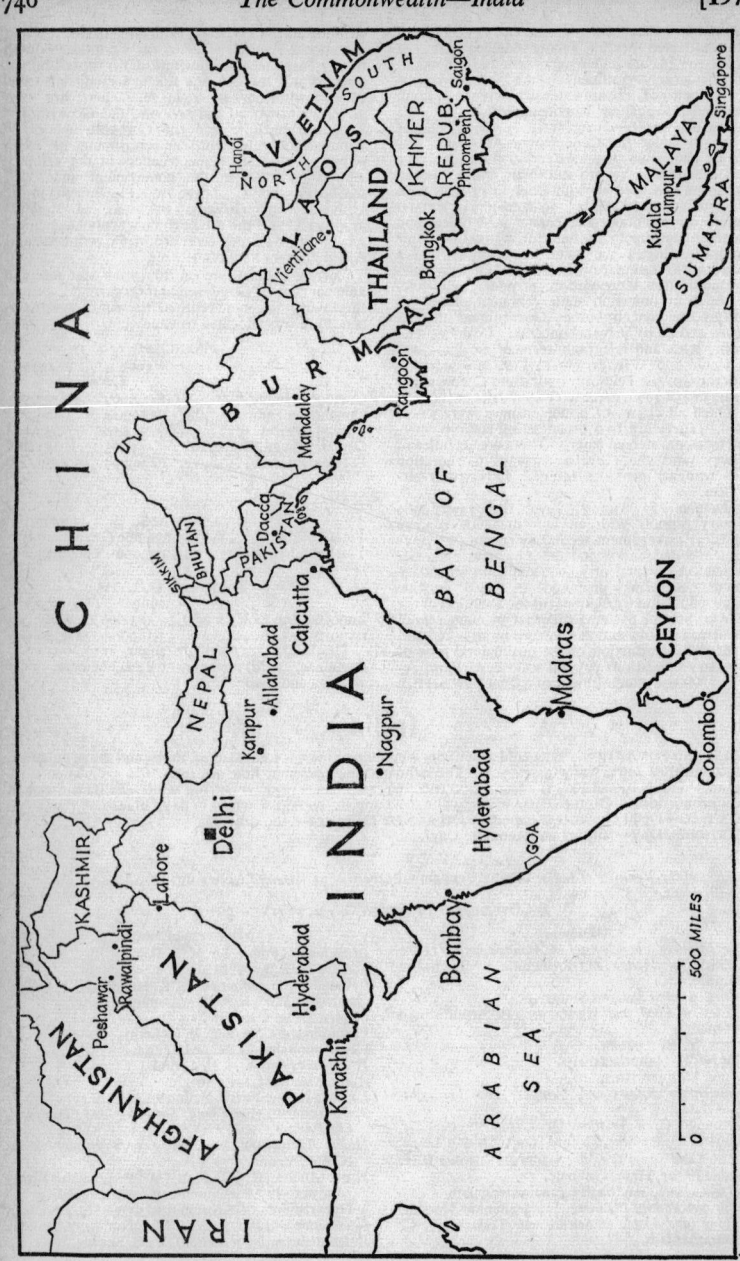

Agriculture, Annasaheb P. Shinde.
Finance, K. R. Ganesh.
Steel and Mines, Shah Nawaz Khan.
Health and Family Planning, Prof. D. P. Chattopadhyaya.
Industrial Development, Ghanshyam Oza.
Planning, Mohan Dharia.
Tourism and Civil Aviation, Dr. Sarojini Mahishi.

Deputy Ministers

Health and Family Planning, A. K. Kisku.
Agriculture, Jagannath Pahadia.
Railways, Mohammed Shafi Qureshi.
Education and Social Welfare, K. S. G. Ramaswamy.
Industrial Development, Sidheshwar Prasad.
External Affairs, Surendra Pal Singh.
Parliamentary Affairs, B. Shankaranand.
Parliamentary Affairs, Kedar Nath Singh.
Company Affairs, Bedabarata Barua.
Education and Social Welfare, Prof. D. P. Yadav.
Labour and Rehabilitation, Balgovind Verma.
Petroleum and Chemicals, Dalbir Singh.
Irrigation and Power, Baij Nath Kureel.
Information and Broadcasting, Dharam Vir Singh.
Communications, Kartik Oraon.
Foreign Trade, A. C. George.
Finance, Mrs. Sushila Rohatgi.
Home Affairs, F. H. Mohsin.

INDIAN HIGH COMMISSION
India House, Aldwych, W.C.2.
High Commissioner, His Excellency Apa B. Pant.
Deputy High Commissioner, P. N. Kaul.
Ministers, A. Mozoombar (*Accounts Adviser*); B. D. Jayal (*Economics*); H. K. Koochar (*Supplies Adviser*); A. J. Kidwai (*Education and Scientific*).

BRITISH HIGH COMMISSION
Chanakyapuri, New Delhi, 21.
High Commissioner, His Excellency Sir Terence (Willcocks) Garvey, K.C.M.G. (1971) £14,000
Minister, P. J. E. Male, C.M.G., M.C.
Deputy High Commissioners, M. H. G. Rogers (*Bombay*); F. S. Miles, C.M.G. (*Calcutta*); V. C. Martin (*Madras*).
British Council Representative in India, S. E. Hodgson, O.B.E., 21 Jor Bagh, New Delhi. Offices also at *Bombay*, *Madras* and *Calcutta*. There are British Council libraries at these four centres and at *Bangalore*, *Bhopal*, *Lucknow*, *Patna*, *Poona*, *Ranchi* and *Trivandrum*.

CONSTITUTION
The Constitution of India came into force on January 26, 1950. The Constitution provides for a single and uniform citizenship for the whole of India, with the right of vote for every adult citizen.

EXECUTIVE
The executive of the Indian Union consists of the President (*Rashtrapati*), the Vice-President and the Council of Ministers. The President is elected for five years by an electoral college consisting of all elected members of Parliament and of the various State Legislative Assemblies. The Vice-President is also elected for five years by members of the two Houses of Parliament. As head of the State the President exercises his functions with the aid and advice of the Council of Ministers headed by the Prime Minister. The Council is collectively responsible to the House of the People.

LEGISLATURE
The Legislature of the Union is called Parliament. It consists of two Houses known as the Council of States (*Raiya Sabha*) and the House of the People (*Lok Sabha*). The Council of States consists of not more than 250 members, of whom 12 are nominated by the President and the rest are indirectly elected by the Legislative Assemblies of the various States. The Council is not subject to dissolution, one-third of its members retiring every two years. The House of the People consists of not more than 500 members directly elected from territorial constituencies in the States and on the basis of adult franchise and not more than 25 members to represent the Union Territories, chosen in such manner as Parliament provides. The House has a maximum duration of five years.

Subject to the provisions of the Constitution the Union Parliament can make laws for the whole of India and the State legislatures for their respective units. The distribution of legislative powers is governed by a system of three lists—the Union, the State and the Concurrent—under which all legislative activity has been mapped out. The Union Parliament has exclusive powers to legislate on 97 subjects of all-India importance, such as defence, foreign affairs, communications, railways, currency and banking, insurance, customs duties, etc. The State List contains 66 headings, *e.g.* public order and police, justice, education, public health, local government, agriculture, etc. The Concurrent List contains 47 subjects of common interest to the Union and the States.

OFFICIAL LANGUAGE
The Constitution (Art. 343) provides that the official language of the Union shall be Hindi in the Devanagari script and the form of numerals for official purposes shall be the international form of Indian numerals. English, which was originally to continue as the official language for a period of 15 years from the commencement of the Constitution (January 1950), will, under the Official Language Act, 1963, still be used after that time in addition to Hindi.

THE JUDICATURE
The Supreme Court of India, consisting of a Chief Justice and not more than 13 associate judges, is the highest court in respect of constitutional matters. It is also the final Court of Appeal in the country.
Chief Justice, Sarv Mittra Sikri (1971) ...Rs.60,000
Judges, J. C. Shah; J. M. Shelat; V. Bhargava; G. K. Mitter; C. A. Vaidialingam; K. S. Hegde; A. N. Grover; A. N. Ray; P. Jaganmohan Reddy; I. D. Dua .... each Rs.48,000

DEFENCE
The supreme command of the armed forces is vested in the President. Administrative and operational control resides in the Army, Navy and Air Headquarters under the supervision of the Ministry of Defence.

The Army has 4 Commands, Southern, Eastern, Western and Central, with headquarters at Poona, Calcutta, Simla and Lucknow respectively. A Territorial Force was inaugurated in Oct. 1949. A National Cadet Corps, with senior, junior, and girls' divisions, has also been raised.

The *Indian Navy* consists of an aircraft-carrier, two cruisers and a number of destroyers, frigates, minesweepers, submarines and auxiliary vessels. A Naval aviation wing and a hydrographic office have also been set up.

The *Indian Air Force* is organized in five major formations, the Western, Eastern and Central Air Commands, and the Training and Maintenance Commands. Aircraft in use include Vampire, Mystère, Hunter, Gnat, Mig 21 and HF24; Canberra bomber; helicopter and training planes.

EDUCATION

In 1968–69, there were 3,712 pre-primary schools, 399,109 primary schools, 32,433 High/Higher Secondary schools, 83,943 Middle schools and 2,163 Arts/Sciences/Commerce colleges. There were 75 universities at the end of 1969.

PRODUCTION

About 70 per cent. of the inhabitants of India are dependent on agricultural pursuits. Most of the agricultural holdings are less than 5 acres. Food crops occupy four-fifths of the cultivated land. There are about 176,000,000 cattle, or about a quarter of the world's cattle population.

Production of Principal Crops, 1968–69

Crop	Production (lakh tonnes)
Rice	397·6
Jowar	98·0
Bajra	38·0
Maize	57·0
Wheat	186·5
Barley	24·2
Ragi	16·5
Small millets	18·1
Pulses	104·23
Total food grains	940·13
Ground-nuts	44·8
Castor seed	1·1
Sesame	4·2
Rape and mustard	15·7
Linseed	3·52
Cotton	52·7*
Jute	30·5*
Sugar-cane	1,175·7
Tobacco	3·5
Tea	3·8

* Lakh bales.

Industrial

The output of coal in 1968–69 was 7,45 lakh tonnes; iron ore 2,12 lakh tonnes; finished steel 47 lakh tonnes; aluminium 125,300 tonnes; cement 122 lakh tonnes; machine tools Rs.24,78 lakhs; automobiles (commercial vehicles, passenger cars, etc.) 78,000; diesel engines (stationary) 119,500; sewing machines, 429,000; sulphuric acid 1,034,000 tonnes; fertilizers 751,000 tonnes; petroleum products (refined), 154 lakh tonnes; cotton cloth 79,050 lakh metres; cotton yarn, 9,580 lakh kg.; rayon yarn, 99,200 tonnes.

TRADE

Distribution of Trade, 1968–69

	Imports Rs. lakhs	Exports Rs. lakhs
U.K.	1,27,87	2,01,51
U.S.A.	5,75,06	2,34,27
U.S.S.R.	1,85,51	1,48,31
Western Germany	1,19,74	26,50
Italy	49,50	18,06
Netherlands	17,75	15,37
France	36,39	20,05
Japan	1,15,30	1,58,23
Australia	25,72	25,50
Canada	98,72	29,70
Kenya	6,71	8,12
Czechoslovakia	35,27	31,77
U.A.R.	41,41	21,82
Burma	16,51	11,94

Trade with U.K.

	1969	1970
Imports from U.K.	£65,528,000	£72,900,000
Exports to U.K.	107,064,000	106,044,000

(Board of Trade figures series.)

Imports from All Countries, 1968–69

	Rs. lakhs
Petroleum products	29,43
Copper	39,17
Metal manufactures	13,52
Electric machinery and appliances	81,07
Medicinal and pharmaceutical products	17,50
Transport equipment	65,36
Crude minerals (excluding coal, petroleum, fertilizer materials and precious stones)	24,40
Chemical elements and compounds	82,70
Textile yarn and thread	4,19
Raw cotton	90,18
Rice	57,47
Wheat, milled	2,59,49

Exports to All Countries, 1968–69

	Rs. lakhs
Iron and steel	17,96
Cotton manufactures (excluding twist and yarn)	87,97
Iron ore and concentrates	88,40
Textile yarn and thread	24,30
Fresh fruits and nuts (excluding oil nuts)	64,77
Vegetable oils (non-essential)	11,71
Leather	71,99
Jute manufacture (excluding twist and yarn)	2,16,94
Coffee	5,04
Tea	1,56,51
Tobacco, unmanufactured	31,16
Floor coverings	10,65
Petroleum products	9.43

FINANCE

Total net revenue of the Government of India estimated in the Budget for 1970–71 is Rs.35,20,38 lakhs as compared to Rs.32,86,99 lakhs (revised estimates) for 1969–70. Expenditure in 1970–71 is estimated at Rs.35,20,38 lakhs; 1969–70 revised estimate, Rs.32,97,93 lakhs. The major heads of revenue and expenditure were as follows:

Revenue

	1969–70 (Rs. lakhs)	1970–71 (Rs. lakhs)
Tax-Revenue		
Customs	4,15,00	4,45,00
Union excise duties	15,25,76	16,79,34
Corporation tax	3,20,00	3,42,00
Taxes on income	4,00,00	4,23,00
Estate Duty	7,50	7,50
Taxes on wealth	14,00	18,00
Expenditure tax	1	1
Gift tax	1,50	1,50
Other heads	48,26	50,62
Total	27,32,03	29,66,97
Non-tax Revenue		
Debt services	5,73,46	6,11,27
Administrative services	10,37	10,34
Social and Developmental services	32,05	32,94
Multipurpose river schemes	5,32	15,48
Transport and communications	13,37	14,19
Public works	6,39	7,11
Currency and mint	94,84	98,07
Miscellaneous	63,50	48,04
Contribution and miscellaneous adjustments	45,83	45,91
Extraordinary items	9,99	16,40
Deduct States' share on income tax	−2,93,18	−3,39,17

Expenditure

	1969–70 (*Rs.* lakhs)	1970–71 (*Rs.* lakhs)
Taxes and duties........	43,93	48,55
Debt services...........	5,68,56	5,97,48
Administrative services...	1,77,32	1,89,70
Social and developmental services.............	2,66,53	3,19,85
Multipurpose river schemes	5,89	14,56
Public works, etc........	38,68	42,63
Transport and communications..............	18,35	20,80
Currency and mint......	26,86	26,00
Miscellaneous...........	2,42,37	2,21,26
Contributions and miscellaneous adjustments...	9,24,27	10,35,63
Extraordinary items.....	5,85	6,63
Defence services (net)....	9,79,32	10,17,84

Banks and Banking.—The number of scheduled banks was 73 and the number of offices of scheduled banks was 1,387 in Dec., 1969. Advances by scheduled banks totalled *Rs.*358,530 ·lakhs at Dec. 31, 1969.

COMMUNICATIONS

Civil Aviation.—India occupies an important place in civil aviation among the nations of the world. All air lines were nationalized in 1953 and two corporations formed, Indian Airlines Corporation and Air India International (now Air India). At the end of 1969, 85 aerodromes were maintained by the Civil Aviation Department of the Government.

Railways.—The railways are grouped into nine administrative zones, Southern, Central, Western, Northern, North-Eastern, North-East Frontier, Eastern, South-Eastern and South-Central.

Gross Traffic Receipts (1969–70), *Rs.* lakhs 95,055. Working expenses, *Rs.* lakhs 68,304. Net railway revenues, *Rs.* lakhs 14,589.

Ψ*Ports.*—The chief seaports are Bombay, Calcutta, Madras, Mormagao, Cochin, Visakhapatnam, Kandla and Paradip. There are over 150 minor working ports with varying capacity.

Shipping.—On April 1, 1970, 258 ships totalling 23·29 lakh gross tons were on the Indian Register.

Postal.—In 1968–69 there were 102,477 post offices, 14,594 telegraph offices, and 1,119,457 telephones.

Broadcasting.—In 1969 there were 66 radio stations in India; receiver licences in force on Dec. 31, 1969, totalled 10,034,960 (Provisional).

STATES AND ADMINISTRATIONS OF THE REPUBLIC OF INDIA

ANDHRA PRADESH

Governor, Pattom A. Thanu Pillai.

The State of Andhra, consisting of the Telugu-speaking areas of the old Madras State, with Kurnool as capital, was inaugurated on Oct. 1, 1953. The Telangana area of Hyderabad State was added in 1956, when the enlarged State, comprising 20 districts, assumed the name of Andhra Pradesh.

Andhra Pradesh has an area of 106,286 sq. miles with a population of 35,983,447.

The Legislature consists of two chambers, the Legislative Assembly and the Legislative Council. *Chief Minister,* K. Brahmananda Reddi.

CHIEF CITY, Hyderabad. Population 1,251,119.

ASSAM

Governor, B. K. Nehru.

Assam, which has an area of 47,094 sq. miles (exclusive of the North-East Frontier area); pop. 11,872,772 (1961 census) first became a British territory in 1826 and was constituted a separate administration in 1874. It was combined in 1905 with part of Bengal to form a new province, Eastern Bengal and Assam, but again became a separate administration in 1912. By the terms of the Indian Independence Act, 1947, the district of Sylhet (except a portion of the Karimganj Subdivision of that district) was detached from Assam and amalgamated with East Bengal (Pakistan).

A range of mountains divides Assam into the Surma and Brahmaputra valleys, of which the chief towns are Silchar and Gauhati respectively. The people are mainly Hindus, Moslems and Tribals. The North-East Frontier railway serves the state. Tea, petroleum, coal, timber, jute and rice are the principal products.

CAPITAL.—Shillong.

CABINET

M. M. Choudhury (*Chief Minister*); K. P. Tripathi; B. Sarma; M. N. Hazaraki; R. C. Barooah; C. S. Teron; J. B. Hagjer; A. Rahman; Mrs. P. K. Gohain; A. H. Mazumder; P. K. Choudhuri; R. Basumatari; A. Thanglura; J. N. Saikia; S. A. Ali.

LEGISLATIVE ASSEMBLY.

Speaker, M. K. Das.

HIGH COURT.

Chief Justice, P. K. Goswami.

Judges, M. C. Pathak; D. M. Sen; B. N. Sarma.

By the terms of the Assam Reorganization (Mehgalaya) Act, 1969 an Autonomous State within the State of Assam, *viz.* the Autonomous State of Mehgalaya, came into being on April 2, 1970 comprising two districts of Assam, United Khasi-Jaintia and Garo Hills.

CAPITAL.—Shillong.

Cabinet of Meghalaya

Capt. W. A. Sangma (*Chief Minister*); S. D. D. Nichols Roy; B. B. Lyngdoh; E. Bareh; S. K. Marak.

BIHAR

Governor, Deva Kant Barooah.

This state has an area of 67,197 sq. miles and a population (1961 census) of 46,455,610. It comprises 4 administrative divisions, Patna, Bhagalpur, Tirhut and Chota-Nagpur. Bihar is notable for extreme temperatures and for high density of population—694 to the square mile in 1961. The highlands of Chota-Nagpur are thinly peopled and contain a large aboriginal population. Rice, wheat, barley, jute, oilseeds, sugar-cane and tobacco are cultivated. 84·7 per cent. of the people are Hindus. The majority of the population speak Hindi, of which there are various dialects. The railway systems are the Eastern, North-Eastern, South-Eastern and North-East Frontier Railways. *Chief Minister,* B. P. Shastri (June 2, 1971).

CHIEF CITIES, Patna. Population 364,594 (1961); Jamshedpur (303,516) and Ranchi (140,253).

CABINET.

Chief Minister, Daroga Prasad Pai.
Ministers, Kedar Pande; Ram Jaipal Singh Yadav;
Zawar Husain; Baleshwar Ram; Lahtan Choud-
hary; Nagendra Jha; Shatrughan Sharan Singh;
T. Mochi Rai Munda; Md. Hussain Azad; Bagun
Sombrui; Chandra Shekhar Singh; Rameshwar
Paswan; Shankar Dayal Singh; Set Hembram;
J. P. Sahi.

In addition there are 7 Ministers of State and 2
Parliamentary Secretaries.

GUJARAT

Governor of Gujarat, Shriman Narayan.

On May 1, 1960, the new state of Gujarat,
consisting of the northern part of Bombay State,
was set up with a temporary capital at Ahmedabad,
the remainder of the former Bombay state
adopting the name of Maharashtra (*see* col. 2).
Gujarat, consisting of the districts of Kutch,
Banaskantha, Mehsana, Sabarkantha, Ahmedabad,
Kaira, Panchmahals, Baroda, Broach, Surat, Rajkot,
Surendranagar, Junagadh, Jamnagar, Bhavnagar,
Amreli, Dangs, Bulsar and Gandhinagar has a total
area of 72,226 square miles and a population of
20,633,350 (1961 census). Gujarat came under
direct Presidential rule on May 13, 1971.

HARYANA

Governor, B. N. Chakravarty.

The most recent State of India to be created,
Haryana was formed on a linguistic basis from part
of the former State of Punjab on Nov. 1, 1966.
Haryana has an area of 17,010 sq. miles and a
population of 9,971,165.

12,721,000 acres of land under crops out of a
total of 30,300,000 acres in the former Punjab is
included in the new State.

Government.—Ministries were formed by Mr.
B. D. Sharma (Nov. 1966 and March 10, 1967),
and by Mr. Rao Birendra Singh on March 24, 1967,
the latter holding office as Chief Minister until the
United Front majority was lost on Nov. 20, 1967.
Following a short period of direct Presidential rule,
elections were held in May, 1968, and Mr. Bansi
Lal installed as Chief Minister on May 21, 1968.

On May 25, 1971, a Cabinet consisting of 15
Ministers and 4 Deputy Ministers was in office.

CAPITAL.—Chandigarh (also capital of Punjab
State) (99,262).

KERALA

Governor, V. Viswanathan, *appointed* April 27,
1967.

The State of Kerala, constituted in 1956, consists
of most of the territories of Travancore-
Cochin and the Malabar district of Madras.
Bounded by Madras and Mysore, the State brings
together the majority of the Malayalam-speaking
peoples. The State stretches along the Arabian
Sea for 360 miles. The North-Eastern part of
Kerala is rich in plantations producing rubber, tea
and pepper. Area, 15,002 sq. miles. Population,
(Census of 1971, provisional), 21,280, 397.

In recent years ministries have been formed by
E. M. S. Namboodiripad (1967–69) and C. Acutha
Menon (Nov., 1969 and Oct., 1970).

CAPITAL, Ψ Trivandrum.

MADHYA PRADESH

Governor, K. C. Reddy.

The State of Madhya Pradesh was formed on
November 1, 1956. Madhya Pradesh has an area
of 171,210 sq. miles and a population of 32,372,408.
It is composed of the former Madhya Bharat,
Vindhya Pradesh and Bhopal States together with
17 Hindi-speaking districts of former Madhya

Pradesh and the Sironj sub-division of Kotah district of Rajasthan, excluding the Sunel enclave of
Mandsaur district from former Madhya Bharat.

The chief crops are wheat, paddy, cotton,
sugar cane, oilseeds, pulses, juwar and bajra.
Nearly 31 per cent. of the State's area is covered
by forests. Hindi is the chief language.

The State has extensive belts of mineral deposits,
possessing coal, iron ore, manganese, bauxite,
diamond, limestone, dolomite, fireclay, ochres,
silica sand, marble, fluorspar and shale. It is also
rich in forest and agricultural resources.

There are 28 cotton mills, 4 cement factories, 5
sugar mills, a newsprint mill, a steel plant, a heavy
electrical equipment factory, 2 strawboard factories
and several other large and small industries.

CAPITAL, Bhopal.

MAHARASHTRA

Governor.—Shri Ali Yawar Jung.

Chief Minister.—Shri V. P. Naik. There are 14
other Ministers, 10 Ministers of State and 5
Deputy Ministers.

The State of Maharashtra was formed on May 1,
1960, as a result of the bifurcation of the former
Bombay State into Gujarat and Maharashtra States.

It lies on the west coast of India between
22·1° and 16·4° N. latitude and 72·6° and 80·9° E.
longitude. The State is bounded by the Arabian
Sea on the west, Gujarat in the north-west,
Madhya Pradesh in the north, Andhra Pradesh in
the south-east and Mysore and Goa in the south.
The region is drained by a number of rivers, large
and small, most of them forming tributaries of
the Tapi, Godavari, Bhima, Krishna, Wardha and
Wainganga. The relief of the land shows high
plateaux with plains on the western coast and along
the river basins. Maharashtra has a coastline of
720 kilometres with 49 minor ports and one major
international port, Ψ Bombay.

Area and Population.—Maharashtra State contains
118,717 square miles, with a population of
39,553,718 at the Census of 1961; (estimated, 1971,
51,420,000). It is a predominantly urban and
industrial state. According to the 1961 Census,
28·2 per cent. of the population is urban. Marathi
is the principal language.

According to the 1961 Census 69·91 per cent. of
the population are engaged in agriculture, 2·16 per
cent. in mining, forestry and quarrying, etc., 4·39
per cent. in household industry, 6·88 per cent. in
manufacture other than household industry, 1·24
per cent. in construction, 4·52 per cent. in trade
and commerce, 2·36 per cent. in transport, storage
and communication and the remaining 8·54 per cent.
in other services.

Maharashtra has four main administrative
divisions containing the 26 districts into which
the State is divided:

Bombay Division.—Greater Bombay, Thana,
Kolaba, Ratnagiri, Nasik, Dhulia and Jalgaon.

Poona Division.—Ahmednagar, Poona, Satra,
Sangli, Sholapur and Kolhapur.

Aurangabad Division.—Aurangabad, Parbhani, Nan-
ded, Bhir, Osmanabad.

Nagpur Division.—Buldhana, Akola, Amravati,
Yeotmal, Wardha Nagpur, Bhandara and
Chanda.

Communications.—Bombay is an international air-
port used by all the main airlines. Poona,
Aurangabad and Nagpur are used for local services.
Three railways pass through Maharashtra. The
Western and Central railways (whose headquarters
are in Bombay) serve western, northern, north-
eastern, central and southern parts of India. The
Southern railway which starts from Poona runs to
Bangalore in the southern part of India. Road

transport in Maharashtra State has been nationalized. During 1969–70 the average number of passengers carried per day was 1,608,450. Motor vehicles in use on Jan. 1, 1970, numbered 257,539 compared with 89,127 in 1960. The 60,694 km. of roads in use in 1969, included 2,378 km. national highways, 11,603 km. state highways, 13,311 other major roads and 33,402 km. minor roads.

Public Health.—In Maharashtra State there are 411 general hospitals (39,525 beds), 997 dispensaries and 4 mental hospitals (5,646 beds), 52 tuberculosis hospitals (5,616 beds) and 392 primary health centres (2,292 beds). The total number of doctors in Maharashtra is 15,982. There are 11 medical colleges (capacity, 1,460 students) and 2 dental colleges (210 students).

Education.—Literacy in the State of Maharashtra according to the 1961 population census, is 29·8 per cent. There are 6 universities with 311 affiliated colleges and 68 post-graduate departments with 237,607 students. There are also two agricultural universities. In 1969–70 there were 44,223 primary schools (with 6,509,587 pupils) and 4,816 secondary schools (1,943,055 pupils).

Production.—Maharashtra is a highly industrialized State. On Dec. 31, 1968 there were 9,116 factories with an average daily employment of 887,174 persons, including 95 cotton textile mills with an installed capacity of 454,927 spindles and 78,351 looms. There are 17 woollen mills and 2 viscose filament yarn factories. Other important industries are sugar and the oil industry. The engineering industry is also expanding. Owing to the absence of consuming factories the mines are not being developed fully. Iron ore, coal, manganese, bauxite and salt are found.

Electricity Production.—Installed capacity was 1,771,147 kW in 1969–70 and consumption totalled 8,362,000,000 kWh, including 4,878,000,000 kWh by industry.

CAPITAL.— Ψ Greater Bombay (estimated, 1971, 5,850,000). Eleven other cities in the State, had a population of more than 100,000 at the 1961 Census, Poona (597,562), Nagpur (643,659), Sholapur (337,585), Kolhapur (187,442), Amravati (137,875), Nasik (131,103), Malegaon (121,408), Ahmednagar (119,010), Akola (115,760), Ulhasnagar (107,760) and Thana (101,107).

MYSORE

Governor, Shri Dharma Vira, *appointed* Oct. 23, 1969.

The Mysore State, formed in 1956, consists of territories of the former State of Mysore, Coorg and parts of the former Madras, Bombay and Hyderabad States. The State brings together the Kannada speaking people, previously distributed in five States. Its area is 74,210 sq. miles and population (1971 Census, provisional) 29,263,334. The State consists largely of an elevated table land. It is rich in hydro-electric power and fairly rich in minerals; it is the major gold producing state of the Republic of India. Direct Presidential rule was introduced on March 27, 1971, and the House of Assembly suspended.

CAPITAL, Bangalore.

NAGALAND

The State of Nagaland, inaugurated on Dec. 1, 1963, has an area of 6,366 sq. miles and a population of 370,000. It has a Legislative Assembly of 46 members, 40 of whom are popularly elected, and 6 elected by the Regional Council of Tuensang District. The Governor of Assam is also Governor of Nagaland.

CAPITAL, Kohima.

ORISSA

Governor, Dr. S. S. Ansari.

Area, 60,136 sq. miles; pop. (1961) 17,548,846, constituted on April 1, 1936, comprises the Orissa Division, transferred from the Province of Bihar and Orissa and areas transferred from the Central Provinces and Madras. 24 States were merged with Orissa in 1948 and 1949. A large majority of the population is Hindu. It is an agricultural State with few towns. The Hirakud dam across the Mahanadi river is now irrigating 3·80 lakh acres of land and generating about 100 MW. of power. Paradeep is being developed as a port. Direct Presidential rule in Orissa (in force from Jan. 11, 1971) was lifted on April 26, 1971, upon the formation of a government by Mr. Biswanath Das.

CAPITAL, Bhubaneswar.

PUNJAB

Governor, **Dr. D. C. Pavate**, *appointed* Aug. 26, 1967.

On November 1, 1966, the former State of Punjab was divided into three on a linguistic basis. That part of the State retaining the name of Punjab has an area of 19,450 (out of the original 47,304) sq. miles and a population of 11,135,069. A new State under the name of Haryana was formed and the remaining part of the undivided Punjab was added to the Union Territory of Himachal Pradesh.

The new Punjab retained some 12,054,000 acres of the total area under crops in the former State (25,010,000 acres) and 75 per cent. of the former industrial capacity. Income per head of population in the Punjab greatly exceeds the all-India average.

Government.—The Government headed by Mr Prakash Singh Badal fell on June 13, 1971, and direct Presidential rule was introduced on June 15.

CAPITAL.—Chandigarh (90,000), the common capital of the States of Punjab and Haryana, was raised to the status of a Union Territory at the time of the reorganization of the Punjab in 1966.

RAJASTHAN

Governor, Sardar Hukam Singh, *assumed office* April 16, 1967.

The State of Rajasthan was formed between March 1948 and Nov. 1956 through the integration of 22 former princely States, including 3 Chiefships, the former state of Ajmer and parts of the former States of Bombay and Madhya Bharat. The State has an area of 132,152 sq. miles and a population (estimated, 1971) of 25,724,142.

The State is divided for administrative purposes into 26 districts, 195 *Tehsils* and 232 Development Blocks. It has rich mineral reserves, the important minerals being gypsum, mica, lead, zinc, manganese, copper, rock phosphate and tungsten. The economy is predominantly based on agriculture. In recent years, the pace of industrial development has gained momentum.

Government.—Mr. Mohanlal Sukhadia, who had held office as Chief Minister of Rajasthan since 1954, resigned on July 8, 1971, and Mr Bankatullah Khan formed a ministry of 9, all but one of the members having served under Mr. Sukhadia.

CAPITAL, Jaipur (613,000).

TAMIL NADU

Governor, Thiru K. K. Shah.
Chief Minister, Thiru M. Karunanidhi.

Tamil Nadu (*formerly* Madras) has an area of 50,331 sq. miles and population of 41,106,125. In spite of its long coast-line the state has no natural harbour but a deep-sea harbour is under construction at Tuticorin. The state is not naturally fertile, though irrigation systems in the river deltas have enormously increased the produce of the soil. Rice

millet, tobacco, tea, etc., are cultivated. The production of electricity has been greatly intensified. Tamil Nadu is served by the Southern Railway. About 91 per cent. of the people are Hindus. The language principally spoken is Tamil, though Telugu, Malayalam, Kannada and Urdu are also spoken. Madurai (424,810) and Tiruchirapalli (249,862), famous for their Hindu temples, and Coimbatore (286,305), an important industrial centre, are the chief cities after the capital.

Government.—Following elections for the Tamil Nadu Assembly held on March 5, 1971, Mr. M. Karunanidhi, leader of the *Dravida Munnetra Kaghagam* party, formed a Government on March 15, 1971.

CAPITAL, Madras. Population (Census 1971), 2,470,289.

UTTAR PRADESH
Governor, Dr. B. Gopala Reddi.

Uttar Pradesh, called the United Provinces until 1949 (formerly the United Provinces of Agra and Oudh) (area, 113,654 sq. miles; est. pop. (1961) 73,746,401), forms the upper part of the great Ganga plain to the W. of Bengal, lying between the Himalayas and the hilly border of the central plateau. The Province is now a State in which the former three princely States, Rampur, Tehri-Garhwal and Benares have been merged and certain areas of the Vindhya Pradesh and Rajasthan States have also been absorbed.

A new Ministry was formed on April 4, 1971, by Mr. Kamlapati Tripalthi, leader of the Ruling Congress Party.

Agriculture employs 72 per cent. of the population, the chief products being wheat, rice, barley, pulse, tobacco, millet, cotton, sugar, and oilseeds. About 84·7 per cent. of the population are Hindus and 14·6 per cent. Muslims. Hindi is the chief language. The State is served by the Northern Railway and the North-Eastern Railway.

CAPITAL.—Lucknow (595,440). Other cities of importance are: Agra (462,020), containing the Taj Mahal and other great works of architecture, the sacred Hindu city of Varanasi (Benares) (471,258), the great manufacturing centre, Kanpur (Cawnpore) (881,177), Allahabad (411,955) and Bareilly (254,409).

WEST BENGAL
Governor, S. S. Dhawan, *appointed* 1969.

West Bengal has an area of 33,829 sq. miles and a population (1971 Census, provisional) of 44,440,095.

The State of West Bengal has sixteen districts including Calcutta, which is considered a separate administrative unit. The Metropolitan area around Calcutta covers about 400 sq. miles with a population of 7,040,345 (1971). It is one of the most densely populated areas in the world.

Government.—West Bengal was under direct rule from New Delhi from March, 1970, until April 2, 1971. Following mid-term elections on March 10, 1971, a Coalition Government was formed by Mr. A. K. Mukerjee, but direct Presidential rule was resumed following his resignation on June 18, 1971. On June 29, Mr. S. S. Ray, Minister of Education in the Central Government, was appointed Minister without Portfolio to deal with the problems of West Bengal, in particular that of the pressing refugee situation in the State.

LEGISLATURE
In the West Bengal Legislative Assembly there are 280 members elected by adult franchise and 1 member nominated by the Governor from the Anglo-Indian Community. The largest number of seats was won at the 1971 elections by the Communist Party of India (*Marxist*) with 113 members. Congress (R), the leading partner of the Democratic Coalition, has 105 members.

HIGH COURT OF JUDICATURE, CALCUTTA
Chief Justice, P. B. Mukherjee (and 33 other puisne judges).
Advocate-General, B. Das.

West Bengal produces India's largest foreign exchange earners, jute and the world famous Darjeeling tea. Its other products are good quality coal in Asansol area, steel in Durgapur and engineering goods in Calcutta's industrial belt. Durgapur also has a number of other industries under the State Sector: a coke-oven plant, a fertilizer factory, an alloy steel plant and an ophthalmic glass plant. A locomotive factory at Chittaranjan and a cable factory at Rupnarayanpur are also under the State Sector.

The port of Calcutta, the main port in eastern India and connected by railways, roads, and airways with other parts of India, will have a new subsidiary port at Haldia, which is halfway between the present port and the sea, for handling bulk cargo. In the port of Haldia a refinery and a fertilizer factory are under construction. A huge petro-chemical complex will also be built.

CAPITAL.—Ψ Calcutta with a population of 3,141,180 (1971 census). Other main towns are Durgapur (282,593); Kharagpur (161,919); Asansol (157,388); and Burdwan (144,970). Howrah, on the west side of the river Hooghly, has a population of 740,662.

TERRITORIES
Delhi.—The Union Territory of Delhi (area 573 sq. miles; pop. (estimated, 1969), 3,780,423. Under the Delhi Administration Act, 1966, a 61-member Metropolitan Council (56 elected and 5 nominated), with legislative functions, has been set up. Four executive councillors, headed by a Chief, assist and advise the Lieut.-Governor in the exercise of his administrative functions.
Lieut.-Governor, A. N. Jha.

Andaman and Nicobar Islands.—The Andamans are a group of 204 islands of various sizes, lying between the 6th and 14th parallels in the Bay of Bengal. The main part of the group is composed of five large islands, *viz.*, North Andaman, Middle Andaman, South Andaman, Baratang and Rutland Islands, generally known as the Great Andamans. There are several good harbours—Port Blair, Port Cornwallis, Mayabunder and Port Elphinstone.

The Nicobar Islands, from Car Nicobar in the north to Great Nicobar in the south, lie between Little Andaman and Sumatra. The most important harbour in the area is Nancowrie.

The total area of the Territory is 3,215 sq. miles, with a population (estimated, 1969) of 84,754.

The Andaman Islands are administered by the President acting through a Chief Commissioner.
Chief Commissioner, H. S. Butalia.
CHIEF CITY, Ψ Port Blair. Population (1961), 14,075.

Chandigarh.—A new Territory created in 1966 to serve as the capital area for the two States of Punjab and Haryana under their 1966 constitution. The Territory surrounds the city of Chandigarh to a distance of about 10 miles. The city was inaugurated in 1953 and built to the plans of Le Corbusier to replace the former capital, Lahore, now in Pakistan. An outstanding example of modern town-planning, it is still under construction. Population (estimated, 1969), 148,070.

Dadra and Nagar Haveli.—A territory formed in 1961 from Portuguese territory, formerly administered as part of Damão. Area, 189 sq. miles. Population (estimated, 1969), 68,557. An Administrator appointed by the Government of India resides at Silvassa.

Administrator, Nakul Sen.

Goa, Daman and Diu.—Three widely separated areas on the west coast of India, formerly Portuguese enclaves since the 16th century, which were taken over by the Indian Government in December, 1961, and have since been centrally administered. Total area of the Territory, 1,431 sq. miles, of which Goa (1,394 sq. miles), with a coastline of 65 miles, forms the largest part. Population (estimated, 1969), 626,667 (Goa, 585,997). Diu is an island with a small mainland area on the south-east coast of Gujarat. Daman (Damão) lies on the Gujarat coast, 70 miles north of Bombay.

CAPITAL (of the Territory).—Panaji (*Nova Goa*).

Himachal Pradesh.—Himachal Pradesh came into being in 1948. Its area is 10,879 sq. miles and population (estimated, 1969), 3,400,879. The territory is divided into six administrative districts, Mahasu, Sirmur, Mandi, Chamba, Bilaspur and Kinnaur.

Lieut.-Governor, Lt.-Gen. Bahadur Singh.

CAPITAL, Simla.

Laccadive, Minicoy and Amindivi Islands.—A group of small islands 100–200 miles off the south-west coast of India, formerly administered by the State of Madras. Total area, 11 sq. miles. Population (estimated, 1969), 26,720.

CAPITAL.—Kavaratti.

Manipur.—Manipur is an inland territory in the extreme east of India and having a common boundary with Burma. The former Princely State was taken over by the Government of India on Oct. 15, 1949, and since then has been centrally administered through a Chief Commissioner. There is a Legislative Assembly of 30 elected members, and 3 nominated members, but this remained dissolved in 1970 and the Territory was under direct Presidential rule.

CAPITAL.—Imphal.
Lt.-Governor, D. R. Kohli.

Pondicherry.—The former French establishments in India, Pondicherry, Karaikal, Yanam and Mahé, ceded to the Government of India in 1956 by treaty, having been administered by India since 1954. The Territory has a total area of 186 sq. miles; population, 369,079.

Lt.-Governor, B. D. Jatti.

Tripura.—A small territory north-east of the Ganges delta, Tripura has common boundaries with Assam on the east and with East Pakistan. An ancient Hindu Princely State, Tripura came under Indian Government administration on Oct. 15, 1947. Area, 4,000 sq. miles; population, (estimated, 1969), 1,409,504. CAPITAL.—Agartala.
Lt.-Governor, A. L. Dias.
Chief Minister, S. L. Singh.

PROTECTORATE

Sikkim.—A small Himalayan State, Sikkim is bounded by Tibet on the north and east, by Bhutan on the south-east, by Assam on the south and by Nepal on the west. It has an area of 2,744 sq. miles and at the Census of India, 1961, had 161,080 inhabitants. Sikkim has internal autonomy and the Government of India is responsible for its external relations, defence and communications.

Ruler of Sikkim, H.H. the Maharaja of Sikkim, O.B.E., *b.* 1923; *s.* Dec. 2, 1963.

CAPITAL.—Gangtok.

FLAG.—White with narrow red border; yellow and red emblem in centre.

Jammu and Kashmir.—A Himalayan State with an area of 86,000 sq. miles, having common boundaries with both India and West Pakistan on the south. The Maharajah of Jammu and Kashmir acceded to the Dominion of India in 1947, but in view of Pakistan claims, the matter of sovereignty is still in dispute, and has been under discussion by the United Nations since 1948. There is a cease-fire line between India and Pakistan forces in the state and the latter occupy some 31,250 sq. miles of Kashmir territory.

Jamaica

Jamaica is situated in the Caribbean Sea south of the eastern extremity of Cuba and lies between latitudes 17° 43′ and 18° 32′ North, and longitude 76° 11′ and 78° 21′ West. The island was discovered by Columbus on May 4, 1494, and occupied by the Spanish from 1509 until 1655 when a British expedition, sent out by Oliver Cromwell, under Admiral Penn and General Venables, attacked the island, which capitulated after a trifling resistance. In 1670 it was formally ceded to England by the Treaty of Madrid. Jamaica became an independent state within the British Commonwealth on August 6, 1962.

Area and Population.—Jamaica is 4,411 square miles in area and is divided into three counties (Surrey, Middlesex and Cornwall) and 14 parishes. The surface of the island is extremely mountainous, the highest peak being 7,402 ft. above sea level. The greatest length from east to west Morant Point to Negril Point) is 146 miles and the extreme breadth 51 miles. At the end of 1978, Jamaica's population was estimated to be 1,861,300. Jamaica for climatic and other reasons is a popular tourist resort, attracting visitors mainly from the U.S.A. The total number of visitor arrivals in 1970 was 414,720. Tourist expenditure in 1969 was estimated at £39,800,000, compared with £38,400,000 in 1969.

Physical Features.—The topography consists mainly of coastal plains, divided by the Blue Mountain Range in the east, and the hills and limestone plateaux which occupy the central and western areas of the interior. The central chain of high peaks of the Blue Mountains is over 6,000 feet above sea level, and the Blue Mountain Peak, the highest of these, reaches an elevation of 7,402 feet. The rivers flow down from the central mountainous area. Most of the rivers are narrow and fast flowing, and some have rapids. In general those flowing south are longer and are fed by more tributaries than those flowing north. None is navigable except the Black River, and that only for small craft.

CAPITAL.—The seat of government is Kingston, the largest town and seaport (estimated population of the Corporate area of Kingston and St. Andrew in 1970, 550,100. Other towns are Montego Bay (42,800) and Spanish Town (41,600).

FLAG.—Gold diagonal cross forming triangles of green at top and bottom, triangles of black at hoist and in fly. NATIONAL DAY.—First Monday in August (Independence Day).

GOVERNMENT

The Legislature consists of a Senate of 21 nominated members and a House of Representatives consisting of 53 members elected by universal adult suffrage. The number of members cannot be fewer than 45 nor more than 60. The Senate has no power to delay money bills for longer than one month or other bills for

longer than seven months against the wishes of the House of Representatives. The Constitution provides for a Leader of the Opposition.

Governor-General, His Excellency Sir Clifford Campbell, G.C.M.G., G.C.V.O.

CABINET

Prime Minister, Minister of External Affairs and Defence, Rt. Hon. Hugh Shearer.
Minister of Finance and Planning, Hon. E. Seaga.
Trade and Industry, Hon. R. C. Lightbourne.
Education, Hon. E. L. Allen.
Public Utilities and Housing, Hon. W. O. Hill.
Development, Youth and Community, Hon. A. M. W. Douglas.
Health, Hon. Dr. H. W. Eldemire.
Labour and National Insurance, Hon. L. G. Newland.
Agriculture and Fisheries, Hon. J. P. Gyles.
Rural Land Development, Hon. W. G. McLaren.
Home Affairs. Hon. R. A. McNeill.
Communications and Works, Hon. N. C. Lewis.
Local Government, Hon. L. A. Lynch.
Minister of Legal Affairs and Attorney-General, Hon. V. B. Grant, Q.C.
Minister without Portfolio, Sen. Hon. Sir Neville Ashenheim, C.B.E.
Ministers of State:—
  Youth and Community Development, Sen. Hon. H. Wynter.
  Education, Sen. Hon. Dr. A. E. Burt.

Speaker, House of Representatives, Hon. E. C. L. Parkinson.

JAMAICAN HIGH COMMISSION
48 Grosvenor Street, W.1
High Commissioner, His Excellency Sir (Henry) Laurence Lindo, C.M.G.

BRITISH HIGH COMMISSION
P.O. Box 628, 58 Duke Street, Kingston
High Commissioner, His Excellency Edward Noel Larmour. C.M.G. (1970)............... £6,875
Deputy High Commissioner, Mrs. M. B. Chitty.

JUDICATURE
Chief Justice and Keeper of Records, Hon. Sir Herbert Duffus.
Judges of the Court of Appeal, Hon. Sir Cyril Henriques, C.B.E. (*President*); Hons. Sir Joseph Luckhoo; H. J. Shelley; L. B. Fox; A. M. Edun; K. G. Smith; C. H. Graham-Parkins.
Puisne Judges, Hons. L. Robinson; U. N. Parnell, H. S. Grannum; E. Zacca; V. L. Lopez; V. C. Melville; L. L. Robotham; I. D. Rowe; W. B. Wilkie; H. V. T. Chambers.

COMMUNICATIONS

There are several excellent harbours, Kingston being the principal port. The island is intersected by 2,700 miles of main road, of which 1,730 are asphalted. There are 241 miles of railway open. Telegraph stations and post offices are established in every town and in very many villages.

There are two international airports capable of handling the largest civil jet aircraft, the Palisadoes Airport on the south coast serving Kingston, and the Montego Bay Airport on the north coast serving the major tourist areas. In addition there are licensed aerodromes at Port Antonio and Ocho Rios which are used by Jamaica Air Service on scheduled domestic flights. There are nearly 40 private airstrips.

Air Jamaica, the national airline formed by the Government of Jamaica in association with Air Canada, operates scheduled services between U.S.A., Nassau and Jamaica. Eleven other international carriers provide air communication with Europe, North, Central and South America and the Caribbean islands. They are:—B.O.A.C., British West Indian Airways, Air Canada, Pan American World Airways, K.L.M., Delta, Lufthansa, Cayman Brac Airways, Mexicana Airlines, Eastern Airlines and TACA International Airlines.

Scheduled internal routes are operated by Jamaica Air Services Ltd. There is also an air taxi service.

PRODUCTION

Most of the staple products of tropical climates are grown. Sugar and rum are manufactured and exported (the latter is still counted the best in the world), and fine quality coffee is grown in certain areas of the Blue Mountains. Sugar production in 1970 amounted to 370,000 tons. There is trade in fruits, chiefly bananas, with U.K. Citrus, cocoa, coffee, pimento and ginger are important export crops. Jamaica has developed a breed of dairy cattle known as Jamaica Hope and a beef breed, the Jamaica Black. Jamaica is now the largest producer of bauxite in the world; output for 1970 was 11,820,000 tons. The bauxite deposits are worked by one Canadian and five U.S. companies; the Canadian company and a consortium of the U.S. companies process bauxite into alumina. Further expansion of the industry is in progress. Gypsum is also mined, production in 1970 being 278,000 tons. Cement is manufactured locally, the output of the factory being 450,000 tons in 1970. The Esso Oil Refinery is designed to process 26,000 barrels of crude oil daily. The Jamaica Industrial Development Corporation is responsible for implementing the Government's industrial development programme. This Corporation administers incentive legislation which was enacted to stimulate the establishment of industries locally. In addition to undertaking promotional activities both locally and abroad, the Corporation maintains branch offices in Montego Bay, Jamaica, in the United States, and the United Kingdom. In the last decade, manufacturing has grown from the processing of a few agricultural products into the production of a whole new range of commodities dependent on both local and foreign raw materials.

FINANCE

	1970–71	1971–72*
Revenue	£125,683,643	£150,634,392
Expenditure	131,814,429	150,488,667
Public Debt	126,360,058	142,481,310

* Estimated.

TRADE

	1969	1970
Total Imports	£181,650,000	£217,000,000
Total Exports	119,000,000	138,950,000

	1969	1970
Imports from U.K.	£34,878,000	£38,203,000
Exports to U.K.	26,174,000	27,480,000

Chief Exports (1970).—Bauxite and alumina, £93,450,000; sugar, rum and molasses, £16,850,000; bananas, £5,900,000; citrus, coffee, cocoa, pimento £5,000,000; manufactured goods, £11,700,000; clothing £3,000,000; mineral fuels etc. lubricants and related products, £3,650,000.

Kenya

Kenya is bisected by the equator and extends approximately from latitude 4° N. to latitude 4° S. and from longitude 34° E. to 41° E. From the coast of the Indian Ocean in the east, the borders of Kenya are with Somalia in the east and Ethiopia and Sudan in the north and north-west. To the west lie Uganda and Lake Victoria. On the south is Tanzania. The total area is 224,960 square miles (including 5,224 square miles of water). At the last census in August, 1969, the population was 10,890,000, including small Asian, European and Arab minorities. The country is divided into 7 Provinces (Nyanza, Rift Valley, Central, Coast, Western, Eastern and North-Eastern).

CAPITAL.—Nairobi, situated at latitude 2° S. and longitude 36°49′ E. at 5,453 feet above sea level, covers an area of 266 sq. miles and has a population of about 480,000. It is 307 miles by road from Mombasa, the country's main port. ΨMombasa (246,000) possesses what is perhaps the finest harbour on the East Coast of Africa and is well served by shipping lines from Europe and Asia besides a frequent coastal service. Other centre ares Nakuru (47,800), Kisumu (30,700), Eldoret (16,900), Thika (18,100) and Nanyuki (11,200).

Nairobi: transit from London about 25 days by sea; by air, 10 hrs.

FLAG.—Three equal horizontal bands of black over red over green; red and white spears and shield device in centre. NATIONAL DAY.—December 12.

GOVERNMENT

Kenya became an independent state and a member of the British Commonwealth on December 12, 1963, after six months of internal self-government. The national assembly consists of a single House of Representatives. Kenya became a Republic on Dec. 12, 1964.

President, His Excellency Jomo Kenyatta, *elected* 1964; *re-elected* 1969.
Vice-President and Minister of Home Affairs, D. T. Arap Moi.

CABINET

Minister of Finance and Economic Planning, M. Kibaki.
Defence, J. S. Gichuru.
Minister of State, Office of the President, M. Koinange.
Agriculture and Animal Husbandry, J. J. M. Nyagah.
Health, I. Omolo-Okero.
Local Government, J. G. Kiano.
Works, J. Nyamweya.
Labour, E. N. Mwendwa.
Education, T. arap Towett.
Tourism and Wildlife, J. Shako.
Lands and Settlement, J. H. Angaine.
Housing, P. J. Ngei.
Power and Communications, R. G. Ngala.
Attorney-General, C. Njonjo.
Information and Broadcasting, Dr. Z. Onyonka.
Foreign Affairs, Dr. N. Mungai.
Co-operatives and Social Services, H. M. Muliro.
Commerce and Industry, J. C. N. Osogo.
Natural Resources, W. O. Omamo.

KENYA HIGH COMMISSION IN LONDON
45 Portland Place, W.1.
[01-636 2371]
High Commissioner, His Excellency Ng'ethe Njoroge (1970).

BRITISH HIGH COMMISSION
Bruce House, Standard Street, P.O. Box 30465 Harambee Avenue, Nairobi.
High Commissioner, His Excellency Sir Eric George Norris, K.C.M.G. (1968)................£9,000
Deputy High Commissioner, R. Walker.
British Council Representative, R. A. Hack, P.O. Box 751, Kenya Cultural Centre, University Way, Nairobi. There are offices at *Kisimu* and *Mombasa.*

JUDICATURE
Chief Justice, J. Wicks.
Puisne Judges, C. B. Madan, Q.C.; E. Trevelyan; Chanan Singh; C. H. E. Miller; A. H. Simpson; L. G. E. Harris; K. G. Bennett; A. A. Kneller; L. P. Mosdell.
Registrar, J. O. Nyarangi.

Production.—Agriculture provides about 35 per cent. of the national income; the principal exports in 1969 were: coffee £16,800,000; tea £11,300,000; petroleum products £7,600,000; meat products, £2,600,000; pyrethrum, £2,800,000; sisal, £1,700,000; hides and skins, £1,900,000; and cement, £1,400,000. The great variation in altitude and ecology provide conditions under which a wide range of crops can

be grown. These include wheat, barley, pyrethrum, coffee, tea, sisal, coconuts, cashew nuts, cotton, maize, and a wide variety of tropical and temperate fruits and vegetables. The total area of high potential land on which concentrated alternate husbandry can be practised, amounts to only 16,761 sq. miles, or 11·9 per cent. of the total land area. The remainder is arid or semi-arid country suitable for stock raising. In the areas of high potential, many of the old, large scale farms, formerly farmed by Europeans, have been bought by the Government for settlement of landless people and for transfer to African large-scale farmers.

In 1967 Kenya's forest area totalled 4,587,000 acres, of which 241,000 acres were under plantation.

Prospecting and mining are carried on in many parts of the country, the principal minerals produced being soda ash, salt and limestone. Small amounts of gold and silver are also mined. Value of all minerals produced in 1968 was £2,200,000.

Hydro-electric power has been developed, particularly on the Upper Tana and Mathioya Rivers. Owen Falls Dam scheme in Uganda is connected to Nairobi and electricity is available throughout the country. The first stage of an important national hydro-electric project was inaugurated by the President in 1965—the Seven Forks Project, which is expected to produce 280 MW on completion within 12 years. Total cost of the project was estimated at £37,000,000.

There has been considerable industrial development over the last 15 years and Kenya has a wide variety of industries processing agricultural produce and manufacturing an increasing range of products from local and imported raw materials. New industries have recently come into being such as an oil refinery, textile mills, dehydrated vegetable processing and motor battery manufacture as well as many smaller schemes which have added to the country's already considerable consumer goods. The market served comprises all the East African territories and the volume of exports to adjoining African and Indian Ocean countries is increasing year by year. Industrial areas have been developed in all the principal towns and light industrial areas exist in many rural areas. The Kenya Government is actively encouraging investment in the industrial sector and has a Foreign Investments Protection Act to protect such investments.

The main imports are manufactured goods, classified chiefly as materials, machinery and transport equipment, mineral fuels, lubricants and related fuels, food and chemicals.

Communications.—The East African Railways and Harbours are a self-contained and self-financing service of the East African Community; the railway, which is metre gauge, has a total route mileage of open line of 3,670 miles (1,270 miles in Kenya). In addition the East African Railways operate a marine service on Lakes Victoria and Tanganyika, with a route mileage of 3,469 miles. There are also 2,367 miles of road services providing regular transport to the Southern Highlands of Tanzania, and beyond the railhead at Pakwach in Uganda. East African Harbours control the four seaports of Mombasa, Tanga, Dar-es-Salaam and Mtwara. Mombasa, Dar-es-Salaam and Mtwara have deep-water berths and Tanga is a lighterage port.

Scheduled trunk airline services are operated to and from Kenya, through Nairobi airport, by East African Airways, B.O.A.C., Air India, Air France, Scandinavian Airlines System, British United Airways, Alitalia, Pan Am, K.L.M., Ethiopian Airlines and El Al Israel Airlines, while regional scheduled services 'were also run by East African Airways, Ethiopian Airlines, Air Congo, Air Malawi and Zambia Airways.

The country has approximately 26,000 miles of road including 3,850 miles of trunk roads and 6,200 miles of secondary roads. There is a total of 1,336 miles of bitumen-surfaced roads, apart from town streets, etc.

FINANCE

	1968–69	1969–70*
Revenue........	£101,710,000	£124,560,000
Expenditure.......	104,980,000	122,710,000

The total public debt at June 30, 1968 was £142,420,000.

* Estimated.

Trade.—A large part of Kenya's trade is with the United Kingdom which in 1969 took 23 per cent. of her exports and supplied 31 per cent. of Kenya's imports (both figures excluding trade with Uganda and Tanzania). The principal exports are coffee, tea, petroleum products, maize, meat products, pyrethrum flowers, powder and extract, and hides and skins.

Trade with U.K.

	1969	1970
Imports from U.K. .	£49,242,000	£52,822,000
Exports to U.K.....	25,706,000	27,064,000

Lesotho

Lesotho (formerly Basutoland) is an enclave within the Republic of South Africa and is bounded north and west by the Orange Free State, east by Natal and East Griqualand, and south by the Cape Province, with an area of 11,716 square miles. The land, which is mountainous, rising to over 11,000 ft. in places, is held in trust for the Basotho by the King. The population of Lesotho was 970,000 at the 1966 Census.

CAPITAL.—Maseru, population (1968), 14,000. Maseru is distant from London 7,668 miles. Transit *via* the Cape about 20 days; by air, 2 days.

FLAG.—Blue, with white Basuto hat device in centre; vertical stripes of red and green (next staff).

Government.—Lesotho consists of nine districts each with its Principal Chief working in close co-operation with an Administrative Secretary. The Constitution was suspended on January 29, 1970. The Lesotho Courts of Law consist of: (*a*) The Court of Appeal, (*b*) The High Court, (*c*) The Subordinate Courts including the Courts of Judicial Commissioners and the Basotho Courts.

Head of State, His Majesty King Moshoeshoe II, *acceded* 1966.

CABINET

Tona Kholo and Minister of Foreign Affairs, Defence and Internal Security, Hon. Leabua Jonathan.

Deputy Prime Minister and Minister of Agriculture, Hon. Sekhonyana 'Maseribane.

Minister of Finance, Commerce, Industry and Labour, Hon. Peete Peete.

Health, Education and Social Welfare, Hon. Benedict M. Leseteli.

Interior, Hon. Matete Majara.

Communications and Works, Hon. A. C. Manyeli.

Justice and Tourism, Hon. P. 'Mota.

Minister to Tona Kholo, Hon. S. M. Letsie.

LESOTHO HIGH COMMISSION

16A St. James's Street (1st Floor), S.W.1

High Commissioner, His Excellency C. M. Molapo.

BRITISH HIGH COMMISSION

P.O. Box 521, Maseru

High Commissioner, His Excellency Harry Godfrey Mitchell Bass (1970)...................£5.765

British Council Representative, G. C. Thomas, P.O. Box 429, Hobson's Square, Maseru. (Also British Council representative for *Botswana* and *Swaziland.*)

Education.—In 1968 there were 1,124 primary schools and 27 secondary schools. The total enrolment at secondary schools in 1969 was 4,141. 287 Lesotho students were undergoing university courses in 1968.

Communications.—There are no railways in Lesotho with the exception of 1 mile of the South African Railways which enters Lesotho at Maseru

from the Orange Free State. A main road runs from Butha Buthe in Northern Lesotho to Quthing in the South. It connects all the Government Stations with the exception of Qacha's Nek and Mokhotlong. Quacha's Nek is accessible by road from Matatiele in East Griqualand and there is a jeep service up the Sani Pass to Mokhotlong. There are 28 air-strips in the Territory, of which 5 are used by a regular internal air service. One of the 5 in Maseru is now being used by a twice weekly external service between Maseru and Jan Smuts Airport. The service began on October 2, 1967. The internal air service carries mail and goods to and from otherwise inaccessible mountain regions and in addition there is a Flying Doctor service. The remaining air-strips are used mainly by traders and missions.

Production, etc.—The economy of Lesotho is mainly agrarian. At the last enumeration (1966) live stock numbers were: Cattle, 278,940; Sheep, 1,477,340; Goats, 817,257; and Horses, 80,000. 10,215,824 lb. of wool, valued at R868,309, and 2,519,243 lb. of mohair, valued at £413,704 were exported in 1968. There is no direct trade between the Territory and the U.K.

FINANCE

Lesotho is a poor and unproductive country. The principal sources of revenue are customs and excise duty, taxes, and wool and mohair export duty.

Total budgetary expenditure for 1968–69 was R11,222,514. Local revenue amounted to R5,653,099 and the difference was met by a U.K. grant.

Malawi

MALAWI, formerly the Nyasaland Protectorate, comprises Lake Malawi (formerly Lake Nyasa) and its western shore, with the high table-land separating it from the basin of the Luangwa River, the watershed forming the western frontier with Zambia; south of the lake Malawi reaches almost to the Zambezi and is surrounded by Portuguese East Africa (Mozambique) the frontier lying on the west on the watershed of the Zambesi and Shire Rivers, and to the east on the Rua, a tributary of the Shire, and Lakes Chiuta and Chilwa. This boundary reaches the eastern shore of Lake Malawi and extends up to the mid-point of the lake for about half its length where it returns to the eastern and northern shores to form a frontier with Tanzania.

Malawi has a total area of 45,411 sq. miles (land area, 36,145). The population of Malawi at the Census of August, 1966, was 4,039,583 (52 per cent. female); estimated, 1970, 4,530,000.

CAPITAL.—Zomba (population 19,666). The city of Blantyre, incorporating Blantyre and Limbe, is the major commercial and industrial centre and headquarters of the Southern region. Other main centres are: Lilongwe, headquarters of the Central Region and the site chosen for the new capital of Malawi for which an initial loan of K9,400,000 (£4,700,000) has been given by the South African Government; Mzuzu, headquarters of the Northern Region; Thyolo, Mulanje, Mangoche, Mzimba and Nkhota-kota.

FLAG.—Horizontal stripes of black, red and green, with rising sun in centre of the black stripe.

Government.—Malawi became a republic on July 6, 1966, having assumed internal self-government on February 1, 1963, and is a member of the Commonwealth. There is a Cabinet consisting of the President and other Ministers. The National Assembly consists of 60 members, each elected by universal suffrage. Under the Constitution Act, 1966, the President exercises power to nominate in addition up to ten members to represent special interests. Being a one-party State (the Malawi Congress Party), all elected members are required to be members of the Party. The Assembly, which usually meets three times a year, is presided over by a Speaker, who need not himself be a member of it.

President, Minister of External Affairs, Works and Supplies, Agriculture and Natural Resources, Hon. Dr. H. Kamuzu Banda, *born* 1907, *sworn in as* President for Life, July 6, 1971.

CABINET

Minister of Trade and Industry, Hon. J. D. Msonthi.
Northern Region, Hon. M. Q. Y. Chibambo.
Ministers of State (President's Office), Hon. A. A. Muwalo; Hon. A. B. J. Chiwanda.
Southern Region, Hon. G. C. Chakuamba.
Finance, Information and Tourism, Hon. A. K. Banda.
Central Region, Hon. J. T. Kumbweza.
Education, Health and Community Development, Hon. M. M. Lungu.
Local Government, Hon. R. J. Sembereka.
Transport, Communications and Labour, Hon. J. W. Gwengwe.

JUDICIARY

Chief Justice, J. J. Skinner.
Puisne Judges, L. Weston, L. A. Chatsikah.
Attorney-General, B. C. Roberts, Q.C.
Solicitor-General, D. R. Barwick.

MALAWI HIGH COMMISSION

47 Great Cumberland Place, W.1
High Commissioner, His Excellency B. W. Katenga.

BRITISH HIGH COMMISSION

Victoria Avenue (P.O. Box 479), Blantyre
High Commissioner, His Excellency Walter Robert Haydon, C.M.G. (1971)................£6,875
Deputy High Commissioner, H. M. S. Reid.
Defence Adviser, Lt.-Col. B. N. Cardozo.

British Council Representative, E. H. Semmens, P.O. Box 456, Glyn Jones Road, Blantyre. Libraries at Blantyre, Lilongwe and Zomba.

Education.—Primary education is the responsibility of local authorities in both urban and rural areas. About 35 per cent. of the population of school age can be taken into schools and only 10 per cent. of those successfully completing primary education can be placed in secondary schools. The Ministry is responsible for policy, school curricula, secondary education teachers' and technical training. Religious bodies, with Government assistance, still play an important part in primary and secondary education and teacher training. Further training is pursued at the University of Malawi, opened in September 1965. In June 1969, there were 308 students studying for degrees and 573 for diplomas at five constituent colleges.

Communications.—A single-track railway runs from the south-western area of Lake Malawi (itself served by two passenger and a number of cargo boats) through Blantyre to the southern frontier into Mozambique, crossing the Zambesi River by a bridge 12,050 feet long, and connecting with the Mozambique port of Beira, which handles the bulk of the country's imports and exports. Work started in May, 1968, on a rail link with the Northern Mozambique port of Nacala. A good-class earth road system covers the whole country and is already tarmacadamized from Mlanje through Blantyre and Zomba to Liwonde where the new Nacala rail link will cross the Shire River and run in an easterly direction, and also from Lilongwe to the lake-shore at Salima, northern terminus of the railway. Construction has already started on a double width bitumen road from Liwonde through Lilongwe.

FINANCE

	1969–70*	1970–71
Revenue	£26,100,000	£22,700,000
Expenditure	26,700,000	22,700,000

* Final accounts for 15 months to Mar. 31, 1970.

Total public debt on Dec. 31, 1969, was £34,200,000, of which £8,600,000 was funded. Decimal currency was introduced on Feb. 15, 1971. The unit is the *kwacha* (=50p. sterling), divided into 100 *tambala*.

TRADE

	1968	1969
Imports	£29,575,000	£30,700,000
Exports	16,928,000	18,300,000

Trade with U.K.

	1969	1970
Imports from U.K.	£7,568,000	£7,983,000
Exports to U.K.	10,658,000	12,135,000

Agriculture is the country's mainstay, the principal exports being tea, tobacco, cotton and groundnuts. The value of exports of these crops in 1969 was: tea, £4,800,000; tobacco, £6,300,000; groundnuts, £3,700,000; maize £1,050,000; cotton, £800,000. Other agricultural exports include tung oil, rice, sisal, casava, coffee and dried vegetables. A total of £17,500,000 of crops was exported in 1969. Sugar production started in the Lower Shire, Southern Region, in August, 1966. Imports are mainly clothing materials, vehicles, fuels and machinery.

2 B+

Malaysia

Malaysia, comprising Malaya, Sabah and Sarawak, forms a crescent well over 1,000 miles long between latitudes 1° and 7° North latitude and longitudes 100° and 119° East. It occupies two distinct regions—the Malay Peninsula which extends from the Isthmus of Kra to the Singapore Strait and the North-West Coastal area of the Island of Borneo. Each is separated from the other by 400 miles of the South China Sea.

Area and Population.—The total area of the 13 states of Malaysia is estimated to be 27,581 sq. miles, containing a population of 10,434,034 at the Census of Housing and Population of Malaysia held in 1970. Details of individual states appear on p. 201.

Climate.—The whole region is open to maritime influences and is subject to the interplay of wind systems which originate in the Indian Ocean and the South China Sea. The year is commonly divided into the Southwest and Northeast monsoon seasons. Rainfall averages about 100 inches throughout the year, though the annual fall varies from place to place. The average daily temperature throughout Malaysia varies from 70° Fahrenheit to 90° Fahrenheit, though in higher areas temperatures are lower and vary widely.

CAPITAL.—Kuala Lumpur, also capital of Selangor (estimated population, 500,000). The chief town Sarawak is Kuching (63,491) and of Sabah is Kota Kinabalu (41,830).

LANGUAGE.—Malay is the national language. In Sabah and Sarawak English continues to be the official language until Parliament decide otherwise. RELIGION.—Islam is the official religion of Malaysia, each Ruler being the head of religion in his State, though the Heads of State of Sabah and Sarawak are not heads of the Muslim religion in their States. The Yang di-Pertuan Agong is the head of religion in Malacca and Penang. There is no State religion in Sabah or Sarawak and the Constitution guarantees religious freedom. NATIONAL DAY —August 31 (*Hari Kebargsaan*).

FLAG.—Equal horizontal stripes of red (7) and white (7); 14 point yellow star and crescent in blue canton.

GOVERNMENT

The Federation of Malaya became an independent country within the Commonwealth on August 31, 1957, as a result of an agreement between H.M. the Queen and the Rulers of the Malay States, whereby Her Majesty relinquished all powers and jurisdiction over the Malay States and over the Settlements of Penang and Malacca which then became States of the Federation. On Sept. 16, 1963, the Federation was enlarged, by the accession of the further states of Singapore, Sabah (*formerly British North Borneo*) and Sarawak, and the name of MALAYSIA was adopted from that date. On Aug. 9, 1965, Singapore seceded from the Federation.

The Constitution was designed to ensure the existence of a strong Federal Government and also a measure of autonomy for the State Governments. It provides for a constitutional Supreme Head of the Federation (His Majesty the *Yang di-Pertuan Agong*) to be elected for a term of 5 years by the Rulers from among their number, and for a Deputy Supreme Head (His Highness the *Timbalan Yang di-Pertuan Agong*) to be similarly elected. The Malay Rulers are either chosen or succeed to their position in accordance with the custom of the particular state. In other states of Malaysia choice of the Head of State is in the discretion of the *Yang di-Pertuan Agong* after consultation with the Chief Minister of the State. Save in certain instances provided in the Constitution, the Supreme Head acts in accordance with the advice of a Cabinet appointed by him from among the members of Parliament on the advice of the Prime Minister. The Supreme Head appoints as Prime Minister the person who in his judgment is likely to command the confidence of the majority of the members of the House of Representatives.

SUPREME HEAD OF MALAYSIA

His Majesty Tuanku Abdul Halim Mu'azam Shah, *b.* 1927, *assumed office for a term of 5 years*, Sept. 21, 1970. *Deputy Supreme Head of State*, His Royal Highness Tuanka Yahya Putra Ibni-Al-Marham Sultan Ibrahim (*Sultan of Kelantan*).

MINISTRY

Prime Minister, Minister of External Affairs and of Defence, Tun Abdul Razak bin Dato Hussein.
Deputy Prime Minister and Home Affairs, Tun Dr. Ismail Al-Haj bin Dato Abdul Rahman.
Finance, Tun Tan Siew Sin.
Works, Posts and Telecommunications, Tun V. T. Sambanthan.
Labour, Tan Sri V. Manickavasagam.
Agriculture and Land, Tuan Sri Haji Mohamed Ghazali bin Haji Jawi.
Education, Enche Hussein Onn.
Health, Tan Sri Haji Sardon bin Haji Jubir.
Commerce and Industry, Mohamed Khir Johari.
Transport, Dato Ganie bin Gilong.
Culture, Youth and Sports, Dato Hamzah bin Haji Abu Samah.
Technology, Research and Local Government, Dato Ong Kee Hui.
Welfare Services, Tan Sri Fatimah binti Haji Hashim.
Sarawak Affairs, Tan Sri Temenggong Juga anak Barieng.
Justice, Tan Sri Abdul Kadir bin Yusoff.
National and Rural Development, Abdul Ghafar bin Baba.
Minister with Special Functions and Minister of Information, Tan Sri Mohammad Ghazali bin Shafie.

Without Portfolio, Tan Sri Ong Yoke Lin; Lee Siok Yew.

In addition there are 6 Deputy Ministers.

NOTE.—The words " Tunku ", " Tun ", " Tan Sri ", and " Dato " are titles. The word " Tunku " is equivalent to " Prince ". "Tun" denotes membership of a high Order of Malaysian Chivalry and " Tan Sri " and " Dato " (" Datu " in Sabah) are each the equivalent of a knighthood. The wife of a " Tun " is styled " Toh Puan ", that of a " Tan Sri " is styled " Puan Sri " and of a " Dato ", " Datin ". The honorific " Tuan " or " Enche " is equivalent to " Mr." and the honorific " Puan " is equivalent to " Mrs." The words " Al-Haj " or " Haji " indicate that the person so named has made the pilgrimage to Mecca.

MALAYSIAN HIGH COMMISSION
45 Belgrave Square, S.W.1
High Commissioner, His Excellency Tan Sri Abdul Aziz bin Yeop (1971).

BRITISH HIGH COMMISSION
Wisma Damansara, Kuala Lumpur.
High Commissioner, His Excellency Sir John (Baines) Johnston, K.C.M.G. (1971) £9,000
Deputy High Commissioner, A. A. Duff, C.M.G., D.S.O.

British Council Representative, J. Goatly, O.B.E., Jalan Bluff, Kuala Lumpur, and offices at *Penang*, *Kota Kinabulu* (Sabah) and *Kuching* (Sarawak).

LEGISLATURE

The Federal Parliament consists of two houses, the Senate and the House of Representatives. The Senate (*Dewan Negara*) consists of 58 members, under a President (*Yang di-Pertua Dewan Negara*), 26 elected by the Legislative Assemblies of the States (2 from each) and 32 appointed by the *Yang di-Pertuan Agong* from persons who have achieved distinction in major fields of activity or are representative of racial minorities, including the Aborigines. The House of Representatives (*Dewan Ra'ayat*), consists of 144 members (States of Malaya, 104; Sarawak, 24; and Sabah, 16). Members are elected on the principle of universal adult suffrage with a common electoral roll. Sabah had its first direct elections in 1967. The House of Representatives is presided over by a Speaker who is either a member of the House or is qualified to be elected as a member. *Speaker*, C. M. Yusoff.

The Constitution provides that each State shall have its own Constitution not inconsistent with the Federal Constitution, with the Ruler or Governor acting on the advice of an Executive Council appointed on the advice of the *Menteri Besar* or Chief Minister and a single chamber Legislative Assembly. Three *ex officio* members sit in the Executive Council besides these elected members. They are the State Secretary, the State Legal Adviser and the State Financial Officer. The State Constitutions provide for the Ruler or Governor to appoint as *Menteri Besar* or Chief Minister, to preside over the Executive Council, a member of the Legislative Assembly who in his judgment is likely to command the confidence of the majority of the members of the Assembly. The Legislative Assemblies are fully elected on the same basis as the Federal Parliament.

Legislative powers are divided into a Federal List, a State List and a Concurrent List, with residual powers vested in the State Legislatures. The Federal List comprises broadly, external affairs, defence, civil and criminal law and justice, the machinery of government, finance, commerce and industry, communications and transport, power, education, medicine and labour and social security. The State List includes land, agriculture and forestry, local government and services and the machinery of state government. In the Concurrent List are, *inter alia*, social welfare, wild-life, animal husbandry, town and country planning, public health and drainage and irrigation.

A State of Emergency was declared after disturbances on May 13, 1969. As Parliament was not then sitting, the *Yang di-Pertuan Agong* did not summon Parliament and instead established the National Operations Council and Y.A.B. Tun Abdul Razak bin Dato Hussein, the then Deputy Prime Minister, was appointed Director of Operations vested with the executive authority of the Federation including the powers to make essential regulations. The *Yang di-Pertuan Agong* remained as the Supreme Head of Federation with powers to promulgate emergency ordinances.

JUDICATURE

The Judicial System consists of a Federal Court and two High Courts, one in West Malaysia and one in East Malaysia. The High Court in West Malaysia known as the High Court in Malaya has its principal registry in Kuala Lumpur while the High Court in East Malaysia known as the High Court in Borneo has its principal registry in Kuching.

The Federal Court comprises a President, the two Chief Justices of the High Courts and other judges.

This court possesses appellate, original and advisory jurisdiction. In its capacity as an appellate court it has exclusive jurisdiction to determine appeals from the decisions of a High Court or of a judge thereof (except decisions of a High Court given by a registrar or other officer of the court and appealable under federal law to a judge of the Court). This appellate jurisdiction is subject to limitations imposed by or under federal law. It also has jurisdiction to determine disputes between the Federation and any of the States within the Federation, any challenge to the competence of the Federal or any State legislature to enact a particular law and any question as to the effect of any of the provisions of the Constitution which question has arisen in proceedings before another court. It also renders advisory opinions on questions referred to it by the *Yang di-Pertuan Agong* as regards the effect of any provision of the Constitution which has arisen or likely to arise.

Each of the High Courts consists of a Chief Justice and not less than 4 other judges. The Federal Constitution allows for a maximum of twelve such judges for Malaya and eight for Borneo. In West Malaysia the Subordinate Courts consist of the Sessions Courts and the Magistrates' Courts. In East Malaysia the Magistrates' Courts constitute the Subordinate Courts.

Lord President of the Federal Court, Tun Azmi bin Haji Mohamed.

Chief Justice of the High Court (*W. Malaysia*), Tan Sri H. T. Ong.

Chief Justice of the High Court (*E. Malaysia*), Tan Sri Ismail Khan.

DEFENCE

The Malaysian Armed Forces consist of the Army, Navy and Air Force, together with volunteer forces for each arm. The defence of the country is largely borne by the army in its role of providing defence against external threat and counter-insurgency operations and also to assist the police in the performance of public order duties. The *Royal Malaysian Navy* (*RMN*) has the responsibility of defending the 3,000 miles of the country's coastline and maintaining constant patrol of 500 miles of the high seas that separate East Malaysia from the mainland. The *Royal Malaysia Air Force* (*RMAF*) is capable of providing close strategic and tactical offensive support to the army and police in the defence and internal security of the country.

FINANCE

	1969	1970†
Revenue	$2,093,000,000	$2,369,000,000
Expenditure	1,929,000,000	2,156,000,000

† Estimates.

PRODUCTION AND TRADE

The agricultural sector continued to be mainstay of the Malaysian economy in 1970. However the rapid growth of the manufacturing sector has to some extent lessened its importance and this is expected to be increasingly so in the future.

Malaysia is the largest exporter of natural rubber, tin, and palm oil. Other major export commodities are timber, manufactured and processed products, petroleum, iron ore, coconut oil, bauxite, copra and tea.

Exports of the six major primary commodities rubber, tin, saw logs, sawn timber, palm oil and iron ore accounted for 76·6 per cent. of total exports in 1970. With the rapid expansion in the manufacturing sector, Malaysia is also increasing her export of manufactured products.

Another commodity which is produced throughout Malaysia is rice, the staple food of Malaysians. Total output of *padi* in 1969–70 season amounted to 1,658,800 tons. The level of self-sufficiency of rice increased to 84 per cent. in West Malaysia in 1970. To achieve self-sufficiency, various measures aimed at increasing output and productivity are being introduced. They include wider use of improved seeds and fertilizers, expansion of double-cropping through the provision of large-scale irrigation schemes and research programmes to improve rice yields.

Imports in 1970 consisted mainly of machinery and transport equipment, manufactured goods, food, mineral fuels, chemicals and inedible crude materials for her growing population and to accelerate the pace of her economic growth and development.

	1969 $M'000,000	1970 $M'000,000
Imports.........	3,611·6	4,265·1
Exports.........	5,051·4	5,150·7
Balance of trade..	+1,439·8	+888·6

Trade with U.K.

	1969	1970
Imports from U.K..	£46,628,000	£60,426,000
Exports to U.K. ...	33,549,000	46,596,000

Malaysia's Trade by Countries ($M'000,000)

Countries	1968 Imports	1968 Exports	1968 Total Trade	1969 Imports	1969 Exports	1969 Total Trade	1970 Imports	1970 Exports	1970 Total Trade
Singapore........	296·8	847·9	1,144·7	289·7	1,076·9	1,366·6	317·7	1,111·4	1,429·1
Japan............	484·2	776·6	1,260·8	575·6	932·1	1,507·5	749·2	942·1	1,691·3
U.K.............	501·5	272·2	773·7	473·1	275·7	748·8	582·6	340·3	922·9
Other, Western Europe........	302·3	388·9	691·2	399·2	563·2	962·4	487·2	691·4	1,178·6
U.S.S.R........	8·3	201·9	210·2	10·1	240·0	250·1	11·1	212·3	223·4
China (Mainland)	243·2	76·4	319·6	243·5	138·1	381·6	227·2	66·7	293·9
Australia........	..	..	..	240·5	131·0	371·5	239·7	115·8	355·5
Indonesia........	..	..	..	183·3	48·2	231·5	207·3	32·5	239·8

Malta, G.C.

Malta lies in the Mediterranean Sea, 58 miles from Sicily and about 180 from the African coast, about 17 miles in length and 9 in breadth, and having an area of 94·9 square miles. Malta includes also the adjoining island of *Gozo* (area 25·9 sq. miles); *Comino* and minor islets. The estimated population on Dec. 31, 1969, was 322,353. Malta's climate, although not tropical, is hot in summer.

Malta was in turn held by the Phœnicians, Greeks, Carthaginians, Romans and Arabs. In 1090 it was conquered by Count Roger of Normandy. In 1530 it was handed over to the Knights of St. John, who made of it a stronghold of Christianity. In 1565 it sustained the famous siege, when the last great effort of the Turks was successfully withstood by Grandmaster La Vallette. The Knights expended large sums in fortifying the island and carrying out many magnificent works, until they were expelled by Napoleon in 1798. The Maltese rose against the French garrison soon afterwards, and the island was subsequently blockaded by the British fleet. The Maltese people freely requested the protection of the British Crown in 1802 on condition that their rights and privileges would be preserved and respected. The islands were finally annexed to the British Crown by the Treaty of Paris in 1814.

Malta was again closely besieged in the last war and again withstood the attacks of all its enemies. From June, 1940, to the end of the war, 432 members of the garrison and 1,540 civilians were killed by enemy aircraft, and about 35,000 houses were destroyed or damaged. In recognition of the part played by the Maltese people, King George VI awarded the George Cross to the island.

Government.—Following the report of a Constitutional Commission under the chairmanship of Sir Hilary Blood, a new Constitution for Malta was introduced by the Malta (Constitution) Order in Council, 1961, under which the Island became known as "the State of Malta". On Sept. 21, 1964 under the Malta Independence Order, 1964, Malta became an independent state within the Commonwealth. Elections under the 1964 Order were held in June, 1971, for the 55 seats in the House of Representatives and they resulted as follows: Nationalist Party, 27 seats; Malta Labour Party, 28 seats. Maltese and English are the official languages of administration and Maltese is ordinarily the official language in all the courts of law and the language of general use in the islands.

CAPITAL.—Ψ Valletta. Population (estimated, Dec., 1970), 15,464. Valletta Grand Harbour is one of the finest in the world; it is very deep, and large vessels can anchor alongside the shore. It is an important port of call and ship repairing centre for vessels, being about half-way between Gibraltar and Port Said.

FLAG.—Equal vertical stripes of white (next staff), and red; a silver George Cross outlined in red in top corner of white stripe.

Governor-General, His Excellency Sir Anthony Joseph Mamo, O.B.E., Q.C. (1971).

CABINET

Prime Minister and Minister of Commonwealth and Foreign Affairs, D. Mintoff.
Minister of Justice and Parliamentary Affairs, A. Buttigieg.
Education and Culture, Miss A. Barbara.
Finance and Customs, Dr. J. Abela.
Development, A. V. Hyzler, M.D.
Health, D. Piscopo, M.D.

Trade, Industry, Agriculture and Tourism, Dr. J. M. Stafrace.
Public Building and Works, L. Sant.
Labour, Employment and Welfare, Dr. J. Cassar.

MALTA HIGH COMMISSION
24 Haymarket, S.W.1
High Commissioner, His Excellency Arthur J. Sceri (1971).

BRITISH HIGH COMMISSION

7 St. Anne Street, Floriana, Malta, G.C.
High Commissioner, His Excellency Sir Noel Duncan Watson, K.C.M.G. (1970)..............£6,875
Deputy High Commissioner, J. S. Arthur.

1st Secretaries, A. G. L. Archer, O.B.E., M.C.; G. S. Forrest (*Labour*); D. W. R. Lewis (*Economic*); R. K. Robertson (*Commercial*).

2nd Secretaries, D. R. Roberts (*Administration and Consular*); R. E. Holloway; T. J. Allison (*Commercial/Information*).

British Council Representative, N. Sutcliffe, Piazza Indipendenza, Valletta.

THE JUDICATURE

Chief Justice and President of the Constitutional Court and of the Court of Appeal (vacant).

Vice President of the Constitutional Court and of the Court of Appeal, Hon. Prof. J. J. Cremona, Q.C., LL.D., D.Litt., Ph.D......£3.748

Judges, Hons. J. Flores, LL.D.; Prof. J. Xuereb, LL.D.; A. P. Gauci Maistre, LL.D.; V. R. Sammut, LL.D.; M. Curuana Curran, LL.D., F.R.S.A.; E. Magri, LL.D...........................each 3,307

Education.—In 1970–71 there were 109 primary and infant schools with 43,925 pupils, 4 grammar schools for girls with 3,412 students, 2 lyceums (grammar schools for boys) with 1,995 students, 4 secondary technical schools (2,638 boys, 1,616 girls), three technical institutes (and 2 annexes) with 1,357 students¹and 2 industrial training centres (and 4 annexes) with 324 trainees; 14 New Secondary Schools for boys with 5,195 students and 16 New Secondary Schools for girls with 5,455 students; a College of Arts, Science and Technology with 1,302 students and two teacher training colleges with an enrolment of 130 men students and 254 women students respectively. During the same year, 1,103 students were registered with the Royal University of Malta. There were 74 private schools (with 7,861 boys and 7,319 girls), of which 26 were subsidized by the Government. Adult education classes had an attendance of 550 in 1970–71. English and Maltese are taught in all classes in Government primary schools.

In religion the Maltese are Roman Catholics. The Maltese language is of Semitic origin, and is held by some to be derived from the Carthaginian and the Phœnician tongues.

Production, etc.—The islands are intensively cultivated. The chief export crops are potatoes, onions, tomatoes and flowers. Wheat, barley, clover and tomatoes are extensively grown on dry lands, while on irrigated land all the usual temperate climate and sub-tropical vegetables are grown. Tomatoes are grown on irrigated and non-irrigated land. Agriculture and ship repairing are among the principal occupations of the inhabitants.

Every effort is being made to increase the productive capacity of industry. An Aids to Industries Scheme was launched in April, 1959, to facilitate and encourage the process of industrialization. A fresh impetus was given to industrial growth by the constitution of the Malta Development Corporation, which took over the responsibility of executing the Aids to Industries Scheme by virtue of an Agency Agreement signed on April 27, 1968. The Corporation is also a development bank, with an equity capital of £1m. provided by the Malta Government.

Since the inception of the scheme, 361 applications for aid from 224 firms were approved; at the end of 1970, 152 of these firms were in operation, of which 71 are operating in Government factories on three fully-serviced industrial estates, 25 are in temporary premises provided by Government and the remainder in private factories; 47 new factories are under construction and are expected to be completed within the next few years.

During the last three years employment in aided units increased from 4,463 in December 1967 to 9,377 by December, 1970, estimated at 9 per cent. of the gainfully occupied population. During the same period sales by aided industries more than doubled from £8.1m. in 1967 to £17.6m. in 1970, with exports increasing from £5·7m. to £11·8m.

FINANCE AND TRADE

	1968–69	1969–70
Public revenue.....	£20,824,991	£24,037,829
Ordinary expenditure	20,116,252	23,986,086
Capital expenditure.	8,180,577	9,538,891

The Central Bank of Malta has the sole right of issuing legal tender currency notes and coins. In addition to its own notes, it continues to be responsible for notes issued under the former Currency Notes Ordinance 1949 and issues United Kingdom coins, of which the following are legal tender ½d., ¼d., 3d., 6d.; 1s., 2s., 2s. 6d.; 5p., 10p. and 50 p.

Trade.—The principal imports for home consumption are foodstuffs—mainly wheat, meat and bullocks, milk and fruit—fodder, beverages and tobacco, fuels, chemicals, textiles and machinery (industrial, agricultural and transport). The chief domestic exports are scrap-metal, hides and skins, potatoes, tomatoes and onions, smoking requisites, gloves, hosiery, beer, mineral waters, edible oil, tallow and fresh flowers. To these may be added exports effected by newly created industries, *viz.* fibres and yarns, rubber seals, flower cuttings, plastic goods, wine, mattresses and knitwear.

Trade with U.K.

	1969	1970
Imports from U.K..	£23,027,000	£25,695,000
Exports to U.K.....	5,382,000	5,760,000

Mauritius

Mauritius is an island group lying in the Indian Ocean, 550 miles east of Madagascar, between 57° 17′–57° 46 E. long. and lat. 10° 58′–20° 33′ S., and comprising with its dependencies an area of 805 square miles. The resident population at the census of 1962 was: Mauritius, 681,619; Rodriguez, 18,335; Lesser Dependencies, 1,062, made up of Europeans (mainly of French extraction), Asiatic races and persons of mixed descent. The total population, including dependencies, was estimated in 1970 at 834,000.

Mauritius was discovered in 1511 by the Portuguese; the Dutch visited it in 1598, and named it Mauritius, in honour of the Stadtholder, Prince Maurice of Nassau. From 1638 to 1710 it was held as a small Dutch colony and in 1715 the French took possession but did not settle it until 1721. Mauritius was taken by a British force in 1810. A British garrison remained on the island until its withdrawal in June 1960. The French language and French law have been preserved under British rule. English is the official language but French is the principal language of communication in the island.

Climate.—Mauritius enjoys a sub-tropical maritime climate, with sufficient difference between summer and winter to avoid monotony; further variation is introduced by the wide range of rainfall and temperature

resulting from the mountainous nature of the island. Humidity is rather high throughout the year and rainfall is sufficient to maintain a green cover of vegetation, except for a brief period in the driest districts.

CAPITAL.— Ψ Port Louis, population (1970), 139,681; other centres are Beau Bassin and Rose Hill (71,285); Curepipe (52,010); Vacoas and Phoenix (49,045) and Quatre Bornes (45,525). FLAG.—Red, blue, gold and green stripes.

Government.—A Crown Colony for 158 years, Mauritius became an independent state within the Commonwealth on March 12, 1968. The Constitution defined by Order in Council in 1964 was slightly altered in 1966 on the recommendation of the Banwell Commission, the effect being to increase the membership of the Legislative Assembly to 70, 62 elected by block voting in multi-member constituencies (including 2 members for Rodriguez) and 8 specially-elected members. Of the latter, 4 seats go to the " best losers " of whichever communities in the island are under-represented in the Assembly after the General Election and the four remaining seats are allocated on the basis of both party and community. The Constitution provides for the appointment of a Governor-General who acts on the advice of the Council of Ministers, collectively responsible to the Legislative Assembly. At the General Election held in August, 1967, the Independence Party led by Sir Seewoosagur Ramgoolam obtained 39 seats and the *Parti Mauricien* led by Mr. Gaetan Duval, 23 seats. After appointment of the specially elected members the composition of the Legislative Assembly was: Independence Party, 43; *Parti Mauricien*, 27. Mauritius became the 124th member of the United Nations on April 24, 1968. In December, 1969, the P.M.S.D. joined the Independence Party to form the Government of National Unity.

Governor-General, His Excellency Sir Arthur Leonard Williams, G.C.M.G. (1968).

COUNCIL OF MINISTERS

Premier and Minister of Defence, Information and Broadcasting, Internal Security and Civil Aviation, Dr. the Rt. Hon. Sir Seewoosagur Ramgoolam.
Minister of External Affairs, Hon. C. G. Duval.
(The Premier receives remuneration of *Rs.* 48,000 and 18 Ministers each *Rs.* 36,000.)

MAURITIUS HIGH COMMISSION
153 Grand Buildings,
Trafalgar Square, W.C.2
High Commissioner, His Excellency Dr. L. Teelock, C.B.E. (1968).
2nd Secretary, D. G. Facknath.

BRITISH HIGH COMMISSION
Cerne House, Chaussée Street,
Port Louis
High Commissioner, His Excellency Peter Anthony Carter, C.M.G. (1970)............... £5,765
1st Secretaries, R. G. Giddens (*Head of Chancery*); J. Quine; E. W. J. Crawley.

British Council Representative, P. J. C. Dart, Royal Road, Rose Hill.

JUDICIARY
Chief Justice, Sir Maurice Latour Adrien
Puisne Judges, W. H. Garrioch; D. Ramphul.

Defence.—A defence agreement signed between Britain and Mauritius on Mar. 12, 1968, provides for joint consultation on any request by the Government of Mauritius for assistance in the event of a threat to the island's internal security. The agreement runs for six years. It provides various rights and defence facilities in Mauritius for the United Kingdom, which agrees to help in training and equipping local police and security forces.

Education.—Regular classes are run up to University entrance level, facilities are available for the preparation of University external degrees. Primary education is provided in 332 schools of which 176 are government and the remainder aided. Secondary education is given in four government schools—one with a technical stream—13 aided and 127 private schools. There are also 3 senior primary schools one of which is co-educational, 5 vocational training centres, and a teacher training college. Education is not yet compulsory but over 89 per cent. of children in the primary age group go to primary school and more than 1 child in 4 in the secondary age group goes to secondary school. Recurrent expenditure on education in 1967–68 totalled *Rs.*31,530,000.

Communications.—There is an excellent harbour on the N.W. coast, on which the capital, Port Louis, stands, and the annual trade of the island passes entirely through Port Louis. The shipping entered in 1969 amounted to 2,487,000 metric tons, and the shipping cleared to 2,436,000 metric tons. There were 78 post-offices and postal agencies, 51 telegraph offices, 22 telephone-exchange offices and 16,793 telephone installations in the island. Mauritius is served by the international airport situated at Plaisance, in the south-east of the island, about 5 miles from Mahébourg. Scheduled services are operated by B.O.A.C., Air France, Qantas, South African Airways, Air India, East African Airways, Air Madagascar, Air Zambia and Lufthansa. There are 9 daily newspapers published, mostly in French with occasional articles in English, and 3 Chinese daily papers. The Mauritian Broadcasting Corporation has a monopoly of radio broadcasting in the country. Television was introduced in February, 1965.

Production, etc.—Of the total cultivable area of about 257,900 acres, in 1969 only 213,400 were under sugar, about 250 under aloe (regular plantations), 450 under maize, 8,400 under tea, 5,000 under tobacco, vegetables and other crops. The sugar crop of 1969 was 668,553 metric tons, 3·13 metric tons per acre.

Finance.—The main sources of revenue are income tax, customs and excise duties (mainly on imports) and there is an export tax on sugar.

	1969–70	1970–71*
Public revenue....	*Rs.*294,000,000	*Rs.*338,700,000
Public expenditure.	284,500,000	338,700,000

*Estimated.

The Public Debt, at June 30, 1969, was *Rs.*320,500,000.

Currency—*Rs.* = *Rupee* = 1s. 6d.

Trade.—Most of the necessities of life have to be imported from abroad. Apart from local consumption (about 26,500 metric tons), the sugar produced is exported, mainly to Britain, Canada and U.S.A.

	1968	1969
Total imports.....	*Rs.*421,100,000	*Rs.*376,700,000
Total exports......	354,018,176	365,741,327

Trade with U.K.

	1969	1970
Imports from U.K...	£4,813,000	£5,899,000
Exports to U.K.....	21,739,000	22,495,000

DEPENDENCIES OF MAURITIUS

Rodrigues, 350 miles east-north-east of Mauritius, area, 40 square miles. Population (1966) 20,600. Cattle, salt fish, sheep, goats, pigs and onions are the principal exports. The island is under the administration of a Magistrate and Civil Commissioner from Mauritius, who takes his orders from the Government of Mauritius. *Magistrate* Y. Pitchen.

Trade with Mauritius

	1968	1969
Total imports.....	Rs.8,481,064	Rs.6,605,388
Total exports......	1,298,845	1,466,343

Other Dependencies.—Two of the scattered groups of coral islands belonging to Great Britain in the Indian Ocean are administered by the Mauritius Government, being visited periodically by two magistrates, whose duty it is to inquire into the condition of the labourers, and settle any disputes which may be referred to them. The chief product is coconut oil. The other islands, including Six Islands, Peros Banhos, Salomon, Diego Garcia and Trois Frères, are now known as British Indian Ocean Territories and are no longer dependencies.

Republic of Nauru

The Republic of Nauru is an island of 8·2 sq. miles in size, situated in 166° 55′ E. longitude and 32′ S. of the Equator. It has a population (U.N. estimate, 1970) of 7,000 of whom two-thirds are Nauruans or other Pacific Islanders. There are Chinese and European minorities. About 43 per cent. of Nauruans are adherents of the Nauruan Protestant Church and there is a Roman Catholic Mission on the island.

Nauru was discovered by Capt Fearn, R.N. in 1798, and was annexed by Germany in 1888. It surrendered to H.M.A.S. *Melbourne* in November, 1914. Until 1968 Nauru was administered by Australia under an international trusteeship agreement which on Nov. 1, 1947, superseded a former League of Nations Mandate.

President, Premier and Minister of Foreign Affairs, Hammer DeRoburt, O.B.E., *born* 1922, *elected* May 19, 1968.

Minister of Health and Education, A. Bernicke.

Works and Community Services, B. Detudamo.

Finance, J. A. Bop.

Justice, D. D. Audoa.

Government.—Under Australian administration a Legislative Council of nine elected and five official members was established in 1966 and a four-member Executive Council. After negotiations at Canberra during 1967 between Mr. DeRoburt, then Head Chief of Nauru, and representatives of the Trusteeship powers Australia, New Zealand and the United Kingdom, and with the concurrence of the U.N. Trusteeship Council, Nauru became an independent State from February 1, 1968. It was announced in November, 1968, that a limited form of membership of the Commonwealth had been devised for Nauru at the request of its Government. A new Parliament was elected on Jan. 26, 1968.

Judiciary.—The Nauruan judiciary consists of a District Court, a Central Court and a Court of Appeal.

Education and Welfare.—Nauru has a hospital service and other medical and dental services. There is also a maternity and child welfare service. Education is available in 9 primary and 2 secondary schools on the island with a total enrolment of 1,797 pupils.

Production, etc.—There are valuable deposits of phosphates on the island which were purchased from the Pacific Phosphate Company in 1919 by the Governments of Australia, New Zealand and the United Kingdom for £3,500,000 and vested in the British Phosphate Commissioners. Royalties on phosphate exports (about £5,000,000 annually) have been paid partly to the Nauruans and partly into a trust fund which used income from investments abroad to pay for Nauru's administrative and social services. Phosphate mining employs 1,369 persons out of a labour force of 2,208.

The assets on Nauru of the British Phosphate Commissioners have been purchased by the Nauruans, control of mining and marketing passing to the Nauru Phosphate Corporation on July 1, 1970.

Trade.—Phosphate exports in 1968–69 amounted to 2,186,000 tons (Australia, 1,424,050; U.K., 73,800; N.Z., 526,950; Japan, 161,200). General imports were valued at $A5,224,924 in 1968–69, including $A212,616 from the United Kingdom.

Finance.—Total revenue in 1968–69 was $A16,447,858, mainly payments by the British Phosphate Commissioners ($A14,337,012); expenditure, $A13,368,774, including Education, $A550,992 and Health, $A242,409.

Trade with U.K.

	1968	1969
Imports from U.K......	£37,000	£1,231,000
Exports to U.K.........	783,000	336,000

Nauru took exports valued at £63,000 from U.K. in 1970.

FLAG.—Twelve-point star (representing the 12 original Nauruan tribes) below a gold bar (representing the Equator), all on a blue ground.

Republic of Nigeria

(*For* MAP, *see* Index).

Area and Population.—The Republic of Nigeria is situated on the west coast of Africa. It is bounded on the south by the Gulf of Guinea, on the west and north by Dahomey and Niger and on the east by the Cameroon Republic. It has an area of 356,669 square miles with a population (U.N. estimate, 1970) of 66,174,000. The population is almost entirely African. There are some 28,000 Europeans, Americans, Lebanese and others engaged in Government posts, commerce and Missionary work.

A belt of mangrove swamp forest 10–60 miles in width lies along the entire coastline. North of this there is a zone 50–100 miles wide of tropical rain forest and oil-palms. North of this the country rises and the vegetation changes to open woodland and savannah. In the extreme north the country is almost desert. There are few mountains, but in Northern Nigeria the central plateau rises to an average level of 4,000 feet. The Niger, Benue, and Cross are the main rivers.

The climate varies with the types of country described above, but Nigeria lies entirely within the tropics and temperatures are high. Temperatures of over 100° in the north are common while coast temperatures are seldom over 90°. The humidity at the coast, however, is much higher than in the north. The rainy season is from about April to October; rainfall varies from under 25 inches a year in the extreme north to 150 inches on the eastern coast line. During the dry season the *harmattan* wind blows from the desert; it is cool and laden with fine particles of dust.

CAPITAL.—ΨLAGOS, estimated population, 700,000. Other important towns are Ibadan (1,000,000), Kano (295,432), Iwo (158,583), Ogbomosho (319,881), Oyo (112,349), Oshogbo (208,966), Onitsha (163,032), Ife (130,050), Abeokuta (187,292), Ilesha (165,822), Enugu (138,457), Aba (131,003), Maiduguri (139,965), Katsina (90,538), Port Harcourt (179,563), Sokoto (89,817), Zaria (166,170). FLAG.—Three equal vertical bands, green, white and green. NATIONAL DAY.—October 1 (Republic Day).

GOVERNMENT

Following the military take-over of January 16, 1966, the Federal and Regional Constitutions were suspended, in relation to the offices of President, Prime Minister, Regional Governors and Regional Premiers, and Parliament and the Regional Legislatures were dissolved. The country was divided into 12 new States by decree in May, 1967—six in the former Northern Region, three in the former Eastern Region, the former Mid-West Region remaining as before, Western Region (*less* the Colony Province), and a new Lagos State, including the Colony Province formerly part of the Western Region. A Federal Military Government, made up of a Supreme Military Council and a Federal Executive Council perform the functions of the former Federal Government and Council of Ministers, while a Military Governor administers each of the 12 States (except East Central State which has a civilian administrator).

SUPREME MILITARY COUNCIL

Head of Federal Military Government and Commander-in-Chief, Maj.-Gen. Yakubu Gowon.
Chief of Staff, Brig. Hassan Usman Katsina.
Head of Navy, Rear Adm. J. E. A. Wey.
Head of Air Force, Lt.-Col. Ikwue.
(and the State Military Governors, see below).
Inspector-Gen. of Police, Kam Selem.
Chief of Staff, Supreme Headquarters, Brig. E. O. Ekpo.
Military Secretary, Col. G. Alley.

STATE MILITARY GOVERNORS

Lagos, Col. M. O. Johnson.
Western, Brig. R. A. Adebayo.
Kwara, Lt.-Col. D. L. Bamigboye.
N. Western, Usman Faruk.
N. Central, Lt.-Col. Abba Kyari.
Kano, Alhaji Audu Bako.
N. Eastern, Lt.-Col. Musa Usman.
Benue-Plateau, J. B. Gonwalk.
S. Eastern, Lt. Col. J. J. Esuene.
Central Eastern, Ukpabi Asika (*Administrator*).
Rivers State, Lt-Cdr. A. Diete-Spiff.
Mid-Western, Lt.-Col. S. O. Obgemudia.

COMMISSIONERS

Commissioner for External Affairs, Dr. Okoi Arikpo.
Works and Housing, Femi Okunnu.
Health, Dr. J. E. Adetoro.
Economic Development, Agriculture and Natural Resources, Alhaji Yahaya Gusau.
Mines and Power, Dr. R. A. Dikko.
Communications, Alhaji Aminu Kano.
Trade and Industry, Alhaji Ali Monguno.
Transport, Joseph Tarka.
Education, Wenike Briggs.
Information and Labour, Chief Anthony Enahoro.

FEDERAL EXECUTIVE COUNCIL

The *ex officio* members of the Federal Executive Council are the Head of the Federal Military Government, who is the Chairman of the Council, the Heads of the Services and the Chief of Staff, the Inspector-General of Police and Deputy Inspector-General of Police and the Attorney-General of the Federation. In addition there are 12 civilian members of the Council representing the 12 States, with Chief Obafemi Awolowo (West) as Vice-Chairman. Each civilian member is designated Commissioner and is responsible for certain government departments.

NIGERIAN HIGH COMMISSION

Nigeria House, 9 Northumberland Avenue, W.C.2
[01-839-1244]
High Commissioner, His Excellency Sule Dede Kolo.

BRITISH HIGH COMMISSION

Kajola House, 62-64 Campbell Street, Lagos.
High Commissioner, His Excellency Sir Cyril Stanley Pickard, K.C.M.G. (1971).........£9,000
Minister, K. A. East, C.M.G.
Deputy High Commissioners, Hon. I. T. M. Lucas (*Kaduna*); J. A. Pugh, O.B.E. (*Ibadan*); A. E. Huttly (*Benin*).
Defence Adviser, Col. D. M. Stileman, O.B.E.

British Council Representative in Nigeria, R. A. F. Sherwood, 8-10 Yakubu Gowon Street, Lagos. Regional centres at *Ibadan, Kano, Kaduna* and *Enugu* with libraries at centres and at *Benin*.

JUDICATURE

Chief Justice, Federal Supreme Court, Rt. Hon. Sir Adetokunbo Ademola, K.B.E. *returned 2/72*
Justices of the Federal Supreme Court, G. B. A. Coker; Sir Ian Lewis; Sir Udo Udoma; C. O. Madarikan; A. Fatayi-Williams.
High Court Judges, G. S. Sowemimo; S. O. Lambo; E. A. Caxton-Martins; J. A. Adefarasin; O. R. I. George; B. A. Adepipe; B. O. Kazeam; J. O. Kassim; S. D. Adebiyi; M. N. Q. Sagoe.

Education.—The University of Ibadan became a fully independent university on Oct. 1, 1962 (3,118 full-time students in 1968-69). The University at Nsukka, E. Central State (1966) had 2,579 full-time students in 1966. The Universities of Lagos, Zaria and Ife were formally established in 1962. In 1968-69 the University of Lagos had 2,062 full-time students, Ife 1,663 and Ahmadu Bello, Zaria, 1,745. Free and universal primary education for all children within the 6-12 year age group is now available in West and East Nigeria and in the Territory of Lagos.

Railways.—The Nigerian railway system, which is controlled by the Nigerian Railway Corporation, is the most extensive in Africa. There are 1,870 route miles of lines. There are two major bridges, one over the Niger at Jebba and one over the Benue at Makurdi. The latter is 2,624 ft. long, and it is believed to be the second longest in Africa. The North-western main line runs from Lagos to Kano (700 miles) through the important towns of Abeokuta, Ibadan, Ilorin, Jebba, Minna, Kaduna and Zaria. From Kano the line continues in a north-easterly direction to its terminus at Nguru. This line is also linked with Sokoto by a scheduled railway-road service from Gusau. The eastern line runs from Port Harcourt deep-water quay on the Bonny river through the thickly populated oil palm area to Enugu, where it serves the collieries. It then crosses the Benue and joins the north-western line at Kaduna, 569 miles from Port Harcourt. A branch line runs to Bauchi, Gombre and Maidugurie.

Roads.—There are 45,000 miles of motorable road. Most of the roads have gravelled or earth surfaces, but about 5,500 miles are tarred. An extensive programme of bituminous surfacing is now being carried out. A road bridge over the lower Niger between Onitsha and Asaba, providing a through trunk road between East and Mid-West Nigeria, was opened on Jan. 4, 1966.

Civil Aviation.—Trunk route services operated by Nigerian and the principal international airlines bring Nigeria within less than 12 hours of the Western European capitals and South Africa. There are also services to other parts of Africa and to the United States. A network of internal air services connects the main centres. Comprehensive radio navigational aids are installed at Kano and Lagos airports, and basic radio navigational facilities are provided at the twelve other aerodromes in regular use. Several flying strips are also in use by light aircraft. There is a network of meteorological reporting stations.

Production and Industry.—Nigeria is mainly an agricultural country. Four of the country's main agricultural products, *viz.* palm-oil and palm kernels, cocoa, cotton and ground nuts are of importance in Nigeria's export trade. Mineral oil is however the principal source of export revenue followed by cocoa and ground-nuts. Other crops include benniseed, capsicums, cassava, coffee, copra, guineacorn, gum arabic, kola-nuts, maize, millet, piassava, rice, rubber, tobacco and yams. There are important tin and coal-mining industries, at Jos and Enugu respectively. The coal is mainly used within the country. Nigeria is the principal source of supply of the world's requirements of columbite. Timber and hides and skins are other major exports. Some of the country's more important industrial installations include a steel rolling mill, a tin smelter, a petroleum refinery, a flour mill, a sugar factory, several cement plants and textile factories. Of growing importance is the local assembly of motor vehicles, bicycles, radio sets, fans and sewing machines. Other major manufactures include soap, cigarettes, beer, soft drinks, vegetable oils, canned food, confectionery, metal containers, plywood, footwear, tyres and tubes, paints, pharmaceuticals, plastic goods, glass containers, cement products, and roofing sheets.

Trade.—The principal imports are cotton piece goods, unmanufactured tobacco and cigarettes, jute bags and sacks, artificial silk piece-goods, motor-vehicles and spares, bicycles and spare parts, other machinery, cement, corrugated iron sheets and stock-fish. The principal exports are cocoa, groundnuts, palm-kernels, palm oil, timber (sawn and logs), hides and skins, cotton, columbite, tin ore, rubber and crude oil.

	1968	1969
Total imports......	£193,190,000	£248,700,000
Total exports......	206,510,000	319,700,000

★ Provisional

Exports to the U.K. include about one-third of the U.K.'s total cocoa imports, one-quarter of her tin imports, one-quarter of her dry hides, and 10 per cent. of her hardwoods.

Trade with U.K.

	1969	1970
Imports from U.K..	£77,904,000	£114,385,000
Exports to U.K.....	104,489,000	123,874,000

Finance.—The Federal Government collects the major part of the national revenue, making the allocations shown below to the States:

	1968–69	1969–70
Revenue..............	£147,710,050	£187,000,000
Expenditure..........	146,408,510	186,800,000
(allotted to States)..	54,437,390	73,000,000

Pakistan

Area and Population.—The Islamic Republic of Pakistan consists of two geographical units of West Pakistan and East Pakistan situated respectively to the north-west and north-east of the Republic of India and separated by about 1,100 miles of Indian territory. Pakistan has a total area of 365,529 sq. miles (W. Pakistan, 310,403 sq. miles; East Pakistan, 55,126 sq. miles). There is a U.N. estimate of the population in 1969 of 111,830,000, but other estimates in 1969 ranged as high as 125,000,000. (For Map, see p. 746.)

Government.—Pakistan was constituted as a Dominion under the Indian Independence Act, 1947, which received the Royal Assent on July 18, 1947.

In terms of the Act the Dominion of Pakistan consisted of former territories of British India. The Punjab States of Bahawalpur and Khairpur, with a Muslim population of almost 80 per cent. and with Muslim rulers, acceded to Pakistan in October, 1947. Boundaries of the Provinces of East Bengal and of Punjab (West Punjab) were defined by a Boundary Commission presided over by Sir Cyril Radcliffe, K.B.E., Q.C. (now Viscount Radcliffe). The following States also acceded to Pakistan: the Baluchistan States of Kalat, Mekran, Las Bela and Kharan, and the North-West Frontier States of Amb, Chitral, Dir and Swat. The States of Junagadh and Manavadar which had acceded to Pakistan, were occupied by India on November 8, 1947.

Pakistan became a Republic on March 23, 1956, when the provisions of the Constitution came into force. On October 7, 1958, however, this Constitution was abrogated and Pakistan came under martial law. General (later Field Marshal) Mohammed Ayub Khan, Commander-in-Chief of the Pakistan Army, was appointed the Chief Martial Law Administrator. On October 28, 1958, General Mohammed Ayub Khan also became President of Pakistan. Following a period of unrest in both East and West Pakistan, marked by rioting and mass strikes, President Ayub Khan on March 24, 1969, announced his resignation and handed over control of the country to the armed forces. The Commander-in-Chief, Gen. Yahya Khan, proclaimed martial law on March 25 and appointed military governors for East and West Pakistan. The Constitution was abrogated, National and Provincial Assemblies dissolved and Provincial Governors dismissed. Law and order were rapidly restored. On March 31, 1969, Gen Yahya Khan assumed the Presidency and formed a Council of Administration.

A *Legal Framework Order* published by the President in March, 1970, laid down the principles on which a new Constitution for Pakistan would be based, including the division of West Pakistan into four provinces—The Punjab, Sind, Baluchistan and the North West Frontier Province.

The first general elections ever held in Pakistan on a basis of " one man, one vote ", were held on Dec. 7, 1970, with a postponement until Jan. 17, 1971, in 9 East Pakistan constituencies which had been severely affected by the cyclone disaster in the Ganges delta. The Awami League in East Pakistan, led by Sheikh Mujibur Rahman, and the Pakistan People's Party in West Pakistan, led by Mr. Zufigar Ali Bhutto, won large majorities, the latter party in Punjab and Sind. Following the elections there was total disagreement between the two main parties on the question of a new Constitution for Pakistan, Sheikh Rahman insisting on almost complete autonomy for East Pakistan. The proposed opening of the National Assembly at Dacca on March 25, 1971, was postponed by the President, East Pakistan was declared an independent republic by the Awami League under the name *Bangla Desh* and civil war broke out. After some heavy fighting in various parts of the Province, the Pakistan Army claimed to be in control of all the important centres by about April 19, 1971.

Sheikh Mujibur Rahman disappeared from East Pakistan after being accused of treason by the President and was believed to be under detention in West Pakistan. (*see also* EVENTS OF THE YEAR.)

CAPITAL.—Rawalpindi (population 1961, 340,175). Pending construction of the proposed new federal capital (Islamabad), Rawalpindi is the seat of Government. FLAG.—The National Flag of Pakistan is dark

green, with white vertical stripe at the mast, the green portion bearing a white crescent in the centre and a five-pointed heraldic star. NATIONAL DAY.—March 23.

President, General Agha Mohammad Yahya Khan, *b.* 1917, *assumed office* March 31, 1969.

PAKISTAN HIGH COMMISSION

35 Lowndes Square, S.W.1

High Commissioner, His Excellency Lt.-Gen. Muhammad Youssuf (1971).

BRITISH HIGH COMMISSION

Diplomatic Enclave, P.O. Box 1122, Islamabad

High Commissioner, His Excellency John Laurence Pumphrey, C.M.G. (1971) £9,000

Deputy High Commissioners. R. A. Burrows, C.M.G.; A. J. Brown (*Karachi*); P. R. Oliver, C.M.G. (*Lahore*); F. C. D. Sargeant (*Dacca*).

Defence Adviser, Brig. G. H. Hoerder, M.B.E.

Counsellors, G. L. Bullard (*Head of Chancery*); R. H. Hobden, D.F.C. (*Economic*); D. F. Duncan (*Information*).

British Council Representative, D. A. Smith, O.B.E., P.O. Box 47, 56a Satellite Town, Rawalpindi. Regional centres at *Dacca, Karachi, Lahore* and *Peshawar*. Libraries at these centres and at *Chittagong, Islamabad, Rajshahi* and *Hyderabad*.

THE JUDICATURE

There is a Supreme Court of Pakistan. In addition the High Court of West Pakistan sits at Lahore, Karachi and Peshawar, and the High Court of East Pakistan at Dacca.

Chief Justice of the Supreme Court, Mr. Justice Hahmood-ur-Rahman.

Education.—School education in Pakistan is organized into 4 stages: Primary stage (5–10); Middle or Lower Secondary stage (10–12); Secondary stage (12–14), Higher Secondary stage (14–16). Institutions of higher education include colleges and universities for general as well as professional and technical education.

Teacher Training institutions are of three levels, turning out teachers for each of the stages above. Examinations for the first two stages are conducted by the Education Department for award of certificates. For the third stage examinations are conducted by the Universities and degrees are awarded upon successful completion of the courses. Funds for the maintenance of the Government institutions and for grants to non-government institutions and the universities are provided in the Provincial budgets.

There are about 61,000 primary and 9,000 secondary schools, 400 arts and science colleges, 18 medical colleges, 130 teachers' training institutions, 44 polytechnics and 12 universities, including 2 engineering and 2 agricultural universities.

Production.—Pakistan's economy is chiefly based on agriculture, which is the occupation of about 85 per cent. of the labour force. The principal crops are rice, wheat, sugar cane, cotton, jute, tobacco and tea. Pakistan has one of the longest irrigation systems in the world. The total area irrigated is about 30·3 million acres.

Other Products: Pakistan also produces burlap, hides and skins, leather, wool, ammonium sulphate, natural gas, soda ash, paper, newsprint, cement, fish, sports goods, surgical appliances and engineering goods, including switchgear, transformers, cables and wires.

Trade.—Pakistan imported manufactured goods and raw materials to the value of Rs.4,870,000,000 in 1968–69 and exported mainly agricultural products valued at Rs.3,305,000,000. Principal imports are listed as: machinery, food grains, iron and steel manufactures, transport equipment, electrical goods, mineral oils, chemicals, drugs and medicines, and vegetable oils. Principal exports are raw jute (Rs.730,000,000 in 1968–69) and jute manufactures (Rs.657,600,000), raw cotton (Rs.365,200,000), twist yarn and thread (Rs.224,300,000) and cotton fabrics (Rs.244,200,000); rice, leather and leather goods, and fish.

Trade with U.K.

	1969	1970
Imports from U.K.	£53,187,000	£49,249,000
Exports to U.K.	39,720,000	35,332,000

Finance.—The exchange rate of the Pakistan rupee is Rs.11·43= £1 (*see also* p. 83).

The State Bank has a capital of about Rs.30,000,000, 51 per cent. of which is held by the State. Total bank deposits in Pakistan on December 31, 1967, were Rs.1,001·87 crores.

The 1968–69 Budget showed income receipts of Rs. 688,930,000 and expenditure (including development expenditure) of Rs. 557,210,000.

Communications.—There are 13,021 post offices, 172,000 telephones, 12,500 miles of metalled roads, 13,300 miles of gravel roads, and over 100,000 miles of earth road, and about 5,000 miles of perennial and seasonable navigable channels in Pakistan. Railways have a total route mileage of 7,115. Roads in West Pakistan and waterways in East Pakistan, together with the railways, are the principal means of transportation.

Main seaports are Karachi (annual handling capacity 4,500,000 tons of cargo) serving West Pakistan and Chittagong (annual handling capacity over 3,000,000 tons of cargo) serving East Pakistan. The Chalna Anchorage, established in East Pakistan in 1960, has a handling capacity of about 1,500,000 tons a year. The main airport at Karachi occupies an important position on international trunk routes and is equipped with modern facilities and equipment. Pakistan International Airlines (P.I.A.) operates air services between the principal cities within the country as well as abroad. It has recently started flights to the U.S.S.R., China, Nepal U.A.R. and Japan.

Post and telegraph facilities are available to every country in the world.

PROVINCES OF PAKISTAN

PROVINCES OF THE ISLAMIC REPUBLIC OF PAKISTAN

1. WEST PAKISTAN

Martial Law Administrator, Lt.-Gen. T. Khan.

Chief Secretary, S. Afzal Agha.

Governor, Lt.-Gen. M. A. Rachman, M.C.

The Establishment of West Pakistan Act, 1955, came into force on October 3, 1955, and incorporated: (1) the former Governors' Provinces of the Punjab, North-West Frontier and Sind; (2) the former Chief Commissioners' Provinces of Baluchistan and Karachi; (3) the States of

Bahawalpur and Khairpur and the Baluchistan States Union; (4) the Tribal Areas of Baluchistan, the Punjab and the North-West Frontier and the States of Amb, Chitral, Dir and Swat, into the Province of *West Pakistan* with effect from October 14, 1955. The Province was reorganized with effect from July 1, 1970, into the four separate Provinces of Punjab (including Bahawalpur), Sind (including Karachi), North West Frontier Province and Baluchistan together with Islamabad Capital Territory and the Tribal Areas.

At the 1961 Census the total population,

excluding the Federal Territory of Karachi, was 42,947,835 (including 97,540 non-Pakistanis).

West Pakistan (including the Federal Territory), has an area of 310,403 square miles; 97·2 per cent. of the population are Muslim; 0·5 per cent. Caste Hindu; 1·0 per cent. Scheduled Caste Hindu and 1·4 per cent. Christian. Running through West Pakistan are five great rivers, the Indus, and its tributaries, Jhelum, Chenab, Ravi, and Sutlej. The upper reaches of these rivers are in Kashmir and their sources are in the lofty Himalayas.

West Pakistan is one of the richest wheat-producing areas populated by a hardy peasantry with great martial traditions. Of the other crops grown, cotton, rice, gram, jowar, oil-seeds, sugar-cane and tobacco are the most important. There are large deposits of rock salt, which with cotton forms the principal export. The Province is served by the Pakistan Western Railway. The Pakistan International Airlines network covers practically the whole of the Province.

Ψ Karachi (estimated population, 1,916,000) is the largest city and seaport; Lahore, the former provincial capital had a population of 1,296,477 at the last Census (1961).

2. EAST PAKISTAN

Governor of East Pakistan, Dr. A. M. Malik, *appointed* August, 1971.
Chief Secretary, S. M. Shafiul Azam.

Dr. Malik was forming a council of Ministers in Sept., 1971, but no details had been announced at the time of going to press.

The Province of East Pakistan: area, 55,126 sq. miles, population (1961 census), 50,840,235 (of whom 80·4 per cent. are Muslim; 8·6 per cent. Caste Hindu; 9·8 per cent. Scheduled Caste Hindu; 0·7 per cent. Buddhist; 0·3 per cent. Christian and 0·1 per cent. others), comprises the Eastern territories of the partitioned province of Bengal and Sylhet, formerly a district of Assam (excluding certain thanas in the Karimganj sub-division).

East Pakistan is the principal producer of raw jute in the world. Other chief agricultural products are rice, tea, oil seeds, pulses, areca nuts and sugar cane. The chief industries are jute and cotton, paper, newsprint and chemical fertilizer.

CHIEF CITY (and Headquarters of East Pakistan): Dacca. Population 556,712 (1961 census).

Sierra Leone

Area and Population, etc.—The peninsula of Sierra Leone, situated on the West Coast of Africa, was ceded to Great Britain in 1787 by the native chiefs to be used as an asylum for the many destitute negroes then in England. At a somewhat later date the Colony was used as a settlement for Africans from North America and the West Indies, and great numbers of Africans rescued from slave ships have from time to time been liberated and settled there. The total area of Sierra Leone is 27,925 sq. miles, and the total population (1963 Census) is 2,183,000, of whom about 2,000 are Europeans, 3,000 Asiatics, 30,000 non-native Africans, and the remainder native Africans (U.N. estimate, 1969, 2,512,000) For administrative purposes, the interior portion of Sierra Leone is divided into 3 Provinces covering 12 Districts, each administered by a Resident Minister. The principal peoples are the Limbas and Korankos in the north, the Temnes in the centre, and the Mendis in the South.

CAPITAL.— Ψ Freetown (population 85,000). Freetown, which possesses the finest and most important harbour in West Africa, is 3,078 miles from Liverpool; transit 9 days by sea; 2 days by air; there are also air connections with most of the capital cities of the world, and an internal air service between Freetown and some of the more important towns in Sierra Leone. FLAG.—Three horizontal stripes of leaf green, white and cobalt blue. NATIONAL DAY.—April 27.

Government.—Sierra Leone became a fully independent state and a member of the British Commonwealth on April 27, 1961. There is a House of Representatives consisting of a Speaker and not fewer than 60 members, elected from constituencies established by an Electoral Commission.

The 1961 Constitution, providing for government by a Governor-General, through a Cabinet of ministers drawn from the House of Representatives, was in force until the General Election held on March 17, 1967. At this Election, the two main political parties obtained almost equal numbers of seats and Mr. Siaka Stevens, leader of the All People's Congress, was appointed Prime Minister by the Governor-General on March 21, 1967. On the same day Brigadier Lansana announced that he had placed the country under martial law to protect the Constitution. Two days later Brigadier Lansana, together with Sir Albert Margai and Mr. Siaka Stevans, was arrested by a group of Army and police officers who on March 25 formed a National Reformation Council. The Council proceeded to suspend the Constitution of 1961 and instituted an enquiry into the conduct of the 1967 General Election, concluding that the elections had been irregular, though the Commission of Enquiry reported that the All People's Congress had won the election and that Mr. Siaka Stevens' appointment as Prime Minister had been correct.

The National Reformation Council affirmed its intention to hand over the administration to a civilian government, but was itself overthrown by an uprising of lower ranks of the Army and police

on April 18, 1968. A National Interim Council succeeded the N.R.C. and the Chief Justice of Sierra Leone was sworn in as Acting Governor-General. Consultations among the successful candidates at the 1967 General Election having resulted in the formation of a National Government under Mr. Siaka Stevens, Parliament reopened on June 26, 1968. 16 Ministers were drawn from the All People's Congress, 2 were independent members and 2 Paramount Chiefs. Further ministerial changes were made on May 12, 1970.

An attempted *coup d'etat* by the Army Commander on March 23, 1971, was unsuccessful, not having the full support of the Army and its leader was arrested and later executed. The Prime Minister announced on March 28 that Guinean troops had been called in to assist his government, in view of the general unrest. The Acting Governor-General was dismissed and was succeeded on March 31, 1971, by the President of the Supreme Court, Mr. Justice Christopher Okoro Cole.

A Bill instituting republican status for Sierra Leone and providing for the appointment of the *interim* Governor-General as its first President was approved on April 19, 1971, and the Prime Minister thereupon declared Sierra Leone a republic. On April 21, Mr. Siaka Stevens was unanimously elected President.

Prime Minister, J. J. Karoma.
Minister of Foreign Affairs, S. A. J. Pratt.

SIERRA LEONE HIGH COMMISSION
33 Portland Place, W.1.
[01-636-6483-6]
High Commissioner, His Excellency Dr. Davidson
Nicol (1971).
Counsellor, Henry M. Lynch-Shyllon.
1st Secretaries, Simeon M. Jonjo; Edison M. Gor-
vie; S. K. Bart-Williams.
2nd Secretaries, Charles E. Logan.
3rd Secretaries, A. Renner-Thomas; Mrs. V. R.
Bart-Williams.

BRITISH HIGH COMMISSION
Standard Bank of West Africa Building,
Oxford Street, Freetown.
High Commissioner, His Excellency Stephen John
Linley Olver, C.M.G., M.B.E. (1969) £6,875
Deputy High Commissioner, J. Brasnett.
Defence Adviser, Lt.-Cdr. A. I. R. Shaw, M.B.E., R.N.
British Council Representative, J. A. B. Smith, P.O.
Box 124, Tower Hill, Freetown.

JUDICATURE
Judges of the Supreme Court, The Hon. Mr. Justice
C. O. E. Cole, C.M.G., O.B.E (*Chief Justice*); Hons.
S. C.W. Betts; C. A. Harding; S. J. Forster; P. R.
Davies, M.B.E; N. E. Browne-Marke; O. B. R.
Tejan.
Acting Judges, The Hon. Mr. Justice R. E. A. Hard-
ing; D. M. A. Macauley; S. Beccles-Davies;
Mrs. A. Macauley; K. O. Omatayo During.

Communications.—A railway runs inland from
Freetown to Pendembu (227½ miles) and a branch
line of 83 miles extends in a north-easterly direction
from Bauya to Makeni. A mining company, the
Sierra Leone Development Company, owns a
railway which runs for 52½ miles from the iron ore
deposits at Marampa to the shipping port of Pepel.
There are about 4,250 miles of road in the country,
of which about 330 miles are bitumen-surfaced.
There is a trunk line network of radio, and overhead
telephone and telegraph routes of approximately
3,000 miles, linking the Western areas with the
other provinces.
The Freetown international airport is situated at
Lungi, across the Sierra Leone River from
Freetown. The main port is Freetown, which
has one of the largest natural harbours in the
world, and where there is a deep water quay,
capable of berthing two large or three small ships.

There are smaller ports at Pepel and Bonthe. The
Sierra Leone Broadcasting Service operates a direct
service, and is responsible for the Freetown Transistor Radio Service. Broadcasts are made daily in
several of the more important indigenous languages,
in addition to English.

Education.—There are 976 primary schools in
Sierra Leone, 23 secondary schools in the Western
Province and 46 in other areas. Technical educa-
tion is provided in the two Government Technical
Institutes, situated in Freetown and Kenema, in two
Trade Centres and in the technical training establish-
ments of the mining companies. Teacher training
is carried out in two Government and four Church
Mission training colleges in the Provinces, and in
the Milton Margai Training College near Freetown.
The University of Sierra Leone (1967) consists of
Fourah Bay College (1960) and Njala University
College (1964).

Production and Trade.—In the Western area, farming is largely confined to the production of cassava
and garden crops, such as maize and vegetables, for
local consumption. In the Provincial areas, the
principal agricultural product is rice, which is the
staple food of the country and export crops such as
palm kernels, cocoa beans, coffee and ginger.
The economy depends largely on mineral exports, principally diamonds and iron ore (80 per
cent.). Diamonds are mined by a British company
at concessions in the Yeugema and Kono districts
and elsewhere by individual operators. Government purchases of diamonds in 1969 totalled
£16,900,000 (1968, £12,700,000). Exports of
iron ore and concentrates in 1969 amounted to
2,400,000 tons (£4,900,000). Some 450,000 tons
of bauxite are produced annually.
Total exports in 1969 were valued at £44,500,000;
imports, £46,350,000.

	1969	1970
Imports from U.K. .	£13,406,000	£12,530,000
Exports to U.K	36,165,000	31,448,000

Finance.—In August, 1964, Sierra Leone adopted
decimal currency. The basic unit is the *leone*
(worth 50p). It is divided into 100 cents.
Total revenue was estimated at £25,500,000 in
1970-71; expenditure on ordinary budget
£23,150,000. Development expenditure was
estimated at £6,600,000

Singapore

The Republic of Singapore consists of the island of Singapore and a number of smaller islands, covering
a total area of 224·5 square miles. Singapore Island is 26 miles long and 14 miles in breadth and is situated
just north of the Equator off the southern extremity of the Malay Peninsula, from which it is separated by
the Straits of Johore. A causeway, carrying a road and railway, crosses the three-quarters of a mile to the
mainland. The highest point of the island is 581 feet above sea level. *Climate.*—The climate is hot and
humid and there are no clearly defined seasons. Rainfall averages 96 inches a year and temperature ranges
from 21°-34° C. (70°-93° F.). *Population.*—Estimated at 2,074,507 on December 31, 1970, the population
is multi-racial with a preponderance of Chinese. The racial groups were estimated in 1970 to be divided
as follows: Chinese—1,579,866; Malays—311,379; Indians and Pakistanis—145,169; Other (Europeans,
Eurasians, etc.), 38,093. At least 6 Chinese dialects are used and Malay, Mandarin, Tamil and English
are the official languages. FLAG.—Horizontal bands of red over white; crescent with five five-point
stars on red band near staff. NATIONAL DAY.—August 9.
Government.—Singapore, where Sir Stamford Raffles had first established a trading post under the East
India Company in 1819, was incorporated with Penang and Malacca to form the Straits Settlements in 1826.
The Straits Settlements became a Crown Colony in 1867. Singapore fell into Japanese hands in 1942 and
civil government was not restored until 1946, when it became a separate colony. Internal self-government
and the title " State of Singapore " were introduced in 1959. Singapore became a state of Malaysia when
the Federation was enlarged in September, 1963, but left Malaysia and became an independent sovereign
state within the Commonwealth on August 9, 1965. Singapore adopted a Republican constitution from
that date, the Yang di-Pertuan Negara being re-styled President. There is a Cabinet collectively responsible
to a fully-elected Parliament of 58 members.

HEAD OF STATE
President, Benjamin Henry Sheares, *assumed office as President*, Jan. 2, 1971.

CABINET

Prime Minister, Lee Kuan Yew, C.H.
Minister for Science and Technology, Dr. Toh Chin Chye.
Finance, Hon. Sui Sen.
Foreign Affairs and Labour, S. Rajaratnam.
Education, Lim Kim San.
Communications, Yong Nyak Lin.
Culture, Jek Yeun Thong.
Social Affairs, Enche Othman bin Wok.
Law and National Development, E. W. Barker.
Health, Chua Sian Chin.
Defence, Dr. Goh Keng Swee.

Speaker of Parliament, Prof. Yeoh Ghim Seng.

Singapore exchanges High Commissioners with Britain, Australia, New Zealand, India and Malaysia, and Canada and Pakistan are represented in Singapore.

SINGAPORE HIGH COMMISSION
2 Wilton Crescent, S.W.1
[01-235-8315]
High Commissioner, His Excellency Dr. Lee Yong Leng (1971).

BRITISH HIGH COMMISSION
Phoenix Park, Tanglin Road, Singapore 10
High Commissioner, His Excellency Samuel Falle, C.M.G., D.S.C. (1970) £6,875
Counsellors, W. J. Watts, O.B.E.; G. F. Finlayson (Commercial).
Defence Adviser, Gp. Capt. A. F. Jenkins.

British Council Representative, K. I. McCallum, Amber Mansions, 1A Orchard Road, Singapore 9.

JUDICATURE
Chief Justice of the High Court, Hon. Mr. Justice Wee Chong Jin.
Judges, Tan Ah Fah; F. A. Chua; A. V. Winslow; T. Kulasekaram; Choor Singh; D. C. D'Cotta.
Communications.—Singapore is one of the largest seaports in the world, with deep water wharves and ship repairing facilities. Ships also anchor in the roads, unloading into lighters. 38,000,000 tons of cargo were handled in 1969. Singapore Airport, 7½ miles from the centre of the city, has a runway 11,000 feet long. There are 28 miles of railway

connected to the Malaysian rail system by the causeway across the Straits of Johore, and 1,204 miles of roads, 847 miles of which are metalled roads maintained by the Government. There are both wireless and wired broadcasting services carrying commercial advertising. Television was introduced in 1963.

Production, etc.—Until 1960 Singapore's trade was primarily based on the distribution and sales of raw materials from surrounding countries and of finished products from developed nations. In the last decade, however, new manufacturing industries have been introduced, including ship building and repairing, iron and steel, textiles, footwear, wood products, micro-electronics, detergents, confectionery, pharmaceuticals, petroleum products, sanitary-ware, building materials, domestic electric appliances, plastic articles, transport equipment, etc.

Future developments include the reclaiming of a further 8,000 acres of marshy land at Jurong Industrial Town which when fully developed will cover 12,000 acres; extensions to other industrial estates, the building of 100,000 low-cost housing units over the next five years by the Housing and Development Board and the building of reservoirs at Kranji and Ulu Pandan together with associated treatment plant ($55m.). Growth industries will include ship building and repairing, metal working, chemicals, electronics, printing and publishing, aerospace engineering and tourism.

FINANCE

	1969–70*	1970–71
Revenue.......	S$1,015,645,000	S$1,041,270,000
Expenditure....	1,024,893,580	1,040,921,780
	*15 months	

Currency.—On June 12, 1967, the Singapore Currency Board began issuing its own currency, the $ *Singapore* (of 100 *cents*), equivalent to 2s. 9d. sterling. The S$ is freely interchangeable with the $ Malaysian and the $ Brunei (also issued on June 12, 1967).

TRADE

	1968	1969
Total imports...	S$5,083,833,546	S$6,243,592,384
Total exports...	3,890,684,596	4,740,681,565

Trade with U.K.

	1969	1970
Imports from U.K..	£49,465,000	£62,518,000
Exports to U.K.....	30,600,000	33,546,000

Swaziland

Swaziland is the smallest of the former three High Commission Territories in Southern Africa. Geographically and climatically, it is divisible into four physiographic provinces; the broken mountainous Highveld of the west, adjacent to the Drakensberg, with altitudes averaging over 4,000 ft., the Middleveld which is mostly farming country, about 2,000 ft. lower and the Lowveld, a hot scrubland region, bounded on the east by the Lubombo mountains, with an average altitude of 1,500 ft. The Lubombo mountains form the fourth physiographic province. Four rivers, the Komati, Usutu, Imbuluzi and Ingwavuma, flow from west to east, cutting their way through the Lubombo mountains to the Indian Ocean. The exploitation of these rivers is particularly important to the agricultural development of the middle and bush veld, where irrigation projects are giving the scenery a different aspect. The total area is 6,704 sq. miles and the population (estimated, May 1970), 451,000.

CAPITAL.—Mbabane (population, 14,000), the headquarters of the Government, is situated on the hills at an altitude of 3,800 ft. There are townships in the districts of Manzini (population 16,000), Hlatikulu (1,000); Siteki (1,400), Nhlangano (1,700), Pigg's Peak (1,400), Havelock Mine (4,100), Big Bend (2,900) and Mhlume (2,200). FLAG.—Five horizontal bands, crimson, bearing shield and spears device, bordered by narrow yellow bands; blue bands at top and foot.

Government.—The Kingdom of Swaziland came into being on April 25, 1967, under a new internal self-government constitution and became an independent kingdom in membership of the Commonwealth on September 6, 1968. Parliament consists of a Senate and House of Assembly. The House of Assembly has 24 elected members and six members who are nominated by the King. The Attorney-General is also a member but has no vote. The Senate has 12 members—six elected by the House of Assembly and six appointed by the King.
King of Swaziland, His Majesty Sobhuza II, K.B.E.

CABINET

Prime Minister and Minister of Foreign Affairs, Prince Makhosini Dlamini.
Deputy Prime Minister, Z. Khumalo.
Minister of Finance, L. Lovell.
Commerce, Industry and Mines, S. S. Nxumalo.
Local Administration, Prince Mfanasibili Dlamini.
Agriculture, A. K. Hlope.
Education, J. M. B. Sukati, M.B.E.
Health, Dr. A. Nxumalo.
Works, Power and Communications, P. L. Dlamini, O.B.E.

SWAZILAND HIGH COMMISSION
58 Pont Street, S.W.1.
[01-589-5447]
High Commissioner, His Excellency the Rev. Dr. A. B. Gamedze (1971).

BRITISH HIGH COMMISSION
Mbabane
High Commissioner, His Excellency Eric George Le Tocq (1971) £5,765

─────────

Education.—In 1970 the primary school enrolment was 69,055; secondary schools, 8,027.

Communications.—Swaziland's first railway was completed in 1964. It is about 140 miles long, starting at Ngwenya, 13 miles north-west of Mbabane, and connecting at the Mozambique frontier with an extension to the existing line between Lourenço Marques and Goba. Principal export traffic on the railway is the iron ore mined at Bomvu Ridge, near Ngwenya, by the Swaziland Iron Ore Development Company. A large part of the country's passenger and goods traffic is carried by privately-owned motor transport services. Besides these, the South African Railways Road Motor Services maintain regular goods and passenger services between Mbabane and Manzini and the main railheads in South Africa which serve Swaziland—Breyton, Piet Retief, Komatipoort, Hectorspruit and Golela. There are post offices, telegraph and telephone offices at all the chief centres.

Production.—Iron ore, which is sold to Japan, is the country's largest single export and in 1970 was worth R.11,041,208. Other major exports in 1970 were sugar, R.11,777,357; asbestos R.5,239,467; and wood pulp and other forest products.

Finance.—Government revenue for 1971–72 was estimated at R.17,241,000 and expenditure at R.16,505,000. Development aid from the United Kingdom was expected to total R.4,100,000 in the form of grants and loans.

Trade with U.K.

	1969	1970
Imports from U.K...	£134,000	£353,000
Exports to U.K.....	£9,830,000	£9,411,000

Tanzania

Tanganyika, the mainland part of the United Republic of Tanzania (Tanganyika and Zanzibar) occupies the east-central portion of the African continent, between 1°–11° 45′ S. lat. and 29° 20′–40° 38′ E. long. It is bounded on the N. by Kenya and Uganda; on the S.W. by Lake Malawi, Malawi and Zambia; on the S. by Mozambique; on the W. it is bounded by Rwanda, Burundi and the Congolese Republic; on the E. the boundary is the Indian Ocean. Tanganyika has a coastline of about 500 miles and an area of 362,820 sq. miles (including 20,650 sq. miles of water). The greater part of the country is occupied by the Central African plateau from which rise, among others, Mt. Kilimanjaro, the highest point on the continent of Africa (19,340 ft.) and Mt. Meru (14,979 ft.). The Serengeti National Park, which covers an area of 6,000 sq. miles in the Arusha, Mwanza and Mara Regions, is famous for its variety and number of species of game.

The African population consists mostly of tribes of mixed Bantu race. The total population of Tanzania at the Census held in August, 1967, was 12,311,991 (estimated, July, 1969, 12,926,000); Africans form a very large majority, while the Europeans, the Asians, and other non-Africans form a small minority. Annual average population growth is 2·7 per cent. The total population of Zanzibar at the 1967 census was 354,815 (estimated, 1969, 369,000). Swahili is the national and official language. English is the second official language, both for educational and government purposes.

Zanzibar.—Formerly ruled by the Sultan of Zanzibar, and a British Protectorate until Dec. 10, 1963, Zanzibar consists of the islands of Zanzibar and Pemba, Lamu, Manda, Patta, and Siu. It has a total area of approximately 1,000 square miles. The islands produce a large part of the world's supply of cloves and clove oil, and coconuts, coconut oil and copra are also produced.

Zanzibar became internally self-governing on June 24, 1963 and fully independent on Dec. 10, 1963. A revolutionary party seized power on Jan. 12, 1964, and the Sultan was forced to leave the country. Later Zanzibar united with Tanganyika (*see* below).

CAPITAL.—Ψ Dar es Salaam (population 272,743). Other towns are Ψ Tanga 61,061); Mwanza (34,861); Arusha (32,452); Moshi (26,853); Morogoro (25,262); Dodoma (23,559); Iringa (21,746); Tabora (20,994) and Mtwara (20,396). In Zanzibar, the chief town and seaport of that name (population, 68,490) provides facilities for shipping and trade. There are also aerodromes at Zanzibar and at Pemba.

FLAG.—Green (above) and blue; divided by diagonal black stripe bordered by gold, running from bottom (next staff) to top (in fly). NATIONAL DAY.—December 9.

President of the United Republic, Julius Kambarage Nyerere, *b.* 1922; *elected* Nov. 1962; *took office* Dec. 9, 1962; *re-elected* Sept., 1965 and Nov., 1970.

Vice Presidents, Sheikh Abeid Amani Karume; R. M. Kawawa.

GOVERNMENT

Following a constitutional conference held in Dar es Salaam in March, 1961, Tanganyika became an independent state and a member of the British Commonwealth on December 9, 1961.

Tanganyika became a Republic, within the Commonwealth, on December 9, 1962, with an executive President, elected by universal suffrage, who is both the Head of State and Head of the Government. A presidential election will be held whenever Parliament is dissolved, and the presidency is closely linked with the official party, the Tanganyika African National Union (TANU), since Tanzania is a one-party state. The National Assembly is composed of 107 elected members from the mainland, 10 members appointed by the President (from both Tanganyika and Zanzibar), 15 National Members (elected by the National Assembly after nomination by various national institutions), 20 Regional Commissioners, up to 32 members of the Zanzibar Revolutionary Council, and up to 20 other Zanzibar members appointed by the President in agreement with the President of Zanzibar.

On April 25, 1964, following a Parliamentary ratification of an agreement signed by the President

of the Republic of Tanganyika and the President of the People's Republic of Zanzibar and Pemba, Tanganyika united with Zanzibar to form a new sovereign state. By this agreement, the President of the United Republic is Julius K. Nyerere; the First Vice-President is Sheikh Abeid Amani Karume (former President of Zanzibar and Pemba) and the Second Vice-President is Rashidi Mfaume Kawawa (of Tanganyika) who is also the leader of the Government business in the National Assembly of the United Republic. The Vice-Presidents and Ministers form the Cabinet of the Union Government, which is presided over by the President. There are 8 Zanzibar Ministers and Junior Ministers in the Union Government and 10 other Zanzibar ministers in the National Assembly of the United Republic.

Zanzibar has its own legislature which legislates for matters which are not under the Union Government, *e.g.* education, agriculture, health and community development.

CABINET

The President.
The Vice-Presidents.
Minister for Agriculture, Food and Co-operatives, Hon. D. N. M. Bryceson.
Commerce and Industries, Hon. P. Bomani.
Communications, Transport and Labour, Hon. J. M. Lusinde.
Economic Affairs and Development Planning, Hon. A. M. Babu.
Finance, Hon. A. H. Jamal.
Health and Social Insurance, Hon. L. N. Sijaona.
Home Affairs, Hon. S. A. Maswanya.
Natural Resources and Tourism, Hon. H. Makame.
Information and Broadcasting, Hon. J. D. Namfua.
Water Development and Power, Hon. Dr. W. K. Chagula.
Lands, Housing and Urban Development, Hon. J. A. Mhaville.
Regional Administration and Rural Development, Hon. P. A. Kisume.
National Education, Hon. C. Y. Mgonja.
Ministers of State, Hons. P. A. Kisumo (*Regional Admin.*); A. Jumbe; I. M. Bhoke Munanka; I. Melinawinga; (*Foreign Affairs*); Shaikh Ali Hassan Masenyi (*President's Office*).

TANZANIA HIGH COMMISSION
43 Hertford Street, W.1.
[01-499-8951]
High Commissioner, His Excellency Philemon Paul Muro (1969).

BRITISH HIGH COMMISSION
Dar es Salaam.
High Commissioner, His Excellency Horace Phillips, C.M.G. (1968) £6,875

British Council Representative, W. M. Emslie, O.B.E. Office and library at *Moshi.*

Chief Justice of Tanzania, Hon. P. T. Georges.

EDUCATION
Education is a joint undertaking by the Government, local authorities and voluntary agencies, including missions. Most schools are either wholly or partly financed by Government or by local authorities.

Technical and vocational education is provided at two Government trade schools and at the Dar es Salaam Technical College. A college has been established at Chang'ombe, Dar es Salaam. For higher education most Tanzanian students go to the University of Dar es Salaam, other East African universities, or to Universities and Colleges outside East Africa—mainly in Britain.

PRODUCTION AND TRADE
The economy is based mainly on the production and export of primary produce and the growing of foodstuffs for local consumption. The chief commercial crops are sisal, cotton, coffee and oilseeds. The most important minerals are diamonds, gold, lead and mica. Hides and skins are another valuable export. Industry is at present largely concerned with the processing of raw materials for either export or local consumption. There is also a healthy growth of secondary manufacturing industries, including factories for the manufacture of leather and rubber footwear, knitwear, razor blades, cigarettes and textiles, and a wheat flour mill.

TRADE WITH U.K.

	1969	1970
Imports from U.K.	£17,985,000	£19,583,000
Exports to U.K.....	23,954,000	23,963,000

Trinidad and Tobago

AREA AND POPULATION

Trinidad, the most southerly of the West Indian Islands, lies close to the north coast of the continent of S. America, the nearest point of Venezuela being 7 miles distant. The island is situated between 10° 3′–10° 50′ N. lat. and 60° 55′–61° 56′ W. long., and is about 50 miles in length by 37 in width, with an area of 1,864 sq. miles. *Population.*—Of the population in 1970 (estimated at 1,010,000), 43 per cent. are African, 36 per cent East Indian, 2 per cent. European, 1 per cent. Chinese, and the rest mixed.

The island was discovered by Columbus in 1498, was colonized in 1532 by the Spaniards, capitulated to the British under Abercromby in 1797, and was ceded to Britain under the Treaty of Amiens (March 25, 1802). Two mountain systems, the Northern and Southern Ranges, stretch across almost its entire width and a third, the Central Range lies somewhat diagonally across its middle portion; otherwise the island is mostly flat. The highest peaks are in the Northern Range (Aripo 3,085 ft., El Tucuche 3,072 ft.). The climate is tropical with temperatures ranging from 82° F. by day to 74° F. by night and a rainfall averaging 82·7 inches a year. There is a well-marked dry season from January to May and a wet season from June to December. The nights are invariably cool. The main tourist season is from December to April.

Tobago lies between 11° 9′ and 11° 21′ N. lat. and between 60° 30′ and 60° 50′ W. long., about 75 miles south-east of Grenada, 19 miles north-east of Trinidad, and 120 miles S.W. of Barbados. It was ceded to the British Crown in 1814 and amalgamated with Trinidad in 1888. The island is 26 miles long, and 7½ wide, and has an area of 116 sq. miles, with a population (Census of 1960) of 33,333. It is one of the healthiest of the West Indies and a popular tourist resort. The main town is Ψ Scarborough.

Other Islands.—Corozal Point and Icacos Point, the N.W. and S.W. extremities of Trinidad, enclose the Gulf of Paria, and west of Corozal Point lie several islands, of which Chacachacare, Huevos, Monos and Gaspar Grande are the most important.

CAPITAL.— Ψ Port of Spain (population 93,954), one of the finest towns in the West Indies, with sewerage, electric lighting, omnibus and telephone services. Other towns of importance are Ψ San Fernando (population, 39,830), about 33 miles south of the capital, and Arima (population, 11,792).

FLAG.—Black diagonal stripe bordered with white stripes, running from top by staff, all on a red field.
NATIONAL DAY.—August 31 (Independence Day).

GOVERNMENT

The Territory of Trinidad and Tobago became an independent state and a member of the British Commonwealth on August 31, 1962, under the Trinidad and Tobago Independence Act, 1962. There is a Parliament consisting of a Senate and a House of Representatives with an elected Speaker and 36 members. The Senate has 24 members of whom 13 are appointed on the advice of the Prime Minister, 4 on the advice of the Leader of the Opposition and 7 on the advice of the Prime Minister after consultation with religious, economic and social organizations.

Governor-General, His Excellency Sir Solomon Hochoy, G.C.M.G., G.C.V.O., O.B.E. (1962).

CABINET

Prime Minister, Dr. the Rt. Hon. Eric Williams, C.H., D.Phil.

Minister of Finance, Planning and Development, G. Chambers.

Industry and Commerce, Petroleum and Mines, Sen. Hon. O. R. Padmore.

External Affairs and West Indian Affairs, Hon. K. Mohammed.

Education and Culture, Mrs. I. Teshea.

Agriculture, Lands and Fisheries, Hon. L. M. Robinson.

Works, Hon. V. L. Campbell.

Interior and Personnel, Hon. G. A. Montano.

Attorney-General and Minister for Legal Affairs, Hon. Karl Hudson-Phillips.

Labour and Social Security, Hon. E. Mahabir.

Health, Sen. Hon. F. C. Prevatt.

Public Utilities and Housing, Sen. Hon. D. Pierre.

Local Government and Social Welfare, Hon. A. Thompson.

National Security, Hon. B. Pitt.

Tobago Affairs, Hon. W. Winchester.

There are in addition 4 Ministers of State.

President of the Senate, Hon. J. H. Maurice.

Speaker of the House of Representatives, Hon. C. A. Thomasos.

Chief Justice (vacant).

TRINIDAD AND TOBAGO HIGH COMMISSION
42 Belgrave Square, S.W.1

High Commissioner (vacant).

Acting High Commissioner, Eustace Seignoret.

Counsellor, J. S. Donaldson.

1st Secretaries, T. Spencer; Mrs. L. Dorset.

BRITISH HIGH COMMISSION
Port of Spain

High Commissioner, His Excellency Roland Charles Colin Hunt, C.M.G. (1970)............£6,875

Deputy High Commissioner, B. A. F. Pennock, O.B.E.

1st Secretary, J. P. B. Simeon (*Commercial*).

Education.—The system of education has been reformed to co-ordinate more closely the nursery, primary, junior secondary, senior secondary and university stages. The system provides for education of the pupils from 4–5 in nursery schools, 5–11

(or 15) in primary schools. Admission to secondary schools (11–18) is by common entrance examination at 11 years. A Primary School leaving Examination can be taken at 15. Junior secondary schools catering for the 11–14 group are being introduced to ease the shortage of places at secondary level. A General Certificate of Education giving admission to the University of the West Indies is taken in senior secondary schools. The Government Polytechnic Institute was established in 1959.

Communications.—There are some 4,000 miles of all-weather roads. The only general cargo port is Port of Spain but there are specialized port facilities elsewhere for landing crude oil, loading refinery products and sugar and for landing, storing and trans-shipping bauxite and cement. Regular shipping services call at Port of Spain, which is also a port for the many small inter-island craft. International scheduled airlines, including the national airline, B.W.I.A., use Piarco International Airport outside Port of Spain. The local Arawak Airline and B.W.I.A. also use Crown Point Airport in Tobago.

There are two commercial broadcasting stations, one rediffusion station and one commercial television station. There is an internal telephone system and good external telephone and telegraph connections.

Production.—Oil is extracted from land and sea wells for refining locally and large quantities of crude oil are also imported. The most important agricultural crop is sugar, but there is a growing diversification into other crops for local use and export. There is considerable industrialization, which already includes the manufacture of cement, chemicals, tyres, clothing, soap, furniture and foodstuffs.

Total exports in 1970 amounted to TT$963 million of which more than three-quarters was on account of exports of crude oil and petroleum products. The other principal exports were sugar and sugar preparations, ammonium compounds, tar oils, coffee and cocoa beans and fertilizer. Total imports in 1970 were TT$1,087 million of which over half was accounted for by imports of crude oil.

FINANCE

The following statistics are from official Trinidad and Tobago publications: figures in TT$ millions (TT$4·80 = £1).

	1969	1970*
Revenue..................	349	348
Expenditure..............	326	389
Gross public debt..........	379	393

*Estimated

TRADE

	1969	1970
Imports............	956	1,087
Exports............	949	963

	1969	1970
Imports from U.K..	£24,866,000	£28,131,000
Exports to U.K.....	21,688,000	19,309,000

Uganda

Situated in Eastern Africa, Uganda is flanked by the Congolese Republic, the Sudan, Kenya and on the south by Tanganyika and Rwanda. Large parts of Lakes Victoria, Edward and Albert are within its boundaries, as are Lakes Kyoga and Salisbury and the course of the River Nile from its outlet from Lake Victoria to the Sudan frontier post at Nimule. Despite its tropical location, Uganda's climate is tempered by its situation some 3,000 ft. above sea level, and well over that altitude in the highlands of the Western and Eastern Regions. Temperatures seldom rise above 85° F. (29° C.) or fall below 60° F. (15° C.). The rainfall averages about 50 inches a year, which means that the country is covered in a lush green cloak for most of the year. Uganda has excellent tourist facilities, including three National Parks with a wide

variety of wildlife and flora good hotels, air and land communications to service these Parks, and a wide range of scenery.

Area and Population.—Uganda has an area of 91,000 square miles (water and swamp 16,400 square miles) and a population (estimated, 1970) of 9,764,000. The total includes some 9,000 Europeans and 93,000 Asians. The official language of Uganda is English. The main local vernaculars are of Bantu, Luo and Hamitic origins. Ki-Swahili is generally understood in trading centres. CAPITAL.—Kampala (population of Greater Kampala, 331,000). FLAG.—Six horizontal stripes of black, yellow and red (repeated) with a crested emblem on a white orb in the centre. NATIONAL DAY.—October 9 (Independence Day).

Government.—Uganda became an independent state and a member of the Commonwealth on October 9, 1962, after some 70 years of British rule. A Republic was instituted on September 8, 1967, under an executive President, assisted by a Cabinet of Ministers.

Early on Jan. 25, 1971, while the President, A. Milton Obote, was in Singapore at the 1971 Commonwealth Prime Ministers' Meeting, the Uganda Army, with the co-operation of the police forces, assumed control of the country. All political activity in Uganda was suspended. On Jan. 26, 1971, Maj.-Gen. Idi Amin, the Army Commander, proclaimed himself Head of State, having previously announced that there would be an early return to civilian rule " after free and fair general elections". There was some short-lived military opposition in northern parts of Uganda, by troops loyal to Dr. Obote. On Feb. 2, Gen. Amin announced the suspension of certain parts of the Constitution, dissolution of Parliament and the formation of a Defence Council under his own Chairmanship. An advisory Council of Ministers was sworn in on Feb. 5, 1971.

Head of State and Commander in Chief of the Armed Forces, Maj.-Gen. Idi Amin, *born* 1926, *assumed office* Jan. 26, 1971.

COUNCIL OF MINISTERS

Minister of Foreign Affairs, W. Kibedi.
Interior, Lt.-Gen. E. A. T. Obitre Gama.
Finance, E. B. Wakhweya.
Education, A. Mayanja.
Minerals and Water Resources, E. W. Oryema.
Agriculture, Forestry and Co-operatives, F. L. Okware.
Commerce, Industry and Tourism, W. Lutara.
Public Service and Local Administration, V. A. Ovonji.
Planning and Economic Development, A. Kironde.
Culture and Community Development, Y. Engura.
Health, Dr. J. H. Gesa.
Works, J. N. M. Zikusoka.
Labour, J. M. Byagagaire.
Animal Industry, Game and Fisheries, Dr. W. B. Banage.
Information, W. Naburi.
Attorney-General, P. J. Nkambo-Mugerwa.
Minister of State for Defence, A.C. K. Oboth-Ofumbi.

UGANDA HIGH COMMISSION
Uganda House, Trafalgar Square, W.C.2
High Commissioner, His Excellency S. E. Luka-kamwa (1971).
Counsellors, S. M. Musoke (*Commercial*); J. C. Katurama (*Education*).
1st Secretary, G. W. Kinuka.
3rd Secretaries, R. E. Okidi; E. L. Ssendaula; B. O. Oywelowo.

BRITISH HIGH COMMISSION
10–12 Parliament Avenue (P.O. Box 7070), Kampala
High Commissioner, His Excellency Richard Mercer Keene Slater C.M.G. (1970)............£6,875
Deputy High Commissioner, A. H. Brind.
Defence Advisor, Lt.-Col. B. H. Bradbrook.

British Council Representative, R. E. Wright, P.O. Box 7014, National Cultural Centre, Kampala. Office and literary at *Fort Portal.*

Education.—Education is a joint undertaking by the Government, Local Authorities and, to some extent, Voluntary Agencies. The education system is divided into three distinct sectors—Primary, Secondary and Post-Secondary. The Primary course covers the first seven years of schooling. There were 434,995 pupils in grant-aided Primary Schools in 1962, which rose to 641,639 pupils in 1967. Education at secondary level falls into four categories—Secondary schools, which are of the Grammar type of school with a course extending over six years to Higher School Certificate; Technical Schools; Farm Schools; and Primary Teacher Training Colleges. Further education is provided at the Uganda Technical College, the National Teachers' College, the Uganda College of Commerce; and Agricultural Colleges. There is also in addition to these, several departmental training schools training staff for different departments. The Medical Department alone has eight such schools training nurses, midwives, medical assistants, health inspectors, and other medical staff.

University level education is available at Makerere University, Kampala; the University College, Nairobi, in Kenya, and the University College, Dar es Salaam, in Tanzania. Uganda students also go to universities and colleges outside East Africa for higher education.

Communications.—There is a first-class international airport at Entebbe, with direct flights to many places in Africa, America, Asia and Europe. There are 10 other state airports in Uganda. There are 3,702 miles of all-weather and 11,230 miles of other roads. Nearly 45 per cent. of the trunk roads are metalled, the remainder and all feeder roads are gravel roads of good standard. A railway network joins the capital to the western, eastern and northern centres. Lake, marine, road and rail services are operated by the E. African Railways and Harbours Administration.

Finance.—Currency is the *Uganda shilling* (Ug. sh. 17·143= £1 sterling). Total revenue in 1970–71 was Ug. sh.1,170,000,000 and expenditure Ug. sh. 1,121,000,000. Development account revenue 1970–71 totalled Ug. sh.414,200,000.

Trade, etc.—The value of the principal foreign export commodities in 1969 were: coffee, Ug. sh.779,900,000; cotton Ug. sh.250,900,000; copper, Ug. sh.120,300,000; tea, Ug. sh.9,300,000; animal feeding-stuffs, Ug. sh.42,100,000; and hides and skins, Ug. sh.26,700,000. Other crops grown include tobacco, sugar and groundnuts. Hydro-electric power is produced from the Owen Falls power station which has a capacity of 150,000 kWh. Plans are under way for the building of a second hydro-electric power station to produce 180,000 kWh.

	1969
Imports............	Ug. sh.910,000,000
Exports............	1,602,000,000

TRADE WITH U.K.

	1969	1970
Imports from U.K. .	£10,058,000	£9,960,000
Exports to U.K.....	17,466,000	17,652,000

Zambia

The Republic of Zambia lies on the plateau of Central Africa between the longitudes 22° E. and 33° 33′ E. and between the latitudes 8° 15′ S. and 18° S. It has an area of 290,587 square miles within boundaries 3,515 miles in length and a population (Census, 1969) of 4,054,000, including about 50,000 non-Africans.

With the exception of the valleys of the Zambesi, the Luapula, the Kafue and the Luangwa Rivers, and the Luano valley, the greater part of Zambia has a flat to rolling topography, with elevations varying from 3,000 to 5,000 feet above sea level, but in the north-eastern districts the plateau rises to occasional altitudes of over 6,000 feet. In many localities the evenness of the plateau is broken by hills, sometimes occurring as chains which develop into areas of broken country.

Although Zambia lies within the tropics, and fairly centrally in the great land mass of the African continent its elevation relieves it from the extremely high temperatures and humidity usually associated with tropical countries. The lower reaches of the Zambesi, Luangwa and Kafue rivers in deeper valleys do experience high humidity and trying extremes of heat, but these areas are remote and sparsely populated.

Government.—At the dissolution of the Federation of Rhodesia and Nyasaland, on December 31, 1963, Northern Rhodesia (as Zambia was then known) achieved internal self-government under a new constitution. Zambia became an independent republic within the Commonwealth on October 24, 1964—75 years after coming under British rule and nine months after achieving internal self-government. The country has a democratic constitution with a President as Head of State and Commander-in-Chief of the armed forces. He must be a citizen of Zambia and be at least 30 years old.

Parliament.—Parliament consists of the President and a National Assembly of 105 members elected for 5 years on a basis of universal suffrage by all citizens of 18 years of age and over. The President has the power to nominate up to five additional special members in order to enhance the representative character of the Assembly, or to obtain services of particular value. President Kaunda, under this section of the constitution, has nominated five members, two of whom have been made members of the Cabinet. The President is not a member of the National Assembly but may address it at any time. The National Assembly is presided over by a Speaker, elected by the Members of the Assembly. The United National Independence Party has 81 of the 105 elected seats. There is also a House of Chiefs, representing 230 chiefs throughout Zambia, with advisory functions.

CAPITAL.—Lusaka, situated in the Central Province. Population (Census, 1969), 238,000. Other centres are Livingstone, Kabwe, Chipata, Mazabuka, Mbala, Kasama, Solwezi, Mongu, Mansa, Ndola, Luanshya, Mufuiira, Chingola, Chililabombwe, Kalulushi and Kitwe, the last six towns being the main centres on the Copperbelt. *FLAG.*—Green with three small vertical stripes, red, black and orange (next fly); eagle device on green above stripes.

President, Dr. Kenneth David Kaunda, *assumed office* October 24, 1964.

CABINET

The President
Vice-President (also *Minister of National Guidance and Development*), Hon. M. Chona.
Minister of Finance, Hon. J. Mwanakatwe.
Foreign Affairs, Hon. E. H. K. Mudenda.
Rural Development, Hon. R. C. Kamanga.
Defence, Hon. A. G. Zulu.
Home Affairs, Hon. L. Changufu.
Provincial and Local Government and Cultural Services (vacant).
Legal Affairs, Hon. H. Chuula.
Information, Broadcasting and Tourism, Hon. S. Wina.
Lands and Natural Resources, Hon. S. Kalulu.
Power, Transport and Works, Hon. H. D. Banda.
Education, Hon. W. Nyirenda.
Labour and Social Services, Hon. F. Mulikita.
Trade and Industry, Hon. A. J. Soko.
Mines, Hon. H. Mulemba.
Central Province, Hon. W. Chakulya.
Copperbelt Province (*formerly Western*), Hon. A. K. Shapi.
Eastern Province, Hon. W. Nkanza.
Luapula Province, Hon. R. Makasa.
Northern Province, Hon. S. C. Mbilishi.
Northwestern Province, Hon. J. Mutti.
Southern Province, Hon. P. Matoka.
Western Province, Hon. J. B. A. Siyomunji.

Secretary-General to the Government, Hon. A. Milner.

ZAMBIA HIGH COMMISSION
7–11 Cavendish Place, W.1
High Commissioner, His Excellency Hon. A. Phiri (1971).

BRITISH HIGH COMMISSION
Lusaka
High Commissioner, His Excellency John Spenser Ritchie Duncan, C.M.G., M.B.E. (1971) £6,875

Counsellor, C. E. Diggines (*Commercial*).
Defence Adviser, Col. A. R. Kettles.

British Council Representative, J. Lawrence, Grosvenor Court, Cairo Road, Lusaka; and an office at Ndola.

JUDICATURE

There is a Chief Justice appointed by the President, all other judges being appointed on the recommendation of the Judicial Service Commission consisting of the Chief Justice, the chairman of the Public Service Commission, a senior Justice of Appeal and one Presidential nominee.
Chief Justice of Zambia, Hon. Brian Doyle.
President, Court of Appeal, T. Pickett.
Justices of Appeal, S. W. Magnus; B. T. Gardener.
Puisne Judges, J. J. Hughes; G. B. Muwo; L. S. Baron; F. M. Chomba; W. S. Bruce-Lyle.

Education.—In 1970 there were 694,469 pupils in primary schools and 52,472 in secondary schools. In 1969 the estimated Government expenditure on education, including both recurrent and capital fund expenditure, was K48,421,000.

Production and Employment.—The total value of marketed farm produce in 1969 was K32,866,596. Principal products were tobacco, maize, groundnuts, cotton, livestock and vegetables.

Mineral production was valued at K674,000,000 in 1970. The production of copper totalled 753,000 short tons. Ore reserves in the Copperbelt exceed 770,000,000 tons. On August 24, 1968, the first diesel fuel arrived by the new pipeline running 1,058 miles through Tanzania and Zambia to Ndola, the terminal. It is planned to switch the

pipeline over to transportation of crude oil when an oil refinery has been constructed in Ndola.

In June, 1970, 337,750 persons were estimated to be in full employment. Included in this figure are: mining and quarrying, 56,510; agriculture, forestry and fishing, 33,930; construction, 69,490; manufacturing, 36,810.

Finance and Currency.—Zambia adopted decimal currency on Jan. 16, 1968, the unit being the *Kwacha*, equivalent to 10s. of the former currency. The *Kwacha*=58p. sterling.

	1970	1971†
Revenue..........	K334,033,000	K421,336,000
Expenditure‡.......	224,315,855	409,184,000
Capital receipts‡....	143,546,000	177,339,000
Capital expenditure .	148,863,150	172,591,000

† estimated; ‡ includes appropriations from revenue to capital fund of K80,000,000 for 1969, and K80,000,000 for 1970.

TRADE WITH U.K.

	1969	1970
Imports from U.K...	£34,454,000	£37,866,000
Exports to U.K......	105,519,000	101,384,000

TONGA

The Tongan or *Friendly Islands*, a British-protected state for 70 years, became independent on June 7, 1970.

These islands are situated in the Southern Pacific some 450 miles to the E.S.E. of Fiji, with an area of 270 sq. miles, and population (estimated, 1970) of 87,000. The largest island, Tongatapu, was discovered by Tasman in 1643. Most of the islands are of coral formation, but some are volcanic (Tofua, Kao and Niuafoou or "Tin Can" Island). The limits of the group are between 15° and 23° 30′ S., and 173° and 177°W. Nuku'alofa, on the island of Tongatapu, is the seat of government. The present King Taufa'ahau Tupou IV, G.C.V.O., K.C.M.G., K.B.E., succeeded his mother, the late Queen Salote Tupou III, on December 16, 1965. The constitution provides for a Government consisting of the Sovereign, a privy council and cabinet, a legislative assembly and a judiciary. The legislative assembly has 22 members, with a Speaker, and includes the Ministers of the Crown, the two Governors of Island groups, and the representatives of the Nobles and of the people (seven of each), who are elected triennially.

Premier, Minister of Foreign Affairs and of Agriculture, H.R.H. Prince Fatafehi Tu'ipelehake, C.B.E.

Soil generally is fertile, the principal exports are copra and bananas. Revenue 1969–70, T$2,714,375; expenditure, T$2,628,841. There is a national debt of T$475,952. Total imports (1970), T$5,539,440; total exports T$2,676,382. The total shipping cleared in 1970 was 425,495 tons. Tongan currency is at parity with Australian currency in relation to sterling.

CAPITAL.—Nuku'alofa (15,455).

FLAG.—Truncated red cross on rectangular white ground (next staff) on a red field.

BRITISH HIGH COMMISSION
Nuku'alofa.

High Commissioner, His Excellency Sir Arthur Norman Galsworthy, K.C.M.G., (*resident at* Wellington N.Z.)

Deputy High Commissioner, H. A. Arthington-Davey, O.B.E.

WESTERN SAMOA

Head of State, H. H. Malietoa Tanumafili II, C.B.E. (April 15, 1963).

Prime Minister, Hon. Tupua Tamasese Leolofi IV (1970).

Formerly administered by New Zealand (latterly with internal self-government), Western Samoa became, on January 1, 1962, the first fully-independent Polynesian State.

The State was treated as a member country of the Commonwealth until its formal admission on August 28, 1970.

Western Samoa consists of the islands of Savai'i (662 sq. miles) and of Upolu, which with nine other islands, has an area of 435 sq. miles. All islands are mountainous. Upolu, the most fertile, contains the harbours of Ѱ Apia and Ѱ Saluafata and Savai'i the harbour of Ѱ Asau. The islanders are mostly Christians of different denominations. A census held on Nov. 21, 1966, showed a total population of 131,377, of whom 88·9 per cent. were Samoans and 10·1 per cent. part-Samoans; estimated population (July 1969), 141,000.

The chief exports are copra, cocoa and bananas. In 1969, the total trade was valued at: exports $4,630,005; imports $7,373,670.

TRADE WITH U.K.

	1969	1970
Imports from U.K......	£293,000	£323,000
Exports to U.K........	71,000	90,000

CAPITAL.—Ѱ Apia (population 25,000). Robert Louis Stevenson died and was buried at Apia in 1894.

FLAG.—Five white stars (depicting the Southern Cross) on a quarter royal blue at top next staff, and three quarters red.

Associated States, Colonies, Protectorates, etc.

Flags of the Dependencies.—Generally the dependencies use the Union Flag (" Union Jack ") or Blue Ensign bearing a badge of arms of the Dependency (with surrounding garland when used with the Union Flag). In a few cases, *e.g.* Bahamas (on ships) and Bermuda, the Red Ensign is used with badge. (*See also* ANTIGUA (W. Indies); BRUNEI; GRENADA (W. Indies); ST. KITTS (W. Indies); ST. LUCIA (W. Indies).

ASCENSION
(*See* ST. HELENA)

COMMONWEALTH OF THE BAHAMAS

The Bahama Islands are an archipelago lying in the Atlantic Ocean between 20° 55′–27° 22′ N. Lat; 72° 40′–79° 20′ W. Long. They extend from the coast of Florida on the north-west almost to Haiti on the south-east. The group consists of 700 islands, of which 30 are inhabited, and 2,400 cays comprising an area of more than 5,380 square miles. The population, at the 1963 census, was 130,220 (estimated, June 1970, 169,000). The principal islands include: Abaco, Acklins, Andros, Berry Islands, Bimini, Cat Cay, Cat Island, Crooked Island, Eleuthera, Exumas, Grand Bahama, Harbour Island, Inagua, Long Cay, Long Island, Mayaguana, New Providence (on which is located the capital, Nassau), Ragged Island, Rum

Cay, San Salvador and Spanish Wells. San Salvador was the first landfall in the New World of Christopher Columbus on October 12, 1492.

The Bahamas were settled by British subjects when the islands were deserted. The ownership of the Bahamas was taken over in 1782 by the Spanish, but the Treaty of Versailles in 1783 restored them to the British.

Tourism is the economic mainstay of the Bahamas, whose salubrious climate and fine beaches attracted 1,298,344 visitors in 1970.

GOVERNMENT

Internal self-government, with Cabinet responsibility, was introduced in Jan. 1964, and a constitutional conference held in London in September, 1968, approved changes giving the Bahamas a further measure of self-government. There are a Senate of 16 members and an elected House of Assembly of 38 members. The Governor retains reserved powers in the sphere of foreign relations, defence and internal security.

Governor and Commander-in-Chief, His
Excellency the Lord Thurlow, K.C.M.G.
(1968) .... B$30,550
Deputy Governor, L. M. Davies, C.M.G., C.B.E.
Prime Minister, Hon. L. O. Pindling.
Deputy Premier and Minister of Home Affairs, Hon.
A. D. Hanna.
Minister of Finance, Hon. C. E. Francis.
Transport, Hon. Dr. Doris L. Johnson.
Education, Hon. C. E. Francis.
Health and Welfare, Tourism and Telecommunications,
Hon. C. T. Maynard.
Labour, Agriculture and Fisheries, Hon. M. B. Butler.
Development, Hon. J. M. Thompson.
Works, Hon. L. Coakley.
Minister of State, Hon. C. Darling.
Chief Justice, Hon. Sir (William) Gordon Bryce,
C.B.E. B$17,250
Puisne Judges, Hon. H. C. Smith; Hon.
J. A. Smith, C.B.E., T.D............... 13,600
Industries.—A plant for the manufacture of cement and an oil refinery have been established in Freeport, Grand Bahama, where there are also a number of light industries. A rum distillery is in operation in New Providence and a multi-million dollar orogonite operation is in progress off the island of Andros. Other industries are those associated with the treatment of local agriculture (including sugar production) and marine produce, salt extraction and handwork, and timber-felling for plywood.

Education.—Education is compulsory between the ages of 5 and 14. There are 321 state-maintained or aided schools with a total roll of 42,806; there are also 76 unaided schools with a total roll of 12,991.

Civil Aviation.—Facilities for external traffic are provided by Pan-American World Airways, B.O.A.C., Air Canada, Air Jamaica, Eastern Air Lines, North-East Air Line and National and International Air Bahama, while Flamingo Airways, Bahamas Air Traders' Island Flying Service and Bahamas Airlines provide internal schedule and charter flights to the outlying islands. There are 16 return flights between Nassau and Miami, several daily flights between Nassau–Palm Beach–Fort Lauderdale and Tampa, and a regular service between Nassau and Montego Bay, Jamaica, besides regular trunk communication with London, New York, Toronto, Montreal, Bermuda and Kingston.

Communications.—There are a General Post Office in Nassau, 4 branch offices in New Providence and 109 sub-offices in the Out Islands. In 1970 more than 35,500,000 letters and prints were handled.

Wireless and telephone services are in operation to all parts of the world. There are 87 radio stations among the islands.

FINANCE AND TRADE

	1969	1970
Public revenue.....	B$78,800,000	B$97,587,191
Expenditure........	78,300,000	97,030,221
Total imports......	302,278,440*	337,116,409
Total exports.......	54,325,928	89,602,498

* Includes duty-free imports at Freeport, Grand Bahama, for the first time.

	1969	1970
Imports from U.K...	£13,446,000	£11,073,000
Exports to U.K.....	1,978,000	2,752,000

The imports are chiefly foodstuffs, manufactured articles, building material, lumber and machinery. The chief exports in 1968 were pulpwood, cement, rum, crawfish and salt.

CAPITAL. — ΨNassau. Estimated population (1970), 110,000. Nassau is distant from Liverpool 4,000 miles.

BERMUDA

The Bermudas, or Somers Islands, are a cluster of about 100 small islands (about 20 only of which are inhabited) situated in the west of the Atlantic Ocean, in 32° 18′ N. lat. and 64° 46′ W. long., the nearest point of the mainland being Cape Hatteras in North Carolina, about 570 miles distant. The total area is now approximately 20.59 sq. miles which includes 2.3 sq. miles leased to, or reclaimed by, the U.S. authorities between 1941 and 1957 under the terms of the 99 year lease. The civil population was 53,000 at the Census taken in October, 1970. The colony derives its name from Juan Bermudez, a Spaniard, who sighted it before 1515, but no settlement was made until 1609, when Sir George Somers, who was shipwrecked here on his way to Virginia, colonized the islands.

Vegetation is prolific, the principal trees being the Bermuda cedar (juniper), formerly of great importance for shipbuilding, but since 1943 almost entirely destroyed by blight. At one time the islands enjoyed a flourishing export in onions, potatoes, and green vegetables, but the imposition of tariffs in U.S.A. and the growing shortage of arable land made further growing for export unprofitable. The lily bud trade with Canada and U.S.A. and locally manufactured concentrates and pharmaceuticals are now the Colony's leading exports. Little food is produced except vegetables and fish, other foodstuffs being imported.

The Colony's economic structure is based on its importance as a tourist resort and as a naval base and from these sources most of its revenue is derived. Bermuda is now within two hours' air travel from New York, and in 1970 a total of 388,914 visitors arrived in Bermuda. The airport is used by B.O.A.C., Pan-American Airways, Air-Canada, Eastern, North-East and Qantas air lines and most cruise ships dock at Hamilton.

Expenditure on education in 1970 was $6,747,152 and was estimated to cost $8,346,794 in 1971. Free elementary education was introduced in May, 1949. Free secondary education was introduced in 1965 for those children in the aided and maintained schools who were below the upper limit of the statutory school age (16 from 1969 onwards). Cost of health and welfare services in 1970 was $2,821,496, and was estimated for 1971 at $5,361,373.

There are 4 radio and 2 television stations, one daily and 3 weekly newspapers and overseas telephone and telegraph services are maintained.

GOVERNMENT

Internal self-government was introduced on June 8, 1968. There are a Legislative Council of

11 Members and an elected House of Assembly of 40 Members. The Governor retains responsibility for external affairs, defence, internal security and the police.

Voters must be British subjects of twenty-one years of age or older at the time of registration, and if they do not possess Bermudian status, they must have been ordinarily resident in Bermuda for the whole of the period of three years immediately before registration. Registration is held every year during the months of February and March. Candidates for election must qualify as electors and must possess Bermudian status.

Governor and Commander-in-Chief, His Excellency The Lord Martonmere, P.C., K.C.M.G. (1964) *(excluding allowances)* ... $28,512

Executive Council

Government Leader, Hon. Sir Henry Tucker, C.B.E., M.C.P.
Labour and Immigration, Hon. Sir Edward Richards, C.B.E., M.C.P.
Finance, Hon. J. H. Sharpe, M.C.P.
Education, Dr. the Hon. E. S. D. Ratteray.
Tourism and Trade, Hon. D. E. Wilkinson, M.C.P.
Public Works and Agriculture, Hon. J. M. S. Patton, G.C., M.C.P.
Health and Welfare, Hon. Mrs. G. McPhee, M.C.P.
Marine and Air Services, Hon. J. E. Pearman, C.B.E., M.C.P.
Planning, Hon. C. V. Zuill, C.B.E., M.C.P.
Transport, Hon. F. J. Barritt, M.C.P.
Organization, Hon. J. R. Plowman, C.B.E.
Member without Portfolio, Hon. L. I. Swan, M.C.P.

President of the Legislative Council, Hon. G. O. Ratteray, C.B.E.
Speaker of the House of Assembly, Lt.-Col. J. C. Astwood, C.B.E., E.D., M.C.P.

Chief Justice, Hon. Sir Myles Abbott.
Puisne Judge, Hon. H. C. Barcilon.
Chief Secretary, I. A. C. Kinnear.
Secretary to Executive Council, W. W. Wallace, O.B.E., D.S.C.

FINANCE

	1970	1971*
Public revenue.....	$36,808,215	$39,591,048
Public expenditure..	34,023,246	40,891,313
Public debt (Dec. 31, 1970)...........	5,205,600	

* Estimated

Currency.—Bermuda Monetary Authority notes ($50, $20, $10, $5 and $1) and metal coinage (50c, 25c, 10c, 5c and 1c) became the currency of Bermuda on Feb. 6, 1970. Exchange Rate: $2·40 = £1.

TRADE

	1969	1970
Imports...........	—	$63,953,773*
Exports...........	—	97,108,168†
Imports from U.K.	£9,814,000	£11,093,000
Exports to U.K.....	11,216,000	15,882,000

* Imports: 1970, eight month Figures April–July not reported. † Exports figures refer to the year to Mar. 31, 1971.

As usual, the adverse balance of trade was offset by substantial compensating revenue from invisible exports such as the tourist trade.

CAPITAL, ΨHamilton, (Population (1966), 3,000). 2,970 nautical miles (3,420 statute miles); transit, 10 days.

BRITISH HONDURAS

British Honduras, in Central America, lies within 18° 29' 50" to 15° 53' N. latitude and 89° 13' 28" to 87° 21' 30" W. longitude. Its extreme length and breadth are approximately 186 m. and 118 m. respectively; it is bounded on the north and north-west by Mexico, on the west and south by Guatemala; and on the east by the Caribbean Sea. The total area (including offshore islands) is about 8,867 sq. miles, with an estimated population (1969) of 122,000. The climate generally is [damp and warm, but not unhealthy. The temperature ranges from 47° to 94° F. The average lies between 75° and 80°, but this is considerably tempered by the prevailing sea-breezes.

The greater part of the country is covered by forest, of which 50 per cent. is high rain forest, 15·5 pine forest and dry savannah, 5·5 wet savannah and mangrove forest, the remaining 20 per cent. being existing or recently abandoned cultivation. The wire grass and sedges of the dry savannahs make very poor pasturage for cattle. The north of the territory and the southern coastal plain (8 to 20 miles wide) are nearly flat. Near the sea the plain is low and swampy. The central mountain mass has a general altitude of 2,000 to 3,000 feet and 20 per cent. of the area of the territory is over 1,000 feet in elevation above mean sea-level.

The staple products are obtained from the forests, and include mahogany, cedar, and *chicle* (the basis of chewing-gum). Agricultural crops which grow readily include sugar cane, coconuts, citrus fruit, plantains, pineapples, mangoes, maize, cucumbers, rice, varieties of beans and peas. Bananas also grow well in certain localities. All varieties of citrus fruits flourish, and in particular grape-fruit, of which a very high grade is exported. Lobster tails and shrimps are also exported.

In 1967 there were 165 Government and grant-aided primary schools and 8 unaided private elementary schools in the country, the total enrolment being 30,000. There are also 18 secondary schools with a total enrolment of 3,000.

There are 37 post offices in the country. A new transmitting and receiving station at Ladyville has been completed. External telegraph and radio telephone services are operated by Cable and Wireless Ltd. Air services are scheduled 4 times weekly to and from the capitals of Panama, Honduras, Mexico, Salvador, Guatemala, Nicaragua, Costa Rica and Jamaica. There is a three times weekly service from and to New Orleans, a six times weekly service from and to Miami and a weekly service to Mexico City. A local scheduled air service links the six districts to which the country is divided.

CAPITAL, Belmopan (estimated population, Dec. 31, 1970, 3,000). The largest city and the former capital is ΨBelize City (population, 1970, 38,000), which was badly damaged by a hurricane in October, 1961. It was announced in 1965 that a new capital would be built, 50 miles inland. Construction was proceeding in 1970 on the new city, Belmopan, with U.K. aid of $24,000,000. Other towns are ΨCorozal (12,319), Cayo (16,484), ΨStann Creek (13,435), Orange Walk (13,266), Toledo (9,804).

FINANCE AND TRADE

	1969	1970
Revenue..........	$22,841,731	$15,460,427
Expenditure......	22,284,741	15,169,658

Estimated revenue and expenditure on capital projects in 1970 balanced at $12,140,416.
Public Debt (Dec. 31, 1970), $9,874,442 (incl. loans, $1,264,700).

TRADE WITH U.K.

	1969	1970
Imports from U.K.	£3,016,000	£3,597,000
Exports to U.K...	2,281,000	2,347,000

GOVERNMENT

Under the Constitution introduced on Jan. 1, 1964, the Governor retains special responsibility for defence, external affairs, internal security and the safeguarding of the terms and conditions of service of public officers. For so long as the Government continues to receive grant-in-aid from the U.K. Government, the Governor also has special responsibility for maintaining or securing financial and economic stability and for ensuring that any condition attached to any financial grant or loan made by the U.K. Government is fulfilled. The Governor appoints as Premier the person who appears to him to be likely to command the support of a majority in the House of Representatives. Ministers are appointed by the Governor on the advice of the Premier.

The National Assembly comprises a House of Representatives and a Senate. The House of Representatives consists of 18 members elected by universal adult suffrage. The Speaker may be elected by the House from among its own members, or from outside; the Deputy Speaker is elected by the House from among its own members. The Senate consists of 8 members appointed by the Governor (5 on the advice of the Premier, 2 on the advice of the leader of the Opposition and 1 after consulting such persons as he considers appropriate).

Governor and Commander-in-Chief, His Excellency Sir John Warburton Paul, G.C.M.G., O.B.E., M.C. (1966)..........	$18,000
Chief Justice, Sir Clifford de Lisle Innis	10,400
Speaker of the House of Representatives, Hon. W. H. Courtenay, O.B.E........	3,750
Premier and Minister of Finance and Economic Development, Hon. G. C. Price.......	7,600
Minister of Works and Communications, Hon. A. E. Arthurs.................	6,900
Trade and Industry, Hon. A. A. Hunter...	6,900
Labour, Hon. D. L. McKoy.............	6,900
Local Government and Community Development, Hon. L. S. Sylvester............	6,900
Education, Housing and Labour, Hon. S. Perdomo.......................	6,900
Home Affairs and Health, Hon. C. L. B. Rogers.......................	6,900
Agriculture, Lands and Co-operatives, Hon. F. H. Hunter.	
Attorney-General, Hon. V. H. Courtenay.	
Without Portfolio, Hon. Sen. J. Gray.	

Leader of the Opposition, Hon. P. S. W. Goldson.
British Council Representative, J. D. T. Hughes, P.O. Box 331, 4 Albert Street, Belize City.

Belize is distant from London about 4,700 miles; transit, 17 days by sea, 2 to 4 days by air.

THE BRITISH VIRGIN ISLANDS

The Virgin Islands are a group of islands at the eastern extremity of the Greater Antilles, divided between Great Britain and the U.S.A. Those of the group which are British number about 42, of which 11 are uninhabited, and have a total area of about 59 square miles. The principal are Tortola, the largest (situate in 18° 27′ N. lat. and 64° 40′ W. long., area, 21 sq. miles), Virgin Gorda (8¼ sq. miles), Anegada (15 sq. miles) and Jost Van Dyke (3½ sq. miles). The 1970 Census of Population showed a total population of 10,500 (Tortola (8,940); Virgin Gorda (1,030); Anegada (290); Jost Van Dyke (130); and other islands (110). Apart from Anegada, which is a flat coral island, the British Virgin Islands are hilly, being an extension of the Puerto Rico and the U.S. Virgin Islands archipelago. The highest point is Sage Mountain on Tortola which rises to a height of 1,780 feet. The

islands are very picturesque and form one of the finest sailing areas in the world on account of their sheltered waters. The sea is rich in gamefish and there are said to be over 400 wrecks off Anegada. Tourism is fast becoming the main industry, but there is some cattle raising and fishing. Rum is distilled on a small scale.

The islands lie within the Trade Winds belt and possess a pleasant and healthy sub-tropical climate. The average temperature varies from 71° to 82° F. in Winter and 78°–88° F. in summer. The summer heat is tempered by sea breezes and the temperature usually falls by about 10° at night. Average rainfall is 67 inches. Hurricanes are very rare—the last occurrence being in 1928.

The principal airport is on Beef Island, linked by bridge to Tortola, and an extended runway of 3,600 feet, opened in 1969, enables larger aircraft to call. There is a second airfield on Virgin Gorda and a third on Anegada. There are direct shipping services to the United Kingdom and the United States and fast passenger services connect the main islands by ferry.

FINANCE AND TRADE

	1969	1970
Revenue......	$U.S.2,355,927	$U.S.6,728,239
Expenditure....	3,672,249	6,352,442
Imports........	8,099,208	10,223,574
Exports........	49,754	42,608

The only legal unit of currency is the U.S. dollar.

GOVERNMENT

The British Virgin Islands are internally self-governing, with a ministerial system. The Administrator, appointed by the Crown, remains responsible for defence and internal security, external affairs, the civil service, administration of the courts and finance, and acts in accordance with the advice of the Executive Council. The Executive Council consists of the Administrator as Chairman, two *ex-officio* members (the Attorney-General and the Financial Secretary), the Chief Minister and two other ministers. The Legislative Council consists of a Speaker chosen from outside the Council, two *ex-officio* members (the Attorney-General and Financial Secretary), one nominated member appointed by the Administrator after consultation with the Chief Minister and seven elected members returned from seven one-member electoral districts. The islands are proud of their tradition of stable government.

Administrator, His Honour Derek George Cudmore, C.B.E. (1971)......	$U.S.9,800
Chief Minister, Hon. W. Wheatley, M.B.E...........................	10,300
Minister of Natural Resources and Public Health, Hon. Q. W. Osborne	8,400
Minister of Communications, Works and Industry, Hon. O. Sills..............	8,400
Financial Secretary, Hon. C. B. Romney	10,800
Attorney-General, Hon. N. Jacobs......	10,800
Chief Education Officer, G. Clough.....	9,000
Chief of Police, B. E. Graves..........	7,800
Chief Medical Officer, P. P. Smith	6,600
Chief Engineer, Public Works, J. L. Steven...........................	6,600
Chief Electrical Engineer, D. Pritchard...	6,600
Chief Agricultural Officer, J. L. M. Winter, M.B.E......................	9,000

CAPITAL.—Ψ Road Town (on the south-east of Tortola). Population, 2,183.

BRUNEI

Sultan, H. H. Hassanal Bolkiah Mu'izzadin Waddaulah, C.M.G., *acceded* 1967, *crowned* Aug. 1, 1968.

Brunei is a British Protected State on the north-west coast of the island of Borneo, total area about 2,226 sq. miles, population (estimated, 1969), 130,000, of whom two-thirds are of Malay or other indigenous race and one-third Chinese. The chief town, Brunei, with its nearby Water Village (groups of houses on stilts on the Brunei River opposite the town) has a population of about 41,000. The country has a humid tropical climate.

On September 29, 1959, the Sultan of Brunei promulgated the first written Constitution, and entered into a new Agreement with H.M. the Queen. The Constitution (since amended) provides for a Privy Council, a Council of Ministers and a Legislative Council. Under the Agreement the British Government continues to be responsible for defence and external affairs, and a High Commissioner is appointed. The post of British Resident was abolished in 1959 and many of his functions were transferred to the Sultan in Council. A *Mentri Besar* (Chief Minister) is appointed by the Sultan, and is responsible to him for the exercise of executive authority. The Sultan presides over the Privy Council, and the Council of Ministers, and the Speaker over the Legislative Council.

FLAG.—Yellow, with diagonal bands of white over narrow black band (from top by staff), with red device on diagonal bands.

H.M. HIGH COMMISSION
Jalan Residency, Brunei.

High Commissioner, His Excellency Arthur Robin Adair, C.V.O., M.B.E. (1967)..............£5,765
1st Secretary, J. E. T. Thorne.

FINANCE

	1968	1969
Revenue.......	B\$191,713,539	B\$222,641,118
Expenditure*...	185,595,958	204,901,056

* Including development expenditure.

Currency.—On June 12, 1967, Brunei started to issue its own currency, the *Brunei dollar* of 100 *cents,* which it was agreed would be fully interchangeable with the currencies of Malaysia and Singapore.

Imports from the U.K. in 1970 totalled £2,882,000 (1969, £2,585,000).

FALKLAND ISLANDS

The Falkland Islands, the only considerable group in the South Atlantic, lie about 300 miles east of the Straits of Magellan, between 52° 15′–53° S. lat. and 57° 40′–62° W. long. They consist of East Falkland (area 2,610 sq. miles), West Falkland (2,090 sq. miles) and upwards of 100 small islands in the aggregate, the estimated population at Dec. 31, 1970, being 2,045. Mount Usborne, the loftiest peak, rises 2,312 feet above the level of the sea. The Falklands were discovered by Davis in 1592, and visited by Hawkins in 1594. A settlement was made by France in 1764; this was subsequently sold to Spain, but the latter country recognized Great Britain's title to a part at least of the group in 1771. The settlement was destroyed by the Americans in 1831. In 1833 occupation was resumed by the British for the protection of the seal-fisheries, and the islands were permanently colonized as the most southerly organized colony of the British Empire. The climate is cool. At Stanley the mean monthly temperature varies between 49°F. in January and 35·5°F in July. The air temperature has never been known to exceed 77°F. or to fall below 12°F.: it is notably windy. The islands are chiefly moorland. The population is almost totally British, and is principally engaged in sheep-farming to which practically all the land in the colony is devoted, 628,690 sheep being carried in 1970. Wool, hides and sheepskins are exported.

The only town is Ψ Stanley on the coast of East Falkland.

GOVERNMENT

The Governor is assisted by a Legislative Council of 8 members, with the Governor as Chairman, 2 *ex officio* (Colonial Secretary and Colonial Treasurer), 2 non-official members (nominated by the Governor) and 4 representatives elected by the people.

Governor and Commander-in-Chief, His
   Excellency Ernest Gordon Lewis, O.B.E., (1970).
          (*+ duty allce.* £680) £3,000
Colonial Secretary, J. A. Jones, O.B.E.
          (*+ duty allce.* £100)   2,490
Colonial Treasurer, L. C. Gleadell, O.B.E...   2,140

FINANCE AND TRADE

	1969–70†	1970–71‡
Public Revenue....	£426,559	£522,521
Expenditure........	480,393	494,608

† Estimated.   ‡ Revised estimates.

	1968	1969
Total imports......	£598,839	£508,977
Total exports	841,671	908,751

Falkland Islands and Dependencies
Trade with U.K.

	1969	1970
Imports from U.K.....	£397,000	£451,000
Exports to U.K.......	937,000	604,000

CHIEF TOWN, Ψ Stanley. Estimated population 1,100. Stanley is distant from England about 8,103 miles; transit by steamer *via* Montevideo. Telegrams by wireless U.K. direct. The journey from U.K. to Falkland Islands can be accomplished in 5 to 7 days travelling to Montevideo by air and thence by local steamer to the Falklands.

DEPENDENCIES.—*South Georgia,* an island 800 miles east-south-east of the Falkland group, with an area of 1,450 square miles. An Administrative Officer and other officials reside there. The South Sandwich Islands group, which is uninhabited and lies some 470 miles S.E. of South Georgia, is the only other dependency.

GIBRALTAR,

a rocky promontory, 3¾ miles in length, ⅜ of a mile in breadth and 1,396 feet high at its greatest elevation, near the southern extremity of Spain, with which it is connected by a low isthmus. It is about 14 miles distant from the opposite coast of Africa. In a total area of 2¼ sq. miles, the population at the census of Oct. 1961 was 24,502 (estimated, Dec., 1969), 28,407.

Ψ Gibraltar is a naval base of strategic importance to Great Britain. It was captured in 1704, during the war of the Spanish Succession, by a combined Dutch and English force, under Sir George Rooke, and was ceded to Great Britain by the Treaty of Utrecht, 1713. Several attempts have been made to retake it, the most celebrated being the great siege in 1779–83, when General Elliot, afterwards Lord Heathfield, held it for 3 years and 7 months against a combined French and Spanish force. The town stands at the foot of the promontory on the W. side. Gibraltar is a free port, and enjoys the advantages of an extensive shipping trade. The chief sources of revenue are the port dues, the rent of the Crown estate in the town, and duties on consumer items. Import duties are low and Gibraltar is a popular shopping centre. The gradual change from a fortress city to an attractive holiday centre has led to a flourishing tourist trade.

A total of 2,399 merchant ships (10,242,149 net tons) entered the port during 1969. Of these 1,828 were deep-sea ships (9,994,152 net tons), including 108 cruise ships. In addition 996 yachts (30,318 net tons) called at the Port. Gibraltar Airport, about 1 mile from the centre of the town, handled 1,404 commercial flights in 1969. There are 19½ miles of roads.

Education is compulsory and free between the ages of 5 and 15 and scholarships are available for university or further education in Britain. There are 10 Government, 2 private and 2 Services primary schools, with 3,239 pupils in Dec. 1969. The six secondary schools had 1,729 pupils in 1969. Government expenditure on education in 1969 was £297,100.

FINANCE AND TRADE

	1968	1969
Revenue	£2,908,703	£2,635,871
Expenditure	2,822,881	2,467,004

	1969	1970
Total imports	£10,000,000	—
Total exports	2,100,000	—

	1969	1970
Imports from U.K.	£5,032,000	£5,739,000
Exports to U.K.	532,000	680,000

GOVERNMENT

The Constitution of Gibraltar, approved in 1969, made formal provision for certain domestic matters to devolve on Ministers appointed from among elected members of the House of Assembly then set up to replace the former Legislative Council. The House of Assembly consists of an independent Speaker, 15 elected members and the Attorney-General and Financial and Development Secretary.

Governor and Commander-in-Chief, His Excellency Admiral of the Fleet Sir Varyl Begg G.C.B., D.S.O., D.S.C. (1968) *(including £750 entertainment allowance and £500 from Army funds)* £6,800

Flag Officer, Gibraltar, and Admiral Supr., H.M. Dockyard, Gibraltar, Rear Admiral A. R. B. Sturdee, C.B., D.S.C.

Chief Minister, Maj. R. Peliza (1969).
Chief Justice, Sir Edgar Unsworth, C.M.G. £4,400
Speaker, A. J. Vasquez.
Permanent Secretary, T. Oates, C.M.G., O.B.E. £4,400
Financial Secretary, E. H. Davis, C.M.G., O.B.E. £4,000
Attorney-General, R. H. Hickling, C.M.G., Q.C. £4,000

Distance 1,209 miles; transit, 3½ days, B.E.A. and B.U.A. operate regular direct air services to the U.K. (Some services are *viâ* Madrid.) Transit times average 3 hours.

HONG KONG

The Crown Colony of Hong Kong, consisting of a number of islands and of a portion of the mainland, on the south-eastern coast of China, is situated at the eastern side of the mouth of the Pearl River, between 22° 9′ and 22° 37′ N. lat. and 113° 52′–114° 30′ E. long.

The capital city, Victoria, situated on the island of Hong Kong, is about 81 miles S.E. of Canton and 40 miles E. of the Portuguese colony of Macau at the other side of the Pearl River. It lies along the northern shore of the island and faces the mainland; the harbour (23 sq. miles water area) lies between the city and the mainland, on which is situated Kowloon with a population equalling that of Victoria. The total area of the Colony is 398½ sq. miles with a population which has varied considerably during recent years owing to unsettled conditions in China: at the Census of 1971 it was 3,950,802.

The island of *Hong Kong* is about 11 miles long and from 2 to 5 miles broad, with a total area of 29 square miles; at the eastern entrance to the harbour it is separated from the mainland by a narrow strait (Lei Yue Min), 500–900 yards in width. It was first occupied by Great Britain in January, 1841, and formally ceded by the Treaty of Nanking in 1842; *Kowloon* was subsequently acquired by the Peking Convention of 1860; and the *New Territories,* consisting of a peninsula in the southern part of the Kwangtung province, together with adjacent islands, by a 99-year lease signed June 9, 1898.

The island is broken in shape and mountainous, the highest point being Victoria Peak, which is 1,805 feet high. The New Territories contain several peaks higher than this, the highest being Tai Mo Shan, 3,140 ft.

Climate.—Although Hong Kong lies within the tropics it enjoys unusually varied weather for a tropical area. The mean monthly temperature ranges from 15° C. in February to 28° C. in July. Spring is cloudy and humid, often with spells of fog and drizzle. Summer days are hot with temperatures exceeding 33° C. several times in most years. The average annual rainfall is 2,168·8 mm., of which nearly 80 per cent. falls between May and September. Tropical cyclones passing at various distances from Hong Kong sometimes cause high winds and heavy rain particularly in July, August and September. Autumn and early winter are the most pleasant seasons with sunny, dry and mild weather. In late winter there is more cloud and strong northerly winds can cause temperatures to drop below 10° C. and frost is not uncommon.

Communications.—Hong Kong, one of the world's finest natural harbours, possesses excellent wharves at which vessels up to 800 ft. in length and 36 ft. draught can be berthed. An ocean terminal pier with an overall length of 1,250 ft. has been constructed. Excellent dockyard facilities are available and the dry docks are capable of taking all classes of vessels up to 35,000 deadweight tons in the case of bulk oil tankers, or 750 ft. in length and 88 ft. beam in the case of passenger liners and large dry cargo vessels. The net tonnage of ocean-going shipping which entered the port in the year to December 31, 1970, amounted to 23,008,320.

Hong Kong International Airport, Kai Tak, situated on the North shore of Kowloon Bay, is an important link on the main air routes of the Far East. It is regularly used by 28 scheduled airlines and many charter airlines, providing frequent services throughout the Far East, to Europe, North America, Africa, Australia and New Zealand.

B.O.A.C. operates 19 passenger services per week, 10 to London, 4 to Sydney and 5 to the U.S.A. Cathay Pacific Airways Ltd., the Hong Kong based airline, provides 152 flights per week on Far East routes.

During the year ending Dec. 31, 1970, 46,841 aircraft on international flights arrived and departed, carrying 2,324,900 passengers, 61,186,740 kg. of freight and 3,783,086 kg. of mail.

Education.—In Sept., 1970, there were 2,804 schools with 1,240,540 pupils. 53·6 per cent. of the pupils are financed wholly or in part by the Government. The University of Hong Kong has a full-time residential student strength of 2,735 in Faculties of Arts, Science, Medicine, and Engineering and Architecture. There is also a Centre of Asian Studies and a Department of Extra-Mural Studies. The Chinese University of Hong Kong, inaugurated in Oct., 1963, has a full time enrolment of 2,260 students in Faculties of Art, Science, and Commerce and Social Science. There is also a Department of Extra-Mural Studies.

FINANCE

	1969-70	1970-71
Public revenue....	$2,480,657,388	$82,980,701,000
Public expenditure.	2,032,183,388	2,472,963,000

$= Hong Kong Dollar= 7 p.

TRADE

Hong Kong is now established as an industrial territory with an economy based on exports rather than the domestic market. Domestic industry, producing mainly light manufactures, has grown rapidly in recent years and now provides the bulk of goods for the export trade; the Colony's traditional role as an *entrepôt*, while still considerable, has become less important, the value of the re-export trade now being 18·9 per cent. of total exports.

Hong Kong produces a wide range of articles, including cotton yarn, cotton piece-goods, garments of all types, woollen knitwear, footwear, wigs, transistor radios, household enamel and aluminium ware, plastic articles (including household ware, toys and artificial flowers), rattan and hardwood furniture, iron and steel bars, photographic equipment, foodstuffs and beverages, cigarettes, jade, jewellery and ivory, and an extensive range of metal products.

Diversification of manufacture continues to be a major feature of recent industrial development, as are industrial partnerships with foreign companies in a wide and varied field of manufactures. New products include air conditioners, automatic telephone dialling equipment, electric household appliances such as rice cookers and toasters, T.V. receiving sets and T.V. tuners, high grade semi-conductors, electronic modules, electronic flash bulbs, and other electronic components, steel pipes, rigid P.V.C. tubes and corrugated sheeting, P.V.C. covered fabrics, mixed cotton-synthetic fabrics, extruded aluminium sections, watches and clocks and fibreglass pleasure craft. Modern manufacturing processes have also been introduced to local industry; these include the permanent press for ready-made garments, soil release processing for garments and the manufacture of polyester fabrics. The marked improvement in both quality and output of items for which precision engineering is required, has continued.

The adverse balance on visible trade is offset by a favourable balance on invisible account—remittances from overseas Chinese, investments, exchange, shipping and insurance profits, and the spending of tourists, etc. In 1970 Hong Kong's principal customers for its domestic products, in order of value of trade, were U.S.A., the United Kingdom, the Federal Republic of Germany, Japan, Canada, Australia, Singapore, Sweden and the Netherlands. Japan was the Colony's principal supplier, followed by China, U.S.A., the United Kingdom, Formosa, the Federal Republic of Germany, Switzerland and Australia.

	1969 H.K.$	1970 H.K.$
Total Exports.	13,197,158,771	15,238,070,653
Total Imports.	14,893,017,707	17,606,714,551

	1969	1970
Imports from U.K.....	£87,134,000	£99,516,000
Exports to U.K........	125,359,000	128,394,000

GOVERNMENT

Hong Kong is administered as a Crown Colony with a Governor, aided by an Executive Council, consisting of 7 official and 8 unofficial members, and a Legislative Council, which consists of 12 official and 13 unofficial members. There is also an Urban Council in which is vested, *inter alia*, power of making bye-laws in respect of certain matters of public health and sanitation.

Governor, His Excellency Sir Crawford Murray MacLehose, K.C.M.G. (1971). (+*allce.* £3,500)	£11,000
General Officer Commanding-in-Chief, Lt.-Gen. Sir Richard Ward, K.C.B., D.S.O., M.C.	10,972
Chief Justice, Hon. Sir Ivo Rigby	10,972
Colonial Secretary, Sir Hugh Norman-Walker, K.C.M.G., O.B.E.	10,972
Deputy Colonial Secretary, M. D. A. Clinton, C.M.G., G.M.	8,085
Puisne Judges, W. A. Blair-Kerr; G. G. Briggs; A. A. Huggins; R. H. Mills-Owen; A. M. McMullin; W. F. Pickering	8,250
Attorney-General, D. T. E. Roberts, C.B.E., Q.C.	9,735
Secretary for Home Affairs, D. C. C. Luddington	9,735
Financial Secretary, Sir John Cowperthwaite, K.B.E., C.M.G.	9,735
Commissioner of Labour, R. M. Hetherington, D.F.C.	8,085
Chairman, Urban Council and Director of Urban Services, D. R. W. Alexander, M.B.E.	8,085
Director of Medical and Health Services, Dr. G. H. Choa.	8,497
Director of Public Works, J. J. Robson.	8,497
Commissioner of Police, C. P. Sutcliffe, O.B.E., Q.P.M.	8,497
Director of Marine, K. Milburn	8,085
General Manager, Kowloon Canton Railway, Lam Po-hon.	7,301
Director of Education, J. Canning.	8,497
District Commissioner, New Territories, D. C. Bray.	8,085
Director of Commerce & Industry, J. Cater, M.B.E.	8,497
Commissioner for Resettlement, K. C. Tsui, O.B.E.	8,085
Director of Social Welfare, G. T. Rowe.	8,085

British Council Representative, G. A. Bridges, Gloucester Building, Hong Kong.

COMMISSIONER OF PRISONS, J.C. PATTERSON

LONDON OFFICE

Hong Kong Government Office, 54 Pall Mall, S.W.1.—*Administrative Commissioner*, A. M. J. Wright, C.M.G......... £8,497

THE NEW HEBRIDES

The New Hebrides Group, in the South Pacific Ocean, situated between the 13th and 21st degrees of South latitude and the 166th and 170th degrees of East longitude. It includes 13 large and some 70 small islands, including the Banks and Torres Islands in the North, and has a total land area of about 6,050 square miles. The principal islands are Vanua Lava and Gaua (Banks), Espiritu Santo, Maewo, Pentecost, Aoba, Malekula, Ambrym, Epi, Efate, Erromango, Tanna and Aneityum.

The Territory is administered by an unique British-French Condominium Government. The British Resident Commissioner, exercising powers delegated to him by the High Commissioner for the Western Pacific, and the French Resident Commissioner, representing the High Commissioner for France in the Pacific Ocean, are the joint heads of the Administration. They each have staffs of national officers to assist them in general administrative work and the running of social services (health and education) financed from national funds. In addition they control the

" joint " public services (posts and telegraphs, public works, mines, meteorology, etc.) which are financed from funds raised in the Territory. The Resident Commissioners are advised regarding policy and legislation by the Advisory Council, a composite body of New Hebrideans, French and British Nationals, some appointed and some elected, which meets twice a year.

The 1967 Census showed a population of 77,988 of whom 72,243 were New Hebrideans. There were 3,841 French Nationals and 1,629 British Nationals but only 1,773 of these were of European ethnic origin. The estimated rate of population increase is 2½ per cent. per annum giving a 1971 population of 86,084.

Principal products are copra, coffee, cocoa, kauri timber, frozen fish, frozen and canned meat, sandalwood and shell. Imports for 1969 totalled $A10,571,952 and exports $A10,021,960. Condominium Budget, 1971, $3,789,459; British National Service Budget $A2,259,704; French National Service Budget $A.717,534. Two currencies are valid in the Territory; 100 New Hebrides Francs= 1 Australian Dollar.

Seat of New Hebrides Administration— Ψ Vila, Efate, population (estimated 1970), 5,500.
British High Commissioner, Sir Michael Gass, K.C.M.G. (see below).
French High Commissioner, L. Verger.
British Resident Commissioner, C. H. Allan, C.M.G., O.B.E.
French Resident Commissioner, R. Langlois.

PACIFIC ISLANDS
(*Western Pacific High Commission*)
High Commissioner, His Excellency Sir Michael David Irving Gass, K.C.M.G. †
(1969) .... (+allce. $A5,000) $A10,875
Chief Justice, Hon. Sir Jocelyn Bodilly, V.R.D. 6,592
Chief Secretary, T. Russell, C.B.E. 6,592
Attorney General, D. R. Davis 5,952
Financial Secretary, J. H. Smith, C.B.E... 5,952
Deputy Chief Secretary, R. Davies, O.B.E. 5,712
† Certain allowances are paid in addition under the Overseas Service Aid Scheme.

The principal groups under the High Commissioner in, over, and for the Western Pacific Islands are (1) The Gilbert and Ellice Islands Colony, including the Central and Southern Line Islands; (2) The British Solomon Islands Protectorate; (3) The New Hebrides (British Service). The headquarters of the High Commissioner are at Honiara in the British Solomon Islands Protectorate.

The Gilbert and Ellice Islands Colony, which includes, in addition, Ocean Island, the Phoenix Islands and the Northern Line Islands, is situated in the south-western Pacific around the point at which the International Date Line cuts the Equator. The Colony consists of 37 coral atolls (of which 28 are permanently inhabited), with a total land area of 283 sq. miles, spread over some 2 million square miles of ocean. Few of the atolls are more than 12 ft. above sea-level or more than half a mile in width. The vegetation consists mainly of coconut palms, breadfruit trees and pandanus. The total population (1968) was 53,517 of whom 44,897 were Micronesians (Gilbertese) and 7,465 Polynesians (Ellice). The Phoenix and Northern Line Islands now have no indigenous populations. Christianity is wide-spread, roughly half the population being Protestants (Congregationalists) and the other half Roman Catholics. Most people still practise a subsistence economy, the main staples of their diet being coconuts and fish.

The Colony is administered, under the general

supervision of the High Commissioner for the Western Pacific, by a Resident Commissioner aided by an Executive Council consisting of 5 officials, a Leader of Government Business elected from among themselves by the members of the Legislative Council and 4 other elected members of the Legislative Council appointed by the Resident Commissioner. The Legislative Council consists of 5 official and 28 elected members. Local government services are provided by elected Island Councils. Under an agreement reached in 1939, Canton and Enderbury Islands, in the Phoenix group, are jointly administered by the United Kingdom and the United States.

The unit of currency is the Australian dollar. Estimated revenue for 1970 was $A5,643,973 and expenditure $A5,621,224. The principal imports are foodstuffs, consumer goods and building materials. The only exports are phosphates from Ocean Island and copra, most of which is produced by small landowners. There are three copra plantations in the Northern Line Islands.

Communication between the islands is mainly by small ships operated by the Wholesale Society, a government-owned trading corporation. There is a weekly air service to Fiji. A few islands are served by an internal air service.

The Government maintains a teacher training college and a secondary school. Three junior secondary schools are maintained by missions. Throughout the Colony there are 55 primary schools and 152 village schools. The total enrolment of children of school age (1970) was 14,646. The Marine Training School at Tarawa trains seamen for service with British and foreign shipping lines.

There is a general hospital at Tarawa in the Gilbert Islands and a smaller one at Funafuti in the Ellice Islands. The British Phosphate Commissioners maintain a general hospital on Ocean Island. The other inhabited islands have dispensaries, the larger ones being in the charge of qualified medical officers.

CAPITAL.— Ψ Tarawa. Estimated population (1968), 10,616
Resident Commissioner, His Hon. Sir John Osbaldiston Field,
K.B.E., C.M.G. (1970) .... (+allce) $A6,592
Asst. Resident Commissioner, A. J. Hunter
(+allce) 5,712
Attorney-General, J. R. Hobbs... (+allce) 5,472
Financial Secretary, D. M. Freegard
(+allce) 5,472
Leader of Government Business, K. Uatioa, M.B.E.

The British Solomon Islands Protectorate, established in 1893, now includes all the islands in the Solomons Archipelago S. and S.E. of the large island of Bougainville. The main islands in the Protectorate are Choiseul, Santa Isabel, the Shortland Group, Vella Lavella, Kolombangara, Ranongga, Gizo, the New Georgia Group, the Florida Group, Guadalcanal, the Russell Islands, Malaita and San Cristobal, and the outlying islands of Bellona, Rennell, Santa Cruz, Vanikolo, Tikopia, Swallow (or Reef Islands) and Duff Groups, the Stewart Islands and the Ontong Java Atoll.

The Protectorate is situated between 5°–13° S. lat. and 155°–170° 20′ E. long. It has a total land area of about 11,500 sq. miles. Distribution of the population at the Census of 1970 was: Melanesian, 149,667; Polynesian, 6,399; Micronesian, 2,362; European, 1,280; Chinese, 577; Others, 713. Total 160,998.

Finance and Trade.—Estimated revenue (1971), $A7,933,200 (including British Development Aid ($A2,693,765) and grant-in-aid of recurrent expenditure from the United Kingdom ($A3,183,765)); The main imports are foodstuffs, consumer goods,

machinery and building materials. Principal exports are copra, timber and trochus shell. Exports of cocoa, though modest in quantity, are increasing annually, and tourism is developing.

Government.—In 1960 an Advisory Council was replaced by a nominated Legislative Council and Executive Council. In 1964 provision was made for a new constitution and the first general elections were held in 1965. In 1967 a general election was held to elect 14 members of the Legislative Council instead of the previous 8. In 1970 a new constitution was introduced providing for a single Governing Council comprising the High Commissioner as President, 3 *ex-officio* members, up to 6 public service members nominated by the High Commissioner and 17 elected members. This constitution provides for the first time for an elected majority in the legislature. In place of the Executive Council the full Governing Council will meet in executive session as well as in legislative session and will be supported by executive committees on which all elected members will serve.

The High Court of the Western Pacific constituted by the Western Pacific (Courts) Order in Council, 1961, consists of a Chief Justice, one Puisne Judge and one Senior Magistrate. The Court is a Superior Court of Record and possesses all the jurisdiction which is vested in Her Majesty's High Court of Justice in England.

PITCAIRN ISLANDS

Pitcairn, a small volcanic island of less than two square miles in area, is the chief of a group of Islands situated about midway between New Zealand and Panama in the South Pacific Ocean at longitude 130° 06′ W. and latitude 25° 04′ S.

The island rises in cliffs to a height of 1,100 feet and access from the sea is possible only at Bounty Bay, a small rocky cove, and then only by whaleboats. Mean monthly temperatures vary between 66° F. in August and 75° F. in February and the average annual rainfall is 80 inches. Moderate easterly and north-easterly winds predominate but short easterly and south-easterly gales occasionally occur from April to September. With an equable climate, the island is very fertile and produces both tropical and sub-tropical trees and crops.

The small community, descendants of the Bounty mutineers and their Tahitian companions who did not wish to remain on Norfolk Island (*see* p. 716) and returned here, numbers about 80. The Islanders live by subsistence farming and fishing, and their limited monetary needs are satisfied by the manufacture of wood carvings and other handicrafts which are sold to passing ships and to a few overseas customers. Other than small fees charged for gun and driving licences there are no taxes and Government revenue is derived almost solely from the sale of postage stamps. Communication with the outside world is maintained by cargo vessels travelling between New Zealand and Panama which call at irregular intervals in each direction; and by means of a telegraphic link with Fiji.

The other three islands of the group (Henderson lying 105 miles E.N.E. of Pitcairn, Oeno lying 75 miles N.W. and Ducie lying 293 miles E.) are all uninhabited. Henderson Island is occasionally visited by the Pitcairn Islanders to obtain supplies of " miro " wood which is used for their carvings. Oeno is visited for excursions of about a week's duration every two years or so.

Under a scheme of co-operation, New Zealand supplies Pitcairn with a teacher for the one-teacher primary school on the Island. Education is compulsory between the ages of five and fifteen. Secondary education in Fiji and New Zealand is encouraged by the Administration which provides scholarships and bursaries for the purpose. Medical care is provided by a registered nurse and additional help is obtained when required from the surgeons of passing ships. Since 1887 the islanders have all been adherents of the Seventh Day Adventist Church.

Pitcairn became a British Settlement under the British Settlements Act, 1887, and was administered by the Governor of Fiji from 1952 until 1970, when a Governor was appointed. The local Government Ordinance of 1964 provides for a Council of ten members of whom four are elected.

Governor of Pitcairn, Ducie, Henderson and Oeno Islands, Sir Arthur (Norman) Galsworthy, K.C.M.G., (*British High Commissioner in New Zealand*) (Oct. 10, 1970).

Commissioner, C. E. Dymond, C.B.E. (*British High Commission,* Auckland, New Zealand).
Island Magistrate and Chairman of Island Council, P. Young.
Education Officer and Government Adviser, R. S. Henry.

RHODESIA

Rhodesia, comprising Matabeleland, Mashonaland, Manicaland, Midlands and Victoria, is that part of the territory named after Cecil Rhodes lying south of the Zambesi River, its political neighbours being Zambia and Portuguese East Africa on the N.; the Transvaal and Botswana on the S. and W.; and Portuguese East Africa on the E. Rhodesia has a total area of 150,820 square miles and a population (estimated, Dec., 1969) of 5,190,000 (Europeans, 234,000; Africans, 4,930,000; Asians and Coloured, 25,400).

The majority of Africans of Rhodesia (members of the so-called Bantu race), are known as Mashona. In the Western portion of the territory are the descendants of the Amandebele who conquered and settled down among the Mashona, and from whom the Province of Matabeleland derives its name.

Rhodesia was administered by the British South Africa Company from the date of occupation (1890) to 1923, when responsible government was granted. On this latter date the Company relinquished all rights and interests in the land of Rhodesia except in those estates which it was already developing on July 10, 1923. A Land and Agricultural Bank grants loans for farm development and acquisition of residential property on easy terms of repayment. Under the Land Tenure Act, operative from March 2, 1970, Rhodesia is divided into three areas—European Area (44,950,000 acres), African Area (44,950,000 acres) and National Area (6,600,000 acres).

FINANCE AND TRADE

	1966–67	1967–68
Revenue	£78,316,850	£82,606,000
Expenditure from revenue funds	61,985,688	66,939,093
Expenditure from loan funds	19,961,643	21,579,651

Revenue for 1969–70 was estimated at $Rh179,500,000.

TRADE WITH U.K.

	1969	1970
Imports from U.K.	£809,000	£503,000
Exports to U.K.	90,000	49,000

EDUCATION

African education comes under the Minister of Education in the Rhodesian Government. The last estimate of annual expenditure is £8,250,000. There are 3,217 primary schools, 97 senior second-

ary schools and 11 junior secondary schools, 6 special schools for physically handicapped, 96 aided farm schools, 9 homecraft schools, 60 part-time evening schools, 122 study groups, 469 unaided schools and 19 teacher training schools. The total enrolment of African pupils in 1969 was 710,148. In 1969 there were 18,044 African teachers and 502 European teachers for African schools. Full secondary schools provide education up to the Cambridge Schools Certificate level, and Junior secondary schools give a vocational schooling up to Junior Certificate level. Five secondary schools offer the Higher School Certificate. Other educational institutes are the Domboshawa School of Social Service and Chibero Agricultural College. At the University College in Salisbury, of the total enrolment of 937 full-time students for 1970, there were 363 Africans. At present 95 per cent. of African children between the ages of 6 to 16 years receive a minimum of 5 years' primary education and over half of this number receive a full 8 years' primary education.

GOVERNMENT

Rhodesia (then *Southern Rhodesia*) obtained self-government in 1923 and has a legislative Assembly of 66 members and a Cabinet of 14 members.

Municipal self-government has been established in the city of Salisbury, the city of Bulawayo, and in the towns of Umtali, Gwelo, Gatooma, Que Que and Fort Victoria. Smaller areas are administered by Town Management Boards. Over the past ten years local self-government among the Africans has been encouraged and at the end of 1968 there were 68 Native Councils.

MINISTRY

The Parliament of Rhodesia, elected on April 10, 1970, consists of 50 Rhodesian Front, 7 Centre Party, 1 National People's Union and 8 Rhodesia Electoral Union Peoples' Party, 2 Democratic Party and 4 Independents.

Prime Minister, Hon. I. D. Smith.
Deputy Prime Minister and Minister of Finance and Posts, Hon. J. J. Wrathall.
Minister of Foreign Affairs, Defence and Public Service, Hon. J. H. Howman.
Justice and Law and Order, Hon. D. W Lardner-Burke.
Local Government and Housing, Hon. M. H. H. Partridge.
Agriculture, Hon. D. C. Smith.
Internal Affairs, Hon. L. B. Smith.
Health, Labour and Social Welfare, Hon. I. F. McLean.
Transport, Power, Roads and Road Traffic, Hon. R. T. R. Hawkins.
Information, Immigration, and Tourism, Hon. P. van der Byl.
Education, Hon. A. P. Smith.
Lands and Water Development, Hon. P. van Heerden.
Mines, Hon. I. B. Dillon.
Commerce and Industry, Hon. B. H. Mussett.

JUDICIARY

The High Court of Rhodesia consists of a Chief Justice, a Judge President of the Appellate Division, a Judge of Appeal and five puisne Judges.
Chief Justice, Rt. Hon. Sir Hugh Beadle, C.M.G., O.B.E.
Judge President, Appellate Division, Hon. H. N. Macdonald.
Judge of Appeal, Hon. J. V. R. Lewis.
Puisne Judges, Hons. E. W. G. Jarvis, C.M.G.; H. E. Davies; B. Goldin; J. M. Greenfield, C.M.G.; J. B. Macaulay.

CAPITAL.—SALISBURY, situated on the Mashonaland plateau, altitude 4,850 ft., population (Dec., 1969), 400,000 (European, 99,900; Asian and Coloured, 9,250; African, 290,000). BULAWAYO, the largest town in Matabeleland, altitude 4,450 ft., population (Dec. 1969), 250,000 (European, 51,300; Asian and Coloured, 8,150; African, 190,000). Other centres are Umtali, Gwelo, Gatooma, Que Que, Fort Victoria and Wankie.

Salisbury is 5,600 miles from London (air route) transit 12 hours; by sea, *viâ* Cape Town, 17 days (approx.).

FLAG.—Vertical stripes of green, white, green; Rhodesian coat of arms in centre of white stripe.

ST. HELENA

Probably the best known of all the solitary islands in the world, St. Helena is situated in the South Atlantic Ocean, 955 miles S. of the Equator, 760 S.E. of Ascension, 1,140 from the nearest point of the African Continent, 1,800 from the coast of S. America and 4,477 from Southampton, in 15° 55′ S. lat. and 5° 42′ W. long. It is 10½ miles long, 6½ broad. and encloses an area of 47 square miles, with an estimated population at June, 1968, of 4,722.

St. Helena is of volcanic origin, and consists of numerous rugged mountains, the highest rising to 2,700 feet, interspersed with picturesque ravines. Although within the tropics, the south-east " trades " keep the temperature mild and equable. St. Helena was discovered by the Portuguese navigator, João de Nova, in 1502 (probably on St. Helena's Day) and remained unknown to other European nations until 1588. It was used as a port of call for vessels of all nations trading to the East until it was annexed by the Dutch in 1633. It was never occupied by them, however, and the English East India Company seized it in 1659. In 1834 it was ceded to the Crown. During the period 1815 to 1821 the island was lent to the British Government as a place of exile for the Emperor Napoleon Bonaparte who died in St. Helena on May 5, 1821. It was formerly an important station on the route to India, but its prosperity decreased after the construction of the Suez Canal. A lacemaking industry has been established. Ψ St. James's Bay, on the north-west of the Island, possesses a good anchorage.

GOVERNMENT

The government of St. Helena is administered by a Governor, with the aid of a Legislative Council, consisting of the Governor, two *ex-officio* members (Government Secretary and Treasurer) and twelve elected members. Five committees of the Legislative Council are responsible for general oversight of the activities of Government Departments and have in addition a wide range of statutory and administrative functions. The Governor is also assisted by an Executive Council of the two *ex-officio* members and the Chairmen of the Council committees.

Governor, His Excellency Sir Dermod Art Murphy, C.M.G., O.B.E. (1968)	£3,250
Government Secretary, I. C. Rose, T.D. ....(+ *allce.*)	1,872
Colonial Treasurer and Collector of Customs, W. Millard ....(+ *allce.*)	1,656
Senior Medical Officer, Dr. J. S. Noaks ....(+ *allce.*)	1,656
Agricultural and Forestry Officer, A. S. Leask................... (+ *allce.*)	1,512

Distance from London: 4,472 miles; transit, 14 days.

FINANCE AND TRADE

	1968	1969
	£	£
Public revenue.......	177,682	515,442*
Expenditure..........	382,629	547,312
Total imports........	375,790	—
Total exports.........	14,710	—

Imports from U.K. in 1970 were valued at £768,000.

* Incl. Grant-in-Aid (£257,000) and Colonial Development and Welfare Grants (£50,147).

CAPITAL, Ψ Jamestown. Population (1966), 1,475.

ASCENSION

The small island of Ascension lies in the South Atlantic (7° 56′ S., 14° 22′ W.) some 700 miles north-west of the island of St. Helena. It is said to have been discovered by João de Nova, on Ascension Day, 1501, and two years later was visited by Alphonse d'Albuquerque, who gave the island its present name. It was uninhabited until the arrival of Napoleon in St. Helena in 1815 when a small British naval garrison was stationed on the island. The population at December 31, 1968, was 1,527 of whom 773 were St. Helenian. The island remained under the supervision of the Board of Admiralty until 1922, when it was made a dependency of St. Helena by Royal Letters Patent and came under control of the Secretary of State for the Colonies.

Ascension is a rocky peak of purely volcanic origin, the highest point (Green Mountain) some 2,817 ft. is covered with lush vegetation, which with each rainy season is slowly creeping down to the lower areas. Cable & Wireless Ltd., maintains a farm of some 10 acres on the mountain, permitting the production of vegetables and livestock. The island is famous for Turtles, which land on the beaches from January to May to lay their eggs. It is also a breeding area for the sooty tern, or wideawake, large numbers of which settle on the southwestern coastal section every eighth month to hatch their eggs. Other wild life on the island includes feral donkeys and cats, rabbits and francolin partridge. All wild life except rabbits and cats is protected by law. The ocean surrounding the island abounds with shark, barracuda, tuna, bonito and many other fish.

Cable & Wireless Ltd., owns and operates a cable station which connects the Dependency with St. Helena, Sierra Leone, St. Vincent, Rio de Janeiro and Buenos Aires. A B.B.C. relay station was opened on the island in 1966.

Administrator, Brig. H. W. D. McDonald, D.S.O.

TRISTAN DA CUNHA

Tristan da Cunha is the chief of a group of islands of volcanic origin lying in lat. 37° 6′ S. and long. 12° 2′ W., discovered in 1506 by a Portuguese admiral (Tristão da Cunha), after whom they are named. They have a total area of 45 square miles. The main island is about 1,500 miles W. of the Cape of Good Hope, 3,600 miles N.E. of Cape Horn, and about 1,320 miles S.S.W. of St. Helena. It was the resort of British and American sealers from the middle of the 18th century, and in 1760 a British naval officer visited the group and gave his name to Nightingale Island. On August 14, 1816, the group was annexed to the British Crown and a garrison was placed on Tristan da Cunha, but this force was withdrawn in 1817, William Glass, a corporal of artillery (*died* 1853), remaining at his own request, with his wife and two children. This party, with five others, formed a settlement. In 1827 five coloured women from St. Helena, and afterwards others from Cape Colony, joined the party.

The islands form a dependency of St. Helena, being administered by the Foreign and Commonwealth Office through a resident Administrator, with headquarters at the settlement of Edinburgh. Under a new constitution introduced in 1969, he is advised by an elected Island Council of 8 members of whom one must be a woman, with universal suffrage at 18. The population numbered about 280 persons in 1970, plus 7 expatriate Government officers and their families.

In October, 1961, a volcano, believed to have been extinct for thousands of years, erupted and mounds of earth were thrown up in some cases to a height of 35 feet. In view of the danger of further volcanic activity, the inhabitants were evacuated and reached the United Kingdom on Nov. 23, 1961, where they remained for nearly two years. An advance party returned to Tristan da Cunha in the spring of 1963, and the main body of the islanders has now returned to the island. Some went back to England in 1966, but most returned in August, 1967.

A boat harbour was completed in 1967. The first freezing factory was re-established in 1966. There are no taxes on Tristan, income being derived from royalties paid by the fishing company and from the sale of stamps. The new Camogli Hospital was opened early in 1971 and a new school was under construction in June, 1971.

Administrator, Maj. J. I. H. Fleming.

Chaplain, Rev. C. J. Jewell.

INACCESSIBLE ISLAND is a lofty mass of rock with sides 2 miles in length; the island is the resort of penguins and sea-fowl. Cultivation was started in 1937, but has been abandoned.

THE NIGHTINGALE ISLANDS are three in number, of which the largest is 1 mile long and ¾ mile wide, and rises in two peaks, 960 and 1,105 ft. above sea-level respectively. The smaller islands, Stoltenhoft and Middle Isle, are little more than huge rocks. Seals, innumerable penguins, and vast numbers of sea-fowl visit these islands.

GOUGH ISLAND (or Diego Alvarez), in 40° 20′ S. and 9° 44′ W., lies about 250 miles S.S.E. of Tristan da Cunha. The island is about 8 miles long and 4 miles broad, with a total area of 40 square miles, and has been a British possession since 1816. The island is the resort of penguins and sea-elephants and has valuable guano deposits. There is no permanent population, but there is a meteorological station maintained on the island by the South African Government and manned by South Africans.

SEYCHELLES

The Colony of Seychelles, in the Indian Ocean, consists of two distinct collections of islands—the Mahé group, 32 islands in all, granitic with high hills and mountains (highest point 2,971 feet) and the out-lying islands, the Coralline group, numbering 57 more and, for the most part, only a little above sea-level. Proclaimed as French territory in 1756, the Mahé group began to be settled as a dependency of Mauritius from 1770, was captured by a British ship in 1794 and was finally assigned to Great Britain in 1810. By Letters Patent of September, 1903, these islands, together with the Coralline group, were erected into a separate Colony.

The total area of the Granitic group is 100 square miles, of which Mahé, the largest island and the seat of Government, claims 55. The next largest island is Praslin, home of the unique double coconut, Coco de Mer. Islands of the Coralline group lie at distances from Mahé varying between 60 and

612 miles and, exclusive of the Aldabra lagoon (50 sq. miles), have a total area of approximately 13 sq. miles. Aldabra is famous for its gigantic land tortoises. These islands have no permanent population and, where worked, are supplied by contract labour from the Granitic group. The population in June, 1969 (U.N. estimate) was 51,000. Although only 4° S. of the Equator, the islands are healthy; the death and birth rates in 1968 were 10·8 and 34·8 per 1,000 respectively. There are 33 primary schools, 10 secondary schools and a teachers' training college.

The new Constitution which was introduced in late 1967 created a single Council with both executive and legislative functions and an unofficial majority. The General Election held under the Constitution in December, 1967, was also significant in that for the first time it was contested on the basis of universal adult suffrage. The Governing Council consists of three *ex-officio* members, eight elected members and up to four nominated members of whom at least two are not public officers, with the Governor as President.

Finance.—Revenue in 1967 totalled £905,544 and recurrent expenditure £1,411,696. Exchange rate: 1 Rupee=1s. 6d. The colony is grant-aided: U.K. grants in 1966 totalled £469,944.

TRADE

	1967	1968
Imports	Rs.24,595,360	Rs.33,875,243
Exports	10,517,737	16,195,706

	1969	1970
Imports from U.K.	£1,306,000	£1,302,000
Exports to U.K.	137,000	51,000

The principal imports are rice, mineral oils, cotton piece goods, vehicles, manufactures and beverages. The chief exports are cinnamon bark, copra, cinnamon leaf oil, guano, vanilla, patchouli leaf and salted fish.

CAPITAL, Ψ Victoria (population, estimated, 1966, 11,000), on the N.E. side of Mahé.

Governor and Commander-in-Chief, His Excellency Sir Bruce Greatbatch, C.M.G., C.V.O., M.B.E. (1968)	Rs.69,000
Chief Justice, Hon. Sir. Louis Georges Souyave	38,004
Chief Secretary, R. V. Rostowski	37,200
Attorney-General, A. F. M. A. Sauzier, O.B.E.	35,400
Administrative Secretary, G. F. Pollard, O.B.E.	34,800
Financial Secretary, A. G. Padgett	35,400
Director of Audit, P. Harrison	32,400
Director of Medical Services, Dr. P. Hossen	33,600
Commissioner of Police, F. D. Marrable	33,600
Director of Public Works, A. S. Boyce	33,600
Director of Education, A. W. Johns	33,600
Director of Agriculture, G. Lionnet, M.B.E.	33,600
Director of Tourism, Information and Broadcasting, J. A. Robinson	31,080

Letters to and from London—5 to 10 days.

VIRGIN ISLANDS,
see BRITISH

THE WEST INDIES

The West Indies are a number of islands and islets, some of them mere rocks, situated between 10° to 27° North and 59° 30′ to 85° West. The whole archipelago extends in a curve from the Florida Channel (North America) to within 7 miles of the coast of Venezuela (South America), and is divided into three main groups: I. GREATER ANTILLES, which contain the largest islands, Cuba (44,000 sq. miles) and *Hispaniola* (Haiti and the Dominican Republic) (30,000 sq. miles), Jamaica and Puerto Rico; II. BAHAMAS, which are entirely British. III. LESSER ANTILLES, which are variously divided; the British islands in the Lesser Antilles are the Leeward and Windward Islands. The total area of the archipelago is nearly 100,000 square miles, of which 72,000 square miles are *Independent*, 12,300 *British*, 3,890 *United States*, 1,350 *French*, 430 *Netherlands*, and 90 *Venezuelan*.

The West India Islands which lie nearest the East have been called the *Windward Islands*; the others the *Leeward Islands*, on account of the winds which in this area generally blow from the east.

COMMISSION FOR THE EASTERN CARIBBEAN GOVERNMENTS
10 Haymarket, S.W.1
Commissioner, N. G. F. Taylor, C.M.G.

The British West Indies were governed under a series of federal arrangements, the last of which, a federation of the Leeward and Windward Islands with Barbados, was abandoned in 1966. The islands of Antigua, Dominica, Grenada, St. Kitts-Nevis-Anguilla and St. Lucia became States in association with Britain in February and March 1967. St. Vincent became an Associated State in October, 1969. Britain's power and responsibilities are limited to defence and external affairs.

West Indies Associated States

The Associated States are described individually in the following sections. The Office of the British Government Representative is at George Gordon Building (P.O. Box 227), Castries, St. Lucia.

British Government Representative, J. E. Marnham, C.M.G., M.C., T.D. (1970)	£5,075
Deputy do., R. A. R. Barltrop.	
Development Adviser, W. L. Bell, C.M.G., M.B.E. (*Resident at* Bridgetown, Barbados).	

Supreme Court

Established by Order in Council (1967), which gives the Court additional jurisdiction in Montserrat and the British Virgin Islands. There are two constituents, a Court of Appeal and a High Court. The Chief Justice is appointed by Her Majesty and puisne judges by the Judicial and Legal Services Commission. Expenses of the Supreme Court, after allowing for contributions from Montserrat and the Virgin Islands, are met by the States in equal shares.

Chief Justice, Hon. Sir Allen Lewis, Q.C.
Justices of Appeal, K. L. Gordon; P. C. Lewis.
Puisne Judges, E. L. St. Bernard (*Grenada*); N. Berridge (*Dominica and Montserrat*); E. H. A. Bishop (*St. Lucia*); E. F. Glasgow (*St. Kitts and Brit. Virgin Islds.*); A. F. L. Louisy (*Antigua*); N. Peterkin (*St. Vincent*).

ANTIGUA

Antigua lies in 17° 6′ N. lat. and 61°45′ W. long., and is nearly 108 square miles in area with a coastline of about 70 miles. Antigua was first settled by the English in 1632, and was granted to Lord Willoughby by Charles II. Population at the census of 1960 totalled 54,304; estimated, 1970, 65,000. Antigua is much less hilly and wooded than the other Leeward Islands, and is largely given up to the cultivation of sugar, for which one central sugar factory has been erected. Exports include petroleum products refined in the island. Cotton and rum are also exported. Tourism is the most important industry, with a good choice of resort hotels mostly built to take advantage of the many fine white sand beaches. There are frequent air services to Canada, U.S.A. and the United Kingdom.

FLAG.—Inverted triangle (centred on a red field)

divided horizontally into three bands of black over blue over white; rising sun device in gold on black band.

Finance and Trade

	1966	1967
Revenue......	\$W.I.11,570,582	\$W.I.17,939,229
Expenditure...	10,311,533	17,924,375
Total imports..	43,913,958	39,094,190
Total exports..	2,369,710	4,968,599

Governor, Sir Wilfred Ebenezer Jacobs, O.B.E., Q.C. (1967) (*plus* £1,000 *allce. and house*)......£3,125

Trade with U.K.

(with St. Kitts-Nevis-Anguilla, Montserrat and Virgin Is.).

	1969	1970
Imports from U.K....	£5,268,000	£6,337,000
Exports to U.K......	1,327,000	1,922,000

Barbuda, formerly a possession of the Codrington family, is situated 30 miles N. of Antigua, of which it is a dependency, 62 square miles in lat. 17° 35′ N., long. 61° 42′ W. Area, 62 square miles. Population, 1,000. The island is flat and mostly stony, producing cotton, corn and ground-nuts. Wild deer are found, and there is good tarpon and other fishing.

Warden (vacant).

Redonda is uninhabited,

CAPITAL Ψ St. John's. Population 25,000.

THE CAYMAN ISLANDS

The Cayman Islands, between 79° 44′ and 81° 26′ W. and 19° 15′ and 19° 46′ N., consist of three islands, Grand Cayman, Cayman Brac, and Little Cayman, with a total area of 100 square miles. Population (Census, 1970), 10,652. The constitution provides for an Administrator, Legislative Assembly and an Executive Council. The Legislative Assembly consists of the Administrator, not fewer than two nor more than three nominated members, not fewer than two nor more than three official members and 12 elected members. The Executive Council consists of the Administrator and two official members appointed by the Administrator, one nominated member appointed from among the nominated members of the Assembly and two elected members, elected by the elected members of the Assembly from among their own number. The normal life of the Assembly is three years. Supervisory powers over the government of the Islands exercised by the Government of Jamaica came to an end in August, 1962.

The principal town is Ψ George Town, in Grand Cayman, population (1970 census) 3,000.

Finance.—(Jamaican Dollars) Total revenue of the Cayman Islands in 1969 was J\$2,286,363, expenditure, J\$1,608,553; public debt, J\$962,263.

TRADE

	1969
Total imports....................	J\$5,733,001
Total exports.....................	11,115

Administrator, His Hon. A. C. E. Long, C.M.G., C.B.E.

MONTSERRAT

Situated in 16° 45′ N. lat. and 61° 15′ W. long., 27 miles S.W. of Antigua, the island is about 11 miles long and 7 wide, with an area of 39 square miles; population (estimated, 1967), 14,468. Discovered by Columbus in 1493, it was settled by Irishmen, conquered and held by the French for some time, and finally assigned to Great Britain in 1783. It is justly considered one of the most healthy and beautiful of the Antilles; it contains three active soufrières and several hot springs, while the scenery is charmingly diversified. About two-thirds of the island is mountainous, the rest

capable of cultivation. The chief exports are sea island cotton, tomatoes and other fruits and vegetables. Exports of fruit and vegetables are expanding and in recent years markets were found in the main tourist areas of the Caribbean, Bermuda and the United Kingdom for the island's production of mangoes and hot peppers. Since 1963 real estate development and tourism have done much to aid the island's economy. Revenue (1970), \$4,060,685; Expenditure, \$4,008,429.

Cabinet government was introduced in Montserrat in 1960. The Executive Council is composed of 4 unofficial members (the Chief, 2 other Ministers and a Member without Portfolio) and two official members (the Attorney-General and the Financial Secretary). The 3 Ministers are appointed from the elected members of the Legislative Council. The present composition of the Legislative Council is the Administrator, who presides, two official members, one nominated unofficial member and 7 elected members.

Administrator, His Hon. Willoughby Harry Thompson, C.B.E. (1971) (+*allowances of* £550 *and* £208 *and quarters*)................................£2,750

EXECUTIVE COUNCIL

President, The Administrator.

Chief Minister, Minister of Finance and Tourism, Hon. P. A. Bramble.

Minister of Social Services, Hon. Mrs. M. Juitt.

Agriculture, Lands and Trade, Hon. J. N. Osborne.

Communications and Works, Hon. E. A. Dyer.

Attorney-General, Hon. B. F. Dias.

Financial Secretary, Hon. J. Taylor, C.M.G.

Without Portfolio, Hon. J. Howe.

Secretary to the Executive Council, T. E. Ryan, O.B.E.

CHIEF TOWN.— Ψ Plymouth (3,000).

ST. KITTS-NEVIS

Governor, His Excellency Milton Pentonville Allen, O.B.E. (1969).

The islands of St. Kitts and Nevis are united to form one Territory, and taken together they have a population (1970) of 45,457. and a total area of about 101 square miles. The climate is decidedly healthy for the tropics, the temperature being from 66° to 88° F.

St. Kitts (population 1970, 34,227), the principal island, was the first possession of the British West Indies to be colonized (1623); it is situated in lat. 17° 18′ N. and long. 62° 48′ W., and has an area of 65 square miles, its greatest length being 28 miles, and greatest breadth about 5 miles. It is one of the most effectively cultivated sugar islands in the West Indies, a continuous line of green sugar estates sweeping up all round the coast from the sea towards the central range, which rises to a height of 3,792 feet (Mount Misery). Cotton is also grown to a considerable extent. The capital, Ψ Basseterre, is a port of registry.

Nevis (population 1970, 11,230) is separated from St. Kitts by a strait 3 miles wide and has an area of 36 sq. miles. Cotton is exported and coconuts are also now exported, mainly to Barbados. The raising of livestock and cultivation of vegetables are also important features of the island's economy. Its greatest elevation is 3,596 feet. The chief town, Ψ Charlestown, is a port of entry.

CAPITAL, Ψ Basseterre (St. Kitts). Population (1970), 13,055. *Flag.*—Tricolour of green (next staff), yellow and blue vertical stripes; palm tree device on yellow stripe.

ANGUILLA

Formerly a part of the Associated State above with St. Kitts and Nevis, Anguilla (population

1960, 5,810) is about 70 miles N.W. of St. Kitts, 16 miles in length, and varies in breadth from 1 to 3 miles, containing an area of 35 square miles. There are no hills. Salt is the principal product, and small stock are raised. H.M. Government intervened to restore legal government on the island on Mar. 19, 1969, and British forces patrolled Anguilla until Sept., 1969, leaving a force of Royal Engineers to complete aid projects such as the building of a school and a jetty and the re-surfacing of roads. The Anguilla Act (July 28, 1971) restored Anguilla to direct British control.
H.M. Commissioner for Anguilla, A. C. Watson.

TURKS AND CAICOS ISLANDS

These West Indian islands geographically form part of the Bahamas group, from which Government they were separated in 1848. From 1873 until 1962 they were annexed to Jamaica, from which they are distant about 450 miles, reverting to U.K. administration on August 6, 1962, upon Jamaica's attainment of independence. On November 5, 1965, the Governor of the Bahamas became also the Governor of the Turks and Caicos. The two Colonies share a Common Bench for their Courts of Appeal. They have an area of about 166 square miles, and a population estimated, June, 30, 1967, of 6,000. Ψ Grand Turk is an important cable station. A tourist industry is rapidly developing as the climate, beaches and sea sports generally are amongst the finest in the world. Trade in salt, for which the island used to be celebrated, has greatly diminished in recent years. Other exports are crawfish and conches. A considerable number of men are employed overseas in the Bahamas. There are a U.S. Air Force missile tracking station and a Naval facility at Grand Turk, and a government-owned airstrip at South Caicos, at which refuelling and other facilities are provided.

FINANCE

	1967	1968
Revenue	£419,853	£512,168
Expenditure	395,286	532,173

                ★ Revised Estimates.

TRADE

	1967	1968
Total imports	£356,943	£442,793
Total exports	50,692	63,133

TRADE WITH U.K. (INCL. CAYMAN ISLDS.)

	1968	1969
Imports from U.K.	£212,000	£320,000
Exports to U.K.	149,000	178,000

The Constitution provides for an Administrator, and a State Council. The State Council consists of a Speaker, three official members, not less than two nor more than three nominated members and nine elected members. The normal life of the State Council is five years.
Administrator, His Hon. R. E. Wainwright,
C.M.G., O.B.E. (1968) (+*duty allce.* £300). £2,450

The Windward Islands

The Windward Islands consist of the four colonies of Grenada, St. Vincent, St. Lucia and Dominica with their dependencies; the Grenadines being divided between Grenada and St. Vincent. The total area is 821 square miles. Since March, 1967, with the attainment of Associated Statehood, there has been a Governor in Grenada, St. Lucia and Dominica and in St. Vincent since October, 1969. Each island has its own elected Parliament and Senate and a Premier. The ministerial form of government was introduced in 1956.

WINDWARD ISLANDS TRADE WITH U.K.

	1969	1970
Imports from U.K.	£6,356,000	£9,735,000
Exports to U.K.	12,727,000	9,473,000

GRENADA AND THE GRENADINES

Grenada is situated between the parallels of 12° 13′–11° 58′ N. lat. and 61° 20′–61° 35′ W. long., and is about 21 miles in length and 12 miles in breadth; it is about 96 miles north of Trinidad, 68 miles S.S.W. of St. Vincent, and 100 miles S.W. of Barbados. Area, about 133 square miles: estimated population (including some of the Grenadines), 105,000 (U.N. estimate, 1969). The country is mountainous and very picturesque, and the climate is healthy. Grenada was discovered by Columbus in 1498, and named Conception. It was originally colonized by the French, and was ceded to Great Britain by the Treaty of Versailles in 1783.

The soil is very fertile, and cocoa, spices, bananas, sugar cane, cotton, coconuts, limes and fruit are grown. The imports are chiefly dry goods, wheat, flour, dried fish, feedstuffs, hardware and rice.

Ψ St. George's (population 8,400) on the southwest coast, is the chief town, and possesses a good harbour.

FLAG.—Tricolour of blue, yellow and green horizontal bands—in centre a nutmeg device on an oval white ground bordered by a brown line.

Finance and Trade

	1965	1966
Public revenue	$10,584,820	$12,286,087
Expenditure	10,350,666	11,955,092
Public debt	10,938,261	11,297,361
Total imports	$19,077,304	$21,724,311
Total exports	10,872,452	10,195,761

Government

Grenada became an Associated State in association with Great Britain on March 3, 1967. The Legislature became bicameral consisting of Her Majesty, a Senate and a House of Representatives. There is a Premier, with four other Ministers. The Principal Law Officer is *ex officio* a member of the Senate.
Governor, Dame Hilda Louisa Bynoe, D.B.E. (1968)
   (+*allce.* £1,925) £2,750
Premier, Eric M. Gairy.

The Grenadines are a chain of small islands lying between Grenada and St. Vincent, within which Governments they are included. The largest island is Carriacou, attached to the Government of Grenada, with area of 13 sq. miles and population of 8,177.

ST. LUCIA,

the second largest and the most picturesque of the Windward group, situated in 13° 54′ N. lat. and 60° 50′ W. long., at a distance of about 90 miles W.N.W. of Barbados, 21 miles N. of St. Vincent, and 24 miles S. of Martinique, is 27 miles in length, with an extreme breadth of 14 miles. It comprises an area of 238 square miles with an estimated population (1968) of 108,000. About 56,000 acres are devoted to agriculture. It possesses perhaps the most interesting history of all the smaller islands. Fights raged hotly around it, and it constantly changed hands between the English and the French. It is mountainous, its highest point being 3,145 feet above the sea, and for the most part it is covered with forest and tropical vegetation. The principal exports are bananas, copra, coconuts, cocoa, edible oil. Over 7,000,000 stems of bananas, valued at $10,800,000, were exported to the U.K. in 1969. The chief imports are flour, machinery, cotton piece goods, sacks and bags.

CAPITAL.—Ψ Castries (estimated population, 40,000) is recognized as being one of the finest ports in the West Indies on account of its reputation as a safe anchorage in the hurricane season. In 1966,

1,708 vessels with a total gross tonnage of 2,011.650 called at Castries. FLAG.—Blue, bearing in centre a device of yellow over black over white triangles having a common base.

Government

There is a Cabinet of Ministers presided over by the Premier and consisting of four other Ministers and the Attorney-General. There is a Legislature which consists of Her Majesty and a House of Assembly, of which the normal life is five years. The House of Assembly consists of a Speaker who may be elected from within or without the House, ten elected and three nominated members and the Attorney General. The Constitution provides for a political Attorney-General if the Legislature or the Premier so decides.

Governor, Sir Frederick Joseph Clarke (1967) (+allce. $3,240)	$15,000
Premier and Minister of Finance and Planning and Development, J. G. M. Compton...	12,000
Education and Health, H. J. François......	9,600
Trade, Industry, Agriculture and Tourism, W. G. Mallet........................	9,600
Communications, Works and Labour, J. A. R. Bousquet...........................	9,600
Housing, Community Development and Social Affairs, J. M. D. Bousquet......	9,600
Attorney-General, L. H. Williams........	9,600

ST. VINCENT

St. Vincent achieved Associated Statehood with the United Kingdom on October 27, 1969. The territory of the State of St. Vincent includes certain of the Grenadines, a group of islands set across the Caribbean sea, stretching 40 miles south, some of the larger of which are Bequia, Canouan, Mayreau, Mustique, Union Island, Petit St. Vincent and Isle-a-Quatre. The territory extends 150 square miles (96,000 acres).

The main island, St. Vincent is situated between 13° 6′ and 14° 35′ N. Latitude and 61° 6′ and 61° 20′ W. Longitude approximately 21 miles South West of St. Lucia and 100 miles West of Barbados. The island is 18 miles long and 100 miles wide at its extremities comprising an area of 133 square miles and an estimated population of 92,000 (1968). St. Vincent was discovered by Christopher Columbus in 1498. It was granted by Charles I to the Earl of Carlisle in 1627 and after subsequent grants and a series of occupations alternately by the French and English, it was finally restored to Britain in 1783. The capital and principal port is Ψ Kingstown, population approximately 23,000.

The economy is based mainly on agriculture but the tourist industry has been rapidly expanding, bringing approximately $4m. to the State in 1969 compared with $2.6m. in 1968. The main products are bananas, arrowroot, coconuts, cocoa, spices, and various kinds of food crops. The main imports are food-stuffs (meat, rice, sugar, flour, butter and pickled and salted fish) textiles, lumber, cement and other building materials, fertilizers and motor vehicles.

The territory's education system provides a general primary and secondary education. Primary education is free but not compulsory. In 1969 there were 58 primary schools with a total enrolment of 27,418; two Government secondary schools and nine (9) privately owned secondary schools with a total enrolment of 3,485 students.

Government.—As an Associated State St. Vincent has a new constitution under which there is a Governor who is Her Majesty's Representative. Except where otherwise provided, the Governor is required to act in accordance with the advice of the Cabinet. Statehood allows St. Vincent the full

self-governing control of its internal affairs including the right to amend its own constitution and the power to end the Association and declare itself independent. The United Kingdom Government accepts the responsibility for the State's external affairs and defence.

Governor, His Excellency Sir Rupert Godfrey John (1971)

CABINET

Premier and Minister of Finance, Hon. R. M. Cato.
Minister for Education and Health, Hon. H. K. Tannis.
Agriculture, Trade and Tourism, Hon. J. F. Mitchell.
Communications, Works and Labour, Hon. L. C. Latham.
Home Affairs, Hon. S. E. Slater.
Housing, Local Government and Community Development, Hon. R. F. Marksman.
Attorney-General, Hon A. T. Warner.

The House of Assembly consists of nine elected members, two nominated members and the Attorney-General, but there is provision for 13 elected seats in the next general election. It is presided over by a Speaker elected by the House from within or without it.

JUDICIARY

Puisne Judge, St. Vincent Circuit, N. Peterkin.
Magistrates, C. E. A. Rawle; S. A. Browne.
Registrar, Supreme Court: A. T. Woods.

Finance and Trade

	1968	1969*
Revenue (including grants)....	EC$9,250,000	EC$10,090,000
Expenditure......	8,650,000	9,250,000
Total Imports....	17,900,000	18,800,000
Total visible Exports..........	8,000,000	8,200,000
G.D.P...........	31,360,000	32,880,000
Public Debt (Dec. 31, 1969)......	—	4,000,000

* Estimated

DOMINICA

Dominica, the loftiest of the Lesser Antilles, was transferred from the Leeward to the Windward Group on Jan. 1, 1940. It is situated between 15° 20 and 15° 45′ N. lat. and 61° 13′ and 61° 30′ W. long., 95 miles S. of Antigua, and is about 29 miles long and 15 broad comprising an area of 290 sq. miles, of which about 37,000 acres are under cultivation. The island is of volcanic origin and very mountainous and picturesque, abounding in streams fairly well stocked with fish, and the soil is very fertile. The temperature varies, according to the altitude, from 55° to 85°F. The climate is healthy, and during the winter months very pleasant. The exports consist almost entirely of agricultural produce, principally bananas, lime oil, lime juice, oranges, bay oil, cocoa, copra and vanilla. Population (U.N. estimate, 1969, 74,000). The principal towns are Ψ Roseau, on the south-west coast, population, 11,924 and Portsmouth, population, 2,566.

Education.—There are 53 elementary schools, of which 50 are Government and 3 assisted. Of the 4 secondary schools, 3 receive a grant-in-aid and one is maintained by the Government.

Finance and Trade

	1968	1969*
Revenue (incl. Grants).	$8,453,931	$8,688,285
Expenditure (do.).....	10,352,163	11,247,445
Public debt.........	2,169,600	2,169,600

Government

On March 1, 1967, Dominica received a new Constitution and became an Associated State of the United Kingdom. The Queen's Representative was renamed the Governor.

The new House of Assembly now comprises 11 elected and 3 nominated members, one nominated on the advice of the Leader of the Opposition. The Cabinet (Executive) presided over by the Premier, consists of 4 other Government Ministers and the Attorney-General (Official Member). The Premier is appointed by the Governor from the elected members of the House of Assembly. The other Ministers are appointed by the Governor on the advice of the Premier. The Speaker is elected from among the members of the House or from outside.

Governor, His Excellency Sir Louis Cools-Lartigue, O.B.E. (1967).

Premier, Hon. E. O. Leblanc.

UNIVERSITIES OF THE COMMONWEALTH
(outside the United Kingdom)

With date of foundation, number of full-time students and name of Executive Head
(*Vice-Chancellor, President or Principal*)

Australia

ADELAIDE (1874). (Full-time students, 5,611).— *Vice-Chancellor,* Prof. G. M. Badger, Ph.D., D.SC.

AUSTRALIAN NATIONAL (1946), Canberra. (2,519).— *Vice-Chancellor,* Emeritus Prof. Sir John Crawford, C.B.E., D.SC.

JAMES COOK, NORTH QUEENSLAND (1970), Townsville. (907).—*Vice-Chancellor,* K. J. C. Back, Ph.D.

FLINDERS, SOUTH AUSTRALIA (1966), Bedford Park (1,661).—*Vice-Chancellor,* (vacant).

LA TROBE (1964), Melbourne. (2,282).—*Vice-Chancellor,* D. M. Myers, D.SC Eng.

MACQUARIE (1964), Sydney. (2,622).—*Vice-Chancellor,* Emeritus Prof. A. G. Mitchell, Ph.D.

MELBOURNE (1853). (10,508).—*Vice-Chancellor,* Prof. D. P. Derham, M.B.E., LL.D.

MONASH (1958), Melbourne. (8,359).—*Vice-Chancellor,* J. A. L. Matheson, M.B.E., Ph.D.

NEWCASTLE (1965). (1,912)—*Vice-Chancellor,* Prof. J. J. Auchmuty, C.B.E., Ph.D.

NEW ENGLAND (1954), Armidale. (2,147).—*Vice-Chancellor,* Prof. A. Lazenby, Ph.D.

NEW SOUTH WALES (1949), Sydney. (11,255).—*Vice-Chancellor,* Prof. R. H. Myers, Ph.D.

WOLLONGONG UNIV. COLL. (1961). (1,337).— *Warden,* Prof. C. A. M. Gray.

W. S. & L. B. ROBINSON UNIV. COLL. (1967), Broken Hill (108).—*Director,* Prof. A. H. Willis, D.SC.(Eng).

QUEENSLAND (1909), Brisbane. (8,210).—*Vice-Chancellor,* Z. Cowen, C.M.G., D.C.I., LL.D.

SYDNEY (1850). (11,018).—*Vice-Chancellor,* Prof. B. R. Williams.

TASMANIA (1890), Hobart. (2,270).—*Vice-Chancellor,* Sir George Cartland, C.M.G.

WESTERN AUSTRALIA (1911), Perth. (5,295).—*Vice-Chancellor,* Emeritus Prof. R. F. Whelan, M.D., Ph.D., D.SC.

Canada

ACADIA (1838), Wolfville. (Full-time students, 2,368).—*President,* J. M. R. Beveridge, M.D., Ph.D., D.SC., LL.D.

ALBERTA (1906), Edmonton. (18,337).—*President,* M. Wyman, Ph.D.

BISHOP'S (1843), Lennoxville. (1,174).—*Vice-Chancellor,* D. M. Healy, Ph.D.

BRANDON (1967). (1,150).—*President,* A. L. Dulmage, Ph.D.

BRITISH COLUMBIA (1908), Vancouver. (20,157).— *President,* W. H. Gage, LL.D.

BROCK (1964), St. Catherines. (2,228).—*President,* J. A. Gibson, D.Phil., LL.D.

CALGARY (1966). (7,962).—*President,* A. W. R. Carrothers, S.J.D.

CARLETON (1942), Ottawa. (7,139).—*President,* A. Davidson Dunton, D.SC., LL.D.

DALHOUSIE (1818), Halifax. (5,545).—*President,* H. D. Hicks, Q.C., LL.D., D.Ed., D.C.L.

UNIV. OF KING'S COLL. (1789), Halifax. (254).—*President,* J. G. Morgan, D.Phil.

GUELPH (1964). (6,045).—*Vice-Chancellor,* W. C. Winegard, Ph.D.

LAKEHEAD (1965), Thunder Bay. (2,546).—*Vice-Chancellor,* W. G. Tamblyn, LL.D.

LAURENTIAN, SUDBURY (1960). (1,780).—*Acting President,* R. J. A. Cloutier, Ph.D.

LAVAL (1852), Quebec. (14,800).—*Rector Magnificus,* Mgr. L.-A. Vachon, D.Th., D.Ph., LL.D.

LETHBRIDGE (1967). (1,335).—*President,* W. A. S. Smith, Ph.D.

McGILL (1821), Montreal. (15,162).—*Principal,* R. E. Bell, Ph.D.

McMASTER (1887), Hamilton. (7,931).—*President,* H. G. Thode, M.B.E., Ph.D., LL.D., D.SC.

MANITOBA (1877), Winnipeg. (13,225).—*President,* E. Sirluck, M.B.E., Ph.D., LL.D.

ST. JOHN'S COLL. (1866), Winnipeg. (320).— *Warden,* Rev. Canon J. R. Brown, D.D.

ST. PAUL'S COLL. (1926), Winnipeg.—*Rector,* Rev. J. E. Page.

MEMORIAL, NEWFOUNDLAND (1949), St. John's. (6,514).—*Vice-Chancellor,* Lord Taylor, M.D.

MONCTON (1963). (2,686).—*Rector,* A. Savoie, Q.C.

MONTREAL (1876). (13,062).—*Rector,* R. Gaudry, D.SC., LL.D., D.U.

COLL. JEAN-DE-BREBEUF (1929), Montreal.

LOYOLA COLL. (1899), Montreal.

MARIANOPOLIS COLL., Montreal.

MOUNT ALLISON (1858), Sackville. (1,363).—*President,* L. H. Cragg, Ph.D., D.SC., D.C.L.

MOUNT ST. VINCENT (1925), Halifax. (944).—*President,* Sister Catherine Wallace, Ph.D., LL.D.

NEW BRUNSWICK (1785), Fredericton. (5,409).— *President,* J. O. Dineen, LL.D., D.SC.

NOTRE DAME, NELSON (1963). (647).—*President,* C. Kaller, Ph.D.

NOVA SCOTIA AGRICULTURAL COLL. (1905), Truro. (355).—*Principal,* W. A. Jenkins, Dr. P.A.

NOVA SCOTIA COLL. OF ART AND DESIGN, Halifax.

NOVA SCOTIA TECHNICAL COLL. (1909), Halifax. (567).—*Acting President,* A. E. Steeves.

OTTAWA (1848). (7,200).—*Rector,* Rev. R. Guindon, D.Th., LL.D.

ST. PAUL (1848), Ottawa.—*Rector,* M. Patry, D.Ph.

PRINCE EDWARD ISLAND (1969), Charlottetown (1,755).—*President,* R. J. Baker, LL.D.

QUEBEC (1968), Chicoutimi, Montreal and Trois-Rivières. (4,597)—*President,* A. Riverin, D.SC.Econ.

QUEEN'S, KINGSTON (1841). (7,868).—*Principal,* J. J. Deutsch, C.C., LL.D., D.SOC.SC., D.U.

ROYAL MILITARY COLL. OF CANADA (1876), Kingston. (557).—*Commandant*, Brig.-Gen. W. K. Lye, M.B.E.

ST. FRANCIS XAVIER (1853), Antigonish. (2,984).—*President*, Rev. M. MacDonell.

ST. MARY'S (1841), Halifax. (2,070).—*President*, D. O. Carrigan, Ph.D.

SASKATCHEWAN (1907), Saskatoon (10,085) and Regina (4,199).—*President*, J. W. T. Spinks, M.B.E., Ph.D., D.SC., LL.D.

SHERBROOKE (1954). (4,135).—*Rector*, Mgr. R. Maltais.

SIMON FRASER (1963), Burnaby. (4,727).—*President*, K. T. Strand, Ph.D.

SIR GEORGE WILLIAMS (1929), Montreal. (5,928).—*Principal*, J. W. O'Brien, Ph.D.

TORONTO (1827). (26,591).—*Acting President*, J. H. Sword, LL.D.
  UNIV. OF ST. MICHAEL'S COLL. (1852), Toronto. (2,326).—*President*, Rev. J. M. Kelly, Ph.D.
  UNIV. OF TRINITY COLL. (1851), Toronto. (759).—*Vice-Chancellor*, Rev. Canon D. R. G. Owen, Ph.D., D.D., D.C.L.
  VICTORIA (1836), Toronto. (2,626).—*President*, J. E. Hodgetts, Ph.D., LL.D.

ONTARIO INSTITUTE FOR STUDIES IN EDUCATION (1965), Toronto. (361).—*Director*, R. W. Jackson, Ph.D., LL.D.

TRENT (1963), Peterborough. (1,688).—*President*, T. H. B. Symons.

VICTORIA (1963), British Columbia. (5,119).—*President*, B. J. Partridge, J.D.

WATERLOO (1959). (10,673).—*Vice-Chancellor*, B. C. Matthews, Ph.D.
  ST. JEROME'S COLL., Waterloo.—*President*, Rev. J. R. Finn, Ph.D.

WATERLOO LUTHERAN (1960). (2,826).—*President*, F. C. Peters, Ph.D.

WESTERN ONTARIO (1878), London. (13,641).—*President*, D. C. Williams, Ph.D., LL.D.
  BRESCIA COLL. (1919), London.—*Dean*, Sister Arleene Walker.
  HURON COLL. (1863), London.—*Principal*, Ven. J. G. Morden, D.D., D.Th.
  KING'S COLL. (1912), London.—*Executive Head*, A. F. McKee, D.U.

WINDSOR (1857). (5,940).—*Vice-Chancellor*, J. F. Leddy, D.Phil., D.Litt., D. ès L., LL.D., D.C.L.

WINNIPEG (1967). (2,416).—*President*, H. E. Duckworth, Ph.D., D.SC.

YORK (1959). (9,787).—*President*, D. W. Slater, Ph.D.

Ceylon

CEYLON (1942), Peradeniya. (Full-time students, 4,137).—*Vice-Chancellor*, S. U. Kodikara, Ph.D.

CEYLON, COLOMBO (1968). (4,532).—*Vice-Chancellor*, B. A. Abeywickrama, Ph.D.

VIDYALANKARA (1959), Kelaniya. (1,420).—*Vice-Chancellor*, K. W. Goonewardena.

VIDYODAYA (1959), Gangodawila. (2,500).—*Acting Vice-Chancellor*, H. Ellawala, Ph.D.

Fiji

SOUTH PACIFIC (1967), Suva. (Full-time students, 417).—*Vice-Chancellor*, C. C. Aikman, Ph.D.

Ghana

GHANA (1961), Legon. (Full-time students, 2,347).—*Vice-Chancellor*, A. A. Kwapong, Ph.D.

UNIV. COLL. OF CAPE COAST (1962). (862).—*Principal*, E. A. Boateng.

UNIV. OF SCIENCE AND TECHNOLOGY (1961), Kumasi. (1,344).—*Vice-Chancellor*, E. Evans-Anfom.

Guyana

GUYANA (1963), Georgetown. (Part-time students, 1,032).—*Vice-Chancellor*, D. H. Irvine, Ph.D.

Hong Kong

CHINESE UNIV. OF HONG KONG (1963). (Full-time students, 2,408).—*Vice-Chancellor*, C. M. Li, C.B.E., Ph.D., LL.D., D.S.SC.

HONG KONG (1911). (2,871).—*Vice-Chancellor*, K. E. Robinson, C.B.E., LL.D.

India

AGRA (1927). (Full-time students, 45,758).—*Vice-Chancellor*, S. Prasad.

AGRICULTURAL SCIENCES (1964), Bangalore. (1,740).—*Vice-Chancellor*, K. C. Naik, Ph.D.

ALIGARH MUSLIM (1920). (7,550).—*Vice-Chancellor*, A. Aleem, Ph.D.

ALLAHABAD (1887). (8,982).—*Acting Vice-Chancellor*, C. M. Bhatia, Ph.D.

ANDHRA (1926), Waltair. (66,641).—*Vice-Chancellor*, L. Bullayya.

ANNAMALAI (1928), Annamalainagar. (6,250).—*Vice-Chancellor*, S. P. Adinarayan, Ph.D.

AWADHESH PRATAP SINGH VISHWAVIDYALAYA (1968), Rewa. (17,351)—*Vice-Chancellor*, L. O. Joshi.

BANARAS HINDU (1915). (10,478).—*Vice-Chancellor*, K. L. Shrimali, Ph.D.

BANGALORE (1964). (39,151).—*Vice-Chancellor*, T. K. Tukol.

BARODA (1949). (15,149).—*Vice-Chancellor*, N. K. Vakil.

BERHAMPUR (1967).—*Vice-Chancellor*, R. P. Padhi.

BHAGALPUR (1960). (39,617).—*Vice-Chancellor*, S. N. Agrawal.

BIHAR (1952), Muzaffarpur. (44,039).—*Vice-Chancellor*, Dr. T. B. Mukherjee.

BOMBAY (1857). (91,227).—*Vice-Chancellor*, P. B. Gajendragadkar, LL.D.

BURDWAN (1960). (37,997).—*Vice-Chancellor*, S. B. Chaudhuri, Ph.D.

CALCUTTA (1857). (196,257).—*Vice-Chancellor*, S. N. Sen, Ph.D.

DELHI (1922). (48,007).—*Vice-Chancellor*, Dr. S. Singh.

DIBRUGARH (1965). (20,003).—*Vice-Chancellor*, B. R. Seth, Ph.D., D.SC.

GAUHATI (1948). (35,532).—*Vice-Chancellor*, M. N. Goswami, Ph.D.

GORAKHPUR (1956). (37,237).—*Vice-Chancellor*, C. B. Rao.

GUJARAT (1949), Ahmedabad. (68,627).—*Vice-Chancellor*, U. J. Joshi.

INDIAN INST. OF TECHNOLOGY, BOMBAY (1958). (2,169).—*Director*, P. K. Kelkar, Ph.D.

INDIAN INST. OF TECHNOLOGY, DELHI (1961). (1,813).—*Director*, R. N. Dogra.

INDIAN INST. OF TECHNOLOGY, KANPUR (1960). (1,950).—*Officiating Director*, M. S. Muthana, Ph.D.

INDIAN INST. OF TECHNOLOGY, KHARAGPUR (1951). (2,380).—*Director*, Prof. S. K. Bose, D.SC.

INDIAN INST. OF TECHNOLOGY, MADRAS (1959). (1,684).—*Director*, A. Ramachandran, Ph.D.

INDORE (1964). (19,736).—*Vice-Chancellor*, K. L. Joshi.

JABALPUR (1957). (16,434).—*Vice-Chancellor*, R. B. Pandey, D.Litt.

JADAVPUR (1955), Calcutta. (4,132).—*Vice-Chancellor*, A. K. Majumder, D.SC.

JAMMU (1969). (9,253).—*Vice-Chancellor*, J. N. Bhan, Ph.D.

JAWAHARLAL NEHRU KRISHI VISHWA VIDYALAYA (1964), Jabalpur. (1,569).—*Vice-Chancellor*, L. S. Negi, Ph.D.

JIWAJI (1964), Gwalior. (29,487).—*Vice-Chancellor*, S. S. Bhandarkar.

JODHPUR (1962). (7,153).—*Vice-Chancellor*, V. V. John.

KALYANI (1960). (2,162).—*Vice-Chancellor*, K. Sen.

KANPUR (1965). (58,328).—*Vice-Chancellor*, R. Krishna.
KARNATAK (1949), Dharwar. (62,819).—*Vice-Chancellor*, A. S. Adke, Ph.D.
KASHMIR (1969), Srinagar. (14,508).—*Acting Vice-Chancellor*, K. Noor-ud-Din.
KERALA (1937). Trivandrum. (112,302).—*Vice-Chancellor*, G. Jacob, Ph.D.
KURUKSHETRA (1956). (4,919).—*Vice-Chancellor*, S. K. Dutta, D.Litt.
LUCKNOW (1921). (24,998).—*Vice-Chancellor*, M.B. Lal, D.Sc.
MADRAS (1857). (116,547).—*Vice-Chancellor*, N. D. Sundaravadivelu.
MADURAI (1966). (53,317).—*Vice-Chancellor*, M. Varadarajan, Ph.D.
MAGADH (1962), Gaya. (37,132).—*Vice-Chancellor*, G. Prasad.
MARATHWADA (1958), Aurangabad. (28,310).— *Vice-Chancellor*, N. R. Tawde, Ph.D.
MEERUT (1966).—*Vice-Chancellor*, Dr. J. N. Kapur.
MYSORE (1916). (73,966).—*Vice-Chancellor*, D. J. Gowda.
NAGPUR (1923). (66,697).—*Vice-Chancellor*, Col. V. B. Kolte, Ph.D.
NORTH BENGAL (1962), Siliguri. (21,979).—*Vice-Chancellor*, Prof. P. C. Mukerji.
OSMANIA (1918), Hyderabad. (47,469).—*Vice-Chancellor*, R. Satyanarayan, Ph.D.
PANJAB (1947), Chandigarh. (151,899).—*Vice-Chancellor*, Suraj Bhan.
PATNA (1917). (12,511).—*Acting Vice-Chancellor*, M. Pratap.
POONA (1948). (58,149).—*Vice-Chancellor*, B. P. Apte.
PUNJABI (1961), Patiala. (21,325).—*Vice-Chancellor*, Kirpal Singh Narang.
RABINDRA BHARATI (1962) Calcutta. (2,409).— *Vice-Chancellor*, Mrs. Roma Chaudhuri, D.Phil.
RAJASTHAN (1947), Jaipur. (49,875).—*Vice-Chancellor*, Prof. A. B. Lal.
RANCHI (1960). (40,824).—*Vice-Chancellor*, B. N. Rohatgi.
RAVISHANKAR (1963), Raipur. (20,528).—*Vice-Chancellor*, B. L. Pandey.
ROORKEE (1949). (2,066).—*Vice-Chancellor*, M. R. Chopra.
SAMBALPUR (1967).—*Vice-Chancellor*, R. K. Kapur.
SARDAR PATEL (1955), Vallabh Vidyanagar. (11,985). —*Vice-Chancellor*, R. H. Mehta.
SAUGAR (1946), Sagar. (21,124).—Acting *Vice-Chancellor*, Dr. W. D. West.
SAURASHTRA (1966), Rajkot.—*Acting Vice-Chancellor*, H. Trivedi.
SHIVAJI (1962), Kolhapur (49,405).—*Vice-Chancellor*, A. G. Pawar, Ph.D.
SHREEMATI N. D. THACKERSEY WOMEN'S (1951), Bombay. (12,613).—*Vice-Chancellor*, Mrs. Sharda Divan.
SOUTH GUJARAT (1966), Surat. (17,105).—*Vice-Chancellor*, V. R. Shah.
SRI VENKATESWARA (1954), Tirupati. (35,203).— *Vice-Chancellor*, D. Jaganatha Reddy, M.D.
UDAIPUR (1962). (6,724).—*Vice-Chancellor*, G. S. Mahajani, Ph.D.
UTKAL (1943), Bhubaneswar. (30,111).—*Vice-Chancellor*, S. Misra, Ph.D.
UTTAR PRADESH AGRICULTURAL (1960), Pantnagar. (1,796).—*Vice-Chancellor*, D. P. Singh.
VARANASEYA SANSKRIT VISHWAVIDYALAYA (1958), Varanasi. (553).—*Vice-Chancellor*, R. G. Chandra, D.Litt.
VIKRAM (1957), Ujjain. (34,007).—*Vice-Chancellor*, S. M. Singh, Ph.D., D.Litt.
VISVA-BHARATI (1951), Santiniketan. (1,133).—*Vice-Chancellor*, P. C. Gupta, Ph.D.

Kenya
NAIROBI (1970). (Full-time students, 2,106).— *Vice-Chancellor*, J. N. Karanja, Ph.D.

Lesotho
BOTSWANA, LESOTHO AND SWAZILAND (1964), Roma; also campuses in Botswana and Swaziland. (Full-time students, 398).—*Vice-Chancellor*, Prof. C. A. Rogers, Ph.D.,

Malawi
MALAWI (1964), Limbe. (929).—*Vice-Chancellor*, Ian Michael, Ph.D.

Malaysia
MALAYA (1962), Kuala Lumpur. (Full-time students, 7,948).—*Vice-Chancellor*, Prof. Ungku A. Aziz, D.Econ.
NATIONAL UNIV. OF MALAYSIA (1970), Kuala Lumpur. (408).—*Vice-Chancellor*, Datuk Dr. Ariffin bin Hj. Ngah Marzuki.
PENANG (1969). (262).—*Vice-Chancellor*, Prof. H. Sendut, D.Sc., LL.D.

Malta
ROYAL UNIV. OF MALTA (1769), Valletta. (864).— *Vice-Chancellor*, Prof. E. J. Borg Costanzi.

Mauritius
MAURITIUS (1965). (564).—*Vice-Chancellor*, P. O. Wiehé, C.B.E., D.Sc.

New Zealand
AUCKLAND (1882). (Full-time students, 6,814).— *Vice-Chancellor*, C. J. Maiden, D.Phil.
CANTERBURY (1873), Christchurch. (5,028).— *Vice-Chancellor*, Emeritus Prof. N. C. Phillips.
  LINCOLN COLL. (1873). (1,028).—*Principal*, M. M. Burns, C.B.E., Ph.D.
MASSEY (1964), Palmerston North. (2,016).—*Vice-Chancellor*, A. Stewart, D.Phil.
OTAGO (1869), Dunedin. (4,280).—*Vice-Chancellor*, R. M. Williams, Ph.D.
VICTORIA, WELLINGTON (1897). (4,251).—*Vice-Chancellor*, D. B. C. Taylor, Ph.D.
WAIKATO (1964), Hamilton. (1,213).—*Vice-Chancellor*, D. R. Llewellyn, D.Phil., D.Sc.

Nigeria
AHMADU BELLO (1962), Zaria. (Full-time students, 2,351).—*Vice-Chancellor*, I. S. Audu, L.H.D.
IBADAN (1948). (3,135).—*Vice-Chancellor*, Prof. T. A. Lambo, O.B.E., M.D., D.Sc.
IFE (1961). (1,803).—*Vice-Chancellor*, H. A. Oluwasanmi, Ph.D.
LAGOS (1962). (2,270).—*Vice-Chancellor*, S. O. Biobaku, C.M.G., Ph.D.
NIGERIA (1960), Nsukka. (1,815).—*Vice-Chancellor* Prof. H. C. Kodilinye.

Pakistan
BALUCHISTAN (1970), Quetta.—*Vice-Chancellor*, Mr. Justice D. Patel.
CHITTAGONG (1966). (Full-time students, 22,364).— *Vice-Chancellor*, U. M. Siddique.
DACCA (1921). (45,191).—*Vice-Chancellor*, Dr. S. S. Hussain.
E. PAKISTAN AGRICULTURAL (1961), Mymensingh. (1,952).—*Vice-Chancellor*, Dr. A. Islam.
E. PAKISTAN U. OF ENGINEERING AND TECHNOLOGY (1961), Dacca. (1,661).—*Vice-Chancellor*, M. A. Naser, Ph.D.
ISLAMABAD (1965), Rawalpindi. (139).—*Vice-Chancellor*, M. Raziuddin Siddiqi, Ph.D., D.Sc.
JAHANGIRNAGAR MUSLIM (1970), Dacca.—*Vice-Chancellor*, M. Ahmed, Ph.D.
KARACHI (1950). (3,506).—*Vice-Chancellor*, Dr. M. Hussain.
PESHAWAR (1950). (20,718).—*Vice-Chancellor*, A. Hashim Khan.

PUNJAB (1882), Lahore. (41,542).—*Vice-Chancellor,* Prof. A. Allama Siddiqui.

RAJSHAHI (1953). (32,507).—*Vice-Chancellor,* Dr. M. A. Bari.

SIND (1947), Hyderabad. (11,951).—*Vice-Chancellor,* H. A. Rehman.

W. PAKISTAN AGRICULTURAL (1961), Lyallpur. (1,565).—*Vice-Chancellor,* Israr-ul-Haq, Ph.D.

W. PAKISTAN UNIVERSITY OF ENGINEERING AND TECHNOLOGY (1961), Lahore. (2,332).—*Vice-Chancellor,* A. Hussan Sheikh.

Papua New Guinea

PAPUA and NEW GUINEA (1965), Port Moresby. (Full-time students, 670).—*Vice-Chancellor,* J. T. Gunther, C.M.G., O.B.E.

Rhodesia

RHODESIA (1955), Salisbury. (Full-time students, 937).—*Principal,* Rev. Prof. R. Craig, Ph.D., D.D.

Sierra Leone

SIERRA LEONE (1966).—*Vice-Chancellor,* Rev. Canon Prof. H. A. E. Sawyerr, C.B.E., D.D.

FOURAH BAY COLL. (1960), Freetown. (Full-time students, 747).—*Principal,* Rev. Canon Prof. H. A. E. Sawyerr, C.B.E., D.D.

NJALA UNIV. COLL. (1964). (303).—*Principal,* S. T. Matturi, C.M.G., Ph.D.

Singapore

NANYANG (1953). (Full-time students, 2,039).—*Vice-Chancellor,* Prof. R. L. Huang, D.Sc., D.Phil.

SINGAPORE (1962). (4,394).—*Vice-Chancellor,* Toh Chin Chye, Ph.D.

Tanzania

DAR ES SALAAM (1970). (Full-time students, 1,989).—*Vice-Chancellor,* P. Msekwa.

Uganda

MAKERERE (1970), Kampala. (Full-time students, 2,645).—*Vice-Chancellor,* F. Kalimuzo.

West Indies

UNIV. OF THE WEST INDIES (1962), Jamaica, with branches in Trinidad and Barbados. (Full-time students, 3,733).—*Vice-Chancellor,* O. R. Marshall, C.B.E., Ph.D.

Zambia

ZAMBIA (1965), Lusaka. (Full-time students, 1,184).—*Vice-Chancellor,* L. K. H. Goma, Ph.D.

H.M. COASTGUARD

Between April 1, 1970, and March 31, 1971, Coastguards saved 3,550 lives and took part in 2,919 rescue operations on British coasts.

There are about 550 full-time Coastguards and 7,000 part-time Auxiliary Coastguards on service to save and safeguard the lives of those at sea and around the 2,500 mile coastline of the United Kingdom. H.M. Coastguard is administered by the Department of Trade and Industry in 10 Divisions, each with three or four Districts within its boundaries. Each District has a number of stations and lookouts of which there are four types.

Constant Watch Stations are manned at all times, keeping a 24-hour watch, the coastguards working six-hour watches. *Day Watch Stations* are manned by three or four coastguards who each keep a four-hour watch in daylight. Additional watch is kept in bad weather. *Auxiliary Lookout Stations* are manned by Auxiliary Coastguards as and when a need arises. *Auxiliary Rescue Stations* are manned by Auxiliary Coastguards as and when a need arises. *Auxiliary Rescue Stations* are comprehensively equipped for all types of rescue.

Coastguard stations and lookouts are frequently located on bleak and isolated clifftops and headlands from which visual and radio watch is kept. The coastguard records the passage of ships at his post or station and informs the next station so that each ship's progress is noted and followed round the coast from station to station. Those intending to make a coastal passage and requiring Coastguard surveillance apply to their Coastguard Rescue Headquarters for a form which, when completed, gives details of the boat's intended passage, a description of the craft and method of identification, enabling the Coastguard stations along the route to keep watch and to organize rescue services should the need arise. As far as local cruising is concerned, H.M. Coastguard advises those making a short trip to leave details of their destination and estimated time of arrival with someone who can contact the local Coastguard station should the boat be overdue. A good description of the boat is vital if a search has to be made. Should a plan be altered, relatives or friends should be told.

Coastguards also watch for oil slicks, hazards and almost anything out of the ordinary, taking all necessary action to warn shipping of hazards.

They are ready to take action on any distress signal and keep all lights in their area under observation, reporting any fault to the appropriate authority. Coastguard radios are tuned to the "distress frequencies" ready to take action if a ship makes a MAYDAY call. A Bad Weather Watch (BWW) is set whenever the wind exceeds Force 6. A Thick Weather Watch (TWW) is set whenever visibility falls to half a mile or less.

Most Coastguard stations give shipping vital information about impending bad weather through the Gale Warning Service. The stations hoist cones on their flag masts, usually black, though at Aberdeen, Cromarty, Kildonan, Ardglass and the Mull of Kintyre Lighthouse they are white so that they can be readily distinguished from the background of dark rocks; for the same reason the cones used at St. Ives and Looe are orange and yellow respectively. The direction of the gale forecast is roughly indicated by the position of the cone; where its apex points upwards, the gale is expected from any point North of the East–West line, and where the apex points downwards the gale is expected from any point South of the East–West line.

Members of the public who urgently require the services of the Coastguard should make an emergency "999" call and ask for "Coastguard." The call will be routed to the nearest Coastguard Rescue Headquarters which is the co-ordinating authority for Search and Rescue operations and which will alert the appropriate Coastguard stations. As the Coastguard Rescue Headquarters is likely to be some way from the scene of the incident, it is important that the person making the call should give as many details as possible (*e.g.* the nature of the emergency, its position, etc.) and should be prepared, if required, to stay near the telephone, in case additional information is required, or to report any change in the situation. On occasions when larger ships need help the Coastguard will alert the lifeboats of the Royal National Lifeboat Institution or inshore rescue boats, Royal Air Force or Royal Navy helicopters, or R.A.F. *Shackleton* aircraft, depending on the circumstances. When ships founder on rocks or beaches the Coastguard commonly organizes a breeches buoy rescue. Coastguard Rescue companies were called out on 460 occasions in the year ending March 31, 1971.

Ireland

See also Northern Ireland, pp. 688–91; Republic of Ireland, pp. 795–797.

Position and Extent.—Ireland lies in the Atlantic Ocean, to the West of Great Britain, and is separated from Scotland by the North Channel and from Wales by the Irish Sea and St. George's Channel. The land area of the island is 32,408 sq. miles and its geographical position between 51° 26' and 55° 21' N. latitude and from 5° 25' to 10° 30' W. longitude. The greatest length of the island, from N.E. to S.W. (Torr Head to Mizen Head), is 302 miles, and the greatest breadth, from E. to W. (Dundrum Bay to Annagh Head), is 174 miles. On the N. coast of Achill Island (Co. Mayo) are the highest cliffs in the British Isles, 2,000 feet sheer above the sea. Ireland is occupied for the greater part of its area by the *Central Plain*, with an elevation of 50 to 350 ft. above mean sea level, with isolated mountain ranges near the coastline. The principal mountains, with their highest points, are the *Sperrin Mountains* (Sawel 2,240 ft.) of County Tyrone; the *Mountains of Mourne* (Slieve Donard 2,796 ft.) of County Down, and the *Wicklow Mountains* (Lugnaquilla 3,039 ft.); the *Derryveagh Mountains* (Errigal 2,466 ft.) of County Donegal; the *Connemara Mountains* (Twelve Pins 2,695 ft.) of County Galway; *Macgillicuddy's Reeks* (Carrantuohill 3,414 ft., the highest point in Ireland); and the *Galtee Mountains* (3,018 ft.) of County Tipperary, and the *Knockmealdown* (2,609 ft.) and *Comeragh Mountains* (2,470 ft.) of County Waterford. The principal river of Ireland (and the longest in the British Isles) is the *Shannon* (240 miles), rising in County Cavan and draining the central plain. The Shannon flows through a chain of loughs to the city of Limerick, and thence to an estuary on the western Atlantic seaboard. The *Slaney* flows into Wexford Harbour, the *Liffey* to Dublin Bay, the *Boyne* to Drogheda, the *Lee* to Cork Harbour, the *Blackwater* to Youghal Harbour, and the *Suir*, *Barrow* and *Nore*, to Waterford Harbour. As in Scotland, the principal hydrographic feature is the *Loughs*, of which Lough Neagh (150 sq. miles) in the north-east is the largest in Ireland and the British Isles, others being the Shannon Chain of *Allen*, *Boderg*, *Forbes*, *Ree* and *Derg*, and the Erne Chain of *Gowna*, *Oughter*, *Lower Erne*, and *Erne*; *Melvin*, *Gill*, *Gara* and *Conn* in the north-west; and *Corrib* and *Mask* (joined by a hidden channel) in the west. In County Kerry, to the east of Macgillicuddy's Reeks, are the famous *Lakes of Killarney*. The climate of Ireland is more equable than that of Great Britain, the extreme range of temperature readings being from 2° F. to 90° F. (compared with − 17° F. to 100° F. over Great Britain). The average annual rainfall varies from 27 inches at Dublin to more than 100 inches in the mountains of Connemara. The rainfall is also more uniform from year to year than in Great Britain.

Primitive Man.—Although little is known concerning the earliest inhabitants of Ireland, there are many traces of neolithic man throughout the island; a grave containing a polished stone axehead assigned to 2,500 B.C. was found at Linkardstown, Co. Carlow, in 1944, and the use of bronze implements appears to have become known about the middle of the 17th century B.C. In the later Bronze Age a Celtic race of *Goidels* appears to have invaded the island, and in the early Iron Age *Brythons* from South Britain are believed to have effected settlements in the south-east, while *Picts* from North Britain established similar settlements in the north. Towards the close of the Roman occupation of Britain, the dominant tribe in the island was that of the *Scoti*, who afterwards established themselves in Scotland.

History.—According to Irish legends, the island of Ierne was settled by a Milesian race, who came from Scythia by way of Spain, and established the *Kingdom of Tara*, about 500 B.C. The supremacy of the *Ardri* (high king) of Tara was acknowledged by eight lesser kingdoms (Munster, Connaught, Ailech, Oriel, Ulidia, Meath, Leinster and Ossory) ruled by descendants of the eight sons of Miled. The basalt columns on the coast of Antrim, eight miles from Portrush, known as the *Giant's Causeway*, are connected with the legendary history of Ireland as the remnants of a bridge built in the time of Finn M'Coul (Fingal) to connect Antrim with Scotland (Staffa).

Hibernia was visited by Roman merchants but never by Roman legions, and little is known of the history of the country until the invasions of *Northmen* (Norwegians and Danes) towards the close of the 8th century A.D. The Norwegians were distinguished as Findgaill (White Strangers) and the Danes as Dubgaill (Black Strangers), names which survive in " Fingall," " MacDougall " and " Mac-Dowell," while the name of the island itself is held to be derived from the Scandinavian *Ira-land* (land of the Irish), the names of the Provinces being survivals of Norse dialect forms (Ulaids-tir, Laigins-tir, Mumans-tir and Kunnak-tir). The outstanding events in the encounters with the Northmen are the *Battle of Tara* (980), at which the Hy Neill

king Maelsechlainn II defeated the Scandinavians of Dublin and the Hebrides under their king Amlaib Cuarán; and the *Battle of Clontarf* (1014) by which the Scandinavian power was completely broken. After Clontarf the supreme power was disputed by the O'Brians of Munster, the O'Neills of Ulster, and the O'Connors of Connaught, with varying fortunes. In 1152 Dermod MacMurrough (Diarmit MacMurchada), the deposed king of Leinster, sought assistance in his struggle with Ruaidhri O'Connor (the high king of Ireland), and visited Henry II, the Norman king of England. Henry authorized him to obtain armed support in England for the recovery of his kingdom, and Dermod enlisted the services of Richard de Clare, the Norman Earl of Pembroke, afterwards known as *Strongbow*, who landed at Waterford (Aug. 23, 1170) with 200 knights and 1,000 other troops for the reconquest of Leinster, where he eventually settled, after marriage with Dermod's daughter. In 1172 (Oct. 18) Henry II himself landed in Ireland. He received homage from the Irish kings and established his capital at Dublin. The invaders subsequently conquered most of the island and a feudal government was created. In the 14th and 15th centuries, the Irish recovered most of their lands, while many Anglo-Irish lords became virtually independent, royal authority being confined to the " Pale," a small district round Dublin. Though under Henry VII, Sir Edward Poynings, as Lord Deputy had passed at the *Parliament of Drogheda* (1494) the act later known as *Poynings' Law*, subordinating the Irish Legislature to the Crown, the Earls of Kildare retained effective power until, in 1534, Henry VIII began the reconquest of Ireland. Parliament in 1541 recognized him as King of Ireland and by 1603 English authority was supreme.

Christianity.—Christianity did not become general until the advent of St. Patrick. *St. Patrick* was born in Britain about 389, and was taken to Ireland as a slave about sixteen years later escaping to Gaul at the age of 22. In 432 he was consecrated Bishop at Auxerre and landed in Wicklow to establish and organize the Christian religion throughout the island.

Republic of Ireland

Area and Population.—The Republic has a land area of 26,600 sq. miles, divided into the four Provinces of LEINSTER (Carlow, Dublin, Kildare, Kilkenny, Laoighis, Longford, Louth, Meath, Offaly, Westmeath, Wexford and Wicklow); MUNSTER (Clare, Cork, Kerry, Limerick, Tipperary and Waterford); CONNACHT (Galway, Leitrim, Mayo, Roscommon and Sligo); and part of ULSTER (Cavan, Donegal and Monaghan). Total population of the Republic at the Census held on April 17, 1966, was 2,884,002 (males, 1,449,032; females 1,434,970), a density of 108 persons per sq. mile (estimated, 1970, 2,944,000). Provisional figures showed 64,092 births, 20,737 marriages and 33,884 deaths in the year 1970.

THE PRESIDENT

Uachtarán na hÉireann (President), Éamon de Valéra, *born* 1882, *assumed office* June 25, 1959; *re-elected for a second term,* June 25, 1966

MEMBERS OF THE GOVERNMENT

Taoiseach, Seán Ó Loinsigh (John Lynch) . . £5,500
Tánaiste and Minister for Health, Erskine H. Childers
External Affairs, An Dr. Pádraig Ó hIrighile (Dr. Patrick J. Hillery).
Transport and Power, Brian Ó Luineacháin (Brian Joseph Lenihan).
Labour and Social Welfare, Seosamh Ó Braoáin (Joseph Brennan).
Finance and Minister for the Gaeltacht, Seoirse Ó Colla (George Colley), T.D.
Lands, Seán Ó Flannagáin (Seán Flanagan).
Education, Pádraig Ó Fachtna (Patrick Faulkner).
Agriculture and Fisheries, Seamús Mac Giobúin (James Gibbons).
Industry and Commerce, Pádraig Ó Leathlobhair (Patrick Joseph Lalor).
Justice, Deasún Ó Máille (Desmond O'Malley).
Defence, Diarmaid Ó Cróinín (Gerrard Cronin).
Local Government, Roibéard Ó Maoildhia (Robert Molloy).
Posts and Telegraphs, Gearóid Ó Coileáin (Gerard Collins). Ministers, *each* £4,500.

Parliamentary Secretaries

Parliamentary Secretary to the Taoiseach and to the Minister for Defence, Daithí Mac Aindriú (David Andrews).
Do. to the Minister for Social Welfare, Seán Mac Eochagáin (John Geoghegan).
Do. to the Minister for Finance, Noel Lemass (Noel T. Lemass).
Do. to the Minister for the Gaeltacht, Mícheál Ó Ceit (Michael Kitt).
Do. to the Minister for Local Government, Liam Mac Cuinneagáin (Liam Cunningham).
Do. to the Minister for Agriculture and Fisheries, Seán Ó Fathaigh (John Fahey).
Do. to the Minister for Education, Mícheál Ó Cinnéide (Michael O'Kennedy).

Attorney-General, Colm Condún, S.C. (Colm Condon, S.C.)
Secretary to the Government, Nioclás Ó Nualláin, Ph.D. (Nicholas G. Nolan).

Irish Embassy
17 Grosvenor Place, S.W.1.
Ambassador Extraordinary and Plenipotentiary, His Excelleney Dr. Donald O'Sullivan.

British Embassy
39 Merrion Square, Dublin
Ambassador Extraordinary and Plenipotentiary, His Excellency Sir John Howard Peck, K.C.M.G. (1970) £6,125
Counsellor, J. T. Williams.
First Secretaries, P. J. C. Evans (*Information*); R. K. McKenzie (*Commercial*); J. White (*Agriculture and Food*).

GOVERNMENT
The Constitution.—The Constitution approved by a plebiscite on July 1, 1937, came into operation on December 29, 1937.

The Constitution declares that Ireland is a sovereign independent democratic State and affirms the right of the Irish Nation to choose its own form of Government, to determine its relations with other nations, and to develop its life, political, economic and cultural, in accordance with its own genius and traditions. The national territory is declared to be the whole island of Ireland, its islands and the territorial seas. Pending the re-integration of the national territory, and without prejudice to the right of the Parliament and the Government established by the Constitution to exercise jurisdiction over the whole of the national territory, the laws enacted by that Parliament shall have the like area and extent of application as those of the Irish Free State, which did not include the six counties of Northern Ireland. The national flag is the tricolour of green, white and orange. The Irish language, being the national language, is the first official language. The English language is recognized as a second official language.

The President.—The President—*Uachtarán na hEireann*—is elected by direct vote of the people for a period of seven years. A former or retiring President is eligible for a second term. The President summons and dissolves Dáil Éireann on the advice of the *Taoiseach* (Head of the Government). He signs and promulgates laws. The supreme command of the Defence Forces is vested in him, its exercise being regulated by law. He has the power of pardon. The President, in the exercise and performance of certain of his constitutional powers and functions, is aided and advised by a Council of State.

The Legislature.—The National Parliament—*Oireachtas*—consists of the President and two Houses: a House of Representatives—*Dáil Éireann* —and a Senate—*Seanad Éireann.*

Dáil Éireann is composed of 144 members elected by adult suffrage on a basis of proportional representation.

Seanad Éireann is composed of 60 members, of whom 11 are nominated by the Taoiseach and 49 are elected; three by the National University of Ireland, three by the University of Dublin, and 43 from panels of candidates, established on a vocational basis.

Members of Dáil Éireann are paid an allowance of £2,500 per annum (and members of Seanad Éireann £1,500); are allowed free travelling facilities between Dublin and their constituencies and are, subject to certain restrictions, granted free telephone and postal facilities from Leinster House and allowances for overnight stays in Dublin.

The Executive.—The executive authority is exercised by the Government subject to the Constitution. The Government is responsible to Dáil Éireann, meets and acts as a collective authority, and is collectively responsible for the Departments of State administered by the Ministers.

The Taoiseach is appointed by the President on the nomination of Dáil Éireann. The other members of the Government are appointed by the President on the nomination of the Taoiseach with the previous approval of Dáil Éireann. The Taoiseach appoints a member of the Government to be the *Tánaiste* who acts for all purposes in the place of the Taoiseach in the event of the death,

permanent incapacitation, or temporary absence of the Taoiseach. The Taoiseach, the Tánaiste and the Minister for Finance must be members of Dáil Éireann. The other members of the Government must be members of Dáil Éireann or Seanad Éireann, but not more than two may be members of Seanad Éireann.

THE LEGISLATURE

The Legislature (*Oireachtas*) consists of the President and two Houses—a House of Representatives (*Dáil Éireann*) and a Senate *Seanad Éireann*). Dáil Éireann has 144 Members, elected on the system of Proportional Representation by means of the single transferable vote. All citizens who have reached the age of 21 years and are not disqualified by law have the right to vote. Each Dáil may continue for a period not exceeding five years from the date of election. The present (19th) Dáil was elected on June 18, 1969, and met on July 2, 1969.

Strengths of the parties in the Dáil on June 1, 1971, were:

Fianna Fáil, 74; *Fine Gael*, 51; *Labour*, 17; *Independent*, 2. Total membership including the *Ceann Comhairle* (Speaker), 144.

THE JUDICIARY

The Judiciary consists of Courts of First Instance and a Court of Final Appeal called the Supreme Court—*Cúirt Uachtarach*. The Courts of First Instance include a High Court—*Ard-Chúirt*—invested with full original jurisdiction in and power to determine all matters and questions, whether of law or fact, civil or criminal, and also Courts of local and limited jurisdiction, with a right of appeal as determined by law. The High Court alone has original jurisdiction to entertain the question of the validity of any law having regard to the provision of the Constitution. The Supreme Court has pellate jurisdiction from all decisions of the High ourt, subject to exceptions and regulations pre bed by law. No law may, however, be enact excepting the question of the validity of any law from the appellate jurisdiction of the Supreme Court.

Chief Justice, Hon. Cearbhall Ó Dalaigh (Daly). £9,360
President of the High Court, Hon. Aindreas O Caoimh (O'Keeffe). 8,190
Judges, Supreme Court, Hon. Brian Walsh; Hon. F. G. Budd; Hon. W. O'B. Fitzgerald; Hon. R. McLoughlin. 8,190
Judges, High Court, Hon. George Murnaghan; Hon. Thomas Teevan; Hon. Seán Kenny; Hon. Seamus Henchy; Hon. Sean Butler; Hon. A. Denis Pringle; Hon. Barra O'Brien (*ex-officio*). . . . . *each* 7,020
Master of the High Court, John O. Leary, S.C.

DEFENCE

Under the direction of the President, and subject to the provisions of the Defence Act, 1954, the military command of the Defence Forces is exercisable by the Government through the Minister for Defence. There is an advisory Council of Defence consisting of the Parliamentary Secretary to the Minister, the Secretary of the Department of Defence, the Chief of Staff, the Adjutant-General and the Quartermaster-General. Establishments provide at present for a Permanent Defence Force of approximately 13,000 all ranks, including the Air Corps and the Naval Service. The Defence Estimates for the year ending March 31, 1972 provide for approximately 23,700 all ranks of the Reserve Defence Force. Recruitment is on a voluntary basis. The Naval Service has three minesweepers and a fishery protection vessel is on order for delivery in 1972. The Air Corps has a small number of Chipmunk, Provost, Vampire and Dove

trainers, and three helicopters. The strength of the Corps is approximately 500 all ranks. The Defence Estimates for the year ending March 31, 1972, provide for an expenditure of £19,165,000.

FINANCE

	1970–71 (Actual)	1971–72 (Estimated)
Revenue.	£481,500,000	£551,900,000
Expenditure.	490,400,000	551,000,000

In addition to the Expenditure figures shown above there were certain services of a capital nature regarded as proper to be met from borrowing. Issues for these services in 1970–71 amounted to £136,900,000, and for 1971–72 are estimated at £121,200,000.

The estimated *Revenue* for 1971–72 includes Customs, £93,400,000; Excise, £99,600,000; Estate etc. Duties, £8,000,000; Income Tax, including Surtax, £144,400,000; Corporation Profits Tax, £21,700,000; Motor Vehicle Duties, £17,900,000; Stamp Duties, £7,000,000; Post Office Services, £36,600,000; Turnover Tax, £48,400,000; Wholesale Tax, £30,700,000.

The principal items of estimated current *Expenditure* for 1971–72 are Debt Service, £113,400,000; Agriculture, etc., £94,100,000; Defence, £19,200,000; Police and Justice, £17,400,000; Education, £72,300,000; Social Welfare, £78,900,000; Health Services, £45,300,000; Transport, £16,800,000; Post Office, £26,800,000; Superannuation, £17,600,000.

The Gross Debt (*provisional*) on March 31, 1971, was £1,197,500,000, with assets £602,700,000, leaving the net total of the debt at £594,800,000.

RELIGION
(Census of 1961)

Catholic.	2,673,473
Church of Ireland.	104,016
Presbyterians.	18,953
Methodists.	6,676
Others.	15,223
Total.	2,818,341

EDUCATION

Primary education is directed by the State. (There are 4,295 State-aided primary schools with an enrolment of 511,219 and average daily attendance 89·4 per cent. in 1968–69). Secondary education is in private hands and is largely conducted by Religious Orders (598 recognized schools with 133,591 pupils 12–20 years of age in 1968–69). Vocational (continuation and technical) education is conducted by 38 Local Committees in 303 permanent schools (excluding 11 residential schools of domestic training and a day trades preparatory school) and a large number of temporary centres. (45,242 full-time day students and 58,718 other students in 1967–68).

The estimated State expenditure on education in 1970–71, excluding administration and inspection, is: Primary £25,258,000; Secondary £19,626,000; Vocational £10,318,000; Science and Art £1,062,000. The vote for Universities and Colleges for 1970/71 amounts to £7,537,000 while, in addition, grants of £1,658,984 are provided in respect of the Faculties of General Agriculture and Dairy Science.

In all cities, principal towns and many rural areas there are vocational schools. These schools are controlled by the local Vocational Educational Committees, and are maintained partly by the rates and partly by state grants.

★ There are two Universities in Dublin, of which the National University has 3 constituent colleges (Dublin, Cork and Galway); and Trinity College Dublin.

PRODUCTION AND INDUSTRY

Agriculture and Livestock.—In 1969 there were 893,500 acres under corn crops, 370,300 under root and green crops, 7,800 under fruit and 2,202,900 under hay, a total of 3,474,400 acres. The principal produce in 1969 was: oats 247,500 tons; wheat 357,100 tons; barley, 775,600 tons; turnips, 1,975,700 tons; potatoes, 1,429,700 tons; sugar beet, 902,400 tons; and hay, 5,218,300 tons. The *livestock* included, 5,687,800 cattle, 4,006,200 sheep, 1,115,500 pigs and 124,900 horses and ponies.

Minerals.—700 persons were employed in the coal mines in 1969 and 152,000 tons of coal won.

Sea Fisheries.—5,443 persons were employed in the fisheries in 1968, the total value of all fish (excluding salmon) landed being £2,404,000.

COMMUNICATIONS

Railways.—In the year ended March 31, 1970, there were 1,333 miles of railway all of standard (5 ft. 3 in.) gauge; 9,957,192 passengers and 3,054,995 tons of merchandise were conveyed; the receipts were £11,909,647 and expenditure £15,020,594. These figures are in respect of railway working by Coras Iompair Éireann, the national transport undertaking which is now the only concern operating a rail service in the State.

Road Motor Services.—In 1970 road motor (omnibus) vehicles carried 281,186,614 passengers, the gross receipts being £12,610,074.

Shipping.—In 1969 the number of ships with cargo and in ballast in the foreign trade which arrived at Irish ports was 14,613 (20,255,339 net registered tons); of these 2,025 (2,098,443 net registered tons) were of Irish nationality.

CIVIL AVIATION

Shannon Airport, 15 miles W. of Limerick, is on the main transatlantic air route. In 1970 the airport handled 831,439 passengers, 28,763 tons of cargo and 933 tons of mail.

Dublin Airport, 6 miles N. of Dublin, serves the cross-channel and European services operated by the Irish national airline *Aer Lingus* and other airlines. During 1970 the airport handled 1,897,917 passengers, 37,835 tons of cargo and 2,319 tons of mail.

Cork Airport, 5 miles S. of Cork, serves the cross-Channel and European services operated by *Aer Lingus* and other airlines. During 1970 the airport handled 198,552 passengers, 1,477 tons of cargo and 5·7 tons of mail.

Licensed private aerodromes are: *Ballyfree* (5 miles west-south-west of Wicklow Town): *Bantry; Castlebar; Castlebridge* (4 miles north of Wexford); *Coonagh* (2 miles west of Limerick); *Dundalk* (5 miles south of Dundalk); *Farranforce* (8 miles southeast of Tralee); *Headfort* (2 miles east-north-east of Kells); *Inishmore* (Aran Islands, 1 mile south-east of Kilronan); *Killarney Race Course* (1 mile south of Killarney); *Kiltullagh* (4 miles east-north-east of Galway); *Letterkenny* (2 miles east of Letterkenny); *Oranmore* (5 miles east of Galway); *Thurles* (Holycross); *Weston* (9 miles west of Dublin).

OVERSEAS TRADE

Year	Imports	Exports	Trade Balance
	£	£	£
1965	371,846,473	220,811,486	− 151,034,987
1966	372,566,792	243,323,022	− 128,243,770
1967	392,259,635	285,086,014	− 107,173,621
1968	496,092,551	332,475,248	− 163,617,303
1969	589,753,079	371,440,598	− 218,312,481
1970	653,721,559	431,203,249	− 222,518,310

Trade With U.K.

	1969	1970
Imports from U.K.	£316,549,000	£381,209,000
Exports to U.K.	293,635,000	341,255,000

PRINCIPAL ARTICLES
Imports (1970)

The principal groups were: live animals, £20,571,183; food, drink and tobacco, £69,434,403; petroleum and petroleum products, £43,012,117; chemicals, £61,395,934; machinery (non-electric), £89,361,084; electrical machinery, £38,302,279; transport equipment, £52,559,277; metal and manufactures, £58,198,985; textiles and clothing, £66,971,287; paper, paperboard and manufactures, £18,217,458.

Domestic Exports (1970)

Principally live animals, £56,885,734, meat and meat preparations, £74,813,037; other food, drink, and tobacco, £74,990,256; machinery and transport equipment, £28,517,649; clothing, headgear and footwear, £22,133,257; textiles, £27,458,363; metal ores and scrap, £20,983,841; metals and manufactures, £9,939,352; non-metallic mineral manufactures, £7,163,459; chemicals, £18,389,839.

CAPITAL.—Dublin *(Baile Atha Cliath)* is a City and County Borough on the River Liffey at the head of Dublin Bay. In April, 1966, its population was 568,772. There are many notable public buildings in the City, among them the two Cathedrals of Christ Church and St. Patrick, the Bank of Ireland (formerly the House of Parliament) and Trinity College (the only constituent College of the University of Dublin). University College is a constituent college of the National University of Ireland. A large export trade of agricultural products passes through the city and there is a considerable brewing industry, while there is an increasing amount of light manufacturing.

Other cities and towns, with populations at the Census of 1966 are ♆ Cork (122,146); ♆ Limerick (55,912); ♆ Dun Laoghaire (51,772); ♆ Waterford (29,842); ♆ Galway (24,597); ♆ Dundalk (20,002); ♆ Drogheda (17,908); Sligo (13,424); Bray (12,699); Wexford (11,542); Tralee (11,213); Clonmel (11,031); Kilkenny (10,052); Athlone (9,623).

FLAG.—Equal vertical stripes of green, white and orange.

NATIONAL DAY.—March 17 (St. Patrick's Day).

The United States of America

Area and Population

Population, 1970.—The total resident population of the United States on May 1, 1970, was estimated at 203,345,000, excluding Armed Forces stationed abroad.   Civilian resident population at the same date was estimated at 201,313,000.   Including Armed Forces stationed abroad (May 1, 1970), 204,437,000.

	Land Area, 1960 (sq. miles)	Population	
		Census 1960	Census 1970
The United States*	3,536,855	179,323,175	203,165,699
Commonwealth of Puerto Rico.....	3,423	2,349,544	2,712,033
Possessions......................	450	123,151	..
Guam..........................	209	67,044	86,926†
Virgin Islands of U.S.............	132	32,099	63,200†
American Samoa.................	76	20,051	27,769†
Midway Islands..................	2	2,356	2,220
Wake Island....................	3	1,097	1,647
Canton Island and Enderbury Island	27	320‡	..
Johnston Island and Sand Island....	—	156‡	1,017
Swan Islands....................	1	28‡	22
Other Outlying areas:			
Panama Canal Zone.............	362	42,122	44,650†
Corn Islands...................	4	1,872	..
Pacific Islands Trust Territory.....	687	70,724‡	101,592†
Population Abroad		1,374,421	1,580,998
Total	3,553,898	183,285,009	..

* The 50 States and the Federal *District of Columbia* (*see* p. 800).
† 1970 Census Preliminary figures.
‡ The islands of Enderbury, Sand, Little Swan and Little Corn were uninhabited at the time of enumeration.

REGISTERED BIRTHS AND DEATHS

Cal-endar Year	Live Births		Deaths	
	Number	Rate per 1,000	Number	Rate per 1,000
1961	4,268,326	23·3	1,701,522	9·3
1962	4,167,362	22·4	1,756,720	9·5
1963	4,098,020	21.7	1,813,549	9.6
1964	4,027,490	21·0	1,798,051	9·4
1965	3,760,358	19·4	1,828,136	9·4
1966	3,606,274	18·4	1,863,149	9·5
1967	3,520,959	17·8	1,851,323	9·4
1968	3,501,564	17·5	1,930,082	9·7
1969*	3,571,000	17·7	1,916,000	9·5
1970*	3,718,000	18·2	1,921,000	9·4

Births based on 50 per cent. sample.   *Provisional.
Note.—Figures tabulated are for the United States.   Deaths exclude fœtal deaths.   Rates are based on the population as estimated on July 1.

IMMIGRATION AND NATURALIZATION

From 1820 to 1970, 45,162,638 immigrants were admitted to the United States.   Of the 373,326 admitted during fiscal year 1970, 65 per cent. were born in Mexico (44,469), the Philippines (31,203), Italy (24,973), Greece (16,464), Cuba (16,334), Jamaica (15,033), the United Kingdom (14,158), China and Formosa (14,093), Canada (13,804),

Portugal (13,195), the Dominican Republic (10,807), India (10,114), Germany (9,684), and Korea (9,314).   During 1970, 110,399 alien residents in the United States were naturalized, and 30,318 persons acquired citizenship status at birth abroad, after birth by the naturalization of parents, through marriage, or by other reasons.

MARRIAGE AND DIVORCE

Laws of marriage and of divorce are within the exclusive jurisdiction of each State.   Each State legislature enacts its own laws prescribing rules and qualifications pertaining to marriage and its dissolution.

Year	Marriages	Per 1,000 Pop.§	Estimated Divorces	Per 1,000 Pop.§
1961	1,548,000	8·5	414,000	2·3
1962	1,677,000	8·5	413,000	2·2
1963	1,654,000	8·8	428,000	2·3
1964	1,725,000	9·0	450,000	2·4
1965	1,800,000	9·3	479,000	2·5
1966	1,857,000	9·5	499,000	2·5
1967	1,927,000	9·7	523,000	2·6
1968	2,069,000	10·4	584,000	2·9
1969	2,145,000	10·6	639,000	3·2
1970*	2,179,000	10·7	715,000	3·5

* Provisional.
§ Population as estimated on July 1.

Increase of the People.

Year of Census	Total Population				Increase over preceding census	Inter-Censal Immigrants*
	White	Negro	Other Races	Total		
1930	110,286,740	11,891,143	597,163	122,775,046	17,064,420	4,107,209
1940	118,214,870	12,864,518	588,887	131,669,275	8,894,229	528,431
1950	134,942,028	15,042,286	713,047	150,697,361	19,028,086	1,035,039
1960‡	158,831,732	18,871,831	1,619,612	179,323,175	28,625,814	2,515,479†
1970	177,612,309	22,672,570	2,880,820	203,165,699	25,861,597	3,321,677

* Includes immigrants to territorial possessions, etc.   † Total for 10 years to June 30, 1960.
‡ Includes Alaska and Hawaii.

THE UNITED STATES

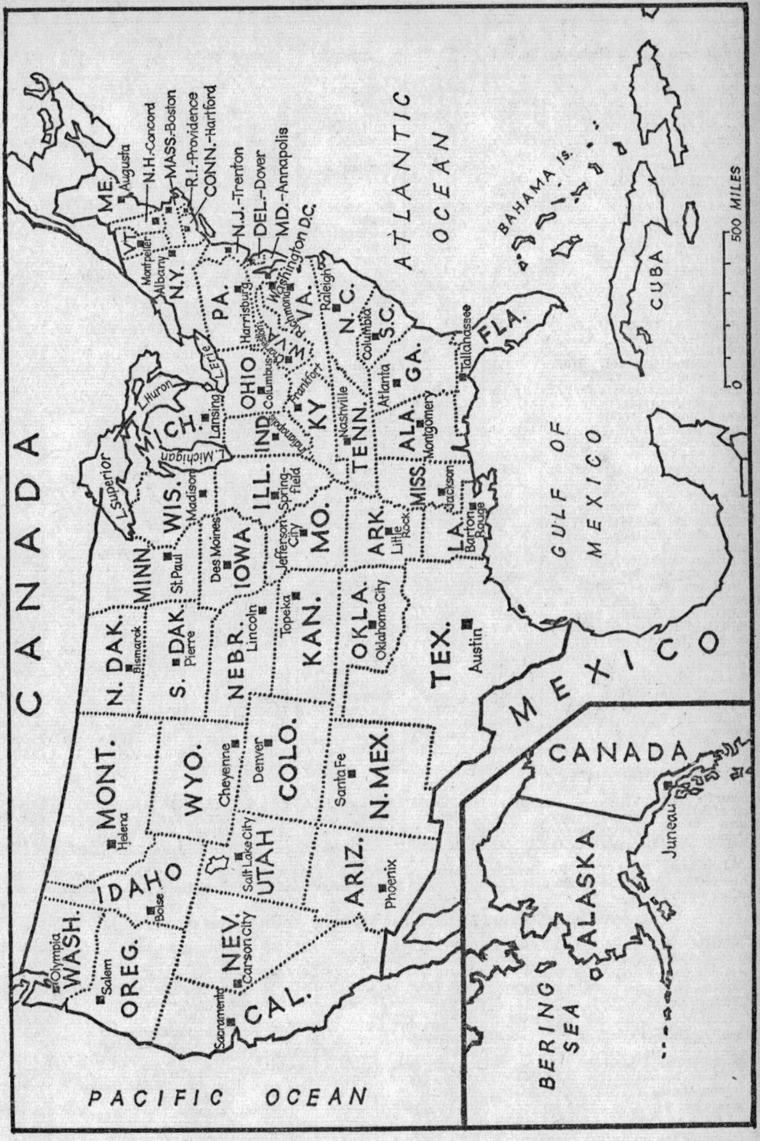

CANADA

CANADA

MEXICO

ME.
N.H.-Concord
MASS-Boston
R.I.-Providence
CONN-Hartford
VT.
Augusta
Montpelier
Albany
N.Y.
N.J.-Trenton
DEL.-Dover
MD.-Annapolis
Washington D.C.
PA.
Harrisburg
Richmond
VA.
W.VA.
OHIO
Columbus
IND.
Indianapolis
Frankfort
KY.
Nashville
TENN.
N.C.
Raleigh
S.C.
Columbia
GA.
Atlanta
ALA.
Montgomery
MISS.
Jackson
FLA.
Tallahassee

L. Superior
L. Huron
L. Michigan
L. Erie

MICH.
Lansing
WIS.
Madison
MINN.
St. Paul
N. DAK.
Bismarck
S. DAK.
Pierre
NEBR.
Lincoln
IOWA
Des Moines
ILL.
Springfield
MO.
Jefferson City
ARK.
Little Rock
LA.
Baton Rouge
KAN.
Topeka
OKLA.
Oklahoma City
TEX.
Austin

MONT.
Helena
WYO.
Cheyenne
COLO.
Denver
N.MEX.
Santa Fe
ARIZ.
Phoenix
IDAHO
Boise
NEV.
Carson City
UTAH
Salt Lake City
WASH.
Olympia
OREG.
Salem
CAL.
Sacramento

ATLANTIC OCEAN

BAHAMA Is.

CUBA

GULF OF MEXICO

PACIFIC OCEAN

BERING SEA

ALASKA
Juneau

500 MILES

THE UNITED STATES

State (with date and *order* of admission)	Area Sq. M.¶	Population, Census 1970	Capital	Governor (term of office in years, and starting year)
Alabama (Ala.) (1819) (*22*)	51,609	3,444,165	Montgomery	George C. Wallace (*D*) (4—1971) $25,000
Alaska (1959) (*49*)	586,400	302,173	Juneau	William A. Egan (*D*) (4—1970) 32,000
Arizona (Ariz.) (1912) (*48*)	113,909	1,772,482	Phoenix	Jack Williams (*R*) (4—1971) 27,500
Arkansas (Ark.) (1836) (*25*)	53,104	1,923,295	Little Rock	Dale Bumpers (*D*) (2—1971) 10,000
California (Cal.) (1850) (*31*)	158,693	19,953,134	Sacramento	Ronald Reagan (*R*) (4—1971) 49,100
Colorado (Colo.) (1876) (*38*)	104,247	2,207,259	Denver	John A. Love (*R*) (4—1971) 20,000
Connecticut (Conn.)§ (1788) (*5*)	5,009	3,032,217	Hartford	Thomas J. Meskill (*R*) (4—1971) 35,000
Delaware (Del.)§ (1787) (*1*)	2,057	548,104	Dover	Russell W. Peterson (*R*) (4—1969) 35,000
Dist. of Columbia (D.C.) (1791)	69	756,510		†
Florida (Fla.) (1845) (*27*)	58,560	6,789,443	Tallahassee	Reubin O'D. Askew (*D*) (4—1971) 36,000
Georgia (Ga.)§ (1788) (*4*)	58,876	4,589,575	Atlanta	Jimmy Carter (*D*) (4—1971) 42,500
Hawaii (1959) (*50*)	6,423	769,913	Honolulu	John A. Burns (*D*) (4—1970) 38,182
Idaho (1890) (*43*)	83,557	713,008	Boise	Cecil D. Andrus (*D*) (4—1971) 17,500
Illinois (Ill.) (1818) (*21*)	56,400	11,113,976	Springfield	Richard B. Ogilvie (*R*) (4—1969) 45,000
Indiana (Ind.) (1816) (*19*)	36,291	5,193,669	Indianapolis	Edgar D. Whitcomb (*R*) (4—1969) 25,000
Iowa (1846) (*29*)	56,290	2,825,041	Des Moines	Robert D. Ray (*R*) (2—1971) 30,000
Kansas (Kan.) (1861) (*34*)	82,276	2,249,071	Topeka	Robert Docking (*D*) (2—1971) 20,000
Kentucky (Ky.) (1792) (*15*)	40,395	3,219,311	Frankfort	Louie B. Nunn (*R*) (4—1967) 30,000
Louisiana (La.) (1812) (*18*)	48,523	3,643,180	Baton Rouge	John J. McKeithen (*D*) (4—1968) 28,374
Maine (Me.) (1820) (*23*)	33,215	993,663	Augusta	Kenneth M. Curtis (*D*) (4—1971) 20,000
Maryland (Md.)§ (1788) (*7*)	10,577	3,922,399	Annapolis	Marvin Mandel (*D*) (4—1971) 25,000
Massachusetts (Mass.)§ (1788) (*6*)	8,257	5,689,170	Boston	Francis W. Sargent (*R*) (4—1971) 35,000
Michigan (Mich.) (1837) (*26*)	58,216	8,875,083	Lansing	William G. Milliken (*R*) (4—1971) 40,000
Minnesota (Minn.) (1858) (*32*)	84,068	3,805,069	St. Paul	Wendell R. Anderson (*D*) (4—1971) 27,500
Mississippi (Miss.) (1817) (*20*)	47,716	2,216,912	Jackson	John Bell Williams (*D*) (4—1968) 25,000
Missouri (Mo.) (1821) (*24*)	69,674	4,677,399	Jefferson City	Warren E. Hearnes (*D*) (4—1969) 37,500
Montana (Mont.) (1889) (*41*)	141,138	694,409	Helena	Forrest H. Anderson (*D*) (4—1969) 23,250
Nebraska (Nebr.) (1867) (*37*)	77,227	1,483,791	Lincoln	J. James Exon (*D*) (4—1971) 18,000
Nevada (Nev.) (1864) (*36*)	110,540	488,738	Carson City	Mike O'Callaghan (*D*) (4—1971) 25,000
New Hampshire (N.H.)§ (1788) (*9*)	9,304	737,681	Concord	Walter Peterson (*R*) (2—1971) 30,000
New Jersey (N.J.)§ (1787) (*3*)	7,836	7,168,164	Trenton	William T. Cahill (*R*) (4—1970) 35,000
New Mexico (N. Mex.) (1912) (*47*)	121,666	1,016,000	Santa Fé	Bruce King (*D*) (4—1971) 20,000
New York (N.Y.)§ (1788) (*11*)	49,576	18,190,740	Albany	Nelson A. Rockefeller (*R*) (4—1971) 50,000
North Carolina (N.C.)§ (1789) (*12*)	52,712	5,082,059	Raleigh	Robert W. Scott (*D*) (4—1969) 35,000
North Dakota (N. Dak.) (1889) (*39*)	70,665	617,761	Bismarck	William L. Guy (*D*) (4—1969) 18,000
Ohio (1803) (*17*)	41,222	10,652,017	Columbus	John J. Gilligan (*D*) (4—1971) 40,000
Oklahoma (Okla.) (1907) (*46*)	69,919	2,559,253	Oklahoma City	David Hall (*D*) (4—1971) 25,000
Oregon (Oreg.) (1859) (*33*)	96,981	2,091,385	Salem	Tom McCall (*R*) (4—1971) 28,500
Pennsylvania (Pa.)§ (1787) (*2*)	45,333	11,793,909	Harrisburg	Milton J. Shapp (*D*) (4—1971) 45,000
Rhode Island (R.I.)§ (1790) (*13*)	1,214	949,723	Providence	Frank Licht (*D*) (2—1971) 30,000
South Carolina (S.C.)§ (1788) (*8*)	31,055	2,590,516	Columbia	John C. West (*D*) (4—1971) 25,000
South Dakota (S. Dak.) (1889) (*40*)	77,047	666,257	Pierre	Richard F. Kneip (*D*) (2—1971) 18,000
Tennessee (Tenn.) (1796) (*16*)	42,244	3,924,164	Nashville	Winfield Dunn (*R*) (4—1971) 18,500
Texas (Tex.) (1845) (*28*)	267,339	11,196,730	Austin	Preston Smith (*D*) (2—1971) 55,000
Utah (1890) (*45*)	84,916	1,059,273	Salt Lake City	Calvin L. Rampton (*D*) (4—1969) 22,000
Vermont (Vt.) (1791) (*14*)	9,609	444,732	Montpelier	Deane C. Davis (*R*) (2—1971) 25,000
Virginia (Va.)§ (1788) (*10*)	40,815	4,648,494	Richmond	Linwood Holton (*R*) (4—1970) 30,000
Washington (Wash.) (1889) (*42*)	68,192	3,409,169	Olympia	Daniel J. Evans (*R*) (4—1969) 32,500
West Virginia (W. Va.) (1863) (*35*)	24,181	1,744,237	Charleston	Arch A. Moore, Jr. (*R*) (4—1969) 35,000
Wisconsin (Wis.) (1848) (*30*)	56,154	4,417,933	Madison	Patrick J. Lucey (*D*) (4—1971) 25,000
Wyoming (Wyo.) (1890) (*44*)	97,914	332,416	Cheyenne	Stanley K. Hathaway (*R*) (4—1971) 25,000
OUTLYING TERRITORIES AND POSSESSIONS				
Puerto Rico (1899)	3,435	2,712,033	San Juan	Luis A. Ferré (*PNP*) (4—1968) 25,000
Guam (1899)	206	86,926	Agaña	Carlos G. Camacho (*R*) (4—1971) 33,495
Samoa (1900)	76	27,769	Pago Pago	John M. Haydon (*R*) (1969) 24,500
Virgin Islands (1917)	133	63,200	Charlotte Amalie	Melvin H. Evans (*R*) (4—1971) 25,899

D.—Democratic Party.　　　*R.*—Republican Party.　　　*PNP*—New Progressive Party.　　　§ The 13 Original States.
† The capital territory is governed by Congress through a Commissioner and City Council (*see* p. 803). ¶ Gross area, including water.

Largest Cities (Standard Metropolitan Statistical Areas: Census 1970 (final)).

Ψ New York, N.Y.	11,528,649	
Ψ Los Angeles–Long Beach, Calif.	7,032,075	
Ψ Chicago, Ill.	6,978,947	
Ψ Philadelphia, Pa.–N.J.	4,817,914	
Ψ Detroit, Mich.	4,199,031	
Ψ San-Francisco–Oakland, Calif.	3,109,519	
Washington, D.C.–Md.–Va.	2,861,123	
Ψ Boston, Mass.	2,753,700	
Pittsburgh, Pa.	2,401,245	
St. Louis, Mo.–Ill.	2,363,017	
Ψ Baltimore, Md.	2,070,670	
Ψ Cleveland, Ohio	2,064,194	
Ψ Houston, Tex.	1,985,031	
Ψ Newark, N.J.	1,856,556	
Minneapolis–St. Paul, Minn.	1,813,647	
Dallas, Tex.	1,555,950	
Ψ Seattle–Everett, Wash.	1,421,869	
Anaheim–Santa Ana–Garden Grove, Calif.	1,420,386	
Ψ Milwaukee, Wis.	1,403,887	
Atlanta, Ga.	1,390,164	
Cincinnati, Ohio	1,384,911	
Paterson–Clifton–Passaic, N.J.	1,358,794	
Ψ San Diego, Calif.	1,357,854	
Ψ Buffalo, N.Y.	1,349,211	
Ψ Miami, Fla.	1,267,792	
Kansas City, Mo.–Kan.	1,256,649	
Denver, Colo.	1,227,529	
San Bernardino–Riverside–Ontario, Calif.	14,143,146	
Indianapolis, Ind.	1,109,882	
San José, Calif.	1,064,714	
Ψ New Orleans, Lar.	1,046,472	
Ψ Tampa–St.Petersburg, Fla.	1,012,594	
Ψ Portland, Oreg.–Wash.	1,009,129	
Phoenix, Ariz.	968,487	
Columbus, Ohio	916,228	
Providence–Pawtucket–Warwick, R.I.–Mass.	914,110	
Ψ Rochester, N.Y.	882,667	
San Antonio Tex.	864,014	
Dayton, Ohio	850,266	
Louisville, Ky.–Ind.	826,553	
Sacramento, Calif.	800,592	
Memphis, Tenn.–Ark.	770,120	
Fort Worth, Tex.	762,086	
Birmingham, Ala.	739,274	

Ψ *Seaport.*

PHYSIOGRAPHY

The conterminous States of the Republic occupy nearly all that portion of the North American Continent between the Atlantic and Pacific Oceans, in latitude 25° 07′-49° 23′ North and longitude 66° 57′-124° 44′ West, its northern boundary being Canada and the southern boundary Mexico. The separate State of Alaska reaches a latitude of 71° 23′ N., at Point Barrow (2,502 miles from the U.S. geographic centre).

The general coastline of the 50 States has a length of about 2,069 miles on the Atlantic, 7,623 miles on the Pacific, 1,060 miles on the Arctic, and 1,631 miles on the Gulf of Mexico.

The principal river is the mighty Mississippi-Missouri-Red Rock, traversing the whole country from north to south, and having a course of 3,710 miles to its mouth in the Gulf of Mexico, with many large affluents, the chief of which are the Yellowstone, Platte, Arkansas, Ohio, and Red Rivers. The rivers flowing into the Atlantic and Pacific Oceans are comparatively small; among the former may be noticed the Hudson, Delaware, Susquehanna, Potomac, James, Roanoke and Savannah; of the latter, the Columbia-Snake, Sacramento, and Colorado. The Nueces, Brazos, Trinity, Pearl, Mobile-Tombigbee-Alabama, Apalachicola-Chattahoochee, Suwannee and Colorado of Texas fall into the Gulf of Mexico, also the Rio Grande, a long river partly forming the boundary with Mexico. The areas of the water-basins have been estimated as follows:—Rivers flowing to the Pacific, 644,040 square miles; to the Atlantic, 488,877; and to the Gulf of Mexico, 1,683,325 square miles, of which 1,257,547 are drained by the Mississippi-Missouri-Red Rock. The chain of the Rocky Mountains separates the western portion of the country from the remainder, all communication being carried on over certain elevated passes, several of which are now traversed by rail-roads; west of these, bordering the Pacific coast, the Cascade Mountains and Sierra Nevada form the outer edge of a high tableland, consisting in part of stony and sandy desert and partly of grazing land and forested mountains, and including the Great Salt Lake, which extends to the Rocky Mountains. Eastward the country is a vast, gently undulating plain, with a general slope southwards towards the partly marshy flats of the Gulf of Mexico, extending to the Atlantic, interrupted only by the Appalachian Highlands, of inferior elevation, in the Eastern States. Nearly the whole of this plain, from the Rocky Mountains to some distance beyond the Mississippi, consists of immense prairies. In the Eastern States (which form the more settled and most thickly inhabited portion of the country) large forests of valuable timber, as beech, birch, maple, oak, pine, spruce, elm, ash, walnut; and in the south, live oak, water-oak, magnolia, palmetto, tulip-tree, cypress, etc., still exist, the remnants of the forests which formerly extended over all the Atlantic slope, but into which great inroads have been made by the advance of civilization. The Mississippi valley is eminently fertile. The mineral kingdom produces much ore of iron, copper, lead, zinc, and aluminium; the non-metallic minerals include immense quantities of coal, anthracite, petroleum, stone, cement, phosphate rock, and salt. Precious metals, gold and silver, have been mined chiefly in Arizona, Colorado, California, Montana, Utah, Idaho and South Dakota. The highest point is Mount McKinley (Alaska), 20,320 ft. above sea level and the lowest point of dry land is in Death Valley (Inyo, California), 282 ft. below sea-level. The mean elevation of the United States is approximately 2,500 ft.

THE PRESIDENTS OF THE UNITED STATES OF AMERICA

	Name (*with Native State*)	Party	Born	Inaug.	Died	Age
1.	George Washington, *Va.*	Fed.	1732, Feb. 22	1789	1799, Dec. 14	67
2.	John Adams, *Mass.*	,,	1735, Oct. 30	1797	1826, July 4	90
3.	Thomas Jefferson, *Va.*	Rep.	1743, April 13	1801	1826, July 4	83
4.	James Madison, *Va.*	,,	1751, Mar. 16	1809	1836, June 28	85
5.	James Monroe, *Va.*	,,	1758, April 28	1817	1831, July 4	73
6.	John Quincy Adams. *Mass.*	,,	1767, July 11	1825	1848, Feb. 23	80
7.	Andrew Jackson, *S.C.*	Dem.	1767, Mar. 15	1829	1845, June 8	78
8.	Martin Van Buren, *N.Y.*	,,	1782, Dec. 5	1837	1862, July 24	79
9.	William Henry Harrison†, *Va.*	Whig	1773, Feb. 9	1841	1841, April 4	68
10.	John Tyler (*a*), *Va.*	,,	1790, Mar. 29	1841	1862, Jan. 17	71
11.	James Knox Polk, *N.C.*	Dem.	1795, Nov. 2	1845	1849, June 15	53
12.	Zachary Taylor† *Va.*	Whig	1784, Nov. 24	1849	1850, July 9	65
13.	Millard Fillmore (*a*), *N.Y.*	,,	1800, Jan. 7	1850	1874, Mar. 8	74
14.	Franklin Pierce, *N.H.*	Dem.	1804, Nov. 23	1853	1869, Oct. 8	64
15.	James Buchanan, *Pa.*	,,	1791, April 23	1857	1868, June 1	77
16.	Abraham Lincoln†§, *Ky.*	Rep.	1809, Feb. 12	1861	1865, April 15	56
17.	Andrew Johnson (*a*), *N.C.*	,,	1808, Dec. 29	1865	1875, July 31	66
18.	Ulysses Simpson Grant, *Ohio.*	,,	1822, April 27	1869	1885, July 23	63
19.	Rutherford Birchard Hayes, *Ohio.*	,,	1822, Oct. 4	1877	1893, Jan. 17	70
20.	James Abram Garfield†§, *Ohio*	,,	1831, Nov. 19	1881	1881, Sept. 19	49
21.	Chester Alan Arthur (*a*), *Vt.*	,,	1830, Oct. 5	1881	1886, Nov. 18	56
22.	Grover Cleveland, *N.J.*	Dem.	1837, Mar. 18	1885	1908, June 24	71
23.	Benjamin Harrison, *Ohio.*	Rep.	1833, Aug. 20	1889	1901, Mar. 13	67
	Grover Cleveland, *N.J.*	Dem.	1837, Mar. 18	1893	1908, June 24	71
24.	William McKinley†§, *Ohio.*	Rep.	1843, Jan. 29	1897	1901, Sept. 14	58
25.	Theodore Roosevelt (*a*), *N.Y.*	,,	1858, Oct. 27	1901	1919, Jan. 6	60
26.	William Howard Taft, *Ohio.*	,,	1857, Sept. 15	1909	1930, Mar. 8	72
27.	Woodrow Wilson, *Va.*	Dem.	1856, Dec. 28	1913	1924, Feb. 3	67
28.	Warren Gamaliel Harding†, *Ohio.*	Rep.	1865, Nov. 2	1921	1923, Aug. 2	57
29.	Calvin Coolidge (*a*), *Vt.*	,,	1872, July 4	1923	1933, Jan. 5	60
30.	Herbert Clark Hoover, *Iowa*	,,	1874, Aug. 10	1929	1964, Oct. 20	90
31.	Franklin Delano Roosevelt†‡, *N.Y.*	Dem.	1882, Jan. 30	1933	1945, April 12	63
32.	Harry S. Truman, (*a*), *Missouri*	,,	1884, May 8	1945	..	..
33.	Dwight D. Eisenhower, *Texas.*	Rep.	1890, Oct. 14	1953	1969, Mar. 28	78
34.	John F. Kennedy, *Mass.*†§	Dem.	1917, May 29	1961	1963, Nov. 22	46
35.	Lyndon B. Johnson (*a*) *Texas*	,,	1908, Aug. 27	1963	..	..
36.	Richard M. Nixon, *California*	Rep.	1913, Jan. 9	1969	..	..

† Died in office.   § Assassinated.   (*a*) Elected as Vice-President.

‡ Re-elected Nov. 5, 1940, the first case of a third term; re-elected for a fourth term Nov. 7, 1944.

GOVERNMENT

The United States of America is a Federal Republic consisting of 50 States and 1 Federal District (of which 13 are Original States, 7 were admitted without previous organization as Territories, and 30 were admitted after such organization), and of 1 organized Territory. Hawaii formally entered the Union as the 50th State on Aug. 21, 1959, from which date the flag of the United States has 13 stripes and 50 stars in 9 horizontal rows of six and five alternately. July 4 (Independence Day) is observed as the National Day.

THE CONSTITUTION.—By the Constitution of Sept. 17, 1787 (to which ten amendments were added on Dec. 15, 1791, and eleventh to twenty-fifth Jan. 8, 1798, Sept 25, 1804, Dec. 18, 1865, July 28, 1868, March 30, 1870, Feb. 25, 1913, May 31, 1913, Jan. 16, 1920, Aug. 26, 1920, Feb. 6, 1933, Dec. 5, 1933, Feb. 26, 1951, March 29, 1961, Jan. 23, 1964 and Feb. 10, 1967), the government of the United States is entrusted to three separate authorities—the Executive, the Legislative, and the Judicial.

THE EXECUTIVE

THE *Executive* power is vested in a President, who is elected every four years, and is eligible for re-election for one additional term. The mode of electing the President is as follows:—Each State appoints, in such manner as the Legislature thereof directs (they are now elected by popular vote on the *first Tuesday after the first Monday in November* of the year preceding the year in which the Presidential term expires), a number of electors, equal to the whole number of Senators and Representatives to which the State may be entitled in the Congress; but no Senator or Representative, or anyone holding office under Government, shall be appointed an elector. The electors for each State meet in their respective States on the *first Monday after the second Wednesday in December* following, and there vote for a President by ballot. The ballots are then sent to Washington, and opened on the *sixth day of January* by the President of Senate in presence of Congress, and the candidate who has received a majority of the whole number of electoral votes cast is declared President for the ensuing term. If no one has a majority, then from the highest on the list (not exceeding three) the House of Representatives elects a President, the votes being taken by States, the representation from each State having one vote. There is also a Vice President, who, on the death of the President, becomes President for the remainder of the term. Under the XXth Amendment to the Constitution the terms of the President and Vice President end at noon on the 20th day of January of the years in which such terms would have ended if the Amendment had not been ratified, and the terms of their successors then begin. In case of the removal or death of both President and Vice President, a statute provides for the succession.

The President must be at least 35 years of age and a native citizen of the United States. He receives a taxable salary of $200,000 with a taxable expense allowance of $50,000 and a non-taxable travelling allowance not exceeding $40,000. Under the XXIInd Amendment to the Constitution, the tenure of the Presidency is limited to two terms. Executive duties:—(1) He is Commander-in-Chief of the Army and of the Navy (and of the Militias when they are in Federal service), and he commissions all officers therein. (2) With the consent of the Senate, he appoints the Cabinet officers and all the chief (and many minor) officials. (3) He exercises a general supervision over the whole Federal Administration and sees that the Federal Laws are duly carried out. Should disorder arise in any State which the authorities thereof are unable to suppress, the aid of the President is invoked. (4) He conducts the Foreign Policy of the Republic, and has power, " by and with the Advice and Consent of the Senate, to make Treaties, provided two thirds of the Senators present concur." The Declaration of War rests with Congress. (5) He makes recommendations of a general nature to Congress, and when laws are passed by Congress he may return them to Congress with a veto. But if a measure so vetoed is again passed by both Houses of Congress by a two-thirds majority in each House, it becomes law, notwithstanding the objections of the President.

President of the United States, RICHARD MILHOUS NIXON, *born* Jan. 9, 1913, *elected President*, Nov. 6, 1968. Republican.

Vice-President, Spiro Theodore Agnew, *born* Nov. 9, 1918, *elected Vice-President*, Nov. 6, 1968.

THE CABINET *(each $60,000)*

Secretary of State, William P. Rogers, of Maryland *(born* June 23, 1913*)*, *appointed* Dec. 11, 1968.
Secretary of the Treasury, John B. Connally, Jr., of Texas *(born* 1917*)*, *appointed* Dec. 14, 1970.
Secretary of Defence, Melvin R. Laird, of Wisconsin *(born* 1922*)*, *appointed* Dec. 11, 1968.
Attorney-General, John N. Mitchell, of New York *(born* 1913*)*, *appointed* Dec. 11, 1968.
Secretary of Interior, Rogers C. B. Morton of Maryland *(born* 1914*)*, *appointed* Nov. 25, 1970.
Secretary of Agriculture, Clifford M. Hardin, of Nebraska *(born* 1915*)*, *appointed* Dec. 11, 1968.
Secretary of Commerce, Maurice H. Stans, of New York *(born* 1908*)*, *appointed* Dec. 11, 1968.
Secretary of Labor, James D. Hodgson, of California *(born* 1915*)*, *appointed* June 10, 1970.
Secretary of Health, Education and Welfare, Elliot L. Richardson, of Massachusetts *(born* 1920*)*, *appointed* June 6, 1970.
Secretary of Housing and Urban Development, George W. Romney, of Michigan *(born* 1907*)*, *appointed* Dec. 11, 1968.
Secretary of Transportation, John A. Volpe, of Massachusetts *(born* 1908*)*, *appointed* Dec. 11, 1968.

REORGANIZATION OF GOVERNMENT DEPARTMENTS.—Details were set out in four Bills presented to Congress by the President on March 25, 1971, of his plan to reorganize the Government Departments, apart from the Departments of State, the Treasury, Defence and Justice. Seven Departments —Interior, Labor, Agriculture, Commerce, Transportation, Housing and Urban Development, and Health, Education and Welfare—are planned to be dismantled and their functions assigned to four new Departments.

Department of Natural Resources.
Department of Human Resources.
Department of Economic Affairs.
Department of Community Development.

UNITED STATES EMBASSY
Grosvenor Square, W.1
[01-499-9000]

Ambassador Extraordinary and Plenipotentiary, His Excellency Walter H. Annenberg (1969).
Minister, Hon. Joseph N. Greene, Jr.
Minister for Economic Affairs, Hon. Robert A. Brand.
Counsellors, J. A. Herfurt *(Consular)*; William E. Weld, Jr. *(Public Affairs)*; William J. Galloway *(Political Affairs)*; Archie M. Andrews *(Commercial)*; Peter J. Skoufis *(Administration)*; Stephen H. Rogers *(Economic)*.
Defence Attaché, Naval Attaché and Naval Attaché for Air, Rear Admiral Fillmore B. Gilkeson, U.S.N.

Air Attaché, Col. John M. Cutler, U.S.A.F.
Army Attaché, Col. Thomas C. Finneran, U.S.A.
1st Secretaries, Irvine S. Lippe; William J. Ford (*Economic*); John J. Ingersoll; Eugene Rosenfeld (*Public Affairs*); Gordon D. King (*Politico-Military Affairs*); C. Thomas Mayfield (*Commercial*); William J. Miller (*Public Affairs*); Thomas M. Gaffney (*Administration*); Julius W. Walker, Jr.; John P. Mulligan (*Commercial*); Allen R. Turner (*Consular*); James E. Kiley (*Consular*).
2nd Secretaries, Gerald G. Oplinger; Bryan H. Baas.
Attachés: David L. Hume (*Agriculture*); John T. Minnich (*Legal*); James A. Griffin (*Finance*); Rolf Kingsley; Robin W. Winks (*Cultural Affairs*); Henry T. Snowdon (*Civil Air*); Robert Montgomery Scott; William L. R. Rice (*Atomic Energy*); Robert J. Murray (*Politico-Military Affairs*); Cameron J. LaClair, Jr.; Edward J. Donnelly (*Administration*); Paul W. Deibel (*Administration*); Alan G. Mencher (*Scientific*); Robert C. Goodell (*Public Affairs*); Marjory J. Fiebig (*Administration*).

CAPITAL OF THE UNITED STATES

In 1790 Congress ratified the cession of 100 sq. miles by the States of Maryland and Virginia as a site for a Federal City to be the national capital of the United States. In 1791 it was decided to name the capital *Washington* and in 1793 the foundation-stone of the Capitol building was laid. In 1800 the seat of government was removed to Washington, which was chartered as a city in 1802. In 1846 the Virginia portion was retroceded and the present area of the *District of Columbia* (with which the City of Washington is considered co-extensive) is 61 square miles, with a population at the Census of 1970 of 756,510.

The District of Columbia is ruled by a Commissioner and assistant and a 9-member City Council, all appointed by the President.

The *City of Washington* is situated on the west central edge of Maryland, opposite the State of Virginia, on the left bank of the Potomac at its confluence with the Anacostia, 107 miles from Chesapeake Bay and 186 from the Atlantic Ocean.

THE CONGRESS

The Legislative power is vested in two Houses, the Senate and the House of Representatives, the President having a *veto* power, which may be overcome by a two-thirds vote of each House. The Senate is composed of two Senators from each State, elected by the people thereof for the term of six years, and each Senator has one vote; and Representatives are chosen in each State, by popular vote, for two years. The number of Representatives for each State is allotted in proportion to its population—at present 1 for 468,972. The *Senate* consists of 100 members. The salary of a Senator is $42,500 per annum, with mileage at 20 cents per mile each session. The *House of Representatives* consists of 435 Representatives, a resident commissioner from Puerto Rico and a delegate from the District of Columbia. The salary of a Representative is $42,500 per annum, with mileage as for Senators. By the XIXth Amendment, sex is no disqualification for the franchise. On Nov. 1, 1970, there were 120,701,000 persons of voting age, excluding members of the armed forces overseas.

THE NINETY-SECOND CONGRESS

Noon of Jan. 21, 1971 to Noon of Jan. 20, 1974.
President of the Senate, Spiro T. Agnew (*Vice-President of the United States*).
Speaker of the House of Representatives, Carl Albert, *Oklahoma*. $62,500
Secretary of the Senate, Francis R. Valeo, *District of Columbia.*

Clerk of the House of Representatives, W. Pat Jennings, *Va.*

Members of the 92nd Congress were elected on Nov. 3, 1970.

The 92nd Congress is constituted as follows:
Senate.—Democrats, 54; Republicans, 44; Independent Democrat, 1; and Conservative Republican, 1. Total, 100. *House of Representatives.*—Democrats, 255; Republicans, 179; (one vacancy). Total, 435.

THE JUDICATURE

The *Federal Judiciary* consists of three sets of Federal Courts: (1) The *Supreme Court* at Washington, D.C., consisting of a Chief Justice and eight Associate Justices, with original jurisdiction in cases affecting Ambassadors, etc., or where a State is a party to the suit, and with appellate jurisdiction from inferior Federal Courts and from the decisions of the highest Courts of the States. (2) The *United States Courts of Appeals*, dealing with appeals from District Courts, and consisting of the Justice of the Supreme Court for the Circuit and all the Circuit Judges within the circuit. (3) The 93 *District Courts* served by 340 District Court Judges.

THE SUPREME COURT

(U.S. Supreme Court Building, Washington, D.C.)
Chief Justice, Warren E. Burger, *Minn.*, *born* Sept. 17, 1907, appointed June 23, 1969....... $62,500

Associate Justices (each $60,000)

Name	Born	Apptd.
Hugo L. Black, *Ala.*	1886	1937
Wm. O. Douglas, *Conn.*	1898	1939
John M. Harlan, *N.Y.*	1899	1955
William J. Brennan, Jr., *N.J.*	1906	1956
Potter Stewart, *Ohio*	1915	1958
Byron R. White, *Colo.*	1917	1962
Thurgood Marshall, *Md.*	1908	1967
Harry Blackmun, *Minn.*	1908	1970

Clerk of the Supreme Court, E. Robert Seaver.

CRIMINAL STATISTICS, U.S.

Crime	No. of Offences	
	1969	1970
Murder	14,590	15,810
Rape	36,470	37,270
Robbery	297,580	348,380
Aggravated Assault	306,420	329,940
Burglary	1,949,800	2,169,300
Larceny ($50 and over)	1,524,600	1,746,100
Thefts of Automobiles	871,900	921,370
Total	5,001,400	5,568,200

DEFENCE

Department of Defence

Secretary of Defence (in the Cabinet), Melvin R. Laird.
  Secretary of the Army, Robert F. Froehlke.
  Secretary of the Navy, John H. Chafee.
  Secretary of the Air Force, Robert C. Seamons, Jr.
  Chairman, Joint Chiefs of Staff, Adm. Thomas H. Moorer, U.S.N. (July 1, 1970).

The Department of Defence includes the Secretary of Defence as its head, the Deputy Secretary of Defence, the Defence staff offices, the Joint Chiefs of Staff and the Joint Staff, the three military departments and the military services within those departments, the unified and specified commands, and other Department of Defence agencies as the Secretary of Defence establishes to meet specific requirements. The Defence staff offices and the Joint Chiefs of Staff, although separately organized, function in full coordination and cooperation. They include the offices of the Director of Defence Research and Engineering, the eight Assistant Secretaries of Defence, the General Counsel of the Department of Defence and such other staff offices

as the Secretary of Defence may establish. The Joint Chiefs of Staff, as a group, are directly responsible to the Secretary of Defence for the functions assigned to them. Each member of the Joint Chiefs of Staff, other than the Chairman, is responsible for keeping the Secretary of his military department fully informed on matters considered or acted upon by the Joint Chiefs of Staff.

Each military department is separately organized under its own Secretary and functions under the direction, authority and control of the Secretary of Defence.

The Department of Defence maintains and employs armed forces: (1) to support and defend the Constitution of the United States against all enemies, foreign and domestic; (2) to insure, by timely and effective military action, the security of the United States, its possessions, and areas vital to its interests; (3) to uphold and advance the national policies and interest of the United States; and (4) to safeguard the internal security of the United States. All functions in the Department of Defence and its component agencies are performed under the direction, authority and control of the Secretary of Defence.

Commanders of unified and specified commands are responsible to the President and the Secretary of Defence for the accomplishment of military missions assigned to them.

Unified Defence Commands
Commanders-in-Chief

U.S. *European Command*, Brussels.—Gen. Andrew J. Goodpaster (concurrently N.A.T.O. *Supreme Allied Commander*).

U.S. *Southern Command*, Quarry Heights, Panama Canal Zone.—Gen. George R. Mather (*U.S. Army*).

Atlantic, Norfolk, Virginia.—Adm. Charles K. Duncan (*U.S. Navy*) (concurrently N.A.T.O. *Supreme Allied Commander, Atlantic*).

Pacific, Hawaii.—Adm. John S. McCain, Jr. (*U.S. Navy*).

†U.S. *Naval Forces, Europe*, London.—Adm. William F. Bringle (*U.S. Navy*).

N. *American Air Defence Command*, Colorado Springs.—Gen. Seth J. McKee (*U.S.A.F.*).

★*Strategic Air Command*, Omaha.—Gen. Bruce K. Holloway (*U.S.A.F.*).

Alaskan Command, Anchorage, Alaska.—Lt.-Gen. Robert G. Ruegg (*U.S.A.F.*).

U.S. *Strike Command*, MacDill, Florida.—Gen. John L. Throckmorton (*U.S. Army*).

★ A Specified Command.

† A subordinate component of U.S. *European Command.*

Army.—The Army of U.S. had a strength of 8,293,766 (including 2,310,436 Air Force) on V.E. Day, reduced by June 30, 1959, to 861,964 (excluding Air Force). The strength on March 31, 1971, was 1,187,485. Stationed in Europe were four divisions and other large combat elements of less than one division size. There were two divisions in Korea. Strong combat units were on duty in the Caribbean area and in Alaska and other combat

units were in Italy as part of the N.A.T.O. force. On June 17, 1971, 194,500 troops were serving in South Vietnam.

Chief of Staff of the Army, Gen. William C. Westmoreland (July 3, 1968).

Navy.—The peak strength of the Navy (including Marine Corps) in August, 1945, was 3,894,180. The strength of the U.S. Navy in March, 1971, was 638,800. Strength of the Marine Corps, 222,000.

The U.S. Navy had in service on April 30, 1971, 697 active fleet ships, including 14 attack carriers, 4 ASW carriers, 9 cruisers, 213 destroyer types, 141 submarines (including 50 nuclear and 41 SSBN), 79 amphibious, 42 mine warfare, and 178 auxiliaries.

Chief of Naval Operations, Adm. Elmo Zumwalt.

Air.—The United States Air Force was established as a separate organization on September 18, 1947. In May 1969, there were more than 2 million people in the Air Force. About 880,000 officers and airmen are on active duty, with more than 340,000 civilian employees and some 455,000 members of the Air Force Reserve and Air National Guard.

There are approximately 14,000 aircraft in the Air Force inventory. To deter aggression the Air Force has 585 strategic bombers maintaining constant alert as well as 1,054 inter-continental ballistic missiles in hardened silos. In addition, the Air Force maintains the capability to carry out limited war and special air warfare operations. In March, 1961, the Air Force was assigned primary responsibility for the Department of Defence space development programmes and projects. By Dec. 1970, the United States had placed 669 spacecraft in orbit round the earth and sent 42 others to the moon and other distant planets. These included Air Force, Army and N.A.S.A. shots.

Chief of Staff of the U.S. Air Force, Gen. John D. Ryan.

NATIONAL ORIGINS OF THE POPULATION

About 75 million of the approximately 200 million persons in the United States reported on a sample survey conducted in November, 1969, that they were of one of seven specific origin categories. Approximately 20·0 million persons reported German origin; 19·1 million, English; 13·3 million, Irish; 9·2 million, Spanish; 7·2 million, Italian; 4·0 million, Polish; and 2·2 million, Russian. About 11 million persons living in the United States at the time of the survey were foreign born. Germany, Italy, Mexico and the United Kingdom were the major contributing countries. Two-thirds of them reported English as the language usually spoken in their homes. They were 23 years older, on the average, than the native population.

Countries of birth of the foreign-born population were: Austria (236,000), Cuba (504,000), Germany (1,004,000), Ireland (277,000), Italy (1,353,000), Mexico (938,000), Poland (550,000), Russia (412,000), Sweden (166,000), United Kingdom (1,006,000); other countries, 4,434,000.

SOCIAL WELFARE EXPENDITURE

The total value of government expenditure on social welfare (federal, state and local government) in 1969 was $126,802,000,000, compared with $112,044,000,000 in 1968 and $52,293,000,000 in 1960. 44·5 per cent. of the 1969 total was Federal expenditure. In 1969 expenditure per person (of the total population of U.S.A.) was $616—social insurance, $236; education, $209; public aid, $65; health and medical services, $43; veterans' welfare, $39; other services, $20 per person. Total expenditure by programmes was:

	1960	1968	$ million 1969
Social insurance......	19,307	42,693	48,720
Education............	17,626	38,757	43,033
Public aid...........	4,101	11,092	13,443
Health and medical...	4,464	8,271	8,817
Veterans.............	5,479	7,362	8,036
Other welfare services.	1,139	3,442	4,196
Housing.............	177	428	556
TOTAL.........	52,293	112,044	126,802

FINANCE

THE UNITED STATES BUDGET [Fiscal years

Description	Actual	
	1970	1971 (preliminary)
Receipts by Source		
Individual income taxes....................................	$90,411,787,000	$86,164,233,000
Corporation income taxes..................................	32,829,330,000	26,805,913,000
Social insurance taxes and contributions:		
Employment taxes and contributions.....................	39,132,959,000	41,699,377,000
Unemployment insurance...............................	3,464,281,000	3,685,607,000
Contributions for other insurance and retirement..........	2,700,653,000	3,201,963,000
Excise taxes..	15,705,490,000	16,629,272,000
Estate and gift taxes......................................	3,644,421,000	3,708,909,000
Customs...	2,430,215,000	2,589,973,000
Miscellaneous receipts....................................	3,424,114,000	3,846,882,000
Total....................................	$193,743,251,000	$188,332,129,000
Outlays by Function		
National defence..	80,296,303,000	77,620,672,000
International affairs and finance............................	3,567,695,000	2,993,668,000
Space research and technology..............................	3,748,927,000	3,382,216,000
Agriculture and rural development..........................	6,187,090,000	5,282,571,000
Natural resources...	2,478,360,000	2,680,631,000
Commerce and transportation..............................	9,316,060,000	11,363,944,000
Community development and housing........................	3,111,006,000	3,383,272,000
Education and manpower...................................	7,438,764,000	8,639,293,000
Health...	12,985,453,000	14,480,410,000
Income security...	43,505,061,000	55,712,507,000
Veterans' benefits and services.............................	8,684,610,000	9,786,730,000
Interest..	18,312,577,000	19,659,607,000
General government.......................................	3,336,608,000	3,964,129,000
Undistributed intrabudgetary transactions..................	−6,380,729,000	−7,375,327,000
Total....................................	$196,587,786,000	$211,574,322,000

PUBLIC DEBT

On June 30, 1971, the total gross *Federal Debt* of the United States stood at $409,467,479,000; the level at the end of the fiscal year 1970 was $382,603,410,000.

COST OF LIVING IN U.S.A.

The Consumer Price Index (for city wage-earner and clerical workers—single persons and families—in 50 cities representative of all cities in the United States) showed a monthly average during the calendar year 1970 of 116·3 (the basic figure of 100 being the 1967 average). The average of consumer prices for the first five months of 1971 were: January, 119·2; February, 119·4; March, 119·8; April, 120·2, and May, 120·8.

According to figures prepared by the Bureau of Labor Statistics, the index of consumer prices (all items) rose from 109·8 in the calendar year 1969 to 116·3 in 1970. Between June, 1970, and June, 1971, food prices rose from 115·2 to 119·2; all other commodities—113·5 to 117·9; rent—109·8 to 115·2; all other services—123·5 to 130·6.

The wholesale price index of all commodities showed a monthly average during 1970 of 110·4 (the average for the year 1967 is 100). The index in June, 1971, was 114·3. Wholesale prices for farm products rose from 108·8 in 1969 to 111·0 in 1970. (The index for June, 1971, was 116·0.) Industrial prices averaged 110·0 in 1970, increasing to 113·9 in June 1971.

PERSONAL INCOMES IN U.S.A.

Personal incomes in the United States rose from $688·9 billion in 1968 to $750·3 billion in 1969 and further to $803·6 billion in 1970. In the year 1970, labour income rose by $34·4 billion, business and professional income by $0·7 billion and personal interest income by $5·5 billion. Dividend income rose by $0·6 billion to $25·0 billion. Personal incomes from all sources other than agriculture rose by $53·7 billion. Preliminary estimates for June, 1971 (seasonally adjusted annual rate) showed personal income at $870·3 billion, an increase of $66·7 billion over the 1970 level. Labour income rose from $572·2 billion in 1970 to $609·0 billion in June, 1971, an increase of $36·8 billion. Business and professional incomes increased from $51·0 billion in 1970 to $52·0 billion in June, 1971, and personal interest income rose from $64·7 billion in 1970 to 67·7 billion in June, 1971.

Disposition of personal incomes.—Of the total of $803·6 billion gross personal income in 1970, $115·9 billion was taken by personal taxes and $615·8 billion was consumed on: Durable goods ($88·6 billion); non-durable goods ($264·7 billion); and services ($262·5 billion), showing personal saving totalling $54·1 billion out of $687·8 disposable personal income. At current prices the latter showed an average of $3,358 per head. Savings amounted to 7·9 per cent. of disposable personal income, as against 6·0 per cent. in 1969.

Private domestic investment.—The total gross private domestic investment rose from $126·0 billion in 1968 to $137·8 billion in 1969 and $139·4 billion in 1970. Fixed investment in new residential construction (excluding farm investment) fell to $29·7 billion in 1970 (1969, $31·2 billion) and other non-farm construction rose to $35·9 billion (1969, $33·7 billion). Investment in producers' durable equipment (excluding farm equipment) rose from $59·2 billion in 1969 to $60·0 billion in 1970.

EXTERNAL TRADE OF THE UNITED STATES

Figures adjusted to include imports of uranium ore and exports of uranium and other nuclear fuels.

Year	General Imports	Total Exports and Re-exports	Excess of Exports over Imports
1966	$25,618,000,000	$30,430,000,000	+ $3,872,000,000
1967	26,889,000,000	31,622,000,000	+ 4,141,000,000
1968	33,226,000,000	34,636,000,000	+ 837,000,000
1969	36,043,000,000	38,000,000,000	+ 1,289,000,000
1970	39,963,000,000	43,226,000,000	+ 2,699,000,000

EXPORTS BY PRINCIPAL COMMODITIES OF DOMESTIC ORIGIN, 1970

Commodity	Value
Food and Live Animals	$4,349,000,000
Meat and Meat Preparations	175,000,000
Dairy Products and Eggs	137,000,000
Wheat and Wheat Flour	1,112,000,000
Rice	306,000,000
Corn and other grains	1,170,000,000
Fruit and Nuts	406,000,000
Vegetables	179,000,000
Animal feedingstuffs	497,000,000
Beverages and Tobacco	702,000,000
Cigarettes	159,000,000
Crude Materials (inedible), except fuels	4,609,000,000
Synthetic rubber	176,000,000
Raw cotton	372,000,000
Mineral fuels, etc.	1,594,000,000
Coal	961,000,000
Petroleum and products	487,000,000
Animal and Vegetable Oils and Fats	493,000,000
Chemicals	3,826,000,000
Machinery and Transport Equipment	17,875,000,000
Other Manufactured Goods	7,638,000,000

UNITED STATES IMPORTS BY PRINCIPAL COMMODITIES, 1970

Commodity	Value
Food and Live Animals	$5,379,000,000
Meat and Meat Preparations	1,014,000,000
Fish	794,000,000
Fruit, Nuts, Vegetables	736,000,000
Sugar	$729,000,000
Coffee (green)	1,160,000,000
Beverages and Tobacco	855,000,000
Whisky	468,000,000
Crude materials (inedible), except fuels	3,312,000,000
Rubber (including latex)	231,000,000
Textile fibres and wastes	202,000,000
Ores and metal scrap	1,149,000,000
Mineral Fuels, etc.	3,081,000,000
Petroleum and Products	2,770,000,000
Animal and Vegetable Oils, Fats	160,000,000
Chemicals	1,450,000,000
Machinery and Transport Equipment	11,171,000,000
Electrical apparatus	2,272,000,000
Motor vehicles and parts	5,067,000,000
Other manufactured goods	13,281,000,000
Paper and manufactures	1,087,000,000
Metals and manufactures	4,509,000,000
Textiles other than clothing	1,135,000,000

UNITED STATES FOREIGN TRADE BY ECONOMIC CLASS, 1970

Class	Imports (1)	Exports (2)
Crude materials	$4,129,000,000	$4,492,000,000
Crude foodstuffs	2,580,000,000	2,748,000,000
Manufactured do.	3,523,000,000	1,921,000,000
Semi-manufactures	7,268,000,000	6,866,000,000
Finished manuf.	22,463,000,000	26,566,000,000
Total	$39,963,000,000	$42,593,000,000

(1) General Imports,
(2) Exports of United States merchandise, including civilian supplies sent to occupied areas.

UNITED STATES FOREIGN TRADE BY PRINCIPAL COUNTRIES, 1970

Country	Exports and Re-exports to	General Imports from	Country	Exports and Re-exports to	General Imports from
Australia	$985,000,000	$611,000,000	Japan	$4,652,000,000	$5,875,000,000
Belgium and Luxemburg	1,195,000,000	696,000,000	Korea	637,000,000	370,000,000
Brazil	841,000,000	669,000,000	Mexico	1,704,000,000	1,222,000,000
Canada	9,084,000,000	11,091,000,000	Netherlands	1,651,000,000	528,000,000
France	1,484,000,000	942,000,000	South Africa	563,000,000	288,000,000
Germany, W.	2,740,000,000	3,130,000,000	Spain	712,000,000	353,000,000
India	573,000,000	298,000,000	Sweden	544,000,000	400,000,000
Israel	594,000,000	150,000,000	Switzerland	700,000,000	459,000,000
Italy	1,353,000,000	1,316,000,000	United Kingdom	2,537,000,000	2,196,000,000
			Venezuela	759,000,000	1,082,000,000

UNITED STATES STOCK OF MONEY $ million

June 30	Gold*	Standard Silver $	Subsidiary Coin	Minor Coin	Silver Certificates	United States Notes	Federal Reserve Notes	Total†
1966	13,434·5	484·7	3,257·2	933·4	602·1	322·5	40,949·6	60,362·0
1967	13,109·8	484·7	4,168·6	979·4	397·6	322·5	41,686·3	61,408·1
1968	10,366·9	484·7	4,554·1	1,022·9	238·4	322·5	44,431·1	61,505·7
1969	10,367·0	484·7	4,538·2	1,085·1	222·8	322·5	47,283·5	64,386·6
1970	10,732·1	484·7	4,821·9	1,221·6	218·6	322·5	53,744·7	71,625·9

* Held by U.S. Treasury only.   † Totals include value of early issue notes in process of withdrawal, not separately shown. Value, June, 1970, $79·7 m. From 1967, totals include silver bullion in excess of amount needed to secure silver certificates. Silver certificates have not been redeemable in silver since June 23, 1968.

AGRICULTURE AND LIVESTOCK

Agriculture.—The total land surface, including Hawaii and Alaska, is 2,280,864,000 acres of which about 50 per cent. is in farms. The total number of farms in 1970 was 2,924,010. The cash income from crops in 1969 was $19,527,000,000, and in 1970, $19,636,000,000. Cash income from livestock and livestock products in 1969 was $28,590,000,000 and in 1970, $29,595,000,000.

Combined production of all crops in 1970 was about 3 per cent. less than in 1969, due largely to lower feed grain and food grain production. Output of oilseeds, hay, tobacco and potatoes set a new high record. Yields per acre were at new high levels for winter wheat, rye, rice, peanuts, tobacco, sugar cane, and potatoes. Farm output of livestock and livestock products was also up in 1970 due to sharp increases in cattle, hogs and chickens. Other classes were relatively unchanged.

Livestock on Farms, Jan. 1

	1969 'ooo head	1970 'ooo head	1971 'ooo head
Cattle	109,585	112,303	114,568
Cows	48,085	48,982	50,002
Hogs*	60,632	56,655	67,540
Stock sheep	18,332	17,411	16,937
Chickens	419,635	433,640	442,783
Turkeys	6,604	6,769	7,462

*Dec. 1, preceding year.

MINERALS

The value of mineral production in the United States in 1970 totalled an estimated $30·0 billion compared with $26·9 billion in 1969 and $25·0 billion in 1968.

The lack of strikes in the copper mining industry also resulted in increased production of gold and silver which are largely by-products of copper production. Lead output rose by 15 per cent. over 1969 and primary aluminium production reached a new peak at 4·0 million tons. Production of zinc, iron and uranium ore also increased.

Nearly 67 per cent. of the mineral production of the United States (in value) consists of fuels. In 1970, U.S. production of crude petroleum amounted to 3,516 billion barrels. Total demand (domestic plus exports) averaged 14·7 million barrels daily, an increase of 1·0 per cent. over 1969.

In the three principal oil-producing states in 1970 daily average production increased as follows: Louisiana, 69,000 barrels (total average daily production, 2,483,000 barrels); Texas, 267,000 barrels (total average daily production 3,423,000 barrels); and California, 8,000 barrels (total average daily production 1,020,000 barrels).

Production of anthracite again decreased in 1970, reflecting continued declines in major markets at home and abroad. Pennsylvania anthracite production fell 9·5 per cent. below the 1969 figure, which was itself a 5·8 per cent. drop from 1968. Anthracite exports to Canada fell 7·4 per cent. below the 1969 tonnage. The quantity shipped to western Europe was 127·2 per cent. above the 1969 level. The continued loss in the domestic market was due to competition from other fuels, principally oil and gas.

Bituminous coal and lignite produced in 1970 totalled 596 million tons, an increase of 6·4 per cent. over 1969. Exports increased by 26·1 per cent. to 70,908,000 tons.

LABOUR

Organized Labour.—On December 5, 1955, the American Federation of Labour (AFL), founded in 1881, and the Congress of Industrial Organizations (CIO), formally established in 1938, merged into an organization called the American Federation of Labour and Congress of Industrial Organizations. The combined membership in 1969 was 15,916,000. There are also 4,778,000 members of unions not affiliated to the AFL–CIO. Of the 20,694,000 members of national and international unions with headquarters in U.S.A., 1,369,000 were employed in Canada. In July, 1968, the large United Auto Workers Union withdrew from the AFL–CIO.

Approximately 27·4 per cent. of the non-agricultural labour force of the United States is estimated to be organized.

Work Stoppages.—There were 5,716 stoppages recorded in 1970. There were 66,412,000 man-days of idleness, representing 0·37 per cent. of estimated working time of all workers.

Employment and Unemployment.—The civilian labour force (working population) was 81,741,000 in May, 1970. This includes self-employed, wage and salary-earners, and unpaid family workers, employed and unemployed. Unemployment was estimated at 3,384,000 in May 1970 (4·1 per cent.).

Wages.—In March, 1971, gross average weekly earnings by industry ranged from $246·91 per week in electrical work to $58·59 in eating and drinking places (30·2 hours and $1·94 average hourly earnings). The average for all manufacturing was $139·83, compared with $131·80 in April, 1970.

Wages Mar. and April 1971	Average Weekly Earnings	Hours per Week	Average Hourly Earnings
Manufacturing	$139·83	39·5	$3·54
Durable	151·18	40·1	3·77
Non-durable	125·32	38·8	3·23
Coal Mining	192·92	40·7	4·74
Bituminous Coal and Lignite Mining	194·95	40·7	4·79
Gen. Bldg. Contractors	194·91	36·5	5·34
Gas, Electricity and Sanitary Services	179·24	41·3	4·34
Wholesale trade	142·63	39·4	3·62
Retail trade (incl. eating and drinking places)	85·17	33·4	2·55
Laundries, Cleaners	79·92	34·9	2·29

On Feb. 1, 1967, the minimum wage set by federal law became $1·40 an hour for employees engaged in interstate commerce or in the production of goods for interstate commerce, or in activities closely related and directly essential to such production. The law requires at least time and a half of an employee's regular rate of pay for all hours over 40 a week. From Feb. 1, 1968, the minimum wage for these employees became $1·60 an hour.

Other employees employed in certain large enterprises having some employees engaged in commerce or the production of goods for commerce, on Feb. 1, 1967, became entitled to a minimum wage of $1·00 an hour increasing by 15 cents each year until it reaches $1·60 after Feb. 1, 1971. Overtime premium—44 hours in a week after Feb. 1, 1967—was reduced to 42 hours one year later and to 40 hours after Feb. 1, 1969.

There are certain exemptions from these monetary requirements in specific occupations and industries.

In addition to cash wages, most workers receive some type of " fringe " benefits—the most common forms being paid vacations, and public holidays, various types of insurance and health funds financed by the employer or by employer and employees jointly.

COMMUNICATIONS

RAILWAYS

Data pertaining to Class I and II Carriers and their non-operating subsidiaries:—

	1968
Capital Stock outstanding	$6,787,692,033
Funded Debt outstanding	8,002,437,818
Total Railway capital actually outstanding	14,577,285,833
Dividends declared	560,048,161
Interest accrued	478,385,806
Total dividends and interest	1,038,433,967
Railway operating revenues	11,061,901,686
Railway operating expenses	8,723,664,216
Number of passengers carried earning revenue	*Number*
	30,1372,150
Number of passenger-train cars in service	14,815
Number of freight-train cars in service	1,488,815
Number of railway employees	602,413
Miles operated	222,924

ROADS

In 1969 there were 3,710,299 miles of roads and streets in the United States, of which 3,161,726 miles were in rural areas and 548,573 miles were in municipal areas. Surfaced roads and streets account for 2,914,131 miles of the total; 796,168 miles were unimproved and graded and drained. State primary roads, including extensions in municipal areas, total 462,432 miles (458,837 surfaced). Other roads and streets under State control total 314,121 miles (283,009 surfaced), 2,751,070 miles are under local control (2,119,679 surfaced); and 182,676 miles (52,606 surfaced) are under Federal control (in national forests and parks).

An estimated total of $18,909,000,000 was spent in 1970 for roads and streets in the United States. Of this total $13,120,000,000 was spent for State highways, $2,574,000,000 was spent for county and local rural roads, $2,770,000,000 was spent for city streets and $445,000,000 was spent on roads in Federal areas. Capital outlay accounts for 59·2 per cent. of the total expenditure; 24·0 per cent. was spent for maintenance, and 6·4 per cent. for administration; 6·4 per cent. for highway police and safety; and 4·0 per cent. for interest on highway bonds.

Motor Vehicles and Taxation.—The number of motor vehicles registered in 1970 in the United States was 108,435,903, an increase of 3·2 per cent. over the 1969 total of 105,098,686. The State governments received $1,468,554,000 in 1941 and $10,277,589,000 in 1969, respectively, from motor-fuel, motor-vehicle,and motor-carrier taxes. In 1970 the Federal Government received $6,932,716,000 from excise taxes on motor vehicles and parts, tyres and tubes, petrol, diesel and special fuels and lubricating oils.

Accidents.—In 1970 there were 54,800 deaths caused by motor vehicle accidents. The death rate

per 100,000,000 vehicle-miles of travel was 4·9 in 1970, compared with 5·3 in 1969.

SHIPPING

The active ocean-going Merchant Marine of the U.S. on June 1, 1971, consisted of 701 vessels of 1,000 gross tons and over, of which 682 were privately owned and 19 were government-owned ships under charter or general agency agreement for operation by private companies, primarily for the carriage of supplies for the Military Sea Transportation Service. Of the active vessels, 444 were freighters, 11 were combination passenger and cargo, and 246 were tankers. There were 710 ships in the National Defense Reserve Fleet of inactive government-owned vessels, of which 395 were to be sold for scrap.

AIR TRANSPORT

United States domestic and international scheduled airlines in 1970 were estimated to have carried 169,668,000 passengers over 131,719,194 revenue passenger miles, over 95 per cent. of which were flown in jets. The freight flown by the scheduled airlines during 1970 totalled 3,407,650,000 ton miles and express 106,521,000 ton miles. In addition, the airlines flew 1,470,176,000 ton miles of mail, an increase of 10·2 per cent. over 1969.

Total operating revenues of all U.S. scheduled airlines reached the record figure of $9,273,426,000 in 1970, an increase of 5·5 per cent. over 1969. Similarly, total operating expenses rose to a record high total of $9,213,475,000 last year, or 9·7 per cent. more than the previous year. The net operating income (*i.e.* before deduction of taxes, interest, etc.) was $59,951,000, a decrease of 84·7 per cent. from the previous year, resulting in a loss of $178,930,000 compared with a profit of $52,752,000 in 1969.

Ten principal classes of commercial air carriers can be distinguished in the United States, (*a*) The Domestic Trunk Lines (11); (*b*) Local Service Carriers, operating routes of lesser traffic density between the smaller traffic centres and between small and large centres (9); (*c*) The International and Territorial Carriers, including all U.S. flag air carriers authorized to operate between the U.S.A. and foreign countries, other than Canada, and over international waters; also between foreign countries and into Mexico, the Caribbean and to Alaska and Hawaii (13); (*d*) Intra-Hawaiian Air Carriers, operating in Hawaii (2); (*e*) Intra-Alaskan Carriers, providing service within Alaska (4); (*f*) All Cargo Carriers (3); (*g*) Helicopter Carriers (4); (*h*) Supplemental Air Carriers (14); (*i*) Air Freight Forwarding Companies (181) and Air Taxi operators; and (*j*) Intra-State Carriers, with operations limited to State boundaries.

In 1970, 297,374 persons were employed by the domestic and international airlines, 4·7 per cent. less than in 1969.

U.S. SCHEDULED AIRLINE INDUSTRY STATISTICS, 1970 (Thousands)

	Domestic Trunk Lines	Local Service Airlines	Intra-Hawaiian Carriers	Helicopter Carriers	Internatl. & Territorial Airlines	Intra-Alaskan Carriers	All Cargo Carriers
Revenue passengers carried	122,866	26,472	2,643	573	16,713	351	..
Revenue passenger miles	95,899,744	7,439,842	355,034	11,341	27,895,289	112,532	..
Air mail ton miles	706,500	24,054	1,038	5	542,738	6,083	225,758
Express ton miles	95,445	8,713	..	25	561	..	1,755
Freight ton miles	1,789,701	53,647	3,314	4	950,196	6,385	604,379
Revenue ton miles	12,589,056	851,547	39,866	1,171	5,253,811	26,073	1,424,327
Revenue plane miles	1,748,729	239,634	8,147	1,427	377,236	7,603	31,979

EDUCATION
State School Systems

Almost every State in the Union has a compulsory school attendance law. In general, children are obliged to attend school from 7 to 16 years of age, and those from 14 to 16 must attend school or be lawfully employed. In the States there are, connected with the local administrative units, officers charged with enforcing the compulsory attendance law, known in the majority of States as the truant or attendance officers.

In the autumn of 1970 the total number of children in the United States of 5 to 17 years of age was 52,988,000, of whom 45,903,371 were enrolled in public elementary and secondary schools. The average daily attendance in the public schools was estimated at 42,495,000 for the 1970–71 school year, the average length of school term was estimated at 179 days, and the average number of days attended by each pupil enrolled at 165. In 1970, 2,061,115 teachers were employed. The estimated average annual salary of all teachers was $9,210.

The 1968–69 total revenue receipts for school purposes, excluding balances on hand, were about $31,903,068,000. Of this amount, about $2,806,469,000 were received from Federal sources, $12,275,536,000 from State sources and $16,821,063,000 from county and local sources. For 1970–71 current expenditures are estimated at $38,026,223,000. It is estimated that $5,061,361,000 were expended for sites, buildings, furniture and equipment, and $1,336,281,000 for interest.

Institutions of Higher Education

In the autumn of 1970 enrolment in institutions of higher education numbered 8,498,117.

Institutions of higher education include universities, colleges, professional schools, and junior colleges. The 1970 survey of enrolments covered 2,556 institutions classified as follows: 1,665 universities, colleges and professional schools enrolling 6,288,196 students; and 891 junior colleges enrolling 2,209,921 students. Publicly controlled institutions of higher education enrolled 75 per cent. (6,371,008) of the students and privately controlled 25 per cent. (2,127,109).

During the school year 1969–70, 833,322 bachelor's and first professional degrees were conferred, 486,949 to men and 346,373 to women; 209,387 master's degrees, 126,146 to men and 83,241 to women; and 29,872 doctorates, 25,892 to men and 3,980 to women. Education, Social Sciences, and Business and Commerce were, in that order, the fields in which most students received first-level degrees. There were 166,423 bachelor's and first professional degrees in Education, 155,235 in Social Sciences, and 106,279 in Business and Commerce. The three leading fields of study for the master's degree were Education (79,841), Social Sciences (23,580) and Business and Commerce (21,417). The most popular fields of study on the doctorate level were Education (5,894), Physical Sciences (4,313) and Social Sciences (3,778).

Particulars of some of the Universities are: *Harvard* (18,465 students, including 5,619 women in 1970), founded at Cambridge, Mass. on Oct. 28, 1636, and named after John Harvard of Emmanuel College, Cambridge, England, who bequeathed to it his library and a sum of money in 1638; *Yale* (8,927 students, including 1,691 women, in 1970), founded at New Haven, Connecticut, in 1701; *Bowdoin*, Brunswick, Me. (founded 1794; 940 men); *Brown*, Providence, R.I. (founded 1764; 5,733 students, including 1,674 women, in 1970); *Columbia*, New York, N.Y. (founded 1754; 23,632 students, including 9,910 women, in 1970); *Cornell* (founded at Ithaca, N.Y., 1865; 19,600 students,

including 5,534 women, in 1970); *Dartmouth* Hanover, N.H. (founded 1769, 3,928 students, including 138 women, in 1970); *Georgetown*, Washington, D.C. (founded 1789; 8,074 students, including 1,836 women, in 1970); *North Carolina*, Chapel Hill, N.C. (founded in 1789; 17,567 students, including 5,765 women, in 1970); *Pennsylvania*, Philadelphia, Pa. (founded 1740; 19,577 students, including 6,044 women, in 1970); *Pittsburgh*, Pa. (founded 1787; 31,650 students, including 9,548 women, in 1970); *Princeton*, N.J. (founded 1746; 5,160 men and 667 women in 1970); *Tennessee*, Knoxville, Tenn. (founded 1794; 38,500 students, including 14,499 women, in 1970); *William and Mary*, Williamsburg, Va. (founded 1693; 9,941 students, including 4,386 women, in 1970); *New York University*, founded in 1831 at New York, had 32,323 students, including 15,806 women, in 1970.

WEIGHTS AND MEASURES

The weights and measures in common use in the United States are of British origin. They date back to the American Revolution when practically all the standards were intended to be equivalent to those used in England at that period. The principal units were the yard, the avoirdupois pound, the gallon, and the bushel. More or less authentic copies of the English standards of the denominations mentioned had been brought over and adopted by the different colonies. Divergencies in these weights and measures were, however, quite common, due no doubt to the fact that the system of weights and measures in England was not itself well established, and hence the copies brought to this country were often adjusted to different standards.

Because of these discrepancies, the system of weights and measures in the United States (U.S. Customary System) is not identical with the British system. The U.S. bushel and the U.S. gallon, and their subdivisions differ from the corresponding British units. Also the British ton is 2,240 pounds, whereas the ton generally used in the United States is the short ton of 2,000 pounds. The American colonists adopted the English wine gallon of 231 cubic inches. The English of that period used this wine gallon and they also had another gallon, the ale gallon of 282 cubic inches. In 1824 these two gallons were abandoned by the British when they adopted the British Imperial gallon, equivalent to 277·42 cubic inches. At the same time, the bushel was redefined as 8 gallons. In the British system the units of dry measure are the same as those of liquid measure. In the United States these two are not the same, the gallon and its subdivisions being used in the measurement of liquids, while the bushel, with its subdivisions, is used in the measurement of certain dry commodities. The U.S. gallon is divided into 4 liquid quarts and the U.S. bushel into 32 dry quarts. All the units of capacity mentioned thus far are larger in the British system than in the U.S. system. But the British fluid ounce is smaller than the U.S. fluid ounce, because the British quart is divided into 40 fluid ounces, whereas the U.S. quart is divided into 32 fluid ounces.

The rapidly diminishing world-wide use of the U.S. Customary and British Systems of measurement and the corresponding rise in metric usage, promoted the passage of Public Law 90-472. This law authorizes the Secretary of Commerce to conduct a programme of investigation, research and survey to determine the impact on U.S.A. of the metric system (SI) and to determine what action, if any, should be taken in the United States as a consequence.

The International System of Units—officially abbreviated SI—is a modernized version of the metric system. It was established by international agreement to provide a logical and interconnected framework for all measurements in science, industry and commerce. SI is built upon a foundation of six base units: Length *Metre*—m; Time, *Second*—s; Mass, *Kilogram*—kg; Temperature, *Kelvin*—K; Electric Current, *Ampere*—A; and Luminous Intensity, *Candela*—cd. All other SI units are derived from these base units. Multiples and submultiples are expressed in a decimal system.

TERRITORIES, ETC. OF THE UNITED STATES

The territories and the principal islands and island groups under the sovereignty of the United States of America comprise: Palmyra Island; Kingman Reef (about 1 sq. mile); Johnston (or Cornwallis) Island and Sand Island (about 1 sq. mile in all); Canton and Enderbury Islands (jointly administered with Great Britain); Midway Islands; Wake Island; Guam, Howland, Baker and Jarvis Islands (about 3 sq. miles in all); American Samoa (including the island of Tutuila, the Manua Islands, and all other islands of the Samoan group east of longitude 171° west of Greenwich together with Swains Island); the Commonwealth of Puerto Rico; the Virgin Islands of the United States, and Navassa Island (2 sq. miles).

The Canal Zone is under the jurisdiction of the United States.

The Trust Territory of the Pacific Islands is under the jurisdiction of the United States pursuant to a trusteeship agreement between the U.S. Government and the Security Council of the United Nations. It consists of the Mariana (except Guam), Caroline and Marshall Islands, with a land area of 687 square miles and a population of 101,592 in 1970. Nine individual languages are spoken in the Territory. Copra is the principal export of importance.

There are certain small guano islands, rocks, or keys which, in pursuance of action taken under the Act of Congress, August 18, 1856, subsequently embodied in Sections 5570–5578 of the Revised Statutes are considered as appertaining to the United States. Responsibility for territorial affairs generally is centred in the Office of Territories, Dept. of the Interior, Washington, D.C.

CANTON AND ENDERBURY

Under the Anglo-American Pact of Aug. 10, 1938, Canton and Enderbury (of the Phoenix Island Group in the Central Pacific) were declared to be for the common use of Great Britain and U.S.A. for aviation and communications. The islands, which are about midway between Hawaii and Australia, extend to a total of 27 sq. miles.

On April 6, 1939, the U.S. and Great Britain agreed to set up a joint regime for Canton and Enderbury Islands. Provision for the joint control of these islands was made by exchange of notes between the two Governments on April 6, 1939.

Canton Island was successively used for aviation support activities and as a missile tracking station by the U.S. National Aeronautics and Space Administration. These activities have been terminated and the island is now uninhabited. Enderbury has been uninhabited since World War II.

GUAM

Guam, the largest of the Ladrone or Mariana Islands in the North Pacific Ocean, lies in 13° 26′ N. lat. and 144° 39′ E long., at a distance of about 1,506 miles east of Manila. The area of the island is estimated at 209 square miles, with an estimated civilian population (1970) of 86,926.

The Guamanians are of Chamorro stock mingled with Filipino and Spanish blood. The Chamorro language belongs to the Malayo-Polynesian family, but has had considerable admixture of Spanish. English is the language used throughout the island, although Chamorro is also used in Guamanian homes.

Guam was occupied by Japanese in Dec., 1941, but was recaptured and occupied throughout by U.S. forces before the end of August, 1944. Under the Organic Act of Guam of August 1, 1950 (Public Law 630 of the 81st Congress), Guam has statutory powers of self-government, and Guamanians are United States citizens. The Governor is popularly elected. A 21-member unicameral legislature is elected biennially. There is also a District Court of Guam, with original jurisdiction in cases under federal law.

Governor, Carlos Comacho, appointed July, 1969; *first elected Governor*, November, 1970.

Secretary, Kurt Moylan.

CAPITAL, Agaña. Port of entry, ♆Apra.

WAKE AND MIDWAY ISLANDS

Wake Island, annexed in 1898, has an area of about 3 sq. miles and lies in the N. Pacific about 2,300 miles from Hawaii on the direct route to Hong Kong. Wake Island was occupied by Japanese, Dec. 27, 1941; it was re-occupied by U.S. on Sept. 15, 1945. Population (1970), 1,647.

Midway Islands, with a total area of 28 sq. miles and a population (1970) of 2,220, lie in the N. Pacific about 1,300 miles from Hawaii. There is no indigenous population. The group is under the jurisdiction of the U.S. Navy.

PUERTO RICO

Puerto Rico (Rich Port) is an island of the Greater Antilles group in the West Indies, and lies between 17° 50′–18° 30′ N. lat. and 65° 30′–67° 15′ W. long., with a total area of 3,435 square miles and a population (1970 Census preliminary) of 2,712,033. The majority of the inhabitants are of Spanish descent and Spanish and English are the official languages. The island is about 100 miles from west to east, and 35 miles from north to south at the western end, narrowing towards the eastern extremity. The capital is 1,399 miles distant from New York, and 963 miles from Key West. Puerto Rico was discovered in 1493 by Christopher Columbus. It was explored by Ponce de León in 1508. It continued a Spanish possession until Oct. 18, 1898, when the United States took formal possession as a result of the Spanish-American War. It was ceded by Spain to the United States by the Treaty ratified on April 11, 1899. Sugar is grown along the coastal plain and tobacco and coffee on the slopes of the hills; fruits, cotton, maize, sweet potatoes, and yams are also grown. The trade is principally with the U.S. Trade with U.K., 1970: Imports £8,139,000; Exports to U.K., £3,004,000. About 7,550 miles of paved roads were in use in 1968. There are good harbours at San Juan, Mayaguez and Ponce.

The Constitution approved by the Congress and the President of the United States, which came into force on July 25, 1952, establishes the Commonwealth of Puerto Rico with full powers of local government. Legislative functions are vested in the Legislative Assembly, which consists of 2 elected houses; the Senate of 27 members (2 from each of 8 senatorial districts and 11 at large) and the House of Representatives of 51 members (1 from each of 40 representative districts and 11 at large). Membership of each house may be increased slightly to accommodate minority representatives. The term of the Legislative Assembly is 4 years. The

Governor is popularly elected for a term of 4 years. A Supreme Court of 9 members is appointed by the Governor, with the advice and consent of the Senate. There are 10 similarly appointed Secretaries at the head of permanent departments, but the selection of the Secretary of State must be approved also by the House of Representatives. The Governor appoints all judges. Puerto Rico is represented in Congress by a Resident Commissioner, elected for a term of 4 years, who has a seat in the House of Representatives, but not a vote. Great improvement has been made in the progress, industrialization and welfare of the island during the last two decades. A programme of tax exemption has raised income from industry to a level higher than that from agriculture. Public schools are established throughout—enrolment in 1971 was 760,908.

CAPITAL.— Ψ San Juan, population (1970) 455,421; Other major towns are: Ψ Ponce (156,498); Bayamón (154,498); Caguas (94,959); Ψ Mayaguez (86,267); and Ψ Arecibo (73,283).

FINANCE

	1968–69	1969–70
Revenue	$754,817,000	$823,327,000
Expenditure	743,400,000	863,000,000

TRADE

	1968–69	1969–70
Total Imports	$2,262,700,000	$2,555,600,000
Total Exports	1,605,500,000	1,729,300,000

Trade with U.K.

	1969	1970
Imports from U.K.	£6,749,000	£8,139,000
Exports to U.K.	3,343,000	3,004,000

Governor, Luis A. Ferré, *elected* 1968.
Resident Commissioner, Jorge L. Córdova (1968).

AMERICAN SAMOA

American Samoa consists of the island of Tutuila, Aunu'u, Ofu, Olosega, Ta'u, Rose and Swains Islands, with a total area of 76·5 square miles and a population of 27,769 in 1970.

Tutuila, the largest of the group, has an area of 52 square miles and contains a magnificent harbour at Ψ Pago Pago (pop. 1960, 1,251), the capital and seat of government. The remaining islands have an area of about 24 square miles. Tuna and copra are the chief exports.

Under an Executive Order of the President, which became effective on July 1, 1951, civilian administration under the Department of the Interior replaced the Naval administration which had existed since 1900. At present the Government consists of an executive, a bicameral legislature and a judiciary. Most of the Samoans are U.S. nationals, but some have acquired citizenship through service in the United States armed forces or other naturalization procedure.
Governor, John M. Haydon.

TRUST TERRITORY OF THE PACIFIC ISLANDS

The Trust Territory of the Pacific Islands consists of the Mariana (excluding Guam), Caroline and Marshall Islands which extend from latitude 1° to 20° north and from longitude 130° to 172° east. They cover an ocean area of 3,000,000 square miles but have a total land area of only 687 square miles. There are 96 separate islands and island groups in the Trust Territory. The population in 1970 was 101,592. The inhabitants of the Trust Territory are broadly classed as Micronesians. The native cultures vary considerably among island groups and even more among islands and atolls in the same geographic area. Nine different languages are spoken in the territory.

Ψ Seaport.

The Trust Territory is administered by the United States pursuant to a Trusteeship Agreement with the Security Council of the United Nations of July 18, 1947, administration being under the general jurisdiction of the Secretary of the Interior. For administrative purposes, the territory is divided into six districts: The Marianas, Palau, Yap, Truk, Ponape and the Marshalls. Local governments exist within each district.
High Commissioner, Edward E. Johnston.
Deputy High Commissioner, Peter T. Coleman.
CAPITAL (Provisional).—Saipan, Mariana Islands.

VIRGIN ISLANDS

Purchased by the United States from Denmark for the sum of $25,000,000, and proclaimed, January 25, 1917. The total area of the islands is 133 sq. miles, with a population (1969) of 63,200. *St. Thomas* (28 sq. miles) had a population of 29,565; *St. Croix* (84 sq. miles) had a population of 31,892; *St. John* (20 sq. miles) had a population of 1,743.

CAPITAL, Ψ Charlotte Amalie contains one of the finest harbours in the West Indies. The government of the Virgin Islands is organized under the provisions of the Revised Organic Act of the Virgin Islands, enacted by the Congress of the United States on July 22, 1954. Legislative power is vested in the Legislature of the Virgin Islands, a unicameral body composed of 15 senators popularly elected for two-year terms. Virgin Islanders are citizens of the United States. A Governor is appointed by the President. From the elections of December, 1970, the Governor will be popularly elected. The Virgin Islands are now a favourite tourist area in the Caribbean. The climate of the Islands is delightful at all times, and particularly so during the winter months.

Trade with U.K.

	1969	1970
Imports from U.K.	£1,686,000	£2,050,000
Exports to U.K.	3,294,000	787,000

Governor, Melvin H. Evans, *appointed* July, 1969; first elected Governor, November, 1970.

THE PANAMA CANAL

The Panama Canal, including the related commercial enterprises in the Canal Zone, are operated by the Panama Canal Company, which was formed on July 1, 1951, under the provisions of the Panama Canal Company Act. The Canal Zone is governed by the Canal Zone Government, which was established simultaneously with the new Canal Company. Both organizations are headed by Major-General David S. Parker, U.S.A., who holds the joint title of Governor of the Canal Zone and President of the Panama Canal Company.

The Canal Zone has an area of 647 sq. miles (about 1 per cent. of the total area of Panama) (land area, 372 sq. miles) and a population in 1970 of 51,000.
Chief Town.—Balboa Heights (population, including Balboa and Ancon, 3,950).

Fiscal Year	No. of Transits	Canal, Net Tons	Cargo Tons
1960	10,795	50,301,926	59,258,219
1961	10,866	61,826,002	63,669,738
1962	11,149	65,378,845	67,524,552
1963	11,017	64,438,115	62,247,094
1964	11,803	69,707,102	70,550,090
1965	11,835	74,853,264	76,573,071
1966	11,926	78,918,013	81,712,940
1967	12,413	88,266,343	86,193,430
1968	13,199	96,487,843	96,550,165
1969	13,150	100,603,265	101,391,132
1970	13,658	108,141,640	119,257,260

Including only ocean-going commercial vessels, 300 Panama Canal net tons measurement or over, against which tolls were collected, the volume of commercial traffic passing through the Canal during each of the last 10 fiscal years is shown on p. 811. In 1970 the 13,658 vessels using the canal carried the highest tonnage so far recorded.

The canal is fifty statute miles long (44·08 nautical miles), and the channel is from 500 to 1,000 feet wide at bottom. It contains 12 locks in twin flights; 3 steps at Gatun on the Atlantic side, 1 step at Pedro Miguel and 2 at Miraflores on the Pacific side. Each lock chamber is 1,000 feet long and 110 feet wide. Transit from sea to sea takes on average 13 to 15 hours. The least width is in Gaillard Cut,

and the greatest in Gatun Lake, where the channel can be made much broader at any time by the cutting down of trees and a small amount of dredging.

The Panama Canal Company is engaged in a Canal improvement programme. The widening of Gaillard Cut from 300 to 500 feet was completed in August, 1970. The maximum draft allowable for ships using the Panama Canal is determined by the level of Lake Gatun, which is an average of 85 feet above sea level. During dry season, from December to April, the lake level drops, imposing draft restrictions. The all-time high maximum tropical fresh water draft was 40 feet for certain types of vessels in 1967.

BRITISH EMBASSY
3100 Massachusetts Avenue, N.W.
Washington, D.C. 200008

Ambassador Extraordinary and Plenipotentiary, His Excellency the Earl of Cromer, P.C., K.C.M.G., M.B.E. (1971) . . . . $\pounds$14,000

Ministers, G. E. Millard, C.M.G., C.V.O.; D. J. Mitchell, C.B., C.V.O. (*Economic*); D. C. Tebbit, C.M.G. (*Commercial*); W. H. Stephens, C.B. (*Defence Research and Development*); T. A. K. Elliott, C.M.G. (*Head of Chancery*).

Head of British Defence Staff and Defence Attaché, Air Marshal Sir John Lapsley, K.B.E., C.B., D.F.C., A.F.C.

Naval Attaché, Rear Admiral C. C. H. Dunlop, C.B.E.

Military Attaché, Brig. G. H. Mills, O.B.E.

Air Attaché, Air Cdre. C. W. Coulthard, A.F.C.

Counsellors, E. Bolland, C.M.G.; J. D. Taylor, C.M.G., O.B.E.; W. M. Drower, M.B.E.; B. Russell Jones; A. H. B. Hermann (*Hong Kong Commercial Affairs*); M. P. J. Lynch (*Overseas Development*); W. R. Lythgo, O.B.E. (*Administration and H.M. Consul-General*); P. G. Hudson (*Civil Aviation*);

J. R. Steele (*Shipping*); R. H. Willmott (*Petroleum*); Dr. J. M. Lock (*Scientific*); J. J. Watson (*Labour*); J. G. Lewis (*Defence Research and Development*); K. J. Uffen (*Economic*); B. W. Meynell (*Commercial*); M. D. Butler; D. P. M. S. Cape; B. Hutchinson; D. B. Janisch (*Defence*); J. G. Taylor (*Information*); J. C. Moberly; E. F. C. Stanford (*Defence Supply*).

1st Secretaries, D. H. Mather, M.B.E. (*Commercial*); H. B. Walker (*Commercial*); A. S. Donkin (*Admin.*); M. R. Melhuish; R. E. F. Walter; J. W. Thorp (*Financial*); L. J. Middleton; J. D. I. Boyd; Miss L. P. Neville-Jones; D. A. Burns (*Information*); B. L. Crowe; M. K. Molloy; J. T. Caff (*Economic*); Miss M. I. Rothwell; J. Ling; W. H. Fletcher; Miss J. F. Veasey, M.B.E.; H. Tansey; A. R. Thomas; W. J. A. Buckley; P. H. Herbert; W. N. Hewson (*Scientific*).

Attaché, (*Defence Supply*), Capt. R. J. D. Glendinning, R.N. (*ret.*).

The United Nations
CHARTER OF THE UNITED NATIONS
The foundations of the Charter of the United Nations were laid at the Conference of Foreign Ministers in Moscow in 1943, and upon those foundations a structure was built at the meetings at Dumbarton Oaks, Washington, D.C., Aug. 21–Oct. 7, 1944. The design was discussed and criticized at San Francisco from April 25 to June 26, 1945, on which date representatives of 50 Allied Nations appended their signatures to the Charter.

The United Nations formally came into existence on October 24, 1945. It was later decided that its seat should be in the United States. Permanent headquarters have been erected at Manhattan, New York. October 24 has been designated " United Nations Day ".

The following 127 states are members of the United Nations:—

Afghanistan, Albania, Algeria, Argentina, Australia, Austria, Barbados, Belgium, Bolivia, Botswana, Brazil, Bulgaria, Burma, Burundi, Belorussian Soviet Socialist Republic, Cameroon, Canada, Central African Republic, Ceylon, Chad, Chile, China, Colombia, Congo (Pop. Repub.), Congolese Republic, Costa Rica, Cuba, Cyprus, Czechoslovakia, Dahomey, Denmark, Dominican Republic, Ecuador, Equatorial Guinea, Ethiopia, Fiji, Finland, France, Gabon, Gambia, Ghana, Greece, Guatemala, Guinea, Guyana, Haiti, Honduras, Hungary, Iceland, India, Indonesia, Iran, Iraq, Republic of Ireland, Israel, Italy, Ivory Coast, Jamaica, Japan, Jordan, Kenya, Khmer Republic, Kuwait, Laos, Lebanon, Lesotho, Liberia, Libya, Luxemburg, Madagascar, Malawi, Malaysia, Maldive Islands, Mali, Malta, Mauritania, Mauritius, Mexico, Mongolia, Morocco, Nepal, Netherlands, New Zealand, Nicaragua, Niger, Nigeria, Norway,

Pakistan, Panama, Paraguay, Peru, Philippines, Poland, Portugal, Rwanda, Rumania, Salvador, Saudi Arabia, Senegal, Sierra Leone, Singapore, Somalia, South Africa, Spain, Sudan, Swaziland, Sweden, Syria, Tanzania, Thailand, Togo, Trinidad and Tobago, Tunisia, Turkey, Uganda, Ukrainian Soviet Socialist Republic, Union of Soviet Socialist Republics, United Arab Republic, United Kingdom, United States of America, Upper Volta, Uruguay, Venezuela, Yemen (Arab Repub.), Yemen (P.D.R.), Yugoslavia, Zambia.

The principal organs of the United Nations are:— (1) The General Assembly; (2) The Security Council; (3) The Economic and Social Council; (4) The Trusteeship Council; (5) The International Court of Justice; (6) The Secretariat.

1. The General Assembly
The General Assembly consists of all the Members of the United Nations. Each Member is entitled to be represented at its meetings by five representatives, but has only one vote. The General Assembly meets once a year in regular session normally beginning on the third Tuesday in September. Special Sessions may also be held. The work of the General Assembly is divided among seven Main Committees, on each of which every Member has the right to be represented:—

✗ Financial Consultant to U. Thant   *Eugene Black.*

(1) Political and Security (including the regulation of armaments); (2) Economic and Financial; (3) Social, Humanitarian and Cultural; (4) Trusteeship (including Non-Self Governing Territories); (5) Administrative and Budgetary; (6) Legal. There is also a Special Political Committee, to relieve the burden on the first Committee.

The Main Committees consider items referred to them by the General Assembly and recommend draft resolutions for submission to the Assembly's plenary meetings.

The Assembly has two procedural committees—a General Committee and a Credentials Committee; and three standing committees—an Advisory Committee on Administrative and Budgetary Questions, a Committee on Contributions and a Disarmament Commission.

The General Assembly appoints such *ad hoc* committees as may be required from time to time for special purposes. The Assembly is also assisted in its work by subsidiary bodies such as a Board of Auditors, an Investments Committee, a United Nations Staff Benefit Committee, and an International Law Commission. In 1964 the General Assembly set up the United Nations Conference on Trade and Development (UNCTAD) as a permanent body.

The United Nations Industrial Development Organization (UNIDO) was set up on Jan. 1, 1967, to promote industrialization and co-ordinate United Nations activities in this field.

President of the United Nations General Assembly, Edvard Hambro (*Norway*), (1970).

2. The Security Council

The Security Council consists of fifteen Members, each of which has one representative and one vote. There are five *permanent Members* (China, France, U.K., U.S.A., U.S.S.R.) and ten non-permanent Members elected for a two-year term.

The Security Council bears the primary responsibility for the maintenance of peace and security. Decisions on procedural questions are made by an affirmative vote of seven Members. On all other matters the affirmative vote of nine Members must include the concurring votes of the *permanent Members*, and it is this clause which makes the *Veto* possible. The only exception to this rule is that with regard to measures for peaceful settlement a party to a dispute may refrain from voting.

The General Assembly, any member of the United Nations, or the Secretary-General, can bring to the Council's attention any matter considered to threaten international peace and security. A non-member State can bring a dispute before the Council provided it accepts in advance the U.N. Charter obligations for peaceful settlement.

A *Committee on the Admission of New Members* was set up by the Security Council on May 17, 1946, for the purpose of examining applications for admission to membership in the United Nations which may be referred to it by the Security Council. It is composed of a representative of each of the members of the Security Council.

The Security Council also establishes *ad hoc* committees and commissions which may be required from time to time for special purposes.

3. The Economic and Social Council

This body is responsible under the General Assembly for carrying out the functions of the United Nations with regard to international economic, social, cultural, educational, health and related matters.

It has established the following Commissions: Statistical, Human Rights, Social, Status of Women, Narcotic Drugs, Population, Regional Economic Commissions for Europe, Asia and the Far East,

Latin America and Africa. The Council also supervises and co-ordinates the work of fourteen related agencies.

United Nations Children's Fund (UNICEF), London Office, 14–15 Stratford Place, W.1.—UNICEF embraces all aspects of child welfare and assists the governments of the developing countries in developing maternal and child health services, the prevention and treatment of disease, nutrition and the preparation of children for adult life. It is financed by voluntary contributions from Governments and from the public and its work is carried out in co-operation with the Specialized Agencies of the United Nations.

4. Trusteeship Council

The Trusteeship Council is composed of countries administering Trust Territories, permanent members of the Security Council, and one other country elected by the General Assembly for a three-year term.

The Trusteeship Council considers reports from administering authorities; examines petitions in consultation with the administering authority; makes periodic inspection visits; and checks conditions with an annual questionnaire on the political, economic, social, and educational advancement of the inhabitants of trust territories.

5. International Court of Justice

The International Court of Justice is the principal judicial organ of the United Nations. The Statute of the court is an integral part of the Charter and all Members of the United Nations are *ipso facto* parties to it. The Court is composed of 15 judges, no two of whom may be nationals of the same State, and meets at The Hague.

If any party to a case fails to adhere to the judgment of the Court, the other party may have recourse to the Security Council.

THE SECRETARIAT

Secretary-General (1966–71), ~~U Thant~~ (*Burma*).   *Dr. KURT WALDHEIM* (*Austria*) 1/1/72 *12/7/*

Under-Secretaries-General

Chef de Cabinet, C. V. Narasimhan (*India*).
Special Political Affairs, Ralph J. Bunche (*U.S.A.*); Roberto Guyer (*Argentina*).
Conference Services, Jiri Nosek (*Czechoslovakia*)
Economic and Social Affairs, P. de Seynes (*France*).
Trusteeship and Information from Non-Self-Governing Territories, I. S. Djermakoye (*Niger*).
Political and Security Council Affairs, L. Kutakov (*U.S.S.R.*).
Director-General, U.N. Office, Geneva, V. W. Guicciardi (*Italy*).
Office for Administration and Management, A. A. Stark (*U.K.*).
Legal Counsel, C. A. Stavropoulos (*Greece*).
Executive Director, U.N. Industrial Development Organization, I. H. Abdel-Rahman (*U.A.R.*).

U.N. Information Centre, 14–15, Stratford Place, W.1.

BUDGET OF THE UNITED NATIONS

The financial year coincides with the calendar year. For the year 1970, the gross appropriation was $168,956,950. The scale of assessments on 1971–73 budget for the British Commonwealth countries was: Australia, 1·47 per cent.; Canada, 3·08 per cent.; Ghana, 0·07 per cent.; India, 1·55 per cent.; Malaysia, 0·10 per cent.; New Zealand, 0·32 per cent.; Pakistan, 0·34 per cent.; United Kingdom, 5·90 per cent. The United States contribution was 31·52 per cent.; U.S.S.R. was 14·18 per cent.; France was 6·0 per cent.; Italy was 3·54 per cent.; Japan was 5·40 per cent.; and China was 4·00 p.c.

UNITED KINGDOM REPRESENTATIVES
845 Third Avenue, New York

Permanent Representative to the United Nations and Representative on the Security Council, Sir Colin Tradescant Crowe, K.C.M.G. (1970)......£5,625

Ministers, K. D. Jamieson, C.M.G. (*Deputy Permanent Representative*); D. J. McCarthy, C.M.G. (*Economic and Social Affairs*); J. I. McK. Rhodes, C.M.G. (*Special duties*).

Counsellors, M. S. Weir (*Head of Chancery*); J. R. Freeland (*Legal Adviser*); D. N. Lane (*Trusteeship Affairs*); C. A. Lovitt, M.B.E. (*Administration*); Miss K. Whalley (*Treasury Adviser*).

1st Secretaries, Miss T. A. H. Solesby; P. C. Petrie; T. N. Haining; N. M. Fenn; M. C. S. Weston; N. C. R. Williams; Miss S. E. Harden, M.B.E.; P. R. M. Hinchcliffe; S. N. P. Hemans; Miss E. C. Wallis.

2nd Secretaries, Miss S. Darling; Miss H. B. Reid.

INTERNATIONAL ATOMIC ENERGY AGENCY

Kärntnerring 11–13, P.O. Box 590, Vienna

Set up on July 29, 1957, to accelerate and enlarge the contribution of atomic energy to peace, health and prosperity throughout the world and to ensure that assistance provided by it or under its supervision is not used to further any military purpose. Agreements have been reached concerning the Agency's working relationship with the United Nations and some of the specialized agencies. In June, 1971, 102 states were members.

A General Conference of all members meets in regular annual session and in such special session as may be necessary. A Board of Governors (25 members) carries out the functions of the Agency and meets usually four times a year. The Budget in 1971 amounted to $17,029,000.

Director-General, Sigvard Eklund (*Sweden*).

INTERNATIONAL AGENCIES

Fourteen other international organizations, having wide responsibilities in economic, social, cultural, educational and other related fields, carry out their functions in co-operation with the United Nations under agreements made with a standing committee of the Economic and Social Council.

International Labour Organisation (ILO) Geneva (London Branch Office, Sackville House, 40 Piccadilly, W.1.). Established with the League of Nations in 1919 under the Treaty of Versailles, the ILO became in 1946 the first specialized agency associated with the United Nations. In June, 1971, the Organisation had 121 member States. The aim of the ILO is to promote lasting peace through social justice, and to this end it works for better economic and social conditions everywhere. It was awarded the Nobel Peace Prize in 1969.

The ILO establishes international labour standards, which set guidelines for improving working conditions and protecting basic human rights; runs a world-wide programme of technical assistance to developing countries (with funds from all sources amounting in 1970 to about £24 million); conducts research and disseminates information on the human aspects of economic activity, with a view to improving social and economic well-being. Through its World Employment Programme, the ILO is attacking unemployment and its associated ills by aiding national and international efforts to provide productive work for the world's fast-growing population.

The International Labour Conference, composed of national delegations of two government delegates, one worker delegate and one employer delegate, meets at least once a year. It formulates international labour standards and broad policies of the Organisation, provides a forum for discussion of world labour and social problems, and approves the ILO's work programme and budget, which is financed by member States.

A 48-member Governing Body, composed of 24 government members, 12 worker members and 12 employer members, acts as the Organisation's executive council. Ten governments hold seats on the Governing Body because of their industrial importance. These are Canada, China, France, the Federal Republic of Germany, India, Italy, Japan, U.S.S.R., the United Kingdom and the United States of America.

The International Labour Office, the secretariat of the Organisation, collects and distributes information, assists governments on request in drafting legislation on the basis of international labour standards, directs technical co-operation activities, and issues publications.

Director-General, Wilfred Jenks (*United Kingdom*).

Food and Agriculture Organization of the United Nations (FAO), Viale delle Terme di Caracalla, Rome.—Established on October 16, 1945, to raise levels of nutrition and standards of living, to secure improvements in the efficiency of the production and distribution of all food and agricultural products and to better the condition of rural populations, thus contributing to the expansion of world economy and ensuring man's freedom from hunger. Among its many activities the Organization promotes the global exchange of information in the fields of agriculture, forestry and fisheries, facilitates international agreement in these fields and provides technical assistance in such subjects as nutrition and food management, soil erosion control, re-afforestation, the establishment of paper industries, irrigation engineering, control of infestation of stored foods, production of fertilizers, control of crop pests and diseases, and improvement of fishing vessels, fish distribution and marketing. As well as its work as an intergovernmental agency the Organization also mobilizes the efforts of private individuals and associations through the world-wide *Freedom from Hunger Campaign.* Jointly with the United Nations it administers a $1,000,000,000 World Food Programme using food as capital backing for development programmes in developing countries. The 1969 session of the governing Conference approved a budget of $70,568,000 for the years 1970–71. In addition, FAO is carrying out field programmes involving expenditure of about $90,000,000 under the U.N. Development Programme and other aid programmes. Through its co-operative programme with the World Bank it is helping to increase international investment in agriculture and allied fields.

The policy of the Organization is directed by a two-yearly Conference of the 119 full member and 2 associate member countries. A council (34 members) acts for the Conference between its sessions.

Director-General, Dr. A. H. Boerma (*Netherlands*).

United Nations Educational, Scientific and Cultural Organization (UNESCO), 9 Place de Fontenoy, Paris 7 ème.—Unesco celebrated its 25th anniversary on November 4, 1971. Under its constitution, the Organization makes its contribution to peace and security by promoting collaboration among its Member States in the fields of education, science, culture and communications. It aims at furthering a universal respect for justice, for the rule of law and for human rights, without distinction of race, sex, language or religion, in accordance with the Charter of the United Nations.

Unesco continues to work for the advancement of mutual knowledge and understanding of peoples ... to give fresh impulse to popular education and

to the spread of culture . . . to maintain, increase and diffuse knowledge.

The Organization is composed of three organs: (i) the *General Conference*, consisting of representatives of Member States, which meets biennially to decide the programme and budget; (ii) the *Executive Board*, composed of 34 members elected by the General Conference to supervise the execution of the approved programme and (iii) the *Secretariat*, which is responsible for Unesco's day-to-day functioning and the execution of the programme. In most Member States National Commissions serve as a link with Unesco and help carry out the programme. Twenty-five years of operation have identified Unesco's broad objectives: in education, its democratization and regeneration; in science, the development of science policy, the application of science and technology to development and the intensification of international programmes of scientific co-operation; in culture, the evolution of cultural policy; in communication, the improvement and development of the mass media in Member States as a means of increasing the flow of information. Member States in June, 1971, 124. *Director-General*, René Maheu (*France*).

World Health Organization (WHO), 1211 Geneva 27. Established on April 7, 1948, the aim of the World Health Organization is the attainment by all peoples of the highest possible level of health. Its services are of two kinds—advisory, to spread knowledge, help to train personnel and assist countries on such subjects as malaria, tuberculosis, venereal diseases and other communicable diseases, maternal and child health, nutrition, and environmental health—and technical services of world-wide interest such as biological standardization and unification of pharmacopœias, collection and dissemination of epidemiological intelligence, medical research and publication of technical and scientific works. Approved budget for 1972, $82,023,000. Membership (June, 1971) 133.

Organs are a *World Health Assembly* meeting annually to frame policy, an *Executive Board* (24 members), meeting at least twice a year, and a *Secretariat*.

Director-General, Dr. M. G. Candau (*Brazil*).

International Bank for Reconstruction and Development (*The World Bank*), 1818 H Street, Washington, D.C.; European office, 66 Ave. d'Iéna, Paris 16e, France.—Established on Dec. 27, 1945, to assist in the reconstruction and development of territories of member countries by facilitating the investment of capital for productive purposes; to promote private foreign investment and, when private capital is not readily available on reasonable terms, to supplement private investment by providing loans for productive purposes out of its own capital, funds raised by it, and its other resources. The 783 loans made by the Bank since its inception to June 30, 1971, totalled $16,493,527,893 to 89 countries. Subscribed capital, June 30, 1971, $23,871,000,000.

The *Board of Governors* consists of one Governor and one alternative appointed by each of the 116 member countries.

Twenty *Executive Directors* exercise all powers of the Bank except those reserved to the Board of Governors. The *President*, selected by the Executive Directors, conducts the business of the Bank, with the assistance of an international staff.

President, Robert S. McNamara (*U.S.A.*).

International Development Association (IDA), 1818 H Street, Washington, D.C.; European office, 66 Ave. d'Iéna, Paris 16e, France.—An affiliate of the World Bank established in September 1960. Its purposes are to promote economic development, increase productivity and thus raise standards of living in the less developed areas of the world included within the Association's membership, in particular by providing finance to meet their important developmental requirements on terms which are more flexible and bear less heavily on the balance of payments than those of conventional loans, thereby furthering the objectives of the World Bank and supplementing its activities. IDA's Board of Governors and Executive Directors are the same as those holding equivalent positions in the World Bank, serving *ex officio* in IDA. By June 30, 1971, IDA had extended 274 development credits totalling $3,406,244,000 in 58 countries for improved transportation, agriculture, electric power facilities, industry, education and municipal water supplies. The credits were for terms of 50 years, free of interest.

International Finance Corporation (IFC), 1818 H Street, Washington, D.C.; European office, 66 Ave. d'Iéna, Paris 16e, France.—The IFC was established in 1956 as an affiliate of the World Bank to assist less developed member countries by promoting the growth of the private sector of their economies. IFC's share capital of $107,000,000 at June 30, 1971, had been subscribed by 96 countries. In addition, IFC is empowered to borrow up to approximately $428,000,000 from the World Bank for use in its lending programme. At the end of June, 1971, IFC had made commitments totalling more than $101,300,000 in 42 countries.

President, Robert S. McNamara (*U.S.A.*).

International Monetary Fund, 19th and H Streets, N.W., Washington, D.C.—Established on Dec. 27, 1945, the Fund exists to promote international monetary co-operation and the expansion of international trade; to promote exchange stability, maintain orderly exchange arrangements and avoid competitive exchange depreciations; and to assist in the establishment of a multilateral system of payments in respect of current transactions between members and in the elimination of foreign exchange restrictions which hamper world trade. 118 countries were in membership of the Fund in June, 1971, their total quota subscriptions being $28,478,000,000. The Fund has an additional arrangement enabling it to borrow up to $6,000,000,000 from ten industrial members.

The $28,397,000,000 which the Fund holds in gold and currencies provides a reserve on which members may draw, with its agreement, to meet foreign obligations during periods of deficit in their international balance of payments. This use of the Fund's resources is linked to its efforts to reduce exchange restrictions and discrimination, and establish currency convertibility.

The Fund's financial assistance takes the form of a foreign exchange transaction. The member pays to the Fund an amount of its own money equivalent, at the par value agreed with the Fund, to the amount of foreign currency it wishes to draw. The member is expected to " repurchase " its own currency from the Fund within three, or at the outside five years, with a payment of gold or dollars or convertible currency acceptable to the Fund. These arrangements are subject to certain charges which rise in proportion to the amount of foreign exchange involved, and the length of time it is held.

Currencies drawn from the Fund may be used in a flexible way to relieve the member's payments difficulty, but its assets are not intended to be used for military purposes, or for programmes of economic development. Countries that are pursuing national development programmes may use the Fund if they experience temporary payments difficulties such as would ordinarily entitle a member to Fund assistance.

× Deputy managing Director, Frank Southard reappointed for further 5/72 4 year term

Each member of the Fund is assigned a quota which approximately determines its voting power and the amount of foreign exchange that it may draw from the Fund. The subscription of each member is equal to its quota, and is payable partly in gold and partly in the member's own currency. On May 31, 1971, the Fund's assets included $4,164,000,000 in gold and $24,233,000,000 in various national currencies. Total drawings from the Fund up to May 30, 1971, amounted to $22,408,000,000.

Managing Director, Pierre-Paul Schweitzer (*France*).

International Civil Aviation Organization (ICAO), 1080 University Street, Montreal 101.— In existence since April 4, 1947, to study problems of international civil aviation and the establishment of international standards and regulations for civil aviation, ICAO encourages the use of safety measures, uniform regulations or operation, and simpler procedures at international airports. It promotes the use of new technical methods and equipment. With the co-operation of members, it has evolved a pattern for meteorological services, traffic control, communications, radio beacons and ranges, search and rescue organization, and other facilities required for safe international flight. It has secured much simplification of government customs, immigration, and public health regulations as they apply to international air transport. 120 states are now members of ICAO.

An *Assembly* of delegates from member states meets at least once every three years. A *Council* of 27 members is elected by the Assembly, taking into account the countries of chief importance in air transport and the need for representation of the main geographical areas of the world. The Council is the executive body, working through subsidiary committees.

President of Council, Walter Binaghi (*Argentina*).
Secretary-General, Dr. A. Kotaite (*Lebanon*).

Universal Postal Union (UPU), Weltpoststrasse 4, 3000 Berne 15.—Established on October 9, 1874, by the postal Convention of Berne and in operation from July 1, 1875, UPU exists to form a single postal territory of all the countries, members of the Union, for the reciprocal exchange of correspondence in order to secure the organization and improvement of the various postal services and to promote in this sphere the development of international collaboration. Every member agrees to transmit the mail of all other members by the best means used for its own mail. The Union includes almost all the countries of the world. Budget, 1971, $U.S.1,900,000. A *Universal Postal Congress* meets at five-yearly intervals, the last Congress was held at Tokyo in 1969. The next is due to be held in Switzerland in 1974.

Director-General, Dr. Michel Rahi (*U.A.R.*).

International Telecommunication Union (ITU), Place des Nations, Geneva.—Founded at Paris in 1865 as the International Telegraph Union, ITU became a U.N. Specialized Agency in 1947 and since 1967 has been governed by the Convention adopted by the Montreux Conference held in 1965. ITU exists to set up international regulations for telegraph, telephone and radio services to further their development and extend their utilization by the public, at the lowest possible rates; to promote international co-operation for the improvement and rational use of telecommunications of all kinds; the development of technical facilities and their most efficient operation. ITU allocates the radio frequency spectrum and registers radio frequency assignments. It studies, recommends, collects and publishes information on telecommunication matters, including space radio communications. The budget for 1972 is 37,317,900 *Swiss francs*.

Secretary-General, M. Mili (*Tunisia*) (*acting*).

World Meteorological Organization (WMO), Geneva.—Established on March 23, 1950, WMO exists to facilitate world-wide co-operation in establishing networks of stations making observations related to meteorology, and to promote the establishment and maintenance of centres providing meteorological services; to promote the establishment of systems for the rapid exchange of weather information; to promote standardization of meteorological observations and to ensure their uniform publication; to further the application of meteorology to aviation, shipping, agriculture, and other human activities; to encourage research and training in meteorology and to co-ordinate their international aspects. Budget (1972–75), $U.S.17,300,000.

A *World Meteorological Congress* meets at least once every four years. An *Executive Committee* (24 members), meeting at least annually carries out the resolutions of the Congress, initiates studies and makes recommendations on matters requiring international action. Other organs are six *Regional Meteorological Associations* (Africa, Asia, S. America, N. and Central America, Europe and South-West Pacific), eight technical commissions and a Secretariat.

Secretary-General, D. A. Davies (*U.K.*).

Inter-Governmental Maritime Consultative Organisation (IMCO), 101–104 Piccadilly, W.1. A United Nations Specialized Agency established on March 17, 1958, to provide means for co-operation and exchange of information among governments on technical matters related to international shipping, especially with regard to safety at sea and preventing marine pollution caused by ships. IMCO is responsible for calling maritime conferences and drafting maritime agreements, *e.g.* Load Line Convention, 1966 and Convention on Tonnage Measurement of Ships. It has produced International Maritime Dangerous Goods Code; Code of Safe Practice for Bulk Cargoes; revised International Code of Signals, and fire safety measures for ships. In June, 1971, 72 nations were in membership. Budget, 1970–71, $2,706,994.

Secretary-General, C. Goad (*U.K.*).

International Trade. *General Agreement on Tariffs and Trade* (GATT), Villa le Bocage, Palais des Nations, 1211 Geneva 10. A multilateral treaty, in operation since 1948, to which 78 countries are parties; a further 15 countries apply GATT *de facto*. Its rules thus govern over four-fifths of the world trade. Objectives of GATT are to lower and stabilize tariffs, expand international trade and promote economic development. Six tariff conferences have been held, through which members have reduced or frozen their tariffs on thousands of items. The most recent and important negotiations, the Kennedy Round, resulted in agreement to reduce world industrial tariffs by January, 1972, by an average of about one-third. Current GATT work is directed towards eventual further reductions in both tariffs and non-tariff barriers to industrial and agricultural trade. Special concern is given to trade problems of developing countries. An International Trade Centre, set up by GATT in 1964 to aid developing countries in export promotion, is now operated jointly by GATT and UNCTAD. GATT also provides a permanent forum for discussion and solution of particular international trade problems.

Director-General, O. Long (*Switzerland*).

Foreign Countries

THE following Articles have been revised under the direction of the various Governments or of the British Representatives at Foreign Capitals, to whom the Editor desires to express his warmest thanks. The Editor is also greatly indebted to the Embassies and Consulates-General in London for various corrections and additions.

Salaries and Allowances.

The Salaries of Officers of H.M. Diplomatic Service are shown below. In addition foreign allowances and furnished accommodation (or rent allowances in lieu thereof) are assigned to officers serving abroad:—

Grade I—£14,000.
Grade II—£9,000.
Grade III—£6,925.
Grade IV—£5,175 to £6,475.
Grade V—£3,425 to £4,575.
Grade VE—£3,383 to £3,998.
Grade VI—£2,950 to £3,575.
Grade VIIA—£2,602 to £3,271.
Grade VIIE—£2,325 to £2,800.
Grade VIII—£1,435 to £2,175.
Grade IX—£975 to £2,175.
Grade X—£682 to £1,560.

NOTE.—Salaries of Ambassadors and of Ministers Plenipotentiary at British Embassies and Legations abroad shown in the following articles are in each case the maximum salary for the post and exclude *Frais de Représentation.*

ABYSSINIA. *See* Ethiopia.
AFGHANISTAN
(Afghānistān)

King of Afghanistan, H.M. Zahir Shah, *born* Oct. 15, 1914, *acceded* Nov. 8, 1933 (on the assassination of his father, Nadir Shah); *married* Nov. 7, 1931, Humaira, daughter of Sardar Ahmad Shah Khan, and has surviving issue five sons and two daughters: H.R.H. Prince Ahmed Shah Khan, *b.* Sept. 23, 1934; H.R.H. Prince Mohammad Nadir, *b.* 1941; H.R.H. Prince Shah Mahmud, *b.* 1946; H.R.H. Prince Daud, *b.* 1949; H.R.H. Prince Mir Wais, *b.* 1957; and H.R.H. Princess Bilqis, *b.* 1931; H.R.H. Princess Maryam, *b.* 1936.

Prime Minister and Minister of Foreign Affairs, Dr. Abdul Zahir.
Deputy Prime Minister, Dr. Abdul Samad Hamed.
Minister of Interior, Amanullah Mansouri.
Defence, Gen. Khan Mohammad Khan.
Foreign Affairs, Mohammad Musa Shafiq.
Justice, Mohammad Anwar Arghandewal.
Finance, Dr. Ghulam Haidar Dawar.
Education, Hamidullah Enayat-Seraj.
Commerce, Mohammad Aref Ghaussi.
Public Works, Lt. Gen. Khwazak Zalmai.
Information and Culture, Mohammad Ibrahim Abbasi.
Communications, Nasratullah Ahmad Macikyar.
Public Health, Dr. Mohammad Ibrahim Majid-Serat.
Mines and Industries, Mohammad Yaqub Lali.
Agriculture, Abdul Hakim.
Planning, Dr. Abdul Wahid Sarabi.
Ministers without Portfolio, Mrs. Shafiqa Ziayee; Dr. Abdul Wakil; Abdul Satar Sirat.

EMBASSY IN LONDON
31 Princes Gate, S.W.7.
[01-589-8891]
Ambassador in London (vacant).
Chargé d'Affaires, Abdul Ali Sulaiman.
1st Secretary, Abdullah Habib Tarzi.

Afghanistan lies to the N. and W. of Western Pakistan. Its ancient name was Aryana, by which title it is referred to by Strabo, the Greek geographer who lived in the 1st century B.C. The estimated area is 250,000 sq. miles, and the population (U.N. estimate, 1969) 16,516,000. The population is very mixed. The most numerous race is the Pathan which predominates in the South and West, the main divisions being the Durranis, from whom the Royal family springs, and the Ghilzais. Then come the Tajiks, an Iranian people mainly cultivators and small traders. There are also Uzbeks and Turkomen in the North, Hazaras in the centre, Baluchis in the South-West and the Nuristanis who live near the Chitral border. All are Sunni Moslems, except the Hazaras and Kizilbashes, who belong to the Shia sect.

Afghanistan is bounded on the W. by Iran (boundary fixed 1857 and 1904), on the S. by Baluchistan (now W. Pakistan) (boundary fixed 1896–7), on the N. by Asiatic Russia (boundary fixed 1886–7 and 1893–5), and on the E. by the N.W. Frontier Province (now W. Pakistan) (boundary fixed 1895). The northern boundary runs from Zulfikar on the Iran frontier to Kushk, the Russian railway terminus, to the Oxus (or Amu Darya, "Mother of Rivers") which forms the boundary from Khamiab to Lake Victoria, whence the line to the Chinese frontier on the branch line from Mary and thence N.E. was fixed by the Pamir agreement of 1895. The Russo-Afghan frontier was demarcated by the Tashkent Boundary Commission in 1948. An Afghan-Chinese border treaty was signed in 1963 and the border demarcated in 1964. The Indo-Afghan frontier was settled by the Durand agreement of 1893.

Mountains, chief among which are the Hindu Kush, cover three-fourths of the country, the elevation being generally over 4,000 feet. There are three great river basins, the Oxus, Helmand, and Kabul. The climate is dry, with extreme temperatures.

Afghanistan is divided into 28 provinces each under a Governor.

Government.—Afghanistan is a constitutional monarchy. By the new constitution which came into effect in October, 1965, sovereign power is vested in the National Assembly of 216 elected members. There is also an Upper House or Senate. Executive Government is carried out by a Cabinet consisting of a Prime Minister and 16 Ministers. Elections were held during 1965 for a new Parliament, consisting of an elected Lower House and a partly-elected Upper House. Further elections were held in 1969. The Prime Minister is chosen by the King. Ministers may be appointed from among members of the Parliament or outside it but they must cease to be members of the Parliament on appointment. Mr. Nur Ahmed Etemadi, Prime Minister from Nov. 1, 1967, resigned on May 17, 1971, in face of a threatened vote of no confidence. Dr. Abdul Zahir was appointed Prime Minister on June 9, 1971. His Government did not receive the necessary vote of confidence until the end of July.

By treaty of Nov. 22, 1921 (renewed in 1930), Great Britain and Afghanistan agreed to respect one another's internal and external independence; to recognize boundaries then existent, subject to a slight re-adjustment near the Khyber; and to establish Legations and consular offices. As successor state to the British Government, Pakistan has agreed that her relations with Afghanistan shall be based on the 1921 treaty.

Judiciary.—Hitherto Afghanistan has been ruled on the basis of Shariat or Islamic law. The new Constitution, however, introduced in 1965, provides for

the creation of a legal code, and for a new structure of courts, consisting of a lower court in each *wuluswal* (sub province), and a court of appeal in each province, with a Supreme Court in Kabul. This system marks the complete separation of executive and judiciary for the first time.

Defence.—The Army has been reorganized and is recruited by twice-yearly calls. Service is for one year for officers and 2 years for other ranks. The peace strength is about 80,000. A military academy and military colleges are located in Kabul; and provision is made for training of regular officers abroad. A small Air Force is maintained. All military and air force equipment is now of Russian pattern.

Production.—Agriculture and sheep raising are the principal industries. There are generally two crops a year, one of wheat (the staple food), barley, or lentils, the other of rice, millet, maize, and *dal*. Sugar beet and cotton are grown. Afghanistan is rich in fruits. Sheep, including the Karakuli, and transport animals are bred. Silk, woollen and hair cloths and carpets are manufactured. Salt, silver, copper, coal, iron, lead, rubies, lapis lazuli, gold, chrome and talc are found.

The following main roads are open to motor traffic. (*a*) Internal: Kabul–Kandahar (310 miles); Kandahar–Herat (350 miles); Herat–Maimana to Mazar-i-Sharif (500 miles); Mazar-i-Sharif–Kabul (380 miles). Also Kabul–Khanabad–Faizabad (450 miles); Kabul–Gardez (80 miles); Kabul–Bamian (140 miles). The road from Kabul to the North has now been shortened by the completion in 1964 of the Salang pass. (*b*) Roads to the frontiers: Kabul–Khyber (175 miles); Kandahar–Chaman (70 miles) and roads from Herat to the Russian and Persian borders. Five of the major roads in Afghanistan have been surfaced by U.S. and Soviet Aid. The Kabul–Khyber, Kandahar–Spin Baldak and Kabul–Kunduz–Qizil Qala roads are also surfaced. Work on the metalling of the Pul-i-Kumhri–Shiberghan road was completed in 1971. Otherwise roads are unmetalled. A network of minor roads fit for motor traffic in fine weather links up all important towns and districts.

Motor transport has taken the place of pack transport as the chief means of conveyance. The chief trade routes to Pakistan and India are the Khyber Pass route, from Kabul to Peshawar (190 miles), and the road from Kandahar to Chaman (70 miles). Internal air services between the main towns are being developed.

Language and Literature.—The languages of the country are Persian and Pushtu, and Turki (spoken by Uzbeks and Turkoman tribes in the North). The Turki language is unwritten in Afghanistan. All schoolchildren learn both Persian and Pushtu. The Government is encouraging the spread of Pushtu, the language of the Pathans. Education is free and nominally compulsory, elementary schools having been established in most centres; there are secondary schools in large urban areas and a university (established in 1932) at the capital.

The annual revenue, of some 2,000,000,000 *Afghanis*, consists largely of payments in kind. There are taxes on land, sales of animals, a grazing tax, customs duties, stamps, fines, receipts from State lands, monopolies, and factories and mining royalties; in addition certain businesses and individuals have become eligible for income-tax.

Trade with U.K.

	1969	1970
Imports from U.K.	£1,963,000	£1,697,000
Exports to U.K.	7,265,000	6,433,000

Exports are mainly Persian lambskins (Karakul), fruits, cotton, raw wool, carpets and spices, while the imports are chiefly cotton yarn and piece goods, metals, leather goods, tea, sugar, jute manufactures, paper and cement.

CAPITAL, Kabul (about 450,000). The chief commercial centres are Kabul and Kandahar (77,000). Other provincial capitals are Herat (75,000), Mazar-i-Sharif (42,000), Jalalabad (22,000).

FLAG.—Vertical stripes of black, red and green, with white device in centre.

NATIONAL DAY.—May 27.

ALBANIA

Head of State, Hadji Lechi, *assumed office*, July 24, 1953.
Chairman, Council of Ministers, Mehmet Shehu.
Labour (= Communist) Party
Politbureau of the Central Committee, R. Alia; B. Balluku; A. Carcani; Enver Hoxha; H. Kapo; S. Koleka; R. Marko; M. Mytfiu; M. Shehu; H. Toska (*full members*); P. Dume; K. Hazbiu; A. Kellezi; P. Peristeri; K. Theodosi (*alternate members*).
Secretariat of the Central Committee, Enver Hoxha. (*First Secretary*); R. Alia; H. Kapo; X. Spahiu.

Situated on the Adriatic Sea, Albania is bounded on the north and east by Yugoslavia and on the south by Greece. The area of the Republic is estimated at 10,050 sq. miles, with a population (U.N. estimate, 1969) of 2,075,000.

On Nov. 10, 1945, the British, U.S.A. and U.S.S.R. governments decided to recognize the Albanian administration under Colonel-General Enver Hoxha as the provisional government of Albania on the understanding that free elections would be held at an early date, in order that a truly representative government could be formed. Elections were held in December, 1945, on Jan. 11, 1946, the Constituent Assembly declared Albania an independent Republic, and on Aug. 7, 1946, Albania applied for admission to the United Nations, but its entry was vetoed by Great Britain and the U.S.A. It was admitted in 1955. United Kingdom diplomatic relations with Albania ceased in 1946.

Albania is almost entirely an agricultural country and the staple crops are wheat and maize.

CAPITAL, Tirana (pop. 50,000).

FLAG.—Black two-headed eagle surmounted by yellow outline star, all on a red field.

ALGERIA
(Republic of Algeria)

President of the Council of Revolution and Minister of National Defence, Houari Boumedienne, *assumed office* June 19, 1965.

CABINET

Minister of State responsible for transport, Rabah Bitat.
Home Affairs and Minister of Finance and National Plan, Ahmed Medeghri.
Foreign Affairs, Abdelaziz Bouteflika.
Information and Culture, Ahmed Taleb.
Health, Dr. Omar Boudjellab.
Justice, Boualem ben Hamouda.
Industry and Energy, Belaid Abdesselam.
Public Works, Abdelkader Zaibek.

Agriculture and Agrarian Reform, Mohamed Larbi Tayebi.

Commerce, Layachi Yaker.

Labour and Social Affairs, Mohand Said Mazouzi.

Higher Education and Scientific Research, Mohamed Benyahia.

Chief of the Party, Ahmed Kaid.

Tourism, Abdelaziz Maoui.

Primary and Secondary Education, Abdelkrim ben Mahmoud.

Religious Affairs, Mouloud Kassim.

Ex-Servicemen, Mahmoud Guennez.

Posts and Telecommunications, Mohamed Kadi.

Youth and Sports, Abdallah Fadel.

Finance, Ismail Mahroug.

ALGERIAN EMBASSY IN LONDON
6 Hyde Park Gate, S.W.7
[01-584-9502-5]

Ambassador Extraordinary and Plenipotentiary, His Excellency Lakhdar Brahimi (1971).

Attachés, Abderahmane Ketem; Kadda Benturquia; Omar Ramoul; Lamri Khelif.

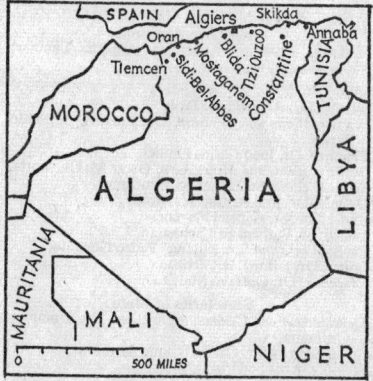

Algeria lies between 8° 45′ W. to 12° E. longitude, 37° 6′ N. to a southern limit about 19° N. Area, 855,900 sq. miles (estimated). The population (U.N. estimate, 1970) is 13,547,000, of which 30 per cent. are urban dwellers.

Government.—Aigiers surrendered to a French force on July 5, 1830, and Algeria was annexed to France in Feb. 1842. From 1881 the three northern departments of Algiers, Oran and Constantine formed an integral part of France. Between 1955 and 1960 these were re-organized to form 13 departments: Algiers, Tizi-Ouzou, Orleansville, (now El-Asnam) Médéa, Constantine, Bône (*now* Annaba), Setif, Batna, Oran, Tlemcen, Mostaganem, Saida and Tiaret. The Southern Territories of the Sahara, formerly a separate colony, became an integral part of Algeria on the attainment of independence, forming the two additional departments of the Saoura and the Oasis. An armed rebellion led by the Moslem *Front de Libération Nationale* (F.L.N.) against French rule broke out on Nov. 1, 1954. French control of Algeria came to an end when President de Gaulle declared Algeria independent on July 3, 1962; by October, 1963, all agricultural land held by foreigners had been expropriated and by 1965 more than 80 per cent. of the French population had left Algeria. More have left since.

Ben Bella was elected President of the Republic in Sept., 1963, but was deposed and a Council of the Revolution presided over by Col. Boumedienne assumed power on June 19, 1965.

At the end of 1969 the Algerian government published an ambitious four-year development plan for 1970 to 1973 based on the full utilization of the country's natural resources in oil, gas and minerals. The plan envisages investment at the rate of about £500 million per year of which about 50 per cent. will be in basic industry, 10 per cent. in agriculture, 20 per cent. in infrastructure and 10 per cent. in education. By the end of 1973, the plan envisages that Algeria should be producing p.a. 440,000 tons of steel, 5 million tons of cement, 2 milliard kWh electricity, 75 million tons of oil and 6·5 milliard cubic metres of natural gas.

Trade with U.K.

	1969	1970
Imports from U.K.	£8,719,000	£16,774,000
Exports to U.K.	22,073,000	21,166,000

Exports are mainly crude petroleum and methane (liquefied natural gas), wine, barley and other cereals, skins, olives, citrus fruits, iron and zinc ores, phosphate rock, corkwood, esparto grass and manufactured tobacco. The principal imports from the United Kingdom are tractors and agricultural machinery, engines, machine tools, rubber and metal manufactures. Natural gas from the Sahara is supplied to a gas liquefaction plant at Arzew and is then exported in specially-designed tankers. A second liquefaction plant is planned for Skikda.

There are 2,450 miles of State Railways. In 1968 the number of ships in foreign trade entering Algerian ports was 7,446. 25,934 civilian aircraft carrying 1,005,727 passengers used the 18 principal Algerian airports in 1968. There are 12,250 miles of national highway, including 2,000 km. of asphalt roads in the Sahara.

Oil, natural gas and iron ore are found in quantity in the Saharan regions. Substantial oil and gas deposits are now being worked. Production of crude oil in 1968 totalled 43m. tons, compared with 39m. tons in 1967. Total production of natural gas in 1968 was 2,478,278,000 cu. metres.

In pursuit of the Government's policy of Algerianization about 80 per cent. of all industrial enterprises are now under state control. State organizations have recently been granted the import monopoly for all mechanical products, paper products and raw material for making paper, pharmaceutical products, medical instruments, sanitary ware and other builders' accessories.

CAPITAL.—Ψ Algiers, population (census of 1966), 943,000. The large numbers of French inhabitants who left the country have largely been replaced by an influx of Algerians to the city. Other towns include Ψ Oran (328,000); Constantine (254,000), Ψ Annaba (*formerly* Bône) (168,000); Blida (99,000); Setif (98,000); Sidi-Bel-Abbès (91,000); Tlemcen (87,000); Mostaganem (75,000); Ψ Skikda (*formerly* Philippeville) (72,000); El Aznam (*formerly* Orleansville) (70,000) and Tizi Ouzou (53,000).

FLAG.—Red crescent and star on a divided green and white background.

NATIONAL DAY.—November 1.

BRITISH EMBASSY
Résidence Cassiopée, 7 Chemin de Glycines, Algiers.

Ambassador Extraordinary and Plenipotentiary, His Excellency Ronald Arthur Burroughs, C.M.G. (1971)..............................£6,925

1st Secretaries, J. R. Johnson (*Head of Chancery*); S. Relton (*Commercial*).

Cultural Attaché, British Council Representative, E. Evans, M.B.E., 6 Avenue Souidani Boudjemaa, Algiers. There is a British Council library in *Algiers.*

Consul, W. F. L. Coleshill.

ANDORRA

A small, neutral principality situated on the southern slopes of the Pyrenees, between Spain and France, with an approximate area of 180 square miles and population (U.N. estimate, 1969) of about 19,000, one-third of whom are native Andorrans. It is surrounded by mountains of 6,500 to 10,000 feet. Historians place the origin between the eighth and ninth centuries. Andorra is divided into six Parishes, each of which has four Councillors elected by vote to the Valleys of Andorra Council of Twenty-four (Heads of families only may vote). The nominal heads of the state are the Bishop of Urgel, Spain, and the President of the French Republic. These two " co-princes " can veto certain decisions of the Council of the Valleys but cannot impose their own decisions without the consent of the Council. Each co-prince nominates his own representative and has a Permanent Delegation and a Supreme Tribune for the hearing of civil causes. These two Tribunes together form the Supreme Courts.

The official language of the country is Catalan. Spanish *pesetas* and French *francs* are the accepted currency. A good road crossing the Valleys from Spain to France is open most of the year. Andorra has deposits of iron and quantities of alum and lead, stone quarries, granite, jasper and marble. Slate is abundant. Timber includes pine, fir, oak, birch and box-tree. Potatoes and cereals are produced in the highlands and tobacco in the plains. The climate is naturally cold for six months, but mild in spring and summer. The mountain slopes are suitable for skiing, and it is estimated that 2,000,000 tourists visit the Valleys during the year.

There are two radio stations in Andorra, one privately-owned and one operated by a French Government corporation. Both pay dues to the Council of the Valleys.

CAPITAL: Andorra la Vella (population 2,500).

FLAG.—Three vertical bands, blue, yellow, red; Andorran coat of arms frequently imposed on central (yellow) band but not essential.

H.M. Consol-General, H. T. Kennedy, O.B.E. (*Resident at Barcelona*).

ARABIA

Arabia is a peninsula in the south-west of the Asiatic continent, forming the connecting link between Asia and Africa, and lies between 30° 30′ —60° E. long. and 12° 45′—34° 50′ N. lat. The north-western limit is generally taken from 'Aqaba at the head of the Gulf of 'Aqaba, to a point in the Syrian Desert about 150 miles north-east, and thence northwards to a point about 50 miles due east of Damascus. The remaining land boundaries are in the form of a horse-shoe, encompassing the Syrian Desert, and descending in a south-easterly direction to the head of the Persian Gulf, and thus excluding the whole of Mesopotamia and the Euphrates Valley. The other boundaries of Arabia are the Red Sea and Gulf of Aden, the Arabian Sea, and the Persian Gulf and Gulf of Oman. Generally speaking, the peninsula consists of a plateau sloping from south-west to north-east towards the Euphrates Valley, except that the broad south-eastern promontory, which encloses the Persian Gulf, contains a coastal range in Oman.

The total area is estimated at 1,200,000 sq. miles (of which nearly one-half is occupied by the Syrian, Nafud, Dahana, and Rub Al Khali deserts), and the total population is believed to be about 10,000,000.

Language and Literature.—Arabic is spoken not only in Arabia, but in many other countries, either as the principal or auxiliary tongue, notably in U.A.R. and the Sudan, Libya, Morocco, Algeria, Iraq, Jordan, Syria, Lebanon; and to some extent also in Nigeria, Madagascar and Zanzibar. Owing to Moorish incursions it was formerly spoken in Spain, the Balearic Islands and Sicily. There are anthologies of pre- and post-Islamic poetry and a considerable prose literature, including popular romances and story cycles (such as " The Thousand Nights and One Night "), historical and biographical studies, and, resulting from the westernizing movement, there is a general revival of learning among Arabic speaking peoples. Many daily newspapers are published in Arabic and there is a native Arabic drama.

See also—BAHRAIN; KUWAIT; OMAN; QATAR; SAUDI ARABIA; TRUCIAL STATES; THE YEMEN REPUBLICS.

ARGENTINE REPUBLIC
(República Argentina)

President, Lt.-Gen. Alejandro Agustín Lanusse, *assumed office* March 26, 1971.

Ministers

Interior, Dr. Arturo Mor Roig.
Foreign Affairs and Worship, Dr. Luis M. de Pablo Pardo.
Treasury, Dr. Juan Carlos Quilici.
Industry, Trade and Mines, Gen. Oscar M. Chescotta.
Social Welfare, Sr. Francisco Manrique.
Defence, Dr. José R. Cáceres Monié.
Agriculture, Sr. Gabriel Perren.
Labour, Sr. Rubens San Sebastian.
Public Works and Services, Ing° Pedro Gordillo.
Justice, Dr. Jaime I. E. Perrieaux.
Education, Dr. Gustavo Malek.

Secretaries of State

Development and Community Welfare, Dr. Omar L. Quintana.
Social Security, Sr. Carlos Roque Argimón.
Housing, Arq° Federico Ugarte.
Public Health, Dr. Horacio R. Castells.
Public Works and Transport, Sr. Alberto Pérez Leirós.
Energy (vacant).
Communications, Brig. Gen. Alberto V. Nieto.
Water Resources, Ing° Jorge A. Simonelli.
Broadcasting, Sr. Edgardo Sajón.
President of Central Bank, Dr. Ricardo Grüneisen.
Commanders-in-Chief, Lt. Gen Alejandro A. Lanusse (*Army*); Admiral Pedro A. J. Gnavi (*Navy*); Brig.Gen. Carlos A. Rey (*Air Force*).

EMBASSY IN LONDON.
9 Wilton Crescent, S.W.1.
[01-235-3717]

Ambassador Extraordinary and Plenipotentiary, His Excellency Gen. Gustavo Martínez-Zuviría (1970)
Minister Plenipotentiary, Juan Carlos Beltramino.
Counsellors, E. Perez Colman; S. N. Martinez.
Naval Attaché, Rear Adm. Carlos G. N. Coda.
Military and Air Attaché, Cdre. Francisco Cabrera.
Economic Minister, Leonardo A. Vartalitis.
Asst. Naval Attachés, Carlos N. A. Guevara; Cdr. J. A. Iriberry.
Asst. Air Attachés, Vice-Cdre. Victor Samuel Aguilar; Vice-Cdre. Raúl A. Valverde; Major Domingo Torea Paz.
1st Secretaries, L. Clarasó de la Vega; E. Perez Tomas.
2nd Secretary, Señorita Graciela L. Grandi.

3rd *Secretaries,* Marcelo F. Colombo Murúa; Federico Mirré.
Attaché, Eduardo Alberto Cotelo.
Consulate-General, 53 Hans Place, S.W.1 (01–584–1701).
Minister Plenipotentiary, José A. del Carril.
1st Secretary, Esteban R. Osorio.

There is also a Consulate in *Liverpool.*

Argentina is a wedge-shaped country, occupying the greater portion of the southern part of the South American Continent, and extending from Bolivia

to Cape Horn, a total distance of nearly 2,300 miles; its greatest breadth is about 930 miles. It is bounded on the north by Bolivia, on the north-east by Paraguay, Brazil, and Uruguay, on the south-east and south by the Atlantic, and on the west by Chile, from which Republic it is separated by the Cordillera de los Andes. On the west the mountainous Cordilleras, with their plateaux, extend from the northern to the southern boundaries : on the east are the great plains. Those in the north are thickly wooded and are known as *El Gran Chaco,* and further south lie the treeless pampas extending from the Bolivian boundary in the north to the Río Negro; and south of the Río Negro are the vast plains of Patagonia. Argentina thus contains a succession of level plains, broken only in Córdoba by the San Luis and Córdoba ranges, in the north-western states by the eastern spurs of the Andes, and in the south-ern portion of the Province of Buenos Aires by the Tandil Hills (about 1,000 ft.) and the Sierra Ventana, near Bahía Blanca (about 3,000 ft.). The Paraná River, formed by the junction of the Upper Paraná with the Paraguay River, flows through the north-eastern states into the Atlantic, and is navigable throughout its course in Argentina; the Pilcomayo, Bermejo, and Salado del Norte are also navigable for some distance from their con-fluence with the Paraná. In the Province of Buenos

Aires the Salado del Sud flows south-east for some 300 miles into Samborombon Bay (Atlantic). In the south the Colorado and Río Negro rise in the extreme west and flow across the pampas into the Atlantic, many similar streams in Patagonia (notably the Chubut and Santa Cruz) traversing the country from the Andes to the Atlantic. The climate ranges from sub-tropical to cold temperate.

The Republic consists of 22 provinces, one territory (Tierra del Fuego) and one federal district (Buenos Aires), comprising in all an area of 1,079,965 square miles, with a population (Census of 1970) of 23,360,000 (male 11,600,000; female 11,760,000).

Government.—The estuary of La Plata was dis-covered in 1515 by Juan Díaz de Solís, but it was not until 1534 that Pedro de Mendoza founded Buenos Aires. This city was abandoned and later founded once more by Don Juan de Garay in 1580. In 1810 (May 25) Spanish rule was defied, and in 1816 (July 9), after a long campaign of liberation conducted by General José de San Martín, the independence of Argentina was declared by the Congress of Tucumán. A revolt in September, 1955, overthrew the Government under the presi-dency of General Juan D. Perón and an interim Provisional Government was formed by the late General Eduardo Lonardi. This Provisional presi-dency passed to General Pedro Aramburu in Nov-ember, 1955.

A Constituent Assembly, elected on July 28, 1957, decided that the country should revert to the 1853 Constitution. General Elections were held in February, 1958, and Dr. Arturo Frondizi was elected President. Following Perónist victories in the partial elections of March, 1962, the armed forces took over the Government and appointed the Chairman of the Senate, Dr. Guido, President. He held office until 1963. After general elections of July 7, Dr. Arturo Illia was elected President in July, 1963, and took office in October, 1963, for a period of six years. But after the bloodless revolution by the Armed Services of June 27–28, 1966, the Presidency was offered to and accepted by General Onganía. Congress was dissolved and the president then ruled by decree. A bloodless *coup* was carried out by the Commanders-in-Chief in June, 1970, and Brigadier General Levingston was appointed President. In March, 1971, another bloodless *coup* took place and the Commander-in-Chief of the Army, General Lanusse, became President. His Cabinet is mainly composed of civilians, expert in their particular fields. The political parties are being restored and the new Government is committed to the return to demo-cratic government not later than 1974.

Agriculture.—Of a total land area of approxi-mately 700,000,000 acres, farms occupy about 425,000,000. About 60 per cent. of the farmland is in pasture, 10 per cent. in annual crops, 5 per cent. in permanent crops and the remaining 25 per cent. in forest and wasteland. A large proportion of the land is still held in large estates devoted to cattle raising but the number of small farms is increasing. The principal crops are wheat. maize, oats, barley, rye, linseed, sunflower seed, alfalfa, sugar, fruit and cotton. Argentina is pre-eminent in the produc-tion of beef, mutton and wool, being self-sufficient in basic foodstuffs and conducting a large export trade in many others. Pastoral and agricultural products provide nearly 90 per cent. of Argen-tina's exports and they originate mainly from the pampas or rich central plain which embraces the provinces of Buenos Aires, Santa Fé, Entre Ríos, Córdoba and La Pampa.

The following table shows the yield of the more important crops:

	1969-70
	metric tons
Wheat	7,020,000
Maize	9,360,000
Linseed	640,000
Oats	425,000
Barley	570,000
Rye	377,000
Rice	407,000
Bird seed	107,000
Cotton (gross bulk production)	444,000
Sugar cane	9,555,000
Millet	25,200
Tobacco	66,000

Livestock.—Livestock population in 1969 was: cattle, 51,000,000; sheep, 51,500,000; and pigs, 4,200,000. Meat exports to U.K. fell from 170,524 tons in 1967 to 83,102 tons in 1968, rising to 164,436 tons in 1969. 12,815,000 cattle were slaughtered in 1970 (1969, 13,791,000).

Mineral Production.—Oil is found in various parts of the Republic and is obtained to a considerable extent at Comodoro Rivadavia (Chubut), Mendoza, Plaza Huincul (Neuquen), Tartagal (Salta) and in other districts. A natural gas pipeline between Comodoro Rivadavia and Buenos Aires has been in operation since 1949. An oil pipeline from Campo Duran (Salta) to a refinery in San Lorenzo (Santa Fé) was put in service in March, 1960, as was also a natural gas pipeline from the same source to the outskirts of Buenos Aires. Another project of importance was the construction of the natural gas pipeline between Neuquén and Bahía Blanca, completed in 1970. The production of oil is of first importance to Argentina's rapidly expanding industries and, to some extent, to her economic and financial development. Total petroleum output for 1970 was 22,802,000 cubic metres compared with 20,681,347 cubic metres in 1969.

Coal, lead, zinc, tungsten, iron ore, sulphur, mica and salt are the other chief minerals being exploited. There are small worked deposits of beryllium, manganese, bismuth, uranium, antimony, copper, kaolin, arsenate, gold, silver and tin. Coal production in 1970 was 615,541 tons, compared with 521,620 tons in 1969; this is produced at the Rio Turbio mine in the province of Santa Cruz. The output of other materials is not large but greater attention is now being paid to the development of these natural resources.

Industries.—Meat-packing is one of the principal industries; flour-milling, sugar-refining, and the wine industry are also important. In recent years great strides have been made by the textile, plastic and machine tool industries and in engineering, especially in the production of motor vehicles and steel manufactures.

Communications.—There are 25,386 miles of railways of which 14,000 miles are broad gauge (5' 6"), 2,000 miles standard (4' 8½"), 8,720 miles of narrow 1 metre, 537 miles of 0·75 metre and 129 miles of 0·60 metre. They are all State property. Plans are in hand for complete re-organization of the railways which is expected to bring a substantial reduction in the lengths of lines operated. The combined national and provincial road network totals approximately 132,659 miles of which 16,449 miles are surfaced. There are air services between Argentina and all the neighbouring republics, Europe, Canada and the U.S.A. Total tonnage entering Argentine ports in 1969 was 12,642,100.

There are 14 short-wave broadcasting stations, 121 medium wave (of which 65 are official). In addition there are 31 television stations, of which 4 are in Buenos Aires. About 3·3 million television receivers were in use in December 1970.

Defence.—The Army is organized in four corps

in which are combined four infantry divisions, one motorized infantry division and one motorized infantry brigade, one mounted infantry division, one armoured division and one cavalry division and numbers about 5,000 officers, 15,000 N.C.O.s and 65-70,000 men on a peace footing.

The Navy consists of 2 cruisers, 1 aircraft carrier, 9 destroyers, 4 frigates/corvettes, 2 submarines, 4 minesweepers, 1 minehunter and ancillary craft.

The Air Force consists of 5 brigades and a training force, with a strength of 1,600 officers, 15,000 other ranks and 20,000 civilians. Aircraft total 321, including Meteor IV's, Skyhawk A.4 BS1, Lockheed C130. Fokker F27 and HS.748.

Education—Primary and Secondary. The new educational programme contemplates free compulsory education between the ages of 6 and 14. There will be a further cycle of three years advanced secondary education from 14 to 17 on a voluntary basis. Primary education is administered at Provincial level and Secondary through the Ministry of Education in Buenos Aires. There are also many private schools in the Argentine. *Teacher-Training.*—2, 3 or 4 year courses will be organized at post-secondary level. *Universities.*—There are National Universities at Buenos Aires, Córdoba, Rosario, San Miguel de Tucumán, Mendoza, La Plate, Bahia Blanca, Resistencia and Corrientes, Sante Fé and Rio Cuarto. In addition a National Technical University has branches all over the country. There are also Provincial Universities and Private Universities are run by the church and other organizations.

Language and Literature.—Spanish is the language of the Republic and the literature of Spain is accepted as an inheritance by the people. There is little indigenous literature before the break from Spain, but all branches have flourished since the latter half of the nineteenth century, particularly journalism. Under the Perón régime many newspapers and reviews were closed down and others turned into Government mouthpieces. Since the 1955 revolution the traditional freedoms have been restored. About 200 daily newspapers are published in Argentina, including 50 in the city of Buenos Aires. The English language newspaper is the *Buenos Aires Herald* (daily). There are several other foreign language newspapers.

TRADE

	1969	1970
	Dollars U.S.	
Total Imports....	1,566,000,000	1,684,639,000
Total Exports....	1,611,000,000	1,773,166,000

Trade with U.K.

	1969	1970
Imports from U.K..	£46,189,000	£44,065,000
Exports to U.K....	78,740,000	65,598,000

For Exchange Rate *see* p. 83.

CAPITAL.—Ψ Buenos Aires, Pop. (Dec. 1960). Metropolitan area 3,200,000; with suburbs, 7,200,000. Other large towns are: Ψ Rosario de Santa Fé (671,976), Córdoba (589,183), Ψ La Plata (400,000), Ψ Mar del Plata (400,000), San Miguel de Tucuman (287,000), Santa Fé (264,413) and Mendoza (109,149).

FLAG.—Horizontal bands of blue, white, blue; gold sun in centre of white band.

NATIONAL DAY.—July 9.

BRITISH EMBASSY
Luis Agote 2412, Buenos Aires.
Ambassador Extraordinary and Plenipotentiary, His Excellency Sir Reginald Michael Hadow, K.C.M.G. (1969)....................£9,000
Minister, J. L. Taylor (*Commercial*).
Counsellor, T. Peters, C.M.G. (*Consul-General*).

1st *Secretaries*, R. W. Whitney, O.B.E.; P. Voller (*Commercial*); H. Fletcher (*Information*); A. J. Sims (*Administration*).

2nd *Secretaries*, E. W. J. Lensh (*Commercial*); B. Attewell; Miss E. P. Ogilvie.

3rd *Secretaries*, R. D. Lavers; C. W. G. Edmonds-Brown (*Commercial*).

Junior Attaché, D. Hay-Edie (*Vice-Consul*).

Defence and Military Attaché, Col. G. W. Croker, M.B.E., M.C.

Naval Attaché, Capt. J. Hood, R.N.

Air Attaché, Gp. Capt. J. F. Melrose, D.F.C.

Veterinary Attaché, R. L . Steele.

Asst. Veterinary Attaché, J. G. S. Boyle.

BRITISH CONSULAR OFFICES

There are British Consular Offices at *Buenos Aires, Cipolletti (Rio Negro), Comodoro Rivadavia, Córdoba, La Plata, Rio Gallegos, Rio Grande, Rosario de Santa Fé, Salta* and *Santa Cruz.*

BRITISH COUNCIL

Representative in Argentine, C. H. Whistler, O.B.E., Lavalle 190, Buenos Aires. There are offices at *Córdoba* and *Rosario* and the Council supplies books to the library of the *Associacion Argentina de Cultura Inglesa* at *Buenos Aires.*

BRITISH CHAMBER OF COMMERCE

Calle Bartolomé Mitre 441. (6 Piso), Buenos Aires.

Buenos Aires is 7,160 miles from Southampton; transit, 19 days by steamship; 18 hours by air.

AUSTRIA

President of the Austrian Republic, Franz Jonas, G.C.B., born 1899; *elected* May 23, 1965; *re-elected* April 25, 1971.

CABINET

Chancellor, Dr. Bruno Kreisky.
Vice-Chancellor and Minister of Social Affairs, Ing. Rudolf Häuser.
Minister for the Interior, Otto Rösch.
Justice, Dr. Christian Broda.
Transport, Erwin Frühbauer.

Foreign Affairs, Dr. Rudolf Kirchschläger.
Finance, Dkfm. Hannes Androsch.
Agriculture, Dip. Ing. Dr. Oskar Weihs.
Defence, Brig. Karl Lütgendorff.
Education, Leopold Gratz.
Trade and Industry, Dr. Josef Staribacher.
Building, Josef Moser.
Science and Research, Frau Dr. Hertha Firnberg.

AUSTRIAN EMBASSY IN LONDON
18 Belgrave Square, S.W.1.
[01-231 3731]

Ambassador Extraordinary and Plenipotentiary, His Excellency Dr. Wilfried Platzer, G.C.V.O. (1970).
Minister-Counsellor, Dr. Erich Hochleitner.
Counsellor, Dr. Alfred Missong.
1st *Secretary*, Dr. Albert Rohan.
Defence Attaché, Brig.-Gen. H. Wingelbauer.
Attachés, Dr. Ernst Menhofer (*Press*); Dr. Karl Schanda, M.B.E. (*Consular Affairs*); Viktor Hauer, M.V.O. (*Administration*).

Austria is a country of Central Europe bounded on the north by Czechoslovakia, on the south by Italy and Yugoslavia, on the east by Hungary, on the north-west by Germany and on the west by Switzerland. Its area is 32,376 square miles and its population (estimated July, 1970), 7,391,000.

Government.—The Austrian Federal Republic comprises nine provinces (Vienna, Lower Austria, Upper Austria, Salzburg, Tyrol, Vorarlberg, Carinthia, Styria and Burgenland) and was established in 1918 on the break-up of the Austro-Hungarian Empire. On March 13, 1938, as a result of the *Anschluss*, Austria (*Oesterreich*) was incorporated into the German *Reich* under the name *Ostmark*. After the liberation of Vienna in 1945, the Austrian Republic was reconstituted within the frontiers of 1937 and, after a period of provisional government, a freely-elected Government took office on December 20, 1945. The country was divided at this time into four zones occupied respectively by the U.K., U.S.A., U.S.S.R. and France, while Vienna was jointly occupied by the four Powers. On May 15, 1955, the Austrian State

Treaty was signed in Vienna by the Foreign Ministers of the four Powers and of Austria. This Treaty recognized the re-establishment of Austria as a sovereign, independent and democratic state, having the same frontiers as on January 1, 1938. It entered into force on July 27, 1955.

There is a National Assembly of 165 Deputies. In the elections of March, 1970, the Socialist Party won the greatest number of seats, and though not obtaining an overall majority, subsequently formed a minority government which is the first Socialist administration in Austrian history.

The state of the parties in June 1971, was:

Socialist Party..................... 81
People's Party..................... 78
Freedom Party (right wing)........ 6

(The date of Oct. 10, 1971, was fixed for a new general election.)

Religion and Education.—The predominant religion is Roman Catholic. Elementary education is free and compulsory between the ages of 6 and 15 and there are good facilities for secondary, technical and professional education. There are Universities at Vienna, Graz, Innsbruck, Salzburg and Linz.

Language and Literature.—The language of Austria is German. but the rights of the Slovene- and Croat-speaking minorities in Carinthia, Styria and Burgenland are protected. The press is free. There are 6 daily papers in Vienna and 24 in the provinces, as well as numerous weeklies and monthlies.

Communications.—Internal communications in Austria are partly restricted because of the mountainous nature of the country, and road and rail routes must, of necessity, follow the river valleys. The railways in Austria are state-owned and have 5,907·6 km. of track of which 2,306·0 km. had been electrified by the end of 1969. While road surfaces in many cases are not up to British standards, the main roads linking the major towns are generally good and relatively fast. The *Westautobahn*, completed in 1967, links Munich, Salzburg, Linz and Vienna. A second major autobahn (*Südautobahn*) linking Vienna with Graz, Klagenfurt and Villach is under construction and part of it is already open for use. There are limited internal air services between some of the major cities.

Production and industry.—Agriculture is an important industry, the arable land producing wheat, rye, barley, oats, maize, potatoes, sugar beet, turnips, and miscellaneous crops. Many varieties of fruit trees flourish and the vineyards produce excellent wine. The pastures support horses, cattle and pigs. Timber forms a valuable source of Austria's indigenous wealth with about 39 per cent. of the total land area consisting of forest areas. Coniferous species predominate and account for more than 80 per cent. of the timber under cultivation. Hardwood trees are mainly confined to Lower Austria. Spruce is the most common among the conifers (about 60 per cent. of the total) and beech is the most prevalent of the broad leaf trees.

Austria has important heavy industries. Production figures for 1970 include (in thousands of metric tons): pig iron 2,964, steel 6,079, rolled products ,2,852. Raw magnesite, nitrogenous fertilizers, paper, chemical pulp and synthetic fibres are produced in quantity. In addition, motor cycles and motor cars, scooters, tractors and motor lorries are produced.

Hydro-electric power offers great possibilities in Austria. Much has already been done to develop it, and a long-term plan has been evolved for further development including greater export of electric current to surrounding countries. Production in 1970 was 30,018 million kWH. Since these resources are limited, however, a contract to construct a 700mW nuclear power station (due to

commence generation of electricity in September, 1976) has been awarded.

Minerals.—There are iron ore deposits and, in Eastern Austria, oil deposits. In addition there are useful deposits of brown coal, magnesite, salt and lead. There are also limited deposits of copper.

FINANCE.	1969	1970
	Schillings '000,000	
Ordinary Budget:		
Expenditure..............	89,608	97,566
Revenue..................	86,021	94,327
Extraordinary Budget:		
Expenditure..............	3,577	4,021

Trade with U.K.

	1969	1970
Imports from U.K..	£69,356,000	£90,706,000
Exports to U.K......	64,123,000	79,596,000

Currency.—The unit of currency is the *Schilling* of 100 *Groschen*, reintroduced in December, 1945. The official rate of exchange (fixed in May 1971) is 59·40 Austrian *schillings* = £1, at par.

CAPITAL, Vienna, on the Danube, population 1,643,100. Other towns are Graz (251,000), Linz (205,700), Innsbruck (115,800), Salzburg (122,100), and Klagenfurt (75,500).

FLAG.—Horizontal stripes of red, white, red, with eagle crest on white stripe. NATIONAL DAY.—October 26.

BRITISH EMBASSY
Vienna.

Ambassador Extraordinary and Plenipotentiary, His Excellency Sir Peter Allix Wilkinson, K.C.M.G., D.S.O., O.B.E. (1970)................£9,000
Counsellor (Commercial) and Consul-General, J. H. Lambert.
Counsellor (IAEA/UNIDO), F. H. Jackson, O.B.E.
1st Secretaries, Hon. E. H. B. Gibbs (*Head of Chancery*); S. Rosdol, O.B.E.; P. G. F. Bryant (*Commercial*); T. J. Trout, M.B.E. (*Information*).
Defence Attaché, Lt.-Col. K. L. Todd.
There are British Consular Offices at *Vienna* and *Innsbruck*.
British Council Representative, C. N. P. Powell, D.S.O., Freyung 1, A1010 Vienna.

BAHRAIN

Emir, H. H. Sheikh Khalifa bin Sulman Al Khalifah, K.C.M.G., *born* 1932; *acceded* Dec. 16, 1961.

COUNCIL OF STATE

Appointed with complete executive powers by the Ruler of Bahrain in January, 1970.
President, H.E. Sheikh Khalifa bin Sulman Al-Khalifa.
Head of Defence, H.E. Sheikh Hamed bin Isa Al-Khalifa (*Heir Apparent*).
Finance, Sayed Mahmud Al-Alawi.
Foreign Affairs and (acting) *Information*, Sheikh Mohammed bin Mubarak Al-Khalifa.
Education, Ahmed Al-Umran.
Justice, Sheikh Khalid bin Mohammed Al-Khalifa.
Development and Engineering Services, Yusuf Ahmed Shirawi.
Labour and Social Affairs, Jawad Salim Al-Arrayedh.
Health, Dr. Ali Fakhroo.
Legal Adviser, Dr. Hussain Al-Baharna.
Police and Public Security (vacant).
Municipalities and Agriculture, Sheikh Abdulla bin Khalid Al-Khalifa.
Secretary to the Council, Saeed Zeera.

Bahrain consists of a group of low-lying islands situated halfway down the Persian Gulf some 20 miles off the east coast of Arabia. The largest of these, Bahrain Island itself, is about 30 miles long and 10 miles wide at its broadest. The two most important towns are Manama (89,608) and Muhar-

raq (49,387). The latter is situated on a separate island of the same name which is connected with Bahrain Island by a causeway 1½ miles long. The population of the islands at the Census held in 1965 was 182,203, of whom about half belong to the Shia Sect, the remainder, including the ruling family being Sunnis. There are 3,135 Europeans and Americans and 38,389 non-Bahrainis of whom about half are Iranians, Indians and Pakistanis. It was estimated that the population had risen to 207,000 by July, 1969. The standard of living is high among the large and influential merchant class and steadily rising among the lower social groups.

Bahrain enjoys a typical Persian Gulf climate with long, mild winters and an annual rainfall of about 3″. Summer extends from May to October, with temperatures between 100° F. and 115° F. and humidity often approaching 100 per cent. The surrounding sea abounds in a variety of fish, and some of the best prawns in the world inhabit the warm sheltered waters.

Local government is the responsibility of six municipalities and the Rural Affairs Department which cares for the villages. Half of the members of the municipal councils (Manama, Muharraq, Rifaa and Hidd) are elected by the public and half nominated by the Government; all the members of the other two, which were created later (Sitra and Jidhafs) are nominated by the Government. In addition to the Department of Rural Affairs, there are a Department of Social Affairs, a Labour Department, a Lands Department and a Public Works Department. There is free primary and secondary education and free medical treatment. The new town of Madinat Isa, planned to rehouse nearly 18 per cent of the population, was formally opened by the Ruler in 1968.

In earlier days the only industry was the pearl trade, of which Bahrain was an important centre, but this has declined since the advent of the cultured pearl and petroleum dominates the scene. Oil was discovered in 1932 and The Bahrain Petroleum Company, Limited (BAPCO), has its headquarters in Awali, some eleven miles from Manama. The company also operates a refinery and about 80 per cent. of the oil refined is piped from Saudi Arabia.

The second source of revenue is that of Bahrain's traditional *entrepôt* trade. The island is conveniently situated to handle goods in transit to the mainland and it is estimated that not less than 70 per cent. of the imports unloaded at Bahrain were, up to a few years ago, destined for onward movement. A decline in this *entrepôt* trade has, however, occurred as there is a growing tendency for eastern Saudi Arabia, Qatar and other places in the Gulf to import direct. This trend was reversed in 1966 when Bahrain re-exported 30 per cent. of its imports compared to the 28·3 per cent. in 1965 and by 1968 re-exports had risen to 35·5 per cent. To encourage the *entrepôt* trade, free transit facilities were introduced in the port of Bahrain on January 1, 1958, and a new harbour, named the Mina Sulman after the late Ruler, was opened in May, 1962.

Bahrain is being developed as a major manufacturing state, the first important enterprise being the Aluminium Bahrain smelter, which will be operated by a company whose shareholders include the Bahrain Government and British, Swedish, German and United States interests. The aluminium operation will be the largest non-oil industry in the Middle East. Ancillary industries being developed around aluminium smelting include the production of aluminium powder and paste. Other projects at present under consideration include the manufacture of magnesium, the further development of marine industries and the expansion of Bahrain's tourist potential.

Bahrain International Airport is the Arabian Gulf's main air communication centre. It is at present being expanded—the runway is being extended to 12,000 feet—and a new terminal building constructed to meet the demands of the Jumbojets that will start using Bahrain as a main stopping point on the routes between the Far East and Australia on one side and Europe and the Middle East on the other. The new terminal building is designed to handle 500 passengers an hour.

The principal imports and re-exports are household goods, foodstuffs, piece-goods, timber and building materials (especially cement), wearing apparel, vehicles and machinery.

Trade with U.K.

	1969	1970
Imports from U.K.	£12,454,000	£24,340,000
Exports to U.K.	2,072,000	1,554,000

Manama, the capital and commercial centre, extends for two miles along the northern shore of Bahrain Island and is a regular port of call for thirty steamship lines. Bahrain is also a port of call for B.O.A.C. and other international airlines, with a modern air terminal and facilities for jet airlines. Banking services are provided by the Bank of Bahrain and by branches of the Eastern Bank, the British Bank of the Middle East, the Arab Bank, the Habib Bank, the United Bank, Rafidainbank, and First National City Bank. There is a radio-telephone service to the United Kingdom and many other parts of the world. Electricity and water supply is available in all towns and most villages.

FLAG: Red, with vertical straight or serrated white bar next to staff.

CAPITAL, Ψ Manama; population, 89,608.

H.M. Political Agent, A. J. D. Stirling (1969).

Bahrain is the headquarters of *H.M. Political Resident in the Persian Gulf*, Sir Geoffrey George Arthur, K. C.M.G., (1970) £9,000

British Council Representative, J. G. Hanson, 1 P.O. Box 452, Manama. There is a Council office at *Dubai* and the Representative at Bahrain is responsible for Council work in Qatar, Trucial States, Muscat and Oman. Libraries at Bahrain and *Dubai*.

BELGIUM
(Royaume de Belgique.)

King of the Belgians, H.M. King Baudouin, K.G., born Sept. 7, 1930; *succeeded* July 17, 1951, on the abdication of his father, King Leopold III, after having acted as Head of the State since August 11, 1950; *married* Dec. 15, 1960, Doña Fabiola de Mora y Aragòn.

Heir Presumptive, H.R.H. Prince Albert, born June 6, 1934, *brother* of the King: *married* July 2, 1959, Donna Paola Ruffo di Calabria, and has *issue* Prince Philippe Léopold Louis Marie, b. April 15, 1960; Princess Astrid Josephine-Charlotte Fabrizia Elisabeth Paola Marie, b. June 5, 1962; Prince Laurent, b. Oct. 20, 1963.

CABINET.

Prime Minister, M. G. Eyskens (CVP).

Deputy Prime Minister and Minister for Economic Affairs, M. A. Cools (PSB).

Scientific Policy and Planning, M. T. Lefevre (CVP).

National Education (Flemish), M. P. Vermeylen (BSP).

National Defence, M. P. W. Segers (CVP).

Foreign Affairs, M. P. Harmel (PSC).

Agriculture, M. C. Heger (PSC).

Posts and Telegraphs, M. E. Anseele (*BSP*).
Budget, M. M. Denis (*PSB*).
Foreign Trade, M. H. Fayat (*BSP*).
Co-operation for Development, M. R. Scheyven (*PSC*).
Communications, M. A. Bertrand (*CVP*).
Justice, M. A. Vranckx (*BSP*).
Public Works, M. J. De Saeger (*CVP*).
Social Security, M. P. De Paepe (*CVP*).
Employment and Labour, M. L. Major (*BSP*).
Finance, Baron ~~J. C. Snoy et d'Oppuers (PSC)~~.
French Culture, M. A. Parisis (*PSC*).
Public Administration, M. R. Petre (*PSC*).
Housing and Families, M. G. Breyne (*BSP*).
Middle Classes, M. C. Hanin (*PSC*).
Public Health, M. L. Nameche (*PSB*).
Interior, M. L. Harmegnies (*PSB*).
National Education (Francophone), M. A. Dubois (*PSB*).
Community Affairs (Flemish), M. L. Tindemans (*CVP*).
Flemish Culture, M. F. Van Mechelen (*CVP*).
Community Affairs (Francophone), M. F. Dehousse (*PSB*).
Flemish Regional Economy, M. A. Vlerick (Non-parliamentary).
Walloon Regional Economy, M. F. Delmotte (*PSB*).

    [*CVP*=Flemish-Speaking Social Christian
    PSC= French-Speaking Social Christian
    BSP=Flemish-Speaking Socialist
    PSB=French-Speaking Socialist]

BELGIAN EMBASSY IN LONDON.
Chancery and Passport Office, 103 Eaton Square, S.W.1.

[01-235-5422]
Ambassador Extraordinary and Plenipotentiary, ~~His Excellency Baron J. van den Bosch (1965).~~
Minister Counsellors, M. S. Frey; M. J. Gerard (*Economic Affairs*).
Counsellors, M. Georges Van der Espt (*Culture and Information*); M. J. Bousse; M. Ch. Raulier; M. P. H. L. Berghs (*Economic Affairs*).
Naval, Military and Air Attaché, Lt.-Gen. Avt. Baron M. Donnet, C.V.O., D.F.C.
1st Secretary, Baron A. Guillaume.
Agricultural Attaché, M. Maurice Cammaerts.
Attachés, M. R. A. P. van Speybrouck; Mlle. F. van Haelewyck.

A Kingdom of Western Europe, with a total area of 11,775 square miles and a population, (estimated Dec., 1970) of 9,691,000. The Kingdom of Belgium is bounded on the N. by the Kingdom of the Netherlands, on the S. by France, on the E. by Germany and Luxemburg, and on the W. by the North Sea.

Belgium has a frontier of 898 miles, and a sea-board of 41 miles. The Meuse and its tributary, the Sambre, divide it into two distinct regions, that in the west being generally level and fertile, while the table-land of the Ardennes, in the east, has for the most part a poor soil. The " polders " near the coast, which are protected by dykes against floods, cover an area of 193 sq. miles. The highest hill, Signal de Botranges, rises to a height of 2,276 feet, but the mean elevation of the whole country does not exceed 526 feet. The principal rivers are the Scheldt and the Meuse. Brussels has a mean temperature of 49° F. (summer 65°, winter 37°).

Belgium is inhabited by two distinct races, the Flemish, of Germanic stock, and the Walloons, of Latin stock. Nearly all the inhabitants are Roman Catholics.

Government.—The kingdom formed part of the "Low Countries " (Netherlands) from 1815 until Oct. 14, 1830, when a National Congress proclaimed its independence, and on June 4, 1831, Prince Leopold of Coburg was chosen hereditary king. The separation from the Netherlands and the neutrality and inviolability of Belgium were guaranteed by a Conference of the European Powers, and by the *Treaty of London* (April 19, 1839), the famous " Scrap of Paper," signed by Austria, France, Great Britain, Prussia, The Netherlands, and Russia. On Aug. 4, 1914, the Germans invaded Belgium, in violation of the terms of the treaty.

The Kingdom was again invaded by Germany on May 10, 1940. The whole Kingdom eventually fell into enemy hands and was occupied by Nazi troops until the victorious advance of the Allies in September, 1944. A monument at Hertain in the province of Hainault (where British forces crossed the frontier on Sept. 3, 1944), set up by the Anglo-Belgian Union, was unveiled on St. George's Day, 1949.

According to the Constitution of 1831 the form of government is a constitutional representative and hereditary monarchy with a bicameral legislature, consisting of the King, the Senate and the Chamber of Representatives. The Senate is partly directly and partly indirectly elected (or co-opted) for 4 years. 106 members out of 175 are directly elected. The Chamber of Representatives consists of not more than 1 per 40,000 inhabitants and is elected directly by all adult nationals.

The elections of March 31, 1968, returned to the Chamber of Deputies 69 Social Christians (Catholics), 59 Socialists, 47 *Parti de la Liberté et du Progrès* (Liberals), 20 *Volksunie*, 12 *Front Démocratique des Bruxellois Francophones* and *Rassemblement Wallon*, and 5 Communists, total 212. The Senate of 179 Members (including H.R.H. Prince Albert) includes 64 Social Christians, 53 Socialists, 37 *Parti de la Liberté et du Progrès* (Liberals), 14 *Volksunie*, 8 *Front Démocratique des Bruxellois Francophones* and *Rassemblement Wallon*, and 2 Communists.

Production.—Belgium is essentially a manufacturing country. With no natural resources except coal, annual production of which formerly averaged some 30,000,000 tons but which dropped to 11,374,000 tons in 1970 following the closing of uneconomic pits, industry is based largely on the processing for re-export of imported raw materials. In 1970 about 5 per cent of the active population was engaged in agriculture and forestry, the former supplying four-fifths of the population's needs. Principal industries are coal, steel and metal products (Mons, Charleroi, Liège, Namur, Hainault, Brabant and Limburg), textiles (Ghent, Bruges,

Courtrai, Verviers, etc.), glass nitrogen, heavy chemicals, sugar, breweries, etc. Crude steel output in 1970 was 12,610,700 metric tons.

Education.—Schools are maintained by communal taxation, with provincial and state grants; many are under ecclesiastical control, Roman Catholic largely predominating. 895 secondary schools, offering a general education, are maintained by the State, 648 by local government authorities, while 2,396 are controlled by independent bodies (largely Roman Catholic) but are mainly eligible for state subsidies. Of primary schools, 565 are controlled by the State, 4,485 by local governments and 3,897 by independent authorities. The Universities of Ghent and Liège are state institutions; the Free University of Brussels and the Catholic University of Louvain are independent though largely subsidized by the State. Starting with the 1969–70 academic year, the two non-state universities were split into four distinct universities—" l'Université Catholique de Louvain ", " de Katholieke Universiteit te Leuven ", " l'Université Libre de Bruxelles " and " de Vrije Universiteit te Brussel ".

Language and Literature.—Flemish is spoken in the provinces of West Flanders, East Flanders, Antwerp, Limburg, and the northern half of Brabant, and French in the provinces of Hainault, Namur, Luxemburg, Liège and the southern half of Brabant. Flemish is recognized as the official language in the northern areas and French in the southern (Walloon) area and there are guarantees for the respective linguistic minorities.

In July, 1971, the Belgian Parliament passed three Bills together implementing the constitutional amendments introduced in December 1970, to ease friction between the French-speaking and Flemish-speaking communities. The first Bill established a cultural council for each linguistic group, in operation from Dec. 1, 1971, all members of the Chamber of Representatives and the Senate being members of one council or the other. The second Bill defined the powers of the cultural councils, providing that the councils would be responsible for certain aspects of cultural life; commissions for co-operation with the other council would be set up, with a statutory obligation to hold at least two meetings with the other council in each Parliamentary session. The third Bill provided for the establishment of five " agglomerations " of municipalities centred on Antwerp, Brussels, Charleroi, Ghent and Liège and the federation of small municipalities, with special provision in respect of the border boroughs of Brussels (which have a predominantly Flemish population) designed gradually to reduce the influence of the French speakers in that area.

The literature of France and the Netherlands is supplemented by an indigenous Belgian literary activity, in both French and Flemish. Maurice Maeterlinck (1862–1949) was awarded the Nobel Prize for Literature in 1911. Emile Verhaeren (1855–1916) was a poet of international standing. Of contemporary Belgian writers, perhaps the most celebrated is Georges Simenon (*born* at Liège in 1903). There are 72 daily newspapers (French, Flemish and some German) in Belgium.

FINANCE

Ordinary Budget	1970	1971
		B. Fr. (millions)
Revenue	290,480	318,900
Expenditure	290,406	318,700
Extraordinary Budget		
Revenue	2,015	800
Expenditure	40,350	56,600

The unit of currency is the Belgian *franc*. On July 1, 1971, the Bank of England official rate of exchange was *frs.* 120 = £1. (*See also* p. 83.)

TRADE

	1969	1970
	('000 *Francs*)	('000 *Francs*)
Total Imports	498,383,000	568,114,922
Total Exports	500,400,000	580,467,451

Trade with U.K.

	1969	1970
Imports from U.K.	£280,844,000	£288,620,000
Exports to U.K.	182,603,000	192,503,000

COMMUNICATIONS.—On Dec. 31, 1970, there were 4,165 kilometres of normal gauge railways operated by the Belgian National Railways, of which 1,217 kilometres were electrified; the length of regional railways operated in 1970 was 378 kilometres. Belgian National Railways also operate 6,981 kilometres of regular bus routes. Other operators run 13,894 km. of bus routes. On Dec. 31, 1970, there were 1,343,541 telephone subscribers in Belgium.

Ship canals include *Ghent-Terneuzen* (18 miles, of which half is in Belgium and half in the Netherlands; constructed 1825–27) which permits the passage to Ghent of ships up to 60,000 tons; the Canal of Willebroek Rupel-Brussels (20 miles, by which ships drawing 18 ft reach Brussels from the sea; opened in 1922); and *Bruges* (from Zeebrugge on the North Sea to Bruges, 6½ miles; opened in 1922). The *Albert Canal* (79 miles), which figured prominently in the fighting (Sept. 1944) for the relief of Belgium and the Netherlands and for the invasion of Germany, links Liège with Antwerp; it was completed in 1939 and accommodates barges up to 1,350 tons. The modernization of the port of Antwerp begun in 1956 is now well advanced. Inland waterway approaches to Antwerp are also to be improved. The river Meuse from the Dutch to the French frontiers, the river Sambre between Namur and Monceau, the river Scheldt from Antwerp-Ghent and the Brussels-Charleroi Canal are being widened or deepened to take barges up to 1,350 tons.

There are 11,972 kilometres of trunk roads of which 485 km. are motorways. Most of the maritime trade of Belgium is carried in foreign shipping, the mercantile marine consisting (1970) of 91 vessels (986,889 tons), in addition to which there are 332 fishing boats (31,185 tons).

The Belgian National Airline *Sabena* operates regular services between Brussels and London, Manchester and many continental centres, as well as overseas services to the United States, the Congo, Canada, Mexico, Guatemala, Middle East, Far East, India, etc. Many foreign airlines call at Brussels. A passenger and mail-carrying helicopter service, the first of its kind in the world, was inaugurated in 1953.

CITIES AND TOWNS.

The Capital, BRUSSELS, had a population (Dec. 31, 1969) of 1,077,035 (with suburbs). Other towns are Ψ Antwerp, the chief port (673,259); Ψ Ghent (229,687), which has large cotton and flax spinning mills, and is the second port of importance after Antwerp, while its flower shows are famous; Liège (446,990), the centre of the iron industry, and Charleroi (218,089), the important coal-mining and metallurgical centre; Ψ Bruges (112,611); Ψ Ostend (57,230); Malines (65,730). Brussels is 224 miles from London; transit, by rail and sea, 8 hrs.; by air, 1 hr.

NATIONAL FLAG.—Three vertical bands, black, yellow, red.

NATIONAL DAY.—July 21 (Accession of King Leopold I, 1831).

BRITISH EMBASSY

28 Rue Joseph II, 1040 Brussels.

Ambassador Extraordinary and Plenipotentiary, His
Excellency Sir John Greville Stanley Beith,
K.C.M.G. (1969)......................£9,000
Counsellors, G. F. Hiller, C.M.G., D.S.O. (*Commercial*);
C. T. E. Ewart-Biggs, C.M.G., O.B.E.; J. E. R.
Little, O.B.E. (*Administration*).
Defence (Military and Naval) Attaché, Col. J. F.
Kenyon, O.B.E., M.C.
Air Attaché, Wing Cdr. R. A. E. Storer.
1st Secretaries, F. J. Bradshaw (*Consul*); E. Pope;
A. E. Heath (*Information*); P. M. S. Corley
(*Commercial*); J. S. Vigors (*Labour*); T. H. Gee;
J. H. Potter (*Administration*); J. Doorbar (*Com-
mercial*); P. L. Morgan.
2nd Secretaries, P. L. Norris (*Commercial*); Miss H.
M. Evans; P. B. Cormack (*Commercial*).

BRITISH CONSULAR OFFICES

There are British Consular Offices at *Brussels,
Antwerp, Ostend, Ghent* and *Liège.*

*British Council Representative to Belgium and
Luxemburg,* P. L. Roussel, 166 Avenue Louise, 1050
Brussels (Council Library at *Brussels*).
BRITISH CHAMBER OF COMMERCE, 30 Rue Joseph II,
1040 Brussels.

BHUTAN

King of Bhutan, Jigme Dorji Wangchuk, *born* 1929;
succeeded his father, March, 1952.

Bhutan, with an area of about 18,000 sq. miles and
a population (U.N. estimate, 1969) of 770,000,
mainly Buddhists, is an independent State bounded
on the North and East by Tibet, on the South by
India, and on the West by Sikkim, which is now a
Protectorate of the Republic of India (*for* MAP
see p. 746). In 1949, a treaty was concluded
with the Government of India under which the
Kingdom of Bhutan agreed to be guided by the
Government of India in regard to its external relations, but it still retains complete independence,
issues its own passports and has diplomatic representatives in Tibet as well as in India. It also receives from the Government of India an annual
payment of about £35,000 as compensation for
portions of its territory annexed by the British
Government in India in 1864. The principal
cottage industries are weaving, metal works and
crafts, and the main exports are timber, rice and
wheat. A motor road runs 107 miles from Paro,
the winter capital, to Phuntsholign in W. Bengal.
Three other roads linking Bhutan with India are
under construction or projected. The Prime
Minister of Bhutan, Lhendup Dorji, succeeded his
brother on July 25, 1964. The Government of
India has a diplomatic representative whose headquarters are situated at Gangtok, capital of the
neighbouring State of Sikkim.

CAPITAL, Punakha. FLAG.—Orange and crimson
divided diagonally, with dragon device in centre.

BOLIVIA

(República de Bolivia)

President, Gen. Hugo Banzer, *assumed office* Aug. 22,
1971.

BOLIVIAN EMBASSY IN LONDON

106 Eaton Square, S.W.1.

[01-235-4248]

Ambassador Extraordinary and Plenipotentiary, His
Excellency Brig. Gen. Juan Lechin Suarez (1970).
Consulate, 106 Eccleston Mews, S.W.1.
Minister-Counsellor, Sr. Victor Mendez Bayá.
1st Secretary, Srta. Marta Bosacoma Bonel.
There are Bolivian Consular Offices in *Liverpool,
Birmingham* and *Hull.*

The Republic of Bolivia extends between lat.
10° and 23° S. and long. 57° 30′ and 69° 45′ W.
It has an area estimated at 415,000 square miles
with an estimated population (estimated, 1970) of
4,658,000. (*For* MAP, *see* p. 830.) The Republic
derives its name from its liberator, Simón Bolívar
(born 1783, died 1830).

The chief topographical feature is the great
central plateau (65,000 square miles) over 500 miles
in length, at an average altitude of 12,500 feet above
sea level, between the two great chains of the
Andes, which traverse the country from south to
north, and contain, in Illampu, Illimani, and
Sajama, three of the highest peaks of the western
hemisphere. The total length of the navigable
streams is about 12,000 miles, the principal rivers
being the Itenez, Beni, Mamore and Madre de Dios.

President Barrientos, who had held office since
his election on July 3, 1966, was killed in a helicopter
accident on April 27, 1969, and in accordance with
the Constitution was succeeded by Vice-President
Dr. Luis Adolfo Siles Salines. On Sept. 26, 1969,
the armed forces overthrew the constitutional
Government and set up a civilian-military government under the Presidency of General Ovando.
On October 7, 1970, Gen. Torres assumed the
Presidency after defeating the right-wing military
group which had overthrown the Government of
Gen. Ovando the day before, and held office
until August 22, 1971.

A *coup d'etat* occurred on Aug. 22, 1971, when,
after reported heavy fighting, the President was
ousted by right-wing Army leaders headed by Gen.
Hugo Banzer, Gen. Florentino Mendieta and Col.
Andres Selich. Gen. Banzer was proclaimed
President in La Paz on Aug. 22. Two co-Ministers
of State were nominated by the military junta—
Mario Gutierrez and Ciro Humbolt.

Mining, petroleum and agriculture are the
principal industries. The ancient silver mines of
Potosí are now worked chiefly for tin, but gold,
partly dug and partly washed, is obtained on the
Eastern Cordillera of the Andes; the tin output is,
after that of Malaya, the largest in the world,
28,921 tons being produced in 1970: copper,
antimony, lead, zinc, asbestos, wolfram, bismuth,
salt and sulphur are found, and petroleum is
also produced.

The Republic has been self-supporting in most
petroleum products since January, 1954. Production of crude oil in 1970 totalled 8,821,517
barrels (of 42 U.S. gallons). The Bolivian Gulf
Oil Company was nationalized on October 17,
1969, and shortly afterwards exports diminished
(4,662,004 barrels in 1970 compared with
8,897,834 barrels in 1969). Exports had again
begun to rise by mid-1971. Bolivia's agricultural produce consists chiefly of rice, barley,
oats, wheat, sugar-cane, maize, cotton, indigo,
rubber, cacao, potatoes, cinchona bark, medicinal
herbs, brazil nuts, etc. The development of
manufacturing industry progresses slowly. However, Bolivia has joined the Latin American Free
Trade Area, and on May 26, 1969, signed the
Andean Pact which is designed to secure economic
integration and co-operation within the Andean
Group of countries. Membership of these
regional groupings may in due course provide
some stimulus to growth.

There are 2,200 miles of railways in operation
including the lines from Corumbá to Santa
Cruz (405 miles) and from Yacuiba to Santa Cruz
(312 miles). There are about 10,950 miles of
telegraphs, and wireless services between Riberalta,
La Paz, Cobija, Capitandi (Chaco). There is direct
railway communication to the sea at Antofagasta

(32 hours), Arica (10 hours), and Mollendo (2 days), and also to Buenos Aires (3½ days); branch lines run from Oruro to Cochabamba, and from Rio Mulato to Potosi, and from Potosi to Sucre, the legal capital. The Antofagasta (Chile) and Bolivia Railroad was formerly an all-British concern, but the Bolivian sector has now been nationalized. Communication with Peru is effected by rail to Guaqui and thence by steamer across Lake Titicaca to the railhead at Puno.

Commercial aviation in Bolivia is conducted by Braniff International Airways (American), Lufthansa, Iberia, Aerolineas Argentinas, and Lloyd Aereo Boliviano (Bolivian), the five former providing international connections with U.S.A., West coast South American countries, Canal Zone, Europe and Argentina; Lloyd Aereo Boliviano, maintaining a service to Lima, São Paulo, Buenos Aires and Arica, and attending to local flights, links with La Paz with Oruro, Cochabamba, Santa Cruz and Trinidad, etc. and connects with LAN of Chile, Argentine Airlines and Cruzeiro do Sul of Brazil.

Bolivia is without a sea-coast, having been deprived of the ports of Tocopilla, Cobija, Mejillones, and Antofagasta by the " Pacific War " of 1879–1884.

Language and Literature.—The official language of the country is Spanish, but many of the Indian inhabitants (about two-thirds of the population) speak Quechua or Aymará, the two linguistic groups being more or less equal in numbers.

The Roman Catholic religion was disestablished in 1961 but relations between it and the State are good. Elementary education is compulsory and free and there are secondary schools in urban centres. Provision is also made for higher education; in addition to St. Francisco Xavier's University at Sucre, founded in 1624, there are six other universities, the largest being the University of San Andres at La Paz. Bolivian literature has not yet produced authors of world-wide renown. There are twelve principal daily newspapers in Bolivia, with an estimated daily circulation of 150,000.

FINANCE

The Budget for 1971, which included State Industrial Organization and local authorities, envisaged an expenditure of $b5,666,671,900, showing a deficit of $b45,302,500. The Central Government expenditure was estimated at $b2,678,197,500, showing a deficit of $b19,651,300.

On December 15, 1956, the *Boliviano* was made freely convertible for all purposes without restriction and from Jan. 1, 1963, the *Boliviano* was replaced by the *Peso Boliviano* at the rate of Bs. 1,000 =*Peso* 1 ($b.1). Exchange rate (1970): $b28·45 = £1. (*See also* p. 83.)

Trade with U.K.

	1969	1970
Imports from U.K..	£2,584,000	£2,201,000
Exports to U.K....	34,212,000	28,460,000

The principal exports are tin ore (most of which is exported to the U.K.), lead and antimony ores, silver, copper, wolfram, zinc, gold, nuts, hides and skins, vicuña wool, cotton and coffee. The chief imports are wheat and flour, sugar, iron and steel products, machinery, vehicles and textiles.

SEAT OF GOVERNMENT, La Paz. Population (estimated 1970) 553,000. Other large centres are Cochabamba (149,900), Oruro (119,700), Santa Cruz (124,900), Potosi, (96,800), Sucre, the legal capital and seat of the judiciary (84,900) and Tarija (35,700).

2 D*

FLAG : Three horizontal bands; Red, yellow, green.
NATIONAL DAY.—August 6 (Independence Day).

BRITISH EMBASSY.
Casilla 694, La Paz.
Ambassador Extraordinary and Plenipotentiary, His Excellency John Gabriel Tahourdin, C.M.G. (1971)
£6,925
1st Secretaries, B. R. Pridham (*Consul and Head of Chancery*); P. A. McLean (*Commercial*).
Defence Attaché, Group Capt. G. D. Fuller (*resident in Lima, Peru*).
2nd Secretary, J. G. Thomas (*Press and Information*).
3rd Secretary, W. H. H. Sanders (*Technical Assistance*).
Attaché, G. Roberts (*Commercial*).

BRITISH CONSULAR OFFICES.
There are British Consular Offices at *La Paz* and *Cochabamba*.

BRAZIL
(The Federative Republic of Brazil)
President, Gen. Emilio Garrastazú Médici, *assumed office* October 30, 1969.
Vice-President, Admiral Augusto Rademaker Grünewald.

BRAZILIAN EMBASSY IN LONDON
32 Green Street, W.1.
[01-629-0155-58]

Ambassador Extraordinary and Plenipotentiary, His Excellency Sérgio Corrêa da Costa, G.C.V.O. (1968).
Minister-Counsellor, F. de Assis Grieco.
Ministers, L. A. P. Souto Maior (*Economic Affairs*); O. de Andrade Mello (*Consular Affairs*).
Air Attaché, Col. D. Almeida Luz.
Naval and Military Attaché, Capt. Hugo R. Veiga.
Counsellor, P. Lindenberg Sette (*Economic Affairs*).
1st Secretaries, P. Pires do Rio; J. A. de Medicis; M. C. de Azambuja, M.V.O. (*Press and Information Affairs*).
2nd Secretaries, R. A. Barbosa, M.V.O. (*Consular*); R. P. F. M. Abdenur (*Consular*); C. L. N. Amorim; A. L. Westphalen (*Commercial Affairs*); J. C. Duvernoy; O. A. Maia (*Economic Affairs*).
Cultural Attaché, A. Olinto.
Attachés, Prof. J. L. da Silva; Sr. S. de Azevedo Lima.
Consular Section, 6 Deanery Street, W.1 (01-499-7441).
Commercial Section, 15 Berkeley Street, W.1 (01-499-6706).
There are also a Brazilian Consulate-General at *Liverpool* and honorary consular offices at *Cardiff* and *Manchester*.

POSITION AND EXTENT
Brazil, the most extensive State of South America, discovered in 1500 by Pedro Alvares Cabral, Portuguese navigator, is bounded on the north by the Atlantic Ocean, the Guianas, Colombia and Venezuela; on the west by Peru, Bolivia, Paraguay, and Argentina; on the south by Uruguay; and on the east by the Atlantic Ocean. Brazil extends between lat. 5° 16′ N. and 33° 45′ S. and long. 34° 45′ and 73° 59′ 22″ W., being 2,685 miles from north to south, and 2,690 from west to east, with a coast-line on the Atlantic of 4,604 miles. The Republic comprises an area of 3,289,440 square miles, with a population (estimated 1970), of 93,000,000.

The northern States of Amazonas and Pará are mainly wide, low-lying, forest-clad plains. The central state of the Mato Grosso is principally plateau land and the eastern and southern states are traversed by successive mountain ranges interspersed with fertile valleys. The principal ranges are

Serra do Mar in São Paulo ; the *Serra Geral* (Caparaó
9,393 feet) between Minas Gerais and Espirito Santo,
the *Serra da Mantiqueira* (Itatiaia, 9,163 feet), and the
Serra do Espinhaço (Itacolumi, 5,748 feet), in the
south-east of Minas Gerais ; the *Serra do Paraná*,
between Goiás and Minas Gerais, the *Serra dos
Aimorés*, which divide Espirito Santo from Minas
Gerais ; and the *Serra do Gurgueia, Branca* and
Araripe, which envelop Piauí.

Brazil is unequalled for its rivers. The River
Amazon has tributaries which are themselves great
rivers, and flows from the Peruvian Andes to the
Atlantic, with a total length of some 4,000 miles.
Its principal northern tributaries are the *Rio Branco,
Rio Negro,* and *Japurá* ; its southern tributaries are the
Jutuá, Purus, Madeira and *Tapajós*, while the *Xingú*
meets it within 200 miles of its outflow into the
Atlantic. The *Tocantins* and *Araguaia* flow north-
wards from the Plateau of Mato Grosso and the
mountains of Goiás to the Gulf of Pará. The
Parnaiba flows from the encircling mountains of
Piauí into the Atlantic. The *São Francisco* rises in
the South of Minas Gerais and traverses Bahía on
its way to the eastern coast, between Alagoas and
Sergipe. The *Paraguai*, rising in the south-west of
Mato Grosso, flows through Paraguay to its confluence with the *Paraná*, which rises in the mountains of that name and divides Brazil from
Paraguay. On the *Iguaçú* or *Iguassú*, which unites

with the Upper Paraná at the Brazil-Argentine-
Paraguay boundary, are the majestic *Falls of the
Iguaçú* (200 ft.), and on the *São Francisco* are the no
less famous falls of *Paulo Afonso* (260 ft.).

Government.—Brazil was colonized by Portugal
in the early part of the sixteenth century, and in
1822 became an independent empire under Dom
Pedro, son of the refugee King João VI. of Portugal.
On Nov. 15, 1889, Dom Pedro II., second of the
line, was dethroned and a republic was proclaimed.

Marshal Arthur da Costa e Silva assumed the
Presidency on March 15, 1967, with a new team of
ministers, and held office until August, 1969. A
triumvirate consisting of the Ministers for the
armed forces then took over the government, the
other Cabinet ministers retaining their portfolios.
On Oct. 14, 1969, the Government decreed that
the President's period of office was terminated
owing to his incapacity through illness. Congress
re-assembled after being suspended since December,
1968, and elected Gen. Emílio Garrastazú Médici
President on Oct. 25, 1969. A new constitution had
been promulgated on Oct. 20, codifying the
extensive powers assumed by the régime since
December, 1968.

Production.—There are large and valuable
mineral deposits including among others, iron ore
(hematite), manganese, bauxite, beryllium, chrome,
nickel, tungsten, cassiterite, lead, gold, monazite

(containing rare earths and thorium) and zirconium. Diamonds and precious and semi-precious stones are also found. The mineral wealth is being exploited to an increasing but still limited extent. The iron ore deposits of Minas Gerais and the untapped ones of the Amazon region are particularly rich. Production is increasing all the time.

In 1970 9,686,000 cubic metres of oil was produced; 5,371,000 metric tons of steel ingots and 24,353,000 cubic metres of refined petroleum (including refining of imported oil).

Licences for new foreign investments amounting to U.S.$20,226,000 were issued in 1967–8, bringing the total since 1955 to U.S.$559,782,000.

In 1970 the Brazilian automobile industry produced 4,259 heavy lorries and buses; 58,431 light and medium weight trucks, 5,176 utility vehicles; 413,202 passenger vehicles and 14,097 tractors.

The main exports of agricultural produce in 1970 were:

	Metric Tons	Value $U.S.
Coffee..........	983,452	981,801,000
Cotton..........	343,000	154,434,000
Sugar..........	1,125,000	126,511,000
Cocoa..........	120,000	77,679,000

Coffee is grown mainly in the States of São Paulo and Paraná and to a lesser extent in Minas Gerais and Espírito Santo.

Defence.—The peace-time strength of the Army is 150,000 of which some 80 to 100,000 are doing military service, with an immediate reserve of 250,000. The Navy consists of 1 Aircraft Carrier, 2 Cruisers, 18 Destroyers and Escorts, 2 Submarines, 4 Minesweepers, 6 Survey Vessels, 10 Corvettes (tugs) and 4 naval transports. The strength of the Navy is 55,000 including marines. The Marine Corps strength is over 10,000. The Air Force, with a strength of 35,000, including approximately 1,500 pilots and aircrew, has 600 aircraft and is the largest in South America.

Education.—*Primary* education is compulsory and is the responsibility of State governments and municipalities. At this level approximately 12 per cent. attend private schools. In 1968, 11,943,506 children were enrolled in primary schools of all types.

Secondary education is largely the responsibility of the State and Municipal Governments, although a small number of very old foundations (the Pedro II Schools) remain under direct Federal control. Over 50 per cent. of all pupils at this level attend Private Schools.

In 1968 a total of 3,205,689 pupils were enrolled in all types of Secondary School—2,404,614 following the basic 4 year course and 801,075 the 3 year superior course leading to university entrance standard.

In 1968 a total of 278,295 students enrolled for courses in 37 Federal and State Universities and other establishments offering courses at university level. In 1968 there were a total of 1,880 Faculties half of which were within universities, the remainder being independent. Of this grand total, 840 were privately run.

Language and Literature.—Portuguese is the language of the country, but Italian, Spanish, German, Japanese and Arabic are spoken by immigrant minorities, and newspapers of considerable circulation are produced in those languages. English and French are currently used by educated Brazilians.

Until the second quarter of the nineteenth century Brazilian literature was dominated by Portugal. French influence is traceable for the next half century, since when a national school has come into existence and there are many modern authors of high standing. Public libraries have been established in urban centres and there is a flourishing national press with widely circulated daily and weekly newspapers.

Communications.—In 1970 there were about 32,015 kilometres of railways in service, largely of 1 metre gauge, but including 3,880 kilometres of other gauges. Traffic carried in 1969 was—Passengers 303,442,000; Freight 31,620,000 metric tons. During 1969, the ports of Brazil were used by 41,042 vessels, shipping a total of 72,591,000 tons.

Varig of Brazil and nine foreign airlines operate services between Brazil and Europe, 3 between Brazil and U.S.A., and there are connections with all Latin American countries. Eight major domestic airlines, as well as the Brazilian Air Force, maintain services throughout the country. During 1970, more than 4 million passengers passed through Brazilian airports; 34 m. kg of cargo were transported and 3m. kg. of mail. The airports of Rio de Janeiro and São Paulo alone handled 2 million passenger arrivals and departures in 1968.

Postal facilities in Brazil include approximately 4,042 post offices and 50,000 miles of telegraph. In 1969, 1,667,225 telephones were in use, of which a large proportion are dial operated.

FINANCE

	1969 Cruzeiros '000	1970 Cruzeiros '000
Revenue.........	14,162,000	19,194,000
Expenditure......	14,812,000	19,932,000

The total internal debt of the Federative Republic at the end of 1968 amounted to NCr$ 3,300,000,000; the States' debt was NCr$ 1,200,000,000. From December, 1968, to March, 1971, the dollar exchange rate rose from Cr$3·38 to Cr$5·11 or Cr$12·5=£1.

TRADE (1968)

Total Imports.............	$U.S.2,840,000,000
Total Exports.............	$U.S.2,711,000,000

Trade with U.K.

	1969	1970
Imports from U.K. .	£43,235,000	£60,769,000
Exports to U.K.....	50,716,000	62,784,000

The principal imports in 1969 and 1970 were machinery and aircraft, foodstuffs, raw materials, oil and chemicals, and manufactured goods. Principal exports were coffee, manufactured goods, iron ore and other minerals, foodstuffs and fruits.

CAPITAL.—Brasilia (inaugurated on April 21, 1960). Population (estimated 1970), 544,862. Other important centres are São Paulo (5,901,553); the former capital Ψ Rio de Janeiro (4,296,782); Ψ Belo Horizonte (1,232,708); Ψ Recife (1,078,819); Ψ Salvador (1,000,647); Ψ Porto Alegre (885,567); and Ψ Fortaleza (842,231).

FLAG.—Green, with yellow lozenge in centre; blue sphere with white band and stars in centre of lozenge.

NATIONAL DAY.—September 7 (Independence Day).

BRITISH EMBASSY.

Rio de Janeiro; and Avenida das Nações, Lote 8, Brasilia, D.F.

Residence, Rua São Clemente 360.

Chancery, Praia do Flamengo 284, 2° andar.

Ambassador Extraordinary and Plenipotentiary, His Excellency Sir David Wathen Stather Hunt, K.C.M.G., O.B.E. (1969)..................£9,000

Minister (Commercial), R. M. John.

Counsellors, A. Brooke-Turner; J. J. Scott.

1st Secretaries C. H. Seaward (*Head of Chancery*); R. L. Joseph (*Information*); M. F. Daly (*Commercial*); W. G. E. Beckmann, O.B.E. (*Consul*); R. A. Wellington, D.S.O., D.F.C.

2nd Secretaries, O. E. Goddard (*Commercial*); Miss I. Stoate; K. Green (*Consular*); R. Westbrook; A. S. Quinn.
Defence and Military Attaché, Col. D. M. Haslehurst.
Naval and Air Attaché, Capt. J. C. Brandt, R.N.
Attachés, M. R. Haselip; M. N. Napier; K. Farnworth; A. T. R. Oaten.

Avenida das Nações, Lote 8, Brasilia.
1st Secretary, R. G. Tallboys.
Attachés, C. A. Gregg; W. Fern.

BRITISH CONSULAR OFFICES
There are British Consular Offices at *Rio de Janeiro, São Paulo, Belém (Para), Belo Horizonte, Vitória, Salvador (Bahia), Manàus, Fortaleza, Pôrto Alegre, Rio Grande, Santos* and *Recife*.

BRITISH COUNCIL.—*Representative in Brazil*, P. R. V. Deed, O.B.E., Avenida Portugal 360, Rio de Janeiro. Offices in *Brasilia, Curitiba* and *São Paulo*. Book supply to libraries of *Sociedade Brasiliera de Cultura Inglesa* at *Rio de Janeiro* and *São Paulo*.

BRITISH AND COMMONWEALTH CHAMBER OF COMMERCE IN SÃO PAULO, Rua Barão de Itapetininga 275, Caixa Postal 1621, São Paulo. (Correspondents at *Santos* and *Porto Alegre*).

Rio de Janeiro, 5,750 miles distant from London: transit, 15 days.

BULGARIA
(Bulgariya)
COUNCIL OF STATE
Chairman of the Council of State, Todor Zhivkov, elected July 7, 1971 (*Head of State*).
First Deputy Chairman, Krustio Trichkov.
Deputy Chairmen, Georgi Andreev; Peko Takov; Georgi Dzhagarov.
Secretary, Mincho Minchev.

COUNCIL OF MINISTERS
Chairman, Stanko Todorov.
First Deputy Chairmen, Tano Tsolov; Peter Tanchev.
Deputy Chairman, Pencho Kubadinski; Zhirko Zhivkov; Prof. Ivan Popov; Sava Dulbokov; Prof. Mako Dakov.
Minister of National Education, Prof. Stefan Vassilev.
National Defence, Dobri Dzhurov (*Army General*).
Internal Trade and Services, Georgi Karamanev.
Foreign Trade, Ivan Nedev.
Light Industry, Dora Belcheva.
Transport, Gregor Stoichkov.
Foreign Affairs, Ivan Bashev.
Internal Affairs, Col. Gen. Angel Tsanev.
Information and Communications, Haralambi Traikov.
Agriculture and Food Industry, Vulkan Shopov.
Forests and Nature Preservation, Yanko Markov.
Machine Building, Prof. Ivan Popov.
Supply and State Reserves, Nikolai Zhisher.
Public Health, Dr. Angel Todorov.
Heavy Industry, Eng. Hristo Penayotov.
Building and Building Materials, Eng. Stamen Stamenov.
Architecture and Public Works, Arch. Georgi Stoilov.
Finance, Dimiter Popov.
Justice, Svetla Daskalova.
Labour and Social Welfare, Misho Mishev.
Chairmen of Committees, Sava Dulbokov (*State Planning*); Ninko Stefanov (*State Control*); Pavel Matev (*Art and Culture*); Nacho Papazov (*Science, Technical Progress and Higher Education*).

THE COMMUNIST PARTY
The Politbureau of the Central Committee, B. Balgaranov; Ts. Dragoycheva; P. Kubadinski; I. Mikhailov; T. Pavlov; I. Popov; S. Todorov; B. Velchev; T. Zhivkov; Zh. Zhivkov; T. Zolov (*full members*); I Abadzhiev; K. Gyaurov; P. Takov; K. Trichov; A. Tsanev; V. Kotsev. (*alternate members*).
The Secretariat of the Central Committee, Todor Zhivkov (*1st*); V. Kotsev; I. Pramov; B. Velchev; I. Abadzhiev; G. Filipov; P. Kiratsov.

BULGARIAN EMBASSY AND CONSULATE IN LONDON
12 Queen's Gate Gardens, S.W.7.
[01–584–9400]
Ambassador Extraordinary and Plenipotentiary, His Excellency Mitko Grigorov (1969).
Counsellors, Ivan Moutafchiev; Maurice Assa (*Commercial*).
Military, Naval and Air Attaché, Lt.-Col. Dimitar Stefanov Simov.
1st Secretary, Vladimir Pchelarov (*Economic*).
2nd Secretary, Tchavdar Damianov (*Cultural Affairs*).
3rd Secretaries, Zhivko Popov (*Consular*); Vladimir Velchev (*Press*).

The Republic of Bulgaria is bounded on the north by Rumania, on the west by Yugoslavia, on the east by the Black Sea, and on the south by Greece and Turkey. The total area is approximately 43,000 square miles, with a population in December, 1970, of 8,524,000. The largest religion of the Bulgarians is the Bulgarian Orthodox Church. The Gregorian (Western) Calendar is in use.

A Principality of Bulgaria was created by the *Treaty of Berlin* (July 13, 1878) and in 1885 Eastern Roumelia was added to the newly-created principality. In 1908 the country was declared to be an independent kingdom, the area at that date being 37,202 square miles, with a population of 4,337,500. In 1912–13 a successful war of the *Balkan League* against Turkey increased the size of the kingdom, but in August, 1913, a short campaign against the remaining members of the League reduced the acquired area, and led to the surrender of Southern Dobrudja to Rumania. On Oct. 12, 1915, Bulgaria entered the War on the side of the Central Powers by declaring war on Serbia. She thus became involved in the defeats of 1918 and, on Sept. 29, 1918, made an unconditional surrender to the Allied Powers. On Nov. 29, 1919, she signed the *Treaty of Neuilly*, which ceded to the Allies her Thracian territories (later handed over to Greece) and some territory on the western frontier to Yugoslavia.

Nazi troops entered the country on March 3, 1941, and occupied Black Sea ports, but Bulgaria was not officially at war with the Soviet Union. On August 26, 1944, the government declared Bulgaria to be "neutral in the Russo-German war" and delegates to Cairo sought terms of peace from Great Britain and the United States. The Soviet Union refused to recognize the so-called "neutrality" and called upon Bulgaria to declare war against Germany, and no satisfactory reply being received on Sept. 5, 1944, the U.S.S.R. declared war on Bulgaria. Bulgaria then asked for an armistice and on Sept. 7 declared war on Germany, hostilities with U.S.S.R. ending on Sept. 10. The armistice with the Allies was signed in Moscow, Oct. 28. On Sept. 9 a *coup d'état* gave power to the Fatherland Front, a coalition of Communists, Agrarians, Social Democrats and Republican officers and intellectuals. In August, 1945, the main body of Agrarians and Social Democrats left the Government. The Peace Treaty with Bulgaria was signed on Feb. 22, 1947, and came into force on Sept. 15, 1947. It recognized the return of Southern Dobrudja to Bulgaria.

On Sept. 8, 1946, a referendum was held, at which, according to the published results, an overwhelming majority declared for the abolition of the Monarchy and the setting up of a Republic. On Oct. 27, a general election to a Grand National Assembly (with power to make a constitution) was held; the Opposition won 101 seats out of 465.

On May 16, 1971 a referendum was held, at which a new Constitution was adopted. According to the Constitution the legislature is a single chamber National Assembly or *Subranie* elected by adult suffrage for a maximum term of 5 years and consisting of 400 deputies representing constituencies of equal size. The 1971 Constitution also established the Council of State, being the supreme permanent body of the National Assembly with both legislative and executive functions. The opposition Agrarian Party was suppressed in 1947, but its remnant was later revived as the Agrarian Union which now constitutionally shares power with the Communist Party.

Production.—Until 1939 Bulgaria was a predominantly agricultural country, but has since pursued an elaborate programme of industrialization. About 90 per cent. of the country's agriculture has been turned over to co-operatives, and a smaller proportion mechanized. The principal crops are wheat, maize, beet, tomatoes, tobacco, oleaginous seeds, fruit, vegetables and cotton. The livestock includes cattle, sheep, goats, pigs, horses, asses, mules and water buffaloes.

There is now a substantial engineering industry producing *inter alia* machine tools, electric trucks of all kinds, agricultural machinery, cranes, electric motors and electronic components, which accounts for about a third of Bulgaria's exports; and considerable production of lead, zinc and copper (1970, 98,100 tons; 76,100 tons and 42,000 tons respectively). Also in 1970 a production of 19,500,000 kW of electricity, 1,800,000 tons of steel, 31,389,000 tons of coal (of which a large proportion is soft coal) was claimed.

There are mineral deposits of varying importance. Bulgaria's heavy industry includes the Kremikovtsi Metallurgical Plant near Sofia, whose first blast furnace, with an annual output of 560,000 tons, was put into operation in 1963, the petrochemical plant at Burgas with an annual capacity of 6 million tons of processed oil (not yet reached in production), a nitrogenous fertilizer plant, and other chemical and metallurgical works.

Defence.—Under the Peace Treaty signed between Bulgaria and the Allies, the Bulgarian Army is limited to 55,000 men, but it is believed at present to be at least 154,000 strong.

Education.—Free basic education is compulsory for children from 7 to 15 years inclusive. The Bulgarian educational system was reorganized on Soviet lines in September, 1950, and in 1968–69 there were 1,468 elementary schools (Grades I–IV), 98 preparatory schools (Grades IV–VIII), 2,902 primary schools (Grades I–VIII), 135 grammar schools (gymnasia), 138 complete secondary schools (Grades I–XI) and 332 vocational training schools; there were 1,560,710 pupils and 81,195 teachers. A reform programme is in progress which includes the lowering of the school age to 6 years and compulsory secondary education.

Bulgaria has one university at Sofia, 26 institutes of higher education and 16 teacher-training and other specialist colleges. In 1971 there were 89,334 students at higher educational establishments.

Language and Literature.—Bulgarian is a Southern Slavonic tongue, closely allied to Serbo-Croat and Russian (*see* U.S.S.R.) with local admixtures of modern Greek, Albanian and Turkish words. There is a modern literature chiefly educational and popular. The alphabet is Cyrillic. In 1967 there were 8 daily newspapers in Sofia.

Finance.—Budget revenue in 1970 was estimated at *leva* 5,226,976,000; expenditure *leva* 5,158,399,000. Currency of Bulgaria is the *lev*. For 1971 rate of exchange, *see* p. 83.

TRADE

The principal imports are industrial and agricultural machinery, industrial raw materials, machine tools, chemicals, dyestuffs, drugs, rubber, paper. The principal exports are cereals, tobacco, fruit, vegetables, livestock, oil seeds, oils, fats, textiles, eggs, chemicals, essential oils including attar of roses, hardwoods, non-ferrous metals, electric trucks and motors, pumps, ships, accumulators and simple machine tools. In 1970, just under 80 per cent. of Bulgaria's foreign trade was with the Soviet bloc, including 55 per cent. with the Soviet Union.

Trade with U.K.

	1969	1970
Imports from U.K.	£4,936,000	£11,118,000
Exports to U.K.	7,333,000	8,307,000

CAPITAL.—Sofia, Pop. (1970), 868,200, at the foot of the Vitosha Range, the capital and commercial centre, is on the main railway line to Istanbul, 338 miles from the Black Sea port of ΨVarna (219,000) and 125 miles from Lom (23,015), on the Danube; ΨBurgas (171,300) is also a Black Sea Port, those on the Danube being ΨRusé (149,600), ΨSvishtov (18,537), Ψ Vidin (23,984). Other important trading and industrial centres are Plovdiv (247,500) Pleven, (57,758) and Stara Zagova (109,000).

FLAG.—3 horizontal bands, white, green, red; national emblem on white stripe near hoist.

NATIONAL DAY.—Sept. 9 (Day of Freedom).

BRITISH EMBASSY

Residence, 69 Boulevard Tolbuhin, Sofia.

Ambassador Extraordinary and Plenipotentiary, His Excellency Donald Arthur Logan, C.M.G. (1970)
£6,875

1st Secretaries, D. K. Jimms (*Consul and Head of Chancery*); G. Feast (*Commercial*).

Defence, Naval and Military Attaché, Lt.-Col. J. Talbot.

2nd Secretary, P. J. Priestley.

3rd Secretary, E. A. Burner.

BURMA
(Republic of the Union of Burma)
Revolutionary Government
Chairman and Member for Defence, General Ne Win.

———

BURMESE EMBASSY AND CONSULATE
19A Charles St., Berkeley Square, W.1.
[01-499-8841]
Ambassador Extraordinary and Plenipotentiary, U.
Chit Myaing (1970).

Area and Population.—Burma forms the western
portion of the Indo-Chinese district of the continent of Asia, lying between 9° 58′ and 28° N.
latitude and 92° 11′ and 101° 9′ E. longitude, with
an extreme length of approximately 1,200 miles
and an extreme width of 575 miles. It has a sea
coast on the Bay of Bengal to the south and west
and a frontier with Pakistan along the Naaf River,
defined in 1964 by a Memorandum of Agreements,
and India to the north-west defined in 1967; in the
north and east the frontier with China was determined by a treaty with the People's Republic in
October, 1960, and has since been demarcated;
there is a short frontier with Laos in the east, while
the long finger of Tenasserim stretches southward
along the west coast of the Malay Peninsula, forming a frontier with Thailand to the east. (*For* MAP,
see p. 746). The total area of the Union is about
262,000 square miles, with an officially estimated
population of 27,584,000 in 1970—about 105 persons
to the square mile.

Political Divisions.—The Union of Burma comprises Burma proper (at about 145,000 sq. miles by
far the largest unit), administered direct by the
Central Government, and also the Shan State (60,155
sq. miles),Kachin State (34,379 sq. miles), Kawthoolei
(formerly Karen) State (11,731 sq. miles) and Kayah
State (4,529 sq. miles) each with its own State
Government. There is also the Special Division
of the Chins (13,907 sq. miles).

Physical Features.—Burma falls into four natural
divisions, Arakan (with the Chin Hills region),
the Irrawaddy basin, the old Province of Tenasserim, including the Salween basin and extending
southwards to the Burma-Siam peninsula, and the
elevated plateau on the east made up of
the Shan States. Mountains enclose Burma on
three sides, the highest point being Hka-kabo Razi
(19,296 ft.) in the northern Kachin hills. Mt.
Popa, 4,981 ft., in the Myingyan district is an
extinct volcano and a well-known landmark in
Central Burma. The principal river systems are
the Kaladan-Lemro in Arakan, the Irrawaddy-
Chindwin and the Sittang in Central Burma, and
the Salween which flows through the Shan Plateau.

Races, Language and Religions.—The indigenous
inhabitants who entered Burma from the north and
east are of similar racial types and speak languages
of the Tibeto-Burman, Mon-Khmer and Thai
groups. The three important non-indigenous elements are Indians, Chinese and Pakistanis. Numbers of resident foreigners have shown a sharp
decline in recent years. Burmese is the official
language, but minority languages include Shan,
Karen, Chin, and the various Kachin dialects.
English is still spoken in educated circles in Rangoon
and elsewhere. Buddhism is the religion of 85 per
cent. of the people, with 5 per cent. Animists, 4 per
cent. Moslems, 4 per cent. Hindus and rather less
than 3 per cent. Christians.

Government.—Burma became an independent
republic outside the British Commonwealth on
January 4, 1948 and remained a parliamentary
democracy for some 14 years.

On March 2, 1962, the army staged a *coup
d'état*, abolished parliament, suspended the Constitution and imprisoned most of the Cabinet, all of
whom were later released. The Revolutionary
Council of senior officers under General Ne Win
have since taken a number of measures to establish
state socialism in Burma in line with the policy
statement " The Burmese Way to Socialism ". A
new political party, the Burma Socialist Programme
Party, was established to take the lead in Burma's
future policies. The problem of insurgency
(minority and Communist groups) remains an
important one for the country.

Education.—The literacy rate is high compared
with other Asiatic countries, there is no caste
system and women engage freely in social intercourse and play an important part in agriculture and
retail trade.

Under the University Education Law of 1964, the
Government reorganized the higher education
system to encourage the expansion of medical and
technical studies. The four existing Universities
(Rangoon, Mandalay, Moulmein and Bassein) have
been decentralized and the faculties of Medicine (at
present there are 2 Medical Institutes in Rangoon
and one in Mandalay), Economics, Engineering,
Agriculture, Veterinary Science and Education have
been reconstituted as independent Institutes. The
remaining faculties are grouped together as the
Arts & Science University of the city concerned.

There are teachers' training colleges in Rangoon,
Moulmein and Mandalay which train junior assistant teachers and 13 State Teachers Training Institutes for primary assistant teachers. The Institute
of Education in Rangoon trains senior assistant
teachers and awards degrees. There are three
Government technical institutes at Insein (near
Rangoon), Mandalay and Kalaw. There are 5
technical high schools, 2 in Rangoon, 1 in Mandalay
1 in Maymo and 1 in Taunggyi. Under the
Colombo Plan, New Zealand financed the construction of a school at Taunggyi at a cost of
£100,000 sterling and Britain provided the school
with equipment valued at £45,000. British aid to
Burma under the Colombo Plan amounts to some
£300,000 annually, over half of this being devoted
to technical assistance awards,

Finance.—The chief sources of revenue are profits
on state trading, income-tax, customs duties, commercial taxes and excise duties; the chief heads of
expenditure are general administration, defence,
education, police and development. The budget
estimates for 1970–71 were: Revenue,
K.8,840,000,000; Expenditure, K.9,036,000,000.

Production, Industry and Commerce.—Three-
quarters of the population depend on agriculture;
the chief products are rice, oilseeds (sesamum and
groundnut), maize, millet, cotton, beans, wheat,
grain, tea, sugarcane, Virginia and Burmese tobacco,
jute and rubber. Rice has traditionally been the
mainstay of Burma's economy but world market
conditions have altered in recent years so that the
relative importance of this crop as an export earner
continues to decline. Exports in 1969–70 amounted to 627,000 tons, including by-products.

The net area sown to all crops in 1969–70 was
19,000,000 acres and reserved forests covered
22,000,000 acres. The principal export after rice is
teak, of which some 200,000 tons were exported
annually before the war. The 1969–70 figure was
114,000 tons.

Burma is rich in minerals, including petroleum,
lead, silver, tungsten, zinc, tin, wolfram and gem-
stones. Of these, petroleum products are the most
important. Oil is now being produced from oilfields in Myanaung, Prome and Shwepyitha and at
Chauk and Yenangyaung. Production of crude oil
in 1969–70 totalled 200,000,000 gallons. There is a
refinery at the main oilfield, Chauk, and another at
Syriam near Rangoon. Their combined output of

petroleum products is sufficient for most of Burma's needs. The production and distribution of petroleum and the importation of oil products is a monopoly of Myanna Oil Corporation (formerly Burmah Oil Company (1954), Ltd.) which is owned by the Government of Burma.

Under the Government's development plan, a cement plant, a brick and tile factory, a steel rolling mill, a jute bag and twine mill, two cotton spinning and weaving mills, a pharmaceutical plant, a large hydro-electric scheme and three sugar factories are in production. West German soft loans have been made available to finance construction of a glass factory, a fertilizer plant and a textile mill; as well as a seismic survey for crude oil sources and technical assistance in the general field of mineral exploitation.

Japan will continue to contribute substantial sums to Burma's development until 1976 under the terms of a technical and economic co-operation agreement. Separate loans for specific projects have also been negotiated.

Burma joined the Colombo Plan in 1952 and is now receiving important assistance from member countries and through the specialized agencies of the United Nations.

Trade with U.K.

	1969	1970
Imports from U.K. .	£6,760,000	£6,346,000
Exports to U.K.	3,055,000	4,274,000

Communications.—The Irrawaddy and its chief tributary, the Chindwin, form important waterways, the main stream being navigable beyond Bhamo (900 miles from its mouth) and carrying much traffic.

¶ The chief seaports are Rangoon, Moulmein, Akyab and Bassein. Transit from London to Rangoon: by sea, 35 days; by air, 16 hours.

The Burma Railways network covers 2,588 route miles, extending to Myitkyina, on the Upper Irrawaddy. The first diesel locomotives were introduced in 1958 and there are now 87 diesel locomotives in service. There were 2,452 miles of Union highways and 5,734 miles of other main roads in 1969–70. Since the war a considerable network of internal air services has come into being. The airport at Mingaladon, about 9 miles north of Rangoon, has been reconstructed and handles international traffic.

CAPITAL.—The chief city of Lower Burma, and the seat of the government of the Union is Rangoon, on the left bank of the Rangoon river, about 21 miles from the sea. The city contains the Shwe Dagon pagoda, much venerated by Burmese Buddhists. Population (1970), 1,758,731.

Mandalay, the chief city of Upper Burma, had a population of 360,000 in 1969, Moulmein of 156,968 and Bassein of 90,006 (1966). Pagan, on the Irrawaddy, S.W. of Mandalay, contains many sacred buildings of interest to antiquaries.

FLAG.—The Union flag is red, with a canton of blue bearing a large white five-pointed star surrounded by 5 smaller stars.

NATIONAL DAY.—January 4.

BRITISH EMBASSY
(80 Strand Road, Rangoon.)
Ambassador Extraordinary and Plenipotentiary, His Excellency Edward Gervase Willan, C.M.G. (1970). £6,925
1st Secretaries, H. E. Rigney (*Head of Chancery and Consul*); W. L. Ward; W. B. J. Dobbs (*Commercial*).
2nd Secretaries, D. Rees (*Information and Colombo Plan*); Miss G. A. Robertson (*Consular*).

BURUNDI
(Republic of Burundi)

President, Col. Micombero Michel, *assumed office*, Nov. 28, 1966.

Formerly a Belgian trusteeship under the United Nations, Burundi was proclaimed an independent State on July 1, 1962. Situated on the east side of Lake Tanganyika, the State has an area of 10,747 sq. miles and a population (estimated, 1969) of 3,475,000. There are some 2,500 Europeans and 1,500 Asians. The population is mainly of the Bahutu and Batutsi tribes.

Burundi became independent as a Constitutional monarchy, but this was overthrown on November 28, 1966. The Constitution and Parliament were also abolished. The President rules through a Cabinet of Ministers and the UPRONA party apparatus. All the Governors of the eight Provinces are Army officers. Burundi is a one-Party State.

The chief crop is coffee, representing about 80 per cent. of Burundi's export earnings, some 87 per cent. of which is exported to the United States. Cotton is the second most important crop. Minerals and hides and skins exports are also important. Joint economic arrangements of Burundi with Rwanda ended in 1964 and each country now has its own national bank, coffee organization, etc.

The currency is the Burundi *Franc*. The rate of exchange is *Fr. Bu.* 210=£1. Government expenditure in 1967 amounted to *Fr. Bu.* 1,650,000,000 and revenue *Fr. Bu.* 1,550,000,000.

CAPITAL.—Bujumbura (*jormerly* Usumbura), with about 70,000 inhabitants. Gitega (7,000 inhabitants) is the only other sizeable town. Official languages are Kirundi, a Bantu language, and French. Kiswahili is also used.

FLAG.—White diagonal cross on green and red quarters, with a circular white panel in the centre.

NATIONAL DAY.—July 1.

British Ambassador, His Excellency Mark Echalaz Allen, C.M.G., C.V.O. (1971) (*resident at* Kinshasa, Congolese Republic).
Hon. British Consul, J. Hussey, P.O. Box 1750, Bujumbura.

CAMEROON REPUBLIC
(Federal Republic of Cameroon)

President, Ahmadou Ahidjo, *elected for* 5 *years*, May 5, 1960; *re-elected for* 5 *years*, May 7, 1965 and Mar. 20, 1970.

Vice-President, Solomon Tandeng Muna.

CAMEROON EMBASSY
84 Holland Park, W.11.
[01–727–0771]
Ambassador Extraordinary and Plenipotentiary, His Excellency Lucas Zaa Nkweta (1965).
Counsellors, P. T. Biloa; J. B. Etame (*Commercial*); E. D. Quan (*Cultural*).

The Federal Republic of Cameroon lies on the Gulf of Guinea between Nigeria to the west, Chad and the Central African Republic to the east and Congo and Gaboon to the south. (*For* MAP, *see* p. 836). It has an area of 183,381 sq. miles (432,000 sq. km.) and a population estimated (1970) at 5,836,000. Principal products of East Cameroon are cocoa, coffee, bananas, cotton, timber, groundnuts and aluminium; of West Cameroon, bananas, rubber, timber, cocoa and palm products. There is an aluminium smelting plant at Edéa in East Cameroon with an annual capacity of 50,000 tons. Annual trade of the Federal Republic is approximately, Exports, £88,000,000; Imports, £80,000,000.

Trade with U.K.

	1969	1970
Imports from U.K.....	£3,696,000	£3,728,000
Exports to U.K........	2,247,000	2,081,000

The whole territory was administered by Germany from 1884 to 1916. From 1916 to 1959, present-day East Cameroon was administered by France as a League of Nations (later U.N.) trusteeship. On Jan. 1, 1960 it became independent as the Republic of Cameroon. The Republic was joined on October 1, 1961, by the former British administered trust territory of the Southern Cameroons (now West Cameroon), after a plebiscite held under United Nations auspices. The Federal government consists of President, Vice-President and 19 Federal Ministers. There are separate East and West Cameroon state governments.

CAPITAL. — Yaoundé (180,000). Ψ Douala (250,000), is an important commercial centre.

FLAG.—Vertical stripes of green, red and yellow with two five-pointed stars in upper half of green band.

NATIONAL DAY.—January 1 (Independence Day).

BRITISH EMBASSY
Yaoundé.

Ambassador Extraordinary and Plenipotentiary, His Excellency Anthony Arthur Golds, C.M.G., M.V.O. (1970) £6,925
1st Secretary, P. J. Barlow.
2nd Secretaries, R. G. Hyde; O. M. O'Brien.
3rd Secretaries, I. McCrory; N. A. Thorne.
British Council Representative, K. Westcott.

CENTRAL AFRICAN REPUBLIC

President, Gen. Jean Bedel Bokassa, *assumed office,* Jan. 1, 1966.

Formerly the French colony of Ubanghi Shari, the Republic lies just north of the Equator between the Cameroon Republic and the southern part of Sudan. It has a common boundary with the Republic of Chad in the north and with the Congolese Republic in the south. The Republic has an area of about 234,000 sq. miles and a population of 2,255,536 (Census of 1968). On December 1, 1958, Ubanghi Shari elected to remain within the French Community and adopted the title of the Central African Republic. It became fully independent on August 17, 1960. The first President of the Central African Republic, M. David Dacko, held office from 1960 until Jan. 1, 1966, when he was replaced by the then Col. Bokassa after a *coup d'état.* Imports from U.K., 1970, £281,000; Exports to U.K., £585,000.

CAPITAL.—Bangui, near the border with the Congolese Republic (301,793).

FLAG.—Four horizontal stripes, blue, white, yellow, green, crossed by central vertical red stripe; a yellow star in centre of blue half-stripe next staff.

CHAD REPUBLIC

President, François Tombalbaye, *elected* August 11, 1960, re-elected June, 1969.

Situated in north-central Africa, the Chad Republic extends from 23° N. latitude to 7° N. latitude and is flanked by the Republics of Niger

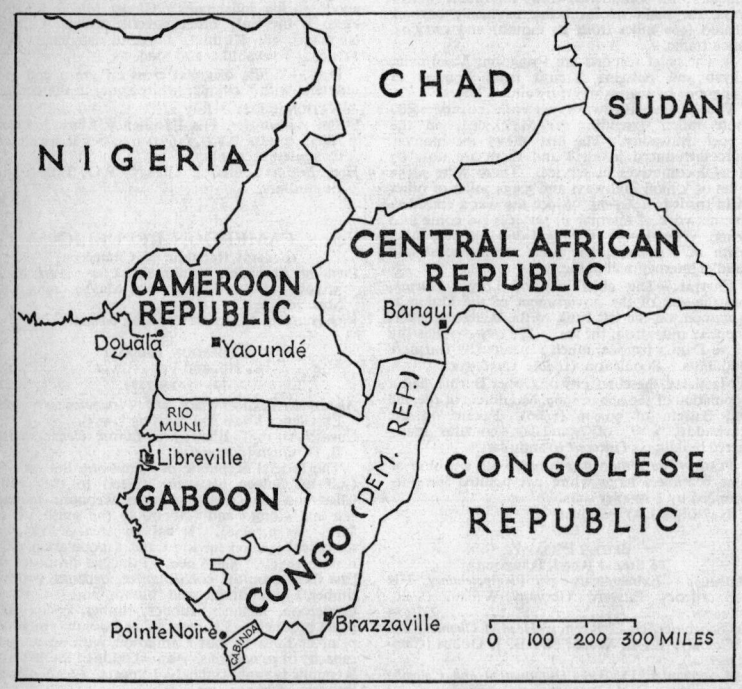

and Cameroon on the west, by the Kingdom of Libya in the north, by the Sudan on the east and by the Central African Republic on the south. (*For* MAP, *see* Index). It has an area of 487,920 sq. miles and a population (U.N. estimate, 1969) of 3,510,000. Chad became a member state of the French Community on Nov. 28, 1958, and was proclaimed fully independent on August 11, 1960. On April 14, 1962, a new Constitution was adopted involving a presidential-type régime. Mr. Tombalbaye accepting the formal title of President on April 23, 1962.

Imports from U.K. in 1970 were valued at £244,000.

CAPITAL.—Fort Lamy, south of Lake Chad (45,600).

FLAG.—Vertical stripes, blue, yellow and red.

CHILE
(República de Chile)

President (1970–76), Dr. Salvador Allende (Gossens), *born* 1908, *elected* Sept. 4, 1970; *assumed office* Nov. 3, 1970.

CABINET

Minister of Foreign Affairs, C. A. Medina (*SP*).
Interior, J. T. Gonzalez (*SP*).
Defence, A. R. Valdivia (*RP*).
Education, M. Astorga (*RP*)
Mines, O. Cantuarias (*RP*)
Agriculture, J. Conchol (*MAPU*).
Housing, C. Cortes (*SP*)
Labour, J. O. Jara (*CP*)
Public Works and Transport, P. Barraza (*CP*).
Finance, A. Z. Rojas (*CP*)
Justice, L. C. Ponce (*API*).
Health, O. J. Pinochet (*SD*).
Lands and Settlement, H. Mantones (*SD*).
Economic Affairs, P. V. Bravo (*IM*).
Minister without Portfolio, *Secretary-General to the Government*, J. S. Bastiadas (*SP*).

SP= Socialist Party; *CP*= Communist Party; *RP*=Radical Party; *SD*=Social Democratic Party; *MAPU*=Action Movement of Popular Unity; *API*=Independent Popular Action Party; *IM*=Independent Marxist.

CHILEAN EMBASSY AND CONSULATE IN LONDON
3 Hamilton Place, W.1.
[01–629–8382]

Ambassador Extraordinary and Plenipotentiary, His Excellency Sr. Alvaro Bunster (1971), 92 Eaton Place, S.W.1.
Minister-Counsellors, Sr. don Jorge Berguño; Sr. don Pedro Buttazzoni.
Counsellor (*Commercial*) Sr. Carlos Fortin.
Naval Attaché, Rear Adm. A. F. Walbaum (Naval Attachés Office : 01–629–8384).
Air Attaché, Col. J. L. Soier, M.V.O.
1st Secretary, Sr. Gonzalo Guerra.
2nd Secretary, Sr. don Juan Enrique Aguirre.
Asst. Naval Attaché, Capt. Carlos Le May; Cdr. Eduardo Angulo.
3rd Secretary, Sr. Herman Montealegre (Consular).
Civil Attachés, Rear-Adm. Don Calixto Rogers; Sr. Juan Allende.
Attachés, Srta. Loreto Herman (*Press*); Sr. Roberto Bravo (*Cultural*); Sr. Carlos Parra (*Legal*); Sr. Miguel Labarca (*Cultural*).

A State of South America, of Spanish origin, lying between the Andes and the shores of the South Pacific, extending coastwise from south north of Arica to Cape Horn south, between lat. 17° 15′ and 55° 59′ S., and long. 66° 30′ and 75° 48′ W. Extreme length of the country is about 2,800 miles, with an average breadth, north of 41°, of 100 miles. The great chain of the Andes runs along its eastern limit, with a general elevation of 5,000 to 15,000 feet above the level of the sea; but numerous summits

attain a greater height. The chain, however, lowers considerably towards its southern extremity. The Andes form a boundary with Argentina, and at the head of the pass where the international road from Chile to Argentina crosses the frontier, has been erected a statue of *Christ the Redeemer*, 26 feet high, made of bronze from old cannon, to commemorate the peaceful settlement of a boundary dispute in 1902. There are no rivers of great size, and none of them is of much service as a navigable highway. In the north the country is arid. (*For* MAP, *see* p. 821)

Among the island possessions of Chile are the *Juan Fernandez group* (3 islands) about 360 miles distant from Valparaiso, where a wireless station has been erected. One of these islands is the reputed scene of Alexander Selkirk's (Robinson Crusoe) shipwreck. *Easter Island* (27° 8′ S. and 109° 28′ W.), about 2,000 miles distant in the South Pacific Ocean, contains stone platforms and hundreds of stone figures, the origin of which has not yet been determined. The area of the island is about 45 sq. miles.

Chile is divided into 25 provinces and the total area of the Republic is estimated at 290,000 square miles, with a population (estimated, 1970) of 8,835,000. Two of these provinces, Arica and Antofagasta, were annexed from Peru and Bolivia respectively after the War of the Pacific (1879–84). The province of Tacna was also annexed but under a treaty signed in 1929 was returned to Peru which at the same time received payment of £1,200,000 for Arica. The Chilean population has four main sources: (*a*) Spanish settlers and their descendants; (*b*) indigenous Araucanian Indians, Fuegians, and Changos; (*c*) mixed Spanish Indians; and (*d*) European immigrants. Only the few remaining indigenous Indians and some originally Bolivian Indians in the north are racially separate. Following extensive inter-marriage there is no effective distinction among the remainder.

Government.—Chile was discovered by Spanish adventurers in the 16th century, and remained under Spanish rule until 1810, when a revolutionary war, culminating in the *Battle of Maipu* (April 5, 1818), achieved the independence of the nation. Under the present Constitution (Aug. 30, 1925), the President is elected by direct choice of all Chilean citizens who have the right to vote. The National Congress consists of a Senate of 50 members, and of a Chamber of 150 Deputies. There is universal suffrage for persons who have attained the age of 21, can read and write, and are on the electoral roll. Chilean women obtained equal voting rights with men on Dec. 21, 1948, before which they only participated in municipal elections.

At a general election held on Sept. 4, 1970, the Marxist candidate Dr. Allende was elected President by a narrow margin. A new Cabinet took office on Oct. 30, 1970 (*see* above).

Production.—About 25 per cent. of the working population is engaged in agriculture which however contributes only 8 per cent. of the country's gross domestic product. Manufacturing and mining, with about 21 and 4½ per cent. respectively of the active population, provide 25 and 11 per cent. of the G.D.P. Wheat, maize, barley, oats, beans, peas, rice, lentils, wines, tobacco, hemp, chili-pepper, potatoes, sugar beet, onions and melons are grown extensively and livestock accounts for some 40 per cent. of agricultural production. The vine and all European fruit-trees flourish in the central zone and fruit is an important export item. Good wines are produced and exported and are becoming more widely known in world markets. Sheep farming predominates in the extreme south (Province of

Magallanes). There are large timber tracts in the central and southern zones of Chile, some types of which are exported to Europe and the Argentine, but the high production costs have caused serious difficulties to this export trade. The mineral wealth is considerable, the country being particularly rich in copper-ore, iron-ore and nitrate. Uranium is also said to have been discovered in small quantities. Copper production in 1968 totalled 666,664 metric tons and extensive investments are being made to raise production to over 1,000,000 tons per annum. Copper provides 70 per cent. of Chile's export earnings, the remainder of which are derived mainly from other minerals, wool, fruit, fish and forestry derivatives. The rainless north is the scene of the only commercial production of nitrate of soda (Chile saltpetre) from natural resources in the world. Production in 1968 (including potassium nitrate) was 679,000 metric tons. Chile also produces iodine, manganese ore, coal, mercury, molybdenum, zinc, lead, and a small quantity of gold. 1,611,304 metric tons of coal, and 11,916,286 metric tons of iron ores were produced in 1968. The country has also large deposits of high grade sulphur, but mostly around high extinct volcanoes in the Andes Cordillera, difficult of access. Production of refined sulphur has hitherto been in relatively small quantities. Annual production is between 25,000 and 50,000 metric tons. Oil was struck in Magallanes (Tierra del Fuego) in December, 1945, and the industry is now self-supporting. Production in 1968 was 2,177,390 cubic metres of crude oil and 6,988,189,000 cu. metres of natural gas—all in the Magallanes area. This total production and some imported crude oil is refined at Concon and San Vicente in the central part of the country. A large steel plant was completed and started operation during 1950 at Huachipato, near Concepción. In 1968 the output of steel ingots from Huachipato totalled 525,818 metric tons.

Most consumer goods are manufactured locally—steel and oil derivatives, pulp and paper, cement and other building materials, tobacco, cutlery, food products and beverages, sugar refining, textiles, clothing and footwear, plastic products, household equipment, tyres and other rubber products, radio and television sets, chemicals, soaps, detergents and cosmetics. New classes of manufacture being developed are in the fields of motor-vehicle assembly, petrochemicals, cellulose, metallurgy and some electrical and mechanical equipment.

Communications.—Most of the country's commerce is distributed along its lengthy sea-board in Chilean ships, which have a virtual monopoly of cabotage, though, with the improvement of the roads, an increasing share of internal transportation is moving to road and rail. Foreign trade continues to be carried on mostly by foreign steamship lines operating either directly to the West Coasts of North and South America, or *viâ* the Panama Canal to Europe or *viâ* the Straits of Magellan. Chilean vessels have also been participating for many years in foreign trade with North America and Europe. The Chilean mercantile marine numbers about 60 vessels (of over 100 tons gross) with a total gross tonnage of about 400,000. Under a law promulgated in June, 1956, 50 per cent. of Chile's foreign trade must be carried by Chilean vessels.

The first railway was opened in 1851 and there are now 6,575 miles of track, of which 5,360 miles are State owned. A metre-gauge line (the *Longitudinal*) runs from La Calera, just north of Santiago, to Iquique. The wide gauge railway (1·676 metres) runs from Valparaiso through La Calera, 60 miles inland, and after passing through Santiago ends at Puerto Montt.

With the completion of a section of 435 miles from Corumba, Brazil, to Santa Cruz, Bolivia, the Trans-Continental Line will link the Chilean Pacific port of Arica with Rio de Janeiro on the Atlantic. Another line from Antofagasta to Salta (Argentine) was opened in 1948. Further south, the Trans-Andine Railway connects Valparaiso on the Pacific with Buenos Aires, crossing the Andes at 11,500 ft.

Chile is served by 15 international airlines. The domestic traffic is carried almost exclusively by the State-owned Linea Aerea Nacional, which also operates internationally. Chile has an extensive system of airports which are being modernized with U.S. financial assistance.

Chile's road system is about 65,000 kilometres in length, but only an estimated 6,000 kilometres are first-class paved highways. At the end of 1968 there were registered 130,225 cars and taxis, 12,614 buses and coaches and 111,721 goods vehicles.

Defence.—Military service is compulsory, but not all those who are liable are required. Recruitment for the Navy is voluntary. In 1966 the Army had 6 infantry divisions, 1 cavalry division and one armoured division with a total strength of 1,900 officers, 11,000 regular other ranks plus 18,000 conscripts. In addition there is a police force of "Carabineros" of 22,500 officers and men. The Air Force had 600 officers and 6,180 other ranks with a strength or 200 aircraft. The Navy consisted of 2 cruisers, 4 destroyers, 2 destroyer escorts, 2 submarines and 4 motor torpedo boats, all operational. There is a support force of transports, tankers, 1 submarine depôt ship and ancillary small craft. The strength of the Navy is 1,002 officers and 11,500 men, plus a Marine Force for coastal defence of 87 officers and 2,200 men.

Education.—Elementary education is free, and has been compulsory since 1920. There are 8 Universities (3 in Santiago, 2 in Valparaiso, 1 in Antofagasta, 1 in Concepción and 1 in Valdivia). The religion is Roman Catholic.

Language and Literature.—Spanish is the language of the country, with admixtures of local words of Indian origin. Recent efforts have reduced illiteracy and have thus afforded access to the literature of Spain, to supplement the vigorous national output. The Nobel Prize for Literature was awarded in 1945 to Señorita Gabriela Mistral, for Chilean verse and prose. There are over 100 newspapers and a large number of periodicals, including some devoted to professional, scientific and social subjects.

Finance.—Total revenue for 1969 was estimated at E° 12,058,587,962 and expenditure at E° 15,842,141,604. Foreign debt in 1969 was estimated at $U.S. 2,819,000,000.

The official rate of exchange, June 2, 1970, was about E° 28= £1 (banker's rate) and E° 33= £1 (brokers' rate).

EXTERNAL TRADE.

	(Final figures)	1968
Total imports	....	$U.S.742,743,000
Total exports	....	940,824,000

Trade with U.K.

	1969	1970
Imports from U.K.	£17,248,000	£20,519,000
Exports to U.K.	72,145,000	64,860,000

The principal exports are metallic and non-metallic minerals (refined copper, ingots and bars, iron ore, etc.), cereals, vegetables, fruit and wool. The principal imports are industrial oils, raw cotton, chemicals, wheat, meat, machinery, tools, electrical and transport equipment and sugar.

CAPITAL, Santiago (December, 1964) 2,100,000 (Greater Santiago). Other large towns are:— Ψ Valparaiso (261,684), Ψ Concepción (158,941),

Temuco (109,141), Viña del Mar (107,563), Chillán (79,461), Talca (75,354), Ψ Antofagasta (74,050), Ψ Valdivia (72,988), Ψ Talcahuano (75,643), Ψ Iquique (47,906), Ψ Punta Arenas (44,597). Punta Arenas, on the Straits of Magellan, is the southernmost city in the world.

FLAG.—2 horizontal bands, white, red; in top sixth a white star on blue square, next staff.

NATIONAL DAY.—September 18 (National Anniversary).

BRITISH EMBASSY.

Calle Bandera 227, Piso 3° Santiago (Casilla 72D).
Ambassador Extraordinary and Plenipoteniary, His Excellency David Henry Thoroton Hildyard, C.M.G., D.F.C. (1970).....................£6,925
1st Secretaries, G. R. Lee (Head of Chancery); W. R. McQuillan (Commercial); A. S. Dyer, O.B.E.; L. Borax, O.B.E. (Consul and Admin.).
Defence Attaché, Capt. F. G. Thatcher, R.N.
2nd Secretaries, K. F. Langham (Commercial); K. Heald (Information), H. McQuade.
3rd Secretary (Information), Miss I. M. Munro.

BRITISH CONSULAR OFFICES.

There are British Consular Offices at *Santiago, Antofagasta, Arica, Iquique, Valparaiso, Concepción, Coquimbo,* and *Punta Arenas.*

BRITISH COUNCIL

Representative in Chile, R. P. H. Davies, Calle Santa Lucía 124, Santiago.

The Council supplies books to the libraries of the *Instituto Chileno-Britanico* in Santiago and in *Viña del Mar/Valparaiso.*

Valparaiso is distant from London 9,000 miles *via* Panama, and 11,000 *via* the Strait; transit 28 to 45 days; by air, 22 hrs.

CHINA

(Zhonghua Renmin Gongheguo—
The People's Republic of China.)

Chairman of the People's Republic of China (vacant)
Vice-Chairmen, Sung Ch'ing-ling (*Mme.* Sun Yat-sen) Tung Pi-wu.
Chairman of the Standing Committee of the 2nd National People's Congress, Chu Teh.
Prime Minister, Chou En-Lai.
Minister of Foreign Affairs, Chi Peng-fei (*acting*).
Vice-Premier and Minister of Defence, Lin Piao.
Chairman of the Chinese Communist Party, Mao Tse-tung.

THE COMMUNIST PARTY

The Standing Committee of the Politbureau of the Central Committee (*elected at the IXth Party Congress in April, 1969*), Mao Tse-tung; Lin Piao; Chou En-lai; Chen Po-ta; K'ang-Sheng.
The Politbureau, Madame Lin Piao (Yeh Ch'un); Yeh Chien-ying; Liu Po-ch'eng; Madame Mao (Chiang Ch'ing); Chu Te; Hsü Shih-yu; Ch'en Hsi-lien; Li Hsien-nien; Li Tso-p'eng; Wu Fa-hsien; Chang Ch'un-ch'iao; Ch'iu Hui-tso; Yao Wen-yuan; Huang Yung-sheng; Tung Pi-wu; Hsieh Fu-chich (*full members*); Chi Teng-kuei; Li Te-sheng; Li Hsueh-feng; Wang Tung-hsing (*alternate members*).

LONDON OFFICE

31 Portland Place, W.1.
Chargé d'Affaires, Pei Tsien-chang.
AREA AND POPULATION.—The area of China is about 4,300,000 square miles. Estimates of the present population vary considerably, but a figure of more than 700,000,000 is generally accepted. According to figures published in 1957 by the

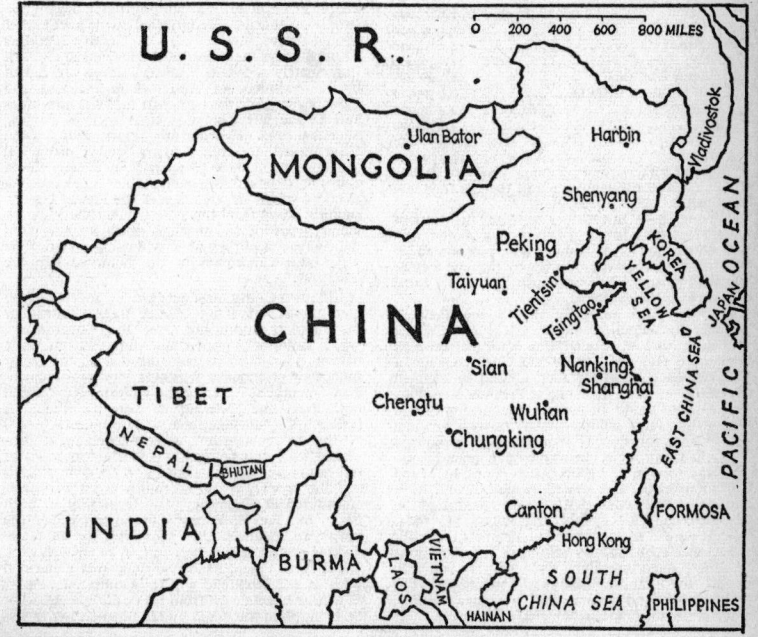

National Bureau of Statistics, the total population of China was 656,630,000, not including Chinese living in Hong Kong, Macau or abroad. Estimates (based on announcements made by the Chinese Revolutionary Committees) show a figure of 732,000,000 for mainland China. A birth-rate of 34 per 1,000 and death rate of 11 per 1,000 are quoted for 1957. In 1953 the percentage distribution of the population was as follows:

Han, 94·13; Mongolian, 0·26; Tibetan, 0·48; Manchu, 0·41; Tribal, 3·57; Others, 1·15. There is no reason to suppose that the proportions have significantly changed.

THE PROVINCES OF CHINA.

According to the National Bureau of Statistics the populations of the Chinese provinces at the end of 1957 were as follows:

Anhwei	33,560,000
Chekiang	25,280,000
Chinghai	2,050,000
Fukien	14,650,000
Heilungkiang	14,860,000
Honan	48,670,000
Hopei	44,720,000
Hunan	36,220,000
Hupeh	30,790,000
Kansu	12,800,000
Kiangsi	18,610,000
Kiangsu	45,230,000
Kirin	12,550,000
Kwangsi Chuang Autonomous Region	19,390,000
Kwangtung	37,960,000
Kweichow	16,890,000
Liaoning	24,090,000
Inner Mongolian Autonomous Region	9,200,000
Ningsia Autonomous Region	1,810,000
Shansi	15,960,000
Shantung	54,030,000
Shensi	18,130,000
Sinkiang Uighur Autonomous Region	6,640,000
Szechuan	72,160,000
Tibet	1,270,000
(Taiwan	10,100,000)
Yunnan	19,100,000

Sinkiang is the largest region or province in area (about 1/6th of the whole area of the country) and Szechuan the most populous.

Government.—On October 10, 1911, the party of reform forced the Imperial dynasty to a "voluntary" abdication, and a Republic was proclaimed at Wuchang. Events leading up to the end of the war with Japan are briefly described in earlier issues of WHITAKER'S ALMANACK.

On September 30, 1949, the Chinese People's Political Consultative Conference (C.P.P.C.C.) met in Peking and appointed the National People's Government Council under the Chairmanship of Mao Tse-tung. On October 1, Mao proclaimed the inauguration of the Chinese People's Republic. The Soviet Union broke off relations with the Nationalists and established relations with the new *régime* on October 2. The *régime* was recognized by all the Communist *bloc* countries in quick succession, and soon after by the Asian countries of the Commonwealth, the United Kingdom and by a number of other countries. France recognized the Chinese People's Republic on January 27, 1964. Canada agreed to recognize the People's Republic in October 1970, and by mid-1971, a further nine countries, including Italy and Austria, had also agreed to establish diplomatic relations. The United States and certain other countries continue to recognize the Nationalist *régime* in Formosa.

The C.P.P.C.C. continued to be the supreme legislative body of the new state until September 20, 1954, when a new constitution was adopted. It was then replaced as the highest organ of state power by the National People's Congress, which exercises legislative power. The Congress can amend the constitution and supervises its enforcement, enacts laws and decides on questions of war and peace. It approves the state budget and adopts the national economic plan. It elects and may remove from office the Chairman and Vice-Chairmen of the Republic. The National People's Congress is supposed to meet only once a year; between sessions its functions are exercised by its Standing Committee, a body made up of a Chairman, 13 Vice-Chairmen, the Secretary-General and more than 100 ordinary members.

With the adoption of the Constitution, the National People's Government Council was replaced by the State Council, composed of the Premier, 16 Vice-Premiers and the heads of ministries and commissions. This body is the supreme administrative body, responsible for the day-to-day running of the country.

Under the Constitution a complicated interlocking hierarchy exists from the bottom to the top. The National People's Congress is not directly elected, but is the peak of a pyramid. Direct elections occur only in rural districts, urban districts and small towns. Local Congresses have two main functions: (1) to appoint as their administrative arm a People's Council; and (2) to elect the next higher level congress, in this case County congresses or large town congresses. The County congresses have a similar twin function: to appoint County People's Councils and to elect the Provincial Congresses. The Provincial Congresses appoint Provincial People's Councils and elect the National People's Congress. The administrative organs, the People's Councils, are controlled by the next higher administrative organ (*e.g.* a County People's Council obeys the orders of the Provincial Council immediately above it). Complications are caused by the existence of Autonomous Regions and Counties set aside for particular national minorities and by the fact that large cities such as Peking, Shanghai and Tientsin are under the Central Government and other towns under provincial governments. Since Congresses meet only rarely and the Councils are responsible for arranging elections of the next Congress, the line of control running down from the State Council through the hierarchy of local Councils is much stronger than the expression of the public will rising up from the basic level Congresses to the National People's Congress.

China is a Communist state but the position of the Communist party is not reflected in the constitution. Its complete dominance over the Government, which includes "united-front" figures from lesser parties, is achieved by ensuring that all the really important positions at whatever level are filled by Party members. During the Cultural Revolution both Party and State organs were disrupted. A system of "Revolutionary Committees" was devised to replace the People's Councils at provincial level and below. These are composed of representatives of the armed forces, civil officials and the people. Party Committees are being reconstituted at all levels. The leadership in both Party and Revolutionary Committees is for the most part identical, thus providing for an interlocking relationship between the two bodies. Until April, 1959, Mao Tse-tung was Chairman both of the Republic and the Communist Party. When he stood down from his position as Head of State his place was taken by Liu Shao-ch'i who was

then First Vice-Chairman of the Party. In October 1968, the Party's Central Committee resolved to strip Liu of all his posts both in the Party and in the State. It has been announced that at an appropriate time a new National People's Congress is to be convened. The Congress is expected to approve a new State Constitution which should clarify the position of the Head of State and the system of government.

Armed Forces.—All three military arms in China are parts of the People's Liberation Army (P.L.A.) The size of this body has not been formally given, but it is estimated that China has between 2½ and 3 million men under arms, with a further 12 million (or perhaps many more) reserves who take part in militia activities. Until 1955 the P.L.A. did not have a rank structure, but one was introduced in that year similar to that of the Russian Army. In the same year compulsory military service was introduced for all men between the ages of 18 and 40. This service was on a selective basis. In January, 1965, the length of service for those conscripted was increased by one year, to four years for the Army, five years for the Air Force and six years for the Navy; and with effect from June 1, 1965, the rank structure was abolished, together with all marks of distinction of branch of service (although members of the services may still be distinguished from one another by the colour of their uniforms). This means a reversion to the previous system by which members of the armed forces are known only by their appointment.

China exploded her first experimental nuclear device on October 16, 1964 and made further tests in 1965 and in May, October and December, 1966. Her first hydrogen bomb was tested in June, 1967, and further tests of nuclear devices were detected up to October, 1970. China launched her first earth-satellite in April, 1970, and a second one in March, 1971.

Religion.—The indigenous religions of China are Confucianism (which includes ancestor worship), Taoism (originally a philosophy rather than a religion) and, since its introduction in the first century of the Christian era, Buddhism. There are also Chinese Moslems and Christians. Since 1949, the practice of all religions has been severely curtailed, although not actually prohibited.

Education.—Although primary education was compulsory under the Nationalists, mass education did not become a fact until after the Communists had taken over. All major educational establishments closed down at the start of the Great Proletarian Cultural Revolution in 1966. Primary and middle school education was interrupted and it was announced that the entire education system was to be reformed. School classes are being resumed, and, among the reforms observable are a reduction in the number of years in primary and middle schools, and the application of the principle of part-work part-study. In the summer of 1970 some of the major institutes of higher education started to enrol new students, and courses started in the autumn. Students are being selected from among workers, peasants, soldiers and also middle-school graduates who have had two–three years experience of manual labour in factories or in the rural areas. The new courses are from 2–3 years duration.

Language and Literature.—The Chinese language has many dialects, Cantonese, Hakka, Swatow, Foochow, Wenchos, Ning-po and Wu (Shanghai). The Common Speech or *Putonghua* (often referred to as " Mandarin ") which is being taught throughout the country is based on the Peking dialect. The Communists, when they came into power, continued the Kuomintang policy of promoting it as the national language and made much more intensive efforts to propagate it throughout the country. Since the most important aspect of this policy is the use of the spoken language in writing, the old literary style of writing has fallen into disuse.

Chinese writing is ideographic and not phonetic. The number of sounds in *Putonghua* is strictly limited; each sound may have a large number of different characters and meanings. Whereas originally the language was monosyllabic and confusion was avoided by the use of different characters, thus producing texts which were visually clear but ambiguous to the ear, with the increasing use of the spoken language for writing people are increasingly making use of polysyllabic compounds both in speech and writing in order to avoid confusion. In 1956, after some 4 years of study, the Government decided to introduce 230 simplified characters with a view to making reading and writing easier. The list was enlarged; there are now about 1,000 simplified characters in use. In January, 1956, all Chinese newspapers and most books began to appear with the characters printed horizontally from left to right, instead of vertically reading from right to left, as previously.

In November 1957, after some experimentation, the Government introduced a system of Romanization, using 25 of the letters of the Latin alphabet (not v). This has been used within the country largely for assisting school children and others to learn the pronunciation of characters in *Putonghua*. It has been announced that there is no intention of using the alphabet to replace characters.

Chinese literature is one of the richest in the world. Paper has been employed for writing and printing for nearly 2,000 years. The Confucian classics which formed the basis of the traditional Chinese culture date from the Warring States period (4th–3rd centuries B.C.) as do the earliest texts of the rival tradition, Taoism. Histories, philosophical and scientific works, poetry, literary and art criticism, novels and romances survive from most periods. Many have been translated into English. In the past all this considerable literature was available only to a very small class of *literati*, but with the spread of literacy in the 20th century, a process which has received enormous impetus since the Communists took over in 1950, the old traditional literature has been largely superseded by modern works of a popular kind and by the classics of Marxism and modern developments from them.

Three daily (and one bi-weekly) newspapers were published in Peking in 1969, of which the most important is the People's Daily, the organ of the Chinese Communist Party.

Currency and Exchange.—The *yuan* was revalued with effect from March 1, 1955, on the basis of 10,000 old *yuan* for one new *yuan*. (*See also* p. 83.)

$$5 \cdot 878 \ yuan = \pounds 1; \ 2 \cdot 46 \ yuan = \$1.$$

Production and Industry.—China is essentially an agricultural and pastoral country: peasants constitute about 80 per cent. of the population. After the establishment of the Chinese People's Government at which time land for the most part was privately owned, there occurred several stages of land reform culminating in the formation of the people's communes in 1958. With the exception of a few State farms, the communes embrace the whole rural population. In all there are 74,000 communes and each is sub-divided into production brigades and teams. Work is assigned on a collective basis and the production team (of about 45 families) is the normal unit of accounting and labour. Wheat, barley, maize, millet and other cereals, with peas and beans, are grown in the northern provinces, and rice and sugar in the south. Rice is the staple food of the inhabitants. Cotton (mostly in valleys

of the Yangtze and Yellow Rivers), tea (in the west and south), with hemp, jute and flax, are the most important crops.

Livestock is raised in large numbers. Silkworm culture is one of the oldest industries. Cottons, woollens and silks are manufactured in large quantities. The mineral wealth of the country is very great. Coal of excellent quality is produced. Iron ore, tin, antimony, wolfram, bismuth and molybdenum are also abundant. Oil is produced in Kansu, Sinkiang, Sining and at a new major oilfield of unspecified location. No reliable figures for industrial production have been published since 1959. The figures given below for 1958 levels are accepted as generally accurate:

Steel, 8,000,000 tons; Pig Iron, 9,530,000 tons; Coal, 270,000,000 tons; Electric Power, 27,530,000,000 kWh.; Crude Petroleum, 2,264,000 tons; Cement, 9,300,000 tons; Timber, 35,000,000 cubic metres; Sulphuric Acid, 740,000 tons; Chemical Fertilizers, 811,000 tons; Machine Tools, 50,000; Motor Vehicles, 16,000; Paper, 1,630,000 tons; and Cotton Cloth 5,700,000,000 metres

Following the Great Leap Forward in 1958 and during three subsequent years of difficult conditions for agriculture, there was a cut back in both agricultural and industrial production which then recovered to its pre-1958 level. During the Cultural Revolution there was some economic dislocation. Industrial policy is governed by the need to build up agriculture, and some branches of industry, especially those such as machine tools and chemical fertilizers which have a direct relevance to agriculture have gone ahead more quickly. China is now virtually self-sufficient in petrol and oil.

A new (third) Five Year Plan began in 1966. No details of the Plan were published, but it was announced in 1970 that it had been completed. The Fourth Five Year Plan began in 1971, but no details of the Plan have as yet been published.

The principal articles of export are animals and animal products; oils; textiles; ores, metals and tea. The principal imports are raw cotton, cotton yarn and thread; motor vehicles; machinery; chemical fertilizer plants; wheat; aircraft; books, paper and paper-making materials; chemicals; metals and ores; and dyes.

Trade with U.K.

	1969	1970
Imports from U.K.	£51,802,000	£44,586,000
Exports to U.K.	37,727,000	33,538,000

Communications.—Of the total area of China about half consists of tableland and mountainous areas where communications and travel are generally difficult. By 1949, the communications system, as a result of years of neglect and civil war, was more or less completely paralysed. In any case such roads and railways as did exist were largely confined to the eastern plains. After the Communists achieved complete control they devoted much attention to restoring and improving the communications system. By the end of 1958 the total length of railways was 19,000 miles (42 p.c. more than 1949), the total length of roads was 250,000 miles (about 5 times as much as in 1949) and of inland waterways about 100,000 miles (twice as much as 1949). In addition, internal civil aviation has been developed; routes total more than 20,000 miles. As a result the communications network now covers most of the country. In the past where roads did not exist the principal means of communications east to west was provided by the rivers, the most important of which are the Yangtze (3,400 miles long), the Yellow River (2,600 miles long) and the West River (1,650 miles). These, together with the network of canals connecting them, are still much used, but their overall importance is less than

it was. In the past 10 years great progress has been made in developing postal services and telecommunications. It is now claimed that 95 p.c. of all rural communes are on the telephone and that postal routes reach practically every production brigade headquarters.

SPECIAL TERRITORY

Tibet, a plateau seldom lower than 10,000 feet, forms the northern frontier of India (boundary imperfectly demarcated), from Kashmir to Burma, but is separated therefrom by the Himalayas. The area is estimated at 463,000 square miles with a population (estimated, 1957) of 1,270,000.

From 1911 to 1950, Tibet was virtually an independent country but its status was never officially so defined. In October, 1950, Chinese Communist forces invaded Eastern Tibet. The Dalai Lama later left Lhasa and set up his Government at Yatung, near the Sikkim frontier. On May 23, 1951, an agreement was reached whereby the Chinese army was allowed entry into Tibet. A Communist military and administrative headquarters was set up. In 1954 the Government of India recognized that Tibet was an integral part of China, in return for the right to maintain trade and consular representation there.

A series of revolts against Chinese rule over several years culminated on March 17, 1959, in a rising in Lhasa. Heavy fighting continued for several days before the rebellion was suppressed by Chinese troops and military rule imposed. The Dalai Lama fled to India where he and his followers were granted political asylum. On May 4, the Indian Government announced that an estimated 9,000 Tibetans had entered India or the Himalayan hill states. On March 28, 1959, the Chinese Prime Minister issued an order dissolving the Tibetan Government. In its place the 16-member Preparatory Committee for the Tibetan Autonomous Region, originally set up in 1955 with the Dalai Lama as Chairman, was to administer Tibet under the State Council. The Preparatory Committee was to have the Panchen Lama as Acting Chairman and also to include 4 Chinese officials. Elections were held to choose local People's Congresses in Tibet, thus indicating that the government organization there no longer differed significantly from that of any ordinary province in China. The Dalai Lama, now exiled in India, announced a "new constitution" in March, 1963.

In December, 1964, the Dalai Lama, although absent, was declared to be a traitor, and both he and the Panchen Lama were dismissed. The position of Acting Chairman of the Preparatory Committee was assumed by Jigme, who had long been the most prominent secular figure in Tibet. This move marked the end of the period of co-operation by the Chinese Government with the traditional religious authorities, and the eclipse of the latter. The Preparatory Committee completed its work with the setting up of Tibet as an Autonomous Region of China on Sept. 9, 1965.

CAPITAL.—Peking, population (estimated, 1957), 4,010,000. The population of the other principal towns in 1957 was estimated as : Ψ Shanghai, 6,900,000; Tientsin, 3,220,000; Shenyang (Mukden), 2,411,000; Wuhan (*formerly* Hankow, Hanyang and Wuchang), 2,146,000; Chungking, 2,121,000; Ψ Canton, 1,840,000; Harbin, 1,552,000; Ψ Port Arthur (Lushun)/Dairen, 1,508,000; Nanking, 1,409,000; Sian, 1,310,000; Ψ Tsingtao, 1,121,000; Chengtu, 1,107,000; Taiyuan, 1,020,000.

FLAG.—Red, with large gold five-point star and four small gold stars in crescent, all in upper quarter next staff.

NATIONAL DAY.—October 1 (Founding of People's Republic).

OFFICE OF THE BRITISH CHARGÉ D'AFFAIRES
5 Kuang Hua Lu,
Chien Kuo Men Wai, Peking.

Chargé d'Affaires, John Boyd Denson, O.B.E. £6,475
1st Secretaries, R. C. Samuel; D. M. March (*Commercial*); G. S. Barrass; K. C. Walker.
2nd Secretary, A. C. Galsworthy (*Consular*).
3rd Secretary, C. O. Hum (*Commercial*).
Attachés, F. R. C. Thomson; W. J. Adsett; N. Bedford; W. Rymer; C. Hosker; Miss V. D. Wright.

FORMOSA
(Taiwan)

President, General Chiang Kai-shek, *born* 1887, *assumed office* 1948.
Prime Minister, Dr. C. K. Yen (Dec. 16, 1963).
Deputy Prime Minister, Gen. Chiang Ching-kuo.

An island of some 13,800 sq. miles in the China Sea, Formosa lies 90 miles east of the Chinese mainland in latitude 21° 45′ N.—25° 38′ N. The population (14,746,375 in Dec., 1970), is almost entirely Chinese in origin and includes about 2,000,000 mainlanders who came to the island with Chiang Kai-Shek in 1947–49. The territory of Formosa includes the Pescadores Islands (50 sq. miles), some 35 miles west of Formosa, as well as Quemoy (68 sq. miles) and Matsu (11 sq. miles) which are only a few miles from the mainland. Settled for centuries by the Chinese, the island has been known as Ryukyu and Taiwan. It was administered by Japan as a province from 1895 to 1945. General Chiang Kai-shek withdrew to Formosa in 1949, towards the end of the war against the Communist *régime* accompanied by 500,000 Nationalist troops, since when the territory has continued under his presidency. A mutual defence treaty between the United States and Formosan Governments was signed in 1954.

The eastern part of the main island is mountainous and forest covered. Mt. Morrison (Yu Shan) (13,035 ft.) and Mt. Sylvia (Tzu'ukaoshan) (12,972 ft.) are the highest peaks. The western plains are watered by many rivers and the soil is very fertile, producing sugar, rice, tea, bananas, pineapples and tobacco. Coal, sulphur, iron, petroleum, copper and gold are mined. There are important fisheries. The principal seaports Ψ Keelung (305,545) and Ψ Kaohsiung (724,222) are situated in the northern and southern sections of the island.

Trade with U.K.

	1969	1970
Imports from U.K.	£4,694,000	£6,630,000
Exports to U.K.	3,979,000	5,869,000

CAPITAL.—Taipei (population 1970, 1,769,568). Other towns are: Ψ Kaohsiung (724,222); Tainan (442,673); Taichung (391,518); and Ψ Keelung (305,545).
FLAG.—Red, with blue quarter at top next staff, bearing a twelve-point white sun.

BRITISH CONSULATES

Tamsui, T. Duffy (*Consul*).
Taipei Branch Office, J. A. Featherstone (*Deputy Consul*).

COLOMBIA
(República de Colombia)

President (1970–74), Misael PASTRANA Borrero, *elected* April 19, 1970: *assumed office* August 7,1970.

EMBASSY AND CONSULATE
3 Hans Crescent, S.W.1
[01–589–9177]

Ambassador Extraordinary and Plenipotentiary, His Excellency Dr. Camilo de Brigard Silva (1970).
Minister-Counsellor, Dr. José María de Guzmán.

Counsellors, Dr. Juan Martínez-Villa; Jorge Ramírez (*Coffee matters*).
1st Secretary, Srta. Ninón Millan.
Consul-General, Sra. María Elena de Crovo.

There is a Columbian Consulate General at Liverpool.

The Republic of Colombia lies in the extreme north-west of South America, having a coastline on both the Atlantic and Pacific Oceans. It is situated between 4° 13′ S. to 12° 30′ N. lat. and 68° to 79° W. long., with an approximate area of 440,000 square miles, and a population (estimated 1970) of 22,000,000.

The Colombian coast was visited in 1502 by Christopher Columbus, and in 1536 a Spanish expedition under Jiménez de Quesada penetrated to the interior and established on the site of the present capital a government which continued under Spanish rule until the revolt of the Spanish-American colonies of 1811–1824. In 1819 Simón Bolívar (born 1783, died 1830) established the Republic of Colombia, consisting of the territories now known as Colombia, Panama, Venezuela and Ecuador. In 1829–1830 Venezuela and Ecuador withdrew from the association of provinces, and in 1831 the remaining territories were formed into the Republic of New Granada. In 1858 the name was changed to the Granadine Confederation and in 1861 to the United States of Colombia. In 1886 the present title was adopted. In 1903 Panama seceded from Colombia, and became a separate Republic.

There are three great ranges of the Andes, known as the Western, Central, and Eastern Cordilleras; the second contains the highest peaks, but the latter is the most important, as it consists of a series of vast tablelands, cool and healthy. This temperate region is the most densely peopled portion of the Republic. The highest mountain in Colombia is the Sierra Nevada de Santa Marta on the Caribbean coast (18,946 feet).

The principal rivers are the Magdalena, Guaviare, Cauca, Atrato, Caquetá, Putumayo and Patia. The Patia flows through the famous *Minima Gorge* of the Western Cordilleras, and one of its tributaries (the Carchi, or Upper Guiatara) is spanned by the Rumichaca Arch, or *Inca's Bridge*, of natural stone. On the Río Bogotá is the great *Fall of Tequendama*, 482 ft. in height.

Government.—During the early nineteen-fifties Colombia suffered a period of virtual civil war between the supporters of the traditional political parties, the Conservatives and the Liberals. The dictatorship of Gen. Rojas Pinilla (1953–57) put an end to the worst of the violence and on May 10, 1957, a military junta took over, preparing the way for a return to democratic government. Congressional elections were held on March 16, 1958, which yielded a Liberal majority. A plebiscite voted on December 1, 1957, had made constitutional changes by which the office of president would during the next sixteen years alternate between candidates of the Liberal and Conservative parties who would hold office for terms of four years, while the two parties would have equal representation in Congress and in the national and departmental governments. This arrangement is known as the National Front.

During the presidency of Dr. Carlos Lleras (May, 1966 to April, 1970) the country made considerable economic advances, but the National Front system was nearly overthrown at the 1970 presidential election, when Gen. Rojas, with his political movement, the National Popular Alliance, almost defeated the Government candidate, Dr. Misael Pastrana.

Production.—The Colombian forests are extensive; among the trees are mahogany, cedar, fustic, and other dye-woods and medicinal plants. The mineral productions are emeralds, gold, silver, platinum, copper, iron, lead, and coal; in 1970 some 80 million barrels of petroleum were produced and prospecting for new sources of production is in progress in many parts of the Republic. The principal agricultural products are coffee (which accounts for 56 per cent. of total exports by value) cotton, bananas, rice, cocoa, sugar, tobacco, maize, wheat and other cereals. Manufactures, mainly for home consumption, consist of woollen, cotton and artificial silk textiles, leather goods, chemicals, asbestos-cement goods, many pharmaceutical products, rubber goods, including motor tyres, furniture boots and shoes, confectionery, cigarettes, beer, cement, glass containers and steel. Successive foreign exchange crises have led to the encouragement by the Government of the rapid development of new industries, including the local assembly and partial manufacture of motor vehicles, radio sets and office machinery. The importation of many consumer goods is prohibited or severely restricted.

Defence.—The Navy consists of 4 destroyers, 3 frigates, some gunboats and some other small craft, with personnel about 5,000, including one battalion of marines; a battalion of the Colombian army served with the United Nations forces in Korea.

Communications.—The first railway was opened in 1855, about 1,014 miles being open in 1949. The "Atlantic Railway" running through the Magdalena Valley, which links the departmental lines running down to the river, and completes the connection between Bogotá and Santa Marta, was opened in July, 1961. There are about 2,200 miles of rail in use at present. The total road network (1964) consists of 35,000 km. of roads of all types, of which 7,000 km. are classified as main trunk and transversal roads. A programme of road improvement and construction is under way, financed by a tax on petrol. The national telephone and telegraph system consists primarily of wireless links between the more important centres. Large appropriations have been made for modernization of the country's telecommunication system. There are daily passenger and cargo air services between Bogotá and all the principal towns. There are daily services to the U.S.A., frequent services to other countries in South America, and services to London daily *viâ* Miami, *viâ* Paris and once a week by B.O.A.C. to London. Air mail is delivered to the United Kingdom 3 to 5 days after leaving Bogotá. There are wireless stations in the main cities, and a television station in Bogotá with relays to most parts of the country.

Roman Catholicism is the established religion.

Language and Literature.—Spanish is the language of the country and education has been free since 1870. Great efforts have been made in reducing illiteracy and it is estimated that about 60 per cent. of those over 10 years of age can read and write. In addition to the National University with headquarters at Bogotá there are 26 other universities. There is a flourishing press in urban areas and a national literature supplements the rich inheritance from the time of Spanish rule.

Finance.—For rate of exchange, *see* p. 83.

	1968	1969
	$U.S.	$U.S.
Total imports.........	643,259,000	686,047,000
Total exports*.........	558,278,000	607,506,000

* Excluding petroleum.

Trade with U.K.

	1969	1970
Imports from U.K. .	£12,173,000	£12,942,000
Exports to U.K.......	7,481,000	8,904,000

CAPITAL, Bogotá, pop. (estimated, 1968) 2,000,000. Bogotá is an inland city in the Eastern Cordilleras, at an elevation of 8,600 to 9,000 feet above sea level. Other centres are Medellin (950,000); Cali (800,000); Barranquilla (700,000); Bucaramanga (290,000); Manizales (250,000); Pereira (250,000); Ψ Cartagena (240,000).

FLAG.—Broad yellow band in upper half, surmounting equal bands of blue and red.

NATIONAL DAY.—July 20 (National Independence Day).

BRITISH EMBASSY

Carrera 10, No. 19–65, Bogotá.

Ambassador Extraordinary and Plenipotentiary, His Excellency Thomas Edward Rogers, C.M.G., M.B.E. (1970)..........................£6,925
1st Secretaries, C. McLean, M.B.E. (*Head of Chancery and Consul*); R. G. Marlow (*Commercial*).
Defence Attaché, Cdr. G. D. H. Sample, R.N.
2nd Secretaries, J. R. H. Evans (*Commercial*); D. H. Parker (*Technical Assistance*); S. T. Nash.
There are British Consular Offices at *Bogotá, Barranquilla, Medellin* and *Cali.*
British Council Representative, T. F. Hibbett, Carrera 10, 19–65 Bogotá.

CONGO
(Popular Republic of the Congo)

President, Council of State, Maj. Marien Ngoabi.
Vice-President, Maj. Alfred Raoul.
Minister of Foreign Affairs, M. Auxence Ikonga.

The Republic lies on the Equator between Gaboon on the west and the Congolese Republic on the east, the River Congo and its tributary the Ubanghi forming most of the eastern boundary of the state. The Congo has a short Atlantic coastline. Area of the Republic of Congo is 129,960 sq. miles, with a population (U.N. estimate, 1969) of 915,000. Formerly the French colony of Middle Congo, it became a member state of the French Community on November 28, 1958, and was proclaimed fully independent on August 17, 1960.

M. Fulbert Youlou held office as President of the Republic from Aug. 7, 1960. Growing discontent with the *régime* culminated in riots in Brazzaville and led to the President's resignation on Aug. 15, 1963, and the dissolution by the Army of the National Assembly. A provisional Government led by M. Alphonse Massemba-Débat took office on Aug. 16, and a new constitution, giving the provisional Government full powers, came into operation in December, 1963.

On Jan. 12, 1968, the President dismissed the Prime Minister, M. Noumazalay, with three other members of his Cabinet and himself assumed office as Prime Minister with a reformed Ministry. He was himself arrested after heavy fighting during the last few days of August and resigned on Sept. 4, 1968. Conduct of affairs was assumed by a National Council of Army officers.

Trade with U.K.

	1969	1970
Imports from U.K. ..	£1,448,000	£2,433,000
Exports to U.K.......	1,609,000	1,782,000

CAPITAL.—Brazzaville (136,000); Ψ Pointe Noire (54,000). FLAG.—Red, with hammer and sickle in centre.

THE CONGOLESE REPUBLIC
(Democratic Republic of the Congo)

President and Prime Minister, Gen. Joseph-Desiré Mobutu, *born* Oct. 30, 1930, *assumed office* November 25, 1965; *elected for 2nd term* Nov. 5, 1970.

CABINET

Interior, Edouard Bulundwe.
Foreign Affairs and Co-operation, Mario Cardoso.
Justice, André Tshibangu.
Finance, Louis Namwisi.
National Economy, Joseph Mbeka.
Transport and Communications, Gaston Kisanga.
Mines, Jean Theodore Umba-di-Lutete.
Energy, Joseph Kahamba.
Information, Dominique Sakombi.
Education, Claude Mafema.
Agriculture, Pierre André.
Labour, Raphael Binton.
Culture and Arts, Charles Bokonga.
Social Affairs, Maurice Nyoka.
Urban Development and Land, Thomas Lwango.
Public Works, Léon Engulu.
Public Service, Ntite Tshisambo.
Posts and Telecommunications, Paul Mushiete.
Public Health, Dr. Paul Kalonda.
Youth and Sports, Godefroid-Maximilien Sampassa.

CONGOLESE EMBASSY

26, Chesham Place, S.W.1

[01-235-6137]

Ambassador, His Excellency Gervais Bahizi.
Minister Counsellor, Joseph Kalume.

The State of the Congo, founded in 1885, became a Belgian Colony on Nov. 15, 1908, and was administered by Belgium until June 30, 1960. Situated between long. 12°–31° E. and lat. 5° N.–13° S., the Congolese Republic comprises an area of 905,582 sq. miles, with a population (U.N. estimate, 1969) of 17,100,000. The State was divided into 21 provinces by July 1963, the number being reduced to 8 in 1966 (*see* below).

Government.—On June 30, 1960, the Belgian Congo became an independent unitary state under the Presidency of M. Kasavubu with a provisional constitution, the *Loi Fondamentale*, drawn up by the metropolitan Belgian Parliament. On July 11, M. Moise Tshombe announced the independence of the State of Katanga and although he failed to obtain international recognition he continued to act in an independent manner with the creation of a visa system, a Katanga franc, etc. Katanga did not come under the Government at Leopoldville until January 14, 1963.

The constitutional and political situation remained unsettled, the United Nations having mixed forces in the country until 1964. By the middle of 1965, the Congolese Government formed by M. Tshombe in July, 1964, had succeeded in gaining control of

all the towns from the rebels and depriving them of military aid from outside the Congo. At elections held in the spring of 1965 the Government party won an overall majority of 86, but the elections in three provinces were annulled on the grounds that they had been irregularly conducted. Following fresh elections held in these provinces in August, 1965, M. Tshombe's Government was dismissed by the President. A new Cabinet was formed by M. Evariste Kimba on October 19 and held office until the deposition on Nov. 25 of the President.

General Joseph-Desiré Mobutu, Commander-in-Chief of the Congolese National Army, announced on November 25, 1965, that he had assumed the Presidency and issued a 13-point proclamation appointing a Prime Minister with the task of forming a 21-member Cabinet, one member being drawn from each Province. After re-organizations in Dec., 1966, and Oct. 5, 1967, a new Cabinet, with the President again as Prime Minister, took office on Mar. 5, 1969.

Climate.—Apart from the coastal district in the West which is fairly dry, the rainfall averages between 60 and 80 inches. The average temperature is about 80° F., but in the South the winter temperature can fall nearly to freezing point. There has been some increase in sleeping-sickness since independence. Malaria, formerly under control in Leopoldville (*now* Kinshasa) and Matadi, has also begun to increase.

Extensive forest covers the central districts.

Provinces.—On Dec. 24, 1966, the provinces of the Republic were re-organized, the total number being reduced to 8. Previously various towns whose names were of European origin had been renamed, notably Leopoldville—now Kinshasa. Following are the eight provinces with names of capitals: Central Congo (*Matadi*), Bandundu (*Bandundu, formerly* Banningville); Equateur (*Mbendaka, formerly* Coquilhatville); Orientale (*Kisangani, formerly* Stanleyville); Kivu (*Bukavu*); Katanga (*Lubumbashi, formerly* Elisabethville); East Kasai (*Mbuji-Mayi, formerly* Bakwanga); and West Kasai (*Luluabourg*). The city of Kinshasa is an administrative unit by itself.

Production.—The cultivation of oil palms is widespread, palm oil being the most important agricultural cash product. Rubber, coffee and timber are the next most important agricultural exports. The production of cotton, pyrethrum, copal and fibres production continues to be severely reduced. The country is rich in minerals, particularly Katanga province. Extensive radium deposits exist near Lubumbashi and reef-gold exists in the north-east of the country.

There is a wide variety of small but flourishing secondary industries, the main products being: cotton fabrics, blankets, sacks, footwear, beer, cigarettes, cement, paint and sugar. There are very large reserves of hydro-electric power.

The chief exports are copper, palm-oil and palm-kernels, coffee, diamonds, rubber, cobalt and cassiterite.

Currency.—In November, 1963, the Congolese *Franc* was devalued from 180 C.F. = £1 to 420 C.F. = £1, for persons selling foreign exchange to obtain Congolese *francs* and 504 to the £ for persons buying foreign exchange with Congolese *francs*. In June, 1967, a new currency was introduced, the unit of which, the *Zaire*, replaced 1,000 old *francs*. At the same time the currency was revalued at £1 = Z1·2. (*See also* p. 83.)

Trade with U.K.

	1969	1970
Imports from U.K. ..	£11,229,000	£12,033,000
Exports to U.K.	22,834,000	18,872,000

Language, Religion and Education.—The people are mainly of Bantu-Negro stock, divided into semi-autonomous tribes, each speaking a Bantu tongue. Swahili, a Bantu dialect with an admixture of Arabic, is the nearest approach to a common language in the East and South, and Lingala along the river. It is estimated there are 5,000,000 African Christians in the Republic (Roman Catholic 4,200,000, Protestant 800,000).

CAPITAL, Kinshasa (*formerly* Leopoldville), population (estimated, 1971) 1,300,000. Principal towns, Lubumbashi (*formerly* Elisabethville) (182,638); Kisangani (*formerly* Stanleyville) (79,941); Jadotville (74,478); Luluabourg (59,935); Ψ Matadi (59,184); Kolwezi (47,712); Mbandaka (*formerly* Coquilhatville) (37, 587); and Ψ Boma (31,598).

FLAG.—Blue with diagonal red band flanked by narrow yellow stripes; 5-point star on blue next staff. NATIONAL DAY.—June 30.

BRITISH EMBASSY
Kinshasa.
Ambassador Extraordinary and Plenipotentiary, His Excellency Mark Echalaz Allen, C.M.G., C.V.O. (1971).................................£6,925
Counsellor, W. E. H. Whyte.
Defence, Military and Air Attaché, Col. J. C. Davis.
1st Secretaries, G. W. Baker, O.B.E., V.R.D. (*Head of Chancery*); A. L. Kettles (*Consul*); T. H. Steggle (*Commercial*); A. Rellie. There is a British Consulate at Lubumbashi.

COSTA RICA
(República de Costa Rica)
President (1970–74), Señor José Figueres Ferrer, *elected* February 1, 1970, *assumed office* May 8, 1970.

COSTA RICAN EMBASSY AND CONSULATE
8 Braemar Mansions, Cornwall Gardens, S.W.7.
[01-937-7883]
Ambassador Extraordinary and Plenipotentiary, His Excellency Sr. don Manuel Escalante-Durán (1970).
Minister-Counsellor, Sr. don Gaston Fournier Facio.

The Republic of Costa Rica, in Central America, extends across the isthmus between 8° 17′ and 11° 10′ N. lat. and from 82° 30′ to 85° 45′ W. long., contains an area of 19,653 English sq. miles, and a population (estimated, 1969) of 1,685,000. The population is basically of European stock, in which Costa Rica differs from most Latin American countries. The Republic lies between Nicaragua and Panama and between the Caribbean Sea and the Pacific Ocean.

For nearly three centuries (1530–1821) Costa Rica formed part of the Spanish-American dominions, the seat of government being at Cartago. In 1821 the country joined in the War of Independence, and from 1824 to 1839 it was one of the United States of Central America.

On Dec. 1, 1948, the Army was abolished, the President declaring it unnecessary, as the country loved peace.

The coastal lowlands by the Caribbean Sea and Pacific have a tropical climate but the interior plateau, with a mean elevation of 4,000 feet, enjoys a temperate climate. The capital is 103 miles from the Atlantic and 72 miles from the Pacific by rail.

The principal agricultural products are coffee (of a high quality), bananas, rice, maize, sugar-cane, potatoes, cocoa beans and hemp, the soil being extremely fertile. Increasing attention is being paid to cattle raising.

The chief ports are Ψ Limón, on the Atlantic coast, through which passes most of the coffee exported, and Ψ Puntarenas on the Pacific coast. Bananas are exported from Golfito, on the Pacific Coast, by the United Fruit Co., and from Limón by the Standard Fruit Co. In 1968, 1,126 ships of a gross tonnage of 5,144,207 entered at Costa Rican ports. About 500 miles of railroad are open. The country is well provided with airways, and Pan-American Airways, TACA, SAHSA and COPA call at San José, while feeder services link the main centres of population with the capital. LACSA is the national airline with BAC-111 flights to Miami, Mexico, Central American capitals and internal flights to local airports.

Spanish is the language of the country. Education is compulsory and free. The literacy rate is the highest in Latin America. In post-war years there has been a big advance in the provision of social services.

FINANCE

	1969	1970
	Colones	Colones
Revenue..............	945,700,000	883,200,000
Expenditure...........	889,300,000	994,600,000
Public Debt (Dec. 1970)		1,876,000

Currency is the *colon* of 100 *centimos*. Exchange rate in 1969 was *Colones* 15·888 = £1 (*see also* p. 83).

TRADE.

	1969	1970
Total imports	$U.S. 245,100,000	$U.S. 229,000,000
Total exports	189,700,000	217,300,000

Trade with U.K.

	1969	1970
Imports from U.K. ..	£5,748,000	£4,745,000
Exports to U.K.	365,000	367,000

The chief exports (1969) were coffee, bananas, meat, sugar, cacao, and fertilizers. The imports, 40 per cent. from U.S.A., 19 per cent. from other Central American Common Market countries, 9 per cent. from Germany and 7·9 per cent. from Japan, consisted of machinery, motor vehicles, bicycles, chemicals, textiles, fuel and lubricants, rubber manufactures, non-ferrous metals, etc.

CAPITAL, San José, pop. (Jan., 1970), 205,650 (city); Alajuela (79,997); Ψ Puntarenas (70,276); Cartago (57,950); Ψ Limón (50,442); Heredia (38,781); Liberia (25,307). (Populations shown are of the Central Cantons of provincial capitals at January, 1969.)

FLAG.—Five horizontal bands, blue, white, red, white, blue (the red band twice the width of the others with emblem near staff).

NATIONAL DAY.—September 15.

BRITISH EMBASSY.
San José

Ambassador Extraordinary and Plenipotentiary and Consul-General, His Excellency Ian Murray Hurrell, M.V.O. (1967).................£6,475
1st Secretary and Consul, M. L. Creek.
3rd Secretary, S. N. Lee.
Commercial Attaché, J. M. Bowden.

San José is 5,687 miles from London; sea transit direct 18 days; *viâ* New York, 20 days; Air Mails (*viâ* New York), 3 to 10 days from London. Ocean Mail, 4 to 10 weeks.

CUBA
(Republica de Cuba)

President, Dr. Osvaldo Dorticós Torrado, *appointed* July 17, 1959.

COUNCIL OF MINISTERS

Prime Minister, Dr. Fidel Castro Ruz.
Vice-Premier and Armed Forces, Major Raúl Castro Ruz.
Minister of Foreign Affairs, Dr. Raúl Roa Garcia.
Justice, Dr. Alfredo Yabur Maluf.
Interior, Maj. Sergio del Valle.
Communications, Maj. Jesus Montané Oropesa.
Public Works, Levi Fara.
Foreign Trade, Marcelo Fernandez Font.
Internal Trade, Capt. Serafín Fernández Rodríguez.
Basic Industry, Joel Domenech.
Light Industry, Mrs. Nora Frometa Silva.
Mining and Metallurgy, Maj. Pedro Miret.
Public Health, Dr. Heliodoro Martinez Junco.
Education, Maj. Bellarmina Castilla Mas.
Labour, Capt. Jorge Risquet Valdes.
Merchant Marine and Posts, Capt. Angel Joel Chaveco Hernández.
National Economy, Dr. Osvaldo Dorticós Torrado.
Transport, Maj. Enrique Lussón Battle.
Sugar Industry, Ing. Marcos Lage Cuello.
Food Industry, José Naranjo.
Without Portfolio, Dr. Carlos Rafael Rodriguez.
President, National Bank, Dr. Orlando Perez.

CUBAN EMBASSY IN LONDON
57 Kensington Court, W.8
[01–937–8226]

Ambassador Extraordinary and Plenipotentiary, Her Excellency Señorita Alba Griñan Nuñez (1965).

Counsellors, Sr. D. Arranz-Tremols (*Commercial*); Sr. F. I. Iglesias (*Commercial*).
1st Secretaries, Sr. Jorge Solís García; Srta. Ana Irma Sarmiento.
2nd Secretaries, Sr. Miguel Alvarez Gomez; Sr. Gerardo Peraza Amechazurra.

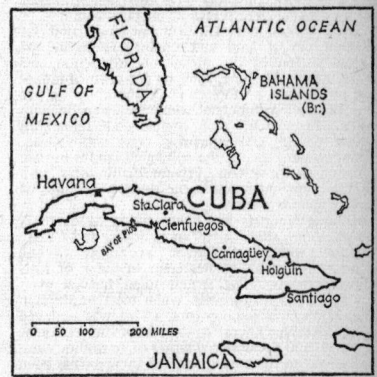

Cuba (the largest of the " West India " Islands) lies between 74° and 85° W. long., and 19° and 23° N. lat., with a total area of 44,178 sq. miles and a population at the Census of 1970 of 8,553,395.

The island of Cuba was visited by Christopher Columbus during his first voyage, on October 27, 1492, and was then believed to be part of the Western mainland of India. Early in the 16th century the island was conquered by the Spaniards, to be used later as a base of operations for the conquest of Mexico and Central America, and for almost four centuries Cuba remained under a Spanish Captain-General. [The island was under British rule for one year, 1762–1763, when it was returned to Spain in exchange for Florida.] Separatist agitation culminated in the closing years of the 19th century in a fierce and blood-thirsty war. In 1898 the government of the United States intervened and despatched the battleship *Maine* to Havana harbour, where in February of that year the vessel was sunk by an explosion, the cause of which remains an unsolved mystery. On April 20, 1898, the U.S. Government demanded the evacuation of Cuba by the Spanish forces, and a short Spanish–American war led to the abandonment of the island, which was occupied by U.S. troops. From Jan. 1, 1899, to May 20, 1902, Cuba was under U.S. military rule, and reforms of the widest and most far-reaching character were instituted. On May 20, 1902, an autonomous government was inaugurated with an elected President, and a legislature of two houses. The island was, however, again the prey of revolution from Aug. to Sept., 1906, when the U.S. Government resumed control. On Jan. 28, 1909, a republican government was again inaugurated. In 1933 a revolution was followed by provisional government until May, 1936, when a constitutional government was elected. A new Constitution was promulgated in 1940, but its operation was suspended for various periods until February 24, 1955, when the Government elected on November 1, 1954, took office.

A revolution led by Dr. Fidel Castro overthrew the Government of General Batista on January 1, 1959. A provisional government was set up and elections were promised within four years. Dr.

Castro has since proclaimed the revolution to be Socialist and himself to be a Marxist-Leninist.

In October, 1965, the Communist Party of Cuba was formed to succeed the United Party of the Socialist Revolution. It is the only authorized political party. Elections are no longer to be held. A new Socialist constitution has also been promised, but no date has been set for its introduction.

The Revolutionary Government has carried out programmes of land and urban reform and of nationalization of the means of production and distribution. By June, 1963, 90 per cent. of industrial production, all foreign trade and about 50 per cent. of small commercial companies were in state hands. In March, 1968, virtually all remaining private commercial enterprises were nationalized. About 70 per cent. of the cultivated land is in state farms or co-operatives. Private smallholders, who own the remainder, also come under a measure of Government control.

Although efforts are being made to diversify the economy, sugar is still its mainstay and Cuba's principal source of foreign exchange. It still accounts for some 80 per cent. in value of total Cuban exports. The largest sugar harvest ever, was produced in 1969/70, when total production reached about 8,500,000 tons. This was achieved at considerable expense to the rest of the economy, however, and the declared target of 10 million tons, which was to have been reached in 1970, has been delayed. Cuba's other main exports are nickel, tobacco and rum, while increases are expected shortly in the availability of fish, meat and citrus fruit.

Despite increased trade with Western Europe and Japan, the Communist countries, particularly the Soviet Union, form Cuba's main trading partners, covering about 80 per cent. of imports and exports. In addition, the U.S.S.R. offers substantial aid from an imbalance in the annual trade profits in Cuba's favour which has recently been in the region of 250 to 350 million roubles.

11,915 miles of railway are open (public service 4,880; sugar plantations and mining areas 7,035) and about 12,000 miles of telegraph line. There are about 8,291 miles of road. At present scheduled international air services run to Mexico City, Moscow, Prague, Madrid, Rabat and Algiers.

Language and Literature.—Spanish is the language of the island, but English is widely understood. Education is compulsory and free. The University of Havana was founded in 1728, but until its enlargement under American auspices in the first quarter of the twentieth century no great progress was made in secondary or higher education. There are universities at Santiago de Cuba and Santa Clara. Public libraries have been established. The daily press and broadcasting and television are under the control of the Government.

Finance.—The public revenue rose from an estimated $365,247,946 in 1958 to $2,399,006,000 for 1964, including profits from State trading concerns, etc. No up-to-date figures are available for the public debt—at the end of 1958 this stood at $760,300,000.

Nominally. $=U.S. $1. U.S. currency ceased to be legal tender in Cuba on June 30, 1951 (*see also* p. 83).

Trade.—Exports in 1968 were valued at $649,900,000, compared with $710,800,000 in 1967; imports, 1968, $1,094,000,000 (1967, $997,800,000). No statistics are available for subsequent years.

Trade with U.K.

	1969	1970
Imports from U.K.	£13,053,000	£20,559,000
Exports to U.K.	5,410,000	5,702,000

The exports are principally molasses and tobacco; the imports are mainly machinery.

CAPITAL. Ψ Havana (pop., Census 1970), 1,755,360; other towns are Ψ Santiago (292,251), Santa Clara (213,296), Camagüey (196,854), Holguín (183,115), and Ψ Cienfuegos (164,061).

FLAG.—Five horizontal bands, blue and white (blue at top and bottom) with red triangle, close to staff, charged with 5-point white star.

NATIONAL DAY.—January 1 (Day of Liberation).

BRITISH EMBASSY

(Chancery: Edif. Bolívar, Capdevila No. 101, 8th Floor. Postal address: P.O. Box N 1229, Nassau, Bahamas).

Ambassador Extraordinary and Plenipotentiary, His Excellency Richard Adam Sykes, C.M.G., M.C. (1970) £6,925
Counsellor, E. A. W. Bullock (*Head of Chancery*).
1st Secretaries, D. F. Ballentyne (*Commercial*); Miss Z. Hawson (*Consul*).
2nd Secretary, R. Murphy (*Commercial*).
3rd Secretaries, S. J. L. Wright; S. A. Saunders, M.V.O. (*Vice-Consul*).
Defence Attaché, Lt.Col. G. R. D. Kennedy (*Resident at Mexico City*).
Cultural Attaché (*British Council Representative*), Miss M. E. Platon.

BRITISH CONSULAR OFFICES.

There are British Consular Offices at *Havana* and *Santiago de Cuba.*

CZECHOSLOVAKIA
(Československá Socialistická Republika)
President, Ludwig Svoboda, *born* Nov. 25, 1895, *elected* March 30, 1968.

Federal Government
Prime Minister, Lubomír Štrougal.
Deputy Prime Ministers, Petr Colotka; Jan Gregor; František Hamouz; Václav Hůla; Josef Korčak; Karol Laco; Matej Lúčan; Jindřich Zahradnik.

Ministers
Agriculture and Food, Bohuslav Večeřa.
Finance, Rudolf Rohlíček.
Foreign Affairs, Ján Marko.
Foreign Trade, Andrej Barčák.
Fuel and Power, Jaromír Murušek.
Interior, Radko Kaska.
Labour and Social Affairs, Michal Štancel.
Metallurgy and Engineering, Josef Šimon.
National Defence, Martin Dzúr.
State Planning Commission, Vaclav Hůla.
Telecommunications, Vlastimil Chalupa.
Technical and Investment Development, Ladislav Šupka.
Transport, Štěpán Šutka.
Peoples Control, Drahomír Kolder.
Prices, Ignác Rendek; Karol Martinka; Bohuslav Kučera.

Prime Minister of the Czech Socialist Republic, Josef Korčák.
Prime Minister of the Slovak Socialist Republic, Dr. Petr Colotka.

CZECHOSLOVAK COMMUNIST PARTY
Secretariat of the Central Committee, G. Husák (*Secretary-General*); V. Bilák; J. Fojtik; M. Hruskovič; A. Indra; J. Kempny; O. Svěstka.
Presidium of the Central Committee, Vasil Bilák; Petr Colotka; Evžen Erban; Gustáv Husák; Antonín Kapek; Josef Kempný; Josef Korčák; Jozef Lenárt; Jan Piller; Ludvík Svoboda; Lubomír Štrougal.

CZECHOSLOVAK EMBASSY AND CONSULATE
25 Kensington Palace Gardens, W.8.
[01-229-1255]

Ambassador Extraordinary and Plenipotentiary, His
Excellency Dr. Miloslav Růžek (1966).
Minister-Counsellor, Dr. Jan Snobl.
Commercial Counsellor, K. Jiráček.
Military and Air Attaché, Col. Jiří Boušek.
1st Secretaries, Josef Konecký; Dr. Miroslav Stoje;
Josef Brabec; Bohuslav Laška.
Commercial Attachés, Ottol Kykal; Karel Parma.
2nd Secretaries, Pavel Stulrajter; Dr. R. Král.
3rd Secretary, Josef Lébl.
Attachés, Stanislav Melichar (*Labour and Head
of Consular Dept.*); Josef Procháska; Miss Vlasta
Basetlíková; Jiří Balšánek; Vilém Pardubský;
Jiří Staněk; Bohumil Karkan; Pavel Šiška.

Area and Population.—Czechoslovakia, formerly
part of the Austro-Hungarian Monarchy, declared
its independence on Oct. 28, 1918 (Czechoslovak
Independence Day), the territory affected having an area of 53,700 square miles, reduced, by
the cession of Ruthenia to U.S.S.R. in 1945, to
49,700 square miles. The population of Czechoslovakia (U.N. estimate) was 14,467,000 in July,
1970.

Government.—The Communist Party, with the
aid of Action Committees, seized power in Czechoslovakia in February, 1948, and Communist control
of the country is now unqualified. On July 11,
1960, a new constitution was proclaimed, replacing
that of 1948. Its purpose was to express the fact
that Czechoslovakia is now deemed to have completed the construction of Socialism and to be
on the road to true Communism. The official
title of the State was accordingly changed to " The
Czechoslovak Socialist Republic ".

A major economic re-organization was approved
by the Central Committee of the Czechoslovak
Communist Party in January, 1965. The main
features of this new system were—a reduction in
central planning and a greater devolution of responsibility to individual enterprises and factories;
increased emphasis on profitability and competition;
recognition of the value of the market, coupled
with a more flexible price policy and greater
participation by all production units in foreign
trade. During 1965 and 1966, some rationalization
of industry took place and minor elements of the
new economic system were introduced experiment-
ally. In June, 1966, the XIIIth Congress of the
Party determined that the new system as such

should be introduced from 1967. The fourth 5-
Year Plan, 1966–70, and the annual plan for 1966
were drawn up on the basis of the old system and
modifications will be undertaken from time to time.

Following Novotný's removal from the post of
First Secretary in January, 1968, there developed a
wave of pressure for legal and political reform.
During the ensuing months Novotný's supporters
were removed from leading positions, and the programme of reform was embodied in a Party Action
Programme adopted in April. Shortly afterwards
the National Assembly began work on new legislation. The reforms envisaged the democratization of the country's political life, greater guarantees
of fundamental liberties and the establishment of a
federal system.

By the summer of 1968 it was evident that the
more liberal policies of the Czechoslovak Government did not meet with Soviet approval. The
Government and party leaders of U.S.S.R.,
Poland, Hungary and Eastern Germany met at
Warsaw on July 14 and 15 and warned Czechoslovakia in a joint letter against the activities of
" anti-socialist and revisionist forces " in Czechoslovakia. Meetings of the Czechoslovak Presidium
with the Soviet Politburo at Cerna and with representatives of the Warsaw powers at Bratislava on
August 3 followed, and the Czechoslovak and
Rumanian Governments signed a 20-year treaty of
friendship and mutual assistance during the
Rumanian President's visit to Prague on August
15–16. At the same time fresh accusations of the
stepping-up of subversive activities in Czechoslovakia appeared in the Soviet press. On the night
of August 20, Czechoslovakia was invaded by
Soviet, Polish, East German, Hungarian and
Bulgarian troops, the capital and all major towns
and cities being occupied.

Dubček and other leaders were immediately
taken to Moscow. President Svoboda, who took
part in discussions there, stoutly resisted Soviet
attempts to impose a quisling government and the
Russians were forced to negotiate with Dubček. On
August 26 the Moscow Agreements were signed;
the Czechoslovak side agreed to the continued
presence of Soviet forces in Czechoslovakia and to
modify their policies. The majority of the troops
were soon withdrawn.

A federal system of government was set up in
Czechoslovakia on Oct. 30, 1968, and some adjustments in its operation were made in the winter of
1970–71.

Language and Literature.—Czech and Slovak are

the official languages, each having its own literature. The Reformation gave a wide-spread impulse to Czech literature, the writings of Jan Hus (who was martyred in 1415 as a religious and social reformer) familiarizing the people with Wyclif's teaching. This impulse endured to the close of the 17th century when Jan Amos Komenský or Comenius (1592–1670) was expelled from the country. He is still recognized as an outstanding educationist and a thinker of first magnitude. Under Austrian repression and with the persistent pursuit of Germanization, there was a period of stagnation until the national revival in the first half of the 19th century. Modern prose, drama and fiction, penned between the Wars, are represented by several authors, of international reputation, notably K. M. Čapek-Chod (1860–1927), Viktor Dyk (1877–1931), Jaroslav Hašek (1883–1923), Karel Čapek (1890–1938), Vladimír Vančura (1891–1942), and Ivan Olbracht (1882–1952). Liberty of the press ceased with the loss of independence and the Nazi occupation in 1939. It was temporarily restored on the liberation of the country. After the Communist take-over of February, 1948, however, freedom of the press was curtailed. All papers and periodicals were forced to follow the Party line and a number of publications were banned. Following the thaw of 1956 and after the relapse into dogmatism after the Hungarian Revolution, the new wave of freedom started in 1962–1963 and led to increased recognition of Czech and Slovak literature in the world. Greater international recognition is hampered by translation difficulties. In 1966 nearly 250 Czech and Slovak books were published abroad, including roughly one-third in non-Socialist countries. The prominent writers include František Hrubín (b. 1910), Bohumil Hrabal (b. 1914), Václav Havel (b. 1936), Ladislav Mňačko (b. 1919), Ladislav Novomeský (b. 1904), Arnošt Lustig (b. 1926), Jiří Mucha (b. 1915), and others. Poetic writing ranges from traditional lyric (Jaroslav Seifert) to "concrete" and typographic modernism (Jiří Kolář, Josef Hiršal).

Education.—The number of pupils in basic nine-year schools is 2,052,526 (Dec. 31, 1968). There are 108,000 students in the secondary grammar schools and the number given for technical schools of all kinds is 278,685. Education is compulsory and free for all children from the ages of 6 to 15. There are five universities in Czechoslovakia of which the most famous is Charles University in Prague (founded 1348), the others being situated at Bratislava, Brno, Olomouc and Košice. In addition there are a considerable number of other institutions of university standing, technical colleges, agricultural colleges, etc. On Dec. 31, 1968, there were 137,654 full-time students in centres of higher education and 46,000 adults part-time.

Finance.—The Czechoslovak currency is the Czechoslovak *Koruna* (*Kčs* = Czechoslovak crown) of 100 *heller*. The present Czechoslovak rate of exchange is Kčs. 17·12 = £1 with a bonus of Kčs. 20 for non-commercial travellers (*see also* p. 83).

Trade with U.K.

	1969	1970
Imports from U.K.	£17,654,000	£20,736,000
Exports to U.K.	21,508,000	22,774,000

CAPITAL, Prague (Praha), on the Vltava (Moldau), the former capital of Bohemia with a population (1966) of 1,030,330. Other towns are Brno (Brünn), capital of Moravia (333,004), Bratislava (Pressburg), capital of Slovakia (276,519), Ostrava (269,642) and Plzen (Pilsen) (142,694).

FLAG.—Two equal horizontal stripes, white (above) and red; a blue triangle next to staff.

NATIONAL DAY.—May 9.

BRITISH EMBASSY.
Thunovská ulice 14, Prague 1.
Ambassador Extraordinary and Plenipotentiary, His Excellency Ronald Stratford Scrivener, C.M.G. (1971)................................. £6,925
Counsellor, J. R. Rich.
Defence Attaché, Col. T. A. Cave.
Air Attaché, Wing-Cdr. R. M. Sparkes.
1st Secretaries, C. Mays (*Commercial*); J. R. Banks.
2nd Secretaries, J. S. S. Beels; R. H. Alford (*Cultural*).
3rd Secretaries, W. B. Swinton (*Commercial*); A. R. Lance; P. Nicholson; C. N. Nies; E. Clapham (*Commercial*).
H.M. Consul, A. White.
Cultural Attaché, A. Mackenzie-Smith, O.B.E., M.C.

DAHOMEY
(Republic of Dahomey)

President of the Presidential Council and Head of State, Hubert Maga; *assumed office,* May 7, 1970.

A republic situated in West Africa, between 2° and 3° W. and 6° and 12° N., Dahomey has a short coast line of 78 miles on the Gulf of Guinea but extends northwards inland for 437 miles. It is flanked on the west by Togo, on the north by Upper Volta and Niger and on the east by Nigeria. It has an area of about 47,000 square miles and a population (U.N. estimate, 1969) of 2,640,000. Although poor in resources, Dahomey is one of the most thickly populated areas in West Africa, with a high level of education. It is divided into four main regions running horizontally: a narrow sandy coastal strip, a succession of inter-communicating lagoons, a clay belt and a sandy plateau in the north.

The first treaty with France was signed by one of the kings of Abomey in 1851 but the country was not placed under French administration until 1892. Dahomey became an independent republic within the French Community on Dec. 4, 1958; full independence outside the Community was proclaimed on August 1, 1960. In October, 1963, a popular revolution led to the fall of the government of the first President of Dahomey, Hubert Maga. The Army held power until Sourou-Migan Apithy was elected President and Justin Ahomadegbé Chief of Government in January, 1964, after a new constitution had been agreed. This government was overthrown in November, 1965, following a long-standing disagreement between Maga and Apithy. It was replaced by President Tahirou Congacou, who was in turn dismissed in December of the same year by the Army. Christophe Soglo then assumed control and dismissed the Assembly. Soglo was in his turn overthrown by an Army *coup d'état* on December 17, 1967. Seven months later Dr. Zinsou was installed, with the support of the Army, as President, an appointment which was confirmed by a national referendum on July 28, 1968.

Dr. Zinsou was overthrown by a military coup on December 10, 1969 and for five months the country was ruled by a military "Directoire". Following abortive elections in March, 1970, a Presidential Council was set up in May, 1970 consisting of MM. Maga, Ahomadégbé and Apithy, with M. Maga as President of the Council and Head of State. Under the terms of the Charter, the Presidency of the Council will revolve every two years between the three members of the Council.

Dahomey is a member of the *Conseil de l'Entente*, the *Organisation Commune Africaine et Malgache* (OCAM) and the Organization of African Unity (O.A.U.). The official language is French.

Finance.—The currency of Dahomey is the *Franc*

CFA (*Francs CFA* 50 = 1 French *Franc*) (*Francs CFA* 666 = £1).

Trade.—The principal exports are palm products (80 per cent.) followed by ground nuts, shea-nuts and coffee. Small deposits of gold, iron and chrome have been found. Imports from U.K., 1970 £1,265,000.

CAPITAL.—Porto Novo (85,000). Principal commercial town and port, Ψ Cotonou (120,000).

FLAG.—Three stripes, one vertical, green, two horizontal yellow and red.

NATIONAL DAY.—August 1.

British Embassy (see Togo).

DENMARK
(Kongeriget Danmark)

King, Frederik IX, K.G., elder son of King Christian X, *born* March 11, 1899; *suc.* April 20, 1947; *married* May 24, 1935, Princess Ingrid (born March 28, 1910), daughter of H.M. King Gustav VI Adolf, King of Sweden; and has issue Princess Margrethe, *born* April 16, 1940 (*Heir Presumptive*), *married* June 10, 1967, Count Henri de Monpezat (Prince Henrik of Denmark) and has issue, 2 sons; Princess Benedikte, *born* April 29, 1944, *married* Feb. 3, 1968, Prince Richard of Sayn-Wittgenstein-Berleburg; and Princess Anne-Marie, *born* Aug. 30, 1946, *married* Sept. 18, 1964, Constantine XIII, King of the Hellenes.

CABINET

Prime Minister, Hilmar ~~Baunsgaard.~~ J. O. KRAG 10/71

Minister of Foreign Affairs, Poul Hartling.

Finance, ~~Erik Ninn-Hansen.~~ K. B. Andersen 10/71

Fisheries and Greenland, A. C. Normann.

Cultural Affairs, Technical Co-operation with Emerging Countries and Disarmament, K. Helveg Petersen.

Interior, H. C. Toft.

Justice, Knud Thestrup.

Defence, Lt.-Col. Knud Østergaard.

Agriculture, Henry Christensen.

Commerce, Knud Thomsen.

Communications, Ove Guldberg.

Housing, Aage Hastrup.

Social Affairs, Mrs. Nathalie Lind.

Education, Helge Larsen.

Labour, Lauge Dahlgaard.

Economics, Nordic Affairs and European Market Affairs, P. Nyboe Andersen.

Ecclesiastical Affairs, Arne Fog Pedersen.

ROYAL DANISH EMBASSY IN LONDON
29 Pont Street, S.W.1
[01-584-0102]

Ambassador Extraordinary and Plenipotentiary, His Excellency Erling Kristiansen (1964).

Minister-Counsellor, H. Kühne.

1st Secretary, A. C. Jönsson.

2nd Secretary, C. Sode Mogensen.

Agricultural Counsellor, M. Munch.

Counsellor for Press and Cultural Affairs, H. Agerbak.

Military Attaché, Lt.-Col. H.H. Prince Georg of Denmark, C.V.O.

Asst. Press and Cultural Attaché, N-P. Albertsen.

Commercial and Consular Section.
67 Pont Street, S.W.1. [01-584-0102]

Economic Counsellor (in charge of Consular Affairs), Sv. A. Nielsen.

Commercial Counsellor, N. Buch Hansen.

Commercial Secretary, P. H. Gideon.

1st Secretary, C. U. Haxthausen.

Consul, T. F. Germer.

Vice-Consul, Niels Kristensen.

Fisheries Attaché, J. C. Bogstad.

Scientific Attaché, K. Kristiansen.

Area and Population.—A Kingdom of Northern Europe, consisting of the islands of Zeeland, Funen, Lolland, etc., the peninsula of Jutland, and the outlying island of Bornholm in the Baltic, the Faroes

and Greenland. Denmark is situated between 54° 34′–57° 45′ N. lat., and 8° 5′–15° E. 12′ long., with an area of 17,000 square miles, and a population estimated (Jan., 1969), of 4,879,187. In 1968 there were 74,543 births, 47,290 deaths and 39,457 marriages.

Government.—Under the Constitution of the Kingdom of Denmark Act of June 5, 1953, the legislature consists of one chamber, the *Folketing*, of not more than 179 members, including 2 for the Faröes and 2 for Greenland. In the 1968 elections the Social Democrats obtained 62 seats, Conservatives 37, Venstre 34, Radicals 27, Socialist People's Party 11, Left-Socialists 4, Faröes 2, Greenland 2. Voting age has been 21 since May, 1961. The *Folketing* passed a proposal to reduce the voting age to 18, on which a referendum was planned to be held late in 1971.

Education is free and compulsory, the schools being maintained by taxation. Special schools are numerous, technical and agricultural predominating. There are Universities at Copenhagen (founded in 1478), Aarhus (1933), and Odense (1966).

Language and Literature.—The Danish language is akin to Swedish and Norwegian. Danish literature, ancient and modern, embraces all forms of expression, familiar names being Hans Christian Andersen (1805–1875), Sören Kierkegaard (1813–1855) and Georg Brandes (1842–1927), with Henrik Pontoppidan (1857–1943) and Karl Gjellerup (1857–1919), who shared the Nobel Prize for Literature in 1917, and Johannes V. Jensen (1873–1950), who received the same award in 1944. Some 61 newspapers are published in Denmark; 10 daily papers are published in Copenhagen.

Production and Industry.—Nine per cent. of the population lives exclusively by agriculture, and about 52 per cent. by manufactures and trade. The chief agricultural products are pigs, cattle, dairy products, poultry and eggs, seeds, cereals and sugar beef; manufactures are mostly based on imported raw material but there are also considerable imports of finished goods.

COMMUNICATIONS.—Mercantile marine (ships above 100 gross tonnage) (January, 1970 948 ships, with a gross tonnage of 3,194,000. On

March 31, 1967, there were 2,354 kilometres of railway and 3,252,234 kilometres of telegraph and telephone lines.

FINANCE 1971–72

Revenue (*Budget estimate*)..... Kr. 40,097,418,000
Expenditure (*Budget estimate*).. 36,811,792,000

Denmark's balance of payments showed a deficit for 1970 of Kr.4,043,000,000 (1969,—Kr. 3,143,000,000).

Rate of Exchange—Kr. 18=£1 (*see also* p. 83).

TRADE

	1969	1970
	Kr. million	
Total Imports.............	28,501	32,885
Total Exports.............	22,182	24,672

Trade with U.K.

	1969	1970
Imports from U.K.	£191,897,000	£220,208,000
Exports to U.K...	245,104,000	275,038,000

The principal imports are machinery, liquid and solid fuels, base metals, vehicles, textile products, chemicals, fertilizers, cereals, feeding stuffs and wood and cork. The chief exports are agricultural produce, fish products, butter, bacon, eggs, meat and livestock, ships, machinery, pharmaceuticals and ready made clothing.

CAPITAL.— Ψ Copenhagen. Population (1969), 835,246; Greater Copenhagen, 1,199,010. Other centres are: Ψ Aarhus 112,750; Ψ Odense 104,174; Ψ Aalborg, 83,519; Ψ Esbjerg, 57,309; Ψ Randers, 41,809; Roskilde, 39,751; Ψ Kolding, 36,995; Ψ Horsens, 36,123; Ψ Fredericia, 34,078; Ψ Vejle, 32,171.

FLAG.—Red, with white cross

NATIONAL DAY.—June 5 (Constitution Day).

Copenhagen, distant from London 728 miles; transit 36 hours by sea.

BRITISH EMBASSY.

Offices, Kastelsvej 38–40, Copenhagen.
Residence, Bredgade 26, Copenhagen.

Ambassador Extraordinary and Plenipotentiary, His Excellency Andrew Alexander Steel Stark, C.M.G., C.V.O. (1971).................£6,925

Counsellor, K. R. C. Pridham.

Counsellor (Commercial), G. W. Marshall, M.B.E.

Defence, Naval, Military and Air Attaché, Cdr. T. M. B. Firth, R.N.

Scientific Attaché, Dr. M. H. Proctor (*resident in Stockholm*).

1st Secretaries, R. F. Browning; E. G. B. Allen (*Consular*); W. Jones (*Information*); D. Mellor (*Commercial*); D. F. Roberts (*Agric. and Food Attaché*); G. D. Cossar (*Labour*) (*resident in Stockholm*).

Asst. Military Attaché, Major I. F. B. Tytler.

Asst. Air Attaché, Sqn. Ldr. D. S. Lennox, (*resident in Stockholm*).

2nd Secretaries, P. V. Rollitt (*Commercial*); R. N. Dales; W. H. Freeman (*Commercial*).

Attaché, J. L. Katzaros.

Chaplain, Rev. H. Picton.

There are Consulates at *Aabenraa*, *Aalborg*, *Esbjerg*, *Aarhus*, *Odense*, *Thorshavn* and *Klaksvig* (Faröes).

———

British Council Representative (vacant). Møntergade 1, Copenhagen.

Outlying Parts of the Kingdom

The outlying parts of Denmark have about 81,000 inhabitants. The FARÖES, or Sheep Islands (540 sq. m.; pop. (1969) 38,000), capital, Thorshavn, are governed by a *Lagting* of 26 members. a *Landstyr* of 4 members which deals with special Faröes affairs, and send 2 representatives to the *Folketing* at Copenhagen. On Sept. 14, 1946, the *Lagting*, with the consent of the Danish Government, for its own guidance held a plebiscite on the Faröes. About one-third of the electors did not, however, take part in the voting: of the rest a little more than half the votes cast were in favour of separation from Denmark and the establishment of a republic. At a subsequent general election for the *Lagting* a great majority voted in favour of remaining part of the Kingdom of Denmark with a certain measure of home rule and in 1948 the Faröes received this. Trade with U.K. in 1970 totalled: Imports, £941,000; Exports, £1,221,000. GREENLAND (ice-free portion about 132,000 sq. m., total area about 840,000 sq. m., population, 1965, 48,792), is divided into 3 provinces (West, North and East). Greenland (capital, Godthaab) has a *Landsraad* of 17 members and sends 2 representatives to the *Folketing* at Copenhagen. The trade of Greenland is mainly under the management of the Royal Greenland Trade Department. Mineral and oil prospecting revealed deposits of lead, zinc, iron ore, oil and gas. Commercial exploitations of these resources has not yet begun. The United States of America has acquired certain rights to maintain air bases in Greenland.

DOMINICAN REPUBLIC
(República Dominicana)

President, Joaquin Balaguer, *born* Sept. 1, 1907; *elected* June 1, 1966; *re-elected* May 16, 1970; *assumed office* July 1, 1970.

EMBASSY AND CONSULATE.

4 Braemar Mansions, Cornwall Gardens, S.W.7
[01–937–1921; 7116 (*Consulate*)]

Ambassador Extraordinary and Plenipotentiary, His Excellency Lic. Porfirio Herrera Báez (1969).

There are also Consular Offices at *Liverpool*, *Birmingham*, *Manchester*, *Nottingham*, *Grimsby*, *Southampton*, *Plymouth*, *Cardiff*, *Edinburgh*, *Glasgow* and *Belfast*.

The Dominican Republic, formerly the Spanish portion of the island of Hispaniola, is the oldest settlement of European origin in America. The western part of the island forms the Republic of Haiti. (*For Map, see* Index.)

The island lies between Cuba on the west and Puerto Rico on the east and covers an area of about 19,322 square miles, with a population (U.N. estimate, 1970) of 4,012,000. The climate is tropical in the low lands and semi-tropical to temperate in the higher altitudes.

Government.—Santo Domingo was discovered by Christopher Columbus in December, 1492, and remained a Spanish Colony until 1821. In 1822 it was subjugated by the neighbouring Haitians who remained in control until 1844 when the Dominican Republic was proclaimed. The country was occupied by American marines from 1916 until the adoption of a new Constitution in 1924. In July, 1924, a properly elected Constitutional Government was installed. From 1930 until May 30, 1961 (when he was assassinated) Generalissimo Rafael Trujillo ruled the country.

A Council of State headed by Rafael F. Bonnelly was set up in 1962, and Professor Juan Bosch, elected President in December 1962, held office until September, 1963, when he was deposed by a military junta. A revolt in favour of ex-President Bosch in April, 1965, developed into civil war lasting until September the same year when a provisional President was elected. At a further election on June 1, 1966, Dr. Joaquin Balaguer was elected President; re-elected May 16, 1970.

Communications.—According to local classification there are 2,932 miles of first class and 1,392 miles of second class and inter-communal roads in the Republic. There is a direct road from Santo

Domingo to Port-au-Prince, the capital of Haiti, but that part of it in the border area has fallen into disuse and it is no longer possible to travel direct between the two capitals except by air. The frontier has been closed since Sept., 1967. A telephone system connects practically all the principal towns of the republic and there is a telegraph service with all parts of the world. There are more than 90 commercial broadcasting stations and there is a television station operated by Radiotelevision Dominicana, which with the help of relay stations provides receptions of its programmes in the major cities. A second television station in Santo Domingo-Rahintel transmits to the local area.

Spanish is the language of the Republic.

The Republic is served by five airlines, and an international airport 18 miles to the east of the capital is in operation.

Sugar, coffee, cocoa, and tobacco are the most important crops. Other products are peanuts, maize, rice, bananas, molasses, salt, cement, bauxite, cattle, sisal products, honey and chocolate. There is a growing number of light industries producing beer, tinned foodstuffs, glass products, cotton textiles, soap, cigarettes, construction materials, plastic articles, shoes, paper, rum, matches, peanut oil and other products.

FINANCE

Budget	1969	1970
Revenue.....	RD\$232,000,000	RD\$267,100,000
Expenditure..	236,700,000	262,900,000

One *Dominican Peso*=\$1·00 U.S.

TRADE

	1969	1970
Imports......	RD\$210,400,000	RD\$206,800,000
Exports......	184,100,000	213,600,000

Trade with U.K.

	1969	1970
Imports from U.K.....	£2,835,000	£3,552,000
Exports to U.K.......	685,000	1,144,000

The chief imports are machinery, foodstuffs, iron and steel, cotton textiles and yarns, mineral oils (including petrol), cars and other motor vehicles, chemical and pharmaceutical products, electrical equipment and accessories, construction material, paper and paper products, and rubber and rubber products; the chief exports are sugar, coffee, cocoa, tobacco, chocolate, molasses and bauxite.

The principal exports to U.K. over a number of years have been sugar and sugar preparations.

CAPITAL.—Santo Domingo (formerly called Ciudad Trujillo), population of the Capital District (estimated, 1969), 823,000. Other centres, with populations (estimated) 1967: Santiago de los Caballeros (205,635); La Vega (143,205); San Francisco de Macoris (128,657); San Juan (114,232); and San Cristóbal (112,996).

FLAG.—Red and blue, with white cross bearing an emblem at centre.

NATIONAL DAY.—February 27 (Independence Day, 1844).

BRITISH EMBASSY

Avenida Independencia 84, Santo Domingo.
Ambassador Extraordinary and Plenipotentiary, His Excellency Leslie Boas, O.B.E. (1969)..... £6,475
1st Secretary, G. Cheesman (*Consul*).

BRITISH CONSULAR OFFICES

There are British Consular Offices at *Santo Domingo, Puerto Plata* and *San Pedro de Macoris.*

ECUADOR

(Republica del Ecuador)

President, Dr. José Mariá Velasco (Ibarra), *elected* June 2, 1968; *assumed office* Sept. 1, 1968.

2 E+

EMBASSY AND CONSULATE.

Flat 3B, 3 Hans Crescent, S.W.1
[01-584-1367]
Ambassador Extraordinary and Plenipotentiary, His Excellency Dr. Antonio Parra-Velasco (1969).
2nd Secretary, Señor Diego Paredes.
Counsellor (*Commercial*), Sr. Edwin Marchan Carrasco.
Naval Attaché, Capt. Guillermo Jarrín N.
Air Attaché; Col. Luis Morejon.
There are consulates at *Liverpool, Birmingham* and *Glasgow.*

Area and Population.—Ecuador is an equatorial State of South America, the mainland extending from lat. 1° 38′ N. to 4° 50′ S., and between 75° 20′ and 81° W. long., comprising an area reduced by boundary settlements with Peru (Jan. 29, 1942) to about 226,000 sq. miles. (*For* MAP, *see* Index.)

The Republic of Ecuador is divided into 19 provinces and one territory. It has a population estimated (1970) at 5,890,000, mostly descendants of the Spaniards, aboriginal Indians, and Mestizoes. The territory of the Republic extends across the Western Andes, the highest peak of which is Aconcagua, in the Chilean sector (22,976 ft.), the highest peaks in Ecuador being Chimborazo (20,498 ft.), Iliniza (17,405 ft.), Carihuairazo (16,515 ft.), Cotocachi (16,301 ft.), and Pichincha (16,000 ft.) in the Western Cordillera; and Cotopaxi (19,612 ft.), Antisana (18,864 ft.), Cayambe (19,160 ft.), Altar (17,730 ft.), Sangay (17,464 ft.), Tungurahua (16,690 ft.), and Sincholagua (16,365 ft.) in the Eastern Cordillera. Ecuador is watered by the Upper Amazon, and by the rivers Guayas, Mira, Santiago, Chone, and Esmeraldas on the Pacific coast. There are extensive forests, and the cinchona bark tree is common.

The *Galápagos* (Tortoise) *Islands* forming the territory of Colon, were annexed by Ecuador in 1832. The archipelago lies in the Pacific, about 500 miles from Saint Elena peninsula, the most westerly point of the mainland. There are 12 large and several hundred smaller islands with a total area of about 3,000 sq. miles and an estimated population (1970) of 3,600. The capital is San Cristobal, on Chatham Island. Although the archipelago lies on the equator, the temperature of the surrounding water is well below equatorial average owing to the *Antarctic Humboldt Current.* The islands export guano, orchilla moss and cattle. There is an increasing amount of fishing, mainly for the North American market.

Government.—The former *Kingdom of Quito* was conquered by the Incas of Peru in the latter part of the 15th century. Early in the 16th century Pizarro's conquests led to the inclusion of the present territory of Ecuador in the Spanish Viceroyalty of Peru. The independence of the country was achieved in a revolutionary war which culminated in the battle of Mount Pichincha (May 24, 1822). The constitution of 1946 was suspended in 1963, when Dr. Carlos Arosemena, President of Ecuador from Nov. 8, 1961, was deposed by the Armed Forces on July 11, 1963. His powers were taken over by a junta of officers who stayed in power until March 29, 1966, when a caretaker government took office. A new Government was formed in November, 1966, after elections for a constituent assembly and a new constitution came into force on May 19, 1967. At elections held on June 2, 1968, Dr. José Mariá Velasco (Ibarra) was elected President and assumed office on Sept. 1, 1968. He dismissed Congress on June 22, 1970, and assumed supreme power.

Production and Industry.—The chief products are

bananas, cocoa, coffee, sugar, rice, petroleum, straw hats, pyrethrum, vegetable ivory and balsa wood. The petroleum is insufficient to meet the whole of Ecuador's needs, but the recent discovery of oil in commercial quantities in the eastern part of Ecuador may lead eventually to the country having an exportable surplus, when the problem of transporting the oil across the Andes has been solved. In the highlands the principal crops are maize, wheat, potatoes and other temperate products. Small amounts of gold, silver and lead are mined, and emeralds and rubies are occasionally found. There is little industry, the textile industry being the most important.

Communications.—There are 11,741 km. of permanent roads and 5,044 km. of roads which are only open during the dry season. There are about 750 miles of railway, including the railway from Quito to Guayaquil. Nine commercial airlines operate international flights, linking Ecuador with New York, Miami, Lima, Santiago, Rio de Janeiro, Paris, Frankfurt, etc. There are internal services between all important towns.

Defence.—The standing Army has a strength of about 15,000. There is an Air Force of some 40 aircraft of various kinds and a small Navy. All are being advised by U.S. missions.

Language and Literature.—Spanish is the language of the country. The electorate is confined to adult male and female citizens who can read and write, and in recent years considerable headway has been made in reducing the high figure of illiteracy. 3 daily newspapers are published at Quito and 4 at Guayaquil. Elementary education is free and compulsory. In 1970 there were 7,142 primary schools with 928,687 pupils and 655 high schools with 173,614 pupils. The 10 Universities (at Quito (2), Guataquil (3), Cuenca, Loja and Portoveijo and the Polytechnic Schools at Quito and Guayaquil) had 22,637 students in the same year.

FINANCE   1969

Revenue (*Budget Estimates*) ...	Sucres 5,147,197,000
Expenditure (*Budget Estimates*) .	5,147,197,000
Internal Debt (Sept. 30, 1967).	5,570,000
External Debt, Dec. 31, 1967....	$U.S.163,700,000

The official rate of Exchange: *Sucres* 43·63 = £1, is used for most legal imports and exports. There is also a free rate of exchange. *See also* p. 83.

TRADE

Import licences are required for all merchandise and these are issued by the Central Bank of Ecuador.

	1967	1968
Imports*.....	$U.S.165,165,000	$U.S.103,417,000
Exports*.....	166,035,000	176,804,000
	*Permits cleared	

Trade with U.K.

	1969	1970
Imports from U.K.....	£4,136,000	£7,027,000
Exports to U.K.......	399,000	588,000

The chief exports are bananas, cocoa, coffee and sugar. Other exports are rice, balsa wood, castoroil seeds, hats, pharmaceuticals, fish, ivory nuts and pyrethrum. Manufactured goods and machinery are the main imports.

CAPITAL.—Quito. Population (estimated 1968), 483,847; Ψ Guayaquil (716,617) is the chief port; other centres are Cuenca (73,407); Ambato (69,766); Riobamba (50,710); Esmeraldas (51,573); and Manta (42,750). The foregoing figures of urban populations have been revised by the Census and Statistics Office to exclude from 1968 figures for rural areas of the cities (*i.e.* areas not supplied by city fuel or water services).

FLAG.—Three horizontal bands, yellow, blue and red (the yellow band twice the width of the others); emblem in centre.

NATIONAL DAY.—August 10 (*Dia de la Independencia*).

BRITISH EMBASSY

Calle G. Suarez, 111 (P.O. Box No. 314), Quito.

Ambassador Extraordinary and Plenipotentiary, His Excellency Peter Mennell, M.B.E. (1970). £6,475
1st Secretary, D. P. Small, M.B.E. (*Commercial, Head of Chancery*).
Vice-Consul, A. E. Clarke.
There is a British Consular Office at *Guayaquil*.

EGYPT. *See* United Arab Republic

EQUATORIAL GUINEA

President, Francisco Macias (Nguema), *elected* October 12, 1968.

Formerly the territory of " Spanish Guinea ", Equatorial Guinea consists of the island of Fernando Póo, an island in the Bight of Biafra about 20 miles from the west coast of Africa, Annobon Island in the Gulf of Guinea, the Corisco Islands (Corisco, Elobey Grande and Elobey Chico) and Rio Muni, a coastal settlement lying between the Cameroon Republic and Gaboon and extending about 125 miles inland. It has a total area of about 11,000 sq. miles and a population (U.N. estimate, 1969) of 286,000.

Fernando Póo is a mountainous island with forests of oil palm, ebony, mahogany and oak, and sugarcane, cotton and indigo. Cocoa, coffee, sugar, tobacco, vanilla nut and kola nut are cultivated and large quantities of cocoa and other products are exported.

Government.—Former colonies of Spain, the territories now forming the Republic of Equatorial Guinea were from April 1, 1960, constituted as two provinces of Metropolitan Spain, the inhabitants having the same rights as Spanish citizens. As a result of a plebiscite held on Dec. 15, 1963, an autonomous *régime* was instituted on June 2, 1964 with the approval of the Spanish Government. Equatorial Guinea became fully independent on October 12, 1968, after a referendum on the new constitution held in August, 1968, and presidential elections on Sept. 22, 1968. The latter were supervised by a U.N. Mission. The first President, Señor Francisco Macias, assumed office on Independence Day, having two days earlier formed a coalition ministry. The President took the Defence portfolio and appointed Ministers of Commerce and Foreign Affairs.

Severe disorders occurred during February and March, 1969, following incidents at the town of Bata (in Rio Muni). Spanish residents left Equatorial Guinea in large numbers, having had to seek the protection of residual Spanish forces while awaiting evacuation to Spain. In a statement to the United Nations Security Council on April 4, the Secretary-General reported that all Spanish troops had left Equatorial Guinea by March 28, together with all civilians who wished to leave. Some 600 Spanish civilians elected to remain in Fernando Póo and about 80 in Rio Muni.

CAPITAL.—Ψ Santa Isabel, on the island of Fernando Póo (population, 9,000). Ψ Bata is the principal town and port of Rio Muni. FLAG.—Three horizontal bands, green over white over red; blue triangle next staff; coat of arms in centre of white band.

British Ambassador, His Excellency Anthony Arthur Golds, C.M.G., C.V.O. (1970) (Resident at *Yaoundé, Cameroon*).

ETHIOPIA
(Ye Ityopia Nigusa Negist Mengist—The Imperial Ethiopian Government)

Emperor of Ethiopia, His Imperial Majesty Hailé Selassié I, K.G., G.C.B., G.C.M.G., G.C.V.O., LL.D., son of the late Ras Makonnen, Governor of Harar; *born* July 23, 1892; *married* in July, 1911, Woizero (*Lady*) Menan, (*who died* February, 1962) daughter of Jantrar Asfaw of Ambassal and Woizero (*Lady*) Sehin Mikael, daughter of King Mikael of Wollo; *crowned as Negus*, Oct., 1928; *proclaimed Emperor*, April 2, 1930; *crowned as Emperor*, Nov. 2, 1930; *in exile*, 1936–1940; *led his patriot army*, 1940–41; *returned to his capital*, May 5, 1941.

Crown Prince, H.I.H. Prince Asfa Wossen, G.C.V.O., G.B.E., eldest son of the Emperor, *born* July 27, 1916; *married* May 9, 1932, Walatta Israel daughter of Ras Seyoum, whom he divorced in 1945, when he married Woizero Medferiash Worq, daughter of Major-General Ababa Damtaw.

Prime Minister, Aklilou Habte-Wold.

EMBASSY IN LONDON
17 Princes Gate, S.W.7
[01–589–7212]

Ambassador Extraordinary and Plenipotentiary, His Excellency Lt.-Gen. Iyassu Mengesha (1970).
Counsellor, Ato Engeda Abbebe.
1st Secretary, Ato Zaudie Makuria.
2nd Secretary, Ato Teferra Guebre-Christos.
3rd Secretary, Ato Zelleke Bellete.

Position and Extent.—The Empire of Ethiopia, with which Eritrea was federated from 1952 to 1962 when it was incorporated as a province, is in North-Eastern Africa, bounded on the north west by the Sudan; on the south by Kenya; on the east by Afars and Issas Territory and the Republic of Somalia; and on the north-east by the Red Sea. The area is estimated at 400,000 square miles, with a population (U.N. estimate, 1969) of 24,769,000 of whom about one-third are of the ruling race of Semitic origin (Amharas and Tigres) and the remainder mainly Gallas, Guraghi, Sidama, Agao, negro tribes on the west and south frontiers, and Danakil and Somalis on the east.

Ethiopia is mainly a mountainous country, volcanic in origin, with several peaks of about 14,000 ft., notably in the centre and in the Simien range in the north; many other mountains exceed 10,000 ft. Eritrea consists of a mountainous hogsback range up to 10,000 ft., interposed between the Red Sea and the Sudan, flanked on east and west

by flatter territory. The lower country and valley gorges are very hot; the higher plateaux are well watered, with a genial climate. On the high plateaux there are two main seasons in the year, a dry winter, October to May, and a rainy summer from June to September, with a season of "small rains" occurring generally in March. The chief river is the Blue Nile, issuing from Lake Tana; the Atbara and many other tributaries of the Nile also rise in the Ethiopian highlands.

Those of Semitic origin (Amharas and Tigres), who inhabit the southern highlands of Eritrea, provinces of Tigre, Begemdir, Gojjam, parts of Shoa, and many of the Gallas, are Christians of the Ethiopian Orthodox Church, which was formerly led by the head of the Coptic Church, the Patriarch at Alexandria. Since 1959, however, the Ethiopian Church has been autocephalous and the new Patriarch, Abuna Theophilos, was enthroned by the Ethiopian archbishops in May, 1971. Moslems predominate in some areas, notably northern Eritrea, Harar and Jimma and Arussi, the Moslem centre being at Harar. The province of Gamu Gofa and parts of Sidamo and Arussi have considerable pagan elements.

Government.—The Empire is governed by a Council of Ministers, responsible to the Emperor, and a Parliament consisting of a Senate and a Chamber of Deputies, in accordance with the revised constitution promulgated in 1955. Elections, on a basis of universal suffrage, were held in 1957, and the Chamber of Deputies met for the first time at the end of that year. General elections have since been held in 1961, 1965 and 1969. The Chamber enjoys greater fiscal control than the previous Assembly and there is a limited degree of ministerial responsibility to Parliament. The Senate continues to be nominated by the Emperor.

Eritrea.—Eritrea was administered by Great Britain from the end of the Second World War until September 15, 1952, when in accordance with a resolution of the United Nations Assembly of December 2, 1950, it was federated with Ethiopia under the Ethiopian Crown, becoming a province of Ethiopia in 1962.

Production and Industry.—The principal pursuits are agriculture and cattle breeding. In the hotter regions, sugar-cane, cotton, &c., flourish; in the middle zone maize, wheat, barley, coffee, oranges and other fruit trees, tobacco, potatoes and oil seeds are cultivated; and above 6,000 feet are excellent pastures with some corn cultivation. Coffee provided approximately 58 per cent. of the country's total exports by value in 1969. The forests are a potential source of wealth. Horses, mules, donkeys, cattle, oxen, goats, and sheep, and camels in the lowlands, form a large portion of the wealth of the people. Industry is small, the main products being textiles, foodstuffs, beer and cement. Hydro-electric power production and telecommunications are expanding rapidly, however, mainly with loans from the World Bank, which in 1971 had approved a number of loans for agricultural development.

Communications.—A railway links Addis Ababa, the capital, *viâ* Dire-Dawa, with Jibouti, 486 miles away. It carried 457,729 passengers and 411,460 tons of freight in 1969–70. In Eritrea a narrow gauge line runs from Massawa to Asmara and on to Agordet. Several roads were constructed before and during the Italian occupation; the principal road runs from Addis Ababa to Dessie and on to Asmara, with a branch from Dessie to Assab on the Red Sea Coast. Addis Ababa and Asmara are linked also by a road running through Gondar and along Lake Tana. Others run from Addis Ababa west to Lekempti, south-west to Jimma, Gore

and Gambela, south to the Kenya frontier, and in the East to Dire Dawa, Harar and the northern region of the Somali Republic. Partly financed by large loans from the International Bank for Reconstruction and Development, much further improvement and extension of roads is being undertaken. The Ethiopian Air Lines maintain regular services from Addis Ababa to most of the provincial towns. External services are operated to Athens, Frankfurt, Rome, Paris, Aden Jibouti, Taiz, Cairo, Khartoum, Nairobi, Dar-es-Salaam, Entebbe, Lagos, Accra, New Delhi and Karachi.

Defence.—A Ministry of Defence has been instituted. The armed forces comprise the Imperial Army, including the Imperial Bodyguard, the Imperial Air Force and the Imperial Navy. The Army consists of four infantry divisions, including one mechanized brigade with armour, with normal artillery, engineer units and supporting arms including a parachute formation. An American Military Advisory and Assistance Group (MAAG) assists the forces, mainly the Army, with training and advice, under an agreement signed with the Ethiopian Government, There is a military academy at Harar and a military training centre at Holleta with a specialist training wing. The Imperial Air Force comprises a transport squadron, a bomber squadron, three fighter squadrons, a training squadron, a jet conversion squadron, a reconnaissance unit and an elementary training unit. The Imperial Air Force Headquarters is situated at Debre Zeit. The aircraft are mostly of American manufacture but also include Canberras.

The Imperial Navy has a headquarters in Addis Ababa with a main base at Massawa and a smaller one at Assab. The principal units are an ex-U.S. seaplane tender (*Ethiopia*), a patrol craft squadron of 5 and a MTB squadron of 4.

Education.—Elementary education is provided without religious discrimination by Government schools in the main centres of population; there are also Mission schools, and cadet-schools for the Army, Air Force, and Police. Government secondary schools are found mainly in Addis Ababa, but also in most of the provincial capitals. In 1961 the Hailé Selassié I University was founded to co-ordinate the existing institutions of higher education (University College, Engineering, Building and Theological Colleges in Addis Ababa, Agricultural College at Alemaya, near Harar, and Public Health Centre in Gondar, etc.) and to provide a framework for future development. Amharic is the official language of instruction, with English as the first foreign language. Arabic is taught in Koran Schools; and Ge'ez (the ancient Ethiopic) in Christian Church Schools, which abound. Adult education is met to some extent by institutes which provide evening classes in Addis Ababa. In 1971 the International Development Agency granted a loan of U.S. $95 million for the development of secondary education.

Finance.—Total revenue for 1969-70 was estimated at £100 m., while expenditure was expected to reach £105 m., 9 per cent. more than in 1968-69. The Ethiopian dollar has a value of 5·52 grains of fine gold and is divided into 100 cents. At Mar. 31, 1971, the combined note and coin issue amounted to £73,100,000. Foreign exchange and gold reserves of the National Bank and Commercial Banks amounted to £31,100,000 at the same date. Eth. $6=£1. (*See also* p. 83.)

Trade.—The chief imports by value are machinery and transport equipment, manufactured goods, chemicals, beverages and tobacco (from U.K.); the principal exports by value being coffee, oilseeds, hides and skins, and pulses.

TRADE

	1969	1970
Total Imports......	£72,060,000	£64,710,000
Total Exports......	44,337,000	£49,680,000

Trade with U.K.

	1969	1970
Imports from U.K.....	£4,813,000	£4,834,000
Exports to U.K.......	1,950,000	1,963,000

CAPITAL, Addis Ababa (population, estimated July, 1967, 644,190), also capital of the province of Shoa; Asmara (population 178,537) is the capital of the Province of Eritrea. Dire Dawa is the most important commercial centre after Addis Ababa and Asmara, Ψ Massawa and Ψ Assab (recently enlarged) are the two main ports. There are ancient architectural remains at Aksum, Gondar, Lalibela and elsewhere.

ETHIOPIAN FLAG.—Three horizontal bands; green, yellow, red; bearing crowned lion at centre.

NATIONAL DAY.—July 23.

BRITISH EMBASSY
(Addis Ababa)

Ambassador Extraordinary and Plenipotentiary, His Excellency Alan Hugh Campbell, C.M.G. (1969) £6,925

Counsellor, R. B. Dorman.

Defence Attaché, Lt.-Col. R. M. Holman, M.B.E.

Air Attaché, Wing Cdr. V. K. Metcalfe, D.F.C. (resident at Nairobi).

1st Secretary, R. C. Robinson, M.B.E. (*Commercial and Consul*).

2nd Secretaries, J. R. Backhouse; R. J. Miller (*Information*).

3rd Secretary, J. S. Wall.

BRITISH CONSULAR OFFICES

There are British Consular Offices at *Addis Ababa* and *Asmara*.

Hon. Consul, Asmara, B. H. Burwood-Taylor.

British Council Representative, J. A. Barnett, Artistic Building, Hailé Selassié Avenue, Addis Ababa.

FINLAND
(Suomi)

President, Dr. Urho Kaleva Kekkonen, G.C.B., *born 1900, elected* Feb. 15, 1956; re-elected 1962 and 1968, for a term of six years.

CABINET

Prime Minister, Dr. Ahti Karjalainen (*C.P.*).
Minister of Labour, Veikko Helle (*S.D.P.*).
Foreign Affairs, Väino Leskinen (*S.D.P.*).
Justice, Mikko Laaksonen (*S.D.P.*).
Interior, Eino Uusitalo (*C.P.*).
Defence, Kristian Gestrin (*S.P.P.*).
Finance, C. O. Tallgren (*S.P.P.*), *Deputy Minister of Finance*, Valto Käkelä (*S.D.P.*).
Education, Jaakko Itälä (*L.P. associate*); *Deputy Minister*, Mrs. Meeri Kalavainen (*S.D.P.*).
Agriculture, Nestori Kaalsalainen (*C.P.*).
Communications and Public Works, Kalervo Haapsalo (*S.D.P.*).
Trade, Arne Berner (*L.P.*).
Industry, Olavi Salonen (*S.D.P.*).
Social Affairs, Pekka Kuusi (*S.D.P.*). *Deputy Minister of Social Affairs*, Mrs. K. H. Eskelinen (*C.P.*).
Development, Olavi Mattila (*C.P.* associate).

[*C.P.*=Centre Party; *S.D.P.*=Social Democratic Party; *S.P.P.*=Swedish People's Party; *L.P.*=Liberal Party.]

✗ WHOLE GOV. RES. 18/3/71

FINNISH EMBASSY AND CONSULATE
66 Chester Square, S.W.1
[01–730–9771–5]
Ambassador Extraordinary and Plenipotentiary, His
Excellency Otso Wartiovaara (1968).
Counsellors, M. Göran Stenius; M. Esko Rajakoski;
M. Juhani Peitsara (*Commercial*).
1st Secretary, M. Risto Kauppi.
Attachés, M. Pekka Harttila; M. Olli Pekkarinen;
M. Jaakko Bergquist (*Press*).
Military, Naval and Air Attaché, Capt. Kai Ruusu-
vuori.
Asst. do., Maj. Hans Christensen.

Area and Population.—A country situated on the
Gulfs of Finland and Bothnia, with a total area of
130,165 square miles, of which 70 per cent. is forest,
9 per cent. cultivated, 9 per cent. lakes and 12 per
cent. waste and other land, population (1970),
4,706,000. In 1967 the birth rate was 16·6, death
rate 9·4 per 1,000. The infant mortality rate was
14·8 per 1,000 live births. 92·6 per cent. of the
people are Lutherans, 1·3 per cent. Greek Orthodox
and 6·1 per cent. others.

The Aland Archipelago (Ahvenanmaa), a group of
small islands at the entrance to the Gulf of Bothnia,

covers about 572 square miles, with a population
(1967) of 21,532 (97 per cent. Swedish-speaking).
The islands have a semi-autonomous status.

Government.—Under the Constitution there is a
single Chamber (*Eduskunta*) for which women are
eligible, composed of 200 members, elected
by universal suffrage of both sexes. The legislative
power is vested in the Chamber and the President.
The highest executive power is held by the President who is elected for a period of 6 years.

Negotiations for the formation of a broadly-based
coalition government on lines proposed by the President lasted from May 15, 1970, until July 15, 1970,
when a five-party coalition government was
formed by Dr. Karjalainen. The Finnish People's
Democratic League left the Coalition in March,
1971.

Defence.—By the terms of the Peace Treaty
(Feb. 10, 1947) with U.K. and U.S.S.R., the Army

is limited to a force not exceeding 34,400. The
Navy is limited to a total of 10,000 tons displacement with personnel not exceeding 4,500. The
Air Force, including naval air arm, is limited to
60 machines with a personnel not exceeding 3,000.
Bombers or aircraft with bomb-carrying facilities
are expressly forbidden. The Defence Forces contain a cadre of regular officers and N.C.O.'s, but
their bulk is provided by conscripts who serve for
8–11 months. None of the Defence Forces has the
full complement permitted.

Education.—Primary education is compulsory
and free for all children from 7 to 16 years, and in
1966–67 there were 523,493 in attendance at primary
schools, with 282,147 in secondary schools; and
91,718 in colleges for vocational training. In
1966–67 there were 8 Higher Schools with 9,066
students, and 6 universities; the State University of
Helsinki (20,578 students); 2 at Turku (one
Swedish-speaking); and new universities at Oulu,
Jyväskylä and Tampere. Combined enrolment at
Higher Schools and Universities was 45,251.

Language and Literature.—Most Finns are bilingual. 92·4 per cent. speak Finnish as their first
language, 7·4 Swedish and the remaining 0·2 per
cent. other languages (mainly Lapps living a
nomadic life in the North). Since 1883 Finnish has
been on an equal footing with Swedish as the official
language of Finland, but since independence in 1917
Finnish has slowly been displacing Swedish. In
literature also, until the close of the eighteenth century, Swedish was dominant, but awakening Finnish nationalism in the early years of the nineteenth
century and the establishment of an association for
the promotion of Finnish literature in 1831 gave
Finnish the status of a literary language. There is
a vigorous modern literature. Eemil Sillanpää was
awarded the Nobel Prize for Literature in 1939.
There are 70 daily newspapers in Finland which
appear on 4 or more days per week (60 Finnish
language, and 10 Swedish).

Production and Industry.—Finland has a greater
area covered in forest than any other European
country except the Soviet Union. Consequently
the national economy is based on the timber, pulp
and paper industries. These industries employ a
large proportion of the working population and
accounted in 1968 for 61 per cent. of Finland's
foreign exchange earnings. The metal and engineering industries, producing 23 per cent. of
Finland's export income in 1968, form the second
important group. Exports of agricultural and
dairy products amounted to 5 per cent. of total
exports in 1968. The remaining export revenue
came from the glass, ceramics and furniture industries. To a large extent domestic requirements in
the textile, rubber, plastics, chemical and pharmaceutical, footwear and foodstuff trades, are met by
local factories.

Communications.—There are 5,556 miles of railroad and a well-developed telegraph and telephone
system. There is railway connection with Sweden
and U.S.S.R., passenger boat connection with
Sweden, Denmark and West Germany. Vessels
on the London to Leningrad route call at Helsinki.
There are also passenger/cargo boat connections
with most countries in the world. External civil
air services are maintained by BEA, Aero Oy
(Finnish Airlines), Kar Air, Scandinavian Airlines,
Malev and Czech Airlines. Finnair and Aeroflot
each maintain services to Moscow and to Leningrad. The merchant fleet (Dec, 1968) consists
of 78 steamships (108,960 tons gross), 414 motor
vessels (971,930 tons gross), and 14 sailing ships
with auxiliary engine (1,776 tons gross).

Finance.—On Jan. 1, 1963, all values expressed
in *Finnmarks* were divided by 100, in a reform of the

currency. *Finnmark* figures below are expressed in terms of the New *Finnmark*.

Finnmarks 10·00 = £1 (*see also* p. 83).

	1968 Finnmarks	1969 Finnmarks
Revenue (*Budget*)	9,276,000,000	9,222,000,000
Expenditure (*do.*)	9,275,000,000	9,221,000,000
Debt (Dec., 1968)	4,431,000,000	4,995,000,000

TRADE

	1967 Finnmarks	1968 Finnmarks
Total Imports	5,794,694,000	6,710,886,000
Total Exports	5,230,295,000	6,874,237,000

Trade with U.K.

	1969	1970
Imports from U.K.	£99,079,000	£128,901,000
Exports to U.K.	173,608,000	195,005,000

The principal imports are raw materials, food-stuffs, machinery and manufactured goods. The exports are principally the output of the timber mills (timber, cellulose and paper).

CAPITAL.—Ψ Helsinki (Helsingfors). Population (Dec., 1967), 526,896; other towns are Tampere (Tammerfors), 150,065; Ψ Turku (Abo), 148,399; Lahti, 85,515; Ψ Oulu (Uleaborg) 83,378; Ψ Pori (Björneborg) 71,010; Jyväskylä, 55,440; Kuopio, 55,183; Lappeenranta, 50,049; and Ψ Vaasa (Vasa) 48,660.

NATIONAL DAY.—December 6 (Day of Independence).

FLAG.—White with blue cross.

BRITISH EMBASSY
Helsinki

British Ambassador's Residence, It. Kaivopuisto 8B. *Chancery Offices,* Uudenmaankatu 16-20.

Ambassador Extraordinary and Plenipotentiary, His Excellency William Bernard John Ledwidge, C.M.G. (1969)............................£6,925

Counsellor (*Commercial*), R. Fox, O.B.E. (*and Consul-General*).

1st Secretaries, A. C. Stuart; C. Fletcher (*Information*); G. T. Burgess, M.B.E. (*Commercial*); D. Stuart.

Defence and Military Attaché, Col. J. W. Lloyd.

Naval Attaché, Capt. H. M. Ellis, R.N.

2nd Secretaries, A. H. Banks (*Commercial*); A. B. Gundersen (*Commercial*); H. O. Spankie; T. H. Moran, M.B.E.; P. Lever.

3rd Secretaries, D. Chambers (*Vice-Consul*); B. J. McDowell.

There are British Consular offices at *Helsinki, Tampere, Turku, Pori, Kotka, Oulu, Hamina* and *Vaasa.*

British Council Representative, J. Makin, M.B.E., E. Esplanaadikatu 22A, Helsinki 13.

FRANCE
(La République Française)

President of the French Republic, Georges Jean Raymond Pompidou, *born* July 5, 1911, *elected* June 15, 1969, *assumed office,* June 20, 1969.

Secretary-General of the President's Office, M. Michel Jobert.

Secretary-General of the French Community, M. Jacques Foccart.

President of the Senate, M. Alain Poher.

President of the National Assembly, M. Achille Peretti.

CABINET

Prime Minister, M. ~~Jacques Chaban-Delmas.~~ + MESSMER

Ministers of State:

Defence, M. Michel Debré.

Administrative Reform, M. Roger Frey.

Cultural Affairs, M. Jacques Duhamel.

Relations with Parliament, M. Jacques Chirac.

Justice, M. René Pleven.

Foreign Affairs, M. Maurice Schumann. ✓

Interior, M. Raymond Marcellin.

Education, M. Oliver Guichard.

Economy and Finance, M. Valéry Giscard d'Estaing. ✓

Planning and Regional Development, M. André Bettencourt.

Overseas Departments and Territories, M. Pierre Messmer.

Industrial Development and Scientific Research, M. François Xavier Ortoli.

Equipment and Housing, M. Albin Chalandon.

Post and Telecommunications, M. Robert Galley.

Agriculture, M. Michel Cointat.

Transport, M. Jean Chamant.

Environment, M. Robert Poujade.

Labour, Employment and Population, M. Joseph Fontanet.

Health and Social Security, M. Robert Boulin.

Veterans, M. Henri Duvillard.

Secretaries of State (Prime Minister's Office), M. Léo Hamon (*Government Spokesman*); M. Joseph Comiti (*Youth and Sport*); M. Philippe Malaud (*Civil Service*); M. Jacques Baumel (*Public Relations*).

Other Secretaries of State, M. André Fanton (*Defence*); M. Jean-Louis Tinaud (*Relations with Parliament—Senate*); M. Jacques Limouzy (*Relations with Parliament—National Assembly*); M. Yvon Bourges (*Foreign Affairs*); M. Jean de Lipkowski (*Foreign Affairs*); M. André Bord (*Interior*); M. Jean Taittinger (*Economy and Finance*); M. Jean-Marie Bailly (*Commerce*); M. Pierre Billecocq (*Education*); M. Gabriel Kaspereit (*Small Industry*); M. Bernard Lafay (*Industrial Development and Scientific Research*); M. Marcel Anthonioz (*Tourism*); M. Robert-André Vivien (*Housing*); M. Bernard Pons (*Agriculture*); M. Philippe Dechartre (*Labour, Employment and Population*); Mlle. Marie-Madeleine Dienesch (*Health and Social Security*).

FRENCH EMBASSY IN LONDON

Residence: 11 Kensington Palace Gardens, W.8 [01-229-9411]

Chancery: 58 Knightsbridge, S.W.1. [01-235-8080]. *Consulate-General:* 24 Rutland Gate, S.W.7 [01-584-9628].

Ambassador Extraordinary and Plenipotentiary, His Excellency Monsieur Geoffroy de Courcel, G.C.V.O., M.C. (1962).

Minister-Counsellor, M. Jean-Paul Anglès.

1st Counsellor, M. René Ziller.

2nd Counsellors, M. Victor Garès (*Press Affairs*); M. André Jouanin.

1st Secretaries, M. Jean-Pierre Angremy; M. Jean-Bernard Mérimée.

2nd Secretaries, M. Samuel Le Caruyer de Beauvais; M. Jean Guéginou; M. Christian Prettre.

3rd Secretary, M. Jean-François Lionnet.

Attachés, M. Paul Poli; Mme. Geneviève Rocheteau; M. Jean-François Massoni.

Naval Attaché, Contre Amiral Paul Delahousse.

Assistant Naval Attaché, Capitaine de Frégate Jean-Hugues de la Forcade.

Military Attaché, Col. Pierre Bonnafont.

Assistant Military Attaché, Ing. en Chef de l'Armement Gérard Mesnet.

Air Attaché, Col. Jean Chenet.

Assistant Air Attaché, Cdt. Christian Sapin.

Attaché, M. Paul Blondel.

Minister Financial Counsellor, ~~M. Jacques Dulière.~~

Financial Attaché, M. Claude Hernandez.

Minister Commercial Counsellor (Head of Dept.), M. Jean Wahl.

Commercial Counsellor (Asst. Head), M. André Rigaillaud.

Commercial Counsellor, M. Francois Padovani.

Commercial Attachés, M. Francis Lohéac; M. Guy Lombard.

+7/72

Cultural Counsellor, M. Pierre de Boisdeffre.
Cultural Attachés, M. Jean-Marie Benoist; M. André Zavriew; Mme. Brigitte Oudiette-Marger.
Maritime Counsellor, M. Michel Jacquier.
Scientific Counsellor, M. Francois Miquel.
Scientific Attaché, M. Jacques Labbé.
Counsellor, Paymaster and Financial Comptroller, M. Jean Lescêne.
Consul-General, M. Robert Fabre.

Area and Population.—The largest state in Central Europe, extending from 42° 20' to 51° 5' N. lat., and from 7° 85' E. to 4° 45' W. long., bounded on the north by the English Channel and the Straits of Dover (*Pas de Calais*), which separate it from England. Its circumference is estimated at about 3,000 miles and its area at 210,038 sq. miles divided into 95 departments, including the island of Corsica, in the Mediterranean, off the west coast of Italy. The population of France (U.N. estimate) in 1970 was 50,770,000. During 1969 there were 838,000 live births, 568,000 deaths and 380,000 marriages. Principal groups of foreigners living in France are: (approximate numbers at the end of 1969), Spaniards 618,200; Italians 585,880; Algerians 471,020; Portuguese 303,160. There are 18,760 Brtish living in France. The total number of foreigners living in France is 2,664,060.

DEPARTMENTS AND REGIONS
(Estimated March 1, 1968)

Paris........	2,590,000	Calvados.....	532,897
Seine-et-		Manche.....	451,939
Marne...	604,340	Orne.....	288,524
Yvelines....	854,382		
Essonne....	674,157	*Basse-Nor-*	
Hauts-de-		*mandie..*	1,294,145
Seine....	1,461,619		
Seine-Saint-		Côte-d'Or...	421,192
Denis....	1,249,606	Nièvre.....	247,702
Val-de-		Saône-et-	
Marne...	1,121,340	Loire.....	550,364
Val-d'Oise ..	693,269	Yonne.....	283,376
Paris			
Region..	9,248,713	*Bourgogne..*	1,502,632
Ardennes....	309,380	Nord.......	2,417,899
Aube.......	270,325	Pas-de-	
Marne.....	485,388	Calais.....	1,397,159
Marne			
(Haute)....	214,336	*Nord..*	3,815,058
Champagne	1,273,429	Meurthe-et-	
		Moselle...	705,413
Aisne.......	526,346	Meuse.....	209,513
Oise.......	540,988	Moselle.....	971,314
Somme.....	512,113	Vosges.....	388,201
Picardie....	1,519,447	*Lorraine..*	2,274,441
Eure.......	383,385	Rhin (Bas)...	827,367
Seine-		Rhin (Haut) .	596,633
Maritime..	1,113,977		
		Alsace..	1,412,385
Haute-Nor-			
mandie..	1,497,962	Doubs.....	426,363
		Jura.....	233,547
Cher.......	304,601	Saône (Haute)	214,176
Eure-et-Loir..	302,207	Belfort (Terr.	
Indre.....	247,118	de)	118,450
Indre-et-			
Loire.....	447,132	*Franche-*	
Loir-et-Cher..	267,896	*Comté...*	992,536
Loiret.......	430,629		
		Loire-Atlan-	
Centre.....	1,990,381	tique......	861,452

Maine-et-		Vienne	
Loire.....	556,272	(Haute) ...	341,589
Mayenne....	252,762		
Sarthe.....	461,839	*Limousin ..*	736,323
Vendée.....	421,250		
		Ain.......	339,262
Pays de la		Ardèche.....	256,927
Loire..	2,582,012	Drôme.....	342,891
		Isère........	768,450
Côtes-du-		Loire.....	722,443
Nord....	506,102	Rhône.....	1,325,611
Finistère....	768,929	Savoie.....	288,921
Ille-et-		Savoie	
Vilaine....	652,722	(Haute)...	378,550
Morbihan...	540,474		
		Rhône-	
Bretagne..	2,468,200	*Alpes ...*	4,422,995
Charente.....	331,016		
Charente-			
Maritime..	483,622	Allier.......	386,533
Sèvres (Deux)	326,462	Cantal......	169,330
Vienne.....	340,256	Loire (Haute)	208,337
		Puy-de-Dôme	547,743
Poitou-Char-			
entes..	1,481,356	*Auvergne ..*	1,311,943
Dordogne...	374,073		
Gironde....	1,009,390	Aude.......	278,323
Landes.....	277,381	Gard.......	478,544
Lot-et-		Hérault.....	591,397
Garonne ..	290,592	Lozère.....	77,258
Pyrénées		Pyrénées-	
(*Atlantiques*)	508,734	Orientales..	281,976
Aquitaine ..	2,460,170	*Languedoc-*	
		Roussillon	
Ariège.....	141,768		1,707,500
Aveyron....	281,568		
Garonne			
(Haute) ..	690,712	Alpes-de-	
Gers........	181,577	Haute-	
Lot........	151,198	Provence ..	104,813
Pyrénées		Alpes (Hautes)	91,790
(Hautes)..	225,730	Alpes-Mari-	
Tarn.......	332,011	times.....	722,070
Tarn-et-Gar-		Bouches-du-	
onne.....	183,572	Rhône..	1,470,271
		Var........	555,926
Midi-Py-		Vaucluse...	353,966
renees ..	2,184,846		
		Provence-Côte-	
Corrèze.....	237,858	*d'Azur ..*	3,298,836
Creuse.....	156,876	Corsica....	273,173

Government.—The monarchical system of government was overthrown by the *French Revolution* (1789–1793), and the *First Republic* lasted until the Great Napoleon (born Aug. 15, 1769, died May 5, 1821) founded the First Empire in 1804. The monarchy was restored in 1814, and also after the "Hundred Days" of Napoleon (March 20–June 29, 1815), until the *Second Republic* of 1848, which became the Second Empire on Nov. 22, 1852. On Sept. 4, 1870, the Emperor Napoleon III (nephew of the Great Napoleon) was deposed, and the *Third Republic* was set up. The constitution of the Third Republic vested the legislative power in a Chamber of Deputies and a Senate. The executive was vested in the President, who was elected for 7 years by the Senate and Chamber assembled in Congress.

On Sept. 1, 1939, Germany invaded Poland thus precipitating war with France and Great Britain, which had (March 31, 1939) given an open pledge to support Poland against aggression.

On June 17, 1940, the late Maréchal Pétain sought

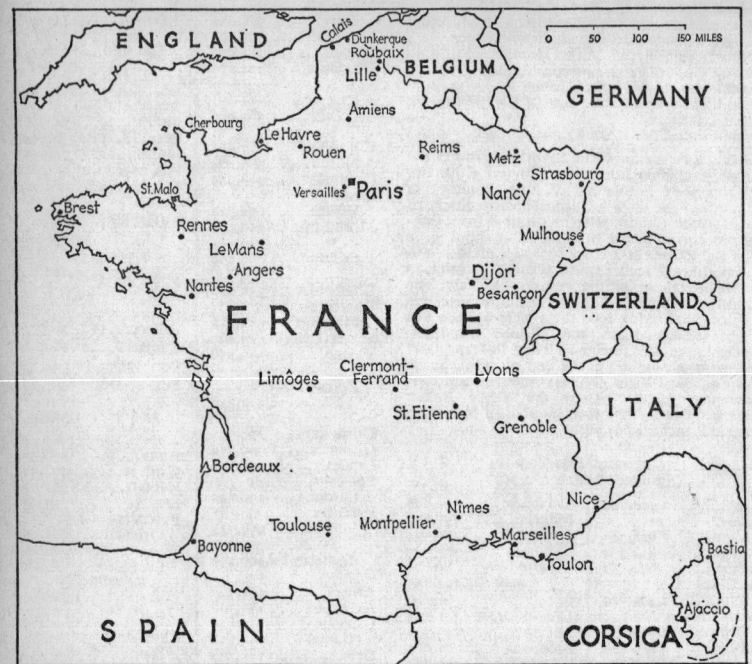

terms of surrender from the Germans. A number of French troops had reached British ports after the evacuation of the British Expeditionary Force from Dunkirk and St. Valéry, and on June 23, 1940, after stating that the French Government had capitulated before all means of resistance had been exhausted, General Charles de Gaulle announced the formation of a Provisional National Committee "to defend that part of the French Empire which has not yet been conquered by Germany and to free that part of France still under the yoke of the invader."

On June 3, 1943, after prolonged negotiation, there was set up a *French Committee of National Liberation*, which was recognized by the allied nations on August 26, 1943.

Paris was liberated on August 25, 1944, and on October 13, 1944, the de Gaulle administration was recognized by the allied nations as the government of France.

Under the de Gaulle administration there was a single chamber legislature (The National Consultative Assembly) which met at Algiers until France was liberated. The enlarged Consultative Assembly met in the Luxemburg Palace (Paris), formerly the Senate House, on Nov. 7, 1944.

Following a national referendum on Oct. 21, 1945, a Constituent Assembly was elected with the task of drafting a new constitution. This was duly drawn up and adopted at a further referendum on Oct. 13, 1946. A National Assembly and Council of the Republic, elected on a territorial basis, were set up. With amendments made in 1954, the Constitution of the Fourth Republic was in force from 1946 until Oct. 5, 1958. From the liberation

of Paris in 1944 until the Fourth Republic came to an end in 1958, 26 Cabinets were formed with an average life of 5½ months. The Government of M. Mollet for 16 months in 1956–57 was the longest in office, that of M. Queuille in 1950 the shortest, being in office for only three days.

Insurrections took place in Algeria and in the Metropolitan Department of Corsica in May, 1958, and, faced by a threat of imminent insurrection among the armed forces at home, President Coty warned the nation that it was on the brink of civil war and invited General de Gaulle to form a Government. M. Pflimlin formally resigned the office of Prime Minister on May 31. On June 1, by 329 votes to 224, Gen. de Gaulle was invested in the National Assembly as Prime Minister, with power to govern by decree for a period of six months during which time proposals for constitutional reform would be submitted to a national referendum.

The Fifth Republic.—The Constitution of the Fifth Republic, embodying important changes, was adopted by an overwhelming majority at a referendum held on Sept. 28 in Metropolitan France and all overseas departments and territories.

The *President* was elected for a term of 7 years by an electoral college consisting of both Houses of Parliament, the departmental general councils, overseas assemblies and elected representatives of the municipal councils. As the result of a referendum in October, 1962, future Presidents are to be elected by direct universal suffrage. Presidents are eligible for re-election. The President appoints the Prime Minister. He may dissolve the National

Assembly after consultation with the Prime Minister and Presidents of both Houses, but may not do so more than once in twelve months. He may submit disputed legislation to a national referendum at the request of the Government or of both Houses of Parliament. The President may assume special powers in an emergency. At the presidential elections held on Dec. 21, 1958, General de Gaulle was elected President by an overwhelming majority and took office on Jan. 8, 1959, as first President of the Fifth French Republic. He was re-elected in December, 1965, for a second presidential term. In May, 1968, a major internal crisis was precipitated by a student rebellion, which led to a generalized strike and the virtual collapse of the Government. General de Gaulle then held parliamentary elections at which the Gaullists won the largest majority in living history. Strengths of the party groups in the National Assembly (after the elections held on June 23 and June 30, 1968) were established on July 13 as follows:—

Union of Democrats for the Republic	292
Independent Republican	61
Federation	57
Communist	34
Progress and Modern Democracy	33
Others	10

The General remained President until April 27 1969, when a referendum on regional and Senate reform on which he had staked his personal future as President, was lost. Alain Poher (*Centrists and President of the Senate*) became interim President and stood for election against MM. Pompidou (*Gaullist*), Duclos (*Communist*), Defferre (*Socialist*) and three other candidates. On the second round M. Pompidou was elected with 58 per cent. of the vote and assumed office as President on June 20, 1969.

Parliament consists of the National Assembly and the Senate. Bills may be presented in either House, except money bills, which must originate in the National Assembly. The normal session of Parliament is confined to 5½ months each year and it may also meet in extraordinary session for 12 days at the request of the Prime Minister or a majority of the Assembly. Voting rights are personal and can only be delegated in special circumstances.

The *Prime Minister* is appointed by the President, as is the Cabinet on the Prime Minister's recommendation. They are responsible to Parliament. But the executive is constitutionally separate from the legislature and Ministers may not sit in Parliament. The Prime Minister is assumed to have the Assembly's confidence unless the Opposition moves a censure motion signed by not less than one-tenth of the deputies; such motion must be approved by an absolute majority; if defeated, its sponsors must not introduce another no-confidence motion in the same session.

A *Constitutional Council* is responsible for supervising all elections and referenda and must be consulted on all constitutional matters and before the President of the Republic assumes emergency powers. At the request of the Government, the *Economic and Social Council* gives advice on bills, ordinances or decrees referred to it. Any economic or social plan or bill must be submitted to it.

Production.—The chief agriculture products are wheat, barley, rye, maize, oats, potatoes, beetroot (for the manufacture of sugar), hops, &c. Rice is being grown in parts of the Camargue (Rhône delta). Fruit trees abound, and are very productive, the principal being the olive, chestnut, walnut, almond, apple, pear, citron, fig, plum, &c.

The harvest in 1970 was:—

	(Quintals)
Wheat	129,221,000
Oats	20,703,000
Barley	80,090,000
Rye	3,015,000
Maize	74,198,000

Forestry is an important industry, the principal forests being those of the Ardennes, Compiègne, Fontainebleau, and Orléans, consisting chiefly of oak, birch, pine, beech, elm, chestnut and the corktree in the south. The vine is cultivated to a very great extent, as the names Bordeaux, Burgundy, Champagne, &c., universally testify. Production of wine in 1970 was 74,373,000 hectolitres. Cider-making is also an important industry. The livestock (1970) included 21,621,000 cattle, 10,106,000 sheep and lambs. 11,215,000 pigs, 672,000 horses and 923,000 goats. The mineral resources include coal, natural gas, pig iron, bauxite, lead, silver, antimony and salt. In 1970 coal production amounted to 40,139,000 tons. The most important manufactures are of metals, cars, aircraft, watches, jewellery, cabinet-work, carving, pottery, glass, chemicals, dyeing, paper making, cottons, woollens, carpets, linen, silk and lace.

Language and Literature.—French is the universal language of France and of a large proportion of the people of Belgium, Luxemburg, Switzerland, Italy, Tunisia, Algeria, Mauritius, Haiti and the Province of Quebec, Canada, to whom the almost inexhaustible literature of France is a treasured heritage. The work of the *French Academy*, founded by Richelieu in 1635, has established *le bon usage*, equivalent to " The King's English " in Great Britain. French authors have been awarded the Nobel Prize for Literature on 10 occasions—R.F.A. Sully-Prudhomme (1901), F. Mistral (1904), Romain Rolland (1915), Anatole France (1921), Henri Bergson (1937), Roger M. du Gard (1937), André Gide (1947), François Mauriac (1952), Albert Camus (1957) and St. John Perse (Alexis Léger) (1960).

Defence.—The personnel of the Defence Forces at the end of 1970 totalled: ARMY 323,344; AIR FORCE, 103,709; NAVY, 70,438; Common Services, 73,617 (including GENDARMERIE of 65,267). National nuclear forces include medium range ballistic missiles (1971) and *Mirage* IV medium bombers. The Army has a variety of new French-made equipment coming into service, including medium tanks, field and air defence guns, trucks and radio sets. A tactical nuclear weapon will enter service in the period 1973–75. The Air Force is equipped with *Mirage* IV nuclear bombers, KC135 tanker/transports, *Mirage* IIIE fighters and *Transall* transports, supported by a large number of older operational aircraft. The Navy includes 2 cruisers, 3 aircraft carriers, 17 fleet escorts, 18 fast escorts, 18 submarines, 15 ocean minesweepers, 1 helicopter carrier, 2 GW frigates, 9 tropical duty frigates, 2 LSD, 7 LST, 80 coastal and inshore minesweepers, and 5 logistic support ships.

Education.—The educational system is highly developed and centralized. It is administered by the Ministry of National Education, comprising (a) the *Direction des Enseignements Supérieurs; Direction de la Pédagogie, des Enseignements Scholaires et de l'Orientation; Direction des Personnels d'Enseignement Général Technique et Professionnel; Direction des Services Administratifs et Sociaux; Direction de l'Equipement Scolaire, Universitaire et Sportif; Direction des Bibliothèques et de la Lecture Publique; Direction de la Coopération*; (b) the Superior Council of National Education (consultative); and (c) the Inspectorate. *Local Administration* comprises 23 Territorial Academies, with inspecting staff for

all grades, and Departmental Councils presided over by the *Préfet*, and charged especially with *primary* education. There is a separate Ministry dealing with Youth and Sport.

Primary and secondary education are compulsory, free and secular, the school age being from 6 to 16. Schools are for boys, for girls, or mixed. (i) *Primary* education is given in *écoles maternelles* (nursery schools), *écoles primaires élémentaires* (primary schools) and *collèges d'enseignement général* (4-year modern course); (ii) *Secondary* education in *collèges d'enseignement technique*, *collèges d'enseignement secondaire* and *lycées* (7-year course leading to one of the five *baccalauréats*). *Baccalauréat A* consists largely of philosophy and languages with a little mathematics, and provides entry into the faculties of Letters and Law. *Baccalauréat B* groups languages, mathematics and economics with philosophy classes oriented towards psychology and sociology. It provides entry to the faculties of Letters for the social sciences and to the faculty of Law for economics. *Baccalauréat C*, consisting of mathematics and physics with some languages, provides entry to the faculty of Sciences for those studying for a degree in mathematics and physics. *Baccalauréat D* has the same language component as *Baccalauréat C*, but its main feature is the natural sciences. It provides entry to the faculty of Sciences for natural science degrees, and also to the Medicine and Pharmacy Faculties. *Baccalauréat E* is largely scientific and technical with a language element, and provides entry to engineering schools and the Faculty of Science. (iii) *Special schools* are numerous. (iv) There are numerous *Grandes Ecoles* in France which award diplomas in many subjects not taught at university, especially applied science and engineering. Most of them are State institutions but have a competitive system of entry, unlike the universities. (v) The reform of the French university structure continues, and there are now universities in twenty-four towns in France. In the major provincial towns the existing university has been reorganized to form two, or three universities, and in Paris and the immediate surrounding district there are, since autumn 1970, thirteen universities.

Archæology, etc.—There are dolmens and menhirs in Brittany, prehistoric remains and cave drawings in Dordogne and Ariège, and throughout France various megalithic monuments erected by primitive tribes, predecessors of Iberian invaders from Spain (now represented by the Basques), Ligurians from northern Italy and Celts or Gauls from the valley of the Danube. Julius Cæsar found Gaul " divided into three parts " and described three political groups—Aquitanians south of the Garonne, Celts between the Garonne and the Seine and Marne, and Belgae from the Seine to the Rhine. Roman remains are plentiful throughout France in the form of aqueducts, arenas, triumphal arches, &c., and the celebrated Norman and Gothic Cathedrals, including Notre Dame in Paris, and those of Chartres, Reims, Amiens (where Peter the Hermit preached the First Crusade for the recovery of the Holy Sepulchre), Bourges, Beauvais, Rouen, etc., have survived invasions and bombardments, with only partial damage, and many of the renaissance and the XVIIth and XVIIIth century châteaux survived the French Revolution.

Roads.—The length of the *Routes Nationales* at the end of 1970 was 81,000 km. and of motorways 1,576 km. The principal rivers of France are the Seine, Loire, Garonne, and Rhône, the navigable waterways in general use in 1970 were: canals, 4,400 km.; navigable rivers, 3,121 km.

Railways.—The system of railroads in France is very extensive. The length of lines of general interest, exclusive of local lines, open for traffic in 1969 was 37,221 km., of which 8,967 km. were electrified. Traffic in 1970 totalled 41,000,000,000 passenger-km. and 70,400,000,000 ton-km.

Shipping.—The French mercantile marine consisted on Jan. 1, 1971, of 538 ships of 5,921,425 tons gross, of which 30 were passenger vessels (286,572 tons gross), 129 tankers (3,359,596 tons gross) and 379 cargo vessels (2,275,257 tons gross).

FINANCE

	1969	1970
	F. millions	
Total revenue (*Budget*)	144,675	159,999
Total expenditure (*do.*)	149,311	158,069

The *Public Debt* on Dec. 31, 1970, was F.103,530,000,000 of which the external debt amounted to F.9,690,000,000.

Currency.—The unit of currency is the *franc* of 100 *centimes*, which was devalued on Aug. 10, 1969. Bank notes in 10, 50 and 100 *franc* denominations and coins in 5 *francs* are issued.

EXCHANGE RATE (at Sept. 17, 1971).—F.13.63 = £1 (*see also* p. 83).

COMMERCE

The principal imports are wool, cotton, chemicals, coke, crude oil, oleaginous fruits and seeds, machinery, raw skins, timber, rubber, copper and coffee. The principal exports are chemical products, iron and steel, textiles (silk and cotton), automobiles, wine and other agricultural products, soaps and perfumes, and glass.

FRENCH FOREIGN TRADE

		1969	1970
		Francs	*Francs*
Imports	....	90,023,000,000	106,190,000,000
Exports	....	77,759,000,000	99,641,000,000

Trade with U.K.

	1969	1970
Imports from U.K.	£290,954,000	£339,229,000
Exports to U.K...	324,448,000	368,243,000

OVERSEAS DEPARTMENTS

With effect from Jan. 1, 1947, the colonies of Guyane (French Guiana), Martinique, Guadeloupe and La Réunion with its dependencies have been theoretically administered in exactly the same way as the Metropolitan Departments, but in practice somewhat greater discretion is allowed to the Prefects and the locally elected bodies.

La Réunion.—Formerly Ile de Bourbon, about 420 miles E. of Madagascar, Réunion has been a French possession since 1643. Area, about 1,000 sq. miles. Population (U.N. estimate, 1969), 436,000. Capital, St. Denis (65,614). Assigned to the administration of Réunion are the distant islands of St. Paul (3 sq. miles), New Amsterdam (27 sq. miles) and Kerguelen containing whaling and fishing stations (1,100 sq. miles). The Crozet Islands (200 sq. miles) and Adélie Land in the Antarctic Continent are also dependencies of Réunion. Imports from U.K., 1970, £539,000.

Martinique.—An island situated in the Windward Islands group of the West Indies, between the British colonies of Dominica in the north and St. Lucia in the south. Population (U.N. estimate, 1969), 332,000. Capital ΨFort de France (60,600). Other towns are ΨTrinité (39,173) and ΨMarin (31,369).

Guadeloupe.—In the Leeward Islands of the West Indies, the island of Guadeloupe, together with Marie Galante, the Ile des Saintes, Petite Terre, St. Barthélemy and St. Martin, form the other West

Indian Department of France. Population (U.N. estimate, 1969), 323,000. Capital Ψ Pointe à Pitre 39,000). Other towns are Ψ Basse Terre (16,000) in Guadeloupe and Ψ Grand Bourg (12,827) in Marie Galante.

French Guiana.—Area, 35,000 sq. miles. Population (U.N. estimate, 1969), 48,000. Capital, Ψ Cayenne (20,000). Situated on the north-eastern coast of South America, French Guiana is flanked by Netherlands Guiana on the west and by Brazil on the south and east. Under the administration of French Guiana is a group of islands (St. Joseph, Ile Royal and Ile du Diable), known as Iles du Salut. On Devil's Isle, Captain Dreyfus was imprisoned from 1894 to 1899. Imports from U.K. in 1970 were valued at £2,549,000.

CAPITAL OF FRANCE. Paris, on the Seine.
Population (estimated, 1969), 2,590,000.

District of Paris.—Created by legislation promulgated on August 10, 1966, the District consists of 8 Departments one of which is the City of Paris (*see* list of Departments, p. 857).

Paris is administered by the Council of Paris which is composed of 90 members elected for six years by popular vote within the city/Department. The President and four Vice-Presidents of the Council are elected for one year by the members. The President presides over the meetings of the Council and is the representative of Paris on all official occasions. The administrative functions exercised in all other towns by the Mayor are exercised in Paris by two Government nominees: the Prefect of Paris, and the Prefect of Police. But Mayors are elected in each of the 20 arrondissements of Paris to carry out local civil duties.

At the Census of 1968 nineteen towns had a population of over 150,000 inhabitants:—Paris (2,590,000); Ψ Marseilles (893,771); Ψ Lyons (535,000); Toulouse (380,340); Ψ Nice (325,400); Ψ Bordeaux (270,996); Ψ Nantes (265,009); Strasbourg (254,038); Saint-Etienne (216,020); Ψ Le Havre (200,940); Lille (194,948); Rennes (188,515); Ψ Toulon (178,489); Montpelier (167,211); Grenoble (165,902); Ψ Brest (159,857); Reims (158,634); Clermont-Ferrand (154,110); Dijon (150,791). 37 towns in France have a population of over 100,000.

The chief towns of Corsica are Ψ Ajaccio (44,659) and Ψ Bastia (51,022).

Paris is distant from London 267 miles; transit by air, 1 hr.

FLAG.—The "tricolour," three vertical bands, blue, white, red (blue next to flagstaff).

NATIONAL DAY.—July 14.

BRITISH EMBASSY
(35 rue du Faubourg St. Honoré, Paris 8e)
Ambassador Extraordinary and Plenipotentiary, His Excellency the Rt. Hon. Arthur Christopher Iohn Soames, C.B.E. (1968).................£14,000
Minister, A. M. Palliser, C.M.G.
Minister (Economic), J. S. Rooke, C.M.G., O.B.E.
Minister (European Economic Affairs), J. E. Galsworthy, C.M.G.
Counsellor and Consul-General, J. McAdam Clark.
Counsellors, R. W. H. Du Boulay; H. S. Colchester, C.M.G., O.B.E.; G. W. Harding (*Press*); J. A. Honeyford (*Administration*); A. G. Wallis, D.F.C. (*Labour*); R. Hibbert (*Defence Supply and Civil Air*); D. Thomas (*Financial*); P. Goodman (*Scientific*).
1st Secretaries, M. K. O. Simpson-Orlebar; Hon. H. J. Maud; J. N. T. Spreckley; C. P. H. T. Isolani, M.V.O., O.B.E.; M. St. E. Burton (*Information*); R. J. Alston (*Economic*); G. E. Howe; R. M. Graham (*Scientific*); C. B. Shakespeare

(*Economic*); B. H. Wilcox, M.B.E. (*Commercial*); Miss T. M. Cullis (*Consular*); J. White (*Defence Supply*).
2nd Secretaries, J. A. Fortescue; D. L. Stephens; E. G. Markee (*Visa*); A. R. Clark (*Economic*); J. A. Graham (*Commercial*); R. O. Barnes (*Commercial*); B. J. Stenning, M.B.E. (*Commercial*); K. Grant; P. Hartnack (*Civil Aviation*); Miss M. Hankins, M.B.E. (*Administration*).
3rd Secretary, I. A. Roberts.
Defence and Air Attaché, Air Cdre. N. E. Hoad, C.B.E., A.F.C.
Naval Attaché, Capt. C. R. P. C. Branson, R.N.
Military Attaché, Brig. W. M. Wingate-Gray.
Asst. Naval Attaché, Cdr. G. A. A. G. Edleston, O.B.E., R.N.
Asst. Military Attaché, Maj. J. K. Chater, R.E.
Asst. Air Attaché, Wing Cdr. P. D. H. Nichols.
Chaplain of the British Embassy Church, Rev. E. M. T. McLellan.

BRITISH CONSULAR OFFICES
There are British Consular Offices in Metropolitan France at *Paris, Bordeaux, Boulogne, Calais, Cherbourg, Dieppe, Dunkirk, Epernay, Le Havre, Lille, Lyons, Marseilles, Nice, St. Malo* and *Strasbourg.*

BRITISH CHAMBER OF COMMERCE
6 Rue Halévy, Paris 9
President, D. H. Goodchild.
Vice-Presidents, P. T. Simpson-Jones; O. G. Longley, M.C.

BRITISH COUNCIL
Representative in Paris, M. H. Cardiff, O.B.E., rue des Ecoles 36, Paris 5e.
There is a British Council office at *Toulouse*; British Council libraries at *Paris, Bordeaux, Lille, Lyons* and *Strasbourg.*

THE FRENCH COMMUNITY
The Constitution of the Fifth French Republic promulgated on Oct. 6, 1958, envisaged the establishment of a French Community of States closely linked with common institutions. A number of the former French States in Africa have seceded from the Community but for all practical purposes continue to enjoy the same close links with France as those that remain formally members of the French Community. The Community Institutions in fact never operated as envisaged. Nevertheless, with the exception of Guinea, which opted out of the Community in the 1958 referendum, all the former French African colonies are closely linked to France by a series of financial, technical and economic agreements.

Francophone Countries.

In the following countries French is either the official or national language or the language of instruction; where there is another national language the name of it is shown after the name of the country:—Algeria (*Arabic*); Belgium (*Flemish*); Burundi (*Kirundi*); Khmer Republic (*Khmer*); Cameroon (*English*); parts of Canada (in Quebec, parts of Ontario and New Brunswick) (*English*); Central African Republic (*Sangho*); Chad; Congo (P.D.R.); Congolese Republic; Dahomey; France; Gabon; Guinea; Haiti (*Creole*); Ivory Coast; Laos (*Laotian*); Lebanon (*Arabic*); Luxemburg (*German* and *Letzeburgesch*); Madagascar (*Malagasy*); Mali; Morocco (*Arabic*); Mauritania (*Arabic*); Niger; Rwanda (*Kinyarwanda*); Senegal; Switzerland (1,000,000 French speaking); Togo; Tunisia (*Arabic*); Upper Volta; Vietnam (*Vietnamese*). French is also spoken in the Overseas Departments (*see* above).

OTHER TERRITORIES

French Territory of the Afars and Issas.—Situated on the north-east coast of Africa, the Territory has an area of 9,000 sq. miles with a population (U.N. estimate, 1969) of about 81,000.

Formerly French Somaliland, the Territory was renamed on July 6, 1967, to emphasize the existence of the two main ethnic groups in the population. A renamed Chamber of Deputies succeeded the former territorial assembly to which a governing council is responsible for the administration of the territory. The French High Commissioner retains responsibility for foreign policy, defence, currency, credit, citizenship and law, other than traditional civil law. Capital, Ψ Jibouti (62,000).

New Caledonia.—Area, 7,200 sq. miles. Population (U.N. estimate, 1969), 98,000. Capital, Ψ Noumea (12,000). A large island in the Western Pacific, 700 miles E. of Queensland. Dependencies are the Isle of Pines, the Loyalty Islands (Mahé, Lifou, Urea, etc., the Huon islands and Alofis). New Caledonia was discovered in 1774 and annexed by France in 1854; from 1871 to 1896 it was a convict settlement. It is the world's third largest producer of nickel, after Canada and U.S.S.R.

Wallis and Futuna Islands.—Following a request from local kings and chiefs, it was decided by referendum (Dec. 27, 1959) that the islands would become the sixth Overseas Territory of France. Population of the islands, formerly dependencies of New Caledonia, is about 9,500, mostly Polynesians.

French Polynesia.—Area, 2,500 sq. miles. Population (U.N. estimate, 1970), 109,000. Capital, Ψ Papeete (15,220), in Tahiti. Includes the Society Islands (Tahiti, Moorea, Makatea, etc.), the Marquesas (Nukahiva, Hiva-oa, etc., 500 sq. miles, population, 3,000); the Leeward Isles (Huahine, Raiatea, Tahaa, Bora Bora, Maupiti, etc.); the Gambier Islands (Mangareva, etc.); the Tubuai Islands (Tubuai, Rurutu, Raivavae, Rimatara and Rapa Island; and Maiao Island).

Comoro Archipelago.—Area, 800 sq. miles. Population (1968), 244,000. Capital, Dzaoudzi. Includes the islands of Great Comoro, Anjouan, Mayotte and Mohilla and certain islets in the Indian Ocean.

St. Pierre and Miquelon.—Area, 93 sq. miles. Population (1967), 5,000. Two small groups of Islands off the coast of Newfoundland.

GABOON
(Gabonese Republic)
(For MAP, *see* p. 836).

President, Albert-Bernard Bongo, *assumed office* December, 1967.

Gaboon lies on the Atlantic coast of Africa at the Equator and is flanked on the north by the Spanish territory of Rio Muni and the Cameroon Republic and on the east and south by the Republic of Congo. It has an area of 101,400 sq. miles and a population (estimated, 1970) of 630,000. Gaboon elected on Nov. 28, 1958, to remain an autonomous republic within the French Community and was proclaimed fully independent on August 17, 1960.

Trade with U.K.

	1969	1970
Imports from U.K.	£975,000	£960,000
Exports to U.K.	1,681,000	1,152,000

CAPITAL.—Libreville (31,000).

FLAG.—Horizontal bands, green, yellow and blue.

NATIONAL DAY.—August 17.

British Ambassador, His Excellency Anthony Arthur Golds, C.M.G., M.V.O. (1970) (Resident at *Yaoundé, Cameroon*).

GERMANY
★ Deutsches Reich (German Realm)

THE HISTORY OF GERMANY from 1863–1945 is marked by wars of aggression. In 1864, Prussia, in company with Austria, attacked Denmark, and after a short campaign annexed the peninsula of Schleswig-Holstein. In 1866, as a result of war with Austria (the Seven Weeks' War), Prussia acquired the hegemony of the North Germanic Confederation from Austria. After the Franco-Prussian War of 1870, when Prussia wrested Alsace-Lorraine from France, the North Germanic Confederation and three South German States became the Germanic Confederation, the King of Prussia being proclaimed German Emperor at Versailles on Jan. 18, 1871.

At the outbreak of the War of 1914–1918, Germany was a Confederate League bearing the name German Empire under the hereditary presidency of the King of Prussia holding the title of German Emperor. At the close of the war, Germany lost most of the gains she had acquired since 1863, including all her colonies.

GERMANY BETWEEN THE TWO WARS.—On Nov. 9, 1918, two days before Germany sued for an Armistice from the victorious Allies, the German Emperor abdicated, and the Government of the country was taken over by the Council of the People's Commissioners in Berlin. In January, 1919, elections were held to a National Assembly on the basis of universal adult suffrage (male and female). The Assembly met at Weimar (Feb. 6, 1919), and elected Friedrich Ebert President of the Republic, a position he occupied until his death (Feb. 28, 1925) when Field Marshal Paul von Hindenburg was elected in his stead. Von Hindenburg was re-elected April 10, 1932, the rival candidate being Adolf Hitler, who was born at Braunau, Austria (April 20, 1889) and had migrated as a young man to Bavaria. A General Election of 1933 provided Hitler's party, the *Nationalsozialistische Deutsche Arbeiter Partei* (National Socialist German Workers' Party, or *Nazis*) with an absolute majority in the legislature (*Reichstag*) and Hitler became Prime Minister (Chancellor), a position which became fused with that of President at the death of von Hindenburg (Aug. 2, 1934), and Adolf Hitler exercised supreme and uncontrolled authority in the Reich.

THE WAR OF 1939–1945.—After concluding a Treaty of Non-Aggression with Soviet Russia (Aug. 24, 1939), Germany invaded Poland (Sept. 1, 1939), thus precipitating war with France and Great Britain, which had (March 31) given a pledge to support Poland against aggression.

Germany invaded and occupied Denmark and Norway (April, 1940), Belgium, the Netherlands, Luxemburg and France (May, 1940). Norway capitulated on June 9, France sued for peace in mid-June. The lightning war against Britain began on August 11, 1940, but the *Luftwaffe* attack, which was to prepare the way for invasion, was defeated. In April, 1941, Yugoslavia was invaded and Germany joined Italy in attacking Greece and Crete. On June 22, 1941, the U.S.S.R. was invaded. In 1942 the Nazi empire reached its height. The boundaries of Greater Germany included Alsace-Lorraine, Luxemburg, Eupen-Malmédy, large

★ Nazi historians referred to the National Socialist régime as *Drittes Reich*. The *First* was the Holy Roman Empire, established in A.D. 962 by Otto I of Saxony, enduring until 1806. The *Second* was established by Prince Otto von Bismarck, after the Franco-Prussian War in 1871, and endured until 1918. The *Third* was established by Adolf Hitler in 1933.

areas of Poland, Memelland and Slovenia; Germany and her satellites controlled all European countries except the British Isles, Spain, Portugal, Switzerland, Sweden and parts of European Russia, as well as large tracts of North Africa. The turning point came in November, 1942, with the Soviet victory at Stalingrad and the British at El Alamein. In 1943 a Soviet offensive threw the invader back almost to the Polish frontier, and the Western Allies after defeating the Axis in North Africa, landed in Italy. In June, 1944, the Second Front opened on the Normandy beaches and by September, 1944, Germany itself was the battlefield. On May 8, 1945, the unconditional surrender of all German forces was accepted by representatives of the Western Allied and Soviet Supreme Commanders.

Hitler committed suicide on April 30, 1945.

In 1962 the Federal Statistical Office reported that during the course of the war from 1939 to 1945, 593,000 persons were killed during allied air attacks on Germany and 403,000 dwellings were destroyed. 537,000 civilians were killed, some 15 per cent. children under 14, and 56,000 foreign civilians, members of the police and armed forces. In the area now covered by the Federal Republic persons injured numbered 486,000, including 16,000 foreigners and prisoners of war.

THE POST WAR PERIOD.—After the surrender the Allied Powers assumed supreme authority in Germany. Power was to be exercised by the Commanders-in-Chief, each in his own zone of occupation and jointly in matters affecting Germany as a whole through a Control Council. Berlin was to be governed jointly by the four occupying powers. The guiding lines of policy were laid down in the agreement reached between the U.K., U.S. and U.S.S.R. Governments at Potsdam in August, 1945, which was to remain in force until a Peace Treaty should confirm or revise its directives. It was decided that " for the time being no Central German Government shall be established," but that central German administrative departments acting under the direction of the Control Council should be established in the fields of finance, transport, communications, foreign trade and industry. The Eastern frontier of Germany was provisionally redrawn (pending final settlement in the Peace Treaty) to transfer the northern area of East Prussia, including Königsberg (now Kaliningrad), to the U.S.S.R. and the rest of East Prussia and all the area lying east of the Oder and Western Neisse rivers to Polish control. On Oct. 15, 1947, the Saar, enlarged at the expense of German territory, voted for economic union with France, but following a plebiscite was incorporated in the

Federal Republic of Germany on Jan. 1, 1957. The Potsdam agreement also laid down that Germany should be disarmed and prohibited from producing armaments, that production of certain other goods should be limited to the amount needed to support a peacetime economy and that existing capital equipment surplus to these requirements should be removed as reparations and distributed by the Inter Allied Reparations Agency among the nations who had suffered war damage, in proportion to their losses. (The proportions were fixed by the Paris Conference of November, 1945.) The agreement further dealt with denazification, democratization, refugees, restitution, decartelization, etc.

Though certain details of the Potsdam agreement (not yet superseded by a Peace Treaty) have been carried out, differences in interpretation among the Allies have made it impossible to apply the provisions in full. Quadripartite control became a dead letter when the Russians withdrew from the Control Council in March, 1948.

Federal Republic of Germany

President, Dr. Gustav W. Heinemann, *born* July 23, 1899, *elected* July 1, 1969, *for five years*.

CABINET

Federal Chancellor, Willy Brandt (*SPD*).
Foreign Minister and Vice-Chancellor, Walter Scheel (*FDP*).
Interior, Hans Dietrich Genscher (*FDP*).
Justice, Gerhard Jahn (*SPD*).
Economic Affairs and Finance, Prof. Dr. Karl Schiller (*SPD*). HELMUT SCHMIDT 7/72
Agriculture, Josef Ertl (*FDP*).
Labour, Walter Arendt (*SPD*).
Defence, Helmut Schmidt (*SPD*).
Housing, Dr. Lauritz Lauritzen (*SPD*).
Transport, Posts and Telegraphs, Georg Leber (*SPD*).
Inter-German Relations, Egon Franke (*SPD*).
Health, Family and Youth Questions, Frau Käte Strobel (*SPD*).
Scientific Research, Prof. Dr. Hans Leussink.
Minister at the Federal Chancellery, Prof. Dr. Horst Ehmke (*SPD*).
Economic Co-operation, Dr. Erhard Eppler (*SPD*).
FDP=Free Democrats; *SPD*=Social Democrats.

EMBASSY IN LONDON
23 Belgrave Square, S.W.1.
[01-235-5033]
6 Rutland Gate, S.W.7 (*Passport and Visa Section and Commercial Information Service*)
[01-584-1271]
Ambassador Extraordinary and Plenipotentiary, His Excellency Karl-Günther von Hase, K.C.M.G. (1970).
Minister Plenipotentiary, Dr. Erwin Wickert.
Minister-Counsellors, Dr. Wolf von Arnim; Dr. Heinz Naupert (*Economic Affairs*).
Counsellors, Dr. Alfons Böcker (*Legal and Consular*); Hans-Werner Graf Finck von Finckenstein (*Press*); Frau Dr. Brigitte Lohmeyer (*Cultural*).

NOTE.—Except where otherwise indicated statistical data on the Federal Republic of Germany include Berlin (West).

Area and Population.—The area of the Federal Republic is approximately 95,935 sq. miles. Total population of the Federal Republic on May 26, 1970, was 59,378,000, excluding Western Berlin, compared with 43,008,300 in 1939. Distribution of the population among the *Länder* on May 26, 1970, was:

Schleswig-Holstein	2,567,000
Hamburg	1,812,000
Lower Saxony	7,125,000
Bremen	757,000
North Rhine Westphalia	17,207,000
Hessen	5,461,000
Rhineland Palatinate	3,684,000
Baden-Württemberg	8,996,000
Bavaria	10,644,000
Saarland	1,127,000
Berlin (West)	2,130,000

The population of the principal cities and towns in the Federal Republic on Dec. 31, 1969, was:

Berlin (West)	2,134,256	Aachen	177,642
ΨHamburg	1,817,073	Mainz	176,720
Munich	1,326,331	Solingen	175,895
Cologne	866,308	Ludwigshafen	174,698
Essen	699,905	Bielefeld	169,347
Düsseldorf	680,806	Freiburg	165,960
Frankfurt/Main	660,410	München-	
Dortmund	648,883	gladbach	152,172
Stuttgart	628,412	ΨBremerhaven	148,793
ΨBremen	607,184	Darmstadt	141,075
Hanover	517,783	Osnabrück	141,000
Nuremberg	477,783	Remscheid	137,374
Duisburg	457,891	Oldenburg	131,434
Wuppertal	413,996	Saarbrücken	130,765
Gelsenkirchen	348,620	Regensburg	128,083
Bochum	346,886	Recklinghausen	125,535
Mannheim	330,920	Heidelberg	121,929
Bonn	299,376	Würzburg	120,317
ΨKiel	269,106	Offenbach/	
Wiesbaden	260,614	Main	118,754
Karlsruhe	257,144	Salzgitter	118,020
Oberhausen	249,045	Neuss	117,599
ΨLübeck	242,191	Göttingen	115,227
Krefeld	227,754	Leverkusen	111,588
Brunswick	225,168	Bottrop	108,161
Augsburg	214,376	Koblenz	106,189
Kassel	213,494	Trier	103,412
Münster	204,571	Wilhelmshaven	103,150
Hagen	201,721	Herne	100,798
Mülheim/Ruhr	191,080	Rheydt	100,633

Vital Statistics.—There were 13·2 live births per 1,000 inhabitants in the Federal Republic in 1970, compared with 19·5 per 1,000 for the same area in 1938. There was an excess of live births over deaths in 1970 of 1·2 per 1,000 and in 1938 of 8·0.

Government.—The Federal Republic grew out of the fusion of the three western zones. The economic union of the U.K. and U.S. zones followed the Fusion Agreement of December, 1946. The Bizone was later joined by the French zone and in 1948-49 a Parliamentary Council, elected by the Diets of the three zones, drafted a provisional democratic federal constitution for Germany. This Basic Law came into force in the three western zones on May 23, 1949. It provides for a President, elected for a five-year term, a Lower House, with a four-year term of office, elected by direct universal suffrage, and an Upper House composed of delegates of the *Länder*, without a fixed term of office.

The results of the elections held for the lower House (*Bundestag*) on September 28, 1969, were as follows:

Party	Numbers
Christian Democratic and Christian Social Unions	242
Social Democrats	224
Free Democrats	30
Total	496

with an additional 22 representatives of Berlin elected by the Berlin Chamber of Deputies (Christian Democrats, 8; Social Democrats, 13; Free Democrats, 1). The Social Democrats form a

coalition with the Free Democrats. The Christian Democratic and the Christian Social Unions are the Parliamentary Opposition.

When the Federal Government took office the Allied Military Governors were replaced by High Commissioners. In 1952 a contractual agreement was signed between the Federal Republic and the western Allies, whereby the Republic, in return for certain promises regarding a defence contribution, a foreign debt settlement, and the continuation of allied policies concerning decartelization, democratization, restitution, etc., regained virtual sovereignty in May, 1955, after ratification by all the parties concerned. The High Commissioners then became Ambassadors.

The Prime Ministers of the *Länder* governments in June, 1971, were:—

Ministers-President

Baden-Württemberg.—Dr. Hans Filbinger.
Bavaria.—Dr. Alfons Goppel.
Berlin.—Klaus Schütz (*Governing Mayor*).
Bremen.—Hans Koschnick (*Mayor*).
Hamburg.—Prof. Dr. Herbert Weichmann (*Mayor*).
Hessen.—Albert Osswald.
Lower Saxony.—Alfred Kubel.
North Rhine-Westphalia.—Heinz Kühn.
Rhineland-Palatinate.—Dr. Helmut Kohl.
Saarland.—Dr. Franz-Josef Röder.
Schleswig-Holstein.—Dr. Gerhard Stoltenberg.

Economic position.—Despite the difficulties arising from the division of Germany, which cut off from the Federal Republic the main food producing areas of Eastern Germany and some of the principal centres of light industry, German economic recovery has made rapid strides since the currency reform of 1948. As a result of United States and British economic aid and of successful economic policies pursued by the Federal Government, Germany has regained her position as the main industrial power on the Continent, and is the most economically powerful member of the European Common Market. The Gross National Product at current prices in 1970 was estimated at *DM*.679·0 milliard, an increase of *DM*.76·2 milliard or 12·6 per cent. over 1969.

Agriculture.—In 1970 total area of farmland was 13,578,200 hectares of which 7,539,300 hectares were arable land. Forest areas cover 7,169,500 hectares. The 1970 harvest yielded 8,446,600 metric tons of bread grains, 8,344,200 metric tons of feeding grains and 16,250,000 metric tons of potatoes. The livestock population at the end of 1970 included 14,025,983 cattle, 252,537 horses, 842,503 sheep, 20,968,908 pigs and 101,545,177 fowl.

Industrial Production.—The index of industrial net production adjusted for irregularities of the calendar (1962=100) has developed in the Federal Republic, including Berlin, as follows:—

	1968	1969	1970
Mining	93·4	96·6	99·1
Manufacturing industry	133·3	151·5	160·5
(i) Basic materials	151·6	170·0	178·6
(ii) Capital goods	122·7	146·5	160·1
(iii) Consumer goods	129·5	144·2	147·7
(iv) Foodstuffs	128·2	134·4	138·6
Power (electricity and gas)	153·4	175·3	193·4
Building Industry	121·8	127·5	138·6
Total industry	131·2	148·2	157·2

Productivity of labour in industry (excluding electricity, gas and building industries) per manhour: 1967, 138·2; 1968, 150·1; 1969, 160·7; 1970, 166·2 per cent.

Some production figures are shown below (monthly averages):

	1969	1970
	Number	
Passenger cars	250,339	260,966
Commercial vehicles	22,865	24,688
	Tons	
	1969	1970
Sulphuric acid (SO_3)	304,827	301,695
Chlorine	131,120	143,867
Artificial plastic material	328,203	360,536
Man-made fibres	59,603	60,276
Cotton yarn	20,965	19,883
Woollen yarn	7,264	6,566

477,900 new dwellings were completed in 1970 in the Federal Republic (1969, *499,696*).

Labour.—Of 27,204,000 employed in 1970, 17,535,000 were men. The average number of unemployed was 148,846, of whom 92,899 were men (1969=*178,579* and *124,591*). In 1970, an average number of 1,806.805 foreign workers was employed in the Federal Republic. An average of 8,603,435 (1969=*8,308,267*) were employed in industry (establishments employing 10 and more persons)

	1969	1970
Coal mining	283,248	277,418
Iron and steel production	327,570	334,594
Mechanical engineering	1,687,738	1,726,000
Chemicals	566,741	595,745
Textiles and clothing	890,411	880,523

Finance.—As from January 1, 1970, the distribution of taxes in the Fed. Rep. of Germany between Federation, Länder, communities and local authorities has been regulated by an amendment of the Basic Law (Constitution) as follows:—

(1) Of the yields of wage tax and assessed income tax, Federation and Länder receive 43 per cent. each, and the communities 14 per cent. The yields of capital yield tax and corporation tax are distributed to Federation and Länder with 50 per cent. each.

(2) The turnover taxes have been made joint taxes of which the Federation obtains 70 per cent. and the Länder 30 per cent.

(3) Of the trade tax which so far had been fully allocated to the communities, the Federation and the Länder receive equal shares (about 20 per cent. of the trade tax receipts).

(4) The yields of capital transactions taxes, insurance and bill taxes, which so far went to the Länder, now accrue to the Federation.

Customs and excise duties, other than the beer tax accrue to the Federal Government, all other taxes (with the exception of local taxes, *i.e.* particularly taxes on land and buildings) to the *Länder*.

Preliminary figures of budgetary expenditure in 1971 are: Total expenditure *DM*.100,125,000,000 (*1970, 87,269,000,000*); Defence *DM*.22,412,000,000 (*1970, 20,558,000,000*); Social expenditure *DM*.29,999,000,000 (*1970, 26,777,000,000*); (about 30 per cent.); Agriculture and food, *DM*.5,852,000,000 (*1970, 6,461,000,000*) (about 6 per cent.); Transport, *DM*.7,831,000,000 (*1970, 7,049,000,000*).

Currency.—The currency of the Federal Republic is the *Deutsche Mark* of 100 *Pfennig*, the rate of exchange with sterling being *DM*.8·78 = £1. Limited exchange fluctuations are permitted. (*See also p.* 83.)

Foreign Trade.—In 1970, imports were valued at *DM*.109,605,908,000 (1969, *97,972,434,000*); and exports at *DM*. 125,276,249,000; 19·1 per cent. of imports consisted of foodstuffs and 13·5 per cent. of industrial raw materials; 44·2 per cent. came from

the Common Market⋆ countries; 15·2 per cent. from the E.F.T.A.† and 12·7 per cent. from the United States and Canada. The Common Market countries took 40·1 per cent. of all exports, the E.F.T.A. 22·6 per cent. and the United States and Canada 10·1 per cent.

Trade with U.K.

	1969	1970
Imports from U.K...	£366,498,000	£502,903,000
Exports to U.K.....	466,129,000	548,934,000

Communications.—In December, 1970, the state-owned railways of the Federal Republic measured 18,383 miles of which 5,340 miles were electrified, and the privately owned railways 2,488 miles, a total of 20,871 miles. In 1970 the railways handled 394,000,000 tons of goods and the inland waterways 239,958,688 tons. Railway rolling stock (*Deutsche Bundesbahn*) included, in 1970, 1,636 steam locomotives, 2,260 electric locomotives, 2,550 diesel locomotives, 18,114 passenger coaches, 829 rail buses and 284,212 goods waggons. Classified roads measure 100,876 miles. On Jan. 1, 1971, there were registered 14,376,500 cars, 1,191,807 commercial vehicles (incl. buses) and 1,370,862 tractors. Ocean-going shipping under the German flag in Dec., 1970, amounted to 8,434,000 tons gross (2,690 ships). Civil aircraft in service at the same date totalled 155 aircraft.

Social Welfare.—There is compulsory insurance against sickness, accident, old age and unemployment. Children's allowances are payable in respect of the second and subsequent children. Pension schemes for widows and orphans of public servants are in operation. Public assistance is given to persons unable to earn their living, or with insufficient income to maintain a decent standard of living.

Law and Justice.—Judicial authority is exercised by the Federal Constitutional Court, the Supreme Federal Court, and the courts of the *Länder*. Judges are independent and subject only to the law. The death sentence has been abolished.

Language and Literature.—Modern (or New High) German has developed from the time of the Reformation to the present day, with differences of dialect in Austria and Alsace and in the German-speaking cantons of Switzerland. The literary language is usually regarded as having become fixed by Luther and Zwingli at the Reformation, since which time many great names occur in all branches, notably philosophy, from Leibnitz (1646–1716) to Kant (1724–1804), Fichte (1762–1814), Schelling (1775–1854) and Hegel (1770–1831); the drama from Goethe (1749–1832) and Schiller (1759–1805) to Gerhart Hauptmann (1862–1946); and in poetry, Heine (1800–1856). German authors have received the Nobel Prize for Literature on five occasions—Theodore Mommsen (1902), R. Eucken (1908), P. Heyse (1909), Gerhart Hauptmann (1912), and Thomas Mann (1929). In 1969 there were 1,305 daily papers.

Education.—School attendance is compulsory for all children and juveniles between the ages of 6 and 18. Compulsory education comprises 9 years of schooling at primary schools (*Volksschulen*)—full-time compulsory education—and 3 years of compulsory vocational education on a part-time basis. Preliminary figures showed that in autumn, 1969, there were in the Federal Republic 23,057 primary schools (*Volksschulen*) with 181,000 teachers and 6,112,327 pupils. Intermediate schools (*Real-*

⋆ Common Market: W. Germany, Belgium and Luxemburg, France, Italy, Netherlands.

† E.F.T.A. (European Free Trade Association): Austria, Denmark, Iceland, Norway, Portugal, Sweden, Switzerland, U.K.

schulen) numbered 2,057 with 31,710 teachers and 826,201 pupils. There were 2,235 secondary schools (*Gymnasien*) with 66,108 teachers and 1,352,065 pupils.

There were also 2,191 special schools (*Sonderschulen*) for retarded, physically and mentally handicapped and socially maladjusted children in the Federal Republic with 16,823 teachers and 290,846 pupils.

The secondary school leaving examination (*Abitur*) entitles the holder to a place of study at a university or another institution of higher education. The number of examinations passed in 1969 was 77,190.

Juveniles below the age of 18 who are not attending an intermediate school, a secondary or a full-time vocational school (*Berufsfachschule*) are obliged to take a three-year course (part-time) at a vocational school. In November, 1969, there were 1,770 part-time vocational schools (*Berufsschulen*) and 748 vocational extension schools (*Berufsaufbauschulen*) with 25,752 teachers and 1,683,545 pupils, 2,575 full-time vocational schools with 9,303 teachers and 203,630 pupils, 3,075 advanced vocational schools (*Fachschulen*) with 7,060 teachers and 178,270 pupils; 147 engineering schools (*Ingenieurschulen*) with 5,666 teachers and 69,322 students and 531 schools for secondary technical studies with 20,749 students. [State expenditure for primary schools per annum amounted to DM.1,237 per pupil, for intermediate schools DM.1,683, and for grammar schools DM.2,235. State expenditure per pupil for part-time vocational, full-time vocational and advanced vocational schools per annum amounted to DM.1,075.] In the winter term 1969–70 there were 25 universities (262,546 students; 10,814 on leave), 9 technical universities (*Technische Hochschulen*) (63,908 students; 1,146 on leave), 18 other scientific colleges (9,123 students; 119 on leave), 25 colleges of fine arts and music (*Kunst- und Musikhochschulen*) (9,328 students; 222 on leave), 1 college for physical education (*Sporthochschule*) (878 students; 16 on leave); a college for television and cinema (109 students; 2 on leave); a total of 321,636 German and 24,256 foreign students (including students on leave). In the winter term 1969–70 there were also 99 teachers' training colleges (*Pädagogische Hochschulen und entsprechende Eintrichtungen*) (57,870 students). The largest universities are in Munich, Cologne, Hamburg, West Berlin, Münster (Westf.), Frankfurt-am-Main, Bonn, Freiburg and Heidelberg. There were 1,194 adult education centres. The attendance figure for 1969 was 4,397,900.

Religion.—In 1966 there were 29,079,000 Protestants in the Republic, 27,816,000 Roman Catholics and (Dec., 1967), 26,241 Jews.

CAPITAL, Bonn, in North Rhine Westphalia, on the left bank of the Rhine, 15 miles distant from Cologne. Population, 299,376 (Dec. 31, 1969).

FLAG.—Horizontal bars of black, red and gold.

BRITISH EMBASSY
Friedrich-Ebert Allee 77, Bonn

Ambassador Extraordinary and Plenipotentiary, His Excellency Sir Roger William Jackling, K.C.M.G. (1968) £14,000

Ministers, F. B. Richards, C.M.G., D.S.C.; D. D. Brown, C.M.G., M.M.

Counsellors, C. J. Audland (*Head of Chancery*); D. W. Hennessy, O.B.E. (*Administration*); H. Carless (*Information*); D. P. Thomson (*Economic*); A. L. Pope, C.V.O., O.B.E.; D. K. Womersley; C. A. Alldis, C.B.E., D.F.C., A.F.C. (*Defence Supply*); E. C. M. Cullingford, C.M.G. (*Labour*); W. F. G. Drury (*Scientific*).

1st Secretaries, N. P. Bayne; R. J. O'Neill; J. D. Campbell, M.B.E., M.C.; P. L. Noble; W. Cohn; R. C. Fisher (*Commercial*); Miss H. N. P. Harrison; W. D. Symington (*Information*); K. G. Cumberbeach (*Defence Supply*); J. O. S. Wilde (*Defence Supply*); Dr. K. C. Wright (*Economic*); D. H. Anderson; M. R. H. Jenkins; D. J. A. Kirk (*Civil Air*); G. W. Hopcroft; G. H. Pecover (*Administration*); N. R. H. A. Broomfield; J. H. A. Emck (*Information*); Dr. J. K. Duxbury; G. Brook.

2nd Secretaries, A. P. Ceurvorst, M.B.E.; Miss E. McCay (*Accountant*); R. E. Palmer; Miss S. Lambert; A. Mineeff; R. Tempest; T. G. Longdon-Griffiths; Miss N. B. Low.

3rd Secretaries, A. Ford; J. B. Rawlings; T. T. Macan.

Defence and Military Attaché, Brig. F. L. Clarkson, M.B.E.

Asst. Military Attaché, Maj. C. J. C. Delamain.

Naval Attaché, Capt. J. M. H. Cox, R.N.

Asst. Naval Attaché, Lt.-Cdr. J. M. Castle, R.N.

Air Attaché, Air Cdre. C. G. Maughan, C.B.E., A.F.C.

Head of Visa Section (*Düsseldorf*), A. E. Higgs.

Chaplain, Rev. A. Nin.

There are British Consulates-General at *Berlin, Hamburg, Hanover, Düsseldorf, Frankfurt, Munich* and *Stuttgart*; and a British Vice-Consulate at *Bremen*.

BRITISH COUNCIL

Representative, J. McDonaugh, C.B.E., Hahnenstrasse 6, Cologne. Offices at *Berlin, Hamburg, Frankfurt* and *Munich* and British Council libraries at *Berlin, Cologne, Frankfurt* and *Munich*.

BERLIN

G.O.C. British Sector, Maj.-Gen. the Earl Cathcart, D.S.O., M.C.

Deputy Commandant (*Minister*), J. C. W. Bushell.

Counsellor, J. E. Jackson (*Political Adviser*.)

EASTERN GERMANY
(For MAP, *see* p. 865)

Area and Population.—The territory of East Germany, an area 41,380 sq. miles in extent, is that of the five former German *länder* of Brandenburg, Mecklenburg, Saxony, Saxony-Anhalt and Thuringia and includes Eastern Berlin, the walled-off former Russian zone of the city. The population of Eastern Germany (U.N. estimate, 1969) is 15,993,000. The former *länder* were abolished in July 1952, and divided into the 14 *Bezirke* (regions) of Potsdam, Cottbus and Frankfurt (*formerly* Brandenburg); Rostock, Schwerin and Neubrandenburg (*formerly* Mecklenburg); Karlmarxtadt, Dresden and Leipzig (*formerly* Saxony); Halle and Magdeburg (*formerly* Saxony-Anhalt); Erfurt, Gera and Guhl (*formerly* Thuringia).

Government.—The Constitution of the "German Democratic Republic" in force from Oct. 7, 1949, came to an end with the approval of a new "socialist draft constitution" by the East German *Volkskammer* (People's Chamber) on March 26, 1968. The supreme organ of State power is the *Volkskammer*, which has power to elect and dismiss the State Council, the Council of Ministers, the Chairman of the National Defence Council, the Supreme Court and the Procurator-General. The State Council is, between sessions, responsible to the *Volkskammer* for the execution of all its laws and decisions and must convene the Chamber on the demand of one-third of the Deputies. Decrees and decisions of the State Council confirmed by the Chamber have the force of law. The executive, with collective responsibility, is the *Council of Ministers*. Among items of the 1949 Constitution omitted from that of 1968 were the former rights of the trade unions to strike, of citizens to emigrate, and of newspapers to publish without censorship.

The German Democratic Republic is not recognized by the governments of Western countries.

The present *Volkskammer* is that elected on July 2, 1967. The office of President having been abolished on Sept. 12, 1960, presidential powers are exercised by the Council of State.

Council of State

Chairman, Herr Walter Ulbricht.

Deputy Chairmen, Herr Willi Stoph; Prof. Johannes Dieckmann; Herr Gerald Götting; Dr. Heinrich Homann; Dr. Manfred Gerlach; Herr Hans Rietz.

Members, Prof. E. Correns; Herr F. Ebert; Herr E. Grützner; Frau B. Hanke; Prof. Lieselott Herfurth; Herr F. Kind; Frau Else Merke; Dr. G. Mittag; Frau A. Neumann; Herr K. Rieke; Prof. H. Rodenberg; Herr H.-H. Simon; Herr K. Sorgenicht; Frau M. Schneider; Herr H. Schumann; Herr P. Strauss.

Council of Ministers

Prime Minister, Herr Willi Stoph.

1st Deputy Prime Minister, Herr Horst Sindermann.

Total membership of the Council is 38, including 10 other Deputy Prime Ministers, 13 holding principal portfolios and 13 holding portfolios of a mainly technical nature.

GERMAN SOCIALIST UNITY (=*Communist*) PARTY

Politbureau of the Central Committee, H. Axen; G. Grüneberg; H. Hagen; E. Honecker; G. Mittag; E. Mückenberger; A. Neumann; H. Sindermann; W. Stoph; P. Verner; H. Warnke (*full members*); G. Ewald; W. Halbritter; W. Jarowinsky; G. Kleiber; M. Müller (*alternate members*).

Secretariat of the Central Committee, E. Honecker (*First*); H. Axen; G. Grünberg; K. Hagen; W. Jarowinsky; W. Lamberz; G. Mittag; A. Norden; P. Verner.

Economic Position.—From the economic point of view the Eastern zone is a more unbalanced area than the Federal Republic. It is more nearly self-sufficient in food, but has few industrial raw materials apart from brown coal and copper ore. Before the war its highly developed secondary industries were dependent on Ruhr coal and steel.

The U.S.S.R. claimed reparations from Germany to a value of $(1938) 10 milliard. Between 1945 and March, 1948, they removed considerable quantities of capital equipment to the U.S.S.R. and took over a number of important plants as Soviet State Concerns (S.A.G.). S.A.G.'s now account for perhaps one-eighth of all industrial production in Eastern Germany. Their products are sold partly in Germany and partly to the U.S.S.R. and other foreign countries. In addition the zone paid reparations from current production to the U.S.S.R. until 1965. Economic control has been centralized, industry subjected to rigid central planning, state ownership and trading greatly expanded at the expense of private interests and the basic industries given priority over secondary industries. Large steel plants have been erected at Füstenberg/ Oder and at Calbe, and crude steel production is now greater than before the war.

The East German Government announced on April 14, 1960, that collectivization of agriculture in East Germany had been completed, the only exceptions being a few small areas unsuitable for large-scale farming.

Trade with U.K.

	1969	1970
Imports from U.K.	£12,131,000	£16,901,000
Exports to U.K.	14,620,000	16,082,000

Principal cities and towns: Dresden (467,966); Leipzig (607,655); Magdeburg (236,326); Halle (222,505); Erfurt (174,633); Rostock (114,869); Zwickau (122,862), and Karlmarxstadt (Chemnitz) (250,188). Eastern Berlin, an integral part of the

zone and its capital city, has a population of approximately 1,200,000.

FLAG.—Horizontal bands of black, red, gold; hammer, compasses and corn device at centre.

GREECE
(Hellas)

King of the Hellenes, Constantine XIII, *born* June 2, 1940; *acceded* (on the death of his father King Paul), March 6, 1964; *married* Sept. 18, 1964, H.R.H. Princess Anne-Marie of Denmark (*born* Aug. 30, 1946); and has issue:—

Crown Prince Paul, *born* May 20, 1967; H.R.H. Princess Alexia, *born* July 10, 1965; H.R.H. Prince Nicholaus, *born* Oct. 1, 1969.

CABINET

Prime Minister and Minister of Defence and Foreign Affairs, George Papadopoulos.
Deputy Prime Minister and Minister of the Interior, Stylianos Patakos.
Co-ordination, Nikolaos Makarezos.
Finance, Adamantios Androutsopoulos.
Commerce, Spyridon Zappas.
Industry, Constantine Kypriaios.
Public Works, Constantine Papadimitriou.
Communications, George Vallis.
Agriculture, Ioannis Papavlachopoulos.
Social Services, George Douvalopoulos.
Merchant Marine, Prof. Ioannis Holevas.
Justice, Angelos Tsoulakas.
Labour, Paul Manalopoulos.
Public Order, Panayotis Tzevelekos.
Education, Nikitas Sioris.
Without Portfolio, Prof. Loukas Patras (acting Minister of Northern Greece); Nikolaus Ephessios.
Alternate Ministers, Ioannis Agathangelou (*Prime Minister's Office*); Emmanuel Phthenakis (*Co-ordination*).

ROYAL GREEK EMBASSY IN LONDON
51 Upper Brook Street, W.1
[01-629-0694]

Ambassador Extraordinary and Plenipotentiary, His Excellency Ioannis A. Sorokos (1969).
Minister Plenipotentiary (Special Adviser), M. Cosmetatos.
Counsellors, N. Diamantopoulos; A. Exarchos (*Consular*); A. Zaphiropoulos (*Commercial*); C. Kondoyiannis (*Agricultural*); G. Angeloglou (*Press and Information*).
Armed Forces Attaché, Capt. Glykis, 71 Park Street, W.1.

1st Secretary, E. Stoforopoulos.
2nd Secretary, P. Apostolides (*Consular*).
Tourist Adviser, B. Iatrides, 195 Regent Street, W.1.
Shipping Attaché, Capt. Eleftherios Photiadis, 96 Gloucester Place, W.1.
Attachés (Press and Information), A. Kovatsis; G. Assimacopoulos; C. Tsikos; E. Kofos (*Cultural*).
Attachés, C. Lambropoulos, M.V.O.; J. Villiotis, M.V.O.; Mme. H. Koutsomitopoulou.
Commercial Secretary, Mrs. A. S. Zachariadou.
Consulate General, Department of Information and Commercial Department, 49 Upper Brook Street, W.1.

There are Honorary Consulates at Birmingham, Bradford, Bristol, Falmouth, Hull, Immingham, Leeds, Liverpool, Newcastle, Plymouth, Portsmouth, Southampton, Cardiff, Edinburgh and Glasgow, and at Belfast.

A maritime Kingdom in the south-east of Europe, bounded on the N. by Albania, Yugoslavia and Bulgaria, on the S. and W. by the Ionian and Mediterranean seas, and on the E. by Turkey, with an estimated area of 51,182 sq. miles. A census held throughout the country on March 14, 1971, recorded a population of 8,736,367 (provisional).

The area of the mainland is 41,328 sq. miles, and of the islands 9,854 sq. miles. The main divisions are: *Macedonia* (which includes Mt. Athos and the island of *Thasos*), *Thrace* (including the island of *Samothrace*), *Epirus*, *Thessaly*, *Continental Greece* (which includes the island of *Euboea* and the *Sporades*, or " scattered islands," of which the largest is *Skyros*), the *Peloponnese* (or *Morea*), the *Dodecanese* or *Southern Sporades* (12 islands occupied by Italy in 1911 during the Italo-Turkish War and ceded to Greece by Italy in 1947) consisting of Rhodes, Astypalaia, Karpathos, Kassos, Nisyros, Kalymnos, Leros, Patmos, Kos, Symi, Khalki and Tilos, the *Cyclades* (a circular group numbering about 200, with a total area of 923 sq. miles ; the chief islands are Syros, Andros, Tinos, Naxos, Paros, Santorini, Milos and Serifos), the *Ionian Islands* (Corfu, Paxos, Levkas, Ithaca, Cephalonia, Zante and Cerigo), the *Aegean Islands* (Chios, Lesbos, Limnos and Samos). In *Crete* there was for over 1,500 years (3000 to 1400 B.C.) a flourishing civilization which spread its influence far and wide throughout the Aegean, and the ruins of the palace of Minos at Cnossos afford evidence of astonishing comfort and luxury. Greek civilization emerges about 1300 B.C. and the poems of Homer, the blind poet of Chios, which were probably current about 800 B.C., record the 10-year struggle between the Achaeans of Greece and the Phrygians of Troy (1194–1184 B.C.).

Government.—Four successive Governments of the National Radical Union Party under M. Karamanlis held office from October, 1955, to June, 1963, when M. Karamanlis resigned after King Paul had refused to accept his advice that the state visit to Britain should be postponed in view of incidents in London. A Government of the Centre Union Party under M. Papandreou was returned at the elections of November, 1963, but did not have an overall majority in Parliament. At the elections of February 16, 1964, the Centre Union was returned to power with a comfortable majority. After a disagreement with the King, however, M. Papandreou resigned in July, 1965. A Cabinet formed in September, 1965, by M. Stephanopoulos consisted of Centre Union deputies who had broken with M. Papandreou and was dependent for its majority on the tolerance of the National Radical Union.

In December, 1966, a caretaker government was appointed and the way seemed clear for elections to be held in May, 1967. A military *coup* on April 21, 1967, however, suspended parliamentary govern-

ment and, following an unsuccessful royal counter *coup* on December 13, 1967, the King went into voluntary exile. He now lives in Rome. The Government is gradually applying a new constitution approved in a national referendum in Sept., 1968, in fulfilment of its declared intention to return the country to parliamentary rule. Martial law was still in force in the autumn of 1971 and no date for parliamentary elections had then been set.

Defence.—The Navy has 65 major war vessels, almost all of U.S. origin, and is mainly a fleet of landing ships supported by destroyers and other escort vessels. The strength of the Army is 116,000. The Air Force consists of 28,000 men, eleven offensive squadrons, two transport squadrons and one helicopter, together with the necessary support, training and maintenance organizations.

Communications.—The 2,650 kilometres of Greek railways are State-owned with the exception of the Athens–Piraeus Electric Railway. The railway from Athens to the Peloponnese, serving Patras and southern Greece, is metre gauge, but the other lines, except one or two minor ones, are standard gauge. Greek roads total somewhat over 50,000 kilometres, of which about 30 per cent. are classified as national highways and 30,000 km. are classified as provincial roads.

On December 31, 1970, the Greek Mercantile fleet numbered 2,101 ships with a total tonnage of 12,849,778 tons gross. On the same day Greek-owned ships registered under foreign flags numbered 1,219 with a total tonnage of 18,049,396 tons gross. Athens has direct airline links with Australasia, North America, most countries in Europe, Africa and the Middle East.

Religion.—Over 97 per cent. of the people are adherents of the Greek Orthodox Church, which is the State religion, all others being tolerated and free from interference. The Church of Greece recognizes the spiritual primacy of the Œcumenical Patriarch of Constantinople, but is otherwise a self-governing body administered by the Holy Synod under the Presidency of the Archbishop of Athens and All Greece. It has no jurisdiction over the Church of Crete, which has a degree of autonomy under the Œcumenical Patriarch, nor over the Monastic Community of Mount Athos and the Church in the Dodecanese, both of which come directly under the Œcumenical Patriarch.

Education is free and compulsory from the age of 6 to 12 and is maintained by State grants. There are three Universities, Athens, Salonika (which also has departments of Philosophy and Mathematics at Ioannina) and Patras. There are several other institutes of higher learning, mostly in Athens.

Language and Literature.—The *spoken* language of modern Greece is descended by a process of natural development from the " Common Greek " of Alexander's empire. Official and technical matter is mostly composed in *Katharevousa*, a conservative literary dialect evolved by Adamantios Corais (Diamant Coray), who lived and died in Paris (1748–1833), but novels and poetry are mostly composed in *dimotiki*, a progressive literary dialect which owes much to John Psycharis (1854–1929). The poets Solomos, Palamas, Cavafis, Sikelianos and Seferis have won a European reputation.

Production.—Though there has in recent years been a substantial measure of industrialization, Greece is still predominantly an agricultural country. Agriculture employs about half the working population, the most important product and export being tobacco, which still accounts for about one-fifth of the value of total visible exports from Greece. Since the war the production of wheat, cotton and rice has been greatly increased, partly in an attempt to make the country's economy less dependent upon tobacco. The most important of the fruit trees are the olive, vine, orange, lemon, fig, almond, pomegranate and currant-vine, and considerable efforts have lately been made to develop exports of Greek fresh fruit and vegetables as well as currants and other dried fruits. Currants, grown mainly around Patras, remain one of Greece's main exports, the United Kingdom being the principal purchaser.

The principal minerals mined in Greece are bauxite, iron ore, iron pyrites, manganese, magnesite, chrome, lead, zinc and emery, and prospecting for petroleum is being carried on. Oil refineries are in operation near Athens and at Salonika, where there is also a petro-chemical plant. The chief industries are textiles (cotton, woollen, silk and rayon), chemicals, cement, glass, metallurgy, shipbuilding, domestic electrical equipment and footwear. In recent years new factories have been opened for the production of aluminium, nickel, iron and steel products, tyres, chemicals fertilizers and sugar (from locally-grown beet). Food processing and ancillary industries have also grown up throughout the country. The development of the country's electric power resources, irrigation and land reclamation schemes, and the exploitation of Greece's lignite resources for fuel and industrial purposes are also being carried out, and the television network is being expanded. Efforts are also being made to develop tourism more rapidly. Greece continues to receive limited aid from the United States mainly in the form of military equipment and foodstuffs. She also receives grants from N.A.T.O. countries to assist her defence programme and loans from member countries of the O.E.C.D. consortium.

Currency.—The Greek *drachma* has an official exchange rate of 72= £1 sterling and 30= $1. U.S.
(*See also* p. 83.)

TRADE

	1969	1970
Total imports....	£597,000,000	£710,000,000
Total exports....	221,000,000	255,000,000

Trade with U.K.

	1969	1970
Imports from U.K....	£57,943,000	£57,239,000
Exports to U.K.......	16,626,000	19,604,000

CAPITAL, Athens. Population (including ΨPiraeus and suburbs), 1,852,709 (1961 Census). Other large towns are: ΨSalonika (373,635); ΨPatras (95,364), ΨVolos (67,424); Larissa (55,391); and ΨCavalla (44,517); in Crete—ΨHeraklion or Candia (63,458), ΨCanea (38,467), and ΨRethymnon (14,999); in the Ionian Islands—ΨCorfu (26,991); in the Dodecanese—ΨRhodes (27,393); in the Cyclades—ΨSyros Hermoupolis (14,402); in Lesbos—ΨMytilene (25,758); in Chios—ΨChios (24,053).

FLAG.—9 horizontal bands, alternately blue and white, with white cross, on blue ground, at top next hoist.

NATIONAL DAY.—March 25 (Independence Day).

BRITISH EMBASSY
(Ploutarchou 1, Athens)

Ambassador Extraordinary and Plenipotentiary, His Excellency Sir Robin William John Hooper, K.C.M.G., D.S.O., D.F.C. (1971)............£9,000
Counsellors, S. Y. Dawbarn (*Commercial*); J. E. Powell-Jones (*Consul-General*).
1st Secretaries, P. L. O'Keeffe; J. D. M. Blyth; A. G. R. Butler (*Information*); R. Burns (*Labour*); N. W. Lomas (*Commercial*).
2nd Secretaries, W. G. Winter, M.B.E. (*Administration*); W. H. Swan (*Consul*); J. F. R. Martin.
3rd Secretary, L. G. Davies (*Commercial*).

Defence and Military Attaché, Brig. H. J. P. Baxter, O.B.E., G.M.

Naval and Air Attaché, Capt. J. A. F. Lawson.

Attachés, E. C. Duckworth, M.B.E. (*Commercial*); E. Tragoutsi, M.B.E.; H. Byatt (*Press*).

Embassy Chaplain, Rev. P. Renshawe.

Hon. Attaché, P. M. Fraser, M.C., F.B.A. (*Director, British School of Archæology*).

BRITISH CONSULAR OFFICES

There are British Consular Offices at *Athens, Crete, Piraeus, Corfu, Samos, Rhodes* and *Salonika*.

BRITISH COUNCIL

17 Filikis Etairias 17, Kolonika Square, Athens 138

Representative (vacant).

There is also an office at *Salonika*; British Council libraries at both centres.

GUATEMALA
(República de Guatemala)

President, Col. Carlos Araña (Osorio), *born* 1918, *elected for* 4 *years*, March 21, 1970; *assumed office*, July 1, 1970.

Guatemala, the most northerly of the Republican States of Central America, is situated in N. lat. from 13° 45′ to 17° 49′, and in W. long. from 88° 12′ 49″ to 92° 13′ 43″, and has an area of 42,042 square miles, and a population (U.N. estimate, 1969) of 5,014,000 (*for* MAP, *see* p. 875). The constitutionally elected president, Gen. Miguel Ydigoras Fuentes, who had taken office on March 3, 1958, was overthrown on March 31, 1963, by the Army, which handed executive and legislative powers to the Minister of Defence, Col. Enrique Peralta Azurdia. Important changes were included in a new constitution promulgated on Sept. 15, 1965, including the reduction of the presidential term from 6 to 4 years and the establishment of a Council of State under the chairmanship of a Vice-President. Elections for a new Congress and for President and Vice-President took place on March 6, 1966. Dr. Mendez was chosen as President at the first meeting of the new Congress and was succeeded by Col. Araña in 1970.

The Republic is divided into 22 departments, and is traversed from W. to E. by an elevated mountain chain, containing several volcanic summits rising to 13,000 feet above the sea; earthquakes are frequent, and the capital (which is at an altitude of 4,800 ft.) was destroyed by an upheaval in Dec. 1917. The country is well watered by numerous rivers; the climate is hot and malarial near the coast, temperate in the higher regions. The rainfall in the capital is 57 in. per annum. The chief seaports are San José de Guatemala and Champerico on the Pacific and Livingston, Matías de Gálvez (*formerly* Santo Tomás) and Puerto Barrios on the Atlantic side.

Language and Literature.—Spanish is the language of the country, and since the establishment of the University in the capital, education has received a marked impulse and the high figure of illiteracy is being reduced. The National library contains about 80,000 volumes in the Spanish tongue.

Finance.—Revenue and expenditure balanced at Quetzales 178,000,000 in 1968, compared with Quetzales 190,600,000 in 1967.

At par 1 *Quetzal* = $1 U.S. (*See also* p. 83.)

TRADE

	1965 Quetzales	1966 Quetzales
Imports (c.i.f.)	229,300,000	207,000,000
Exports (f.o.b.)	185,800,000	226,000,000

Trade with U.K.

	1969	1970
Imports from U.K.	£3,505,000	£4,150,000
Exports to U.K.	799,000	859,000

The principal export is coffee, other articles being bananas, cotton, *chicle* (chewing gum), essential oils, zinc and lead. The chief imports are textiles, petroleum, vehicles, machinery and foodstuffs.

CAPITAL, Guatemala. Population: 770,000. Quezaltenango (second city of the Republic), has a pop. of 38,400. Other towns are Ψ Puerto Barrios (32,100), Mazatenango (32,400), and Antigua (22,000).

FLAG.—Three vertical bands, blue, white, blue; coat of arms on white stripe.

BRITISH EMBASSY
(Diplomatic relations suspended, July 31, 1963.)

GUINEA
(Republic of Guinea)

President, Ahmed Sékou Touré, *elected for a term of* 7 *years*, January, 1961; *re-elected*, 1968.

President of National Assembly, Léon Maka.

CABINET

Minister of External Affairs, El Hadj Diallo Saifoulaye.

Economic Affairs, Dr. Louis Lansana Beavogui.

Interior, Gen. Diane Lansana.

Finance, Ismael Touré.

Trade Exchanges, Dr. Touré Mamouna.

Social Affairs, Kéita N'Famara.

15 Secretaries of State and 4 Ministers-Delegate for the regions (Forestal, Upper, Middle and Maritime Guinea) were also appointed in January, 1968.

Formerly part of French West Africa, Guinea has a coastline on the Atlantic Ocean between Portuguese Guinea and Sierra Leone and in the interior is adjacent to Senegal, Mali, Ivory Coast, Liberia and Sierra Leone (*see* below). Area, 96,865 sq. miles. The population (U.N. estimate, 1969), is 3,890,000, mostly the Fullah, Malinké and Soussou tribes. It is estimated that there are about 2,000 Europeans in the country.

Government.—Guinea was separated from Senegal in 1891 and administered by France as a separate colony until 1958. In the referendum held in Metropolitan France and the overseas territories on Sept. 2, 1958, Guinea rejected the new French Constitution. Accordingly, on Sept. 28, it was declared that Guinea had separated itself from the other territories of French West Africa which had adopted the Constitution. French administrative and financial assistance was terminated; and Guinea left the French Community. On October 2, 1958, Guinea became an independent republic governed by a Constituent Assembly. M. Sékou Touré, Prime Minister in the Territorial Assembly, assumed office as head of the new Government.

A provisional constitution, adopted on Nov. 12, 1958, declared Guinea " a democratic, secular and social republic ", powers of government being exercised by a president assisted by the Cabinet. The President, eligible for a term of 7 years and for re-election, is head of state and of the armed forces. M. Sékou Touré was elected President of the Republic by an overwhelming vote in an election (in which he was the sole candidate) in January, 1961 and re-elected in 1968. General recognition of Guinea as an independent state was followed by her admission to membership of the United Nations in December, 1958.

Guinea withdrew from the Franc Zone on March 1, 1960, and established her own currency, the Guinea franc (at par with the franc C.F.A.). This led to the rupture of commercial relations with France, hitherto her most important supplier and

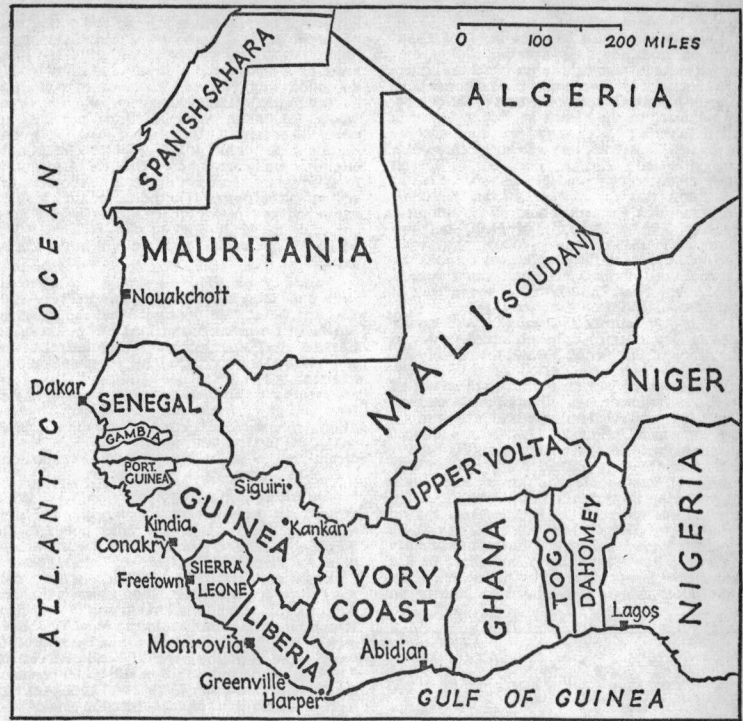

purchaser. Guinea is in receipt of economic aid and technical assistance from a number of countries, including the United States, Federal Republic of Germany, Yugoslavia, the Soviet Union and China. The Government's foreign policy is one of " positive neutralism " and non-alignment. In May, 1963, Guinea signed agreements with France covering *inter alia* the settlement of Governmental claims and technical co-operation. Diplomatic relations with U.K., suspended in December, 1965, were resumed on Feb. 20, 1968.

Production, etc.—The principal products of Guinea are alumina, iron-ore, palm kernels, millet, rice, coffee, bananas, pineapples and rubber. Principal imports are cotton goods, manufactured goods, tobacco, petroleum products, sugar, rice, flour and salt; exports, alumina, iron-ore, diamonds, coffee, hides, bananas, palm kernels and pineapples. In the mountains in the hinterland of Guinea (Fouta Djalon, 4,970 feet), where the rivers Senegal, Gambia and Niger have their sources, large deposits of bauxite (the raw material of aluminium) are worked and alumina is produced for export. Bauxite has been worked and exported from the Conakry area where there are also rich deposits of iron-ore and large-scale mining is carried on. There are a British-built cotton mill and a Chinese-built cigarette and match factory. Guinea imported goods to the value of £1,258,000 from U.K. in 1970 (1969, £1,041,000).

CAPITAL.—Ψ Conakry (120,000). Other towns

are Kankan (29,000), which is connected with Conakry by a railway, Kindia (25,000), N'Zérékoré, Mamou, Siguiri and Labé.

FLAG.—Three vertical stripes of red, yellow and green.

NATIONAL DAY.—October 2 (Anniversary of Proclamation of Independence).

BRITISH EMBASSY
Conakry.

Ambassador Extraordinary and Plenipotentiary, His Excellency Ivor Forsyth Porter, C.M.G. (*resident at Dakar*).

Hon. British Consul, J. Buhagiar, c/o Paterson Zochonis Guinée S.A., B.P. 598, Conakry.

HAITI
(République d'Haiti)

President, Jean Claude Duvalier, *installed as President for life*, April 21, 1971.

EMBASSY AND CONSULATE
1st Secretary, (*Chargé d'Affaires*), Molière Duplan.

The Republic of Haiti occupies the western third of the island of Hispaniola, which, next to Cuba, is the largest island in the West Indies.

The area of the Republic, including off-shore islands, is about 10,700 sq. miles with a population (estimated, 1969) of 4,768,000. The people are mainly negroes but there are numbers of mulattoes and others with some admixture of European

blood. About 250 British subjects, many of West Indian origin, reside in Haiti.

A French colony under the name of Saint-Domingue from 1697, the slave population, estimated at 500,000, revolted in 1791 under the leadership of Toussaint L'Ouverture, who was born a slave and made himself Governor-General of the colony. He capitulated to the French in 1802 and died in captivity in 1803. Resistance was continued by Jean Jacques Dessalines, also a former negro slave, who, on January 1, 1804, declared the former French colony to be an independent state. It was at this time that the name Haiti, an aboriginal word meaning mountainous, was adopted. Dessalines became Emperor of Haiti, but was assassinated in 1806. In 1915, following a period of political upheaval, the country was occupied by a force of U.S. marines. The occupation came to an end in 1934, and U.S. control of the revenue of Haiti officially ended on October 1, 1947.

The six-year term of General Magloire having ended in December 1956, he attempted to stay in power for a further period but was forced to resign and go into exile. A period of political upheaval followed and for many months there was no effective government. A military junta took over in June, 1957, and elections were held in September, following which Dr. François Duvalier was installed as the new President of the Republic. He began a second term in 1961 and in May, 1964, a new constitution granting absolute power to the President was adopted by the National Assembly. Dr. Duvalier was re-elected as President for life on June 15, 1964. He died on April 21, 1971. He was succeeded as President for life on the same day by his son, Jean Claude Duvalier, whom he had nominated as his successor under Article 102 of the Constitution of 1964 as amended on January 14, 1971.

Production, Industry, etc.—In French colonial times, Haiti was one of the most productive countries in the world and the richest French possession. Improvident methods of peasant agriculture succeeded the plantation system and resulted in the gradual impoverishment of natural resources through exhaustion of the soil, deforestation and erosion. In recent years measures for agricultural rehabilitation have been taken with the aim of a gradual restoration of productivity. The main project is a scheme for the irrigation of more than 70,000 acres of the Artibonite valley.

The principal products are coffee, sugar, essential oils, sisal, cocoa and cotton. Coffee accounts for about one third of total exports and is still a mainstay of the country's economy though exports now rarely exceed 300,000 bags (of 60 kg.). Exports of bauxite began in 1957 and production of copper in the Terre Neuve area started in 1960. Industry is still on a small scale but the last three years or so have seen a steady and considerable expansion of light industry (the so-called transportation industries) taking advantage of cheap local labour (minimum wage $US1.00 per day) to assemble or manufacture labour-intensive goods for the U.S. market (baseballs, brassieres, simple electronic equipment, etc.). Exports of manufactures now rank second after coffee at about 20 per cent. of total exports. The tourist industry is again expanding and many French Canadians are now attracted to Haiti for winter holidays. The country is one of the most beautiful in the Caribbean.

Communications.—There are very few asphalted roads and internal communications are very bad. Air services between the capital and the principal provincial towns are maintained by the Aviation Corps of the Haitian Army. The principal towns and villages are connected by telephone and/or telegraph. The telephone company has been acquired by a Canadian enterprise and the service both in Port-au-Prince and Inter-urban has been greatly improved. External telegraph, telephone and postal services are normal. There are several commercial radio stations and a television station—at Port-au-Prince.

Haiti is very well served by air from New York, Miami and Kingston to the North and from Martinique, Puerto Rico and other points to the South, with daily services by one line or another in both directions. The airlines touching Port-au-Prince International Airport include Pan American, Air France, American Air Lines, Caribair (Eastern Airlines), K.L.M., and Cia. Dominicana de Aviación. Regular passenger liner services to New York have ceased, but cruise ships call regularly, one Norwegian line operating a weekly cruise service to Kingston and Miami. Freight sailings are frequent for the U.S.A., Canada, Europe and Latin America (except Cuba) but sailings between Haiti and Jamaica are infrequent. (Airmail: UK/Port-au-Prince, 4–14 days—extremely variable).

Climate.—The climate is tropical with comparatively little difference in the temperatures between the summer (March–Oct.) and the winter (Nov.–Feb.). The temperature at Port-au-Prince rarely exceeds 95° F., but the humidity is high, especially in the autumn.

Language and Literature.—French is the language of the government and the press, but it is only spoken by the educated minority. The usual language of the people is Creole. Education is free but estimates of illiteracy are as high as 90 per cent. There are 3 French daily newspapers and one fortnightly in English. The total circulation is very small.

Finance.—The International Monetary Fund has granted Haiti a stand-by credit of $U.S.2,200,000 renewable annually.

	1969–70 $U.S.	1970–71* $U.S.
Revenue......	28,013,560	28,217,105
Expenditure...	28,013,560	28,217,105

* Haitian budget figures: there is also non-fiscal revenue—e.g. from the Tobacco Monopoly.

Exchange Rate: 5 *Gourdes* = $1 (U.S.). (*See also* p. 84.)

Trade.—Estimated value of imports, 1970, $U.S.40,000,000; exports $U.S. 38,000,000.

Trade with U.K.

	1969	1970
Imports from U.K.......	£812,000	£976,000
Exports to U.K..........	178,000	144,000

The principal exports are listed above; the principal imports are foodstuffs, machinery, vehicles, chemicals and miscellaneous manufactured goods.

CAPITAL, Ψ Port-au-Prince. Population (estimated, 1971), 300,000. Other centres are: Ψ Cap Haitien (24,957); Ψ Gonaives (13,534); Ψ Les Cayes (11,835); Jérémie (11,138); Ψ St. Marc (10,485); Ψ Jacmel (8,545); Ψ Port de Paix (6,309) (1960 Census figures).

FLAG.—Two vertical bands, black (next staff) and red; arms in centre on a white background.

NATIONAL DAY.—January 1.

BRITISH EMBASSY
(Port-au-Prince)

Ambassador Extraordinary and Plenipotentiary, His Excellency Edward Noel Larmour, C.M.G. (1970) *(resident at Kingston, Jamaica)*..........£6,925
1st Secretary and Consul, J. D. Murray, C.M.G. (Port-au-Prince).

HEJAZ, *see* Saudi Arabia

HONDURAS
(Republica de Honduras)

President, Dr. Ramon Ernesto Croz, *assumed office* June 6, 1971.

HONDURAS EMBASSY AND CONSULATE
48 George Street, W.1.
[01-486-4880]

Chargé d'Affaires, Sr. Ramon Humberto España Nini.

Honduras, one of the five Republican States of Central America, lies between lat. 13° and 16° 30′ N. and long. 83° and 89° 41′ W. with a seaboard of about 400 miles on the Caribbean Sea and an outlet, consisting of a small strip of coast 77 miles in length on the Pacific. Its frontiers are contiguous with those of Guatemala, Nicaragua and El Salvador.

The Republic contains a total area of approximately 43,278 square miles and a population of 1,884,765 (Census of 1961); estimated, 1969, 2,535,000 of mixed Spanish and Indian blood. There is a strong foreign negro (British West Indian) element in Northern Honduras. The country is very mountainous, being traversed by the Cordilleras. Most of the soil is poor and acid, except for a few areas along the North coast and in the interior. Rainfall is seasonal, May to October being wet and November to April dry. The climate varies with the altitude, being tropical throughout the year in the coastal belts and temperate and mainly healthy in the uplands.

Originally discovered and settled by the Spaniards at the beginning of the sixteenth century Honduras formed part of the Spanish American Dominions for nearly three centuries until 1821 when independence was proclaimed.

On March 28, 1971, the Nationalist Party won the Presidential election and nominated Dr. Croz

to head a Coalition Government which took office on June 8, 1971.

The Republic is divided into 18 departments, the newest of which, Gracias a Dios, formed in Feb. 1957, covers all the territory previously known as La Mosquitia, together with portions of the Departments of Olancho and Colón. It is inhabited by Indian tribes and largely unexplored.

The chief industry is the production of bananas. Other products are coffee, tobacco, beans, maize, rice, cotton, sugar cane, cement and tropical fruits. Cattle raising is becoming an increasingly important industry, a large number of cattle being exported to the neighbouring countries every year. Honduras is also a timber producing country, the most important woods being pine, mahogany and cedar. There are large tracts of uncultivated land.

The mineral resources of the country are reputed to be considerable, but only a small portion is at present exploited owing to transport difficulties.

There are about 730 miles of railway in operation, chiefly to serve the banana plantations and the Caribbean ports. The total road mileage is approximately 2,260, the greater part of which is in poor condition, but improvements are now being made and new roads built. There are 33 unpretentious airports and three international airports in use in Honduras. A new international airport suitable for jet aircraft has been built near San Pedro Sula. There are numerous small landing and emergency fields. There are four international air services (AVIATECA, SAHSA, PAA and TAN) and 3 domestic air services (SAHSA, Aero Servicios and LANSA). There are 1,646 miles of telephone lines, 5,324 miles of telegraph lines and 488 post-offices.

Ψ The chief ports are Puerto Cortes, Tela and La Ceiba on the North Coast, through which passes the bulk of the trade with the United States and Europe, and Amapala, situated on Tiger Island in the Gulf of Fonseca, on the Pacific side.

Language and Literature.—The language of the country is Spanish. Primary and secondary education is free, primary education being compulsory, and, although there is still a great deal of illiteracy, it is gradually diminishing. There is no recognized native literature.

FINANCE 1971

Revenue (*Budget estimate*)	Lempiras 251,260,700
Expenditure	„ 251,260,700

Public Debt:—

External	Lempiras 12,231,818
Internal	18,567,385

The currency is the *Lempira* (named after a native chief), value of 50 cents, U.S. and *Lps.* 4·80 to the *£.* (*See also* p. 84.)

TRADE 1970

Imports	Lempiras 441,318,756
Exports	„ 339,111,155

Trade with U.K.

	1969	1970
Imports from U.K.	£1,282,000	£1,506,000
Exports to U.K.	347,000	260,000

CAPITAL.—Tegucigalpa. Pop. 225,000 (approximate, including the contiguous town of Comayaguela); other towns are San Pedro Sula (120,000), Ψ La Ceiba (31,000), Ψ Puerto Cortes (30,000), Choluteca (25,000) and Ψ Tela (20,000).

FLAG.—Three horizontal bands, blue, white, blue (with five blue stars on white band).

NATIONAL DAY.—September 15.

BRITISH EMBASSY
(Tegucigalpa.)

Ambassador Extraordinary and Plenipotentiary and Consul-General, His Excellency Laurence Percy Farrer L'Estrange, O.B.E. (1969) £6,475
1st Secretary and Consul, K. H. Jones.
3rd Secretary, T. H. Butlin (*Vice Consul*).

BRITISH CONSULAR OFFICES

There is a British Consular Office at *Tegucigalpa*. Tegucigalpa is 5,930 miles from London; transit, *viâ* New York, 14 days; *viâ* Panama 20 days. By air *viâ* New York or Miami 2 days.

HUNGARY
(Magyarország)

President of the Presidential Council of the Republic, Pál Losonczi, *elected* April, 1967.

COUNCIL OF MINISTERS

Prime Minister, Jenö Fock.
Deputy Prime Ministers, Miklós Ajtal; Lajos Fehér; Mátyás Timár; Péter Vályi.
Foreign Affairs, János Péter.
Home Affairs, András Benkei.
Defence, Lajos Czinege.
Finance, László Faluvégi.
Justice, Mihály Korom.
Metallurgy and Machine Industry, Gyula Horgos.
Heavy Industry, Gyula Szekér.
Light Industry, János Keserü.
Foreign Trade, József Biró.
Internal Trade, István Szurdi.
Agriculture and Food, Imre Dimény.
Health, Dr. Zoltán Szabó.
Education, Pál Ilku.
Building and Town Planning, Jozsef Bondor.
Labour, György Lázár.
Transport and Communications, György Csanádi.
President, National Planning Office, Imre Párdi.
President, Technical Development Committee, Miklos Ajtai.

THE COMMUNIST PARTY

Politbureau of the Central Committee, G. Aczél; A. Apró; V. Benke; B. Biszku; L. Feher; J. Fock; S. Gáspar: J. Kádár; G. Kállai; Z. Komócsin; D. Nemes; K. Németh; R. Nyers; (*full members*); M. Ajtai; L. Czinege; P. Ilku (*candidate members*).
Secretariat of the Central Committee, Janos Kádár (*1st Secretary*); G. Aczél; B. Biszku; Z. Komócsin; R. Nyers; M. Ovari; A. Pullai.

HUNGARIAN EMBASSY AND CONSULATE
35 Eaton Place, S.W.1

[01-235-4048, 7191; Consulate: 01-235-4462]
Ambassador Extraordinary and Plenipotentiary, His Excellency Dr. Vencel Házi (1970).
Counsellors, Dr. László Ujházy (*Commercial*); M. Kálmán Dóczé.
Military and Air Attaché, Col. Géza Pászka.
1st Secretaries, M. András Halász; M. Zoltán Komornik.
2nd Secretaries, M. Sandor Igaz; M. János Zentai; M. Károly Beszédes.
3rd Secretaries, M. G. Szombathelyi; Dr. J. Foder (*Consul*); M. G. Kótai.
Asst. Military and Air Attaché, Lt.-Col. Ferenc Esztergomi.
Attaché, M. P. Trunk.
Area and Population.—The area of Hungary may be stated as approximately 36,000 sq. miles with a population (U.N. estimate, Sept. 1970) of 10,344,000.

Government.—Hungary was reconstituted a kingdom in 1920 after having been declared a republic on Nov. 17, 1918. She joined the Anti-Comintern Pact on Feb. 24, 1939, and entered the 1939–45 War on the side of Germany in 1941. On Jan. 20, 1945, a Hungarian provisional government of liberation, which had been set up during the preceding December, signed an armistice under the terms of which the frontiers of Hungary were withdrawn to the limits existing in 1937.

For the first four years after the liberation, Hungary was governed by a coalition of the Smallholder, National Peasant, Social Democrat and Communist parties. During this time land reform was carried out, the great landowners being dispossessed and their estates partitioned among peasants; mines, heavy industry, banks and schools were nationalized. By 1949 the Communists, under the leadership of Mr. Rákosi, having compelled the Social Democrat Party to merge with them, and having disrupted the peasant parties, had succeeded in gaining a monopoly of power. Elections in that year, in which candidates for the National Assembly were drawn from a single list, resulted in 95.6 per cent. of the votes cast being obtained by the Communist-dominated People's Front. A campaign was opened to collectivize agriculture and by 1952 practically the entire economy had been "socialized."

In mid-1953 Mr. Imre Nagy replaced Mr. Rákosi as Prime Minister, though the latter continued to hold his post as First Secretary of the Party. Mr. Nagy introduced a more moderate policy based largely on the development of agriculture rather than heavy industry; but in April, 1955, Mr. Rákosi succeeded in turning the tables on his rival who was removed from his position as Prime Minister and subsequently expelled from the Party. But after the 20th Congress of the Soviet Communist Party, opposition to Mr. Rákosi within the Hungarian Communist Party mounted and on July 18, 1956, he was removed from his post as First Secretary and succeeded by Mr. Gerö, who had been one of his closest associates.

The period from July to the outbreak of the national revolution on Oct. 23, 1956, was marked by growing ferment in intellectual circles and increased discord within the Party. The immediate signal for the revolt was a series of students' demonstrations, first in Szeged on Oct. 22 and in Budapest a day later. The chief demands put forward by students and other demonstrators were for the return of Mr. Nagy as Prime Minister, for the withdrawal of Soviet troops from the country and for free elections. Fighting broke out on the night of Oct. 23 between demonstrators, who had been joined by large numbers of factory workers, and the State Security Police (A.V.H.). Soviet forces intervened in strength early the next morning. By Oct. 30 Soviet troops had withdrawn from Budapest and on Nov. 3 Mr. Nagy formed an all-party coalition government. This government was overthrown and the revolution suppressed as the result of a renewed attack by Soviet forces on Budapest in the early hours of Nov. 4. Simultaneously the formation of a new Hungarian Revolutionary Worker Peasant Government under the leadership of Mr. Kádár, Mr. Gerö's successor as First Secretary of the Party, was announced. The trial and execution of Imre Nagy and three of his associates was announced on June 17, 1958.

Dr. Ferenc Münnich succeeded as President of the Council of Ministers on Jan. 27, 1958, and held office until Sept. 13, 1961, being replaced by Mr. Kádár. Several other Ministers were replaced at the same time. Mr. Kádár relinquished the post of President of the Council of Ministers in June, 1965, and was succeeded by Mr. Kállai. In April, 1967, Mr. Fock replaced Mr. Kállai as Prime Minister and two new Deputy Prime Ministers were appointed. Mr. Kádár continues as First Secretary of the Hungarian Socialist Workers' Party.

Production, Industry, etc.—Though industrialization has made considerable progress in the last decade, agriculture still occupies an important place in the Hungarian economy and 54.2 per cent. of the total area of the country is arable land. 10.7 per cent. of this arable land is owned by state farms and 63.6 per cent. by co-operative farms. Production of the most important crops in 1970 was as follows (1,000 tons): Wheat, 2,718; rye, 155; barley, 552; maize, 4,005; rice, 45; oats, 57; potatoes, 1,429; sugar beet, 2,174; green maize and silage maize, 3,832; lucerne, 1,971.

Industry is mainly based on imported raw materials, but Hungary has her own coal (mostly brown), bauxite, considerable deposits of natural gas (some not yet under full exploitation), some iron ore and oil. Output figures in 1970 (1,000 tons): coal, 27,800; bauxite, 2,022; steel, 3,110; crude oil, 1,937; cement, 2,771. Natural gas production totalled 3,469,000,000 cubic metres.

In 1970 most Plan targets were met or exceeded, with the exception of agricultural production (which fell by 6 per cent.) largely owing to unfavourable weather and flooding. In industry production per worker (an index of productivity) rose by 7 per cent. The Hungarian economy is now run according to a new system of economic management introduced on Jan. 1, 1968, which provides for greater decentralization, profitability and profit-sharing.

Religion and Education.—About two-thirds of the Magyars are Roman Catholics, and the remainder mostly Calvinist. There are five types of schools under the Ministry of Education—infant schools 3–6, general schools 6–14 (compulsory), vocational schools (15–18), secondary schools (15–18), universities and adult training schools (over 18). In the academic year 1970–71 there were 80,536 students at institutions of higher learning, 347,165 (incl. 113,874 part-time) at secondary schools and 1,116,000 at general schools.

Language and Literature.—Magyar, or Hungarian, is one of the Finno-Ugrian languages. Hungarian literature began to flourish in the second half of the sixteenth century. Among the greatest writers of the nineteenth and twentieth

centuries are Mihály Vörösmarty (1800–1855), Sándor Petöfi (1823–1849), János Arany (1817–1882), Endre Ady (1877–1918), Attila József (1905–1937), Mihály Babits (1883–1941) and Dezsö Kosztolányi (1885–1936).

Finance.—The budget estimates for the year 1970–71 were: Revenue, Forints 193,061,000,000; Expenditure, Forints 195,226,000,000. The Forint (of 100 Filler) has an official exchange value of 28·18 Forints = £1. The tourist exchange rate is 71·93 Forints = £1.

TRADE

	1969 Forints	1970 Forints
Imports	22,631,100,000	29,410,000,000
Exports	24,462,200,000	27,196,000,000

Trade with U.K.

	1969	1970
Imports from U.K.	£12,744,000	£18,995,000
Exports to U.K.	9,408,000	10,629,000

CAPITAL: Budapest, on the Danube; population (estimated, Jan. 1, 1969), 2,007,000. Other large towns are: Miskolc (144,000); Debrecen (136,719); Pécs (125,104); and Szeged (104,506).

FLAG.—Red, white green (horizontally).

NATIONAL DAY.—April 4 (Anniversary of Liberation, 1945).

BRITISH EMBASSY
6 Harmincad Utca, Budapest V

Ambassador Extraordinary and Plenipotentiary, His Excellency Derek Sherborne Lindsell Dodson, C.M.G., M.C. (1969)..................£6,925
1st Secretaries, O. R. Blair (*Head of Chancery*); P. D. R. Davies; J. E. Reeve (*Commercial*),
2nd Secretary (*Information*), D. M. Bell.
Consul and Visa Officer, Miss A. M. Wood.
Military Attaché, Lt.-Col. M. H. Burge.
Air Attaché, Wing Cdr. J. H. Rogers, A.F.C.
Cultural Attaché, C. R. Hewer.
Budapest is distant 1,126 miles from London, transit by rail 34 hours; by air 2 hrs. 10 mins.

ICELAND
(Island)

President, Dr. Kristjan Eldjarn, *born* 1917, *elected* July 1, 1968, *for a term of 4 years; assumed office* Aug. 1, 1968.

Prime Minister, Prof. Olafur Jóhannesson.
Foreign Affairs, Einar Augústsson.

EMBASSY IN LONDON
1 Eaton Terrace, S.W.1
[01–730–5131–2]

Ambassador Extraordinary and Plenipotentiary, His Excellency Gudmundur Gudmundsson, K.B.E. (1965)
Counsellor, M. Eirikur Benedikz.

Iceland is a large volcanic island in the North Atlantic Ocean, extending from 63° 23′ to 66° 33′ N. lat., and from 13° 22′ to 24° 35′ W. long., with an estimated area of 40,500 square miles, or about one-sixth greater than that of Ireland. The population was 204,000 on Dec. 1, 1970.

Iceland was uninhabited before the ninth century, when settlers came from Norway. For several centuries a form of republican government prevailed, with an annual assembly of leading men called the *Althing*, but in 1241 Iceland became subject to Norway, and later to Denmark. During the colonial period, Iceland maintained its cultural integrity but a deterioration in the climate, together with frequent volcanic eruptions and outbreaks of disease led to a serious fall in the standard of living and to a decline in the population to little more than 40,000. In the nineteenth century a

struggle for independence began which led first to home-rule for Iceland under the Danish Crown (1918), and later to complete independence under a republican form of rule in 1944.

The Icelandic Cabinet normally consists of seven Ministers, responsible to the *Althing*, a Parliamentary assembly of 60 members. The government elected in June, 1967, was a coalition of Conservatives and Social Democrats, with the Progressive and Communist parties forming the Opposition. After the General Election of June 13, 1971, Prof. Jóhannesson formed a new coalition government of Progressives, Liberal Left and People's Union members.

The principal exports are frozen fish fillets, aluminium, saltfish, fishmeal and oil, skins and lamb; the imports consist of almost all the necessaries of life, the chief items being petroleum, transportation equipment, textiles, machinery, base metals, wood and cork and cereals.

At January 1, 1971, the mercantile marine consisted of 571 vessels of under 100 gross tons and 278 ships of 100 gross tons and over; a total of 849 vessels (159,305 gross tons), of which 199 were fishing boats, 24 deep sea trawlers and 31 freighters. There is a regular shipping service between Reykjavik and Felixstowe and frequent but irregular services run between Reykjavik, Hull, Weston Point on the Mersey and the Continent.

A regular air service is maintained between Glasgow and London and Reykjavik. There are also air services from the island to Scandinavia, U.S.A., Germany and Luxemburg.

Road communications are adequate in summer but greatly restricted by snow in winter. Only roads in town centres are well surfaced. The State highways and side roads are non-metalled (gravel and lava dust). The climate and terrain make first-class surfaces for highways out of the question. Iceland changed to right-hand driving on May 26, 1968. Total number of vehicles licensed is 47,000 (private cars, 40,000).

Language and Literature.—The ancient Norraena (or Northern tongue) presents close affinities to Anglo-Saxon and as spoken and written in Iceland to-day differs little from that introduced into the island in the ninth century. There is a rich literature with two distinct periods of development, from the middle of the eleventh to the end of the thirteenth century and from the beginning of the nineteenth century to the present time.

FINANCE

	1969	1970
	Krónur	*Krónur*
Revenue	7,096,482,000	8,396,000,000
Expenditure	7,000,607,000	8,187,384,000
External Debt. (Jan. 1, 1969)	3,002,400,000	3,600,500,000
Internal Debt. (Jan. 1, 1969)	2,145,400,000	2,518,200,000

TRADE

	1969	1970
	Krónur	*Krónur*
Exports	9,466,368,000	12,896,627,000
Imports	10,855,863,000	13,842,850,000

Trade with U.K.

	1969	1970
Imports from U.K.	£5,891,000	£9,284,000
Exports to U.K.	6,774,000	8,951,000

The Icelandic *Krona* was devalued on Nov. 24, 1967, with the concurrence of the International Monetary Fund and again in Nov., 1968, the new par value being expressed as *Krónur* 88 = $U.S. 1. (*See also* p. 83.)

CAPITAL: ΨReykjavik. Population (Dec. 1, 1969), 81,354.

Other centres in approximate order of importance are Akureyri, Akranes, Hafnafjord, Kopavogur, Siglufjord, Keflavik, Isafjordhur and Westmann Islands.

FLAG.—Blue, with white-bordered red cross.

NATIONAL DAY.—June 17.

BRITISH EMBASSY
Laufasvegur 49, Reykjavik

Ambassador Extraordinary and Plenipotentiary and Consul-General, His Excellency John McKenzie, C.M.G., M.B.E. (1970).....................£6,925
1st Secretary, D. H. Fowler, M.B.E.
Consul, B. D. Holt, M.B.E.

BRITISH CONSULAR OFFICES
There are Consular Offices at *Reykjavik*, *Akureyri* and *Isafjordhur*.

INDONESIA
(Republic of Indonesia)

President, General Soeharto, *born* June 9, 1921. *Acting President*, March 12, 1967; *confirmed as President*, Mar. 28, 1968.

DEVELOPMENT CABINET
Ministers of State

Economic, Financial and Industrial Affairs, Sri Sultan Hamengku Buwono IX.
People's Welfare, K. H. Dr. Idham Chalid.
Perfecting and Purging State Apparatus, H. Harsono Tjokroaminoto.
Minister of State, Development Operations, Prof. Dr. Soenawar Soekowati.
In charge of Relations between the Government, Congress, Parliament and Supreme Advisory Council, H. Mintaredja.

Ministers

Home Affairs, Lt.-Gen. Amir Machmud.
Foreign Affairs, Hadji Adam Malik.
Defence/Security, Gen. Soeharto.
Justice, Prof. Oemar Seno Adji.
Information, Air Vice Marshal Boediardjo.
Finance, Prof. Dr. Ali Wardhana.
Trade, Prof. Dr. Soemitro Djojohadikusumo.
Agriculture, Prof. Dr. Ir. Thojib Hadiwidjaja.
Industry, Maj.-Gen. M. Jusuf.
Mining, Prof. Ir. Soemantri Brodjonegoro.
Public Works and Electricity, Ir. Sutami.
Communications, Drs Frans Seda.
Education and Culture, Mashuri S.H.
Health, Prof. Dr. G. A. Siwabessy.
Religion, K. H. Mohamad Dahlan.
Manpower, Rear Admiral Mursalin.
Social Affairs, K. H. Dr. I. Chalid.
Transmigration/Co-operatives, Lt.-Gen. Sarbini.

INDONESIAN EMBASSY AND CONSULATE
38 Grosvenor Square, W.1.
[01-499-7661]

Ambassador Extraordinary and Plenipotentiary, His Excellency Roesmin Nurjadin (1970).
Minister-Counsellors, Munawir Sjadzali; Jusuf Natanegara (*Economic*).
Military Attaché, Col. Edi Sugardo.
Air Attaché, Col. Sunaryo.
Naval Attaché and Attaché for Air, Cdre. A. Dipo.
Defence Attaché, Col. Srijono.
1st Secretaries, M. Samsi Abdullah (*Press and Public Relations*); Mme. T. D. Soemolang.
3rd Secretaries, M. Tjahjono; M. Mohammad Seng (*Economic*); M. Endoeng Sasmito; Sri Narjadi.
Attachés (Administration), M. Bachtiar S. Yamil; M. Soerjo Buwono Sudijatno.
Attachés, M. Mazhar Abdullah; Doddy Soegijanto.

Situated between latitudes 6° North and 11° South and between longitudes 95° and 141° East, Indonesia comprises the islands of *Java* and *Madura*, the island of *Sumatra*, the *Riouw-Lingga Archipelago* (which with Karimon, Anambas, Natuna Islands, Tambelan, and part of Sumatra, forms the province of Riau), the islands of *Bangka* and *Billiton*, part of the island of *Borneo* (Kalimantan), *Sulawesi* (*formerly* Celebes) *Island*, the *Molucca Islands* (Ternate, Halmahera, Buru, Seram, Banda, Timor-Laut, Larat, Bachiam, Obi, Kei, Aru, Babar, Leti and Wetar), part of *Timor Island*, the islands of *Bali* and *Lombok* and the western half of the island of New Guinea (*West Irian*), with a total area of 735,000 sq. miles, and a population (estimated, 1969) of 118,000,000.

From the early part of the 17th century much of the Indonesian Archipelago was under Netherlands rule. Following the World War 1939-45, during which the Archipelago was occupied by the Japanese, a strong nationalistic movement manifested itself and after sporadic fighting the formal transfer of sovereignty by the Netherlands of all the former Dutch East Indies except W. New Guinea took place on December 27, 1949.

Dr. Sukarno was elected President of Indonesia and held office until his deposition in 1967. He died on June 21, 1970.

Following the establishment of Malaysia (including Sabah and Sarawak) in 1963, President Sukarno pursued a policy of " confrontation " against it, involving border incursions in both West and East Malaysia. Commonwealth forces assisted Malaysian resistance. Western New Guinea became part of Indonesia in 1963 under the name West Irian, this interpretation being confirmed in an "Act of Free Choice " in July, 1969, of which the United Nations took note in November, 1969.

On Sept. 30, 1965, an attempted *coup d'état* assisted by the Palace Guard resulted in the murder of six generals. The Indonesian Communist Party was charged with plotting to destroy the power of the Army and to set up a Peking-oriented régime, nominally under President Sukarno. The coup was swiftly crushed and a widespread massacre of Communists and their supporters followed. Sukarno remained in office but his Foreign Minister, Dr. Subandrio, among others, was arrested and later sentenced to death. The sentence had not been carried out by the summer of 1971.

Following a three-week period of unrest and violent student demonstrations the Minister of the Army, General Soeharto, took over effective political power in March, 1966, and announced the banning in Indonesia of the Communist Party. The new régime concluded an agreement ending the " confrontation " with Malaysia on Aug. 11, 1966, and Indonesia resumed membership of the United Nations Organization which it had left in 1965. General Soeharto was made Acting President with full powers, on March 12, 1967.

Using his powers as Acting President, General Soeharto revised the membership of the two Houses of Parliament, and on March 28, 1968, the MPRS (Provisional People's Consultative Congress), the highest constitutional body, appointed him full President for a period of five years, and instructed him to arrange for general elections to be held not later than July 5, 1971; the last general elections were held in 1955.

In accordance with another instruction General Soeharto on June 6 replaced the Ampera Cabinet with the Development Cabinet, *i.e.* one which was intended to reflect the emphasis to be placed henceforward on the development of the country, economic affairs, efficiency and expertise in general,

and to reduce the direct influence of the military in the Government.

Finance.—Following new measures introduced by the Government in October, 1966, inflation declined from the rate of 600 per cent. in 1966 to about 110 per cent. for 1967 and 85 per cent. for 1968. In 1969 and 1970 the rate of inflation was about 109 per cent. Bank notes in circulation rose from *rupiahs* 180,000,000,000 at the beginning of 1969 to 205,900,000,000 in May 1970. Following the agreement on the re-scheduling of Indonesia's debts in 1966, Western creditor nations agreed to make available aid amounting to $200 million as balance of payments support and in 1969 undertook further commitments totalling $36,500,000 in respect of non-food aid.

The new measures adopted by the Government in October, 1966, included the abolition of State controls and the introduction of a free market policy with more realistic exchange rates geared to a floating rate for the purchase of foreign exchange in the form of bonus export certificates for essential imports. The rate had risen to a peak of *Rps.*480= $1 by mid-1968, but fell to *Rps.*378 = $1 by mid-1969. It has remained stable since then even though on April 17, 1970, the Government abolished the bonus exports certificate system and introduced a free market for foreign exchange.

Production.—Nearly 70 per cent. of the population of Indonesia is engaged in agriculture and related production. Copra, kapok, nutmeg and pepper cloves are produced, mainly by smallholders; palm oil, sugar, fibres and cinchona are produced by large estates. Rubber, tea, coffee and tobacco are also produced by both in large quantities. Rice is a traditional staple food for the people of Indonesia and the islands of Java and Madura are important producers, but production is insufficient to meet home demands and substantial imports of rice are necessary.

Indonesia is rich in minerals; petroleum, tin, coal and bauxite are the principal products; gold, silver, manganese phosphates, nickel and sulphur were produced in quantity before the Second World War and there are considerable deposits.

A five-year development programme announced on Dec. 30, 1968, concentrating particularly on agriculture and communications, was inaugurated on April 1, 1969.

Trade with U.K.

There was a progressive decline in British exports to Indonesia after 1960. This became more marked during Indonesia's policy of " confrontation " against Malaysia which resulted in a disruption of normal commercial relations and stringent import controls due to lack of foreign currency, but exports improved in 1967 following the restoration of normal commercial relations.

	1969	1970
Imports from U.K.	£8,793,000	£11,840,000
Exports to U.K.	6,599,000	7,273,000

Principal exports to the United Kingdom are rubber, tea, coffee, spices and sugar. Imports from the United Kingdom are mainly of machinery, chemicals, electrical equipment, motor vehicles, cycles, lubricating and heavy oils, and metal goods.

Transport.—In Java a main line connects Djakarta with Surabaya in the East of Java and there are several branches, including a line from Semarang on the North coast to Djogjakarta in the South. In Sumatra the important towns of Medan, Padang and Palembang are the centres of short railway systems.

Sea communications in the archipelago are maintained by the State-run shipping companies Djakarta-Lloyd (ocean-going) and Pelni (coastal

and inter-island) and other smaller concerns. Transport by small craft on the rivers of the larger islands plays an important part in trade. Air services in Indonesia are operated by Garuda Indonesian Airways and Djakarta is served by various international services. There are approximately 49,000 miles of roads.

CAPITAL.—Ψ Djakarta, formerly Batavia (population 4,750,000). Other important centres are: (Java) Surabaya, Ψ Semarang, Bandung, Ψ Tjirebon, Ψ Surakarta and Jogjakarta; (1961 populations) (Madura) Pamekesan (180,000); (Sumatra) Palembang (500,000), Medan (500,000) and Ψ Padang; (Sulawesi) Ψ Makassar (450,000) and Ψ Menado; (Kalimantan, Borneo) Bandjarmasin, Ψ Balikpapan and Ψ Pontianak; (Moluccas) Ternate (9,000); (Bali) Denpasar and Singaradja (120,000); (W. Timor) Kupang (10,000); (W. Irian) Djajapura.

NATIONAL DAY.—August 17 (Anniversary of Proclamation of Independence).

FLAG.—Equal bands of red over white.

BRITISH EMBASSY
Djakarta

Ambassador Extraordinary and Plenipotentiary, His Excellency Willis Ide Combs, C.M.G. (1970)
£6,925

Counsellor, M. P. Preston.
Defence and Military Attaché, Col. M. P. F. Jones, C.B.E., D.S.O.
Naval Attaché, Cdr. R. E. Hoskin, R.N.
Air Attaché, Wing Cdr. C. T. K. Cody.
1st Secretaries, R. M. Hunt (*Head of Chancery*); J. von M. Lister; E. W. Cook; G. Dickson; L. J. Watling.
2nd Secretaries, J. R. de Fonblanque; Miss S. M. Bull (*Information*).
3rd Secretaries, R. N. E. Smith; Miss C. Shepherd (*Commercial*); R. F. Cornish.

BRITISH CONSULAR OFFICES
There are British Consular Offices at *Djakarta* and *Medan*.

BRITISH COUNCIL
Representative, J. M. Ure, O.B.E., Djalan Imam Bondjol, 57–59 Djakarta. There is also an office at *Bandung*.

IRAN
(Persia)

Shahanshah of Iran, H.I.M. Mohammed Reza Pahlevi, *born* Oct. 26, 1919; *acceded* Sept. 16, 1941 (on abdication of his father Reza Shah Pahlevi); *married* (March 15, 1939), Princess Fawzich, sister of ex-King Farouk of Egypt (marriage dissolved Nov. 17, 1948), and has issue a daughter *born* 1940. The Shah *married* (Feb. 12, 1951) Suraya Esfandiari Bakhtiari (marriage dissolved, April 6, 1958); *married* Dec. 21, 1959, Farah Dibah (Empress Farah Pahlevi) and has issue Crown Prince Reza, *born* Oct. 31, 1960; Princess Farahnaz, *b.* March, 1963; Prince Ali Reza, *b.* April 28, 1966; Princess Leila, *b.* Mar. 27, 1970.

Prime Minister, Amir Abbas Huvaïda.

IRANIAN EMBASSY IN LONDON
16 Princes Gate, S.W.7
[01–584–8101]
Consular and Cultural Sections:
50 Kensington Court, W.8.
[01–937–5225]
Consular Section: [01–937–6540]
Ambassador Extraordinary and Plenipotentiary, His Excellency Amir Khosrow Afshar, K.C.M.G. (1969).
Minister-Counsellors, Ahmad Minai; Dr. Mostafa Elm.

Armed Forces Attaché, Col. Hossein Reshad.
Counsellors, Nasser Majd; Khosrow Gharai; Ali Asghar Emami Ahari (*Cultural*); Kazem Shiva; Djamchid Tavallali; Morteza Mortezaie; Gholam Hossein Kazemian (*Cultural*).
1st Secretaries, Abdol Ali Jahanbin; Bahram Rezvani.
Military Attaché, Lt.-Col. Esmail Hodjat-Kashani.
Naval Attaché, Lt.-Cdr. Djamshid Pourzand.
2nd Secretaries, Ebrahim Mokalla; Eskandar Rastegar.
3rd Secretaries, Miss Chirine Tahmasseb; Iradj Amini; Mahmoud Hedjazi; Feryctoon Novrnia.
Attachés, Dariush Pirnia; Ali Mohammad Shapurian (*Press*); Ebrahim Nabavi; Manoochehr Razmjoo.

Area and Population.—Iran has an area of 628,000 sq. miles, with a population of 25,781,090 (Census of 1966); U.N. estimate, March, 1970, 28,448,000. It is mostly an arid table-land, encircled, except in the east, by mountains, the highest in the north rising to 18,934 ft. The central and eastern portion is a vast salt desert.

The Iranians are mostly Shi'ah Moslems but among them are a few hundred thousand Zoroastrians, Bahais, Sunni Moslems and Armenian and Assyrian Christians. There is also a substantial Jewish community. Civil and Penal codes based on those of France and Switzerland are in force.

Government.—Iran was ruled from the end of the 18th century by Shahs of the Qajar Dynasty, with despotic power, subject only to the influence of interpreters of the sacred law. A nationalist movement became active in Dec., 1905, and in Aug., 1906, the Shah, Muzaffer-ud-Din, admitting the need for reforms, granted a Constitution. After the war of 1914–18, the subsequent troubles and the signature of the Soviet-Iranian Treaty of 1921, a vigorous Prime Minister, Reza Khan, formerly an officer of the Persian Cossack Regiment, re-established general order. On Oct. 31, 1925, the last representative of the Qajar Dynasty, Sultan Ahmed Shah, who had been absent from the country for some time, was deposed by the National Assembly, which handed over the government to the Prime Minister, Reza Khan, who was elected Shah on Dec. 13, 1925, by the Constituent Assembly, and took the title Reza Shah Pahlevi.

Owing to Nazi German penetration before and during the early part of the war of 1939–45, the

Shah and his Government tended so far to favour the Axis powers that, after the German invasion of the U.S.S.R. in 1941, counter-measures became necessary; British and Soviet Forces entered the country from south and north on August 25, 1941, and expelled the agents of the Axis. On September 16, 1941, Reza Shah abdicated and left the country, nominating the Crown Prince as his successor. The Prince ascended the throne under the title of Mohammed Reza Shah Pahlevi.

In March, 1949, the Shah issued an Imperial Firman convoking a Constituent Assembly to make certain revisions to the Constitution and the Assembly was duly elected and convened on April 21. After this Assembly the Senate was formed for the first time.

On February 26, 1963, the Shah announced his six point " White Revolution ". The six points are: 1. A land reform designed to redistribute land and place it in the hands of the peasants. 2. Nationalization of all forest land. 3. The sale of government shares in factories and industrial enterprises to raise money for the implementation of the land reform. 4. The distribution of factory profits among the factory employees. 5. The granting of the vote to women. 6. The creation of a Literacy Corps to bring basic education to the rural areas. Six additional points have since been added.

For the purposes of local government the country is divided into 14 Provinces *Ustans*) and 8 Counties (*Farmandariye Kol*), comprising 147 Sub-Provinces (*Shahristans*), under Governors-General and Governors, respectively.

Defence.—The Ground Forces, which have a strength of about 60,000 regulars and 100,000 conscripts, are made up of 5 infantry and 2 armoured divisions grouped under three Army Headquarters. Their equipment is modern and includes the latest American tanks and some Russian vehicles. The Air Force has a strength of about 14,000. It is equipped with some 140 American aircraft including 100 jets. The Navy consists of a small fleet of frigates, minesweepers, patrol boats, hovercraft and a cruiser in the Persian Gulf, and some small craft in the Caspian Sea. The personnel of the Navy amounts to about 6,000 all ranks. The Gendarmerie is an all regular, para-military force of about 32,000 men which provides frontier guards and mans small posts throughout the country.

Education.—Since 1943 primary education has been compulsory and free. The establishment in 1963 of the Literacy Corps (a body of National Servicemen who are seconded to the Ministry of Education to work as Primary School teachers in rural districts) has brought schooling to hitherto deprived villages and is making a valuable contribution in increasing educational opportunities for country people. During the academic year 1970–71 there were 4,200,000 pupils attending 21,800 schools. About 2,500,000 of these were at Primary School. There are in Iran eight universities (Tehran 3, Tabriz, Meshed, Isfahan, Shiraz and Ahwaz) and attending these and other institutes of higher education there are over 50,000 students.

Language and Literature.—Persian, or Farsi, the language of Iran, and of some other areas formerly under Persian rule, is an Indo-European tongue with many Arabic elements added; the alphabet is mainly Arabic, with writing from right to left. Among the great names in Persian literature are those of Abu'l Kásim Mansúr, or Firdausi (A.D. 939–1020), Omar Khayyám, the astronomer-poet (died A.D. 1122), Muslihu'd-Din, known as Sa-di (born A.D. 1184) and Shems-ed-Din Muhammad, or Hafiz (died A.D. 1389).

Press.—In Iran about 140 newspapers and magazines are published, over half of them in Tehran. Three papers in the capital have the status of national dailies. Two English and one French daily are also published in Tehran. Provincial publications have very small circulations.

Finance.—The budget for the Iranian year beginning March 21, 1971, including development expenditure, balanced at Rls. 481,000,000,000 an increase of 18 per cent. over 1970–71. The development budget showed an increase of 30 per cent. and defence expenditure increased by 32 per cent.

Following the devaluation of sterling in November, 1967, the rate of exchange was fixed at Rials 182 = £1 (*see also* p. 84).

Production and Industry.—While petroleum is the principal product and by far the greatest export, Iran, except for its desert areas, is essentially an agricultural country and three-quarters of the inhabitants depend for their living on the land. Wheat is the principal crop, using about half the area under cultivation. Other important crops are barley, rice, cotton, sugar beet, fruits and vegetables. Wool is also produced—sheep, as well as goats, being numerous. There are extensive forests in the north and west, the conservation of which is an urgent problem. Rapid progress has been made in the development of industry. Apart from oil, the principal industrial products are carpets, textiles (mainly cotton), sugar, cement and other construction materials, ginned cotton, vegetable oil and other food products, leather and shoes, metal manufactures, pharmaceuticals, automobiles, fertilizers, plastics, matches and cigarettes. A steel mill is under construction at Isfahan. There are now three petrochemical plants in operation, producing fertilizers, plastics, detergents, sulphur and liquid petroleum gas. Large-scale copper deposits have been found in the south-eastern part of the country.

The oilfields had produced over 200,000,000 metric tons of oil from their first output to Dec. 31, 1946. Production had risen to a total of 35,000,000 metric tons in 1950, the last full year before nationalization. Oil shipments ceased in 1951 and were not resumed until Oct. 30, 1954.

The former functions of A.I.O.C. (now renamed "British Petroleum Company") in Iran were taken over for an initial period of 25 years by a consortium of 8 oil companies (including A.I.O.C., one French, one Dutch and five U.S.), A.I.O.C. receiving from Iran £25,000,000 cash in the 10 years from Jan. 1, 1957, in compensation for its oil assets in Northern Iran and in settlement of losses since 1951; and from the other members of the consortium for their shares, about £214,000,000 payable over 20–25 years. The consortium is responsible for the production, refining and sale of Iranian oil through two operating companies, while "non-basic" operations are undertaken by the National Iranian Oil Company.

Oilfields outside the Consortium area are being developed by several oil companies formed jointly by N.I.O.C. with western oil companies, notably S.I.R.I.P., I.P.A.C., L.A.P.C.O. and I.M.I.N.C.O. Production from offshore oil wells in the Persian Gulf developed by these companies is increasing rapidly.

Recent oil production figures are (in long tons): 1966, 105,100,000; 1967, 129,300,000; 1968, 142,200,000; 1969, 168,100,000; 1970, 194,000,000.

Communications.—The principal roads are from the frontier of Iraq at Khosravi to Tehran; from Tehran *viâ* Saveh and Hamadan to Ahwaz and Khorramshahr; from Tehran *viâ* Qum, Isfahan and Shiraz to Bushire; from Tehran into Azerbaijan, through Tabriz to Julfa (on the Soviet frontier) with a branch road into Turkey; from Tehran to Meshed; three roads through the Elbruz mountains to the Caspian coast and the Soviet borders

east and west of the Caspian Sea; and from Isfahan, *viâ* Yezd and Kerman to Zahidan and thence to Meshed. Zahidan is connected by road with Quetta (Pakistan). Meshed is connected by road with Herat (Afghanistan). Some of these roads traverse extremely difficult mountainous country; others are desert tracks. Railways have been constructed since 1927. The *Trans-Iranian Railway,* from Bandar Shah, on the Caspian Sea, to Bandar Shahpur, on the Persian Gulf, was inaugurated in 1938; this line has a total length of 872 miles, the total cost, after eleven years' work, being approximately £30,000,000. The branch lines from Tehran to Meshed and to Tabriz have now been completed. There are also railroads from Tabriz to Julfa and from Zahidan to Mirjawa and thence to Quetta and branch lines from Ahwaz to Khorramshahr and Khorramshahr to Tanuma in Iraq (on the Shatt el Arab, opposite Basrah) were opened during the war. An extension from Qum to Yazd *viâ* Kashan is now in operation as is one from Bandar Shah to Gorgan. Extensions from Yazd to Kerman and from Tabriz to Van (Turkey) are being built. It is hoped to connect the Iranian rail system with the Turkish and with the Pakistan systems, thereby offering a through route from Europe to Asia.

Civil Aviation.—In May, 1946, a Department of Civil Aviation was created, subordinate to the Ministry of Roads. Progress has been made towards establishing first-class International Airports at Tehran and Abadan, with secondary airfields in accordance with ICAO standards. The *Iranian National Airlines Corporation* was formed from the former *Iranian Airways* and *Persian Air Services* in February, 1962. The Company is 51 per cent. Government-owned and operates internal and international routes. Air France, K.L.M., S.A.S., Iraqi, M.E.A., P.A.A., Lufthansa, B.O.A.C., Qantas, P.I.A., Aeroflot, Alitalia, Aryana Airways and El Al operate services to Tehran.

TRADE

	1968–69	1969–70
Imports.	*Rials* 106,723,875,715	*Rials* 115,567,000,000
Exports.	16,268,001,537	18,533,000,000

These figures are calculated at the commercial rate of exchange and exclude oil exports. Total exports, including oil exports for 1969–70, *Rials* 612,357,000,000.

Trade with U.K.

	1969	1970
Imports from U.K.	£70,844,000	£66,335,000
Exports to U.K.	73,768,000	76,054,000

Imports into Iran consist mainly of industrial and agricultural machinery, iron and steel (including manufactures), electrical machinery and goods, sugar, chemicals and pharmaceuticals, motor vehicles and certain textile fabrics and yarns. The principal exports, apart from oil, are cotton, carpets, dried fruits and nuts, hides and skins, mineral ores, wool, gums, caviare, cummin seed and animal casings. West Germany, the U.S.A. and the U.K. are Iran's three leading suppliers. West Germany, the U.S.S.R., the U.K. and the U.S.A. are the main customers for non-oil exports.

CAPITAL: Tehran, population (1970), 3,150,000. Other large towns are Isfahan (388,000), Meshed (340,000), Shiraz (206,000), Resht (119,000), Kerman (73,000), Hamadan (115,000), Yezd (74,000), Kermanshah (152,000), Ψ Abadan (273,000), Ahwaz (145,000).

FLAG.—Equal horizontal bands of green, white and red; with arms (lion and sun) in centre.

NATIONAL DAY.—October 26 (Anniversary of Birthday of the Shahanshah).

BRITISH EMBASSY
Avenue Ferdowsi, Tehran

Ambassador Extraordinary and Plenipotentiary, His Excellency the Hon. Peter Edward Ramsbotham, C.M.G. (1971).....£14,000/

Counsellors, D. F. Murray (*Political*); J. C. Cloake (*Commercial*).

Defence and Military Attaché, Col. F. J. T. Durie, M.B.E.

Naval Attaché, Capt. C. R. A. O'Brien, R.N.

Air Attaché, Gp. Capt. P. D. Thorne.

1st Secretaries, H. J. Arbuthnott (*Head of Chancery*); W. J. R. G. P. Dawson, O.B.E.; D. J. Makinson (*Information*); D. M. Edwards, D.S.C. (*Consul*); J. W. H. O'Regan, O.B.E. (*Development*); A. R. Wood; G. Lello (*Civil Aviation*); M. R. F. Noel-Clarke.

2nd Secretaries, E. D. O. Maltman (*Vice-Consul*); G. Fallon (*Administration*); S. Prince (*Commercial*); N. W. Browne.

BRITISH COUNCIL

Representative, R. A. Simcox, M.B.E., 58 Avenue Ferdowsi, Tehran. Centres and libraries at Isfahan, Meshed, Shiraz, Tabriz and Tehran.

IRAQ

REVOLUTIONARY COMMAND COUNCIL

Chairman, President of the Republic, and Supreme Commander of the Armed Forces, Field Marshal Ahmad Hasan al Bakr, *assumed* office July 17, 1968.

Members, General Hammad Shihab (*Minister of Defence*); General Sa'dun Ghaidan (*Minister of the Interior*); (*Minister of Foreign Affairs*) (vacant); Dr. Izzat Mustafa (*Minister of Health*); Sd Abdul Khaliq al Samarra'ie; Sd Izzat al Duri (*Minister of Agrarian Reform*); Sd Murtadha al Hadithi (*Minister of Economy*); Sd Taha [al Jazrawi (*Minister of Industry*).

[*The Vice-President* (Gen. Ammash) *and Foreign Minister* (Abdel Karim al-Shaikhli) *were dismissed on Sept. 28, 1971, by Presidential decree.*]

In addition to those members of the R.C.C. holding departmental portfolios listed above, there are 19 other ministers and one minister of state.

IRAQ EMBASSY
21–22 Queen's Gate, S.W.7
[01–584–7141]

Ambassador Extraordinary and Plenipotentiary, His Excellency Kadhim M. Khalaf (1968).

Area, etc.—Traversed by the Rivers Euphrates and Tigris, Iraq extends from Turkey on N. and N.E. to the Persian Gulf on the S. and S.E. and from Iran on E. to Syria and Arabian Desert on W., the approximate position being between $37\frac{1}{2}°$ to $48\frac{1}{2}°$ E. long., and from $37\frac{1}{2}°$ to $30°$ N. lat. (*see* MAP, p. 881). The area of Iraq is officially estimated at 168,000 sq. miles of which 37 per cent. is desert land. About 35 to 40 per cent of the remainder is potentially cultivable either by rainfall or by irrigation.

Population.—At the Census of 1965 Iraq had a total population of 8,261,527; estimated 1970, 9,465,800.

The *Euphrates* (which has a total length of 1,700 miles from its source to its outflow in the Persian Gulf) is formed by two arms, of which the Murad Su (415 miles) rises in the slopes of the Ala Dagh, a mountain of Eastern Erzerum, and flows westwards to a junction with the Kara Su, or Frat Su (275 miles); the other arm rises in the north-west of Erzerum in the Dumlu Dagh. The *Tigris* has a total length of 1,150 miles from its source to its junction with the Euphrates at Qurna, 70 miles from the Persian Gulf, and rises in two arms south of the Taurus mountains, in Kurdistan,

uniting at Til, where the boundaries of the districts of Diarbekir, Van and Bitlis conjoin.

Antiquities.—In 1944 excavations at Tell Hassuna, near Shura (on the Tigris in North Iraq) unearthed abundant traces of culture dating back to 5000 B.C. Excavations in 1948 at Tel Abu Shahrain, 14 miles south of " Ur of the Chaldees," confirm Eridu's claim to be the most ancient city of the Sumerian world. Hillah, the ancient city on the left bank of the Shatt el Hillah, a branch of the Euphrates, about 70 miles south of Baghdad, is near the site of Babylon and of the " house of the lofty-head " or " gate of the god " (Tower of Babel). Mosul *Liwa* covers a great part of the ancient kingdom of *Assyria*, the ruins of Nineveh, the Assyrian capital, being visible on the banks of the Tigris, opposite Mosul. Qurna, at the junction of the Tigris and Euphrates, is the traditional site of the *Garden of Eden.* The " *Tree of Knowledge*," which had stood there " from time immemorial," withered and died in December, 1946. It has been replaced by a shoot said to be from the original tree.

Government.—Under the Treaty of Lausanne (1923), Turkey renounced the sovereignty over Mesopotamia. A provisional Arab Government was set up in Nov., 1920, and in Aug., 1921, the Emir Faisal was elected King of Iraq. The country was a monarchy until July, 1958, when King Faisal II was assassinated. From 1958 Iraq has been under Presidential rule with a succession of republican Cabinets: President Kassem (Qasim),1958–63 (executed); President Abdul Salam Arif, 1963–66 (killed in an air accident); President Abdul Rahman Arif, 1966–68 (overthrown and exiled).

President Arif's régime ended in a bloodless military *coup d'état* on July 17, 1968, when Maj.-Gen. Ahmed Hassan al-Bakr was elected President by the Revolutionary Command Council.

Diplomatic relations with the United Kingdom which were broken off by Iraq after the war of June, 1967, were resumed in May, 1968.

Language.—The language is mainly Arabic (*see* Arabia) and English is widely used in commerce, science and the arts.

Education.—In 1968–69 Iraq had 130 infant schools, with 619 teachers and 15,697 pupils; 5,172 primary schools, with 48,290 teachers and 1,040,968 pupils; and 863 intermediate and preparatory secondary schools, with 10,116 teachers and 302,611 full-time students. There were 5 universities and 4 other public institutes of higher education, with 49 teachers and lecturers and 1,146 students. In 1968–69 there were 48 vocational schools (agriculture, commerce and industry, home economics).

Communications and Trade.—New roads are being rapidly built, and communications between Baghdad and the provincial capitals are being improved and secured. The port of Basrah is well equipped and able to handle expeditiously all seaborne traffic. Continuous dredging of the Shatt-al-Arab has provided a navigable channel of 22½ feet at low water (as compared with 9 feet before dredging was begun) giving easy access to the Port at all times. A new channel across the Fao Bar has been dredged. The desert route between Baghdad and the Mediterranean carries an increasing amount of traffic, particularly since the closing of the Suez Canal route.

Airports for the use of international air traffic have been provided at Baghdad and Basrah (Maqil). BOAC provides a weekly service between London and Baghdad, which is also served by Iraqi Airways and other European, Middle Eastern and Far Eastern Airlines. Iraqi Airways operates services from Baghdad to Basra and Mosul, and to other Middle Eastern countries, Europe, and India and Pakistan. Iraqi Republican Railways provide regular passenger and goods services on a standard gauge line between Basra, Baghdad and Mosul, which links up through Syria and Turkey with the Mediterranean and the Bosphorus. There is also a metre gauge line connecting Baghdad with Khannaqin, Kirkuk and Arbil.

Agriculture and Industry.—Iraq is capable of supporting a considerably greater population if irrigation is developed and extended. Apart from the valuable revenues to be derived from oil the wealth of the country depends upon agricultural development and two harvests can usually be gathered in the year. Production fluctuates from year to year according to rainfall, but in 1969 the following crops were produced in sufficient quantities to allow a margin for export: barley, millet, rice, wheat, dates, cotton and tobacco.

Few industries are yet established on any scale but an increasing industrialization is taking place under both private enterprise and Government action. Existing industries include cement, building materials, flour milling, cigarettes, soap, beer, steel fabrications, furniture, tanning, textiles, footwear and vegetable oils. In 1968 there were 1,432 industrial establishments employing an average number of 90,027 persons annually. Turnover of these establishments was *ID*166,863,000. Iraq's major industry is oil production, and this accounts for approximately four-fifths of the country's foreign exchange receipts, two-thirds of total government revenue and one-fifth of the Gross National Product. Production figures in long tons are:

| 1967 | 58,939,000 | 1969 | 73,309,000 |
| 1968 | 72,137,000 | 1970 | 75,241,000 |

Total revenues from exports of crude oil in 1969 were *ID*346 millions. Half the government revenue from oil is allocated by law to development projects under the 5-year Development Plan although actual expenditure under the Development Budget has, in the past, fallen to below 50 per cent. of the sum budgeted. International and internal oil agreements between the government and the oil producing companies in 1971 are expected substantially to increase the government's revenues from oil.

FINANCE

	1970–71*	1971–72*
Total revenue....	*ID*257,474,430	*ID*332,755,560
Total expenditure....	257,474,430	332,755,560

* Budget estimates.

The Iraqi *Dinar* of 1,000 *Fils*= £1 sterling. Exchange rate (June, 1971), 857 *Fils*= £1 (*see also* p. 85).

TRADE
(Excluding oil)

	1969	1970
Total imports....	*ID*157,169,147	*ID*181,651,464
Total exports.....	22,001,947	22,565,565

Trade with U.K.

	1969	1970
Imports from U.K.....	£21,332,000	£23,774,000
Exports to U.K.......	31,129,000	18,729,000

The principal imports are iron and steel, mechanical and electrical machinery, motor cars, cotton and rayon piecegoods, sugar and tea; and the chief exports are crude petroleum, dates, cement, raw wool, raw hides and skins and raw cotton.

CAPITAL.—Baghdad. Population of the governorate (estimated 1970), 2,696,000. Other towns of importance are Ψ Basrah and Mosul.

FLAG.—Horizontal stripes of red, white and black, with three green stars on the white stripe.

BRITISH EMBASSY
Sharia Salah Ud-Din,
Karkh, Baghdad

Ambassador Extraordinary and Plenipotentiary, His Excellency Hugh Glencairn Balfour-Paul, C.M.G. (1969)............................£6,925
Counsellor, J. W. Hutson, O.B.E. (*Commercial*).
Defence and Military Attaché, Col. L. A. D. Harrod, O.B.E.
Air Attaché (vacant).
1st Secretaries, A. C. D. S. MacRae, J. R. Clube (*Economic*); D. M. Mitchell (*Consul*); J. D. Perris; R. K. Hamilton (*Commercial*).
Asst. Military Attaché, Maj. J. S. Hay.
2nd Secretaries, D. I. Lewty; D. Cartwright (*Commercial*).
Attachés, D. A. Wright (*Commercial*); W. I. Rae (*Vice-Consul*); R. C. Mansfield.
In 1971 there were no British Consular Offices outside Baghdad.

British Council Representative, J. F. C. Springford, O.B.E, 7/2/9 Waziriya, Baghdad.

ISRAEL
(Yisrael)

President of the Republic, Zalman Shazar, *born* 1889, *elected President of Israel*, May 22, 1963.

CABINET

Prime Minister, Mrs. Golda Meir.
Deputy Prime Minister and Minister of Education and Culture, Yigal Allon.

Foreign Affairs, Abba Eban.
Agriculture and Development, Haim Gvati,
Labour, Joseph Almogi.
Defence, Moshe Dayan.
Justice, Yaakov Shapiro.
Police, Shlomo Hillel.
Interior, Yosef Burg (*N.R.P.*).
Health, Victor Shemtov (*Mapam*).
Finance, Commerce and Industry, Pinhas Sapir.
Transport and Communications, Shimon Peres.
Housing, Ze'ev Sharef.
Social Welfare, Michael Hazani (*N.R.P.*).
Religious Affairs, Dr. Zerah Warhftig (*N.R.P.*).
Immigration Absorption, Natan Peled (*Mapam*).
Tourism, Moshe Kol (*I.L.P.*).
Without Portfolio, Israel Galilee.

Apart from Ministers marked otherwise, members of the Cabinet belong to the Israel Labour Party, a merger (Jan. 21, 1968) of the former *Mapai Ahdut Avodah* and *Rafi* parties. *N.R.P.* = National Religious Party; *Mapam* = Unified Workers Party; *I.L.P.* = Independent Liberal Party.

EMBASSY IN LONDON
2 Palace Green, Kensington, W.8
[01-937-8091]

Ambassador Extraordinary and Plenipotentiary, His Excellency Michael Comay (1970).
Consular Section, 2A Palace Green, W.8.
Consul-General, Matityan Dagan.

Area and Population.—Israel lies on the western edge of the continent of Asia at the eastern extremity

of the Mediterranean Sea, between lat. 29° 30'–33° 15' N. and long. 34° 15'–35° 40' E. Its political neighbours are Lebanon on the North, Syria on the North and East, Jordan on the East and the Egyptian province of Sinai on the South.

The area is estimated at 7,992 square miles out of the 10,429 square miles comprised in the whole of Palestine (the remainder being occupied by Israel since the Six Day War in June, 1967, together with the Sinai Peninsula and the Golan Heights in Syria). The population was estimated in 1970 at 2,919,000. Jewish immigration has made rapid progress since the establishment of the State. In 1912 there were only 83,790 Jews in Palestine out of a total population of 752,048. During the upheavals of 1948–49 some 600,000 Arabs left the country as refugees and settled in neighbouring countries. Since 1948 the population of Israel has more than trebled.

Hebrew is the official language of Israel. Arabic is also used extensively in Government publications and on currency and stamps. Arabs are entitled to transact all official business with Government Departments in Arabic, and provision is made in the *Knesset* for the simultaneous translation of all speeches into Arabic.

Physical Features.—Israel comprises four main regions: (*a*) the hill country of Galilee and Judæa and Samaria, rising in places to heights of nearly 4,000 feet; (*b*) the coastal plain from the Gaza strip to North of Acre, including the plain of Esdraelon running from Haifa Bay to the south-east, and cutting in two the hill region; (*c*) the Negev, a semi-desert triangular-shaped region, extending from a base south of Beersheeba, to an apex at the head of the Gulf of 'Aqaba; and (*d*) parts of the Jordan valley, including the Hula Region, Tiberias and the south-western extremity of the Dead Sea. The principal river is the Jordan, which rises from three main sources in Israel, the Lebanon and Syria, and flows through the Hula valley and the canals which have replaced Lake Hula, drained in 1958. Between Hulata and Tiberias (Sea of Galilee) the river falls 926 ft. in 11 miles and becomes a turbulent stream. Lake Tiberias is 696 ft. below sea-level and liable to sudden storms. Between it and the Dead Sea the Jordan falls 591 ft. The other principal rivers are the Yarkon and Qishon. The largest lake is the *Dead Sea* (shared between Israel and Jordan); area 393 sq. miles, 1,286 feet below sea-level, 51·5 miles long, with a maximum width of 11 miles and a maximum depth of 1,309 ft.; it receives the waters of the Jordan and of six other streams, and has no outlet, the surplus being carried off by evaporation. The water contains an extraordinarily high concentration of mineral substances. The highest mountain peak is Mount Meron, 3,962 feet above sea-level, near Safad, Upper Galilee.

Climate.—The climate is variable, similar to that of Lower Egypt, but modified by altitude and distance from the sea. The summer is hot but tempered in most parts by daily winds from the Mediterranean. The winter is the rainy season lasting from November to April, the period of maximum rainfall being January and February.

Antiquities.—The following are among the principal historic sites in Israel: Jerusalem: the Church of the Dormition and the Cœnaculum on Mount Zion; Ein Karem: Church of the Visitation, Church of St. John the Baptist. Galilee: The Sea; Mount and Mount of the Beatitudes, ruins of Capernaum and other sites connected with the life of Christ. Mount Tabor: Church of the Transfiguration. Nazareth: Church of the Annunciation and other Christian shrines associated with the childhood of Christ. There are also numerous sites dating from biblical and mediæval days, such as Ascalon, Cæsarea, Atlit, Massada, Megiddo and Hazor. Other antiquities in the West Bank of Jordan, Sinai or the Golan Heights at present occupied by Israel can now be visited from Israel.

Government.—There are a Cabinet and a single-chamber Parliament (*Knesset Israel*) of 120 members. A general election is held at least once every four years. The last took place on Oct. 29, 1969.

A "Government of National Unity" was formed on December 11, 1969, headed by Mrs. Golda Meir. It was a broad coalition and with one exception, embraced the same parties as were in the two previous governments formed in June, 1967, and March, 1969, by the late Mr. Levi Eshkol and Mrs. Meir respectively. In August, 1970, the *Gahal* bloc left the Government because they were opposed to a resumption of the Jarring negotiations. The present coalition government commands 76 seats in the Knesset, as follows:—*Alignment*, 56; *Arab & Druse Lists* (affiliated to Labour Party), 4; *National Religious*, 12; *Independent Liberals*, 4. The Opposition commands 44 seats in the Knesset as follows:— *Gahal*, 26; *State List*, 4; *Agudat Israel*, 4; *Poalei Agudat Israel*, 2; *New Communists*, 3; *Israel Communists*, 1; *Free Centre*, 2; *Ha'olam Ha'ze*, 2.

Immigration.—The Declaration of Independence of May 14, 1948, laid down that "the State of Israel will be open to the immigration of Jews from all countries of their dispersion." The Law of Return, passed by the *Knesset* on July 5, 1950, provides that an immigrant visa shall be granted to every Jew who expresses his desire to settle in Israel. From the establishment of the State until 1970, 1,400,000 immigrants had entered Israel from over 100 different countries.

Education.—Elementary education for all children from 5 to 15 years is compulsory. The Law also provides for working youth, age 15–18 who, for some reason, have not completed their primary education, to be exempted from work in order to do so.

In 1969–70 enrolment in all educational establishments was 811,300, including 96,600 non-Jews; kindergartens, 118,000; primary schools, 468,700; post-primary, 134,500; teachers' training colleges, 5,500; institutions of higher learning, 37,000; and elsewhere, at all stages, 47,660. This means 5,878 establishments, 36,088 classes, and 30,010 women and 16,855 men teachers.

Finance.—Government expenditure for the fiscal year 1969–70 totalled I£8,788,000,000, with revenue at I£8,824,000,000.

The unit of account is the Israel pound of 100 *agorot*. Exchange rate, *see* p. 84.

COMMUNICATIONS

Railways and Roads.—Israel State Railways started operating in August, 1949. Towns now served are Haifa, Tel Aviv, Jerusalem, Lod, Nahariya, Beersheba, Dimona, Ashdod and intermediate stations. In March, 1970, the total railway network amounted to 793 km. There were approximately 9,086 km. of paved road and 262,700 licensed vehicles.

Shipping.—Israel's merchant marine had reached a total of 1,948,534 tons deadweight by December, 1969.

The chief ports are Haifa, a modern harbour, with a depth of 30 ft. alongside the main quay; the new harbour on the Red Sea at Eilat, inaugurated in September, 1965, has a capacity of 10,000 tons a day; Acre has an anchorage for small vessels; the deep-water port at Ashdod, 20 miles south of Tel Aviv, which started operations at the end of 1965, was designed to handle 1,000,000 tons of cargo in the first year, 2·5 m. annually until 1970, and 4 m. tons

later, after deepening. In 1907–71 Israel's three main ports handled 7,682,000 tons of cargo (excluding petroleum.

Civil Aviation.—In the year to March, 1971, El Al carried 497,000 passengers. El Al operates Boeing jets exclusively and is buying two Boeing 747's. Arkia, the internal airline has had a steep increase in traffic since the Six Day War and in 1970 carried about 250,000 passengers. Arkia uses five Heralds and two Viscounts.

PRODUCTION AND INDUSTRY

Agriculture.—The country is generally fertile and climatic conditions vary so widely that a large variety of crops can be grown, ranging from temperate crops, such as wheat and cherries, to subtropical crops such as sorghum, millet and mangoes. The famous " Jaffa " orange is produced in large quantities mostly in the coastal plain for export; other kinds of citrus fruits are also grown and exported. The citrus yield during the 1069–70 season was 1,221,600 tons. Of this total, 815,000 tons were exported, of which 244,162 tons went to the U.K. Olives are cultivated, mainly for the production of oil used for edible purposes and for the manufacture of soap. The main winter crops are wheat and barley and various kinds of pulses, while in summer sorghum, millet, maize, sesame and summer pulses are grown. Large areas of seasonal vegetables are planted; potatoes can be grown in autumn and in the winter. Since the establishment of the State of Israel, beef, cattle and poultry farming have been developed and the production of mixed vegetables and dairy produce has greatly increased. Tobacco and medium staple cotton are now grown. Fishing has also been extended, and production (mostly from fish ponds) reached 23,000 tons in 1970. All kinds of summer fruits such as figs, grapes, plums and apples are produced in increasing quantities for local consumption. Water supply for irrigation is the principal limiting factor to greater production. The area under cultivation during 1969–70 was 4,231,000 dunams, of which 1,711,000 were under irrigation. The largest of these is the Kinneret-Negev Project. Much of the dairy industry is dependent on the production of fodder crops under irrigation; areas under fodder crops have doubled. The Israel land measure is the *dunam*, equivalent to 1,000 square metres (approximately a quarter of an acre).

Industry.—Among the more important industries are citrus and by-products, manufactured food products, pharmaceuticals, textiles and wearing apparel, artificial teeth, polished diamonds, plywood, cement, plastics, light engineering and the assembly of motor cars and trucks.

TRADE

	1969	1970
Imports...	$U.S.1,318,000,000	$U.S.1,438,000,000
Exports.....	723,000,000	780,555,000

Trade with U.K.

	1969	1970
Imports from U.K.	£101,086,000	£96,157,000
Exports to U.K.....	39,304,000	45,079,000

The principal imports are foodstuffs, crude oil, machinery and vehicles, iron, steel and manufactures thereof, and chemicals. The principal exports are citrus fruits and by-products, polished diamonds, plywood, cement, tyres, minerals, finished and semi-finished textiles.

CAPITAL.—Most of the Government departments are in Jerusalem (population, estimated 1969, 283,100). A resolution proclaiming Jerusalem as the capital of Israel was adopted by the Israel parliament on Jan. 23, 1950. It is not, however, recognized as the capital by the United Nations.

Other principal towns are ΨTel Aviv-Jaffa (382,900); ΨHaifa and district (214,500); Ramat Gan (112,600) and Beersheba (74,500).

FLAG.—White, with two horizontal blue stripes, the Shield of David in the centre. NATIONAL DAY (1971).—April 30.

JERUSALEM

Until 1967 Jerusalem was divided between Israel and Jordan, two of the 36 recognized Christian Holy Places (in the New City) being under Jewish administration, the remainder under Arab administration in the Old City. At the conclusion of hostilities between Israel and the surrounding Arab countries in 1967 the entire city was under Israeli control.

BRITISH EMBASSY

192 Hayarkon Street, Tel Aviv.

Ambassador Extraordinary and Plenipotentiary, His Excellency Ernest John Ward Barnes (1969)
£6,925

Counsellor, P. M. Foster (*Head of Chancery and Consul-General*).

Defence and Air Attaché, Group-Capt. A. D. Boyle.

British Council Representative, R. Twite, 140 Hayarkon Street, Tel Aviv. There are an office and library in *Tel Aviv*; libraries at *Haifa* and *Jerusalem*.

ITALY
(Repubblica Italiana)

PRESIDENT OF THE ITALIAN REPUBLIC, Giuseppe Saragat, G.C.B., *born* at Turin in 1898. *Elected* Dec. 28, 1964.

COUNCIL OF MINISTERS

Prime Minister and (interim) Minister of Justice, Emilio Colombo (*CD*).

Deputy Prime Minister, Francesco de Martino (*PSI*).

Minister for Foreign Affairs, Aldo Moro (*CD*).

Interior, Franco Restivo (*CD*).

Budget and Economic Planning, Antonio Giolitti (*PSI*).

Finance, Luigi Preti (*PSDI*).

Treasury, Mario Ferrari Aggradi (*CD*).

Defence, Mario Tanassi (*PSDI*).

Education, Riccardo Misasi (*CD*).

Public Works, Salvatore Lauricella (*PSI*).

Agriculture, Lorenzo Natali (*CD*).

Transport and Civil Aviation, Senator Italo Viglianesi (*PSI*).

Posts and Telecommunications, Senator Giacinto Bosco (*CD*).

Industry, Commerce and Arts and Crafts, Senator Silvio Gava (*CD*).

Labour and Social Security, Carlo Donat-Cattin (*CD*).

Foreign Trade, Mario Zagari (*PSI*).

Merchant Marine (vacant).

State Participation, Flaminio Piccoli (*CD*).

Health, Senator Luigi Mariotti (*PSI*).

Tourism and Entertainment, Matteo Matteotti (*PSU*).

Ministers without Portfolio:—

Relations with Parliament, Carlo Russo (*CD*).

Regional Problems, Eugenio Gatto (*CD*).

Scientific and Technological Research, Sen. Camillo Ripamonti (*CD*).

Special politital assignments, Giuseppe Lupis (*PSU*).

Administrative Reform, Remo Gaspari (*CD*).

CD=Christian Democrat; *PSI*=Socialist; *PSU* =Socialist; *PRI*=Republican.

ITALIAN EMBASSY IN LONDON

14 Three Kings Yard, Davies Street, W.1

[01–629–8200]

Ambassador Extraordinary and Plenipotentiary, His Excellency Signor Raimondo Manzini, G.C.V.O. (1968).

Minister, Signor Pasquale Ricciulli, K.C.V.O., C.M.G.

Minister-Counsellor, Signor Ernesto Toti Lombardozzi (*Commercial*).

First Counsellors, Signori Ugo Barzini; Vittorio Farinelli.

Counsellors, Francesco Pulcini (*Labour*); Paolo Galli; Sergio Berlinguer, M.V.O. (*Press*).

1st Secretaries, Italo di Muccio (*Commercial*); Umberto Vattani (*Commercial*).

2nd Secretaries, Signori Gianfranco F. Bonetti; Roberto di Leo, M.B.E.

Defence and Naval Attaché, Capt. Corrado Vittori.

Asst. Naval Attaché, Lt.-Cdr. Gian Paolo Berengan.

Military Attaché, Col. Mario Bucalossi, M.V.O.

Asst. Military Attaché, Lt.-Col. Aldo Papadia.

Air Attaché, Col. Stelio Nardini.

Asst. Air Attaché, Capt. Filippo Castania.

Financial Attaché, Signor Giovanni Magnifico.

Cultural Attaché, Prof. Filippo Donini, M.V.O.

Administrative Attaché, Signor Amedeo Baroni, M.V.O.

Italian Consulate General, 38 Eaton Place, S.W.1. (01–235–4831).

Consul General, Signor Giovanni Battista Crosetti, M.V.O.

Consul, Signor Mario Fuggazzola.

Italy is a Republic in the South of Europe, consisting of a peninsula, the large islands of Sicily and Sardinia, the island of Elba and about 70 islands (with certain dependencies noted below). Italy is bounded on the N. by Switzerland and Austria, on the S. by the Mediterranean, on the E. by the Adriatic and Yugoslavia, etc., and on the W. by France and the Ligurian and Tyrrhenian Seas. The total area is about 324,000 sq. kilometres (131,000 sq. miles).

The peninsula is for the most part mountainous, but between the Apennines, which form its spine, and the East coastline are two large fertile plains; of Emilia/Romagna in the north and of Apulia in the south. The Alps form the northern limit of Italy, dividing it from France, Switzerland, Austria and Yugoslavia. *Mont Blanc* (15,782 feet), the highest peak, is in the French Pennine Alps, but partly within the Italian borders are Monte Rosa (15,217 feet), Matterhorn (14,780 feet) and several peaks from 12,000 to 14,000 feet.

The chief rivers are the Po (405 miles), which flows through Piedmont, Lombardy and the Veneto and the Adige (Trentino and Veneto) in the north, the Arno (Florentine Plain) and the Tiber (flowing through Rome to Ostia). The *Rubicon*, a small stream flowing into the Adriatic near Rimini (and now usually identified with the Fiumicino) formed the boundary between Italy and Cisalpine Gaul: " crossing the Rubicon " (as Cæsar did in

49 B.C., thus "invading" Italy in arms) is used to indicate definite committal to some course of action.

Population.—Italy has a resident population estimated at 54,683,136 in October, 1970, about 417 persons per sq. mile. Live births in 1970 totalled 917,496 deaths, 528,622 and marriages 395,321 (estimated).

Government.—Italian unity was accomplished under the House of Savoy, after an heroic struggle from 1848 to 1870, in which the great patriots Mazzini (1805-72), Garibaldi (1807-82) and Cavour (1810-61) were the principal figures. It was completed when Lombardy was ceded by Austria in 1859 and Venice in 1866, and through the evacuation of Rome by the French in 1870. In 1871 the King of Italy entered Rome, and that city was declared to be the capital.

Benito Mussolini, known as *Il Duce* (The Leader), was born July 29, 1883, and was continuously in office as Prime Minister from June 30, 1925, until July 25, 1943, when the Fascist *régime* was abolished. He was captured by Italian partisans while attempting to escape across the Swiss frontier and was put to death on April 28, 1945.

In fulfilment of a promise given in April, 1944, that he would retire when the Allies entered Rome a decree was signed on June 5, 1944, by the late King Victor Emmanuel III under which Prince Umberto, the King's son, became "Lieutenant-General of the Realm." The King remained head of the House of Savoy and retained the title of King of Italy until his abdication on May 9, 1946, when he was succeeded by the Crown Prince.

A general election was held on June 2, 1946, together with a referendum on the question of Republic or Monarchy. The Referendum resulted in 12,717,923 votes for a Republic and 10,719,284 for a Monarchy. The Royal Family left the country on June 13, and on June 28, 1946, a Provisional President was elected.

Constitution.—On Dec. 22, 1947, the Constituent Assembly approved the Constitution, Article I of which states "Italy is a Democratic Republic founded on work. Sovereignty belongs to the people who exercise it in the forms and within the limits of the Constitution."

Since the General Election of 1948, governments have been formed by Signor de Gasperi (1948-53, coalition); Signor Pella (1953-54, *Christian Democrat*); Signor Scelba (1954-55, coalition); Signor Segni (July, 1955-May, 1957, coalition); Signor Zoli (June, 1957-May, 1958, *Christian Democrat*); Signor Fanfani (May, 1958-Feb., 1959, coalition); S. Segni (Feb., 1959-Feb., 1960, *Christian Democrat*, with *Liberal* support). Signor Tambroni (March 25-July 1960, *Christian Democrat*, with Neo-Fascist support); Signor Fanfani (July 27, 1960-Feb., 1962, *Christian Democrat*); Signor Fanfani (Feb. 1962-June, 1963, coalition); Signor Leone (June-Nov., 1963, *Christian Democrat*); Signor Moro (coalitions formed, Nov., 1963; July, 1964; Feb., 1966); Sen. Leone (May, 1968-December, 1968, *Christian Democrat*); Sig. Rumor (December, 1968-June, 1969, Centre Left coalition); Sig. Rumor (second Government) (August, 1969) (*Christian Democrat*); Sig. Rumor (third Government, centre left coalition); Sig. Colombo (Aug. 6, 1970, coalition).

Signor Moro took office in November, 1963, at the head of a coalition consisting of the four parties of the centre-left, *i.e.*, the Christian Democrats, the Republicans, the Socialist and Social Democrat Parties (united in October, 1966, to form the United Socialist Party). This coalition remained in being until the General Election of May 19, 1968, at which the Communists and their left-wing allies gained votes at the expense of the United Socialists. Since then there have been a caretaker Christian Democrat Government, a centre left coalition under Sig. Rumor which fell in July, 1969, when the Socialist Party split once more, a one party Christian Democrat Government, again under Sig. Rumor, and, after a long political crisis, a further centre left coalition under Sig. Rumor which took office in March, 1970. Sig. Rumor's third government fell in July, 1970, and was replaced by the present coalition formed by Sig. Emilio Colombo on Aug. 6, 1970 (*see above*).

The shares of the total vote and the number of seats in the Chamber of Deputies won by each party in the May, 1968 elections were as follows:—

	Percentage of Votes	Seats
PCI (*Communist*)	26·9	177
PSIUP (*Proletarian Unity*)	4·5	23
PSI } *PSU (Socialist)* PSDI	14·5	91
PRI (*Republican*)	2·0	9
DC (*Christian Democrat*)	39·1	266
PLI (*Liberal*)	5·8	31
MSI (*ex-Fascist*)	4·5	24
Monarchist	1·3	6
Other	—	3
Total	100	630

On June 7, 1970, elections were held for the first time to elect regional councils in the 15 so-called "Ordinary Statute" regions, as opposed to the "Special Statute" regions of Sicily, Sardinia Valle d'Aosta, Trentino Alto Adige and Friuli Venezia-Guilia, where such councils already existed. The voting in these elections was as follows: P.C.I. (Communist), 27·9 per cent., P.S.I.U.P. (Proletarian Unity), 3·2; P.S.I. (Socialist)★, 10·4; P.S.U. (*now* P.S.D.I.) (Social Democrat)★, 7·0; P.R.I. (Republican) 2·9; D.C. (Christian Democrat), 37·9; P.L.I. (Liberal), 4·7; M.S.I. (ex-Fascist), 5·2; Monarchist, 0·7 per cent.

Defence.—The period of conscription is 15 months for the Army and Air Force and 24 months for the Navy. The *Army* consists of 254,000 men including 21,000 officers. It has two armoured divisions, five infantry divisions, five Alpine brigades, one independent armoured brigade, one missile brigade and one parachute brigade. There is also a para-military force, the Carabinieri, about 80,000 strong. The *Navy* consists of 4 carriers, 45 escorts including a G.W. destroyers, 9 submarines, 60 minesweepers and also coastal craft and fleet auxiliaries. Approximate strength; officers, 4,700; men, 36,000. The *Air Force* consists of 500 aircraft; approximate strength: officers, 7,500 men, 62,500, with some 1,500 under training.

REGIONS OF ITALY

Rome and Central Italy.—Rome was founded, according to legend, by Romulus in the year now known as 753 B.C. It was the focal point of Latin civilization and dominion under the Republic and afterwards under the Roman Empire and became the capital of Italy when the Kingdom was established in 1871. With a metropolitan population of 2,778,872, Rome has been recreating herself as a major capital in the 100 years since Italy's reunification. The capital is concerned mainly with tourism and government, but due partly to the fact that the power of the Central Government is increasingly felt by industry, and that the headquarters of the giant State and parastatal companies are located there, Rome's importance as a business centre, although far from rivalling that of Milan, is steadily increasing.

★ Stood together as a single party in the May, 1968, Parliamentary elections.

Lombardy and Milan.—In the small area around Milan, which has a metropolitan population of 1,713,539, are to be found some 22 per cent. of Italy's commercial and banking services and some 30 per cent, of her industry. Here too, a market for consumer goods greatly exceeds that of any other comparable area in Italy. Lombardy's population of some 8·3 million is growing fast, both naturally and by immigration, and enjoys a *per capita* income some 40 per cent. above the national average. The whole range of Italian industry is there. Most important are the steel, machine tool and motor car factories.

Turin and Piedmont.—Turin between 1861 and 1865 was Italy's first capital as the home of the Piedmontese Royal Family. Now with a metropolitan population of 1,190,688 it is famous as the headquarters of Europe's largest manufacturer of motor cars, produces 75 per cent of Italy's motor vehicles and over 80 per cent. of its roller bearings. Turin is also Italy's second largest steel producing city Piedmont is the centre of the Italian textile industry, based mainly on Biella.

Genoa and the Liguruan Riviera.—Genoa, with a metropolitan population of 842,114, is Europe's fourth largest port and handles one-third of Italy's foreign trade. About 80 per cent. of the goods handled are imports. Anglo-Genoese trade goes back to the 13th century and 20 per cent. of Genoa's imports still come from Britain. Genoa is Italy's third most important industrial city.

Venice and the North-East.—Venice, with a metropolitan population of 367,528 is primarily a tourist attraction of unique beauty. It was founded in the middle of the 5th century by refugees from the mainland fleeing from Barbarian attacks. At the beginning of the 16th century it was one of the strongest and richest states of Europe, dominating Eastern Mediterranean trade. It lost its independence in 1797 when Napoleon handed it over to Austria. Industry is now developing in the Venice area, particularly on the autostrada linking Venice with her historical and now developing rivals Verona, Vicenza, Padua and in the areas around Pordenone. Padua is known for mechanical equipment. Verona for paper and stationery, Treviso for consumer goods, and Valdagno for its woollen industry. An important electrical appliance industry is based near Treviso and at Pordenone. Near Trieste which has a population of 277,133, is the modern Monfalcone shipyard. Present-day Trieste itself consists of Zone A, the area which was administered by the Allied Military Government from June 12, 1945, to October 26, 1954, when it was handed over to the Italian authorities. The remainder of the area of Trieste was administered by Yugoslavia after the War and handed over to that country in 1954 after the free territory of Trieste, an arrangement agreed in the Italian Peace Treaty of 1947, had proved to be unworkable.

Tuscany, Emilia and Romagna.—In 1940–45 this area was the agricultural centre of Italy and there was little industry. Now there are large industrial centres at Bologna (metropolitan population, 493,070), Florence (metropolitan population, 460,944), Modena, Pistoia and Ravenna. Most of the new firms are small or medium-sized. In Prato there are about 1,000 textile firms. The footwear industry is based on Florence, reproduction furniture at Cascina and Poggibonsi, ceramics at Sassuolo, and glass and pottery at Empoli and Montelupo. Bologna is an important centre for the food industry. Florence, the capital of Tuscany was one of the greatest and most creative cities in Europe from the 11th to the 16th centuries. Under the Medici family in the 15th century flourished many of the greatest names in Italian art, including Filippo Lippi, Botticelli, Donatello and Brunelleschi. In the 16th century the tide turned to Rome where great Florentine artists like Michelangelo and Leonarda da Vinci flourished.

Naples and the Toe of Italy.—Naples (metropolitan population 1,278,051), formerly the capital and administrative centre of the Kingdom of Naples and Sicily, remains the dominant city in the area, but it is beset with great problems of unemployment and the need for modernization. Around it, however, helped by Government incentives, industry is slowly developing, northwards to Caserta, southwards to Salerno and eastwards to Benevento. The most important industrial decision was taken in 1967, when the Government announced that a large new car factory would be built on the outskirts of Naples.

Puglia.—Bari (metropolitan population, 356,250) has always been a commercial centre. Fairly rapid industrial development is now taking place in the areas of Taranto, Bari, Brindisi and Foggia. At Taranto there are a highly-mechanized steel-works and a modern oil refinery. The Bari industrial zone has factories producing electronic and pneumatic valves, specialized vehicle bodies and tyres, etc. The main industry of Brindisi is a petro-chemical plant. At Foggia there is a textile factory.

Sicily.—Sicily is an autonomous region with a considerable measure of self-government. The main source of income is agriculture, particularly citrus fruits, almonds and tomatoes, but this faces severe competition. Oil and oil products have recently supplanted citrus fruits as Sicily's main exports. The island is the scene of intense activity in the fields of oil, natural gas and petro-chemicals. Small and medium-sized industries, benefiting from the Government incentives, are developing. Of the island's 279 factories, some 90 are in the Catania area and 60 around Palermo (metropolitan population, 663,694), the capital of the island. Tourism is bringing an increasing amount of revenue to Sicily.

Sardinia.—Sardinia is another autonomous region, with its capital at Cagliari (metropolitan population, 225,812). Six main industrial development areas have been officially designated; they are at Cagliari, Porto Vesme, Oristano, Sassari, Olbia and Arbatax. Lead and zinc mining are important. At Porto Vesme, a large smelting plant is being constructed. In tha same area, a company plans to invest some £60 million in an aluminium plant. There is a flourishing tourist industry.

THE ECONOMY

Italian total net national income in 1970 was the equivalent of £38,829 million, an increase of 11·6 per cent. over 1969. The economy has been developing very fast since the 1950's with an average real annual increase in the gross national output of about 7 per cent. But its recovery after a setback caused by labour unrest in the last quarter of 1969, has been slower than was expected.

Currency.—The market rate of exchange on July 26, 1971, stood at lire 1,507 = £1.

Industry.—The general index of industrial production (1966 = 100) stood at 127·4 in 1970 (an increase of 6·6 per cent. over 1969). Some of the faster growing sectors of industry are precision instruments (up 21·1 per cent., 1969–70) electrical machinery and apparatus (up 18·7 per cent.), mechanical industry in general (up 11·9 per cent.), petroleum and coal products (up 11·7 per cent.), rubber manufacturing industry (up 9 per cent.), furniture (up 8·7 per cent.) and clothing (up 8·4 per cent.).

The State-owned sector of Italian industry is important, dominated by the holding companies IRI (mechanical, steel, airlines), ENI (petro-chemicals) and ENEL (electricity).

Mineral Production.—Italy is generally poor in mineral resources but since the war deposits of natural methane gas and smaller deposits of oil have been discovered and rapidly exploited. Production of lignite has also increased. Sulphur production, in Sicily and Calabria, is important although declining in volume. Other minerals produced in significant quantities include iron ores and pyrites, mercury (over one-quarter of the world production), lead, zinc and aluminium. Marble is a traditional product of the Massa Carrara district. Salt and tobacco are Government monopolies.

Agriculture.—Agriculture accounted for 10·9 per cent. of gross domestic product in 1968, and at the beginning of 1971 employed about 18·2 per cent. of the working population. Some three-quarters of the 3,785,000 farms and small holdings are privately owned and operated. Considerable structural improvement is required to increase the efficiency of Italian agriculture; the Piano Verde law of 1966 set aside £140,000,000 a year for this purpose, particularly by means of 2 per cent. loans for investment in new plant and machinery. In the period 1964–70 Italy was a net exporter of rice, vegetables, fresh and dried fruit and wine, but a net importer of nearly all other agricultural products.

Tourist Traffic.—About 32,000,000 visitors entered Italy in 1970, compared with about 30,000,000 in 1969.

Communications.—The main railway system is State-run by the *Ferrovia dello Stato.* A network of motorways (*autostrade*) covers the country, built and operated mainly by the IRI State-holding company and ANAS the State highway authority. The autostrada network covered 3,967 km. in May, 1970, with a further 1,263 km. under construction and another 1,430 km. to be built in the near future. *Alitalia,* the principal international and domestic airline, is also State-Controlled by the IRI group. Other smaller companies, including ATI (an *Alitalia* subsidiary) and *Itavia* operate on domestic routes. The Italian mercantile marine total of 7,332,000 tons in August, 1970, compared with 3,500,000 tons before the War.

FOREIGN TRADE

Total Italian imports in 1970 were 9·337 milliard *Lire* and exports were 8·256 milliard *Lire.* The main markets for Italian exports were West Germany, France and the United States, and the main commodities exported were machinery, textiles and clothing, motor vehicles, chemicals and fruit and vegetables. The main commodities imported were petroleum products, machinery, chemicals, iron and steel, meat, cereals, copper, wool and cotton. The main sources of imports in 1970 were West Germany (19·8 per cent.), U.S.A. (10·3 per cent.), France (13·2 per cent.), U.K. (3·8 per cent.). The tendency in recent years has been for Italy's EEC partners to provide a larger share of Italy's imports. Between 1953 and 1970 the EEC's share increased from 22·1 per cent. to 41·1 per cent. while the United Kingdom's share, for example, has decreased from 6·1 per cent. in 1963 to 3·8 per cent. in 1970.

Trade with U.K.

	1969	1970
Imports from U.K.	£190,994,000	£239,663,000
Exports to U.K.	222,920,000	249,176,000

Language and Literature.—Italian is a Romance language derived from Latin. It is spoken in its purest form at Siena (Tuscany), but there are numerous dialects, showing variously French, German, Spanish and Arabic influences. Sard, the dialect of Sardinia, is accorded by some authorities the status of a distinct Romance language. Italian literature (in addition to Latin literature, which is

the common inheritance of the civilized world) is one of the richest in Europe, particularly in its golden age (Dante, 1265–1321; Petrarch, 1304–1374; and Boccaccio, 1313–1375) and in the renaissance during the fifteenth and sixteenth centuries (Ariosto, 1474–1533; Machiavelli, 1469–1527; Tasso, 1544–1595). Modern Italian literature has many noted names in prose and verse, notably Manzoni (1785–1873), Carducci (1835–1907) and Gabriele d'Annunzio (1864–1938). The Nobel Prize for Literature has been awarded to Italian authors on four occasions—G. Carducci (1906), Signora G. Deledda (1926), Luigi Pirandello (1934) and Salvatore Quasimodo (1959). In 1965, there were 85 daily newspapers published in Italy, of which 16 were published in Rome and 9 in Milan.

Education.—Education is free and compulsory between the ages of 6 and 14; this comprises five years at primary school and three in the " middle school ", of which there are about 3,000. Pupils who obtain the middle school certificate may seek admission to any " senior secondary school ", which is roughly equivalent to a U.K. grammar school but may be a lyceum with a classical or scientific or artistic bias, or may be an institute or school for teacher training, or may be an institute directed at technology (of which there are eight different types) or trade or industry (including vocational schools). Courses at the lyceums and technical institutes usually last for five years and success in the final examination qualifies for admission to university. There are 32 State and 17 private universities, some of ancient foundation; those at Bologna, Genoa, Macerata, Naples, Padua and Perugia were started in the thirteenth century. University education is not free, but entrants with higher qualifications are charged reduced fees according to a sliding scale. In general, schools, lyceums and universities are financed by local taxation and central government grants.

CAPITAL, Rome. Metropolitan population (estimated Dec. 31, 1970), 2,778,872.

Recent estimates of the metropolitan population of the principal cities and towns are Milan, 1,713,539; Ψ Naples 1,278,051; Turin, 1,190,688; Ψ Genoa, 842,114; Bologna, 493,007; Florence, 460,944; Ψ Venice, 367,528; Ψ Bari, 356,250; Verona, 262,014; Padua, 228,854; Ψ Taranto, 223,392; Brescia, 209,659; Modena, 170,450; Ψ Reggio Calabria, 167,087; Ψ Salerno, 152,780; and Bergamo, 126,504; in *Sicily*; Ψ Palermo, 663,694; Ψ Catania, 414,619; Ψ Messina, 274,740; in *Sardinia*: Ψ Cagliari, 225,812.

ISLANDS.—*Pantelleria Island* (part of Trapani Province) in the Sicilian Narrows, has an area of 31 sq. miles and a population of 9,601. The *Pelagian Islands* (Lampedusa, Linosa and Lampione) are part of the Province of Agrigento and have an area of 8 sq. miles, pop. 4,811. The Tuscan Archipelago (including Elba), area 293 sq. km., pop. 31,861; Pontine Archipelago (including Ponza, area 10 sq. km., pop. 2,515); Flegrean Islands (including Ischia, area 60 sq. km., pop. 51,883); Capri; Eolian Islands (including Lipari, area 116 sq. km., pop. 18,636); Tremiti Islands (area 3 sq. km., pop., 426).

FLAG.—Vertical stripes of green, white and red.
NATIONAL DAY.—June. 2.

BRITISH EMBASSY
Via Venti, Settembre 80a, Rome.

Ambassador Extraordinary and Plenipotentiary, His Excellency Sir Patrick Francis Hancock, K.C.M.G. (1969).............................. £14,000
Minister, R. W. Selby, C.M.G.
Defence and Military Attaché, Col. G. L. Wathen.

Ast. Defence Attaché, Sqn.-Ldr. B. E. Hogan.
Naval Attaché, Capt. J. J. Phillips, R.N.
Air Attaché, Group-Capt. R. G. Churcher, D.S.O.,
M.V.O., D.F.C.
Counsellors, P. A. Rhodes (*Head of Chancery*);
W. G. Lamarque (*FAO*); C. W. Wallace
(*Commercial*) (*resident in* Milan); S. J.G.Cambridge
(*Economic*); K. Kenney, O.B.E. (*Labour*).
1st Secretaries, M. W. Ponsonby, C.B.E.; A. R.
Sinclair (*Information*); E. A. F. Seaman (*Adminis-
tration*); G. E. FitzHerbert; J. A. Shorten; T. C.
Wood; J. H. Bailey (*Consul*); A. A. C. Nash,
M.B.E. (*Commercial*); Sir Joseph Cheyne, Bt.;
A. R. Hughes.
2nd Secretaries, P. J. F. Barrett (*Administration*); J. A.
Shepherd (*Commercial*).
3rd Secretaries, Miss M. E. Hunt (*Private Secretary to
the Ambassador*) Miss M. E. Gutsell (*Information*).
Chaplain, Rev. Canon D. Davies.

BRITISH CONSULAR OFFICES
There are British Consular Offices at *Milan* (from
which all official trade promotion work in Italy is
controlled), *Rome, Genoa, Florence, Palermo, Turin,
Venice, Trieste, Messina* and *Cagliari* (*Sardinia*).

British Council Representative, M. Dodderidge,
O.B.E., Palazzo del Drago, Via delle Quattro
Fontane 20, 00184, Rome.
There are *British Council Institutes* at Milan and
Naples, and an office at Bologna, each with a library.

IVORY COAST
(Republic of the Ivory Coast)
President and Minister of Foreign Affairs, Félix
Houphouët-Boigny, *elected* for five years on
November 27, 1960; *re-elected* November 7, 1965.
President of National Assembly, Philippe Yacé.
President of Economic and Social Council, Mamadou
Coulibaly.
President of Supreme Court, Alphonse Boni.
Ministers of State, Auguste Denise; Mathieu Ekra;
Blaise N'Dia Koffi.
Minister for Foreign Affairs, Arsène Usher Assouan.

IVORY COAST EMBASSY IN LONDON
2 Upper Belgrave Street, S.W.1
Ambassador Extraordinary and Plenipotentiary, His
Excellency Honoré Polneau (1969).
Counsellors, M. Collet Vieira; M. Georges N'Dia
(*Commercial*).
1st Secretary, M. Daba Daniel Agoussi.
Attaché, M. Alloh Blaise Mobio.

The Ivory Coast is situated on the Gulf of Guinea
between 5° and 10° N. and 3° and 8° W. and is
flanked on the West by Guinea and Liberia, on
the North by Mali and Upper Volta and on the
East by Ghana. It has an area of about 189,029 square
miles—tropical rain forest in the southern half and
savannah in the northern—and a population (U.N.
estimate, 1969) of 4,195,000 divided into a large
number of ethnic and tribal groups. (*For* MAP, *see*
p. 873.)

Although official French contact was made in
the first half of the 19th century, the Ivory Coast
became a Colony only in 1893 and was finally
pacified in 1912. It decided on December 5, 1958
to remain an autonomous republic within the
French Community; full independence outside
the Community was proclaimed on August 7, 1960.
Special agreements with France, covering financial
and cultural matters, technical assistance, defence,
etc., were signed in Paris on April 24, 1961. The
Ivory Coast was a founder member of the *Conseil
de l'Entente*, established on May 29, 1959, as a loose
union embracing also, without abrogation of
sovereignty, Dahomey, Niger and Upper Volta.
Togo also adhered in June, 1966. The Ivory Coast

is also an Associated State of E.E.C. and a member
of the *Organisation Commune Africaine et Malgache*
(O.C.A.M.) and of the Organization of African
Unity (O.A.U.). The official language is French.
The Ivory Coast has a presidential system of
government modelled on that of the United States
and the French Fifth Republic. The single
Cnamber National Assembly of 85 members was
elected on November 7, 1965, for five years.
The defence of the Constitution. which was
promulgated on Nov. 3, 1960, is vested in a
Supreme Court.
Finance.—The currency of the Ivory Coast is the
Franc CFA (*Francs CFA* 661= £1). In 1968, the
Ivory Coast Budget balanced at *Francs CFA*
43,200,000,000.
Trade.—The principal exports are coffee, cocoa,
timber and bananas. The United Kingdom imports Ivory Coast timber and a small quantity of
her coffee. Diamonds and manganese are exported.
There are a few deposits of minerals including manganese. Trade in 1969 was valued at: Imports,
Francs CFA 86,283,623,143; Exports, *Francs CFA*
118,223,105,101.

Trade with U.K.
	1969	1970
Imports from U.K.....	£2,944,000	£3,122,000
Exports to U.K.......	10,107,000	9,637,000

CAPITAL, Ψ Abidjan (population, 400,000) which
is also the main port.
FLAG.—3 vertical stripes, orange, white and green.
NATIONAL DAY.—August 7 (Proclamation of
Independence).

BRITISH EMBASSY
Immeuble Shell, Abidjan, B.P. 2581.
Ambassador Extraordinary and Plenipotentiary, His
Excellency Peter Murray, C.M.G. (1970)..£6,475
(also Ambassador to *Niger* and *Upper Volta*).
1st Secretary, P. Eyers (*Consul*).
2nd Secretary, H. B. Herring (*Commercial*).
2nd Secretary, J. K. Radford (*Information*).
3rd Secretary, P. C. E. Davies (*Admin. and Vice-
Consul*).

JAPAN
(Nippon Koku—Land of the Rising Sun)
Emperor of Japan, His Majesty Hirohito, *born* April
29, 1901; *succeeded* Dec. 25, 1926; *married* (1924)
Princess Nagako (*born* March 6, 1903), daughter
of the late Prince Kuniyoshi Kuni, and has issue
two sons and four daughters.
Heir-Apparent, His Imperial Highness Prince
Akihito, *Crown Prince, born* Dec. 23, 1933;
married April 10, 1959, Miss Michiko Shoda and
has issue Prince Naruhito Hironomiya, *born*
Feb. 23, 1960, Prince Fumihito, *born* Nov. 30,
1965 and Princess Sayako, *born* April 18, 1969.

CABINET
Prime Minister, ~~Eisaku Sato~~. KAKUEI TANAKA
7/72
Minister of Justice, Shigesaburo Maeo.
Foreign Affairs, Takeo Fukudu.
Finance, ~~Mikio Mizuta~~. KOSHIRO UEKI *7/72*
Education, Saburo Takami.
Health and Welfare, Noboru Saito.
Agriculture and Forestry, Munenori Akagi.
International Trade and Industry, Kakuei Tanaka.
Transport, Kyoshiro Niwa.
Posts and Telecommunications, Masao Hirose.
Labour, Kenzaburo Hara.
Construction, Eiichi Nishimura.
Home Affairs, Motosaburo Tokai (and *Director-
General, Hokkaido Development Agency*) (in charge
of 1972 Winter Olympics).
Chief Cabinet Secretary, Noboru Takeshita.
Director-General, Prime Minister's Office, Sadanori
Yamanaka.

Director-General, Administrative Management Agency, Torata Nakamura. (and *Chairman, National Public Safety Commission*).

Director-General Science and Technology Agency and *Chairman Atomic Energy Commission,* Wataru Hiraizumi.

Director-General, Defence Agency, Naomi Nishimura.

Director-General, Economic Planning Agency, Toshio Kimura.

Director-General, Environment Agency, Buichi Oishi.

JAPANESE EMBASSY AND CONSULATE
46 Grosvenor Street, W.1,
Information Centre: 9 Grosvenor Square, W.1
[01-493-6030]

Ambassador Extraordinary and Plenipotentiary, His Excellency Morio Yukawa (1968).

Minister Plenipotentiary, Nobuyuki Nakashima.

Counsellors, Hidezo Hara (*Financial*); Kumao Okazaki (*Press and Information*); Toshihiko Nishiwaki (*Commercial*).

1st Secretaries, Ken-ichi Yanagi; Akira Matsuura (*Agriculture*); Hiroshi Sawano (*Financial*); Hideaki Sagara (*Transport*); Toshihiko Kubota (*Consular*); Koji Saka (*Home*); Tadashi Mano (*Transport*); Toshiyuki Hiraga (*Labour*); Keijiro Matsumura (*Commercial*); Hidero Maki (*Agriculture*); Takehiro Togo; Captain Keizo Ohashi (*Defence Attaché*); Masahiko Kashiwagi (*Commercial*); Habuki Sasaki (*Scientific*).

2nd Secretaries, Mamoru Funakoshi (*Information*); Yasutaro Ishikawa; Shunji Maruyama; Tadashi Ogawa (*Financial*); Akimasa Kuwagata; Tomoji Mutoh; Akio Ijuin.

3rd Secretaries, Yukio Takeuchi; Gunkatsu Kano; Hiroshi Yamada.

Area and Population.—Japan consists of 4 large and many small islands situated in the North Pacific Ocean between longitude 128° 6′ East and 145° 49′ East and between latitude 26° 59′ and 45° 31′ N., with a total area of 142,812 square miles and a population (estimated, Dec. 1970) of 103,265,000, excluding Okinawa (945,000).

Japan Proper consists of *Honshū* (or Mainland), 230,448 sq. k. (88,839 sq. m.), *Shikoku,* 18,757 sq. k. (7,231 sq. m.), *Kyūshū,* 42,079 sq. k. (16,170 sq. m.), *Hokkaido,* 78,508 sq. k. (30,265 sq. m.).

Formosa and the Kwantung Province, which had been throughout the years of Japanese expansion and aggression leased or annexed, reverted to Chinese sovereignty after the War of 1939–45.

After the unconditional surrender to the Allied Nations (Aug. 14, 1945), Japan was occupied by Allied forces under General MacArthur (Sept. 15, 1945). A Japanese peace treaty conference opened at San Francisco on Sept. 4, 1951, and on Sept. 8, 48 nations signed the treaty, which became effective on April 28, 1952. Japan then resumed her status as an independent power.

British participation in the occupation of Japan was virtually over by May, 1950. However, the outbreak of hostilities in Korea in June, 1950, resulted in the despatch to Korea of British Forces, from the United Kingdom, Australia, New Zealand and Canada to participate in the United Nations action. The main base of this force was established in Japan at Kure. On July 1, 1956, the base was moved to Inchon, Korea, and all Commonwealth troops had left Japan by the middle of 1957.

Under the terms of the Japan–U.S.A. Security Treaty of Sept. 8, 1951, United States forces remained to assist in the defence of Japan. However, as Japan's own Self Defence Forces have been built up, U.S. ground troops have been withdrawn. A revised version of the security treaty, which went into effect on June 23, 1960, was the subject of considerable controversy in the summer of that year.

Vital Statistics.—The birth rate in 1969 was 18·5 per 1,000 (1947, 34 per 1,000; 1967, 19·7 per 1,000). It has been stated that a considerable part in reducing the birth rate to its present level was played by drastic methods, induced abortion and sterilization, the legal grounds for which had been extended by the Eugenics Law, 1948, to include economic and social hardship. The improving standard of living has also played an important part in keeping the birthrate down.

The death rate in 1967 was 6·8 per 1,000, compared with 17 per 1,000 in pre-war years, natural increase of the population being 1,185,050 in 1968.

Physiography.—The coastline exceeds 17,000 miles and is deeply indented, so that few places are far from the sea. The interior is very mountainous, and crossing the mainland from the Sea of Japan to the Pacific is a group of volcanoes, mainly extinct or dormant. Mount Fuji, the loftiest and most sacred mountain of Japan, about 60 miles from Tokyo, is 12,370 ft. high and has been dormant since 1707, but there are other volcanoes which are active, including Mount Aso in Kyūshū. There are frequent earthquakes, mainly along the Pacific coast near the Bay of Tokyo. Japan proper extends from sub-tropical in the south to cool temperate in the north. Heavy snowfalls are frequent on the western slopes of Hokkaidō and Honshū, but the Pacific coasts are warmed by the Japan current. There is a plentiful rainfall and the rivers are short and swift-flowing, offering abundant opportunities for the supply of hydro-electric power.

Government.—According to Japanese tradition, Jimmu, the First Emperor of Japan, ascended the throne on Feb. 11, 660 B.C. Under the constitution of Feb. 11, 1889, the monarchy was hereditary in the male heirs of the Imperial house. A new constitution approved by the Supreme Allied Commander was published on March 6, 1946, superseding the "*Meiji Constitution*" of 1889, and containing many radical changes based on the constitutional practices of the United Kingdom, U.S.A. and France.

The new constitution came into force on May 3, 1947. Legislative authority rests with *The Diet,*

which is bicameral, consisting of a *House of Representatives* and a *House of Councillors*, both Houses being composed of elected members. Executive authority is vested in the Cabinet which is responsible to the Legislature.

A General Election was held on December 21, 1969, in which the Liberal Democratic Party was once more returned to power. The strength of the parties in the House of Representatives on June 1, 1970, was: Liberal Democratic Party, 302; Japan Socialist Party, 90; Komeito, 47; Democratic Socialist Party, 32; Japan Communist Party, 14; Independent, 1.

A regular election for the House of Councillors was held in June, 1971. The Liberal Democratic Party maintained their overall majority in the Upper House. The state of the parties there is now: Liberal Democratic Party, 136; Japan Socialist Party, 67; Komeito, 23; Democratic Socialist Party, 14; Japan Communist Party, 10; Niin Club, 3; Independent, 1.

Ryukyu Islands.—Since World War II the appointment of a Chief Executive, chosen by the local legislature, has been subject to the approval of the United States High Commissioner. On Nov. 10, 1968, elections were held in Okinawa and the other Ryukyu Islands and Mr. Chobyu Yara (*Socialist*) was elected Chief Executive. Control of the legislature remained with the Liberal Democratic Party which in 1971 had 20 of the 32 seats.

Elections were held in late 1970 for 5 seats for Okinawa in the House of Representatives and 2 seats for Okinawa in the House of Councillors. The decision to hold these elections followed a meeting between Prime Minister Sato and President Nixon in November, 1969, when it was agreed that the Administration of Okinawa should revert to the Japanese Government in 1972. The agreement for the reversion of Okinawa was signed on June 17, 1971, and final reversion is expected to take place during 1972. Until reversion the Diet seats for Okinawa carry limited privileges.

Agriculture and Livestock.—Owing to the mountainous nature of the country not more than one-sixth of its area is available for cultivation. There were in February, 1970 25,284,000 hectares of forest, which include the Cryptomeria japonica, Pinus massoniana, Zelkowa keaki, and Pawlonia imperialis in addition to camphor trees, mulberry, vegetable wax tree and a lacquer tree which furnishes the celebrated lacquer of Japan. The soil is only moderately fertile, but intensive cultivation secures good crops. In February, 1970, there were 6,355,000 hectares under cereals (rice, 2,923,000 hectares). The tobacco-plant, tea-shrub, potato, rice, wheat and other cereals are all cultivated: rice is the staple food of the people, about 12,689,300 metric tons being produced in 1970. The floral kingdom is rich, beautiful, and varied. Fruit is abundant, including the mandarin, persimmon, loquat and peach; European fruits such as apples, strawberries, pears, grapes and figs are also produced. Mulberry trees are now cultivated on only 163,100 hectares (1970) compared with 577,525 in 1935.

Minerals.—The country has mineral resources, including gold and silver, and copper, lead, zinc, iron chromite, white arsenic, coal, sulphur, petroleum, salt and uranium, but iron ore, coal and crude oil are among the principal post-war imports to supply deficiencies at home.

Industry.—Japan is the most highly industrialized nation in the Far East, with the whole range of modern light and heavy industries, including mining, metals, machinery, chemicals, textiles (cotton, silk, wool and synthetics), cement, pottery, glass, rubber, lumber, paper, oil refining and shipbuilding. The labour force of Japan in 1970, was 51,530,000, of which only 590,000 were unemployed. Of the total labour force, some 42,510,000 were engaged in non-agricultural industries, 8,860,000 in agriculture, forestry and fisheries.

Communications.—There were 27,236 kilometres of Government and private railroad (steam and electric) in March, 1970. The merchant fleet (ocean-going ships over 3,000 tons gross) consisted of 1,261 vessels totalling 22,564,359 tons gross in April, 1971.

Armed Forces.—After the unconditional surrender of August, 1945, the Imperial Army and Navy were disarmed and disbanded and all aircraft confiscated by the occupying forces.

Although the Constitution of Japan prohibits the maintenance of armed force, an internal security force, known as the National Police Reserve, came into being in August, 1950, and a Maritime Safety Force was established in April, 1952. In August, 1952, these Forces were renamed the National Safety Force and the Coastal Safety Force and were placed under a National Safety Agency. In July, 1954, the Agency was renamed the Defence Agency, the Forces under it the Ground Self Defence Force and the Maritime Self Defence Force respectively, and a new arm, the Air Self Defence Force, was created. At the same time the mission of the forces was extended to include the defence of Japan against direct and indirect aggression.

A Treaty of Mutual Co-operation and Security between Japan and the U.S.A. was signed in January, 1960, replacing an earlier Security Treaty signed in 1951 at the same time as the Peace Treaty. By this Treaty each country recognized that an armed attack against either in the territories under the administration of Japan would be dangerous to its own safety and declared that it would act to meet the counter danger

By 1970 the authorized uniformed strength of the three Self Defence Forces was 179,000 in the GSDF, 38,323 in the MSDF and 41,657 in the ASDF. The Combined Defence Agency vote for 1970–71 was Yen 589,019,000,000.

At the end of November, 1970, the GSDF was organized as five armies totalling 12 infantry divisions, one armoured division, one airborne brigade, one artillery brigade and two Hawk (SAM) battalions. 7 of the infantry divisions have an authorized strength of about 9,000 (4 combat teams) and 6 have a strength of about 7,000 (3 combat teams). Major equipment includes about 709 tanks, 605 armoured cars, 4,600 artillery pieces (field, 900; mobile 444, anti-tank, 75, Hawk missiles, 65, Type 30 rocket launchers, 25) and 352 aircraft (219 helicopters and 133 fixed-wing aircraft). Equipment is now largely of Japanese manufacture.

The MSDF has 206 warships totalling 138,450 tons and including one TARTAR-equipped GMD, 39 escort ships, 10 submarines and 157 others. Principal AS weapons include ASROC and DASH. The MSDF has a total of 251 aircraft (63 helicopters, 42 S2F-1, 51 P2U-7 and 85 others).

The ASDF has about 961 aircraft (192 F-104J, 287 F-86F, 36 helicopters and 446 others). The principal fighter is the F.104S. There are also 2 battalions of Nike-Ajax missiles (70 launchers).

Religion.—All religions are tolerated. The principal religions of Japan are Mahayana Buddhism and Shinto. The Roman Catholic Church has 1 Cardinal, 1 archbishop and 14 bishops. The Nippon Seikokai (Holy Catholic Church of Japan) has 11 Japanese bishops (1968) and is an autonomous branch of the Anglican communion. There is also a United Protestant Church.

Education.—According to the laws passed in 1947.

education on elementary level (6-year course) and lower secondary level (3-year course) is free, compulsory and co-educational. Upper secondary schools (3-year course) are mainly established and maintained by prefectures, and are co-educational. They have several courses in general, agricultural, commercial, technical, mercantile marine, radio-communication and home-economics education, etc. There are 2- or 3-year junior colleges and 4-year universities. Some of the 4-year universities have graduate schools. In May, 1970, the total number of these junior colleges and universities was 909, of which 128 were established and maintained by the State, while 80 were established and maintained by prefectures and cities, and 701 were private institutions. The most prominent universities are the seven State Universities of Tokyo, Kyoto, Tohoku (Sendai), Hokkaidō (Sapporo), Kyūshū (Fukuoka), Osaka and Nagoya, and the two private universities, Keio and Waseda.

Language and Literature.—Japanese is said to be one of the Uro-Altaic group of languages and remained a spoken tongue until the fifth-seventh centuries A.D., when the Chinese characters came into use. Japanese who have received school education (99·8 per cent. of the population) can read and write the Chinese characters in current use (about 1,800 characters) and also the syllabary characters called Kana. English is the best known foreign language. It is compulsory in almost all middle and high schools. By March, 1972, the number of libraries open to the public was expected to have risen to 806 (The National Diet Library and 805 public libraries) with 28,571,925 volumes. In addition there are 916 University libraries with 57,900,975 volumes. There were 100 daily newspapers in Japan of which 25 were published in Tokyo and 75 locally. Japan's total newspaper circulation was estimated at 33,792,078 copies and 1·25 per household at the end of 1970.

FINANCE

The Budget for the financial year 1971–72, ending on March 31, is estimated to balance at Yen 9,414,315,000,000 for revenue and expenditure on the general account, an increase of 18·4 per cent. over the preceding financial year.

The official rate of exchange with Sterling in July, 1971, was Yen 864 = £1. (*See also* p. 83.)

PRODUCTION AND TRADE

Being deficient in natural resources, Japan has had to develop a complex foreign trade. Principal imports consist of raw materials (cotton, wool, mineral oils, rubber, iron ore, coking coal, salt, wood pulp, hides), foodstuffs (wheat, barley, soya beans, sugar), petroleum, chemicals and specialized machinery. Principal exports consist of cotton and rayon textiles, machinery, ships, metals and products, canned fish, chemicals and a wide variety of manufactured goods, including chinaware, toys, motor cars, bicycles, sewing machines, cameras and transistor radios.

FOREIGN TRADE

	1969 $1,000	1970 $1,000
Total Imports.........	15,230,536	18,881,168
Total Visible Exports....	15,990,014	19,317,687
Surplus/Deficit.........	+966,478	+436,519

Trade with U.K.

	1969	1970
Imports from U.K..	£124,678,000	£147,841,000
Exports to U.K.....	104,453,000	134,414,000

CAPITAL.—TOKYO. Population (estimated March 1, 1971), 11,403,744. The other chief cities had the following populations at the beginning of

1971: Ψ Osaka (2,980,409); Ψ Nagoya (2,037,952); Ψ Yokohama (2,273,029); Kyoto, the ancient capital (1,415,880); Ψ Kobé (1,294,373); Kita-Kyushu (1,042,319); Ψ Sapporo (1,010,123); Ψ Kawasaki (973,486); Ψ Fukuoka (853,270).

FLAG.—White, charged with sun (red).

NATIONAL DAY.—April 29 (Birthday of the Emperor).

Yokohama, by sea *viâ* Cape Town, 14,653 miles (50 days); *viâ* Panama, 12,544 miles (35 days); Tokyo, by air (B.O.A.C., polar route), 8,382 miles distant from London: transit, 17 hrs.; (B.O.A.C. trans-Siberia route (13 hrs.)).

BRITISH EMBASSY

(Ichiban-cho, Kojimachi, Chiyoda-ku, Tokyo.)

Ambassador Extraordinary and Plenipotentiary, His Excellency Sir John Pilcher, K.C.M.G. (1967)
             £14,000

Minister, P. A. G. Westlake, M.C.
Counsellors, P. G. A. Wakefield (*Commercial*); J. R. Greenwood (*Information*); J. H. Morley, C.B.E.
1st Secretaries, L. Pickles (*and Consul-General*), B. Hitch (*Head of Chancery*); A. F. R. Harvey, O.B.E. (*Commercial*); E. Williamson (*Atomic Energy*); P. J. L. Popplewell (*Commercial*); R. S. Gorham; R. G. Farrar (*Commercial*); J. C. A. Rundall (*Scientific*); D. E. H. Hellings, M.B.E. (*Administration*).
2nd Secretaries, D. W. F. Warren-Knott (*Commercial*); E. A. Owen (*Commercial*); N. A. Smith (*Commercial*); M. R. J. Guest; J. W. Hodge (*Information*); D. J. Wright (*Commercial*); A. N. R. Millington.
Defence and Military Attaché, Col. W. A. E. Todd., M.C.
Naval and Air Attaché, Capt. H. J. Abraham, R.N.
Asst. Defence Attaché, Lt.-Cdr. S. K. Grove, R.N.
Scientific Attaché, Dr. D. I. Packham.
There is a British Consulate-General at *Osaka* and Consulates at *Yokohama, Nagoya* and *Kita Kyushu.*

BRITISH COUNCIL

Iwanami Building, 1 Jinbo-cho 2-chome, Kanda, Chiyoda-ku, Tokyo, 101.

Representative and Counsellor (*Cultural*), *British Embassy,* R. A. H. Duke, C.B.E.
Deputy do., F. H. Beatty, M.B.E.
There is a British Council office with library at *Kyoto.*

JORDAN

(The Hashemite Kingdom of The Jordan)

King of the Jordan, Hussein, G.C.V.O., *born* November 14, 1935, *succeeded* on the deposition of his father, King Talal, Aug. 11, 1952, *assumed constitutional powers,* May 2, 1953, on coming of age.

Crown Prince, Prince Hassan, third son of King Talal of Jordan, *born* 1948, *appointed* Crown Prince, April 1, 1965.

CABINET

Prime Minister and Minister of Defence, Wasfi al-Tel.
Minister of Development and Reconstruction, Dr. Subhi Amin Amro.
Finance, Ahmad al Lozi.
Foreign Affairs, Abdullah Salah.
Justice, Fawwaz al Rusan.
Interior, Ibrahim al Habashneh.
Information, Culture, Tourism and Antiquities, Adnan Abu Audeh.
Interior (Rural and Municipal Affairs), Dr. Yacub Sa'id Abu Ghosh.
Agriculture, Omar Abdullah.
National Economy, Omar al Nabulsi.
Communications, Muhammed Khalaf.

Transport, Anis Mansour Mou'asher.
Health, Dr. Muhammed al Beshir.
Education and Minister of Wakfs, Islamic Affairs and Shrines, Dr. Ishak Farhan.
Social Welfare and Labour, Mustafa Dudin.
Public Works, Muhammed al Farnan Muhd Abeidat.
Ministers of State for Prime Minister's Office Affairs, Emil al Ghori; Dr. Abdul Salam al Majali.

JORDANIAN EMBASSY AND CONSULATE
6 Upper Phillimore Gardens, W.8
[01-937-3685]

Ambassador Extraordinary and Plenipotentiary, His Excellency Zaid al-Rifa'i.
Military, Naval and Air Attaché, Brig. Rakan Jazi.
1st Secretary, Nabih N. Nimr.
2nd Secretaries, Miss Zein Rifai; Kasim Ghazzawi.
Finance Officer, Capt. Yahai Hasan Moh'd Irsan.
Service Attaché's Office, 18 Upper Phillimore Gardens, W.8 [01-937-9611].

Area and Population.—The Kingdom is bounded on the north by Syria, on the west by Israel, on the south by Saudi Arabia and on the east by Iraq. Since the hostilities of June, 1967, that part of the country lying to the west of the Jordan River has been under Israeli occupation. The majority of the population are Sunni Moslems and Islam is the religion of the State. Total population (U.N. estimate, Dec., 1969) is 2,300,000, of whom 1,600,000 live in East Jordan and the remainder on the West Bank and in East Jerusalem. (*For* MAP, *see* p. 885.)

History and Government.—After the defeat of Turkey in the First World War the Amirate of Transjordan was established in the area east of the River Jordan as a state under British mandate. The mandate was terminated after the Second World War and the Amirate, still ruled by its founder, the Amir Abdullah, became the Hashemite Kingdom of Jordan. Following the 1948 war between Israel and the Arab States, that part of Palestine remaining in Arab hands (but excluding Gaza) was incorporated into the Hashemite Kingdom. King Abdullah was assassinated in 1951; his son Talal ruled briefly but abdicated in favour of the present King, Hussein, in 1952. All of Jordan west of the River has been under Israeli occupation since 1967. As a result of the wars of 1948 and 1967 there are about 750,000 refugees and displaced persons living in East Jordan, about 200,000 of whom live in refugee and displaced persons camps established by the U.N. Relief and Works Agency (UNRWA). It was largely among this refugee population that the Palestinian *fedayeen* (commando) movement which had come into existence some years earlier grew considerably in strength during 1969 and 1970. The *fedayeen* organizations conducted a number of operations against Israel but during 1970 came more and more into conflict with the Jordanian Government. The severe crisis which followed the spectacular multiple hijackings of aircraft in September, 1970, led directly to civil war between the Jordan army and the *fedayeen*. The army came off best, and following the conclusion of a series of agreements between the Government and the *fedayeen*, the Jordan Government re-established effective authority.

The present constitution of the Kingdom came into force in 1952. It provides for a senate of 30 members (all appointed by the King) and an elected House of Representatives of 60 persons. The King himself appoints the other members of the Council of Ministers. Crown Prince Hassan normally acts as Regent when King Hussein is away from Jordan.

Production and Industry.—West Jordan is fertile,

though many areas have suffered from soil erosion. In East Jordan the main agricultural areas are the east part of the Jordan Valley, the hills overlooking the Valley and the flatter country to the south of Amman and around Madaba and Irbid. The rest of the country is desert and semi-desert. The principal crops are wheat, barley, vegetables, olives and fruit (mainly grapes and citrus fruits). Agricultural production in the Jordan Valley has suffered from the continued hostilities in the area, though the East Ghor Canal, vital to the irrigation of the area, has now been restored and is being extended. The only important industrial product is raw phosphates (production 1970: 938,900 tons), most of which is exported. Tourism was a major industry and foreign currency earner before the 1967 war but has now dwindled considerably as most of the tourist sites are in Israeli occupied territory. The Trans-Arabian oil pipeline (Tapline) runs through North Jordan on its way from the eastern province of Saudi Arabia to the Lebanese coast of Sidon. A branch pipeline feeds a refinery at Zerqa (production 1970: 445,800 tons) which meets most of Jordan's requirements for refined petroleum products.

Communications.—The trunk road system is good. Amman is linked to Damascus, Baghdad and Jedda by tarred roads which are of considerable importance in the overland trade of the Middle East. The former Hejaz Railway enters Jordan east of Ramtha and runs through Zerqa and Amman to Ma'an with a spur to the top of the Raz al-Naqb escarpment. The formerly abandoned section from Ma'an to Medina in Saudi Arabia has been partially reconstructed. The only port is 'Aqaba which handled 220 vessels and 381,900 tons of imports and exports in 1970. Much of Jordan's trade moves overland to or from ports in Syria and Lebanon. The Royal Jordanian Airline (ALIA) operates from Amman Airport to other cities in the Middle East and to Rome, London, Paris, Frankfurt, Athens and Istanbul. A new airport is under construction at 'Aqaba.

FINANCE

	1969	1970 (Revised estimates)
	JD	JD
Expenditure	88,410,000	84,826,000
Domestic Revenue	33,168,000	30,415,000
Budgetary Support Grants	37,553,000	33,070,000
Economic and Technical Aid	824,000	279,000
Development Loans	4,837,000	1,042,000
Domestic Borrowing	8,400,000	4,200,000
Deficit	3,628,000	15,820,000

Trade with U.K.

Since 1966 Britain has been the leading source of supply of imported goods to Jordan. Jordan's exports to U.K. are negligible.

	1969	1970
Imports from U.K.	£16,410,000	£12,266,000
Exports to U.K.	202,000	217,000

CAPITAL.—Amman. Population, 542,000 (1968).
FLAG.—Black, white and green horizontal stripes, surcharged with white seven-point star on red triangle.
NATIONAL DAY.—May 25 (Independence Day).

BRITISH EMBASSY, AMMAN

Ambassador Extraordinary and Plenipoteniary, His Excellency John Fleetwood Stewart Phillips, C.M.G. (1970) £6,925
Counsellor, J. S. Champion, O.B.E. (*Head of Chancery*).

Defence Attaché, Col. R. N. Harrison, O.B.E.
Asst. Military Attaché, Maj. F. J. Goddard.
Air Attaché, Wing-Cdr. J. M. A. Parker, A.F.C.
1st Secretaries, J. A. Speares, O.B.E.; A. W. B. Strachan, O.B.E. (*Consul, Development and Commercial*); P. S. Allfree (*Information*).
2nd Secretaries, C. P. Carter, M.B.E.; P. D. D. Warden (*Commercial*).
3rd Secretary, F. B. T. Martin (*Admin.*).

BRITISH COUNCIL
Representative, L. K. Lovett-Taylor, Box 634. Jebel Amman, Amman.

KHMER REPUBLIC
(*formerly* Cambodia)
Head of State, Cheng Heng, *assumed office* March 1970.

Prime Minister, Marshal Lon Nol, *appointed* August, 1969.

KHMER EMBASSY
26 Townshend Road, N.W.8.
[01-722-8802]
Ambassador Extraordinary and Plenipotentiary, His Excellency Samreth Soth.
Counsellor, So Yandara.
1st Secretary, Nguon Pytoravuth.
2nd Secretary, Penn Nhach (*Cultural and Press Affairs*).

Area and Population.—Situated between Thailand and South Vietnam and extending from the border with Laos on the north to the Gulf of Siam, the Khmer Republic covers an area of some 70,000 square miles. It has a population (estimated, 1969) of 6,701,000. (*For* MAP, *see* Index.)

History.—Once a powerful kingdom, which, as the Khmer Empire, flourished between the tenth and fourteenth centuries, Cambodia became a French protectorate in 1863 and was granted independence within the French Union as an Associate State in 1949. Two years earlier Prince (then King) Norodom Sihanouk had promulgated a constitution providing for parliamentary government. Full independence was proclaimed on November 9, 1953. The Geneva Conference of 1954 took Cambodia further along the road to independence by ensuring the withdrawal of French and Vietminh forces from the country, and the process was completed when, in January, 1955, the Kingdom of Cambodia became financially and economically independent not only of France but also of Laos and Vietnam. For the next fifteen years the political life of the country was dominated by Prince Norodom Sihanouk, first as King, then as Head of Government after he had abdicated in favour of his father and finally (following his father's death in 1960) as Head of State. Although the *Sangkum Reastr Nyum* or Popular Socialist Community, which he set up to embody his political views still won all the seats in the National Assembly elections of September, 1966, his initial popularity was, towards the end of the sixties, increasingly dimmed by criticism both of his management of the economy and of the pro-communist slant of the neutralist policy he proclaimed, which condoned extensive use of Cambodian territory by the North Vietnamese in their military operations against South Vietnam.

Prince Sihanouk left Cambodia during January, 1970, on a health cure, and on March 18 was dismissed as Head of State by the National Assembly. The monarchy was replaced by a Republic on October 9, 1970, since when the official name of the country has been The Khmer Republic. Preparations for the adoption of a republican constitution and for new elections to the National Assembly were included in the Government's programme in May, 1971.

In April, 1970, the Communist Vietnamese invaded Cambodia and fighting in various parts of the country has continued since then. With considerable assistance from abroad and in particular from the United States, the armed forces have been increased from some 35,000 to nearly 200,000 and, in frequent co-operation with South Vietnamese forces, have succeeded in regaining all the main centres of population, although security outside the main towns remains precarious..

Geography, Economy and Communications.—Cambodia has an economy based on agriculture, fishing and forestry, the bulk of its people being rice-growing farmers living in the basins of the Mekong and Tonlé Sap rivers. In addition to rice, which is the staple crop, the major products are rubber, livestock, maize, timber, pepper, palm sugar, fresh and dried fish, kapok, beans, soya and tobacco. Rice and rubber are normally the main exports though rubber production was brought to a standstill by the hostilities and rice exports much reduced by transport difficulties. Fifty per cent. of the total land area is forest or jungle abounding in wild life of all kinds, including big game. The climate is tropical monsoon with a rainy season from May to October.

The country has over 5,000 kilometres of roads, of which nearly half are hard-surfaced and passable in the rainy season. There are two railways (both in 1971 interrupted by enemy damage). One runs from Phnom-Penh to the Thai border; the other from Phnom-Penh to Kampot and on to Kompong Som (formerly Sihanoukville). Phnom-Penh is a river port capable of receiving ships of up to 2,500 tons all the year round. The main installations of a deep water port at Kompong Som on the Gulf of Thailand have been completed and can receive ships up to 10,000 tons. The port is linked to Phnom-Penh by a modern highway. There is as yet no large-scale industry, but textile mills, plywood, cement, sugar, and paper factories have been set up with Communist aid. Jute, bottle and tyre factories, a lorry and tractor plant, an oil refinery and a brewery have been set up, but production has been reduced or suspended during the hostilities.

Cambodia's foreign aid previously came mainly from France and the Communist bloc, but much of this aid has been suspended since the deposition of Prince Sihanouk. U.S. economic aid was instituted late in 1970 at a rate of $78 million for 1970–71. Other committed non-military aid from Japan, Australia and other non-communist countries in grants and loans, stood at some U.S. $40 million. U.S. *military* aid in 1970–71 was running at about $200 million a year. State control of foreign trade and banking which had been nationalized since 1963 was slowly being liberalized in the months prior to the overthrow of Prince Sihanouk.

The national airline Air Cambodge at present operates services to Singapore, Hong Kong and South Vietnam. There are several internal airlines connecting the main cities under government control. It is still possible to fly to Siamreap but not to visit the famous ruins of Angkor. Cargo boats from Singapore and Hong Kong visit Kompong Som on the Gulf of Siam and also come up the Mekong River to Phnom-Penh.

Religion and Education.—The state religion is Buddhism of the "Little Vehicle". There is also a small Christian community. The national language is Khmer, although French is widely spoken and is still largely the official language of government and commerce. In recent years considerable

efforts have been devoted to the development of education and new schools, colleges and technical institutes have been established.   There is a Buddhist University in Phnom-Penh, where there are also Faculties of Arts, Medicine and Law and a Technological Institute.   Several residential teachers' training colleges are now in operation.

Trade with U.K.

	1969	1970
Imports from U.K.	£1,538,000	£1,067,000
Exports to U.K.	651,000	328,000

CAPITAL, Phnom-Penh.   Population (estimated, 1971), 1,500,000.

FLAG.—Blue, with three white stars arranged horizontally in right top quarter; left top quarter red, bearing emblem (Temple of Angkor Wat in white).   NATIONAL DAY.—November 9.

BRITISH EMBASSY

96 Moha Vithei Preah Bat Norodom, Phnom-Penh.

Ambassador Extraordinary and Plenipotentiary and Consul-General, His Excellency Anthony James Williams C.M.G. (1970)................£6,475

Defence and Military Attaché, Lt.-Col. J. Moore.

1st Secretaries, J. A. Davidson; M. C. B. Greig (*Commercial and Consul*).

3rd Secretary, W. O'Hara.

Vice-Consul, Miss M. Maxwell.

KOREA

Korea is situated between 124° 11″ and 130° 57″ E. long., and between 33° 7″ and 43° 1″ N. lat.   It has an area of 85,256 sq. miles with an estimated population of about 42,484,000, of whom about 30,000,000 live south of the present dividing line. The southern and western coasts are fringed with innumerable islands, of which the largest, forming a province of its own, is Chejudo (Quelpart).

Agriculture.—The soil is fertile, but the arable land is limited by the mountainous nature of the country.   The staple agricultural products are rice, barley, and other cereals, beans, cotton, tobacco and hemp.   Fruit-growing and seri-culture are also practised.   Gingseng, a medicinal root much affected by the Chinese, is largely grown at Kaesong (now in North Korean hands) but also in parts of South Korea.   It forms a rich source of revenue.

Minerals.—Gold, copper, coal, iron, graphite, tungsten and other minerals are distributed throughout the country but are more abundant in the north.

In pre-war days the south was mainly agricultural and most of the limited industries were in the north.   Since 1966, however, rapid industrialization has taken place in the south.

History.—The last native dynasty (Yi) ruled from 1392 until 1910, in which year Japan formally annexed Korea.   The country remained an integral part of the Japanese Empire until the defeat of Japan in 1945, when it was occupied by troops of the U.S.A. and the U.S.S.R.; the 38th parallel being fixed as the boundary between the two zones of occupation.   The U.S. Government endeavoured to reach agreement with the Soviet Government for the creation of a Korean Government for the whole country and the withdrawal of all Russian and American troops.   These efforts met with no success, and in September, 1947, the U.S. Government laid the whole question of the future of Korea before the General Assembly of the United Nations.   The Assembly in November, 1947, resolved that elections should be held in Korea for a National Assembly under the supervision of a temporary Commission formed for that purpose by the United Nations and that the National Assembly when elected should set up a Government.   The Soviet Government refused to allow the Commission to visit the Russian Occupied

Zone and in consequence it was only able to discharge its function in that part of Korea which lies to the south of the 38th parallel.

The Korean War.—The country remained effectively divided into two along the line of the 38th parallel, until the aggression of June 25, 1950, when the North Korean forces invaded South Korea.   On the same day, at an emergency meeting of the United Nations Security Council, a resolution was adopted calling for immediate cessation of hostilities, and the withdrawal of the North Korean armed forces to the 38th parallel.   The Communist forces ignored this demand and continued their advance.   In response to a Security Council recommendation that United Nations members should furnish assistance to repel the attack, 16 nations, including the United States of America and the United Kingdom, came to the aid of the Republic of Korea.   A unified command under the leadership of the United States was established on July 8. Shortly afterwards U.S. troops were landed in Korea but were at first unable to stem the Communists' onslaught.   Finally the United Nations and South Korean forces were able to stabilize a front around the Pusan perimeter.   On September 15, U.S. Marines made a successful surprise landing at Inchon which was quickly followed by a breakout from the Pusan perimeter and a general advance to the north.   The Communist forces had been pushed back almost to the Manchurian frontier, when, at the beginning of November, hordes of Chinese " Volunteers " began to pour over the Yalu River and by sheer weight of numbers forced the U.N. troops to withdraw once again south of Seoul.   However, the latter quickly regrouped and threw the Communist forces back to approximately the old dividing line.

The fighting was ended by an armistice agreement signed by the U.N. Commander-in-Chief and the commanders of the North Korean army and the Chinese People's " Volunteers " on July 27, 1953. By this agreement (which was not accepted by the government of the Republic of Korea) the line of division between North and South Korea remained in the neighbourhood of the 38th parallel.   The Geneva Conference discussed Korea from April 26 to June 15, 1954, but failed to agree on measures for reunifying the country.

Republic of Korea

President, Park, Chung Hee, *assumed office,* March 22, 1962; *re-elected for four years* 1963, 1967 *and* 1971.
Prime Minister, Kim, Jong Pil (1971).

KOREAN EMBASSY
36 Cadogan Square, S.W.1
[01–581–0247/40]

Ambassador Extraordinary and Plenipotentiary, His Excellency Ei Whan Pai (1967).
Ministers, Keun Park; Keun Sup Chang.
Counsellor, Jae Won Roh.
Naval, Military and Air Attaché, Col. Dong Ho Kim.
Attachés, In Yong Chung (*Financial*); In Shik Chung (*Cultural and Press Affairs*).
1st Secretary, Choo Nyun Chung.
2nd Secretary, Duk Soo Oh.
3rd Secretaries, In Hyuk Kwon (*Vice Consul*); Soo Whan Lee.

The Republic of Korea has been officially recognized by the Governments of the United States, France, Great Britain, and most other countries except the U.S.S.R. and its satellites. It has an area of 38,022 sq. miles and a population of 29,207,856 (Census of 1966; estimated, 1970, 31,738,000.

A general election was held on May 10, 1948, and the first National Assembly met in Seoul on May 31. The Assembly passed a Constitution on July 12, and on July 20 elected the late Dr. Syngman Rhee as the first President of the Republic of Korea, an office which he held until 1960. On August 15, 1948, the Republic was formally inaugurated and American Military Government came to an end.

President Syngman Rhee was succeeded as President by Dr. John M. Chang whose Government was, however, overthrown by a revolution led by army officers. On March 22, 1962, General Park, Chung Hee, took over as acting President, retaining his post as Chairman of the Supreme Council. Elections were originally promised for May and August, 1963, respectively, but when political activities were allowed to start again at the beginning of that year there was considerable confusion, so that the military government decided to retain power until December, 1963. Elections were then held in which General Park was elected and the Democratic Republican Party secured a majority. At further elections held in 1967, Pres. Park was returned to a comfortable majority for a new four-year term. In 1969 a constitutional amendment was passed to enable Pres. Park to stand for a third term and he was re-elected on April 27, 1971.

The Republic of Korea has an army of about 550,000 men, a small navy mainly for coast protection duties, a small air force and a Marine Corps which includes one division trained in amphibious operations.

Finance.—The Budget for 1971 totalled *Won* 508,420,727,000, of which 23 per cent. was for defence.

The unit of Korean currency is the *Won.* On March 24, 1965, a unitary fluctuating rate of exchange was introduced and stood in 1971 at about *Won* 780 = £1. The *Won* was devalued by 13 per cent. on June 26, 1971.

Trade.—The Republic of Korea's main exports are tungsten and iron ores, graphite, anthracite, fish and fish products, agar-agar, seaweed, raw silk, textile yarns, fabric, plywood, tobacco and human hair goods. Her main customers are Japan and the U.S.A. Imports greatly exceed exports. In 1970 exports totalled \$U.S. 835,185,000; imports amounted to \$U.S. 1,983,974,000.

Trade with U.K.

	1969	1970
Imports from U.K.	£12,042,000	£11,393,000
Exports to U.K.	4,099,000	6,239,000

CAPITAL.—Seoul, population (1966), 3,794,959. Other main centres are ΨPusan (pop. 1,425,703), Taegu (pop. 845,073) and ΨInchon (pop. 525,072). Pusan on the south-east coast, and Inchon on the west coast, only 28 miles from Seoul, are the main ports but the development of Inchon is hampered by a tide variation of 28–30 feet.

FLAG.—White, with red over blue device in centre, three black parallel bars, some broken, in each quarter.

NATIONAL DAY.—August 15 (Independence Day).

BRITISH EMBASSY
Seoul

Ambassador Extraordinary and Plenipotentiary, His Excellency Jeffrey Charles Petersen, C.M.G (1971).................................£6,925
1st Secretary, P. J. George (*Commercial*).
Defence Attaché, Brig. A. B. Taggart, M.C.
2nd Secretary, A. F. Blake-Pauley (*Head of Chancery and Consul*).
Vice-Consul, N. C. MacKenzie.

Democratic People's Republic of Korea.—Meanwhile in the Russian-occupied zone north of the 38th parallel the Democratic People's Republic had been set up with its capital at Pyongyang; a Supreme People's Soviet was elected in September 1948, and a Soviet-style Constitution adopted. Recognition had been given by the U.S.S.R. and its satellites. The population (U.N. estimate, 1969) is 13,300,000.

FLAG.—Broad red horizontal band bordered by white lines bearing a five-point red star on a white disc in centre; blue horizontal bands at top and bottom.

Korean Workers (= Communist) Party

Presidium of the Political Committee, Choe Yong-kun; Kim Il-song; Kim Il; Kim Kwang-hyop; Pak Kum-chol; Yi Hyo-sun.
Secretariat, Kim Il-Song (*Secretary-General*); Choe Yong-kun; Ho Pong-hak; Kim Il; Kim Kwang-hyop; Kim To-man; Kim Yong-chu; Pak Kum-chol; Pak Yong-kuk; Sok San; Yi Hyo-sun.

KUWAIT
(The State of Kuwait)

Amir, H.H. Shaikh Sabah as-Salem as-Sabah, *born* 1915; acceded Nov. 24, 1965.
Crown Prince and Prime Minister, (Dec., 1965), H.H. Shaikh Jabir al-Ahmed as-Sabah; *appointed Crown Prince,* May 31, 1966.

KUWAIT EMBASSY IN LONDON
40 Devonshire Street, W.1
[01–580–8471]

Ambassador Extraordinary and Plenipotentiary, His Excellency Ahmad Abdulwahab Al-Nakib (1971).

Area and Population.—Kuwait extends along the shore of the Persian Gulf from Iraq to Saudi Arabia, with an area of about 5,800 square miles and a population (Census, 1969) of 733,000. It is officially estimated that about 44 per cent. of this total are Kuwaitis, the remainder being large numbers of other Arab peoples, Persians, Indians and Pakistanis. The total European and American population is about 5,000. Kuwait has a hot, dry climate with a summer season extending from April to September. During the coldest month (January) the temperatures can fall below freezing, but normally range between 50° to 60°F. Shade temperatures are about 85°F.; and can reach 125°F.; 180°F. has been recorded in the sun. Humidity rarely exceeds 60 per cent. except in July and August.

Government.—Although Kuwait had been inde-

pendent for some years, the "exclusive agreement" of 1899 between the Shaikh of Kuwait and the British Government was formally abrogated by an exchange of letters dated June 19, 1961. This exchange was immediately followed by Iraqi claims to sovereignty over Kuwait and, in accordance with the terms of the exchange, the Amir requested British military assistance to help him maintain his sovereignty and independence, which was immediately supplied. British troops were withdrawn in October, 1961, and replaced by the Arab League Security Force composed of contingents from various Arab States. The withdrawal of this Force was completed in January, 1963. On May 7, 1963, Kuwait was admitted to the United Nations and on Oct. 4, 1963, Iraq recognized Kuwait's independence. On May 13, 1968, an exchange of Notes was signed giving notice that the 1961 defence agreement with the United Kingdom would end on May 13, 1971.

Elections were held in December, 1961, for a Constituent Assembly, which held its first meeting in January, 1962. A council of Ministers including non-members of the ruling family was formed in January, 1962, to replace the former Supreme and Joint Councils. Under the Constitution drafted by the Constituent Assembly, the first 50-member National Assembly was elected in January, 1963. The present National Assembly was elected for four years in January, 1967. The Constitution provides that the Assembly must pass all laws and approve the Heir Apparent nominated by the Amir. The Prime Minister is appointed by the Amir and can appoint his Ministers from the members of the Assembly or from outside. The Assembly has the right to pass a vote of no confidence in any Minister except the Prime Minister.

Education, etc.—As a result of the very considerable oil revenues, the Kuwait Government embarked on a large scale development scheme and plans for social services. Education and medical treatment are free. New hospitals and schools continue to be built. Kuwait University was opened in 1966. In 1967 there were 58,702 boys and 43,026 girls in 172 government schools.

Public Utilities.—Kuwait has a domestic water supply from water distillation plants which operate on waste natural gas from the oil fields. These plants can produce over 25,000,000 gallons of fresh water daily. For storage there are two 15,000,000 gallon reservoirs and one of 3,000,000 gallons. There is also a 7,500,000 gallon reservoir at Shuaiba attached to the power station there and a 10,000,000 gallon storage reservoir at Hawalli.

In 1961 a natural source of fresh water was discovered at Raudhatain in the north of the State. This has been developed to produce 5,000,000 gallons per day for at least 20 years and a pipeline has been built to carry the water to Kuwait town. Kuwait signed an agreement with Iraq on Feb. 11, 1964, allowing her to draw up to 120,000,000 gallons of sweet water a day from the Shatt-al-Arab, but this has yet to be implemented. Electricity is produced by three power stations in Kuwait (160 MWh) and one at Shuaiba (350 MWh). The town is served by a network of dual carriageway roads and more are under construction.

Communications.—Ships of British, Dutch, Kuwaiti and other lines make regular calls at Kuwait. B.O.A.C., Kuwait Airways, K.L.M., Lufthansa and several international and Middle Eastern airlines operate regular air services, and other companies make non-scheduled flights to Kuwait under charter. Wireless communications, telephone and postal services are conducted by the Kuwait Government, which has built an earth satellite station.

Finance.—Banking is carried out by the British Bank of the Middle East, the National Bank of Kuwait, the Commercial Bank, the Gulf Bank and the Ahli Bank. The banking system is controlled by the Central Bank of Kuwait.

Revenue for the financial year 1969–70 was budgeted at KD303,000,000. Expenditure included KD67,000,000 on construction projects and land purchases, in addition to ordinary expenses of KD232,000,000 (including nearly KD38,000,000 on Education, KD16,000,000 on Public Health, KD 11,000,000 for Public Works and KD25,000,000 for Defence).

Production and Trade.—The centre of the Kuwait Oil Company's production is at Burgan, south of Kuwait town. An oil port has been constructed by the company at Mina-al-Ahmadi, about five miles from Ahmadi, the company's administrative and residential centre. Production of crude oil in 1969 totalled 127,502,503 long tons. The Company is jointly owned by the British Petroleum Company and the American Gulf Oil Corporation. It has about 5,123 employees, including British, Americans, Indians, Pakistanis, Kuwaitis and Arabs from neighbouring territories. In May, 1962, the Company relinquished about half of its original concession area. Oil was also struck in the Kuwait-Saudi Arabian Neutral Zone to the South of the State early in 1953. Concessions for this area are held by the American Independent Oil Co. (Aminoil) from Kuwait and the Getty Oil Company from Saudi Arabia. Aminoil's production for 1969 (*i.e.*, Kuwait's share from the Neutral Zone) was 1,828,112 long tons.

The Arabian Oil Company, of Japan, having been awarded in 1958 the oil concession for the Partitioned Zone offshore sea-bed by Kuwait and Saudi Arabia for their respective half shares, commenced exploratory drilling in the summer of 1959 and struck oil in commercial quantity early in 1960. The first shipment of crude oil was made in March, 1961; production in 1969 was 7,885,144 long tons. A concession covering the off-shore area of Kuwait proper was awarded to the Shell Company in November, 1960, and the concession agreement in the name of The Kuwait Shell Petroleum Development Co. was signed in Kuwait on January 15, 1961. Exploratory drilling began in 1962 but was suspended in the autumn of 1963. The establishment of a Kuwait company, The Kuwait National Petroleum Co., was authorized by an Amiri Decree on October 5, 1960. This company took over the distribution of petroleum products in Kuwait from the Kuwait Oil Co., on June 1, 1961, and was, in partnership with the Spanish Company Hispanoil, awarded the concession to exploit the area relinquished by the K.O.C. Ltd. in 1962.

In addition to petroleum products, skins and wool are also exported. Trade in 1969 (Jan.–Sept.) amounted to: Imports £200,325,000; Exports (including re-exports), £15,815,000, excluding oil.

Trade with U.K

	1969	1970
Imports from U.K..	£40,888,000	£36,224,000
Exports to U.K.....	171,982,000	165,397,000

CAPITAL.— Ψ Kuwait (population, excluding suburbs, 300,000).

FLAG.—Three horizontal stripes of green, white and red, with black trapezoid next to staff.

NATIONAL DAY.—February 25.

BRITISH EMBASSY
Kuwait
Arabian Gulf Street, Kuwait

Ambassador Extraordinary and Plenipotentiary, His Excellency Arthur John Wilton, C.M.G., M.C. (1970).................................£6,925

Counsellor, C. T. McGurk, O.B.E. (*Commercial*).
1st Secretaries, P. G. de C. Ireland (*Head of Chancery*); M. J. Moore; H. Halilwell (*Consul*); S. Muir.
2nd Secretaries, J. J. Beale (Economic); D. Wigan; G. A. Tantum; G. S. Burton (*Commercial*); J. Khoury (*Commercial*); R. J. Newell (*Commercial*); G. J. Gillespie (*Admin.*).

British Council Office in the Persian Gulf, P.O. Box 345 Kuwait. *Representative*, R. F. Hitchcock. There is a library in *Kuwait*.

LAOS

(For MAP, *see* Index).

King, H.M. Sri Savang Vatthana, *born* 1907, proclaimed King, Nov. 1, 1959.
Prime Minister, Prince Souvanna Phouma (June 23, 1962).

EMBASSY IN LONDON
5 Palace Green, W.8

Ambassador Extraordinary and Plenipotentiary, His Excellency Phagna Inp-èng Suryadhay (1971).

Position and Extent.—Laos is a kingdom in the northerly part of Indo-China, lying between Vietnam, on the north and east, and Burma and Thailand on the west. Laos has a common boundary with the Khmer Republic to the south. The area of the kingdom is approximately 90,000 sq. miles, with a population (estimated, 1970) of about 2,700,000, of which 160,000 live in the capital, Vientiane.

History.—The Kingdom of Lane Xang, the Land of a Million Elephants, was founded in the 14th century, but broke up at the beginning of the 15th century into the separate kingdoms of Luang Prabang and Vientiane and the Principality of Champassac, which together came under French protection in 1893. In 1945 the Japanese executed a *coup de force* and suppressed the French administration. Under a new Constitution of 1947 Laos became a constitutional monarchy under King Sisavang Vong of the House of Luang Prabang, father of the present King, and an independent sovereign state in 1949.

The past twenty years in Laos have been marked by power struggles and civil war. Attempts by international commissions in 1954–58 and in 1961–62 to secure the withdrawal of foreign forces and the pacification and neutralization of Laos met with no lasting success. Personalities involved include the present Prime Minister, Prince Souvanna Phouma, who in 1957 formed a short-lived Government of National Union, including *Pathet Lao* (Communist) ministers, and has held office as Prime Minister with intervals since 1962; Prince Boun Oum of Champassac who formed a rightist Government in December 1960; and Prince Souvannouvong, a *Pathet Lao* leader, who took part in a later coalition with Souvanna Phouma and Boun Oum in 1962–63. Attempts to seize power by Capt. Kong Le (1960), Gen. Phoumi Nosavan (1965) and Gen. Thao Ma (1966) were unsuccessful.

Recent Events.—Since 1967 North Vietnam has steadily increased its military activities in Laos. Early in 1968 N. Vietnam troops captured a number of government positions in northern Laos, but the government's forces retaliated by occupying the town of Xieng Khouang. In June, 1967, the North Vietnamese army took the neutralist stronghold at Muong Soui, but lost it again when Major-General Vang Pao's guerrilla forces overran the Plain of Jars, destroying large communist caches

and recovering territory that had not been under government control for 5 years. The N. Vietnamese army recaptured the Plain of Jars in February, 1970, and occupied and destroyed Vang Pao's guerrilla base at Sam Thong to the south-west. In October, Vang Pao went over to the offensive again, re-occupying Muong Soui and high ground to the west of the Plain of Jars.

The provincial capitals of Attopeu and Saravane in the south fell to the communists in April and June, 1970, and there was heavy fighting around government positions on the eastern edge of the Bolovens Plateau as the N. Vietnamese sought to strengthen their supply lines through Laos into South Vietnam and Cambodia. In June Prince Souvannouvong sent Tiao Souk Vongsak, titular Secretary of State for Public Works and Transport, to Vientiane as his special emissary to discuss with Souvanna Phouma the modalities of a conference to be held between the two sides at Khang Khay to negotiate a peaceful settlement. No agreement was reached on the security arrangements for the talks, and Souk Vongsak returned to Sam Neua in January, 1971. The North Vietnamese army captured Muong Phalane on Route 7 in the south on January 26 and Muong Soui on February 3, threatening Luang Prabang. In February South Vietnamese forces attacked North Vietnamese supply routes in southern Laos. On February 12 the Government declared a state of emergency throughout Laos. In May Souk Vongsak returned and contacts between the two sides reopened. Later that month the North Vietnam troops overran the Bolovens Plateau in the south and consolidated their grip on the trails area.

Laos is in effect divided into two parts, with the *Pathet Lao* controlling the northern and eastern portion with the backing of approximately 70,000 North Vietnamese troops, whose principal interests are to safeguard supply lines between North and South Vietnam along the Ho Chi Minh trail, and to back up *Pathet Lao* administration of areas outside the government's control.

Finance.—Budget estimates for the fiscal year 1970–71 were: Revenue, K9,048,000,000; Expenditure, K18,248,000,000, of which the military budget absorbed K8,869,000,000. The unit of currency is the *Kip* (K). In July 1971, the official rate of exchange was K564= £1; K240=U.S.$1. There is also a free rate of exchange (approx. K1,200= £1; K500=U.S.$1) for non-official dealings.

CAPITAL.—Vientiane, population (estimated, 1962), 162,297.

FLAG.—Three-headed white elephant on 5 steps, surmounted by parasol, all on a red ground.

NATIONAL DAY.—May 11 (Independence Day).

BRITISH EMBASSY
Vientiane

Ambassador Extraordinary and Plenipotentiary, His Excellency John Owen Lloyd, C.B.E. (1970)
£6,925

1st Secretaries, C. Wilson (*Head of Chancery and Consul*); J. G. Wallace (*Aid*); D. R. Gallwey.
Defence, Military and Air Attaché, Lt.-Col. D. H. Thursby-Pelham.
Asst. Defence Attaché, Maj. A. S. Calder.
2nd Secretaries, W. A. Lees (*Administration*); P. C. Barnes (*Commercial and Vice-Consul*).
3rd Secretary, R. P. Ralph.
3rd Secretaries, M. J. Pawley (*Information*); Miss E. M. Garland (*Vice-Consul*).

LEBANON

President of the Republic of Lebanon, Suleiman
Franjieh, *elected* Aug. 17, 1970.

CABINET

Prime Minister and Minister of the Interior, Saeb
Salam.
*Vice Premier and Minister of Finance and National
Defence,* Elias Saba.
Foreign Affairs, Kabil Abu Hamad.
National Economy and Tourism, Saeb Jaroudi.
Public Works, Transport and Agriculture, Henri Eddé.
General Planning, Hassan Meshrifrieh.
Justice and Communications, Jamil Kebbeh.
Public Health, Emile Bitar.
Labour and Social Affairs, Mounir Hamdan.
Hydro-electric Resources, Jaafan Sharafuddine.
Education, Nagib Abu-Haidar.
Information, Henri Torbey.

LEBANESE EMBASSY IN LONDON
21 Kensington Palace Gardens, W.8
[01-229-7265]

Ambassador Extraordinary and Plenipotentiary, His
Excellency Nadim Dimechkie (1966).
Counsellor, Dr. Khalil Makkawi.
1st Secretary, Chawki Choueri.
Consular Section, 15 Palace Gardens Mews, W.8
(01-229-8485).

Area and Population.—Lebanon forms a strip
about 120 miles in length and varying in width
from 30 to 35 miles, along the Mediterranean littoral, and extending from the Israel frontier on
the south to the Nahr al Kebir (15 miles north of
Tripoli) on the north; its eastern boundary runs
down the Anti-Lebanon range and then down the
Great Central depression, the *Beqaa,* in which flow
the rivers Orontes and Litani. It is divided into 5
districts, North Lebanon, Mount Lebanon, Beirut,
South Lebanon and Beqaa. The seaward slopes of
the mountains have a Mediterranean climate and
vegetation. The inland range of Anti-Lebanon
has the characteristics of steppe country. There is
a mixed Arabic-speaking population of Christians,
Moslems and Druses. The total area of Lebanon
is about 4,300 sq. miles, population (U.N. estimate,
1969), 2,645,000. (*For* MAP, *see* p. 885.)

Production.—Fruits are the most important products and include citrus fruit, apples, bananas and
olives. Industry is on a small scale, the most
important industries being those connected with
food and drinks (sugar refining, flour milling,
confectionery, wines and beer, etc.), building
materials, furniture and the textile industry. There
is little remaining of the famous cedars of Lebanon.

Railways.—A narrow-gauge railway runs from
Beirut to Damascus, connecting at Rayak with a
branch of the standard-gauge line which runs
from Tripoli through Homs, Hama and Aleppo
to the Turkish frontier, from Nusaybin to the
Iraq frontier at Tel Kotchek. A standard gauge
railway also runs up the coast from Beirut to
Tripoli.

Civil Aviation.—Beirut International Airport is
one of the most important traffic centres in the
Middle East. Numerous international air services
to all parts of the world pass through it, and local
services connect with all Middle Eastern capitals
except Tel Aviv. Lebanon has two international
airlines of its own, Middle East Airlines/Air Liban,
primarily a passenger carrier, and Trans Mediterranean Airways, specializing in freight.

Archæology, etc.—Lebanon has some important
historical remains, notably Baalbek (Heliopolis)
which contains the ruins of first to third century
Roman temples and Jubail (Biblos), one of the
oldest continuously inhabited towns in the world,
and ancient Tyre which is in course of excavation.

Language and Literature.—Arabic is the principal
language (*see* Arabia), and French is also widely
used. The use of English is increasing. About
40 daily papers are published, including 3 in French,
1 in English and 4 in Armenian; and a further 30
periodicals.

Education.—There are four universities in Beirut,
the American and the French (R.C.) Universities
established in the last century, and the Lebanese
National University and the Arab University which
are recent foundations in the early stages of development. There are several institutions for vocational
training and there is a good provision throughout
the country of primary and secondary schools,
among which are a great number of private schools.

Finance.—Revenue and Expenditure, 1968 (Estimated) £L68,500,000. The monetary unit is the
Lebanese £(L); official rate £L7·58=£1. There
is also an officially recognized free market in foreign
currencies, which is used for nearly all commercial transactions. The free market rate for
sterling is variable, but averages about £L7·80=£1.
(*See also* p. 84.)

Principal Imports.—Gold and precious metals,
cereals, cotton and woollen textiles, artificial and
cotton yarns, iron and steel goods, wood, pharmaceuticals, raw hides, sugar, motor-vehicles, livestock, wheat, flour, machinery, crude oil, chemicals
and domestic electric appliances, and paper.

Principal Exports.—Gold and precious metals, citrus
fruits, onions, textiles, apples and pears, scrap metal,
vegetables, hides and skins, soap, butter, cereals, oil-
seed, cement products, wooden and steel furniture,
tobacco and wines.

Trade with U.K.

	1969	1970
Imports from U.K.	£20,874,000	£23,013,000
Exports to U.K.	3,995,000	3,124,000

There is also a considerable transit trade through
Beirut, mainly in gold and crude oil. Lebanon is
the terminal for two oil pipe lines, one belonging
to the Iraq Petroleum Company, debouching at
Tripoli, the other belonging to the Trans-Arabian
Pipeline Company, at Sidon. There are refineries
at the end of each pipeline which can supply
Lebanon's needs.

CAPITAL.—ΨBeirut (population, excluding suburbs, about 555,000). Other towns are ΨTripoli
(210,000), Zahlé (45,000), ΨSidon (42,000), Aley
(14,500), ΨTyre (12,000).

FLAG.—Horizontal bands of red, white and red
with a green cedar of Lebanon in the centre of
the white band.

NATIONAL DAY.—November 22.

BRITISH EMBASSY
Beirut

Ambassador Extraordinary and Plenipotentiary, His
Excellency Paul Hervé Giraud Wright, C.M.G.,
O.B.E. (1971)..........................£6,925
Counsellor, E. F. Given, C.M.G.
1st Secretaries, N. M. Darbyshire, O.B.E.; A. J.
Sindall; R. L. Morris, O.B.E. (*Labour*); Hon. M. S.
Buckmaster (*Information*); P. Joy, O.B.E. (*Inform-
mation*); N. G. S. Beckett (*Commercial*); R.
Bland; J. A. Bryan (*Consul*).
Defence, Naval and Military Attaché, Lt.-Col. S. A. R.
Cawston.
Civil Air Attaché, B. Lello.
The British Embassy houses the Office of the
Middle East Development Division of the Over-
seas Development Administration.
British Council Representative, P. B. Gotch; Fawzi
Acar Building, Sidani Street, Ras Beirut.

LIBERIA
(Republic of Liberia)

Acting President, William R. Tolbert.★
Secretary of State, J. Rudolph Grimes.
Treasury, James M. Weeks.
Attorney-General, James A. A. Pierre.
Postmaster-General, McKinley A. Deshield.
Defence, Allan H. Williams.
Education, G. Flamma Sherman.
Internal Affairs, E. Jonathan Goodridge.
Public Works and Utilities, G. Tucker.
Agriculture, J. T. Phillips, Jr.
Commerce and Industry, A. Magnus Jones.
Information and Cultural Affairs, E. R. Townsend.
Planning and Economic Affairs, Cyril Bright.
Public Utilities Authority, Taylor E. Major.
Director-General, Public Health Services, Edwin M.
  Barclay; *Chairman, Special Commission on Government
  Operations,* James T. Phillips, Sr.
★Under the Constitution the Vice-President succeeded
Pres. Tubman in 1971, beginning a 4-year term
on Jan. 1, 1972, under the title "Acting President".

LIBERIAN EMBASSY IN LONDON
21 Princes Gate, S.W.7
[01-589-9405]

Ambassador Extraordinary and Plenipotentiary, His
  Excellency J. Dudley Lawrence (1964).
Counsellor, R. B. King.
2nd Secretaries, Julia B. Wesley, M.V.O.; William
  Knuckles (*Consular*).
Attaché, Mrs. L. Tucker (*Educational*).
Counsellor (Consular Section), C. Birch.

An independent republic of Western Africa,
occupying that part of the coast between Sierra
Leone and the Ivory Coast, which is between the
rivers Mano in the N.W. and Cavalla in the
S.E., a distance of about 350 miles, with an area
of about 43,000 square miles, and extending to the
interior to latitude 8° 50′, a distance of 150 miles
from the seaboard. It was founded by the
American Colonization Society in 1822, and has
been recognized since 1847 as an independent State.
The population at the Census of 1962 was 1,000,000
(U.N. estimate, 1969, 1,150,000). (*For* MAP, *see*
p. 873.)

The executive power is vested in a President
elected for 4 years (8 years in the first instance)
assisted by a Cabinet; there are two houses of
Legislature, the Senate and the House of Representatives. The Senate is composed of eighteen
members elected from each of the nine Counties.
They hold office for a period of six years. The
House of Representatives is composed of fifty-two
members, each member holding office for four years.
William V. S. Tubman, President of Liberia since
1944, died on July 23, 1971, and was succeeded by
Mr. Tolbert (*see* above). The Army of Liberia consists of one division of 2 brigades of militia, three
regular infantry battalions, one engineer battalion
and a small coastguard. The artificial harbour and
free port of Monrovia was opened on July 26, 1948.
There are 9 ports of entry, including 3 river ports.

Liberia is receiving assistance from the U.S.
A.I.D. (successor to I.C.A.), particularly in the field
of education, and technicians have been sent from
U.S.A. to advise on various projects. Technical
assistance is also being provided by several other
countries, including the United Kingdom.
UNESCO, WHO and FAO have missions in the
country providing technical assistance. The U.S.A.
has also made loans for the improvement of power
and water supplies, roads and hospitals.

FINANCE

	1968	1969
Revenue	$55,917,000	$61,862,009
Expenditure	55,917,000	60,749,665

$ = U.S. Dollar.

TRADE

	1967	1968
Imports	$125,200,000	$108,500,000
Exports	152,800,000	169,000,000

Trade with U.K.

	1969	1970
Imports from U.K.	£13,655,000	£13,628,000
Exports to U.K.	8,693,000	11,972,000

The principal exports are iron ore, crude rubber,
uncut diamonds, palm kernels, cocoa and coffee.
The chief imports are manufactured goods of all
kinds, transport and iron-ore mining equipment and
foodstuffs.

The language of the Republic is English. American weights and measures are used.

CAPITAL, Ψ Monrovia. Est. Pop. 110,000. Other
ports are Ψ Buchanan, Ψ Greenville (Sinoe) and
Ψ Harper (Cape Palmas).

FLAG.—Alternate horizontal stripes (5 white,
6 red), with 5-pointed white star on blue field in
upper corner next to flagstaff.

NATIONAL DAY.—July 26.

BRITISH EMBASSY.
Monrovia

*Ambassador Extraordinary and Plenipotentiary and
  Consul-General,* His Excellency Martin John
  Moynihan, M.C. (1970)................£6,475
1st Secretary and Consul, R. G. Osborn.
3rd Secretary and Vice-Consul, A. N. Grant.

Monrovia, 3,650 miles distant; transit by
English steamers from Liverpool, 11 to 20 days;
also by French, Netherlands, German and U.S.
vessels from Continent and U.S.A. U.T.A., Pan
American Airways, Ghana Airways, Nigerian Airways, K.L.M., Sabena, S.A.S., Swissair, Middle
East Airlines and Air Afrique aircraft call at
Robertsfield, 35 miles from Monrovia.

LIBYA

King Idris I, who had ruled Libya since its independence in 1951, was deposed on September 1,
1969, by a group of Army officers, who formed a
Revolutionary Command Council and declared
the country a Republic. The Revolutionary
Command Council is the highest authority in
Libya. The Cabinet, containing several members
of the Revolutionary Command Council, formed
on Sept. 16, 1969, included:—

*Chairman of the R.C.C.: Prime Minister and Minister
  of Defence,* Col. Muammer El Qadhafi.
*Deputy Prime Minister for Production and Minister of
  Economy and Industry,* Major Abdussalam Jalud.
Deputy Prime Minister for Services, Maj. Abdul
  Munim al Huni.

LIBYAN EMBASSY IN LONDON
58 Princes Gate, S.W.7
[01-589-5235]

Ambassador, His Excellency Khain Mohammed Ben
  Amer (1971).

Libya, on the Mediterranean coast of Africa, is
bounded on the East by Egypt and the Sudan, on
the South by the Republics of Chad and Niger,
and on the West by Algeria and Tunisia. It
consists of the three former provinces of Tripolitania, Cyrenaica and the Fezzan, with a combined
area of approximately 810,000 square miles and a
population (U.N. estimate, 1969) of 1,869,000.
The people of Libya are principally Arab with some
Berbers in the West and aboriginal tribes in the
Fezzan. Islam is the official religion of Libya, but
all religions are tolerated. The official language is
Arabic.

Vast sand and rock deserts, almost completely
barren, occupy the greater part of Libya. The
Southern part of the country lies within the Sahara
Desert. There are no rivers and, as rainfall is

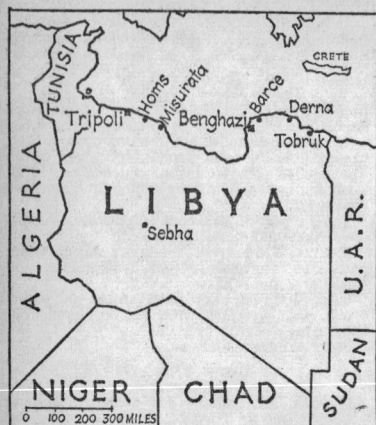

precarious, a good harvest is infrequent. Agriculture is confined mainly to the coastal areas of Tripolitania and Cyrenaica, where barley, wheat, olives, almonds, citrus fruits and dates are produced, and to the areas of the oases, many of which are well supplied with springs supporting small fertile areas. Among the important oases are Jagabub, Gadames, Jofra, Sebha, Murzuch, Brach, Gat, Jalo and the Kufra group in the South-East. Exports from Libya include crude oil, wool, cattle, sheep and horses, esparto grass, olive oil, sponges and hides and skins. Principal imports are foodstuffs, including sugar, tea and coffee and most constructional materials and consumer goods. There are now some thirty-five oil companies prospecting in Libya. The major producing companies are Esso, Oasis, Mobil, Amoseas, B.P., Occidental, Aquitane and Libyan National Oil Co. In addition to the Esso main pipeline from Zelten to the terminal at Mersa Bregha and the Oasis Company's pipeline from Dahra to Ras-es-Sidre. Mobil operates a 176-mile pipeline from Amal to Ras Lanuf, the B.P. line runs from Serir to Tobruk and the Occidental line from Intisar field to Zveitina. A new gas liquefaction plant run by Esso was opened at Mersa Bregha in June, 1970. Production of crude oil in 1970 was approximately 159 million tons (3·2 million barrels per day) which was an increase of 6·6 per cent. over 1969.

The ancient ruins in Cyrenaica, at Cyrene, Ptolemais (Tolmeta) and Apollonia, are outstanding, as are those at Leptis Magna near Homs, 70 miles from Tripoli and at Sabratha, 40 miles west of Tripoli. An Italian expedition has found in the S.W. of the Fezzan a series of rock-paintings more than 5,000 years old. The Museum in the Castello at Tripoli has been completely re-organized and is of great interest to visitors.

Communications in Libya are good in the coastal area where a motor road (now under reconstruction to international standards) runs from the Tunisian frontier through Tripoli to Benghazi, Tobruk and the Egyptian border, serving the needs of the main population centres. A road from the coast to Sebha, in the Fezzan, was completed in October, 1962. Elsewhere roads are poor and the transport inland is confined to caravan and occasional motor bus routes. There are airports at Tripoli and Benghazi (Benina), Tobruk (El Adem), Marsa Brega, Sebha, Gadames and Kufra regularly used by commercial airlines and military airfields at El Adem and Okba ben Nafi' (formerly Wheelus Field near Tripoli).

Government.—Libya was occupied by Italy in 1911-12 in the course of the Italo-Turkish War, and under the Treaty of Ouchy (Oct., 1912) the sovereignty of the province was transferred by Turkey to Italy. In 1939 the four Provinces of Libya (Tripoli, Misurata, Benghazi and Derna) were incorporated in the national territory of Italy as *Libia Italiana*. After the Second World War Tripolitania and Cyrenaica were placed provisionally under British and the Fezzan under French administration, and in conformity with a resolution of the General Assembly on Nov. 21, 1949, Libya became on Dec. 24, 1951, the first independent state to be created by the United Nations. The monarchy was overthrown by a revolution on Sept. 1, 1969, and the country was declared a republic.

Local Government.—Until the amendment of the Constitution in 1963, Libya was a Federal State, each of the three Provinces, Tripolitania, Cyrenaica and Fezzan, being administered by a Governor assisted by Executive and Legislative Councils. In April, 1963, however, comprehensive unity was proclaimed and the Federal system (together with the Governors and the Executive and Legislative Councils) abolished. The country is now divided into ten divisions, each administered by a Commissioner (*Muhafidh*).

Currency.—The £ Libyan equal to £1·70. Sterling was abolished in August, 1971, and a new currency the Libyan *dinar* of 1,000 *dirham* was introduced (*see also* p. 83).

Technical assistance is being provided by the United Nations, the United States and the United Kingdom to foster Libya's economic development.

A treaty of alliance and friendship between the United Kingdom and Libya, together with military and financial agreements, was signed at Benghazi on July 29, 1953.

Trade with U.K.

	1969	1970
Imports from U.K.	£42,465,000	£24,346,000
Exports to U.K.	151,557,000	166,876,000

CAPITAL.—Tripoli and Benghazi are the joint capitals of Libya, but the Government departments are situated in Tripoli.

The principal towns with the latest available estimates of populations are: Ψ Tripoli (331,947); Ψ Misurata (70,015); Ψ Benghazi (107,657); Khoms-Cussabat (66,559); Derna (21,432); Barce (10,645); Ψ Tobruk (15,867); Sebha (9,804).

FLAG.—The Libyan National flag is a tricolour of red, white and black. NATIONAL DAY—Sept. 1.

BRITISH EMBASSY IN LIBYA

Ambassador Extraordinary and Plenipotentiary, His Excellency John Peter Tripp, C.M.G. (1970) £6,925

Tripoli

Counsellor, M. P. V. Hannam.
1st Secretary, D. K. Haskell (*Head of Chancery*); D. A. Marston (*Commercial*); D. H. G. Rose (*Consul*).
2nd Secretaries, R. F. Sharp (*Information*); R. A. Kealy; L. E. Walker (*Commercial*); C. Lord (*Administration*).

Benghazi

1st Secretary, C. J. H. Keith (*Consul*).
2nd Secretaries, M. K. Jenner (*Commercial and Vice-Consul*).

3rd Secretaries, D. E. Tarling (*Vice-Consul*); A. Brown (*Commercial*).

There are British Consular Offices at *Benghazi* and *Tripoli.*

British Council Representative, W. R. Keight, M.B.E., Khweildi Bldg., Maidan Septimus Severus, Tripoli. There is a British Council Institute at *Benghazi*; libraries at *Benghazi* and *Tripoli.*

LIECHTENSTEIN
(Fürstentum Liechtenstein)

Prince, Franz Josef II., *b.* Aug. 16, 1906; *suc.* Aug. 25, 1938; *married* March 7, 1943, Countess Gina von Wilczek. *Heir,* Crown Prince Hans Adam, *b.* Feb. 14, 1945; *married* July 30, 1967, Countess Marie Kinsky.

Prime Minister, Dr. Alfred Hibe.

Liechtenstein is represented in diplomatic and consular matters in the United Kingdom by the Swiss Embassy, *q.v.*

At a General Election on Feb. 1, 1970, the Progressive Citizens' Party lost the majority in Parliament which they had enjoyed for 42 years and Dr. Alfred Hibe was asked to form a new Government.

A Principality on the Upper Rhine, between Vorarlberg (Austria) and Switzerland, with an area of 65 square miles and a population (U.N. estimate, 1969) of 22,000. The main industries are metal goods, cotton spinning and weaving, measuring instruments, coating of lenses, manufacture of vacuum apparatus, electronic microscopes, ceramics, artificial teeth and sausage casings, textiles, various apparatus, foodstuffs, leatherware and woodwork. The chief products are cotton yarn, cotton material, screws, bolts and bolt-shooting apparatus, needles, knitting machinery, ceramics, artificial teeth, precision measuring instruments, vacuum pumps, coated lenses, shoes, leather gloves, bed down, conveyor belts, boilers, preserves, damask cloth, socks and stockings, and furniture. Revenue (1969), *Swiss francs* 53,833,560. Expenditure (1969) *Swiss francs* 51,041,556.

The language of the Principality is German.

CAPITAL, Vaduz. Pop. (1968), 4,070.

FLAG.—Equal horizontal bands of blue over red; gold crown on blue band near staff.

British Consul-General, Patrick Desmond Stobart, M.B.E. (*office at* Bellerivestrasse 5, 8008 Zürich, Switzerland). *Consul (Commercial),* H. I. Duck.

LUXEMBURG
(Grand-Duché de Luxembourg)

Grand Duke, H.R.H. Jean, *born* Jan 5, 1921, *married,* April 9, 1953, Princess Joséphine-Charlotte of Belgium, and has issue, 3 sons and 2 daughters; *succeeded* (on the abdication of his mother) Nov., 1964. *Heir Apparent,* Prince Henri, *born* April 16, 1955.

Prime Minister and Minister of the Treasury, M. Pierre Werner.

Deputy Prime Minister, Minister of the Interior, Justice and Armed Forces, M. Eugène Schaus.

Minister of Foreign Affairs, Physical Education and Sport, M. Gaston Thorn.

Agriculture and Viticulture, and Public Works, M. Jean-Pierre Buchler.

Education, Labour and Social Security, M. Jean Dupong.

Family, Youth, Health, Culture, Religion, Mme. Madeleine Frieden-Kinnen.

Economic Affairs, Middle Classes, Tourism and Transport, M. Marcel Mart.

State Secretaries, Dr. Camille Ney; M. Emile Krieps.

EMBASSY AND CONSULATE
27 Wilton Crescent, S.W.1
[01-235-6961]

Ambassador Extraordinary and Plenipotentiary and Consul-General, His Excellency André J. Clasen, G.C.V.O. (1955). (*Doyen of the Diplomatic Corps in London*).

A Grand Duchy in Western Europe, bounded by Germany, Belgium, and France. Established as an independent State under the sovereignty of the King of the Netherlands and Grand Duke by the Congress of Vienna in 1815, it formed part of the Germanic Confederation, 1815–66, and was included in the German "Zollverein". In 1867 the Treaty of London declared it a neutral territory. On the death of the King of the Netherlands in 1890 it passed to the Duke of Nassau. The territory was invaded and overrun by the Germans at the beginning of the war in 1914, but was liberated in 1918. By the *Treaty of Versailles,* 1919, Germany renounced her former agreements with Luxemburg in respect of the customs union, etc., and in 1921 an economic union was made with Belgium (B.L.E.U.). The Grand Duchy was again invaded and occupied by Germany on May 10, 1940. The constitution of the Grand Duchy was modified on April 28, 1948, and the stipulation of permanent neutrality was then abandoned. Luxemburg is now a fully effective member of the Western association of powers and a signatory of the Brussels and North Atlantic Treaties. She is also a member of the European Economic Community.

Besides B.L.E.U., Luxemburg is also a member of the Belgium–Netherlands–Luxemburg Customs Union (Benelux). The Court of the European Community has its seat in Luxemburg, as does the Secretariat of the European Parliament and the European Investment Bank.

The area is 1,000 square miles; the population (Dec., 1970) 339,848, nearly all Roman Catholics. There is a Chamber of 56 Deputies, elected by universal adult suffrage for 5 years. Legislation is submitted to the Council of State. The Grand Duchy is rich in iron-ore and possesses an important iron and steel industry with an annual productive capacity over 5,000,000 tons (1970, 5,462,000 metric tons). The revenue for 1970 was estimated at L.F.11,592,600, expenditure L.F.11,911,000,000. The Luxembourg *franc* has at present the same value as the Belgian *franc* and the latter is legal tender in the Grand Duchy. Exchange Rate, 120 *Francs*= £1. There are 212 miles of railway.

Trade with U.K.

	1969	1970
Imports from U.K.	£2,020,000	£5,653,000
Exports to U.K.	4,657,000	4,306,000

The capital, Luxemburg, pop. (1970), 76,143, is a dismantled fortress. The country is well wooded, with many deer and wild boar. The language is Letzeburgesch but French is the official language: all speak German and many English.

FLAG.—Three horizontal bands, red, white and blue. NATIONAL DAY.—June 23.

BRITISH EMBASSY
Luxemburg

Ambassador Extraordinary and Plenipotentiary, His Excellency John Charles Abercromby Roper, C.M.G., M.C. (1970).....................£5,925

1st Secretary and Consul, J. N. Allan.

MADAGASCAR
(Ny Repoblika Malagasy)

President and Head of Government, M. Philibert Tsiranana, *elected,* 1959; *re-elected,* 1965.

Vice-President of the Government, M. Calvin Tsiebo.

Minister of Foreign Affairs, M. Jacques Rabemananjara.

MALAGASY EMBASSY IN LONDON
33 Thurloe Square, S.W.7.
[01-584-3714]
Ambassador Extraordinary and Plenipotentiary, His Excellency Dr. Alfred Rajaonarivelo.
Counsellor (Economic), R. Rambahiniarison.

Area 228,000 sq. miles. Population (U.N. estimate, 1969), 6,600,000. Madagascar is 240 miles distant from the S.E. coast of Africa and is the fifth largest island in the world. It became a French protectorate in 1895. In 1896 the Hova dynasty was suppressed and the administration entrusted to a Governor-General. Constitutional reforms were introduced in 1957 giving the island internal autonomy and Madagascar adopted republican status on Oct. 14, 1958, while remaining within the French Community. Complete independence was proclaimed on June 26, 1960, and immediately thereafter the President of the Republic, M. Philibert Tsiranana, signed formal agreements with the French Government confirming Madagascar's continued membership of the French Community and establishing co-operation with the French Republic on defence, monetary, judicial and educational matters, etc.

The island's economy is still mainly agricultural. A first development plan (1964-68) was put into operation in 1965, with emphasis on increased agricultural production and creation of small industries. A second development plan was expected to start in 1971. The principal exports in 1969 in order of value were: coffee (28½ per cent. of total), vanilla (10 per cent.), rice, sugar, meat and meat products, petroleum products, clove oil, sisal, tobacco and cigarettes, pepper, butter beans, raffia, graphite, fish and shell-fish, hides and skins, cinnamon, cloves and mica. Cattle raising is an important activity and scientific breeding has been started. A livestock development project is being financed by a World Bank loan. Minerals mined and exported, which until recently comprised mainly graphite and mica, now include chromium ore. Several foreign companies are prospecting for oil.

Total exports in 1969 were *FMG*29,134,000,000 compared with *FMG*28,607,900,000 in 1968. The main imports in 1969, totalling *FMG*46,187,600,000 (1968, *FMG*42,024,100,000) were machinery, transport equipment, metal products, chemical and semi-chemical goods, crude and other petroleum products, textiles, food products, electrical equipment, clothing, paper and paper products.

Trade with U.K.

	1969	1970
Imports from U.K....	£945,000	£923,000
Exports to U.K.......	1,718,000	1,338,000

The average rate of exchange is *Malagasy francs* (FMG) 660= £1. (*See also* p. 84.)

CAPITAL.—Antananarivo (364,496). Other towns with 1968 populations are: ΨTamatave (54,665), the chief port; ΨMajunga (49,798); Fianarantsoa (47,348); Diego-Suarez (41,218); Tuléar (33,842); Antsirabe (28,108).

The former dependencies of Madagascar in the Mozambique Channel, Juan de Nova, Europa Island and Bassas da India (uninhabited), are integral parts of the French Republic and, as such, are administered by the Ministry of Overseas Territories and Departments of the French Government. The Island of Saint-Marie, off the east coast of Madagascar is recognized as a dependency of the Malagasy Republic but its inhabitants enjoy dual (French/Malagasy) nationality.

FLAG.—Equal horizontal bands of red (above) and green, with vertical white band by staff.

NATIONAL DAY.—October 14 (Proclamation of Republic).

BRITISH EMBASSY
41 Rue Choiseul, Antananarivo.
(P.O. Box 167)
Ambassador Extraordinary and Plenipotentiary, His Excellency Timothy Leland Crosthwait, C.M.G., M.B.E. (1970)...........................£5,925
1st Secretary and Consul, S. E. Warder.
3rd Secretary, D. Herbert.
Commercial Attaché and Vice-Consul, M. J. M. Pitchen, M.B.E.
There is an Honorary British Vice-Consul at *Tamatave*.

THE MALDIVES

President, His Excellency Amir Ibrahim Nasir.

Area, etc.—The Maldives are a chain of coral atolls, some 400 miles to the south-west of Ceylon, stretching from just south of the equator for about 600 miles to the north. There are 12 clearly defined atolls, separated from each other by deep channels, through which the currents run strongly. The total number of islands is over 1,067, some being very small; 193 of them are inhabited. The population of the islands (estimated, 1970) is 114,469. The people are Moslems and the Maldivian language is akin to Elu or old Sinhalese. They are highly civilized and are great navigators and traders.

Government.—The Maldives form a Republic which is elective. There is a Parliament (the *Citizens' Majlis*) with representatives elected from all the atolls. The life of the Majlis is 5 years. The Government consists of the President and the Cabinet, who are responsible to the Majlis. By the agreement signed with the British Government in 1965, the Maldives form a composite sovereign and fully independent state, free to conduct their own external relations with other countries.

With the agreement of the Maldivian Government, an R.A.F. staging post has been constructed on Gan Island, in Addu Atoll, the most southerly atoll, lying just south of the equator.

Production, etc.—The islands are thickly covered with coconut palms, and coir and ropes are exported. The principal industry is fishing and considerable quantities of dried fish are exported to Ceylon, where it is in great demand.

CAPITAL.—Malé (population, estimated 1970, 13,610). Communications are by steam or sailing ship, and an air strip has been constructed on Hulule Island about 1 mile from Malé.

FLAG.—Green field bearing a white crescent, with wide red border.

BRITISH REPRESENTATION
Ambassador Extraordinary and Plenipotentiary, His Excellency A. M. MacKintosh, C.M.G. (1969) (*concurrently British High Commissioner in Ceylon*).

MALI
(Republic of Mali)

Chairman, National Liberation Committee, Lt. Moussa Traore, *born* 1937, *assumed office* Nov. 20, 1968.
Prime Minister, Capt. Yoro Diakité, *appointed* Nov. 23, 1969.

The Republic of Mali, an inland state in northwest Africa has an area of 465,000 square miles and a population (U.N. estimate, 1969) of 4,929,000.

Formerly the French colony of Soudan, the territory elected on Nov. 24, 1958, to remain as an autonomous republic within the French Community. It associated with Senegal in the Federation of Mali which was granted full independence on June 20, 1960. The Federation was effectively dissolved on August 22 by the secession of Senegal.

The title of the Republic of Mali was adopted on Sept. 22, 1960. The Republic is no longer a member of the French Community. On July 1, 1962, a Mali *franc* equal in value to the *Franc CFA* was introduced and a new State bank set up.

The *régime* of Modibo Keita was overthrown on Nov. 19, 1968, and the President arrested by a group of Army officers, who formed a National Liberation Committee and appointed a Prime Minister. Lieut. Traore assumed the functions of Head of State.

Mali's principal exports are groundnuts (raw and processed), cotton fibres, meat and dried fish. The principal rivers are the Niger and the Senegal. Goods to the value of £284,000 were imported from the United Kingdom in 1970 (1969, £65,000); Exports to U.K. 1970, £318,000.

CAPITAL.—Bamako (150,000). Other towns are Gao, Kayes, Mopti, Sikasso and Segou (all regional capitals), and Timbuktu.

FLAG.—Vertical stripes of green (by staff), yellow and red. NATIONAL DAY.—September 22.

BRITISH EMBASSY

Ambassador Extraordinary and Plenipotentiary, His Excellency Ivor Forsyth Porter, C.M.G., O.B.E. (resident at *Dakar*).

MAURITANIA
(Islamic Republic of Mauritania)
President and Prime Minister, Moktar Ould Daddah, assumed office Nov. 28, 1958; *re-elected for 5 years*, Aug. 7, 1966.

Mauritania lies on the north-west coast of Africa between Spanish Sahara and the Republic of Senegal. It is bounded on the east and south by the Republic of Mali. Area 419,000 sq. miles. The population of Mauritania was estimated at 1,140,000 in 1969. (*For* MAP, *see* p. 873.) The Republic of Mauritania elected on November 28, 1958, to remain within the French Community as an autonomous republic. It became fully independent on Nov. 28, 1960. Mauritania's main source of potential wealth lies in rich deposits of iron ore around Fort Gouraud, in the north of the country. These are being exploited by an international company, the Société de Mines de Fer de Mauritanie, with the aid of a loan from the I.B.R.D. Exports began in June, 1963, by a new railway built to link the mine with the Mauritanian coast at Nouadhibou. A company has been set up to exploit copper deposits at Akjoujit.

Trade with U.K.

	1969	1970
Imports from U.K.	£1,720,000	£1,234,000
Exports to U.K.	9,338,000	8,586,000

FLAG.—Yellow star and crescent on green ground.
NATIONAL DAY.—November 28.
CAPITAL.—Nouakchott. (18,000).
British Ambassador, His Excellency Ivor Forsyth Porter, C.M.G., O.B.E. (*Resident at Dakar*).

MEXICO
(Estados Unidos Mexicanos)
President (1970–76), Lic. Luis Echeverria Alvarez, assumed office, Dec. 1, 1970.

CABINET

Minister of the Interior, Lic. Mario Moya Palencia.
Foreign Affairs, Lic. Emilio O. Rabasa.
National Defence, Dr. Hermenegildo Cuenca Díaz.
Navy and Marine, Almirante C. G. Luis M. Bravo Carrera.
Finance, Lic. Hugo B. Margáin.
National Patrimony, Lic. Horacio Flores de la Peña.
Industry and Commerce, Lic. Carlos Torres Manzo.
Agriculture and Livestock, Manuel Bernardo Aguirre.
Communications and Transport. Ing. Eugenio Méndez Docurro.
Public Works, Ing. Luis Enriquez Bracamontes.
Hydraulic Resources, Ing. Leandro Rovirosa Wade.
Education, Ing. Victor Bravo Ahuja.
Labour and Social Affairs, Lic. Rafael Hernández Ochoa.
Secretariat of the Presidency, Lic. Hugo Cervantes del Río.
Agrarian Affairs, Lic. Augusto Gómez Villanueva.
Federal District, Lic. Octavio Senties Gomez.
Health and Public Welfare, Dr. Jorge Jiménez Cantu.
Attorney-General, Lic. Julio Sánchez Vargas.
Tourism, Adolfo de la Huerta.

MEXICAN EMBASSY IN LONDON
48 Belgrave Square, S.W.1
[01-235-6393]

Ambassador Extraordinary and Plenipotentiary, His Excellency Vicente Sanchez Gavito (1970).
Naval Attaché, Vice-Adm. Diego Múgica-Naranjo.
Counsellor (Cultural Affairs), Señor Lic. Don Hugo Gutiérrez Vega.
Counsellor, Señora doña Francisca Celis-Campes (*Information*).
1st Secretary, Señor Don Luis Wybo Alfaro (*Consular Affairs*).
Attachés, Señor Lic. Don Román Millán Morales (*Commercial*); Señor Gustavo Luders de Negri.

Area and Population.—Mexico occupies the southern part of the continent of North America, with an extensive seaboard to both the Atlantic and Pacific Oceans, extending from 14° 33' to 32° 43' N. lat. and 86° 46' to 117° 08' W. long., and comprising one of the most varied zones in the world. It contains 29 states, 2 territories, and the federal district of Mexico, making in all 32 political divisions, covering an area of 758,000 square miles. At the Mexican General Census taken on Jan. 28, 1970, the total population was 48,313,000.

The two great ranges of North America, the Sierra Nevada and Rocky Mountains, are prolonged from the north to a convergence towards the narrowing Isthmus of Tehuantepec, their course being parallel with the west and east coasts. The surface of the interior consists of an elevated plateau between the two ranges, with steep slopes both to the Pacific and Atlantic (Gulf of Mexico). In the west is the Peninsula of Lower California, with a mountainous surface, separated from the mainland by the Gulf of Lower California. The Sierra Nevada, known in Mexico as the *Sierra Madre*, terminates in a transverse series of volcanic peaks, from Colima on the west to Citlaltepetl

("El Pico de Orizaba") on the east. The low-lying lands of the coasts form the *Tierra Caliente*, or tropical regions (below 3,000 ft), the higher levels form the *Tierra Templada*, or temperate region (from 3,000 to 6,000 ft.), and the summit of the plateau with its peaks is known as *Tierra Fria*, or cold region (above 6,000 ft.). The only considerable rivers are the *Río Grande del Norte* which forms part of the northern boundary, and is navigable for about 70 miles from its mouth in the Gulf of Mexico, and the *Río Grande de Santiago*, the *Río Balsas* and *Río Papaloapan*. The remaining streams are governed by the formation of the land, and run in mountain torrents between deep-cut cañons or "barrancas". The largest fresh-water lakes are *Chapala* (70 miles long and 20 miles wide), and *Pátzcuaro*. In the north-west are saline lakes amid bare and dry regions. The climate varies according to the altitude, the rainy season lasting from June to October.

History and Archæology.—The present Mexico and Guatemala were once the centre of a remarkable indigenous civilization, which had unknown beginnings in the centuries before Christ, flowered in the periods from A.D. 500 to 1100 and A.D. 1300 to 1500 and collapsed before the little army of Spanish adventurers under Hernán Cortés in the years following 1519. Pre-Columbian Mexico was divided between different but connected Indian cultures, each of which has left distinctive archæological remains: the best-known of these are Chichén Itzá, Uxmal, Bonampak and Palenque, in Yucatan and Chiapas (Maya); Teotihuacán, renowned for the Pyramid of the Sun (216 feet high) in the Valley of Mexico (Teotihuacáno); Monte Albán and Mitla, near Oaxaca (Zapotec); El Tajín in the State of Vera Cruz (Totonac); and Tula in the State of Hidalgo (Toltec). The last and most famous Indian culture of all, the Aztec, based on Tenochtitlán, suffered more than the others from the Spaniards and only very few Aztec monuments remain.

A few years after the Conquest, the Spaniards built Mexico City on the ruins of Tenochtitlán, and appointed a Viceroy to rule their new dominions, which they called New Spain. The country was largely converted to Christianity, and a distinctive colonial civilization, representing a marriage of Indian and Spanish traditions, developed and flourished, notably in architecture and sculpture. In 1810 a revolt began against Spanish rule. This was finally successful in 1821, when a precarious independence was proclaimed. Friction with the United States in Texas led to the war of 1845–48, at the end of which Mexico was forced to cede the northern provinces of Texas, California

and New Mexico. In 1862 Mexican insolvency led to invasion by French forces which installed Archduke Maximilian of Austria as Emperor. The empire collapsed with the execution of the Emperor in 1867 and the austere reformer, Juárez, restored the republic. Juárez's death was followed by the dictatorship of Porfirio Díaz, which saw an enormous increase of foreign, particularly British and United States, investment in the country. In 1910 began the Mexican Revolution which reformed the social structure and the land system, curbed the power of foreign companies and ushered in the independent industrial Mexico of today.

Government.—Under the Constitution of Feb. 5, 1917 (as subsequently amended), Congress consists of a Senate of 60 members, elected for six years, and of a Chamber of Deputies, at present numbering 213, elected for three years. Presidents, who wield full executive powers, are elected for six years; they cannot be re-elected.

There are four political parties registered in Mexico, of which by far the largest and most influential is the *Partido Revolucionario Institucional* (P.R.I.) which has for many years constituted the government party.

Communications.—Veracruz, Tampico and Coatzacoalcos are the chief ports on the Atlantic, and Guaymas, Mazatlán, Acapulco and Salina Cruz on the Pacific. The total tonnage of registered merchant marine at the end of 1969 was 650,000 tons. There were 24,119 kilometres of railway track open in Mexico in 1968. Work is proceeding on the reorganization, rehabilitation and re-equipment of the whole system; help in this has been forthcoming from the World Bank, the Export-Import Bank and private sources in the United States. The railways were completely nationalized in 1970.

The total length of road at the end of 1969 was 75,331 kilometres, of which 40,523 kilometres were paved, 23,934 dressed and 10,874 gravelled. Mexico City may be reached by at least three excellent roads from the United States, and work is complete on roads southward from Mexico City to Yucatán and the Guatemalan border.

At the end of 1969 the national telegraph system's lines were 200,000 kilometres in length. International telegraph services to the United States frontier are provided by the Government-owned Mexican Telegraph Company and then through the United States to Canada and Europe. Telephone communications are similar, with over 3,000,000 km. of long distance lines.

There is a good national and international network of air services. There are 1,202 airports and landing fields in Mexico. 24 airfields are equipped to receive turbojets and 26 to receive medium sized aircraft. There are 77 Mexican airlines including two trunk lines *Aeronaves de Mexico S.A.* and *Mexicana de Aviacion S.A.* which both have turbojets.

Production.—The total area of arable land is estimated at 24,000,000 hectares, of which an increasing amount is under cultivation. The principal agricultural crops are maize, beans, wheat, sugar cane, coffee, cotton, tomatoes, chili, tobacco, rice, chick-peas, groundnuts, sesame, alfalfa, vanilla, cocoa and many kinds of fruit, both tropical and temperate. The maguey, or Mexican cactus yields several fermented drinks, mezcal and tequila (distilled) and pulque (undistilled). Another species of the same plant supplies sisal-hemp (henequen). The forests abound in mahogany, rosewood, ebony and chicle trees.

The principal industries (apart from agriculture) are mining and petroleum, but during recent years there has been very considerable expansion of both light and heavy industries, over 80 per cent. of

all consumer goods now being made in Mexico. Most of the remaining 20 per cent. is in fact made up of bulk imports of industrial equipment and motor vehicles for assembly, so that the true figure for local manufacture of consumer goods is nearer to 95 per cent. The steel industry has expanded rapidly and produced 3,420,000 tons of steel in 1969. The mineral wealth is great, but in recent years the low world market prices have caused a slump in the mining industry. The principal minerals are gold, silver, copper, lead, zinc, quicksilver, iron and sulphur. Substantial reserves of uranium have been found. Production in 1969 amounted to: gold, 5,614 kilograms; silver, 1,334 tons; copper, 66,167 tons; lead, 170,894 tons.

The total petroleum reserves were said to be 5,574 m. U.S. barrels in 1969. Total production of petroleum and natural gasoline reached 150,626,000 barrels and 17,218 million cubic metres respectively in 1969.

Woollen and cotton spinning and weaving, the making of footwear and clothing and of domestic appliances of all kinds have made such progress in recent years that all these industries are protected by high import duties and import licence restrictions.

An indication of the rapid industrial expansion of Mexico is that output of electricity increased from 4,423 million kWh in 1950 to 25,758 million kWh in 1969.

Defence.—The regular army has a strength of 52 infantry battalions, one infantry brigade and a Presidential Guard of three battalions, 20 cavalry regiments, a parachute battalion and a small number of artillery and engineer units. There is also a conscript army of about 250,000 men organized into National Service divisions, each 6,000–7,000 strong. The Navy has some 50 ships of all kinds and the Air Force some 200 aircraft.

Language and Literature.—Spanish is the official language of Mexico and is spoken by about 95 per cent. of the population. About 1,005,000 inhabitants speak Indian languages only (about 0·3 per cent.) and of those about 30 per cent. speak Nahuatl, 9 per cent. Maya, 8 per cent. Zapotec, 7 per cent. Otomi and 10 per cent. Mixtec, the remainder speaking other varieties of the minor linguistic families. The National Library in the capital contains about 600,000 volumes. The Press of Mexico is in a flourishing condition with many daily newspapers in the capital and in other urban centres. The first printing press and the first regularly issued newspaper in the New World were established by the Spaniards in Mexico City.

Education.—Education is divided into primary, secondary and university. Primary education is free, secular and nominally compulsory. In 1970 there were 47,756 primary schools with 9,387,000 pupils, 3,403 secondary schools with 1,024,237 pupils. Other schools (preparatory, vocational, normal (for teachers), technical and commercial) numbered 1,985, with 478,350 students. The National University of Mexico (1533) had 100,000 students in 1970. There were 323 professional schools including universities, with 194,090 students. The prevailing religion is Roman Catholic. In 1965, 21 per cent. of the population above 6 years old were illiterate; while progress in reducing illiteracy has been steady over the last few years, it has barely kept pace with the rapidly increasing population. Between 1964 and 1970 the number of schools increased by 22 per cent. and the number of pupils by 43 per cent.

FINANCE (*Pesos*)

Budget expenditure in 1970 rose to 72,229·3 million *pesos*, 9·4 per cent. over 1969. The direct expenditure of the Federal Government amounted to 28,133·8 million *pesos*, while that of the decentralized agencies amounted to 44,095·4 million *pesos*. The proposed budget expenditure for 1971 amounts to 79,656,·2 million *pesos*, 30,762,800,000 from the Federal Government and 48,893,400 from the decentralized agencies. 51·7 per cent is to be spent on economic growth, 32·7 per cent. on investment and social welfare, 10·0 per cent. on public debt and the remainder on administration and military expenses.

As from April 19, 1954, by agreement with the International Monetary Fund, the Rate of Exchange has been fixed at 12·50 *pesos*=1 $U.S. (*See also* p. 84.)

TRADE   1969

Total Imports	Pesos 29,975,000,000
Total Exports	„ 17,311,876,000

Trade with U.K.

	1969	1970
Imports from U.K.	£29,170,000	£34,170,000
Exports to U.K.	14,525,000	6,343,000

The imports (mainly from U.S.A.) consist largely of machinery and implements for industry, mining and agriculture, and raw materials for industry. Principal exports are cotton, coffee, sisal (henequen), sugar, tomatoes and shrimps, lead, silver, zinc and other metals, tobacco, sulphur and heavy fuel oil.

CAPITAL.—Mexico City, population (estimated 1970) 8,000,000. Other towns (with estimated populations) are: Guadalajara (1,500,000); Monterrey (1,200,000); Ciudad Juarez (522,000); Mexicali (440,000); Puebla (390,000); Léon (347,000); Chihuahua (347,000); Ψ Merida (240,900) and San Luis Potosi (190,000).

FLAG.—Three vertical bands, green, white, red, with shield of Mexico in centre. NATIONAL DAY.—September 16 (Proclamation of Independence).

BRITISH EMBASSY

(Calle del Río Lerma 71, Colonia Cuauhtémoc, Mexico 5, D.F.)

Ambassador Extraordinary and Plenipotentiary, His Excellency Charles Peter Hope, C.M.G., T.D. (1967) £6,695

Counsellor, D. I. Dunneff, C.M.G., O.B.E.

Defence, Naval, Military and Air Attaché, Lt.-Col. G. R. D. Kennedy.

1st Secretaries, J. L. Y. Sanders (*Head of Chancery*); F. S. E. Trew (*Information*); C. N. Horton (*Cultural*); A. White (*Commercial*).

2nd Secretaries, E. F. Barrett (*Consul*); R. H. G. Davies (*Information*); W. G. Doherty.

Attachés, L. R. Elborn (*Cultural*); J. O'Brien (*Administration*).

Vice-Consul, A. D. Morales.

There are British Consular Offices at *Mexico City, Guadalajara, Acapulco, Mazatlán, Mérida, Monterrey, Pachuca, Tampico, Tapachula* and *Veracruz*.

British Council Representative.—R. A. C. du Vivier, M.B.E., Calle M. Antonio Caso 127, Mexico 4, D. F. The Council supplies books to the *Instituto Anglo-Mexicano de Cultura* in Mexico City.

BRITISH CHAMBER OF COMMERCE, Calle Tiber 103, 6th Floor, Mexico, D.F.—*Manager*, T. A. Blench.

Transit from London to Mexico City:—By air, 13 hours; By sea, U.K.–New York, 5 to 10 days; New York–Mexico City, by rail, 3 days; by air, 6 hours. There is a direct freight service from Liverpool to ports on both the Mexican Gulf and the Pacific Coast.

MONACO
(Principauté de Monaco)
Sovereign Prince, H.S.H. Rainier III-Louis-Henri-Maxence Bertrand, *born* May 31, 1923, *succeeded his grandfather* (H.S.H. Prince Louis II), May 9, 1949; *married* April 19, 1956, Miss Grace Patricia Kelly and has issue Prince Albert Alexandre Louis Pierre, *born* March 14, 1958, Princess Caroline Louise Marguerite, *born* January 23, 1957; and Princess Stephanie Marie Elisabeth, *born* Feb. 1, 1965.

President of the Crown Council, M. Pierre Blanchy.
President of the National Council, M. Auguste Medecin.

President of the Council of Government, M. Francois-Didier Gregh (*Minister of State*), *appointed* 1969.

CONSULATE-GENERAL IN LONDON
4 Audley Square, W.1.
[01–629–0734]
Consul-General, I. S. Ivanović.
Consul, A. J. Hucker, 3 Gray's Inn Square, W.C.1 [01–242–5323].

A small Principality on the Mediterranean, with land frontiers joining France at every point, and consisting of the old town of Monaco, La Condamine, and Monte Carlo, where is the famous casino. The Principality comprises a narrow strip of country about 2 miles long and half-a-mile broad (area approx. 360 acres), with (1970) 24,000 inhabitants and a yearly average of over 650,000 visitors. The whole available ground is built over, so that there is no cultivation, though there are many public and private gardens. Monaco has a small harbour (20 ft. alongside quay) and the import duties are the same as in France. The National Council consists of 18 members and the Council of Government of the Minister of State and three State Counsellors. There is a local police force of 160 men.

A new constitution was promulgated by Prince Rainier on Dec. 17, 1962, which is subject to modification only with the approval of the elected National Council. It maintains the traditional hereditary monarchy and gives guarantees for the right of association, trade union freedom and the right to strike.

CAPITAL.—Monaco-ville (2,422).
FLAG.—Red and white

British Consul-General, D. G. Crichton, M.V.O. (*Resident at Nice*).

(OUTER) MONGOLIA
(Mongolian People's Republic— Bugd Nairamdakh Mongol Ard Uls)
Prime Minister, Yu Tsedenbal (May, 1952).

Mongolian People's Revolutionary Party
(= Communist)
Politbureau of the Central Committee, Ts. Dugersuren; S. Luvsan; D. Maidar; D. Molomzhants; Zh Sambu; Yu. Tsendenbal; N. Zhagvaral (*full members*); B. Lkhamsuren; N. Luvsanravdan (*alternate members*).
Secretariat of the Central Committee, Yu. Tsedenbal (*1st*); Ts. Dugersuren; B. Lkhamsuren; D. Molomzhants; N. Zhagvaral.

MONGOLIAN EMBASSY
7 Kensington Court, W.8.
[01–937–0150]
Ambassador Extraordinary and Plenipotentiary, His Excellency Sonomdorjiin Dambadarjaa (1969).
1st Secretary, Sh. Hashid.
Attaché, Dambin Myagmar.

Area and Population.—The Mongolian People's Republic (Outer Mongolia) is a large and sparsely populated country to the North of China. Its area is over 600,000 square miles. Its population, (U.N. estimate, 1969) is about 1,240,000. However, this total constitutes only part of the Mongolians of Asia, the greater number of whom are to be found in China and in the neighbouring regions of the Soviet Union (especially the Mongolian Buryat Autonomous Region). This country, which is almost nowhere below 1,000 feet above sea level, forms part of the Central Asiatic Plateau and rises towards the west in the high mountains of the Mongolian Altai and Khanggai Ranges. The Khentai Mountain Range, situated to the northeast of the capital Ulan Bator, is less high. The Gobi region covers the southern half of the country. It contains some sand deserts, but between these less hospitable areas there is steppe land which provides pasture for great numbers of cattle, sheep, goats, camels and horses (the latter is still the characteristic means of transport for the population). There are several long rivers and many lakes, but good water is scarce since much of the water is salty. The climate is hard, with a short mild summer giving way to a long winter when temperatures can drop as low as minus 50° Centigrade.

History.—Mongolia, under Genghis Khan the conqueror of China and much of Asia, was for many years a buffer state between Tsarist Russia and China, although it was under general Chinese suzerainty. The outbreak of the Chinese Revolution in 1911 was the signal for a declaration of independence which was confirmed by the Sino-Russian Treaty of Kiakhta (1915), but cancelled by a unilateral Chinese declaration in 1919. Later the country became a battleground of the Russian Civil War, and Soviet and Mongolian troops occupied Ulan Bator in 1921: this was followed by another declaration of independence. However, in 1924 the Soviet Union in a Treaty with China again recognized the latter's sovereignty over Mongolia: but this was never properly exercised because of China's pre-occupation with internal affairs, and later by the anti-Japanese war. The Mongolian People's Republic was formally established in 1924. Under the Yalta Agreement, Chiang Kai-shek agreed to a plebiscite, held in 1945, in which the Mongolians declared their desire for independence; this was granted. The country entered the United Nations in 1961. The heroes of Mongolian history during the earlier part of the century were Sukhebator, who died in 1923, and the Communist Choibalsang (died 1952), who did much to turn the country into the Communist state it is today, and carried out a systematic destruction of the power of the Lamas and the old princely houses which had previously been the dominant force in both the economy and the government.

Production, etc.—The total of Mongolia's livestock was estimated at about 21,000,000 in 1971. There had been severe losses from the herds during the 1968–69 winter. Traditionally the Mongolian is a herdsman, tending his flock of sheep, goats and horses, cows and camels and leading a totally nomadic life. With the coming of the Communist régime (under the Mongolian People's Revolutionary Party) and especially since 1952, great efforts have been made to settle the population, but 80 per cent. or more still live nomadically or semi-nomadically in the traditional *yurt* (circular tent). The pastoral population was collectivized at the end of the 1950's into huge *negdels* (co-operatives) which have hastened the process of settlement, but within a *negdel* or state farm the herdsmen and their families still move with their *yurts* from pasture to pasture as the seasons change. The country, except for the capital, is today divided into 18 *aimaks* (provinces) and beneath these into more than 300 *somons*

(counties), and these form the basis of the State organization of the country, parallel with which runs the apparatus of the Revolutionary Party.

Membership of the Communist bloc has brought Mongolia considerable quantities of aid from other Socialist countries, especially the Soviet Union and China, the last of which has supplied many thousands of workers to help with various construction projects. Mongolia's support of the Soviet Union in the Sino-Soviet dispute resulted in the cessation of Chinese aid and a halt in the supply of Chinese workers. Mongolia is now relying much less on Chinese and more on eastern European, especially Czech, Polish and East German aid to supplement the massive assistance received from the Soviet Union. Soviet and Bloc aid is hastening the process of industrialization; for although the economy remains based on the herds of animals, and the principal exports of the country are still animal by-products (especially wool, hides and furs) and cattle, factories serving the needs of the country have been started up and the coal and electricity industries are being developed to provide an industrial base.

Ulan Bator, which contains a quarter of the country's population, is the main seat of industry. Under the third 5-year plan, a new industrial centre was founded at Darkhan, north of the capital near the Soviet frontier. This was being continued in the fourth 5-year plan (1966–70), and a start has been made with the development of Choibalsan in the east as a third industrial town (mostly for the processing of animal and agricultural products). There are mineral resources which are beginning to be exploited. Agriculture, formerly little practised, is now being extended. Communication is still difficult in the country as there are virtually no roads. The trans-Mongolian railway, following the line of the old north–south trade route, was opened in 1955 and links Mongolia with both China and Russia. Mongolia's fundamental difficulty is its very small population and labour force.

Foreign trade is dominated by the Soviet Union, with the eastern European countries taking most of what is left. The Government hopes to build up some trade with western countries, but this is developing very slowly.

CAPITAL.—Ulan Bator (195,300).

FLAG.—Vertical tri-colour red, blue, red and in the hoist the traditional Soyombo symbol in gold.

NATIONAL DAY.—July 11 (Anniversary of the Mongolian People's Republic).

BRITISH EMBASSY
Ulan Bator

Ambassador Extraordinary and Plenipotentiary, His Excellency John Horace Ragnar Colvin, C.M.G. (1971).................................£4,575
3rd Secretary, P. Shaw.
Attaché, W. B. Sylvester.

MOROCCO
(Kingdom of Morocco)

King, H.M. King Hassan II, *born* July 9, 1929; *acceded* February 26, 1961, *on the death of his father,* King Mohammad V. *Heir,* Crown Prince Sidi Muhammad, *b.* 1963.

CABINET
(August, 1971)

Prime Minister, in charge of Economic Affairs, Mohamed Karim Lamrani.
Minister of Justice and General Secretary of the Government, Hadj M'Hamed Bahnini.
Defence and Major-General of the Royal Armed Forces, General Mohamed Oufkir.
Interior, Ahmed Benbouchta.
Foreign Affairs, Dr. Abdellatif Filali.

Secondary, Technical and Further Education, Ahmed Laski.
Primary Education, Haddou Echiguer.
Posts, Telegraph and Telephone, General Driss Benomar Alami.
Habbous and Islamic Affairs, Hadj Ahmed Bargach.
Agriculture and Promotion Nationale, Maati Jorio.
Public Works and Transport, Mohamed Bernoussi.
Public Health, Abdelmajid Belmahi.
Public Administration, Ahmed Majid Benjelloun.
Information, Abdelkader Sahraoui.
Youth, Sports, Employment and Social Affairs, Arsalan Jadidi.
Under Secretaries of State:—
  Secondary Technical and Further Education, Mohamed Chafik.
  Finance, Mohamed M'Daghri.
  Commerce and Industry, Abdelaziz Benjelloun.
  Tourism, Abdelmalek Reghai.
  (There are also five Under Secretaries of State.)

ROYAL MOROCCAN EMBASSY AND CONSULATE
49 Queen's Gate Gardens, S.W.7
[01–584–8827]

Ambassador (vacant).
Minister-Counsellor (*Chargé d'Affaires*), M. Aissa Benchekroun.
1st Secretary, M. Mustapha Mzabi (*Consular and Cultural Affairs*).
Military, Naval and Air Attaché, Cdt. Mustapha Jabrane.
Attachés, Rashid Bouzid; Abdel 'Illah Marcil; Mohamed Fenzar (*Commercial*).

Area and Population.—Morocco is situated in the north-western corner of the African continent between latitude 27°40′–36° N. and longitude 2°–11° W. with an area estimated at approximately, 180,000 sq. miles, and a population (U.N. estimate, 1970) of 15,525,000. It is traversed in the north by the Riff Mountains and in a general S.W. to N.E. direction, by the Middle Atlas, the High Atlas, the Anti-Atlas and the Sarrho ranges. The northern flanks of the Middle and High Atlas Mountains are well wooded but their southern slopes, exposed to the dry desert winds, are generally arid and desolate, as are the whole of the Anti-Atlas and Sarrho ranges. The north-westerly point of Morocco is the peninsula of Tangier which is separated from the continent of Europe by the narrow strait of Gibraltar. The Jebel Mousa dominates the promontory and, with the rocky eminence of Gibraltar, was known to the ancients as the *Pillars of Hercules,* the western gateway of the Mediterranean.

Climate.—The climate of Morocco is generally good and healthy, especially on the Atlantic coast, (where a high degree of humidity is, however, prevalent) the country being partially sheltered by the Atlas mountains from the hot winds of the Sahara. The rainy season may last from November to April. The plains of the interior are intensely hot in summer. Average summer and winter temperatures for Rabat are 81° F. and 45° F.; for Marrakesh 101° F. and 40° F. respectively.

Government.—Morocco became an independent sovereign state in 1956, following joint declarations made with France on March 2, 1956, and with Spain on April 7, 1956. The Sultan of Morocco, Sidi Mohammed ben Youssef, adopted the title of King Mohammed V.

A constitution, adopted by referendum on December 7, 1962, was in force from December 14, 1962, until June 7, 1965.

Following serious disturbances in Casablanca in March, 1965, attempts were made by King Hassan, in consultation with all political parties, to form a government of national union. These efforts were unsuccessful and on June 7, 1965, the King proclaimed a " state of exception " and suspended Parliament. Assuming himself the office of Prime Minister, he announced the formation of a new government and indicated that constitutional changes were to follow. A revised Constitution was approved by a national referendum on July 24, 1970. It provides that not only political parties, but trade unions, chambers of commerce and professional bodies will participate in the organization of the State and representation of the people; specifies that the King is the supreme representative of the people; makes changes in the composition of the Regency Council and the Sovereign's rights; establishes a unicameral legislature in which members' tenure of office is six years. The new Chamber is to have 240 members, 90 elected by direct universal suffrage and 50 members elected by electoral colleges representing local government, industry, agriculture and working class groups.

Defence.—The Moroccan army, formed in 1956, is about 50,000 strong. A Moroccan air force was also formed in 1959 and a navy in 1960. The armed forces possess quantities of French, Soviet and American equipment, including aircraft.

Production and Trade.—Morocco's main sources of wealth are agricultural and mineral. The current Five Year Plan (1968–72) for economic development places particular emphasis on agricultural development. Other priority sectors are education and training and tourism.

Agriculture employs some 70 per cent. of the working population and accounts for about 45 per cent. of Morocco's exports. The main agricultural products are cereals, citrus fruits, olives, grapes, tomatoes and vegetables. Dates and figs are also grown and exported. Cork is the most important commercial forest product. Esparto grass is also produced. There is a fishing industry and substantial quantities of canned fish, mainly sardines, are exported. Livestock in 1967 included about 11,000,000 sheep, 6,500,000 goats, 2,900,000 horned cattle and smaller numbers of donkeys, camels, horses and pigs.

Morocco's mineral exports are phosphates, anthracite, manganese, iron ore, lead and zinc, while the following are also produced: petroleum, cobalt, graphite, copper, molybdenum, tin, antimony, ochre and gypsum. Production of phosphates totalled 11,294,000 tons in 1969. There are oil refineries at Mohammedia and Sidi Kacem, total output of which in 1969 was 1,469,616 tons. Production of crude oil in 1969 amounted to 58,560 tons.

Morocco's main import requirements are petroleum products, motor vehicles and tyres, building materials, fabrics, agricultural and other machinery, chemical products, clothing, household-ware, sugar, green tea and other foodstuffs.

The trade of Morocco, which is chiefly with France and the *franc* area, the U.S.A., Germany, the United Kingdom and Italy, was valued in 1969 at Imports, DH 2,884,421,000; Exports, DH 2,278,049,000.

Trade with U.K.

	1969	1970
Imports from U.K.	£12,617,000	£12,609,000
Exports to U.K.	15,690,000	16,250,000

There is a British Chamber of Commerce at Casablanca (c/o B.B.M.E., 80 Avenue Lalla Yacout).

Finance and Currency.—The unit of currency is the *dirham.* Exchange rate (*see* p. 84).

The 1970 Ordinary Budget amounted to DH 2,608,680,000, and the Development Budget to DH1,132,860,000.

Communications.—The railway runs south from Tangier to Sidi Kacem. From this junction, one line runs eastwards through Fez and Oujda to Algeria, and another continues southwards, through Rabat and Casablanca, to Marrakesh. A line running due south from Oujda skirts the Morocco-Algeria frontier and reaches Colomb-Bechar in Algeria, the beginning of the Mediterranean–Niger project. Moroccan railroads cover 1,250 miles and traction is electric or diesel. An extensive network of well-surfaced roads covers all the main towns in the kingdom.

Tangier is distant from London about 1,200 miles or a matter of hours by air, 4 days by sea. Royal-Air-Maroc operates services between Casablanca and London. There are air services between Tangier and Gibraltar connecting with B.E.A. services to London. Air France and Royal-Air-Maroc operate internal services and many between Morocco and towns in France and Spain. There are also regular services to other European and North African countries and to Senegal and the Canaries.

Language.—Arabic is the official language. Berber is the vernacular mainly in the mountain regions. French and Spanish are also spoken, mainly in the towns. The foreign population is estimated at 170,000 (1969). The national daily press consists of 3 Arabic, 4 French and one Spanish newspapers.

Education.—There are government primary, secondary and technical schools. At Fez there is a theological university of great repute in the Moslem world. There is a secular university at Rabat. Schools for special denominations, Jewish and Catholic, are permitted and may receive government grants.

CAPITAL.— Ψ Rabat (population 469,000). On Jan. 2, 1962, it was decreed that Tangier (166,000) would be the summer capital of Morocco, the King and the Government residing there for two months each year from 1962. Tangier was on the same date declared a " free zone " primarily for commercial purposes. The other chief towns are (1969): Ψ Casablanca (1,363,000); Marrakesh (264,300); Fez (1,048,000); Meknès (769,000); Oujda (149,300); Tetuan (117,000). Ψ Kenitra (99,380). The towns of Fez, Marrakesh and Meknes were capitals at various times in Morocco's history.

FLAG.—Red, with green pentagram (the Seal of Solomon). NATIONAL DAY.—March 3 (Anniversary of the Throne).

Ambassador Extraordinary and Plenipotentiary, His
Excellency Thomas Richard Shaw, C.M.G. (1969)
£6,925

BRITISH CONSULAR OFFICES
There are British Consular Offices at *Tangier, Fez*
and *Casablanca* and an Honorary Consul at *Larache.*

British Council Representative, W. E. M. Kensdale,
P.O. Box 427, 6 Avenue Moulay Youssef, Rabat
(Library).

NEJD. *See* Saudi Arabia

NEPAL

Sovereign, King Mahendra Bir Bikram Shah Deva,
born 1920, *succeeded* March 13, 1955.

COUNCIL OF MINISTERS
*Prime Minister and Minister for Palace Affairs, Finance,
Defence and General Administration,* Kirtinidhi
Bista.
Minister for Foreign Affairs and Health, Gehendra
Bahadur Rajbhandari.
*Forest, Industry, Commerce, Power and Water Re-
sources,* Nava Raj Subedi.
Home, Panchayat, Information and Broadcasting, Rudra
Prasad Giri.
Education, Land Reform, Food and Agriculture,
Gyanendra Bahadur Karki.
Public Works, Transport and Communications,
Chaturbhuj Prasad Singh.
Law and Justice, Sambhu Prasad Gyawali.
There are also three State Ministers and four
Assistant Ministers.

ROYAL NEPALESE EMBASSY IN LONDON
12A, Kensington Palace Gardens, W.8.
[01–229–6231]
Ambassador Extraordinary and Plenipotentiary, His
Excellency Upendra Bahadur Basnyat (1969).
1st Secretary, Ishwari Raj Pandey.
Military Attaché, Lt.-Col. N. C. Malla.
Attaché, M. P. Sharma.

Nepal lies between India and Tibet on the slopes
of the Himalayas, and includes Mt. Everest (29,028
ft.). It has a total area of 54,362 sq. miles and a
population (estimated, 1969) of 10,845,000. Amid
the mountains lie many fertile valleys. The lower
hills and Terai Plains are covered with jungle, in
which wild animals abound. Rice, wheat, maize,
etc., are grown. (*For* MAP, *see* p. 746.) Katmandu,
the capital, is connected with India by a road,
the mountain section of which was built by India
under the Colombo Plan, and to Tibet by a road
from Katmandu to Kodari on the border, which
was built by the Chinese and opened on May 26,
1967. The Indian-aided Sunauli Pokhara road
(128 miles) was expected to be completed in 1972
and construction by the Chinese of a road between
Katmandu and Pokhara has been started. The
East–West Highway (*Mahendra Raj Marg*) to run
the length of the country, is now under construction
in the following sections: Jhapa to Janakpur (173
miles) by Indian aid team; Janakpur–Simra (73
miles) by Russian aid team; Narayanghat–Butwal
(75 miles) by British aid team.

Nepal exports rice and other grains, hides, oilseeds, *ghi*, cattle, jute, large quantities of timber,
etc., and imports cotton goods and yarn, sugar,
salt, spices, petrol, metals, etc. Nepalese imports
from U.K. were valued at £1,767,000 in 1970
(1969, £526,000); exports to U.K., £857,000
(1969, £702,000).

Finance.—Revenue for the fiscal year 1970–71,
mainly from land rent and taxes, was estimated at
N.Rs.494,940,000, compared with a revised figure
of N.Rs 435,890,000 in 1969–70. A State Bank was
inaugurated on April 26, 1956, to issue bank notes,
regulate the Nepalese currency, fix foreign exchange
rates and help in the preparation of a national
budget. The exchange rate is N.Rs.24·20 = £1.
There are 3 commercial banks with branches
throughout Nepal.

The inhabitants are of mixed stock with Mongolian characteristics prevailing in the north and Indian
in the south, and their religions are Hinduism and
Buddhism. They were originally divided into
numerous hill clans and petty principalities, one
of which, Gorkha, whose ruler founded the present
Nepalese dynasty, became predominant in 1768.
During the 1914–18 and the 1939–45 wars, the
Nepalese Government rendered unstinted and unconditional assistance to the British Government.

From the middle of the nineteenth century,
Nepal was ruled by the Rana family which provided the hereditary prime ministers of the country.
After the Second World War, a revolutionary
movement in 1950 and 1951 achieved the aim of
breaking the hereditary power of the Ranas and of
restoring to the monarchy the powers which it had
lost 104 years before. After ten years, during
which various parties and individuals tried their
hand at government, King Mahendra resumed
direct powers on December 16, 1960, with the
object of leading a united country to basic democracy.

The state of emergency ended on April 13,
1963, the King appointing a Cabinet consisting of
a Prime Minister and seven other ministers, all of
whom have seats in the indirectly elected
Rashtriya Panchayat (Parliament). A State Council
(*Raj Sabha*) of 69 members, to advise the King on
state affairs, constitutional matters and on the choice
of the heir to the throne was also appointed on
April 2, 1963. An Act was passed at the same time
maintaining the existing ban on political parties.

CAPITAL.—Katmandu, population (1961) 224,867.
Other towns of importance are Biratnagar (325,645).
Lalitpur (145,301) and Bhaktapur (89,822). These
population figures include some adjacent rural
areas.

FLAG.—Double pennant of crimson with blue
border on peaks; white moon with rays in centre of
top peak; white quarter sun, recumbent in centre of
bottom peak. NATIONAL DAY.—February 18.

Ambassador Extraordinary and Plenipotentiary, His
Excellency Terence John O'Brien, C.M.G., M.C.
(1970)....................................£6,475
1st Secretaries, W. D. Wilson, O.B.E., M.C. (*Head of
Chancery and Consul*); D. A. Spain (*Information*).
Defence Attaché, Lt.-Col. D. F. Neill, O.B.E., M.C.
2nd Secretary, Miss M. K. Dean.
Vice-Consul, D. A. Dunford.

British Council Representative, R. Arbuthnott, P.O.
Box 640, Kanti Path, Katmandu.
Libraries at *Katmandu, Dharan and Pokhara.*

NETHERLANDS (or HOLLAND)
(Koninkrijk der Nederlanden)
Queen of the Netherlands, Her Majesty JULIANA,
K.G., *born* April 30, 1909; *married* January 7, 1937,
Prince Bernhard of Lippe Biesterfeld, G.C.B.,
G.C.V.O., G.B.E. (THE PRINCE OF THE NETHERLANDS),
born June 29, 1911; *succeeded,* September 4, 1948,
upon the abdication of her mother Queen Wil-
helmina who died Nov. 28, 1962. Issue:
(1) H.R.H. Princess Beatrix Wilhelmina Arm-
gard, G.C.V.O., *born* Jan. 31, 1938; *married*
March 10, 1966, H.R.H. Prince Claus

George Willem Otto Frederik Geert of the Netherlands, Jonkheer van Amsberg; and has issue, Prince Willem Alexander, b. April 27, 1967; Prince Johan Friso, b. Sept. 25, 1968; and Prince Constantijn Christof, b. Oct. 11, 1969.

(2) H.R.H. Princess Irene Emma Elizabeth, born Aug. 5, 1939; married April 29, 1964, Prince Hugo Carlos of Bourbon-Parma and has issue, Prince Carlos, b. Jan. 27, 1970.

(3) H.R.H. Princess Margriet Francisca, born (at Ottawa, Canada), Jan. 19, 1943; married Jan. 10, 1967, Mr. Peter van Vollenhoven; and has issue, Prince Maurits, b. April 17, 1968; and Prince Bernhard, b. Dec. 25, 1969.

(4) H.R.H. Princess Maria Christina, born Feb. 18, 1947.

CABINET

Prime Minister and Minister of General Affairs, B. W. Biesheuvel (*Anti-Revolutionary*).

Vice-Premier and Minister of Finance, R. J. Nelissen (*Catholic*).

Vice-Premier and Minister of Home Affairs, W. J. Geertsema (*Liberal*).

Transport and Waterways, Dr. W. Drees (*Democratic Socialist*).

Foreign Affairs, W. K. N. Schmeltzer (*Catholic*).

Justice, Prof. A. A. M. van Agt (*Catholic*).

Culture, Recreation and Social Welfare, P. J. Engels (*Catholic*).

Social Affairs, J. Boersma (*Anti-Revolutionary*).

Defence, H. J. de Koster (*Liberal*).

Economic Affairs, Prof. H. Langman (*Liberal*).

Development Aid, Dr. C. Boertien (*Anti-Revolutionary*).

Housing and Planning, B. J. Udink (*Christian Historical*).

Education, C. van Veen (*Christian Historical*).

Agriculture and Fisheries, P. J. Lardinois (*Catholic*).

Public Health and Environmental Hygiene, L. B. J. Stuijt (*Catholic*).

Science and Higher Education, Jhr. W. M. de Brauw (*Democratic Socialist*).

NETHERLANDS EMBASSY IN LONDON
38 Hyde Park Gate, S.W.7
[01–584–5040]

Ambassador Extraordinary and Plenipotentiary, His Excellency Baron W. J. G. Gevers, C.V.O. (1971).

Minister Plenipotentiary, Jhr. J. L. R. Huydecoper.

Counsellor, P. A. van Buuren.

1st Secretary, Count L. de Marchant et d'Ansembourg.

2nd Secretaries A. J. A. M. Nooy; Miss A. H. M. Nierman; J. Huisman (*Administration*).

Naval Attaché and Naval Attaché for Air, Capt. F. de Blocq van Kuffeler.

Assistant Naval Attaché and Naval Attaché for Air, Cdr. G. A. M. van Wermeskerken.

Air Attaché, Col. Y. J. Beek.

Military Attaché, Col. C. A. de Regt.

Counsellor (Cultural Affairs), J. H. Braaksma.

Counsellor (Press Affairs), D. J. van Wijnen.

Minister Plenipotentiary (Economic Affairs), P. C. Witte.

Counsellor (Economic), C. H. A. Plug.

2nd Secretaries, J. H. W. Fietelaars; J. W. Jansen.

Civil Air Attaché, Dr. D. Goedhuis.

Agricultural Attaché. W. G. F. van Oosten

Asst. Agricultural Attachés, J. P. Tripplaar; A. van der Struik.

Consular Section.
38 Hyde Park Gate, S.W.7.

Consul-General, A. U. W. van Werven.

1st Secretary (Consular), Jhr. R. de Beaufort, M.V.O.

3rd Secretary, F. Racké.

Area and Population.—The Kingdom of the Netherlands is a maritime country of Western Europe, situated on the North Sea, in lat. 50° 46'– 53° 34' N. and long. 3° 22'–7° 14' E., consisting of 11 provinces plus the North-East Polder and Eastern and Southern Flevaland (reclaimed parts of the Zuider Zee) and containing a total area of 13,500 sq. miles (34,830 sq. km.). The population in Oct. 1970, was estimated at 13,077,000. The live birth rate in 1968 was 18·6 per 1,000 of the population, and the death-rate was 8·2.

The land is generally flat and low, intersected by numerous canals and connecting rivers—in fact, a network of water courses. The principal rivers are the Rhine, Maas, Yssel and Scheldt.

The chief agricultural products are potatoes, sugar beet, cattle, horses, pigs, butter, wheat, rye, barley, oats, beans, peas, flax-seed, cheese, poultry, eggs, vegetables, fruit and flower bulbs and there is an important fishing industry. Among the principal industries are engineering, both mechanical and electrical, electronics, nuclear energy, petro-chemicals and plastics, shipbuilding, steel, textiles of all types, leather goods, electrical appliances, metal ware, furniture, paper, cigars, sugar, liqueurs, beer, clothing, rubber products, etc.

Production of coal (1969) was 5,564,000 metric tons; oil, 2,020,000 metric tons; steel, 4,713,000 metric tons and natural gas, 21,848,000,000 cu. metres. Diamond-cutting, though still an important industry, has declined considerably in importance, employing about 540 hands at the end of 1967.

Government.—In 1815 the Netherlands became a constitutional Kingdom under King William I, a Prince of Orange-Nassau, a descendant of the house which has taken a leading part in the destiny of the nation since the 16th century. The States-General comprise the *Eerste Kamer* (First Chamber) of 75 members, elected for 6 years by the Provincial Diets; and the *Tweede Kamer* (Second Chamber) of 150 members, elected for 4 years by men and women voters of 21 years and upwards. Members of the *Tweede Kamer* are paid.

General elections were held on April 28, 1971 for the Second Chamber of the States-General. Party Representation is: Catholic People's Party,

35; Labour Party, 39; Liberal, 16; Anti-Revolutionary, 13; Christian Historical Union, 10; Democrats 66, 11; Communists, 6; Pacifist Socialists, 2; Farmers Party, 1; Political Reformed, 3; Reformed Political Union, 2; Radicals, 2; Democratic Socialists '70, 8; Retailers Party, 2.

The Upper House of the States General was elected by the Provincial Councils in May, 1971. Party Representation is: Catholic Peoples Party, 22; Labour, 18; Liberal, 8; Anti-Revolutionary, 7; Christian Historical, 7; Pacificist Socialists, 1; Communists, 3; Democrats 66, 6; Radicals, 2; Political reformed, 1.

Defence.—The armed forces are all fully committed to N.A.T.O. The Royal Netherlands Navy consists of a modern balanced anti-submarine force centred on 18 escorts. The Royal Netherlands Army has recently reorganized at all staff levels, with the rôle of the ground forces remaining unchanged in N.A.T.O. The Air Force, which since 1953 has been independent of the Army with the title " Royal Netherlands Air Force ", has been reconstituted since the war, and now forms an integral part of the air defence of N.A.T.O. After a period of reorganization and expansion it has now attained a considerable strength consisting mainly of jet-fighters which are divided between an air defence and a tactical air command. The latter is integrated into the N.A.T.O. tactical air force.

Language and Literature.—Dutch is a West-Germanic language of Saxon origin, closely akin to Old English and Low German. It is spoken in the Netherlands and the northern part of Belgium. It is also used by many people in the Netherlands West Indies. Afrikaans, one of the two South African languages, has Dutch as its origin, but differs from it in grammar and pronunciation. There are ten national papers, four of which are morning papers, and there are many regional daily papers.

Education.—Illiteracy is practically non-existent. Primary and secondary education is given in both denominational and State schools, the denominational schools being eligible for State assistance on equal terms with the State schools. Attendance at primary school is compulsory. Secondary schools are numerous, well equipped and well attended. The principal Universities are at Leiden, Utrecht, Groningen, Amsterdam (2), Nijmegen (R.C.), and there are technical Universities at Delft (polytechnic); Eindhoven (polytechnic), Enschede (polytechnic) and Rotterdam (economics), Wageningen (agriculture), Tilburg (R.C., economics) and a medical faculty in Rotterdam.

Communications.—The total extent of navigable rivers is 6,044 km. and of roads approximately 71,418 km. On January 1, 1967, the total length of the railway system amounted to 3,232 km., of which 1,641 km. were electrified. The mercantile marine on Jan. 1, 1969, consisted of 1,218 ships of total 4,256,000 gross registered tons, excluding tugs and contractors' equipment. The total length of air routes covered by K.L.M. (Royal Dutch Airlines) in the course of 1968 was 253,000 miles.

FINANCE
Estimates, 1971

Current Revenue	*Fl.*29,499,000,000
Current Expenditure	27,684,000,000
Capital Revenue	1,164,000,000
Capital Expenditure	5,041,000,000
Aggregate Budget Revenue	30,663,000,000
„ „ Expenditure	32,725,000,000
Funded Internal Debt, June 30, 1970	22,427,000,000
Internal Floating Debt (June 30, 1970	10,449,000,000
Foreign Debt	97,000,000

The official rate of exchange permits of fluctuation between 8·58 and 8·62 *florins*=£1.
See also p. 83.

TRADE
The Dutch are traditionally a trading nation. *Entrepôt* trade, banking and shipping are of particular importance in their economy. The geographical position of the Netherlands, at the mouths of the Rhine, Meuse and Scheldt, brings a large volume of transit trade to and from the interior of Europe to Dutch ports.

Principal trading partners are the Federal Republic of Germany and Belgium/Luxemburg. Britain supplied 5·8 per cent. of Netherlands imports in 1970 (*Fls.*2,766,112,000) and took 7·6 per cent. of Netherlands exports (*Fls.*2,978,556,000).

In common with other members of the European Economic Community, the Netherlands on July 1, 1968, removed remaining duties on imports from EEC countries and brought down duties on imports from other countries into line with the Common External Tariff of the EEC.

The index of industrial production in the Netherlands (1963=100) rose from 129 in 1967 to 175 in 1970 and the index of industrial production per worker (1963=100) rose from 132 in 1967 to 180 in 1970.

In 1970 Dutch imports amounted to *Fl.*48,482,478,000 and exports to *Fl.*42,594,554,000.

Trade with U.K.

	1969	1970
Imports from U.K.	£278,929,000	£377,767,000
Exports to U.K.	409,140,000	459,102,000

SEAT OF GOVERNMENT, The Hague (Den Haag or, in full, 's-Gravenhage). Pop. (Jan. 1, 1969) 576,160.

PRINCIPAL TOWNS.—ΨAmsterdam, 845,821; ΨRotterdam, 699,245; Utrecht, 276,328; Eindhoven, 187,230; Haarlem, 172,941; Groningen, 167,670; Tilburg, 151,205; Nijmegen, 147,201; Enschede, 136,883; Arnhem, 134,252; Breda, 119,954; Apeldoorn, 120,946; Leiden, 102,534; Hilversum, 100,404.

FLAG.—Three horizontal bands of red, white and blue. NATIONAL DAY.—April 30 (The Queen's Birthday).

BRITISH EMBASSY
(Lange Voorhout, 10, The Hague)

Ambassador Extraordinary and Plenipotentiary, His Excellency Sir Edward (Emile) Tomkins, K.C.M.G., C.V.O. (1970) ... £9,000
Counsellors, R. S. Faber; L. E. M. Taylor (*Commercial*).
Defence and Naval Attaché, Capt. P. J. Shaw, R.N.
Air Attaché, Gp.-Capt. E. S. Chandler, A.F.C.
Military Attaché, Lt.-Col. B. B. Houghton-Berry.
1st Secretaries: Miss J. J. d'A. Collings (*Chancery*); E. Patterson, M.B.E. (*Commercial*); J. D. Blakeway (*Information*); J. S. Vigors (*Labour*); D. Roberts (*Agriculture*); J. M. C. Vivian (*Chancery*).

BRITISH CONSULAR OFFICES
Amsterdam, Herengracht 460.—*Consul-General*, A. H. Hughes, O.B.E.
Rotterdam, Parklaan 18.—*Consul-General*, Miss F. M. Young, O.B.E.
There is an Honorary British Consul at *Curaçao*, Netherlands Antilles.

British Council Representative, N. S. Whitworth, Keizergracht 343, Amsterdam (Library).

OVERSEAS TERRITORIES
The *Netherlands West Indies* comprise *Surinam* (Dutch Guiana) in South America, and certain islands in the West Indies known as the *Netherlands Antilles* (Curaçao, Bonaire, Aruba, part of St. Martin, St. Eustatius and Saba). The area of

Surinam is about 54,000 sq. miles, with a population (U.N. estimate, 1969) of 389,000; area of Netherlands Antilles, 394·1 sq. miles with a population of 220,000 at December 31, 1969. Under the Realm Statute which took effect on December 29, 1954, Surinam and the Netherlands Antilles received autonomy in domestic affairs as parts of the Netherlands Realm under the Crown. Agreement on their new status was reached after prolonged negotiations between the Netherlands Government and representatives of the territories concerned. Bauxite is an important export of Surinam.

Governors
Netherlands Antilles, Dr. B. M. Leito (1970).
Surinam, Dr. J. H. E. Ferrier (1968).

Trade with U.K.

	1969	1970
Netherlands Antilles		
Imports from U.K....	£6,448,000	£8,260,000
Exports to U.K.......	13,062,000	13,137,000
Surinam		
Imports from U.K....	£2,671,000	£3,135,000
Exports to U.K.......	410,000	718,000

The administrative capital of Surinam is Ψ Paramaribo (population, 1962, 120,000); the capital of Curaçao is Ψ Willemstad (pop. 45,000), of Aruba, Ψ Oranjestad; of Bonaire, Ψ Kralendijk; of St. Martin, Philipsburg; of Statius (St. Eustatius), Oranjestad; and of Saba, Bottom.

NICARAGUA
(República de Nicaragua)
President, Gen. Anastasio Somoza Debayle, *assumed office*, May 1, 1967.
Foreign Affairs, Dr. Lorenzo Guerrero.

NICARAGUAN EMBASSY AND CONSULATE GENERAL
8 Gloucester Road, S.W.7
[01–584–3231]
Ambassador Extraordinary and Plenipotentiary, His Excellency Señor Lic. Ricardo Parrales Sánchez.
Counsellor, Señor Don Lorenzo Guerrero-Mora.
1st Secretary, Señor Lic. B. M. Abaúnza.
Commercial Attaché, Señor M. G. Horvilleur.

Area and Population.—Nicaragua is the largest State of Central America, with a long seaboard on both the Atlantic and Pacific Oceans, situated between 9° 45′–15° N. lat. and 83° 40′–87° 38′ W. long., containing an area of 57,145 English square miles (*see* MAP, p. 875). It has a population (U.N. estimate, 1970) of 1,984,000, of whom about threequarters are of mixed blood. Another 15 per cent. are white, mostly of pure Spanish descent, and the remaining 10 per cent. are Indians or negroes. The latter group includes the Mosquitos, who live on the Atlantic coast and were formerly under British protection.

Government.—The eastern coast of Nicaragua was touched by Columbus in 1502, and in 1519 was overrun by Spanish forces under Davila, and formed part of the Spanish Captaincy-General of Guatemala until 1821, when its independence was secured. The present constitution took effect on May 1, 1951. The President is elected by direct suffrage. Congress comprises a Senate of 16 members (together with ex-Presidents of the Republic) and a Chamber of Deputies of 54 members.

Agriculture and Industry.—The country is mainly agricultural. The major crops are cotton, coffee, sugar, sesame and bananas. Beans, rice, maize and ipecacuanha are also important. Livestock and timber production, already considerable, are capable of unlimited expansion. Nicaragua possesses deposits of gold and silver, both of which are mined and exported by United States and Canadian concessionaires.

Communications.—There are 252 miles of railway, all on the Pacific side, 4,218 miles of telegraph and 4,485 miles of telephone lines and 14,943 telephones. There are several powerful wireless stations and two television stations at Managua. An automatic telephone system has been installed in the capital and extended to the provincial towns of León, Granada, Matagalpa and Chinandega. Transport except on the Pacific slope, is still attended with difficulty but many new roads have either been opened or are under construction. The Inter-American Highway runs from the Honduras frontier in the north to the Costa Rican border in the south; the interoceanic highway runs from Corinto on the Pacific coast viâ Managua to Rama, where there is a natural waterway to Bluefields on the Atlantic.

Language and Literature.—The official language of the country is Spanish. In 1969 there were 2 daily newspapers published at Managua, apart from the official Gazette (*La Gaceta*) and 4 in the provinces. Education is backward, about 50 to 60 per cent. of the population being illiterate. There are universities at León and Managua.

Trade with U.K.

	1969	1970
Imports from U.K....	£2,939,000	£2,724,000
Exports to U.K.......	996,000	821,000

Considerable quantities of foodstuffs are imported as well as cotton goods, jute, iron and steel, machinery and petroleum products. The chief exports are cotton, coffee, beef, gold, sugar, cottonseed, bananas, meat, copper and soluble coffee.

CAPITAL, Managua, population (1967), 300,000; León, 62,019; Granada, 40,104; Masaya, 34,158; Chinandega, 36,885; Ψ Bluefields, 17,706; Matagalpa, 61,520; Jinotepe, 15,957. Ψ Corinto (9,650), on the Pacific, is the chief port, handling about 70 per cent. of the total trade; Bluefields and Puerto Cabezas on the E. coast are mainly concerned in the fish, banana and timber trade to the United States.

FLAG.—Three horizontal bands, blue, white, blue (the arms of the Republic on the white band, displaying five volcanoes surmounted by a cap of liberty under a rainbow).

BRITISH EMBASSY
Managua
Ambassador Extraordinary and Plenipotentiary and Consul-General, His Excellency Ivor Francis Sutherland Vincent, C.M.G., M.B.E. (1970). £6,475
1st Secretary, J. K. B. Davenport, M.B.E. (*Head of Chancery and Consul*).

NIGER
(Republic of Niger)
President and Minister for Foreign Affairs, Diori Hamani, G.C.M.G. *elected* for five years, November 9, 1960; *re-elected* Sept. 30, 1965.
President, National Assembly, Boubou Hama.
President, Supreme Court, Diallo Ousmane Bassarou.
Situated in West Central Africa, between 12° and 24° N. and 0° and 16° E., Niger has common boundaries with Algeria and Libya in the north, Chad, Nigeria Dahomey, Mali and Upper Volta.
It has an area of about 484,000 square miles with a population (U.N. estimate, 1970) at 4,016,000. Apart from a small region along the Niger Valley in the south-west near the capital the country is entirely savannah or desert. The main races in Niger are the Haussas in the east, the Djermas in the south-west and the nomadic Touaregs in the north.

The first French expedition arrived in 1891 and the country was fully occupied by 1914. It decided on December 18, 1958, to remain an autonomous republic within the French Community; full independence outside the Community was proclaimed on August 3, 1960. Special agreements with France, covering financial and

cultural matters, technical assistance, defence, etc., were signed in Paris on April 24, 1961.

The constitution of Niger, adopted on November 8, 1960, provides for a presidential system of government, modelled on that of the United States and the French Fifth Republic, and a single Chamber National Assembly. The present Assembly of 50 members was elected on October 21, 1965. Niger is a member of the United Nations, the *Conseil de l'Entente* and of the Organization for African Unity (O.A.U.) (*see* Ivory Coast). The official language is French.

Finance.—The currency of Niger is the *franc CFA* (*Francs CFA* 50=1 *French Franc*). In 1968 the operating budget amounted to *Francs CFA* 9,570,100,000 and the development budget to *Francs CFA* 858,800,000.

Trade.—The cultivation of ground-nuts and the production of livestock are the main industries and provide the two main exports. A company has been formed by the Government, the French Atomic Energy Authority and private interests to exploit uranium deposits. There are indications of other mineral deposits but only tin is being mined at present. Total value of trade in 1968 was: Imports, £16,710,000; Exports, £9,275,000 of which ground-nuts and ground-nut oil accounted for 70 per cent. and livestock 13 per cent.

CAPITAL.—Niamey (60,000).

FLAG.—Three horizontal stripes, orange, white and green with an orange disc in the middle of the white stripe. NATIONAL DAY.—December 18. *British Ambassador*, His Excellency Peter Murray, C.M.G. (*resident at Abidjan*).

NORWAY
(Norge)

King, Olav V, K.G., K.T., G.C.B., G.C.V.O., *b.* July 2, 1903; *succeeded*, Sept. 21, 1957, on death of his father King Haakon VII; *married* March 21, 1929, Princess Märtha of Sweden (*born* March 29, 1901; *died* April 5, 1954); having issue, Harald (*see below*) and two daughters.

Heir-Apparent, H.R.H. Prince Harald, G.C.V.O., *b.* Feb. 21, 1937; *m.* Aug. 29, 1968, Sonja Haraldsen, and has issue Princess Martha Louise, *b.* Sept. 22, 1971.

CABINET

Prime Minister, Trygve Bratteli.
Foreign Affairs, Andreas Cappelen.
Finance, Ragnar Christiansen.
Municipal Affairs, Oddvar Nordli.
Trade, Per Kleppe.

Church and Education, Bjartmar Gjerde.
Social Affairs, Odd Højdahl.
Justice, Oddvar Berrefjord.
Communications, Reiulf Steen.
Industry, Finn Lied.
Prices and Incomes, Olav Gjærevoll.
Agriculture, Torstein Treholt.
Defence, Alv Jakob Fostervoll.
Fisheries, Knut Hoem.
Family and Consumer Affairs, Mme. Inger Louise Valle.

ROYAL NORWEGIAN EMBASSY IN LONDON
Offices: 25 Belgrave Square, S.W.1
[01-235-7151]

Ambassador Extraordinary and Plenipotentiary, His Excellency Paul Gruda Koht (1968).
Minister-Counsellor, Tore Bøgh.
Counsellors, Herman Pedersen (*Press and Information*), Kåre Dæhlen; Semund Remøy (*Fisheries*); Svein Halland (*Consular*); Iacob Chr. Prebensen (*Commercial*).
1st Secretaries, John E. Grieg (*Press and Information*); Helge Vindenes; Lars Tangeraas.
Defence Attaché, Capt. O. A. Aslaksrud.
Asst. Defence Attaché, Maj. A. R. Thorn.
2nd Secretaries, Dag. M. Ulnes; Ole F. Knudsen (*Commercial*).
Consulate, 42 Lancaster Gate, W.2.
Consul-General, Aage F. Bothner.
Consular Attachés, Thor Torvik; Kåre Bryn.

Area and Population.—Norway (" The Northern Way "), a kingdom in the northern and western portion of the Scandinavian peninsula, was founded in 872. It is 1,752 km. in length, its greatest width about 430 km. The length of the coastline is 2,650 km., and the frontier between Norway and the neighbouring countries is 2,531 km. (Sweden 1,619 km., Finland 716 km. and U.S.S.R. 196 km.). It is divided into 20 counties (*fylker*) and comprises an area of 323,877 sq. km. (125,016 sq. miles) with a population (estimated, Jan., 1971) of 3,891,739. In 1968 there were for every 1,000 inhabitants: 17·6 live births; 9·9 deaths; 13·7 deaths during first year of age (per 1,000 live births); 7·7 marriages.

The Norwegian coastline is extensive, deeply indented with numerous fiords, and fringed with an immense number of rocky islands. The surface is mountainous, consisting of elevated and barren tablelands, separated by deep and narrow valleys. At the North Cape the sun does not appear to set from the second week in May to the last week in July, causing the phenomenon known as the *Midnight Sun*; conversely, there is no apparent sunrise from about Nov. 18 to Jan. 23. During the long winter nights are seen the multiple coloured *Northern Lights* or *Aurora Borealis*, which have a maximum intensity in a line crossing North America from Alaska to Labrador and Northern Europe to the Arctic coast and Siberia. A similar phenomenon occurs in the Antarctic and is known as *Aurora Australis*.

Production.—The cultivated area is about one-fortieth part of the country; forests cover nearly one-fourth; the rest consists of highland pastures or uninhabitable mountains.

The *Gulf Stream* pours from 140 to 170 million cubic feet of warm water per second into the sea around Norway and causes the temperature to be higher than the average for the latitude. It brings shoals of herring and cod into the fishing grounds and causes a warm current of air over the west coast, making it possible to cultivate potatoes and barley in latitudes which in other countries are perpetually frozen

The chief industries are manufactures, agriculture and forestry, fisheries, mining and shipping. In January, 1971, 378,701 persons were

employed in Norwegian industry. Manufactures are aided by great resources of water power, estimated at 11,870 MW. Actual production in 1968 amounted to 60·2 GW*. In normal years the quantity of fish caught by Norwegian fishing vessels is greater than that of any other European country except U.S.S.R. In 1968 the total catch amounted to 2,590,590 metric tons. In 1969 fish oil production amounted to 203,520 metric tons and fish liver ("tran") production to 30,333 metric tons.

Government.—From 1397 to 1814 Norway was united with Denmark, and from Nov. 4, 1814, with Sweden, under a personal union which was dissolved on June 7, 1905, when Norway regained complete independence. Under the constitution of May 17, 1814, the *Storting* (Parliament) itself elects one-quarter of its members to constitute the *Lagting* (Upper Chamber), the other three-quarters forming the *Odelsting* (Lower Chamber). Legislative questions alone are dealt with by both parts in separate sittings.

On April 8–9, 1940, Germany invaded Norway, and it was not until June 7, 1945, that the late King Haakon was able to return from Great Britain to Oslo.

Defence.—Norway is a member of the North Atlantic Treaty Organization, and the Headquarters of Allied Forces, Northern Europe, is situated near Oslo. Extensive reorganization of the Norwegian armed forces is in progress. The period of compulsory national service is 15 months (without refresher training) in the Navy and Air Force, and 12 months (with refresher training) in the Army.

Education is compulsory and free between the ages of 7 and 16, schools being maintained by local taxation with State grants in aid. Secondary schools are provided by the State, by local authorities, and privately. There are many special schools and industrial and technical institutes. The University of Oslo (opened in 1811) was

attended by 14,000 students and the University of Bergen (opened in 1948) by 4,100 students in 1968. Plans for new universities were announced on March 28, 1968, by the *Storting*—at Tromsö (for 2,200 students) in faculties of medicine, science, political science and the humanities; and at Trondheim (for 7,000 students) by a merger of the State Institute of Technology (3,500 students in 1968), the State College for Teachers and the Museum of the Royal Norwegian Society of Science. The latter university is expected to have facilities in engineering, architecture, the sciences, medicine, the humanities and political sciences by 1975.

Language and Literature.—Norwegian is one of the Scandinavian languages and is the language of the mainland and of Svalbard. Old Norse literature is among the most ancient (and the richest) in Europe. Modern Norwegian became formed in the time of the Reformation and Ludvig Holberg (1684–1754) is regarded as the founder of Norwegian literature, although modern Norwegian literature dates from the establishment of a national university at Christiania (Oslo) in 1811 and with the writings of Henrik A. Wergeland (1805–1845). Some of the famous names are Henrik Ibsen (1828–1906) the dramatist, Björnstjerne Björnson (1832–1910) journalist, dramatist and novelist and Nobel Prizewinner in 1903, Jonas Lie (1833–1908) novelist, Knut Hamsun (1859–1952) novelist and Nobel Prizewinner in 1920, and Sigrid Undset (1882–1949), champion of Norwegian womanhood and herself a Nobel Prizewinner in 1928. In 1969 there were 81 daily newspapers in the country with a total circulation of 1,466,423, and 76 newspapers published 1 to 5 times a week with a total circulation of 309,182.

Communications.—The total length of railways open at the end of 1969 was 4,242 km., excluding private lines. The extension of the main line from Fauske to Bodö, 60 miles north of the Arctic Circle, was completed in 1962 and opened on June 7 by King Olav. The number of telephones at the end of 1970 was 1,144,795, which is 29·4 telephones per 100 inhabitants. There are 71,100 km. of public roads in Norway (including urban streets). At the end of 1970, 1,188,973 road motor vehicles were registered, equivalent to 2·1 inhabitants per passenger car.

Civil Aviation.—Scheduled airlines are operated by Scandinavian Airlines System (SAS) on behalf of Det Norske Luftfartselskap (DNL), by Braathens South American and Far East Airtransport (SAFE), and by Wideröes Flyveselskap A.S.

Mercantile Marine.—The Mercantile Marine, December 31, 1970, consisted of 2,177 vessels of 19,708,000 gross tons (vessels above 100 gross tons, excluding fishing boats, floating whaling factories, tugs, salvage vessels, icebreakers and similar types of vessel). The fleet ranks fourth among the merchant navies of the world.

FINANCE

	1970	1971*
	million *Kroner*	
Revenue	16,760	20,574
Expenditure	20,780	20,452
National Debt	12,143	18,879
*Budget Estimate		

Rate of Exchange (Sept. 27, 1971) *Kr.*17·02 = £1.
See also p. 83.

TRADE

	1969	1970
	million *Kroner*	
Total imports	21,011	26,443
Total exports	15,741	17,549

---

* Gigawatt = 1,000 million watts.

Trade with U.K.

	1969	1970
Imports from U.K.	£140,781,000	£173,834,000
Exports to U.K.	179,656,000	198,637,000

The chief imports are raw materials, motor vehicles, chemicals, motor spirit, fuel and other oils; coal, ships and machinery; together with manufactures of silk, cotton and wool. The exports consist chiefly of fish and products of fish (as canned fish, whale oils); pulp, paper, iron ore and pyrites, nitrate of lime, stone, calcium carbide, aluminium, ferro-alloys, zinc, nickel, cyanamide, etc.

CAPITAL.— Ψ Oslo (incl. Aker). Pop. (Jan. 1, 1970), 486,972. Other towns are ΨTrondheim, 126,170; ΨBergen, 115,590; ΨStavanger, 81,579; ΨKristiansand, 56,152; ΨDrammen, 49,271; ΨTromsø, 38,064; ΨAalesund, 39,390; ΨHauge-sund, 27,603; Moss, 24,580.

FLAG.—Red, with white-bordered blue cross.
NATIONAL DAY.—May 17 (Constitution Day).
AIR TRANSIT FROM U.K.—London–Bergen or Oslo, 2 hrs.

BRITISH EMBASSY
(8 Thomas Heftyes Gate, Oslo 2; Postuttak, Oslo 1.)

Ambassador Extraordinary and Plenipotentiary, His Excellency Thomas Frank Brenchley, C.M.G. (1968)..................................£6,925
Counsellor, G. A. Crossley (*Economic and Commercial*).
1st Secretaries, T. Quinlan (*Commercial*); R. G. Young.
Defence Attaché, Lt.-Col. J. H. Vaughan-Johnson.
Naval Attaché, Cdr. C. J. L. Croft.
Chaplain, Rev. B. W. Horlock.

BRITISH CONSULAR OFFICES
There are British Consular Offices at *Bergen* and *Oslo* and Honorary Vice-Consulates at *Tromsø, Aalesund, Kristiansund N., Narvik, Stavanger, Trond-heim, Tønsberg, Kristiansand S.* and *Haugesund*.

BRITISH COUNCIL
Representative, J. D. Edmondston, O.B.E., Fridtjof Nansen Plass 5, Oslo 1.

SVALBARD
(*Spitsbergen and Bear Island*)

By Treaty (Feb. 3, 1920) the sovereignty of Norway over the Spitsbergen (" Pointed Mountain ") Archipelago was recognized by the Great Powers and other interested nations, and on Aug. 14, 1925, the Archipelago was officially taken over by Norway. In September, 1941, Allied forces (British, Canadian and Norwegian) landed on the main island. After destruction of the accumulated stocks of coal and dismantling of mining machinery and the wireless installation, the Norwegian inhabitants (about 600) were evacuated to a British port and the Russians (about 1,500) to the U.S.S.R. After the war the Norwegian mining plants were rebuilt. 843,149 metric tons of coal were shipped from Norwegian and Russian mines in Svalbard in 1969 (Norwegian mines, 385,263 metric tons).

The Svalbard Archipelago lies between 74°–81° N. lat. and between 10°–35° E. long., with an estimated area of 24,295 square miles. The archipelago consists of a main island, known as West Spitsbergen (15,200 sq. miles); North East Land, closely adjoining and separated by Hinlopen Strait; the Wiche Islands, separated from the mainland by Olga Strait; Barents and Edge Islands, separated from the mainland by Stor Fjord (or Wybe Jansz Water); Prince Charles Foreland, to the W.;

Hope Island, to the S.E.; Bear Island (68 square miles) 127 miles to the S.; with many similar islands in the neighbourhood of the main group. In addition to those engaged in coal-mining, the archipelago is also visited by hunters for seal, foxes and polar bears.

South Cape is 360 miles from the Norwegian Coast. Ice Fjord is 520 miles from Tromsö, 650 miles from Murmansk, and 1,300 miles from Aberdeen. Transit from Tromsö to Green Harbour 2 to 3 days; from Aberdeen 5 to 6 days.

JAN MAYEN, an island in the Arctic Ocean (70° 49'–71° 9' N. lat. and 7° 53'–9° 5' W. long.) was joined to Norway by law of Feb. 27, 1930.

Norwegian Antarctic
BOUVET ISLAND (54° 26' S. lat. and 3° 24' E. long.) was declared a dependency of Norway by law of Feb. 27, 1930.

PETER THE FIRST ISLAND (68° 50' S. lat. and 90° 35' W. long.), was declared a dependency of Norway by resolution of Government, May 1, 1931.

PRINCESS RAGNHILD LAND (from 70° 30' to 68° 40' S. lat. and 24° 15' to 33° 30' E. long.) has been claimed as Norwegian since Feb. 17, 1931.

QUEEN MAUD LAND.—On Jan. 14, 1939, the Norwegian Government declared the area between 20° W. and 45° E., adjacent to Australian Antarctica, to be Norwegian territory.

OMAN
(The Sultanate of Oman)
Sultan, Qabas bin Said, *succeeded* on deposition of Sultan Said Bin Taimur, July 23, 1970.

Prime Minister, Sayid Tarig bin Taimur, *appointed by the Sultan*, Aug. 9, 1970.

The independent Sultanate of Oman is situated at the easterly corner of Arabia. Its seaboard is nearly 1,000 miles long and extends from near Tibat on the west coast of the Musandam Peninsula round to Ras Darbat Ali, with the exception of the stretch between Dibba and Kalba on the east coast of the peninsula which belongs to the Trucial Shaikhdom of Sharjah. Ras Darbat Ali marks the boundary between the Sultanate and the territory of Southern Yemen. The Sultanate extends inland to the borders of the Rub'al Khali or " Empty Quarter " as the South-Eastern Arabian Desert is called.

Physically, the Sultanate consists of 3 divisions, a coastal plain, a range of hills and a plateau. The coastal plain varies in width from 10 miles in the neighbourhood of Suwaiq to practically nothing in the vicinity of Matrah and Muscat towns, where the hills descend abruptly into the sea. The mountain range runs generally from north-west to south-east, reaching its greatest height in the Jebel Akhdar region where heights of over 9,000 feet occur. The hills are for the most part barren, but in the high area round Jebel Akhdar they are green and there is considerable cultivation. The plateau has an average height of 1,000 feet. With the exception of oases there is little or no cultivation.

North-west of Muscat the coastal plain is known as the Batinah. It is fertile and prosperous, the date gardens extending for over 150 miles, Batinah dates (which ripen in the first half of July, well before the Basrah dates) being famous for their flavour. The coast-line between Muscat and the province of Dhofar is barren and forbidding. The fertile province of Dhofar lies on the south-eastern coast of Arabia. Sugar cane is grown and cattle can be raised in this province, which is the only part of the Arabian peninsula to receive the

benefit of the monsoon. Frankincense is also exported. Its principal town is Salalah on the coast, while Ψ Murbat is the port. Ψ *Gwadur*, situated on the Baluchistan coast, formerly belonged to the Sultanate, but was transferred to Pakistan on September 8, 1958.

The town of Muscat is the capital and seat of Government of the Sultanate of Oman. Possessing a natural harbour, though exposed to the north-west wind (*Shumal*), and at one time a town of some commercial importance, it has lost most of its trade, which has been transferred to the adjacent town of Matrah. Matrah is the starting point for the trade routes into the interior. Other ports on the Gulf of Oman are Sohar, Khaburah and Sur. None, however, provides sheltered anchorage.

The area of the Sultanate has been estimated as about 82,000 square miles and the population at 750,000 (1970). The Kuria Muria Islands have less than 100 inhabitants. The inhabitants are for the most part Arab, but there is a strong infusion of negro blood, especially along the coast. The inhabitants of the towns of Muscat (pop. 7,650) and Matrah (pop. 17,000) are mostly of Baluchi and Negro stock. The Baluchis have mostly migrated from Mekran and the Negroes from Zanzibar. There are few Arab residents in these two towns. In the valleys of the interior, as well as on the Batinah, date cultivation has reached a high level, and there are possibilities of agricultural development if the water supply were more certain. The inland tribes breed large numbers of camel, which are prized in Arabia for their quality. There are no industries of importance.

The only port of call for steamers is Ψ Muscat (one of the ports on the mail route between Bombay and Basrah). Frequency of the mail service between Muscat and Basrah is three or four times a month and twice monthly from Basrah to Muscat. 182 vessels of all nationalities, including 108 British, with a total tonnage of 1,057,128, entered the port in 1969. In addition 12 tankers with a tonnage of 262,010 tons called in for medical attention to members of their crews. 218 tankers called at the oil company port of Mina-al-Fahl in 1969 and carried to various destinations just under 120,000,000 barrels of crude oil. In addition Mina-al-Fahl provided bunkering facilities for 120 tankers. 46 other vessels (gross tonnage of 389,875) discharged cargo for the oil company.

Cable and Wireless, Ltd., operates the telegraph office, an automatic telephone service in Muscat and Matrah and an international telephone service.

Inland transport is by pack animals. The towns of Muscat and Matrah and the airfield at Bait-al-Falaj are linked by a concrete road. Outside the towns of Muscat and Matrah and the airfield there are only tracks ranging from good ones which have been cleared and graded, to ravines containing large boulders or stretches of soft sand. Land-Rovers and similar types of truck are the only vehicles which can be relied on. The Sultanate Development Department has completed over 500 miles of motorable tracks so far.

Finance.—On May 7, 1970, a new currency was brought into circulation. The main unit is the *Rial Saidi*= £1. Each *Rial* is divided into 1,000 new *Baiza*. There are notes of *Rials* 10, 5, 1, ½, ¼ and 100 *Baiza* and coins of *Baiza* 100, 50, 25, 10, 5 and 2. The Indian External Rupee ceased to be legal tender from May 21, 1970. The weights in use are one *kiyas*=the weight of six dollars or 5·9375 oz.; 24 *kiyas*=one Muscat *maund*; 10 *maunds*=one *Farasala*; 200 *maunds*=1 *Bahar*. Rice is sold by the bag, other cereals by the following measurement: 40 *Palis*=one *Farrah*; 20 *Farrahs*=one *Khandi*.

Trade with U.K.

	1969	1970
Imports from U.K.....	£5,280,000	£7,791,000
Exports to U.K........	10,368,000	7,813,000

Commerce and Trade.—Trade is mainly with India, Pakistan, the Persian Gulf States, Australia, the United Kingdom, the Netherlands and Japan. Imports for the year 1969 amounted to £5,619,167 (1968, £4,044,761) (excluding duty-free imports); exports (other than crude oil) remained at about £750,000. Chief imports in 1969 were: rice, about £828,000; wheat and wheat flour, £312,000; coffee, £389,000; textiles and fabrics, £547,000. The U.K. share of these imports amounted to £800,000; total imports, about £11,000,000.

Petroleum Development (Oman) Ltd., a subsidiary of Shell began exporting oil on Aug. 1, 1967. Exports are currently at a rate of 340,000 barrels a day. A German company, Wintershall A.-G. has an off-shore concession in the Gulf of Oman.

Development.—For many years the Sultanate was a poor country with a total annual income of less than £1,000,000. The advent of oil revenues since 1967 has enabled the Sultan to commission a comprehensive development plan for the region of Muscat and Matrah. Its cost is likely to be several million pounds and it will be carried out in phases over a number of years. Several public buildings had been completed or were under construction in 1970. They include a new Post Office, a Secretariat, a girls' school and hospitals at Rui and Tana'am. In addition a number of flats for Government officials have been completed. A fresh water pipeline from Sib to Muscat (33 miles) has been completed at a cost of £1,500,000. A new port and harbour at Muttrah is expected to cost £10,000,000.

CAPITAL.— Ψ Muscat, population (estimated), 7,650.

FLAG.—Red.

BRITISH EMBASSY
Muscat

Ambassador Extraordinary and Plenipotentiary, His Excellency Donald Frederick Hawley, C.M.G. (1971).

PANAMA
(República de Panama)

President of the Provisional Government Council, Ing. Demetrio Lakas, *appointed* Dec. 18, 1969.
Member of the Junta, Lic. Arturo Sucre Pereira.

CABINET
Minister of Interior and Justice, J. M. Vasquez.
Foreign Affairs, J. A. Tack.
Finance, J. G. Aizpú.
Commerce and Industry, H. Porras.
Public Works, E. Fábrega.
Agriculture and Livestock, N. Espino.
Health, Dr. J. R. Esquivel.
Education, M. B. Moreno.
Labour, Dr. J. de la R. Castillo.
Minister to the Presidency, P. Rognoni.

PANAMANIAN EMBASSY AND CONSULATE
23–25 Billiter Street, E.C.3.
[01–709–9833]

Ambassador (vacant).
Chargé d'Affaires, Sr. A. Cuevas (3rd *Secretary*) 34 Bristol House, Lower Sloane Street, S.W.1.
Attachés, Señorita Ines V. Zarak; Señora Brunilda Garcia Navarro; Sr. Fernando Perez Bedolla; Señora C. G. Revilla de Prudhoe.
There are Consular Offices of the Republic at Glasgow and Liverpool.

Panama lies on the isthmus of that name which connects N. and S. America (*see* MAP, p. 846). After a revolt (Nov. 3, 1903) it declared its independence from Colombia and established a separate Government. The constitution provides for a single chamber legislature of 42 members elected every four years. In October, 1968, however, a military *coup* resulted in the deposition of the President, Dr. Arnulfo Arias, who had been in office only 11 days, and the suspension of the National Assembly.

Since 1969 control of Panama has been increasingly taken over by Gen. Omar Torrijos, Commander of the National Guard (which had overthrown Dr. Arias in 1968). The latter appointed a President and one member to a new provisional Government Council and also appointed a small Cabinet which was reorganized in April 13, 1971 (*see* above).

The area of the Republic is 31,890 sq. m., the population (1970 Census), 1,425,343. The birth rate in 1969 was 37·9 and the death rate 7·3 per thousand. The soil is extremely fertile, but nearly one-half of the land is uncultivated. The chief crops are bananas, coconuts, cacao, coffee and cereals. The shrimping industry plays an important rôle in the Panamanian economy. A railway 47 miles in length joins the Atlantic and Pacific oceans.

Education is compulsory and free from 7 to 15 years. In 1969 there were 1,613 official primary schools and 75 private primary schools; 48 official secondary and 115 private secondary schools. Primary students numbered 238,027 in 1969; secondary students, 79,904. The average number of students at Panama University in 1969 was 6,527 and at the Catholic University (*Universidad Santa María La Antigua*) about 725.

Language and Literature.—The official language is Spanish. There are 4 daily newspapers published in the capital, 2 of which print editions in English. There are one English newspaper and one Spanish weekly newspaper.

Finance.—Budget estimates for 1971 showed revenue and expenditure in balance at *B.*400,000,000.

The monetary unit is the *Balboa* (= $1 U.S.); no Panamanian paper currency is issued, and U.S. dollar bills of all values are in circulation in the Republic and in the Canal Zone.

TRADE

	1968*	1969*
	Balboas	Balboas
Imports	243,459,715	267,664,000
Exports	93,807,085	108,948,000

* Final figures.

Trade with U.K. †

	1969	1970
Imports from U.K.	£7,575,000	£8,765,000
Exports to U.K.	2,699,000	1,839,000

† Including Canal Zone.

The imports are mostly manufactured goods, machinery, lubricants, chemicals and foodstuffs; exports are bananas, petroleum products, shrimps, sugar, meat and fishmeal. The exports are bananas, cacao, fresh shrimps, mahogany and cement.

CAPITAL, ΨPanama City. Population (1970 Census, preliminary), 418,000.

FLAG.—Four quarters; white with red star (top, next staff), red (in fly); blue (below, next staff) and white with red star. NATIONAL DAY.—November 3.

Dependencies of Panama.—Taboga Island (area 4 sq. miles) is a popular tourist resort some 12 miles from the Pacific entrance to the Panama Canal. Tourist facilities are also being developed in the Las Perlas Archipelago in the Gulf of Panama. There is a penal settlement at Guardia on the island of Coiba (area 19 sq. miles) in the Gulf of Chiriqui.

BRITISH EMBASSY
(120 Via España, Panama)

Ambassador Extraordinary and Plenipotentiary, His Excellency Dugald Malcolm, C.M.G., C.V.O. T.D. (1971).....................................£6,475
1st Secretary and Consul, G. C. O. Key, O.B.E., D.F.C.

There is a British consular office at *Panama City*, and an honorary consul at *Colon*.

Panama, 4,650 miles; transit from Liverpool, 15 to 19 days; from Southampton 15 days; *via* N.Y., 14 days.

PARAGUAY
(República del Paraguay)

President, General Alfredo Stroessner, *inaugurated* Aug. 15, 1954, *re-elected* 1958, 1963 and 1968.
Foreign Affairs, Dr. Raúl Sapena Pastor.
Finance, General César Barrientos (*ret.*).
Interior, Dr. Sabino A. Montanaro.
Defence, General Leodegar Cabello.
Justice and Labour, Dr. Saúl González.
Education and Worship, Dr. Raúl Peña.
Public Health and Social Welfare, Dr. Adán Godoy Gimenez.
Public Works and Communications, General Marcial Samaniego (*ret.*).
Agriculture and Livestock, Eng. Hernando Bertoni.
Industry and Commerce, Sr. José Antonio Moreno González.
Without Portfolio, Arq. Tomás Romero Pereira.
President of Central Bank, Dr. César Romeo Acosta.

PARAGUAYAN EMBASSY IN LONDON
Braemar Lodge, Cornwall Gardens, S.W.7
[01–937–1253]

Ambassador Extraordinary and Plenipotentiary, His Excellency Numa Alcídes Mallorquin (1969).
Minister-Counsellor, I. A. Pane (*Consul General*).
1st Secretary, Jorge A. Colmán.
2nd Secretary, Mrs. G. S. de Jauregui.
Consulate-General, Braemar Lodge, Cornwall Gardens, S.W.7 [01–937–6629].
Consular Official, Mrs. T. Castill.

There is also a Paraguayan Consulate in *Liverpool*.

Area and Population.—Paraguay is an inland subtropical State of South America, situated between Argentina, Bolivia and Brazil (*see* MAP, p. 828). The area is computed at 157,000 square miles, with a population (U.N. estimate, 1969) of 2,314,000.

Eastern Paraguay consists of a series of plains, intersected by abrupt ranges of hills, none of which exceeds 2,300 feet above sea level. The Paraguay and Alto Paraná rivers are normally navigable for vessels of 6 to 7 feet draught. Some of the tributary streams are also navigable. The Pilcomayo river is navigable for small craft for 180 miles from Asunción. Paraguay is a country of grassy plains and dense forest, the soil being marshy in many parts and liable to floods; while the hills are covered for the most part with immense forests. The streams flowing into the Alto Paraná descend precipitously into that river. In the angle formed by the Paraná-Paraguay confluence are extensive marshes, one of which, known as "Ñeembucú," or "endless," is drained by *Lake Ypoa*, a large lagoon, south-east of the capital. The *Chaco*, lying between the rivers Paraguay and Pilcomayo and bounded on the north by Bolivia, formed the subject of a long-standing dispute with that country and led to war between Paraguay and Bolivia from 1932 to 1935. The Chaco is a flat plain, rising uniformly towards its western boundary to a height of 1,140

feet; it suffers much from floods and still more from drought.

Government.—In 1535 Paraguay was settled as a Spanish possession. In 1811 it declared its independence of Spain.

The 1967 constitution provides for a two-chamber parliament consisting of a 30-member Senate and a 60-member Chamber of Deputies. Two-thirds of the seats in each chamber are allocated to the majority party and the remaining one-third shared among the minority parties in proportion to the votes cast. Voting is compulsory for all citizens over 18.

The President is elected for 5 years and may be re-elected for a further term. He appoints the Cabinet, which exercises all the functions of government. During parliamentary recess it can govern by decree through the Council of State, the members of which are representative of the Government, the armed forces and various other bodies.

The first elections under the new constitution were held on Feb. 11, 1968.

Production.—About three-quarters of the population are engaged in agricultural and pastoral pursuits, cattle breeding being the principal industry. In addition to canned and frozen meat, timber, quebracho extract, cotton, hides, *yerba maté*, tobacco, sugar, citrus fruits, vegetable oils and *petit grain* essence (which are the principal exports), manioca, maize, rice and edible oils are also produced for home consumption. The production of rice, wheat, soya and ground-nuts is being encouraged by the government. The forests contain many varieties of timber, but only Spanish Cedar (Cedrela species) and a few of the best known hardwoods find a market abroad.

Communications.—A railway, 985 miles in length, connects Asunción with Buenos Aires. The journey takes 55 hours. Train ferries enable the run to be accomplished without break of bulk. River steamers also connect Buenos Aires and Asunción (3 to 5 days). This service is liable to cancellation without warning when the river is low or in flood. There are direct shipping services between Hamburg, Antwerp, Amsterdam and Asunción; New York, Philadelphia, Baltimore and Asunción; and Liverpool, London and Asunción. Eight airlines operate services from Asunción.

There are 500 miles of asphalted roads in Paraguay, connecting Asunción with São Paulo (26 hrs.) *viâ* the Bridge of Friendship and Foz de Yguazú and with Buenos Aires (24 hrs.) *viâ* Pilcomayo, and about 4,050 miles of earth roads in fairly good condition, but liable to be closed or to become impassable in wet weather. Bus services connect the principal towns and there are services to Buenos Aires, São Paulo and Paranaguá, a port on the Brazilian coast.

Defence.—There is a permanent military force of about 14,000 all ranks, most of whom are conscripts doing their military service; and about 6,500 armed police (again mostly conscripts). Three gunboats and a number of small armed launches patrol inland waters.

Language and Literature.—Spanish is the official language of the country but outside the larger towns *Guaraní*, the language of the largest single unit of original Indian inhabitants, is widely spoken. Three morning and one weekly newspapers are published in Asunción; and one daily in Encarnación.

Education.—Primary education is free and compulsory. In 1969 there were 2,592 Government primary schools and 304 private schools with about 415,000 pupils and 12,951 teachers; 498 secondary schools with 50,000 pupils, a national university and a Catholic university in Asunción and branches of

the Catholic University in three provincial towns. There are about 5,500 university students.

FINANCE

	1970 *Guaranies*	1971* *Guaranies*
Revenue	9,994,348,278	10,255,000,000
Expenditure	10,441,775,884	10,522,000,000

* Estimated

Currency.—A free exchange system was introduced in August, 1957. The rate of exchange in May, 1971 was Gs.295–305 = £1. (*See also* p. 84.)

Trade.—The imports are chiefly articles of food and drink, consumer goods, textiles, vehicles and machinery. Main exports: Meat and by-products, tobacco, seeds, yerba maté, maize, fruit (lemons, grapefruit, oranges), coffee, cotton fibre, essential oils, vegetable oil, castor seed oil, skins, pelts, and timber.

Trade with U.K.

	1969	1970
Imports from U.K.	£2,412,000	£2,210,000
Exports to U.K.	2,122,000	2,271,000

CAPITAL, Ψ Asunción, about 1,000 miles up the River Paraguay from Buenos Aires. Pop. (estimated, 1970), 437,000; other centres being Ψ Encarnación, 39,000; Concepción, 52,800; and Villarica 38,000.

FLAG.—Three horizontal bands, red, white, blue with the National seal on the obverse white band and the Treasury seal on the reverse white band.

NATIONAL DAY.—May 14.

BRITISH EMBASSY
(25 de Mayo 171, Casilla de Correo 404, Asunción)

Ambassador Extraordinary and Plenipotentiary and Consul-General, His Excellency Brian Charles MacDermot, C.B.E., M.V.O. (1968)......£6,475
1st Secretary and Consul, E. V. Nelson.
Defence Attaché, Col. G. W. Croker, M.B.E., M.C. (resident in *Buenos Aires*).
Attaché, J. E. Kingsbury (*Vice-Consul*).

Asunción is approximately 4,000 miles distant from London by air. Transit by sea 25 days. By air approximately 21 hours flying time *viâ* Rio de Janeiro.

PERSIA *See* IRAN

PERU
(República del Perú)

President, Lt.-Gen. Juan Velasco (Alvarado), *born* 1910, *appointed by a revolutionary junta,* Oct. 3, 1968.

Prime Minister, Gen. Ernesto Montagne Sánchez.
Minister of Foreign Affairs, Lt.-Gen. Edgardo Mercado Jarrín.

PERUVIAN EMBASSY AND CONSULATE
52, Sloane Street, S.W.1
[01–235–1917/2545]; *Consulate* [01–235–6867]

Ambassador Extraordinary and Plenipotentiary, His Excellency Señor Don Adhemar Montagne (1969).
Counsellor, Señor Don Ricardo Walter Stubbs.
Air Attaché, Lt.-Gen. Jesús Gabilondo.
Naval Attaché, Rear-Adm. Alberto Benvenuto.
1st Secretary, Señor Don Gerardo Balbuena;
2nd Secretaries, Señor Don Alfonso Rivero (*Consular*); Señorita Iris Valverde.
Commercial Attaché, Señor Don Jack Gubbins.

There are a Consulate-General at *Liverpool* and Consulates at *Birmingham, Hull,* and *Glasgow.*

Area and Population.—Peru is a maritime Republic of South America, situated between 0° 00′ 48″ and 18° 21′ 00″ S. latitude and between 68° 39′ 27″ and 81° 20′ 13″ W. longitude. The area of the Repub-

lic including 4,440 square kilometres of the Peruvian section of Lake Titicaca and 32 square kilometres of the coastal islands, is about 531,000 square miles with a total population (estimated, 1970) of 13,600,000.

Physical Features.—The country is traversed throughout its length by the Andes, running parallel to the Pacific coast, the highest points in the Peruvian sector being *Huascaran* (22,211 feet), *Huandoy* (20,855 feet), *Ausangate* (20,235 feet), *Misti* volcano (18,364 feet), *Hualcan* (20,000 feet), *Chachani* (19,037 feet), *Antajasha* (18,020 feet), *Pichupichu* (17,724 feet), and *Mount Meiggs* (17,583 feet).

There are three main regions, the *Costa*, west of the Andes, the *Sierra* or mountain ranges of the Andes, which include the *Punas* or mountainous wastes below the region of perpetual snow and the *Montana*, or *Selva*, which is the vast area of jungle stretching from the eastern foothills of the Andes to the eastern frontiers of Peru. The coastal area, lying upon and near the Pacific, is not tropical, though close to the Equator, being cooled by the Humboldt Current; its chief products are cotton, sugar, and petroleum. It contains the capital, Lima, and most of the white population.

In the mountains, where most of the Indians live, are to be found minerals in great richness and variety, and cattle, sheep, llamas and alpacas are bred there. In the mountain valleys maize, potatoes and wheat are grown. Upon the eastern slopes of the Andes are to be found very large tracts suitable for cultivation and stock raising. The main products of the jungle are timber, barbasco and leche caspi.

Government.—Peru was conquered in the early 16th century by Francisco Pizarro (born 1478, died 1541). He subjugated the Incas (the ruling caste of the Quechua Indians), who had started their rise to power some 500 years earlier, and for nearly three centuries Peru remained under Spanish rule. A revolutionary war of 1821–1824 established its independence, declared on July 28, 1821. The constitution rests upon the fundamental law of Oct. 18, 1856 (amended in 1860, 1919, 1933, 1936 and in 1939), and is that of a democratic Republic. The President is elected for six years by direct vote of the people. Congress is composed of a Senate and of a Chamber of Deputies, both Houses being elected for six years.

Presidential and Congressional elections on a basis of proportional representation were held on June 9, 1963, and a new President, Sr. Belaúnde Terry, held office from July 28 until deposed by a revolutionary junta on Oct. 3, 1968, and sent out of the country. The junta appointed a Cabinet composed of officers from the three armed services and named General Velasco as President. The all-military character of this Cabinet has been retained.

Production.—Agriculture employing about 40 per cent. of the labour force accounted for only 15 per cent. of the Gross Domestic Product in 1970. The chief crops are cotton, potatoes and other vegetables, sugar, fruit, maize, rice, wheat, barley, grapes and coffee. Mineral exports in 1970 were valued at U.S. $500,000,000 and included lead, zinc, copper, iron ore, petroleum and silver.

Peru is the world's largest exporter of fish meal. The value of fishmeal exports in 1970 was U.S. $315,000,000, compared with U.S. $220,000,000 in 1969.

Communications.—In recent years the coastal and sierra zones have been opened up by means of roads and air routes and there is air communication, as well as communication by protracted land routes, with the tropical eastern zones, which lie east of the Andes towards the borders of Brazil, and consist mainly of unexplored or little known country inhabited by Indians in a savage state. The completion in 1944 of the trunk road of the *Andean Highway* from the Pacific port of Callao, *viâ* Lima, Oroya, Cerro de Pasco (14,700 ft.), Huanuco, Tingo Maria, to Pucallpa, the river port on the Ucayali, forms a link between the Pacific, the Amazon and the Atlantic. The trunk road runs through the *Boqueron del Padre Abad*, a pass rediscovered on July 22, 1937, in the backbone of the Blue Cordillera. The Peruvian section of the Pan American highway is complete and is asphalted throughout.

The first railway was opened in 1850 and of the 2,400 miles of railways now operating, Government lines and the Peruvian Corporation account for 1,674 miles and private enterprises about 726 miles. There is also steam navigation on the eastern rivers such as the Ucayali (*see* Andean Highway above) and Huallaga, and in the south on Lake Titicaca. Air services are maintained throughout Peru, and a number of international services call at Lima.

Defence.—The Army is recruited by voluntary enlistment, supplemented by conscription (2 years), and numbers about 35,000 of all ranks. Armoured units are equipped with American and French vehicles. Engineer units are employed on the reconstruction of roadways in North Eastern Peru using American equipment. *Navy.*—The Navy consists of 2 cruisers; 5 destroyers; 2 frigates; 4 submarines completed in the United States of America in 1954–57; 4 LST's; 7 river gunboats; 4 fleet oilers; 4 fleet auxiliaries; 2 river transports; 6 patrol boats; 4 launches; 1 floating dock; 3 tugs. 2 Daring Class Destroyers being modernized in Cammell Laird's, Birkenhead, will join the fleet during 1972. The main Naval base is in Callao and supports all ships of the Fleet. There are training establishments in Callao and at La Punta. *Air Force.*—The Air Force is equipped with British Hunter and Canberra aircraft; American training, fighter and transport aircraft plus helicopters; French *Mirage* aircraft and Alouette helicopters; Russian helicopters. There are military airfields at Talara, Piura, Chiclayo, Lima, Pisco and Iquitos plus a seaplane base at Iquitos.

Education.—Elementary education is compulsory and free for both sexes between the ages of 7 and 14. In 1961 there were 1,495,047 pupils undergoing primary education, 184,849 attending ordinary secondary schools and 42,978 attending

technical secondary schools. There were 13,510 state primary schools with 36,503 teachers and 450 state secondary schools with 10,900 teachers (of which 191 schools and 4,200 teachers provided technical education). In addition there were 1,350 private schools providing primary education, with 7,050 teachers, and 420 private secondary schools (of which 70 technical) with 7,490 teachers (990 technical); and 306 schools conducted by religious orders. The State provides rural agricultural schools for Indians, and mining schools and polytechnics in the more populated centres. There are now 21 state and 12 private universities in Peru. The University of San Marcos at Lima, founded in 1551, has about 14,000 students.

Language and Literature.—Spanish is the official language of the country and notably of the original Spanish stock from which the governing and professional classes are mainly recruited, but more than half the nation is composed of Indians, whose principal languages (Quechua and Aymara) are widely spoken. Before the arrival of Pizarro, the Incas had attained a high state of culture, some traces of which survived three centuries of Spanish rule. Modern Peruvian literature includes a national drama in the Spanish tongue and many Peruvian writers have attained international fame. The national library founded at Lima in 1821 was pillaged by Chileans in the Pacific War of 1879–1882, but many of the scattered manuscripts and books have since been recovered. The greater part of the historical section of the library was destroyed by fire in 1943. The first printed news-sheet in South America was issued at Lima in 1594 and in 1971 there were 7 main morning papers, including the official gazette *El Peruano*, four afternoon papers daily and about 50 provincial papers.

Finance.—The rate of exchange with sterling in June, 1971, was *Soles* 104=£1 (*see also* p. 84).

	1970
Public revenue......... *Soles*	45,394,000,000
Public expenditure........	45,531,000,000

Peru's balance of payments surplus amounted to $U.S.243,000,000 in 1970 (provisional).

Trade.—Import trade of Peru in 1970 totalled $U.S.619,000,000 and exports $U.S.1,048,000,000.

Trade with U.K.

	1969	1970
Imports from U.K. .	£11,569,000	£9,905,000
Exports to U.K....	13,903,000	15,197,000

The principal imports are machinery and vehicles, foodstuffs, metal and manufactured metal goods, chemicals, and pharmaceutical products. The chief exports are minerals and metals (48 per cent.), fishmeal (32), sugar (6), cotton (5) and coffee (4 per cent.).

CAPITAL.—Lima. Population (estimated 1969), 2,500,000; other large towns are Ψ Callao (161,286), Arequipa (156,657), Ψ Iquitos (55,695), Ψ Chiclayo (86,904).

FLAG.—Three vertical bands, red, white, red; coat of arms on white band. NATIONAL DAY.—July 28 (Anniversary of Independence).

BRITISH EMBASSY

Offices; Edificio Washington, Plaza Washington, Lima; Residence: Esquina Arenales y Bermudez, Lima.)

Ambassador Extraordinary and Plenipotentiary, His Excellency Hugh Travers Morgan, C.M.G. (1970)
£6,925
Counsellor, S. F. Campbell, O.B.E., T.D. (*Head of Chancery*).

1st Secretary, M. D. W. McCann, M.B.E. (*Commercial*).

BRITISH CONSULAR OFFICES

There are British Consular Offices at *Lima, Arequipa, Callao* and *Iquitos.*

British Council Representative, H. R. H. Salmon, Apartado 1608, Edif. Pacifico-Washington, Ave Arequipa, Lima.

Lima, 7,020 miles; transit, *viâ* New York and Colon, 21–27 days: *viâ* Liverpool and Colon, 17–30 days. Direct BOAC service Lima–London.

THE PHILIPPINES
(República ng Pilipinas)

President, Ferdinand Marcos, *b.* 1917, *elected* Nov. 10, 1965, *assumed office* Dec. 30, 1965; re-elected for 4 years, Nov. 11, 1969.

CABINET
Foreign Affairs, Carlos P. Romulo.
Justice, Felix Makasiar.
Finance, Cesar Virata.
Defence, Juan Ponce Enrile.
Education, Onofre D. Corpuz.
Labour, Blas F. Ople.
Commerce and Industry, Leonides S. Virata.
Executive Secretary, Alejandro Melchor.
Public Services, Constancio E. Castañeda.
[The above are the principal appointments following a reorganization of the Cabinet on February 8, 1971, in which the number of Secretaries of State was reduced from 26 to 14.]

PHILIPPINE EMBASSY
9a Palace Green, W.8
[01–937–3646]

Ambassador Extraordinary and Plenipotentiary, His Excellency Jaime Zobel de Ayala (1971).
Minister-Counsellor, Pablo A. Araque (*Consular*).
Armed Forces Attaché, Col. Pedro L. Los Banos.
Asst. do., Cdr. Jaime V. Francisco.
3rd Secretaries, Raul ch. Rabe (*Vice-Consul*); Lauro L. Baja; Miss Anita P. Soliongco.
Commercial Attaché, Francisco J. Santos, Jr.
Science Attaché, Dr. Justo de la Paz.

Area and Population.—The Philippines are situated between 21° 20′–4° 30′ N. lat. and 116° 55′–126° 36′ E. long., and are distant about 500 miles from the south-east coast of the continent of Asia.

The total land area of the country is 114,834 square miles, of which total 106,914 square miles are contained in the eleven largest islands, the 7,079 other islands having a combined area of 7,929 square miles.

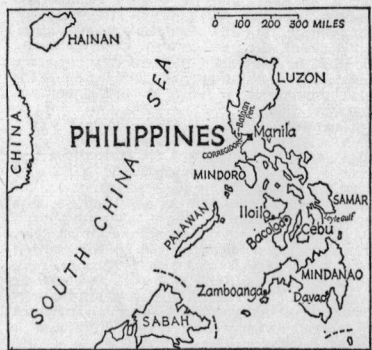

The principal islands are:—

Name	sq. miles	Name	sq. miles
Luzon.....	40,422	Mindoro.....	3,759
Mindanao..	36,538	Leyte........	2,786
Samar.....	5,050	Cebu........	1,703
Negros....	4,906	Bohol	1,492
Palawan...	4,550	Masbate......	1,262
Panay....	4,446		

Other groups in the Republic are the Sulu islands (Capital, Jolo), Babuyanes and Batanes; the Catanduanes; and Culion Islands.

The population of the Philippines was estimated in November, 1970, at 39,079,000.

The inhabitants, known as Filipinos, are basically all of Malay stock, with a considerable admixture of Spanish and Chinese blood in many localities, and over 90 per cent. of them are Christians, predominantly Roman Catholics. Most of the remainder are Moslem Moros in the south, and Pagans, mainly in the north. There is a Chinese minority estimated at 350,000, and other much smaller foreign communities, notably Spanish, American and Indian.

The Portuguese navigator Magellan came to the Philippines in 1521 and was slain by the natives of Mactan, a small island near Cebu. In 1565 Spain undertook the conquest of the country which was named " Filipinas ", after the son of the King of Spain, and in 1571 the city of Manila was founded by the conquistador Legaspi, who subdued the inhabitants of almost all the islands, their conversion from barbarism and paganism being undertaken by the Augustinian friars in Legaspi's train. In 1762 Manila was occupied by a British force, but in 1764 it was restored to Spain. In the nineteenth century there were frequent disturbances in the islands, and at the outbreak of the Spanish-American War of 1898 a rebellion under Aguinaldo, a native leader, had just died down. After the Spanish fleet had been destroyed in Manila Bay (May 1, 1898), Manila was captured by American troops with the help of Filipinos, on Aug. 13, 1898, and the Islands were ceded to the United States by the *Treaty of Paris* of Dec. 10, 1898. However, the Filipinos, under Aguinaldo, rose up in arms on Feb. 4, 1899, against the U.S. Government, maintaining a desultory rebellion until it was quelled in 1902. Following this, the Philippine Commission was established, consisting of a Governor-General and Commissioner appointed by the President of the United States, who exercised a large measure of executive and legislative authority.

A measure of local independence was granted under the Jones Act of August 29, 1916. On March 24, 1934, the Tydings-McDuffie Law, gave the Philippines a " Commonwealth " Status. The Republic of the Philippines came into existence on July 4, 1946. The Constitution provides for a President elected for a term of four years, and a bi-cameral Congress, consisting of a Senate composed of 24 Senators and a House of Representatives of not more than 120 members. No person may serve as President for more than eight consecutive years. The term of office of Senators is six years and of Representatives four years.

Language and Literature.—The official languages are Pilipino, English and Spanish. Pilipino, the national language, is based on Tagalog, one of the Malay-Polynesian languages which according to the 1960 census is spoken by 44 per cent. of the population. English, which is the language of government and of instruction in secondary and university education, is spoken by at least 40 per cent. of the population, while Spanish, which is on the decline, is now spoken by only 2 per cent.

73 per cent. of the population are literate. There is a National Library in the capital with branches in other urban centres and a flourishing press. Education accounts for about 30 per cent. of total expenditure in the national budget. Secondary and higher education is extensive and there are 33 private universities recognized by the Government, including the Dominican University of Santo Thomas (founded in 1611), the first in the Far East and 25 years older than Harvard; there are also 6 State-supported universities including the University of the Philippines, founded 1908. It is estimated that students at private universities number 232,797; State universities, 23,357.

Roads and Railways.—Communications suffered serious damage during the War of 1941–45 owing to the lack of proper maintenance during the Japanese occupation and destruction by bombardment. The highway system is undergoing rehabilitation and extension and, including all types of services, covered 60,526 kilometres in June, 1968. In 1967 there were 436,149 road vehicles registered. Before the war the railways, which were largely Government owned, operated approximately 845 miles of track of which some 642 miles are still operated. The Manila railway, on Luzon island, has been converted to diesel traction.

Shipping.—There are over 30 ports of entry in the Philippines and 3,551 vessels of various types, totalling 732,231 tons, are engaged in inter-island traffic. There are 108 ocean-going vessels registered in the Philippines, totalling 725,123 gross tons.

Civil Aviation.—Air transport plays a key part in inter-island travel and an important one in communications overseas. Philippine Air Lines have regular flights to Hong Kong, Taipei, Sydney, Singapore, Saigon, Bali, and Tokyo and operate four trans-Pacific flights a week to San Francisco, in addition to inter-island services. Air Manila (Inc.) and Filipinas Orient Airways (Inc.) also operate internal air services.

FINANCE

	1968–69†	1969–70†
Receipts.......	P.3,155,800,090	P.3,502,282,700
Expenditure....	3,012,963,000	3,196,657,000

† Estimated.

P.=Philippine *Peso*. Official rate of exchange: *P* 3·90 = $U.S.1. Rate of exchange for imports is *P*.3·82=U.S.$1; exports *P*.3·43=U.S.$1. (*See also* p. 84.)

TRADE

	1967	1968
Total imports...	P.4,125,017,389	P.4,470,424,771
Total Exports...	3,476,860,161	3,721,949,112

Trade with U.K.

	1969	1970
Imports from U.K..	£27,911,000	£25,087,000
Exports to U.K.....	4,333,000	7,480,000

The Philippines is a predominantly agricultural country, the chief products being rice, coconuts, maize, sugar-cane, abaca (manila hemp), fruits, tobacco and lumber. There is, however, an increasing number of manufacturing industries and it is the policy of the Government to diversify its economy.

The principal Philippine exports in both natural and manufactured states are coconuts, sugar, abaca, base metals, lumber, pineapples, embroideries and tobacco.

CAPITAL.— Ψ Manila, in the island of Luzon: population (1969): City area, 1,550,000; Manila with suburbs (incl. Quezon City, Pasay City, Caloocan City, Makati, Parañaque, San Juan Mandaluyong and Navotas), 2,989,300. Quezon City has been designated as the future capital of the Philippines, but pending completion of government building projects, the Executive, Legislative and

Judicial departments of the government are still located in Manila. The next largest cities are ΨCebu (343,900), ΨDavao (298,300), ΨIloilo (201,000), ΨZamboanga (183,800), and Bacolod (162,200).

FLAG.—Equal horizontal bands of blue (above) and red; gold sun with three stars on a white triangle next staff. NATIONAL DAY.—June 12 (Independence Day).

BRITISH EMBASSY
Manila

Ambassador Extraordinary and Plenipotentiary, His Excellency John Noel Ormiston Curle, C.M.G., C.V.O. (1970)......................................£6,875

CONSULAR OFFICES

There are honorary British Vice-Consuls at *Cebu* and *Iloilo*.

POLAND
(Polska Rzeczpospolita Ludowa)
COUNCIL OF STATE

Chairman, Jósef Cyrankiewicz, *elected* Dec. 23, 1970.
Deputy Chairmen, Z. Moskwa; Prof. M. Klimaszewski; B. Ruminski; S. Gucwa.
Secretary, L. Stasiak.

CABINET

Prime Minister, Piotr Jaroszewicz.
Deputy Premiers, Stanislaw Majewski; Eugeniusz Szyr; Zdzislaw Tomal; Mieczyslaw Jagielski; Wincenty Krásko; Franciszek Kaim; Jan Mitrega.
Foreign Affairs, Dr. Stefan Jedrychowski.
Defence, Gen. Wojciech Jaruzelski.
Foreign Trade, Kazimierz Olszewski.
Finance, Jozef Trendota.
Mining and Power, Jan Mitrega.
Heavy Industry, Wlodzimierz Lejczak.
Home Trade, Edward Sznajder.
Transport, Mieczyslaw Zajfryd.
Culture and Art, Lucjan Motyka.
Forestry and Timber Industry, Jerzy Popko.
Education and Higher Education, Prof. Henryk Jablonski.
Communications, Edward Kowalczyk.
Chemical Industry, Edward Zawada.
Engineering, Tadeusz Wrzaszczyk.
Light Industry, Tadeusz Kunicki.
Food Industry, Emil Kolodziej.
Agriculture, Jozef Okuniewski.
Justice, Stanislaw Walczak.
Shipping, Jerzy Szopa.
Health and Social Welfare, Jan Kostrzewski.
Home Affairs, Franciszek Szlachcic.
Building and Building Materials, Andrzej Giersz.
Chairmen of Committees, Witold Trąmpczyński (*Planning Commission*); Michal Krukowski (*Labour and Wages*); Prof. Jan Kaczmarek (*Science and Technology*); Jerzy Kusiak (*Small-scale Industry and Handicrafts*).

UNITED WORKERS' (=Communist) PARTY

Politbureau of the Central Committee, E. Babiuch; J. Cyrankiewicz; E. Gierek; P. Jaroszewicz; J. Jedrychowski; W. Kruczek; M. Moczar; S. Olszowski; J. Szydlak; J. Tejchma; (*full members*); H. Jablonski; M. Jagielski; W. Jaruszewski; J. Kepa (*alternate members*).
Secretariat of the Central Committee, E. Gierek (*First*); E. Babiuch; K. Barczikowski; S. Olszowski; A. Starewicz; J. Sydlak; J. Techma; S. Kania.

POLISH EMBASSY IN LONDON
47 Portland Place, W.1
[01–580–4324]

Ambassador Extraordinary and Plenipotentiary (vacant).

Counsellors, Janusz Zablocki; Wlodzimierz Wisniewski (*Commercial*); Pawel Cieślar (*Press*).
1st Secretaries, Narczy Grzechowiak; Dr. Antoni Knychala; Juliusz Bialy.
Attachés, Jan Janowski (*Commercial*); Ireneusz Kubiczek (*Economic*); Wojciech Opalko (*Commercial*).
Military, Air and Naval Attaché, Col. Witold Lokuciewski.
Consulate-General in London, 19 Weymouth Street, W.1. [01–580–4324]

Area and Population.—In 1939 the area of the Polish Republic was 150,572 square miles with a population of about 35,000,000, of whom 30 per cent. were national minorities (including over 3,000,000 Jews). Frontier changes took place at the end of the war as foreshadowed at the Tehran Conference in 1943. About 69,000 square miles of territory in the east were ceded to the Soviet Union. In exchange Poland received in the west 39,000 square miles of Eastern Germany. The southern boundary was not affected except for minor adjustments to that part formerly dividing Poland from Ruthenia (Czechoslovakia). The western boundary is formed by the Rivers Oder and Neisse. Poland now has a maritime frontier stretching from west of Kaliningrad (formerly Königsberg) to west of Szczecin (formerly Stettin). As a result of the change of frontier and of very

great war-time losses, at the census of December 3, 1950, the population had fallen to 24,977,000 in an area of 121,000 square miles; on Oct. 31, 1970, it was estimated at 32,889,000. Roman Catholicism is the religion of the vast majority of the inhabitants.

Government.—The Republic of Poland (reconstituted within the limits of the old Polish Commonwealth) was proclaimed at Warsaw in November, 1918, and its independence guaranteed by the signatories of the Treaty of Versailles. The Polish Commonwealth had ceased to exist in 1795 after three successive partitions in 1772, 1793 and 1795, in which Prussia, Russia and Austria shared. During the Napoleonic wars, the small Grand Duchy of Warsaw was created but was dissolved by the final act of the Congress of Vienna. The so-called " Congress Kingdom " was then established on the Polish territory which had fallen to Russia's share and the Tsar assumed the title of King of Poland. Prussia acquired Poznania and Polish Pomerania, Austria acquired Galicia and the

small Republic of Cracow came into existence under the joint control of Prussia, Russia and Austria. In 1831, after an insurrection, the Congress Kingdom was dissolved and annexed by Russia and in 1848 the Austrians absorbed the Cracow Republic, Poland as an independent state ceasing to exist until the end of the War of 1914–18, when she became independent once again, after 150 years of foreign rule.

In March, 1939, Great Britain entered into a treaty with Poland (France had done so in 1921) guaranteeing Polish territory against aggression, and on Hitler's invasion France and Britain implemented their guarantee. On September 17, 1939, Russian forces invaded eastern Poland and on September 21, 1939, Poland was declared by Germany and Russia to have ceased to exist. A line of demarcation was established between the areas occupied by German and Russian forces. At the end of the war a Coalition Government was formed in which the Polish Workers' Party played a large part. In December, 1948, the Polish Workers' Party and the Polish Socialist Party fused in the new Polish United Workers' Party. This is a Communist Party which closely controls every branch of State activity. A new Constitution modelled on the Soviet Constitution of 1936 was adopted on July 22, 1952. It changed the title of the country to the Polish People's Republic (*Polska Rzeczpospolita Ludowa*). It made no provision for a President of the Republic, whose functions were to be jointly exercised by a Council of State. Private ownership of land and freedom of religion were recognized. Church and State were to be separate.

Despite the guarantee of religious freedom in the Constitution, a campaign of encroachment in 1953 culminated in the arrest of the Primate of the Roman Catholic Church, Cardinal Wyszyński. Dissatisfaction with the *régime* and conditions of life led to riots in Poznań in June, 1956, and subsequently M. Władysław Gomułka, who had been expelled from the Party in 1949, was reinstated and elected First Secretary of the Party. At the same time Cardinal Wyszyński was allowed to resume his functions. In Jan., 1957, elections to the *Sejm* were held and in Feb., 1957, a reconstructed Government, still led by M. Cyrankiewicz, took office. Elections to the *Sejm* have been held in 1961, 1965 and 1969. The expression of severe popular discontent in December, 1970, in the form of rioting in the northern parts of Gdansk, Gdynia and Szczecin led to the ousting of Gomulka, and substantial Government and Party changes followed.

Education.—Elementary education is compulsory and free. There are universities at Kraków, Warsaw, Poznań, Łódź, Wrocław, Lublin and Toruń and a considerable number of other towns.

Language and Literature.—Polish is a western Slavonic tongue (*see* U.S.S.R.), the Latin alphabet being used. Polish literature developed rapidly after the foundation of the University of Cracow (a printing press was established there in 1474 and there Copernicus died in 1543). A national school of poetry and drama survived the dismemberment and the former era of romanticism was followed by realistic and historical fiction, including the works of Henryk Sienkiewicz (1846–1916), Nobel Prize-winner for Literature in 1905, Boleslaw Prus (1847–1912), and Stanislaw Reymont (1868–1925), Nobel Prize-winner in 1924. There are now 42 daily papers published in Poland, 11 of them in Warsaw.

Production and Industry.—On January 3, 1946, a decree was issued to provide for the nationalization of mines, petroleum resources, water, gas and electricity services, banks, textile factories and large retail stores. At present over 99 per cent. of Polish industry is stated to be "socialized", but 84·6 per cent. of agricultural land is privately farmed.

FINANCE

	1967 '000 Zloty	1968 '000 Zloty
Revenue†	326,700,000	320,700,000
Expenditure†	321,600,000	326,200,000

† Estimated.

The basic exchange rate is 9·60 zloty= £1 but this is not used in practice. A special rate of 57·40 zloty= £1 is in force for non-commercial transactions with western countries. All foreign trade is conducted in foreign currencies. (*See also* p. 84.)

Trade with U.K.

	1969	1970
Imports from U.K.	£54,175,000	£59,695,000
Exports to U.K.	57,001,000	63,025,000

CAPITAL.—Warsaw, on the Vistula, pop. (December, 1970) 1,308,100. Other large towns are Łódź (761,800); Kraków (583,400); Wrocław (523,300); Poznań (469,100); Ψ Gdansk (364,300); Ψ Szczecin (337,000); Katowice (303,300); Bydgoszcz (280,500); Lublin (236,500); Zabrze (197,000); Częstochowa (188,000).

FLAG.—Equal horizontal stripes of white (above) and red. NATIONAL DAY—July 22.

BRITISH EMBASSY
(No. 1 Aleja Róz, Warsaw)

Ambassador Extraordinary and Plenipotentiary, His Excellency John Nicholas Henderson, C.M.G. (1968).....................£6,925

Counsellor, M. J. E. Fretwell (*Commercial*).
Defence and Air Attaché, Gp.-Capt. K. J. Barrett.
Naval and Military Attaché, Lt.-Col. D. J. Lear.
1st Secretaries, R. H. Baker; I. P. Chambers; N. MacPhee.
Consul, Miss I. Hogg.

British Council Representative. P. G. Lloyd, O.B.E., 59 Al Jerozolmskie, Warsaw (Library).

PORTUGAL
(República Portuguesa)

President of the Republic, Rear-Admiral Américo Deus Rodrigues Tomás, *inaugurated President* August 9, 1958, *re-elected for 7 years*, July 25, 1965.

CABINET

Prime Minister, Prof. Marcello Caetano, *appointed* Sept. 26, 1968.
Minister of Defence, Gen. H. de Sá V. Rebelo.
Interior, Dr. António M. G. Rapazote.
Justice, Prof. Dr. Mario de Almeida Costa.
Finance, Dr. João A. D. Rosas.
Marine, Cdre. Manuel P. Crespo.
Foreign Affairs, Dr. Rui M. de M. d'Espiney Patrício.
Public Works and Communications, Eng. Rui A da S. Sanches.
Overseas, Prof. Dr. Joaquim Moreira da Silva Cunha.
Education, Prof. Dr. José Veiga Simão.
Corporations, Social Security, Health and Assistance, Dr. Baltazar Rebelo de Sousa.

In addition there are 12 *Secretaries of State* and 8 *Under Secretaries*.

EMBASSY IN LONDON
Chancery: 11 Belgrave Square, S.W.1
[01-235-5331]

Ambassador Extraordinary and Plenipotentiary, His Excellency Senhor Antonio Leite de Faria (1968).
Counsellors, Senhor Luís Soares de Oliveira, M.V.O.; Senhor Luís de Oliveira Nunes (*Economic and Consular*); Senhor António Potier (*Press*).

1st Secretary, Senhor Dr. Francisco Manuel Baltazar Moita.

2nd Secretary, Dr. Carlos Teixeira da Motta.

Naval Attaché, Cdr. José Baptista Pinheiro de Azevedo.

Military and Air Attaché, Lt.-Col. Renato Fernando Marques Pinto.

Commercial Attachés, Senhor Jorge Goncalves Dias; Senhor Alexandre Castro Freire.

Asst. Commercial Attaché, Senhor José Agnelo de Vaz Carreiro.

Consulate-General, 47 Wilton Crescent, S.W.1 (01-235-6216).

Area and Population.—Continental Portugal occupies the western part of the Iberian Peninsula (*for* MAP, *see* p. 939). It contains an area of 34,500 square miles, with a population (including the Azores and Madeira) (estimated, June 1969) of 9,560,000. It lies between 36° 58'–42° 9' 12" N. lat. and 6° 11' 48"–9° 29' 45" W. long., being 302 miles in length from N. to S., and averaging about 117 in breadth from E. to W. The Azores and Madeira Islands in North Atlantic are treated as parts of continental Portugal for administrative purposes.

Government.—From the eleventh century until 1910 the government of Portugal was a monarchy, and for many centuries included the Vice-Royalty of Brazil, which declared its independence in 1822. In 1910 an armed rising in Lisbon drove King Manoel II and the Royal family into exile, and the National Assembly of Aug. 21, 1911, sanctioned a Republican form of government. The President is elected for seven years by indirect vote of the electors, who vote for members of an electoral college to select the President. The Prime Minister is appointed by the President, who also appoints the other Ministers on the recommendation of the Prime Minister. Dr. Salazar, Prime Minister from 1932, died on July 27, 1970.

The Government is responsible only to the President. There is a single Chamber Legislature (*Assembleia Nacional*) of 130 members elected by direct vote of the electors. There is also a "Corporative Chamber" consisting of representatives of local authorities and industrial, commercial, cultural and religious interests, to which all bills introduced into the Chamber must be submitted for its opinion. The Legislature is in session for three months in the year. In the recess the Government legislates by decrees or decree-laws, of which the latter only must be confirmed by the legislature. Both men and women enjoy the franchise; but there are certain educational or tax-payment qualifications.

Portugal is still essentially an agricultural country and over 40 per cent. of the working population are engaged in agriculture, forestry and animal husbandry.

Defence.—Military service is compulsory for all men who are physically fit and very few are exempted. The present strength of the Army is about 200,000 of which a large proportion is serving in Portuguese Africa. Much of the Army's old British equipment is now being replaced by French, German and American material. The Navy consists of 1,280 officers and 13,200 men manning a total of over 130 craft. The serving strength of the Air Force is about 1,000 officers and 12,500 other ranks (including some 2,500 parachutists) and about 800 aircraft of all types.

Education is free and compulsory for four years from the age of 7 and is being extended to six years. Secondary education is mainly conducted in State lyceums, but there are also private schools. There are also military, naval, technical and other special schools. There are Universities at Coimbra (founded in 1290), Lisbon (1911) and Oporto (1911).

Language and Literature.—Portuguese is a Romance language with admixtures of Arabic and other idioms. It is the language of Portugal and Brazil.

Portuguese language and literature reached the culminating point of their development in the *Lusiadas* (dealing with the voyage of Vasco da Gama) and other works of Camoens (Camões), born in 1524, died in 1580. Until the second quarter of the nineteenth century Portuguese literature dominated that of Brazil. Modern literature, both prose and verse, is in a flourishing condition and there are more than twenty daily newspapers, of which 9 are published in Lisbon.

Civil aviation is controlled by the Ministry of Communications. There is an international airport at Portela, about 5 miles from Lisbon, and the airport of Pedras Rubras near Oporto is also used for some international services. A new airfield at Faro in the Algarve now takes direct flights from London. There are a civil airline, an inter-island service and services in Portuguese Africa. British European Airways and *Transportes Aereos Portugueses* operate a daily service between London and Lisbon by agreement between them which calls at Oporto twice weekly in both directions. There are altogether 19 airlines operating a total of about 400 services a month through Lisbon airport.

Agriculture.—The chief agricultural products are cork, maize, wheat, rye, rice, oats, barley, potatoes, beans, onions, olives, oranges, lemons, figs, almonds, tomatoes, timber, port wine and table wines. There are extensive forests of pine, cork, eucalyptus and chestnut covering about 20 per cent. of the total area of the country.

Industry.—The country is so far only moderately industrialized, but is fairly rapidly extending its industries. The principal manufactures, most of which are still protected by high tariffs, are textiles (cotton, woollen and rayon), furniture, pottery, glassware, cork goods, leather, paper pulp, tomato concentrates, canned fish, cement, fertilizers, chemicals and hardware. There is a modern steelworks; several British and foreign motor-car manufacturers assemble their vehicles in Portugal and lately the tourist industry has become an important earner of foreign exchange. There are several hydro-electric power stations and a new thermal power station. *Minerals.*—The principal mineral products are pyrites, wolfram, tin, iron ores and some copper.

Finance.—Portugal is a member of the European Monetary Agreement, the World Bank, the International Monetary Fund and the International Finance Corporation. The country has large gold and foreign exchange reserves, which amounted to Escudos 24,317,488,067 in April, 1969. The 1969 State budget showed a surplus of *Escudos* 1,900,000. Total revenue, Escudos 25,327,100,000; expenditure Escudos 25,325,200,000.

Currency.—*Escudo* (of 100 *Centavos*). *Conto* consists of 1,000 escudos. Since devaluation of the £ sterling in 1967 the rate of exchange has fluctuated around the level Escudos 68·50 = £1 (*see also* p. 83).

Trade.—Total trade of Portugal in 1969 amounted to imports valued at *Escudos* 37,261,000,000 and exports valued at *Escudos* 24,525,000,000. The British share of the Portuguese import market amounted to 13·8 per cent. and the United Kingdom imported 21·09 per cent. of all Portuguese exports.

Portugal is a member of E.F.T.A., G.A.T.T. and O.E.C.D. The principal imports are raw and semi-manufactured iron and steel of the types that are not produced by the national steel-works, in-

dustrial machinery, chemicals, crude oil, motor vehicles, wool, dried cod fish and raw material for textiles.

The principal exports in 1969 were textiles, foodstuffs, timber, cork and respective manufactures, diamonds, electrical and other machinery, and chemicals

Trade with U.K.

	1969	1970
Imports from U.K...	£74,850,000	£86,776,000
Exports to U.K.....	75,907,000	85,630,000

CAPITAL, Ψ Lisbon. Population (estimated, 1966), 820,000. Ψ Oporto 310,000; Ψ Setubal 44,030.

Lisbon, distance 1,110 miles; transit, 50 hours; by air, 2½ hours.

FLAG.—Vertical band of green (next staff) and square of red, bearing arms of the Republic, framed. NATIONAL DAY.—June 10 (Portugal Day).

BRITISH EMBASSY
Ambassador's Residence—Rua S. Francisco de Borja 63, Lisbon. *Chancery Offices*, Rua São Domingos à Lapa 37, Lisbon.
Ambassador Extraordinary and Plenipotentiary, His Excellency David Francis Muirhead, C.M.G., C.V.O. (1970).........................£6,925

BRITISH CONSULAR OFFICES
There are British Consular Offices at *Lisbon, Oporto, Portimao* and *Vila Real de Santo Antonio, Figuera da Foz* (Portugal), St. *Vincent* (*Cape Verde Islands*), *Funchal* (*Madeira*), *Lourenço Marques* and *Beira* (*Portuguese East Africa*), *Luanda* (*Portuguese West Africa*) and *Macau*.

BRITISH COUNCIL
Representative, A. M. Welsh, O.B.E., The British Institute, Rua de Luis Fernandes 3, Lisbon 2.

There is a British Institute at *Coimbra* (Rua Alexandre Herculano 34) and the Council has libraries at *Lisbon, Coimbra* and *Oporto.*

ROYAL BRITISH CLUB, Rua da Estrela 8, Lisbon.
BRITISH-PORTUGUESE CHAMBER OF COMMERCE, Rua da Estrela 8, Lisbon (Branch at Rua de Sá da Bandeira, 784 2° EF, *Oporto*).
ANGLO-PORTUGUESE ASSOCIATION, Rua de Breyner 79, Oporto.

MADEIRA AND THE AZORES
Madeira and The Azores are administratively parts of metropolitan Portugal.

The *Madeiras* are a group of islands in the Atlantic Ocean about 520 miles west of Lisbon, and consist of Madeira, Porto Santo and 3 uninhabited islands (Desertas). The total area is 314 square miles, with a population of 269,769. Ψ Funchal in Madeira, the largest island (270 square miles), is the capital, with a population of 43,301; Machico (4,734). Trade with U.K., 1969: Imports from U.K., £1,307,000; Exports, £516,000.

The *Azores* are a group of 9 islands (Flores, Corvo, Terceira, São Jorge, Pico, Fayal, Graciosa, São Miguel and Santa Maria) in the Atlantic Ocean, with a total area of 922 square miles and a population of 318,558. Ψ Ponta Delgada the capital of the group, has a population of 22,448. Other ports are Ψ Angra, in Terceira, (13,501) and Ψ Horta (7,109). Trade with U.K., 1970: Imports from U.K., £557,000; Exports, £227,000.

PORTUGUESE OVERSEAS PROVINCES
CAPE VERDE ISLANDS, off the west coast of Africa, consist of two groups of islands, Windward (Santo Antao, São Vicente, Santa Luzia, São Nicolao, Boa Vista and Sal, the last-named having a South Atlantic air base, opened in 1949) and Leeward (Maio, São Tiago, Fogo and Brava) with a total area of 1,516 square miles and a population (U.N. estimate, 1969) of 250,000. Revenue (1964), *Escudos* 135,411,000. Capital, Ψ Praia (6,000). Vessels take coal and oil at Ψ Mindelo, Sao Vicente (pop. 20,000).

SÃO TOMÉ and PRÍNCIPE ISLANDS, in the Gulf of Guinea (area 372 square miles, population (1969), 66,000). Capital Ψ São Tomé (3,187).

PORTUGUESE GUINEA, area 14,000 sq. miles, population (estimated, 1969), 530,000; (capital Ψ Bissau, population 6,000). Revenue (1964), *Escudos* 202,012,000.

ANGOLA has an area of 488,000 sq. miles, population (U.N. estimate, 1969), 5,430,000, with present capital Ψ St. Paul de Luanda (pop. 346,763), and capital designate Nova Lisbôa, and includes also Kabinda and Portuguese Zaire (N. of Congo). Angola was restored to Portugal by the Netherlands in 1648.

Angola's Trade with U.K.

	1969	1970
Imports from U.K....	£11,101,000	£13,819,000
Exports to U.K......	3,639,000	8,920,000

A transcontinental railway from *Benguela* (Lobito Bay) in Angola, traverses the Katanga mineral district of the Congo and then runs southwards through Rhodesia to Bulawayo and eastwards to Beira. This line makes through communication from Lobito Bay on the Atlantic to Beira on the Indian Ocean.

PORTUGUESE EAST AFRICA, OR MOZAMBIQUE, Lourenço Marques, Inhambane, Quelimane, Tete, Mozambique, Cape Delgado and Nyasa, together with the territory of Manica and Sofala, has a total area of 297,657 square miles, with a population (estimated, 1969) of 7,376,000. Capital Ψ Lourenço Marques (441,363).

Trade with U.K.

	1969	1970
Imports from U.K....	£11,597,000	£13,131,000
Exports to U.K......	4,019,000	5,859,000

Ψ MACAU, in China, on an island in the Canton River, has an area of 5 square miles and a population (U.N. estimate, 1969) of 260,000.

PORTUGUESE TIMOR (the eastern portion of the island), in the Malay Archipelago, has an area of 7,329 square miles, with a population (estimated, 1967) 566,000. Capital, Ψ Dili, pop. 7,000.

QATAR
Ruler of Qatar, Shaikh Ahmed bin Ali bin Abdullah Al Thani; *succeeded* Oct. 24, 1960.
Deputy Ruler, Heir Apparent, Prime Minister and Minister of Finance and Petrol, Shaikh Khalifa bin Hamad Al Thani.

COUNCIL OF MINISTERS
Minister of Education, Shaikh Jassem bin Hamad Al Thani.
Health, Shaikh Abdul Aziz bin Ahmad Al Thani.
Economy and Commerce, Shaikh Naser bin Khaled Al Thani.
Justice, Shaikh Abdul Rahman bin Saoud Al Thani.
Electricity and Water, Shaikh Jasem bin Moh'd Al Thani.
Industry and Agriculture, Shaikh Faisal bin Thani Al Thani.
Public Works, Sayed Khaled bin Abdullah Al-Attiyah.
Labour and Social Welfare Affairs, Sayed Ali bin Ahmed Al-Ansari.
Communications and Transport, Sayed Abdullah bin Naser Al-Suwaidi.

Until 1971, Qatar was one of the nine independent Emirates in the Persian Gulf in special treaty relations with the Government of the United Kingdom. In that year, with the withdrawal of H.M. Forces from the area, these special treaty relations were terminated. On April 2, 1970 a Provisional Constitution for Qatar was proclaimed, providing for the establishment of a Council of Ministers and for the formation of a 33-member Consultative Council (of which 20 members are elected) to assist the Council of Ministers in running the affairs of the State. The first Cabinet was formed of 10 members on May 29, 1970. A permanent constitution will be formulated in the light of experience gained during the current transitional stage to supersede the Provisional Constitution. Qatar is also a member of the Union of Arab Emirates.

The state of Qatar covers the peninsula of Qatar from approximately the Northern shore of Khor al Odaid to the Eastern shore of Khor al Salwa. The area is about 4,000 sq. miles, with a population estimated at about 130,000 (May, 1970).

The great majority of the population is concentrated in the urban district of the capital Doha. Only a small minority still pursue the traditional life of the semi-nomadic tribesmen and fisherfolk. There are townships on the coast at Khor, Dukhan, Wakra and Umm Said. There are many gardens and farms near Doha and to the North and encouragement is being given to the development of agriculture. Qatar is self-sufficient in most vegetables, exporting a large surplus to the other Gulf states.

Doha is an expanding town with good shopping facilities and services and an airport built to international standards. Work on the extension of the runway to a total length of 15,000 feet began in 1970. Regular air services connect Qatar with Bahrain and the Trucial States, Kuwait, Muscat, Iran, Saudi Arabia, Jordan, Lebanon, U.A.R., the Indian sub-continent and Europe.

In September, 1966, the new Qatar/Dubai Riyal was introduced.

Further development projects include a cement factory, inaugurated in May, 1969, a factory for processing and freezing prawns which began operations in 1968 and a £15,000,000 fertilizer project under construction at Umm Said. The daily productive capacity of this plant will be 990 tons of ammonia and 1,100 tons of urea. The plant is expected to begin production by 1972. A fully automated flour mill is also under construction at Umm Said and this was scheduled to go into operation in 1972 with a daily output of 50 tons of flour.

In 1970 a new £10,000,000 5 berth deep water port was opened to ocean going ships.

The Qatar Broadcasting Station has been transmitting on medium and short-wave bands since 1968. In 1969 the Marconi Company began constructing a television station which was due to be completed in 1972. A pilot television station began transmitting in September 1970.

Oil deposits on land are being exploited by the Qatar Petroleum Company, a subsidiary of I.P.C. under a concession granted by the Ruler, and the first oil shipment was made on December 31, 1949. The Company is following an agreed policy of levelling off annual production at about 9,000,000 long tons. An offshore concession is held by the Shell Company of Qatar which is exporting oil from its terminal on Halul Island at a rate of about 7,000,000 long tons per annum. Following the withdrawal of the Continental Oil Company of Qatar from the country part of its offshore concession area was awarded to the Qatar-Japan Oil

Company. In March, 1970, another offshore concession area was awarded to The South East Asia Oil and Gas Company. Extension of the Doha water distillation plant raised its total capacity to nearly 4,000,000 gallons daily in 1969.

Trade with U.K.

	1969	1970
Imports from U.K.	£5,815,000	£7,430,000
Exports to U.K.	24,743,000	30,581,000

CAPITAL.—Doha. Population (estimated) 100,000.

FLAG.—White and maroon, white portion nearer the mast; vertical indented line comprising 17 angles divides the colours.

British Political Agent, E. F. Henderson.
Asst. Political Agent, P. J. F. Mansley.
2nd Secretary, P. J. Hurr (*Commercial*).
3rd Secretary, J. Martin (*Consular*).

RUMANIA
(Republica Socialistă România)
STATE COUNCIL

President, Nicolae Ceauşescu. *assumed office* Dec. 9, 1967; *re-elected* March 16, 1969.
Vice-Presidents, Emil Bodnăraş; Manea Mănescu; Vasile Vîleu; Ştefan Peterfi.

COUNCIL OF MINISTERS

President, Ion Gheorghe Maurer.
First Vice-President, Ilie Verdet.
Vice-Presidents, Iosif Banc; Janos Fazekas; Gheorghe Gaston Marin; Gheorghe Radulescu; Emil Draganescu; Leonte Răutu; Mihai Marinescu; Ion Pătan.
Minister of the Armed Forces, Gen. Ion Ioniţă.
Internal Affairs, Cornel Onescu.
Foreign Affairs, Corneliu Manescu.
President of the Economic Council, Mănea Mănescu.
President of the State Planning Committee, Maxim Berghianu.
Minister of Finance, Florea Dumitrescu.
Metallurgic Industry, Nicolae Agachi.
Machine-Building, Ioan Avram.
Chemical Industry, Alexandru Boabă.
Petroleum Industry, Nicolae Toader.
Transport, Pavel Stefan.
Light Industry, Ion Crăciun.
Industrial Construction, Matei Ghigiu.
Timber Industry, Mihai Suder.
Food Industry, Gheorghe Moldovan.
Health, Dan Enăchescu.
Labour, Petre Lupu.
Internal Trade, Nicolae Bozdog.
Foreign Trade, Cornel Burtică.
Education, Mircea Maliţa.
Justice, Teodor Vasiliu.
Presidents of:—
State Committee for Problems of Organization and Wages, Petre Lupu.
Agriculture and Silviculture, Angelo Miculescu.
Committee for Prices, Gheorghe Gaston Marin.
Local Economy and Administration, Petre Blajovici.
State Committee for Culture and Art, Pompiliu Macovei.
Central Council of the General Union of Trade Unions, —*Minister*, Florian Dănălache.
National Union of Agricultural Production Co-operatives, Virgil Trofin.
Minister, Youth Problems, Ion Iliescu.

THE COMMUNIST PARTY

Standing Presidium Central Committee, E. Bodnăras; N. Ceausescu; M. Mănescu; J. G. Maurer; P. Niculescu-Mizil; G. Pana; G. Radulescu; V. Trofin; I. Verdet.
Secretariat of the Central Committee, Nicolae Ceauş-

sescu (*First*); M. Gere; I. Iliescu; M. Mănescu; P. Niculescu-Mizil; G. Pana; V. Patilinet; D. Popescu.

RUMANIAN EMBASSY IN LONDON
4 Palace Green, W.8
[01-937-9666-9]
Ambassador Extraordinary and Plenipotentiary, His Excellency Vasile Pungan (1966).
Counsellors, Constantin Rădulescu (*Commercial*); Vasile Tilincă.

Area and Population.—Rumania is a republic of South-Eastern Europe, formerly the classical *Dacia* and *Scythia Pontica*, having its origin in the union of the Danubian principalities of *Wallachia* and *Moldavia* under the *Treaty of Paris* (April, 1856). The area in October, 1945, was estimated at 91,600 sq. miles, with a population (U.N. estimate, July, 1969) of 20,010,000.

Government.—The principalities remained separate entities under Turkish suzerainty until 1859, when Prince Alexandru Ion Cuza was elected Prince of both, still under the suzerainty of Turkey. Prince Cuza abdicated in 1866 and was succeeded by Prince Charles of Hohenzollern-Sigmaringen, in whose successors the crown was vested. By the *Treaty of Berlin* (July 13, 1878) the Principality

was recognized as an independent State, and part of the *Dobrudja* (which had been occupied by the Rumanians) was incorporated. On March 27, 1881, it was recognized as a Kingdom.

The outcome of the War of 1914–18 added Bessarabia, the Bukovina, Transylvania, The Banat and Crişana-Maramureş, these additions of territory being confirmed in the Treaty of St. Germain, 1919, and the Treaty of Petit Trianon, 1920.

On June 27, 1940, in compliance with an ultimatum from U.S.S.R., Bessarabia and Northern Bukovina were ceded to the Soviet Government, the area affected being about 20,000 sq. miles, with a population of about 4,000,000.

In August, 1940, Rumania ceded to Bulgaria the portion of Southern Dobrudja (about 3,000 sq. miles) taken from Bulgaria in 1913. Rumania became "The Rumanian People's Republic" in December, 1947, on the abdication of King Michael.

A new Constitution, modelled on the Soviet Constitution of 1936, was adopted unanimously on September 24, 1952, by the Grand National Assembly. The Assembly was later dissolved and elections were held for a new Grand National Assembly on November 30, 1952; in each constituency there was only one candidate for election,

representing the People's Democratic Front. Further elections on similar lines were held in February, 1957; in March, 1961, and in March, 1965. A new Constitution was approved by the Grand National Assembly in 1965 when the name of the state was changed to The Socialist Republic of Rumania. The Constitution states (Art. 3) that the leading political force of the whole of society is the Rumanian Communist Party.

Agriculture.—The soil of Wallachia and Moldavia is among the richest in Europe producing wheat, maize, millet, oats, barley, rye, beans, peas and other vegetables. Grape vines and fruits are abundant. The fertile plain of Transylvania yields large crops of maize, wheat, rye, oats, flax and hemp. Agriculture and sheep and cattle raising are the principal industries of Rumania, but the climate of this part of South-Eastern Europe is of the Continental character, and the intense winter cold and summer heat, and fierce summer drought sometimes defeat these principal industries. The forests of the mountainous regions are extensive (17,851,401 acres), and the timber industry is important. The total arable land under cultivation in 1968 was 9,743,100 hectares.

Socialization of agriculture was completed when plans for collectivization were fulfilled in the spring of 1962, some three years ahead of the planned date.

Natural Resources and Industry.—Before the war petroleum and agriculture were the backbone of the Rumanian economy. Though the production of both industries has increased, they no longer hold the same dominant position. Rumania's oil resources now enable her to produce about 13,000,000 tons of crude oil a year and there are plentiful supplies of natural gas, together with various mineral deposits including coal, iron ore, bauxite, lead, zinc, copper and uranium in quantities which allow a substantial part of the requirements of industry to be met from local resources. Since 1948 industrialization has proceeded rapidly and the State is well on the way to establishing a mixed industrial economy. Heavy investments have been made in electric power, the chemical industry, the metallurgical industry and the engineering industry and growing attention is being paid to light industry. The economy is centrally organized on the basis of Five-Year Plans which cover all branches of national activity including investment and production. The current Five-Year Plan (1966 to 1970) calls for an average annual increase of 11 per cent. in industrial output, a figure which has been exceeded in the first two of the five years.

1968 production figures were: crude oil, 13,285,000 tons; coal, 17,020,000 tons; electric power, 27,828 million kWh; natural gas, 17,226 million cubic metres; steel, 4,751,000 tons; pig iron, 2,992,000 tons; wheat, 4,847,900 tons; maize, 7,105,300 tons; sunflower seed, 729,900 tons; sugar beet, 3,936,400 tons.

Language and Literature.—Rumanian is a Romance language with many archaic forms and with admixtures of Slavonic, Turkish, Magyar and French words. The folk-songs and folk-lore, composed by the people themselves, and transmitted orally through many centuries (and collected in the 19th century), form one of the most interesting of such collections. The publication of all books and reviews is controlled and authorized by the State Committee for Culture and Art, which has the status of a Ministry. In 1968 57 daily newspapers were published. The leading religion is that of the Rumanian Orthodox Church; the Roman Catholics and some Protestant denominations are of importance numerically. The Jewish community has declined through emigration.

Education is free and nominally compulsory, with 3,902,347 in attendance in 1967–68, including 141,589 in higher education. There are 5 Universities, at Bucharest, Iasi, Cluj, Timisioara and Craiova. A " Marxist–Leninist " University was opened in Bucharest in 1951. There are polytechnics at Bucharest, Timisioara, Cluj, Brasov, Galaţi and Iasi, two commercial academies at Bucharest and Brasov, and agricultural colleges at Bucharest, Iasi, Cluj, Craiova and Timisioara.

Communications.—In 1967 there were 11,023 miles of railway open for traffic. The mercantile marine, as a result of war losses, seizure and reparations, was reduced to a few moderate-sized sea-going steamers and a number of coastal and river craft. The number of sea-going ships had been increased by 1970. The principal ports are Constantza (on the Black Sea), Sulina (on the Danube Estuary), Galaţi, the most important, Brăila, Giurgiu and Turnu Severin. Rumania is a member of the Danube Commission whose seat is at Budapest.

FINANCE

	1967 Lei	1968 Lei
Revenue....	129,307,000,000	138,757,013,826
Expenditure..	124,322,000,000	131,920,728,882

Up-to-date figures of the Public Debt are not available. No foreign loans (other than short-term commercial loans) are known to have been contracted since March, 1947. The internal debt was virtually wiped out by stabilization in August, 1947; there has been no internal loan issue since that date.

The Rumanian *Leu* (of 100 *Bani*) had been re-valued three times since the war by Feb. 1, 1954. With a 200 per cent. premium on all " capitalist " currencies for non-commercial transactions, the effective exchange rate after devaluation of sterling in 1970, was *Lei* 43·20= £1 and *Lei* 18= $U.S.1. (*See also* p. 84.)

TRADE

	1967 Lei	1968 Lei
Imports.........	9,276,500,000	9,653,800,000
Exports.........	8,372,100,000	8,811,400,000

No complete figures for foreign trade have been published since the start of the Communist *régime*. Imports are chiefly semi-manufactured goods, raw materials, machinery and metals; exports consist principally of maize, wheat, barley, oats, petroleum, timber, cattle, machines and industrial equipment. Trade with U.K., although relatively small, has increased notably since the signature of an Anglo-Rumanian trade arrangement in 1960.

Trade with U.K.

	1969	1970
Imports from U.K. ...	£28,637,000	£29,077,000
Exports to U.K......	24,970,000	23,188,000

About 50 per cent. of Rumania's foreign trade is now with the Soviet Union and the other countries of Eastern Europe. Rumania is a member of the Soviet-sponsored " Council for Mutual Economic Assistance ".

CAPITAL, Bucharest, on the Dimbovita, population (1966), 1,511,388. Other towns with a population of over 100,000 in 1966 are: Brasov (263,201); Cluj (222,652); Ψ Constantza (199,356); Iasi (194,835); Timisioara (193,030); Ploiesti (190,687); Craiova (173,315); Ψ Galaţi (151,349); Ψ Braila (144,341); Arad (136,912); Oradea (134,939); Reşiţa (121,458); Sibiu (109,546); Baia Mare (108,709); Tîrgu-Mureş (104,922); and Hundedoara (100,953).

FLAG.—Three vertical bands, blue, yellow, red, with the emblem of the Republic in the centre band. NATIONAL DAY.—August 23 (Liberation Day, 1944).

BRITISH EMBASSY

24 Strada Jules Michelet, Bucharest 22

Ambassador Extraordinary and Plenipotentiary, His Excellency Denis Seward Laskey, C.M.G., C.V.O. (1968)....................................£6,925

Counsellor, R. M. Russell (*Commercial*).

Defence, Naval and Military Attaché, Lt.-Col. C. U. Blascheck, M.C.

1st Secretaries, P. Yarnold (*Head of Chancery*); A. A. Rowell.

2nd Secretaries, N. A. McGregor (*Consul*); D. Reed (*Commercial*).

RWANDA
(Republic of Rwanda)

President, Grégoire Kayibanda, *born* 1925; *elected* Oct. 26, 1961; *assumed office,* July 1, 1962; *re-elected,* 1965 and 1969.

Rwanda became an independent republic on July 1, 1962. Formerly part of the Belgian-administered trusteeship of Ruanda-Urundi, it has an area of 10,169 sq. miles and a population (estimated, 1969) of 3,500,000, mainly of the Bahutu tribe, with Batutsi and Batwa minorities. Coffee, cotton and tea are grown and there is some mineral production. Hides, extract of quinine and pyrethrum flowers are also exported.

The currency is the *Rwanda franc.* In 1968 total imports were valued at $U.S. 17,200,000; total exports, $U.S. 16,100,000; imports from U.K. 1970, £261,000; exports to U.K., £974,000. Revenue in 1968 totalled: *Rw.Fr.* 1,313,000,000; Expenditure *Rw.Fr.* 1,505,000,000.

At a referendum held in September, 1961, under supervision of the United Nations, a large majority voted against the retention of the monarchy which was accordingly abolished on Oct. 2, 1961. Elections for a new Legislative Assembly were also held in September, 1961, and the Assembly elected M. Kayibanda as President of the National Council, to hold office as Head of State and Head of the Government Admission of Rwanda to membership of the United Nations was approved on July 26, 1962.

CAPITAL.—Kigali (4,273).

FLAG.—Three vertical bands, red, yellow and green with letter R on yellow band.

British Ambassador, His Excellency Richard Mercer Keene Slater, C.M.G. (1970) (*resident at* Kampala, Uganda).

EL SALVADOR
(República de El Salvador)

President, Fidel Sanchez Hernandez; *elected* March 5, 1967; *assumed office* July 1, 1967, *for a five-year term.*

Vice-President, Humberto Guillermo Cuestas.

Minister of Foreign Affairs, Dr. Francisco José Guerrero.

SALVADOREAN EMBASSY AND CONSULATE
9B Portland Place, W.1.
[01–636–9563]

Ambassador, His Excellency Don Rafael Alfonso Quiñonez-Meza (1968).

Secretary and Consul, Señor Lic. Jorge Saguer-Saprissa.

Attaché, Don René A. Machon-Rivera.

Area and Population.—The Republic of El Salvador extends along the Pacific coast of Central America for 160 miles with a general breadth of about 50 miles, and contains an area of 7,722 square miles with a population (U.N. estimate, 1969) of 3,390,000. El Salvador is therefore a densely populated country with some 424 persons per square mile. It is divided into 14 Departments. (*For* MAP, *see* p. 875.)

The surface of the country is very mountainous, many of the peaks being extinct volcanoes. The

highest peaks are the Santa Ana volcano (7,700 ft.) and the San Vincente volcano (7,200 ft.). Much of the interior has an average altitude of 2,000 feet. The lowlands along the coast are generally hot, but towards the interior the altitude tempers the severity of the heat. Much has been done in recent years to improve sanitary conditions and services. There is a wet season from May to October, and a dry season from November to April. Earthquakes have been frequent in the history of El Salvador, the most recent being that of May 3, 1965, when considerable damage was done to San Salvador.

The principal river is the Rio Lempa. There is a large volcanic lake (Ilopango) a few miles to the east of the capital, while farther away and to the west lies the smaller but very picturesque lake of Coatepeque, which appears to have been formed in a vast crater flanked by the Santa Ana volcano.

Government.—El Salvador was conquered in 1526 by Pedro de Alvarado, and formed part of the Spanish vice-royalty of Guatemala until 1821. Under a new Constitution adopted in 1950, the President is elected for six years and the Legislature for two. New legislative elections under proportional representation held in March, 1970, resulted in a chamber composed of 34 deputies of the official party and 18 opposition deputies. In the Presidential elections held on March 5, 1967, the candidate of the Government Party, Colonel Fidel Sanchez Hernandez, won by 54·4 per cent. of the votes against three opposition candidates.

Agriculture.—The principal cash crops are coffee, which is grown under shade-trees principally on the slopes of the volcanoes, cotton, which is cultivated on the coastal plains, and cane sugar. Also cultivated are maize, sesame, indigo, rice, balsam, etc. In the lower altitudes towards the east, sisal is produced and used in the manufacture of coffee and sugar bags. Diversification and modernization of agriculture are in progress, including plans for a meat export industry.

Industry.—There is growing industrialization and existing factories make textiles, constructional steel, furniture, cement and household items. El Salvador is a leading exporter to the Central American Common Market, of which she is a member.

Education.—The illiteracy rate is about 50 per cent. Primary education is nominally compulsory, but the number of schools and teachers available is too small to enable education to be given to all children of school age. In recent Budgets, however, a high percentage of the national revenue has been devoted to education and great efforts are being made to eliminate the existing shortage of schools and teachers.

Language and Literature.—The language of the country is Spanish. Indigenous literature has not yet produced work of international repute. There are 4 daily newspapers published at the capital, and 4 in the provinces.

Communications.—The El Salvador Railway, nearly 100 miles in length, connects Acajutla with the capital and with the important coffee centre of Santa Ana. The International Railways of Central America have a line from the port of La Union (on the Gulf of Fonseca) to the capital and another one in the opposite direction which taps the richest coffee growing region in the country and proceeds to Zacapa (in Guatemala) thereby affording continuous railway communication between San Salvador and Guatemala City and Puerto Barrios on the Caribbean coast. The roads are paved and in good condition. There is a good motor road between Acajutla, the principal port, and the capital (23 miles), while motor transportation is possible throughout the year between the capital and Guatemala City. The Pan-American Highway from the

Guatemalan frontier follows this route and continues to the Honduran frontier. Pan-American Airways, TACA, TAB, LANICA, SAHSA and LACSA connect El Salvador with the rest of the world. The Ilopango international airport can receive jet aircraft.

There are post and telegraph offices throughout the country. There are many broadcasting stations and two television stations.

FINANCE

	1969 Colones	1970 Colones
Revenue (*Budget*)...	279,266,000	313,932,000
Expenditure (*do.*)....	255,831,000	312,480,000
Public Debt (Dec. 31, 1970):		
External Debt......		329,238,000
Internal Debt		231,000,000
Direct Governmental.............49,015,000		
Guaranteed by Government.........48,451,000		

TRADE

	1969 Colones	1970 Colones
Imports..............	537,600,000	535,900,000
Exports..............	506,200,000	573,500,000

Trade with U.K.

	1969	1970
Imports from U.K....	£1,768,000	£2,338,000
Exports to U.K.......	172,000	340,000

Par of Exchange 2·50 *Colones* = $1 (U.S.) (*see also* p. 84).

Coffee to the value of ₡223,364,000 was exported in 1969. Exports of cotton were valued at ₡36,200,000 in 1968 and ₡48,700,000 in 1969. Other exports are shrimps (₡12,401,000) sisal (in the form of the bags used for exporting coffee, sugar, etc.), gold, sugar indigo, sesame, balsam, hides and skins. The chief imports are iron and steel goods, motor cars, fertilizers, manufactured goods, chemical products and petrol.

CAPITAL.—San Salvador. Population (Census of 1968), 340,000. Other towns are Santa Ana (73,864); San Miguel (38,330), ΨLa Union (Cutoco), ΨLa Libertad and ΨAcajutla.

FLAG.—Three horizontal bands light blue, white, light blue; coat of arms on white band. NATIONAL DAY.—September 15.

BRITISH EMBASSY
13A Avenida Norte (Continuación), Colonia Dueñas, (Apartado 601), San Salvador
Ambassador Extraordinary and Plenipotentiary and Consul-General, His Excellency Donovan Harold Clibborn, C.M.G. (1971)................£6,475
1st *Secretary,* P. Pendleton (*Consul*).
San Salvador is 5,700 miles from London.

SAN MARINO
(Repubblica di San Marino)
Regents, Two " Capitani Reggenti ".
CONSULATE GENERAL IN LONDON
Saxone House, 74A Regent Street, W.1
Consul General, C. Forte.
Vice-Consul, R. E. Rudge.

A small Republic in the hills near Rimini, on the Adriatic, founded, it is stated, by a pious stonecutter of Dalmatia in the 4th century. The Republic always resisted the Papal claims and its integrity is respected by Italy. The Republic is governed by a State Congress of 10 members, under the Presidency of two Captains-Regent. The Great and General Council, a legislative body of 60 members is elected by a universal suffrage for a term of 5 years. A Council of Twelve forms in certain cases a Supreme Court of Justice. The area is approximately 23 square miles, the population (U.N. estimate, 1970) is 19,000. There is a

ceremonial guard of about 180. The city of San Marino, on the slope of Monte Titano, has three castles, a fine church and Government palace, a theatre and a museum. The principal industries are wine, cereals, and cattle, and the main industries are ceramics, lime, concrete, cotton yarns, colour and paints. A Treaty of Extradition between the Governments of Great Britain and the Republic of San Marino has been in force since 1899.

FLAG.—Two horizontal bands, white, blue (with coat of arms of the Republic in centre).

SAUDI ARABIA
(al Mamlaka al Arabiya as-Sa'udiya.)

King of Saudi Arabia, H.M. King Faisal bin Abdul Aziz, G.B.E., *born* 1904, *ascended the throne*, Nov. 2, 1964.

Crown Prince, H.R.H. Amir Khalid bin Abdul Aziz, *born* 1912.

COUNCIL OF MINISTERS

President of the Council and Foreign Minister, H.M. King Faisal bin Abdul Aziz.

Deputy President, H.R.H. Amir Khalid bin Abdul Aziz.

2nd Deputy President and Minister of Interior, H.R.H. Amir Fahd bin Abdul Aziz.

Defence and Aviation, H.R.H. Amir Sultan bin Abdul Aziz.

Finance and National Economy, H.R.H. Amir Musa'id bin Abdul Rahman.

Agriculture, Shaikh Hassan al Mishari.

Education, Shaikh Hassan Al al-Shaikh.

Trade and Industry, Shaikh Abid Shaikh.

Communications, Shaikh Mohammad Omar Tawfiq.

Petroleum and Mineral Resources, Shaikh Ahmad Zaki Yamani.

Justice, Shaikh Mohamed Ali Al Harakan.

Labour and Social Affairs, Shaikh Abdul Rahman Aba Khail.

Information, Shaikh Ibrahim Augary.

Health, Shaikh Jamil al-Hujailan.

Pilgrimage and Trusts, Shaikh Hassan Kutbi.

Foreign Affairs, Shaikh Umar Saqqaf (*Minister of State*).

SAUDI ARABIAN EMBASSY
27 Eaton Place, S.W.1
[01-235-8431]

Ambassador Extraordinary and Plenipotentiary, His Excellency Sheikh Abdul Rahman Al Helaissi, G.C.V.O. (1966).

Minister-Counsellor, Mohamed Nouri Ibrahim, C.V.O.

Counsellor, Salem Azzam, C.V.O.

2nd Secretaries, Saleh Al-Fouzan; Yasien Khalil Allaf; Hassan M. Attar.

3rd Secretary, Hassan M. Enany.

Defence Attaché, Col. Abdulla I. Al-Saheal.

Commercial Counsellor, Ibrahim Malaika, C.V.O.

Cultural Counsellor, Abdulaziz Mansour Al-Turki.

The Kingdom of Saudi Arabia, so named since Sept. 20, 1932, is a personal union of two countries, the Sultan of Nejd being also King of the Hejaz.

By the *Treaty of Jedda* (May 20, 1927) Great Britain recognized Ibn Saud as an independent ruler, King of the Hejaz and of Nejd and its Dependencies.

The total area of the Kingdom is about 927,000 sq. miles, with a population (U.N. estimate, 1969) of 7,200,000.

In the 18th century Nejd was an independent State and the stronghold of the Wahhabi sect. It subsequently fell under the Turkish yoke, but in 1913 Ibn Saud threw off Turkish rule and captured from the Turks the Province of Hasa. In 1921 he added to his dominions the

territories of the Rashid family of Jebel Shammar, which he captured by force of arms; in 1925 he completed the conquest of the Hejaz, and in 1926 accepted the surrender of the greater part of Asir, the whole of which is now part of the Kingdom.

Nejd (" Plateau ") has no definite frontiers, but may be said to extend over about 800,000 square miles of Central Arabia, including the Nafud and Dahana Deserts, and reaches eastward to the Persian Gulf (Hasa). The population is largely nomadic and is estimated at about 3,500,000, the majority being Moslems of the Wahhabi persuasion. There is little agriculture, but wheat and barley are grown, and there is an experimental farm, irrigated from natural deep pools and covering 3,000 acres, at al-Kharj, about 50 miles south of Riyadh. The principal occupation of the bulk of the population is camel and sheep raising, but oil makes by far the largest contribution to the economy of the country. Oil was found in commercial quantities at Dammam, near Dhahran in the Hasa in 1938, and by mid-1970 total production of crude oil for the whole country, including off-shore concessions, was running at a rate of some 3,400,000 barrels per day. Exports other than oil are negligible. The capital is Riyadh (300,000) and the principal trading centres are Hofuf (the chief town of the Hasa province) (100,000), Ψ Al Khobar and Ψ Dammam on the Persian Gulf littoral, Anaiza, Buraida, Hail (20,000), and Jauf. The old ports (Persian Gulf) were Ψ Qatif, Ψ Uqair and Ψ Al Khobar, which were suitable only for sailing craft, but the Arabian-American Oil Company, which is exploiting the Hasa oil under a 60 years' lease, has built a deep-water port for its own purposes at Ψ Ras Tannura, and a civil deep-water port, with a pier seven miles long, was brought into use at Ψ Dammam in 1950. A railway is in operation from Dammam through Hofuf to Riyadh.

The *Hejaz* (" The Boundary "—between Nejd and Tihama) extends from Asir in S. to Jordan in N., and from the Red Sea, the Gulf of 'Aqaba in the W. to the ill-defined boundaries of Central Arabia. The coastline on the Red Sea is about 800 miles, and the total area is about 112,500 sq. miles, with a population of from 1,000,000 to 1,500,000, including many nomad tribes. On the coast are the small ports of El Wejh, Yanbu', Rabegh and Gizan. Jedda contains the ruins of the reputed " tomb of Eve, the mother of mankind "; and inland are many settlements through which runs the course of the disused Saudi-Arabian section of the Hejaz Railway

which is under reconstruction. The *Oasis of Khaibar*, east of the railway, contains a considerable population, descendants of former negro slaves, with a centre at Kasr el Yahudi. The importance of the Hejaz depends upon the pilgrimages to the holy cities of Medina and Mecca. *Medina (al Madinah al Munawwarah, "* The City of Light "), once the terminus of the Hejaz Railway, 820 miles from Damascus, has a permanent population of about 20,000 and is celebrated as the burial place of Muhammad, who died in the city on June 7, 632 (12 Rabia, A.H. 11). The Mosque of the Prophet (500 feet in length and over 300 in breadth) contains the sacred tomb of Muhammad. *Mecca*, the birth-place of the Prophet, is 45 miles east of the sea-port of Jedda, by road, and about 200 miles south of Medina, and has a population estimated at 200,000. The city contains the great mosque surrounding the *Kaaba*, or sacred shrine of the Muhammadan religion, in which is the black stone " given by Gabriel to Abraham ", placed in the south-east wall of the Kaaba at such a height that it may be kissed by the devout pilgrim. Ψ *Jedda* (250,000) is the principal port and commercial centre of Saudi Arabia. A new deep-water port was due to be completed in 1971.

Asir (" The Inaccessible ") extends, geographically, from a line drawn inland from Birk on the southern limit of Hejaz to the northern boundary of the Yemen, some 12 miles N. of the port of Meidi. Its breadth extends about 180 miles eastwards to Bisha in the north and to the boundary of the Beni Yam in the south. According to ancient Arab geographers, Asir used to be considered as a part of the Yemen. The territory includes the Farsan Islands, where prospectors have searched for oil, but without success. The maritime lowland is interspersed with fertile areas near the wadis, which afford pasturage and bear grain. Capital, Abha.

Finance and Trade.—Oil is the main source of the country's wealth, though customs revenues and other taxes, as well as the foreign exchange accruing from the annual Pilgrimage to Mecca, also bring in a significant income. In the fiscal year 1970–71 the budget was balanced at SR.6,380,000,000 of which 85 per cent. was derived from oil. 40 per cent. of total Government expenditure is allocated to development projects. The rate of exchange is SR.10·80= £1. (*See also* p. 84) The currency is strong, and backed by gold and foreign exchange reserves of over £300,000,000. With few exceptions, such as the ban on alcohol, there are no restrictions on trade or payments. There is no public debt. Imports in 1970 were over £350,000,000, compared with an annual rate of £2,500,000 before 1939. The United States of America is the leading supplier, followed in 1969 by the United Kingdom, Japan and W. Germany.

Trade with U.K.

	1969	1970
Imports from U.K....	£56,161,000	£35,249,000
Exports to U.K.......	86,796,000	104,231,000

Communications.—The railway from the port of Dammam to the oilfields at Abqaiq and through Hofuf to Riyadh was opened late in 1951. Metalled roads connect Mecca with its Port of Jedda (45 miles), and with Riyadh and Dhahran. A 7,658 km. (4,760 miles) programme of new road construction is largely complete. It provides the first stage of a country-wide network. The Government-owned Saudi Arabian Airlines in association with Transworld Airlines, operate Dakota, Skymaster, Convair, Boeing 720, Douglas DC9 and Boeing 707 aircraft. Scheduled services are flown to all the main towns of the country.

There are first class airports at Dhahran, where a new airport was opened in 1962, and at Jedda. A new airfield for Jedda is planned. Riyadh Airport is to be brought up to international standards and 13 other internal airfields are to be constructed. Saudi Arabian Airlines have an extensive overseas operation including a weekly direct flight to London. A large and increasing number of international airlines operate into Jedda and Dhahran.

Education.—There are 1,419 Government schools, mostly primary or intermediate, but including 30 secondary schools. There is an Islamic University at Medina, a college of Islamic law at Mecca, a college of Petroleum and Minerals at Dhahran, and universities at Riyadh and Jedda. Government education is free. With three exceptions all schools are maintained by the Government. Education at all levels is free.

CAPITAL.—Riyadh, population about 300,000.

SAUDI ARABIAN FLAG.—Green oblong, white Arabic device in centre: " There is no God but God, Muhammad is the Prophet of God," and a white scimitar beneath the lettering.

BRITISH EMBASSY

Kilo 5, Medina Road, Jedda

Ambassador Extraordinary and Plenipotentiary, His Excellency Willie Morris, C.M.G. (1968). £6,925

Counsellor, I. S. Winchester.

1st Secretaries, D. A. Hamley (*Commercial*); H. St. J. B. Armitage, O.B.E.; H. R. Leach, M.B.E.

2nd Secretaries, C. O. Wood (*Consul*); I. S. Lockhart, M.B.E. (*Commercial*).

3rd Secretaries, V. J. Henderson (*Commercial*); A. M. Leyden.

Defence and Military Attaché, Col. R. M. Begbie.

Air Attaché, Cp.-Capt. W. J. Ives.

Asst. Air Attaché, Sqn. Ldr. M. R. S. Wismark.

British Council Representative, K. S. Ferguson, P.O. Box 2701, Riyadh.

SENEGAL
(République du Sénégal)

President and Head of Government, Léopold Senghor, elected President, Sept. 5, 1960.

Prime Minister, Abdou Diouf.

A Cabinet of thirteen other Ministers and four Secretaries of State was appointed on Feb. 28, 1970 and reorganized, April 10, 1971.

Ambassador in London, His Excellency Alioune Badara M'Bengue (1970), 10 Gloucester Place W.1. [01–935–0313].

Senegal lies on the west coast of Africa between Mauritania in the north and the Republic of Guinea in the south. (*For* MAP, *see* p. 873.) It has an area of 77,814 sq. miles and a population (estimated, 1969) of 3,780,000.

Formerly a French colony, Senegal elected on Nov. 25, 1958, to remain within the French Community as an autonomous State. Foundation of a Federation of Mali, to consist of the State of Senegal, (French) Soudan, Dahomey and Upper Volta, was announced in January, 1959, and the Federation came into existence on April 4, consisting of Senegal and the Sudanese Republic only, the others having meanwhile withdrawn. Mali was proclaimed fully independent by the President of the Federal Assembly, M. Léopold Senghor, on June 20, 1960. However, these arrangements proved short-lived as on August 22, 1960, the Senegal Legislative Assembly formally approved measures to secede from the Federation and continue as an independent state. In March, 1963 (after an attempted *coup d'état* by the then Prime Minister in the previous December) a new constitution was

approved giving executive powers to the President, on the lines of the present French constitution. Senegal's principal exports are ground-nuts (raw and processed) and phosphates.

Trade.—Total trade of Senegal in 1968 amounted to: Imports *Francs CFA.* 44,680,498,111; Exports, *Francs CFA.* 37,358,288,515.

Trade with U.K.

	1969	1970
Imports from U.K. .	£1,454,000	£1,503,000
Exports to U.K.	1,783,000	2,109,000

CAPITAL.— Ψ Dakar (500,000).

FLAG.—Three vertical bands, green, yellow and red; a green star on the yellow band. NATIONAL DAY.—April 4.

BRITISH EMBASSY
B.P. 6025, Dakar.
British Ambassador, His Excellency Ivor Forsyth Porter, C.M.G., O.B.E. (1971) £6,925

SIAM. *See* Thailand

SOMALIA
(Somali Democratic Republic)
Chairman of the Revolutionary Council, Gen. Mohammed Siyad, *assumed office* Oct. 21, 1969.

EMBASSY
60 Portland Place, W.1.
[01–580–7148]
Ambassador Extraordinary and Plenipotentiary, His Excellency Ahmed Haji Dualeh (1970).
Counsellor, Mohamed Sheikh Ahmed.
2nd Secretary, Mohamed Hussein Abby.
Attaché, Abdi Hazy Ahmed Liban.

The Somali Republic occupies part of the northeast horn of Africa, with a coast-line on the Indian Ocean extending from the boundary with Kenya (2° South latitude) to Cape Guardafui (12° N.); and on the Gulf of Aden to the boundary with the Territory of the Afars and Issas. (*For MAP, see* p. 855.) Somalia is bounded on the west by the Territory of the Afars and Issas, Ethiopia and Kenya and covers an area of approximately 246,000 sq. miles. The population, of which a large proportion is nomadic, is estimated (June, 1969) at 2,730,000. Livestock raising is the main occupation in Somalia and there is a modest export trade in livestock on the hoof, skins and hides. Italy imports the bulk of the banana crop, the second biggest export, under agreement with the Somali Government. Imports from U.K. in 1970 totalled £1,224,000.

Government.—The Somali Republic, consisting of the former British Somaliland Protectorate and the former Italian trust territory of Somalia, was set up on July 1, 1960. British rule in Somaliland lasted from 1887 until June 26, 1960, with the exception of a short period in 1940–41 when the Protectorate was occupied by Italian forces. Somalia, formerly an Italian colony, was occupied by the United Kingdom from 1941 until the end of 1950, when it was placed under Italian administration by resolution of the United Nations. This trusteeship came to an end on July 1, 1960, when Somalia became independent and united with the former British Somaliland Protectorate under the title of the Somali Republic. Aden Abdulle Osman was returned to office as the first substantive President of the Republic in 1961, after a year as provisional President. Following national elections on June 10, 1967, Dr. Shermarke suceeded to the Presidency and on July 6 appointed Mr. Egal as Prime Minister. On October 16, 1969, the President was assassinated and Army commanders assisted by the police took over the Government without resistance. Mr. Mohammed Egal was placed under

arrest. A revolutionary council under Gen. Siyad assumed full control of the State and on Nov. 1, 1969, nominated a 14-member Cabinet.

CAPITAL.— Ψ Mogadishu (Mogadiscio), population (estimated 1969), 200,000. Other towns are Hargeisa (50,000), Kisimayu (18,000), Ψ Berbera (19,000) and Burao (10,000).

FLAG.—Five-pointed white star on blue ground. NATIONAL DAY.—October 21.

BRITISH EMBASSY
Ambassador Extraordinary and Plenipotentiary, His Excellency James Bourn (1970) £6,475
1st Secretary and Consul, J. Plant (*Head of Chancery*)
2nd Secretary, D. C. Lees (*Consular and Information*).
Attaché, J. C. White (*Vice-Consul*).

British Council Representative, D. A. Latter, P.O. Box 989, Jirdeh Hussein Building, Corso Somalia, Mogadishu (Library).

SOUTH AFRICA
(Republiek van Suid-Afrika)
State President, Johannes Jacobus Fouché, *born* 1898; *elected President,* Feb. 19, 1968; *inaugurated* April 10, 1968.

CABINET
Prime Minister, B. J. Vorster.
Minister of Foreign Affairs, Dr. H. Muller.
Information, Immigration, Social Welfare and Pensions, Dr. Mulder.
Justice and Prisons, P. C. Pelser.
Transport, B. J. Schoeman.
Finance, Dr. N. Diederichs.
Economic Affairs and Police, S. L. Muller.
National Education, Sen. J. P. van der Spuy.
Agriculture, Sen. D. C. H. Uys.
Defence, P. W. Botha.
Community Development and Public Works, B. Coetzee.
Water Affairs and Forestry, S. P. Botha.
Labour and Posts and Telegraphs, M. Viljoen.
Indian Affairs, Tourism and Sport, F. W. Waring.
Interior, T. Gerdener.
Bantu Affairs, M. C. Botha.
Planning and Coloured Affairs, J. J. Loots.
Mines and Health, Dr. C. de Wet.

EMBASSY AND CONSULATE
South Africa House, Trafalgar Square, W.C.2
[01–930–4488]
Ambassador Extraordinary and Plenipotentiary, His Excellency Dr. Hendrik G. Luttig (1967).
Ministers, P. R. Killen; D. S. Franklin (*Consul-General*).
Counsellors, P. A. Grobbelaer; G. du T. Roux (*Administration*).
1st Secretary, A. B. du Preez; J. J. Swart.
2nd Secretaries, S. W. Wentzel; A. H. Bouwer; W. Scholtz.
3rd Secretaries, J. D. Filmalter; J. R. Mostert.
Armed Forces Attaché, Rear Adm. M. R. Terry-Lloyd.
Naval Attaché, Capt. R. D. Kingon.
Army Attaché, Cdt. A. J. Liebenberg.
Air Force Attaché, Cdt. T. P. Stegemann.

Area and Population.—The Republic occupies the southernmost part of the African continent from the courses of the Limpopo, Molopo and Orange Rivers (34° 50′ 22″ South latitude) to the Cape of Good Hope, with the exception of Lesotho, Botswana and Swaziland, and part of Mozambique. It has a total area of 472,359 square miles, and a total population (census of May, 1970, preliminary) of 21,282,000 (White 3,779,000; African, 14,893,000; Coloured, 1,996,000; and Asian, 614,000). Populations of the Provinces at the 1960 census were: Cape Province (278,380 sq.

miles), 5,360,234; Natal (33,578 sq. miles), 2,977,084 Transvaal (109,621 sq. miles), 6,270,711; Orange Free State (49,866 sq. miles), 1,386,202.

Zululand, annexed in 1897, comprises about two-thirds of the country formerly under Zulu kings, and is bounded on the south and south-west by the Tugela River; on the south-east by the Indian Ocean; on the north by the Portuguese possessions; and on the west by the districts of Babanango, Vryheid and Ngotshe and by Swaziland. In 1951, the appointment was confirmed of Cyprian Bekuzulu, grandson of Dinizulu and great-grandson of Cetewayo, as Paramount Chief of the Zulus in Natal.

The southernmost province contains many parallel ranges, which rise in steps towards the interior. The south-western peninsula contains the famous *Table Mountain* (3,582 feet), while the *Great Swartberg* and *Langeberg* run in parallel lines from west to east of the Cape Province. Between these two ranges and the *Roggeveld* and *Nieuwveld* ranges to the north is the Great Karroo Plateau, which is bounded on the east by the *Sneeuberg*, containing the highest summit in the province (Kompasberg, 7,800 feet). In the east are ranges which join the *Drakensberg* (11,000 feet) between Natal and the Orange Free State.

The Orange Free State presents a succession of undulating grassy plains with good pasture-land, at a general elevation of some 3,800 feet, with occasional hills or kopjes. The Transvaal is also mainly an elevated plateau with parallel ridges in the *Magaliesberg* and *Waterberg* ranges of no great height. The veld or plains of this northernmost province is divisible into the High Veld of the south, the Bankenveld of the centre, and the Low Veld of the north and east, the first and second forming the grazing and agricultural region of the Transvaal and the last a fertile sub-tropical area. The eastern province of Natal has pastoral lowlands and rich agricultural land between the slopes of the Drakensberg and the coast, the interior rising in terraces as in the southern provinces. The *Orange*, with its tributary the *Vaal*, is the principal river of the south, rising in the Drakensberg and flowing into the Atlantic between the Territory of South West Africa and the Cape Province. The *Limpopo*, or Crocodile River, in the north, rises in the Transvaal and flows into the Indian Ocean through Portuguese East Africa. Most of the remaining rivers are furious torrents after rain, with partially dry beds at other seasons.

Government.—The self-governing colonies of the Cape of Good Hope, Natal, the Transvaal and the Orange River Colony became united on May 31, 1910, under the South Africa Act, 1909, in a legislative union under the name of the Union of South Africa, the four colonies becoming Provinces of the Union. The Union of South Africa continued as a member of the British Commonwealth until 1961. A referendum held among white voters on October 5, 1960, decided by a narrow majority in favour of Republican status. 1,633,772 votes were cast—a poll of 90·73 per cent.—with 52·05 per cent. in favour. The Union of South Africa became a republic on May 31, 1961, and withdrew from the Commonwealth. Mr. C. R. Swart was elected the first President of the Republic on May 10 and assumed office on May 31, 1961. He retired on May 31, 1967, a year before his term of office was due to expire. The former Minister of Finance, Dr. T. E. Dönges, was elected to the Presidency but fell seriously ill before his inauguration. The Leader of the Senate Senator J. F. T. Naudé was Acting President during 1967 and until the inauguration of Mr. Fouché on April 10, 1968.

The *Senate* as reconstituted by the Senate Act, 1960, consists of 54 members, appointed or elected for a term of five years. Eleven are appointed by the Government (8 for the Republic, 2 for South West Africa and a Coloured representative). Forty-three are elected (Transvaal, 14; Cape Province, 11; Natal and Orange Free State, each 8; and South West Africa, 2). The Act of 1960 reintroduced proportional representation at elections to the Senate and excluded Native representation.

The *House of Assembly* consists of 166 elected members, 54 of whom represent the Cape of Good Hope, 18 Natal, 73 Transvaal, 15 the Orange Free State, and 6 South West Africa. Members of both Houses must be South African citizens of white descent. White female franchise was introduced under the provision of Act No. 18 of 1930. Cape Bantu voters ceased to be entitled to elect 3 members in Nov. 1959.

After the General Election on April 22, 1970, the party representation in the House of Assembly was as follows: Nationalist Party, 116; United Party, 48; National Union, 1; Progressive Party, 1; by-elections pending, 1. Total 166.

Defence.—The South Africa Defence Act, 1957, became law on Nov. 1, 1958. This Act, as amended in 1961, provides that every citizen between the ages of 17 and 65 is liable to render personal service in time of war, and those between 17 and 25 are liable to undergo a prescribed course of peace training with the Citizen Force or Commandos spread over a period of four consecutive years. Thereafter citizens are required to serve with the Reserve for a prescribed period of time.

Education.—The Provinces have been relieved of all vocational education (technical and industrial), and the Departments of Cultural Affairs and Higher Education under the Minister are concerned with 9 Universities, 11 technical colleges, schools of industries, reformatories and State technical, housecraft and commercial high schools, State-aided vocational schools and State and State-aided special schools for the physically handicapped. There are two non-white university colleges and three Bantu university colleges, students of these taking the examinations of the University of South Africa.

Communications.—The total open mileage of Government-owned railway lines at the end of March, 1969, was 13,287 miles, of which 2,512 miles were electrified. Working expenditure (excluding depreciation) amounted to R.794,704,000 (railways, harbours. airways and pipelines). Internal air services are operated between all the major centres in South and South West Africa. Regional air services are operated between Johannesburg and Rhodesia, East Africa, Central Africa and Portuguese East Africa. The "Springbok

Service" is operated jointly by South African Airways and the British Overseas Airways Corporation, providing a regular service between Johannesburg and London and a weekly flight in each direction between Cape Town and London.

Production and Trade.—Final figures for the principal crops produced in 1968–69 (1,000 bags of 200 lbs. each) were: Wheat, 13,445 (1967–68, 107,607); Maize, 57,158; Kaffir corn, 2,200; Barley, 314; Oats, 644 (150 lb. bags). Estimated production of ground nuts in 1969 was 245,000 metric tons, shelled. Sales of wool during the 1968–69 season amounted to 321,542,747 lbs. (1967–68, *309,122,260 lbs.*).

Mineral production is of the greatest importance in the South African economy, value of production in 1969 being: gold, R.829,126,084; diamonds, R.103,919,149; coal, R.106,082,024; copper, R.115,464,275; tin, concentrates and metallic, R.4,293,075; silver, R.4,392,365; asbestos, R.30,947,934.

Value of trade in 1969 (with 1968 figures in *italic* type) was: R.2,136,800,000 (*R.1,876,800,000*); Exports R.1,528,300,000 (*R.1,502,400,000*).

Trade with U.K.★

	1969	1970
Imports from U.K.	£285,797,000	£332,896,000
Exports to U.K.	302,322,000	258,266,000

★Excluding gold bullion and specie.

Currency.—The South African £ reached parity with the £ sterling in 1946. A new decimal currency the *Rand* (R.) was introduced in South Africa on Feb. 14, 1961, with a par value of 10s. Sterling. Since devaluation of the £ sterling in Nov., 1967, the rate of exchange has been R.1·72 = £1 (*see also* p. 83). Coins are one silver coin, the Rand (11s. 8d.); four nickel coins, 50 cents; 20 cents; 10 cents; 5 cents; three bronze coins, 2 cents 1 cent and ½ cent (minted for the first time in 1970). In addition the yellow bronze ½ cent, though no longer minted, will remain in circulation for an unspecified period.

Finance.—Total revenue for the year ended December 31, 1969 was R.1,562,332,000 (1968, *R.1,549,835,000*); total expenditure, R.1,465,765,000 (1968, *R.1,404,341,000*). The gross Public Debt of the Republic on March 31, 1969 was R.4,879,000,000 (1968, *R.4,218,000,000*).

CAPITAL.—The administrative seat of the Government is PRETORIA, Transvaal; population (census of 1960), 422,590; the seat of the Legislature is ΨCAPE TOWN, population (1961), 807,211. Cape Town is 5,979 miles from Southampton; transit by mail steamship 11 days, and by air mail two days. There is a modern and well-equipped aerodrome seventeen miles by road from the centre of the city. Cape Town's harbour and docking facilities, existing and projected, are in keeping with its status as a world port of commercial and strategic importance. Other large towns are Johannesburg, Transvaal (1,110,905); ΨDurban, Natal, the largest seaport (659,934); ΨPort Elizabeth, Cape (274,180); Germiston, Transvaal (213,642); BLOEMFONTEIN, capital of Orange Free State (145,273); Springs, Transvaal (137,253); Benoni, Transvaal (136,476); ΨEast London, Cape (115,677); Welkom, O.F.S. (67,614); and PIETERMARITZBURG, capital of Natal (96,236).

FLAG.—Three horizontal stripes of equal width; from top to bottom, orange, white, blue; in the centre of the white stripe, the old Orange Free State flag hanging vertical, towards the pole the Union Jack horizontal, away from the pole the old Transvaal Vierkleur, all spread full. The national flag was adopted by the Union in 1927 and was flown side by side with the Union Jack. This practice was expected to be continued in Natal.

NATIONAL DAY.—May 31.

BRITISH EMBASSY
Hill Street, Pretoria

91 Parliament Street, Cape Town (Jan.–June)
Ambassador Extraordinary and Plenipotentiary, His Excellency Sir Arthur Wendell Snelling, K.C.M.G., K.C.V.O. (1969) £14,000
Minister, S. G. Gross, C.M.G.
Counsellor, M. H. Morgan (*Head of Chancery*; A. H. Reed (*Economic*).
Defence and Air Attaché, Air Cdre. E. W. Wright, C.B.E., D.F.C., D.F.M.
Naval Attaché, Cdre. O. N. A. Cecil.
Military Attaché, Col. B. A. Fargus, O.B.E.
Cultural Attaché and British Council Representative, D. E. Frean, O.B.E., 6 Hill Street, Pretoria.

There are British Consular Offices at *Cape Town, Johannesburg, Durban* and *Port Elizabeth.*

South West Africa.
Administrator, W. C. du Plessis.

South West Africa stretches from the southern border of Angola (lat. 17°23′ S.) to part of the northern (Orange River) and north-western borders of the Cape Province of the Republic of South Africa; and from the Atlantic Ocean in the west to Botswana in the east.

The territory has an area of 318,261 sq. miles, including the area of Walvis Bay (434 sq. miles) which, although part of the Republic of South Africa, is for convenience administered as part of South West Africa. The population was estimated at 610,100 in 1966 and the main population groups are: Ovambo (270,900), Whites (96,000), Damara (50,200), Herero (40,000), Nama (39,400), Okavango (31,500), East Caprivians (17,900) Coloureds (15,400), Basters (13,700), Bushmen (13,300), Kaokovelders (10,500), Tswana and others (11,300).

Government.—A German protectorate from 1880 to 1915, South West Africa was administered until the end of 1920 by the Union of South Africa. In terms of the Treaty of Versailles the Territory was declared a "C" Mandate and entrusted to South Africa with full powers of administration and legislation over the Territory. After the dissolution of the League of Nations and in the absence of a trusteeship agreement, South Africa informed the United Nations that she would continue to administer South West Africa in the spirit of the Mandate. Since the establishment of the United Nations, South West Africa has been the subject of dispute.

The South African Government announced on Oct. 2, 1968, the formation of a Legislative Council of 42 members for Ovamboland, six members nominated by each of the seven tribal authorities in the territory and a nominated Executive Council of seven members, with a Chief Councillor elected by the Legislative Council. Certain administrative powers held in South West Africa were in February, 1969, transferred to the South West African Government.

On June 21, 1971, the International Court of Justice at The Hague delivered an advisory opinion as requested by the U.N. Security Council on the legal consequences for States of the continued presence of South Africa in "Namibia" (South West Africa). The Court decided by 13 votes to 2, that (*inter alia*) "the continued presence of South Africa being illegal, South Africa is under obligation to withdraw its administration from Namibia immediately and thus put an end to its occupation of the Territory". Dissenting opinions were

submitted by the British and French judges; several other judges issued separate opinions in respect of parts of the Court's advisory opinion. A member of the South African legal team had contended at the hearings that South Africa had no obligation to submit to general international supervision of its administration of South West Africa, as the Mandate by the League of Nations had come to an end at the dissolution of that organization. The South African Prime Minister rejected the Court's majority opinion in a statement also made on June 21, 1971.

Production and Communications.—Mining, agriculture and fisheries are important. In 1965, animal husbandry accounted for 99 per cent. of the total gross output of commercial agriculture which was estimated at £22·2 million. The average rainfall over 70 per cent. of the Territory is below 400 mm. per annum. 1,453 miles of railway line have been laid; 810 miles of road have been tarred; 41,526 motor vehicles were registered in 1966; air links exist between Windhoek and major cities of the Republic. Lüderitz is the only harbour in the Territory proper. 118 telephone exchanges serve the 16,491 telephone subscribers in the Territory. In 1966 the school attendance for the indigenous groups was 62 per cent.; in 1960 there were 37 Native pupils to one teacher and it was estimated that 56 per cent. of the adult indigenous population was literate.

Development.—Under the current five-year plan of the Department of Bantu Administration and Development £30 million will be spent on the indigenous groups (£11·065 million for community centres, schools, offices and other buildings; £6·595 million for water and electricity supplies; £2·28 million for internal roads; £2·46 million for residential housing; £1·675 million for the control of animal diseases and stock improvements).

Trade with U.K.

	1969	1970
Imports from U.K....	£1,615,000	£1,883,000
Exports to U.K.	26,429,000	26,052,000

CAPITAL.—Windhoek (estimated population, 60,000). The ports are Ψ Walvis Bay and Ψ Lüderitz.

SPAIN
(España)

Head of the Spanish State, Generalisimo Don Francisco Franco Bahamonde, *born* Dec. 4, 1892, *assumed office,* Oct. 1, 1936.

Vice-President of the Government, Rear-Adm. Don Luis Carrero Blanco, *appointed* Sept. 14, 1967.

CABINET

Minister for Foreign Affairs, Sr. Don Gregorio Lopez Bravo.
Interior, Don Tomás Garicano Goñi.
Army, Teniente General Don Juan Castañón de Mena.
Marine, Almirante Don Adolfo Baturone Colombo.
Air, Teniente General Don Julio Salvador y Díaz-Benjumea.
Justice, Sr. Don Antonio de Oriol y Urquijo.
Finance, Sr. Don Alberto Monreal Luque.
Industry, Sr. Don José María Lopez de Letona y Nunez del Pino.
Agriculture, Sr. Don Tomas Allende y García-Baxter.
Labour, Sr. Don Licinio de la Fuente y de la Fuente.
Education, Sr. Don José Villar Palasí.
Public Works, Sr. Don Fernando González de la Mora y Mon.
Commerce, Sr. Don Enrique Fontana Codina.
Information and Tourism, Sr. Don Alfredo Sánchez Bella.

Minister Secretary-General of the Movimiento, Don Torcuato Fernández Miranda y Hevia.
Minister of Housing, Sr. Don Vicente Mortes Alfonso.
Minister without Portfolio and Commissioner of the Development Plan, Sr. Don Laureano López Rodó.

SPANISH EMBASSY IN LONDON
24 Belgrave Square, S.W.1
[01-235-5555]

Ambassador Extraordinary and Plenipotentiary, His Excellency El Marqués de Santa Cruz (1958).
Minister Counsellor, Don Manuel Gómez Acebo.
Ministers Plenipotentiary, Don Ernesto Barnach Calbó (*Consul General*); El Marqués de Espinardo (*Economic and Commercial*).
Counsellors, Don José María Alonso Gamo (*Cultural*); El Conde de Campo Rey (*Consular*); Don Javier Chapa, Marqués de los Arcos.
1st Secretaries, Don José J. Puig de la Bellacasa; Don Gil Armanqué; Don Miguel Angel García-Mina; Don Antonio Oyarzábal.
2nd Secretary, Don Fernando Schwartz y Giron (*Consular*).
Military Attaché, Lt.-Col. Don Juan Cano Hevia.
Asst. Military Attaché, Captain Don Alejandro Pareja.
Naval Attaché, Capt. Don Salvador Moremo.
Air Attaché, Lt.-Col. Don Enrique Tapias Curbera.
Labour Attaché, Don Mario Jiménez de la Espada y Suarez.
Agricultural Attaché, Don Alberto González Quijano.
Asst. Commercial Counsellors, Don Victor Audera; Don Julio Cisneros.
Information Counsellor, Don Francisco José Mayans.
Attachés, Don Luis Fernández-Cid (*Information*); Don Andrés Vazquez de Prada (*Tourism*); Don Eduardo Propper de Callejón.
Hon. Attachés, Don Rafael de Romero; Don Francisco Xavier de Salas.
Consular Section, 3 Hans Crescent, S.W.1.
Commercial Office, 3 Hans Crescent, S.W.1.
Spanish Institute, 102 Eaton Square, S.W.1.

Area and Population.—A National State in the south-west of Europe, between 36°-43° 45′ N. lat. and 4° 25′ E.-9° 20′ W. long., bounded on the south and east by the Mediterranean, on the west by the Atlantic and Portugal, and on the north by the Bay of Biscay and France, from which it is separated by the Pyrenees. Continental Spain occupies about eleven-thirteenths of the Iberian

peninsula, the remaining portion forming the Republic of Portugal. Its coast-line extends 1,317 miles—712 formed by the Mediterranean and 605 by the Atlantic—and it comprises a total area of 196,700 square miles, with a population (estimated, 1970) of 33,290,000. Returns for 1969 gave 657,449 births, 297,126 deaths and 238,102 marriages.

Physical Features.—The interior of the Iberian Peninsula consists of an elevated tableland surrounded and traversed by mountain ranges—the Pyrenees, the Cantabrian Mountains, the Sierra Guadarrama, Sierra Morena, Sierra Nevada, Montes de Toledo, &c. The principal rivers are the Douro, the Tagus, the Guadiana, the Guadalquivir, the Ebro and the Minho.

Government.—In April, 1931, the last monarch of Spain, Alfonso XIII, left the country; a Republic was immediately proclaimed and a Provisional Government, drawn from the various Republican and Socialist parties, was formed. The Republican Assembly (*Cortes*) was a single Chamber Congress of Deputies. On July 18, 1936, a counter-revolution broke out in many military garrisons in Spanish Morocco and spread rapidly throughout Spain. The principal leader was General Francisco Franco Bahamonde, formerly Governor of the Canary Islands. The struggle, in its later phases, threatened to embroil some of the European Powers, those of Nazi-Fascist tendency lending aid to General Franco (leader of the Military-Fascist fusion, or *Falange*) while those of Communist views supported the Azaña (*Popular Front*) government. In October, 1938, many of the supporting troops were withdrawn, and on March 29, 1939, the Civil War was declared to have ended, the Popular Front Governments in Madrid and Barcelona surrendering to the *Nationalists* (as General Franco's followers were then named). On June 5, 1939, the Grand Council of the *Falange Española Tradicionalista y de las Juntas Ofensivas Nacional-Sindicalistas*, which replaced the former *Cortes*, met at Burgos to legislate for the reorganization of the country under the Presidency of General Franco, who had assumed the title of *Caudillo* (*Leader*) of the *Empire and Chief of the State.* In the Civil War of 1936–39 over 1,000,000 lives were lost.

On July 1, 1942, General Franco announced the reinstatement of the *Cortes de España*. This was re-organized by an Organic Law of 1967 and is composed of approximately 564 members—ministers, 19; members of the National Council of the Movement, 109; Presidents of various State bodies, 5; representatives of the national syndicates, 150; 100 members elected by heads of families and married women; university rectors, 12; representatives of professional, academic and scientific bodies, 28; representatives of local administration, 116; and 25 members directly appointed by the Head of State.

A referendum held in 1967 approved an Organic Law of the State introducing a number of changes in state institutions. The offices of Head of State and Head of Government were separated, but General Franco still holds both offices.

On July 22, 1969, General Franco nominated Prince Juan Carlos (Alfonso) of Bourbon (*born* Jan. 5, 1938; grandson of the late King Alfonso XIII) to succeed him as head of state at his death or retirement. The nomination was approved in the *Cortes* by a large majority.

Defence.—*Army:* There are in Spain one armoured, one mechanized, one motorized, two mountain and one parachute divisions; one cavalry brigade; one artillery brigade, one air-transportable brigade and nine territorial brigades. The *Guardia Civil* also forms part of the Army though it oper-ates as a gendarmerie in the rural areas under the control of the Ministry of the Interior.

The active Spanish *Navy* consists of 1 cruiser, 1 helicopter carrier, 8 destroyers, 24 frigates and corvettes, 2 attack transports, 4 minelayers, 25 mine-sweepers, 4 submarines, 2 midget submarines, 3 landing ships, 4 squadrons of helicopters, a large number of auxiliary and small craft. A further destroyer is being completely rebuilt and a building programme of 5 large destroyers and 2 submarines is well in hand.

The *Air Force* is divided geographically into 3 Regions covering Spain plus an Air Zone for the Canaries. There are also separate functional Air Defence, Tactical and Transport Commands. The Air Force consists of 4 Fighter Squadrons, 3 Fighter Bomber Squadrons and 2 transport groups with 5 Squadrons. There is also a variety of training and miscellaneous aircraft and some helicopters. Strength in front-line aircraft, about 300 planes.

Education.—Primary education is free, but compulsory attendance cannot be enforced because of the inadequate number of schools. There are 12 Universities in continental Spain and 1 at La Laguna in the Canary Islands. The University of Sala-manca was founded in 1230, Valencia (1245), Oviedo (1317), Valladolid (1346), Barcelona (1450), Zaragoza (1474), Santiago (1501), Seville (1502), Granada (1526), Madrid (1590), Murcia (1915). The Catholic University of Pamplona (1953) is the only University in Spain not subject to government control. Small autonomous universities were formed in Madrid and Barcelona in 1969.

Language and Literature.—Castilian is the language of more than three-quarters of the population of Spain and is the form of Spanish spoken in Mexico, Central and (except in Brazil) Southern America. Basque, reported to have been the original language of Iberia, is spoken in the rural districts of Vizcaya, Guipuzcoa and Alava. Catalan is spoken in Provençal Spain, and Galician, spoken in the north-western provinces, is allied to Portuguese. The literature of Spain is one of the oldest and richest in the world, the *Poem of the Cid*, the earliest and best of the heroic songs of Spain, having been written about A.D. 1140. The outstanding writings of its golden age are those of Miguel de Cervantes Saavedra (1547–1616), Lope Felix de Vega Carpio (1562–1635) and Pedro Calderón de la Barca (1600–1681). The Nobel Prize for Literature has three times been awarded to Spanish authors—J. Echegaray (1904), J. Benavente (1922) and Juan Ramón Jimenez (1956).

FINANCE

	1970 million Pesetas	1971 million Pesetas
Estimated Revenue....	309,758	370,169
Estimated Expenditure.	309,758	370,169

Public Debt (Dec. 31, 1964) excluding parastatal organizations and State-guaranteed issues: *Pesetas* 186,928,600,000.

The rate of exchange for the *peseta* in June, 1971, was 168 *pesetas*= £1 sterling (*see also* p. 83).

Production and Industry.—The country is generally fertile, and well adapted to agriculture and the cultivation of heat-loving fruits—olives, oranges, lemons, almonds, pomegranates, bananas, apricots and grapes. The agricultural products include wheat, barley, oats, rice, hemp and flax. The orange crop is exported mainly to Germany, France and the United Kingdom. The vine is cultivated widely; in the south-west, Jerez, the well-known sherry and tent wines are produced.

Spain's mineral resources of coal, iron, wolfram, copper, zinc, lead and iron ores are variously exploited. Many of the richer and more easily

worked deposits have been exhausted, but the authorities are actively engaged in stimulating the exploitation of hitherto unworked or lower grade deposits. In 1970 the coal output amounted to 13,150,000 metric tons. 4,150,000 metric tons of iron ore and 7,366,000 metric tons of steel were produced in 1970. Other production figures included ('000 metric tons): cement, 16,500; sulphuric acid, 2,015; cotton yarn, 117 and wool yarn, 37. Production of electric power was 56,484 million kWh. The fishing industry is important.

The principal goods produced are manufactured goods, textiles, chemical products, footwear and other leather goods, ceramics, sewing machines and bicycles. 24,105,000 tourists visited Spain in 1970 and spent £700,000,000. The Gross National Product was approximately £13,400 million.

Communications.—In 1970 there were over 13,400 km. of railways in service and 138,670 km. of paved roads. The sea-going mercantile marine in 1970 (excluding fishing boats) registered a total of 3,338,190 gross tons. Civil aviation is under the control of the Air Ministry; there are several inland and international services in operation.

TRADE

	1969 $ million	1970 $ million
Imports (c.i.f.)......	4,233	4,747
Exports (f.o.b.).....	1,900	2,387

The balance of payments surplus in 1970 was $600 (provisional) and reserves stood at $1,730 m. at the end of the year.

Trade with U.K.

	1969	1970
Imports from U.K...	£115,254,000	£123,169,000
Exports to U.K....	98,774,000	108,490,000

Inclusion of the Canary Islands trade with U.K. raises the 1970 figures to: Imports from U.K., £142,695,000; Exports, £126,524,000.

The principal imports are cotton, tobacco, cellulose, timber, coffee and cocoa, fertilizers, dyes, machinery, motor vehicles and agricultural tractors, wool and petroleum products. The principal exports include iron ore, cork, salt, vegetables, citrus fruits, wines, olive oil, potash, mercury, pyrites, tinned fruit and fish, bananas and tomatoes.

CAPITAL, Madrid. Population 3,150,000. Other large cities are Ψ Barcelona (1,750,000), Valencia (600,000), Ψ Seville (650,000), Zaragoza (440,000), Ψ Málaga (350,000), Bilbao (800,000); Murcia (260,000).

FLAG.—Three horizontal bands, red, yellow and red, with coat of arms on yellow band. NATIONAL DAY.—July 18 (*Fiesta Nacional Española*).

AIR TRANSIT FROM U.K.—London–Barcelona (713 miles) 2 *hrs.* 25 *mins.*; Madrid (775 miles), 2 *hrs.* 5 *mins.*; Valencia, 2 *hrs.* 10 *mins.*

BRITISH EMBASSY

(Calle Fernando el Santo, 16, Madrid)

Ambassador Extraordinary and Plenipotentiary, His Excellency Sir John Russell, G.C.V.O., C.M.G. (1969)..£9,000

Minister, R. A. Farquharson.

Counsellor (*Commercial*), A. H. Spire.

1st Secretaries, M. W. Atkinson, M.B.E. (*Head of Chancery*); D. I. Morphet (*Information*); S. E. Croft, T.D. (*Consul-General*), D. J. Melliar-Smith; K. E. L. Barton, M.B.E.; A. St. J. H. Figgis.

2nd Secretaries, C. J. R. Meyer; M. Sullivan; C. Hampton, M.B.E. (*Consul*).

Commercial Attaché, Miss B. Cawood.

Defence and Military Attaché, Col. T. P. O'H. Pollock, M.B.E.

Naval Attaché, Cdr. J. G. Nelson, R.N.

Air Attaché, Wing-Cdr. A. R. Scott, D.F.C.

Archivist, J. Quinn.

Chaplain, Rev. R. B. Ney, M.B.E.

BRITISH CONSULAR OFFICES

There are Consular Offices at *Alicante, Barcelona, Palma de Mallorca, Tarragona, Valencia, Granada, Seville, Cadiz, Ibiza, Jerez, Algeciras, Gijon, Vigo, Bilbao, San Sebastian, Malaga, Tenerife, Las Palmas, Ceuta (Morocco)* and *Madrid.*

British Council Representative, N. N. Tett, O.B.E., Calle Almagro 5, Madrid, 4.

There are a British Institute at *Barcelona* and libraries at both cities.

BRITISH CHAMBER OF COMMERCE OF SPAIN, Marqués de Valdeigiesias 3, *Madrid*; Paseo de Gracia 11 (Segundo), *Barcelona*; Pascual y Genis 22, *Valencia*; Alameda de Mazarredo 5, 30, *Bilbao.*

The BALEARIC ISLES form an archipelago off the east coast of Spain. There are four large islands (Majorca, Minorca, Ibiza and Formentera), and seven smaller (Aire, Aucanada, Botafoch, Cabrera, Dragonera, Pinto and El Rey). The islands were occupied by the Romans after the destruction of Carthage and provided contingents of the celebrated Balearic slingers. The total area is 1,935 square miles, with a population of 441,842. The archipelago forms a province of Spain, the capital being Ψ Palma in Majorca, pop. 149,921; Ψ Mahon (Minorca), pop. 16,547.

The CANARY ISLANDS are an archipelago in the Atlantic, off the African coast, consisting of 7 islands and 6 uninhabited islets. The total area is 2,807 square miles, with a population of 908,718. The Canary Islands form two Provinces of Spain.—*Las Palmas* (Gran Canaria, Lanzarote (38,500), Fuerteventura (19,500) and the islets of Alegranza, Roque del Este, Roque del Oeste, Graciosa, Montaña Clara and Lobos), with seat of administration at Ψ Las Palmas (pop. 177,746) in Gran Canaria, where major oil companies have installations for re-fuelling shipping; and *Santa Cruz de Tenerife* (Tenerife, La Palma (76,000), Gomera (31,829), and Hierro (10,000)), with seat of administration at Ψ Santa Cruz in Tenerife, pop. 140,000.

Trade with U.K.

	1969	1970
Imports from U.K....	£15,715,000	£19,526,000
Exports to U.K......	16,225,000	18,034,000

ISLA DE LOS FAISANES is an uninhabited Franco-Spanish condominium, at the mouth of the Bidassoa in La Higuera bay.

Ψ CEUTA is a fortified post on the Moroccan coast, opposite Gibraltar. The total area is 5 square miles, with a population (estimated, 1970) of 88,000.

Ψ MELILLA is a town on a rocky promontory of the Rif coast, connected with the mainland by a narrow isthmus. Melilla has been in Spanish possession since 1492. Population (estimated, 1970) 77,000. Ceuta and Melilla are parts of Metropolitan Spain.

OVERSEAS TERRITORIES

The former provinces of Spanish Guinea, Fernando Póo and Rio Muni achieved independence on October 12, 1968, under the title of Equatorial Guinea.

Ifni, the former enclave in Morocco, was incorporated in the latter state by treaty, on June 30, 1969.

SPANISH SAHARA.—The province of Spanish Sahara extends from 27° 40′ N. lat. in the north to La Agüera (Cape Blanco) in the south, though the main southern boundary runs along latitude 21° 20′. The land area is approximately 125,000 square

miles. Spanish Sahara is divided into two regions separated by latitude 26° which passes south of Cape Bojador. The northern region is the Seguia el Hamra (Río Rojo) of which the capital is Aaiun. It extends eastward to approximately 8° 40′ W. long. The southern region is the Rio de Oro, of which the capital is Villa Cisneros. Its eastern boundary is approximately 12° W. long. Total population was estimated in 1969 at 63,000. There are rich deposits of potash.

Spain has accepted, but not implemented, a series of United Nations resolutions enjoining her to determine the wishes of the inhabitants as to their future. Both Morocco and Mauritania have claims on the territory.

SPANISH MOROCCO.—In addition to Ceuta and Melilla, Spain exercised until 1956 a protectorate over a part of Northern Morocco. Moroccan independence was proclaimed after negotiations with France and Spain in 1956 (*see* "Morocco"). Remaining Spanish settlements on the Moroccan seaboard are :—

Alhucemas, the bay of that name includes six islands : population 366.

Peñon de la Gomera (or *Peñon de Velez*) is a fortified rocky islet about 40 miles west of Alhucemas Bay : population 450.

The *Chaffarinas* (or Zaffarines) are a group of three islands near the Algerian frontier, about 2 miles north of Cape del Agua ; population 610.

SUDAN
(Democratic Republic of the Sudan)

Chairman of Revolutionary Council, Col. Jaafar Mohammed al Nemery, *assumed office* May 25, 1969.

Minister of Foreign Affairs, Manswar Khalid.

SUDANESE EMBASSY IN LONDON
3 Cleveland Row, S.W.1.
[01–839–8080]
Ambassador Extraordinary and Plenipotentiary, His Excellency Abdin Ismail (1970).
Counsellors, Sayed Ahmed Mohammed Nur; Sayed Phillip Obang.
1st Secretary, Sayed Mohamed Ahmed Mirghani.
Military, Naval and Air Attaché, Brig. Saleh El Din Mohamed Saeed.
3rd Secretary, Musa Ismail Saied.

Area and Population.—The Sudan extends from the southern boundary of U.A.R. 22° N. lat., to the northern boundary of Uganda, 3° 36′ N. lat., and reaches from the Republic of Chad about 21° 49′ E. (at 12° 45′ N.) to the north-west boundary of Ethiopia in 38° 35′ E. (at 18° N.). The greatest length from north to south is approximately 1,300 miles, and from east to west 950 miles.

The northern boundary is the 22nd parallel of North latitude; on the east lie the Red Sea and Ethiopia; on the south lie Kenya, Uganda and the Congolese Republic; and on the west the Central African Republic, Chad and Libya.

The *White Nile* enters from Uganda at the Sudan frontier post of Nimule in Equatoria Province, as the *Bahr el Jebel,* and leaves the Sudan at Wadi Halfa. The *Blue Nile* flows from Lake Tana on the Ethiopian Plateau. Its course in the Sudan is nearly 500 miles long, before it joins the White Nile at Khartoum. The next confluence of importance is at Atbara where the main Nile is joined by the River Atbara. The total length of the Nile, now accepted as the longest river in the world, is estimated to be 4,160 miles from its source to the Mediterranean Sea. Between Khartoum and Wadi Halfa occur five of the six *Cataracts.*

The estimated area is about 976,750 sq. miles, with a population (estimated, 1970) of 15,312,000, partly Arabs, partly Negroes, and partly of mixed Arab-Negro blood, with a small foreign element, including some 8,000 Europeans. The Arabs and other Northern peoples are all Moslems. The Nilotics of the Bahr el Ghazal and Upper Nile Valleys are generally pagans, but some have been converted to Christianity and others are beginning to go over to Islam.

Government.—The Anglo-Egyptian Condominium over the Sudan which had been established in 1899 ended when the Sudan House of Representatives on Dec. 19, 1966, voted unanimously a declaration that the Sudan was a fully independent sovereign state. A Republic was proclaimed on Jan. 1, 1956, and was recognized by Great Britain and Egypt, a Supreme Commission being sworn in to take over sovereignty. The Sudan was under military rule from Nov., 1958, until 1964 when a new civilian Cabinet was appointed. Following a crisis in the coalition Cabinet of Mr. Mahgoub, the Prime Minister resigned on April 23, 1969, and was unable to form a new coalition. Government of the country was taken over on May 25, 1969, by a ten-man revolutionary council headed by Col. Jaafar Mohammed al Nemery. A *coup d'état* by a Communist group on July 19, 1971, was short-lived. The leader of the group, Lt.Col. Babikr al Noor, had been in London for medical treatment when power was seized by Maj. Hashem Atta. The B.O.A.C. plane in which the former was returning to Khartoum on July 22 was forced down at Benghazi by Libyan fighter aircraft and Lt.-Col. Noor and an aide were arrested. Later reports from Khartoum indicated that Col. Nemery had resumed office as Chairman of the Revolutionary Council and that a number of leaders of the Communist group had been summarily tried and executed.

Education.—Government education is heavily subsidized or free according to means, beginning at the age of seven and passing through elementary, intermediate and secondary stages, each of four years. University degree courses vary from 4 to 6 years. Arabic is the normal language of instruction in schools throughout the Sudan, although English is the main language of instruction in higher education. English is taught in intermediate and secondary schools as the first foreign language. In 1968–69 the University of Khartoum had over

3,500 students of whom 400 graduated in 1968 in nine faculties. There were about 700 students at the Khartoum Technical Institute, which is divided in eight vocational schools and about 300 at the Senior Trade School. The Higher Teacher Training Institute at Omdurman had about 500 students. B.Ed. degrees will be awarded from 1971 after affiliation with the University of Khartoum. Non-governmental higher education was offered by Cairo University, Khartoum Branch (three faculties with about 1,600 students), and at the newly established Islamic University of Omdurman (600 students).

There were two training colleges for intermediate teachers with 200 men and 50 women, and 14 training colleges for elementary school teachers with 1,400 students. 42 academic secondary schools, with a total first year entry of 114 streams with 40 pupils each (90 for boys and 24 for girls), had a total of 14,000 boys and 4,000 girls. There was one secondary technical school with 4 class entry and 11 post-intermediate two-year technical schools with 4 class entry, making a total of 1,642 boys. 7 Government religious secondary schools also had about 1,200 boys. There were 228 streams in academic intermediate schools, making a total of 37,800 boy pupils and 12,400 girls, an increase of about 10 per cent. over 1967–68.

In 1967–68 there were 455,000 pupils receiving elementary education. In addition, 107,600 were enrolled in private schools at all levels, an increase of nearly two-thirds in a single year. The percentage of the age-group enrolled in all schools is: elementary, 31 per cent.; intermediate, 4·5 per cent.; secondary, 2·2 per cent.

Production.—The principal grain crop is *dura* (great millet), the staple food of the people in the Sudan. Sesame and ground-nuts are other important food crops, which also yield an exportable surplus and a promising start has been made with castor seed. The principal export crop is cotton. Main production is of long-staple (mainly Egyptian type) cotton of which the Sudan is a major producer, but increasing quantities of short and medium staple (American) type cotton are being grown. Production in 1965–66 totalled 790,180 bales, an increase over the figure of 541,963 for 1963–64, but less than the 1961–62 level of 1,142,392 bales. Much of the high quality, long-staple cotton is provided by the Sudan Gezira Scheme (a Government-controlled project irrigated from the Sennar Dam on the Blue Nile) and its extension, the Managil Scheme. The Sudan also produces the bulk of the world's supply of gum arabic. Livestock is the mainstay of the nomadic Arab tribes of the desert and the negro tribes of the swamp and wooded grassland country in the South. A new dam at Khashm el Girba began to store water in May, 1964, and will eventually provide irrigation to about 500,000 acres, most of which is being used to resettle the population of the Wadi Halfa area which is being flooded by the reservoir of the Egyptian High Dam. Another dam at Roseires on the Blue Nile will enable new or increased irrigation on a further 3,000,000 acres as well as providing hydro-electric power.

Communications.—The railway system (3 ft. 6 in. gauge) has a route length of about 3,200 miles, linking Khartoum with Wadi Halfa, Port Sudan, Wad Medani, Sennar, Kosti, El Obeid and Nyala. A line branches out southwards to Wau from the Sennar/Nyala western line. Regular rail and Nile steamer services connect Khartoum with Juba in Equatoria Province which in turn is connected by a bus service with Nimule on the Uganda border. The river service between Wadi Halfa and Shellal in the U.A.R. was withdrawn in 1964 and it has not yet been decided finally what form of trans-port, if any, will replace it. ΨPort Sudan is a well-equipped modern seaport. Sudan Airways fly regular services from Khartoum to many parts of the Sudan and to Egypt, Greece, Italy, the Lebanon, the United Kingdom, Ethiopia, Uganda and W. Germany and are equipped with a Comet 4C and 4 Fokker F27 aircraft as well as some smaller machines.

FINANCE

	1968–69
Revenue	£113,000,000
Expenditure	100,000,000

£S = Sudanese *Pound* of 100 *Piastres.*
Exchange Rate 83·23 *Piastres* = £1 sterling (*see also* p. 84).

TRADE

	1969
Total imports	£92,500,000
Exports	85,600,000

Trade with U.K.

	1969	1970
Imports from U.K.	£21,558,000	£18,181,000
Exports to U.K.	7,310,000	7,624,000

The principal exports are cotton and cotton seed, ground-nuts and gum arabic. The chief imports are cotton piece goods, base metals, vehicles and transport equipment, machinery, petroleum products, sugar, tea, coffee, chemicals and pharmaceuticals.

CAPITAL.—Khartoum. The town contains many mosques, an Anglican Cathedral, and the University, with extensive Government buildings. Estimated population, 124,000. Khartoum North and Omdurman have estimated populations of 53,000 and 154,000 respectively.

FLAG.—3 horizontal stripes of blue, yellow and green. NATIONAL DAY.—January 1 (Independence Day).

BRITISH EMBASSY
Khartoum

Ambassador Extraordinary and Plenipotentiary, His Excellency (Raymond) Gordon (Antony) Etherington-Smith, C.M.G. (1970) £6,925

British Council Representative, M. S. Dalziel, 32 Barlaman Street, P.O. Box 1253, Khartoum. There are British Council libraries at *Khartoum, El Fasher, El Obeid, Omdurman* and *Wad Medani.*

SWEDEN
(Sverige)

King of Sweden, of the Goths and the Wends*, Gustaf VI Adolf, K.G., elder son of the late King Gustaf V, *born* Nov. 11, 1882; *married* (1) June 15, 1905, H.R.H. the late Princess Margaret of Connaught (*died* May 1, 1920), (2) Nov. 3, 1923, the late Lady Louise Mountbatten, Princess of Battenberg (*died* March 7, 1965); *succeeded* Oct. 29, 1950.

Heir Apparent, Crown Prince Carl Gustaf, Duke of Jämtland, *grandson* of the King, *born* April 30, 1946.

CABINET
Prime Minister, Olof Palme.
Justice, Lennart Geijer.
Foreign Affairs, Krister Wickman.
Defence, Sven Andersson.
Social Affairs, Sven Aspling.
Local Government and Planning, Svante Lundqvist.
Communications, Bengt Norling.
Finance, Gunnar Sträng.
Education, Ingvar Carlsson.
Agriculture, Ingemund Bengtsson.
Interior, Eric Holmqvist.
Industry, Rune Johansson.

---

*This is the official title of the King of Sweden.

Trade, Kjell-Olof Feldt.
Ministers without Portfolio, Sven-Eric Nilsson; Carl Lidbom (with special responsibility for the *drafting of legislation*); Alva Myrdal (with special responsibility for *disarmament*); Camilla Odhnoff (with special responsibility for *family affairs*); Sven Moberg (with special responsibility for *education*); Bertil Löfberg (with special responsibility for *Civil service wages and salaries*).

SWEDISH EMBASSY IN LONDON

Residence, 29 Portland Place, W.1; *Chancery*, 23 North Row, W.1 (and Consulate-General)
[01-499-9500]
Ambassador Extraordinary and Plenipotentiary, His Excellency Leif Belfrage, G.B.E. (1967).
Minister Plenipotentiary, G. Fagrell.
Counsellors, O. Ternström (*Press*); Arne Feltheim (*Economic and Financial*).
1st Secretary, G. Ekholm.
2nd Secretaries, J. Kronholm; S. Danielsson;
Naval Attaché, Capt. N. Rydström.
Military Attaché, Col. Å. Hultin.
Air Attaché, Lt.-Col. L. H. Sonesson.
Press Attaché, K. Holm.
Cultural Attaché, N-G. Hildeman.
Labour Attaché, B. Carlson.
Attaché, B. Petraeus (*Administration*).
Chaplain, Rev. S. Evander.
Consul-General, Baron G. F. von Otter.
Consuls, A. Lundqvist; G. Luthman, M.V.O.

Area and Population.—Sweden occupies the eastern area of the Scandinavian peninsula in N.W. Europe and comprises 24 local government districts, "*Län*," with an area of 173,436 sq. miles, and a population Jan. 1, 1970 of 8,013,696. In 1969 there were 107,622 births (13·5 per 1,000 inhabitants); death rate was 13·5 per 1,000 inhabitants and infant mortality rate (under one year of age) 1·17 per cent. of all live births.

Government.—Under the Constitution of June 6, 1809 (with amendments) the throne is hereditary in the House of Bernadotte. Jean-Baptiste Jules

Bernadotte, Prince of Ponte Corvo, a Marshal of France, was invited to accept the title of Crown Prince, with succession to the throne. He landed at Helsingborg on Oct. 20, 1810, and succeeded Charles XIV in 1818. There is a unicameral Diet (*Riksdag*) of 350 members elected for 3 years. The Council of Ministers (*Statsråd*) is responsible to the *Riksdag*.

Production and Industry.—Since the end of the First World War Sweden has become one of the leading industrial nations of Europe. Agriculture is still one of the main activities, but its relative importance is declining and in 1969 less than 7 per cent. of the working population was engaged in farming and forestry. The country's rising industrial prosperity is based on an abundance of natural resources in the form of forests, mineral deposits and water power. The forests are very extensive, covering about half the total land surface, and sustain flourishing timber, pulp and paper milling industries. The mineral resources include iron ore of excellent quality, lead, zinc, sulphur, granite and marble. There are also extensive deposits of low grade uranium ore. Important industries based on mining include iron and steel, aluminium, and copper. The engineering industry has expanded largely on the basis of products invented or developed by Swedish engineers. Sweden has now one of the most important shipbuilding industries in the world. Motor car manufacturing is a major industry. The establishment of a petro-chemicals industry has led to a rapid expansion in the output of chemicals and plastics.

Communications.—The total length of Swedish railroads is about 7,800 miles. At the beginning of 1971 there were 557 telephones for every 1,000 of the population, and in January, 1971, the number of broadcast receiving licences issued had reached 2,513,000. On Sept. 3, 1967, right-hand traffic rules were introduced on the roads in Sweden. The number of private cars in use on January 1, 1971, was 2,287,700 (283 per 1,000 population) (1970, 2,193,600).

The Mercantile Marine (June, 1971) consisted of 751 vessels of 100 tons gross and over with a total tonnage of 4,784,000. The Board of Civil Aviation under the control of the Ministry of Communications handles civil aviation matters. Regular domestic air traffic is maintained by the Scandinavian Airlines System and by A. B. Linjeflyg. Regular European and inter-continental air traffic is maintained by the Scandinavian Airlines System.

Defence.—A period of service in the Defence Forces is compulsory and about 40,000 National Servicemen are called up each year. In addition some 45,000 reservists receive training each year. However, the regular strength of the *Army* is only about 12,400 all ranks. There are some 500,000 trained reserves. Weapons and equipment are modern and the Army is highly mechanized. The *Navy* has 1 cruiser, 8 destroyers, 7 frigates, 24 submarines, 42 F.P.S.'s and a large number of minor craft and auxiliaries. Only about ⅓ of this force is commissioned in normal times. The *Air Force* is equipped with modern supersonic jet fighters, attack and reconnaissance aircraft of Swedish manufacture. There are 7 fighter, 4 attack and 2 reconnaissance wings. These wings are backed by an efficient control and reporting organization and air base system.

Religion.—The State religion is Lutheran Protestant, to which over 95 per cent. of the people adhere.

Language and Literature.—As one of the Scandinavian languages, Swedish is closely allied to Norwegian, Danish and Icelandic. Swedish literature

dates back to King Magnus Eriksson, who codified the old Swedish provincial laws in 1350. With his translation of the Bible, Olaus Petri (1493–1552) formed the basis for the modern Swedish language. In 1643 Georg Stiernhielm wrote his first poem, dedicated to Queen Christina, the first in a series of works which earned him the title of "The father of Swedish poetry". Literature flourished during the reign of Gustavus III, who founded the Swedish Academy in 1786, and Swedish drama was born. 19th century Swedish literature was studded by names such as Atterbom, Almquist, Levertin, Rydberg, and was enriched by Finnish writers such as Topelius and Runeberg. At the culmination of this tradition came Strindberg and Lagerlöf. The modern tone was set by the so-called Proletarian School, the most famous authors of which were Ivar Lo-Johansson and Martinsson. There followed a proliferation of young writers among whom Moberg, Lagerquist, Dagerman and Frans G. Bengtsson have won international repute. The Swedish scientist Alfred Nobel (1833–96) founded the Nobel Prizes for Literature, Science and Peace. In 1969 there were 148 daily newspapers with a total circulation of 4,420,000 copies, 4 major papers being published at Stockholm, 3 at Göteborg and 4 at Malmö.

Education.—Well developed and recently reorganized to provide (i) 9 years' compulsory schooling from the age of 7 to 16 in the *Grundskolan*; (ii) further education from 16 to 18/19 in the *Gymnasia*, which offer a number of courses preparing for entry to the universities, other centres of higher education, the professions, etc.; (iii) Vocational and continuation schools following upon the *Grundskolan* and offering both practical and theoretical courses. These may be said to stand between the *Grundskolan* and the *Gymnasia*. (iv) the universities. There are five State universities—Uppsala (founded 1477); Lund (founded 1668); Stockholm (founded 1878); Göteborg (founded 1887); Umeå (founded 1963). Tuition within the State system, which is maintained by the State and by local taxation, is free.

FINANCE

	1970–71 '000 *Kronor*
Revenue (Total Budget).........	44,839,000
Expenditure (Operational Budget).	45,630,000
National Debt..................	33,401,000

The Swedish *Krona* (of 100 *Ore*) exchanges at 12·40–12·50 *Kronor* = £1 sterling. (*See also* p. 83.)

TRADE

	1969 '000 *Kronor*	1970 '000 *Kronor*
Imports........	30,517,000	36,239,300
Exports........	29,425,800	35,083,600

Trade with U.K.

	1969	1970
Imports from U.K...	£294,766,000	£364,065,000
Exports to U.K.....	332,805,000	371,047,000

The chief imports from Britain are machinery and engineering goods, transport equipment, petroleum products, chemicals, plastics, raw materials, iron and steel and other metals, textile fabrics, clothing, instruments and some foodstuffs. Sweden's chief exports to Britain are timber, pulp and paper, machinery, motor vehicles, iron ore, and iron and steel.

CAPITAL.—Ψ Stockholm. Population (1970): City 747,490; Greater Stockholm, 1,306,762; Ψ Gothenburg (Göteborg) (446,875); Ψ Malmö (258,311); Västerås (113,389); Uppsala (101,696); Ψ Norrköping (95,851); Örebro (90,930); Ψ Hel-

singborg (82,137); Linköping (80,767); Ψ Gävle (72,987); Borås (71,227); Eskilstuna (67,536).

FLAG.—Yellow cross on a blue ground. NATIONAL DAY.—June 6 (Day of the Swedish Flag).

BRITISH EMBASSY

(*Residence*, Laboratoriegatan 8; *Chancery*, Skarpögatan 8, Stockholm.)

Ambassador Extraordinary and Plenipotentiary, His Excellency Sir Archibald David Manisty Ross, K.C.M.G. (1966) £14,000
Counsellors, J. I. McGhie (*Commercial*); Miss P. M. Hutchinson.
1st Secretaries, O. G. Griffith (*Commercial*); J. P. Davies; G. D. Cossar (*Labour*); J. C. Longbotham, M.B.E. (*Economic*); P. G. L. Gould (*Consul*).
2nd Secretaries, M. Cederlund (*Information*); W. P. Hartshorne; Miss M. M. Ramsay.
Defence and Air Attaché, Gp. Capt. R. H. B. Dixon.
Naval Attaché, Cdr. J. R. Symonds-Taylor.
Military Attaché, Lt.-Col. D. G. Raschen.
Assist. Air Attaché, Sqn.-Ldr. D. S. Lennox.
Scientific Attaché, Dr. M. H. Proctor.
Cultural Attaché (*British Council Representative*), D. H. Spencer.
Archivist, R. I. White.

BRITISH CONSULAR OFFICES

There are British Consular Offices at *Gävle*, *Göteborg*, *Helsingborg*, *Luleå*, *Malmö*, *Norrköping*, *Stockholm* and *Sundsvall*.

British-Swedish Chamber of Commerce in Sweden: Hovslagaregatan 5B, Stockholm.

SWITZERLAND
(Schweizerische Eidgenossenschaft—Confédération Suisse—Confederazione Svizzera.)

CABINET

President* (1971) and Defence, M. Rudolf Gnägi.
Vice-President (1971) and Finance and Customs, Dr. Nello Celio.
Foreign Affairs, M. Pierre Graber.
Justice and Police, M. Ludwig von Moos.
Interior, Prof. Dr. Hans-Peter Tschudi.
Public Economy, M. Ernst Brugger.
Transport, Communications and Power, M. Roger Bonvin.

SWISS EMBASSY IN LONDON

77 Gloucester Place, W.1.
[01–723–0701]

Ambassador Extraordinary and Plenipotentiary, His Excellency Albert Weitnauer.
Counsellors, Jurg Iselin; Charles Bruggman (1971).
Defence Attaché, Col. Helmut von Frisching.
Secretaries, Carlo Jagmetti; Franz Birrer; Anton Greber; René Serex.
Asst. Defence Attaché, Capt. Matthey-de-l'Endroit Marcel.
Consular Section, 1 Montagu Place, W.1.
Consul and Head of Administration, Fritz Adams.
There is a Swiss Consulate in *Manchester*.

Area and Population.—The Helvetia of the Romans, a Federal Republic of Central Europe, situated between 45° 50′–47° 48′ N. lat. and 5° 58′–10° 3′ E. long. It is composed of 22 Cantons, 3 subdivided, making 25 in all, of very dissimilar size, united under a Constitution dated May 29, 1847, and comprises a total area of 15,950 square miles, with a population (estimated Dec. 1, 1970) of 6,269,783. In 1969 there were 102,520 live births, 58,002 deaths and 46,886 marriages. The infant

---

* The President is elected in December and remains in office from Jan. 1 to Dec. 31; he is *generally* succeeded by the Vice-President.

mortality rate was 15 per 1,000 live births. In 1960, out of a total of 5,492,061, 52·6 per cent. of the population was Protestant, 45·6 per cent. Roman Catholic and 0·4 per cent. Jewish.

Physical Features.—Switzerland is the most mountainous country in all Europe. The Alps, covered with perennial snow and from 5,000 to 15,217 feet in height, occupy its southern and eastern frontiers, and the chief part of its interior; and the Jura mountains rise in the north-west. The Alps occupy 61 per cent., and the Jura mountains 12 per cent., of the country. The *Alps* are a crescent-shaped mountain system situated in France, Italy, Switzerland, Bavaria and Austria, covering an area of 80,000 square miles from the Mediterranean to the Danube (600 miles). The highest peak, Mont Blanc, Pennine Alps (15,732 feet) is partly in France and Italy; Monte Rosa (15,217 feet) and Matterhorn (14,780 feet) are partly in Switzerland and partly in Italy. The highest wholly Swiss peaks are Dufourspitze (15,203 ft.), Finsteraarhorn (14,026), Aletschhorn (13,711), Jungfrau (13,671), Mönch (13,456), Eiger (13,040), Schreckhorn (13,385), and Wetterhorn (12,150) in the Bernese Alps, and Dom (14,918), Weisshorn (14,803) and Breithorn (13,685).

The Swiss lakes are famous for their beauty and include Lakes Maggiore, Zürich, Lucerne, Neuchâtel, Geneva, Constance, Thun Zug, Lugano, Brienz and the Walensee. There are also many artificial lakes.

Production and Industry.—Agriculture is followed chiefly in the valleys, where wheat, oats, maize, barley, flax, hemp, and tobacco are produced, and nearly all English fruits and vegetables as well as grapes are grown. Dairying and stock-raising are the principal industries, about 3,000,000 acres being under grass for hay and 2,000,000 acres pasturage. The forests cover about one-quarter of the whole surface. The chief manufacturing industries comprise engineering and electrical engineering, metal-working, chemicals and pharmaceuticals, textiles, watchmaking, woodworking, foodstuffs and footwear. Banking, insurance and tourism are major industries.

Government.—The legislative power is vested in a Parliament, consisting of two Chambers, a National Council (*Nationalrat*) of 200 members, and a Council of States (*Ständerat*) of 44 members; both Chambers united are called the Federal Assembly, and the members of the National Council are elected for four years, an election taking place in October. The executive power is in the hands of a Federal Council (*Bundesrat*) of 7 members, elected for four

years by the Federal Assembly and presided over by the President of the Confederation. Each year the Federal Assembly elects from the Federal Council the President and the Vice-President. Not more than one of the same canton may be elected member of the Federal Council; on the other hand, there is a tradition that Italian and French-speaking areas should between them be represented on the Federal Council by at least two members.

Defence.—All Swiss males must undertake military service in the Army. *Elite* (ages 20 to 32) initial training, 118 days. Subsequently 8 training periods of 21 days; then *Landwehr* (33–42) and *Landsturm* (43 to 50). Flying personnel of the Air Force, which is part of the Army (ages 20–36): Initial training 1 year, totalling 200 hours of flying. 6 weeks with squadron each year and completion of 70 hours of flying. After 36 revert to ground duties with Air Force or Army. Swiss Army equipment includes many British items, notably Centurion tanks, Bloodhound missiles, and Venom, Vampire and Hunter aircraft.

Communications.—By the end of 1969 there were 3,129 miles of railway tracks (Swiss Federal Railways, 1,823 miles, Swiss privately owned railways, 1,306 miles); the whole system is electrified. At the end of 1970, there were 51,640 miles of telegraph and telephone lines. By December, 1970, the number of telephone subscribers amounted to 1,945,168 and the network was fully automatic throughout the country. There were 1,851,612 licensed radio receivers and 1,273,893 television receivers.

At the end of 1967, the total length of first-class roads was 36,378 miles. The number of motor vehicles licensed at the end of 1969 was 2,039,236 (1,146,033 private cars, 624,353 motor cycles, motor scooters and bicycles with auxiliary motor, 4,921 motor buses, 237,584 motor lorries, 26,345 special vehicles and tractors).

A merchant marine, established in 1940, consisted in 1970 of 31 vessels with a total displacement of 209,151 tons (gross). In addition 445 vessels with a total tonnage of 450,716 were engaged in Rhine shipping. In 1970, goods handled at the Basle Rhine Port amounted to 8,924,820 tons. 121 lake vessels transported 9,729,000 passengers and 382,326 tons of freight in 1969. The national airline, Swissair, has a network covering 134,741 miles and in 1970 carried a total of 3,867,576 passengers. Its fleet of 36 aircraft includes 2 Jumbojets. In 1970 net profit was 34,310,000 francs. It flies to and from the Swiss airports at Zurich, Geneva and Basle.

Education.—Control by cantonal and communal authorities. No central organization. Illiteracy practically unknown. (i.) *Primary*: Free and compulsory. School age varies, generally 7 to 14. (ii) *Secondary*: Age 12–15 for boys and girls. Schools numerous and well-attended, and there are many private institutions. (iii) *Special schools* make a feature of commercial and technical instruction. (iv) *Universities*: Basle (founded 1460), Berne (1834), Fribourg (1889), Geneva (1873), Lausanne (1890), Zürich (1832), and Neuchâtel (1909), and the technical University of Zürich and commercial University of St. Gall.

Language and Literature.—There are three official languages: French, German and Italian. In addition Romansch is recognized as a national, but not an official language. German is the dominating language in 19 of the 25 cantons; French in Fribourg, Geneva, Neuchâtel, Valais and Vaud; Italian in Ticino, and Romansch in parts of the Grisons.

Many modern authors, alike in the German school and in the Suisse Romande, have achieved

international fame. Karl Spitteler (1845–1924) and Hermann Hesse (1877–1962) were awarded the Nobel Prize for Literature, the former in 1919, the latter in 1947.

FINANCE

	Budget 1970	Budget 1971
	Swiss Francs	*Swiss Francs*
Revenue.....	5,842,000,000	8,517,000,000
Expenditure .	5,637,000,000	8,609,000,000
Federal Public Debt (Dec. 31, 1970): Internal consolidated....		6,361,000,000

Following the revaluation of the *Swiss Franc* in May, the rate of exchange in 1971 was *Sw. Frs.* 9·89 = £1 (*see also* p. 83).

TRADE

	1969	1970
	Sw. Frs.	*Sw. Frs.*
Total Imports..	22,734,361,000	27,873,477,193
Total Exports ..	20,009,061,000	22,140,267,645

Trade with U.K. (including Liechtenstein)

	1969	1970
Imports from U.K.	£167,716,000	£209,298,000
Exports to U.K...	174,462,000	198,839,000

The principal imports are metals, machinery, instruments and apparatus; motor vehicles, chemical and pharmaceutical raw materials and products; fuel oil, petrol and coal; timber; cereals, fruit and vegetables. The principal exports are machinery, watches, chemicals and pharmaceuticals, textiles and foodstuffs. Switzerland is a member of E.F.T.A.

CAPITAL, Berne. Population (estimated 1968), 166,800. Other large towns are Zürich (432,400), Basle (213,200), Geneva (169,500), Lausanne (138,300), St. Gallen (78,600), Winterthur (92,500), Lucerne (73,000), Biel (66,900) and La Chaux-de-Fonds (43,100).

FLAG.—Red, with white cross. NATIONAL DAY. —August 1.

AIR TRANSIT FROM U.K.—London–Basle (446 miles), 1 hr. 20 mins.; Geneva (468 miles), 1 hr. 20 mins.; Zürich (491 miles), 1 hr. 20 mins.

RAIL TRANSIT FROM U.K.—London–Berne, 16 hrs.

BRITISH EMBASSY
(Thunstrasse 50, 3005 Berne)

Ambassador Extraordinary and Plenipotentiary, His Excellency Eric Atkinson Midgley, C.M.G., M.B.E. (1970) £6,925

Counsellor, Miss G. G. Brown, C.M.G.

1st Secretary, H. R. W. Latham.

2nd Secretaries, C. K. Woodfield; E. H. L. Ellis (Consul).

Defence, Naval, Military and Air Attaché, Col. J. I. G. Capadose.

Asst. Air Attaché, Wing Cdr. P. D. A. Nichols.

Attachés, W. F. G. Drury (*Scientific*); E. G. Collier; D. L. Wetton, M.B.E. (*Commercial*); P. Arengo-Jones (*Press*).

BRITISH CONSULAR OFFICES

There is a Consular Section at H.M. Embassy, Berne; British Consular Offices at *Basle, Geneva, Lugano* and *Montreux;* and a Directorate of British Export Promotion in Switzerland and Consulate-General in *Zürich.*

BRITISH COUNCIL.—Rämistrasse 34, 8001, *Zürich* (*Representative,* M. H. S. Everett).

BRITISH–SWISS CHAMBER OF COMMERCE FOR SWITZERLAND, Dufourstrasse 51, 8008 *Zürich* (Branch at 1 Galeries Benjamin Constant, 1,000 *Lausanne*).

SWISS-BRITISH SOCIETY, Berne.—*President,* Prof. R. Fricker.

SWISS-BRITISH SOCIETY, Zürich.—*President,* Dr R. Schneebeli.

SYRIA
(Syrian Arab Republic)

President, Lt.-Gen. Hafez el Assad, *b.* 1930, *assumed office* March 14, 1971, *for a term of 7 years.*

[Following the outbreak of hostilities between Israel and the surrounding Arab States, Syria broke off diplomatic and consular relations with the United Kingdom on June 6, 1967.]

Area and Population.—Syria is in the Levant, covering a portion of the former Ottoman Empire, with an estimated area of 70,800 sq. miles and a population (Census of 1970) of 6,294,000, Arabic speaking and mainly Moslems. (*For* MAP, *see* p. 885.) The Orontes flows northwards from the Lebanon range across the northern boundary to Antakya (Antioch, Turkey). The Euphrates crosses the northern boundary near Jerablus and flows through north-eastern Syria to the boundary of Iraq.

Archæology, etc.—The region is rich in historical remains. Damascus (*Dimishq ash-Sham*) is the oldest continuously inhabited city in the world, having an existence as a city for over 4,000 years. It is situated on the river Abana (now known as Barada), in an oasis at the eastern foot of the Anti-Lebanon, and at the edge of the wide sandy desert which stretches to the Euphrates. The city contains the Omayyed Mosque, the Tomb of Saladin, and the "Street Called Straight" (Acts ix. 11), while to the North-East is the Roman outpost of Dmeir and further east is Palmyra.

On the Mediterranean coast at Amrit are ruins of the Phœnician town of Marath, where the *tell* has been found and is being excavated and also ruins of Crusaders' fortresses at Markab, Sahyoun, and Krak des Chevaliers. At Tartous (also on the coast) the cathedral of Our Lady of Syria, built by the Knights Templars in the 12th and 13th centuries has been restored as a museum.

Hittite cities, dating from 2,000 to 1,500 B.C., have recently been explored on the west bank of the Euphrates at Jerablus and Kadesh.

Government.—Syria, which had been under French mandate since the 1914–18 war, became an independent Republic during the 1939–45 war. The first independently elected Parliament met on August 17, 1943, but foreign troops were in part occupation until April, 1946. Syria remained an independent Republic until February, 1958, when it became part of the United Arab Republic. It seceded from the United Arab Republic on Sept. 28, 1961.

In May, 1969, a new Constitution was promulgated, declaring that "the Syrian Arab Region will constitute a democratic, popular and socialist republic " in which the only political party would be the *Baath.* Supreme power in the State would lie with the People's Assembly which would elect the Chief of State and ratify laws. The Constitution provides for a planned socialist economy, with safeguards for private property.

Dr. Nureddin Atassi held office as President of Syria from Feb. 25, 1966, until his dismissal by the former Minister of Defence, Lt.-Gen. Hafez el Assad, on Nov. 13, 1970. The Constitution was amended by decree on Feb. 16, 1971, which provided for the selection of a President with extended powers and the establishment of a People's Council of 173 nominated members. The Council met for the first time on Feb. 22, 1971, and nominated Gen. Assad as President for 7 years on March 1.

Production and Industry.—Agriculture is the principal source of production; wheat and barley are the main cereal crops, but the cotton crop is the highest in value. Tobacco is grown in the maritime plain in Sahel, the Sahyoun and the Djebleh

district of Lattakia; skins and hides, leather goods, wool and silk, textiles, cement, vegetable oil, glass, soap, sugar, plastics and copper and brass utensils are locally produced. There are also some light assembly plants. Mineral wealth is small but oil has been found at Karachuk in the north-eastern corner of the country and drilling is continuing. A pipeline is to be built to the Mediterranean port of Tartous, *via* Homs. An oil refinery is in production at Homs and revenue is derived from the Kirkuk-Banias oil pipeline and the pipeline from the oilfields of Saudi-Arabia to Sidon in Lebanon (Tapline). Syria also has deposits of phosphate and rock salt.

Language and Literature.—Arabic is the principal language (*see* Arabia), but a few villages still speak Aramaic, the language spoken by Christ and the Apostles. There are a daily newspapers and several periodicals in Arabic published in Damascus and one daily newspaper in Aleppo.

Education.—Education in Syria is under State control and, although a few of the schools are privately owned, they all follow a common system and syllabus. Elementary education is free at State Schools, and is compulsory from the age of seven. Secondary education is not compulsory and is free only at the State Schools. Because of the shortage of places, entry to these State Schools is competitive. Damascus University, founded in 1924, has faculties of law, medicine, engineering, science, arts, commerce, agriculture, divinity, fine arts, and a Higher Teachers' Training College. The number of students has risen from a few hundred in 1943 to about 20,000. There are also over 4,500 students at Aleppo University (founded 1961). Approximately 10 per cent. of all students receive scholarships, and at the present time Palestinian refugees are admitted free. The rest pay fees.

Communications.—A narrow-gauge railway runs from Beirut in the Lebanon to Damascus, connecting at Rayak (Lebanon) with the standard-gauge line which runs from Beirut and Tripoli (in the Lebanon) through Homs, Hama and Aleppo to the Turkish frontier, from Nusaybin to the Iraq frontier at Tel Kotchek. From Damascus the Hejaz railway runs southwards to Jordan. Railway lines are under construction to link the ports of Lattakia and Tartous with Aleppo and Qamishli. All the principal towns in the country are connected by roads of varying quality. An internal air service operates between Damascus and Aleppo, and between Aleppo and Qamishli. There are also flights from Damascus to Palmyra and Deir-ez-Zor. Damascus is also on international air routes.

Currency.—The monetary unit is the Syrian paper pound (*£Syr.*). Exchange rate, *see* p. 84.

Trade.—The principal imports are foodstuffs (fruit, vegetables, cereals, meat and dairy products, tea, coffee and sugar), mineral and petroleum products, yarn and textiles, iron and steel manufactures, machinery, chemicals, pharmaceuticals, fertilizers and timber.

Principal Exports.—Raw cotton, cereals, fruit, livestock and dairy products, other foodstuffs, textiles and raw wool.

Trade with U.K.

	1969	1970
Imports from U.K.	£7,128,000	£5,995,000
Exports to U.K.	1,235,000	489,000

CHIEF TOWNS.—Damascus (population (1965), 599,000) is the capital of Syria, other important towns being Aleppo (population 562,000), Homs (189,000) and Hama (135,000), and the principal port is Ψ Lattakia (82,000).

FLAG.—Red over white over black horizontal bands, with three green stars on central white band. NATIONAL DAY.—April 17.

BRITISH EMBASSY
[Diplomatic relations suspended, June 6, 1967.]

THAILAND (Siam)

King, His Majesty Bhumibol Adulyadej, *born* 1927; *succeeded his brother,* June 9, 1946; *married* Princess Sirikit Kityakara, April 28, 1950; *crowned* May 5, 1950; daughter *born,* April 6, 1951; son and heir *born,* July 28, 1952; second daughter *born* April 2, 1955; third daughter *born* July 4, 1957.

Prime Minister, Field Marshal Thanom Kittikachorn.
Foreign Minister, Nai Thanat Khoman.

ROYAL THAI EMBASSY IN LONDON
30 Queen's Gate, S.W.7
[01-589 0173]
Ambassador Extraordinary and Plenipotentiary, His Excellency Konthi Suphamongkhon (1970).

Area and Population.—The Kingdom of Thailand, or Muang Thai, formerly known as Siam, has an area of 198,247 sq. miles with a population (estimated 1969) of 34,738,000. For position, *see* MAP, p. 746. It has a common boundary with Malaysia in the south, and is bounded on the west and north-west by the Union of Burma and in the north-east and east by the Kingdoms of Laos and Cambodia, which were formerly part of the French Colony of Indo-China. Although there is no common boundary between Thailand and China, the Chinese province of Yunnan is separated from the Thai northern border only by a narrow stretch of Burmese and Laotian territory.

The country slopes southwards from the north-west and from the great mountains of Tibet. The principal rivers are the Salween (which forms a boundary with Burma for 200 miles), the Menam Chao Phraya with its tributary the Meping (which are Thai throughout) and the Mekong and its tributaries, which water the eastern plateau.

Government.—Thailand is a sovereign independent state. Under the new Constitution promulgated in June, 1968, the King exercises legislative power by and with the advice and consent of the National Assembly, executive power through the Council of Ministers and judicial power through the courts established by law. He is advised by a Privy Council appointed by himself. The National Assembly is bi-cameral, consisting of the Senate, whose 120 members are appointed by the government, and the House of Representatives, whose 219 members were elected by universal suffrage in a General Election held in February, 1969. The government *Saha Pracha Thai* (United Thai People's) Party has 120 seats in the House of Representatives and the major opposition party, the Democratic Party, 53. The other seats are held by independents and the members of small parties, large numbers of whom vote with the government.

Language, Religion and Education.—Thai is basically a monosyllabic, tonal language, a branch of the Indo-Chinese linguistic family, but its vocabulary especially has been strongly influenced by Sanskrit and Pali. It is written in an alphabetic script derived from ancient Indian scripts. The principal religion is Buddhism, its followers numbering 24,563,523 in 1964, with 1,025,569 Moslems and 150,053 Christians. Primary education is compulsory and free and secondary education in Government Schools is free. In 1964 there were 28,264 schools of all kinds with 5,007,430 pupils and 158,920 teachers. There are 7 Universities attended by 45,000 students, 34 training colleges and 196 vocational schools (all types). New uni-

versities were opened at Chiengmai and Khon Kaen in 1966 and another in the southern part of the country was planned.

Production and Industry.—The country's most important products are agricultural or forest; rice (about 13,000,000 tons a year), rubber (about 280,000 tons a year) and timber (about 4,000,000 cubic metres a year of which only 300,000 are of teak, traditionally the important timber product). Other crops of some importance are sugar cane, tapioca, kenaf, groundnuts, tobacco, maize, soya beans, cotton and coconuts

As regards mineral wealth, tin ore (production in 1970, 29,731 tons) is important, and small amounts of wolfram, iron and lead are mined, and nearly 400,000 tons of lignite. Most of the output of tin concentrates is now processed in a smelter in South Thailand which began operation in 1965.

Before the war industry was mainly confined to the basic processing industries—sawmilling, rice-milling, etc. After the war the Government set up a number of factories, run by the Civil Service or the Armed Forces. The Government still has a sizeable stake in industry—notably the tobacco monopoly and factories for the manufacture of cement, glass, paper, jute, textiles, sugar and beer and spirits.

The present Government in 1962 instituted a policy of encouraging the private sector to invest in industry, by means of tax reliefs and other incentives. The private sector industries are almost entirely of a secondary nature; soap products, gunny bags, textiles, car assembly, pharmaceutical preparations and packaging, dry batteries, etc. Nevertheless, more advanced organizations have recently started, such as a tyre factory, an aluminium rolling mill, a third glass factory, food processing plants and the manufacture of asbestos cement products. A fertilizer plant and a kraft paper factory have also been established.

Communications.—About 2,250 miles of State-owned railways were open to traffic in 1966. The track is metre gauge. Main lines run from Bangkok to Aranya Pradet, linking up with the Cambodian state railway at this border town (160 miles E.); *via* Korat to Ubol (about 352 miles E.) and to Nongkhai (415 miles N.E.) the ferry terminal on the River Mekong opposite Vientiane, capital of Laos; to Chiengmai (411 miles N.); and to Haadyai (600 miles S.), whence lines go down the eastern and western sides of the Malay Peninsula, *via* Sungei Golok and Penang respectively, to Singapore.

Thailand has about 10,000 kilometres of highways, of which about 45 per cent. are paved. An additional 1,500 kms. of highway is under construction or planned. The development of roads is being given top priority in the Government's development plans and substantial extensions and improvements are being financed mainly by World Bank funds.

Bangkok is an international airport of importance, and services connect it with Europe, America, India, Pakistan, Japan and Australasia, as well as other parts of S.E. Asia. Thai Airways International (THAI), was formed in 1960 in association with SAS to operate international routes. Domestic routes are operated by Thai Airways Corporation. There are about 14,500 miles of telegraph lines and parts of a countrywide micro-wave communications system are coming into operation The harbour at Bangkok, which can take vessels up to 10,000 tons dead weight, is becoming congested, but an expansion programme is under study.

FINANCE	1965	1969
	millions of *Baht*	
Total revenue	12,160	16,881
Total expenditure	14,355	23,960

Since 1950 Thailand has received amounts in excess of U.S. $380,000,000 in external loans for rehabilitation and development of railways, the port of Bangkok, irrigation, hydro-electric and other projects.

Thailand receives economic and technical assistance from many sources. The largest civil sector contribution is that of the United States which amounts to approximately U.S. $31,000,000 annually. Substantial military aid is also received from U.S. sources.

The exchange rate for the *Baht* was officially fixed at *Baht* 20·8 = $1 U.S. (*See also* p. 84.)

TRADE

	1969	1970
	millions of *Baht*	
Total imports	25,966	26,992
Total exports	14,712	14,768

Trade with U.K.

	1969	1970
Imports from U.K.	£30,758,000	£32,112,000
Exports to U.K.	5,705,000	5,509,000

The main exports are rice and rubber which normally account for about 50 per cent. of the total. Principal exports in 1970 (millions of *Baht*) were: Rice, 2,474·4; Rubber, 2,304; Maize 1,846·3. Other exports, whose levels vary more are jute and kenaf, teak, and tapioca products. The main imports are machinery, petroleum products, iron and steel, cotton fabrics and vehicles.

CAPITAL, Ψ Bangkok (population, 1966, 1,577,003); in the delta of the Menam Chao Phraya. Other centres are Chiengmai, Nakorn Sawan and Korat, but no other town approaches Bangkok in size or importance.

FLAG.—Five horizontal bands, red, white, dark blue, white, red (the blue band twice the width of the others). NATIONAL DAY.—December 5 (King's Birthday).

BRITISH EMBASSY
(Bangkok)

Ambassador Extraordinary and Plenipotentiary, His Excellency Sir Arthur James de la Mare, K.C.M.G., (1970) £9,000
Counsellor, B. G. Smallman.
Defence and Military Attaché, Col. W. V. G. Smith.

CONSULAR OFFICES
There is a Consular Office at *Bangkok*.

BRITISH COUNCIL
Representative, T. J. Rutter, 428 Rama I Road, Siam Square, Bangkok (Library).

TOGO
(Republic of Togo)

President and Minister of Defence, Gen. Etienne Eyadéma, *born* 1937, *assumed office as Head of State,* April 14, 1967.
Minister for Foreign Affairs, M. Joachim Hunlédé.

The Republic is situated in West Africa between 0°–2°W. and 6°–11°N., with a coastline only 35 miles long on the Gulf of Guinea, and extends northward inland for 350 miles. It is flanked on the west by Ghana, on the north by Upper Volta and in the east by Dahomey (*see* MAP, p. 957). It has an area of 21,000 sq. miles and a population (U.N. estimate, 1970) of 1,857,000, including people of several African races.

The first President of Togo, Sylvanus Olympio, assassinated on January 13, 1963, was succeeded by Nicolas Grunitzky, who was himself overthrown by an army *coup d'état* on January 13, 1967. On April 14, 1967, the Commander-in-Chief of the Togolese army, Lt. Colonel (later promoted General) Etienne Eyadéma named himself Presi-

dent. Togo is a member of the *Conseil de l'Entente*, the *Organisation Commune Africaine et Malgache* (O.C.A.M.), and the Organization of African Unity (O.A.U.). The official language is French.

Finance.—The currency of Togo is the *Franc C.F.A.* (Francs C.F.A. 50 = 1 French Franc) (Francs C.F.A. 666 = £1).

Production and Trade.—The economy of Togo is largely agricultural, the main exports being coffee, cocoa, palm kernels, copra, cotton and manioc. Production of phosphates by a Franco-American consortium begun in 1955 contributed 33 per cent. to Togo's export revenue in 1968 and cocoa a further 25 per cent.

Trade with U.K.

	1969	1970
Imports from U.K.....	£3,149,000	£3,395,000
Exports to U.K.......	553,000	463,000

CAPITAL.—Ψ Lomé, population (1968), 100,000.

FLAG.—Five alternating green and yellow horizontal stripes; a quarter in red at top next staff bearing a white star. NATIONAL DAY.—April 27 (Independence Day).

BRITISH EMBASSY

Ambassador Extraordinary and Plenipotentiary, His Excellency Frank Smitherman, M.B.E. (1970)
£6,475

3rd Secretary, D. R. Emsley (*Vice-Consul*).

TRUCIAL STATES

Seven independent Arab Shaikhdoms (Abu Dhabi, Ajman, Dubai, Fujairah, Ras al Khaimah, Sharjah and Umm el Qaiwain), known collectively as the Trucial States, have treaty relations with the British Government originating in treaties to prevent slavery and the piracy which formerly gave the name of " The Pirate Coast " to this area, and to maintain a perpetual maritime truce. The earliest treaty dates from 1820.

The British Government, by virtue of a treaty made in 1892, is responsible for the external affairs of the states through the British Political Resident in the Persian Gulf and the British Political Agents in the Trucial States. Six of the states lie on the coast of the Gulf between the Musandam peninsula in the East and the Qatar peninsula in the West and one, Fujairah, lies on the Gulf of Oman.

Agreement on a federal Constitution for the Trucial States was announced in Dubai on July 18, 1971. The proposed " Union of Arab Emirates " includes six of the seven Trucial States, the Ruler of Ras al Khaimah, though attending the latest meeting of Rulers, having refused to agree to the Constitution at this stage.

Area and Population.—The approximate combined area of the states is 32,000 square miles and the population (estimated, 1969) is about 185,000. Security in the area is maintained by the Trucial Oman Scouts, the force having headquarters at Sharjah, and in Abu Dhabi by the Abu Dhabi Defence Force. There are police forces in all seven states.

Revenue is chiefly derived from customs dues on imports and oil concession payments. The export of dried fish is also a significant source of revenue and some pearling is still carried on.

On Sharjah's west coast the offshore oil concession is held by Buttes Gas & Oil Co. and the onshore concession by Shell Hydrocarbons, while on Sharjah's east coast both the onshore and offshore concessions are held by Shell Minerals. In Ajman, Occidental of Ajman Inc. hold both the onshore and offshore concessions. In Umm al Qaiwain the offshore concession is held by Occidental of Umm al Qaiwain Inc. and the onshore by Shell Hydro-

carbons. In Ras al Khaimah, Union Oil has the offshore and Shell Hydrocarbons the onshore concession. In Fujairah Shell Minerals have the onshore and offshore concessions. (For Abu Dhabi and Dubai, *see* below).

From 1956 to 1965 the British Government financed a Trucial States Development Scheme to contribute to the material welfare of the people, including an Agricultural Trials Station in the Shaikhdom of Ras al Khaimah, trade schools in Sharjah and Dubai, a hospital in Ras al Khaimah and a number of dispensaries in the smaller towns and villages. In 1965 this scheme was amalgamated with the Trucial States Council's Development Office, which was founded to manage a fund for development, established with contributions from Britain, Qatar, Bahrain and Abu Dhabi. In recent years Abu Dhabi has been the principal contributor to the fund which has financed numerous development projects: roads, jetties, piped water and electricity supplies, flood and sea protection, soil, water and mineral surveys, a trade school at Ras al Khaimah, and clinics, dispensaries and anti-malaria work.

Kuwait, U.A.R., Bahrain and Qatar contribute educational assistance to the states. Her Majesty's Government has jurisdiction over certain categories of foreigners, though this is gradually being transferred to the Rulers. The Rulers of all the states meet together in the Trucial States Council to discuss matters of mutual interest three or four times a year. The currency in Abu Dhabi is the Bahraini *dinar*; in the other Trucial States, the Qatar and Dubai *riyal*.

Abu Dhabi is the largest of the Trucial States in area, stretching from the Khor el Odaid in the West to the borders with Dubai in the region of Jebel Ali. It includes six villages of the Buraimi oasis and a number of settlements in the series of oases known as the Liwa.

Ruler of Abu Dhabi, Shaikh Zaid bin Sultan al-Nahayan.

Prime Minister and Minister of Defence and Finance, Shaikh Khalifa bin Zaid (*Crown Prince*).

Deputy Prime Minister and Minister of Public Works, Shaikh Hamdan bin Mohamed.

Abu Dhabi's first Cabinet was formed on July 1, 1971, and legislation providing for a National Consultative Council of 50 members (max.) was initiated.

Two oil companies are operating in Abu Dhabi territory, Abu Dhabi Petroleum Co. Ltd. on land and Abu Dhabi Marine Areas Ltd. in the Abu Dhabi off-shore concession area. Oil has been discovered off Das Island, where Abu Dhabi Marine Areas has its headquarters and production started in 1962. Production from the on-shore Murban oil field commenced in December 1963. There are airfields at Abu Dhabi and at Das Island and an air strip at Buraimi. Work has started on a substantial development plan for the town of Abu Dhabi and the first stage has been completed.

Trade with U.K.

	1969	1970
Imports from U.K....	£14,918,000	£10,802,000
Exports to U.K.......	16,624,000	18,730,000

Ψ *Dubai* is by far the largest town in the Trucial States and has a population estimated at about 70,000. It is the main port for the import of goods into the Trucial States and the interior of Oman, and there is also a lively *entrepôt* trade. The value of imports in the year 1969 was £80,635,000 and in 1970, £83,980,400. Oil was discovered offshore in 1966 and production began in September, 1969. This concession is held by Dubai Marine Areas Ltd. The production facilities are entirely offshore and include a giant underwater storage tank, the first of

its kind in the world. The certainty of oil revenue enabled a start to be made on a number of development projects. The onshore oil concession is held by Dubai Petroleum Company. The first four berths of a 15-berth deep water harbour were opened in 1970 and a new international airport terminal in May, 1971. Other projects are a new sewage scheme, a £6m. hospital and a new police headquarters. The State continues to derive an increasing income from import duties. Telegraphic and telex communications are good and managed by Cable & Wireless Ltd. Ten international airlines fly regular scheduled services into Dubai and two have regular freight services. Fifteen banks are now operating in Dubai.

Ruler of Dubai, Shaikh Rashid bin Sa'id al Muktum, K.C.M.G.

Sharjah has begun to import some items, mainly rice and cement, through its new deep water jetty and a £1 million scheme to improve the creek and harbour is almost complete. The town is linked to Dubai, Ras al Khaimah and the oasis of Dhaid by metalled roads and the number of new businesses is increasing rapidly. A small international air terminal is served by Gulf Aviation and Syrian Arab Airlines. Two new hospitals, one built by the Trucial States Council and the Government of Sharjah, and the other by the Kuwait Government for tuberculosis patients, are under construction in the State. Sharjah has dependencies on the Batinah coast at Khorfakkhan, which forms a good natural harbour, Kalba and Dibba. The headquarters of the Trucial Oman Scouts is near Sharjah. British Army and Royal Air Force units based at Sharjah were expected to withdraw before the end of 1971.

Ajman is the smallest state, having a population of only about 5,000. It has inland enclaves at Manama and Masfut. *Umm el Qaiwain* does a small trade in dried fish. It has an oasis at Falaj al Mu'alla where palms and some fruit are grown. *Ras al Khaimah* has a population of about 25,000, of whom about half live in the town. It is an ancient seaport near which some remains of archaeological interest have been found. Dates, vegetables, fruit and tobacco are grown. The seat of government has now moved from its present exposed position on the shore to the inland side of the Creek. *Fujairah* was recognized as one of the Trucial States in 1952. Its inhabitants (about 9,000) are spread between the inland hills and the town of Fujairah, which is on the comparatively fertile plain of the Batinah Coast.

Trucial States Trade with U.K.
(excluding Abu Dhabi, see above)

	1969	1970
Imports from U.K.	£13,258,000	£13,748,000
Exports to U.K.	13,632,000	13,378,000

British Political Agent, Trucial States, J. F. Walker, M.B.E. *(resident at Dubai)*.
British Political Agent, Abu Dhabi, C. J. Treadwell.

TUNISIA
(Tunisian Republic)

President, Habib Bourguiba, *elected* July 25, 1957; *re-elected* 1959, 1964 and 1969.

CABINET

Prime Minister, Hedi Nouira.
Minister of National Economy, Tijani Chelli.
Foreign Affairs, Mohamed Masmoudi.
Justice, Mohamed Fitouri.
Interior, Ahmed Mestiri.
Defence, Hassib ben Ammar.
Finance, Abderrazak Rassaa.
Agriculture, Abdallah Farhat.
Education, Youth and Sport, Chedli Ayari.
Cultural Affairs and Information, Habib Boularès.

Health, Driss Guiga.
Public Works, Nassaed Ben Osman.
Plan, Mansour Moalla.
Agriculture, Abdullah Ferhet.
Youth and Sport, Teher Belkhadja.
In addition there are 6 Secretaries of State.

TUNISIAN EMBASSY IN LONDON
29 Princes Gate, S.W.7
[01-584 8117]

Ambassador, His Excellency Ismail Khelil (1969).
2nd Secretaries, Mustapha Mizouni; Hamid Zaouche.
3rd Secretary, Hamid Zardi.
Attaché, Hassen Sediri; Belgacem Gabchoug.

Area and Population.—Tunisia lies between Algeria and Libya and extends southwards to the Sahara Desert, with a total area of 45,000 sq. miles and a population (U.N. estimate, 1969) of 5,027,000.

Government.—A French Protectorate from 1881 to 1956, Tunisia became an independent sovereign State with the signing on March 20, 1956, of an agreement whereby France recognized Tunisia's independence and right to conduct her own foreign policy and to form a Tunisian Army. The United Kingdom formally recognized Tunisia as an independent and sovereign state on May 10, 1956.

Following a first general election held on March 25, 1956, a Constituent Assembly met for the first time on April 8. On July 25, 1957, the Constituent Assembly deposed the Bey, abolished the monarchy and elected M. Bourguiba first President of the Republic. On June 1, 1959, the Constitution was promulgated and on December 7, 1959, the National Assembly held its first session.

Important changes in the system of local government were decreed on June 16, 1956. The country was divided into 13 regions each administered by a Governor.

Production, Trade, etc.—The valleys of the northern region support large flocks and herds, and contain rich agricultural areas, in which wheat, barley, and oats are grown. The vine and olive are extensively cultivated.

The chief exports are olive oil, phosphates, cereals and wine. The chief imports are machinery, foodstuffs, iron and steel, textiles and crude petroleum, etc. Some oil has been discovered in Tunisia and production is running at about 4,000,000 tons a year. In 1970 Tunisia's imports totalled in value 191,400,000 *dinars* and exports 148,400,000 *dinars*. The volume of Tunisia's trade with France is diminishing but France still remains Tunisia's main trading partner. In 1969 France supplied 33 per cent. of Tunisia's total imports and she bought 26·7 per cent. of Tunisia's total exports.

Trade with U.K.

	1969	1970
Imports from U.K.	£3,488,000	£4,306,000
Exports to U.K.	2,835,000	2,487,000

Currency.—The Tunisian *dinar* was adopted on Nov. 3, 1958. At the same time a new Central Bank of Tunisia became responsible for the issue of notes. Although Tunisia remains in the Franc Zone the *dinar* is not tied to the French *franc*. The current rate of exchange is *dinars* 1·25 = £1.

So far as trade is concerned Tunisia was effectively part of metropolitan France until September, 1959, when she abrogated the Customs Union with the latter and a new trade and payments agreement was negotiated. This reduced or eliminated the tariff advantages enjoyed by certain French goods. Under commercial agreements concluded in November, 1962, and February, 1964, import quotas were established for certain French goods. In June, 1964, however, following Tunisian measures regarding the take-over of foreign-owned lands in Tunisia, France gave notice

that she would not renew the 1959 Trade Agreement, due to expire on Sept. 30, 1964. In May, 1966, France opened import quotas for a wide range of Tunisian goods (but excluding wine). Within these quota limits these goods can be admitted into France customs-free. In 1966 a policy of severe import restriction was adopted in order to reduce the country's chronic imbalance of trade. An ambitious programme of co-operative schemes for most areas of the economy was reversed in September, 1969, and gave way to a more orthodox economic policy. Tunisia became an associate member of EEC early in 1969.

CAPITAL, Ψ Tunis, connected by canal with La Goulette on the coast, had a population (Municipal Council area) of 784,787 at the Census of 1966. The ruins of ancient Carthage lie a few miles from the city. Other towns of importance are: Ψ Sfax (249,991); Ψ Bizerta (95,023); Ψ Sousse (82,666); Kairouan (82,299).

FLAG.—Red crescent and star in a white orb, all on a red ground. NATIONAL DAY.—June 1.

BRITISH EMBASSY
Place de la Victoire, Tunis

Ambassador Extraordinary and Plenipotentiary and Consul-General, His Excellency Archibald Robert Kerr Mackenzie, C.B.E. (1970) £6,925
1st Secretary, J. B. Wright (_Consul and Commercial_).
1st Vice-Consul, G. Cardona, M.B.E.
2nd Secretary, R. J. S. Muir (_Commercial_).
Vice-Consul, E. J. Hazou.

British Council Representative, E. T. H. Fitzsimmons, O.B.E. There is a British Council Library in Tunis.

TURKEY
President of the Republic, General Cevdet Sunay, G.C.B., _born_ 1900; _elected President,_ March 28, 1966.

COUNCIL OF MINISTERS (March 26, 1971)
(_Names as spelt in Turkish characters_)
Prime Minister, Nihat Erim.
Deputy Prime Minister (_Political and Administrative_), Sadi Koçaş.
Deputy Prime Minister (_Economic_), Atilla Karaosmanoğlu.
Ministers of State, Mehmet Özgüneş; Doğan Kitapli.
Justice, Ismail Arar.
Defence, Ferit Melen.

Interior, Hamdi Ömeroğlu.
Foreign Affairs, Osman Olcay.
Finance, Sait Naci Ergin.
Education, Şinasi Orel.
Culture, Talat Halman.
Public Works, Cahit Karakaş.
Foreign Economic Relations, Özer Derbil.
Industry and Trade, Ayhan Çilingiroğlu.
Health, Türkân Akyol.
Customs and Monopolies, Haydar Özalp.
Agriculture, Orhan Dikmen.
Communications, Halûk Arik.
Energy and Natural Resources, Ihsan Topaloğlu.
Tourism, Erol Yilmaz Akçal.
Reconstruction, Selahâttin Babüroğlu.
Rural Affairs, Cevdet Aykan.
Youth and Sport, Sezai Ergun.
Forestry, Selahattin Inal.

TURKISH EMBASSY IN LONDON
Chancery: 43 Belgrave Square, S.W.1
[01-235 5252]

Ambassador Extraordinary and Plenipotentiary, His Excellency Zeki Kuneralp (1969).
Minister, Sadi Akarcalioğlu.
Counsellors, Celil Vayisoğlu (_Commercial_); Yalçin Tuğ; Zeki Arsan (_Medical_); Galip Balkar; Hayrettin Ozansoy (_Financial_); Nejat Sönmez.
1st Secretary, Tugay Ozçeri.
2nd Secretary, Umit Pamir.
Armed Forces Attaché, Brig.-Gen. Hasan Saglam.
Military Attaché, Col. Selahattin Dayicioğlu.
Air Attaché, Wing Cdr. Yüksel Aykut.
Naval Attaché, Capt. Hasan Sarioğlu.
Consulate-General: 46 Rutland Gate, S.W.7.
Consul-General, Savlet Aktuğ.
Consuls, Aydin Tosun; Bilal Şimşir.

Area and Population.—The Turks belong to the Turanian Race, which comprises the Manchus and Mongols of North China, the Finns, and the Turks of Central Asia. Their numbers probably exceed 50,000,000, with the same language, religion and culture, but the actual Turkish State occupies only a small part of the area inhabited by the Turkish Race, the remainder being in Soviet Russia, China, Afghanistan and Iran.

Turkey extends from Edirne (Adrianople) to Transcaucasia and Iran, and from the Black Sea to

the Mediterranean, Syria and Iraq. Total population at the Census of October, 1970 was 35,666,549.

Turkey in Europe consists of Eastern Thrace, including the cities of Istanbul and Edirne, and is separated from Asia by the Bosphorus at Istanbul and by the *Dardanelles*—about 40 miles in length with a width varying from 1 to 4 miles—the political neighbours being Greece and Bulgaria on the west. Population (Census, 1970), 3,165,629.

Turkey in Asia comprises the whole of Asia Minor or *Anatolia* ("Land of the Rising Sun" or Orient), and extends from the Aegean Sea to the western boundaries of Georgia, Soviet Armenia and Iran, and from the Black Sea to the Mediterranean and the northern boundaries of Syria and Iraq. Population (Census, 1970), 32,500,920.

Government.—On October 29, 1923, the National Assembly declared Turkey a Republic and elected Gazi Mustafa Kemal (later known as Kemal Ataturk) President. Following the introduction of a multi-party régime in 1945, the Democratic Party was returned to power in 1950 and re-elected in 1954 and 1957. On May 27, 1960, the D.P. Government was overthrown by the Turkish Armed Forces which ruled through the Committee of National Union, a body of military officers. The committee ruled from January to November, 1961, in conjunction with a civilian House of Representatives, the two bodies together forming the Constituent Assembly.

At elections held in October, 1969, the Justice Party obtained 256 seats, the People's Republican Party 143 and the Reliance Party 15. Mr. Demirel's Justice Party Government (in office since Oct., 1965) resigned on March 12, 1971, following a memorandum to the President by the Chiefs of Staff of the Armed Forces. A new all-party Government, including a number of technocrats, was formed by Dr. Nihat Erim on March 26, 1971.

Turkey is divided for administrative purposes into 67 *vilayet* with subdivisions into *kaza* and *nahiye*. Each *vilayet* has a governor (*vali*) and elective council.

Religion and Education.—98·99 per cent. of the population are Moslems. The main religious minorities, which are concentrated in Istanbul and on the Syrian frontier, are: Orthodox, 107,000; Armenian Apostolic, 71,000; Catholic, 25,000; Protestant, 17,000; others, 10,000 (Total Christians, 230,000); Jewish, 44,000. On April 10, 1928, the Grand National Assembly passed a law in virtue of which Islam ceased to be the State religion of the Republic. Education is compulsory, free, and secular. There are elementary, secondary and vocational schools.

In 1969–70 there were 37,177 primary schools, with 4,906,712 pupils. There are two universities at Istanbul (one being a Technical University), three at Ankara (including the new Hacetteppe University), one each at Izmir, Erzurum and Trabzon. There is also a Faculty of Agriculture at Adana. The expenditure allocated to education in the 2nd Five Year Plan (1968–72) is *TL* 7,500,000,000, but this level of expenditure is unlikely to be realized. Expenditure so far (in *TL*'000,000): 1968, 1,150·6; 1969, 1,129·6; 1970, 1,083.

Language and Literature.—Osmanli or Ottoman Turkish is one of the Turanian languages spoken from Macedonia to Siberia. Until 1928 this language was written in Arabic script, but in that year the Roman alphabet was substituted for use in official correspondence and in 1928 for universal use, with Arabic numerals as used throughout Europe. Mainly as a consequence of this change the number of Turks who can read and write is rising steadily (although the proportion is constant at about 40 per cent.). Ancient Turkish literature

aped the Arabic manner, but the revolution of 1908 was followed by a popular reaction against the writings of the past (which appealed only to a small class) and led to the introduction of a native literature free from foreign influences and adapted to the understanding of the people. The vehicle first employed was the newspaper, printed in the neo-Latin alphabet, with supplements for prose and dramatic fiction, poetry and literary criticism. The leading Turkish newspapers are centred in Ankara and Istanbul, although most provincial towns have their own daily papers. There are foreign language papers in French, Greek, Armenian and English and numerous magazines and weeklies on various subjects, but few trade or commercial publications.

Agricultural Production.—In 1970, agriculture accounted for 31·1 per cent. of gross domestic income, while exports of agricultural commodities represented 75·2 per cent. of total exports. About 10,000,000, 77·6 per cent. of the working population, are in the rural sector, but agriculture is still primitive and agricultural productivity is low. Production figures for the principal crops in 1969 were ('000 tons): Cereals, 17,091; Sugar beet, 4,254; Cotton, 407; Tobacco, 147; Olives, 680; Hazel nuts, 250; Figs, 50; Tea (dry), 33; Sultanas, 128. With the important exception of wheat, which is mostly grown on the arid Central Anatolian Plateau, most of the crops are grown on the fertile littoral. Tobacco, sultana and fig cultivation is centred around Izmir, where substantial quantities of cotton are also grown. The main cotton area is in the Çukurova Plain around Adana. In 1969 it was estimated that there were 75,000,000 head of livestock, including sheep, 36,351,000; goats, 20,267,000; and cattle, 14,367,000. The forests which lie between the littoral plain and the Anatolian Plateau, contain beech, pine, oak, elm, chestnut, lime, plane, alder, box, poplar and maple. During recent years the Government has attempted, so far not altogether successfully, to combat the depredations of peasant and goat which threaten to destroy the existing forests within the next 25 years.

Industry.—After agriculture, Turkey's second most important industry is based on her considerable mineral wealth which is, however, as yet comparatively unexploited. The most important developments are in coal, of which over 13,650,000 metric tons are produced annually (of which 9,000,000 metric tons are lignite) for domestic needs. The main export mineral is chromite. Production of iron ore in 1970 was 2,646,133 tons; chrome ore, 696,870 tons; manganese, 9,494 tons; sulphur, 26,760 tons; blister copper, 18,955 tons and boracite, 523,650 tons. The research and exploitation of the principal mineral deposits are mainly in the hands of the Mineral Research and Exploration Institute of Turkey and the State-owned Etibank respectively. The latter controls directly, on behalf of the Government, all the copper, sulphur and pyrite output of Turkey, as well as much of the colemenite and chrome production. Since State-sponsored industrialization began in 1935, industry has played an increasing part in the Turkish economy. Here, also, as in the case of minerals, much of the industry of the country is controlled by the Government.

The progress made in the manufacture of sugar, cotton, woollen and silk textiles, and cement, has been such that the bulk of the country's requirements can now be produced locally, while other industries contributing substantially to local needs include paper, glass and glassware, iron and steel, leather and leather goods, sulphur refining, canning and rubber goods, soaps and cosmetics, pharmaceutical products, prepared foodstuffs and a host of minor industries. Legislation was passed in 1954 to encourage the investment of foreign

capital in Turkey and to promote the exploitation of Turkey's petroleum resources by foreign countries. Local production of crude petroleum in 1970 totalled 3,544,466 tons.

General Economic Factors.—Turkey's balance of payments continues to be burdened with the servicing of her large external debts (the total of public and private external debts repayable in foreign currencies totalled TL38,265,000,000 on Feb. 28, 1971), and the difficulty of increasing exports, which are mainly agricultural products, and minor raw materials for which world markets are rather weak. At the same time, Turkey's population is growing at an estimated rate of about 2·6 per cent. per annum. Since the Second World War the United States Government has given Turkey financial aid totalling over 5 billion dollars, half of which has been for military and half for economic purposes. The other main official sources of foreign aid have been the O.E.C.D. and the I.M.F., which have made medium term loans for balance of payment support. The United Kingdom has pledged nearly £60,000,000 of aid to Turkey since 1963.

The second of Turkey's three Five-Year Development Plans, for the years 1968–72, began in January, 1968. The basic economic objective of the second plan is to achieve an aggregate growth rate of around 40·3 per cent. in the gross national product.

COMMUNICATIONS

Railways.—The complete network became the property of the State Railways Administration in 1948. The total length of lines in operation at the end of 1970 was 8,126 kilometres. In 1970, the railways carried 104,040,847 passengers, 14,998,978 metric tons of freight and 1,727,000 head of livestock.

Roads.—At the end of 1969, there were 36,266 km. of national roads (15,546 of which were hard-surfaced). All-weather roads accounted for 26,322 km. The number of motor vehicles in use at the end of 1969 was 137,345 passenger cars, 118,133 trucks, 36,049 buses and 96,407 tractors.

Posts.—On Dec. 31, 1970, the number of telephone subscribers in Turkey was 376,987. There is a considerable shortage of telephone lines in some of Turkey's major cities.

Shipping.—At the end of 1968, the Turkish Merchant Navy consisted of 2,235 dry cargo ships of 300 tons gross and over totalling 489,492 tons, 154 passengers ships of a gross tonnage of 116,105 tons and 75 tankers with a gross tonnage of 140,247 tons.

Civil Aviation.—The State Airlines (T.H.Y.) operate all internal services and have services to London, Paris, Athens, Beirut, Brussels, Amsterdam, Zurich, Frankfurt, Munich, Rome, Nicosia, Tel Aviv and Vienna. Most of the leading foreign airlines operate services to Istanbul and some also to Ankara, including British European Airways. The T.H.Y. fleet is composed of Vickers Viscounts, D.C.9's, Fokker Friendships and Boeing 707's.

FINANCE
(Financial year, March 1 to February 28)

	1970–71	1971–72
	TL'000,000	
Estimated Expenditure...	29,893	37,093
Estimated Revenue.....	29,293	36,293

The deficit is to be covered by domestic borrowing.

Currency.—The Turkish *Lira* (*TL*) is divided into 100 *Kurus*. The official rate of exchange is TL36 = £1 and TL15 = U.S.$1. A special tourist rate of exchange was introduced in 1968. (*See also* p. 84.)

TRADE

	1969	1970
Total imports....	$801,226,000	$947,664,000
Total exports.....	536,834,000	598,526,000

All imports are subject to licence and the issue of licences is limited to goods considered necessary for the country's economy. Lists of permitted imports are published annually at the beginning of January. The main imports are machinery, crude oil and petroleum products, iron and steel, vehicles, medicines and dyes, fabrics and yarns. The principal exports are cotton, tobacco, fruits, minerals, livestock, cereals and oil seeds.

Trade with U.K.

	1969	1970
Imports from U.K..	£33,890,000	£35,932,000
Exports to U.K.....	15,658,000	15,609,000

CAPITAL OF TURKEY, ANKARA (Angora), an inland town of Asia Minor, about 275 miles E.S.E. of Istanbul, with a population (Census, Oct 1970) of 1,440,779. Ankara (or Ancyra) was the capital of the Roman Province of *Galatia Prima*, and a marble temple (now in ruins), dedicated to Augustus, contains the *Monumentum* (*Marmor*) *Ancyranum*, inscribed with a record of the reign of Augustus Caesar. A new city has been laid out on modern lines, with parks, statues and avenues. ΨISTANBUL (2,312,751), the former capital, was the Roman city of Byzantium. It was selected by Constantine the Great as the capital of the Roman Empire about A.D. 328 and renamed Constantinople. Istanbul contains the celebrated Mosque of St. Sophia, since 1934 a museum of Byzantine and Turkish art. Other cities are ΨIzmir (753,443); Adana (529,926); Bursa (415,348); Gaziantep (329,087); and Eskişehir (246,071).

FLAG.—Red, with white crescent and star.
NATIONAL DAY.—October 29 (Republic Day).

BRITISH EMBASSY
(Ankara)

Ambassador Extraordinary and Plenipotentiary, His Excellency Sir Roderick Francis Gisbert Sarell, K.C.M.G. (1969).........................£9,000
Counsellors, A. G. Elgar, O.B.E. (*Commercial*); J. C. Edmonds.
1st Secretaries, J. M. Brown; A. F. Davidson; Miss A. E. Stoddart; J. C. Harrison; B. V. White; B. R. Berry.
2nd Secretaries, Miss J. M. Murdoch; R. G. Short.
Naval Attaché, Cdr. G. M. A. James, R.N.
Defence and Military Attaché, Brig. D. S. Sole, O.B.E.
Air Attaché, Wing-Cdr. F. C. P. Elliot.
Information Officer, M. C. A. Large, M.B.E.
Administrative Officer and Consul, P. J. Kirchner, M.B.E.

BRITISH CONSULAR OFFICES
There are British Consular Offices at *Istanbul, Izmir* and *Iskenderun.*

BRITISH COUNCIL.—27 Adakale Sokak, Yenisehir, Ankara. *Representative*, H. G. Wayment, O.B.E.—There are also a centre and library at *Istanbul* and a library at *Ankara.*

BRITISH CHAMBER OF COMMERCE OF TURKEY INC., Meşrutiyet Caddessi No. 34, Tepebaşi Beyoğlu, Istanbul (Postal Address, P.K.190 Karaköy, Istanbul). *Chairman*, R. G. Lawson, O.B.E.

UNITED ARAB REPUBLIC
(Egypt)

President, Anwar Sadat *elected* Oct. 15, 1970.
Vice-President, Husain al Shafei.
Prime Minister, Dr. Mahmud Fawzi.

Deputy Prime Ministers

For Production and Trade, and Minister of Industry, Petroleum and Mining, Dr. Aziz Sidqi.

Minister of Information, Dr. Muhammad Abdul Qadir Hatim.

For Agriculture and Irrigation, and Minister of Agriculture, Agrarian Reform and Land Reclamation, Eng. Sayyid Marei.

Minister of Foreign Affairs, Mahmud Riad.

Minister of Economy and Foreign Trade and (Acting) Supply and Home Trade, Muhammad Abdulla Mirzaban.

Planning, Dr. al Sayyid Gaballa.

Treasury, Dr. Abdul Aziz Higazi.

Education, Dr. Muhammad Hafiz Ghanim.

Waqfs and al Azhar Affairs, Dr. Abdul Aziz Kamil.

Local Government, Muhammad Hamdi Ashur.

Scientific Research, Dr. Abdul Wahab al Burullussi.

Health, Dr. Abdu Mahmud Salam.

Presidential Affairs, Muhammad Ahmad Muhammad.

Justice, Hassan Fahmi al Badawi.

Tourism, Dr. Ahmad al Sayyid Darwish.

Labour, Abdul Latif Bultia.

Interior, Mamduh Salim.

War, Gen. Muhammad Ahmad Sadiq.

Higher Education, Dr. Muhammad Mursi Ahmad.

Power, Eng. Ahmad Sultan Ismail.

Housing and Utilities, Eng. Ali al Sayyid Muhammad.

Transport, Eng. Suliman Abdul Hai.

Irrigation, Eng. Muhammad Abdul Rakib.

Petroleum and Mining, Eng. Ali Wali.

Youth, Dr. Mustafa Kamal Tulba.

Culture, Dr. Ismail Ghanim.

Social Affairs, Dr. Muhammad Fathalla al Khatib.

Communications, Eng. Abdul Malik Saad.

Ministers of State, Muhammad Hafiz Ismail (Foreign Affairs); Dr. Ahmad Ismat Magid (Cabinet Affairs); Ahmad Nuh (Civil Aviation); Muhammad Abdul Salam al Zayyat (National Assembly Affairs).

Ministers, Samir Ahmed; Dr. Mohamed Mustafa El-Alaily (Scientific and Cultural Affairs); Mahmoud Abdel-Hamid Shalaby (Commercial Affairs).

Counsellors, Omran El-Shafei; Dr. Kamal M. Hagras; Dr. Hamdi El Tahri (Consular); Moheb El-Samra (Consular); Ahmed I.K.A. Anis (Information).

1st Secretaries, Mohamed Sharara; Rafik Salah El Din Hassan.

2nd Secretaries, Shawkat Fahmy Yanny (Commercial); Abdel Meguid Abdel Fattah Hassan (Commercial); Ibrahim Abd El Fattah (Commercial).

3rd Secretaries, Fouad Cherif; Mohamed A. Abdel Wahab.

Attachés, Dr. Roushdy Mohammed El-Sherbini (Medical); Mohamed Sayed Ahmed Sherif (Cultural); Anwar Galal Mohamed Shawky (Press); Salah Eldin Mohamed Kamel Selim.

AREA AND POPULATION.—The total area of the United Arab Republic is estimated at 1,000,000 square kilometres (385,110 square miles), the inhabited area being only 35,168 square kilometres (13,578 square miles), with a population (estimated May, 1971) of 34,000,000.

There are three distinct elements in the native population. The largest, or "Egyptian" element, is a Hamito-Semite race, known in the rural districts as Fellahin (fellâh—ploughman, or tiller of the soil). The Fellahin have been mainly of the Moslem faith since the conquest of the country in the 7th century. A second element is the Bedouin, or nomadic Arabs of the Libyan and Arabian deserts, of whom about one-seventh are real nomads, and the remainder semi-sedentary tent-dwellers on the outskirts of the cultivated end of the Nile Valley and the Fayûm. The third element is the Nubian of the Nile Valley between Aswân and Wadi-Halfa of mixed Arab and negro blood. The Bedouin and Nubians are Moslems.

The territory of Egypt comprises (1) Egypt Proper, forming the N.E. corner of the African continent, divisible into (a) the valley and delta of the Nile, (b) the Libyan or Western Desert, and (c) the Arabian or Eastern Desert; (2) The Peninsula of Sinai, forming part of the continent of Asia; and (3) a number of Islands in the Gulf of Suez and Red Sea, of which the principal are Jubal, Shadwan, Gafatin and Zeberged (or St. John's Island). This territory lies between 22° and 32° N. lat. and 24° and 37° E. long. The northern boundary is the Mediterranean, and in the south Egypt is conterminous with the Sudan. The western boundary runs from a point on the coast 10 kilometres N.W. of Sollûm to the latitude of Siwa and thence due S. along the 25th meridian to the parallel of 22° N. (the N. boundary of the Sudan) at 'Uweinat Mountain. The E. boundary follows a line drawn from Rafa on the Mediterranean (34° 15' E. long.) to the head of the Gulf of 'Aqaba, from which point the remainder of the E. boundary is washed by the waters of the Gulf of 'Aqaba and the Red Sea. The "settled land area" is stated officially at 7,667,000 feddâns (12,431 square miles) and the area of lakes at 641,000 feddâns (1,039 square miles), a total of 8,308,000 feddâns (13,470 square miles).

Physical Features.—The Nile valley varies in width from less than half a mile in the southern granitic region to over 10 miles in the northern limestone region, and the cliffs in some places rise to heights of over a thousand feet above the river. The fertile lands, on which the prosperity of the country depends, occupy the floor of the valley between the river and the bounding cliffs, while to the north of Cairo they spread out into the irregular fan-shaped formation of the Delta which

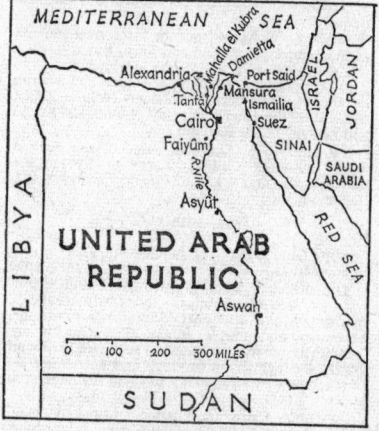

EMBASSY IN LONDON
26 South Street, W.1
[01–499 2401]
Ambassador Extraordinary and Plenipotentiary, His Excellency Kamal Eddin Reifaat (1971).

comprises the six provinces of Lower Egypt, with the richest soil in the country.

The *Nile* has a total length of 4,160 miles. In the 960 miles of its course through Egypt it receives not a single tributary stream. The river formerly had a regular yearly rise and fall of about 13 feet at Cairo, but since the commencement of storage in the reservoir of the Aswan High Dam in 1965, there has been no flood downstream of the Dam and the water level remains almost constant throughout the year. Westward from the Nile Valley into Tripolitania stretches the *Libyan Desert*, an arid region, containing some depressions, whose springs irrigate small areas known as *Oases*, of which the principal, from S.E. to N.W., are known as Kharga, Dakhla, Farafra, Baharia and Siwa.

On the eastern edge of the Libyan Desert, a few miles south-west of Cairo stand the Pyramids of Gizeh, of which the highest, the *Great Pyramid*, is 451 feet high. Close to the pyramids is the *Great Sphinx*, 189 feet long. In the Eastern Desert a great backbone of high and rugged mountains extends north-westwards from Ethiopia to near Suez, and reappears as a detached mass in the Peninsula of Sinai. Flanking this mountain chain on the west, between the axis of the range and the Nile, are plateaux of sandstones and limestones, dissected by *wadis* (dry water-courses), often of great length and depth, with some wild vegetation and occasional wells and springs. The roads follow the course of the main *wadis* from well to well, and here and there are to be found small encampments of wandering Arabs.

Religions.—The predominant religion is Islam but there are about 2,000,000 Christians (mainly Copts). By 1968 nearly all the Jews had left the country. The chief Moslem religious authorities in Egypt are the *Sheik el Gami el Azhar* and the *Mufti al Gumhuriya al Arabiya al Muttahida*.

Government.—From 30 B.C. to A.D. 639 Egypt was a province of the Roman Empire, but in A.D. 640 the Christian inhabitants were subjugated by Moslem invaders and Egypt became a province of the Eastern Caliphate. In 1517 the country was incorporated in the Ottoman Empire under which it remained until early in the 19th century.

A British Protectorate over Egypt declared on Dec. 18, 1914, lasted until Feb. 28, 1922, when Sultan Ahmed Fuad was proclaimed King of Egypt. Following closely on the accession of King Farouk, the *Anglo-Egyptian Treaty* was signed in London (Aug. 26, 1936) and the military occupation by British troops was terminated.

The security of Egypt was threatened after the outbreak of war in 1939 and reinforcements were sent from Britain and the Dominions. Axis troops invading Egypt in 1940 and fierce fighting ensued, with Allied victories and reverses, until the decisive victory in " The Battle of Egypt " (Oct.–Nov. 1942) drove the enemy out of the country. In July, 1952, following a military *coup d'état*, King Farouk abdicated in favour of his infant son, who became King Ahmed Fuad II. In June, 1953, however, Gen. Neguib's military council deposed the young king, and declared Egypt a Republic, Gen. Neguib himself assuming the Presidency. In November, 1954, General Neguib was deposed by Lt.-Col. Gamai Abdel Nasser and the military council. On June 23, 1956, Col. Nasser assumed office as President, after an election at which voting was compulsory, and he was the only candidate.

A union with Syria was effected in 1958 and lasted until September, 1961, when Syria seceded after a *coup d'état*. The title and flag of the United Arab Republic were, however, retained for Egypt.

President Nasser died suddenly on Sept. 28, 1970, and the duties of Head of State were assumed by

Mr. Anwar Sadat who as elected President in a referendum on Oct. 15. After initially making few Ministerial changes, President Sadat took the opportunity of an alleged plot against him in April, 1971, to remove many of the Ministers and officials he had inherited from Nasser.

Agriculture.—Despite increased industrialization and the discovery of new oil fields, agriculture continues to provide the most substantial contribution to the national economy. Cotton (10 million *kanbars* in 1970) and rice are by far the most important exports, but sugar cane, onions, potatoes and citrus fruits are also sold extensively to overseas markets. Nearly all cultivation is carried out by peasant farmers whose operations are funded and generally controlled by co-operative organizations. Productivity is usually good. Irrigation and land reclamation schemes have contributed to a small increase in the cultivable area, and a $147 million drainage project, financed partly by the International Bank for Reconstruction and Development, is intended ultimately to irrigate nearly one million acres.

Railways.—The principal lines radiate from Cairo to Alexandria (and on to Rosetta), Damietta and Ismailia (continuing northwards to Port Said and southward to Suez). From Cairo the line runs southwards for a distance of 554 miles to a new port being constructed upstream of the High Dam. At this point a steamer connection runs to New Halfa, connecting the U.A.R. with the Sudan Government Railways. Westwards from Alexandria (and close to the coast) runs a line to the frontier at Sollûm, thus joining Tripoli to Egypt. The gauge is standard (4 ft. 8½ in.).

Roads and Caravan Routes.—A sea coast motor road exists from Alexandria to Mersa Matruh, with an extension along the coast to Sollûm and thence to connect with the coast road in Libya. A bitumen road leads to Kharga and Dakhla, from the former of which there is a route, known as the Darb el 'Arbain, leading to Dar Fûr and the south of the Sudan. There are many well-known routes across the Arabian Desert to the Red Sea, that from Qena to Qoseir, a metalled road, being probably the most frequently used.

Shipping.— Ψ Apart from the three great seaports of Alexandria, Port Said and Suez, Egypt has but few harbours and anchorages adapted for large craft ; the principal are those of Sollûm and Matruh on the Mediterranean, Tor, Abu Zenima, Zeitia, Jemsa and Hurghada in the Gulf of Suez, and Safaga and Qoseir on the Red Sea.

Currency.— £E (Egyptian *pound* of 100 *piastres*) =96p sterling. Official Rate of Exchange— (*Buying*) £E1·032 = £1; (*Selling*) £E1·075 = £1. (*See also* p. 84.)

Trade with U.K.

	1969	1970
Imports from U.K. .	£15,036,000	£18,724,000
Exports to U.K.	9,302,000	10,852,000

The principal imports are metals, and manufactures thereof, chemicals and pharmaceuticals, machinery and transport equipment, foodstuffs, beverages and textile fibres. The exports are principally raw cotton, textile yarns, rice, fruit and vegetables, petroleum products and a growing list of secondary exports, many of them manufactured goods.

CAPITAL.—Cairo (population, estimated May, 1971, 5,126,000), stands on the E. bank of the Nile, about 14 miles from the head of the Delta. Its oldest part is the fortress of Babylon in old Cairo, with its Roman bastions and Coptic churches. The earliest Arab building is the Mosque of 'Amr, dating from A.D. 643, and the most conspicuous is the Citadel,

built by Saladin towards the end of the 12th century and containing in its walls the Mosque of Mohamed Ali built in the 19th century.

Ψ ALEXANDRIA (estimated population, 1,900,000), founded 332 B.C. by Alexander the Great, was for over 1,000 years the capital of Egypt and a centre of Hellenic culture which vied with Athens herself. Its great *pharos* (lighthouse), 480 feet high, with a lantern burning resinous wood, was one of the " Seven Wonders of the World." Other towns are: Ismailia; Ψ Port Said; Mansura (102,709); Asyût (284,000); Faiyûm (162,000); Tanta (139,965); Mahalla el Kubra (115,509); Ψ Suez; Ψ Damietta (97,000). Ismailia, Port Said and Suez had been almost totally evacuated by 1969.

CAIRO is 2,520 miles from London: transit *viâ* Trieste, 5 days; *viâ* Marseilles, 6 days.

FLAG.—Horizontal bands of red, white and black, with two 5-point green stars in white band. NATIONAL DAY.—July 23 (Anniversary of Revolution in 1952).

BRITISH EMBASSY

Kasr el Doubara, Garden City, Cairo

Ambassador Extraordinary and Plenipotentiary, His Excellency Sir Richard Ashton Beaumont, K.C.M.G., O.B.E. (1968)................£9,000

Counsellor, A. B. Urwick.

Defence and Military Attaché, Col. A. D. Lewis.

1st Secretaries, M. I. Goulding (*Head of Chancery*); M. R. Postgate (*Information*); M. J. Wilmshurst (*Commercial*); R. L. Morris, O.B.E. (*Labour*);

T. J. Sigsworth (*Consul and Administration Officer*); P. J. Monk (*Claims*).

2nd Secretaries, D. F. B. Edye (*Commercial*); H. W. J. Coates (*Vice-Consul*); J. R. Young.

Attachés, Miss B. R. Griffiths (*Vice-Consul*); R. Fawkes (*Vice-Consul*); R. D. Baird-Fraser.

Cultural Attaché, N. A. Daniel, O.B.E.

British Consulate-General, Alexandria

Consul-General, F. W. Hall.

Vice-Consul, M. J. Cooper.

UPPER VOLTA
(République de Haute Volta)

Head of State (provisional Government) and *Minister of Foreign Affairs,* Lt.-Col. Sangoulé Lamizana, *assumed power* January 3, 1966.

Prime Minister, Gérard Kango Ouedraogo (Feb, 13, 1971).

Upper Volta is an inland, savannah state in West Africa, situated between 9° and 15°N and 2°E and 5°W with an area of about 100,000 square miles and a population estimated in 1969 at 5,330,000. It has common boundaries with Mali on the west, Niger and Dahomey on the east and Togo, Ghana and the Ivory Coast on the south. The largest tribe is the Mossi whose king, the Moro Naba, still wields a certain moral influence.

Upper Volta was annexed by France in 1896 and between 1932 and 1947 was administered as part of the Colony of the Ivory Coast. It decided on December 11, 1958, to remain an autonomous republic within the French Community; full

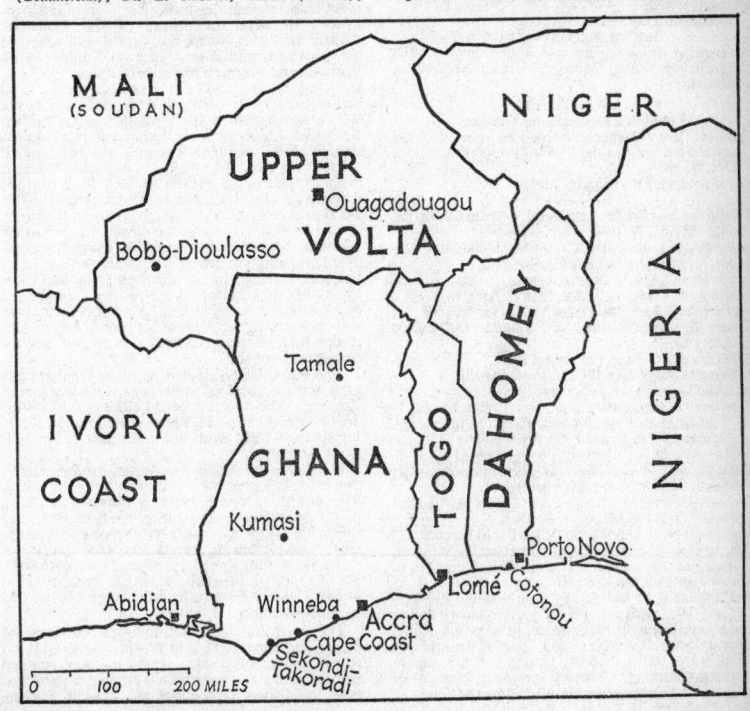

independence outside the Community was proclaimed on August 5, 1960. Special agreements
with France, covering financial and cultural
matters, technical assistance, etc., were signed in
Paris on April 24, 1961. Upper Volta is a
member of the *Conseil de l'Entente*, *OCAM*, the
Organization of African Unity, etc. The official
language is French. The constitution, adopted by
referendum on November 27, 1960, provides for a
presidential form of government with a single
chamber National Assembly, but the Constitution
was suspended and the National Assembly dissolved
in January, 1966, when the Army assumed power
after popular demonstrations in Ouagadougou
against the *régime* of the former President Yaméogo.
A new constitution allowing for a partial return to
civilian rule but with the Army still in effective
control was adopted by a referendum held on June
14, 1970.

Finance and Trade.—The currency of the Republic
is the *Franc CFA* (*Francs CFA* 50=1 French Franc)
(*Francs CFA* 661 = £1). The 1968 Budget totalled
Francs CFA 8,563,610,000.

The principal industry is the rearing of cattle
and sheep and the chief exports are livestock,
groundnuts, shea-nuts and cotton. Small deposits
of gold, manganese, copper, bauxite and graphite
have been found. Value of trade in 1969 (Jan.–
June) amounted to: Imports, *francs CFA*
6,281,942,000; Exports, *francs CFA* 2,884,245,000.

CAPITAL.—Ouagadougou (110,000). Other principal town: Bobo-Dioulasso (68,000).

FLAG.—Three horizontal stripes, black over
white over red.

NATIONAL DAY.—December 11.

BRITISH REPRESENTATION
Ambassador Extraordinary and Plenipotentiary, His
Excellency Peter Murray, C.M.G. (*resident at
Abidjan*).

URUGUAY
(República Oriental del Uruguay)

President, Jorge Pacheco Areco, *born* 1920, *succeeded
to the Presidency on the death of* President Gestido,
Dec. 6, 1967.

Vice-President, Dr. Alberto Abdala.

Minister of Interior, Dr. Santiago De Brum Carabajal.
Foreign Affairs, Dr. José A. Mora Otero.
Economy and Finance, Dr. Carlos Mario Fleitas.
Public Works, Arq. Walter Pintos Risso.
Public Health, Dr. Walter Ravenna.
Industry and Commerce, Ctdr. Juan P. Amestoy.
Livestock and Agriculture, Juan María Bordaberry.
Transport, Communications and Tourism. Dr. Carlos
Queraltó.
Education and Culture, Dr. Angel Rath.
Labour and Social Security, Dr. Jorge Sapelli.
National Defence, Dr. Federico García Capurro.
Director of Planning and Budget, Dr. Aquiles Lanza.

URUGUAYAN EMBASSY AND CONSULATE
Chancery: 48 Lennox Gardens, S.W.1
[01–589 8835; Consulate 01–589 8735]

Ambassador Extraordinary and Plenipotentiary, His
Excellency Dr. Jorge Barreiro (1970).
Minister-Counsellors, Señor Don Carlos A. Ghirin-
ghelli; Dr. Don Miguel J. Berthet.
Consul-General, Señor Don Pedro Pablo Lerena.
Adjoint Consul, Señora Doña Diva Batello Meneses.

Area and Population.—The smallest Republic in
South America, on the east coast of the Río de la
Plata situated in lat. 30°–35°S. and long. 53° 25'–
57° 42' W., with an area of 72,172 square miles,
and a population (U.N. estimate, 1969) of 2,852,000,
almost entirely white and predominantly of
Spanish and Italian descent. Many Uruguayans are
Roman Catholics. There is complete freedom of
religion and no church is established by the State.

Physical Features.—The country consists mainly
(and particularly in the south and west) of undulating grassy plains. The principal chains of
hills are the Cuchilla del Haedo, which cross the
Brazilian boundary and extend southwards to the
Cuchilla Grande of the south and east. In no case
do the peaks exceed 2,000 feet.

The principal river is the *Rio Negro* (with its
tributary the Yi), flowing from north-east to south-
west into the *Rio Uruguay*. The boundary river
Uruguay is navigable from its estuary to Salto,
about 200 miles north, and the Negro is also
navigable for a considerable distance. Smaller
rivers are the Cuareim, Yaguaron, Santa Lucia,
Queguay, and the Cebollati. On the south-east
coast are several lagoons, and the north-east boundary crosses (the Brazilian) Lake Merin.

The climate is reasonably healthy. The summer
is warm, but the heat is often tempered by the
breezes of the Atlantic. The winter is, on the
whole, mild, but cold spells, characterized by
winds from the South Polar regions, are experienced
in June, July and August. Rainfall is regular
throughout the year, but there are occasional
droughts.

Government.—Uruguay—or the *Banda Oriental*,
as this territory lying on the eastern bank of the
Uruguay River was then called—resisted all
attempted invasions of the Portuguese and Spaniards
until the beginning of the 17th century, and 100
years later the Portuguese settlements were captured
by the Spaniards. From 1726 to 1814 the country
formed part of Spanish South America and under-
went many vicissitudes during the Wars of Independence. In 1814 the armies of the Argentine
Confederation captured the capital and annexed
the province, and it was afterwards annexed by
Portugal and became a province of Brazil. In 1825,
the country threw off the Brazilian yoke. This
action led to war between Argentina and Brazil
which was settled by the mediation of the United
Kingdom, Uruguay being declared an independent
state in 1828. In 1830 a Republic was inaugurated.

Elections were held on Nov. 27, 1966, together
with a referendum which decided in favour of
Uruguay's return to a presidential system. The
election gave the Colorado Party a narrow majority.

The President appoints a council of 11 ministers
and the Vice-President presides over Congress.
The legislature consists of a Chamber of 99 deputies and a Senate of 30 members (plus the Vice-
President), elected for five years by a system of
proportional representation. Voting is obligatory
and extends to all citizens of good repute and
certain long standing residents who are not citizens,
from the age of 18.

The Republic is divided into 19 Departments
each with a chief of police and a Departmental
Council. The most important cities of the interior
are Salto and Paysandú, both situated on the River
Uruguay, which forms the main line of division
from Argentina.

Production and Industry.—Wheat, barley, maize,
linseed, sunflower seed and rice are cultivated.
The wealth of the country is obtained from its
pasturage, which supports large herds of cattle and
sheep, the wool of which is of excellent quality.
The 1966 livestock census showed figures of
8,187,676 cattle, 23,078,537 sheep, 460,467 horses,
382,921 hogs. In addition to the meat packing
industry, other foodstuffs, wine, beer and textiles
are of importance.

The development of local industry continues and
during and since the Second World War, in addition
to the greatly augmented textile industry, marked
expansion in local production is notable in respect of
tyres, sheet-glass, three-ply wood, cement, leather-

curing, beet-sugar, plastics, household consumer goods, edible oils and the refining of petroleum and petroleum products. There are no mineral deposits of importance.

Communications.—There are about 5,000 miles of national highways, and about 7,508 miles of telegraph, with 48,375 miles of telephones.

There are about 1,873 miles of standard gauge railway in use in Uruguay. A State Autonomous Entity was formed to administer the railway systems purchased by the Government from four British companies in 1948.

An internal airline, PLUNA, which is owned by the State, runs a daily passenger service and limited freight service to the principal capitals of the interior, and also runs services to Southern Brazil, Paraguay and Argentina. International passenger and freight services are maintained by American, South American and European airlines. The airport of Carrasco lies 12 miles outside Montevideo.

Education and Social Services.—Uruguay is one of the most advanced of the South American states, with old-age pensions, maternity and child welfare centres, accident insurance, etc. Primary education is compulsory and free, with about 293,900 pupils in 2,362 state schools and technical and trade schools and evening courses for adult education. In 1969 there were 140,700 pupils in secondary schools. The University at Montevideo (founded in 1849) had, in 1969, 18,000 students enrolled in its ten faculties.

Language and Literature.—Spanish is the language of the Republic. Modern literature has provided some authors with international reputations and the literature of Spain is accessible in all public libraries. 10 daily newspapers are published in Montevideo with an estimated total circulation of 200,000. Most of them are distributed throughout the country.

Finance.—No recent figures of revenue and expenditure are available. The public debt at June 30, 1969, amounted to $Ur.10,737,625,290.

Currency.—The monetary unit is the *peso*. In May, 1963, the gold content of the *peso* was fixed at 0·059245 grammes of pure gold. After several devaluations the *peso* stood in 1970 at $Ur.250= $U.S.1 in the official markets. Quotations in the parallel markets fluctuate, within 10 per cent, of the official rate. Sterling exchange, *see p.* 84.

TRADE

	1969	1970
Total imports	$U.S.197,325,000	$U.S.233,078,574
Total exports	200,236,000	232,708,699

Trade with U.K.

	1969	1970
Imports from U.K. ...	£4,709,000	£6,401,000
Exports to U.K. ...	13,119,000	8,556,000

The exports are principally animal and agricultural products, and include chilled, frozen and canned meat, wool, hides and oleaginous products; the imports are principally machinery, motor vehicles, fuels and lubricants, raw materials, construction materials, timber and foodstuffs.

The principal imports from the U.K. are vehicles (including omnibus chassis, tractors and spares and accessories), iron sheets, tinplate, raw materials, industrial machinery spare parts, paper money, road-making machinery, chemical products and tea.

CAPITAL, Ψ Montevideo, Pop. (1963), 1,173,114. Other centres are Ψ Salto (60,000), Ψ Paysandú (60,000), Ψ Mercedes (34,000), Minas (34,000), Melo (30,000), and Rivera (22,000).

FLAG.—Four blue and five white horizontal stripes surcharged with sun on a white ground in the top corner, next flagstaff. NATIONAL DAY.—August 25 (Declaration of Independence, 1825).

Time of transit from London to Montevideo, by air, 20–22 hours.

BRITISH EMBASSY

Chancery, Calle Cerrito, 420, Montevideo.
Ambassador Extraordinary and Plenipotentiary. His Excellency Sir Geoffrey Holt Seymour Jackson, K.C.M.G. (1969)........................£6,925
1st Secretaries, J. P. I. Hennessy (*Head of Chancery*); D. R. Collard (*Commercial*).
2nd Secretary, C. J. Sharkey.
Naval Attaché, Capt. I. Hood, R.N. (*resident at* Buenos Aires).
Defence and Military Attaché, Col. G. W. Croker, M.B.E., M.C. (*resident at* Buenos Aires).
Air Attaché, Group-Capt. J. F. C. Melrose., D.F.C. (*resident at* Buenos Aires).

BRITISH CONSULAR OFFICES

There is a British Consular Office at *Montevideo.*

BRITISH COUNCIL.—*Representative,* R. A. Martin, San José 1426, Montevideo. The Council supplies books to the:
ANGLO-URUGUAYAN CULTURAL INSTITUTE, San José 1426, Montevideo.
There are branch Institutes at Salto, Paysandú, Fray Bentos, Rivera, Las Piedras, Melo, Mercedes, Trinidad and Treinta y Tres.
BRITISH–URUGUAYAN CHAMBER OF COMMERCE, Avenida Agraciada 1641, Piso 2°, *Montevideo.*

U.S.S.R.

Soyuz Sovetskikh Sotsialisticheskikh Respublik = Union of Soviet Socialist Republics)

THE COMMUNIST PARTY OF THE SOVIET UNION

(K.P.S.S.=Kommunisticheskaya Partiya Sovetskogo Soyuza)

Constitutionally, the highest executive organ of the C.P.S.U. is its *Central Committee,* as elected by the *Party Congress.* The present Central Committee (elected at the XXIVth Party Congress in April, 1971) consists of 241 members; there are also 155 "candidates for membership" with a consultative voice and 81 members of the *Central Auditing Commission.* The real power in the Party is vested, however, in the *Politbureau,* the *Secretariat* and the permanent Departments of the Central Committee:
Politbureau, L. I. Brezhnev; V. V. Grishin; A. P. Kirilenko; A. N. Kosygin; F. D. Kulakov; D. A. Kunayev; K. T. Mazurov; A. J. Pelše; N. V. Podgorny; D. S. Polyansky; P. E. Shcherlitsky; A. N. Shelepin; P. Ye. Shelest; M. A. Suslov; G. T. Voronov (*full members*); Yu. V. Andropov; P. M. Masherov; V. P. Mzhavanadze; Sh. R. Rashidov; D. F. Ustinov (*candidates for membership*).
Secretariat, Leonid Ilyich Brezhnev (*General Secretary*) (*since* October 14, 1964); P. N. Demichev; I. V. Kapitonov; K. F. Katushev; A. P. Kirilenko; F. D. Kulakov; B. N. Ponomarev; M. S. Solomentsev; M. A. Suslov; D. F. Ustinov.
Committee of Party Control, A. J. Pelše (*Chairman*).
Komsomol (*Young Communist League*), Ye. M. Tyazhelnikov (*1st Secretary*).

GOVERNMENT OF THE U.S.S.R.
The Presidium of the Supreme Soviet of the U.S.S.R.

Chairman (=President of the U.S.S.R.), Nikolay Viktorovich Podgorny (*since* December 9, 1965).
Secretary, M. P. Georgadze.
The Supreme Soviet (=Parliament) consists of two chambers.
Chairman (=*Speaker*) of the Council of the Union, A. P. Shitikov.
Chairman (=*Speaker*) of the Council of Nationalities, Mrs. S. Nasriddinova.

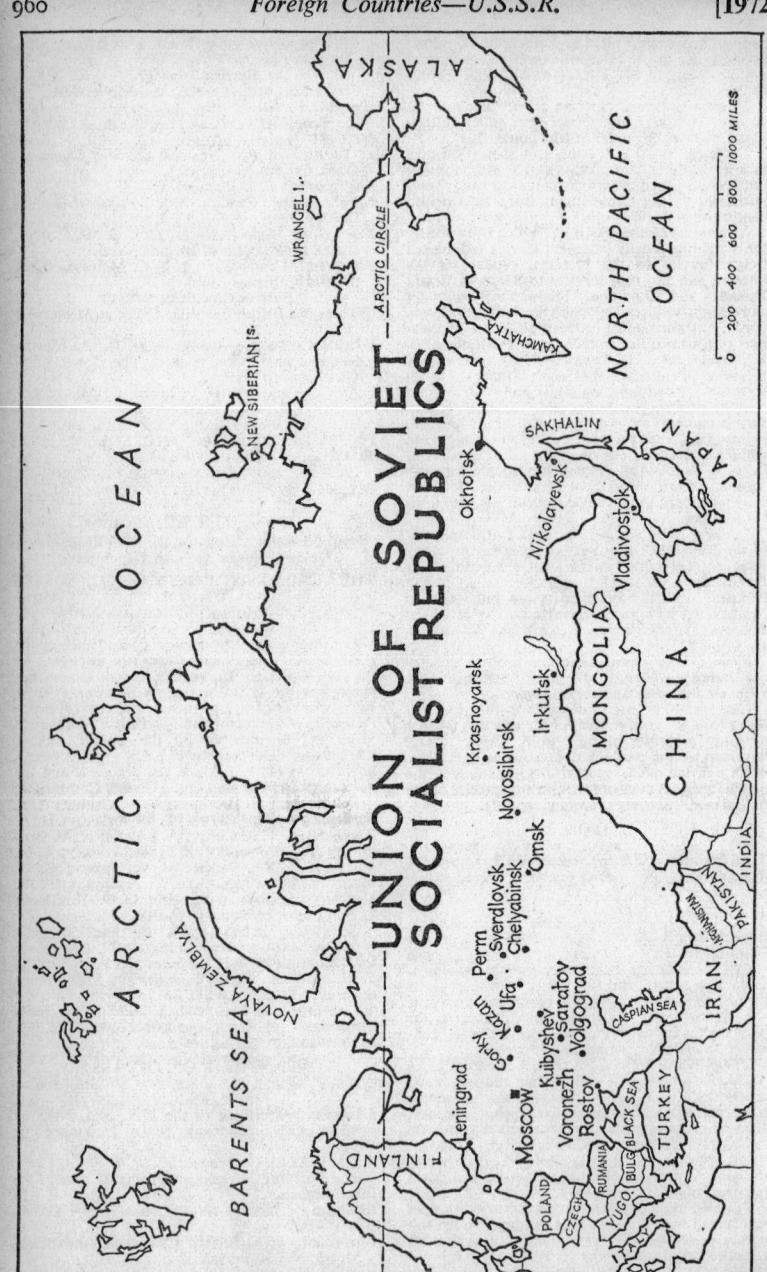

The Council of Ministers of the U.S.S.R.
Chairman (=*Prime Minister*), Alexei Nikolayevich Kosygin (*since* October 14, 1964).
1st Vice-Chairmen, K. T. Mazurov: D. S. Polyansky.
Vice-Chairmen, N. K. Baybakov; V. E. Dymshits; V. A. Kirillin; M. A. Lesechko; I. T. Novikov; V. N. Novikov; L. V. Smirnov; N. A. Tikhonov: M. T. Yefremov.
Ministries.—There are three groups of departmental ministries, with a total of 70 ministers—25 All Union Ministries, *i.e.* federal ministries, 31 Union Republican Ministries (co-ordinating ministries of individual republics) and 14 Chairmen of State committees, etc., ranking as Ministers. The more important posts are occupied by:
Foreign Affairs, A. A. Gromyko.
Defence, Marshal A. A. Grechko.
Foreign Trade, N. S. Patolichev.
Internal Affairs, N. A. Shchelokov.
Planning, N. K. Baybakov.
Science and Technology, V. A. Kirillin.
Building, I. T. Novikov.
State Security, Yu V. Andropov.
The Prime Ministers of the 15 constituent republics belong to the Council *ex officio.*

EMBASSY OF THE U.S.S.R. IN LONDON
13 Kensington Palace Gardens, W.8.
[01–229 2666; 36289; 6412.]
Ambassador Extraordinary and Plenipotentiary, His Excellency Mikhail N. Smirnovsky (1966).
Minister-Counsellor, I. I. Ippolitov.
Counsellors, I. D. Biryukov; I. A. Gavva; Y. N. Voronin; Y. F. Sepelev; B. G. Kolodyazhny; I. B. Puchkov; V. G. Filatov; V. V. Karyagin; A. I. Akimov; Y. B. Kashlev.
1st Secretaries, I. P. Azarov; Y. E. Chernetsov; L. A. Rogov; Y. V. Skoptsov; A. D. Chikvaidze; B. S. Nikitin; Y. A. Kondratenko; P. N. Filatov; I. K. Laptev; S. N. Semenko; S. R. Gologev; V. M. Tsaregradsky; P. I. Gamov.
Military Attaché, Col. Y. A. Chelpanov.
Naval Attaché, Rear-Adm. B. D. Yashin.
Air Attaché, Col. V. P. Konobeev.
Trade Representative, V. M. Ivanov, 32 Highgate West Hill, N.6.
Deputy Trade Representatives, G. I. Sakulin; K. D. Tikhomirov.
Consulate, 5 Kensington Palace Gardens, W.8.
[01–229 3215]

AREA AND POPULATION

The U.S.S.R. is composed of 15 Union Republics (*see below*). Before the outbreak of the war of 1939–45 the U.S.S.R. consisted of 11 Republics—the Russian Socialist Federal Soviet Republic (R.S.F.S.R.) and the Ukrainian, Belorussian, Armenian, Azerbaidjan, Georgian, Turkmen, Uzbek, Tadjik, Kazakh and Kirghiz Soviet Socialist Republics. After the collapse of Poland in September, 1939, the Soviet Government by agreement with Germany seized five-eighths of Poland's territory, the so-called *Western Ukraine* and *Western Belorussia*, subsequently incorporated into the Ukrainian and Belorussian Republics respectively.

In March, 1940, some territories ceded by Finland under the 1940 Treaty were joined to the Karelian Autonomous Soviet Socialist Republic to form a Karelo-Finnish S.S.R. which became the 12th constituent Republic of the U.S.S.R., while others, including the town of Viipuri (Vyborg), were added to the R.S.F.S.R. Similarly, in August of the same year, the major part of *Bessarabia* ceded by Rumania in June was joined to the Moldavian A.S.S.R. to form a Moldavian S.S.R. as the 13th Soviet Republic, while a smaller part of Bessarabia, including the

Danube estuary port of Izmaïl, and *Northern Bukovina*, also ceded by Rumania, became part of the Ukraine. The new Soviet-Rumanian frontier was confirmed by the 1947 Peace Treaty with Rumania.

In August, 1940, the three independent Baltic States, *Estonia, Latvia* and *Lithuania*, were forcibly incorporated into the Soviet-Union to form the 14th, 15th and 16th Republics respectively. In June, 1945, *Ruthenia* was ceded by Czechoslovakia and became part of the Ukrainian S.S.R under the name of *Transcarpathia*. After the defeat of Germany, a part of *East Prussia* with its capital Königsberg (renamed Kaliningrad in July, 1946) became part of the R.S.F.S.R., while the port and district of *Memel* (Klaipeda) was incorporated into the Lithuanian S.S.R. By the 1947 Peace Treaty with Finland, the district of *Petsamo* (Pechenga) was added to the territory of the R.S.F.S.R. In the Far East, the southern half of *Sakhalin* and the whole of the *Kurile Islands* were incorporated into the last-named Republic in 1945, after the defeat of Japan. In October, 1944, *Tannu-Tuva*, until the war of 1939–45 a nominally independent state lying to the N.W. of Outer Mongolia, became the autonomous province of *Tuva* and, in 1961, the Autonomous Republic of Tuva, within the R.S.F.S.R.

In July, 1956, the Karelo-Finnish Republic reverted to the status of an Autonomous (*Karelian*) Republic within the R.S.F.S.R.

Area and population (January 1, 1970) of the constituent Republics of the U.S.S.R. with their capitals—

Republic (Capital)	Sq. miles	Population
I. R.S.F.S.R. (Moscow)	6,593,391	130,079,000
II. Ukraine (Kiev)	252,046	47,126,000
III. Belorussia (Minsk)	20,154	9,002,000
IV. Uzbekistan (Tashkent)	158,069	11,960,000
V. Kazakhstan (Alma-Ata)	1,064,092	12,849,000
VI. Georgia (Tbilisi)	26,911	4,686,000
VII. Azerbaidjan (Baku)	33,436	5,117,000
VIII. Lithuania (Vilnius)	26,173	3,128,000
IX. Moldavia (Kishinev)	13,012	3,569,000
X. Latvia (Riga)	24,695	2,364,000
XI. Kirghizia (Frunze)	76,642	2,933,000
XII. Tadjikistan (Dushanbe)	54,019	2,900,000
XIII. Armenia (Erevan)	11,306	2,492,000
XIV. Turkmenistan (Ashkhabad)	188,417	2,159,000
XV. Estonia (Tallinn)	17,413	1,356,000
Total	8,599,806	241,720,000

A striking demographic feature is the rapid urbanization. While in 1939 the proportion of urban population was 32 per cent. of the total, in 1970 it reached 56 per cent., owing to migration to the towns, growth of new towns, incorporation of villages into conurbations and a higher birth-rate in urban areas. There are now 33 towns with over 500,000 (11 in 1939).

The proportion of women to men is 53·9 to 46·1. (In 1966 the birth-rate was 17·4; the mortality rate, 7·6; the natural increase, 9·8 per 1,000.

More than four-fifths of the people were born after the 1917 Revolution.

Main Nationalities
(1965 Estimate)

The most numerous national groups of U.S.S.R. are: Russian, 129 m and Ukrainian, 41 m. There are between 5 and 9 million Belorussians, Uzbeks, Kazakhs, and Tartars respectively. Azerbaidjanis, Armenians and Georgians number between 3 and

5 million each group. There are some 2·5 million Lithuanians, Jews, Moldavians and Tadjiks respectively. In each of the remaining nationality groups the population numbers between 1·05 and 1·8 million: Germans, Chuvashes, Latvians, Poles, Mordovians, Turkmens, Kirghizians, Bashkirs and Estonians.

The 1970 census revealed a remarkable difference between the growth rates of individual nationalities: while the Slav nations showed an annual increase of roughly one per cent., certain Central-Asian and Caucasian (mostly Moslem) nations recorded an annual net growth of three to five per cent.

CONSTITUTION

Under the 1936 ("Stalin") Constitution, the *Union of Soviet Socialist Republics* is "a socialist state of workers and peasants" (§ 1) in which "all power belongs to the working people as represented by the Soviets [Councils] of Working People's Deputies "(§ 3), while its economy is based on "the socialist ownership of the instruments and means of production" (§ 4). "The land, its mineral wealth, waters, forests, mills, factories, mines, rail, water and air transport, banks, communications, large state-organized agricultural enterprises, as well as municipal enterprises and the bulk of dwelling-houses in the cities and industrial localities, are state property" (§ 6), while "the joint enterprises of collective farms and co-operative organizations . . . constitute the common, socialist property of the collective farms and co-operative organizations" (§ 7). "The law [also] permits the small private economy of individual peasants and handicraftsmen based on their own labour and precluding the exploitation of the labour of others" (§ 9). "The personal property right of citizens in their incomes and savings from work, in their dwelling-houses and subsidiary home enterprises, in household articles . . . as well as the right of citizens to inherit personal property, is protected by law" (§ 10). The whole economic life, however, is subordinated to the state economic plan (§ 11).

The U.S.S.R. is a federal state, "formed on the basis of a voluntary union of equal Soviet Socialist Republics" (§ 13); every Republic has "the right to secede from the U.S.S.R." (§ 17).

"The highest organ of state power in the U.S.S.R. is the Supreme Soviet of the U.S.S.R." (§ 30) which exercises exclusively the legislative power (§ 32). It consists of two Chambers, the *Soviet of the Union* (elected on the basis of one deputy for every 300,000 of the population) and the *Soviet of Nationalities* (elected at the ratio of 25 deputies from each Union Republic, 11 from each Autonomous Republic, 5 from each Autonomous Province and 1 from each National Territory) (§§ 33–35). At elections held on June 14, 1970, for the two Chambers, approximately 153 million persons voted *for* candidates (99·96 per cent. of voters) and under 400,000 against. The *Supreme Soviet* which, as a rule, meets four to five times a year for about a week, delegates most of its power to its *Presidium* which acts as a kind of collective President of the U.S.S.R. between the sessions.

"The highest executive and administrative organ of state power is the Council of Ministers of the U.S.S.R." (§ 64). It is appointed by the Supreme Soviet (§ 70) and is accountable to it, or, in the intervals between the sessions, to its Presidium (§ 65).

The Supreme Court of the U.S.S.R. and the Special Courts of the U.S.S.R. are elected by the Supreme Soviet for a term of five years (§ 104). Similarly, the Procurator-General, who exercises "supreme supervisory power to ensure the strict observance of law" (§ 113), is appointed by the Supreme Soviet for a term of seven years.

Citizens of the U.S.S.R. have the right to work, to rest and leisure, to maintenance in old age and sickness and disability relief and to education (§§ 118–121). "Women are accorded equal rights with men" (§ 122). Citizens are accorded equal rights irrespective of their nationality or race (§ 123). The citizens are also guaranteed freedom of speech, of the press, of assembly and of street processions and demonstrations, "in conformity with the interests of the working people and in order to strengthen the socialist system" (§ 125).

Section 126 of the Constitution is remarkable for containing the only reference to the real master of the country, the Communist Party. It says that "the most active and politically conscious citizens in the ranks of the working class and other sections of the working people unite in the Communist Party of the Soviet-Union, which is the vanguard of the working people in their struggle to strengthen and develop the socialist system and is the leading core of all organizations of the working people, both public and state." The new Party programme, adopted in November, 1961, envisages a great increase of the economic capacity of the country and promises the transition to "full Communism" some time after 1980.

A special committee was set up in November, 1961, to draft a new constitution, but has been in abeyance ever since.

Local Government.—The State power in regions, provinces, autonomous provinces, territories, districts, towns and rural localities is vested in the *Soviets of Working People's Deputies* (§ 94), elected by the working people of the respective administrative units for a term of two years (§ 95). The executive and administrative organ of a Soviet is its Executive Committee elected by it (§ 99). The Union Republics and the Autonomous Republics have Supreme Soviets and Councils of Ministers of their own (§§ 57–63 and 79–88), although their jurisdiction is severely circumscribed in favour of the central Government. Since February, 1944, the Union Republics have had the right to enter into direct relations with foreign states and to conclude agreements and exchange diplomatic and consular representatives with them (§ 18A). So far, however, the only important activity of this kind has been the individual membership of the Ukraine and of Belorussia in the United Nations Organization. Similarly, the 1944 law allowing each Union Republic to possess its own Republican military formations (§ 18B) seems to have remained a paper provision.

The Union Republics possess Ministries of their own for internal affairs, certain branches of heavy and light industry, agriculture, public health, trade, finance and the like. The work of these Ministries is co-ordinated by respective federal Ministries and/or the *Gosplan*. Nominally, the Union Republics possess exclusive jurisdiction over such matters as motor transport, housing, social security, municipal affairs, local industry, education and, since 1956, inland water transport and justice.

Religion.—Section 124 of the Constitution lays down that "in order to ensure to citizens freedom of conscience, the church in the U.S.S.R. is separated from the state, and the school from the church," and that "freedom of religious worship and freedom of anti-religious propaganda is recognized for all citizens." Churches have remained open in virtue of contracts concluded between the congregations and the local authorities. The clergy live on voluntary donations from their parishioners. A new *modus vivendi* between the

Government and the religious communities was created during the War of 1939–1945. In September, 1943, Stalin agreed to the election of the Patriarch of Moscow and All Russia, a post which had been vacant since the death of Patriarch Tokhon in 1925. Patriarch Sergius, elected by the Council of the Russian Church in 1943, died in May, 1944, and was succeeded in February, 1945 by Patriarch Alexius (*d.* 1970). A new Patriarch, Pimen, was elected in 1971.

The proselytizing successes of the religious communities have become of great concern to the authorities; there has been a great increase of anti-religious articles in the press since 1959, and a number of religious institutions were once again closed or banned.

Education.—Under the Constitution, citizens of the U.S.S.R. have the right to education. Since 1956 the entire educational course, including higher education at universities, technical colleges, etc., has been free.

The state controls all educational institutions, theatres, cinemas, museums, libraries and picture galleries, as well as the press and the radio. The main centre of research and learning is the Academy of Sciences of the U.S.S.R., which is in effect a vast government-controlled pool of scientists.

President, M. V. Keldysh.

Chronological System.—On February 14, 1918, the Soviet Government adopted the Gregorian (Western) Calendar, and by a decree of June 16, 1930, the Soviet Government advanced all the clocks in the Union by one hour, thus adopting permanent Summer Time. The country is divided into several time zones (Moscow time is 3 hours ahead of G.M.T.).

LANGUAGE, LITERATURE AND ARTS

Language and Literature.—Russian is a branch of the Slavonic family of languages which is divided into the following groups: *Eastern,* including Russian, Ukrainian and White Russian; *Western,* including Polish, Czech, Slovak and Soroish (or Lusatian Wendish); and *Southern,* including Serbo-Croat, Slovene, Macedonian and Bulgarian. The Western group and part of the Southern group are written in the Latin alphabet, the others in the Cyrillic, said to have been instituted by SS. Cyril and Methodius in the ninth century, and largely based on the Greek alphabet. Before the Westernization of Russia under Peter the Great (1682–1725), Russian literature consisted mainly of folk ballads (*byliny*), epic songs, chronicles and works of moral theology. The eighteenth and particularly the nineteenth centuries saw a brilliant development of Russian poetry and fiction. Romantic poetry reached its zenith with Alexander Pushkin (1799–1837) and Mikhail Lermontov (1814–1841). The 20th century produced great poets like Alexander Blok (1880–1921), the Nobel Prize laureate of 1958 Boris Pasternak (1890–1960), Vladimir Mayakovsky (1893–1930) and Anna Akhmatova (1888–1966). Realistic fiction is associated with the names of Nikolai Gogol (1809–1852), Ivan Turgenev (1818–1883), Fedor Dostoyevsky (1821–1881) and Leo Tolstoy (1828–1910), and later with Anton Tchekhov (1860–1904), Maxim Gorky (1868–1936), Ivan Bunin (1870–1953) and Alexander Solzhenitsyn (*b.* 1918).

Great names in music include Glinka (1804–1857), Borodin (1833–87), Mussorgsky (1839–1881), Rimsky-Korsakov (1844–1908), Rubinstein (1829–1894), Tchaikowsky (1840–1893), Rakhmaninov (1873–1943), Skriabin (1872–1915), Prokofiev (1891–1953), Stravinsky (1882–1971) and Shostakovich (*b.* 1906).

FINANCE

A new, "heavy" Rouble was introduced on January 1, 1961. Prices and wages have been changed accordingly at the rate of 10 old Roubles = 1 new Rouble. The official exchange rate is now £1 = R.2·16. It bears little relation to the actual purchasing power of the two currencies. Banknotes in circulation are those valuing R. 1, 3, 4, 25, 50 and 100. There are also coins valuing Kopecks 1, 2, 3, 5, 10, 20 and 50 and R. 1.

DEFENCE

No official returns concerning the services are made in the U.S.S.R. It may be said, however, that the general trend over the last years has consisted in a growing emphasis on nuclear missiles and in a steady reduction of conventional arms.

The basic military service is two years in the Army and four years in the Air Force and the Navy.

The total size of the Soviet regular forces is now estimated to be about 3,150,000 men.

Operational ICBM's now total around 270, an increase of about 40 per cent. on the 1964 figure. The number of MRBM's and IRBM's launchers still appears to be between 700 and 750. The operational personnel of the Strategic Rocket Forces totals about 180,000.

The Air Forces comprise about 10,500 operational aircraft. The total strength of the Air Forces, excluding the Naval Air Force, is about 510,000 men. The total personnel of the separate Air Defence Command is estimated at 250,000 men.

The total size of the Soviet Army is estimated at 2,000,000 men. It is thought to be organized in 140 divisions, distributed as follows: 75 divisions in European U.S.S.R., 22 in Central U.S.S.R., 17 in the Far East, 26 in Eastern Europe.

The total strength of the Soviet Navy and Naval Air Force is 450,000 men. In total tonnage, it is the second largest navy in the world, and its main strength still lies in the submarine fleet. There are now 370 conventionally-powered and 40 nuclear-powered submarines. At least 40 can fire ballistic missiles and carry an average of three each. Over 300 are ocean-going.

There are no aircraft-carriers in the Soviet Navy. The land-based Naval Air Force comprises about 400 bombers and 400 other aircraft. The surface ships comprise 20 cruisers and 80 destroyers.

The security and border troops number some 230,000. There are also about 1½ million DAAFSO members who participate in such activities as shooting, athletics and parachuting.

Minister of Defence, Marshal A. A. Grechko.

Chief of General Staff, Marshal M. V. Zakharov.

Chief, Political Administration, Soviet Armed Forces, Army Gen. A. A. Yepishev.

On May 14, 1955, a Treaty of Friendship, Co-operation and Mutual Assistance was signed in Warsaw between the Soviet Union and its European associates (Bulgaria, East Germany, Hungary, Poland, Rumania and Czecho-Slovakia) to serve as a counter-poise to NATO. A united military command was set up in Moscow (*Secretary-General,* N. P. Firyubin; *C.-in-C.,* Marshal I. I. Yakubovsky.

Industry and Agriculture

One of the most remarkable aspects of Soviet economy has been the transformation of an essentially agricultural country into the second-strongest industrial power in the world. The 1969 output amounted to 81,600,000* tons of pig-iron, 110,300,000* tons of steel, 87,500,000* tons of rolled metal, 608,000,000* tons of coal, 328,000,000* tons of crude oil, 87,500,000* tons of cement, 689,000 million kW/h of electricity and 800,900 motor vehicles.

* Metric.

Agricultural development has been far slower, mainly owing to lack of incentives among peasants organized in *kolkhozy* (collective farms). Repeated droughts, such as in 1965, were a contributing factor to a permanent shortage of grain. Stock breeding has also suffered from the general mis-management of farming. The livestock in 1969 included 95,200,000 cattle, including 40,500,000 cows, and 135,700,000 sheep and goats. The level of productivity remains very low. It remains to be seen whether new incentives for peasants intro-duced in 1966 and 1970 will bring about a radical change in the situation. *Forests* cover nearly 40 per cent. of the whole area of the Union and form a considerable source of wealth.

Trade with U.K.

	1969	1970
Imports from U.K. .	£96,403,000	£102,132,000
Exports to U.K.....	197,155,000	220,054,000

COMMUNICATIONS

European Russia is relatively well served by railways, Leningrad and Moscow being the two main focal points of rail routes. The centre and south have a good system of north-south and east-west lines, but the eastern part (the Volga lands), traversed as it is by trunk lines between Europe and Asia which enter Siberia *viâ* Sverdlovsk, Chelya-binsk, Magnitogorsk and Ufa, lacks north-south routes. In Asia, there are still large areas of the U.S.S.R., notably in the Far North and Siberia, with few or no railways. Railways built since 1928 include the Turkestan-Siberian line (*Turksib*) which has made possible a large-scale industrial exploit-ation of Kazakhstan, a number of lines within the system of the *Trans-Siberian Railway* (Magnito-gorsk-Kartaly-Troitsk, Sverdlovsk-Kurgan, Novo-sibirsk-Proyektnaya, etc.), which are of great importance for the industrial development in the east, the Petropavlovsk-Karaganda-Balkhash line which has made possible the development of the Karaganda coal basin and of the Balkhash copper mines, and the Moscow–Donbass trunk line. In the northern part of European Russia, the North Pechora Railway has been completed, while in the Far East a second Trans-Siberian line is under con-struction; it will follow a more northerly alignment than the existing Trans-Siberian and will terminate in the Pacific port of Sovetskaya Gavan.

Sea Ports and Inland Waterways.—The most im-portant ports (Odessa, Nikolayev, Batuum, Tagan-rog, Rostov, Kerch, Sebastopol and Novorossiisk) lie around the Black Sea and the Sea of Azov. The northern ports (Leningrad, Murmansk and Arch-angel) are, with the exception of Murmansk, ice-bound during winter. Several new ports have been built along the Arctic Sea route (between Murmansk and Vladivostok) and are now in regular use every summer. The great Far Eastern port of Vladivostok, the Pacific naval base of the U.S.S.R., is kept open by icebreakers all the year round. Inland waterways, both natural and artificial, are of great importance in the country, although all of them are icebound in winter (from 2½ months in the south to 6 months in the north). The great rivers of European Russia flow outwards from the centre, linking all parts of the plain with the chief ports, an immense system of navigable waterways which carries about 239,000,000 tons of freight per year. They are supplemented by a system of canals which provide a through traffic between the White, Baltic, Black and Caspian Seas. The most notable of them, built largely by forced labour, are the *White Sea-Baltic Stalin Canal*, and the *Moscow-Volga Canal*. The 63-miles long *Volga-Don* Canal linking the Baltic and the White Seas in

the North to the Caspian, the Black Sea and the Sea of Azov in the South, was completed in May 1952.

FLAG OF THE U.S.S.R.—Red, with five-pointed star above hammer and sickle.

NATIONAL DAY OF THE U.S.S.R.—November 7 (Commemorating the October Bolshevist Revolu-tion of 1917).

BRITISH EMBASSY
(Naberezhnaya Morisa Toreza 14, Moscow)
Ambassador Extraordinary and Plenipotentiary, Sir John Edward Killick, K.C.M.G. (1971)... £9,000
Minister, J. A. Dobbs.
Counsellors, N. E. Cox (*Commercial*); K. B. A. Scott (*Head of Chancery*); H. G. T. P. Doyne-Ditmas; G. L. Scullard, O.B.E. (*Admin.*); T. Garrett (*Scientific*).
1st Secretaries, D. J. E. Ratford (*Commercial*); B. L. Barder; E. J. Field (*Cultural*); A. Burwood-Smith (*Scientific*); M. B. Nicholson; R. R. B. Baxendine (*Medical Officer*).
2nd Secretaries, D. H. Cooper (*Commercial*); R. J. Griffiths (*Consul*); N. H. Livingston; R. H. Smith; Miss A. W. Lewis; M. H. Hewitt (*Admin.*); J. Q. Davies (*Commercial*); R. S. Reeve; M. Tickner; N. Duckett; D. P. Hanks.
Defence and Air Attaché, Air Cdre. R. P. Harding, C.B.E.
Asst. Air Attachés, Sqn. Ldr. P. Watton; Flt-Lieut. O. J. A. Knight.
Military Attaché, Brig. H. L. B. Salmon.
Asst. Military Attaché, Major A. J. Smith.
Naval Attaché, Capt. H. M. Ellis, R.N.
Asst. Naval Attachés, Lt. Cdr. J. E. Dyes, R.N.; Lt.-Cdr. A. Wolstenholme, R.N.
There are no British Consulates in the U.S.S.R. apart from the Consular Section attached to the Embassy.

I.—R.S.F.S.R.
(The Russian Soviet Federal Socialist Republic)
Chairman of the Presidium of the Supreme Soviet, M. A. Yasnov.
Chairman of the Council of Ministers, M. S. Soloment-sev.
The R.S.F.S.R. has no Communist Party Central Committee of its own.

The R.S.F.S.R., the largest and the most im-portant of the Republics, occupies the major half of the European part of the U.S.S.R. and the major northern half of its Asiatic part and makes up 77 per cent. of the total territory of the U.S.S.R. with 53 per cent. of the total population. It consists of 16 Autonomous Republics (the Bashkir, Buryat, Checheno-Ingush, Chuvash, Daghestan, Kabardin-Balkar, Kalmyk, Karelian, Komi, Mari, Mordovian, North-Osetian, Tartar, Tuva, Udmurt and Yakut A.S.S.R.'s); 6 regions (Altai, Khabarovsk, Krasnodar, Krasnoyarsk, Mari-time and Stavropol) containing in their turn 5 auto-nomous provinces; 49 provinces (Amur, Arch-angel, Astrakhan, Belgorod, Bryansk, Chelyabinsk, Chita, Gorky, Irkutsk, Ivanovo, Kalinin, Kalinin-grad, Kaluga, Kamchatka, Kemerovo, Kirov, Kos-troma, Kuibyshev, Kurgan, Kursk, Leningrad, Lipetsk, Magadan, Moscow, Murmansk, Nov-gorod, Novosibirsk, Omsk, Orel, Orenburg, Penza, Perm, Pskov, Rostov, Ryazan, Sakhalin, Saratov, Smolensk, Sverdlovsk, Tambov, Tomsk, Tula, Tyumen, Ulyanovsk, Vladimir, Volgograd, Vologda, Vorenezh and Yaroslavl).

Physical Features.—The R.S.F.S.R. may be con-veniently divided into three areas, a low-lying flat Western part stretching eastwards up to the Yenisei and divided in two by the Ural ridge; an eastern part, between the Yenisei and the Pacific, consisting of a number of tablelands and ridges,

and a southern mountainous part. Climatically, the R.S.F.S.R. extends over all zones, except the tropics, and may be divided into the following belts (from north to south): Arctic, Tundra, Forest, Mixed Forest-Steppe, Steppe, Sub-Tropics.

The Republic has a very long coast-line, including the longest Arctic coast-line in the world (about 17,000 miles). The most important rivers in the European Part of the R.S.F.S.R. are the Volga with its tributaries Kama and Oka, the Northern Dvina and the Pechora, the short but wide Neva, the Don and the Kuban, and in the Asiatic part, the Obi with the Irtysh, the Yenisei, the Lena and the Amur, and, further north, Khatanga, Olenek, Yana, Indigirka, Kolyma and Anadyr. Lakes are abundant, particularly in the north-west. The huge Baikal Lake in Eastern Siberia is the deepest lake in the world. There are also two large artificial water reservoirs within the Greater Volga canal system, the Moscow and Rybinsk " Seas."

Minerals.—The Republic occupies one of the first places in the world for mineral wealth. Coal is mined in the Kuznetsk area, in the Urals, south of Moscow, in the Donets basin (its Eastern part lies in the R.S.F.S.R.) and in the Pechora area in the North. Oil is produced in the Northern Caucasus and in the area between the Volga and the Ural (the so-called " Second Baku "). The Ural mountains contain a unique assortment of minerals—high-quality iron ore, manganese, copper, aluminium, gold, platinum, precious stones, salt, asbestos, pyrites, coal, oil, etc. Iron ore is mined, in addition to the Urals, near Kursk, Tula, Lipetsk, Khoper, in several areas in Siberia and in the Kola Peninsula. Non-ferrous metals are found in the Altai, in Eastern Siberia, in the Northern Caucasus, in the Kuznetsk Basin, in the Far East and in the Far North. Nine-tenths of all U.S.S.R. forests are located in the R.S.F.S.R.

Production and Industry.—The vastness of the territory of the Republic and the great variety in climatic conditions cause great differences in the structure of agriculture from north to south and from west to east. In the Far North stag breeding, hunting and fishing are predominant. Further south, timber industry is combined with grain growing. In the southern half of the forest zone and in the adjacent forest-steppe zone, the acreage under grain crops is far larger and the structure of agriculture more complex. In the eastern part of this zone, between the Volga and the Urals, cericulture is predominant (particularly summer wheat), with cattle breeding next. Beyond the Urals, we find another important grain-growing and stock-breeding area in the southern part of the Western-Siberian plain. The southern steppe zone is the main wheat granary of the U.S.S.R., containing also large acreages under barley, maize and sunflower. In the extreme South (Krasnodar region, Stavropol region) cotton is now cultivated. Vine, tobacco and other Southern crops are grown on the Black Sea shore of the Caucasus.

Industrially, the R.S.F.S.R. occupies the first place among the Soviet Republics. Major changes in the location of industry have occurred since the revolution and again since the war with two new industrial areas being developed in the Urals and in the Kuznetsk basin, although Moscow and Leningrad are still the two largest industrial centres in the country. Most of the oil produced in the U.S.S.R. now comes from two areas in the R.S.F.S.R.—the Bashkir and Tartar Autonomous Republics. All industries are represented in the R.S.F.S.R., including iron and steel and engineering. Industrial centres include Magnitogorsk, Chelyabinsk, Novokuznetsk, Tula, Komsomolsk, Perm, Ufa, Irkutsk, Kuibyshev, Krasnoyarsk, Nizh-

ny-Tagil, Novosibirsk, Omsk, Volgograd, Gorky, Saratov, Grozny, Rostov and Taganrog.

CAPITAL, MOSCOW. Population 7,061,000. Moscow, founded about A.D. 1147 by Yuri Dolgoruki, became first the centre of the rising Moscow principality and, later, in the 15th century, the capital of the whole of Russia (Muscovy). In 1325, it became the seat of the Metropolitan of Russia. In 1703 Peter the Great transferred the capital to the newly built St. Petersburg, but on March 14, 1918, Moscow was again designated as the capital. ΨLeningrad (before the First World War " St. Petersburg " and from 1914-1924 " Petrograd ") has a population of 3,950,000.

Other towns with populations exceeding 500,000 are:—

Gorky (Nizhny-Novgorod)	1,170,000
Novosibirsk (Novonikolayevsk)	1,161,000
Kuibyshev (Samara)	1,047,000
Sverdlovsk (Yekaterinburg)	1,026,000
Chelyabinsk	874,000
Kazan	869,000
Perm (Molotov)	850,000
Omsk	821,000
Volgograd (Stalingrad; Tsaritsyn)	818,000
ΨRostov-on-Don	789,000
Ufa	773,000
Saratov	758,000
Voronezh	660,000
Krasnoyarsk	648,000
Yaroslavl	517,000

Ψ Seaport.

About 83 per cent. of the population are Russians.

II.—UKRAINE

First Secretary of the Party Central Committee, P. Ye. Shelest.

Chairman of the Presidium of the Supreme Soviet, A. P. Lyashko.

Chairman of the Council of Ministers, V. V. Shcherbitsky.

This Republic, second largest in population, lying in the south-western part of the European half of the U.S.S.R., was formed in December, 1917. It consists of 25 provinces—Cherkassy, Chernigov, Chernovtsy, Crimea, Dnepropetrovsk, Donetsk, Ivano-Frankovsk, Kharkov, Kherson, Khmelnitsky, Kiev, Kirovograd, Lvov, Nikolayev, Odessa, Poltava, Rovno, Sumy, Ternopol, Transcarpathia, Vinnitsa, Volhynia, Voroshilovgrad, Zaporozhye and Zhitomir.

Physical Features.—The larger part of the Ukraine forms a plain with small elevations. The Carpathian mountains lie in the south-western part of the Republic. The climate is moderate, with relatively mild winters (particularly in the south-west) and hot summers. The main rivers are the Dnieper with its tributaries, the Southern Bug and the Northern Donets (a tributary of the Don).

Production and Industry.—The main centre of Soviet coal mining and iron and steel industry is situated in the southern part of the Ukraine. Engineering and chemical industry have been greatly developed under the Soviet régime. In 1955, the Ukraine provided 37 per cent. of the total Soviet steel, 39 per cent. of metal goods and 32 per cent. of coal. The central forest-steppe region (mainly on the right bank of the Dnieper) is the greatest sugar-producing area in the U.S.S.R. The Ukraine also leads in grain-growing and stock-raising.

There are large deposits of coal and salt in the Donets Basin, of iron ore in Krivoy Rog and near Kerch in the Crimea, of manganese in Nikopol, and of quicksilver in Nikitovka.

CAPITAL (since 1934), Kiev, the oldest city in the U.S.S.R. founded in the 9th century A.D., was

the capital of the Russian State from 865 to 1240. Population 1,632,000. Other towns with population over 500,000 are:—

Kharkov	1,223,000
Ψ Odessa	892,000
Donetsk (Stalino; Yuzovka, *i.e.* Hughesovka)	879,000
Dnepropetrovsk (Yekaterinoslav)	863,000
Zaporozhye (Aleksandrovskaya)	658,000
Krivoy-Rog	573,000
Lvov (Lviv; Lwow; Lemberg)	553,000

III.—BELORUSSIA
(White Russia)

First Secretary of the Party Central Committee, P. M. Masherov.

Chairman of the Presidium of the Supreme Soviet, F. A. Surganov.

Chairman of the Council of Ministers, T. Ya. Kiselev.

The Belorussian S.S.R., lying in the western part of the European half of the U.S.S.R., was formed early in 1919. It now consists of six provinces (Brest, Gomel, Grodno, Minsk, Mogilev and Vitebsk). It is largely a plain with many lakes, swamps and marshy land. Before the revolution of 1917 the area was one of the most backward parts of European Russia. Since then, agriculture has been greatly developed, thanks to draining of swamps. Most of the Republic's industry is also of recent growth. Woodworking is of great importance, but engineering has also been greatly extended with several major plants built in Gomel and Minsk.

The main rivers are the upper reaches of the Dnieper, of the Niemen and of the Western Dvina.

CAPITAL, Minsk. Population 916,000.

Belorussians make up four-fifths of the population, with Russians and Poles coming next.

IV.—UZBEKISTAN

First Secretary of the Party Central Committee, Sh. R. Rashidov.

Chairman of the Presidium of the Supreme Soviet N. M. Matchanov.

Chairman of the Council of Ministers, N. D. Khudayberdyev.

The Uzbek S.S.R. was formed in 1924 and consists of the Kara-Kalpak A.S.S.R. and of 10 provinces (Andizhan, Bokhara, Ferghana, Kashka-Darya, Khorezm, Namangan, Samarkand, Surkhan-Darya, Syr-Darya and Tashkent). It lies between the high Tienshan Mountains and the Pamir highlands in the east and south-east and sandy lowlands in the west and north-west. The major part of the territory is a plain with huge waterless deserts and several large oases, which form the main centres of population and economic life. The largest is the Ferghana valley, watered by the Syr-Darya. Other oases include Tashkent, Samarkand, Bokhara and Khorezm. The climate is continental and dry. Minerals include oil (in the Ferghana valley and in Khaudag), coal (Angren) and sulphur (Shorsu).

The Uzbeks, a Turkic people, make up 64 per cent. of the population, the Russians (12·5 per cent.) and Tartars (five per cent.) come next.

There is a major agricultural machinery plant at Tashkent and a chemical combine at Chirchik. Uzbekistan is the main cotton-growing area of the U.S.S.R. producing more than 60 per cent. of all Soviet cotton. Irrigation has always been of decisive importance in this area, and the Soviet Government has done much in this field, including the construction of the Great Ferghana Canal (230 miles).

CAPITAL, Tashkent. Population 1,385,000. Samarkand contains the Gur-Emir (Tamerlane's Mausoleum), completed A.D. 1400 by Ulug-bek, Tamerlane's astronomer-grandson, and a 15th-

century observatory. Heavy damage was done to this ancient city by the series of severe earthquakes in April and May, 1966.

V.—KAZAKHSTAN.

First Secretary of the Party Central Committee, D. A. Kunayev.

Chairman of the Presidium of Supreme Soviet, S. B. Niyazbekov.

Chairman of the Council of Ministers, B. A. Ashimov.

The Kazakh S.S.R., the second-largest Union-Republic, stretching from the lower reaches of the Volga and the Caspian in the west to the Altai and Tienshan in the east, and bordering on China, was formed in 1920 as an autonomous republic (under the name of the Kirghiz A.S.S.R.) within the R.S.F.S.R., and was constituted a Union Republic in 1936. It consists of the 15 Provinces (Aktyubinsk, Alma-Ata, Chimkent, Djambul, East-Kazakhstan, Guryev, Karaganda, Kokchetav, Kustanay, Kzyl-Orda, Semipalatinsk, Taldy-Kurgan, Tselinograd, Turgay and Uralsk.

Kazakhstan is a country of arid steppes and misedeserts, flat in the west, hilly in the east and mountainous in the south-east (Southern Altai and Tienshan). The climate is continental and very dry. The main rivers are the (Upper) Irtysh, the Ural, the Syr-Darya and the Ili. Kazakhstan contains rich deposits of non-ferrous metals: copper in Kounrad, Djezkazgan and Boshchekul, other metals in the Altai, in the Kara-Tau Mounts, and elsewhere. It also contains an important coal-producing area (Karaganda) ranking third in the U.S.S.R. and an oil-bearing area (near Emba). Major centres of metal industry exist now in the Altai Mountains, in Chimkent, North of the Balkhash Lake and in Central Kazakhstan. Stockraising is highly developed, particularly in the central and south-western parts of the Republic. Grain is grown in the north and north-east and cotton in the south and south-east. In 1954 an ambitious programme of development of " virgin " lands in the steppes was launched by the Government to increase grain production.

The Kazakhs (a Turkic people) are now in a minority in the Republic named after them; they constitute only 32 per cent. of its population. Russian settlers make up 42 per cent. and Ukrainians 7 per cent.

CAPITAL, Alma-Ata (formerly Verny). Population, 730,000. Karaganda, a major mining centre, has a population of 522,000.

VI.—GEORGIA

First Secretary of the Party Central Committee, V. P. Mzhavanadze.

Chairman of the Presidium of the Supreme Soviet, G. S. Dzotenidze.

Chairman of the Council of Ministers, G. D. Djavakhishvili.

The Georgian S.S.R., occupying the north-western part of Transcaucasia, lies on the shore of the Black Sea and borders in the south-east on Turkey. It was formed in 1921; in 1922 it joined the Transcaucasian Federation which, in its turn, adhered to the U.S.S.R. in the same year. After the liquidation of the Transcaucasian S.F.S.R. in 1936 Georgia became a Union Republic. It contains two Autonomous Republics (Abkhazia and Adjaria) and the South-Osetian Autonomous Province. Georgia is a country of mountains, with the Greater Caucasus in the north and the Smaller Caucasus in the south. A relatively lowlying land between these two ridges is divided into two parts by the Sura Ridge: Western Georgia with a mild and damp climate and Eastern Georgia with a more continental and dry climate. The Black Sea shore and the Rion lowlands are subtropical in their climatic character. The most

Important mineral deposits are manganese (Chiatury) coal (Tkibuli and Tkvarcheli) and oil (Kakhetia). Georgia is leading as regards production of manganese in the U.S.S.R. There are also many oil refineries. Viniculture and tobacco-growing are the two main agricultural industries. The Black Sea coast harbours many famous holiday resorts. Georgians make up 66 per cent. of the population, the remainder being composed of Armenians, Russians, Azerbaidjani and Osetians.

CAPITAL, Tbilisi (Tiflis), population 889,000.

VII.—AZERBAIDJAN

First Secretary of the Party Central Committee, G. A. Aliev.

Chairman of the Presidium of the Supreme Soviet, K. A. Khalilov.

Chairman of the Council of Ministers, A. I. Ibragimov.

The Azerbaidjan S.S.R. occupies the eastern part of Transcaucasia, on the shore of the Caspian Sea, and borders on Iran. It was formed in 1920. Between 1922 and 1936 it formed part of the Transcaucasian Federation. In 1936 it became a Union Republic. It contains the Nakhichevan Autonomous Republic and the Nagorno-Karabakh Autonomous Province.

The north-eastern part of the Republic is taken up by the south-eastern end of the main Caucasus ridge, its south-western part by the smaller Caucasus hills, and its south-eastern corner by the spurs of the Talysh Ridge. Its central part is a depression irrigated by the Kura and by the middle reaches of its tributary Aragva. Sheltered by the mountains from the humid west winds blowing from the Black Sea, Azerbaidjan has a continental climate. The land requires artificial irrigation. The Republic is very rich in minerals, particularly in oil. The Baku oilfields form the second-largest oil-producing area in the U.S.S.R. A large power station on the Kura (Mingechaur) was completed in 1954. Azerbaidjan is also important as a cotton growing area. The Azerbaidjani (Turks) make up three-quarters of the population of the Republic, Armenians, about 9 per cent., and Russians, about 10 per cent.

CAPITAL, ΨBaku. Population 1,261,000.

VIII.—LITHUANIA

First Secretary of the Party Central Committee, A. J. Snieckus.

Chairman of the Presidium of the Supreme Soviet, M. J. Šumauskas.

Chairman of the Council of Ministers, I. A. Maniušis.

Lithuania, formerly a Province of the Russian Empire, was declared an independent Republic at Vilna in 1918 and was incorporated into the U.S.S.R. in August, 1940. It was occupied by German forces from June, 1941 until the autumn of 1944. The Republic forms a plain with a large number of lakes and swamps. The forests occupy 19 per cent. of the whole area. The main river is the Niemen with its tributaries.

The chief industries are agriculture and forestry, the chief products being rye, oats, wheat, barley, flax, sugar-beet and potatoes. Before its incorporation into the Soviet Union, Lithuania exported a large quantity of meat and dairy produce.

The Lithuanians make up four-fifths of the population, Russians and Poles, 8–9 per cent. each.

CAPITAL, Vilnius (Vilna, restored to Lithuania by U.S.S.R. after the collapse and partition of Poland in 1939, and recaptured by Soviet forces in 1944). Population 372,000.

IX.—MOLDAVIA

First Secretary of the Party Central Committee, I. L. Bodyul.

Chairman of the Presidium of the Supreme Soviet, K. F. Ilyashenko.

Chairman of the Council of Ministers, P. A. Paskar.

Moldavia, occupying the south-western corner of the U.S.S.R., borders in the west on Rumania with the Pruth forming the frontier. In 1918, Rumania seized the Russian Province of Bessarabia. In 1924 a Moldavian Autonomous Republic was formed within the Ukraine, and in 1940 the U.S.S.R. forced Rumania to give back Bessarabia, the major part of which was merged with the Moldavian A.S.S.R. to form a Moldavian Union Republic. Moldavia was occupied by the Germans and Rumanians from 1941 to 1944.

The northern part of the Republic consists of flat steppe lands, now all under plough. Some forests skirt the Dniester. Further south, around Kishinev, there are woody hills and further south again, low-lying steppe lands. The climate is moderate. The main river is the Dniester, navigable along the whole course.

The main industry is agriculture (viniculture, fruit-growing and market-gardening). Industry is insignificant in both parts of Moldavia, but the Republic has the densest population in the U.S.S.R. Moldavians make up 64 per cent. of the population, with Ukranians, and Russians next.

CAPITAL, Kishinev (Chisinau). Population, 357,000.

X.—LATVIA

First Secretary of the Party Central Committee, A. E. Voss.

Chairman of the Presidium of the Supreme Soviet, V. P. Ruben.

Chairman of the Council of Ministers, J. J. Ruben.

The Latvian S.S.R., lying on the shores of the Baltic and of the Gulf of Riga, was formerly a Baltic Province of the Russian Empire. It was proclaimed an independent state in 1918 and was forcibly incorporated into the U.S.S.R. in August 1940. Between 1941 and 1944 the Republic was occupied by the German forces.

The surface of the country is generally flat, interspersed by occasional chains of hills. The climate is moderately-continental. The main rivers are the lower reaches of the Western Dvina and its tributaries. Forests occupy 20 per cent. of the total territory.

The Latvians make up 57 per cent. of the Republic's population, Russians 28 per cent.

Latvian industry was always highly developed, with shipbuilding, engineering, chemical industry, textile industry, wood-working and dairying being the chief occupations. Both Riga and Liepaja (Libava, Liebau) are important sea-ports.

As in other newly-acquired Republics an agrarian reform was carried out in Latvia in 1940–41 and again after 1944.

CAPITAL, ΨRiga. Population, 733,000.

XI.—KIRGHIZIA

First Secretary of the Party Central Committee, T. U. Usubaliyev.

Chairman of the Presidium of the Supreme Soviet, T. Kulatov.

Chairman of the Council of Ministers, A. S. Suyumbayev.

The Kirghiz S.S.R. occupies the north-eastern part of Soviet Central Asia and borders in the south-east on China. In 1924, a Kara-Kirghiz Autonomous Province was formed within the R.S.F.S.R. In 1926 it became a Kirghiz Autonomous Republic, and in 1936 a Union Republic. It contains three provinces, Issyk-Kul, Naryn and Osh. The Kirghiz Republic is a mountainous country, the major part being covered by the ridge of the Central Tienshan, while mountains of the Pamir-Altai system occupy its southern part. There are

a number of spacious mountain valleys, the Alai, Susamyr, the Issyk-kul lake and others. The majority of the population is concentrated in plains, lying at the foot of mountains—Chu, Talass, part of the Ferghana Valley where agriculture prospers. Industry is insignificant, but some mining is done. A number of railways have been built under the Five Year Plans. The Kirghiz now constitute only 44 per cent. of the population, the Russians, 30 per cent. The Uzbeks (in Eastern Ferghana) amount to 11 per cent.

CAPITAL, Frunze (formerly Pishpek). Population, 431,000.

XII.—TADJIKISTAN

First Secretary of the Party Central Committee, D. Rasulov.
Chairman of the Presidium of the Supreme Soviet, M. Kholov.
Chairman of the Council of Ministers, A. Kakharov.

The Tadjik S.S.R. lies in the extreme south-east of Soviet Central Asia and borders in the south on Afghanistan and in the east on China. It was originally formed in 1924 as an Autonomous Republic within the Uzbek S.S.R. and became a Union Republic in 1929. It includes the Gorno-Badakhshan Autonomous Province and the Lenina-bad Province.

The country is mountainous: in the east lie the Pamir highlands with the highest point in the U.S.S.R., Pik Communizmu (24,500 feet), in the centre the high ridges of the Pamir-Altai system. Plains are formed by wide stretches of the Syr-Darya valley in the north and of the Amu-Darya in the south.

Like the other Central-Asiatic Republics, Tadji-kistan is a cotton-growing country. Its climatic conditions favour the cultivation of Egyptian cotton. Irrigation is of great importance. Fifty-six per cent. of the population are Tadjiks (linguistically and culturally akin to the Persians), about 23 per cent. Uzbeks, the rest Russians and others.

CAPITAL, Dushanbe (formerly Stalinabad; Dyu-shambe). Population, 374,000.

XIII.—ARMENIA

First Secretary of the Party Central Committee, A. E. Kochinyan.
Chairman of the Presidium of the Supreme Soviet, N. Kh. Arutyunyan.
Chairman of the Council of Ministers, B. A. Murad-yan.

The Armenian S.S.R. occupies the south-western part of Transcaucasia: it was formed in 1920. In 1922 it joined the Transcaucasian Federation, and on its liquidation in 1936 became a Union Republic. In the south it borders on Turkey. It is a mountainous country consisting of several vast table lands surrounded by ridges. The population and the economic life are concentrated in the low-lying part of Armenia, the Aras valley and the Erevan hollow; the climate is continental, dry and cold, but the Aras valley has a long, hot and dry summer. Irrigation is essential for agriculture. At the junction of the former Turkish, Persian and Russian boundaries is *Mount Ararat* (17,160 ft.), the traditional resting place of "Noah's Ark." Industrial and fruit crops are grown in the low-lying districts, grain in the hills. Armenia is traditionally noted for her wine. There are large copper ore and molybdenum deposits and other minerals. The Armenian Church centred in Etchmiadzin is the oldest established Christian Church, Christianity having been recognized as the State religion in A.D. 300.

Nearly 90 per cent. of the population is Armenian.

CAPITAL, Erevan. Population, 767,000.

XIV.—TURKMENISTAN

First Secretary of the Party Committee, M. Gapurov.
Chairman of the Presidium of the Supreme Soviet, A. Klychev.
Chairman of the Council of Ministers, O. N. Oraz-mukhamedov.

Turkmenia occupies the extreme south of Soviet Central Asia, between the Caspian and the Amu-Darya and borders in the south on Iran and Afghanistan. It was formed in 1924 and contains three Provinces (Chardjou, Mary and Tashauz). The country is a low-lying plain, fringed by hills in the south. Ninety per cent. of the plain is taken up by the arid Kara-Kum desert. Of all Central-Asiatic Republics, Turkmenia is the lowest and driest. The principal industries are agriculture and stock-raising, cotton, wool, astrakan furs, carpets and horses being the principal products. Minerals include oil and sulphur. Most of the land under plough is artificially irrigated. Silk industry is of an old standing. There are also some fisheries in the Caspian.

Turkmens, nomadic in the past, make up two-thirds of the population, with Russians coming second, and Uzbeks, third.

CAPITAL, Ashkhabad (formerly Askhabad, Poltoratsk). Population, 253,000.

XV.—ESTONIA

First Secretary of the Party Central Committee, I. G. Käbin.
Chairman of the Presidium of the Supreme Soviet, A. P. Vader.
Chairman of the Council of Ministers, W. J. Klauson.

Estonia, formerly a Baltic province of the Russian Empire, was proclaimed an independent Republic in 1918. In 1940, it was forcibly in-corporated into the U.S.S.R. It lies on the shores of the Baltic and of the Finnish Gulf in the north and of the Gulf of Riga in the south-west. Some 800 islands, among them Dagö and Ösel, form part of Estonian territory. Between 1941 and 1944, Estonia was occupied by the German forces.

The country forms a low-lying plain with many lakes, among them the Chud (or Pskov) Lake, on the border with the R.S.F.S.R. Forests take up about one-fifth of the territory. Agriculture and dairy-farming are the chief industries, rye, oats, barley, flax and potatoes being the chief crops, and butter, bacon and eggs the chief products of dairy farming. There are important manufactures, in-cluding textiles, engineering, shipbuilding, wood-working, etc.

The population consists of Estonians (66 per cent.) and Russians (24 per cent.).

CAPITAL, Ψ Tallinn (formerly Reval). Population, 363,000.

THE VATICAN CITY STATE
(Stato della Città del Vaticano)

Sovereign Pontiff, His Holiness Pope Paul VI (Giovanni Battista Montini), *born* at Concesio (Brescia), Sept. 26, 1897, *elected* Pope (in succession to John XXIII), June 21, 1963.
Secretary of State, Cardinal Jean Marie Villot, *appointed* April 30, 1969.

The office of the ecclesiastical head of the Roman Catholic Church (*Santa Sede* or Holy See) is vested in the Pope of Rome, the Sovereign Pontiff. For many centuries the Sovereign Pontiff exercised temporal power, and in 1859 the Papal States had an area of 17,218 square miles, with a population of 3,124,688. During the reign of Pius IX (1846–1878), the Papal States of Romagna, Umbria and the Marches were incorporated in the Kingdom of Sardinia and with the remaining States (Rome, Comacchio, Viterbo, Civita Vecchia, Velletri and Frosinone) became

part of unified Italy in 1870. The territory of the Papacy was confined to the palaces of the Vatican and the Lateran and the Villa of Castel Gandolfo and the temporal power of the Pope was in suspense until the treaty of Feb. 11, 1929, which recognized the full and independent sovereignty of the Holy See in the City of the Vatican. Accompanying the treaty were conventions regulating the condition of religion and the Catholic Church in Italy and agreeing to pay 750,000,000 *lire* in cash and the income at 5 per cent. on 1,000,000,000 *lire* State bonds as a final settlement of the claims of the Holy See against Italy for the loss of temporal power. The population of the Vatican City in 1969 was 1000.

FLAG.—Square flag; equal vertical bands of yellow (next staff), and white; crossed keys and triple crown device on white band.

BRITISH LEGATION
(91 Via Condotti, Rome)

Envoy Extraordinary and Minister Plenipotentiary to the Holy See, His Excellency Desmond John Chetwode Crawley, C.M.G., C.V.O. (1970) £6,925
1st Secretary, A. G. L. Turner.
Attaché, J. P. Blackledge.

VENEZUELA
(La Republica de Venezuela)

President, Dr. Rafael Caldera (Rodriguez), *elected* Dec. 1, 1968, *assumed office* March 11, 1969.

CABINET
Home Affairs, Dr. Lorenzo Fernández.
Foreign Affairs, Dr. Arístides Calvani.
Finance, Dr. Pedro R. Tinoco.
Defence, Vice Almirante Luis Carbonell.
Development, Dr. Hector Fernández Carabaño.
Public Works, Ing. José Curiel Rodríguez.
Education, Dr. Enrique Pérez Olivares.
Health and Social Welfare, Dr. Jesus Maiz-Lyon.
Agriculture and Stockbreeding, Dr. Daniel Scott Cuervo.
Labour, Dr. Nectario Andrade Labarca.
Communications Dr. Enrique Bustamante Luciani,
Justice, Dr. Edilberto Escalante.
Mines and Hydrocarbons, Dr. Hugo Pérez La Salvia.

VENEZUELAN EMBASSY IN LONDON
3 Hans Crescent, S.W.1.
[01-584-4206]

Ambassador Extraordinary and Plenipotentiary, His Excellency Dr. Carlos Perez de la Cova (1970).
Minister-Counsellor, Dr. Anibal Valero.
1st Secretary, Señorita Esther Meneses.
2nd Secretary, Señor Lic. Alberto Dominguez Roche.
3rd Secretaries, Señor Lic. John Velasco de Armas; Dr. Francisco Alvarez Gorsira.
Counsellor, Señor Francisco Rodríguez Reggeti *(Commercial)*.
Naval Attaché, Rear Adm. Pablo Cohen Guerrero.
Military Attaché, Col. Pedro José Tejera.
Air Attaché, Col. Fernández Paredes Bello.
Special Attaché, Señora Miriam Blanco-Fombona de Hood.

Consulate-General: 71A Park Mansions, S.W.1.
Minister-Counsellor, Señor Guillermo Espinosa (Consul).
There is also a Consulate-General at *Liverpool*.
Area and Population.—A South American Republic, situated approximately between 0° 45′ S. lat. and 12° 12′ N. lat. and 59° 45′–73° 09′ W. long. It consists of one Federal District, 20 states and 2 territories. Venezuela has a total area of 352,150 square miles and a population (U.N. estimate, 1970)

of 10,399,000, increasing annually at a rate of 35 per 1,000.

Venezuela lies on the north of the South American continent, and is bounded on the north by the Caribbean Sea, west by the Republic of Colombia, east by Guyana, and south by Brazil. Included in the area of the Republic are 72 islands off the coast, with a total area of about 14,650 square miles, the largest being *Margarita*, which is politically associated with Tortuga, Cubagua and Coche to form the State of *Nueva Esparta*. Margarita has an area of about 400 square miles. In 1942 Great Britain ceded to Venezuela the small island of *Patos* (170 acres) about 3 miles from the mainland.

Physical Features.—The Eastern Andes from the south-west cross the border and reach to the Caribbean Coast, where they are prolonged by

the Maritime Andes of Venezuela to the Gulf of Paria on the north-east. The main range is known as the Sierra Nevada de Merida, and contains the highest peaks in the country in Pico Bolívar (16,411 feet) and Picacho de la Sierra (15,420 feet), the maritime ranges containing the Silla de Caracas (8,531 feet). Near the Brazilian border the Sierras Parima and Pacaraima, and on the eastern border the Sierras de Rincote and de Usupamo, enclose the republic with parallel northward spurs, between which are valleys of the Orinoco tributaries. The Sierra Parima contains Yaparana (7,175 feet) and Duida (8,120 feet), and Pacaraima contains Maraguaca (8,228 feet) and Roraima (9,000 feet), the latter being on the Venezuela-Guyana boundary. The slopes of the mountains and foothills are covered with dense forests, but the basin of the Orinoco is mainly *llanos*, or level stretches of open prairie, with occasional woods.

The principal river of Venezuela is the *Orinoco*, with innumerable affluents, the main river exceeding 1,600 miles in length from its rise in the southern highlands of the republic to its outflow in the deltaic region of the north-east.

A Franco-Venezuelan Expedition, led by Major Frank Risquez, claimed to have discovered the source of the Orinoco, on Nov. 27, 1951, at 63° 15′ W. long., 2° 18′ N. lat., and about 1,100 metres above sea-level.

The Orinoco is navigable for large steamers from its mouth for 700 miles, and by smaller vessels

as far as the Maipures Cataract, some 200 miles farther up-stream. Dredging operations completed at the beginning of 1954 opened the Orinoco to ocean-going ships, of up to 40 ft. draft, as far as Puerto Ordaz (about 150 miles up-stream), which with the adjacent town of San Felix is now officially known as Ciudad Guayana. Among the many tributaries of the main stream are the Ventuari, Caura and Caroni from the south, and the Apure (with its tributary the Portuguesa), Arauca, Meta, and Guaviare from the west, the Meta and Guaviare being principally Colombian rivers. The upper waters of the Orinoco are united with those of the Rio Negro (a Brazilian tributary of the Amazon) by a natural river or canal, known as the *Casiquiare*. A British scientific expedition travelled in April–May, 1968, by Hovercraft from Manaos in Brazil *viâ* the Rio Negro, Casquiare canal and Orinoco River to Trinidad. The coastal regions of Venezuela are much indented and contain many lagoons and lakes, of which *Maracaibo*, with an area of 8,296 square miles, is the largest lake in South America. Other lakes are Zulia (290 square miles), south-west of Maracaibo, and Valencia (216 square miles) about 1,400 ft. above sea-level in the Maritime Andes. The *llanos* also contain lakes and swamps caused by the river floods, but they are dry in the summer seasons.

The climate is tropical and, except where modified by altitude or tempered by sea breezes, is unhealthy, particularly in the coastal regions and in the neighbourhood of lowland streams and lagoons. The hot, wet season lasts from April to October, the dry, cooler season from November to March.

Government.—On January 23, 1958, the military dictatorship of Maj.-Gen. Marcos Pérez Jiménez, which had lasted since 1953 and covered a period of remarkable economic expansion due to the Venezuelan oil boom, was overthrown by a popular and military uprising. Since 1958 Venezuela has had a freely-elected democratic government. In elections in December, 1958, *Accion Democratica* (A.D.) gained a clear majority and Sr. Rómulo Betancourt of A.D. was elected President. For most of his five-year term of office Sr. Betancourt governed in coalition with the Christian Socialist Party, *Copei.* Further national elections were held on December 1, 1963, in which A.D. retained a reduced majority. Dr. Raúl Leoni of A.D. was elected President. The inauguration of the new Government took place on March 11, 1964. Formation of a broad-based coalition government composed of A.D., U.R.D. (*Union Republicana Democratica*) and F.N.D. (*Frente Nacional Democratico*) was announced on Nov. 5, 1964. The F.N.D. left the Government in 1965 and U.R.D. in April, 1968. A general election held in Dec., 1968, was narrowly won by *Copei* and Dr. Rafael Caldera assumed the Presidency in March, 1969.

Language and Literature.—Spanish is the language of the country. Some Venezuelan literature is of international repute. There are 39 daily newspapers in Venezuela, of which 8 are published in Caracas, 75 weeklies and 23 fortnightlies. There are also 233 other periodicals, mostly monthlies, but including also some appearing once, twice or three times a week.

Education is free and primary education compulsory from the age of 7 years. There are ten universities in Venezuela, five in Caracas and the others in Maracaibo, Mérida, Valencia, Cumaná and Barquisimeto.

Production and Industry.—The produce of Venezuelan forest and fields includes the following: (*a*) Tropical forest region: orchids, wild rubber, timber, mangrove bark, balata gum and tonka beans. (*b*) Agricultural areas: cocoa beans, coffee, cotton, rice, maize, sugar, sesame, groundnuts, potatoes, tomatoes, other vegetables, sisal and tobacco. There is an extensive beef and dairy farming industry. The country does not produce all the grain it requires but is practically self-sufficient for its other food requirements.

The principal industry is that of *Petroleum.* Daily production of the oilfields had declined slightly to 3,708,000 barrels (42 gallons) in 1970. Before the war of 1939–45 over 80 per cent. of the crude oil was exported to Netherlands Antilles refineries. In 1942 small refineries were established in Venezuela, capable of handling about 200,000 barrels daily. The large Shell plant at Punta Cardon went into production in February, 1949, and the Creole refinery at Amuay a year later. Both companies have invested heavily in desulphurization plant to satisfy anti-pollution measures in Eastern U.S.A., whither most of their product goes in the form of fuel oil. Other refineries are being operated at Caripitó, San Lorenzo, Puerto La Cruz, Tucupitó, El Chaure and El Palito. New contracts have been signed for exploitation of petroleum resources in parts of the Maracaibo region. The Venezuelan Government has unified income tax on firms involved in mining and petroleum at 60 per cent. and reformed the basis on which tax is calculated.

Rich iron ore deposits in Eastern Venezuela have been developed and production was 22,000,000 metric tons in 1970. Secondary processes for pelletizing and briqueting ore for export have been installed. The government-owned steel mill at Matanzas in the Guayana uses local iron ore and obtains its electric power from hydro-electric installations on the Caroni River. It produces seamless steel tubes, billets, wire and profiles. The production of more steel products is planned over the next few years. A new mill at Ciudad Guayana for the production of centrifugally-cast iron pipe came into operation at the end of 1970, with an annual capacity of 30,000 tons.

Other industries include petrochemicals, gold, diamonds and asbestos; textiles and clothing; plastics; manufacture of paper, cement, glass and plate glass; beer and other alcoholic beverages; tyres, cigarettes, soap, animal feeding concentrates, non-alcoholic drinks, simple steel products, shoes, tins, jewellery, rope, metal and wooden furniture, sacks, paint and motor-vehicle assembly; preparation of pharmaceutical goods, lard, powdered milk, vegetable oil, flour, biscuits and other foods; fishing and fish-canning; pearl fishing, sanitary ware, electric home appliances, pumps, aluminium products, toys, agricultural machinery, bicycles, electronic components, cosmetics and many others.

Communications.—There are about 39,563 km. of all-weather roads. The State has now acquired all but a very few of the railway lines, whose total length is only some 372 kilometres. Road and river communications have made railways of negligible importance in Venezuela except for carrying iron-ore in the south-east. British, U.S. and European airlines provide Venezuela with a wide range of services. There are three Venezuelan airlines (two of them state-owned) which between them have a comprehensive network of internal lines and also connect Caracas with the United States, Central America, South America, the Caribbean and Europe. In 1971 the Venezuelan state-owned merchant fleet had 14 ships with a total deadweight tonnage of 87,826. Foreign vessels are not permitted to engage in the coast trade. The telegraph, radio-telegraph and radio-telephone services are state-owned. There are one government-controlled and 96 commercial broadcasting stations.

There are four television stations in Venezuela, all in Caracas. One is government controlled. Three television stations have relay transmitters in the interior of the country.

FINANCE

	1969	1970†
	(in millions of *Bs.*)	
Revenue	10,080	10,647
Expenditure	9,689	9,739
† Revised estimates		

National income per head in Venezuela is $U.S.860, the highest in Latin America.

Currency.—The unit of currency is the gold *Bolívar* of 100 *centimos*. The selling rate for foreign exchange for all purposes is *Bs.* 4·50 = U.S. $1. The rates for other currencies fluctuate according to their quotations against the U.S. dollar. Importers of wheat and dried powdered milk can obtain a subsidy of *Bs.* 1·15 per U.S. dollar. There are special buying rates for the proceeds of petroleum, iron ore, coffee and cocoa exports.

TRADE

	1968	1969
Imports	*Bs.*6,699,582,752	*Bs.*6,865,135,557
Exports	13,564,287,405	13,719,104,889

The principal imports are machinery, foodstuffs, durable and non-durable consumer goods, iron, steel and chemicals. The principal exports are petroleum and petroleum products, iron ore, coffee and cocoa, and diamonds.

Trade with U.K.

	1969	1970
Imports from U.K.	£31,035,000	£33,706,000
Exports to U.K.	56,653,000	50,825,000

CAPITAL.—Caracas (3,000 ft.). Population, 1968, 2,064,000. Other principal towns are Ψ Maracaibo (500,000), Barquisimeto (300,000), Valencia (300,000), Maracay (200,000), San Cristobal (150,000), Cumaná (120,000) and Ciudad Guayana (150,000).

FLAG.—Three horizontal bands, yellow, blue, red (with seven white stars on blue band and coat of arms next staff on yellow band). NATIONAL DAY.—July 5.

BRITISH EMBASSY

Edificio La Estancia, Apartado 1246, Ciudad Comercial Tamanaco, Caracas.
Ambassador Extraordinary and Plenipotentiary, His Excellency Sir Donald Charles Hopson, K.C.M.G., D.S.O., M.C., T.D. (1969) £6,925
Counsellors, T. C. Barker; C. T. Brant (*Commercial*).
Defence Attaché, Cdr. D. L. J. Corner, R.N.
1st Secretaries, T. Pidgeon; M. J. F. Duncan (*Information*); M. Alan-Smith (*Commercial*).
Consul, E. Cade-Hughes.
Vice-Consul, G. Hall.

BRITISH CONSULAR OFFICES

There are British Consular Offices at *Caracas*, *Cardon*, *Maracaibo*, *Puerto La Cruz* and *Valencia*.

British Council Representative, S. C. Alexander, Venezuelan-British Cultural Institute, Avenida de Los Jabillos 21, La Florida (Apartado 1246), Caracas.

VIETNAM
SOUTHERN ZONE

President, Nguyen van Thieu, *appointed* June 19, 1965; re-elected Sept. 3, 1967.
(*Presidential election pending* (Oct. 3, 1971) *with no other candidate*).
Vice-President, Air Vice Marshal Nguyen cao Ky.
Prime Minister, Gen. Tran Thiem Khiem.

VIETNAM EMBASSY AND CONSULATE
18 Victoria Road, W.8
[01–937–3765]
Ambassador Extraordinary and Plenipotentiary, His Excellency Le-Ngoc-Chan (1967).
Counsellor, Than Trong Nghia.
Defence Attaché, Lt.-Col. Cao Xuan Ve.
1st Secretary, Duong Hong Duc (*Cultural and Consular*).
2nd Secretary, Vinh Ninh.
3rd Secretaries, Miss Nguyen Minh Nguyet (*Economic*); Le Trung Nghia; Miss Nguyen-Thi Phong-Lan (*Protocol*).
Attaché, Nguyen Van Dieu.

The Southern Zone has an area of 66,281 sq. miles and a population (U.N. estimate, 1969) of 17,867,000. Rice and rubber are the chief products. Trade in 1968 (excluding trade financed or assisted under American aid programmes) was: Imports £158,600,000; Exports £9,160,000.

Trade with U.K.

	1969	1970
Imports from U.K.	£4,372,000	£4,382,000
Exports to U.K.	615,000	446,000

Following the devaluation of sterling in 1967 exchange rates for the *piastre* were: Official rate *VN*$192=£1, but most transactions attract a subvention for economic consolidation, making the overall rate *VN*$283=£1.

On October 23, 1955, a referendum showed a large majority in favour of the deposition of the former Chief of State, Bao Dai, and the election of Ngo dinh Diem to his place. The latter was accordingly proclaimed Chief of State on October 26, and his first act was to declare South Vietnam a Republic of which he became the President. An elected constituent assembly became the first Legislative Assembly of the Republic of Vietnam on Oct. 26, 1956. A new national assembly was elected on August 31, 1963, President Diem having been re-elected for a second term of 5 years in April, 1961. On November 1, 1963, the Government of President Diem was overthrown by a military *coup d'état* during which the President was killed. General Duong-Van-Minh assumed power as Chairman of the Military Revolutionary Council and Head of State, but the former position was wrested from him on January 30 by General Nguyen-Khanh who assumed the function of Prime Minister and on Aug. 17 the Presidency.

The Military Revolutionary Council was dissolved on August 27, to be followed by the Provisional Steering Committee led by three Army generals. This Committee in turn dissolved on October 26 and on November 4 Tran van Huong became Prime Minister and Phan Khac Suu Head of State.

On December 18, the Armed Forces Council was created under General Khanh and became the real power. On December 20, the A.F.C. dissolved the High National Council and on Jan. 27, 1965, Huong was forced to resign under pressure from the A.F.C. and the Buddhists. On February 16, the A.F.C. nominated Phan Huy Quat as Prime Minister. Then on February 22 General Khanh himself was overthrown by a *coup d'état* and, under the temporary leadership of General Nguyen van Thieu, the A.F.C. lasted only until May 5 before dissolving itself and handing back control of the country to the civilian government under Mr. Quat. The latter, with the Head of State (Mr. Suu) resigned under pressure on June 12 and on June 19, full power reverted to the armed forces in the form of a National Leadership Committee led by General Thieu. Elections to a constituent assembly were held on Sept. 11, 1966, and a new democratic constitution was promulgated on April 1, 1967. Presidential elections were held on Sept. 3, 1967.

INDO-CHINA

At his presidential inauguration on October 30, 1967, President Nguyen Van Thieu proclaimed the Second Republic of Vietnam. Mr. Tran Van Huong, Prime Minister since May 25, 1968, was succeeded in office by Gen. Tran Thiem Khiem on Sept. 1, 1969. The Government of the Republic of Vietnam in Saigon is recognized by the United Kingdom, the United States and other members of the United Nations as the legal government of Vietnam.

CAPITAL.— Ψ Saigon, population (1968), 2,500,000, of which 25,000 were thought to be foreigners. Other principal towns are Ψ Danang (500,000) and Hué (150,000). Saigon and Danang are the main ports.

FLAG.—Orange with three horizontal red stripes in centre. NATIONAL DAY.—November 1.

BRITISH EMBASSY
25 Dai Lo Thong Nhut, Saigon
Ambassador Extraordinary and Plenipotentiary, His Excellency John Oscar Moreton, C.M.G., M.C. (1969) £6,925
Counsellor, C. M. James (*Consul-General*).
Defence, Naval and Military Attaché, Col. J. L. Waddy, O.B.E.
Air Attaché, Gp. Capt. J. W. J. Leggatt, O.B.E.
1st Secretaries, D. K. Middleton (*Head of Chancery*); M. J. Thompson; N. F. J. Mercer.
2nd Secretaries, A. J. Ward (*Commercial and Consul*); F. D. Robins; D. V. Odgear; R. A. Fulton.
NORTHERN ZONE
President, Ton Duc Thang, *elected* Sept. 24, 1969
Prime Minister, Pham Van Dong (1955).
Minister of Foreign Affairs, Nguyen duy Trinh.

VIETNAMESE WORKERS' (= Communist) PARTY
Chairman, Le Duan.
Politbureau of the Central Committee, Hoang Van Hoan; Le Duc Tho; Hoang Quoc Viet; Le Duan; Le Thanh Nghi; Nguyen Chi Thanh; Nguyen Duy Trinh; Pham Hung; Pham Van Dong; Truong Chinh (*full members*); Tran Quoc Hoan; Van Tien Dung (*alternate members*).
Secretariat of the Central Committee, Le Duan (*1st*); Hoang Anh; Le Duc Tho; Nguyen Van Tran; To Huu; Le Van Luong; Pham Hung.

The Northern Zone (north of the 17th parallel) has an area of approximately 63,000 sq. miles and a population (U.N. estimate, 1969) of 21,340,000. The capital is Hanoi (800,000) and the chief port is Ψ Haiphong (367,000). The chief crop is rice, of which the production in 1961 was claimed to be 4,600,000 tons. No figures have been given since. The chief industrial products are coal and cement. The production of apatite (phosphate) is increasing, and with Chinese and Soviet aid some new factories have been built to produce consumer goods.

The *régime* in the north styles itself the Government of the Democratic Republic of Vietnam. Power is wielded by the *Lao Dong* (or Workers') Party which is Communist in character, and which can exert its influence through another mass organization known as the Fatherland Front (which some years ago superseded the "Vietminh"). The policy of the northern *régime* is to work for unification of north and south, whilst in the meantime it strives to remould the political and economic life of the north on Communist lines. A five-year plan started in 1961. Elections to the "Second National Assembly" were held in the north in April 1964. The *régime* has diplomatic relations with the U.S.S.R., China and other states of the Sino-Soviet bloc, but very few other countries recognize it. FLAG.—Red, with yellow five-point star in centre.

There is a British Consulate General at Hanoi.

YEMEN
(Yemen Arab Republic)
Council of the Presidency, Qadi Abdul Rahman al-Iriani (*Chairman*); Ahmad Muhammad Noman; Muhammad Ali Othman.
Prime Minister, Muhsin al Aini.

YEMENI EMBASSY
41 South Street, W.1
[01-499-5246]
Minister (vacant).
Counsellor (*Chargé d'Affaires*), Assayed Abdul Wahab Al-Shamy.

Yemen, "the land on the right hand" (of Syria) and the *Arabia Felix* of the ancients, occupies the S.W. corner of Arabia between Asir and Southern Yemen, with an estimated area of 74,000 square miles and a population of 5,000,000 (1969). It extends inland to the borders of the Hadramaut. The highlands and central plateau of Yemen, and the highest portions of the maritime range, form the most fertile part of Arabia, with an abundant and regular rainfall.

Trade.—The main exports are coffee, cotton, oil-grains, salt, hides, and raisins. Trade agreements have been concluded with a number of countries. Aden is an important centre for Yemeni exports and imports. The chief port of the Yemen is Ψ Hodeida (Ahmedia) which now has deep water quays, able to accommodate ocean going vessels. Imports from U.K. in 1970 were valued at £1,887,000.

The ruins of Marib, the ancient Sabæan capital and its dam are in the Yemen.

Government.—Under the first permanent constitution for the Yemen Arab Republic (Dec. 28, 1970) there are a President and a Consultative Council of 179 members, 20 chosen by the President and the remainder elected by general franchise. The Council is responsible for the election of a Presidential Council of not more than 5 members, which selects the Prime Minister. Elections under the new constitution were planned to be held in 1971.

A 14-member Cabinet headed by Muhsin al Aini took office on Feb. 5, 1970.

CAPITAL.—Taiz (pop. about 20,000); Sana'a has about 60,000 inhabitants. Other cities of the Yemen are Ψ Hodeida, Ibb, Mocha and Beidha.

FLAG.—Horizontal bands of red, white and black, with 5-point green star in centre of white band. (Adopted Dec., 1962).

BRITISH EMBASSY
Sana'a
Ambassador Extraordinary and Plenipotentiary, His Excellency John Michael Edes (1971).
1st Secretary, E. H. Noble (*Head of Chancery*).

YEMEN
(People's Democratic Republic of Yemen)
Presidential Council, Salim Robaya Ali (*Chairman*); Ali Nasser Hassaniya; Abdul Fattah Ismail.

Prime Minister, Ali Nasser Hassaniya.
Deputy Prime Minister and Minister of Finance, Mahmoud Abdullah Oshaish.
Foreign Affairs, Mohammed Saleh al Aulaqi.
There are 9 other departmental Ministers.

EMBASSY
95 Park Lane, W.1
[01-499-2536]
Ambassador Extraordinary and Plenipotentiary, His Excellency Fadhle Ahmed Sallami (1970).
Minister Plenipotentiary (*Cultural*), Abdullah Ahmed Muheirez.
2nd Secretary, Hussein Saleh Fadhli.
3rd Secretaries, Saeed Hadi Awad Aulaqi; Ali As'ad Muthana (*Consular*).
Attaché, Abdullah Awad Aulaqi.

Area and Population.—The Democratic Republic of Yemen lies at the southern end of the Arabian peninsula, having a frontier with the Yemen Arab Republic, and a coastline extending 700 miles from the Red Sea eastwards along the Gulf of Aden. The area is largely composed of mountains and desert. Rainfall is generally scarce and unpredictable. The population outside Aden is concentrated in the fertile districts. In the more extensive desert and near-desert areas nomadic communities depend on their livestock for a livelihood.

Included in the State are the offshore islands of Perim (in the Bab-el-Mandeb Straits), Kamaran (area, 70 sq. miles) in the Red Sea, and Socotra, formerly part of the sultanate of Qishn and Socotra, now merged in the People's Republic. The area of the People's Democratic Republic is 117,000 sq. miles, with a population estimated at 1,250,000 in 1970. The population of Aden alone (75 sq. miles) is about 150,000. The twin volcanic peninsulas of Aden and Little Aden are linked by a sandy strip of coastline. The towns are Tawahi, Crater, Maalla (built on land reclaimed from the sea), Khormaksar and Sheikh Othman and Madinet al Shaab (the administrative capital).

Government.—The People's Republic of South Yemen was set up on Nov. 30, 1967, bringing to an end 129 years of British rule in Aden and some years of protectorate status in the hinterland. Its name was changed to People's Democratic Republic of Yemen on Nov. 30, 1970. Territory of the Re-

public is that of the former Federation of South Arabia and the Eastern Aden Protectorate, consisting of the State of Aden and some 17 sultanates and amirates in which effective power had passed to the National Liberation Front during August and September, 1967. It is now divided into six Governorates. Negotiations held between the British Government and representatives of the N.L.F. at Geneva from Nov. 21–29, 1967, ended in agreement on financial aid to South Yemen for civil and military purposes for a period of six months from the date of independence. Evacuation of British military forces which had begun in April, 1967, was completed on Nov. 29.

The Secretary-General of the National Liberation Front, Mr. Qahtan as-Shaabi, who had been appointed President from Nov. 30, 1967, held office until June 22, 1969, when he was deposed in a bloodless *coup d'état* and replaced by a Presidential Council led by Salem Robeya Ali. Under a constitution promulgated on Nov. 30, 1970, a Supreme People's Council of 101 members was appointed in May, 1971.

Kuria Muria Islands.—The Kuria Muria Islands, which had been administered by Gt. Britain from Aden although 200 miles distant from Yemen territory, were retroceded to the Sultanate of Oman on Nov. 30, 1967.

Production.—Agriculture is the main occupation of the inhabitants of the 60,000 square miles of the Republic, outside Aden State. This is largely of a subsistence nature, sorghum, sesame and millets being the chief crops, and wheat and barley widely grown at the higher elevations. Of increasing importance, however, are the cash crops which have been developed since the Second World War, by far the most important of which is long-staple cotton, which is now the country's major export, and revenue from which averages about £2,000,000 annually.

Owing to lack of rainfall, cultivation is largely confined to fertile valleys and flood plains on silt built up and irrigated in the traditional manner. Of recent years, however, these traditional methods have been augmented and replaced by the use of modern earth-moving machinery and pumps. Irrigation schemes, designed to replace some of the more important traditional structures with permanent installations, are now being undertaken. Nearly all the fruit and vegetables grown in the Republic are marketed in Aden, through which passes annually some 30,000 tons of locally produced fruit and vegetables worth up to £600,000. The trade of Aden is mainly transhipment and *entrepôt*, the port serving as a centre of distribution to and from neighbouring territories. Transit trade is mainly in textiles, gums and resins; grains and flour; coffee; tea; hides and skins; raw cotton and cotton-seed and cheap consumer goods. The traditional status of free port was abolished in December, 1970.

Trade with U.K.

	1966	1970
Imports from U.K...	£6,650,000	£4,978,000
Exports to U.K.....	14,619,000	9,626,000

Before the closure of the Suez Canal, because of its favourable geographical position and its efficient service to ships, Aden was one of the busiest oil bunkering ports in the world, handling some 500 ships a month. The closing of the Canal has reduced this to about 120 ships a month. The British Petroleum refinery exports about 5,600,000 tons of petroleum products annually. In the main harbour, cargo handling for larger vessels is by lighter, but wharves at Maalla can accommodate alongside vessels up to 300 feet in length and 18 feet in draught. Aden has 140 miles of good roads.

Finance and Currency.—In the financial year 1969–70 revenue was estimated at about £14,000,000 and expenditure £19,000,000. Currency is the South Yemen *dinar* (SYD), the total circulation of which is about £25,000,000.

Communications.—There are no railways in the Republic. A system of undeveloped but motorable roads links the towns and villages outside Aden. There is an international airport at Aden (Khormaksar) into which nine international airlines operate.

CAPITAL.—Aden (population, 150,000).

FLAG.—A tricolour, red, white and black horizontal bands, with a triangle of light blue at the hoist pointing towards the fly and charged with a five pointed red star.

NATIONAL DAYS.—Independence Day, Nov. 30; Revolution Day, Oct. 14.

BRITISH EMBASSY
Khormaksar, Aden.

Ambassador Extraordinary and Plenipotentiary, His Excellency Arthur Roy Handasyde Kellas, C.M.G. (1970)...............................£6,925
1st Secretaries, J. A. N. Brehony; W. H. Harper (*Consul*).
2nd Secretary, D. R. MacLennan.
Vice-Consul, B. A. Lane.

YUGOSLAVIA
(Socijalistička Federativna Republika Jugoslavije)

President of the Republic, President of the League of Communists of Yugoslavia, Chairman of the National Defence Council and Supreme Commander of the Armed Forces, Josip Broz Tito, *assumed office,* Jan. 14, 1953, *re-elected for 4 years,* 1954, 1958, 1963, 1967 and July 29, 1971 (5 yrs.).
President of the Federal Assembly, Dr. Marjan Brecelj (*acting*).
President of the Federal Executive Council, Mitja Ribičič.
President of the Socialist Alliance of the Working People of Yugoslavia, Veljko Milatović.
Vice-Presidents of the Federal Assembly, Blazo Djuričić; Peko Dapčević; Milos Minić; Džavid Nimani; Josip Djerdja.
Vice-Presidents of the Federal Executive Council, Alexsandar Grličkov; Dr. Jakov Sirotković; Mišo Pavićević
Secretary of the Federal Executive Council, Rajko Gagović.
Foreign Affairs, Mirko Tepavac.
Defence, Nicola Ljubičić.
Internal Affairs, Luka Banović (*acting*).
Finance, Muhamed Hadžić (*acting*).
Economy, Dr. Borivoje Jelić.
Foreign Trade, Muhamed Hadžić.
President of the Constitutional Court, Blazo Jovanović.

LEAGUE OF YUGOSLAV COMMUNISTS
President, Josip Broz Tito.
Presidium, J. Broz Tito; K. Avramović; V. Bakarić; D. Belovski; S. Bijelić; J. Blažević; B. Borojević; R. Bugarin; K. Crvenkovski; D. Culafić; N. Dizdarević; E. Dobardžić; S. Dolanc; I. Dolničar; S. Dorojnski; R. Dugonjić; P. Gaži; K. Gligorov, F. Hodža; E. Kardelj; S. Kavčić; M. Kelemen; L. Koliševski; S. Krajger; S. Kranjc; Z. Liker; N. Ljubičić; C. Mijatović; S. Milosavlevski; M. Pečuljić; J. Pečenović; L. Perović; H. Pozderac; M. Ribičič; P. Stambolić; M. Stanojević; B. Šiljegović; K. Siroka, B. Soškić; M. Todorović; S. Tomić; M. Tripalo; V. Vlahović; A. Zulfićari; V. Žarković.

Executive Bureau, J. Broz Tito; V. Bakarić; K. Crvenkovski; N. Dizdarević; S. Dolanc; S. Dorojnski; K. Gligorov; F. Hodža; E. Kardelj; C. Mijatović; M. Pečuljić; B. Šoškić; M. Todorović; M. Tripalo; V. Vlahović.

YUGOSLAV EMBASSY IN LONDON
25 Kensington Gore, S.W.7
[01–589–3400]
Ambassador Extraordinary and Plenipotentiary, His Excellency Dobrivoje Vidić (1970).
Minister-Counsellor, Vojislav Pekić.
Counsellors, Svetozar Marković (*Economic*); Milan Zupan (*Press*); Milenko Ristić (*Consular*).
Defence Attaché, Col. Svetozar Oro.
Asst. Defence Attaché, Capt. Dragoljub Milanović.
1st Secretary, Branko Vuletić.
2nd Secretary, Tomislav Janković.
3rd Secretary, Jovan Premeru (*Press*).
Consulate, 19 Upper Phillimore Gardens, W.8.

Area and Population.—Yugoslavia is a Federation comprising the Socialist Republics of Serbia, Croatia, Slovenia, Montenegro, Bosnia and Herzegovina, and Macedonia. Serbia includes the Socialist Autonomous Provinces of the Vojvodina and Kosovo. In July, 1946, Pelagosa and adjacent islands with all territory east of the line known as the *French Line* in Istria (including Pola and Fiume) were ceded by Italy to Yugoslavia. By an agreement concluded in London on Oct. 5, 1954, between Yugoslavia, Italy, the United Kingdom and the United States, Zone B of the Trieste Territory was transferred to the civil administration of Yugoslavia, under whose military administration it had been since 1945. Zone B, an area of 200 square miles with a population of 73,500, included the towns of Kopar (Capodistria) Pitan (Pirano) and Novi Grad (Cittanuova). The area has now been divided between the Republics of Slovenia and Croatia. The area of Yugoslavia is estimated at 255,804 square kilometres (98,725 square miles) and the population in April, 1971, at 21,500,000. As a result of the war there was a decrease of nearly 2,000,000 in the population of Yugoslavia, and this loss has only recently been made up.

Government.—On Nov. 29, 1945, the Constituent Assembly of Yugoslavia at a joint session of the Skupšatina and the House of Nationalities, proclaimed Yugoslavia a Republic. In January, 1953, a new Constitution became effective, under which two houses (the Federal Council and Council of Producers) were established. Elections to these houses were held in November, 1953 and March, 1958.

On April 7, 1963, a new Constitution was proclaimed under which the official name of the country was changed to "The Socialist Federal Republic of Yugoslavia." The existing two Councils of the Federal Assembly were replaced by five Chambers of 120 members each (Federal Chamber, Economic Chamber, Educational-Cultural Chamber, Social Welfare and Health Chamber, and Organizational/Political Chamber), plus a Chamber of Nationalities of 70 members. A Constitutional Court was created. Elections to the new Federal Assembly were held in 1963 and in April, 1967.

In 1969 the Federal Assembly was reconstructed by the abolition of the Federal and Organizational/Political Chambers and the addition of one new chamber, the Social/Political. All Chambers continued to have 120 members each except the Chamber of Nationalities which doubled its size to 140. Elections to this Assembly were held in April, 1969. Several amendments to the Constitution were made in 1971. The most important formed a new ruling body called the Presidency. The intention is that its members, three from each republic and two from each of the two provinces, will take it in turns to become President of the Republic for a period of 12 months each. President Tito will however have the title of Life President.

Defence.—The Army, Navy and Air Force on a peace footing consist of 289,000 officers and men.

Religion and Education.—The Orthodox, Roman Catholic, Protestant, Islamic and Judaic faiths are recognized by the State. The 1953 Census revealed that 2,127,875 of the population were without religion, 6,984,686 were Orthodox, 5,370,760 Catholic, 157,702 Protestant, 61,274 other Christians, 2,090,380 Moslem, 2,565 Jews, 495 other non-Christians, 10,096 undecided and 130,740 unknown. The Church is separated from the State. All religious instruction in schools has been forbidden since January 1952. Priests are allowed to teach in churches. Eight years' elementary education is compulsory and all education is free. In 1969–70 there were 14,043 elementary schools with 116,895 teachers and 2,854,579 pupils and 2,974 secondary schools (including adult and special schools) with 33,702 teachers and 801,169 pupils. In addition, in the 1970–71 academic year there were 13 art academies with 483 teachers and 2,225 pupils, 10 high schools with 557 teachers and 7,456 pupils, and 119 higher schools with 3,986 teachers and 79,325 pupils. There are eight universities: Belgrade, Zagreb, Ljubljana, Sarajevo, Skopje, Novi Sad, Niš and Priština.

Language and Literature.—The languages of the country are Serbo-Croat, Slovenian and Macedonian, all South-Slav tongues. Serbo-Croat predominates and is the language of the Federal Government. In Serbia, Macedonia and Montenegro the Cyrillic script is used and in the rest of the country the Latin; Hungarian, Rumanian, Albanian, Italian, Slovak and Ruthenian are also used in certain districts. The desire for the political union of the South Slavs led to a cultural unity and a revival of Slav literature. There are 4 Serbian daily newspapers in Belgrade, 2 Slovene dailies in Ljubljana (Laibach), 2 Croat dailies in Zagreb, 2 dailies in Novi Sad, one in Hungarian, 2 dailies in Rijeka, one in Italian and daily papers at Skopje, Sarajevo, Priština, Split, Maribor and Osijek.

Production and Industry.—About 50 per cent. of the population is engaged in agriculture, although in recent years industry has expanded rapidly and in-

dustrial production has grown sevenfold since 1939. Recent emphasis has been on the integration of small industrial enterprises into more efficient complexes. In agriculture the main emphasis is on increased investment in mechanization and fertilizers in the large socially-owned agricultural combines but now the private sector is being encouraged to mechanize and become more efficient and small size tractors, farm machinery and implements are being supplied.

The main crops are wheat and maize, of which the yields in 1970 were 3,790,000 and 6,961,000 tons respectively. The forest areas produced 17,051,000 cubic metres of timber in 1969. According to Yugoslav official estimates, the livestock population at the beginning of 1970 was approximately as follows: cattle, 5,029,000; sheep, 8,974,000; pigs 5,544,000; poultry, 40,854,000. Minerals are an important source of wealth, particularly in the central and south-eastern regions. Estimated production in 1970 included the following ('000 tons): Hard coal 650; brown coal 9,900; lignite 17,600; electrolytic copper 90; refined lead 98; iron ore. 2,700; pig iron 1,268; steel (total) 2,224; aluminium 47; zinc 63; mercury 540 and crude petroleum 2,900.

Communications.—In 1970 there were approximately 6,562 miles of standard and narrow gauge railway and approximately 56,315 miles of roads of widely varying quality. There were also 506,000 telephones in use in the country. The principal Ψports on the long Adriatic seaboard of Yugoslavia are Rijeka, Šibenik, Split, Zadar, Ploče, Dubrovnik, Bar, Kotor (Carraro) and Koper. A new port is still under construction at Bakar. The Danube forms a great commercial highway and the tributary rivers Sava and Tisa provide other shipping routes.

FINANCE

	1968	1969
	'000 Dinars	
Revenue	10,829,000	8,905,000
Expenditure	11,554,000	9,399,000

Since Jan. 24, 1971, the rate of exchange has been 36 *dinars=* £1 (*see also* p. 84).

Trade with U.K.

	1969	1970
Imports from U.K.	£31,251,000	£45,608,000
Exports to U.K.	24,799,000	21,725,000

The chief exports to the United Kingdom are meat and meat products, furniture and timber. The main imports from the United Kingdom are machinery of all kinds, iron and steel, chemicals, wool tops and metal manufactures.

CAPITAL.—Belgrade, population (Greater Belgrade, 1971), 1,204,000. Other towns are Zagreb (602,000); Skopje (388,000); Ljubljana (258,000); Sarajevo (292,000); Novi Sad (214,000); Priština (153,000); Ψ Split (152,000); Ψ Rijeka (133,000); Titograd (99,000).

FLAG.—Five-point red star outlined by narrow yellow stripe, on a ground of three horizontal bars, blue, white and red. NATIONAL DAY.—November 29.

BRITISH EMBASSY

Generala Ždanova 46, Belgrade.

Ambassador Extraordinary and Plenipotentiary, His Excellency Dugald Leslie Lorn Stewart, C.M.G. (1971).....................................£9,000
Counsellors, P. McKearney (*Economic and Commercial*); W. Bentley.
Defence Attaché, Col. C. M. Moir, O.B.E.
Naval and Air Attaché, Wing-Cdr. D. O. Luke.
1st Secretaries, T. J. Clark; (*Information*); M. L. Tait; G. C. Gullan (*Commercial*); R. Burns (*Labour*) (*resident at Athens*); Miss D. A. Garton, M.B.E. (*Admin. and Consular*).
2nd Secretaries, P. A. Rennie; P. R. Bull (*Commercial*).
3rd Secretaries, D. W. Berry; P. A. McDermott; W. J. Robertson.
Attaché, N. P. Carter.

BRITISH CONSULAR OFFICES
There are British Consular Offices at *Belgrade, Zagreb* and *Split.*

────

British Council Representative, C. W. Fyfield, O.B.E. Generala Ždanova 34, Belgrade. There are also a centre and library at *Zagreb.*

EUROPEAN FREE TRADE ASSOCIATION (EFTA)

Member States: Austria, Denmark, Norway, Portugal, Sweden, Switzerland, The United Kingdom.

Following the unsuccessful attempt to create a European Free Trade Area linking the E.E.C. with other members of the O.E.E.C., the seven European states above came together in 1959 to form the European Free Trade Association. The EFTA Convention became effective on May 3, 1960, and just over a year later, on June 26, 1961, Finland became an associate member. The Faröe Islands sponsored by Denmark, were included in the EFTA area from January 1, 1968. Iceland applied for full membership in November, 1968, and acceded to the Association and to the Finland—EFTA Agreement on March 1, 1970.

The Convention defines the objects of the Association as (1) to promote economic expansion in the area of the Association and in each member state; (2) to ensure that trade between member states takes place in conditions of fair competition; (3) to avoid significant disparity between member states in the conditions of supply of raw materials produced within the area; and (4) to contribute to the harmonious development and expansion of world trade and to the progressive removal of barriers to it.

Members agreed to reduce progressively their tariffs on imports of industrial goods originating in the Area with a view to their complete elimination by January 1, 1970. They also undertook to abolish quantitative restrictions on imports of goods from the free trade area. Provision was made for alterations in these timetables and in May, 1963, when tariffs had been reduced to 50 per cent. of the original rates, members agreed to bring forward the date when tariffs and quotas would be finally eliminated to December 31, 1966. Since that date therefore the member countries of the Association have constituted a virtually complete industrial free trade area. There is no common external tariff for the Association, each member country being free to fix the level of its tariffs against countries outside the area. The Convention includes rules governing the origin of goods manufactured in the area. It also contains provisions relating to the " rules of competition "—government subsidies, restrictive business practices, etc. There are special provisions relating to trade in agricultural and fish products.

EFTA Trade With U.K.

	1969	1970
Imports from U.K.	1,041,379,000	£1,283,535,000
Exports to U.K.	1,247,443,000	1,411,861,000

The Council of EFTA consists of one ministerial or official representative from each member country. Each state has a single vote and recommendations must normally be unanimous. Decisions of the Council are binding on member countries.

Secretary-General, Sir John Coulson, K.C.M.G.(*U.K.*)
9–11 rue de Varembé, 1211 Geneva 20.

EUROPEAN COMMUNITY

The Six Member States: Belgium, France, Germany, Italy, Luxemburg, The Netherlands.

The beginnings of the European Community date from May 9, 1950, when Robert Schuman, France's Foreign Minister, proposed that France and Germany should pool their coal and steel industries under an independent (" supranational ") High Authority, in a Community open to the membership of any other European country wishing to join. Not only Germany, but also Italy, Belgium, the Netherlands, and Luxemburg accepted this invitation.

The Coal and Steel Community (ECSC), Common Market and Euratom share a single institutional framework: a Commission, Council of Ministers, Parliament and Court of Justice. The core of the Community policymaking process is the " dialogue " between the Commission, which initiates and implements policy, and the Council of Ministers, which takes major policy decisions. The beginnings of democratic control are exercised by the European Parliament, while the Court of Justice ensures the rule of law and is the final arbiter in all matters arising from the Community Treaties.

Since the start of the Common Market and Euratom in 1958, the Parliament and Court of Justice have been common to all three Communities. Up to July, 1967, each Community had its own executive body (the EEC and Euratom Commissions, and the ECSC High Authority) and its own Council of Ministers.

In April, 1965, the Six signed a treaty providing for the merger of the three executive bodies in a single Commission and the three Councils in a single Council, with a view to the eventual merger of the three Communities themselves. The merger treaty came into force on July 1, 1967; the single Commission and single Council then took office. They enjoy the same powers under the three Community Treaties as did their predecessors.

On December 1 and 2, 1969, the Heads of State or Government of the Six met at the Hague and decided on the completion, strengthening, and, provided that other European countries wished to accept the Treaties of Rome, enlargement of the Community. They instructed the Commission to draw up a plan for economic and monetary union, and the Foreign Ministers to report by the end of July on possible moves towards political unification. They also resolved to intensify the co-ordination of research and development programmes.

In accordance with the Hague decisions the Council of Ministers agreed in April, 1970, that as from 1975 the Community would have its own revenue, independent of national contributions. The Foreign Ministers agreed (May, 1970) to hold formal political consultations twice a year.

In June, 1970, the Six invited Britain, the Irish Republic, Denmark and Norway to open negotiations on June 30 at Luxemburg on their applications to join the Community. Negotiations continued in 1971 and were concluded with the United Kingdom Government for all major questions by the end of June; on July 8, H.M. Government issued a White Paper on the results. Negotiations with the other applicant countries continued.

The Commission

On July 1, 1970, the Commission was reduced from 14 members to nine, two each from Germany, France and Italy, and one each from Belgium, the Netherlands, and Luxemburg. If the four applicant countries join, the number will be brought back to 14, with two seats each for Britain, France, Germany, and Italy and one each for the other members.

The members of the Commission are appointed by agreement among the six member governments for a four-year renewable term; the president and vice-presidents are appointed from among the members for a two-year term, also renewable.

The members of the Commission are pledged to independence of the governments and of national or other particular interests. They accept joint responsibility for their decisions, which are taken by majority vote.

In addition to being the initiator of Community action and having specific powers, the Commission acts as a mediator between the member governments in Community affairs and is the guardian of the Community Treaties.

Commission of the European Communities

23–27 Avenue de la Joyeuse Entrée, Brussels 4.

President, ~~Franco Malfatti~~ (*Italian*). DR SICCO MANSH

Vice-Presidents, Sicco Mansholt (*Dutch*); R. Barre (*French*); Wilhelm Haferkamp (*German*).

Members, Albert Coppé (*Belgian*); Jean-François Deniau (*French*); Albert Borschette (*Luxemburger*); Ralf Dahrendorf (*German*); Altiero Spinelli (*Italian*).

The Commission maintains information offices in London (23 Chesham Street, S.W.1), Washington (Suite 707, 2100 M Street, N.W., Washington, D.C. 20037), New York (2207 Commerce Building, 155 East 44th Street, N.Y. 10017) and in other cities.

The Council of Ministers

2 Rue Ravenstein, Brussels 1.

This consists of ministers from each member government, the ministers concerned depending on the subject under discussion. It is the Community's main decision-taking body but its authority is not as great in ECSC matters as in those relating to the Common Market and Euratom. The powers of the Commission are proportionately greater under the ECSC Treaty. For coal and steel, decisions are usually by majority vote; on Common Market and Euratom matters decisions usually had to be unanimous in the early stages, but most decisions can now be taken by a qualified majority vote. For certain vital questions, however, unanimity is still required. (Admission of new members is not decided by the Council, but by a unanimous decision of the member governments.) Although the Council is the Community's ultimate decision-taking body, in almost all cases it can act only on the basis of proposals submitted by the Commission. The Council acts by issuing (*a*) " regulations " which are generally and directly binding throughout the Community; (*b*) " decisions " which bind only those addressed (normally member states); and (*c*) " recommendations ", which have no binding force. The meetings of the Council are prepared by a Committee of Permanent Representatives of the member states.

The Presidency of the Council is held in rotation for periods of six months. The presidency was held by Italy during the last six months of 1971, and was due to pass to Luxemburg for the first half of 1972, and to the Netherlands for the second half of 1972.

European Parliament

Secretariat: Centre Européen, Kirchberg, Luxemburg.

The European Parliament consists of 142 members nominated by the national parliaments of the member countries—36 members each from France, Germany and Italy, 14 each from Belgium and the Netherlands and 6 from Luxemburg. Set up under the terms of the ECSC Treaty of 1952, its authority

was extended by the Treaty of Rome 1957 to cover also the European Economic Community and Euratom. The Parliament must be consulted on all major issues and can force the dismissal of the Commission by a vote of no confidence. In April, 1970, the Council agreed that as part of the completed financial arrangements giving the Community its own direct revenue, the Parliament would have after 1975 a degree of control over the Community's budget, the exact degree of such control to be reviewed in 1972. The Treaty provides for the Parliament's direct election and a scheme for this was drawn up by the Parliament in May, 1960. For nearly ten years little progress was made in this field but in 1970 the question again came under active consideration. The members of the Parliament have formed four political groups— *Christian Democrat* (52 in March 1970), *Socialist* (38), *Liberal* (24), and *European Democratic Union* (French Gaullist), 18. There are also seven Italian Communists and three independents.

If the four applicant countries join, the Parliament will be enlarged to 208, the "Big Four" having 36 seats each, Belgium and the Netherlands 14 each, the other three candidates ten each and Luxemburg six.

President, Mario Scelba (*Italian Christian Democrat*) (1970).

European Court of Justice

12, Rue de la Côte d'Eich, Luxemburg.

The European Court superseded the Court of Justice of ECSC and is common to the three European Communities. It exists to safeguard the law in the interpretation and application of the Community treaties, to decide on the legality of decisions of the Council of Ministers or the Commission and to determine violations of the Treaties. Cases may be brought to it by the member States, the Community institutions, firms or individuals. Its decisions are directly binding in the member countries. The seven judges of the court are appointed by the member Governments in concert and hold office for 6 years, being eligible for re-appointment.

Judges, R. Lecourt (*President*); R. Monaco; A. Trabucchi; A. Donner; J. J. Mertens de Wilmars; P. Pescatore; J. Kutscher.

Advocates-General, K. Roemer; A. Dutheillet de Lamothe.

Registrar, A. Van Houtte.

If the enlargement of the Community to include the United Kingdom, Ireland, Denmark and Norway is ratified it was expected that these countries would join the Community on Jan. 1, 1973. In that event they will each hold one seat on the Council of Ministers; the United Kingdom will nominate two members of the Commission and the other three countries one each; the United Kingdom will send 36 members to the European Parliament and the other three countries 10 each. The size of the Court of Justice had not been settled by July, 1971.

EUROPEAN COAL AND STEEL COMMUNITY

This, the first of the European Communities, was established in 1952. Since then it has abolished for coal, steel, iron ore and scrap, customs duties, quantitative restrictions, the dual pricing system whereby prices charged on exported coal or steel differed from those charged to home consumers, currency restrictions and discrimination in transport rates based on the nationality of customers and the special frontier charges which made international transport of these goods within the Community dearer than transport within national frontiers. It

has applied rules for fair competition and a harmonized external tariff for the whole Community.

In the period 1952 to 1968 Community steel production rose rapidly from 41·9 to 99 million tons. The coal industry, however, after expanding initially in conditions of acute energy shortage, found that a growing share of the energy market was being won by oil. The task of the ECSC thus came to be to ensure the orderly retreat of coal at a price which would avoid social or economic dislocation. So far, since the start of the crisis in 1957, the Community's coal industry has lost a third of its labour force. The ECSC has been especially active in meeting the social problems raised by such changes. Its adaptation aid from 1958 to end-1970 amounted to $150 million and was matched by an equivalent contribution from the six governments and had by that time helped to re-train and resettle 429,000 ex-miners and steelworkers. It has also made grants and loans for industrial redevelopment, increasing this activity sharply during the coal and steel crises of 1967. Its housing programmes have provided 113,000 houses for coal and steel workers.

Decisions of the European Commission in ECSC matters are directly binding on the industries concerned. The Commission now supervises the smooth working of the common market in ECSC products, ensures that the Treaty rules of fair competition are observed, stimulates investment and research, and aids workers threatened with unemployment. The Council of Ministers instructed the Commission in Nov., 1969, to work out proposals for a Community energy policy as soon as possible.

EUROPEAN ECONOMIC COMMUNITY (THE COMMON MARKET)

Discussions were held at Messina, Sicily, in 1955 between the foreign ministers of the six member states of ECSC (Belgium, France, Germany, Italy, Luxemburg and The Netherlands) on proposals for further advances towards economic integration in Europe, and after intensive study of these proposals, a treaty was signed at Rome on March 25, 1957, setting up the European Economic Community.

The Treaty aimed to lay the foundations of an enduring and closer union between the European peoples by gradually removing the economic effects of their political frontiers. The Common Market was established during a transition period of twelve years which ended on Dec. 31, 1969. The Treaty provides for the elimination of customs duties and quotas in trade between member states; the establishment of a common customs tariff and a common trade policy towards third countries; the abolition of the obstacles to free movement of persons, services and capital between member states; the inauguration of common policies for agriculture and transport; the establishment of a system ensuring that competition shall not be distorted in the Common Market; the co-ordination of economic policies; the harmonization of social and economic legislation to the extent necessary in order to enable the Common Market to work; the creation of a European Social Fund in order to improve the possibilities of employment for workers and to contribute to the raising of their standard of living; the establishment of an Economic and Social Committee which must be consulted on major proposals, consisting of representatives of employers, workers, consumers and other groups; the establishment of a European Investment Bank intended to aid investment in underdeveloped areas and help to finance modernization; and the association of overseas countries and territories with the Community with a view to increasing trade and to

x British representative on steering e/tte
Sir Douglas Allen

pursuing jointly their effort towards economic and social development.

To date, this programme has been put into effect as follows:

Reduction of trade barriers.—A first 10 per cent. reduction in customs duties between member countries took place on January 1, 1959. Decisions taken by the Council of Ministers in May, 1960, and July, 1963, resulted in a speeding up of the rate of tariff cutting. On May 11, 1966, the Council of Ministers agreed that the abolition of internal duties should be completed on July 1, 1968, and this advanced target date was met. Quota restrictions on trade within the Common Market were completely removed on January 1, 1962. A determined effort is being made to speed up the removal of non-tariff barriers to trade, *e.g.* different safety regulations and technical specifications.

E.E.C. Trade with U.K.

	1969	1970
Imports from U.K.	£1,410,239,000	£1,753,835,000
Exports to U.K.	1,609,896,000	1,822,264,000

Common external tariff.—The Common Market has a common external tariff which came fully into effect on July 1, 1968. A first 30 per cent. move of notional duties towards the common external tariff was made at the end of 1960, on the basis of a notional common tariff reduced by 20 per cent. A second 30 per cent. move towards the common tariff took place on July 1, 1963.

In international tariff and trade negotiations in the GATT framework (such as the Kennedy Round), the Community is represented by the Commission, which negotiates under a mandate from the Council of Ministers.

Trade between the member countries of the Common Market increased from $6,864 million in 1958 to $43,301 million in 1970, an increase of 548 per cent. Community exports to the rest of the world increased from $15,911 million in 1958 to $45,198 million in 1970, an increase of 184 per cent. Imports from the rest of the world in 1970 were $45,621 million, leaving the Community as a whole with a deficit of $423 million, against $25 million in 1969 and a surplus of $1,725 million in 1968.

Free movement of labour.—Freedom of movement for workers has been achieved within the Common Market, and those who work in member countries other than their own are ensured of rights equal to those of local workers, and of full transferability of social security benefits. They enjoy equal treatment in applying for jobs and receive priority over workers from non-member countries. There is, however, a shortage of trained labour in all Community countries at present.

Services.—The right of Community firms to establish businesses in member countries other than their own is being progressively freed, as is the right of Community citizens to engage in professional activities in member countries other than their own. In parallel with this programme, the harmonization of professional qualifications is being achieved.

Capital.—So far unconditional and complete freedom of movement has been achieved for direct investments, transfers of personal funds and emigrants' remittances, short and medium term commercial loans and the buying and selling of stocks and shares. For other transactions, such as capital issues, there is conditional liberalization. Progress is being made towards equalizing access to domestic capital markets within the Six.

Rules for Fair Competition.—The Common Market Treaty bans agreements which prevent, restrain or distort competition and, in particular, price-fixing, market-sharing, restriction of production or of technical development and discriminatory supply conditions if they are likely to affect trade between member states. The abuse of a dominant position in the market by a firm or firms is also banned. Implementing regulations adopted by the Council have caused some 36,000 restrictive agreements to be registered with the Commission. Decisions banning or authorizing particular agreements have begun to be taken, and a body of case-law is being established.

Agriculture.—The basic machinery for a common organization of agricultural markets throughout the Community was established by decision of the Council of Ministers in January 1962. It involved the setting of target prices, support buying, levies on imports, and export rebates. Community funds can be allotted for the modernization of farming and the improvement of agricultural productivity in the Community. The common agricultural policy came into effect in July, 1962, for grains, eggs and poultry, pigmeat, fruit and vegetables, and wine. It was extended in September, 1964, to rice, and in November 1964 to beef, veal, and dairy produce, thus covering 90 per cent. of total Community agricultural output.

Under a decision reached in December, 1964, common price levels throughout the Community came into effect in July, 1967, for grains, pigmeat, and eggs and poultry. Further decisions taken on July 24, 1966, established common marketing regulations and common price levels for fruit and vegetables, sugar, dairy produce and fats and oils; to come into force between July 1, 1967, and July 1, 1968. On July 24, also, common price levels were fixed for beef and veal, milk and other dairy produce.

On July 1, 1967, grains, pigmeat, eggs and poultry reached the full single-market stage, thus bringing half the Community's farm production under the common agricultural policy's marketing and financial provisions. On May 29, 1968, the Six agreed on the pricing system for dairy produce and beef and veal in the single-market stage from July 1, 1968, having failed to agree by the original planned date of May 1. The Ministers of Agriculture did not accept the Commission's recommendation that the common prices for milk and butter be reduced in order to diminish the Community's mounting surplus of butter; they did, however, agree on measures to limit the common commitment to finance the dairy policy and to maintain differential prices between some member states as a temporary measure.

In December, 1968, the Commission published medium-term proposals (the " Mansholt Plan ") for restoring supply/demand balance in the dairy, sugar, fruit, vegetable, and oil and fats markets, and long-term proposals for the reform of Community farming. The latter plan provided for extended pensions for older farmers, retraining programmes for younger men, grants to enable land to be taken out of production and for co-operative holdings, extensive improvements in farm capital and in the provision of new industries and services in regions affected by the decline of farming. Under these plans the Community farm population would be halved by 1980 to 5,000,000.

In March, 1971, the Council agreed on Community part-financing of pensions for farmers retiring between the ages of 55 and 65 and other measures to reduce the number of small, scattered farms and to improve agricultural efficiency. In May the Commission tabled other proposals to hasten retraining of younger farmers and farm workers and their children, and to encourage the establishment of industry in agricultural areas.

Economic Policy.—Member States are required by the Treaty to consider their economic policies as matters of common interest, and to consult with each other and the Commission in order to concert

these policies. The Commission undertakes annual economic forecasts, quarterly economic surveys, and monthly business surveys to help towards this end. A strong tradition of consultation between those responsible for economic policy in the member countries has been established. A Monetary Committee bringing together senior officials from national treasuries and central banks has met regularly since 1959 to discuss Community monetary and economic problems. Similar Committees on Short Term Economic Policy and Budgetary Policy have been established, as has a Committee of Governors of Central Banks, and a Committee on Medium Term Economic Policy, which in May, 1966, published its first 5-year programme, covering the period 1966–1970; this programme was adopted by the member states in February, 1967. In April 1964, the Council of Ministers adopted for the first time a series of recommendations to member governments on short term economic policy to meet the current threat of inflation in the Community. Steps are being taken to harmonize the tax policies of the member states. In February, 1967, the Council agreed to adopt a single system of value-added tax from 1970 with the harmonization of the applicable rate to be introduced later. In June, 1967, the E.E.C. Commission published a draft plan for the harmonization of direct taxes on debenture interest and dividend.

In February, 1970, the Six set up a common $2 billion reserve fund to provide help for up to six months to a member state in short-term economic difficulties, and later in the year agreed to set up a fund of similar amount for medium-term assistance (for up to five years). In February, 1971, the Council agreed to Commission proposals drawn up in the light of the Werner Report (Oct., 1970) by a committee set up under the chairmanship of the Luxemburg Prime Minister. In the first phase of the plan, to run to December 31, 1973, the Six agreed to narrow the margins of fluctuation of their currencies, to set up a $2,000 million medium-term reserves pool, to co-ordinate short and medium-term budget policies to move towards a joint position in international money questions, to step up the harmonization of some taxes and to encourage regional development. In May, 1971, a surge of speculation led to the temporary floating of the *Deutschemark* and *guilder*.

Industrial Policy.—On March 21, 1970, the Commission published proposals (the " Colonna Plan ") for a joint industrial policy calling for the removal of technical barriers to trade; the throwing open of public contracts to any firm in the Community; the creation of a European company statute; the encouragement, where efficiency would be improved, of industrial mergers across Europe's frontiers; the strengthening of Community regional policy; the extension of the European Social Fund; and the improvement of business education.

Transport.—The Treaty aims to establish a common policy on transport, with common rules for international transport within the Common Market, covering road, rail and inland water transport. Rates for freight which discriminate as to the national origin or destination of goods transported are to be eliminated within the transitional period. In June, 1965, the Council adopted a Commission proposal setting out the principles of a common policy to be put into force by the end of the transition period. The member governments did not agree on the implementation of these principles, but late in 1967 and early in 1968 a number of steps were agreed, on controlling social and economic conditions in intra-Community transport, especially road-haulage. Other mea-

sures covering railways were agreed by the Commission later in 1968 and early in 1969.

Social Policy.—Under the Treaty, member states agree upon the necessity to promote improvement of the living and working conditions of labour so as to permit the equalization of such conditions in an upward direction. They also cooperate closely on matters relating to employment, labour legislation and working conditions, occupational training, social security, industrial accidents and diseases, industrial hygiene and trade union law. Equal pay for men and women is also required and a regulation was agreed in December, 1961, by which all discrimination was to be abolished by the end of 1964. The Commission's most important instrument of social policy is the European Social Fund which promotes employment facilities and the mobility of workers within the community by means of vocational retraining, resettlement and other aids. It provides 50 per cent. of expenditure undertaken by the Six governments in the productive re-employment of workers. In July 1970, the Council agreed to reform the fund and to increase its size and scope for action. An ultimate expenditure of $250 million annually is envisaged, against $55 million in 1971.

Regional development policy. Proposals have been made by the Commission for an overall policy on regional development in the Community. A major instrument of this policy is the European Investment Bank with a capital of $1,000 million, which aids investment in the Community's underdeveloped regions and helps modernization projects or new activities of general Community interest. While recognizing that regional development must remain chiefly a matter for national governments, in October, 1969, the Commission proposed that there should be an annual review of the situation in those regions where development plans are needed; that a permanent committee on regional development should be set up, composed of representatives of the Six and the Commission; and that there should be a Community interest rebate fund for regional development and a loan guarantee system. In June, 1971, the Commission published proposals to hasten the retraining of farmers and their children and to encourage the establishment of industry in farming areas.

The Community's external relations.—Trade or association agreements have been made with Greece (1962), Turkey (1964), Spain (1970), Yugoslavia (1970), Iran (1970), Tunisia and Morocco (1969), Israel (1970) and Malta (1971). Talks have begun with Lebanon, Algeria, U.A.R., Argentina and Uruguay.

The 1963 agreement between Community member countries and 18 independent African states was replaced in July, 1969, with another, also signed at Yaoundé and in broadly similar terms; it came into effect on Jan. 1, 1971, and will expire on Jan. 31, 1975. Under the new agreement the Community is providing $1,000 million in grants and loans for the five-year period for these countries and dependencies of Community countries. In 1968 the Community signed association agreements with Kenya, Uganda and Tanzania; these were renewed in 1969 and came into effect on Jan. 1, 1971 (expiring Jan. 31, 1975).

Scientific and technical collaboration.—In March, 1970, Britain and eight other European countries accepted an invitation by the Six to start discussing concrete projects for Europe-wide scientific and technical collaboration. Seven working parties have so far been set up covering data-processing, telecommunications, new forms of transport, metallurgy, pollution, meteorology and oceanography.

Enlargement.—The question of possible enlargement of the Community has played an important part in its development since the Autumn of 1961 when Britain, the Irish Republic, Denmark and Norway first sought membership, and Austria, Sweden, Switzerland, Spain and Cyprus sought association with the Community. The negotiations were vetoed by France in January, 1963. In May, 1967, Britain, the Irish Republic and Denmark formally submitted applications for Community membership. In July Norway followed suit and Sweden announced that it would seek to participate in the enlargement of the Community on terms compatible with its neutrality. These applications made very slow progress and appeared to come to a standstill when in December, 1967, France declared that Britain's economy would have to be strengthened before negotiations could begin. But shortly after taking office as President of France, Georges Pompidou stated in July, 1969, that there was no objection in principle to the admission of Britain to the Community. At the Hague "summit" meeting in December 1969 (*see above*) the Six decided that provided that the completion of the Community was not prejudiced, and provided that the Community was strengthened to provide for enlargement, then the entry of other European countries would be desirable. After deciding on a common negotiating position, the Six invited Britain and the other applicants to begin negotiations for membership, and these were opened in Luxemburg on June 30, 1970.

Contributions to the EEC budget were originally fixed in the following proportions: France, Italy and Germany, each 28 per cent.; Belgium and Netherlands, each 7·9 per cent.; Luxemburg 0·2 per cent.

As from January 1, 1971, the Six will pay all their farm levies (less 10 per cent. to cover administrative costs) and a part of their customs duties into the Community fund. The scale, starting at 50 per cent. of the total of levies and customs duties in 1971, will gradually increase so that in 1975 100 per cent. of both duties and levies will be paid in. From 1971 to 1974 inclusive, any deficit will be made up under a national percentage key as follows: Belgium, 6·8;

Germany, 32·9; France, 32·6; Italy 20·2; Luxemburg, 0·2 and Netherlands, 7·3 per cent. From 1975 onwards, the Six will finance the deficit by turning over to the Community fund the revenue from a rate up to a maximum of 1 per cent. of the value-added tax. Nevertheless, the total contributions of the member states will continue to be limited under a "moving key" until the end of 1977. The application of these arrangements to Britain and the other candidate countries was one of the main issues in the membership negotiations.

For 1970 alone, Community financing was covered by percentage contributions as follows: Belgium, 8·25; Germany, 31·70; France, 28·00; Italy 21·50; Luxemburg, 0·20; Netherlands, 10·35. These will also form the basis of the "moving key" referred to above.

EUROPEAN ATOMIC ENERGY COMMUNITY   (EURATOM)

A second treaty, arising from the Messina discussions between the ECSC powers on additional means of co-operation, was signed in Rome on March 25, 1957, setting up the European Atomic Energy Community. The task of *Euratom*, defined in detail in the Treaty, is to create within a short period the technical and industrial conditions necessary to utilize nuclear discoveries and especially to produce nuclear energy on a large scale. Other sections of the Treaty cover the establishment and growth of nuclear industries, the procurement, ownership and control of nuclear materials, matters affecting health and safety, including training, and external relations, the stimulation of scientific research and the training of specialists, to assure through a Supply Agency adequate supplies of nuclear fuels, the supervision of the nuclear common market, inspection and control of the use of fissile material, and the safeguarding of both workers and the population at large by laying down basic standards for the protection of health.

U.K. DELEGATION TO THE EUROPEAN COMMUNITIES

51–52 Avenue des Arts, 1040 Brussels.
Ambassador (vacant).
Minister, K. C. Christofas, C.M.G., M.B.E.

NORTH ATLANTIC TREATY ORGANIZATION

Headquarters: Brussels 1110, Belgium.
The North Atlantic Treaty was signed on April 4, 1949, by the Foreign Ministers of twelve nations. The twelve are Belgium, Canada, Denmark, France, Iceland, Italy, Luxemburg, the Netherlands, Norway, Portugal, the United Kingdom and United States. Greece and Turkey acceded to the Treaty in 1952 and the Federal Republic of Germany in 1955. The North Atlantic Council is the highest authority of the Alliance and is composed of permanent representatives of the fifteen member countries. It meets at ministerial level at least twice per year. The permanent representatives head national delegations of advisers and experts.
Permanent U.K. Representative, His Excellency Sir Edward (Heywood) Peck, K.C.M.G. (1970)
£14,000
The senior military authority in NATO is the Military Committee composed of a Chief-of-Staff of each member country except France. The Military Committee, which is assisted by an international military staff, functions in permanent session with permanent military representatives and is responsible for higher strategic direction throughout the North Atlantic Treaty area.

Secretary General, J. M. A. H. Luns (*Netherlands*).
Deputy Secretary General, M. Pansa Cedronio (*Italy*).
Assistant Secretaries General, Jörg Kastl (*Fed. Republic of Germany*) (*Political Affairs*); Kenneth Nash (U.K.) (*Defence Planning and Policy*); A. Tyler Port (U.S.A.) (*Defence Support*); Prof. Gunnar Randers (*Norway*) (*Scientific Affairs*).
Supreme Allied Commander, Europe, Gen. Andrew J. Goodpaster (U.S.).
Supreme Allied Commander, Atlantic, Admiral Charles K. Duncan (U.S.).
Allied Commander-in-Chief, Channel, Admiral Sir Edward Ashmore, K.C.B., D.S.C. (U.K.).

SOUTH-EAST ASIA TREATY ORGANIZATION

Headquarters: Bangkok, Thailand.

A *South-East Asia Collective Defence Treaty* was signed on Sept. 8, 1954, by representatives of Australia, New Zealand, Pakistan, the Philippines, Thailand, France, the United Kingdom and the United States. The Treaty consists of eleven Articles. The parties undertake mutual defence responsibilities in the area of the Treaty. Other articles deal with mutual economic assistance, including technical assistance, designed to promote economic progress and social well-being; the rights and obligations of

the parties under the Charter of the United Nations; accession of further states; and define the area to which the Treaty applies. Member countries are represented on a Council of Ministers which meets annually to review and determine policy. The meetings are held in a different member nation capital each year. Between Council Meetings, Council Representatives meet at least monthly in Bangkok to supervize the work of the Organization. The Council Representatives are the Ambassadors to Thailand of 7 member countries and a Thai Foreign Affairs Officer of ambassadorial rank. The United States executed the Treaty with the understanding that its recognition of the effect of aggression and armed attack apply only to Communist aggression, but agreed to consult with the other signatories in the event of any other armed attack.

In a declaration of principles, *The Pacific Charter*, the Treaty powers uphold the principle of equal rights and self-determination of peoples. They will earnestly strive by every peaceful means to promote self-government and to secure the independence of all countries whose peoples desire it and are able to undertake its responsibilities. They will continue to co-operate in the economic, social and cultural fields in order to promote higher living standards, economic progress and social well-being in the region. They are determined to prevent or counter by appropriate means any attempt in the Treaty area to subvert their freedom or destroy their sovereignty or territorial integrity.

Secretary-General, Lt.-General Jesus M. Vargas.

CENTRAL TREATY ORGANIZATION

Headquarters: Ankara, Turkey

A mutual security and defence treaty was concluded between Turkey and Iraq at Baghdad on Feb. 24, 1955. Three further states, the United Kingdom, Iran, and Pakistan signed the *Baghdad Pact* later in the same year. The United States, although not a full member of the Council, participates in an observer capacity, is a member of all major committees, and contributes an equal share to the international staff and budget, as well as a large share of economic and military assistance. Iraq formally withdrew from the Pact on March 24, 1959, and the title Central Treaty Organization (C.E.N.T.O.) was adopted on Aug. 21, 1959.

Secretary-General, Turgut Menemencioğlu (1968).

U.K. MEMBERSHIP OF INTERNATIONAL ORGANIZATIONS

Estimated total cost of United Kingdom subscriptions, etc., to international organizations in 1971–72 was £44,669,379, compared with a total estimate in 1970–71 of £41,266,908.

To Political and Military Organizations.—Central Rhine Commission, £11,370; Central Treaty Organization, £55,000; C.E.N.T.O. Military Agencies, £18,000; Commonwealth Secretariat, £195,000; Council of Europe, £776,000; International Supervisory Commissions on Indo-China, £315,000; N.A.T.O. Secretariat, £1,093,000; N.A.T.O. Military Agencies, £8,600,000 (1970–71 £7,300,000); South East Asia Treaty Organization, £80,000; S.E.A.T.O. Military Agencies, £16,000; South Pacific Commission, £76,260; United Nations Organization, £4,000,000; Western European Union, £80,000.

To Economic and Social Organizations.—European Free Trade Association, £225,000; General Agreement on Tariffs and Trade, £150,300; International Bureaux (Protection of Industrial, Literary and Artistic Property, and Weights and Measures), £64,930; Colombo Plan Bureau, £4,510; Customs Co-operation Council, £34,000; International Criminal Police Organization, £20,550; International Telecommunications Union, £160,000; International Labour Organization, £1,189,000; Organization for Economic Co-operation and Development, £807,689; UNESCO, £945,000; World Health Organization, £1,886,000; Universal Postal Union, £25,000.

To Scientific Organizations.—European Nuclear Energy Agency, £75,000; European Organization for Nuclear Research, £8,215,000; European Organization for Space Research, £5,100,000 and Space Application Studies, £2,265,000; International Atomic Energy Agency, £399,000; Atomic Energy Projects, £1,240,000 (1970–71, £995,000); N.A.T.O. Scientific Schemes, £415,000; World Meteorological Organization, £81,300; European Molecular Biology Conference, £80,000; International Cancer Research Agency, £100,000.

To Transport Organizations.—Eurocontrol (traffic control of high-flying aircraft), £3,000,000; Inter-Governmental Maritime Consulative Organization, £183,000; International Civil Aviation Organization, £258,000; South Pacific Air Transport Council, £560,000; and smaller subscriptions.

To Agricultural, Fishery and Food Organizations.—Commonwealth Agricultural Bureaux, £208,000; International Sugar Council, £22,000; Wheat Council, £15,000; Coffee Organization, £12,500; U.N. Food and Agriculture Organization, £1,175,000; and a number of smaller subscriptions.

THE ARCTIC OCEAN

The Arctic Ocean consists of a deep sea over 2,000 fathoms, on the southern margin of which there is a broad continental shelf with numerous islands. Into this deeper sea there is only one broad channel, about 700 miles, between Greenland and Scandinavia. Behring Strait is only 49 miles wide and 27 fathoms deep. The southern boundary of the Arctic Ocean is the Wyville-Thomson and Faeroe-Icelandic submarine ridge, which separates the North Atlantic from the Norwegian and Greenland Seas. The Norwegian Deep lies between Norway and Jan Mayen and Iceland; it exceeds 1,500 fathoms. The Greenland Deep, of similar depth, lies between Spitsbergen and Greenland. These two depressions are separated by a somewhat deeply submerged ridge from the east of Jan Mayen to Bear Island, south of Spitsbergen. A shallow ridge from the north-west of Spitsbergen to Greenland separates the Greenland Sea from the deep North Polar Basin. This extends from the north of Spitsbergen and Franz Josef Land to the north of the New Siberia Islands and of the North American Arctic Archipelago. Another more shallow depression is Baffin Bay, less than 1,000 fathoms. This is separated from the North Atlantic by a submarine ridge. Barent's Sea, between Spitsbergen, Norway and Novaya Zemlya, and the Kara Sea, between Novaya Zemlya and the Siberian coast, are respectively below 200 and 100 fathoms. The total area of the Arctic Sea is about 5·5 million square miles, of which 2·3 million square miles are probably covered with floating ice.

BRITISH PASSPORT REGULATIONS

Applications for United Kingdom passports must be made on the forms obtainable at any of the Passport Offices (addresses given below) or at any Employment Exchange. Applications for passports required in less than ten days should not be taken to such local offices.

London.—Clive House, Petty France, S.W.1.
Liverpool.—India Buildings, Water Street, Liverpool, 2.
Newport, Mon.—Olympia House, Dock Street.
Peterborough.—Passport Office, Westwood, Peterborough.
Glasgow.—1st Floor, Empire House, 131 West Nile Street, Glasgow, C.1.

Hours. The above offices are open Mon-Fri. 9 a.m. to 4.30 p.m. The Passport Offices are also open for cases of special emergency (e.g. death or serious illness) arising outside normal office hours between 4.30 p.m. and 5.30 p.m. (6.30 p.m. in London); Saturdays 10.00–12.00, and in London on Sundays and Public Holidays between 10 a.m. and noon (except Christmas Day).

To facilitate the issue of passports applicants are recommended to make personal application to any one of the above mentioned offices. If it is not possible to make personal application at one of the Passport Offices or Employment Exchanges, completed forms of application should be sent to one of the five Passport Offices, with photographs, supporting documents and the fee of £5, in the form of a Cheque or Postal Order which should be crossed and made payable to the Passport Office.

Persons resident in Northern Ireland may apply in person to the Foreign and Commonwealth Office Passport Agency, 1st Flr., Marlborough House, 30 Victoria Street, Belfast, or by post to the Passport Office, Glasgow; citizens of the United Kingdom and Colonies resident in the Irish Republic should make applications to the Visa Section, British Embassy, 30 Merrion Square, Dublin.

A Passport cannot be issued or renewed by the Foreign and Commonwealth Office on behalf of a person already abroad; such person should apply, in a foreign country, to the nearest British Mission or Consulate, or, within the British Commonwealth outside the United Kingdom of Great Britain and N. Ireland, to the nearest British Passport issuing authority.

United Kingdom Passports are granted:—
(i) To citizens of the United Kingdom and Colonies.
(ii) To British subjects without citizenship.
(iii) To British Protected Persons.

Passports are available for ten years unless otherwise stated. They are not available beyond ten years from the original date of issue. Thereafter, or if at any time the Passport contains no further space for visas, a new Passport must be obtained.

A Passport including particulars of the holder's wife is not available for the wife's use when she is travelling alone. A wife's particulars may only be added at the time of issue of a passport.

Children who have reached the age of sixteen years require separate Passports. Their applications must be signed by one of their parents.

The application must be countersigned by a Member of Parliament, Justice of the Peace, Minister of Religion, Doctor, Lawyer, Bank Officer, established Civil Servant, Public Official, Police Officer or any person of similar standing personally acquainted with the applicant. The applicant's birth certificate and other evidence in support of the statements made in the application must be produced.

In the case of children under the age of 16 requiring a separate passport, an application should be made by one of the parents on form (B).

If the applicant for a Passport be a British subject by naturalization or registration, the Certificate of Naturalization or registration must be produced with the application.

British Passports are generally available for travel to all countries. The possession of a Passport does not, however, exempt the holder from compliance with any Immigration Regulations in force in British or foreign countries, or from the necessity of obtaining a visa where required.

PHOTOGRAPHS

Duplicate unmounted photographs of applicant (and his wife, if to be included in the Passport) must be sent. These photographs should be printed on thin paper and must not be glazed on the reverse side. They should measure not more than 2½ in. by 2 in. or less than 2 in. by 1½ in., and should be taken full face without a hat.

RENEWAL OF PASSPORTS

Applications for the renewal of United Kingdom passports must be made on Form D.

British Visitors' Passports

A simplified form of travel document is available for British subjects (Citizens of the United Kingdom and Colonies) wishing to pay short visits (not exceeding three months) to certain foreign countries, viz.

ANDORRA; AUSTRIA; BELGIUM; DENMARK†; FINLAND†; FRANCE (incl. CORSICA); GREECE (& THE GREEK ISLANDS); W. GERMANY (incl. West Berlin by air only); ICELAND; ITALY; LIECHTENSTEIN; LUXEMBURG; MONACO; NETHERLANDS; NORWAY†; PORTUGAL (incl. MADEIRA & AZORES); SAN MARINO; SPAIN(incl.BALEARIC & CANARY ISLANDS); SWEDEN†; SWITZERLAND; TURKEY.

†Length of stay restricted to three months in any nine months in Nordic Group Countries (including Finland and Iceland) as a whole. Holders may also pay short visits to Canada, Gibraltar and Malta. A British Visitor's Passport must be valid for three months beyond the last day on which the visitor will be in Canada.

A fee of £1·50 is charged for the issue of a British Visitors' Passport, which is valid for 12 months, cannot be amended and is not renewable; on expiry application should be made for a new passport if required. Particulars of an applicant's wife and/or children under 16 years can be included at the time of issue at no extra cost. A child of 8 years of age and over is eligible to hold a British Visitors' Passport. Applications for, or including, a person under 18 years of age (unless married or serving in H.M. Forces) must be countersigned by the legal guardian.

British Visitors' Passports are obtainable by application on Form VP (from any Employment Exchange). Applicants in England, Scotland and Wales should take the completed form in person to any Employment Exchange which will normally issue the passport without further delay ; applicants in Northern Ireland to any local office of the Ministry of Health and Social Services. British Visitors' Passports are not obtainable from the Passport Offices. Two recent passport photographs will be required of the applicant and of his wife, if to be included; photographs of children are not required. Size of photographs must be 2 in × 1½ in. (see also PHOTOGRAPHS above). No visas are required on British Visitors' Passports.

Applicants must also produce for the purpose of identification a N.H.S. Medical Card, birth certificate or retirement pension book.

984

CURRENCIES OF THE WORLD

Country	Monetary Unit	Denominations in Circulation	
		Notes	Coins
Afghanistan	Afghani of 100 Puls	Afghanis 1,000, 500, 100, 50, 20, 10	Afghanis 5, 2, 1; Puls 50, 25
Albania	Lek of 100 Qintar	Leks 100, 50, 25, 10, 5, 3, 1	Lek 1; Qintars 50, 20, 10, 5
Algeria	Dinar of 100 Centimes	Dinars 100, 50, 10, 5	Dinars 1; Centimes 50, 20, 10, 5, 2, 1
Angola	Escudo of 100 Centavos	Escudos 1,000, 500, 100, 50, 20	Escudos 20, 10, 2½, 1; Centavos 50, 20, 10
Argentina	Peso of 100 Centavos or 100 Old Pesos	Pesos 1,000, 500, 100, 50, 10, 5, 1	Old Pesos 25, 10, 5, 1; Centavos 50, 20, 10, 5, 1
Australia	Dollar of 100 Cents	$A 20, 10, 5, 2, 1	Cents 50, 20, 10, 5, 2, 1
Austria	Schilling of 100 Groschen	Schillings 1,000, 500, 100, 50, 20	Schillings 50, 25, 10, 5, 1; Groschen 50, 10, 5, 2, 1
Bahamas	Bahamian Dollar of 100 Cents	B.$ 100, 50, 20, 10, 5, 3, 1; Cents 50	B.$ 5, 2, 1; Cents 50, 25, 15, 10, 5, 1
Bahrain	Dinar of 1,000 Fils	Dinars 10, 5, 1, ½, ¼; Fils 100	Fils 500, 250, 100, 50, 25, 10, 5, 1
Belgium	Belgian Franc of 100 Centimes	Frs. 5,000, 1,000, 500, 100, 50, 20	Frs. 100, 50, 10, 5, 1; Centimes 50, 25
Bermuda	Dollar of 100 Cents	$50, 20, 10, 5, 1	Cents 50, 25, 10, 5, 1
Bolivia	Peso of 100 Centavos	Pesos 100, 50, 20, 10, 5, 1	Peso 1; Centavos 50, 20, 10, 5
Brazil	Cruzeiro of 100 Centavos	Cruzeiros 100, 50, 10, 5, 1	Cruzeiro 1; Centavos 50, 20, 10, 5, 2, 1
British Honduras	British Honduras Dollar of 100 Cents	$20, 10, 5, 2, 1	Cents 50, 25, 10, 5, 1
Brunei	Brunei Dollar of 100 Sen	$100, 50, 10, 5, 1	Sen 50, 20, 10, 5, 1
Bulgaria	Lev of 100 Stotinki	Léva 20, 10, 5, 2, 1	Léva 2, 1; Stotinki 50, 20, 10, 5, 2, 1
Burma	Kyat of 100 Pyas	Kyats 20, 10, 5, 1	Pyas 50, 25, 10, 5, 1
Burundi	Burundi Franc	Frs. 5,000, 1,000, 500, 100, 50, 20, 10	Frs. 10, 5, 1
Cameroon (Federal Republic of)	Franc C.F.A.	Frs. 5,000, 1,000, 500, 100	Frs. 100, 50, 25, 10, 5, 2, 1
Canada	Dollar of 100 Cents	Dollars 1,000, 100, 50, 20, 10, 5, 2, 1	Dollars 1; Cents 50, 25, 10, 5, 1
Cape Verde Islands	Escudo of 100 Centavos	Esc 500$00, 100$00, 50$00, 20$00	Esc 10$00, 5$00, 2$50, 1$00, 50$, $20, $10, $05
Ceylon	Rupee of 100 Cents	Rupees 100, 50, 10, 5, 2	Rupees 5, 2, 1; Cents 25, 10, 5, 2, 1
Chile	Escudo of 100 Cóndores or 100 Centésimos (=1,000 Pesos or 1,000 Milésimos)	Escudos 100, 50, 10, 5, 1, 0·50	Escudos 0·10, 0·05, 0·02
China	Renminbi or Yuan of 10 Jiao or 100 Fen	Yuan 10, 5, 2, 1; Jiao 5, 2, 1	Fen 5, 2, 1
Colombia	Peso of 100 Centavos	Pesos 500, 50, 20, 10, 5, 2, 1	Centavos 50, 20, 10, 5, 1
Comoro Archipelago	Franc C.F.A.	Frs. 5,000, 1,000, 500, 100, 50	Frs. 20, 10, 5, 2, 1
Congolese Republic	Zaire of 100 Makuta or 10,000 Sengi	Zaires 5, 1; Makuta 50, 20, 10	Makuta 5, 1; Sengi 10
Costa Rica	Colon of 100 Céntimos	Colones 1,000, 500, 100, 50, 10, 5	Colones 2, 1; Céntimos 50, 25, 10, 5
Cuba	Peso of 100 Centavos	Pesos 100, 50, 20, 10, 5, 1	Centavos 40, 20, 5, 2, 1
Cyprus	Cyprus Pound of 1,000 Mils	£5, £1; Mils 500, 250	Mils 500, 100, 50, 25, 5, 3, 1
Czechoslovakia	Koruna (Crown) of 100 Halérů (Heller)	Korunas 100, 50, 25, 20, 10, 5, 3	Korunas 5, 3, 1; Heller 50, 25, 10, 5, 3, 1
Dahomey (Republic of)	Franc C.F.A.	Frs. 5,000, 1,000, 500, 100, 50	Frs. 100, 25, 10, 5, 2, 1
Denmark	Krone of 100 Öre	Kroner 500, 100, 50, 10	Kroner 5, 1; Öre 25, 10, 5, 2, 1
Dominican Republic	Peso of 100 Centavos	Pesos 100, 500, 100, 50, 20, 10, 5, 1	Peso 1; Centavos 50, 25, 10, 5, 1
Ecuador	Sucre of 100 Centavos	Sucres 1,000, 500, 100, 50, 20, 10, 5	Sucre 1; Centavos 50, 20, 10, 5
Ethiopia	Ethiopian Dollar of 100 Cents	Dollars 500, 100, 50, 20, 10, 5, 1	Cents 50, 25, 10, 5, 1
Falkland Islands	Pound of 100 Pence	£5, £1; 50p	As in U.K.
Faröe Islands	Krone	Kr. 100, 50, 10*	As in Denmark
Fiji	Fiji Dollar of 100 Cents	$20, 10, 5, 2, 1; Cents 50	Cents 20, 10, 5, 2, 1
Finland	Markka of 100 Penniä	Markkas 100, 50, 10, 5, 1	Markkas 10, 5, 1; Penniä 50, 20, 10, 5, 1

* Danish notes are also legal tender.

Country	Monetary Unit	Denominations in Circulation	
		Notes	Coins
Formosa.........	New Taiwan Dollar	NT$ 100, 50, 10, 5, 1; Cents 50, 10, 5, 1	$5; $1; Cents 50, 20, 10
France	Franc of 100 Centimes (1 Franc = 100 old Francs)	Francs 500, 100, 50, 10, 5	Francs 10, 5, 1, ½; Old Francs 2, 1; Centimes 20, 10, 5, 1
French Community (Republics of Gabon, Congo, Central Africa and Chad)	Franc C.F.A.	Frs. 5,000, 1,000, 500, 100, 50, 20, 10, 5	Frs. 100, 50, 25, 10, 5, 2, 1
French Guiana....	Franc of 100 Centimes	Frs. 100, 50, 10, 5	Frs. 10, 5, 1, ½; Centimes 20, 10, 5, 1
Gambia (The).....	Dalasi of 100 Bututs	Dalasis 25, 5, 1	Dalasi 1; Bututs 50, 25, 10, 5, 1
Germany (East)....	Mark der Deutschen Demokratischen Republik (M.) of 100 Pfennig	M. 100, 50, 20, 10, 5	M. 20, 10, 5, 2, 1; Pfennig 50, 20, 10, 5, 1
Germany (Federal Republic of)	Deutsche Mark of 100 Pfennig	D.M. 1,000, 500, 100, 50, 20, 10, 5	D.M. 10, 5, 2, 1; Pfennig 50, 10, 5, 2, 1
Ghana	New Cedi of 100 Pesewa	New Cedis 10, 5, 1	New Pesewas 20, 10, 5, 2½, 1, ½
Gibraltar.........	Pound of 100 pence	£5, £1	As in U.K.
Greece...........	Drachma of 100 Lepta	Drachmae 1,000, 500, 100, 50	Drachmae 20, 10, 5, 2, 1; Lepta 50, 20, 10, 5
Guadeloupe.......	Franc of 100 old Metropolitan Francs or 100 Centimes	Frs. 100, 50, 10, 5	As in France
Guatemala........	Quetzal of 100 Centavos	Quetzales 100, 50, 20, 10, 5, 1; Centavos 50	Centavos 25, 10, 5, 1
Guinea (Republic of)	Guinean Franc of 100 Centimes	F.G. 1,000, 500, 100, 50	F.G. 50, 25, 10, 5, 1
Guyana...........	Guyana Dollar of 100 Cents	Dollars 20, 10, 5, 1	Cents 100, 50, 25, 10, 5, 1
Haiti.............	Gourde of 100 Centimes*	Gourdes 100, 50, 10, 5, 2, 1	Centimes 50, 20, 10, 5
Honduras........	Lempira of 100 Centavos	Lempiras 100, 50, 20, 10, 5, 1	Lempira 1; Centavos 50, 20, 10, 5, 2, 1
Hong Kong......	Hong Kong Dollar of 100 Cents	Dollars 500, 100, 50, 10, 5; Cents 1	Dollar 1; Cents 50, 10, 5
Hungary.........	Forint of 100 Fillér	Forints 100, 50, 20, 10	Forints 25, 20, 10, 5, 2, 1; Fillér 50, 20, 10, 5, 2
Iceland...........	Króna of 100 Aurar	Króna 5,000, 1,000, 500, 100, 25	Króna 50, 10, 5, 1; Aurar 50, 10
India.............	Rupee of 100 Paise	Rupees 10,000, 5,000, 1,000, 100, 10, 5, 2, 1	Rupees 10, 1, ½, ¼; Paise 50, 25, 20, 10, 5, 3, 2, 1
Indonesia.........	Rupiah of 100 Sen	Rupiahs 10,000, 5,000, 1,000, 500, 100, 50, 25, 10, 5, 2½, 1; Sen 50, 25, 10, 5, 1	Rupiahs 10, 5, 2, 1
Iran..............	Rial of 100 Dinars	Rials 5,000, 1,000, 500, 200, 100, 50, 20, 10, 5	Rials 10, 5, 2, 1; Dinars 50, 25, 10, 5
Iraq..............	Iraqi Dinar of 1000 Fils	Dinars 10, 5, 1, ½, ¼	Dinars 5, 1; Fils 500, 250, 100, 50, 25, 10, 5, 1
Ireland (Republic of)	Pound of 100 Pence	£100, 50, 20, 10, 5, 1	10s., 2s., 1s.; 6d., 3d., 1d.; 50 new pence, 10 new pence, 5 new pence, 2 new pence, 1 new penny, ½ new penny
Israel............	Israel Pound of 100 Agorot (formerly 1,000 Prutot)	Pounds 100, 50, 10, 5, 1, ½; Prutot 500, 250, 100, 50	Pounds 1, ½; Agorot 25, 10, 5, 1; Prutot 250, 100, 50, 25, 10, 5, 1
Italy.............	Lira of 100 Centisimi	Lire 100,000, 50,000, 10,000, 5,000, 1,000, 500	Lire 1,000, 500, 100, 50, 20, 10, 5, 2, 1
Ivory Coast (Republic of)	Franc C.F.A.	Frs. C.F.A. 5,000, 1,000, 500, 100, 50	Frs. C.F.A. 100, 25, 10, 5, 2, 1
Jamaica..........	Jamaican Dollar of 100 Cents	$10, 2, 1; Cents 50	Cents 25, 20, 10, 5, 1
Japan............	Yen	Yen 10,000, 5,000, 1,000, 500, 100	Yen 1,000, 100, 50, 10, 5, 1
Jordan (Hashemite Kingdom of)	Jordanian Dinar of 1,000 Fils	J. Dinars 10, 5, 1, ½	Fils 250, 100, 50, 25, 20, 10, 5, 1
Kenya...........	Kenya Shilling of 100 Cents	Shillings 100, 50, 20, 10, 5	Shillings 2, 1; Cents 50, 25, 10, 5

* U.S.A. Currency also used.

Country	Monetary Unit	Denominations in Circulation	
		Notes	Coins
Khmer Republic (*formerly* Cambodia)	*Riel* of 100 *Sen*	*Riels* 500, 100, 50, 20, 10, 5, 1	*Sen* 50, 20, 10
Korea, Republic of (South Korea)	*Won* of 100 *Jeon*	*Won* 500, 100, 50, 10, 5, 1; *Jeon* 50, 10	*Won*, 100 10, 5, 1
Korea (North)....	*Won* of 100 *Jeon*	*Won* 100, 50, 10, 5, 1; *Jeon* 50	*Jeon* 10, 5, 1
Kuwait..........	*Kuwaiti Dinar* of 1,000 *Fils*	*Dinars* 10, 5, 1, ½, ¼	*Fils* 100, 50, 20, 10, 5, 1
Laos............	*Kip* of 100 *Ats*	*Kips* 1,000, 500, 200, 100, 50, 20, 10, 5, 1	—
Lebanon.........	*Lebanese Pound* of 100 *Piastres*	*Pounds* 100, 50, 25, 10, 5, 1	*Piastres* 50, 25, 10, 5, 2½, 1
Liberia..........	*Liberian $* of 100 *Cents*	*Dollars* 20, 10, 5, 1 (U.S. notes)	*Dollar* 1; *Cents* 50, 25, 10, 5, 1*
Libya...........	*Libyan Dinar* of 1,000 *Dirhams*		
Luxemburg.......	*Franc* of 100 *Centimes*†	*Francs* 100, 50, 20, 10	*Francs* 250, 100, 5, 1; *Centimes* 25
Macau...........	*Pataca* of 100 *Avos*	*Patacas* 500, 100, 50, 10	*Patacas* 5, 1; *Avos* 50, 10, 5
Madagascar.......	*Franc Malgache* (*F.M.G.*)	*Frs.* 5,000, 1,000, 500, 100, 50	*Frs.* 20, 10, 5, 2, 1
Malawi..........	*Malawi Kwacha* of 100 *Tambala*	*KM.* 10, 2, 1; *Tambala* 50	*Tambala* 20, 10, 5, 2, 1
Malaysia.........	*Malaysian Dollar* (*Ringgit*) of 100 *Cents* (*Sen*)	*Dollars* 1,000, 100, 50, 10, 5, 1	*Dollar* 1; *Cents* 50, 20, 10, 5, 1
Mali (Republic of)	*Franc Malien*	*Frs.* 10,000, 5,000, 1,000, 500, 100, 50	*Frs.* 25, 10, 5
Malta............	*Maltese Pound* of 20 *Shillings* or 240 *Pence*	£5, £1; 10*s.*	As in U.K. except 2, 1, ½p
Martinique.......	*Franc* of 100 *old Metropolitan Francs* or 100 *Centimes*	*Frs.* 100, 50, 10, 5	*Frs.* 10, 5, 1, 0·50, 0·20, 0·10, 0·05, 0·01
Mauritania (Islamic Republic of)	*Franc C.F.A.*	*Frs. C.F.A.* 5,000, 1,000, 500, 100, 50	*Frs. C.F.A.* 100, 25, 10, 5, 2, 1
Mauritius.........	*Rupee* of 100 *Cents*	*Rs.* 50, 25, 10, 5	*R.* 1; *Cents* 50, 25, 10, 5, 2, 1
Mexico..........	*Peso* of 100 *Centavos*	*Pesos* 10,000, 1,000, 500, 100, 50, 20, 10, 5, 1	*Pesos* 25, 5, 1; *Centavos* 50, 25, 20, 10, 5. 1
Mongolian People's Republic	*Tugrik* of 100 *Mongo*	*Tugriks* 100, 50, 25, 10, 3, 1	*Mongo* 20, 15, 10, 2, 1
Morocco.........	*Dirham* of 100 *Francs*	*Dirham* 100, 50, 10, 5; *Francs* 10,000	*Dirham* 5, 1; *Francs* 500, 200, 100, 50, 20, 10, 5, 2, 1
Mozambique......	*Escudo* of 100 *Centavos*	*Escudos* 1,000, 500, 100, 50	*Escudos* 20, 10, 5, 2½, 1; *Centavos* 50, 20, 10
Nepal............	*Rupee* of 100 *Paisa*	*Rupees* 1,000, 100, 10, 5, 1	*Rupee* 1; *Paisa* 50, 25, 10, 5, 2, 1
Netherlands (The).	*Florin* (*Guilder*) of 100 *Cents*	*Florins* 1,000, 100, 25, 10, 5, 2½, 1	*Florins* 10, 2½, 1; *Cents* 25, 10, 5, 1
Netherlands Antilles (The)	*N.A. Guilder* of 100 *Cents*	*Guilders* 500, 250, 100, 50, 25, 10, 5, 2½, 1	*Guilders* 2½, 1, ¼, $\frac{1}{10}$; *Cents* 5, 2½, 1
New Zealand.....	*New Zealand Dollar* of 100 *Cents*	N.Z.$ 100, 20, 10, 5, 2, 1	*Cents* 50, 20, 10, 5, 2, 1
Nicaragua........	*Córdoba* of 100 *Centavos*	*Córdobas* 1,000, 500, 100, 50, 20, 10, 5, 1	*Centavos* 50, 25, 10, 5
Niger (Republic of)	*Franc C.F.A.*	*Frs. C.F.A.* 5,000, 1,000, 500, 100, 50	*Frs. C.F.A.* 100, 25, 10, 5, 2, 1
Nigeria (Federal Republic of)	*N. Pound* of 20 *Shillings* or 240 *Pence*	£5, £1; 10*s.*, 5*s.*	2*s.*, 1*s.*; 6*d.*, 3*d.*, 1*d.*, ½*d.*
Norway..........	*Krone* of 100 *Öre*	*Kroner* 1,000, 500, 100, 50, 10, 5	*Kroner* 5, 1; *Öre* 50, 25, 10, 5, 2, 1
Oman	*Rial Saidi* of 1,000 *Baiza*	*Rial Saidis* 10, 5, 1, ½, ¼; *Baiza* 100	*Baiza* 100, 50, 25, 10, 5, 2
Pakistan.........	*Rupee* of 100 *Paisa*	*Rupees* 500, 100, 50, 10, 5, 2, 1	*Rupee* 1, ½, ¼; *Paisa* 50, 25, 10, 5, 2, 1
Panama..........	*Balboa* of 100 *Cents* (= *U.S.$*)	As in U.S.A.	*Balboa*, 1, ½, ¼, $\frac{1}{10}$, $\frac{1}{20}$; *Cent* 1.*
Paraguay.........	*Guarani* of 100 *Céntimos*	*Guaranies* 10,000, 5,000, 1,000, 500, 100, 50, 10, 5, 1	—
Peru.............	*Gold Sol* of 100 *Centavos*	*Soles* 1,000, 500, 200, 100, 50, 10, 5	*Soles* 10, 5, 1; *Centavos* 50, 25, 20, 10, 5, 2, 1
Philippines........	*Philippine Peso* of 100 *Centavos*	*Pesos* 100, 50, 20, 10, 5, 2, 1	*Peso* 1; *Centavos* 50, 25, 20, 10, 5, 1

*U.S. coins also circulate. † Belgian currency is also legal tender.

Country	Monetary Unit	Denominations in Circulation	
		Notes	Coins
Poland	*Zloty* of 100 *Groszy*	*Zlotys* 1,000, 500, 100, 50, 20	*Zlotys* 100, 10, 5, 2, 1; *Groszy* 50, 20, 10, 5, 2, 1
Portugal	*Escudo* of 100 *Centavos*	*Escudos* 1,000, 500, 100, 50, 20	*Escudos* 20, 10, 5, 2½, 1, ½; *Centavos* 20, 10
Portuguese Guinea	*Escudo* of 100 *Centavos*	*Escs.* 1,000, 500, 100, 50	*Escs.* 20, 10, 2·50, 1; *Centavos* 50, 20, 10
Portuguese Timor	*Escudo* of 100 *Centavos*	*Escs.* 1,000, 500, 100, 50, 20	*Escs.* 10, 5, 2½, 1; *Centavos* 50, 20, 10
Qatar	*Qatar & Dubai Riyal* of 100 *Dirhams*	*Q.D.R.* 100, 50, 25, 10, 5, 1	*Dirhams* 50, 25, 10, 5, 1
Rumania	*Leu* of 100 *Bani*	*Lei* 100, 50, 25, 10, 5, 3, 1	*Lei* 3, 1; *Bani* 25, 15, 10, 5, 3, 1
Rwanda	*Rwanda Franc*	*Frs.* 1,000, 500, 100, 50, 20	*Frs.* 10, 5, 2, 1, ½
St. Tomé and Principé	*Escudo* of 100 *Centavos*	*Escs.* 1,000, 500, 100, 50, 20	*Escs.* 10, 5, 2½, 1; *Centavos* 50, 20, 10
El Salvador	*Colón* of 100 *Centavos*	*Colones* 100, 25, 10, 5, 2, 1	*Centavos* 50, 25, 10, 5, 1
Saudi Arabia	*Riyal* of 20 *Qursh* or 100 *Halalas*	*Riyals* 100, 50, 10, 5, 1	*Qursh* 4, 2, 1; *Halala* 1
Seychelles	*Rupee* of 100 *Cents*	*Rs.* 100, 50, 20, 10, 5	*Rupees* 5, 1; *Cents* 50, 25, 10, 5, 2, 1
Sierra Leone	*Leone* of 100 *Cents*	*Leone* 5, 2, 1	*Cents* 20, 10, 5, 1, ½
Singapore	*S. Dollar* of 100 *Cents*	$1,000, 100, 50, 10, 5, 1	$1; *Cents* 50, 20, 10, 5, 1
Somalia	*Somali Shilling* of 100 *Cents*	*S. Shillings* 100, 20, 10, 5	*Shilling* 1, ½; *Cents* 10, 5, 1
South Africa (Republic of)	*Rand* of 100 *Cents*	*Rands* 20, 10, 5, 2, 1; *£SA* 100, 20, 10, 5, 1; 10*s.*	*Rand* 1; *Cents* 50, 20, 10, 5, 2, 1, ½
Spain	*Peseta* of 100 *Céntimos*	*Pesetas* 1,000, 500, 100, 50, 25, 5, 1	*Pesetas* 100, 50, 25, 5, 2½, 1; *Céntimos* 50, 10
Sudan	*Sudanese Pound* of 100 *Piastres* or 1,000 *Milliemes*	*£S* 10, 5, 1; *Piastres* 50, 25	*Piastres* 10, 5, 2; *Milliemes* 10, 5, 2, 1
Surinam	*Guilder* of 100 *Cents*	*Guilders* 1,000, 100, 25, 10, 5, 2½, 1	*Guilder* 1; *Cents* 25, 10, 5, 1
Sweden	*Krona* of 100 *Öre*	*Kronor* 10,000, 1,000, 100, 50, 10, 5	*Kronor* 5, 2, 1; *Öre* 50, 25, 10, 5, 2, 1
Switzerland	*Franc* of 100 *Centimes*	*Francs* 1,000, 500, 100, 50, 20, 10, 5	*Francs* 5, 2, 1; *Centimes* 50, 20, 10, 5, 2, 1
Syria	*Syrian Pound* of 100 *Piastres*	*Pounds* 500, 100, 50, 25, 10, 5, 1	*Pound* 1, ½; *Piastres* 50, 25, 10, 5, 2½
Tanzania	*T. Shilling* of 100 *Cents*	*Shillings* 100, 20, 10, 5	*Shilling* 1; *Cents* 50, 20, 5
Thailand	*Baht* of 100 *Stangs*	*Bahts* 100, 20, 10, 5, 1; *Stangs* 50	*Baht* 1; *Stangs* 50, 25, 20, 10, 5, 1, ½
Togo (Republic of)	*Franc C.F.A.*	*Frs. C.F.A.* 5,000, 1,000, 500, 100, 50	*Frs. C.F.A.* 100, 25, 10, 5, 2, 1
Tonga	*Pa'anga* (*T$*) of 100 *Seniti*	*Pa'anga* 10, 5, 2, 1, ½	*Pa'anga* 2, 1; *Seniti* 50, 20, 10, 5, 2, 1
Trinidad and Tobago	*Trinidad and Tobago Dollar* of 100 *Cents*	*Dollars* 20, 10, 5, 1	*Dollar* 1; *Cents* 50, 25, 10, 5, 1
Tunisia	*Tunisian Dinar* of 1,000 *Millimes*	*Dinars* 10, 5, 1, ½	*Dinar* ½; *Millimes* 100, 50, 20, 10, 5, 2, 1
Turkey	*Turkish Lira* of 100 *Kuruş*	*TL* 1,000, 500, 100, 50, 20, 10, 5	*TL* 10, 2½, 1; *Kuruş* 50, 25, 10, 5, 1
Uganda	*U. Shilling* of 100 *Cents*	*Shillings* 100, 20, 10, 5	*Shillings* 5, 2, 1; *Cents* 50, 20, 10, 5
United Arab Republic	*Egyptian Pound* of 100 *Piastres* or 1,000 *Millièmes*	*£E* 10, 5, 1, ½, ¼; *Piastres* 10, 5	*Piastres* 10, 5; *Millièmes* 20, 10, 5, 2, 1
United Kingdom (*See* pp. 1210–11)	*Pound* of 100 *new pence*	£20, £10, £5, £1	*Pence* 50, 10, 5, 2, 1, ½; 5*s.* (25*p*); 6*d.* (2½).
United States of America	*Dollar* of 100 *Cents*	$100, 50, 20, 10, 5, 1	$1; *Cents* 50, 25, 10, 5, 1
Upper Volta (Republic of)	*Franc C.F.A.*	*Frs. C.F.A.* 5,000, 1,000, 500, 100, 50	*Frs. C.F.A.* 100, 25, 10, 5, 2, 1
Uruguay	*Peso* of 100 *Centésimos*	*Pesos* 10,000, 5,000, 1,000, 500, 100, 50, 10, 5, 1	*Pesos* 10, 5, 1
U.S.S.R.	*Rouble* of 100 *Copecks*	*Roubles* 100, 50, 25, 10, 5, 3, 1	*Rouble* 1; *Copecks* 50, 20, 15, 10, 5, 3, 2, 1
Venezuela	*Bolívar*	*Bolívares* 500, 100, 50, 20, 10, 5	*Bolívares* 100, 20, 10, 5, 2, 1, ½, ¼, ⅛, 1/20
Vietnam (North)	*Dong* of 10 *Hào* or 100 *Xu*	*Dong* 10, 5, 2, 1; *Hào* 5, 2, 1; *Xu* 2	*Xu* 5, 2, 1

Country	Monetary Unit	Denominations in Circulation	
		Notes	Coins
Vietnam (South) ..	*Dong* of 100 *Cents*	*Dong* 500, 200, 100, 50, 20, 10, 5, 2, 1	*Dong* 20, 10, 5, 1; *Cents* 50, 20, 10
West Indies (The)★.	*East Caribbean Dollar* of 100 *Cents*	$100, 20, 5, 1	*Cents* 50, 25, 10, 5, 2, 1
Yemen (Arab Republic)	*Riyal* of 40 *Bugshas*	*Riyals* 50, 20, 10, 5, 1; *Bugshas* 20, 10	*Bugshas* 2, 1, ½
Yemen (People's Democratic Republic)	*Southern Yemen Dinar* (£*SY*) of 1,000 *Fils*	£*SY* 10, 5, 1; *Fils* 500, 250	*Fils* 50, 25, 5, 1
Yugoslavia........	*Dinar* of 100 *Old Dinars* or 100 *Paras*	*Dinars* 100, 50, 10, 5	*Old Dinars* 50, 20, 10; *Dinar* 5, 2, 1; *Paras* 50, 20, 10, 5
Zambia..........	*Kwacha* of 100 *Ngwee*	*Kwacha* 20, 10, 2, 1; *Ngwee* 50	*Ngwee* 20, 10, 5, 2, 1

★ Barbados and Leeward and Windward Islands.

THE COUNCIL OF EUROPE
Headquarters: Strasbourg 67, France.   *Secretary-General*, M. L. Toncic-Sorinj.

A European organization founded in 1949 whose aim is to achieve a greater unity between its Members to safeguard their European heritage and to facilitate their economic and social progress. The aim of the Council is pursued through discussion and common action in economic, social, cultural, educational, scientific, legal and administrative matters and in the maintenance and furtherance of human rights and fundamental freedoms.

The following 17 countries belong to the Council: Austria, Belgium, Cyprus, Denmark, France, the Federal Republic of Germany, Iceland, the Republic of Ireland, Italy, Luxemburg, Malta, Netherlands, Norway, Sweden, Switzerland, Turkey and the United Kingdom. Greece withdrew from membership in December, 1969, but with legal effect from Dec. 31, 1970.

The organs are the Committee of Ministers, consisting of the Foreign Ministers of member countries; and the Consultative Assembly of 147 members, elected or chosen by the national parliaments of member countries in proportion to the relative strength of political parties. There is also a Joint Committee of Ministers and Representatives of the Consultative Assembly.

The Committee of Ministers is the executive organ of the Council. Certain of its conclusions take the form of international agreements or recommendations to governments. On certain major matters the Committee votes by unanimity but abstentions are permitted. Decisions of the Ministers may also be embodied in partial agreements to which a limited number of member governments are party. The Committee of Ministers meets twice yearly. All Ministers have appointed Deputies to act on their behalf. The Committee of Deputies meets monthly to transact business and to take decisions on behalf of Ministers. Member governments accredit Permanent Representatives to the Council in Strasbourg, who are also the Ministers' Deputies.

The Committee is a forum for discussion between member governments on political and other matters, supervises the work of the technical expert committees and considers recommendations received from the Consultative Assembly. The Assembly's conclusions may take the form of recommendations to the Committee of Ministers or resolutions. Ministers, including Ministers other than those for Foreign Affairs, may address the Assembly and take part in its debates.

The Assembly holds three week-long sessions a year. It debates reports on, *inter alia*, political, economic, agricultural, social, educational, legal and regional planning affairs. The Chairman in office of the Committee of Ministers presents a report at each session. The Assembly also debates reports received annually from the O.E.C.D., other European organizations and certain specialized agencies of the United Nations. It holds an annual joint meeting with the members of the European Parliament of the "Six". Matters of mutual interest to the Committee of Ministers and the Assembly are discussed in the joint Committee. The Council's budget is voted annually in December and is met by agreed contributions of member countries.

One of the principal achievements of the Council of Europe is the European Convention on Human Rights (1950) under which was established the European Commission and the European Court of Human Rights. These organs have built up a valuable system of European jurisprudence in the field of Human Rights. Other major achievements of the Council of Europe are the European Cultural Convention (1953) and the European Social Charter (1960). Over 60 conventions and agreements have been concluded by the Council covering matters in all the fields of its competence, such as social insurance, equivalence of European diplomas for university entrances, equivalence of university degrees, public health patents, extradition, etc.

The Council's cultural and educational programme is administered by the Council for Cultural Co-operation to which in addition to members of the Council of Europe belong Finland, Greece, Spain and the Holy See. A European Committee for Legal Co-operation administers the Council's legal programme. A few non-member states take part as observers in several of the Council's intergovernmental activities.

The Committee of Ministers approves annually the Council of Europe Programme of Work handled by the intergovernmental committees of experts. The Work Programme lists the various projects on which the Council is working and thus provides a guide to the intergovernmental work of the Council.

Permanent U.K. Representative, His Excellency Douglas John Brett Robey, C.M.G. (1969) £6,475
Deputy Representative, P. A. Grier, O.B.E.

RETROSPECT OF SPORT 1970-71

THE OLYMPIC GAMES

The Modern Olympic Games were revived in 1896 and meetings have been held as follows:—

I	1896	Athens	VII	1920	Antwerp	XIV	1948 London
II	1900	Paris	VIII	1924	Paris	XV	1952 Helsinki
III	1904	St. Louis	IX	1928	Amsterdam	XVI	1956 Melbourne
IV	1908	London	X	1932	Los Angeles	XVII	1960 Rome
V	1912	Stockholm	XI	1936	Berlin	XVIII	1964 Tokyo
VI	1916	Berlin**	XII	1940	Tokyo, Helsinki**	XIX	1968 Mexico City
			XIII	1944	London**		

** The Games of 1916 were allotted to Berlin, but were not held owing to the war. The Games of 1940 were allotted first to Tokyo, then in 1938 to Helsinki, but also were not held owing to the war. The Games of 1944 were awarded to London in 1939, but again were not held owing to the war. It is a rule of the Olympic Charter that the cancellation of any Meeting must not alter the numbered sequence.

Olympic Games, 1972.—The Games of the Olympiad are scheduled to take place in Munich from August 26 to September 10, 1972, and will consist of the following sports:

ARCHERY	BOXING	EQUESTRIAN	GYMNASTICS	JUDO	ROWING	VOLLEYBALL
ATHLETICS	CANOEING	FENCING	HANDBALL	MODERN	SHOOTING	WEIGHTLIFTING
BASKETBALL	CYCLING	FOOTBALL	HOCKEY	PENTATHLON	SWIMMING	WRESTLING

The following are the Olympic records for the track and field events:—

Men's Events

Distance Metres	Name	Country	Time hr.min.sec.			Year
100	J. Hines	U.S.A.	9·9			1968
200	T. Smith	U.S.A.	19·8			1968
400	L. Evans	U.S.A.	43·8			1968
800	R. Doubell	Australia	1 44·3			1968
1,500	K. Keino	Kenya	3 34·9			1968
5,000	V. Kuts	U.S.S.R.	13 39·6			1956
10,000	W. Mills	U.S.A.	28 24·4			1964
110 Hurdles	W. Davenport	U.S.A.	13·3			1968
400 Hurdles	D. Hemery	G.B.	48·1			1968
Steeplechase	G. Roelants	Belgium	8 30·8			1964
20,000 Walk	K. Matthews	G.B.	1 29 34·0			1964
50,000 Walk	A. Pamich	Italy	4 11 12·4			1964
Marathon	A. Bikila	Ethiopia	2 12 11·2			1964
			metres	ft.	in.	
High Jump	R. Fosbury	U.S.A.	2·24	7	4	1968
Pole Vault	B. Seagren	U.S.A.	5·40	17	8½	1968
,,	C. Schiprowski	Germany				
,,	W. Nordwig	G.D.R.				
Long Jump	B. Beamon	U.S.A.	8·90	29	2½	1968
Triple Jump	V. Saneyev	U.S.S.R.	17·39	57	0½	1968
Shot	R. Matson	U.S.A.	20·68	67	10½	1968
Discus	A. Oerter	U.S.A.	64·78	212	6	1968
Hammer	G. Zsivotzky	Hungary	73·36	240	8	1968
Javelin	J. Lusis	U.S.S.R.	90·10	295	7	1968
Decathlon	W. Toomey	U.S.A.	8,193 points			1968
4×100 Relay	United States		38·2 sec.			1968
4×400 Relay	United States		2 min. 56·1 sec.			1968

Women's Events

Distance	Name	Country	Time min. sec.			Year
100	W. Tyus	U.S.A.	11·0			1968
200	L. Szewinska	Poland	22·5			1968
400	B. Cuthbert	Australia	52·0			1964
,,	C. Besson	France	52·0			1968
800	M. Manning	U.S.A.	2 00·9			1968
80 Hurdles*	M. Caird	Australia	10·3			1968
4×100 Relay	United States		42·8			1968
			metres	ft.	in.	
High Jump	I. Balas	Roumania	1·90	6	2¾	1964
Long Jump	V. Viscopoleanu	Roumania	6·82	22	4½	1968
Shot	M. Gummel	G.D.R.	19·61	64	4	1968
Discus	L. Manoliu	Roumania	58·28	191	2	1968
Javelin	E. Gorchakova	U.S.S.R.	62·40	204	8	1964
Pentathlon**	L. Press	U.S.S.R.	5,246 points			1964

NOTE—Olympic Swimming Records are on pp. 1012-13.
* Changed to 100 metres hurdles for 1972.
** 100 metres hurdles substituted for 80 metres and scoring tables changed.

2 I*

WORLD'S ATHLETIC RECORDS

* (All the world records given below have been accepted by the International Amateur Athletic Federation with the exception of those marked thus (*) which await ratification and are likely to be accepted.)

Running

Distance	Time hr. min. sec.	Name	Nation	Year
100 yards	9·1	R. Hayes	U.S.A.	1963

Equalled in 1966 by H. Jerome (*Canada*); in 1967 by J. Hines (*U.S.A.*) and C. Greene (*U.S.A.*); and in 1969 by J. Carlos (*U.S.A.*).

Distance	Time	Name	Nation	Year
100 metres	9·9	C. Greene	U.S.A.	1968

Equalled in 1968 by J. Hines (*U.S.A.*) and R. R. Smith (*U.S.A.*).

Distance	Time	Name	Nation	Year
200 metres (straight)	19·5	T. Smith	U.S.A.	1966
” (turn)	19·8	T. Smith	U.S.A.	1968
”	19·8*	D. Quarrie	Jamaica	1971
220 yards (straight)	19·5	T. Smith	U.S.A.	1966
” (turn)	20·0	T. Smith	U.S.A.	1966
400 metres	43·8	L. Evans	U.S.A.	1968
440 yards	44·7	C. Mills	U.S.A.	1969
”	44·5*	J. Smith	U.S.A.	1971
800 metres	1 44·3	P. G. Snell	New Zealand	1962
”	1 44·3	R. Doubell	Australia	1968
880 yards	1 44·9	J. Ryun	U.S.A.	1966
1,000 metres	2 16·2	J. May	Germany	1965
”	2 16·2	F. Kemper	Germany	1966
1,500 metres	3 33·1	J. Ryun	U.S.A.	1967
One Mile	3 51·1	J. Ryun	U.S.A.	1967
2,000 metres	4 56·2	M. Jazy	France	1966
3,000 metres	7 39·6	K. Keino	Kenya	1965
2 miles	8 19·6	R. Clarke	Australia	1968
”	8 17·8*	E. Puttemans	Belgium	1971
3 miles	12 50·4	R. Clarke	Australia	1966
5,000 metres	13 16·6	R. Clarke	Australia	1966
6 miles	26 47·0	R. Clarke	Australia	1965
10,000 metres	27 39·4	R. Clarke	Australia	1965
10 miles	46 37·8	J. Drayton	Canada	1970
20,000 metres	58 06·2	G. Roelants	Belgium	1966
15 miles	1 12 48·2	R. Hill	G.B.	1965
25,000 metres	1 15 22·6	R. Hill	G.B.	1965
30,000 metres	1 31 30·4	J. Alder	G.B.	1970
12 miles 1,478 yards (20,664 metres)	1 hour	G. Roelants	Belgium	1966
3,000 metres steeplechase	8 22·0	K. O'Brien	Australia	1970

Hurdling

Distance	Time	Name	Nation	Year
120 yards (3 ft. 6 in.)	13·2	M. Lauer	Germany	1959

Equalled in 1960 by L. Calhoun (*U.S.A.*); in 1967 by E. McCulloch (*U.S.A.*); and in 1969 by E. Hall (*U.S.A.*).

Distance	Time	Name	Nation	Year
120 yards (3ft. 6in.)	13·0*	R. Milburn	U.S.A.	1971
110 metres	13·2	M. Lauer	Germany	1959

Equalled in 1960 by L. Calhoun (*U.S.A.*) and in 1967 by E. McCulloch (*U.S.A.*).

Distance	Time	Name	Nation	Year
200 metres (2 ft. 6 in.) (straight)	21·9	D. Styron	U.S.A.	1960
200 metres (turn)	22·5	M. Lauer	Germany	1959
”	22·5	G. Davis	U.S.A.	1960
220 yards (straight)	21·9	D. Styron	U.S.A.	1960
400 metres (3 ft.)	48·1	D. Hemery	G.B.	1968
440 yards	48·8	R. Mann	U.S.A.	1970

Relay Racing

Distance	Time	Nation	Year
4 × 100 metres	38·2	United States	1968
4 × 110 yards	38·6	United States	1967
4 × 200 metres	1 22·7	United States	1970
4 × 220 yards	1 22·7	United States	1970
4 × 400 metres	2 56·1	United States	1968
4 × 440 yards	3 02·8	Trinidad and Tobago	1966
4 × 800 metres	7 08·6	West Germany	1966
4 × 880 yards	7 11·6	Kenya	1970
4 × 1,500 metres	14 49·0	France	1965
4 × 1 mile	16 09·0	U.S.A.	1962

Jumping and Throwing

Distance	ft.	in.	metres	Name	Nation	Year
High Jump	7	5¾	2·28	V. Brumel	U.S.S.R.	1963
”	7	6¼*	2·29	P. Matzdorf	U.S.A.	1971
Pole Vault	18	0	5·49	C. Papanikolaou	Greece	1970

World Jumping and Throwing Records—*continued*

	ft.	in.	metres	Name	Nation	Year
Long Jump	29	2½	8·90	B. Beamon	U.S.A.	1968
Triple Jump	57	0¾	17·39	V. Saneyev	U.S.S.R.	1968
" "	57	1*	17·40	P. Perez	Cuba	1971
Shot	71	5½	21·78	R. Matson	U.S.A.	1967
Discus	224	5	68·40	L. Silvester	U.S.A.	1968
"	229	9*	70·04	L. Silvester	U.S.A.	1971
"	230	11*	70·38	L. Silvester	U.S.A.	1971
Hammer	245	0	74·68	A. Bondarchuk	U.S.S.R.	1969
"	245	9*	74·90	U. Beyer	Germany	1971
"	250	8*	76·40	W. Schmidt	Germany	1971
Javelin	304	1	92·70	J. Kinnunen	Finland	1969
Decathlon	8,417 pts.			W. Toomey	U.S.A.	1969

Walking

Distance	hr.	min.	sec.			
20,000 metres	1	25	50·0	P. Frenkel	G.D.R.	1970
30,000 metres	2	17	16·8	A. Yegorov	U.S.S.R.	1959
" "	2	15	16·0*	C. Hohne	G.D.R.	1971
20 miles	2	31	33·0	A. Vedyakov	U.S.S.R.	1958
30 miles	4	00	06·4	C. Höhne	Germany	1969
"	3	56	12·6	P. Selzer	G.D.R.	1971
50,000 metres	4	08	05·0	C. Höhne	Germany	1969
" "	4	04	19·8*	P. Selzer	G.D.R.	1971
26,658 metres	Two hours			P. Frenkel	G.D.R.	1971
(16 miles 993 yards)						

WOMEN'S EVENTS
Running

				Name	Nation	Year
60 metres			7·2	B. Cuthbert	Australia	1960
"			7·2	I. Bochkareva	U.S.S.R.	1960
100 yards			10·3	M. Willard	Australia	1958

Equalled in 1965 by W. Tyus (U.S.A.) and in 1970 by Chi Cheng (Formosa).

100 metres			11·0	W. Tyus	U.S.A.	1968
"			11·0	Chi Cheng	Formosa	1970
200 metres			11·0	R. Meissner	G.D.R.	1970 and 1971*
"			22·4	Chi Cheng	Formosa	1970
220 yards			22·9	M. Burvill	Australia	1964
400 metres			51·0	M. Neufville	Jamaica	1970
440 yards			52·4	J. Amoore	Australia	1965
800 metres	2		00·5	V. Nikolic	Yugoslavia	1968
"	1		58 3*	H. Falck	Germany	1971
880 yards	2		02·0	D. Willis	Australia	1962
"	2		02·0	J. Pollock	Australia	1967
1,500 metres	4		09·6	K. Burneleit	G.D.R.	1971
One mile	4		36·8	M. Gommers	Netherlands	1969
"	4		35·4*	E. Tittel	Germany	1971
100 metres hurdles (2ft. 9in.)			12·9	K. Balzer	G.D.R.	1970
"			12·7	T. Sukniewicz	Poland	1970
"			12·6*	K. Balzer	G.D.R.	1971
200 metres hurdles (2ft. 6in.)			25·8	P. Kilborn	Australia	1969

Equalled in 1970 by A. Jahns (G.D.R.) and T. Sukniewicz (Poland).

Relays

						Year
4 × 100 metres		42·8	....	U.S.A.		1968
4 × 110 yards		45·0	....	G.B.		1968
" "		44·7*	....	U.S.A.		1971
4 × 200 metres	1	33·8	....	G.B.		1968
" "	1	33·6*	....	G.B.		1971
4 × 220 yards	1	35·8	....	Australia		1969
3 × 800 metres	6	15·5	....	Netherlands		1968
3 × 880 yards	6	25·2	....	G.B.		1967
4 × 400 metres	3	29·3	....	G.D.R.		1971
4 × 440 yards	3	47·8	....	U.S.A.		1970
" "	3	38·8*	....	U.S.A.		1971
" "	3	38·7*	....	U.S.A.		1971
4 × 800 metres	8	25·0	....	G.B.		1970
"	8	16·8*	....	Germany		1971

Women's Jumping and Throwing

	ft.	in.	metres	Name	Nation	Year
High Jump	6	3¼	1·91	I. Balas	Rumania	1964
" "	6	3½*	1·92	I. Gusenbauer	Austria	1971
Long Jump	22	5¼	6·84	H. Rosendahl	Germany	1970
Shot Putt	67	0¼	20·43	N. Chizhoua	U.S.S.R.	1969 and 1971
Discus	210	8	64·22	F. Melnik	U.S.S.R.	1971
"	212	10*	64·88	F. Melnik	U.S.S.R.	1971
Javelin	204	8	62·40	E. Gorchakova	U.S.S.R.	1963
Pentathlon	5,406 pts.			B. Pollak	G.D.R.	1970

UNITED KINGDOM (ALL COMERS') RECORDS
(Records made in the United Kingdom of Great Britain and Northern Ireland by any athlete.)

Distance	Time hr. min. sec.	Name	Nation	Year
100 yards	9·4	K. A. Gardner	Jamaica	1958
,,	9·4	P. F. Radford	G.B.	1960
100 metres	10·3	W. H. Dillard	U.S.A.	1948
,,	10·3	P. F. Radford	G.B.	1960
200 metres (t)	20·5	D. Quarrie	Canada	1970
,,	20·5	P. F. Radford	G.B.	1960
220 yards (t)	20·5	P. F. Radford	G.B.	1960
400 metres	45·0	C. Asati	Kenya	1970
440 yards	45·9	W. Mottley	Trinidad	1966
800 metres	1 46·5	J. Boulter	G.B.	1966
880 yards	1 47·2	C. Carter	G.B.	1968
1,500 metres	3 36·6	K. Keino	Kenya	1969
1 mile	3 53·4	K. Keino	Kenya	1966
2 miles	8 17·8	E. Puttemans	Belgium	1971
3 miles	12 52·4	R. Clarke	Australia	1965
5,000 metres	13 22·2	D. Bedford	G.B.	1971
6 miles	26 51·6	D. Bedford	G.B.	1971
10,000 metres	27 47·0	D. Bedford	G.B.	1971
10 miles	46 44·0	R. Hill	G.B.	1968
12 miles 1268 yards	One hour	R. Hill	G.B.	1968
15 miles	1 12 48·2	R. Hill	G.B.	1965
3,000 metres steeplechase	8 26·2	T. Manning	Australia	1970
120 yards hurdles	13·7	G. W. Davenport	U.S.A.	1967
110 metres hurdles	13·7	G. W. Davenport	U.S.A.	1967
220 yards hurdles (straight)	23·3	P. B. Hildreth	G.B.	1955
220 yards hurdles (curve)	23·3	E. Gilbert	U.S.A.	1957
400 metres hurdles	49·6	D. Hemery	G.B.	1968
440 yards hurdles	49·7	G. A. Potgieter	S. Africa	1958
4 × 100 metres	39·4	——	Jamaica	1970
4 × 110 yards	40·0	——	G.B.	1963
4 × 220 yards	1 26·0	——	London Team	1959
4 × 400 metres	3 03·6	——	Kenya	1970
4 × 440 yards	3 06·4	——	U.S.A.	1960
4 × 880 yards	7 16·0	——	U.S.S.R.	1966
4 × 1 mile	16 28·2	——	England Team	1961

	Time ft. in.			
High Jump	7 3	V. I. Brumel	U.S.S.R.	1961
Pole Vault	17 4¾	C. Papanicalaou	Greece	1971
Long Jump	26 10	R. Boston	U.S.A.	1965
Triple Jump	54 11	J. Schmidt	Poland	1965
Shot	66 11	R. Matson	U.S.A.	1967
Discus	200 2	L. Danek	Czechoslovakia	1965
Hammer	230 9	R. Theimer	G.D.R.	1970
Javelin	279 9	J. Lusis	U.S.S.R.	1966
Decathlon	7,985 pts.	W. Toomey	U.S.A.	1968

Walking	hr. min. sec.			
3,000 metres	11 51·2	P. Nihill	G.B.	1971
10,000 metres	41 55·6	P. Embleton	G.B.	1971
20 miles	2 42 25·2	D. J. Thompson	G.B.	1959
30 miles	4 19 50·8	D. J. Thompson	G.B.	1956
16 miles 315 yards	Two hours	R. Wallwork	G.B.	1971

WOMEN

Distance	Time min. sec.	Name	Nation	Year
100 yards	10·6	M. Willard	Australia	1958

Equalled in 1958 by H. J. Young (*G.B.*); by W. Rudolph (*U.S.A.*) in 1960; in 1962 and 1964 by D. Hyman (*G.B.*); in 1964 by D. Arden (*G.B.*) and M. Rand (*G.B.*); and in 1968 by V. Peat (*G.B.*).

100 metres	11·4	V. Peat	G.B.	1968
200 metres	23·2	I. Kirszenstein	Poland	1965
220 yards	23·6	M. Willard	Australia	1958
,,	23·6	D. Arden	G. B.	1964
400 metres	51·0	M. Neufville	Jamaica	1970
440 yards	54·2	G. Kraan	Netherlands	1962
800 metres	2 00·5	V. Nikolic	Jugoslavia	1968
880 yards	2 04·2	A. Smith	G.B.	1966
1,500 metres	4 14·0	E. Tittel	Germany	1971
3,000 metres	9 23·4	J. Smith	G.B.	1971
4 × 100 metres	44·1	Australia	Australia	1970
4 × 110 yards	45·0	——	G.B.	1968
4 × 200 metres	1 33·8	——	G.B.	1968
4 × 220 yards	1 37·6	——	G.B.	1968

U.K. (ALL COMERS') RECORDS: Women's Events—*continued*

3 × 800 metres	6 20·0	——	G.B.	1967
3 × 880 yards	6 27·4	——	G.B.	1968
4 × 400 metres	3 34·5	——	G.D.R.	1971
4 × 800 metres	8 27·0	——	G.B.	1970
100 metres hurdles	13·2	P. Kilborn	Australia	1970
	ft. in.			
High Jump	6 0¾	R. Schmidt	G.D.R.	1970
Long Jump	22 0¾	S. Sherwood	G.B.	1970
Shot	59 3½	M. Lange	G.D.R.	1970
Discus	201 0	G. Hinzmann	G.D.R.	1970
Javelin	189 11	R. Fuchs	G.D.R.	1970
Pentathlon	5,148 pts.	M. Peters	G.B.	1970

UNITED KINGDOM (NATIONAL) RECORDS

(Records made anywhere by athletes eligible to represent Great Britain and Northern Ireland)

100 yards.—9·4 sec. (P. F. Radford, 1960).
100 metres.—10·2 sec. (M. Campbell, 1967).
200 metres.—20·5 sec. (P. F. Radford, 1960).
220 yards.—20·5 sec. (P. F. Radford, 1960).
400 metres.—45·5 sec. (D. A. Jenkins, 1971).
440 yards.—45·9 sec. (R. I. Brightwell, 1962).
800 metres.—1 min. 46·2 sec. (A. Carter, 1971).
880 yards.—1 min. 47·2 sec. (C. Carter, 1968).
1,000 metres.—2 min. 18·2 sec. (J. P. Boulter, 1969).
1,500 metres.—3 min. 39·0 sec. (P. Stewart, 1970).
1 mile.—3 min. 55·7 sec. (A. Simpson, 1965).
2,000 metres.—5 min. 08·2 sec. (C. Robinson, 1968).
3,000 metres.—7 min. 47·6 sec. (R. G. Taylor, 1969).
2 miles.—8 min. 24·8 sec. (B. Foster 1971).
3 miles.—58·2 sec. (D. Bedford, 1971).
5,000 metres.—13 min. 22·2 sec. (D. Bedford, 1971).
6 miles.—26 min. 51·6 sec. (D. Bedford 1971).
10,000 metres.—27 min. 47·0 sec. (D. Bedford, 1971).
10 miles.—46 min. 44·0 sec. (R. Hill, 1968).
20,000 metres.—58 min. 39·0 sec. (R. Hill, 1968).
12 miles 1,268 yards.—1 hr. (R. Hill, 1968).
15 miles.—1 hr. 12 min. 48·2 sec. (R. Hill, 1965).
25,000 metres.—1 hr. 15 min. 22·6 sec. (R. Hill, 1965).
30,000 metres.—1 hr. 31 min. 40·4 sec. (J. Alder, 1970).
3,000 metres Steeplechase.—8 min. 28·6 sec. (D. Bedford, 1971).
120 yards Hurdles.—13·6 sec. (D. P. Hemery, 1969).
110 metres Hurdles.—13·6 sec. (D. P. Hemery, 1969).
220 yards Hurdles (straight).—23·3 sec. (P. B. Hildreth, 1955).
220 yards Hurdles (curve).—23·7 sec. (P. A. L. Vine, 1955).
400 metres Hurdles.—48·1 sec. (D. P. Hemery, 1968).
440 yards Hurdles.—50·2 sec. (D. P. Hemery, 1968).
4 × 100 metres Relay.—39·3 sec. (British Team, 1968).
4 × 110 yards.—40·0 sec. (British Team, 1963).
4 × 200 metres.—1 min. 24·1 sec. (British Team, 1961).
4 × 220 yards.—1 min. 26·0 sec. (London Team, 1959).
4 × 400 metres.—3 min. 01·2 sec. (British Team, 1968).
4 × 440 yards.—3 min. 06·5 sec. (English Team, 1966).
4 × 800 metres.—7 min. 17·4 sec. (British Team, 1970).
4 × 880 yards.—7 min. 20·4 sec. (British Team, 1967).
4 × 1,500 metres.—15 min. 06·6 sec. (G.B. Team, 1970).
4 × 1 mile.—16 min. 24·8 sec. (English Team, 1963).
High Jump.—6 ft. 10 in. (G. A. Miller, 1964; M. Campbell, 1971).
Pole Vault.—16 ft. 8¾ in. (M. R. Bull, 1970).
Long Jump.—27 ft. 0 in. (L. Davies, 1968).
Triple Jump.—53 ft. (F. J. Alsop, 1964).
Shot.—64 ft. 2 in. (A. Rowe, 1961).
Discus.—189 ft. 11 in. (J. Watts, 1971).

Hammer.—225 ft. 9 in. (A. H. Payne, 1970).
Javelin.—273 ft. 9 in. (D. Travis, 1970).
Decathlon.—7,903 pts. (P. Gabbett, 1971).
Walking
3,000 metres.—11 min. 51·2 sec. (P. Nihill, 1971).
2 miles.—13 min. 02·4 sec. (S. F. Vickers, 1960).
5 miles.—34 min. 21·2 sec. (K. J. Matthews, 1960).
10,000 metres. 41 min. 55·6 sec. (P. B. Embleton, 1971).
7 miles.—48 min. 22·2 sec. (K. J. Matthews, 1964).
10 miles.—1 hr. 9 min. 40·6 sec. (K. J. Matthews, 1964).
20,000 metres.—1 hr. 28 min. 45·8 sec. (K. J. Matthews, 1964).
20 miles.—2 hr. 42 min. 25·2 sec. (D. J. Thompson, 1959).
30 miles.—4 hr. 8 min. 11·6 sec. (D. J. Thompson, 1960).
50,000 metres.—4 hr. 17 min. 29·8 sec. (D. J. Thompson, 1964).
8 miles 1,151 yards.—1 hr. (K. J. Matthews, 1964).
16 miles 315 yards.—(R. Wallwork, 1971).

Women

100 yards.—10·6 sec. (H. Young, 1958; D. Hyman, 1962, 1964; D. Arden, M. Rand, 1964; V. Peat, 1968).
100 metres.—11·3 sec. (D. Hyman, 1963; D. James, V. Peat, 1968; A. Neil, 1971).
200 metres.—23·2 sec. (D. Hyman, 1963; M. C. Critchley, 1970).
220 yards.—23·6 sec. (D. Arden, 1964).
400 metres.—52·1 sec. (L. Board, 1968).
440 yards.—54·1 sec. (D. Watkinson, 1966).
800 metres.—2 min. 01·1 sec. (A. Packer, 1964).
880 yards.—2 min. 04·2 sec. (A. Smith, 1966).
1,500 metres.—4 min. 12·7 sec. (R. Ridley, 1971).
1 mile.—4 min. 37·0 sec. (A. Smith, 1967).
3,000 metres.—9 min. 23·4 sec. (J. Smith, 1971).
100 metres Hurdles.—13·4 sec. (C. Bell, 1970).
200 metres Hurdles.—26·7 sec. (S. Colyear, 1971).
4 × 100 metres Relay.—43·7 sec. (G.B. Team, 1968).
4 × 110 yards Relay.—45·0 sec. (G.B. Team, 1968).
4 × 200 metres Relay.—1 min. 33·8 sec. (G.B. Team, 1968).
4 × 220 yards Relay.—1 min. 33·6 sec. (L.O.A.C. 1971).
4 × 400 metres.—3 min. 30·8 sec. (G.B. Team, 1969).
3 × 800 metres Relay.—6 min. 20·0 sec. (G.B. Team, 1967).
4 × 800 metres. Relay.—8 min. 23·8 sec. (G.B. Team, 1971).
3 × 880 yards Relay.—6 min. 25·2 sec. (G.B. Team, 1967).
High Jump.—6 ft. 0¾ in. (B. Inkpen, 1971).
Long Jump.—22 ft. 2¼ in. (M. Rand, 1964).
Shot.—53 ft. 6½ in. (M. Peters, 1966).
Discus.—180 ft. 7 in. (R. Payne, 1970).
Javelin.—182 ft. 5 in. (S. Platt, 1968).
Pentathlon.—5,148 pts. (M. Peters, 1970).

EUROPEAN INDOOR CHAMPIONSHIPS

Held in Sofia, March 13 and 14, 1971.

Metres MEN'S EVENTS	min.	sec.
60—V. Borzov (U.S.S.R.)		6·7
400—A. Badenski (Poland)		46·8
800—Y. Arzhanov (U.S.S.R.)	1	48·7
1,500—H. Szordyskowski (Poland)	3	41·4
3,000—P. Stewart (G.B.)	7	53·6
60 *Hurdles*—E. Berkes (Germany)		7·8
1,600 *Relay*—Poland	3	11·1
	ft.	in.
High Jump—L. Major (Hungary)	7	1½
Pole Vault—W. Nordwig (G.D.R.)	17	8¾
Long Jump—H. Baumgartner (Germany)	26	7¾
Triple Jump—V. Taneyev (U.S.S.R.)	55	2½
Shot—H. Briesenick (G.D.R.)	66	3

Metres WOMEN'S EVENTS	min.	sec.
60—R. Meissner-Stecher (G.D.R.)		7·3
400—V. Popkova (U.S.S.R.)		53·7
800—H. Falcke (Germany)	2	06·1
1,500—M. Beacham (G.B.)	4	17·2
60 *Hurdles*—K. Balzer (G.D.R.)		8·1
800 *Relay*—U.S.S.R.	1	37·1
1,600 *Relay*—U.S.S.R.	3	36·6
High Jump—M. Karbanova (Czechoslovakia)	5	11
Long Jump—H. Rosendahl (Germany)	21	9½
Shot—N. Chizhova (U.S.S.R.)	64	7½
	ft.	in.

Xth EUROPEAN ATHLETIC CHAMPIONSHIPS, HELD IN HELSINKI

August 10 to 15, 1971

Men's Events

Metres		min.	sec.
100—V. Borzov (U.S.S.R.)			10·3
200—V. Borzov (U.S.S.R.)			20·3
400—D. Jenkins (G.B.)			45·5
800—E. Arzhanov (U.S.S.R.)		1	45·6
1,500—F. Arese (Italy)		3	38·4
5,000—J. Vaatainen (Finland)		13	32·6
10,000—J. Vaatainen (Finland)		27	52·8
Marathon—K. Lismont (Belgium)	2 hr	13	09·0
20,000 *Walk*—N. Smaga (U.S.S.R.)	1 hr	27	20·2
50,000 *Walk*—V. Soldatenko (U.S.S.R.)	4 hr	02	22·0
400 *Relay*—Czechoslovakia			39·3
1,600 *Relay*—Germany		3	02·9
110 *Hurdles*—F. Siebeck (G.D.R.)			14·0
400 *Hurdles*—J. Nallet (France)			49·2
Steeplechase—J. Villain (France)		8	25·2
		ft.	in.
High Jump—K. Shapka (U.S.S.R.)		7	2¾
Pole Vault—W. Nordwig (G.D.R.)		17	6¾
Long Jump—M. Klauss (G.D.R.)		25	11½
Triple Jump—J. Drehmel (G.D.R.)		56	3¾
Shot—H. Briesenick (G.D.R.)		69	2
Discus—L. Danek (Czechoslovakia)		209	8
Hammer—U. Beyer (Germany)		237	5
Javelin—J. Lusis (U.S.S.R.)		297	6
Decathlon—J. Kirst (G.D.R.)		8,196	pts.

Women's Events

Metres	min.	sec.
100—R. Stecher (G.D.R.)		11·4
200—R. Stecher (G.D.R.)		22·7
400—H. Seidler (G.D.R.)		52·1
800—V. Nikolic (Yugoslavia)	2	00·0
1,500—K. Burnleit (G.D.R.)	4	09·6
400 *Relay*—Germany		43·3
1,600 *Relay*—German Democratic Republic	3	29·3
100 *Hurdles*—K. Balzer (G.D.R.)		12·7
	ft.	in.
High Jump—I. Gusenbauer (Austria)	6	1¾
Long Jump—I. Becker (Germany)	22	2¼
Shot—N. Chizhova (U.S.S.R.)	66	2
Discus—F. Melnik (U.S.S.R.)	210	8
Javelin—D. Jaworska (Poland)	200	1
Pentathlon—H. Rosendahl (Germany)	5,299	pts.

The First European Championships were held in 1934, the men in Turin, the women in Vienna. Since then combined championships have been held in Paris (1938), Oslo (1946), Brussels (1950), Berne (1954), Stockholm (1958), Belgrade (1962), Budapest (1966), Athens (1969) and in 1974 will be held in Rome.

GT. BRITAIN v. GERMAN DEMOCRATIC REPUBLIC (INDOOR)

Held in East Berlin on February 20, 1971

Men's Events

Metres	min.	sec.
50—M. Kokot (G.D.R.)		5·6
400—C. Rudolph (G.D.R.)		48·1
800—J. Davies (G.B.)	1	49·1
1,500—W. Wilkinson (G.B.)	3	49·0
3,000—W. Scholz (G.D.R.)	7	55·0
50 *Hurdles*—J. Wehnert (G.D.R.)		6·5
8 *laps relay*—Great Britain	2	12·6
	ft.	in.
High Jump—P. Hertel (G.D.R.)	7	0¾
Pole Vault—W. Nordwig (G.D.R.)	17	6¾
Long Jump—M. Klauss (G.D.R.)	25	10¼
Triple Jump—J. Drehmel (G.D.R.)	56	1¾
Shot—H. Briesenick (G.D.R.)	65	2¼

German Democratic Republic beat Great Britain by 76 pts to 52

Women's Events

Metres	min.	sec
50—R. Meissner (G.D.R.)		6·0
400—R. Kuhne (G.D.R.)		55·7
800—W. Pohland (G.D.R.)	2	08·5
1,500—M. Beacham (G.B.)	4	17·4
50 *Hurdles*—K. Balzer (G.D.R.)		6·8
8 *laps relay*—Great Britain	2	29·4
	ft.	in.
High Jump—R. Schmidt (G.D.R.)	6	1¾
Long Jump—R. Martin-Jones (G.B.)	21	0½
Shot—M. Gummel (G.D.R.)	63	6

German Democratic Republic beat Great Britain by 54 pts. to 41.

G. BRITAIN v. FRANCE (INDOOR)

Held at Cosford, February 27, 1971

Men's Events

Metres	min.	sec.
60—B. Kelly (G.B.)		6·8
400—J. Aukett (G.B.)		48·7
800—J. Davies (G.B.)	1	48·1
1,500—W. Wilkinson (G.B.)	3	44·2
3,000—P. Stewart (G.B.)	7	56·8
4×400 *Relay*—Great Britain	3	21·0
60 *Hurdles*—G. Drut (F.)		7·7
	ft.	in.
High Jump—H. Elliott (F.)	6	11½
Pole Vault—M. Bull (G.B.)	16	0¾
Long Jump—J. Pani (F.)	25	3½
Triple Jump—A. Wadhams (G.B.)	50	5½
Shot—P. Colnard (F.)	60	10½

Great Britain beat France by 71½ pts. to 55½.

Women's Events

Metres	min.	sec.
60—S. Telliez (F.)		7·4
400—C. Leclerq (F.)		56·3
800—C. Besson (F.)	2	06·3
1,500—M. Beacham (G.B.)	4	26·4
4×200 *Relay*—Great Britain	1	29·7
60 *Hurdles*—J. Andre (F.)		8·7
	ft.	in.
High Jump—A. Wilson (G.B.)	5	6½
Long Jump—R. Martin-Jones (G.B.)	20	1
Shot—G. Porter (G.B.)	47	9

Great Britain beat France by 56 pts. to 36.

GREAT BRITAIN v. FRANCE

Held at Portsmouth, July 9 and 10, 1971

Metres	min.	sec.
100—R. Metz (F.)		10·8
200—D. Jenkins (G.B.)		21·1
400—D. Jenkins (G B.)		46·5
800—A. Carter (G.B.)	1	47·9
1,500—J.P. Dusfresne (F.)	3	40·6
5,000—A. Rushmer (G.B.)	13	46·6
10,000—D. Bedford (G.B.)	27	47·0
Steeplechase—J-P. Villain (F.)	8	28·2
400 *Relay*—France		40·0
1,600 *Relay*—France	3	06·8
110 *Hurdles*—G. Drut (F.)		13·9
400 *Hurdles*—J. Sherwood (G.B.)		51·1
	ft.	in.
High Jump—H. Elliott (F.)	6	10¼
Pole Vault—J-M. Bellot (F.)	16	0¾
Long Jump—L. Davies (G.B.)	26	0
Triple Jump—S. Firca (F.)	50	10¼
Shot—A. Beer (F.)	62	3¼
Discus—J. Watts (G.B.)	189	7
Hammer—V. Prikhodko (F.)	223	1
Javelin—D. Travis (G.B.)	263	3

France beat Great Britain by 206½ pts. to 201½.

GT. BRITAIN v. GERMANY

Held at Crystal Palace on August 28 and 30, 1971

Men's Events

Metres	min.	sec.
100—G. Wücherer (G.)		10·6
200—D. Jenkins (G.B.)		21·4
400—H. Schlöske (G.)		46·4
800—A. Carter (G.B.)	1	48·2
1,500—H. Norpoth (G.)	3	43·9
5,000—D. Bedford (G.B.)	13	40·0
10,000—L. Philipp (G.)	28	51·0
400 *Relay*—Germany		40·2
1,600 *Relay*—Great Britain	3	06·0
110 *Hurdles*—A. Pascoe (G.B.)		14·0
400 *Hurdles*—D. Friedrich (G.)		51·1
Steeplechase—W. Wagner (G.)	8	35·0
	ft.	in.
High Jump—G. Spielvogel (G.)	7	1½
Pole Vault—H. Engel (G.)	16	4¾
Long Jump—H. Baumgartner (G.)	26	4¼
Triple Jump—J. Kugler (G.)	53	4¼
Shot—G. Capes (G.B.)	63	9
Discus—K. Hennig (G.)	200	1
Hammer—E. Klein (G.)	229	7
Javelin—H. Schlechter (G.)	256	10

Germany beat Great Britain by 118 pts. to 94.

Women's Events

Metres	min.	sec.
100—I. Becker (G.)		11·8
400—I. Bödding (G.)		53·2
800—H. Falck (G.)	2	05·1
1,500—E. Tittel (G.)	4	14·0
400 *Relay*—Germany		44·6
1,600 *Relay*—Germany	3	34·5
Hurdles—H. Rosendahl (G.)		14·1
	ft.	in.
High Jump—B. Inkpen (G.B.)	6	0
Long Jump—S. Sherwood (G.B.)	21	9½
Shot—S. Kogink (G.)	52	11¾
Discus—L. Westermann (G.)	191	0
Javelin—A. Kolowska (G.)	187	2

Germany beat Great Britain by 81 pts. to 54.

INTERNATIONAL DECATHLON AND PENTATHLON

Held at Leicester, May 22 and 23, 1971.

Decathlon

		Points
1	P. Gabbett (G.B.)	7,639
2	R. Ghesquiere (Belgium)	7,341
3	E. de Noorlander (Netherlands)	7,196

Team Competition

(Total of three)

1, Netherlands, 21,503, 2, Great Britain, 21, 406 (only two Belgians completed the ten events).

Women's Pentathlon

		Points
1	A. Wilson (G.B.)	4,894
2	M. Sterk (Netherlands)	4,804
3	M. Walls (G.B.)	4,600

Team Competition

(Total of two)

1, Great Britain (9,494), 2, Netherlands (9,278), 3, Belgium (8,472).

International Marathon

(Held in Manchester, June 13, 1971.

		hr.	min.	sec.
1	R. Hill (Bolton)	2	12	39
2	T. Wright (Hallamshire)	2	12	27
3	J. Busch (East Germany)	2	14	03

Team Match

(Aggregate times of three)

1	Great Britain	6	44	28
2	Germany (Team A)	7	07	15
3	Germany (Team B)	7	12	07

A.A.A. CHAMPIONSHIPS

Held at Crystal Palace, July 23 and 24, 1971.

Metres	min.	sec.
100—B. Green (Pilkingtons)		10·6
200—A. Pascoe (Polytechnic)		21·1
400—D. Jenkins (Edinburgh Univ.)		47·1
800—P. Browne (Q.P.H.)	1	47·5
1,500—A. Polhill (New Zealand)	3	40·0
5,000—M. Baxter (Leeds)	13	39·6
(a) 10,000m—D. Bedford (Shaftesbury)	27	47·0
(b) *Marathon*—R. Hill (Bolton) 2 hr	12	39·0
3,000 *Walk*—P. Nihill (Surrey)	12	08·4
(c) 10,000 *Walk*—P. Embleton (Met. W.C.)	45	26·2
(d) *Ten miles*—J. Wright (Hallamshire)	46	51·6
110 *Hurdles*—A. Pascoe (Polytechnic)		14·5
400 *Hurdles*—J. Sherwood (Birchfield)		51·4
Steeplechase—A. Holden (Preston)	8	38·0
	ft.	in.
High Jump—M. Campbell (Hillingdon)	6	8¼
Pole Vault—M. Bull (Albert Foundry)	16	6¾
Long Jump—H. Hines (U.S.A.)	26	3½
Triple Jump—A. Wadhams (Blackheath)	49	9
Shot—L. Mills (New Zealand)	63	2¾
Discus—L. Mills (New Zealand)	192	4
Hammer—H. Payne (Birchfield)	218	0
Javelin—D. Travis (Surrey)	252	7

(a) Held at Portsmouth on July 10.
(b) Held at Manchester on June 13.
(c) Held at Leicester on July 3.
(d) Held at Leicester on April 3.

WOMEN'S A.A.A. CHAMPIONSHIPS

Held at Crystal Palace, July 16 and 17, 1971.

Metres	min.	sec.
100—S. Berto (Canada)		11·4
200—S. Berto (Canada)		23·5
400—J. Roscoe (Stretford)		53·9
800—A. Hoffman (Canada)	2	04·0
1,500—R. Ridley (Essex)	4	14·3
3,000—J. Smith (Barnet)	9	23·2
100 *Hurdles*—V. Bufanu (Roumania)		13·5
200 *Hurdles*—S. Colyear (Stretford)		26·7
1,500 *Walk*—B. Cook (Wolverhampton)	12	39·8
	ft.	in.
High Jump—D. Brill (Canada)	6	0
Long Jump—S. Sherwood (Sheffield)	21	4¾

Shot—J. Roberts (Australia)	51	10½
Discus—L. Westermann (Germany)	191	9
Javelin—I. Fallo (Norway)	156	5
*Pentathlon**—J. Honour (Woking)	4,571 pts	

*Held at Birmingham on July 3.

A.A.A. INDOOR CHAMPIONSHIPS

Held at Cosford, January 29 and 30, 1971.

Men's Events

Metres	min.	sec.
60—D. Halliday (R.A.F.)		6·8
400—J. Auckett (Wolverhampton)		48·2
800—P. Lewis (Wolverhampton)	1	50·2
1,500—J. Davies (Sale)	3	46·9
3,000—P. Stewart (Birchfield)	8	00·4
Steeplechase—B. Hayward (Cardiff)	5	34·8
60 *Hurdles*—B. Price (Cardiff)		7·9
	ft.	in.
High Jump—D. Livesey (Newham)	6	10¼
Pole Vault—M. Bull (N. Ireland)	15	6¼
Long Jump—A. Lerwill (Queen's Park)	25	0½
Triple Jump—A. Wadhams (Blackheath)	50	7½
Shot—G. Capes (Birchfield)	59	3½

Women's Events

Metres	min.	sec.
60—S. Lannaman (Solihull)		7·5
400—J. Roscoe (Stretford)		56·1
800—R. Stirling (Wolverhampton)	2	08·0
1,500—M. Beacham (Barnet)	4	20·5
60 *Hurdles*—A. Wilson (Southend)		8·9
	ft.	in.
High Jump—A. Wilson (Southend)	5	7
Long Jump—R. Martin-Jones (Birchfield)	19	9
Shot—B. Bedford (Mitcham)	46	4¾

A.A.A. JUNIOR CHAMPIONSHIPS

Held at Wolverhampton on August 6 and 7, 1971

Metres	min.	sec.
100—R. Munns (Northampton)		10·8
200—R. Munns (Northampton)		22·0
400—D. Coneys (Blackburn)		49·1
800—J. Carroll (Liverpool)	1	53·5
1,500—D. Moorcroft (Coventry)	3	51·9
2,000 *Steeplechase*—D. Coates (Middlesborough)	5	38·4
3,000 *Walk*—B. Laver (Essex)	13	39·0
110 *Hurdles*—P. Kelly (Wolverhampton)		14·5
400 *Hurdles*—P. Kelly (Wolverhampton)		53·4
	ft.	in.
High Jump—C. Boreham (Bournemouth)	6	4¾
Pole Vault—B. Hooper (Woking)	12	5¾
Long Jump—J. Gangadeen (London)	23	2½
Triple Jump—D. Johnson (Hallamshire)	47	0¾
Shot—A. Satchwell (Jersey)	52	3¾
Discus—G. Dirkin (Stretford)	165	3
Hammer—K. Lasis (Crawley)	176	4
Javelin—B. Kawalko (Cambridge)	203	9

INTERCOUNTIES CHAMPIONSHIPS

Held at Leicester, May 30 and 31, 1971

Metres	min.	sec.
100—I. Matthews (Surrey)		10·8
200—I. Matthews (Surrey)		21·5
400—M. Bilham (Sussex)		46·7
800—J. Kirkbride (Cumberland)	1	50·2
Mile—W. Wilkinson (Yorkshire)	3	56·6
5,000—D. Black (Staffordshire)	13	46·2
10,000—M. Freary (Lancashire)	28	33·0
Steeplechase—D. Camp (Northumberland)	8	40·6
110 *Hurdles*—G. Gower (Kent)		14·5
400 *Hurdles*—J. Sherwood (Yorkshire)		51·2
3,000 *Walk*—R. Hughes (Worcestershire)	12	15·6
	ft.	in.
High Jump—A. Lerwill (Middlesex)	6	6¾
Pole Vault—M. Bryant (Essex)	15	1
Long Jump—A. Lerwill (Middlesex)	26	7¾
Triple Jump—A. Wadhams (Essex)	50	2¾
Shot—G. Capes (Cambridge)	60	0¼
Discus—J. Watts (Kent)	183	5
Hammer—H. Payne (Warwickshire)	212	10
Javelin—M. Wooton (Staffordshire)	243	2
20 *Miles Road Race*—A. Moore (Middlesex)	1 hr. 40 min 44 sec.	

Championship: 1, Surrey (70 pts); 2, Yorkshire and Middlesex (50 pts).

ENGLISH SCHOOLS

Held at Crystal Palace, July 9 and 10, 1971.

Boys' Events

Metres	min.	sec.
100—R. Munns (Northants)		10·8
200—A. Gershuny (Herts.)		21·7
400—P. Beaven (Lancs.)		48·5
800—A. Settle (Cheshire)	1	52·5
1,500—D. Glassbrow (Warwick)	3	48·7
5,000—J. Davies (Middlesex)	14	47·2
Steeplechase—I. Kilpatrick (Bucks.)	5	46·0
110 *Hurdles*—R. Parker (Hants.)		14·8
400 *Hurdles*—G. Wood (Rutland)		53·9
5,000 Walk—P. Le Bas (Hants.)	24	08·0
	ft.	in.
High Jump—P. Hambley (Lancs.)	6	5
Pole Vault—B. Hooper (Surrey)	15	3
Long Jump—I. Anderson (Yorks.)	23	11¾
Triple Jump—R. Heward-Mills (Som.)	50	9
Shot—J. Corbett (Lancs.)	52	8¾
Discus—G. Dirkin (Cheshire)	160	3
Hammer—S. Douglas (Durham)	184	8
Javelin—H. Frobisher (Yorks.)	195	10
400 *Relay*—Warwickshire		42·7

Girls' Events

Metres	min.	sec.
100—J. Rowell (Durham)		12·0
200—A. Lynch (London)		24·2
400—D. Webster (Yorks.)		55·4
800—S. Marquis (Herts.)	2	11·0
100 *Hurdles*—D. Toon (Somerset)		14·3
	ft.	in.
High Jump—S. Rampton (Middlesex)	5	4½
Long Jump—L. Beverley (Bucks.)	18	8
Shot—V. Redford (London)	40	2
Discus—J. Elsmore (Berks.)	143	4
Javelin—C. Johnson (Somerset)	141	1
400 *Relay*—Essex		48·3

OXFORD v. CAMBRIDGE

Held at Crystal Palace, May 15, 1971.

Metres	min.	sec.
100—A. Conteh (C.)		10·9
200—S. White (O.)		22·3
400—D. Knight (C.)		49·1
800—P. Lewis (O.)	1	53·2
1,500—R. Steele (O.)	3	50·7
5,000—A. Moore (O.)	14	43·8
110 *Hurdles*—P. Thompson (C.)		15·6
200 *Hurdles*—S. Nussey (O.)		24·4
400 *Hurdles*—S. Nussey (O.)		54·3
	ft.	in.
High Jump—J. Ellicock (C.)	6	7½
Pole Vault—P. Thompson (C.)	11	11¾
Long Jump—S. White (O.)	23	3½
Triple Jump—R. Gyles (O.)	46	7½
Shot—L. Daniels (C.)	40	10½
Discus—N. Nops (O.)	140	6
Javelin—P. Greenwood (O.)	197	3

Oxford won by 96 pts to 91. Sports first held in 1864. Oxford have won on 48 occasions, Cambridge on 43. There have been six ties.

OXFORD v. CAMBRIDGE, 1970

Relays, held at Oxford on November 11, 1970. Cambridge beat Oxford by 4 events to 3.
Field Events, held at Cambridge on November 18, 1970, Cambridge beat Oxford by 6 events to 1.
Cross Country, held at Roehampton on December 5, 1970, Cambridge beat Oxford by 29 pts to 57.

INTERNATIONAL CROSS COUNTRY RACES

Held at San Sebastian, March 20, 1971
Senior Race

		min.	sec.
1	D. Bedford (England)	38	42·8
2	T. Wright (England)	39	05·2
3	E. Gray (New Zealand)	39	11·6
4	J. Alvarez Salgado (Spain)	39	15·4
5	P. Standing (England)	39	19·4
6	M. Thomas (Wales)	39	22·8

	TEAM RESULT	points
1	England (1, 2, 5, 15, 16, 17)	56
2	Belgium (12, 14, 22, 23, 50, 53)	174
3	France (7, 13, 33, 34, 35, 63)	185

Junior Race

		min.	sec.
1	N. Rose (England)	23	12·4
2	R. Smedley (England)	23	17·4
3	J. Brown (Scotland)	24	02·0

	TEAM RESULT	points
1	England (1, 2, 4)	7
2	Scotland (3, 13, 14)	30
3	Italy (6, 8, 25)	39

Women's Race

		min.	sec.
1	D. Brown (U.S.A.)	11	08·4
2	B. Boxem-Lenferink (Netherlands)	11	21·2
3	J. Smith (England)	11	23·2

	TEAM RESULT	points
1	England (3, 4, 10, 12)	29
2	New Zealand (7, 8, 9, 18)	42
3	United States (1, 5, 11, 33)	50

NATIONAL CROSS COUNTRY CHAMPIONSHIPS

Held at Norwich, March 6, 1971

	Senior (9 miles)	min.	sec.
1	D. Bedford (Shaftesbury)	47	04
2	M. Thomas (T.V.H.)	47	44
3	T. Wright (Hallamshire)	47	58
4	J. Caine (Gateshead)	48	03
5	P. Standing (Brighton)	48	04
6	A. Simmons (Luton)	48	05

	TEAM RESULT	points
1	Shettleston H. (11, 19, 24, 32, 65, 131)	282
2	Tipton H. (14, 31, 42, 53, 62, 88)	287
3	Reading A.C. (37, 38, 40, 54, 86, 91)	346

Junior (6 miles)
Won by J. Lane (Feltham) in 31 min. 11 sec. Team: Birmingham University, 64 pts.

Youths (4 miles)
Won by D. Black (Small Heath) in 20 min. 39 sec. Team: Liverpool Pembroke, 112 pts.

NATIONAL ROAD RELAY

Held at Sutton Coldfield, May 1, 1971
1, Birchfield Harriers, 4 hrs. 10 mins. 58 secs.;
2. Coventry Godiva, 4 hrs. 11 mins. 31 secs.;
3. Tipton Harriers, 4 hrs. 13 mins. 17 sec.

WOMEN'S NATIONAL CROSS COUNTRY

Held at Wolverhampton, February 27, 1971

1	R. Ridley (Essex Ladies)	18	43
2	J. Smith (Barnet)	18	53
3	G. Tivey (Derby)	19	01

Team: Coventry Godiva (4, 7, 29, 55) 95 pts.
Intermediates.—Won by M. Stewart (Birchfield) in 14 min. 30 sec. Team: Stretford, 96 pts. *Juniors.*—Won by C. Boxer (Aldershot) in 10 min. 39 sec. Team: Sale, 91 pts. *Minors.*—R. Taylor (Birchfield).

NATIONAL TEN MILES WALK

Held at Redditch, March 20, 1971

		min.	sec.
1	P. Embleton (Met W.C.)	69	29
2	P. Nihill (Surrey W.C.)	71	42
3	R. Wallwork (Lancs. W.C.)	72	49

TEAM EVENT
1, Belgrave Harriers (5, 10, 13, 25), 53 points; 2, Lancashire Walking Club, 65 points; 3, Southend, 68 points.

NATIONAL 20 KM. WALK

Held at Luton, May 8, 1971

1	P. Nihill (Surrey W.C.)	92	06
2	S. Lightman (Met W.C.)	94	14
3	R. Wallwork (Lancs W.C.)	94	27

TEAM EVENT
1, Surrey Walking Club (1, 5, 19, 21), 46 points; 2, Basildon, 48 points; 3, Lancashire Walking Club, 74 points.

NATIONAL 20 MILES WALK

Held at Sheffield, June 12, 1971

		hr	min.	sec.
1	P. Nihill (Surrey W.C.)	2	30	35
2	R. Wallwork (Lancs. W.C.)	2	35	18
3	I. Brooks (Surrey W.C.)	2	35	54

TEAM EVENT
1, Surrey Walking Club, 23 points; 2, Sutton Coldfield, 49 points; 3, Belgrave Harriers, 60 points.

NATIONAL 50 KM. WALK

Held at Redditch, July 17, 1971

		hr.	min.	sec.
1	P. Nihill (Surrey W.C.)	4	15	05
2	R. Dobson (Basildon)	4	17	4.
3	C. Lawton (Belgrave)	4	19	00

TEAM EVENT
1, Surrey Walking Club, 29 points; 2, Belgrave Harriers, 32 points; 3, Sutton Coldfield, 71 points.

THE TURF

The Turf in Great Britain is under the control of the Jockey Club.

Flat Racing. The *Jockey Club,* H.Q. at Newmarket. Stewards are: Maj.-Gen. Sir Randle Feilden, K.C.V.O., C.B., C.B.E. (*Senior Steward*); Major W. D. Gibson; The Viscount Allendale (*Deputy Senior Stewards*); Lt.-Col. J. D. Hornung, O.B.E., M.C. *Steeplechasing.* The Earl Cadogan, M.C.; The Hon. J. J. Astor, M.B.E.; Brigadier F. B. B. Noble, O.B.E.; Capt. J. Macdonald-Buchanan, M.C.; Col. the Hon. Julian Berry.

Leading Owners and Trainers, 1971
(Flat Season up to Oct. 8)

Winning Owners	
P. Mellon...	£138,132
D. Robinson..	87,279
F. R. Hue-Williams....	58,055
Mrs. J. Hislop..	53,962
Mrs. J. Rogerson....	49,212
H. J. Joel....	37,703
Mrs. C. W. Engelhard....	36,817
Mrs. S. Joel..	30,208
Mrs. J. Benskin.	27,154
Lady Beaverbrook.......	23,690
Lord Rosebery..	22,006

D. Prenn......	20,564

Winning Trainers	
I. Balding...	£156,830
N. Murless...	145,118
W. R. Hern...	116,251
B. van Cutsem.	80,305
Douglas Smith .	66,821
H. Thomson Jones.......	65,490
P. Walwyn...	56,981
A. M. Budgett .	56,742
Denys Smith..	47,501
M. A. Jarvis ..	46,127
H. Cecil....	43,238
B. Hobbs......	42,447

Leading Breeders, 1971
(Up to Oct. 8)

	Horses	Races won	Value
P. Mellon............	7	15	£133,249
Col. and Mrs. F. R. Hue-Williams..............	9	16	78,176
J. Hislop..............	2	6	54,445
Kilcarn Stud	8	14	52,407
Mrs. J. Benskin..........	3	9	27,676
H. J. Joel............	13	20	27,532
Lord Rosebery...........	12	20	22,501
Cragwood Estates.........	9	16	21,490
Mereworth Farm.........	4	11	21,171
New England Stud......	3	7	20,912
Col. P. L. M. Wright.....	6	14	20,032
Ballymacoll Stud Farm....	6	9	20,031

Winning Jockeys, 1971
(Up to Oct. 8)

	1st	2nd	3rd	Unpl.	Total Mts.
L. Piggott	155	112	89	241	597
W. Carson.........	136	100	93	396	725
G. Lewis..........	110	77	62	224	473
A. Murray........	106	103	94	405	708
J. Mercer........	82	59	57	281	479
G. Starkey.......	77	64	45	222	408
E. Hide..........	77	79	73	283	512
F. Durr...........	67	43	38	205	353
B. Taylor.........	66	56	62	244	428
P. Eddery........	66	57	57	417	597
P. Waldron.......	62	47	47	272	428
J. Seagrave........	62	62	75	238	437

Winning Sires, 1971
(Up to Oct. 8)

	Horses	Races won	Value
Never Bend (1960), by Nasrullah..............	3	9	£125,021
Saint Crespin III (1956), by Aureole...............	12	16	82,593
Baldric (1961), by Round Table...............	4	5	76,469
Queen's Hussar (1960), by March Past.............	11	20	63,805
Celtic Ash (1957), by Sicambre...............	10	15	53,470
Pirate King (1953), by Prince Chevalier...........	19	35	40,906
St. Paddy (1957), by Aureole	18	29	39,995
Fortino II (1959), by Grey Sovereign...............	13	27	37,576
Tudor Melody (1956), by Tudor Minstrel.............	17	23	37,296
Le Levanstell (1957), by Le Lavandou...............	26	45	36,803
Relko (1960), by Tanerko..	13	27	34,797
Primera (1954), by My Babu..................	14	26	33,994

THE DERBY, 1961–1971
For particulars of the Derby from 1780–1960 see 1921–61 editions.

The *Distance* of the Derby course at Epsom is 1½ mile. Lord Egremont won Derby in 1782, 1804, 5, 7, 26 (also, 5 Oaks); Duke of Grafton, 1802, 9, 10, 15 (also, 9 Oaks); Mr. Bowes, 1835, 43, 52, 3; Sir J. Hawley, Teddington (1851), Beadsman (1858), Musjid (1859), and Blue Gown (1868), the 1st Duke of Westminster, Bend Or (1880), Shotover (1882), Ormonde (1886), and Flying Fox (1899). Lady James Douglas was the first lady to win the Derby—War Substitute at Newmarket (1918); at Epsom, Mrs. G. B. Miller (1937). First winner was Sir Charles Bunbury's Diomed in 1780. From 1940 to 1945 a substitute Derby was run at Newmarket. By winning his 5th Derby, the late Aga Khan equalled Lord Egremont's record. He also won 2 Oaks.

Year	OWNER AND NAME OF WINNER	Betting	Jockey	Trainer	No. of Run'rs
1961	Mrs. A. Plesch's Psidium	66 to 1	R. Poincelet...	H. Wragg....	28
1962	Mr. R. R. Guest's Larkspur (Ir.)........	22 to 1	N. Sellwood...	M. V. O'Brien	26
1963	M. F. Dupré's Relko (Fr.)............	5 to 1 F.	Y. Saint-Martin	F. Mathet....	26
1964	Mr. J. Ismay's Santa Claus (Ir.)........	15 to 8 F.	A. Breasley...	J. Rogers.....	17
1965	M. J. Ternynck's Sea Bird II (Fr.).....	7 to 4 F.	T. P. Glennon ..	E. Pollet	22
1966	Lady Zia Wernher's Charlottown......	5 to 1	A. Breasley...	G. Smyth......	25
1967	Mr. H. J. Joel's Royal Palace*........	7–4 F.	G. Moore....	N. Murless ...	22
1968	Mr. R. R. Guest's Sir Ivor*(Ir.).......	4–5 F.	L. Piggott.....	M. V. O'Brien	13
1969	Mr. A. M. Budgett's Blakeney........	15–2	E. Johnson....	A. M. Budgett	26
1970	Mr. C. W. Engelhard's Nijinsky*° (Ir.)..	11–8 F.	L. Piggott.....	M. V. O'Brien	11
1971	Mr. P. Mellon's Mill Reef...........	100–30 F.	G. Lewis.....	I. Balding....	21

Marked* also won the Two Thousand Guineas; ° the St. Leger.
Record times, 2 min. 34 secs. by Hyperion in 1933; Windsor Lad in 1934; 2 min. 33·8 sec. Mahmoud in 1936.

TWO THOUSAND GUINEAS. First Run, 1809. Rowley Mile. Newmarket. 9 st.

Year	Owner and Name of Winner	Betting	Jockey	Trainer	No. of Run'rs
1967	Mr. H. J. Joel's Royal Palace.........	100 to 30 Jt. F.	G. Moore......	N. Murless......	18
1968	Mr. R. R. Guest's Sir Ivor (Ir.).....	11 to 8 F.	L. Piggott......	M. V. O'Brien...	10
1969	Mr. J. R. Brown's Right Tack.......	15 to 2	G. Lewis......	J. Sutcliffe......	13
1970	Mr. C. W. Englehard's Nijinsky.....	4 to 7 F.	L. Piggott......	M. V. O'Brien...	14
1971	Mrs. J. Hislop's Brigadier Gerard.....	11 to 2	J. Mercer......	D. Hern.........	6

ONE THOUSAND GUINEAS. 1814. Rowley Mile. Newmarket. Fillies. 9 st.

Year	Owner and Name of Winner	Betting	Jockey	Trainer	No. of Run'rs
1967	Mr. R. C. Boucher's Fleet...........	11 to 2	G. Moore......	N. Murless......	16
1968	Mrs. N. Murless's Caergwrle........	4 to 1 F.	A. Barclay......	N. Murless......	14
1969	Mr. R. B. Moller's Full Dress II.....	7 to 1	R. Hutchinson..	H. Wragg......	13
1970	Jean, Lady Ashcombe's Humble Duty.	3 to 1 Jt.F.	L. Piggott......	P. Walwyn......	12
1971	Mr. F. Hue-Williams's Altesse Royale	25 to 1	Y. Saint-Martin.	N. Murless......	10

OAKS. 1779. Epsom. 1½ Mile. Fillies. 9 st.

Year	Owner and Name of Winner	Betting	Jockey	Trainer	No. of Run'rs
1967	Countess Margit Batthyany's Pia.....	100 to 7	E. Hide........	W. Elsey......	12
1968	M. H. Berlin's La Lagune (Fr.)......	11 to 8 F.	G. Thiboeuf....	F. Boutin......	14
1969	Lord Rosebery's " Sleeping Partner ".	100 to 6	J. Gorton......	D. Smith......	15
1970	Mrs. S. Joel's Lupe...............	100–30 F.	A. Barclay......	N. Murless......	16
1971	Mr. F. Hue-Williams's Altesse Royale	6 to 4 F.	G. Lewis......	N. Murless......	11

ST. LEGER. 1776(8). Doncaster. 1¾ mile, 132 yards.

Year	Owner and Name of Winner	Betting	Jockey	Trainer	No. of Run'rs
1967	Mr. C. W. Englehard's Ribocco.....	7 to 2 Jt.F.	L. Piggott......	R. F. J. Houghton	9
1968	Mr. C. W. Englehard's Ribero.......	100 to 30	L. Piggott......	R. F. J. Houghton	8
1969	Mr. G. A. Oldham's Intermezzo.....	7 to 1	R. Hutchinson..	H. Wragg......	11
1970	Mr. C. W. Englehard's Nijinsky.....	2–7 F.	L. Piggott......	M. V. O'Brien...	9
1971	Mrs. J. Rogerson's Athens Wood.....	5 to 2	L. Piggott......	T. Jones......	8

	Lincolnshire Handicap. Doncaster—1 mile	Free Handicap. Newmarket—3 yrs.—7f.	Jockey Club Stakes. Newmarket 1½ miles.	Coronation Cup. Epsom 1½ miles.
1968	Frankincense 4y 9st 6lb....	Panpiper 7st 13lb........	Crozier 5y 9st..........	Royal Palace 4y 8st 10lb.
1969	Foggy Bell 4y 7st 11lb....	Welsh Pageant 8st 10lb....	Torpid 4y 9st 6lb.......	Park Top 5y 9st.........
1970	New Chapter 4y 8st 1lb....	Shiny Tenth 8st 3lb........	Queen of Twilight 4y 8st 11lb	Caliban 4y 9st..........
1971	Double Cream 4y 8st 9lb..	No Mercy 8st 5lb........	Meadowville 4y 9st 6lb....	Lupe 4y 8st 11lb........

	Ascot Stakes. 2½ miles.	Gold Cup. Ascot 2½ miles.	Coventry Stakes. Ascot—2 yrs—5 furlongs.	Grand Prix de Paris. 1 mile 7 furlongs.
1968	King of Peace 5y 7st 12lb..	Pardalio II 5y 9st........	Murrayfield 9st........	Dhaudevi.........
1969	Lexicon 5y 8st 11lb......	Levmoss 4y 9st........	Prince Tenderfoot 9st....	Chaparral.........
1970	Magna Carta 4y 8st 4lb....	Precipice Wood 4y 9st.....	Mill Reef 9st........	Roll of Honour......
1971	Celtic Cone 4y 8st 13lb....	Rock Roi 4y 9st*........	Sun Prince 8st 11 lb....	Basileus.........

	Chester Cup. Chester—2¼m, 77yd.	Jubilee Handicap. Kempton Park—1¼m.	Eclipse Stakes. Sandown Park—1¼m.	King George VI and Queen Elizabeth Stakes. Ascot—1½ miles.
1968	Major Rose 6y 8st 7lb....	Pally's Double 4y 6st 11lb..	Royal Palace 4y 9st 5lb..	Royal Palace 4y 9st 7lb.
1969	(Abandoned)............	Sovereign Ruler 4y 7st.....	Wolver Hollow 5y 9st 5lb	Park Top 5y 9st 4lb....
1970	Altogether 4y 7st 5lb....	Blue Yonder 4 y 8st 2lb....	Connaught 3y 8st 7lb....	Nijinsky (Ir.) 3y 8st 7lb.
1971	Random Shot 4y 8st 1lb..	Welsh Rarebit 4y 7st 11lb..	Mill Reef 3y 8st 7lb....	Mill Reef 3y 8st 7 lb....

	Prix de L'Arc de Triomphe Longchamp—1½ m.	Cheltenham Gold Cup. abt. 3¼ m.	Cambridgeshire. Newmarket—9 f.	Middle Park Stakes. Newmarket—2 yrs.—6 f.
1968	Vaguely Noble 3y 8st 10lb.	Fore Leney 11y 12st......	Emerilo 4y 7st 9lb......	Right Tack 9st..........
1969	Levmoss 4y 9st 6lb......	What A Myth 12y 12st....	Prince de Galles 3y 7st 12lb	Huntercombe 9st.........
1970	Sassafras 3y 8st 10lb....	L'Escargot 7y 12st......	Prince de Galles 4y 9st 7lb.	Brigadier Gerard 9st.....
1971	Mill Reef 3y 8st 10lb....	L'Escargot 8y 12 st......	King Midas 3y 7st 9lb....	Sharpen Up 8st 11lb.....

	Cesarewitch. Newmarket 2¼ m.	Washington Int'national Laurel Park—1½ m.	Champion Stakes. Newmarket 1¼ m.	Grand National. Liverpool 4m. 856 yds.
1968	Major Rose 6y 9st 4lb.....	Sir Ivor (England).........	Sir Ivor (Ir.) 3y 8st 7lb....	Red Alligator 9y 10st. [4lb
1969	Floridian 5y 7st 7lb......	Karabas (England)........	Flossy (Fr.) 3y 8st 4lb....	Highland Wedding 12y 10st
1970	Scoria 4y 7st...........	Fort Marcy (U.S.A.)......	Lorenzaccio 5y 9st......	Gay Trip 11st 5 lb.......
1971	Orosio 4y 8st 2lb........		Brigadier Gerard 3y 8st 7lb	Specify 9y 10st 13 lb....

* Race awarded at end of August to Random Shot.

CRICKET

Cricket is played under the "Laws of Cricket" and is governed by the Committee of the Marylebone Cricket Club (1787), Lord's, N.W.8. *Pres.*—F. R. Brown, *Sec.*, S. C. Griffith, D.F.C., T.D. *Asst. Secs.*, J. G. Dunbar; D. B. Carr; J. A. Bailey.

TEST MATCHES

Australia v. England, 1970–71

First Test.—(Brisbane, Nov. 27–Dec. 2). Drawn. Australia 433 and 214; England 464 and 39 for 1.

Second Test.—(Perth, Dec. 11–16). Drawn. England 397 and 287 for 6 (dec.); Australia 440 and 100 for 3.

Third Test.—(Melbourne, Dec. 31–Jan. 5). Abandoned.

Fourth Test.—(Sydney, Jan. 9–14). England won by 299 runs. England 332 and 319 for 5 (dec.); Australia 236 and 116.

Fifth Test.—(Melbourne, Jan. 21–26). Drawn. Australia 493 for 9 (dec.) and 169 for 4 (dec.); England 392 and 161 for no wicket.

Sixth Test.—(Adelaide, Jan. 29–Feb. 3). Drawn. England 470 and 233 for 4 (dec.); Australia 235 and 328 for 3.

Seventh Test.—(Sydney, Feb. 12–17). England won by 62 runs. England 184 and 302; Australia 264 and 160.

ENGLAND BATTING

Batsmen	Innings	Times not out	Runs	Highest Score	Average
G. Boycott	10	3	657	142*	93·85
J. H. Edrich	11	2	648	130	72·00
B. W. Luckhurst	9	1	455	131	56·87
R. Illingworth	10	1	333	53	37·00
B. L. d'Oliveira	10	0	369	117	36·90
A. P. E. Knott	9	2	222	73	31·71
K. W. R. Fletcher	9	0	225	80	25·00
J. A. Snow	7	1	141	38	23·50
J. H. Hampshire	4	0	92	55	23·00
M. C. Cowdrey	4	0	82	40	20·50
M. G. D. Willis	5	3	37	15*	18·50
P. Lever	6	0	83	36	13·83
D. L. Underwood	6	3	16	8*	5·33

Also batted: K. Shuttleworth, 7, 2. *Signifies not out.*

BOWLING

Bowlers	Overs	Maidens	Runs	Wickets	Average
J. A. Snow	225·5	47	708	31	22·83
R. G. D. Willis	88	16	329	12	27·41
D. L. Underwood	194·6	50	520	16	32·50
P. Lever	143·5	25	439	13	33·76
K. Shuttleworth	75·5	13	242	7	34·57
R. Illingworth	132	43	349	10	34·90
B. L. d'Oliveira	114	29	290	6	48·33
K. W. R. Fletcher	20	1	101	1	101·00

Also bowled: G. Boycott, 1–0–7–0; M. C. Cowdrey 6–0–36–0.

AUSTRALIA BATTING

Batsmen	Innings	Times not out	Runs	Highest score	Average
K. R. Stackpole	12	0	627	207	52·25
I. R. Redpath	12	2	497	171	49·70
W. M. Lawry	10	2	324	84	40·50
I. M. Chappell	12	0	452	111	37·66
K. D. Walters	12	2	373	112	37·30
G. S. Chappell	8	1	243	108	34·71
R. W. Marsh	9	1	215	92*	26·87
A. L. Thomson	5	4	22	12*	22·00
G. D. McKenzie	5	3	28	11*	14·00
K. J. O'Keeffe	3	0	42	27	14·00
A. A. Mallett	3	0	38	28	12·66
A. P. Sheahan	3	0	38	36	12·66
T. J. Jenner	4	0	36	30	9·00
J. W Gleeson	7	0	42	16	6·00
D. K. Lillee	3	0	16	10	5·33

Also batted: K. H. Eastwood 5, 0; A. N. Connolly 14, 0; J. R. F. Duncan 3; A. Dell 3*, 3* *Signifies not out.*

BOWLING

Bowlers	Overs	Maidens	Runs	Wickets	Average
D. K. Lillee	62·3	5	199	8	24·87
K. D. Walters	61·5	8	181	7	25·85
T. J. Jenner	65·6	15	176	6	29·33
A. A. Mallett	56·7	8	188	6	31·33
J. W. Gleeson	221	57	605	14	43·21
K. J. O'Keeffe	100	30	260	6	43·33
G. D. McKenzie	110·4	14	351	7	50·14
G. S. Chappell	193	15	255	5	51·00
A. L. Thomson	190	33	654	12	54·50
K. R. Stackpole	92·5	33	261	2	130·50

Also bowled: I. M. Chappell 3–0–10–1, J. R. F. Duncan 14–4–30–0; K. H. Eastwood 5–0–21–1; A. Dell 42·7–11–97–5; A. N. Connolly 27–3–81–1.

New Zealand v. England, 1971

First Test.—(Christchurch, Feb. 25–March 1). England won by 8 wickets. New Zealand 65 and 254; England 231 and 89 for 2.

Second Test.—(Auckland, March 5–8). Drawn. England 321 and 237; New Zealand 313 for 7 (dec.) and 40 for no wicket.

West Indies v. India, 1971

First Test.—(Kingston, Feb. 19–23.) Drawn. India 387; West Indies 217 and 385 for 5.

Second Test.—(Port of Spain, March 6–10.) India won by 7 wickets. West Indies 214 and 261; India 352 and 125 for 3.

Third Test.—(Georgetown, March 19–24.) Drawn. West Indies 363 and 307 for 3 (dec.); India 376 and 123 for no wicket.

Fourth Test.—(Bridgetown, April 1–6.) Drawn. West Indies 501 for 5 (dec.) and 180 for 6 (dec.); India 347 and 221 for 5.

Fifth Test.—(Port of Spain, April 13–19.) Drawn. India 360 and 427; West Indies 526 and 165 for 8.

WEST INDIES BATTING

Batsmen	Innings	Times not out	Runs	Highest Score	Average
C. A. Davis	8	4	531	125*	132·75
M. L. C. Foster	4	2	175	99	87·50
D. Lewis	5	2	259	88	86·33
G. S. Sobers	10	2	594	187*	74·25
R. B. Kanhai	9	1	433	158*	54·12
R. C. Fredericks	8	0	242	80	30·25
C. H. Lloyd	10	0	295	64	29·50
D. A. J. Holford	2	0	53	44	26·50
L. R. Gibbs	1	0	25	25	25·00
M. C. Carew	5	0	121	45	24·20
T. M. Findlay	3	1	37	30*	18·50
G. S. Camacho	4	0	68	35	17·00
V. A. Holder	3	0	35	14	11·66
K. D. Boyce	1	0	9	9	9·00
A. Barrett	4	0	33	19	8·25
G. Shillingford	4	0	31	25	7·75
J. N. Shepherd	3	0	12	9	4·00
J. Noreiga	5	2	11	9	3·66
U. Dowe	2	1	3	3	3·00

Did not bat: I. Ali. *Signifies not out.*

BOWLING

Bowlers	Overs	Maidens	Runs	Wickets	Average
J. Noreiga	200.2	47	493	17	29.00
K. D. Boyce	22.2	5	59	2	29.50
J.N. Shepherd	103	26	223	7	31.85
V. A. Holder	82	28	192	6	32.00
G. S. Sobers	219	69	402	11	36.54
D. A. J. Holford	55	8	131	3	43.66
A. Barrett	80.4	19	194	4	48.50
U. Dowe	84	14	244	5	48.80
M. L. C. Foster	39	14	52	1	52.00
G. Shillingford	75	9	217	4	54.25
I. Ali	38	5	125	1	125.00

Also bowled: R. B. Kanhai, 1—0—1—0; M. C. Carew, 14—4—20—0; C. H. Lloyd, 12—4—46—0; L. R. Gibbs, 40—17—65—0; C. A. Davis, 31—5—69—0; R. C. Fredericks, 5—0—10—0.

INDIA BATTING

Batsmen	Innings	Times not out	Runs	Highest Score	Average
S. M. Gavaskar	8	3	774	220	154.80
D. N. Sardesai	8	0	642	212	80.25
E. D. Solkar	7	1	224	65	37.33
A. V. Mankad	6	1	180	53*	36.00
E. A. S. Prasanna	4	2	61	25	30.50
G. R. Viswanath	5	0	135	50	27.00
S. Abid Ali	7	2	119	50*	23.80
A. L. Wadekar	7	0	151	54	21.57
S. Venkataraghavan	6	0	105	51	17.50
B. S. Bedi	6	2	37	20*	9.25
M. L. Jaisimha	5	0	43	23	8.60
A. S. Durani	4	0	24	13	6.00
P. Krishnamurthy	6	0	33	20	5.50
K. Jayantilal	1	0	5	5	5.00

BOWLING

Bowlers	Overs	Maidens	Runs	Wickets	Average
S. Venkataraghavan	289.3	67	774	22	33.81
E. A. S. Prasanna	160.5	40	395	11	35.90
B. S. Bedi	300.3	105	656	15	43.73
A. S. Durani	61	13	141	3	47.00
S. Abid Ali	164.1	29	523	11	47.54
E. D. Solkar	124	19	363	4	90.75

Also bowled: S. M. Gavaskar, 1—0—9—0; A. L. Wadekar, 3—0—12—0; M. L. Jaisimha, 24—4—63—0.

England v. Pakistan, 1971

First Test.—(Birmingham, June 3–8.) Drawn. Pakistan 608 for 7 (dec.); England 353 and 229 for 5.

Second Test.—(Lord's, June 17–22.) Drawn. England 241 for 2 (dec.) and 117 for no wicket; Pakistan 148.

Third Test.—(Leeds, July 8–13.) England won by 25 runs. England 316 and 264; Pakistan 350 and 205.

ENGLAND BATTING

Batsmen	Innings	Times not out	Runs	Highest Score	Average
G. Boycott	3	1	246	121*	123.00
B. W. Luckhurst	6	2	242	108*	60.50
B. L. d'Oliviera	4	0	241	74	60.25
A. P. E. Knott	4	1	137	116	45.66
R. A. Hutton	3	1	90	58*	45.00
D. L. Amiss	5	1	124	56	31.00
P. Lever	3	0	74	47	24.66
J. H. Edrich	5	0	87	37	17.40
R. Illingworth	4	0	67	45	16.75

Also batted: M. C. Cowdrey 16, 34; N. Gifford, 3*, 2*; R. N. S. Hobbs, 6, 0; K. Shuttleworth, 21; D. L. Underwood, 9; A. Ward, 0.

BOWLING

Bowlers	Overs	Maidens	Runs	Wickets	Average
B. L. d'Oliveria	99	47	162	8	20.05
N. Gifford	99.4	46	133	6	22.16
R. A. Hutton	63	13	126	5	25.20
R. Illingworth	87	36	162	6	27.00
P. Lever	88.3	20	239	7	34.14

Also bowled: R. N. S. Hobbs, 24—5—70—0; J. S. E. Price, 11.4—5—29—3; Shuttleworth, 23—2—83—0; Underwood, 41—13—102—0; A. Ward 29—3—115—0.

PAKISTAN BATTING

Batsmen	Innings	Times not out	Runs	Highest Score	Average
Zahir Abbas	4	0	386	274	96.50
Asif Iqbal	4	1	160	104*	53.33
Mushtaq Mohammad	4	0	164	100	41.00
Sadiq Mohammad	4	0	164	91	41.00
Salim Altaf	3	2	30	22	30.00
Aftab Gul	4	0	106	33	26.50
Wasim Bari	4	1	77	63	25.65
Intikhab Alam	4	0	48	18	12.00
Asif Masood	3	0	1	1	0.33

Also batted: M. J. Khan, 35, 9; Pervez Sajjad, 9*, 0; Saeed Ahmed, 22, 5; Imran Khan, 5.

* Signifies not out.

BOWLING

Bowlers	Overs	Maidens	Runs	Wickets	Average
Salim	58.4	20	110	6	18.33
Masood	119.5	26	344	13	26.46
Iqbal	50	11	108	4	27.00
Pervez	71.5	71	201	5	40.20
Saeed	19	4	43	1	43.00
Intikhab	143.1	46	366	8	45.75

Also bowled: Zahir, 1—0—1—0; Aftab, 1—0—4—0; Sadiq, 5—1—17—0; M. J. Khan, 14—3—31—0; Imran 28—9—55—0.

England v. India, 1971

First Test.—(Lord's, July 22–27.) Drawn. England 304 and 191; India 313 and 145 for 8.

Second Test.—(Old Trafford, Aug. 5–10.) Drawn. England 386 and 245 for 3 (dec.); India 212 and 65 for 3.

Third Test.—(The Oval, Aug. 19–24). India won by 4 wickets. England 355 and 101; India 284 and 174 for 6.

ENGLAND BATTING

Batsmen	Innings	Times not out	Runs	Highest Score	Average
A. P. E. Knott	5	0	223	90	44.00
B. W. Luckhurst	6	0	244	101	40.66
J. A. Jameson	4	0	141	82	35.25
R. Illingworth	5	0	175	107	35.00
R. A. Hutton	5	1	129	81	32.25
J. H. Edrich	6	0	180	62	30.00
J. A. Snow	4	0	85	73	21.25
B. L. d'Oliviera	6	1	88	30	17.60
N. Gifford	3	1	32	17	16.00
K. W. R. Fletcher	4	1	30	28	10.00
J. S. E. Price	5	2	9	5	3.00

Also batted: D. L. Amiss, 9, 0; G. Boycott, 3, 33; D. L. Underwood, 22, 11; P. Lever, 88.

BOWLING

Bowlers	Overs	Maidens	Runs	Wickets	Average
N. Gifford	64·3	18	127	8	15·88
P. Lever	33	7	84	5	16·80
J. S. E. Price	81	21	207	8	25·87
B. L. d'Oliveira	58	28	83	3	27·66
J. A. Snow	74	21	169	6	28·16
R. Illingworth	118·3	43	202	7	28·85
D. L. Underwood	63	20	121	4	30·25
R. A. Hutton	60	14	131	4	32·75

Also bowled: B. W. Luckhurst, 2–0–9–1.

INDIA BATTING

Batsmen	Innings	Times not out	Runs	Highest Score	Average
F. M. Engineer	5	1	172	59	43·00
E. D. Solkar	5	1	168	67	42·00
A. L. Wadekar	6	0	204	85	34·00
D. N. Sardesai	6	1	147	54	29·40
G. R. Viswanath	6	1	128	68	25·60
S. M. Gavaskar	6	0	144	57	24·00
S. Venkataraghavan	4	0	62	24	15·50
S. Abid Ali	5	1	50	26	12·50
A. V. Mankad	6	0	42	11	7·00
B. S. Bedi	3	1	12	8	4·00

Also batted: B. S. Chandrasekhar, 0, 4, 0.

BOWLING

Bowlers	Overs	Maidens	Runs	Wickets	Average
E. D. Solkar	58	16	137	6	22·83
S. Venkataraghavan	150·3	38	350	13	26·92
B. S. Chandrasekhar	146·1	32	379	13	29·15
B. S. Bedi	151·3	46	325	11	29·54
S. Abid Ali	97·4	14	269	5	53·80

Also bowled: S. M. Gavaskar, 15–3–42–0.

MISCELLANEOUS CRICKET RECORDS

Highest Individual Scores.—In first-class cricket in England: A. C. MacLaren, 424, for Lancashire *v.* Somerset at Taunton, July, 1895. In Australia: D. G. Bradman (Australia), 452 (not out) for N.S.W. *v.* Queensland, Sydney, 1929–30. In India: B. B. Nimbalkar (Maharashtra *v.* W. Indian States), Poona, 1948–49, 443 (not out). In Pakistan: Hanif Mohammad, 499, Karachi *v.* Bahawalpur, 1959. In a minor inter-county match: F. E. Lacey (Hampshire *v.* Norfolk), Southampton, 1887, 323 (not out). In other minor matches: A. E. J. Collins, aged 13, scored 628 (not out) in a Junior House match playing for Clarke's House *v.* North Town at Clifton College in 1899.

Highest Team Innings.—Australia, Victoria 1,107 *v.* N.S.W., Melbourne, 1926; England, England 903 (for 7 dec.) *v.* Australia, 1938.

Smallest Totals.—Oxford University (one man absent), 12 *v.* M.C.C. at Oxford, May 1877; Northamptonshire *v.* Gloucestershire, June 11, 1907.

Highest Aggregate.—Bombay, 651 and 714 for 8 dec. *v.* Maharastra. 407, 604, Poona, 1948–49. Total 2,376 (38 wkts.).

Highest Partnership.—Gul Mahomed (319) and V. S. Hazare (288) made 577 for 4th wkt. for Baroda *v.* Holkar, March 7, 1947.

County Championship Table, 1971

County Order for 1971. 1970 in brackets	Played	Won	Lost	Drawn	No Decision	Bonus Btg.	Bonus Blng.	Points
Surrey (5)	24	11	3	10	0	63	82	255
Warwickshire (8).	24	9	6	9	0	73	92	255
Lancashire (3)	24	9	4	11	0	76	75	241
Kent (1)	24	7	6	11	0	82	82	234
Leicestershire (15)	24	6	2	16*	0	74	74	215
Middlesex (16)	24	7	6	11	0	61	81	212
Somerset (13)	24	7	4	13	0	50	89	209
Gloucestershire (17)	24	7	3	13	1	50	81	201
Hampshire (10)	24	4	6	14	0	70	82	192
Essex (12)	24	6	5	13	0	43	84	187
Sussex (9)	24	5	9	10	0	55	77	182
Nottinghamshire (11)	24	3	7	14	0	58	83	171
Yorkshire (4)	24	4	8	12	0	47	75	162
Northamptonshire (14)	24	4	8	12	0	36	83	159
Worcestershire (6)	24	3	7	14	0	46	76	152
Glamorgan (2)	24	2	5	15	0	55	63	148
Derbyshire (7)	24	1	4	19	0	51	81	142

* Leicestershire's record includes five points in drawn match when scores finished level and they were batting.

County Knock-Out Competition (Gillette Cup)

Final.—Lancashire beat Kent by 24 runs. Kent 200; Lancashire 224 for 7.

Worcestershire won the 1971 John Player Sunday League Competition on faster run rate with 44 points from 16 games.

Universities.—Oxford University drew with Cambridge University. Cambridge 180 for 7 (dec.) and 266 for 5 (dec.); Oxford 203 and 180 for 9.

Eton v. Harrow.—Drawn. Harrow 183 and 148 for 8 (dec.); Eton 195 for 9 (dec.) and 70 for 4.

JOHN PLAYER SUNDAY LEAGUE TABLE, 1971

	Played	Won	Lost	No Res.	Pts.
Worcestershire	16	11	5	0	44
Essex	16	11	5	0	44
Lancashire	16	10	6	0	40
Leicestershire	16	10	6	0	40
Somerset	16	9	5	2	38
Hampshire	16	9	7	0	36
Kent	16	8	8	0	32
Surrey	16	8	8	0	32
Sussex	16	8	8	0	32
Glamorgan	16	7	7	2	30
Derbyshire	16	7	8	1	29
Nottinghamshire	16	6	9	1	25
Middlesex	16	6	10	0	24
Northants	16	6	10	0	24
Gloucestershire	16	5	9	2	22
Yorkshire	16	5	9	2	22
Warwickshire	16	5	11	0	20

Worcestershire won on faster run rate.

BATTING AND BOWLING AVERAGES

English Batting Averages, 1971
(Qualifications, 8 Innings)

Batsmen	Number of Innings	Times not out	Total Runs	Highest Innings	Average
G. Boycott	30	5	2,503	233	100·12
K. W. R. Fletcher	41	12	1,490	164*	51·37
M. J. Harris	45	1	2,238	177	50·86
M. J. Smith	48	9	1,951	127	50·02
B. W. Luckhurst	41	3	1,861	155*	48·97
R. B. Kanhai	41	9	1,529	135*	47·78
B. A. Richards	45	4	1,938	141*	47·26
J. H. Edrich	44	1	2,031	195*	47·23
G. S. Sobers	38	6	1,485	151*	46·40
Asif Iqbal	34	6	1,294	120	46·21
R. C. Fredericks	33	3	1,377	145*	45·90
M. J. Procter	43	4	1,786	167	45·79
R. G. A. Headley	42	2	1,805	187	45·12
G. R. J. Roope	46	9	1,641	171	44·35
M. C. Cowdrey	16	1	655	132	43·66
A. J. Harvey-Walker	8	1	304	110*	43·42
D. B. Close	42	10	1,389	116*	43·40
A. R. Lewis	44	9	1,501	111	42·88
C. C. Inman	38	5	1,404	147	42·54
G. M. Turner	31	4	1,126	179	41·70
A. P. E. Knott	35	6	1,209	128*	41·68
Majid J. Khan	40	2	1,542	113	40·57
J. A. Jameson	48	1	1,906	231	40·55
W. E. Russell	49	5	1,743	118	39·61
P. H. Parfitt	52	4	1,901	130	39·60
C. A. Milton	20	2	700	90	38·88
R. T. Virgin	46	3	1,668	179*	38·79
C. H. Lloyd	33	4	1,124	217*	38·75
H. Pilling	43	8	1,351	126*	38·60
R. E. Marshall	47	7	1,543	142*	38·57
P. J. Watts	45	11	1,311	102*	38·55
B. C. Francis	45	4	1,577	140	38·46
M. H. Denness	42	3	1,494	111	38·30
B. Wood	43	4	1,492	165*	38·25
M. J. Smedley	49	4	1,718	131*	38·17
J. Whitehouse	36	2	1,295	173	38·08
D. L. Amiss	37	3	1,294	124	38·05
C. T. Radley	42	10	1,202	110*	37·56
Younis Ahmed	47	6	1,485	138*	36·21
J. H. Hampshire	40	5	1,259	183*	35·97
S. J. Storey	40	7	1,187	164	35·87
C. P. Wilkins	47	4	1,517	156	35·27
D. S. Steele	48	3	1,577	140	35·04
A. G. E. Ealham	45	6	1,363	104	34·94
B. Dudleston	44	4	1,366	101*	34·75
K. G. Suttle	16	1	521	120	34·73
P. D. Johnson	16	4	416	66	34·66
J. Balderstone	13	1	415	63	34·58
D. R. Owen-Thomas	34	3	1,065	146	34·35
B. L. d'Oliveira	38	5	1,130	136	34·24
Mushtaq Mohammad	51	2	1,660	108	33·87
R. W. Tolchard	36	10	877	105*	33·73
I. W. Hall	47	4	1,449	95	33·69
B. Davison	40	2	1,280	102	33·68
H. M. Ackerman	46	1	1,504	123	33·42
P. J. Sharpe	26	2	801	172*	33·37
P. J. Sainsbury	39	10	959	72*	33·06
M. G. Griffith	43	15	905	142*	32·32
M. J. Kitchen	43	2	1,325	120	32·31
J. F. Harvey	43	5	1,226	94	32·26
D. Nicholls	33	2	1,000	135	32·25
K. L. Snellgrove	37	6	991	71*	31·96
J. B. Bolus	49	3	1,468	131	31·91
J. F. Steele	41	5	1,147	195	31·86
M. A. Buss	46	4	1,337	140	31·83
J. M. Brearley	35	4	979	81*	31·58
R. A. Hutton	40	8	1,009	189	31·53
D. A. Livingstone	18	2	501	91	31·41
D. M. Lewis	16	4	374	62*	31·16
N. G. Featherstone	37	6	965	120*	31·12
P. J. K. Gibbs	45	3	1,307	127	31·11
M. H. Page	38	3	1,050	111	30·91
B. S. Crump	44	14	915	133*	30·50
T. J. Yardley	39	4	1,066	104*	30·45
G. Frost	31	0	941	104	30·35
R. M. C. Gilliat	45	4	1,231	79	30·02
F. M. Engineer	35	4	930	141	30·00
D. Lloyd	45	1	1,316	92	29·90
R. B. Nicholls	45	2	1,276	81	29·67
R. D. V. Knight	47	3	1,305	102*	29·65

English Bowling Averages, 1971
(Qualifications, 10 Wickets in 10 Innings)

Bowlers	Overs	Maidens	Runs	Wickets	Average
G. G. Arnold	632	171	1,421	83	17·12
P. J. Sainsbury	845·5	332	1,874	107	17·51
T. W. Cartwright	976·4	407	1,852	104	17·80
D. Wilson	572·2	210	1,095	60	18·25
N. G. Featherstone	131·3	34	336	18	18·66
L. R. Gibbs	1024·1	296	2,475	131	18·89
M. J. Procter	535	149	1,232	65	18·95
D. L. Underwood	945·5	368	1,986	102	19·47
J. C. Balderstone	162·5	59	354	18	19·66
R. Illingworth	633	230	1,269	64	19·82
G. D. McKenzie	716·4	196	1,666	82	20·31
R. A. Hutton	738·3	181	1,628	80	20·35
P. Lever	452·3	122	1,142	56	20·39
D. S. Steele	304·5	101	818	40	20·45
J. N. Graham	638·4	176	1,648	78	21·12
M. Llewellyn	121	31	275	13	21·15
C. E. Waller	377·4	127	914	43	21·25
R. N. S. Hobbs	604·4	130	1,702	78	21·82
R. M. H. Cottam	848·2	260	1,784	80	22·30
J. K. Lever	528·3	93	1,535	68	22·57
K. V. Jones	702·1	242	1,676	74	22·64
F. J. Titmus	1065·1	341	2,355	104	22·64
R. A. Woolmer	321	82	770	34	22·64
P. Willey	195·1	58	478	21	22·76
J. Birkenshaw	917·4	269	2,059	90	22·87
N. Gifford	629·5	213	1,275	55	23·18
P. H. Edmonds	479	153	1 045	45	23·22
B. L. d'Oliveira	464·4	164	999	43	23·23
J. A. Jameson	113·5	19	398	17	23·41
K. J. O'Keefe	653·1	217	1,815	77	23·57
G. F. Cross	124·2	22	332	14	23·71
S. J. Storey	444	129	1,000	42	23·80
R. E. East	738·1	223	1,623	67	24·22
J. A. Spencer	569·3	138	1,471	60	24·51
R. J. Hadley	172·4	39	519	21	24·71
J. F. Steele	461·2	149	1,091	44	24·79
K. Shuttleworth	583	163	1,468	59	24·88
E. J. O. Hemsley	127·3	30	326	13	25·07
K. Ibadulla	264	79	634	25	25·36
J. Davey	437·3	99	1,251	49	25·53
J. W. Swinburne	351·1	97	1,066	39	25·79
S. Turner	426·3	136	913	35	26·08
M. A. Nash	671·2	170	1,701	65	26·16
H. C. Latchman	717	172	2,123	81	26·20
N. M. McVicker	697·2	153	1,942	74	26·24
A. S. Brown	329	73	893	34	26·26
A. G. Nicholson	678·5	195	1,476	56	26·35
R. D. Jackman	490·1	93	1,561	59	26·45
P. H. Parfitt	254	60	608	26	26·46
M. A. Buss	570·1	178	1,649	62	26·59
J. Simmons	624·5	184	1,758	66	26·63
H. R. Moseley	382·5	73	1,042	39	26·71
J. S. E. Price	660·3	164	1,790	67	26·71
D. A. Allen	271	51	803	30	26·76
D. J. Shepherd	820·3	253	1,878	70	26·82
M. K. Bore	538·3	192	1,184	44	26·90
P. I. Pocock	907	266	2,216	82	27·02
D. Breakwell	376·5	111	975	36	27·08
J. C. Dye	377·2	93	1,003	37	27·10
V. A. Holder	788·1	192	2,064	76	27·15
Mushtaq Mohammad	504·2	127	1,417	52	27·25
M. Bissex	532·2	135	1,562	57	27·40
J. B. Mortimore	952·3	248	2,448	89	27·50
J. W. Holder	164·2	30	524	19	27·57
C. M. Old	497	114	1,337	48	27·85
M. St. J. Burton	323·4	109	781	28	27·89
K. Wilkinson	247·5	50	675	24	28·12
R. A. White	780·5	191	2,288	81	28·24
B. Julien	398·1	88	1,244	44	28·27
U. C. Joshi	782·5	197	2,096	74	28·32
Intikhab Alam	1007·4	245	2,950	104	28·36
A. Ward	551·2	110	1,730	61	28·36
K. D. Boyce	621·1	116	1,831	64	28·60
D. J. Brown	273	70	801	28	28·60
R. G. D. Willis	370	83	1,011	35	28·88
C. T. Spencer	314	95	726	25	29·04
A. W. Greig	799·4	168	2,239	77	29·07
A. E. Cordle	531·3	123	1,429	49	29·16
T. E. Jesty	472·2	115	1,226	42	29·19
D. P. Hughes	871·2	302	2,409	82	29·37

* Denotes not out

LIST OF COUNTY CRICKET CHAMPIONS.

1934	Lancashire		1956	Surrey	1964	Worcestershire
1935	Yorkshire	1949 { Middlesex / Yorkshire	1957	Surrey	1965	Worcestershire
1936	Derbyshire		1958	Surrey	1966	Yorkshire
1937	Yorkshire	1950 { Lancashire / Surrey	1959	Yorkshire	1967	Yorkshire
1938	Yorkshire	1951 Warwickshire	1960	Yorkshire	1968	Yorkshire
1939	Yorkshire	1952 Surrey	1961	Hampshire	1969	Glamorgan
1946	Yorkshire	1953 Surrey	1962	Yorkshire	1970	Kent
1947	Middlesex	1954 Surrey	1963	Yorkshire	1971	Surrey
1948	Glamorgan	1955 Surrey				

RUGBY FOOTBALL
International Union Table, 1970–71

Country	Played	Won	Drawn	Lost	Points Scored		Points
					For	Against	
Wales	4	4	0	0	73	38	8
France	4	1	2	1	41	40	4
England	4	1	1	2	44	58	3
Ireland	4	1	1	2	41	46	3
Scotland	4	1	0	3	47	64	3

CALCUTTA CUP
England v. Scotland
1967 England 27–14
1968 England 8–6
1969 England 8–3
1970 Scotland 14–5
1971 Scotland 16–15

COUNTY CHAMPIONSHIP
Surrey and Durham.
Middlesex.
Lancashire.
Staffordshire.
Surrey.

INTERNATIONAL MATCHES, 1970–71
1970
Oct. 3   Twickenham. England and Wales 14; Scotland and Ireland 14.
1971
Jan. 16   Cardiff. Wales 22; England 6.
Jan. 16   Colombes. France 13; Scotland 8.
Jan. 30   Dublin. Ireland 17; France 9.
Feb. 6   Edinburgh. Scotland 18; Wales 19.
Feb. 13   Dublin. Ireland 6; England 9.
Feb. 27   Twickenham. England 14; France 14.
Feb. 27   Edinburgh. Scotland 5; Ireland 17.
Mar. 13   Cardiff. Wales 23; Ireland 9.
Mar. 20   Twickenham. England 15; Scotland 16.
Mar. 27   Paris. France 5; Wales 9.
Mar. 27   Edinburgh. Scotland 26; England 6.
June 26   Dunedin. New Zealand 3; British Isles 9.
July 10   Christchurch. New Zealand 22; British Isles 12.
July 31   Wellington. New Zealand 3; British Isles 13.
Aug. 14   Auckland. New Zealand 14; British Isles 14.
Sept. 24   Osaka. Japan 19; England 27.
Sept. 28   Tokyo. Japan 3; England 6.

COUNTY CHAMPIONSHIP FINAL
Surrey beat Gloucestershire 14–3.
OTHER CHIEF MATCHES, 1970–71
Universities. 1970. Oxford University beat Cambridge University 14–3 at Twickenham on Dec. 8.
Hospitals Cup Final.—Guy's beat St. Mary's 14–3.
Services.—Army and R.A.F. drew 6–6; Royal Navy beat Army 11–9; R.A.F. beat Royal Navy 17–6.

RUGBY FOOTBALL LEAGUE (Est. 1895)
International Matches
1971
Feb. 7   Toulouse. France 16; Great Britain 8.
Mar. 17   St. Helens. Great Britain 24; France 2.

World Cup Competition
1970
Oct. 21   Wigan. Australia 47; New Zealand 11.
24   Leeds. Great Britain 11; Australia 4.
25   Hull. France 15; New Zealand 16.

Oct. 28   Castleford. Great Britain 6; France 0.
31   Swinton. Great Britain 27; New Zealand 17.
Nov. 1   Bradford. Australia 15; France 17.
FINAL
Nov. 7   Leeds. Great Britain 7; Australia 12.

Rugby League Challenge Cup.—Final. Leigh beat Leeds by 24–7 pts. at Wembley Stadium on May 15, 1971. *Semi-Finals.* Leeds beat Castleford 19–5; Leigh beat Huddersfield 10–4.
County Champions.—Yorkshire.
Northern League Champions.—St. Helens beat Wigan 16–12 at Swinton.

HOCKEY, 1970–71
MEN'S HOCKEY
INTERNATIONAL CHAMPIONSHIP

					Goals		
	P.	W.	D.	L.	F.	A.	P.
England	3	3	0	0	4	0	4
Scotland	3	2	0	1	2	1	3
Wales	3	1	0	2	2	2	2
Ireland	3	0	0	3	0	5	1

INTERNATIONAL MATCHES
England and France drew 0–0; England beat Scotland 1–0; England beat West Germany 1–0; England and Holland drew 0–0; Wales beat Ireland 2–0; Scotland beat Ireland 1–0; England beat Wales 1–0; England beat Ireland 2–0; Scotland beat Wales 1–0.
Universities.—Cambridge University beat Oxford University 1–0.
County Championship Final.—Staffordshire beat Lancashire 2–1.
Services Championship.—R.A.F. and Army.

WOMEN'S HOCKEY
LEADING MATCHES, 1970–71
England and West Germany drew 2–2; England beat Ireland 1–0; England beat Scotland 1–0; England and Wales drew 0–0; England beat Wales 2–0.

LACROSSE, 1970–71
Annual Territorial Match.—North beat South 15–5.
English Club Championship (Iroquois Cup).—South Manchester and Wythenshawe beat Lee 15–6.
North of England Senior Flags—South Manchester and Wythenshawe beat Urmston (replay).
South of England Senior Flags.—Lee beat Hampstead 19–6.
Northern Counties Championship.—Lancashire beat Cheshire.
University.—Oxford University beat Cambridge University 16–10.

ASSOCIATION FOOTBALL
International Table 1970-71

Country	Played	Won	Drawn	Lost	Goals		Points
					For	Against	
England...............	3	2	1	0	4	1	5
Ireland...............	3	2	0	1	2	1	4
Wales................	3	0	2	1	0	1	2
Scotland.............	3	0	1	2	1	4	1

ENGLAND *v.* SCOTLAND.

	g. g.
1966 England....	4—3
1967 Scotland ...	3—2
1968 Draw......	1—1
1969 England....	4—1
1970 Draw......	0—0
1971 England....	3—1

LEAGUE COMPETITION, 1970-71

Div. I.—Arsenal, 65 pts. Runners-up, Leeds United, 64 pts. Relegated: Burnley, 27 pts., and Blackpool, 23 pts.

Div. II.—Promoted: Leicester City, 59 pts. and Sheffield United, 56 pts. Relegated: Blackburn Rovers, 27 pts. and Bolton Wanderers, 24 pts.

Div. III.—Promoted: Preston, 61 pts. and Fulham, 60 pts. Relegated: Reading, 39 pts., Bury, 37 pts., Doncaster Rovers, 35 pts. and Gillingham 33 pts.

Div. IV.—Promoted: Notts. County, 69 pts., Bournemouth, 60 pts., Oldham, 59 pts. and York City, 56 pts.

SCOTTISH LEAGUE.—Div. I Champions: Celtic, 56 pts; Div. II Champions: Partick Thistle, 56 pts.

REPRESENTATIVE MATCHES, 1970-71
HOME INTERNATIONALS

1971
May 15   Cardiff. Wales 0; Scotland 0.
         Belfast. Ireland 0; England 1.
May 18   Hampden Park. Scotland 0; Ireland 1.
May 19   Wembley. England 0; Wales 0.
May 22   Wembley. England 3; Scotland 1.
         Belfast. Ireland 1; Wales 0.

OTHER INTERNATIONALS

1970
Nov. 25 Wembley. England 3; East Germany 1.

European Nations Cup
1971
Feb. 3   Valletta. Malta 0; England 1.
April 21 Wembley. England 3; Greece 0.
May 12   Wembley. England 5; Malta 0.

INTER-LEAGUE MATCHES

1970
Sept. 2 Celtic Park. Scottish League 1; League of Ireland 0.
Sept. 23 Norwich. Football League 5; Irish League 0.

1971
Mar. 17 Hampden Park. Scottish League 0; Football League 1.

UNDER-23 INTERNATIONALS

1970
Oct. 14 Leicester. England 3; West Germany 1.
Nov. 11 Hull. England 2; Sweden 0.
Dec. 2   Wrexham. Wales 0; England 0.

1971
Feb. 24 Hampden Park. Scotland 2; England 2.

CUP FINALS, 1970-71

F.A. CUP.—*S.F.:* March 27 (Old Trafford), Liverpool beat Everton 2–1. Attendance 62,144.

FOOTBALL ASSOCIATION CUP.

	g. g.
Everton *b.* Sheffield W.	3—2
Tottenham H. *b.* Chelsea...	2—1
W.B.A. *b.* Everton	1—0
Manchester C. *b.* Leicester.	1—0
Chelsea *b.* Leeds U.	2—1
Arsenal *b.* Liverpool	2—1

Final: May 8 (Wembley Stadium), Arsenal beat Liverpool 2–1 (after extra time). Attendance 100,000. Receipts £187,000 (record).

FOOTBALL LEAGUE CUP. *Final,* Feb. 27 (Wembley Stadium), Tottenham Hotspur beat Aston Villa 2–0. Attendance 100,000. Receipts £132,000 (record).

F.A. AMATEUR.—*S.F.:* March 20 (Bolton), Skelmersdale United beat Leatherhead 2–0. March 27 (Fulham), Dagenham beat Slough 2–1 (after 3–3 draw).

Final: April 24 (Wembley Stadium), Skelmersdale United beat Dagenham 4–1. Attendance 45,000.

F.A. CHALLENGE TROPHY.—*F.:* Telford United beat Hillingdon 3–2 at Wembley Stadium.

SCOTTISH CUP.—*S.F.:* (Hampden Park) Celtic beat Airdrie 2–0 (after 3–3 draw). (Hampden Park) Rangers beat Hibernian 2–1 (after 0–0 draw).

Final: May 12 (Hampden Park) Celtic beat Rangers 2–1 (after 1–1 draw). Attendance 103,332.

SCOTTISH LEAGUE CUP.—*F.:* Rangers beat Celtic 1–0.

ARTHUR DUNN CUP.—*F.:* Old Malvernians beat Old Brentwoods 4–2.

EUROPEAN CUP.—*S.F.* Ajax Amsterdam beat Athletico Madrid (on aggregate) 3–1; Panathinaikos and Red Star Belgrade (on aggregate) drew 4–4. Panathinaikos won on away goals. *F.:* Ajax beat Panathinaikos 2–0 at Wembley Stadium.

CUP-WINNERS CUP.—*S.F.:* Chelsea beat Manchester City (on aggregate) 2–0; Real Madrid beat PSV Eindhoven (on aggregate) 2–1. *F.:* Chelsea beat Real Madrid 2–1 at Athens (after 1–1 draw).

INTER-CITIES' FAIRS CUP.—*F.:* Leeds United beat Juventus (on away goals after 3–3 on aggregate).

AMATEUR HOME INTERNATIONALS

1970
Oct. 2   Woking. England 4; Ireland 1.
Dec. 5   Hendon. England 3; Wales 0.
1971
Feb. 6   Rhyl. Wales 3; Scotland 1.
Feb. 19 Belfast. Ireland 1; Scotland 1.
April 2 Falkirk. Scotland 0; England 2.
April 17 Llanelli. Wales 1; Ireland 0.

Universities.—Cambridge University beat Oxford University 1–0.
Services Championship.—Army.

WORLD CUP WINNERS, 1930-1970

1930 *(Played in Uruguay)*............Uruguay
1934 *(Italy)*..........................Italy
1938 *(France)*........................Italy
1950 *(Brazil)*......................Uruguay
1954 *(Switzerland)*...........West Germany
1958 *(Sweden)*.......................Brazil
1962 *(Chile)*........................Brazil
1966 *(England)*.....................England
1970 *(Mexico)*.......................Brazil

GOLF, 1970–72

CHAMPIONSHIPS.

OPEN
(Instituted 1860.)
1964 A. Lema (U.S.A.), 279.
1965 P. W. Thomson (Australia) 285.
1966 J. W. Nicklaus (U.S.A.), 282.
1967 R. de Vicenzo (Argentina), 278.
1968 G. Player (S. Africa), 289.
1969 A. Jacklin, (G.B.), 280.
1970 J. W. Nicklaus (U.S.A.) beat D. Sanders (U.S.A.), after tie 283.
1971 L. Trevino (U.S.A.) 278.

PROFESSIONAL MATCH PLAY TOURNAMENT
1964 N. C. Coles.
1965 N. C. Coles.
1966 P. W. Thomson (Aust.)
1967 P. W. Thomson (Aust.)
1968 B. G. C. Huggett.
1969 M. Bembridge.
1970 T. Horton.

AMATEUR
(1885.)
1964 G. J. Clark.
1965 M. F. Bonallack.
1966 R. Cole (S. Africa).
1967 B. Dickson (U.S.A.).
1968 M. F. Bonallack.
1969 M. F. Bonallack.
1970 M. F. Bonallack.
1971 S. N. Melnyk (U.S.A.).

LADIES
(1893.)
1964 Miss C. Sorenson (U.S.A.).
1965 Mlle. B. Varangot (France).
1966 Miss D. E. Chadwick.
1967 Miss D. E. Chadwick.
1968 Mlle. B. Varangot (France).
1969 Mlle. C. Lacoste (France).
1970 Miss D. L. Oxley.
1971 Miss M. Walker

WALKER CUP
(St. Andrews, May 1971)
Great Britain and Ireland won by 13 matches to 11.
Winners—
Great Britain and Ireland.—Singles—H. B. Stuart (2); W. Humphreys; C. W. Green; R. J. Carr; G. MacGregor; D. M. Marsh.
Foursomes—M. F. Bonallack and Humphreys; Green and Carr; Marsh and MacGregor; J. S. Macdonald and R. Foster; Stuart and Carr.
U.S.A.—Singles—J. L. Wadkins (2); M. M. Giles; A. L. Miller; S. N. Melnyk; J. R. Gabrielsen; T. O. Kite (2).
Foursomes—Melnyk and Giles; Miller and J. Farquhar.

RYDER CUP
(St. Louis, Sept. 1971)
U.S.A. won by 16 matches to 11, with 5 halved.
Winners—
Singles—U.S.A.—L. Trevino (2); G. Dickinson; D. Stockton; J. W. Nicklaus (2); J. C. Snead.
British Isles—P. A. Oosterhuis (2); B. Barnes (2); H. Bannerman; B. Gallacher.
Foursomes—U.S.A.—A. Palmer and Dickinson (2); Nicklaus and Snead.
British Isles—N. C. Coles and C. O'Connor; B. G. C. Huggett and A. Jacklin; M. Bembridge and P. J. Butler; Bannerman and Gallacher.
Fourballs—U.S.A.—Trevino and M. Rudolph; Palmer and Dickinson; Snead and F. Beard; Nicklaus and G. Littler; Littler and Snead; Palmer and Nicklaus.
British Isles—Gallagher and Oosterhuis.

OTHER CHIEF GOLF EVENTS, 1970–71
Australian Open.—G. Player, 280.
President's Putter.—G. T. Duncan beat D. L. Baxter.
Halford Hewitt Cup (Final).—Charterhouse beat Marlborough 3 to 2.
English Amateur.—W. Humphreys.
Piccadilly Medal Tournament. P. A. Oosterhuis.
Penfold Tournament.—N. C. Coles, 284.
Brabazon Trophy.—M. F. Bonallack.
World Senior Championship.—K. Nagle (Australia).
Wills Tournament.—B. J. Hunt, 276.
Wills Women's International Tournament.—Miss D. L. Oxley.

Australian P.G.A. Championship.—B. Devlin, 275.
World Cup Championship (Buenos Aires, Nov. 1970) —1, Australia, 545; 2, Argentina, 554; 3, S. Africa, 563.
Golf Illustrated Gold Vase.—M. F. Bonallack.
Agfa-Gevaert Tournament.—P. A. Oosterhuis, 276.
Daks.—N. C. Coles and B. G. C. Huggett, 284.
Martini—B. Gallacher, 282.
Hovis Women's Stroke Play.—Mrs. C. Barclay, 223.
Gallacher Ulster Tournament.—T. Horton, 274.
Uniroyal Southern Championship.—P. A. Oosterhuis.
Scottish Amateur.—S. Stephen.
Irish Amateur.—R. Kane.
Welsh Amateur.—C. Brown.
Welsh Women.—Mrs. A. Briggs.
Under 23 Professional.—D. J. Vaughan.
Carroll's Tournament.—N. C. Coles, 276.
U.S.A. Masters.—C. Coody, 279.
U.S.A. Open.—L. Trevino (U.S.A.).
U.S.A., P.G.A. Championship.—J. W. Nicklaus, 281.
Universities.—Oxford beat Cambridge 11–4.
English County Championship.—Staffordshire.
Women's County Championship.—Kent.
British Youth Open.—P. Elson, 277.
Youth's International.—Great Britain and Ireland beat Continent of Europe 10–5.
Boys' International.—England and Scotland drew 7½–7½.
British Boys' Championship.—H. K. Clark.
English Girls' Championship.—Miss C. Eckersley.
British Girls' Championship.—Miss J. Mark.
Girls' International Championship Series.—England.
HomeAmateur International Championship.—Scotland.
Dunlop Masters.—M. Bembridge, 273.
English Women's Championship.—Miss D. L. Oxley.
Women's Home International Championship.—England.
New Zealand Open.—R. J. Charles (N.Z.).
French Open.—Liang Huan Lu (Formosa).
Spanish Open.—D. Hayes (S. Africa).
Sunningdale Foursomes.—A. Bird and H. Flatman.
Lytham Trophy.—W. Humphreys.
Benson and Hedges Tournament.—A. Jacklin, after play off with P. J. Butler.
British Women's Stroke Play, Mrs. I. C. Robertson, 302.
Piccadilly World Match Play Tournaments. (Oct. 1971).—J. W. Nicklaus (U.S.A.) beat Liang Huan Lu (Formosa); N. C. Coles (G. B.) beat C. Coody (U.S.A.); G. Player (S. Africa) beat A. Jacklin (G.B.); R. J. Charles (N.Z.) beat A. Palmer (U.S.A.); *Semi-Finals.*—Nicklaus beat Coles; Player beat Charles. *Final.* Player beat Nicklaus.
German Open.—N. C. Coles, 279.
Vagliano Trophy.—British Isles beat Europe 17½ to 12½.
Swiss Open.—P. Townsend, 270.
Italian Open.—R. Sota (Spain).
Dutch Open.—R. Sota (Spain).
Classic International Tournament.—P. J. Butler, 277.
Southern Professional.—L. Platts.
Scottish Professional.—E. C. Brown.
Scottish Women.—Mrs. I. C. Robertson.
Irish Women—Miss E. Bradshaw.
Midland Professional.—R. A. Beattie.
Midland Amateur.—J. A. Fisher.
Midland Women's Championship.—Miss J. Stuart.
Northern Women's Championship.—Mrs. V. Stone.
Grafton Morrish Trophy.—Dulwich College.
County Champions' Championship.—M. Lee (Yorkshire).
Coca-Cola Young Professionals Tournament.—J. R. Garner.

LAWN TENNIS

THE DAVIS CUP CHALLENGE ROUNDS
(Founder—Dwight Filley Davis (1879-1945), First Played, 1900.)

1930 France beat U.S.A. 4–1	1948 U.S.A. beat Australia.......5–0	1960 Australia beat Italy 4–1
1931 France beat Great Britain ...3–2	1949 U.S.A. beat Australia.......4–1	1961 Australia beat Italy.........5–0
1932 France beat U.S.A. 3–2	1950 Australia beat U.S.A 4–1	1962 Australia beat Mexico.......5–0
1933 Great Britain beat France...3–2	1951 Australia beat U.S.A......3–1	1963 U.S.A. beat Australia 3–2
1934 Great Britain beat U.S.A....4–1	1952 Australia beat U.S.A. 4–1	1964 Australia beat U.S.A.........3–2
1935 Great Britain beat U.S.A. ...5–0	1953 Australia beat Australia 3–2	1965 Australia beat Spain........4–1
1936 Great Britain beat Australia..3–2	1954 U.S.A. beat Australia.......3–0	1966 Australia beat India 4–1
1937 U.S.A. beat Great Britain ...4–1	1955 Australia beat U.S.A. 5–0	1967 Australia beat Spain........4–1
1938 U.S.A. beat Australia.......3–2	1956 Australia beat U.S.A. 5–0	1968 U.S.A. beat Australia........4–1
1939 Australia beat U.S.A........3–2	1957 Australia beat U.S.A 3–2	1969 Australia beat Rumania......5–0
1946 U.S.A. beat Australia.......5–0	1958 U.S.A. beat Australia 3–2	1970 U.S.A. beat W. Germany 5–0
1947 U.S.A. beat Australia.......3–1	1959 Australia beat U.S.A........3–2	1971 U.S.A. beat Rumania........3–2

THE CHAMPIONSHIPS (WIMBLEDON)
1971

Men's Singles.—J. D. Newcombe (Australia) beat S. R. Smith (U.S.A.), 6–3, 5–7, 2–6, 6–4, 6–4.

Women's Singles.—Miss E. F. Goolagong (Australia) beat Mrs. B. M. Court (Australia), 6–4, 6–1.

Men's Doubles.—R. S. Emerson and R. Laver (Australia) beat A. R. Ashe and R. D. Ralston (U.S.A.), 4–6, 9–7, 6–8, 6–4, 6–4.

Women's Doubles.—Miss R. Casals and Mrs. L. W. King (U.S.A.) beat Mrs. B. M. Court and Miss E. F. Goolagong (Australia), 6–3, 6–2.

Mixed Doubles.—O. K. Davidson (Australia) and Mrs. L. W. King (U.S.A.) beat M. C. Riessen (U.S.A.) and Mrs. B. M. Court (Australia), 3–6, 6–2, 15–13.

All-England Plate:

Men's Singles.—R. D. Crealy (Australia) beat P. Cornejo (Chile), 6–3, 6–4.

Women's Singles.—Mrs. M. R. Wainwright (G.B.) beat Miss B. F. Stove (Holland), 6–4, 0–6, 6–2.

Junior International Invitation Tournament:

Boys' Singles.—R. Kreiss (U.S.A.) beat S. A. Warboys (G.B.), 2–6, 6–4, 6–3.

Girls' Singles.—Miss M. Kroshina (U.S.S.R.) beat Miss S. Minford (Ireland), 6–4, 6–4.

Veterans' Doubles.—G. Mulloy and A. Vincent (U.S.A.) beat L. S. Clark and E. V. Seixas (U.S.A.), 6–2, 6–4.

WIGHTMAN CUP
(Cleveland, Ohio, August)

U.S.A. won by 4 matches to 3.

Results:

Singles.—Miss C. Evert (U.S.A.) beat Miss W. M. Shaw (G.B.), 6–0, 6–4; Miss S. V. Wade (G.B.) beat Miss J. M. Heldman (U.S.A.), 7–5, 7–5; Mrs. G. M. Williams (G.B.) beat Miss K. Pigeon (U.S.A.), 7–5, 3–6, 6–4; Miss V. Ziegenfuss (U.S.A.), beat Miss Shaw 6–4, 4–6, 6–3; Miss Evert beat Miss Wade 6–1, 6–1.

Doubles.—Miss Ziegenfuss and Mrs. P. W. Curtis (U.S.A.) beat Mrs. C. C. Janes and Miss N. Truman (G.B.), 6–1, 6–4; Miss Wade and Mrs. Williams beat Miss Evert and Miss C. Graebner (U.S.A.), 10–8, 4–6, 6–1.

BRITISH HARD COURT CHAMPIONSHIPS
(Bournemouth)

Men's Singles.—G. Battrick (G.B.).

Women's Singles.—Mrs. B. M. Court (Australia).

Doubles.—*Men's:* W. W. Bowrey and O. K. Davidson (Australia). *Women's:* Mrs. P. W. Curtis (U.S.A.) and Miss F. Durr (France). *Mixed:* F. D. McMillan (S. Africa) and Mrs. D. E. Dalton (Australia).

U.S.A. Championships:

Men's Singles.—S. R. Smith (U.S.A.).

Women's Singles.—Mrs. L. W. King (U.S.A.).

Men's Doubles.—J. D. Newcombe (Australia) and R. Taylor (G.B.).

Women's Doubles.—Miss R. Casals (U.S.A.) and Mrs. J. Dalfoy (Australia).

Mixed Doubles.—Mrs. L. W. King (U.S.A.) and O. K. Davidson (Australia).

French Championships:

Men's Singles.—J. Kodes (Czechoslovakia).

Women's Singles.—Miss E. F. Goolagong (Australia).

Men's Doubles.—A. Ashe and M. Riessen (U.S.A.).

Women's Doubles.—Miss F. Durr and Mrs. G. Chanfreau (France).

Mixed Doubles.—J. C. Barclay and Miss F. Durr (France).

Federation Cup.—Australia beat Gt. Britain 3–0.

Public Schools.—*Youll Cup:* University College School beat Stowe 3–0.

Clark Cup.—Millfield beat University College School 2–1.

County Championship.—*Men:* Surrey; *Women:* Surrey.

Inter-Services Tournament.—Royal Air Force.

Services.—*Royal Navy Championship:* Lt.-Cdr. R. E. Tayler. *Army Championship:* Capt. R. Green. *R.A.F. Championship:* Flt.-Lt. M. P. Hann. *W.R.N.S. Championship:* 2nd Off. M. J. MacColl. *W.R.A.C. Championship:* Maj. D. J. Temple. *W.R.A.F. Championship:* Sgt. P. A. Kemp.

Universities.—Cambridge University beat Oxford University 11–10.

BRITISH JUNIOR CHAMPIONSHIPS
(Wimbledon)

Boys' Singles.—C. J. Mottram beat S. A. Warboys, 6–3, 7–5.

Girls' Singles.—Miss G. L. Coles beat Miss C. M. Panton, 1–6, 6–2, 6–1.

Boys' Doubles.—M. J. Farrell and J. M. Lloyd beat C. Dowdeswell and M. D. Wayman, 6–8, 6–2, 6–4.

Girls' Doubles.—Miss S. Barker and Miss N. Salter beat Miss G. L. Coles and Miss D. Y. Staniszewski, 6–2, 7–5.

Mixed Doubles.—R. A. Leslie and Miss C. M. Panton beat J. R. Smith and Miss V. J. Leiper, 3–6, 6–3, 6–1.

TENNIS, 1971

Amateur Singles Championship: H. R. Angus beat R. Bloomfield, 3–0.

Open Doubles Championship.—N. A. R. Cripps and F. R. Hughes beat H. R. Angus and N. W. Smith, 3–2.

Universities.—Cambridge University beat Oxford University 2–1.

Henry Leaf Cup.—Harrow beat Eton 2–1.

BADMINTON, 1971

ALL-ENGLAND CHAMPIONSHIPS, 1971

Men's Singles.—R. Hartono (Indonesia) beat Muljadi (Indonesia), 2–0.

Ladies' Singles.—Mrs. E. Twedberg (Sweden) beat Miss A. Berglund (Denmark), 2–1.

Men's Doubles.—P. Gunalan and Ng Boon Bee (Malaysia) beat R. Hartono and Indra Gunawan (Indonesia), 2–0.

Ladies' Doubles.—Miss N. Takagi and Miss H. Yuki (Japan) beat Mrs. M. A. Gilks and Mrs. G. C. K. Hashman (England), 2–0.

Mixed Doubles.—S. Pri and Mrs. U. Strand (Denmark) beat D. Talbot and Mrs. Gilks (England), 2–1.

Inter-County Championship Final.—Surrey beat West of Scotland 14–3.

Universities.—Cambridge University beat Oxford University 9–6.

SQUASH RACKETS, 1970–71

Open Championship.—J. P. Barrington (Ireland) beat A. Jawaid (Pakistan) 3–0.

Amateur Championship.—G. Alauddin (Pakistan) beat W. Reedman (Australia) 3–0.

Women's Championship.—Mrs. H. McKay (Australia) beat Mrs. J. Irving (Australia) 3–0.

Inter-County Championship.—*Men:* Middlesex. *Women:* Lancashire.

Services Championship.—*Royal Navy:* Lt. R. M. H. Bawtree beat Lt. B. Taft 3–0. *Army:* Capt. I. C. Mackay-Dick beat Capt. J.W. Beattie 3–1. *R.A.F.:* Sqdn. Ldr. P. D. Stokes beat Flt. Lt. M. H. A. Eggleton 3–0.

Inter-Services Championship.—R.A.F.

University Match.—Oxford University beat Cambridge University 4–1.

Londonderry Cup.—Lancing Old Boys beat Barnard Castle Old Boys 3–2.

Drysdale Cup.—Mohibullah (Pakistan) beat P. G. Verow 3–0

Harp Lager National Competition.—P. E. Millman.

World Team Championship.—Australia.

FENCING, 1970–71

Amateur Championships:

Foil.—G. Paul (Salle Paul).
Epée.—G. Paul (Salle Paul).
Sabre.—D. L. Acfield (Salle Boston).
Ladies' Foil.—Mrs. J. Wardell-Yerburgh (London Fencing Club).

Corble Cup.—G. Ganchev (London Fencing Club).

Magrini Cup.—Salle Boston.

Public Schools Championship:

Foil.—I. Paretti (King's, Taunton).
Epée.—R. J. Maurer (Brentwood).
Sabre.—P. Mather (Brentwood).

Inter-Schools (Graham Bartlett Cup).—Belfast Royal Academical Institute.

Universities.—Cambridge University beat Oxford University 16–11.

RACKETS, 1970–71

Amateur Singles Championship.—M. G. M. Smith beat H. R. Angus 3–2.

Amateur Doubles Championship.—R. M. K. Gracey and M. G. M. Smith beat C. T. M. Pugh and C. J. Hue-Williams 4–0.

Public Schools Championship.—*Singles (H. K. Foster Cup):* R. W. Drysdale (Eton) beat J. P. Willcocks (Clifton) 3–0. *Doubles:* Harrow (M. Thatcher and J. A. N. Prenn) beat Clifton (J. P. Willcocks and D. G. Parsons) 4–2.

Noel Bruce Cup.—Tonbridge beat Marlborough 4–0.

Universities.—Oxford University beat Cambridge University 3–0.

ETON FIVES, 1971

Amateur Championships.—*Kinnaird Cup:* A. Hughes and R. J. G. Campbell beat M. F. Hayes and A. E. Bundy.

Public Schools Competition.—Highgate (G. P. T. Bond and C. D. Gilbert) beat Repton (P. C. J. Gould and R. S. Scott) 3–1.

Alan Barber Cup.—Old Olavians beat Old Edwardians 3–0.

RUGBY FIVES, 1971

Amateur Singles Championship.—*(Jesters' Club Cup):* T. A. Cowie beat J. H. M. East 2–0.

Amateur Doubles Championship (Cyriax Cup).—D. E. Gardner and S. H. Reid beat E. Marsh and S. Holt 2–1.

Universities.—Cambridge University beat Oxford University by 282 to 189 pts.

Schools Competition.—*Singles (Jesters' Cup):* M. I. McLaren (Bedford) beat M. Morgan (Denstone) 2–0. *Doubles (Mappin Cup):* Denstone beat Bedford 2–0.

POLO, 1971

Queen's Cup.—Stowell Park beat Jersey Lilies 5–4.

Cowdray Gold Cup.—Pimms beat Columbia (U.S.A.) 11–10.

Cowdray Park Challenge Cup.—Pimms beat Stowell Park 11–8.

Royal Windsor Gold Cup.—Oakbrook (U.S.A.) beat Windsor Park 6–3.

Harrison Cup.—Columbia (U.S.A.) beat Oakbrook (U.S.A.) 9–8.

Smith's Lawn Cup.—San Flamingo beat Buckethill 6–4.

Argentine Ambassador's Cup.—Jersey Lilies beat Greenhill Farm (U.S.A.) 4½–3.

Aotea Cup.—Friar Park beat Peover Park 7–4½.

Tyro Cup.—Cowdray Park beat Amersham 4–3.

Maidensgrove Cup.—Jersey Lilies beat Greenhill Farm (U.S.A.) 4–2

Universities.—Oxford University beat Cambridge University 3–2.

Benson Cup.—Jersey Lilies beat Maidensgrove 4–3.

Coronation Cup.—U.S.A. beat England 9–6.

Rodney Moore Cup.—Eaglesfield beat Friar Park 7½–5.

West Sussex Cup.—Polo Cottage beat Jersey Lilies 5½–3.

Jersey Lilies Cup.—Maidensgrove beat Jersey Lilies 10–2½.

Farewell Cup.—Cowdray Park beat Polo Cottage 6–4½.

TABLE TENNIS, 1971
ENGLISH OPEN CHAMPIONSHIPS
(Brighton)

Singles.—*Men's:* T. Klampar (Hungary) beat I. Jonyer (Hungary).

Women.—Mrs. M. Alexandru (Rumania) beat Mrs. D. Scholer (W. Germany).

Doubles—*Men:* S. Bengston and B. Pearson (Sweden) beat G. C. Barnes and D. Neale (G.B.). *Women:* Mrs. M. Alexandru and Miss E. Mihalca (Rumania) beat Miss J. Shirley (G.B.) and Miss B. Kishazi (Hungary).

Mixed: A. Stipancic (Yugoslavia) and Mrs. M. Alexandru (Rumania) beat D. Neale and Mrs. K. Matthews (G.B.).

Swaythling Cup.—China.

Corbillon Cup.—Japan.

WRESTLING, 1971
British Amateur Championships

Light Flyweight.—D. Urquhart (Scotland); Flyweight.—A. Eslami (London); Bantamweight.—A. Singh (Bradford); Featherweight.—T. Brett (Kent); Lightweight.—K. Dawes (London); Welterweight.—A. Shacklady (Manchester); Middleweight.—R. Mitchell (Scotland); Light-Heavyweight.—R. Barraclough (Huddersfield); Mid-Heavyweight.—G. Page (Kent); Heavyweight.—W. Robertson (Scotland).

ANGLING
National Championship

Year	Venue	No. of teams	Individual Winner	Weight	Team winners	Weight	Total Weight in match
				lb. oz.		lb. oz.	
1967	R. Ouse, Downham Market.	111	E. Townsin (Cambridge)	40 6½	Derby Railway Institute	83 4½	17 cwt. 31 lb. 5½ oz.
1968	Rivers Ant, Bure and Thurne, Gt. Yarmouth	112	D. Groom (Leighton Buzzard)	37 6	Leighton Buzzard A.C.	74 0	26 cwt. 68lb.1½oz.
1969	R. Trent, Newark	114	R. Else (Lincoln)	9 7	Stoke and District	38 2	8 cwt. 88 lb. 13½ oz.
1970	Middle Level, Norfolk	114	B. Lakey (Cambridge)	35 4½	Cambridge F.P.S.	97 2	23cwt.94 lb. 1½ oz.
1971	R. Severn, Stourport	116	R. Harris (Peterborough)	40 5	Leicester A.S.	124 8½	42 cwt. 19lb.

SWIMMING

World's Amateur Swimming Records
(as at June 1. 1971)
MEN—FREE STYLE
100 metres.—M. Spitz, U.S.A., 51·9 s.
200 metres.—M. Spitz, U.S.A., 1 m. 53·5 s.
400 metres.—T. McBreen, U.S.A., 4 m. 2·1 s.
800 metres.—G. Windeatt, Australia, 8 m. 28·6 s.
1,500 metres.—J. Kinsella, U.S.A., 15 m. 57·1 s.
Free Style Relay:
4 × 100 metres.—U.S.A., 3 m. 28·8 s.
4 × 200 metres.—U.S.A., 7 m. 43·3 s.
Medley Relay:
4 × 100 metres.—U.S.A., 3 m. 50·4 s.
Individual Medley:
200 metres.—G. Larsson, Sweden, 2 m. 9·3 s.
400 metres.—G. Hall, U.S.A., 4 m. 31·9 s.

MEN—BACK STROKE
100 metres.—R. Matthes, E. Germany, 56·7 s.
200 metres.—R. Matthes, E. Germany, 2 m. 5·6 s.
MEN—BREAST STROKE
100 metres.—M. Pamkin, U.S.S.R., 1 m. 5·8 s.
200 metres.—B. Job, U.S.A., 2 m. 23·5 s.
MEN—BUTTERFLY STROKE
100 metres.—M. Spitz, U.S.A., 55 s.
200 metres.—H. Fassnacht, W. Germany, 2m. 3·9 s.

WOMEN—FREE STYLE
100 metres.—Miss D. Fraser, Australia and Miss S. Gould, Australia, each 58·9 s.
200 metres.—Miss S. Gould, Australia, 2 m. 6·5 s.
400 metres.—Miss S. Gould, Australia, 4 m. 21·2 s.
800 metres.—Miss A. Simmons, U.S.A., 8 m. 59·3 s.
1,500 metres.—Miss C. Calhoun, U.S.A., 17 m. 19·2 s.

WOMEN—BREAST STROKE
100 metres.—Miss C. Ball, U.S.A., 1 m. 14·2 s.
200 metres.—Miss C. Ball, U.S.A., 2 m. 38·5 s.

WOMEN—BUTTERFLY STROKE
100 metres.—Miss A. Jones, U.S.A., 1 m. 4·1 s.
200 metres.—Miss E. Daniel, U.S.A., 2 m. 18·4 s.

WOMEN—BACK STROKE
100 metres.—Miss K. Muir, S. Africa, 1 m. 5·6 s.
200 metres.—Miss S. Atwood, U.S.A., 2 m. 21·5 s.
Free Style Relay:
4 × 100 metres.—U.S.A., 4 m 0·7 s.
Individual Medley:
200 metres.—Miss C. Kolb, U.S.A., 2 m. 23·5 s.
400 metres.—Miss C. Kolb, U.S.A., 5 m. 4·7 s.
Medley Relay:
4 × 100 metres.—U.S.A., 4 m. 27·3 s.

AMATEUR SWIMMING ASSOCIATION CHAMPIONSHIPS
(Leeds, Aug.1971)
Men:
110 yards Free Style.—M. B. Windeatt, 55·2 s.
110 yards Back Stroke.—M. Richards, 62·6 s.

110 yards Butterfly.—B. Robertson, 58·4 s.
110 yards Breast Stroke.—M. O'Connell, 69·8 s.
220 yards Back Stroke.—M. Richards, 2m. 15·7 s.
220 yards Free Style.—B. Brinkley, 2 m. 2·6 s.
220 yards Breast Stroke.—M. O'Connell, 2 m. 33·7 s.
220 yards Butterfly.—J. Mills, 2m. 10·1 s.
220 yards Medley.—B. Brinkley, 2 m. 19·5 s.
440 yards Free Style.—B. Brinkley, 4m 18·5 s.
400 yards Medley.—S. Roxborough, Canada, 4 m. 58·1 s.
1,650 yards Free Style.—J. Hills, 17. m. 21·5 s.
Free Style 4 × 110 yards Team Relay.—1, Nottingham Northern, 3 m. 49·6 s.; 2, St. James's, 3 m. 54·8 s.; 3, Royal Navy, 3 m. 58·4 s.
Ladies:
110 yards Free Style.—Miss L. Hill, 62·2 s.
110 yards Back Stroke.—Miss J. Brown, 70·7 s.
110 yards Butterfly.—Miss J. Jearons, 70 s.
110 yards Breast Stroke.—Miss D. Harrison, 1 m. 18·8 s.
220 yards Free Style.—Miss L. Allardice, 2 m. 13·9 s.
220 yards Breast Stroke.—Miss D. Harrison, 2 m. 51·2 s.
220 yards Back Stroke.—Miss D. Ashton, 2 m. 30·7 s.
220 yards Butterfly.—Miss C. Stockley, 2 m. 37·2 s.
220 yards Medley.—Miss D. Banks, 2 m. 34·9 s.
440 yards Free Style.—Miss L. Allardice, 4 m. 44·6 s.
440 yards Medley.—Miss D. Banks, 5 m. 26·9 s.
880 yards Free Style.—Miss J. Green, 10 m. 0·1 s.
Free Style 4 × 110 yards Team Relay.—Havering, 4 m. 21·9 s.
Medley Relay.—Southampton, 4 m. 53·5 s.

DIVING CHAMPIONSHIPS
Men.—*Springboard:* C. Walls, 478·30 pts; *High Diving:* A. Gill, 421·20 pts.
Ladies—Springboard: Miss A. Drake, 358·6 pts.; *High Diving:* Miss B. Williams, 318·3 pts.

THE UNIVERSITIES
Oxford University and Cambridge University drew 42–42 pts.

HENLEY REGATTA, 1971
Grand Challenge Cup.—Tideway Scullers beat Cairo Police (U.A.R.) by 2½ lengths, 6 m. 46 s.
Ladies' Challenge Plate.—University of London beat Trinity College, Hartford (U.S.A.) by 1½ lengths, 7 m. 0 s.
Princess Elizabeth Cup.—Pangbourne College beat St. Andrews School (U.S.A.) by 2 lengths, 7 m. 4 s.
Thames Cup.—Harvard University (U.S.A.) beat Kingston by ¾ length, 6 m. 48 s.

Stewards' Cup.—Thames Tradesmen beat Cambridge University by 1 length, 7 m. 12s.
Prince Philip Cup.—London R.C. and University of London beat Leander by 1¾ lengths, 7 m. 37 s.
Visitors' Cup.—University of London beat Keble College, Oxford by 1½ lengths, 7 m. 34 s.
Wyfold Cup.—Harvard University (U.S.A.) beat Marlow by 2 lengths, 7 m. 37 s.
Britannia Challenge Cup.—Hereford beat Nottingham and Union by 2½ lengths, 7 m. 45 s.
Silver Goblets.—G. A. S. Locke & T. J. Crooke (Leander) beat C. J. Dailey and R. N. Winckless (Quintin), easily, 8 m. 7 s.
Double Sculls.—M. A. Brigden and C. A. Brigden (Walton) beat B. Balmer and G. G. Parsonage (Scottish Argonauts) by 1 length, 8 m. 21 s.
Diamond Sculls.—A. Demiddi (Argentina) beat J. W. Dietz (New York) by 2½ lengths, 8 m. 8 s.

THE UNIVERSITY BOAT RACE

(Putney-Mortlake, 4m. 1f. 180 yds)

Year	Winner	m. s.	Won by
1960	Oxford	18 59	1¼ lengths
1961	Cambridge ...	19 22	4¼ lengths
1962	Cambridge ...	19 46	5 lengths
1963	Oxford	20 47	5 lengths
1964	Cambridge ...	19 18	6½ lengths
1965	Oxford	18 45	4 lengths
1966	Oxford	19 12	3¾ lengths
1967	Oxford.......	18 52	3¼ lengths
1968	Cambridge ...	18 22	3½ lengths
1969	Cambridge ...	18 4	4 lengths
1970	Cambridge ...	20 22	3½ lengths
1971	Cambridge ...	17 58	10 lengths

Cambridge have won 65 times, Oxford 51, and there has been 1 dead-heat.

OTHER AQUATIC EVENTS

Head of the River (Thames, Mortlake-Putney).—1, Tideway Scullers II, 17 m. 37 s.; 2, Tideway Scullers I, 17 m. 39 s.; 3, Leander, 17 m. 41 s.
Oxford Torpids.—Balliol College.
Oxford Summer Eights.—Christ Church.
Cambridge Lents.—1st and 3rd Trinity.
Cambridge Mays.—Fitzwilliam College.
Wingfield Sculls (Putney-Mortlake).—1, K.V. Dwan (Poplar, Blackwall and Dist.), 23 m. 45 s.; 2, T. Crookes (Leander), 24 m. 43 s.; 3, J. T. McCarthy (Argosy), 24 m. 56 s.
Doggett's Coat and Badge (Estab. 1715, 257th Race) (London Bridge–Chelsea, 4½ miles), 1, K. V. Dwan (Gravesend); 2, B. R. Cole (Erith); 3, C. T. Andrews (Bermondsey).

SKATING, 1970–71

WORLD CHAMPIONSHIPS

(Lyons)

Men's Figure.—O. Nepela (Czechoslovakia).
Ladies' Figure.—Miss B. Schuba (Austria).
Pairs.—A. Ulanov and Miss I. Rodnina (U.S.S.R.).
Ice Dancing.—A. Gorschkov and Miss L. Pakhomova (U.S.S.R.).

EUROPEAN CHAMPIONSHIPS

(Zurich)

Men's Figure.—O. Nepela (Czechoslovakia).
Ladies Figure.—Miss B. Schuba (Austria).
Pairs.—A. Ulanov and Miss I. Rodnina (U.S.S.R.).
Ice Dancing.—A. Gorschkov and Miss L. Pakhomova (U.S.S.R.).

World Speed Skating Championship.—A. Schenk (Netherlands).
European Championship.—D. Fornaess (Norway).

BRITISH CHAMPIONSHIPS (Ice)

Men's Figure.—J. A. Curry.
Ladies' Figure.—Miss P. A. Dodd.
Pairs.—C. Taylforth and Miss L. Connolly.
Dancing.—R. Bradshaw and Miss S. Getty.

(Roller)

Men's Figure.—G. Cubitt.
Ladies' Figure.—Miss J. Gray.
Pairs.—K. Evans and Miss S. Pagett.
Dancing.—P. Hicks and Mrs. M. Gibbs.

SHOOTING–BISLEY, 101st N.R.A., 1971

Queen's Prize.—1, R. Stevens, 292 pts. (record); 2, M. J. Brister, 291; 3, F. A. Bird, 289.
St. Georges' Challenge Vase.—J. H. Bagnell-Oakley, 149 (record).
Grand Aggregate.—1, M. T. Heathcote, 594 (record); 2, G. F. Arnold, 593; 3, C. F. O. Sullivan, 592.
Elcho Challenge Shield.—1, Scotland, 1,602; 2, England, 1,585; 3, Ireland, 1,497.
Kolapore Cup.—1, Mother Country, 1,159 (record); 2, Canada, 1,159; 3, Jersey, 1,142; 4, Guernsey, 1,141.
Universities.—Chancellor's Challenge Plate.—1, Cambridge University, 1,140; 2 Oxford University, 1,124.
Inter-Services Long Range.—1, R.A.F., 577 (record); 2, Regular Army, 573; 3, R.N., 571.
United Service.—1, R.N., 1,336; 2, Regular Army, 1,326; 3; Canadian Forces, 1,296.
Ashburton Shield.—1, Merchant Taylors, 512; 2, Uppingham, 509; 3, St. Peters, York, 508.
National Match.—1, England, 2,032; 2, Scotland, 2,016; 3, Ireland, 1,998; 4, Wales, 1,976.

CLAY PIGEON SHOOTING, 1971

International Cup.—1, England, 7,081/7,500; 2, Scotland, 7,016; 3, Ireland, 6,978.
Mackintosh Trophy.—1, Canada, 7,314/7,500; 2, S. Africa, 7,274; 3, Australia, 7,223.
British Open Down-the-Lines Championship.—B. Bailey (Shropshire), 297/300.
British Open Skeet Championship.—D. Seabrook (Northants.), 98/100.
British Open Sporting Championship.—J. Wheater (Hull), 87/100.
Coronation Cup.—R. Townroe (Notts.), 371/400.
Grand Prix of Britain (Olympic Trench).—B. W. Bailey (Salop.), 195/200.
Grand Prix of Britain (International Skeet).—J. M. Neville (Derbys.), 192/200.
European Sporting Championship.—W. J. Sykes (Suffolk), 176/200.

BOXING, 1971

A.B.A. CHAMPIONSHIPS

(Winners)

Light-Flyweight.—M. Abrams (Battersea); *Flyweight.*—P. Wakefield (Leeds); *Bantam.*—G. Turpin (Liverpool); *Feather.*—T. Wright (Doncaster); *Light.*—J. Singleton (Kirkby); *Light-Welter.*—M. Kingwell (Robert Browning); *Welter.*—D. Davies (Bangor); *Light-Middle.*—A. Edwards (Worcester); *Middle.*—A. Minter (Crawley); *Light-Heavy.*—J. Conteh (Kirkby); *Heavy.*—L. Stevens (Reading).

UNIVERSITIES

Cambridge University beat Oxford University by six bouts to three.

PROFESSIONAL BOXING WORLD CHAMPIONS

Title Holders in Oct. 1971

Flyweight.—E. Salvarria (Philippines); *Bantamweight.*—R. Olivares (Mexico); *Featherweight.*—K. Shibata (Japan); *Lightweight.*—K. Buchanan (Scotland); *Welterweight.*—J. Napoles (Mexico); *Middleweight.*—C. Monzon (Argentina); *Light-Heavyweight.*—B. Foster (U.S.A.); *Heavy-weight.*—J. Frazier (U.S.A.).

BRITISH CHAMPIONS

Title holders in Oct. 1971

Flyweight.—J. McCluskey (Scotland); *Bantamweight.*—A. Rudkin (England); *Featherweight.*—

E. Armstrong (Scotland); *Lightweight.*—K. Buchanan (Scotland); *Welterweight.*—R. Charles (England); *Middleweight.*—B. Sterling (England); *Light-
Heavyweight.*—C. Finnegan (England); *Heavyweight.*—J. Bodell (England).

BRITISH EMPIRE CHAMPIONS
Title holders in Oct. 1971
Flyweight.—H. Nissen (Australia); *Bantamweight.*
—A. Rudkin (England); *Featherweight.*—T. George
(N. Zealand); *Lightweight.*—P. Hales (Jamaica);
Welterweight.—R. Charles (England); *Middleweight.*
—B. Sterling (Jamaica); *Light-Heavyweight.*—
C. Finnegan (England); *Heavyweight.*—J. Bodell;
(England).

EUROPEAN CHAMPIONS
Title holders in Oct. 1971
Flyweight.—F. Atzori (Italy); *Bantamweight.*—
A. Senin (Spain); *Featherweight.*—J. Legra (Spain);
Lightweight.—M. Velazquez (Spain); *Light-Welter-
weight.*—P. Carraco (Spain); *Welterweight.*—
R. Menetrey (France); *Light-Middleweight.*—
J. Hernandez (Spain); *Middleweight.*—J.-C. Bouttier
(France); *Light-Heavyweight.*—C. Velensek (Ger-
many); *Heavyweight.*—J. Bodell (England).

BILLIARDS AND SNOOKER, 1970–71
World Professional Billiards Championship.—L.
Driffield (England) beat J. Karnehm (England) by
9,027 to 4,342.
World Professional Snooker Championship.—J. Spencer
(England) beat W. Simpson (Australia) 42–31.
World Amateur Snooker Championship.—J. Barron
(England) beat S. Hood (England) 11–7 frames.
English Amateur Billiards Championship.—N. Dagley
beat W. Dennison by 3,672 to 2,019.
English Amateur Snooker Championship.—J. Barron
beat D. French by 11–9 frames.
Women (Amateur).—Billiards: Mrs. V. Selby;
Snooker: Miss M. Hazeldine.

BOWLS, 1971
English Bowling Association Championship (Mortlake).
Fours.—S.F.: Clevedon Park beat St. Austell
15–14; Spalding Mail Cart beat Rainworth
Miners Welfare 17–16. *F.:* Clevedon Park
beat Mail Cart 27–13.
Triples.—S.F.: Banbury Chestnuts beat Mid-
Surrey 17–14; Marlow beat Huntingdon St.
Peters 20–11. *F.:* Marlow beat Banbury
Chestnuts 16–15.
Pairs.—S.F.: Stoke (Warwickshire) beat Princes
Gardens (Devon) 22–17; Livesey Memorial
(Kent) beat St. Austell 24–8. *F.* Livesey
Memorial (D. Cross and D. Crocker) beat
Stoke 23–17.
Singles.—S.F.: J. Blewett (Penlee, Cornwall) beat
F. Summers (Brotherhood, Worcs.) 21–7;
D. J. Bryant (Clevedon) beat T. Brown
(Woking Park) 21–9. *F.:* D. J. Bryant beat
J. Blewett 21–18.
Inter-County Championship (Middleton Cup).—S.F.:
Middlesex beat Northumberland 129–101;
Hampshire beat Northamptonshire 134–111.
F.: Hampshire beat Middlesex 110–104.
International Championships.—Winners.—Scotland.
Results.—Scotland beat Ireland 98–89; England
beat Wales 107–87; Scotland beat England 110–
93; Ireland and Wales drew 97–97; England beat
Ireland 109–72; Scotland beat Wales 103–80.

BRITISH SHOW JUMPING, 1971
ROYAL INTERNATIONAL HORSE SHOW, HICKSTEAD
AND WEMBLEY
Country Life and Riding Cup.—1, A. Oliver on
Sweep III; 2, R. Ridland (U.S.A.) on Charles
Stewart; 3, G. Fletcher on Buttevant Boy.
Prince of Wales Cup.—1, Great Britain; 2, West
Germany; 3, U.S.A.

King George V Gold Cup.—1, G. Wiltfang on
Askan (Germany); 2, C. Homfeld on Triple
Crown (U.S.A.); 3, W. Steinkraus on Fleet
Apple (U.S.A.).
Daily Mail Cup (Victor Ludorum).—1, H. Steenken
(W. Germany) on Der Lord; 2, Capt. R.
d'Inzeo (Italy) on Bellevue; 3, N. Shapiro
(U.S.A.) on Sloopy.
Horse and Hound Cup.—1, N. Shapiro (U.S.A.) on
Sloopy; 2, G. Fletcher on Buttevant Boy;
3, G. Wiltfang (W. Germany).
Moss Bros. Puissance Trophy.—Capt. R. d'Inzeo
(Italy) on Bellevue and Miss A. Drummond-Hay
on Sporting Ford, equal first; H. Steenken (West
Germany) on Der Lord and G. Wiltfang (West
Germany) on Abadan, equal third.
British Grand Prix (John Player Trophy).—1, W.
Steinkraus (U.S.A.) on Fleet Apple; 2, L. Cervera
(Spain) on Acorne; 3, S. Hadley on No Reply.
Queen Elizabeth II Cup.—1, Mrs. M. Mould on
Stroller; 2, Miss A. Moore on April Love;
3, Miss A. Ferguson on Freelance IV.

CANOEING, 1971
Devizes—Westminster Race (124 miles) Senior Class.—
1, P. S. Lawler and C. J. Baker (Richmond C.C.),
19 hr. 22 m. 26 s.; 2, B. J. Kidston and A. G.
Wheeler (63 Para. Sqn. R.C.T.), 20 hr. 4 m. 56 s.;
3, M. Bosher and B. Greenaway (Richmond C.C.)
20 hr. 8 m. 37. s.

OXFORD AND CAMBRIDGE
Principal Events and Winners, 1970–71

Event (with date of first meeting)	Summary of Results			Results 1970–71
	Ox.	Camb.	Drawn	
Cricket (1827).........	44	50	33	Draw
Boat Race (1829)......	51	65	1	Camb.
Rackets (1858)........	60	32	19	Oxford
Tennis (1859).........	25	58	15	Camb.
Athletics (1864).......	47	44	6	Camb.
Football—				
Association (1873–4)..	31	40	17	Camb.
Rugby (1871–2).......	41	35	13	Oxford
Golf (1878)...........	33	42	5	Oxford
Lawn Tennis (1881)....	25	44	—	Camb.
Hockey (1890)........	24	31	13	Camb.
Boxing (1897).........	24	58	6	Camb.

OTHER UNIVERSITY EVENTS AND WINNERS
1970–71

Cross-Country....................Cambridge
Relays...........................Cambridge
Fencing..........................Cambridge
Lacrosse............................Oxford
Rugby Fives.....................Cambridge
Shooting.........................Cambridge
Squash Rackets ....Oxford
Polo................................Oxford
Swimming..........................Draw
Ski-ing.........................Cambridge
Badminton.......................Cambridge

CYCLING, 1971
Tour de France.—E. Merckx (Belgium).
Tour of Britain.—F. Den Hertog (Netherlands).
World Championships:
   Professional Sprint.—L. Lovesisn (Netherlands).
   Professional Pursuit.—D. Baert (Belgium).
   Amateur Road Race.—R. Ovion (France).
   Professional Road Race.—E. Merckx (Belgium).
   Ladies Sprint.—G. Tsareva (U.S.S.R.).
   Ladies' Pursuit.—T. Garkushkina (U.S.S.R.).
   Ladies' Road Race.—A. Konkina (U.S.S.R.).
National Championships:
   Amateur Sprint.—E. Crutchlow.

Ladies' Sprint.—B. Swinnerton.
Amateur Pursuit.—I. Hallam.
Ladies' Pursuit.—B. Burton.
Amateur Road Race.—D. Rollinson.
Ladies' Road Race.—B. Burton.

MOTOR CYCLING, 1971

Senior T.T., Isle of Man.—1, G. Agostini, (M.V.), 2 hr. 12 m. 24·4 s. (102·59 m.p.h.); 2, P. J. Williams (Arter Matchless), 2 hr. 18 m. 3 s. (98·4 m.p.h.); 3, F. Perris (Suzuki), 2 hr. 20 m. 45·4 s. (96·51 m.p.h.).

Junior 350 c.c. Race, Isle of Man.—1, A. Jeffries (Yamsel), 2 hr. 5 m. 48·6 s. (89·98 m.p.h.); 2, G. Pantall (Padgett-Yamaha), 2 hr. 6 m. 25 s. (89·55 m.p.h.); 3, W. Smith (Honda), 2 hr. 7 m. 4·8 s. (89·09 m.p.h.).

250 c.c. Lightweight T.T., Isle of Man.—1, P. Read (Yamaha), 1 hr. 32 m. 23·6 s. (98·02 m.p.h.); 2, B. Randle (Yamaha), 1 hr. 34 m. 27·6 s. (95·87 m.p.h.); 3, A. Barnett (Yamsel), 1 hr. 35 m. 2 s. (95·29 m.p.h.).

Manx Grand Prix (Isle of Man).—*Senior:* 1, N. G. A. Rollason (Yamaha), 2 hr. 23 m. 52·8 s. (94·42 m.p.h.); 2, K. J. Huggett (Norton), 2 hr. 23 m. 58·6 s. (94·35 m.p.h.); 3, P. N. Elmore (Norton), 2 hr. 24 m. 21·8 s. (94·10 m.p.h.).

MOTOR RACING, 1970–71

24-hours (Le Mans).—1, H. Marko and J. van Lennep (Porsche), 396 laps (138·1 m.p.h.); 2, R. Attwood and H. Muller (Porsche), 394 laps; 3, S. Posey and A. Adamovicz (Ferrari), 365 laps.

Monaco Grand Prix.—1, J. Stewart (Tyrrell-Ford), 1 hr. 52 m. 21·3 s. (83·48 m.p.h.) (record); 2, R. Peterson (March-Ford), 1 hr. 52 m. 46·9 s.; 3, J. Ickx (Ferrari), 1 hr. 53 m. 14·6 s.

French Grand Prix.—1, J. Stewart (Tyrrell-Ford), 1 hr. 46 m. 41·68 s. (111·66 m.p.h.); 2, F. Cevert (Tyrrell-Ford), 1 hr. 47 m. 9·8 s.; 3, E. Fittipaldi (Lotus-Ford), 1 hr. 47 m. 15·75 s.

British Grand Prix (Silverstone).—1, J. Stewart (Tyrrell-Ford), 130·48 m.p.h.; 2, R. Peterson (March-Ford), 129·63 m.p.h.; 3, E. Fittipaldi (Lotus-Ford), 129·29 m.p.h.

German Grand Prix.—1, J. Stewart (Tyrrell-Ford), 1 hr. 29 m. 15·7 s. (114·4 m.p.h.); 2, F. Cevert (Tyrrell-Ford), 1 hr. 29 m. 45·8 s.; 3, C. Regazzoni (Ferrari), 1 hr. 29 m. 52·8 s.

Spanish Grand Prix.—1, J. Stewart (Tyrrell-Ford), 1 hr. 49 m. 3·4 s. (97·19 m.p.h.); 2, J. Ickx (Ferrari), 1 hr. 49 m. 6·8 s.; 3, C. Amon (Matra-Simca), 1 hr. 50 m. 1·5 s.

Mexican Grand Prix.—1, J. Ickx (Ferrari) (107·4 m.p.h.); 2, C. Regazzoni (Ferrari); 3, D. Hulme (McLaren-Ford).

Dutch Grand Prix.—1, J. Ickx (Ferrari), 1 hr. 56 m. 20·09 s. (94·06 m.p.h.); 2, P. Rodriguez (B.R.M.), 1 hr. 56 m. 25·08 s.; 3, C. Regazzoni (Ferrari).

South African Grand Prix.—1, M. Andretti (Ferrari), 1 hr. 47 m. 35·5 s. (112·36 m.p.h.); 2, J. Stewart (Tyrrell-Ford), 1 hr. 47 m. 56·4 s. (112·05 m.p.h.); 3, C. Regazzoni (Ferrari), 1 hr. 48 m. 6·9 s. (111·95 m.p.h.).

U.S. Grand Prix.—(1970) 1, E. Fittipaldi (Lotus-Ford), 1 hr. 57 m. 32·79 s. (126·79 m.p.h.) (record); 2, P. Rodriguez (B.R.M.), 1 hr. 58 m. 9·18 s.; 3, R. Wissell (Lotus-Ford), 1 hr. 58 m. 17·95 s. (1971) 1, F. Cevert (Tyrrell-Ford), 1 hr. 43 m. 51 s. (115·09 m.p.h.); 2, J. Siffert (B.R.M.), 1 hr. 44 m. 32 s.; 3, R. Peterson (March-Ford), 1 hr. 44 m. 36 s.

Italian Grand Prix.—1, P. Gethin (B.R.M.), 1 hr. 18 m. 12·6 s. (150·8 m.p.h.); 2, R. Peterson (March-Ford), 1 hr. 18 m. 12·61 s.; 3, F. Cevert (Tyrrell-Ford), 1 hr. 18 m. 12·69 s.

Austrian Grand Prix.—1, J. Siffert (B.R.M.), 1 hr. 30 m. 23·91 s. (132·3 m.p.h.); 2, E. Fittipaldi (Lotus-Ford), 1 hr. 30 m. 28·03 s.; 3, T. Schenken (Brabham-Ford), 1 hr. 30 m., 42·68 s.;

Canadian Grand Prix.—1, J. Stewart (Tyrrell-Ford), 1 hr. 55 m. 12·9 s.; 2, R. Peterson (March-Ford), 1 hr. 55 m. 51·2 s.; 3, M. Donohue (McLaren-Ford), 1 hr. 56 m. 48·7 s'.

OLYMPIC SWIMMING RECORDS
(*To 1968*)

Men

Distance Metres	Name	Country	Time min. sec.	Year
100 Free style	M. Wenden	Australia	52·2	1968
200 Free style	M. Wenden	Australia	1 55·2	1968
400 Free style	M. Burton	U.S.A.	4 09·0	1968
1,500 Free style	M. Burton	U.S.A.	16 38·9	1968
100 Breaststroke	R. Mathes	G.D.R.	1 01·9	1968
200 Backstroke	R. Mathes	G.D.R.	2 09·6	1968
100 Backstroke★	D. McKenzie	U.S.A.	1 07·7	1968
200 Breaststroke	I. O'Brien	Australia	2 27·8	1964
100 Butterfly★	D. Russell	U.S.A.	55·9	1968
200 Butterfly	K. Berry	Australia	2 06·6	1964
200 Individual Medley★	C. Hickcox	U.S.A.	2 12·0	1968
400 Individual Medley	C. Roth	U.S.A.	24 45·4	1964
4 × 100 Free style		United States	3 31·7	1968
4 × 200 Free style		United States	7 52·1	1964
4 × 100 Medley		United States	3 54·9	1968

Women's Events

100 Free style	D. Fraser	Australia	59·5	1964
200 Free style★	D. Meyer	U.S.A.	2 10·5	1968
400 Free style	D. Meyer	U.S.A.	4 31·8	1968
800 Free style★	D. Meyer	U.S.A.	9 24·0	1968
100 Backstroke	K. Hall	U.S.A.	1 06·2	1968
200 Backstroke	L. Watson	U.S.A.	2 24·8	1968
100 Breaststroke★	B. Bjedov	Yugoslavia	1 15·8	1968
200 Breaststroke	S. Wichman	U.S.A.	2 44·4	1968
100 Butterfly	S. Stouder	U.S.A.	1 04·7	1964
200 Butterfly★	A. Kok	Netherlands	2 24·7	1968

SWIMMING—Women's Events—*continued*

Distance Metres	Name	Country	Time min. sec.	Year
200 Individual Medley	C. Kolb	U.S.A.	2 24·7	1968
400 Individual Medley	C. Kolb	U.S.A.	5 08·5	1968
4 × 100 Freestyle		United States	4 02·5	1968
4 × 100 Medley		United States	4 28·1	1968

★ First held in 1968.

SPORTS REPRESENTATIVE BODIES

ANGLING.—National Federation of Anglers. *Hon. Sec.,* J. W. Warner, 56 Ward Street, Derby.

ASSOCIATION FOOTBALL.—The Football Association. *Sec.,* D. Follows, C.B.E., 16 Lancaster Gate, W.2.

ATHLETICS.—Amateur Athletic Association. *Hon. Sec.,* B. E. Willis, 26 Park Crescent, W.1.

—— Women's Amateur Athletic Association. *Hon. Sec.,* Miss G. M. Hartman, M.B.E., 41 Hayward Court, Levehurst Way, S.W.4.

BADMINTON.—Badminton Association of England. *Sec.,* J. B. H. Bisseker, 81A High Street, Bromley, Kent.

BASKET BALL.—Amateur Basket Ball Association. *Sec.,* K. K. Mitchell, Dept. of Physical Education, The University, Leeds, 2.

BILLIARDS.—Billiards and Snooker Control Council. *Chairman,* L. Oldham, 1–5 Salisbury Promenade, Green Lanes, Haringey, N.8.

BOBSLEIGH.—British Bobsleigh Association. *Hon. Sec.,* G. Renwick, 515 Watford Way, N.W.7.

BOWLS.—English Bowling Association. *Sec.,* J. F. Elms, Merville Hotel, Exeter Road, Bournemouth, Hants.

BOXING.—Amateur Boxing Association. Clutha House, 10 Storey's Gate, S.W.1.—*Hon. Sec.,* W. T. Lovett.

—— British Boxing Board of Control, Ramillies Buildings, Hills Place, W.1.—*Gen. Sec.,* E. J. Waltham.

CANOEING.—British Canoe Union. *Gen. Sec.,* Major G. E. Tomlinson, 26–29 Park Crescent, W.1.

CLAY PIGEON SHOOTING.—Clay Pigeon Shooting Association. *Dir.,* A. P. Page, Angel Road, N.18.

CRICKET.—Marylebone Cricket Club, Lord's Ground, N.W.8. *Sec.,* S. C. Griffith, D.F.C., T.D.

CYCLING.—British Cycling Federation, 26 Park Crescent, W.1.—*Sec.,* L. Unwin.

FENCING.—Amateur Fencing Association. *Sec.,* L. A. Mowlam, 83 Perham Road, W. Kensington,W.14.

GOLF.—Royal and Ancient Golf Club, St. Andrews. *Sec.,* K. R. T. Mackenzie, M.C.

—— English Golf Union. *Sec.,* Lt.-Col. K. A. Nash, 12A Denmark Street, Wokingham, Berks.

—— Ladies' Golf Union, 2 Fairways, Sandwich Bay, Kent.

GYMNASTICS.—British Amateur Gymnastics Association. *Gen. Sec.,* R. G. Taylor, 23A High Street, Slough, Bucks.

HOCKEY.—Hockey Association. *Sec.,* R. J. W. Struthers, 26 Park Crescent, W.1.

—— All England Women's Hockey Association. *Sec.,* Miss A. G. Browne, 45 Doughty Street, W.C.1.

JUDO.—British Judo Association, 26–29 Park Crescent, W.1. *Gen. Sec.,* A. J. Reay.

LACROSSE.—English Lacrosse Union. *Sec.,* C. D. Coppock, 3 Chessington Avenue, Bexley Heath, Kent.

LAWN TENNIS.—Lawn Tennis Association. *Sec.,* S. B. Reay, O.B.E., Palliser Road, Barons Court, West Kensington, W.14.

MOTOR CYCLING.—Auto-Cycle Union, 31 Belgrave Square, S.W.1. *Sec.* K. E. Shierson.

MOUNTAINEERING.—British Mountaineering Council, Room 314, 26 Park Crescent, W.1. *Hon. Sec.,* J. P. Ledeboer.

NETBALL.—All England Netball Association. *Sec.,* Miss A. Cairncross, 26–29 Park Crescent, W.1.

RACING.—The Jockey Club (incorporating National Hunt Committee), 42 Portman Square, W.1. *Sec.,* D. Weatherby.

RIFLE SHOOTING.—National Rifle Association. *Sec.,* Air Commodore A. B. Riall, C.B.E., R.A.F. (ret.), Bisley Camp, Brookwood, Woking, Surrey.

—— National Small-bore Rifle Association. *Sec.,* R. C. Russell, Codrington House, 113 Southwark Street, S.E.1.

ROWING.—Amateur Rowing Association. *Sec.,* J. H. Page, O.B.E., 160 Great Portland Street, W.1.

RUGBY FIVES.—Rugby Fives Association. *Sec.,* A. V. Maltby, 28 Devonshire Road, Bexhill-on-Sea, Sussex.

RUGBY FOOTBALL.—The Rugby Football Union, Whitton Road, Twickenham, Middx. *Sec.,* R. E. Prescott.

—— The Rugby Football League. *Sec.,* W. Fallowfield, O.B.E., 180 Chapeltown Road, Leeds, 7.

SKATING.—National Skating Association of Great Britain. *Sec.,* A. R. Drake, Charterhouse, E.C.1.

SKI-ING.—National Ski Federation of Great Britain. *Sec.,* Maj. Gen. I. R. Graeme, C.B., O.B.E., 118 Eaton Square, S.W.1.

SQUASH RACKETS.—Squash Rackets Association. *Sec.,* J. H. Horry, 26 Park Crescent, W.1.

—— Women's Squash Rackets Association. *Hon. Sec.,* Miss J. Wilson, 4 Denbigh Gardens, Richmond upon Thames, Surrey.

SUB-AQUA.—British Sub-Aqua Club. *Director,* R. Vallintine, 160 Great Portland Street, W.1.

SWIMMING.—Amateur Swimming Association. *Sec.,* N. W. Sarsfield, M.C., Acorn House, 314 Gray's Inn Road, W.C.1.

TABLE TENNIS.—English Table Tennis Association. *Gen. Sec.,* D. R. Tremayne, 26–29 Park Crescent, W.1.

TOBOGANNING.—British Racing Tobogganing Association.—*Pres.,* Dr. R. Liversedge, 42 Portland Place, W.1.

WATER SKI-ING.—British Water Ski Federation. *Hon. Sec.,* T. Richardson, B.W.S.F., Virginia Water, Surrey.

WEIGHT-LIFTING.—British Amateur Weight Lifters Association. *Hon. Sec.,* W. W. R. Holland, 3 Iffley Turn, Iffley, Oxford.

WRESTLING.—British Amateur Wrestling Association. *Sec.,* A. Wishart, 60 Calabria Road, N.5.

YACHTING.—Royal Yachting Association. *Sec.-Gen.,* N. Hacking, 5 Buckingham Gate, S.W.1.

TOPICS OF THE DAY

INDUSTRIAL RELATIONS ACT 1971

The Act, which received the Royal Assent on August 5, 1971, comes into force on a day to be appointed. It does not apply to Northern Ireland. The following is a summary of the main innovations contained in the Act, but for points of detail reference should be made to the Act itself.

General Principles

The Act's stated purpose is to promote good industrial relations in accordance with four general principles:—

(a) the principle of collective bargaining freely conducted on behalf of workers and employers and with due regard to the interests of the community;

(b) the principle of developing and maintaining orderly procedures for the peaceful and expeditious settlement of disputes by negotiation, conciliation or arbitration, with due regard to the general interests of the community;

(c) the principle of free association of workers in independent trade unions and of employers in employers' associations, so organized as to be representative, responsible and effective bodies for regulating relations between employers and workers; and

(d) the principle of freedom and security for workers, protected by adequate safeguards against unfair industrial practices, whether on the part of employers or others (s. 1).

Rights of Workers

Trade Union Membership.—Section 5 declares that, *vis-à-vis* his employer, every worker shall have the right to belong to a trade union, *i.e.* registered trade union, of his choosing and to participate in its activities whether as ordinary member or official. He has also the right to belong to no trade union if he so desires, although this right is modified if an agency shop or closed shop agreement is in force.

Agency Shop Agreements (ss. 11–16).—An employer and trade union are free to enter into an agency shop agreement, *i.e.* that all workers of a specified description must as a condition of their employment either be a member of the trade union or pay appropriate contributions to its funds instead of being a member or, in the case of conscientious objectors, pay equivalent contributions to a charity. Where the employer is unwilling to enter into such an agreement, the trade union may apply to the Industrial Court for a secret ballot to be held. If on such ballot the majority of the workers concerned, or two-thirds of those who vote, are in favour of an agency shop, the employer must enter into such an agreement with the union. Provision is also made for a ballot on similar terms, on the application of one-fifth of the workers concerned, to determine whether they are in favour of the continuance of an existing agency shop agreement. At least two years must elapse between any such applications.

Closed Shop Agreements (ss. 17 & 18).—Where in any particular type of employment it appears that an agency shop agreement would give inadequate protection to the workers engaged in it, it is possible for the Industrial Court, on the recommendation of the Industrial Relations Commission, to approve a closed shop agreement made between an employer and a trade union. In such case, all workers (except conscientious objectors) must be members of the trade union. Again, the Act provides for a ballot to be held to determine whether the workers concerned are in favour of a

closed shop, or, once it is in force, of its continuance.

Contracts of Employment (ss. 19–21).—The minimum periods of notice specified in the Contracts of Employment Act, 1963, now apply where an employee has completed thirteen weeks' employment, instead of 26 as previously. Other amendments are that employees of ten years' standing are to be entitled to six weeks' notice, and of fifteen years' standing, to eight weeks' notice. The written statement of his terms of employment to be given to each employee under that Act must inform him of his rights under section 5 of the Industrial Relations Act and include details of a grievance procedure operated by his employer.

Unfair Dismissal (ss. 22–33).—The Act introduces a new concept, that of unfair dismissal. Broadly, all employees, under retiring age, are given the right not to be unfairly dismissed. Every dismissal (whether with or without notice, or on the expiry of a fixed term contract) is deemed to be unfair unless the employer can show that it was because of physical or mental incapacity, misconduct, redundancy, a statutory restriction against continuance, or some other substantial reason justifying the dismissal. A dismissal is deemed to be unfair if the reason for it is that the employee had sought to exercise his rights under section 5 of the Act. Dismissals by way of lock-outs are not to be regarded as unfair provided the employee is offered re-engagement; dismissals in connection with strikes are not unfair provided they are not discriminatory. Employees excluded from these provisions include persons who have been employed for less than two years, close relatives of the employer and part-time employees (less than 21 hours weekly). Contracting out is permitted only in the case of fixed term contracts for two years or more, or where the Industrial Court has approved a procedure agreement between the management and workers' organization concerned giving equivalent rights.

Compensation.—Any employee who has been unfairly dismissed, or who has been refused the rights given to him under section 5, may within four weeks apply to an industrial tribunal for compensation, independently of any other right of action he may possess (s. 106). The industrial tribunal will then award him such compensation as it considers just and equitable, though subject to a maximum limit of 104 weeks' pay or £4,160, whichever is less. Conciliation officers will be appointed to try to promote settlements of complaints without the need for them to be determined by the industrial tribunal (s. 146).

Collective Bargaining

Collective Agreements (ss. 34–36).—A "collective agreement" is any agreement made between an employer or employers' organization and a workers' organization which prescribes (wholly or in part) the terms and conditions of employment of workers, or which is a procedure agreement (s. 166). Under the Act, every written collective agreement, except in so far as it expressly states that it is not intended to be legally enforceable, is conclusively presumed to have been intended to be a legally enforceable contract. It is an unfair industrial practice (for which compensation may be ordered, *see post*) for any party to such a contract to break it, or to fail to take all such steps as are reasonably practicable to prevent its agents or members from breaking it.

Procedure Agreements (ss. 37–43).—A "procedure agreement" is so much of a collective agreement

as relates to machinery for the settlement of disputes between employers and workers regarding the terms and conditions of employment, negotiating rights, disciplinary and grievance procedures etc. Where in any particular unit of employment, *i.e.* any business etc., there is no procedure agreement, or the procedure agreement is defective, then either an employer or trade union may apply to the Industrial Court, which in turn will refer the matter to the Industrial Relations Commission for it to prepare a report setting out new or revised provisions. In default of agreement between the parties, the Industrial Court may order such new or revised provisions to constitute a legally enforceable contract, as if made by the parties themselves.

Sole Bargaining Agents (ss. 44–55).—An employer or trade union may apply to the Industrial Court for it to determine whether, in relation to a specified group of employees, sole bargaining rights for the making of collective agreements should be given to one particular workers' organization or joint negotiating panel. The question will then be referred to the Industrial Relations Commission for its report. On the recommendation of the Commission and after the conduct of a ballot to determine whether a majority of the employees are in favour of it, the Industrial Court will order that a specified trade union or joint negotiating panel shall be recognized as sole bargaining agent. Provision is made for the possibility of subsequent ballots regarding the continuance of sole bargaining rights.

Disclosure of Information (s. 56).—In all the stages of collective bargaining between an employer and trade union representatives, it is the duty of the employer to disclose all such information relating to his business as it would be in accordance with good industrial relations practice to disclose and without which the trade union representatives would be materially impeded in carrying on collective bargaining with him.

Registration & Conduct of Trade Unions, Employers' Associations, etc. (ss. 61–95)

Guiding Principles.—Every organization of workers, whether registered as a trade union or not, is subject to certain guiding principles set out in section 65. These are:—

(a) no person who applies for membership shall be excluded by way of arbitrary or unreasonable discrimination;

(b) every member shall have the right to terminate his membership;

(c) no member shall by way of arbitrary or unreasonable discrimination be excluded from playing a full part in union affairs;

(d) voting in any ballot shall be kept secret and every member shall have a fair and reasonable opportunity of voting without interference or restraint;

(e) no member shall be subjected to any unfair or unreasonable disciplinary action, *e.g.* for refusing to participate in an unfair industrial practice;

(f) every member shall be afforded a full and fair hearing in any disciplinary action and his membership shall not be terminated without reasonable notice giving him the reason for it;

(g) no restriction shall be placed on a member's right to take any proceedings before any court or tribunal.

A similar set of guiding principles is prescribed for organizations of employers (s. 69). Any action or threat of action in contravention of these principles is an unfair industrial practice, which may be made the subject of a complaint to an industrial tribunal (s. 107).

Registration.—Any independent organization of workers may apply to a new officer, called the Registrar of Trade Unions and Employers' Associations, for registration as a trade union, whereupon its name will be placed on the register. The Registrar will as soon as practicable examine the rules of the organization to check that they are not inconsistent with the "guiding principles" and that they comply with the requirements set out in the 4th Schedule to the Act. If there is any such defect which the organization refuses to amend, the Registrar may apply to the Industrial Court for an order cancelling the registration. Again, similar provisions exist for the registration of organizations of employers or employers' associations. A provisional register will be maintained during the transitional period.

Investigation by the Registrar.—Where a member of a trade union or employers' association claims that there has been a breach of its rules or an infringement of the " guiding principles ", the Registrar will investigate the matter (s. 81). He also has power to investigate on his own initiative (s. 83). If the matter cannot be resolved amicably, then the Registrar may refer it to an industrial tribunal, or, in a more serious case, to the Industrial Court, for its adjudication of the matter and an order for compensation (not exceeding 104 weeks' pay or £4,160, whichever is less). The Industrial Court also has jurisdiction to make an injunction against the trade union or employers' association concerned.

Unfair Industrial Practices

In addition to the unfair industrial practices referred to already, there are many other miscellaneous unfair industrial practices defined by the Act, these broadly being acts done for the purpose of putting pressure on persons or organizations to refrain from exercising rights given to them under the Act, or from carrying out duties imposed by it. By section 96, it is an unfair industrial practice for any person, except a registered trade union or employers' association or their authorised agent, in furtherance of an industrial dispute knowingly to induce or threaten to induce another person to break a contract to which he is a party. It is also an unfair industrial practice for any person, in furtherance of an industrial dispute, to take or threaten any steps, such as organizing or procuring a strike, go-slow or lock-out, in support of action which constitutes an unfair industrial practice, or with the intention of inducing third parties to break their contracts with a party to the dispute (ss. 97 & 98).

Compensation.—Except where the Act makes specific provision, any person may complain to the Industrial Court that action which constitutes an unfair industrial practice has been taken against him. If the Court finds the complaint well-founded, it may make a declaration as to the rights of the parties and order an injunction and compensation against the party in default (s. 101). If the party in default is a registered trade union, the maximum compensation that can be ordered is limited in accordance with its size, *i.e.* £5,000 if its membership is less than 5,000, £25,000 if less than 25,000, £50,000 if less than 100,000, and £100,000 in any other case (s. 117). A trade union official is protected if he was acting in his official capacity, any liability being that of the trade union which authorized him. There is no limit to the amount of compensation that may be ordered against a non-registered organization of workers.

Miscellaneous

Industrial Court.—The Act establishes an entirely new court, the National Industrial Relations Court (the " Industrial Court "), having equal status with the High Court and composed of a High Court judge sitting with between two and four other persons with special knowledge and experience of industrial relations. It has sole jurisdiction over questions involving the construction and enforcement of collective agreements. An appeal on points of law lies from its decisions to the Court of Appeal.

First appointments of judges to the Industrial Court were announced on Sept. 28, 1971. It was expected that the Court would be in operation before the end of 1971.

NATIONAL INDUSTRIAL RELATIONS COURT
President, Mr. Justice (Hon. Sir John Francis) Donaldson.
Judges, Mr. Justice (Hon. Sir John Anson) Brightman; Lord Thomson (Alexander Thomson).

Industrial Tribunals.—The existing system of industrial tribunals is retained and their jurisdiction greatly extended. An appeal from their decision lies to the Industrial Court on points of law. The Lord Chancellor is given power, at a future date, to confer jurisdiction on the industrial tribunals in respect of damages for breach of contracts of employment (s. 113).

Industrial Relations Commission.—This is now put on a statutory basis. It consists of between six and fifteen members. In addition to the functions specifically given to it under the Act, the Secretary of State may refer to it any question relating to industrial relations generally.

Industrial Arbitration Board.—The former Industrial Court is renamed the Industrial Arbitration Board. It has a limited jurisdiction relating to certain breaches of duty by employers.

Proceedings in Contract.—The present law is re-affirmed that no court can specifically enforce a contract for personal service against an employee, nor can it force anyone to take part in a strike (s. 128).

Proceedings in Tort.—Wherever there is an overlap between a tort and an unfair industrial practice, any proceedings in tort may be stayed (s. 131). In relation to acts done in furtherance of an industrial dispute, the torts of procurement of breach of contract and intimidation cease to be actionable (s. 132).

Picketing.—The right to picket peacefully is confirmed, but is limited so as to exclude picketing a person's home (s. 134).

Emergency Procedures

Cooling-off Period (ss. 138–140).—On the application of the Secretary of State, the Industrial Court may order a cooling-off period of not exceeding 60 days in respect of any proposed strike or lock-out. Before making any order, the Court must be satisfied that the industrial action in question is likely to cause grave injury to the national economy, imperil national security, create a serious risk of public disorder, or endanger the lives or health of a substantial number of persons.

Secret Ballot (ss. 141–145).—A similar application may be made by the Secretary of State on any of the grounds mentioned above for a secret ballot to be taken, if he has reason to doubt whether the workers concerned are in favour of a proposed strike. An additional ground for such application is that the proposed industrial action would be seriously injurious to the livelihood of a substantial number of workers employed in that industry.

Code of Practice

In furtherance of the principles of the Act stated in section 1, the Secretary of State has the duty of preparing a Code of Industrial Relations Practice for approval by Parliament (s. 2). This Code, which is advisory only, deals in general terms with the responsibilities of management, trade unions and shop stewards, employers' associations and the individual employee. It states the need for clear and comprehensive employment policies and the establishment of individual grievance procedures. Lastly, it gives advice on collective bargaining, consultation and communication machinery.

INDEPENDENT RADIO

In a White Paper published in February, 1971, the Government made known its intentions on an alternative service of radio broadcasting. The Government started with the assumption that, despite the controversy aroused at the time by the legislation which established independent television in 1954, there were few who would now wish to see monopoly restored in television. It was now generally accepted as desirable that there should be more than one source of programmes, particularly in news and current affairs, and the case which was largely accepted for competition in television was no less strong in radio.

The Government had consulted a wide body of interests, and though there was a great divergence of views, there was a consensus of opinion, with which the Government warmly associated itself, that radio financed from advertisements must offer a truly public service; there would be no place for a system of broadcasting which did little more than offer a vehicle for advertisements. The Government was anxious to ensure that a new service should maintain high standards, not least in the provision of news and news commentaries.

Control by renamed I.T.A.

The Government considered whether the Independent Television Authority should assume responsibility for the new radio service or whether a separate authority should be established. It was felt that the functions required of a radio authority would be broadly the same as those discharged by the I.T.A. for television, and that differences would be differences of degree only. It was also thought that considerations of cost and speed in starting the new service argued in favour of giving the task to the I.T.A., and that the Authority's regional organisation would be well suited to the requirements of independent radio. It was also thought desirable to avoid adding unnecessarily to the number of public authorities.

It was therefore proposed to entrust the new service to the I.T.A., which would be renamed the Independent Broadcasting Authority (I.B.A.). The I.B.A. would co-operate with local authorities and other local organizations in a system of advisory committees. The duty to share masts and sites already imposed on the B.B.C. and the I.T.A. would be applied on a reciprocal basis to the radio transmissions of the B.B.C. and I.T.A.

The B.B.C. had confirmed that they could finance out of licence revenue the 20 stations for which the Government had given provisional authority in August 1970, and the Government had concluded that the B.B.C. stations should continue.

The IBA Radio Stations

A network of up to 60 stations throughout the United Kingdom was envisaged for the I.B.A., and it was thought essential that the stations, if they were to be available to as many people as possible,

within a reasonable period, should start both on mf and vhf. It would be necessary to supplement the frequencies already assigned to the United Kingdom, by proposing under Article 8 of the Copenhagen Convention and Article 9 of the I.T.U. Radio Regulations the use of further mf channels. The allocation of medium frequencies in the European Broadcasting Area is to be reviewed and the broadcasting organisations cannot count on the use of as many medium frequency channels after 1976, but there may ultimately be room for more stations in the vhf band.

The precise number and disposition of local stations would be a matter for the I.B.A. It would inevitably take some years to establish the full network. The stations should, so far as possible, serve recognisable communities, and there would therefore be great variations in the size of population covered. Stations to serve the big conurbations would be among the first to be provided but the I.B.A. would be encouraged to experiment in the early stages with the establishment of relatively small stations, and there were various possibilities for linking small stations in a joint operation. The I.B.A. stations must be firmly rooted in their locality, and that should be reflected in the choice of station operators and subsequently in the output. The stations would be linked by a network in order to exchange news, music and other programmes, but a major ingredient of the output of the stations would be local news and information.

A central news company was envisaged to supply a service of national and international news; the White Paper outlined a number of different ways in which such a company could be organized and said that the Government would consider the various possibilities further in the light of public reaction.

Financial Arrangements and Programme Contracts

The income for the new radio stations would be derived from spot advertising, and no other kinds of advertising, such as sponsored programmes, would be permitted.

Estimates of potential revenue would vary very widely, but in the larger conurbations local stations might well attract very substantial income. Excessive profits must not be allowed to result from the exploitation of radio frequencies which are a scarce national asset. Equally, the financial arrangements must be such as to attract able broadcasters and support programmes of quality. The terms of the contracts would take local factors into account.

Each local radio company would have the right and duty to provide the local programmes and sell advertising time in its local service. The I.T.A's franchise would end in 1976 and the same limitation would apply to the I.B.A. franchise. But, subject to the renewal of the franchise, it was intended that the I.B.A. should have the right to grant, at the end of the first and each subsequent year, extensions for a further year. The Authority and the Minister of Posts and Telecommunications would also have the same rights to suspend or terminate contracts as already existed in relation to television programme contractors.

The Government believed that the system of " rolling " three-year contract periods was best suited to the needs of radio. It would allow the I.B.A. to make a continuous assessment of the worth of the contractors in a new field. The Authority's power to offer or withhold extension of the contracts would provide a warning system for the contractors. It would help them to keep their own performance under continual surveillance, and it would also assure them of a year's grace after a first occasion of non-renewal in which

to bring their standards up to the requirements of the I.B.A.

The same company would not necessarily be precluded from providing a service at more than one place, but no individual would be allowed an excessive aggregate interest. The I.B.A. would be expected to aim at a wide diversity of ownership.

Implications for Local Press

The Government considered the possible impact of independent radio on the press, but concluded that radio would be a relatively small contender for advertising and did not believe that its effects would necessarily be damaging to local newspapers. But the Government accepted the need for giving special consideration to the local and provincial press, believing that providing safeguards could be secured against undue concentration of the ownership of means of communication, the existing media could make a valuable contribution to independent radio.

It was therefore proposed:

(i) that local newspapers with a significant circulation in a local station's transmission area should have the right to acquire an interest in the station, whether or not they form part of the company awarded the contract.

(ii) that where a local newspaper has a monopoly in an area it should not be allowed to acquire a controlling interest.

(iii) that a television company should not be allowed a controlling interest in the area of its television franchise.

THE BRITISH LIBRARY

In January 1971, the Government announced details of a scheme to set up a British Library, combining into a single organization the British Museum Library (including the National Reference Library of Science and Invention), the National Central Library, the National Lending Library for Science and Technology and the British National Bibliography. The British Museum Library will retain its name and the National Library of Science and Invention will be renamed the Science Reference Library. A White Paper outlined the steps to be taken, subject to the approval of Parliament, to establish the British Library as a national institution.

Objective and Scope

The objective will be to provide the best possible central library services for the United Kingdom. These services include preserving and making available for reference at least one copy of every book and periodical of domestic origin and of as many overseas publications as possible, providing an efficient central lending and photocopying service in support of other libraries and information systems, and providing central cataloguing and other bibliographical services related to the needs of the central libraries and other libraries and information centres throughout the country and in close co-operation with central libraries overseas.

A new national library for reference and research can only be built round the British Museum Library and the National Reference Library of Science and Invention, both of which urgently need rehousing. The site for the new buildings will be the seven acres lying between New Oxford Street and Great Russell Street, immediately adjacent to the British Museum. It will also be necessary to expand the lending facilities at Boston Spa in Yorkshire so that all the lending activities of the British Library may be concentrated there. There will therefore be two centres, one for reference, research and bibliographical services in London and one for lending services at Boston Spa.

The National Libraries of Scotland and Wales, the Science Museum Library and other libraries of national importance will remain independent of the British Library, but the British Museum Library and the Science Reference Library must have close working relations with the other national libraries and specialist collections. Consideration will be given to a proposal that the national organization should give financial support to specialist libraries on terms which assured the accessibility of their collections.

Constitution and Administration

The British Library will be an independent body corporate, enjoying the maximum freedom over its internal affairs consistent with the broad objectives of government policy and employing its own staff. Apart from income derived from its own services and from independent sources, it will be financed by an annual grant-in-aid from the Department of Education and Science linked to a three-year " rolling programme " covering both capital and current expenditure. The library will not have power to borrow and specific authorization will have to be obtained from the Secretary of State for Education and Science for large items of capital expenditure or the undertaking of major new services.

The Board of the British Library will consist of a Chairman, who will probably be full-time, not more than four other full-time members, and not more than seven part-time members. The appointments will be made for periods of three to seven years and will be renewable. Of the part-time members, one will be appointed by the Queen with special responsibility to the Board for the Library of King George III which was presented to the British Museum, and four will be appointed after consultation respectively with the Secretaries of State for Trade and Industry, for Scotland and for Wales, and the Trustees of the British Museum.

In the interim period before the Board is established, a committee under Ministerial chairmanship will be established to plan the new organization and to develop and co-ordinate policy. The interim period is likely to last at least two years.

The first tasks of the Committee and later of the Board itself will be staffing, planning the buildings, establishment of policy, and research and development. There will be separate directorates, each equally under the management of the Board, for the British Museum Library, the Science Reference Library, Bibliographical Services and Lending Services. An Advisory Council will be appointed for each Directorate within the British Library to ensure that account is taken of users' needs. A special council will be appointed to give advice on the acquisition of rare books, maps and manuscripts. Members of all these bodies will be appointed by the Board in conjunction with the Department of Education and Science, the Chairman's appointment in each case being subject to the approval of the Secretary of State. The special interest of industry and commerce in the Science Reference Library will be fully recognized.

Publishers are under a legal obligation to deposit at the British Museum one copy of each item they publish. Arrangements will be made to amend this to an obligation to deposit the material with the British Library.

Staff and Costs

The staff of the various organizations to be incorporated in the British Library will be transferred to the new organization in their existing or equivalent posts, and it is intended to employ members of the staff on terms and conditions which, taken as a whole, will be no less favourable than those which they have enjoyed in the past.

The establishment of the Board of the British Library will involve additional headquarters costs of £150,000 to £200,000 a year. As against this, gains in efficiency are expected, notably by economies which will be achieved through the concentration of lending services at Boston Spa.

Major capital expenditure will be essential on new buildings in Bloomsbury and at Boston Spa. It has been established that it will be possible to erect new buildings on the Bloomsbury site to meet the needs of both the British Museum Library and the Science Reference Library, while preserving all the more important listed buildings, including St. George's Church and all the buildings along the west side of Bloomsbury Square. The project is expected to take about 13 years to complete and to cost about £36,000,000. At Boston Spa, a start has already been made on an urgently needed extension of the National Lending Library for Science and Technology which is likely to cost £940,000. A further comparable extension will be needed to provide not only for growth but for accommodating the services to be transferred from London.

LOCAL GOVERNMENT IN UNITED KINGDOM

The Government made its considered proposals for local government reform in White Papers published in February 1971, and it was made clear that these plans, superseding in many respects the Redcliffe–Maud recommendations, would be embodied in legislation to be introduced before the end of the year.

The scheme provides for a two-tier structure of county councils and district or borough councils, each with clearly defined functions. Greater London, which was reorganized in 1963–65, is unaffected.

Altogether 44 new counties will be set up, comprising all the urban and rural areas within their boundaries. County Councils will be responsible for major services such as education, highways, traffic and transport, refuse disposal, police and fire.

The bigger cities and towns will retain their identities as district councils, but smaller towns will be merged with surrounding rural areas. In some cases new districts will be formed by the amalgamation of rural areas. These new districts will have populations of not less than 40,000, except in sparsely populated areas. Housing will primarily be the responsibility of district councils, which will also deal with planning applications.

Six of the new counties are referred to as Metropolitan counties. They are Merseyside, South-East Lancashire and North-East Cheshire (to which the White Paper saw fit to give the designation Selnec), the West Midlands, West Yorkshire, South Yorkshire, and the Tyne and Wear area. These six areas will be treated as entities for the purposes of planning, transport and certain other services. The districts into which they divide will be big enough in population and resources, and sufficiently compact in size, to be responsible for education and personal social services, as well as the more local functions.

A Local Government Boundary Commission will be established to make recommendations for the final pattern of the new districts, and the Commission will take account of local proposals. The Boundary Commission will be kept in being, and should form part of the permanent machinery for keeping local government areas and electoral divisions up-to-date.

The White Paper says that the whole question of borough status requires consideration, and that the Government will seek ways in which the office of mayor and other traditional attributes and dignities of boroughs can be retained, as well as special honours granted to particular towns, including the style " city " and the right of the Mayor of certain cities to the title " Lord Mayor".

The Government expressed a wish to give every encouragement to existing rural parishes outside metropolitan counties, but suggested that there are many places where small parishes could, with advantage, be amalgamated to form fewer units. In urban areas it was suggested that in some cases parish councils might be replaced by what the White Paper referred to as " non-statutory bodies", and that district authorities should have power to assist those bodies financially and in other ways.

The New Counties

Eleven counties will either retain entirely their existing geographical area, or will undergo only very minor alteration. They are: Shropshire, Derbyshire, Nottinghamshire, Cornwall, Devon, Wiltshire, Norfolk, Bedfordshire, Hertfordshire, Essex and Kent.

The other counties, in addition to the Metropolitan Counties already listed, will be broadly as follows:—

Northumberland, apart from the area included in Tyneside–Wearside.

Durham, apart from the area included in Tyneside–Wearside, but including Darlington and part of the North Riding of Yorkshire.

An enlarged Teesside, including Hartlepool, and extending into the North Riding as far as Whitby.

The remainder of the North Riding together with York and some parts of the East and West Ridings; this county will stretch from Sedbergh in the west to Scarborough in the east.

Hull and the remainder of the East Riding, with some parts of the West Riding, including Goole.

Cumberland, Westmorland and the Furness part of Lancashire.

North Lancashire, with the Settle and Skipton areas of the West Riding of Yorkshire.

Warrington and those parts of Cheshire not included in the two Metropolitan Counties.

North Staffordshire.

Worcestershire and Herefordshire.

Worcestershire, less those areas, including Coventry and Solihull, taken into the West Midlands Metropolitan County.

Leicestershire and Rutland.

Lincolnshire, forming one administrative county instead of three, and including Newark.

South Somerset.

North Somerset and South Gloucestershire, including Bath and Bristol.

North and West Gloucestershire.

Dorset, with the addition of the Bournemouth and Christchurch areas.

Cambridgeshire, Huntingdonshire and Peterborough, and the Isle of Ely; also including Newmarket.

Suffolk, forming one administrative county, and losing Newmarket and also a small area on the north-east, included in Norfolk.

Oxfordshire and North Berkshire, with the Brackley area of Northamptonshire.

Northamptonshire, minus the Brackley area.

Buckinghamshire, apart from the area of Slough and Eton.

Berkshire, other than the parts included with Oxfordshire, but taking in Slough and Eton.

Surrey, including the Aldershot district, but less a small area round Dorking and Horley.

Hampshire and the Isle of Wight, apart from the Bournemouth and Christchurch and Aldershot areas.

West Sussex, with Dorking and Horley taken from Surrey and East Grinstead from East Sussex.

East Sussex, minus the East Grinstead area.

The Government expects the necessary Bill to be passed by the summer of 1972, and the Orders giving effect to the new pattern of districts to go through by the end of that year. Councils for the new counties and metropolitan districts would then be elected in the spring of 1973 and other district councils in November 1973, and all new authorities would take over on April 1, 1974.

Wales

In place of 13 counties, four county boroughs and 164 other authorities, Wales will have seven counties and 36 districts. The new counties will be, in general terms, as follows:—

Gwynedd, consisting of Anglesey, Caernarvonshire, Merioneth and part of Denbighshire.

Clwyd, taking in the rest of Denbighshire and Flintshire.

Dyfed, incorporating Cardiganshire, Carmarthenshire and Pembrokeshire.

Powys, covering Brecon, Radnorshire and Montgomeryshire.

West Glamorgan.

East Glamorgan.

Gwent, being the present county of Monmouthshire.

Most of the new counties will have a population of between 200,000 and 430,000, although East Glamorgan will have 900,000. The boundaries of Cardiff will be largely extended, causing an increase in its population from 284,000 to 316,000.

Scotland

The proposals for Scotland follow in broad terms the recommendations of the Royal Commission on Local Government in Scotland (the Wheatley Commission). The Government, however, concluded that the role of the district authorities should be enlarged.

The main modifications to the Wheatley Report which the new White Paper put forward are: that there should be one more region (the Borders); that both Orkney and Shetland should be given separate status, with independent control over almost all local government services; that the number of districts should be increased from 35 to 49, and that additional functions, notably in relation to housing, should be conferred on the district authorities.

The geographical division of the regions follows largely the proposals of the Wheatley Commission, except that the greater part of Argyllshire will be included in the West Region rather than the Highlands, that Kincardineshire, instead of being divided between East and North-East, will all be placed in the North-East Region, and the Girvan area of Ayrshire will be transferred from the West Region to the South-West.

Edinburgh, Glasgow, Aberdeen and Dundee will cease to be all-purpose authorities and will constitute district authorities within their respective regions.

BUILDING SOCIETIES INTEREST RATES

Per cent. per annum

	Average rates				New rates recommended by the Building Societies Association		
	Paid on shares	Paid on deposits and loans	Received on mortgage advances		Shares	Deposits	New mortgages to owner-occupiers
1961	3·54	3·11	6·28	1963 February	3¾	3½	6
1962	3·70	3·26	6·61	April	3½	3¼	6
1963	3·56	3·15	6·27	1965 February	3¾	3½	6¾
1964	3·50	3·11	6·16	July	4	3¾	6¾
1965	3·78	3·39	6·63	1966 May	4	3¾	7⅛
1966	4·01	3·62	6·95	December	4¼	4	7⅛
1967	4·20	3·80	7·20	1968 April	4½	4¼	7⅝
1968	4·37	3·94	7·46	1969 April	5	4¾	8½
1969	4·82	4·42	8·07	1971 November	—	—	8
1970	4·94	4·53	8·58	1972 January	4¾	4½	8

MORTGAGE REPAYMENT TABLE

Calendar monthly subscriptions required to pay off principal and interest of mortgages at 8 per cent. interest* over various periods of years. Intermediate amounts can be determined by addition of subscription rates, *e.g.*, Calendar monthly subscription for a mortgage of £3,500 over 20 years—£25·50+ £4·25 = £29·75.

Period of Years	£100	£200	£300	£500	£1,000	£2,000	£3,000
	£	£	£	£	£	£	£
5	2·09	4·18	6·27	10·45	20·90	41·80	62·70
10	1·25	2·50	3·75	6·25	12·50	25·00	37·50
15	0·98	1·96	2·94	4·90	9·80	19·60	29·40
20	0·85	1·70	2·55	4·25	8·50	17·00	25·50
25	0·79	1·58	2·37	3·95	7·90	15·80	23·70
30	0·75	1·50	2·25	3·75	7·50	15·00	22·50
35	0·72	1·44	2·16	3·60	7·20	14·40	21·60

* Most of the Building Societies were charging 8½ per cent. on mortgages to owner-occupiers at the time of going to press. A rate of 8 per cent. was recommended on October 8, 1971, by the Council of the Building Societies Association and it was expected that this would be adopted by all the larger building societies from Nov. 1, 1971, for new borrowers; and from Jan. 1, 1972, for existing borrowers. Certain smaller societies were expected to adopt a rate of 8·1 per cent.

RELATIVE RANK—SEA, LAND AND AIR

Officers of the Royal Navy, The Army, and The Royal Air Force rank with one another according to Seniority or Date of Appointment, as shown in the following table. Recognized abbreviations are shown in brackets. Comparable ranks in the Women's Royal Naval Service appear in *italics*. Commissioned ranks of the Women's Royal Army Corps are named as for the Army, the Director holding the rank of Brigadier. Commissioned ranks of the Women's Royal Air Force are named as for the R.A.F., the Director holding the rank of Air Commodore.

Royal Navy

1. Admiral of the Fleet.
2. Admiral.
3. Vice Admiral (Vice-Adm.).
4. Rear-Admiral (Rear-Adm.).
5. Commodore (1st & 2nd Class) (Cdre.) (*Commandant*).
6. Captain (Capt.) *Superintendent*) (*Supt.*).
7. Commander (Cdr.) (*Chief Officer*).
8. Lieutenant-Commander (Lt.-Cdr.) (*First Officer*).
9. Lieutenant (Lt.) (*Second Officer*).
10. Sub-Lieutenant (Sub-Lt.) (*Third Officer*).
11. Acting Sub-Lieutenant.

Army

1. Field-Marshal (FM).
2. General (Gen.).
3. Lieutenant-General (Lt.-Gen.).
4. Major-General (Maj.-Gen.).
5. Brigadier (Brig.).
6. Colonel (Col.).
7. Lieutenant-Col. (Lt.-Col.).
8. Major (Maj.).
9. Captain (Capt.).
10. Lieutenant (Lt.).
11. Second Lieutenant (2-Lt.).

Royal Air Force

1. Marshal of the R.A.F.
2. Air Chief Marshal.
3. Air Marshal.
4. Air Vice-Marshal.
5. Air Commodore (Air Cdre.)
6. Group Captain (Gp. Capt.)
7. Wing Commander (Wing Cdr.).
8. Squadron Leader (Sqn. Ldr.)
9. Flight-Lieutenant (Flt. Lt.)
10. Flying Officer (F.O.)
11. Pilot Officer (P.O.)

Commissioned Officers of the Royal Marines rank at all times, when serving on shore, according to seniority, with Army Officers of the same titles. When serving afloat a Major, R.M., ranks with a Commander, R.N., a Captain, R.M., with 12 years' service from his First Commission ranks with a Lieutenant-Commander, R.N., and a Lieutenant, R.M., with four years' service ranks with a Lieutenant, R.N.

LITERATURE OF THE YEAR

As in 1970, when the centenary of the death of Charles Dickens was marked by exhibitions of manuscripts and the publication of relevant books, so in 1971 was celebrated the bicentenary of the birth of Sir Walter Scott. He was born in Edinburgh on August 15, (though some writers suggest other dates) in 1771, in a house off a lane called College Wynd which ran steeply up from the Cowgate to the 16th century college which was the University of Edinburgh—built on the site of the Kirk-o'-Field where Darnley was murdered and the house he occupied blown up in 1567. Scott's birthplace no longer exists, but he knew little of it anway because soon after his arrival his father, a lawyer, moved to George Square. Shortly after Scott's marriage in 1797 he and his wife settled at 39 Castle Street, which remained their town house until 1826, when they made their last home at Abbotsford. There Lady Scott died in the same year, and Sir Walter in 1832. Much of his writing was done in his study in Castle Street, and this was reproduced in one of the two commemorative exhibitions which were staged in Edinburgh in the summer.

One exhibition, held in the Parliament House, home of the Court of Session, provided a particularly appropriate setting for the display of manuscripts, portraits and prints to illustrate Scott's life and work, the First Division Court Room being itself part of the exhibition. For here he had sat daily for some years as the Clerk of Session and according to Robert Louis Stevenson, " wrote many a page of Waverley novels to the drone of judicial proceeding. " The other exhibition, in Waverley Market, included the reproduction of Scott's Castle Street study, with some of the historical relics he collected, portraits of friends, and a kind of *son et lumière* presentation of scenes and figures associated with his writings. The programme brochure of this exhibition was an artistic publication, worthy of its subject.

NEW BIOGRAPHY.—Among books about Scott published during his bicentenary year the most notable was Prof. Edgar Johnson's *Sir Walter Scott: The Great Unknown*, in two volumes. We are told that this had taken 9 years to write and contains half a million words, and it is as valuable and as readable as it is prodigious in size and comprehensive in range. Many lives of Scott have been written since 1837–38, when John Gibson Lockhart, his son-in-law, published his large and not always reliable biography. Until now, perhaps the best was by the late John Buchan (Lord Tweedsmuir) which appeared in 1932 for the centenary of Scott's death; but that was 40 years ago, and more recent discoveries have enabled Prof. Johnson to give us this definitive Life of Scotland's greatest poet and novelist. A smaller biographical study was *Sir Walter Scott and his World* by David Daiches, in which the author described places and people associated with Scott and his work in a book copiously and well illustrated.

Prof. John Hayden edited *Scott: The Critical Heritage*, a collection of 19th century writings about him by contemporary or near-contemporary writers which were gathered together to make an interesting volume. Another collection of essays was edited by Prof. A. Norman Jeffares in *Scott's Mind and Art*, the contributors ranging from Coleridge to Colvin. Particularly interesting is the contribution of Prof. Frederick A. Pottle, editor of Boswell's papers, who wrote about the remarkable powers of memory enjoyed by both Boswell and Scott. Moray McLaren discussed one aspect of Scott and his work in *Sir Walter Scott: The Man*

and *Patriot*, which should interest everyone, especially remembering Scott's early martial activities as a militia officer and his monumental biography of Napoleon—who was born on the same date two years earlier than Scott. Another book having some bearing on Scott's life was *Lessudden House, Sir Walter Scott, and the Scotts of Raeburn*, by the present occupant of the house, Sir Tresham Lever. It was formerly the home of Scott's first cousin, the inadequate Wille, whom he often tried to help, and the book contains hitherto unpublished letters.

QUANTITY WITH QUALITY.—A prolific writer of the quill pen age was Jeremy Bentham, political scientist and sociologist, the whole of whose works are being published in a uniform edition planned to fill 38 large volumes. The first two, containing about one-third of his correspondence, appeared in 1968 (*see* WHITAKER 1969). Now we have the first two books he wrote: *An Introduction to the Principles of Morals and Legislation*, edited by Profs. J. H. Burns and H. L. A. Hart, and *Of Laws in General*, edited by Prof. Hart. They were continuously written, and Bentham reluctantly published the first part in 1789, but could not be persuaded to publish the second, and in fact it was first printed as recently as 1945. The *Introduction* set out a plan for a penal code based on the utilitarian philosophy, and showed how this applied to the principles of legislation and of ethics. Europe's largest collection of Shakespeareana, comprising about 40,000 volumes, was made more accessible to scholars and students by the publication of the *Catalogue of the Birmingham Shakespeare Library*, in 7 volumes. It contains 4,300 pages carrying about 100,000 entries and, to quote the publishers, it provides an index that is " unrivalled in scope and depth to every aspect of Shakespeare's life and work and to the literature generated by more than 300 years of Shakespeare studies. " The items listed include 1,200 concerning the Shakespeare-Bacon argument, and more than 2,000 pieces of music.

Among works of reference a large and leading place is occupied by one which was further enlarged during the year by the publication of *The Dictionary of National Biography 1951–1961* edited by E. T. Williams and Helen M. Palmer. The sixth of the supplements to the original work to appear in this century, it runs to 1,178 pages and adds biographies of 760 eminent people who died during the decade. The first volume of the *DNB* was issued in 1885 and 63 volumes appeared between then and 1900, subsequently combined into the 22 which now form the main work. Among those included in this newest supplement are Queen Mary and King George VI, Christabel Pankhurst and Marie Stopes, Gilbert Murray, scholar, Gilbert Jessup, cricketer, and Gilbert Harding, radio personality. Another great multi-volume work reached a notable milestone with the publication of the 150th volume in the *Victoria History of the Counties of England*. The first appeared in 1900 and Queen Victoria, almost at the end of her long life, gave permission for the series to bear her name, since when each volume has been dedicated to her memory. Each county is described in a set of several prehistory down to the history of each parish. So far, 14 of the 26 English counties have been completed, and work on others is in progress. The latest to appear were the 3rd volume on Staffordshire, the 9th on Wiltshire and the first, on the city of Hull, in the East Riding of Yorkshire series. To mark the completion of 150 volumes a separate *General Introduction* was published, providing a useful index to the

contents of each volume; and Queen Elizabeth the Queen Mother attended a reception held in November (1970) to celebrate this achievement of English scholarship. The general editor since 1949, Prof. R. B. Pugh, and his many collaborators deserve the gratitude of all inquirers into local English history.

POLITICS AND PEPYS.—Further progress in another publishing marathon was evident during the year when two more volumes were added to *The History of Parliament*, which deals with both local and national history, often amusingly. These volumes, entitled *The House of Commons, 1715–1754* edited by Romney Sedgwick, contain 2,041 biographies of those who sat during that period of 40 years, and electoral histories of 314 constituencies. Uninhibited by any libel laws the 12 contributors have been free to detail the eccentricities of many of their subjects, of whom 12 were expelled for financial frauds, 82 went bankrupt (19 of them ruined by their election expenses), 9 committed suicide, 13 became insane, at least two were poachers (and for that were adjudged guilty of breach of privilege) and one was a pirate and a smuggler in his spare time. He was Thomas Benson, M.P. for Barnstaple, who contracted to transport convicts to Virginia but shipped them to Lundy Island instead, where he employed them like slaves on building work. Yet the government of the country was carried on, useful legislation was passed, and parliamentary rule continued to evolve. For modern parliamentarians there was a new edition of the book generally styled *Erskine May*—its full title *A Treatise on the Law, Privileges, Proceedings and Usage of Parliament*. It was first published in 1844 by (Sir) Thomas Erskine May, who was Clerk of the House of Commons from 1871 to 1886; and this 18th edition was edited by Sir (Thomas) Barnett Cocks, who fills the same office today. This is the authoritative rule-book and guide for the parliaments of the United Kingdom and many overseas countries, and an indispensable adjunct for all who serve and rule. For the more general reader who is concerned with our Parliament came a 3rd edition of *Abraham and Hawtrey's Parliamentary Dictionary*, edited by S. C. Hawtrey and H. M. Barclay. This book sets out without too much technical and legal phraseology the rules and procedures, up to date. More studies of parliamentary activities announced for publication in September (1971) were the first 6 titles (making 10 volumes) of a *Parliamentary and Congressional Series* under the general editorship of David C. L. Holland, Librarian of the House of Commons.

From contemplating all these great works on the machinery of the legislature some readers may turn with a great feeling of relief to the writings of one famous M.P. already widely known and enjoyed in various truncated editions, but now presented in full with notes and commentaries: Samuel Pepys, Esquire, M.A., F.R.S., M.P. for Castle Rising and for Harwich. For there appeared the first three handsome volumes of an entirely new edition of *The Diary of Samuel Pepys*, newly edited by Robert Latham and William Matthews, and " mighty pleasant " books they are, both to read and to admire on the shelf. Each volume contains one year of the Diary, so there are 6 more to come, to be followed by a volume of additional commentary and a final index volume which will complete the fullest edition yet conceived of the approximately 1,250,000 words of the world's most famous and entertaining diary. Another large-scale publishing programme, of special value to politicians and economists, was introduced with the announcement of the first 4 volumes of the complete works of the late Lord Keynes, expected to run to not fewer than

24 volumes in all. In another series was the 2nd volume of *The Bodley Head Bernard Shaw*, edited by Dan H. Laurence. It contains 6 plays and a sketch; and there are 4 or 5 more to come.

CAMBRIDGE CELEBRATION.—An interesting event occurred at Cambridge in July when the University Press celebrated its 450th anniversary with an exhibition of books printed in England before 1521, and the performance of a masque written by John Rastell about the same time as the Press printed its first book. Printing was brought to the University by Johann Lair von Sieburg, whose name became more or less anglicized as Siberch; and his first production was a tactful choice—the text of an oration by his patron, Henry Bullock, a Fellow of Queens' College. Siberch soon after departed from Cambridge without having repaid a £20 loan made to him by the University Chest, and the debt remained on the books for these 450 years. The central point of the 1971 celebrations was its solemn repayment (but without interest) by Siberch's successor, Mr. Brooke Crutchley, the present University Printer, who also contributed an essay on Siberch and 16th century printing to a commemorative book.

LIBRARIES OF THE WORLD.—In another sector of the literary field we had a handsome, generously illustrated book, *Great Libraries* by Anthony Hobson, which described and depicted 32 of the world's greatest public libraries, ranging from the Capitular Library at Verona, dating from the 5th century, to the Humanities Research Center at Austin, Texas, dating from 1956. The geographical coverage is as wide as the chronological, with 5 examples each in the United Kingdom, the United States and Italy, 3 each in Germany and Spain, and others in Greece, Austria, Switzerland, Belgium and Portugal. One looks forward hopefully to having a similar volume recording the resources and glories of the great private libraries of the world.

SCHOOLS NEED BOOKS.—Public reference libraries in the provinces needed government aid, said Dr. George Chandler, Liverpool city librarian, in his presidential address to the Public Libraries Conference at Blackpool in September (1971). Pointing out that special grants were made for symphony orchestras, theatres, museums and sports centres, he said surely some libraries giving special services should be helped. There should also be more spending on books for schools, which was not enough to meet their needs, according to a survey published by the National Book League and the Association of Education Committees, thus reinforcing a similar complaint made in 1970 by the Educational Publishers' Council (*see* WHITAKER 1971). The National Book League showed that spending by local authorities in 1969–70 on books for schools rose only to £13·15m. from the 1968–69 figure of £12·24m., this small rise being partly due to the growth of school population and partly to cost inflation of at least 10 per cent. In real terms, spending had been barely stationary for primary schools and had declined for secondary schools. Local education authority expenditure of all kinds had continued to rise, but the proportion of it spent on school class and library books had fallen, from 0·85 per cent. in 1966–67 to 0·77 per cent. in 1969–70. Mr. Martyn Goff, director of the National Book League, said it was " a national scandal " that children were not getting the books they needed; and Mr. Martin Ballard, director of the Educational Publishers' Council, asked what was the good of spending money on new school buildings if there were no books inside them.

There was a considerable fall in the number of new Children's Books titles published during 1970,

from 1,987 in the previous year to 1,831, according to the *Bookseller*. This fall of 156 titles added to the steep rise in book prices may have accounted to some degree for the decline in local authority provision of books for children. The total number of titles published in 1970 was 33,489, an increase of 1,096 on the previous year, but nearly 10,000 of these were new editions, not new books. Of the increase, 871 were new editions and only 225 were new titles. But Poetry accounted for 709 of the new titles, an increase of 91.

JOHNSONIANS RALLY.—Although the birthplaces of Scott and Pepys have disappeared, that of Doctor Johnson at Lichfield remains, and it was reopened to visitors after extensive repairs and rearrangement on the 262nd anniversary of his birth on September 18 (Sept. 7, O.S.), 1709. It is a house of 4 storeys and about 15 rooms which was built by his bookseller father in 1707–08. In recent years it had become somewhat dilapidated, but with money given by Johnsonians all over the world it has been redecorated, rooms that had been blocked off and become damp have been restored and usefully adapted, and the exhibition of furniture, pictures, manuscripts and books has been redeployed and amplified to make a worthy place of pilgrimage for all admirers. A fine new edition of Johnson's *Account of the Life of Mr. Richard Savage* revived interest in the mysterious Savage (or Smith), a minor figure in Johnson's literary London but the subject of one of the best short " lives " in the language. Edited by Prof. Clarence Tracy and based mainly on the first (1744) edition, it traces Savage's turbulent life from unknown birth to death in jail, providing clear testimony to Johnson's rather than Savage's quality.

Three more volumes in the monumental Yale Edition of *The Works of Samuel Johnson* appeared during the year. They were devoted to the complete republication of Johnson's *Rambler*, the twice-weekly paper which he produced in 1750–52, edited and annotated by W. J. Bate and Albrecht B. Strauss. These moral and critical essays, sermons and tales which poured from Johnson's pen even while he was working on his *Dictionary* had but a small circulation in their periodical form, but the two bound volumes in which they were reissued became a best-seller in Johnson's lifetime. Prof. Bate also published a volume of *Essays from the Rambler, Adventurer and Idler*, containing a selection of Johnson's ventures into periodical publication. For this book Prof. Bate chose and edited, with full and scholarly notes, 79 of these essays (69 of them are given in full) on literary and moral subjects, to make a volume of value to students and the general reader alike. Another useful publication for Johnsonians was *Samuel Johnson: A Survey and Bibliography of Critical Studies*, by James L. Clifford and Donald J. Greene, which lists almost every book or separately printed pamphlet concerning Johnson that has been printed. The basis of this work is the two volumes of *Johnsonian Studies* by Mr. Clifford, previously published, which covered the years from 1887 to 1960. Mr. Greene is mainly responsible for the century before and the decade after that period.

DICKENS AND KEATS.—Among books by Charles Dickens which appeared in good time for the 1970 Christmas gift period was the first new edition of *The Life of Our Lord* which he wrote in 1849 for his own children. It remained in manuscript until 1934, when it was at last released and sold for serial publication in the world's press. In the United Kingdom it was published in a well illustrated book which had a large sale, but no new edition was issued until 36 years later. This re-telling of the Gospel story is simple and straightforward, in language well suited to young readers (generally speaking), or to Victorian children at least. One of Dickens's pleasantest and most popular stories is *A Christmas Carol*, and it was a pleasing idea to publish a new edition, comprising a facsimile of the manuscript, each page faced by the corresponding page of the first printed edition, with reproductions of Leech's original illustrations. As with Scott, so with Dickens, opinions of his books expressed by contemporaries were gathered into an interesting volume, *Dickens, The Critical Heritage*, edited by Philip Collins. Some thought his books would not live after his death!

John Keats was only 25 when he died in Rome on February 23, 1821, but he had written some poetry of beauty which has ever since been widely admired. The sesquicentenary of his death was marked by publication of *The Poems of John Keats*, edited by Miriam Allott, a splendid complete edition; *Keats and his World*, a good critical study by Timothy Hilton; and two small volumes dealing with parts of his work: *The Odes of Keats and their Earliest Known Manuscripts*, edited by Robert Gittings, and *Keats at Wentworth Place*, introduced by Dorothy Hewlett. The latter contains much of his best work, all written between Dec. 1818 and Sept. 1820 while his home was in one of two neighbouring houses (later joined into one) called Wentworth Place, in John Street, Hampstead. The street was renamed Keats Grove in 1920, when the house was bought and entrusted to the local authority, and Wentworth Place was reopened as Keats House, museum and library, five years later. Most of the purchase price of the house came from the United States, where Keats has long had many devotees, and this 150th anniversary of his death was marked by an exhibition at Harvard University which included about 60 of his manuscripts.

POETICAL FRIENDSHIPS.—Poets were numerous, and many of them prosperous, in the late 18th and early 19th centuries, and their relations with each other were in the main cordial. Scott and Byron were on especially friendly terms and corresponded often, although they met only on a few occasions. Although both were fine and famous poets, and both were lame, in most other respects they were opposites—perhaps a foundation for friendship. In *Byron: A Portrait* Prof. Leslie A. Marchand gave us a brilliantly written volume which provides for the general reader a handier, more concentrated study of the poet to supplement the author's earlier 3-volume biography. He discusses with clarity and tolerance the puzzle of Byron's marriage. Another poetical friend of Scott was James Hogg, known as " The Ettrick Shepherd," a selection of whose best work appeared in *James Hogg: Selected Poems*, well chosen and edited by Douglas S. Mack. Hogg's character and qualities were as different from Scott's as Byron's were, but Hogg helped Scott to compile his *Minstrelsy of the Scottish Border*, and he had a sense of humour which made him popular with Scott and many others.

Scott was an admirer of the work of another contemporary, Jane Austen, although she, like the Author of *Waverley*, was a " Great Unknown," the four novels appearing in her lifetime appearing anonymously. Students and others not familiar with her work would welcome *Jane Austen* by Yasmine Gooneratna, an excellent short biography and study of the author and her six novels, published *Letters* and minor works. For more sophisticated students there was *Jane Austen's English* by K. C. Phillipps, in which her vocabulary is analysed and her syntax and sentence structure are studied. Jane's favourite authors included Scott, Johnson and Richardson, and a new biography entitled *Samuel*

Richardson, by T. C. Duncan Evans and Ben D. Kimpel, was a welcome contribution to the year's literature. It presents a scholarly study of the author and his work which must have been long and carefully researched, but it is also pleasantly readable. Largely unpublished work by Charlotte Brontë was included in one handsome volume, *Five Novelettes*, edited by Winifred Gérin, who had transcribed them from the original manuscripts. Only one of the five, *Mina Laury*, had been previously published. Fresh light was thrown on the life of a favourite children's author by Prof. Leslie Linder in *A History of the Writings of Beatrix Potter*, in which he details her various kinds of writing and includes some new work hitherto unpublished. A remarkable first book, by a centenarian author, was *Portrait of a Victorian Youth*, by Alice Pollock, who is 102. She gives a wonderfully lively account of her childhood and youth and the way of life of upper middle class people.

POLITICAL AFFAIRS.—Political reminiscences and biographies loomed large and heavy in the year's publishing, beginning with weighty tomes by or about four former prime ministers. From Mr. Harold Macmillan came the 4th portion of his autobiography, entitled *Riding the Storm 1956–1959*, the period between the end of the Suez affair and his ascent to the premiership. It is as rich in perception, humour and personal revelation as its predecessors. Mr. Harold Wilson was quickly off the mark after his electoral defeat with *The Labour Government 1964–1970*, which he described as a personal record, in a book that was longer than Mr. Macmillan's and no less self-revealing. Two books appeared concerning the life and premiership of Mr. David (briefly Earl) Lloyd George. Many notable events in his life were recalled in *Lloyd George: A Diary* by Frances Stevenson (now the Dowager Countess), which gives an intimate, though not continuous, account of political events between 1914 and 1944 as seen by his secretary, constant companion and second wife. The book was edited by A. J. P. Taylor, who also edited *Lloyd George: Twelve Essays* contributed by writers with differing viewpoints on aspects of Lloyd George's activities. Associated with these books was *Politicians at War, July 1914 to May 1915*, by Cameron Hazlehurst, which is sub-titled "Prologue to the Triumph of Lloyd George." Dr. Hazlehurst has researched the puzzling period between the ultimatum to Serbia and the formation of our first coalition government, during which the hitherto radical pacificist Chancellor became accepted as a war leader. The 4th prime minister who attracted an author was studied afresh in *Lord Palmerston* by Jasper Ridley, who gave us a highly readable biography of that lively, prudent and long-lived statesman.

Autobiographical books came from several politicians who never reached the top of the ladder but contributed much of value to the political scene. Notable among them was Lord (" Rab ") Butler whose volume of memoirs, *The Art of the Possible*, was itself a work of literary art. He filled many high offices, and was at times deputy prime minister, in fact if not in name; but he seems especially proud of what he was able to do in the education field. Another possible prime minister *manqué* was George Brown, now also a life peer, whose *In My Way* was a piquant piece of good writing. Lord George-Brown's views on the mechanics of Labour government reflect his ebullient personality and many political gifts. A new biography by Keith Robbins, *Sir Edward Grey*, shed some fresh light on the enigmatic foreign secretary from 1905 to 1916, which sought to explain why he wielded so much influence in the

Cabinet and the public mind. A mixture of qualities characterized Sir Winston Churchill's son according to those to knew him, and the opinions of some of them were capably edited by Kay Halle to make *Randolph Churchill: The Young Unpretender* the fascinating book it is. His last and unfinished activity, the writing of his father's biography, redeemed many of his own earlier failures.

MILITARY MATTERS.—Army surgeons, especially those who worked before the coming of antisepsis and anaesthetics, saw much of the grimmest side of war, and probably few saw more than did Baron Dominique Jean Larrey, whose story was re-told, partly in his own words, in *Napoleon's Surgeon* by J. Henry Dible. Larrey served through all Napoleon's campaigns and was also his personal surgeon. His most notable innovations were the introduction of " flying ambulances "—light horsed carts to collect wounded and carry them swiftly to the rear for treatment while fighting continued; and his insistence on the earliest possible treatment of wounds, against the then idea that surgical treatment should be delayed. During one battle in Russia Larrey did about 200 amputations in 24 hours, he asserted in his memoirs, which Prof. Dible has used extensively in this excellent book. An English doctor's activities and observations during the Indian Mutiny as recorded in his diaries make *Cavalry Surgeon* an equally interesting book, perhaps more suited to the lay reader. Sub-titled " The Recollections of Deputy Surgeon-General John Henry Sylvester, FGS, Bombay Army "—who seems to have done as much fighting as operating—it is well edited by A. McKenzie Annand.

One of the gay and lively women in the fashionable world of the late 18th century was Lady Sarah Lennox, a great-granddaughter of Charles II, who became the mother of three generals by her (second) marriage to Colonel George Napier. Her story and theirs is attractively told in *The Sword Dance* by Priscilla Napier, which takes its title from an incident in the Peninsular War—the war of which Lady Sarah Napier's 3rd son, Sir William, was the famous historian. His *History of the War in the Peninsula* is a standard book for students of military history. His eldest brother, Sir Charles, later became the leading general in India, and has a statue in Trafalgar Square. India was the scene of many conflicts during the last 200 years, not least important of which for Great Britain was the war of 1814–16 against the Gurkhas, thousands of whom have since served in the British Army and have endeared themselves to the British people. The war was graphically described by John Pemble in *The Invasion of Nepal*.

It was in India that Lord Cornwallis achieved the success that his character and talents deserved, but he had previously been most unfortunate in America, where his surrender at Yorktown in 1781 ensured the loss of our colonies and the birth of the United States, and is better remembered than his later good work in India. The American period of his service is sympathetically depicted in *Cornwallis and the War of Independence* by Franklin and Mary Wickwire, an American husband and wife team who give the highest praise and credit to one of England's greatest defeated generals. From America came the 3rd volume of *The Papers of Ulysses S. Grant*, edited by John Y. Simon, which covers the three months from Oct. 1861 to January 1862. Grant, like Eisenhower, was a successful commanding general who later became President of the republic. There are evidently many more volumes to come in this valuable series. What has been called our most unnecessary war was stirringly described in *The Thin Red Line* by John Selby, who

uses many eye-witness accounts to give us a vivid picture of the campaign in the Crimea. Of topical and continuing interest was Ernle Bradford's *Gibraltar: The History of a Fortress*, a detailed history of the Rock and the sieges it has experienced. One of England's greatest military humiliations (before the fall of Singapore in 1942) occurred in 1667, as readers of Pepys's Diary know. It was fully described by P. G. Rogers in *The Dutch in the Medway*, for which he drew on Dutch accounts as well as our own to produce an admirable book.

NOTABLE NOVELS.—A large-scale project in fiction writing was completed by the publication of *Last Things*, the 11th and last volume in the " Strangers and Brothers " series of novels by C. P. (Lord) Snow which has occupied the author for 30 years. The series deals with the life and times of Lewis Eliot, born poor, who rises to affluence by way of the law, politics and books. Ernest Raymond, in his 83rd year, achieved wide success with his 42nd novel, *A Georgian Love Story*; and it was announced that he had completed another, entitled *Our Late Member*, which would be published on February 16, 1972, the 50th anniversary of the publication of his famous first novel, *Tell England*; and by the same publishers (Cassell) who have published all his books.

Another remarkable literary partnership is that of Manfred B. Lee and Frederic Dannay, cousins and collaborators who are better known under their pen-name of Ellery Queen. Their first book was *The Roman Hat Mystery*, which appeared 41 years and 77 books ago, during which period of quarrelsome but highly profitable partnership they are estimated to have sold 125 million copies of their books, besides producing a dozen films, several television series, a radio programme that has run non-stop for 9 years, and a monthly crime story magazine which has run for 30 years. Their latest book, *The Last Woman in his Life*, was published in November 1970, and was well up to their invariable high standard. But no " hero " of Ellery Queen's creation has held popular interest and affection for as long a time as Sherlock Holmes has and, while Conan Doyle's stories about him continue to delight old friends and gain new ones, books about the books continue to appear. The latest was *The Late Mr Sherlock Holmes* by Trevor H. Hall, in which some more interesting and amusing theories were put forward to entertain Holmesians. One is that Holmes retired because of failing eyesight caused, of course, by his excessive smoking—a topical idea, but what about his early drug addition? Another essay seeks to show that Doctor Watson had not two, but five wives! Perhaps over the years a similar body of mythical commentary will grow around the late C. S. Forester's notable naval hero. A start, at least, was

made by C. Northcote Parkinson with *The Life and Times of Horatio Hornblower* in which he purports to have found two boxes of family papers which enable a full biography to be constructed. Prof. Parkinson makes a delightful job of it.

SOCIAL STUDIES.—A hard-working social investigator and writer of last century was Henry Mayhew, and in the middle of that century, when cholera was rife, he observed and wrote much about London's squalor. In *The Unknown Mayhew*, edited by E. P. Thompson and Eileen Yeo, they have reprinted a selection of his contributions to the " Morning Chronicle " in 1849-50, when he was at his best as observer and chronicler, with two essays describing his life and the background of his writing. Another scourge of that time besides cholera was the heavy drinking practised by people of all classes, and in *Drink and the Victorians* Brian Harrison wrote well about this and the struggle for temperance between 1815 and 1872. Giles St. Aubyn, in *Infamous Victorians*, retold the stories of two notorious medical poisoners, Doctors Palmer and Lamson, who are among the immortal villains of criminology. An earlier period of social history was dealt with by George Rude in *Hanoverian London 1714–1808*, which gives a good all-round account of the growth of the capital and its social and administrative life. At the height of that hard-drinking period, we are told, London contained 450 taverns, 6,000 beerhouses, and 8,650 gin or brandy shops, to serve a population much smaller than today's. An earlier chronicler, and one of the greatest, was John Stow, and many readers were glad to have a revised edition in two fine volumes of his *A Survey of London*, edited by Charles Lethbridge Kingsford, completed in 1598. It remains a standard guide to old London life.

Among other books published during the year were the following:

The European Discovery of America, by Samuel Eliot Morison; *Charles II: The Man and the Statesman*, by Maurice Ashley; *A Sort of Life*, by Graham Greene; *The Conservative Party from Peel to Churchill*, by Robert Blake; *The Napoleonists*, by E. Tangye Lean; *Oxford Now and Then*, by Daeve Balsdon; *The Pinkertons* by James D. Horan; *Sarah Siddons*, by Roger Manvell; *Queen Anne*, by David Green; *Fanfare for a Tin Hat*, by Eric Linklater; *Anne of Denmark*, by Ethel Carleton Williams; *Frederick the Great*, by Nancy Mitford; *The Courtiers of Henry VIII*, by David Mathew; *The Drovers*, by K. J. Bonser; *The Ladies of Llangollen*, by Elizabeth Mavor; *Motive for a Mission*, by James Douglas-Hamilton; *Robert, Earl of Essex*, by Robert Lacey; *Wren* by Margaret Whinney; *The Girl in Blue*, by P. G. Wodehouse; *Books do Furnish a Room*, by Anthony Powell.

DRAMATIC SUMMARY, 1970–71

Among London productions between Oct. 1, 1970 and Sept 30, 1971 were the following:—

ADELPHI, Strand, W.C.2.—(1971) *July* 29. Revival of Kern and Hammerstein's *Show Boat* (Thomas Carey, Kenneth Nelson, André Jobin, Miguel Godreau, Cleo Laine, Jan Hunt and Ena Cabayo).

ALDWYCH, Aldwych, W.C.2.—Royal Shakespeare Company's London Season (1970). *Oct.* 19. Shaw's *Major Barbara* (Brewster Mason, Roger Rees, Richard Pasco, Miles Anderson, Judi Dench, Elizabeth Spriggs and Anne Dyson). *Dec.* 22. *The Two Gentlemen of Verona* (Ian Richardson, Clement McCallin, Terence Taplier, Sebastian Shaw, Patrick Stewart and Estelle Kobler). (1971)

March 24. World Theatre Season opened with production by Théâtre Michel of Paris. *June* 1. *Old Times*, by Harold Pinter (Colin Blakeley, Dorothy Tutin and Vivien Merchant). *June* 10. *A Midsummer Night's Dream* (Alan Howard, David Waller, Sara Kestelman, Dame Margaret Rutherford and Frances la Tour). *July* 22. *Enemies*, by Gorky (John Wood, Alan Howard, Patrick Stewart, Philip Locke, Sebastian Shaw, Helen Mirren and Mary Rutherford). Royal Shakespeare Company productions. *Sept.* 14. Etherege's *The Man of Mode* (Alan Howard, John Wood, David Waller, Helen Mirren and Vivien Merchant).

APOLLO, Shaftesbury Avenue, W.1.—(1971). *March* 31. *Children of the Wolf*, by John Peacock

(Shane Briant, Yvonne Mitchell and Sheelagh Cullen). *April* 28. *Forget-Me-Not Lane*, by Peter Nichols (Michael Bates, Anton Rogers and Sandra Payne).

CAMBRIDGE, Earlham Street, W.C.2.—National Theatre productions (1970) *Oct.* 27. Rostand's *Cyrano de Bergerac* (Edward Woodward, Gerald James, Anthony Nicholls, Charles Kay and Anna Carteret). (1971) *Feb.* 18. Shaw's *Captain Brassbound's Conversion* (Joss Ackland, John Robinson, Kenneth Williams and Ingrid Bergman). *Aug.* 5. *Hamlet* (Ian McKellar, John Woodvine, James Cairncross, Faith Brook and Susan Fleetwood).

CRITERION, Piccadilly, W.1.—(1970) *Dec.* 29. *The High Bid*, by Henry James (Gary Watson, Hugh Manning, Charles Carson and Eartha Kitt). (1971) *Feb.* 4. *After Haggerty*, by David Mercer (Frank Finlay, Leslie Sands, John White, David Wood and Billie Whitelaw). *July* 14. *Batley*, by Simon Gray (Alan Bates, Richard O'Callaghan and Michael Byrne).

DUCHESS, Catherine Street, W.C.2.—(1971). *Feb.* 25. *Mister*, by Stanley Eveling (Freddie Jones, Esmond Knight, Andrew Robertson and Delia Lindsay).

DUKE OF YORK'S, St. Martin's Lane, W.C.2.—(1971). *Jan.* 21. *Meeting at Night*, by James Bridie (Wilfrid Hyde White, Jonathan Newth, Sydney Tafler, David Battley and Renee Houston). *Sept.* 28. *Romance!*, musical by John Spurling and Charles Ross (Bill Simpson, Jess Conrad, Joyce Blair and Roberta D'Este).

FORTUNE, Drury Lane, W.C.2.—(1971). *Sept.* 30. *Suddenly at Home*, by Francis Durbridge (Gerald Harper, Terence Longden, Jennifer Daniel, Veronica Strong and Penelope Keith).

GARRICK, Charing Cross Road, W.C.2.—(1971). *Feb.* 10. *Don't Start Without Me*, by Joyce Rayburn (Paul Daneman, Brian Cox, Jan Waters and Lucy Fleming). *Sept.* 15. *Don't Just Lie There, Say Something*, by Michael Pertwee (Brian Rix, Alfred Marks, Leo Franklyn, Peter Bland, Joanna Lumley and Deborah Grant).

GLOBE, Shaftesbury Avenue, W.1.—(1971). *Jan.* 28. *Kean*, by Jean-Paul Sartre (Alan Badel and Felicity Kendal).

HAYMARKET, Haymarket, S.W.1.—(1971). *Feb.* 24. *Spoiled*, by Simon Gray (Jeremy Kemp, Simon Ward and Anna Massey). *April* 27. Enid Bagnold's *The Chalk Circle* (Peter Bayliss, Michael Goodlife, Dame Gladys Cooper, Joan Greenwood and Vanessa Miles). *August* 4. *A Voyage Round My Father*, by John Mortimer (Sir Alec Guinness, Jeremy Brett, Richard Fraser, Leueen MacGrath, Nicola Pagett and Phyllida Law).

MERMAID, Puddle Dock, E.C.—(1970). *Nov.* 12. *Exiles*, by James Joyce (John Wood, Timothy West, Vivien Merchant and Lynn Farleigh). *Dec.* 30. *The Watched Pot*, by "Saki" (Alan Dobie, Timothy Carlton, John Tordoff, Lally Bowers and Moira Redmond). (1971) *Feb.* 15. *The Licentious Fly*, by Huntly Harding (Christopher Benjamin and Antonia Pemberton). *April* 1. *Hanky Park*, by Walter Greenwood (Jack Tweddle, Bernard Padden, Sally Miles and Penny Ryder). *July* 29. *The Old Boys*, by William Trevor (Sir

Michael Redgrave, Bernard Hepton, Norman Shelley, Sylvia Coleridge and Margaret Courtenay).

NEW, St. Martin's Lane, W.C.2.—(1970) *Nov.* 5. Terence Rattigan's *The Winslow Boy* (Kenneth More, Laurence Naismith, Steven Pacey, Peter Gale and Annette Crosbie). (1971) National Theatre productions. *June* 15. Pirandello's *The Rules of the Game* (Paul Scofield, Edward Hardwicke, Paul Carron and Joan Plowright). *July* 20. *Tyger*, musical celebration of William Blake, by Adrian Mitchell, with music by Mike Westbrook (Gerald James, John Moffatt, Bill Fraser and Isabelle Lucas). *Aug.* 3. *Danton's Death*, by Georg Büchner (Christopher Plummer, Charles Kay, Ronald Pickup, Frank Barrie, Michael Tudor Barnes, Anna Carteret and Jo Maxwell Muller).

OLD VIC (National Theatre), Waterloo Road, S.E.1.—(1970) *Dec.* 30. Shaw's *Mrs. Warren's Profession* (Ronald Pickup, Edward Hardwicke, Bill Fraser, Coral Browne and Sarah Badel). (1971) *Feb.* 3. *The Architect and the Emperor of Austria*, by Fernando Arrabal (Jim Dale and Anthony Hopkins). *March* 9. Zuckmayer's *The Captain of Köpernick*, translated by John Mortimer (Paul Schofield, Jim Dale, John Moffatt, Bill Fraser and Kenneth Mackintosh). *April* 7. Heywood's *A Woman Killed with Kindness* (Anthony Hopkins, Frank Barrie, Derek Jacobi, Paul Curran, Dai Bradley and Joan Plowright). *May* 6. *Coriolanus* (Anthony Hopkins, Denis Quilley, John Moffatt, Charles Kay, Bernard Gallagher, Kenneth Mackintosh and Constance Cummings). *Aug.* 24. Production by Octagon Theatre, Bolton, of Strindberg's *The Father*. *Sept.* 6. Theatre Royal, York, Company in *The Last Sweet Days of Isaac*, musical.

PICCADILLY, Denman Street, W.1.—(1970) *Oct.* 8. *Vivat! Vivat! Regina!* by Robert Bolt (Richard Pearson, Edward Atienza, David McKail, Eileen Atkins and Sarah Miles).

PRINCE OF WALES, Coventry Street, W.1.—(1971) *Aug.* 2. *The Avengers*, by Terence Feely and Brian Clemens (Simon Oates, Paul McDowell and Sue Lloyd). *Sept.* 14. Revival of *Big Bad Mouse* (Jimmy Edwards and Eric Sykes).

QUEEN'S, Shaftesbury Avenue, W.1.—(1971) *March* 16. *Child's Play*, by Robert Marasco (Laurence Harvey, Rupert Davies, Derek Fowlds and Richard Heffer). *June* 17. *The Patrick Pearse Motel*, by Hugh Leonard (Godfrey Quigley, Norman Rodway, May Cluskey and Moira Redmond). *Aug* 31. *Jump!*, by Larry Gelbert (Warren Mitchell, Linal Haft, Sheila Steafel and Sheila Scott Wilkinson).

STRAND, Aldwych, W.C.2.—(1970) *Nov* 17. J. B. Priestley's *When We Are Married* (Fred Emney, Frank Thornton, Hugh Lloyd, William Moore, Peggy Mount, Freda Jackson, Gwen Cherrell and Gretchen Franklin). (1971) *June* 3. *No Sex, Please—We're British* by Anthony Marriott and Alistair Foot (Michael Crawford, Anthony Valentine, Linda Thorson and Evelyn Laye).

VAUDEVILLE, Strand, W.C.2.—(1971) *March* 17. *Move Over, Mrs. Markham*, by Roy Cooney and John Chapman (Tony Britton, Terence Alexander, Cicely Courtneidge, Moira Lister and Lana Morris).

POETS LAUREATE

Samuel Daniel	1599	Nicholas Rowe	1715	Robert Southey	1813
Ben Jonson	1619	Rev. Laurence Eusden	1718	William Wordsworth	1843
Sir William D'Avenant	1637	Colley Cibber	1730	Lord Tennyson	1850
John Dryden	1670	William Whitehead	1757	Alfred Austin	1896
Thomas Shadwell	1688	Rev. Thomas Warton	1785	Robert Bridges	1913
Nahum Tate	1692	Henry James Pye	1790	John Masefield	1930

Cecil Day Lewis...1967

SCIENCE, DISCOVERY AND INVENTION IN 1971.

The narrowness of the divide between triumph and tragedy in space exploration was doubly emphasised during the year. America's Apollo 15 mission to the Moon, bedevilled by a succession of mechanical faults which could have brought it to a premature close and to failure, if not disaster, ended as an overwhelming success and proved the most rewarding of all attempts at Moon exploration. Russia's first attempt at a manned station, which had gone so smoothly that the stay of the three man crew had been extended, ended in calamity because of what may have been a small mechanical fault, aided by human error.

The *Soyuz* 11 supply craft docked with the *Salyut* space station, launched nearly seven weeks earlier, on June 7, just over 24 hours after take-off from the Baikonur cosmodrome. After the two craft had been connected mechanically, hydraulically and electrically the three Russian cosmonauts, Lt.-Col. Georgi Dobrovolsky (43), flight commander, Viktor Patsayev (38), test engineer, and Vladislav Volkov (36), flight engineer transferred to *Salyut* through an inter-connecting tunnel. Thus came what could reasonably be described as the birth of the first manned space-station, the prototype orbiting laboratory, factory, space-ship station of the future.

Just over three weeks later, on June 29, after surpassing the previous space flight endurance record of 17 days, 17 hours, set a year before by their compatriots Vitaly Sevastianov and Andrian Nikolayev, the cosmonauts transferred back to the *Soyuz* craft with the results of their experiments. After they had reported that everything was well the retro-rockets fired, early on June 30, to initiate earth landing. Soon afterwards and earlier than expected radio communication was lost, though the landing proceeded perfectly. Silence continued and when the helicopter recovery crew went into the *Soyuz* landing module they found the three cosmonauts dead. The craft had taken itself through the whole complicated landing procedure automatically with the lifeless bodies of the three men in their seats before the controls.

Their deaths were the first due directly to a space environment. Three Americans, Virgil Grissom, Edward White and Roger Chafee, who died in 1967, had died during ground testing of an Apollo moonship on top of its rocket. The Russian cosmonaut, Vladimir Komarov, who perished the same year, died from the excessive landing impact after the parachutes on his craft became tangled. Among the early suggestions put forward to account for the deaths of the three Russians was that their bodies, weakened by the long period of weightlessness to which they had been exposed, may have succumbed to the strain of the overload forces as the atmosphere slowed their craft. The Russians, with experience of longer space flights even than the American journeys to the Moon, had earlier reported adverse effects of weightlessness on the heart, the composition of the blood, the bones and the body's balancing mechanism. The *Soyuz* 11 crew had been given special exercise suits—" penguin suits " they nicknamed them from their appearance—to simulate some of the strains of gravity and counter the effects of weightlessness.

If the after-effects of prolonged flight were responsible they were only indirectly so, it turned out. The three men were reported to have died of embolism, gas bubbles in the blood, produced by sudden depressurization of their spacecraft. They were the first victims of a space version of the " bends ", the decompression sickness which is a hazard of sea diving. The Russians, in their rather guarded comment later, did not disclose exactly how this had happened. Although there had been no structural failure of the craft, it was stated, there had been a " loss of sealing ". A number of possible causes of this were being examined. Why the defect in sealing had not shown up on instruments, or why the cosmonauts had ignored it if it had, remained a mystery. One irony was that, because descent from orbit had now become almost a routine measure, the men were not wearing space suits and were breathing the air of their cabin at the time. If they had had space suits on and had been breathing oxygen they would have come through unharmed.

Because of the Soyuz mishap the American astronauts of *Apollo* 15, Col. David Scott, the Commander, Major Alfred Worden, Command Module Pilot, and Lt.-Col. James Irwin, Lunar Module Pilot, did wear space suits at similar points in their voyage. Before it began, it was revealed later, the Russians were asked if the *Soyuz* 11 experience indicated it should be put off. The Russians gave the Americans the go-ahead. In fact the Americans seemed to suffer a similar mechanical problem for a leak as indicated in the tunnel connecting two parts of their craft. The astronauts were wearing their space suits at the time and any sealing problems there may have been were put right.

The *Apollo* journey, taking place in the greater blaze of publicity which surrounds American efforts, seemed to the Earthbound spectator to be continually subject to troubles which belied the reputation of American space engineering for superlative workmanship. Cancellation seemed probable almost at the outset when trouble was indicated in the main service engine on which all operations for going into orbit about the Moon and return to Earth depended. This was found, however, to be a fault in an indicator unit, due to a short circuit, not in the engine itself. Water leaks appeared in the spacecraft, broken glass in the lunar module. There was trouble with the separation of the moon craft and service module in orbit about the Moon and a near collision on docking again. The first car designed to carry men around the moon had its own faults, with unstable battery indicators and no front steering when first tested—these were put right by the mechanical improvisations of the astronauts. The journey on the Moon's surface had to be cut short. Finally one of the three landing parachutes failed to open. The bump as the spaceship plunged into the ocean at the end of the voyage was harder than planned but not too hard for the men inside to withstand. After their journey the men reported dizziness, minor heart irregularities and unusual difficulty in adapting again to gravity. Though none of these was of serious medical concern consideration was given to shortening the amount of activity of the next *Apollo* team.

Apollo Success

Despite this the eventual outcome of the mission was an undoubted triumph. Scientists at the NASA base at Houston claimed that more had been learned from that one flight than from all previous ones manned or unmanned. Information gathered by Worden, in the command module orbiting the Moon and by Scott and Irwin, on the surface, indicated that the Moon had had a prolonged, tumultuous period of development in which vulcanism had played a large part. Cinder cones seen by Worden indicated that vulcanism

had gone on for longer than had been generally believed and some of the craters he reported seemed to be relatively young. The terraced appearance of mountains, described by Scott and Irwin, and the similar layering in the Hadley Rille, a 1,000 foot cleft in a *mare* basin, also support the idea that a series of cataclysmic events, with outpourings of lava, took place on the Moon and go against the theory that it was always a cold body with its surface features solely the result of battering by meteorites.

One hope had been that the *Apollo* 15 mission would bring back some " genesis " rock, the oldest exposed material on the Moon. From this it should be possible to deduce more about the original condition and formation of the Moon and perhaps the Earth, but the excited cry of Scott, as he gathered one piece of rock, " This is what we came for," appeared later to have been premature. Nevertheless it was of great value and the total bag of 60 odd rocks brought ecstatic feelings to geologists on Earth because of their wide variety. How valuable and how extensive the information was still a matter of surmise, only because it would take long to unravel. Apollo 15's success also meant that the U.S. now had three experimental stations on the Moon recording " moonquakes ". This should make it possible to triangulate and locate the events. One surprising discovery has been that swarms of quakes occur, yielding the possibility of discovering more of the interior structure of the Moon. One quake was located at almost 500 miles below the surface—the deepest on Earth occurs at about 450 miles. This implied that the Moon's structure was rigid enough to support considerable sheer forces at considerable depth.

The 1,000 foot Hadley Rille provides its own puzzle. Pickering, the original discoverer of the rilles, suggested that they had been cut out of the surface by water. Unlikely as it might seem, the Rille still appeared at least possibly to have been formed in some such way by some such agency. For water to flow, even if it was ejected from the rocks, there would have to be some atmosphere, otherwise it would vaporise immediately. A considerable atmosphere, and water, after the hundreds or millions or thousands of millions of years needed for laying down the *mare* basins would take more explaining than is possible at the moment.

Space Stations

Space stations, in orbit for long periods, if not permanently, manned by a succession of crews of astronauts and scientists ferried to them for stays of one to three months, now seem to have had priority in the Russian manned space programme for some time. They are due to become the main feature of American plans as the impetus goes out of the Apollo programme. From space stations, say their advocates, it will be possible, in the future, to prospect for minerals more successfully than on the surface, to watch crops for the optimum time for harvesting, as well as for the first signs of pests. Meteorologists will be able to watch weather formations and the spread of ice and snow, astronomers to make their observations at all wavelengths, not just at those which can penetrate Earth's atmospheric curtain. Industrial processes carried out in conditions of weightlessness and high vacuum will yield products of a refinement impossible or extremely difficult to achieve on Earth. The actual objects of the *Salyut-Soyuz* mission were stated to be, (1) checking space equipment; (2) trial of new methods of station orientation and navigation; (3) study of geological and geographical objects on Earth and atmospheric formations and

snow and ice " with the aim of using this information in the solution of economic problems "; (4) study of physical and chemical processes and phenomena in the atmosphere and outer space in various regimes of the electromagnetic spectrum; and (5) biomedical studies including the effects of spaceflight on the human system.

All this was carried out successfully, it appeared. Part of the equipment of *Salyut* was an " Orion " observatory, described as a complex and highly accurate optical-electronic system. One telescope and spectrograph were outside the cosmonaut's pressurized working area and another telescope inside. Patsayev became the first extra-terrestrial astronomer when he studied a star in the constellation of Centaurus, obtaining spectrograms at wavelengths not possible from the Earth. He also staked a claim to be regarded as the first "space gardener ", tending plants on Salyut to observe changes in their structure in conditions of weightlessness and test their nutritional value.

Drawings of *Salyut* showed it as being 65 feet long with a maximum diameter of about 13 feet. The volume available for working in was over 3,500 cubic feet, and the spherical orbiting module of *Soyuz*, docked against *Salyut*, was used as a rest and sleeping area. Together *Salyut* and *Soyuz* weighed over 25 tons. *Soyuz* 11, it appeared, had been intended to be just the first of a number of craft ferrying crews to *Salyut*. The space station, orbiting relatively close to the Earth at a height at which it would quickly descend into the atmosphere, was put into a higher orbit the day after the tragedy and again just over a month later. It was unofficially reported that *Soyuz* 12 was being made ready at Baikonur to ferry the next crew when the tragedy took place.

American space station plans feature initially around Skylab, due to be launched in 1972 by a Saturn 5 rocket, of the type used to send Apollo spacecraft to the Moon. The workshop would be 48 ft. long and 21·6 ft. in diameter, with a total volume of over 10,000 cubic feet. Crews would be carried to it by an Apollo command and service module, launched by the smaller Saturn 1B rocket. The total length of the space station, including the docked Apollo craft would be almost 120 ft. and the weight over 80 tons, more than three times that of the docked *Soyuz-Salyut* combination. Skylab, developed from one stage of a Saturn rocket, was to be only a preliminary experimental venture. More ambitious plans for the late 1970's, if NASA's budget can support them, are for a 12 man station and leading ultimately to 450 ton spaceports, a hundred yards or more across.

Automatic Moon Exploration

Russia had her own space triumphs, including *Lunakhod* 1, the first robot mobile Moon explorer, landed by *Luna* 17 to follow up the success of *Luna* 16, the automatic craft for returning rock samples to Earth. *Luna* 16 opened up a new phase in space exploration, with the possibility of samples being returned from the planets by unmanned craft something for which NASA has no plans. After extracting a core of rock, by an electric drill, it blasted straight off into a ballistic trajectory for Earth, without going into orbit around the Moon, and with no provision for any mid-course correction. For this remarkable feat of navigation to be carried out the spacecraft had to be landed accurately at the planned point on the Moon and, on its return, accelerated to precisely the required speed. This was achieved and it landed in the planned recovery area at Kazakhstan.

Lunakhod 1, however Heath Robinsonian a contraption it appeared, proved to be designed

perfectly for its job. Looking like an inverted bath on eight metal wheels, it trundled down its landing ramp under the power of its electric motors and at once began a number of experiments from the analysis of moon rock to the study of X-rays from remote parts of the Universe. With five men controlling it from Earth, using T.V. cameras installed in the robot as their eyes, it moved steadily over the Sea of Rains until the long night of the Moon began. Even then it continued to perform a scientific function, through the French built laser reflector it carried. Laser beams reflected from this were observed by Russian astronomers in the Crimea and by French in the Pyrenees.

Ten months later *Lunakhod* was still functioning, having covered a total distance of about seven miles —to the delight, if not, indeed, to the surprise, of its designers and builders.

Unmanned automatic stations were best for Moon exploration, claimed Russian scientists. They provided information at a fraction of the cost of manned expeditions—the official cost for the Apollo 15 mission alone was £168 million. This comment provoked exercises in cost analysis by supporters of manned exploration, to show that Luna 16's moon rock cost more per gram than Apollo rock. But cost was becoming an ever more vital factor. Shortage of funds at NASA had curtailed the Apollo programme and the priority of Skylab meant the cancellation of at least one Moon mission, so that the Saturn 5 rocket would be available to launch it, instead of the two Saturn 1B rockets which would otherwise be required at extra cost.

Cancer Research

While space exploration was feeling its pocket pinched the strained American economy was being pressed to spend comparable sums on other research which, thought some, would yield more valuable results for mankind and yield them more speedily. Senator Edward Kennedy wanted a moon-shot sized financial boost for cancer research to solve that problem in the decade or so it had taken to put a man on the Moon—or less. One resolution put before the U.S. Congress called, to the more than little amazement of their own scientists, for the solution of cancer by 1976. The comment of Prof. John Watson, the American microbiologist and Nobel Prizewinner, was that it was no good just calling such people " gooses ". Science should accept the money. Much might be spent on sheer idiocy but if some went in the right direction it would be better than none. In the event President Nixon proposed an increase of $122 million for the U.S. National Institute of Health in the following year, of which $100 million was earmarked for cancer research—an amount equivalent to six or seven times the total British expenditure. But this was too much for U.S. institutes to absorb on their own immediately, because of the shortage of skilled manpower. Hopes were high that some might find its way to the United Kingdom.

In Europe there were proposals for multi-national collaboration in molecular biology, on the lines of the joint work on particle physics at CERN in Geneva. Cancer was a stimulus for this in the minds of many who believed that further unravelling of the secrets of the cell and the gene could provide the answer. Prof. Watson's own view was that the next decade could see the answer to the fundamental problem, by revealing the biochemistry of the process by which a gene might alter a cell to make it cancerous—though whether this would lead to a cure most workers in the field would doubt, he added.

Cancer Viruses and "Genes"

The successes of tumour virologists were responsible for the excitement in the field of cancer research and the belief that at last we might be getting near an understanding of the disease. Just how the viruses identified in chick and animal tumour cells might affect the cell was shown by the discovery of reverse transcriptase. This is an enzyme which reverses the normal method of synthesis of cellular nucleic material, which had previously been thought to proceed from double-stranded DNA to single stranded RNA. Now the RNA of the virus was shown to produce a DNA molecule which could be stably incorporated into the cell and, according to the theory, maintain it in a malignant state. The enzyme was found in four tumour viruses at Wisconsin University, by Dr. Howard Temin who had been arguing for years that it must exist, and independently by Dr. David Baltimore of the Massachusetts Institute of Technology. Quickly the finding was confirmed by Prof. Sam Spiegelman, of the Institute of Cancer Research, who found the enzyme in as many tumour viruses as he and his team could lay hands on. At once the search began for the enzyme in human tumour cells in the hope that it would reveal a human tumour virus. Soon success was reported, by Spiegelman and others. The enzyme had been found in leukaemic cells. But the jubilation was premature. For convenience the RNA used had not been taken from tumour viruses and though an enzyme which could perform reverse transcription had been found it proved to be by no means limited to cancer cells. So the search for human cancer virus continues, with perhaps the closest possibility, so far, coming with the detection of a virus in samples of human milk which, in structure, closely resembles mouse breast cancer virus.

Not all researchers are so optimistic about the promise of virus research. Although viruses have been shown to transform cells and even induce tumours in some susceptible animals cancer rarely, if ever, presents the characteristic of an infectious disease. There is a school of thought which holds that the seeds of cancer lie dormant in all cells, in the form of genes which can produce malignant proliferation of the cells when switched on by some outside agency, such as a chemical carcinogen—or a virus—or even, some might say, by the natural process of ageing. Some support for this has come with the isolation of what appeared to be tumour virus from the cells of healthy chick embryos. Most biologists would give as much weight, in cancer research, to the study of the cell surface as to its nucleus, though this is likely to be even more difficult. After all the surface seems to be involved in both aspects of malignancy, uncontrolled growth of the primary tumour and the appearance of secondaries. The cancerous cell continues to grow when, normally, contact with other cells inhibits growth. It also breaks away from its correct site and migrates to other parts of the body to produce those secondary growths which are often the cause of death. Plant proteins which make cells clump together have been found to return some cancerous cells to normal behaviour in the laboratory, presumably by blocking some changed site on the cell surface.

More immediate, so far as the cancer patient, or the man in the street fearful of becoming a cancer patient, is concerned, is work which could lead to

an earlier diagnosis of the disease, when treatment might be more effective, and also to possible new ways of treatment. An early warning system for cancer of the cervix, from the study of cells, has been in use for some years, though with somewhat contradictory views about its effect on the incidence and outcome of the disease. A ten year study of women in the Channel Islands has indicated that the presence of hormones could provide a good guide to the risk of breast cancer, though here, again there was controversy over the value of early diagnosis.

A possible blood test for cancer revealed itself at the Medical Research Council's Demyelinating Diseases Unit in Newcastle. A test devised to pick out patients with certain nervous diseases by recording sensitization of white blood corpuscles against brain and sciatic nerve proteins was found also to pick out people with cancer.

It could also select those with malignant tumours from those with benign tumours. This discovery, it was thought, apart from yielding a possible test, might cast fresh light on the cell surface changes which may lie behind malignancy.

Also from the U.K. came reports of two pieces of work which might lead to more effective treatment. A drug synthesized at the laboratories of the Imperial Cancer Research Fund in London proved able to prevent the formation of metastases, the secondary growths, in animals, apparently by preventing the release of cancerous cells from the primary tumour. Dr. K. Hellman, Head of the Cancer Chemotherapy Department said that if this could be done in humans then the malignant circle which made cancer so feared might be broken. Secondary growths, which had developed, could be removed in the confident belief that no others would form. If the primary tumour was not itself fatal it could be dealt with as a benign tumour.

At the Cancer Research Campaign Laboratories at Nottingham University injections of the anti-tuberculous vaccine, BGG, were also shown to affect the growth of secondary cancers, by stimulating the body's own natural defences. In tests on a strain of rats which develop fatal secondaries in the lung from their own strain of skin cancer the use of BCG had doubled the animals' lives. Tumours had either not grown at all or grown less rapidly and the appearance of secondaries in the lungs had been reduced.

ANCIENT ASTRONOMY.—The antiquity of man's study of the stars is shown by rock carvings found in the Armenian highlands. The most elaborate, dating back about 5,000 years, show not only how detailed were man's own observations but also how some of his pictorial impressions of the constellations have endured, according to Dr. B. Tumanyan, Director of the Observatory of the State University of Erevan. This is in the Martuni region of the Sevkar foothills. One small part of the carving shows the three bright stars of Cygnus in a line, with the sizes of the stars, as shown, roughly proportional to their brightness. Beside them is a carving of two men holding a serpent above their heads, so the imagination which first saw the picture in the stars which provoked the constellation name of the Serpent-Bearer existed at least as long ago as the rock carver. Other pictograms indicate that early man was in the habit of grouping stars and giving them names. Amongst numerous dots and dashes representing stars of part of the Milky Way are pictures of a sword, a shield and crosses and a triangle. Other carvings in the area date back even earlier, perhaps to 8,000 B.C. Altogether they show considerable knowledge and indicate that the people living in those mountain highlands —chosen, nowadays, for the sites of new Soviet observatories—divided the year into twelve parts.

APPETITE MECHANISM FOUND.—Three French physiologists at the Faculté de Médecine de Lyon claimed to have found evidence for the " ponderostat ", a previously hypothetical body mechanism for controlling food intake. Normally a sensory feedback affects the senses of taste and smell after eating, making food less attractive. When one is below normal weight, however, they reported in *Nature*, that mechanism appears not to work—hungry or not hungry, food is just as delicious.

The three men, in good health, who had kept their bodyweights virtually unchanged for two years, tested themselves by assessing the pleasantness of the taste of various sucrose solutions and the smell of dilutions of orange syrup before and one hour after drinking 200 ml of water solution containing 50 g of glucose. First the tests were made on two control trials while the men were at normal bodyweight. They set about losing weight, going on a reduced calorie diet of 500 to 800 calories a day, aiming at losing 8 per cent. or 10 per cent. of bodyweight. The trials were repeated when half that weight had been lost, when the desired minimum weight had been reached, after two weeks and one month of resting on a 1600 to 2000 calorie diet, at the minimum weight, after two days of overeating to caloric levels of up to 8000 cals. a day and after recovering control bodyweight.

At normal bodyweight there was a highly significant decrease in the pleasantness of both taste and odour of sweet substances after the glucose syrup had been taken. Thereafter, during weight loss and even after beginning to gain weight no subject showed any significant decrease in taste response after taking the glucose, though smell response did begin to reappear as weight was regained. By the time the initial bodyweight had been regained, however, responses were almost identical to those at the beginning of the experiment. The results have been repeated with other subjects.

Non-obese subjects become psychologically " obese " when they are underweight and the Frenchmen, M. Cabanac, R. Duclaux and N. H. Spector, hazard the supposition that obesity could be a resetting of the ponderostat at a higher value, making the obese less subject to some internal signal for satiety. *Anorexia nervosa*, loss of appetite which can lead to death by starvation, may be a resetting of the ponderostat at a lower value.

AUTOMATIC SAFETY BELT.—A car safety belt which automatically wraps itself around a car's occupants as they close the doors was developed at the Road Research Laboratory. The belt, in either diagonal or lap and diagonal form, has one end fastened to the door and is held taut by an inertia reel. The action of closing the door brings it into its proper protective position, around driver or passenger, instead of hanging uselessly onto the floor, as do four out of five ordinary present-day belts according to the Laboratory's surveys. The door-mounted belt has a further advantage. It holds the door closed and so guards against ejection in a sideways impact.

Air bags of the type which will have to be fitted to American cars by mid-1972 have been assessed by the Laboratory as being likely to prevent 50 per cent. of the more serious injuries, on the most favourable view of their effectiveness and assuming that they work correctly every time—the requirement being that they should inflate automatically within forty milliseconds of a crash, activated by

high pressure reservoir or from a chemical generator set off by the impact. Even ignoring the complexity of the airbag system and the possibility that it would not work correctly every time, safety belts appear to offer the same amount of protection at far lower cost, if only people could be persuaded or manoeuvred into wearing them. The door-mounted wrap-around belt is a possible solution to the problem and arrangements were made with an industrial company to take the project further.

BACTERIA STOP MINE FIRES.—A permanent self-repairing blanket to seal off disused coal faces was developed by three Georgian mining engineers. The material they used consisted solely of bacteria. Methane consuming bacteria have been used for some years in Russian mines to keep down the gas concentration and reduce the risk of fire but they cannot prevent direct interaction between oxygen and the coal face, which can lead to a spontaneous combustion. Films of latex sprayed on the face can provide a barrier, but only until the coal moves and splits the protective film. Pondering the problem the mining engineers, Academician A. Dzidziguri, L. Mchedlishvili and Y. Tsintsadze, thought it might be possible to use another attribute of bacteria, to make a living film able to grow over any crack or hole which might develop. After a number of trials as the engineers turned themselves into microbiologists they succeeded in breeding special strains of *aspergillus* and *bacillis* species which quickly adapted themselves to underground life. All that needs to be done is to spray the coal face well with a solution containing the bacteria. At once they begin to grow into a film several millimetres thick, solid enough not to be penetrated by a finger. The film penetrates into all the crevices, like the skin of a walnut. No oxygen can get at the coal so there is no spontaneous ignition. Other self-igniting materials can also be protected in the same way, it is claimed.

BEATING THE DESERT.—Horses sweat, men perspire, ladies only glow may have been the old saying, before the cosmetic manufacturers decided there was money to be made from telling ladies they perspired but shouldn't. The truth of sweating, or perspiring, is that it is probably the best way of keeping cool, except for living in the sea, devised by any animal. Man's own heat control mechanism is probably better than that of any other animal—far better to sweat than to pant like his pet dog. How one other creature goes about keeping cool was described at a Zoological Society symposium on desert animals in London, by Knut Schmidt-Neilson, of Duke University, USA. He and his colleagues investigated an unusual snail. Unlike other snails which hanker after cool, moist places and satisfy their hankerings, their particular snail, *sphincterochila boissieri*, lives in the deserts of the Near East, coping with high temperature, lack of water and, in the summer, lack of food. The snail, they found, will die at a temperature of 50–55 degrees Centigrade, lower than the temperatures it may meet on the sun-baked ground. One obvious precaution is to avoid that sun-baked ground if possible, either by burrowing below the surface or clambering above it on a branch. This it does when it can. But it also has its own built-in insulation system. Between the living creature and its shell is an air space which provides a circulating barrier against the high surface temperature. Its habit of remaining dormant in the summer also helps by reducing its own oxygen consumption and consequent heat production.

Sphincterochila Boissieri also overcomes that lack of water and food in the desert summer by just going without. All its eating and drinking has to be crammed into the short rainy season. Each snail apparently contains 1·4 grams of water but as it only loses half a milligram a day it will have lost barely a tenth of its reserves even after a year-long drought.

BIRTHWEIGHT HAZARD FOR THE POOR.—Mental subnormality can be a penalty for being born undersized when the baby's parents are poor and come from the lower social class, but not when they are prosperous, professional people, according to an Aberdonian survey. Sociologists from the Medical Sociology Unit at the University there compared the ante-natal and birth records of 11,000 children born in 1950 to 1955 with their later I.Q. performance to come to this conclusion. They found virtually no relationship between I.Q. and birth weight in upper class babies while in the lower class the relationship was marked and continuous—I.Q. fell steadily as birthweight declined from the well above average figure of 9½ lbs. One possible explanation is that the weight of babies in better off families does not depend on food and social conditions but in those with small incomes it indicates poorer nutrition and deprivation for the mother, affecting the child. Severe subnormality with neurological damage was spread equally across the social classes but while every mentally subnormal child in the higher social class families showed neurological damage this was so with only one in three of those in the lower class families, an indication that some environmental factor was at work in these. A massive clustering of children with mild subnormality in the lowest social classes made mental subnormality of all degrees ten times as common in the families of unskilled workers as in the non-manual section of the population. In families with severely adverse environmental factors it was thirty times as frequent.

Babies delivered with forceps or by Caesarean section proved to be brighter than average when tested later in life, showing I.Q. scores of 110 to 113, compared with the Aberdonian mean of 107, itself above the accepted general standard of 100. But this is apparently the result of such techniques being used more often on older professional women having their first babies and just reflects the advantage of being the firstborn of such a woman.

One factor which could be relevant in the development of a child and its I.Q. scoring has shown up in a study of twenty-five firstborn children from top and bottom social groups. These are fitted with jackets equipped with microphones and radio transmitters so that every word spoken by mother and child is recorded. Twice as many words, even three or four times as many, can pass between mother and child in the Class I or Class II family as in a Class V family. The total can reach 10,000 or 15,000 a day, the equivalent of a novel in a week. It is not just the number of subjects talked about which accounts for the difference but the amount of time devoted to a subject. The upper class mother uses less baby talk, more precise language and is more likely to explain than to adopt a " take it or leave it " attitude in her answers.

BRITISH ASSOCIATION.—The 133rd meeting of the British Association for the Advancement of Science took place at Swansea under the presidency of Sir Alexander Cairncross. In his presidential address Sir Alexander gave his audience of scientists, academics, students and teachers an economist's view of the role of science in the national economy, warning that they should not put too much faith in finding in it the solution to Britain's economic ills. Industry, he said, was felt to be falling down

on the job. What was more natural than to turn to science, in which Britain had such an outstanding record and press the Government to let it come to the rescue. Technological change had, indeed, been the mainspring of social progress over two centuries, but the part played by science in producing technological change could be exaggerated. Scientific knowledge was only one ingredient in the solution of engineering problems and very often by no means the most important. There was no correlation between a country's expenditure on research and development and its rate of economic growth. Japan, which spent only half as much as Britain, had had a fantastically rapid improvement in productivity.

Post-war policy on innovation in Britain had been wrong, he declared, because "the problem was misconceived, the strategy mistaken, the tactics unsatisfactory". Post-war discussions had been dominated by what was thought to be the achievements of science in wartime. In fact the achievements were largely the achievements not of science but of scientists acting as technologists, creating engineering knowhow. It had been a serious error in strategy for the United Kingdom to have put so much effort into research-intensive industries. We had measured ourselves against the United States. In nuclear energy, aero-space, computers and so on our achievements might stand out in comparison with Continental countries but they had not enabled us to meet American competition with much success abroad or, very often, even at home. It might have been wiser to have concentrated on less ambitious targets and to spread our limited scientific manpower more evenly. Sweden and the Netherlands had been remarkably successful in limited sectors of high technology industry.

The emergence of research and development on the grand scale, amounting in the U.S.A. to 22,500 million dollars in 1966 had not really transformed the situation. We could not match American expenditure, but while the U.S. dominated world markets in many of the research-intensive industries such as aircraft, computers and drugs the American share of total world trade and manufacture had been falling not rising.

It could be positively injurious to economic development, he declared, to concentrate on educating a higher proportion of the top talent of the country as scientists. What was needed was not so much *more* technologists as *better* technologists and better training for them.

With financial problems still facing the British Association it looked as if the 133rd meeting might have been the last in the traditional form, running from mid-week to mid-week, with a weekend set aside for scientific and economic exploration of the surrounding area. The 1972 meeting, under the presidency of Sir Vivian Fuchs, to take place in Leicester, will run from Monday to Friday. Despite that it promises to provide as much intellectual meat as earlier meetings. After 1972 the prospect was uncertain, but a proposal, from a committee on reforms, that annual meetings should alternate between London and provincial centres, with some meetings lasting only two days or so (in effect, conferences on scientific-social issues) met with opposition. Future meetings, it seemed the general view, should continue to provide an opportunity for different centres to meet leading scientists and hear of their work on as broad a scale as possible. A heartening feature in 1971 was the number of young people who attended.

The presidents of sections and the titles of their addresses were: *Physics and Mathematics*, Prof. R. V. Jones, " Some problems in optical measurement "; *Chemistry*, Prof. C. C. Addison, " The chemistry of liquid metals "; *Geology*, Dr. A. W. Woodland, " Geological maps in a changing Britain "; *Zoology*, Prof. G. C. Varley, " The ecology of insect parasites and predators "; *Geography*, Dr. S. R. Eyre, " Population, production and pessimism "; *Economics*, H. D. N. Worswick, " Is progress in economic science possible ?"; *Engineering*, Sir Robert Cockburn, " Scientists or engineers "; *Anthropology*, G. Ewart Evans, " The relevance of oral tradition "; *Biomedical Sciences*, Prof. R. R. Porter, " The contribution of the biological and medical sciences to human welfare "; *Psychology*, Principal J. Drever, " Specialists and generalists 1971–81 "; *Botany*, Prof. R. Brown, " Plant growth "; *Forestry*, J. W. L. Zehetmayr, " The future of forestry "; *Education*, Prof. W. J. G. Beynon, " Innovation in education "; *Agriculture*, Dr. G. D. H. Bell, " Biological productivity and environment "; *Sociology*, Prof. J. A. Rex, " Race class and the city "; *General*, John Maddox, " The Doomsday Syndrome ".

BUILDING ON PARAFFIN.—Liquid foundations for more solidly based buildings were proposed by a Leningrad engineer, Stepan Gapayev. He put forward his suggestion for dealing with one of Russia's main construction problems, the permafrost which covers vast areas of Siberia and the Far North where lie the mineral riches which are attracting new towns. Frozen ground may make firm foundations but the difficulty is to make certain that it will stay frozen during the summer. Although air temperatures in winter may drop to minus 75 degrees Centigrade the ground itself does not become nearly so cold. Though frozen it may only be a few degrees below zero and when summer comes the foundations, which seemed so firm, may subside. Gapayev's answer is to freeze the ground more thoroughly by using paraffin filled pipes in the foundations. The pipes are sunk half way into the ground. The top halves are exposed to the cold winter air and the paraffin, cooled by that air, in its turn cools the ground to a similar temperature. The extensive super-cooled area surrounding the foundation which this causes can defy any summer warmth and the foundations stay firm. His idea was first tried out successfully with a five storey block of flats. After that it was adopted for five bridges to be built in Norilsk and for a housing settlement in Magadan, both in the industrial areas of the Far North.

CLEAN TYRE BURNER.—An answer to a dirty and malodorous problem of the affluent society, how to get rid of used tyres and plastics without adding to pollution, was provided by the engineering firm of Redman, Heenan Froude. This Worcester company developed a device to burn them without spilling excessive smokes and noxious gases into the atmosphere. Called an Aeropur Electrostatic Filter it can be coupled directly to industrial incinerators, boilers, dust extractors and similar equipment when, it is claimed, it proves 99·4 per cent. effective in eliminating smoke and dust down to particles under a micron, one millionth of a metre, across and to reduce emissions of sulphur trioxide, chlorine and hydrochloric acid as well as sulphur dioxide. The filter is designed to handle 8,000 cubic metres of smoke and gases an hour at a maximum temperature of 400° C. Three dust removal techniques are used in the one device, centrifugal separation, gas scrubbing and electrostatic precipitation. Dust laden gases are directed on a spiral path through the Aeropur's tower. A central mast inside the tower carries banks of point electrodes which produce a corona discharge to ionize the dust particles. This central mast is at the high potential of 150,000 volts, the tower acting as

an earth return, but the current is so small that electricity costs are no greater than those of a half kilowatt fire. As dust particles are charged they are attracted to the side plates and washed by water to the base of the tower. They are allowed to settle in a tank and the water recirculated. At higher temperatures than 400 degrees a water cooling system, using spray injection, can be added, resulting in increased reaction and higher efficiency.

EXTRA-TERRESTRIAL LIFE?—The first real evidence that life might exist outside the Earth was reported from NASA, America's space exploration agency. It came, however, not from space exploration but by examination of a visitor from space, a meteorite. Amino acids, the basic materials of proteins and life, found on the Murchison meteorite, which fell near Murchison, Victoria, Australia, in September 1969, were claimed to be the first of definitely extra-terrestrial origin identified by man. Previous claims of such finds on meteorites have been rejected, because the amino acids could have resulted from contamination, they followed too closely the pattern of those found in fingerprints. But contamination could be ruled out in this case, according to Dr. Cyril Ponnamperuma, of the space agency's Ames Research Center, California—some of the molecules could not be of Earthly origin, he declared.

The molecular structure of amino acids can be of right-handed or left-handed form, but biologists agree that only one form is likely in any biological system. On Earth all biological amino-acids are of the left-handed variety. About half those found on the meteorite were left-handed, including some found on Earth in living cells, so these could have been due to contamination. The remainder, however, were right-handed, mirror images of the biological form and so could not have originated on Earth.

The finding of a mixture of right- and left-handed molecules on the meteorite virtually rules out the chances of the meteorite coming from some place where life exists but gives strong new support for the theories of the origin of life produced independently by the Russian Oparin and the Englishman Haldane in the 1920's. This was that energy discharges could produce complex molecules from simpler compounds, to evolve, eventually, into molecules able to reproduce themselves and so form the basis of life. Laboratory experiments based on the Oparin-Haldane hypothesis have produced mixtures of right- and left-handed molecules in the proportions found on the Murchison meteorite. Since the two scientists put forward their theory radio-astronomy has detected in space the raw materials of the "primaeval soup" in which the reaction could take place, including water, ammonia, formaldehyde, carbon monoxide and hydrogen cyanide.

The Murchison meteorite is of a type believed to have originated in the asteroid belt and to be around 4,500 million years old. The finding of amino acids on it suggests that complex chemicals may have been present on the Earth from its formation, ready for evolution into life. Conceivably they could be present at the formation of other planetary bodies in our own and other solar systems, to evolve similarly where conditions are suitable.

FEELING THE UNBORN BABY'S PULSE.—A machine to monitor an unborn baby's heartbeat and give early warning of danger during labour successfully completed its trials at a million pound maternity unit at St. Peter's Hospital, Chertsey, Surrey. Picking up electrical signals from the baby's scalp or from its buttocks in a breech presentation, it can keep an unrelenting watch for any change in heart rate. Normally a baby's heart beats just twice as fast as its mother's. A sudden change, particularly during the mother's labour contractions, is a signal of distress, indicating, for example, that the umbilical cord is caught and the extra pressure of a contraction may be cutting off the baby's blood supply. Doctors at the hospital claimed that babies' lives had been saved by emergency action being taken more quickly when trouble developed and was revealed by the machine.

Information is presented in graph form and also by a digital printout, the heartrate being shown in fluorescent numbers on a screen. In future one ward sister might be able to keep her eye on a whole series of patients with possible problems, each woman having her own machine connected to a display panel on the sister's table.

Another version of the machine, using ultrasonics to pick up the foetal heartbeat by doppler effects, as the heart movements change the frequency of the reflected signal, completed its trials in the year, at a London teaching hospital. Ultrasonics can provide information through the later stages of pregnancy without interference with the mother; electrocardiograph monitoring provides a more direct reading of the heartrate but has to await the rupturing of the amniotic sac before the electrodes can be attached to the baby. The machines, made by Sonicaid of Bognor, were claimed to have advantages in safety and performance over an American rival and to be only half the price. Gynaecologists forecast that every maternity hospital would want them but four-fifths of production was to go to export—inquiries were received from North and South America, Europe, Japan and from Russia, where it was displayed at a Moscow medical exhibition.

FINGER MYSTERY SOLVED.—A combined assault by doctors and engineers at Leeds University solved one of the long-standing mysteries of mankind, the cracking finger joint. The ability to produce an audible snapping noise by stretching the fingers is possessed by about one third of humanity, perhaps to their own satisfaction but often to the annoyance of those of the other two-thirds who find the sound unpleasant. Delightful or nauseating it was inexplicable until the Leeds team took high speed X-ray films while volunteers had their fingers gradually stretched by machine. That showed that the cause lies in the sudden formation and collapse of gas bubbles in the spaces in the joints, in a manner, explained the engineers, similar to cavitation, the production of gas bubbles around a ship's propeller.

Of seventeen people tested five had joints which cracked. In these the bones on either side of the joint separated gradually until the gap suddenly increased and a gas bubble appeared. Stretching the fingers apparently lowers the inside of the joint, allowing the formation of the bubble of gas. The condition is unstable, the pressure inside the bubble being lower than that in the liquid surrounding it, so the bubble collapses again, causing the sound. One other discovery was that twenty minutes' rest is needed between cracks, or the phenomenon cannot be repeated.

HIGH-TEMPERATURE MOTOR.—A small electric motor that runs literally red-hot, at temperatures of more than $1,400°$ F was designed and tested by scientists of the U.S. General Electric Company. This is believed to be the highest temperature at which an electric motor has ever operated, comparable to the temperature generated by the coil of

an electric stove at its reddest and hottest and one at which such metals as aluminium, tin, magnesium and zinc would become liquid. The previous record of 900° was set in 1957 by another General Electric motor. The new high-temperature device is a synchronous motor measuring four inches long by three wide and three high. The field windings of such high temperature motors need special insulation, conventional materials beginning to melt or burn at above 150°, causing the motor to fail. The new record temperature was made possible by a special wire fabricated from a silver-palladium alloy coated with nickel. When run at high temperatures in air the wire creates its own electrical insulation as the nickel changes to nickel oxide.

HILLSIDE AGRICULTURE.—The Valley of a Thousand Hills, on the Transkei Zulu Reserve in South Africa, has seen an agricultural innovation which is claimed by its admirers to be as valuable as the compost heap and to promise fresh fertility and more food for the tropics. Known as the Mazibuko Trench it is the invention of the son of a Zulu chief. Mr. R. T. Mazibuko, trained at a missionary agricultural college, turned his white man's training, in conjunction with his native genius, to rescuing his countrymen from the troubles that have come from an over-refined white man's diet, including sugar and white flour.

The trenches are dug, six feet wide and four deep, in the side of the hillside with native hoes. Into them goes first a sprinkling of topsoil. This is followed by alternate one foot layers of waste and soil. Waste includes virtually everthing the Zulus discard in their plastics-less and tin-less community, chopped millet and maize stems, cut grass, feathers and chicken bones from the deep litter poultry units, though the manure has other uses, and even worn-out clothing. The first sowing, on the final capping which is heaped high enough to allow for sinkage, is of a legume, Sunn Hemp. The nitrogen released by the nodule bacteria in its long roots provides the activator for the breakdown of the buried waste. Meanwhile the hemp foliage is cut as cattle feed. When the rains come the water, instead of rushing down the hillside, tearing away the surface soil and eroding gullies, sinks into the trench and soaks into the sponge of the humus to provide a store of moisture for year-round cropping.

The second crop is madumbe, a kind of taro with edible leaves that taste like the potted meat "Gentleman's Relish", according to the agronomist Lawrence Hills, writing in *The Ecologist*. More to the point, perhaps, in that area, it also has highly nutritious roots. After that come maize, millet, carrots, pumpkins and many native vegetables, cropping right through the dry season.

Trials conducted by the University of Natal have established that the system provides far higher yields than plots treated by chemical fertilizers without the underground compost. Chemical fertilizers could increase the yield of the trench still further, by another 10 per cent, but it is the original trench system, not fertilizers, which seems to hold the key to the problem of food shortages in many parts of the world, wherever men try to scrape a living from dry steep hillsides, suffering erosion from the seasonal rains which they see quickly flow away.

The Valley of a Thousand Hills has no stone to build retaining walls as are used in hillside terrace cultivation elsewhere. Instead, a further touch of genius on the part of Mr. Mazibuko, a lucerne is used to hold the slopes. Not only does its strong web of roots hold the soil but it also provides nitrogen for the soil as well as cattle fodder. People can learn to chew the foliage to obtain rich supplies of vitamins.

Mr. Mazibuko joined a white man, Dr. Halley Stott in the Valley. Dr. Stott, a South African who qualified at Edinburgh, went to the Valley to attend to the medical needs of the Zulu Reserve but quickly found that health problems arose from the abandonment of the original native Zulu diet for white man's food. So his first main onslaught on sickness was to build a mill at which the Zulus could grind their own maize to wholemeal, doubling or quadrupling their intake of certain essential proteins. Then he and Mr. Mazibuko took the next step, teaching the natives to build ponds large enough to rear fish to provide other missing amino acids for their diet. In so doing they have also shown the way for millions more living far from the sea to get fish protein—and get it fresher than it is often available in traditional sea-fishing countries.

MATRIMONIAL MATHS.—Girls at university who hope, one day, to be the wives of eminent men, should move over to the science side. Disappointment on the arts side is much more likely. For male arts specialists are five times as likely as scientists to remain single, reported Dr. L. Hudson and Dr. B. Jacot, of the Research Unit on Intellectual Development, Edinburgh University, in *Nature*. There are also differences within the science side which the matrimonially ambitious girl should know. If the prospective wife of the eminent man wants the best chance of her marriage lasting then she had better look out for a physicist boy friend; biologists are particularly prone to divorce, especially those from public schools. Dr. Hudson and Dr. Jacot did their research between the covers of *Who's Who*, studying the entries of men eminent enough for an entry there. They found that 14·8 per cent. of 216 philosophers, classicists, historians and other arts specialists were unmarried, compared with only 2 per cent. of 147 biologists and 3·6 per cent. of physicists. They were also more likely, when they did marry, to marry late in life, further reducing their attractions to their college contemporaries.

When arts specialists do get married their marriages often prove less fruitful, 16·2 per cent. having no children. Biologists, as might be expected, prove to be the most successful by this standard. Only 6·1 per cent. have childless marriages and, altogether, only 8·1 per cent. fail to hand on their talents to the next generation by marrying and having children against 31 per cent. of the arts specialists and 15·1 per cent. of physicists. Mathematicians, it turns out, are more like artists than scientists in their family lives. Surprisingly social scientists, psychologists, sociologists and others, who might be thought more experienced in human relations and their problems are distinguished in one respect only—their divorce rate is the highest of all, 23·3 per cent.

The net result of all this is that biologists are reproducing themselves more rapidly than their fellow intellectuals, producing on average 2½ children each, compared with 1·83 children per arts specialist and 2·05 per physicist. But for those fearful that the world is going to be overpopulated with biologists with the dead languages becoming even more dead for lack of children to follow in their fathers' footsteps, Drs Jacot and Hudson warn that their results are no basis for hasty generalization. The men they studied are the eminent few, who, presumably, dedicated their lives to academic success. Those who do not qualify for *Who's Who* may appear in quite different proportions in other registers.

MECHANICAL CURRANT PICKING.—Anyone who grows—and harvests—his own black or other coloured currants knows why they are so dear in the shops. It is not so much the growing but the picking which swallows up the man-hours. Cotton bolls may be sucked up by machines like giant vacuum cleaners, tea plants have their tastiest leaves delicately snipped off by other ingenious devices. Even special varieties of strawberries have been grown to hold their fruit well away from the leaves to be cut off and garnered by machine—with, unfortunately, the disadvantage, minor for the grower but major for the consumer, that breeding in such accommodating qualities usually means breeding out the taste. But blackcurrants remained unamenable to anything but the discriminating fingers of the human being until the National Institute of Agricutural Engineering and the St. Albans firm of Smallford Planters Ltd. got to work, backed by a grant from the National Research and Development Corporation. The outcome is a machine which shakes the currants off. Half the branches are spread at a time over the shaker. The shaking has to be vigorous, as any human picker knows it takes a good pull or a strong thumb-nail to sever a sprig of currants. But, claim the makers, all but five per cent. of the leaves remain fast, to continue feeding the bush for the next year's crop and the fruit, despite its shaking, suffers less bruising than at the hands of the commercial fruit picker. The cost of the machine is £3500 but it raises its operator's output to a ton of fruit an hour compared with the 80 lbs. a day which an experienced picker can manage. The black currant market for the machine may not be large, ten thousand acres of bushes produce up to 20,000 tons of fruit a year, but it is planned to modify the shaking picker to pick gooseberries and olives.

"MONSTER" SUBMARINE KILLER.—The mysterious sinkings of the U.S. nuclear submarine *Thresher* and of French submarines in the Mediterranean may be laid at the door of a Loch Ness Monster, it was disclosed at the British Association meeting. The monster, a hundred feet high, swims slowly up and down the loch in the autumn, at a rate of a mile an hour, regularly observed by scientists. But it is not the sea-serpent, as reported in the newspaper silly season. It is a giant wave which occurs deep in the Loch, with no noticeable effect at the surface, in favourable conditions of wind and water.

The Monster Internal Wave of Loch Ness, as described by Dr. Steve Thorpe of the National Institute of Oceanography, is caused by temperature differences in the waters of the 24 mile long, 800 feet deep Loch and by the wind which blows along it. By the autumn the top 100 feet of the Loch has been heated to a temperature of around 13 degrees Centigrade but below this there is a region where the temperature falls rapidly and the water density increases. As the wind blows the warm surface water is pushed to the far end of the Loch and the thermocline, the line dividing lighter from heavier water, tilts. Under the force of gravity it attempts to return to the horizontal and this causes the wave to surge up and down the Loch. Autumn winds may blow in rhythm with the wave, reaching a peak every 2½ days, the time the wave takes for a return journey. When this happens the wave is strengthened and reaches its maximum height of 100 feet, though its effect on the surface is to cause only a half inch rise.

Similar waves may occur whenever weather conditions force a thermocline to tilt. The Americans, it appears, have accepted that such a wave over-whelmed the *Thresher* and the French are seeking the phenomenon in the Mediterranean where their submarines vanished. The Straits of Gibraltar is one site where such surges have been found.

Apart from warning of dangers to submarines, studies of the wave may help to prevent aircraft disasters. It resembles the clear air turbulence which still causes many aircraft accidents and could be a greater hazard to *Concorde* and other high-flying aircraft, said Dr. Thorpe.

NEW SOURCE OF GOLD?—The economic recovery of precious noble metals such as gold and platinum from base metal ores could become possible with an ion exchange resin developed at the Technion-Israel Institute of Technology in Haifa. When a solution of metals in acid is passed along a conventional ion exchange column containing the resin base metals pass through freely while precious metals are retained. The initial discovery was made in 1964 but Dr. Gabriella Schmukler, of the Institute's Department of Chemistry has developed it considerably since then. During the year the U.S. Bureau of Mines reported favourably on its properties. Although small quantities of precious metals are often found in base metal ores it is usually far too costly to be worthwhile attempting their recovery by conventional means. The new resin, known commercially as Srafion NMRR, promises to make extraction feasible. It is relatively cheap, has a long life and the value of metals extracted by it would be many times its original cost. Its more immediate use, however, is likely not to be in mining but in recovering spent catalysts from solution and the silver from used photographic " fixing " baths. As well as producing an economic return it will also help combat pollution, by preventing dangerous concentrations being discharged into sewage systems.

NEW TYPE AUTOMOBILE.—Electric cars, steam cars and, no doubt, pedal cars have their advocates for helping the drive against pollution. The idea of an American engineer was the flywheel car, a car in which all the energy needed for a journey is stored in the flywheel before the start. David W. Rabenhorst, an engineer at Johns Hopkins University's Applied Physics Laboratory in Silver Spring, Maryland, designed the super flywheel needed to drive an emission free car. Measuring 30 inches in diameter and weighing 222 pounds it should be sufficient to propel a mini-sized car with two or three passengers at a cruising speed of 55 mph for two hours, with a top speed of 70 mph and an acceleration of 0–60 mph in 15 seconds. After one 110 mile journey it would need a 24 minutes, electric meal to gain the energy for another, similar drive.

The flywheel has an electric motor which, plugged into the supply system either at home or at a wayside garage would bring the rotor up to its full speed of 23,700 revolutions a minute, spinning in a vacuum can at the back of the car. When it has reached peak energy storage it reverses its nature to become an electric generator instead of a consumer, supplying current to electric motors driving each of the car's wheels. Braking would see the energy flow reversed again, to recharge the flywheel. A simple dial would indicate how much energy remained in the flywheel. Should it run down, however, and the car become stranded then, plans Mr. Rabenhorst, a small solid fuel turbine or a reserve flywheel could provide the main flywheel with enough energy to reach an electric supply point.

Theoretically a flywheel's energy depends on how fast it is being driven. The faster it rotates the more work it can do. There comes a limit, how-

ever, when the centrifugal force just tears it apart and converts it into dangerous missiles, unwelcome as fellow travellers in the back of the car. Mr. Rabenhorst and his associates were experimenting with a number of materials to produce a safe wheel capable of storing the maximum energy. Wheel is probably a misnomer, for the device is most likely to be in the form of a bar rotating around its centre of gravity. The need is for a material that is strongest in one direction, to oppose the outward stresses that tend to pull a fast-spinning wheel apart. High-strength piano wire, with a tensile strength of 600,000 pounds to the square inch is one such material. Another is the British invented carbon fibre, or the American boron fibre, or whiskers of pure crystals imbedded in plastic or metal.

The filaments would fan out during rotation.

One possibility is to combine the flywheel with a normal heat engine. It would provide extra power for overtaking, acceleration and hill-climbing. The heat engine would run at its optimum speed for minimum pollution, providing enough power for cruising and recharging the flywheel. Not only would the flywheel powered engine be emission-free, it would also be noise-free. It may have a future in silent lawn-motors, silent portable tools, silent speed boats, as well as silent, pollution-free cars. Mechanical hammers powered by such a motor would have none of the compressor noise of present pneumatic hammers. Even miniature submarines could have a place for a simple, fume-free motor able to store more energy in a light-weight device than any electric battery and capable of being re-charged time and time again without losing efficiency.

POCKET LIBRARY.—A library literally in one's pocket or, at most, in the traveller's brief case, will be possible in the age of micro-publishing heralded by the invention of two Channel Islanders, George Davies and Hedda Wertheimer, described in the *New Scientist*. Their "micro-books" provide the equivalent of one ordinary book on ten five inch by five and a half inch sheets. With ten books making up a "micro-library" inside one single PVC cover, the equivalent of 3000 foolscap pages, it could also mean a halt to the paper explosion which can only be satisfied by the destruction of Earth's forests. The magic lantern approach of retrieving information from conventional microfilming was hardly a convincing way of saving those forests, they decided, after working on American lines seeking something the Americans have sought for years, a small, easily portable, cheap device for reading microfilms. Instead they have shown that printing only one tenth the size of conventional print size can be achieved successfully, using a standard offset press, provided a little extra care is taken. The paper to be used is PVC paper, durable, waterproof, difficult to tear and, although only two thousandths of an inch thick, so opaque that it can carry print on both sides. To read his book the user would take out a pair of binocular lenses in a holder which folds up little thicker than a bookmark. This fits magnetically to the book so that micro reading is no more trouble than reading an ordinary book or magazine. As the reading device opens the focus of the lenses is adjusted to suit different people's vision. A binocular reader means that everything has to be printed twice, but this is compensated by the fact that printing can be done on both sides of the paper compared with the single side of ordinary microfilms. The double display also has the advantage that it makes full 3D illustrations possible with the binocular reader.

A binocular reader, the two inventors believe, is necessary for ease and comfort in reading. But if the book is not intended to be read continuously, if, for example, it contains reference data, then ordinary monocular magnification on the lines of the Victorian reading glass should be sufficient. A library in this form can be readily updated. The lithoprinting is easily erased from PVC paper and, as the paper can be stuck to and separated from adhesive tape, it means it can be kept conveniently in looseleaf form.

Mr. Davies admits that he has a chicken and egg problem to face, people will not start reading microbooks until there are microbooks to be read and publishers will not start publishing them until they are sure of a readership. But he hopes some technical journal may take the plunge in order to put out the specialized material for which it might not have room in a normally printed journal. One day, he believes, every local library will be able to hold as much as today's British Museum library and every home as much as today's local library.

One other idea he and his colleagues are working on is the "cine book", a book of microfilmed motion pictures with the equipment to read it in the form of a private cinema show, a challenge to play-back T.V.

PORCINE PROTECTION FOR THE PATIENT.—A slice of bacon is a new treatment for burns, able to spare the patient both physical and mental anguish. But it has to be a special slice of bacon, divided up in an unusual way for its unsual use. Only the rind is wanted, the rest can be sent back to the farmer to supply the breakfast table.

The bacon or pigskin treatment was reported to be working well at a children's hospital in Galveston, Texas, as an additional source of skin covering for bad burn cases. The size of the problem in Britain is shown by the fact that about 10,000 people are admitted to hospital each year with burns and about 1000 die, 15 to 20 per cent. of them children, Mr. M. E. J. Hackett of the Queen Victoria Hospital, East Grinstead, told the British Medical Association's scientific meeting. In those who recover treatment can take three months, bringing considerable physical and psychological suffering. Skin grafts can save lives and suffering—lives by reducing the loss of fluids, proteins and heat and by reducing infection, the biggest single hazard in burns, suffering by speeding up healing, reducing pain, increasing the mobility of the patient and boosting his morale by hiding the burns under a natural looking covering, preventing his seeing and smelling his own sepsis.

The best skin comes from the patient's own body but there is not enough available if the burns involve more than a quarter of the body. Some patients may need to grow five lots of skin to provide enough to cover the burns and this takes two months.

The Galveston answer, also used elsewhere in the States, is to provide a temporary cover of pigskin while the patient grows successive crops of his own skin for permanent grafts. In the basement of the hospital are facilities for keeping six pigs, borrowed from a local farmer on the understanding that they are cared for and fed. When skin is required the pig is anaesthetised and skin stripped from one side. Two weeks later the other side is stripped. When the pig is fully healed it is returned to the farmer, who is well content with having had it fattened for him while the hospital has a constant supply of material for its novel treatment.

Pigskin may not be so good as human skin for the job but taking it is a lot less painful for all involved, except, perhaps, for the pig. Skin can only be taken from corpses after complying with

the same regulations about notification and obtaining permission as cover taking organs for grafts. Live skin is no better than corpse skin, it will be sloughed off eventually, and means ten fairly painful days in hospital for the donor. But even that, the psychologists believe, can be good at times. For a parent to give skin for a burned child can assuage the feeling of guilt he or she may have over the accident.

POTATOES FROM POLLUTION.—Making money out of muck has traditionally been the recipe for success. A new meaning for the phrase, found by the Henry Doubleday Research Association should bring joy to the heart of any cost-conscious borough engineer and also to those who worry about pollution and waste. It was that pulverized refuse spread in a layer one foot thick will grow at least three 16 ton-an-acre crops of potatoes. Modern refuse consists of 50 per cent. waste paper by weight—far more by volume as the piles that mount during dustman strikes show. Britain's boy scouts enable part to be saved, selling it to waste paper merchants for funds, but most has to be destroyed, which usually means incineration and an extra problem in air pollution and smoke. Paper defeats the household compost heap but when it goes through the modern refuse pulveriser it is broken down into a size small enough to be vulnerable to the composting organisms. Pulverized compost will compost where it is spread, without reaching a temperature high enough to produce a fire risk. Councils wanting to fill pits with good soil to make recreation grounds can easily see the advantages over unsightly tip heaps. Now the Henry Doubleday findings mean income as well. A ten acre site spread with a foot of the material will produce £2,000 worth of potatoes annually for three years, when another foot can be added and the process repeated, until everything levels off into playing fields, complete with pavilions paid for by the potatoes.

In a year when official reports showed sizeable areas of England in danger of becoming agriculturally unproductive, because lack of humus had made the soil liable to pack under farm machinery in rainy weather or blow away in dust in drought, farmers were seeing the value of composted refuse. Many gardeners with views on natural food need no convincing of the value of the compost. Horley council, in Surrey, was enlightened enough to make money directly from its muck, composting its refuse with sewage sludge. Sludge, though rich in organic matter, nitrogen and phosphorus and ideal, according to previous work, for growing cabbages and beetroot, contains only a trace of potash. Horley compost, however, contains more potash than ordinary farmyard manure, for it preserves all there was in the wood which originally went to make that waste paper.

ROBOT AT WORK.—A "thinking" industrial robot was claimed to be operational in Tokyo. Its robot powers of thought were reported enough for it to work out how to assemble a number of parts into a product after studying blue-prints. Two television "eyes", focussing independently on the diagram and the parts, a computer system and a manipulating hand made up the robot. Using the eye studying the diagram the computer works out a stereoscopic image of what the product should be. It then analyses that image and compares it with the information about the parts given to it by its other eye. A careful study, according to rules impressed on its memory, results in its deciding just how the parts should be fitted together to produce the object deduced fom the diagram. Then it instructs its mechanical hand to fit the pieces together, according to a set of assembly rules also imprinted on its memory. These include, according to its Japanese inventors, knowledge of seven different movements of its hand, enough to imitate the basic actions of a human assembly line operator.

SAVING THE SEABIRDS.—The chances of saving seabirds contaminated by oil from leaking or wrecked tankers were improved by work reported from Sweden. The Torrey Canyon disaster and other pollution episodes have shown that it is not so much the oil which makes life impossible for the birds but the results of removing it from their feathers. The detergents usually used for cleaning fouled plumage also remove the natural waxes on which the bird depends to remain waterproof, afloat and warm. The prospects of successfully cleaning badly oiled plumage are regarded as so small by some animal organizations that they have claimed it is more humane to destroy the birds, that if released they only vanish quite quickly, presumably dead. Keeping birds until their wax is replaced naturally after detergent degreasing can be a long job. The preen glands of a bird may only manufacture it at the rate of fifty milligrammes a day while total covering may amount to several grammes.

Two Swedish chemists, Goran Odham and Einar Stenhagen of the University of Goteborg, investigated the possibility of replacing the wax with a synthetic material and claimed success from their findings. Waxes are complicated substances but modern laboratory techniques have made it possible to analyse them. Those of individual birds differ enormously, the two Swedes found; some might contain only two or three components, others might contain several hundred. This seemed to rule out any hope of synthesising a bird's own wax. Even if it were possible to do this economically, too wide a range would be required. What was possible, however, was to find out the main characteristics these waxes held in common, look for them among other waxes, decide which of possible synthetics was most suitable and then try the effects of that.

First attempts revealed another problem, how to get the wax onto the feathers in a reasonably natural fashion. Over waxing, it proved, can be as harmful as under-waxing, having much the same effect. The answer lay in that modern technique so dear to the housewife with little time on her hands and even dearer to the manufacturer who sells to her. The wax was mixed in with the detergent so that, in modern advertising parlance, the birds could be "polished as they are cleaned". In the first trials, it was claimed, seventy-five birds were successfully cleaned, rewaxed and released within a fortnight.

SCIENTIFIC WATER DIVINER.—The dowser's aim of finding underground water without digging deeply in search of it was reported realized by a young U.S. geologist. The essential equipment proved not to be the traditional twigs but a series of thermometers. For two years of experiments by Philip J. O'Brien, at Pennsylvania State University, confirmed his belief that subterranean water signals its presence by temperature changes detectable near the surface. His system is to stake out scores of temperature-measuring stations, inserting thermistors, or electronic thermometers, into narrow six foot shafts. By analysing the measurements he can determine whether an accumulation of underground water, known as an aquifer, is present and, if one is, where is the most favourable site to drill and tap it. Straightforward

measurements are not enough. Allowance has to be made for other factors which can alter soil temperature, rain and snow, the heat seeping from the interior of the Earth, normal seasonal changes. But the system could eventually be used to detect underground water supplies from space, provide another economic prospecting task for the space-station. Infra-red sensing should be sensitive enough to build up the necessary heat maps of the Earth's surface.

SEABED WASTE SINK.—Radioactive and poisonous chemical wastes could be safely dealt with by letting them sink naturally deep into the Earth, Dr. T. Francis, of the Institute of Geological Sciences suggested in *Nature*. Natural waste dumps, he argued, occur in those ocean trenches, which are earthquake zones and where part of the Earth's crust is thought to be steadily swallowed up. Others have pointed out the possibility of waste disposal in these trenches but, according to Dr. Francis, the process would be far more rapid than anyone had previously thought and rapid enough to end all the worries about contamination of the sea bed which hang around current methods of dumping waste at sea. This, he argued, was because the sediments in the trenches possess the "thixotropic" qualities best known to the laymen in the jelly paint which liquefies on stirring. The sediments are stirred by earthquakes and during earthquakes, he argued, they would present no more resistance to the sinking of drums containing waste than would thick soup.

Studies of continental drift have shown, in recent years, that the ocean floor of the Pacific is being forced down into the interior of the earth beneath the continents of North and South America—the cause, on the one hand of the earthquakes which afflict that part of the world and, on the other, of the upthrusting of the Rocky Mountains and the Andes. One puzzle has been that the beds of sediment in these trenches show none of the buckling which would be expected. It is only puzzling, argued Dr. Francis, if it is supposed that the sediment behaves like a solid. In fact unconsolidated sediments have been shown, in laboratories, to be thixotropic, changing from a semi-solid, jelly-like state, a "gel", to a liquid state, a "sol", on being shaken, reverting back to the jelly like state on standing. A strong earthquake could shake an area of 14,000 square miles with forces of one tenth of gravity and the shaking could last half a minute. While the sediments are behaving like a liquid they redistribute themselves and at these times, also, solid objects would sink through them. The average yearly shaking, at any point would amount to only a few seconds, but this would be long enough to allow a spherical container to sink about 20 metres a year. The sediments, he believes, retain their thixotropic quality down to a seabed depth of at least a kilometre and a container would reach this depth in 50 years.

Wastes are being dumped at sea with remarkably little thought given to the consequences, declared Dr. Francis. No one really knows how long the containers will last before they allow their contents to seep out. Apart from the permanently poisonous nature of some chemicals, radioactive wastes can retain their dangers for very long periods. If natural geological processes do allow such packages to bury themselves to a depth of a kilometre in sediment beneath five kilometres of seawater in 50 years then a 50 year lifetime for the package will suffice, any effects of leakage then would probably be undetectable. Whether or not this theory about sinkage through the sediment is sound could be found by a few years' experiment.

"SEE-THROUGH" PATIENTS.—A machine for producing three dimensional X-ray pictures, giving the effect of a solid but transparent patient, had its first public showing during the year. When it becomes hospital equipment a doctor using it will be able to look into his patient's body from any angle he wishes, peering around ribs, for example, to examine organs behind. The system, developed jointly by workers at the Royal Postgraduate Medical School, Hammersmith, and the Aldermaston nuclear research establishment, uses the technique of holography. This post war invention produces true three dimensional pictures by "freezing" light waves on to a photographic plate. When stimulated by light of the same wavelength as that used for recording the picture the original pattern of light waves is released, to reach an observer in the exact form in which they came from the original scene pictured. Not only is a stereoscopic view given but movement of the head produces parallax, the different angular movement of objects at different distances, revealing what was originally hidden behind those in front.

The light has to be very pure, of a single wavelength, such as is emitted by a laser. Lasers cannot be used to scan a patient's body, even if they had any X-ray effect. Instead a succession of X-ray pictures are taken on ordinary film, as a camera is rotated around the patient, to be combined in the holograph. As the machine rotates through 90° it takes one thousandth of a second exposures every fifteen minutes of arc, 360 pictures altogether, in a matter of seconds. These pictures are then exposed in turn, by laser light, on to a single photographic plate. The plate is rotated between each pair of exposures by the same angular amount as separated the successive X-ray views of the body. When the radiologist views the finished product, available about half an hour after the patient has been X-rayed, he sees just the picture imprinted on the plate from the angle at which he is looking at it. Movement of his head brings successive pictures into view, enabling him to see into the patient from any angle he wishes. Each eye receives a slightly different impression, exactly as in real life, to give a stereoscopic view.

Early work was done with a small scale simulator using sixteen millimetre film, because a full scale machine would cost £30,000 to £40,000 to construct as a prototype. Although a three dimensional effect was clearly shown, according to Mr. E. Shuttleworth, of the Department of Medical Physics at the Royal Postgraduate Medical School, it was marred by a shimmer, rather like that produced by the shop window advertising devices which have two pictures hidden in them to flash into view when looked at from different angles. Scaling up the machine with thirty-five millimetre film reduced the shimmer and gave rise to hopes that it would be possible to eliminate it altogether in full-scale models. Already, claimed Mr. Shuttleworth and his co-operator, Mr. David Redman of Aldermaston, a view of a skull was so realistic that it was like looking into an actual skull through the eye holes.

SHRIMPS' DEPTH DETECTOR.—Shrimps and other sea creatures which need to live at one particular level in the sea sometimes have an electrically operated depth detector in their shells, the British Association meeting was told. Once again Nature has proved to have forestalled man—the apparatus uses the thin film semi-conductor techniques which have transformed electronics in the past decade.

Professor Peter Digby, of McGill University Montreal, described how he found the device and then confirmed its working by building a depth

detector himself on the same principles. Certain marine animals were found just after the war to be sensitive to water pressure and so able to choose the depth at which they lived. The most likely way a sense organ would do this is by detecting pressure changes through the compression of a gas but no gas could be seen, even in the completely transparent plankton animals that show the ability. The hint how it works in some shellfish came when he bubbled oxygen into the water in which he was keeping some brine shrimps and found that their pressure sensitivity disappeared. The oxygen would have removed hydrogen—if hydrogen had been present—and one way hydrogen might be produced by a sea animal was by electrolysis of water. So he looked for evidence for this and found minute electric currents were flowing through the shells of the shrimps, which contained semi-conductor materials. The amount of hydrogen is too small to be seen, but enough for the animal to note pressure changes and enough, though still invisible, to do the same in Prof. Digby's copy of the shrimp's apparatus. The discovery of electric currents in shells is throwing fresh light on their formation and also on how bone is laid down in animals and man, he reported.

SOLUBLE PLASTIC COUNTERS POLLUTION.—Russia's answer to the problem of plastic pollution is a material which dissolves in water, but only when the weather is warm enough. This means that Russian farmers can happily leave their fertilizer bags lying around the fields in the winter, secure in the knowledge that they will fall foul of no pollution laws or inspectors—when spring comes with its warm rains the bags just disappear. In fact, it is claimed, the fertiliser bags can be dumped in the fields complete with contents. As the bags disappear in the spring the fertilisers are washed into the ground at the time they can do most good.

One other use of the synthetic film in areas of extreme winter cold is to cover whole fields. It keeps the soil relatively warm during the winter and disappears as warmer weather spreads before the first plant shoots appear. Wheat harvests are said to be half as large again and three weeks earlier than normal when this technique is used. The plastic has been developed by Leningrad chemists.

STAR CHAMPIONS.—The heavyweight record for the most massive body in the Universe now stands to a galaxy 600 million light years away, according to the Canadian astronomer, Dr. Sidney van den Bergh, of the University of Toronto. It weighs in at 45 times the mass of our own galaxy, the Milky Way.

The heavyweight galaxy is associated with a powerful radio source which aroused astronomers' interest when it proved to have its peak power emission at an unusual wavelength. Dr. van den Bergh studied it through the 200 inch telescope at Mount Palomar, the biggest in the world until the Russians' new 234 inch telescope becomes fully operational in the Caucasus. He found that the galaxy, 4C31.04, is really a double object, like a binary star, with the two parts circulating around each other. Careful measurement of their relative speeds and the distance separating them, he reported in the Publications of the Astronomical Society of the Pacific, showed that the smaller galaxy was moving at 800 miles a second relative to the larger and that the distance separating them was 150,000 light years. The laws of celestial mechanics demand that for this to be so the total mass must be around six million times as great as that of our own Sun. Our own Milky Way has a total mass of 140,000 million Suns and is itself no

dwarf. It is one of the largest of the spiral galaxies though elliptical galaxies are generally five times as massive. The new record holder is just over twice as massive as the previous owner of the title, the elliptical M87.

Another title, that of the most luminous star in our Galaxy, was allotted during the year to a star known as HR 5171. Three American astronomers, R. M. Humphreys, D. W. S. Trecker and E. P. Ney, working at the Cerro Tololo Inter-American Observatory, noted its supremacy during a study of supergiants. It is, they reported in the Astrophysical Journal, 600,000 times as luminous as our own Sun, though its actual brightness in the sky is nil, it is invisible to the naked eye because of its great distance. The brightest object in the sky to us is, of course, our own Sun but it is really a very nondescript object as stars go. HR 5171 is a G-type supergiant, one of a number of young stars found in the spiral arms of our galaxy. But a neighbouring galaxy, the Large Megallanic Cloud, can boast two stars pouring out even more energy than the Milky Way's champion. These are also supergiants but of different classes. One pours out almost as much energy in the visual part of the spectrum alone as HR 5171 does over its total energy spectrum and the total energy of the other is around ten times as great.

TAMING THE TSETSE.—The side-effects of insecticides on animals are usually unpredictable, unwanted and to be abhorred. Work done at Edinburgh, reported in the *Bulletin of Entomological Research*, however, pointed to the possibility that one effect could be beneficial, at least to man and some of his animals. If predictable it could be something much to be desired for it showed the way to making effective use of insecticide against that scourge of Central Africa, the notorious tsetse fly. A colony of *Glossina morsitans orientalis*, the carrier of the disease to animals and man, from the Zambesi Valley in Rhodesia, which was kept in the University's Department of Zoology, suddenly stopped breeding though things had been well with them for eighteen months. More flies, living healthily at Bristol, were imported to Edinburgh. Although the first generation of imported flies bred normally their own offspring did very badly in reproducing themselves. The trouble proved to be something in the food. At Edinburgh the flies were fed by being allowed to browse on the ears of rabbits. When the reproduction trouble arose some were then fed on human blood, to be compared with those on a rabbit blood diet. The human blood flies proved quite healthy, so the trouble was narrowed down to something in a rabbit.

It turned out that the rabbit's own diet had been changed shortly before. New trials were carried out to compare Bristol flies on the new diet with others on the old. The results were quite definite. The offspring of flies fed on rabbits given the new diet died early and only a few reached an effective age for reproduction. Of 65 flies only three produced larvae. In contrast the progeny of flies fed on blood from rabbits given the original diet were 90 per cent. successful in reproducing themselves during their very first reproductive cycle.

The outstanding difference between the two rabbit diets was the presence of more of the insecticide malathion in the "poisonous" one. Though no direct proof had been shown of an effect on the flies' reproductive systems by insecticide contaminated blood there was the hope that the findings could lead to some new way of controlling this dangerous disease carrying insect without embarking on widespread destruction of insect life in

the area—the rabbits were not noticeably affected by their diet.

TASTY DANGERS.—More evidence for the truth of the adage " A short life but a merry one " came during the year. For more of life's pleasures went through what now seems the inevitable process of condemnation—condemnation not from Puritanical motives but in the interests of health. Coffee joined the long list of those other joys such as smoking, sex and even eating charged with causing the dreaded disease of our times, cancer. Even Worcester Sauce was accused of producing less innocent effects than the addition of interest to the teetotaller's tomato juice at a cocktail party or exciting the jaded appetite confronted with yesterday's leftovers—it has been associated with kidney troubles.

It was Dr. Philip Cole, of the Harvard School of Public Health at Boston who showed that T. S. Eliot may have been speaking more literally than he knew when he declared in his " Love Song of J. Alfred Prufrock " that " I have measured out my life in coffee spoons ". Coffee, he suggested in the *Lancet,* may lead to cancer of the bladder and other parts of the urinary system. Women appear to be most at risk from his analysis of local statistics, though whether this was due to the prevalence of the coffee-morning among the leisured female Bostonians he did not indicate. His study of 668 cases in the Boston area showed that half the cases of cancer of the bladder in women could be caused by coffee drinking. For men the extra risk was halved, but that still left a significant increase of cancer cases in coffee drinking men, after taking account of the effects of cigarette smoking, also implicated in bladder cancer, and occupational risks. The work of other researchers supported his case, he claimed, for caffeine, which gives to coffee its apparently life-restoring " kick " has, in fact, been found to damage cells. A known cancer-causing substance, benz-pyrene, has been found in soot from coffee roasting plants.

The evidence against Worcester sauce was reported from Australia, but it also showed just how excessive is the delight of some people in it. A little of what you fancy undoubtedly may do you good, but an excess can be positively harmful, as an Australian found who took it literally by the glassful. Like some others whose liking for it was extreme he developed kidney trouble. Another man who had been taking half to one bottle of sauce a day developed similar trouble. The trouble usually clears up when the excessive consumption is curtailed. Worcester sauce is mostly vinegar but also contains garlic, black pepper and a variety of other spices. Which, if any, has the effect on the kidneys is uncertain, but if too much sauce harms the kidneys then it is a failing shared with too much milk, too much vitamin D, too many purgatives and too much of some painkillers.

Dr. Cole pointed out that further research into an association between coffee and cancer should include an investigation of the part played by artificial sweeteners, which have also been charged with harmful effects. The banning of cyclamates, following suggestions that they might cause cancer, left saccharine as the only available artificial sweetener and many people find this leaves a bitter after-taste. Fresh hope of reducing the dangers and improving the palatability of artificial sweeteners came from other American work, a new sweetener, 160 times sweeter than cane sugar, was tested at the Department of Food Science and Nutrition, University of Missouri. This substance, aspartyl-phenylalanine methyl ester, was found not to differ from cane sugar in bitterness, after-taste or

general acceptability in concentrations equivalent to two teaspoonfuls of sugar in one cup of tea or coffee. Off-flavours appeared in higher concentrations but not when the substance was mixed with sucrose, saccharine or cyclamate to give sweetness levels equivalent to six spoonfuls in a cup, amply sweet enough for it to be used for carbonated soft drinks. A cocktail of artificial sweeteners appears sweeter than would be expected from the sweetening effect of each individual one, so the American scientists recommend the use of blends as reducing any possible toxic hazard.

TELL-TALE BOLTS.—Every do-it-yourself motorist knows that trouble goes with vibration. Bolts can shake loose and failure to fasten a critical bolt which is subjected to vibration can be fatal. Not only bolts in vehicles are liable to be loosened by vibration, this can happen on bridges and railway lines also. Not all bolts can be locked permanently and checking and tightening bolts at risk can be costly and time-consuming, essential as this obviously is. An anonymous scientist at the U.S. Bureau of Standards, however, had one of those bright ideas which can transform a situation. Why not get the bolt to signal the news when it needs tightening? He found a way of doing so, getting the bolt to show red for danger, through a little window, when it needed attention.

An ordinary bolt can be modified by drilling a hole straight into the bolt head and the neck of the bolt. Into this goes a flat-headed pin plus a blue silicone fluid, the whole being covered with a transparent window. The pinhead, coloured red, is flush with the window, the other end of the pin being fastened solidly into the body of the bolt. Normally, when unstressed, the bolt shows the red pinhead in the window. When it is under tension, however, it is stretched but the pin, free at its upper end and unstressed, remains its same length This results in the pinhead being pulled away from the window and the silicone liquid seeping around the pinhead to cover it. The bolt, under strain, shows a blue colour in its window. When tension falls below a certain, preset critical level the pinhead returns to the window, forcing the liquid away and the bolt shows red again. With this bolt checking just becomes a simple matter of looking at the bolts and tightening those showing red until they are blue again. The company licensed to market the bolts has labelled it " Tell-Torq " with the additional, predictable description " the bolt with a brain ". (*New Scientist.*)

ULTRASONIC SOLDERING.—Ultrasonics, already put to work at a host of jobs from cleaning cars to detecting foetal heartbeats, found a new use during the year, in the solder pot. An American firm, Branson Sonic Power Company, of Danbury, Connecticut, claimed that high frequency sound waves made it possible to solder aluminium without a flux or using high temperatures. The oxide film which forms on the surface of aluminium prevents normal soldering and scraping it off does no good, for the film reforms before the solder can be applied. The answer is to provide a continual scraper, by ultrasonics, using the solder as the scraper. A transducer vibrating at 20,000 Herz, inserted into the solder pot, sends high-frequency waves through the melted solder. As the aluminium part to be soldered is dipped into the pot the waves scrub away at the surface, removing the oxide and allowing the solder to reach pure metal. The part can then be withdrawn coated with solder and ready for the next stage of the soldering process. The thickness of the coat depends on the speed at which the part is withdrawn and the temperature of the

solder. Their recommended temperature is 600 to 900 degrees Fahrenheit, compared with the 900 to 1200 degrees needed for soldering with flux.

UNDERWATER DIESEL.—A diesel engine able to run on the seabed, breathing its own exhaust gas with added oxygen, was demonstrated in the waters of Shoreham Harbour to possible foreign buyers from Europe, America and Japan. Claimed to be the world's first self-contained source of power for underwater use to be made available commercially, it should transform offshore oil and gas industries and sea-bed prospecting by making divers independent of surface ships for their power supply.

The unit was developed by Ricardo and Company Engineers (1927) Ltd. under a £20,000 contract from the National Research Development Corporation. It had grown from an earlier investigation, after the war, when the Navy wanted an underwater power unit for submarines which would be more powerful than battery powered electric motors and not dependent on a Schnorkel breathing tube to the surface. That investigation came to an end with the appearance of the nuclear submarine but the growth of sea-bed industry—and the appearance of the submersible, the small privately-owned submarine used for industrial surveys or scientific research—reawakened interest.

The device, as demonstrated, consisted of a standard Perkins engine fitted into a pressurised steel vessel. When started above the sea it runs normally, using ordinary air, until it is lowered beneath the surface. Then it is automatically switched over to exhaust gas recycling. The exhaust gas is cooled by injecting water, excess gas ejected by a compressor against the sea pressure and the remainder mixed with a small quantity of uncooled exhaust gas to raise the temperature to about 100°C. A measured amount of oxygen is then added and the mixture passes into the engine intake. Starting underwater has to be carried out on a small supply of pure air until there is enough exhaust gas to operate the changeover, automatically, after about ten seconds.

As nitrogen is bled away with the discharged exhaust gas the engine has to run on a carbon dioxide/oxygen mixture instead of a nitrogen/oxygen one. This reaches a lower temperature under compression, reducing efficiency, but this is offset by warming the gas with uncooled exhaust.

The correct proportion of oxygen is vital. Pure oxygen cannot be used, a conventional engine could not stand the fivefold increase in power which would result. But even a slight change from normal proportions could produce troubles, a deficiency resulting in inefficient running and an excess burning the lubricating oil beneath the piston rings and damaging the engine.

The unit has been designed for working at depths down to 600 feet, where the compressor used for ejecting surplus exhaust gas, would absorb about 5 horsepower, or 15 per cent. of the total engine output. The power take-off is through a pump which delivers it hydraulically to operate the hydraulic tools now available for underwater working. In the demonstration the hydraulic output was returned to the surface to be reconverted to a mechanical output of 20 horsepower.

Despite the obvious and unavoidable power losses, compared with an atmospheric engine, the underwater unit has one advantage. The hot engine cooling water, normally wasted, could be used for warming divers' suits or underwater living quarters.

As demonstrated the unit obtained its oxygen from four cylinders of compressed gas, mounted beneath the pressure vessel and accounting for half the total weight of eight tons. These provided for twelve hours working at full output. One possibility being investigated was the use of high-test peroxide as the oxygen source, particularly when the engine is used in submersibles. This could be stored in plastic bags and delivered under the normal underwater pressure. Compared with lead batteries the underwater diesel delivers three times as much power per pound weight when using oxygen from cylinders, nearly four times when supplied from liquid oxygen containers and over five times when high test peroxide is the oxygen source.

UNHELPFUL HEN.—An unfortunate habit of the hen is perplexing agricultural research scientists, it was disclosed at a Royal Society Conversazione. She stands up when laying.

What may happen to the egg because of this is determined by a simple rule enunciated at the conversazione " an eggshell will crack if the local strength of the shell is less than the strength of an environmental insult to which it is exposed ". In other words, if an eggshell is hit—or hits the floor— too hard it will break. It is a large problem, the percentage of Britain's 15,000,000 eggs produced a year that have to be downgraded, mainly due to eggshell cracking, has risen from four in 1968 to seven.

Not only engineers but geneticists and behaviour scientists are devoting their minds to it. For the vital factor is what might be called the hen's drop height. This varies from hen to hen. It is inherited but each individual hen is remarkably consistent in the drop and the insult she inflicts on her eggs. What is wanted is for engineers to design new shockproof floors and hen breeders to provide more duck-like traits for their hens, so far as that vital factor is concerned.

WEATHER WORRIES FOR WORKERS.—One group of immigrant workers has proved not as good as the native article and the trouble, as might be expected, is the British climate. Because our summers are cold and getting colder output is down—in the honey production field. Mr. G. W. Hurst, of the Meteorological Office, Bracknell, analysed July and August temperatures over the previous thirty years, in the *Meteorological Magazine*, and showed a steady fall that closely paralleled the decline in honey production. The average August temperature is now 1 to 1½° lower than it was in the 1930's. The working offspring of the imported Italian queen bees just don't like it. British beekeepers have, over the years, taken to importing replacement queens from Italy, partly because Italian bees share the national reputation for good looks, vigour, keenness on breeding and, also, hard work. They are also cheaper than the darker home-reared bees which are probably the nearest thing still existing to the native British bee which has been wiped out by disease. Italian queens are precocious, they start breeding early in the year and build up large colonies which, if it is warm, produce a lot of honey. But, if it stays cold, all those would be honey foragers and gatherers just stay in the hive, eating up what supplies they have, until the temperature rises to 55 or 60°. The black bee, even if not so numerous, at least goes out to work in temperatures 10° lower.

The answer to the declining honey production in the South of England, put forward by one group of beekeepers who scorned the " join Europe" trend of 1971, would be to discard those unsatisfactory foreigners and replace them with black bees. The black bee has never been ousted by the Italian variety in the North of England and Scotland but it

would probably take five or ten years to breed enough for restocking the South.

WHY TEETH DECAY.—Everyone knows, or should know, that sugar is bad for the teeth. It hastens the appearance of the disease of caries and causes decayed teeth. Contrary to general opinion, white sugar is no worse for the teeth than brown sugar, according to work carried out at Guy's Hospital in London. Nor is white bread any worse for one's teeth than brown bread—both are virtually harmless compared with sugar. Tests carried out with a strain of rats specially bred for the consistent way their teeth decay showed that starchy foods, mainly wheat products, caused very few caries. Bread is about 60 per cent. starch and only 2 per cent. sugar so its lack of effect on teeth, whether it is white or brown, is easily explained. Further trials showed that the matter is more complicated as brown bread may contain agents which protect the teeth. The enamel-protecting substances in wholemeal bread come from the bran and are phytates, complex phosphorus containing compounds.

But the relative innocuousness of wheat flour, even its protective qualities, vanishes when it is mixed with sugar and baked into biscuits. Not when it is just mixed and not baked, an uncooked 24 per cent. sucrose/42 per cent. flour diet produced only moderate caries, reported Dr. T. H. Grenby, a biochemist working on dental problems at Guy's, writing in *Chemistry in Britain*. When it is baked into biscuits, however, and these are fed to the rats the tooth destruction rises to a very high level, akin to that of sugar itself. Very few of the decay spots appear on the smooth surface of the teeth and the trouble is located where the pieces of biscuit become stuck in the molar fissures. This could explain why Western-style diets are more harmful to teeth than the native diets they are replacing— Eskimos living on fish, seal and walrus meat have sound teeth but around trading posts, where manufactured and sugar foods are available, decay increases.

Whatever the diet, however cariogenic it is, the rats' teeth stay sound, provided there are no germs around. Rats grown in germ-free conditions at Guy's are free from caries. But introducing just one single specific strain of bacteria finds decay following. The development of caries apparently depends on four main factors, the presence of the bacteria, a suitable food base, a suitable environment close to the teeth and susceptible sites on the teeth.

Only carbohydrates provide suitable foods. Instead of being broken down completely into carbon dioxide and water they may, in favourable, or unfavourable, conditions, produce acid which attacks the enamel of the teeth. As wave after wave of sugar reaches the colonies of bacteria so wave after wave of acid is produced. At the Royal College of Surgeons' Dental Laboratories at Farnborough, Kent, vaccination against teeth decay is being tested on monkeys. More immediate, however, is the promise of a new caries preventative, calcium glycerophosphate. Added in only minute quantities to just part of the diet of baboons it effectively prevents tooth decay. Success with baboons may not mean success with humans, scientists working at the Laboratories pointed out, but arrangements were being made for human trials. No trouble was expected in getting permission to use calcium glycerophosphate on humans because it has been used as an ingredient in some tonics for many years. It appears to be at least as effective as the fluoridation of water in preventing caries but no one at the Laboratories would put it forward as an alternative, even though it can be taken or not, as one chooses. Fluoridation has been proved over 25 years and must stay, they say.

WIND AND WOODS.—Spare the rod and spoil the child—a good shaking now and again will make him grow tough and strong. Whether the maxims are true or not for human children they certainly seem to work with trees. Many people, before two University of California scientists did so, have wondered why trees growing in isolation in parkland are so different from those in a wood. It is probably not just a crowding effect caused by reaching up towards the light because the trunk shape is quite different. The sturdy parkland tree has a trunk which is very thick at the base but which rapidly tapers to produce a crown of heavy branches; the tree well within a wood has very little taper to its tall, slender trunk. Trees growing on the edge of a wood resemble those in parkland. Cut them down and those further in prove to be very vulnerable to the wind, and are easily blown over. The two Californian scientists, P. L. Neel and R. W. Harris, considering this, wondered if the sturdiness of the trees on the edge of a wood, protecting their slighter fellows from the wind, was an effect of wind itself, caused by the young seedlings being shaken by it.

They tested the idea with uniform pairs of seedlings of Liquidambar trees, kept in a greenhouse at a controlled temperature. One tree of each pair received a daily shaking, the other did not. Their findings, reported in the American journal *Science*, certainly showed an effect. After 27 days the unshaken trees were over 20 cm taller whose those shaken had lengthened, on average, by only 4·3 cm. Six out of the eight shaken trees had developed a terminal bud at the end of the main shoot. Even in the two shaken trees which did not develop terminal buds growth was only about one-third of that of the unshaken trees. Examination of the internal structure of the trees showed a stunting effect in the shaken trees, wood fibres were both shorter and narrower. The mechanism by which this happens is still a mystery but it looks as if there is a fairly general effect within the tree because leaves may also be smaller than normal in a shaken tree.

YESTERDAY'S T.V. ON RECORD.—The video disc system for play-back television, claimed to be much cheaper than video tape, was tested in black and white by Independent Television and in colour by the B.B.C. The system, developed by Teldec, a German company jointly owned by the British Decca firm and A.E.G. Telefunken of Germany, was tested in the United Kingdom prior to being marketed here in 1973. Black and white playback equipment was expected to cost about £65, exclusive of tax, and colour equipment, with a magazine able to give a three hour show, £125.

ARCHÆOLOGY IN 1970-71

THE CRISIS IN BRITISH ARCHÆOLOGY.—Considerable attention has been devoted in the past year to the accelerating rate of destruction of archæological sites as a consequence of development schemes and an attempt has been made to assess this. In an article entitled " Rescuing Our Past " in *The Observer* for August 22, 1971, Philip Barker and Peter Fowler outlined the problem.

The establishment of new towns, the proliferation of motorways requiring thousands of tons of sand and gravel, the exploitation of peat bogs, the afforestation of marginal land, the deep ploughing of arable land—all these activities destroy archæological remains. For example, in South Dorset nearly 900 Bronze Age round barrows are known but fewer than 5 per cent. of these are now undamaged. Of 360 round barrows in Gloucestershire half have been destroyed, while a survey in 1970 showed that only one barrow cemetery now remains complete and that is covered with trees. In Wiltshire more than 400 of 640 scheduled sites were found to have been damaged or destroyed in the decade 1954 to 1964.

As far as the sites of deserted mediæval villages are concerned, between A.D. 1500 and 1950 about 300 were destroyed, but in the twenty years between 1950 and 1970 another 300 have vanished and others continue to do so at the rate of 20 to 30 a year. A similar tale of destruction may be told for historic town centres and the gravels of the river valleys. The latter, because of the light soils that developed on them, were heavily settled in antiquity, but are now being quarried away at a rate of about 200 million cubic yards a year.

The construction of motorways, which take random routes from an archæological point of view, frequently reveals hitherto unknown sites of importance; for example the 75 miles of the M.5 motorway from North Gloucestershire to Central Somerset revealed 125 sites of which 85 per cent. were previously unknown. The authors of the article draw attention to the very small sums of money spent on archæological investigation compared to the cost of the motorways. They claim that if less than 1 per cent. of the construction cost of £1 million per motorway mile was devoted to archæological purposes, adequate excavation and research could be undertaken.

Emphasising that many of the development projects are desirable and often vitally necessary, the case for adequate research in advance of development is cogently argued and the urgency is stressed —archæological investigations are pointless and indeed impossible after the motorway or the housing estate has been built. The State already has some legislation and the organization to deal with this drastic situation, but " the present crisis, in which the destruction of the greater part of our archæological heritage can be realistically envisaged within the next thirty years, is very largely the result of the State's failure to modernize its provision, to develop and expand its own machinery to keep pace with the great changes in land-use and social attitudes which have occurred in the last thirty years ". In practical terms inadequate financial provision is the main problem and in an attempt to find a solution a fund-raising organization called " Rescue " was formed early in 1971.

" RESCUE ".—On January 23, 1971, some 700 people attended a special meeting at London University—allegedly the largest archæological meeting on record—to discuss the state of British archæology. This gathering was preceded by the meetings of working parties at Barford and Newcastle upon Tyne in 1970.

The London meeting accepted two main recommendations; first, that there should be a unified State Antiquities Service which, through regional centres and with much improved financial provision, would deal efficiently with all archæological contingencies by working closely with planners and developers, as well as maintaining up-to-date records of the archæological situation in different parts of the country. The second recommendation was that an organization called " Rescue " should be established. This new body would be an association of all interested people with direct individual membership; it is this latter characteristic among others which will distinguish " Rescue " from existing national bodies such as the Council for British Archæology. It will actively raise money for archæological purposes by way of subscriptions, bequests, donations and appeals.

The resources of " Rescue " will be used, according to the organisers, " to make the public aware of the rapidly accelerating destruction of our archæological heritage; to encourage the revision and extension of existing legislation concerning archæological remains, and to seek for new legislation where necessary; to obtain greatly increased funds for rescue excavation and its publication; to press for the extension and the improvement of field archæological training at all levels; in general to help to record and conserve the physical remains of Britain's archæological heritage of every age, and with particular reference to the changing character of the natural environment; specifically to support surveys, to acquire sites or areas of archæological importance for permanent conservation, to initiate or support rescue excavations and the consequent work on the results and their publication."

The supporters of " Rescue " see the immediate future, that is the next 20 to 30 years, as the crucial period for archæological recording and excavation; at about the turn of the century the rate of destruction of archæological sites will probably slow down as the major road systems, new towns and similar large-scale undertakings are completed.

ANCIENT MONUMENTS BOARD.—The 17th Annual Report of the Ancient Monuments Board for England, covering the year 1970, was published in June, 1971. After describing the meetings of the Board, and welcoming the information that ancient monuments legislation is in active preparation, the Report details various individual cases with which the Board has been concerned; these included such diverse monuments as an area near the now famous Sutton Hoo ship-burial in Suffolk, the remains of the Augustinian Priory at Dunstable, Bedfordshire, a section of Norwich City Walls and the only surviving tread-wheel crane on the Wey Navigation in Surrey.

The Board states that, " It is our concern to see that the relationship between ancient monuments and their environment should be preserved ", and urges that the upper Plym Valley, " which probably includes the finest representative collection of different types of antiquities on Dartmoor ", should be maintained in such a way as to achieve the preservation of the antiquities in their natural setting. Attention is also drawn to the problem of ancient bridges which are liable to be damaged because of the increasing amount of traffic passing over them. In addition there is another danger in that the lowering of the water level of the rivers passing under the bridges can also harm those old structures constructed of timber.

After noting in a short section that research is in

progress on the effects of sonic booms, the Board welcomes the fact that the 500 yards of the Warden Simonburn and Humshaugh section of Hadrians Wall at Black Carts has been taken into the care of the Department of the Environment, as has Castle Acre Castle in Norfolk. In addition the Ancient Monuments Board recommended 331 monuments for scheduling, of which 76 were in Cornwall, 33 in the North Riding of Yorkshire, and 31 each in Derbyshire and Devon.

The 331 monuments recommended for scheduling during 1970 were divided into the following categories: prehistoric burial mounds or groups of mounds, 128; camps, settlements and other prehistoric sites, 60; Roman sites, 6; Linear earth works, 11; Ecclesiastical sites, 18; castles and other secular buildings, bridges, standing stones and crosses, 94; industrial monuments, 6; deserted villages, 8.

The importance that the Board attaches to the use of aerial photographs for archæological purposes is both stated and emphasized by the publication, as appendices, of a memorandum by Dr. J. K. St. Joseph, Director in Aerial Photography at the University of Cambridge, and comments thereon by the Chief Inspector of Ancient Monuments.

Dr. J. K. St. Joseph reviews the history of the use of aerial photographs for archæological purposes, stressing their basic value as enabling, by viewing from a considerable distance, a more unified and informative picture to be obtained of large scale archæological features such as earthworks, and also providing a distinct outline of lost or unknown remains due to the fact that buried features such as ditches, pits, foundations and roads affect the vegetation covering them.

Although air photographs specifically taken to reveal archæological information have to be taken during different seasons with careful regard to weather, light, time of year, type of crop, and despite handicaps imposed by Air Traffic Control regulations, aerial reconnaissance is unique in the way it can record thousands of previously unknown archæological sites, many of which are not visible at all at ground level; for this reason the use of aerial photographs can prove cheaper and yield better results than employing people on general ground surveys. Its particular value at the present time is that, with the very rapid rate of change in land use with the construction of new towns, motorways, and so on, it is a method of establishing in advance where archæological sites ought to be investigated.

The Chief Inspector in his comments stressed that as the Ancient Monuments Acts form the only framework for safeguarding archæological sites, the Inspectorate of Ancient Monuments should have very close liaison with those responsible for maintaining and augmenting important collections of aerial photographs and that aerial reconnaissance for the Inspectorate should be undertaken.

Bearing in mind the degree of archæological expertise which has been developed in Cambridge over the years, the Chief Inspector felt that there is a good case for giving a financial subvention to the Cambridge Committee to help the latter body undertake the following work in connection with ancient monuments: to notify as a matter of routine to the Inspectorate new discoveries and also the principal results of the preceding flying season, to undertake periodic special surveys for the Department of the Environment particularly in connection with development schemes such as motorways or new towns, and to make some attempt to catch up on the detailing of the more important of the 90,000 archæological sites for which aerial photographic cover is already held at Cambridge.

VINDOLANDA.—Chesterholm, midway between Carlisle and Corbridge, is the site of the Roman fort and *vicus* or civil settlement of Vindolanda. Founded in the mid 80's A.D., it lies on the original Stanegate frontier and was abandoned on the construction of Hadrian's Wall, when its garrison was probably moved forward to the new fort at Housesteads about 2 miles away. Later the site was reoccupied under Calpurnius Agricola and became part of the frontier system of Hadrian's Wall.

In an article in number 23 for November, 1970, of *Current Archæology*, Robin Birley explains the desirability of excavating on a large scale, but in considerable detail, a Hadrianic frontier site, and describes how in 1969 Mrs. Daphne Archibald of Tarset, near Hexham in Northumberland purchased the property to which the remains of Vindolanda belonged so that the site could be preserved for posterity.

The Vindolanda Trust was set up in April, 1970, under the chairmanship of Prof. Eric Birley with the following aims: to excavate and conserve for public display the entire civil settlement covering some 15 acres, to excavate with the permission of the Department of the Environment the fort dating to the 4th century A.D., and to display the finds in a Museum to be built on the site. It is hoped to complete this work within about 10 years and the difficult task of raising the necessary finance has been started. With a grant of £700 from Durham University to cover the payment of staff and the conservation work, and with considerable interest from the public to whom an appeal for funds is being made, a full time Director of Excavations was appointed with effect from April 1, 1971.

Mr. Birley considers the opportunities presented by this site at Vindolanda to include a chance to obtain detailed information about the numerous civilians who lived on the frontier in close proximity to the soldiers and to assess their impact upon the social and economic life of the area. In addition, the fort, which is visible and lies to the east of the civil settlement, was built in about 300 A.D. and has hardly been investigated. A thorough excavation should reveal a considerable amount of information about the organization and standard of living of the Roman Army in the early 4th century. It may also be shown that the occupation by Theodosian forces about 370 A.D. continued without a break until the 5th century.

It is envisaged that the next 10 years will be spent in investigating particularly the 4th and 5th century remains in the 15 acre field; but below the 4th century levels there lie the remains of at least 3 earlier forts and civil settlements, with perhaps a native site below these.

During the 1970 season, the excavation of a 15-roomed courtyard house, identified as a *mansio* was largely finished, as was the excavation of a military bath house; 7 buildings in the civil settlement between these 2 establishments were also investigated.

The *mansio* had its own suite of baths, a communal latrine, a large reception room, and a number of small guest rooms. During the 3rd century minor officials requiring overnight accommodation would have been put up here during their tours of duty on the frontier. Modifications were carried out in the 4th century in that the latrine was filled in and the reception room became a kitchen—perhaps the whole building passed into private hands.

Some of the remains of the military bath house have been visible on the surface for some years. Excavations on the site revealed that it was first built in the 3rd century probably by a detachment of the 6th Legion, if the stamped bricks in the western stoke-hole arch are a reliable guide, and was

rebuilt in the early 4th century before conversion to another use after 370 A.D. The western walls of the building were found to stand to a height of 7 feet above floor level, and in the silt of the cold plunge drain and latrine sewer were found over 20 silver, bronze and bone hairpins, 8 double-sided wooden combs, many beads, pieces of jewellery, gem stones from rings and a child's sandal. The excavators are satisfied that this evidence must indicate civilian usage of this military establishment in the 4th century.

The rest of the 1970 programme was devoted to the buildings in the civil settlement between the bath house and the *mansio* and the excavators were surprised by two things; first, two of the buildings were not strip-houses, one having a range of three rooms on either side of the central corridor, and some rooms had three floor levels dating to after 300 A.D. Secondly, there was a fine abundance of small finds although no rubbish pits were excavated. The former include two stone reliefs, one of which portrays a Celtic god with the dedicators' military figure in the bottom right corner, a silver crescent shaped votive plaque, a rare jet betrothal medallion, three gold rings, and a wide range of bronzes as well as numerous iron and lead objects, pottery and 123 coins. Mr. Birley feels that the evidence indicates " a flourishing 4th century community, with a wide range of sophisticated personal and domestic goods."

LUNT GATEWAY RESTORED.—Near to Coventry on land zoned for recreational use is the Lunt, one of a number of Roman forts along the Fosse Way, but excavations have shown that it is later in date (about 60 to 75 A.D. on pottery evidence) than the others (43 to 47 A.D.) and different in design.

Public imagination was caught by a scheme proposed by Mr. Brian Hobley, Field Officer of the Herbert Museum, Coventry, whereby not only would the site be fully excavated but the fort itself would be rebuilt as an open air museum. An article in *Current Archæology*, number 24 for January, 1971, described how in 1970 the main eastern gateway—the *Porta Principalis Sinistra*—was rebuilt. £6,000 was donated by a benefactor, the excavation undertaken by the local society, the turf ramparts constructed by Borstal and approved school boys, and the gateway erected by the Royal Engineers.

Before the gateway could be erected the archæological evidence had to be evaluated and answers provided to questions such as whether the timber would have been felled locally and the posts erected singly or whether prefabricated structures would have been made in a central depot and then carried to the site. The weight of archæological evidence inclined the organisers of the operation to choose a prefabricated gateway made in army workshops with traditional tools.

Although it was not possible completely to follow the Roman pattern the operations did throw light on some of the problems the Romans would have encountered; for example turf would obviously have to be cut and an experiment in 1967 had proved that the turf at the Lunt had to be cut while the winter moisture was still in the soil— the Romans would no doubt have taken this practical factor into their calculations. Another insight into Roman techniques was provided by the fact that when the prefabricated timbers were erected in the Roman post holes it was found that the bottoms of the latter were so well levelled by the Romans by eye that there was a discrepancy of within a tenth of an inch over the 30 foot distance. Reconstruction of the gateway took from Friday morning to Sunday evening, without the use of

modern equipment—only a single pole with pulley attachments and guys, and a tripod.

THE FIRST BRITISH NAVY.—In an article by Mr. C. E. Dove in *Antiquity* for March, 1971, he suggests from his study of the coins of Allectus that it is possible to determine the nature of the ships in what he calls " The first British Navy ". The author points out that the coins of Allectus with the inscription *Virtus* show " a distinctive type of craft, different from anything to be found elsewhere in the Roman coinage ", and further argues that in the then current political situation with the prospect of invasion, Allectus had every incentive to court the navy and therefore to ensure that the pictorial representation of craft on his coins was correct in detail.

Mr. Dove's argument rests on a careful study of the coins of Allectus including a bronze coin in the British Museum, which shows a small rowing boat containing 4 oarsmen and a steersman; this is thought to be a realistic depiction and relates well to the representation on the Low Ham mosaic. Mr. Dove feels that the *Virtus* vessel is tubby, floating high in the water with bow and stern rounded and bouyant; it probably resembles a large open rowboat with a deck length of approximately 24 to 27 feet, a single square sail and five to seven oars a side. " They are too small for transports. Naval vessels they must be, however, and use as scouts seems most likely ". The author links the use of these boats with the need to patrol the south-eastern coastline in particular, in view of the danger of invasion and the premium on naval defence; he develops this theme by reference to classical authorities, to whom he also looks for suggestions as to the origins of this type of craft. Mr. Dove concludes, " it seems undeniable that in the *Virtus* ship coins of Allectus we have that rare thing in Roman coinage: a vessel realistically portrayed. This being so, these coins at least offer the earliest of all representations of a British naval vessel ".

GLASTONBURY TOR.—Glastonbury Tor in Somerset has been the scene of important excavations during the last decade and a report by Mr. Philip Rahtz appeared in 1971 entitled " Excavations on Glastonbury Tor, Somerset, 1964–6 ", and was published in *The Archæological Journal* for 1970.

The Tor is a very important natural landmark in central Somerset and may be seen from 20 miles away in all directions. The earliest human activity, not necessarily occupation, on the Tor dates from the prehistoric and Roman periods; a scatter of Upper Palaeolithic, Mesolithic and Neolithic flints were recovered, as were 7 sherds of Roman coarse pottery, 4 pieces of Samian, 20 Roman tiles and similar scattered finds; there were no associated structures.

During the 6th century A.D. the whole area was disturbed and the first period of definite occupation recognized by Mr. Rahtz centres on the middle of that century. Traces of perhaps five timber buildings were found as well as two hearths which may have been domestic but may also have been connected with metal working. There is no slag but two crucible fragments were found nearby. Apart from this, there was evidence that the community consumed substantial quantities of meat. Other finds included local grass-tempered pottery, Roman tile, metal objects and traces of possible graves.

The main dating evidence was provided by 10 sherds of imported Mediterranean pottery which is usually assigned to the mid 6th century A.D.; in any case, the absence of Roman pottery other than Samian suggests a date after the 4th century.

In interpreting this first period of occupation Mr. Rahtz seeks to answer the question as to why the Tor was chosen as a settlement; he suggests that the reason is to do with either defence or religion, bearing in mind its remoteness, inaccessibility, inconvenience, and lack of a nearby water supply, as well as its being a good vantage point.

Whether the settlement had a defensive or religious purpose can only be determined on the evidence. The latter includes probable timber buildings set on platforms cut into the rock to provide a level basis, 1½ cwt. of bones from animals not slaughtered on the spot but brought in as joints, Mediterranean wine or olive oil being used on the site, the utilization of Roman tile and probable metal working. All this might perhaps suggest a small Celtic Christian monastic site but the quantity of meat bones does not conform to what is known of early Christian monastic habits, although this in itself is not conclusive evidence either way. On balance Mr. Rahtz feels that the better interpretation of the site is as a local chieftain's stronghold, thus placing the emphasis on the settlement's security from attack.

To the second period of occupation may be assigned four buildings, one of which may be identified as a probable wooden church. In addition the one certain period two feature on the summit, a cross-base was recovered as was a wheel-headed cross—the most important find from this period. Taken together with food remains amongst which fish, bird bones and egg shell predominated, this evidence suggests a Christian bias, and Mr. Rahtz feels that the best interpretation for this period might be that of a Christian hermitage set upon an exposed hill top.

As far as dating is concerned, the wheel-headed cross is thought to be of 10th or 11th century A.D. and the pottery, when compared to parallels from Cheddar, may be assigned to the broad period 1000 to 1200 A.D. In short, period two represents a monastic settlement spanning the late Saxon and early Mediæval periods—probably 10th century A.D. or earlier in origin through to the 11th and possibly 12th centuries.

Much of the interpretation of the third period of occupation of the Tor is tentative according to Mr. Rahtz. The evidence suggests that there could have been a, presumably towerless, church on the summit as early as the late 12th or early 13th century. There is a tradition that the church was destroyed by an earthquake in 1275 and there is no archæological evidence to contradict this. The later church, of which the Tower at the west end still survives, was perhaps built in the 1290's and may have continued in use until the 16th century. In addition to the church complex there was a range of buildings on the shoulder of the hill which dated from the latter part of period three—the finds were of 14th and 15th century date. It is suggested that these buildings perhaps housed a resident priest who would celebrate mass in the church and collect the pilgrims' offerings. Period three was the last major period of occupation of the site, although the post mediæval features indicate human activity on the summit over the last three centuries.

THE GRAVENEY BOAT.—The excavation of a drainage channel on the Graveney Marshes not far from Faversham in Kent revealed by accident in September, 1970, part of a clinker-built boat. Mr. Basil Greenhill, Director of the National Maritime Museum, described in the March 1971 issue of *Antiquity* the circumstances of the discovery and the subsequent excavation.

The remains of the boat were first brought to light by a mechanical excavator driver working for the Kent River Authority and an excavation was undertaken by local archæologists. The find was reported to the National Maritime Museum and to the British Museum by a member of the staff of the Royal Canterbury Museum, and this ultimately resulted in the site being visited by the Keeper of the Institute of Maritime Archæology of the Danish National Museum and Director of the Viking Ship Museum at Roskilde who advised on methods of excavation. With the co-operation of the Kent River Authority, a detailed record of the boat was made and a recovery operation mounted jointly by the National Maritime Museum and the Sutton Hoo Unit of the British Museum.

Although on first examination this clinker-built boat would seem to date between about A.D. 400 and 800 and perhaps be contemporary with the Sutton Hoo vessel, Mr. Greenhill urged caution on this point stating that " There has, perhaps, been a tendency in piecing together the story of the development of the clinker built boat in Northern Europe to assume that a type became extinct as soon as it was improved upon and that, therefore, the finds so far made necessarily represent a process of evolution which can be dated. In fact, old types may have continued to be built for a long period."

The boat is described as being broad and shallow, without evidence of a mast step nor any obvious indication of how she was propelled. The floor timbers, of such a size as to suggest the carrying of heavy cargo, are fixed to the shell with wooden tree-nails; the shell itself is composed of many narrow strakes fastened to each other with iron rivets. The keel-plank, the last piece to be excavated, was a large baulk of timber some 5·4 metres long and 0·6 m. wide at the centre. All in all, Mr. Greenhill is confident that " The boat would have been fully capable of crossing the North Sea."

A further fuller account of the Graveney boat by Miss Angela Evans and Mrs. Valerie Fenwick who directed the work was published in the June 1971 issue of *Antiquity*. From this we learn that most of the keel, the stern post, parts of 8 strakes on each side, and parts of 9 floor frames were found in position. A 3 strand rope was discovered, one end of which was fixed to the stern post while the other disappeared into the side of the section suggesting that the boat was moored, an impression given weight by the fact that series of posts with pointed ends were found alongside. After a consideration of the evidence the excavators felt that the boat had probably been pulled up on to a hard on one side of a creek.

In the very bottom of the boat were discovered " 12 sherds of a fine, hard fabric, buff in colour and ungritted. These all came from one unglazed wide-mouthed vessel ". Mr. J. G. Hurst thinks the latter probably originated in Belgium or France and is " 10th or 11th century in date, perhaps a little earlier ". In addition to this pottery evidence, radio carbon dates of 1080+ or −40 years BP and 1064+ or −54 years BP were obtained from timber samples taken from the shell of the boat; in more conventional terms these dates are equivalent to about A.D. 870 and A.D. 886 respectively. Although these dates relate specifically to the time when the timber was felled, as the boat was free of repairs, they may also suggest the construction of the vessel in the second half of the 9th century. There are no contemporary boats in the British Isles and no obvious continental parallel exists.

AN 18TH/19TH CENTURY GLASSHOUSE.—Gawber, near Barnsley in Yorkshire, was a glass production centre in the 18th and 19th centuries and has been

described in detail by Mr. Denis Ashurst in a paper in *Post-Medieval Archæology* in 1970.

Although no documents survive for the earliest phase of glass making at Gawber, a furnace was excavated which has been given a thermo-remanent magnetic dating of 1690–1735 for its last firing, although no glass was found which could positively be associated with the early furnace to suggest any activity before the year 1700–1710.

Soon after 1732 William Thorpe took the lease of Gawber Hall and from 1734 onwards the parish registers record a large increase in the number of glass makers. Between 1734 and 1818 there are no fewer than 100 entries in the parish registers relating to a total of 22 different families. During the early 19th century however, Samuel Thorpe was transferring his business interests to the coal fields at Barnsley and the Gawber Glasshouse was sold in 1821, when glass making finished on the site.

Of the three sites excavated, Site B revealed a waste heap made up of glass scum and broken crucible, cullet store, workyard and workshops, forming an annexe to the cone furnace of the Thorpe bottle house dating from the 1730's. Site C revealed an early furnace overlaid and partly destroyed by the cone furnace of the Thorpe glasshouse. Although nothing survived above ground level and no documentary evidence has been found, a conical brick superstructure is assumed in the later phase on the basis of another traditional 18th century South Yorkshire glasshouse, together with the evidence of the shape of the outer foundation and the brick dust which had accumulated.

During the early period the Glasshouse probably produced only clear glass, but in the later period phials and wine bottles were made in clear, green and dark brown glass often incorporating seals. Bottles were usually blown in a mould, but the many variations in the phials indicate that they were blown free without the use of a mould.

The evolution of the Gawber bottles may be traced through the evolution of the rim which was originally intended as an aid to tieing in the cork but later became a purely decorative feature. On the Gawber bottles this string rim is found in three forms—round, rectangular, and triangular; also, the mouth of the bottle is either cut off square, marvered out to form a lip, or turned completely over to meet the string rim just below the mouth. During the late 17th and early 18th centuries there was a tendency for bottles to have a plain round string rim, but throughout the 18th century the triangular form predominated, while in the late 18th century the rectangular shape was most typical.

In conclusion, after a thorough review of the evidence, Mr. Ashurst feels that the site is a late survival of a cottage-based industry, retaining features of the old forest Glasshouse, which was subsequently replaced by a works more fitted to the needs of 18th century industrial expansion.

LETTER POST SINCE 1897

The following list shows the cost of sending within the United Kingdom an ordinary letter not exceeding the weight shown:

After June 22, 1897..............4 oz. for 1d.
Nov. 1, 1915................1 oz. for 1d.
　　　　　　　　　　　2 oz. for 2d.
　　　　　　　　　　　4 oz. for 2½d.
June 3, 1918..............4 oz. for 1½d.
　　　　　　　　　　　6 oz. for 2d.
June 1, 1920..............3 oz. for 2d.
May 29, 1922..............1 oz. for 1½d.
　　　　　　　　　　　3 oz. for 2d.
May 14, 1923..............2 oz. for 1½d.
May 1, 1940..............2 oz. for 2½d.
May 1, 1952..............2 oz. for 2½d.
　　　　　　　　　　　4 oz. for 3d.
Jan. 1, 1956..............2 oz. for 2½d.
Oct. 1, 1957..............1 oz. for 3d.
　　　　　　　　　　　2 oz. for 4½d.
May 17, 1965..............2 oz. for 4d.
　　　　　　　　　　　4 oz. for 6d.

Sept. 16, 1968.　Two-Tier Letter Service Introduced

	First-Class		Second-Class
4 oz. for	.. 5d. ..	..	.. 4d.
6 oz. for	.. 9d. ..	..	.. 6d.
8 oz. for	.. 1s. 0d. ..	..	.. 8d.
10 oz. for	.. 1s. 3d. ..	..	.. 10d.
12 oz. for	.. 1s. 6d. ..	..	.. 1s. 0d.
14 oz. for	.. 1s. 9d. ..	..	.. 1s. 2d.
1 lb. for	.. 2s. 0d. ..	..	.. 1s. 4d.

Without limit of weight)　　(Limit of weight 1 lb. 8 oz.)

Feb. 15, 1971		First-Class		Second-class
4 oz.	for	.. 3p	..	2½p
6 oz.	for	.. 5p	..	4½p
8 oz.	for	.. 7p	..	5½p
10 oz.	for	.. 9p	..	6½p
12 oz.	for	.. 11p	..	7½p
14 oz.	for	.. 13p	..	8½p
1 lb.	for	.. 15p	..	9½p
1 lb. 8 oz. for		.. 20p		10½p
2 lb.	for	.. 30p		Limit of weight
Each extra lb.	..	15p		1 lb. 8 oz.

without limit of weight

CORONATION DATES, 1714–1953

Sovereign.	Accession.		Coronation.	
George I.	Aug.	1, 1714	Oct.	20, 1714
George II.	June	12, 1727	Oct.	11, 1727
George III.	Oct.	25, 1760	Sept.	22, 1761
George IV.	Jan.	29, 1820	July	19, 1821
William IV.	June	26, 1830	Sept.	8, 1831
Victoria	June	20, 1837	June	28, 1838
Edward VII.	Jan.	22, 1901	Aug.	9, 1902
George V.	May	6 1910	June	22, 1911
Edward VIII.	Jan.	20, 1936		..
George VI.	Dec.	11, 1936	May	12, 1937
Elizabeth II	Feb.	6, 1952	June	2, 1953

EDUCATION IN THE UNITED KINGDOM

ENGLAND AND WALES

The present pattern of education in England and Wales derives from the Education Act of 1944 (Butler Act) which was modified by nine minor Acts from 1946 to 1968.

Department of Education and Science

The Secretary of State for Education and Science is assisted by two Parliamentary Under-Secretaries of State. Her responsibilities relating to civil science and (exercised through the University Grants Committee) the universities cover the whole of Great Britain, but her functions in connection with schools, further education and teachers relate to England and Wales only, except that responsibility for primary and secondary education in Wales is in the hands of the Secretary of State for Wales. Most of the work of the 550 H.M. Inspectors (who inspect schools and other educational establishments apart from universities, and provide the Secretary of State with information and advice) is in the local education authority areas. The Secretary of State's requirements under the Act are issued, and guidance is given, mainly in the form of regulations, orders and circulars addressed to local education authorities and other bodies, and in booklets. A report and six volumes of statistics are published annually.

Local Education Authorities

Among the main features of the system are:—

(a) Its administration is decentralized, the responsibility for providing state primary, secondary and further education (but not university education) to meet the needs of their areas being that of the 162 local education authorities (L.E.A.'s). These are the elected councils of counties and county boroughs and the outer London boroughs, the Inner London Education Authority being a specially constituted statutory committee of the Greater London Council.

The councils appoint education committees consisting of some of their own members (a majority of the committee) and some other persons with experience in education and knowledge of local educational conditions. The L.E.A.'s maintain schools and colleges and build new ones, pay teachers and provide equipment and materials. Most of the public money spent on education is disbursed by the local authorities. Education is by far the largest item of their expenditure. L.E.A.'s are financed by rate support grants from the Ministry of Housing and Local Government and from the rates; and employ more than one million people, half of them teachers, whose salaries account for almost half of the national expenditure on education.

Voluntary Agencies

(b) Voluntary agencies play an important part in educational provision often in co-operation with the State. Some indication of its nature and extent is given below.

There are separate central advisory councils for education in England and Wales which advise the Secretary of State, usually on subjects referred to them. Their membership changes from one reference to another. Among the subjects on which the Council for England has reported in recent years are the education of boys and girls aged 15 to 18 (the Crowther Report, 1959), the education between 13 and 16 of pupils of average or less than average ability (the Newsom Report on *Half our Future*, 1963), and primary education and the transition to secondary education (the Plowden Report, 1967). The Plowden Report on *Children and their Primary Schools* recommended a national policy of positive discrimination in favour of areas where children are most deprived socially.

SCHOOLS AND PUPILS

Schooling is compulsory for all children between 5 and (from 1972–73) 16 years. No fees are charged in any publicly maintained school.

There are four main categories of school: (a) those *maintained* by local education authorities, the authorities meeting their expenditure partly from local rates and partly from grants made by the Ministry of Housing and Local Government; (b) *direct grant* schools which are assisted by grants from the Department of Education and Science; (c) *recognized independent* schools *i.e.* independent schools which have sought and obtained recognition as efficient after inspection by H.M. Inspectors of Schools; (d) *other independent* schools.

County and Voluntary Schools

Maintained schools are of two types: (i) *county schools* (19,000) which are built, maintained and staffed by local education authorities. Their managers (primary schools) and governors (secondary schools) are appointed by the L.E.A.'s. (ii) *Voluntary schools* (9,500) which although built by voluntary bodies (mainly religious denominations) are maintained by an L.E.A. More than two-thirds of the voluntary schools are Church of England schools and about 2,000 are Roman Catholic. Voluntary schools are of three kinds: controlled, aided, and special agreement. In *controlled* schools the L.E.A. nominates two-thirds of the managers or governors (the rest are nominated by the voluntary body), bears all costs and appoints the teachers.

Aided Schools

In *aided* schools the managers or governors (two-thirds appointed by the voluntary interest and one-third by the L.E.A.) are responsible for repairs to the exterior of the school building and for improvements and alterations to it though the Department of Education and Science may reimburse up to four-fifths of approved expenditure. The L.E.A. meets all running costs. The managers or governors control the appointment of teachers. *Special agreement* schools are those where the L.E.A. may, by special agreement, pay between one-half and three-quarters of the cost of building a new, or extending an existing, voluntary school, almost always a secondary school. Two-thirds of the governors are appointed by the voluntary body and the remainder by the L.E.A. Expenditure is normally apportioned between the authority and the voluntary body as for an aided school.

Direct Grant Schools

A *direct grant grammar school* has an independent governing body with L.E.A. representatives and receives maintenance grants direct from the Department of Education and Science in return for which a quarter of its places ("free places") are offered to pupils who have attended a grant-aided primary school for not less than two years. The remainder of the places may be available for fee-payers, except that up to a further 25 per cent. ("reserved places") may be claimed by the authority. The authority's proportion of the admissions may not, unless the governors agree, exceed one half. Fees are paid by the L.E.A.'s for the places they take up and they pay for about 60 per cent. of direct grant pupils. The fees paid by the parents of all other pupils are assessed according to the parents' means, any balance being paid to the school by the Department of Education and Science. The maintenance grant from the D.E.S. to the school comprises a capitation grant for every boy and girl in the school together with an additional sum for each sixth-former.

Public Schools

By the term *public schools* is usually meant the independent schools in the membership of the

Headmasters' Conference, the Governing Bodies Association or the Governing Bodies of Girls' Schools Association.

Independent schools charge fees and do not receive grants from the State. *Preparatory schools* are mainly for boys from about 8 to 13 years who wish to enter public schools. All independent schools are open to inspection and must register with the Department of Education and Science which lays down certain minimum standards and can make schools remedy any unacceptable features of their buildings or instruction and exclude any unsuitable teacher or proprietor. To be designated " recognized as efficient ", an independent school must satisfy the D.E.S. that its standards are broadly comparable with those of grant-aided schools.

The State System.— *The Primary Stage* begins at 5 years and the transfer to secondary school is made between 10½ and 12 years. About half the primary schools take 5 to 11-year olds; about a quarter are schools for infants (up to 7 years only); and most of the rest take juniors only (7 to 11 year olds). Children under 5 may attend the limited number of nursery schools or nursery classes attached to infant schools.

Secondary Stage.—Secondary schools are for children aged 11 to 15 (from 1972–73) and over. In January, 1969, when there were 2,959,661 pupils in maintained secondary schools the main types were: (*a*) *secondary modern* schools (1,303,751 pupils) providing mainly a general education with a practical bias, with an increasing number of pupils staying on after the school-leaving age; (*b*) *comprehensive* schools (772,612 pupils) catering for the secondary education of all pupils in an area; (*c*) *grammar* schools (631,948 pupils) providing an academic course from 11 to 16–18 years and constituting the main route to the universities and the professions; and (*d*) *technical* schools (56,627 pupils) providing an integrated academic and technical course.

The allocation to (*a*), (*c*) and (*d*) of pupils leaving primary schools at or about the age of 11 often took account of an " eleven plus " examination involving attainment or intelligence tests. The Labour Government aimed to end selection at eleven plus, abolish separatism in secondary education and provide a system of secondary education in comprehensive schools which would cater for all the secondary school level pupils in their areas. Secondary education was consequently in the process of being reorganized and by January 1969 26 per cent. of the maintained secondary school population were in comprehensive schools.

The Conservative Government, however, announced in circular 10/70 in June 1970, its belief that it is wrong to impose a uniform pattern of secondary organization on local education authorities by legislation or other means. Where a particular pattern of organization in an area is working well and commands general support the Secretary of State intimated that she does not wish to cause further change without good reason.

The Further Stage is treated separately below.

Primary and Secondary Schools

In January, 1969, there were 33,077 schools, of which 29,838 were maintained by local education authorities, 315 were direct grant schools, 1,448 were independent schools recognized as efficient, and 1,476 were other independent schools. There were at school in 1969, 8,391,756 children (4,312,803 boys and 4,078,953 girls) of whom 7,846,056 were in maintained schools, 128,451 in direct grant schools, 301,166 in recognized independent schools and 116,083 in other independent schools. Of those in maintained schools, 4,788,591 were in primary, 2,959,661 in secondary schools and the rest in

nursery (17,170) or special (75,884) schools including hospital. Almost all maintained primary schools, and rather more than half of the maintained secondary schools, are for both boys and girls. At secondary level most independent schools are for boys only or girls only.

The total number aged 15 years or over (excluding those under the school-leaving age) was 644,037 (14·5 per cent. of the age-group); of these 535,373 (11·7 per cent. of age-group) were in maintained schools, 38,597 were in direct grant schools, 63,155 in recognized independent schools and 6,912 in other independent schools. 340,895 of the 644,037 were boys.

By January 1970 the total number of pupils in all maintained schools (excluding nursery and special schools) had risen to 7,958,848.

Handicapped Pupils.—In January 1969 there were 75,884 handicapped pupils in 845 maintained special schools (including 3,264 in hospital); 13,780 of them were boarding. Of the 75,884, 50,228 were classified as " educationally sub-normal ".

Class sizes.—In January, 1969, 12·5 per cent. of primary pupils in maintained schools were in classes of over 40 (compared with 19 per cent. in 1963). 44·4 per cent. of secondary pupils in maintained schools were in classes of over 30 (compared with 52·9 per cent. in 1963). 9·5 per cent. of all primary classes were oversize (by January 1970 this had dropped to 6·7 per cent.) and 36·1 per cent. of secondary classes; the corresponding percentages ten years earlier were 17·8 and 54·9.

School Meals.—In September 1970, 5,156,000 school meals were provided, 12·3 per cent. of them free of charge. Free school milk is available to children under 8 years of age, to other junior pupils recommended on health grounds by a school medical officer, and to pupils in special schools.

Immigrant pupils.—By January, 1970, there were nearly 264,000 immigrant pupils in maintained primary and secondary schools; this was 3·3 per cent. of all full-time pupils in those schools and an increase of about 14,000 over the previous year.

Examinations.—Secondary school pupils (and others) can take the General Certificate of Education (G.C.E.) or the Certificate of Secondary Education (C.S.E.). The examinations for the G.C.E., which are conducted by eight examining bodies (most connected with universities) are set at two levels: Ordinary level (" O ") and Advanced level (" A "). " A " level is usually taken after two years in the sixth form following " O " level. The G.C.E. is not a " grouped subject " examination and candidates at either level may take one or more subjects as they wish. At " A " level passes are awarded in five grades. " A " level candidates may take Special papers which are usually set on the same syllabus as the basic " A " level papers but contain more searching questions.

Like the G.C.E. the Certificate of Secondary Education (C.S.E.) can be taken in one or more subjects. It is open to boys and girls in any school completing five years of secondary education. Five grades are awarded. The C.S.E. can be examined in a number of ways, internal and external, and is controlled largely by teachers sitting on the 14 regional examining boards. In 1969 235,000 candidates took the C.S.E. examinations.

Co-ordinating the work of the G.C.E. and C.S.E. examining boards, and advising them, is the *Schools Council for the Curriculum and Examinations* which was established in 1964 by the Secretary of State for Education and Science as an independent advisory body representing all educational interests with teachers forming a majority of its members. It is concerned *inter alia* with maintaining comparability of standards between boards and also between

the two examinations (grade 1 in the C.S.E. is intended to indicate a standard such that a candidate achieving it might reasonably have been expected to obtain a pass at " O " level in the G.C.E. had he followed a course leading to that examination). The Council is also particularly concerned with promoting and encouraging curriculum study and development. Among its major programmes of work are those relating to English teaching at all school stages, preparations for the raising of the school-leaving age to 16, and sixth form curricula and examinations. See also p. 1045.

Of the 260,440 sixth-form pupils at school in January 1969 (142,354 boys and 110,926 girls) 246,484 were following G.C.E. " A " level courses. 127,848 of the 260,440 were in maintained grammar schools, 37,287 in recognized independent schools, 24,737 in direct grant grammar schools, 48,661 in comprehensive schools, 7,872 in technical schools, 7,230 in secondary modern schools and 6,805 in other maintained schools.

Of the boys and girls who left school in 1968–69, 21·3 per cent. gained 5 or more " O " level passes, 15·6 per cent. one or more " A " levels and 12·1 per cent. 2 or more " A " levels.

TEACHERS

Teachers are appointed by local education authorities, school governing bodies or managers. Those in maintained schools must (except temporary and occasional teachers) be approved as " qualified " by the Department of Education and Science. Most teachers become qualified by successfully completing a course at a college of education or university department of education. For many years graduates and holders of certain specialist qualifications were recognized as qualified teachers without having to take a teacher-training course, but the Secretary of State for Education and Science announced in 1969 that new graduates or holders of graduate-equivalent qualifications will not be accepted as teachers in maintained secondary schools after 1973 and in maintained primary schools from 1970 unless they had satisfactorily completed a suitable course of professional training.

A continuing problem relates to the supply of teachers as the number of children at school increases with the birth rate and the number of those staying on at school beyond the statutory leaving age rises. It is estimated that there will be 10,172,900 boys and girls at school in 1980, rising to 11,103,600 in 1990.

In February, 1970, there were 393,672 full-time teachers in maintained schools and establishments, 172,434 of whom were teaching in primary schools and 156,688 in secondary schools; 206,765 of the 393,672 were women. There were also 45,762 part-time teachers. 44,842 of the teachers in grant-aided primary and secondary schools were graduates in March 1969.

In October, 1969, teachers were being trained in a total of 211 institutions of various types: 125 maintained by local education authorities, 53 by voluntary bodies and 33 by universities. These included 30 university departments of education providing mainly one-year courses for graduates; 159 colleges of education providing mainly three- and four-year courses for non-graduates, 5 departments of education in technical colleges which also offered mainly three- and four-year courses, 13 art teacher training centres offering one-year specialist courses, and 4 college of education (technical) providing one-year specialist courses and initial training courses for serving teachers. At the voluntary colleges (provided mainly by religious denominations) up to 80 per cent. of approved capital expenditure and 100

per cent. of running costs are paid by the Government. 10,736 full-time teachers were engaged in teaching the students in the colleges of education, departments of education in technical colleges, and colleges of education (technical).

There were 116,277 students in training in October, 1969 (35,113 men and 81,164 women), of whom 7,114 were in university departments of education and 105,785 in colleges of education. Many colleges now provide for suitably qualified students a four-year course leading to a B.Ed. degree awarded by the university of whose institute of education the college is a member.

In 1969 (provisional figures), 6,690 married, qualified women teachers returned to service after a break of at least one year, 4,800 going to primary schools and 1,890 to secondary. 3,670 of them returned to full-time teaching and 3,020 to part-time; 950 of the 6,690 were graduates. Many local education authorities provide refresher courses which are often open also to graduates with no previous teaching experience.

Salaries.—The payment of full-time teachers in maintained schools is negotiated through a new Burnham Primary and Secondary Committee set up under the Remuneration of Teachers Act 1965. The committee has two sides, one (teachers' panel) representing teachers and the other (management panel) the Secretary of State for Education and Science and the local authorities, with an independent Chairman. Its agreed recommendations are transmitted to the Secretary of State who must give effect to them. If the committee is unable to agree on a new salary award the matter is referred to independent arbitration and the Secretary of State must give effect to the arbitrators' recommendations unless they are set aside by Parliament. The latest agreement involves a new structure based on five separate pay scales; and all teachers received an increase of 10 per cent. from April 1, 1971. This settlement involved an increase of about £63M. or 10·8 per cent. in the salary bill in the first year. There is a superannuation scheme administered by the Department of Education and Science.

FURTHER EDUCATION

Local Education Authorities are responsible, under the 1944 Education Act, for providing full-time and part-time courses of post-secondary education (other than university education) in their areas. There are ten Regional Advisory Councils which co-ordinate further education in their regions and nominate a majority of the members of the National Advisory Council on Education for Industry and Commerce which advises the Secretary of State for Education and Science on national educational policy relating to industry and commerce.

The 7,691 further education establishments (1969 enrolment: 3,099,263 students) other than the colleges of education, may at present be grouped in nine main categories of which all, except the last, are grant-aided:—

1. *National Colleges* (4 in 1969).—Established and financed jointly by the Department of Education and Science and industry to provide advanced technical studies for particular industries. 1,186 students in 1969.

2. *Polytechnics.*—Establishments developed within the further education system to complement the universities and colleges of education, and providing full-time, part-time, and sandwich courses at all levels of higher education (*see* p. 1051).

3. *Regional Colleges* (20)—Providing a substantial amount of advanced study particularly by means of full-time and sandwich courses for students from

several Local Education Authority areas. 65,037 students.

4. *Colleges of Art* (125).—102,097 students.

5. *Agricultural Colleges* (4).—Providing courses mostly of two years' duration. 1,405 students.

6. *Farm Institutes* (41).—Providing mainly non-advanced courses. 13,378 students.

7. *Other Major Establishments* (483).—Including "area" and "local" colleges: technical colleges, colleges of commerce, etc., which provide a substantial number of day courses. 1,505,824 students.

8. *Evening Institutes* (6,895) offering a wide range of courses, many of them recreational, for evening students, and often housed in premises used by day for other educational purposes. 1,352,552 students.

9. *Independent Establishments* which may apply to the Department of Education and Science for recognition as efficient; in 1969 there were 98 such recognized establishments with 16,708 students.

For Colleges of Education, *see* under "Teachers" above.

The number of students taking advanced courses (full-time, part-time, sandwich, or evening only) leading to recognized qualifications at grant-aided establishments was 197,526 (167,763 men and 29,763 women) in 1967. Of these 54,814 were on full-time courses, 28,072 were sandwich course students, 72,068 were taking part-time day courses and 42,572 were attending evening only classes. 31,800 of the total were working for a first degree (university or C.N.A.A. (*see* below)) and 1,296 for a higher degree. 645,272 students were released by their employers during working hours to take part-time day courses at grant-aided establishments. In February 1970 there were 49,884 full-time teachers serving in further education establishments and 7,112 in colleges of education; this compares with 33,802 and 3,856 five years earlier.

A number of the Industrial Training Boards (*see* pp. 535–6) set up following the Industrial Training Act of 1964 have made arrangements with technical colleges for help and in 1969–70 some 264 colleges were providing full-time integrated courses of combined education and training for trainees from industry. About 14,000 students followed such courses.

Polytechnics.—To achieve a greater concentration of the facilities for full-time higher education within the Further Education system, there are being designated as Polytechnics (*see* pp. 534–5 for list) some 30 major centres (some single colleges and others combinations of colleges) in which a wide range of full-time, sandwich and part-time courses can be developed and which can become "comprehensive academic communities" catering for students at all levels of higher education, and entirely or almost entirely for those of 18 years or more. They will have governing bodies with a large measure of autonomy and will be mainly teaching institutions though provision will be made for certain essential research. As part of the sector of higher education within the Further Education system they will complement the universities and colleges of education.

An important body with few, if any, parallels in other countries is the *Council for National Academic Awards* (C.N.A.A.) which awards degrees to students taking courses approved by it in non-university institutions. Following a recommendation of the Robbins Committee it was established by Royal Charter in 1964 as an autonomous body. Nearly 50 colleges in Great Britain conduct courses leading to its degrees: B.A., B.Sc., and the higher degrees of M.A. and M.Sc. (for postgraduate course work) and M.Phil. and Ph.D. (for research which

may be undertaken jointly in industry and college). Although these degrees are mainly in science and applied science subjects they can be awarded in any field and include at present degrees in economics, law, languages and business studies.

A *Further Education Information Service* is provided each summer by the local education authorities in cooperation with the polytechnics and other colleges offering full-time degree and higher national diploma courses, and the Department of Education and Science. Its purpose is to provide up-to-date information and advice about full-time degree and H.N.D. courses in the colleges for those who find themselves, late in the summer, without a place on a course. It operates during August and September each year. A list of local advisory officers is available from the D.E.S.

Adult Education. A wide variety of courses for the education and recreation of adults is provided by local education authorities, the Workers Educational Association, and other voluntary bodies, the extra-mural departments of universities and certain residential colleges. In November, 1969, the total number of students enrolled at evening institutes was 1,352,552; there were also many students engaged in day-time and evening non-vocational and recreational classes at other further educational establishments. In 1969–70 there were 254,258 students attending courses provided by the university extra-mural departments, the W.E.A. and other responsible bodies.

In February 1969 the Secretary of State for Education and Science set up a committee of inquiry, under the chairmanship of Sir Lionel Russell, to examine the purpose and structure of adult education.

The Youth Service.—Provides for the spare-time activities of young people. The Local Education Authorities co-operate with voluntary bodies in their areas and may maintain their own youth clubs. There are various national voluntary youth organizations which receive grants from the Department of Education and Science. By the end of 1970 there were 1,920 full-time youth leaders on the Department's register. In addition there are many thousands of part-time paid leaders and voluntary workers.

SCOTLAND

The educational system of Scotland has developed independently of that of England and has a number of distinctive features. The general supervision of the national system of education, except for the universities, is the responsibility of the Secretary of State for Scotland acting through the Scottish Education Department. The duty of providing education locally rests with the education authorities, *i.e.* the councils of the four cities (Aberdeen, Dundee, Edinburgh and Glasgow) and 31 county councils or joint county councils. Educational facilities of various kinds are also provided by the governing bodies of grant-aided schools, independent schools, "central institutions", and national voluntary organizations in the field of informal further education.

Schools in Scotland fall into three main categories, viz. *public schools*, which in Scotland means schools managed by education authorities; *grant-aided schools*, conducted by voluntary managers who receive grants direct from the department; and *independent schools* which receive no direct grant, but which are subject to inspection and registration. As at January 1970 there were 3,089 public schools with a roll of 948,485, 47 grant-aided schools with a

roll of 20,560 and 111 independent schools attended by 17,315 pupils.

Schooling normally starts at the age of 5, and the primary school course lasts for 7 years. Primary schools usually take both boys and girls. Pupils transfer from the primary course to secondary courses about the age of 12.

A large and increasing proportion of pupils at the secondary stage attend schools which offer a full range of non-certificate courses and of certificate courses leading to the Scottish Certificate of Education at Ordinary and Higher grade. There are also a number of other types of schools—those providing 3-year non-certificate courses, those providing 4-year courses leading to the Ordinary grade of the Scottish Certificate of Education; and senior secondary schools providing 6-year courses leading to the Higher grade of the Scottish Certificate of Education and post-certificate work.

The Scottish Certificate of Education examination is conducted by the S.C.E. Examination Board. Pupils may attempt as many of a wide range of subjects as they are capable of, on either the Ordinary grade which corresponds to the Ordinary level of the General Certificate of Education, or on the Higher grade which is normally taken a year earlier than the G.C.E. Advanced level and is therefore not of so high a standard. The Board grants a Certificate of Sixth Year Studies designed to give direction and purpose to sixth-year work by encouraging pupils who have completed their main subjects at Higher grade to study a particular subject in depth.

Further Education.—Facilities for further education are provided by 13 Central Institutions (grant-aided colleges administered by independent Boards of Governors) and by further education centres managed by education authorities. The Central Institutions provide mainly advanced courses in science and technology, commerce, art, music, domestic science, and other subjects, leading to their own diplomas, to professional qualifications or, in certain cases, to C.N.A.A. degrees.

The further education centres normally provide less advanced courses which are mainly part-time covering vocational and non-vocational subjects, but a few offer courses of degree level. Courses are offered in a wide variety of subjects but to make the most economic use of resources, provision of certain courses is made on a regional or even a national basis.

Teachers.—All teachers in permanent posts in public or grant-aided schools in Scotland are required to be registered with the General Teaching Council for Scotland and normally to hold a teaching qualification awarded by a Scottish college of education. There are ten of these colleges and six, including two Roman Catholic residential colleges for women, provide both one- and three-year courses leading to a teaching qualification (primary education) or a teaching qualification (secondary education). Four of these colleges, in conjunction with local universities, also provide four-year combined courses leading to the degree of B.Ed. and to a teaching qualification (primary and/or secondary education). One of the Roman Catholic colleges also admits men to the three-year non-graduate course for primary teachers. Of the remaining four colleges, one is a residential college of physical education for women and the other three train only non-graduate primary teachers.

The basic scales of teachers' salaries are non-graduate, graduate and honours graduate, with additional payment for posts of special responsibility.

NORTHERN IRELAND

The statutory system of education in Northern Ireland is broadly comparable to that in Great Britain. Under the 1947 Act (and its amendments to 1971) primary education is provided for children up to about 11½ years of age when they are transferred to secondary school. The main types of secondary school are: grammar and secondary (intermediate). Selection for secondary education is based on verbal reasoning tests at eleven-plus combined with teachers' assessments of performance in school subjects. Fees are charged at grammar schools but qualified pupils there receive scholarships from their local education authority.

In January 1971 there were 1,240 primary (including nursery) schools with 213,051 pupils and 7,356 full-time teachers; 171 secondary (intermediate) schools with 84,543 pupils and 4,415 full-time teachers; 13 technical intermediate schools with 484 pupils and 32 full-time teachers; 81 grammar schools with 51,642 pupils and 2,781 full-time teachers; 26 special schools with 2,259 pupils and 209 full-time teachers.

In 1969–70 there were 31 institutions of further education and over 150 centres with 1,256 full-time teachers and an enrolment of 11,748 full-time, 11,913 part-time day and 38,733 evening students. The training of teachers is carried out mainly in 8 colleges, and in the departments of education of the Queen's University of Belfast and the education centre of the New University of Ulster.

Expenditure on education in Northern Ireland during 1971–72 is estimated at £83,834,000, of which £67,194,000 (including university grants) will be provided by the Exchequer and £16,640,000 by rates.

UNIVERSITIES

There are 44 universities in the United Kingdom (*see* pp. 502–11). Of these, 33 are in England, eight in Scotland, two in Northern Ireland and one (a federal institution) in Wales. In addition, there is an " *Open University* " which provides courses leading to degrees by a combination of television, radio, correspondence, tutorials, short residential courses and local audio-visual centres (*see* p. 510). Its Vice-Chancellor is Dr. W. L. M. Perry. It is grant-aided directly by the Department of Education and Science and does not come within the University Grants Committee system.

In 1969–70 there were 226,372 full-time students enrolled at universities in the United Kingdom; of these, 63,927 were women, 39,852 were postgraduates (including 8,760 women). The number of new undergraduate entrants (full-time) in 1969–70 was 64,213; the corresponding figures for 1958–59 and 1965–66 were 29,054 and 52,446. The full-time total of 226,372 in 1969–70 compares with just over 50,000 in 1938–39. In 1968–69, 46,001 first degrees (including honours degrees) and 10,414 higher degrees were awarded by universities. In 1969–70 there were 32,935 full-time teaching and research staff in U.K. universities; 3,374 of them were professors, 5,812 readers or senior lecturers, 21,707 lecturers, or assistant lecturers.

Students applying for admission to a first degree course at a university do so through the Universities Central Council on Admissions (U.C.C.A.) which was set up by the universities in 1961 on the initiative of the Committee of Vice-Chancellors and Principals. All universities now participate fully in the U.C.C.A. scheme except Aberdeen, Dundee and Glasgow, which receive direct applications from candidates resident in Scotland and

from those United Kingdom candidates outside Scotland who are not also applying to other universities within the scheme.

The requirements for entry to first degree courses may vary from one university to another but the universities publish co-operatively an annual Compendium which describes these requirements in detail.

Students who are normally resident in Britain, have certain minimum qualifications and have been admitted to a university in the United Kingdom are entitled to an award from public funds; the amount varies according to the financial circumstances of the students and their parents.

In 1968–69 the total income of universities in the U.K. was £240,815,054 of which 2 per cent. came from endowments and donations, 1 per cent. from grants from local education authorities, 71 per cent. from exchequer grants, 7 per cent. from students' fees, 11 per cent. from payments for research, and 8 per cent. from other sources. Non-recurrent grants for capital expenditure paid by the Exchequer to universities in Great Britain totalled £71,995,557 in 1968–69.

The University Grants Committee advises the Secretary of State for Education and Science on university matters (*see* p. 435). The Comptroller and Auditor General has access to the books and records of the U.G.C. and of the universities.

SCHOOLS COUNCIL FOR CURRICULUM AND EXAMINATIONS
160 Great Portland Street, W.1.

Established in 1964, the Schools Council is an independent body representing all sections of the education service in England and Wales—with a majority of teacher members on its main committees. It undertakes research and development in the curriculum and keeps under review teaching methods and examinations in schools, including aspects of school organization in so far as they affect the curriculum.

The Schools Council is jointly financed by the Department of Education and Science and local education authorities.

Chairman, Dame Muriel Stewart, D.B.E.

Secretaries, G. F. Cockerill; G. W. Cooksey; R. Sibson (*joint*).

STOCK EXCHANGES IN THE UNITED KINGDOM

Notes on the London Stock Exchange are to be found on pp. 648 and 1110.

Other stock exchanges serve most of the major centres of population outside London and are associated in the Council of Associated Stock Exchanges founded in 1890. Individual stock exchanges joined to form regional stock exchanges starting in 1964 when the Scottish Stock Exchange was established. The Northern Stock Exchange was formed in August, 1965, and the Midlands and Western Stock Exchange in October, 1966. Membership of the Associated Stock Exchanges totals about 900. About 1,100 securities are quoted exclusively on these exchanges, besides a very large number of securities which are also quoted elsewhere.

MIDLANDS AND WESTERN STOCK EXCHANGE, Margaret Street, Birmingham 3 (includes the Exchanges of Birmingham, Bristol, Cardiff, Nottingham and Swansea).—*Secretary,* H. L. Rudge.

NORTHERN STOCK EXCHANGE, 4 Norfolk Street, Manchester (includes the Exchanges of Huddersfield, Leeds, Liverpool, Manchester, Newcastle upon Tyne, Oldham and Sheffield, and the Northern Counties Brokers Association).—*Secretary,* A. L. Owen, O.B.E., Exchange Street East, Liverpool.

SCOTTISH STOCK EXCHANGE, P.O. Box 141, 227 Ingram Street, Glasgow, C.1 (includes the Exchanges of Aberdeen, Dundee, Edinburgh and Glasgow, and the Scottish Country Brokers Association, Stirling).—*Secretary,* M. M. Sloan (*joint*). *C.H.M.N. G.M. MILLER DRUMMOND*

BELFAST STOCK EXCHANGE, Northern Bank House, 10 High Street, Belfast, N. Ireland.—*Secretary,* E. S. Mullan.

(The Irish Stock Exchange, Dublin, including the Exchanges of Dublin and Cork, is also a member of the Council of Associated Stock Exchanges). *Secretary,* M. O'Shea.

ASE stockbrokers buy and sell shares for members of the public. This is done for individual investors, for their advisers such as bank managers, solicitors and accountants, and for investing institu-

tions like insurance companies, pension funds, unit trusts and merchant banks. For this the stockbroker is paid a fixed scale of commission based on the value of the securities. In addition to this service, ASE brokers advise their clients, according to their particular circumstances and needs, on how to invest their money to greatest advantage. In addition, they will undertake to review periodically the portfolios of their clients. Often this service is backed up by a regular newsletter, keeping the investors up-to-date with economic developments and current recommendations.

The Associated Stock Exchanges provide facilities for raising capital for industry. Any broker will give advice on how a company can finance its growth by getting a quotation for its shares on one of the Associated Exchanges. For companies already quoted, other methods are possible—such as rights issues and debenture or loan stocks—for obtaining additional funds. Brokers' advice is also available to industrialists on matters such as mergers and acquisitions.

The large majority of companies are incorporated under the Companies' Acts, which contain stringent regulations for their management and control. They are limited liability companies, which means that if you are a shareholder in such a company you cannot be called upon to pay any part of its debt or liabilities if it gets into difficulties, unless, in quite exceptional cases, you are a holder of partly-paid shares, in which event your liability is limited to the amount required to make the shares fully paid. The Associated Stock Exchanges serve investors, whether inexperienced or expert, big or small, and the authorities of the member stock exchanges insist on compliance with stringent regulations to ensure that the public are fully informed of the constitution and record of every company whose securities are admitted to the market.

Furthermore, members of Associated Stock Exchanges contribute to the Compensation Fund maintained by the Federation of Stock Exchanges (representing all stock exchanges in Great Britain and Ireland).

THE NOBEL PRIZES

The Nobel Prizes are awarded each year from the income of a trust fund established by the Swedish scientist Alfred Nobel, the inventor of dynamite, who died on December 10, 1896, leaving a fortune of £1,750,000. They are awarded to those who have contributed most to the common good in the domain of (a) Physics; (b) Chemistry; (c) Physiology or Medicine; (d) Literature; (e) Peace. The first awards were made in 1901 on the fifth anniversary of Nobel's death. The awarding authorities are the Swedish Academy of Sciences—(a) Physics; (b) Chemistry; the Royal Caroline Institute, Stockholm—(c) Physiology or Medicine; the Swedish Academy—(d) Literature; a committee of five persons elected by the Norwegian Storting—(e) Peace. The Trust is administered by the Board of Directors of the Nobel Foundation, Stockholm. The Board consists of five members and three deputy members. The Swedish Government appoints a chairman and a deputy chairman, the remaining members being appointed by the awarding authorities. 405 awards had been made up to December 10, 1970.

The nationality of prizewinners is indicated as follows: (a) Great Britain; (b) U.S.A.; (c) France; (d) Sweden; (e) Belgium; (f) U.S.S.R.; (g) Germany; (h) Netherlands; (i) Switzerland; (k) Denmark; (l) Norway; (m) Spain; (n) Poland; (o) Austria; (p) Italy; (q) India; (r) Hungary; (s) Finland; (t) Canada; (u) Chile; (v) Argentina; (w) Japan; (x) Portugal; (y) Irish Free State; (z) Republic of Ireland; (aa) South Africa; (bb) Iceland; (cc) China; (dd) Czechoslovakia; (ee) Australia; (ff) Yugoslavia; (gg) Greece; (hh) Israel; (ii) Guatemala. The distribution by nationalities is shown at foot of table.

For prize winners for the years 1901–1958, *see* earlier editions of WHITAKER'S ALMANACK.

Year	(a) PHYSICS	(b) CHEMISTRY	(c) PHYSIOLOGY OR MEDICINE	(d) LITERATURE	(e) PEACE
1959	E. Segrè (b) O. Chamberlain (b)	J. Heyrovský (dd)	S. Ochoa (b) A. Kornberg (b)	S. Quasimodo (p)	P. J. Noel-Baker (a)
1960	D. A. Glaser (b)	W. F. Libby (b)	Sir Macfarlane Burnet (ee) P. B. Medawar (a)	St. J. Perse (c)	A. Luthuli (aa)
1961	R. Hofstadter (b) R. Mössbauer (g)	M. Calvin (b)	G. von Békésy (b)	I. Andric (ff)	D. Hammarskjöld (d)
1962	L. D. Landau (f)	M. F. Perutz (a) J. C. Kendrew (a)	F. H. C. Crick (a) J. D. Watson (b) M. H. F. Wilkins (a)	J. Steinbeck (b)	L. Pauling (b)
1963	E. P. Wigner (b) Maria Goeppert-Mayer (b) J. H. D. Jensen (g)	K. Ziegler (g) G. Natta (p)	Sir John Eccles (ee) A. L. Hodgkin (a) A. F. Huxley (a)	G. Seferis (gg)	Int. Ctee. of Red Cross (i) League of Red Cross Socs. (i)
1964	C. H. Townes (b) N. G. Basov (f) A. M. Prochorov (f)	Dorothy Crowfoot Hodgkin (a)	K. Bloch (b) F. Lynen (g)	J. P. Sartre (c)	Rev. M. L. King, Jr. (b)
1965	S. I. Tomonaga (w) J. Schwinger (b) R. P. Feynman (b)	R. B. Woodward (b)	A. Lwoff (c) F. Jacob (c) J. Monod (c)	M. Sjolochov (f)	U.N. Children's Fund
1966	A. Kastler (c)	R. S. Mulliken (b)	P. Rous (b) C. B. Huggins (b)	S. Y. Agnon (hh) N. Sachs (g)	No award
1967	Prof. H. A. Bethe (b)	Prof. M. Eigen (g) Prof. G. Porter (a) Prof. R. Norrish (a)	Prof. R. Granit (d) Prof. H. K. Hartline (b) Prof. G. Wald (b)	M. A. Asturias (ii)	No award
1968	Prof. L. W. Alvarez (b)	Prof. L. Onsager (b)	R. W. Holley (b) H. G. Khorana (b) M. W. Nirenberg (b)	Y. Kawabata (w)	R. Cassin (c)
1969	M. Gell-Mann (b)	D. H. Barton (a) O. Hassel (l)	M. Delbrück (b) A. D. Hershey (b) S. E. Luria (b)	S. Beckett (z)	International Labour Organization
1970	H. Alfven (d) L. Néel (c)	L. F. Leloir (v)	Sir Bernard Katz (a) U. von Euler (d) J. Axelrod (b)	A. Solzhenitsyn (f)	N. E. Borlaug (b)

The awards have been distributed as follows: PHYSICS (90).—*U.S.A.*, 28; *Gt. Britain*, 15; *Germany*, 14; *France*, 9; *U.S.S.R.*, 6; *Netherlands*, 5; *Austria*, 3; *China*, 2; *Italy*, 2; *Japan*, 2; *Sweden*, 3; *Denmark*, 1; *India*, 1; *Ireland*, 1.

CHEMISTRY (79).—*Germany*, 22; *Gt. Britain*, 18; *U.S.A.*, 16; *France*, 6; *Sweden*, 4; *Switzerland*, 3; *Netherlands*, 2; *Austria*, 1; *Czechoslovakia*, 1; *Finland*, 1; *Hungary*, 1; *Italy*, 1; *Norway*, 1; *U.S.S.R.*, 1; *Argentina*, 1.

PHYSIOLOGY OR MEDICINE (104).—*U.S.A.*, 39; *Gt. Britain*, 16; *Germany*, 10; *France*, 6; *Denmark*, 4; *Sweden*, 4; *Switzerland*, 4; *Austria*, 3; *Australia*, 2; *Belgium*, 2; *Canada*, 2; *Hungary*, 2; *Italy*, 2; *Netherlands*, 2; *U.S.S.R.*, 2; *Argentina*, 1; *Portugal*, 1; *South Africa*, 1; *Spain*, 1.

LITERATURE (66).—*France*, 11; *Germany*, 6; *Gt. Britain*, 6; *U.S.A.*, 6; *Italy*, 4; *Sweden*, 4; *U.S.S.R.*, 4; *Denmark*, 3; *Norway*, 3; *Spain*, 3; *Ireland*, 2; *Poland*, 2; *Switzerland*, 2; *Belgium*, 1; *Chile*, 1; *Finland*, 1; *Greece*, 1; *Guatemala*, 1; *Iceland*, 1; *India*, 1; *Israel*, 1; *Japan*, 1; *Yugoslavia*, 1.

PEACE (64).—*U.S.A.*, 15; *Institutions*, 10; *France*, 9; *Gt. Britain*, 7; *Sweden*, 4; *Belgium*, 3; *Germany*, 3; *Switzerland*, 3; *Austria*, 2; *Norway*, 2; *Argentina*, 1; *Canada*, 1; *Denmark*, 1; *Italy*, 1; *Netherlands*, 1; *South Africa*, 1.

BRITISH ARCHITECTURE OF 1970–71

TOWN HALL AND CIVIC CENTRE, SUNDERLAND

The real interest of this new group of buildings which has had the additional satisfaction of receiving one of the year's R.I.B.A. Design Awards, lies in the fact that it suggests a new interpretation of local government which seems basically much closer to the opinions held by most Englishmen of this generation. The architectural expression of this concept has been admirably captured by Sir Basil Spence, Bonnington and Collins in their design, being determined not by the desire to lend prestige to the Council but rather to make the building convenient and attractive to the ordinary citizen. This is expressed in the plan by the openness and accessibility of the building, its modest presence in the landscape and balanced use of materials contrasting sharply with the assertiveness of many large schemes built over the last decade or so.

Built at a cost of over £3,000,000, the building occupies a dominating 15 acres site on high sloping ground to the south of Sunderland's commercial centre from which it is separated by an extensive railway cutting. Formerly waste land, the site faces towards the town's extensive dockland area to the west and solid Victorian residental terraces to the south sheltered by a belt of trees. To the east is Mowbray Park separated from the site by a sunken highway but now linked to the Centre by a new footbridge.

The brief called for accommodation to house eighteen council departments each with easy ground floor access preferably from separate entrances, a civic suite and Council Chamber, an administration centre where about 1,000 people could work, the usual Committee rooms and a small Mayoral suite with extensive car parking and service facilities for staff and visitors.

The whole complex is based on a triangular grid in which the design is expressed as extensions of a hexagonal form permitting the easy addition of any future accommodation that may be required. The two major hexagons, built round hollow courtyards form an interconnected figure of eight containing the local authority departments and the minor Council Chambers, linked to a third smaller but solid hexagon containing the civic suite and Council Chamber. One continuous podium provides this geometrical building form with a unifying base which also houses a small car park and extends to the north as a terrace with the main four storey car park beneath.

Structurally, the building stands on a major grid of 20 ft. equilateral triangles with a subsidiary division into further 5 ft equilateral triangles, supporting floor edge mullions from their apexes. The width of the office building varies according to the pattern of accommodation it contains, the structure following this form changing from two major and two minor triangles at the widest points to the two minor triangles at the narrowest. Floors are flat concrete slabs edge supported on concrete mullions from the minor grid pattern. Pre-cast concrete cladding panels faced with cast in brick tiles rest on the edge of the slab, bolted to the mullions. These panels also house the services at their head and lighting fittings and Venetian blind boxes at their base. The irregular hexagonal form of the Council chamber is constructed of reinforced concrete and load bearing brickwork walls supporting the intermediate floors and a three dimensional tied arched roof truss system in steel, resting on rubber bearings.

Externally, finishes comprise brown brindled engineering bricks with matching tiles for walls, paving and plinth, offsetting the copper clad roof to the Council Chamber and louvres of the main plant roof situated on top of the administration block. Inside the same brown brick tiles are used for hall floors and occasionally for walls and in contrast a light grey wall panelling lines the main corridors throughout the office floors which are carpeted in an orange coloured nylon felt.

In spite of its size, the scale of the centre remains human, parts only of the fairly low buildings being revealed at one time. The hexagonal theme combines the informal and at times almost domestic groups of buildings into an understandable whole resulting in a most satisfying and distinguished contribution to the urban scene.

LLWYCOED CREMATORIUM, WALES

Much of the value of the R.I.B.A. Awards system lies in its balanced recognition that all types of building from rare, exotic multi-million commissions to small, one-off houses, are potential winners. High standards of architectural and environmental design are the only common factors forming a bond between selected buildings which this year ranged from the Civic Centre in Sunderland and Antrim County Hall to offices for the Dorset Water Board and a Crematorium in Wales.

This Crematorium which fits so admirably into the Welsh surroundings will serve the Aberdare and Merthyr Tydfil areas at Llwycoed, high up on the boundary of Brecon National Park overlooking one of the great mining districts of South Wales.

The architects, H. M. R. Burgess and Partners, were asked to provide buildings which would incorporate two chapels, large and small, with a plan arrangement which would permit their concurrent use without confusion. The resulting design provided for four main blocks with hipped single-pitch roofs which are arranged so that their ridge lines converge over the centre of the complex. In this way, the overall composition of the building, while made up of separate units, retains an overall unity symbolized by the pyramid form. No attempt was made by the architects to adopt an " ecclesiastical " form and strong reliance was placed on traditional local materials such as slate, timber and stonework. Within the complex are the two chapels, one seating 120 and the other 50, a small chapel of remembrance, a wreath court, waiting rooms and office accommodation. The whole building fits just as naturally into the landscape as the small farmhouses which are scattered round the slopes of this sweeping countryside. From its approach by a gently curving lane, the crematorium produces a continually changing profile; the apex of what from the main road appears as a complete pyramid of slate being revealed as a group of disconnected triangular segments of monopitched roofs supported off white painted rendered walls.

Two covered courtyards cut deep into the structure between the main elements of the building give access to the two chapels. Both are simply furnished, square on plan; lofty spaces naturally lit only by windows located high in the apex of their triangulated roof structures. The use of traditional materials and well tried details are a refreshing change from the many mundane structures of concrete, steel and glass to be found elsewhere and the architects are to be congratulated in achieving what must surely be regarded as a satisfying and lasting contribution to the Welsh landscape.

YORKSHIRE POST NEWSPAPERS LIMITED—LEEDS

Accommodating in one building complex all the activities associated with the production of a major provincial newspaper, the Leeds headquarters of the *Yorkshire Post* has gained this year's R.I.B.A. Award for the best building in the Yorkshire Region.

The old *Yorkshire Post* offices in Wellington Street were built in 1887 to the design of Chorley and Cannon, when the proprietors were consolidating their position in the centre of the city. Developments in printing, production and distribution dictated a move towards a more commanding site in the same area, where the needs for a functional building of maximum flexibility to take advantage of the latest developments in production techniques, could best be met.

The John Madin Design Group, who as architects for the *Birmingham Post and Mail* offices in 1965, were conversant with the requirements of modern newspaper production, began their designs for the new building in 1966. Work was put in hand some two years later and completed, ready for operational occupation in September, 1970.

The 4·6 acre site, bounded on the south by the River Aire, was formerly occupied by Bean Ing Mills, designed by Benjamin Gott at the end of the eighteenth century as the first woollen factory in the West Riding. Situated at the intersection of Wellington Street and the future ring road, the massing and detailed design of the building were conceived with high regard to the future road pattern which provides immediate connection to major urban and regional roads, and serves to promote the speedy distribution of newspapers.

News is one of the world's most perishable products; every second it loses some of its value and is always produced in a race against time. Meticulous thought was given to the planning of the new building to ensure that every part of the process was most advantageously located so that every second is fully used. Whereas the *Birmingham Post and Mail* had a predominantly vertical production flow, the *Yorkshire Post* premises occupy a more generous site where a horizontal production flow could be used. Here it was possible to plan all production departments at first floor level which is almost unique in newspaper production and can put news into print within half an hour. From the moment the copy and advertisements arrive in the composing room until bundles of newspapers pass down a shute to the vans below, the whole operation takes place on one floor.

The creation of large open planned areas was a policy decision, especially so in the editorial hall where height has been used to give a deliberate monumental quality. The roof form and combination of natural and artificial lighting, which has been varied in different parts of the building, have also been very closely and carefully considered to produce an editorial hall of distinction.

The press hall, with a height of almost 34 ft and a clear span of 108 ft., houses the biggest hybrid newspaper printing complex of this kind in the world. It has a capacity to produce 300,000 forty-eight page newspapers in a little over two hours with pages in full and spot colour, with the dual advantage of being able to print in both the traditional letterpress and in the modern web offset techniques. The highly automated publishing department deals with the flood of newspapers pouring from the press lines and in this huge room papers are stacked, bundled and tied and passed down chutes to the waiting fleet of vans in the despatch area.

Piled foundations of an average depth of 35 ft.

are used to carry the structure of the building which is all of reinforced concrete except the press hall. The column grid of the reinforced concrete part of the building was determined by the machinery layout at first floor level. The large uninterrupted areas required in the public space and editorial hall are obtained by supporting these elements on central cruciform columns with twin columns around the periphery. Structural steel work is used for the press hall because of the long clear spans required and also because this area was required for press erection well before the completion of the contract as a whole. Castellated beams are used for the roof and are supported on steel stanchions encased in concrete.

With the exception of the press hall and publishing blocks, the exterior of the building is faced with precast concrete panels of an exposed Dorset shingle aggregate finish chosen for its weathering properties and its warm colour. The press hall walls are clad externally with a sandwich construction with demountable plastic steel sheets in one length from cill to coping to permit ease of future expansion. Simple finishes are used internally with materials such as the exposed aggregate cladding panels and blue brick paviors being carried through from external to internal areas. Glazing to the ground floor areas, particularly around the public space where exhibitions will be held has been designed to allow uninterrupted reflections on the exterior face. All metal surfaces and ironmongery have a bronze finish and bronze doors have been fitted in more important areas with ash veneers and frames elsewhere.

From the clients' point of view, the architects appear to have found an extremely successful solution to a very complex planning problem. As an Award winner, the R.I.B.A. jury considered that the building will be of immense value in demonstrating publicly the advantages of the closest possible client/architect relationship in the commercial and industrial field.

ALEXANDER BARRACKS—PIRBRIGHT

Winner of the 1971 R.I.B.A. Award for the South Eastern Region, the new guards depot at Pirbright is one of a large number of projects in the War Department's barracks rebuilding programme stemming from the early sixties. In 1963, this department—together with the works organizations of the other services—was merged with the Ministry of Works to become part of the Ministry of Public Building and Works and a private firm of architectural consultants—the Architects' Co-Partnership Incorporated—was briefed to provide a new training establishment for the Household Division of the Guards.

Located at Pirbright in about 50 acres of Surrey heathland, the almost flat site, some outlying areas of which are open and exposed to northerly winds, is well wooded. To the north, scrub oak, pine and birch cover a wide belt of land, much of it used for firing ranges and military training, while to the south, rough woodland conceals a much neglected section of the long since disused Basingstoke canal. The layout of the new buildings has been arranged as far as possible to enable these existing woodland belts to form natural barriers, the conservation of which is reinforced by the new buildings.

The function of the depot is to train recruits for the guards regiments and musicians for guards bands, operate a junior guardsmen unit and provide specialist training courses in drill for senior N.C.O.'s throughout the Army and Commonwealth forces. The new buildings, replacing old hutted accommodation, provide living, training, working and dining facilities for about 1,500 men, a strict order

of military tradition making it essential that separated living accommodation be provided for the varying levels of seniority. The depot provides for the training of boy soldiers as well as for more experienced troops and includes special drill courses for the Ministry of Defence, for which a separate parade ground and mess was required.

The layout of the depot is closely planned as a small community with the central facilities grouped around a small pedestrian square. The junior ranks club for men and visitors, the C. of E. church, swimming pool and squash court, rank and file mess, education and hobbies centre and hairdresser's shop, all converge to this area with streets, seats and paving. Traffic is excluded (except in emergencies) and all servicing is by a ring road system giving access to car parking areas. The parade grounds forming the main working areas for training, which inevitably are large, barren and a considerable source of noise, have been purposely sited as far away from the centre as possible.

Rejecting system building as unsuitable, the architects decided that the buildings should be of load bearing brick construction, using laminated timber beams and steel trusses where the spans are large and in many buildings, leaving the beams exposed. Elevations are simply treated with a dark brown facing brick; some cedar cladding is used at eaves level and above, and windows too are in timber frames.

Standardized barrack blocks were considered unsuitable for recruits and junior guardsmen in training; instead special rooms were provided, representing the biggest departure from tradition and accommodating between 20 and 25 men, with a clear central space in which the recruits could gather at any time and at short notice for group activity. All barrack rooms are in two-storey blocks, most arranged in pairs sharing a staircase and sitting room. Separate rooms are provided for one N.C.O. and one trained man and each unit is equipped with its own ablutions and cleaning accommodation. Corporals and guardsmen are housed in attached four-storey blocks, each of the three upper floors containing four four-man rooms and two corporal's rooms with the administration rooms on the ground floor.

A strong consistency in design and detailing is evident throughout, but it is probably the extremely successful hard and soft landscaping in contrast to the traditional attitude, which contributes so much to the success of this modern guards barracks complex.

PIMLICO MUSIC SCHOOL

Every Saturday in term time, some 120 of the most talented young instrumentalists from London's schools attend all day at Pimlico school for concentrated individual tuition from a corps of 60 top rank professional musicians. The establishment of a special music school has been achieved to provide education specially designed for London's most promising young musicians. Until recently, such special education has been available only at the Yehudi Menuhin School at Stoke D'Abernon and at the Central Tutorial School for Young Musicians. Now, parents of London children will be able to apply for places on the new Pimlico course.

Designed to accommodate 1,725 boys and girls between eleven and eighteen years of age, the new Pimlico school draws upon the Westminster and Chelsea catchment areas. The area was intensively developed in the middle nineteenth century, giving rise on the one hand to the narrow oblong of grass and mature plane trees flanked by tall stuccoed Victorian housing forming St. George's Square, with the matching period domesticity of

Lupus Street and Claverton Street, to the enormous, depressing seven storey block of super flats in Chichester Street, built in the 1930's of red brick with Portland stone dressings. This is the environment within which the school is situated on a site area of only 4½ acres, at a level of between 9 and 10 ft. below that of the surrounding roads.

The bulk of the school, which has in total a superficial area of some 135,000 sq. ft., is accommodated in one four storey building which divides the site longitudinally into two new open spaces extending St. George's Square at right angles to its main axis; both are to be planted with grass and trees to strengthen the link with the Square. The facetted glass form of the building is complementary to the older adjoining buildings and is sufficiently complex to counterbalance their greater bulk. The modelling is continued over the adjoining parts of the site by paving and grass at various levels for walking and sitting.

Circulation areas are scaled to the anticipated volume of traffic. The ground floor concourse, the main horizontal circulation area, has entry for the children from St. George's Square and Claverton Street at the ends. Wide flights of stairs drop from this to the lower ground floor and rise to the first floor gallery round the upper part of the concourse. From this level, smaller stairs ascend to groups of teaching rooms on the second floor. Entry from Lupus Street to the first floor separates the public, administrative staff and sixth form, from the mass movement of children below. All major circulation spaces have a positive character and are scaled to the numbers using them. The ground floor concourse, in particular, can be used in parts for exhibitions and displays, and seats down the sides will encourage leisure use during bad weather.

Social activities and welfare of the pupils will be organized on a yearly basis. Each year group will be in the charge of a head of year and a year tutor who will remain with the group until its members have completed their fifth year in the school. (The sixth form will be divided into tutor groups.) The year rooms are for morning assembly, for dining and for use during break and after school hours. Food from the central kitchen at lower ground level will be transported by lift to the upper floors and distributed from mobile hot cabinets placed for the duration of the meal in each year-room.

For flexibility in drama and music production the assembly hall is designed with a sunk arena floor. A curtain proscenium is formed with a stage constructed of portable rostra units over the stepping when used as a conventional theatre. Stage lighting will be hung from the underside of the crossed portal frame structure in a variety of positions. Adjoining rooms can be used as green rooms.

Sixth form accommodation, grouped round the upper part of the library, is an entity distinct from the rest of the school and is in keeping with the older pupils' status as young adults. On the floor below, the library is at the centre of the building within easy reach of all subject rooms. Its position and shape with top and side lighting should make it attractive and ensure the fullest use of its facilities.

The swimming pool has a pool size of 66 ft × 24 ft. × 5 ft 6 in. deep; changing accommodation for swimmers is provided separately from that for the two gymnasia. The service entrance is from Lupus Street viâ a ramped service road to the service yard/car park at lower ground floor. For easy supervision, the schoolkeeper's single storey house with its walled patio garden is adjacent.

The structure including all external walling is of *in situ* reinforced concrete using lightweight aggre-

gate. External surfaces generally are ribbed either horizontally or vertically, depending on position or cast against a sawn board shutter. Internal faces, including soffits to floor slabs, are smooth finished, decorated directly with textured plastic paint.

The glazing form has been developed to give adequate lighting in the many deep rooms. Constructed of aluminium patent glazing, the roof is double glazed with expanded PVC sheet in the interspace; sidewall glazing is single with mild steel opening lights and horizontal and vertical fabric blinds have been provided to control sunlight.

LONDON GRADUATE SCHOOL OF BUSINESS STUDIES

Designed by B. & N. Westwood, Piet & Partners under the cost control of the University Grants Committee, the London Graduate School of Business Studies is in Regents Park. The site consisted of some two hectares of land with a Nash terrace of 26 houses fronting on to the park, a central mews and a row of houses facing Park Road at the rear. The houses were empty, some dilapidated, but the floor area matched the client's requirements for the first phase of the development and vacant possession of the remainder of the site could gradually be obtained to carry out the second phase.

An essential part was the preservation of the original Nash façade, which now fronts the new building. The land owners, in the belief that the façade was in a poor state, had earlier proposed that it should be rebuilt as a replica. The architects, however, managed to convince them that it was sound and should be saved from demolition.

Holding up this long wall, while demolition work was continued behind it, was no easy problem and eventually the consultant engineers designed tubular steel raking shores, anchored to massive blocks of concrete. A separate steel and concrete framed structure was then erected behind the façade on concrete piled foundations, tie rods, from a flexible link between the old and the new, allowing some settlement of the new block to occur without endangering the stability of the Nash structure.

Along the top of the wall a section of brickwork damaged as a result of leaking roofs and gutters has been removed. New lintels and balconies installed in concrete have given added strength and about 50 of the columns were pressure grouted to give greater structural stability. Ten of the original octagonal cupolas had to be demolished during the course of the work, happily to be replaced with light weight replicas of glassfibre construction, cream in colour, to match the stucco.

The length of the building, according to the architects, presented the biggest problem in planning the accommodation, but an early decision by the clients simplified the circulation. The school caters for two distinct types of student—the younger post-graduate on a two year course and the older manager or director on a six week course. The differences in curriculum and age persuaded the clients to keep each group independent with its own common and dining room facilities, both sharing the same lecture rooms, library and so on. This led to the teaching space being planned centrally in the terrace with two groups of 100 study bedrooms, occupying a curved wing at each end. The end houses were converted (with the exception of the third floor) into the principal's house and the staff house.

This sub-division permitted the architects to consider the structural problems in relation to the specific problems of each unit. The two end

houses have been treated as conversions because of the need to preserve all three elevations. The repetitive and cellular character of the curved wing study bedroom units made possible the structural use of short span beams and columns. In the teaching spaces, however, the great variety of room sizes and the need for flexibility of planning dictated long span beams to give an uninterrupted floor area. Access from both wings to the teaching unit is made externally along a cloister which stretches the length of the new teaching block façade, echoing Nash's arcade on the park elevation.

REGIONAL H.Q. FOR THE NATIONAL WESTMINSTER BANK—MANCHESTER

The original version of the design for this building which this year received the R.I.B.A. Award for the North West Region, was the winning entry in a limited competition held in 1963. At that time, the site was smaller and more constricted, bounded by four roads and by close set neighbours.

The architects, Casson Conder and Partners, felt that the Bank was best served by a building having relatively few levels—each of extensive area, rather than by a taller building split into many levels of small area. It was this thinking, coupled with the tightness of the site, that led to the basic form of the building which was an almost exact model of the "envelope" set up by the light angles relevant to the original site. The splays in both plan and section, the dumb-bell shape, and the off-centre spine were all derived from these considerations and result in a building that is sensed as a carved monolith rather than as an assembly of constructed parts. The maximum floor area is provided within the smallest height—sculpted, tight skinned, totally sealed and air-conditioned.

Shortly after the design was accepted, however, the owners and architects for both this and the adjoining site to the east agreed with the local authority to the closure of Pall Mall—the original street separating the two buildings—so that a piazza could be formed between them and the Bank building could be moved eastwards to widen Cheapside. In the event, therefore, the light angles were less constricting and at this later stage the building was enlarged in both height and girth.

Originally designed as the headquarters of the District Bank, the building is now the North Regional Headquarters of the National Westminster Bank and serves not only as an administrative headquarters for the region but as a major branch bank. Facilities include a 100 ft. counter together with interview rooms and special lift service to the safe deposit area. The walls are deeply undercut at ground floor level, from low entrances through which the public enters the white air-conditioned hall that extends upward through three levels.

The general offices of the regional headquarters are arranged on the first to fifth floors inclusive, the sixth floor housing the senior executive offices, the board room and dining rooms for the directors and senior staff. Above that again, in the sloping blank brow of the building, are further plant rooms and condenser chambers, the whole structure being founded on a 50 ft. deep basement developed on four main levels to house strong-rooms, plantrooms and car parking together with staff restaurants and recreation rooms.

The external walls are of monolithic reinforced concrete which together with the vertical service and lift shafts (and the relatively few columns) support all the loads of the building. The floors are generally of trough-sectioned reinforced concrete cast *in situ* and the whole building is fully air-conditioned, the air outlets in the general office

areas being in linear form combined with the continuous light fittings.

In their summing up, the R.I.B.A. Award Jury commended the appropriate and excellent use of textured granite cladding material and bronze metal used on the outside of the building, commenting that this combination, both physically and aesthetically, could hardly fail to endure as a work of fine architecture. Whatever may be said about the qualities to be seen outside the building, they are surpassed by what is found inside it. The combination of mature and confident detailing and an impeccable sense of space, together with almost perfect workmanship and co-ordination of services, extends throughout all twelve levels of the structure.

GARDNER CENTRE FOR THE ARTS— SUSSEX UNIVERSITY

Recently completed as part of the University of Sussex complex, the Arts Centre caters for the unusual amalgam of visual and aural art expressions. Facilities are provided for student practice of the arts, together with a fellowship programme of artists in residence, professionals working in the whole range of artistic disciplines and establishing, without any formal duties, a link between the academic and artistic worlds. From the very beginning, it has been intended as a centre not just for the University of Sussex but for the entire region.

With collaboration and exchange on a national and international level, it is hoped that the centre will embrace all forms of exhibition, plays and concerts, as well as experimental developments in the arts. In addition to all activities by students and artists in residence, the centre will have its own company and is planning to work as a fully professional theatre during the summer months.

The architects, Sir Basil Spence, Bonnington and Collins, were briefed in 1965 to provide accommodation comprising an experimental theatre workshop with capacity for 500 seats, with ancillary dressing rooms, greenroom and workshop. The theatre workshop has one main and two subsidiary stages and the seating has been designed as a series of movable platforms on hydraulic jacks and wheels to allow all varieties of seating layout from proscenium productions to theatre in the round. The foyer with its bar and cloakrooms leads into an art gallery, and to the subsidiary brick cylinders which surround the main theatre, containing studios for painting, sculpture and music practice as well as administrative offices for the centre.

An extensive investigation was made by the architects and theatre consultant into theatre planning before the unusual shape of the building was conceived. The three traditional theatre forms, proscenium stage, theatre in the round and forestage theatre were examined and discarded, yet all three forms and variations of these themes had certain interesting advantages. It was finally decided that the new centre must achieve a degree of flexibility not found before so that it could be all things or nearly everything to all artistic directors.

It was considered that the theatre was a composition of all the arts; of music and of painting, of sculpture and of poetry and so on, all happening more or less together. For this reason, the building comprises a related group of enclosures, comprising five circular pavilions grouped around a large and also circular core. These pavilions vary in height from one to three storeys, giving rise to an extremely interesting geometrical massing of interlocking circular shapes. The shape has also brought about some unconventional window detailing which makes an important contribution to the design as a whole. Windows do not occur, as perhaps one might expect, as a hole in the curved brick walls, but instead two semi-circular walls of different diameters are juxtaposed so that the smaller faces to the larger and is overlapped by it. Inside the overlap, a very small aluminium channel is set into the face of the brickwork as a concealed frame to carry direct glazing. Fair faced brick work which is used both as an internal and external finish is thus transposed without interruption from the inside to the outside of the building, satisfactorily unifying the interior of the building with its naturally landscaped surrounding.

The money available for the building was severely restricted, and this led to a deliberate policy of constructing as large a shell as possible and leaving some areas to be completed and standards to be raised as and when funds permit.

The structure adopted for the building embodies the slightly unusual combination of fairfaced load-bearing brickwork and *in situ* reinforced concrete with a radial steel lattice roof truss to the theatre. This roof has been likened to a cycle wheel lying flat, the trusses representing the spokes, with a clear span generating from a welded hub, centrally placed over the circular auditorium. Further steel trusses were placed over the openings to the three stages, on the chord lines intersecting the main trusses at a constant radius from the setting out point.

The theatre consultant, Sean Kenny, is reported to have said: " What we must build is a tent, a place to hang things up in." The architects have provided a linked series of tents of the most sophisticated kind.

THE QUEEN'S AWARD TO INDUSTRY

The Queen's Award to Industry was instituted by H.M. the Queen by Royal Warrant published on March 22, 1966, "to recognise outstanding achievements in industry either in increasing exports or in technological innovation."

The Award is related to the production of goods by any branch of British industry, including agriculture and horticulture, and is made to organizations and not to individuals. The Award is normally made to particular industrial units, but units or agencies of central or local government with industrial functions, as well as research associations, educational institutions and bodies of a similar character are eligible provided that they can show they have contributed to industrial efficiency in the field in which the scheme is concerned.

The Award is made for industrial efficiency, assessed in terms of achievement such as: a substantial and sustained increase in total exports over 3 years; a substantial and sustained increase in the percentage of total exports to total business over 3 years; a percentage of exports to total business which is considerably and consistently higher than the average for the applicant's sector of industry; a spectacular increase over a shorter period than three years where there is a reasonable prospect that the performance can be maintained; a breakthrough in a particularly difficult market; the greatest value of export sales by any group or company in a given year; a significant advance in the application of advanced technology to a production or development process in British industry; the production for sale of goods which incorporate new and advanced technological qualities.

Export achievement is based on visible exports, including, where appropriate, construction work by

British companies overseas. In the case of technological achievement, Awards are confined to finished products or processes resulting from or involved in the normal course of commercial production.

Industrial concerns are invited to apply for the Award and the names of winners of the Award are announced each year on the Queen's Birthday, April 21. Holders of the Queen's Award are entitled to display its emblem; they receive a Grant of Appointment and a representation of the emblem cast in stainless steel and embedded in a transparent block. The emblem may appear on the goods themselves.

Increased Exports Awards

In 1971 the Queen's Award was conferred on the following 93 concerns for achievement in increasing exports: Airfix Products Ltd., London SW18; Anderton Springs Ltd., Bingley, Yorks.; Aquascutum and Associated Companies Ltd., London W1; Ashmore, Benson, Pease & Co. Ltd., Stockton-on-Tees, Co. Durham; Associated Television Corporation Ltd., London W1; B.T.I. Chemicals Ltd., Bradford, Yorks.; BTR Leyland Industries Ltd., Belting Division and the Hose Division, Preston, Lancs.; Barclays Bank Ltd., London EC3; Beecham Group Ltd., Pharmaceutical Division, Brentford, Middx.; Berry Bros. & Rudd Ltd., London SW1; Bexford Ltd., Brantham, Suffolk; Bonsoir Ltd., London N16; Boosey & Hawkes Ltd., Edgware, Middx.; Borg-Warner Ltd., Transmission Division, Letchworth, Herts.; British Communications Corporation Ltd., Wembley, Middx.; British Overseas Airways Corporation, Hounslow, Middx.; British Overseas Engineering & Credit Co. Ltd., London EC4; British United Shoe Machinery Co. Ltd., Leicester; David Brown Tractors Ltd., Huddersfield, Yorks.; John Brown Engineering (Clydebank) Ltd., Clydebank, Dunbartonshire; Bull Motors Ltd., Ipswich, Suffolk; Burberrys Ltd., London SW1; James Burrough Ltd., London SE11; Camber International (England) Ltd., Leicester; Cannon Rubber Manufacturers Ltd., London N17; Joseph Cheaney & Sons Ltd., Desborough, Northants; Cincinnati Co. Ltd., East Kilbride, Lanarks.; H. Clarkson and Co. Ltd., London EC2; Colchester Lathe Co. Ltd., Colchester, Essex; Coles Cranes Ltd., Pinner, Middx.; Coseley Buildings Ltd., Lanesfield, Staffs.; Costain Civil Engineering Ltd., London SE1; Coulter Electronics Ltd., Dunstable, Beds.; The Courtelle Division of Courtaulds Ltd., Bradford, Yorks.; John Crossley & Sons Ltd., Halifax, Yorks.; Cummins Ltd., Darlington, Co. Durham; Dale Electric of Great Britain, Filey, Yorks.; Thomas De La Rue & Co. Ltd., Basingstoke, Hants; Dexion-Comino International Ltd., Wembley, Middx.; Dodwell and Co. Ltd., London EC2; Eaton Yale and Towne Inc., Construction Equipment Division in U.K., Telford, Salop; Elliott Flight Automation Ltd., Rochester, Kent; Exquisite Knitwear Ltd., London SW6; Financial Times Ltd., London EC4; Firth Cleveland Fastenings Ltd., Pontypridd, Glam.; Foster Wheeler Ltd., London NW1; GEC-English Electric Gas Turbines Ltd., Whetstone, Leics.; Sir Alexander Gibb and Partners, London SW1; Stanley Gibbons Ltd., London WC2; Gillette Industries Ltd., Isleworth, Middx.; Glacier Metal Co. Ltd., Wembley, Middx.; Glaxo Laboratories Ltd., Greenford, Middx.; Grand Metropolitan Hotels Ltd. (London Hotels Division), London, W1; Harrold Leather Manufacturing Co. Ltd., Harrold, Beds.; John Harvey & Sons Ltd., Bristol, Glos.; Hield Brothers Ltd., Bradford, Yorks; Honeywell Ltd., Brentford, Middx.; Hoover Ltd., Greenford, Middx.; Howard Rotavator Co. Ltd., West Horndon,

Essex; International Sports Co. Ltd., London SW1; James A. Jobling & Co. Ltd. (Process Plant Division), Stoke-on-Trent, Staffs.; Kent Meters Ltd., Luton, Beds.; Lancer Boss Group Ltd., Leighton Buzzard, Beds.; Lansing Bagnall Ltd., Basingstoke, Hants; Lewis & Peat Ltd., London EC3; Lister & Co. Ltd. (Fur Fabric Division), Bradford, Yorks.; Lloyd's Register of Shipping, London EC3; Lygon Arms Ltd., Broadway, Worcs.; Manchester Liners Ltd., Manchester; Manesty Machines Ltd., Liverpool; Performing Right Society Ltd., London W1; Perkin-Elmer Ltd., Beaconsfield, Bucks.; Petbow Ltd., Sandwich, Kent; Edgar Pickering (Blackburn) Ltd., Blackburn, Lancs.; Pringle of Scotland Ltd., Hawick, Roxburghshire; Proprietary Perfumes Ltd., Ashford, Kent; Racal-Mobilcal Ltd., Reading, Berks.; Raleigh Industries Ltd., Nottingham; Rank Xerox Ltd., London NW1; Reid & Taylor Ltd., Langholm, Dumfriesshire; Rose Downs and Thompson Ltd., Hull, Yorks.; Shilton Ltd., London SW6; Short Brothers & Harland Ltd. (Missile Systems Division), Belfast, Northern Ireland; Strand Hotels Ltd., London W1; Swizzels Ltd., Stockport, Ches.; Thermos Ltd., Brentwood, Essex; Thorn Lighting Ltd., London WC2; Timex Corporation (U.K. Branches), Dundee; Tozer Kemsley & Millbourn (Holdings) Ltd., London EC3; Geo Tucker Eyelet Co. Ltd., Birmingham; United Transport Overseas Ltd., London W1; Wedgwood Ltd., Stoke-on-Trent, Staffs.; Wiggins Teape Ltd., London EC4.

Awards for Technological Innovation

In 1971 the following 13 concerns received the Queen's Award for achievement in technological innovation: AEI Scientific Apparatus Ltd., Harlow, Essex (*a 1 million volt electron microscope*); W. H. Allen & Co. Ltd. (Gearing Division), Pershore, Worcs. (*high power epicyclic gears*); BP Chemicals International Ltd., London EC2 (*production of chloroprene for synthetic rubbers*); Brentford Electric Ltd., Crawley, Sussex (*beam transfer magnet power supply system for the intersecting storage ring project at the CERN laboratory*); Decca Radar Ltd., London SE1 (*solid state marine radar; radar velocity sensors for helicopter and fixed-wing aircraft*); Decca Survey Ltd., London SE1 (*the radio position fixing system "Hi-Fix "*); English Clays Lovering Pochin & Co. Ltd., St. Austell, Cornwall (*micro mineral separation techniques*); Fisons Ltd. (Pharmaceutical Division), Loughborough, Leics. (*development and production of the drug " Intal " used in treatment of asthma*); Linotype-Paul Ltd., London NW9 (*a photo-typesetting system*); Marconi Instruments Ltd., St. Albans, Herts. (*radio-frequency power meters*); Metals Research Ltd., Royston, Herts. (*a crystal pulling system; production of gallium phosphide single crystals; an Image Analysing Computer*); Plastic Coatings Ltd., Guildford, Surrey (*automatic plastic dip moulding machinery*); Westwind Turbines Ltd., Poole, Dorset (*precision machine tool spindles incorporating air bearings*).

Double Awards

In 1971 a further 4 concerns received The Queen's Award for achievement both in increasing exports and in technological innovation: Imperial Chemical Industries Ltd. (Dyestuffs Division, Manchester, and Agricultural Division, Billingham) (*export achievement by the Dyestuffs Division and production of methanol by the Agricultural Division*); International Computers Ltd., London SW15 (*a computer integrated design and production system for the ICL 1906A computer*); Turner Brothers Asbestos Co. Ltd., Rochdale, Lancs. (*innovation in asbestos textile technology*); The Wellcome Foundation Ltd., London, NW1 (*development and production of the drug " Septrin "*).

WEATHER IN THE UNITED KINGDOM, 1970-1971

(1970) *August.*—The first two days were generally dry, sunny and very warm. This type of weather continued until the 7th, apart from the east coasts where fog occurred, especially on the 4th and 5th. Temperatures reached 28·0° C (84° F.) at Santon Downham (Norfolk) and 27·2° C. (81° F.) at Usk (Monmouthshire) on the 3rd. Severe thunderstorms spread across the Midlands and southern England on the 7th and 8th, to give 65 mm. (2·6 in.) of rain in 81 min at Harwell (Berks) on the 7th. On the 9th and 10th anticyclonic weather developed in the south-west, but rains occurred in the north-west. Following this sunny spell a cold front moved slowly eastwards between the 11th and 13th bringing rain to most areas. From the 14th to 22nd stormy weather prevailed, with widespread rains. Rain was heavy on the 15th and 16th, especially in the north, continuing in the east of Scotland on the 17th. For the 15th 118 mm. (4·6 in.) fell at Kilroot (Co. Antrim) and for the 16th and 17th 152 mm. (6·0 in.) at Lochindorf Lodge (Moray). From the 15th to 17th strong winds with gales in places occurred in most areas, especially on the 16th when rough coastal waters caused damage to many small craft. On the 16th Valley (Anglesey) recorded a gust of 61 knots (70 m.p.h.). Further rains fell widely on the 19th and 20th, with 98 mm. (3·8 in.) at Timberscombe (Somerset) for the 19th and 95 mm. (3·74 in.) at Birmingham for the 24 hours ending at midday on the 20th. These further rains renewed flooding in east Scotland, where the Rivers Lossie, Spey and Findhorn overflowed causing damage in the towns of Forres and Elgin, widespread silting of fields, and damage to crops and livestock. From the 23rd there was a warm dry spell with morning fogs, but by the 28th light rains occurred in the north-west, followed by further rains spreading across the country from the west.

September—The 1st was windy in Scotland with a few showers; the 2nd brought more widespread rains and the 3rd showers in Scotland. The 4th to 7th gave light rains in the north and west; morning coastal fog in the south-west and warm weather in central and south-east England. Temperatures rose to 26° C. (78° F.) on the 7th at places in the south-east. Thunderstorms developed in the south-west late on the 7th and in other places on the 8th, 9th and 10th. Lightning damaged a church steeple in Dundee on the 8th. A deep depression moved slowly north-eastwards across northern Scotland during the 8th to 10th. Gales were severe along western coasts on the 9th with a gust of 75 knots (86 m.p.h.) at Mull of Galloway (Wigtownshire), and heavy rains occurred in the Western Highlands. Cool weather persisted from the 9th to 16th, snow settled on Ben Nevis and the Cairngorms around the 13th, while temperature fell to 0° C. (32° F.) at a number of places on the 15th or 16th, including parts of Kincardineshire, south Wales and Leicestershire. Belts of heavy rains spread across Wales and the southern half of England from the 11th to 15th, and over northern England on the 13th. On the 11th 58 mm. (2·3 in.) fell at Slapton (Devon) and on the 14th 49 mm. (1·9 in.) at Whitstable (Kent). A ridge of high pressure on the 16th brought a dry spell to central and southern England, giving in places 13 consecutive days without measurable rain, but rain and drizzle occurred in the north-west on the 17th and 18th. Overnight fog was widespread in England and Wales, and in the south-east of Scotland from the 18th to 28th. Maximum temperatures reached 26·7° C. (80° F.) at places in eastern England on the 20th and at Gloucester on the 28th.

Rain occurred during the last two days, mainly in the north.

October—At the beginning of the month an anticyclone to the south-west brought north-west winds over much of the country, with rain in the north. The strong winds caused blowing dust in Suffolk and Norfolk on the 3rd. Colder air spread from the north on the 4th, with slight ground frost in many areas from the 7th to 10th. Over parts of western Scotland 50 mm. (2 in.) of rain was recorded at many stations for the 4th and 152 mm. (6·0 in.) at Dalness (Argyll). Isolated thunderstorms occurred from the 5th to 8th. Air frost occurred in the south early on the 8th and 9th, while early morning temperature on the 10th fell to −5·6° C. (22° F.) at Caldecott (Leicestershire). A ridge of high pressure developed over England and Wales on the 9th and subsequently mild afternoons with winds from the south-east persisted over much of the country. The 11th was wet in the west (with local flooding in south Wales) but in the south-east temperature reached 24·1° C. (75° F.) at East Dereham (Norfolk). 20·0° C. (68° F.) was recorded at Rhyl, on the North Wales coast on the 14th and at a few places in Scotland on the 13th and 14th. Between the 8th and 18th overnight fog was widespread in many parts of England and Wales, especially in Lancashire, Yorkshire, the Midlands and East Anglia. Sea fog was persistent at times from the 11th to 15th along the North Sea coasts of Scotland and northern England. Following a few days of westerly winds, winds from the north affected most areas on the 18th and 19th, a gust of 100 knots (115 m.p.h.) being recorded at 1074 m. in the Cairngorms on the 18th and of 84 knots (97 m.p.h.) near Stirling on the 19th. Westerly winds returned on the 23rd, giving 91 mm. (3·6 in.) at Seathwaite (Cumberland) on the 24th and 80 mm. (3·1 in.) in Merioneth on the 27th. The south remained generally dry, apart from early on the 26th and the end of the month, when more widespread rain occurred on the 30th and 74 mm. (2·9 in.) fell at Blaenau Ffestiniog (Merioneth).

November—Heavy rains occurred on the 1st and 2nd in the north and west, with 84 mm. (3·3 in.) at Clydach (Glamorgan) on the 1st and 50 mm. (2·0 in.) at Greenock (at the mouth of the Clyde) on the 2nd. Exeter recorded a temperature of 17·3° C. (63° F.) on the 2nd. On the 3rd gales caused damage in many areas eg in northern England where a number of vehicles were blown over. A gust of 102 knots (117 m.p.h.) was recorded at 857 m. on Great Dun Fell (northern Pennines) and 80 knots (92 m.p.h.) at Durham. The 6th brought widespread rains to the south and west, which persisted in the south on the 7th. Following morning frost and fog on the 8th, heavy rain spread to south Wales and south-west England followed by showers and gales in the north. Further weak fronts from the west on the 10th and 11th brought widespread rains, followed by cold westerly winds and wintry showers. Lightning damaged a church in the Isle of Wight on the 13th. The coolest period of the month was from the 12th to 17th, when in the northern half of the country air frost was widespread at night, snow was widespread in Scotland and snow occurred further south on the 12th and 16th. Temperature fell to −8·3° C. (17° F.) in parts of Aberdeenshire on the 14th and to −6·1° C. (21° F.) locally in Buckinghamshire and Norfolk on the 14th, 15th or 16th. Thunderstorms spread over England and Wales on the 13th and 14th. A series of depressions moving towards the north-east between the 17th and 23rd

brought heavy rains to most of the country. At Rydal (Lake District) there was a spell of 30 hours of continuous rain commencing in the early hours of the 23rd. The depression on the 23rd brought a mild spell to the south-west with 17·0° C. (63° F.) at Chivenor in North Devon. Fog occurred in many areas at times during the 26th to 30th, persisting all day on the 26th in parts of eastern England and restricting air traffic at the major airports.

December—Westerly winds prevailed over the country during the first six days with rain in the north and west on the 2nd, 3rd and 4th, and showers later. During this mild spell temperature reached 14·4° C. (58° F.) to the north of London on the 4th, while gusts exceeded 50 kt. (57 m.p.h.) in the north-west of Scotland. On the 6th whirlwinds were observed near Portsmouth and Dungeness. An unusually intense anticyclone crossed the British Isles from the 7th to 10th, with overnight fog, freezing in places, mainly in the Midlands and southern England. Air traffic was delayed in the south between the 13th and 15th. On the 16th and 17th widespread rains occurred, with gales in Scotland and northern England, 63 kt. (73 m.p.h.) being recorded at Lerwick (Shetland Islands) on the 17th. Milder weather, with south-westerly winds, prevailed on the 18th and 19th, temperature reaching 14·4° C. (58° F.) in Montgomeryshire on the 19th. A very cold spell, with widespread frost at night, commenced on the 21st. Snow showers occurred over England and Wales on the 24th, to give snow cover on Christmas morning in most areas, apart from the south-west. From the 26th to 31st strong cold east winds occurred at times along the east coast of England. On the 26th the snow spread across southern England and by the 27th snow lay to a depth of 8 cm. (3 in.) on high ground as far north as Huddersfield and of 15 cm. (6 in.) in parts of Kent and east Sussex. On the 28th cold weather extended to much of the remainder of the country, giving −8·3° C. (17° F.) locally in Leicestershire and Berkshire. The 29th brought widespread rain or sleet to much of the southern half of the country, but by the 31st wintry showers were confined mainly to the east coast.

Year (1970)—Rainfall exceeded the 1916–50 average over England and Wales for the sixth consecutive year. The excess was only 0·3 in., almost the same as in 1969. The years 1965–70 gave the wettest period of six consecutive years since that of 1927–1932. Over Scotland and Northern Ireland the excesses amounted to 1·9 in. and 1·2 in. respectively, the deficiencies in 1969 being 7·1 in. and 4·8 in. for these areas. In 1970 the excesses were mainly in the west, parts of the Western Highlands of Scotland recording 130 per cent. of average, where many previous years had had less than the 1916–50 average. Over England and Wales the first four months and also November were wetter than usual, while relatively dry months continued from May to October and occurred again in December. The range in the annual totals was from 4971 mm. (196 in.) on the slopes of Snowdon to 468 mm. (18 in.) at Burnham in the east of Essex. The total duration of bright sunshine was 103, 97 and 94 per cent. of the 1931–60 average over England and Wales, Scotland and Northern Ireland respectively. Sunshine exceeded the monthly averages widely in February, June, November and December; January, April, July, September and October being generally less sunny than usual. March was unusually sunny in central Scotland, while May was dull in the north but sunny in the south. The sunniest stations included Shanklin, Eastbourne, Swanage, Bognor Regis and

Jersey, with 1951, 1918, 1904, 1898 and 1887 hours respectively. The annual mean temperatures were in most districts close to the 1921–50 average, the general values being 0·1° F. above, 0·6° F. below and 0·2° F. above for England and Wales, Scotland and Northern Ireland respectively. The mean temperature was notably below average in February and July over Scotland and Northern Ireland and more generally in March and April, while May and June were generally warmer than usual.

January (1971)—The first week was mainly cold and dry, with widespread air frost at night persisting during the day at times in parts of central and south-east England. Fog was widespread, especially in the east on the 3rd and 4th. Heavy rains occurred in the west and north on the 5th and 6th, 88 mm. (3·5 in.) being recorded in Carmarthenshire for the 6th, as south-west winds spread across the country to give three weeks of generally mild weather. On the 9th 16·7° C. (62° F.) was recorded at Lairg (Sutherland), equal to the highest air temperature recorded in Scotland during January since 1889. The 10th was sunny and mild, except in parts of the south-east where mist and fog persisted. Temperatures reached 18·3° C. (65° F.) at Aber, to the north-east of Snowdon, to give the highest recorded air temperature in the United Kingdom during January. It was the mildest January day in central Manchester since 1877. By the 10th the Cairngorms were mainly free of snow. From the 12th to 14th light winds prevailed, with local rains and drizzle. Wet weather occurred frequently from the 15th to 26th, with some snow on high ground in northern Britain around the 17th and 23rd and heavy rains and local thunderstorms in the south and west between the 21st and 26th. Many areas reported strong winds during the period 23rd to 25th. A gust of 78 kt. (90 m.p.h.) was recorded at Hartland Point (Devon) on the 25th, when strong winds associated with whirlwinds in south-east England and the Isle of Wight caused damage to buildings, trees and cars, especially at Welling (Kent). Snow fell in parts of Wales and south-west England on the 31st, resulting in snow depths of 10–15 cm. (4–6 in.) in the afternoon and local flooding as the snow melted.

February—During the first two days there were showers of sleet or snow, mainly in the north, but also in parts of the south-east. Milder weather spread to most of the country during the 3rd and 4th, especially in the east, and temperatures reached 15° C. (59° F.) on the 3rd at Scarborough, on the east coast of Yorkshire. From the 4th to 11th overnight fog occurred, mainly in England, especially on the 8th and 11th, when air traffic was delayed. Most of the east and south of the country recorded no rain until the middle of the month—*eg.* the 13th at Cleethorpes (Lincolnshire) and the 14th at Sandown (Isle of Wight). From the 11th to 18th rain spells with strong winds were frequent, but mainly in the west and north, as much as 132 mm. (5·2 in.) being recorded locally in the Lake District. The 15th and 16th brought snow and sleet to Northern Ireland and south-west Scotland, which spread to much of England and Wales. On the 16th snow lay to a depth of 7 cm. (3 in.) at Aldergrove (Co. Antrim) and 5–10 cm. (2–4 in.) on high ground in the northern half of England and Wales. Air temperature fell to −11·7° C. (11° F.) at Lanark, to the south-east of Glasgow on the 16th and to −10·0° C. (14° F.) at Shawbury (Shropshire) on the 17th. Rain was widespread on the 19th and 20th, but anticyclonic weather prevailed from the 22nd to 26th, with little rain over

England and Wales and frost and fog in the south-east. Fog was also widespread on the 23rd in south Wales and the west country. Snow and sleet fell in northern England and southern Scotland during the last two days of the month, when snow depths of 5–10 cm (2–4 in.) were measured in the Pennines on the 28th and colder air, with some snow, spread to eastern England.

March—The 1st brought widespread rains, heavy in many western districts, and preceded by snow over England and Wales, where in places the depths reached 5–10 cm. (2–4 in.). Later, easterly winds and wintry showers developed over the south-east to give 13 cm. (5 in.) of snow in parts of Kent on the 4th. The first week was mild in Scotland and Northern Ireland, temperature reaching 15·0° C. (59° F.) at Rothesay (Bute) on the 5th, while on the same day Santon Downham (Norfolk) recorded − 11·7° C. (11° F.). The period 8th to 12th was generally mild, except in the extreme north and west, temperature reaching 16·4° C. (62° F.) at Wrexham (Denbighshire) on the 12th, although light rain and drizzle occurred in places with some snow in the north. From the 13th to 16th showers were frequent, with local outbreaks of heavy rain and snow in places, especially on the 15th in southern England, quickly followed by rain. Thunderstorms occurred over the Hebrides on the 13th. Heavy prolonged rains fell over much of the country between the 17th and 20th, with gales in places, the total measured for these four days at West Baldwin (Isle of Man) being 209 mm. (8·2 in.). During the 18th to 20th snow was widespread over high ground in the Isle of Man and along the Border between England and Scotland. A gust of 67 kt. (77 m.p.h.) was recorded on the 20th at St. Abb's Head (Berwickshire) and of 68 kt. (78 m.p.h.) at Whitby on the coast of Yorkshire on the 21st. The 21st and 22nd were mainly sunny in the west and north, with occasional rain in the south-east. The 24th was mild, temperatures reaching 15° C. (59° F.) at Stonehaven (Kincardineshire) and at Liphook (Hampshire). Thunderstorms were frequent over Scotland on the 24th and in parts of England on the 25th. From the 27th to 29th winds prevailed from the south-west, with rain and drizzle in places, followed by easterly winds and sunny weather in the south.

April—At the beginning of the month winds backed from south-east to north-east, giving snow showers in the north, while some rain occurred in the south-west on the 2nd. During the first half of the month east winds kept areas near the North Sea dull and cold, with slight air frosts in Scotland, but generally dry weather over much of the country. There was widespread rain in southern England on the 9th, but in this area the dry weather continued until the 23rd. In eastern England there were hill and coastal fog patches during the first week and again from the 11th to 16th. The 16th brought wintry showers, with local gale force winds, to the north and outbreaks of thundery rains to parts of the south. From the 17th to 20th westerly winds predominated, with showers in parts of Scotland and gale force winds in the extreme north on the 18th, when a gust of 67 kt. (77 m.p.h.) was recorded at Lerwick (Shetland). Sea fog affected English Channel districts on the 19th and during the night, 19th to 20th, dense fog patches formed widely in southern England. Most inland districts of England became warm on the 23rd, temperature reaching 22·9° C. (73° F.) at Santon Downham (Norfolk). A complex depression moving slowly to eastern Europe brought widespread easterly winds, with persistent rains between the 22nd and 25th, as much as 40·9 mm.

(1·6 in.) being recorded at Watnall (Nottinghamshire) for the 23rd. Hill fog was widespread on the 23rd with sea fog over much of the southern coasts. On the 26th snow fell in south Wales, south-west England and over the hills of south-east England, snow depths of 5–10 cm. (2–4 in.) being reported in the west. This snow soon melted, but air frost was widespread at night during the remainder of the month. On the 27th northerly winds brought showers to the east, but later the weather became dry and sunny in the south with showers in the north.

May—The first four days were generally cool, dry and sunny, with air frost at nights in parts of Scotland and the south-east of England. Rain reached south-west England on the 5th, spreading to most of England, Wales and southern Scotland on the 6th, with thunderstorms and strong winds, and local flooding at Portsmouth, Bath and in the west Midlands. On the 7th rain extended over Scotland and was heavy in places in southern and eastern England, with hailstones at Ilkley, to the north of Bradford, accompanied by some flooding. Dry, sunny weather prevailed in the south-east from the 8th to 10th, but showers occurred in the north and west. Morning fog developed over south-west coastal areas on the 10th, 11th and 12th and along coasts bordering on the North Sea on the 12th, 13th and 15th. The weather of the 15th to 17th was generally changeable with local rains. The 13th and 14th brought air frost to much of Scotland, while there was more widespread ground frost on the 17th and 18th. Anticyclonic weather prevailed over England and Wales from the 18th to 21st with long spells of sunshine, with some rain in the north of Scotland. The 22nd and 23rd brought more widespread outbreaks of rain with thunderstorms in the Midlands, the south-west and in eastern Scotland. Further heavy rains occurred during the night, 24th–25th, in the Midlands and southern England, including London, lightning damaging houses in Harrow and Wembley and large hailstones falling at Uxbridge, where 34 mm. (1·3 in.) of precipitation was recorded in 35 mins. A depression, moving from Iceland to Scotland, gave rain, which spread to south-east England by the 27th. Showers were widespread on the 28th, following a night with ground frost in many places and snow showers on the peaks of Scottish mountains. During the remainder of the month showers were confined mainly to the north.

June—Dry anticyclonic weather predominated during the first 5 days, with sea fog affecting coasts bordering the North Sea, although thundery rains spread across the Midlands on the 3rd, when temperatures reached 25·6 °C. (78° F.) at Littlehampton on the Sussex coast. From the 5th to 22nd, with winds from the north or east, temperatures were mainly below average, especially during the day, with air frost at night in some upland areas around the 10th and 15th. Low cloud or drizzle occurred over eastern districts between the 5th and 7th, with more widespread rain on the 8th. Rainfall amounts for the 10th exceeded 50 mm. (2·0 in.) in southern England, with 81·5 mm. (3·2 in.) at Yarford (Somerset) and 78·8 mm. (3·1 in.) in the Isle of Wight. On the 11th rain spread to the north-west, 60·7 mm. (2·4 in.) being recorded in Co. Antrim, but the next two days brought only light showers. The 14th was wet over the southern half of England and Wales, where at East Hoathly, to the north of Sussex, 54·2 mm. (2·1 in.) fell in 5½ hours. With north-westerly winds the period, 15th to 17th, was generally showery with local hail and thunder. Widespread rains occurred on the 18th and 19th in south-west England and Wales, with 90 mm. (3·5 in.) in Cardiganshire for

the 18th. Rain and drizzle spread south-east between the 23rd and 25th; showery westerlies prevailed from the 26th to 28th with rain in the south during the night 27th to 28th; followed by mainly cloudy weather with light rains during the 29th and 30th, and sea fog along parts of the Cornish coasts. Places in north and west Scotland recorded half their average rainfall, while four times the average occurred along the Sussex coast and in the Isle of Wight, giving at Ryde the wettest June since before 1870. In most parts of the country day temperatures for June were below those for May, while sunshine totals were below average, except for a few places in the west and north of Scotland.

July—Anticyclonic conditions prevailed over most of the country until the 21st, with mainly dry, sunny and warm weather, although heavy thunderstorm rains occurred locally. For the 3rd, with thunderstorms in the west and north, more than 70 mm. (2·8 in.) was recorded in parts of Denbighshire and also in Perthshire, with flooding, especially at Abergele in north Wales. On the 4th a boy was killed by lightning in Oxfordshire. On the 9th thunderstorms affected south-west England and later south Wales, giving 44 mm. (1·7 in.) in about 2 hours at Sturminster Newton (Dorset).

During the first half of the month the nights were often misty, especially in central and eastern England, and occasionally sea fog spread inland, often persisting all day near the North Sea coasts. Day temperatures reached 27·6° C. (82° F.) on the 7th at Turnhouse, near Edinburgh; 27·1° C. (81° F.) on the 8th at Newquay (Cornwall); and 29° C. (84° F.) on the 11th at a few places in England. During the 14th and 15th gales and strong winds occurred in Scotland and the northern half of England. The period, 16th to 18th, was generally cool, especially at night, when ground frost was experienced in many places. The weather of the month was generally dry in southern England until the 21st and there was a water shortage in the south of Westmorland. From the 22nd until the 31st a number of heavy rains resulted in local flooding. On the 27th 44 mm. (1·7 in.) fell in 14 mins. near Watchet, on the north-west coast of Somerset, while heavy rains affected south-east England and East Anglia, continuing in the east of this area during the 28th. During the 24 hours from 21h. G.M.T. on the 27th Gorleston, on the north-east coast of Norfolk, recorded 88·2 mm. (3·5 in.). Heavy rains spread north-east over the country on the 30th and 31st. Plymouth Hoe experienced its sunniest July since 1911.

General Values, 1968–71 (July)

Month	Rainfall (inches)				Temperature at Sea-Level (° F.)				Bright Sunshine (Hrs. per day)			
	1968	1969	1970	1971	1968	1969	1970	1971	1968	1969	1970	1971
					England and Wales							
January........	3·1	3·8	4·2	4·3	41·0	43·2	39·9	41·4	1·2	1·1	1·1	1·3
February......	1·9	2·9	3·2	1·3	37·0	35·1	38·8	41·7	2·2	2·4	3·6	2·4
March.........	2·2	3·0	2·5	2·6	44·6	39·4	39·7	42·3	4·0	2·4	3·7	3·2
April.........	2·6	2·3	3·4	2·1	47·3	46·2	44·8	46·6	5·9	6·3	4·4	4·0
May..........	2·9	4·5	1·0	2·0	50·3	52·9	55·4	53·6	5·0	4·6	6·2	7·2
June..........	3·4	2·2	1·8	4·1	58·8	57·7	61·5	55·2	6·3	8·5	8·2	4·8
July..........	4·1	2·8	2·8	1·7	59·2	62·6	60·1	62·6	4·6	6·7	5·3	7·4
August........	2·9	3·0	3·1	—	60·8	61·9	61·5	—	4·0	4·6	5·5	—
September.....	5·9	1·5	2·6	—	58·1	58·3	58·8	—	3·9	3·4	4·4	—
October......	3·6	0·7	2·2	—	55·6	55·9	52·3	—	2·0	3·3	3·2	—
November.....	2·9	5·6	6·9	—	45·1	43·2	47·1	—	1·4	2·5	1·9	—
December.....	3·1	3·5	2·2	—	39·4	39·6	41·2	—	1·1	0·9	1·6	—
YEAR........	38·6	35·8	35·9	—	50·0	49·8	50·2	—	3·5	3·7	4·1	—
					Scotland							
January........	5·1	5·8	4·6	4·9	39·0	40·5	38·1	40·6	1·2	1·0	0·9	0·8
February......	3·2	3·2	5·5	3·5	36·1	34·0	35·8	41·5	2·6	2·5	3·3	1·9
March.........	5·3	1·7	3·6	3·8	42·1	37·6	39·0	41·7	2·9	3·0	3·8	2·7
April.........	3·1	2·9	3·7	2·3	44·8	43·9	42·6	45·3	5·3	5·3	5·0	4·6
May..........	4·5	4·6	2·9	3·2	46·9	49·1	51·6	51·6	4·7	4·0	3·9	6·5
June..........	2·7	3·4	3·0	2·9	55·8	55·8	57·9	52·3	6·3	6·8	7·5	5·0
July..........	4·5	3·1	5·7	3·6	56·3	59·0	55·6	58·1	4·0	4·8	3·3	5·7
August........	2·7	3·4	4·7	—	57·0	59·5	58·3	—	5·5	4·8	4·1	—
September.....	5·1	4·9	5·7	—	54·5	54·9	54·5	—	3·1	3·3	2·9	—
October......	8·1	4·7	7·2	—	51·4	53·1	49·1	—	1·9	2·2	2·2	—
November.....	3·4	6·7	7·5	—	42·6	38·5	52·6	—	1·3	1·7	1·6	—
December.....	3·5	4·4	3·7	—	38·8	38·7	40·3	—	0·8	0·8	1·1	—
YEAR........	51·2	48·8	57·8	—	46·9	46·9	46·9	—	3·3	3·3	3·3	—

TEMPERATURE AND RAINFALL RECORDS

GENERAL: The *maximum shade temperature* of the air on record is 136° F. (57·8° C.) at San Louis, Mexico, on Aug. 11, 1933; the *extreme lowest recorded temperature* in Antarctica *e.g.*— 127° F. (−88·3° C.) at Vostok on Aug. 24, 1960. In the upper air temperatures as low as− 143° F. (−97·2° C.) have been recorded—*e.g.* over Halley Bay, Antarctica, on Aug. 9, 1959 at about 27 kms.

U.K.: The *maximum shade temperature* recorded in the air at 4 feet above the ground is 100·5 F. (38·1° C.) at Tonbridge, Kent (July 22, 1868).

The *lowest shade temperature* is −17° F. (−27·2° C.) at Braemar (Feb. 11, 1895).

The *greatest rainfall* recorded in a day was at Martinstown, near Dorchester, 11·00 inches in the 24 hours commencing 9 a.m. (July 18, 1955). *Annual totals* exceeding 240 inches were recorded at The Stye, Borrowdale, in 1872, 1923, 1928 and 1954; at Ben Nevis Observatory in 1898 and at Llyn Llydaw, Snowdon, in 1909. The *smallest annual total* is 9·29 inches at Margate in 1921 and the *largest* may be regarded as 257 inches at Sprinkling Tarn in 1954.

TEMPERATURE, RAINFALL AND SUNSHINE

AT VARIOUS PLACES IN GREAT BRITAIN

Mean Temperature of the air (° C.), Rainfall (mm.) and Bright Sunshine (as mean hours per day) at representative British Health Resorts and Towns during the year July, 1970, to June 1971, and the calendar year 1970. Also height of Climatological Station above mean sea level, altitude being given in metres. Fuller details of the weather are given in the *Monthly Weather Report* published by the Meteorological Office. (To convert ° C. to ° F. multiply by 9/5 and add 32).

		1970											
		July			August			September			October		
		Temp.	Rain	Sun	Temp.	Rain	Sun	Temp.	Rain	Sun	Temp.	Rain	Sun
	mtrs.	°C	mm.	hrs.	°C	mm.	hrs.	°C	mm.	hrs.	°C	mm.	hrs.
Aberporth	133	13.9	57	6.1	15.0	43	5.8	14.1	49	4.4	11.1	108	3.3
Aberystwyth	138	14.6	98	4.3	15.5	60	4.8	14.9	68	3.8	11.5	116	2.7
Aldergrove	68	13.7	76	3.2	14.9	107	5.0	13.1	117	3.0	10.3	83	2.1
Ambleside	46	14.1	158	3.4	15.7	114	5.0	13.3	203	2.7	10.1	243	2.3
Balmoral	283	11.4	119	—	13.2	124	—	10.9	65	—	6.8	61	—
Bath	118	15.3	52	—	16.3	67	—	14.9	72	—	11.1	15	—
Birmingham	163	15.2	46	4.9	16.1	148	4.7	14.6	34	4.8	10.9	25	2.8
Bournemouth	40	15.8	42	7.1	16.3	47	6.3	15.1	70	6.3	11.7	28	3.7
Buxton	307	13.0	99	4.3	13.9	134	5.1	12.5	99	3.7	8.7	126	2.9
Cambridge	12	16.1	42	5.9	16.6	39	5.9	15.5	38	5.4	11.5	21	3.4
Cardiff	62	15.8	82	5.6	16.4	85	4.6	15.3	83	4.7	11.2	80	3.0
Cirencester	135	14.9	64	6.1	15.7	63	5.5	13.9	71	4.8	10.1	30	3.1
Douglas	87	13.1	85	5.2	14.8	69	6.4	12.9	82	4.0	10.7	119	3.1
Dovercourt	5	15.9	30	5.3	16.5	16	6.9	14.9	41	5.3	11.5	18	3.7
Dumfries	49	13.5	73	4.3	15.3	51	6.1	12.6	107	2.9	9.9	100	3.0
Dundee	45	13.7	72	3.9	14.7	102	4.3	13.1	107	3.6	9.5	42	3.0
Durham	102	14.6	46	4.9	15.7	64	5.6	13.7	34	4.1	10.1	23	3.9
Eastbourne	7	15.5	59	7.5	16.7	69	7.2	15.4	114	6.5	12.4	28	4.1
East Malling	37	16.3	45	6.2	16.5	55	6.5	14.9	65	5.5	11.3	15	3.9
Edinburgh	134	13.5	74	3.5	14.7	44	4.1	13.2	63	3.8	9.9	55	3.0
Falmouth	51	15.5	79	6.4	15.9	90	6.1	14.7	73	4.1	11.9	34	3.6
Glasgow	107	12.9	75	3.5	15.0	83	4.8	12.5	115	3.0	9.3	140	2.8
Hastings	45	15.3	50	6.2	16.7	55	6.7	15.5	82	6.1	12.4	21	4.1
Huddersfield	99	15.3	51	4.1	15.7	67	4.4	14.4	47	4.4	10.3	65	3.3
Hull	2	15.7	91	4.8	16.6	41	6.0	18.1	27	4.6	11.3	41	3.6
Ilfracombe	8	15.5	102	6.0	16.6	109	5.5	15.5	—	—	12.5	112	2.2
Inverness	4	13.0	78	3.6	14.8	97	3.4	12.7	62	3.3	9.1	80	1.7
Lincoln	7	15.7	46	5.4	15.9	68	6.0	14.3	23	5.3	10.3	33	3.4
Liverpool	60	14.8	68	5.2	16.3	79	5.4	14.4	44	4.5	11.1	71	3.5
Llandrindod Wells	235	14.4	64	4.1	15.0	106	4.3	13.8	76	3.4	9.5	77	2.1
London (Kew)	5	16.3	66	6.1	16.6	54	6.2	14.7	67	5.5	11.4	14	3.3
Lowestoft	25	15.9	39	5.9	16.3	25	6.6	15.3	47	5.3	11.7	33	3.7
Manchester Airport	75	14.9	68	4.3	16.1	93	5.3	14.4	54	3.7	10.7	73	3.5
Margate	16	16.9	39	6.5	17.2	20	6.8	16.3	44	6.0	12.7	9	4.0
Morecambe	7	14.8	95	4.1	16.5	75	5.8	14.5	129	3.9	11.0	109	3.3
Newquay	54	15.7	56	5.6	15.8	85	5.8	15.1	70	4.3	12.1	50	3.1
Nottingham	59	15.7	43	4.9	16.8	70	5.2	15.2	33	5.1	10.9	29	2.7
Oxford	63	16.1	42	6.2	16.5	52	6.0	15.3	40	5.2	11.2	20	3.4
Penzance	19	15.7	66	7.2	15.9	84	6.6	15.3	88	4.6	12.4	35	3.8
Plymouth	36	15.5	69	6.4	16.4	91	5.7	15.3	70	4.8	11.9	25	3.3
Prestwick	16	13.2	87	3.9	14.9	82	5.6	13.1	123	3.4	10.1	127	2.7
Ross-onWye	68	15.6	44	5.3	15.9	98	4.5	14.8	41	4.6	10.9	19	2.6
Sandown	4	16.3	57	7.6	17.1	64	7.1		84	6.4	12.8	36	4.3
Scarborough	36	15.3	74	5.3	15.3	30	5.3	14.5	16	4.7	11.0	40	3.9
Scilly	48	15.7	42	6.4	16.0	41	5.9	15.3	70	4.0	12.7	25	3.7
Sheffield	131	15.5	39	4.9	16.3	73	4.8	14.7	43	4.1	10.8	48	3.3
Shoeburyness	2	16.9	31	6.1	16.7	37	6.2	15.9	44	5.5	12.3	14	4.1
Shrewsbury	56	15.5	44	4.6	15.8	112	5.2	14.5	35	4.4	10.4	33	3.1
Skegness	5	15.6	47	5.5	15.9	37	6.3	14.9	14	5.2	11.1	42	3.0
Southampton	3	16.3	56	6.5	17.2	61	6.3	15.7	69	5.4	12.0	13	3.5
Stornoway	3	11.5	83	3.1	12.8	70	3.7	11.2	101	2.8	8.9	213	1.5
Tiree	9	11.9	136	4.2	13.7	88	4.2	12.2	174	2.9	10.1	126	1.8
Torbay	8	16.2	59	7.9	16.5	114	6.4	15.1	92	5.5	12.1	37	3.7
Weston-super-Mare	9	—	70	6.5	—	90	5.0	15.7	102	4.5	12.0	36	3.2
Weymouth	23	15.1	41	8.4	15.9	70	5.5	15.2	65	6.1	11.9	21	3.7
Worthing	8	16.0	41	7.2	17.1	90	7.1	15.9	74	6.2	12.3	28	4.0
York	20	14.9	93	4.8	16.1	55	6.1	14.0	25	4.2	10.3	21	3.4

TEMPERATURE, RAINFALL AND SUNSHINE AT VARIOUS PLACES IN GREAT BRITAIN

Mean Temperature of the air (° C.), Rainfall (mm.) and Bright Sunshine (as mean hours per day) at representative British Health Resorts and Towns during the year July, 1970 to June, 1971, and the calendar year 1970. Fuller details of the weather are given in the *Monthly Weather Report* published by the Meteorological Office. (To convert ° C. to ° F. multiply by 9/5 and add 32.)

	1970						1970			1971					
	November			December			Year			January			February		
	Temp.	Rain	Sun	Temp.	Rain	Sun	Temp.	Rain	Sun	Temp.	Rain	Sun	Temp.	Rain	Sun
	°C	mm.	hrs.	°C.	mm.	hrs.	°C.	mm.	hrs.	°C.	mm.	hrs.	°C.	mm.	hrs.
Aberporth	8.6	188	1.4	5.4	43	2.2	9.6	884	3.7	5.7	107	1.2	5.1	32	2.0
Aberystwyth	9.9	215	1.4	5.7	43	2.5	—	1,027	—	6.1	111	1.3	5.3	39	1.6
Aldergrove	7.0	91	2.2	4.7	36	1.5	9.1	910	3.5	5.1	52	1.8	5.5	57	1.9
Ambleside	6.3	257	1.1	4.4	94	1.5	8.9	1,894	3.4	—	—	—	—	—	—
Balmoral	3.3	73	—	2.0	45	—	6.1	911	—	2.5	73	—	2.3	15	—
Bath	6.7	173	—	4.0	31	—	9.9	752	—	4.5	121	—	—	—	—
Birmingham	7.9	142	1.7	4.3	34	1.3	9.7	846	3.8	4.3	97	1.1	4.9	18	2.2
Bournemouth	9.5	216	2.2	4.8	32	2.5	10.3	802	5.1	5.7	120	1.6	5.2	23	3.6
Buxton	5.8	208	—	2.8	65	—	7.5	1,393	—	2.9	94	—	3.2	69	—
Cambridge	—	117	2.0	4.1	39	1.2	—	561	4.3	4.6	64	1.3	4.5	11	2.7
Cardiff	8.7	249	1.7	6.9	63	1.5	10.3	1,168	3.8	5.3	166	0.9	—	—	—
Cirencester	—	162	2.1	—	37	1.9	—	797	4.3	4.1	132	—	3.7	33	—
Douglas	7.9	170	2.2	5.7	57	1.8	9.2	1,110	4.4	5.9	75	1.5	5.7	94	2.3
Dovercourt	7.7	103	2.1	4.1	57	1.4	—	—	—	3.9	48	1.2	4.9	26	2.8
Dumfries	6.3	140	2.3	4.1	40	1.9	8.5	941	4.0	3.9	60	1.1	4.9	74	2.1
Dundee	5.7	95	2.4	4.3	28	2.1	8.5	771	3.8	4.3	74	1.2	5.1	20	2.3
Durham	6.1	62	2.2	4.3	72	1.7	8.8	562	4.3	3.7	46	0.9	4.5	17	3.0
Eastbourne	9.5	210	2.3	5.3	66	1.9	10.5	913	5.3	5.9	90	1.8	5.8	25	3.3
East Malling	8.1	139	2.2	3.8	58	1.3	9.9	660	4.4	4.6	61	1.5	5.0	21	2.8
Edinburgh	6.2	77	1.9	4.3	47	1.4	8.5	599	3.4	4.5	30	0.9	4.9	29	2.1
Falmouth	10.1	161	2.6	6.1	63	2.1	10.7	1,053	4.5	7.3	171	—	6.7	29	—
Glasgow	5.5	142	1.7	4.2	59	1.5	8.2	1,025	3.5	3.9	70	1.0	4.9	79	1.6
Hastings	9.4	205	2.4	4.8	56	1.7	10.3	821	4.8	5.5	77	1.7	5.7	24	2.9
Huddersfield	6.8	138	1.5	4.3	47	1.4	—	791	—	4.5	49	1.2	4.9	49	2.0
Hull	7.5	109	1.9	4.9	49	1.5	9.8	654	4.2	4.3	56	1.2	5.3	16	2.0
Ilfracombe	10.7	242	1.3	7.0	49	1.8	—	—	4.1	7.0	156	1.1	6.2	—	—
Inverness	5.6	117	1.7	4.6	49	0.9	8.1	778	3.2	4.5	47	0.8	5.1	36	2.4
Lincoln	7.0	116	1.9	3.4	30	1.6	9.1	577	4.3	4.3	67	1.5	3.9	12	2.2
Liverpool	7.8	138	1.7	5.3	19	1.7	9.9	732	—	4.8	60	1.6	5.3	26	2.2
Llandrindod Wells	7.1	196	0.9	3.1	51	0.7	8.7	1,048	3.1	3.4	151	0.6	3.7	52	1.8
London (Kew)	8.4	157	2.2	4.3	38	1.2	10.2	636	4.5	5.3	68	1.5	5.0	13	2.9
Lowestoft	8.0	136	2.2	4.7	43	1.3	9.6	557	4.4	4.3	71	0.9	4.9	12	2.4
Manchester Airport	7.9	130	1.7	4.5	27	1.7	9.7	819	4.0	4.7	55	1.6	4.9	35	2.0
Margate	9.5	118	2.1	5.5	40	1.3	10.7	505	4.6	5.5	47	1.1	5.7	19	2.5
Morecambe	7.7	154	1.8	5.0	31	1.8	9.8	986	4.1	4.7	67	1.5	5.0	51	2.0
Newquay	10.3	171	2.1	6.2	52	2.4	10.8	872	4.1	7.1	157	1.5	6.5	27	3.3
Nottingham	7.9	101	1.6	4.5	21	1.5	9.9	520	3.9	4.5	74	1.2	5.1	19	1.9
Oxford	8.5	150	2.2	4.3	34	1.4	10.1	640	4.5	4.8	105	1.4	4.7	22	2.5
Penzance	10.6	176	2.6	6.7	62	2.4	11.2	1,057	4.7	7.8	179	1.8	7.3	36	3.5
Plymouth	9.9	166	2.1	5.9	48	2.5	10.7	931	4.5	6.8	153	1.5	6.0	28	3.0
Prestwick	6.9	125	1.8	4.7	40	1.6	8.7	956	3.8	4.9	51	1.1	5.7	81	1.7
Ross-on-Wye	8.7	137	2.0	4.2	22	1.3	9.9	800	3.9	4.9	125	0.8	4.9	18	2.4
Sandown	10.0	233	2.2	5.5	34	2.2	—	—	5.3	5.4	105	1.7	6.5	20	3.4
Scarborough	7.4	89	2.0	5.2	55	1.4	9.5	561	4.2	4.7	48	1.2	5.5	12	2.3
Scilly	10.9	149	2.7	7.7	64	2.4	11.4	868	4.4	8.5	118	2.1	7.9	32	3.3
Sheffield	7.3	142	1.6	4.9	40	1.5	9.7	786	3.8	4.5	69	1.3	5.1	27	2.3
Shoeburyness	9.2	101	2.2	4.7	45	1.1	10.4	494	4.5	4.9	31	1.7	5.7	14	2.8
Shrewsbury	7.8	123	2.1	4.1	23	1.2	9.5	626	4.0	4.2	75	1.2	4.5	24	2.2
Skegness	7.1	110	2.0	4.7	46	1.3	—	519	4.3	4.1	60	1.5	4.5	9	2.0
Southampton	9.6	221	2.1	4.9	27	2.1	10.9	784	4.7	5.7	111	1.5	5.4	27	2.7
Stornoway	5.6	143	1.6	4.9	64	0.8	7.7	1,150	2.9	5.4	107	0.7	5.3	98	1.7
Tiree	7.1	164	1.7	6.1	73	1.1	8.8	1,127	3.5	6.5	87	1.2	6.4	83	1.3
Torbay	9.9	167	2.3	5.9	34	2.3	10.9	960	5.1	6.9	175	1.7	5.9	102	3.6
Weston-super-Mare	9.5	181	1.8	5.1	39	1.7	—	884	4.2	5.6	142	1.0	5.3	23	2.7
Weymouth	10.0	183	2.5	5.1	42	2.6	10.4	794	5.1	5.9	107	1.5	5.7	18	3.9
Worthing	9.3	191	2.1	4.9	29	2.1	10.5	795	5.2	5.7	80	2.0	5.6	15	3.4
York	6.3	98	1.8	4.2	29	1.6	9.2	589	4.2	3.8	57	1.0	4.5	10	2.2

TEMPERATURE, RAINFALL AND SUNSHINE AT VARIOUS PLACES IN GREAT BRITAIN

Mean Temperature of the air (° C.), Rainfall (mm.) and Bright Sunshine (as mean hours per day) at representative British Health Resorts and Towns during the year July 1970. to June, 1971, and the calendar year 1970. Fuller details of the weather are given in the *Monthly Weather Report* published by the Meteorological Office. (To convert ° C. to ° F. multiply by 9/5 and add 32.)

	1971											
	March			April			May			June		
	Temp.	Rain	Sun	Temp.	Rain	Sun	Temp.	Rain	Sun	Temp.	Rain	Sun
	°C.	mm.	hrs.	°C.	mm.	hrs.	°C.	mm.	hrs.	°C.	mm.	hrs.
Aberporth	5.4	63	2.7	7.7	59	4.6	10.7	45	8.4	11.9	117	5.3
Aberystwyth	5.7	50	2.8	8.1	49	4.9	11.5	37	8.6	12.5	85	4.3
Aldergrove	5.4	39	2.6	7.6	106	5.1	10.6	66	6.0	11.9	85	5.4
Ambleside	—	—	—	—	—	—	—	—	—	—	—	—
Balmoral	2.9	60	—	5.1	44	—	8.1	45	—	9.1	47	—
Bath	5.1	57	—	7.9	99	—	11.9	64	—	12.9	136	—
Birmingham	5.1	62	2.7	7.7	53	3.3	11.8	37	7.2	12.2	74	4.3
Bournemouth	5.5	62	4.5	8.5	55	6.1	11.9	31	7.8	13.3	148	6.6
Buxton	3.3	79	2.3	5.8	82	3.3	9.6	52	6.9	10.4	98	4.4
Cambridge	5.0	32	3.3	8.1	33	4.0	12.1	48	7.7	13.1	83	4.4
Cardiff	5.9	67	3.0	8.6	61	3.9	12.9	41	7.2	13.3	151	5.1
Cirencester	4.7	61	—	7.3	54	—	11.3	50	—	12.1	137	—
Douglas	5.5	143	2.7	7.7	85	5.3	10.3	36	7.3	11.3	81	5.9
Dovercourt	5.1	35	3.6	7.5	28	4.2	11.6	20	7.8	13.4	71	5.1
Dumfries	4.9	53	2.8	7.5	39	4.8	10.5	62	6.8	11.7	48	5.1
Dundee	5.6	34	3.5	7.6	65	4.8	11.1	75	7.3	11.6	37	5.5
Durham	5.0	62	2.9	7.1	49	4.0	10.7	48	8.4	11.2	59	4.6
Eastbourne	5.6	57	4.9	8.1	34	5.3	12.1	59	8.7	13.9	182	6.9
East Malling	5.2	56	3.2	7.6	41	3.9	11.8	52	7.0	13.5	122	5.5
Edinburgh	5.3	66	2.8	7.6	25	4.6	11.1	41	7.3	11.3	52	4.2
Falmouth	6.4	86	3.6	8.1	33	4.4	11.9	42	7.2	13.1	81	5.5
Glasgow	5.3	39	2.7	7.4	54	4.5	10.6	68	6.5	11.9	37	5.8
Hastings	5.2	43	4.1	8.3	41	5.2	12.3	42	8.0	13.5	152	6.2
Huddersfield	5.3	45	2.5	7.2	69	2.4	11.3	54	6.1	11.9	72	3.9
Hull	5.7	41	3.1	7.5	51	3.4	11.5	36	7.1	12.5	60	4.6
Ilfracombe	6.4	—	—	8.7	—	—	12.0	—	—	13.1	—	—
Inverness	5.7	34	2.5	7.7	15	4.8	11.7	42	6.8	11.2	63	4.0
Lincoln	5.0	45	3.2	7.3	40	3.5	10.9	41	7.4	11.8	45	4.7
Liverpool	5.5	56	2.6	8.4	68	4.1	12.1	25	7.8	12.7	80	5.1
Llandrindod Wells	4.5	66	2.5	7.1	49	3.2	10.8	57	6.3	11.7	88	3.7
London (Kew)	5.7	42	3.5	8.1	36	3.8	12.1	67	4.8	13.5	131	5.6
Lowestoft	5.2	33	3.2	7.3	16	4.0	11.5	26	7.6	12.7	62	5.8
Manchester Airport	5.3	46	2.3	8.1	64	3.7	11.7	48	7.0	12.4	74	4.2
Margate	5.5	37	3.8	7.8	41	4.0	12.1	40	7.3	13.8	80	5.6
Morecambe	5.1	48	2.5	8.6	39	4.6	12.1	49	8.1	12.9	66	4.8
Newquay	6.3	66	3.6	8.4	22	5.1	11.5	64	7.9	13.2	94	6.6
Nottingham	5.7	42	2.8	8.1	51	2.8	12.0	35	6.7	12.7	79	4.1
Oxford	5.5	43	3.4	8.1	45	4.1	12.3	46	7.4	13.1	136	4.8
Penzance	7.0	76	4.6	8.7	37	4.6	11.7	55	7.4	13.5	89	5.9
Plymouth	6.3	73	3.9	8.9	36	5.1	12.4	50	7.2	14.0	93	5.9
Prestwick	5.3	43	2.6	7.7	19	5.5	10.7	45	7.6	11.5	50	6.1
Ross-on-Wye	5.7	66	3.0	8.1	46	3.4	12.0	49	7.6	12.9	115	4.6
Sandown	6.3	54	4.4	8.5	48	5.9	12.5	29	8.4	14.2	170	7.4
Scarborough	6.7	28	2.8	6.7	64	3.6	10.4	35	6.6	11.3	70	4.1
Scilly	7.6	62	4.2	9.1	51	4.7	11.7	74	7.2	13.2	80	5.9
Sheffield	5.4	47	2.6	7.7	84	2.3	11.7	63	6.7	12.2	67	4.4
Shoeburyness	5.5	36	3.7	7.4	31	4.0	11.6	40	7.6	13.9	105	5.9
Shrewsbury	5.4	41	2.8	7.4	50	3.3	11.4	34	7.2	12.3	74	4.6
Skegness	5.3	36	3.2	7.1	32	4.0	11.5	41	7.5	12.7	38	5.3
Southampton	5.9	72	3.9	9.0	52	5.5	12.9	30	7.7	13.9	130	5.8
Stornoway	5.5	93	3.4	6.9	67	4.0	9.8	79	5.8	10.1	49	4.9
Tiree	6.5	62	3.5	7.8	91	5.8	10.3	48	6.3	11.2	49	8.5
Torbay	6.3	66	4.0	8.3	68	5.4	12.3	14	8.2	13.8	119	6.5
Weston-super-Mare	5.8	65	3.3	—	—	—	—	—	—	—	—	—
Weymouth	5.7	55	4.6	7.9	49	5.9	11.5	18	8.6	13.1	90	7.0
Worthing	5.7	55	4.5	—	—	—	—	—	—	—	—	—
York	5.3	35	2.7	7.1	45	3.0	11.1	33	7.6	12.2	51	4.6

Weather Record, August, 1970 / Weather Record, September, 1970

Day	Temperature Max.	Min.	Wind Speed	Rainfall	Sunshine	Temperature Max.	Min.	Wind Speed	Rainfall	Sunshine	Day
	°C.	°C.	knots	mm.	hours	°C.	°C.	knots	mm.	hours	
1	26.1	8.9	2.3	—	11.1	18.5	9.0	6.6	—	10.6	1
2	25.9	10.0	2.1	—	11.5	16.1	4.9	7.2	2.3	0.1	2
3	27.5	10.8	3.5	—	8.3	19.6	14.0	5.1	—	3.7	3
4	26.9	16.4	6.8	—	5.7	22.6	12.4	7.7	—	5.0	4
5	24.8	17.0	7.7	2.8	2.2	22.4	15.0	6.8	—	6.7	5
6	23.6	16.9	4.2	4.6	4.1	21.5	10.6	3.0	—	5.2	6
7	22.3	14.4	3.6	5.6	2.6	23.3	11.1	5.2	0.4	6.2	7
8	20.6	13.9	3.0	1.4	1.9	20.2	15.6	13.0	8.1	4.9	8
9	22.4	11.5	5.3	1.6	8.9	16.5	13.2	15.1	1.7	0.5	9
10	20.8	14.5	7.5	1.1	0.3	16.6	11.2	13.7	5.9	6.0	10
11	21.5	13.4	3.3	—	13.8	17.9	10.4	8.4	2.5	4.8	11
12	22.2	10.0	5.0	—	7.3	14.7	10.6	5.3	16.4	0.3	12
13	25.7	12.0	5.9	—	7.3	16.1	5.9	7.7	4.3	3.9	13
14	20.8	12.9	5.8	—	11.8	16.5	13.4	2.9	8.5	1.2	14
15	19.1	10.0	5.7	0.5	4.5	16.7	9.8	2.6	4.7	4.7	15
16	17.9	13.4	12.7	—	6.7	16.6	7.4	5.7	—	8.2	16
17	17.3	10.2	8.1	—	6.4	18.7	11.3	8.6	—	10.3	17
18	17.7	3.3	2.4	17.5	5.0	21.9	4.6	1.7	—	9.2	18
19	16.6	12.5	5.8	11.6	—	22.1	6.3	0.5	—	9.9	19
20	16.6	8.2	3.7	3.1	1.3	24.8	9.6	0.9	—	11.0	20
21	17.4	12.7	3.6	3.5	1.0	20.8	10.3	3.7	—	0.2	21
22	17.3	10.9	3.0	0.2	1.8	17.6	14.8	6.5	—	3.9	22
23	18.9	9.7	5.1	—	4.1	21.4	4.8	2.1	—	7.2	23
24	20.8	13.1	5.3	—	6.4	21.0	5.7	0.5	—	10.2	24
25	20.1	13.5	3.6	—	5.0	22.8	5.6	1.8	—	8.6	25
26	21.7	13.0	6.0	—	9.7	20.9	5.3	2.0	—	2.3	26
27	23.8	8.7	3.1	—	8.1	21.3	10.1	0.5	—	3.4	27
28	21.9	7.5	4.1	—	8.7	25.1	10.5	2.8	—	8.6	28
29	22.4	7.7	3.0	—	11.5	21.1	9.7	3.3	1.9	4.6	29
30	25.1	9.1	2.0	—	10.5	17.8	8.7	7.8	—	3.1	30
31	23.3	13.3	7.7	0.1	5.1						
Total ..	—	—	—	53.6	192.6	—	—	—	56.7	164.5	.. Total
Mean ..	21.6	11.6	4.9	—	—	19.8	9.7	5.3	—	—	.. Mean
Temp.°F.	70.9	52.9	—	—	—	67.6	49.5	—	—	—	Temp.°F.
Average ..	70.5	55.6	6.2	57	188	65.5	51.6	6.6	50	142	..Average

Weather Record, October, 1970 / Weather Record, November, 1970

Day	Temperature Max.	Min.	Wind Speed	Rainfall	Sunshine	Temperature Max.	Min.	Wind Speed	Rainfall	Sunshine	Day
	°C.	°C.	knots	mm.	hours	°C.	°C.	knots	mm.	hours	
1	17.0	10.2	7.7	—	6.0	14.7	11.6	9.2	10.6	5.0	1
2	15.4	13.9	12.7	0.5	5.2	16.7	10.6	10.3	9.5	—	2
3	15.6	9.3	9.5	—	7.5	14.0	10.9	12.4	—	6.6	3
4	19.2	9.9	7.8	—	0.7	12.6	7.7	8.6	0.1	3.9	4
5	17.7	13.9	10.9	3.5	2.1	12.6	8.3	7.4	—	7.5	5
6	13.9	8.8	4.7	1.8	4.1	10.5	4.2	2.4	16.8	0.3	6
7	14.1	0.3	3.3	—	8.0	9.5	6.6	8.7	0.2	—	7
8	14.4	0.1	0.7	—	7.3	10.8	-0.8	5.8	0.1	0.5	8
9	15.9	-0.9	2.5	—	9.3	11.7	8.7	8.7	—	5.0	9
10	16.1	6.4	4.0	0.4	—	11.4	6.1	4.6	1.0	0.2	10
11	20.2	11.9	4.9	0.1	0.7	14.7	11.4	13.6	8.6	0.4	11
12	19.2	9.0	1.0	—	1.5	8.4	6.4	6.2	0.1	0.1	12
13	18.1	11.2	1.3	—	0.8	10.2	0.7	6.6	19.6	6.2	13
14	16.4	12.4	3.7	—	—	8.1	4.5	5.7	33.0	—	14
15	14.9	12.5	5.8	—	1.6	6.3	2.0	7.6	—	4.8	15
16	16.5	1.3	3.2	—	6.3	9.5	-3.5	6.0	3.9	—	16
17	17.6	0.9	0.1	—	8.4	12.9	-0.6	6.1	7.3	0.8	17
18	16.4	1.4	5.3	1.7	6.3	13.3	7.0	9.7	13.7	—	18
19	13.7	10.7	11.3	—	6.2	9.5	8.5	9.7	0.8	1.1	19
20	10.0	4.2	9.2	—	5.6	10.6	-0.3	5.5	3.3	0.1	20
21	9.2	3.3	8.7	—	5.6	9.0	5.0	6.5	—	5.0	21
22	10.9	2.5	2.7	0.2	0.1	9.8	-2.4	2.7	8.8	6.4	22
23	10.8	2.8	3.1	—	—	13.9	5.3	9.9	—	—	23
24	14.7	8.7	6.0	—	0.2	14.4	6.8	4.7	—	3.6	24
25	14.5	10.5	11.0	1.2	—	14.1	4.5	2.4	—	4.3	25
26	13.3	10.1	6.2	—	5.8	13.8	1.9	1.6	—	1.3	26
27	12.8	0.8	4.7	1.5	—	12.0	4.2	3.6	0.1	0.5	27
28	16.3	12.8	8.6	—	0.5	13.7	8.4	4.4	12.2	0.1	28
29	15.8	8.4	8.8	—	4.2	13.6	8.7	7.0	6.9	—	29
30	17.1	12.4	12.7	3.4	—	10.1	5.6	5.2	0.3	1.3	30
31	15.4	13.4	12.7	0.2	—						
Total ..	—	—	—	14.5	104.0	—	—	—	156.9	65.0	.. Total
Mean ..	15.3	7.5	6.3	—	—	11.7	5.1	6.8	—	—	.. Mean
Temp.°F.	59.5	45.5	—	—	—	53.1	41.2	—	—	—	Temp.°F.
Average ..	57.6	45.3	6.6	57	97	49.8	40.6	6.8	63	53	..Average

Entries of Maximum Temperature cover day period 9–21 h.; Minimum Temperature night period 21–9 h. and are entered to day of reading; Rainfall the 24 hours commencing at 9 h. on day of entry; Sunshine the 24 hours 0–24 h.; Mean Wind Speed in knots at 50 ft. above ground (100 knots = 110·5 m.p.h.); Rainfall 1000 mm. = 39·37 in.

Weather Record, December, 1970

Day	Temperature Max.	Min.	Wind Speed	Rainfall	Sunshine
	°C.	°C.	knots	mm.	hours
1	8·8	7·4	5·0	—	—
2	11·3	2·6	7·5	1·4	0·8
3	10·9	10·2	4·8	13·0	—
4	12·3	8·8	6·7	0·9	2·1
5	10·3	5·9	7·0	—	5·8
6	10·9	8·7	9·8	3·6	2·6
7	8·0	2·3	7·0	0·1	0·2
8	8·3	4·0	5·2	—	4·6
9	3·2	-3·6	1·0	—	—
10	8·2	3·0	7·9	—	—
11	5·3	4·7	5·3	—	—
12	10·9	4·5	5·6	0·8	1·1
13	5·0	-1·4	0·5	—	—
14	3·9	-0·4	0·8	—	—
15	7·0	-2·7	1·4	—	1·2
16	6·6	2·5	4·7	—	—
17	10·6	4·7	6·5	0·2	—
18	11·4	1·6	6·1	—	0·1
19	10·8	8·2	7·3	—	2·1
20	9·0	2·8	4·3	—	0·1
21	5·5	-1·6	7·7	—	2·5
22	4·2	-1·5	9·0	—	1·9
23	5·7	2·0	8·3	4·0	—
24	2·3	0·6	11·9	1·0	3·5
25	1·0	-2·7	9·1	1·2	3·2
26	1·2	-1·3	10·4	2·4	2·8
27	0·1	-2·4	10·0	—	—
28	2·7	-0·8	12·2	3·6	—
29	1·6	1·1	11·0	6·1	—
30	3·3	0·7	13·0	—	0·6
31	2·1	-1·5	7·5	—	2·0
Total	—	—	—	38·3	37·2
Mean	6·5	2·1	6·9	—	—
Temp.°F.	43·7	35·8	—	—	—
Average	45·7	37·4	7·6	52	40

Weather Record, January, 1971

Temperature Max.	Min.	Wind Speed	Rainfall	Sunshine	Day
°C.	°C.	knots	mm.	hours	
1·9	-1·4	4·5	—	1·2	1
0·2	-6·1	1·0	—	—	2
-0·2	-2·6	1·7	—	—	3
-1·1	-2·1	1·7	—	—	4
0·8	-5·4	6·7	—	3·1	5
6·5	-1·1	6·3	0·4	—	6
11·3	6·5	15·7	4·1	—	7
11·4	9·2	8·7	—	0·1	8
11·6	8·1	10·3	—	—	9
13·7	1·1	3·6	—	4·9	10
6·1	2·4	8·0	—	5·0	11
9·1	-1·0	2·0	—	0·2	12
9·2	3·1	4·7	0·1	1·2	13
5·5	2·0	6·1	1·7	0·8	14
8·1	4·6	6·7	1·2	—	15
7·5	3·6	5·8	6·7	—	16
10·1	4·3	4·6	—	0·3	17
7·5	6·8	11·5	2·1	0·2	18
9·8	7·1	11·5	7·9	0·8	19
8·4	3·9	10·2	8·3	5·0	20
9·7	7·2	12·3	0·9	1·4	21
7·3	6·4	8·0	3·9	—	22
12·5	4·2	14·9	8·4	—	23
9·7	4·7	15·5	1·3	5·6	24
9·3	7·0	14·8	6·1	2·8	25
9·0	6·8	9·5	8·1	—	26
9·6	2·9	8·2	0·7	2·0	27
9·6	5·0	10·6	0·4	3·9	28
7·7	2·5	4·5	1·7	5·7	29
3·7	1·6	5·9	2·4	—	30
5·8	3·0	4·1	1·6	1·6	31
—	—	—	68·0	45·8	Total
7·5	3·0	7·7	—	—	Mean
45·5	37·4	—	—	—	Temp.°F.
43·7	35·2	8·1	55	46	Average

Weather Record, February, 1971

Day	Temperature Max.	Min.	Wind Speed	Rainfall	Sunshine
	°C.	°C.	knots	mm.	hours
1	4·3	0·4	15·4	—	—
2	5·0	-2·9	5·4	—	3·9
3	11·2	2·5	7·9	—	—
4	10·5	-0·2	3·0	—	1·6
5	8·3	6·9	9·8	—	—
6	6·0	5·3	4·7	—	—
7	9·4	4·3	3·6	—	1·6
8	7·5	-0·1	3·3	—	—
9	7·5	5·3	4·0	—	—
10	8·9	-0·7	2·6	—	2·4
11	7·5	-0·6	3·4	—	—
12	10·9	5·7	15·6	2·2	—
13	9·1	5·8	14·3	—	7·7
14	9·4	2·5	12·5	4·7	5·8
15	7·4	2·6	9·6	0·3	4·2
16	5·2	-2·8	5·4	1·6	2·1
17	7·7	-1·6	6·4	2·5	—
18	8·9	5·5	8·7	0·3	2·4
19	9·8	0·2	3·0	0·8	7·9
20	11·6	5·9	8·7	0·6	0·5
21	11·3	4·4	8·7	—	6·3
22	9·9	0·2	3·6	—	8·5
23	9·7	-3·9	3·1	—	8·4
24	10·8	-2·9	4·0	—	7·4
25	8·8	-0·8	3·4	—	4·6
26	8·5	2·7	3·4	—	3·0
27	6·2	0·8	5·7	—	1·1
28	4·4	0·8	4·7	—	1·2
Total	—	—	—	13·0	80·6
Mean	8·4	1·6	6·6	—	—
Temp.°F.	47·1	34·9	—	—	—
Average	44·6	35·1	8·3	39	64

Weather Record, March, 1971

Temperature Max.	Min.	Wind Speed	Rainfall	Sunshine	Day
°C.	°C.	knots	mm.	hours.	
5·0	1·4	4·9	6·9	4·3	1
8·7	0·2	7·9	—	4·9	2
4·1	1·7	12·0	0·1	3·2	3
3·2	-1·9	9·8	—	5·4	4
2·1	-3·4	6·3	—	1·3	5
0·4	-0·7	12·4	—	3·7	6
3·1	-3·9	5·5	0·3	5·5	7
7·7	0·0	5·5	0·6	—	8
10·9	4·1	7·7	—	2·8	9
8·1	-0·4	7·0	—	9·6	10
10·6	5·0	5·2	—	0·9	11
11·0	3·6	7·1	—	3·7	12
10·3	6·6	5·3	0·2	—	13
10·9	-1·3	2·5	13·3	0·9	14
8·5	3·3	6·9	2·5	1·8	15
9·3	-0·7	7·8	—	3·3	16
10·6	2·5	9·9	10·4	6·7	17
10·5	7·6	14·2	3·5	—	18
8·3	6·9	8·8	2·5	—	19
11·2	5·0	6·6	0·5	2·0	20
8·0	5·1	12·7	—	—	21
9·6	5·6	15·0	—	8·6	22
10·6	-1·3	8·5	—	6·5	23
13·2	6·8	10·8	0·2	0·6	24
11·4	7·8	11·8	0·1	6·1	25
10·7	2·7	8·7	—	6·6	26
10·4	4·7	7·0	—	9·2	27
12·3	0·5	7·0	0·4	0·1	28
11·1	6·6	4·3	0·1	—	29
13·2	-1·0	7·6	—	9·5	30
9·9	2·8	7·7	—	2·2	31
—	—	—	41·6	109·4	Total
8·9	2·4	8·2	—	—	Mean
48·0	36·3	—	—	—	Temp.°F.
50·2	37·4	8·0	37	113	Average

See footnote, p. 1068

Weather Record, April, 1971 / Weather Record, May, 1971

Day	Temperature Max.	Min.	Wind Speed	Rainfall	Sunshine	Temperature Max.	Min.	Wind Speed	Rainfall	Sunshine	Day
	°C.	°C.	knots	mm.	hours	°C.	°C.	knots	mm.	hours	
1	7.6	4.5	6.3	—	—	13.9	2.6	11.0	—	12.3	1
2	11.6	5.4	14.7	—	1.5	15.3	1.9	6.9	—	13.3	2
3	8.6	4.2	13.4	—	0.1	16.2	−1.9	3.4	—	12.7	3
4	10.9	5.2	10.6	—	0.6	18.5	−0.3	3.1	—	9.4	4
5	8.4	5.2	5.7	—	—	18.7	6.4	7.9	—	6.6	5
6	9.6	7.1	3.6	—	—	22.0	10.3	8.2	15.4	2.9	6
7	9.6	6.2	6.5	—	—	15.9	8.0	4.2	6.0	—	7
8	9.5	6.3	12.7	4.7	—	18.5	6.8	6.0	—	11.8	8
9	8.4	5.2	14.0	—	—	18.6	6.1	7.5	—	9.1	9
10	12.4	4.8	11.4	—	3.9	20.9	8.6	6.2	—	11.2	10
11	13.6	3.0	9.2	—	10.7	23.4	7.5	3.3	—	9.3	11
12	14.3	0.4	11.0	—	9.9	22.0	6.8	7.1	—	11.0	12
13	9.7	6.5	11.2	—	2.6	19.9	11.8	11.2	—	9.3	13
14	8.7	5.6	9.2	—	—	19.5	7.9	7.3	—	8.6	14
15	16.2	4.9	3.7	—	7.0	18.9	4.9	4.2	7.6	5.3	15
16	12.2	7.3	10.2	0.1	1.2	13.7	6.9	3.9	1.8	3.5	16
17	12.4	2.6	9.1	—	11.9	16.0	8.4	5.2	—	8.5	17
18	12.8	4.6	8.5	—	4.0	18.5	0.6	2.1	—	13.5	18
19	14.1	2.4	2.2	—	0.3	20.0	9.7	6.8	—	12.1	19
20	17.5	1.3	3.3	—	7.8	19.9	4.5	6.1	—	13.2	20
21	17.3	5.1	12.1	—	11.0	18.0	3.6	6.9	—	14.6	21
22	21.6	9.3	6.5	2.5	4.5	16.5	7.0	4.4	0.9	1.6	22
23	14.5	12.7	5.7	20.2	—	17.0	12.1	4.1	4.8	4.0	23
24	10.3	7.4	10.3	2.0	—	18.3	4.7	2.0	23.7	8.9	24
25	9.9	5.1	6.6	3.1	1.8	12.3	9.7	8.1	0.1	0.2	25
26	5.0	3.3	9.8	3.6	0.1	14.0	8.9	3.9	1.0	0.2	26
27	10.3	−0.9	5.8	—	7.7	12.3	9.6	4.9	4.5	2.7	27
28	11.9	0.9	4.1	—	12.3	16.0	2.8	4.0	—	10.4	28
29	13.2	−1.4	5.4	—	6.6	15.5	5.0	8.0	0.4	4.0	29
30	11.3	−1.5	7.1	—	9.4	15.9	11.1	7.3	0.6	0.2	30
31						19.0	9.7	2.5	—	11.0	31
Total ..	—	—	—	36.2	114.9	—	—	—	66.8	241.4	.. Total
Mean ..	11.8	4.4	8.3	—	—	17.6	6.5	5.7	—	—	.. Mean
Temp.°F.	53.2	39.9	—	—	—	63.7	43.7	—	—	—	Temp.°C.
Average ..	55.8		8.1	46	160	62.4	46.4	5.7	46	198	..Average

Weather Record, June, 1971 / Weather Record, July, 1971

Day	Temperature Max.	Min.	Wind Speed	Rainfall	Sunshine	Temperature Max.	Min.	Wind Speed	Rainfall	Sunshine	Day
	°C.	°C.	knots	mm.	hours	°C.	°C.	knots	mm.	hours	
1	21.2	6.7	5.1	—	13.3	22.0	15.0	2.0	—	3.0	1
2	22.3	9.3	10.0	0.1	12.1	24.1	13.3	2.4	—	4.7	2
3	23.4	12.3	11.5	—	9.2	20.0	13.9	6.9	—	8.8	3
4	16.3	9.6	12.7	—	9.7	23.0	14.4	5.0	0.6	1.8	4
5	12.8	9.9	10.5	—	—	21.2	14.3	6.0	—	3.2	5
6	13.4	9.7	4.3	—	—	22.9	13.4	7.0	—	10.1	6
7	15.8	10.5	2.3	—	0.2	24.0	13.6	7.8	—	11.2	7
8	15.9	11.2	4.5	12.9	2.2	27.8	14.4	2.6	—	9.4	8
9	16.5	10.6	6.9	1.3	4.3	27.9	14.2	5.5	—	11.9	9
10	12.5	10.9	10.5	28.4	—	25.5	16.4	5.6	—	8.5	10
11	14.9	9.4	8.0	—	4.2	28.6	10.3	1.0	—	12.7	11
12	15.5	5.6	4.2	—	1.7	23.0	16.8	9.7	—	4.9	12
13	18.5	6.3	3.3	12.6	11.7	21.4	10.5	7.2	—	14.7	13
14	12.7	9.5	10.4	22.0	—	23.8	6.6	4.3	—	10.2	14
15	14.2	7.7	7.7	—	5.4	26.1	14.6	5.9	—	14.0	15
16	15.8	9.3	6.8	0.9	6.2	20.1	12.1	6.4	—	8.1	16
17	15.7	9.1	5.5	1.0	6.4	19.9	6.5	5.0	—	11.1	17
18	13.7	8.9	8.4	28.3	—	18.2	4.8	2.9	—	5.1	18
19	17.8	12.3	6.8	8.5	2.3	21.7	5.1	2.3	—	4.3	19
20	17.5	11.9	9.3	—	3.8	21.0	12.5	2.9	0.6	5.9	20
21	17.0	6.4	8.7	—	3.5	20.7	13.7	2.8	—	2.2	21
22	19.4	12.7	7.3	—	14.5	23.7	8.2	3.0	—	7.4	22
23	20.7	8.2	3.1	—	4.5	22.1	12.2	3.6	1.4	3.3	23
24	22.8	10.9	5.3	—	13.7	21.8	13.6	8.0	0.7	6.6	24
25	19.9	10.2	8.9	0.1	5.1	21.7	12.1	5.8	2.4	5.1	25
26	18.7	13.6	10.0	1.5	5.0	22.6	10.9	7.4	3.8	9.7	26
27	16.9	10.8	8.3	12.5	8.2	20.7	12.2	1.6	12.3	2.4	27
28	18.4	9.0	6.6	1.3	10.8	21.4	14.7	1.6	—	4.5	28
29	17.4	6.2	6.5	—	2.5	24.5	9.3	2.1	—	10.9	29
30	20.0	12.6	3.5	—	7.7	25.6	8.2	4.6	2.8	12.7	30
31						22.1	14.9	9.3	0.1	10.2	31
Total ..	—	—	—	131.4	168.2	—	—	—	24.7	238.6	.. Total
Mean ..	17.3	9.7	7.2	—	—	22.9	12.0	4.8	—	—	.. Mean
Temp.°F.	63.1	49.5	—	—	—	73.2	53.6	—	—	—	Temp.°F.
Average ..	68.5	52.5	7.2	44	213	71.2	56.1	6.8	62	198	..Average

See footnote, p. 1068

Principal Book Publishers and Their Addresses

More than 3,700 firms, individuals and societies have published one or more books in recent years. The list which follows is a selective one comprising, in the main, those firms whose names are most familiar to the general public. An interleaved list containing some 2,000 names and addresses is available, price 60p post free, from the publishers of "Whitaker."

Abelard-Schumann, Intertext House, Stewarts Rd., S.W.8.
Aberdeen University Press, Aberdeen.
Allan (Ian), Terminal House, Shepperton, Mddx.
Allen (J. A.), 1 Lower Grosvenor Pl., S.W.1.
Allen (W. H.), 43 Essex St., W.C.2.
Allen & Unwin, 40 Museum St., W.C.1.
Angus & Robertson, 54 Bartholomew Close, E.C.1.
Architectural Press, 9 Queen Anne's Gate, S.W.1.
Arco, 3 Upper James St. W.1.
Arlington Books, 38 Bury Street, S.W.1.
Arms & Armour Press, 677 Finchley Rd., N.W.2.
Arnold (E.), & Co., 41 Maddox St., W.1
Arnold (E. J.) & Son, Butterley St., Leeds.
Arrow Books, 3 Fitzroy Square, W.1.
Athlone Press, 2 Gower St., W.C.1.
Autopress, 76 Bennett Rd., Brighton.
Baillière & Tindall, 8 Henrietta St., W.C.2.
Baker (John), 5 Royal Opera Arcade, S.W.1.
Barker (Arthur), 5 Winsley St., W.1.
Barrie & Jenkins, 2 Clement's Inn, W.C.2.
Bartholomew & Son, 12 Duncan St., Edinburgh.
Batsford, 4 Fitzhardinge St., Portman Square, W1.
Bell (Geo.) & Sons, 6 Portugal St., W.C.2.
Benn (Ernest), 154 Fleet St., E.C.4.
Bingley (Clive), 16 Pembridge Rd., W.11.
Black (A. & C.), 4 Soho Sq., W1.
Blackie, Glasgow, and 5 Fitzhardinge St., W.1.
Blackwell (Basil), 49 Broad Street, Oxford.
Blackwood, Edinburgh and Buckingham House, Buckingham St., W.C.2.
Blandford Press, 167 High Holborn, W.C.1.
Blond (Anthony), 56 Doughty St., W.C.1.
Bodley Head. 9 Bow St., W.C.2
Bowes & Bowes, 9 Bow St., W.C.2.
Brockhampton Press. Salisbury Rd., Leicester.
Brown, Son & Ferguson, 52 Darnley St., Glasgow.
Brython Press, 350 Stanley Rd., Liverpool.
Burke Pub. Co., 14 John St., W.C.1.
Butterworth & Co., 88 Kingsway, W.C.2.
Calder & Boyars, 18 Brewer St., W.1.
Cambridge Univ. Press, 200 Euston Rd., N.W.1, and Cambridge.
Cape (Jonathan), 30 Bedford Square, W.C.1.
Cassell & Co., 35 Red Lion Sq., W.C.1.
Centaur Press. Fontwell, Arundel, Sx.
Chambers (W. & R.), 11 Thistle St., Edinburgh.
Chapman & Hall, 11 New Fetter Lane, E.C.4.
Chapman (Geoffrey), 18 Wimbledon High St., S.W.19.
Chatto & Windus, 40–42 William IV St., W.C.2.
C.M.S., 157 Waterloo Rd., S.E.1.
Churchill (J. & A.), 104 Gloucester Place W.1.
Clark (T. & T.), 38 George St., Edinburgh, 2.
Clarke (Jas.) & Co., 7 All Saints Passage, Cambridge.
Clowes (Wm.), 14 Lower Regent St., S.W.1.
Collier-Macmillan, 29 Wrights Lane, W.8.
Collingridge, 42 The Centre, Feltham, Mddx.
Collins, Sons & Co., 14 St. James's Place, S.W.1.
Constable & Co., 10 & 12 Orange St., W.C.2.
Cooper (Leo), 196 Shaftesbury Ave., W.C.2.
Corgi Books, 57 Uxbridge Road, W.5.
Country Life, 42 The Centre, Feltham, Mddx.
Darton, Longman & Todd, 85 Gloucester Rd., S.W.7.

David & Charles, South Devon Ho., Railway Stn. Newton Abbot, Devon.
Davies (Peter), 15 Queen St., W.1.
Davis (R. Hart-), 3 Upper James St., W.1.
Dean & Son, 43 Ludgate Hill, E.C.4.
Dent (J. M.) & Sons, 10 Bedford St., W.C.2.
Deutsch (A.), 105 Gt. Russell St., W.C.1.
Dickens Press, 161 Queen Victoria St., E.C.4.
Dobson (Books), 80 Kensington Church St., W.8.
Dryad Press, Northgates, Leicester.
Duckworth & Co., 3 Henrietta St., W.C.2.
Educational Prodns., 17 Denbigh St., S.W.1.
Elek, 2 All Saints St., N.1.
Elliot Right Way Books, Kingswood Bldg., Kingswood, Surrey.
Encyclopædia Britannica, 18 Regent St., S.W.1.
English Universities Press, Warwick Lane, E.C.4.
Epworth Press, 27 Marylebone Rd., N.W.1.
Evans Bros., Montague House, Russell Sq., W.C.1.
Eyre & Spottiswoode, 11 New Fetter Lane, E.C.4.
Faber & Faber, 3 Queen Square, W.C.1.
Focal Press, 31 Fitzroy Square, W.1.
Foulis (G. T.), 50A Bell St., Henley-on-Thames, Oxon.
Foulsham & Co., Yeovil Rd., Slough, Bucks.
Fountain Press, 46 Chancery Lane, W.C.2.
French (Samuel), 26 Southampton St., W.C.2.
Frewin (Leslie), 1 New Quebec St., W.1.
Gale & Polden, Wellington Press, Aldershot.
Gall & Inglis, 12 Newington Road, Edinburgh, 9.
Gee & Co., 151 Strand, W.C.2.
Geographia, 178 Gt. Portland St., W.1.
Gibbons (Stanley), 391 Strand, W.C.2.
Gibson (Robert), 2 West Regent St., Glasgow.
Gifford (John), 125 Charing Cross Road, W.C.2.
Ginn & Co., 18 Bedford Row, W.C.1.
Gollancz (Victor), 14 Henrietta St., W.C.2.
Green (W.), St. Giles St., Edinburgh.
Gresham (John), 63 Old Brompton Rd., S.W.7.
Griffin (Charles), 42 Drury Lane, W.C.2.
Guinness Superlatives, 2 Cecil Court, London Road, Enfield.
H.M. Stationery Office, Atlantic Ho., Holborn Viaduct, E.C.1.
Hachette, 4 Regent Place, W.1.
Hale (Robert), 63 Old Brompton Rd., S.W.7.
Hamilton (Hamish), 90 Gt. Russell St., W.C.1.
Hamlyn, 42 The Centre, Feltham, Mddx.
Harrap (G. G.) & Co., 182 High Holborn, W.C.1.
Harvill Press, 30A Pavilion Rd., S.W.1.
Heffer & Sons, 20 Trinity Street, Cambridge.
Heinemann (Wm.), 15 Queen St., W.1.
Hodder & Stoughton, Warwick Lane, E.C.4.
Hodge & Co., 12 Bank St., Edinburgh.
Hogarth Press, 40–42 William IV St., W.C.2.
Hollis & Carter, 9 Bow St., W.C.2.
Holmes-Macdougall, 30 Royal Terr., Edinburgh.
Hughes & Son, 29 Rivulet Rd., Wrexham.
Hurst & Blackett, 3 Fitzroy Square, W.1.
Hutchinson & Co., 3 Fitzroy Square, W.1.
Iliffe & Sons, Bell Yard, W.C.2.
Independent Press, 86 Tavistock Pl., W.C.1.
Jackdaw Publications, 30 Bedford Sq., W.C.1.
Jarrold & Sons, Barrack Street, Norwich.
Jarrolds, 3 Fitzroy Square, W.1.
Johnson Pubns., 11 Stanhope Mews West, S.W.7.
Johnston & Bacon, 18 High Street, S.W.19.
Jordan & Sons, 82 City Rd., E.C.1.
Joseph (Michael), 52 Bedford Sq., W.C.1.

Kaye & Ward, 194 Bishopsgate, E.C.2.
Kelly's Directories, Neville House, Eden St., Kingston, Surrey.
Kimber (Wm.), 22A Queen Anne's Gate, S.W.1.
Kimpton (Henry), 205 Gt. Portland St., W.1.
Lane (Allen), The Penguin Press, Vigo St., W.1.
Lawrence & Wishart, 46 Bedford Row, W.C.1
Lewis (H. K.), 136 Gower St., W.C.1.
Livingstone (E. & S.), 17 Teviot Pl., Edinburgh.
Lockwood (Crosby), 26 Old Brompton Rd., S.W.7.
Long (John), 3 Fitzroy Square, W.1.
Longman Group, Burnt Mill, Harlow, Essex.
Low (S.), Marston & Co., 52 Poland St., W.1.
Lutterworth Press, Albion House, Woking, Surrey.
Macdonald & Co., 49 Poland St., W.1.
Macdonald & Evans, 8 John St., W.C. 1.
MacGibbon & Kee, 3 Upper James St., W.1.
McGraw-Hill, Shoppenhangers Rd., Maidenhead, Berks.
Machinery Pub. Co., New England St., Brighton.
MacLellan (Wm.), 90 Buccleuch Street, Glasgow.
Macmillan & Co., 4 Little Essex St., W.C.2.
Marshall, Morgan & Scott, 1-5 Portpool Lane, E.C.1.
May Fair Books, 14 St James's Pl., S.W.1
Mayflower, 3 Upper James St., W.1.
Methuen & Co., 11 New Fetter Lane, E.C.4.
Mills & Boon, 17 Foley St., W.1.
Mowbray, The Alden Press, Osney Mead, Oxford.
Muller (F.), 110 Fleet St., E.C.4.
Murray (John), 50 Albemarle St., W.1.
Museum Press, 39 Parker St. W.C.2.
National C.E.C., Robt. Denholm House, Nutfield, Surrey.
Nelson (T.), 36 Park St., W.1.
New Authors, 3 Fitzroy Square, W.1.
Newman Neame, 350 Gray's Inn Road, W.C.1.
Newnes (G.), 42 The Centre, Feltham, Mddx.
Nisbet & Co., Digswell Pl., Welwyn, Herts.
Nonesuch Library, 9 Bow St. W.C.2.
Novello & Co., Borough Green, Sevenoaks, Kent.
Odhams Books, 42 The Centre, Feltham, Mddx.
Oliphants, 1-5 Portpool Lane, E.C.1.
Oliver & Boyd, 14 High Street, Edinburgh.
Owen (Peter), 12 Kendrick Mews, S.W.7.
Oxford Univ. Press, 37 Dover St., W.1.
Pall Mall Press, 5 Cromwell Pl., S.W.7.
Pan Books, 33 Tothill St., S.W.1.
Panther, 3 Upper James St., W.1.
Paul (Kegan), 43 Gt. Russell St., W.C.1.
Paul (Stanley), 3 Fitzroy Square, W.1.
Pearson (C. A.), 42 The Centre, Feltham, Mddx.
Pelham Books, 52 Bedford Sq., W.C.1.
Penguin Books, Harmondsworth, Middlesex.
Pergamon Press, Headington Hill Hall, Oxford.
Phaidon Press, 5 Cromwell Place, S.W.7

Pharmaceutical Press, 17 Bloomsbury Sq., W.C.1.
Philip (George), 12 Long Acre, W.C.2.
Phœnix House, 10 Bedford St., W.C.2.
Pickering & Inglis, 26 Bothwell St., Glasgow, C.2.
Pitkins, 11 Wyfold Rd., S.W.6.
Pitman (Sir Isaac), 39-41 Parker St., W.C.2.
Putnam & Co., 9 Bow St., W.C.2.
Rapp & Whiting, 105 Great Russell Street, W.C.1
Redman (Alvin), 17 Fleet St., E.C.4.
Reinhardt (Max), 9 Bow St., W.C.2.
Religious Education Press, Headington Hill Hall, Oxford.
Rider & Co., 3 Fitzroy Square, W.1.
Rivingtons, Montague House, Russell Sq., W.C.1.
Routledge & Kegan Paul, 68-74 Carter Lane, E.C.4.
Scripture Union & C.S.S.M., 5 Wigmore St., W.1.
Secker & Warburg, 14 Carlisle St., W.1.
Seeley, Service, 196 Shaftesbury Av., W.C.2.
Sheed & Ward, 33 Maiden Lane, W.C.2.
Sidgwick & Jackson, 1 Tavistock Chambers, W.C.1.
S.P.C.K., Holy Trinity Church, Marylebone Rd., N.W.1.
Souvenir Press, 95 Mortimer St., W.1
Spearman (N.), 112 Whitfield St., W.1.
Sphere Books, 30 Gray's Inn Rd., W.C.1.
Spon (E. & F. N.), 11 New Fetter Lane, E.C.4.
Sporting Handbooks, 13 Bedford Square, W.C.1.
Stanford (Edward), 12-14 Long Acre, W.C.2.
Staples Press, 3 Upper James St., W.1.
Stephens (Patrick), 9 Ely Pl., E.C.1.
Stevens & Sons, 11 New Fetter Lane, E.C.4.
Student C. M. P., 58 Bloomsbury St., W.C.1.
Studio Vista, Blue Star House, Highgate Hill, N.19.
Sweet & Maxwell, 11 New Fetter Lane E.C.4.
Tabard Press, 59 Gordon Square, W.C.1.
Talbot Press, 89 Talbot Street, Dublin.
Tavistock Publications, 11 New Fetter Lane, E.C.4.
Technical Press, 112 Westbourne Grove, W.2.
Temple Press Books, 42 The Centre, Feltham, Mddx.
Thames & Hudson, 30 Bloomsbury St., W.C.1.
Tiranti (Alec), 72 Charlotte St., W.1.
University of London Press, Warwick Lane, E.C.4.
University of Wales Press, Cathays Park, Cardiff.
University Tutorial Press, 9 Gt. Sutton St., E.C.1.
Vallentine, Mitchell, 18 Cursitor St., E.C.4.
Ward, Lock, 116 Baker St., W.1.
Warne, 1-4 Bedford Court, Bedford St., W.C.2.
Watts & Co., 39 Parker St., W.C.2.
Weidenfeld & Nicolson, 5 Winsley St., W.1.
Wheaton (A.), Headington Hill Hall, Oxford.
"Whitaker," 13 Bedford Square, W.C.1.
Wills & Hepworth, Derby Sq., Loughborough.
Witherby (H. F. & G.), 15 Nicholas Lane, E.C.4.
World Distributors, 12 Lever St., Manchester
World's Work, Kingswood, Tadworth, Surrey.
Wright (John), 42 Triangle West, Bristol.

Most of the principal book publishers are members of The Publishers Association, whose address is 19 Bedford Square, London, W.C.1.—*President*, Rayner Unwin (Allen & Unwin Ltd.); *Secretary*, R. E. Barker.

BOOK PRODUCTION AND BOOK EXPORTS

Figures issued by The Publishers Association (based on information supplied to its Chartered Accountants by individual publishers) show a marked and continuing increase in book exports in recent years. The totals for the years 1959 to 1970 are shown below :—

Year	Total value of Books produced in U.K.	Total value of Books exported from U.K.	Year	Total value of Books produced in U.K.	Total value of Books exported from U.K.
1959	66,945,183	25,393,960	1965	104,876,998	46,123,190
1960	75,426,683	29,833,866	1966	119,578,145	51,417,786
1961	78,911,506	31,738,057	1967	125,782,262	53,838,418
1962	81,376,301	34,493,754	1968	137,748,324	61,741,160
1963	90,142,709	39,043,851	1969	145,693,000	68,523,000
1964	£98,489,220	£43,225,649	1970	£154,615,000	£68,306,000

BOOKS PUBLISHED IN GREAT BRITAIN IN 1970

This table, from *The Bookseller* of January 2, 1971, shows the books published in 1970 with the number of new editions, translations and limited editions.

Books and pamphlets priced at less than 10p have been omitted, as are also all Government publications except the more important issued by H.M. Stationery Office.

	Total	Reprints and New Editions	Translations	Limited Editions
Aeronautics	151	34	2	—
Agriculture and Forestry	235	66	3	—
Architecture	340	78	17	2
Art	967	217	49	9
Astronomy	91	22	5	—
Bibliography and Library Economy	464	94	1	1
Biography	940	265	61	11
Chemistry and Physics	803	125	23	—
Children's Books	2,406	575	77	—
Commerce	759	199	5	1
Customs, Costume, Folklore	116	46	7	1
Domestic Science	354	142	3	1
Education	973	206	8	—
Engineering	1,015	252	20	—
Entertainment	295	57	21	1
Fiction	4,449	2,129	213	11
General	102	45	2	—
Geography and Archæology	371	122	13	3
Geology and Meteorology	187	34	9	—
History	1,556	568	56	2
Humour	148	61	—	—
Industry	481	126	9	—
Language	337	104	7	—
Law and Public Administration	960	367	10	1
Literature	1,320	375	107	7
Mathematics	530	99	13	—
Medical Science	1,285	313	12	—
Military Science	141	29	5	5
Music	272	96	9	3
Natural Sciences	928	216	33	—
Occultism	165	40	12	1
Philosophy	405	120	59	4
Photography	51	17	2	—
Plays	287	112	45	1
Poetry	840	133	50	100
Political Science and Economy	2,575	815	70	1
Psychology	399	103	10	—
Religion and Theology	1,245	375	101	2
School Textbooks	1,875	293	24	—
Science, General	115	37	9	—
Sociology	699	168	16	1
Sports and Outdoor Games	534	159	7	—
Stockbreeding	167	51	4	—
Trade	350	144	2	—
Travel and Guidebooks	637	316	16	1
Wireless and Television	169	32	2	—
Totals	**33,489**	**9,977**	**1,229**	**170**

COPYRIGHT

The Government Department dealing with Copyright is the *Industrial Property and Copyright Dept., Department of Trade and Industry,* 25 Southampton Bldgs., W.C.2.

Subject to the provisions of the Copyright Act, 1956, copyright subsists automatically in every original literary, dramatic, musical and artistic work and continues to subsist until the end of the period of fifty years from the end of the calendar year in which the author died and shall then expire. *No registration nor other formalities are required in order to obtain the protection of the Act.* Protection is conferred not only against reproduction but also against the public performance of a work without permission. Copyright may also subsist in sound recordings, cinematograph films and television and sound broadcasts. Libraries entitled, under a provision still in force of the Copyright Act, 1911, to receive free copies of books published in the United Kingdom are the British Museum, the Bodleian Library, Oxford, University Library, Cambridge, the National Library of Wales, the National Library of Scotland and Trinity College, Dublin.

Voluntary Registration at Stationers' Hall.—Compulsory registration at Stationers' Hall was terminated by the Copyright Act of 1911, but in 1924 the Stationers' Company established a *new* Register in which Books and Fine Arts can be registered. A copy has to be filed at Stationers' Hall and certified copies of the entries are issued, the fees being £2 for a Book, or a Fine Art; certified copies £2 in either case. The fee for a search is 50p.

ANNUAL REFERENCE BOOKS

Advertiser's Annual.—Mercury House, 103–119 Waterloo Road, S.E.1. (May). £6·00

Advertising Directory.—25 Breams Bldgs., E.C.4. £25·00

Amateur Gardening Annual.—Tower House, Southampton St., W.C.2. (Oct.). 40p

Anglers' Annual.—Link Ho., Dingwall Ave., Croydon, CR9 2TA. (Nov.). 37½p

Annual Register of World Events.—74 Grosvenor St., W.1. (May). £7·00

Antiques in Britain.—2 High St., Wendover, Bucks. (Nov.). £1·50

Astronomical Ephemeris.—H.M. Stationery Office, Atlantic House, Holborn Viaduct, E.C.1. (Jan.). £3·00

Automobile Year.—9 Ely Place, E.C.1. (Feb.). £4·75

Aviation Year Book, British.—4 Mill St., Hanover Sq., W.1. (Jan.). £3·15

Baily's Hunting Directory.—1 Lower Grosvenor Place, Buckingham Palace Rd., S.W.1. (Oct.). £6·00

Banker's Almanac & Year Book.—30 Finsbury Square, E.C.2. (Feb.). £11·50

Benn's Hardware Directory.—154 Fleet St., E.C.4. (Dec.). £12·70

Bloodstock Breeders Review.—26 Charing Cross Rd., W.C.2. £8·50

Boat World Annual.—39 East St., Epsom, Surrey. (Jan.). £1·25

Boxing News Annual.—81 Aldwych, W.C.2. (Feb.). 75p

Brassey's Annual.—14–16 Lower Regent St., S.W.1. £4·20

Brewers Almanack.—19 Briset St., E.C.1. £5·25

Brewery Manual.—258 Gray's Inn Road, W.C.1. (Mar.). £2·50

British Books in Print.—13 Bedford Square, W.C.1. £15·00

British Commonwealth & International Trades Index.—39 East St., Epsom, Surrey. £3·00

British Film & Television Year Book.—142 Wardour St., W.1. (Jan./Feb.). £3·00

British Plastics Yearbook.—33 Bowling Green La., E.C.1. £4·00

British Rubber Industry, Directory of.—9 Whitehall, S.W.1. (Aug.). £2·50

British Textile Industry.—30 Finsbury Sq., E.C.2. (Oct.). £2·00

Brown's Nautical Almanack.—52 Darnley St., Glasgow S.1. (Sept.). £2·50

Building Societies Yearbook.—2–3 Burgon St., E.C.4. (July). £4·50

Caravan Sites and Mobile Home Parks.—Link Ho., Dingwall Ave., Croydon CR9 2TA. (Feb.). 25p

Carpet Annual.—5 Winsley St., W.1. (Jan.). £5·25

Catholic Directory.—25 Ashley Place, S.W.1. (Jan.). £2·25

Charities Digest.—88 Kingsway, W.C.2. (Jan.). £1·20

Chemical Industry Directory & Who's Who.—154 Fleet St., E.C.4. (Nov.). £7·00, £6·50

Church of England Year Book.—Church House, Dean's Yard, Westminster, S.W.1. (Jan.). £2·10

Church of Scotland Year Book.—121 George St., Edinburgh 2. (Apr.). 50p

Clean Air Year Book.—Field House, Bream's Buildings, E.C.4. (May). 60p

Commercial Growers' Directory & Buyers' Guide.—154 Fleet St., E.C.4. (Nov.). £3·75

Commercial Television Yearbook & Directory.—103–119 Waterloo Road, S.E.1. £4·00

Commonwealth Universities Year Book.—36 Gordon Square, W.C.1. (Sept.). £8·50

Computer and Information System Services, International Dictionary of.—18 Bedford Sq., W.C.1. (June). £5·00

Congregational Year Book.—86 Tavistock Pl., W.C.1. (Sept.). £2·10

Connoisseur Art Sales Annual.—Chestergate House, Vauxhall Bridge Rd., S.W.1. (Nov.). £11·00

Consulting Engineers Who's Who.—100 Gray's Inn Rd., W.C.1. £3·75

Contractors and Public Works Annual, Directory of.—68 High St., Northwood, Middx. (Apr.). £4·50

Corn Trade Year Book.—65–66 Turnmill St., E.C.1. £2·00

Cotton and Man-made Fibres Directory.—30 Finsbury Square, E.C.2. (Dec.). £6·00

Coventry Evening Telegraph Year Book and Who's Who.—Coventry Newspapers Ltd., Corporation St., Coventry. (Nov.). £1·25

Cricketer Spring Annual.—178–202 Great Portland St., W.1. (March). 62½p

Cricketer Winter Annual.—178–202 Great Portland St., W.1. (Nov.). 67½p

Current Law Year Book.—11 New Fetter La., E.C.4. £9·45

"Daily Mail" Year Book.—Carmelite House, Fleet St., E.C.4. (Dec.). 40p, 30p

Debrett's Peerage.—Neville House, Eden St., Kingston-on-Thames. (May). £15·75

Diplomatic Service List.—H.M.S.O., Atlantic House, Holborn Viaduct, E.C.1. (April). £2·00

Directory of Directors.—30 Finsbury Square, E.C.2. (Apr.). £6·00

Dod's Parliamentary Companion.—39 East St., Epsom, Surrey. (Sept.) £3·15

Do-it-Yourself Annual.—Link House, Dingwall Ave., Croydon. (Jan.). 20p

Education Authorities' Directory and Annual.—Derby Ho., Bletchingley Rd., Merstham, Surrey. (Jan.). £3·50

Electrical & Electronic Trader Year Book.—33 Bowling Green La., E.C.1. £2·00

Electrical Trades Directory.—154 Fleet St., E.C.4. (Feb.). £9·00

Electrical Contractor's Yearbook.—145 Charing Cross Road, W.C.2. (Feb.). £2·50

Europa Year Book.—18 Bedford Square, W.C.1. 2 vols. (Apr.). £18·00

Exporters Year Book.—154 Fleet St., E.C.4. (Dec./Jan.). £6·00

Fabric & Clothing Trades Index.—299–301 Gray's Inn Road W.C.1. (Mar.). £2·50

Finishing Handbook & Directory.—4 Ludgate Circus, E.C.4. (Sept.). £3·00

Fire Protection Directory.—154 Fleet St., E.C.4. (Nov.). £8·00

Fishing Industry Index International.—5 Winsley St., W.1. (Oct.). £2·00

"Flight" Directory of British Aviation.—Neville Ho., Eden St., Kingston-upon-Thames, Sy. (Mar.). £2·75

Food Trades Directory.—68 Welbeck St., W.1. (April). £9·25

Frozen Foods Yearbook.—17 John Adam St., W.C.2. (Dec.). £1·50

Fruit Trades World Directory.—5 Winsley St., W.1. (Jan.). £4·20

Furnishing Trade, Directory to the.—154 Fleet St., E.C.4. (Jan.). £7·50

Furnishing World Buyer's Guide.—103-119 Waterloo Rd., S.E.1. (Jan.). £1·00

G. B. Commart.—39 East St., Epsom, Surrey. (July). £3·00

Games & Toys Yearbook.—30-31 Knightrider St., E.C.4. (Dec.). £2·00

Gas Industry Directory.—154 Fleet St., E.C.4. (Jan.). £5·00

Gibbons' Stamps of the World Catalogue.—391 Strand, W.C.2. (Oct.). £3·50

Girls' School Year Book.—4-6 Soho Square, W.1. (May). £1·25

Government & Municipal Contractors Register.—39 East St., Epsom, Surrey. (Jan.). £3·00

Guild of Agricultural Journalists Year Book.—41 Parliament St., S.W.1. £1·50

Guinness Book of Records.—2 Cecil Court, London Rd., Enfield. (Oct.). £1·10

Hard's Yearbook for Clothing Industry.—9 Gough Sq., Fleet St., E.C.4. (Apr.). £4·00

Hardware Directory.—154 Fleet St., E.C.4. £5·50

Harpers Directory & Manual of Wine & Spirit Trades.—22 Cousin Lane, E.C.4. (May). £2·00

Harper's Guide to the Sports Trade.—22 Cousin Lane, E.C.4. (Jan.). £1·25

Historical Literature Annual Bulletin.—59a Kennington Park Road, S.E.11. 50p

Hollis Press and P.R. Annual.—3 Old Orchard, Sunbury-on-Thames. (Oct.). £2·25

Horse & Hound Yearbook.—Tower Ho., Southampton St., W.C.2. (Winter). £1·25

Horseman's Year.—52 Bedford Sq., W.C.1. (Apr.). £2·10

Hospitals Yearbook.—75 Portland Place, W.1. (Nov.). £7·25

Hotel and Restaurant Managers, Directory for.—124 Regent St., W.1. (Nov.). 75p

Hydraulic Handbook.—Crown House, Morden, Surrey. £7·00

Independent Schools Assn. Year Book.—49 Gordon Rd., Whitstable, Kent. (Mar.). 25p

Industrial Finishing Yearbook.—65-66 Turnmill St., E.C.1. (Jan.). £3·25

Insurance Directory & Yearbook.—12-13 Henrietta St., W.C.2. (April). £4·20

International Antiques Yearbook.—Bracken Ho., Cannon St., E.C.4. (Oct.). £1·50

International Model.—5 Winsley St., W.1. (Dec.). £3·37½

International Shipping & Shipbuilding Directory—154 Fleet St., E.C.4. £7·00

International Who's Who.—18 Bedford Sq., W.C.1. (Sept.). £9·50

International Yearbook & Statesmen's Who's Who.—103-119 Waterloo Rd., S.W.1. (Apr.). £12·00

International Yearbook of Education.—H.M.S.O., Atlantic House, Holborn Viaduct, E.C.1. (Sept.). £3·90

Iron & Steel Works of World.—46 Wigmore St., W.1. £10·50

Iron & Steel Year Book.—Atlantic Ho.. Holborn Viaduct, E.C.1. £1·09

Jane's All The World's Aircraft.—8 Shepherdess Walk, N.1. (Sept.). £10·50

Jane's Fighting Ships.—8 Shepherdess Walk, N.1. (Aug.). £10·50

Jane's Major Companies of Europe.—8 Shepherdess Walk, N.1. £15·00

Jane's Surface Skimmer Systems.—8 Shepherdess Walk, N.1. (Sept.). £5·25

Jane's World Railways.—8 Shepherdess Walk, N.1. (Nov.). £12·50

Jewish Year Book.—25 Furnival Street, E.C.4. (Jan.). £1·75

Journal of Commerce Annual Review.—19 James St., Liverpool 2. 50p

Kelly's Handbook to the Titled, Landed and Official Classes.—Neville Ho., Eden St., Kingston-upon-Thames, Sy. £7·50

Kelly's Post Office London Directory.—Neville Ho., Eden St., Kingston-upon-Thames, Sy. (Jan.). £7·00

Kempe's Engineers Year Book.—Summit Ho., Glebe Way, West Wickham, Kent. £8·00

Kemp's Directory.—299-301 Gray's Inn Road, W.C.1. (Sept.). £7·50

Kemp's International Film & T.V. Directory.—299-301 Gray's Inn Road, W.C.1. (May). £5·00

Kime's International Law Directory.—107 St. Alban's Rd., Watford, Herts. (June). £1·50

Kine & T.V. Yearbook.—161-166 Fleet St., E.C.4. (Spring). £2·10

Law List.—11 New Fetter Lane, E.C.4. (May). £4·75

Law List: Commonwealth and International.—88 Kingsway, W.C.2. (Jan.). £4·25

Laxton's Building Price Book.—Neville Ho., Eden St., Kingston-upon-Thames, Sy. £2·50

Libraries, Museums & Art Galleries Yearbook.—7 All Saints Passage, Cambridge. £4·75

Library Association Yearbook.—7 Ridgmount St., Store St., W.C.1. (May). £2·50

Lloyd's Calendar.—71 Fenchurch St., E.C.3. (Oct.). £1·15

Local Government Manual & Directory.—Shaway House, Lower Sydenham, S.E.26. (Nov.). £7·50

London Directory & International Register of Manufacturers, Wholesalers, & Shippers.—338 Kilburn High Rd., N.W.6. (Jan.). £6·50

Manufacturers & Merchants Directory.—Neville Ho., Eden St. Kingston-upon-Thames, Sy. £7·00

Manufacturers Manual.—Worcester Press, Worcester. (Jan.). £3·50

Markets (Retail) Yearbook.—Union St., Oldham. 90p

Mason's Publishers.—13-14 Homewell, Havant, Hants. (Feb.). £3·15

Master Printers Annual.—11 Bedford Row, W.C.1. (Jan.). £4·00, £3·50

Medical Annual.—42-44 Triangle West, Bristol. (Sept.). £4·50

Medical Directory.—104 Gloucester Place, W.1. (Apr.). £8·00

Medical Register.—44 Hallam St., W.1. (Mar.). £8·00

Metal Bulletin Handbook.—46 Wigmore St., W.1. £5·00

Middle East & North Africa.—18 Bedford Sq., W.C.1. £7·00

Mining Annual Review.—15 Wilson St., Moorgate, E.C.2. (May). £2·00

Mining Yearbook.—Vintry House, Queen St. Place, E.C.4. (June). £5·00

Modern Publicity.—Blue Star House, Highgate Hill, N.18. (Sept.). £4·20

Motor Industry of Great Britain.—Forbes House, Halkin St., S.W.1. (Oct.). £5·00

Municipal Yearbook & Public Utilities Directory.—3 Clements Inn, Strand, W.C.2. (Dec.). £8·40

Music Trade Directory.—64A Lansdowne Rd., E.18 (June). £1·25, £2·00

Nautical Almanac.—H.M.S.O., Atlantic House, Holborn Viaduct, E.C.1. (Oct.). £1·05

Newspaper Press Directory.—154 Fleet St., E.C.4. (Feb.). £9·00

Oil & Petroleum Yearbook.—Vintry House, Queen St. Place, E.C.4. (Nov.). £5·00

Old Moore's Almanac.—Yeovil Rd., Slough, Bucks. (July). 5p

Packaging Directory.—75 Carter La., E.C.4. £4·20

Paint Trade Manual of Raw Materials.—4 Ludgate Circus, E.C.4. (Feb.). £3·00

Paper Makers' & Merchants Directory of all Nations.—Mercury House, Waterloo Rd., S.E.1. £4·00

Paper Trade Directory of the World, Phillips'.—50–51 Fetter Lane, E.C.4. (Jan.). £6·30

Paton's List of Schools and Tutors.—63 Queen Victoria St., E.C.4. (Feb.). 75p

Pears Cyclopedia.—52 Bedford Square, W.C.1. £1·50

Penrose Annual.—12 Bedford Square, W.C.1. (Apr.). £3·50, £5·00

Photography Year Book.—46–47 Chancery Lane, W.C.2. £2·50

Plastics Materials Guide, 33–39 Bowling Green Lane, E.C.1. (Jan.). £3·00

Ports of the World.—154 Fleet St., E.C.4. (June). £8·50

Printing Trades Directory.—154 Fleet St., E.C.4. £6·00

Process Engineering, Directory of.—Summit Ho., Glebe Way, West Wickham. £7·00

Public and Preparatory Schools Year Book.—4–6 Soho Square, W.1. (Apr.). £1·75

Publishers in the United Kingdom and their Addresses.—13 Bedford Square, W.C.1. (Feb.). 60p

Publishing, Directory of.—35 Red Lion Square, W.C.1. (Oct.). £3·15

Pumping Manual.—Crown House, Morden, Surrey. £7·35

R.A.C. Guide & Handbook.—85 Pall Mall, S.W.1. (Apr.). £1·00

Raceform Annual.—29–31 York Rd., S.W.11. (Dec.). £1·50

Radio & Television Year Book.—Dorset Ho., Stamford St., S.E.1. £1·00

Reeds Nautical Almanac.—39 St. Andrew's Hill, E.C.4. (Sept.). £2·40

Register of Defunct & Other Companies.—30 Finsbury Sq., E.C.2. £3·00

RIBA Directory.—Royal Institute of British Architects, 66 Portland Place, W.1. (Oct.). £8·50

Ruff's Guide to the Turf.—12–16 Dryden St., W.C.2. (Dec.). £4·20

Salvation Army Year Book.—117–121 Judd St., W.C.1. (Nov.). 50p, 75p

Scottish Episcopal Church Year Book and Directory.—13 Drumsheugh Gdns., Edinburgh 3. (May). 75p

Scottish Law Directory.—12 Bank St., Edinburgh. £2·10

Scottish Current Law Year Book.—St. Giles St., Edinburgh. £10·50

Sell's Automation Electronics & Nuclear Engineering.—39 East St., Epsom, Surrey. £2·50

Sell's British Aviation.—39 East St., Epsom, Surrey. 50p

Sell's British Exporters Register & National Directory.—39 East St., Epsom, Surrey. £3·50

Sell's Building Index.—39 East St., Epsom, Surrey. £4·00

Sell's Directory of Registered Telegraphic Addresses.—39 East St., Epsom, Surrey. (Apr.). £5·80

Shipowners, Shipbuilders & Marine Engineers, Directory of.—33–39 Bowling Green La., E.C.1. (Apr.). £4·00

Shipping & Shipbuilding Directory, International.—154 Fleet St., E.C.4. £7·00

Shoe Trades Directory & Diary.—84 Great Eastern St., E.C.2. (Jan.). £3·50

Shop Equipment & Shopfitting Directory.—Crown House, Morden, S.W.19. (Dec.). £2·50

Skinners Hosiery & Knit Goods Directory.—30 Finsbury Square, E.C.2. (May). £4·00

Skinners Wool Trade Directory of the World.—30 Finsbury Square, E.C.2. (Aug.). £6·00

Soap, Perfumery & Cosmetics Yearbook & Buyers Guide.—9 Gough Sq., E.C.4. (Mar.). £4·00

Specification.—9–13 Queen Anne's Gate, S.W.1. (May). £2·00

Spon's Architects' & Builders' Price Book.—11 New Fetter La., E.C.4. (Oct.). £3·00

Spon's Mechanical & Electrical Services Prices Book.—11 New Fetter La., E.C.4. £3·00

Stage Yearbook.—19–21 Tavistock St., W.C.2. (Dec.). £1·75

Statesman's Yearbook.—Little Essex St., W.C.2. (Aug.). £3·50

Statistical Review Advertising Directory.—25 Breams Buildings, E.C.4. £15·75

Stone's Justices' Manual.—88 Kingsway, W.C.2. 2V. (May). £10·50

Stores and Shops Retail Directory.—68 Welbeck St., W.1. £10·50

Tanker Register.—52 Bishopsgate, E.C.2. (May). £12·50

Technical Education, Yearbook of.—4 Soho Sq., W.1. (Mar.). £2·50

Textile Directory of Brands and Trade Marks.—33–39 Bowling Green Lane, E.C.1. 75P

Theatre.—178–202 Gt. Portland St., W.1. (Oct.). £3·80

Times Issuing House Year Book.—Printing House Square, E.C.4. £12·00

Trader Handbook.—33 Bowling Green La., E.C.1. £2·25

Trades Register of London.—299–301 Gray's Inn Road, W.C.1. (Jan.). £4·00

Travel Trade Directory.—Adelphi, John Adam St., W.C.2. (July). £3·50

U.K. Kompass Register of British Industry & Commerce.—R.A.C. House, Lansdowne Rd., Croydon. £15·75

Veterinary Annual.—42–44 Triangle West, Bristol. (Dec.). £3·25

Whitaker's Almanack.—13 Bedford Sq., W.C.1. (Dec.). 95p, £2·00, £3·00

Who Owns Whom.—14 Gt. College St., S.W.1. £14·00

Who's Who.—4 Soho Sq., W.1. (May). £9·00

Who's Who, International.—18 Bedford Sq., W.C.1. £9·00

Who's Who in the Gas Industry.—154 Fleet St., E.C.4. (Mar.). £1·00

Who's Who in Motor & Commercial Vehicle Industry.—Neville Ho., Eden St., Kingston-upon-Thames. (Sept.). £2·50

Willing's Press Guide.—3–4 Holborn Circus, E.C.1. (Apr.). £4·20

Wine & Spirit Trade Diary.—12 Norfolk St., W.C.2. (May). £4·00

Wire Industry Yearbook.—157 Station Rd., E., Oxted, Sy. (Jan.). £2·20

Wisden Cricketers' Almanack.—13 Bedford Square, W.C.1. (Apr.). £1·65, £1·95

Woodworker Annual.—Montague House, Russell Sq., W.C.1. (Dec.). £2·10

World of Learning.—18 Bedford Square, W.C.1. (Jan.). £10·50

Writers' & Artists' Year Book.—4 Soho Square, W.1. (Mar.). 90p

The *Newspaper Press Directory*, 1971 shows that there are published in the United Kingdom 144 daily and Sunday newspapers, 1,225 weekly newspapers, 5,019 periodicals of all types and 1,392 directories and other annuals. Circulation figures at June 30, 1971, are in brackets.

LONDON

The Times (*Ind.*), Printing House Sq., E.C.4 (341,242).

Daily Express (*Ind.*) Fleet St., E.C.4 (3,436,214).

Daily Mail (*Ind.*) Northcliffe House, E.C.4 (2,007,000).

Daily Mirror (*Ind.*) Holborn Circus, E.C.1 (4,380,470).

Daily Telegraph and Morning Post (*Cons.*) 135 Fleet St., E.C.4 (1,454,581).

Financial Times (*Ind.*) 10 Cannon St., E.C.4 (167,500).

The Guardian (*Lib.*), 192 Grays Inn Rd., W.C.1 (327,897).

Lloyd's List, Lloyd's, E.C.3.

Morning Advertiser (*Ind.*) 18-20 St. Andrews St., E.C.4.

Morning Star (*Communist*), 75 Farringdon Rd., E.C.1.

Sporting Life, 9 New Fetter Lane, E.C.4 (87,519).

The Sun, 30 Bouverie St., E.C.4 (2,082,686).

Evening News and Star (*Ind.*), Carmelite House, E.C.4 (987,232).

Evening Standard (*Ind*), 47 Shoe Lane, E.C.4 (527,951).

ABERDEEN.......Press and Journal (*Cons.*)
Evening Express (*Ind.*)
BARROW.........North-Western Evening Mail (*Ind.*)
BATH............Bath and Wilts. Evening Chronicle (*Cons.*)
BELFAST.........News Letter (*Un.*)
Belfast Telegraph (*Cons.*)
Irish News (*Nat.*)
BIRMINGHAM....Birmingham Post (*Ind.*)
Evening Mail (*Ind.*)
BLACKBURN.....Lancs. Evening Telegraph (*Ind.*)
BLACKPOOL......W. Lancs. Ev. Gazette (*Ind.*)
BOLTON.........Evening News (*Ind.*)
BOURNEMOUTH..Evening Echo, Bournemouth (*Ind.*) (64,132).
BRADFORD......Telegraph and Argus (*Ind.*)
BRIGHTON.......Evening Argus (*Ind.*) (110,529).
BRISTOL.........Western Daily Press (*Ind.*)
Bristol Evening Post (*Ind.*)
BURNLEY........Evening Star (*Ind.*)
BURTON.........Burton Daily Mail (*Un.*)
CAMBRIDGE.....Cambridge Evening News (*Ind.*) (50,033).
CARDIFF.........South Wales Echo (*Ind.*)
Western Mail (*Ind.*)
CARLISLE........Cumberland Evening News (*Cons.*)
CHELTENHAM....Gloucestershire Echo (*Ind.*)
COLCHESTER.....Evening Gazette (*Ind.*)
COVENTRY.......Coventry Evening Telegraph (*Ind.*)
DARLINGTON....Northern Echo (*Ind.*)
Evening Despatch (*Ind.*)
DERBY...........Derby Evening Telegraph and Express (*Ind.*) (97,000).
DONCASTER.....Doncaster Evening Post (*Ind.*)
DUNDEE.........Courier and Advertiser (*Ind.*)
Evening Telegraph and Post (*Ind.*)

EDINBURGH......Scotsman (*Ind.*)
Evening News (*Ind.*)
EXETER.........Express and Echo (*Ind.*)
GLASGOW........Glasgow Herald (*Ind.*)
Daily Record (*Ind.*) (528,045).
Evening Citizen (*Ind.*)
Evening Times (*Ind.*)
Scottish Daily Express (*Ind.*)
GLOUCESTER.....Citizen (*Ind.*). (39,000).
GREENOCK......Greenock Telegraph (*Lib.*)
GRIMSBY.........Evening Telegraph (*Ind.*) (75,000).
GUERNSEY.......Guernsey Evening Press and Star (*Ind.*)
HALIFAX........Halifax Evening Courier and Guardian (*Ind.*)
HARTLEPOOL.....Northern Daily Mail (*Ind.*)
HUDDERSFIELD...Huddersfield Daily Examiner (*Lib.*)
HULL............Daily Mail (*Ind.*). (133,000).
IPSWICH.........East Anglian Daily Times (*Ind.*)
Evening Star (*Ind.*)
JERSEY..........Evening Post (*Ind.*)
KETTERING......Northants Evening Telegraph (*Ind.*)
LEAMINGTON SPA.Leamington Spa Morning News (*Ind.*)
LEEDS...........Yorkshire Post (*Cons.*)
Yorkshire Evening Post and News (*Ind.*)
LEICESTER.......Leicester Mercury (*Ind.*)
LINCOLN.........Lincolnshire Echo (*Ind.*) (37,000).
LIVERPOOL......Liverpool Daily Post (*Ind.*)
Liverpool Echo (*Ind.*)
Journal of Commerce (*Ind.*)
LUTON..........Evening Post (*Ind.*)
MAIDSTONE.....Kent Evening Post (*Ind.*)
MANCHESTER....Manchester Evening News & Chronicle (*Ind.*) (416,363).
Sporting Chronicle
NEWCASTLE......Newcastle Journal (*Cons.*)
Evening Chronicle (*Cons.*)
NEWPORT, MON..South Wales Argus (*Ind.*)
NORTHAMPTON...Chronicle and Echo (Northampton) (*Ind.*)
NORWICH........Eastern Daily Press (*Ind.*)
Eastern Evening News (*Ind.*)
NOTTINGHAM....Guardian Journal (*Cons.*)
Evening Post & News (*Ind.*)
NUNEATON.......Nuneaton Evening Tribune (*Ind.*)
OLDHAM.........Oldham Evening Chronicle (*Lib.*)
OXFORD.........Oxford Mail (*Ind.*)
PAISLEY.........Paisley Daily Express (*Ind.*)
PETERBOROUGH..Peterborough Evening Telegraph (*Ind.*)
PLYMOUTH.......Western Morning News (*Ind.*)
Western Evening Herald (*Ind.*)
PORTSMOUTH....Portsmouth News (*Ind.*)
PRESTON........Lancashire Evening Post (*Ind.*).
READING........Evening Post (*Ind.*)
SCARBOROUGH....Scarborough Evening News (*Ind.*)
SHEFFIELD.......Morning Telegraph (*Ind.*)
Star (*Ind.*)
SHIELDS.........Shields Gazette and Shipping Telegraph (*Ind.*)

SLOUGH.........Evening Mail (*Ind.*)
SOUTHAMPTON....Southern Evening Echo (*Ind.*) (101,733).
SOUTHEND.......Evening Echo (*Ind.*) (50,498).
STOKE..........Evening Sentinel (*Ind.*)(125,000).
SUNDERLAND.....Sunderland Echo (*Ind.*)
SWANSEA........South Wales Evening Post (*Ind.*) (72,000).
SWINDON........Evening Advertiser (*Ind.*)
TEESSIDE........Evening Gazette (*Ind.*)
TELFORD........Shropshire Star (*Ind.*)
TORQUAY........Herald Express (*Ind.*)¹
WATFORD........Evening Echo (*Ind.*)
WEYMOUTH......Dorset Evening Echo (*Ind.*)
WOLVERHAMPTON.Express and Star (*Ind.*)
WORCESTER......Worcester Evening News (*Ind.*)
YORK...........Yorkshire Evening Press (*Ind.*)

SUNDAY NEWSPAPERS

Independent—55-57 Exeter St., Plymouth.
Island Sun—13 Burrard St., St. Helier, Jersey.
News of the World (*Ind.*)—30 Bouverie St., E.C.4. (6,170,890).
Observer (*Ind.*)—160 Queen Victoria St., E.C.4. (796,528).
People (*Ind.*)—9 New Fetter Lane, E.C.4 (4,941,738).
Sunday Express (*Ind.*)—Fleet St., E.C.4. (4,163,105)
Sunday Mail (*Ind.*)—Record House, Glasgow (760,438).
Sunday Mercury (*Ind.*)—Colmore Circus, Birmingham.
Sunday Mirror (*Ind.*)—Holborn Circus, E.C.1. (4,686,564).
Sunday News (*Ind.*)—51-59 Donegall St., Belfast.
Sunday Post (*Ind.*)—144 Port Dundas Road, Glasgow.
Sunday Sun (*Cons.*)—Groat Market, Newcastle-on-Tyne.
Sunday Telegraph (*Cons.*)—135 Fleet St., E.C.4. (751,673).
Sunday Times (*Ind.*)—200 Gray's Inn Rd., W.C.1. (1,432,946).

RELIGOUS PAPERS

[*W.*=Weekly; *M.*=Monthly; *Q.*=Quarterly]
Baptist Times—4 Southampton Row, W.C.1. *W.*
British Weekly—69 Fleet St., E.C.4. *W.*
Catholic Herald—67 Fleet St., E.C.4. *W.*
Challenge—Revenue Buildings, Chapel Rd., Worthing, Sussex. *M.*
Christian Herald—4 Western Esplanade, Portslade, Brighton, Sussex. *W.*
Church of England Newspaper and Record—69 Fleet St., E.C.4. *W.*
Church of Ireland Gazette—20 High St., Belfast 1. *W.*
Church Times—7 Portugal St., W.C.2. *W.*
Crusade—30 Bedford Place, W.C.1. *M.*
English Churchman—St. Mark's Church Chmbrs, Kennington Park Rd., S.E.11. *W.*
Friend—46 Chancery Lane, W.C.2. *W.*
Inquirer—1-6 Essex St., W.C.2. *W.*
Jewish Chronicle—25 Furnival St., London, E.C.4. *W.*
Jewish Gazette—18 Cheetham Parade, Manchester, 8. *W.*
Jewish Telegraph—Levi House, Bury Old Road, Manchester, 8. *W.*
Life and Work—121 George St., Edinburgh 2. *M.*
Methodist Recorder—176 Fleet St., E.C.4. *W.*
Sunday—P.O. Box 80, Leicester. 5. *M.*
Tablet—48 Great Peter St., S.W.1. *W.*
Universe and Catholic Times—Universe House, 21 Fleet St., E.C.4. *W.*
War Cry—101 Queen Victoria St., E.C.4. *W.*

PERIODICALS, MAGAZINES AND REVIEWS

[*W.*=Weekly; *M.*=Monthly; *Q.*=Quarterly]
Aeromodeller—13-35 Bridge St., Hemel Hempstead. Herts. *M.*
Air Pictorial—142 Sloane St., S.W.1. *M.*
Amateur Gardening—189 High Holborn, W.C.1. *W.*
Amateur Photographer—161 Fleet St., E.C.4. *W.*
Angler's Mail—Fleetway House, Farrington St., E.C.4. *W.*
Angling—81 Aldwych, W.C.2. *M.*
Angling Times—Park House, Park Rd., Peterborough. *W.*
Animals—21-22 Great Castle St., W.1. *M.*
Antiquaries' Journal—Oxford U. Press, Press Rd., N.W.10. *Twice a year.*
Antique Collector—16 Strutton Ground, S.W.1. *Six times a year.*
Apollo—10 Cannon St., London, E.C.4. *M.*
Argosy—Fleetway House, Farringdon St., E.C.4. *M.*
Art and Antiques Weekly—2 Arundel St., W.C.2.
Art and Artists—75 Victoria St., S.W.1. *M.*
Asia and Africa Review—38 Kennington Lane, S.E.11. *M.*
Autocar—Dorset House, Stamford St., S.E.1. *W.*
Birds and Country Magazine—79 Surbiton Hill Park, Surrey. *Q.*
Blackwood's Mag.—6 Buckingham St., W.C.2. *M.*
Books & Bookmen and John O'London's Books of the Month—75 Victoria St., S.W.1. *M.*
Boxing News—81 Aldwych, W.C.2. *W.*
Brain—Macmillan (Journals) Ltd., 4 Little Essex St., W.C.2.
Brides—Vogue House, Hanover Sq., W.1. *Alt. M.*
British Birds—10 Merton Rd., Bedford. *M.*
British Book News—The British Council, 59 New Oxford St., W.C.1. *M.*
Bunty—186 Fleet St., E.C.4. *W.*
Burlington Mag.—49 Park Lane, W.1. *M.*
Buses—Terminal House, Shepperton. *M.*
Cage and Aviary Birds—161 Fleet Street, E.C.4. *W.*
Caravan—Link House, Dingwall Ave., Croydon, Surrey. *M.*
Charles Buchan's Football Monthly—161 Fleet St., E.C.4.
City Press—4 Moorfields, E.C.2. *W.*
Classical Quarterly—Oxford U. Press, Press Rd., N.W.10.
Classical Review—Oxford U. Press, Press Rd., N.W.10. *Three times a year.*
Coal News—Hobart House, Grosvenor Place, S.W.1. *M.*
Coin Monthly—Sovereign House, High St., Brentwood, Essex.
Coins—Link House, Dingwall Ave., Croydon, Surrey. *M.*
Collectors Weekly—81 Aldwych, W.C.2.
Connoisseur—Chestergate House, Vauxhall Bridge Road, S.W.1. *M.*
Contemporary Review—38 Farringdon St., E.C.4. *M.*
Cornhill—50 Albemarle St.,W.1. *Q.*
Country Life—Tower House, Southampton St., W.C.2. *W.*
Countryman—23/27 Tudor St., E.C.4. *Q.*
Cricketer—Mercury House, Waterloo Rd., S.E.1. *M.*
Cricket Quarterly—The Lantern, Mullion, Helston, Cornwall.

Criminologist—9 Old Bailey, E.C.4. Q.

Cycling—161 Fleet Street, E.C.4. W.

Dalton's Weekly—Windsor Ave., Merton, S.W.19. W.

Dance and Dancers—75 Victoria St., S.W.1. M.

Dancing Times—18 Hand Court, W.C.1. M.

Disc and Music Echo—161-166 Fleet St., E.C.4. W.

Discovering Antiques—49/50 Poland St., W.1. W.

Dog World—Press House, Wotton Rd., Ashford Kent. W.

Do It Yourself—Link House, Dingwall Ave, Croydon. M.

Drama—9 Fitzroy Sq.,W.1. Q.

Drive—Berkeley Sq. House, Berkeley Sq., W.1. Q.

Economic Journal—4 Little Essex St.,W.C.2. Q.

Economica—Lond. Sch. of Economics, Houghton St., Aldwych,W.C.2. Q.

Edinburgh Gazette (Official)—Exchequer Chambers, 102 George St., Edinburgh 2. Twice a week.

Elizabethan—355 Ashford Rd., Staines, Middx. M.

Encounter—25 Haymarket, S.W.1. M.

English Historical Review—5 Bentinck St., W.1. Q.

Exchange and Mart—Pembroke House, Wellesley Rd., Croydon, Surrey. W.

Family Circle—100 Gray's Inn Rd., W.C.1. (1,202,805).

Field—8 Stratton St., W.1. W.

Films and Filming—75 Victoria St., S.W.1. M.

Flair—Fleetway House, Farringdon St., E.C.4. M.

F.A. News—Football Association, 22 Lancaster Gate, W.2. M.

Freethinker—103 Borough High St., S.E.1. W.

Fur and Feather—Idle, Bradford. Alt. W.

Gardeners' Chronicle—5 Winsley St., W.1. W.

Garden News—Park House, Park Rd., Peterborough. W.

Geographical Journal—Kensington Gore, S.W.7. Q.

Geographical Magazine—128 Long Acre, W.C.2 M.

Golf Illustrated—8 Stratton St., W.1. W.

Golf Monthly—113 St. Vincent St., Glasgow, C.2 M.

Good Health—Stanborough Press, Ltd., Alma Park, Grantham. Alt. M.

Good Housekeeping—Chestergate House, Vauxhall Bridge Road, S.W.1. M.

Good Motoring—2 Ellis St., Sloane St., S.W.1. M.

Gramophone—179 Kenton Road, Kenton, Mx. M.

Greece and Rome—Oxford U. Press, Press Rd., N.W. 10. Twice a year.

Guider—17-19 Buckingham Palace Rd., S.W.1. M.

Harper's and Queen—Chestergate House, Vauxhall Bridge Rd., S.W.1. Sixteen times a year.

Health & Strength—20-23 Holborn. E.C.1. M.

Health Education Journal—Tavistock House, Tavistock Square, W.C.1. Alt. M.

Hers—Fleetway House, Farringdon St., E.C.4. M.

History—59A Kennington Park Road, S.E.11. Three times a year.

History Today—10 Cannon St., E.C.4. M.

Homefinder—199 Strand, W.C.2. M.

Homemaker—189 High Holborn, W.C.1. M.

Homeopathy—27A Devonshire St., W.1. M.

Homes and Gardens—Tower House, Southampton St.,W.C.2. M.

Honey—Fleetway House, Farringdon St., E.C.4. M.

Horse and Hound—Tower House, Southampton St., W.C.2. W.

House and Garden—Vogue House, Hanover Sq., W.1. M.

Ideal Home—189 High Holborn, W.C.1. M.

Illustrated London News (Ind.)—100 Gray's Inn Rd., W.C.1. M.

In Britain—239 Old Marylebone Rd., N.W.1.— M.

International Affairs—Chatham House, St. James's Square, S.W.1. Q.

Jazz Journal—27 Willow Vale, W.12. M.

June and Schoolfriend—Fleetway House, Farringdon St., E.C.4. W.

Kennel Gazette—1-4 Clarges St., Piccadilly, W.1. M.

Labour Monthly—134 Ballards Lane, N.3.

Lady—39-40 Bedford St.,W.C.2. W.

Land and Liberty—177 Vauxhall Bridge Rd., S.W.1. Alt. M.

Lawn Tennis—Lowlands, Wenhaston, Suffolk. M.

Liberal News—Exchange Ct., Strand, W.C.1. W.

Light (Psychic)—16 Queensberry Place, S.W.7. Q.

Light Horse—19 Charing Cross Rd., W.C.2. M.

Lion and Eagle—Fleetway House, Farringdon St., E.C.4. W.

Listener—35 Marylebone High St., W.1. W.

Living—100 Gray's Inn Rd., W.C.1. M. (575,221).

Local Government Chronicle (Ind.)—11-12 Bury St., St. Mary Axe, E.C.3. W.

London Gazette (Official)—First Avenue House, Warwick Court, High Holborn, W.C.1. Three times a week.

London Magazine—30 Thurloe Place, S.W.7. Six times a year.

London Weekly Advertiser—Classified House, New Bridge St., E.C.4.

London Weekly Diary of Social Events—39 Hertford St., W.1.

Look and Learn—Fleetway House, Farringdon St., E.C.4. W.

Look and Listen—75 Victoria St., S.W.1. M.

Man—21 Bedford Square, W.C.1. Q.

Mayfair—95A Chancery Lane, W.C.2. M.

Meccano Magazine—13-15 Bridge St., Hemel Hempstead. M.

Melody Maker—161 Fleet Street, E.C.4. W.

Meteorological Magazine—Atlantic House, Holborn Viaduct, E.C.1. M.

Mind—108 Cowley Rd., Oxford. Q.

Mirabelle—Fleetway House, Farringdon St., E.C.4. W.

Model Boats—13-35 Bridge St., Hemel Hempstead, Herts. M.

Model Cars—13-35 Bridge St., Hemel Hempstead, Herts. M.

Model Railway Constructor—Terminal House, Shepperton. M.

Model Railway News—13-35 Bridge St., Hemel Hempstead, Herts. M.

Modern Caravan—Heathcock Press, P.O. Box 200, Croydon. M.

Modern Languages—2 Manchester Sq., W.1. Q.

Month, The—114 Mount St., W.1. M.

Monthly Digest of Statistics (Official)—Atlantic House, Holborn Viaduct, E.C.1.

Mother—189 High Holborn, W.C.1. M.

Motor Cycle News—Dryland St., Kettering. W.

Movie Maker—46-47 Chancery Lane, W.C.2. *M.*

Municipal Engineering—3 Clements Inn, W.C.2. *W.*

Municipal and Public Services Journal—3 and 4 Clement's Inn, W.C.2. *W.*

Municipal Review—36-38 Old Queen St., Westminster, S.W.1. *M.*

Museums Journal—87 Charlotte St., W.1. *Q.*

Music and Letters—Oxford University Press, Press Rd., N.W.10. *Q.*

Music and Musicians—75 Victoria St., S.W.1. *M.*

My Home and Family—Fleetway House, Farringdon St., E.C.4. *W.*

My Weekly—186 Fleet St., E.C.4.

National Advertiser—Classified House, New Bridge St., E.C.4. *W.*

Nature—4 Little Essex St., W.C.2. *W.*

Nautical Magazine—52 Darnley Street, Glasgow, S.1. *M.*

Navy—Broadway House, S.W.19. *M.*

Needlewoman and Needlecraft—School St., Bromley Cross, Bolton, Lancs. *Q.*

New Homes and Conversions—203-209 North Gower St., N.W.1. *W.*

New Middle East—68 Fleet St., E.C.4. *M.*

New Musical Express—Fleetway House, Farringdon St., E.C.4. *W.*

New Scientist—128 Long Acre, W.C.2. *W.*

New Society—128 Long Acre, W.C.2. *W.*

New Statesman (*Ind.*)—10 Great Turnstile, High Holborn, W.C.1. *W.*

19—Fleetway House, Farringdon St., E.C.4. *M.*

Notes and Queries—Oxford U. Press, Press Rd., N.W.10. *M.*

Nova—Fleetway House, Farringdon St., E.C.4. *M.*

Nursery World—2 Salisbury Ct., Fleet St., E.C.4. *W.*

Opera—334 Brixton Rd., S.W.9. *M.*

Our Dogs—Oxford Road, Station Approach, Manchester. *W.*

Oxford—18 Museum Rd., Oxford. *Twice a year.*

Parade—81 Aldwych, W.C.2. *W.*

Parliamentary Debates (Lords) (Hansard)—Atlantic House, Holborn Viaduct, E.C.1. *Daily.*

Parliamentary Debates (Commons) (Hansard)—Atlantic House, Holborn Viaduct, E.C.1. *Daily.*

Penthouse—2 Bramber Rd., W.14. *M.*

People's Friend—186 Fleet St., E.C.4. *W.*

Philosophy—4 Little Essex St., W.C.2. *Q.*

Photography—46-47 Chancery Lane, W.C.2. *M.*

Photoplay—12-18 Paul St., E.C.2. *M.*

Pins and Needles—100 Gray's Inn Rd., W.C.1. *M.*

Playhour and Robin—Fleetway House, Farringdon St., E.C.4. *W.*

Plays and Players—75 Victoria St., S.W.1. *M.*

Poetry Review—21 Earls Court Square, S.W.5. *Q.*

Political Quarterly—49 Park Lane, W.1.

Polytechnic Magazine—309 Regent St., W.1. *M.*

Pony—19 Charing Cross Rd., W.C.2. *M.*

Popular Gardening—Tower House, Southampton St., W.C.2. *W.*

Poultry World—161 Fleet St., E.C.4. *W.*

Practical Boat Owner—Tower House, Southampton St., W.C.2. *M.*

Practical Camper—5 Winsley St., W.1. *M.*

Practical Caravan—5 Winsley St., W.1. *M.*

Practical Home-Building and Decorating—Fleetway House, Farringdon St., E.C.4. *M.*

Practical Householder—Fleetway House, Farringdon St., E.C.4. *M.* (191,547).

Princess Tina—Fleetway House, Farringdon St., E.C.4. *W.*

Progress (*Braille Type*)—224-8 Great Portland St., W.1. *M.*

Punch (*Ind.*)—23-27 Tudor St., E.C.4. *W.*

Racing Calendar—42 Portman Sq., W.1. *W.*

Radio Control Models—13-35 Bridge St., Hemel Hempstead, Herts. *M.*

Radio Times—35 Marylebone High St., W.1. *W.* (3,380,500).

Railway Magazine—Dorset House, Stamford St., S.E.1. *M.*

Railway World—Terminal House, Shepperton. *M.*

Reader's Digest—25 Berkeley Sq., W.1. *M.*

Records and Recording—75 Victoria St., S.W.1. *M.*

Red Star Weekly—186 Fleet St., E.C.4.

Reveillé—33 Holborn, E.C.1. *W.* (925,608).

Riding—Tower House, Southampton St., W.C.2. *M.*

Round Table—18 Northumberland Ave. W.C.2., *Q.*

Saturday Titbits—Tower House, Southampton St., W.C.2. *W.*

Scotland—1 Castle St., Edinburgh. *M.*

Scotland's Magazine—24-28 Elder St., Edinburgh. *M.*

Scots Independent—16 Upper Bridge St., Stirling. *W.*

Scottish Field—70 Mitchell St., Glasgow, C.1. *M.*

Scouting—25 Buckingham Palace Rd., S.W.1. *M.*

Sea Breezes—19 James St., Liverpool. *M.*

Seafarer—207 Balham High Rd., S.W.17. *Q.*

She—Chestergate House, Vauxhall Bridge Road, S.W.1. *M.*

Shoot!—Fleetway House, Farringdon St., E.C.4. *W.*

Shooting Times and Country Magazine—Clivemont Rd., Maidenhead. *W.*

Socialist Leader—197 King's Cross Rd., W.C.1. *W.*

Sociological Review—University of Keele, Staffs. *Three times a year.*

Spectator (*Ind.*)—99 Gower Street, W.C.1. *W.*

Sporting Chronicle Handicap Book and Sporting Life Guide—Thomson House, Manchester 4. *W.*

Sporting Chronicle Racing Up To Date.—Thomson House, Manchester, 4. *W.*

Stamp Weekly—Link House, Dingwall Ave., Croydon.

Stitchcraft—76 Grosvenor St., W.1. *M.*

Strad—27 Soho Sq., W.1. *M.*

Studio International—37 Museum St., W.C.1. *M.*

Sunny Stories—Fleetway House, Farringdon St., E.C.4. *W.*

Tatler and Bystander—15 Berkeley St., W 1. *M.*

Tennis World—Lancaster Rd., Hinckley, Leics. *M.*

Theatre Quarterly—North Way, Andover, Hants.

Time (British Isles)—Time and Life Bldg., New Bond St., W.1. *W.*

Time & Tide (*Ind.*)—Classified House, New Bridge St., E.C.4. *W.*

Times Educational Suppl't.—Printing House Sq., E.C.4. *W.* (111,093).

Times Higher Education Suppl't.—Printing House Sq., E.C.4. *W.*

Times Literary Suppl't.—Printing House Sq., E.C.4. *W.*

Tribune—24 St. John St., E.C.1. *W.*

Trout and Salmon—Park House, Park Rd. Peterborough. *M.*

True Magazine—Fleetway House, Farringdon St., E.C.4. *M.*

True Romances and True Story Magazine—12-18 Paul St., E.C.2. *M.*

TV Times—247 Tottenham Court Rd., W.1. *W.* (3,129,381).

Twentieth Century—3 Clement's Inn, W.C.2. *Q.*

Universities Quarterly—10 Gt. Turnstile, W.C.1.

Vacher's Parliamentary Companion—67 Clerkenwell Rd., E.C.1. *Q.*

Vanity Fair—Chestergate House, Vauxhall Bridge Road, S.W.1. *M.*

Vogue—Vogue House, Hanover Square, W.1. *Sixteen times a year.*

Weather—49 Cromwell Rd., S.W.7. *M.*

Weekend—Northcliffe Gouse, E.C.4. *W.*

Weekly Star and Competitors' Journal—81 Aldwych, W.C.2.

Welsh Nation—8 Queen St., Cardiff. *M.*

West Africa (*Ind*).—Cromwell House, Fulwood Pl., W.C.1. *W.*

Woman—189 High Holborn, W.C.1. *W.*

Woman and Home—Tower House, Southampton St., W.C.2. *M.*

Woman, Bride and Home—Tower House, Southampton St., W.C.2. *Six times a year.*

Woman's Journal—Tower House, Southampton St., W.C.2. *M.*

Woman's Own—Tower House, Southampton St., W.C.2. *W.*

Woman's Realm—Tower House, Southampton St., W.C.2. *W.*

Woman's Realm Home Sewing and Knitting—Tower House, Southampton St., W.C.2. *Six times a year.*

Woman's Weekly—Tower House, Southampton St., W.C.2.

World Archæology—68-74 Carter Lane, E.C.4. *Three times a year.*

World Today—Chatham House, St. James's Sq., S.W.1. *M.*

Yachting & Boating Weekly—100 Gray's Inn Rd., W.C.1.

Yachting Monthly—Tower House, Southampton St., W.C.2.

Yachting World (*Ind.*)—Dorset House, Stamford St., S.E.1. *M.*

Yachts and Yachting—196 Eastern Esplanade, Southend-on-Sea. *Alt. W.*

TRADE, PROFESSIONAL AND BUSINESS JOURNALS

[*W.*=Weekly; *M.*=Monthly; *Q.*=Quarterly]

Accountancy—56 Goswell Rd., E.C.1. *M.*

Accountant—151 Strand, W.C.2. *W.*

Accountants' Magazine—27 Queen St., Edinburgh. *M.*

Achievement—Classified House, New Bridge St., E.C.4. *M.*

Advertiser's Weekly—110 Fleet St., E.C.4.

Advertising Quarterly—1 Bell Yard, W.C.2.

Agricultural Machinery Journal—161 Fleet St., E.C.4. *M.*

Air Cushion Vehicles—P.O. Box 39, Bagshot, Surrey. *Alt. M.*

Ambassador—49 Park Lane, W.1. *M.*

Anti-Corrosion—4 Ludgate Circus, E.C.4. *M.*

Antique Dealer—81 Aldwych, W.C.2. *M*

Architects' Journal—9-13 Queen Anne's Gate, S.W.1. *W.*

Architectural Review—9-13 Queen Anne's Gate, S.W.1. *M.*

Artist—33 Warwick Sq., S.W.1. *M.*

Automobile Engineer—Dorset House, Stamford St., S.E.1. *M.*

Baker and Bakery Management—17-19 John Adam St., W.C.2. *M.*

Baker, Confectioner and Caterer—65-66 Turnmill St., E.C.1. *M.*

Bakers Review—Queen's House, Holly Rd., Twickenham, Middx. *W.*

Banker—10 Cannon St., E.C.4. *M.*

Banker's Magazine—12 Vandy St., E.C.2. *M.*

Bookseller—13 Bedford Square, W.C.1. *W.*

Brewers' Guardian—Elm House, Elm St., W.C.1. *M.*

Brewing Trade Review—19 Briset St., E.C.1. *M.*

British Baker—69-77 High St., Croydon, Surrey. *W.*

British Clayworker—65-66 Turnmill St., E.C.1 *M.*

British Clothing Manufacturer—20 Soho Sq., W.1. *M.*

British Dental Journal—64 Wimpole St., W.1. *Twice a month.*

British Export Gazette—1F Oval Rd., N.W.1. *M.*

British Farmer and Stockbreeder—25-31 Knightsbridge, S.W.1. *Alt. Weeks.*

British Food Journal—Peterson House, Livery St., Birmingham, 3. *Alt. M.*

British Jeweller—27 Frederick St., Birmingham. *M.*

British Journal for Philosophy of Science—200 Euston Rd., N.W.1. *Q.*

British Journal of Photography—24 Wellington Street, W.C.2. *W.*

British Knitting Industry—1 Ford Lane, Salford, Lancs. *M.*

British Medical Journal—Tavistock Square, W.C.1. *W.*

British Plastics—33 Bowling Green Lane, E.C.1. *M.*

British Printer—30 Old Burlington St., W.1. *M.*

British Steelmaker—65-66 Turnmill St., E.C.1. *M.*

British Sugar Beet Review—134 Piccadilly, W.1. *Q.*

British Tax Review—11 New Fetter Lane, E.C.4. *Alt. M.*

British Veterinary Journal—7-8 Henrietta St., W.C.2. *M.*

Brushes—157 Hagden Lane, Watford. *M.*

Building—4 Catherine St., W.C.2. *W.*

Building Societies' Gazette—2-3 Burgon St., E.C.4. *M.*

Cabinet Maker—154 Fleet St., E.C.4. *W.*

Cage and Aviary Birds—161 Fleet St., E.C.4. *W.*

Campaign—5 Winsley St., W.1. *W.*

Canoe-Camper—11 Lower Grosvenor Pl., S.W.1 *Q.*

Carpet Review—5 Winsley St., W.1. *M.*

Caterer and Hotel Keeper—1 Dorset Buildings, Salisbury Square, E.C.4. *W.*

Caterers' Association Bulletin—Victoria House Vernon Place, Southampton Row, W.C.1. *M.*

Catering and Restaurant Management—167 High Holborn, W.C.1. *M.*

Catering Times—Elm House, 10-16 Elm Street, W.C.1. *W.*

Chemical Age—154 Fleet St., E.C.4. *W.*

Chemist and Druggist—154 Fleet St., E.C.4. *W.*

Chemistry and Industry—14 Belgrave Sq., S.W.1. *W.*

Child Education—Montague House, Russell Sq., W.C.1. *M.*

Chiropodist—8 Wimpole St., W.1. *M*

Civil Engineering—8 Buckingham St., W.C.2. *M.*

Club Mirror—48 Goodge St., W.1. *M.*

Coal Merchant and Shipper—17-19 John Adam St., W.C.2. *W.*

Colliery Guardian—17-19 John Adam St., W.C.2. *M.*

Commerce International—69 Cannon St., E.C.4. *M.*

Commercial Grower—154 Fleet St., E.C.4. *W.*

Commercial Motor—Dorset House, Stamford St., S.E.1. *W.*

Computer Survey—9 Gough Sq., E.C.4. *Alt. M.*

Concrete—52 Grosvenor Gdns., S.W.1. *M.*

Confectionery & Tobacco News—33-39 Bowling Green Lane, E.C.1. *Alt. W.*

Contract Journal—32 Southwark Bridge Rd., S.E.1. *W.*

Control and Instrumentation—28 Essex St., W.C.2. *M.*

Cordage, Canvas and Jute World—157 Hagden Lane, Watford. *M.*

C.S.E. News (Camping and Sports Equipment)—4 Spring St., W.2. *M.*

Dairy Farmer—Lloyds Chambers, Ipswich. *M.*

Dairy Industries—9 Gough Sq., E.C.4. *M.*

Decorating Contractor—17-19 John Adam St., Adelphi, W.C.2. *M.*

Design—8 Haymarket, S.W.1. *M.*

Display—167 High Holborn, W.C.1. *M.*

Dock and Harbour Authority—19 Harcourt St., W.1. *M.*

Draper's Record—20 Soho Sq., W.1. *W.*

Drapery and Fashion Weekly—29-32 Finsbury Sq., E.C.2.

Education—10 Queen Anne St., W.1. *W.*

Education Equipment—125 High St., S.W.19. *M.*

Electrical & Electronic Trader—Dorset House, Stamford St., S.E.1. *W.*

Electrical and Electronics Technician Engineer—2 Savoy Hill, W.C.2. *Alt. M.*

Electrical and Radio Trading—Dorset House, Stamford St., S.E.1. *W.*

Electrical Review—Dorset House, Stamford St., S.E.1. *W.*

Electrical Times—Dorset House, Stamford St., S.E.1. *W.*

Electronic Engineering—28 Essex St., W.C.2. *M.*

Electronics Weekly—Dorset House, Stamford St., S.E.1.

Embroidery—73 Wimpole St., W.1. *Q.*

Employment and Productivity Gazette (*Official*)—Atlantic House, Holborn Viaduct, E.C.1. *M.*

Engineer—28 Essex St., Strand, W.C.2. *W.*

Engineering—33-39 Bowling Green Lane, E.C.1. *W.*

Engineer's Digest—120 Wigmore St., W.1. *M.*

Estates Gazette—151 Wardour St., W.1. *W.*

Export Management—125 High St., S.W.19. *M.*

Fairplay International Shipping Journal—51 Bishopsgate, E.C.2. *W.*

Far East Trade & Development—3 Belsize Crescent., N.W.3. *M.*

Farmer and Stockbreeder—161-166 Fleet St., E.C.4. *W.*

Farmers' Weekly—161-168 Fleet St., E.C.4.

Financial World—79 Temple Chambers, Temple Ave., E.C.4. *Alt. W.*

Fire (British Fire Service)—34 Dudley Rd., Tunbridge Wells, Kent. *M.*

Fire Protection Review—125 High St., S.W.19. *M.*

Fish Friers' Review—289 Dewsbury Road, Leeds. *M.*

Fish Trades Gazette—17-19 John Adam St., Adelphi, W.C.2. *W.*

Flight International—Dorset House, Stamford St., S.E.1. *W.*

Food Trade Review—7 Garrick St., W.C.2. *M.*

Foundry Trade Journal—17-19 John Adam St., Adelphi, W.C.2. *W.*

Free Trade Review & Club Management—Wheatsheaf House, Carmelite St., E.C.4. *M.*

Frozen Foods—17 John Adam St., W.C.2. *M.*

Fruit Trades Journal—6-7 Gough Square, E.C.4. *W.*

Fuel—32 High St., Guildford. *Q.*

Funeral Service Journal—Hillingdon Press, Uxbridge, Mx. *M.*

Furnishing World—109-119 Waterloo Rd., S.E.1. *Alt. W.*

Furniture and Bedding Production—33 Furnival St., E.C.4. *M.*

Fur Review—27 Garlick Hill, E.C.4. *M.*

Fur Weekly News—87 Lamb's Conduit St., W.C.1.

Games and Toys—30-31 Knightrider St., E.C.4. *M.*

Garage—277 Gray's Inn Rd., W.C.1. *W.*

Gas Journal—100 Gray's Inn Rd., W.C.1. *W.*

Gas World—154 Fleet St., E.C.4. *W.*

Glass—17-19 John Adam St., W.C.2. *M.*

Grocer—Eastcheap Buildings, E.C.3. *W.*

Grocer's Gazette—1-2 Pudding Lane, E.C.3. *W.*

Grower—49 Doughty St., W.C.1. *W.*

Hair and Beauty—54 Wilton Rd., S.W.1. *M.*

Hairdressers' Journal—33-39 Bowling Green Lane, E.C.1. *W.*

Handy Shipping Guide—12-16 Laystall St., E.C.1. *W.*

Hardware Trade Journal—154 Fleet St., E.C.4. *W.*

Harper's Sports and Games—Southbank House, Black Prince Rd., S.E.1. *Alt. W.*

Harper's Wine and Spirit Gazette—Southbank House, Black Prince Rd., S.E.1. *W.*

Heating and Ventilating Engineer—11-13 Southampton Row, W.C.1. *M.*

Hosiery Trade Journal—11 Millstone Lane, Leicester. *M.*

Hospital—75 Portland Place, W.1. *M.*

Hospital Management—29 Palace St., S.W.1. *M.*

Ice Cream & Frozen Confectionery—90 Grays Inn Rd., W.C.1. *M.*

Illustrated Carpenter and Builder—Elm House, Elm Street, W.C.1. *W.*

Industrial Daily News—Pear Tree Court, Farringdon Rd., E.C.1.

Industrial Society—48 Bryanston Square, W.1. *M.*

Insurance Mail, 44 Fleet St., E.C.4. *M.*

Insurance Record—75 Carter Lane, E.C.4. *M.*

Investor's Chronicle and Stock Exchange Gazette—30 Finsbury Sq., E.C.2. *W.*

Investors' Guardian—13-14 Charterhouse Sq., E.C.1. *W.*

Investors' Review—Wardrobe Chambers, Queen Victoria St., E.C.4. *Alt. W.*

Jeweller and Metalworker—Victoria Rd., N.W.10. *Alt. W.*

Journalist—8 Regent's Park Terrace, N.W.1. *M.*

Journal of the Institute of Bankers—10 Lombard St., E.C.3. *Alt. M.*

Journal of the Chemical Society—Burlington House, W.1. *M.*

Junior Age—167 High Holborn, W.C.1. *M.*

Justice of the Peace and Local Govt.—Little London, Chichester. *W.*

Jute and Synthetics Review—222 Strand, W.C.2. *M.*

Kinematograph Weekly—161 Fleet St., E.C.4.

Knitting and Haberdashery Review—222 Strand, W.C.2. *Ten a year.*

Lancet—7 Adam Street, W.C.2. *W.*

Law Quarterly Review—11 New Fetter Lane, E.C.4.

Law Reports—3 Stone Buildings, Lincoln's Inn, W.C.2. *M.*

Law Society's Gazette—Chancery Lane, W.C.2. *M.*

Leather—125 High St., S.W.19. *M.*

Leathergoods—125 High St., S.W.19. *M.*

Library Review—98-100 Holm St., Glasgow. *Q.*

Library World—10 New Fetter Lane, E.C.4. *M.*

Light and Lighting—York House, Westminster Bridge Road, S.E.1. *M.*

Litho-Printer—5 Winsley St., W.1. *M.*

Lloyd's Loading List—Lloyd's, E.C.3. *W.*

Local Government Chronicle—11-12 Bury St., E.C.3. *W.*

Local Government Finance—1 Buckingham Place, Westminster, S.W.1. *M.*

Locomotive Journal—9 Arkwright Rd., N.W.3. *M.*

London Corn Circular—52 Mark Lane, E.C.3. *W.*

Machinery Market—146A Queen Victoria St., E.C.4. *W.*

Maker-Up—42 Gerrard St., W.1. *M.*

Management Accounting—63 Portland Place, W.1. *M.*

Management Decision—32 High St., Guildford. *Q.*

Management Today—5 Winsley St., W.1. *M.*

Manufacturing Chemist—28 Essex St., W.C.2. *M.*

Manufacturing Clothier—42 Gerrard St.. W.1. *M.*

Marine and Air Catering—125 High St., S.W.19. *M.*

Marine Engineer and Naval Architect—Wrotham Place, Wrotham, Kent. *M.*

Marketing—5 Winsley St., W.1. *M.*

Master Builders Journal—33 John St., Holborn, W.C.1. *M.*

Materials Reclamation Weekly—69-77 High St. Croydon. *W.*

Meat Industry—1 Dorset Buildings, Salisbury Square, E.C.4. *M.*

Meat Trades Journal—5 Charterhouse Square, E.C.1. *W.*

Mechanical Handling—33-39 Bowling Green Lane. E.C.1. *M.*

Medical Officer—Little Essex St., W.C.2. *W.*

Medico-Legal Journal—104 Hills Rd., Cambridge. *Q.*

Men's Wear (incorporating Outfitter)—20 Soho Sq., W.1. *W.*

Mercantile Guardian—125 High St., S.W.19. *M.*

Metal Bulletin—46 Wigmore St. W.1. *Twice a week.*

Metallurgia—31 King St. West, Manchester, 3. *M.*

Milk Industry—37 Queen's Gate, S.W.7. *M.*

Milling—65-66 Turnmill St., E.C.1. *W.*

Mining Journal—15 Wilson St., Moorgate, E.C.2. *W.*

Mining Magazine—15 Wilson St., Moorgate, E.C.2. *M.*

Model Engineer—13-15 Bridge St., Hemel Hempstead, Herts. *Twice a month.*

Modern Law Review—11 New Fetter Lane, E.C.4. *Alt. M.*

Modern Railways—Terminal House, Shepperton. *M.*

Motor—Dorset House, Stamford St., S.E.1. *W.*

Motor Boat and Yachting—Dorset House, Stamford St., S.E.1. *Twice a Month.*

Motor Cycle—161 Fleet St., E.C.4. *W.*

Motor Cycle and Cycle Trader—161 Fleet St., E.C.4. *Alt. W.*

Motor Industry—17-19 John Adam St., Adelphi, W.C.2. *M.*

Motor Trader—Dorset House, Stamford Street, S.E.1. *W.*

Motor Transport—Dorset House, Stamford St., S.E.1. *W.*

Muck Shifter—28 Essex St., W.C.2. *M.*

Musical Times—27 Soho Square, W.1. *M.*

National Builder—82 New Cavendish St., W.1. *M.*

National Guardian—113 St. Vincent St., Glasgow, C.2. *W.*

National Newsagent—Lennox House, Norfolk St., W.C.2. *W.*

New Commonwealth—4-5 Fitzroy Sq., W.1. *M.*

New Law Journal—11-12 Bell Yard, W.C.2. *W.*

Nuclear Energy—147 Victoria St., S.W.1 *Six times a year*

Nuclear Engineering International—Dorset House, Stamford St., S.E.1. *M.*

Nurseryman & Garden Centre—154 Fleet St., E.C.4. *W.*

Nursing Mirror—161 Fleet St., E.C.4. *W.*

Nursing Times—4 Little Essex St., W.C.2. *W.*

Off Licence Journal—1 Dorset Bldgs., Salisbury Sq., E.C.4. *14 times a year.*

Off Licence News—19 Eastcheap, E.C.3. *W.*

Official Architecture and Planning—4 Catherine St., W.C.2. *M.*

Official Journal (Patents)—25 Southampton Bldgs., Chancery Lane, W.C.2. *W.*

Ophthalmic Optician—65 Brook St., W.1. *Alt. W.*

Optician—69 Aldwych, W.C.2. *W.*

Packaging—75 Carter Lane, E.C.4. *M.*

Packaging Review—33-39 Bowling Green Lane, E.C.1. *M.*

Paint Manufacture—28 Essex St., W.C.2. *M.*

Paint, Oil and Colour Journal—17 John Adam St., W.C.2. *W.*

Paint Technology—4 Ludgate Circus, E.C.4. *M.*

Painting and Decorating Journal—30 Princes St., Southport, Lancs. *M.*

Paperbacks in Print—13 Bedford Sq., W.C.1. *Twice a year.*

Paper Maker—50-51 Fetter Lane, E.C.4. *M.*

Parish Councils Review—99 Gt. Russell St., W.C.1. *Q.*

Personnel and Training Management—Mercury House, Waterloo Rd., S.E.1. *M.*

Petroleum Times—Bowling Green Lane, E.C.1. *Alt. W.*

Pharmaceutical Journal—17 Bloomsbury Square, W.C.1. *W.*

Philatelic Magazine—42 Maiden Lane, W.C.2. *Alt. W.*

Philatelic Trader—42 Maiden Lane, W.C.2. *Alt. W.*

Plumber and Heating Engineer—103 Brigstock Rd., Thornton Heath, Surrey. *M.*

Police Review—67 Clerkenwell Rd., E.C.1. *W.*

Policy Holder—Waterloo Rd., Stockport. *W.*

Post Magazine—The Butts, Half Acre, Brentford. *W.*

Power Farming—161 Fleet St., E.C.4. *M.*

Power Laundry + Cleaning News—40 Bowling Green Lane, E.C.1. *Alt. W.*

Practical Wireless—Fleetway House, Farringdon St., E.C.4. *M.*

Practical Woodworking—Fleetway House, Farringdon St., E.C.4. *M.*

Practitioner—5 Bentinck St., W.1. *M.*

Printing Trades Journal—154 Fleet St., E.C.4. *M.*

Printing World—125 High St., S.W.19. *W.*

Product Finishing—4 Ludgate Circus, E.C.4. *M.*

Professional Administration—388/389 Strand, W.C.2. *M.*

Public Law—11 New Fetter Lane, E.C.4. *Q.*

Public Ledger (Commercial)—11 Tokenhouse Yard, E.C.2. *Daily*

Public Service—Nalgo House, 8 Harewood Row, N.W.1. *M.*

Quarry Manager's Journal—62–64 Baker St., W.1. *M.*

Quarterly Journal of Experimental Physiology, 5 Bentinck St., W.1.

Quarterly Journal of Experimental Psychology, Berkeley Sq. House, Berkeley Sq., W.1.

Quarterly Journal of Medicine, Oxford U. Press, Press Rd., Neasden, N.W.10.

Railway Review—205 Euston Rd., N.W.1. *W.*

Rating and Valuation Reporter—2 Paper Bldgs., Temple, E.C.4. *W.*

Resale Weekly—Unit 4, Sewell Street Industrial Colony, Plaistow, E.13.

Retail Jeweller—Elm House, Elm St., W.C.1. *Alt. W.*

Retail Newsagent—15 Charterhouse St., E.C.1. *W.*

Review (Insurance)—9 Gough Square, E.C.4. *Alt. W.*

Review of Economic Studies—5 Bentinck St., W.1. *Q.*

Review of English Studies, Oxford U. Press, Press Rd., Neasden, N.W.10 *Q.*

Ridley's Wine and Spirit Trade Circular—Wheatsheaf House, Carmelite St., E.C.4. *M.*

Roads and Road Construction—Blenheim House, S.W.11. *M.*

Safety at Sea International—54–55 Wilton Rd., S.W.1. *Alt. M.*

School Government Chronicle and Education, Review—Darby House, Bletchingley Rd., Merstham, Redhill, Surrey. *M.*

Scottish Farmer—39 York St., Glasgow. *W.*

Scottish Grocer—34–6 North Frederick St., Glasgow, *W.*

Scottish Schoolmaster—41 York Place, Edinburgh 1. *Alt. M.*

Self Service and Supermarket—1 Dorset Bldgs., Salisbury Sq., E.C.4. *W.*

Service Station—3 Clement's Inn, W.C.2. *M.*

Sheet Metal Industries—17–19 John Adam St., Adelphi, W.C.2. *M.*

Shipbuilding and Shipping Record—33 Bowling Green Lane, E.C.1. *W.*

Shipping World and Shipbuilder—125 High St., S.W.19. *W.*

Shoe and Leather News—84–88 Great Eastern St., E.C.2. *W.*

Shoe Manufacturers' Monthly—4 Market Place, Leicester.

Soap, Perfumery and Cosmetics—9 Gough Square, E.C.4. *M.*

Solicitors' Journal—Oyez House, Bream's Bldgs., E.C.4. *W.*

Sports Trader—125 High St., S.W.19. *M.*

Stage—19 Tavistock St., W.C.2. *W.*

Structural Engineer—11 Upper Belgrave Sq., S.W.1. *M.*

Surveyor and Local Government Technology—32 Southwark Bridge Rd., S.E.1.

Tableware International + Pottery Gazette—17 John Adam St., W.C.2. *M.*

Tailor and Cutter—42 Gerrard St., W.1. *W.*

Taxation—98 Park St., W.1. *W.*

Teacher—Derbyshire House St. Chad's St., W.C.1. *W.*

Teacher's World—Montague House, Russell Sq., W.C.1. *W.*

Teaching History—59A Kennington Park Rd., S.E.11. *Twice a year.*

Television—Fleetway House, Farringdon St., E.C.4. *M.*

Textile Institute and Industry—10 Blackfriars St,, Manchester, 3. *M.*

Textile Manufacturer—31 King St. West, Manchester 3. *M.*

Textile Month—30 Finsbury Sq., E.C.2. *M.*

Textile Production—222 Strand, W.C.2. *M.*

Timber and Plywood—194–200 Bishopsgate, E.C.2. *W.*

Timber Trades Journal—154 Fleet St., E.C.4. *W.*

Tobacco—17–19 John Adam St., Adelphi, W.C.2. *M.*

Today's Cinema—142 Wardour St., W.1. *Thrice a week.*

Tooling—4 Ludgate Circus, E.C.4. *M.*

Town and Country Planning—28 King St., W.C.2. *M.*

Town Planning Review—123 Grove St., Liverpool, 7. *Q.*

Toy Trader—157 Hagden Lane, Watford. *M.*

Trade and Industry (Official)—1 Victoria St., S.W.1. *W.*

Trade Marks Journal—25 Southampton Bldgs., W.C.2. *W.*

Traffic Engineering and Control—26–30 Holborn Viaduct, E.C.1. *M.*

U.K. Press Gazette—2–3 Salisbury Ct., Fleet St., E.C.4. *W.*

Ultrasonics—32 High St., Guildford. *Q.*

Underwater Science Technology Journal—32 High St., Guildford. *Q.*

Universities Quarterly—10 Great Turnstile, W.C.1.

Watchmaker, Jeweller and Silversmith—40 Bowling Green Lane, E.C.1. *M.*

Water and Water Engineering—17 John Adam St., W.C.2. *M.*

Weekly Law Reports—3 Stone Buildings, Lincoln's Inn, W.C.2.

Welding and Metal Fabrication—33 Bowling Green Lane, E.C.1. *M.*

Which?—14 Buckingham St., W.C.2. *M.*

Whitaker's Books of the Month and Books to Come—13 Bedford Sq., W.C.1. *M.*

Whitaker's Cumulative Book List—13 Bedford Sq., W.C.1. *Q.*

Wine and Spirit Trade Record—12 Norfolk St., W.C.2. *M.*

Wire Industry—33 Furnival St., E.C.4. *M.*

Wireless World—Dorset House, Stamford St., S.E.1. *M.*

Wood—154 Fleet St., E.C.4. *Q.*

Woodworker—12–18 Paul St., E.C.4. *M.*

Wool Record—30 Finsbury Sq., E.C.2. *W.*

World Crops—Riverside House, Hough St., S.E.18. *Alt. M.*

World Sports—23–27 Tudor St., E.C.4. *M.* (33,013).

World's Fair—Union St., Oldham. *W.*

World's Paper Trade Review—125 High St., S.W.19. *W.*

COMMONWEALTH, NORTHERN IRISH AND AMERICAN NEWSPAPERS

LONDON OFFICES:

Australia:—

Adelaide Advertiser—107 Fleet St., E.C.4.
Adelaide Chronicle—107 Fleet St., E.C.4.
Adelaide Sunday Mail—35 Dover St., W.1.
Adelaide News—35 Dover St., W.1.
Australian Financial Review—85 Fleet St., E.C.4
Brisbane Courier-Mail—107 Fleet St., E.C.4.
Brisbane Telegraph—107 Fleet St., E.C.4.
Canberra Times—85 Fleet St., E.C.4.
Hobart Mercury—110 Fleet St., E.C.4.
Illawarra Daily Mercury (Woollongong)— 85 Fleet St., E.C.4.
Melbourne Age—Times Building, Printing House Sq., E.C.4.
Melbourne Australasian Post—107 Fleet St., E.C.4.
Melbourne Herald—107 Fleet St., E.C.4.
Melbourne Sun News-Pictorial—107 Fleet St., E.C.4.
Melbourne Weekly Times—107 Fleet St., E.C.4.
Newcastle Herald—85 Fleet St., E.C.4.
Newcastle Sun—85 Fleet St., E.C.4.
Perth Daily News—107 Fleet St., E.C.4.
Perth West Australian—107 Fleet St., E.C.4.
Sydney Bulletin—107 Fleet St., E.C.4.
Sydney Mirror—Keystone House, Red Lion Court, E.C.4.
Sydney Morning Herald—85 Fleet St., E.C.4.
Sydney Sun-Herald—85 Fleet Street, E.C.4.
Sydney Telegraph—107 Fleet St., E.C.4.
The Barrier Miner (Broken Hill)—35 Dover St., W.1.

Canada:—

Albertan (Calgary)—Times Building, Printing House Sq., E.C.4.
Globe and Mail (Toronto)—Times Building, Printing House Sq., E.C.4.
Montreal Gazette—35 Dover St., W.1.
Ottawa Journal—Times Building, Printing House Sq., E.C.4.
Toronto Daily Star—Times Building, Printing House Sq., E.C.4.
Vancouver Province—Times Building, Printing House Sq., E.C.4.
Vancouver Sun—Times Building, Printing House Sq., E.C.4.
Victoria (B.C.) Times, and Daily Colonist—Times Building, Printing House Sq., E.C.4.
Winnipeg Free Press—Times Building, Printing House Sq., E.C.4.

New Zealand:—

Christchurch Press—107 Fleet St., E.C.4.
Christchurch Star—5 Winsley St., W.1.
Dominion (Wellington)—41-42 Shoe Lane, E.C.4
Dunedin Evening Star—Bredon Cottage, Ditchling, Sussex.
New Zealand Evening Post (Wellington)—107 Fleet Street, E.C.4.
New Zealand Herald (Auckland)—107 Fleet St., E.C.4.
Otago Daily Times and Witness (Dunedin)—107 Fleet St., E.C.4.

Northern Ireland:—

Ballymena Guardian—63 Fleet St., E.C.4.
Ballymena Observer—200 Gray's Inn Rd., W.C.1.
Banbridge Chronicle—30 Fleet St., E.C.4.
Belfast Telegraph (and Weekly Telegraph)—Thomson House, 200 Grays Inn Road, W.C.1.
Coleraine Chronicle—30 Fleet St., E.C.4.
Derry Journal—30 Fleet St., E.C.4.
Down Recorder—30 Fleet St., E.C.4. [E.C.4.
Impartial Reporter (Enniskillen)—30 Fleet St.,
Irish News—177 Fleet St., E.C.4.
Irish Weekly and Ulster Examiner—177 Fleet St., E.C.4.
Londonderry Sentinel—54-55 Wilton Rd., S.W.1.
Lurgan Mail—54-55 Wilton Rd., S.W.1.
Mid Ulster Mail—27 Chancery Lane, W.C.2.
Northern Constitution (Coleraine)—63 Fleet St., E.C.4.
Portadown News—30 Fleet St., E.C.4.
Portadown Times—54-55 Wilton Rd., S.W.1.
Strabane Weekly News—30 Fleet St., E.C.4.
Tyrone Constitution—30 Fleet St., E.C.4.
Tyrone Courier—30 Fleet St., E.C.4.
Ulster Gazette (Armagh)—30 Fleet St., E.C.4.
Ulster Herald (Omagh)—Drayton House, Gordon St., W.C.1.

U.S.A.:—

Baltimore News American, 72-78 Fleet St., E.C.4.
Baltimore Sun—85 Fleet St., E.C.4.
Chicago Daily News—69 Fleet St., E.C.4.
Chicago Tribune—54 Burton Ct., S.W.3.
New York News—54 Burton Ct., S.W.3.
New York Times—5 Winsley St., W.1.
New York Wall Street Journal—Printing House Square, 162 Queen Victoria St., E.C.4.

REPORTING AND NEWS AGENCIES IN LONDON

ASSOCIATED NEWS SERVICE,
9 Linthorpe Rd., N.16. 01-800 9595.

ASSOCIATED PRESS LTD.,
83-86 Farringdon Street, E.C.4. 01-353 1515.

BRENARD PRESS LTD.,
London Airport, Hounslow, Middx. 01-759 1325.

CAPEL COURT PRESS AGENCY LTD., 20 Copthall Avenue, E.C.2. 01-628 3580.

CENTRAL PRESS FEATURES,
80 Fleet Street, E.C.4. 01-353 7792.

EXCHANGE TELEGRAPH CO., LTD.,
Extel House, East Harding Street, E.C.4. 01-353 1080.

2 M*

NATIONAL PRESS AGENCY LTD.,
Newspaper House, 8-16 Great New Street, E.C.4. 01-353 1030.

NEWSPAPER FEATURES LTD.,
80 Fleet Street, E.C.4. 01-353 7888.

PARLIAMENTARY NEWS SERVICES,
92 Fleet Street, E.C.4. 01-583 7848.

PRESS ASSOCIATION LTD.,
85 Fleet Street, E.C.4. 01-353 7440.

REUTERS LTD.,
85 Fleet Street, E.C.4. 01-353 6060.

UNITED PRESS INTERNATIONAL, LTD., 8 Bouverie St., E.C.4. 01-353 2282.

UNIVERSAL NEWS SERVICES, LTD., 11 New Fetter Lane, E.C.4. 01-353 5200

THE PRESS COUNCIL

In April, 1947, a Royal Commission was appointed to enquire into the control, management and ownership, etc., of the Press and news agencies and to make recommendations thereon. The Commission, in its report of June, 1949, recommended *inter alia* that a voluntary Press Council be formed.

A constitution ultimately set up provided for the establishment of such a council on July 1, 1953. This constitution was materially amended in 1963 by the introduction of an independent chairman and up to 20 per cent. lay membership. The objects of the Council are (1) to preserve the established freedom of the British Press; (2) to maintain the character of the British Press in accordance with the highest professional and commercial standards; (3) to consider complaints about the conduct of the Press or the conduct of persons and organizations towards the Press; to deal with these complaints in whatever manner might seem practical and appropriate and record resultant action; (4) to keep under review developments likely to restrict the supply of information of public interest and importance; (5) to report publicly on developments that may tend towards greater concentration or monopoly in the Press (including changes in ownership, control and growth of Press undertakings) and to publish statistical information relating thereto; (6) to make representations on appropriate occasions to the Government, organs of the United Nations and Press organizations abroad; and (7) to publish periodical reports recording the Council's work and to review, from time to time, developments in the Press and the factors affecting them.

The membership of the Council consists of editorial and managerial nominees of The Newspaper Publishers Association Ltd. (5), The Newspaper Society (3), The Periodical Publishers Association Ltd. (2), The Scottish Daily Newspaper Society (1), Scottish Newspaper Proprietors' Association (1), The Guild of British Newspaper Editors (2), The National Union of Journalists (4) and The Institute of Journalists (2).

Chairman, The Lord Pearce, P.C.

Vice-Chairman, H. Bate, O.B.E.

Professional Members, G. B. Allan; W. D. Barnetson; Sir Eric Clayson; R. Deadman; Sir Trevor Evans, C.B.E.; D. C. Flatley; P. W. Gibbings; D. Greenslade; C. D. Hamilton, D.S.O.; W. Heald; S. Jacobson, M.C.; A. A. Jenner; F. M. Johnston; J. C. Jones; C. Kilner; A. M. Lee; E. Pickering; D. W. Rees.

Lay Members, W. R. Buckley, M.B.E.; D. Ellis, O.B.E., T.D.; A. Glen; The Rev. M. R. Hollings, M.B.E.; Lady Littlewood.

Secretary, N. S. Paul, New Mercury House, 81 Farringdon Street, E.C.4.

THE ARTS COUNCIL
105 Piccadilly, W.1

The Arts Council of Great Britain is incorporated under Royal Charter with the following objects, (a) to develop and improve the knowledge, understanding and practice of the arts; (b) to increase the accessibility of the arts to the public throughout Great Britain; and (c) to advise and cooperate with Departments of Government, local authorities and other bodies on any matters concerned directly or indirectly with the foregoing objects.

The members of the Council, who may not exceed twenty in number, are appointed by the Secretary of State for Education and Science after consultation with the Secretary of State for Scotland and the Secretary of State for Wales. With their approval the Council appoints separate committees for Scotland and Wales known as the Scottish Arts Council and the Welsh Arts Council respectively.

The Council receives a grant-in-aid from the Government, and for the year 1971-72 the amount was £11,900,000.

Chairman, The Lord Goodman.

Secretary-General, R. H. Willatt.

WEATHER INFORMATION AND FORECASTS

Recorded weather forecasts for the areas listed below are available by telephoning the numbers shown:

Bedford area	Bedford 8091	Lancs. Coast	Blackpool 8091	South Devon and	
	01-246 8099		Southport 9541	East Cornwall	Exeter 8091
	Peterborough 8091	Leeds/Bradford area			Plymouth 8091
	Luton 8091		Bradford 8091		Torquay 8091
Belfast area	Belfast 8091		Huddersfield 8091	Southern Hants.	
Birmingham area	021-246 8091		Leeds 8091	(including I.O.W.	
	Coventry 8091	London area	01-246 8091	and Poole Harbour)	
Bristol area	Bristol 8091		Tunbridge Wells 8091		Bournemouth 8091
	Swindon 8091		Guildford 8091		Portsmouth 8091
Cardiff area	Cardiff 8091	North Lincs. and			Southampton 8091
Central Lancs.	Blackburn 8091	Retford area	Grimsby 8091	South Lancs. and	
Edinburgh area	031-246 8091		Lincoln 8091	North Cheshire	051-275 8091
Essex Coast	Chelmsford 8091	North Wales Coast			061-246 8091
	01-246 8096	and Chester	051-275 8093	South-West Midlands	
	Colchester 8091		061-246 8093		Cheltenham 8091
	Southend 8091		Chester 8091		Gloucester 8091
Glasgow area	041-246 8091		Colwyn Bay 8091		Hereford 8091
Kent Coast	01-246 8098	Notts., Leics. and		Sussex Coast	01-246 8097
	Canterbury 8091	Derby	Nottingham 8091		Brighton 8091
	Medway 8091		Leicester 8091	Thames Valley	01-246 8090
Lancs. Coast	051-275 8092		Derby 8091		Oxford 8091
	061-246 8092	Sheffield area	Sheffield 8091		Reading 8091
	Blackburn 8092		Doncaster 8091	Tyne-Tees	Newcastle 8091
					Middlesbrough 8091

Principal London Clubs

Club and Address	Secretary	Subscription		Remarks
		Entr.	Ann.	
		£	£	
Alpine (1857), 74 S. Audley St., W.1	M. H. Westmacott (Hon.)	4·20	5·00	Mountaineering.
American (1919), 95 Piccadilly, W.1.	A. Saynes............	45·00	Various	Americans in London.
American Women's (1899) 1 Cadogan Gardens, S.W.3.	Mrs. K. E. Hayward...	5·00	18–11	American Women in London.
Anglo-Belgian (1955), 6 Belgrave Square, S.W.1.	Cdr. R. M. Fell, R.N.	10·50	15·00–7·50	Social.
Army and Navy (1837), 36–39 Pall Mall, S.W.1.	J. Gordon.............	Nil	25·00	Regular officers of H.M. Forces.
Arts (1863), 40 Dover Street, W.1.	Cdr. E. Laurie, R.N.....	··	30·00–5·00	Art, Literature, Science.
The Athenæum (1824), 107 Pall Mall, S.W.1.	A. C. C. Peebles, C.V.O.	52·50	40·00	Literature and Science, Public Services, The Arts.
Authors' (1891), 1 Whitehall Place, S.W.1	M. S. Lindsay.........	··	25·00 to 10·00	Literary and Social.
The Bath (1896), 43 Brook St., W.1	Cdr. C. E. L. Sclater, D.S.O., R.N.	31·50	50·00	Social: non-political.
Beefsteak (1876), 9 Irving St., W.C.2.	W. E. Usher..........	21·00	30·00	Dining and Social.
Boodle's (1762), 28 St. James's St., S.W.1.	R. J. Edmonds........	52·50	60·00	Social: non-political.
Brooks's (1764), St. James's St., S.W.1.	Lt.-Col. D. A. St. G. Laurie, O.B.E., M.C.	42·00	55·00	Social: non-political.
Buck's (1919), 18 Clifford Street, W.1.	K. J. Hunn...........	Nil	42·00	Social: non-political.
Caledonian (1897), 9 Halkin St., S.W.1.	Capt. G. G. Wilson, C.B.E., R.N.	Nil	37·00 to 4·00	Strictly Scottish.
Canning (1910), 42 Half Moon Street, W.1.	R. B. Baker..........	15·00	27·00	Social: S. American.
Carlton (1832), 69 St. James's St., S.W.1.	M. R. D. Lord........	32·00	55·00	Conservative.
Cavalry (1891), 127 Piccadilly, W.1.	Sqn.-Ldr. A. F. O'Connor (Hon.)	31·50	26·25	Officers of Mounted Services.
Challoner (1949), 59–61 Pont St., S.W.1.	Brig. P. B. Cuddon, C.B.E., M.C.	2·10	6·30 to 3·15	Social: Roman Catholic.
Chemical (1918), 1 Whitehall Place, S.W.1.	M. S. Lindsay.........	Nil	20·00 & 15·00	Social.
City Livery (1914), Sion College, E.C.4.	B. L. Morgan, M.B.E. (Hon.)	15·75	10·50	Liverymen of City only.
City of London (1832), 19 Old Broad Street, E.C.2.	A. C. Woollard.......	105·00	48·30	Merchants, Bankers, &c.
City University (1885), 50 Cornhill, E.C.3.	C. Lazenby...........	26·25	29·40	Oxford and Cambridge Graduates.
Civil Service (1953), 13–15 Great Scotland Yard, S.W.1.	E. G. Roberts (Manager)	Nil	1·50	Serving or pensioned Civil Servants.
Constitutional (1883), 86 St. James's Street, S.W.1.	S. F. Head............	Nil	30·00	Social and Political.
Cowdray (1922), 20 Cavendish Sq., W.1.	R. S. Low............	5·25	10·00 to 5·00	Ladies.
Devonshire (1874), 50 St. James's St., S.W.1.	C. J. Gibling........	Nil	42·00	Social.
East India and Sports' (1849), 16 St. James's Square, S.W.1.	J. Gledhill............	Nil	31·50 to 5·25	Social and Residential.
Eccentric (1890), 9 Ryder Street, S.W.1.	Cdr. C. H. Tyers, R.N. (ret.).	10·50	31·50	Social.
Farmers' (1842), 3 Whitehall Ct., S.W.1.	Lt.-Col. R. L. Henson, M.B.E.	20·00 to 5·00	20·00 to 5·00	Agricultural Interests.
Flyfishers' (1884), 86 St. James's Street, S.W.1.	H. A. Rickett........	10·50	18·90 to 8·00	Flyfishing and Social.
Garrick (1831), 14 Garrick Street, W.C.2.	Cdr. E. S. Satterthwaite, R.N.	52·50	52·50	Dramatic and Literary.
Golfers' (1893), 4 Arlington Street, S.W.1.	Mrs. M. A. Pearse.....	Nil	10·50 to 6·30	Members of Golf Clubs.
Green Room (1877), 9 Adam Street, W.C.2.	R. Gosse (Hon.).......	5·00	20·00	Dramatic Profession.
Gresham (1843), 15 Abchurch Lane, E.C.4.	Maj. C. A. E. Parker...	75·00	42·00	Bankers, Merchants, Social.

Club and Address	Secretary	Subscription Entr. £	Subscription Ann. £	Remarks
Guards (1810), 16 Charles St., W.1.	J. E. Savage	Nil	40·00	Guards Officers only.
Hurlingham (1869), Ranelagh Gardens, S.W.6.	C. J. L. Reynolds......	55·00	40·00	Tennis, Swimming, Croquet, Squash, Bowls, Social.
Irish (1948), 82 Eaton Sq., S.W.1.	J. Sheehy (Hon.).......	1·05	10·50 & 6·30	Social: Non-political.
Junior Carlton (1864), 30 Pall Mall, S.W.1.	W. A. Jolly...........	30·00	40·00	Conservative.
Kempton Park (1879) Sunbury-on-Thames.	S. H. Hyde...........	..	25·00	Racing.
Kennel (1873), 1–4 Clarges St., W.1.	Lt.-Cdr. J. S. Williams.	Nil	10·50	For improving breed of dogs.
Ladies' Alpine (1907), c/o National Book League, 7 Albemarle St., W.1.	Miss C. M. Ramsay (Hon.)	1·00	3·00	Mountaineering.
Lansdowne (1935), 9 Fitzmaurice Place, Berkeley Sq., W.1.	Brig. R. F. B. Hensman, C.B.E.	15·75	32·00 to 10·00	Social, Sports and Residential.
London Fencing (1848), 83 Perham Road, W.14.	E. J. Morten (Hon.)....	Nil	12·00	Fencing.
London Rowing (1856), Embankment, Putney, S.W.15.	A. J. Tressidder (Hon.)..	2·00	Various	Amateur Rowing.
M.C.C. (Marylebone Cricket Club) (1787), Lord's Cricket Ground, N.W.8.	S. C. Griffith, D.F.C., T.D.	5·00	9·00	Headquarters of Cricket.
Mining (1910), 3 London Wall Bldgs, E.C.2.	G. Sumner...........	5·25	12·60 to 3·15	Mining and metallurgical interests.
National (1845), c/o Constitutional Club (q.v.)	E. Scott (Hon.)........	Nil	20·00	Clerical and social.
National Liberal (1882), Whitehall Place, S.W.1.	C. Billson...........	Nil	20·00 to 14·00	Social and political.
Naval (1943), 38 Hill Street, W.1.	Lt.-Cdr. L. A. d'E. Lloyd, M.B.E., R.N.	Nil	8·00 to 2·00	Officers of R.N., R.M., R.N.R., R.N.V.R., and yacht club members.
Naval and Military (1862), 94 Piccadilly, W.1.	Maj. W. E. Anderson, M.B.E., M.C.	15·00	27·00 to 3·50	Officers of R.N., Army, Marines, R.A.F.
Oriental (1824), Stratford House, Stratford Place, W.1.	R. N. Rapson, M.V.O.	50·00	26·25 to 3·15	Social.
Oxford and Cambridge University (1830), 71–7 Pall Mall, S.W.1.	J. Harper............	Nil	39·90 to 10·50	Oxford and Cambridge Univ.
Portland (1816), 42 Half Moon Street, W.1.	H. E. Pretyman.......	52·50	31·50	Social: Non-political.
Pratt's (1841), 14 Park Place, S.W.1	Maj. G. C. Hackett, M.B.E.	Nil	7·50	Social.
Press (1882), St. Bride's House, Salisbury Sq., E.C.4.	T. H. McArthur.......	5·00 & 2·00	20·00 & 6·50	Strictly Journalistic.
Public Schools (1909), 100 Piccadilly, W.1.	H. L. Bugbee.........	Nil	25·00 to 5·00	Social: Public Schools.
Queen's (1886), W. Kensington, W.14.	R. J. Ritchie.........	15·75	33·60 & 29·40	Lawn Tennis, Tennis, Rackets and Squash Racquets.
Railway (1899), 112 High Holborn, W.C.1.	D. R. A. Whitnell (Hon.)	0·50	3·15	Railway interests.
Reform (1832), 104–5 Pall Mall, S.W.1.	Cdr. A. C. Mathews, O.B.E., R.N.	26·25	42·00	Social.
Roehampton (1901), Roehampton Lane, S.W.15.	J. Maples............	40·00 & 10·00	65·00 to 25·00	Golf, Lawn Tennis, Squash Racquets, Croquet, Swimming.
Royal Air Force (1917), 128 Piccadilly, W.1.	E. A. Jeffreys.........	Nil	6·30*	Officers of R.A.F., R.A.F.V.R., R.F.C., R.N.A.S., etc.
Royal Automobile (1897), 89–91 Pall Mall, S.W.1.	Lt.-Col. J. D. Nixon, M.C.	25·00 to 7·00	35·00 to 13·00	And at Woodcote Park, Epsom.
Royal Cruising (1880), 42 Half Moon Street, Piccadilly, W.1.	A. P. Gray (Hon.).....	6·30	4·20	Cruising and social.
R.A.F. Reserves (1948), c/o Naval Club, 38 Hill Street, W.1.	Sqn. Ldr. H. C. Room, M.B.E. (Hon.)	Nil	5·25 to 1·05	Officers of R.A.F., R.A.F.V.R., R.A.F. Reserve and ex-officers.

*or half a day's pay.

Club and Address	Secretary	Subscription Entr.	Subscription Ann.	Remarks
		£	£	
Royal Ocean Racing (1925), 20 St. James's Place, S.W.1.	A. H. Paul, O.B.E.	6·00	16·00 & 8·00	Off-shore Yacht Racing.
Royal Societies (1894), 100 Piccadilly, W.1.	V. S. Gregg (Hon.)	Nil	21·00	Learned Societies, Professional, Social.
Royal Thames Yacht (1775), 60 Knightsbridge, S.W.1.	Lt.-Col. D. W. Browne, M.C.	52·50 & 26·25	60·00 & 40·00	Yachting and Social.
Royal Water Colour Society Art (1884), 26 Conduit Street, W.1.	M. Fry	2·00	4·00	Exhibiting Art Club only.
St. James' (1859), 106 Piccadilly, W.1.	P. K. Hiller	26·25	52·50	Diplomatic and Social.
St. Stephen's (1871), 34 Queen Anne's Gate, S.W.1.	L. H. Coleman	Nil	31·50 to 5·25	Conservative and Social.
Sandown Park (1875), Esher, Surrey.	F. J. Bates	Nil	18·00	Racing.
Savage (1857), 86 St. James's Street, S.W.1.	A. Wykes (Hon.)	21·00	26·25 to 13·13	Drama, Literature, Art, Music, Science, Law.
Savile (1868), 69 Brook Street, W.1	H. G. Vevers, M.B.E.	21·00	42·00 & 25·00	Social: Non-political.
Service Women's (1922), 52 Lower Sloane St., S.W.1.	(vacant)	4·00	6·30 & 5·25	Social and Residential.
Sesame Pioneer and Lyceum, 49 Grosvenor Street, W.1.	Miss C. Sutton	Nil	15·75 to 6·30	Social and Residential: Men and Women.
Ski Club of G.B. (1903), 118 Eaton Square, S.W.1.	Gp.-Capt. R. D. May	Nil	Various	Ski-ing and Social.
Spanish (Centro Español de Londres) (1913), 5 Cavendish Sq., W.1.	J. R. Roca	Nil	0·75 to 1·50	Social and Residential.
Thames Rowing (1860), Embankment, Putney, S.W.15.	A. J. H. Pollitt (Hon.)	2·00	10·50	Amateur Rowing and Sculling.
Travellers' (1819), 106 Pall Mall, S.W.1.	R. P. McDouall	Nil	48·00 to 24·00	Social: non-political.
Turf (1868), 5 Carlton House Terrace, S.W.1.	J. D. Thomson	31·50	52·00 to 15·00	Racing and Social.
United Nursing Services (1921), 40 South Street, W.1.	W. Oakes	3·15	8·40	Ladies; Nursing Services and Social.
United Service and Royal Aero (1815), 116–19 Pall Mall, S.W.1.	Cdr. J. C. Allan	Nil	30·00	Regular Officers.
United University (1821), 1 Suffolk Street, S.W.1.	J. D. McDougall	Nil	39·90 to 2·10	Oxford and Cambridge Univ.
United Wards (1877), 92 Avenue Chambers, Vernon Pl., Southampton Row, W.C.1.	L. C. Roberts	1·05	4·20	Freemen, Liverymen, Ward Club members in City: Civic.
University Women's (1867), 2 Audley Square, W.1.	Miss L. Lindsay	4·20	10·50 to 5·25	University Graduates.
V.A.D. Ladies (1920) 44 Gt. Cumberland Place, W.1.	Miss R. M. Knibb	2·00	8·50	Red Cross and St. John.
Victoria (1860), 150–162 Edgware Road, W.2.	G. Bailie	26·25	36·75	Sporting and Social.
Victory Ex-Services (1907), 63–79 Seymour Street, W.2.	Lt.-Cdr. J. B. Williams, R.N.	Nil	1·50	Social: Serving and Ex-Service Men and Women.
West Indian (1906) 18 Northumberland Avenue, W.C.2.	J. N. D. Bettley (Hon.).	3·00	16·00 to 5·00	Social: West Indian.
White's (1693), 37–8 St. James's St. S.W.1.	H. L. Webb	100·00	60·00	Social: Non-political.
Wig and Pen (1908), 229–230 Strand, W.C.2.	R. A. Brennan	5·00	6·00	Law and Journalism.
Women's Press Club Ltd., c/o The Arts Theatre Club, 6 Great Newport Street, W.C.2.	Mrs. W. Crum Ewing (Administrator)	Nil	7·00	Writers, Journalists and Authors. (Men and Women.)

CLUB AND LIBRARY EDITION OF WHITAKER, 1972

The Club and Library Edition of Whitaker's Almanack, 1972, contains 1,220 pages, illustrations and additional coloured maps (The World, The British Isles, Baltic States, Russia and her neighbours, Germany and her neighbours, France and Spain, The Far East, India, Pakistan and Burma, Africa, Canada, and Newfoundland, The United States, South America, Australia, New Zealand) in strong leather binding, with gilt top and silk headband. Price £3·00 net.

PRINCIPAL CLUBS OUTSIDE LONDON

Club and Address (with date of foundation)	Secretary or *Hon Sec.	Subscription	
		Entr.	Ann.
		£	£
Aldershot (Officers) (1855), Farnborough Road.	B. A. Harvey.........	10·00†	9·90 to 7·65
Bath (Bath and County) (1858), 21–22 Queen Square.	*R. A. L. Belben......	Nil	17·00 to 4·20
(Bath and County Ladies) (1895), 25 Queen Square.	*Mrs. M. C. Osborne..	1·05	5·25
Birmingham—			
(Chamber of Commerce) (1921), 75 Harborne Road.	J. R. Dixon...........	Nil	14·00
(Conservative) (1872), Winston Churchill House, Ethel Street.	*J. R. Bettinson.......	Nil	31·50
(Midland) (1868), 5 Ethel Street.	*F. B. Murray.........	..	30·00
(St. Paul's) (1859), 34 St. Paul's Square.	*R. J. Allen..........	..	26·25
(Union) (1856), 87 Colmore Row.	*M. N. W. Wilcox....	Nil	Various
Bishop Auckland (The Club) (1866), 1 Victoria Street.	*J. McM. Moore......	5·25	7·35
Bolton (Constitutional) (1870), 25 Mawdsley Street.	*R. B. Walker........	Nil	14·70 & 6·30
Bradford (The Club) (1870), 41 Bank Street.	*W. E. B. Holroyd; G. R. Turner	5·00	28·50
Union (1857), Piece Hall Yard.	*C. P. Wightman....	10·50	30·00
Bridport and West Dorset (1921), 12 South Street.	*W. Gibson..........	Nil	5·25
Bristol (Clifton) (1882), 22 The Mall.	Lt.-Col. C. T. Ingle....	Nil	16·80 to 3·15
(Constitutional) (1885), Marsh Street.	Brig. H. A. Hardy, M.B.E., M.C.	10·50	16·80 to 5·25
(The Bristol Club) (1889), 38a Corn Street.	*M. G. Sinclair........	Nil	17·85
Buxton (Union) (1887), 3 St. John's Road.	W. H. Finney........	3·15 to 1·05	11·55 to 2·60
Cambridge (Amateur Dramatic) (1855), Park Street.	*H. B. Frayman.......	Nil	3·00
(Hawks) (1874), Jesus Lane.	*S. P. Berry.........	..	9·00
(Union) (1815), Bridge Street.	R. F. Thompson (Chief Clerk).	1·05	5·25
(University Pitt) (1835), Jesus Lane.	*J. G. Norman........	5·25	15·75
Canterbury (Kent and Canterbury) (1868), 17 Old Dover Road.	D. F. Andrews........	3·15	8·40
Cardiff (Cardiff and County) (1866), 2 Westgate Street.	*W. H. Williams......	21·00	23·10
Cheltenham (The New Club) (1874), Mountpellier Parade.	*J. V. Venn...........	Nil	18·90
Chester (Grosvenor) (1866) 3 Vicars Lane.	*G. N. S. Mitchell.....	Nil	18·90
(City) (1807), St. Peter's Church Yd.	H. Dodd.............	21 to 4·20	10·50 to 2·10
Chichester (W. Sussex County) (1872), 38 East Street.	*E. W. Cornell	Nil	5·25
Colchester (The Club) (1874), 67–69 Culver Street.	P. A. Witard........	Nil	8·40 & 7·35
Devizes (Devizes & District) (1930), 27 St. John Street.	*C. S. D. Hall........	5·00	4·20 to 2·10
Douglas, Isle of Man (Ellan Vannin Club) (1893), 20 Finch Road.	*Capt. N. Wood......	1·05	10·50
Dudley (Conservative) (1884), 6 Castle Hill.	*(vacant).............	4·20	6·30
Durham (County) (1890), 52 Old Elvet.	*Cdr. D. A. Bickmore, R.N.	Nil	6·30 to 2·10
Exeter (Exeter and County) (1871), 5 Cathedral Close.	*A. V. Weaver........	4·00	14·60
Folkestone (Radnor Club) (1874), 136 Sandgate Road.	K. N. G. Foster.......	5·00	12·00
Harrogate (The Club) (1848), Royal Sq., St. Helier.	*C. L. Leslie..........	..	20·00 & 5·25
Haverfordwest (Pembrokeshire County) (1877), 48 High Street.	*T. G. Jones..........	3·70	3·15
Henley-on-Thames (Leander) (1818), Remenham Village, Henley.	*J. D. Cazes, D.F.C....	10·00 & 5·00	8·00 & 6·00
(Phyllis Court) (1906), Marlow Road.	D. C. Ferguson.......	Nil	21·00
Hove (The Hove Club) (1882), 28 Fourth Avenue.	*S. Carr.............	Nil	15·75
Jersey (United) (1848), Royal Sq., St. Helier.	*R. W. Le Sauter.....	12·00	12·00
(Victoria) (1853), Beresford St., St. Helier.	*H. A. Ham..........	10·00 & 6·30	12·60 & 6·30
Leamington (Tennis Court) (1837), 50 Bedford Street.	*J. Camkin..........	Nil	15·00
Leeds (The Leeds Club) (1850), 3 Albion Place.	*J. W. Bosomworth....	..	31·50
(Leeds & County Conservative) (1881), 13 South Parade.	P. Jones.............	Nil	18·90
Leicester (Constitutional) (1880), 1 Pocklington's Walk.	A. O. Hallam.........	1·55	10·50
(Leicestershire Club) (1873), 9 Welford Place.	A. B. Proctor.........	10·00	26·25

† For civilian members only.

Club and Address (with date of foundation)	Secretary or *Hon. Sec.	Subscription	
		Entr.	Ann.
		£	£
Liverpool (Artists) (1889), 5 Eberle Street.	*D. T. Miller........	10·00	21·00
(Athenæum) (1797), Church Alley.	*W. M. Richardson...	Nil	25·00 to 5·00
(Lyceum) (1801), 1 Bold Street.	Cdr. A. S. Smith, R.N. (ret.).	Nil	30·00
(Old Hall, Exchange and Palatine) (1909), Cotton Exchange Bldgs.	*P. W. Bullivant	10·00	31·50
(Racquet) (1874), 102 Upper Parliament Street.	*R. L. Packer.........	Nil	30·00
Manchester (The Manchester Club) (1871), 81 King Street.	J. Elliott.............	Nil	35·00
(The Old Rectory) (1912), 90 Deansgate.	*J. E. Wilkinson.....	Nil	18·00
(St. James's) (1961), 7 Charlotte Street.	*M. Pattinson; R. J. Skelton (joint)	21·00	32·55
Newbury (South Berks) (1881), 5 Bridge Street.	*A. L. Osborne......	Nil	6·30
Newcastle upon Tyne (Northern Constitutional) (1882), 29 Pilgrim Street.	Mrs. G. Whitham.....	Nil	22·05
(Union) (1862), 48 Westgate Road.	B. Collins............	Nil	Various
Northampton (Northampton and County) (1873), George Row.	Sqdn. Ldr. K. W. Hadland, D.F.C. (ret.).	5·25	18·00 to 5·00
Norwich (Norfolk) (1864), 17 Upper King Street.	H. C. Boardman......	10·00	30·00 to 5·00
Nottingham (Nottinghamshire) (1840), Bottle Lane.	*Lt.-Col.G.A.Wharton, C.B.E., T.D.	21·00	21·00
Oxford (Clarendon) (1863), 121 High Street.	*B. Jefferson..........	16·80	16·80
(Frewen) (1869), 98 St. Aldate's.	*W. H. Miller........	5·25	7·35
(O.U.D.S.) (1884), O.U.D.S., Oxford.	T. Maby.............	Nil	0·30
(Union Society) (1833), Frewin Court.	L. W. Crawte (Steward)	Nil	15·00
(Vincent's) (1863), 1a King Edward Street.	*R. L. Laurence-Nairae.	5·00	21·00
Peterborough (City and Counties) (1867), 12 Priestgate.	F. R. Southgate......	2·00	15·75
Portsmouth (Royal Naval and Royal Albert Yacht) (1867), 17 Pembroke Road.	*Capt. H. S. P. Watch, O.B.E., R.N. (ret.).	Nil	6·30 to 1·05
Preston (Conservative) (1878), Guildhall Street.	*L. M. C. Waller......	Nil	2·25
Reading (Athenæum) (1842), 28 Friar Street.	*M. Beer.............	Nil	10·50
Berkshire Club (1776), 53A Blagrave Street.	Col. L. R. C. Watson .	Nil	12·60
Rochester (Castle) (1865), 3 Esplanade.	*B. H. Dyer.........	5·25	15·75
Rugby (The Rugby) (1865), 35 North Street.	*V. M. Roberts, O.B.E.	4·20	10·50
Rye (Dormy House) (1895), Landgate, Rye.	*H. A. Fowler........	2·50	6·30 & 4·20
St. Leonards on Sea (East Sussex) (1893), 1 Warrior Square.	*S. G. Bradbury.......	1·05	10·50
Sheffield (The Club) (1843), George Street.	Lt. Col. H. Brown.....	21·00	28·00
Shrewsbury (Shropshire) (1872), 6 The Square.	Lt.-Col. M. V. Sowerby M.C., T.D.	..	10·50
Southwold (The Blyth Club) (1929), 81 High Street.	*Brig. A. J. le G. Jacob	2·50	6·00 to 3·00
Teddington (Royal Canoe) (1866), Trowlock Island.	Mrs. M. N. Shepherd..	2·10	4·20
Torbay (The Paignton Club) (1882), The Esplanade.	R. Down.............	5·00	7·00
(Torbay) (1906), Hyde Road.	F. Greenwood........	3·15	4·20
Tunbridge Wells (Tunbridge Wells and Counties) (1872) 40 London Road.	*Miss S. Richardson...	Nil	6·30
Winchester (Hampshire Club) (1857), 32 Southgate Street.	*R. Dudley-Utting....	4·20 & 2·10	12·60 to 4·20
Worcester (Union and County), (1861) 40 Foregate Street.	*J. D. Schooling; E. C. Lancey (joint).	..	10·50
Yeovil (Ivel Club) (1884), Frederick Place.	B. A. Collins.........	3·15	9·45 to 3·15
York (Yorkshire) (1839), 17 Museum Street.	F. H. Godfrey.........	Nil	21·00
(City) (1876), 4 Museum Street.	*J. R. Richardson.....	2·10	10·50
Scotland			
Ayr (County) (1872), Savoy Park Hotel.	*Col. W. W. McHarg, O.B.E., M.C., T.D.	Nil	4·00
Dundee (Eastern) (1865), 2 Euclid Street.	A. G. Adamson......	10·00	18·90
Edinburgh (Caledonian) (1825), 112 Princess Street.	Mrs. M. W. Hutton...	Nil	25·00 to 5·00
(Ladies' Caledonian) (1908), 13–14 Charlotte Square.	Miss P. D. Bremner...	10·50	18·90 to 4·20
(New) (1787), 85 Princes Street.	Maj. G. E. Thomas...	35·00	36·00 to 8·00
(Queen's) (1897), 7 Frederick Street.	Mrs. A. MacRae......	10·50	15·75 to 14·70
(University Union) (1889), Teviot Row.	E. W. Turberville....	Nil	0·50
Glasgow (Art) (1867), 185 Bath Street.	G. Cowan............	5·00	21·00 & 16·50
(Conservative) (1880), 33 Bothwell Street.	D. Cameron..........	18·90	26·25 to 7·35
(Kelvin) (1897), 19 Royal Exchange Square.	Miss W. Hamilton....	8·40	16·80
(Royal Scottish Automobile) (1899), 11 Blythswood Square.	Maj. R. T. Reid, M.C. .	26·25	16·80

Club and Address (with date of foundation)	Secretary or *Hon. Sec.	Subscription Entr.	Ann.
		£	£
Glasgow—*continued.*			
(The Western Club) (1825), 32 Royal Exchange Square.	Lt.-Col. A. Gordon, M.C.	25·00	40·00
Inverness (Highland) (1870), 39 High Street.		*Nil*	15·75
Stirling (Stirling and County), (1877), 5 Melville Terrace.	*R. Heathwood.......	10·50	10·50

Northern Ireland

Belfast (Ulster) (1837), 23 Castle Place.	*Capt. E. S. Robinson	10·50	32·00
(Ulster Reform) (1885), 4 Royal Avenue.	*R. C. Arnold........	10·50	24·15

YACHT CLUBS

Club and Address (with date of foundation)	Secretary or *Hon. Sec.	Subscription Entr.	Ann.
		£	£
Beaumaris (Royal Anglesey) (1802), 6–7 Green Edge.	*R. R. M. Jones......	5·25 & 4·20	5·25 to 1·05
Bembridge, I. of W. (Sailing) (1886), Isle of Wight.	S. Browne...........	12·60	12·60
Birkenhead (Royal Mersey) (1844), 8–10 Bedford Road, Rock Ferry.	*R. E. Buckley.......	10·00	10·00
Bridlington (Royal Yorks) (1847), 1 Windsor Crescent.	*D. P. Elliker.........	6·30	8·40 & 7·35
Burnham-on-Crouch (Royal Burnham) (1895), The Quay.	*G. C. Paddison......	6·00	20·00
(Royal Corinthian) (1872), Burnham-on-Crouch, and The Parade, Cowes.	Lt.-Col. D. C. Mahoney M.C., R.M. (*ret.*).	*Nil*	23·60 to 6·60
Caernarvon (Royal Welsh) (1847), Porth-yr-Aur.	*H. M. Catlin........	3·15	5·25 to 3·25
Cowes (Royal Yacht Squadron) (1815), The Castle, Cowes.	Maj. J. D. Dillon, D.S.C., R.M.	150·00	50·00
(Royal London) (1838), The Parade.	*Sqn.-Ldr. C. A. A. Davis (*ret.*).	10·50	20·00
Dover (Royal Cinque Ports) (1872), Waterloo Crescent.	*Mrs. E. A. Parker....	5·00	12·00 to 1·00
Fishbourne, I. of W. (Royal Victoria) (1844), Fishbourne.	*Mrs. A. Gilbert......	3·15	5·00
Fowey (Royal Fowey) (1894), Fowey.	*Capt. D. M. Fyfe.....	5·00	8·00
Harwich (Royal Harwich) (1843), Woolverton, nr. Ipswich.	Cdr. R. D. S. Bennett, R.N.	9·45	9·45
Jersey (R.C.I.) (1862), Le Boulevard, St. Aubin, Jersey.	Maj. H. Petch, M.B.E. ..	5·00	5·00
Kingswear (Royal Dart.) (1866), Kingswear, S. Devon.	*Miss A. M. Hine-Hay-cock, M.B.E.	10·00	5·25 to 1·05
Leigh-on-Sea (Essex) (1890), Leigh-on-Sea.	Capt. H. J. Patterson; Lt.-Cdr. C. Stokes, M.B.E. (*joint*).	8·00	8·00
London (Cruising Association) (1908), Chiltern Court, Baker Street, N.W.1.	Miss B. Wenmoth.....	4·20	5·25 to 1·05
(Royal Cruising) (1880), 42 Half Moon Street, W.1.	*A. P. Gray..........	6·30	4·20
Lowestoft (Royal Norfolk and Suffolk) (1859), Royal Plain.	Cdr. M. R. E. Faning, O.B.E., D.S.C., (*ret.*).	10·00	20·00
Penarth (Penarth) (1880), The Esplanade.	D. E. Morse..........	2·10	8·00
Plymouth (Royal Western) (1827), West Hoe.	*Capt. T. W. B. Shaw, D.S.C., R.N. (*ret.*).	10·50	10·50
(Royal Plymouth Corinthian) (1877), Madeira Road.	*C. N. P. Nicholson...	2·10	5·25
Poole (East Dorset Sailing) (1875), Witley Pier, Parkstone.	Miss A. Bailey........	10·50	8·40
(Parkstone) (1895), Pearce Avenue, Parkstone.	Col. T. A. Hunt.......	10·50	10·50
(Poole Harbour) (1948), Salterns Way, Lilliput.	Mrs. E. M. Perry......	Various	10·50 to 7·35
(Royal Motor Yacht) (1905), Sandbanks, Pano-rama Rd., Poole.	Mrs. M. C. Hardie....	26·25	21·00
(Yacht) (1865), New Quay Road, Hamworthy.	G. E. Thornton.......	15·00	8·00
Ramsgate (Royal Temple) (1857), 6 West Cliff Mansions.	J. Baker..............	Various	Various
Southampton:			
(Royal Air Force) (1932), Riverside Ho., Hamble.	Sqn.-Ldr. K. H. F. Sol-man.	10·00	10·00
(Royal Southern) (1837), Hamble, Hants.	*Maj. G. H. King.....	16·80 to 5·25	15·75 to 1·05

Club and Address (with date of foundation)	Secretary or *Hon. Sec.	Subscription Entr. £	Subscription Ann. £
Southampton—*continued*.			
(Royal Southampton) (1867), Northlands Road and Beaulieu.	Sqn. Ldr. W. C. Marshall (*ret.*).	*Nil*	Various
(Royal Thames) (1775), Shore House, Warsash, Hants.	Lt.-Col. D. W. Browne, M.C.	52·50 & 26·25	60·00 & 40·00
Southend (Alexandra) (1873), The Cliffs.	*A. H. Smirk........	5·00	8·40
Southsea (Royal Naval and Royal Albert) (1864), 17 Pembroke Road, Portsmouth; 62 Clarence Esplanade.	Capt. H. S. P. Watch, O.B.E., R.N. (*ret.*).	*Nil*	6·30 to 1·05
Swansea (Bristol Channel) (1875), Southend, Mumbles.	P. G. Cawker.........	10·50	15·75 & 10·50
Torbay (Royal Torbay) (1863), Beacon Hill.	*R. A. Edwards.......	8·50	8·50
Westcliff-on-Sea (Thames Estuary) (1947), 3 The Leas.	*A. D. Tomkins.......	3·50	7·00
Weymouth (Royal Dorset) (1875), 6 Charlotte Row.	*J. C. T. Plummer.....	5·00	6·30
Windermere (Royal Windermere) (1860), Bowness-on-Windermere, Westmorland.	*A. Murdoch..........	18·00	10·50 & 8·50
Yarmouth (Royal Solent) (1878), Yarmouth, I.O.W.	Cp.-Capt. F. R. Drew, C.B.E.	Various	Various
Scotland			
Edinburgh (Royal Forth) (1868), 1 Boswall Road, Edinburgh, 5.	*D. J. S. Miller	5·00	12·60
Glasgow (Royal Clyde) (1856), Rhu, Dunbartonshire.	J. Colville, 147 Blythswood St., Glasgow, C.2.	5·25	4·20
(Royal Western) (1875), (None).	*P. J. F. Henderson, 120 St. Vincent St., Glasgow, C.2.	1·00	1·00
Oban (Royal Highland) (1881), Gt. Western Hotel.	A. B. Wilson, Fernfield, Crinan, Argyll.	*Nil*	2·10
Rhu (Royal Northern) (1824), Rhu, Dunbartonshire.	S. L. Revett, D.S.C., V.R.D.	20·00	Various
Northern Ireland			
Bangor (Royal Ulster) (1866), Clifton Road, Bangor, Co. Down.	*K. Smyth...........	12·00	20·00

PRESIDENTS OF THE THE ROYAL SOCIETY

The Royal Society received a charter from Charles II on April 22, 1662, when it was incorporated as a body politic and corporate under the appellation of The President, Council and Fellowship of the Royal Society of London, for improving Natural Knowledge.

Sir Robert Moray......................	1660	Earl of Rosse............................	1848
Viscount Brouncker....................	1662	Lord Wrottesley.........................	1854
Sir Joseph Williamson.................	1677	Sir Benjamin Brodie, Bt...............	1858
Sir Christopher Wren..................	1680	Maj.-Gen. Sir Edward Sabine.............	1861
Sir John Hoskins, Bt..................	1682	Sir George Biddell Airy.................	1871
Sir Cyril Wyche.......................	1683	Sir Joseph Dalton Hooker................	1873
Samuel Pepys..........................	1684	William Spottiswoode....................	1878
Earl of Carbery.......................	1686	Thomas Henry Huxley....................	1883
Earl of Pembroke......................	1689	Sir George Stokes, Bt...................	1885
Sir Robert Southwell..................	1690	Lord Kelvin.............................	1890
Earl of Halifax.......................	1695	Lord Lister.............................	1895
Lord Somers...........................	1698	Sir William Huggins....................	1900
Sir Isaac Newton......................	1703	Lord Rayleigh..........................	1905
Sir Hans Sloane, Bt...................	1727	Sir Archibald Geikie....................	1908
Martin Folkes.........................	1741	Sir William Crookes....................	1913
Earl of Macclesfield..................	1752	Sir Joseph John Thomson................	1915
Earl of Morton........................	1764	Sir Charles Scott Sherrington............	1920
Sir James Burrow......................	1768	Lord Rutherford........................	1925
James West............................	1768	Sir Frederick Gowland Hopkins...........	1930
Sir John Pringle, Bt..................	1772	Sir William Henry Bragg................	1935
Sir Joseph Banks, Bt..................	1778	Sir Henry Hallett Dale..................	1940
William Hyde Wollaston................	1820	Sir Robert Robinson....................	1945
Sir Humphry Davy, Bt.................	1820	Lord Adrian............................	1950
Davies Gilbert........................	1827	Sir Cyril Hinshelwood	1955
The Duke of Sussex	1830	Lord Florey............................	1960
Marquess of Northampton...............	1838	Lord Blackett..........................	1965

Principal British and Irish Societies and Institutions

THE ROYAL ACADEMY OF ARTS (1768), Burlington House, W. 1.—*President*, Sir Thomas Monnington (1966); *Keeper*, Peter Greenham, R.A.; *Treas.*, Marshall A. Sisson, C.V.O., C.B.E., R.A.; *Sec.*, Sidney C. Hutchison, M.V.O., F.S.A.; *Reg.*, K. J. Tanner; *Librarian*, Philip James, C.B.E.

Royal Academicians

1963 Aldridge, John.	1938*Lawrence, A. K.
1970 Ardizzone, Edward	1962*Lowry, L. S.
1949*Austin, Robert S.	1963 McFall, David.
1955 Bawden, Edward, C.B.E.	1955 Machin, Arnold, O.B.E.
1937‡Brockhurst, G. L.	1933*McMillan, W., C.V.O.
1971 Bratby, John R.	
1955 Buhler, Robert.	1947*Maufe, Sir Edward.
1962 Burn, Rodney J.	1959*Methuen, Lord.
1970 Casson, Sir Hugh.	1938 Monnington, Sir Thomas.
1968 Cowern, Raymond T.	1951 *Nash, John, C.B.E.
	1967 Nimptsch, Uli.
1944 *Cundall, Charles.	1955 O'Rorke, Brian.
1969 de Grey, Roger.	1953*Pitchforth, R. V.
1955 Dring, William.	1942*Procter, Mrs. Dod.
1950 *Dunlop, R. O.	1966*Roberts, William.
1968 Dunstan, Bernard.	1969 Rosoman, Leonard.
1967 Elwes, Simon.	
1964 Erith, Raymond C.	1961 Sanders, Christopher C.
1953 Eurich, Richard.	
1954 Fitton, James.	1968 Schilsky, Eric.
1942‡Frampton, Meredith.	1963 Sisson, Marshall A., C.V.O., C.B.E.
1965 Freeth, H. Andrew.	1959 Skeaping, John R.
1969 Gibberd, Sir Frederick, C.B.E.	1969 Soukop, Willi.
1971 Gillies, Sir William, C.B.E.	1954 Spear, Ruskin.
1960 Greenham, Peter G.	1960 Spence, Sir Basil, O.M., O.B.E., T.D.
1970 Hayes, Colin.	1945 *Thomson, A. R.
1961 Hepple, Norman.	1954 Tunnicliffe, C. F.
1971 Hermes, Miss Gertrude.	1965 Ward, John.
1967 Hillier, Tristram.	1965 Weight, Carel, C.B.E.
1968 Holford, Lord.	1940*Wheeler, Sir Charles, K.C.V.O., C.B.E.
1965*Jones, Allan Gwynne, D.S.O.	
1930*Kelly, Sir Gerald F., K.C.V.O.	1945*Woodford, James, O.B.E.

Associates

1967 Adams, Norman.	1969 Fell, Miss Sheila.
1966 †Armstrong, John.	1966 Fry, E. Maxwell, C.B.E.
1970 Blamey, Norman.	
1970 Bowey, Miss Olwyn.	1964 Gore, Frederick.
1971 Blackadder, Miss Elizabeth V.	1971 Green, Anthony
	1969 Jones, Ivor Roberts.
1971 Brown, H. T. Cadbury, O.B.E.	
1968 Brown, Ralph.	1970 Kneale, Bryan.
1964 Butler, James.	1968 MacTaggart, Sir William.
1970 Clarke, Geoffrey.	
1968 Clatworthy, Robert.	1968 Middleditch, Edward.
1965 Coker, Peter.	1966 Sheppard, Richard, C.B.E.
1965 Cooke, Miss Jean E.	
1969 Cuming, Frederick.	1967 Tunnard, John.
1966 Darwin, Sir Robin, C.B.E.	1968 Wakeford, Edward.
1970 Dickson, Miss Jennifer.	1970 Williams, Kyffin.
	1967 Wolfe, Edward.

* Senior Academician.   † Senior Associate.
‡ Honorary Retired Academician.

Former Presidents of the Royal Academy

Sir J. Reynolds, 1768.	Sir E. Poynter, 1896.
Benjamin West, 1792.	Sir A. Webb, 1919.
James Wyatt, 1805.	Sir F. Dicksee, 1924.
Benjamin West, 1806.	Sir W. Llewellyn, 1928.
Sir T. Lawrence, 1820.	Sir E. Lutyens, 1938.
Sir M. A. Shee, 1830.	Sir A.J. Munnings, 1944.
Sir C. Eastlake, 1850.	Sir G. F. Kelly, 1949.
Sir F. Grant, 1866.	Sir A. E. Richardson, 1954.
Lord Leighton, 1878.	
Sir J. Millais, 1896.	Sir C. Wheeler, 1956.

ROYAL CAMBRIAN ACADEMY OF ART (1881), Plas Mawr, Conway.—*Hon. Sec.*, Mrs. M. della R. Whitehead; *Curator and Sec.*, Frederic Lees.

THE ROYAL SCOTTISH ACADEMY (1826), Princes Street, Edinburgh.—*Pres.*, W. H. Kininmonth, R.S.A.; *Sec.*, R. Philipson, R.S.A.; *Treas.*, H. Lorimer, R.S.A.; *Librarian*, D. Peploe, R.S.A.; *Asst. Sec.*, W. Keith.

Hon. Academician, H.R.H. the Prince Philip, Duke of Edinburgh, K.G., K.T.

Honorary Retired Academicians

1936 Sutherland, D. M.	
1937 Cursiter, Stanley, C.B.E.	
1944 Bone, Phyllis M.	
1949 Wilson, William, O.B.E.	
1946 Thomson, Adam B., O.B.E.	
1964 Miller, James.	

Royal Scottish Academicians

1958 Armour, Mrs.Mary	1971 McClure, David.
1966 Armour, William.	1946 MacDougall, Leslie Grahame.
1970 Burns, W. A.	
1971 Cameron, Gordon S.	1939 McGlashan, Arch. A.
1962 Coïa, J. A., C.B.E.	1948 MacTaggart, Sir William.
1956 Crawford, H. Adam	
1970 Cumming, James	1966 Miller, John.
1962 Donaldson, David A.	1963 Morrocco, Alberto.
	1957 Patrick, J. McIntosh.
1956 Fleming, Ian.	
1947 Gillies, Sir William, C.B.E.	1966 Peploe, Denis.
	1962 Philipson, Robin.
1967 Gordon, Esmé.	1956 Schilsky, Eric.
1964 Hislop, Mrs. Margaret.	1937 Schotz, Benno.
	1970 Sutherland, Scott.
1966 Johnston, Ninian.	1957 Thomson, J. Murray.
1956 Kininmonth, W. H.	
1957 Lorimer, Hew.	1954 Whalen, Thomas.

Associates

Baillie, W. J. L.	Littlejohn, William.
Blackadder, Elizabeth.	Malcolm, Ellen.
Bone, W. Drummond.	Matthew, Prof.Sir Robert H., C.B.E.
Campbell, Alex.	
Clark, James H.	Michie, David.
Collins, Peter.	Morrocco, Leon.
Crosbie, William.	Reeves, Philip.
Dick, Miss Alix.	Reiach, Alan, O.B.E.
Dods, Andrew.	Robertson, R. Ross.
Fraser, Alexander.	Steedman, Robert R.
Glover, John Hardie, O.B.E.	Stewart, S. Birnie.
	Thomson, Sinclair.
Henderson, Ann.	Walker, Frances.
Houston, John.	Wheeler, H. Anthony.
Johnstone, Miss Dorothy.	Whiston, Peter.
	Womersley, Peter.

Hon. Retired Associates, C. d'O. Pilkington-Jackson; N. J. Forrest; Miss Elizabeth Dempster; *Non-Resident Associates*, Mrs. Josephine Miller; Charles Pulsford; Sir Basil Spence, O.M., O.B.E., T.D., R.A.; Ancell Stronach.

ROYAL IRISH ACADEMY (1786), 19 Dawson Street, Dublin.—*Pres.*, V. C. Barry, D.SC.; *Treas.*, W. O'Sullivan, D.ECON.SC.; *Sec.*, J. R. McConnell, D.SC.

ROYAL ULSTER ACADEMY (1950), 7 College Square N., Belfast.—*Pres. and Chairman*, Patric Stevenson; *Hon. Sec.*, F. C. Maguire.

ACCOUNTANTS, INSTITUTE OF CHARTERED, in England and Wales (1880), Chartered Accountants' Hall, Moorgate Place, E.C.2.—*Pres.* (1971–72), A. H. Walton; *Secretary*, C. A. Evan-Jones, C.B.E.

ACCOUNTANTS, THE INSTITUTE OF COMPANY (1928), 11 Portland Road, Edgbaston, Birmingham, 16.—*Exec. Offr.*, J. H. Tresman.

ACCOUNTANTS AND AUDITORS, BRITISH ASSOCIATION OF (1923), Stamford House, W.4.—*Sec.*, G. F. Garrad.

ACCOUNTANTS, ASSOCIATION OF CERTIFIED (1904), 22 Bedford Square, W.C.1.—*Pres.*, R. P. Crout; *Sec.*, F. C. Osbourn, M.B.E.

ACCOUNTANTS OF SCOTLAND, INSTITUTE OF CHARTERED (1854), 27 Queen Street, Edinburgh 2.—*Pres.*, G. C. Patterson; *Sec.*, E. H. V. McDougall.

ACCOUNTANTS IN IRELAND, INSTITUTE OF CHARTERED (1888), 7 Fitzwilliam Place, Dublin 2, and 6 Callender Street, Belfast 1.—*Sec.*, R. L. Donovan (Dublin).

ACCOUNTANTS, SOCIETY OF COMMERCIAL, 40 Tyndalls Park Road, Clifton, Bristol 8.—*Sec.*, R.H.S. Beacham.

ACTORS' BENEVOLENT FUND (1882), 6 Adam Street, W.C.2.—*Sec.*, Miss A. G. Marks.

ACTORS' CHARITABLE TRUST (incorporating DENVILLE HALL), Gloucester House, 19 Charing Cross Road, W.C.2.—Assists children of theatrical parentage who are in need; home for elderly and infirm actors and actresses.—*Pres.*, The Lord Olivier; *Admin. Sec.*, Miss M. M. Brisley.

ACTORS' CHURCH UNION (1899), St. Paul's Church, Covent Garden, W.C.2.—*Senior Chaplain*, Rev. J. Hester.

ACTUARIES IN SCOTLAND, THE FACULTY OF (1856), Hall and Library, 23 St. Andrew Square, Edinburgh.—*Sec.*, G. C. Train.

ACTUARIES, INSTITUTE OF (1848), Staple Inn Hall, W.C.1.—*Pres.*, R. S. Skerman; *Secretaries*, C. J. Cornwall; D. R. Spackman.

ADDICTION (TO ALCOHOL AND OTHER DRUGS), SOCIETY FOR THE STUDY OF (1884).—*Sec.*, T. H. Bewley, M.D., Tooting Bec Hospital, S.W.17.

ADDITIONAL CURATES SOCIETY; HOME MISSIONS OF CHURCH OF ENGLAND AND THE CHURCH IN WALES (1837), 14 Rothamsted Avenue, Harpenden, Herts.—*Sec.*, Rev. Canon C. J. Read, M.A.

ADVERTISING ASSOCIATION, Chantrey House, Eccleston Street, S.W.1.—*Director-General*, J. S. Williams. *Sec.*, R. C. G. Hunt-Taylor.

ADVERTISING BENEVOLENT SOCIETY, NATIONAL (1913), 3 Crawford Place, W.1.—*Dir.*, R. Rivers.

ADVERTISING, INSTITUTE OF PRACTITIONERS IN, 44 Belgrave Square, S.W.1.—*Dir.*, J. P. O'Connor.

ADVERTISING MANAGERS' ASSOCIATION, INCORPORATED (founded 1932, inc. 1938), 45 Hertford Street, W.1. *Admin. Offr.*, D. St.C. McBride.

AERONAUTICAL SOCIETY, ROYAL (1866) (incorporating the Institution of Aeronautical Engineers and the Helicopter Association of Great Britain), 4 Hamilton Place, W.1.—*Pres.* (1971–72), S. D. Davies, C.B.E.; *Sec.*, Dr. A. M. Ballantyne, O.B.E.

AFRICA BOARD, JOINT (1926), 25 Victoria Street, S.W.1.—*Sec.*, S. Stanley-Smith.

AFRICAN INSTITUTE, INTERNATIONAL (1926), St. Dunstan's Chambers, 10–11 Fetter Lane, E.C.4.—*Administrative Director*, Prof. Daryll Forde; *Sec.*, W. Hardcastle.

AGED PILGRIMS' FRIEND SOCIETY (1807), Morley House, 26–30 Holborn Viaduct, E.C.1.—*Sec.*, F. R. Clifford.

AGED POOR SOCIETY (1708) AND ST. JOSEPH'S HOUSE, 39 Eccleston Square, S.W.1.—*Sec.*, Miss M. Flood.

AGRICULTURAL BENEVOLENT INSTITUTION, ROYAL, Vincent House, Vincent Square, S.W.1.—*Hon. Treas.*, W. T. Gauntlett; *Sec.*, Cdr. O. C. Wright.

AGRICULTURAL BENEVOLENT INSTITUTION, ROYAL SCOTTISH (1897), 8 Dublin Street, Edinburgh.—*Sec.*, K. M. Campbell, W.S.

AGRICULTURAL BOTANY, NATIONAL INSTITUTE OF (1919), Huntingdon Road, Cambridge.—*Director*, P. S. Wellington, D.S.C., Ph.D.; *Sec.*, G. D. Ginn.

AGRICULTURAL ENGINEERS ASSOCIATION, LIMITED (1877), 6 Buckingham Gate, S.W.1.—*Dir.-Gen.*, F. D. Swift, O.B.E.

AGRICULTURAL SOCIETY, GLASGOW (1860).—*Sec.*, S. Gilmour, 24 Beresford Terrace, Ayr.

AGRICULTURAL SOCIETY, ROYAL ULSTER (1826), The King's Hall, Balmoral, Belfast 9.—*Sec.*, J. T. Kernohan, O.B.E.

AGRICULTURAL SOCIETY OF THE COMMONWEALTH, ROYAL (1959).—*Hon. Sec.*, F. R. Francis, 17 Devonshire Street, W.1.

AGRICULTURE, ASSOCIATION OF (1947), 78 Buckingham Gate, S.W.1.—*Gen. Sec.*, Miss J. Bostock.

AIRBROKERS ASSOCIATION (1949), 25 Bury Street, E.C.3.—*Sec.*, J. L. Logan.

AIRCRAFT NOISE, BRITISH ASSOCIATION FOR THE CONTROL OF, 30 Fleet Street, E.C.4.—*Chairman*, D. A. Morris.

AIR LEAGUE, THE (1909), 142 Sloane Street, S.W.1.—*Dir.*, J. Motum.

ALEXANDRA ROSE DAY FUND, 1 Castelnau, Barnes, S.W.13.—*Organizer*, Mrs. Edward Day.

ALLOTMENTS AND GARDENS SOCIETY, NATIONAL, 22 High Street, Flitwick, Beds.

ALMSHOUSES, NATIONAL ASSOCIATION OF, Billingbear Lodge, Wokingham, Berks.—*Gen. Sec.*, L. A. Hackett, O.B.E.

ANALYTICAL CHEMISTRY, THE SOCIETY FOR, 9–10 Savile Row, W.1.—*Hon. Sec.*, W. H. C. Shaw.

ANCIENT BUILDINGS, SOCIETY FOR THE PROTECTION OF (1877), 55 Great Ormond Street, W.C.1.—*Sec.*, Mrs. M. Dance, M.B.E.

ANCIENT MONUMENTS SOCIETY (1924).—*Sec.*, W. Oddie, 11 Alexander Street, W.2.

ANGLO-ARAB ASSOCIATION (1961), West End House, Hills Place, W.1.

ANGLO-BELGIAN UNION (1918), 6 Belgrave Square, S.W.1.—*Hon. Sec.*, Mrs. M. Taylor.

ANGLO-BRAZILIAN SOCIETY (1943), 2 Belgrave Square, S.W.1.—*Sec.*, Mrs. E. C. Skinner.

ANGLO-DANISH SOCIETY (1924), 5 St. Helen's Place, Bishopsgate, E.C.3.—*Chairman*, The Countess Beauchamp.

ANGLO-NORSE SOCIETY, c/o Royal Norwegian Embassy, 25 Belgrave Square, S.W.1.

ANGLO-SWEDISH SOCIETY, 4 Staple Inn, High Holborn, W.C.1.

ANGLO-THAI SOCIETY (1962).—*Hon. Sec.*, C. Sophonpanich, 59–67 Gresham Street, E.C.2.

ANIMAL HEALTH TRUST, 24 Portland Place, W.1.—*Chief Exec. Offr.*, Brig. J. Clabby, C.B.E., M.R.C.V.S.

ANTHROPOLOGICAL INSTITUTE, ROYAL (1843), 21 Bedford Square, W.C.1.—*Hon. Sec.*, J. Waechter.

ANTHROPOSOPHICAL SOCIETY IN GREAT BRITAIN, Rudolf Steiner House, 35 Park Road, N.W.1.—*Chairman*, A. C. Harwood.

ANTIQUARIES, SOCIETY OF (1717), Burlington House, W.1.—*Pres.*, J. N. L. Myres, LL.D., D.Litt., F.B.A.; *Treas.*, R. M. Robbins; *Director*, A. J. Taylor; *Sec.*, K. S. Painter.

ANTIQUARIES OF SCOTLAND, SOCIETY OF (1780), National Museum of Antiquities of Scotland, Queen Street, Edinburgh.—*Sec.*, B. C. Skinner; *Treas.*, W. H. T. Harris.

ANTI-SLAVERY SOCIETY FOR THE PROTECTION OF HUMAN RIGHTS (1839), 49 Denison House, 296 Vauxhall Bridge Road, S.W.1.—*Sec.*, Col. J. R. P. Montgomery, M.C.

ANTI-VIVISECTION: BRITISH UNION FOR THE ABOLITION OF VIVISECTION (INC.) (1898), 47 Whitehall, S.W.1.—*Gen. Sec.*, S. Hicks.

ANTI-VIVISECTION SOCIETY, THE NATIONAL (1875), 51 Harley Street, W.1.

ANTI-VIVISECTION SOCIETY, SCOTTISH, 121 West Regent Street, Glasgow, C.2.—*Sec.*, A. Cormack.

APOSTLESHIP OF THE SEA (1921). For active seafarers; Atlantic House, Hardman Street, Liverpool, and Stella Maris, New Strand, Bootle; for retired seafarers; Gateacre Grange, Rose Brow, Liverpool 20.—*Dir.*, Very Rev. B. R. Boardman.

APOTHECARIES, SOCIETY OF (1617).—Black Friars Lane, Queen Victoria Street, E.C.4.—*Clerk and Registrar*, Ernest Busby, M.B.E.

ARAB HORSE SOCIETY.—*Sec.*, Brig. F. H. V. Purcell M.B.E., Loughmoe, Shelley Close, Itchen Abbas Winchester, Hants.

ARBITRATORS, THE INSTITUTE OF (1915), 16 Park Crescent, W.1.— *Sec.*, G. Darling.

ARCHÆOLOGICAL ASSOCIATION, BRITISH (1843), History of Art Dept., Birkbeck College, Malet Street, W.C.1.—*Hon. Sec.*, P. Draper.

ARCHÆOLOGICAL ASSOCIATION, CAMBRIAN (1846)— *President* (1971–72), C. E. V. Owen; *Treas.*, W. H. Howells, National Westminster Bank, 2/4 Belle Vue Way, Swansea; *Gen. Sec.*, H. D. Rees, Llyswen, Bow Street, Cardiganshire.

ARCHÆOLOGICAL INSTITUTE, ROYAL (1843).— *Hon. Sec.*, S. D. T. Spittle, M.A., F.S.A., A.R.I.B.A.; *Asst. Sec.*, Mrs. H. J. Saunders, 9 Somerset Road, New Barnet, Herts.

ARCHÆOLOGY, COUNCIL FOR BRITISH (1944), 8 St. Andrew's Place, N.W.1.—*President*, Prof. A. C. Thomas; *Hon. Sec.*, P. J. Fowler, F.S.A.; *Sec.*, Miss B. de Cardi, B.A., F.S.A.

ARCHITECTS, THE ROYAL INSTITUTE OF BRITISH (1834), 66 Portland Place, W.1.—*Pres.* (1971–73), A. J. Gordon; *Sec.*, P. K. Harrison.

ARCHITECTS, INSTITUTE OF REGISTERED (1933), 68 Gloucester Place, W.1.—*Pres.*, G. B. A. Williams; *Sec.*, A. E. Ward.

ARCHITECTS REGISTRATION COUNCIL OF THE UNITED KINGDOM, 73 Hallam Street, W.1.—*Chairman*, P. D. B. Groves; *Registrar*, Mrs. N. Dawson, M.B.E.

ARCHITECTS AND SURVEYORS, INCORPORATED ASSOCIATION OF (1925), 29 Belgrave Square, S.W.1.—*Pres.*, F. D. Entwisle; *Sec.*, K. Hay.

ARCHITECTS' BENEVOLENT SOCIETY (1850) 66 Portland Place, W.1.—*Hon. Sec.*, Howard Lobb, C.B.E.

ARCHITECTS IN SCOTLAND, ROYAL INCORPORATION OF (1922), 15 Rutland Square, Edinburgh.— *Sec. and Treas.*, P. G. D. Clark.

ARCHITECTURAL ASSOCIATION (INC.) (1847), 34–36 Bedford Square, W.C.1.—*Pres.*, J. Smith; *Sec.*, E. Le Maistre.

ARCHIVISTS, SOCIETY OF (1946), *Hon. Sec.*, P. Walne, County Hall, Hertford.

ARLIS (Art Libraries Society) (1969).—*Sec.*, C. Phillpot, Chelsea School of Art Library, Manresa Road, S.W.3.

ARMY BENEVOLENT FUND (1944), "G" Block, Duke of York's H.Q., Chelsea, S.W.3.—*Controller*, Maj.-Gen., D. N. H. Tyacke, C.B., O.B.E.

ARMY CADET FORCE ASSOCIATION (1930), 58 Buckingham Gate, S.W.1.— *Sec.*, W. F. L. Newcombe, O.B.E., T.D.

ARMY HISTORICAL RESEARCH, SOCIETY FOR (1921). —*Hon. Sec.*, Maj. N. P. Dawnay, c/o The Library, Old War Office Building, Whitehall, S.W.1.

ART-COLLECTIONS FUND, NATIONAL (1903), Hertford House, Manchester Square, W.1.—*Sec.*, Miss M. Shapland.

ART EDUCATION, NATIONAL SOCIETY FOR (1888), 37A East Street, Havant, Hants.—*Gen. Sec.*, W. J. L. Gaydon.

ART WORKERS GUILD (1884), 6 Queen Square Bloomsbury, W.C.1.—*Master*, Joan Hassal *Sec.*, R. Murry.

ARTHRITIS AND RHEUMATISM COUNCIL FOR RESEARCH, Faraday House, 8–10 Charing Cross Road, W.C.2.—*Gen. Sec.*, M. C. G. Andrews.

ARTISTS' GENERAL BENEVOLENT INSTITUTION (1814) AND ARTISTS' ORPHAN FUND (1871), Burlington House, Piccadilly, W.1.—*Sec.*, Miss D. P. Laidman.

ARTS COUNCIL OF GREAT BRITAIN, 105 Piccadilly, W.1.—*Chairman*, The Lord Goodman; *Secretary-General*, R. H. Willatt.

ASLIB (1924). (Formerly Association of Special Libraries and Information Bureaux), 3 Belgrave Square, S.W.1.—*Director*, L. Wilson, M.A.

ASSISTANT MASTERS IN SECONDARY SCHOOLS INCORPORATED ASSOCIATION OF (1891), 29 Gordon Square, W.C.1.—*Sec.*, A. W. S. Hutchings, M.A.

ASSISTANT MISTRESSES IN SECONDARY SCHOOLS, ASSOCIATION OF, 29 Gordon Square, W.C.1.— *Sec.*, Miss S. D. Wood.

ASTHMA RESEARCH COUNCIL, 28 Norfolk Place, W.2.—*Chairman*, D. M. Walters, M.B.E., M.P.

ASTRONOMICAL ASSOCIATION, BRITISH—*Office*, Burlington House, Piccadilly, W.1. Meetings at 23 Savile Row, W.1.—*President*, Dr. V. Barocas, F.R.A.S.; *Secs.*, N. J. Goodman;. A. C. Curtis; *Asst. Sec.*, J. L. White.

ASTRONOMICAL SOCIETY, ROYAL (Incorporated 1820), Burlington House, W.1.—*Pres.*, Prof. F. Hoyle, F.R.S.; *Secs.*, Dr. T. F. Gaskell; Dr. D. McNally; Prof. R. J. Tayler.

A.T.S. AND W.R.A.C. BENEVOLENT FUNDS (1964), Block E. Duke of York's H.Q., Chelsea, S.W.3. —*Sec.*, Mrs. J. W. Aggleton.

AUDIT BUREAU OF CIRCULATIONS LTD. (1931), 19 Dunraven Street, W.1.—*Dir.*, K. Derbyshire.

AUTHORS, PLAYWRIGHTS AND COMPOSERS, INCORPORATED SOCIETY OF, 84 Drayton Gardens, S.W.10.—*Secs.* G. D. Astley; V. Bonham-Carter; Philippa MacLiesh.

AUTOMOBILE ASSESSORS, INSTITUTE OF (1939), 16 17 Pudding Lane, E.C.3.—*Sec.*, P. G. Redfern.

AUTOMOBILE ASSOCIATION (1905), Fanum House, Leicester Square, W.C.2.—*Chairman*, The Viscount Brentford; *Dir.-Gen.*, A. C. Durie; *Sec.*, W. Lynch.

AVICULTURAL SOCIETY (1894).—*Hon. Sec.*, H. J. Horswell, Sladmore Farm, Cryers Hill, nr. High Wycombe, Bucks.

AYRSHIRE CATTLE SOCIETY OF GREAT BRITAIN AND IRELAND (1877), 1 Racecourse Road, Ayr.—*Gen. Sec.*, J. Lawson.

BALTIC EXCHANGE (1903), St. Mary Axe, E.C.3.— *Chairman*, A. H. D. Granger; *Sec.*, D. J. Walker.

BANKERS' ASSOCIATION, BRITISH (1920), 10 Lombard Street, E.C.3.—*Sec.*, R. K. C. Giddings, M.C.

BANKERS, THE INSTITUTE OF (1879), 10 Lombard Street, E.C.3.—*Pres.*, A. H. Carnwath; *Sec.-Gen.*, G. H. Dix.

BANKERS IN SCOTLAND, THE INSTITUTE OF (1875). 62 George Street, Edinburgh.—*Sec.*, F. S. Taylor.

BAPTIST MISSIONARY SOCIETY (1792), 93–97 Gloucester Place, W.1.—*Secs.*, Rev. A. S. Clement, B.A., B.D. (*Home*); Rev. E. G. T. Madge, B.A., B.D. (*Overseas*).

BAR, GENERAL COUNCIL OF THE, Carpmael Building, Temple, E.C.4.—*Chairman*, John Arnold, Q.C.; *Sec.* W. W. Boulton, C.B.E., T.D.

(DR.) BARNARDO'S (1866), *Head Offices*, Tanner's Lane, Barkingside, Essex. More than 212,000 children have been helped. Nearly 7,000 boys and girls are helped in residential and non-residential settings.—*Director-General,* H. Ellis.

BARONETAGE, STANDING COUNCIL OF THE (1898), Kent House, Telegraph Street, E.C.2.—*Sec. and Regr.,* P. L. Forwood.

BARRISTERS' BENEVOLENT ASSOCIATION (1873), King's Bench Walk, Temple, E.C.4.—*Hon. Treasurers,* H. H. Monroe, Q.C.; Peter Curry; *Sec.,* Mrs. B. D. G. Rickards.

BEIT MEMORIAL FELLOWSHIPS (for Medical Research) (1909).—*Sec.,* Prof. W. G. Spector, Pathology Dept., St. Bartholomew's Hospital, E.C.1.

BIBLE AND MEDICAL MISSIONARY FELLOWSHIP (formerly Zenana Bible and Medical Mission) (1852), 352 Kennington Road, S.E.11.—*Gen. Sec.,* A. M. S. Pont.

BIBLE CHURCHMEN'S MISSIONARY SOCIETY (1922), 157 Waterloo Road, S.E.1.—*Gen. Sec.,* Rev. Canon A. S. Neech.

BIBLE SOCIETY, BRITISH AND FOREIGN (1804), 146 Queen Victoria Street, E.C.4. Has published or circulated all or parts of the Bible in 1,431 languages and distributes 173 million copies a year.

BIBLIOGRAPHICAL SOCIETY (1892), c/o British Academy, Burlington House, W.1.—*Pres.,* J. C. T. Oates; *Hon. Sec.,* R. J. Roberts.

BIBLIOGRAPHICAL SOCIETY, EDINBURGH (1890), c/o National Library of Scotland, Edinburgh, 1.—*Hon. Sec.,* J. R. Seaton.

BIOCHEMICAL SOCIETY, THE (1911), 7 Warwick Court, W.C.1.—*Sec.,* A. I. P. Henton.

BIOLOGICAL ENGINEERING SOCIETY.—*Hon. Sec.,* K. Copeland, Biophysics Dept., Faculty of Medical Sciences, University College, London, Gower Street, W.C.1.

BIOLOGISTS, ASSOCIATION OF APPLIED.—*Hon. Gen. Sec.,* A. J. Cooper, Glasshouse Crops Research Institute, Rustington, Littlehampton, Sussex.

BIOLOGY, INSTITUTE OF, 41 Queen's Gate, S.W.7.—*Pres.,* Sir Frederick Bawden; *Gen. Sec.,* D. J. B. Copp.

BIRD PRESERVATION, INTERNATIONAL COUNCIL FOR (BRITISH SECTION), c/o Natural History Museum, Cromwell Road, S.W.7.—*Hon. Sec.,* Miss Phyllis Barclay-Smith, M.B.E.

BLIND, GARDNER'S TRUST FOR THE (1882), 8 Bloomsbury Square, W.C.1.—*Sec.,* W. J. D. Cooper, C.B.E.

BLIND, GREATER LONDON FUND FOR THE, 2 Wyndham Place, W.1.—*Pres.,* The Lord Mayor of London; *Gen. Sec.,* A. C. Jay, D.S.C.

BLIND, GUIDE DOGS FOR THE, ASSOCIATION, 113 Uxbridge Road, Ealing, W.5.—*Gen. Manager,* R. E. Forrester, O.B.E.

BLIND, INCORPORATED ASSOCIATION FOR PROMOTING THE GENERAL WELFARE OF THE (1854), 8–22 Curtain Road, E.C.2.

BLIND, LONDON ASSOCIATION FOR THE (1857), Pelican House, 88–92 Peckham Road, S.E.15. A national voluntary organization helping the blind and partially-sighted both in London and country. Training and employment; homes and hostels; self-contained flats; benevolent and pensions fund.—*Gen. Sec.,* G. W. Guy.

BLIND, METROPOLITAN SOCIETY FOR THE, AND INDIGENT BLIND VISITING SOCIETY, 51 Denison House, 296 Vauxhall Bridge Road, S.W.1.—Residential Homes for blind men and women at Maldon, Essex (45) and Worthing, Sussex (50); 12 flats in Hackney. Objects include visiting the blind, installation and maintenance of radio sets, social clubs and grants for a wide variety of needs.

BLIND, ROYAL COMMONWEALTH SOCIETY FOR THE (1950), Heath Road, Haywards Heath, Sussex.—*Dir.,* J. Wilson, C.B.E.

BLIND, ROYAL NATIONAL INSTITUTE FOR THE (1868), 224 Great Portland Street, W.1.—*Director-General,* J. C. Colligan, C.B.E. Branches of the Institute: *Queen Elizabeth Homes of Recovery, Homes for Blind and Deaf Blind, School of Physiotherapy, Schools for Blind Girls and Boys, School for Shorthand-Typing and Telephony, Sunshine Home Nursery Schools, Braille and Moon Periodicals and Books, Braille Music, Talking Books, Students' Library, Professional, Commercial and Industrial Placement, Vocational Assessment Centre for Blind Adolescents, Apparatus and Appliances, Personal Services, Prevention of Blindness, etc.*

BLIND, NATIONAL LIBRARY FOR THE (1882), 35 Great Smith Street, S.W.1.—Books in embossed and large type are sent free on loan and post free to blind and partially-sighted readers. Stock of volumes, 350,000.—*Director-General,* W. A. Munford, M.B.E., Ph.D.

BLIND PENSION SOCIETY, ROYAL (1863), 145–7 North End, Croydon, Surrey.—*Sec.,* L. E. Watts.

BLIND, ROYAL LONDON SOCIETY FOR THE (1838), *Head Office and Workshops,* 105–9 Salusbury Road, Brondesbury, N.W.6; *School,* Dorton House, Seal, nr. Sevenoaks, Kent; *Home Workers' Scheme* and *Residential Clubs.*—*Hon. Sec.,* W. W. Woods.

BLIND, ROYAL NORMAL COLLEGE (1872), Albrighton Hall and Rowton Castle, nr. Shrewsbury.—*Princ. and Sec.,* A. W. Laurie.

BLIND, ROYAL SCHOOL FOR THE INDIGENT (1799), Leatherhead.—*Resident Principal and Chaplain,* Rev. B. G. Bartlett.

BLIND, SOCIETY FOR GRANTING ANNUITIES TO THE POOR ADULT, c/o The Clothworkers' Company, Clothworkers' Hall, Dunster Court, Mincing Lane. E.C.3.

BLIND (LONDON) SPORTS CLUB FOR THE (1932), *Chairman,* R. D. Birrell, Grants, Grants Lane, Limpsfield, Oxted, Surrey.

BLOOD TRANSFUSION. *See* GREATER LONDON RED CROSS BLOOD TRANSFUSION SERVICE.

BLUE CROSS, THE (Incorporating Our Dumb Friends' League) (1897), Animals' Hospital, Hugh Street, Victoria, S.W.1.—*Sec.,* Peter Carpmael.

BODLEIAN, FRIENDS OF THE, Bodleian Library, Oxford.—*Sec.,* D. H. Merry.

BOOK-KEEPERS, INSTITUTE OF (1916), Walter House, 418–422 Strand, W.C.2.—*Sec.,* D. W. Bradley.

BOOKSELLERS ASSOCIATION OF GREAT BRITAIN AND IRELAND (1895), 152 Buckingham Palace Road, S.W.1.—*Dir.,* G. R. Davies.

BOOK TRADE BENEVOLENT SOCIETY (1967), 19 Bedford Square, W.C.1, formerly the National Book Trade Provident Institution (1962).—*Pres.,* J. D. Newth; *Hon. Sec.,* R. E. Barker, O.B.E.

BOTANICAL SOCIETY OF THE BRITISH ISLES (1836), c/o Dept. of Botany, British Museum (Natural History), S.W.7.

BOTANICAL SOCIETY OF EDINBURGH, Royal Botanic Garden, Edinburgh.—*Hon. Gen. Sec.,* R. Watling.

BOY SCOUTS ASSOCIATION, *see* SCOUT ASSOCIATION, THE.

BOYS' BRIGADE, THE (INCORPORATED) (1883), Brigade House, Parsons Green, S.W.6. Membership: British Isles, 163,042; Overseas, 89,072 in 66 countries; World strength, 252,114.—*Sec.,* I. G. Neilson, D.F.C., T.D.

BOYS' CLUBS, NATIONAL ASSOCIATION OF, INCOR-PORATED (1925), 17 Bedford Square, W.C.1. Responsible for the development and co-ordination of boys' club work throughout the country, and has affiliated to it, either directly or through local organizations, 1,996 clubs.—*Gen. Sec.,* Sir Reginald Goodwin, C.B.E.

BOYS' CLUBS, NORTHERN IRELAND ASSOCIATION OF (1940), 28 Bedford Street, Belfast.—*Gen. Sec.,* V. J. Dunlop.

BREWING, INSTITUTE OF (1886), 33 Clarges Street, W.1.—*Sec.,* Capt. S. Le H. Lombard-Hobson, C.V.O., O.B.E., R.N.

BRIDEWELL ROYAL HOSPITAL, King Edward's School, Witley, Surrey (1553).—*Treas.,* Gerald Coke; *Clerk to the Governors,* Lt.-Col. S. A. Faith.

BRITISH ACADEMY, THE (1901), Burlington House, Piccadilly, W.1.—*President,* Prof. Sir Denys Page, F.B.A.; *Council,* T. S. R. Boase, M.C.; Prof. H. C. Darby, O.B.E.; Prof. A. G. Dickens; Prof. O. R. Gurney; Prof. G. S. Kirk; Prof. W. C. Kneale; Prof. F. H. Lawson; Prof. S. Piggott; C. H. Roberts; Prof. E. A. G. Robinson, C.M.G., O.B.E.; A. N. Sherwin-White; Prof. G. R. Elton; P. M. Fraser, M.C.; Prof. C. A. Moser, C.B.E.; Dr. R. Shackleton; Miss B. Smalley; *Treas.,* Sir Roy Allen, C.B.E.; *Sec.,* D. F. Allen, C.B.; *Foreign Sec.,* Prof. A. G. Dickens.

BRITISH AND FOREIGN SCHOOL SOCIETY (1808). 7 Stone Buildings, Lincoln's Inn, W.C.2.—*Sec.,* G. G. G. Robb.

BRITISH ASSOCIATION FOR THE ADVANCEMENT OF SCIENCE (1831), 3 Sanctuary Buildings, 20 Great Smith Street, S.W.1.—*President,* Sir Vivian Fuchs, Ph.D.; *Gen. Secs.,* Prof. G. E. Fogg, F.R.S.; H. M. Finniston, F.R.S.; Sir Gordon Cox, K.B.E., F.R.S.; *Gen. Treas.,* Sir Eric Mensforth, C.B.E.; *Sec.,* J. A. V. Willis.

BRITISH ASSOCIATION OF THE HARD OF HEARING.—*Hon. Sec.,* C. H. Mardell, M.B.E., Briarfield, Syke Ings, Iver, Bucks.

BRITISH BEE-KEEPERS' ASSOCIATION (1874), 55 Chipstead Lane, Riverhead, Sevenoaks, Kent.—*Gen. Sec.,* O. Meyer.

BRITISH BOARD OF FILM CENSORS, 3 Soho Square, W.1.—*Sec.,* S. Murphy.

BRITISH COLOUR COUNCIL (1930), 10A Chandos Street, Cavendish Square, W.1.—*Sec.,* K. B. Robinson.

BRITISH COMMONWEALTH EX-SERVICES LEAGUE, 92 New Bond Street, W.1.—*Sec.-Gen.,* Air Commodore B. J. R. Roberts.

BRITISH COMMONWEALTH GAMES FEDERATION.—*Hon. Sec.,* K. S. Duncan, M.B.E., 12 Buckingham Street, W.C.2.

BRITISH COTTON GROWING ASSOCIATION (1904), 334–350 Royal Exchange, Manchester 2.—*Pres.,* The Earl of Derby, M.C.; *Sec.,* I. G. Fisher.

BRITISH COUNCIL, THE (1934), 65 Davies Street, W.1.—*Chairman,* Sir Leslie Rowan, K.C.B., C.V.O.; *Director-General,* Hon. Sir John Henniker, K.C.M.G., C.V.O., M.C.

BRITISH CYCLING FEDERATION (1878), 26 Park Crescent, W.1.—*Sec.,* L. Unwin.

BRITISH DENTAL ASSOCIATION (1880), 64 Wimpole Street, W.1.—*Pres.,* R. H. Chapman; *Sec.,* J. N. Peacock.

BRITISH DIABETIC ASSOCIATION (1934), 3–6 Alfred Place, W.C.1.—*Sec.-Gen.,* J. G. L. Jackson.

BRITISH DRAMA LEAGUE (1919), 9–10 Fitzroy Square, W.1.—*Dir.,* W. Lucas.

BRITISH FIELD SPORTS SOCIETY (1930), 26 Caxton Street, S.W.1.—*Sec.,* Lt.-Gen. Sir Richard Goodwin, K.C.B., C.B.E., D.S.O.

BRITISH FILM INSTITUTE (1933), 81 Dean Street, W.1.—*Director,* S. Reed; *Deputy do. and Curator, National Film Archive,* E. H. Lindgren, O.B.E.; *Sec.,* V. Saunders; *Controller, National Film Theatre,* L. Hardcastle.

BRITISH GLIDING ASSOCIATION (1930), affiliated to Royal Aero Club. Artillery Mansions, 75 Victoria Street, S.W.1.—*Gen. Sec.,* B. Rolfe.

BRITISH GOAT SOCIETY (1879). *Sec.,* Mrs. T. T. F. May, Lion House, Rougham, Bury St. Edmunds, Suffolk.

BRITISH HORSE SOCIETY, National Equestrian Centre, Kenilworth, Warwicks.—*Dir.-Gen.,* Maj.-Gen. J. R. Reynolds, O.B.E.

BRITISH INDUSTRY, CONFEDERATION OF, 21 Tothill Street, S.W.1.—*Director-General,* W. O. C. Adamson.

BRITISH INSTITUTE OF ARCHÆOLOGY AT ANKARA, 140 Cromwell Road, S.W.7.—*Hon. Sec.,* Prof. S. Lloyd, C.B.E., F.B.A., F.S.A.

BRITISH INSTITUTE OF INTERNATIONAL AND COMPARATIVE LAW, 32 Furnival Street, E.C.4.—*Sec.,* Mrs. A. J. Lang.

BRITISH INSTITUTE OF PERSIAN STUDIES (1961), *Hon. Sec.,* J. E. F. Gueritz, 85 Queen's Road, Richmond, Surrey.

BRITISH INSTITUTE OF RADIOLOGY, 32 Welbeck Street, W.1.—*Gen. Sec.,* Miss B. J. Bashford.

BRITISH INSTITUTE OF RECORDED SOUND (1955), 29 Exhibition Road, S.W.7.—*Dir.,* P. Saul.

BRITISH INTERPLANETARY SOCIETY (1933), 12 Bessborough Gardens, S.W.1.—*Sec.,* L. J. Carter.

BRITISH ISRAEL WORLD FEDERATION (1919) 6 Buckingham Gate, S.W.1.—*Sec.,* H. E. Stough.

BRITISH LEGION, ROYAL. *Headquarters,* Pall Mall, S.W.1. *Pres.,* Gen. Sir Charles Jones, G.C.B., C.B.E., M.C.; *Gen. Sec.,* D. E. Coffer, O.B.E.—*British Legion Poppy Fund,* £1,229,229 raised on Poppy Day, 1970, exclusive of Scotland. Grand total for years 1921 to 1970, £40,001,787.

BRITISH LEGION SCOTLAND, ROYAL, Haig House, 23 Drumsheugh Gardens, Edinburgh, 3.—*Gen. Sec.,* Col. MacLeod of Glendale, O.B.E., T.D.

BRITISH MEDICAL ASSOCIATION (1832), B.M.A. House, Tavistock Square, W.C.1.—*President,* Sir John Peel, K.C.V.O., F.R.C.S., F.R.C.O.G.; *Sec.,* D. P. Stevenson, Ll.D., M.R.C.S., L.R.C.P.

BRITISH MUSIC INFORMATION CENTRE, 10 Stratford Place, W.1.—*Librarian,* L. Glaze,

BRITISH OPTICAL ASSOCIATION, THE, 65 Brook Street, W.1.—*Sec.,* G. M. Dunn.

BRITISH RECORDS ASSOCIATION (1932), The Charterhouse, Charterhouse Square, E.C.1.—*Pres.,* The Master of the Rolls; *Hon. Sec.* (vacant).

BRITISH RECORD SOCIETY (1888), 38 Finsbury Square, E.C.2.—*Hon. Sec.,* P. Spufford, Dept. of History, The University, Keele, Staffs.

BRITISH RED CROSS SOCIETY (1870). *National Headquarters,* 9 Grosvenor Crescent, S.W.1.—*Dir.-Gen.,* A. B. Hodgson, C.M.G.

BRITISH SCHOOL AT ATHENS—*Chairman of the Managing Committee,* V. R. d'A. Desborough, F.B.A., F.S.A.; *Director,* H. W. Catling, D. Phil.; *Sec.,* Mrs. M. J. Thornton, 31–34 Gordon Square, W.C.1.

BRITISH SCHOOL AT ROME (1901).—*Chairman of Executive Committee,* T. S. R. Boase, M.C.; *Director,* J. B. Ward Perkins, C.B.E.; *Hon. Sec.,* C. A. H. James, 1 Lowther Gardens, S.W.7.

BRITISH SCHOOL OF ARCHÆOLOGY IN JERUSALEM (1919), 2 Hinde Mews, Marylebone Lane, W.1.—*Pres.,* Sir Mortimer Wheeler, C.H., C.I.E., M.C.; *Dir.,* Mrs. C. M. Bennett.

BRITISH SEAMEN'S BOYS' HOME, Rock House, Brixham.—*Supt.,* Capt. W. G. Parry, R.N.

BRITISH SHIP ADOPTION SOCIETY (1936), H.Q.S. *Wellington*, Temple Stairs, Victoria Embankment, W.C.2.—*Sec.*, B. D. Emson.

BRITISH SOCIAL BIOLOGY COUNCIL, 69 Eccleston Square, S.W.1.—*Sec.*, R. Weatherall.

BRITISH STANDARDS INSTITUTION, 2 Park Street, W.1.—*Dir.-Gen.*, G. B. R. Feilden, C.B.E., F.R.S.

BRITISH THORACIC AND TUBERCULOSIS ASSOCIATION (1928), 59 Portland Place, W.1.—*Sec.*, L. D. Booker, M.B.E.

BRITISH UNITED PROVIDENT ASSOCIATION LIMITED (1947), Essex Street, Strand, W.C.2.—*Chief Exec.*, E. D. Roberts.

BRITISH VETERINARY ASSOCIATION (1881), 7 Mansfield Street, W.1.—*Sec.*, P. B. Turner.

BUILDING, INSTITUTE OF (1834), Englemere, Ascot, Berks.—*Exec. Dir.*, D. A. Neale, M.C.

BUILDING SOCIETIES ASSOCIATION, 14 Park Street, W.1.—*Sec.-Gen.*, N. E. Griggs.

BUILDING SOCIETIES INSTITUTE, 6 Cavendish Place, W.1.—*Sec.*, E. C. L. Butler.

BUSINESS AND PROFESSIONAL WOMEN'S CLUBS OF GREAT BRITAIN AND NORTHERN IRELAND, NATIONAL FEDERATION OF (1938), 54 Bloomsbury Street, W.C.1.—*Gen. Sec.*, Mrs. I. G. Rayner.

BUSINESS ARCHIVES COUNCIL, 37–45 Tooley Street, S.E.1.—*Hon. Sec.*, Maj. T. L. Ingram.

BUTCHERS' CHARITABLE INSTITUTION (1828).—*Sec.*, J. A. Fordyce, 61 West Smithfield, E.C.1.

CALOUSTE GULBENKIAN FOUNDATION, LISBON, United Kingdom and British Commonwealth Branch (1956), 98 Portland Place, W.1.—*Dir.*, A. Dunbar.

CAMBRIDGE FUND AND WILLIAM WOODMAN CHARITY. (Applicants must be ex-soldiers who served as Regulars before the 1914–18 War.) *Address*, The Deputy Under-Secretary of State (C.2(AD)), Ministry of Defence, Old War Office Building, Whitehall, S.W.1.

CAMBRIDGE PRESERVATION SOCIETY (1929).—*Chairman*, M. N. Bradford; *Sec.*, N. Clark, 21 Northampton Street, Cambridge.

CAMERA CLUB (1885), 8 Great Newport Street, W.C.2.—*Hon. Sec.*, F. J. Reid

CANADIAN-UNITED KINGDOM CHAMBER OF COMMERCE (1921). 1–3 Lower Regent Street, S.W.1.—*Pres.*, G. Roberge; *Sec.*, K. R. S. Leadlay.

CANCER RESEARCH CAMPAIGN (Brit. Empire Cancer Campaign for Research), 2 Carlton House Terrace, S.W.1. For research into the disease of cancer in all its forms.—*Sec. Gen.*, Brig. K. D. Gribbin, M.B.E.

CANCER COUNCIL, BRITISH (1968).—*Sec.*, Dr. Graham Bennette, 2 Harley Street, W.1.

CANCER RELIEF, NATIONAL SOCIETY FOR (1911), Michael Sobell House, 30 Dorset Square, N.W.1. —*Gen. Sec.*, G. F. Tredwell.

CANCER RESEARCH FUND, IMPERIAL (1902), Lincoln Inn Fields, W.C.2. Research into causes, prevention, treatment and cure of all forms of cancer; assists research in hospitals and other institutions.—*Sec.*, A. B. L. Clarke, O.B.E.

CANCER RESEARCH, INSTITUTE OF: ROYAL CANCER HOSPITAL (1911), Fulham Road, S.W.3.—*Sec.*, N. P. Hadow, O.B.E.

CARAVAN MISSION TO VILLAGE CHILDREN (1893), 47 Marylebone Lane, W.1.—*Sec.*, H. P. M. Warde.

CARNEGIE DUNFERMLINE TRUST (1903) (social and cultural purposes in Dunfermline).—*Sec.*, F. Mann, Abbey Park House, Dunfermline, Fife.

CARNEGIE HERO FUND TRUST (1908). Income £33,000. Makes grants and allowances to people injured or the dependants of people killed in saving human life within the British Isles and territorial waters.—*Sec.*, F. Mann, Abbey Park House, Dunfermline, Fife.

CARNEGIE UNITED KINGDOM TRUST (1913), Comely Park House, Dunfermline, Fife.—*Object*, The improvement of the well-being of the masses of the people of Great Britain and Ireland by means which are "charitable" in law and are to be selected by the Trustees themselves The Trust is particularly concerned with social welfare schemes of a pioneer or experimental kind; grants are not made to individuals or in response to general appeals for subscriptions. Management—By trustees. *Sec.*, M. Holton.

CATHEDRALS ADVISORY COMMITTEE, 83 London Wall, E.C.2.—*Sec.* (vacant).

CATHOLIC MARRIAGE ADVISORY COUNCIL (National Office), 15 Lansdowne Road, W.11; (London Centre), 33 Willow Place, Francis Street, S.W.1. —*Chairman*, Rev. M. O'Leary, S.T.L.

CATHOLIC RECORD SOCIETY (1904).—*Hon. Sec.*, Miss R. Rendel, 48 Lowndes Square, S.W.1

CATHOLIC TRUTH SOCIETY (1868), P.O. Box 422, 38–40 Eccleston Square, S.W.1.—*Gen. Sec.*, T. H. Rittner.

CATHOLIC UNION OF GREAT BRITAIN.—*Pres.*, The Duke of Norfolk, K.G., P.C., G.C.V.O., G.B.E.; *Sec.*, The Lord Craigmyle, 18 The Boltons, S.W.10.

CATTLE BREEDERS' CLUB, BRITISH (1949), Lavenders, Isfield, nr. Uckfield, Sussex.—*Sec.*, C. R. Stains.

CATTLE VETERINARY ASSOCIATION, BRITISH.—*Sec.*, M. H. Hinton, Veterinary Investigation Centre, Job's Well Road, Johnston, Carmarthen.

CAXTON CONVALESCENT HOME (1895), The Chart, Limpsfield, Surrey. (For Printing, and Kindred Trades, Men and Women). *London Office*, 1 Gough Square, E.C.4.—*Sec.*, A. C. Oram.

CECIL HOUSES (Inc.), 190–192 Kensal Road, W.10. —*Sec.*, Mrs. E. Gordon Phillips.

CEREALS AND BALTIC FRIENDLY SOCIETY (1908). 24 St. Mary Axe, E.C.3.—*Sec.*, C. W. Stevens, M.B.E.

CERAMIC SOCIETY, BRITISH (1900), Shelton House, Stoke Road, Shelton, Stoke-on-Trent, Staffs.— *Pres. and Hon. Sec.*, A. Dinsdale.

CERAMICS, INSTITUTE OF (1955), Shelton House, Stoke Road, Shelton, Stoke-on-Trent, Staffs.— *Sec.*, K. C. J. Seabridge.

CEYLON ASSOCIATION IN LONDON, 2/3 Crosby Square, Bishopsgate, E.C.3.—*Dir.*, Capt. A. S. Webb, R.N.(ret.).

CHADWICK TRUST (1895) (for the promotion of health and prevention of disease), 90 Buckingham Palace Road, S.W.1.—*Clerk*, P. A. Wells.

CHAMBERS OF COMMERCE.—*See* COMMERCE.

CHANTREY BEQUEST (1875).—*Sec. to the Trustees*, The Secretary, Royal Academy of Arts, Burlington House, W.1.

CHEMICAL ENGINEERS, INSTITUTION OF (1922), 16 Belgrave Square, S.W.1.—*Pres.*, J. F. Davidson; *Gen. Sec.*, D. H. Sharp.

CHEMICAL INDUSTRY, SOCIETY OF, 14 Belgrave Square, S.W.1.—*Pres.*, G. H. Beeby; *Sec.*, D. H. Sharp.

CHEMICAL SOCIETY, Burlington House, Piccadilly, W.1.—*Pres.*, Prof. G. Porter, F.R.S.; *Gen. Sec.*, J. R. Ruck Keene, M.B.E., T.D., M.A.

CHEMISTRY, THE ROYAL INSTITUTE OF, 30, Russell Square, W.C.1.—*Pres.*, Sir Ewart Jones, F.R.S.; *Sec. and Registrar*, R. E. Parker, ph.D.

CHESS FEDERATION, BRITISH, 9A Grand Parade, St. Leonards-on-Sea, Sussex.—*Sec.*, G. H. Simmons.

CHEST AND HEART ASSOCIATION (1899), Tavistock House North, Tavistock Square, W.C.1.—*Dir. Gen.*, J. H. Harley Williams, O.B.E., M.D.

CHILDREN, THOMAS CORAM FOUNDATION FOR, *see* CORAM FOUNDATION.

CHILDREN'S COUNTRY HOLIDAYS FUND, 1 York Street, W.1.—*Sec.*, Miss Z. de Zouche.

CHILDREN'S RELIEF INTERNATIONAL (1959), Overstream House, Cambridge.—*Dir.*, B. Faithfull-Davies.

CHINA ASSOCIATION (1889), 18 Diamond House, Hatton Garden, E.C.1.—*Sec.*, E. S. Bush.

CHIROPODISTS, THE SOCIETY OF, 8 Wimpole Street, W.1.—*Sec.*, G. C. Jenkins.

CHOIR SCHOOLS ASSOCIATION (1921).—*Hon. Sec.*, Rev. D. Thomson, Cathedral Choir School, Ripon, Yorks.

CHRISTIAN ACTION (1949), 2 Amen Court, E.C.4. —*Dir.*, Rev. C. Hodgetts.

CHRISTIAN EDUCATION MOVEMENT (1965), Annandale, North End Road, N.W.11.—*Gen. Sec.*, Rev. J. P. Lee-Woolf.

CHRISTIAN EVIDENCE SOCIETY (1870), St. Margaret Pattens, Eastcheap, E.C.3.—*Hon. Sec.*, Rev. S. E. Alford.

CHRISTIAN KNOWLEDGE, SOCIETY FOR PROMOTING (1698), Holy Trinity Church, Marylebone Road, N.W.1.—*Gen. Sec.*, P. N. G. Gilbert.

CHRISTIANS AND JEWS, COUNCIL OF (1942), 41 Cadogan Gardens, S.W.3.—*Gen. Sec.*, Rev. W. W. Simpson, O.B.E., M.A.

CHURCH ARMY, 185 Marylebone Road, N.W.1.— *Chief Sec.*, Rev. Preb. D. M. Lynch, M.A.

CHURCH BUILDING SOCIETY, INCORPORATED (1818), 7 Queen Anne's Gate, S.W.1.—*Sec.*, W. A. Carter.

CHURCH EDUCATION CORPORATION, 35 Denison House, S.W.1.—*Sec.*, W. F. Holmes.

CHURCH HOUSE, Dean's Yard, Westminster, S.W.1.—*Sec.*, Maj. G. C. Hackett, M.B.E.

CHURCH LADS' BRIGADE (1891), *National Headquarters*, 185 Marylebone Road, N.W.1.—*Gen. Sec.*, Maj. H. S. Forbes, M.B.E., M.C.

CHURCH MISSIONARY SOCIETY (1799), 157 Waterloo Road, S.E.1. Income, 1970, £1,132,405.—*Secs.*, Rev. Canon J. V. Taylor, D.D. (*General*); A. P. F. Paton (*Depy. Gen. Sec.*); J. J. Hillman (*Africa*); Rev. J. B. Carden (*Asia*); A. D. Iliff (*Medical*); Rev. W. F. Curtis (*Home*); Miss M. Pritchard (*Candidates*); G. A. Hill (*Financial*).

CHURCH OF ENGLAND CHILDREN'S SOCIETY (1881) (formerly Waifs and Strays), Old Town Hall, Kennington Road, S.E.11.—*Gen. Sec.*, Rev. R. C. M. Beeny.

CHURCH OF ENGLAND MEN'S SOCIETY (1899), 185 Marylebone Road, N.W.1.—*Gen. Sec.*, Rev. C. D. S. Woodhouse.

CHURCH OF ENGLAND PENSIONS BOARD (1926), 53 Tufton Street, S.W.1.—*Sec.*, L. J. Sillito, O.B.E.

CHURCH OF ENGLAND SOLDIERS', SAILORS' AND AIRMEN'S CLUBS (1891), Trafalgar Services Club, 16 Edinburgh Road, Portsmouth, Hants.—*Chairman*, Rear-Adm. J. L. Blackham, C.B.; *Gen. Sec.*, Group Capt. J. A. S. Brown.

CHURCH OF SCOTLAND DEPT. OF SOCIAL SERVICE, 121 George Street, Edinburgh 2.—*Dir.*, L. B. Garden.

CHURCH PASTORAL AID SOCIETY (1836), Falcon Court, 32 Fleet Street, E.C.4.—*Sec.*, Rev. T. Dudley-Smith.

CHURCH UNION (1859), 199 Uxbridge Road, W.12. —*Sec.*, Rev. D. Carter.

CHURCHES, BRITISH COUNCIL OF (1942), 10 Eaton Gate, S.W.1.—*Gen. Sec.*, Rt. Rev. C. K. Sansbury, D.D.

CHURCHES, COUNCIL FOR THE CARE OF, 83 London Wall, E.C.2.—*Sec.* (vacant).

CHURCHES, FRIENDLESS, FRIENDS OF (1957), 12 Edwardes Square, W.8.—*Hon. Dir.*, I. Bulmer-Thomas; *Hon. Sec.*, L. E. Jones.

CHURCHES MAIN COMMITTEE (1941), 7 Little College Street, S.W.1.—*Sec.*, Sir Thomas Bromley, K.C.M.G.

CIRCUS PROPRIETORS OF GREAT BRITAIN, ASSOCIATION OF, 24 Denmark Street, W.C.2.—*Sec.*, R. Walker.

CIVIC TRUST FOR THE NORTH WEST, 56 Oxford Street, Manchester 2.—*Dir.*, G. Ashworth.

CIVIL DEFENCE OFFICERS, ASSOCIATION OF, 8 Meadow Road, Harborne, Birmingham 17.— *Hon. Gen. Sec.*, E. E. Alley.

CIVIL ENGINEERS, INSTITUTION OF (1818), Great George Street, S.W.1.—*Pres.*, G. A. Wilson, C.B.E.; *Sec.*, J. G. Watson, C.B.

CIVIL LIBERTIES, NATIONAL COUNCIL FOR (1934), 152 Camden High Street, N.W.1.—*Sec.*, T. Smythe.

CIVIL SERVANTS, SOCIETY OF, 124–126 Southwark Street, S.E.1.—*Gen. Sec.*, J. R. M. Dryden.

CIVIL SERVICE COUNCIL FOR FURTHER EDUCATION.— *Sec.*, M. L. Winspear, 11 Belgrave Road, S.W.1.

CLASSICAL ASSOCIATION (1903).—*Hon. Treas.*, Prof. L. A. Moritz, D.PHIL., University College, Cardiff.

CLASSICAL TEACHERS, JOINT ASSOCIATION OF (1962), 31–34 Gordon Square, W.C.1—*Hon. Sec.*, M. R. F. Cunningham.

CLAY TECHNOLOGY, INSTITUTE OF (1927), Stamford House, 65/66 Turnmill Street, E.C.1.— *Gen. Sec.*, J. E. Roberts, F.R.S.A.

CLERGY FRIENDLY SOCIETY (1882), Aldwych House, Aldwych, W.C.2.

CLERGY ORPHAN CORPORATION (1749), 5 Verulam Buildings, Gray's Inn, W.C.1.—*Sec.*, Miss V. B. Warters.

CLERKS OF THE PEACE OF COUNTIES AND OF CLERKS OF COUNTY COUNCILS, SOCIETY OF.—*Hon. Sec.*, A. R. Davis, County Hall, West Bridgford, Nottingham.

CLERKS OF THE PEACE OF SCOTLAND, ASSOCIATION OF (1908).—*Hon. Sec.*, J. B. McGowan, 135 Irish Street, Dumfries.

CLERKS OF DISTRICT COUNCILS, SOCIETY OF (1926). —*Sec.*, R. E. C. Jewell, White Oak, Swanley, Kent.

CLERKS OF WORKS OF GREAT BRITAIN INCORPORATED, INSTITUTE OF (1882), 6 Highbury Corner, N.5.—*Sec.*, A. P. Macnamara.

CLYDESDALE HORSE SOCIETY OF GREAT BRITAIN AND IRELAND (1877), 24 Beresford Terrace, Ayr.

COACHING CLUB (1871), 65 Medfield Street, S.W.15.—*Sec.*, R. A. Brown, O.B.E.

COAL TRADE BENEVOLENT ASSOCIATION (1888), 63 Narrow Street, Limehouse, E.14.—*Sec.*, R. W. Porcas.

COAL UTILISATION COUNCIL (1932), 19 Rochester Row, S.W.1.—*Director*, W. C. Moss, M.B.E.

COKE OVEN MANAGERS' ASSOCIATION, Waveney House, Adwick Road, Mexborough, Yorks.

COLLEGE OF THE SEA (Seafarers Education Service) (1938), Mansbridge House, 207 Balham High Road, S.W.17.

COMBINED CADET FORCE ASSOCIATION (1952), 58 Buckingham Gate, S.W.1.—*Sec.*, W. F. L. Newcombe, O.B.E., T.D.

COMMERCE, ASSOCIATION OF BRITISH CHAMBERS OF (1960).—*Pres.*, H. Eccles-Williams, C.B.E.; *Dir.*, A. C. F. Hey, 68 Queen Street, E.C.4.

COMMERCE AND INDUSTRY, LONDON CHAMBER OF (1881), 69 Cannon Street, E.C.4.—*Pres.*, R. E. Brook, C.M.G., O.B.E.; *Dir.*, W. J. Luxton, C.B.E.

COMMERCE, SCOTTISH CHAMBER OF, 30 George Square, Glasgow, C.2.—*Dir.*, W. G. Buchan.

COMMERCE AND MANUFACTURES, EDINBURGH CHAMBER OF (1786), 20 Hanover Street, Edinburgh 2.—*Sec.*, D. M. Mowat.

COMMERCE AND MANUFACTURES, GLASGOW CHAMBER OF (1783), 30 George Square, Glasgow C.2.—*Sec.*, M. Neil.

COMMERCIAL AND INDUSTRIAL EDUCATION, BRITISH ASSOCIATION FOR (BACIE), 16 Park Crescent, Regent's Park, W.1.—*Dir.*, P. J. C. Perry, O.B.E.

COMMERCIAL TRAVELLERS' BENEVOLENT INSTITUTION (1849), Wax Chandlers' Hall, Gresham Street, E.C.2.—*Sec.*, E. B. Auger.

COMMISSIONAIRES, THE CORPS OF (1859), founded by the late Captain Sir Edward Walter; for the employment of ex-Soldiers, Sailors and Airmen and ex-police, fire service and merchant navy servicemen. *Headquarters,* Exchange Court, 419A Strand, W.C.2. *Outquarters,* 124 Donegall Street, Belfast; Room 53, Guildhall Buildings, Navigation Street, Birmingham; 90 Colston Street, Bristol; 99 Shandwick Place, Edinburgh; 230 W. Regent Street, Glasgow; Room 23, 10-12 East Parade, Leeds; 21 Dale Street, Liverpool; 2 St. John Street, Deansgate, Manchester; 10 Bigg Market, Newcastle-upon-Tyne 1. Total strength, 4,200.—*Commandant,* Lt.-Col. R. F. Walter; *Adjutant,* Wing Cdr. E. Holden, D.F.C.

COMMONS, OPEN SPACES AND FOOTPATHS PRESERVATION SOCIETY (1865), Suite 4, 166 Shaftesbury Avenue, W.C.2.—*Sec.*, I. S. Campbell.

COMMONWEALTH AND CONTINENTAL CHURCH SOCIETY (1823), 7 York Buildings, Adelphi, W.C.2.—*Sec.*, Rev. F. H. Crook.

COMMONWEALTH INDUSTRIES ASSOCIATION, LTD., 60 Buckingham Gate, S.W.1.—*Dir.*, E. Holloway.

COMMONWEALTH PARLIAMENTARY ASSOCIATION.—*Sec., U.K. Branch,* P. G. Molloy, M.C., Westminster Hall, S.W.1.

COMMONWEALTH PRESS UNION (1909), 154 Fleet Street, E.C.4.—*Sec.*, Lt.-Col. T. Pierce-Goulding, M.B.E., C.D.

COMMONWEALTH PRODUCERS' ORGANIZATION (1916), 25 Victoria Street, S.W.1.—*Dir.*, S. Stanley-Smith.

COMMONWEALTH SETTLEMENT, CHURCH OF ENGLAND COUNCIL FOR (1925), Church House, Dean's Yard, S.W.1.—*Gen. Sec.,* Rev. Canon J. Oates.

COMMONWEALTH SOCIETY FOR THE DEAF (1959), 75 Kinnerton Street, S.W.1.—*Exec. Chairman,* Lady Templer.

COMMONWEALTH UNIVERSITIES, ASSOCIATION OF, 36 Gordon Square, W.C.1.—*Sec.-Gen.*, Sir Hugh Springer, K.C.M.G., C.B.E.

COMMUNIST PARTY OF GREAT BRITAIN EXECUTIVE COMMITTEE (1920), 16 King Street, W.C.2.—*Gen. Sec.,* J. Gollan.

COMPOSERS' GUILD OF GREAT BRITAIN, THE (1945), 10 Stratford Place, W.1.—*Sec.*, Miss E. Yeoman.

COMPUTER SOCIETY, BRITISH (1957), 29 Portland Place, W.1.—*Sec.-Gen.*, M. C. Ashill.

CONGREGATIONAL COUNCIL FOR WORLD MISSION (1966), Livingstone House, Carteret Street, S.W.1.—previously the London Missionary Society and the Commonwealth Missionary Society.—*Gen. Sec.,* The Rev. B. G. Thorogood.

CONSERVATIVE AND UNIONIST ASSOCIATIONS, NATIONAL UNION OF (1867), 32 Smith Square, S.W.1.—*Sec.*, S. A. Cooke, M.B.E.; *Women's National Advisory Committee.—Sec.,* Miss B. A. Cribb; *Young Conservative and Unionist National Advisory Committee.—Sec.,* R. Boaden.

CONSERVATIVE AND UNIONIST CENTRAL OFFICE, 32 Smith Square, S.W.1.—*Chairman,* Rt. Hon. P. J. M. Thomas, Q.C., M.P.; *Deputy Chairman,* Sir Michael Fraser, C.B.E.; *Vice-Chairmen,* R. W. Elliott, M.P.; Mrs. C. Morrison; Hon. Mrs. M. K.

Macmillan; *Treasurers,* The Lord Chelmer, M.C., T.D.; Sir Tatton Brinton, M.P.; *Dir. of Organization,* Sir Richard Webster, D.S.O.

CONSERVATIVE CLUBS, LTD., ASSOCIATION OF (1894), 32 Smith Square, S.W.1.—*Sec.*, L. G. Waterman.

CONSTRUCTION SURVEYORS' INSTITUTE (1952), 189-193 Temple Chambers, Temple Avenue, E.C.4.—*Gen. Sec.,* S. L. J. Cook.

CONSULTING ENGINEERS, ASSOCIATION OF (1913), Abbey House, 2 Victoria Street, S.W.1.—*Sec.,* Maj.-Gen. M. W. Prynne, C.B., C.B.E.

CO-OPERATIVE SOCIETIES AND ASSOCIATIONS:—

Co-operative Party, 158 Buckingham Palace Road, S.W.1.—*Sec.*, T. E. Graham.

Co-operative Productive Federation (1882), 42 Western Road, Leicester.—*Sec.*, J. Leonard.

Co-operative Union (1869), Holyoake House, Hanover Street, Manchester, 4.—*Gen. Sec.,* Sir Robert Southern, C.B.E.

Co-operative Wholesale Society (C.W.S.) (1863), New Century House, Manchester 4.—*Chief Exec. Offr.,* A. Wilson.

Co-operative Women's Guild, 342 Hoe Street, Walthamstow, E.17.—*Gen. Sec.,* Mrs. K. Kempton.

Fisheries Organization Society, Ltd. (1914), Denison House, 296 Vauxhall Bridge Road, S.W.1.—*Sec.*, E. B. Hamley.

International Co-operative Alliance (1895), 11 Upper Grosvenor Street, W.1.—*Dir.*, S. K. Saxena.

Plunkett Foundation for Co-operative Studies (1919), 31 St. Giles, Oxford.—*Sec.*, F. H. Webster.

Scottish Agricultural Organisation Society Ltd. (1905), 18-19 Claremont Crescent, Edinburgh 7.—*Sec.*, J. B. Robb.

Welsh Agricultural Organisation Society, Ltd., (1922), P.O. Box 8, Brynawel, Great Darkgate Street, Aberystwyth.—*Dir.*, E. R. Thomas.

COPYRIGHT COUNCIL, BRITISH (1953), 29-33 Berners Street, W.1.—*Sec.*, R. Wreford.

(THOMAS) CORAM FOUNDATION FOR CHILDREN (formerly FOUNDLING HOSPITAL) (1739) AND CORAM NURSERY. All inquiries to 40 Brunswick Square, W.C.1.—*Sec.*, F. C. Brown.

CORONERS' SOCIETY OF ENGLAND AND WALES (1846).—*Hon. Sec.,* J. Burton, Coroner's Court, 77 Fulham Palace Road, W.6.

CORRESPONDENCE COLLEGES, ASSOCIATION OF BRITISH (1955), 4-7 Chiswell Street, E.C.1.—*Sec.*, C. Nuttall.

COST ACCOUNTANTS' ASSOCIATION (1937), 60A Station Road, Upminster, Essex.—*Sec.*, K. D. Gilpin.

COST AND WORKS ACCOUNTANTS, INSTITUTE OF (1919), 63 Portland Place, W.1.

COTTON RESEARCH CORPORATION (1921), 12 Chantrey House, Eccleston Street, S.W.1.—*Dir.*, M. A. Choyce, O.B.E.

COUNTRY LANDOWNERS' ASSOCIATION (1907), Swallow Street, W.1.—*Sec. Gen.,* J. M. Douglas.

COUNTY COUNCILS ASSOCIATION (1890) Eaton House, 66A Eaton Square, S.W.1.—*Sec.*, A. C. Hetherington, C.B.E.

COUNTY PLANNING OFFICERS' SOCIETY.—*Hon. Sec.,* M. W. Robinson, Talbot Cottage, Minster Lovell, Oxon.

COUNTY SURVEYORS' SOCIETY (1884).—*President,* D. Farrar, County Offices, Cardiff; *Hon. Sec.,* P. C. Gane, County Offices, Lincoln.

COUNTY TREASURERS, SOCIETY OF (1903), County Hall, Taunton, Som.—*Hon. Sec.,* W. Hollinrake.

CRAFT EDUCATION, INSTITUTE OF.—*Gen. Sec.,* T. E. Atkinson, Hillside, Little Weighton, Hull.

CRAFTS CENTRE OF GREAT BRITAIN (1948), 43 Earlham Street, W.C.2.—*Dir.*, Rosalind Sutton.

CRUELTY TO ANIMALS, ROYAL SOCIETY FOR THE PREVENTION OF. *See* "ROYAL."

CRUELTY TO ANIMALS, CENTRAL COUNCIL OF SOCIETIES IN SCOTLAND FOR PREVENTION OF (1950), 19 Melville Street, Edinburgh 3.—*Hon. Sec.*, G. F. S. Brian.

CRUELTY TO ANIMALS, ULSTER SOCIETY FOR THE PREVENTION OF, 65–67 May Street, Belfast, 1.—*Sec.*, Mrs. M. L. Pitt.

CRUELTY TO CHILDREN. *See* "NATIONAL" and "ROYAL SCOTTISH."

CULTURAL EXCHANGE, ASSOCIATION FOR (1958), 9 Emmanuel Road, Cambridge.—*Sec.* P. B. Barnes.

CURATES' AUGMENTATION FUND (1866), East Wing, Fulham Palace, S.W.6.—*Sec.*, Rev. M. L. Nicholas.

CYCLISTS TOURING CLUB (1878), Cotterell House, 69 Meadrow, Godalming, Surrey.—*Sec.*, Leslie C. Warner.

CWMNI URDD GOBAITH CYMRU (Welsh League of Youth) (1922), Aberystwyth.—*Dir.*, R. E. Griffith, O.B.E.

CYMMRODORION, THE HONOURABLE SOCIETY OF (1751).—*Hon. Sec.*, B. G. Jones, 118 Newgate Street, E.C.1.

DAIRY ASSOCIATION, UNITED KINGDOM (1950), Giggs Hill Green, Thames Ditton, Surrey.—*Sec.*, R. D. Lemmer.

DAIRY TECHNOLOGY, SOCIETY OF (1943), 17 Devonshire Street, W.1.—*Sec.*, M. Sonn.

D DAY FELLOWSHIP.—*Hon. Sec.*, Cdr. A. D. Gilbert, R.N. (*ret.*), Cathedral House, St. Thomas's Street, Portsmouth, Hants.

DATA PROCESSING, INSTITUTE OF (1966), Walter House, 418–422 Strand, W.C.2.—*Sec.*, D. W. Bradley.

DEAF, ROYAL NATIONAL INSTITUTE FOR THE (1911) 105 Gower Street, W.C.1.—*Sec. Gen.*, R. Sydenham.

DEAF AND DUMB, ROYAL ASSOCIATION IN AID OF. To promote the general, social and spiritual welfare of deaf and blind/deaf people in London and the south-east. 7–11 Armstrong Road, W.3. —*Sec.*, M. Thompson.

DEAF AND DUMB WOMEN, BRITISH HOME FOR, 26 Clapton Common, E.5.—*Matron and Sec.*, Miss E. Cheverall.

DEAF CHILDREN, ROYAL SCHOOL FOR (1792), Margate. *Office*, 90 Queen Street, E.C.4.—*Sec.*, J. Coombs.

DEAF WELFARE EXAMINATION BOARD.—*Hon. Registrar*, Rev. A. F. Mackenzie, 10 Treves Road, Dorchester, Dorset.

DECORATORS AND INTERIOR DESIGNERS, INCORPORATED INSTITUTE OF BRITISH (1899), 30 Baker Street, W.1.—*Sec.*, Mrs. A. E. Gordois.

DEER SOCIETY, BRITISH—*Sec.*, F. J. T. Page, Nature Reserve and Deer Museum, Low Hay Bridge, Bouth, by Ulverston, Lancs.

DELINQUENCY, INST. FOR THE STUDY AND TREATMENT OF (1931), 8 Bourdon Street, W.1.—*Gen. Sec.*, Miss E. Saville, M.B.E.

DENTAL COUNCIL, GENERAL, 37 Wimpole Street, W.1.—*Registrar*, D. Hindley-Smith.

DENTAL HOSPITALS OF GREAT BRITAIN AND NORTHERN IRELAND, ASSOCIATION OF (1942),—*Hon. Sec.*, Dr. R. G. Mitchell, Dental Hospital, St. Mary's Row, Birmingham 4.

DESIGN AND INDUSTRIES ASSOCIATION (1915) 12 Carlton House Terrace, S.W.1.—*Hon. Sec.*, R. Plummer.

DESTITUTE SAILORS' FUND (1827), c/o The Red Ensign Club, Dock Street, E.1.

DEVON AND CORNWALL RECORD SOCIETY (1904).— c/o Devon and Exeter Institution, 7 The Close, Exeter.

DEVONIAN ASSOCIATION, LONDON (1888).—*Hon Sec.*, Mrs. D. Gunzi, 59 Elms Road, Clapham Common, S.W.4.

DICKENS FELLOWSHIP, Dickens House, 48 Doughty Street, W.C.1.

DIRECTORS, INSTITUTE OF (1903), 10 Belgrave Square, S.W.1.—*Dir. Gen.*, Sir Richard Powell, Bt., M.C.

DISABLED, BRITISH COUNCIL FOR REHABILITATION OF THE (1944), Tavistock House (South), Tavistock Square, W.C.1.—*Sec.-Gen.*, I. R. Henderson.

DISABLED, CENTRAL COUNCIL FOR THE (1919), 34 Eccleston Square, S.W.1.—*Dir.*, D. Guthrie.

DISPENSING OPTICIANS, ASSOCIATION OF (1925), 22 Nottingham Place, W.1.—*Sec.*, M. G. Aird.

DISTRESS, SOCIETY FOR THE RELIEF OF (1860), 51 The Chine, N.21.—*Hon. Sec.*, Miss W. F. Piper.

DISTRESSED GENTLEFOLKS' AID ASSOCIATION (1897), (Headquarters and London Nursing Home), Vicarage Gate House, Vicarage Gate, Kensington, W.8.

DITCHLEY FOUNDATION, Ditchley Park, Enstone, Oxford.—*Provost*, Sir Michael Stewart, K.C.M.G., O.B.E.

DR. GRAHAM'S HOMES LIMITED (1968) (formerly Dr. Graham's Homes, Kalimpong), 9 Brackendale Gardens, Upminster, Essex.—*Chairman*, Sir John Jardine Paterson; *Hon. Sec.*, J. F. d'A. Willis, O.B.E.

DOGS HOME BATTERSEA, THE (1860), Battersea Park Road, S.W.8. *Hours*: Monday to Friday, 9.30–5. Claims only, Saturday and Sunday and Public Holidays, 2–4 p.m.—*Sec.*, Lieut.-Cdr. B. N. Knight, R.N.

DOMESTIC SERVANTS' BENEVOLENT INSTITUTION (1846), Royal Bank of Scotland, Burlington Gardens, W.1.—*Sec.*, P. M. Clements.

DOMINION STUDENTS' HALL TRUST, London House, Mecklenburgh Square, W.C.1.

DOWSERS, BRITISH SOCIETY OF (1933).—*Hon. Sec.*, P. B. Smithett, High Street, Eydon, Daventry, Northants.

DRAINAGE AUTHORITIES, ASSOCIATION OF (1937).— *Sec.*, H. E. G. Wells, 12 The Plain, Thornbury, Bristol.

DRAMATISTS, LEAGUE OF, 84 Drayton Gardens, S.W.10.—*Sec.*, Julia Jones.

DRINKING FOUNTAIN ASSOCIATION (formerly Metropolitan Drinking Fountain and Cattle Trough Association) (1859) 426 Lewisham High Street, S.E.13.—*Sec.*, Brig. J. M. Rymer-Jones, C.B.E., M.C., Q.P.M.

DRUG DEPENDENCE, INSTITUTE FOR THE STUDY OF, Chandos House, 2 Queen Anne Street, W.1.— *Hon. Dir.*, F. Logan.

DUKE OF EDINBURGH'S AWARD, 2 Old Queen Street, S.W.1.—*Director*, A. L. Blake, M.C.; *Gen. Sec.*, H. Robinson, M.B.E., 6 Derwentwater Terrace, Leeds 6.

DYERS AND COLOURISTS, SOCIETY OF (1884), Perkin House, P.O. Box 244, 82 Grattan Rd, Bradford, Yorks.—*Gen. Sec.*, M. Tordoff, Ph.D., F.R.I.C.

EARL HAIG'S (BRITISH LEGION) APPEAL FUND. *See* "BRITISH LEGION."

EARL HAIG FUND (SCOTLAND). Established for the relief of distress among ex-service personnel of all ranks and their dependants in Scotland. Applicants may apply to either of the following: *North, South and East Area.* 23 Drumsheugh Gardens, Edinburgh 3.—*Gen. Sec.*, Col. J. M. Grant, O.B.E.; or *Glasgow and South-West Area*, 1 Fitzroy Place, Glasgow, C.3.—*Sec.*, Lt. G. B. Steel, R.N.R.

EARLY ENGLISH TEXT SOCIETY (1864).—*Hon. Director*, Prof. N. Davis, F.B.A.; *Exec. Sec.*, Dr. A. Hudson, Lady Margaret Hall, Oxford.

ECCLESIASTICAL HISTORY SOCIETY.—*Sec.*, Prof. R. M. T. Hill, Westfield College, N.W.3.

ECCLESIOLOGICAL SOCIETY (Founded in 1839 as the Cambridge Camden Society).—*Hon. Sec.*, S. Chapman, C.B.E., c/o St. Ann's Vestry Hall, Carter Lane, E.C.4.

EDUCATION COMMITTEES, ASSOCIATION OF, 10 Queen Anne Street, W.1.—*Sec.*, Sir William Alexander, Ph.D.

EDUCATION COUNCIL OF THE SOCIETY OF FRIENDS, Friends House, Euston Road, N.W.1.—*Sec.*, J. E. Brigham.

EDUCATION, NATIONAL COMMITTEE FOR AUDIO-VISUAL AIDS IN, 33 Queen Anne Street, W.1.—*Dir.*, Dr. J. A. Harrison.

EDUCATION OFFICERS, SOCIETY OF.—*Sec.*, C W. W. Read, 10 Queen Anne Street, W.1.

EDUCATION OFFICERS' SOCIETY, COUNTY.—*Hon. Sec.*, G. V. Cooke, County Offices, Lincoln.

EDUCATION, SCOTTISH COUNCIL FOR RESEARCH IN, 46 Moray Place, Edinburgh, 3.

EDUCATION THROUGH ART, SOCIETY FOR, 29 Great James Street, W.C.1.—*Sec.*, Miss F. Bacon.

EDUCATIONAL CENTRES ASSOCIATION, Walthamstow Adult Education Centre, Greenleaf Road, E.17.—*Sec.*, Ray Lamb.

EDUCATIONAL FOUNDATION FOR VISUAL AIDS, 33 Queen Anne Street. W.1.—*Dir.*, Dr. J. A. Harrison.

EDUCATIONAL INSTITUTE OF SCOTLAND (1847), 46 Moray Place, Edinburgh.—*Gen. Sec.*, G. S. Bryden, M.B.E.

EDUCATIONAL RESEARCH IN ENGLAND AND WALES, NATIONAL FOUNDATION FOR, The Mere, Upton Park, Slough, Bucks.; 79 Wimpole Street, W.1.—*Director*, S. Wiseman.

EDUCATIONAL VISITS AND EXCHANGES, CENTRAL BUREAU FOR, 43 Dorset Street, W.1.

ELDERLY INVALIDS FUND AND OLD PEOPLES INFORMATION SERVICE, 10 Fleet Street, E.C.4.

ELECTORAL REFORM SOCIETY (founded 1884 as Proportional Representation Soc.), 6 Chancel Street, S.E.1.—*Dir.*, Miss E. Lakeman.

ELECTRICAL AND ELECTRONICS TECHNICIAN ENGINEERS, INSTITUTION OF (1965), 2 Savoy Hill, W.C.2.—*Sec.*, E. A. Bromfield.

ELECTRICAL ENGINEERS, INSTITUTION OF (1871), Savoy Place, W.C.2.—*Sec.*, Dr. G. F. Gainsborough.

ELECTRONIC AND RADIO ENGINEERS, INSTITUTION OF (1925), 8–9 Bedford Square, W.C.1.—*Sec.*, G. D. Clifford, C.M.G.

EMPLOYMENT FELLOWSHIP (formerly WINTER DISTRESS LEAGUE) (1922), Drayton House, Gordon Street, W.C.1. Assists in the setting-up of sheltered workrooms for the elderly.—*Dir.*, T. H. Oakman.

ENGINEERING DESIGNERS, INSTITUTION OF (1945), 38 Portland Place, W.1.—*Gen. Sec.*, W. E. Walters.

ENGINEERING INDUSTRIES ASSOCIATION (1940), 3–7 Portman Square, W.1.—*Dir.*, Air Cdre. L. K. Jarman, D.F.C.

ENGINEERING INSPECTION, INSTITUTION OF (1919), 10 Chesterfield Street, W.1.—*Sec.*, R. J. Miskin.

ENGINEERS AND SHIPBUILDERS IN SCOTLAND, INSTITUTION OF (1857), 183 Bath Street, Glasgow, C.2.—*Pres.*, W. M. Cormie, O.B.E.; *Sec.*, W. McLaughlin.

ENGINEERS AND SHIPBUILDERS, N.E. COAST INSTITUTION OF (1884), Bolbec Hall, Newcastle on Tyne 1.—*Sec.*, Capt. H. G. S. Brownbill, D.S.C., R.N.

ENGINEERS' GUILD, LTD. (for Chartered Engineers), 400–403 Abbey House, 2 Victoria Street, S.W.1.

ENGINEERS, INSTITUTION OF BRITISH (1928), Windsor House, 46 Victoria Street, S.W.1.—*Sec.*, Mrs. D. Henry.

ENGINEERS, SOCIETY OF (Incorporated) (1854) Abbey House, Victoria Street, S.W.1.—*Sec.*, L. T. Griffith.

ENGLISH ASSOCIATION (1906), 29 Exhibition Road, S.W.7.—*Sec.*, Mrs. K. Sales.

ENGLISH FOLK DANCE AND SONG SOCIETY (1932), Cecil Sharp House, 2 Regent's Park Road, N.W.1.—*Gen. Sec.*, K. F. Goode.

ENGLISH PLACE-NAME SOCIETY (1923).—*Hon. Director*, Prof. K. Cameron, Ph.D., The University, Nottingham.

ENGLISH-SPEAKING UNION OF THE COMMONWEALTH (1918), 37 Charles Street, Berkeley Square, W.1.—*Chairman*, Sir John Benn, Bt.; *Exec. Dir.*, Miss K. Graham, C.B.E.

ENHAM VILLAGE CENTRE (1918), The White House, Enham Alamein, Andover, Hants. For rehabilitation of the physically handicapped.—*Sec.-Gen.*, D. Benwell.

ENTOMOLOGICAL SOCIETY OF LONDON, ROYAL (1833), 41 Queen's Gate, S.W.7.—*Hon. Sec.*, H. L. G. Stroyan.

ENTOMOLOGY, COMMONWEALTH INSTITUTE OF (1913), 56 Queen's Gate, S.W.7.—*Director*, R. G Fennah, Sc.D.

EPILEPSY ASSOCIATION, BRITISH, 3–6 Alfred Place, W.C.1.—*Gen. Sec.*, O. M. Jones.

EPILEPTICS, THE NATIONAL SOCIETY FOR (1892), Chalfont Centre for Epilepsy, Chalfont St. Peter, Bucks.—*Sec.*, R. W. Garratt.

ESPERANTO ASSOCIATION (INC.), BRITISH (1907), 140 Holland Park Avenue, W.11.—*Sec.*, H. E. Platt.

EUGENICS SOCIETY (1907), 69 Eccleston Square, S.W.1.—*Gen. Sec.*, Miss F. B. Schenk.

EVANGELICAL ALLIANCE (1846), 19 Draycott Place, S.W.3.—*Gen. Sec.*, G. J. T. Landreth.

EVANGELICAL LIBRARY, THE, 78A Chiltern Street, W.1.—*Sec.*, Geoffrey Williams.

EXAMINERS UNDER SOLICITORS (SCOTLAND) ACTS (1933–1965), Law Society's Hall, 26–27 Drumsheugh Gardens, Edinburgh.—*Clerk*, R. B. Laurie W.S.

EXECUTIVES ASSOCIATION OF GREAT BRITAIN (1929), 5A Westminster Bridge Road, S.E.1.—*Sec.*, M. C. Waddilove.

EXPORT, INSTITUTE OF, Export House, 14 Hallam Street, W.1.—*Director*, A. J. Day.

EX-SERVICES MENTAL WELFARE SOCIETY (for ex-Service men and women suffering from psychoses and neuroses arising from active or long regular service), 37–39 Thurloc Street, S.W.7.

FABIAN SOCIETY (1884), 11 Dartmouth Street, S.W.1.—*Gen. Sec.*, T. Ponsonby.

FAIRBRIDGE SOCIETY (1909) (formerly Fairbridge Farm Schools), 119–126 Bush House (N.E.), Aldwych.—*Dir.*, Maj.-Gen. W. T. Campbell, C.B.E.

FAIR ISLE BIRD OBSERVATORY TRUST, 21 Regent Terrace, Edinburgh.—*Hon. Sec.*, George Waterston, O.B.E., F.R.S.E.

FAMILY PLANNING ASSOCIATION, 27–35 Mortimer Street, W.1.—*Dir.*, C. Brook.

FAMILY SERVICE UNITS, 207 Old Marylebone Road, N.W.1.—*Dir.*, J. R. Halliwell.

FAMILY WELFARE ASSOCIATION (Founded 1869 as CHARITY ORGANISATION SOCIETY), Denison House, Vauxhall Bridge Road, S.W.1.—*Dir.*, Miss J. Lacey, C.B.E.

FAUNA PRESERVATION SOCIETY (1903).—*Office*, c/o Zoological Society of London, Regent's Park, N.W.1.—*Hon. Sec.*, R. S. R. Fitter.

FAWCETT SOCIETY (1866), 27 Wilfred Street, S.W.1.—*Sec.*, Mrs. J. Kitching.

FEEDING STUFFS TRADE BENEVOLENT SOCIETY OF GREAT BRITAIN (1923), 24 St. Mary Axe, E.C.3.—*Sec.*, R. T. Wheelans.

FELLOWSHIP HOUSES TRUST (Flatlets for the elderly) (1937), Clock House, Byfleet, Surrey.—*Sec.*, L. P. Leech.

FIELD LANE INSTITUTION (1841), Vine Hill, Clerkenwell Road, E.C.1; HOMES FOR OLD PEOPLE; COMMUNITY CENTRE, 32 Cubitt Street, W.C.1.—*Gen. Sec.*, A. C. Ash.

FIRE ENGINEERS, INSTITUTION OF, 148 New Walk, Leicester.—*Gen. Sec.*, D. S. Ramsey.

FIRE PROTECTION ASSOCIATION, Aldermary House, Queen Street, E.C.4.—*Dir.*, N. C. Strother Smith.

FIRE SERVICES ASSOCIATION, BRITISH, 86 London Road, Leicester.—*Gen. Sec.*, Cdr. A. C. Pitman, R.N. (ret.)

FIRE SERVICES ASSOCIATION, NATIONAL (1940), 12–13 Bow Lane, E.C.4.—*Hon. Sec.*, J. J. Ellis.

FIRE SERVICES NATIONAL BENEVOLENT FUND (1943), 4 Altyre Road, Croydon.—*Hon. Organizing Sec.*, R. W. Greene, M.B.E.

FOLKLORE SOCIETY, c/o University College London, Gower Street, W.C.1.—*Hon. Sec.*, Mrs. V. J. Newall.

FORCES HELP SOCIETY AND LORD ROBERTS'S WORKSHOPS (1899), 118–122 Brompton Road, S.W.3. *Comptroller*, Maj. L. F. E. James, M.B.E.

FOREIGN BONDHOLDERS, COUNCIL OF (1873), 68 Queen Street, E.C.4.—*Director-General*, C. E. N. Wyatt, M.C.

FOREIGN PRESS ASSOCIATION IN LONDON, 11 Carlton House Terrace, S.W.1.—*Pres.*, H. A. Van Der Zee.

FORENSIC SCIENCES, BRITISH ACADEMY OF (1959).—*Secretary-General*, F. E. Camps, M.D., 190 Andrewes House, Barbican, E.C.2.

FORESTERS OF GREAT BRITAIN, SOCIETY OF (1925), Newton House, Freuchie, Fife.—*Sec. and Treas.*, A. Foggie.

FORESTRY ASSOCIATION, COMMONWEALTH (1921). Royal Commonwealth Society, Northumberland Avenue, W.C.2.—*Editor-Sec.*, E. W. March.

FORESTRY ASSOCIATION LTD., ENGLISH (1926), The Knowle Nurseries, Caversham Heights, Reading.

FORESTRY SOCIETY OF ENGLAND, WALES AND NORTHERN IRELAND, ROYAL (1882), 102 High Street, Tring.—*Sec.*, P. S. Leathart, M.B.E.

FORESTRY SOCIETY, ROYAL SCOTTISH (1854), 26 Rutland Square, Edinburgh.—*Sec. and Treas.*, W. B. C. Walker.

FRANCO-BRITISH SOCIETY, 1 Old Burlington Street, W.1.—*Sec.*, Miss M. Coate, M.B.E.

FREE CHURCH FEDERAL COUNCIL, 27 Tavistock Square, W.C.1.—*Moderator*, Rev. L. G. Champion; *Gen. Sec.*, Rev. G. A. D. Mann, H.C.F.

FREEMASONS, GRAND LODGE OF SCOTLAND (1736), Freemasons' Hall, Edinburgh.—*Grand Master Mason of Scotland*, D. Liddell-Grainger of Ayton, F.S.A.(Scot.); *Grand Sec.*, E. S. Falconer.

FREEMASONS, UNITED GRAND LODGE OF ENGLAND, Freemasons' Hall, Great Queen Street, W.C.2.—*Grand Master*, H.R.H. the Duke of Kent, G.C.M.G., G.C.V.O.; *Pro Grand Master*, The Earl Cadogan, M.C.; *Deputy Grand Master*, Maj.-Gen. Sir Allan Adair, Bt., K.C.V.O., C.B., D.S.O., M.C.; *Asst. Grand Master*, F. W. R. Douglas; *Grand Wardens*, The Earl of Eglinton and Winton; Lt.-Col. the Lord Burnham; *Grand Chaplain*, The Bishop of Penrith; *Grand Sec.*, J. W. Stubbs.

FREEMEN OF CITY OF LONDON, GUILD OF (1908), 4 Dowgate Hill, E.C.4.—*Master*, C. F. W. Dyer; *Clerk*, D. Reid.

FREIGHT FORWARDERS LTD., INSTITUTE OF, Suffield House, Paradise Road, Richmond, Surrey.

FRESHWATER BIOLOGICAL ASSOCIATION (1932), The Ferry House, Far Sawrey, Ambleside, Westmorland.—*Sec. and Director of Laboratories*, H. C. Gilson, C.B.E., M.A.

FRIEND OF THE CLERGY CORP. (1849), 27a, Medway Street, S.W.1.—*Sec.*, J. M. Terry.

FRIENDLY SOCIETIES, NATIONAL CONFERENCE OF —*Hon. Sec.*, D. H. Roper, O.B.E., Charnwood, Mount Park, Harrow-on-the-Hill, Middx.

FRIENDS OF CATHEDRAL MUSIC (1956), The Faith House, 7 Tufton Street, S.W.1.—*Hon. Gen. Sec.*, N. T. Barnes.

FRIENDS OF THE NATIONAL LIBRARIES, c/o The British Museum, W.C.1.—*Chairman*, The Lord Kenyon; *Hon. Sec.*, T. S. Blakeney.

FRIENDS OF THE POOR & GENTLEFOLK'S HELP (1905), and DISABLED SOLDIERS EMBROIDERY INDUSTRY, 42 Ebury Street, S.W.1.—*Gen. Sec.*, Miss P. M. Lethbridge.

FROEBEL FOUNDATION, NATIONAL, 2 Manchester Square, W.1.—*Sec.*, Miss D. C. Clark.

FUEL, INSTITUTE OF (1927), 18 Devonshire Street, Portland Place, W.1.—*Sec.*, R. Jackson, Ph.D.

FURNITURE HISTORY SOCIETY (1964).—*Hon. Sec.*, Dr. L. Boynton, c/o Dept. of Furniture, Victoria and Albert Museum, S.W.7.

GAME CONSERVANCY (1960), Fordingbridge, Hants.—*Dir.*, C. L. Coles.

GARDENERS' ROYAL BENEVOLENT SOCIETY (1839), Palace Gate, Hampton Court, East Molesey, Surrey.—*Sec.*, W. J. Hayward.

GAS ENGINEERS, INSTITUTION OF (1863), 17 Grosvenor Crescent, S.W.1.—*Sec.*, A. G. Higgins.

GEMMOLOGICAL ASSOCIATION OF GREAT BRITAIN (1931), St. Dunstan's House, Carey Lane, E.C.2.—*Sec.*, G. F. Andrews.

GENEALOGICAL RESEARCH SOCIETY, IRISH.—*Hon. Sec.*, Mrs. L. Rosbottom, 82 Eaton Square, S.W.1.

GENEALOGISTS AND RECORD AGENTS, ASSOCIATION OF (1968).—*Sec.*, G. B. Greenwood, 2 Burhill Road, Walton on Thames, Surrey.

GENEALOGISTS, SOCIETY OF (1911), 37 Harrington Gardens, S.W.7.—*Sec.*, Mrs. C. M. Mackay.

GENERAL PRACTITIONERS, ROYAL COLLEGE OF (1952), 14 Princes Gate, S.W.7.—*Sec.*, J. Wood, D.S.C.

GENTLEPEOPLE, GUILD OF AID FOR (1904), 280 Earls Court Road, S.W.5.—*Sec.*, Miss M. R. Scott.

GEOGRAPHICAL ASSOCIATION, 343 Fulwood Road, Sheffield.—*Joint Hon. Secs.*, W. R. A. Ellis; S. Gregory.

GEOGRAPHICAL SOCIETY, ROYAL (1830), Kensington Gore, S.W.7.—*Pres.*, The Lord Shackleton, P.C., O.B.E.; *Hon. Secs.*, Prof. W. R. Mead; Dr. G. C. L. Bertram; *Hon. Foreign Sec.*, Prof. M. J. Wise, M.C.; *Hon. Treas.*, Sir Duncan Cumming, K.B.E., C.B.; *Director and Sec.*, L. P. Kirwan, C.M.G., T.D.; *Keeper of the Map Room*, Brig. R. A. Gardiner, M.B.E.; *Librarian*, G. S. Dugdale.

GEOGRAPHICAL SOCIETY, MANCHESTER (1884), 16 St. Mary's Parsonage, Manchester.—*Sec.*, Mrs. A. Wood.

GEOGRAPHICAL SOCIETY, ROYAL SCOTTISH (1884). 10 Randolph Crescent, Edinburgh 3.—*Sec.*, D. G. Moir.

GEOLOGICAL SOCIETY (1807), Burlington House, Piccadilly, W.1.—*Pres.*, Prof. W. A. Deer, Ph.D., F.R.S.; *Secs.*, H. W. Ball, Ph.D.; W. W. Bishop, Ph.D.; Prof. W. S. Pitcher, D.SC.; *Foreign Sec.*, Prof. D. Williams, D.SC., Ph.D.; *Exec. Sec.*, D. G. Clayton.

GEOLOGISTS' ASSOCIATION.—*Hon. Gen. Sec.*, F. H. Moore, B.SC., Ph.D., F.G.S., 278 Fir Tree Road, Epsom, Surrey.

GEORGIAN GROUP (1937), 2 Chester Street, S.W.1.

GIFTED CHILDREN, NATIONAL ASSOCIATION FOR (1966), 27 John Adam Street, W.C.2.—*Dir.*, Brig. A. C. E. Devereux.

GILBERT AND SULLIVAN SOCIETY.—*Hon. Sec.*, Miss C. Lambert, 273 Northfield Avenue, W.5.

GIRL GUIDES ASSOCIATION.—An organization founded by the first Lord Baden-Powell as a sister movement to the Scouts and incorporated by Royal Charter in 1922. In 1971 the total membership in Great Britain and Northern Ireland was 744,509 and the world membership was over 6,000,000 in 87 countries. *Commonwealth Headquarters*, 17-19 Buckingham Palace Road, S.W.1.

GIRLS' BRIGADE, THE, Brigade House, 8 Parsons Green, S.W.6.—*Brigade Sec. for Eng. & Wales*, Miss M. I. Taylor.

GIRLS' FRIENDLY SOCIETY AND TOWNSEND FELLOWSHIP (1875), Townsend House, Greycoat Place, S.W.1.

GIRLS OF THE REALM GUILD (1900).—Educational grants towards schooling or initial training of single girls. Applications before March for ensuing academic year to: *Sec.*, Mrs. L. Jennens, Wistaria, Church Street, Chiswick W.4.

GIRLS' VENTURE CORPS, 33 St. George Drive, S.W.1. A uniformed youth movement for girls.

GLASS TECHNOLOGY, SOCIETY OF (1916), 20 Hallam Gate Road, Sheffield.—*Hon. Sec.*, T. S. Busby.

GORDON BOYS' SCHOOL (1885), West End, Woking.—*Headmaster*, G. Leadbeater.

GORDON SMITH INSTITUTE FOR SEAMEN (INCORPORATED) (1820) (Gordon Smith Seamen's Club), 96 Paradise Street, Liverpool, 1.—*Sec. and Supt.*, N. A. Williams,

GRAPHIC ARTISTS, SOCIETY OF (1919), 17 Carlton House Terrace, S.W.1.—*Sec.*, M. Bradshaw.

GREATER LONDON RED CROSS BLOOD TRANSFUSION SERVICE (1921), 4 Collingham Gardens, S.W.5 [01-373-1056/7]. Hours, 9 a.m. to 10 p.m. every day.

GRENFELL ASSOCIATION OF GREAT BRITAIN AND IRELAND, P.O. Box 349, Hope House, 45 Great Peter Street, S.W.1. For medical and social work among the fishermen of Labrador and N. Newfoundland.—*Sec.*, Miss S. A. Yates.

GULBENKIAN FOUNDATION, see CALOUSTE.

HANSARD SOCIETY FOR PARLIAMENTARY GOVERNMENT (1944), 162 Buckingham Palace Road, S.W.1.—*Dir.*, E. Macalester.

HARLEIAN SOCIETY (1869), Ardon House, Mill Lane, Godalming, Surrey.—*Hon. Sec.*, J. P. Heming.

HARVEIAN SOCIETY OF LONDON.—*Hon. Sec.*, H. White, F.R.C.S., 11 Chandos Street, Cavendish Square, W.1.

HEADMASTERS' CONFERENCE. See p. 539.

HEAD MASTERS, INCORPORATED ASSOCIATION OF, 29 Gordon Square, W.C.1.—*Pres.*, (1971), L. H. Shave; *Joint Hon. Secs.*, H. Anderson; D. P. M. Michael; *Hon. Treas.*, J. S. Robinson; *Sec.*, R. St. J. Pitts-Tucker; *Deputy Sec.*, B. C. Harvey.

HEAD MISTRESSES ASSOCIATION OF, 29 Gordon Square, W.C.1.—*President*, Miss J. R. Glover; *Sec.*, Miss L. Spalding.

HEADMISTRESSES OF PREPARATORY SCHOOLS, ASSOCIATION OF.—*Hon. Sec.*, Miss M. Barclay, Leelands School, Walmer, Kent.

HEAD TEACHERS, NATIONAL ASSOCIATION OF.—*Gen. Sec.*, R. J. Cook, Maxwelton House, 41-43 Boltro Road, Haywards Heath, Sussex.

HEALTH EDUCATION COUNCIL, THE (1927), Middlesex House, Ealing Road, Wembley, Middlesex.—*Dir.-Gen.*, W. T. Jones.

HEALTH EDUCATION, INSTITUTE OF.—*Sec.*, F. St. D. Rowntree, 35 Victoria Road, Sheffield.

HEALTH, GUILD OF (1904), Edward Wilson House, 26 Queen Anne Street, W.1.—*Chairman*, Rev. A. B. Clark.

HEALTH SERVICE ADMINISTRATORS, INSTITUTE OF (1902), 75 Portland Place, W.1.— *Sec.*, J. F. Milne.

HEART FOUNDATION, BRITISH (1963), 57 Gloucester Place, W.1.—*Dir.-Gen.*, Brig. E. B. W. Cardiff, C.B., C.B.E.

HEATING AND VENTILATING ENGINEERS, INSTITUTION OF (1897), 49 Cadogan Square, S.W.1.—*Sec.*, B. A. Hodges, B.A.

HELLENIC STUDIES, SOCIETY FOR THE PROMOTION OF (1879), 31-34 Gordon Square, W.C.1.—*Pres.*, Prof. K. J. Dover, F.B.A.; *Hon. Sec.*, Prof. R. P. Winnington-Ingram, F.B.A.

HENRY GEORGE SCHOOL OF SOCIAL SCIENCE, 177 Vauxhall Bridge Road, S.W.1.—*Dir. of Studies*, V. H. Blundell.

HERALDIC AND GENEALOGICAL STUDIES, INSTITUTE OF (1961), 81-82 Northgate, Canterbury, Kent.—*Dir.*, C. R. Humphery-Smith.

HERALDRY SOCIETY, THE (1947), 28 Museum Street, W.C.1.—*Sec.*, Maj. J. C. Riley.

HIGHWAY ENGINEERS, INSTITUTION OF (1930), 14 Queen Anne's Gate, S.W.1.—*Sec.*, M. J. Hall.

HISPANIC COUNCIL (1943), Canning House, 2 Belgrave Square, S.W.1.—*Dir. Gen.*, S. M. Mackenzie, C.B.E.

HISTORIC AND ARTISTIC WORKS, INTERNATIONAL INSTITUTE FOR CONSERVATION OF, 608 Grand Buildings, Trafalgar Square, W.C.2.—*Pres.*, A. E. Werner; *Sec. Gen.*, N. Brommelle.

HISTORICAL ASSOCIATION (1906), 59A Kennington Park Road, S.E.11.—*Hon. Sec.*, H. L. Freakes.

HISTORICAL SOCIETY, ROYAL (1868), University College, London, Gower Street, W.C.1.—*Pres.*, R. W. Southern, D.Litt., F.B.A.; *Sec.*, A. G. Watson, F.S.A.

HISTORY OF SCIENCE, BRITISH SOCIETY FOR THE.—*Pres.*, W. P. D. Wightman; *Hon. Sec.*, Dr. M. P. Earles, 393 Cowley Road, Oxford.

HOMELESS CHILDREN'S AID AND ADOPTION SOCIETY, and F. B. Meyer Children's Home (1920), 54 Grove Avenue, Muswell Hill, N.10.—*Gen. Sec.*, Rev. R. H. Johnson.

HONG KONG ASSOCIATION (1961), 18 Diamond House, Hatton Garden, E.C.1.—*Sec.*, E. S. Bush.

HORATIAN SOCIETY (1933).—*Hon. Sec.*, Mrs. S. Templeman, Manor Heath, Knowl Hill, The Hockering, Woking, Surrey.

HOROLOGICAL INSTITUTE, BRITISH (1858), 35 Northampton Square, E.C.1.—*Sec.*, F. West, M.B.E., F.R.A.S.

HOROLOGICAL SOCIETY, ANTIQUARIAN (1953), 35 Northampton Square, Clerkenwell, E.C.1.—*Hon. Sec.*, J. C. Stevens.

HORTICULTURAL ADVISORY BUREAU, INTERNATIONAL, Arkley Manor, Arkley, nr. Barnet, Herts.—*Dir.*, W. E. Shewell-Cooper, M.B.E., D. Litt.

HOSPITAL FEDERATION, INTERNATIONAL (1947), The Hospital Centre, 24 Nutford Place, W.1.—*Dir. Gen.*, D. G. H. Hawes.

HOSPITALS CONTRIBUTORY SCHEMES ASSOCIATION, BRITISH (1948), 87 Lord Street, Liverpool 2.—*Hon. Sec.*, R. G. Whitehead.

HOSPITAL SATURDAY FUND THE (1873).—*Head Office*, 192-198 Vauxhall Bridge Road, S.W.1.—*Sec.*, Miss I. Gleeson.

HOSPITAL SAVING ASSOCIATION, THE, 30 Lancaster Gate, W.2.—*Gen. Sec.*, Air Vice-Marshal A. A. Case, C.B., C.B.E.

HOTELS AND RESTAURANTS ASSOCIATION, BRITISH, 20 Upper Brook Street, W.1.

HOUSE OF HOSPITALITY LTD., Holy Cross Priory, Cross-in-Hand, Heathfield, Sussex. Fourteen homes for old people.—*Sec.*, Sister Mary Garson.

HOUSE OF ST. BARNABAS IN SOHO (House of Charity for Distressed Women in London) (1846), 1 Greek Street, Soho Square, W.1.

HOUSECRAFT (EMPLOYMENT AND TRAINING) LTD., NATIONAL INSTITUTE FOR, Boston Manor House, Boston Manor Road, Brentford, Middlesex.

HOUSING AID SOCIETY, CATHOLIC (1956), 189a Old Brompton Road, S.W.5.—*Hon. Sec.*, The Lord Hylton.

HOUSING AND TOWN PLANNING COUNCIL, NATIONAL (1900), 11 Green Street, W.1.—*Dir.*, F. J. Berry.

HOUSING ASSOCIATION FOR OFFICERS' FAMILIES (1916), The Manor House, 341 London Road, Mitcham, Surrey.—*Gen. Sec.*, R. Davis.

HOUSING MANAGERS, INSTITUTE OF, Victoria House, Southampton Row, W.C.1.—*Sec.*, H. Key.

HOWARD LEAGUE FOR PENAL REFORM (1866), 125 Kennington Park Road, S.E.11. For the advancement of knowledge of constructive penal and social policies.—*Dir.*, M. Wright.

HUGUENOT SOCIETY OF LONDON (1885), c/o Barclays Bank, Ltd., 1 Pall Mall East, S.W.1.—*Hon. Sec.*, Miss I. Scouloudi, M.SC., F.S.A., F.R.Hist.S.

HUNTERIAN SOCIETY.—*Secs.*, A. Kingley Brown, M.B.E., F.R.C.S., 52 King's End, Ruislip, Middx; D. D. L. Woolf, 2 The Green, Woodford Green, Essex.

HUNTERS' IMPROVEMENT AND NATIONAL LIGHT HORSE BREEDING SOCIETY (1885), 17 Devonshire Street, W.1.—*Sec.*, G. W. Evans.

ILLUMINATING ENGINEERING SOCIETY (1909), York House, Westminster Bridge Road, S.E.1.—*Sec.*, G. F. Cole.

INCOME TAX PAYERS' SOCIETY, 5 Plough Place, Fetter Lane, E.C.4.—*Dir.*, E. C. L. Hulbert-Powell.

INDEXERS, SOCIETY OF, c/o Barclays Bank, 1 Pall Mall East, S.W.1.—*Hon. Sec.*, Miss P. M. Trew.

INDIA, PAKISTAN AND CEYLON, ROYAL SOCIETY FOR (1966), 3 Temple Chambers, Temple Avenue, E.C.4.—*Hon. Sec.*, J. W. N. Baldock.

INDUSTRIAL ARTISTS AND DESIGNERS, SOCIETY OF (1930), 12 Carlton House Terrace, S.W.1.—*Sec.*, G. V. Adams.

INDUSTRIAL CHRISTIAN FELLOWSHIP (1877), St. Katharine Cree Church, Leadenhall Street, E.C.3.—*Gen. Sec.*, Rev. N. F. P. Brown.

INDUSTRIAL CO-PARTNERSHIP ASSOCIATION (1884), 60 Buckingham Gate, S.W.1.—*Sec.*, Mrs. I. S. Ramsey, M.B.E.

INDUSTRIAL MARKETING RESEARCH ASSOCIATION.—*Admin. Sec.*, 28 Bore Street, Lichfield, Staffs.

INDUSTRIAL SAFETY OFFICERS, INSTITUTION OF (1953), 23 Queen Square, W.C.1.—*Sec.*, W. H. Welstead.

INDUSTRIAL SOCIETY, THE (1918), Robert Hyde House, 48 Bryanston Square, W.1.—*Dir.*, W. J. P. M. Garnett, C.B.E.; *Sec.*, D. Fazakerley.

INLAND WATERWAYS ASSOCIATION LTD., 114 Regent's Park Road, N.W.1.—*Gen. Sec.*, R. W. Shopland.

INNER WHEEL CLUBS IN GREAT BRITAIN AND IRELAND, ASSOCIATION OF (1934), Berners Hotel, Berners Street, W.1.—*Sec.*, Miss J. Dobson.

INSTITUTIONAL MANAGEMENT ASSOCIATION INCORPORATED (1960), Swinton House, 324 Gray's Inn Road, W.C.1.—*Sec.*, B. H. Catchpole.

INSURANCE AGENTS, CORPORATION OF (1906), 63 Gt. Cumberland Place, W.1.—*Sec.*, G. Leigh.

INSURANCE ASSOCIATION, BRITISH (1917), Aldermary House, Queen Street, E.C.4.—*Dir.*, R. T. D. Wilmot.

INSURANCE INSTITUTE, CHARTERED (1897), 20 Aldermanbury, E.C.2.—*Sec.*, D. C. McMurdie.

INTERNATIONAL LAW ASSOCIATION (1873), 3 Paper Buildings, Temple, E.C.4.—*Chairman*, The Lord Wilberforce, P.C., C.M.G., O.B.E.; *Sec.-Gen.*, J. B. Edwards.

INTERNATIONAL POLICE ASSOCIATION (British Section).—*National Headquarters*, 1 Fox Road, West Bridgford, Nottingham.—*Sec.-Gen.*, K. Robinson.

INTERNATIONAL SHIPPING FEDERATION (1909), 146–150 Minories, E.C.3.—*President*, R. A. Huskisson; *Gen. Manager*, J. K. Rice-Oxley; *Sec.*, J. Lusted.

INTERNATIONAL SOCIETY FOR THE PROTECTION OF ANIMALS (1959), *Headquarters*, 106 Jermyn Street, S.W.1.—*Exec. Dir.*, T. H. Scott.

INTERNATIONAL STUDENTS TRUST (1962), 1–6 Park Crescent, W.1.—*Chairman*, The Duke of Grafton; *Dir.*, H. A. Shaw, O.B.E.

INTERNATIONAL UNION FOR LAND VALUE TAXATION AND FREE TRADE, 177 Vauxhall Bridge Road, S.W.1.—*Sec.*, V. H. Blundell.

INTERNATIONAL VOLUNTARY SERVICE (1920), 91 High Street, Harlesden, N.W.10.

INTER-PARLIAMENTARY UNION. *See* p. 317.

INVALID CHILDREN'S AID ASSOCIATION (LONDON), INCORPORATED (1888), 126 Buckingham Palace Road, S.W.1.—Family social work, 4 special schools, World Blind Centre, information service on all problems connected with child handicap.—*Gen. Sec.*, Miss E. Hilton.

INVALIDS-AT-HOME (1966).—*Hon. Sec.*, Mrs. J. Pierce, 23 Farm Avenue, N.W.2. Helps seriously disabled people living at home.

IRISH LINEN MERCHANTS' ASSOCIATION (1872), Lambeg, Lisburn, N. Ireland.—*Sec.*, E. O. L. Seccombe.

IRISH SOCIETY, THE HONOURABLE THE (1613), Irish Chamber, Guildhall Yard, E.C.2.—*Sec.*, E. H. Shackcloth; *Gen. Agent and Solicitor (Ireland)*, Peter W. Dickson.

IRON AND STEEL INSTITUTE (1869), 39 Victoria Street, S.W.1.—*Sec.*, A. Post, T.D.

JAPAN ASSOCIATION (1950), 18 Diamond House, Hatton Garden, E.C.1.

JAPAN SOCIETY OF LONDON (1891), 630 Grand Buildings, Trafalgar Square, W.C.2.—*Hon. Sec.*, Mrs. E. F. Dobson.

JERUSALEM AND THE EAST MISSION (1887), 12 Warwick Square, S.W.1.—*Gen. Sec.*, J. B. Wilson.

JEWISH ASSOCIATION FOR THE PROTECTION OF GIRLS, WOMEN AND CHILDREN (administered by the Jewish Welfare Board) (1885).

JEWISH WELFARE BOARD (1859), Lionel Cohen House, 74A Charlotte Street, W.1.

JEWISH HISTORICAL SOCIETY OF ENGLAND, Mocatta Library, University College, W.C.1.—*Hon. Sec.*, E. Ettinghausen, 33 Seymour Place, W.1.

JEWISH RELIGIOUS EDUCATION, CENTRAL COUNCIL OF, Woburn House, Upper Woburn Place, W.C.1.—*Sec.*, S. Cohen.

JEWISH YOUTH, ASSOCIATION FOR (1899), 33 Henriques Street, E.1.—*Gen. Sec.*, Michael Goldstein, M.B.E.

JEWS, LONDON SOCIETY FOR PROMOTING CHRISTIANITY AMONGST THE (1809), 16 Lincoln's Inn Fields, W.C.2.—*Secs.*, Rev. W. F. Barker; Rev. J. Ayre.

JEWS AND CHRISTIANS, LONDON SOCIETY OF (1927), 28 St. John's Wood Road, N.W.8.—*President*, The Dean of Westminster; *Joint Chairmen*, Rabbi Leslie I. Edgar, M.A., D.D.; The Ven. E. F. Carpenter, Ph.D., M.A., D.D.; *Sec.*, Mrs. E. Nathan.

JOHN INNES INSTITUTE (1910), Coiney Lane, Norwich.—*Director*, Prof. R. Markham, Ph.D., F.R.S.

JOHNSON SOCIETY OF LONDON (1928).—*Hon. Sec.*, A. G. Dowdeswell, 92 St. Paul's Road, N.1.

JOURNALISTS, THE INSTITUTE OF, 2–4 Tudor Street, E.C.4.—*Gen. Sec.*, R. F. Farmer.

JUSTICES' CLERKS' SOCIETY (1839).—*Hon. Sec.*, J. B. Horsman, 32 Chapel Lane, Wigan, Lancs.

KEEP BRITAIN TIDY GROUP (1954), 76 Strand, W.C.2.—*Dir. Gen.*, D. J. Lewis.

KING EDWARDS' HOSPITAL FUND FOR LONDON (1897), 14 Palace Court, W.2.—A charity which uses its annual income to help hospitals improve the effectiveness and efficiency of their service to patients. The Fund divides its income between several major activities: making grants to hospitals both within and outside the National Health Service but confined to those in or serving the Greater London Area; providing education for hospital staffs through its College of Hospital Management; sponsoring experiment and enquiry and providing information through its various experts and through the Hospital Centre; providing the special service of the Emergency Bed Service.—*Chairman of Management Committee*, The Lord Hayter; *Treasurer*, A. H. Carnwath; *Secretary*, G. A. Phalp.

KING GEORGE'S FUND FOR SAILORS (1917), 1 Chesham Street, S.W.1 (the central fund for the Marine Benevolent Institutions in the Commonwealth). About £250,000 is given annually to Marine Benevolent Institutions, working for the Royal Navy, the Merchant Navy and Fishing Fleets.—*Gen. Sec.*, Capt. l. M. Clegg, R.N.

KING GEORGE'S JUBILEE TRUST, 166 Piccadilly, W.1.—Inaugurated in 1935 in commemoration of the Silver Jubilee of King George V. Its objects are the advancement of the physical, mental and spiritual welfare of the younger generation.—*Sec.*, D. S. Miller, C.B.E.

KING'S FUND THE (1940), Ivybridge House, 1 Adam Street, W.C. 2.—To give temporary assistance in directions which are beyond the province of State liability to war-disabled members of the Navy, Army, Air Force, Auxiliary Services, Home Guard, Merchant Navy and Civil Defence organizations and to widows, children and other dependants of those who lost their lives through war service.

LABOUR PARTY, Transport House, Smith Square, S.W.1.—*Gen. Sec.*, Sir Herbert Nicholas, O.B.E.

LADIES IN REDUCED CIRCUMSTANCES, SOCIETY FOR THE ASSISTANCE OF (1886), Lancaster House, Malvern, Worcs.—*Sec.*, Mrs. A. R. White.

LANCASTRIANS IN LONDON, ASSOCIATION OF (1892), Burnley House, 129 Kingsway, W.C.2.—*Hon. Sec.*, W. H. Butler.

LANDSCAPE ARCHITECTS, INSTITUTE OF (1929), 12 Carlton House Terrace, S.W.1.—*Sec.*, Miss A. C. Dale.

LAND-VALUE TAXATION LEAGUE, 177 Vauxhall Bridge Road, S.W.1.—*Pres.*, V. G. Saldji.

LANDS VALUATION ASSESSORS OF SCOTLAND, ASSOCIATION OF.—*Sec.*, S. A. Jack, County Buildings, Hamilton, Lanarks.

LAW AGENTS SOCIETY, SCOTTISH.—*Sec.*, J. W. Barty, 61 High Street, Dunblane, Perthshire.

LAW REPORTING FOR ENGLAND AND WALES, INCORPORATED COUNCIL OF (1865), 3 Stone Buildings, Lincoln's Inn, W.C.2.

LEAGUE OF THE HELPING HAND, Edgeleys, Manor Farm, Alton, Hants.—*Sec.*, Mrs. L. E. M. Stacey.

LEAGUE OF REMEMBRANCE, 48 Great Ormond Street, W.C.1.—*Hon. Administrator*, Miss M. Marriott, O.B.E.

LEAGUE OF WELLDOERS (incorporated) (1893), 119 & 133 Limekiln Lane, Liverpool, 5.—*Warden and Sec.*, W. J. Horn.

LEATHER AND HIDE TRADES' BENEVOLENT INSTITUTION (1860) 9 St. Thomas Street, S.E.1.—*Sec.*, H. G. Forward.

LEPROSY GUILD (St. Francis) (1895), 20 The Boltons, S.W.10.

LEPROSY MISSION, THE (*formerly* The Mission to Lepers) (1874), 50 Portland Place, W.1.—*Chairman*, Sir Harry Greenfield, C.S.I., C.I.E.; *Gen. Sec.*, G. N. Fox.

LEUKAEMIA RESEARCH FUND (1962), 61 Great Ormond Street, W.C.1.—*Dir.*, G. J. Piller.

LIBERAL CENTRAL ASSOCIATION, 7 Exchange Court, Strand, W.C.2.—*Hon. Sec.*, T. D. Nudds.

LIBERAL PARTY ORGANIZATION, 7 Exchange Court, Strand, W.C.2.—*Head of Organization*, E. Wheeler.

LIBERAL PUBLICATION DEPARTMENT (1887), 7 Exchange Court, Strand, W.C.2.—*Sec.*, Mrs. E. Hill.

LIBRARY ASSOCIATION (1877), Ridgmount Street, W.C.1.—*Sec.*, H. D. Barry.

LIFEBOATS. *See* " ROYAL NATIONAL."

LIFE OFFICES' ASSOCIATION, THE (1889), Aldermary House, Queen Street, E.C.4.—*Dir.*, R. W. Boss.

LINGUISTS, INSTITUTE OF (1910), 91 Newington Causeway, S.E.1.—*Sec.*, G. H. Smith, O.B.E.

LINNEAN SOCIETY OF LONDON, Burlington House, W.1.—*Pres.*, Prof. A. J. E. Cave, M.D., D.SC.; *Treas.*, F. R. Goodenough; *Secs.*, J. P. M. Brenan (*Botany*); Prof. R. D. Purchon, D.SC. (*Zoology*); Dr. Doris M. Kermack (*Editorial*); *Exec. Sec.*, T. O'Grady.

LLOYD'S, Lime Street, E.C.3.—*Chairman* (1971), Sir Henry Mance; *Deputy Chairman*, H. H. T. Hudson; L. R. Dew; *Principal Clerk*, C. G. Wastell; International Insurance Market, Office of *Lloyd's List, Shipping Index, Loading List, etc.*

LLOYD'S PATRIOTIC FUND (1803), Lloyd's Building, 5 Lime Street, E.C.3.—*Sec.*, A. J. Carter.

LLOYD'S REGISTER OF SHIPPING (1760), 71 Fenchurch Street, E.C.3.—*Chairman*, A. C. Grover; *Deputy Chairman and Chairman of the Sub-Committees of Classification*, R. M. Turnbull; *Deputy Chairman and Treas.*, G. Milling; *Executive Director*, C. M. Glover; *Technical Director*, B. Hildrew; *Chief Ship Surveyor*, J. McCallum; *Chief Engineer Surveyor*, J. E. Martin; *Secretary*, J. Huxster; Office of *Lloyd's Register Book, Lloyd's Register of Yachts, etc.*

LOCAL AUTHORITIES, INTERNATIONAL UNION OF (1913), British Section, 36 Old Queen Street, S.W.1.—*Sec.*, R. M. Franklin.

LOCAL GOVERNMENT ADMINISTRATORS, INSTITUTE OF.—*Hon. Sec.*, B. J. N. Gleave, 3 Vermont Close, Clacton-on-Sea, Essex.

LOCAL GOVERNMENT BARRISTERS, SOCIETY OF.—*Hon. Sec.*, N. A. L. Rudd, Clerk of the Council, Tarvin Rural District Council, Tower Wharf, Chester.

LOCAL GOVERNMENT LEGAL SOCIETY.—*Hon. Sec.*, J. B. Chirnside, County Hall, Oxford.

LOMBARD ASSOCIATION (1930), 54 Lombard Street.—*Hon. Sec.*, W. L. Cockburn.

LONDON AND MIDDLESEX PLAYING FIELDS ASSOCIATION (1926), Playfield House, 57B Catherine Place, S.W.1.—*Sec.*, Capt. D. N. Forbes, D.S.C., R.N.(ret.).

LONDON APPRECIATION SOCIETY (1932), 8 Scarsdale Villas, Kensington, W.8. Visits to places of historic and modern interest in and around London.—*Hon. Sec.*, H. L. Bryant Peers.

LONDON BOARD OF CONGREGATIONAL MINISTERS, City Temple, Holborn Viaduct, E.C.1.—*Chairman*, Rev. L. C. K. French; *Sec.*, Rev. J. R. Plowman, M.A.

LONDON BOROUGHS ASSOCIATION (1964), City Hall, Westminster, S.W.1.—*Hon. Sec.*, A. G. Dawtry, C.B.E., T.D. (*Town Clerk of Westminster*).

LONDON CITY MISSION (1835), The Mission House, 6 Eccleston Street, S.W.1.—*Gen. Sec.*, Rev. D. M. Whyte.

LONDON CORNISH ASSOCIATION (1898), *Hon. Gen. Sec.*, N. S. Bunney, 119 Warwick Road, N.11.

LONDON COURT OF ARBITRATION (1892), 69 Cannon Street, E.C.4.—*Chairman*, A. W. Last; *Registrar*, H. F. Hoare.

LONDON DIOCESAN FUND AND LONDON DIOCESAN HOME MISSION, 33 Bedford Square, W.C.1.—*Sec.*, Ven. M. M. Hodgins.

LONDON LIBERAL PARTY, St. Margaret's Mansions, 51–53 Victoria Street, S.W.1.—*Hon. Sec.*, George B. Patterson.

LONDON LIBRARY, THE (1841), 14 St. James's Square, S.W.1.—*Librarian*, S. G. Gillam.

LONDON MISSIONARY SOCIETY, *see* CONGREGATIONAL COUNCIL.

"LONDON OVER THE BORDER" CHURCH FUND (1878), Guy Harlings, New Street, Chelmsford.—*Sec.*, H. J. Matthews.

LONDON PLAYING FIELDS SOCIETY (1891), 45 Denison Road, Vauxhall Bridge Road, S.W.1.

LONDON SOCIETY, THE (1912), 3 Dean's Yard, S.W.1.—*Hon. Sec.*, Miss E. B. Ashford.

LONDON SOLICITORS AND FAMILIES ASSOCIATION (formerly LAW ASSOCIATION) (1817), Maesgwyn, 52 Orchard Close, Normandy, Guildford, Surrey.—*Sec.*, K. M. Hugh-Jones.

LONDON TOPOGRAPHICAL SOCIETY, 50 Grove Lane, S.E.5.—*Hon. Sec.*, S. N. P. Marks.

LORD KITCHENER NATIONAL MEMORIAL FUND. *See* p. 514.

LORD MAYOR TRELOAR TRUST (incorporating Lord Mayor Treloar College and Florence Treloar School). Froyle, nr. Alton, Hants.—*Sec. and Bursar*, B. E. T. Roberts.

LORD'S DAY OBSERVANCE SOCIETY (1831), 55 Fleet Street, E.C.4.—*Gen. Sec.*, H. J. W. Legerton.

LORD'S TAVERNERS, THE, 1 St. James's Street, S.W.1.—*Sec.*, D. A. L. Camm.

LUSO BRAZILIAN COUNCIL (1943), Canning House, 2 Belgrave Square, S.W.1.—*Dir.-Gen.*, S. M. Mackenzie, C.B.E.

MAGISTRATES' ASSOCIATION (1920), 28 Fitzroy Square, W.1.—*Pres.*, The Lord Chancellor; *Sec.*, A. J. Brayshaw, O.B.E.

MALAYSIA-SINGAPORE COMMERCIAL ASSOCIATION INC. (1955), 5th Flr., Grand Buildings, Trafalgar Square, W.C.2.—*Sec.*, W. C. S. Corry, C.B.E.

MALONE SOCIETY (for the study of Early English Drama).—*Hon. Sec.*, Miss K. M. Lea, Lady Margaret Hall, Oxford.

MANAGEMENT, BRITISH INSTITUTE OF, Parker Street, W.C.2.—*Dir.-Gen.*, H. J. Marsh, C.B.E., D.SC.

MANAGEMENT RESEARCH GROUPS LTD. (1926), Mansfield House, 376 Strand, W.C.2.—*Dir.*, Brig. W. R. Holman.

MARINE BIOLOGICAL ASSOCIATION OF THE U.K. (1884), The Laboratory, Citadel Hill, Plymouth.—*Sec. to Council and Director of Plymouth Laboratory*, J. E. Smith, SC.D., F.R.S.

MARINE ENGINEERS, INSTITUTE OF (1889), Memorial Building, 76 Mark Lane, E.C.3.—*Dir. and Sec.*, J. Stuart Robinson.

MARINE SOCIETY (1756), Hanway House, Clark's Place, E.C.2. Ensures as far as possible that no boy is prevented by lack of means from going to sea in the capacity for which he is suited. Advice on training and entry of boys for the sea services.

MARKET AUTHORITIES, NATIONAL ASSOCIATION OF BRITISH, Cattle Market, Gloucester.

MARKETING, INSTITUTE OF (1911), Marketing House, Richbell Place, Lamb's Conduit Street, W.C.1.—*Sec.*, D. A. Chatt.

MARK MASTER MASONS, GRAND LODGE OF (1856), Mark Masons' Hall, 40 Upper Brook Street, W.1.—*Grand Master*, The Lord Harris, M.C.; *Deputy Grand Master*, The Earl of Stradbroke; *Grand Sec.*, Lt.-Col. Hon. M. G. Edwardes, M.B.E.

MASONIC BENEVOLENT INSTITUTION, ROYAL (1842), 20 Great Queen Street, W.C.2.—*Sec.*, Sqn.-Ldr. D. A. Lloyd, D.F.C., D.F.M.

MASONIC BENEVOLENT INSTITUTIONS IN IRELAND; *Masonic Girls' School* (1792); *Masonic Boys' School* (1867); *Victoria Jubilee Masonic Annuity Fund* (1887).—*Sec.*, R. J. Clinton, 19 Molesworth Street, Dublin, 2.

MASONIC DEGREES—ORDER OF THE TEMPLE, Mark Masons' Hall, 40 Upper Brook Street, W.1.—*Grand Master*, The Lord Harris, M.C.; *Great Vice-Chancellor*, Lt.-Col. Hon. M. G. Edwardes, M.B.E.

MASONIC INSTITUTION FOR BOYS, ROYAL (Incorporated) (1798), 26 Great Queen Street, W.C.2—*Sec.*, A. R. Jole.

MASONIC INSTITUTION FOR GIRLS, ROYAL (1788). *Schools*, Rickmansworth and Weybridge; *Offices*, 31 Great Queen Street, W.C.2.—*Sec.*, A. A. Huckle.

MASTER BUILDERS, FEDERATION OF (1941), 33 John Street, W.C.1.—*Sec.*, E. L. E. Whitehead.

MASTERS OF FOXHOUNDS ASSOCIATION (1856), The Elm, Chipping Norton, Oxon.—*Hon. Sec.*, Lt.-Col. J. E. S. Chamberlayne.

MATERNAL AND CHILD WELFARE, NATIONAL ASSOCIATION FOR (1911), Tavistock House (North), Tavistock Square, W.C.1.—*Gen. Sec.*, W. Rice.

MATHEMATICAL ASSOCIATION (1871), 150 Friar Street, Reading.—*Pres.*, B. T. Bellis; *Hon. Secs.*, Miss R. K. Tobias; A. G. Howson.

MATHEMATICAL SOCIETY, LONDON (1865), Burlington House, W.1.—*Hon. Secs.*, D. E. Cohen; S. J. Taylor; J. A. Tyrrell.

MATHEMATICS AND ITS APPLICATIONS, INSTITUTE OF (1964), Maitland House, Warrior Square, Southend, Essex.—*Sec.*, N. Clarke.

MEASUREMENT AND CONTROL, INSTITUTE OF (1944), 20 Peel Street, W.8.—*Sec.*, E. Eden.

MECHANICAL ENGINEERING FEDERATION (1912), 25 Victoria Street, S.W.1.

MECHANICAL ENGINEERS, INSTITUTION OF, 1 Birdcage Walk, S.W.1.—*Pres.*, R. L. Lickley; *Sec.*, K. H. Platt, C.B.E.

MEDICAL AUXILIARIES, THE BOARD OF REGISTRATION of (1936), B.M.A. House, Tavistock Square, W.C.1.—*Sec. and Registrar*, A. E. Vince.

MEDICAL COUNCIL, GENERAL, 44 Hallam Street, W.1.—*Registrars*, M. R. Draper (*General Council of England and Wales*); A. B. Brown, M.C., (*Branch Council for Scotland*), 8 Queen Street, Edinburgh 2; Miss M. Hoolan (*Branch Council for Ireland*), 20 Fitzwilliam Square, Dublin 2.

MEDICAL OFFICERS OF HEALTH, SOCIETY OF (1856), Tavistock House South, W.C.1.—*Pres.*, W. G. Harding; *Sec.*, N. G. T. Taylor.

MEDICAL OFFICERS OF HEALTH, GROUP AND ASSOCIATION OF COUNTY (England and Wales).—*Hon. Sec.*, G. Ramage, M.D., County Health Dept., Martin Street, Stafford.

MEDICAL SOCIETY OF LONDON (1773), 11 Chandos Street, Cavendish Square, W.1.—*Pres.*, H. R. Thompson; *Hon. Sec.*, F. G. Ellis, F.R.C.S.; *Registrar*, Maj. H. R. Mitchell, T.D.

MEDICAL WOMEN'S FEDERATION (1917), Tavistock House (North), Tavistock Square, W.C.1.—*Pres.*, Dame Albertine Winner, D.B.E., M.D., F.R.C.P.; *Hon. Sec.*, Dr. Jean Lawrie.

MEDICO-PSYCHOLOGICAL ASSOCIATION, ROYAL (1841), Chandos House, Queen Anne Street, W.1.—*Hon. Gen. Sec.*, A. B. Monro, M.D., Ph.D.

MEN OF THE TREES (1922), Crawley Down, Crawley, Sussex.

MENTAL AFTER CARE ASSOCIATION (1897), for the care and rehabilitation of those recovering from mental illness.—*Sec.*, Mrs. E. Clifton, 110 Jermyn Street, S.W.1.

MENTAL HEALTH, NATIONAL ASSOCIATION FOR, 39 Queen Anne Street, W.1.—*Gen. Sec.*, Miss M. Applebey, O.B.E.

MENTAL HEALTH RESEARCH FUND (1949), 38 Wigmore Street, W.1.—*Dir.*, Maj.-Gen. C. M. F. Deakin, C.B., C.B.E.

MERCANTILE MARINE MASTERS AND OFFICERS BENEVOLENT FUND, Shipping Federation House, 146 Minories, E.C.3.—*Sec.*, Miss G. E. Lanham.

MERCANTILE MARINE SERVICE ASSOCIATION (1857) (Shipmasters in command). Affiliated to the Officers (Merchant Navy) Federation. Nautilus House, Mariners' Park, Wallasey, Cheshire.— *Gen. Sec.*, W. L. S. Harrison; *London Office*, 133 Whitechapel High Street, E.1.

MERCHANT NAVY WELFARE BOARD (1948), 19 Lancaster Gate, W.2.—*Sec.*, R. E. Haerle.

MERSEY MISSION TO SEAMEN (1857). *Headquarters, Hostel and Registered Office*, Kingston House, James Street, Liverpool 2. Indian and Pakistani Seamen's Clubs at Bootle and Birkenhead.—*Gen. Sec.*, L. M. Robertson.

METALLURGISTS, THE INSTITUTION OF, 17 Belgrave Square, S.W.1.—*Registrar-Sec.*, D. W. Harding.

METALS, INSTITUTE OF (1908), 17 Belgrave Square, S.W.1.—*Pres.*, G. Campbell; *Sec.*, R. E. Moore.

METEOROLOGICAL SOCIETY, ROYAL (1850), Cromwell House, High Street, Bracknell, Berks.— *Pres.*, F. Pasquil, D.Sc.; *Hon. Secs.*, T. J. Chandler, Ph.D.; G. R. R. Benwell.

METHODIST MISSIONARY SOCIETY (1786), 25 Marylebone Road, N.W.1. Income, 1970, £1,299,147.

METROPOLITAN AND CITY POLICE ORPHANS FUND (1870), 30 Hazlewell Road, Putney, S.W.15— *Sec.*, E. R. Hall.

METROPOLITAN HOSPITAL-SUNDAY FUND (1872), Mansion House, E.C., and 18 Queen Victoria Street, E.C.4. In 1970, £32,275 was distributed as maintenance grants and grants for specific purposes to Hospitals and Homes not controlled by the State; £18,550 to State Hospital Boards and Management Committees for the use of their medical and psychiatric social workers; £2,100 to other medical charities.—*Sec.*, Miss V. A. Miles.

METROPOLITAN PUBLIC GARDENS ASSOCIATION (1882), 58 Denison House, 296 Vauxhall Bridge Road, S.W.1.

MIDDLE EAST ASSOCIATION (1961), Bury House, 33 Bury Street, S.W.1.—*Dir.-Gen.*, Sir Roger Allen, K.C.M.G.

MIDWIVES, ROYAL COLLEGE OF (1881), 15 Mansfield Street, W.1.—*Gen. Sec.*, Miss B. D. Mee.

MIGRAINE TRUST (1965), 23 Queen Square, W.C.1. —*Dir.*, D. R. Mullis.

MILITARY HISTORICAL SOCIETY.—*Hon. Sec.*, J. Gaylor, Duke of York's Headquarters, Chelsea, S.W.3.

MINERALOGICAL SOCIETY (1876).—*Pres.* (1970), M. H. Hey; *Hon. Gen. Sec.*, A. C. Bishop, Ph.D., 41 Queen's Gate, S.W.7.

MINIATURE PAINTERS, SCULPTORS AND GRAVERS, ROYAL SOCIETY OF (1895), 17 Carlton House Terrace, S.W.1.—*Pres.*, S. Shepherd, O.B.E.; *Sec.*, C. de Winter.

MINIATURISTS, SOCIETY OF (1895), R. W. S. Galleries, 26 Conduit Street, W.1.—*Sec.*, M. Fry.

MINING AND METALLURGY, INSTITUTION OF (1892), 44 Portland Place, W.1.—*Pres.*, M. G. Fleming; *Sec.*, B. W. Kerrigan.

MINING ENGINEERS, THE INSTITUTION OF (1889), 3 Grosvenor Crescent, S.W.1.—*Pres.* (1971–72), E. J. Kimmins; *Sec.*, G. R. Strong.

MINING INSTITUTE OF SCOTLAND, c/o National Coal Board, Green Park, Greenend, Edinburgh 9.— *Sec.*, E. R. Rodger.

MISSIONS TO SEAMEN, THE, AND ST. ANDREW'S WATERSIDE CHURCH MISSION FOR SAILORS, St. Michael Paternoster Royal, College Hill, E.C.4.—*Gen. Sec.*, Rev. T. P. Kerfoot, M.B.E.

MODERN CHURCHMEN'S UNION (1898), for the Advancement of Liberal Religious Thought— *Pres.*, Ven. E. F. Carpenter, Ph.D., D.D.; *Hon. Sec.*, Rev. F. E. Compton, Caynham Vicarage, Ludlow, Salop.

MODERN LANGUAGE ASSOCIATION, 2 Manchester Square, W.1.—*Hon. Sec.*, S. R. Ingram.

MONUMENTAL BRASS SOCIETY (1887), *Hon. Sec.*, J. Coales, 90 High Street, Newport Pagnell, Bucks.

MORAVIAN MISSIONS, LONDON ASSOCIATION IN AID OF (1817), 639 Grand Buildings, Trafalgar Square, W.C.2.—*Sec.*, W. J. Enright.

MORDEN COLLEGE (1695), Blackheath, S.E.3. *Clerk to the Trustees*, M. S. Graham, M.B.E.

(WILLIAM) MORRIS SOCIETY AND KELMSCOTT FELLOWSHIP (1918).—*Hon. Sec.*, R. C. H. Briggs, 25 Lawn Crescent, Kew, Surrey.

MOTOR INDUSTRY, THE INSTITUTE OF THE (1920), Fanshaws, Brickendon, Hertford.—*Dir.*, E. V. Tipper.

MOUNTBATTEN (EDWINA) TRUST, 1 Grosvenor Crescent, S.W.1.

MULTIPLE SCLEROSIS SOCIETY, 4 Tachbrook Street, S.W.1.—*Gen. Sec.*, A. C. Waine, M.B.E., T.D.

MUNICIPAL CORPORATIONS, ASSOCIATION OF (1873), 36 Old Queen Street, S.W.1.—*Sec.*, J. C. Swaffield, C.B.E., R.D.

MUNICIPAL ENGINEERS, INSTITUTION OF (1873), 25 Eccleston Square, S.W.1.—*Sec.*, A. Banister, O.B.E., B.SC.

MUNICIPAL TREASURERS AND ACCOUNTANTS, INSTITUTE OF (1885).—*Sec.*, M. F. Stonefrost, 1 Buckingham Place, S.W.1.

MUSEUMS ASSOCIATION (1889), 87 Charlotte Street, W.1.—*Sec.*, Miss B. Capstick.

MUSICIANS' BENEVOLENT FUND, St. Cecilia's House, 16 Ogle Street, W.1. *Convalescent Home*, Westgate-on-Sea.

MUSICIANS, INCORPORATED SOCIETY OF (1882), 48 Gloucester Place, W.1.—*Gen. Sec.*, D. H. R. Brearley.

MUSICIANS OF GREAT BRITAIN, ROYAL SOCIETY OF (1738), 10 Stratford Place, W.1.—*Hon. Treas.*, E. Cruft, M.V.O., O.B.E.

MUSIC SOCIETIES, NATIONAL FEDERATION OF (1935), 29 Exhibition Road, S.W.7.—*Sec.*, Capt. T. A. K. Maunsell, R.N. (*ret.*).

MUTUAL HOUSEHOLDS ASSOCIATION LTD., 41 Kingsway, W.C.2.—*Hon. Sec.*, Mrs. J. McMillan.

MYCOLOGICAL SOCIETY, BRITISH.—*Sec.*, R. L. Lucas, M.B.E., Ph.D., Keble College, Oxford.

NATIONAL ADULT SCHOOL UNION (1899), Drayton House, Gordon Street, W.C.1.—*Sec.*, W. A. Hall.

NATIONAL ALLIANCE OF PRIVATE TRADERS (1943), 388 Corn Exchange, Hanging Ditch, Manchester 4.

NATIONAL AND UNIVERSITY LIBRARIES, STANDING CONFERENCE OF (1950).—*Hon. Sec.*, R. J. Bates, c/o The Library, University College, P.O. Box 78, Cardiff.

NATIONAL ASSOCIATION FOR THE CARE AND RESETTLEMENT OF OFFENDERS, 125 Kennington Park Road, S.E.11—*Dir.*, R. L. Morrison.

NATIONAL ASSOCIATION OF ESTATE AGENTS (1962), Victoria House, Southampton Row, W.C.1.—*Sec.*, A. R. Taylor.

NATIONAL ASSOCIATION OF FIRE OFFICERS, 5–6 Palace Chambers, Bridge Street, S.W.1.—*Gen. Sec.*, W. R. J. Hitchin.

NATIONAL ASSOCIATION OF PARISH COUNCILS (1947), 100 Great Russell Street, W.C.1.—*Sec.*, C. Arnold-Baker, O.B.E.

NATIONAL BENEVOLENT INSTITUTION (1812), 61 Bayswater Road, W.2.—*Sec.*, Lt.-Col. G. G. Robson.

NATIONAL BIRTHDAY TRUST FUND (1928), 57 Lower Belgrave Street, S.W.1. For Extension of Maternity Services.—*Sec.*, Miss D. V. Riddick, M.B.E.

NATIONAL BOOK LEAGUE (1944), 7 Albemarle Street, W.1.—*Dir.*, M. Goff.

NATIONAL CATTLE BREEDERS' ASSOCIATION, Archer House, 15 Market Place, Ely, Cambs.—*Sec.*, J. A. Taylor.

NATIONAL CHILDREN'S HOME (1869). *Chief Office,* Highbury Park, N.5.—*Principal,* Rev. G. E. Barritt.

NATIONAL CHRISTIAN EDUCATION COUNCIL (*formerly* National Sunday School Union), Robert Denholm House, Nutfield, Redhill, Surrey.

NATIONAL CORPORATION FOR THE CARE OF OLD PEOPLE, Nuffield Lodge, Regent's Park, N.W.1.—*Sec.*, M. R. F. Simson, O.B.E.

NATIONAL COUNCIL OF LABOUR COLLEGES, 10 Mount Boone, Dartmouth, Devon.—*Gen. Sec.*, J. P. M. Millar.

NATIONAL COUNCIL OF SOCIAL SERVICE, 26 Bedford Square, W.C.1.—*Dir.*, J. K. Owens.

NATIONAL COUNCIL OF WOMEN OF GREAT BRITAIN, 36 Lower Sloane Street, S.W.1.—*Gen. Sec.* (vacant).

NATIONAL FEDERATION OF OLD AGE PENSIONS ASSOCIATIONS, 91 Preston New Road, Blackburn, Lancs.—*Sec.*, Mrs. M. Green.

NATIONAL FEDERATION OF OWNER-OCCUPIERS' AND OWNER-RESIDENTS' ASSOCIATIONS.—*Hon. Sec.*, J. W. Clark, 29 Norview Drive, East Didsbury, Manchester 20.

NATIONAL FEDERATION OF YOUNG FARMERS' CLUBS, Y.F.C. Centre, National Agricultural Centre, Kenilworth, Warwicks.

NATIONAL FUND FOR RESEARCH INTO CRIPPLING DISEASES (1952), Vincent House, Vincent Square, S.W.1.—*Dir.*, D. Guthrie.

NATIONAL MARITIME BOARD (1919), 110 Cannon Street, E.C.4.

NATIONAL MARKET TRADERS' FEDERATION (1899).—*Pres.*, H. Evans; *Gen. Sec.*, J. Coates, 87 Spital Hill, Sheffield 4.

NATIONAL MARRIAGE GUIDANCE COUNCIL, Church Street, Rugby, Warwicks.—*Chief Officer*, N. J. Tyndall.

NATIONAL MONUMENTS RECORD (*incorporating* the National Buildings Record) (1941), Fielden House, 10 Great College Street, S.W.1.—*Curator,* C. Farthing, O.B.E., F.S.A.

NATIONAL PEACE COUNCIL (1908), 29 Great James Street, W.C.1.—*Gen. Sec.*, A. E. Tomlinson.

NATIONAL PURE WATER ASSOCIATION (1960).—*Hon. Sec.*, R. G. J. Maitland Earl, Holcombe House, Oakley, Hants.

NATIONAL SECULAR SOCIETY (1866), 103 Borough High Street, S.E.1.—*Gen. Sec.*, M. Page.

NATIONAL SOCIETY FOR CLEAN AIR (1899), 134–136 North Street, Brighton, Sussex.—*Director,* Rear-Adm. P. G. Sharp, C.B., D.S.C.

NATIONAL SOCIETY FOR PROMOTING RELIGIOUS EDUCATION IN ACCORDANCE WITH THE PRINCIPLES OF THE CHURCH OF ENGLAND (1811), 69 Great Peter Street, S.W.1.—*Gen. Sec.*, Rev. Canon R. T. Holtby.

NATIONAL SOCIETY FOR THE PREVENTION OF CRUELTY TO CHILDREN (1884) (Incorporated), *Headquarters*, 1 Riding House Street, W.1.—*Chairman,* Lady Holland-Martin, O.B.E.; *Treas.*, G. Edmiston; *Director,* Rev. Arthur Morton, O.B.E.

NATIONAL TRUST for places of Historic Interest or Natural Beauty (1895), 42 Queen Anne's Gate, S.W.1.—*Dir. Gen.*, F. A. Bishop, C.B., C.V.O.

NATIONAL TRUST FOR SCOTLAND for places of historic interest or natural beauty (1931), 5 Charlotte Square, Edinburgh 2.—*Sec.*, J. C. Stormonth Darling, M.C., T.D., W.S.

NATIONAL UNION OF STUDENTS, 3 Endsleigh Street, W.C.1.—*Admin. Sec.*, D. G. Metheringham.

NATIONAL VIEWERS' AND LISTENERS' ASSOCIATION.—*Hon. Gen. Sec.*, Mrs. M. Whitehouse, Triangle Farm House, Far Forest, Kidderminster, Worcs.

NATIONAL WOMEN CITIZENS' ASSOCIATION (1918), Incorporating the National Council for Equal Citizenship and Women for Westminster, 83 Denison House, 296 Vauxhall Bridge Road, S.W.1.—*Pres.*, Mrs. M. S. Sprunt; *Gen. Sec.*, Mrs. N. E. Copp.

NATION'S FUND FOR NURSES, 1 Vere Street, W.1.—*Sec.*, Mrs. M. Wynne Williams.

NATURAL RUBBER PRODUCERS' RESEARCH ASSOCIATION (1938), 19 Buckingham Street, Adelphi, W.C.2.—*Sec.*, P. O. Wickens.

NATURE RESERVES, SOCIETY FOR PROMOTION OF (1912).—*Hon. Sec.*, A. E. Smith, O.B.E., The Manor House, Alford, Lincs.

NAUTICAL RESEARCH, SOCIETY FOR (1911), National Maritime Museum, Greenwich, S.E.10.—*Hon. Sec.*, G. P. B. Naish.

NAVAL, MILITARY AND AIR FORCE BIBLE SOCIETY (1780), Radstock House, Eccleston Street, S.W.1. Copies and portions of the Scriptures circulated to the Forces (1970), 193,630.—*Sec.*, J. M. Smith.

NAVAL ARCHITECTS, ROYAL INSTITUTION OF (1860), 10 Upper Belgrave Street, S.W.1.—*Sec.*, P. W. Ayling.

NAVIGATION, INSTITUTE OF, c/o Royal Geographical Society, 1 Kensington Gore, S.W.7.—*Sec.*, M. W. Richey, M.B.E.

NAVY LEAGUE (INC.) (1895), Broadway House, S.W.19.—*Pres.*, The Earl Cairns, K.C.V.O., C.B.; *Dir.-Gen.*, Rear Adm. B. C. Durant, C.B., D.S.O., D.S.C.

NAVY RECORDS SOCIETY, Royal Naval College, Greenwich, S.E.10.—*Hon. Sec.*, Hon. D. Erskine.

NEWCOMEN SOCIETY (1920), for the Study of the History of Engineering and Technology, Science Museum, S.W.7.—*Hon. Sec.*, R. J. Law.

NEW ENGLISH ART CLUB (1886), 17 Carlton House Terrace, S.W.1.—*Sec.*, M. B. Bradshaw.

NEWMAN ASSOCIATION (1942), Newman House, 15 Carlisle Street, W.1.

NEWSPAPER EDITORS, GUILD OF BRITISH (1946), Whitefriars House, Carmelite Street, E.C.4.—*Pres.*, P. H. Harland (*Telegraph and Argus, Bradford*); *Sec.-Treas.*, C. Gordon Page.

NEWSPAPER PRESS FUND (1864), Bouverie House, Fleet Street, E.C.4.—*Sec.*, S. C. Reynolds, O.B.E.

NEWSPAPER PUBLISHERS ASSOCIATION LTD. (1906), 6 Bouverie Street, E.C.4.—*Dir.*, N. Reeves.

NEWSPAPER SOCIETY (1836), Whitefriars House, Carmelite Street, E.C.4.—*Pres.*, E. Cheadle (*Thomson Organization*); *Dir.*, D. Lowndes.

NEWSVENDORS' BENEVOLENT INSTITUTION (1839), Broadway Chambers, 7 Ludgate Broadway, E.C.4.—*Sec.*, J. E. Llewellyn-Jones.

NEW TOWNS ASSOCIATION (1970), Glen House, Stag Place, S.W.1.—*Sec.*, G. Philipson, D.F.C.

NOISE ABATEMENT SOCIETY, 6 Old Bond Street, W.I.—*Chairman*, John Connell.

NORE R.N. AND R.M. CHILDREN'S TRUST (formerly R.N. and R.M. Children's Home, The Nore, Gillingham), H.M.S. *Pembroke*, Chatham.—*Sec.*, Lt.-Cdr. H. Blease, R.N.(ret.).

NORTHERN IRELAND TOURIST BOARD, River House, 48 High Street, Belfast I—*Chief Executive*, R. C. C. Hall.

NORTHUMBERLAND AND DURHAM ASSOCIATION IN LONDON (1920).—*Hon. Sec.*, H. J. Luxton, 36 Hedley House, Stewart Street, E.14.

NORWOOD HOME FOR JEWISH CHILDREN (Jewish Orphanage) (1795), Knights Hill, West Norwood, S.E.27.—*Sec.*, H. Altman.

NUCLEAR ENERGY SOCIETY, BRITISH (1962), 1–7 Great George Street, S.W.I.—*Sec.*, J. G. Watson, C.B.

NUCLEAR ENERGY SOCIETY, BRITISH (1962), c/o Institution of Civil Engineers, 1–7 Great George Street, S.W.I.—*Sec.*, J. G. Watson, C.B.

NUFFIELD CENTRE FOR FORCES OF THE CROWN (1943), 8 Adelaide Street, W.C.2.—*Sec.*, F, D. Stead.

NUFFIELD FOUNDATION (1943), Nuffield Lodge, Regent's Park, N.W.I.—*Dir.*, C. C. Butler, F.R.S.

NUFFIELD PROVINCIAL HOSPITALS TRUST (1939). 3 Prince Albert Road, N.W.I.—*Gen. Sec.*, G. McLachlan. C.B.E.

NUMISMATIC SOCIETY, BRITISH.—*Hon. Sec.*, W. Slayter, 63 West Way, Edgware, Middx.

NUMISMATIC SOCIETY, ROYAL, c/o Dept. of Coins and Medals, The British Museum, W.C.I.—*Pres.*, C. M. Kraay, D.Phil., F.S.A.; *Hon. Sec.*, Miss M. M. Archibald.

NURSERY SCHOOL ASSOCIATION OF GT. BRITAIN AND N. IRELAND, 89 Stamford Street, S.E.I.—*Sec.*, Miss D. E. Warren.

NURSES', ELDERLY, NATIONAL HOME, Riverside Avenue, Holdenhurst, Bournemouth.

NURSES, ROYAL NATIONAL PENSION FUND FOR, 15 Buckingham Street, W.C.2.—*Manager and Actuary*, C. M. O'Brien, M.A.

NURSING COUNCIL FOR ENGLAND AND WALES, GENERAL, 23 Portland Place, W.I.—*Registrar*, Miss M. Henry, C.B.E.

NURSING COUNCIL, GENERAL, for Scotland, 5 Darnaway Street, Edinburgh 3.—*Registrar*, Miss J. G. M. Main, R.G.N.

NURSING, ROYAL COLLEGE OF, IA Henrietta Place, W.I.—*Gen. Sec.*, Miss C. M. Hall, C.B.E.

NUTRITION SOCIETY (1941).—*Hon. Sec.*, G. L. S. Pawan, Middlesex Hospital Medical School, W.I.

OBSTETRICIANS AND GYNAECOLOGISTS, ROYAL COLLEGE OF (1929), 27 Sussex Place, Regent's Park, N.W.I.—*Pres.*, Sir Norman Jeffcoate; *Sec.*, N. Catterall, M.B.E.

OFFICE MANAGEMENT, INSTITUTE OF (1915), 205 High Street, Beckenham, Kent.—*Sec.*, J. L. Cousins.

OFFICERS' ASSOCIATION, THE (1920), 28 Belgrave Square, S.W.I. Affords relief to ex-officers of the Royal Navy, Army and R.A.F. or their widows and dependants in distress; assists such persons with disability pension and other claims, and to find accommodation in homes for the elderly; helps unemployed ex-officers to find employment.—*Gen. Sec.*, Maj.-Gen. J. K. Shepheard, C.B., D.S.O., O.B.E.

OFFICERS' FAMILIES FUND (1899), 56 Regency Street, S.W.I.—*Sec.*, Mrs. E. R. Sword.

OFFICERS' PENSIONS SOCIETY, LTD., 15 Buckingham Gate, S.W.I.—*Gen. Sec.*, Rear Adm. F. B. P. Brayne-Nicholls, C.B., D.S.C.

OIL PAINTERS, ROYAL INSTITUTE OF (1883), 17 Carlton House Terrace, S.W.I.—*Pres.*, A. Hill; *Sec.*, M. Bradshaw.

OLYMPIC ASSOCIATION, BRITISH (1905), 12 Buckingham Street, W.C.2.—*Gen.-Sec.*, K. S. Duncan, M.B.E.

OPEN-AIR MISSION (1853), 19 John Street, Bedford Row, W.C.I.—*Sec.*, E, W. Jealous.

OPTICAL COUNCIL, GENERAL, 41 Harley Street, W.I. —*Registrar*, J. D. Devlin.

ORDERS AND MEDALS RESEARCH SOCIETY.—*Gen. Sec.*, N. G. Gooding, 11 Maresfield, Chepstow Road, Croydon.

ORIENTAL CERAMIC SOCIETY (1921), 31B Torrington Square, W.C.I.—*Sec.*, Brig. J. R. I. Platt, D.S.O., O.B.E.

ORNITHOLOGISTS' CLUB, THE SCOTTISH, 21 Regent Terrace, Edinburgh.—*Sec.* Maj. A. D. Peirse-Duncombe.

ORNITHOLOGISTS' UNION, BRITISH, c/o Zoological Society of London, Regent's Park, N.W.I.—*Hon. Sec.*, J. F. Monk, D.M.

ORNITHOLOGY, BRITISH TRUST FOR (1932), Beech Grove, Tring, Herts.—*Administrator*, C. W. N. Plant.

ORNITHOLOGY, FIELD, THE EDWARD GREY INSTITUTE OF (1938), Dept. of Zoology, South Parks Road, Oxford.—*Director*, David Lack, F.R.S.

ORTHOPÆDIC ASSOCIATION, BRITISH (1918), c/o Royal College of Surgeons, Lincoln's Inn Fields, W.C.2.—*Hon. Sec.*, D. R. Sweetnam, F.R.S.

OUTWARD BOUND TRUST, Iddesleigh House, Caxton Street, S.W.I. Administers six schools for character-building through adventure using mountains and sea to produce challenging situations at: Aberdovey, Wales, Eskdale and Ullswater, Cumberland, Burghead, Morayshire, Ashburton, Devon (boys) and Towyn, Wales (girls).—*Exec. Dir.*, Cdr. H. E. B. Jenkinson, R.N.

OVERSEAS DEVELOPMENT INSTITUTE LTD. (1960), 10–11 Percy Street, W.I.—*Dir.*, A. G. Tasker, C.B.E.

OVER-SEAS LEAGUE, ROYAL (1910), Over-Seas House, Park Place, St. James's Street, S.W.I.— *Dir.-General*, P. Crawshaw, C.B.E.

OVERSEAS SERVICE PENSIONERS' ASSOCIATION (1960), 408-412 Coastal Chambers, 172 Buckingham Palace Road, S.W.I.—*Sec.*, K. M. Cowley, C.M.G., O.B.E.

OWNERS OF CITY PROPERTIES. ASSOCIATED.—*Sec.*, M. Scott, 14–16 Bressenden Place, S.W.I.

OXFORD AND CAMBRIDGE SCHOOLS EXAMINATION BOARD (1873). *Offices*, 10 Trumpington Street, Cambridge and Elsfield Way, Oxford.— *Secs.*, J. M. Todd, Oxford; H. F. King, Cambridge.

OXFORD PRESERVATION TRUST (1927), The Painted Room, 3 Cornmarket Street, Oxford.—*Sec.*, R. S. W. Malcolm.

OXFORD SOCIETY (1932), 8 Wellington Square, Oxford.—*Sec.*, Mrs. D. M. Lennie.

PAINTER-ETCHERS AND ENGRAVERS, ROYAL SOCIETY OF (1880), 26 Conduit Street, W.I.—*Pres.*, Paul Drury; *Sec.*, M. Fry.

PAINTERS IN WATER COLOURS, ROYAL INSTITUTE OF (1831), 17 Carlton House Terrace, S.W.I. —*Pres.*, R. Hilder; *Treas.*, E. Wesson; *Sec.-Gen.*, M. B. Bradshaw.

PAINTERS IN WATER COLOURS, ROYAL SOCIETY OF (1804), 26 Conduit Street, W.I.—*Pres.*, R. S. Austin, R.A.; *Sec. and Curator*, M. Fry.

PAINTERS, SCULPTORS AND ENGRAVERS, NATIONAL SOCIETY OF (1930), 17 Carlton House Terrace, S.W.I.—*Pres.*, B. Mathews; *Sec.*, M. Bradshaw.

PALÆONTOGRAPHICAL SOCIETY (1847). *Sec.*, F. G. Dimes. c/o Institute of Geological Sciences, Exhibition Road, S.W.7.

PALÆONTOLOGICAL ASSOCIATION (1957).—*Sec.*, Dr. W. D. I. Rolfe, Hunterian Museum, The University, Glasgow, W.2.

PALESTINE EXPLORATION FUND (1865), 2 Hinde Mews, Marylebone Lane, W.1.—*Chairman*, Sir Alec Kirkbride, K.C.M.G., O.B.E., M.C., F.S.A.

PARENTS' NATIONAL EDUCATIONAL UNION, P.N.E.U. (1888), Murray House, Vandon Street. S.W.1.— *Sec.*, Miss P. P. Gilmour.

PARLIAMENTARY AND SCIENTIFIC COMMITTEE.—*Sec.*, Lt.-Cdr. C. Powell, 14 Buckingham Palace Road, S.W.1.

PARLIAMENTARY LABOUR PARTY.—*Leader*, Rt. Hon. J. H. Wilson, O.B.E., M.P.; *Deputy Leader*, Rt. Hon. R. H. Jenkins, M.P.; *Chief Whip*, Rt. Hon. R. J. Mellish, M.P.; *Chairman*, Rt. Hon. D. Houghton, C.H., M.P.; *Leader of Labour Peers*, The Lord Shackleton, P.C., O.B.E.; *Sec.*, F. H. Barlow, C.B.E.

PASTEL SOCIETY (1899), 17 Carlton House Terrace, S.W.1.—*Pres.*, A. Sykes; *Sec. Gen.*, M. B. Bradshaw.

PASTORAL PSYCHOLOGY, GUILD OF (1936).—*Sec.*, Miss N. Fardon, 41 Redcliffe Gardens, S.W.10.

PATENT AGENTS, CHARTERED INSTITUTE OF (1882) Staple Inn Buildings, W.C.1.—*Sec.*, P. E. Lincroft, M.B.E.

PATENTEES AND INVENTORS, INSTITUTE OF (1919), 207–208 Abbey House, Victoria Street, S.W.1.—*Sec.* A. L. T. Cotterell.

PATHOLOGISTS, ROYAL COLLEGE OF, 2 Carlton House Terrace, S.W.1.

PATIENTS ASSOCIATION (1963), 335 Gray's Inn Road, W.C.1.—*Sec.*, Mrs. U. Miller.

PEACE SOCIETY, INTERNATIONAL (1816), Fellowship House, Browning Street, S.E.17. (*Continental Offices*, 5 rue Charles Bonnet, Geneva).—*Director and Sec.*, Rev. H. Rathbone Dunnico, Ll.D.

PEARSON'S FRESH AIR FUND, 81 Denison House, 296 Vauxhall Bridge Road, S.W.1.—*Gen. Sec.*, G. Franklin, O.B.E.

PEDESTRIANS' ASSOCIATION FOR ROAD SAFETY, 4 College Hill, E.C.4.—*Sec.*, Mrs. M. Gray.

P.E.N., INTERNATIONAL (1921), 62–3 Glebe Place, S.W.3. World association of writers.—*Gen. Sec.*, D. Carver, O.B.E.

PENSION CONSULTANTS, C.I.B. SOCIETY OF (1958), 15 St. Helen's Place, E.C.3.—*Sec.*, G. L. Necker.

PENSION FUNDS, NATIONAL ASSOCIATION OF (1923) —*Sec.*, J. D. Cran, 14 Queen Anne's Gate, S.W.1.

PEOPLE'S DISPENSARY FOR SICK ANIMALS (1917), P.D.S.A. House, South Street, Dorking, Surrey. —*Gen. Sec.*, E. Rowling.

PERFORMING RIGHT SOCIETY LTD. (1914), 29–33 Berners Street, W.1.—*Gen. Manager*, M. J. Freeguard; *Sec.*, D. A. S. de Freitas.

PERIODICAL PUBLISHERS ASSOCIATION LTD., Imperial House, Kingsway, W.C.2.—*Sec.*, H. MacDougall.

PERSONNEL MANAGEMENT, INSTITUTE OF (1913), 5 Winsley Street, W.1.—*Dir.*, E. Tonkinson.

PESTALOZZI CHILDREN'S VILLAGE TRUST, Sedlescombe, Battle, Sussex.—*Sec.*, G. Chambers.

PETROLEUM, INSTITUTE OF (1913), 61 New Cavendish Street, W.1.—*Gen. Sec.*, D. A. Hough, M.B.E., T.D.

PHARMACEUTICAL SOCIETY OF GREAT BRITAIN. 17 Bloomsbury Square, W.C.1.—*Pres.*, W. M. Darling; *Sec.*, D. F. Lewis.

PHARMACOLOGICAL SOCIETY, BRITISH.—*Gen. Sec.*, Prof. J. R. Vane, Dept. of Pharmacology, Royal College of Surgeons, Lincoln's Inn Fields, W.C.2.

PHILOLOGICAL SOCIETY (1842), University College, Gower Street, W.C.1.—*Hon. Secs.*, C. J. E. Ball; Prof. R. H. Robins.

PHILOSOPHY, ROYAL INSTITUTE OF, 14 Gordon Square, W.C.1.—*Director*, Prof. G. N. A. Vesey.

PHOTOGRAPHERS, INSTITUTE OF INCORPORATED. (1901), Amwell End, Ware, Herts.—*Gen. Sec.*, E. I. N. Waughray.

PHYSICAL EDUCATION ASSOCIATION OF GREAT BRITAIN AND N. IRELAND, Ling House, 10 Nottingham Place, W.1.—*Hon. Sec.*, P. Sebastian.

PHYSICAL RECREATION, CENTRAL COUNCIL OF (1935), 26 Park Crescent, W.1.—*Gen. Sec.*, W. Winterbottom, O.B.E.

PHYSICIANS, ROYAL COLLEGE OF (1518), 11 St. Andrew's Place, N.W.1.—*Pres.*, The Lord Rosenheim, K.B.E., M.D.; *Treas.*, N. D. Compston, M.D.; *Registrar*, Sir Kenneth Robson, C.B.E., M.D.; *Sec.*, G. M. G. Tibbs.

PHYSICIANS AND SURGEONS, ROYAL COLLEGE OF (Glasgow) (1599), 242 St. Vincent Street, Glasgow.—*Pres.*, Prof. E. M. McGirr; *Hon. Sec.*, T. J. Thomson.

PHYSICIANS OF EDINBURGH, ROYAL COLLEGE OF (1681), *Hall and Library*, 9 Queen Street, Edinburgh 2.—*Sec.*, A. J. Keay.

PHYSICS, INSTITUTE OF (1874), 47 Belgrave Square, S.W.1.—*Pres.*, J. W. Menter, SC.D., F.R.S.; *Sec.*, L. Cohen, Ph.D.

PHYSIOLOGICAL SOCIETY (1876), Norwoods, Rectory Lane, Heswall, Wirral, Cheshire.—*Hon. Sec.* J. Gillespie, Ph.D.

PIG BREEDERS ASSOCIATION, NATIONAL (1884), 51a Clarendon Road, Watford, Herts.—*Sec.*, E. G. Wake.

PILGRIM TRUST, THE (1930), Millbank House, 2 Great Peter Street, S.W.1.—*Sec.*, Sir Edward Ford, K.C.B., K.C.V.O.

PILGRIMS OF GREAT BRITAIN, THE (1902), Savoy Hotel, W.C.2.—*Chairman*, Hon. Gavin Astor; *Hon. Sec.*, Lt.-Col. S. W. Chant-Sempill, O.B.E., M.C.

PILGRIMS OF THE U.S., THE (1903).—*Pres.*, Hugh Bullock, K.B.E., 74 Trinity Place, New York, N.Y., 10006 U.S.A.

PIT PONIES PROTECTION SOCIETY (1927).—*Sec.*, D. Jeffrey Williams, 120 Loudoun Road, N.W.8.

PLANT ENGINEERS, INSTITUTION OF, 138 Buckingham Palace Road, S.W.1.—*Sec.*, C. L. Baxter.

PLASTICS INSTITUTE, THE (1931), 11 Hobart Place, S.W.1.—*Sec.*, J. N. Ratcliffe.

PLAYING FIELDS ASSOCIATION, NATIONAL (1925), 57B Catherine Place, S.W.1.—*Chairman*, The Lord Luke, T.D.; *Gen. Sec.*, Maj.-Gen. Sir John Nelson, K.C.V.O., C.B., D.S.O., O.B.E., M.C.

POETRY SOCIETY (1909), 21 Earls Court Square, S.W.5.—*Gen. Sec.*, M. S. Mackenzie.

POLAR RESEARCH INSTITUTE, SCOTT (1920), Cambridge.—*Director*, G. de Q. Robin.

POLIO FELLOWSHIP, BRITISH (1939), Bell Close, West End Road, Ruislip, Middlesex.—*Gen. Sec.*, D. S. Powell. A national voluntary organization for polio disabled persons.

POLITICAL AND ECONOMIC PLANNING (PEP) (1931), 12 Upper Belgrave Street, S.W.1.—*Dir.*, J. Pinder.

POOR CLERGY RELIEF CORPORATION (1856), 27 Medway Street, S.W.1.—*Sec.*, C. L. Talbot.

POULTRY STOCK ASSOCIATION, LTD., 52–54 High Holborn, W.C.1.—*Gen. Sec.*, T. J. Aley.

POULTRY CLUB, THE (1877), (incorporating the British Bantam Association).—*Gen. Sec.*, Mrs. S. Jones, 72 Springfields, Gt. Dunmow, Essex.

PRECEPTORS, COLLEGE OF, 2 & 3 Bloomsbury Square. W.C.1. All persons engaged in education who have obtained a Diploma of the College or have passed an examination satisfactory to the Council are admissible as members.—*Secretary*, J. V. Chapman.

PREHISTORIC SOCIETY (1908).—*Hon. Sec.*, I. H. Longworth, PH.D., F.S.A., Dept. of Prehistoric and Romano-British Antiquities, British Museum, W.C.1.

PRESBYTERIAN HISTORICAL SOCIETY OF ENGLAND (1913), Presbyterian Church House, 86 Tavistock Place, W.C.1.

PRESBYTERIAN HOUSING LIMITED (1929), 86 Tavistock Place, W.C.1.—*Sec.*, C. M. Manning.

PRESS ASSOCIATION (1868), 85 Fleet Street, E.C.4.—*Chairman* (1971–72), J. G. S. Linacre (*Yorkshire Post Newspapers*); *General Manager*, G. C. Bloom; *Sec.*, J. Purdham.

PRIMROSE LEAGUE (1883), Abbey House, Victoria Street, S.W.1.—*Grand Master*, Rt. Hon. Sir Alec Douglas-Home, K.T., M.P.; *Chancellor*, The Lord Tweedsmuir, C.B.E.; *Sec.*, Miss E. M. Killby, O.B.E.

PRINCESS LOUISE SCOTTISH HOSPITAL FOR LIMBLESS SAILORS AND SOLDIERS (1916), Erskine, Bishopton, Renfrewshire.—*Sec. and Tres.*, Maj. G. A. Rankin, 201 W. George Street, Glasgow, C.2.

PRINTERS' PENSION CORPORATION (1827), 61 Doughty Street, W.C.1. Homes for elderly printers and widows at Basildon and Bletchley.—*Sec.*, A. Reynolds.

PRINTING HISTORICAL SOCIETY (1964), St. Bride Institute, Bride Lane, E.C.4.—*Hon. Sec.*, D. Chambers.

PRINTING, INSTITUTE OF (1961), 10–11 Bedford Row, W.C.1.—*Sec.*, M. A. Smith.

PRISON VISITORS, NATIONAL ASSOCIATION OF (1922), 47 Hartington Street, Bedford.—*Gen. Sec.*, Mrs. A. G. McKenna.

PRISONERS' AID SOCIETY, ROYAL LONDON (1939), Hayward House, 56–58 East India Dock Road, E.14.—*Sec.*, H. C. Bennett.

PRIVATE LIBRARIES ASSOCIATION (1957), 41 Cuckoo Hill Road, Pinner, Middlesex.—*Hon. Sec.*, W. Forster.

PRIVATE PATIENTS PLAN (The London Association for Hospital Services), Eynsham House, Tunbridge Wells, Kent.—*Gen. Manager*, J. H. Dyter.

PROCURATORS IN GLASGOW, ROYAL FACULTY OF (1600).—*Treas., Clerk and Fiscal*, A. F. Ferguson, T.D., 55 West Regent Street, Glasgow, C.2.

PRODUCTION ENGINEERS, INSTITUTION OF, 10 Chesterfield Street, W.1.—*Sec.*, W. F. S. Woodford, O.B.E.

PROFESSIONAL CIVIL SERVANTS, INSTITUTION OF (1919), 3–7 Northumberland Street, W.C.2.—*Gen. Sec.*, W. McCall.

PROFESSIONAL CLASSES AID COUNCIL, 10 St. Christopher's Place, W.1.—*Sec.*, Miss P. Roden.

PROFESSIONAL WORKERS, NATIONAL FEDERATION OF (1920), Lord Alexander House, Waterhouse Street, Hemel Hempstead, Herts.

PROFESSIONS SUPPLEMENTARY TO MEDICINE, COUNCIL FOR, York House, Westminster Bridge Road, S.E.1.—*Registrar*, J. S. Tapsfield.

PROPAGATION OF THE GOSPEL, UNITED SOCIETY FOR THE (U.S.P.G.), 15 Tufton Street, S.W.1.—*Sec.*, Rt. Revd. I. W. A. Shevill.

PROPERTY OWNERS, NATIONAL ASSOCIATION OF.—*Sec.*, M. Scott, 14–16 Bressenden Place, S.W.1.

PROTECTION OF LIFE FROM FIRE, SOCIETY FOR THE (1836), Chichester House, 278–82 High Holborn, W.C. 1.—*Sec.*, W. E. Chantler.

PROTESTANT ALLIANCE, THE (1845), 119 Earlsfield Road, S.W.18.—*Hon. Sec.*, O. T. Taylor.

PROTESTANT REFORMATION SOCIETY (1827), 1 Lawn Mansions, 7F High Street, Barnet, Herts.—*Sec.*, W. H. Gaze.

PROVINCIAL NOTARIES SOCIETY (1907), 132 High Street, Portsmouth, Hants.—*Sec.*, G. E. Delafield.

PSYCHICAL RESEARCH, SOCIETY FOR (1882), 1 Adam and Eve Mews, W.8.—*Pres.*, Prof. C. W. K. Mundle.

PSYCHOLOGICAL SOCIETY, THE BRITISH (1901), 18–19 Albemarle Street, W.1.—*Pres.*, Prof. H. Kay; *Hon. Gen. Sec.*, R. M. Farr.

PUBLIC ADMINISTRATION, ROYAL INSTITUTE OF (1922), 24 Park Crescent, W.1.—*Dir.*, R. Nottage, C.M.G.

PUBLIC HEALTH AND HYGIENE, THE ROYAL INSTITUTE OF (1937), Postgraduate Medical School, 28 Portland Place, W.1.; Harben Laboratories, 23 Queen Square, W.C.1.—*Sec.*, A. R. Horsham.

PUBLIC HEALTH ENGINEERS, INSTITUTION OF (1895), 32 Eccleston Square, S.W.1.—*Sec.*, I. B. Muirhead.

PUBLIC HEALTH INSPECTORS, ASSOCIATION OF (1883), 19 Grosvenor Place, S.W.1.—*Sec.*, R. Johnson.

PUBLIC RELATIONS, INSTITUTE OF (1948), 1 Great James Street, W.C.1.—*Gen. Sec.*, Mrs. A. Wood.

PUBLIC ROAD TRANSPORT ASSOCIATION, 172 Buckingham Palace Road, S.W.1; *Sec.*, R. L. Howlett.

PUBLIC SCHOOLS, ASSOCIATION OF GOVERNING BODIES OF (BOYS) (1941).—*Hon. Sec.*, M. H. Glover, Skinners' Hall, 8 Dowgate Hill, E.C.4. *Sec.*, Brig. A. J. Knott, O.B.E. West Rood, West Hill, Harrow, Middx.

PUBLIC SCHOOLS, ASSOCIATION OF GOVERNING BODIES OF GIRLS' (1942), 26 Queen Anne's Gate, S.W.1.—*Hon. Sec.*, W. L. Lister.

PUBLIC SCHOOLS APPOINTMENTS BUREAU, 17 Queen Street, W.1.—*Dir.*, R. F. B. Campbell.

PUBLIC SCHOOLS BURSARS' ASSOCIATION (1932).—*Sec.*, D. M. Sherwood, Badminton School, Westbury-on-Trym, Bristol.

PUBLIC TEACHERS OF LAW, SOCIETY OF (1908).—*Pres.*, Prof. P. S. James; *Hon. Sec.*, Prof. J. F. Wilson, Faculty of Law, The University, Southampton.

PUBLISHERS ASSOCIATION (1896), 19 Bedford Square, W.C.1.—*Pres.*, R. Unwin; *Sec.*, R. E. Barker, O.B.E.

PURCHASING AND SUPPLY, INSTITUTE OF (1967), York House, Westminster Bridge Road, S.E.1.—*Dir.*, P. F. H. Emery, M.P.

QUANTITY SURVEYORS, INSTITUTE OF, 98 Gloucester Place, W.1.—*Dir.*, Brig. F. H. Lowman.

QUARRIER'S HOMES (1871), Bridge of Weir, Renfrewshire, Scotland.

QUARRYING, INSTITUTE OF (1917), 62–64 Baker Street, W.1.—*Sec.*, Miss Mary Roberts, M.B.E.

QUEEN ELIZABETH'S FOUNDATION FOR THE DISABLED (1967), Leatherhead Court, Leatherhead Surrey.—*Dir.*, R. N. Smith, M.C., T.D. Incorporating Queen Elizabeth's Training College (1934), Banstead Place Rehabilitation Centre (1956), Dorincourt Residential Sheltered Workshop (1958) and Lulworth Court Holiday and Convalescent Home (1959).

QUEEN VICTORIA CLERGY FUND (1897), *Central Fund*, Church House, Dean's Yard, S.W.1.—*Sec.*, Maj. G. C. Hackett, M.B.E.

QUEEN VICTORIA SCHOOL, Dunblane, Perthshire.—*Headmaster*, Lt.-Col. A. K. Evans.

QUEEN'S INSTITUTE OF DISTRICT NURSING (1887), 57 Lower Belgrave Street, S.W.1.—*Gen. Sec.*, Miss M. Faulkner.

RACE RELATIONS, INSTITUTE OF (1958), 36 Jermyn Street, S.W.1.—*Chairman*, The Lord Walston; *Dir.*, Prof. H. Tinker.

RADIO SOCIETY OF GREAT BRITAIN (Incorporated), 35 Doughty Street, W.C.1.—*Gen. Manager*, D. A. Findlay.

RADIOLOGISTS, FACULTY OF (1934), c/o Royal College of Surgeons, Lincoln's Inn Fields, W.C.2.—*Hon. Sec.*, R. Morrison.

RAILWAY AND CANAL HISTORICAL SOCIETY.—*Hon. Sec.*, J. R. Harding, 174 Station Road, Wylde Green, Sutton Coldfield, Warwicks.

RAILWAY BENEVOLENT INSTITUTION (1858), 29 John Street, W.C.1; Railway Children's Home at Derby.—*Gen. Sec.*, R. A. Scott.

RAILWAY OFFICERS' AND SERVANTS' ASSOCIATION, UNITED KINGDOM (1861), Room 9, 17 Crosswall, E.C.3.

RAINER FOUNDATION, 2 Hobart Place, Eaton Square, S.W.1. A voluntary society providing residential and remedial help for children and young people.—*Gen. Sec.*, R. Howell.

RAMBLERS' ASSOCIATION (1935), 1–4 Crawford Mews, York Street, W.1.—*Sec.*, C. Hall.

RATEPAYERS' ASSOCIATIONS, NATIONAL UNION OF, 47 Victoria Street, S.W.1.

RATING AND VALUATION ASSOCIATION (1882), 29 Belgrave Square, S.W.1.—*Sec.*, Frank L. Othick.

RED CROSS SOCIETY, BRITISH. *See* BRITISH.

RED ENSIGN CLUB, SAILORS' HOME AND (1830), Dock Street, E.1.—*Gen. Manager*, Capt. J. C. Young, R.D., R.N.R. (*ret.*).

RED POLL CATTLE SOCIETY AND BRITISH DANE CATTLE SOCIETY, Suffolk Showground, Bucklesham Road, Ipswich.—*Sec.*, K. V. Cousins.

REEDHAM SCHOOL (Incorporated) (1844), Purley, Surrey.—*Sec.*, H. W. Richardson.

REED'S SCHOOL (1813), *Offices*, 8 Little Trinity Lane, E.C.4.—*Sec.*, Philip Horton.

REFRIGERATION, INSTITUTE OF (1899), 272 London Road, Wallington, Surrey.—*Sec.*, D. T. Lee.

REGULAR FORCES EMPLOYMENT ASSOCIATION (1885), 4 Buckingham Palace Mansions, Buckingham Palace Road, S.W.1. Finds employment for non-commissioned ex-Regulars.—*General Manager*, Maj.-Gen. P. F. Claxton, O.B.E.

REINDEER COUNCIL OF THE UNITED KINGDOM (1949), Newton Hill, Harston, Cambridge.—*Hon. Sec.*, Dr. E. J. Lindgren, M.A.

RELIGION AND MEDICINE, INSTITUTE OF (1964).—*Organizing Sec.*, Miss M. C. Kidson, 58A Wimpole Street, W.1.

RENT OFFICERS, INSTITUTE OF.—*Hon. Sec.*, D. A. G. Sargent, D.F.C., Clarendon House, Friars Place, Chelmsford, Essex.

RESEARCH DEFENCE SOCIETY, 11 Chandos Street, Cavendish Square, W.1.—*Hon. Sec.*, A. D. Macdonald, M.D.; *Sec.*, Mrs. C. Ewen.

RETAIL ALLIANCE, 4 Harley Street, W.1.—*Sec.*, J. Ramage, O.B.E.

RETIRED NAVAL OFFICERS, ASSOCIATION OF (Trafalgar Day, 1925), 72 Princes Square, W.2. *Gen. Sec.*, Lt.-Cdr. C. G. Scott Bevis, R.N.

RHEUMATISM AND ARTHRITIS ASSOCIATION (1947), 1 Devonshire Place, W.1.—*Gen. Sec.*, T. E. Riches.

RICHARD III SOCIETY.—*Gen. Sec.*, Miss V. A. Giles, 72 Heathfield Road, Croydon, Surrey.

RIVER AUTHORITIES, ASSOCIATION OF, Grosvenor Gardens House, Grosvenor Gardens, S.W.1.—*Sec.*, D. J. Kinnersley.

RIVERS PROTECTION, CENTRAL COUNCIL FOR, Fishmongers' Hall, E.C.4.—*Joint Hon. Secs.*, Cdr. O. S. M. Bayley, R.N.; Leonard Millis, C.B.E.

ROADS IMPROVEMENT ASSOCIATION, Ruebilder House, Havelock Road, Southall, Middlesex.—*Gen. Sec.*, L. Bailey.

ROAD TRANSPORT ENGINEERS, INSTITUTE OF (1945), 1 Cromwell Place, S.W.7.—*Sec.*, J. A. Fletcher, M.B.E.

ROMAN AND MEDIAEVAL LONDON EXCAVATION COUNCIL.—*Hon. Sec.*, R. A. Woods, F.S.A., c/o Bank of England, E.C.2.

ROMAN STUDIES, SOCIETY FOR PROMOTION OF, 31–34 Gordon Square, W.C.1.—*Pres.*, A. H. McDonald, F.B.A.; *Sec.*, Mrs. P. Gilbert.

ROTARY INTERNATIONAL IN GREAT BRITAIN AND IRELAND (1914), Sheen Lane House, Sheen Lane, S.W.14.—*Sec.*, V. Dover, M.C.

ROYAL AFRICAN SOCIETY (1901), 18 Northumberland Avenue, W.C.2.—*Sec.*, H. Heather.

ROYAL AGRICULTURAL SOCIETY OF ENGLAND (1838), National Agricultural Centre, Kenilworth, Warwicks.—*Dir.*, W. D. Draffan, M.B.E.

ROYAL AIR FORCE BENEVOLENT FUND (1919), 67 Portland Place, W.1.—*Controller*, Air Marshal Sir William Coles, K.B.E., C.B., D.S.O., D.F.C., A.F.C.

ROYAL AIR FORCES ASSOCIATION, 43 Grove Park Road, W.4.—*Gen. Sec.*, G. R. Boak, O.B.E.

ROYAL ALEXANDRA AND ALBERT SCHOOL (1758). *Offices*, Gatton Park, Reigate, Surrey.—*Sec.*, Eric A. Corner.

ROYAL ALFRED MERCHANT SEAMEN'S SOCIETY (1865), Weston Acres, Woodmansterne Lane, Banstead, Surrey. Home for aged seamen, Belvedere, Kent; Flatlets for retired seafarers and widows at Banstead, Surrey. Out-pensions for retired seamen of limited means. Samaritan and War Fund for general relief. Allowances for widows in distress and Home for widows and retired stewardesses, Eastbourne.—*Gen. Sec.*, D. J. Lafferty, M.B.E.

ROYAL ARMOURED CORPS BENEVOLENT FUND, *Headquarters*, R.A.C. Centre, Bovington Camp, Wareham, Dorset; *Sec.*, Lt.-Col. C. H. Rayment, M.B.E.

ROYAL ARTILLERY ASSOCIATION, 58 Woolwich Common, S.E.18.—*Gen. Sec.*, Maj. F. C. Emery, M.B.E.

ROYAL ARTILLERY EMPLOYMENT BUREAU FOR FINDING WORK FOR EX-ARTILLERYMEN, 2 Lower Sloane Street, S.W.1.

ROYAL ASIATIC SOCIETY, 56 Queen Anne Street, W.1.—*Sec.*, Miss D. Crawford.

ROYAL ASSOCIATION OF BRITISH DAIRY FARMERS (1876), 17 Devonshire Street, W.1.—*Sec.*, F. R. Francis.

ROYAL BRITISH NURSES ASSOCIATION, 194 Queen's Gate, S.W.7.—*Sec.*, Miss E. G. Campbell.

ROYAL CALEDONIAN SCHOOLS (1815), Bushey, Herts.—*Sec.*, George Deans.

ROYAL CAMBRIDGE HOME FOR SOLDIERS' WIDOWS, 82–84 Hurst Road, East Molesey, Surrey.—*Sec.*, Miss E. M. Bennett, M.B.E.

ROYAL CENTRAL ASIAN SOCIETY (1901), 42 Devonshire Street, W.1.—*Pres.*, The Earl of Selkirk, P.C., G.C.M.C., G.B.E., A.F.C.; *Sec.*, Miss M. FitzSimons.

ROYAL CHORAL SOCIETY (1871), Royal Albert Hall, S.W.7.—*Sec.*, Phyllis G. Dabbs.

ROYAL COLLEGE OF VETERINARY SURGEONS, 32 Belgrave Square, S.W.1.—*Pres.*, J. McC. Ingram; *Registrar*, A. R. W. Porter.

ROYAL COMMONWEALTH SOCIETY (1868), Northumberland Avenue, W.C.2.—*Chairman*, F. H. Tate (30,000 members).—*Secretary-General*, A. S. H. Kemp, O.B.E.

ROYAL DESIGNERS FOR INDUSTRY, FACULTY OF (1936), (Royal Society of Arts), John Adam Street, W.C.2.—*Master*, F. H. K. Henrion, M.B.E., R.D.I.; *Sec.*, G. E. Mercer.

ROYAL DRAWING SOCIETY (1902), 17 Carlton House Terrace, S.W.1.—*Pres.*, R. R. Tomlinson, O.B.E.; *Sec.*, W. Manston.

ROYAL ECONOMIC SOCIETY (1890), The Marshall Library, Sidgwick Avenue, Cambridge.—*Sec.*, C. F. Carter, F.B.A.

ROYAL ENGINEERS ASSOCIATION (1960), *Headquarters*, R.S.M.E., Chatham, Kent.—*Controller*, Col. R. R. L. Harradine, T.D.

ROYAL ENGINEERS, THE INSTITUTION OF (1875), Chatham.—*Sec.*, Brig. J. H. S. Lacey, C.B.E.

ROYAL HIGHLAND AND AGRICULTURAL SOCIETY OF SCOTLAND (1784), Ingliston, Newbridge, Midlothian.—*Sec.*, T. W. M. Alder.

ROYAL HORTICULTURAL SOCIETY (1804).—*Offices*, Vincent Square, S.W.1. *Garden*, Wisley, Ripley, Woking, Surrey.—*Sec.*, J. Hamer, M.B.E.

ROYAL HOSPITAL AND HOME FOR INCURABLES, PUTNEY (1854), West Hill, S.W.15.—*Sec.*, Col. N. F. Gordon-Wilson, M.B.E.

ROYAL HOSPITAL SCHOOL, Holbrook, nr. Ipswich, Suffolk.—*Headmaster*, N. A. York.

ROYAL HUMANE SOCIETY (1774).—In 1970, 896 persons were rewarded by the R.H.S. for saving 616 lives, and attempting to save the lives of 94 others.—*Offices*, Watergate House, York Buildings, Adelphi, W.C.2.—*Sec.*, Lt.-Col. R. W. C-Charlton, M.B.E.

ROYAL INSTITUTE OF INTERNATIONAL AFFAIRS (1920), Chatham House, St. James's Square, S.W.1.—*Director*, A. Shonfield.

ROYAL INSTITUTION OF GREAT BRITAIN (1799), 21 Albemarle Street, W.1.—*Pres.*, The Lord Kings Norton, PH.D., D.SC., D.TECH.; *Dir.*, Prof. G. Porter, F.R.S.; *Sec.*, M. A. T. Rogers, PH.D., F.R.I.C.

ROYAL INSTITUTION OF SOUTH WALES, Swansea (1835).—*Hon. Sec.*, F. M. Gibbs.

ROYAL LIFE SAVING SOCIETY, THE (1891), Desborough House, 14 Devonshire Street, W.1.—*Dir.*, Brig. P. de C. Jones, O.B.E.

ROYAL LITERARY FUND (1790), 11 Ludgate Hill, E.C.4. Grants to necessitous authors of some published work of approved literary merit or to their immediate dependants.—*Pres.*, J. Lehmann, C.B.E.; *Sec.*, V. Bonham-Carter.

ROYAL LONDON AID SOCIETY (1939), Hayward House, 56–58 East India Dock Board, E.14.—*Sec.*, H. C. Bennett.

ROYAL MEDICAL BENEVOLENT FUND (1836), 24 King's Road, Wimbledon, S.W.19.—*Sec.*, Mrs. G. Roosmale-Cocq.

ROYAL MEDICAL SOCIETY (1737), 3 Hill Square, Edinburgh 8.—*Secs.*, R. Branford; R. Simpson.

ROYAL MICROSCOPICAL SOCIETY, Canterbury House, 393 Cowley Road, Oxford.—*Exec. Sec.*, R. Pennington.

ROYAL MUSICAL ASSOCIATION (1874) c/o British Museum, W.C.1.—*Sec.*, M. Turner.

ROYAL NATIONAL LIFE-BOAT INSTITUTION, THE (1824).—*Income* (1970), £2,012,678, expenditure £1,766,340; total number of lives rescued, over 93,000; rescued in 1970, 1,250. 138 life-boats and 109 fast inshore rescue boats are maintained on the coasts of Great Britain and Ireland. *Offices*, 42 Grosvenor Gardens, S.W.1.—*Sec.*, Capt. N. Dixon, R.N.

ROYAL NATIONAL MISSION TO DEEP SEA FISHERMEN (1881), 43 Nottingham Place, W.1.—*Sec.*, J. C. Lewis, O.B.E.

ROYAL NATIONAL ROSE SOCIETY, Chiswell Green Lane, St. Albans, Herts.—*Sec.*, L. G. Turner.

ROYAL NAVAL AND ROYAL MARINE CHILDREN'S HOME (1834), Portsmouth. *Sec.*, Miss B. H. W. Nimmo, M.B.E., Royal Naval Barracks, Portsmouth.

ROYAL NAVAL BENEVOLENT SOCIETY (1739), 1 Fleet Street, E.C.4.—*Sec.*, Capt. R. C. Steele, R.N. (*ret.*).

ROYAL NAVAL BENEVOLENT TRUST (1922) (Grand Fleet and Kindred Funds), High Street, Brompton, Gillingham, Kent (Local Committees at Devonport and Portsmouth).—*Gen. Sec.*, Lt.-Comdr. H. B. Binks, O.B.E., D.S.C., R.N. (*ret.*).

ROYAL NAVAL FUND (1891). Administered by the Royal Naval Benevolent Trust. *See above.*

ROYAL PATRIOTIC FUND CORPORATION (1904), Wellington House, Buckingham Gate, S.W.1. Administers funds for the benefit of widows, children and other dependants of deceased officers and servicemen of the Armed Forces; also the Royal Victoria Patriotic School, Bedwell Park, Essendon, Hatfield, Herts., for daughters of Sailors, Soldiers, Marines and Airmen.—*Sec.*, Brig. H. E. Boulter, C.B.E., D.S.O.

ROYAL PHILANTHROPIC SOCIETY'S SCHOOL, Redhill, Surrey.—*Princ.*, L. H. Crew.

ROYAL PHILATELIC SOCIETY, LONDON (1869), 41 Devonshire Place, W.1.—*Hon. Sec.*, G. South, M.B.E.

ROYAL PHILHARMONIC SOCIETY (1813), 29 Exhibition Road, S.W.7.—*Hon. Sec.*, W. Cole, M.V.O., D.MUS., F.R.A.M., F.R.C.O.

ROYAL PHOTOGRAPHIC SOCIETY (1853), 14 South Audley Street, W.1.—*Sec.*, K. R. Warr.

ROYAL PINNER SCHOOL FOUNDATION, 110 Old Brompton Road, S. Kensington, S.W.7. Assists in the education of children (primarily orphans) of commercial travellers in adverse circumstances. —*Sec.*, W. H. Drayton.

"ROYAL SAILORS' RESTS" (Miss Agnes Weston's) (1876). *Head Office*, 32 Western Parade, Southsea, Hants. Rests for naval personnel, at Portsmouth, Devonport, Weymouth and Singapore; Christian Community centres for Naval families at Gosport, Tipner and Plymouth.

ROYAL SCHOOL OF NEEDLEWORK (1872), 25 Princes Gate, S.W.7.—*Sec.*, Miss V. Beames.

ROYAL SCOTTISH COUNTRY DANCE SOCIETY (1923), 12 Coates Crescent, Edinburgh 3.—*Sec.*, Miss E. R. Grubb.

ROYAL SCOTTISH SOCIETY FOR PREVENTION OF CRUELTY TO CHILDREN (1884), 16 Melville Street, Edinburgh, 3.—*Sec.*, A. M. M. Wood.

ROYAL SCOTTISH SOCIETY OF ARTS (1821) (Science and Technology).—*Sec.*, A. D. C. Simpson Royal Scottish Museum, Chambers Street, Edinburgh 1.

ROYAL SEAMEN'S PENSION FUND (Incorporated) (1919), 58 High Street, Sutton, Surrey—*Sec.*, R. F. Van Houten.

ROYAL SIGNALS INSTITUTION (1950), Cheltenham Terrace, S.W.3.—*Sec.*, Lt.-Col. E. G. Day, O.B.E., T.D.

ROYAL SOCIETY, THE (1660), 6 Carlton House Terrace, S.W.1.—*Pres.*, Prof. A. L. Hodgkin; *Treas.* and *Vice-Pres.*, Sir Frederick Bawden; *Secretaries and Vice-Presidents*, Sir Bernard Katz; Sir Harrie Massey; *Foreign Secretary and Vice-Pres.*, Sir Harold Thompson, C.B.E.; *Executive Sec.*, Sir David Martin, C.B.E.

ROYAL SOCIETY FOR THE PREVENTION OF ACCIDENTS, Terminal House, 52 Grosvenor Gardens, S.W.1. —*Dir.-Gen.*, W. G. Alexander, M.B.E.; *Sec.* R. F. B. Fenn.

ROYAL SOCIETY FOR THE PREVENTION OF CRUELTY TO ANIMALS (1824), 105 Jermyn Street. S.W.1. —*Sec.*, Major R. F. Seager.

ROYAL SOCIETY FOR THE PROTECTION OF BIRDS (1889), The Lodge, Sandy, Beds.—*Dir.*, P. J. Conder.

ROYAL SOCIETY OF ARTS (1754), 6–8 John Adam Street, Adelphi, W.C.2.—*Chairman*, Sir James Taylor; *Sec.*, G. E. Mercer.

ROYAL SOCIETY OF BRITISH ARTISTS (1823), 17 Carlton House Terrace, S.W.1.—*Pres.*, E. I. Halliday; *Hon. Sec.*, D. J. Winfield; *Keeper*, M. B. Bradshaw.

ROYAL SOCIETY OF BRITISH SCULPTORS (1904), 8 Chesham Place, S.W.1.—*Pres.*, M. Clark; *Sec.*, Mrs. O. H. D. Churchill.

ROYAL SOCIETY OF EDINBURGH (1783), 22 George Street, Edinburgh 2.—*Pres.*, Sir Maurice Yonge, F.R.S.; *Gen. Sec.*, Prof. A. E. Ritchie, M.D.; *Treas.*, The Lord Balerno, C.B.E., T.D., D.SC.; *Curator*, H. E. Butler, PH.D.

ROYAL SOCIETY OF HEALTH (1876), to promote the health of the people, 90 Buckingham Palace Road, S.W.1.—*Sec.*, P. Arthur Wells, M.A., M.SC.

ROYAL SOCIETY OF LITERATURE (1823), 1 Hyde Park Gardens, W.2.—*Sec.*, Mrs. J. M. Patterson.

ROYAL SOCIETY OF MEDICINE (1805), 1 Wimpole Street, W.1.—*Pres.*, Prof. Sir Hedley Atkins, K.B.E.; *Sec.*, R. T. Hewitt, O.B.E.

ROYAL SOCIETY OF PORTRAIT PAINTERS (1891), 17 Carlton House Terrace, S.W.1.—*Pres.*, E. Halliday, P.R.B.A.; *Sec.*, M. B. Bradshaw.

ROYAL SOCIETY OF ST. GEORGE (1894), 4 Upper Belgrave Street, S.W.1.—*Gen. Sec.*, Sir Ian Hogg, K.C.B., D.S.C.

ROYAL STATISTICAL SOCIETY (1834), 21 Bentinck Street, W.1.—*Pres.*, Prof. G. A. Barnard; *Sec.*, I. H. Blenkinsop.

ROYAL TANK REGIMENT ASSOCIATION and BENEVOLENT FUND, H.Q. R.A.C. Centre, Bovington Camp, Wareham, Dorset.—*Sec.*, Lt.-Col. C. H. Rayment, M.B.E.

ROYAL UNITED KINGDOM BENEFICENT ASSOCIATION (1863), Aldine House, 13 Bedford Street, W.C.2. —*Gen. Sec.*, Maj.-Gen. R. D. Houghton, C.B. O.B.E., M.C.

ROYAL UNITED SERVICE INSTITUTE FOR DEFENCE STUDIES, Whitehall, S.W.1.—*Dir.-Gen.*, Air Vice-Marshal S. W. B. Menaul, C.B., C.B.E., D.F.C., A.F.C.

RURAL DISTRICT COUNCILS ASSOCIATION (1895), Eggington House, 25 Buckingham Gate, S.W.1. —*Sec.*, S. Rhodes, O.B.E.

RURAL ENGLAND, COUNCIL FOR THE PROTECTION OF (1926), 4, Hobart Place, S.W.1.—*Secs.*, M. V. Osmond; A. F. Holford-Walker.

RURAL SCOTLAND, ASSOCIATION FOR PRESERVATION OF (1927), 39 Castle Street, Edinburgh, 2.—*Sec.*, K. Macrae, W.S.

RURAL WALES, COUNCIL FOR THE PROTECTION OF (1928), Meifod, Montgomeryshire.—*Gen. Sec.*, S. Meade.

SAILORS' CHILDREN'S SOCIETY, THE (1821), Newland, Hull. Cares for British seamen's children who have lost a parent and for short periods during a mother's illness if father is at sea. Provides welfare facilities for seamen in Humber area, including Homes for aged seafarers at Hull, Goole, Grimsby, S. Shields, Fleetwood and Lowestoft.—*Sec.*, L. Hartley.

ST. CHRISTOPHER'S FELLOWSHIP (incorporating Homes for Working Boys in London (1870)) 53 Warwick Road, S.W.5.

ST. DUNSTAN'S, for men and women blinded on War Service, P.O. Box 58, 191 Old Marylebone Road, N.W.1. In March 1971, the number of blinded men and women in the care of the organization was 1,909.—*Pres.*, Sir Neville Pearson, Bt.; *Chairman*, The Lord Fraser of Lonsdale, C.H., C.B.E.; *Hon. Treas.*, I. G. Orme; *Sec.*, A. D. Lloyds.

ST. GILES CHRISTIAN MISSION 1860), 60 Bride Street, N.7.—*Sec.* (vacant).

ST. JOHN AMBULANCE ASSOCIATION AND BRIGADE, 1 Grosvenor Crescent, S.W.1.—*Chief Commander and Commissioner-in-Chief*, Lt.-Gen. Sir William Pike, K.C.B., C.B.E., D.S.O. *Brigade Strengths* (U.K., 1970). Men, 27,073; Women, 17,338; Boy Cadets, 21,611; Girl Cadets, 35,021. —*Registrar*, G. W. Woodhill.

SALES ENGINEERS, INSTITUTION OF (1966), Queensway, Leamington Spa, Warwicks.—*Natl. Sec.*, J. E. Fenton.

SALMON AND TROUT ASSOCIATION (1903), Fishmongers' Hall, E.C.4.—*Hon. Sec.*, Cdr. O. S. M. Bayley, R.N.

SALTIRE SOCIETY (1936), Gladstone's Land, 483 Lawnmarket, Edinburgh 1.

SALVAGE CORPS (FIRE)—

London (1866), 140 Aldersgate Street, E.C.1. *Chief Officer*, R. V. Seels.

Liverpool (1842), 46 Derby Road, Liverpool, 20. *Chief Officer*, K. G. Smith.

Glasgow (1873) 201-203 Albion Street, Glasgow, C.1.—*Chief Officer*, A. S. Edmiston.

SANITARY ENGINEERS, INSTITUTION OF. *See* PUBLIC HEALTH ENGINEERS.

SAVE THE CHILDREN FUND (1919), 29 Queen Anne's Gate, S.W.1.—*Dir. Gen.*, Sir Colin Thornley, K.C.M.G., C.V.O.

SAVINGS BANKS INSTITUTE, Knighton House, 52-66 Mortimer Street, W.1.—*Sec.* A. J. F. Miller.

SCHOOL LIBRARY ASSOCIATION, Premier House, 150 Southampton Row, W.C.1.—*Hon. Sec.*, E. L. Moor.

SCHOOL NATURAL SCIENCE SOCIETY, 2 Bramley Mansions, Berrylands Road, Surbiton, Surrey.— *Hon. Gen. Sec.*, M. Jenny Sellers.

SCHOOLMASTERS' ASSOCIATION, SCOTTISH, 41 York Place, Edinburgh.—*Gen. Sec.*, R. McClement.

SCHOOLMASTERS, NATIONAL ASSOCIATION OF, Swan Court, Waterhouse Street, Hemel Hempstead, Herts.—*Sec.*, T. A. Casey.

SCHOOLMASTERS, SOCIETY OF (1798) (for the relief of Necessitous Schoolmasters and of their Widows and Orphans), 308 Galpins Road, Thornton Heath, Surrey.—*Sec.*, Mrs. H. E. Closs.

SCHOOLMISTRESSES AND GOVERNESSES BENEVOLENT INSTITUTION, 39 Buckingham Gate, S.W.1. For the benefit of all kinds of women private teachers. working and retired; annuities; temporary assistance; homes for the retired.—*Sec.*, J. W. Beattie.

SCHOOLS MUSIC ASSOCIATION, THE (1938), 4 Newman Road, Bromley, Kent.—*Sec.*, S. S. Moore.

SCIENCE AND LEARNING, SOCIETY FOR THE PROTECTION OF, 3 Buckland Crescent, N.W.3.— *President*, Prof. A. V. Hill, C.H., O.B.E., F.R.S.; *Sec.*, Miss E. Simpson, O.B.E.

SCIENCE EDUCATION, ASSOCIATION FOR (1963), College Lane, Hatfield, Herts.

SCOTTISH CONSERVATIVE AND UNIONIST ASSOCIATION, 72 Waterloo Street, Glasgow, C.2.

SCOTTISH CONSERVATIVE AND UNIONIST CENTRAL OFFICE, 11 Atholl Crescent, Edinburgh 3.

SCOTTISH GENEALOGY SOCIETY (1953).—*Hon. Sec.*, Miss J. P. S. Ferguson, 21 Howard Place, Edinburgh 3.

SCOTTISH HISTORY SOCIETY (1886).—*Hon. Sec.*, T. I. Rae, PH.D., c/o National Library of Scotland, George IV Bridge, Edinburgh 1.

SCOTTISH LANDOWNERS' FEDERATION (1906).—*Sec.*, A. F. Roney Dougal, 26 Rutland Square, Edinburgh.

SCOTTISH LIBERAL PARTY (1946), 2 Atholl Place, Edinburgh 3.—*Sec.*, W. Mackenzie.

SCOTTISH NATIONAL BLOOD TRANSFUSION ASSOCIATION (1940), 5 St. Colme Street, Edinburgh, 3.— *Sec.*, Neil A. Milne, W.S.

SCOTTISH NATIONAL PARTY, 14 Manor Place, Edinburgh.—*Sec.*, Lt.-Col. M. Muriel Gibson.

SCOTTISH RECORD SOCIETY, Scottish Record Office, Edinburgh 2.—*Hon. Sec.*, A. L. Murray.

SCOTTISH SECONDARY TEACHERS' ASSOCIATION, 15 Dundas Street, Edinburgh, 3.—*Gen. Sec.*, J. Docherty.

SCOTTISH SOCIETY FOR PREVENTION OF CRUELTY TO ANIMALS (1839), 19 Melville Street, Edinburgh, 3.—*Sec.*, G. F. S. Brian.

SCOTTISH SOCIETY FOR THE PROTECTION OF WILD BIRDS (1927), 125 Douglas Street, Glasgow, C.2.—*Sec.*, James M. MacKellar.

SCOTTISH TOURIST BOARD (1945), Rutland Place, Edinburgh 1.—*Chief Executive*, L. Borley.

SCOTTISH WOMEN'S RURAL INSTITUTES (1917), 42 Heriot Row, Edinburgh 3.—*Gen. Sec.*, Miss H. B. Ramage, M.B.E.

SCOUT ASSOCIATION, THE, *Headquarters*, 25 Buckingham Palace Road, S.W.1.—*Chief Scout*, The Lord Maclean, K.T., K.B.E.; *Sec.*, E. W. Hayden. Membership in U.K. (1970), 539,340; World Membership over 12,000,000 in over 100 countries.

SCRIBES AND ILLUMINATORS, THE SOCIETY OF.—*Hon. Sec.*, J. M. Cackett, 270 Trinity Road, S.W.18.

SCRIPTURE GIFT MISSION (1888), Radstock House, Eccleston Street, S.W.1. Copies and selections of the Scriptures circulated (1970), 17,897,024.—*Sec.*, J. M. Smith.

SCRIPTURE UNION (1867), 5 Wigmore Street, W.1.—*Gen. Dir.*, N. W. H. Sylvester.

SEAFARERS EDUCATION SERVICE (1919), Mansbridge House, 207 Balham High Road, S.W.17.—*Director*, Ronald Hope, O.B.E., M.A., D.Phil.

SEAMEN'S CHRISTIAN FRIEND SOCIETY (1846), 87 Brigstock Road, Thornton Heath, Surrey.

SECRETARIES, CHARTERED INSTITUTE OF (1891), 16 Park Crescent, W.1.—*Sec.*, J. F. Phillips, O.B.E., Ll.M.

SELBORNE SOCIETY (1885). Founded in memory of Gilbert White of Selborne.—*Hon. Sec.*, A. H. Austin, 10 Sunbeam Cottages, Limpsfield, Oxted, Surrey.

SELDEN SOCIETY (1887), Faculty of Laws, Queen Mary College, Mile End Road, E.1.—*Pres.*, Rt. Hon. Lord Diplock; *Sec.*, V. Tunkel.

SHAFTESBURY HOMES AND *Arethusa* (secondary boarding school in a ship, founded 1843 in River Medway, Kent); *Headquarters*, 229A Shaftesbury Avenue, W.C.2.—*Gen. Sec.*, Lt.-Cdr. A. D. England, R.N.

SHAFTESBURY SOCIETY (1844), Shaftesbury House, 112 Regency Street, S.W.1.—Engaged in social service among the physically handicapped and the poor. Maintains Residential Schools for physically handicapped children, Hostels for Muscular Dystrophy sufferers over 16 years, Holiday centres for the disabled and Missions in Greater London.—*Sec.*, G. A. Franklin, O.B.E.

SHAW SOCIETY (1941), 3 Chestnut Court, Middle Lane, N.8.—*Hon. Gen. Sec.*, Miss T. Block.

SHELLFISH ASSOCIATION OF GREAT BRITAIN, Fishmongers' Hall, E.C.4.—*Hon. Sec.*, Cdr. O. S. M. Bayley.

SHELTER (National Campaign for the Homeless), 86 Strand, W.C.2.

SHERLOCK HOLMES SOCIETY (1951), The Studio, 39 Clabon Mews, S.W.1.—*Hon. Sec.*, C. Prestige.

SHIPBROKERS, INSTITUTE OF CHARTERED (1911), 25 Bury Street, E.C.3.—*Sec.*, N. C. Cowland.

SHIPPING OF THE UNITED KINGDOM, CHAMBER OF, 30–32 St. Mary Axe, E.C.3.—*Pres.* (1971–72), J. H. Kirby; *Dir.*, L. J. H. Horner, O.B.E.

SHIPWRECKED FISHERMEN AND MARINERS' ROYAL BENEVOLENT SOCIETY (1839), 1 North Pallant, Chichester, Sussex.—*Sec.*, Lt.-Cdr. H. E. Pinchin, R.N.

SHIRE HORSE SOCIETY (1878), East of England Showground, Peterborough.—*Sec.*, R. W. Bird.

SIR OSWALD STOLL FOUNDATION, 446 Fulham Road, S.W.6.—*Sec.*, Miss J. M. Buckle-Pickett.

SMALL INDUSTRIES COUNCIL for Rural Areas of Scotland, 27 Walker Street, Edinburgh.—*Sec.*, T. I. Geddes.

SMALL INDUSTRIES IN RURAL AREAS, COUNCIL FOR, 11 Cowley Street, S.W.1.—*Sec.*, B. E. Lincoln.

SOCIAL CREDIT CO-ORDINATING CENTRE.—*Hon. Sec.*, V. R. Hadkins, Montagu Chambers, Mexborough, Yorkshire.

SOCIAL WORKERS, BRITISH ASSOCIATION OF (1970), 42 Bedford Square, W.C.1.—*Gen. Sec.*, K. H. Brill.

SOCIALIST PARTY OF GREAT BRITAIN (1904), 52 Clapham High Street, S.W.4.—*Gen. Sec.*, V. Phillips.

SOIL ASSOCIATION, Walnut Tree Manor, Haughley, Stowmarket Suffolk.—*Pres.*, E. F. Schumacher; *Gen. Sec.*, Brig. A. W. Vickers, D.S.O., O.B.E.

SOLDIERS' AND AIRMEN'S SCRIPTURE READERS ASSOCIATION (1838), Havelock House, 35 Catherine Place, S.W.1.—*Gen. Sec.*, Lt.-Col. T. A. Dick, M.B.E.

SOLDIERS' DAUGHTERS' SCHOOL, ROYAL (1855) 65 Rosslyn Hill, Hampstead, N.W.3.—*Sec.*, Col. J. W. Bell.

SOLDIERS', SAILORS' AND AIRMEN'S FAMILIES ASSOCIATION (1885), 27 Queen Anne's Gate, S.W.1.—*Chairman*, Lieut.-Gen. Sir Reginald Denning, K.B.E., C.B.; *Controller*, M. H. Nisbet, M.B.E.; *Sec.*, Lt.-Cdr. R. G. Brown, V.R.D., R.N.R.

SOLDIERS, SAILORS AND AIRMEN'S HELP SOCIETY (Incorporated) (1899), *see* FORCES HELP SOCIETY.

SOLICITORS' BENEVOLENT ASSOCIATION (1858), Clifford's Inn, Fetter Lane, E.C.4.—*Sec.*, Miss M. Gold.

SOLICITORS IN THE SUPREME COURTS, SCOTLAND.—*Sec.* (vacant); *Treas.*, A. Stewart, 27 Chester Street, Edinburgh.

SONS OF THE CLERGY, CORPORATION OF THE (1655), 1 Dean Trench Street, S.W.1.—*Regr.*, Brig. G. O. N. Thompson, D.S.O., O.B.E.

S.O.S. SOCIETY, THE (1929), 14 Culford Gardens, S.W.3. Old people's homes (6), Mental Rehabilitation Units (2), Ex-offenders hostel (1), Boys' Hostel (1).—*Gen. Sec.*, E. A. Burrus.

SOUTH AMERICAN MISSIONARY SOCIETY, 157 Waterloo Road, S.E.1.—*Gen. Sec.*, Rev. Canon H. Sutton.

SOUTH WALES INSTITUTE OF ENGINEERS (1857), Institute Buildings, Park Place, Cardiff.—*Sec.*, Mrs. E. M. Rees.

SPASTICS SOCIETY, THE (1952), 12 Park Crescent, W.1.—*Sec.*, R. C. E. Cumplen.

SPURGEON'S HOMES (1867), Park Road, Birchington, Kent.—*Sec.*, P. E. Johnson.

STAFFORDSHIRE SOCIETY, THE.—*Hon. Sec.*, Mrs. A. C. Thwaites, 9 Burnham Way, Ealing, W.13.

STAIR SOCIETY (to encourage the study and advance the knowledge of the history of Scots Law).—*Sec.*, G. R. Thomson, T.D., Ph.D., 2 St. Giles' Street, Edinburgh 1.

STAR AND GARTER HOME FOR DISABLED SAILORS, SOLDIERS, AND AIRMEN (1916), Richmond-upon-Thames.—*Sec.*, Maj.-Gen. J. Sheffield, C.B., C.B.E.

STATISTICIANS, INSTITUTE OF (1949), 55 Park Lane, W.1.—*Hon. Sec.*, B. O. Longman.

STEWART SOCIETY (1899), 48 Castle Street, Edinburgh.—*Hon. Sec.*, D. F. Stewart, W.S.

STOCK EXCHANGE, THE, Threadneedle Street, E.C.2.—*Chairman*, Sir Martin Wilkinson; *Deputy Chairmen*, K. H. M. Crabbe, T.D.; G. A. Loveday, T.D.; The Lord Ritchie of Dundee, P.C.; *Sec.-Gen.*, G. W. R. Brind.

STRUCTURAL ENGINEERS, INSTITUTION OF (1908), 11 Upper Belgrave Street, S.W.1.—*Sec.*, C. D. Morgan, O.B.E.

STUDENT CHRISTIAN MOVEMENT OF GREAT BRITAIN AND IRELAND (1889), Annandale, North End Road, N.W.11.—*Gen. Sec.*, Rev. D. Head.

SURGEONS OF ENGLAND, ROYAL COLLEGE OF (1800), Lincoln's Inn Fields, W.C.2.—*Pres.*, Sir Thomas Sellors, D.M.; *Sec.*, R. S. Johnson-Gilbert.

SURGEONS OF EDINBURGH, ROYAL COLLEGE OF (1505). 18 Nicolson Street, Edinburgh.—*Sec.*, J. Cook, F.R.C.S.E., F.R.S.E.

SURGICAL AID SOCIETY, ROYAL (1862), 1 Dorset Buildings, Salisbury Square, E.C.4.—*Sec.*, Capt. F. D. G. Challis, R.N.

SURGICAL TECHNICIANS, BRITISH INSTITUTE OF, 21 Tothill Street, S.W.1.—*Sec.*, R. Nunn.

SURVEYORS, ROYAL INSTITUTION OF CHARTERED (1868), 12 Great George Street, S.W.1.—*Pres.*, (1971–72), J. B. George, M.B.E., T.D.; *Sec.*, R. Steel.

SUSSEX CATTLE SOCIETY (1887), 12 Lonsdale Gardens, Tunbridge Wells, Kent.—*Sec.*, H. J. Hancorn.

SUTTON DWELLINGS TRUST (1901), Swan Court, Hemel Hempstead, Herts.—*Gen. Manager*, C. V. Baker.

SWEDENBORG SOCIETY (1810), 20–21 Bloomsbury Way, W.C.1.—*Hon. Sec.*, Freda G. Griffith, Ph.D., B.SC.

TAIL WAGGERS' CLUB (GREAT BRITAIN), LTD., Old Change House, Cannon Street, E.C.4.—*Sec.*, A. S. C. Michell.

TAVISTOCK INSTITUTE OF HUMAN RELATIONS, Tavistock Centre, Belsize Lane, N.W.3.—*Sec.*, S. G. Gray.

TAXATION, INSTITUTE OF (1930), Cliffords Inn, E.C.4.—*Sec.*, A. A. Arnold.

TEACHERS IN COLLEGES AND DEPARTMENTS OF EDUCATION, ASSOCIATION OF, 3 Crawford Place, W.1.—*Gen. Sec.*, S. Hewett.

TEACHERS IN COMMERCE LTD., FACULTY OF, 12 Crampton Drive, Halebarns, Altrincham, Cheshire.—*Sec.*, J. Snowdon.

TEACHERS IN TECHNICAL INSTITUTIONS, ASSOCIATION OF (1904), Hamilton House, Mabledon Place, W.C.1.—*Sec.*, T. Driver.

TEACHERS OF DOMESTIC SCIENCE, ASSOCIATION OF, Hamilton House, Mabledon Place, W.C.1.—*Sec.*, Miss A. M. Crawley.

TEACHERS OF MATHEMATICS, ASSOCIATION OF.—c/o *Sec.*, Market Street Chambers, Nelson, Lancs.

TEACHERS OF SPEECH AND DRAMA, SOCIETY OF, St. Bride Institute, Fleet Street, E.C.4.—*Hon. Sec.*, E. J. Burton.

TEACHERS OF THE DEAF, NATIONAL COLLEGE OF.—*Hon. Sec.*, E. Brown, Needwood School, Rangemore Hall, Burton-on-Trent.

TEACHERS' UNION, ULSTER (1919), 72 High Street, Belfast.—*Sec.*, B. K. Toms.

TEACHING HOSPITALS ASSOCIATION, 121–3 Edgware Road, W.2.—*Sec.*, S. C. Merivale, C.B.E.

TELEPHONE USERS' ASSOCIATION (1965), 35 Connaught Square, W.2.—*Sec.*, M. Elwes.

TELEVISION SOCIETY, ROYAL, 166 Shaftesbury Avenue, W.C.2.—*Hon. Sec.*, C. A. Marshall.

TEMPERANCE SOCIETIES:—
  British National Temperance League (1834), Livesey-Clegg House, 44 Union Street, Sheffield, 1.—*Sec.*, Miss M. Daniel.
  British Women's Temperance Association, S.C.U. (1876), 8 North Bank Street, Edinburgh 1.—*Sec.*, Miss M. I. D. Smith.

  Church of England Council for Social Aid, Church House, Dean's Yard, S.W.1.—*Gen. Sec.*, Rev. J. B. Harrison.
  Church of Scotland Women's Committee on Social Service and Moral Welfare, 121 George Street, Edinburgh 2.—*Sec.*, Mrs. R. Gray.
  Congregational Church in England and Wales, Committee on Temperance, Drug Dependence and Gambling, Livingstone House, Carteret Street, S.W.1.
  Department of Christian Citizenship of the Methodist Church, Central Buildings, Matthew Parker St., S.W.1.—*Gen. Sec.*, Rev. Edward Rogers.
  Independent Order of Rechabites, Salford Unity Friendly Society, London District (1870), No. 30, 18 Doughty Street, W.C.1.
  National Association of Temperance Officials (1897), 5 Kirby Avenue, Swinton, Manchester, 3.—*Hon. Sec.*, J. Harrison.
  National Temperance Federation (1884), 12 Caxton Street, S.W.1.—*Hon. Sec.*, G. T. Brake.
  National Unitarian and Free Christian Temperance Association (1893), 35 Oakington Manor Drive, Wembley.—*Hon. Sec.*, Rev. W. M. Long.
  Order of the Sons of Temperance, 21 Victoria Avenue, Harrogate.—*Sec.*, K. Unsworth.
  Royal Naval Temperance Society (auxiliary of Royal Sailors' Rests), 32 Western Parade, Southsea, Hants.
  Scottish Temperance Alliance, 244 Bath Street, Glasgow, C.2.—*Sec.*, Colin Palmer.
  Social Service Board of the Episcopal Church in Scotland (1919).—*Sec.*, I. D. Stuart, 21 Grosvenor Crescent, Edinburgh.
  South Wales Temperance Union, Temperance Collegiate Association, 112 Albany Road, Cardiff.—*Sec.*, A. C. Davey.
  Temperance Council of the Christian Churches (1915) (incorporating the Overseas Temperance Council), Drayton House, Gordon Street, W.C.1.—*Gen. Sec.*, Rev. A. C. Davies.
  Temperance Education Board (Ireland) (1918), 12 Lombard Street, Belfast.—*Sec.*, H. C. Jones.
  United Kingdom Band of Hope Union, Hope House, 45 Great Peter Street, S.W.1.—*Gen. Sec.*, Robert Tayler.

TERRITORIAL, AUXILIARY AND VOLUNTEER RESERVE ASSOCIATIONS, COUNCIL OF (1908), Duke of York's Headquarters, Chelsea, S.W.3.—*Sec.*, Brig. A. C. Tyler, C.B.E., M.C.

TEXTILE INSTITUTE (1910), 10 Blackfriars Street, Manchester, 3.—*Gen. Sec.*, D. B. Moore, M.A.

THEATRE MUSEUM, BRITISH, Leighton House, 12 Holland Park Road, Kensington, W.14.—*Curator*, Miss J. Aylmer.

THEATRE PRESS REPRESENTATIVES, ASSOCIATION OF LONDON (1950), 3rd Floor, West End House, Hills Place, W.1.

THEATRE RESEARCH, SOCIETY FOR (1948).—*Hon. Secs.*, Miss K. M. Barker, J. Reading, 14 Woronzow Road, N.W.8.

THEATRICAL FUND, ROYAL GENERAL (1839), 11 Garrick Street, W.C.2.—*Sec.*, Mrs. A. Copland.

THEATRICAL LADIES' GUILD OF CHARITY (1892), Gloucester House, 19 Charing Cross Road, W.C.2.—*Sec.*, Mrs. G. Hammill.

THEATRICAL MANAGEMENT ASSOCIATION, Gloucester House, 19 Charing Cross Road, W.C.2.—*Sec.*, C. R. L. Thompson.

THEOSOPHICAL SOCIETY IN ENGLAND (1875), 50 Gloucester Place, W.1.—*Gen. Sec.*, G. A. Farthing.

THISTLE FOUNDATION, THE (1945), 22 Charlotte Square, Edinburgh 2.—*Secs.*, Graham, Smart and Annan, Chartered Accountants.

THORACIC SOCIETY, THE.—*Hon. Sec.*, P. D. B. Davies, M.D., Whittington Hospital, Highgate, N.19.

TIBET SOCIETY OF THE UNITED KINGDOM AND TIBET RELIEF FUND (1959), 58 Eccleston Square, S.W.1. —*Sec.*, Mrs. V. Potter.

TIN RESEARCH INSTITUTE (1932), Fraser Road, Perivale, Greenford, Middlesex.—*Dir.*, W. E. Hoare, D.SC.

TOC H (TALBOT HOUSE) (1915), *British Headquarters*, 15 Trinity Square, E.C.3.—*Gen. Sec.* G. A. Francis.

TOWN AND COUNTRY PLANNING ASSOCIATION, 17 Carlton House Terrace, S.W.1.—*Dir.*, D. Hall.

TOWN CLERKS, SOCIETY OF (1928).—*Hon. Sec.*, T. Foord (*Worthing*).

TOWN PLANNING INSTITUTE, ROYAL (1914), 26 Portland Place, W.1.—*Sec.*, P. R. Rathbone.

TOWNSWOMEN'S GUILDS, NATIONAL UNION OF (1929), 2 Cromwell Place, S.W.7.—*Nat. Sec.*, Mrs. M. Erskine-Wyse.

TRADE MARK AGENTS, INSTITUTE OF (1934), 69 Cannon Street, E.C.4.—*Sec.*, H. F. Hoare.

TRADE, NATIONAL CHAMBER OF (1897), Enterprise House, 3 Hyde Park Place, W.2.—*Gen. Sec.*, J. B. Pegnall.

TRADES UNION CONGRESS (T.U.C.)—*See* p. 1125.

TRAFFIC ADMINISTRATION, INSTITUTE OF (1944), 8 Cumberland Place, Southampton.—*Sec.*, F. R. Pywell.

TRANSPORT, CHARTERED INSTITUTE OF (1919), 80 Portland Place, W.1.—*Sec.*, A. G. Griffiths.

TRANSPORT MANAGERS, NATIONAL GUILD OF, 53 Hainton Avenue, Grimsby, Lincs.—*Gen. Sec.*, F. P. Coult.

TRAVEL AGENTS, ASSOCIATION OF BRITISH (1950), 50–57 Newman Street, W.1.—*Chief Exec.*, M. A. Elton.

TRAVELLERS' ASSOCIATIONS JOINT COMMITTEE.— *Hon. Sec.*, D. J. Bowen, Thurston Cottage, Thurston Park, Whitstable, Kent.

TROPICAL MEDICINE AND HYGIENE, ROYAL SOCIETY OF (1907), Manson House, 26 Portland Place, W.1.—*Pres.*, Lt.-Gen. Sir Robert Drew, K.C.B., C.B.E., F.R.C.P.; *Sec.*, Miss N. Hopper, M.B.E.

TRUSTEE SAVINGS BANKS ASSOCIATION (1887), Knighton House, 52–66 Mortimer Street, W.1.— *Sec.*, J. F. D. Miller, M.B.E.

TUTORS IN ADULT EDUCATION, ASSOCIATION OF. —*Hon. Sec.*, K. Jackson, Dept. of Adult Education and Extra-Mural Studies, The University, P.O. Box 147, Liverpool.

UFAW (Universities Federation for Animal Welfare) (1926), 230 High Street, Potters Bar, Herts.— *Sec.*, Mrs. C. Brockhurst.

ULSTER SOCIETY IN LONDON, THE, 11 Berkeley Street, W.1.—*Pres.*, The Lord Rathcavan, P.C.; *Hon. Sec.*, Capt. J. Lindsay.

UNIT TRUST MANAGERS, ASSOCIATION OF (1959), 306–8 Salisbury House, Finsbury Circus, E.C.2.— *Sec.*, W. J. Burnett.

UNITED COMMERCIAL TRAVELLERS' ASSOCIATION OF GREAT BRITAIN AND IRELAND (U.K.C.T.A.), (1883) (Incorporated), Bexton Lane, Knutsford, Cheshire.—*Gen. Sec.*, J. Maguire.

UNITED KINGDOM ALLIANCE FOR TOTAL SUPPRESSION OF LIQUOR TRAFFIC (1853), Alliance House, 12 Caxton Street, S.W.1.—*Pres.*, G. E. Macpherson.

UNITED NATIONS ASSOCIATION OF GREAT BRITAIN AND NORTHERN IRELAND (1945), 93 Albert Embankment, S.E.1.—*Sec.*, D. W. Tweddle.

UNITED SERVICES CORPS (1908), for employment of ex-regular Soldiers, Sailors and Airmen of exemplary character. *Headquarters*, 19 Hand Court, W.C.1.

UNITED SOCIETY FOR CHRISTIAN LITERATURE, THE, Albion House, Woking, Surrey; *Africa*, Lusaka, Zambia.—*Gen. Secs.*, Rev. E. H. Wade; Rev. D. R. Chesterton; *Gen. Manager*, M. E. Foxell.

UNITED SYNAGOGUE (1870).—*Pres.*, Sir Isaac Wolfson, Bt.—*Sec.*, N. Rubin, Woburn House, Upper Woburn Place, W.C.1.

UNIVERSITIES CENTRAL COUNCIL ON ADMISSIONS (1961), P.O. Box 28, Cheltenham, Glos.—*Sec.*, L. R. Kay.

UNIVERSITY TEACHERS, ASSOCIATION OF (1919), Bremar House, Sale Place, W.2.—*Sec.*, L. J. Sapper.

UNIVERSITY WOMEN, BRITISH FEDERATION OF (LTD.) (1907), Crosby Hall, Cheyne Walk, S.W.3.—*Sec.*, Mrs. E. Bianco.

UNIVERSITY WOMEN, INTERNATIONAL FEDERATION OF (1919), 17A King's Road, Sloane Square, S.W.3.—*Exec. Sec.*, Miss J. B. Robinson.

UNMARRIED MOTHER AND HER CHILD, NATIONAL COUNCIL FOR THE (INCORPORATED), 255 Kentish Town Road, N.W.5.—*Dir.*, Mrs. M. E. Bramall, O.B.E.

VALUERS AND AUCTIONEERS, INCORPORATED SOCIETY OF, 3 Cadogan Gate, S.W.1.—*Sec.*, J. A. Crockett.

VEGETARIAN SOCIETY (U.K.) LTD., Parkdale, Dunham Road, Altrincham, Cheshire.—*Gen. Sec.*, G. L. Rudd.

VENEREAL DISEASES, MEDICAL SOCIETY FOR THE STUDY OF, 11 Chandos Street, W.1.—*Hon. Sec.*, J. L. Fluker, M.D., F.R.C.P., West London Hospital, W.6.

VICE-CHANCELLORS AND PRINCIPALS OF THE UNIVERSITIES OF THE UNITED KINGDOM, COMMITTEE OF, 29 Tavistock Square, W.C.1.—*Chairman*, T. A. F. Noble, M.B.E., Ll.D.; *Sec.*, A. A. Bath.

VICTORIA LEAGUE FOR COMMONWEALTH FRIENDSHIP (1901), 38 Chesham Place, Belgrave Square, S.W.1.—*Gen. Sec.*, Vice-Adm. Sir John Gray, K.B.E., C.B.

VICTORIAN SOCIETY (1958), 29 Exhibition Road, S.W.7.—*Sec.*, Mrs. E. Fawcett.

VICTORY (SERVICES) ASSOCIATION LTD. AND CLUB, THE, 63–79 Seymour Street, W.2.—*Sec.*, Lt.-Cdr. J. B. Williams, R.N.

VIKING SOCIETY FOR NORTHERN RESEARCH, University College, Gower Street, W.C.1.—*Hon. Secs.*, Prof. G. Turville-Petre, M.A., B.Litt.; Prof. P. G. Foote, M.A.

VITREOUS ENAMELLERS, INSTITUTE OF, Ripley, nr. Derby.—*Sec.*, J. D. Gardom.

VOLUNTARY SERVICE OVERSEAS (1958), 14 Bishop's Bridge Road, W.2.—*Dir.*, D. H. Whiting, O.B.E.

WAR BLINDED, SCOTTISH NATIONAL INSTITUTION FOR THE. Workshops at Edinburgh, Glasgow and Linburn. *Appeals Director*, Maj. D. F. Callander, M.C., P.O. Box 304, 38 Albany Street, Edinburgh 1.

WATER ENGINEERS, INSTITUTION OF, 6–8 Sackville Street, W.1.—*Pres.*, (1971–72), G. M. Swales; *Sec.*, J. P. Banbury, M.B.E.

WEIGHTS & MEASURES ADMINISTRATION, INSTITUTE OF.—*Hon. Sec.*, O. W. Barnes, Weights and Measures Office, Tredegar Street, Cardiff.

WELDING INSTITUTE, THE (1968), Abington Hall, Cambridge and 54 Princes Gate, S.W.7.—*Dir.-Gen.*, R. Weck, C.B.E.

WELLCOME TRUST (1936), 52 Queen Anne Street, W.1.—*Dir.*, P. O. Williams.

WELSH JOINT EDUCATION COMMITTEE (1949), 245 Western Avenue, Cardiff.—*Sec.*, D. A. Davies.

WELSH NATIONAL PARTY (Plaid Cymru), 8 Queen Street, Cardiff.—*Gen. Sec.*, D. Williams.

WESLEY HISTORICAL SOCIETY (1893).—*Gen. Sec.*, Rev. T. Shaw, The Manse, St. Keverne, Helston, Cornwall.

WEST END THEATRE MANAGERS, SOCIETY OF, 19 Charing Cross Road, W.C.2.—*Sec.*, C. R. L. Thompson.

WEST INDIA COMMITTEE (1750), 18 Grosvenor St., W.1.—*Sec.*, Lt.-Col. M. R. Robinson, D.S.O.

WEST LONDON MISSION (1887), Kingsway Hall, W.C.2.—*Supt.*, Rev. The Lord Soper, M.A. Ph.D.

WIDOWS, SOCIETY FOR THE RELIEF OF DISTRESSED (1823) (residing within five miles of Charing Cross and applying within two months of widowhood), 39 Buckingham Gate, S.W.1.—*Sec.*, P. A. Marno.

WINE AND SPIRIT ASSOCIATION OF GREAT BRITAIN (1824), 68½ Upper Thames Street, E.C.4.—*Sec.*, R. H. Insoll, E.R.D.

WOMEN ARTISTS, SOCIETY OF (1855), 195 Piccadilly, W.1.—*Sec.*, Diana Spencer Russell.

WOMEN, NATIONAL ADVISORY CENTRE ON CAREERS FOR (formerly Women's Employment Federation) (1933), 251 Brompton Road, S.W.3.—*Sec.*, Miss I. F. Hilton.

WOMEN PILOTS' ASSOCIATION, BRITISH, (1955), c/o P.O. Box 13, B.O.A.C. Air Terminal, S.W.1.

WOMEN, SOCIETY FOR PROMOTING THE TRAINING OF (1859) (Women's Loan Training Fund), Court Farm, Hedgerley, Bucks.—*Sec.*, Mrs. W. M. Golding.

WOMEN'S ADVISORY COUNCIL ON SOLID FUEL (1943), 18 South Molton Street, W.1.

WOMEN'S ENGINEERING SOCIETY (1920), 25 Foubert's Place, W.1.—*Sec.*, Mrs. E. H. Kane.

WOMEN'S HOLIDAY FUND (1895), 76 Denison House, Vauxhall Bridge Road, S.W.1.—*Sec.*, Mrs. U. Muirhead.

WOMEN'S INSTITUTES, NATIONAL FEDERATION OF (1915), 39 Eccleston Street, S.W.1.—*Gen. Sec.*, Miss M. R. Withall, M.B.E.

WOMEN'S INTERNATIONAL LEAGUE FOR PEACE AND FREEDOM (1915), British Section, 29 Great James Street, W.C.1.—*Sec.*, Mrs. J. Le Grand.

WOMEN'S LIBERAL FEDERATION, 7 Exchange Court, Strand, W.C.2.—*Pres.*, Mrs. P. Jessel; *Sec.*, Mrs. C. Niman.

WOMEN'S PROTESTANT UNION (INC.), WORLD PROTESTANT UNION, and THE SENTINELS' UNION, Clive Court, Ashdown Avenue, Saltdean, Sussex.

WOMEN'S ROYAL NAVAL SERVICE BENEVOLENT TRUST (1942), 2 Lower Sloane Street, S.W.1.—*Gen. Sec.*, Miss E. G. W. Young.

WOMEN'S ROYAL VOLUNTARY SERVICE (WRVS) (1938), 17 Old Park Lane, W.1.

WOMEN'S TRANSPORT SERVICE (FANY) (1907), Duke of York's H.Q., King's Road, S.W.3.—*Corps Commander*, Mrs. S. Y. Parkinson.

WOOD PRESERVING ASSOCIATION, BRITISH, 62 Oxford Street, W.1.—*Dir.*, W. E. Bruce.

WORCESTERSHIRE ASSOCIATION (1926),—*Hon. Treas.*, R. L. Spalding, The White Cottage, Star Hill, Woking, Surrey.

WORK STUDY PRACTITIONERS, INSTITUTE OF (1965), 9-10 River Front, Enfield, Middx.—*Dir.*, E. A. King.

WORKERS' EDUCATIONAL ASSOCIATION, 9 Upper Berkeley Street, W.1.—*Gen. Sec.*, R. J. Jefferies.

WORKING MEN'S CLUB AND INSTITUTE UNION, Club Union House, 251-256 Upper Street, N.1. —*Gen. Sec.*, J. B. Holmes.

WORKS AND HIGHWAYS SUPERINTENDENTS, INSTITUTE OF (1938), 26 Bloomsbury Way, W.C.1.— *Sec.*, Lt.-Col. W. H. Bush.

WORKS MANAGERS, INSTITUTION OF, 34 Bloomsbury Way, W.C.1.—*Dir.*, R. Chichester-Clark.

WORLD CONGRESS OF FAITHS (1934), Younghusband House, 23 Norfolk Square, W.2.—*Chairman*, The Lord Sorensen.

WORLD EDUCATION FELLOWSHIP (1921), *International Headquarters*, 55 Upper Stone Street, Tunbridge Wells, Kent.

WORLD ENERGY CONFERENCE (1924). *Central Office*, 5 Bury Street, S.W.1.—*Sec.-Gen.*, *International Executive Council*, E. Ruttley.

WORLD PROHIBITION FEDERATION (1909), 2 Caxton Street, S.W.1.—*Sec.*, Mark H. C. Hayler.

WRITERS TO H.M. SIGNET, SOCIETY OF, Parliament Square, Edinburgh.—*Deputy Keeper of the Signet*, P. J. Oliphant, T.D.; *Sub-Keeper and Clerk*, P. C. Millar.

YEOMANRY BENEFIT FUND, 206 Brompton Road, S.W.3.—*Sec.*, Mrs. L. Bernard.

YORKSHIRE AGRICULTURAL SOCIETY (1837), Cliftonfield, Shipton Road, York.—*Sec.-Gen.*, F. M. Baldwin, O.B.E., B.SC.

YORKSHIRE FIELD STUDIES LTD.—*Gen. Sec.*, D. H. Smith, Westland, Westfields, Kirbymoorside, York.

YORKSHIREMEN IN LONDON, SOCIETY OF (1899), AND THE YORKSHIRE SOCIETY (1812), 200 High Street, Brentford, Middx.—*Sec.*, G. G. Prince.

YOUNG MEN'S CHRISTIAN ASSOCIATION, *National Council*, 83 Endell Street, W.C.2.—*Gen. Sec.*, R. E. Roberts.

YOUNG WOMEN'S CHRISTIAN ASSOCIATION (1855), *National Headquarters*, 2 Weymouth Street, W.1. —*Nat. Gen. Sec.*, Miss B. Cowderoy.

YOUTH CLUBS, NATIONAL ASSOCIATION OF, 30 Devonshire Street, W.1.—*Gen. Sec.*, S. A. Fox.

YOUTH CLUBS, NORTHERN IRELAND ASSOCIATION OF, 26 Wellington Place, Belfast 1.—*Dir.*, M. A. Brown.

YOUTH HOSTELS ASSOCIATION (ENGLAND AND WALES) (1930), *National Office*, Trevelyan House, St. Albans, Herts.—*Sec.*, H. B. Livingstone.

YOUTH HOSTELS ASSOCIATION (SCOTTISH) (1931), *National Office*, 7 Glebe Crescent, Stirling.

YOUTH HOSTEL ASSOCIATION OF NORTHERN IRELAND LTD. (1931), 28 Bedford Street, Belfast.— *Organizing Sec.*, R. G. Carinduff.

ZOOLOGICAL SOCIETY OF LONDON, Regent's Park, N.W.1.—*Sec.*, The Lord Zuckerman, O.M., K.C.B., D.SC., F.R.S. Attendances (1970), Regent's Park 1,794,000, and Whipsnade Park, 474,800.

ZOOLOGICAL SOCIETY OF SCOTLAND, ROYAL, Scottish National Zoological Park, Murrayfield, Edinburgh 12.—*Dir.*, G. D. Fisher.

THE CIVIC TRUST
18 Carlton House Terrace, S.W.1
[01-930-0914]

Founded in 1957 with the object of improving the appearance of town and country. The Trust is an independent organization which is supported financially by leading industrial and commercial companies. Four Associate Trusts are linked with it in Scotland, Wales, the North West and the North East.

The Trust gives support and advice to some 800 local civic and amenity societies throughout Britain. It has initiated hundreds of schemes to brighten and tidy up drab streets. It has moved over 650 semi-mature trees into London as part of a wider campaign to plant more trees. It stimulates voluntary action to remove eyesores which mar town and countryside. It makes awards annually for good development of all kinds. Its scheme for a 20-mile regional park alongside the River Lea in East London is now being implemented by the Lee Valley Regional Park Authority. It makes available on loan films, photographs, slides and exhibitions. By conferences, projects and reports, it focuses attention on major issues in town planning and architecture.

LOCAL ARCHAEOLOGICAL SOCIETIES
England and Wales

Anglesey.—ANGLESEY ANTIQUARIAN SOCIETY. Hon. Sec., D. O. Jones, County Library, Llangefni, Anglesey.

Bedfordshire.—SOUTH BEDFORDSHIRE ARCHÆOLOGICAL SOCIETY. Hon. Sec., D. H. Kennett, 55 Mount Grace Road, Stopsley, Luton.

Berkshire.—BERKSHIRE ARCHÆOLOGICAL SOCIETY. Hon. Sec., F. M. Underhill, F.S.A., "Turstins", High Street, Didcot, Berks.

Berkshire.—NEWBURY DISTRICT FIELD CLUB, Donnington Dene, Newbury. Hon. Sec., M. E. Kaines-Thomas, D.Lit., F.S.A.

Buckinghamshire.—BUCKS ARCHÆOLOGICAL SOCIETY. Hon. Sec., E. Viney, County Museum, Church Street, Aylesbury, Bucks.

Cambridgeshire. — CAMBRIDGE ANTIQUARIAN SOCIETY. Hon. Sec., Miss J. Liversidge, 20 Manor Court, Grange Road, Cambridge.

Cardiganshire. — CARDIGANSHIRE ANTIQUARIAN SOCIETY. Hon. Sec., D. M. Jones, 26 Alban Square, Aberaeron.

Cheshire.—CHESTER ARCHÆOLOGICAL SOCIETY. Grosvenor Museum, Chester.—Hon. Sec. (vacant)

Cornwall.—ROYAL INSTITUTION OF CORNWALL, County Museum and Art Gallery, Truro. Hon. Sec., A. J. Lyne.

Cumberland and Westmorland.—CUMBERLAND AND WESTMORLAND ANTIQUARIAN AND ARCHÆOLOGICAL SOCIETY. Hon. Sec., W. Rollinson, Dept. of Extension Studies, The University, 1 Abercromby Square, Liverpool 7.

Derbyshire.—DERBYSHIRE ARCHÆOLOGICAL SOCIETY, 35 St. Mary's Gate, Derby. Hon. Sec., M. A. B. Mallender.

Devonshire.—DEVON ARCHÆOLOGICAL SOCIETY. Hon. Sec., J. Bosanko, c/o The Museum, Queen Street, Exeter.

Dorset.—DORSET NATURAL HISTORY AND ARCHÆOLOGICAL SOCIETY, Dorset County Museum, Dorchester. Curator and Sec., R. N. R. Peers.

Durham. — DURHAM AND NORTHUMBERLAND ARCHITECTURAL AND ARCHÆOLOGICAL SOCIETY. Hon. Sec., Miss J. Kewley, Ph.D., F.S.A.(Scot.), Neville's Cross College, Durham.

SUNDERLAND ANTIQUARIAN SOCIETY.—Hon. Sec., A. Stewart, 9 Keswick Avenue, Sunderland.

Essex.—ESSEX ARCHÆOLOGICAL SOCIETY, Little Pitchbury, Brick Kiln Lane, Great Horkesley, Colchester. Hon. Sec., J. S. Appleby.

Gloucestershire.—BRISTOL AND GLOUCESTERSHIRE ARCHÆOLOGICAL SOCIETY, Council House, Bristol, 1. Hon. Sec., Miss E. Ralph.

UNIVERSITY OF BRISTOL SPELÆOLOGICAL SOCIETY, The University, Bristol 8.—Hon. Secs., A. Boycott; R. A. Churcher.

Hampshire.—HAMPSHIRE FIELD CLUB AND ARCHÆOLOGICAL SOCIETY. Hon. Sec., Prof. B. W. Cunliffe, Dept. of Archæology, The University, Southampton.

Herefordshire.—WOOLHOPE NATURALISTS' FIELD CLUB. Hon. Sec., c/o The City Library, Broad Street, Hereford.

Hertfordshire.—EAST HERTFORDSHIRE ARCHÆOLOGICAL SOCIETY. Hon. Sec., G. Moodey, F.S.A., 27 West Street, Hertford.

ST. ALBANS AND HERTFORDSHIRE ARCHITECTURAL AND ARCHÆOLOGICAL SOCIETY.—Hon. Sec., O. J. Weaver, 17 Ridgmont Road, St. Albans.

Kent.—KENT ARCHÆOLOGICAL SOCIETY, Gen. Sec., c/o The Museum, Maidstone.

Lancashire.—LANCASHIRE AND CHESHIRE ANTIQUARIAN SOCIETY.—Hon. Sec., A. G. Rose, c/o Central Library, St. Peter's Square, Manchester 2.

HISTORIC SOCIETY OF LANCASHIRE AND CHESHIRE.—Hon. Sec., V. J. Andrews, c/o Central Public Library, Liverpool 3.

Leicestershire.—LEICESTERSHIRE ARCHÆOLOGICAL AND HISTORICAL SOCIETY, The Guildhall, Guildhall Lane, Leicester. Hon. Sec., Miss M. P. Rippin.

Lincolnshire.—LINCOLNSHIRE LOCAL HISTORY SOCIETY (incorporating Lincolnshire Architectural and Archaeological Society).—Hon. Sec., Miss F. A. R. Murray, 86 Newland, Lincoln.

Middlesex.—LONDON AND MIDDLESEX ARCHÆOLOGICAL SOCIETY, Bishopsgate Institute, E.C.2. Hon. Sec., E. E. F. Smith.

Norfolk.—NORFOLK AND NORWICH ARCHÆOLOGICAL SOCIETY. Hon. Gen. Sec., I. Cresswell, F.S.A., The Old Rectory, Shelton, Norwich.

Nottinghamshire.—THOROTON SOCIETY OF NOTTINGHAMSHIRE, Bromley House, Angel Row, Nottingham. Hon. Sec., M. G. Dobbin.

Oxfordshire.—OXFORD ARCHITECTURAL AND HISTORICAL SOCIETY.—Hon. Sec., Mrs. J. C. Cole, Ashmolean Museum, Oxford.

Radnorshire.—RADNORSHIRE SOCIETY. Hon. Secs., E. V. Howells, The White House, Cefnllys Lane, Llandrindod Wells; C. W. Newman, County Library, Cefnllys Road, Llandrindod Wells.

Salop.—SHROPSHIRE ARCHÆOLOGICAL AND PARISH REGISTER SOCIETY. Hon. Sec., H. Beaumont, Silverdale, Severn Bank, Shrewsbury.

Somerset.—SOMERSET ARCHÆOLOGICAL AND NATURAL HISTORY SOCIETY, Taunton Castle, Taunton. Secretary, L. A. Haldane.

Staffordshire.—NORTH STAFFORDSHIRE FIELD CLUB, Hon. Sec., R. A. Tribbeck. Dept. of Chemistry, North Staffordshire Polytechnic, Stoke-on-Trent.

CITY OF STOKE-ON-TRENT MUSEUM ARCHÆOLOGICAL SOCIETY, City Museum, Stoke-on-Trent. Chairman, A. R. Mountford.

SOUTH STAFFORDSHIRE ARCHÆOLOGICAL AND HISTORICAL SOCIETY.—Hon. Sec., J. Gould, F.S.A., 307 Erdington Road, Aldridge.

Suffolk.—SUFFOLK INSTITUTE OF ARCHÆOLOGY.—Hon. Sec., D. G. Penrose, Westwood, Constitution Hill, Ipswich.

Surrey.—SURREY ARCHÆOLOGICAL SOCIETY, Castle Arch, Guildford.—Hon. Sec., D. J. Turner, F.S.A., F.S.A.(Scot.).

Sussex.—SUSSEX ARCHÆOLOGICAL SOCIETY, Barbican House, High Street, Lewes.—Hon. Secs., T. T. Harris; H. S. Martin, C.B.E.

Warwickshire.—BIRMINGHAM AND WARWICKSHIRE ARCHÆOLOGICAL SOCIETY, Birmingham and Midland Institute, Margaret Street, Birmingham 3.—Hon. Sec., Mrs. R. Taylor.

Wight.—ISLE OF WIGHT NATURAL HISTORY AND ARCHÆOLOGICAL SOCIETY.—Sec., Miss H. Blount, 50 Queen's Road, Ryde, I.o.W.

Wiltshire.—WILTSHIRE ARCHÆOLOGICAL AND NATURAL HISTORY SOCIETY, The Museum, 41 Long Street, Devizes.—Sec. and Treas., Brig. A. R. Forbes.

Worcestershire.—WORCESTERSHIRE ARCHÆOLOGICAL SOCIETY.—Hon. Sec., R. F. Panton, Birchdale, 4 Orchard Road, Gt. Malvern.

Yorkshire.—HUNTER ARCHÆOLOGICAL SOCIETY. Hon. Sec., Miss D. Greene, F.S.A., Sitwell Villa, Moorgate, Rotherham.

YORKSHIRE ARCHÆOLOGICAL SOCIETY.—Hon. Sec., Miss L. Wordingham, Claremont, 23 Clarendon Road, Leeds.

HALIFAX ANTIQUARIAN SOCIETY. Hon. Sec., R. L. Sutherland, 37 Lombard Street, King Cross, Halifax.

THORESBY SOCIETY, Claremont, 23 Clarendon Road, Leeds 2.—*Hon. Sec.*, D. Keighley.

Isle of Man and Channel Islands

ISLE OF MAN NATURAL HISTORY AND ANTIQUARIAN SOCIETY, c/o The Manx Museum, Douglas.

SOCIÉTÉ JERSIAISE, The Museum, Pier Road, St. Helier, Jersey. *Hon. Sec.*, Mrs. W. E. Macready.

Scotland

AYRSHIRE ARCHÆOLOGICAL AND NATURAL HISTORY SOCIETY, Carnegie Library, Ayr.—*Hon. Sec.*, R. W. Brash, 54 Midton Road, Ayr.

DUMFRIESSHIRE AND GALLOWAY NATURAL HISTORY AND ANTIQUARIAN SOCIETY. *Hon. Sec.*, Mrs. P. Williams, Hills Tower, Lochfoot, nr. Dumfries

GLASGOW ARCHÆOLOGICAL SOCIETY. *Hon. Secs.*, Miss A. S. Robertson, D.Litt., F.S.A., Hunterian Museum, University of Glasgow; A. Morrison, F.S.A. scot., Dept. of Archæology, University of Glasgow.

HAWICK ARCHÆOLOGICAL SOCIETY. *Hon. Sec.*, T. I. Storie, 3 Rinkvale Cottages, Hawick.

SHETLAND ARCHÆOLOGICAL AND NATURAL HISTORY SOCIETY, County Museum, Lerwick.—*Hon. Sec.*, Miss A. M. Sutherland.

EMPLOYERS' ASSOCIATIONS

AEROSPACE COMPANIES, SOCIETY OF BRITISH (1916), 29 King Street, S.W.1.—*Dir.*, Vice-Adm. Sir Richard Smeeton, K.C.B., M.B.E.

ALUMINIUM FEDERATION, Broadway House, Calthorpe Road, Five Ways, Birmingham 15.—*Dir.*, H. R. Murray Shaw.

BAKERS, CONFECTIONERS AND CATERERS, NATIONAL ASSOCIATION OF MASTER, Queen's House, Holly Road, Twickenham, Middx.—*Dir.*, M. F. Zimmerman.

BAKERS, THE FEDERATION OF.—*Dir.*, A. Kinch, 52 Lincoln's Inn Fields, W.C.2.

BANK EMPLOYERS, FEDERATION OF, 10 Lombard Street, E.C.3.—*Dir. and Sec.*, E. S. Richards.

BISCUIT MANUFACTURERS, NATIONAL ASSOCIATION OF, Scottish Union House, 25 Bucklersbury, E.C.4.—*Sec.*, C. T. Digby-Jones.

BOOT TRADES ASSOCIATION, LTD., ST. CRISPINS, St. Crispin's House, Desborough, nr. Kettering, Northants.—*Gen. Sec.*, Mrs. P. J. Copley.

BRUSH MANUFACTURERS' ASSOCIATION, BRITISH, 90–93 Cowcross Street, E.C.1.—*Sec.*, R. F. Knox, M.B.E.

BUILDING AND ALLIED HARDWARE MANUFACTURERS FEDERATION, NATIONAL, 5 Greenfield Crescent, Edgbaston, Birmingham 15.—*Dir. and Sec.*, T. B. Jackson, M.B.E.

BUILDING TRADES EMPLOYERS, NATIONAL FEDERATION OF (1878), 82 New Cavendish Street, W.1.—*Sec.*, H. L. Foster.

CARPET MANUFACTURERS, FEDERATION OF BRITISH (1960), 55–61 Moorgate, E.C.2.—*Sec.*, W. R. P. Adams.

CATERERS' ASSOCIATION OF GREAT BRITAIN (1917), Victoria House, Vernon Place, Southampton Row, W.C.1.—*Sec.*, J. D. G. Hooper.

CEMENT MAKERS' FEDERATION, Terminal House, 52 Grosvenor Gardens, S.W.1—*Dir.*, Rear Adm. C. K. T. Wheen, C.B.

CHEMICAL INDUSTRIES ASSOCIATION LTD. (1966), Alembic House, 93 Albert Embankment, S.E.1.—*Dir.-Gen.*, D. B. Kimber, O.B.E.

CHINA AND GLASS RETAILERS' ASSOCIATION, 17–19 John Adam Street, W.C.2.—*Sec.*, W. E. V. Burch, T.D.

CINEMATOGRAPH EXHIBITORS' ASSOCIATION OF GREAT BRITAIN AND IRELAND, 22–25 Dean Street, W.1.—*Gen. Sec.*, R. S. Camplin.

CIVIL ENGINEERING CONTRACTORS, FEDERATION OF, Romney House, Tufton Street, S.W.1.—*Dir.*, D. V. Gaulter.

CLAY INDUSTRIES, NATIONAL FEDERATION OF, Drayton House, 30 Gordon Street, W.C.1.—*Dir.*, G. K. Timperley, M.B.E., F.R.S.A.

CLOTHING MANUFACTURERS' FEDERATION OF GREAT BRITAIN LTD., 14–16 Cockspur Street, S.W.1.—*Dir.*, M. K. Reid, O.B.E.

COAL MERCHANTS' FEDERATION OF GREAT BRITAIN, Victoria House, Southampton Row, W.C.1.—*Dir.*, L. R. Chambers, O.B.E.

COCOA, CHOCOLATE AND CONFECTIONERY MANUFACTURERS' INDUSTRIAL GROUP, 11 Green Street, W.1.—*Sec.*, E. T. Beauchamp.

COLD STORAGE AND ICE TRADES, NATIONAL FEDERATION OF, 272 London Road, Wallington, Surrey.—*Sec.*, D. T. Lee.

CONFECTIONERS ASSOCIATION, THE RETAIL, 53 Christchurch Avenue, North Finchley, N.12.—*Sec.*, C. J. Southam.

COOPERAGE FEDERATION, NATIONAL, 27 Queen Charlotte Street, Leith, Edinburgh 6.—*Sec.*, J. Steven.

CUTLERY AND SILVERWARE MANUFACTURERS ASSOCIATION, UNITED KINGDOM, Light Trades House, Melbourne Avenue, Sheffield, 10.—*Gen. Sec.*, I. D. Sutherland.

CYCLE AND MOTOR CYCLE TRADERS, NATIONAL ASSOCIATION OF, 31A High Street, Tunbridge Wells, Kent.—*Gen. Sec.*, C. F. Mayo.

DRAPERS' CHAMBER OF TRADE, 4 Harley Street, W.1.—*Dir.*, H. G. Mounsey.

ELECTRICAL AND ALLIED MANUFACTURERS ASSOCIATION, BRITISH (1905), 8 Leicester Street, W.C.2.—*Man. Dir.*, J. P. Waterfield.

ELECTRICAL APPLIANCE ASSOCIATION (R.T.R.A.) LTD., 19–21 Conway Street, Fitzroy Square, W.1.

ELECTRICAL CONTRACTORS' ASSOCIATION, 55 Catherine Place, S.W.1.—*Dir.*, B. E. Gray.

ENGINEERING EMPLOYERS' FEDERATION, Broadway House, Tothill Street, S.W.1.—*Sec.*, H. K. Mitchell.

FARMERS' UNION, NATIONAL (1908), Agriculture House, Knightsbridge, S.W.1.—*Dir. Gen.*, G. H. B. Cattell.

FILM PRODUCTION ASSOCIATION OF GREAT BRITAIN, 27 Soho Square, W.1.—*Gen. Sec.*, J. P. H. Walton.

FISH FRIERS, NATIONAL FEDERATION OF, 289 Dewsbury Road, Leeds 11.—*Gen. Sec.*, P. Worthington.

FISHMONGERS, NATIONAL FEDERATION OF, Sherwood House, Matlock, Derbyshire.—*Sec.*, J. A. Claypole.

FLAT GLASS ASSOCIATION, THE, 6 Mount Row, W.1.—*Sec.*, L. F. Brett.

FOOTWEAR MANUFACTURERS FEDERATION, BRITISH, Royalty House, 72 Dean Street, W.1.—*Dir.*, P. Glennie-Smith, O.B.E.

FRESH MEAT WHOLESALERS, FEDERATION OF, District Bank Buildings, 236 Telegraph Road, Heswall, Wirral, Cheshire.—*Sec.*, J. F. Moore.

FURNISHERS, NATIONAL ASSOCIATION OF RETAIL, 42–44 Sun Street, E.C.2.—*Dir.*, H. S. S. Few.

GLASS MANUFACTURERS FEDERATION, 19 Portland Place, W.1.—*Dir.*, O. C. T. R. Normandale.

GRAIN, SEED, FEED AND AGRICULTURAL MERCHANTS, BRITISH ASSOCIATION OF, Cereal House, 58 Mark Lane, E.C.3.—*Sec.*, H. S. Leech.

GROCERS' FEDERATION, NATIONAL, 24A High Street, Camberley, Surrey.—*Chief Exec.*, L. E. Reeves-Smith.

GROCERS AND PROVISION MERCHANTS, NATIONAL FEDERATION OF WHOLESALE, 18 Fleet Street, E.C.4.—*Sec.*, D. Ellam.

HAIRDRESSERS' FEDERATION, NATIONAL, Britannia House, 958–964 High Road, Finchley, N.12.—*Gen. Sec.*, L. J. Dodd.

HYDRAULIC EQUIPMENT MANUFACTURERS LTD., ASSOCIATION OF (1959), 54 Warwick Square, S.W.1.—*Dir.*, J. F. Nosworthy.

IRON ORE INDUSTRY, NATIONAL JOINT BOARD FOR THE, 41 Meadow Road, Kettering, Northants.—*Sec.* P. T. M. Wilson.

JEWELLERY AND GIFTWARE FEDERATION LIMITED, BRITISH, St. Dunstan's House, Carey Lane, E.C.2.—*Dir.-Gen.*, F. W. Bibb.

JUTE SPINNERS AND MANUFACTURERS ASSOCIATION, Kandahar House, 71 Meadowside, Dundee.—*Dir.*, D. A. Borrie.

LAUNDERERS AND CLEANERS, ASSOCIATION OF BRITISH, LTD., 22 Lancaster Gate, W.2.—*Dir.*, E. W. Swetman.

LEATHER PRODUCERS' ASSOCIATION, Leather Trade House, 9 St. Thomas Street, S.E.1.—*Sec.*, P. A. T. Smith.

LINOLEUM AND FELT BASE EMPLOYERS' FEDERATION, c/o Nairn-Williamson Ltd., Victoria Road, Kirkcaldy.—*Sec.*, J. H. Reid.

MALTSTERS' ASSOCIATION OF GREAT BRITAIN, 75 Cannon Street, E.C.4.—*Sec.*, Group Capt. V. Fairfield, O.B.E.

MEAT TRADERS' ASSOCIATIONS INCORPORATED, NATIONAL FEDERATION OF, 29 Linkfield Lane, Redhill, Surrey.

MENSWEAR ASSOCIATION OF BRITAIN LTD., 293 Regent Street, W.1.—*Dir.*, K. E. Smith.

MILK DISTRIBUTIVE COUNCIL, Freeth House, 37 Queens Gate, S.W.7.—*Sec.*, P. O'Neill.

MILLERS, NATIONAL ASSOCIATION OF BRITISH AND IRISH, LTD. (1878), 21 Arlington Street, S.W.1.—*Sec.*, E. T. J. Hurle.

MINES OF GREAT BRITAIN, FEDERATION OF SMALL, 30 King Street, Wigan, Lancs.—*Chairman and Sec.*, J. Wainwright.

MOTOR AGENTS' ASSOCIATION, LTD., 201 Great Portland Street, W.1.—*Dir.-Gen.* F. E. Higham, O.B.E.

MOTOR MANUFACTURERS AND TRADERS, SOCIETY OF (1902), Forbes House, Halkin Street, S.W.1.—*Sec.*, M. G. Feather.

PAINTERS AND DECORATORS OF ENGLAND AND WALES, NATIONAL FEDERATION OF MASTER, 6 Haywra Street, Harrogate, Yorks.—*Dir.*, K. A. C. Blease.

PAINTING AND DECORATING TRADE EMPLOYERS, CONFEDERATION OF, 6 Haywra Street, Harrogate, Yorks.—*Sec.*, K. A. C. Blease.

PAINTMAKERS ASSOCIATION OF GREAT BRITAIN LIMITED, Prudential House, Wellesley Road, Croydon, Surrey.—*Dir.*, K. S. Flory.

PAPERMAKERS AND BOARDMAKERS, EMPLOYERS' FEDERATION OF, 1 Clements Inn, W.C.2.—*Dir.*, M. Lambert.

PAPER MERCHANTS, NATIONAL ASSOCIATION OF, 35 New Bridge Street, E.C.4.—*Gen. Sec.*, S. R. W. Bailey.

PLUMBERS AND DOMESTIC HEATING ENGINEERS, NATIONAL FEDERATION OF, 6 Gate Street, W.C.2.—*Sec.*, H. Leighton.

PLYWOOD AND VENEER MANUFACTURERS, ASSOCIATION OF BRITISH, 25–35 City Road, E.C.1.—*Sec.*, T. P. G. Neale.

PORT EMPLOYERS, NATIONAL ASSOCIATION OF, Three Quays, Tower Hill, E.C.3.—*Gen. Manager*, E. Bainbridge.

POTTERY MANUFACTURERS' FEDERATION, BRITISH, Federation House, Station Road, Stoke-on-Trent.—*Sec.*, D. Turner.

PRECAST CONCRETE FEDERATION, BRITISH, 9 Catherine Place, S.W.1.—*Dir.*, R. W. Parks.

PRINTERS, BRITISH FEDERATION OF MASTER, 11 Bedford Row, W.C.1.—*Dir.*, L. E. Kenyon, C.B.E.

PROPRIETARY ASSOCIATION OF GREAT BRITAIN, 519 Victoria House, Southampton Row, W.C.1.—*Dir.*, J. P. Wells.

RADIO AND TELEVISION RETAILERS' ASSOCIATION, 19–21 Conway Street, Fitzroy Square, W.1.

ROAD HAULAGE ASSOCIATION LTD., 22 Upper Woburn Place, W.C.1.—*Dir.-Gen.*, G. K. Newman.

ROOFING CONTRACTORS, NATIONAL FEDERATION OF, West Bar Chambers, 38 Boar Lane, Leeds 1.—*Sec.*, A. K. Davidson, M.B.E.

SAND AND GRAVEL ASSOCIATION LIMITED, 48 Park Street, W.1.—*Gen. Sec.*, F. W. Parsley.

SAWMILLING ASSOCIATION, NATIONAL, Clareville House, Oxendon Street, S.W.1.—*Sec.*, J. Bick.

SCIENTIFIC INSTRUMENT MANUFACTURERS' ASSOCIATION OF GREAT BRITAIN. 20 Peel Street, W.8.

SCOTCH WHISKY ASSOCIATION, 77 George Street, Edinburgh 2.—*Sec.*, P. J. Woodhouse. *Information Office*, 17 Half Moon Street, W.1.

SHIPBUILDERS AND REPAIRERS NATIONAL ASSOCIATION, 21 Grosvenor Place, S.W.1.—*Dir.*, N. A. Sloan, Q.C.

SHIPPING FEDERATION, LTD., BRITISH (1890), 146–150 Minories, E.C.3.—*Dir.*, J. K. Rice-Oxley.

TAILORS, FEDERATION OF MERCHANT, 19 Hanover Square, W.1.—*Sec.*, P. Barron.

TEXTILE EMPLOYERS' ASSOCIATION, BRITISH, 5th Flr., Royal Exchange, Manchester.—*Sec.*, J. Platt.

TIMBER TRADE FEDERATION OF THE U.K., Clareville House, Whitcomb Street, W.C.2.—*Sec.*, H. J. Bocking.

TOBACCONISTS, NATIONAL UNION OF RETAIL, 546–548 Commercial Road, E.1.—*Sec.*, G. H. Scott.

TRAWLERS FEDERATION LTD., BRITISH, Trinity House Chambers, 12 Trinity House Lane, Hull.—*Sec.*, I. C. Thorburn.

TYRE DISTRIBUTORS ASSOCIATION, NATIONAL, Broadway House, The Broadway, S.W.19.—*Sec.*, M. Thomas.

VEHICLE BUILDERS AND REPAIRERS ASSOCIATION, Belmont House, 102 Finkle Lane, Gildersome, Leeds.—*Gen. Sec.*, A. L. Sunderland.

WATER COMPANIES ASSOCIATION, THE, 15 Great College Street, S.W.1.—*Sec.*, M. A. Liddell, O.B.E.

WATERWORKS ASSOCIATION (INCORPORATED), BRITISH, 34 Park Street, W.1.—*Dir.*, L. W. F. Millis, C.B.E.

CLUB AND LIBRARY EDITION OF WHITAKER, 1972

CONFEDERATION OF BRITISH INDUSTRY
21 Tothill Street, London, S.W.1.

The Confederation of British Industry was founded in August 1965 to promote the prosperity of British industry and those elements of British business closely associated with it. It combines in a single, democratic and voluntary association the rôles previously played by the British Employers' Confederation, the Federation of British Industries and the National Association of British Manufacturers.

The C.B.I. is recognized nationally and internationally as the representative organization of the management side of industry for the United Kingdom. It acts as a national point of reference for all those who seek the views of industry and management and it advises the Government on all aspects of Government policy which affect the interests of industry and business, both at home and abroad.

Membership of the C.B.I. consists of some 11,500 companies and over 200 trade associations and employers' organizations. In addition to these the nationalized industries are able to apply for membership as public sector members and thereby to work with the C.B.I. on problems that are the concern of all management.

The governing body of the C.B.I. is the Council, which meets monthly in London. It is assisted by some 30 expert standing committees which advise on the main aspects of policy. There is a C.B.I. Regional Council and C.B.I. office in each of the administrative regions of England and offices and councils covering Scotland, Wales and Northern Ireland. These Regional Councils send their representatives to the governing body. The C.B.I.

is represented in more than 100 centres overseas.

The C.B.I. provides its members with a wide range of services and practical advice on economic, industrial relations, commercial, technical, social and export questions. Company members pay subscriptions, fixed according to a scale based on wages and salaries paid.

President, J. Partridge *SIR VAL DUNCAN (CHMN)*
Vice-Presidents, Sir Arthur Norman, K.B.E., D.F.C.; *9/72*
   Sir Stephen Brown, K.B.E.
Director-General, C. Adamson.
Secretary, J. Gough.

NATIONAL BUILDING AGENCY
N.B.A. House, Arundel Street, W.C.2
(3 North St. Andrew Street, Edinburgh 2; Bedford House, Bedford Street, Belfast 2.)

The N.B.A. is a technical semi-public agency whose job is to promote new and improved methods of building and building management. Initially concerned with the appraisal of building systems it is currently involved in liaison with the Department of the Environment and Government Departments in Scotland and Northern Ireland, in promoting the application of dimensional co-ordination and metrication in the construction industry; with pilot schemes in housing improvement areas; and with management techniques suited to works programmes for design offices, for public authorities and for private contractors. It receives a Government grant for services to housing authorities but charges fees for its consultancy work.

Chairman, Gen. the Lord Bourne, G.C.B., K.B.E.,
   C.M.G. .... *(part-time)* £4,000
Managing Director, A. W. Cleeve Barr
                               (full-time) £6,300

HOME-GROWN CEREALS AUTHORITY
Haymarket House, Oxendon Street, S.W.1.

Constituted under the Cereals Marketing Act, 1965, the Authority consists of 9 members representing cereal growers, 9 representing dealers in, or processors of, grain and 5 independent members. The purpose of the Authority is to improve the marketing of home-grown cereals. Production has increased to the level of 14 million tons per annum, worth £400,000,000. The Authority is empowered by the Act to provide a market intelligence service; to operate schemes for the encouragement of forward sales, and the orderly phasing of supplies according to market needs; and to undertake research aimed at the expansion of the market for home-grown cereals. The Authority has reserve buying powers by which it can support the market in certain circumstances and subject to Parliamentary

and Ministerial approval. It submits advice to Ministers on matters affecting cereals marketing.

Chairman, Sir Henry Hardman, K.C.B.
Deputy Chairman, Dr. Clare Burgess.

Members (Independent), The Lord Collison, C.B.E.;
   Prof. D. K. Britton; O. G. Williams.
   (Cereal Growers), G. E. Daniels; R. Farquharson,
   O.B.E.; J. Macaulay; H. D. Maidment; Lt.-Col.
   A. Robinson, T.D.; E. Richards; P. Savory;
   S. Shaw; J. Stobo.
   (Merchants, Dealers & Processors), K. J. Arnott;
   F. S. D. Brown; J. Gray, O.B.E., T.D.; P. H.
   Griffiths; A. O. Hutchison; P. A. Metaxa;
   J. M. C. Parry; B. C. Read; L. J. Wright.
General Manager and Secretary, J. W. Pugsley.

PERIODS OF GESTATION AND INCUBATION
The table shows approximate periods of gestation or incubation for some common animals and birds. In some cases the periods may vary and where doubt arises professional advice should be sought.

Species	Shortest Period. Days	Usual Period. Days	Longest Period. Days	Species	Shortest Period. Days	Usual Period. Days	Longest Period. Days
Human	240	273	313	Turkey	25	28	28
Mare	305	336	340	Duck	28	28	32
Ass	365	—	374	Goose	28	30	32
Cow	273	280	294	Pigeon	17	18	19
Ewe	140	147–50	160	Canary	12	14	14
Goat	147	151	155	Guinea Pig	63	—	70
Sow	109	112	125	Mouse	18	—	19
Bitch	55	63	70	Rat	21	—	24
Cat	53	56	63	Elephant		2 years	
Rabbit	30	32	35	Camel		45 weeks	
Hen	20	21	22	Zebra		56 weeks	

TRADES UNION CONGRESS (T.U.C.)

Congress House, 23–28 Great Russell Street, W.C.1.

[01–636–4030]

The Trades Union Congress, founded in 1868, is a voluntary association of Trade Unions, the representatives of which meet annually to consider matters of common concern to their members. The Congress has met annually since 1871 (with the exception of 1914) and in recent years has met normally on the first Monday in September, its sessions extending through the succeeding four days. Congress is constituted by delegates of the affiliated unions on the basis of one delegate for every 5,000 members, or fraction thereof, on whose behalf affiliation fees are paid. Affiliated unions (in 1970–71) totalled 142 with an aggregate membership of 10,002,204.

The main business of the annual Congress is to consider the report of its General Council dealing with the activities of the Congress year, along with motions from affiliated societies on questions of policy and organization. Although 142 trade union organizations are affiliated to Congress, some of these, especially in cotton, are themselves federal bodies including in total 150 more unions. All the large British unions are affiliated to the T.U.C.

One of the important responsibilities of the annual Congress is to elect a General Council to keep watch on all industrial movements, legislation affecting labour and all matters touching the interest of the trade union movement, with authority to promote common action on general questions, and to assist trade unions in the work of organization. The General Council is elected by Congress and is composed of 37 members (35 representing 18 trade groups and two representing women workers). Following is a list of these trade groups with the aggregate membership of unions in each group and with the number of representatives each group is entitled to have on the General Council. *Women Members.*—In 1971, a total of 2,394,915 women were members of unions in the T.U.C. The largest groups were members of the Transport and General Workers Union (222,866), National Union of General and Municipal Workers (245,685), Union of Shop, Distributive and Allied Workers (170,742), National and Local Government Officers' Association (167,797), National Union of Teachers (228,855), and National Union of Public Employees (220,768).

Among the powers vested in it by consent of the Unions in Congress is the responsibility of adjusting disputes and differences between affiliated organizations; such cases being dealt with by a Disputes Committee of the General Council which investigates matters referred to it and issues its findings thereon, which are invariably accepted by the parties to the dispute. The General Council has power also if there appears to be justification, to institute an investigation into the conduct of any affiliated organization on the ground that its activities are detrimental to the interests of the trade union movement or contrary to the declared principles and policy of the Congress; but membership of the Congress is voluntary and Unions retain full control of their own affairs, and a penalty of suspension from membership of the Congress or exclusion from membership is the only measure that can be taken to enforce Congress decisions. Through the General Council, the trade union movement maintains systematic relations with the Government and Government Departments, with the Confederation of British Industry and with a large number of other bodies. A major instrument for Government relations is the National Joint Advisory Council which functions at Ministerial level; in this body the Confederation of British Industry and the boards of nationalized industries are represented along with the T.U.C. for purposes of consultation and advice on matters of governmental policy and administration, affecting industry. The General Council is represented on the National Economic Development Council, established to examine problems associated with faster economic growth. The Council includes Ministers dealing with economic and industrial affairs, representatives of public and private industry and independent members. The General Council nominates members to serve on numerous other bodies, *e.g.* Central Training Council, and National Insurance Advisory Committee.

Chairman (1971–72), G. F. Smith, C.B.E.
General Secretary, V. Feather, C.B.E.
Asst. Gen. Secretary, L. Murray.

Trade Group (with numbers of unions)	Total Membership
Mining and Quarrying (2)	302,842
Railways (3)	302,790
Transport (other) (9)	1,761,998
Shipbuilding (2)	127,285
Engineering, Founding and Vehicle Building (12)	1,539,995
Technical Engineering and Scientific (5)	359,949
Electricity (1)	420,588
Iron and Steel and Minor Metal Trades (11)	158,432
Building, Woodworking and Furnishing (9)	375,628
Printing and Paper (7)	403,199
Textiles (24)	149,173
Clothing, Leather and Boot and Shoe (7)	268,866
Glass, Pottery, Chemicals, Food, Drink, Tobacco, Brushmaking, and Distribution (11)	476,269
Agriculture (1)	100,000
Public Employees (11)	1,358,403
Civil Servants (14)	689,213
Professional, Clerical and Entertainment (11)	350,002
General Workers (2)	857,572
TOTAL (142)	10,002,204

SCOTTISH TRADES UNION CONGRESS

12 Woodlands Terrace, Glasgow, C.3.

The Congress was formed in 1897 and acts as a national centre for the trade union movement in Scotland. In 1971 it consisted of 84 unions with a membership of 880,319 and 47 directly affiliated Trades Councils. The majority of the unions organize throughout Britain and affiliate on their membership in Scotland.

The Annual Congress in April elects a 17-member General Council on the basis of 10 industrial sections. Congress has been prominent in pressing for economic expansion and full employment in Scotland and the development of the social services, most of which are separately organized in Scotland.

Chairman (1971–72), R. MacDonald.
General Secretary, J. Jack, C.B.E.

TRADE UNIONS

A list of the Trade Unions affiliated to the Trades Union Congress in September, 1971. The number of members of each Union is shown in parenthesis.

ACTORS' EQUITY ASSOCIATION, BRITISH (incorporating The Variety Artistes' Federation).—(17,983).—*Sec.* G. Croasdell, O.B.E., 8 Harley Street, W.1.

AGRICULTURAL AND ALLIED WORKERS, NATIONAL UNION OF (100,000).—*Sec.*, R. N. Bottini, 308 Gray's Inn Road, W.C.1.

ASPHALT WORKERS, THE AMALGAMATED UNION OF (2,924).—*Sec.*, H. M. Wareham, Jenkin House, 173A Queen's Road, Peckham, S.E.15.

BAKERS UNION (48,784), Station House, Darkes Lane, Potters Bar, Herts.—*Gen. Sec.*, S. Gretton.

BAKERS AND ALLIED WORKERS, SCOTTISH UNION OF (11,713).—*Sec.*, W. Mowbray, O.B.E., Baxterlee, 127 Fergus Drive, Glasgow, N.W.

BANK EMPLOYEES, NATIONAL UNION OF (89,144).—*Gen. Sec.*, A. G. Brooks, 2 Holly Road, Twickenham, Middlesex.

BASKET, CANE, WICKER AND FIBRE FURNITURE MAKERS OF GREAT BRITAIN AND IRELAND, NATIONAL UNION OF (48).—*Sec.*, T. Burrows, 9 District Road, Wembley, Middlesex.

BEAMERS, TWISTERS AND DRAWERS (HAND AND MACHINE), AMALGAMATED ASSOCIATION OF (1,640).—*Gen. Sec.*, G. Barrett, 27 Every Street, Nelson, Lancs.

BLASTFURNACEMEN, ORE MINERS, COKE WORKERS AND KINDRED TRADES, THE NATIONAL UNION OF (18,585).—*Sec.*, H. C. Smith, 93 Borough Road West, Middlesbrough.

BLIND AND DISABLED OF GREAT BRITAIN AND IRELAND, NATIONAL LEAGUE OF THE (4,250).—*Sec.*, T. J. Parker, 262 Langham Road, N.15.

BOILERMAKERS, SHIPWRIGHTS, BLACKSMITHS AND STRUCTURAL WORKERS, AMALGAMATED SOCIETY OF (126,830).—Lifton House, Eslington Road, Newcastle-upon-Tyne 2.—*Pres.*, D. McGarvey, C.B.E.

BOOT, SHOE AND SLIPPER OPERATIVES, ROSSENDALE UNION OF (5,842).—*Sec.*, T. Whittaker, 7 Tenterfield Street, Waterfoot, Rossendale, Lancs.

BRITISH AIR LINE PILOTS ASSOCIATION (4,005).—*Gen. Sec.*, A. F. Sherman, 81 New Road, Harlington, Hayes, Middlesex.

BROADCASTING STAFF, ASSOCIATION OF (11,235), King's Court, 2 Goodge Street, W.1.—*Gen. Sec.*, G. T. Rhys.

BRUSHMAKERS, NATIONAL SOCIETY OF (2,495).—*Sec.*, T. B. Thomas, M.B.E., 18–20 High Street, Watford, Herts.

BUILDING TECHNICIANS, ASSOCIATION OF (2,125).—*Sec.*, F. E. Shrosbree, 9–11 Macaulay Road, S.W.4.

CARD SETTING MACHINE TENTERS' SOCIETY (174).—*Sec.*, G. Priestley, 36 Greenton Avenue, Scholes, Cleckheaton, Yorks.

CARPET TRADE UNION, NORTHERN (1,907).—*Sec.*, R. Townsend, 9 St. James Street, Halifax, Yorks.

CERAMIC AND ALLIED TRADES UNION (34,085).—*Sec.*, A. Dulson, 5 Hillcrest Street, Hanley, Stoke-on-Trent.

CHAIN MAKERS AND STRIKERS' ASSOCIATION (216)—*Sec.*, A. E. Head, M.B.E., Unity Villa, Sidney Road, Cradley Heath, Warley, Worcs.

CHEMICAL WORKERS' UNION (15,100).—*Sec.*, R. J. Edwards, M.P., 155 Kennington Park Road, S.E.11.

CIGARETTE MACHINE OPERATORS' SOCIETY (376).—R. E. Williams, 3 Mascot Road, Bedminster, Bristol 3.

CINEMATOGRAPH, TELEVISION AND ALLIED TECHNICIANS, ASSOCIATION OF (16,545).—*Sec.*, A. Sapper, 2 Soho Square, W.1.

CIVIL AND PUBLIC SERVICES ASSOCIATION (184,935).—*Sec.*, W. L. Kendall, 215 Balham High Road, S.W.17.

CIVIL SERVICE UNION (35,247).—*Sec.*, J. O. N. Vickers, 17–21 Hatton Wall, E.C.1.

CLERICAL AND ADMINISTRATIVE WORKERS' UNION (125,541).—*Gen. Sec.*, R. Grantham, 22 Worple Road, S.W.19.

CLOTH PRESSERS' SOCIETY (120).—*Sec.*, G. Kaye, 34 Southgate, Honley, Yorks.

COLLIERY OVERMEN, DEPUTIES AND SHOTFIRERS, NATIONAL ASSOCIATION OF (23,389).—*Sec.*, J. Crawford, O.B.E., Argyle House, 29–31 Euston Road, N.W.1.

COMMERCIAL MOTORMEN'S UNION, SCOTTISH (21,000).—*Sec.*, A. H. Kitson, 308 Albert Drive, Glasgow, S.1.

CO-OPERATIVE OFFICIALS, NATIONAL ASSOCIATION OF (6,742).—*Sec.*, A. W. Potts, 56 Market Street Manchester, 1.

COOPERS' FEDERATION OF GREAT BRITAIN AND IRELAND (1,866).—*Sec.*, T. Bain, 13 Gayfield Square, Edinburgh 1.

COUNTY COURT OFFICERS' ASSOCIATION (5,151).—*Sec.*, F. Humphries, c/o Westminster County Court, 82 St. Martin's Lane, W.C.2.

CUSTOMS AND EXCISE FEDERATION (4,300).—*Hon. Sec.*, H. E. Buckingham, M.B.E., Bloomsbury Mansions, 26 Bloomsbury Way, W.C.1.

CUSTOMS AND EXCISE PREVENTIVE STAFF ASSOCIATION (2,845).—*Sec.*, R. J. Lowe, Peek House, 20 Eastcheap, E.C.3.

DOMESTIC APPLIANCE & GENERAL METAL WORKERS, NATIONAL UNION OF (5,999).—*Sec.*, J. Higham, M.B.E., Stove Grate Offices, Imperial Bldgs, Corporation Street, Rotherham.

DYERS, BLEACHERS AND TEXTILE WORKERS, NATIONAL UNION OF (56,986), National House, Sunbridge Road, Bradford 1.—*Sec.*, J. A. Peel.

ELECTRICAL, ELECTRONIC, TELECOMMUNICATION UNION/PLUMBING TRADES UNION (420,588).—*Sec.*, F. J. Chapple, Hayes Court, West Common Road, Hayes, Bromley, Kent.

ELECTRICAL POWER ENGINEERS' ASSOCIATION (29,612).—*Gen. Sec.*, H. Norton, O.B.E., Station House, Fox Lane North, Chertsey, Surrey.

ENGINEERING WORKERS, AMALGAMATED UNION OF (1,202,218) 110 Peckham Road, S.E.15.—*Gen. Sec.*, J. Conway.

CONSTRUCTIONAL SECTION (CEU) (27,726).—*Sec.*, E. Marsden, 140 Lower Marsh, S.E.1.

FOUNDRY SECTION (65,000).—*Sec.*, W. Simpson, 164 Chorlton Road, Manchester 16.

TECHNICAL AND SUPERVISORY SECTION (DATA) (105,418).—*Sec.*, G. H. Doughty, Onslow Hall, Little Green, Richmond, Surrey.

ENGINEERS' AND FIREMEN'S UNION, GRIMSBY STEAM AND DIESEL FISHING VESSELS (220).—*Acting Sec.*, 10 Orwell Street, Grimsby.

ENGINEER SURVEYORS' ASSOCIATION (2,194).—*Sec.*, A. Thompson, Bermuda House, 4 Hall Street, Manchester 2.

ENGRAVERS, UNITED SOCIETY OF (454).—*Sec.*, D. Hill, 34 Anson Road, Manchester, 14.

FELT HATTERS AND ALLIED WORKERS, AMALGAMATED SOCIETY OF JOURNEYMEN (900).—*Sec.*, H. Walker, 14 Walker Street, Denton, nr. Manchester.

FELT HAT TRIMMERS, WOOL FORMERS AND ALLIED WORKERS, AMALGAMATED (800).—*Sec.* H. Walker, 14 Walker Street, Denton, nr. Manchester.

FILM ARTISTES' ASSOCIATION, THE (2,175).—*Sec.*, S. Brannigan, 61 Marloes Road, W.8.

FIRE BRIGADES UNION, THE (30,000).—*Sec.*, T. Parry, O.B.E., 59 Fulham High Street, S.W.6.

FOOTWEAR, LEATHER AND ALLIED TRADES, NATIONAL UNION OF (78,630). The Grange, Earls Barton, Northampton.—*Sec.*, T. A. Moore.

FUNERAL SERVICE OPERATIVES, NATIONAL UNION OF (1,025).—*Sec.*, D. R. Coates, 42–44 Wellington Street, Woolwich, S.E.18.

FURNITURE TRADE OPERATIVES, NATIONAL UNION OF (60,754).—*Sec.* A. G. Tomkins, C.B.E., Fairfields, Roe Green, Kingsbury, N.W.9.

GENERAL AND MUNICIPAL WORKERS UNION (853,353), Ruxley Towers, Claygate, Esher, Surrey.—*Gen. Sec.*, The Lord Cooper of Stockton Heath.

GOLD, SILVER AND ALLIED TRADES, NATIONAL UNION OF (3,837).—*Gen. Sec.*, B. H. Bridge, Kean Chambers, 11 Mappin Street, Sheffield 1.

GOVERNMENT SUPERVISORS AND RADIO OFFICERS, ASSOCIATION OF (10,777).—*Sec.*, P. L. Avery, 90 Borough High Street, S.E.1.

GRAPHICAL ASSOCIATION, NATIONAL (107,360). *Gen. Sec.*, J. M. Bonfield, Graphic House, 63–67 Bromham Road, Bedford.

GREATER LONDON COUNCIL STAFF ASSOCIATION (14,096).—*Sec.*, F. T. Hollocks, 164–8 Westminster Bridge Road, S.E.1.

HEALDERS AND TWISTERS TRADE AND FRIENDLY SOCIETY, HUDDERSFIELD (256).—*Sec.* H. S. Fillingham, Room 8, Friendly and Trade Societies Club, Huddersfield.

HEALTH SERVICE EMPLOYEES, CONFEDERATION OF (89,550).—*Gen. Sec.*, F. J. Lynch, Glen House, High Street, Banstead, Surrey.

HEALTH VISITORS' ASSOCIATION (5,432).—*Sec.*, Mrs. J. Wyndham-Kaye, 36 Eccleston Square, S.W.1.

HOSIERY AND KNITWEAR WORKERS, NATIONAL UNION OF (64,407).—*Sec.*, H. L. G. Gibson, M.B.E., 55 New Walk, Leicester.

INLAND REVENUE STAFF FEDERATION (49,735).—*Sec.*, C. T. H. Plant, O.B.E., 7 St. George's Square, S.W.1.

INSURANCE WORKERS, NATIONAL UNION OF (35,028).—*Sec.*, J. P. Brown, 59A St. John's Road, S.W.11.

IRON AND STEEL TRADES CONFEDERATION (116,632).—*Sec.*, D. H. Davies, Swinton House, 324 Gray's Inn Road, W.C.1.

IRON, STEEL AND WOOD BARGE BUILDERS' AND HELPERS' ASSOCIATION (455).—*Sec.*, W. H. Harris, 32 Woolwich Road, S.E.10.

JOURNALISTS, NATIONAL UNION OF (24,503).—*Sec.*, K. Morgan, Acorn House, 314–320 Gray's Inn Road, W.C.1.

JUTE, FLAX AND KINDRED TEXTILE OPERATIVES, UNION OF (3,380).—*Sec.*, R. Doyle, 93 Nethergate, Dundee.

LAMINATED AND COIL SPRING WORKERS' UNION (270).—*Sec.*, F. M. Hynes, 144 Rural Lane, Wadsley, Sheffield.

LITHOGRAPHIC ARTISTS, DESIGNERS, ENGRAVERS AND PROCESS WORKERS, SOCIETY OF (16,519).—*Sec.*, L. Knapp, 54 Doughty Street, W.C.1.

LOCK AND METAL WORKERS, NATIONAL UNION OF (5,205).—*Sec.*, J. Martin, Bellamy House, Wilkes Street, Willenhall, Staffs.

LOCOMOTIVE ENGINEERS AND FIREMEN, ASSOCIATED SOCIETY OF (29,277).—*Sec.*, R. W. Buckton, 9 Arkwright Road, N.W.3.

LOOM OVERLOOKERS, THE GENERAL UNION OF ASSOCIATIONS OF (3,920).—*Gen. Sec.*, A. Howcroft, Derby Chambers, 6 The Rock, Bury.

MACHINE CALICO PRINTERS, TRADE SOCIETY OF (473).—*Sec.*, D. J. Barr, Room 43, 62 George Street, Manchester 1.

MANAGERS AND OVERLOOKERS' SOCIETY (1,997).—*Sec.*, L. Smith, Textile Hall, Westgate, Bradford 1.

MEDICAL PRACTITIONERS' UNION (5,502).—*Sec.*, H. Faulkner, 10–26 Jamestown Road, N.W.1.

MERCHANT NAVY AND AIRLINE OFFICERS' ASSOCIATION (21,000).—*Sec.*, J. W. Slater, Oceanair House, 133–137 Whitechapel High Street, E.1.

METALWORKERS' SOCIETY, ASSOCIATED (5,280).—*Sec.*, E. Tullock, Lord's Chambers, 26 Corporation Street, Manchester 4.

METAL MECHANICS, NATIONAL SOCIETY OF (45,896).—*Sec.*, F. Briggs, 70 Lionel Street, Birmingham 3.

MILITARY AND ORCHESTRAL MUSICAL INSTRUMENT MAKERS TRADE SOCIETY (130).—*Gen. Sec.*, J. Barker, 11 Bideford Close, Edgware, Middx.

MINEWORKERS, NATIONAL UNION OF (279,453).—*Sec.* L. Daly, 222 Euston Road, N.W.1.

MINISTRY OF LABOUR STAFF ASSOCIATION (15,899).—*Gen. Sec.*, J. L. Tindall, 244 Tolworth Rise South, Tolworth, Surbiton, Surrey.

MUSICIANS' UNION (32,892).—*Gen. Sec.*, J. Morton, 29 Catherine Place, Buckingham Gate, S.W.1.

NATIONAL AND LOCAL GOVERNMENT OFFICERS ASSOCIATION (439,887).—*Sec.*, W. C. Anderson, C.B.E., Nalgo House, 8 Harewood Row, N.W.1.

PATTERNMAKERS AND ALLIED CRAFTSMEN, ASSOCIATION OF (12,093).—*Sec.*, G. Eastwood, 15 Cleve Road, W. Hampstead, N.W.6.

PATTERN WEAVERS' SOCIETY (200).—*Sec.*, W. Lockwood, 572 Wakefield Road, Huddersfield.

POST OFFICE ENGINEERING UNION (116,559).—*Sec.* Lord Delacourt-Smith, P.C., Greystoke House, Hanger Lane, Ealing, W.5.

POST OFFICE EXECUTIVES, ASSOCIATION OF (14,187).—*Sec.*, J. K. Glynn, 345 Upper Richmond Road, West, S.W.14.

POST OFFICE MANAGEMENT STAFFS ASSOCIATION (17,109).—*Sec.*, L. F. Pratt, 52 Broadway, Bracknell, Berks.

POST OFFICE WORKERS, UNION OF (209,479).—*Sec.*, T. Jackson, U.P.W. House, Crescent Lane, Clapham Common, S.W.4.

POWER LOOM CARPET WEAVERS AND TEXTILE WORKERS' ASSOCIATION (4,975).—*Sec.*, C. S. Yarsley, Callows Lane, Kidderminster.

POWER LOOM OVERLOOKERS, YORKSHIRE ASSOCIATION OF (1,808).—*Sec.*, E. D. Sleeman, Textile Hall, Westgate, Bradford.

POWER LOOM OVER-LOOKERS, SCOTTISH UNION OF (500).—*Sec.*, J. McCann, 33 Glenclova Terrace, Dundee.

PRISON OFFICERS' ASSOCIATION (13,658).—*Sec.*, F. G. Castell, Cronin House, 245 Church Street, N.9.

PROFESSIONAL FOOTBALLERS' AND TRAINERS' ASSOCIATION (2,160).—*Sec.*, C. Lloyd, 124 Corn Exchange Buildings, Manchester 4.

PUBLIC EMPLOYEES, NATIONAL UNION OF (372,709).—*Sec.*, A. W. Fisher, Civic House, Aberdeen Terrace, Blackheath, S.E.3.

RADIO AND ELECTRONIC OFFICERS UNION (2,963), 4–6 Branfill Road, Upminster, Essex.—*Sec.*, K. A. Murphy.

RAILWAYMEN, NATIONAL UNION OF (198,319).—*Sec.*, Sir Sidney Greene, C.B.E., Unity House, Euston Road, N.W.1.

RETAIL BOOK, STATIONERY AND ALLIED TRADES EMPLOYEES' ASSOCIATION, THE (3,584) —*Sec.*, A. J. Johnson, 152–3 Temple Chambers, Temple Avenue, E.C.4.

ROLL TURNERS' TRADE SOCIETY, BRITISH (1,000).—*Sec.*, B. W. Johnson, 44 Collingwood Avenue, Corby, Northants.

RUBBER WORKERS OF GREAT BRITAIN, THE UNITED (4,219).—*Sec.*, L. Walsh, 219 Bury New Road, Whitefield, Prestwich, Manchester.

SAWMAKERS' PROTECTION SOCIETY, SHEFFIELD (326). —*Sec.*, A. Marples, 43 Witney Street, Sheffield 8.

SCALEMAKERS, NATIONAL UNION OF (2,350).—*Gen. Sec.*, S. W. Parfitt, 2, 4 & 6 St. John Street, E.C.1.

SCHOOLMASTERS, NATIONAL ASSOCIATION OF (56,899).—*Sec.*, T. A. Casey, Swan Court, Waterhouse Street, Hemel Hempstead, Herts.

SCIENTIFIC, TECHNICAL AND MANAGERIAL STAFFS, ASSOCIATION OF (220,600).—*Gen. Sec.*, C. Jenkins, 10–26A Jamestown Road, N.W.1.
  INSURANCE STAFFS' SECTION, Wardrobe Court, 146A Queen Victoria Street, E.C.4.—*Sec.*, M. W. Reynolds.

SCREW, NUT, BOLT AND RIVET TRADE SOCIETY (2,524).—*Sec.*, H. Cater, 368 Dudley Road, Birmingham 18.

SEAMEN, NATIONAL UNION OF (50,000).—*Gen. Sec.*, W. Hogarth, Maritime House, Old Town, Clapham, S.W.4.

SHEET METAL WORKERS, COPPERSMITHS AND HEATING AND DOMESTIC ENGINEERS, NATIONAL UNION OF (78,281).—*Gen. Sec.*, L. W. Buck, 75–77 West Heath Road, N.W.3.

SHEET METAL WORKERS' SOCIETY, BIRMINGHAM AND MIDLAND (8,775).—*Sec.*, A. E. Cooper, 134 Bromsgrove Street, Birmingham, 5.

SHOP, DISTRIBUTIVE AND ALLIED WORKERS, UNION OF (329,890).—*Sec.*, A. W. H. Allen, C.B.E., "Oakley," 188 Wilmslow Road, Fallowfield, Manchester 14.

SHUTTLEMAKERS, SOCIETY OF (170).—*Pres.*, E. V. Littlewood, 21 Buchan Towers, Manchester Road, Bradford.

SIGN AND DISPLAY TRADES UNION (3,919), 67 Albert Road, S. Woodford, E.18.—*Gen. Sec.*, A. C. Torode.

SPINNERS AND TWINERS, THE AMALGAMATED ASSOCIATION OF OPERATIVE COTTON (1,362).—*Sec.*, J. Richardson, 115 Newton Street, Manchester.

SPRING TRAPMAKERS' SOCIETY (90).—*Sec.*, J. Martin, Bellamy House, Wilkes Street, Willenhall, Staffs.

TAILORS AND GARMENT WORKERS, NATIONAL UNION OF (117,573), 14 Kensington Square, W.8. —*Gen. Sec.*, J. Macgougan.

TEACHERS, NATIONAL UNION OF (310,536).—*Sec.*, E. Britton, C.B.E., Hamilton House, Mabledon Place, W.C.1.

TEACHERS IN TECHNICAL INSTITUTIONS, ASSOCIATION OF (29,740).—*Gen. Sec.*, T. Driver, Hamilton House, Mabledon Place, W.C.1.

TEXTILE AND ALLIED WORKERS, NATIONAL UNION OF (24,222).—*Sec.*, J. King, O.B.E., 81 Fountain Street, Manchester 2.

TEXTILE CRAFTSMEN, YORKSHIRE SOCIETY OF (1,068). —*Sec.*, C. Hall, Textile Hall, Westgate, Bradford, 1.

TEXTILE WAREHOUSEMEN, AMALGAMATED (4,502). —*Sec.*, F. Walker, 80 St. George's Road, Bolton.

TEXTILE WORKERS AND KINDRED TRADES, AMALGAMATED SOCIETY OF (6,820).—*Sec.*, H. Lisle, Foxlowe, Market Place, Leek, Staffs.

THEATRICAL, TELEVISION AND KINE EMPLOYEES, THE NATIONAL ASSOCIATION OF (15,643).—*Gen. Sec.*, R. L. Keenan, 20 Bedford Street, Strand, W.C.2.

TOBACCO WORKERS' UNION, THE (19,250).—*Sec.*, C. D. Grieve, 218 Upper Street, Islington, N.1.

TRANSPORT AND GENERAL WORKERS' UNION (1,638,686).—*Sec.*, J. L. Jones, M.B.E., Transport House, Smith Square, S.W.1.

TRANSPORT SALARIED STAFFS' ASSOCIATION (75,194), —*Gen. Sec.*, A. P. Coldrick, Walkden House, 10 Melton Street, N.W.1.

TRANSPORT UNION, UNITED ROAD (21,580).—*Sec.*, J. Moore, 76 High Lane, Manchester 21.

TYPOGRAPHICAL ASSOCIATION, SCOTTISH (6,906).—*Sec.*, F. Smith, 136 West Regent Street, Glasgow, C.2.

VEHICLE BUILDERS, NATIONAL UNION OF (83,553). —*Gen. Sec.* (vacant), 44 Hathersage Road, Manchester 13.

WALL PAPER WORKERS' UNION (4,010).—*Gen. Sec.*, D. A. McIntosh, 223 Bury New Road, Whitefield, Manchester.

WARPDRESSERS, TWISTERS AND KINDRED TRADES ASSOCIATIONS, LEEDS AND DISTRICT (132).—*Sec.*, B. Jowett, 34 Greenhill Drive, Bramley, Leeds 13.

WATERMEN, LIGHTERMEN, TUGMEN AND BARGEMEN'S UNION (2,544).—*Sec.*, W. A. Lindley, 33 East India Dock Road, E.14.

WATER WORKS EMPLOYEES, NATIONAL UNION OF (4,052).—*Sec.*, A. R. Bevan, 484 London Road, Mitcham, Surrey.

WEAVERS' AND WOOLLEN TEXTILE WORKERS' ASSOCIATION. SADDLEWORTH AND DISTRICT (1,458). —*Sec.*, F. G. Battye, 4 Grains Road, Delph, nr. Oldham.

WEAVERS' ASSOCIATION, AMALGAMATED (29,446)— *Gen. Sec.*, H. C. Kershaw, Chronicle Buildings, 74 Corporation Street, Manchester 4.

WIRE DRAWERS AND KINDRED WORKERS, THE AMALGAMATED SOCIETY OF (12,252).—*Sec.*, L. Carr, Prospect House, Alma Street, Sheffield 3.

WOODCUTTING MACHINISTS, AMALGAMATED SOCIETY OF (23,100).—*Sec.*, C. Stewart, 8 Fairfield Street, Manchester 1.

WOODWORKERS AND PAINTERS, AMALGAMATED SOCIETY OF (incorporating Amalgamated Union of Building Trade Workers) (220,895).—*Sec.*, G. F. Smith, C.B.E., 9–11 Macaulay Road, S.W.4.

WOOL SHEAR WORKERS' TRADE UNION, SHEFFIELD (19).—*Sec.*, J. Billard, 19 Rivelin Park Drive, Sheffield 6.

WOOL SORTERS' SOCIETY, NATIONAL (1,373).—*Sec.*, N. Newton, M.B.E., 40 Little Horton Lane, Bradford 5.

WRITERS' GUILD OF GREAT BRITAIN (1,656).—*Sec.*, A. Griffiths, 430 Edgware Road, W.2.

PRINCIPAL LAND AREAS OF THE WORLD BELOW SEA LEVEL
(With approx. greatest depth in feet below Mean Sea Level.)

Europe: Netherlands coastal areas (15).

Asia: Jordan Valley, Dead Sea (1290).*
China: Sinkiang, Turfan Basin (980).
U.S.S.R.–Persia: Caspian Sea (85).*
Arabia: Trucial Oman–Qatar (70).

Africa: Libyan Desert Depressions:—
Qattara (440), Faiyum (150).
Wadi Rayan (140), Sittra (110).

Africa: Libyan Desert Depressions (*continued*) —
Areg (80), Wadi Natrun (75).
Melfa (60), Siwa (55), Bahrein (50).
Eritrea: Salt Plains depression (385).
Algeria–Tunisia: Shott Melghir and El Gharsa (90).*

America: Death Valley (275), Salton Sea (245).

Australia: Lake Eyre (40).

* Water surface.

INDUSTRIAL RESEARCH ASSOCIATIONS

A notable development in modern industry is the growth in numbers and importance of Industrial Research Associations and their increasing influence on the scientific and economic life of the country. The total income of these Associations exceeds £15,000,000 per annum. In 1971–72, £4,070,000 is being provided by the Department of Trade and Industry, Department of the Environment, and the Ministry of Agriculture, Fisheries and Food (1970–71) approximately £4 million), and the remainder by subscriptions of individual members or through other sources.

The Government Scheme for Co-operative Industrial Research was launched by the Department of Scientific and Industrial Research in 1917. Its aim was to stimulate the industries of the United Kingdom to undertake co-operative research as a means of increasing their efficiency.

Research Associations formed under this scheme are registered companies, limited by guarantee of a nominal sum and working without the division of profits in the form of dividends. To assist the formation of such Associations the Department of Trade and Industry keeps a model Memorandum and Articles of Association, to which Research Associations under the scheme conform in all essential points.

The Research Associations are autonomous bodies free to determine their own policy for the development of their research programmes and the use to be made of the results of their research. Membership is open to any British firm in the particular industry, subject to the approval of the Councils of the Research Associations.

There are now 41 Research Associations and 2 other organizations in receipt of grants from the Ministry. They cover most of the principal industries of the country, as follows:—

Brushes.
BRITISH BRUSH MANUFACTURERS' RESEARCH ASSOCIATION, 90 Cowcross Street, E.C.1.—*Dir.*, D. I. Fothergill.

Cast Iron.
BRITISH CAST IRON RESEARCH ASSOCIATION, Bordesley Hall, Alvechurch, Birmingham.—*Dir.*, H. Morrogh, C.B.E., F.R.S.

Ceramics.
BRITISH CERAMIC RESEARCH ASSOCIATION, Queen's Road, Penkhull, Stoke-on-Trent.—*Dir.*, N. F. Astbury, C.B.E., Sc.D.

Civil Engineering.
CONSTRUCTION INDUSTRY RESEARCH AND INFORMATION ASSOCIATION, Old Queen Street House, 6 Storey's Gate, S.W.1.—*Dir.*, A. R. Collins, M.B.E., D.SC., Ph.D.

Coke.
BRITISH COKE RESEARCH ASSOCIATION, Coke Research Centre, Chesterfield, Derbyshire.—*Dir.*, J. P. Graham.

Cotton, Silk, etc.
COTTON, SILK AND MAN-MADE FIBRES RESEARCH ASSOCIATION, Shirley Institute, Didsbury, Manchester, 20.—*Dir.*, L. A. Wiseman.

Cutlery.
CUTLERY AND ALLIED TRADES RESEARCH ASSOCIATION, Doncaster Street, Sheffield, 3.—*Dir.*, E. A. Oldfield.

Drop Forging.
DROP FORGING RESEARCH ASSOCIATION, Shepherd Street, Sheffield, 3.—*Director*, S. E. Rogers, Ph.D.

Electrical.
ELECTRICAL RESEARCH ASSOCIATION, Cleeve Road, Leatherhead, Surrey.—*Dir.*, B. C. Lindley, Ph.D.

Flour Milling and Baking
FLOUR MILLING AND BAKING RESEARCH ASSOCIATION, Research Station, Chorleywood, Rickmansworth, Herts.—*Dir.*, G. A. H. Elton, D.SC., Ph.D., F.R.I.C.

Food Manufacture.
BRITISH FOOD MANUFACTURING INDUSTRIES RESEARCH ASSOCIATION, Randalls Road, Leatherhead, Surrey.—*Dir. of Research*, A. W. Holmes, Ph.D.

Fruit and Vegetable Canning.
FRUIT AND VEGETABLE PRESERVATION RESEARCH ASSOCIATION, Chipping Campden, Glos.—*Dir.*, H. R. Hinton.

Furniture.
FURNITURE INDUSTRY RESEARCH ASSOCIATION, Maxwell Road, Stevenage, Herts.—*Dir.*, D. M. Heughan.

Glass.
BRITISH GLASS INDUSTRY RESEARCH ASSOCIATION, Northumberland Road, Sheffield 10.—*Dir.*, R. G. Newton, O.B.E., D.SC., Ph.D.

Heating and Ventilating.
HEATING AND VENTILATING RESEARCH ASSOCIATION, Old Bracknell Lane, Bracknell, Berks.—*Dir.*, N. S. Billington, O.B.E.

Hosiery.
HOSIERY AND ALLIED TRADES RESEARCH ASSOCIATION, Thorneywood, 7 Gregory Boulevard, Nottingham.—*Dir.*, W. A. Dutton.

Hydromechanics.
BRITISH HYDROMECHANICS RESEARCH ASSOCIATION, Cranfield, Bedford.—*Dir.*, L. E. Prosser, O.B.E.

Industrial Psychology.
NATIONAL INSTITUTE OF INDUSTRIAL PSYCHOLOGY, 14 Welbeck Street, W.1.—*Dir.*, R. B. Buzzard.

Instrumentation.
BRITISH SCIENTIFIC INSTRUMENT RESEARCH ASSOCIATION, South Hill, Chislehurst, Kent.—*Dir.*, S. S. Carlisle.

Jute and Polypropylene.
SCOTTISH TEXTILE RESEARCH ASSOCIATION, Kinnoull Road, Kingsway West, Dundee.—*Dir.*, H. P. Stout, Ph.D.

Lace.
LACE RESEARCH ASSOCIATION, Glaisdale Drive West, Bilborough, Nottingham.—*Dir.*, D. I. Griggs.

Laundering.
BRITISH LAUNDERERS' RESEARCH ASSOCIATION, The Laboratories, Hill View Gardens, Hendon, N.W.4.—*Dir.*, J. Leicester.

Leather.
BRITISH LEATHER MANUFACTURERS' RESEARCH ASSOCIATION, Milton Park, Egham, Surrey.—*Dir.*, R. L. Sykes, Ph.D.

Linen.
LAMBEG INDUSTRIAL RESEARCH ASSOCIATION, Research Institute, Lambeg, Lisburn, Co. Antrim, N. Ireland.—*Dir.*, H. A. C. Todd.

Machine Tools.
MACHINE TOOL INDUSTRY RESEARCH ASSOCIATION, Hulley Road, Hurdsfield, Macclesfield, Cheshire.—*Dir.*, A. E. De Barr.

Motor Vehicles.
MOTOR INDUSTRY RESEARCH ASSOCIATION, Lindley, nr. Nuneaton, Warwickshire.—*Dir.*, R. H. Macmillan.

Mycology.

COMMONWEALTH MYCOLOGICAL INSTITUTE, Ferry Lane, Kew, Surrey.—*Dir.*, A. Johnston.

Non-Ferrous Metals.

BRITISH NON-FERROUS METALS RESEARCH ASSOCIATION, Euston Street, N.W.I.—*Dir.*, A. J. Kennedy, D.SC., Ph.D.

Paint.

RESEARCH ASSOCIATION OF BRITISH PAINT, COLOUR AND VARNISH MANUFACTURERS, Paint Research Station. Waldegrave Road, Teddington, Middlesex.—*Dir.*, G. de W. Anderson, Ph.D.

Paper, Board, Printing and Packing.

RESEARCH ASSOCIATION FOR THE PAPER AND BOARD, PRINTING AND PACKAGING INDUSTRIES, Randalls Road, Leatherhead, Surrey.—*Dir.*, G. L. Riddell, Ph.D.

Production Engineering.

PRODUCTION ENGINEERING RESEARCH ASSOCIATION OF GREAT BRITAIN, Melton Mowbray, Leics.—*Dir.*, D. F. Galloway, C.B.E., Ph.D.

Rubber and Plastics.

RUBBER AND PLASTICS RESEARCH ASSOCIATION OF GREAT BRITAIN, Shawbury, Shrewsbury, Shropshire.—*Dir.*, W. F. Watson, D.SC., Ph.D.

Ships.

BRITISH SHIP RESEARCH ASSOCIATION, Research Station, Wallsend, Northumberland.—*Dir.*, R. Hurst, G.M., Ph.D.

Shoes.

SHOE AND ALLIED TRADES RESEARCH ASSOCIATION, Satra House, Rockingham Road, Kettering, Northants.—*Dir.*, A. R. Payne, D.SC.

Springs.

SPRING RESEARCH ASSOCIATION, Doncaster Street, Sheffield 3.—*Dir.*, J. A. Bennett.

Steel Castings.

STEEL CASTINGS RESEARCH AND TRADE ASSOCIATION, East Bank Road, Sheffield 2.—*Director*, H. T. Hall, Ph.D.

Tar.

COAL TAR RESEARCH ASSOCIATION, Oxford Road, Gomersal. Cleckheaton, Yorks.—*Dir.*, D. McNeil, O.B.E., Ph.D.

Timber.

TIMBER RESEARCH AND DEVELOPMENT ASSOCIATION, Hughenden Valley, High Wycombe, Bucks.—*Dir.*, J. S. McBride.

Toxicology.

BRITISH INDUSTRIAL BIOLOGICAL RESEARCH ASSOCIATION, Woodmansterne Road, Carshalton, Surrey.—*Dir.*, R. F. Crampton, Ph.D.

Water.

WATER RESEARCH ASSOCIATION, Ferry Lane, Medmenham, Marlow, Bucks.—*Dir.*, R. G. Allen, Ph.D.

Welding.

WELDING INSTITUTE, Abington Hall, nr. Cambridge.—*Dir.*, R. Weck, C.B.E., Ph.D.

Whiting, Chalk and Lime.

WELWYN HALL RESEARCH ASSOCIATION, The Hall, Church Street, Welwyn, Herts.—*Dir.*, R. R. Davidson.

Wool.

WOOL INDUSTRIES RESEARCH ASSOCIATION, Headingley Lane, Leeds 6.—*Dir.*, B. E. King, Ph.D.

AGRICULTURAL RESEARCH INSTITUTES AND UNITS

The following research institutes are under the direct control of the Agricultural Research Council (see p. 368):—

Unit of Animal Genetics, University of Edinburgh, King's Buildings, West Mains Road, Edinburgh 9.—*Director*, Prof. D. S. Falconer, B.SC., Ph.D.

Unit of Developmental Botany, 181A Huntingdon Road, Cambridge.—*Director* Prof. P. W. Brian, F.R.S.

Unit of Experimental Agronomy, Department of Agricultural Science, University of Oxford.—*Hon. Director*, Prof. G. E. Blackman, F.R.S.

Unit of Flower Crop Physiology, Horticultural Research Laboratories, Shinfield Grange, Shinfield, Reading, Berks. *Hon. Dir.*, Prof. O. V. S. Heath, D.SC., F.R.S.

Unit of Invertebrate Chemistry and Physiology, University of Sussex, The Chemical Laboratory, Falmer, Brighton.—*Hon. Director*, Prof. A. W. Johnson, F.R.S.

Unit of Invertebrate Chemistry and Physiology (Subgroup), University of Cambridge, Zoology Dept., Downing Street, Cambridge.—*Associate Director*, Dr. J. E. Treherne.

Unit of Muscle Mechanism and Insect Physiology, Dept. of Zoology, University of Oxford, South Parks Road, Oxford.—*Hon. Dir.*, Prof. J. W. S. Pringle, M.B.E., SC.D., F.R.S.

Unit of Nitrogen Fixation, University of Sussex, Brighton.—*Director*, Prof. J. Chatt, Ph.D., SC.D., F.R.S.

Unit of Plant Physiology, Imperial College of Science and Technology, Prince Consort Road, S.W.7.—*Director*, Prof. C. P. Whittingham, Ph.D., D.SC.

Unit of Reproductive Physiology and Biochemistry, 307 Huntingdon Road, Cambridge.

—*Director*, Prof. T. R. R. Mann, C.B.E., M.D., SC.D., Ph.D., F.R.S.

Unit of Soil Physics, 219C Huntingdon Road, Cambridge.—*Hon. Dir.*, E. C. Childs, SC.D., Ph.D.

Unit of Statistics, University of Edinburgh, 21 Buccleuch Place, Edinburgh 8.—*Hon. Director*, Prof. D. J. Finney, SC.D., F.R.S., F.R.S.E.

Unit of Structural Chemistry, Inveresk House, Strand, London, W.C.2.—*Hon. Dir.*, Prof. Sir Ronald Nyholm, D.SC., Ph.D., F.R.I.C., F.R.S.

Systemic Fungicide Unit, Wye College, Ashford, Kent.—*Hon. Director*, Prof. R. L. Wain, C.B.E., D.SC., Ph.D., F.R.S.

Institute for Research on Animal Diseases, Compton, Newbury, Berks.—*Director*, W. M. Henderson, D.SC., M.R.C.V.S.

Institute of Animal Physiology, Babraham, Cambs.—*Director*, R. D. Keynes, Ph.D., SC.D., F.R.S.

Animal Breeding Research Organisation, King's Buildings, West Mains Road, Edinburgh, 9.—*Dir.*, Prof. H. P. Donald, Ph.D., D.SC., F.R.S.E.

Poultry Research Centre, King's Buildings, West Mains Road, Edinburgh, 9.—*Director*, T. C. Carter, O.B.E., D.SC., F.R.S.E.

Statistics Group, Dept. of Agricultural Science and Applied Biology, Downing Street, Cambridge.—*Officer-in-Charge*, R. C. Campbell, Ph.D.

Letcombe Laboratory, Letcombe Regis, Wantage, Berks.—*Director*, R. Scott Russell, D.SC., Ph.D.

Weed Research Organization, Begbroke Hill, Sandy Lane, Yarnton, Oxford.—*Director*, J. D. Fryer.

Food Research Institute, Colney Lane, Norwich.—*Director*, Prof. S. R. Elsden, B.A., Ph.D.

Meat Research, Institute, Langford, nr. Bristol.—*Director*, Prof. M. Ingram, Ph.D.

GRANT-AIDED RESEARCH INSTITUTES

In addition to the above there are other institutes which, while retaining their own individuality, are financed wholly or in the main by grants made from Government funds. Most of these Institutes have governing bodies of their own to which they are directly responsible. The maintenance grants for Institutes in England and Wales are met from funds voted by Parliament and administered by the Agricultural Research Council; the Scottish Institutes are borne on the vote of the Department of Agriculture and Fisheries for Scotland.

Long Ashton Research Station, Bristol.—*Director*, Prof. J. P. Hudson, M.B.E., G.M., Ph.D.

Animal Diseases Research Association, Moredun Institute, 408 Gilmerton Road, Edinburgh.—*Dir.*, J. T. Stamp, D.SC., M.R.C.V.S., F.R.S.E.

Animal Virus Research Institute, Pirbright, Surrey. —*Director*, J. B. Brooksby, D.SC., Ph.D., M.R.C.V.S., F.R.S.E.

East Malling Research Station, Maidstone, Kent.— *Director*, H. C. Pereira, D.SC., F.R.S.

Glasshouse Crops Research Institute, Worthing Road, Rustington, Littlehampton, Sussex.— *Director*, D. Rudd-Jones, Ph.D.

Grassland Research Institute, Hurley, nr. Maidenhead, Berks.—*Director*, Prof. E. K. Woodford, O.B.E., Ph.D.

Hannah Dairy Research Institute, Ayr.—*Director*, Prof. J. A. F. Rook, Ph.D., D.SC., F.R.I.C.

Hill Farming Research Organisation, 29 Lauder Road, Edinburgh 9.—*Director*, J. M. M. Cunningham, Ph.D.

Hop Research Centre, Wye College, Ashford, Kent. *Head of Dept.*, R. A. Neve, B.SC., Ph.D.

Houghton Poultry Research Station.* Houghton Grange, Huntingdon.—*Director*, R. F. Gordon, D.SC., M.R.C.V.S.

John Innes Institute, Colney Lane, Norwich.— *Director*, Prof. R. Markham, Ph.D., F.R.S.

Macaulay Institute for Soil Research, Craigiebuckler, Aberdeen.—*Director*, R. L. Mitchell, Ph.D., F.R.I.C., F.R.S.E.

National Institute of Agricultural Engineering, Wrest Park, Silsoe, Bedford.—*Director*, C. J. Moss, B.SC.

National Institute of Agricultural Engineering. Scottish Station, Bush Estates, Penicuik, Midlothian.—*Director*, W. J. West, F.R.S.E.

National Institute for Research in Dairying, Shinfield, nr. Reading.—*Director*, Prof. B. G. F. Weitz, O.B.E., D.SC., M.R.C.V.S.

National Vegetable Research Stn. Wellesbourne, Warwick.—*Director*, Prof. D. W. Wright.

Plant Breeding Institute, Maris Lane, Trumpington, Cambridge.—*Director*, Prof. R. Riley, F.R.S.

Welsh Plant Breeding Station, Plas Gogerddan, nr. Aberystwyth.—*Director*, Prof. P. T. Thomas, C.B.E., B.SC., Ph.D.

Scottish Plant Breeding Station, Pentlandfield, Roslin, Midlothian.—*Director*, N. W. Simmonds, SC.D., F.R.S.E.

Rowett Research Institute, Bucksburn, Aberdeen. —*Director*, J. L. Blaxter, Ph.D., D.SC., F.R.S., F.R.S.E.

Rothamsted Experimental Station, Harpenden, Herts.—*Director*, Sir Frederick Bawden, F.R.S.

Scottish Horticultural Research Institute, Invergowrie, Dundee.—*Director*, C. H. Cadman, Ph.D., F.R.S.E.

* Financed jointly by the Agricultural Research Council and the Animal Health Trust.

DISTANCES FROM LONDON BY AIR

A list of the distances in statute miles from London to various places abroad. Distances given are those of the shortest routes in use by the British Airways Corporations—B.O.A.C. services(O); B.E.A. services(E).

To	Miles	To	Miles	To	Miles
Abadan (O)	2,937	Detroit (O)	3,901	Nairobi (O)	4,261
Ajaccio (E)	791	Doha (O)	3,248	Naples (E)	1,012
Algiers (E)	856	Dublin (E)	279	Nassau (O)	4,361
Amsterdam (E)	231	Düsseldorf (E)	311	New York (O)	3,456
Ankara (E)	1,771	Entebbe (O)	4,026	Nice(E)	646
Athens (E)	1,501	Frankfurt (E & O)	400	Nicosia (Cyprus) (E & O)	2,001
Auckland (O)	12,992	Geneva (E)	468	Oslo (E)	723
Baghdad (O)	2,970	Gibraltar (E)	1,085	Palermo (E)	1,129
Bahrain (O)	3,199	Gothenburg (E)	651	Palma (Majorca) (E)	837
Bangkok (O)	6,132	Hamburg (E)	463	Paris (E) ... 215; (Orly, 227)	
Barbados (O)	4,198	Hanover (E)	437	Perth, Australia (O)	9,612
Barcelona (E)	712	Helsinki (E)	1,148	Prague (E)	649
Basle (E)	446	Hong Kong (O)	7,022	Rangoon (O)	6,087
Beirut (E & O)	2,154	Honolulu (O)	8,470	Rome (E & O)	892
Bergen (E)	648	Istanbul (E)	1,561	Salzburg (E)	652
Berlin (E)	593	Johannesburg (O)	6,053	Shannon (E)	369
Bermuda (O)	3,437	Karachi (O)	4,159	Singapore (O)	6,936
Bombay (O)	4,655	Khartoum (O)	3,063	Stockholm (E)	907
Bordeaux (E)	458	Kingston (Jamaica) (O)	4,687	Sydney (O)	11,537
Brisbane (O)	11,229	Kuala Lumpur (O)	6,976	Tangier (E)	1,121
Brussels (E)	217	Kuwait (O)	2,898	Teheran (O)	2,738
Budapest (E)	924	Lisbon (E)	972	Tel Aviv (E & O)	2,222
Cairo (O)	2,185	Madrid (E)	774	Tokyo (O)	6,224
Calcutta (O)	5,135	Malaga (E)	1,042	Toronto(O)	3,557
Chicago (O)	3,953	Malta (E)	1,306	Trinidad (O)	4,412
Cologne (E)	331	Mauritius (O)	6,314	Tripoli (E)	1,457
Colombo (O)	5,495	Milan (E)	609	Turin (E)	570
Copenhagen (E)	608	Montego Bay (O)	5,007	Valencia (E)	827
				Venice (E)	715
Dar-es-Salaam (O)	4,685	Montreal (O)	3,251	Vienna (E)	791
Darwin (O)	9,457	Moscow (E)	1,558	Warsaw (E)	913
Delhi (O)	4,324	Munich (E)	588	Zürich (E & O)	480

PRINCIPAL CHARITABLE BEQUESTS OF THE YEAR

The following alphabetical list showing the estates of 27 men and 28 women, details principal charitable bequests since our last issue. Death duties, bequests and other charges are deductible from the gross estates shown. The Treasury is again the main beneficiary taking over £2,600,000 in estate duty. The Finance Act, 1971, raised the death duty limit to £12,500, thus enlarging charitable bequests to some extent.

Capt. Philip Saltmarshe, a former A.D.C. to the Governor of New South Wales and later to the Governor of Newfoundland, left the residue of his £102,032 gross estate, after life interests, to the R.S.P.C.A. Home at York, for the upkeep of its cats' home and for the care of strays. Animal charities also benefit in the Will of Miss Rosina E. Leicester, who left her £30,000 residue equally between the R.S.P.C.A. and the Royal Society for the Protection of Birds. The Secretary of State for Social Services is left £16,000 to be equally divided among four hospitals of his own choice in the Will of Mr. Henry Seher; and London hospitals benefit under the wills of Miss Freda MacKenzie, who left the residue (£43,000) for research purposes at The London Hospital, Whitechapel, and a retired dental surgeon Mr. Albert B. Kennedy, a former Governor of Guy's Hospital, left the ultimate residue of his estate to that hospital for the foundation of a Kennedy Scholarship.

Nailsworth U.D. Council receives £11,700 under the Will of a bachelor, Mr. William J. Mortimer, to benefit the town; and Canon Percy F. Bateson left his £7,000 residue to St. Ambrose Church, Leyland, where he was vicar for 16 years. £93,000 is left for charitable purposes in England at their executors' discretion in the compounded estates of Lady Colina E. Hussey, sister of the 9th Earl of Breadalbane, Miss Mabel K. Davis and Mr. Harold D. M. Hutton, who left his £48,000 residue for distribution in £500 lots.

Lincoln College, Oxford, receives £48,000 under the Will of Mr. Arthur C. Gamble and two other Oxford Colleges are beneficiaries, Balliol receiving £55,000—£45,000 under the Will of Rev. John S. MacArthur, and St. Hugh's £10,000 from that of Miss Edith M. Watson. £20,000 to reduce the National Debt (of £33,420,000,000) passes under the Will of Miss Marjorie W. Jesson, of Bournemouth, and 86-year-old Mrs. Louise Wright left £125,000 for the benefit of the Pestalozzi Children's Village, Trogen, Switzerland, while £60,000 goes equally between The Children's Society and Dr. Barnardo's in the Will of Mr. Bertram G. Ewens.

The R.N.L.I. receives a total of £29,000 for lifeboats under the Wills of Miss Edith M. Linton and Mrs. Elizabeth G. Holland. Sir Robert Hart, 3rd Baronet, the last of his line, left his residuary estate to the National Gallery, to be used if possible " in or towards the purchase of a picture or pictures for the Gallery," and the Tate Gallery received a Vlaminck landscape under Sir Robert's Will. Mr. Harry Crook, founder of the Kleen-e-Ze Brush Co. left the ultimate residue of his £199,160 estate to the Harry Crook Charitable Trust.

Sir Allen Lane, founder of Penguin books, left his £1,216,474 estate on trusts previously arranged with his executors. A few months before his death he made a gift of £500,000 to the Allen Lane Charity (which aids the Friends of the Young Deaf, mentally handicapped children and other organizations), but this was reduced to about a quarter of its original value by the Inland Revenue, since it was made within a year of his death.

The principal figure in the list below is that of the gross estate.

Mrs. Hettie Ball, of Ilkley £23,578
(The residue to Girton College, Cambridge.)

Canon Percy Frederick Bateson, of Leyland
£10,707
(Several small charitable bequests and the residue to St. Ambrose Church, Leyland.)

Mrs. Agnes Greig Blake, of London £201,337
(The residue equally between Imperial Cancer Research Fund and the Institute of Cancer Research.)

Mr. Charles William Clark, of East Leake. £82,886
(The residue equally between St. Dunstan's and Dr. Barnardo's.)

Mrs. Alice Blanche Frances Colten, of Eastbourne £217,300
(All of her property equally between Miss Shephard's Annuitants Homes, The Wireless for the Bedridden Society, British Limbless Ex-Servicemen's Association, the Distressed Gentlefolks' Aid Association, and the Searchlight Cripples' Workshops, Newhaven)

Mrs. Charlotte Susanah Cooke, of Bexley Heath
£54,070
(All her property equally between Dr. Barnardo's and the People's Dispensary for Sick Animals.)

Mr. Donald Ifould Craig, of Camberley... £33,721
(The residue to the R.N.L.I.)

Mr. Harry Crook, of Westbury on Trym
£199,160
(Ultimate residue to the Harry Crook Charitable Trust.)

Mr. Alexander Cross, of Shillingstone, Dorset
£83,027
(The residue equally between Dr. Barnardo's and St. Dunstan's.)

Miss Mabel Kate Davis, of London £43,866
(The residue for charitable purposes in England as her executors decide.)

Miss Dorothy Dixon, of Eastbourne.... £446,252
(Several small charitable bequests and the residue equally between the British and Foreign Bible Society, the British Red Cross Society, the Royal Masonic Hospital, the Clergy Friendly Society, the Friend of the Clergy Corporation, St. Dunstan's and the Women's Holiday Fund.)

Mr. Bertram George Ewens, of Torquay . £178,894
(Several small charitable bequests and the residue equally between The Children's Society and Dr. Barnardo's.)

Mr. Alan Calverley Fielding, of London... £70,684
(The residue to OXFAM.)

Julia Morrison Fleming, of Exmouth..... £117,168
(Several small charitable bequests and the residue to the National Trust.)

Mr. Gerald Rowland Fothergill, of Reading
£54,512
(The residue to the Association for the Propagation of the Faith.)

Mr. Arthur Christopher Gamble, of Ashburton
£144,083
(The residue to Lincoln College, Oxford.)

Mr. Thomas Ernest Garratt, of London.... £68,107
(The residue to St. Dunstan's.)

Mrs. Jane Gauden, of Durham £57,461
(The residue to the Fleming Memorial Fund for Medical Research.)

Miss Lily Hargreaves, of Bacup £30,707
(The residue to the Baptist Missionary Society.)

Sir Robert Hart, Bt., of London £553,600
(The residue to The National Gallery.)

Mrs. Elizabeth Gagie Holland, of Hexham. £14,212
(The residue to the R.N.L.I.)

Lady Colina Elwy Hussey, of Tipton St. John, Devon.............................£58,476
(The residue for charitable purposes in England as her executors decide.)

Mr. Harold Maxwell D'Arcy Hutton, of Bucklebury........................£111,821
(The residue for charitable purposes as his executors decide.)

Mrs. Maria Camilla Theresa Jenkins, of London
£99,921
(The residue equally between the Salvation Army, Cecil Houses Incorporated, and the R.N.L.I.)

Mrs. Mary Claire Jensen, of Pinner......£25,886
(The residue to the Imperial Cancer Research Fund.)

Miss Marjorie Wilhelmina Jesson, of Bournemouth............................£36,164
(The residue for the reduction of the National Debt.)

Mr. Albert Bernard Kennedy, of Sunbury-on-Thames...........................£27,734
(Ultimate residue to Guy's Hospital.)

Mrs. Katharine Agnes Gertrude Ker, of London
£60,566
(The residue to the Imperial Cancer Research Fund.)

Mr. Fiennes Thomas Lambert, of Bournemouth
£230,354
(The residue equally between the National Institute for the Blind, St. Dunstan's, and the Wireless for the Blind Society.)

Mr. John Grimmer Lamming, of Streatley, Beds.
£33,408
(All of his property to the Family Welfare Association.)

Miss Rosina Emily Leicester, of Ferring... £38,165
(The residue equally between the R.S.P.C.A. and the Royal Society for the Protection of Birds.)

Mr. Robert Albert Likeman, of London.. £15,683
(All of his property to the Cancer Research Campaign.)

Miss Edith Maud Linton, of Tilehurst.....£21,300
(The residue to the R.N.L.I.)

Manon Diana Liveing, of Alverstoke.....£94,559
(£5,000 to The National Trust and the residue equally between War on Want and the R.S.P.C.A.)

Mrs. Florence Ellen Lyall, of Canterbury. £17,784
(The residue to British Limbless Ex-Servicemen's Association.)

Rev. John Stewart MacArthur, of Burnham-on-Sea................................£135,493
(The residue to Balliol College, Oxford.)

Miss Freda MacKenzie, of London......£101,395
(The residue to The London Hospital, Whitechapel.)

Mrs. Ethel May MacKie, of Thurston, Suffolk
£27,722
(All her property equally between The National Trust and the First Church of Christ Scientist, Boston, Mass.)

Miss Sheila Frances Magenis, of Felbridge
£122,430
(The residue equally between the R.S.P.C.A. and Blue Cross.)

Mr. William John Mortimer, of Watledge, Nailsworth..............................£12,249
(All of his property to Nailsworth U.D.C.)

Miss Norah Katherine Mounsey, of Hoylake
£418,871
(A third of the residue each to The National Trust for Scotland, Sherborne School for Girls, and a third for the welfare of old people residing in Hoylake U.D.C. area as her executors decide.)

Dr. Edgar David Maurice Neumann, of Brighton
£601,148
(Ultimate residue to the Murphy-Neumann Charity Co. Ltd.)

Mrs. Mary Ann Pattison, of Birmingham. £93,204
(The residue equally between the National Spastics Society and the British Rheumatism and Arthritis Association.)

Capt. Philip Saltmarshe, of Saltmarshe, Yorks.
£102,032
(Ultimate residue to the R.S.P.C.A., York.)

Mr. Henry Seher, of London........... £40,479
(Bequests to charities including £16,000 equally between four hospitals selected by the Secretary of State for Social Services and the residue to orphanages as his executor selects.)

Mr. Leslie Charles Thomas Sharpe, of Uxbridge
£19,008
(All of his property to Dr. Barnardo's.)

Miss Gertrude Annie Skerritt, of Draycott, Derbyshire.................................£118,741
(The residue to Nottingham Council of Social Service.)

Mr. Edmund Rowland Thompson, of Long Marton..............................£86,598
(£10,000 to the Marie Curie Memorial Foundation.)

Mr. Sydney Percy Turner, of Hove......£18,220
(All of his property to the Imperial Cancer Research Fund.)

Mrs. Elsie Ward, of Bournemouth.......£82,998
(The residue equally between the R.N.L.I., Dr. Barnardo's and the Save the Children Fund.)

Mr. Francis Leon Warner, of Dover......£21,099
(The residue to Dr. Barnardo's.)

Major Charles Lisle Watson, M.B.E., of London
£46,959
(The residue to the Pitt Street Settlement, London.)

Miss Edith Marion Watson, of London.. £104,130
(£10,000 to St. Hugh's College, Oxford.)

Mr. Joseph Austen Williams, of Camborne
£51,434
(All of his property to the Wesley Chapel, Camborne.)

Mrs. Louise Margaret Wright, of Eastbourne
£338,339
(All of her property to the Pestalozzi Children's Village, Trogen, Switzerland.)

CLUB AND LIBRARY EDITION OF WHITAKER, 1972

The Club and Library Edition of Whitaker's Almanack, 1972, contains 1,237 pages, including illustrations and coloured maps (The World, The British Isles, Baltic States, Russia and her neighbours, Germany and her neighbours, France and Spain, The Far East, India, Pakistan and Burma, Africa, Canada and Newfoundland, The United States, South America, Australia, New Zealand) in strong leather binding, with gilt top and silk headband. Price £3·00 net.

LIFE ASSURANCE AND FIRE AND GENERAL INSURANCE

LIFE ASSURANCE

THE list on the following two pages contains the names of all the more important British Life offices, and of Commonwealth companies (marked C), all of which transact business in this country.

CLASS OF BUSINESS.—The second column shows whether the company is conducted on the Mutual system whereby the whole of the divisible profit is allotted to participating policy-holders (M), or whether the company has proprietors by whom part (usually a very small proportion) of such profit is received (P). Life offices transacting other insurance business are marked (O) in this column. In such cases the Life funds are kept separately, and are not liable for the claims of other departments. The Share Capital is usually liable for the claims of all branches. Those having an Industrial branch are indicated by letter (I).

FIGURES.—These are taken from the latest annual accounts available at date of going to press, and in the majority of cases refer to annual reports for the financial year ended December 31, 1970.

LIFE FUNDS.—The amounts of these funds, though interesting, are not in themselves a sufficient indication of the financial stability of a company, which cannot be judged unless liabilities are actuarially compared with assets.

PREMIUM INCOME.—The annual premium income is in all cases stated after deduction of the amount paid to other companies for reassuring parts of the risks.

CONSIDERATION FOR ANNUITIES.—These are the amounts received to provide various types of Annuities.

INTEREST.—The rate of interest earned is important for comparison with the rate assumed in valuing liabilities, since the greater the margin

between these rates the greater is the surplus available from this source for bonus. The rate of interest given is before deduction of Income Tax except where marked (N)—net.

VALUATION.—The valuation returns which are required to be made by the companies to the Board of Trade indicate liability under existing policies, after making allowance for the amounts to be paid and received. It is assumed that deaths will occur in accordance with a mortality table (various tables are used), and that interest will be earned at a certain rate. If a company assumes that it will earn a high rate of interest in the future the net liability will appear less than if it assumes a low rate, while the liability on account of mortality appears greater by some tables than by others. The position of an office is most satisfactory when a stringent basis of valuation is adopted, because the margin between the calculated and experienced liability is larger and the surplus available for bonuses is greater. The lower the rate of interest assumed the more stringent is the valuation. The foregoing remarks, however, do not apply in the case of an office which has adopted a Bonus Reserve Valuation.

It is not possible to include details of all the various types of Policy which come under the heading of Life Assurance and only the basic Whole Life and Endowment are, therefore, dealt with in the following pages. Most Life Offices, however, issue Contracts which cover Mortgages, provision for Children's Education, etc., Pensions and Unit Trust linked with Life Assurance, and advice on the kind of Policy most suitable to the needs of an enquirer would be best obtained through a qualified Insurance Broker or an Office transacting Life business.

FIRE INSURANCE RATES

Many large fire offices belong to the tariff association, charging identical rates of premium. There are, however, a number of non-tariff offices which claim to assess individual risks independently on merits. Tariff rates of premium per £100 insured against fire for the more common classes of risk are as follows:—

Private Dwelling Houses, built of brick or stone and tiled or slated and in no hazardous proximity £0·075.

Household goods therein, usually £0·10.

A number of companies issue " Householders " policies embracing in one contract all risks incidental to private houses and contents.

Shops and Warehouses, similarly built and circumstanced, in which no hazardous goods are deposited nor hazardous trades carried on, from £0·225 for Saleshops and from £1·20 for Wholesalers' Warehouses.

Stock and Utensils in trade fixtures, and household furniture in such shops and warehouses, at the same rates. Some offices require an extra premium if Storm and Tempest cover is to be included. A minimum premium ranging from £1·50 to £3·00 is required under all of these Insurances.

Most fire insurance companies transact accident (including Motor) and miscellaneous business and if a strong company be selected it will probably be found to the advantage of an insurer that he should effect with it all such policies as he may require, in place of dividing them amongst several companies. The "Householders" policies, previously referred to, combine in one contract protection against damage by fire to the contents of a house, or from burglary, housebreaking, larceny, theft, etc. and insurance against domestic servants' employers' liability, third party risks, and other hazards. This can usually be arranged for an annual premium of around £0·25 per £100 of the full value of the contents of the house. Insurance of the house itself is not included, however, in this estimate, but can be included under the same policy, if desired. The advantage of a policy of this description is that it obviates the inconvenience of payments of small amounts in insurance premiums at different dates, and that in one comprehensive form it supplies protection at a moderate cost for all a householder's ordinary insurance requirements.

NOTE.—As Insurance is highly technical, particularly where business risks are involved, the advice and assistance of a qualified Insurance Broker can be utilized with considerable advantage.

PRINCIPAL LIFE ASSURANCE COMPANIES

Established	Class	Name of Office	Life and Annuity Funds	Life Premium Income	Consideration for Annuities	Rate of Interest % Earned	Interest % assumed at Valuation
			£	£	£	£	£
1961	P	Abbey Life....................	99,804,000	31,275,000	1,526,000	4·34	3·0
1849	M	Australian Mutual (C)..........	1,117,999,547	136,254,394	3,829,222	6·55	—
1925	PO	Avon........................	4,148,101	558,886	68,396	7·99	2·50 & 3·50
1961	P	Bedford Life.................	4,490,432	705,175	1,123,689	34·00	3·00
1839	PIO	Blackburn (Ord.).............	4,792,568	628,237	—	7·78	2·50
1866	PIO	Britannic (Ord.).............	80,484,989	7,548,687	109,976	7·68	2·50
1896	P	British Life.................	3,309,022	879,097	62,485	4·30	3·00
1920	PO	British National.............	3,820,629	438,803	106,231	—	2·50 to 4·00
1847	M	Canada Life (C)†.............	430,644,947	38,447,940	11,344,233	6·32	1·75 to 5·50
1862	MI	City of Glasgow (Ord.)........	2,767,828	315,487	—	6·17	2·50
1824	M	Clerical, Medical and General...	129,735,737	9,559,718	8,674,871	6·56	4·00
1873	M	Colonial Mutual (C)..........	429,809,192	53,372,696	362,114	6·89	3·00
1861	PO	Commercial Union★...........	565,022,032	66,961,879	7,188,594	6·97	2·50
1871	P	Confederation (C)............	271,581,586	37,059,278★	—	6·50	2 to 3·50
1867	MIO	Co-operative (Ord.)..........	217,806,000	25,698,000	192,000	7·00	2·50
1900	PO	Crown Life..................	286,171,325	40,512,244	11,112,550	6·41	Various
1899	PO	Crusader....................	49,155,040	7,908,904	2,691,279	7·46	2·50 to 8·00
1904	PO	Eagle Star★.................	406,453,307	47,056,418	7,981,819	6·69	2·50
1887	PO	Ecclesiastical★.............	4,271,156	467,326	128,162	5·51(N)	2·00 & 3·00
1901	PO	Economic....................	3,350,117	323,273	406,673	—	—
1762	M	Equitable...................	113,138,372	6,236,146	5,857,419	7·03	7·00 Bonus Reserve
1844	P	Equity & Law................	260,115,215	12,390,628	7,226,713	6·32	6·25
1925	M	Federation Mutual...........	1,190,642	141,230	6,832	7·24	2·00, 2·75 & 3·50
1832	M	Friends Prov. & Cent.........	261,668,000	27,106,000	1,370,000	7·42	2·75
1848	P	Gresham.....................	62,665,393	7,339,067	400,018	6·80	2·50 & 2·75
1821	PO	Guardian★..................	585,371,000	54,012,000	16,819,000	7·24	Various
1932	PO	Ideal......................	1,192,677	127,971	1,366	7·78	3·00
1897	P	Imperial Life of Canada (C)....	194,965,537	24,422,794	—	6·38	2·50 & 3·00
1939	PI	Irish Life (Ord.)............	59,837,657	9,375,186	2,879,089	6·26(N)	2·50
1836	PO	Legal & General.............	1,080,138,000	110,282,000	3,746,000	—	2·50 to 3·50
1838	M	Life Assoc. of Scotland.......	32,925,532	4,319,432	282,593	7·69	2·50, 2·75 & 3·00
1843	MI	Liverpool Victoria (Ord.)......	49,481,500	4,703,163	—	6·28	3·00 Bonus Reserve
1869	PIO	London & Manchester (Ord.) ·..	76,447,267	7,646,500	1,770,147	7·52	2·50
1964	P	London Indemnity & General†..	6,383,219	113,872	4,275,807	—	3·00 to 4·00
1806	M	London Life.................	118,017,490	12,467,707	1,678,575	6·71	3·00 & 3·50 Bonus Res.
1887	M	Manufacturers Life (C)........	750,326,142	56,557,345	29,613,535	6·40(N)	2·00 to 6·25
1852	M	Marine & General............	28,913,083	3,541,884	638,678	6·85	2·50 & 2·75
1884	M	Medical Sickness Ann. & Life...	12,268,280	952,135	11,264	5·31(N)	2·50
1886	P	Mutual Life & Citizens (C)	340,359,457	40,368,051	17,226	6·61	3·00 & 3·50
1890	M	Nalgo Assoc.................	3,999,000	416,000	Nil	7·50	2·50
1925	M	Nation Life★................	1,768,337	1,514,003	1,897	—	3·50
1935	P	Natl. Employers' Life.........	11,553,584	3,531,874	1,136,654	8·52	3·50
1910	MO	Natl. Farmers' Union.........	55,265,777	4,817,836	1,026,645	7·98	3·00, 3·50 & 4·00
1830	M	Natl. Mutual................	50,764,649	3,654,296	3,164,800	6·33	4·00 & 4·50
1869	M	Natl. Mutual of Australasia (C)★	442,458,000	60,174,000★	—	6·89	Various
1835	M	Natl. Provident.............	106,143,354	12,589,813	980,621	6·71	2·50 & 3·00
1925	PI	New Ireland (Ord.)...........	22,305,444	2,630,719	—	6·76	3·00 & 3·50
1960	P	Noble Lowndes Annuity........	57,390,719	2,166,734	16,579,606	8·38	2·50 & 3·50
1808	M	Norwich Union Life...........	622,620,272	72,901,188	3,179,081	6·27	2·25 to 6·00
1864	PIO	Pearl (Ord.).................	271,426,329	27,414,600	5,997,726	7·77	3·00
1782	PO	Phœnix......................	136,221,575	16,958,144	518,403	7·36	2·50 & 2·25
1877	M	Prov. Life Assoc. of London....	55,618,648	5,365,638	2,221,300	5·85	2·50 & 3·50
1840	M	Provident Mutual............	78,511,733	10,569,027	1,271,898	7·28	4·00 Bonus Reserve
1848	PIO	Prudential (Ord.)	1,398,579,611	161,941,327	4,558,600	6·93	2·75 & 3·00
1864	PIO	Refuge (Ord.)...............	127,997,924	11,937,899	624,586	7·65	2·50
1911	MI	Reliance Mutual (Ord.)........	4,527,226	682,208	14,555	6·30	2·75
1845	PO	Royal★.....................	305,136,000	21,702,000	12,023,000	6·29	2·00 & 3·50
1850	MI	Royal Liver (Ord.)...........	28,332,694	3,308,677	2,827	6·72	2·50
1861	MIO	Royal London (Ord.)..........	73,676,000	5,572,000	31,000	7·48	2·25
1867	PI	Salvation Army (Ord.)........	8,372,648	811,955	1,365	5·11(N)	2·50

PRINCIPAL LIFE ASSURANCE COMPANIES—*continued*

| Established | Class | Name of Office | ANNUAL ACCOUNTS | | | | Interest % assumed at Valuation |
			Life and Annuity Funds	Life Premium Income	Consideration for Annuities	Rate of Interest % Earned	
			£	£	£	£	£
1826	M	Scottish Amicable............	225,469,000	22,884,500	401,000	8·16	2.50
1831	M	Scottish Equitable...........	86,112,996	8,950,346	5,635,104	6·97	2·25 & 3·00
1852	MI	Scottish Legal (Ord.)†........	2,838,433	343,873	—		2·50
1881	P	Scottish Life.................	87,773,727	9,709,451	1,015,115	7·00	2·50 & 3·00
1883	MO	Scottish Mutual.............	69,110,292	8,257,172	1,120,168	7·49	2·50 & 3·00
1837	M	Scottish Provident...........	135,604,307	11,749,348	2,843,718	7·48	2·50 & 2·75
1815	M	Scottish Widows.............	377,751,063	37,288,211	6,858,077	7·75	2·25
1904	P	Sentinel★...................	11,378,246	1,186,960	66,230	7·48	3·50 Bonus Reserve
1964	P	Southampton, The............	5,525,891	1,252,065	29,172		Various
1899	M	Stamford Mutual (Ord.).......	2,186,472	428,367	—	5·10(N)	3·25
1825	M	Standard★...................	829,948,452	83,532,819	7,268,412	7·22	2·00 & 2·25
★	PO	Sun Alliance & London........	191,504,000	21,442,000	913,000	7·03	2·00 & 3·00
1810	P	Sun Life....................	414,814,000	50,592,000	6,503,000	7·32	2·00 & 5·75
1865	M	Sun Life of Canada (C)........	970,000,000	118,000,000	8,600,000	5·90(N)	2·50, 3·00 & 3·50
1839	M	Tunstall & District (Ord.).....	2,661,160	56,387	Nil	6·53	2·50
1908	P	United Friendly.............	15,520,154	3,159,490	Nil	6·78	3·00
1804	P	United Kingdom Prov..........	145,345,021	10,713,891	2,295	8·26	2·25, 2·50 & 3·00
1825	P	University..................	20,566,509	986,658	2,810,310	6·85	6·00 Bonus Reserve
1952	P	Welfare....................	10,013,058	2,256,612★	—	—	3·50
1841	MIO	Wesleyan & General (Ord.).....	30,379,035	3,066,233	186,692	7·41	2·75
1837	P	Yorkshire General............	239,259,159	22,497,623	6,582,828	6·79	3·00

INDUSTRIAL COMPANIES

Established	Class	Name of Office	Life Funds	Life Premium Income	Rate of Interest% Earned	Interest % assumed at Valuation
			£	£	£/p	£/p
1839	PO	Blackburn....................	12,526,640	1,476,091	8·85	2·50
1866	PO	Britannic....................	127,053,703	15,595,294	7·40	2·50
1862	M	City of Glasgow..............	7,121,912	893,663	6·17	3·00
1867	MO	Co-operative.................	290,317,000	42,693,000	7·00	3·00
1939	P	Irish Life....................	27,262,085	4,193,456	6·78	3·00
1843	M	Liverpool Victoria............	244,897,108	25,875,988	6·25	2·50
1869	PO	London & Manchester.........	62,602,066	6,772,999	7·52	2·50
1925	P	Nation Life★.................	1,493,734	379,636	—	3·50
1925	P	New Ireland.................	9,871,487	2,496,815	6·95	3·50
1864	PO	Pearl.......................	281,639,763	37,448,768	7·80	2·50
1848	PO	Prudential...................	743,665,104	88,161,414	7·80	2·75
1864	PO	Refuge......................	130,121,732	17,176,572	7·65	2·75
1911	MO	Reliance Mutual..............	4,269,726	913,275	6·30	2·75
1850	M	Royal Liver.................	108,262,480	14,292,541	6·72	2·50 & 3·00
1861	MO	Royal London................	181,021,000	15,412,000	7·69	2·25
1867	P	Salvation Army...............	19,885,775	2,455,018	6·28(N)	2·50
1852	M	Scottish Legal†..............	29,314,335	2,636,445	—	2·50
1899	M	Stamford Mutual.............	8,736,490	1,389,869	5·40(N)	3·25
1841	MO	Wesleyan & General...........	31,821,996	4,116,755	7·51	3·00

LIFE ASSURANCES IN FORCE

Figures published by the life offices' associations show that 13,500,000 ordinary assurance policies to the amount of £27,800,000,000 were in force at the end of 1970, with total yearly premiums of £583,000,000 compared with 12,900,000, £24,000,000,000 and £527,000,000,000 respectively in 1969. These figures include the Ordinary Branch business of Friendly Societies.

IMMEDIATE ANNUITIES (payable half-yearly, in arrear) FOR EVERY £1,000 PAID (*See notes*, p. 1138)
These rates may vary from month to month according to current conditions.

	MALES				FEMALES			
	Age 50	Age 60	Age 65	Age 70	Age 50	Age 60	Age 65	Age 70
	£	£	£	£	£	£	£	£
Abbey Life	94·80	112·20	126·90	148·00	89·80	102·20	112·90	128·40
Australian Mutual★	103·20	120·40	135·00	156·20	100·40	112·50	123·00	138·40
Avon★	113·00	129·00	144·00	166·00	107·00	120·00	130·00	146·00
Bedford Life★	108·70	128·55	143·65	165·95	102·80	117·40	129·45	146·35
Britannic★	105·00	123·00	137·00	159·00	100·00	113·00	123·00	139·00
British National★	111·00	130·00	145·20	166·00	105·40	119·40	130·80	146·80
Canada Life★	108·46	125·00	139·28	160·00	103·84	115·60	125·78	140·84
City of Glasgow★	101·60	119·90	134·60	155·20	95·10	109·10	120·60	137·50
Clerical, Medical and General★	109·60	124·80	137·70	156·10	105·30	116·10	125·30	138·80
Colonial Mutual★	100·40	117·80	131·50	152·00	95·20	107·20	117·40	132·30
Confederation★	87·00	102·20	114·60	132·40	83·00	94·80	104·20	117·60
Co-operative Ins.★	106·20	123·80	138·60	159·80	101·20	113·80	124·40	140·20
Crown Life★	82·80	100·30	113·50	132·50	75·80	89·40	100·20	115·70
Crusader★	108·00	130·20	144·70	165·90	103·50	120·40	130·70	146·20
Eagle Star★	111·65	129·40	144·05	165·05	106·40	119·35	130·20	145·65
Ecclesiastical★	110·40	126·40	140·40	160·40	106·00	117·20	126·80	141·60
Economic★	118·50	133·90	147·40	167·00	114·40	124·90	134·40	148·50
Equitable★	113·40	131·40	146·20	167·60	108·20	121·20	132·20	148·00
Equity & Law★	109·10	125·90	140·80	160·70	105·00	116·90	127·60	142·10
Federation Mutual	107·00	125·00	139·00	161·00	102·00	115·00	125·00	141·00
Friends Prov. & Cent.★	104·80	121·60	136·00	156·40	100·00	112·00	122·40	137·40
Gresham★	107·00	124·30	138·60	159·00	103·10	115·70	126·00	141·10
Guardian★	110·00	127·10	141·70	162·90	105·30	117·30	127·70	143·20
Imperial Life	108·00	125·00	139·40	160·40	103·40	115·20	125·60	140·80
Irish Life★	111·10	129·90	143·60	164·30	106·50	120·60	130·50	145·90
Legal & General★	111·00	128·30	142·60	163·00	108·10	120·70	131·00	146·10
Life Assoc. of Scotland★	103·30	120·60	135·90	157·20	98·30	110·70	121·80	137·40
London and Manchester	106·40	125·20	139·80	160·90	101·40	115·20	125·90	141·40
London Indemnity and General★	112·85	130·35	145·05	166·20	107·85	120·40	131·10	146·65
London Life★	108·40	126·60	142·00	164·00	103·20	116·20	127·20	143·60
Marine & General★	110·88	128·75	143·46	164·46	105·84	118·75	129·59	145·09
Medical Sickness Ann. & Life★	102·60	120·10	134·90	156·20	97·60	110·10	120·80	136·50
National Employers Life	106·40	122·40	136·60	157·20	102·00	113·00	123·00	137·80
National Farmers' Union★	113·00	129·00	144·00	166·00	107·00	120·00	130·00	146·00
National Mutual	102·50	119·00	134·50	155·50	97·50	110·00	120·50	136·00
National Provident★	106·00	127·50	141·50	163·00	101·00	118·00	128·50	144·50
New Ireland★	112·10	129·80	144·50	165·90	107·20	119·80	130·60	146·20
Noble Lowndes★	112·30	129·20	143·80	164·90	107·70	119·40	129·80	145·20
Norwich Union Life★	104·60	123·30	137·80	158·20	99·90	112·60	124·10	139·10
Pearl★	114·50	130·50	144·50	165·20	110·20	121·10	131·00	145·70
Phœnix★	110·80	125·70	138·30	156·60	106·70	117·10	126·20	139·40
Prov. Life Assoc. of London★	102·70	120·40	135·00	155·80	95·90	109·00	119·80	135·20
Provident Mutual★	109·65	127·25	141·90	162·75	104·55	117·35	128·00	143·50
Prudential★	108·00	125·40	139·80	160·80	105·20	117·20	128·00	143·00
Refuge	102·50	120·00	134·50	156·00	97·50	110·00	120·50	136·00
Reliance	96·10	113·50	128·20	149·30	91·20	103·60	114·60	129·70
Royal★	110·10	127·60	142·40	163·50	105·00	117·70	128·40	143·90
Royal London★	100·80	118·40	132·80	154·00	96·00	108·40	118·80	134·40
Scottish Equitable★	103·70	122·10	137·40	157·80	98·60	111·40	122·90	139·00
Scottish Life★	101·50	119·20	133·90	155·00	96·30	109·20	120·10	135·60
Scottish Mutual★	102·90	120·30	135·10	156·10	97·90	110·30	121·00	136·50
Scottish Provident	111·40	128·00	142·00	162·60	105·10	117·40	128·00	143·60
Scottish Widows★	108·20	126·00	141·20	163·20	103·30	115·80	126·70	142·70
Sentinel★	105·00	122·00	136·00	156·50	100·50	113·00	123·50	138·50
Southampton, The	95·70	115·30	130·70	152·20	89·70	104·30	116·30	132·30
Stamford Mutual★	101·80	119·30	134·50	155·60	97·00	109·20	120·00	134·80
Standard★	112·08	128·92	143·44	164·56	106·92	118·58	128·88	144·14
Sun Alliance and London★	111·20	129·00	143·60	164·60	106·00	119·00	129·80	145·20
Sun Life★	109·90	127·40	142·10	163·30	105·00	117·40	128·10	143·60
United Kingdom★	100·85	118·70	133·45	154·50	95·70	108·70	119·50	135·05
University★	113·60	132·40	147·80	169·60	108·20	122·00	133·40	149·40
Welfare	117·50	134·20	148·70	169·85	112·95	124·45	134·75	150·10
Wesleyan & General★	104·30	119·90	133·30	152·60	100·00	110·90	120·40	134·50
Yorkshire General★	104·00	121·50	136·00	157·00	99·00	111·50	122·50	137·50

Note P.P.—Purchase Price. ★ Deduction required or increase in Annuity rate as shown. Australian Mutual—Deduct £3 per contract. Avon—Deduct £2 per contract. Bedford Life—Deduct £2 per contract. Britannic—Deduct £3 per contract. British National—Deduct £2·50 per contract. City of Glasgow—Deduct £2 per contract. Clerical, Med. & Gen.— Minimum P.P. £500—Deduct £2·50 per contract. Colonial Mut.—Rates for P.P. £1,000–£10,000. Confederation—Deduct £15 from P.P. Co-operative—10p% if P.P. over £2,000. Crown—Deduct £18 per contract. Crusader—Deduct £2 per contract. Eagle Star—Deduct £2·50 per contract. Ecclesiastical—Deduct £1·50 per contract. Economic—Deduct £1·50 per contract. Equitable—Deduct £3 per contract. Equity & Law—Rates for P.P. up to £2,499. Increased for more. Friends Prov. & Cent.—Deduct £3 per contract. Gresham—Deduct £3 per contract. Guardian—Deduct £2 per contract. Irish Life—Deduct £3 per contract. Legal & General—Deduct £3 per contract. Life Assoc. of Scotland—Deduct £2.50 per contract. London Indemnity—Deduct £2 per contract. London Life—Deduct 2·50 per contract. Marine & General—Deduct £2 per contract. Medical Sickness An. & Life—Deduct £2 per contract. Natl. Farmers' Union—Deduct £2 per contract. Nat. Provident—Deduct £2 per contract. New Ireland—Deduct £2·50 per contract. Noble Lowndes—Deduct 15p per annuity payment. Norwich Union—Deduct £4 per contract. Pearl—Deduct £3 per contract. Phœnix—Deduct £3 per contract. Prov. Life Assoc. of London—Rates increased if P.P. £2,000 or over. Provident Mutual—Rates for P.P. £2,000. Reduced for less. Prudential—Deduct £3 per contract. Royal—Deduct £2 per contract. Royal London—Deduct £2 per contract. Scottish Equitable—Deduct £2 per contract. Scottish Life—Deduct £3 per contract. Scottish Mutual—Deduct £2 per contract. Scottish Widows—Deduct £1·25 per contract. Sentinel—Deduct £2·50 per contract. Stamford Mutual— Deduct £2·50 per contract. Standard—Deduct £3 per contract. Sun Alliance & Lond.—Deduct £3 per contract. Sun Life— Deduct £2 per contract. United Kingdom—Deduct £1·50 per contract. University—Deduct £3 per contract. Wesleyan & General—Deduct £2 per contract. Yorkshire General—Rates increased if P.P. £2,500 or over.

BONUSES

The following table gives examples of Bonus last declared on Whole Life and Endowment Assurances for £100. In most cases the rate given is in respect of a policy effected at age 30 next birthday and the Endowment Bonus is based on a Policy maturing at the end of 30 years.

Office	Last★ Valuation	Bonus declared on Whole Life Assurances	Bonus declared on Endowment Assurances	Interim Bonus
Australian Mutual.......	1970A	£2·55 compound	£2·35 compound	At rate last declared
Avon.................	1968Q	£3·75	£3·75	£3·75‡
Bedford Life............	1968★	£1·37 up to Dec. 31. 1968	£1·00 from Jan. 1. 1969	At rate last declared
Blackburn..............	1970A	£3·50	£3·50	£3·50
Britannic..............	1970A	£3·50	£3·50	£3·50
British National........	1968★	£2·50	£2·50	£2·50
Canada Life............	1970A	Vary with age, plan and duration		Allowed on death after 1 year
City of Glasgow Friendly.	1969Q	£2·50	£2·50	£2·50
Clerical, Medical & Gen. .	1968★	£4·25‡	£4·25‡	£4·00‡
Colonial Mutual........	1970A	£3·40★	£3·10★	At rate last declared‡
Commercial Union.......	1969★	£4·25 compound	£4·25 compound	£4·00 compound
Confederation..........	1970A	Vary with age, plan and duration		
Co-operative...........	1970A	£3·40	£3·40	£3·40†
Crown Life............	1970Q	Vary with age, plan and duration		Allowed on death after 2 years
Crusader..............	1970A	£3·80 compound	£3·60 compound	At rate last declared
Eagle Star.............	1969★	£3·15 compound†	£3·15 compound†	£3·15 compound†
Ecclesiastical..........	1969★	£4·00 compound★	£4·00 compound★	£3·50 compound
Economic	1968★	£3·25 compound	£3·25 compound	£3·25 compound
Equitable.............	1970★	£1·00 to £5·00 according to years in force	£5 plus £2·50 on existing Bonus	W.L.—£5·00 and upwards Endmt.—£5·00 plus £2·50
Equity & Law..........	1970★	£3·50	£3·50	£3·50
Federation Mutual.......	1970★	£3·50	£3·50	£3·50
Friends Prov. & Century★	1970★	£4·00 compound	£4·00 compound	£3·80 compound‡
Gresham..............	1970A	£2·90	£2·90	£2·90
Guardian..............	1970A	£4·25	£4·00	At rate last declared‡
Ideal Life.............	1968★	£3·00	£3·00	£3·00
Imperial Life of Canada..	1970A	Vary with age, plan and duration		Allowed at death
Irish Life..............	1970A	£4·50	£4·50	At rate last declared
Legal and General.......	1970A	£3·15†	£3·15†	At rate last declared
Life Assoc. of Scotland...	1970★	£3·00 compound	£3·00 compound	£3·00 compound
Liverpool Victoria.......	1967★	£3·60	£3·60	£3·60
London & Manchester ...	1970A	£3·25‡	£3·25‡	—
London Life............	1970A	£3·90 compound for year	beginning July 1, 1971	
Marine & General.......	1970A	£4·00★	£3·75★	At rate last declared‡
Med. Sickness, An. & Life	1970★	£4·00	£4·00	£4·00
Mutual Life............	1970A	£2·25 compound	£2·25 compound	£2·25
Nalgo.................	1968★	£5·00	£5·00	£5·00‡
Nation Life	1970★	£3·40	£3·40	£3·40‡
National Employers Life .	1970A	£1·00	£1·00	£1·00
Nat. Farmers' Union	1970★	£3·75	£3·75	£3·75
National Mutual	1970★	£3·00 compound	£2·75 compound	At rate last declared†
Natl. Mut. of Austr......	1970★	£2·52 compound	£2·52 compound	At rate last declared
National Provident......	1969★	£3·87	£3·25	£3·62 & £3·00‡
New Ireland	1970A	£2·30†	£2·12†	At rate last declared
Noble Lowndes Annty ..	1970★	£2·75 compound	£2·75 compound	£2·75 compound

Office	Last* Valuation	Bonus declared on Whole Life Assurances	Bonus declared on Endowment Assurances	Interim Bonus
Norwich Union	1970A	£3·35 compound*	£3·35 compound*	At rate last declared
Pearl*	1970A	£3·35‡	£3·35‡	—
Phœnix	1970A	£3·75‡	£3·75‡	£3·75
Prov. Life Assoc. of Lond	1970A	£3·90	£3·90	—
Provident Mutual	1968*	{ £4·00—Age 65 or over { £3·50—Under age 65	£3·00	At rate last declared†
Prudential	1970A	£3·25	£3·25	At rate last declared‡
Refuge	1970A	£3·60†	£3·60†	£3·60†
Reliance Mutual	1968*	£3·00 compound	£3·00 compound	£3·00 compound
Royal	1968Q	£3·60 compound	£3·60 compound	£4·00 compound
Royal Liver Friendly	1970A	£3·50‡	£3·50‡	£3·50
Royal London	1968*	£4·00†	£4·00†	£4·00†
Salvation Army	1970A	£3·10	£3·10	—
Scottish Amicable	1968*	£3·62 compound	£3·62 compound	£3·80 compound
Scottish Equitable	1968*	£3·25 compound	£3·25 compound	£3·25 compound
Scottish Legal Life	1969Q	£3·60	£3·60	£3·60
Scottish Life*	1968*	{ Old series £4·25† { New series £2·87½	Old series £4·25† New series £2·87½	Old series £3·25.† New £2·75
Scottish Mutual	1970*	£3·00†	£3·00†	£3·00†
Scottish Provident	1968	£4·20 compound†	£4·20 compound†	£4·00 compound
Scottish Widows	1968Q	£4·00 compound	£4·00 compound	£3·50 compound†
Sentinel	1970*	—	—	£2·50
Southampton, The	1970*	£2·70 compound	£2·70 compound	£2·70
Stamford Mutual	1970A	£3·00	£3·00	£3·00
Standard	1970*	£3·50 on sum assured and £5·00 on vested bonuses		£3·00 and £4·50 on vested bonus†
Sun Alliance & London	1969*	£3·25 compound	£3·25 compound	£3·25 compound†
Sun Life	1969*	£4·50‡	£4·00‡	At rate last declared
Sun Life of Canada	1970A	Vary with age, plan and duration		—
Tunstall & District	1970Q	£4·25	£4·25	£4·25
United Friendly	1970A	£3·50	£3·50	—
United Kingdom	1968*	{ £3·45 compound Temperance Section† { £3·40 compound all other Policies†		£3·55 Temperance Section† £3·50 Others†
University	1969*	£4·50†	£4·00†	At rate last declared†
Welfare	1968*	£3·00 compound	£3·00 compound	£3·25
Wesleyan & General	1970A	£3·50	£3·50	£3·50
Yorkshire General	1970*	£4·25	£4·25	£4·25

* NOTE.—A—Annual Valuation. Q—Quinquennial Valuation. The Valuation period ends December 31, in the year shown unless otherwise indicated. † Plus special additions. ‡ Plus Terminal Bonus.

Bedford Life.—Three years ending Dec. 31, 1968.

British National.—Three years ending Dec. 31, 1968.

Clerical Med. & Gen.—Three years ending Dec. 31, 1968.

Colonial Mutual.—On an increasing scale.

Commercial Union.—Three years ending Dec. 31, 1969.

Eagle Star.—Three years ending December 31, 1969.

Ecclesiastical.—Five years ending February 28, 1969. Plus 20% of existing Bonus.

Economic.—Three years ending Dec. 31, 1968.

Equitable.—Three years ending Dec. 31, 1970.

Equity & Law.—One year ending Dec. 31, 1970.

Federation Mutual.—Three years ending Dec. 31, 1970.

Friends Prov. & Century—United Kingdom Policies and closed Republic of Ireland series. Three years ending December 31, 1970.

Gresham.—Three years ending December 31, 1970.

Ideal Life.—Three years ending December 31, 1968.

Life Assoc. of Scot.—Compound Series from Oct. 1, 1970.

Liverpool Victoria.—Two years ending Dec. 31, 1967.

Marine & Genl.—Increasing to £4·50 after 12 years—Whole Life and to £4·25—Endowment.

Med. Sickness An. & Life.—Three years ending December 31, 1970.

Naglo.—Three years ending December 31, 1968.

Nation Life.—15 months ending March 31, 1970.

Nat. Farmers Union.—Four years ending Dec. 31, 1970.

National Mutual.—Two years ending December 31, 1970.

National Mut. of Austr.—One year ending Sept. 30, 1970.

National Provident.—Three years ending Dec. 31, 1969.

Noble Lowndes.—Two years, five months ending March 31, 1970.

Norwich Union.—Compound Series from Jan. 1, 1965.

Pearl.—Policies effected since 1965.

Provident Mutual.—Three years ending Dec. 31, 1968.

Reliance Mutual.—Three years ending Dec. 31, 1968.

Royal London.—Three years ending Dec. 31, 1968.

Scottish Amicable.—Three years ending Dec. 31, 1968.

Scottish Equitable.—Three years ending Dec. 31, 1968.

Scottish Life.—Old series—Simple. New series Compound Bonus. Three years ending Dec. 31, 1968.

Scottish Mutual.—Three years ending Dec. 31, 1970.

Sentinel.—One year ending March 31, 1970.

Southampton.—Three years ending Dec. 31, 1970

Standard.—One year ending Nov. 15, 1970.

Sun Alliance & London.—Three years ending Dec. 31, 1969.

Sun Life.—Three years ending Dec. 31, 1969.

United Kingdom.—Three years ending December 31, 1968.

University—Three years ending Dec. 31, 1969.

Welfare.—Three years ending Dec. 31, 1968.

Yorkshire General.—Two years ending Dec. 31, 1970. Rates as from November 9, 1970.

ANNUAL PREMIUMS FOR WHOLE LIFE ASSURANCE

Life assurance may be effected either with or without participation in profits. If with participation then a higher premium is charged and the Policy is entitled to a Bonus, which is a share in the profits made by the Office, as and when declared. Valuations are made by Offices at periods varying from one to five years and the rate of Bonus then declared is usually in respect of each year since the previous valuation. These Bonuses are normally payable with the Sum Assured for their full amount, but, if desired, they can be applied to reduce the premium or surrendered for a cash payment. If a Policy is effected without participation the Sum Assured only is payable.

The ages applicable to the life and endowment assurance (but not the annuity) rates as hereafter given are " next birthday " unless otherwise stated

AVERAGE ANNUAL PREMIUMS FOR WHOLE LIFE ASSURANCE OF £1000

Age at Entry	With Profits	Without Profits	Age at Entry	With Profits	Without Profits	Age at Entry	With Profits	Without Profits
	£	£		£	£		£	£
30	22·50	11·41	40	29·54	17·16	50	42·41	27·32
31	23·12	11·91	41	30·34	17·84	51	44·21	28·98
32	23·79	12·42	42	31·20	18·56	52	46·01	30·65
33	24·47	12·94	43	32·16	19·34	53	47·81	32·33
34	25·16	13·48	44	33·22	20·14	54	49·63	34·02
35	25·86	14·04	45	34·42	20·98	55	51·47	35·72
36	26·57	14·62	46	35·82	21·88	56	53·37	37·44
37	27·29	15·22	47	37·32	22·88	57	55·27	39·17
38	28·02	15·86	48	38·92	24·18	58	57·67	40·91
39	28·76	16·51	49	40·62	25·68	60	63·49	44·57

The next table shows the annual premiums for a policy of £1000 payable at death, with and without profits. Normally premiums are payable throughout life but with some Offices they cease at age 85 (see note † on p. 1136). It is not sufficient to judge a life office by premium rates only. An office charging a high premium may give higher bonuses than one charging a low premium, and therefore bonus results and prospects as well as premiums have to be considered. Most offices grant interim bonuses between valuation periods, and it is important to ascertain if this is the case before an assurance is effected, and how such interim bonuses compare with valuation bonuses, especially in cases of endowment assurance. A without profit Insurance provides the maximum amount of cover at the lowest cost and if an Office as in some cases, is prepared to allow the option of converting the Insurance at any time to " with " profits either for whole of Life or on the Endowment plan, this gives an attractive contract. The change would, of course, entail a higher premium being paid but under this arrangement the highest cover can be obtained in the early years and the alteration made when the increased cost can be met.

ANNUAL PREMIUMS FOR ASSURANCE OF £1000 PAYABLE AT DEATH
MALE LIVES (lower premiums are quoted by many offices for female lives)

NAME OF OFFICE	WITH PROFITS					WITHOUT PROFITS			
	Age 30	Age 35	Age 40	Age 50	Age 60	Age 30	Age 40	Age 50	Age 60
	£	£	£	£	£	£	£	£	£
★Abbey Life	Not available					11·55	17·55	27·85	45·75
★Australian Mutual	21·70	25·10	29·30	41·80	64·50	Not available			
★Avon†	20·60	24·00	28·60	41·40	62·60	10·90	16·90	27·40	46·30
★Bedford Life	15·15	18·15	22·00	33·60	53·30	10·75	16·45	26·65	43·00
★Blackburn	21·70	25·10	29·50	41·90	62·50	13·80	20·30	31·40	50·80
★Britannic	21·90	25·40	29·90	42·80	64·50	13·30	19·80	31·10	51·10
★British National	23·40	26·70	30·80	43·00	64·70	14·60	20·20	30·10	47·60
★Canada Life	18·75	22·00	20·17	38·83	62·33	13·42	19·42	30·00	48·92
City of Glasgow Friendly	20·75	24·08	28·50	42·00	67·42	Not issued			
★Clerical, Medical & General	23·30	27·10	31·70	44·60	67·40	10·90	16·70	26·90	46·10
Colonial Mutual†	23·65	27·25	31·80	44·10	67·60	14·10	20·15	31·00	50·70
★Commercial Union	27·83	30·97	35·02	46·92	66·58	13·34	18·84	29·02	47·33†
★Confederation	15·90	18·90	22·75	33·90	52·84	11·30	17·10	27·05	44·30
★Co-operative	23·00	27·50	32·50	48·00	71·00	Not issued			
★Crown Life	16·55	19·45	23·35	35·25	56·05	12·30	18·35	28·85	47·15
★Crusader	28·30	32·10	36·70	50·30	74·35	13·20	19·50	30·70	51·28
★Eagle Star	23·80	27·00	31·00	42·60	61·60	10·40	16·20	26·30	44·00
★Ecclesiastical†	21·90	25·20	29·40	42·00	64·70	9·60	15·00	24·90	42·60
★Economic	25·50	28·80	33·00	45·30	67·30	12·90	18·40	28·40	47·20
★Equitable	28·52	31·00	34·52	45·00	64·00	12·96	18·44	28·20	45·96
Equity & Law	27·50	31·23	35·42	48·47	68·51	13·05	18·64	28·90	46·14
★Federation Mutual	23·90	27·40	31·75	44·45	66·80	11·35	17·30	27·55	45·40
★Friends' Provident & Century	24·50	27·80	32·20	44·60	65·80	12·60	18·50	29·10	48·40
★Gresham	25·80	29·16	33·24	45·72	67·32	13·68	19·20	29·76	49·56
★Guardian	22·35	25·86	30·30	43·06	64·35	11·12	17·08	27·38	45·28
Ideal	24·70	28·30	32·70	45·40	66·00	15·10	21·50	32·40	51·40

NAME OF OFFICE	WITH PROFITS					WITHOUT PROFITS			
	Age 30	Age 35	Age 40	Age 50	Age 60	Age 30	Age 40	Age 50	Age 60
	£	£	£	£	£	£	£	£	£
★Imperial Life of Canada	18·55	21·75	25·70	37·90	60·95	12·45	18·40	29·05	47·40
★Irish Life	23·63	27·63	32·37	45·87	67·50	13·00	19·25	30·13	48·25
★Legal and General†	24·23	27·40	31·40	44·57	67·10	10·47	15·88	26·22	45·63
★Life Association of Scotland	23·65	26·93	31·19	43·66	63·46	11·35	16·97	27·15	44·65
Liverpool Victoria	23·05	26·75	31·35	44·95	67·55	15·75	22·35	33·95	54·45
★London & Manchester	23·70	27·60	32·50	46·40	69·40	14·00	20·00	30·70	49·90
★London Indemnity & General			Not quoted			11·25	16·00	25·30	42·25
★London Life	20·20	23·40	27·60	40·00	60·40	9·60	15·00	24·80	42·60
★Manufacturers	17·24	20·48	24·70	37·29	59·27	10·89	16·57	26·16	42·99
★Marine & General	24·90	28·40	32·70	45·60	68·40	12·40	18·10	28·30	46·10
★Medical Sickness	21·30	24·90	29·50	42·70	63·90	11·00	16·70	27·00	45·80
Mutual Life	19·09	22·26	26·28	38·34	59·33	13·74	19·83	30·71	50·40
Nalgo Association	20·95	25·61	30·26	44·23	68·68	12·80	18·62	30·26	51·22
★Nation Life	24·00	28·00	33·00	46·00	69·00	10·20	15·65	23·35	42·25
★National Employers Life	14·40	17·20	20·80	32·00	52·00	11·40	16·80	26·40	43·60
★National Farmers' Union†	18·40	21·80	26·00	38·20	58·80	10·30	16·20	26·60	45·40
★National Mutual†	28·00	31·50	36·00	48·00	68·00	15·00	22·50	33·50	53·50
★National Mutual of Australasia†	19·35	22·55	26·70	38·95	60·05	12·40	18·20	28·40	46·20
★National Provident	21·70	25·40	30·00	43·20	64·80	12·60	18·20	28·20	45·90
★New Ireland	21·90	25·40	29·80	42·90	66·10	15·10	21·10	31·80	50·50
★Noble Lowndes Annty.	18·60	21·70	25·70	37·25	56·55	10·15	15·57	25·16	41·90
★Norwich Union†	26·10	29·20	33·15	44·45	65·35	14·05	19·50	29·90	49·10†
★Pearl	20·40	23·92	28·34	40·92	61·34	11·78	17·70	28·04	46·10
★Phœnix	21·20	24·70	29·00	41·80	63·00	10·40	15·80	25·40	42·60
★Provident Life Association of London†	23·80	27·20	31·40	43·90	67·30	13·50	19·50	29·00	46·00†
★Provident Mutual	20·30	23·90	28·30	41·20	62·20	10·40	16·00	25·80	43·00
★Prudential	21·00	24·80	29·50	42·90	65·30	10·70	16·70	27·30	46·30
★Refuge	23·50	27·00	31·50	44·50	66·50	14·50	21·00	32·50	53·00
★Reliance	21·88	25·30	29·40	42·18	61·78	11·40	17·40	27·64	45·63
★Royal	25·64	29·28	33·63	45·39	64·68	10·23	15·88	27·75	43·75†
Royal Liver Friendly	24·00	27·50	32·20	45·90	70·60	15·60	23·00	35·90	58·90
★Royal London	21·50	25·10	29·70	42·80	65·10	—	19·50	30·50	50·40
Salvation Army	23·00	26·80	31·40	45·10	69·80	15·90	23·00	35·60	57·70
★Scottish Amicable	23·60	26·70	30·80	43·70	64·40	12·00	18·10	28·20	47·00†
★Scottish Equitable	24·80	28·08	32·20	44·40	64·70	11·23	15·91	26·21	44·93†
★Scottish Legal	20·80	24·80	29·90	44·90	72·20			Not Issued	
★Scottish Life	25·90	29·10	33·20	44·80	64·00	12·60	18·50	26·80	45·80
★Scottish Mutual	24·12	27·42	30·46	44·34	66·22	12·00	17·64	27·88	46·22†
Scottish Provident	25·60	29·00	33·25	45·40	65·15	11·60	17·15	27·25	45·00
★Scottish Widows	24·40	27·80	32·00	44·20	64·30	10·60	16·50	27·00	45·90†
★Sentinel	20·35	23·90	28·35	41·15	62·20	10·20	15·70	25·40	42·35
★Southampton, The	22·43	25·88	29·67	41·17	60·15	11·85	17·71	27·83	45·43
Stamford Mutual	22·10	26·00	31·00	45·90	70·30	12·00	18·20	28·90	47·60
★Standard	26·20	29·11	32·86	43·98	62·78	11·10	17·15	27·60	45·00
Sun Alliance and London	26·30	29·60	33·90	46·30	68·40	13·40	19·40	30·00	48·60
★Sun Life	24·40	27·80	32·00	44·40	64·90	12·80	18·60	28·70	46·50
Sun Life of Canada	25·20	28·25	32·25	44·30	66·60	16·65	23·30	34·70	56·40
Tunstall and District	20·80	24·50	29·20	41·50	64·30			Not Issued	
United Friendly	22·90	26·50	31·00	44·20	65·80	15·00	21·54	33·10	53·40
★United Kingdom Provident	24·30	27·60	31·80	43·85	63·90	11·00	17·05	27·65	46·55
★University Life	19·70	23·40	28·00	40·00	60·00	9·10	14·60	24·30	42·20
Welfare	23·71	27·02	31·24	42·75	61·90	9·35	14·36	23·60	40·13
★Wesleyan & General	22·44	25·92	30·36	43·20	65·76	12·12	18·24	29·16	48·48
★Yorkshire General	23·10	26·70	31·10	43·90	65·10	11·90	17·50	27·10	44·30

* † For notes see p. 1143.

ENDOWMENT ASSURANCES.

Endowment Assurances are very popular, and are extremely attractive to persons who desire to combine a provision for their dependants, in event of premature death, with the investment of savings for the realization of a fund for their own personal enjoyment in later life. For the investment of small annual sums there is no medium promising more satisfactory results than an Endowment assurance participating in profits in a good bonus-paying life office. The selection of such an office is all-important, as so much depends upon profit-earning capacity—*see* first page of Life Assurance.

Under endowment assurances the sum assured is paid after a given number of years, or on the attainment of a fixed age. Should the life assured, however, die during the endowment period, the sum assured is paid at death together with any Bonuses attaching under a "with profit" Policy.

The following table shows the annual premiums, for various ages at entry, charged by the offices named, to secure £1000 at the end of 15, 20 and 25 years, or at death, if previous, with profits.

MALE LIVES (lower premiums are quoted by many offices for female lives)

NAME OF OFFICE	SUM ASSURED PAYABLE AT DEATHS, OR AT THE END OF									
	15 YEARS			20 YEARS			25 YEARS			
	Age 35	Age 40	Age 45	Age 30	Age 35	Age 40	Age 25	Age 30	Age 35	Age 40
	£	£	£	£	£	£	£	£	£	£
★Australian Mutual	66·00	66·70	68·10	48·20	48·80	49·80	37·60	38·00	38·70	40·00
★Avon	70·50	71·50	72·50	52·50	53·00	54·00	41·00	41·50	42·00	43·50
★Bedford Life	58·75	59·65	61·05	41·35	41·95	43·00	31·50	31·85	32·60	34·00
★Blackburn	70·00	70·70	72·10	52·00	52·50	53·50	41·00	41·30	42·00	43·40
★Britannic	70·40	71·10	72·40	52·30	52·80	53·80	41·30	41·60	42·40	43·80
★British National	71·10	71·90	73·20	52·90	53·50	54·60	41·90	42·40	43·30	44·70
★Canada Life	65·50	66·33	67·75	46·92	47·58	48·71	35·92	36·37	37·25	38·75
City of Glasgow	64·75	65·83	67·58	46·58	47·42	48·75	35·92	36·42	37·50	39·33
★Clerical, Medical & General	73·70	74·40	75·60	55·60	56·00	57·00	44·30	44·60	45·30	46·70
Colonial Mutual	70·55	71·40	72·65	52·15	52·75	53·90	41·05	41·60	42·45	44·10
★Commercial Union	73·48	74·06	75·70	56·05	56·51	57·80	45·52	45·87	46·56	47·85
★Confederation	63·05	64·00	65·65	44·55	45·25	46·45	33·85	34·35	35·30	36·75
★Co-operative	72·00	73·00	74·00	53·50	54·00	55·00	42·50	42·50	43·50	45·00
★Crown Life	61·95	62·85	64·45	43·40	44·05	45·30	32·60	33·05	33·95	35·60
★Crusader	74·30	75·20	76·60	56·10	56·80	57·90	45·00	45·60	46·50	48·00
★Eagle Star	70·10	70·70	71·90	52·90	53·30	54·20	42·40	42·70	43·30	44·60
★Ecclesiastical	67·60	68·40	69·60	50·10	50·70	51·70	39·50	40·00	40·80	42·20
★Economic	71·80	72·60	74·00	54·30	54·80	55·80	43·70	44·00	44·70	46·00
★Equitable	73·00	73·60	74·60	55·40	55·60	56·40	44·40	44·60	45·20	46·20
Equity & Law	75·96	76·89	77·83	57·56	58·02	58·95	46·60	47·07	47·54	48·93
★Federation Mutual	69·70	70·40	71·70	51·85	52·45	53·45	41·05	41·50	42·30	43·65
★Friends' Provident & Century	71·30	72·10	73·50	52·70	53·20	54·30	42·10	42·50	43·30	44·80
★Gresham	73·92	74·40	75·84	55·08	55·56	56·64	44·16	44·40	45·00	46·44
★Guardian	71·60	72·42	73·71	52·65	53·35	54·40	40·60	41·07	41·89	43·29
Ideal Life	73·70	74·40	75·80	55·70	56·10	57·20	44·50	44·90	45·70	47·10
★Imperial Life of Canada	67·55	68·50	70·10	48·45	49·15	50·40	37·80	38·35	39·25	40·95
★Irish Life	75·00	75·75	77·13	56·37	56·87	58·00	44·75	45·13	46·00	47·50
★Legal & General	71·38	71·97	72·91	52·21	52·68	53·39	41·75	42·22	42·81	43·86
★Life Assoc. of Scotland	71·68	72·28	73·46	54·07	54·46	55·34	43·36	43·64	44·25	45·48
Liverpool Victoria Friendly	72·25	73·05	74·45	53·85	54·35	55·45	42·55	42·95	43·75	45·25
★London & Manchester	71·60	72·30	73·50	53·80	54·40	55·40	43·00	43·58	44·30	45·60
★London Life	67·80	68·50	69·70	50·10	50·50	51·30	39·80	40·00	40·60	41·90
★Manufacturers	63·15	64·29	66·13	44·75	45·58	47·02	33·85	34·45	35·52	37·33
★Marine & General	73·60	74·40	75·60	54·40	54·90	56·10	43·20	43·70	44·50	46·00
★Medical Sickness Annuity & Life	71·40	72·20	73·50	53·00	53·50	54·50	41·70	42·00	42·70	44·00
Mutual Life	64·58	65·26	66·61	47·25	47·70	48·66	36·82	37·12	37·79	39·12
★Nalgo Assoc.	72·17	73·33	75·66	53·54	53·54	54·71	41·90	41·90	41·90	44·23
Nation Life	72·00	73·00	74·00	53·00	54·00	55·00	42·00	43·00	43·00	45·00
★Natl. Employers	57·40	58·20	59·60	40·40	40·80	41·80	30·40	30·60	31·40	32·60
★Natl. Farmers' Union	66·50	67·50	68·50	49·00	49·50	50·50	38·00	38·50	39·00	40·50
★Natl. Mutual	72·00	72·50	74·00	54·50	55·00	56·00	44·00	44·50	45·50	46·50
★Natl. Mutual of Australasia	64·90	65·65	67·00	47·40	47·90	48·95	36·90	37·25	37·95	39·40
★Natl. Provident	67·00	68·40	70·50	48·80	49·90	51·60	37·50	38·40	39·80	42·40
★New Ireland	69·10	70·00	71·30	50·40	51·00	52·10	39·10	39·60	40·40	42·00
★Noble Lowndes Annuity	65·70	66·35	67·50	47·50	47·95	48·80	36·90	37·15	37·85	39·15
★Norwich Union	71·75	72·30	73·40	54·20	54·60	55·40	43·60	43·85	44·45	45·55
★Pearl	70·68	71·32	72·56	52·40	52·84	53·76	41·10	41·40	42·08	43·38
★Phœnix	72·90	73·50	74·50	54·30	54·60	55·40	42·70	42·90	43·40	44·60
★Provident Life Assoc. of London	70·30	71·10	72·40	52·30	53·00	54·00	41·50	41·90	42·70	44·10
★Provident Mutual	67·70	68·30	69·50	49·70	50·10	59·90	38·60	38·90	39·50	40·70
★Prudential	70·20	70·90	72·40	52·00	52·60	53·60	40·80	41·20	42·00	43·50
★Refuge	71·50	72·50	73·50	53·50	54·00	55·00	42·50	43·00	43·50	45·00
★Reliance	68·64	69·26	70·44	50·70	51·28	52·34	39·98	40·45	41·28	42·69
★Royal	71·62	72·21	73·62	54·45	54·80	55·74	43·98	44·22	44·81	46·23
Royal Liver Friendly	71·70	72·80	74·30	53·00	53·60	55·00	41·20	41·70	42·60	44·30
★Royal London	71·10	71·90	73·10	52·50	53·10	54·20	41·30	41·70	42·50	43·90
Salvation Army	71·70	72·50	73·80	53·30	53·90	55·00	42·20	42·60	43·50	45·00
★Scottish Amicable	71·60	72·30	73·60	53·30	53·80	54·70	41·90	42·30	42·90	44·20
★Scottish Equitable	71·60	72·54	73·94	53·82	54·29	55·22	43·06	43·52	43·99	45·40
Scottish Legal	71·70	72·60	74·10	51·60	52·30	53·50	39·70	40·20	41·20	42·80
★Scottish Life	71·05	71·70	72·95	53·70	54·10	55·05	43·15	43·45	44·10	45·40
★Scottish Mutual	71·62	72·34	73·74	54·44	54·85	55·52	43·52	43·76	44·34	45·64
★Scottish Provident	72·95	73·60	74·85	55·40	55·80	56·80	44·70	45·00	45·70	47·00
★Scottish Widows	72·90	73·60	74·90	54·60	55·10	56·10	43·60	43·90	44·70	46·10
★Sentinel	68·50	69·25	70·65	50·50	51·00	52·05	39·40	39·75	40·45	41·90
★Southampton, The	71·76	72·45	73·95	53·48	54·05	55·09	42·44	42·78	43·59	45·08
Stamford Mutual	72·50	73·35	75·00	53·35	54·00	55·65	41·15	41·65	43·00	45·35
★Standard	71·54	72·19	73·47	52·71	53·15	54·10	42·66	42·96	43·63	44·92

NAME OF OFFICE	SUM ASSURED PAYABLE AT DEATH OR AT THE END OF									
	15 YEARS			20 YEARS			25 YEARS			
	Age 35	Age 40	Age 45	Age 30	Age 35	Age 40	Age 25	Age 30	Age 35	Age 40
	£	£	£	£	£	£	£	£	£	£
Sun Alliance and London..........	72·60	73·30	74·60	54·60	55·10	56·20	43·90	44·20	44·90	46·30
★Sun Life............................	71·60	72·30	73·70	53·80	54·30	55·40	43·00	43·40	44·10	45·50
Sun Life of Canada................	72·10	72·85	74·35	53·75	54·30	55·35	42·90	43·25	44·00	45·40
Tunstall & District................	71·00	72·00	73·70	51·70	52·30	53·60	40·00	40·40	41·30	43·10
United Friendly..................	72·10	72·90	74·30	53·60	54·20	55·30	42·30	42·60	43·50	45·00
★United Kingdom Provident........	71·00	71·70	73·00	53·55	54·00	55·00	43·05	43·40	44·10	45·40
★University Life..................	68·50	69·00	70·00	49·00	50·00	51·00	38·00	38·50	39·50	41·00
Welfare........................	71·36	72·16	73·53	53·47	54·04	54·95	42·75	42·98	43·66	45·03
★Wesleyan & General..............	69·96	70·68	71·64	51·72	52·20	53·04	40·80	41·16	41·88	42·96
★Yorkshire General................	72·50	73·50	74·50	54·50	55·00	56·00	43·50	43·50	44·50	45·50

★ Reductions allowed and additions required, are as shown, and some offices allow further reductions for sums assured of £5,000 and over. † Premiums cease at age 85.

Australian Mut.—£0·50 £2,000–£4,999.

Avon—Add £3·00 per policy.

Bedford—Add £3·00 per policy.

Blackburn—Add £1·50 per policy.

Britannic—Add £1·50 per policy.

British National—£1·50 per mille £2,000–£2,999. £2·50 p.m. £3,000–£3,999. £3·50 p.m. £4,000–£4,999.

Canada Life—Ages nearest birthday. £1·00 per mille £2,500–£9,999.

Clerical Medl. & Gen.—Add £2·50 per policy.

Commercial Union—Rates include Policy charge.

Confederation—Add £3·00 per policy. Whole life, minimum policy £5,000.

Co-operative—£1·20 per mille in excess of £2,000.

Crown Life—Ages last birthday—Whole Life, with profits, minimum Sum Assured £2,000—add £3·00 per policy. Without profits, minimum £5,000—add £5·00. Endowment—add £3·00.

Crusader—Rates include Policy charge of £2·00.

Eagle Star—Add £2·00 per policy.

Ecclesiastical—Add £1·50 per policy.

Economic—Without profit rates include Policy charge of £1·50.

Equitable—Rates include Policy charge of £3·00 and assume payment quarterly by Bankers' order.

Fedn. Mutl.—Whole Life rates reduced by £1·00 per mille over £5,000. Add £2·00 per policy.

Friends' Prov. & Cent.—Under £1,000 add £0·50 to rates shown. £2,500–£4,999 deduct £0·50 per mille.

Gresham—Premiums quoted include Policy charge and would be slightly lower if paid yearly.

Guardian—Add £2·00 per policy.

Imp. Life of Can.—Rates reduced for Whole Life £5,000 and over. Endowment £2,000 and over.

Irish Life—£0·50 per mille £2,000–£4,999.

Legal and General—Add £2·44 per policy.

Life Assn. of Scotland—Add £2·50 per policy.

Lond. & Man.—£1·00 per mille £2,500–£4,999.

London Indemnity & Gen.—Add £3·00 per policy.

London Life—Add £2·50 per policy.

Manufacturers'—Add £3·00 per policy.

Medical Sickness—Add £2·00 per policy. Reduction £0·50–£2,500 to £4,999.

Nation Life—Add £2·00 per policy.

Natl. Employers—Special profit-sharing scheme. £0·50 per mille £2,000–£4,999.

National Farmers' Union—Add £3·00 per policy.

National Mutual—£0·50 per mille £2,500–£3,999. £1·00 per mille £4,000–£4,999.

Natl. Mut. of Aust.—Ages nearest birthday. £0·50 per mille £2,000–£4,999.

Nat. Prov.—Add £2·00 per policy.

New Ireland—£0·50 per mille £2,000–£2,999. £1·00 per mille £3,000–£3,999. £1·50 per mille £4,000–£4,999.

Noble Lowndes Annty.—Policy charge £0·15 per premium payment.

Norwich Union—£1·50 per mille £2,000–£4,999.

Pearl—Add £3·00 per policy.

Phœnix—Add £3·00 per policy.

Prov. Life Assoc. of London—Under £1,500 add £1·50 per policy. Reductions made for £2,500 or more.

Prov. Mut.—Add £2·00 per policy.

Prudential—Add £1·50 per policy.

Refuge—£0·50 per mille £2,500–£4,999.

Reliance—Rates include policy fee.

Royal—Add £2·40 per policy.

Royal London—add £1·50 per policy.

Scottish Amicable—Add £2·50 per policy.

Scottish Equitable—Add £3 per policy under £5,000.

Scottish Legal—Add £1·50 per policy.

Scottish Life—Add £3·00 per policy.

Scottish Mut.—Add £3·00 per policy. Rebates allowed to non-smokers or total abstainers.

Scottish Widows—Add £2·50 per policy.

Sentinel—Add £3·00 per policy.

Southampton—Add £3·00 per policy.

Standard—Add £2·50 per policy.

Sun Life—Rates include Policy charge of £2·00.

United K. Prov.—Add £1·50 per policy.

University Life—Add £3·00 per policy.

Wes. & Gen.—Add £1·50 per policy.

Marine & Genl.—Rates include Policy charge of £2·00 p.a.

Yorkshire General.—£0·50 per mille £2,000–£4,999.

LIFE INSURANCE NEW BUSINESS, 1970

The following tables show the new business (after allowing for amount reassured) and net annual and single premiums received during the year ended December 31, 1970, unless otherwise stated.

Name of Office	No. of policies issued	Net sums assured	Net annual premiums	Net single premiums
		£	£	£
Abbey Life	64,064	170,951,000	5,074,000	23,032,000
Australian Mutual Provident	258,681	1,115,425,679		
Avon	3,266	9,814,636	337,872	3,181
Bedford	6,680	13,427,582	182,421	3,881
Blackburn (Ord.)	1,769	2,356,835	69,899	1,284
Britannic (Ord.)	22,391	31,588,957	960,705	114,254
British Life	15,141	36,959,452	736,118	2,500
British National	1,348	4,921,643	101,567	1,636
Canada Life†	34,045	297,893,949	3,491,175	413,116
City of Glasgow Friendly	843	965,000	38,586	44,984
Clerical, Medical & General	24,558	91,843,451	1,507,774	32,733
Colonial Mutual	—	358,888,898	8,921,575	—
Commercial Union★	88,799	719,369,329	6,986,103	1,187,052
Confederation	38,500	556,488,000	14,348,000★	
Co-operative (Ord.)	93,139	173,072,000	3,248,000	13,000
Crown Life	36,536	657,162,954	6,755,178	171,064
Crusader	12,896	102,033,503	1,029,839	1,076,595
Eagle Star★	39,201	319,862,267	6,289,783	12,401,484
Ecclesiastical	1,547	3,894,925	66,276	2,478
Economic	1,188	4,905,200	89,137	1,167
Equitable	27,100	28,828,589	1,475,954	2,839,463
Equity & Law	37,508	196,185,481	2,244,106	123,563
Federation Mutual	501	966,135	23,752	1,557
Friends' Provident & Century	30,239	200,805,157	2,931,247	168,124
Gresham Life	12,706	40,486,754	863,757	5,500
Guardian	87,613	674,405,000	8,753,000	8,775,000
Ideal	220	748,556	5,156	49
Imperial Life of Canada	22,063	196,601,168	2,334,631	1,991,051
Irish Life	18,468	56,847,969	1,656,389	4,725,836
Legal and General	110,043	689,118,000	20,155,000★	1,993,000
Life Assoc. of Scotland	7,677	34,056,709	485,180	29,596
Liverpool Victoria	18,216	14,184,855	573,783	Nil
London & Manchester (Ord.)	12,819	24,598,189	1,032,222	113,984
London Indemnity & General†	872	3,101,002	50,148	1,436
London Life	19,852	53,871,170	1,442,652	31,050
Manufacturers	47,638	476,952,876	7,236,213	1,728,283
Marine & General	5,886	26,671,390	988,155	2,654
Medical Sickness	2,008	11,726,790	72,071	7,153
Mutual Life	97,620	285,994,789	—	706,974
Nalgo Association	2,045	4,958,574	60,000	Nil
Nation Life†	5,501	6,036,830	186,929	1,209,356
Natl. Employers	11,426	86,402,641	1,100,560	4,483
Natl. Farmers' Union	7,312	30,233,657	616,987	21,535
Natl. Mutual of Australasia★	—	602,430,000	16,800,000	—
Natl. Mutual	11,707	34,164,822	747,179	8,273
Natl. Provident	11,496	43,819,635	968,754	58,221
New Ireland (Ord.)	11,549	20,671,983	404,069	38,695
Noble Lowndes Annuity	13,717	37,461,906	754,737	510,467
Norwich Union	122,814	423,210,000	8,052,000	260,000
Pearl (Ord.)	70,228	140,870,461	3,602,646	6,648,590
Phoenix	30,998	279,303,757	3,362,747	401,584
Provident Life Assoc. of London	14,197	45,149,600	912,217	2,235,404
Provident Mutual	27,635	101,532,979	1,202,641	78,348
Prudential (Ord.)	268,660	1,434,873,403	24,338,119	11,166,285
Refuge (Ord.)	28,917	37,529,483	1,207,483	598,516
Reliance Mutual	3,445	8,432,114	143,100	45,651
Royal★	74,755	507,548,000	5,287,000	6,568,000
Royal Liver (Ord.)	15,006	12,415,317	503,484	18,819
Royal London (Ord.)	25,367	46,744,545	1,406,476	76,208
Salvation Army (Ord.)	2,653	1,482,975	66,286	496
Scottish Amicable	18,367	132,619,000	1,966,000	9,000
Scottish Equitable	14,113	63,024,233	1,599,023	5,654,934
Scottish Legal (Ord.)†	3,104	2,311,913	96,996	6,099
Scottish Life	12,421	69,743,663	1,281,447	23,137
Scottish Mutual	15,206	50,381,056	1,457,438	35,979
Scottish Prov.	28,600	102,397,996	1,959,393	202,723
Scottish Widows	—	250,411,895	3,231,548	87,628
Sentinel★	5,976	19,503,617	333,337	3,835

Name of Office	No. of policies issued	Net sums assured	Net annual premiums	Net single premiums
		£	£	£
Southampton, The.........................	4,538	5,589,243	292,572	Nil
Stamford Mutual..........................	797	1,171,767	27,148	3,886
Standard★................................	62,074	540,130,227	7,427,423	124,950
Sun Alliance & London....................	38,958	204,233,184	2,661,894	904,620
Sun Life of Canada.......................	97,338	696,000,000	10,000,000	558,000
Sun Life.................................	29,740	264,444,231	3,441,006	278,484
Tunstall & District......................	151	69,400	4,378	Nil
United Friendly..........................	17,496	43,165,040	629,389	2,554
United Kingdom..........................	15,313	54,979,012	1,272,830	45,328
University Life...........................	5,560	7,636,018	269,019	257,779
Welfare.................................	36,303	96,374,826	1,255,520	45,531
Wesleyan & Gen. (Ord.)..................	7,224	13,715,727	392,663	9,805
Yorkshire General........................	44,218	257,788,612	2,881,114	166,243

Industrial Companies

Office	Policies Issued	Net sums Assured	Office	Policies Issued	Net sums Assured
		£			£
Blackburn.......................	25,824	2,821,528	Prudential......................	1,128,727	263,857,857
City of Glasgow Friendly..........	22,200	3,135,000	Refuge.........................	284,591	48,832.539
Co-operative....................	628,626	123,231,000	Reliance Mutual................	20,246	3,165 735
Irish Life.......................	71,298	8,672,726	Royal Liver....................	281,015	30,102,196
Liverpool Victoria................	526,961	68,315,617	Royal London..................	219,725	39,465,394
London and Manchester...........	90,840	18,382,106	Salvation Army................	35,000	3,239,372
New Ireland....................	40,612	5,210,245	Stamford Mutual..............	24,932	3,120,578
Pearl..........................	541,366	98,294,346	Wesleyan and General.........	53.756	8,145,262

★ Commercial Union, including figures of associated companies. Confederation—Combined Annual and Single premiums Eagle Star Group figures. Legal & General—including Annuity Annual premiums. Natl. Mutual of Australasia, year ending September 30, 1970. Royal Group figures. Sentinel, year ending March 31, 1970. Standard, year ending November 15, 1970. † 1969 figures.

DIRECTORY OF INSURANCE COMPANIES

The class of Insurance undertaken is shown in the second column as follows: A—Accident (which includes Motor, Employers' Liability, etc.); F—Fire (including Burglary); L—Life; and M—Marine. A number of offices are now included in a Group—the initials of which appear after the name. The main Groups are as follows—E.S.—Eagle Star; C.U.—Commercial Union; G.R.E.—Guardian Royal Exchange; G.A.—General Accident; N.U.—Norwich Union; R—Royal; S.A.—Sun Alliance & London.

Est'd	Nature of Business	Name of Company	Address of Head and London Offices
1961	L	Abbey Life....................	1–3 St. Paul's Churchyard, E.C.4.
1960	AFLM	Ansvar.......................	24–28 London Rd., Wembley, Middx.
1904	Annuities	African Life..................	*Johannesburg:* 1, Kingsway, W.C.2.
1951	AFM	Albion.......................	Albion House, 34–35 Leadenhall St., E.C.3.
1824	AFM	Alliance.................S.A.	1 Bartholomew Lane, E.C..
1921	L	American Life................	*Delaware, U.S.A.:* Paramount Ho., 75 Uxbridge Rd., W.5.
1904	AFM	Army, Navy & General....E.S.	1 Threadneedle St., E.C.2.
1808	ALFM	Atlas................G.R.E.	Royal Exchange, E.C.3.
1849	L	Australian Mutual Provident....	*Sydney:* A.M.P. Ho., Dingwall Rd., Croydon.
1925	AFL	Avon.........................	1 Church St., *Stratford-upon-Avon*; 88–89 Gracechurch St., E.C.3.
1905	AFM	Baptist.......................	4 Southampton Row, W.C.1.
1883	AFM	Beacon.................S.A.	1 Bartholomew Lane, E.C.2. [W.C.1.]
1894	AFM	Bedford General..............	Fairfax Ho., Fulwood Pl., High Holborn,
1961	L	Bedford Life.................	Fairfax Ho., Fulwood Pl., High Holborn, [W.C.1.]
1839	L	Blackburn Assurance...........	151 Dale St., *Liverpool.*
1925	AFM	Black Sea and Baltic..........	106 Fenchurch St., E.C.3.
1959	AFLM	Bradford.....................	Peckover St., *Bradford,* 1.
1866	AFL	Britannic....................	Moor Green, *Birmingham* 13.
1863	M	British & Foreign Marine......	Liverpool & London Chambers, Exchange, *Liverpool* 2: Lime St., E.C.3.
1878	Machinery	British Engine, &c............	Longbridge House, *Manchester* 4; 17 Mincing Lane, E.C.3.
1854	AFL	British Equitable .......G.R.E.	Royal Exchange, E.C.3.

Est'd.	Nature of Business	Name of Company	Address of Head and London Offices
1904	AFM	British General......... C.U.	St. Helen's, 1 Undershaft, E.C.3.
1888	AFM	British Law ............S.A.	1 Bartholomew Lane, E.C.2.
1896	L	British Life.................	Reliance House, *Tunbridge Wells*, Kent; 123–127 Cannon St., E.C.4.
1920	AFL	British Nat. Life............	4 South Place, Moorgate, E.C.2.
1920	AF	British Merchants	92–94 Gracechurch St., E.C.3.
1908	AFM	British Oak......... G.R.E.	81–82 Cornhill, E.C.3.
1881	A	Builders' Accident...........	31 & 32 Bedford St., Strand, W.C.2.
1805	AFLM	Caledonian .... G.R.E.	13 St. Andrew Sq., *Edinburgh*; Royal Exchange
1934	AFM	Cambrian .... G.R.E.	68 King William St., E.C.4. [E.C.3.
1847	AL	Canada Life.................	*Toronto:* 6 Charles II St., S.W.1.
1932	Dog Ins.	Canine Ins. Assoc............	24–26 Spring St., W.2.
1903	AFM	Car & General .... G.R.E.	Royal Exchange, E.C.3.
1899	AFM	Central.....................	1 Cornhill, E.C.3.
1885	AFM	Century....................	7 Leadenhall St., E.C.3.
1922	AFMex-motor	Chemists' Mutual............	321 Chase Rd., Southgate, N.14.
1862	L	City of Glasgow Friendly	200 Bath Street, *Glasgow* C.2.
1824	L	Clerical, Medical & Gen......	15 St. James's Square, S.W.1.
1873	L & Pers. Acc.	Colonial Mutual.............	330 Collins St., *Melbourne*, C.1; 24 Ludgate Hill,
1919	AFM	Comrcl. Ins. Co. of Ireland....	10 Donegall Square, S., *Belfast*, N.Ireland [E.C.4.
1861	AFLM	Commercial Union	St. Helen's, 1 Undershaft, E.C.3.
1871	L	Confederation................	*Toronto:* 120 Regent St., W.1.
1891	AF	Congregational..............	21–22 Apsley Crescent, *Bradford* 8.
1867	AFLM	Co-operative................	Miller St., *Manchester*; Rochdale Ho.,Theobald's
1905	AFM	Cornhill....................	32 Cornhill, E.C.3. [Road, W.C.1.
1807	AFM	County Fire ...........S.A.	50 Regent St., W.1.
1900	L	Crown Life..................	*Toronto:* 130 Jermyn St., S.W.1. [E.C.3.
1899	AFLM	Crusader....................	Woodhatch, *Reigate*, Surrey; Tower Place,
1908	AFM	Dominion...................	41 Melville St., *Edinburgh*; 18 Finsbury Circus, E.C.2.
1904	AFLM	Eagle Star..................	1 Threadneedle St., E.C.2.
1887	AFL	Ecclesiastical	Aldwych House, W.C.2.
1901	AFLM	Economic...................	Lloyd's Building, 19 Leadenhall St., E.C.3.
1823	AFM	Edinburgh............C.U.	St. Helen's, 1 Undershaft, E.C.3.
1880	AFM	Employers' Liability.....C.U.	St. Helens, 1 Undershaft, E.C.3.
1762	L	Equitable Life...............	4 Coleman St., E.C.2.
1844	L	Equity & Law...............	20 Lincoln's Inn Fields, W.C.2.
1802	AF	Essex & Suffolk .......G.R.E.	Royal Exchange, E.C.3.
1894	AFM	Excess.....................	13 Fenchurch Avenue, E.C.3.
1904	AF	Federated Employers'.........	77 Whitworth St., *Manchester* 1; 34–35 Leadenhall St., E.C.3.
1925	AFL	Federation Mutual...........	29 Linkfield Lane, *Redhill*, Surrey; Terminus Ho., Holborn Viaduct, E.C.1.
1890	AF	Fine Art & General .....C.U.	St. Helen's, 1 Undershaft, E.C.3.
1832	L	Friends' Prov. & Century....	*Dorking*, Surrey; 7 Leadenhall St., E.C.3.
1885	AFM	General Accident............	General Buildings, *Perth*, Scotland; Becket House, 36–37, Old Jewry, E.C.2.
1848	L	Gresham Life...............	Barrington Ho., 59 Gresham St., E.C.2.
1910	AFM	Gresham Fire & Accident.....	11 Queen Victoria St., E.C.4.
1840	AFM	Guarantee Society ... . .G.A.	38 Eastcheap, E.C.3.
1821	AFLM	Guardian .............G.R.E.	Royal Exchange, E.C.3.
1908	AFM	Hibernian..................	Hawkins St., *Dublin*, 2.
1966	AF	Household & General	107 Cheapside, E.C.2.
1932	FL	Ideal......................	Pitmaston, *Birmingham*, 13.
1897	L	Imperial Life of Canada.......	*Toronto:* London Road, Guildford, Surrey.
1824	M	Indemnity Marine...........	4 Fenchurch Avenue, E.C.3.
1935	AFM	Insurance Corpn. of Ireland...	33–36 Dame St., *Dublin* 2; 40 Lime St., E.C.3.
1939	L	Irish Life..................	Mespil Road, *Dublin* 4.
1880	A	Iron Trades Employers'.......	Iron Trades Ho., 21–24 Grosvenor Pl., S.W.1.
1845	AF	Law Fire...............S.A.	114 Chancery Lane, W.C.2.
1806	AFM	Law Union & Rock......R.	7 Chancery Lane, W.C.2.
1907	AFM	Legal .... R.	24–28 Lombard St., E.C.3.
1836	AFLM	Legal and General...........	Temple Court, 11 Queen Victoria St., E.C.4.
1890	AFLM	Licenses & General....G.R.E.	Royal Exchange, E.C.3.
1838	L	Life Assoc. of Scotland.......	10 George St., *Edinburgh*; 1 Finsbury Sq., E.C.2.
1836	AFM	L'pool & London & Globe..R.	1 Dale St., *Liverpool*; 24 Lombard St., E.C.3.
1918	AFM	Liverpool Marine & General .	7 Leadenhall St., E.C.3.
1843	L	Liverpool Victoria Friendly...	Victoria House, Southampton Row, W.C.1.
1890	AFM	Local Government Guarantee G.R.E.	Royal Exchange, E.C.3.
1836	AFM	Lombard Insurance...........	3 & 4 Lime St., E.C.3.
1720	AFLM	London Assurance........S.A.	1 Bartholomew Lane, E.C.2.
1869	AFM	London Guar. & Accident....	4 King William St., E.C.4.

Est'd.	Nature of Business	Name of Company	Address of Head and London Offices
1964	L	London Indemnity & General	Stevinson Ho., 155 Fenchurch St., E.C.3.
1861	AFM	London & Lancashire......R.	45 Dale St., *Liverpool*; 24 Lombard St., E.C.3.
1806	L	London Life................	81 King William St., E.C.4.
1919	AFLM	London & Edinburgh........	1 Seething Lane, E.C.3.
1869	AFL	London & Manchester.......	50 Finsbury Square, E.C.2.
1860	AFM	London & Provincial Marine G.A.	4 Fenchurch Avenue, E.C.3.
1862	AFM	London & Scottish..... C.U.	1 Moorgate, E.C.2.
1887	L	Manufacturers Life..........	*Toronto:* 197 Knightsbridge, S.W.7.
1836	M	Marine................R.	159 Leadenhall St., E.C.3.
1852	L	Marine & General..........	1 St. Swithin's Lane, E.C.4.
1864	M	Maritime............N.U.	Water St., *Liverpool*, 2. 51 Fenchurch St., E.C.3.
1884	L Sickness A	Med., Sickness, Ann. and Life.	7–10 Chandos St., Cavendish Sq., W.1.
1907	Reinsurance	Mercantile & General.......	Moorfields House, Moorfields, E.C.2.
1871	M	Merchants' Marine ......C.U.	4 Fenchurch Ave., E.C.3.
1872	AF	Methodist..................	51 Spring Gardens, *Manchester*.
1934	L	Migdal-Binyan	*Tel-Aviv*, Israel; Migdal Ho.,Finsbury Sq.,E.C.2
1940	AFM	Minster...................	Minster House, Arthur St., E.C.4.
1906	AFM	Motor Union ........G.R.E.	Royal Exchange, E.C.3.
1903	AF	Municipal Mutual..........	22 Old Queen St., Westminster. S.W.1.
1886	L	Mutual Life & Citizens'.....	P.O. Box 200 *North Sydney*, N.S.W., 2060 Australia; 1 Lancaster Place, Strand, W.C.2.
1890	AFL	Nalgo Insurance Association..	8 Harewood Row, N.W.1.
1925	L	Nation Life	40 Hampton Rd., Teddington, Mdx.
1864	Boilers, etc.	National Boiler.........S.A.	{St. Mary's Parsonage, *Manchester* 3; Empire House, St. Martin's-le-Grand, E.C.1.}
1935	L	National Employers' Life.....	Milton Court, *Dorking*, Surrey.
1914	AFM	National Employers' Mutual..	National Employers House, Bury Street, E.C.3.
1910	AFL	National Farmers' Union.....	Church St., *Stratford-upon-Avon*; 25 Knightsbridge, S.W.1.
1863	Fidelity Guar.	Natl. Guaran. & Suretyship C.U.	17 Charlotte St., *Edinburgh*: St. Helens, 1 Undershaft, E.C.3.
1894	AF	National Ins. & Guarantee Cor.	11–13 Holborn Viaduct, E.C.1.
1830	L	National Mutual Life.......	5 Bow Churchyard (off Cheapside), E.C.4.
1869	L	National Mutual of Australasia	*Melbourne:* Austral Ho., Basinghall Ave., E.C.2.
1835	L	National Provident........	48 Gracechurch St., E.C.3.
1854	Plate Glass	National Provincial....G.R.E.	Royal Exchange, E.C.3.
1921	{Naval Officers risks, etc. }	Navigators & General,...E.S.	1 Threadneedle St., E.C.2.
1924	L	New Ireland	11/12 Dawson St., *Dublin*, C.2.
1960	L	Noble Lowndes Annuities....	N.L.A. Tower, 12–16 Addiscombe Rd., Croy-[don.
1809	AFLM	North British & Mercantile C.U.	St. Helen's, 1 Undershaft, E.C.3.
1862	FM	North Pacific.........G.R.E.	*Hong Kong:* 78–80 Cornhill, E.C.3.
1836	AFLM	Northern............C.U.	St. Helen's, 1 Undershaft, E.C.3.
1797	AFM	Norwich Union Fire........	Surrey St., *Norwich*; 51–54 Fenchurch St., E.C.3.
1808	L	Norwich Union Life........	P.O. Box 4, *Norwich*; 51 Fenchurch St., E.C.3.
1871	AFM	Ocean Accident........C.U.	St. Helen's, 1 Undershaft, E.C.3.
1859	M	Ocean Marine...........C.U.	37–39 Lime St., E.C.3.
1931	AFM	Orion	70–72 King William St., E.C.4.
1886	AF	Palatine..................C.U.	St. Helen's, 1 Undershaft, E.C.3.
1824	AF	Patriotic .... S.A.	40–43 Nassau St., *Dublin* 2.
1864	AFLM	Pearl......................	High Holborn, W.C.1.
1958	Sickness A	Permanent	7–10 Chandos Street, Cavendish Sq., W.1.
1782	AFLM	Phœnix.....................	Phœnix House, King William St., E.C.4.
1920	AFM	Planet Assurance..........	63 Threadneedle St., E.C. 2.
1877	L	Prov. Life Assocn. of London.	246 Bishopsgate, E.C.2.
1840	L	Provident Mutual Life.......	25–31 Moorgate, E.C.2.
1903	AFM	Provincial.................	*Kendal:* Provincial Ho., 100 Cannon St., E.C.4.
1848	AFLM	Prudential.................	Holborn Bars, E.C.1.
1886	AFM	Queensland................	*Sydney:* Trent House, St. Mary Axe, E.C.3.
1849	AF	Railway Passengers......C.U.	St. Helen's, 1 Undershaft, E.C.3.
1864	AFL	Refuge....................	Oxford St., *Manchester* 1. [Cannon St., E.C.4.
1911	L	Reliance Mutual.............	Reliance Ho., *Tunbridge Wells*, Kent; 123–7
1906	AF	Reliance Fire & Accident....	Reliance Ho., *Tunbridge Wells*, Kent; 123–7 Cannon St., E.C.4.
1881	AFM	Reliance Marine.... G.R.E.	Reliance Ho., Water St., *Liverpool*; 51 Lime
1823	Reversions	Reversionary Interest Society	4 Coleman St., E.C.4. [St., E.C.3.
1918	AF	Road Transport & General G.A.	77 Upper Richmond Rd., S.W.15. [E.C.3.
1845	AFLM	Royal.....................	1, North John St., Liverpool, 2; 24, Lombard St.,
1720	AFL	Royal Exchange.............	Royal Exchange, E.C.3.
1850	L	Royal Liver Friendly	Royal Liver Building, *Liverpool* 3.

Est'd.	Nature of Business	Name of Company	Address of Head and London Offices
1861	AFL	Royal London..............	Royal London House, Finsbury Square, E.C.2.
1887	L	Royal Nat. Pensions (Nurses).	15 Buckingham St., W.C.2.
1867	L	Salvation Army.............	220–226 Tottenham Court Road, W.1.
1909	AFM	Salvation Army Fire.........	4 Holywell Hill, St. Albans, Herts.
1826	L	Scottish Amicable............	35 St. Vincent Place, *Glasgow*, C.1.; 17 Token-house Yard, E.C.2. [E.C.2.
1881	FM	Scottish Boiler..........G.A.	22 Queen St., *Glasgow*, C.1.; 36 Old Jewry,
1831	L	Scottish Equitable...........	28 St. Andrew Sq., *Edinb.*: 13 Cornhill, E.C.3.
1919	AFM	Scottish General........G.A.	100 West Nile St., *Glasgow*, C.2.; The Broadway, W.5.
1852	L	Scottish Legal...............	95 Bothwell St., *Glasgow*, C.2. [E.C.2.
1881	L	Scottish Life................	19 St. Andrew Sq., *Edinburgh*, 2; 36 Poultry,
1876	AF	Scottish Metropolitan...C.U.	St. Helen's, 1 Undershaft, E.C.3. [W.C.2.
1883	AL	Scottish Mutual.............	109 St. Vincent St., *Glasgow*, C.2.; 6 Bell Yard,
1837	L	Scottish Provident...........	6 St. Andrew Sq., *Edinburgh*; 3 Lombard St., E.C.3.
1824	AFLM	Scottish Union & National N.U.	Surrey St., *Norwich*; 51–54 Fenchurch St. E.C.3. [E.C.3
1815	L	Scottish Widows'...........	9 St. Andrew Sq., *Edinburgh*, 2; 28 Cornhill,
1875	AFM	Sea....................S.A.	1 Bartholomew Lane, E.C.2.
1904	AFL	Sentinel	11–13 Holborn Viaduct, E.C.1.
1872	AFM	South British................	Shortland St., *Auckland*, N.Z.; 4 Fenchurch Avenue, E.C.3.
1964	L	Southampton, The	Number One, Kingsway, W.C.2.
1899	L	Stamford Mutual............	23 Stamford St., S.E.1.
1825	L	Standard Life................	3 George St., *Edinburgh*; 3 Abchurch Yard, Cannon St., E.C.4.
1871	M	Standard Marine ....R.	Exchange, Liverpool,2; 159 Leadenhall St. E.C.3.
1891	AFM	State...................G.R.E.	Royal Exchange, E.C.3.
1710	AFM	Sun....................S.A.	1 Bartholomew Lane E.C.2.
*	AFLM	Sun Alliance & London......	1 Bartholomew Lane, E.C.2; Life Dept., North St., Horsham, Sussex.
1810	AFL	Sun Life....................	107 Cheapside, E.C.2.
1865	L	Sun Life of Canada..........	*Montreal*: 2, 3 & 4 Cockspur St., S.W.1.
1936	FL	Teachers' Assurance.........	Hamilton Ho., Mabledon Pl., W.C.1.
1860	M	Thames & Mersey ....R.	Liverpool & London Chambers, Exchange, *Liverpool*, 2; 3–6 Lime St., E.C.3.
1894	FM	Thistle....................	3 Lombard St., E.C.3.
1916	AF	Timber & General...........	Moor Ho., London Wall, E.C.2.
1850	FM	Triton....................	*Calcutta:* 3–4 Lime St., E.C.3.
1839	L	{Tunstall & District Assurance {Collecting Society.........)	Station Chambers, Tunstall, *Stoke on Trent.*
1867	M	Ulster Marine ..........G.A.	1 Linen Hall St., *Belfast*, N. Ireland
1714	AFM	Union Assurance............	St Helen's, 1 Undershaft, E.C.3
1835	AFM	Union Ins. Soc. of Canton G.R.E.	*Hong Kong:* 78 Cornhill. E.C.3.
1863	M	Union Marine	4–5, King William St. E.C.4.
1915	AFM	United British ........G.R.E.	Royal Exchange, E.C.3.
1908	AFL	United Friendly.............	42 Southwark Bridge Road, S.E.1.
1840	L	United Kingdom Prov.......	33–36 Gracechurch St., E.C.3.
1912	AFM	United Scottish.............	118/119 Fenchurch St., E.C.3.
1825	L	University..................	4 Coleman St., E.C.2.
1919	Reinsurance	Victory Insurance...........	122 Leadenhall St., E.C.3.
1859	Machinery	Vulcan Boiler and General.S.A.	14 St. Mary's Parsonage, Manchester 3; Empire Ho., St. Martin's-le-Grand, E.C.1.
1875	AFM	Warden ....R..	24–28 Lombard St., E.C.3.
1952	AFLM	Welfare	The Leas, Folkestone, Kent.
1911	AF	Welsh Insurance Corpn..C.U.	1 Moorgate, E.C.2.
1841	AFL	Wesleyan & General.........	Colmore Circus, Ringway, *Birmingham*, 4; 116 Cannon St., E.C.4.
1886	AF	West of Scotland....... C.U.	26 George St., *Edinburgh*, 2; St. Helen's, 1 Undershaft, E.C.3.
1851	AFM	Western Assurance....... R.	*Toronto:* 24 Lombard St., E.C.3.
1912	AFLM	Western Australian..........	I.O.O.F. Building, 224 St. George's Terrace, *Perth*, W. Australia; 107–111 Fleet St., E.C.4
1717	AF	Westminster Fire........S.A.	50 Regent St., W.1.
1865	AF	White Cross....... C.U.	St. Helen's, 1, Undershaft, E.C.3.
1894	AFM	World Marine & General.C.U.	4 & 7 Fenchurch Avenue, E.C.3.
1837	L	Yorkshire General Life...G.A.	Rougier St., *York*; 9 Bishopsgate, E.C.2.
1872	AF	Zurich	*Zurich:* Fairfax Ho., Fulwood Place, W.C.1.

★ Sun Alliance & London—Incorporating Funds established 1720, 1824 and 1883.

EXPECTATION OF LIFE

(English Life Table No. 12, 1960–62)

Expectation of life at under 1 year of age is: Males, 68·09 years; Females, 74·00 years.

Age	Male	Female	Age	Male	Female	Age	Male	Female	Age	Male	Female
1	68·80	74·43	26	44·89	50·11	51	21·84	26·69	76	6·66	8·27
2	67·90	73·52	27	43·93	49·14	52	21·02	25·81	77	6·28	7·77
3	66·97	72·58	28	42·98	48·17	53	20·21	24·95	78	5·92	7·28
4	66·02	71·62	29	42·02	47·20	54	19·42	24·09	79	5·57	6·83
5	65·06	70·66	30	41·06	46·23	55	18·65	23·24	80	5·25	6·39
6	64·09	69·69	31	40·11	45·26	56	17·89	22·39	81	4·94	5·98
7	63·13	68·71	32	39·16	44·30	57	17·16	21·56	82	4·66	5·60
8	62·16	67·73	33	38·21	43·34	58	16·44	20·73	83	4·39	5·24
9	61·18	66·75	34	37·26	42·38	59	15·74	19·91	84	4·14	4·90
10	60·21	65·77	35	36·31	41·42	60	15·06	19·11	85	3·90	4·58
11	59·23	64·79	36	35·37	40·47	61	14·40	18·31	86	3·68	4·29
12	58·25	63·80	37	34·43	39·52	62	13·76	17·53	87	3·48	4·01
13	57·28	62·82	38	33·49	38·57	63	13·14	16·76	88	3·30	3·76
14	56·30	61·83	39	32·55	37·63	64	12·54	16·00	89	3·13	3·53
15	55·33	60·85	40	31·62	36·69	65	11·95	15·26	90	2·97	3·32
16	54·36	59·87	41	30·70	35·75	66	11·39	14·53	91	2·83	3·12
17	53·40	58·89	42	29·77	34·82	67	10·84	13·81	92	2·70	2·94
18	52·45	57·91	43	28·86	33·90	68	10·31	13·12	93	2·58	2·78
19	51·51	56·93	44	27·95	32·98	69	9·79	12·44	94	2·47	2·63
20	50·57	55·95	45	27·05	32·06	70	9·29	11·78	95	2·38	2·49
21	49·63	54·98	46	26·15	31·15	71	8·81	11·14	96	2·29	2·37
22	48·69	54·00	47	25·27	30·25	72	8·35	10·52	97	2·21	2·26
23	47·74	53·03	48	24·40	29·35	73	7·90	9·93	98	2·14	2·16
24	46·80	52·06	49	23·53	28·46	74	7·47	9·35	99	2·07	2·07
25	45·84	51·08	50	22·68	27·57	75	7·05	8·80	100	2·00	1·99

Comparative Table

	Males				Females			
Age	England and Wales	England	Wales	Greater London	England and Wales	England	Wales	Greater London
0	68·1	68·2	66·8	68·7	74·0	74·1	73·2	75·0
10	60·2	60·3	59·2	60·6	65·8	65·9	65·1	66·6
20	50·6	50·7	49·6	51·0	56·0	56·0	55·3	56·7
30	41·1	41·2	40·2	41·4	46·2	46·3	45·6	47·0
40	31·6	31·7	30·8	32·0	36·7	36·8	36·1	37·5
50	22·7	22·7	21·9	23·0	27·6	27·6	27·1	28·3
60	15·1	15·1	14·5	15·2	19·1	19·2	18·7	19·8
70	9·3	9·3	8·9	9·4	11·8	11·8	11·4	12·3
80	5·2	5·3	5·1	5·4	6·4	6·4	6·2	6·8

EXPECTATION OF LIFE IN YEARS: VARIOUS COUNTRIES

	ENGLAND AND WALES 1965–67		SCOTLAND 1968		NORTHERN IRELAND 1966–68		UNITED STATES 1967		AUSTRIA 1968	
Age	Male	Female	Male	Female	Male	Female	Male	Female	Male	Female
0	68·7	74·9	66·9	73·0	68·1	73·4	67·0	74·2	66·7	73·5
1	69·1	75·1	67·5	73·3	69·0	74·1	67·7	74·6	67·6	74·1
5	65·4	71·3	63·8	69·5	65·2	70·3	63·9	70·9	63·9	70·4
10	60·5	66·4	58·9	64·7	60·4	65·4	59·1	66·0	59·1	65·5
15	55·6	61·5	54·1	59·7	55·5	60·5	54·2	61·1	54·2	60·7
20	50·9	56·6	49·3	54·8	50·7	55·6	49·6	56·3	49·6	55·8
30	41·4	46·9	39·8	45·0	41·2	45·8	40·5	46·7	40·3	46·1
40	31·9	37·3	30·5	35·6	31·8	36·3	31·4	37·3	31·2	36·6
50	23·0	28·2	21·8	26·6	22·9	27·2	23·1	28·4	22·6	27·4
60	15·3	19·8	14·5	18·5	15·3	18·8	16·0	20·2	14·9	18·9
70	9·5	12·4	9·0	11·4	9·5	11·6	10·4	13·0	9·2	11·5
75	7·3	9·4	6·9	8·5	7·3	8·8	8·3	10·0	6·9	8·5
80	5·5	6·9	5·3	6·2	5·3	6·5	6·4	7·3	5·2	6·1
85	4·0	5·0	3·8	4·2	3·9	4·6	4·7	5·0	3·9	4·4

Friendly Societies—Great Britain

Acts 1896-1971

Friendly societies are mutual insurance societies in which the members subscribe for provident benefits, in particular sickness, death, endowment and old age benefits. Those friendly societies that are known as "collecting societies" because they collect members' premiums for life assurance by house-to-house visits of collectors or agents are subject to the provisions of the Industrial Assurance Acts as well as the Friendly Societies Acts. The totals in ordinary type in the table below relate to registered friendly societies proper (including both centralized societies and the Orders with their branches); those in italics relate to collecting societies.

End of Year	No. of Societies on Register		Member-ship	Assurances or Policies	Total Funds	
			Thousands		£000	
1969............	7,342	*75*	4,978	27,446	333,743	*469,976*
1938............	19,600	*149*	8,491	*25,733*	151,613	*84,837*
1913	25,475	*71*	6,783	*7,481*	51,489	*11,165*

The first column headed "No. of Societies on Register" in the above table includes (for 1969) 727 societies without branches and 31 societies with branches ("Orders"), the remainder being the separately registered branches of the Orders.

Although recent years have seen the growth of societies registered for such specific purposes as the provision of Institutional treatment or assuring annuities and pensions, most friendly societies continue to provide the customary benefits in sickness and at death. During 1969 Friendly Societies proper paid out £5.8 millions in sickness benefit and £2.5 millions in death benefit.

As compared with the previous year the number of societies without branches decreased by 35 and the number of branches by 405. Total membership fell to just below 5 millions.

Many societies still operate mainly on the old system of accumulating funds on a mutual basis. Others, usually termed deposit societies, allocate all or the greater part of their funds annually to the individual credit of the members to be withdrawn by them as the rules provide. Apart from the National Deposit Society's method of a uniform contribution throughout membership there are several systems operated on individual account lines, one of which (known as the "Holloway" principle) is worked by a contribution increasing with each year of attained age after the member reaches age 30 up to age 65.

The latest available figures of membership and funds set out below indicate the relative strength of several leading old established societies, including the three largest Orders which operate through registered districts and branches subject to a central body :—

FRIENDLY Socs.—Name with (in brackets) Year Established	Membership	Total Funds
		£000
National Deposit Friendly Society (1868).................................	413,000	25,564
Hearts of Oak Benefit Society (1842).....................................	317,000	19,473
Independent Order of Odd Fellows, Manchester Unity (1810)..............	314,000	30,891
Ancient Order of Foresters (1834).......................................	259,000	22,461
Independent Order of Rechabites, Salford Unity (1835)..................	126,000	7,413

COLLECTING Socs.—Name and Year Established	No. of Industrial Assurances		Total Funds
	Premium Paying	Free Paid-up	
			£000
Liverpool Victoria Friendly Society (1843)..................	9,958,000	4,087,000	233,969
Royal Liver Friendly Society (1850)........................	6,225,000	2,266,000	103,944
Scottish Legal Life Assurance Society (1852)................	1,926,000	1,013,000	29,510

Long before the term "Friendly Society" came into use, the seeds of voluntary mutual insurance had been sown in the ancient religious and trade "Guilds." As is evident from the many extant parchment returns detailing their rules and possessions under a decree of Richard II, Guilds had become widespread in Britain by the 14th century. By then, the purely charitable character of the original Guilds had largely changed with the emergence of numerous small institutions adopting primitive mutual insurance methods of a regular flat rate contribution to insure relief when sick or in old age and a payment to the widow in the event of death.

The present register of Friendly Societies includes several societies which have been in existence for upwards of 200 years, the oldest, operating in Scotland, being the "Incorporation of Carters in Leith" established as long ago as 1555. The oldest

society now on the register in England is the Bottesford Friendly Society established in Leicestershire in 1747.

The first Act for the encouragement and protection of "Friendly Societies" in this country was not passed until 1793, but various amending Acts were put on the Statute Book during the next century as the result of the recommendations of successive Select Committees (including a Royal Commission in 1871). For example, it was not until the 1829 Act that all registered Friendly Societies were required to keep proper records of individual sickness and mortality amongst their members, which data enabled the construction of standard actuarial tables showing the expected (average) duration of sickness at successive ages, and also (with data from the Census) the corresponding mortality rates.

The rules and other documents of societies

deposited with local justices passed into the custody of the Registrar following the Act of 1846 and are of considerable interest to social historians. Those relating to some societies no longer on the register have been transferred to the Public Record Office for permanent preservation.

The present consolidating Act of 1896 allows various specific classes other than "Friendly Societies" to be registered thereunder, but tax exemption (irrespective of the extent of interest income) is enjoyed only by registered "Friendly Societies."

Important changes in the conditions under which friendly societies enjoy tax exemption were made by the Finance Act, 1966. In general, societies registered after May 3, 1966 are not entitled to any tax exemption on their life or endowment business. The same restriction applies to any society registered after December 31, 1957, which during the period of three months ending May 3, 1966 entered into a life or endowment contract on payment of a single premium. Other societies continue to enjoy tax exemption on life and endowment business which satisfies the requirements of Schedule 8 of the Act. These conditions are broadly that the term of an endowment assurance must not be less than ten years and the premiums must be of equal or rateable amounts payable at yearly or shorter intervals over the whole term of the policy. At the same time by Part II of the Schedule the limits of assurance imposed on friendly societies were raised. The limits for tax exempt business remained unchanged at £500 gross and £104 per annum by way of annuity, but in addition a society is now permitted to insure up to £3,500 as lump sum (£5,000 under a mortgage protection policy) and £350 per annum by way of annuity. All these limits are exclusive of bonuses. Profits arising from the business under the new limits are liable to tax.

The Friendly Societies Act, 1971 received the Royal Assent on July 27, 1971. Its main purpose is to simplify the procedures for amalgamation, transfer of engagements and dissolution of societies registered under the principal Act. It also makes a large number of minor amendments to the earlier Acts in order to facilitate the consolidation of all statutes relating to friendly societies.

In future a society wishing to amalgamate with or transfer its engagements to another society will not be obliged to attempt to obtain the written consents of a substantial portion of its members. It will be sufficient for the society to pass a special resolution at a general meeting or meeting of delegates provided that it has sent a notice of the proposed terms in a form approved by the Chief Registrar to all its members or, with his approval, has advertised them in the press. Any member is given the right to complain to the Chief Registrar of an alleged breach in procedure and any person (whether a member or not) can complain on the ground that he is one of a class of persons who to a substantial extent is adversely affected by the proposed amalgamation or transfer.

In regard to dissolution friendly societies are placed in the same position as societies in other classes of registration under the Act in that the consent in writing to an instrument of dissolution of three-quarters of the members is sufficient to dissolve the society.

The Act empowers the Chief Registrar if he considers it expedient to do so in the interests of members or the public to forbid a society to admit new members or to enter into any new contracts with existing members.

Another section of the Act makes it easier for societies to carry on group insurance business by removing the obligation to include the tables of contributions and benefits for such business in the rules provided the form of policy has been approved by the Chief Registrar. This will enable a society to offer " tailor made " schemes (especially for sickness benefit) to an individual employer for his employees. The limits on life assurance business (including the tax exempt limits) referred to above apply separately to group insurance and other business. Thus a society can offer life cover to an employee in a group scheme irrespective of other friendly society assurances he may have.

Building Societies—Great Britain
Act 1962.

Building Societies are associations incorporated with limited liability under the Building Societies Act. All Building Societies are required to register their rules and file their accounts with the Registry of Friendly Societies. The following particulars showing the growth of Building Societies (as also that of Friendly and Co-operative Societies tabulated on pp. 1143 and 1078) are based on the Chief Registrar's Annual Reports. The Editor is also indebted to the publishers of the " Building Societies Year Book " for details of individual societies from which the second table hereunder has been compiled.

During 1970 the total assets of all building societies passed the £10,000 million mark and by the end of the year had reached £10,819 millions. The increase of £1,530 millions over 1969 was the highest annual increase ever attained and represented a growth rate of 16·5 per cent.

The amount advanced on mortgage was £1,954 millions 25 per cent more than in 1969. The number of advances increased by only 14·5 per cent. The size of the average advance continues to increase. However 87 per cent of the advances were for amounts of less than £5,000 and the bulk of the money advanced by building societies is to owner-occupiers to assist them to buy their homes.

The number of societies on the register dropped from 504 at the beginning of 1970 to 481 at the end of the year. Twenty-seven societies were removed from the register during the year, twenty-four of them as a result of mergers. Of four societies added to the register during the year only two were new organizations.

Shareholders added £3,027 million to their accounts during 1970. Withdrawals (at £1,867 millions) represented 62 per cent of the new subscriptions compared with 71 per cent. in 1969.

Mortgage balances amounted to £8,752 millions at the end of 1970 as compared with £7,705 millions at the end of 1969. The remainder of the total assets consisted mainly of investments and cash. The investments in which societies may invest their surplus funds are restricted to those authorized by the Building Societies (Authorised Investments) Orders.

For the year 1970 interest received by societies from borrowers amounted to £706 millions. Interest paid or credited to shareholders and depositors totalled £465 millions. Expenses at £68 millions for 1970 averaged only about 68p per £100 of the mean total assets.

The rate of interest usually charged on mortgage advances to new borrowers who are owner-occupiers is at present 8½ per cent. Interest rates paid on share and deposit accounts are usually 5 and

4¾ per cent. respectively (income tax on both share and deposit interest being paid by the societies).

Section 1 of the House Purchase and Housing Act 1959, empowered the Chief Registrar to designate building societies for the purposes of the section. Societies that had been designated up to the time of going to press were marked " D " in the list which follows. Deposits in a designated building society rank as " narrower-range investments requiring advice " and shares in such a society as " wider-range investments " under the First Schedule to the Trustee Investments Act, 1961.

The basic requirements for designation are contained in the Building Societies (Designation for Trustee Investment) Regulations, 1964 (as amended by The Building Societies (Designation for Trustee Status) (Amendment) Regulations, 1968). These regulations prescribe £1 million as the minimum asset requirement and lay down a scale of reserves required to be held by designated societies ranging from 1¾ per cent. of assets exceeding £1,000 million to 2½ per cent. of assets not exceeding £100 million. At the end of 1970 there were 241 designated societies. Two societies were designated during the year and two were removed from

the list on transfer of their engagements to other designated societies. The total asset s of designated societies amount to 98·9 per cent. o f the assets of all building societies.

Under the Building Societies Acts, the Chief Registrar exercises certain power of control over building societies. Section 11 of the Prevention of Fraud (Investments) Act, 1958, under which the Registrar had prohibited certain societies from inviting investments was repealed by the Building Societies Act, 1960 (but without prejudice to any order currently in force) and the Chief Registrar was empowered to direct that a building society shall not advertise at all or to give directions to a particular society as to the matter included in its advertisements. In addition he may make an order prohibiting a building society from accepting further investments. The Chief Registrar's Report to Parliament for 1970 disclosed that at the end of that year 5 orders under the 1958 Act were still in force while 6 orders under the 1960 and 1962 Acts prohibiting the acceptance of further investments were in force at the end of 1970. Directions controlling advertising were in force in respect of 5 societies at the end of the year.

BUILDING SOCIETIES, GREAT BRITAIN, 1970—with 1969 in italics.

Class	Number	Share Investors	Advances during Year	Amount due to Shareholders	Amount due to Depositors	General Reserve and Bal'es C/fd.	Mortgage Assets	Total Assets
Assets over		000	£000	£000	£000	£000	£000	£000
£1 m.......	250	10,200	1,943,602	9,731,387	379,278	388,517	8,697,195	10,754,359
Other Socs......	*231*	*65*	*10,106*	*56,357*	*2,329*	*3,860*	*54,324*	*64,413*
1970 TOTALS	481	10,265	1,953,708	9,787,744	381,607†	392,376	8,751,519*	10,818,772
1969 ,,	*504*	*9,085*	*1,558,715*	*8,376,238*	*347,386*	*340,461*	*7,705,302*	*9,289,270*

† Total Depositors, 618,000.   * Total Borrowers, 3,655,000.

SOCIETIES WITH TOTAL ASSETS EXCEEDING £500,000—AT END OF FINANCIAL YEAR, 1970

Year Estabd.	★ Name of Society (abbreviated) Head Office	Share Investors	Assets Total £'000
1849D	Abbey National, Abbey House, Baker St., London, N.W.1..........	1,785,352	1,522,054
1879	Aberavon Mut P., 2 Forge Road, Port Talbot, Glam...............	526	674
1869D	Accrington Savings and Bldg. Soc., 15 Dutton St., Accrington, Lancs...	2,627	2,338
1875	Accrington Victoria, 7 St. James's St., Accrington, Lancs..........	665	711
1866D	Alfreton, 103 High St., Alfreton, Derby...........................	1,420	1,330
1863D	Alliance, Alliance House, Hove Park, Hove, Sussex.................	237,974	377,336
1886	Anchor 8 Coronation St., South Shields, Co. Durham.............	641	623
1848D	Anglia, Abington St., Northampton..............................	254,056	207,705
1870D	Argyle, Argyle House, 105 Seven Sisters Rd., Holloway, London, N.7	3,925	4,370
1945	Ashton-Stamford, Booth St. Chambers, Ashton-u-Lyne..........	493	690
1965	Banner, Banner Cross Hall, Sheffield.............................	11	7,628
1853D	Barnsley P., Regent St., Barnsley, Yorks..........................	11,763	13,989
1850D	Barnstaple and North Devon, 17 Joy St., Barnstaple, Devon..........	1,878	1,784
1922D	Barry Mutual, Lombard Bldgs., Barry, Glam......................	1,108	1,336
1953D	Bath Investment and Bldg. Soc., 20 Charles St., Bath, Som........	6,910	3,773
1870D	Bath Liberal, 1 South Parade, Bath, Som..........................	2,315	2,361
1863	Bede P., 5, Grange Road West, Jarrow, Co. Durham...............	675	613
1881D	Bedford Crown, 117 Midland Rd., Bedford.......................	2,025	1,497
1879D	Bedford P., 65 Midland Rd., Bedford.............................	6,345	4,880
1924D	Bedfordshire, Kingsway, Bedford	51,875	50,343
1905	Berkhamsted Dt. P., 322 High Street, Berkhamsted, Herts..........	538	579
1866D	Beverley, 16 Lairgate, Beverley, Yorks............................	2,561	1,346
1914D	Bexhill-on-Sea, 2 Devonshire Sq., Bexhill-on-Sea, Sussex..........	1,563	2,042

★P.=Permanent: B.=Benefit. The words "Building Society" are the last words in every society's name.

Year Established	Name of Society (abbreviated) Head Office	Share Investors	Assets Total £'000
1853D	Bideford and North Devon, 5 The Quay, Bideford, Devon..........	2,590	3,017
1889D	Birmingham Citizens, 20 Bennetts Hill, Birmingham, 2..............	10,770	15,046
1847D	Birmingham Incorporated, 42–44 Waterloo St., Birmingham........	21,552	30,356
1857D	Bishop Auckland P., 56 North Bondgate, Bishop Auckland, Co. Durham	937	1,063
1903D	Blackheath, Cranford House, 14, Long Lane, Rowley Regis, Warley, Worcs..	8,397	5,693
1873	Blyth and Morpeth Dt P. B., 3, Stanley St., Blyth, Nbld............	657	629
1864D	Bolton, 213 Baker St., London, N.W.1............................	1,613	2,769
1866D	Bournemouth and Christchurch, 162 Old Christchurch Rd., Bournemouth, Hants..	4,193	7,443
1851D	Bradford and Bingley, P.O. Box 2, Bingley, Yorks..................	231,029	260,039
1885D	Bradford P., 57-63 Sunbridge Rd., Bradford, 1....................	63,211	90,061
1921D	Bridgwater, 1 King Sq., Bridgwater, Som..........................	43,852	39,041
1849D	Brierley Hill and Stourbridge Incorporated, 12 Hagley Rd., Stourbridge, Worcs...	6,415	5,529
1867D	Brighton and Shoreham, 115 Western Rd., Brighton, Sussex........	612	985
1853D	Bristol Econ., 40 Broad St., Bristol..............................	2,153	2,858
1850D	Bristol and West, Broad Quay, Bristol............................	103,213	150,146
1883D	Bromley, 182 High St., Bromley, Kent............................	1,700	1,804
1907D	Buckinghamshire, High St., Chalfont St. Giles, Bucks..............	4,899	3,653
1850D	Burnley, 12 Grimshaw St., Burnley, Lancs..........................	193,987	222,178
1866D	Bury St. Edmunds P. B., 87 Guildhall St., Bury St. Edmunds, Suffolk..	1,647	2,176
1850D	Cambridge, 32, St. Andrew's St., Cambridge......................	11,565	13,142
1865D	Cardiff, Old Vestry Hall, 75 St. Mary St., Cardiff	1,791	3,174
1960D	Catholic, 48 Gt. Peter St., London, S.W.1........................	1,149	859
1899	Century, 21–23 Albany St., Edinburgh, 1..........................	1,186	1,898
1862	Chatham, 27 Lord St., Liverpool................................	597	559
1898D	Chatham Reliance, Reliance House, Manor Rd., Chatham, Kent......	13,821	10,731
1845	Chelmsford and Essex, 48, Duke St., Chelmsford, Essex............	1,210	1,533
1878D	Chelsea, 110/112, Kings Road, London, S.W.3	41,459	58,932
1850D	Cheltenham and Gloucester, 37–43 Clarence St., Cheltenham, Glos.....	131,946	140,732
1845D	Chesham, 15 Market Sq., Chesham, Bucks..........................	3,532	3,220
1888D	Chesham and Dt. Mut. & P., Norfolk Hse., Station Rd., Chesham, Bucks...	1,161	1,272
1870D	Cheshire and Northwich, Castle St., Macclesfield	26,381	24,414
1861D	Cheshunt, 100 Crossbrook St., Waltham Cross, Herts..............	5,796	11,272
1859D	Chorley and Dt., 51 St. Thomas's Rd., Chorley, Lancs..............	2,433	2,504
1866	Chorley P. B. 41, Chapel St, Chorley, Lancs.	604	625
1905D	Citizens Regency, Citizens Hse., Marlborough Pl., Brighton, Sussex...	9,938	12,507
1946D	City and Metropolitan, 37 Ludgate Hill, London, E.C.4	6,156	8,459
1862D	City of London, 34 London Wall, London, E.C.2....................	13,060	21,686
1931D	Civil Service, 26 Caxton St., London, S.W.1......................	6,126	7,518
1894D	Clacton, 72 Station Rd., Clacton-on-Sea, Essex....................	720	844
1859D	Clay Cross Benefit, 42 Thanet St., Clay Cross, Derbyshire..........	1,589	1,076
1912D	Coalville P., 42 High St., Coalville, Leics........................	1,526	1,457
1869D	Colchester Eq., 1–3 Pelhams Lane, Colchester, Essex..............	2,773	3,398
1856D	Colchester P. B., 11 Sir Isaac's Walk, Colchester, Essex..........	1,791	2,548
1866D	Colne, Albert Rd., Colne, Lancs..................................	4,263	5,577
1906	Consett Reliance, 44 Medomsley Rd., Consett, Co. Durham........	706	600
1884D	Coventry Economic, 19 and 20 High St., Coventry, Warws..........	91,867	70,976
1872D	Coventry Provident Provident Hse., 25 Warwick Rd., Coventry, Warws...	16,114	17,015
1848	Coventry and Warwickshire B, 23 Bayley Lane, Coventry, Warws.....	591	588
1906D	Cradley Heath, 194 High St., Cradley Heath, Warley, Worcs.	3,865	3,394
1850D	Cumberland, 38 Fisher St., Carlisle..............................	23,131	21,223
1946D	Darlington, Tubwell Row, Market Place, Darlington, Co. Durham...	18,976	18,767
1847D	Deal and Walmer, 7 Victoria Rd., Deal, Kent......................	597	824
1865	Denton, 13, Hyde Rd., Denton, Manchester........................	540	646
1859D	Derbyshire P.O. Box No. 48, 7 Iron Gate, Derby..................	63,934	61,409
1866D	Dewsbury and West Riding P.O. Box 19 Church St., Dewsbury, Yorks.	18,777	22,437
1923	Dillwyn P., 11 Cradock St., Swansea, Glam......................	1,142	1,382
1879	Dorking, 124 High St., Dorking, Surrey..........................	710	1,136
1861	Dover Dt., 3 Market Sq., Dover, Kent............................	596	705
1883	Dover and Folkestone, 27–29 Castle St., Dover, Kent..............	458	559
1858D	Dudley, Dudley Hse., Stone St., Dudley, Worcs....................	4,866	5,731
1869	Dunfermline P.O. Box 4, East Port, Dunfermline, Fife..............	20,350	23,455
1852D	Dunstable, 13A West St., Dunstable, Beds........................	2,578	2,716
1956	Eagle, Chancery House, Chancery Lane, London, W.C.2............	528	512
1927D	Ealing and Acton, 55 The Mall, Ealing, London, W.5..............	2,217	3,777
1857D	Earl Shilton, 22 The Hollow, Earl Shilton, Leicester..............	4,866	3,807
1903D	East Surrey, 54 Station Rd., Redhill, Surrey	4,643	4,336
1877D	Eastbourne Mut., 147 Terminus Rd., Eastbourne, Sussex..........	15,488	20,842

Year Established	Name of Society (abbreviated) Head Office	Share Investors	Assets Total £'000
1855D	Eastern Counties, 13 and 15 Queen St., Ipswich, Suffolk	27,030	30,152
1870D	Edinburgh, 32 Castle St., Edinburgh	4,180	5,707
1880D	Enfield, 47 London Rd., Enfield, Middx.	14,142	13,547
1899D	Essex and Kent P., 1 Orsett Rd., Grays, Essex	1,445	1,874
1874D	Essex Eq., 13, Orsett Rd., Grays, Essex	2,290	2,310
1876D	Failsworth P., 546 Oldham Rd., Failsworth, Manchester	1,085	971
1966	Falkirk, Manse Place, Falkirk, Stirlingshire	2,750	1,224
1902D	Finchley, 767 High Rd., North Finchley, London, N.12	7,140	11,056
1860D	Frome Selwood P., Bath St., Frome, Som.	3,200	3,253
1865D	Furness, 36 Cornwallis St., Barrow-in-Furness, Lancs.	19,049	14,712
1911D	Gainsborough, 26 Lord St., Gainsborough, Lincs.	1,055	1,338
1906D	Glantawe P., 47 Mansel St., Swansea, Glam.	712	1,544
1876D	Goldhawk 15–17 High Rd., Chiswick, London, W.4	11,149	15,790
1899	Govanhill, 160 Hope St., Glasgow, C.2	676	550
1957D	Grainger and Percy, Hood St., Newcastle upon Tyne	15,504	20,778
1880D	Grays, 22 New Rd., Grays, Essex	6,751	6,467
1852D	Greenwich, 281 Greenwich High Rd., London, S.E.10	8,570	10,403
1848D	Grimsby and North Lincolnshire, Osborne Chambers, Osborne St., Grimsby, Lincs.	964	1,486
1871D	Guardian, Guardian House, 120 High Holborn, London, W.C.1.	37,478	72,104
1928D	Hadrian, 30 Fowler St., South Shields, Co. Durham	2,113	2,237
1849	Halesowen B., 20 Stourbridge Rd., Halesowen, Worcs.	1,498	1,422
1853D	Halifax, Permanent Bldgs, Halifax, Yorks.	1,792,510	1,995,661
1866D	Hampshire, 44 Commercial Rd., Portsmouth, Hants	4,329	5,463
1854D	Hanley Econ., 42 Cheapside, Hanley, Stoke-on-Trent, Staffs.	15,670	11,096
1953	Harpenden and Dt., 15A, Station Rd., Harpenden, Herts.	846	818
1882D	Harrow, Cunningham Hse., Bessborough Rd., Harrow, Middx.	3,757	4,881
1866	Hartlepool and Dt., 17 Scarborough St., Hartlepool, Co. Durham	454	569
1851D	Hasbury and Cradley, 5 Summer Hill, Halesowen, Worcs.	2,862	2,298
1931	Haslemere, 17 Petworth Rd., Haslemere, Surrey.	557	590
1851D	Hastings and East Sussex, 12–13 Wellington Place, Hastings, Sussex	27,804	27,666
1849D	Hastings and Thanet, 12/14 Wigmore St., London, W.1	147,241	151,330
1800D	Haywards Heath and Dt., 33 The Broadway, Haywards Heath, Sussex	9,078	8,706
1875D	Hearts of Oak P., 47–49 Oxford St., London, W.1.	9,426	17,820
1884D	Hemel Hempstead, 43 Marlowes, Hemel Hempstead, Herts.	5,601	5,857
1926D	Hendon, Central Circus, Hendon, London, N.W.4	4,507	3,618
1888	Herne Bay, 39 William St., Herne Bay, Kent.	2,028	2,528
1888D	Herts and Essex P., 4 Market Sq., Bishop's Stortford, Herts.	2,361	2,935
1874D	Hibernian P., 49 Churchill Way, Cardiff, Glam.	1,354	1,400
1860D	Highgate, Northway Hse., High Rd., Whetstone, London, N.20	431	936
1853D	Hinckley and Country, 9 Castle St., Hinckley, Leics.	8,876	11,328
1865D	Hinckley P., Upper Bond St., Hinckley, Leics.	11,669	11,509
1881D	Holloway, 246 Upper St., London, N.1	3,865	4,370
1855D	Holmesdale B., 43 Church St., Reigate, Surrey.	5,065	5,864
1856D	Horsham, 30 Carfax, Horsham, Sussex.	2,487	2,630
1864D	Huddersfield, Britannia Bldgs., Huddersfield, Yorks.	92,093	111,654
1868	Hyde, 5 Corporation St., Hyde, Cheshire.	974	1,430
1853D	Ilkeston P., Queen St., Ilkeston, Derby.	2,014	1,082
1891D	Inverness, 21–23 Union St., Inverness	3,426	3,682
1876D	Ipswich and Dt., 8, Northgate St., Ipswich.	3,362	2,632
1849D	Ipswich and Suffolk, 44 Upper Brook St., Ipswich.	10,877	7,944
1847	Kent and Canterbury P.B., 3 The Parade, Canterbury, Kent	421	560
1869D	Kettering P. B., Norwich Union Chambers, Market Place, Kettering.	650	738
1961	Kidderminster Eq., 30 Church St., Kidderminster.	539	540
1851	Kidderminster P. B., 29 Church St., Kidderminster, Worcs.	1,212	1,301
1864	Kilmarnock Bldg. and Investment Soc., P.O. Box 16, Royal Bank Bldgs., The Cross, Kilmarnock.	694	894
1917	King Edward, 19 Castle St., Liverpool	362	588
1865D	Kingston, 6 Eden St., Kingston-on-Thames, Surrey.	5,253	6,395
1852D	Lambeth, 118/120 Westminster Bridge Rd., London, S.E.1	21,371	30,855
1867D	Lancashire, 127 Union St., Oldham, Lancs.	2,230	2,734
1853D	Leamington Spa, 24 Warwick New Road, Leamington Spa, Warws.	5,083	5,629
1875D	Leeds and Holbeck, 105 Albion St., Leeds.	56,216	63,432
1848D	Leeds P. Permanent Hse., The Headrow, Leeds, 1.	535,475	555,645
1856D	Leek and Westbourne, P.O. Box 20, Newton Hse., Leek, Staffs.	280,970	299,138
1863D	Leek United and Midlands, 50 St. Edward St., Leek, Staffs.	26,814	23,662
1853D	Leicester, P. Oadby, Leics.	211,382	282,741
1875D	Leicester Temperance, Halford Hse., Charles St., Leicester.	74,910	88,787
1875	Leigh P., Lonsdale Hse., Cook St., Leigh, Lancs.	613	957
1870D	Lewes 11 High St., Lewes, Sussex.	8,749	8,048
1877D	Liverpool P.O. Box 831 107 Duke St., Liverpool	27,584	33,025
1859	London B., St. Bride's Hse., Salisbury Sq., E.C.4	998	1,248

Year Established	Name of Society (abbreviated) Head Office	Share Investors	Assets Total £'000
1863D	London Commercial, Guilford Hse., Gray's Inn Rd., London, W.C.1..	1,595	1,847
1883D	London and Essex, Security Hse., 2 Romford Rd., London, E.15.....	3,360	4,180
1878	London Grosvenor and Middlesex, 5 Old Brompton Rd., S.W.7....	833	692
1879D	London Investment, 54 Goldhawk Rd., London, W.12.............	10,465	13,234
1848	London P., 231–232 Strand, London W.C.2.....................	996	1,648
1867D	Loughborough P., 16 Baxter Gate, Loughborough, Leics...........	3,721	5,139
1877	Louth, Mablethorpe and Sutton P. B., 3 Eastgate, Louth, Lincs........	612	722
1866D	Luton, 24 King St., Luton, Beds.	5,347	7,940
1868D	Magnet, North West Hse., Marylebone Rd., London, N.W.1.......	40,896	49,556
1922D	Manchester, 18–20 Bridge St., Manchester...................	1,928	3,622
1956	Mancunian, 22, Dickinson St., Manchester...................	972	1,215
1870D	Mansfield, Regent Hse., Regent St., Mansfield. Notts.............	7,776	9,572
1867	Margam P.B., 51, Tydran St., Port Talbot	322	563
1870D	Market Harborough, Welland Hse, The Square, Market Harborough, Leics.	12,529	9,023
1860D	Marsden, 6–20 Russell St., Nelson, Lancs.	21,465	19,218
1875D	Melton Mowbray, 43 Nottingham St., Melton Mowbray, Leics......	7,896	9,844
1875D	Mercantile, 75 ,Howard St., North Shields....................	6,497	7,071
1882	Mersey P., 41 North John St., Liverpool, 2...................	437	049
1886D	Metrogas, 709 Old Kent Rd., London, S.E.15.................	1,857	1,143
1872D	Middleton, 99 Long St., Middleton, Manchester	12,015	10,625
1933	Midland, P., 3 Lower High St., Cradley Heath, Warley, Worcs......	437	519
1880D	Mid-Sussex, Mid-Sussex Hse., 66 Church Rd., Burgess Hill, Sussex ...	1,982	1,862
1883	Mitcham, 173 London Rd., Mitcham, Surrey.	1,473	709
1866D	Mornington P., 158 Kentish Town Rd., London, N.W.5.........	8,296	8,151
1869D	Monmouthshire, Friars Chambers, Dock St., Newport, Mon.......	5,336	7,308
1896D	National Post Office, Waterloo Hse., High St., Epsom, Surrey	21,606	39,669
1884D	Nationwide, New Oxford Hse., High Holborn, London, W.C.1	932,556	771,044
1877	Nelson and Premier, 3 Westoe Village, South Shields, Co. Durham..	2,118	2,436
1866D	New Cross, 470 New Cross Rd., London, S.E.14...............	2,740	3,769
1958	New Homes, 342 Richmond Rd., Twickenham, Middx............	745	958
1882D	New Swindon, 36 Regent Circus, Swindon, Wilts...............	1,324	1,884
1856D	Newbury, 17/20 Bartholomew St., Newbury, Berks.............	9,661	10,864
1863D	Newcastle and Gateshead, St. Nicholas Sq., Newcastle upon Tyne....	3,034	3,048
1861D	Newcastle upon Tyne P., 37–41 Grainger St. (P.O. Box No. 1DT), Newcastle upon Tyne...................................	15,120	20,965
1876D	North East Globe, 218 Ridley Place, Newcastle upon Tyne	2,118	2,777
1866D	North Kent, North Kent Hse., Windmill St., Gravesend, Kent......	7,879	5,756
1886	North London, 407 Holloway Rd., London, N.7...............	574	1,195
1877D	North of England, 57 Fawcett St., Sunderland, Co. Durham......	12,274	16,047
1899D	North Wilts Eq., 18 and 19 Commercial Rd., Swindon, Wilts......	2,836	3,247
1888D	Northampton and Midlands, 60 Gold St., Northampton..........	13,374	11,465
1850D	Northern Rock, Northern Rock Hse., Gosforth, Newcastle upon Tyne.	134,430	133,164
1868D	Northumbria P. B., 11 Beaconsfield St., Blyth, Nbld..............	1,039	1,118
1852D	Norwich, St. Andrew's Hse., St. Andrew St., Norwich, Norfolk.....	18,428	29,339
1850D	Nottingham, Nottingham Hse., Nottingham, Notts...............	21,496	27,838
1935D	Nottingham Oddfellows, Imperial Bldg., Victoria St., Nottingham....	2,876	1,618
1849	Nuneaton and Warwickshire, 9 Queen's Road, Nuneaton, Warws. ...	871	766
1909	Oldbury Britannia, Britannia Hse., 19 High St., West Bromwich, Staffs.	835	754
1848D	Otley, 34 Boroughgate, Otley, Yorks..........................	4,916	6,012
1869D	Over Darwen, 24 Railway Rd., Darwen	2,032	1,687
1860D	Oxford Prov., 154 Cowley Rd., Oxford.......................	1,836	1,513
1879D	Paddington, 17–19 Gt. Western Rd., London, W.9..............	1,287	2,612
1877D	Padiham, 34 Burnley Rd., Padiham, Lancs.....................	3,630	4,548
1853D	Paisley, 7 Glasgow Rd., Paisley, Renfrew	4,801	5,845
1879D	Peckham Mut., Hanover Park Hse. London, S.E.15.............	4,517	4,319
1855D	Peckham P., 6–8 Queens Rd., London, S.E.15.	1,520	1,753
1870	Peebleshire Savings Inv., National Commercial Bank Bldgs, Peebles ..	935	778
1880	Pelham P., 110 St. James's St., Brighton, Sussex................	454	522
1877D	Penrith, King Street, Penrith, Cumb..........................	1,647	2,053
1860D	Peterborough, 5 Cathedral Sq., Peterborough...................	15,428	18,422
1884	Pioneer P., 8 Breams Bldgs., Fetter Lane, London, E.C.4........	459	639
1848D	Planet, Planet Hse., 215, Strand, London, W.C.2...............	19,524	28,647
1866D	Pontypridd, 4, Gelliwastad Rd. Pontypridd, Glam..............	1,174	2,321
1881D	Portman, 40 Portman Sq., London, W.1......................	36,750	50,328
1896D	Portsmouth, 176 London Rd., North End, Portsmouth...........	6,816	9,286
1860D	Principality, Principality Bldgs., Queen St., Cardiff	32,965	39,581
1941D	Property Owners, 4 Cavendish Place, London W.1..............	13,205	24,891
1849D	Provincial, Provincial Hse., Market St., Bradford, 1, Yorks..........	272,099	320,140
1933D	Prudential Inv., 1 Leopold Place, Edinburgh, 7................	1,007	1,415
1868D	Queen Anne, Queen Anne Chambers, The Strand, Barnstaple, Devon..	1,934	1,806
1886D	Queen Victoria Street, Pearl Assurance Hse., 1A Katherine St., Croydon	916	1,493

Year Established	Name of Society (abbreviated) Head Office	Share Investors	Assets Total £'000
1846D	Ramsbury, The Square, Ramsbury, Marlborough, Wilts............	18,853	17,066
1859D	Redditch and Worcester, Church Green West, Redditch, Worcs.	30,083	26,308
1883	Rowland Hill, P., Victoria House Southampton Row, London, W.C.1	715	971
1888D	Rowley Regis, 223 Halesowen Rd., Cradley Heath, Warley, Worcs.	6,705	6,242
1870D	Royal Arcade, 25 Grey St., Newcastle upon Tyne..................	671	807
1906	Royston and Dt., P., John St., Royston, Herts....................	683	935
1854D	Rugby and Warwick, Temple Bldgs, Rugby, Warws.	33,021	24,871
1861D	Rugby Prov., 34 North St., Rugby, Warwicks.	2,812	2,333
1840D	Saffron Walden and Dt., Market Place, Saffron Walden, Essex........	3,410	4,251
1867D	St. Andrew's 26 , Ridley Place, Newcastle upon Tyne...............	1,123	1,255
1937	St. Pancras, 200 Finchley Rd., London, N.W.3...................	2,541	3,551
1850	St. Philip's B., Queens College Chambers, 38A Paradise Street, Birmingham, 1..	553	936
1852	Sandbach, 5 Middlewich Rd., Sandbach, Ches.	1,608	1,849
1875D	Sandy, 6 Bedford Rd., Sandy, Beds..........................	1,994	2,165
1846D	Scarborough, York Hse., York Place, Scarborough, Yorks...........	9,089	10,349
1848D	Scottish, 4 York Place, Edinburgh, 1.........................	3,392	4,355
1035D	Sheffield, 66 Campo Lane, Sheffield, Yorks.....................	1,571	2,272
1879D	Shepshed P. B., Bull Ring, Shepshed, Loughborough, Leics.........	3,189	2,592
1875D	Shields Commercial, Barrington St., South Shields, Co. Durham.....	1,883	2,375
1853D	Skipton, 59 High St., Skipton, Yorks.........................	45,207	61,796
1855D	Smethwick, 346 High St., Smethwick, Warley, Worcs..............	2,412	2,236
1849	Somersetshire, 9 Market Place, Glastonbury, Som.	664	696
1859D	South of England, 58 King St., Maidenhead, Berks.	59,150	75,562
1876	South Shields Sun P., Sun Bldgs, Beach Rd., Sth. Shields, Durham ...	397	648
1902D	South Staffordshire, 3 Princess St., Wolverhampton, Staffs........	29,851	26,849
1875D	South West Wales, 17 The Kingsway, Swansea, Glam...............	1,455	2,224
1876D	South Western, 11–13 Regent Parade, Brighton Rd., Sutton, Surrey..	6,261	4,764
1867D	Stafford and County P., 2 Martin St., Stafford...................	3,359	4,957
1877D	Stafford Railway, 4 Market Sq., Stafford.......................	3,787	4,277
1875D	Standard, 64 Church Way, North Shields, Nbld...................	2,089	1,951
1970	Stanley and N.W. Durham, Cromarty Hse., Front St., Stanley, Co. Durham..	1,080	1,029
1878D	Steyning and Sussex County, Bank Hse., 62 High St., Steyning, Sussex.	7,762	10,105
1877	Stockport and County P., Carlyle Hse., 109 Wellington Rd. Sth., Stockport, Ches..	570	548
1898D	Stockport Mersey 72/74 Wellington Rd. South, Stockport, Ches.	825	1,157
1852D	Stoke-on-Trent P., 66–68 Liverpool Rd., Stoke-on-Trent, Staffs......	1,117	1,549
1889D	Stourbridge, Lye and Dt. P., Victoria Chambers, 94 High St., Stourbridge, Worcs..	3,568	3,417
1850D	Stroud, 4 Rowcroft, Stroud, Glos............................	9,038	7,893
1901D	Summers, Shotton Steel Works, Shotton, Deeside, Flint............	7,346	2,772
1853D	Sunderland and Shields, 51 Fawcett St.. Sunderland, Co. Durham....	23,415	26,144
1872D	Sussex Mutual, Sussex Hse., 126/127 Western Rd., Hove, Sussex....	10,762	18,537
1887	Swansea Albion and Gower, 60 Mansel St., Swansea, Glam.........	430	661
1868D	Swindon P., 1 Commercial Rd., Swindon, Wilts..................	2,403	3,334
1854D	Tamworth P. B., 6 Victoria Rd., Tamworth, Staffs................	2,601	2,573
1966	Teachers, Hamilton Hse, Mabledon Place, London W.C.1	7,650	8,675
1854D	Temperance P., P.O. Box 18, Worthing, Sussex..................	89,347	130,640
1883D	Tewkesbury and Dt. 142–143 High St., Tewkesbury, Glos.	1,850	1,890
1901D	Tipton and Coseley P., 57–60 High St., Tipton, Staffs............	7,316	4,501
1866D	Tyldesley, 213–215 Elliott St., Tyldesley, Lancs..................	3,364	3,526
1877D	Tyne Commercial, 10 Grange Rd. West, Jarrow, Co. Durham.......	2,457	2,622
1855D	Tynemouth, 53–55 Howard St., North Shields, Nbld..............	3,367	2,827
1887D	Tynemouth Victoria, 23 West Percy St., North Shields, Nbld.......	2,497	3,033
1863D	Universal, 36 Grey St., Newcastle upon Tyne...................	11,696	12,250
1924D	Vernon, 26 St. Petersgate, Stockport, Ches.	2,799	3,866
1919D	Victory, Victory Hse., Burrow St., South Shields, Co. Durham......	547	835
1846D	Wakefield, 57 Westgate, Wakefield, Yorks.	16,034	13,385
1863D	Walsall Mut., 41–45 Bridge St., Walsall, Staffs.................	14,774	14,377
1847D	Waltham Abbey, 5 Church St., Waltham Abbey, Essex............	4,275	5,683
1877D	Walthamstow, 223/7 Hoe St., London, E.17....................	16,403	19,182
1851D	Wednesbury, 52 Lower High St., Wednesbury, Staffs..............	16,123	11,989
1878D	Welsh Economic, Old Bank Chambers, Pontypridd, Glam..........	742	1,205
1949D	Wessex P., 115 Old Christchurch Rd.,Bournemouth, Hants.........	7,496	9,367
1849D	West Bromwich, 321 High St., West Bromwich, Staffs........[S.W.14	52,828	50,235
1850D	West London, 246 Upper Richmond Rd. West, East Sheen, London,	1,717	2,002
1907	Westbury and Dt. P., Laverton Institute, Westbury, Wilts..........	514	657
1862D	Western Counties, 20 The Quay, Bideford, Devon	15,970	16,033
1873D	Wigan, 1 Library St., Wigan, Lancs..........................	1,914	1,848
1875D	Wimbledon, 22A Wimbledon Bridge, London, S.W.19.............	645	880
1877D	Wolverhampton and Dt., 37–41 Lichfield St., Wolverhampton, Staffs..	13,609	18,234

Year Estab-lished	Name of Society (abbreviated) Head Office	Share Investors	Assets Total £'000
1849D	Wolverhampton Freeholders' P., 37 Queen Square, Wolverhampton	19,403	20,043
1847D	Woolwich Eq., Equitable Hse., London, S.E.18..................	493,226	572,049
1882D	Workington and West Cumberland P. B., Gray St., Workington, Cumb.	1,546	1,721
1878D	Wotton-under-Edge and Dursley, 11 Long St., Wotton-under-Edge...	1,654	1,390

NATIONAL HEALTH SERVICE STATISTICS

	England and Wales			Scotland		
	1968	1969	1970	1968	1969	1970
HOSPITAL SERVICES:—						
In-patients Departments:—						
Beds staffed*...........	464,900	461,100	455,700	63,300	63,100	63,000
Average daily occupation of beds	385,200	380,500	372,200	54,000	55,300	53,500
Discharges and deaths ...	5,150,000	5,282,200	5,329,000	679,000	693,000	699,000
Patients on waiting list* ..	534,900	561,400	555,900	52,900	53,300	51,500
Out-patients Departments:—						
Consultant Departments .	32,429,000	32,846,000	34,013,600	—	—	—
Accident and emergency departments..........	13,866,000	14,271,000	14,082,900	—	—	—
Total Attendances	46,824,000	47,661,000	48,096,500	8,358,000	8,488,000	8,619,000
EXECUTIVE COUNCIL SERVICES:—						
Prescriptions dispensed by chemists	267,378,000	264,172,000	266,581,207	28,498,000	28,167,000	28,881,000
Dental treatment courses completed†............	20,066,000	20,226,000	20,748,000	1,833,000	1,841,000	1,890,000
Ophthalmic services:—						
Sight Tests paid for	6,633,000	6,722,000	6,767,000	579,000	584,000	595,000
Pairs of glasses paid for ..	5,688,000	5,783,000	5,663,000	557,000	571,000	550,000

* At end of period.   † Including emergency treatments.

CHILDREN IN THE CARE OF LOCAL AUTHORITIES, 1970

On March 31, 1970, there were 71,210 children in the care of local authorities in England and Wales. During the year ended March 31, 1970, 51,542 were received into care. Of the total received during the year, 17,047 children were taken into care through short term illness of the parent or guardian, 5,798 because of the confinement of the mother and 5,241 children deserted by the mother, the father being unable to care for them. 2,709 of the children were illegitimate, the mother being unable to provide a home. 2,693 children were in care because the family was homeless (through eviction, 1,353) and in 3,074 cases home conditions were unsatisfactory. 4,998 children were in care under fit persons orders (1,641 offenders)

Manner of Accommodation of Children in Care	On March 31, 1969			On March 31, 1970		
	Boys	Girls	Total	Boys	Girls	Total
Boarded out.............................	15,545	14,929	30,474	15,448	14,836	30,284
In lodgings..............................	641	608	1,249	665	635	1,300
In residential employment..................	167	232	399	152	205	357
Local authority children's homes:						
Reception homes with special facilities.....	999	642	1,641	1,045	675	1,720
Other reception homes...................	328	224	552	393	253	646
Residential nurseries...................	1,545	1,220	2,765	1,420	1,101	2,521
Homes for not more than 12 children......	4,688	3,673	8,361	4,796	3,761	8,557
Other children's homes..................	4,543	2,885	7,428	4,478	2,798	7,276
Total....................	12,103	8,644	20,747	12,132	8,588	20,720
Voluntary homes........................	2,760	2,466	5,226	2,856	2,555	5,411
Boarding homes/special schools for handicapped children...............................	1,688	594	2,282	1,594	571	2,165
Hostels.................................	644	515	1,159	693	513	1,206
Subject of fit person order, but placed under charge and control of parent, etc.......	3,095	2,279	5,374	3,696	2,700	6,396
Other accommodation....................	1,952	1,326	3,278	2,073	1,298	3,371
Total number of children in care............	38,595	31,593	70,188	39,309	31,901	71,210
Percentage boarded out....................	45	52	48	44	52	48

UNIT TRUSTS

A Unit Trust is a method of investment by which money subscribed in varying amounts by individual investors is pooled in a fund, the investment and management of which is subject to the strict legal provisions of a Trust Deed. The fund is invested in carefully-selected stocks and shares by a management company and the investments so acquired are held by a Trustee (normally a bank or insurance company). Therefore, through his subscription to the Trust Fund, each subscriber acquires a fractional interest in the block of securities in which the Fund is invested, while the dividends received from the investments form the income of the trust. The net income is paid to all investors in the Trust Fund in proportion to the size of their holdings. The management company and the Trustee, who must be effectively independent of each other, are parties to the Trust Deed which must be authorized by the Department of Trade and Industry (or the Ministry of Commerce in Northern Ireland) before any public offer of units for sale may be made.

Although the record of unit trusts has been good in recent years, investment of this nature neither guarantees an increasing income nor ensures continual capital appreciation. They are essentially a medium to long-term form of investment—the rate of repurchases of units by the management companies of all authorized unit trusts in 1970 being only about 5½ per cent. of the average value of funds invested.

Units are readily marketable, being bought or sold at the price (based on the value of the underlying securities) ruling at the time the order for sale or repurchase is received by the Management Company. The Department of Trade and Industry regulates the charges which Unit Trust managers may make. These charges are taken by way of an initial service charge (which is included in the sale price of a unit), and a semi-annual management fee levied on the value of the fund and taken out of either income or capital. Over a 20-year life of a Trust, the initial service charge, together with management fees, may not total more than 13¼ per cent. In order to avoid the need for quoting unit prices with awkward fractions of a penny the managers are also entitled to round off the price of a unit by 1·25p or 1 per cent, whichever is the lower.

Savings Schemes

Most management companies operate savings schemes whereby an investor is able to make contributions at intervals which are utilized to purchase units at the current price, the cash balance remaining from any such purchase being carried forward and added to the next contribution. The dividend income is either paid directly to the investor every six months, or, more generally, is used by arrangement to purchase further units for his account. In either case any unit-holder who is not liable to tax at the standard rate of tax deducted can claim appropriate relief from the Inland Revenue. Without doubt, the Savings schemes linked with life assurance have provided one of the most rapid growth sectors of the Unit Trust movement in recent years. These schemes enable a person to accumulate a sum of money for retirement, etc. with the protection of life assurance cover for the duration of the planned period of saving. At the end of this period, the investor receives all the units acquired or their cash value. If death occurs beforehand, the dependants receive all the units bought up to date, plus a cash sum equivalent to the total remaining contributions necessary to have completed the savings programme. Tax relief is available on these contributions as with other life assurance premiums.

Arrangements for Children

In general, units cannot be registered in the name of a child but they can be registered in the name of a parent or any other adult, and the registered holding can be designated with the initials of the child. Alternatively, money can be settled on a child under one of the various children's gift plans operated and the units held in trust. Income distributions, less income tax, are invested in further units, and additional units may be purchased at any time. When the child reaches 18 or some chosen later age, the units become his property absolutely, and, until the 1969 Finance Act, he was able, in most cases, to reclaim income tax deducted from the income distributions. From the point of view of the settlor, income from the gift did not give rise to any liability on him for income tax or surtax. Since the 1969 Finance Act, however, the income from a children's gift plan is not aggregable with that of the parents and it is not now possible to reclaim income tax deducted from income which arose on or after April 6, 1969.

The unit trust movement, which has been in operation for some thirty years, has experienced an upsurge in business in recent years. At the end of 1960 holdings in Unit Trusts numbered 654,520 valued at £201·4 million. This had risen to 1,419,100 (value £522 m.) by 1965 and further to 2,374,932 holdings valued at £1,658·42 m. by May 31, 1971. Allowing for duplication, there were over 1,250,000 separate investors at the end of 1970.

The Association of Unit Trust Managers of 306–8 Salisbury House, Finsbury Circus, E.C.2 was formed on October 13, 1959 and membership is open to any management company of an authorized unit trust scheme. It publishes an annual directory of members who represent approximately three-quarters of the funds invested in the movement. The Association's main object is to act as a consulting body amongst its members in order to agree strict standards of unit trust practices for the protection of the interest of unit holders and management companies, and to maintain the good name of the Unit Trust Movement.

The following details as at December 31, 1970, relating to the management groups operating in Great Britain and Northern Ireland have been extracted from the *Unit Trust Year Book* 1971, published by Fundex Ltd., and the *Directory of Unit Trusts* published by the Association of Unit Trust Managers.

Unit Trusts, 1970–71

(With value of funds managed and number of unit holdings.)

*ABACUS UNIT TRUST MANAGEMENT CO. LTD., 26 Pall Mall, Manchester 2.—*Funds Managed*, £2,114,587; *Holdings*, 8,330.

*ALLIED INVESTORS TRUSTS LTD., 41 Bishopsgate, London, E.C.2.—*Funds Managed*, £54,916,507; *Holdings*, 112,970.

*ANSBACHER UNIT MANAGEMENT CO. LTD., 1 Noble Street, Gresham Street, London, E.C.2.—*Funds Managed*, £436,842; *Holdings*, 1,156.

*ARCHWAY UNIT TRUST MANAGERS LTD., 24 St. Mary Axe, London, E.C.3.—*Funds Managed*, £789,023; *Holdings*, 415.

*BARCLAYS UNICORN LTD., Unicorn House, 252 Romford Road, London, E.7.—*Funds Managed*, £85,975,844; *Holdings*, 231,340.

BISHOPSGATE PROGRESSIVE UNIT TRUST MANAGEMENT CO. LTD., 9 Bishopsgate, London, E.C.2.—*Funds Managed*, £1,500,000; *Holdings*, 650.

WM. BRANDT'S SONS & CO. LTD., 36 Fenchurch Street, London, E.C.3.—*Funds Managed*, £1,156,328; *Holdings*, 283.

BRIDGE TRUST MANAGEMENT CO. LTD., Canoe House, Monument Street, London, E.C.3.

*BRITISH LIFE OFFICE LTD., (THE), 16 Coleman Street, London, E.C.2.—*Funds Managed*, £1,457,988; *Holdings*, 678.

*CABOT UNIT TRUST MANAGEMENT CO. LTD., The Bristol & West Building, Broad Quay, Bristol 1.—*Funds Managed*, £418,000; *Holdings*, 142.

CARLIOL UNIT FUND MANAGERS LTD., A Floor, Milburn House, Newcastle upon Tyne.—*Funds Managed*, £421,000; *Holdings*, 250.

*CAVALIER SECURITIES LTD., 117 Old Broad Street, London, E.C.2.—*Funds Managed* £382,000; *Holdings*, 1,081.

CHARTERHOUSE JAPHET UNIT MANAGEMENT LTD., 1 Paternoster Row, St. Paul's London, E.C.4.—*Funds Managed*, £1,563,508; *Holdings*, 463.

DISCRETIONARY UNIT FUND MANAGERS LTD., 1-4 Copthall Chambers, London, E.C.2.—*Funds Managed*, £1,350,216; *Holdings*, 747.

*DOWGATE FUND MANAGERS LTD., Dowgate Hill House, London, E.C.4.— *Funds Managed*, £150,000; *Holdings*, 105.

*EDINBURGH SECURITIES CO. LTD. (THE), 4 Melville Cres., Edinburgh.—*Funds Managed*, £1,509,998; *Holdings*, 1,766.

EMBLEM FUND MANAGEMENT COMPANY LTD. (THE), 20 Copthall Avenue, London, E.C.2.— *Funds Managed*, £614,379; *Holdings*, 263.

*E.P. FUND MANAGERS LTD., 37-45 Tooley Street, London, S.E.1.—*Funds Managed*, £389,803; *Holdings*, 1,414.

EQUITY AND LAW UNIT TRUST MANAGERS LTD., Amersham Road, High Wycombe, Bucks.— *Funds Managed*, £684,450; *Holdings*, 541.

FAMILY FUND MANAGERS, 16 Coleman Street, London, E.C.2.—*Funds Managed*, £781,308; *Holdings*, 566.

*FIRST PROVINCIAL UNIT TRUST LTD., 21 Spring Gardens, Manchester.—*Funds Managed*, £11,474,781; *Holdings*, 19,528.

FOUNDERS COURT MANAGEMENT SERVICES LTD., Founders Court, Lothbury, London, E.C.2.— *Funds Managed*, £220,000; *Holdings*, 111.

FRAMLINGTON UNIT MANAGEMENT LTD., Spencer House, 4 South Place, London, E.C.2.—*Funds Managed*, £406,100; *Holdings*, 480.

*FRIENDS' PROVIDENT UNIT TRUST MANAGERS LTD., 7 Leadenhall Street, London, E.C.3.—*Funds Managed*, £440,000; *Holdings*, 784.

*G. AND A. UNIT TRUST MANAGERS LTD., 41 Bishopsgate, London, E.C.2.—*Funds Managed*, £2,532,402; *Holdings*, 12,770.

G.T. UNIT MANAGERS, LTD., 16 St. Martins-le-Grand, London, E.C.1.—*Funds Managed*, £216,987; *Holdings*, 605.

JOHN GOVETT UNIT MANAGEMENT LTD., Winchester House, 77 London Wall, London, E.C.2.— *Funds Managed*, £6,800,000; *Holdings*, 6,300.

*GUARDIAN-HILL SAMUEL UNIT MANAGERS LTD., 100 Wood Street, London, E.C.2.—*Funds Managed*, £6,177,540; *Holdings*, 2,853.

*HAMBRO ABBEY SECURITIES LTD., 41 Bishopsgate, London, E.C.2.—*Funds Managed*, £20,459,805; *Holdings*, 16,790.

*HAMBROS UNIT TRUST MANAGERS LTD., 41 Bishopgate, London, E.C.2.—*Funds Managed*, £8,931,368; *Holdings*, 1,986.

HENDERSON GROSS FUND MANAGEMENT LTD., 28 Austin Friars, London, E.C.2.—*Funds Managed*, £2,205,000; *Holdings*, 45.

*HILL SAMUEL UNIT TRUST MANAGERS LTD., 100 Wood Street, London, E.C.2.—*Funds Managed*, £53,688,286; *Holdings*, 57,773.

*INTEL FUNDS (MANAGEMENT) LTD., 15 Christopher Street, London, E.C.2.—*Funds Managed*, £3,250,000; *Holdings*, 1,531.

IONIAN UNIT TRUST MANAGEMENT LTD., 64 Coleman Street, London, E.C.2.—*Funds Managed*, £186,103; *Holdings*, 46.

*JANUS SECURITIES LTD., 117 Old Broad Street, London, E.C.2.—*Funds Managed*, £4,169,778; *Holdings*, 15,895.

*JASCOT SECURITIES LTD., 21 Young Street, Edinburgh.—*Funds Managed*, £1,052,032; *Holdings*, 1,486.

*JESSEL BRITANNIA GROUP LTD., 37-45 Tooley Street, London, S.E.1.—*Funds Managed*, £37,358,533; *Holdings*, 121,673.

*KEY FUND MANAGERS LTD., 1 Angel Court, London, E.C.2.—*Funds Managed*, £192,000; *Holdings*, 113.

L.S. FUND MANAGERS LTD., Canoe House, Monument Street, London, E.C.3.—*Funds Managed*, £290,000; *Holdings*, 125.

LLOYDS BANK UNIT TRUST MANAGERS LTD., 71 Lombard Street, London, E.C.3.—*Funds Managed*, £34,788,944; *Holdings*, 98,728.

*LONDON WALL GROUP OF UNIT TRUSTS LTD., 6 Angel Court, London, E.C.2.—*Funds Managed*, £17,504,115; *Holdings*, 43,000.

M. AND G. SECURITIES LTD., Lee House, London Wall, London, E.C.2.—*Funds Managed*, £122,269,773; *Holdings*, 109,176.

*MALLET AND WEDDERBURN UNIT TRUST MANAGERS LTD., 82 Lombard Street, London, E.C.3.— *Funds Managed*, £2,568,750; *Holdings*, 6,275.

*MINSTER FUND MANAGERS LTD., Minster House, Arthur Street, London, E.C.4.—*Funds Managed*, £653,617; *Holdings*, 173.

*MORGAN GRENFELL FUNDS (MANAGEMENT) LTD., 15 Christopher Street, London, E.C.2.—*Funds Managed*, £2,116,000; *Holdings*, 310.

*MUTUAL UNIT TRUST MANAGERS LIMITED, 4 Token House Buildings, Kings Arms Yard, London, E.C.2.—*Funds Managed*, £7,200,000; *Holdings*, 20,100.

N.E.L. TRUST MANAGERS LTD., Milton Court, Dorking, Surrey.—*Funds Managed*, £1,338,200; *Holdings*, 1,721.

THE NATIONAL GROUP OF UNIT TRUSTS, National Group House, 3/5 Norwich Street, Fetter Lane, London, E.C.4.—*Funds Managed*, £90,143,270; *Holdings*, 192,995.

NATIONAL PROVIDENT INVESTMENT MANAGERS LTD., 48 Gracechurch Street, London, E.C.3.—*Funds Managed*, £657,544; *Holdings*, n.a.

*OCEANIC-HODGE MANAGERS, 16 Finsbury Circus, London, E.C.2.—*Funds Managed*, £16,774,642; *Holdings*, 80,747.

*PEARL MONTAGU TRUST MANAGERS, LTD., 114 Old Broad Street, London, E.C.2.—*Funds Managed*, £854,100; *Holdings*, 3,690.

*PELICAN UNITS ADMINISTRATION LTD., 21 Spring Gardens, Manchester.—*Funds Managed*, £620,137; *Holdings*, 125.

PICCADILLY UNIT TRUST MANAGERS LTD., 1 Love Lane, London, EC2.—*Funds Managed*, £366,000; *Holdings*, 850.

PORTFOLIO FUND MANAGERS LTD., 31 Gresham Street, London, E.C.2.—*Funds Managed*, £350,000; *Holdings*, 433.

PRACTICAL INVESTMENT CO. LTD., London House, Crutched Friars, London, E.C.3.—*Funds Managed*, £25,715,745; *Holdings* 4,344.

PROVINCIAL LIFE INVESTMENT CO. LTD., 100 Cannon Street, London, E.C.4.—*Funds Managed*, £993,973; *Holdings*, 462.

PRUDENTIAL UNIT TRUST MANAGERS LTD., 142 Holborn Bars, London, E.C.1.—*Funds Managed*, £4,500,000; *Holdings*, 2,650.

ROTHSCHILD AND LOWNDES MANAGEMENT LTD., New Court, St. Swithin's Lane, London, E,C.4.—*Funds Managed*, £1,747,689; *Holdings*, 66.

*SAVE AND PROSPER GROUP LTD., 4 Great St. Helen's, London, E.C.3.—*Funds Managed*, £452,416,660; *Holdings*, 768,657.

J. HENRY SCHRODER WAGG AND CO. LTD., 120 Cheapside, London, E.C.2.—*Funds Managed*, £31,806,115; *Holdings*, 10,132.

SLATER WALKER TRUST MANAGEMENT LTD., 16 Coleman Street, London, E.C.2.—*Funds Managed*, £24,109,000; *Holdings*, 45,123.

SOUTHERN CROSS MANAGEMENT LTD., 65 London Wall, London, E.C.2.—*Funds Managed*, £11,500,000; *Holdings* 22,000.

*STRATTON TRUST MANAGERS LTD., 8 Bishopsgate, London, E.C.2.—*Funds Managed*, £1,443,224; *Holdings*, 456.

*SURINVEST FUND MANAGERS LTD., Berendsen House, 31/33 High Street, Carshalton, Surrey.—*Funds Managed*, £1,874,000; *Holdings*, 6,590.

*TARGET TRUST MANAGERS LTD., Bartlett House, 9 Basinghall Street, London, E.C.2.—*Funds Managed*, £36,530,000; *Holdings*, 91,562.

*TRADES UNION UNIT TRUST MANAGERS LTD. 100 Wood Street, London, E.C.2.—*Funds Managed*, £16,952,318; *Holdings*, 687.

TRUSTEES AND PROFESSIONAL FUNDS, 37/45 Tooley Street, London, S.E.1.—*Funds Managed*, £312,319; *Holdings*, 261.

*TRUSTEE SAVINGS BANKS UNIT TRUST MANAGERS LTD., 16 Coleman Street, London, E.C.2.—*Funds Managed*, £19,065,833; *Holdings*, 68,489.

TYNDALL MANAGERS LTD., 18 Canynge Road, Bristol, 8.—*Funds Managed*, £75,536,000; *Holdings*, 29,907.

TYNDALL ULSTER MANAGERS LTD., 140/142 Great Victoria Street, Belfast.—*Funds Managed*, £198,000; *Holdings*, 118.

*ULSTER HAMBRO TRUST MANAGERS LTD., P.O. Box 233, Waring Street, Belfast, Northern Ireland.—*Funds Managed*, £1,451,817; *Holdings*, 3,430.

*VAVASSEUR GROUP OF UNIT TRUSTS, 15/16 America Square, London, E.C.3.—*Funds Managed*, £16,440,767; *Holdings*, 70,491.

*WESTMINSTER HAMBRO TRUST MANAGERS LTD., 41 Bishopsgate, London, E.C.2.—*Funds Managed*, £33,016,480; *Holdings*, 71,830.

★ Members of the Association of Unit Trust Managers Limited.

BANKRUPTCIES

Large Failures.—In 570 cases of bankruptcy starting in 1970, estimated liabilities exceeded £40,000; in 35 of these cases the estimated liabilities were between £40,000 and £100,000 and in 22 between £100,000 and £500,000. In 1969 there were 19 cases where the estimated liabilities exceeded £40,000, the largest being £1,020,000.

In 1970 there were thirteen cases of arrangement with estimated liabilities over £40,000; of these, the liabilities in one case were about £134,000, in three others between £80,000 and £100,000 and in the remaining 9 up to £80,000.

Failures in some of the principal trades in 1970

were: Construction, 1,027 (*Liabilities*, £3,347.309; *Assets*, £1,133,313); (Non-food) Retailing, 548 (*Liabilities*, £1,950,332; *Assets*, £487,307); Food Retailing, 398 (*Liabilities*, £1,309,640; *Assets*, £248,939); Restaurants, cafes, etc., 268 (*Liabilities*, £824,915; *Assets*, £192,996); Directors and promoters of companies, 258 (*Liabilities*, £4,707,170; *Assets*, £1,280,892); Garages, motor dealers, etc., 216 (*Liabilities*, £1,123,501; *Assets*, £366,482); Farming, 200 (*Liabilities*, £1,655,167; *Assets*, £501,436); Employees, no occupation and unemployed, 760 (*Liabilities*, £1,005,588; *Assets*, £426,677).

Insolvency, 1962-1970

	Under the Bankruptcy Acts			Under Deeds of Arrangement Act		
Year	Number of Receiving Orders and Administration Orders	Liabilities as estimated by debtors	Assets as estimated by debtors	Number of Deeds	Liabilities as estimated by debtors	Assets as estimated by debtors
		£	£		£	£
1962	4,145	14,449,281	3,173,463	315	3,778,676	2,349,131
1963	3,968	13,145,890	2,687,696	235	1,352,908	654,113
1964	3,359	13,353,285	3,701,968	205	1,773,555	613,726
1965	3,404	17,711,865	4,046,856	198	1,463,370	669,025
1966	3,706	17,006,097	3,496,993	194	2,280,419	1,146,270
1967	4,029	19,600,242	4,705,192	160	1,946,747	1,012,834
1968	3,926	17,728,053	4,679,386	138	1,379,626	744,954
1969	4,369	19,308,485	6,689,211	212	2,874,731	1,522,397
1970	4,656	22,158,811	6,621,644	174	2,540,426	1,140,562

TELEVISION VIEWING IN THE UNITED KINGDOM

	February				August			
	1967	1968	1969	1970	1967	1968	1969	1970
Average weekly hours viewed by:								
Males aged 5–14	19·2	19·8	21·8	22·8	15·9	15·3	16·2	18·0
Females aged 5–14	17·6	19·1	20·6	21·3	14·8	14·3	14·7	15·9
Males aged 15 and over	14·5	15·8	16·0	16·9	11·9	10·7	12·2	13·3
Females aged 15 and over	17·0	18·4	19·2	20·0	13·1	12·1	13·9	14·0
Average weekly hours of viewing	16·2	17·6	18·2	13·4	13·4	12·1	13·5	14·2

Legal Notes

ADOPTION OF CHILDREN

In England and Wales the adoption of children is regulated mainly by the Adoption of Children Acts, 1926 to 1949, and the Adoption Act, 1958. An order of court is necessary to legalize the adoption. Adoption puts the child adopted practically on the same footing as a child born to the adopter in lawful wedlock, in all matters of custody, education and maintenance; further, it is provided by the Act of 1958 that an adopted child shall be treated as the child of the adopter (and not the child of its natural parents) for the purpose of the devolution of property on an intestacy occurring, or under any disposition made, after the date of the adoption order. Applications are made to the High Court (Chancery), County Court, or Magistrates Court. Orders will not usually be made for a man to be *sole* adopter of a girl, and the applicant must be either:—

(a) Twenty-five years of age or over; or

(b) Twenty-one years of age or over and a relative (as defined in the Act of 1958) of the infant; or

(c) the mother or father of the infant.

Two spouses may jointly adopt an infant, but unless one of them is the mother or father of the infant, condition (a) or (b) above must be satisfied in respect of one of the applicants and the other spouse must have attained the age of twenty-one.

Except in relation to an infant who is not a United Kingdom national (where special provisions apply), the consent of the child's parents or guardian is required before an adoption order will be made, but in certain circumstances (e.g., where the parent or guardian has ill-treated or neglected the child) the Court may dispense with this consent. Since the 1949 Act, marriage between the adopter and the adoptee is prohibited, but marriages of that kind, solemnized before the passing of the Act, are not thereby invalidated.

The 1958 Act places restrictions on societies which make arrangements for the adoption of children.

The Adoption Act, 1964, provides for effect to be given to adoption orders made in Northern Ireland, the Isle of Man and the Channel Islands.

The Adoption Act 1968 (which applies to Scotland) enables an adoption order to be made on the application of a person who is either habitually resident in Great Britain or possesses British nationality. The Act also provides for the recognition of certain overseas adoptions.

Scotland.—The Adoption of Children (Scotland) Acts, 1930 to 1949, and the Adoption Act, 1958, cover the law relating to the adoption of children in Scotland, where an Adopted Children Register is maintained. Applications are made to the Court of Session, or the Sheriff Court within whose jurisdiction either the applicant or the child resides at the date of application. The Adoption Act, 1958, which is a consolidating Act, also applies, with modifications, to Scotland, and reference is also made to the Adoption Act, 1960 which amends the law with respect to revocation of adoption orders and to the Adoption Act, 1968 (*see* above). The Succession (Scotland) Act, 1964, gives the adopted child the same rights of succession as a child born to the adopter in wedlock, but deprives him of any such rights in the estates of his natural parents.

All adoptions in Great Britain are registered in the Registers of Adopted Children kept by the Registrars General in London and Edinburgh respectively. Certificates from these registers including short certificates which contain no reference to adoptions, can be obtained on conditions similar to those relating to birth certificates. (See below.)

BIRTHS (REGISTRATION)

When a birth takes place, personal information of it must be given to the Registrar of Births and Deaths for the sub-district in which the birth occurred, and the register signed in his presence, by one of the following persons:—

1. The father or mother of the child. If they fail; 2. the occupier of the house in which the birth happened; 3. a person present at the birth; or, 4. the person having charge of the child. The duty of attending to the registration therefore rests firstly on the parents. The mother is responsible for the registration of the birth of an illegitimate child. The registration is required to be made within 42 days of the birth. Failure to do this, without reasonable cause, involves liability to a penalty of twenty pounds. The registration of a birth is free. In England or Wales, the informant, instead of attending before the registrar of the sub-district where the birth occurred, may make a declaration of the particulars required to be registered in the presence of any registrar. Under the Public Health Act, 1936, notice of every birth must be given by the father, or person in attendance on the mother, to the district medical officer of health by post within 36 hours of the birth. *This is in addition to the registration already mentioned.*

A "Stillbirth" must be registered and a certificate signed by the doctor or midwife who was present at the birth or has examined the body of the child must be produced to the registrar. The certificate must, where possible, state the cause of death and the estimated duration of the pregnancy.

The re-registration of the birth of a person legitimated by the subsequent marriage of the parents is provided for in the Births and Deaths Registration Act, 1953.

Birth at Sea : The master of a British ship must record any birth on board and send particulars to the Registrar General of Shipping.

Birth Abroad : Consular Officers are authorized to register births of British subjects occurring abroad. Certificates are procurable in due course at Registrar General's Office, London.

The registration of births occurring out of the United Kingdom among members of the armed forces, or occurring on board H.M. ships and aircraft, is provided for by the Registration of Births, Deaths and Marriages (Special Provisions) Act, 1957, applicable also to Scotland.

SCOTLAND

New provisions are included in the Registration of Births, Deaths and Marriages (Scotland) Act, 1965, which amends and re-enacts provisions in former Acts. Personal notification within 21 days of any birth, must be given to the registrar of (a) the registration district in which the birth took place, or (b) any registration district in which the mother of the child was ordinarily resident at the time of the birth and (c) in the case of a foundling child, dead or alive, when the place of birth is not known, the registration district in which the child, or the body was found. When a child is born (in or out of Scotland) in a ship, aircraft or land vehicle during a journey and the child is conveyed therein to any place in Scotland, the birth shall, unless the Regis-

trar General otherwise directs, be deemed to have occurred at that place.

The register must be signed in the presence of the registrar by the father or mother of the child, and if they fail, by one of the following: (a) any relative of either parent who has knowledge of the birth; (b) the occupier of the premises in which the child was, to the knowledge of that occupier, born; (c) any person present at the birth; (d) any person having charge of the child. Failure without reasonable cause involves a penalty not exceeding £20.

The name of the father of an illegitimate child may be entered in the register of births at the time of registration if jointly requested by the mother and father, and the latter's name may also be recorded at a later date on declarations by both parents. A free abbreviated certificate of birth will be issued to the informant at the time of registration. Provision is made for the re-registration of the birth of a person made legitimate by the subsequent marriage of the parents or whose birth entry is affected by any matter respecting status or paternity, or has been so made as to imply that he is a foundling.

A still-birth must be registered and a certificate, signed by the doctor or certified midwife present at the birth or who has examined the body of the child, must be produced.

CERTIFICATES
OF BIRTHS, MARRIAGES, OR DEATHS

England and Wales.—Certificates of Births, Deaths, or Marriages can be obtained at the General Register Office, Somerset House or from the Superintendent Registrar having the legal custody of the register containing the entry of which a certificate is required on payment of fees amounting to 40p.(When application is made by post [Somerset House only] the charges are 65p). Certificates of marriages can also be obtained from the incumbent of the church in which the marriage took place; or from the Nonconformist minister (or other "authorized person") where the marriage takes place in a registered building (*see post* under Marriage).

Certificates at reduced rates can be obtained for the purposes of certain Acts of Parliament, and under Births and Deaths Registration Act, 1953, a modified form of birth certificate, showing the names, sex and date of birth and certain other particulars, but not the parentage, may be obtained from the Registrar General, or the appropriate Superintendent Registrar or Registrar, on payment of a fee of 15p and on furnishing certain particulars.

English Registers.—Records of births, deaths and marriages registered in England and Wales since 1837 are kept at the General Register Office, Somerset House, W.C.2. The Society of Genealogists 37 Harrington Gardens, S.W.7, possess many records of Baptisms, Marriages and Deaths prior to 1837, including copies, in whole or in part of about 4,000 Parish Registers.

Scottish Registers of Births, Deaths and Marriages.—Certificates of births, deaths or marriages registered from 1855 when compulsory registration commenced in Scotland can be obtained personally at the General Register Office, New Register House, Edinburgh, or from the appropriate local Registrar, on payment of the fee of 50p for a full extract entry of birth, death, or marriage, and 20p for a short certificate of birth. When the period searched is over 20 years additional fees are payable. A short certificate of registration of deaths is issued free of charge for National Insurance purposes in certain cases.

There are also available at the General Register Office old parish registers of date prior to 1855,

which were formerly kept under the administration of the Established Church of Scotland. An extract of an entry in these registers may be obtained at the fee of 50p. A fee of £1 per day is payable for a general search of all the Scottish registers.

BRITISH NATIONALITY AND CITIZENSHIP OF THE UNITED KINGDOM AND COLONIES

General.—The law as to British Nationality is now to be found mainly in the British Nationality Act 1948, which came into force on Jan. 1, 1949. The Act introduces a new term, "citizenship." Every person who under the Act is a citizen of the United Kingdom and Colonies, or any citizen (by virtue of legislation in that country) of Canada, Australia, New Zealand, India, Pakistan, Southern Rhodesia, Ceylon, Ghana, Malaysia, Cyprus, Nigeria, Sierra Leone, Tanzania, Jamaica, Trinidad and Tobago, Uganda, Kenya, Malawi, Zambia, Malta, Gambia, Guyana, Botswana, Lesotho, Singapore, Barbados, Mauritius, Swaziland, Tonga, and Fiji (hereafter referred to as "the Dominions") has by virtue of that citizenship the status of a British subject and may be known either as a British subject or as a Commonwealth citizen. Under s. 2 of the Newfoundland (Consequential Provisions) Act 1950, potential citizens of Newfoundland under the British Nationality Act 1948, are deemed to have been potential citizens of Canada.

Nationality before Jan. 1, 1949, was determined mainly by the British Nationality and Status of Aliens Acts 1914–1943, though these Acts did not affect the status of any person born *before* Jan. 1, 1915.

Retention of nationality by persons born in or who are citizens of Eire (now by virtue of the Ireland Act 1949, styled the Republic of Ireland).

By the Ireland Act 1949, a person who was born before Dec. 6, 1922, in what is now the Republic of Ireland (Eire) and was a British subject immediately before Jan. 1, 1949, is not deemed to have ceased to be a British subject unless either (i) he was domiciled in the Irish Free State on Dec. 6, 1922, or (ii) was on or after April 10, 1935, and before Jan. 1, 1949, permanently resident there, or (iii) had before Jan. 1, 1949, been registered as a citizen of Eire under the laws of that country.

In addition, by the British Nationality Act 1948, any citizen of Eire who immediately before Jan. 1, 1949, was also a British subject can retain that status by submitting at any time a claim to the Home Secretary on any of the following grounds: (a) he has been in the service of the United Kingdom government; (b) he holds a British passport issued in the United Kingdom or in any colony, protectorate, United Kingdom mandated or trust territory; (c) he has associations by way of descent, residence or otherwise with any such place; or on complying with similar legislation in any of the "Dominions."

Citizenship of the United Kingdom and Colonies

In the majority of cases, a person who is a British subject becomes also a "citizen," either of one of the "Dominions" by virtue of legislation in that country, or of the United Kingdom and Colonies under the 1948 Act. In the latter case, citizenship is acquired by:—

1. *Birth* on or after Jan. 1, 1949, in the United Kingdom and Colonies (which term does not include the "Dominions"), except

    (a) children born to non-citizen fathers enjoying diplomatic immunity from suit or legal process;

(b) children born to fathers who are enemy aliens in enemy occupied territory.

2. *Descent*, if the father was a citizen by *birth*. If the father was a citizen by *descent* only, the child acquires citizenship by descent if either:—

(a) the child is or his father was born in a protectorate, protected state, mandated territory or trust territory, or in a foreign country where Her Majesty then had jurisdiction over British subjects; or

(b) the birth (occurring elsewhere than (a)) is registered at a United Kingdom consulate within one year; or

(c) the father is at the time of birth in the service of the Crown under Her Majesty's United Kingdom government; or

(d) the child is born in one of the "Dominions" in which a citizenship law has then taken effect and does not become a citizen thereof by birth.

3. *Registration* by the Home Secretary upon application by:—

(a) a citizen of one of the "Dominions" or of the Republic of Ireland who can show that he has been (a) ordinarily resident in the United Kingdom; or (b) in Crown service under Her Majesty's Government in the United Kingdom; or (c) partly the one and partly the other throughout the period of five years ending with the date of his application, or such shorter period so ending as the Home Secretary may in the special circumstances of any particular case accept; or, in certain circumstances, if he is serving under an international organization of which the United Kingdom government is a member, or is in the employment of a body established in the United Kingdom;

(b) a woman married to a United Kingdom, etc. citizen. If she is a British protected person or an alien she must take an oath of allegiance. (A woman who marries on or after Jan. 1, 1949, does not by virtue of that marriage acquire citizenship.)

A minor child of a citizen can be registered upon application being made by his parent or guardian

A person in respect of whom a recommendation for deportation or a deportation order is in force under the Commonwealth Immigrants Act 1962, is not entitled to be registered, although the Home Secretary may register such a person.

4. *Naturalization.*—In order to be eligible for a certificate of naturalization an alien must:—

(a) during the eight years preceding his application have resided for not less than five years (of which not less than one year immediately preceding the application *must* have been spent in the United Kingdom) in the United Kingdom or in any colony, protectorate, United Kingdom mandated or trust territory, or have been for five years in the service of the Crown; and

(b) be of good character and have a sufficient knowledge of the English language; and

(c) intend to reside in the United Kingdom or any colony, etc., or to enter or continue in the service of the Crown or in the service of certain organizations.

A British protected person who satisfies (b) and (c) above can apply for naturalization if he can show that he has been (a) ordinarily resident in the United Kingdom; or (b) in Crown service under Her Majesty's Government in the United Kingdom; or (c) partly the one and partly the other throughout the period of five years ending with the date of

his application, or such shorter period as the Home Secretary may in a particular case accept.

Instructions for the guidance of persons desiring to apply for a Certificate of Naturalization are supplied with the form of application which may be obtained from H.M. Stationery Office.

5. *Incorporation of Territory* when citizenship is granted to such persons as are specified by Order in Council.

6. *Transitional provisions*, which confer citizenship on a person who was a British subject immediately before Jan. 1, 1949, if either:—

(i) (a) he would, if born after that date, have qualified for citizenship by birth; or

(b) he is a person naturalized in the United Kingdom and Colonies; or

(c) he became a British subject by reason of annexation of territory which on Jan. 1, 1949, was included in the United Kingdom and Colonies; or

(ii) at the time of his birth his father was a British subject and possessed any of the above qualifications; or

(iii) he was born within territory comprised on Jan. 1, 1949, in a protectorate, protected state or United Kingdom trust territory; or

(iv) he was not on that date a citizen or potential citizen of one of the "Dominions"; or

(v) being a woman, had before Jan. 1, 1949, been married to a man who becomes, or would but for his death have become, a citizen.

A British subject who is merely a potential citizen of one of the "Dominions" continues as a British subject without citizenship until he becomes a citizen of such "Dominion" or of the Republic of Ireland, or an alien. If none of these has happened at the date when a citizenship law is passed in the country of which he is potentially a citizen, he becomes a citizen by descent of the United Kingdom and Colonies.

A woman who lost British nationality by reason of marriage to an alien regained it on Jan. 1, 1949.

By the Adoption Act 1958 an adopted child becomes a citizen of the United Kingdom and Colonies as from the date of the adoption order if the adopter or, in the case of a joint adoption, the male adopter, is a citizen of the United Kingdom and Colonies.

Citizenship of the United Kingdom and Colonies can be lost —

(i) by declaration in the prescribed manner by a person who is also a citizen of a "Dominion" or of the Republic of Ireland or a national of a foreign country. The Home Secretary can withhold registration of the declaration in time of war. Under the British Nationality Act 1964 a person who has ceased to be a citizen of the United Kingdom and Colonies as a result of a declaration of renunciation is entitled to registration as a citizen of the United Kingdom and Colonies if he can satisfy the Home Secretary on a number of matters;

(ii) where the Home Secretary is satisfied that citizenship by registration or naturalization was obtained by fraud, false representation, etc.;

(iii) by the Home Secretary depriving a *naturalized* person of citizenship if such person has:—

(a) shown himself by act or speech to be disloyal or disaffected towards Her Majesty; or

(b) in time of war, traded with the enemy; or

(c) within five years after becoming naturalized, been sentenced in any country to a term of twelve months' imprisonment; or

(d) continuously resided in foreign countries for seven years, and during that period has neither at any time been in the service of the Crown or of certain international organizations, nor registered annually at a United Kingdom consulate his intention to retain citizenship;

and the Home Secretary is satisfied that it is not conducive to the public good that such person should retain his citizenship;

(iv) where a naturalized person is deprived of citizenship of a " Dominion " or of the Republic of Ireland, the Home Secretary can also deprive him of citizenship of the United Kingdom and Colonies.

(v) Under a series of Acts, 1958-1968, which contain special provisions relating to Ghana, Cyprus, Nigeria, Sierra Leone, Tanzania, Jamaica, Trinidad and Tobago, Uganda, Malaysia, Kenya, Malawi, Zambia, Malta, Gambia, Guyana, Botswana, Lesotho, Barbados, Aden, Perim and Kuria Muria Islands, Mauritius, Swaziland and Fiji.

STATUS OF ALIENS.—Property may be held by an alien in the same manner as by a natural-born British subject, but he may not hold public office, exercise the franchise or own a British ship or aircraft. The Republic of Ireland Act 1949 declares that the Republic, though not part of H.M. Dominions, is not a foreign country, and any reference to an Act of Parliament to foreigners, aliens, foreign countries, etc., shall be construed accordingly.

CROWN—PROCEEDINGS AGAINST

Before 1947 proceedings against the Crown were generally possible only by a procedure known as a petition of right, which placed the litigant at a considerable disadvantage and which was not normally available at all in cases of tort (i.e., civil wrongs other than breach of contract). Thus, no proceedings would normally lie against the Government if a subject were injured by the negligent driving of a Government vehicle (although the driver could be sued) or if a Government employee were injured by the defective condition of the Crown premises on which he worked. Now, however, by the Crown Proceedings Act 1947, which came into operation on Jan. 1, 1948, the Crown, in its public capacity, is largely placed in the same position as a subject, although some procedural disadvantages remain. Exceptions to the Act include the immunity of the Crown and any member of the armed forces from liability in tort in respect of death of, or personal injury to, another member of the armed forces on duty, provided that the death or injury is attributable to service for purposes of pension.

Scotland.—The Act extends to Scotland and has the effect of bringing the practice of the two countries as closely together as the different legal systems will permit. While formerly actions against the Crown, when permissible, were confined to the Court of Session, proceedings may now be brought in the Sheriff Court.

The Act lays down that arrestment of money in the hands of the Crown or of a Government Department is competent in any case where arrestment in the hands of a subject would have been competent, but an exception is made in respect of National Savings Bank deposits. Section 2 (1) of the Law Reform (Miscellaneous Provisions) (Scotland) Act 1966 removes the privilege whereby the wages of Crown servants, other than serving members of the armed forces, are exempt from assessment in execution.

DEATHS, BURIAL AND CREMATION
DEATHS
(For Certificates, *see* under BIRTHS)

In England and Wales.—When a death takes place, personal information of it must be given to the local Registrar of Births and Deaths, and the register signed in his presence, by one of the following persons: (1) A relative of the deceased present at the death, or in attendance during the last illness. If they fail (2) some other relative of the deceased. In default of any relatives (3) a person present at the death; or, the occupier of the house in which the death happened. If all the above-named fail (4) an inmate of the house, or the person causing the disposal of the body. Relatives present or in attendance are first required to attend to the registration. The registration must be made within five days of the death, or within the same time when notice of the death sent to the Registrar. If the deceased was attended during his last illness by a registered medical practitioner, a certificate of cause of death must be sent by the doctor to the Registrar. The doctor must give to the informant of the death a written notice of the signing of the certificate, which must be delivered to the Registrar. It is essential that a certificate for disposal should be obtained from the Registrar before the funeral and delivered to the clergyman or other person in charge of the churchyard or cemetery. No fee is chargeable for this certificate. If the death is not registered within five days (or fourteen days if written notice of the occurrence of the death is sent to him) the Registrar may require any one of the above-mentioned persons, to attend to register at a stated time and place. Failure to comply involves a penalty of ten pounds. The registration of a death is free of charge. After twelve months no death can be registered without the Registrar General's consent.

A body must not be disposed of until (1) either the Registrar has given a certificate to the effect that he has registered or received notice of the death, or (2) until the Coroner has made a disposal order (*Births and Deaths Registration Act 1926*, s.1).

A person disposing of a body must within ninety-six hours deliver to the Registrar a notification as to the date, place, and means of the disposal of the body (*ib.*, s. 3).

" Still-born " child (*see* under Births (Registration), p. 1161).

Death at Sea.—The master of a British ship must record any death on board and send particulars to the Registrar General of Shipping.

Death Abroad.—Consular Officers are authorized to register deaths of British subjects occurring abroad. Certificates are procurable at the Registrar General's Office, London. If the deceased was of *Scottish* domicile, particulars are sent to the Registrar General for Scotland.

With regard to the registration of deaths of members of the armed forces, and deaths occurring on H.M. ships and aircraft, *see* the Registration of Births, etc. Act 1957.

Deaths (Registration) in Scotland.—New provisions are included in the Registration of Births, Deaths and Marriages (Scotland) Act 1965 which amends and re-enacts provisions in former Acts.

Personal notification within 8 days must be given to the registrar of (a) the registration district

in which the death took place or (b) any registration district in which the deceased was ordinarily resident immediately before his death, and (c) when a body is found and the place of death is not known, either the registration district in which the body was found or any other registration district appropriate by virtue of the preceding paragraph. When a person dies (in or out of Scotland) in a ship, aircraft or land vehicle during a journey and the body is conveyed therein to any place in Scotland the death shall, unless the Registrar General otherwise directs, be deemed to have occurred at that place.

The register must be signed in the presence of the registrar by one of the following: (a) any relative of the deceased; (b) any person present at the death; (c) the deceased's executor or other legal representative; (d) the occupier, at the time of the death, of the premises where the death took place; (e) if these fail, any other person having knowledge of the particulars to be registered. Failure to comply involves a penalty not exceeding £20.

The medical practitioner who attended the deceased during his last illness must sign a certificate of the cause of death. If there is no such medical practitioner, any medical practitioner who is able to do so, may sign the certificate. At the time of registering the death the registrar shall, without charge, give the informant a certificate of registration, and the person to whom the certificate is given must hand it to the undertaker previous to interment or cremation.

BURIAL

The duty of burial is incumbent on the deceased person's Executors (if any appointed); it is also a recognized obligation of the husband of a woman, and the parent of a child, also of a householder where the body lies. Funeral expenses of a reasonable amount will be repayable out of deceased's estate in priority to any other claims. Directions as to place and mode of burial are frequently contained in the deceased's will or in some memorandum placed with private papers, or may have been communicated verbally to a relative. Consequently steps should immediately be taken to ascertain the deceased's wishes from the above sources. If the wishes are considered objectionable, they are not necessarily enforceable: legal advice should be taken. A person may legally leave directions for the anatomical examination of his body. As to the place of burial—unless closed by Order in Council—the parish churchyard is the normal burying place for parishioners, or any person dying in the Parish, but nowadays this will apply only in villages and the smaller towns. In populous districts cemeteries and crematoria have been established either by the local council or a private company, and burials will take place there in accordance with the regulations. For an exclusive right to a burial space in the churchyard a faculty is required from the Ecclesiastical Court. Poor persons may be buried at the public expense by the local authority. As to the necessity for obtaining a registrar's certificate or authority from the Coroner for disposal, *see* above

CREMATION

Under the Cremation Acts, 1902 and 1952, regulations are made by the Home Secretary dealing fully with the cremation of a body, disposal of ashes, etc., and containing numerous essential safeguards. If Cremation is desired it is advisable for instructions to be left in writing to that effect.

To arrange for Cremation the Executor or near relative should instruct the undertaker to that effect and obtain from him the Statutory Forms required as given in the Cremation Regulations issued in 1930 (Statutory Rules and Orders, 1930, No. 1016),

as amended by the Cremation Regulations 1965 (No 1146).

DIVORCE, ETC.

Preliminary.—Matrimonial Suits may be conveniently divided into two classes, viz. (1) those in which a declaration that there has never been a marriage is sought; and (2) those in which, the marriage being admitted, it is sought to end the marriage or the duties arising from it. By virtue of the Matrimonial Causes Act, 1967, all matrimonial causes are now commenced in one of the divorce county courts designated by the Lord Chancellor. If they remain undefended, they are tried by a county court judge in one of these courts which has also been designated as a court of trial, or in the Royal Courts of Justice in London. If the suit becomes defended, it must be transferred to the High Court.

(1) *Nullity of Marriage.*—Marriage is void *ab initio* if the parties were in the prohibited degrees of affinity, if it was bigamous, if there was no sufficient consent on the part of one or both of the parties, if one of the parties was insane, or if one of the parties was under the age of consent, *i.e.,* 16 —Marriage Act, 1949. Where the *formalities* of the marriage were defective, the marriage is generally void if *both* parties knew of the defect (*e.g.,* where marriage took place otherwise than in an authorized building). But absence of the consent of parents or guardians (or of the Court or other authority, in lieu thereof) in the case of minors does not invalidate the marriage. Inability to consummate a marriage may also be a ground for a nullity decree; but in this case, the marriage is only voidable and remains valid until the decree is made.

Under the Matrimonial Causes Act, 1965, which in this context has no application to Scotland, a marriage is also voidable (*i.e.,* a decree of nullity may be obtained) on the following grounds—(a) respondent's wilful refusal to consummate the marriage; (b) that either party at the time of marriage was a mentally disordered person or subject to recurrent attacks of insanity or epilepsy; (c) that at the time of marriage the respondent was suffering from communicable venereal disease; (d) that at the time of the marriage the respondent was pregnant by another man. In cases, (b), (c) and (d), the petitioner must have been ignorant of the grounds at the date of the marriage and must not have agreed to intercourse taking place since his discovering the grounds, and proceedings must be instituted within a year of the marriage.

By the Matrimonial Causes Act, 1965, and, as to Scotland, by the Law Reform (Miscellaneous Provisions) Act, 1949, it is provided that a decree of nullity in respect of a voidable marriage shall not operate so as to bastardize any child, who would have been the legitimate child of the parties to the marriage if the marriage had been dissolved instead of annulled. Further, even if a marriage is void, a child of such a union can sometimes be treated as legitimate if at the time of conception or of the marriage (if later) either or both of the parties reasonably believed that the marriage was valid (Legitimacy Act, 1959).

A spouse's insistence upon the use of contraceptives will not constitute wilful refusal to consummate within (a) above, even though there has been no normal intercourse, but it may in certain circumstances constitute unreasonable behaviour for the purposes of divorce (as to which *see* below). Further it has been allowed as a *defence* to a charge of desertion against the aggrieved party.

In one High Court case the judge held that a husband's insistence on the practice of *coitus interruptus* amounted to wilful refusal to consummate

the marriage, where there had been no other inter-course. In other High Court cases the judges have disagreed with this view, but held that, in the circumstances of the particular cases, a divorce could be granted on the ground of legal cruelty.

(2) *Judicial Separation and Divorce.*—The second class of suit includes a suit for judicial separation (which does not dissolve a marriage) and a suit for divorce (which, if successful, dissolves the marri-age altogether and leaves the parties at liberty to marry again). Either spouse may petition for judi-cial separation on the same ground as for divorce.

Divorce.—With effect from January 1, 1971, the sole ground on which a divorce is obtainable by either husband or wife is the irretrievable break-down of the marriage. However, the court is pre-cluded from holding that a marriage has irretriev-ably broken down unless it is satisfied of one or more of the following facts: (a) that the respondent has committed adultery since the marriage and the petitioner finds it intolerable to live with the re-spondent; (b) such behaviour by the respondent that the petitioner cannot reasonably be expected to continue co-habitation; (c) desertion by the re-spondent for 2 years immediately before the peti-tion; (d) 5 years separation immediately before the petition (but only 2 years where the respondent consents to the decree). Divorce Reform Act 1969.

The foregoing is subject to a clause prohibiting any petition for divorce (but not for judicial separation) before the lapse of three years from the date of marriage, except in the case of ex-ceptional hardship (upon petitioner) or of excep-tional depravity of respondent.

Desertion may be defined as a voluntary with-drawal from cohabitation by one spouse without just cause and against the wishes of the other. Where one spouse is guilty of conduct of a serious nature which forces the other to leave, the party at fault is said to be guilty of constructive desertion.

Provisions designed to encourage reconciliation.—The 1969 Act envisages that before proceedings are commenced, the petitioner shall have discussed with his or her solicitor the possibility of a recon-ciliation, and been informed of available marriage guidance services.

A total period of less than six months during which the parties have resumed living together is to be disregarded in determining whether the pre-scribed period of desertion or separation has been continuous. Similar provision for effecting a recon-ciliation exists in relation to the other proofs of break-down, but a petitioner cannot claim that it is intolerable to live with the other party if they have lived together for more than six months after dis-covery of the respondent's adultery.

Intervention by Queen's Proctor.—At any time during the progress of a suit, and before the decree *nisi* is made absolute, the Queen's Proctor may intervene.

Decree Absolute.—Every decree of dissolution or nullity is in the first instance a decree *nisi*. The marriage subsists until the decree is made absolute, usually three months after decree *nisi*. After that date either spouse may marry again; but as to marriage within " Prohibited Degrees " *see* Marriage—Miscellaneous Notes, p. 1176. Under the Matrimonial Proceedings and Property Act, 1970, a decree *nisi* cannot normally be made absolute until the court is satisfied that arrange-ments have been made for the welfare of every child of the family who has not attained the age of sixteen which are satisfactory or the best which can be devised in the circumstances or that it is impracticable for the parties before the court to make any such arrangements.

Maintenance, etc.—The court has wide powers to order either party to the marriage to make financial provision (e.g. periodical payments, a lump sum, the transfer of property) for the other party or any child of the family, having regard to the party's means, the recipient's needs and all the important aspects of the case. The husband can be ordered to pay his wife's costs, even if she is unsuccessful in her suit or defence. A guilty co-respondent may be ordered to pay costs.

The court may, where the husband has wilfully neglected to provide reasonable maintenance for the wife or children, order the husband to make pro-vision for them, *even though* no matrimonial suit is pending between the parties to the marriage, and while such an order is in force the court may also deal with custody of and access to the children.

CUSTODY OF CHILDREN

In suits for nullity, divorce or judicial separation, whether the suit succeeds or is dismissed, the court can make orders as to the custody of and access to the children and as to their upkeep and education, and these orders can be made not only in respect of children of the marriage but also in respect of a child of one party who has been accepted as one of the family by the other party. Either spouse may be awarded custody, the paramount consideration being always the welfare of the child.

A spouse who has been deprived of the custody of a child will not thereby be deprived of his other rights as the child's *guardian* unless the court expressly so orders.

SEPARATION BY AGREEMENT

Husband and wife may agree, with or without consideration, to separate and live apart, but the agreement, to be valid, must be followed by an immediate separation. It is most desirable to consult a solicitor in every such case.

MAGISTRATES' SEPARATION AND MAINTENANCE ORDERS

When a husband has been guilty of adultery or has been convicted of certain assaults or has deserted his wife, or has been guilty of persistent cruelty to her or to an infant child of the family, or of wilful neglect to maintain her or such a child, or where he is an habitual drunkard or drug addict, or insists on having intercourse while suffering from a venereal disease, or compels her to submit herself to prostitu-tion, the wife may obtain relief from the local magis-trates' court. A husband may apply on similar grounds, so far as they are applicable to him. In particular a wife can sometimes be guilty of the offence of wilful neglect to provide reasonable maintenance for her husband or children and an order can be made against her. The court may declare that the complainant is no longer bound to cohabit with the defendant. It may order the hus-band to pay a weekly sum in its discretion to the wife and may order her to make a similar payment to him if his earning capacity is impaired by age or illness. Provision may be made for legal custody of and access to any child of the family who is under the age of 16 years and for payment by either or both of the spouses of a weekly sum to the person entrusted with legal custody in respect of each child of the family up to the age of 16. If the court thinks the child would still be a dependant although over that age, similar payments may be ordered for sup-port of the child up to the age of 21. The court cannot make an order that the parties need no longer cohabit or that either spouse shall support the other where the complainant has committed adultery during the marriage, unless the defendant has con-doned or connived at, or by wilful neglect or misconduct conduced to, that act of adultery. The court has wide powers of revocation, revival and

variation of orders already made. The order must be revoked if the parties have resumed cohabitation, and must be revoked, except so far as the order relates to the children, if the complainant is subsequently proved to have committed adultery since the marriage and the defendant has not condoned or connived at or by wilful neglect or misconduct conduced to that act of adultery. Complaints based on desertion or failure to maintain can be made whilst the offence continues. Complaints based on adultery must usually be made within 6 months of the complainant discovering it, all other complaints within 6 months of the offence itself. The Magistrates' Courts Act, 1952, separates the hearing of matrimonial disputes from ordinary court business; specifies the persons allowed to be present; limits newspaper reports, etc., etc.

SCOTLAND
DIVORCE

Proceedings are brought in the Court of Session and it is necessary that the husband be domiciled in Scotland, or, he not being domiciled in the United Kingdom or in the Channel Islands or the Isle of Man, that the wife is resident in Scotland and has been ordinarily resident there for a period of three years immediately preceding commencement of proceedings.

The following are grounds for divorce:—

1. *Adultery.*—A mere confession by the defender is of itself insufficient; there must be proof of the facts. Direct evidence is not required, if facts can be established which give rise to an inevitable inference of adultery. There must be no collusion between the parties, and the pursuer is required to swear to this. It is not collusion, however, for a guilty spouse to give information of an act of adultery already committed. It is a defence to an action of divorce for adultery to plead that the innocent spouse has condoned the misconduct on which the action is founded, but the adultery shall not be held to have been condoned if cohabitation was continued or resumed with a view to effecting a reconciliation, for any one period not exceeding three months; Divorce (Scotland) Act, 1964.

2. *Desertion.*—The defender must have wilfully and without reasonable cause deserted the pursuer and persisted in such desertion for a period of not less than three years, but in calculating the period no account is taken of any one period not exceeding three months during which the parties resumed cohabitation with a view to reconciliation. It must be shown that the desertion was without reasonable cause, and it is a defence to an action on this ground that during that period the pursuer has refused a genuine and reasonable offer by the defender to adhere; Divorce (Scotland) Act, 1964. Refusal by one spouse to have marital relations with the other for any period of three years without any overt act of desertion does not constitute desertion. Here also, collusion is fatal to the success of the action.

3. *Incurable Insanity.*—The defender must, for five years preceding the raising of the action, have been under care and treatment as an insane person.

4. *Cruelty.*—The degree of cruelty to be established depends on the circumstances of each individual case, but the test, generally speaking, is that the conduct complained of must be such as to endanger the health of the pursuer. Cruelty may take the form of habitual drunkenness on the part of one of the spouses. The fraudulent activity of one spouse involving the other may amount to cruelty. There must be no condonation but, as in the case of an action on the ground of adultery, the Divorce (Scotland) Act, 1964 provides a reconciliation period not exceeding three months.

5. *Unnatural Sexual Offences.*—An extract of the criminal conviction is sufficient proof.

Maintenance etc. Under the Succession (Scotland) Act, 1964, legal rights are not exigible on divorce as was formerly the case. The Act gives the Court power to order the guilty spouse to pay either a capital sum or a periodic allowance or both. The latter may be varied by the Court where there is a change in the circumstances of either party after the divorce.

A husband, being liable for his wife's debts, may be ordered to pay her costs, even though he has successfully defended the action. A guilty co-respondent, if named as a defender, may be required to pay costs and damages.

Nullity of Marriage.—A declaration of nullity of marriage may be obtained on the ground of any impediment, viz., consanguinity and affinity, subsistence of a previous marriage, non-age of one of the parties, incapacity or insanity of one of the parties, or by the absence of genuine consent.

SEPARATION

A decree of judicial separation may be obtained by one spouse against the other on the grounds of (a) adultery, (b) cruelty. This entitles the parties to live apart, but does not dissolve the marriage. The husband, if the guilty party, is liable for aliment.

CUSTODY OF CHILDREN

In actions for divorce and separation, the Court has a discretion in awarding the custody of the children of the parties. The welfare of the children is the paramount consideration, and the mere fact that a spouse is the guilty party in the action does not of itself deprive him or her of the right to claim custody, though where the considerations of welfare are equally balanced the Court will have regard to the element of guilt.

HIRE-PURCHASE
ENGLAND AND WALES

Protection of the hirer against unscrupulous dealings and against delivery of shoddy goods is given by the Hire-Purchase Act, 1965, which applies to hire-purchase agreements under which the hire-purchase price, *i.e.*, the total sum payable by the hirer to complete the purchase of the goods, does not exceed £2,000. The Act also provides that where the hirer is a body corporate, the Act is not to apply at all.

Before any agreement is made, the owner of the goods must state in writing to the hirer the cash price at which the goods can be purchased, and the agreement must be in writing signed by the hirer himself and by or on behalf of the owner and any guarantor. The agreement must contain (i) the cash price, (ii) the hire-purchase price, (iii) the amount of each instalment, (iv) when each instalment falls due, (v) a list of the goods, and (vi) a notice informing the hirer of his right to terminate the agreement (*below*), and of the restrictions on the owner's right to recover the goods (*below*). If the agreement is complete as soon as the hirer signs it he must be given a copy there and then; in all other cases he must be given one copy when he signs and another within seven days of the completion of the agreement. There are also Board of Trade regulations dealing with such matters as the size of the print. In breach of any of these conditions the owner can neither recover the goods from the hirer nor enforce the agreement or any security given, although the Court can dispense with any of the conditions save that as to the signed agreement. The same result ensues (while default continues) if the owner fails without reasonable cause within four days after written request (with a tender of 12½ p. for expenses) to supply to the hirer a copy of the agreement and a statement of amounts paid, in

arrear, and not yet payable. Before the last instalment becomes due, the hirer may by writing determine the agreement, and, although he remains liable for any instalments already due, he will be under no further obligation *under the agreement*. Under the Act, however, he must allow the owner to retake the goods and, if one-half of the hire-purchase price exceeds the total of the sums paid and due he must pay the difference to the owner unless the court considers that a lesser sum is sufficient to compensate the owner. These rights of the hirer cannot be taken away from him, but he can enforce more favourable rights (if any) under the agreement.

An important new provision in the Act gives the hirer the right to cancel the agreement and recover all sums paid if he signed it at a place other than trade premises. This right (which was designed to cover the activities of door-step salesmen) must be exercised within 4 days of receiving the second copy.

Any provision in the agreement giving the owner a right to enter any premises for the purpose of seizing the goods is invalidated by the Act. Further, even though the agreement may have been terminated because the hirer has broken it, or because the owner has exercised a right to terminate it, if one-third of the hire-purchase price has been paid or tendered, the owner cannot recover the goods otherwise than by action in a County Court, in which the Court can ensure that the hirer is fairly treated. If the owner disregards this provision, the hirer cannot recover the goods, but can recover all sums paid under the agreement.

The Trade Descriptions Act, 1968, further protects the consumer by making it a criminal offence for traders falsely to describe or advertise the quantity or price of goods or services; prosecutions are brought by Inspectors of Weights and Measures. The Act provides no civil remedies.

SCOTLAND

Formerly the provisions governing hire-purchase in Scotland were very different from England, but a change was made by the Hire Purchase Act, 1964, which in effect extended to Scotland the English code. Now, the Hire Purchase (Scotland) Act, 1965, provides a Scots code corresponding to, but not identical with, the English enactments found in the Hire Purchase Act, 1965, referred to above.

ILLEGITIMACY AND LEGITIMATION
ENGLAND AND WALES

A man may be summoned to petty sessions on the application of the mother of a bastard child, or by the Supplementary Benefits Commission where the child becomes chargeable to the local authority, and the Justices, on his being proved to be the father of the child, may make an order requiring him to pay for its maintenance and education a sum in their discretion. The evidence of the woman must be *corroborated* in a material particular. The mother has the custody of her bastard children. *Prima facie* every child born of a married woman during a marriage is legitimate; and this presumption can only be rebutted by strong, distinct, satisfactory and conclusive evidence. However, under the Family Law Reform Act, 1969, any presumption of law as to the legitimacy (or illegitimacy) of any person may in civil proceedings be rebutted by evidence showing that it is more probable than not that the person is illegitimate (or legitimate). If however the husband and wife are separated under an Order of the Court, a child conceived by the wife during such separation is presumed not to be the husband's child.

LEGITIMATION.—By the *Legitimacy Act*, 1926, which came into force on Jan. 1, 1927, where the parents of an illegitimate person marry, or have married, whether before or after that date, the marriage, if the father is at the date thereof domiciled in England or Wales, renders that person, if living, legitimate as from Jan. 1, 1927, or from the date of the marriage, whichever last happens. Under the Act of 1959, marriage legitimates a person even though the father or mother was married to a third person at the time when the illegitimate person was born. It is the duty of the parents to supply to the Registrar-General information for re-registration of the birth of a legitimated child.

Declarations of Legitimacy.—A person claiming that he, his parent, or any remoter ancestor has become legitimated, may petition the High Court or the County Court for the necessary declaration.

Rights and Duties of Legitimated Persons.—A legitimated person, his spouse or issue may take property under an intestacy occurring after the date of legitimation, or under any disposition (*e.g.*, a will) coming into operation after such date, as if he had been legitimate.

He must maintain all persons whom he would be bound to maintain had he been born legitimate, and he is entitled to the benefit of any Act of Parliament which confers rights on legitimate persons to recover damages or compensation. The Act specially provides that nothing therein contained is to render any person capable of succeeding to or transmitting a right to any dignity or title.

Property Rights of Illegitimate Children.—By the Family Law Reform Act, 1969, the rights of an illegitimate child on an intestacy are now equated with those of a legitimate child. Also, in any disposition made after January 1, 1970, any reference to children and other relatives shall, unless the contrary intention appears, be construed as including references to, and to persons related through, illegitimate children.

SCOTLAND

Illegitimate Children (Scotland) Act, 1930.—The mother of an illegitimate child may raise an action of affiliation and aliment against the father, either in the Court of Session or, more usually, in the Sheriff Court. Where in any such action the Court finds that the defender is the father of the child, the Court shall, in awarding inlying expenses, or aliment, have regard to the means of the parties, and the whole circumstance of the case. The Court may, upon application by the mother or by the father of any illegitimate child, or in any action for aliment for an illegitimate child, make such order as it may think fit regarding the custody of such child and the right of access thereto of either parent, having regard to the welfare of the child and to the conduct of the parents and to the wishes as well of the mother as of the father and may on the application of either parent recall or vary such order. The obligation of the mother and of the father of an illegitimate child to provide aliment for such child shall (without prejudice to any obligation attaching at common law) endure until the child attains the age of sixteen years.

By Scots Law an illegitimate child is legitimated by and on the date of the subsequent marriage of its parents and there is now no objection to there having been an impediment to the marriage of the parents at the time of the child's conception—*see* the Legitimation (Scotland) Act, 1968, which came into operation on June 8, 1968, on which date thousands of existing illegitimate children were regarded as legitimated. By the Registration of Births, Deaths and Marriages (Scotland) Act, 1965, a child so legitimated, who has already been regis-

tered as illegitimate, may be re-registered as legitimate. The consent of the father of an illegitimate child to its adoption is not required.

The Law Reform (Miscellaneous Provisions) (Scotland) Act, 1968, gives an illegitimate child full rights of succession (including legitim, *see* next section) in the estate of both parents, while the father and mother share equally in the estate of their illegitimate child. Unless expressly excluded, a reference in a deed to a relationship, *e.g.* " issue " or " children ", is presumed to include illegitimate children.

INTESTACY
ENGLAND AND WALES

As regards deaths on or after January 1, 1967, the position is governed by the Administration of Estates Act, 1925, as amended by the Intestates' Estates Act, 1952, and the Family Provision Act, 1966. The 1952 and 1966 Acts increased the benefits of a surviving spouse of an intestate, and the 1952 Act extended the provisions of the Inheritance (Family Provision) Act, 1938 (*see under* " Wills "), to intestacies. These notes deal with the position under the 1966 Act, so that if the death occurred before 1967 reference must be made elsewhere. If the intestate leaves a spouse and issue, the spouse takes (i) the " personal chattels "; (ii) £8,750 with interest at 4 per cent. from death until payment; and (iii) a life interest in half of the rest of the estate. This life interest can be capitalized at the option of the spouse. " Personal chattels " are articles of household use or ornament (including motor-cars), not used for business purposes. The rest of the estate goes to the issue. If the intestate leaves a spouse and no issue, but leaves a parent or brother or sister of the whole blood or issue of such brothers and sisters the spouse takes (i) the " personal chattels "; (ii) £30,000 with interest at 4 per cent. from death until payment, and (iii) half of the rest of the estate absolutely. The other half of the rest of the estate goes to the parents, equally if more than one, or, if none, to the brothers and sisters of the whole blood. If the intestate leaves a spouse, but no issue, no parents and no brothers or sisters of the whole blood or their issue, the spouse takes the whole estate absolutely. If resident therein at the intestate's death, the surviving spouse may generally require the personal representatives to appropriate the interest of the intestate in or towards satisfaction of any absolute interest of the spouse, including the capitalized value of a life interest. In certain cases, leave of Court is required. On a partial intestacy any benefit (other than personal chattels specifically bequeathed) received by the surviving spouse under the will must be brought into account against the statutory legacy of £8,750 or £30,000 as the case may be. If there is no surviving spouse, the estate is distributed among those who survive the intestate in the following order (those entitled under earlier numbers taking to the exclusion of those entitled under later numbers):—(1) issue; (2) father or mother (equally, if both alive); (3) brothers and sisters of the whole blood; (4) brothers and sisters of the half blood; (5) grandparents (equally, if more than one alive); (6) uncles and aunts of the whole blood; (7) uncles and aunts of the half blood; (8) the Crown.

In cases (1), (3), (4), (6) and (7) the persons entitled lose their interests unless they or their issue not only survive the intestate, but also attain eighteen or marry under that age, their shares going to the other persons (if any) within the same group who do attain eighteen or marry. Moreover, in the same cases, succession is not *per capita*, but *per stirpes, i.e.,* by stocks or families. Thus, if the

intestate leaves one child and two grandchildren being the children of a child of the intestate, who pre-deceased the intestate, the two grandchildren represent their deceased parent and take between them one-half of the issue's share, the remaining half going to the surviving child. Similarly, nephews and nieces represent a deceased brother, and so on.

When the deceased died partially intestate (*i.e.,* leaving a will which disposed of only part of his property), the above rules apply to the intestate part.

Children must bring into account (hotchpot) any substantial advances received from the intestate during his lifetime before claiming any further share under the intestacy. Special hotchpot provisions apply to partial intestacy.

For further details, *see* Administration of Estates Act, 1925, as amended by the Intestates' Estates Act, 1952, and the Family Provision Act, 1966.

By the Family Law Reform Act, 1969, the position of an illegitimate child is equated with that of a legitimate child in respect of all deaths occurring after January 1, 1970.

SCOTLAND

The Succession (Scotland) Act, 1964, provides that the whole estate of any person dying intestate after the commencement of the Act shall devolve without distinction between heritable and moveable property, besides altering the law of succession in other respects. By that Act the surviving spouse of an intestate may, as a prior right (in addition to legal rights, *see* below), claim the matrimonial home (or in certain circumstances the value thereof), with its furniture and plenishings not exceeding £5,000 in value, plus the sum of £2,500 if the deceased left issue or, if no issue, the sum of £5,000.

The Act has been modified by the Law Reform (Miscellaneous Provisions) (Scotland) Act, 1968, as to the status of illegitimate children (*see* preceding section). The succession rights of an illegitimate child are however confined to the estate of his parents. He cannot claim from the estate of a grandparent, either legitim or a share in intestacy, even though such would have fallen to his pre-deceasing parent.

Legal rights, referred to above, are:—

Jus reliciti: right of surviving husband to one-half or one-third of deceased's net moveable estate, after satisfaction of prior rights.

Jus relictae: the corresponding right of a surviving wife in her deceased husband's estate.

Legitim: right of surviving children to one-half or one-third of the net moveable estate of deceased parents after satisfaction of prior rights—*see* p. 1179. There are no legal rights in heritage.

In general, the lines of succession are: (1) descendants; (2) collaterals; (3) ascendants and their collaterals, and so on in the ascending scale, but the Act of 1964 has made important modifications. The right of representation, *i.e.,* the right of the issue of a person, who would have succeeded if he had survived the intestate, is open to any line of succession where previously it was limited to apply only when there were next of kin or the issue of predeceasing next of kin. The surviving mother of an intestate now has equal rights of succession with the surviving father, where formerly these were restricted. The intestate's maternal relations, who prior to the Act had no rights of succession, are now on an equal footing with his paternal relations. A surviving spouse, if there are no children, succeeds to the whole estate. Where the intestate is survived only by parents, and by brothers and sisters (collaterals) half of the estate is taken by the parents and the other half by the brothers and sisters, those of the whole blood being preferred to

those of the half blood; where, however, succession opens to collaterals—(which expression can include the brothers and sisters of an ancestor of the intestate)—of the half blood, they shall rank equally amongst themselves, whether related to the intestate (or his ancestor) through their father or their mother.

JURY SERVICE

Liability to Jury Service depends upon inclusion in the local Jury Book. This is compiled from the Electors Lists for each year *see, post, under* "Voters' Qualifications"). The names of all persons who are on October 10 qualified and liable to serve as jurors are marked with the letter " J " on the Electors Lists. The marked Electors Lists are published, and anyone whose name is improperly marked may before the following 17th December claim that, although *qualified* to serve [see below] he is *exempt* from service [see below]; the marks will be removed from the names of exempted persons. The remaining marked names are thereafter included in the Jury Book. No one whose name actually appears in the Jury Book may claim exemption on any ground whatever except illness or, if a woman, for medical reasons.

QUALIFICATIONS

England and Wales.—Every man and woman between 21 and 60 years of age residing in England or Wales being the owner, legally or under a trust, of freehold land worth £10 a year or more, or of leasehold land worth £20 a year or more (if the lease is for at least 21 years) in the county in which they live; or being a householder rated in respect of premises of a net annual value of at least £20 (or in London or Middlesex £30); is qualified and liable to serve on juries in the superior courts (civil and criminal) and at Assizes in their own county, and on petty juries in the local County Court or Quarter Sessions. Also all burgesses of boroughs having separate quarter sessions or a borough civil court are qualified and liable to serve on juries therein. Special regulations govern the qualifications and method of listing common jurors in the City of London; and jurors for a coroner's inquest. By the Juries Act, 1954, a person attending for jury service is entitled to be paid travelling and subsistence allowances together with compensation for loss of earnings and other loss of expenses (*see* col. 2).

Disqualifications.—The disqualification of ex-prisoners is dealt with by section 74 of the Criminal Justice Act, 1967.

Exemptions.—The persons who are exempt from serving on juries (including coroner's juries) include: peers; M.P.s; judges; ministers of religion (Christian and Jewish); practising lawyers; officers of the Courts; coroners; prison, etc., officers; keepers of public mental hospitals; practising M.R.C.S.s, M.R.C.P.s and L.R.C.P.s; practising apothecaries, doctors and chemists, registered practising dentists, registered practising veterinary surgeons; midwives; members of the armed forces; members of the Territorial Army Volunteer Reserve (in certain cases) or the Royal Auxiliary Air Force; members of the Mersey Docks and Harbour Board, and of the Port of London Authority; certain members of Trinity House, Deptford Strond; masters of buoy and light vessels under the Trinity Houses, and all licensed water pilots; household servants of the Crown; officers of the Post Office, customs and excise; sheriff's officers; police officers; special constables; metropolitan magistrates and their court clerks and servants; officers of the Houses of Parliament.

As to their own counties: members of the G.L.C., and commissioners of income tax.

As to their local counties: borough councillors and J.P.s, town clerks and borough treasurers; burgesses of boroughs having separate Quarter Sessions are exempt from serving on the County Sessions.

As to their own area of jurisdiction: J.P.s.

Moreover a juror can never be called upon to serve oftener than once in each year; this period of exemption is longer in certain counties.

Section 13 of the Criminal Justice Act, 1967, provides that the verdict of a jury in criminal proceedings need not be unanimous.

ALLOWANCES TO JURORS AND WITNESSES

Maximum allowances payable to jurors, witnesses in indictable cases and witnesses in Coroners' Courts proceedings were increased from February 15, 1971. In respect of all three categories the subsistence allowance maxima are:—

Day Subsistence Allowances.—In respect of any period other than a period in respect of which an overnight allowance is payable, the allowance shall not exceed:—

(a) if the period on any one day during which a witness or juror is necessarily absent from his place of residence, business or employment for the purpose of attending to give evidence or serving as a juror, does not exceed four hours, 45p in respect of that day;

(b) if the said period on any one day exceeds four hours but does not exceed eight hours, 95p in respect of that day;

(c) if the said period on any one day exceeds eight hours but does not exceed twelve hours, £1·75 in respect of that day;

(d) if the said period on any one day exceeds twelve hours but does not exceed sixteen hours, £2·50 in respect of that day;

(e) if the said period on any one day exceeds sixteen hours, £2·95 in respect of that day.

Overnight Allowances.—If a witness or juror is necessarily absent from his place of residence overnight for the purpose of attending to give evidence or serving as a juror, the subsistence allowance shall not exceed £5·50 in respect of each period in twenty-four hours or fraction thereof during which he is so absent overnight.

The maximum overnight allowance in respect of professional and expert witnesses is increased to £3·75 a night.

Mileage Allowances.—Where a witness or juror travels to or from Court by a private conveyance and the court is satisfied that the use of the vehicle results in substantial saving of time or is otherwise reasonable, there may be allowed in respect thereof a sum not exceeding:—

(i) in the case of a vehicle of engine capacity not exceeding 1000 c.c., 3½p a mile each way;

(ii) in the case of a vehicle of engine capacity exceeding 1000 c.c. but not exceeding 1750 c.c., 4½p a mile each way;

(iii) in the case of a vehicle of engine capacity exceeding 1750 c.c., 5p a mile each way.

In any other case, a sum not exceeding 2p a mile each way.

All other fees and allowances remain unchanged (*See* Juries Act, 1954; Jurors' Allowances Regulations, 1971).

JURY SERVICE IN SCOTLAND

It is the duty of the Sheriff in each county to make up a list of persons qualified and liable to serve as jurors. The list is compiled from information which every householder is required to

provide. From this list the General Jury Book is made up. Part II of the Juries Act, 1949 (amended by the Juries Act, 1954 with Regulations following thereon), applies only to Scotland and provides, *inter alia*, for the payment of travelling expenses and subsistence allowances to jurors, and for compensation for loss of earnings, recently increased.

The number of a jury in a civil cause in the Court of Session is twelve. In a criminal trial the number is fifteen, and in inquiries by Sheriff and jury under the Fatal Accidents Inquiry (Scotland) Act, 1895, or the Fatal Accidents and Sudden Deaths Inquiry (Scotland) Act, 1906 the number is seven. In Scotland there is no Coroner's Inquest.

QUALIFICATIONS

Every man or woman between the ages of 21 and 60 is qualified, who is possessed of heritable property of the yearly value of at least £5, or of moveable property of the value of at least £200 sterling.

Exemptions.—The persons who are exempt from serving on juries include: peers, judges of the supreme courts, sheriffs, magistrates of Royal Burghs, ministers of religion, parochial schoolmasters, practising lawyers, clerks and officers of court, prison officers, university professors, physicians, surgeons and dentists, officers in the Navy or Army on full pay, customs officers messengers-at-arms and other officers of the law, lighthouse keepers and their assistants, soldiers, members of the Territorial Army and the Auxiliary Air Force (in certain circumstances), Inland Revenue officials and officers of the Post Office.

Jurors failing to attend without good cause are liable to a penalty.

LANDLORD AND TENANT

ENGLAND AND WALES

Although basically the relationship between the parties to the lease is governed by the lease itself, the position is complicated by numerous statutory provisions. The few points dealt with may show the desirability of seeking professional assistance in these matters. Important provisions include:—

(1) As to agricultural holdings—the Agricultural Holdings Act, 1948. Among other things, this Act regulates the length of notice necessary to determine an agricultural tenancy, the tenant's right to remove fixtures on the land, his right to compensation for damage done by game, for improvements and for disturbance, and his right to require the consent of the Agricultural Land Tribunal to the operation of a notice to quit.

(2) As to business premises—the Landlord and Tenant Acts, 1927 and 1954, and the Law of Property Act 1969, Pt. I. Part II of the 1954 Act gives security of tenure to the tenant of most business premises, and in effect he can only be ousted on one or more of the seven grounds set out in the Act. In some cases, where the landlord can resume possession, the tenant is entitled to compensation.

(3) As to unfurnished dwelling houses—the complicated mass of legislation now embodied in the Rent Act, 1968, which does not extend to Scotland or Northern Ireland. If a house is within this Act, the tenant may have a personal right to reside in the house and can only be ousted on certain grounds. Further, each house within the Act has a rent limit, and the rent recoverable by the landlord is limited to this rent.

Houses let at a rent which includes board or substantial attendance or furniture are also governed by the Rent Act 1968.

The Rent Act, 1957, made considerable inroads into the importance of rent control by removing many houses from control altogether and fixing new maximum rent limits for all houses which remain subject to control. The principal changes effected by this Act were:

1. Any house whose rateable value on November 7, 1956, exceeded £40 in London and elsewhere £30, was automatically decontrolled.

2. No tenancies beginning on or after July 6, 1957, were subject to control unless the person to whom the tenancy was granted was already a protected tenant of that house.

3. For all houses remaining subject to control the maximum rent was determined by reference to the gross value shown in the rating valuation list on November 7, 1956.

Important changes were made by the Rent Act, 1965, without immediately affecting the system of control and determination of rents of property let before July 6, 1957, within the £40/30 limits of rateable value on the 1956 rating lists. If a tenancy of a dwelling-house was not already subject to Rent Act control immediately before December 8, 1965, the 1965 Act brought that tenancy within the Rent Acts provided the rateable value in March, 1965, did not exceed £400 in London and £200 elsewhere in Great Britain. Such a tenancy is known as a regulated tenancy. Broadly, the maximum rent recoverable from the tenant under such a tenancy is the rent payable under the terms of the agreement between landlord and tenant, save that if within the previous three years the house has been the subject of another regulated tenancy, then the limit is the rent payable under that earlier tenancy. However, provision is made by the Act for the registration of rents, and if a rent is registered under the Act that is the maximum rent which can be recovered. The Act provides for the appointment of rent officers and rent assessment committees to determine a fair rent to be registered.

The Act also provides that if any person with intent to cause the residential occupier of any premises to give up the occupation thereof does any act calculated to interfere with the peace or comfort of the residential occupier or members of his household, he shall be guilty of an offence. A further provision prevents a landlord enforcing a right to possession against a tenant (who is not already protected by any security of tenure legislation) without a court order, and there are special rules in such cases relating to agricultural employees.

(4) Part I of the Landlord and Tenant Act, 1954, applies to most tenancies of houses for over twenty-one years at a ground rent. Where it applies, the contractual tenancy is continued until brought to an end in the manner prescribed by the Act, and in effect the landlord can only get possession on limited grounds.

Further, under the Leasehold Reform Act, 1967, tenants of houses under leases for over twenty-one years at a rent less than two-thirds of the rateable value of the house are in most cases given a right to purchase the freehold or to take an extended lease for a term of fifty years, provided the tenant at the time when he seeks to exercise the right has been occupying the house as his residence for the last five years or for periods amounting to five years in the last ten years.

(5) A notice to quit *any* dwellinghouse must be given at least four weeks before it is to take effect.

(6) Under the Housing Act, 1961 (which does not extend to Scotland), in a lease of a dwellinghouse granted after October 24, 1961, for a term of less than 7 years, there is implied a covenant by the landlord (a) to keep in repair the structure and exterior of the house and (b) to keep in repair and proper working order the installations in the house (i) for the supply of water, gas and

electricity, and for sanitation, and (ii) for space heating or heating water.

SCOTLAND

A Lease is a Contract, the relationship of the parties being governed by the terms thereof. As is also the case in England (see the foregoing Section) legislation has played an important part in regulating that relationship. Thus, what at Common Law was an Agreement binding only the parties to the deed, becomes in virtue of Statute 1449 c. 17, a contract binding the landlord's successors, as purchasers or creditors, provided the following four conditions are observed; (1) the lease, if for more than one year, must be in writing, (2) there must be a rent, (3) there must be a term of expiry, and (4) the tenant must have entered into possession.

It would be impracticable in a brief section of these Notes to enter upon a general discussion of this branch of the law and, accordingly, the plan adopted in the preceding Section of quoting a few important Statutes is followed here.

The Agricultural Holdings (Scotland) Act, 1949 (amended by the Agriculture Act, 1958), which is a consolidating Act applicable to Scotland, contains provisions similar to those in the English Act, alluded to in the preceding Section. It cannot here be analysed in detail.

It is of interest to note that the Small Landholders Act, 1911, provided for the setting up of the Land Court which has jurisdiction over a large proportion of agricultural and pastoral land in Scotland.

In Scotland business premises are not controlled by Statute to so great an extent as in England, but the Tenancy of Shops (Scotland) Acts, 1949 and 1964 give a measure of security to tenants of shops. These Acts enable the tenant of a shop who is threatened with eviction to apply to the Sheriff for a renewal of the tenancy. If the landlord has offered to sell the subjects to the tenant at an agreed price the application for a renewal of the tenancy may be dismissed. Reference should be made to Section 1 (3) of the 1949 Act for particulars of other circumstances under which the Sheriff has a discretion to dismiss an application. The Acts apply to premises held by the Crown or Government Departments, either as landlord or tenant.

The series of complicated statutes known as The Rent and Mortgage Interest (Restrictions) Acts, 1920 to 1939, largely govern the relations between landlord and tenant in regard to certain unfurnished houses—including parts thereof if let as separate dwellings—and it is important to note that notwithstanding conditions in the lease of a controlled house providing for the removal of the tenant, it is not possible to contract out of the Acts. Employees occupying premises by virtue of their employment are not tenants and so cannot claim protection. The Housing (Repairs and Rents) (Scotland) Act, 1954, provides for increase in rent of a controlled dwelling house on which repairs of a certain value have been carried out. The Rent of Furnished Houses Control (Scotland) Act, 1943 contains provisions applicable to houses or parts of houses let with furniture and with or without services, as also to unfurnished premises let with services. These Acts were subsequently altered or modified by the Rent Act, 1957. Under it (1) Dwelling houses, the rateable value of which was on November 7, 1956, over £40, were released from control. (2) All tenancies coming into operation on or after July 6, 1957, were free from control, except where a new tenancy was granted to a statutory tenant already in occupation. (3) Provision was made for the increase of rent by a maximum of one quarter of all controlled houses. (4) The repairs increase of

two-fifths provided for in the 1954 Act was increased to one-half.

However, the main provisions of the Rent Act, 1965 (see above) apply to Scotland and substantially extend the application of the Rent Acts.

The Rent Act, 1957, further provides that a notice to quit a dwelling house (furnished or unfurnished) must be sent at least four weeks before the date on which it is to take effect.

Neither the Landlord and Tenant Act, 1954, nor the Law of Property Act, 1969, referred to in the preceding section, applies to Scotland.

LEGAL AID

LEGAL AID IN CIVIL PROCEEDINGS

The Legal Aid and Advice Act, 1949, is designed to make legal aid and advice more readily available for persons of small and moderate means. The main structure of the new service is contained in the Act itself and the Regulations made thereunder but the administrative details are embodied in a scheme made by the Law Society.

Legal aid is available for proceedings (including matrimonial causes) in the House of Lords, Court of Appeal, High Court, County Courts, Lands Tribunal, certain local courts, and civil proceedings in Magistrates Courts. In any event, an application for legal aid will not be approved if it appears that the applicant would gain only a trivial advantage from the proceedings. Further, proceedings wholly or partly in respect of defamation are excepted from the scheme, as are also relator actions, election petitions and proceedings by way of judgment summons.

Where a person is concerned in proceedings only in a representative, fiduciary or official capacity, his personal resources are not to be taken into account in considering eligibility for legal aid. Apart from this, eligibility in civil proceedings depends upon an applicant's " disposable income " and " disposable capital". Legal aid cannot be granted if the former exceeds £950 per annum, and a person may be refused assistance if he has a disposable capital of more than £500 and it appears that he can afford to proceed without legal aid. Even so, the applicant *may* be required to contribute up to one third the excess of his disposable income above £300, together with the whole excess of his disposable capital above £125. Disposable income is calculated by making deductions from gross income in respect of certain matters such as dependants, interest on loans, income tax, rates, rent and other matters for which the applicant must or reasonably may provide. Disposable capital is calculated by excluding from gross capital the value of the house in which the applicant resides, of furniture and household possessions; a deduction of up to £75 may be made in respect of dependants. Except in cases where the spouses are living apart, or have a contrary interest, any resources of a person's wife or husband are to be treated as that person's resources. These figures will be assessed by the Ministry of Social Security, and will be certified to a Local Committee, who will determine whether reasonable grounds exist for the grant of a civil aid certificate. Appeal from refusal of a certificate lies to an Area Committee. A person resident in England or Wales desiring legal aid may apply for a certificate to any Local Committee; if resident elsewhere application should be made to the Local Committee for London. However, if the application is made in respect of proceedings in an *appellate* court and the applicant is resident in England or Wales, application should generally be made to any *Area* Committee—if resident elsewhere, to the *Area* Committee for London. If a certificate is granted, the applicant may select his solicitor, and,

if necessary, counsel, from a panel. The costs of the assisted person's solicitor and counsel will be paid out of the legal aid fund. Under the Legal Aid Act, 1964, the court may order that the costs of a successful unassisted party shall be paid out of the legal aid fund.

LEGAL ADVICE

Legal advice from a solicitor on the Legal Aid Panel is now available to anyone over the age of sixteen. Persons on Supplementary Benefits can get it free of charge, whilst those whose means are within the limits set out below can get it for 12½p. An application form should be obtained from a Citizens' Advice Bureau, Court Office or from one of the Law Society's Legal Aid Offices, or from a solicitor whose name is on the panel, and, after completing the form, it should be taken to a solicitor on the panel and an interview requested. A person is entitled to advice on any one legal question only from one solicitor; and for not more than one hour and thirty minutes, but application for further advice may be made to the Area Committee. Lists of solicitors concerned may be consulted at the places mentioned above.

Legal advice is available for 12½p. to a person whose capital is £125 or less and whose income has not been more than £9·50 during the seven days up to and including the day of application for legal advice. Capital and income of husband and wife must be added together for this purpose, unless they are living apart or the applicant seeks advice on a matter in which the spouse has a contrary interest. In working out capital, the value of the applicant's house, its contents and the value of clothing and tools can be ignored. In working out income, the following deductions may be made:—

For a spouse living with or maintained by the applicant, £3·05; for any child maintained by the applicant and aged under 5, £1·40; for any child maintained by the applicant and aged 5–11, £1·65; for any child maintained by the applicant and aged 11–13, £2·05; for any child maintained by the applicant and aged 13–16, £2·20; for any other adult person maintained by the applicant, £3·05. There may also be deducted any income tax and any National Insurance, Industrial Injuries or National Health contributions paid by the applicant during the week immediately before the date of obtaining legal advice.

Quite apart from the above statutory scheme for legal advice, there exists a voluntary scheme under which any person may apply to a solicitor who is on the panel for advice for a fee of £1 for up to thirty minutes. If the matter cannot be disposed of in thirty minutes, the solicitor should give an estimate of the approximate cost of any further advice or steps which may be necessary.

It should be mentioned that under both schemes a solicitor, even though he is on the panel, is entitled to decline to give advice to the applicant without giving any reason to the applicant.

OTHER LEGAL AID

Neither of the advice schemes covers further action such as writing letters. If however a person wants something more than advice but something less than proceedings, he may obtain a certificate to take steps to assert or dispute a claim where the question of proceedings has not yet arisen, but if it did arise legal aid could be granted for those proceedings. This type of legal aid could cover writing letters, obtaining evidence, and negotiating settlements. The certificate limits the amount to be spent under it, and does not cover any step in proceedings, nor can counsel be instructed. It is available to a person whose disposable capital does not exceed £125 and who was either receiving

supplementary benefits under the Ministry of Social Security Act, 1966 or has a disposable income not exceeding £325 per annum. In assessing disposable capital deductions are made in respect of dependants, and further deductions for them are made in assessing disposable income. Where the applicant's disposable income exceeds £253 he must pay a contribution of up to £1 for each £3 above £250.

LEGAL AID IN CRIMINAL CASES

The Criminal Justice Act, 1967, Part IV provides for legal aid in criminal proceedings. A criminal court (e.g., magistrates' court, Assizes, Quarter Sessions) has power to order legal aid to be granted where it appears desirable to do so in the interests of justice. The court shall make an order in certain cases, e.g., where a person is committed for trial on a charge of murder. However, the court may not make an order unless it appears to the court that the person's means are such that he requires assistance in meeting the costs of the particular proceedings in question. Application should be made to the appropriate court where proceedings are to take place.

An applicant may be required to make a contribution towards the costs of the action. In order to ascertain the amount of this contribution he will have to produce written evidence of his means. Any assessment of means will be carried out by the Supplementary Benefits Commission, which will report to the court. No contribution will be required from a person who has insufficient means.

Any practising barrister or solicitor may act for a legally aided person in criminal proceedings unless excluded by reason of misconduct. In general where legal aid is given it will normally include representation by both counsel and solicitor. However, in connection with magistrates' courts, representation will be by solicitor alone unless it is a serious offence.

Where any doubt arises about the grant of a legal aid order that doubt is to be resolved in favour of the applicant. The court also has power to amend or revoke a legal aid order. Legal aid may also be granted in connection with appellate proceedings, e.g., on appeal to the Criminal Division of the Court of Appeal under the Criminal Appeal Act, 1968.

SCOTLAND

Civil Proceedings

The Legal Aid and Solicitors (Scotland) Acts, 1949 and 1960 provide a scheme which is limited to civil actions in the Court of Session and in the Sheriff Courts except actions in respect of defamation or verbal injury, breach of promise of marriage, the inducement of one spouse to leave or remain apart from the other, election petitions (under the Representation of the People Act, 1949), and small debt proceedings (i.e., under £50) and proceedings for summary removing, in both of which liability for the debt and the amount thereof are admitted.

As to those to whom legal aid is available, the same considerations as to income and capital apply in Scotland as in England. (*See* the preceding paragraph.) A person believing himself to be eligible may instruct any solicitor of his own choice who is on the official lists, or he may apply for a solicitor to one of the various Legal Aid Committees which are set up to administer the scheme. Application for a certificate granting legal aid is thereafter made to the appropriate Committee by the applicant's solicitor, who is required to prepare, for the signature of the applicant, a memorandum setting forth the grounds of the proposed action. Investigation into the applicant's financial means is

carried out by the Supplementary Benefits Commission after the Committee has considered the memorandum and, on a suitable contribution, if any, by the applicant being approved, a Certificate is granted enabling the applicant to proceed with his action. The Legal Aid Act, 1964, which applies to Scotland with certain modifications, provides for the payment (to a limited extent) out of the legal aid fund of costs incurred by successful opponents of legally aided litigants.

LEGAL ADVICE

Since March, 1959, legal advice, as distinct from legal aid in proceedings, is available to anyone in Scotland on terms similar to those stated in a preceding paragraph dealing with legal advice in England. Application forms are available in the offices of all Legal Aid Committees and Citizens' Advice Bureaux.

Criminal Proceedings

Legal Aid (Scotland) (Criminal Proceedings) Regulations, 1964, which came into operation in October 1964, provide for the administration of criminal legal aid.

MARRIAGE

A.—MARRIAGE ACCORDING TO RITES OF THE CHURCH OF ENGLAND

1. MARRIAGE BY BANNS.—The Marriage Act, 1949, prescribes audible publication according to the rubric, on three Sundays preceding the ceremony during morning service or, if there is no morning service on a Sunday on which the banns are to be published, during evening service. Where the parties reside in different parishes, the banns must be published in both. Under the Act, banns may be published and the marriage solemnized in the parish church, *which is the usual place of worship* of the persons to be married or either of them, although neither of such persons dwells in such parish; but this publication of banns is *in addition* to any other publication required by law and does not apply if the church or the residence of either party is in Wales. The Act provides specially for the case where one of the parties resides in Scotland and the other in England, the publication being then in the parish in England in which one party resides, and, according to the law and custom in Scotland, in the place where the other party resides. After the lapse of three months from the last time of publication, the banns become useless, and the parties must either obtain a licence (*see below*), or submit to the republication of banns.

2. MARRIAGE BY LICENCE.—Marriage licences are of two kinds:—

(i) *A Common Licence,* dispensing with the necessity for banns, granted by the Archbishops and Bishops through their Surrogates, for marriages in any church or chapel duly licensed for marriages. A Common Licence can be obtained in London by application at the Faculty Office (1 The Sanctuary, Westminster, S.W.1) and (for marriages in London) at the Bishop of London's Diocesan Registry (1 The Sanctuary, S.W.1), by one of the parties about to be married. In the country there may be obtained at the offices of the Bishops' Registrars, but licences obtained at the Bishop's Diocesan Registry only enable the parties to be married in the diocese in which they are issued; those procured at the Faculty Office are available for *all* England and Wales. No instructions, either verbal or in writing, can be received, except from one of the parties. Affidavits are prepared from the personal instructions of one of the parties

about to be married, and the licence is delivered to the party upon payment of fees amounting to four pounds fifty pence. *No previous notice is required and the licence is available as soon as it is issued.* Before a licence can be granted one of the parties must make an affidavit that there is no legal impediment to the intended marriage; and also that one of such parties has had his or her usual place of abode for the space of fifteen days immediately preceding the issuing of the licence within the parish or ecclesiastical district of the church in which the marriage is to be solemnized, or the church in which the marriage is to be solemnized is the usual place of worship of the parties or one of them. In the country there may generally be found a parochial clergyman (Surrogate) before whom the affidavit may be taken, and whose office it is to deliver the licence personally to the applicant. (In some dioceses it is necessary for the Surrogate to procure the licence from the Bishop's Registry.) The licence continues in force for three months from its date.

(ii) *A Special Licence* granted by the Archbishop of Canterbury, under special circumstances, for marriage at any place with or without previous residence in the district, or at any time, etc.; but the reasons assigned must meet with his Grace's approval. Application must be made to the Faculty Office. Fees for licence, etc., £25.

3. MARRIAGE UNDER SUPERINTENDENT REGISTRAR'S CERTIFICATE.—A marriage may be performed in church on the Superintendent Registrar's Certificate (as to which see below) without banns, provided that the incumbent's consent is obtained. One of the parties must be resident within the ecclesiastical parish of the church in which the marriage is to take place unless the church is the usual place of worship of the parties or one of them.

MARRIAGE FEES.—The Church Commissioners settle tables of fees for all parishes. The usual fees are paid although a stranger-clergyman may be invited to perform the service.

B.—MARRIAGE UNDER SUPERINTENDENT REGISTRAR'S CERTIFICATE

The following marriages may be solemnized on the authority of a Superintendent Registrar's Certificate (either with or without a licence):—

(a) A marriage in a registered building (*e.g.,* a nonconformist church registered for the solemnization of marriages therein).

(b) A marriage in a register office.

(c) A marriage according to the usages of the Society of Friends (commonly called Quakers).

(d) A marriage between two persons professing the Jewish religion according to the usages of the Jews.

(e) A marriage according to the rites of the Church of England (*see* above—in this case the marriage can only be *without* licence).

NOTICE.—Notice of the intended marriage must be given as follows:—

(i) Marriage by certificate (*without* licence)—If both parties reside in the same registration district, they must both have resided there for seven days before the notice can be given. It may then be given by either party. If the parties reside in different

registration districts, notice must be given by each to the Superintendent Registrar of the district in which he or she resides, and the preliminary residential qualification of seven days must be fulfilled by each before either notice can be given.

(ii) Marriage by certificate (*with licence*)—One notice only is necessary, whether the parties live in the same or in different registration districts. Either party may give the notice, which must be given to the Superintendent Registrar of any registration district in which one of the parties has resided for the period of fifteen days immediately preceding the giving of notice, but both parties must be resident in England or Wales on the day notice is given.

The notice (in either case) must be in the prescribed form and must contain particulars as to names, marital status, occupation, residence, length of residence, and the building in which the marriage is to take place. The notice must also contain or have added at the foot thereof a solemn declaration that there is no legal impediment to the marriage, and, in the case of minors, that the consent of the person whose consent to the marriage is required by law (*see below*) has been duly given, and that the residential qualifications (mentioned above) have been complied with. A person making a false declaration renders himself or herself liable to prosecution for perjury. The notice is entered in the marriage notice book.

ISSUE OF CERTIFICATE:

(i) *Without* licence.—The notice (or an exact copy thereof) is affixed in some conspicuous place in the Superintendent Registrar's office for 21 days next after the notice was entered in the marriage notice book. After the lapse of this period the Superintendent Registrar may, provided no impediment is shown, issue his certificate for the marriage, which can then take place at any time within three months from the date of the entry of the notice.

(ii) *With* licence.—The notice in this case is not affixed in the office of the Superintendent Registrar. After the lapse of one whole day (other than a Sunday, Christmas Day or Good Friday) from the date of entry of the notice, the Superintendent Registrar may, provided no impediment is shown, issue his certificate and licence for the marriage, which can then take place on any day within three months from the date of entry of the notice.

SOLEMNIZATION OF THE MARRIAGE:

(i) *In a Registered Building.*—The marriage must generally take place at a building within the district of residence of one of the parties, but if the usual place of worship of either is outside the district of his or her residence, it may take place in such usual place of worship. Further, if there is not within the district of residence of one of the parties a registered building within which marriages are solemnized according to the rites and ceremonies which the parties desire to adopt in solemnizing their marriage, it may take place in an appropriate registered building in the nearest district.

The presence of a Registrar of Marriages is not necessary at marriages at registered buildings which have adopted the provisions of section 43 of the Marriage Act, 1949. This section provides for the appointment of an " authorized person " (a person, usually the minister or an official of

the building, certified by the trustees or governing body as having been duly authorized for the purpose) who must be present and must register the marriage.

The marriage must be solemnized between the hours of 8 a.m. and 6 p.m. with open doors in the presence of two or more witnesses. The parties must at some time during the ceremony make the following declaration—" I do solemnly declare that I know not of any lawful impediment why I, A. B., may not be joined in matrimony to C. D." Also each of the parties must say to the other: " I call upon these persons here present to witness that I, A. B., do take thee, C. D., to be my lawful wedded wife [or husband]," *or*, if the marriage is solemnized in the presence of an authorized person without the presence of a Registrar, each party may say in lieu thereof: "I, A. B., do take thee, C. D., to be my wedded wife [or husband]."

(ii) *In a Register Office.*—The marriage may be solemnized in the office of the Superintendent Registrar to whom notice of the marriage has been given. The marriage must be solemnized between the hours of 8 a.m. and 6 p.m., with open doors in the presence of the Superintendent Registrar or a Registrar of the registration district of that Superintendent Registrar, and in the presence of two witnesses. The parties must make the following declaration: "I do solemnly declare that I know not of any lawful impediment why I, A. B., may not be joined in matrimony to C. D.," and each party must say to the other: "I call upon these persons here present to witness that I, A. B., do take thee, C. D., to be my lawful wedded wife [or husband]." No religious ceremony may take place in the Register Office, though the parties may, on production of their marriage certificate, go through a subsequent religious ceremony in any church or persuasion of which they are members.

(iii) *Other Cases.*—If both parties are members of the Society of Friends (Quakers), or if, not being in membership, they have been authorized by the Society of Friends to solemnize their marriage in accordance with its usages, they may be married in a Friends' meeting-house. The marriage must be registered by the registering officer of the Society appointed to act for the district in which the meeting house is situated. The presence of a Registrar of Marriages is not necessary.

If both parties are Jews they may marry according to their usages in a synagogue, which has a certified marriage secretary, or private dwelling-house at any hour ; the building may be situated within or without the district of residence. The marriage must be registered by the secretary of the synagogue of which the man is a member. The presence of a Registrar of Marriages is not necessary.

FEES OF SUPERINTENDING REGISTRARS

For entering notice of a marriage by certificate (with or without licence) in the marriage notice book	£0·75
For a licence for marriage	3·00
For a marriage by certificate (with or without licence) in the presence of a Registrar (including cost of certificate)	1·25

C.—MARRIAGE UNDER REGISTRAR GENERAL'S LICENCE

The main purpose of the Marriage (Registrar General's Licence) Act 1970, which came into force on January 1, 1971, is to enable non-Anglicans to be married in unregistered premises where one of the persons to be married is seriously ill, is not expected to recover and cannot be moved to registered premises. A fee of £15 is payable to the Registrar General for the licence, though he has power to remit this in whole or in part to avoid hardship.

MISCELLANEOUS NOTES

Consanguinity and Affinity.—A marriage between persons within the prohibited degrees of consanguinity or affinity is void. Relaxations have, however, been made by various statutes which have now been replaced by the Marriage Act, 1949 (see the 1st Schedule to the Act) and the Marriage (Enabling) Act, 1960. It is now permitted to contract a marriage with:—

Sister, aunt or niece of a former wife (whether living or not). Former wife of brother, uncle or nephew (whether living or not).

No clergyman can be compelled to solemnize any of the foregoing marriages, but he may allow his church to be used for the purpose by another minister.

Minors.—Persons under 18 years of age are generally required to obtain the consent of certain persons (see Marriage Act, 1949, section 3 and 2nd Schedule as amended by the Family Law Reform Act, 1969). Where both parents are living, both must consent, where one is dead, the survivor, or, if there is a guardian appointed by the deceased parent, the guardian and the survivor. No consent is required in the case of an infant's second marriage. In certain exceptional cases consent may be dispensed with, *e.g.*, the insanity of a parent. If consent is refused the Court may, on application being made, consent to the marriage; application can be made for this purpose to the High Court, the County Court, or a Court of Summary Jurisdiction. The Act *prohibits* any marriage where either party is under 16 years of age.

D.—MARRIAGE IN ENGLAND OR WALES WHEN ONE PARTY LIVES IN SCOTLAND OR NORTHERN IRELAND

Notice for a marriage by a Superintendent Registrar's certificate in a register office or registered building may be given in the usual way by the party resident in England. As regards Scotland, the party there, after a residence of fifteen days, should either apply to the session clerk to publish banns or give notice of marriage to the registrar; as regards Northern Ireland, the party there, after a residence of seven days, must give notice to the District Registrar of Marriages. Notice cannot be given for such marriages to take place by Certificate *with* licence of the Superintendent Registrar.

Marriage of such parties may take place in a church of the Church of England after the publication of banns, or by Ecclesiastical licence.

MARRIAGES IN SCOTLAND

According to the law of Scotland, marriage is a contract which is completed by the mutual consent of parties.

Impediments to marriage: These render the marriage null and void. (*a*) Age: If either party is under the age of 16. (*b*) Forbidden Degrees: If the parties are within certain degrees of relationship. (*c*) Subsisting previous marriage. (*d*) Impotency of either party. (*e*) Non-residence, *i.e.*, if the legal requirement of prior residence of one or other of the parties in Scotland have not been complied with. (*f*) Insanity of either party.

No consent of parents or guardians is necessary. Marriages may be regular or " irregular."

Regular Marriages.

A regular marriage is one which is celebrated by a Minister of religion or authorized Registrar after due notice by the proclamation of banns or publication by the Registrar, or by a Sheriff's licence. Any Minister of any denomination (including a person officiating at a Quaker wedding) who performs the ceremony is reckoned to be a minister of religion. It must be performed before two witnesses and one of the parties must either have his or her usual residence in the Registration District, or have resided there for at least 15 days before the ceremony or have a parent so residing there. No form, place or hours are prescribed by law. There are no canonical hours as in England. Public proclamation is made by (*a*) banns, or (*b*) notice by the Registrar. Banns must be proclaimed in a parish church situated within the registration district of the qualifying address of each party. It is ordered that the proclamation of banns should be made twice, but by immemorial practice proclamation on one Sunday is sufficient. The Clerk of the Kirk Session of the Parish takes in notices of banns and issues certificates of proclamation. The fee for proclamation may not exceed 35p. A certificate of proclamation of banns is only valid for three months.

Under the Marriage Notices (Scotland) Act, 1878, amended by the Marriage (Scotland) Act, 1956, a notice posted up in a conspicuous or accessible place on the board or outer wall of the Registrar's office is equivalent to the proclamation of banns, but a minister of the Church of Scotland is not bound, although he is entitled, to celebrate a marriage not preceded by banns. The statute is limited to persons with qualifying residence in Scotland or having parents so residing. Exhibition is made for 7 consecutive days, during which time any person may appear personally and lodge an objection in writing subscribed by him. If no objections are lodged the Registrar issues a certificate. Such certificate of publication is only valid for three months. Regulations made under the Births, Deaths and Marriages (Scotland) Act, 1965 provide that the cost of publication is 35p and the extract certificate, 50p. The Naval Marriages Act 1908, regulates the publication of banns or of notice on board H.M. ships and the granting of certificates by the Officer-Commanding.

Marriage before Registrar: After obtaining a certificate of due publication as above, it is competent for the parties to contract the marriage in the office of the authorized Registrar in his presence and in the presence of two witnesses. The fee for the ceremony is £1. Such a marriage is regular and valid in all respects.

Marriage by Licence: In unforeseen and exceptional circumstances—*see* Section 2 of the Marriage (Scotland) Act, 1939—where normal method of publication cannot be carried through, the Sheriff, on application by the parties may grant a licence (valid for ten days) which is otherwise deemed in all respects to be equivalent to a certificate of publication.

Irregular Marriages

Since the passing of the Marriage (Scotland) Act, 1939, only one form of irregular marriage is recognized, *viz.* marriage by co-habitation and habit and repute. If parties live together constantly as husband and wife, and if they are held to be such by the general repute of the neighbourhood, then there may arise a presumption from which

marriage can be inferred. Before such marriage can be registered, however, a decree of declarator of marriage must be obtained from the Court of Session.

MASTER AND SERVANT
WAGES AND HOLIDAYS

Under the Truck Acts, it is in general forbidden for an employer to pay wages other than in current coin of the realm, and it is illegal for an employer to deduct from the employee's wages sums alleged to be due to the employer. However, the application of these Acts is confined to manual workers, and domestic servants are specifically excluded from their operation. Even in the case of payments to workmen, certain deductions, including rent and the price of food to be consumed on the employers' premises, are not forbidden where the employee's written consent is obtained. Further, under the Payment of Wages Act, 1960, it is permissible for wages to be paid otherwise than in cash at the request of the employee, *e.g.*, by cheque, money order, postal order or into a banking account. The Truck Acts did not relate to the amount of wage to be paid to the employee, but today minimum wage rates for particular trades are prescribed by numerous statutes. The Wages Councils Act, 1945 (now Act of 1959) established Wages Councils, which are given power to fix minimum wages in respect of a number of trades and industries. The Councils may also direct as to the length of holidays for workers in such trades and industries, and for payment of wages during holidays, under the Holidays with Pay Act, 1938. Subject to this Act, a servant's right to a holiday is a matter of contract. The terms of the contract may be express or implied; but if there is a right to a holiday once in a year and if the servant is rightfully dismissed before the end of that year, he cannot successfully claim pay in respect of the loss of the holiday.

The Equal Pay Act 1970, which extends to Scotland, but does not come into force until December 29, 1975, prevents discrimination, as regards terms and conditions of employment between men and women.

OFFICES, SHOPS AND RAILWAY PREMISES

The Offices, Shops and Railway Premises Act, 1963, which extends to Scotland with minor modifications, applies to office premises, shop premises and railway premises being, in each case, premises where persons are employed to work. Shop premises include a building which is not a shop but of which the main use is the carrying on there of a retail trade or business; a building occupied by a wholesaler where goods are kept for sale wholesale (except a warehouse belonging to the owner of a dock, wharf or quay); and a building to which the public can resort for the purpose of having goods repaired. However, the Act does not apply to premises if the only employees are the spouse, parent, grandparent, child, grandchild or brother or sister of the employer, and it does not apply to premises if the period of time worked there during each week does not normally exceed 21 hours.

The following is a very brief summary of the main provisions affecting premises to which the Act applies—

1. The premises and all furniture etc., must be kept clean, and no dirt or refuse must be allowed to accumulate.

2. No overcrowding so as to cause risk of injury to health is permitted.

3. Provisions must be made for maintaining a reasonable temperature in rooms, and a thermometer must be provided on each floor of a building.

4. Provision must be made for securing adequate ventilation.

5. Provision must be made for securing sufficient and suitable lighting.

6. Suitable and sufficient sanitary conveniences and washing facilities (including a supply of clean, running hot and cold or warm water and, in addition, soap and clean towels or other suitable means of cleaning or drying) must be provided at accessible places; and also an adequate supply of wholesome drinking water.

7. Accommodation must be provided for clothing which is not in use.

8. For each sedentary worker there must be provided a seat of a design, construction and dimensions suitable for that worker.

9. Where persons employed to work in shop premises eat meals there, suitable and sufficient facilities for eating them must be provided.

10. All floors, stairs and passages must be of sound construction and properly maintained.

11. Every dangerous part of any machinery must be securely fenced, unless it is in such a position or of such construction as to be as safe as if it were fenced. No person under 18 can clean machinery if he is thereby exposed to risk of injury from a moving part.

12. No person can be required to lift or carry a load so heavy as to be likely to injure him.

13. A first-aid box or cupboard must be provided.

14. Means of escape in case of fire must be provided, as must appropriate fire-fighting equipment.

15. Where an accident occurs which causes death to an employee or disables him from working for more than 3 days, the occupier of the premises must at once send notice of the accident to the appropriate authority.

RECEIPTS

Receipts should be kept for six years from the date of payment, after which period no action can be brought concerning the goods, etc., received.

In *Scotland*, as in England, inability to produce receipts does not necessarily bar defence to an action for payment.

TOWN AND COUNTRY PLANNING

The Town and Country Planning Act, 1962, contains very far-reaching provisions affecting the liberty of an owner of land to develop and use it as he will. A person has generally to get planning permission before carrying out any development on his land from the Local Planning Authority. Development charge is not payable in respect of operations begun or uses of land instituted on or after November 18, 1952. By the Land Commission (Dissolution) Act 1971, betterment levy, which was formerly payable on the realization of the development value of land, is not chargeable on any transactions carried out after July 23, 1970. This Act extends to Scotland.

What is Development:—

(*a*) Carrying out of building, engineering, mining or other operations.

(*b*) Making a material change in use.

It is expressly provided that if one dwelling-house is converted into two or more dwelling-houses, this involves a material change in use.

Examples of what is not deemed Development:—

(*a*) Maintaining, improving or altering the interior of a building (except works for making good war damage), provided there is no material change to the exterior, with the exception that on and after January 1, 1969, any expansion of a building below ground level will constitute development (Town and Country Planning, Act, 1968).

(*b*) Change of use of property within the curtilage of a dwelling-house for a purpose incidental to the use of the dwelling-house as such. (It will, however, be development if building operations are carried out.)

Application can be made to the Local Planning Authority to determine whether or not an operation or change of use constitutes development.

Planning Permission.—Application for such permission is not always necessary, as the Minister may make Development Orders giving general permission for a specified type of development. Thus a General Development Order of 1963 specified a number of types of development for which no permission is required *e.g.*, enlargement of a dwelling-house (including erection of a garage), so long as the cubic content of the original dwelling (external measurement) is not exceeded by more than 1,750 cubic feet or one-tenth whichever is greater, subject to a maximum of 4,000 cubic feet.

Appeal against refusal of permission lies to the Minister, and from the Minister, in limited circumstances, to the High Court. If the result of the appeal is unsatisfactory, an applicant may in certain circumstances require the Council to purchase the land.

Enforcement Notice.—If development is carried out without permission, or in defiance of conditions attached to such permission, the Local Planning Authority may serve an enforcement notice on the owner of the land calling upon him to demolish or alter any building, or to discontinue the use of land, or to comply with the said conditions. If the notice is not complied with, the Local Planning Authority may take appropriate steps to enforce it, recovering their expenses from the owner for the time being of the land. Appeal against an enforcement notice lies to the Minister. *See* also the Act of 1968.

Scotland.

In Scotland special provisions, on similar lines, have been made by the Town and Country Planning (Scotland) Act, 1947, which incorporates certain provisions of the Town and Country Planning (Scotland) Act, 1945, all other earlier planning Acts being repealed. The financial provisions of the 1947 Act, have, however, been amended by the Town and Country Planning Act, 1953, which abolished development charges, and by the Town and Country Planning (Scotland) Act, 1954, which set up a new Scheme of compensation. *See also* the Town and Country Planning (Scotland) Act, 1959. The Highlands and Islands Development (Scotland) Act, 1965 is concerned with the promotion of the economic and social development of parts of Scotland.

VOTERS' QUALIFICATIONS

The franchise is governed by the Representation of the People Acts, the latest of which is the Act of 1969. Those entitled to vote as electors at a parliamentary election in any constituency are all persons resident there on the qualifying date who, at that date and on the date of the poll, are British subjects of at least 18 years of age and not subject to any legal incapacity to vote. In addition, a person who is of voting age on the date of the poll at a parliamentary or local government election is entitled to vote, whether or not he is of voting age on the qualifying date. Accordingly, a qualified person will be entitled to be registered in a register of parliamentary electors or a register of local government electors if he will attain voting age within twelve months from the date on which the register is required to be published. Since the Electoral Registers Act of 1949, the registers are prepared once in each year only. Under the

Electoral Registers Act, 1953, the Register (of parliamentary and local government electors or, in Northern Ireland, of parliamentary electors) is published not later than February 15 in each year and is for use in the period of 12 months commencing on February 16. The qualifying date referred to is, in England, Wales and Scotland the preceding October 10, and in Northern Ireland the preceding September 15.

The Register is prepared by the Registration Officer in each constituency in Great Britain. It is the registration officer's duty to have a house to house or other official inquiry made as to the persons entitled to be registered and to publish preliminary electors lists showing the persons appearing to him to be entitled to be registered. Any person whose name is omitted may claim registration, and any person on the list may object to the inclusion therein of other persons' names: the registration officer determines the claims and objections. The procedure is slightly different for Northern Ireland.

Special provision is made for " Service voters," (and persons employed by the British Council in posts outside the United Kingdom), who include wives of Service voters resident with their husbands outside the United Kingdom. Such persons may make a Service declaration in a prescribed form and are then treated as resident at the address specified in the declaration. Service voters may vote by post or by proxy, on making the necessary application to the registration officer.

Certain other persons (*e.g.*, those unable to go in person to the polling station owing to the general nature of their occupation, blindness or other physical incapacity, etc.) may vote by post or, in some cases, by proxy as " absent voters ", and Section 3 of the 1969 Act deals specifically with merchant seamen. Section 5 extends to certain married persons the right to vote by proxy or by post.

The local government franchise now depends solely upon residence in the area, the previous non-resident qualification for owners of property having been abolished by the Representation of the People Act, 1969, with effect from February 16, 1970. There are provisions, similar to those relating to the parliamentary franchise, for the preparation of registers, etc., and in fact the same register is used, as far as possible, with a mark indicating those persons entitled to vote for local government purposes only.

The Acts apply generally to Scotland where certain matters relating to local government and parliamentary elections are further regulated by Representation of the People (Scotland) Regulations, 1949.

WILLS

IMPORTANT NOTE.—*The following notes must be read subject to the provisions of the Inheritance (Family Provision) Act, 1938, which is liable to affect or modify the will of any person (domiciled in England) dying after July 13, 1939.* This Act empowers the Court to order maintenance out of the testator's estate for the benefit of certain " dependants," *i.e.*, a surviving wife or husband; an unmarried (or invalid) daughter; an infant (or invalid) son. Such order can be made if the will does not itself make " reasonable provision " for the maintenance of the dependant who seeks the order. An application must normally be made within six months of probate. A legally adopted child comes within the definition of a " son " or " daughter " under the Act. For further details as to the limits of an order, the Act, as amended by the Family Provision Act, 1966, and the Family Law Reform Act, 1969, s. 18, should be consulted.

Since the object of the Act is to provide *maintenance* for dependants, an application is not likely to be successful where the estate is very small, *e.g.* two or three hundred pounds.

There are similar provisions under the Matrimonial Causes Act, 1965, whereby the court may order provision out of a deceased's estate for the support of a *former* husband or wife where the marriage has been dissolved or annulled.

REASONS FOR MAKING A WILL.—Every person should make a will. However small the estate, it is safer in every case to protect the interests of the survivors by a will, and by the appointment of one or more trustworthy persons as executors to carry the testator's wishes into effect. The help of a lawyer in making a will is not in every case essential, but it is always advisable, particularly where there is a desire on a testator's part to provide for his property being " settled " as it is called—*e.g.*, the income being paid to his widow and the capital being ultimately divided among his children, for this requires the skill of a practised lawyer. When property is thus " settled," there may be a saving in death duties. Assuming a lawyer is not employed, a person having resolved to make a will must remember that it is only after a person is dead, and cannot explain his meaning, that his will can be open to dispute. It is the more necessary, therefore, to express what is meant in language of the utmost clearness, avoiding the use of any word or expression that admits of another meaning than the one intended. Avoid the use of " legal terms," such as " heirs " and " issue," when the same thing may be expressed in plain language. If in writing the will a mistake be made, it is better to rewrite the whole. Before a will is executed (*see below*) an alteration *may* be made by striking through the words with a pen, but opposite to such alteration the testator and witnesses should write their names or place their initials. Never scratch out a word with a knife or other instrument, and no alteration *of any kind whatever* must be made after the will is executed. If the testator afterwards wishes to change the disposition of his estate, it is best to make a new will, revoking the old one. The use of *codicils* should be left to the lawyer. *A will should be written in ink and very legibly, on a single sheet of paper.* Although, of course, forms of wills must vary to suit different cases, the following forms may be found useful to those who, in cases of emergency, are called upon to draw up wills, either for themselves or others.

Nothing more complicated should be attempted. The forms should be studied in conjunction with the notes following.

This is the last will and testament of me [*Thomas Smith*] of [*Vine Cottage, Silver Street, Reading, Berks*] which I make this [*thirteenth*] day of [*February*, 1970] and whereby I revoke all previous wills and testamentary dispositions.

1. I hereby appoint [*John Green of —— and Richard Brown of ——*] to be the executor(s) of this my will.

2. I give all my property real and personal to [*my wife Mary* or *my sons Raymond and David equally* or as the case may be].

Signed by the testator in the presence of us both present at the same time who, at his request, in his presence and in the presence of each other have hereunto set our names as witnesses.

Thomas Smith
Signature of Testator;

William Jones (*signed*) of Green Gables, South Street, Reading, tailor.

Henry Morgan (*signed*) of 16, North Street, Reading, butcher.

Should it be desired to give legacies and/or gifts of specific property, instead of giving the whole estate to one or more persons, the form about should be used with the substitution for clause 2 of the following clauses:—

2. I give to —— of —— the sum of £—— and to —— of —— the sum of £—— and to —— of —— all my books (*or as the case may require*).

3. All the residue of my property real and personal I give to —— of ——.

TERMS.—Real property includes freehold land and houses; while personal property includes debts due, arrears of rents, money, leasehold property, house furniture, goods, assurance policies, stocks and shares in companies, and the like. The words " my money," apart from the context, will normally only include actual real money. The expression " goods and chattels " should not be used. In giving *particular* property, ordinary language is sufficient, *e.g.*, " my house, Vince Cottage, Silver Street, Reading, Berks." Such specific gifts fail if not owned by the testator at his death.

RESIDUARY LEGATEES.—It is well in all cases where legacies or specific gifts are made, to leave to some person or persons " the residue of my property," although it may be thought that the whole of the property has been disposed of in legacies, etc., already mentioned in the will. *It should be remembered that a will operates on property acquired after it has been made.*

EXECUTION OF A WILL, AND WITNESSES.—The testator should sign his name at the foot or end of the will, in presence of two witnesses, who will immediately afterwards sign their names in his and in each other's presence. A person who has been left any gift or share of residue in the will, or whose wife or husband has been left such a gift, should not be an attesting witness. Their attestation would be good, but they would forfeit the gift. It is better that a person named as executor should not be a witness. Husband and wife may both be witnesses, provided neither is a legatee. If a solicitor be appointed executor, it is lawful to direct that his ordinary fees and charges shall be paid; but in this case he (as an interested party) must not be a witness to the will.

It is desirable that the witnesses should be fully described, as they may possibly be wanted at some future time. If the testator should be too ill to sign, even by a mark, another person may sign the testator's name to the will for him, in his presence and by his direction, and in this case it should be shown that the testator knew the contents of the document. The attestation clause should therefore be worded: " Signed by Thomas Brown, by the direction and in the presence of the testator, Thomas Smith, in the joint presence of us, who thereupon signed our names in his presence and in the presence of each other, the will having been first read over to the testator, who appeared fully to understand the same."

A *blind person* may make a will in Braille. If the testator be blind the will should be read aloud to him in the presence of the witnesses, and the fact mentioned in the attestation clause. A blind person cannot witness a will.

If by inadvertence the testator should have signed his will without the witnesses being present, then the attestation should be:—" The testator acknowledged his signature already made as his signature to his last will and testament, in the joint presence," etc. Any omission in the observance of these details may invalidate the will. *The stringency of the law as to signature and witnessing of a will is only relaxed in favour of soldiers, sailors and airmen in certain circumstances.*

EXECUTORS.—It is usual to appoint two executors, although one is sufficient; any number up to and including four may be appointed. The name and address of each executor should be given in full. An executor may be a legatee. Thus a child of full age or wife to whom the whole or a portion of the estate is left may be appointed sole executor, or one of two executors. The addresses of the executors are not essential; but it is desirable here as elsewhere, to avoid ambiguity or vagueness.

LAPSED LEGACIES.—If a legatee dies in the life-time of the testator, the legacy generally lapses and falls into the residue. Where a residuary legatee predeceases the testator, his share of the residuary estate will not generally pass to the other residuary legatees, but will pass to the persons entitled on the deceased's intestacy. In all such cases it is desirable to make a new will.

TESTAMENTARY CAPACITY.—A minor, i.e. a person under 18, cannot make a will except, in certain circumstances, if he be a soldier, sailor or airman. A married woman may dispose by will of any real or personal property as if she were a man.

REVOCATION.—A will is revoked by a subsequent will (but, if it does not expressly revoke former wills, only so far as such subsequent will operates as an implied revocation as by making other provisions inconsistent with the previous will, for this reason a will should always have a clause revoking previous testamentary dispositions), or by burning, tearing or otherwise *destroying* the will with the intention of revoking it. Such destruction must either be by the testator or by some other person in his presence and at his direction. *It is not sufficient to obliterate the will with a pen.* Marriage in every case acts as the revocation of a will, unless, in the case of a will made on or after Jan. 1, 1926, it is expressed to have been made in contemplation of a particular marriage (Law of Property Act, 1925, s. 177); so that after marriage a new will should be made, except in this last case.

PERSONAL APPLICATION FOR PROBATE OR LETTERS OF ADMINISTRATION

Application for probate or for letters of administration may be made *in person* at the Principal Probate Registry, a district probate registry or sub-registry, or a probate office by the executors or persons entitled to a grant of administration (*see* list of probate offices, pp. 1181–2). Applicants should bring (1) the will, if any; (2) a certificate of death; (3) particulars of property liable to estate duty; and (4) generally, a list of debts and funeral expenses. In an application for administration, the applicant will be required to enter into a bond for due administration, generally with two sureties who must attend at the Registry, although they need not do so at the same time as the applicant.

Intending applicants, before attending at a registry or probate office, should write or telephone to the nearest probate registry or sub-registry for the necessary forms. Postal or telephone applications cannot be dealt with at the local probate offices, which are part-time only.

Certain property can be disposed of on death without a grant of probate or administration, or in pursuance of a nomination made by the deceased, provided the amount involved does not exceed £500. *See* the Administration of Estates (Small Payments) Act, 1965.

WHERE TO FIND A PROVED WILL

A will proved since 1858 must have been proved either at the Principal Registry at Somerset House, or a District Registry. In the former case the original will itself is carefully preserved at Somerset House, the copy of which probate has been granted is in the hands of the executors who proved the will, and another copy for Parliament is bound up in a folio volume of wills made by testators of that initial and date; the indices to these volumes fill a room of considerable size at Somerset House, where the indices may be examined and a copy of any will read. In the latter case, the original will proved in the District Registry, is kept there, and may be seen or a *copy* obtained, but a copy is sent to and filed at Somerset House, where also it may be seen. A general index of grants, both probates and administrations, is prepared and printed annually in lexicographical form, and may be seen at either the Principal or a District Registry. This index is usually ready by about October of the following year.

SCOTS LAW OF WILLS

A domiciled Scotsman, unlike a domiciled Englishman, cannot in certain circumstances dispose effectively of the entirety of his estate. If he leave a widow and children, the widow is entitled to a one-third share in the whole of the moveable estate (her *jus relictae*), and the children are entitled to another one-third share equally between them (their *legitim*). If he leave a widow but no children —or children but no widow—the *jus relictae* or *legitim* is increased to a one-half share of the estate. The remaining portion is known as the *dead's part.* A surviving husband and children have comparable rights (*jus relicti* and *legitim*) in the wife's estate. It should be noted that the amount of any claim of *jus relicti, jus relictae* or *legitim* out of an estate shall be calculated by reference to so much of the net moveable estate as remains after the satisfaction of any prior claims under the Succession (Scotland) Act, 1964,—*see* Illegitimacy, Scotland and Intestacy, Scotland, *supra.* The *dead's part* is the only portion of which the testator can freely dispose. All burdens falling upon the representatives in moveables are payable out of the whole of the moveables before any division. Burdens in the nature of legacies are payable out of the *dead's part.* Pupils cannot make wills. Formerly a minor could dispose only of moveables but since the passing of the Succession (Scotland) Act, 1964 he has a like capacity to test on heritable property. A will must be in writing (except that a person may leave a legacy verbally if the amount of that legacy does not exceed 100 pounds Scots (£8·33 sterling)) and may be typewritten or even in pencil. A will may be either (1) *holograph*, i.e. written by the testator himself, in which case no witnesses are necessary; a printed form filled up by the testator is not necessarily *holograph* but may be made effectual when it has clearly been adopted as *holograph.* Words written on erasure or marginal additions or interlineations in *holograph* writings, if proved to be in the handwriting of the maker of the deed, are valid; (2) *tested*, i.e., signed in presence of two witnesses. It is not necessary that these witnesses should sign in presence of one another, or even that they should see the testator signing so long as the testator acknowledges his signature to the witnesses. The Conveyancing and Feudal Reform (Scotland) Act 1970 whilst altering generally the rules for the description of deeds, specifically (s. 44 (2)) makes no change in the rules applying to wills which must still be signed by the testator on every page. If the testator cannot write, or is blind, his will may be authenticated by a notary and two witnesses. It is better that the will be not witnessed by a beneficiary thereunder, although this circumstance will not invalidate the attestation of the will or (as it would in England) the gift. A parish minister may act as a notary for

the purpose of subscribing a will in his own parish. Wills are registered in the Books of the Sheriffdom in which the deceased died domiciled, and in the Books of Council and Session, H.M. General Register House, Edinburgh. The original deed may be inspected on payment of a small fee and a certified official copy may be obtained. A Scottish will is not revoked by the subsequent marriage of the testator. The subsequent birth of a child, no testamentary provision having been made for him, may revoke a will in whole or in part. A will is revoked by a subsequent will, either expressly or by implication; but in so far as the two can be read together both wills have effect.

"Confirmation," the Scottish equivalent of Probate, is obtained in the Sheriff Court of the County in which the deceased was domiciled at the date of his death or, where he had no fixed domicile or died abroad, in the commissariat of Edinburgh. Executors are either "nominate" or "dative." An Executor nominate is one nominated by the deceased in his will or, where such person has predeceased the testator, by the residuary beneficiary. An Executor dative is one appointed by the Court (1) in the case of intestacy or (2) where the deceased had failed to name an executor in his will. In the former case the deceased's next-of-kin are all entitled to be declared executors dative. An inventory of the deceased's estate and a schedule of debts, together with an affidavit, must first be given up. In estates under £1,000 nett confirmation is obtained under a simplified procedure at reduced fees.

Presumption of Survivorship.—The Succession (Scotland) Act, 1964, referred to above provides that where two persons die in circumstances indicating that they died simultaneously or if it is uncertain which was the survivor, the younger will be deemed to have survived the older; but if the persons so dying were husband and wife, neither shall be presumed to have survived the other.

PROBATE OFFICES
(See pp. 461–2)
The Principal Registry of the Family Division, S.W. Wing, Bush House, Strand, London, W.C.2.
[08-836 7366] Mon.–Fri. 9.30–4.30
District Probate Registries and Sub-registries (Mon.–Fri., 9.30–4).

BANGOR, Caerns.—Garth Road.
BIRMINGHAM.—Cavendish House, Waterloo Street.
BODMIN, Cornwall.—Market St.
BRIGHTON.—28 Richmond Place.
BRISTOL.—37–41 Prince Street.
CARLISLE.—2 Victoria Place.
CARMARTHEN.—King Street.
CHESTER.—17 Cuppin Street.
COVENTRY.—4 Copthall House, Eaton Road.
EXETER.—94 Fore Street.
GLOUCESTER.—3 Pitt Street.
IPSWICH.—15 Museum Street.
KINGSTON-UPON-HULL.—Commerce House, Paragon Street.

LANCASTER.—3 Cable Street.
LEEDS.—Devereux House, East Parade.
LEICESTER.—Govt. Bldgs., Newarke Street.
LINCOLN.—Guildhall Street.
LIVERPOOL.—India Bldgs., Water Street.
LLANDAFF.—Probate Registry of Wales, 49 Cardiff Road
MAIDSTONE, Kent.—5–11 London Road
MANCHESTER.—9th Flr., Astley House, 23 Quay Street.

NEWCASTLE UPON TYNE.—Prudhoe House, Prudhoe Street.
NORWICH.—65 Cathedral Close.
NOTTINGHAM.—Castle Gate Ho.
OXFORD.—10A New Road.
PETERBOROUGH.—Clifton House, Broadway.
SHEFFIELD.—24 Castle Square.
STOKE ON TRENT.—Norwich Union Ho., Trinity St., Hanley.
TEESSIDE.—91 Albert Road, Middlesbrough.
WINCHESTER.—4 St. Peter Street.
YORK.—Duncombe Place.

Local Probate Offices (with days and hours of opening)
(A=10.30–1; 2–4; B=11–3; C=11–1; 2–3; D=10–1; 2–4; E=10–1; 2–3.30; F=10.30–1; 2–3.30)
BEDFORDSHIRE: Bedford, 42–44 Ashburnham Road (W.A); Luton, Phoenix House, 2 Mill Street (M.A).
BERKSHIRE: Reading, 16–18 Friar Street (Tu.A).
BUCKINGHAMSHIRE: Aylesbury, 49 Buckingham Street (M.B); High Wycombe, 7 Queen Victoria Road (W.A); Slough, Prudential Buildings, High Street (Tu. & Th.A).
CAMBRIDGE: 20 Station Road (M.A).
CARDIGANSHIRE: Aberystwyth, 30 Pier Street (1st & 3rd F. monthly, C).
CHESHIRE: Crewe, 6 Nile Street (Th.D); Stockport, 54 St. Petersgate (F.A); Wallasey, Dominick House, St. Albans Road (Tu.A).
CORNWALL: Truro, Rm 12, Public Rooms, Quay Street (W.E).
CUMBERLAND: Workington, Langdale House, Gray Street (Tu.B).
DENBIGHSHIRE: Wrexham, 24 Grosvenor Road (M.B).
DERBYSHIRE: Chesterfield, 22 Knifesmithgate (M.A); Derby, St. Mary's Gate (F.A).
DEVON: Barnstaple, Queen's House, Queen Street (1st & 3rd Th. monthly, F.); Newton Abbot, 1 Courtenay Park (W.F); Plymouth, Pearl Assurance Bldg., Royal Parade (Tu. & Th., 10.30–1; 1.45–3.45).
DORSET: Dorchester, 59–60 High West Street (2nd & 4th Th. monthly, 11.30–3).

DURHAM: Darlington, 1 Victoria Road (Th.E); Durham, Elvet House (W. & F.D); South Shields, Wouldhave House, Market Place (Th.D); Sunderland, Dunn House, North Bridge Street (Tu.D).
ESSEX: Chelmsford, London House, New London Road (F.A); Colchester, 11 Pelhams Lane (M.A); Harlow, Beaufort House, Crown Gate (W.B); Romford, 16–18 North Street (M. & Th.A); Southend-on-Sea, Baryta House, Victoria Avenue (W.B).
FLINTSHIRE: Rhyl, New Lessor Bldg., 64 Brighton Road (F.B).
GLAMORGAN: Bridgend, Garth Celyn, Merthyr Mawr Road (T.E); Pontypridd, 37–38 Mill Street (W.D); Swansea, Custom House, Cambrian Place (Tu. & Th.D).
GLOUCESTERSHIRE: Cheltenham, 55 Clarence Street (F.A).
HAMPSHIRE: Bournemouth, Crown Chambers, Richmond Hill (M.F); Newport, I. of Wight, Broadlands House (1st & 3rd Th. monthly, F.); Portsmouth, 47 Kingston Crescent (Tu. & W.F); Southampton, Hanover House, Hanover Buildings (Tu. & W.A).
HEREFORDSHIRE: Hereford, 27 Castle Street (W.B).
HERTFORDSHIRE: Watford, Rigby House, 14A High Street (W. & F.A).
KENT: Canterbury, 22–23 St. Margaret's Street (Tu.F); Folkestone, Old Council Offices, Church Street (Th.F); Ramsgate, New Court House, Cavendish Street (W.B); Rochester, 6 New Road (M.F); Tunbridge Wells, 47 London Road (M.A).

LANCASHIRE: Barrow-in-Furness, Rm. 22, Employment Exchange, Duke Street (*W*.B); Blackpool, Rm. 118, 22 Plymouth Road (*Th*.A); Bolton, Knowsley House, Knowsley Street (*M*. & *W*.A); Burnley, Rm. 414, Brun House, Kingsway (*Tu*. B); Oldham, Rm. 14, County Court Bldg., Church Lane (*Tu*. & *Th*.A); Preston, Arndale House, Lancaster Road (*Tu*.A); St. Helens, County Court Bldgs., East Street (*W*.A.); Southport, Coronation Bldgs., Lord Street (*Th*. A); Warrington, Bold Street Methodist Church Rms., Palmyra Square North (*W*.A.); Wigan, 71/73 King Street (*M*.A).

LINCOLNSHIRE: Boston, Crown Bldg., Nelson Way (1st & 3rd *Th*. monthly, 11–1; 2–4); Grantham, Spitalgate House, London Road (*M*.A); Grimsby, 202 Victoria Street (*W*.A.); Scunthorpe, 28 Laneham Street (*M*.B).

LONDON: Woolwich, 26/28 Powis Street, S.E.18 (*Tu*. & *F*.A).

MIDDLESEX: Enfield, Embassy Bldg., Eaton Road (*M*.A).

MONMOUTHSHIRE: Newport, Olympia House, Dock Street (*Th*.D).

NORFOLK: King's Lynn, County Court Offices, London Road (*Tu*. 11–1; 2–4).

NORTHAMPTONSHIRE: Kettering, Northampton House, Station Road (*M*.B); Northampton, 15 Castilian Street (*W*.B).

NORTHUMBERLAND: Alnwick, U.D.C. Offices, Wagonway Road (2nd & 4th *M*. monthly, F); Ashington, Government Bldgs., Woodhorn Road (1st & 3rd *M* monthly, F).

NOTTINGHAMSHIRE: Mansfield, Bentinck Chmbrs., Market Street (*Th*.A).

OXFORDSHIRE: Banbury, 3 West Bar (*Th*.B).

PEMBROKESHIRE: Haverfordwest, 7 Goat Street (*W*.A).

SHROPSHIRE: Shrewsbury, 1 Barker Street (*Tu*.B).

SOMERSET: Bath, 7 Pulteney Street (*Tu*.A); Taunton, Quantock House, Paul Street (*F*.F); Weston-super-Mare, 39A Oxford Street (*Th*.A); Yeovil, 20 Kingston (1st & 3rd *M* monthly, 9.30–12.30; 1.30–3).

STAFFORDSHIRE: Lichfield, Municipal Offices, Wade Street (*W*.D); Stafford, Employment Exchange, Millbank (*W*.D); Wolverhampton, Govt. Bldgs., Bath Avenue (*Tu*. D).

SUFFOLK: Bury St. Edmunds, Triton House, St. Andrews Street North (*W*.A); Lowestoft, Sea View, Battery Green Road (*Th*.A).

SURREY: Croydon, 454/458 London Road (*W*. & *F*. A); Guildford, Stoke House, Leapole Lane (*M*.F); Surbiton, 19 Upper Brighton Road (*Tu*. & Th. A).

SUSSEX: Crawley, 8 The Broadway (*W*.A); Hastings, 10B Queen's Road (*Th*.A); Worthing, Revenue Chambers, Chapel Road (*F*.A).

WILTSHIRE: Salisbury, Lloyds Bank Chambers, Blue Boar Row (*Th*.B); Swindon, Park House, Church Place (*F*.B).

WORCESTERSHIRE: Kidderminster, 99 New Road (*M*.D); Worcester, 3 Sansome Place (*M*.A).

YORKSHIRE: Bradford, Forster House, Forster Square (*M*. & *Th*.A); Doncaster, Y.M.C.A. Bldg., Wood Street (*Tu*.E); Harrogate, 35 Victoria Avenue (*F*.A); Huddersfield, 1/5 Cloth Hall Street (*W*., 10.30–1; 2–3.45); Scarborough, Arundel House, Arundel Place (*Th*.A); Wakefield, 49 King Street (*Th*.D).

TAXES AND STAMP DUTIES
SELECTIVE EMPLOYMENT TAX

This new tax was imposed by the Finance Act 1966, section 44, but the details regarding repayment to certain employers and a number of other matters are contained in the Selective Employment Payments Act 1966, the Finance Acts 1967, 1968 and 1969 and the Revenue Act 1968. The Finance Act 1966 imposes on the employer the liability to pay selective employment tax " in respect of each person in respect of whom the employer is liable to pay an employer's insurance contribution for that week "—the reference to the week is because the tax is imposed in respect of each contribution week beginning on or after September 5, 1966. The result of the above is that all employers must pay the tax in respect of all employees who work for the employers for more than eight hours in a week; the only exceptions relate to the Forces and certain seamen. The weekly amount of the tax is now as follows:—

Male over 18........................ £1·20
Female over 18...................... 60p
Male under 18....................... 60p
Female under 18..................... 40p

The tax is collected together with the employer's insurance contributions (*i.e.*, contributions payable by him under the National Insurance Acts), but, in so far as collected in Great Britain, is paid by the Minister of Social Security into the Exchequer.

The tax is collected from all employers, but to certain manufacturing employers it was to be repaid with a premium, to certain other employers the tax is repaid without a premium, the third group of employers pay the tax but obtain no repayment. However, since the Revenue Act, 1968, the premium is only payable in respect of establishments within a development area.

It was announced in the 1971 budget proposals that the tax will be abolished in its entirety in April, 1973, and, together with Purchase Tax, replaced by Value Added Tax.

SELECTIVE EMPLOYMENT PREMIUM

Section 1 provides for repayment by the Secretary of State for Employment and Productivity of selective employment tax and payment of a premium to certain employers; the weekly amount of the premium varies with the tax paid as follows:—

Tax	Premium
£1·20	£1·50
60p	75p
40p	47½p

The tax and premium are payable in respect of employment in an establishment in a development area engaged by way of business in certain activities, research or training, set out in more detail below, but in order to qualify for repayment of tax and payment of premium more than half of the employees must be employed wholly or mainly in connection with such activities, research or training, and must not be employed wholly or mainly in non-qualifying activities, *i.e.*, broadly, activities carried on for office purposes, or activities by way of carriage of goods by road in connection with a business by the owner of the business, or activities by way of the sale of goods.

The activities which qualify for repayment of tax and payment of premium are set out in detail in Orders III to XVI of the Standard Industrial Classification—the main headings are as follows:—

Food, Drink and Tobacco—including grain milling, making bread, etc., curing bacon, making butter, manufacturing sugar, jam, etc., preserving fruit, manufacturing animal food, brewing ale and

distilling gin and whisky, and manufacturing tobacco.

Chemicals and Allied Industries, including manufacturing coke, refining petroleum, tar distillation, compounding patent medicines, and production of crude oil from seeds and fish.

Metal Manufacture, including smelting, refining and alloying. Engineering and Electrical goods.

Shipbuilding and Marine Engineering, including repair of ships.

Vehicles—including repair of locomotives.

Metal goods not elsewhere specified, including assaying, smelting and refining of gold, silver and platinum.

Textiles, including preparation of fabrics.

Leather, leather goods and fur, including curing skins and dressing furs.

Clothing and footwear.

Bricks, pottery, glass, cement, etc.

Timber, furniture, etc., including saw milling.

Paper, printing and publishing, including printing of wallpaper, printing and publishing newspapers and magazines.

Other manufacturing industries—not otherwise specified.

Also included are activities by way of the manufacture from exposed film of cinematograph films for public exhibition and the production thereof including television presentation, certain specified activities in relation to scrap metal and waste paper, industrial photography and slaughter of animals, as set out in the Selective Employment Payments Variation Order, 1969, and any scientific research related to any of the activities specified above.

SELECTIVE EMPLOYMENT REFUND

Section 2 deals with repayment by the appropriate Minister—the Secretary for Employment and Productivity—of selective employment tax, but without payment of any premium. The repayment is payable in respect of employment in an establishment engaged by way of business in certain activities set out below, but in order to qualify more than half of the employees must be employed wholly or mainly in connection with those activities and must not be employed wholly or mainly in non-qualifying activities. Non-qualifying activities are defined above, but in this context do not include the carriage of goods by road in connection with a business by the owner of the business (except in relation to road haulage contractors).

The main activities which qualify for repayment of the tax are as follows: Sea fishing and whaling; Fishing in inland waters and the operation of fish farms; Mining and quarrying; Production and distribution of electricity and water; Railways; Road passenger transport, including taxis and car hire; Road haulage contracting; Sea transport; Port and inland water transport; Air transport; Postal services and tele-communications; Extraction of coal from open-cast workings; Agriculture, horticulture and forestry; milk processing and delivering; and relevant scientific research or training.

PAYMENTS TO CERTAIN PUBLIC BODIES

Section 3 enables "the designated Minister" (*i.e.*, designated by the Treasury) to repay the tax to certain public bodies with, in certain cases, a premium as well, except in respect of employees employed in National Coal Board depots which are outside the curtilage of a colliery and wholly or mainly engaged in wholesale or retail dealing in coal, or employed in premises occupied by British Transport Hotels Ltd., or employed by Thos. Cook and Son Ltd., any wholly-owned subsidiary, or employed by the National Savings Bank, N.C.B. Computer Power, the National Data Processing Service of the Post Office, a shop, room or other place used by an Area Electricity Board, the North of Scotland Hydro-Electric Board or the South of Scotland Electricity Board wholly or mainly for the sole display or demonstration of apparatus or accessories for the use of consumers of electricity, and similar provisions in respect of an Area Gas Board.

The public bodies within section 3 are as follows:

1. The National Coal Board.
2. The Electricity Council.
3. The Central Electricity Generating Board.
4. An Area Electricity Board.
5. The North of Scotland Hydro-Electric Board.
6. The South of Scotland Electricity Board.
7. The Gas Council.
8. An Area Gas Board.
9. The British Railways Board.
10. The London Transport Board.
11. The British Transport Docks Board.
12. The British Waterways Board.
13. The Transport Holding Company.
14. Any company which is a wholly-owned subsidiary of any of the bodies specified in paragraphs 9 to 13 or which would be such a subsidiary if any two or more of those bodies constituted a single body corporate.
15. Cable and Wireless Ltd.
16. The Commonwealth Development Corporation.
17. The British Overseas Airways Corporation.
18. B.O.A.C. Associated Companies Ltd.
19. B.E.A.
19A. B.E.A. Airtours Ltd.
20. B.E.A. Helicopters Ltd.
21. The British Airports Authority.
22. The United Kingdom Atomic Energy Authority so far as its activities are financed out of the United Kingdom Atomic Energy Authority Trading Fund.

The parts of the undertakings set out above which qualify for the payment of the premium are as follows, but only if situate in a development area—The Brickworks Executive of the National Coal Board; The Coal Products Division of the National Coal Board; The Tredomen and Cowdenbeath workshops of the National Coal Board; The London Transport Railway Overhaul Workshops at Acton; Workshops of the British Waterways Board which are wholly or mainly engaged in manufacturing or repairing waterway equipment; Workshops and railway signal works of the British Railways Board which are wholly or mainly engaged in manufacturing or repairing railway equipment; Star Bodies (B.R.S.) Ltd.; The Engineering and Maintenance Division of the British Overseas Airways Corporation; The Engineering Department of: British European Airways Corporation; BEA Helicopters Limited. Activities financed out of the United Kingdom Atomic Energy Authority Trading Fund.

PAYMENTS TO LOCAL AUTHORITIES, ETC.

Section 4 enables "the appropriate Minister" (*i.e.*, in relation to an employer in Scotland or in Wales or Monmouthshire, the Secretary of State; in any other case, the Secretary of State for the Environment) to make payments to certain employers by reference to the amounts paid by way of selective employment tax. The employers within the section include local authorities, development corporations, statutory water undertakers and internal drainage boards.

REFUNDS TO CHARITIES

Section 5 provides for the refund by the Minister of Labour of selective employment tax paid by

charities, subject to certain conditions, including production to the Minister of records of the payment of the tax. For this purpose, in England and Wales, "charity" means a body registered under the Charities Act, 1960 or certified as a charity not requiring registration or as an ecclesiastical corporation, and includes Greenwich Hospital. In the application of this section to Scotland, "charity" has the same meaning as in the Income Tax Acts, and the Minister is not bound to make any payment unless the Secretary of State certifies that the employer is a charity within that meaning.

REFUNDS FOR CERTAIN HOUSEHOLDS

Section 6 deals with repayment by the Minister of Social Security to certain employers (not being charities as above defined) of selective employment tax paid in respect of an employee in a qualified household for more than eight hours a week in giving domestic or nursing assistance, subject to the Supplementary Benefits Commission being satisfied that the requirements of section 6 are fulfilled. A qualified household is a private household which includes a person (not being the employee) over the age of seventy, or which includes a person in need of such assistance by reason of infirmity, sickness or other incapacity (including pregnancy) or which includes a child under sixteen (not being a child of the family of the employee). However, no repayment can be made in respect of the child under sixteen if the household includes both parents of the child, although the household must contain one (but not more) member who is either a parent or a spouse of a parent of the child and who is normally engaged for more than eight hours in the week in work other than domestic work of the household. If the household includes no such parent or spouse but includes a person (fulfilling the eight-hour qualification) who appears to the Supplementary Benefits Commission to be discharging the function of a parent with respect to the child, and does not include a spouse of such person, then repayment will be made.

Other Refunds—Finance Acts 1967 and 1968

1. Where an employer has paid the tax in respect of an employee for any contribution week beginning on or after September 4, 1967 in which the employee worked in that employment for less than 21 hours, the Minister shall refund to that employer a sum equal to half the tax paid, except where (a) the employee was for the purposes of the tax a boy or girl under the age of 18, or (b) the contract normally involved that employee's working for 21 or more hours weekly. If the contribution week begins on or after September 2, 1968, the refund is two-thirds of the tax paid.

2. Where an employer has paid the tax in respect of an employee who, during a continuous period of more than 13 contribution weeks, has been employed by him wholly outside the U.K., the Minister shall refund to that employer the tax paid in respect of that employee for those weeks, provided that the 14th of such weeks began on or after September 4, 1967.

3. There are further detailed restrictions on the payment of the above refunds, and the Finance Act 1968 deals with payments in respect of a person over 65.

REGISTERS AND ENFORCEMENT

In the case of employments within section 1 or 2, the Minister required to make repayments must compile registers of establishments falling within the repayment and premium provisions; registration is made on application by the employer in a prescribed form. The Minister is not bound to make any payment before registration of the establishment, nor in respect of any contributions week as respects which the employer does not produce records of payment of selective employment tax. An establishment is deemed to have been registered as from the date on which the application for registration was received by the Minister or such earlier date as it appears to the Minister to be equitable to allow.

Any person authorized by the Minister may enter on registered business premises, or any premises occupied by a charity who have claimed repayment of the tax, in order to examine and make copies of records of payment of the tax, and such person may require anyone on the premises to give him such information as he may reasonably request as to the activities carried on in the establishment.

TABLE OF INCOME OR WAGES
(Based on the official *whole new penny* conversion table.)

Per Year	Per Month	Per Week	Per Day	Per Year	Per Month	Per Week	Per Day	Per Year	Per Month	Per Week	Per Day
£	£	£	£	£	£	£	£	£	£	£	£
0·50	0·04	0·01	—	8·00	0·67	0·15	0·02	18·00	1·50	0·35	0·05
1·00	0·08	0·02	—	8·40	0·70	0·16	0·03	18·90	1·57	0·36	0·05
1·50	0·13	0·03	—	8·50	0·71	0·16	0·03	19·00	1·58	0·37	0·05
2·00	0·17	0·04	—	9·00	0·75	0·17	0·03	20·00	1·67	0·38	0·05
2·10	0·17	0·05	—	9·45	0·79	0·18	0·03	30·00	2·50	0·58	0·08
2·50	0·21	0·05	—	10·00	0·83	0·19	0·03	40·00	3·33	0·77	0·11
3·00	0·25	0·06	0·01	10·50	0·87	0·20	0·03	50·00	4·17	0·96	0·14
3·15	0·26	0·06	0·01	11·00	0·92	0·21	0·03	60·00	5·00	1·15	0·17
3·50	0·29	0·07	0·01	11·55	0·96	0·23	0·03	70·00	5·83	1·35	0·19
4·00	0·33	0·07	0·01	12·00	1·00	0·23	0·03	80·00	6·67	1·54	0·22
4·20	0·35	0·08	0·01	12·60	1·05	0·24	0·04	90·00	7·50	1·73	0·25
4·50	0·37	0·09	0·01	13·00	1·08	0·25	0·04	100·00	8·33	1·92	0·27
5·00	0·42	0·10	0·01	13·65	1·14	0·26	0·04	200·00	16·67	3·85	0·55
5·25	0·44	0·10	0·01	14·00	1·17	0·27	0·04	300·00	25·00	5·77	0·82
5·50	0·46	0·12	0·02	14·70	1·23	0·28	0·04	400·00	33·33	7·69	1·10
6·00	0·50	0·12	0·02	15·00	1·25	0·29	0·04	500·00	41·67	9·62	1·37
6·30	0·53	0·13	0·02	15·75	1·31	0·30	0·04	600·00	50·00	11·54	1·64
6·50	0·54	0·13	0·02	16·00	1·33	0·31	0·05	700·00	58·33	13·46	1·92
7·00	0·58	0·13	0·02	16·80	1·40	0·32	0·05	800·00	66·67	15·38	2·19
7·35	0·61	0·14	0·02	17·00	1·42	0·33	0·05	900·00	75·00	17·31	2·47
7·50	0·63	0·15	0·02	17·85	1·49	0·34	0·05	1000·00	83·33	19·23	2·74

INCOME TAX 1971–72

By the Finance Act, 1965, a new tax, the Corporation Tax, was introduced and applies to the income and profits of bodies corporate. The Corporation Tax is outside the scope of this article which must therefore be read throughout as not applying to bodies corporate. Income Tax remains chargeable on the income of all individuals and persons other than bodies corporate, as in previous years.

Income Tax is a tax on annual income, represented by money, or money's worth. In general, the charge to tax is on the full amount of income arising for the year of assessment, the fiscal year which runs from April 6 in one year to April 5 in the next, subject to the deductions authorized by the Income Tax Acts. Under Schedule D, however, the assessment is made on the profits or gains of a continuing trade or profession for the year preceding the year of assessment, which is called the "basis year." The profits are arrived at on ordinary accountancy principles and then adjusted for tax purposes. The profits for the accounting year of the trade or profession which ends in the year preceding the year of assessment, are the profits of the "basis year."

Broadly, the charge to tax is on income arising in the United Kingdom, or on income received from home or abroad, by residents in the United Kingdom. An individual is resident and ordinarily resident in the United Kingdom if he is living here in the ordinary course of his life, or for an extended period; also, though normally he lives here, if he is abroad for occasional residence only; or if he visits the United Kingdom year by year, even though his main home is abroad.

The income of a married woman living with her husband is aggregated with his income. Separate assessment may be claimed, but the tax due remains the same. From April 1971, the earned income of a married woman may be assessed as if she were not married provided that on the balance of their joint income the husband is assessed as a single man.

Income Tax is imposed at the rates specified by the annual Finance Acts. There are graduated rates of tax the principal rate being called the "Standard Rate," which for 1971–72 is 38·75 per cent. (39p in the £). There is an additional income tax on higher incomes called "Sur-tax." The enactments relating to income tax were consolidated in the Income and Corporation Tax Act 1970, as amended by subsequent Finance Acts.

The Tables which follow show the income tax payable for 1971-72 and surtax (if any) for 1971-72, payable on Jan. 1, 1973 by an individual on the amount of income specified, after deduction of the personal allowance, children's allowance (where appropriate) and, in the case of earned income, the earned income relief. The taxpayer, however, may be entitled to further reliefs which would reduce the tax payable below the amounts shown in the Tables.

Assessment.—The Income Tax Acts provide for tax to be assessed and collected under a number of Schedules which deal with separate sources of income:—

Schedule A—Under this schedule are assessed those receipts previously dealt with under case VIII of Schedule D, *viz:* ground rents, certain other receipts from land (other than mineral rents and Royalties) rents (less expenditure on maintenance insurance and repairs) and premiums on leases for less than fifty years. Such premiums are assessed on the amount received less 2 per cent. for every year

Income	Income all Earned		All Investment Income	
Ann. (Wkly.)	Income Tax and Surtax (if any)	Average Rate per cent.	Income Tax and Surtax (if any)	Average Rate per cent.
£	£		£	
416 (£8)...	Nil		Nil	
468 (£9)...	15	3·2	19	4·0
520 (£10)..	30	5·7	48	9·2
572 (£11)..	44	7·6	76	13·2
624 (£12)..	62	9·9	105	16·8
676 (£13)..	77	11·3	133	19·6
728 (£14)..	93	12·7	156	21·4
780 (£15)..	109	13·9	176	22·5
832 (£16)..	124	14·9	196	23·4
900........	145	16·1	222	24·6
1,000........	175	16·9	261	26·1
1,100........	205	18·7	300	27·3
1,200........	235	19·6	339	28·2
1,300........	265	20·5	377	29·0
1,400........	296	21·1	416	29·7
1,500........	326	21·7	455	30·3
1,600........	356	22·3	494	30·8
1,700........	386	22·7	532	31·3
1,800........	416	23·1	571	31·7
1,900........	446	23·5	610	32·1
2,000........	476	23·8	649	32·4
2,250........	552	24·5	745	33·1
2,500........	627	25·1	842	33·7
2,750........	702	25·5	1,020	37·0
3,000........	778	25·9	1,148	38·2
3,500........	928	26·5	1,429	40·8
4,000........	1,079	27·0	1,711	42·7
4,500........	1,243	27·6	2,017	44·8
5,000........	1,408	28·2	2,324	46·4
6,000........	1,827	30·5	2,986	49·7
7,000........	2,239	31·9	3,699	52·7
8,000........	2,799	35·0	4,411	55·1
9,000........	3,248	36·0	5,174	57·4
10,000........	3,911	39·1	5,936	59·3
12,000........	5,117	42·6	7,561	63·0
15,000........	7,085	47·2	10,149	67·6
20,000........	10,674	53·4	14,586	72·9
25,000........	14,439	57·7	19,024	76·0
30,000........	18,211	60·7	23,461	78·2
40,000........	25,754	64·3	32,336	80·8
50,000........	33,298	66·6	41,211	82·4
100,000........	71,017	71·0	85,586	85·5

after the first year. "Lease" includes any tenancy. Furnished letting income is normally assessed under case VI Schedule D without distinguishing the receipts as between the space let and the furniture hire. But rent for the space can be distinguished and assessed under Schedule A, the profit on hire being assessed under case VI schedule D.

Under Schedule B.—Assessment under this Schedule is now restricted to woodlands in the U.K. managed on a commercial basis and with a view to the realization of profits. The assessment on woodlands will be based on one-third of the annual value of the land arrived at on the normal rating basis on the assumption that the lands were let and occupied in their natural and unimproved state. The taxpayer has the option to be assessed under Schedule D Case I on the results shown by accounts instead.

Under Schedule C.—Assessed on the paying agent. Not of concern to the individual tax payer.

Under Schedule D.—This schedule is divided into six cases as follows:—Cases I and II—Profits of

trades, businesses, commercial activities on land including farming, professions or vocations.

Case III—Interest on Government stocks not taxed at source (*e.g.* War Loan, Defence Bonds, National Development Bonds), bank deposit interest, discounts, etc. Interest on National Savings Bank and Trustee Savings Bank accounts up to £21 is exempt from income tax but assessable to Surtax grossed at standard rate. This exemption applies to both husband and wife separately. Interest on the new Post Office Investment Deposits and also Trustee Savings Bank Special Investment Accounts is, however, not exempt.

Cases IV and V.—Interest from foreign or Commonwealth securities, rents, dividends and all other unearned income: assessed on full amount arising, whether remitted or not, where person domiciled and ordinarily resident in the U.K. But on amount remitted, where person not domiciled in the U.K. or a British subject not ordinarily resident. In cases of Income earned abroad (*e.g.* from businesses,

trades, and professions) and pensions, assessed only on amount remitted and only where person entitled is resident in U.K.

Case VI.—Sundry profits and casual receipts not assessed under any other case, *e.g.* insurance commission, post cessation receipts, certain premiums paid to persons other than landlords and numerous other receipts treated as income and specifically charged hereunder. As to furnished lettings, *see* under Schedule A.

Case VII—*Short-term gains.*—This tax (previously chargeable on gains realised within twelve months of acquisition) ceased to have effect for and from 1971/72. Capital gains realized after April 5, 1971 are subject only to capital gains tax. Short term losses unapplied as at April 5, 1971 may be used for set off against capital gains arising after April 5, 1971.

Case VIII—On the previous tax acts being consolidated into the Income and Corporation Taxes Act 1970, Case VIII, Schedule D was renamed Schedule A. (*See* above).

Losses.—Under Cases I, II, VI, losses can in general be carried forward and allowed against corresponding income or profits of subsequent fiscal years without time limit. Losses under Cases I and II can alternatively be set off against other income of the same fiscal year and the year next following.

Capital Gains.—A separate long-term gains tax was introduced in the Finance Act, 1965, and this applies to gains realized on chargeable assets disposed of after April 6, 1965. In the case of assets owned on April 6, 1965 and disposed subsequently, only the proportion of the gains attributable to the period after that date is chargeable. These gains are not charged to income tax and surtax as income, but in accordance with separate rules. The detailed rules of this new tax are outside the scope of this article.

For 1967/68 onwards exemption is given where the total gains in the year do not exceed £50. For and from 1970/71 where the combined sales of husband and wife do not produce more than £500 such sales will not attract capital gains tax. From April 1971 however the £50 gain exemption referred to above will cease to have effect.

The calculation of gains and losses on quoted securities held at April 6, 1965, which are disposed of after March 19, 1968, may be made solely by reference to the market value at April 6, 1965, if the taxpayer elects to deal with all his holdings in this way. Separate elections may, however, be made in relation to fixed interest stocks and preference shares and/or other quoted shares.

The rate of Capital Gains Tax payable by an individual is 30 per cent. but one half the net gains may be charged at the taxpayer's marginal rate of tax (including Surtax) where this produces a lower charge. From April 15, 1969, gains on disposal of securities issued or guaranteed by the British Government are not subject to Capital Gains Tax. This exemption does not, however, apply where such stocks are sold within twelve months after being acquired.

Under Schedule E.—Income from all offices, employments and pensions, including salaries, wages, emoluments, directors' fees, etc. Assessed on the actual earnings for the year of assessment. If, however, the individual is (*a*) not resident (or resident but not ordinarily resident) then the assessment is confined to the emoluments for services performed in the U.K. Or (*b*) although resident, the duties were performed wholly abroad when the assessment

(2) Married Couples Without Children

Income	Income all earned		All investment income	
Ann. (Wkly.)	Income Tax and Surtax (if any)	Average Rate per cent.	Income Tax and Surtax (if any)	Average Rate per cent.
£	£		£	
468 (£9)..	Nil		1	0·2
520 (£10)..	Nil		21	4·0
572 (£11)..	Nil		41	7·1
624 (£12)..	7	1·1	61	9·7
676 (£13)..	23	3·4	81	11·9
728 (£14)..	39	5·3	101	13·8
780 (£15)..	54	7·0	122	15·6
832 (£16)..	70	8·4	142	16·9
900........	91	10·1	168	18·6
1,000........	121	12·1	207	20·7
1,100........	151	13·8	246	22·3
1,200........	181	14·0	285	23·7
1,300........	211	16·3	323	24·8
1,400........	241	17·3	362	25·8
1,500........	271	18·1	401	26·7
1,600........	302	18·9	440	27·5
1,700........	332	19·5	478	28·1
1,800........	362	20·1	517	28·7
1,900........	392	20·7	556	29·2
2,000........	422	21·1	593	29·6
2,250........	497	22·0	691	30·7
2,500........	573	22·9	788	31·5
2,750........	648	23·5	929	33·7
3,000........	723	24·1	1,077	35·9
3,500........	874	24·9	1,351	38·5
4,000........	1,025	25·6	1,632	40·7
4,500........	1,190	26·4	1,932	42·9
5,000........	1,354	27·1	2,238	44·7
6,000........	1,752	29·2	2,893	48·2
7,000........	2,217	31·4	3,599	51·4
8,000........	2,713	33·9	4,311	53·8
9,000........	3,245	36·0	5,067	56·3
10,000........	3,811	38·1	5,829	58·2
12,000........	5,023	41·8	7,449	62·0
15,000........	6,972	46·5	10,028	66·8
20,000........	10,553	52·8	14,462	72·3
25,000........	14,315	57·2	18,899	75·5
30,000........	18,086	60·3	23,337	77·7
40,000........	25,630	64·0	32,212	80·5
50,000........	33,174	66·3	41,987	82·1
100,000........	70,893	70·8	85,462	85·4

(3) Married Couples with One Child

Income	All Earned Income					
	One Child not over 11		One Child over 11, but not over 16		One Child over 16	
	Income Tax (and Surtax, if any)	Average Rate %	Income Tax (and Surtax, if any)	Average Rate %	Income Tax (and Surtax, if any)	Average Rate %
£	£		£		£	
700	Nil		Nil		Nil	
800	Nil		Nil		Nil	
900	31	3·4	21	2·3	11	1·2
1,000	60	6·0	51	5·1	41	4·1
1,100	91	8·2	81	7·3	71	6·4
1,200	121	10·0	111	9·2	101	8·4
1,300	151	11·6	141	10·8	132	10·1
1,400	181	12·9	171	12·2	161	11·5
1,500	211	14·0	201	13·4	192	12·8
1,600	241	15·0	232	14·5	222	13·8
1,700	272	16·0	262	15·4	252	14·8
1,800	302	16·7	292	16·2	282	15·6
1,900	332	17·4	322	16·9	312	16·4
2,000	362	18·1	352	17·6	342	17·1
2,250	437	19·4	428	19·0	418	18·5
2,500	513	20·5	503	20·1	493	19·7
2,750	588	21·3	578	21·0	568	20·6
3,000	663	22·1	654	21·8	644	21·4
3,500	814	23·2	804	22·9	795	22·7
4,000	965	24·1	955	23·8	945	23·6
4,500	1,129	25·0	1,120	24·8	1,110	24·6
5,000	1,294	25·8	1,284	25·6	1,275	25·5
6,000	1,630	27·1	1,614	26·9	1,604	26·7
7,000	2,129	30·4	2,115	30·2	2,101	30·0
8,000	2,618	32·7	2,603	32·5	2,588	32·3
9,000	3,142	34·9	3,126	34·7	3,109	34·5
10,000	3,705	37·0	3,689	36·8	3,672	36·7
12,000	4,912	40·9	4,895	40·7	4,877	40·6
15,000	6,846	45·6	6,826	45·5	6,805	45·3
20,000	10,432	52·1	10,402	52·0	10,380	51·9
25,000	14,177	56·7	14,155	56·6	14,133	56·5
30,000	17,949	59·8	17,927	59·7	17,905	59·6
40,000	25,493	63·7	25,471	63·6	25,448	63·6
50,000	33,037	66·0	33,014	66·0	32,992	65·9
100,000	70,755	70·7	70,733	70·7	70,711	70·7

is confined to the amount remitted to the U.K. Necessary expenses are allowable, including fees and subscriptions to certain professional bodies and learned societies and within strict limits, depreciation allowances.

Expense allowances and payments in kind (less expenses incurred in performance of duties) to directors and employees enjoying emoluments of £2,000 p.a. or more are assessable. From 1965–66 onwards expenses incurred in providing business entertainment (including hospitality of any kind and gifts) are not allowable except when provided for an overseas customer. Where any person has premises available for his use by reason of his employment and either pays no rent or pays less than the annual value he will be charged to tax on the annual value less any rent paid. Certain payments made on retirement or removal from a person's office or employment (in excess of £5,000) are assessable to tax on him.

Exemptions.—Unemployment, sickness and maternity benefit and grant, and death grant payable under the National Insurance Acts are not assessable to income tax, but (retirement, widows, etc.) pensions and family allowances are included in the charge under this schedule. Under Finance Act, 1966, statutory redundancy payments are exempt from tax.

Where the emoluments are paid by an employer in the U.K. deduction of income tax is made by the employer, at the time of payment, in accordance with employee's code number. As to P.A.Y.E. (pay as you earn) see further below.

Under Schedule F.—From April 6, 1966, onwards income tax will be charged on all dividends and distributions of a U.K. resident company. Tax will be deducted at standard rate and has to be accounted for monthly by the Company to the Inland Revenue.

ALLOWANCES.—The following allowances and deductions are given, in calculating the income tax payable:—

Personal Allowance.—To single person.... £325

To married man living with or normally maintaining his wife (but in year of marriage allowance is reduced by 1/12 of £140 for each fiscal month (*i.e.*, ending May 5, June 5, etc.) which ended before the date of marriage).. £465

When either husband or wife is absent from United Kingdom throughout a complete fiscal year they are treated as separate entities for tax purposes, each entitled to Single Personal Allowance. A married woman permanently separated from her husband is treated as a single woman.

Children.—For each child under 16 (or over that age at the beginning of the fiscal year and receiving full time instruction at a recognized educational establishment, or who is articled or apprenticed) and who does not have income in that year

(4) Married Couples with Two Children

Income	All Earned Income					
	Two Children not over 11		Two Children over 11, but not over 16		Two Children over 16	
	Income Tax (and Surtax, if any)	Average Rate %	Income Tax (and Surtax, if any)	Average Rate %	Income Tax (and Surtax, if any)	Average Rate %
£	£		£		£	
800	*Nil*		*Nil*		*Nil*	
900	*Nil*		*Nil*		*Nil*	
1,000	*Nil*		*Nil*		*Nil*	
1,100	31	2·8	11	1·0	*Nil*	
1,200	61	5·0	41	3·4	22	1·8
1,300	91	7·0	72	5·5	52	4·0
1,400	121	8·6	101	7·2	82	5·8
1,500	151	10·0	132	8·8	112	7·4
1,600	181	11·3	162	10·1	142	8·8
1,700	211	12·3	192	11·2	173	10·1
1,800	242	13·4	222	12·3	203	11·2
1,900	272	14·3	252	13·2	233	12·2
2,000	302	15·1	282	14·1	263	13·1
2,250	377	16·7	358	15·9	339	15·0
2,500	452	18·0	433	17·3	414	16·5
2,750	528	19·2	508	18·4	489	17·7
3,000	603	20·1	583	19·4	564	18·8
3,500	754	21·5	735	21·0	715	20·4
4,000	905	22·6	885	22·1	866	21·6
4,500	1,069	23·7	1,050	23·3	1,031	22·9
5,000	1,234	24·6	1,215	24·3	1,195	23·9
6,000	1,563	26·0	1,544	25·7	1,525	25·4
7,000	2,042	29·1	2,014	28·7	1,986	28·3
8,000	2,523	31·5	2,493	31·1	2,464	30·8
9,000	3,044	33·8	3,013	33·4	2,983	33·1
10,000	3,603	36·0	3,570	35·7	3,536	35·3
12,000	4,802	40·0	4,766	39·7	4,731	39·4
15,000	6,720	44·8	6,681	44·5	6,643	44·2
20,000	10,290	51·4	10,247	51·2	10,203	51·0
25,000	14,040	56·1	13,995	55·9	13,951	55·8
30,000	17,811	59·3	17,767	59·2	17,723	59·0
40,000	25,355	63·3	25,311	63·2	25,266	63·1
50,000	32,899	65·7	32,877	65·7	32,855	65·7
100,000	70,618	70·6	70,573	70·5	70,529	70·5

NOTE:—These tables do not take into account the loss of child relief due to family allowance " clawback " (*see* under " Reliefs for Children ").

exceeding £115 in his or her own right, the allowances are:—

(a) Child over 16 at commencement of fiscal year.......................... £205
(b) Child over 11 at commencement of fiscal year.......................... £180
(c) Other children (each).............. £155

Scholarship or bursary does not count for this purpose. Marginal relief is given where a child's income exceeds £115. The child relief will then be reduced by £1 for each £1 by which the child's income exceeds £115. "Child" includes step-child and adopted child. Child allowance is due to the person who has the custody of and maintains the child. If more than one person could claim the allowance; *e.g.* if a husband and wife are divorced or separated, the allowance will be apportioned between them, as necessary. These allowances are reduced by £42 for each child for whom Family Allowance is due for the whole year 1971-72 and by an appropriately smaller amount where the allowance is received for only part of the year.

For and from the year 1969–70 the income of children under the age of 18 not regularly working (other than earned income and income arising from compensation for personal injury to the child) is to be aggregated with the parents' income and treated for tax purposes as the parents' income. The 1971 Finance Act, however, provides that as from April, 1972 such income shall cease to be regarded as the parents' income.

The "Family Allowance" for children is payable to the mother but ranks only for the Earned Income Allowance.

Dependent Relatives.—The maximum deduction for each dependent relative is normally £75. By the Finance Act, 1967, where the claimant is a woman (other than a married woman living with her husband) the maximum deduction is £110. These allowances are reduced by £1 for every £1 by which the relative's own income (excluding voluntary allowances) exceeds £289. Claimant must maintain relative who must be incapacitated by old age or infirmity from maintaining himself or herself, except in the case of his or his wife's widowed mother (which includes any woman living apart from her husband, or whose marriage has been dissolved or annulled). If more than one person gives support to the dependent relative then allowance is divided *pro rata*.

Daughter.—A person who by reason of his or her old age or infirmity, has to retain the services of a daughter resident with him or her is entitled to an allowance of £40.

Housekeeper or person looking after children.—An allowance to:—

(a) Widows and Widowers: Housekeeper allowance of £75 in respect of a house-

keeper as such or a female relative or female employee engaged to look after children. These females must be resident.

(b) Unmarried man: Housekeeper allowance of £75 in respect of a female relative living with and maintained by him, to look after brothers or sisters for whom he is entitled to child allowance.

(c) All other claimants: An allowance of £100 where entitled to child allowance whether or not employing or maintaining a resident housekeeper. From April, 1971, housekeeper relief cannot also be claimed.

Blind persons.—An allowance of £100 less 7/9ths of any tax free disability receipts may be claimed by a registered blind person, provided that the Daughter's allowance of £40 is not also claimed. Where both spouses are blind the maximum allowance is £200 less 7/9ths of any free disability receipts. Proportionate relief for persons registered as blind during part only of the year of assessment was contained in the Finance Act, 1965.

Earned Income.—Allowance of the following fractions of earned income (after deducting allowances for necessary expenses, superannuation, etc.):—

Up to £4,005—Two-ninths.
In excess of £4,005—15 per cent.

Married woman earning income in her own right has deduction of earned income relief and, in addition, an allowance equal to seven-ninths of her earnings subject to a maximum of £325.

Small Income Relief.—All incomes up to £450 are treated as earned income; *i.e.* relief of two-ninths of income is allowed. Marginal relief is given where income slightly exceeds £450 up to a maximum of £750.

Age Relief.—Allowance of two-ninths of unearned income where taxpayer (or his wife) attains 65 years subject to total income not exceeding £1,200. Where the total income exceeds £1,200, marginal relief is given so that the full tax on the investment income scale is not payable until the marginal relief runs out. For single persons relief is given only on income up to £1,000.

Age exemption.—Persons over 65 years of age are exempt from tax if their total incomes do not exceed :—

Single person.............................£504
Married couple (either being over 65).......£786

Marginal relief is given where income slightly exceeds these amounts.

Pension Contributions.—Contributions by both employed and self-employed persons to officially approved superannuation funds, or premiums paid (within certain limits) to provide for *retirement annuities* are allowed as deductions.

Life Assurance Premiums.—Relief is given for premiums paid under assurance policies on life of taxpayer or his wife. A capital sum must be payable at death. Where the total premiums available for relief to taxpayer and his wife do not exceed £25 an amount of £10 or total premiums, whichever is less, may be deducted from assessable income. Where total premiums exceed £25 the deduction is two-fifths of the premiums. Where annual premium exceeds 7 per cent. of capital sum assured, the allowable premium is restricted to 7 per cent. of capital sum. The amount on which relief is given must not exceed one-sixth of net total income. Relief is also given on sums paid under Act of Parliament or under terms of employment for securing deferred annuity to widow or provision for children after death of the taxpayer.

In order to qualify for the relief outlined above, policies effected after March 19, 1968 must also satisfy certain conditions which are in general as follows: (a) The policy is for a term of at least 10 years; (b) The premiums are spread reasonably evenly; and (c) where the policy is an endowment policy the capital sum payable on death is not less than 75 per cent. of the total premiums payable. Where a policy is caught by the provisions of the 1968 Finance Act the proceeds less premiums paid will be subject to Surtax assessment.

Purchased Life Annuities.—The capital element of annuities for a term referable to a life, which are purchased for money or money's worth from a person whose business is to grant annuities (with certain exceptions) is not taxable as income.

Reduced Rate Relief.—Abolished by Finance Act 1970, personal allowances being increased to compensate for this loss.

Repayment Claims.—Where relief or allowance due has not been given in the assessment of the taxpayer, or where tax has been deducted from income received in excess of the amount of tax due in respect of total income, repayment may be claimed in general, within six years after the end of the year of assessment.

Error or Mistake.—Relief may be claimed if an assessment is excessive because of some error or mistake in the return or statement made by the taxpayer. Application for relief must be made to the Inspector within six years after the end of the fiscal year in which the assessment was made.

Building Society Interest.—Majority of societies operate under special arrangement with Inland Revenue and interest is paid to depositors and shareholders " free of income tax." But such interest must be included in taxpayer's total income for assessment to surtax, grossed at the standard rate.

Victoria Cross and George Cross.—Annuities paid to holders of the Victoria Cross and George Cross, and (from 1968) the Albert Medal and the Edward Medal, as such are disregarded for income tax purposes.

Surtax is an additional duty of income tax, chargeable on total income (the amount of income chargeable to income tax by deduction or assessment) of individuals. Less the following deductions: (a) approved pension and superannuation contributions including retirement annuity premiums paid by self-employed persons: (b) losses on trading activities for which relief against income tax allowed for the same year: (c) earned income relief as allowed for income tax. Where the earned income less earned income relief exceeds £2,000, a further deduction is allowed of the excess over £2,000, with a limit for this purpose of £2,000: (d) interest paid on loans, mortgages, overdrafts, etc., but from March 19, 1968, in general, interest on sums borrowed to pay life assurance premiums is not deductible; (e) payments under certain Deeds of Covenant as to which see below; (f) all personal allowances as granted for income tax excluding relief on life assurance premiums, to the extent that the total exceeds £325.

Also as provided by the 1969 Finance Act from 1969–70 interest paid will no longer qualify either for income tax or surtax relief unless it is a proper business expense or is paid on money borrowed for the purchase or improvement of land or buildings in the United Kingdom or the Irish Republic. Special provisions, however, apply in the case of borrowing (including borrowing on bank loan account) before April 15, 1969, interest on such borrowing being in general allowable until April 5, 1975.

The net sum is chargeable on a sliding scale as follows:—

On first £2,000   *Nil*
On each £ of first £500 at 10%
       "   next £500   "   12·5%
       "   £1,000   "   17·5%
       "   £1,000   "   22·5%
       "   £1,000   "   27·5%
       "   £2,000   "   32·5%
       "   £2,000   "   37·5%
       "   £2,000   "   42·5%
       "   £3,000   "   47·5%
On each £ above £15,000   "   50%

Surtax is payable on January 1 following year of assessment, so that surtax for 1971/72 is payable on January 1, 1973.

Surtax will not be charged for 1971/72 where surtaxable income does not exceed £2,500 and where income exceeds £2,500 but not £2,681, the surtax payable will be limited to 40% of the excess of income over £2,500.

Seven-year Covenants.—Where covenant to pay annual sums of money is made for other than valuable and sufficient consideration, the period of the covenant must be for a term which can exceed six years if the Covenantor wishes to divest himself of such income for income tax purposes. Any such covenant entered into after April 6, 1965, whether in favour of a charitable body or in favour of an individual, may no longer be deducted from the covenantor's total income for surtax purposes. There are three exceptions to this: payments under a partnership agreement to a former partner, his widow or dependants, similar payments in connection with the acquisition of a business made under liability incurred for full consideration; and settlements made by one party to a marriage for the other or for the children of the marriage, in consequence of divorce, nullity or separation. A separation may be under a court order or by agreement or in such circumstances that the separation is likely to be permanent.

Settlements in favour of taxpayer's own infant children.—The Income of any such Settlement made since April 22, 1936, is treated as that of the Settlor for all income tax purposes if:—

(a) the settlement can be revoked within a period of six years (unless the child becomes Bankrupt).

(b) the income is paid to or for the benefit of the child during the lifetime of the settlor. This ceases to apply after the child attains 21 or marries (or from 1969-70 has reached the age of 18 and is in full employment).

Double Taxation Relief.—Agreements for the avoidance of Double Taxation have been made between the United Kingdom and Antigua, Australia, Austria, Barbados, Belgium, Botswana, British Honduras, British Solomon Islands, Brunei, Burma, Canada, Cyprus, Denmark, Dominica, Falkland Islands, Faröe Islands, Fiji, Finland, France, Gambia, Germany (Federal Rep.), Ghana, Gilbert and Ellice Islands, Grenada, Guernsey, Guyana, Ireland (Rep.), Isle of Man, Israel, Italy, Jamaica, Japan, Jersey, Kenya, Lesotho, Luxemburg, Malawi, Malaysia, Malta, Mauritius, Montserrat, Netherlands, Netherlands Antilles, New Zealand, Nigeria, Norway, Pakistan, Portugal, Rhodesia (*suspended*), St. Christopher and Nevis, St. Lucia, St. Vincent, Seychelles, Sierra Leone, Singapore, South Africa, South West Africa, Swaziland, Sweden, Switzerland, Trinidad and Tobago, United States of America, Virgin Islands and Zambia.

Persons Resident Abroad.—Persons normally resident outside the United Kingdom are liable, in general, in respect of income from United Kingdom sources.

Certain Double Taxation agreements, however, exempt or partially exempt U.K. interest. Some agreements (*e.g.* that with Malta) exempt dividends from U.K. tax altogether while others (*e.g.* that with United States) provide for a modified rate of U.K. tax deduction (usually 15 per cent.) from U.K. dividend income.

All persons not ordinarily resident are exempt from U.K. tax on interest from beneficial holdings of:

3½% War Stock 1952 or after; 4% Victory Bonds; 4% Funding Loan 1960-90; 3% Savings Bonds (all issues); 5½% Funding Loan 1982-84; 5% Exchequer Stock 1976-78; 5½% Funding Stock 1978-80; 5½% Treasury Stock 2008-12, 5¾% Funding Loan 1987-91; 8¾% Treasury Stock 1997; 6% Funding Loan 1993; 6½% Treasury 1976; 6¾% Treasury 1995-98; 6½% Exchequer 1972; 6½% Funding Loan 1985-87; 6¾% Exchequer 1973; 9% Treasury Stock 1994; 8½% Treasury Loan 1980-82; 8½% Treasury Loan 1984-86; 6½% Exchequer Stock 1976; 6¾% Treasury Loan 1974; 9% Treasury Loan 1992-96; and 6% Treasury Stock 1975.

Such persons become resident in the United Kingdom if they visit for a period or periods exceeding six months in any fiscal year. Also if they visit for any period in a year in which they have retained a place of abode in the United Kingdom, except such persons as are engaged in full-time employment abroad. They would then be liable to United Kingdom Tax on all remittances of income arising abroad. If they visit the United Kingdom in four consecutive years for periods averaging three months or more per annum they would be regarded as ordinarily resident here.

A person who is not resident in the United Kingdom who has income which is liable to United Kingdom tax cannot claim any of the normal income tax allowances unless he is:

(a) a British subject;

(b) a present or former servant of the Crown; or widow of a former Crown servant;

(c) employed by any missionary society controlled from the United Kingdom or a servant of a native State under British protection;

(d) a resident of the Isle of Man or the Channel Islands; or

(e) was previously resident in the United Kingdom but resides abroad for the sake of his health or the health of a member of his family;

(f) entitled to such allowances under the Double Tax Agreement with the country of his residence.

Post War Credits.—Those Credits arising out of the temporary reduction of certain income tax allowances during the years 1941-42 to 1945-46 inclusive are repayable to women over 55 and men over 60 years of age, and to widows entitled to Credits in their own right. Where a man or woman has died, repayment is made to personal representatives or beneficiaries, irrespective of age.

Holders of Credits are also entitled to repayment if certified as blind persons or in-patients of hospitals or nursing homes, or if in receipt of any of the following: National Assistance, Constant Attendance Allowance or Unemployability Supplement, Sickness or Injury Benefit, Disablement Pensions, Workmen's Compensation 1956 Supplement; or if registered as unemployed. There is a qualifying period of 26 weeks in certain categories (12 weeks for National Assistance). Interest from October 1, 1959 will be added to the sum repayable.

INCOME TAX ADMINISTRATION

Income Tax under Schedules B, D and E, is assessed by H.M. Inspectors of Taxes. Schedule B assessments are made by the Inspector for the district in which the woodlands are situated. Assessments under Schedules D and E are made by the Inspector of Taxes for the district in which the Trade, Profession or Employment is carried on, or from which the Pension is paid, otherwise assessments are made in the district in which the taxpayer resides. Notices of Assessment are sent to taxpayer who should make a formal appeal against any assessment which he disputes direct to H.M. Inspector by whom the notice was issued within the time limit for such appeals, as stated on the notice. The grounds of appeal should be given. If the assessment cannot be agreed with H.M. Inspector, the appeal will be heard by the General Commissioners. Alternatively, certain appeals are made to the Special Commissioners. An appeal may be made by way of Case Stated from the Appeal Commissioners' decision to the High Court on points of law.

Income Tax is payable to the Collector of Taxes.

Surtax is assessable by the Commissioners of Inland Revenue. Returns of total income are made to the Controller of Surtax except where a full return of income is made to H.M. Inspector of Taxes. Appeals are made to the Special Commissioners and thence to the Courts by way of Case Stated.

Surtax is payable to the Accountant and Comptroller General.

Penalties may be incurred for failure to make proper returns of income or false claims for allowances.

Every person chargeable to income tax must give notice of chargeability within one year (unless an income tax return has already been made).

Interest at 6 per cent. simple (previously 4 per cent.) is charged where tax assessed under Schedule " D ", Surtax or Capital Gains Tax is unpaid two months after it has become due, where the amount of tax charged exceeds £1,000 and where the interest payable exceeds £5.

Tax Reserve Certificates—Provision for future tax liabilities may be made by the purchase of Tax Reserve Certificates. When surrendered in payment of income tax (other than Schedule " E "), Surtax or Capital Gains Tax, interest is allowed for a maximum period of two years, provided the certificates tendered were purchased more than one month before the date the tax became payable. Such interest is not subject to tax.

P.A.Y.E.

Income Tax payable under Schedule E is deducted by employer, who accounts for it to the Collector of Taxes. The amount of tax deduction from each payment of salary, wage, pension, etc., is determined by reference to Tax Tables issued by H.M. Inspector of Taxes to employer, in conjunction with the taxpayer's Code Number. This Code Number is an interpretation of the taxpayer's Allowances and Reliefs. Notices of Coding are issued by H.M. Inspector of Taxes and they may take into account income assessable under other Schedules. Notice of Coding should be checked on receipt and H.M. Inspector of Taxes informed of any necessary amendment in order that no considerable over or under-deduction of income tax may take place. The tax deductions are on a cumulative basis and can be carried on by successive employers should changes in employment take place during fiscal year. When leaving one employment a statement (Form P45) showing code number, remuneration, and tax deductions to date should be obtained from old employer and handed, in due course, to new employer. At the end of fiscal year employer should give employee a statement (Form P60) showing total remuneration and tax deductions for the year. Form P.60 should be preserved in case it is needed in connection with any application for earnings-related supplements to sickness or unemployment benefits. Provided the correct allowances are given in determining the code number and the income from which the deduction is made is the correct amount assessable, the Inspector is not required to make a formal assessment under Schedule E, unless the taxpayer is also liable to Surtax. Where assessments are required (and the taxpayer may call for his assessment) any over-deduction of tax is repaid or under-deduction recovered in a later year: under-deductions of less than £1 are ignored.

OTHER TAXES AND STAMP DUTIES

The Commissioners as a general rule allow deeds, etc., to be stamped after execution:—

WITHOUT PENALTY, ON PAYMENT OF DUTY ONLY. Deeds and instruments not otherwise excepted. within 30 days of *first* execution.

NOTE.—Where wholly executed *abroad*, the period begins to run from the date of arrival here.

PENALTIES ENFORCEABLE ON STAMPING, IN ADDITION TO DUTY:—

Instruments presented after the proper time (subject to special provisions in some cases)............................... £10

AGREEMENT for Lease, *see* LEASES.

AGREEMENT FOR SALE OF PROPERTY—charged with *ad val.* duty as if an actual conveyance on sale (see *post*, p. 1192) with certain exceptions, *e.g.* agreements for the sale of land, stocks and shares, goods, wares or merchandise, or a ship (see s. 59 (1), Stamp Act 1891). If *ad val.* duty is paid on an agreement in accordance with this provision, the subsequent conveyance or transfer is not chargeable with any *ad val.* duty and the Commissioners will upon application either place a denoting stamp on such conveyance or transfer or will transfer the

ad val. duty thereto. Further, if such an agreement is rescinded, not performed, etc., the Commissioners will return the *ad val.* duty paid.

AGREEMENT, not otherwise charged with duty, under seal or with clause of registration.. 50p

APPOINTMENT of a new trustee or in exercise of a power over property, not being by a will; also on retirement of trustee, although no new trustee be appointed............. 50p

ASSIGNMENT:

By way of sale—*see* Conveyance.

By way of gift—*see* Voluntary Disposition.

ASSURANCE—*see* Insurance Policies.

BANK NOTE for money payable on demand, (Scotland only):

Not exceeding £1.......................		2p
„ „ 2.......................		4p
„ „ 5.......................		6p
„ „ 10.......................		9p
„ „ 20.......................		10p
„ „ 30.......................		15p
„ „ 50.......................		25p
„ „ 100.......................		43p

BEARER INSTRUMENT:

Inland bearer instrument, i.e. share warrant, stock certificate to bearer or any other

instrument to bearer by which stock can be transferred, issued by a company or body formed or established in U.K. Duty of an amount equal to three times the transfer duty (usually £3% of the market value).

Overseas bearer instrument, *i.e.*, such an instrument issued in G.B. by a company formed out of the U.K. Duty equal to twice the transfer duty (usually £2% of the market value). Even if issued out of G.B. the instrument must be stamped before transfer in G.B. The issue or transfer of a bearer instrument relating to stock expressed in the currency of a territory outside the Scheduled territories is exempt from duty.

BILL OF SALE, Absolute, *see* CONVEYANCE ON SALE.

CAPITAL DUTY (Share).—Companies and Corporations with limited liability, on every £100 or fraction of £100 of the nominal capital..........................   50p

Statement of amount of any increase of registered capital shall be delivered duly stamped within fifteen days after the resolution of the company authorizing the increase (Companies Act 1948).

CAPITAL DUTY (Loan).—Per £100 or part of £100...................................   50p

(Subject to deduction of 95p for each £200 which is applied in conversion or consolidation of existing Loan Capital.) The issue or transfer of an instrument securing the loan capital of a local authority is exempt from duty.

CONTRACT, *see* AGREEMENT.

CONTRACT NOTE for the sale or purchase of any stock or marketable security; where the value of the stock or marketable security—

Exceeds £100 and does not exceed £500...   10p
 „   £500 „   „   „   „   £1,500.....   30p
 „ £1,500..............................   60p
          (Special adhesive stamps)

Option Contract Notes are chargeable with half the above rates only, unless the option is a double one.

Contract Note following a duly stamped option contract note chargeable with half the above rates only.

CONTRACT OR GRANT FOR PAYMENT OF A SUPERANNUATION ANNUITY: for every £10 or fractional part of £10...............   5p

CONVEYANCE OR TRANSFER on sale or by way of gift *inter vivos* of Stock or Marketable Securities: where the purchase money (or in the case of a gift the middle market value on the date of the transaction) does not exceed £5.......................   5p

Exceeding £5 but not exceeding £100, 10p for every £10 or part of £10.

Exceeding £100 but not exceeding £300, 20p per £20 or part.

Exceeding £300 per every £50 or part.....   50p
NOTE.—The rate chargeable in respect of a transfer of commonwealth government stock is 5p for every £20 or part if not exceeding £300 and in every other case 25p for every £100 or part.

"Marketable Security" includes the Registered Bonds and Debentures generally of Companies, Corporations, and Public Bodies.

CONVEYANCE OR TRANSFER ON SALE (in the case of a Voluntary Disposition, *see* below, p. 1194) of any property (*except* stock or marketable securities for which, *see* above),

where the consideration for the sale does not exceed £5,500....................   nil

Exceeds £5,500 but does not exceed £7,000 for every £50 and any fraction of £50..   25p

Exceeds £7,000, for every £50 and any fraction of £50........................   50p

If the consideration does not exceed £5,500 (or £7,000, as the case may be) the Conveyance or Transfer on Sale must contain a certificate of value certifying that the transaction does not form part of a larger transaction or series of transactions in respect of which the amount or value of the aggregate amount or value of the consideration exceeds £5,500 (or £7,000, as the case may be).

If the Conveyance or Transfer on Sale does not contain the appropriate statement duty at the full rate of 50p for every £50 or fraction of £50 will be payable whatever the amount of the consideration.

However, if the consideration does not exceed £300, and the instrument does not contain a certificate of value, then:
Where the consideration:
Does not exceed £5.................   5p

Exceeds £5 but does not exceed £100 10p per £10 or part.

Exceeds £100 but does not exceed £300, 20p per £20 or part.

If in such a case the instrument is certified at £7,000 it is stamped at ½ the above rates, with a minimum of 5p

CONVEYANCE OR TRANSFER of any other kind ....fixed duty   50p

Included under this head are Transfers for nominal consideration within any of the following categories:—

(*a*) Transfers vesting the property in trustees on the appointment of a new trustee of a pre-existing trust, or on the retirement of a trustee.

(*b*) Transfers, where no beneficial interest in the property passes, (i) to a mere nominee of the transferor; (ii) from a mere nominee of the transferee; (iii) from one nominee to another nominee of the same beneficial owner.

(*c*) Transfer to a residuary legatee of stock, etc., forming part of the residue divisible under a will.

(*d*) Transfers to a beneficiary under a will of a specific legacy of stock, etc. (*Note.*—Transfers by executors in discharge, or partial discharge, of a pecuniary legacy (unless made under an express power of appropriation) are chargeable with *ad valorem* duty on the amount of the legacy so discharged.)

(*e*) Transfers of stock, etc., forming part of an intestate's estate to the person entitled to it.

(*f*) Transfers to a beneficiary under settlement on a distribution of the trust funds of stock, etc., forming the share or part of the share of those funds to which the beneficiary is entitled in accordance with the terms of the settlement.

(*g*) Transfers on the occasion of a marriage to trustees of stocks, etc., to be held on the terms of a settlement made in consideration of marriage.

(h) Transfers by the liquidator of a company of stocks, etc., forming part of the assets of the company to the persons who were shareholders, in satisfaction of their rights on a winding-up.

The evidence necessary to establish that a transfer is liable to the fixed duty of 50p should take the form of a certificate setting forth the facts of the transaction. In cases falling within (b) such a certificate should be signed by (1) both transferor and transferee or (2) a member of a Stock Exchange or a solicitor acting for one or other of the parties or (3) an accredited representative of a bank; in the last case when the bank or its official nominee is a party to the transfer, the certificate, instead of setting out the facts, may be to the effect that "the transfer is excepted from Section 74 of the Finance (1909–10) Act 1910." A certificate in other cases should be signed by a solicitor or other person (e.g., a bank acting as trustee or executor) having a full knowledge of the facts.

Registering Officers will in any case in which a Marking Officer's certificate has not been given require such evidence in order to satisfy themselves that a transfer stamped with the 50p fixed duty is duly stamped.

COVENANT—For original creation and sale of any annuity, *see* CONVEYANCE.

Separate Deed of, made on occasion of sale, but not being an instrument chargeable with *ad valorem* duty as a Conveyance: same duty as a Conveyance on sale, but not to exceed.......................... 50p

DEATH DUTIES, *see* ESTATE DUTY.

DECLARATION OF TRUST, not being a Will or Settlement............................. 50p

DEED of any kind not charged under some special head............................ 50p

DEMISE, *see* LEASE.

DUPLICATE OR COUNTERPART
Same duty as original, but not to exceed.. 25p

ESTATE DUTY:
In the case of every person dying on or after March 31, 1971 the total duty payable on an estate is found by adding up the amounts of duty payable on various slices of the estate, according to a scale laid down in F.A. 1969, Schedule 17, as amended.

The rates of duty are as follows:

On the first £12,500—*Nil*
On the next £5,000—25 per cent
On the next £12,500—30 per cent
On the next £12,500—30 per cent
On the next £10,000—45 per cent
On the next £40,000—60 per cent
On the next £70,000—65 per cent
On the next £150,000—70 per cent
On the next £200,000—75 per cent
On the next £250,000—80 per cent
On the excess over £750,000—85 per cent

The rate of duty for any particular asset is found by dividing the total duty by the aggregate value of the estate.
The amount of duty is in no case to exceed 80 per cent of the principal value.

The amount of duty payable in certain circumstances on property passing on two deaths occurring within 5 years of one another is reduced. (Finance Act 1958.)

A *reduction* of 45 per cent. is applied to the "agricultural value" of agricultural property; and (as respects deaths on and after July 30, 1954) to certain business assets, viz.: "industrial hereditaments" and "machinery or plant" (Finance Act 1954, s. 28).

Gifts made by deceased during his life for public or charitable purposes are liable for duty, unless made more than twelve months before death; other gifts are liable for duty, unless made more than seven years before death (although if the donor dies at any time within the fifth year after making the gift, the value of the property the subject of the gift is for estate duty purposes reduced by 15 per cent.; if he dies within the sixth year it is reduced by 30 per cent.; and if he dies within the seventh year it is reduced by 60 per cent.). Gifts made in consideration of marriage by a parent or grandparent to either spouse or by one spouse to the other excepted as to the first £5,000 (or £1,000 if made by any other person). Gifts forming part of deceased's reasonable normal expenditure and gifts not exceeding £100 in value or amount (or in certain circumstances £500) also excepted.

Payment of Estate Duty may, by agreement with the Commissioners, be made, wholly or in part, in the form of real or leasehold property comprised in the estate.

Interest at 3 per cent. per annum is also payable on the Estate Duty on personalty from the day after the death up to that of delivery of the affidavit or account.

The Estate Duty on real property, leasehold property, shares in certain companies and a business or interest therein may be paid, if desired, by eight yearly or sixteen half-yearly instalments, and 3 per cent. interest is charged on all unpaid instalments from twelve months after death.

FEES are taken in all Public Departments by means of Stamps: such payments are accounted for to the Exchequer under the heading of Miscellaneous Revenue.

GIFT (*see* VOLUNTARY DISPOSITION, p. 1194).

GUARANTEE:
If under seal............................. 50p

HIRE-PURCHASE AGREEMENTS:
Under seal.............................. 50p
(Finance Act 1907, s. 7)
N.B.—If the agreement amounts to a "credit-sale" the position is the same.

INSURANCE POLICIES:
Life:—
Exc. £50 and not exc. £1,000 for every £100 or part of £100............... 5p
Excl. £1,000, for every £1,000 or any fractional part of £1,000............. 50p
Made after 1 August 1966 for period not exceeding 2 years.................... 5p

LEASES:—Lease or tack for any definite term less tan a year of any furnished dwelling-house or apartments where the rent for such term exceeds £100, 50p; of any lands, tenements, etc., in

consideration of any rent, according to the following table:—

Annual rent not exceeding	★ Term not exceeding			Term exceeding 100 years
	7 years	35 years	100 years	
£				
5	Nil	5p	30p	6op
10	Nil	10p	60p	£1·20
15	Nil	15p	90p	£1·80
20	Nil	20p	£1·20	£2·40
25	Nil	25p	£1·50	£3
50	Nil	50p	£3	£6
75	Nil	75p	£4·50	£9
100	Nil	£1	£6	£12
Exceeding £100, for every £50 or fraction of £50	25p	50p	£3	£6

★ If the term is indefinite the same duty is payable as if the term did not exceed 7 years. Agreement for lease not exceeding 35 years, same as actual lease.

Where a consideration other than rent is payable and duty is charged on that consideration at conveyance rates, the same graduation applies where the consideration does not exceed £7,000 as under Conveyance or Transfer on Sale (except stock or marketable securities), provided that any rent payable does not exceed £50 a year.

MORTGAGES are exempt.

POWER OF ATTORNEY, etc., for receiving certain prize-money or wages......... 5p
For the receipt of any money, or bill, or note, not exceeding £20, or of any periodical payments not exceeding £10 annually............................ 25p

For the receipt of dividends or interest of any stock, if for one payment only..... 5p
Ditto in any other case.................. 25p
Power of attorney for any other kind...... 50p
PROCURATION, Deed, etc., of.............. 50p
RECEIPTS FOR SALARIES, Wages and Superannuation, and other like allowances are exempt.
REVOCATION of any TRUST of Property not being a Will.......................... 50p
TRANSFER OF STOCK, *see* CONVEYANCE.
UNIT TRUST INSTRUMENT—Any trust instrument of a unit trust scheme—For every £100, and also for any fractional part of £100, of the amount or value of the property subject to the trusts created or recorded by the instrument............. 25p
VOLUNTARY DISPOSITION *inter vivos*:—
On any instrument being a voluntary disposition (*inter vivos*) of any property (except stock or marketable securities, *see ante*, under Conveyance or Transfer) where the value of the property conveyed or transferred does not exceed £5,500........... nil
Exceeds £5,500, but does not exceed £7,000, for every £50 and fraction of £50..... 25p.
Exceeds £7,000, for every £50 and fraction of £50................................ 50p
The instrument must contain similar certificates of value as a Conveyance or Transfer on Sale (*see* pp. 1192), with the substitution of the words "property conveyed or transferred" for the word "consideration."
If the value of the property does not exceed £300, the same graduated rates apply as under Conveyance or Transfer on Sale (except Stock or marketable securities).
N.B.—The instrument is not deemed to be duly stamped unless it has been lodged with the Commissioner who will adjudge the value of the property and the duty payable.

PURCHASE TAX
(*Rates with effect from July 20, 1971*)

Purchase tax is an *ad valorem* tax which is imposed, in general, at the wholesale stage in the distribution of goods. The tax is expressed as a percentage of the statutory wholesale value of goods supplied under *chargeable purchases*. This value is, briefly, the price (exclusive of the tax) which the goods would fetch, on a sale made at the time when the tax becomes due, by a person selling by wholesale in the open market to a retail trader. Broadly speaking, there is a *chargeable purchase* when a *registered* wholesaler or manufacturer sells *chargeable goods* to a retailer or appropriates or applies them to retail trading or to any other purpose other than a sale as stock or materials to another registered trader. A registered wholesaler can buy goods as stock for resale, and a registered manufacturer can buy goods as materials for manufacture, tax-free, from a registered seller.

The tax is levied on chargeable goods imported into the United Kingdom unless they are imported by a registered wholesaler as stock or by a registered manufacturer as materials for manufacture, in which case they are brought within the scope of the internal tax law. Registered persons may export chargeable goods free of tax, and certain purchases made by foreign tourists in this country may be exported tax-free under the Personal Export Scheme. Arrangements exist under which registered traders may supply chargeable goods tax-free to certain Government Departments.

The list below indicates in general terms, and subject to the free list which follows it, the principal kinds of goods which are chargeable with tax:—

11¼ per cent.—Garments, headgear, footwear, gloves; haberdashery and minor articles of apparel; cushions, pillows, bolsters and mattresses; narrow fabrics; most floor coverings; wallpaper; most domestic, garden and office furniture; domestic hardware, ironmongery, table-ware, kitchen-ware, toilet-ware and most hand-operated domestic appliances; cutlery, spoons, forks, etc.; sewing and dressmaking requisites and knitting wool; paper handkerchiefs and table-ware; household textiles and cloth.

18 per cent.—Confectionery, soft drinks and ice cream; salted and roasted nuts; potato crisps; and prepared pet foods.

30 per cent.—Cuff links and studs, hat-pins, tie-pins and similar articles not of precious metal; most gas and electric space and water heating appliances; domestic refrigerators, washing machines and vacuum cleaners; electric irons and electric kettles; domestic oil-burning space heaters; sewing machines.

Lighting fittings, mantles and bulbs; hand lamps and hand torches; clocks and watches not of precious metal; radio and television sets and valves; musical instruments; gramophones; radio-gramophones and tape recorders; toys; fireworks; sports requisites; umbrellas.

Trunks, bags wallets, purses, etc.; stationery and office requisites; motor cars, motor cycles and bicycles; mirrors; brushes, combs, razors, sponges and certain other toilet requisites; soap, shaving cream, shampoos, dentifrices and certain other

toilet preparations; hair waving and hair drying machines; drugs and medicines.

45 per cent.—Fur garments, fur headgear, fur rugs and fur skin; jewellery and imitation jewellery; articles of precious metal worn on the person; clocks and watches of precious metal; gramophone records and pre-recorded tape; smokers' requisites; cameras, projectors and photographic goods; prints, frames, figures, greeting cards, etc.; ornaments and most fancy goods; hairdressing goods, waving and curling outfits; perfumery and cosmetics; toilet requisites and preparations other than those charged at 30 per cent.

Goods which are free of tax include:—
Foodstuffs (except confectionery, soft drinks and ice cream); fuel; books; young children's garments, gloves and footwear; sanitary ware, household brushes, brooms and mops; most tissues and fabrics, domestic textile articles and soft furnishings; plastic sheeting; cooking stoves; pianos and organs; school satchels; toilet paper and tooth brushes; certain essential or non-proprietary drugs and medicines; omnibuses, ambulances, invalid carriages and perambulators; goods vehicles; office machinery; most industrial and building materials and appliances; most articles (e.g. spirits, tobacco) subject to indirect taxation.

THE COST OF LIVING

The first cost-of-living index to be calculated in Great Britain was the one which took July, 1914, as 100 and was based on the pattern of expenditure of working-class families in 1904. Since 1947 the Index of Retail Prices has superseded the cost-of-living index, although the older term is still often popularly applied to it. This index is designed to reflect the month-by-month changes in the average level of retail prices of goods and services purchased by the *majority* of households in the United Kingdom, including practically all wage-earners and most small and medium salary-earners. For spending coming within the scope of the index, a representative list of items is selected and the prices actually charged for these items are collected at regular intervals. In working out the index figure, the price changes are " weighted "—that is, given different degrees of importance—in accordance with the pattern of consumption of the average family.

Consumer Price Index

However, a more useful guide when considering changes in the average level of prices of all consumer goods and services, particularly over a number of years, is the consumer price index. This index, which has been calculated back to 1938, covers the expenditure of *all* consumers as defined for national income purposes, and compares the price of goods and services actually purchased in a given year with the prices of the same goods and services in the base year. It is a by-product of calculations of changes in expenditure at constant prices and is derived by dividing the annual estimates of total consumers' expenditure at current prices by the corresponding estimates at 1963 prices.

The consumer price index and the retail price index therefore give slightly different results because of the differences both in method of construction and in coverage.

Purchasing Power of the £

The purchasing power of money varies inversely with prices. For example, if prices are doubled over a period of time the purchasing power is halved; if prices rise by 50 per cent., the purchasing power falls by 33⅓ per cent.; and so on. The consumer price index, which is devised annually, is normally used for estimating changes in the internal purchasing power of the pound, although for years prior to 1938 it is necessary to fall back on the original cost-of-living index. Over short periods of time (*e.g.* a few months) or when interest is centred particularly upon the purchasing power of the pound for households such as those of wage earners and medium salary earners, the index of retail prices is used.

The following cost-of-living tables have been compiled by using the Cost of Living Index, 1914–1938 and the Consumer Price Index, 1938 to date. The centre column shows the equivalent cost in other years of goods costing £1 in 1963.

	Price Index 1963=100	Equivalent cost in other years	Purchasing Power of £1 1963=£1
		£	£
1914	21	485	4·85
1920	51	195	1·95
1930	33	307	3·07
1938	32	311	3·11
1946	55	184	1·84
1950	66	152	1·52
1951	72	139	1·39
1952	76	131	1·31
1953	78	129	1·29
1954	79	127	1·27
1955	82	122	1·22
1956	85	117	1·17
1957	88	114	1·14
1958	90	111	1·11
1959	91	110	1·10
1960	92	109	1·09
1961	95	106	1·06
1962	98	102	1·02
1963	100	100	1·00
1964	103	97	0·97
1965	108	93	0·93
1966	112	89	0·89
1967	115	87	0·87
1968	120	83	0·83
1969	127	79	0·79
1970	133	75	0·75

There are no official figures for the years 1939–1945.

The method employed to estimate the rise in the cost of living in a given period is illustrated by the following example. To find the rise in the cost of living between 1950 and 1959:

From consumer price index (1963 = 100)

$$\left.\begin{array}{l}1950 = 66 \\ 1959 = 91\end{array}\right\} \text{ Then if } 1950 = 100,$$

$$1959 = \frac{91}{66} \times 100 = 138.$$

The purchasing power of money varies inversely with prices. Thus, if the cost-of-living index (1963 = 100) is 127 in 1969, then the purchasing power of the £1 compared with 20s. in 1963:—

$$£\frac{100}{127} = £0·79$$

It should be noted that these figures can only be approximate.

POSTAL REGULATIONS

For full conditions, exceptions, etc., *see* Post Office Guide, price 20p. Associated volumes are London Post Offices and Streets 10p, Post Offices in the United Kingdom 20p and Postal Addresses 7½p.

CHIEF POSTAL SERVICES

LETTERS AND CARDS

Inland (U.K., Channel Islands and Irish Republic):—

Weight not exceeding *lb. oz.*	1st class *p*	2nd class *p*
4	3	2½
6	5	4½
8	7	5½
10	9	6½
12	11	7½
14	13	8½
1 0	15	9½
1 8	20	10½
2 0	30	Not admissible
Each extra 1 lb.	15	over 1½ lb.

British Commonwealth and Foreign:—

(*a*) *British Commonwealth:*

Not over 1 oz. 3p; 2 oz. 5p; 4 oz. 7½p; 8 oz. 10p; 1 lb. 20p; 2 lb. 35p; 4 lb. 70p.

(*b*) *Elsewhere:—*

Not over 1 oz. 5p; 2 oz. 9p; 4 oz. 12p; 8 oz. 30p; 1 lb 50p; 2 lb. 80p; 4 lb. £1·30.

WEIGHT LIMITS:—Inland, First Class, none. Second Class 1½ lb. Elsewhere, 4 lb.

SIZE LIMITS: (A) If in roll form:—Inland and elsewhere (35 in. for the greatest dimension); length + twice diameter, 41 in. (B) not in roll form:—(i) United Kingdom, Irish Republic, British Commonwealth; 24 × 18 × 18 in.; (ii) Elsewhere, length 24 in. length + width + depth, 36 in. Envelopes must be at least 5½ × 3½ in. for inland destinations but items weighing up to 4 oz., sent in envelopes which do not conform to the preferred range of sizes will eventually be charged extra. To all overseas destinations the minimum limits for letters in the form of a roll are 6¾ inches for the length and twice the diameter combined (at least 4 inches for the greatest dimension), unless provided with a strong address label at least 4 inches in length and 2¾ inches in width. For letters other than in the form of a roll the minimum limits are one surface 5½ inches in length, 3½ inches in width, unless provided with a strong address label of 4 × 2¾ ins.

POST CARDS (p. 1201).

To all destinations overseas:—3p.

Limit of size for destinations abroad: maximum, 5⅞ inches in length, 4⅛ inches in width; minimum, 5½ inches in length, 3½ inches in width.

PRINTED PAPERS, BOOKS

British Commonwealth and Foreign:—

Single packets

Not over: 1 oz. 3p; 2 oz. 4p; 4 oz. 5p; 8 oz. 8p; 1 lb. 15p; 2 lb. 25p; 4 lb. 40p.

Posted in bulk: 20p per 2 lb. for the total weight of the bag.

Exceptionally, newspapers, periodicals, books, pamphlets, maps and musical scores which comply with the conditions shown in the Post Office Guide under *Printed Papers at Reduced Rates* may be sent abroad at the postage rate of: Single packets,

Not over: 1 oz. 1½p; 2 oz. 2p; 4 oz. 2½p; 8 oz. 4p; 1 lb. 8p; 2 lb 15p; 4 lb. 25p. Posted in bulk, 12p per 2 lb. for the total weight of each bag.

LIMITS: Size, as for Letters; Weight: 4 lb.; but a packet of books or booklets up to 11 lb. may be sent abroad.

NEWSPAPERS

(*See also* p. 1201).

Inland (Newspapers "Registered at P.O."):—

Not over: 4 oz. 2½p; 6 oz. 4½p; 8 oz. 5½p; 10 oz. 6½p; 12 oz. 7½p; 14 oz. 8½p; 1 lb. 9½p; 1 lb. 8 oz. 10½p.

Publications registered at the P.O. as newspapers will be given First Class service at the newspaper postage rate, but *only* if posted by publishers or their agents, and prominently marked *Newspaper Post*. All other newspapers are transmitted as first or second class letters. Limit of weight 1½ lb. Limit of size as Letters.

British Commonwealth and Foreign: See printed papers.

SMALL PACKETS (*See also* p. 1201).

British Commonwealth and Foreign—(certain countries only)

Not exceeding 4 oz. 5p; 8 oz. 10p; 1 lb. 15p; 2 lb. 30p.

LIMITS: Maximum size, as for letters A and B ii. Minimum limits of size as for letters; Weight, 2 lb. in general but some countries only accept Small Packets weighing up to 1 lb.

INSURED BOXES (*See also* p. 1200).

British Commonwealth and Foreign—(certain countries only)

Not over 8 oz. 15p; 1 lb. 25p; 2 lb. 50p.

Plus appropriate fee for insurance.

LIMITS: Maximum size, 12 × 8 × 4 in. Minimum size limits as for letters other than in the form of a roll; weight, 2 lb.

PARCELS

Should be marked "Parcel Post," and must be handed across the counter; postage must be prepaid by stamps, affixed by the sender. On Sundays parcels are not accepted or delivered. The name and address of sender should be inside and (not too prominent) on the outside of every parcel, and preferably be to the left of and at right angles to the name and address of the addressee.

A rural postman will accept any packets he can conveniently carry, except overseas letters intended for insurance or any parcels for abroad; but if on foot or cycle not more, without notice, than 22 lb. from one person. He may weigh parcels on request. Mail-drivers need not accept between regular stopping points.

Parcels to or from Irish Republic, Channel Is. or I. of Man are liable to customs duty: except in last case, the sender must declare contents when posting. Addressee must pay a clearance fee if any duty be payable. Senders can undertake to pay customs charges of Irish Republic, Channel Islands, and some overseas countries (a deposit is required).

Inland:—(Limit of size: length, 3 ft. 6 in.; length and girth combined, 6 ft.):—

U.K. and Irish Republic:—

(1) Ordinary Parcels		(2) Local Parcels
Not over 1½ lb.	15p	As in (1) less 5p at each step.
" " 2 lb.	20p	Note: The Local Parcel Delivery Area comprises all places which have in their postal address the same post town as the office of posting.
" " 4 lb.	24p	
" " 6 lb.	27½p	
" " 10 lb.	35p	
" " 14 lb.	45p	
" " 18 lb.	55p	
" " 22 lb. (limit)	65p	

AIR MAIL SERVICES
For mode of packing, prohibitions, limits of size, &c., see Post Office Guide.

Normal regulations as to make-up and acceptance of various categories of postal packets and parcels apply equally to air mail items. A blue air-mail label, obtainable free from post offices, must be affixed to each air mail item except letters, letter packets and postcards for Europe, for which no special air mail marking is required. Special air-mail rates apply to correspondence for members of H.M. Forces overseas (*see* leaflet PL(B)3043).

Air letter forms, postage 5p, may be sent to all countries. Enclosures are not permitted. You may get the special forms at post offices or use privately-manufactured forms which bear a statement that they have been approved by the Post Office, with the approval number. Unapproved forms will be treated as ordinary air mail letters.

Printed papers. Small Packets and Newspapers may be sent by air to countries outside Europe at the rates shown in col. 3 below. NEWSPAPERS: Publications registered at the P.O. as newspapers may be sent at the reduced rates indicated in col. 4 below. There is no air mail service to Europe for these items. If the quickest transmission is desired, the letter post rate should be paid.

European Countries (and *The Azores*)

Letters, letter packets and postcards for all European countries, prepaid at the ordinary international postage rates, are in general despatched daily by air or surface transport, whichever offers earlier delivery. The rates are:—

Letters—Not over: 1 oz. 5p; 2 oz. 9p; 4 oz. 12p; 8 oz. 30p; 1 lb. 50p; 2 lb. 80p; 4 lb. £1·30.
Postcards, 3p.

For *Cyprus*, *Gibraltar* and *Malta* the rates are:

Letters—Not over: 1 oz. 3p; 2 oz. 5p; 4 oz. 7½p; 8 oz. 10p; 1 lb. 20p; 2 lb. 35p; 4 lb. 70p.
Postcards, 3p.

Air mail labels should not be used.
Air Parcel Post to Europe. Rates are included in the Overseas Parcel Post tables, see pp. 1206-9.

Countries Outside Europe

Rates for letters, postcards and printed papers, etc. appear below; for air parcel rates *see* pp.1206-9.

COUNTRIES OUTSIDE EUROPE

For air mail services to Europe, see above; Air Parcel Rates, pp. 1206-9. For details of insurance and times of posting at London Chief Office and of transmission to principal cities, consult P.O. Air Mail Leaflet at any Post Office.

Destination	Rates of Postage				Destination	Rates of Postage			
	Letters per ½ oz.	Post Cards	Printed Papers etc. per ½ oz.	Newspapers regd. at P.O. per ½ oz.		Letters per ½ oz.	Post Cards	Printed Papers, etc. per ½ oz.	Newspapers regd. at P.O. per ½ oz.
	p	p	p	p		p	p	p	p
Abu Dhabi	5	3	3	1½	Ecuador	7½	4	4	2
Afghanistan	7½	4	4	2	Equatorial Guinea	7½	4	4	2
Algeria	5	3	3	1½	Ethiopia	5	3	3	1½
Antigua	7½	4	4	2	Falkland Islands	7½	4	4	2
Argentina	7½	4	4	2	Fiji	9	5	5	2½
Australia	9	5	5	2½	Formosa (Taiwan)	9	5	5	2½
Bahamas	7½	4	4	2	French Guiana	7½	4	4	2
Bahrain	5	3	3	1½	French Polynesia	9	5	5	2½
Barbados	7½	4	4	2	French Territory of the				
Bermuda	7½	4	4	2	Affars and Issas	5	3	3	1½
Bolivia	7½	4	4	2	Gaboon	7½	4	4	2
Botswana	7½	4	4	2	Gambia	7½	4	4	2
Brazil	7½	4	4	2	Ghana	7½	4	4	2
British Honduras	7½	4	4	2	Gilbert and Ellice Islds.	9	5	5	2½
Brunei	7½	4	4	2	Grenada	7½	4	4	2
Burma	7½	4	4	2	Guatemala	7½	4	4	2
Cameroon (E. and W.)	7½	4	4	2	Guinea	7½	4	4	2
Canada	7½	4	4	2	Guyana	7½	4	4	2
Canary Islands‡	—				Haiti	7½	4	4	2
Cape Verde Islands‡	—	—	—	—	Honduras (Republic)	7½	4	4	2
Caroline Islands	9	5	5	2½	Hong Kong	7½	4	4	2
C. African Republic	7½	4	4	2	India	7½	4	4	2
Ceylon	7½	4	4	2	Indonesia	7½	4	4	2
Chile	7½	4	4	2	Iran (Persia)	5	3	3	1½
China	9	5	5	2½	Iraq	5	3	3	1½
Christmas Is. (Ind. Oc.)	7½	4	4	2	Israel	5	3	3	1½
Cocos (Keeling) Islds.	7½	4	4	2	Ivory Coast	7½	4	4	2
Colombia	7½	4	4	2	Jamaica	7½	4	4	2
Congo (People's Rep.)	7½	4	4	2	Japan	9	5	5	2½
Congolese Republic	7½	4	4	2	Jordan	5	3	3	1½
Costa Rica	7½	4	4	2	Kenya	7½	4	4	2
Cuba	7½	4	4	2	Khmer Republic	7½	4	4	2
Cyprus‡	—	—	—	—	Korea, all parts	9	5	5	2½
Dahomey	7½	4	4	2	Kuwait	5	3	3	1½
Dominica	7½	4	4	2	Laos	7½	4	4	2
Dominican Republic	7½	4	4	2	Lebanon	5	3	3	1½

For mode of packing, prohibitions, limits of size, &c., see Post Office Guide.

Destination	Rates of Postage				Destination	Rates of Postage			
	Letters per ½ oz.	Post Cards	Printed Papers etc. per ½ oz.	News-papers regd. at P.O. per ½ oz.		Letters per ½ oz.	Post Cards	Printed Papers etc. per ½ oz.	News-papers regd. at P.O. per ½ oz.
	p	p	p	p		p	p	p	p
Lesotho	7½	4	4	2	Rwanda	7½	4	4	2
Liberia	7½	4	4	2	St. Helena	7½	4	4	2
Libya	5	3	3	1½	St.Kitts–Nevis–Anguilla	7½	4	4	2
Macau	7½	4	4	2	St. Lucia	7½	4	4	2
Madeira‡	—	—	—	—	St. Pierre and Miquelon	7½	4	4	2
Madagascar	7½	4	4	2	St. Vincent	7½	4	4	2
Malawi	7½	4	4	2	El Salvador	7½	4	4	2
Malaysia†	7½	4	4	2	Samoa (U.S.A. Terr.)	9	5	5	2½
Maldives (Republic)	7½	4	4	2	Saudi Arabia	5	3	3	1½
Mali	7½	4	4	2	Senegal	7½	4	4	2
Marian Islands	9	5	5	2½	Seychelles	7½	4	4	2
Marshall Islands	9	5	5	2½	Sharjah	5	3	3	1½
Mauritania	7½	4	4	2	Sierra Leone	7½	4	4	2
Mauritius	7½	4	4	2	Singapore	7½	4	4	2
Mexico	7½	4	4	2	Solomon Islands	9	5	5	2½
Mongolia	9	5	5	2½	Somalia	7½	4	4	2
Montserrat	7½	4	4	2	South Africa	7½	4	4	2
Morocco	5	3	3	1½	Spanish N. and W.				
Nauru Island	9	5	5	2½	Africa	5	3	3	1½
Nepal	7½	4	4	2	Sudan	5	3	3	1½
Netherlands Antilles	7½	4	4	2	Surinam (Neth. Guiana)	7½	4	4	2
New Caledonia	9	5	5	2½	Swaziland	7½	4	4	2
New Guinea Territory	9	5	5	2½	Syria	5	3	3	1½
New Hebrides	9	5	5	2½	Tanzania	7½	4	4	2
New Zealand (and					Thailand (Siam)	7½	4	4	2
Island Territories)	9	5	5	2½	Tibet	7½	4	4	2
Nicaragua	7½	4	4	2	Togo	7½	4	4	2
Niger (Republic)	7½	4	4	2	Tonga	9	5	5	2½
Nigeria	7½	4	4	2	Trinidad and Tobago	7½	4	4	2
Norfolk Island	9	5	5	2½	Tunisia	5	3	3	1½
Oman	5	3	3	1½	Turks and Caicos Is.	7½	4	4	2
Pakistan	7½	4	4	2	Uganda	7½	4	4	2
Panama (Republic of)	7½	4	4	2	United Arab Republic	5	3	3	1½
Panama Canal Zone	7½	4	4	2	United States	7½	4	4	2
Papua	9	5	5	2½	Upper Volta	7½	4	4	2
Paraguay	7½	4	4	2	Uruguay	7½	4	4	2
Peru	7½	4	4	2	U.S.S.R. (Asia)‡	—	—	—	—
Philippines	9	5	5	2½	Venezuela	7½	4	4	2
Pitcairn Island	9	5	5	2½	Vietnam (N. and S.)	7½	4	4	2
Portuguese East Africa	7½	4	4	2	Virgin Islds. of U.S.A.	7½	4	4	2
Portuguese Timor	9	5	5	2½	Wake Island	9	5	5	2½
Portuguese W. Africa	7½	4	4	2	Western Samoa	9	5	5	2½
Puerto Rico	7½	4	4	2	Yemen (Arab Repub.)	5	3	3	1½
Qatar	5	3	3	1½	Yemen (P.D.R.)	5	3	3	1½
Réunion	7½	4	4	2	Zambia	7½	4	4	2
Rhodesia	7½	4	4	2					

‡ Rates as for Europe, see page 1195.   † Malaya, Sabah and Sarawak.

GENERAL REGULATIONS

EXPORT RESTRICTIONS.—Under Department of Trade and Industry regulations the exportation of some goods by post is prohibited except under Department of Trade and Industry licence. Enquiries in the matter should be addressed to the Controller, Export Licensing Branch, Board of Trade, Broadway Buildings, 54 Broadway, S.W.1.

PROHIBITED AND DUTIABLE ARTICLES.—Among prohibitions are offensive or dangerous things, packets likely to impede the P.O. sorters, and certain kinds of advertisement. To Channel Islands, dutiable articles must be sent in Parcels. Abroad generally they may be sent in Parcels, in Insured Boxes, and Small Packets (to those countries which accept them) or in Letters.

CERTIFICATE OF POSTING.—Given as a matter of course for registered and insured items. May also be obtained for ordinary parcels (no charge) and other unregistered packets (fee, 1p).

RECORDED DELIVERY (inland, *not to Irish Republic*). Charge: 4p.—This service provides for a record of posting and delivery. Advice of delivery, a further 7½p at time of posting, 10p after time of posting. Money and jewellery are not allowed, and contents must not exceed £2 in value. The service does not apply to parcels, railex or railway letters.

UNPAID PACKETS, except Business Reply packets and redirected parcels are charged *double postage* on delivery; UNDERPAID PACKETS, *double the deficiency.*

UNDELIVERABLE POSTAL PACKETS.—Inland packets

chargeable with a postage exceeding 2½p, undelivered, are returned to sender without charge, if his address is found either outside or inside. If the sender's address is not available, letters containing nothing of importance are destroyed; packets containing anything of importance, and parcels, if not applied for, are generally disposed of after 3 months, or if perishable are dealt with as requisite. *Packets chargeable with postage not exceeding* 2½p. (1) Those bearing on the outside the name and address of the sender are returned direct and unopened. (2) Those not bearing on the outside the name and address of the sender and not marked "Newspaper Post" or posted subject to the special conditions under which rebate of postage has been allowed, are opened by an officer deputed for the purpose. If they contain the sender's address, they are returned to him unless the contents consist only of newspapers, magazines or commercial advertising material. (3) Those not bearing on the outside the name and address of the sender and marked "Newspaper Post" or posted subject to the special conditions under which rebate of postage has been allowed, are destroyed unopened. (4) Those not bearing on the outside the name and address of the sender which when opened are found to contain only newspapers, magazines or commercial advertising material are destroyed. *British packets undelivered abroad* are returned to sender here on payment of charges due; printed papers of no value only if request for return appears outside in a language known in the country of destination. Parcels further incur other charges unless abandonment is requested *at the time of posting.*

REPLY COUPONS, for the purpose of prepaying replies to letters, are exchangeable abroad for stamps representing the minimum letter postage rate by surface route from the country concerned to the U.K. International Reply Coupons (valid in most countries) 10p; Commonwealth Reply Coupons (valid within most countries of the British Commonwealth and the Irish Republic) 4p. Sold at chief offices.

POSTE RESTANTE (solely for the convenience of travellers, and for three months only in any one town).—A packet may be addressed as a rule to any Post Office except Town Sub-Offices, and should have the words "Poste Restante" or "to be called for" in the address. If addressed to initials, fictitious names, or Christian name only, it is treated as undeliverable. Applicants must furnish sufficient particulars to ensure delivery to the proper person. Redirection from a Poste Restante is not undertaken for more than 14 days unless longer (up to 3 months) is applied for. Letters at a seaport for an expected ship are kept 2 months; otherwise letters are kept for 2 weeks—or for 1 month if originating from abroad—at the end of which time they are treated as undeliverable, unless bearing a request for return at or before the end of the period.

REDIRECTION.—(1) By agent of addressee: *Packets other than parcels and business reply* may be reposted free not later than the day after delivery (not counting Sundays and public holidays) if unopened and not tampered with, and if original addressee's name is unobscured. *Parcels* may be redirected free of charge, within the same time limits, only if the original and the corrected addresses are both within the same local parcel delivery area (or within the London Postal Area). *Registered packets,* which must be taken to a Post Office, are *re-registered* free only up to day after delivery. (2) By the Post Office: Requests for redirection of *letters,* etc., should be on printed forms, obtainable from any post office, and must be signed by the persons to whom the letters are to be addressed.

The fees for redirection are as follows:—Redirection for a period not exceeding one month 50p; redirection or renewal for a period not exceeding three months 75p; redirection or renewal for a period not exceeding twelve months £2. A fee is payable for each different surname on the application form. Additional postage is generally due on redirected parcels (*see* above). Separate forms must be filled in for the forwarding of *telegrams.*

REGISTRATION, INLAND.—All kinds of postal packets intended for registration should be marked "Registered" in bottom left-hand corner, and *must be handed to an officer of the Post Office, and a receipt taken.* The packets must be made up in a reasonably strong cover appropriate to their contents. Parcels (or the string with which they are tied) and letters must be fastened with adhesive (if tape is used it must be transparent and each piece must be signed or distinctively marked), or sealed with wax, lead, etc. Minimum fee: Letters 20p, parcels 25p, exclusive of postage. Advice of delivery, a further 7½p at time of posting, 10p after time of posting. The latest time for registering is usually half an hour before the latest time for posting ordinary packets. Compulsory registration is applied to (a) any packet apparently meant for registration and wrongly posted (minimum fee less any prepaid excess postage); (b) packets found open (or undeliverable) and containing any bank or currency note, coin, jewellery, stamps, uncrossed bearer cheques, uncrossed postal orders without payee's name, etc., in each case £2 or more in value.

COMPENSATION, INLAND.—Subject to certain prescribed regulations which are fully set forth in the Post Office Guide, the Post Office pays compensation for (i) loss of or damage to registered letters and parcels, (ii) though not as a legal right, for loss of or damage to recorded delivery packets, unregistered parcels and for unregistered packets conveyed by Express Messenger all the way. The onus of making up properly any packet sent by post and of packing adequately any article or articles enclosed therein lies on the sender, and the Post Office does not accept any responsibility for loss arising from faulty or inadequate packing. No compensation is paid for consequential injury or damage arising in respect of anything sent by post. *Registered letters and parcels (including items sent to the Irish Republic and the Channel Islands):* The fees for registration are: Letters, 20p covering compensation up to £150; 22½p, £300; 25p, £500 (maximum). Parcels 25p, covering compensation up to £150; 27½p, £300; 30p, £500 (maximum). (No legal right to compensation exists in respect of registered letters and parcels sent to and from Irish Republic or the Channel Islands.) *Recorded delivery packets:* maximum compensation £2 provided no contents inadmissible. *Unregistered parcels and unregistered packets* conveyed by Express Messenger all the way: Maximum compensation £5.

Compensation in respect of money of any kind (coin, notes, orders, cheques, stamps, etc.) is only given if the money is sent by *registered letter* post in one of the special envelopes sold officially (see p. 1201) and, in the case of paper money, if particulars (for identification) are kept; the maximum compensation for coin, which must be packed so as not to move about, will not exceed £5 except in a case where the value of each coin exceeds its face value. Compensation cannot be paid for loss or damage in the case of any packet containing anything not legally transmissible by post; and for fragile articles only if they have been adequately packed and the cover is conspicuously marked "Fragile, with care." No compensation is paid

for deterioration due to delay of perishable articles or for damage to exceptionally fragile articles, liquids or semi-liquids sent by letter or parcel post to or from Irish Republic whether registered or not.

REGISTRATION, OVERSEAS (except for parcels and printed paper items posted in bulk), is in force to all countries with the exception of Chagos Islands, Republic of Maldives, or North Vietnam. No compensation is payable for the loss of or damage to valuable articles or other items sent in an unregistered letter. Fee 20p. If claimed within a year, compensation (in the U.K., £5·50) is paid to the sender for entire loss of registered packets while in the custody of a country in the Universal Postal Union, subject to certain conditions. Compensation is also payable for the partial or complete loss of or damage to the contents of registered items in the service with certain countries (*see* Post Office Guide for list).

INSURANCE, OVERSEAS, may be effected on packets to many countries at the following rates:— 21p for £28; 1p each further £14 up to 55p for £500. For H.M. Ships abroad and also members of H.M. Army and Air Force overseas using closed Forces addresses (*e.g.*, British Forces Post Office followed by a number) only parcels are insurable, up to £50. Packets containing no articles (besides correspondence) but valuable papers (banknotes, &c.) or valuable documents (plans, &c.) can be insured as *letters*; other valuable articles should be sent as insured parcels, or as " insured boxes."

INSURED BOX POST.—Jewellery and precious articles (*not* letters or paper valuables) may be sent in insured boxes to certain countries. Customs declarations must be filled in.

The Post Office Guide should be consulted for details of the conditions of Insurance.

COMPENSATION up to a maximum of £8·20 may be given for loss or damage in the U.K. to *uninsured* parcels to or from most overseas countries, if certificate of posting is produced.

No compensation will be paid for any loss or damage due to the act of the Queen's Enemies.

CASH ON DELIVERY SERVICE, INLAND (*not* to or from Irish Republic, nor to H.M. Ships).—A sum (Trade Charge) up to £50 can, under certain conditions, be collected from addressee and remitted to sender of a parcel or registered letter posted at a Money Order Office. Fee (extra to first class postal charge): 25p.

CASH ON DELIVERY, OVERSEAS.—Applicable to parcels only, but not to all countries, nor to H.M. Naval and Military Forces and R.A.F. serving overseas. A fee of 50p per parcel must be prepaid in addition to the postage. The Trade Charge (amount to be collected) may not exceed £50, but to some countries the limit is lower. Addressee has also to pay on delivery, besides Customs, if any, a further fee (10p in U.K.) not prepayable. If Trade Charge cannot be collected, special rules for undeliverable C.O.D. parcels apply.

EXPRESS and SPECIAL SERVICES (INLAND).— In general the express services are limited to the hours of telegraph business, but the times vary according to the service used and local conditions. (1) *All the way*, by P.O. messenger, of packets, conspicuously marked "Express" above the address, handed over the counter. Inclusive charge, 20p per mile, or part of a mile, with 3p on each *separate* packet after the first. Live animals, liquids, and money may be delivered by this service. Waiting fees: 10 minutes free, each further 10 minutes or less, 5p:—(*a*) *After transmission by post*, on addressee's application (20p per mile, or part of a mile, and 2½p for every ten or less additional packets). (3) *After transmission by post*, at *sender's* request "Special Delivery" from the

ordinary delivery office, if messengers are available (20p.+postage). This service is restricted to First Class letters and to parcels. Packets must be marked " Special Delivery," and letters bear a broad blue or black vertical line back and front. A similar line must be drawn completely round a packet or parcel. (4) *Special delivery on Sunday of postal packets* (*except parcels*) *handed in on Saturdays*. Limited inter-city services, for London, Belfast, and certain provincial cities (except that the service is not in operation from Southampton to Belfast) are available *only*: (1) Sundays: reciprocally between certain towns as shown in the Post Office Guide; (2) Good Friday: *to* London only *from* towns in (1). Delivery is made from offices only during periods when they are open for telegraphic business. The handing-in offices in London are:—The London Chief Office, King Edward St., E.C.1., W. and S.W. District Offices, and Camberwell Green, Clapham Common, Hammersmith Broadway, Holloway, Trafalgar Square, Stratford, and Swiss Cottage (Branch Offices). Packets marked "Express: Sunday Delivery," must be handed in in time to catch *preceding* night mails (in London 12.45 p.m.-5.0 p.m. for provincial towns). The latest time of posting to Belfast should be ascertained at selected office of posting. Fee is 50p in addition to postage. Not available for parcels. (5) (*Railex.*) Postal packets which cannot be registered are despatched by rail, met, and specially delivered in Great Britain, Douglas (I.O.M.), Northern Ireland (Belfast, Larne and Londonderry only). Inclusive charges irrespective of weight but not exceeding 1 lb, £1, but packets handed in in Northern Ireland for destinations in Great Britain, Douglas or Northern Ireland may not exceed 2 oz. (6) *A Railway Parcel* is similarly accelerated at the cost of a telegram, of railway charges, and of Service (1) at both ends of its journey. It should be marked "Railway Parcel, to be handed to Post Office messenger at .... Station."

RAILWAY LETTERS, &C.—A First Class letter, not liable to registration, may be handed in at the parcel or passenger booking office of a railway station, at any time when the station is open to the public, for conveyance by the next available train. A railway letter may either be addressed to be called for at a station, or to the residence of the addressee in which case it is posted at the station named in the address. The service is available between any two stations in Great Britain and Northern Ireland, between Great Britain and Douglas (I.O.M.), and from Great Britain and Northern Ireland to the Irish Republic. It is not available at or to stations of the London Transport Executive. Fees (besides postage): Between stations in Great Britain: not over 2 oz. 15p; not over 4 oz., 20p; not over 1 lb. (maximum) 25p. From stations and ports in Great Britain, to stations in Northern Ireland or Douglas (Isle of Man); not over 2 oz., 20p; not over 4 oz., 25p; not over 1 lb. (maximum) 30p. From Douglas (Isle of Man) to a station in Northern Ireland: not over 2 oz., 20p; not over 4 oz., 25p; not over 1 lb. (maximum) 30p. From stations and ports in Great Britain, Douglas (Isle of Man) to stations in the Republic of Ireland: not over 2 oz. (maximum) 20p. For railway letters handed in at stations in Northern Ireland the railway fee is: not over 2 oz. (maximum) 10p. Except on Sundays, or in Irish Republic, the letter can be delivered Express under Service (3), or directly from the station (Service (1)) by wiring for messenger to meet it. For other combinations of rail and express, *see* preceding paragraph, Services (5) and (6).

AIRWAY LETTERS.—On certain internal air routes operated by the British European Airways Corporation, First Class letters may be handed in at the

airport or town terminal for conveyance by the next available direct air service to be transferred to the post at the distant airport or town terminal or to be called for at the airport or town terminal. Fees (besides postage): 2 oz., 18p; 4 oz., 21p; 1 lb. (maximum), 26p. The conditions on which this service operates are, in general, similar to those applying to the Railway Letter Service. The service is not available to the Irish Republic or to any country overseas. Full information can be obtained from any office of B.E.A.

INTERNATIONAL EXPRESS SERVICE.—From the office of delivery by special messenger is available to or from certain countries. In some countries the service is restricted to certain towns. 20p is paid by the sender, the rest, if any, by addressee, according to the local regulations. (*See* P.O. Guide.)

DATAPOST.—This service offers a door-to-door overnight service to most parts of the country on a contract basis. Charges are negotiated with individual customers and reflect the services performed. Head Postmasters will provide full information on request.

This service is also available to the U.S.A.

POST CARDS (Inland).—Minimum size $3\frac{1}{2} \times 5\frac{1}{2}$ in., maximum $4\frac{3}{4} \times 9\frac{1}{4}$ in. Cards outside these sizes will eventually be charged extra. The left-hand half of the address side may be used for correspondence, inland or abroad. Plain cards, if as stiff as official cards and not under $\frac{1}{100}$th inch thick, may also be used both inland and abroad.

BUSINESS REPLY AND FREEPOST (Inland, excluding Irish Republic).—These services enable a person or firm to receive replies to advertisements, letters from clients, etc. without prepayment of postage, the addressee paying the postage together with a handling charge of $\frac{1}{2}$p per item delivered. A licence costing £5 p.a. must be obtained to use either service and these are available from Head Postmasters who will also provide any further information required.

POSTAGE FORWARD PARCEL SERVICE.—This service enables a person or firm to receive parcels from clients without prepayment of postage. A special label is used for this service. A licence costing £5 p.a., to use the service must first be obtained from the local Head Postmaster.

ARTICLES FOR THE BLIND (Inland, including Irish Republic). Books, papers, literature and specified articles specially adapted for the use of the blind are admissible subject to certain conditions. A packet should bear on the outside the indication " Articles for the Blind " and the name and address of the sender. Packets must be capable of easy examination in the post. Postage free.

BLIND LITERATURE, OVERSEAS (in other respects treated as Printed Papers):—Papers, periodicals and books, if printed in special type (also plates for embossing blind literature, and voice recordings and special paper intended solely for the use of the blind) subject to certain conditions of posting, marked outside " Literature for the Blind ", with name and address of sender. Packets must be capable of easy examination in the post. Packets may be sent post free by surface route to all parts.

SMALL PACKETS POST (OVERSEAS).—For the transmission of goods (including trade samples) in the same mails as Printed Papers up to 2 lb. Registration is allowed; not insurance. Available to all countries, but to some countries there is a limit of 1 lb. A customs declaration is required.

NEWSPAPER POST (INLAND).—For newspapers " registered at the P.O." (p. 1196).

Copies of registered newspapers may be posted by the publishers or their agents in wrappers open at both ends, in unsealed envelopes approved by the Post Office for the purpose or without covers and tied with string which can be removed without cutting. Wrappers and envelopes must be prominently marked NEWSPAPER POST in the top left-hand corner and be easily removable for the purpose of examination. No writing or additional printing is permitted, other than the words " with compliments ", name and address of sender, request for return if undeliverable and a reference to a page.

Newspapers posted by the public or supplements to registered newspapers despatched apart from their ordinary publications are transmitted under the conditions governing the First or Second Class Letter Services.

STAMPS, ENVELOPES, POST CARDS, &c.

Stamps of reigns before that of King George V are no longer valid.

POSTAGE STAMPS (used also for receipts, telegrams, and certain Inland Revenue duties) are sold for the respective values of $\frac{1}{2}$p, 1p, 1$\frac{1}{2}$p, 2p, 2$\frac{1}{2}$p, 3p, 3$\frac{1}{2}$p, 4p, 5p, 6p, 7$\frac{1}{2}$p, 9p, 10p, 20p, 50p and £1. Books containing 2 at $\frac{1}{2}$p, 2 at 1p, 2 at 1$\frac{1}{2}$p, 2 at 2p, 10p; 5 at $\frac{1}{2}$p, 9 at 2$\frac{1}{2}$p, 25p; 10 at 3p, 30p; 5 at $\frac{1}{2}$p, 7 at 2$\frac{1}{2}$p, 10 at 3p, 50p. Rolls of 1p, 2$\frac{1}{2}$p or 3p stamps are sold. There are also mixed value rolls made up of strips of 2p, $\frac{1}{2}$p, 1p, 1p; 5p.

REGISTERED LETTER ENVELOPES with a 23p embossed stamp (20p for registration and 3p for postage) are of three sizes: G, $6\frac{1}{2}'' \times 3\frac{3}{4}''$ 24$\frac{1}{2}$p each; H, $8'' \times 4\frac{3}{4}''$ 25p each; K $11\frac{1}{2}'' \times 6''$ 27p each.

FORCES AIR LETTER FORMS issued against purchase of 2$\frac{1}{2}$p stamp.

LETTER CARDS with 2$\frac{1}{2}$p stamp, 3$\frac{1}{2}$p each; with 3p stamp, 4p each.

POST CARDS with impressed 2$\frac{1}{2}$p stamp, 3p each.

EMBOSSED ENVELOPES with 2$\frac{1}{2}$p stamp: A ($5\frac{3}{4}'' \times 3\frac{3}{4}''$) 3$\frac{1}{2}$p each; B ($9\frac{1}{4}'' \times 4\frac{1}{4}''$) 3$\frac{1}{2}$p each. With 3p stamp: A ($5\frac{3}{4}'' \times 3\frac{3}{4}''$) 4p each; B ($9\frac{1}{4}'' \times 4\frac{1}{4}''$) 4p each.

Air Letter Forms impressed with 5p stamp, 5p each.

Embossed or impressed postage stamps cut out of envelopes, post cards, letter cards, air letter forms or newspaper-wrappers may be used as adhesive stamps in payment of postage or telegrams provided they are not imperfect, mutilated, or defaced in any way.

MONEY ORDERS

Advice of Payment: 7$\frac{1}{2}$p inland (and to Irish Republic), 7$\frac{1}{2}$p overseas orders (to certain countries). Payment may be stopped (fee 7$\frac{1}{2}$p); or deferred up to 10 days in case of Ordinary Inland Money Orders. Inland orders (including those for Irish Republic) may be crossed for payment through a bank.

Inland Ordinary Money Orders (and to Irish Republic).

The fee is 25p per order (maximum value £50). No order may contain a fractional part of 1p. The rules and regulations are on the forms issued. No fee is charged for M.O. in payment of certain Excise Duties and Licences if demand note is produced (*see* Post Office Guide).

Inland Telegraph Money Orders (and to Irish Republic).

Money may be transmitted by this means from most Money Order offices which despatch telegrams, and paid at most of those which also deliver telegrams, and at some other offices. On Sundays, Christmas Day, Boxing Day and Good Friday special arrangements apply (*see* Post Office Guide).

The fee is 25p per order (maximum value £50) plus cost of official Telegram of Advice, 25p minimum for Inland Orders and 30p minimum for Irish Republic Orders and where applicable the charge for any private message sent with the order, 2p per word.

Ordinary Money Orders for Abroad.

The fee is 40p per order. Limits of amount vary according to destination but in any case may not exceed £50; validity varies between one and twelve months (*see* Post Office Guide).

Telegraph Money Orders for Abroad.

The fee is 50p per order, *plus* cost of official Telegram of Advice (at Letter Telegram rate, if desired, to certain countries).

Application to remit money orders to countries outside the Scheduled Territories (formerly known as the Sterling Area) must be made on a special declaration form upon which the purpose of the remittance must be stated. This form is obtainable at any money order office, where it may be ascertained whether any particular country with which a money order service is in operation is outside the Scheduled Territories.

POSTAL ORDERS

Postal Orders (British pattern) are issued and paid at nearly all post offices in the United Kingdom during the ordinary hours of business on weekdays. They are also issued and/or paid in many countries within the Commonwealth and in a few other countries. Transmission of postal orders to any country outside the Scheduled Territories (formerly known as the Sterling Area) is prohibited except to members of H.M. Forces under special arrangements, particulars of which may be obtained at any Post Office transacting Postal Order business. They are *paid* (but not *issued*) in Channel Islands and Irish Republic. They are printed with a counterfoil, for 5p, then for 7½p and every multiple of 2½p up to 25p, then 30p and every multiple of 5p up to £1, then by every multiple of £1 to £5. Adhesive unmarked current British Postage Stamps not exceeding two in number, if affixed in the two spaces provided, increase the value of the order by not more than 4½p. Poundage, 5p to £1; 2½p, £2, £3, £4 or £5; 5p. The name of payee must be inserted. If not presented within six months of the last day of the month of issue, Orders must be sent to the local Head Postmaster, or in London to the District Postmaster to ascertain whether the order may still be paid.

INLAND TELEGRAMS

Telegrams are accepted during counter business hours at any post office at which telegraph business is transacted. They may also be handed with the necessary payment to messengers delivering telegrams or express letters. Telegrams may be tendered by telephone at all times. Rate, 12 words or less 25p (to Irish Republic 12 words or less 30p), each further word 2p. Standard Greetings telegrams on appropriately designed forms in golden decorative envelopes cost 27½p for 12 words or less, each extra word 2p. Greetings telegrams for special occasions on a large *de luxe* folded card with matching envelope cost 35p for 12 words or less, each extra word 2p. Greetings telegrams may be tendered by telephone or handed in any day prior to day of delivery. Priority rate (not available to or from Irish Republic) 10p extra.

Overnight Telegram

An Overnight telegram may be sent between 8 a.m. and 10.30 p.m. for delivery, normally by first post, the following morning. On days when there is no postal delivery, Overnight telegrams are held until the next postal delivery. The charge is 12½p for 12 words or less and 1p for each extra word. The Overnight service is not available to the Irish Republic. A redirection charge of 25p per telegram is made if the original and new addresses are in the same delivery area or London Postal District. In all other cases the redirection charge is at the ordinary inland rate. Telegrams, except Press telegrams, handed in on *Sundays* and (exc. Scotland) *Good Friday* or *Christmas Day* are charged 12½p extra. Replies may be prepaid within the limits of 12½p (minimum) and £1 (maximum) (Irish Republic 45p (minimum)

and £1 (maximum); the reply vouchers may be used in payment or part payment of any Post Office telegram or any telegraph, telex or telephone account rendered by the Post Office, or its value refunded to sender, the addressee or person applying on behalf of the sender of the original telegram, on completion of the declaration on the back of the voucher. Receipt for charges free on request. Certified copy 12½p; application to the local Head Postmaster must be within 3 months of the date of sending. There is no charge for delivery in the United Kingdom. In the Irish Republic delivery is free to addresses within 1 mile of the delivery office; beyond that any necessary charge will be collected on delivery.

TELEGRAPH OFFICE ALWAYS OPEN IN LONDON: — Trafalgar Sq., 24–28 William IV Street, WC2N 4DL.

INTERNATIONAL TELEGRAMS

The charges for ordinary or FULL RATE telegrams from the United Kingdom to places abroad are shown below and on pp. 1206-9. The minimum charge for an ordinary telegram is as for 7 words. To any place in the British Commonwealth the full rate does not exceed 9p per word. Urgent telegrams may be sent at double the ordinary rate.

For telegrams of a social character the GLT (Commonwealth Social Telegram) service is available to Commonwealth countries. The charge is 45p for 11 words or less (including the indication=GLT=) and 4½p for each additional word except to Bermuda, Canada, Cyprus, Jamaica, Trinidad and Tobago and certain Commonwealth points in the Caribbean to which lower charges apply, and they are normally delivered the day following the day of handing in.

Most countries admit Letter Telegrams at half the full rate for messages in plain language of a lengthy though less urgent character for which the minimum charge is as for 22 words including the appropriate indication=ELT= for European countries and =LT= for countries outside Europe. ELT messages are not delivered until at least 5 hours from the time of handing in and LT messages normally during the day following.

Phototelegrams, i.e. pictures, photographs, drawings, plans, printed, typed or written documents may be telegraphed in facsimile to many places in the world. Full particulars of all telegraph charges and services available to any country will be given on enquiry at any Post Office or International Telegraph Office.

RADIOTELEGRAMS

Radiotelegrams for transmission to ships at sea in any part of the world may be handed in at any Postal Telegraph Office or dictated over the telephone. The charge for radiotelegrams is 8½p per word (standard rate) for all vessels other than (1) British trawlers and (2) British vessels REGULARLY engaged in voyages not exceeding 1,000 miles to or from a port in the British Isles. Radiotelegrams at the Standard rate should be addressed Portishead Radio unless the sender nominates another coast station. Radiotelegrams for British trawlers should be charged at the reduced rate of 5p per word and addressed Wick Radio unless the sender nominates another coast station. Radiotelegrams for British vessels REGULARLY engaged in voyages not exceeding 1,000 miles to or from a port in the British Isles should also be charged at the reduced rate of 5p per word and addressed to the nearest coast station unless the sender nominates another coast station. The address should contain (1) the name or rank of the addressee, (2) the name of the ship and (3) the name of the coast station in the British Isles if the sender knows that the ship is within range of that station; or the name of a foreign

coast station if the message is to be routed through such a station.

Radiotelegrams may be sent to H.M. Ships in the Home Fleet or based on the Home Station at a reduced rate of 3½p a word. Total charge is rounded down to nearest 1p. The charge for messages to H.M. Ships in foreign waters or proceeding to and from a foreign naval station is 5½p a word. The address should contain (1) the name of the addressee and his rank or rating, (2) the word " Warship " (or " Submarine "), (3) the name of the ship (or identifying letters and number) and (4) the word " Admiraltyradio " (or in the case of the Home Fleet, the words " Homewaters Admiraltyradio ").

Radiotelegrams may also be sent to R.A.F. vessels in Home Waters at a reduced rate of 3½p per word. Total charge is rounded down to nearest 1p. Such radiotelegrams should be addressed in the same way as for commercial vessels and in addition should include the words " R.A.F. Vessel " before the name of the ship.

The minimum charge is as for seven words.

RADIOTELEPHONE SERVICE

Radiotelephone services are available between telephone subscribers (but not from coin-box telephones or call offices unless the caller is a holder of a telephone credit card) in Great Britain, Northern Ireland, the Channel Islands and the Isle of Man and suitably equipped ships. The service is generally available at all hours of the day and night, but the periods of communication with a particular ship vary with the ship's position and are dependent on radio conditions.

Calls are normally made through the coast stations, listed below, and callers should ask the local exchange telephone operator for SHIPS' TELEPHONE SERVICE adding, if known, the telephone number and name of the coast station through which the call should be made. If the name of the coast station is not known the caller will be connected to Portishead Radio. When connected to the coast station operator, the caller should ask for SHIPS' RADIO TELEPHONE CALL giving the name of the ship and the name (or designation) of the person required.

Anglesey Radio.........	0407 83 0541
Cullercoats Radio........	0894 4 23479
Humber Radio...........	Mablethorpe 3447
Ilfracombe Radio........	Ilfracombe 3453
Land's End Radio........	0736 77 493
Niton Radio.............	0983 73 495
North Foreland Radio....	0843 20592
Oban Radio.............	0631 2059
Portishead Radio........	027 878 3291
Portpatrick Radio........	0776 81 311
Stonehaven Radio........	0569 2 2917
Thames Radio (restricted short range VHF services)	0843 20592
Wick Radio.............	0955 2271

There is also a restricted short range radiotelephone VHF service available through Clyde Radio. To obtain calls through this service subscribers should ask the local exchange telephone operator for CLYDE RADIO VHF RADIOTELEPHONE SERVICE 0475 22255.

Charges vary according to the position of the ship. Ships in Zone A (All waters within the limits 13°W, 9°E, 45°N and 63°N) the charge is 63p for a 3 minute call (minimum charge) and 21p per additional minute. Ships in Zone B (All Northern waters beyond Zone A) and within the limits 35°W, 35°E and 35°N and the whole of the Mediterranean Sea) the charge is £1·80 for a 3 minute call (minimum charge) and 60p per additional minute. Ships in Zone C (All waters

beyond those defined in Zones A and B) the charge is £3 for a 3 minute call (minimum charge) and £1 per additional minute.

The service is available, for calls to and from H.M. Ships, subject to the approval of the Duty Commander M.O.D. Navy, through whom all calls to H.M. Ships should be booked. The charges are the same as those for merchant ships but as H.M. Ships do not normally keep watch for private radiotelephone calls from the shore, no attempt should be made to book a call to one of H.M. Ships unless prior arrangements have been made with the person concerned on the ship. The caller must be able to give the name of the coast station through which the call is to be made, or the approximate position of the ship at the time the call is required.

The holder of a telephone credit card issued in Great Britain, Northern Ireland, the Channel Islands or the Isle of Man may use it to make radiotelephone calls to ships at sea from any telephone in this country (including coin-box telephones and call offices) and have the charges debited to his own account.

INLAND TELEPHONES

The quarterly rental for an exclusive business exchange line is £6 and £5 for any other exclusive exchange line. For shared service, in which two subscribers share one line but have practically the same facilities as those provided by individual lines, each customer pays £4 per annum less than for exclusive line service. A condition of telephone service is that all new and removing residential customers since January, 1948, are liable to share their lines if called upon to do so. Subscriber trunk dialling (STD) facilities are provided at an increasing number of exchanges. Local and dialled trunk calls from these exchanges are charged in 1p units, 2p units from pay on answer coin-box lines: the length of time per unit depends on the distance of the call, from six minutes for a local call to eight seconds for distances over 50 miles. Additional time is allowed during the cheaper rates period.

From other exchanges local calls are charged 1½p from ordinary lines and 2p from a call office or coin-box line. All trunk calls are obtained via the operator. Operator-controlled trunk calls from any exchange have a three minute minimum charge which varies with the distance but does not exceed 25½p (34½p to Irish Republic from non-coin-box telephones). Operator-controlled calls made from coin-box lines are charged in 3 minute periods at the coin-box tariff. Trunk calls via the operator are cheaper if made after 6 p.m. or at weekends. Personal calls (to specified person) 10p extra, if the person cannot be found nothing further is charged. For fuller information *see* Preface to Telephone Directory, Dialling Instruction Booklet (where appropriate) and Post Office Guide.

TELEX SERVICE

Annual rental of teleprinter, associated equipment and line to Telex exchange is from £160 per annum (depending upon the equipment required). Charges for inland calls are about half equivalent charges for daytime telephone calls. International calls to European countries are less than charges for telephone calls; to extra-European countries the charges are generally the same as for telephone calls, *e.g.* £1 or £1·25 per minute. The minimum call charge is three minutes except for subscriber-dialled calls to some extra-European countries, where the minimum call charge is one minute, and subscriber-dialled calls to Europe which are charged

in 1p units. Automatic equipment allowing messages to be sent at the maximum speed of 400 characters (60–70 words) per minute can be rented in addition. Descriptive booklet available from all Telephone Managers: for local address see Telephone Directory.

DATEL SERVICES

Data transmission facilities are provided to cater for transmission speeds ranging from 50 to 48,000 bits per second. They are:

Datel 100: This service uses private telegraph circuits and the public telex network with maximum transmission speeds of 110 and 50 bits per second respectively. The service has been extended internationally using the public telex network for transmission to a number of countries.

Datel 200: This service provides for the transmission of data in both directions simultaneously at speeds up to 200 bits per second and on certain connections, 300 bits per second on telephone circuits using Post Office modems. Service is available to several countries in Europe and beyond.

Datel 600: This provides for transmission of data on telephone circuits at speeds up to 600 bits per second, and on certain connections, 1200 bits per second, using Post Office modems. The service is available to several countries in Europe and beyond.

Datel 2400: This service, using Post Office modems, enables transmission at a rate of 2,400 bits per second over private speech type circuits with improved characteristics. The modem has optional facilities to send at speeds of 600 or 1,200 bits per second over the public telephone network.

48 Kbit/s Service. This service using Post Office modems was opened in 1970 and can be provided either as private links between customers' premises or viâ a new switched network which has been set up between London, Birmingham and Manchester.

INTERNATIONAL TELEPHONES

The same charges are made for calls from any part of Great Britain, Northern Ireland and the Isle of Man. Callers on exchanges with the STD facility in Birmingham, Edinburgh, Glasgow, Liverpool, London and Manchester should consult their Dialling Instructions booklets for information about how to make calls. They can dial directly to subscribers in Belgium, France, Germany, Italy, Monaco, the Netherlands, Norway, San Marino, Switzerland, Vatican City and the U.S.A. Directly-dialled calls are charged in units of time costing 1p. Elsewhere, callers should ask the local operator for an international call, specifying the country required.

The charges for calls viâ an operator based on a three-minute minimum. Each additional minute or part of a minute is charged at one third of this minimum charge. Transferred charge (collect) calls are available with some countries and British

Post Office credit cards can be used in many countries for calls to the U.K.; charges for such calls incoming to this country may be higher than those for outgoing calls. A personal call service is available at an extra charge on calls to the Continent and certain extra-European countries and will be extended as the introduction of modern conditions on extra-European services permits. A person-to-person service is available on calls to all other countries; the cost of this facility is included in the call charge. At night (10 p.m. to 10 a.m.) and on Sundays a reduced rate is available on services with Canada, the U.S.A., and Cuba. Reduced Sunday rates apply also for calls to certain other countries.

Calls to Ships

For calls to ships at sea, *see* p. 1203, col. 2.

GENERAL SUNDAY AND HOLIDAY ARRANGEMENTS

(For Express Services see p. 1200).

On SUNDAY *THROUGHOUT THE U.K.* there is no general delivery of letters and parcels. There is a collection for night despatch in most places. *IN LONDON*, the Trafalgar Square Branch Office is open always. *OUTSIDE LONDON*, some Head Offices and a few country telegraph sub-offices open 9–10.30 a.m. (Scotland 9–10 a.m.) for stamps, telegrams, registration and with some exceptions telegraph money orders up to £5, Savings Bank withdrawals up to £20, and National Savings Stamps encashment up to £3; all other offices are closed.

Christmas Day, Boxing Day and Good Friday

London: There are no deliveries of letters and parcels on Christmas Day, Boxing Day or Good Friday. All offices except Trafalgar Square Branch office are closed.

Outside London: In Scotland, normal weekday deliveries except on Christmas Day when there are no deliveries of letters and parcels; offices open as usual on Boxing Day and Good Friday; on Christmas Day some town sub-offices are shut, and after noon many chief offices are open only for telegraph business. In England, Wales and Northern Ireland there are no deliveries of letters and parcels on Christmas Day or Boxing Day; on Good Friday there is one delivery; offices are closed on Christmas Day; Head Offices and some country telegraph sub-offices are open from 9 a.m. to 10.30 a.m. for all classes of business on Boxing Day and for " Sunday " business on Good Friday.

Other Public Holidays

In Scotland on New Year's Day office hours and classes of business are as on Sundays; no delivery of letters and parcels and no collection. Post Office counter and postal services on other public holidays in the U.K. vary in accordance with local conditions—details may be obtained from the local Head Postmaster.

BROADCAST RECEIVING LICENCES

Television.—Broadcast receiving licences (for television) are obtainable at most post offices for £7 (excluding colour) and £12 (including colour). The colour television licence includes reception of television programmes in black and white.

Blind Persons.—Blind persons who produce the required certificates of registration may obtain concessionary television (excluding colour) licences for £5·75 and a television (including colour) licence for £10·75.

Licensing Requirements.—One licence (which needs to be a colour television licence if a colour tele-

vision set is used anywhere in the household) covers any number of sets in a single household; but lodgers, paying guests and occupiers of flats (even if not self-contained) count as separate householders and require separate licences. Licences are also required by those using apparatus which is rented or hired.

Period of Validity.—An initial licence (except a demonstration licence) is dated to expire twelve months from the last day of the month preceding that of issue. A renewal licence covers a period of twelve months from the date on which the previous licence expires.

INTERNATIONAL TELEPHONE CHARGES

Services to countries within Europe are marked (A); remaining services are to countries outside Europe.

Country	Minimum	Country	Minimum	Country	Minimum
	£		£		£
French territory of the Afars and Issas	3·39	Gibraltar (A)	0·84	Paraguay	3·75
Afghanistan	3·75	Gilbert and Ellice Islds.	3·75	Peru	2·49
Alaska★	3·75	Greece (A)	1·20	Philippines★	3·75
Albania (A)	1·89	Grenada	3·00	Poland (A)	0·75
Algeria (A)	1·26	Guatemala★	3·75	Portugal (A)	0·84
Andorra (A)	0·45	Guinea	3·39	Principe (Island)	3·00
Angola	3·00	Guyana	3·00	Puerto Rico	3·75
Antigua	3·00	Haiti★	3·75	Qatar	3·00
Argentina	2·49	Hawaii Islands★	3·75	Réunion	3·39
Ascension	3·00	Honduras★	3·75	Rhodesia	3·00
Australia	3·00	Hong Kong	3·75	Rumania (A)	1·20
Austria (A)	0·60	Hungary (A)	0·99	Rwanda	3·00
Azores (A)	1·59	Iceland (A)	1·35	Ryukyu Islands	3·75
Bahamas★	3·75	India	3·75	Sabah (including Labuan)	3·75
Bahrain	3·00	Indonesia	3·75	St. Helena	3·00
Balearic Islands (A)	1·35	Iran (Persia)φ	2·49	St. Kitts	3·00
Barbados	3·00	Iraq	3·00	St. Lucia	3·00
Belgium (A)	0·45	Israelφ	2·49	St. Pierre and Miquelon	3·39
Bermuda	3·00	Italy (A)	0·60	St. Vincent (West Indies)	3·00
Bolivia	3·75	Ivory Coast	3·39	Samoa (U.S.A. Territory)	4·26
Botswana	3·00	Jamaica	3·00	Samoa (Western)	3·75
Brazilφ	2·49	Japanφ (No reduced rate)	2·49	San Marino (A)	0·60
British Honduras	3·75	Jordan	3·00	Sarawak	3·75
British Virgin Islds.	3·75	Kenyaφ	2·49	Saudi Arabia	3·75
Brunei	3·75	Khmer Republic	4·41	Jedda only	3·39
Bulgaria (A)	1·20	Kuwaitφ	2·49	Senegal	3·39
Burma	3·75	Laos	4·41	Seychelles	3·75
Burundi	3·00	Lebanon	3·39	Sierra Leone	3·00
Cameroon	3·39	Leeward Islands (Nevis)	3·00	Singapore	3·75
Canada¢	2·25	Lesotho	2·49	Solomon Islands	3·75
Canary Islands (A)	1·59	Liberia	3·39	Somali Republic	4·89
Cape Verde Islands	3·00	Libya (A)	3·00	South and S.W. Africaφ	2·49
Cayman Islands	3·00	Liechtenstein (A)	0·54	South Korea★	3·75
Central African Republic	3·00	Luxemburg (A)	0·45	South Vietnam	4·41
Ceylon	3·00	Macau	3·75	Spain (A)	0·84
Chad	3·00	Madeira (A)	1·59	Sudan	3·00
Chileφ	2·49	Malagasy Republic	3·39	Surinam	3·00
China	3·75	Malawi	3·00	Swaziland	2·49
Christmas Isld. (Indian Oc.)	3·00	Malaya	3·75	Sweden (A)	0·69
Colombia★	3·75	Mali	3·39	Switzerland (A)	0·54
Congo D.R. (Brazzaville)	3·00	Malta (A)	1·11	Syria	3·75
Congolese Republic	3·00	Mariana Islands★	3·75	Tanzaniaφ	2·49
Cook (or Hervey) Islds.	3·75	Martinique	3·39	Thailandφ	2·49
Costa Rica★	3·75	Mauritania	3·39	Tobago	3·00
Cuba†	3·75	Mauritius	3·75	Togo	3·39
Cyprus	2·25	Mexico	3·75	Tonga	3·75
Czechoslovakia (A)	0·66	Midway Island	3·75	Trinidad	3·00
Dahomey	3·39	Monaco (A)	0·45	Trucial States	3·00
Denmark (A)	0·54	Montserrat	3·00	Tunisia (A)	1·35
Dominica	3·00	Morocco (A)	1·35	Turkey (A)	1·50
Dominican Republic★	3·75	Mozambique	3·00	Turks Island	3·00
Ecuador★	3·75	Nauru Island	3·00	Ugandaφ	2·49
El Salvador★	3·75	Nepal	3·75	United Arab Republic	3·00
Equatorial Guinea	4·11	Netherlands (A)	0·45	Upper Volta	3·39
Ethiopia	3·00	New Caledonia	3·39	Uruguay★	3·75
Falkland Islands	3·00	New Guinea Territory	3·00	U.S.A.¢ (except Alaska and Hawaii)	2·25
Faroe (A)	0·75	New Hebrides	3·00	U.S.S.R. (A)	1·05 to 2·25
Fiji Islands‡	3·00	New Zealand	2·49	Vatican City (A)	0·60
Finland (A)	1·05	Nicaragua★	3·75	Venezuela‡	3·00
Formosa★	3·75	Niger	3·39	Virgin Islds. (of the U.S.A.)	3·75
France (A)	0·45	Nigeria	3·00	Wake Island	3·75
French Guiana	3·39	Norway (A)	0·69	Windward Islands	3·00
French Polynesia	3·39	Oman	3·00	Yemen (Arab Republic)	3·00
Gaboon	3·00	Pakistan	3·00	Yemen (P.D.R.)	3·00
Gambia	3·00	Panamaφ	2·49	Yugoslavia (A)	0·99
Germany (A)	0·54	Panama Canal Zone	2·49	Zambia	3·00
Ghana	3·00	Papua	3·00		

¢ Night and Sundays 57p less.   Personal calls £1·75 additional.   ‡ Personal calls £1·50 additional.
★ Sundays only, 75p less.   † Night and Sundays, 75p less.   φ Personal calls £1·51 additional.

For mode of packing, prohibitions, etc., *see* Post Office Guide.

Telegrams (see pp. 1202–3)	DESTINATION	SURFACE MAIL Each parcel not over:—				AIR MAIL Each parcel	
		2 lb	7 lb	11 lb	22 lb	First 1b	Each 1b after
p		£	£	£	£	£	£
16½	Abu Dhabi....................	0·80	1·10	1·60	2·45	1·05	0·40
11	Afghanistan...........(Direct)	1·25	1·60	2·15	3·35	} 1·30	0·50
	(via U.S.S.R.)	1·20	1·70	2·40	3·90		
5	Albania......................	0·95	1·20	1·65	2·40	0·90	0·20
5	Algeria......................	0·90	1·15	1·50	2·30	1·00	0·25
7	Antigua.....................	0·90	1·10	1·50	2·30	1·25	0·45
14½	Argentina...................	1·00	1·30	1·80	2·65	1·65	0·85
9	Ascension...................	0·65	0·90	1·20	1·80	No service	
9	Australia....................	0·90	1·30	1·90	2·95	1·60	1·20
5	Austria.....................	0·85	1·05	1·40	2·10	0·75	0·15
5	Azores......................	0·75	0·95	1·30	1·95	0·85	0·20
7	Bahamas....................	0·80	1·05	1·40	2·20	1·20	0·50
11	Bahrain.....................	1·05	1·40	2·00	2·70	1·25	0·40
7	Barbados....................	0·85	1·10	1·50	2·25	1·25	0·50
5	Belgium.....................	0·70	0·90	1·25	1·80	0·90	0·10
7	Bermuda....................	0·75	0·95	1·30	1·80	1·00	0·40
17	Bolivia.....................	1·00	1·25	1·75	2·60	1·45	0·80
9	Botswana....................	0·80	1·20	1·75	2·75	} 1·30	0·65
	Kazungula and Kasane only.....	1·05	1·40	2·05	3·20		
13½	Brazil.......................	1·25	1·55	2·00	2·90	1·75	0·65
	British Antarctic Territory—*see* Falkland Islands Dependencies.						
9	British Solomon Islands............	0·90	1·20	1·75	2·55	1·90	1·20
7	British Honduras..............	0·80	1·05	1·45	2·20	1·30	0·55
7	British Virgin Islands (Tortola)......	0·85	1·10	1·45	2·25	1·20	0·55
9	Brunei......................	1·20	1·55	2·15	3·15	1·80	0·80
5	Bulgaria....................	0·95	1·20	1·70	2·60	0·90	0·20
11	Burma......................	0·90	1·20	1·65	2·55	1·50	0·70
10	Burundi.....................	1·10	1·45	2·00	2·95	1·25	0·50
	Cambodia, *see* Khmer Republic.						
13½	Cameroon...................	1·00	1·25	1·75	2·55	1·10	0·40
7	Canada.....................	0·80	1·20	1·75	2·70	1·15	0·45
5	Canary Islands...............	0·90	1·05	1·40	2·05	0·85	0·20
9	Cape Verde Islands............	0·80	1·05	1·50	2·25	1·05	0·35
18	Caroline Islands...............	0·95	1·65	2·65	4·35	1·90	1·15
7	Cayman Islands..............	1·00	1·35	1·80	2·50	1·20	0·55
20½	Central African Republic............	1·05	1·40	2·10	3·20	1·10	0·45
9	Ceylon.....................	0·90	1·30	1·80	2·75	1·40	0·60
20½	Chad.......................	0·80	1·10	1·60	2·40	1·05	0·45
14½	Chile.......................	1·00	1·30	1·85	2·80	1·65	0·85
17	China (People's Republic of)						
	(via U.S.S.R.)	1·00	1·50	2·25	3·60	1·30	0·65
9	Christmas Island (Indian Ocean)....	0·90	1·30	1·90	2·95	No service	
9	Christmas Island (Pacific Ocean)....	0·90	1·35	1·95	3·00	1·70	1·15
9	Cocos (Keeling) Islands...........	0·90	1·30	1·90	2·95	1·60	1·20
16	Colombia....................	1·20	1·50	2·25	3·15	1·70	0·70
13½	Comoro Islands...............	0·95	1·35	2·00	3·00	1·35	0·65
20½	Congo (People's Republic).........	0·80	1·10	1·60	2·40	1·05	0·45
10	Congo (Democratic Republic)......	0·85	1·20	1·80	2·80	1·15	0·55
9	Cook (or Hervey) Islands...........	0·85	1·15	1·65	2·45	2·15	1·45
5	Corsica.....................	0·85	1·05	1·45	2·15	1·20	0·10
16	Costa Rica..................	1·05	1·35	1·90	3·00	1·40	0·60
10★	Cuba— (a) Direct to all places except Guantanamo Bay................	0·85	1·10	1·45	2·10	} 1·35	0·70
	(b) Guantanamo Bay (U.S. Naval Station)..........(via U.S.A.)	0·80	1·25	1·95	3·15		
5	Cyprus......................	0·90	1·10	1·40	2·00	1·10	0·25
5	Czechoslovakia................	0·90	1·15	1·60	2·45	0·85	0·15
10½	Dahomey....................	1·05	1·45	1·85	2·80	1·50	0·60
5	Denmark.............(Direct)	0·70	0·85	1·15	1·60	} 0·80	0·10
	(via Netherlands)	0·75	1·00	1·40	2·10		
7	Dominica...................	0·80	1·05	1·45	2·25	1·15	0·55
17★	Dominican Republic...........	0·80	1·10	1·55	2·25	1·20	0·55
14½	Dubai......................	0·95	1·25	1·80	2·70	1·20	0·40
19½★	Ecuador.....................	0·95	1·25	1·70	2·50	1·45	0·65
19½	El Salvador..................	1·10	1·35	1·80	2·70	1·60	0·60
18	Equatorial Guinea.............	0·85	1·10	1·55	2·25	1·15	0·45
9	Ethiopia....................	1·00	1·35	1·95	3·15	1·30	0·50
9	Falkland Islands and Falkland Islands Dependencies........	0·80	1·10	1·55	2·35	1·35	0·75
5	Faroe Islands................	0·70	0·85	1·15	1·60	No service	
9	Fiji........................	0·90	1·25	1·80	2·70	1·80	1·10
5	Finland.....................	0·75	0·95	1·20	1·70	0·90	0·20
5	France.....................	0·85	1·00	1·30	1·85	1·20	0·10
14	French Guiana...............	0·90	1·15	1·65	2·55	1·30	0·60
16	French Polynesia..............	1·15	1·75	2·65	4·25	2·15	1·25
11	French Territory of the Afars and Issas (formerly Fr. Somali Coast).	0·95	1·20	1·75	2·70	1·10	0·45
14	French West Indies (Guadeloupe and Martinique)................	0·90	1·15	1·65	2·50	1·25	0·50

★ Variable rates for some parts.

For mode of packing, prohibitions, etc., *see* Post Office Guide.

Telegrams (see pp. 1202–3) p	DESTINATION	SURFACE MAIL Each parcel not over:— 2 lb £	7 lb £	11 lb £	22 lb £	AIR MAIL Each parcel First lb £	Each lb after £
20½	Gabon	0·90	1·35	2·05	2·90	1·25	0·50
9	Gambia	0·95	1·20	1·55	2·10	1·15	0·40
—	Gaza and Khan Yunis	0·90	1·15	1·65	2·30	1·05	0·30
5	German Federal Republic and Western Sectors of Berlin	0·85	1·05	1·40	2·10	0·80	0·15
5	Germany—Soviet Zone and Eastern Sector of Berlin	0·85	1·05	1·40	2·10	0·80	0·15
9	Ghana	0·95	1·20	1·65	2·45	1·30	0·40
5	Gibraltar	0·70	0·95	1·30	1·80	0·80	0·15
9	Gilbert and Ellice Islands Colony, including Line Islands (Fanning, Christmas (Pacific Ocean) and Washington Islds.), Ocean Isld. and Phoenix Islds	0·90	1·35	1·95	3·00	1·70	1·15
5	Greece ....(Direct)	0·90	1·10	1·55	2·30	} 0·95	0·25
	(via France)	0·95	1·20	1·65	2·55		
7½	Greenland— By sea to Denmark	0·70	0·85	1·15	1·60	} 0·95	0·35
	Via Netherlands to Denmark	0·75	1·00	1·40	2·10		
7	Grenada	0·85	1·10	1·65	2·25	1·35	0·55
18	Guatemala	0·90	1·15	1·60	2·35	1·40	0·60
11½	Guinea	0·85	1·10	1·60	2·35	1·20	0·50
7	Guyana	1·00	1·25	1·70	2·45	1·45	0·50
17★	Haiti	0·80	1·05	1·50	2·30	1·30	0·60
18	Honduras (Republic of)	0·85	1·10	1·50	2·40	1·35	0·60
9	Hong Kong	0·75	1·00	1·45	2·25	1·25	0·65
5	Hungary	0·90	1·15	1·55	2·30	0·90	0·15
5	Iceland	0·80	0·95	1·25	1·80	0·85	0·20
9	India	1·00	1·30	1·75	2·65	1·40	0·60
13	Indonesia	0·90	1·45	1·60	2·50	1·60	0·85
9½	Iran	1·05	1·65	2·45	4·00	1·00	0·35
11½	Iraq ....(via Lebanon)	1·10	1·55	2·20	3·60	} 1·15	0·35
	(All sea route)	0·95	1·35	1·85	2·85		
9	Israel	0·85	1·15	1·65	2·30	1·05	0·30
5	Italy	0·85	1·05	1·45	2·15	0·95	0·15
10½	Ivory Coast	0·85	1·15	1·70	2·55	1·20	0·50
7	Jamaica	0·95	1·25	1·65	2·35	1·45	0·50
17	Japan (Islands of Honshu, Kyushu, Shikoku and Hokkaido only) and Ryukyu Islands ....(Direct)	1·00	1·25	1·75	2·65	} 1·50	0·65
	(Via U.S.S.R.)	1·30	1·90	2·75	4·45		
9	Jordan ....(Direct)	0·85	1·10	1·50	2·25	} 1·05	0·30
	(Via Lebanon and Syria)	0·90	1·15	1·55	2·40		
9	Kenya	0·90	1·20	1·70	2·45	1·25	0·50
16	Khmer Republic (formerly Cambodia)	0·90	1·25	1·75	2·60	1·40	0·70
17	Korea ....(a)	0·95	1·30	1·90	3·00	1·40	0 75
11½	Kuwait ....(Direct)	0·85	1·15	1·65	2·65	} 1·05	0·35
	(Via Lebanon)	1·10	1·55	2·15	3·75		
16	Laos	1·00	1·40	1·95	3·10	1·45	0·70
7	Lebanon	0·85	1·10	1·45	2·20	1·05	0·30
9	Lesotho	1·05	1·45	2·10	3·10	1·55	0·65
11	Liberia	0·85	1·10	1·50	2·25	1·15	0·45
6½	Libyan Arab Republic (Cyrenaica, Tripolitania and the Fezzan)	0·85	1·05	1·45	2·15	1·05	0·30
5	Liechtenstein	0·75	0·95	1·30	1·90	0·70	0·10
5	Luxemburg	0·75	0·90	1·25	1·90	0·70	0·10
19	Macao	0·85	1·25	1·80	2·80	1·35	0·65
5	Madeira ....(Direct)	0·75	0·95	1·25	1·90	} 0·85	0·20
	(Via Portugal (May to Aug. only))	0·80	1·00	1·40	2·15		
12½	Madagascar	0·95	1·35	2·00	3·00	1·35	0·65
9	Malawi ....(Via Beira)	0·85	1·15	1·65	2·60	} 1·30	0·60
	(Via Capetown)	1·15	1·70	2·45	3·90		
9	Malaya	0·80	1·05	1·55	2·25	1·30	0·75
—	Maldives (Republic of)	0·90	1·30	1·95	2·90	1·20	0·60
10½	Mali	1·05	1·45	2·10	3·50	1·20	0·40
5	Malta	0·85	1·05	1·40	2·05	0·90	0·20
11★	Marian Islands	0·95	1·65	2·65	4·30	1·90	1·15
	Marquesas Islnds. (see Fr. Polynesia).						
18	Marshall Islands	0·95	1·65	2·65	4·35	1 90	1·15
10½	Mauritania	0·90	1·20	1·65	2·65	1·20	0·55
9	Mauritius (incl. Rodriguez Island) (Direct)	0·80	1·10	1·55	2·40	} 1·35	0·70
	(Via France)	0·85	1·20	1·70	2·65		
12½	Mexico— (a) all places except Chetumal	0·80	1·05	1·40	2·00	} 1·35	0·65
	(b) Chetumal	0·90	1·10	1·50	2·25		
5	Monaco	0·85	1·00	1·30	1·85	1·20	0·10
19	Mongolia		No service			No service	
7	Monserrat	0·75	1·00	1·45	2·10	1·20	0 55
6½	Morocco	0·85	1·10	1·50	2·35	0·90	0·20

★ Variable rates for some parts. (a) Parcels, S. Korea only.

For mode of packing, prohibitions, etc., *see* Post Office Guide.

Telegrams (*see* pp. 1202–3)	DESTINATION	SURFACE MAIL Each parcel not over:—				AIR MAIL Each parcel	
		2 lb	7 lb	11 lb	22 lb	First lb	Each lb after
p		£	£	£	£	£	£
9	Nauru Island	0·90	1·30	1·85	2·85	1·65	1·15
9	Nepal	0·95	1·30	1·85	3·05	1·15	0·55
5	Netherlands	0·75	0·90	1·25	1·80	0·80	0·10
14	Netherlands Antilles	0·80	1·05	1·50	2·30	1·20	0·60
16	New Caledonia	1·10	1·50	2·10	3·30	2·05	1·15
9	New Guinea Territory	0·90	1·30	1·90	2·95	1·60	1·20
9	New Hebrides (incl. Banks and Torres Islands)	0·95	1·35	1·90	3·00	1·85	1·10
9	New Zealand	0·85	1·15	1·65	2·45	1·90	1·20
9	New Zealand Island Territories	0·85	1·15	1·65	2·45	2·15	1·45
16★	Nicaragua	0·85	1·10	1·55	2·35	1·35	0·65
9	Nigeria	0·95	1·25	1·70	2·40	1·25	0·40
10½	Niger Republic	1·05	1·45	2·15	3·55	1·00	0·40
9	Norfolk Island	0·90	1·30	1·90	2·95	1·60	1·20
5	Norway	0·85	1·00	1·35	1·90	1·00	0·15
11	Oman (Sultanate of)	0·75	1·05	1·50	2·35	1·05	0·40
9	Pakistan	0·90	1·35	1·70	2·65	1·25	0·55
15½★	Panama (Republic of)	0·95	1·25	1·70	2·65	1·40	0·60
15½★	Panama Canal Zone (*Direct*)	0·75	1·15	1·70	2·70	} 1·20	0·65
	(*Via* U.S.A.)	0·80	1·30	2·05	3·35	}	
9	Papua	0·90	1·30	1·90	2·95	1·60	1·20
17½	Paraguay	0·90	1·30	1·90	2·90	1·45	0·70
17½	Peru	1·10	1·45	1·90	2·75	1·75	0·75
15½★	Philippines	0·85	1·15	1·60	2·20	1·35	0·75
9	Pitcairn Island	0·75	1·05	1·55	2·35	1·75	1·15
5	Poland	0·75	0·95	1·25	1·90	0·85	0·15
5	Portugal	0·70	0·90	1·20	1·80	0·85	0·20
9½	Portuguese East Africa	0·75	1·00	1·40	2·15	1·30	0·70
14½	Portuguese Timor	0·90	1·20	1·70	2·70	1·70	0·95
9	Portuguese West Africa—						
	(*a*) Provinces of Angola and the Islands of Principe and São Tomé	0·80	1·05	1·50	2·30	1·25	0·55
	(*b*) Portuguese Guinea	0·80	1·05	1·50	2·30	1·10	0·40
11	Puerto Rico	0·80	1·30	2·05	3·35	1·20	0·60
13	Qatar, State of	0·80	1·10	1·55	2·45	1·05	0·40
11½	Réunion	0·90	1·20	1·75	2·65	1·40	0·65
9	Rhodesia (*Via* Beira)	0·75	1·05	1·50	2·35	} 1·15	0·65
	(*Via* Capetown)	0·95	1·40	2·10	3·20	}	
5	Rumania	0·95	1·20	1·70	2·55	0·90	0·20
10	Rwanda	1·05	1·40	1·90	2·85	1·15	0·50
9	Sabah	0·80	1·05	1·55	2·25	1·40	0·80
9	St. Helena	0·65	0·90	1·20	1·80	No service	
7	St. Kitts–Nevis–Anguilla	0·65	0·90	1·35	2·00	1·05	0·50
7	St. Lucia	0·85	1·15	1·55	2·10	1·30	0·55
7	St. Pierre and Miquelon	1·05	1·50	2·10	3·50	1·15	0·45
9	St. Vincent	0·85	1·05	1·50	2·05	1·30	0·55
11	Samoa (U.S.A. Territory)	0·95	1·60	2·20	4·25	1·90	1·15
5	San Marino	0·85	1·05	1·45	2·15	0·95	0·15
9	Sarawak	0·80	1·05	1·55	2·25	1·40	0·80
10★	Saudi Arabia	0·90	1·20	1·65	2·55	1·10	0·45
10½	Senegal	0·85	1·10	1·50	2·25	1·20	0·45
9	Seychelles	0·75	0·95	1·35	2·00	1·15	0·50
15½	Sharjah	1·20	1·55	2·10	3·10	1·50	0·40
9	Sierra Leone	0·95	1·20	1·60	2·20	1·20	0·45
9	Singapore	0·80	1·05	1·55	2·25	1·30	0·75
9	Somali Democratic Republic	1·00	1·35	1·85	2·90	1·30	0·55
	South Africa (Republic of)—						
9	(*a*) Republic of South Africa	0·75	1·05	1·60	2·35	1·30	0·70
9	(*b*) South-West Africa	0·85	1·35	2·05	3·10	1·45	0·70
	Spain—						
5	(*a*) all places except Balearic Is.	0·90	1·10	1·50	2·20	} 0·85	0·20
5	(*b*) Balearic Islands	0·85	1·10	1·45	2·10	}	
	Spanish Guinea (Rio Muni and Fernando Po)—*see* Equatorial Guinea.						
5	Spanish Territories of North Africa (Ceuta, Chafarinas, Jadu and Melilla)	0·90	1·10	1·45	2·10	0·95	0·20
—	Spanish West Africa	0·90	1·10	1·45	2·25	1·05	0·30
—	Spitzbergen (Svalbard)	0·85	1·00	1·35	1·90	No service	
8	Sudan (Democratic Republic of)	1·00	1·35	1·90	3·05	1·20	0·45
14	Surinam	0·80	1·05	1·45	2·20	1·20	0·55
9	Swaziland	0·80	1·30	2·00	3·05	1·20	0·65
5	Sweden	0·85	1·05	1·30	1·85	0·85	0·15
5	Switzerland	0·75	0·95	1·30	1·90	0·70	0·10
7	Syria	0·85	1·05	1·50	2·25	1·00	0·30
17	Taiwan (Formosa)	0·85	1·15	1·65	2·60	1·45	0·85
9	Tanzania—						
	(*a*) Tanganyika	0·90	1·20	1·70	2·45	} 1·30	0·55
	(*b*) Zanzibar	0·90	1·20	1·70	2·45	}	

★ Variable rates for some parts.

For mode of packing, prohibitions, etc., see *Post Office Guide*.

Telegrams (See pp. 1202–3) p	DESTINATION	SURFACE MAIL Each parcel not over:—				AIR MAIL Each parcel	
		2 lb £	7 lb £	11 lb £	22 lb £	First 1b £	Each 1b after £
13½	Thailand (Siam)...................	1·00	1·35	1·80	2·85	1·50	0·70
	Tibet............................	No service				No service	
10½	Togo............................	1·05	1·35	1·85	2·85	1·25	0·55
9	Tonga (Friendly Islands)...........	1·10	1·45	2·05	3·05	1·90	1·15
7	Trinidad and Tobago..............	0·90	1·10	1·45	2·00	1·25	0·50
9	Tristan da Cunha.................	0·80	1·25	1·95	3·05	1·30	0·70
5	Tunisia..........................	0·80	1·05	1·45	2·25	0·85	0·20
5	Turkey...................(Direct)	0·90	1·15	1·60	2·45	} 1·05	0·25
	(Via France)	1·05	1·35	1·95	3·05		
7	Turks and Caicos Islands..........	0·80	1·05	1·45	2·20	1·15	0·55
9	Uganda.........................	0·90	1·20	1·70	2·45	1·25	0·50
6½	U.S.S.R. in Europe...............	0·80	1·05	1·45	2·20	1·05	0·35
6½	in Asia.............	1·05	1·40	1·90	3·10	1·30	0·40
6½	United Arab Republic.............	0·85	1·10	1·45	2·20	1·05	0·30
7 (m)	U.S.A...........................	0·80	1·00	2·05	3·35	1·00	0·55
10½	Upper Volta......................	0·90	1·25	1·85	3·05	1·25	0·50
18★	Uruguay.........................	0·90	1·15	1·65	2·45	1·40	0·75
5	Vatican City State................	0·75	0·95	1·35	2·05	0·95	0·15
18½	Venezuela.......................	1·05	1·30	1·70	2·50	1·50	0·60
16	Vietnam.........................	0·95	1·30	1·80	2·80	1·50	0·75
11	Virgin Islands of the U.S.A. (St. Croix, St. John and St. Thomas)...	0·85	1·30	1·95	3·10	1·25	0·60
11	Wake Island.....................	0·95	1·60	2·20	4·25	1·70	0·95
9	Western Samoa.........(Via U.S.A)	1·05	1·65	2·55	4·00	} 1·85	1·15
	(Via New Zealand)	0·85	1·15	1·65	2·45		
13½	Yemen (Arab Republic)...........	1·00	1·35	1·90	3·05	No service	
11	Yemen (People's Democratic Rep. of) (Southern)...................	0·90	1·20	1·70	2·65	1·25	0·45
5	Yugoslavia.......................	0·90	1·15	1·55	2·30	0·90	0·20
9	Zambia...............(Via Beira)	1·05	1·40	2·00	3·10	} 1·45	0·65
	(Via Capetown)	1·25	1·75	2·55	3·95		

(*m*) Alaska 11p. ★ Variable rates for some parts.

MOTOR VEHICLE AND DRIVING LICENCES

Road licences and driving licences for mechanically-propelled vehicles are issued in England and Wales by county councils and by county borough councils (Scotland, 4 cities and Greenock, Motherwell, Paisley, Coatbridge and Kirkcaldy), on behalf of the Minister for Transport Industries. Renewal licences are issued in certain circumstances by the Post Office. Details of the excise duties chargeable on motor vehicles are set out in the Vehicles (Excise) Act, 1971, which provides *inter alia* that any vehicle *kept* on a public road but not used on roads is chargeable to excise duty as if it were in use.

Rates of duty for motor car and motor cycle licences taken out after March 19, 1968, are shown below. For Hackney Carriages the rates of duty are: Hackney carriage with seating capacity not exceeding 20 persons, £12·00; additional for each person above 20 (excluding the driver) for which the vehicle has seating capacity, 50p.

MOTOR CARS, MOTOR CYCLES, ETC.

Type of vehicle	Exceeding	Not Exceeding	12 months	4 months
			£	£
MOTOR CARS				
Electric and those first registered before January 1, 1947......................	—	7 h.p.	18·00	6·60
Other than the above	—		25·00	9·15
MOTOR CYCLES				
With or without sidecar...............	—	150 c.c.	2·50	—
With or without sidecar...............	150 c.c.	250 c.c.	5·00	—
With or without sidecar...............	250 c.c.	—	10·00	3·65
THREE WHEELERS				
Other than pedestrian controlled.........	—	—	10·00	3·65
PEDESTRIAN-CONTROLLED VEHICLES	—	—	5·00	

Driving Licence Rates

	£
Three-year Driving Licence........	1·00
Replacement of lost or defaced licence,.........................	0·12½
Amendment of licence (*e.g.* for additional Group of vehicles), for the unexpired period..............	0·25
Provisional Driving Licence: 12 months	1·00
Public Service Vehicle Driving Licence: 3 years★.........................	0·15

★Additional to ordinary driving licence.

Permanent Driving Licences, 1973

The Minister for Transport Industries announced on Oct. 6, 1971, proposals for a £5 driving licence (to replace existing three-year licences) valid for life. The permanent licences will be issued (from late in 1973) to new drivers immediately on passing the driving test and to current licence holders upon the renewal of their licences. The proposals do not apply to licences issued for limited periods on medical grounds or to heavy goods vehicle licences. A small sheet or card suitable for computer processing may replace the red book licences.

BRITISH MONETARY UNITS

COIN

GOLD COINS	CUPRO-NICKEL (SILVER)
†Five Pound £5	Crown 5s. (25p)
†Two Pound £2	Florin 2s. (10p)
†Sovereign £1	Shilling 1s. (5p)
†Half-Sovereign 10s.	Sixpence 6d. (2½p)
† Discontinued	*50 New Pence 50p
	*10 New Pence 10p
BRONZE COINS	*5 New Pence 5p
*2 New Pence 2p	
*1 New Penny 1p	
*½ New Penny ½p	

*For further details of decimal coins, see p. 1211.

SILVER
Maundy Money‡

Fourpence 4p	Twopence 2p
Threepence 3p	Penny 1p

‡ Gifts of special money distributed by the Sovereign annually on Maundy Thursday to the number of aged poor persons corresponding to the Sovereign's own age.

Gold Coin.—Gold ceased to circulate during the First World War. An Order of April 27, 1966, made it illegal for U.K. residents to continue holding more than 4 gold coins minted after 1837, or to acquire such coins unless they had been licensed as genuine collectors by the Bank of England. This Order was revoked on April 1, 1971, by the Exchange Control (Gold Coins Exemption) Order, 1971, whereby residents of the United Kingdom, Channel Islands and the Isle of Man may freely buy and sell and hold gold coins.

The English sovereign, however, is still used as currency in certain Middle East countries and to meet foreign demand during the years 1958–1968 the Royal Mint struck some 44·5 million sovereigns.

Silver.—Prior to 1920 our silver coins were struck from standard silver—an alloy of which 925 parts in 1,000 were silver. In 1920 the proportion of silver was reduced to 500 parts. From January 1, 1947 all 'silver' coins, except Maundy money, have been struck from cupro-nickel—an alloy of copper 75 parts and nickel 25 parts. Maundy coins since 1947 have been struck from standard silver.

Bronze, introduced in 1860 to replace copper, is an alloy of copper 97 parts, zinc 2½ parts and tin ½ part. These proportions are subject to slight variation.

The 'Remedy' is the amount of variation from standard permitted in weight and fineness of coins when first issued from the Mint.

Legal tender of coin.—Gold, dated 1838 onwards, if not below least current weight, is legal tender to any amount. Since Decimal Day cupro-nickel (silver) coins with values up to and including the 10p have been legal tender up to £5. The 50p coin has been legal tender up to £10 from the date of its introduction. Bronze coins are legal tender for amounts up to 20p. Farthings ceased to be legal tender on December 31, 1960, the halfpenny on August 1, 1969, the halfcrown on January 1, 1970, and the threepence and penny on August 31, 1971.

Royal Mint Output in 1970.—Production of coins at the Royal Mint reached a new peak in 1970 with 2,976 million pieces being minted, of which the mint at Llantrisant accounted for 71 per cent. Coinage for domestic use showed a slight decline to 2,202 million pieces. Decimal coinage accounted for 95 per cent. of domestic production, the figures being: 50 pence 40,000,000; 10 pence 130,000,000; 5 pence 123,000,000; 2 pence 786,000,000; 1 penny 444,000,000; half-penny 558,000,000. Some £ s. d. coins were minted, the figures for these are: threepences 12,000,000; pennies 109,000,000.

Coinage for overseas governments represented some 21 per cent. of the year's total production and among the 594,000,000 pieces supplied were new coinage for the Bahama Islands, Bahrain, Bermuda, Brunei, Ceylon, Cyprus, Dominican Rep., Fiji, Gambia, Guyana, Iceland, Iraq, Irish Republic, Jamaica, Jordan, Kenya, Kuwait, Lebanon, Malawi, Mauritius, Rwanda, El Salvador, Seychelles Is., Somalia, Switzerland, Tanzania, Trinidad and Tobago, Uganda and South Vietnam.

BANK NOTES

Bank of England notes are issued in denominations of £1, £5, £10 and £20 for the amount of Fiduciary Note Issue. All notes are legal tender in England and Wales, and notes of denominations less than £5 are legal tender in Scotland and Northern Ireland. The Bank of England is the only bank legally obliged to change a note on demand for the equivalent in other notes and coin.

The last of the old white £5 notes, dated up to September 20, 1956, and the £5 notes issued between 1957 and 1963, bearing a portrait of Britannia, ceased to be legal tender on March 13, 1961 and June 27, 1967, respectively. The old series of £1 notes issued during the years 1928 to 1960 and the 10s. notes of the same type issued from 1928 to 1961—those without the portrait of the Queen—ceased to be legal tender on May 28 and October 29, 1962, respectively. Bank notes which are no longer legal tender are payable when presented at the head office of the Bank of England in London.

The £10 note—after an interval of 21 years—was restored on February 21, 1964. This completed the original series bearing portraits of the Queen, plans for which were announced in November, 1959.

Notes for £50, £100, £500 and £1,000 which were issued until April 22, 1943, ceased to be legal tender on May 1, 1945. However, on February 28, 1971, notes of these values were still outstanding to a total of some £796,000.

A new series of bank notes, generally smaller in size than the notes at present in issue, is to be introduced over the next few years. The first of the series is a £20 note, which the Bank of England introduced on July 8, 1970. It will be followed in due course by new £1, £5 and £10 denominations. There will be no 10s. note in the new series as the former 10s. note was replaced by the 50 new penny coin in October 1969, and ceased to be legal tender on November 20, 1970.

Note circulation is highest at the two peak spending periods of the year—around Christmas and the beginning of August. On December 22, 1970, it reached a peak of £3.705 million, which was £137 million more than the previous peak of £3,568 million reached on July 28, 1970.

£5 notes continue to enjoy popularity and now represent almost 57 per cent. of the total value of notes in circulation as against 14 per cent. in 1956. On the other hand, the proportion of £1 notes has dropped from 76 per cent. to under 27 per cent. The percentage of £10 notes in circulation has increased steadily since 1965 and now represents over 9½ per cent. of the total. On February 28, 1971, the values of notes in circulation were:—£20: £76,678,000; £10: £354,015,000; £5: £2,079,724,000; £1: £977,334,000; 10s.: £15,267,000.

Partly because of a rapidly-growing preference by the public for new notes rather than used ones, the demand for new bank notes has increased greatly

in recent years. Between 1957 and 1971 the average life of a £1 note fell from nineteen months to ten, and consequently it has been necessary for the Bank of England to print more notes per head of the population than in comparable countries abroad.

In an attempt to alleviate the high cost of note replacement the 50 new penny coin was introduced in October, 1969, in place of the 10s. note. The Bank of England has been conducting a campaign in conjunction with the commercial banks to encourage the public to accept more used but clean notes and this has been successful in reducing the public's requirements of new notes of the lower denominations. The success of a further campaign to stimulate the use of higher sum notes is evidenced by the continued increase in the number of £5 and £10 notes issued and the £20 note has been introduced to encourage this trend further.

Other bank notes.—Bank Notes are issued by three Scottish banks—Bank of Scotland, Clydesdale Bank Ltd., Royal Bank of Scotland Ltd. Notes of the latter's constituent banks—Royal Bank of Scotland and National Commercial Bank of Scotland Ltd.—are being withdrawn from circulation, as are those of the former British Linen Bank. These banks issue notes for £1, £5, £10, £20 and £100. There are no Scottish 10s. notes. Scottish notes are not legal tender, but in Scotland they enjoy a status equal to that of the Bank of England note.

Channel Isles and the Isle of Man.—The States of Jersey and Guernsey issue notes for £5 and £1, and are now issuing 50 new penny coins of their own design, to replace their 10s. notes which are no longer being issued and, in the case of Jersey, are gradually being withdrawn from circulation. The Government of the Isle of Man issues notes for £5, £1, and 50 new pence. These are legal tender only in their respective islands.

Although none of the series of notes specified above are legal tender in the United Kingdom they are generally accepted by the banks irrespective of their place of issue. At one time English banks made a small commission charge for handling Scottish and Irish notes but this was abolished some years ago.

Currency Notes.—Under the provision of the Currency and Bank Notes Act, 1928, Currency Notes (popularly known as Treasury Notes) of the value of 10s and £1 were replaced by the issue of Bank of England notes of the same denominations as from November 22, 1928.

Denomination	Metal	Standard Weight (grams)	Standard Diameter (centimetres)
New halfpenny	bronze	1·78200	1·7145
New penny	bronze	3·56400	2·0320
2 New pence	bronze	7·12800	2·5910
5 New pence	cupro-nickel	5·65518	2·3595
10 New pence	cupro-nickel	11·31036	2·8500
50 New pence	cupro-nickel	13·5	3·0

WIND FORCE MEASURES

The *Beaufort Scale* of wind force has been accepted internationally and is used in communicating weather conditions. Devised originally by Admiral Sir Francis Beaufort in 1805, it now consists of the numbers 0–17, each representing a certain strength or velocity of wind at 10 m. (33 ft.) above ground in the open.

Scale No.	Wind Force	M.p.h.	Knots	Scale No.	Wind Force	M.p.h.	Knots
0	Calm	1	1	9	Strong gale	47–54	41–47
1	Light air	1–3	1–3	10	Whole gale	55–63	48–55
2	Slight breeze	4–7	4–6	11	Storm	64–72	56–63
3	Gentle breeze	8–12	7–10	12	Hurricane	73–82	64–71
4	Moderate breeze	13–18	11–16	13	—	83–92	72–80
5	Fresh breeze	19–24	17–21	14	—	93–103	81–89
6	Strong breeze	25–31	22–27	15	—	104–114	90–99
7	High wind	32–38	28–33	16	—	115–125	100–108
8	Gale	39–46	34–40	17	—	126–136	109–118

BUCHAN'S WEATHER PERIODS OR RECURRENCES OF WEATHER

Dr. Alexander Buchan, F.R.S., Secretary of the Scottish Meteorological Society, published in 1867 a paper in the Journal of that Society entitled "Interruptions in the regular rise and fall of temperature in the course of the year." Buchan gave six cold periods and three warm periods, based on his examination of the mean daily temperature as recorded at stations in Scotland covering long periods. The cold periods were February 7–14, April 11–14, May 9–14, June 29–July 4, August 6–11, November 6–13, and the warm periods July 12–15, August 12–15, and December 3–14. This early work aroused considerable interest later. It should be noted, however, that Buchan claimed no more than the existence of tendencies for short spells of relatively cold or warm weather to occur at certain times of the year.

In recent years these smaller fluctuations of weather super-imposed on the normal seasonal changes have been examined from the aspect of tendencies to stormy or anticyclonic spells over the British Isles and have been referred to as "singularities." Stormy periods are relatively warm in winter and cool in summer. The following tendencies have been given:—Jan. 5–17 stormy; Jan. 18–24 anticyclonic; Jan. 24–Feb. 1 stormy; Feb. 8–16 anticyclonic; Feb. 21–25 cold; Feb. 26–Mar. 9 stormy; Mar. 12–19 anticyclonic; Mar. 24–31 stormy; April 10–15 stormy; April 23–26 unsettled; June 1–21 summer monsoon; July 10–24 warm; Aug. 20–30 stormy; September 1–17 anticyclonic; Sept. 17–24 stormy; Sept. 24–Oct. 4 anticyclonic; Oct. 5–12 stormy; Oct. 16–20 anticyclonic; Oct. 24–Nov. 13 stormy; Nov. 15–21 anticyclonic; Nov. 24–Dec. 14 stormy; Dec. 18–24 anticyclonic; Dec. 25–Jan. 1 stormy.

HALL-MARKS ON GOLD AND SILVER WARES

London (Goldsmiths' Hall) Date-Marks
From 1478 to 1976.

	Lombardic, double cusps	1478–9 to 1497–8	Roman letter, small	1736–7 to 1755–6
	Black letter, small......	1498–9 ,, 1517–8	Old English, capitals	1756–7 ,, 1775–6
	Lombardic	1518–9 ,, 1537–8	Roman letter, small...	1776–7 ,, 1795–6
	Roman and other capitals...............	1538–9 ,, 1557–8	Roman letter, capitals	1796–7 ,, 1815–6
	Black letter, small ...	1558–9 ,, 1577–8	Roman letter, small...	1816–7 ,, 1835–6
	Roman letter, capitals	1578–9 ,, 1597–8		
	Lombardic, external cusps	1598–9 ,, 1617–8	Old English, capitals	1836–7 ,, 1855–6
	Italic letter, small ...	1618–9 ,, 1637–8	Old English, small ...	1856–7 ,, 1875–6
	Court hand	1638–9 ,, 1657–8	Roman letter, capitals [A to M *square* shield N to Z as shown.]	1876–7 ,, 1895–6
	Black letter, capitals	1658–9 ,, 1677–8	Roman letter, small...	1896–7 ,, 1915–6
	Black letter, small ...	1678–9 ,, 1696–7	Black letter, small ...	1916–7 ,, 1935–6
	Court hand	1697 ,, 1715–6 (From March 1697 only.)	Roman letter, capital	1936–7 ,, 1955–6
	Roman letter, capitals	1716–7 ,, 1735–6	Italic letter, small ...	1956–7 ,, 1975–6

Hall-marks are the symbols stamped on gold or silver articles to indicate that they have been chemically tested and that they conform to one of the legal standards. With certain exceptions, all gold or silver articles are required by law to be hall-marked before they are offered for sale. Hall-marking was instituted in 1300 under a statute of Edward I.

Normally a complete modern hall-mark consists of four symbols—the maker's mark, assay office mark, standard mark and date letter. Additional marks have been authorized from time to time.

Maker's Mark.—Instituted in 1363, the maker's mark was originally a device such as a bird or *fleur-de-lys* and now consists invariably of the initials of the Christian and surnames of the maker or of the firm.

Assay Office Mark.—The existing assay offices and their distinguishing marks are:—

LONDON (Goldsmiths' Hall).

A leopard's head (uncrowned from 1300 to 1478–9, when it became crowned until 1821, since when it has been uncrowned). From

1697–1720 this mark was used in London for gold only and not for silver.

BIRMINGHAM......................An anchor.
SHEFFIELD......................A York rose.
EDINBURGH.........................A castle.

Offices formerly existed in other towns, *e.g.* Chester, Glasgow, Newcastle, Exeter, York and Norwich, each having its own distinguishing mark.

Standard Mark.—Instituted in 1544. The current legal standards and their marks are as follows:—

SILVER.—Sterling silver (92·5 per cent. silver) is marked by English assay offices with a *lion passant* and by the Edinburgh Assay Office with a *thistle*. A full-length figure of *Britannia* was impressed on

fine silver plate (95·84 per cent. silver) between 1697 and 1720 and this mark is still used occasionally by all British assay offices.

GOLD.—22 carat articles (91·6 per cent. gold) are marked by English offices with a crown followed by the figure 22; by the Edinburgh office with the figure 22 following the standard mark as for sterling silver (*see* above).

18 carat articles (75 per cent. gold) are marked by English assay offices with a crown followed by the figure 18.

All British assay offices mark 14 carat gold (58·5 per cent. gold) with the figures 14·585 and 9 carat gold (37·5 per cent. gold) with the figures 9·375.

Date Letter.—Instituted in 15th Century. The date letter denotes the year in which an article was assayed or hall-marked. Each alphabetical cycle

has a distinctive style of lettering or shape of shield. The date letters are different at the various assay offices and the particular office must be established from the assay office mark before reference is made to tables of date letters. The date letter is changed at the London Office in May each year and at Birmingham and Sheffield in July. Specimen shields and letters used by the London Office in each period from 1438 to date are shown on p. 1212.

OTHER MARKS

Duty Mark.—In 1784 an additional mark of the reigning sovereign's head was introduced to signify that the excise duty had been paid. The mark became obsolete on the abolition of the duty in 1890.

Silver Jubilee and Coronation Marks.—Voluntary marks were authorized to be used at manufacturers' request to commemorate the silver jubilee of King George V and Queen Mary and the

 Coronation of Her Majesty Queen Elizabeth II. The Jubilee Mark was used on silver made in 1933, 1934 and 1935 and the Coronation Mark on gold and

silver with date letter 1952/3 or 1953/4.

Foreign Wares.—Since 1842 foreign wares imported into Great Britain have been required to be hall-marked before sale. The marks consist of the importer's mark, a special assay office mark (*see* below), the decimal figures denoting fineness (together with the carat figure in the case of gold) and the annual date letter. The current assay office marks for foreign wares are as follows:—

LONDON.—The sign of the Constellation Leo.
BIRMINGHAM.—Equilateral triangle.
SHEFFIELD.—The sign of the Constellation Libra.
EDINBURGH.—St. Andrew's Cross.

CLOSE TIMES

Wild Birds.—The *Protection of Wild Birds Act*, 1954, lays down a close season for wild birds (other than Game Birds) from February 1 to August 31 inclusive, each year. Exceptions to these dates are made for—

Capercaillie and (except Scotland) *Woodcock*, Feb. 1—Sept. 30.

Snipe, Feb. 1—Aug. 11.

Wild Duck and Wild Goose (in or over water areas), Feb. 21—Aug. 31.

Birds which may be killed or taken outside the close season (except in Scotland on Sundays, on Christmas Day or in a prescribed area) are the above and coot, curlew (other than stone curlew), bar-tailed godwit, moorhen, plover (golden or grey), common red-shank, certain wild duck (common pochard, gadwall, mallard, pintail, shoveller, teal, tufted duck, wigeon) and certain wild geese (bean, Canada, pink-footed and white-fronted).

Certain wild birds may be killed or taken at any time by authorized persons—cormorant, crow, gull (black-backed or herring), jackdaw, jay, magpie, rook, shag, sparrow, starling, stock-dove and wood pigeon; and, in Scotland only, goosander, red-breasted merganser and rock-dove. The sale of Wild Bird's Eggs is prohibited, except that gulls' eggs may be sold at any time and those of the lapwing (green or black plover) from Jan. 1—

April 14 inclusive.

Game Birds—In each case the dates are inclusive:—

Black Game—Dec. 11 to Aug. 19 (Aug. 31 in Somerset, Devon, and New Forest).

*Grouse—Dec. 11 to Aug. 11.

*Partridge—Feb. 2 to Aug. 31.

*Pheasant—Feb. 2 to Sept. 30.

*Ptarmigan—(Scotland only) Dec. 11 to Aug. 11.

It is also unlawful (in *England* and *Wales*) to kill the game marked * on a Sunday or Christmas Day.

Hunting and Ground Game.—There is no statutory close-time for fox-hunting or rabbit-shooting, nor for hares: but by an Act passed in 1892 the *sale* of hares or leverets in Great Britain is prohibited from March 1 to July 31 inclusive under a penalty of a pound. The First of November is the recognized date for the opening of the *fox-hunting* season, which continues till the following April. *Otter-hunting* lasts from mid-April to mid-September.

Deer.—The *Deer Act*, 1963, effective from Nov. 1, 1963, imposed the following close times. *Red Deer and Sika Deer*: Stags, May 1–July 31; Hinds, March 1–Oct. 31. *Fallow Deer and Roe Deer*: Buck, May 1–July 31; Doe, March 1–Oct. 31. Under the Act it is an offence to take or wilfully kill deer of any species from one hour after sunset to one hour before sunrise.

WEIGHTS AND MEASURES

The Weights and Measures Act of 1963 enacts the legal measures for Great Britain, basing them upon "United Kingdom primary standards" in the custody of the Standards Department of the Dept. of Trade. The primary standards are the yard, pound, metre and kilogramme. The GALLON, the capacity standard, wet or dry, is based upon the Pound. The Act of 1963 defines the GALLON as the space occupied by 10 pounds weight of distilled water of density 0·998 859 gramme per millilitre weighed in air of density 0·001 217 gramme per millilitre against weights of density 8·136 grammes per millilitre. The METRE and the LITRE have the meanings assigned by order of the Dept. of Trade to reproduce in English the international definition of these measures in force at the time of making of the orders.

New definitions for an *international yard* and *pound* were adopted on Jan. 1, 1959, by the standards laboratories of the United Kingdom, Canada, Australia, New Zealand, South Africa and the United States:
international yard = 0·914 4 metre.　　　　*international pound* = 0·453 592 37 kilogramme.

The following list shows the definitions of measures set out in the Weights and Measures Act, 1963 and some useful conversions.　*See also* Conversion Tables, p. 1218.

Measurement of Length

Imperial Units

Mile = 1,760 yards.	1 mil = 1/1000 inch.
Furlong = 220 yards.	12 inches (*in.*) = 1 foot (*ft.*).
Chain = 22 yards.	3 feet = 1 yard (*yd.*).
YARD = 0·914 4 metre.	6 feet = 1 fathom.
Foot ' = ⅓ yard.	22 yards = 1 chain = 100 links.
Inch " = 1/36 yard.	10 chains = 1 furlong.
	8 furlongs = 1 mile = 1,760 yards.

Metric Units

Kilometre = 1,000 metres.	10 millimetres (*mm.*) = 1 centimetre (*cm.*) = 0·393 701 inch.
METRE (*see above*) = 1·094 yards.	10 centimetres = 1 decimetre (*dm.*) = 3·937 011 inches.
Decimetre = 1/10 metre.	10 decimetres = 1 METRE (*m.*) = 1·093 614 yards.
Centimetre = 1/100 metre.	10 metres = 1 dekametre (*dam.*) = 10·936 143 yards.
Millimetre = 1/1000 metre.	10 dekametres = 1 hectometre (*hm.*) = 109·361 43 yards.
	10 hectometres = 1 kilometre (*km.*) = 0·621 371 mile.

A kilometre is approximately *five-eighths* of a mile, so that 8 kilometres may be regarded as 5 miles.

Measurement of Area

Imperial Units

Square mile = 640 acres	144 sq. inches = 1 sq. foot.
Acre = 4,840 square yards.	9 sq. feet = 1 sq. yard.
Rood = 1,210 square yards.	4 roods = 1 acre.
SQUARE YARD = a superficial area equal to that of a square each side of which measures one yard	10 square chains = 1 acre = 4,840 sq. yards.
	640 acres = 1 square mile.
Square foot = 1/9 square yard	
Square inch = 1/144 square foot.	

Metric Units

Hectare = 100 ares.	1 sq. centimetre = 0·155 sq. inch.
Dekare = 10 ares.	1 sq. METRE = 10·763 9 sq. feet = 1·195 99 sq. yds.
Are = 100 square metres	1 are (*a.*) = 0·098 8 rood.
SQUARE METRE = a superficial area equal to that of a square each side of which measures one metre.	1 hectare (10,000 sq. metres) (*ha.*) = 2·471 05 acres.
Square decimetre = 1/100 square metre.	1 sq. kilometre = 0·386 102 sq. mile.
Square centimetre = 1/100 square decimetre.	
Square millimetre = 1/100 square centimetre.	

Measurement of Volume

Imperial Units

CUBIC YARD = a volume equal to that of a cube each edge of which measures one yard.	1,728 cubic inches = 1 cubic foot.
	27 cubic feet = 1 cubic yard.
Cubic foot = 1/27 cubic yard.	
Cubic inch = 1/1728 cubic foot.	

Metric Units

CUBIC METRE = a volume equal to that of a cube each edge of which measures one metre.	1 cubic metre (*cbm.* or *m³.*) = 35·314 7 cu. ft. = 1·307 95 cu. yds.
Cubic decimetre = 1/1000 cubic metre.	(1 stere (= 1 cu. metre) is used as a unit of measurement of timber.)
Cubic centimetre = 1/1000 cubic decimetre.	1 cubic cm. (water) = 1 gram; 1,000 cubic cm. (water) or 1 litre = 1 kilogram; 1 cubic metre (1,000 litres, 1,000 kilograms) = 1 metric ton.

Measurement of Capacity

Imperial Units

GALLON (*see above*)	4 gills = a pint.
Quart = ¼ gallon.	2 pints = 1 quart.
Pint = ½ quart.	4 quarts = 1 GALLON.
Gill = ¼ pint.	1 gallon = 160 fluid ounces.
Fluid ounce = 1/20 pint.	= 277·274 cubic inches.

Bushel = 8 gallons.	2 gallons = 1 peck.	1 hectolitre = 2·749 69 bushels.
Peck = 2 gallons.	4 pecks = 1 bushel.	1 hectolitre per hectare = 1·11 bushels per acre.
	8 bushels = 1 quarter.	1 quintal = 3·674 3 bushels.
	A chaldron is 36 bushels = 4½ quarters.	1 quintal per hectare = 1·49 bushels per acre.

Measurement of Capacity—*continued*

Fluid drachm = ⅛ fluid ounce. | *See* Apothecaries' Weight (*below*)
Minim = 1/60 fluid drachm. |

Metric Units

Hectolitre = 100 litres.
LITRE = The volume occupied by the mass of 1 kilogramme of pure water at its temperature of maximum density and under a pressure of one standard atmosphere (14·696 lb. per sq. inch).
Decilitre = 1/10 litre.
Centilitre = 1/100 litre.
Millilitre = 1/1000 litre.

1 centilitre (*cl.*) = 0·070 4 gill.
1 decilitre (*dl.*) = 0·175 98 pint.
1 LITRE* (1/1,000 cubic metre) (*lit.*) = 1·759 8 pints
= 0·88 Imp. quart = 0·22 Imp. gallon = 61·025 5 cu. inch = 0·035 315 7 cu. ft.
1 hectolitre (*hl.*) = 21·997 5 Imp. gallons = 26·417 1 U.S. gallons = 2·749 Imp. bushels = 2·837 7 U.S. bushels.

Measurement of Mass or Weight

Imperial Units

Ton = 2,240 pounds.
Hundredweight = 112 pounds.
Cental = 100 pounds.
Quarter = 28 pounds.
Stone = 14 pounds.
POUND = 0·453 592 37 kilogram.
Ounce = 1/16 pound.
Dram = 1/16 ounce.
Grain = 1/7000 pound.

7000 grains (*gr.*) = 1 pound (*lb.*).
16 drams (*dr.*) = 1 ounce (*oz.*).
16 ounces = 1 POUND (*lb.*).
14 pounds = 1 stone.
28 pounds = 1 quarter (of a *cwt.*).
4 quarters (112 *lb.*) = 1 hundredweight (*cwt.*).
20 hundredweight (2,240 *lb.*) = 1 ton.

20 pennyweights (*dwt.*) = 1 Troy ounce.

Ounce Troy = 480 grains
Pennyweight = 24 grains

For gold and silver the ounce, divided decimally, and *not* into grains, is the sole unit of weight. The Troy ounce is the same as the Apothecaries' ounce = 480 Avoirdupois grains (31·1035 *Grammes*) in weight. A Troy POUND (= 5,760 grains) is legalized in the United States.

Ounce apothecaries' = 480 grains. | *See* Apothecaries' Weight (*below*)
Drachm = ⅛ ounce apothecaries. |
Scruple = ⅓ drachm. |

Metric Units

Metric ton = 1,000 kilograms.
Quintal = 100 kilograms.

1 centigram (*cg.*) = 0·154 32 grains.
1 decigram (*dg.*) = 1·543 2 grains.
1 gramme (*grm.*) = 15·432 4 grains.
1 dekagram (*dag.*) = 5·643 8 drams.
1 hectogram (*hg.*) = 3·527 4 oz.
1 KILOGRAM (*kg.*) = 32·150 7 oz.   Troy = 35·273 4 oz. Avoirdupois = 2·204 62 lb. Avoirdupois.
1 myriagram = 22·046 2 lb. Avoirdupois.
1 quintal (*q.*) = 100 kg. = 220·5 lb.   Avoirdupois = 1·968 4 cwt.
1 tonne (*t.*) = 0·984 207 U.K. or long ton = 1·102 31 U.S. or short ton.

Measurement of Electricity

Units of measurement of electricity, the AMPERE (unit of electrical current), the OHM (unit of electrical resistance), the VOLT (unit of difference of electrical potential) and the WATT (unit of electrical power) have the meanings assigned to them respectively by order of the Dept. of Trade, to reproduce in English the international definitions in force at the date of the making of the order.

Kilowatt = 1000 watts.   Megawatt = 1,000,000 watts.

Apothecaries' Weight
Measures of Weight.

20 grains   = 1 scruple (℈1).
3 scruples = 1 drachm (ℨ1).
8 drachms = 1 ounce.

Measures of Capacity.

60 minims (*min.*) = 1 fluid drachm.
8 fluid drachms = 1 fluid ounce.
5 fluid ounces = 1 gill.
4 gills = 1 pint.
8 pints = 1 GALLON.

The Apothecaries' grain is the Avoirdupois grain, and the Apothecaries' ounce is the Troy ounce, of 480 grains. The Apothecaries' *drachm* is not the same as the Avoirdupois *dram*, and is spelled differently. A fluid ounce of distilled water at a temperature of 62° Fahrenheit is equal in weight to the Avoirdupois ounce (437·5 grains). A fluid *drachm* (54·6875 grains) is equal in weight to TWO Avoirdupois *drams*.

Angular or Circular Measure

60 seconds (″) = 1 minute (′).
60 minutes = 1 degree (°).

90 degrees = 1 right angle or quadrant.
Diameter of circle × 3·141 6 = circumference.
Diameter squared × ·7854 = area of circle.
Diameter squared × 3·141 6 = surface of sphere.
Diameter cubed × ·523 6 = solidity of sphere.
One degree of circumference × 57·3 = radius.*
Diameter of cylinder × 3·141 6; product by length or height, gives the surface.
Diameter squared × ·7854; product by length or height, gives solid content.

* Or, one radian (the angle subtended at the centre of a circle by an arc of the circumference equal in length to the radius) = 57·3 degrees, nearly.

Note.—A circle of 7 yards diameter has, in practice, a circumference of 22 yards = 1 chain.

Water Measures.

Cubic inch .... = 252·458 grains.
Gallon (277·274 cu. in.) ... = 10 lb. (distilled).
Cubic foot .... = 62·321 lb.
35·943 cubic ft. (224 gals.) . = 1 ton.
Water for Ships: Tun, 210 gals., Butt 110, Puncheon 72, Barrel 36, Kilderkin 18 gals.

THERMOMETER COMPARISONS

Comparison between Scales of Fahrenheit, Réaumur and Centigrade.

CENT.	FAH'T.	RMR.	CENT.	FAH'T	RMR.
°	°	°	°	°	°
100B.	212B.	80B.	25	77	20·0
99	210·2	79·2	24	75·2	19·2
98	208·4	78·4	23	73·4	18·4
97	206·6	77·6	22	71·6	17·6
96	204·8	76·8	21	69·8	16·8
95	203	76	20	68	16
94	201·2	75·2	19	66·2	15·2
93	199·4	74·4	18	64·4	14·4
92	197·6	73·6	17	62·6	13·6
91	195·8	72·8	16	60·8	12·8
90	194	72	15	59	12
89	192·2	71·2	14	57·2	11·2
88	190·4	70·4	13	55·4	10·4
87	188·6	69·6	12	53·6	9·6
86	186·8	68·8	11	51·8	8·8
85	185	68	10	50	8·0
84	183·2	67·2	9	48·2	7·2
83	181·4	66·4	8	46·4	6·4
82	179·6	65·6	7	44·6	5·6
81	177·8	64·8	6	42·8	4·8
80	176	64	5	41	4
79	174·2	63	4	39·2	3·2
78	172·4	62·4	3	37·4	2·4
77	170·6	61·6	2	35·6	1·6
76	168·8	60·8	1	33·8	0·8
75	167	60	*zero*	32	*zero*
74	165·2	59·2	1	30·2	0·8
73	163·4	58·4	2	28·4	1·6
72	161·6	57·6	3	26·6	2·4
71	159·8	56·8	4	24·8	3·2
70	158	56	5	23	4
69	156·2	55·2	6	21·2	4·8
68	154·4	54·4	7	19·4	5·6
67	152·6	53·6	8	17·6	6·4
66	150·8	52·8	9	15·8	7·2
65	149	52	10	14	8
64	147·2	51·2	11	12·2	8·8
63	145·4	50·4	12	10·4	9·6
62	143·6	49·6	13	8·6	10·4
61	141·8	48·8	14	6·8	11·2
60	140	48	15	5	12
59	138·2	47·2	16	3·2	12·8
58	136·4	46·4	17	1·4	13·6
57	134·6	45·6	18	0·4	14·4
56	132·8	44·8	19	2·2	15·2
55	131	44	20	4	16
54	129·2	43·2	21	5·8	16·8
53	127·4	42·4	22	7·6	17·6
52	125·6	41·6	23	9·3	18·4
51	123·8	40·8	24	11·2	19·2
50	122	40	25	13	20
49	120·2	39·2	26	14·8	20·8
48	118·4	38·4	27	16·6	21·6
47	116·6	37·6	28	18·4	22·4
46	114·8	36·8	29	20·2	23·2
45	113	36	30	22	24
44	111·2	35·2	31	23·8	24·8
43	109·4	34·4	32	25·6	25·6
42	107·6	33·6	33	27·4	26·4
41	105·8	32·8	34	29·2	27·2
40	104	32	35	31	28
39	102·2	31·2	36	32·8	28·8
38	100·4	30·4	37	34·6	29·6
37	98·6	29·6	38	36·4	30·4
36	96·8	28·8	39	38·2	31·2
35	95	28	40	40	32
34	93·2	27·2	41	41·8	32·8
33	91·4	26·4	42	43·6	33·6
32	89·6	25·6	43	45·4	34·4
31	87·8	24·8	44	47·2	35·2
30	86	24	45	49	36
29	84·2	23·2	46	50·8	36·8
28	82·4	22·4	47	52·6	37·6
27	80·6	21·6	48	54·4	38·4
26	78·8	20·8	49	56·2	39·2

NOTE.—The *normal* temperature of the *human body* is 98·4° F., or 37° (36·9°) C., or 29·5° R. *Freezing* point=32° F.=0° C.=0° R.; *Boiling* point=212° F.=100° C.=80° R. "*Absolute*" *Temperature* is Temperature reckoned from "*Absolute Zero*," which is at 273° C. below 0° C., 459·4° below 0° F., and 218·4° below 0° R. and is denoted by the letter "K."

* Below 32° F. *subtract* 32.

CONVERSION.
Let F = Fahr.
" C = Cent.
" R = Réaum.

$$^{*}F = \frac{9C}{5} + 32 \qquad C = \frac{5(F-32)}{9}$$

$$F = \frac{9R}{4} + 32$$

F C+R+32

$$R = \frac{4(F-32)}{9}$$

An *Inch of Rain* on the surface of an acre (43,560 sq. feet)=3,630 cubic feet=100·992 tons.

Cisterns: A cistern 4 feet by $2\frac{1}{2}$ and 3 deep will hold brimful 186·963 gallons, weighing 16 cwt. 2 qrs. 21·6 lbs. in addition to its own weight.

Million, Billion, etc.

Value in the United Kingdom

Million................thousand × thousand (10^6)
Billion................million × million (10^{12})
Trillion...............million × billion (10^{18})
Quadrillion............million × trillion (10^{24})

Value in U.S.A

Million..............thousand × thousand (10^6)
Billion..............thousand × million (10^9)
Trillion.............million × million (10^{12})
Quadrillion..........million × billion U.S. (10^{15})

United Kingdom (and other European) usage above follows the decision of the 9th Gen. Conference on Weights and Measures, 1948.

PAPER AND BOOK MEASURES

Writing Paper	*Printing Paper*
480 sheets = 1 ream	516 sheets = 1 ream
24 sheets = 1 quire	2 reams = 1 bundle
20 quires = 1 ream	5 bundles = 1 bale

Sizes of Writing and Drawing Papers

Emperor..............	=	72 × 48	inches
Antiquarian............	=	53 × 31	"
Double Elephant.........	=	40 × $26\frac{3}{4}$	"
Grand Eagle............	=	42 × $28\frac{3}{4}$	"
Atlas..................	=	34 × 26	"
Colombier..............	=	$34\frac{1}{2}$ × $23\frac{1}{2}$	"
Imperial...............	=	30 × 22	"
Elephant...............	=	28 × 23	"
Cartridge..............	=	26 × 21	"
Super Royal............	=	27 × 19	"
Royal..................	=	24 × 19	"
Medium.................	=	22 × $17\frac{1}{2}$	"
Large Post.............	=	21 × $16\frac{1}{2}$	"
Copy or Draft..........	=	20 × 16	"
Demy...................	=	20 × $15\frac{1}{2}$	"
Post...................	=	19 × $15\frac{1}{4}$	"
Pinched Post...........	=	$18\frac{1}{2}$ × $14\frac{3}{4}$	"
Foolscap...............	=	17 × $13\frac{1}{2}$	"
Sheet and $\frac{1}{3}$ Foolscap....	=	22 × $13\frac{1}{2}$	"
Sheet and $\frac{1}{2}$ Foolscap....	=	$24\frac{1}{2}$ × $13\frac{1}{2}$	"
Double Foolscap........	=	$26\frac{1}{2}$ × $16\frac{1}{2}$	"
Double Post............	=	$30\frac{1}{2}$ × 19	"
Double Large Post......	=	33 × 21	"
Double Demy............	=	31 × 20	"
Brief..................	=	$16\frac{1}{2}$ × $13\frac{1}{4}$	"
Pott...................	=	15 × $12\frac{1}{2}$	"

Sizes of Printing Papers

Foolscap...............	=	17 × $13\frac{1}{2}$	inches
Double Foolscap........	=	27 × 17	"
Crown..................	=	20 × 15	"
Double Crown...........	=	30 × 20	"
Quad Crown.............	=	40 × 30	"
Double Quad Crown......	=	60 × 40	"
Post...................	=	$19\frac{1}{4}$ × $15\frac{1}{2}$	"
Double Post............	=	$31\frac{1}{2}$ × $19\frac{1}{2}$	"
Double Large Post......	=	33 × 21	"
Sheet and $\frac{1}{2}$ Post.......	=	$23\frac{1}{2}$ × $19\frac{1}{2}$	"
Demy...................	=	$22\frac{1}{2}$ × $17\frac{1}{2}$	"
Double Demy............	=	35 × $22\frac{1}{2}$	"
Quad Demy..............	=	45 × 35	"
Music Demy.............	=	20 × $15\frac{1}{2}$	"
Medium.................	=	23 × 18	"
Royal..................	=	25 × 20	"
Super Royal............	=	$27\frac{1}{2}$ × $20\frac{1}{2}$	"
Elephant...............	=	28 × 23	"
Imperial...............	=	30 × 22	"

Sizes of Brown Papers

Casing..................	=	46 × 36	inches
Double Imperial.........	=	45 × 29	„
Elephant................	=	34 × 24	„
Double Four Pound......	=	31 × 21	„
Imperial Cap............	=	29 × 22	„
Haven Cap..............	=	26 × 21	„
Bag Cap................	=	24 × 19½	„
Kent Cap...............	=	21 × 18	„

Sizes of Bound Books

Demy 16mo.............	=	5⅝ × 4⅜	inches
Demy 18mo.............	=	5¾ × 3¾	„
Foolscap Octavo (8vo)..	=	6¾ × 4¼	„
Crown 8vo..............	=	7½ × 5	„
Large Crown 8vo........	=	8 × 5¼	„
Demy 8vo...............	=	8⅜ × 5⅝	„
Medium 8vo.............	=	9½ × 6	„
Royal 8vo..............	=	10 × 6¼	„
Super Royal 8vo........	=	10¼ × 6⅞	„
Imperial 8vo...........	=	11 × 7½	„
Foolscap Quarto (4to)...	=	8½ × 6¾	„
Crown 4to..............	=	10 × 7½	„
Demy 4to...............	=	11¼ × 8¾	„
Royal 4to..............	=	12½ × 10	„
Imperial 4to...........	=	15 × 11	„
Crown Folio............	=	15 × 10	„
Demy Folio.............	=	17½ × 11¼	„
Royal Folio............	=	20 × 12½	„
Music..................	=	14 × 10¼	„

NOTE.—*Folio* means a sheet folded in half, *quarto* folded into four, and so on; thus, a crown 8vo page is one-eighth the size of a crown sheet. Books are usually bound up in sheets of 16 or 32 pages. *Octavo* books are generally printed 64 pages at a time (32 pages on each side of a sheet of quad); a crown octavo book of 320 pages will therefore require 5 sheets of quad crown, or 10 reams per 1,000 copies, the odd 16 sheets in each ream being allowed as waste. Newspapers (and some books in editions of 50,000 or over) are printed on rotary presses, for which the paper is supplied in continuous reels.

INTERNATIONAL PAPER SIZES

Simplification of the large number of stock paper sizes in use in the United Kingdom has been proceeding since publication of British Standard 730 in 1937. Recommendations made by the International Organization for Standardization were accepted by the United Kingdom in 1959 and it is considered that general adoption of the international or A size will bring great economies to users of paper.

The basis of the international series of paper sizes is a rectangle having an area of one square metre, the sides of which are in the proportion of $1:\sqrt{2}$. In other words, taking one side as X and the other as Y, this basic size provides the equation—$X:Y = 1:\sqrt{2}$; and $X \times Y = 1$. It may be noted that the proportions $1:\sqrt{2}$ have a geometrical relationship, the side and diagonal of any square being in this proportion. As the basic size is one square metre in area, this means that $X = 841$ millimetres and $Y = 1{,}189$ millimetres. The effect of this arrangement is that if the short side is doubled or the longer side halved, *i.e.*, if the area of the sheet is doubled or halved, the shorter side and the longer side of the new sheet are still in the same proportion $1:\sqrt{2}$. This feature is particularly useful where photographic enlargement or reduction is used, as the proportions remain the same.

Description of the A series is by the capital A followed by a figure. The basic size has the description A0 and the higher the figure following the letter, the greater is the number of sub-divisions and therefore the smaller the sheet. Half A0 is A1 and half A1 is A2. Where larger dimensions are required the A is *preceded* by a figure. Thus 2A means twice the size of A0; 4A is four times the size of A0.

It is an essential feature of these series that the dimensions are of the trimmed or finished sizes.

'A' SERIES OF TRIMMED SIZES

Designation	SIZE	
	mm	inches
A 0	841 × 1189	33·11 × 46·81
A 1	594 × 841	23·39 × 33·11
A 2	420 × 594	16·54 × 23·39
A 3	297 × 420	11·69 × 16·54
A 4	210 × 297	8·27 × 11·69
A 5	148 × 210	5·83 × 8·27
A 6	105 × 148	4·13 × 5·83
A 7	74 × 105	2·91 × 4·13
A 8	52 × 74	2·05 × 2·91
A 9	37 × 52	1·46 × 2·05
A 10	26 × 37	1·02 × 1·46

Subsidiary Series.—A series of B sizes has been devised for use in exceptional circumstances when sizes intermediate between any two adjacent sizes of the A series are needed.

'B' SERIES OF TRIMMED SIZES

Designation	SIZE	
	mm	inches
B 0	1000 × 1414	39·37 × 55·67
B 1	707 × 1000	27·83 × 39·37
B 2	500 × 707	19·68 × 27·83
B 3	353 × 500	13·90 × 19·68
B 4	250 × 353	9·84 × 13·90
B 5	176 × 250	6·93 × 9·84
B 6	125 × 176	4·92 × 6·93
B 7	88 × 125	3·46 × 4·92
B 8	62 × 88	2·44 × 3·46
B 9	44 × 62	1·73 × 2·44
B 10	31 × 44	1·22 × 1·73

In addition there is a series of C sizes which is used much less. A is for magazines and books, B for posters, wall charts and and other large items, C for envelopes particularly where it is necessary for an envelope (in C series) to fit into another envelope. The size recommended for business correspondence is A4.

Long Sizes.—Long sizes are obtainable by dividing any appropriate sizes from the two series above into three, four or eight equal parts parallel with the shorter side in such a manner that the proportions mentioned in paragraph 2 (above) are not maintained, the ratio between the longer and the shorter sides being greater than $\sqrt{2}:1$. In practice long sizes should be produced from the A series only.

CONVERSION TABLES FOR WEIGHTS AND MEASURES

NOTE.—The central figures in heavy type represent either of the two columns beside them, as the case may be. *Examples:*—1 centimetre = 0·394 inch and 1 inch = 2·540 centimetres. 1 metre = 1·094 yards and 1 yard = 0·914 metre. 1 kilometre = 0·621 mile and 1 mile = 1·609 kilometres.

Length			Area			Volume			Weight (Mass.)					
Centimetres.		Inches.	Square Centimetres.		Square Inches.	Cubic Centimetres.		Cubic Inches.	Long Tons.		Short Tons.	Metric Tonnes.		Short Tons.
2·540	1	0·394	6·452	1	0·155	16·387	1	0·061	0·893	1	1·120	0·907	1	1·102
5·080	2	0·787	12·903	2	0·310	32·774	2	0·122	1·786	2	2·240	1·814	2	2·205
7·620	3	1·181	19·355	3	0·465	49·161	3	0·183	2·679	3	3·360	2·722	3	3·307
10·160	4	1·575	25·806	4	0·620	65·548	4	0·244	3·571	4	4·480	3·629	4	4·409
12·700	5	1·969	32·258	5	0·775	81·936	5	0·305	4·464	5	5·600	4·536	5	5·512
15·240	6	2·362	38·710	6	0·930	98·323	6	0·366	5·357	6	6·720	5·443	6	6·614
17·780	7	2·756	45·161	7	1·085	114·710	7	0·427	6·250	7	7·840	6·350	7	7·716
20·320	8	3·150	51·613	8	1·240	131·097	8	0·488	7·143	8	8·960	7·257	8	8·818
22·860	9	3·543	58·064	9	1·395	147·484	9	0·549	8·036	9	10·080	8·165	9	9·921
25·400	10	3·937	64·516	10	1·550	163·871	10	0·610	8·929	10	11·200	9·072	10	11·023
50·800	20	7·874	129·032	20	3·100	327·742	20	1·220	17·857	20	22·400	18·144	20	22·046
76·200	30	11·811	193·548	30	4·650	491·613	30	1·831	26·786	30	33·600	27·216	30	33·069
101·600	40	15·748	258·064	40	6·200	655·484	40	2·441	35·714	40	44·800	36·287	40	44·092
127·000	50	19·685	322·580	50	7·750	819·355	50	3·051	44·643	50	56·000	45·359	50	55·116
152·400	60	23·622	387·096	60	9·300	983·226	60	3·661	53·571	60	67·200	54·431	60	66·139
177·800	70	27·559	451·612	70	10·850	1147·097	70	4·272	62·500	70	78·400	63·503	70	77·162
203·200	80	31·496	516·128	80	12·400	1310·968	80	4·882	71·429	80	89·600	72·575	80	88·185
228·600	90	35·433	580·644	90	13·950	1474·839	90	5·492	80·357	90	100·800	81·647	90	99·208
254·000	100	39·370	645·160	100	15·500	1638·710	100	6·102	89·286	100	112·000	90·719	100	110·231

Metres.		Yards.	Square Metres.		Square Yards.	Cubic Metres.		Cubic Yards.	Metric Tonnes.		Long Tons.	Kilograms.		Av. Pounds.
0·914	1	1·094	0·836	1	1·196	0·765	1	1·308	1·016	1	0·984	0·454	1	2·205
1·829	2	2·187	1·672	2	2·392	1·529	2	2·616	2·032	2	1·968	0·907	2	4·409
2·743	3	3·281	2·508	3	3·588	2·294	3	3·924	3·048	3	2·953	1·361	3	6·614
3·658	4	4·374	3·345	4	4·784	3·058	4	5·232	4·064	4	3·937	1·814	4	8·819
4·572	5	5·468	4·181	5	5·980	3·823	5	6·540	5·080	5	4·921	2·268	5	11·023
5·486	6	6·562	5·017	6	7·176	4·587	6	7·848	6·096	6	5·905	2·722	6	13·228
6·401	7	7·655	5·853	7	8·372	5·352	7	9·156	7·112	7	6·889	3·175	7	15·432
7·315	8	8·749	6·689	8	9·568	6·116	8	10·464	8·128	8	7·874	3·629	8	17·637
8·230	9	9·843	7·525	9	10·764	6·881	9	11·772	9·144	9	8·858	4·082	9	19·842
9·144	10	10·936	8·361	10	11·960	7·646	10	13·080	10·161	10	9·842	4·536	10	22·046
18·288	20	21·872	16·723	20	23·920	15·291	20	26·159	20·321	20	19·684	9·072	20	44·092
27·432	30	32·808	25·084	30	35·880	22·937	30	39·239	30·481	30	29·526	13·608	30	66·139
36·576	40	43·745	33·445	40	47·840	30·582	40	52·318	40·642	40	39·368	18·144	40	88·185
45·720	50	54·681	41·806	50	59·799	38·228	50	65·398	50·802	50	49·210	22·680	50	110·231
54·864	60	65·617	50·168	60	71·759	45·873	60	78·477	60·963	60	59·052	27·216	60	132·277
64·008	70	76·553	58·529	70	83·719	53·519	70	91·557	71·123	70	68·894	31·752	70	154·324
73·152	80	87·489	66·890	80	95·679	61·164	80	104·636	81·284	80	78·737	36·287	80	176·370
82·296	90	98·425	75·251	90	107·639	68·810	90	117·716	91·444	90	88·579	40·823	90	198·416
91·440	100	109·361	83·613	100	119·599	76·455	100	130·795	101·605	100	98·421	45·359	100	220·462

Kilometres.		Miles.	Square Kilometres.		Square Miles.	Litres.		Gallons.	Bushels U.S.		Bushels U.K.	Hectares.		Acres.
1·609	1	0·621	2·590	1	0·386	4·546	1	0·220	1·032	1	0·969	0·405	1	2·471
3·219	2	1·243	5·180	2	0·772	9·092	2	0·440	2·064	2	1·938	0·809	2	4·942
4·828	3	1·864	7·770	3	1·158	13·638	3	0·660	3·096	3	2·907	1·214	3	7·413
6·437	4	2·485	10·360	4	1·544	18·184	4	0·880	4·128	4	3·876	1·619	4	9·884
8·047	5	3·107	12·950	5	1·931	22·730	5	1·100	5·160	5	4·845	2·023	5	12·355
9·656	6	3·728	15·540	6	2·317	27·276	6	1·320	6·192	6	5·814	2·428	6	14·826
11·265	7	4·350	18·130	7	2·703	31·822	7	1·540	7·224	7	6·783	2·833	7	17·297
12·875	8	4·971	20·720	8	3·089	36·368	8	1·760	8·256	8	7·752	3·237	8	19·769
14·484	9	5·592	23·310	9	3·475	40·914	9	1·980	9·288	9	8·721	3·642	9	22·240
16·093	10	6·214	25·900	10	3·861	45·460	10	2·200	10·321	10	9·689	4·047	10	24·711
32·187	20	12·427	51·800	20	7·722	90·919	20	4·400	20·641	20	19·379	8·094	20	49·421
48·280	30	18·641	77·700	30	11·583	136·379	30	6·599	30·962	30	29·068	12·140	30	74·132
64·374	40	24·855	103·600	40	15·444	181·839	40	8·799	41·282	40	38·758	16·187	40	98·842
80·467	50	31·069	129·499	50	19·305	227·298	50	10·999	51·603	50	48·447	20·234	50	123·553
96·561	60	37·282	155·399	60	23·166	272·758	60	13·199	61·923	60	58·137	24·281	60	148·263
112·654	70	43·496	181·299	70	27·027	318·217	70	15·398	72·244	70	67·826	28·328	70	172·974
128·748	80	49·710	207·199	80	30·888	363·677	80	17·598	82·564	80	77·516	32·375	80	197·684
144·841	90	55·923	233·099	90	34·749	409·137	90	19·798	92·885	90	87·205	36·422	90	222·395
160·934	100	62·137	258·999	100	38·610	454·596	100	21·998	103·205	100	96·895	40·469	100	247·105

SYMBOLS FOR CORRECTING PROOFS

Supplied by WILLIAM CLOWES & SONS LTD, Beccles, Suffolk, Printers of "WHITAKER"

Letter(s) or word(s) requiring alteration should be struck through IN INK in the text and the substitution should be written in the nearest margin followed by / (the symbol used to denote that the marginal mark is concluded). Insertions should be indicated by ⋏ or ∧ at the conclusion of the marginal mark *and* at the desired place in the text.

Alteration required	Mark in margin	Mark in text	Alteration required	Mark in margin	Mark in text
Delete (take out)	∂ or ∂⏋	/ or ──── Vertical stroke to delete one or two letters; horizontal line to delete more	Take letter(s) or word(s) from beginning of one line to end of preceding line	(back) or (take back)	⏋
Delete and close up	∂ or ∂⏋	Strike out letter(s) not required and add "close up" mark above and below	Begin a new paragraph	n.p.	⌐ before first word of new paragraph
Close up: delete space between letters	⌣	linking letters or words	No new para. here or run on with previous matter with later matter	run on	between paras. or other matter
Use ligature (fi, fl, ffl, etc.) or diphthong (æ, œ)	⌣ *enclosing ligature or diphthong required*	enclosing letters to be altered	Spell out in full the abbreviation, contraction, or figure	spell out	Encircle words, etc., or figures concerned
Insert space between letters or words	#⋏	⋏	Insert omitted portion of copy	(out - see copy)	⋏ Attach the relevant copy to the proof, indicating omitted portion
Leave as printed (i.e. a cancellation of previous marking)	stet	.... under letter(s) or word(s) crossed out but to be retained	Inserted or substituted letter(s), figure(s), or sign(s) under which this is placed to be superscript (i.e. high alignment) [1]	⏋ (see footnote)	⋏ for insertions For substitutions encircle letter(s), figure(s), or sign(s) to be altered
Invert type (of letter(s) upside down)	∂	Encircle letter(s) to be altered	Inserted or substituted letter(s), figure(s), or sign(s) over which this is placed to be subscript (low alignment) [2]	⏋ (see footnote)	⋏ for insertions For substitutions encircle letter(s), figure(s), etc., to be altered
"Battered" letter(s) to be replaced by similar but undamaged characters	✕	Encircle letter(s) or word(s) to be replaced and write the correct letter(s) in the margin	Change to lower case	l.c.	Encircle letter(s) to be altered
Push down space or "high" letter(s) or word(s)	⊥	Encircle space, letter(s), or word(s) affected	Replace "wrong fount" by letter(s) of correct fount	w.f.	Encircle letter(s) or word(s) to be altered
Transpose	tr. or trs.	⊐⏌ between letters or words, numbered when necessary	Change to capital letters	caps.	══ under letter(s) or word(s) to be altered
Take letter(s) or word(s) from end of one line to beginning of next line	(take over) or (over)	⌐	Change to small capitals	s.c.	══ under letter(s) or word(s) to be altered

⋎ indicates a superior (superscript) figure one   ⏋₂ indicates an inferior (subscript) figure two

Alteration required	Mark in margin	Mark in text	Alteration required	Mark in margin	Mark in text
Use capital letters for initial letter(s) (as desired) and small capitals for rest of word(s)	*caps* *s.c.*	≡ under initial letter(s) and = under the remainder of the word(s)	Move lines to the left	⌐ ⌐	at right side of group of lines to be moved (indicating approx. position)
Change to bold type	*bold*	∿ Draw wavy line under letter(s) or word(s) to be altered	Move portion of matter so that it is positioned as indicated	[ ]	at limits of required position
Change to roman type	*rom.*	Encircle letter(s) or word(s) to be altered	Raise lines	*raise*	↗ over lines to be raised
Change to italic type	*italic*	Draw this straight line under letter(s) or word(s) to be altered	Lower lines	*lower*	↓ under lines to be lowered
Letter(s) or word(s) to be underlined	*underline*	under letter(s), word(s), etc., to be underlined	Correct the vertical alignment	‖	‖
			Straighten lines	—	through lines to be straightened
Equalize space between words	*eq. #*	between words	Insert parentheses (round-shaped brackets)	(/) or (/)|	⋏ ⋏⋏
Reduce space	*less #*	between words	Insert [square] brackets	[/] or [/]	⋏ ⋏⋏
Space to be inserted between lines or paragraphs	*#>*	Amount of space should be indicated	Insert hyphen	-/	⋏
To be placed in centre of line, etc.	*centre*	Position to be indicated by	Insert en (=half-em) rule (*see above*)	*en*/	⋏
Indent one en (approx. space occupied by n of type in use)	*en* □⋏	indicating approximate position	Insert one-em rule (*see above*)	*em*/	⋏
Indent one em (approx. space occupied by M of type in use)	*em* □⋏	Ditto	Insert two-em rule (*see above*)	*2-em*/	⋏
Indent two ems (approx. space occupied by MM of type in use)	□□⋏	Ditto	Insert apostrophe	᾿	⋏
Move to the left	⌐	Ditto	Insert single quotation marks	⸲ ᾿	⋏ ⋏
Move to the right	⌐	Ditto	Insert double quotation marks	⸲⸲ ᾿᾿	⋏ ⋏
Move lines to the right	⌐ ⌐	at left side of group of lines to be moved (indicating approx. position)	Insert ellipsis	.../	⋏
			Insert leader (*visual guide to alignment in contents pages, etc.*)	●●●	⋏ (*three, two, or one dot*)
			Insert shilling stroke (oblique)	(/)	⋏

Punctuation   ⋏/   ⸴/   ⋏   ;/   ⊙   ⊙   ?⋏   ?/   !⋏   !/

THE WORLD